Foreword

The New Scofield Study Bible, New King James Version, is the latest edition of a trusted publication first issued in 1909. Its study system, familiar to millions of Christians around the world, is the masterpiece of evangelist and Bible conference leader Cyrus I. Scofield (1843–1921). He saw the need for a Bible with helps that would display the great orthodox teachings that had been emphasized during the period of doctrinal awakening in which he lived—and to present those teachings in a form that could be easily grasped by the average reader. Scofield resigned his pastoral ministry in 1903, assembled a team of scholars, traveled to Europe for research, and spent countless hours perfecting his notes, chain references and other study aids.

The Scofield Reference Bible was an outstanding success, and it was followed by an improved edition in 1917. After many printings, an extensive revision was begun in 1954 by a new generation of scholars headed by E. Schuyler English, all of whom were in firm sympathy with Scofield's approach. That became the *New Scofield Reference Bible,* first published in 1967. It is the basis for the current adaptation.

No Bible student or teacher should ever claim to be able to present new doctrinal truth or material supposedly given from God and on a par with the Bible. If he were living C. I. Scofield would probably be the first to acknowledge that his study system should never be taken as a substitute for the pages of the Bible itself. But it is for this very reason that the Scofield Bible is significant. It announces that its purpose is to permit the Bible to speak for itself, by allowing the Bible student to compare parts of the Bible with each other, working from what is more easily understood to what is more difficult. The whole system is designed to open up as much Scripture as possible to the individual. In order to accomplish this the Scofield Bible not only offers study helps such as cross references and chain references, but also espouses a theological position that gives a comprehensive picture of the Bible. It is this combination of theological frankness and extensive mechanical helps that makes the Scofield unique.

Can a study Bible take a particular stand and not be accused of bias? Yes, if it seeks to allow the Bible to demonstrate its own teachings. It should be remembered that every translation reflects the theological position of the individual or committee that shaped it. And every work on biblical interpretation espouses some position, with some assumptions. For Scofield there were two overriding guidelines that directed him in his study: (1) The most accurate understanding of the Bible comes when it is allowed to shed light on itself, and (2) in the final analysis all Scripture is to be related to the work of the Lord Jesus Christ. This is in keeping with the biblical principle enunciated in Rev. 19:10: "The testimony of Jesus is the spirit of prophecy" (see the Scofield note at Rev. 19:10).

The resulting stress on orthodox doctrines of the faith and vital prophetic truths, especially the premillennial return of Christ (see Rev. 20:4), caused the Scofield study system to be of great value for millions. It enabled them to appropriate for their faith and service a unified biblical message. Bible students could see the Scriptures as a progressive revelation of varying dealings of God with humanity, comprising *dispensations* (see Gen. 1:28). And they could recognize that although God's purposes at different times in human history might not all have the same facets, all of His acts were ultimately to be related to the Cross and all of His blessings for humanity were to be mediated through *covenants* (see Gen. 2:16). This emphasis on dispensations and covenants is indeed a doctrinal distinctive of the Scofield. But it is one that lies at the heart of dispensationalism, the most fruitful approach to the Bible known until now. In a real sense the Bible is a history of the making of covenants by God. It encourages us to formulate a theology of covenants. And the understanding that dispensationalism gives as an *approach* to the Bible makes it a significant framework for biblical study. Frank Gaebelein, one of the consulting editors for the *New Scofield Reference Bible,* notes:

> That [Scofield] himself would have equated this particular dispensational system with intimate and absolute truth is doubtful. But that it is a useful tool for comprehending

the inspired unfolding of the divine plan for the ages is undeniable, as multitudes of users of this edition of the Bible know.

In other words, then, the very theology of the Scofield Bible is one that is based on the assumption that the best approach to the Bible is one which allows the reader to understand the greatest portion of the Bible. The dispensational framework does this. Many people have attested to the fact that this feature, emphasizing as it does the great network of prophetic truth in the Bible, much of it yet unrealized, opened the Bible to them in a sensible and fruitful way. This has often been in great contrast to teaching they had previously received to the effect that many parts of the Bible could not be understood, were merely repetitive of each other, or were to be taken as non-literal.

Finally, it is not without significance that Scofield's emphasis on service in his own life and in the formulation of the annotations has led so many to appreciate the Scofield Bible for its assistance in their own personal walk with God. A presentation of doctrinal understanding of the Bible is incomplete without an accompanying encouragement to lead a fruitful and Christ-like life. In the final analysis, sound biblical doctrine actually accomplishes that. It takes the teachings of the Bible as they are intended to be applied to the lives of real people and by its reasonableness and exaltation of Christ leads individuals to serve a gracious God. We can see this link between doctrine and practice clearly in such passages as Titus 2:11, where an understanding of God's purposes centered in Christ brings godly living while believers await His return. Correct doctrine leads to correct behavior, just as incorrect doctrine leads to incorrect behavior. Sound interpretation of the Bible is the prerequisite to pleasing God. Scofield knew this, and has helped millions to see it confirmed in their own lives.

Paul S. Karleen

Table of Contents

THE NAMES AND ORDER
OF THE

Books of the Old and New Testaments

with abbreviations of their names, and the number of chapters in each

The Old Testament

		PAGE	CHS.			PAGE	CHS.
Genesis	Gen.	1	50	Ecclesiastes	Eccl.	757	12
Exodus	Ex.	74	40	Song of Solomon	Song	768	8
Leviticus	Lev.	131	27	Isaiah	Isa.	778	66
Numbers	Num.	173	36	Jeremiah	Jer.	858	52
Deuteronomy	Dt.	224	34	Lamentations	Lam.	933	5
Joshua	Josh.	267	24	Ezekiel	Ezek.	941	48
Judges	Jud.	297	21	Daniel	Dan.	1003	12
Ruth		327	4	Hosea	Hos.	1028	14
1 Samuel	1 Sam.	332	31	Joel		1042	3
2 Samuel	2 Sam.	368	24	Amos		1048	9
1 Kings	1 Ki.	401	22	Obadiah	Obad.	1058	1
2 Kings	2 Ki.	438	25	Jonah	Jon.	1061	4
1 Chronicles	1 Chr.	473	29	Micah	Mic.	1065	7
2 Chronicles	2 Chr.	507	36	Nahum	Nah.	1073	3
Ezra		548	10	Habakkuk	Hab.	1077	3
Nehemiah	Neh.	561	13	Zephaniah	Zeph.	1082	3
Esther	Est.	579	10	Haggai	Hag.	1087	2
Job		589	42	Zechariah	Zech.	1090	14
Psalms	Ps.	627	150	Malachi	Mal.	1106	4
Proverbs	Prov.	724	31				

The New Testament

		PAGE	CHS.			PAGE	CHS.
Matthew	Mt.	1121	28	1 Timothy	1 Tim.	1462	6
Mark	Mk.	1182	16	2 Timothy	2 Tim.	1468	4
Luke	Lk.	1213	24	Titus	Ti.	1473	3
John	Jn.	1267	21	Philemon	Phile.	1476	1
Acts		1308	28	Hebrews	Heb.	1478	13
Romans	Rom.	1365	16	James	Jas.	1496	5
1 Corinthians	1 Cor.	1390	16	1 Peter	1 Pet.	1502	5
2 Corinthians	2 Cor.	1412	13	2 Peter	2 Pet.	1509	3
Galatians	Gal.	1425	6	1 John	1 Jn.	1514	5
Ephesians	Eph.	1434	6	2 John	2 Jn.	1520	1
Philippians	Phil.	1443	4	3 John	3 Jn.	1522	1
Colossians	Col.	1449	4	Jude		1523	1
1 Thessalonians	1 Th.	1454	5	Revelation	Rev.	1526	22
2 Thessalonians	2 Th.	1459	3				

In-Text Maps and Charts

Introduction to the 1989 Edition

The New Scofield Study Bible, New King James Version is the first Bible to combine the unparalleled accuracy and beauty of the New King James Version of the Bible (NKJV) with the time-tested usefulness of the Scofield study system. A few minutes spent reading the following introduction will greatly increase the reader's potential benefit.

Some of the distinctive features of this study Bible are:

The New King James Version

A detailed preface to the New King James Version of the Holy Bible begins on page xiv. Although this is not the first attempt to wed a current English translation to the study features of the *New Scofield Reference Bible,* it is uniquely appropriate for several reasons:

(1) The New King James Version is an accurate translation of the Scriptures based on the principle of faithfully rendering into current English the words and meanings found in the original languages. The Scofield approach to Bible study is built on the same premise of careful attention to the words of Scripture, resulting in a consistent treatment of Bible text and study system.

(2) The policy of the New King James translators was to keep important theological words such as "sanctification," "propitiation" and "atonement" the same as they were in the King James Version, wherever principles of precise translation allowed. This practice makes the NKJV compatible with Scofield's language and style.

(3) While making reference to the ancient versions and manuscripts, and supplying variant textual readings where significant (see section entitled "New King James Footnotes" in the Preface to The New King James Version), the New King James Version is based on the same Hebrew and Greek manuscript sources as the King James Version used by Dr. Scofield. Thus, agreement between the Bible text and the Scofield study system is ensured in the process of adaptation for this edition.

Maps

To further illustrate the events of scriptural history, *The New Scofield Study Bible, New King James Version* contains more than forty in-text maps and charts. These are placed at appropriate locations where they can be conveniently consulted by the Bible user. A full-color map supplement with index to place names is included at the back of the volume.

Subheadings

The entire Bible is provided with subheadings to guide the reader. The subheadings outline the major divisions of each book of the Bible, in harmony with the book outlines that appear after the book introductions. Beyond the major divisions, detailed subheadings identify subjects throughout the Scriptures. The subheadings are easily distinguished from the text of the inspired Scriptures.

Chronology

In the references no dates before 2100 B.C. are given, because of the lack of evidence on which to fix such dates (cp. Gen. 1:1; 5:3; 11:10, *notes*). Between 2100 and 1000 B.C. approximate dates are given. After 1000 B.C. events are dated with more precision in cases where the present state of knowledge makes this possible, but even here most dates are tentative and may need revision if required by new evidence.

INTRODUCTION

Reference Columns

The center-column and side-column references of the 1967 *New Scofield Reference Bible* have been retained in this edition, including those which offer alternative readings or interpretations of the text based on the findings of Dr. Scofield's editorial team and the revision committee. In certain cases, what was an alternative reading for the King James Version has become the accepted rendering in the New King James text, and such material has been allowed to drop from the reference column.

Chain references, showing the first and last appearances of important subjects (such as Inspiration, Holy Spirit, Israel, etc.) and carrying the reader through the major references to them in the Old and New Testaments, are invaluable for comparing Scripture with Scripture in order to better understand the great truths of divine revelation.

Book Introductions

The author, theme, and date of writing are shown immediately below each book title. Then every book of the Bible is provided with an introduction, an analysis, and an outline, of which the subheadings throughout the text are an expansion. Wherever possible, the person or persons addressed are identified in the introduction.

Annotations

The annotations elucidate obscure and difficult passages of Scripture. The great words and doctrines of the Bible are defined in understandable terms. Such subjects as adoption, atonement, death, election, eternal life, faith, grace, justification, kingdom, and sanctification are given a full explanation with numerous Scripture references. Notes summarizing the subject chain references are integrated with the annotations. These summary notes may be located quickly by consulting either the Brief Index to Subject Chain References or the Complete Index to Subject Chain References at the back of this volume.

Scriptural typology is designated, with care being taken to distinguish between types on the one hand, and illustrations or examples on the other. An Old Testament type usually has a New Testament antitype; otherwise Old Testament experiences are examples (1 Cor. 10:6) or may be used as illustrations.

Archaeological discoveries in Egypt, Mesopotamia, Palestine, and other Bible lands have provided a mass of material that illustrates biblical statements and corroborates biblical accuracy. Certain of the more important of these have been summarized in annotations at suitable places. The Qumran documents—better known as the Dead Sea Scrolls—the tablets from Ugarit, from Nuzi, from Mari, and elsewhere have been winnowed for appropriate facts.

The position of the 1967 editorial committee concerning our Lord's return and related events in Bible prophecy has been preserved intact in this work of adaptation. Their exposition of the dispensational and premillennial viewpoint was based on the notes of Dr. Scofield and his associates in the original work, which were strengthened and clarified to take into account controversies and differing opinions that had developed in the field of prophetic interpretation during the preceding fifty-year period.

The style of the 1967 revisers concerning capitalization has been followed as consistently as possible in the adapted annotations. Additionally, pronouns that refer to God the Father, the Son, or the Holy Spirit are capitalized to maintain conformity with the style of the New King James Version.

Covenants

The greater covenants of God which bear upon human life and divine redemption, and around which the entire Bible gathers, are analyzed, and their relationships to each other and to Christ are clarified.

Dispensations

The dispensations are distinguished, exhibiting the progressive order of God's dealings with humanity and the purpose which runs through and links together time periods during which man has been responsible for specific and varying tests as to his obedience to God, from the beginning of human history to its end. Although not all

Bible students agree in every detail of the dispensational system presented in this study Bible, it is generally recognized that the distinction between law and grace is basic to the understanding of the Scriptures. As a further aid to comprehending the divine economy of the ages, a recognition of the dispensations is of highest value, so long as it is clearly understood that throughout all the Scriptures there is only one basis of salvation, that is, by grace through faith. Strict limits cannot be placed upon the terminations of all the dispensations because (1) there is some overlapping, and (2) the divinely-given stewardship may continue after the time-era of special testing has ended.

Concordance

The Concise Concordance, a key feature of the 1967 *New Scofield Reference Bible,* has been fully revised for the first time in this edition. This useful reference tool contains key words, proper names and subject entries, all blended together in one alphabetical listing. The substance and analytical approach of the subject entries have been maintained, with only such changes as were needed to conform them to the language of the New King James Version.

Indexes

In addition to the Concise Concordance, *The New Scofield Study Bible, New King James Version* contains three indexes to make the Scofield study system more accessible than ever: (1) the Index to Annotations and (2) the Brief Index to Subject Chain References (both of which have been adapted from the 1967 edition); and (3) a new feature—the Complete Index to Subject Chain References.

The Index to Annotations provides quick access to the wealth of material contained in the Scofield notes. The index includes historical terms (such as Apollos, Gomer, Egypt, Nineveh) as well as doctrinal entries (such as judgment, man, sin, world), with verse references directing the reader to the annotations containing pertinent material. Entries concerning such deep topics as Christ, Holy Spirit, Israel, and Kingdom are extensively subdivided.

The Brief Index to Subject Chain References gives the names of the Subject Chains with the locations of first and last references and summary footnotes. It provides direct access for the reader who wants to trace a chain from start to finish, or who merely wishes to read the summary material.

The Complete Index to Subject Chain References is a new addition to the Scofield study system. It gives a chapter and verse for every subject chain reference. Someone wanting to trace the verses that deal with grace in the writings of John, for example, will no longer have to follow the chain references from Acts through 2 Peter to get from John to 2 John; the Complete Index shows the relevant verses at a glance.

New King James Notes

The scholarly value of this edition of the Scofield Study Bible is enhanced by the footnotes of the New King James Version. These notes, which show important textual variants and offer comments on the translation, have contributed greatly to the popularity of the NKJV, and they form a very helpful complement to the Scofield study system.

The New Scofield Study Bible, New King James Version, has a rich heritage. Millions have been led to a deeper understanding of the Word of God through Dr. Scofield's approach to Bible study. This edition is offered for the same purpose as its predecessors:

"The completed work is now dedicated to the service amongst men of that Loving and Holy God, whose marvellous grace in Christ Jesus it seeks to exalt."

—C. I. Scofield, 1909

"May the Lord of the Book be dearer to each reader of it."

—E. Schuyler English, 1967

A Panoramic View of the Bible

The Bible, the most widely circulated book ever published, is both attractive and puzzling to those who try to study it. Even people who deny the Bible's authority admit that it is a sign of ignorance not to be familiar with its contents. And yet, even sincere believers are quick to give up any attempt to master Bible doctrine. The reason is that no part of Scripture can be understood apart from its place in the whole. The Bible message is like a mosaic. Each piece has its appointed place, and is appreciated only when seen in relation to the other pieces around it. Therefore, a general knowledge of the Bible is essential to anyone who would understand a part of it.

The Bible—One Book

First, the Bible is one Book. The unity of Scripture is evidenced in a number of ways. (1) Throughout its pages the Bible bears witness to one God who is consistent with Himself and the revelation concerning Him. (2) The Bible gives one continuous account of humanity in relation to God. (3) The Bible makes predictions about future events that are quite unlikely, then records their fulfillment when they have come to pass. (4) The Bible is a progressive unfolding of truth. Several writers, moved by the Holy Spirit but separated by centuries, add new details until the whole revelation takes form. (5) From beginning to end the Bible testifies to one redemption. (6) The Bible has one great theme throughout—the person and work of Jesus Christ. And (7) finally, some forty-four writers have produced a perfect harmony of doctrine over a two-thousand-year period. This, to every unprejudiced mind, is proof of the divine inspiration of the Bible.

The Bible—Many Books

Second, the Bible is a collection of books. The one Book is made up of sixty-six books, each complete in itself with its own theme and analysis. Each book, therefore, needs to be studied in the light of its own unique character. Genesis, for example, is the book of beginnings, initiating all that comes after it; Matthew is the book of the King, and so forth.

The Plan of the Bible

Third, the books of the Bible are arranged in groups. Generally speaking, there are five great divisions in the Scriptures, with Christ being the great overall theme. The divisions are:

PREPARATION
The OT

MANIFESTATION
The Gospels

PROPAGATION
Acts

EXPLANATION
The Epistles

CONSUMMATION
Revelation

The Old Testament is the preparation for Christ; He is manifested to the world in the Gospels; in Acts He is preached and the Gospel is propagated to the world; the Epistles explain Him; and the purposes of God in Christ are consummated—brought to a climax—in Revelation.

In turn, the Old Testament may be further divided into four well-defined categories:

The Law	History	Poetry and Wisdom	Prophecy	
Genesis	Joshua	Job	Isaiah	Obadiah
Exodus	Judges	Psalms	Jeremiah	Jonah
Leviticus	Ruth	Proverbs	Lamentations	Micah
Numbers	1 and 2 Samuel	Ecclesiastes	Ezekiel	Nahum
Deuteronomy	1 and 2 Kings	Song of Solomon	Daniel	Habakkuk
	1 and 2 Chronicles		Hosea	Zephaniah
	Ezra		Joel	Haggai
	Nehemiah		Amos	Zechariah
	Esther		Malachi	

Again, we should not overlook, in these general groupings, the distinctive messages of the individual books. For example, while redemption is the general theme of the Pentateuch, as it tells the story of the redemption of Israel out of bondage and into "a good and large land," each of the five books has its own distinctive part in the whole. Genesis is the book of beginnings and explains the origin of Israel. Exodus tells of the deliverance of Israel; Leviticus of the worship of Israel as a delivered people; Numbers of the wanderings and failures of the delivered people; and Deuteronomy warns and instructs the people as they prepare to enter into their inheritance.

The poetical books record the spiritual experiences of the redeemed people in the various scenes and events through which the providence of God led them. The prophets were inspired preachers, and the prophetic books consist of sermons with brief connecting and explanatory passages. Two prophetic books, Ezekiel and Daniel, have a different character and are largely apocalyptic.

The Human Story

Fourth, the Bible tells the human story. Beginning with the creation of the earth and of man, the story of the human race descended from Adam and Eve continues through the first eleven chapters of Genesis. In the twelfth chapter begins the history of Abraham and of the nation of which he was the ancestor. It is that nation—Israel—with which the Bible narrative is chiefly concerned from the eleventh chapter of Genesis to the second chapter of Acts. The Gentiles are mentioned, but only in connection with Israel. It is made increasingly clear, however, that Israel fills the scene this way only because entrusted with the accomplishment of great worldwide purposes (Dt. 7:7).

The appointed mission of Israel was (1) to be a witness to the unity of God in the midst of universal idolatry (Dt. 6:4; Isa. 43:10); (2) to illustrate to the nations the greater blessedness of serving the one true God (Dt. 33:26–29; 1 Chr. 17:20–21; Ps. 102:15); (3) to receive and preserve the divine revelation (Rom. 3:1–2); and (4) to produce the Messiah, earth's Savior and Lord (Rom. 9:4–5). The prophets foretell a glorious future for Israel under the reign of Christ.

The biblical story of Israel, past, present, and future, falls into seven distinct periods: (1) from the call of Abram (Gen. 12) to the Exodus (Ex. 1—20); (2) from the Exodus to the death of Joshua (Ex. 21—Josh. 24); (3) from the death of Joshua to the establishment of the Hebrew monarchy under Saul; (4) the period of the kings from Saul to the captivities; (5) the period of the captivities; (6) the restored commonwealth from the end of the Babylonian captivity of Judah to the destruction of Jerusalem in A.D. 70; and (7) the present dispersion.

The Gospels record the appearance in human history and within the Hebrew nation of the promised Messiah, Jesus Christ, and tell the wonderful story of His manifestation to Israel, His rejection by that people, His crucifixion, resurrection, and ascension.

Acts records the descent of the Holy Spirit, and the beginning of a new thing in human history, the Church. The division of the race now becomes threefold: the Jew, the Gentile, and the Church of God. Just as Israel is in the foreground from the call of Abram to the resurrection of Christ, so now the Church fills the scene from the second chapter of Acts to the fourth chapter of Revelation. The remaining chapters of that book complete the story of humanity and the final triumph of Christ.

Christ the Central Theme

Fifth, the central theme of the Bible is Christ. It is this manifestation of Jesus Christ, His person as God manifest in the flesh (1 Tim. 3:16), His sacrificial death, and His resurrection, which constitute the Gospel. All preceding Scripture leads to it and all subsequent Scripture flows from it. The Gospel is preached in Acts and explained in the Epistles. Christ—Son of God, Son of Man, Son of Abraham, Son of David—thus binds the many books into one Book. As Seed of the woman (Gen. 3:15), He is the ultimate destroyer of Satan and his works; as Seed of Abraham, He is benefactor of the world; as Seed of David, He is Israel's King, "Desire of All Nations." Exalted to the right hand of God, He is Head over all the Church, which is His body; while to Israel and the nations the promise of His return forms the one and only rational expectation that humanity will yet fulfill itself. Meanwhile the Church looks momentarily for the fulfillment of His special promise, "I will come again, and receive you to Myself" (Jn. 14:3). To Him the Holy Spirit throughout this Church Age bears testimony. The last book of all, the consummation book, is "The Revelation of Jesus Christ" (Rev. 1:1).

Preface
to
The New King James Version

Purpose

In the preface to the 1611 edition, the translators of the Authorized Version, known popularly as the King James Bible, state that it was not their purpose "to make a new translation . . . but to make a good one better." Indebted to the earlier work of William Tyndale and others, they saw their best contribution to consist in revising and enhancing the excellence of the English versions which had sprung from the Reformation of the sixteenth century. In harmony with the purpose of the King James scholars, the translators and editors of the present work have not pursued a goal of innovation. They have perceived the Holy Bible, New King James Version, as a continuation of the labors of the earlier translators, thus unlocking for today's readers the spiritual treasures found especially in the Authorized Version of the Holy Scriptures.

A Living Legacy

For nearly four hundred years, and throughout several revisions of its English form, the King James Bible has been deeply revered among the English-speaking peoples of the world. The precision of translation for which it is historically renowned, and its majesty of style, have enabled that monumental version of the Word of God to become the mainspring of the religion, language, and legal foundations of our civilization.

Although the Elizabethan period and our own era share in zeal for technical advance, the former period was more aggressively devoted to classical learning. Along with this awakened concern for the classics came a flourishing companion interest in the Scriptures, an interest that was enlivened by the conviction that the manuscripts were providentially handed down and were a trustworthy record of the inspired Word of God. The King James translators were committed to producing an English Bible that would be a precise translation, and by no means a paraphrase or a broadly approximate rendering. On the one hand, the scholars were almost as familiar with the original languages of the Bible as with their native English. On the other hand, their reverence for the divine Author and His Word assured a translation of the Scriptures in which only a principle of utmost accuracy could be accepted.

In 1786 Catholic scholar Alexander Geddes said of the King James Bible, "If accuracy and strictest attention to the letter of the text be supposed to constitute an excellent version, this is of all versions the most excellent." George Bernard Shaw became a literary legend in our century because of his severe and often humorous criticisms of our most cherished values. Surprisingly, however, Shaw pays the following tribute to the scholars commissioned by King James: "The translation was extraordinarily well done because to the translators what they were translating was not merely a curious collection of ancient books written by different authors in different stages of culture, but the Word of God divinely revealed through His chosen and expressly inspired scribes. In this conviction they carried out their work with boundless reverence and care and achieved a beautifully artistic result." History agrees with these estimates. Therefore, while seeking to unveil the excellent *form* of the traditional English Bible, special care has also been taken in the present edition to preserve the work of *precision* which is the legacy of the 1611 translators.

Complete Equivalence in Translation

Where new translation has been necessary in the New King James Version, the most complete representation of the original has been rendered by considering the history of usage and etymology of words in their contexts. This principle of complete equivalence seeks to preserve *all* of the information in the text, while presenting it in good literary form. Dynamic equivalence, a recent procedure in Bible translation, commonly results in paraphrasing where a more literal rendering is needed to reflect a specific and vital sense. For example, complete equivalence truly renders the original text in expressions such as "lifted her voice and wept" (Gen. 21:16); "I gave you cleanness of teeth" (Amos 4:6); "Jesus met them, saying, 'Rejoice!' " (Mt. 28:9); and " 'Woman, what does your concern have to do with Me?' " (Jn. 2:4). Complete equivalence translates fully, in order to provide an English text that is both accurate and readable.

In keeping with the principle of complete equivalence, it is the policy to translate interjections which are commonly omitted in modern language renderings of the Bible. As an example, the interjection *behold,* in the older King James editions, continues to have a place in English usage, especially in dramatically calling attention to a spectacular scene, or an event of profound importance such as the Immanuel prophecy of Isaiah 7:14. Consequently, *behold* is retained for these occasions in the present edition. However, the Hebrew and Greek originals for this word can be translated variously, depending on the circumstances in the passage. Therefore, in addition to *behold,* words such as *indeed, look, see,* and *surely* are also rendered to convey the appropriate sense suggested by the context in each case.

In faithfulness to God and to our readers, it was deemed appropriate that all participating scholars sign a statement affirming their belief in the verbal and plenary inspiration of Scripture, and in the inerrancy of the original autographs.

Devotional Quality

The King James scholars readily appreciated the intrinsic beauty of divine revelation. They accordingly disciplined their talents to render well-chosen English words of their time, as well as a graceful, often musical arrangement of language, which has stirred the hearts of Bible readers through the years. The translators, the committees, and the editors of the present edition, while sensitive to the late-twentieth-century English idiom, and while adhering faithfully to the Hebrew, Aramaic, and Greek texts, have sought to maintain those lyrical and devotional qualities that are so highly regarded in the Authorized Version. This devotional quality is especially apparent in the poetic and prophetic books, although even the relatively plain style of the Gospels and Epistles cannot strictly be likened, as sometimes suggested, to modern newspaper style. The Koine Greek of the New Testament is influenced by the Hebrew background of the writers, for whom even the Gospel narratives were not merely flat utterance, but often song in various degrees of rhythm.

The Style

Students of the Bible applaud the timeless devotional character of our historic Bible. Yet it is also universally understood that our language, like all living languages, has undergone profound change since 1611. Subsequent revisions of the King James Bible have sought to keep abreast of changes in English speech. The present work is a further step toward this objective. Where obsolescence and other reading difficulties exist, present-day vocabulary, punctuation, and grammar have been carefully integrated. Words representing ancient objects, such as *chariot* and *phylactery,* have no modern substitutes and are therefore retained.

A special feature of the New King James Version is its conformity to the thought flow of the 1611 Bible. The reader discovers that the sequence and selection of words, phrases, and clauses of the new edition, while much clearer, are so close to the traditional that there is remarkable ease in listening to the reading of either edition while following with the other.

In the discipline of translating biblical and other ancient languages, a standard method of transliteration, that is, the English spelling of untranslated words, such as names of persons and places, has never been commonly adopted. In keeping with the design of the present work, the King James spelling of untranslated words is retained, although made uniform throughout. For example, instead of the spellings *Isaiah* and *Elijah* in the Old Testament, and *Esaias* and *Elias* in the New Testament, *Isaiah* and *Elijah* now appear in both Testaments.

King James doctrinal and theological terms, for example, *propitiation, justification,* and *sanctification,* are generally familiar to English-speaking peoples. Such terms have been retained except where the original language indicates need for a more precise translation.

Readers of the Authorized Version will immediately be struck by the absence of several pronouns: *thee, thou,* and *ye* are replaced by the simple *you,* while *your* and *yours* are substituted for *thy* and *thine* as applicable. *Thee, thou, thy* and *thine* were once forms of address to express a special relationship to human as well as divine persons. These pronouns are no longer part of our language. However, reverence for God in the present work is preserved by capitalizing pronouns, including *You, Your,* and *Yours,* which refer to Him. Additionally, capitalization of these pronouns benefits the reader by clearly distinguishing divine and human persons referred to in a passage. Without such capitalization the distinction is often obscure, because the antecedent of a pronoun is not always clear in the English translation.

In addition to the pronoun usages of the seventeenth century, the *-eth* and *-est* verb endings, so familiar in the earlier King James editions, are now obsolete. Unless a speaker is schooled in these verb endings, there is common difficulty in selecting the correct form to be used with a given subject of the verb in vocal prayer. That is, should we use *love, loveth,* or *lovest? do, doeth, doest,* or *dost? have, hath,* or *hast?* Because these forms are obsolete, contemporary English usage has been substituted for the previous verb endings.

In older editions of the King James Version, the frequency of the connective *and* far exceeded the limits of present English usage. Also, biblical linguists agree that the Hebrew and Greek original words for this conjunction may commonly be translated otherwise, depending on the immediate context. Therefore, instead of *and,* alternatives such as *also, but, however, now, so, then,* and *thus* are accordingly rendered in the present edition, when the original language permits.

The real character of the Authorized Version does not reside in its archaic pronouns or verbs or other grammatical forms of the seventeenth century, but rather in the care taken by its scholars to impart the letter and spirit of the original text in a majestic and reverent style.

The Format

The format of the New King James Version is designed to enhance the vividness and devotional quality of the Holy Scriptures:

—Words or phrases in *italics* indicate expressions in the original language which require clarification by additional English words, as also done throughout the history of the King James Bible.

—Verse numbers in **bold type** indicate the beginning of a paragraph.

—*Oblique type* in the New Testament indicates a quotation from the Old Testament.

—Poetry is structured as contemporary verse to reflect the poetic form and beauty of the passage in the original language.

—The covenant name of God was usually translated from the Hebrew as "LORD" or "GOD" (using capital letters as shown) in the King James Old Testament. This tradition is maintained. In the present edition the name is so capitalized whenever the covenant name is quoted in the New Testament from a passage in the Old Testament.

The Old Testament Text

The Hebrew Bible has come down to us through the scrupulous care of ancient scribes who copied the original text in successive generations. By the sixth century A.D. the scribes were succeeded by a group known as the Masoretes, who continued to preserve the sacred Scriptures for another five hundred years in a form known as the Masoretic Text. Babylonia, Palestine, and Tiberias were the main centers of Masoretic activity; but by the tenth century A.D. the Masoretes of Tiberias, led by the family of ben Asher, gained the ascendancy. Through subsequent editions, the ben Asher text became in the twelfth century the only recognized form of the Hebrew Scriptures.

Daniel Bomberg printed the first Rabbinic Bible in 1516–17; that work was followed in 1524–25 by a second edition prepared by Jacob ben Chayyim and also published by Bomberg. The text of ben Chayyim was adopted in most subsequent Hebrew Bibles, including those used by the King James translators. The ben Chayyim text was also used for the first two editions of Rudolph Kittel's *Biblia Hebraica* of 1906 and 1912. In 1937 Paul Kahle published a third edition of *Biblia Hebraica*. This edition was based on the oldest dated manuscript of the ben Asher text, the Leningrad Manuscript B19a (A.D. 1008), which Kahle regarded as superior to that used by ben Chayyim.

For the New King James Version the text used was the 1967/1977 Stuttgart edition of the *Biblia Hebraica*, with frequent comparisons being made with the Bomberg edition of 1524–25. The Septuagint (Greek) Version of the Old Testament and the Latin Vulgate also were consulted. In addition to referring to a variety of ancient versions of the Hebrew Scriptures, the New King James Version draws on the resources of relevant manuscripts from the Dead Sea caves. In the few places where the Hebrew was so obscure that the 1611 King James was compelled to follow one of the versions, but where information is now available to resolve the problems, the New King James Version follows the Hebrew text. Significant variations are recorded in footnotes.

The New Testament Text

There is more manuscript support for the New Testament than for any other body of ancient literature. Over five thousand Greek, eight thousand Latin, and many more manuscripts in other languages attest the integrity of the New Testament. There is only one basic New Testament used by Protestants, Roman Catholics, and Orthodox, by conservatives and liberals. Minor variations in hand copying have appeared through the centuries, before mechanical printing began about A.D. 1450.

Some variations exist in the spelling of Greek words, in word order, and in similar details. These ordinarily do not show up in translation and do not affect the sense of the text in any way.

Other manuscript differences such as omission or inclusion of a word or a clause, and two paragraphs in the Gospels, should not overshadow the overwhelming degree of *agreement* which exists among the ancient records. Bible readers may be assured that the most important differences in English New Testaments of today are due, not to manuscript divergence, but to the way in which translators view the task of translation: How literally should the text be rendered? How does the translator view the matter of biblical inspiration? Does the translator adopt a paraphrase when a literal rendering would be quite clear and more to the point? The New King James Version follows the historic precedent of the Authorized Version in maintaining a literal approach to translation, except where the idiom of the original language cannot be translated directly into our tongue.

The King James New Testament was based on the traditional text of the Greek-speaking churches, first published in 1516, and later called the Textus Receptus or Received Text. Although based on the relatively few available manuscripts, these were representative of many more which existed at the time but only became known later. In the late nineteenth century, B. Westcott and F. Hort taught that this text had been officially edited by the fourth-century church, but a total lack of historical evidence for this event has forced a revision of the theory. It is now widely held that the Byzantine Text that largely supports the Textus Receptus has as much right as the Alexandrian or any other tradition to be weighed in determining the text of the New Testament. Those readings in the Textus Receptus which have weak support are indicated in the footnotes as being opposed by both Critical and Majority Texts (see "New King James Footnotes").

Since the 1880s most contemporary translations of the New Testament have relied upon a relatively few manuscripts discovered chiefly in the late nineteenth and early twentieth centuries. Such translations depend primarily on two manuscripts, Codex Vaticanus and Codex Sinaiticus, because of their greater age. The Greek text obtained by using these sources and the related papyri (our most ancient manuscripts) is known as the Alexandrian Text. However, some scholars have grounds for doubting the faithfulness of Vaticanus and Sinaiticus, since they often disagree with one another, and Sinaiticus exhibits excessive omission.

A third viewpoint of New Testament scholarship holds that the best text is based on the consensus of the majority of existing Greek manuscripts. This text is called the Majority Text. Most of these manuscripts are in substantial agreement. Even though many are late, and none is earlier than the fifth century, usually their readings are verified by papyri, ancient versions, quotations from the early church fathers, or a combination of these. The Majority Text is similar to the Textus Receptus, but it corrects those readings which have little or no support in the Greek manuscript tradition.

Today, scholars agree that the science of New Testament textual criticism is in a state of flux. Very few scholars still favor the Textus Receptus as such, and then often for its historical prestige as the text of Luther, Calvin, Tyndale, and the King James Version. For about a century most have followed a Critical Text (so called because it is edited according to specific principles of textual criticism) which depends heavily upon the Alexandrian type of text. More recently many have abandoned this Critical Text (which is quite similar to the one edited by Westcott and Hort) for one that is more eclectic. Finally, a small but growing number of scholars prefer the Majority Text, which is close to the traditional text except in the Revelation.

In light of these facts, and also because the New King James Version is the fifth revision of a historic document translated from specific Greek texts, the editors decided to retain the traditional text in the body of the New Testament and to indicate major Critical and Majority Text variant readings in the footnotes. Although these variations are duly indicated in the footnotes of the present edition, it is most important to emphasize that fully eighty-five percent of the New Testament text is the same in the Textus Receptus, the Alexandrian Text, and the Majority Text.

New King James Footnotes

Significant textual variations, explanatory notes, alternate translations, and cross-references, as well as New Testament citations of Old Testament passages, are supplied in the footnotes below the right text column, in a box indicated by an asterisk.

Important textual variants in the Old Testament are identified in a standard form.

The textual notes in the present edition of the New Testament make no evaluation of readings, but do clearly indicate the manuscript sources of readings. They objectively present the facts without such tendentious remarks as "the best manuscripts omit" or "the most reliable manuscripts read." Such notes are value judgments that differ according to varying viewpoints on the text. By giving a clearly defined set of variants the New King James Version benefits readers of all textual persuasions.

Where significant variations occur in the New Testament Greek manuscripts, textual notes are classified as follows:

1. NU-Text
   These variations from the traditional text generally represent the Alexandrian or Egyptian type of text described previously in "The New Testament Text." They are found in the Critical Text published in the twenty-sixth edition of the Nestle-Aland Greek New Testament (N) and in the United Bible Societies' third edition (U), hence the acronym, "NU-Text."

2. M-Text
   This symbol indicates points of variation in the Majority Text from the traditional text, as also previously discussed in "The New Testament Text." It should be noted that M stands for whatever reading is printed in the first edition of *The Greek New Testament According to the Majority Text*, whether supported by overwhelming, strong, or only a divided majority textual tradition.

The textual notes reflect the scholarship of the past 150 years and will assist the reader to observe the variations between the different manuscript traditions of the New Testament. Such information is generally not available in English translations of the New Testament.

Miscellaneous Abbreviations

Aram.	—	Aramaic
c.	—	(L. *circa*) about
ch(s).	—	chapter(s)
contra.	—	contrast
cp.	—	compare
e.g.	—	(L. *exempli gratia*) for example
f.	—	single verse following Scripture reference
ff.	—	two or more verses following Scripture reference
Gk.	—	Greek
Heb.	—	Hebrew
i.e.	—	(L. *id est*) that is
KJV	—	King James Version
L.	—	Latin
lit.	—	literally
LXX	—	Septuagint, an early Greek translation of the Old Testament (the roman numeral seventy representing the traditional number of its translators)
marg.	—	margin
ms(s).	—	manuscript(s)
M-Text	—	the Majority Text of the Greek New Testament
NKJV	—	New King James Version
NT	—	New Testament
NU-Text	—	Nestle-Aland/United Bible Societies text of the Greek New Testament
OT	—	Old Testament
ref(s).	—	reference(s)
Syr.	—	Syriac
transl.	—	translated
v.	—	verse
vv.	—	verses
Vul.	—	Vulgate, a Latin translation of the Scriptures

How to Use
The New Scofield Study Bible
New King James Version

The Gospel According t

MATTHEW

Read the **book introductions** to acquaint yourself with the author, purpose, and main themes of the book.

Author: Matthew *Theme:* Christ, the King

MATTHEW, called also Levi, was the writer of the First Gospel.
eighth in the NT lists of the apostles (Mt. 10:3; Mk. 3:18; L
who collected taxes for the Roman government. He was thus
Written originally for the Jews, the Gospel of Matthew p
David and the Son of Abraham. Because He is portrayed as I
to King David; and the place of His birth, Bethlehem, the hc
Seven times in this Gospel Christ is spoken of as "the Son of I
20:30; 21:9; 22:42). Only in Matthew does Christ speak of "th
cp. 25:31). Moreover, only here in the Gospels is Jerusalem
(4:5) and "the city of the great King" (5:35). Since it is the Gc
also the Gospel of the kingdom; in it the word "kingdom" a
and the expression "the kingdom of heaven," which is found nc
about thirty times.
Matthew, more than any of the Gospel writers, identifies
life of our Lord with OT predictions, e.g. 1:22; 2:15,17,23; 4:1
27:9,35.
Matthew may be divided as follows:

An **outline** for each book shows you the book "at a glance."

I. The King Introduced: His Genealogy, Birth, and Ear
II. The Principles of the Rule of the King: the Sermon
III. The Authority of the King Manifested and Rejected,
IV. The Mysteries of the Kingdom: the Period Between t
13.
V. The Ministry of the Rejected King, 14—23.
VI. The Predicted Return of the King: the Olivet Discou
VII. The Death and Resurrection of the King, 26—28.

Subheadings identify the themes of the Bible. This helps you organize and outline your Bible study.

CHAPTER 1

1
a vv. 1–17
b 1 Sam. 16:1–14; 2 Sam. 7:12–29; Ps. 132:11
c Gen. 12:1–4; 13:15–18; 15:1–6; 17:1–8; 22:15–18

2
d Gen. 21:1–8; 26:1–5
e Gen. 25:19–28; 28:1–4, 10–15
f Gen. 29:35

3
g Gen. 38:24–30;

I. The King Introduced: His Genealogy, Birth, and Early Life, 1—4

Genealogy of Jesus through Solomon (v. 7) and foster father, Joseph (v. 16; cp. Lk. 3:23–38)

1 THE book of the [1a]geneal-
ogy of Jesus Christ, the Son
of [b]David, the Son of [c]Abra-
ham:
2 Abraham begot [d]Isaac,
Isaac begot [e]Jacob, and Jacob
begot [f]Judah and his brothers.
3 Judah begot [g]Perez and
Zerah by Tamar, Perez begot
Hezron, and Hezron begot
Ram.
4 Ram begot Amminadab,

Amminadab
and Nahshon
5 Salmon
Rahab, Boaz
Ruth, Obed be
6 and Jess
king.
David th
omon by her w
*wife** of [i]Uria
7 Solomo
boam, Rehob
jah, and Abija
8 Asa beg
Jehoshaphat b
Joram begot [2]

* 1:6 Words in italic ty for clarity. They are original Greek. 1: *Asaph.*

17 Then was fulfilled what
was [d]spoken by Jeremiah the
prophet, saying:
18 *"A voice was heard in*
Ramah,
Lamentation, weeping,
and great mourning,
Rachel weeping for her
children,
Refusing to be
comforted,
Because they are no
more."

Return from Egypt to Nazareth
(cp. Lk. 2:39–40; also read
Lk. 2:41–52)

19 Now [f]when Herod was
dead, behold, an [g]angel of the
Lord appeared in a dream to Joseph in Egypt,
20 [h]saying, "Arise, take the
young Child and His mother,
and go to the land of Israel, [i]for
those who [j]sought the young
Child's life are dead."
21 Then he arose, took the
young Child and His mother,
and came into the land of Israel.
22 But when he heard that
[k]Archelaus was reigning over
Judea instead of his father
Herod, he was afraid to go
there. And being warned by
God in a [l]dream, he turned
aside into the region of Galilee.
23 And he came and dwelt in
a city called Nazareth, that it
might be fulfilled which was
[d]spoken by the prophets, [2]"He
shall be called a Nazarene."

Ministry of John the Baptist
(Mk. 1:1–8; Lk. 3:1–20;
Jn. 1:6–8,15–37)

3 IN those days John the Baptist came [m]preaching in the
wilderness of Judea,
2 and [n]saying, [o]"Repent,
for [p]the [3]kingdom of heaven is
[q]at hand!"

19
f c. 4 B.C. See Mk. 6:14, *note*
g See Heb. 1:4, *note*
20
h Lk. 2:14
i Cp. Ex. 4:19
j v. 16
22
k Son of Herod the Great. See Mt. 2:1, *note*
l Mt. 2:13,19
CHAPTER 3
1
m *Gospel:* vv. 1–2; Mt. 4:17. (Gen. 12:3; Rev. 14:6)
2
n See Acts 17:30, *note*
o *Repentance:* vv. 2, 8,11; Mt. 4:17. (Mt. 3:2; Acts 17:30, *note*)
p *Kingdom (NT):* v. 2; Mt. 4:17. (Mt. 2:2; 1 Cor. 15:24, *note*)
q See Mt. 4:17, *note*

A raised letter in the Bible text leads you to the reference column, where the most carefully prepared **subject chain reference system** in any Bible is found.

The name of the subject chain is given first, for example, "Gospel." Then several references lead you forward to other Scripture references in the same subject chain. The last reference given before the parentheses is the next reference on a following page.

In parentheses are found the first reference in the subject chain and the reference for the Summary Note on the subject of the chain. For example, Genesis 12:3 is the first reference in the subject chain "Gospel."

The last reference in parentheses is always the location of the **Summary Note** for that subject. If the last reference appears by itself (without the word *note*), then that reference is both the last reference in the chain and the location of the Summary Note. For example, a note summarizing "Gospel" is found at Revelation 14:6.

If the Summary Note is not located at the last reference in the chain, then the word *note* appears with the reference.

For more information, see the Complete Index to Subject Chain References, page 1565.

A raised number in the Bible text keys you to an **annotation** at the foot of the page. A matching number at the beginning of each annotation tells you where to read for insights into God's message.

12:9 **GENESIS**

pitched his tent *with* Bethel on the
west and Ai on the east; there he built
an altar to the LORD and called on the
name of the LORD.
9 So Abram journeyed, going on
still toward the [1]South.

Under trial Abram fails, forsaking the place of blessing

10 Now there was a famine in the
land, and Abram went down to Egypt
to dwell there, for the famine *was* severe in the land.
11 And it came to pass, when he
was close to entering Egypt, that he
said to Sarai his wife, "Indeed I know
that you *are* a woman of beautiful
countenance.
12 "Therefore it will happen, when
the Egyptians see you, that they will
say, 'This *is* his wife'; and they will kill
me, but they will let you live.

13
a Cp. Gen. 20:1–18; 26:6–11
16
b Gen. 20:14
c Gen. 13:2
17
d Miracles (OT): v. 17; Gen. 15:17. (Gen. 5:24; Jon. 1:17, *note*)

(1 Ki. 13:1–5; 2 Ki. 23:15–17; Amos 3:14–15). Althou
against that which is contrary to His character, what
is accompanied by the sorrow of His divine compa:
[1](12:9) "The South" translates the Hebrew word N
"to be dry." It is a geographical term which refers to
13:1) located between Debir and the Arabian Desert.
this area was south of the larger part of Israel, the v
direction (cp. Gen. 13:14; Dan. 8:4,9; 11:5, etc.).
[2](12:13) Abram's proposal was partial truth, for S
what was told was with intent of deception. Cp. Ge

More than 40 **in-text maps** throughout the Old and New Testaments orient you to the land of the Bible, helping you to "see" the biblical narrative unfold.

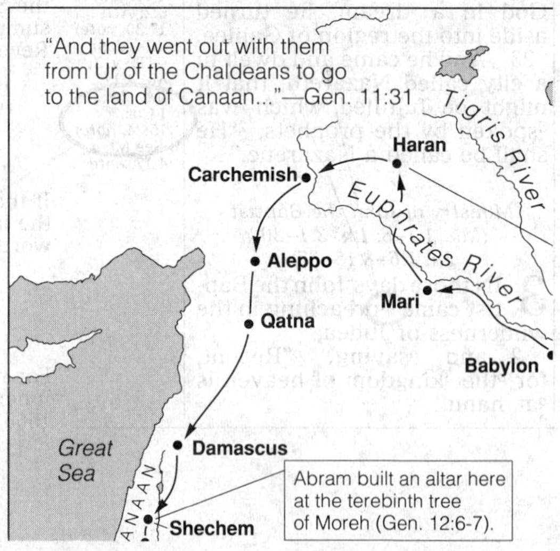

THEW 19:26

17 So He said to him, "Why
do you call Me good?* No one *is*
[j]good but One, *that is,* God.*
But if you want to enter into life,
[k]keep the commandments."
18 He said to Him, [l]"Which
ones?" Jesus said, "'*You shall
not murder,' 'You shall not
commit adultery,' 'You shall not
steal,' 'You shall not bear false
witness,'*
19 *'Honor your father and
your mother,'** and, *'You shall
love your* [m]*neighbor as yourself.'* "
20 The young man said to
Him, "All these things I have
[n]kept from my youth.* What do
I still lack?"
21 Jesus said to him, "If you
want to be [o]perfect, go, sell
what you have and give to the
poor, and you will have treasure
in heaven; and come, follow
Me."
22 But when the young man
heard that saying, he went
away sorrowful, for he had
great possessions.
23 Then Jesus said to His disciples, "Assuredly, I say to you
that it is hard for a [p]rich man to
[q]enter the [d]kingdom of heaven.
24 "And again I say to you, it
is easier for a camel to go
through the eye of a [r]needle
[s]than for a rich man to enter the
kingdom of God."
25 When His disciples heard
it, they were greatly astonished,
saying, "Who then can be
[t]saved?"
26 But Jesus looked at *them*

19:9 Or *fornication* **19:16** NU-Text omits *Good.* **19:17** NU-Text reads *Why do you ask Me about what is good?* • NU-Text reads *There is One who is good.* **19:19** Exodus 20:12–16 Deuteronomy 5:16–20 **19:20** NU-Text omits *from my youth.*

17
j Ps. 25:8; 34:8; Nah. 1:7; Rom. 2:4
k Lev. 18:5; Dt. 4:40; 6:17; 7:11; 11:22; 28:9; Gal. 3:10; cp. Rom. 3:19; 10:1–5
18
l *Law* (of Moses): vv. 18–20; Mt. 22:24. (Ex. 19:1; Gal. 3:24, *note*)
19
m Lev. 19:18; Mt. 5:43; 22:39; Lk. 10:29–37; Rom. 13:9; Gal. 5:14; Jas. 2:8
20
n Phil. 3:6–7; contrast vv. 7–9
21
o See Mt. 5:48, *note*
23
p Mt. 13:22; 1 Tim. 6:9–10; Jas. 5:1–3; cp. Jas. 2:5
q Cp. Jn. 3:5
24
r Gk. *raphis, a sewing needle*
s Cp. Mt. 7:13–14
25
t Cp. Mt. 13:3–9; see Rom. 1:16, *note*

An asterisk in the Bible text tells you to look at the lower right-hand column of text on that page to find **textual information:** significant textual variations, explanatory notes, alternate translations, and key cross references. The textual footnotes give you special information about the original language texts of the Bible. The New King James Version contains the most objective and complete set of textual footnotes of any English Bible.

Verse markers in the reference column provide milestones for the cross references and subject chain references. By giving you the verse numbers which coordinate with the raised letters in the Bible text, the verse markers make it easier to move from the Bible text to the reference column, and back again.

Cross references lead you to Bible verses which help clarify the meaning of the present verse.

takes, each of which was met by the Lord with
Person of Christ, thinking Him only a good
nma—either He is God or He is not a good man
al life, supposing it could be earned by works,
ands of divine law (v. 17). (3) His mistake about
was answered by testing him as to works of
s failure (v. 22). And (4) his most tragic mistake
ome, follow Me" (v. 21); for therein was offered

THE OLD TESTAMENT

The Pentateuch

CERTAIN critics have denied that Moses wrote Genesis to Deuteronomy despite the fact that they were attributed to Moses by the Lord Jesus Christ. The arguments against Mosaic authorship are chiefly based on the variation of the names of God (*Elohim* and *Jehovah*; see Mal. 3:18, *note*), the differences in style and vocabulary, and the presence of more than one account of the same event, e.g. the creation of man in Gen. 1:26 and 2:7.

These contentions have been adequately answered in that the variation in divine names is for the purpose of revealing certain aspects of God's character; the style is dependent on the subject matter; and the so-called parallel accounts, well known in ancient Near Eastern literature, are intended to add details to the first account.

Some theologians, rejecting the actuality of the events recorded in the early chapters of Genesis, yet at the same time recognizing their religious value, call such accounts as those of Eden and the fall "myths," meaning by "myth" not merely legend but, rather, a "supra-historical" story that conveys spiritual teaching of permanent significance. However, the historicity of the Genesis record is so related to the authority of Christ that it cannot be assigned to a mythical category without impugning the perfection of His knowledge.

These five books have a unique place in the structure of the Bible, and an order which is undeniably the order of the experience of the people of God in all ages. Genesis is the book of origins—of the beginning of life, and of ruin through sin. Its first words, "In the beginning God," are in striking contrast with the end, "in a coffin in Egypt." Exodus is the book of redemption, the first need of a ruined race. Leviticus is the book of worship and communion, the proper exercise of the redeemed. Numbers speaks of the experiences of a pilgrim people, the redeemed passing through a hostile scene to a promised inheritance. Deuteronomy, retrospective and prospective, is a book of instruction for the redeemed about to enter that inheritance.

That Babylonian and Assyrian literature contain records bearing a grotesque resemblance to the majestic account of the creation and of the flood is true, as also that these antedate Moses. But this confirms rather than invalidates the inspiration of the Mosaic account. Some tradition of creation and the flood would inevitably be handed down in the ancient cradle of the race. Such a tradition, following the order of all tradition, would take on incongruous and mythological features, and these abound in the Babylonian records. Of necessity, therefore, the first task of inspiration would be to supplant the often absurd and childish tradition with a revelation of the true history, and such a history we find in words of matchless grandeur, and in an order which, rightly understood, is absolutely scientific.

In the Pentateuch, therefore, we have a true and logical introduction to the entire Bible; and, in type, an epitome of the divine revelation.

The First Book of Moses Called

GENESIS

Author: Moses *Theme:* Beginnings [a]*Date of writing:* c. 1450–1410 B.C.

GENESIS is the book of beginnings. It records not only the beginning of the heavens and the earth, and of plant, animal, and human life, but also of all human institutions and relationships. Typically, it speaks of the new birth, the new creation, where all was chaos and ruin. (See also The Pentateuch, p. xxvi.)

With Genesis begins also the progressive self-revelation of God which culminates in Christ. The three primary names of Deity—*Elohim, Jehovah,* and *Adonai*—and the five most important of the compound names occur in Genesis, and these in an ordered progression which could not be changed without confusion.

The problem of sin as affecting man's condition on the earth and his relationship to God, and the divine solution of that problem, are here in essence. Of the eight great covenants which condition human life and progressively unfold the divine redemption, four—the Edenic, Adamic, Noahic, and Abrahamic Covenants—are in this book, and these are the fundamental covenants to which the other four—the Mosaic, Palestinian, Davidic, and New Covenants—are related chiefly as adding detail or development.

Genesis enters into the very structure of the New Testament, in which it is quoted above sixty times in seventeen books. In a profound sense, therefore, the roots of all subsequent revelation are planted deep in Genesis, and whoever would truly comprehend that revelation must begin here.

The inspiration of Genesis and its character as a divine revelation are authenticated by the testimony of Jesus Christ (Mt. 19:4–6; 24:37–39; Mk. 10:4–9; Lk. 11:49–51; 17:26–29,32; Jn. 7:21–23; 8:44,56) and supplemented by the testimony of history. As indicated in notes throughout the book, archaeology bears witness to the historical reliability of Genesis.

Genesis may be divided into five parts:

I. Creation, 1:1—2:25.
II. The Fall and the Promise of Redemption, 3:1—4:7.
III. The Diverse Seeds, Cain and Seth, to the Flood, 4:8—7:24.
IV. The Flood to Babel, 8:1—11:9.
V. From the Call of Abram to the Death of Joseph, 11:10—50:26.

I. Creation, 1:1—2:25

Creation of the heavens and earth

1 [1]IN the [2b]beginning [3c]God [4]cre-
ated the heavens and the earth.

Earth waste and empty

2 The earth was [5]without form,
and void; and darkness *was** on the
face of the deep. And [d]the [e]Spirit of
God was hovering over the face of the
waters.

a See Intro., p. ix

CHAPTER 1

1

b Jn. 1:1
c Deity (names of): v. 1; Gen. 2:4. (Gen. 1:1; Mal. 3:18)

1:2 *d Holy Spirit* (OT): v 2; Gen. 6:3. (Gen. 1:2; Zech. 12:10) *e* Job 26:13

*

1:2 Words in italic type have been added for clarity. They are not found in the original Hebrew or Aramaic.

---

[1](1:1) The Bible begins with God, not with philosophic arguments for His existence.

[2](1:1) Scripture gives no data for determining how long ago the universe was created. See *notes* on Gen. 5:3; 11:10. Cp. Introduction, p. ix.

[3](1:1) *Elohim* (English form "God"), the first of the names of Deity, is a plural noun in form but is singular in meaning when it refers to the true God. Emphasis in Gen. 1:26 is on the plurality in Deity; in v. 27, on the unity of the divine Substance. (Cp. Gen. 3:22.) The plural form of the word suggests the Trinity. See Gen. 2:4; 14:18, *note;* 15:2, *notes;* 17:1, *note;* 21:33, *note;* Ex. 34:6, *note;* 1 Sam. 1:3, *note;* Mal. 3:18, *note.*

[4](1:1) Only three creative acts of God are recorded in this chapter: (1) the heavens and the earth, v. 1; (2) animal life, vv. 20–21; and (3) human life, vv. 26–27. The first creative act refers to the dateless past.

[5](1:2) Two main interpretations have been advanced to explain the expression "without form, and void" (Heb. *tohu* and *bohu*). The first, which may be called the Original Chaos interpretation, regards these words as a description of an original formless matter in the first stage of the creation of the universe. The second, which may be called the Divine Judgment interpretation, sees in these words a description of the earth only, and that in a condition subsequent to its creation, not as it was originally (see Isa. 45:18, *note;* cp. also *notes* at Isa. 14:12; Ezek. 28:12).

First day: light diffused

3 Then God said, "Let there be
[1]light"; and there was light.
4 And God saw the light, that *it
was* good; and God divided the light
from the darkness.
5 God called the light [2]Day, and
the [a]darkness He called Night. So the
[3]evening and the morning were the
first day.

Second day: vapor above, water below

6 Then God said, "Let there be a
[b]firmament in the midst of the waters,
and let it divide the waters from the
waters."
7 Thus God made the firmament,
and [c]divided the waters which *were*
under the firmament from the [d]waters
which *were* above the firmament; and
it was so.
8 And God called the firmament
Heaven. So the evening and the morning were the second day.

Third day: land and sea;
plant life appears

9 Then God said, "Let the waters
under the heavens be [e]gathered together into one place, and let the [f]dry
land appear"; and it was so.
10 And God called the dry *land*
Earth, and the gathering together of
the waters He called Seas. And God
saw that *it was* good.
11 Then God said, "Let the earth
bring forth grass, the herb *that* yields
seed, *and* the fruit tree *that* yields fruit
according to its kind, whose seed *is* in
itself, on the earth"; and it was so.
12 And the earth brought forth
grass, the herb *that* yields seed according to its kind, and the tree *that*
yields fruit, whose seed *is* in itself according to its kind. And God saw that
it was good.

5
a Ps. 104:20
6
b Lit. *expanse* (i.e. *of waters beneath, of vapor above*)
7
c Prov. 8:27–29
d Ps. 148:4
9
e Job 26:10
f Ps. 95:5
14
g Ps. 136:5–9
h Ps. 104:19
17
i i.e. *the heaven of the stars;* cp. Gen. 15:5
22
j v. 28; 8:17

13 So the evening and the morning
were the third day.

Fourth day: sun, moon, and stars
become visible

14 Then God said, [g]"Let there be
lights in the firmament of the heavens
to divide the day from the night; and
let them be for signs and [h]seasons,
and for days and years;
15 "and let them be for lights in the
firmament of the heavens to give light
on the earth"; and it was so.
16 Then God made two great lights:
the greater light to rule the day, and
the lesser light to rule the night. *He
made* the stars also.
17 God set them in the firmament of
the [i]heavens to give light on the
earth,
18 and to rule over the day and over
the night, and to divide the light from
the darkness. And God saw that *it was*
good.
19 So the evening and the morning
were the fourth day.

Fifth day: animal life
(see Gen. 2:19)

20 Then God said, "Let the waters
abound with an abundance of living
creatures, and let birds fly above the
earth across the face of the firmament
of the heavens."
21 So God created great sea creatures and every living [4]thing that
moves, with which the waters
abounded, according to their kind,
and every winged bird according to its
kind. And God saw that *it was* good.
22 And God blessed them, saying,
[j]"Be fruitful and multiply, and fill the
waters in the seas, and let birds multiply on the earth."
23 So the evening and the morning
were the fifth day.

---

[1](1:3) Neither here nor in vv. 14–18 is an original creative act implied. A different word is used. The sense is *made to appear, made visible.* The sun and moon were created "in the beginning." The light came from the sun, of course, but the vapor diffused the light. Later the sun appeared in an unclouded sky.

[2](1:5) The word "day" is used in Scripture in four ways: (1) that part of the solar day of twenty-four hours which is light (Gen. 1:5,14; Jn. 11:9); (2) a period of twenty-four hours (Mt. 17:1; Lk. 24:21); (3) a time set apart for some distinctive purpose, as "Day of Atonement" (Lev. 23:27); and (4) a longer period of time, during which certain revealed purposes of God are to be accomplished (cp. 2 Pet. 3:10).

[3](1:5) The use of "evening" and "morning" may be held to limit "day" to the solar day; but the frequent parabolic use of natural phenomena may warrant the conclusion that it simply means that each creative day was a period of time marked off by a beginning and ending (cp. Ps. 90:6). In any event the sun did not become a measure of time before the fourth day, as seen in vv. 14–18.

[4](1:21) The theme "every living thing that moves," as distinguished from fish merely, is taken up again in v. 24 ("living creature"), showing that in the second creative act all animal life is included.

Sixth day: (1) living creatures brought forth

24 Then God said, "Let the earth bring forth the living [1]creature according to its kind: cattle and creeping thing and beast of the earth, *each* according to its kind"; and it was so.

25 And God made the beast of the earth according to its kind, cattle according to its kind, and everything that creeps on the earth according to its kind. And God saw that *it was* good.

Sixth day: (2) man created and given dominion

26 Then God said, "Let Us make [2]man in Our image, according to Our likeness; let them have [3][a]dominion over the fish of the sea, over the birds of the air, and over the cattle, over all* the earth and over every creeping thing that creeps on the earth."

27 So God created man in His *own* image; in the image of God He created him; [b]male and female He created them.

First [4]Dispensation: Innocence (Gen. 1:28—3:6)

28 [c]Then God blessed them, and God said to them, "Be fruitful and

26
a Kingdom (OT): vv. 26–28; Gen. 9:6. (Gen. 1:26; Zech. 12:8, *note*)

27
b Cp. Mt. 19:4; Mk. 10:6–8

28
c Gen. 5:2

* 1:26 Syriac reads *all the wild animals of.*

[1](1:24) "Creature" (Heb. *nephesh*). In itself *nephesh,* or soul, implies conscious life, as distinguished from plants which have unconscious life. In the sense of conscious life an animal also has a soul. See vv. 26 (with *note* 2)–27.

[2](1:26) Man. Gen. 1:26–27 gives the general account of the creation of man, and Gen. 2:7,21–23 the particular. The revealed facts are:

(1) Man was *created,* not evolved. This is expressly declared, and the declaration is confirmed by Christ (Mt. 19:4; Mk. 10:6); it is also confirmed by the unbridgeable chasm between man and beast; the highest beast has no God-consciousness (religious nature).

(2) Man was made in the "image [and] likeness" of God. This image is found chiefly in the fact that man is a personal, rational, and moral being. While God is infinite and man finite, nevertheless man possesses the elements of personality similar to those of the divine Person: thinking (Gen. 2:19–20; 3:8); feeling (Gen. 3:6); willing (Gen. 3:6–7). That man has a moral nature is implicit in the record and is further attested by NT usage (Eph. 4:23–24; Col. 3:10). Man is also according to 1 Th. 5:23 (cp. *note*) a triunity, made up of body, soul, and spirit; but, because "God is Spirit" (Jn. 4:24), this tripartite nature of man is not to be confused with the original "image [and] likeness" of God which, being spiritual, relates to the elements of personality.

[3](1:26) Dominion. The Bible is a unity and the purpose of God is one. Man created in God's image (vv. 26–27) was placed in sovereignty over the earth (vv. 28–30), crowned with glory and honor (Ps. 8:5–8), yet subject to God his Creator (Gen. 2:15–17). The divine intention was and is that man should have fellowship with God in obedience. Sin came, the essence of which is rebellion against the will of God, and man became separated from God (Gen. 3:8–10) and lost sovereignty over the earth (Gen. 3:17–19). The goal of God is to restore sinning man to His likeness, fellowship, and dominion (Rom. 8:29; Rev. 21:3; 20:6; 22:5). "But now we do not yet see all things put under him [mankind]. But we see Jesus . . . crowned with glory and honor" in anticipation of many sons sharing His fellowship and dominion (Heb. 2:8–10; Rom. 8:17–19). This is in accordance with the first promise of redemption (Gen. 3:15). In the meantime, we wait with patient assurance for God's complete victory on the earth (Rom. 8:19–25; 1 Cor. 15:24–28; Rev. 11:15–18). For the working out of God's purpose of total redemption, see *note* on Dispensations at 1:28.

[4](1:28, heading) A dispensation is a period of time during which man is tested in respect to his obedience to some specific revelation of the will of God.

Three important concepts are implied in this definition: (1) a *deposit* of divine revelation concerning God's will, embodying what God requires of man as to his conduct; (2) man's *stewardship* of this divine revelation, in which he is responsible to obey it; and (3) a *time-period,* often called an "age," during which this divine revelation is dominant in the testing of man's obedience to God.

The dispensations are a progressive and connected revelation of God's dealings with man, given sometimes to the whole race and at other times to a particular people, Israel. These different dispensations are not separate ways of salvation. During each of them man is reconciled to God in only one way, i.e. by God's grace through the work of Christ that was accomplished on the cross and vindicated in His resurrection. Before the cross man was saved in prospect of Christ's atoning sacrifice, through believing the revelation thus far given him. Since the cross man has been saved by believing on the Lord Jesus Christ in whom revelation and redemption are consummated.

On man's part the continuing requirement is obedience to the revelation of God. This obedience is a stewardship of faith. Although the divine revelation unfolds progressively, the deposit of truth in the earlier time-periods is not discarded; rather it is cumulative. Thus multiply; [1]fill the earth and [2]subdue it; have dominion over the fish of the sea, over the birds of the air, and over every living thing that moves on the earth."

29 And God said, "See, I have given you every herb *that* yields seed which *is* on the face of all the earth, and every tree whose fruit yields seed; to you it shall be for [a]food.

30 "Also, to every beast of the earth, to every bird of the air, and to everything that creeps on the earth, in which *there is* life, *I have given* every green herb for [a]food"; and it was so.

31 Then God saw everything that He had made, and indeed *it was* very good. So the evening and the morning were the sixth day.

29
a Gen. 9:3

CHAPTER 2
2
b Heb. 4:4; cp. Heb. 4:8–9
3
c Sabbath: v. 3; Ex. 16:25. (Gen. 2:3; Mt. 12:1, *note*)
d Sanctification (OT): v. 3; Ex. 19:23. (Gen. 2:3; Zech. 8:3)

God's seventh-day rest (Sabbath)

2 THUS the heavens and the earth, and all the host of them, were finished.

2 And on the seventh day God ended His work which He had done, and He [b]rested on the seventh day from all His work which He had done.

3 Then God blessed the [c]seventh day and [3d]sanctified it, because in it He rested from all His work which [4]God had created and made.

Further detail (vv. 4–25) about creation of man

4 This *is* the history* of the heavens and the earth when they were [5]created, in the day that the

*
2:4 Hebrew *toledoth,* literally *generations*

conscience (moral responsibility) is an abiding truth in human life (Rom. 2:15; 9:1; 2 Cor. 1:12; 4:2), although it does not continue as a dispensation. Similarly, the saved of this present dispensation are "not under the law" as a specific test of obedience to divine revelation (Gal. 5:18; cp. Gal. 2:16; 3:11), yet the law remains an integral part of the Holy Scriptures which, to the redeemed, are profitable for "instruction in righteousness" (2 Tim. 3:16–17; cp. Rom. 15:4).

The purpose of each dispensation, then, is to place man under a specific rule of conduct, but such stewardship is not a condition of salvation. In every past dispensation unregenerate man has failed, and he has failed in this present dispensation and will in the future. But salvation has been and will continue to be available to him by God's grace through faith.

Seven dispensations (see Introduction, p. x) are distinguished in this edition of the Bible: Innocence (Gen. 1:28); Conscience or Moral Responsibility (Gen. 3:7); Human Government (Gen. 8:15); Promise (Gen. 12:1); Law (Ex. 19:1); Church (Acts 2:1); Kingdom (Rev. 20:4), where see *notes;* also important *note* at Gen. 11:10, relating to God's dealings with mankind.

[1](1:28) *The First Dispensation: Innocence.* Man was created in innocence, placed in a perfect environment, subjected to a simple test, and warned of the consequences of disobedience. He was not compelled to sin but, tempted by Satan, he chose to disobey God. The woman was deceived; the man transgressed deliberately (1 Tim. 2:14). The stewardship of Innocence ended in the judgment of the expulsion from Eden (Gen. 3:24). For *notes* on the other dispensations, see: Conscience or Moral Responsibility (Gen. 3:7); Human Government (Gen. 8:15); Promise (Gen. 12:1); Law (Ex. 19:1); Church (Acts 2:1); Kingdom (Rev. 20:4); also Gen. 11:10, *note.*

[2](1:28) This is the divine magna charta for all true scientific and material progress. Man began with a mind that was perfect in its finite capacity for learning, but he did not begin knowing all the secrets of the universe. He is commanded to "subdue," i.e. acquire a knowledge and mastery over his material environment, to bring its elements into the service of the race.

[3](2:3) The Hebrew word *(qdsh)* means *to set apart,* hence, *to make holy.*

[4](2:3) Up to this point the general term "God" has been used. "LORD" is added to "God" in verse 4, and continues to be used for several chapters. "LORD" is perhaps pronounced *Yahweh (YHWH)* in Hebrew, though traditionally *Jehovah* in English. (Here please read *notes* on LORD at Ex. 3:14; 6:3; 34:6; see also Preface, p. xvi.) The documentary theory of the authorship of the Pentateuch was built in part on the basis of this change in the name of God. See *note* at Mal. 3:18. Cp. also *notes* at Gen. 1:1; 15:2(2); 17:1; 21:33; 1 Sam. 1:3.

[5](2:4) It is often said that Gen. 2:4–25 is a second account of creation differing from that in Gen. 1:1—2:3. In point of fact, however, Gen. 1 tells of the creation of the whole universe, including man and woman; while Gen. 2 specifically describes the origin of man and woman without repeating the story of the creation recorded in Gen. 1. Thus Gen. 2 says nothing of the creation of light, of the separation of the waters, or of the formation of sun, moon, and stars. Nor does it actually describe the creation of vegetation or of animals.

Genesis 2:8 is sometimes erroneously interpreted as describing the creation of vegetation, but it only mentions the planting of a particular garden. Verse 19, often misinterpreted as another description of the creation of animals coming after rather than before the creation of man, actually refers back to the creation of the animals that were brought before Adam. To think that the planting of the garden described in v. 8 was not done until after man had

[1a]LORD God made the earth and the heavens,

5 before any plant of the field was in the earth and before any herb of the field had grown. For the LORD God had not caused it to [b]rain on the earth, and *there was* no man to [c]till the ground;

6 but a mist went up from the earth and watered the whole face of the ground.

God forms man and prepares Eden for him

7 And the LORD God [d]formed man *of* the [e]dust of the ground, and breathed into his nostrils the breath of life; and man became a living being.

8 The LORD God planted a garden eastward in [f]Eden, and there He put the man whom He had formed.

9 And out of the ground the LORD God made every tree grow that is pleasant to the sight and good for food. The [g]tree of life *was* also in the midst of the garden, and the tree of the knowledge of good and evil.

10 Now a river went out of Eden to water the garden, and from there it parted and became four riverheads.

11 The name of the first *is* Pishon; it *is* the one which skirts the whole land of Havilah, where *there is* gold.

12 And the gold of that land *is* good. Bdellium and the onyx stone *are* there.

13 The name of the second river *is* Gihon; it *is* the one which goes around the whole land of Cush.

14 The name of the third river *is* [h]Hiddekel; it *is* the one which goes toward the east of Assyria. The fourth river *is* the Euphrates.

First, or Edenic Covenant (v. 16, note): test of obedience. Cp. Gen. 1:28

15 Then the LORD God took the [i]man and put him in the garden of Eden to tend and keep it.

16 And the LORD God [2j]commanded the [3]man, saying, "Of every tree of the garden you may freely eat;

4
a Deity (names of): vv. 4ff; Gen. 14:18. (Gen. 1:1; Mal. 3:18)

5
b Gen. 7:4; Job 5:10
c Gen. 3:23

7
d Mt. 19:4; Mk. 10:6; 1 Cor. 15:45
e v. 19; Gen. 3:19

8
f Lit. *delight*

9
g Gen. 3:22, 24

14
h Ancient name of the Tigris

15
i Heb. *'adam*

16
j Eight Covenants: vv. 15–17 (cp. 1:26–28); Gen. 3:15. (Gen. 2:16; Heb. 8:8)

---

been formed, as stated in v. 7, is unnecessary. In both cases (the "planting" of the garden and the "forming" of the animals) the Hebrew verb could be more correctly translated by the English "had planted" and "had formed."

[1](2:4) For the use of "LORD God" instead of "God," see *note* on "God" at v. 3, and references.

[2](2:16) A covenant is a sovereign pronouncement of God by which He establishes a relationship of responsibility (1) between Himself and an individual (e.g. Adam in the Edenic Covenant, Gen. 2:16ff.), (2) between Himself and mankind in general (e.g. in the promise of the Noahic Covenant never again to destroy all flesh with a flood, Gen. 9:9ff.), (3) between Himself and a nation (e.g. Israel in the Mosaic Covenant, Ex. 19:3ff.), or (4) between Himself and a specific human family (e.g. the house of David in the promise of a kingly line in perpetuity through the Davidic Covenant, 2 Sam. 7:16ff.). A covenant of one category may overlap others; e.g. the Davidic Covenant, where a continuing kingly house is promised with ultimate blessing, not only to David but also to the whole world in the reign of Jesus Christ.

The covenants are normally unconditional in the sense that God obligates Himself in grace, by the unrestricted declaration, "I will," to accomplish certain announced purposes, despite any failure on the part of the person or people with whom He covenants. The human response to the divinely announced purpose is always important, leading as it does to blessing for obedience and discipline for disobedience. But human failure is never permitted to abrogate the covenant or block its ultimate fulfillment.

In the case of the Mosaic Covenant, the fulfillment of all the promises was made conditional upon Israel's obedience, as implied by the words, ". . . *if you will indeed obey* . . . then . . . you shall be . . ." followed by "All the people answered together . . . 'All that the LORD has spoken we will do' " (Ex. 19:5,8).

The three universal and general covenants are: the Adamic, the Noahic, and also the Edenic in that the whole race is represented as present in Adam in his failure. All the other covenants are made with Israel or Israelites and apply primarily to them, although with ultimate blessing to the whole world. See next *note*.

[3](2:16) There are eight major covenants of special significance in explaining the outworking of God's purposes with man. They are: the Edenic (Gen. 2:16); the Adamic (Gen. 3:15); the Noahic (Gen. 9:16); the Abrahamic (Gen. 12:2); the Mosaic (Ex. 19:5); the Palestinian (Dt. 30:3); the Davidic (2 Sam. 7:16); and the New Covenant (Heb. 8:8). See *notes* at the above Scriptures.

The first or Edenic Covenant required the following responsibilities of Adam: (1) to propagate the race; (2) to subdue the earth for man; (3) to have dominion over the animal creation; (4) to care for the garden and eat its fruits and herbs; and (5) to abstain from eating of one tree, the tree of the knowledge of good and evil, on penalty of death for disobedience.

17 "but of the [1]tree of the knowledge of good and evil you shall not eat, [a]for in the day that you eat of it you shall surely [b]die."

God creates a wife for Adam (cp. 1:27)

18 And the LORD God said, "*It is* not good that man should be alone; I will make him a [c]helper comparable to him."

19 Out of the ground the LORD God formed every beast of the field and every bird of the air, and brought *them* to Adam to see what he would call them. And whatever Adam called each living creature, that *was* its name.

20 So Adam gave names to all cattle, to the birds of the air, and to every beast of the field. But for Adam there was not found a helper comparable to him.

21 And the LORD God caused a deep sleep to fall on Adam, and he slept; and He took one of his ribs, and closed up the flesh in its place.

22 Then the rib which the LORD God had taken from man He made into a woman, and He brought her to the man.

God institutes marriage

23 And Adam said:

[2]"This *is* now [d]bone of my bones
And flesh of my flesh;
She shall be called [3e]Woman,
Because she was taken out of
Man."

24 Therefore a man shall leave his father and mother and [f]be joined to his wife, and they shall become one flesh.

25 And they were both naked, the man and his wife, and were not ashamed.

II. The Fall and the Promise of Redemption, 3:1—4:7

The temptation and fall

3 NOW the [4g]serpent was more cunning than any beast of the field which the LORD God had made.

17
a Cp. Rom. 5:12; 1 Cor. 15:21–22
b *Death* (spiritual): v. 17; 3:3; Mt. 8:22. (Gen. 2:17; Eph. 2:5, *note*). *Death* (physical): v. 17; Gen. 3:19. (Gen. 2:17; Heb. 9:27, *note*)

18
c 1 Cor. 11:8–9

23
d Gen. 29:14
e Heb. *Ishshah*, because she was taken out of the man *(Ish)* (Hos. 2:16)

24
f i.e. *hold fast* or *cling*. Mt. 19:5; Mk. 10:7–8; 1 Cor. 6:16; Eph. 5:31

3:1 *g* *Satan*: vv. 1–2,4, 13–14; 1 Chr. 21:1. (Gen. 3:1; Rev. 20:10)

---

[1](2:17) Apart from the seven references to trees in general in the first three chapters of Genesis, frequently called fruit trees (1:11,12,29; 3:2,3; etc.), two particular trees are assigned great importance in this narrative:

(1) "The tree of the knowledge of good and evil" (2:9), said to be "in the midst of the garden" (3:3), was good for food as well as pleasant to the eyes (3:6), the fruit of which God forbade Adam and Eve to eat on the pain of death (2:17; 3:11,17). The tree was real, not mythical (cp. The Pentateuch, p. xxvi); it was not, however, any magical or psychological effect of eating the fruit that brought upon man moral disaster and death, but rather his disobedience to God.

(2) Of the "tree of life" (2:9) there are no details except that it was also "in the midst of the garden." The tree acquires significance because of the words in 3:22, that Adam must be expelled from the garden lest he "put out his hand and take also of the tree of life, and eat, and live forever." Adam and Eve were already in a state of sinfulness and in them, because of sin, the seeds of death were planted. There was, evidently, some virtue in the fruit of this tree which would prolong physical life indefinitely. It would have been tragic for men to live endlessly in a state of sin and approaching death. True life is now made available to all mankind, however, through Christ's death upon another tree (Acts 5:30; 10:39; 1 Pet. 2:24). This tree of life obtains an even richer meaning for the redeemed, according to Rev. 2:7; 22:2, in an eternal paradise prepared by God for sinners saved by His grace.

[2](2:23) A type (e.g. see next *note*) is a divinely purposed illustration of some truth. It may be: (1) a person (Rom. 5:14); (2) an event (1 Cor. 10:11); (3) a thing (Heb. 10:19–20); (4) an institution (Heb. 9:11–12); or (5) a ceremonial (1 Cor. 5:7). Types occur most frequently in the Pentateuch, but are found, more sparingly, elsewhere. The antitype, or fulfillment of the type, is found generally in the NT.

Two warnings are necessary: (1) nothing may be insisted upon as a type without explicit NT authority; and (2) all types not so authenticated must be recognized as having only the authority of analogy, of spiritual congruity.

[3](2:23) The woman is a type of the Church, the bride of Christ (Eph. 5:25–32; 2 Cor. 11:2–3; cp. Jn. 3:28–29; Rev. 19:7–8).

[4](3:1) The serpent, in his Edenic form, is not to be thought of as a writhing reptile. That is the effect of the curse (Gen. 3:14). The creature which lent itself to Satan may well have been the most beautiful as it was the most "cunning" of creatures less than man. Traces of that beauty remain despite the curse. Every movement of a serpent is graceful, and many species are beautifully colored. In the serpent, Satan appeared as "an angel of light" (2 Cor. 11:14). Satan is called "serpent" in Rev. 12:9,14,15; 20:2. For the record of the fall of Satan, see Isa. 14:12–14, and read carefully *note* at v. 12.

And he said to the woman, [a]"Has God
indeed said, 'You shall not eat of every
tree of the garden'?"
2 And the woman said to the serpent, "We may eat the fruit of the trees
of the garden;
3 "but of the fruit of the tree which
is in the midst of the garden, God has
said, 'You shall not eat it, [b]nor shall
you [c]touch it, lest you die.' "
4 Then the serpent said to the
woman, "You will not surely die.
5 "For God knows that in the day
you eat of it your eyes will be opened,
and you will be like God, knowing
good and evil."
6 So when the [d]woman saw that
the tree *was* good for food, that it *was*
pleasant to the eyes, and a tree desirable to make *one* wise, she took of its
fruit and [1]ate. She also gave to her
husband with her, and he ate.

Second Dispensation: Conscience
(Moral Responsibility) (Gen. 4:1—8:14)

7 Then the eyes of both of them
were opened, and they [2]knew that
they *were* naked; and they sewed fig
leaves together and made themselves
coverings.

The divine interrogation

8 And they heard the sound of the
LORD God walking in the garden in the
cool of the day, and Adam and his wife
[e]hid themselves from the presence of
the LORD God among the trees of the
garden.
9 Then the LORD God called to
Adam and said to him, "Where *are*
you?"
10 So he said, "I heard Your voice
in the garden, and I was [f]afraid because I was naked; and I hid myself."
11 And He said, "Who told you that
you *were* naked? Have you eaten from
the tree of which I commanded you
that you should not eat?"
12 Then the man said, "The woman
whom You gave *to be* with me, she
gave me of the tree, and I ate."
13 And the LORD God said to the
woman, "What *is* this you have done?"
The woman said, "The serpent [g]de-
ceived me, and I ate."

Second, or Adamic Covenant
(v. 15, note)

14 So the LORD God said to the serpent:

"Because you have done this,
You *are* cursed more than all
cattle,
And more than every beast of
the field;
On your belly you shall go,
And you shall eat [h]dust
All the days of your life.

CHAPTER 3

1
a Test/tempt: vv. 1–6, 12–13; Gen. 22:1. (Gen. 3:1; Jas. 1:14, *note*)

3
b Cp. Gen. 2:17
c Cp. Ex. 19:12,13

6
d 1 Tim. 2:14

8
e Job 31:33

10
f Ex. 3:6; Dt. 9:19

13
g 2 Cor. 11:3

14
h Isa. 65:25

[1](3:6) The tragic consequence of the temptation and fall was nothing less than the universal sinfulness of all humanity. The Holy Spirit's commentary in the NT clearly states that the woman was deceived, whereas the man was not deceived; but both transgressed (1 Tim. 2:14). Satan's assault was threefold (cp. Mt. 4:1–11; 1 Jn. 2:16). The temptation was initiated by Satan's introducing doubt and denial of God's Word (Gen. 3:1–5; Jn. 8:44). The fall brought a consciousness of sin, of condemnation, and of separation from God, as indicated by the fact that Adam and Eve "hid themselves from the presence of the LORD God" (Gen. 3:8; see also vv. 9–13). Man's nature became evil and inimical to God (Rom. 5:19; 8:7–8). This state of spiritual death issued in eventual physical death, both being implied in Gen. 2:17 (cp. Rom. 5:12–14, where see *notes*). See also Gen. 3:15, *note 1*.

[2](3:7) *The Second Dispensation: Conscience (Moral Responsibility)*. Man had now sinned (3:6–7), the first promise of redemption was to be given (3:15), and our first parents were to be expelled from Eden (3:22–24). Man's sin was a rebellion against a specific command of God (2:16–17) and marked a transition from theoretical to experiential knowledge of good and evil (3:5–7,22). Man sinned by entering the realm of moral experience by the wrong door when he could have entered by doing right. So man became as God through a personal experience of the difference between good and evil, but also unlike God in gaining this experience by choosing the wrong instead of the right. Thus he was placed by God under the stewardship of moral responsibility whereby he was accountable to do all known good, to abstain from all known evil, and to approach God through blood sacrifice here instituted in prospect of the finished work of Christ. The result is set forth in the Adamic Covenant (Gen. 3:14–21, see v. 15, *note*). Man failed the test presented to him in this dispensation (witness Gen. 6:5), as in others. Although, as the specific test, this time-era ended with the flood, man continued in his moral responsibility as God added further revelation concerning Himself and His will in succeeding ages (e.g. Acts 24:14–16; Rom. 2:15; 2 Cor. 4:2).

For *notes* on the other dispensations, see: Innocence (Gen. 1:28); Human Government (Gen. 8:15); Promise (Gen. 12:1); Law (Ex. 19:1); Church (Acts 2:1); Kingdom (Rev. 20:4); also Gen. 1:28 and 11:10, *notes*.

15 [1][a]And I will put [2]enmity
Between you and the woman,
And between [b]your seed and [c]her Seed;
He shall bruise your head,
And [3]you shall [d]bruise His [e]heel."

16 To the woman He said:
"I will greatly multiply your sorrow and your conception;
In pain you shall bring forth children;
Your desire *shall be* for your husband,
And he shall [f]rule over you."

17 Then to Adam He said, "Because you have heeded the voice of your wife, and have eaten from the tree of which I commanded you, saying, 'You shall not eat of it':

"Cursed *is* the ground for your sake;
In toil you shall eat *of it*
All the days of your life.
18 Both thorns and thistles it shall bring forth for you,
And you shall eat the herb of the field.
19 In the sweat of your face you shall eat bread
Till you return to the ground,
For out of it you were taken;
For dust you *are*,
And to [g]dust you shall return."

Adam's faith; God's provision of sacrifice

20 And Adam [h]called his wife's name [i]Eve, because she was the mother of all living.

21 Also for Adam and his wife the LORD God made [4]tunics of skin, and [j]clothed them.

15
a Eight Covenants: vv. 14–20; Gen. 9:16. (Gen. 2:16; Heb. 8:8)
b Cp. Mt. 3:7
c Isa. 7:14; Mt. 1:18,25
d Sacrifice (prophetic): v. 15; Gen. 4:4. (Gen. 3:15; Heb. 10:18, *note*)
e Christ (first advent): v. 15; Gen. 12:3. (Gen. 3:15; Acts 1:11, *note*)

16
f 1 Cor. 11:3; Eph. 5:22; Ti. 2:5; 1 Pet. 3:1

3:19 *g Death* (physical): v. 19; Gen. 5:5. (Gen. 2:17; Heb. 9:27, *note*) 3:20 *h Faith:* v. 20; Gen. 4:4. (Gen. 3:20; Heb. 11:39, *note*) *i* Lit. *lifegiver*
3:21 *j Righteousness* (garment): v. 21; Job 29:14. (Gen. 3:21; Rev. 19:8)

[1](3:15) The Adamic Covenant conditions the life of fallen man—conditions which must remain till, in the kingdom age, "the creation itself also will be delivered from the bondage of corruption into the glorious liberty of the children of God" (Rom. 8:21). The elements of the covenant are:

(1) The serpent, Satan's tool, is cursed (v. 14; Rom. 16:20; 2 Cor. 11:3,14; Rev. 12:9) and becomes God's graphic warning in nature of the effects of sin—from the most beautiful and subtle of creatures to a loathsome reptile. The deepest mystery of the cross of Christ is strikingly pictured by the bronze serpent, a type of Christ "made . . . to be sin for us" in bearing the judgment we deserved (Num. 21:5–9; Jn. 3:14–15; 2 Cor. 5:21).

(2) The first promise of a Redeemer (v. 15). Here begins the "highway of the Seed": Abel, Seth, Noah (Gen. 6:8–10), Shem (Gen. 9:26–27), Abraham (Gen. 12:1–4), Isaac (Gen. 17:19–21), Jacob (Gen. 28:10–14), Judah (Gen. 49:10), David (2 Sam. 7:5–17), Immanuel-Christ (Isa. 7:10–14; Mt. 1:1,20–23; Jn. 12:31–33; 1 Jn. 3:8).

(3) The changed state of the woman (v. 16), in three particulars: (a) multiplied conception; (b) pain in motherhood; (c) the headship of the man (cp. Gen. 1:26–27). Sin's disorder makes necessary a headship; it is vested in man (Eph. 5:22–25; 1 Cor. 11:7–9; 1 Tim. 2:11–14).

(4) The light occupation of Eden (Gen. 2:15) changed to burdensome labor (3:18–19), because of the earth's being cursed (3:17).

(5) The inevitable sorrow of life (v. 17).

(6) The brevity of life and the tragic certainty of physical death to Adam and all his descendants (v. 19; Rom. 5:12–21). See also Death (spiritual), Gen. 2:17; Eph. 2:5; and *notes*. Nevertheless, the curse upon the ground is for man's sake. It is not good for man to live without toil.

For *notes* on other major covenants, see: Edenic (Gen. 2:16); Noahic (Gen. 9:16); Abrahamic (Gen. 12:2); Mosaic (Ex. 19:5); Palestinian (Dt. 30:3); Davidic (2 Sam. 7:16); New (Heb. 8:8). Follow also the chain references on this subject. See *a* in center margin.

[2](3:15) As the English word "enmity" comes from the same root as "enemy," so also the Greek word used in the Septuagint at this verse, and the Greek word in the NT commonly rendered "enemy," derive from the same root. Our Lord specifically designates Satan as the "enemy" (Mt. 13:25,28, cp. v. 39; probably also Lk. 10:19). All men outside of Christ are enemies of God (Rom. 5:10; Col. 1:21; Jas. 4:4); the carnal mind is at enmity with God (Rom. 8:7). This enmity, which is particularly manifested in those who are "enemies of the cross of Christ" (Phil. 3:18), will develop in great intensity in the end times (Rev. 12:13–17).

[3](3:15) The chain of references which begins here includes the promises and prophecies concerning Christ which were fulfilled in His birth and works at His first advent. See, for line of unfulfilled promises and prophecies: Christ (second advent) (Dt. 30:3 to Acts 1:11); Kingdom (OT) (Gen. 1:26–28 to Zech. 12:6–8); Kingdom (NT) (Lk. 1:31–33 to 1 Cor. 15:24–28); Day of the LORD (Isa. 2:10–22 to Rev. 19:11–21).

[4](3:21) Tunics of skin: a type of Christ, who became for us righteousness (1 Cor. 1:30)—a

Expulsion from Eden

22 Then the LORD God said, "Behold, the man has become like one of Us, to know good and evil. And now, lest he put out his hand and take also of the tree of life, and eat, and live forever"—

23 therefore the LORD God sent him out of the garden of Eden to till the ground from which he was taken.

24 So He drove out the man; and He placed [a]cherubim at the east of the garden of Eden, and a flaming sword which turned every way, to guard the way to the tree of life.

Birth of Cain and Abel

4 NOW Adam knew Eve his wife, and she conceived and bore [1]Cain, and said, "I have acquired a man from the LORD."

2 Then she bore again, this time his brother [2]Abel. Now Abel was a keeper of sheep, but Cain was a tiller of the ground.

3 And in the process of time it came to pass that Cain brought an offering of the fruit of the ground to the LORD.

4 Abel also [b]brought of the [3]firstborn of his flock and of their fat. And the LORD [c]respected Abel and his [d]offering,

5 but He did not respect Cain and his offering. And Cain was very angry, and his countenance fell.

24
a Cp. Ezek. 1:5, *note*

CHAPTER 4

4
b Faith: v. 4; Gen. 5:22. (Gen. 3:20; Heb. 11:39, *note*)
c Heb. 11:4
d Sacrifice (typical): v. 4; Gen. 8:20. (Gen. 3:15; Heb. 10:18, *note*)

8
e Mt. 23:35; Lk. 11:51; 1 Jn. 3:12

9
f 1 Cor. 8:11–13

Cain exhorted even yet to bring a sin offering

6 So the LORD said to Cain, "Why are you angry? And why has your countenance fallen?

7 "If you do well, will you not be accepted? And if you do not do well, [4]sin lies at the door. And its desire *is* for you, but you should rule over it."

III. The Diverse Seeds, Cain and Seth, to the Flood, 4:8—7:24

First murder: history of Cain (cp. Gen. 4:23)

8 Now Cain talked with Abel his brother;* and it came to pass, when they were in the field, that Cain rose up against Abel his brother and [e]killed him.

9 Then the LORD said to Cain, "Where *is* Abel your brother?" He said, "I do not know. *Am* I [f]my brother's keeper?"

10 And He said, "What have you done? The voice of your brother's blood cries out to Me from the ground.

11 "So now you *are* cursed from the earth, which has opened its mouth to receive your brother's blood from your hand.

12 "When you till the ground, it shall no longer yield its strength to you. A fugitive and a vagabond you shall be on the earth."

*
4:8 Samaritan Pentateuch, Septuagint, Syriac, and Vulgate add *"Let us go out to the field."*

divinely provided garment that the first sinners might be made fit for God's presence. See Righteousness, garment (Rev. 19:8).

[1](4:1) Cain is a type of the mere man of the earth. His religion was destitute of any adequate sense of sin or need of atonement. This religious type is described in 2 Pet. 2. Seven things are said of him: he (1) worships in self-will; (2) is angry with God; (3) refuses to bring a sin offering; (4) murders his brother; (5) lies to God; (6) becomes a wanderer; and (7) is, nevertheless, the object of the divine solicitude.

[2](4:2) Abel *(exhalation* or *that which ascends)* is a type of the spiritual man. His sacrifice, in which atoning blood was shed (Heb. 9:22), was therefore at once his confession of sin and the expression of his faith in the interposition of a substitute (Heb. 11:4).

[3](4:4) Type of Christ the Lamb of God, the most constant type of the suffering Messiah,"the Lamb of God who takes away the sin of the world" (Jn. 1:29). A lamb fitly symbolizes the unresisting innocence and harmlessness of the Lord Jesus (Isa. 53:7; Mt. 26:52–54; Lk. 23:9). This type is brought into prominence by contrast with Cain's bloodless offering of the fruit of the ground and proclaims, in the very infancy of the race, the primal truth that "without shedding of blood there is no remission" (Heb. 9:22; 11:4). Cain acknowledged God as the source of all natural good but rejected His revealed way of worship; Abel, in conformity with that revelation, brought a blood offering, thus confessing himself a sinner. In Cain began all false religion, the essence of which is man's coming to God in his own way.

[4](4:7) Or, "sin offering." In Hebrew the same word is used for "sin" and "sin offering," thus emphasizing in a remarkable way the complete identification of the believer's sin with his sin offering (cp. Jn. 3:14 with 2 Cor. 5:21). Here both meanings are brought together. "Sin lies at the door," but so also "a sin offering lies at [your tent] door." It is "where sin abounded" that "grace abounded much more" (Rom. 5:20). Abel's offering implies a previous instruction (cp. Gen. 3:21), for it was "by faith" (Heb. 11:4), and faith is taking God at His word; so that Cain's unbloody offering was a refusal of the divine way. But the LORD made a last appeal to Cain even yet to bring the required offering (Gen. 4:7).

13 And Cain said to the LORD, "My
punishment *is* greater than I can bear!
14 "Surely You have driven me out
this day from the face of the ground;
I shall be hidden from Your face; I
shall be a fugitive and a vagabond on
the earth, and it will happen *that* anyone who finds me will kill me."
15 And the LORD said to him,
"Therefore,* whoever kills Cain, vengeance shall be taken on him sevenfold." And the LORD set a [a]mark on
Cain, lest anyone finding him should
kill him.

Cainite civilization

16 Then Cain went out from the
[b]presence of the LORD and dwelt in the
land of [c]Nod on the east of Eden.
17 And Cain knew his wife, and she
conceived and bore Enoch. And he
[1]built a city, and [d]called the name of
the city after the name of his son—
Enoch.
18 To Enoch was born Irad; and
Irad begot Mehujael, and Mehujael
begot Methushael, and Methushael
begot Lamech.
19 Then Lamech took for himself
two wives: the name of one *was* Adah,
and the name of the second *was* Zillah.
20 And Adah bore Jabal. He was
the father of those who dwell in tents
and have livestock.
21 His brother's name *was* Jubal.
He was the father of all those who play
the harp and flute.
22 And as for Zillah, she also bore
Tubal-Cain, [e]an instructor of every
craftsman in bronze and iron. And the
sister of Tubal-Cain *was* Naamah.
23 Then Lamech said to his wives:

"Adah and Zillah, hear my
voice;
Wives of Lamech, listen to my
speech!
For I have killed a man for
wounding me,
Even a young man for hurting
me.
24 If Cain shall be avenged
sevenfold,
Then Lamech
seventy-sevenfold."

Birth of Seth

25 And Adam knew his wife again,
and she bore a son and named him
[f]Seth, "For God has appointed another seed for me instead of Abel,
whom Cain killed."
26 And as for Seth, to him also a
son was born; and he named him
[g]Enosh. Then *men* began to call on
the name of the LORD.

Reign of death (Rom. 5:12)

5 THIS is the book of the [h]geneal-
ogy of [2]Adam. In the day that God
created man, He made him [i]in the
likeness of God.
2 He created them [j]male and female, and [k]blessed them and called
them Mankind in the day they were
created.
3 And Adam lived one hundred
and thirty [3]years, and begot *a son* in
his [l]own likeness, after his image,
and named him [m]Seth.
4 [n]After he begot Seth, the days of
Adam were eight hundred years; and
he had sons and daughters.
5 So all the days that Adam lived
were nine hundred and thirty years;
and he [o]died.

Seth's family

6 Seth lived one hundred and five
years, and begot [p]Enosh.
7 After he begot Enosh, Seth lived
eight hundred and seven years, and
had sons and daughters.
8 So all the days of Seth were nine
hundred and twelve years; and he
died.

15
a i.e. *for Cain's protection.* The law of Gen. 9:6 was not yet enacted. Cp. Ex. 12:23
16
b Jon. 1:3
c Lit. *wandering*
17
d Ps. 49:11
22
e Lit. *the forger of all instruments of bronze and iron*
25
f Heb. *Sheth,* meaning *appointed*
26
g Lit. *mortal*
CHAPTER 5
1
h Gen. 2:4; 6:9
i Gen. 1:27
2
j Mk. 10:6
k Gen. 1:28; 9:1
3
l v. 1
m Gen. 4:25
4
n vv. 4–32; cp. 1 Chr. 1:1–4; Lk. 3:36–38
5
o *Death* (physical): v. 5; Gen. 6:17. (Gen. 2:17; Heb. 9:27, *note*)
6
p Gen. 4:26

*4:15 Following Masoretic Text and Targum; Septuagint, Syriac, and Vulgate read *Not so.*

[1](4:17) This early civilization, which perished in the judgment of the flood, was Cainitic in origin, character, and destiny. Many elements of material civilization are mentioned in vv. 16–22—city and pastoral life, and the development of arts and manufactures. But they deliberately excluded God from their thoughts (Rom. 1:18–23). Observe the boastful speech of Lamech (vv. 23–24). The Cainitic civilization may have been as splendid as that of Greece or Rome, but the divine judgment is according to the moral state, not the material (Gen. 6:5–7). No traces of this advanced civilization have yet been found, nor is the geographic location known. Some day evidences may be uncovered by the archaeologist's spade.

[2](5:1) Adam, as the natural head of the race (Lk. 3:38) is a contrasting type of Christ, the Head of the new creation. Cp. Rom. 5:14; 1 Cor. 15:21–22,45–47.

[3](5:3) Scripture does not reveal the date of Adam's creation. For the relation of the early genealogies to this and similar questions, see Gen. 11:10, *note.*

9 Enosh lived ninety years, and begot Cainan.*

10 After he begot Cainan, Enosh lived eight hundred and fifteen years, and had sons and daughters.

11 So all the days of Enosh were nine hundred and five years; and he died.

12 Cainan lived seventy years, and begot Mahalalel.

13 After he begot Mahalalel, Cainan lived eight hundred and forty years, and had sons and daughters.

14 So all the days of Cainan were nine hundred and ten years; and he died.

15 Mahalalel lived sixty-five years, and begot Jared.

16 After he begot Jared, Mahalalel lived eight hundred and thirty years, and had sons and daughters.

17 So all the days of Mahalalel were eight hundred and ninety-five years; and he died.

18 Jared lived one hundred and sixty-two years, and begot Enoch.

19 After he begot Enoch, Jared lived eight hundred years, and had sons and daughters.

20 So all the days of Jared were nine hundred and sixty-two years; and he died.

21 Enoch lived sixty-five years, and begot Methuselah.

22 After he begot Methuselah, [1]Enoch [a]walked with God three hundred years, and had sons and daughters.

23 So all the days of Enoch were three hundred and sixty-five years.

24 And Enoch walked with God; and he *was* not, for God [b]took him.

25 Methuselah lived one hundred and eighty-seven years, and begot Lamech.

26 After he begot Lamech, Methuselah lived seven hundred and eighty-two years, and had sons and daughters.

27 So all the days of Methuselah were nine hundred and sixty-nine years; and he died.

28 Lamech lived one hundred and eighty-two years, and had a son.

29 And he called his name Noah, saying, "This *one* will comfort us concerning our work and the toil of our hands, because of the ground which the LORD has cursed."

30 After he begot Noah, Lamech lived five hundred and ninety-five years, and had sons and daughters.

31 So all the days of Lamech were seven hundred and seventy-seven years; and he died.

32 And Noah was five hundred years old, and Noah begot Shem, Ham, and Japheth.

The flood (Gen. 6:1—8:14):
(1) continuation of the race

6 NOW it came to pass, when men began to multiply on the face of the earth, and daughters were born to them,

2 that the sons of God saw the daughters of men, that they *were* beautiful; and they took wives for themselves of all whom they chose.

(2) Warning of the LORD

3 And the LORD said, "My [c]Spirit shall not [d]strive* with man forever, for he *is* indeed flesh; yet his days shall be one hundred and twenty years."

(3) Antediluvian civilization
(see Lk. 17:27)

4 There were giants on the earth in those [e]days, and also afterward, when the [2]sons of God came in to the daughters of men and they bore *chil-*

22
a Faith: vv. 22–24; Gen. 6:22. (Gen. 3:20; Heb. 11:39, *note*)

24
b Miracles (OT): v. 24; Gen. 7:11. (Gen. 5:24; Jon. 1:17, *note*)

CHAPTER 6

3
c Holy Spirit (OT): v. 3; Gen. 41:38. (Gen. 1:2; Zech. 12:10). Cp. 1 Pet. 3:19–20
d 2 Th. 2:7

4
e Cp. Num. 13:32–33

*5:9 Hebrew *Qenan* 6:3 Septuagint, Syriac, Targum, and Vulgate read *abide.*

[1](5:22) Enoch, "taken away so that he did not see death" (Heb. 11:5) before the judgment of the flood, is a type of those saints who are to be translated before the apocalyptic judgments (1 Th. 4:14–17).

[2](6:4) Some hold that the "sons of God" were fallen angels "who did not keep their proper domain" (Jude 6–7, cp. "as Sodom and Gomorrah"; 2 Pet. 2:4–9). Accordingly, this intrusion into the human sphere produced a race of wicked giants (Gen. 6:4–6). Others hold that since angels are spoken of in a sexless way (cp. Mt. 22:30), and because the words "took wives" signify a lasting marriage, the reference has to do with the breakdown of the separation of the godly line of Seth by intermarriage with the godless line of Cain. A refinement of the latter view holds that the expression "sons of God" refers to all the godly, and "daughters of men" to all the ungodly, irrespective of their natural paternity. Whichever view is held, it is obvious that Satan attempted so to corrupt the race that the Messiah could not come to redeem man. But God salvaged a remnant (Gen. 6:8ff.), and a godly line was preserved. However, there is no remedy for rebellion against God; the judgment predicted by Noah's ancestor fell (Jude 14–15; cp. Gen. 7:11; Isa. 1:2–7,24–25).

dren to them. Those *were* the mighty
men who *were* of old, men of renown.

(4) Purpose of the LORD *in judgment*

5 Then the LORD* saw that the
wickedness of man *was* great in the
earth, and *that* every [a]intent of the
thoughts of his heart *was* only evil
continually.
6 And the LORD [b]was sorry that He
had made man on the earth, and He
[c]was grieved in His heart.
7 So the LORD said, "I will [d]destroy
man whom I have created from the
face of the earth, both man and beast,
creeping thing and birds of the air, for
I am sorry that I have made them."

(5) Purpose of the LORD *in grace*

8 But Noah found grace in the
eyes of the LORD.
9 This is the genealogy of Noah.
Noah was a [e]just man, [f]perfect in his
generations. Noah [1]walked with God.
10 And Noah begot three sons:
Shem, Ham, and Japheth.
11 The earth also was corrupt before God, and the earth was [g]filled
with violence.
12 So God looked upon the earth,
and indeed it was corrupt; for all flesh
had corrupted their way on the earth.
13 And God said to Noah, "The end
of all flesh has come before Me, for the
earth is filled with violence through
them; and behold, I will destroy them
with the earth.
14 "Make yourself an [2]ark of
gopherwood; make rooms in the ark,
and cover it inside and outside with
pitch.
15 "And this is how you shall make
it: The length of the ark *shall be* three
hundred [h]cubits, its width fifty cubits,
and its height [3]thirty cubits.

5
a Lit. *the whole imagination,* i.e. *including purposes and desires.* Cp. Gen. 8:21

6
b Zech. 8:14, *note*
c Cp. Ps. 78:40; Eph. 4:30

7
d Gen. 7:4, 23

9
e Righteousness (OT): v. 9; 7:1; Gen. 15:6. (Gen. 6:9; Lk. 2:25, *note*)
f Lit. *upright,* or *sincere*

11
g Ezek. 8:17

15
h See Weights and Measures (OT), 2 Chr. 2:10, *note*

16
i An opening one cubit high, perhaps running round the ark

17
j Death (physical): v. 17; Mk. 5:39. (Gen. 2:17; Heb. 9:27, *note*)

16 "You shall make a [i]window for
the ark, and you shall finish it to a
cubit from above; and set the door of
the ark in its side. You shall make it
with lower, second, and third *decks.*
17 "And behold, I Myself am bringing floodwaters on the earth, to destroy from under heaven all flesh in
which *is* the breath of life; everything
that *is* on the earth shall [j]die.
18 "But I will establish My [k]cov-
enant with you; and you shall go into
the ark—you, your sons, your wife,
and your sons' wives with you.
19 "And of every living thing of all
flesh you shall bring [4]two of every *sort*
into the ark, to keep *them* alive with
you; they shall be male and female.
20 "Of the birds after their kind, of
animals after their kind, and of every
creeping thing of the earth after its
kind, two of every *kind* will come to
you to keep *them* alive.
21 "And you shall take for yourself
of all food that is eaten, and you shall
gather *it* to yourself; and it shall be
food for you and for them."
22 Thus Noah [l]did; according to all
that God commanded him, so he did.

(6) Judgment of the flood

7 THEN the LORD said to Noah,
[5]"Come into the ark, you and all
your household, because I have seen
that you *are* [e]righteous before Me in
this generation.
2 "You shall take with you seven
each of every clean animal, a male
and his female; two each of animals

6:18 *k* Gen. 8:20–9:17 **6:22** *l Faith:* v. 22; Gen. 12:5. (Gen. 3:20; Heb. 11:39, *note*)

*
6:5 Following Masoretic Text and Targum; Vulgate reads *God;* Septuagint reads *LORD God*

[1](6:9) Noah and Enoch are the two antediluvians of whom it is said that they "walked with God" (Gen. 5:24).

[2](6:14) Ark: a type of Christ as the refuge of His people from judgment (Heb. 11:7).

[3](6:15) The dimensions of the ark are themselves an evidence of the accuracy of the Scriptures. On the basis of a cubit as 18 inches, the ark was 450 ft. long with a beam of 75 ft. and a depth of 45 ft. Similar to the proportions of a modern ocean liner, these dimensions are in marked contrast with descriptions of the ark found in ancient mythology. Compare the cuneiform representation of it as shaped like a six-storied cube of 262 ft. with a mast and pilot on top; or the Greek legend, according to Berosus, that it was 3000 ft. long and 1200 ft. wide.

[4](6:19) Compare Gen. 7:2. In addition to two animals, etc., commanded here to be preserved for future increase ("male and female"), the further command was given to take of clean animals, i.e., animals acceptable for sacrifice, seven each. Exodus gives ten such animals, or but seventy in all. Modern ships carry hundreds of live animals, with their food, besides scores of human beings.

[5](7:1) Here God's beckoning embraces the basic meanings of this gracious invitation occurring again and again in the Scriptures, even down to the last page (Rev. 22:17). This invitation (1) is extended by God to man; (2) urges him to avail himself of the perfect provision God has made for his preservation; and (3) is given in a time of overwhelming judgment and doom.

that *are* [a]unclean, a male and his female;

3 "also seven each of birds of the air, male and female, to keep the species alive on the face of all the earth.

4 "For after seven more days I will cause it to rain on the earth forty days and forty nights, and I will destroy from the face of the earth all living things that I have made."

5 And [b]Noah did according to all that the LORD commanded him.

6 Noah *was* six hundred years old when the floodwaters were on the earth.

7 So [c]Noah, with his sons, his wife, and his sons' wives, [d]went into the ark because of the waters of the flood.

8 Of clean animals, of animals that *are* unclean, of birds, and of everything that creeps on the earth,

9 two by two they went into the ark to Noah, male and female, as God had commanded Noah.

10 And it came to pass after seven days that the waters of the [1]flood were on the earth.

11 In the six hundredth year of Noah's life, in the second month, the seventeenth day of the month, on [e]that day all the fountains of the [f]great deep were [g]broken up, and the [h]windows of heaven were opened.

12 And the rain was on the earth forty days and forty nights.

13 On the very same day Noah and Noah's sons, Shem, Ham, and Japheth, and Noah's wife and the three wives of his sons with them, entered the ark—

14 they and every beast after its kind, all cattle after their kind, every creeping thing that creeps on the earth after its kind, and every bird after its kind, every bird of every sort.

15 And they went into the ark to Noah, two by two, of all flesh in which *is* the breath of life.

16 So those that entered, male and female of all flesh, went in as God had commanded him; and the LORD shut him in.

17 Now the flood was on the earth forty days. The waters increased and lifted up the ark, and it rose high above the earth.

18 The waters prevailed and greatly increased on the earth, and the ark moved about on the surface of the waters.

19 And the waters prevailed exceedingly on the earth, and all the high hills under the whole heaven were covered.

20 The waters prevailed fifteen [i]cubits upward, and the mountains were covered.

21 And all flesh [j]died that moved on the earth: birds and cattle and beasts and every creeping thing that creeps on the earth, and every man.

22 All in whose nostrils *was* the breath of the spirit* of life, all that *was* on the dry *land,* died.

23 So He destroyed all living things which were on the face of the ground: both man and cattle, creeping thing and bird of the air. They were destroyed from the earth. Only Noah and those who *were* with him in the ark remained *alive.*

24 And the waters prevailed on the earth one hundred and fifty [2]days.

IV. The Flood to Babel, 8:1—11:9

(7) Flood subsides

8 THEN God [k]remembered Noah, and every living thing, and all the animals that *were* with him in the ark. And God made a wind to pass over the earth, and the waters subsided.

2 The fountains of the deep and the [l]windows of heaven were also [g]stopped, and the rain from heaven was restrained.

3 And the waters receded continually from the earth. At the end of the hundred and fifty days the waters decreased.

4 Then the ark rested in the seventh month, the seventeenth day of the month, on the mountains of [m]Ararat.

5 And the waters decreased continually until the tenth month. In the tenth *month,* on the first *day* of the month, the tops of the mountains were seen.

CHAPTER 7

2
[a] See Gen. 6:19, *note*

5
[b] Gen. 6:22

7
[c] See Gen. 6:9, *note*
[d] Mt. 24:38

11
[e] Mt. 24:39; Lk. 17:27; 2 Pet. 2:5; 3:6
[f] Isa. 51:10
[g] *Miracles* (OT): v. 11; 8:2; Gen. 11:7. (Gen. 5:24; Jon. 1:17, *note*)
[h] Lit. *floodgates*

20
[i] See Weights and Measures (OT), 2 Chr. 2:10, *note*

21
[j] Gen. 7:4

CHAPTER 8

1
[k] Gen. 19:29

2
[l] Lit. *floodgates*

4
[m] The name of a country, Armenia; Isa. 37:38

*7:22 Septuagint and Vulgate omit *of the spirit.*

[1](7:10) The NT refers to the flood under three aspects: (1) our Lord said that, as it was in the days of Noah, so it will be at the end of this age (Mt. 24:37–39; Lk. 17:26–27); (2) Noah himself is used as an illustration of saving faith (Heb. 11:7); and (3) the flood is used as a type of baptism (1 Pet. 3:19–21).

[2](7:24) The number (150) suggests the use of a 30-day month—5 months of 30 days each. Cp. Gen. 7:11 and 8:4; also see 8:14, *note.*

6 So it came to pass, at the end of
forty days, that Noah opened the window of the ark which he had made.
7 Then he sent out a raven, which
kept going to and fro until the waters
had dried up from the earth.
8 He also sent out from himself a
dove, to see if the waters had receded
from the face of the ground.
9 But the dove found no resting
place for the sole of her foot, and she
returned into the ark to him, for the
waters *were* on the face of the whole
earth. So he put out his hand and took
her, and drew her into the ark to himself.
10 And he waited yet another seven
days, and again he sent the dove out
from the ark.
11 Then the dove came to him in the
evening, and behold, a freshly
plucked olive leaf *was* in her mouth;
and Noah knew that the waters had
receded from the earth.
12 So he waited yet another seven
days and sent out the dove, which did
not return again to him anymore.
13 And it came to pass in the six
hundred and first year, in the first
month, the first *day* of the month, that
the waters were dried up from the
earth; and Noah removed the covering of the ark and looked, and indeed
the surface of the ground was dry.
14 And in the second month, on the
twenty-seventh [1]day of the month, the
earth was dried.

Third Dispensation: Human Government (Gen. 8:15—11:32)

15 [2]Then God spoke to Noah, saying,
16 "Go out of the ark, you and your

---

[1](8:14) The flood began in the 600th year, 2nd month, 17th day of Noah's life (7:11). It rained 40 days and nights (7:12); the waters continued to increase (7:18), reaching their highest point on the 150th day (7:24), which figure includes the 40 days of 7:12. The ark rested somewhere in the mountain range known as Ararat (i.e. Armenia, 8:4) on the 7th month, 17th day (i.e. 74 more days). There followed 40 days before Noah sent out the raven (8:6–7), and three periods of 7 days related to the three releasings of the dove (8:8–12, cp. v. 10 "another seven days"). Thus far there were 285 days. The period between the removal of the covering of the ark (601st year, 1st month, 1st day, v. 13) and the third sending forth of the dove is 29 days (deduced by comparing 8:13 with the date of entering the ark, 7:11). Finally, a comparison of 8:13 with vv. 14–16 indicates a further 57 days' wait before Noah and his family went forth to the dry earth, or 371 days in all, which figure agrees when 7:11 is deducted from 8:14—12 months of 30 days plus 11 days. (The Jews count both the beginning and ending day of a sequence). But the actual elapsed time was exactly a solar year. This is established by multiplying the 12 months, of 7:11 and 8:14, by the 29½ days which comprise a lunar month. The total is 354 days. Add 11 days (17th to 27th of 2nd month, 7:11 and 8:14)—a total of 365 days, one solar year.

[2](8:15) *The Third Dispensation: Human Government*. This dispensation began when Noah and his family left the ark. As Noah went into a new situation, God (in the Noahic Covenant) subjected humanity to a new test. Before this no man had the right to take another man's life (cp. Gen. 4:10–11,14–15,23–24). In this new dispensation, although man's direct moral responsibility to God continued ("Render . . . . to God the things that are God's," Mt. 22:21), God delegated to him certain areas of His authority, in which he was to obey God through submission to his fellow man ("Render . . . to Caesar the things that are Caesar's," Mt. 22:21). So God instituted a corporate relationship of man to man in human government.

The highest function of government is the protection of human life, out of which arises the responsibility of capital punishment. Man is not individually to avenge murder but, as a corporate group, he is to safeguard the sanctity of human life as a gift of God which cannot rightly be disposed of except as God permits. "The authorities that exist are appointed by God," and to resist the authorities is to resist God (Rom. 13:1–2). Whereas in the preceding dispensation restraint upon men was internal (Gen. 6:3) as God's Spirit worked through moral responsibility, now a new and external restraint was added, i.e. the power of civil government.

Man failed to rule righteously. That both Jew and Gentile have governed for self, not for God, is sadly apparent. This failure was seen racially in the confusion of Babel (Gen. 11:9); in the failure of Israel in the period of the theocracy, which closed with captivity in Babylon (2 Chr. 36:15–21); and in the failure of the nations in the "times of the Gentiles" (Lk. 21:24; cp. Dan. 2:31–45). Man's rule will finally be superseded by the glorious reign of our Lord Jesus Christ, whose right to reign is incontestable (Isa. 9:6–7; Jer. 23:5–6; 33:17; Ezek. 21:27; Lk. 1:30–33; Rev. 11:15–18; 19:16; 20:4–6). The dispensation of Human Government was followed as a specific test of obedience by that of Promise, when God called Abram as His instrument of blessing to mankind. However, man's responsibility for government did not cease but will continue until Christ sets up His kingdom.

For *notes* on other dispensations, see: Innocence (Gen. 1:28); Conscience or Moral Responsibility (Gen. 3:7); Promise (Gen. 12:1); Law (Ex. 19:1); Church (Acts 2:1); Kingdom (Rev. 20:4); also *notes* on Gen. 1:28; 2:16; and 11:10.

wife, and your sons and your sons'
wives with you.
17 "Bring out with you every living
thing of all flesh that *is* with you: birds
and cattle and every creeping thing
that creeps on the earth, so that they
may abound on the earth, and be
[a]fruitful and multiply on the earth."
18 So Noah went out, and his sons
and his wife and his sons' wives with
him.
19 Every animal, every creeping
thing, every bird, *and* whatever creeps
on the earth, according to their families, went out of the ark.
20 Then Noah built an [b]altar to the
LORD, and took of every clean animal
and of every clean bird, and offered
[c]burnt offerings on the altar.
21 And the LORD smelled a soothing
aroma. Then the LORD said in His
heart, "I will never again curse the
ground for man's sake, although the
imagination of man's heart *is* evil
from his youth; nor will I again destroy every living thing as I have done.
22 "While the earth remains,
Seedtime and harvest,
Cold and heat,
Winter and summer,
And day and night
Shall not cease."

17
a Gen. 1:22; 9:1,7
20
b Gen. 12:7
c *Sacrifice* (typical): v. 20; Gen. 12:7. (Gen. 3:15; Heb. 10:18, *note*)
CHAPTER 9
1
d v. 7; 8:17
2
e Gen. 1:26; Ps. 8:6
4
f Lev. 17:11–14
6
g *Kingdom* (OT): v. 6; Ex. 3:1. (Gen. 1:26; Zech. 12:8, *note*)
h Gen. 42:22; cp. Gen. 4:9–10; Ex. 21:12, 14

Third, or Noahic Covenant
(Gen. 9:16, note)

9 SO God blessed Noah and his
sons, and said to them: [d]"Be fruitful and multiply, and fill the earth.*
2 "And the [e]fear of you and the
dread of you shall be on every beast of
the earth, on every bird of the air, on
all that move *on* the earth, and on all
the fish of the sea. They are given into
your hand.
3 "Every moving thing that lives
shall be food for you. I have given you
all things, even as the green herbs.
4 "But you shall not eat flesh with
its [f]life, *that is,* its blood.
5 "Surely for your lifeblood I will
demand *a reckoning;* from the hand of
every beast I will require it, and from
the hand of man. From the hand of
every man's brother I will require the
life of man.

6[g]"Whoever sheds [h]man's blood,
By man his blood shall be
shed;
For in the image of God
He made man.

*9:1 Compare Genesis 1:28

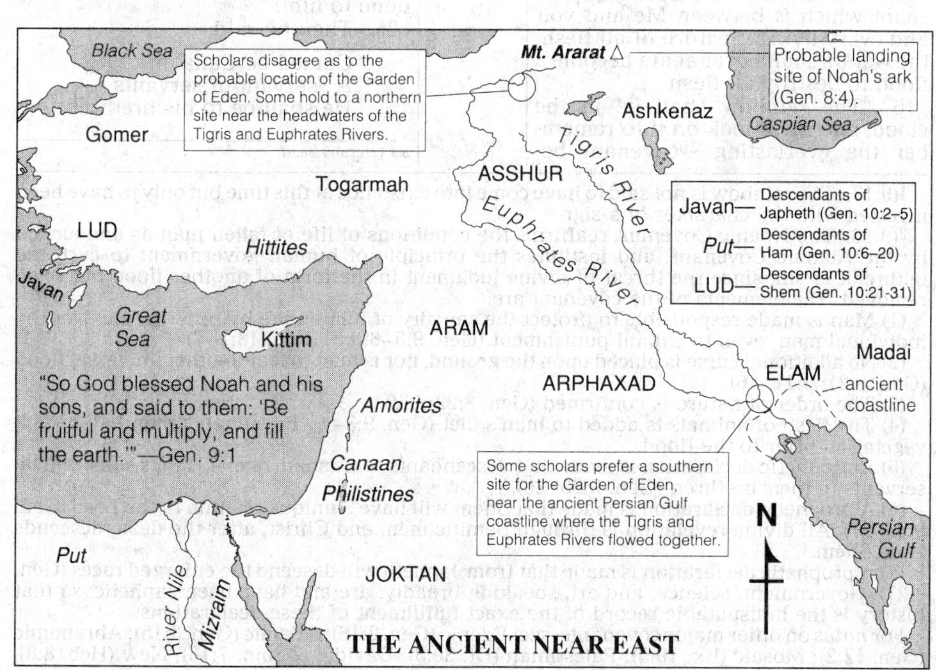
Black Sea
Scholars disagree as to the probable location of the Garden of Eden. Some hold to a northern site near the headwaters of the Tigris and Euphrates Rivers.
Mt. Ararat
Probable landing site of Noah's ark (Gen. 8:4).
Ashkenaz
Caspian Sea
Gomer
Tigris River
Togarmah
ASSHUR
Euphrates River
Javan— Descendants of Japheth (Gen. 10:2–5)
Put— Descendants of Ham (Gen. 10:6–20)
LUD— Descendants of Shem (Gen. 10:21-31)
LUD
Hittites
Javan
Great Sea
Kittim
ARAM
Madai
ELAM
ARPHAXAD
ancient coastline
"So God blessed Noah and his sons, and said to them: 'Be fruitful and multiply, and fill the earth.'"—Gen. 9:1
Amorites
Canaan
Philistines
Some scholars prefer a southern site for the Garden of Eden, near the ancient Persian Gulf coastline where the Tigris and Euphrates Rivers flowed together.
N
Persian Gulf
Put
JOKTAN
River Nile
Mizraim
THE ANCIENT NEAR EAST

7 And as for you, be fruitful and
multiply;
Bring forth abundantly in the
earth
And multiply in it."

8 Then God spoke to Noah and to
his sons with him, [a]saying:
9 "And as for Me, behold, I establish My covenant with you and with
your descendants* after you,
10 "and with every living creature
that *is* with you: the birds, the cattle,
and every beast of the earth with you,
of all that go out of the ark, every
beast of the earth.
11 "Thus I establish My covenant
with you: Never again shall all flesh
be cut off by the waters of the flood;
never again shall there be a flood to
destroy the earth."
12 And God said: "This *is* the sign
of the covenant which I make between
Me and you, and every living creature
that *is* with you, for perpetual generations:
13 "I set My [1]rainbow in the cloud,
and it shall be for the sign of the covenant between Me and the earth.
14 "It shall be, when I bring a cloud
over the earth, that the rainbow shall
be seen in the cloud;
15 "and I will remember My covenant which *is* between Me and you
and every living creature of all flesh;
the waters shall never again become a
flood to destroy all flesh.
16 "The rainbow shall be in the
cloud, and I will look on it to remember the everlasting [2b]covenant between God and every living creature
of all flesh that *is* on the earth."
17 And God said to Noah, "This *is*
the sign of the covenant which I have
established between Me and all flesh
that *is* on the earth."
18 Now the sons of Noah who went
out of the ark were Shem, Ham, and
Japheth. And Ham *was* the father of
Canaan.
19 These three *were* the sons of
Noah, and from these the whole earth
was populated.

Noah's sin

20 And Noah began *to be* a farmer,
and he planted a vineyard.
21 Then he drank of the wine and
was drunk, and became uncovered in
his tent.
22 And Ham, the father of Canaan,
saw the nakedness of his father, and
told his two brothers outside.
23 But Shem and Japheth took a
garment, laid *it* on both their shoulders, and went backward and covered
the nakedness of their father. Their
faces *were* turned away, and they did
not see their father's nakedness.

Noah's prophecy

24 So Noah awoke from his wine,
and knew what his younger son had
done to him.
25 Then he said:

[c]"Cursed *be* Canaan;
A [d]servant of servants
He shall be to his brethren."

8
a See Gen. 8:15 and 9:16, *notes*
16
b *Eight Covenants:* 8:21–9:17, 24–27; Gen. 12:2. (Gen. 2:16; Heb. 8:8)
25
c See v. 16, *note*, pars. (5)–(7)
d Josh. 9:23

* 9:9 Literally *seed*

[1](9:13) The rainbow is not said to have come into existence at this time but only to have been invested with the character of a sign.

[2](9:16) The Noahic Covenant reaffirms the conditions of life of fallen man as announced by the Adamic Covenant, and institutes the principle of human government to curb the outbreak of sin, since the threat of divine judgment in the form of another flood has been removed. The elements of the covenant are:

(1) Man is made responsible to protect the sanctity of human life by orderly rule over the individual man, even to capital punishment (Gen. 9:5–6; cp. Rom. 13:1–7).

(2) No additional curse is placed upon the ground, nor is man to fear another universal flood (Gen. 8:21; 9:11–16).

(3) The order of nature is confirmed (Gen. 8:22; 9:2).

(4) The flesh of animals is added to man's diet (Gen. 9:3–4). Presumably man had been a vegetarian prior to the flood.

(5) A prophetic declaration is made that descendants of Canaan, one of Ham's sons, will be servants to their brethren (Gen. 9:25–26).

(6) A prophetic declaration is made that Shem will have a unique relation to the LORD (Gen. 9:26–27). All divine revelation is through Semitic men, and Christ, after the flesh, descends from Shem.

(7) A prophetic declaration is made that from Japheth will descend the enlarged races (Gen. 9:27). Government, science, and art, speaking broadly, are and have been Japhetic, so that history is the indisputable record of the exact fulfillment of these declarations.

For *notes* on other major covenants, see: Edenic (Gen. 2:16); Adamic (Gen. 3:15); Abrahamic (Gen. 12:2); Mosaic (Ex. 19:5); Palestinian (Dt. 30:3); Davidic (2 Sam. 7:16); New (Heb. 8:8).

26 And he said:

"Blessed *be* the LORD,
The God of Shem,
And may Canaan be his
servant.
27 May God enlarge Japheth,
And may he dwell in the tents
of Shem;
And may Canaan be his
servant."

28 And Noah lived after the flood
three hundred and fifty years.
29 So all the days of Noah were
nine hundred and fifty years; and he
died.

Noah's family (Gen. 9:28—10:32)

10 NOW this *is* the [1]genealogy of
the sons of Noah: Shem, Ham,
and Japheth. And sons were born to
them after the flood.
2 The [a]sons of Japheth *were* [2]Go-
mer, [3]Magog, [4]Madai, [5]Javan, [6]Tubal,
[7]Meshech, and [8]Tiras.

CHAPTER 10
2
a 1 Chr. 1:5–7
6
b 1 Chr. 1:8–16
8
c Mic. 5:6

3 The sons of Gomer *were* [9]Ashke-
naz, [10]Riphath,* and Togarmah.
4 The sons of Javan *were* [11]Elishah,
[12]Tarshish, Kittim, and [13]Dodanim.*
5 From these the coastland *peoples* of the Gentiles were separated
into their lands, everyone according
to his language, according to their
families, into their nations.
6 The [b]sons of Ham *were* [14]Cush,
[15]Mizraim, [16]Put, and Canaan.
7 The sons of Cush *were* Seba,
Havilah, Sabtah, Raamah, and Sabte-
chah; and the sons of Raamah *were*
Sheba and Dedan.
8 Cush begot [c]Nimrod; he began
to be a mighty one on the earth.
9 He was a mighty hunter before
the LORD; therefore it is said, "Like
Nimrod the mighty hunter before the
LORD."
10 And the beginning of his king-

*
10:3 Spelled *Diphath* in 1 Chronicles 1:6
10:4 Spelled *Rodanim* in Samaritan Pentateuch and 1 Chronicles 1:7

[1](10:1) This chapter contains the earliest ethnological table in the literature of the ancient world, compiled centuries before the Homeric writings. In this table of nations there is a remarkable perception of the ethnic and linguistic situation of the age of Noah and his descendants. Virtually all the names here have been found in archaeological discoveries of the past century.

Many of these names reappear subsequently in Hebrew literature in Isa. 13–27; Jer. 46–51; Ezek. 25–32. Eleven of the names reappear in Ezek. 27: Javan, Tubal, Meshech, Togarmah, Kittim, Dedan, Lud, Sidon, Tarshish, Arvad, and Mizraim, which is (Egypt). Kittim (Cyprus) is named also in Isa. 23; Sidon, in Isa. 23:4ff.; Jer. 47:4; Egypt, in Isa. 19; Jer. 46; Ezek. 29–32. Babel, or Babylon, is prophetically discussed in Isa. 13,47; Jer. 50,51; as well as Rev. 17,18. Elam reappears in Isa. 21:2; Jer. 49:34–39; and Tarshish in Isa. 23:1,6. Magog is dominant in Ezek. 38,39. Some of these prophecies have not yet been completely fulfilled; thus some of these areas and tribes will have a history in God's program thousands of years after their names first appeared.

[2](10:2) Progenitor of the ancient Cimmerians and Cimbri, from whom are descended the Celtic family.

[3](10:2) From Magog may be descended the ancient Scythians (Josephus, *Ant.* 1,vi,i), who lived north of the Black Sea. For Magog in prophecy, cp. Ezek. 38:2; 39:6; Rev. 20:8.

[4](10:2) Progenitor of the ancient Medes.

[5](10:2) Progenitor of those who peopled Greece, Syria, etc.

[6](10:2) Some believe that Tubal's descendants peopled the region south of the Black Sea, from whence they spread north and south. It is quite possible that Tobolsk perpetuates the tribal name.

[7](10:2) Progenitor of a race mentioned in connection with Tubal, Magog, and other northern nations (Ezek. 38:2; 39:6). Many think Russia is modern Magog, Tubal, and Meshech.

[8](10:2) According to ancient opinion, progenitor of the Thracians, more recently the Tyrsenoi, a people occupying the coast lands of the Aegean Sea.

[9](10:3) Jeremiah 51:27 reveals that the Ashkenaz lived in the vicinity of Ararat, Armenia. In later Jewish literature Ashkenaz is employed as a designation of Germany. The *Ashkenazim* were Jews who had their abode in Germanic countries, just as the *Sephardim* denote Jews of Portugal and Spain.

[10](10:3) Riphath and Togarmah were inhabitants of Asia Minor.

[11](10:4) Perhaps peoples from Sicily or Cyprus.

[12](10:4) Tarshish is frequently mentioned in the OT as a flourishing seaport (cp. 1 Ki. 10:22; Jon. 1:3). This may well be a reference to Tartessus in ancient Spain.

[13](10:4) This name may allude to the people of the Rhodian islands in the Aegean Sea.

[14](10:6) Ethiopia.

[15](10:6) Egypt.

[16](10:6) Sometimes written "Phut," Put refers to Libya.

dom was [a]Babel, Erech, Accad, and
Calneh, in the land of Shinar.
11 From that land he went to Assyria and built [b]Nineveh, Rehoboth Ir,
Calah,
12 and Resen between Nineveh and
Calah (that *is* the principal city).
13 Mizraim begot Ludim, Anamim,
Lehabim, Naphtuhim,
14 Pathrusim, and Casluhim (from
whom came the Philistines and Caphtorim).
15 Canaan begot [1]Sidon his firstborn, and [2]Heth;
16 the [3]Jebusite, the Amorite, and
the Girgashite;
17 the Hivite, the Arkite, and the Si-
nite;
18 the Arvadite, the Zemarite, and
the Hamathite. Afterward the families
of the Canaanites were dispersed.
19 And the border of the Canaanites was from Sidon as you go toward
Gerar, as far as Gaza; then as you go
toward Sodom, Gomorrah, Admah,
and Zeboiim, as far as Lasha.
20 These *were* the sons of Ham, according to their families, according to
their languages, in their lands *and* in
their nations.
21 And *children* were born also to
Shem, the father of all the children of
Eber, the brother of Japheth the elder.
22 The [c]sons of Shem *were* [4]Elam,
[5]Asshur, [d]Arphaxad, Lud, and Aram.
23 The sons of Aram *were* [6]Uz, Hul,
Gether, and Mash.*
24 Arphaxad begot Salah,* and Salah begot Eber.
25 To Eber were born two sons: the
name of one *was* Peleg, for in his days
the earth was divided; and his
brother's name *was* Joktan.
26 Joktan begot Almodad, Sheleph,
Hazarmaveth, Jerah,
27 Hadoram, Uzal, Diklah,
28 Obal,* Abimael, Sheba,
29 [7]Ophir, Havilah, and Jobab. All
these *were* the sons of Joktan.
30 And their dwelling place was
from Mesha as you go toward Sephar,
the mountain of the east.
31 These *were* the sons of Shem,
according to their families, according
to their languages, in their lands, according to their nations.
32 These *were* the families of the
sons of Noah, according to their generations, in their nations; and from
these the nations were divided on the
earth after the flood.

Man's failure at Babel. Life continues under the Adamic and Noahic Covenants

11

NOW the whole earth had [8]one
language and one speech.
2 And it came to pass, as they journeyed from the east, that they found a
plain in the land of Shinar, and they
dwelt there.
3 Then they said to one another,
"Come, let us make bricks and bake
them thoroughly." They had brick for
stone, and they had asphalt for mortar.
4 And they said, "Come, let us
build ourselves a city, and a [9]tower
whose [e]top *is* in the heavens; let us
make a name for ourselves, lest we be
scattered abroad over the face of the
whole earth."
5 But the LORD came down to see
the city and the tower which the sons
of men had built.
6 And the LORD said, "Indeed the
people *are* one and they all have one
language, and this is what they begin
to do; now nothing that they propose
to do will be withheld from them.
7 "Come, let Us go down and there
[f]confuse their language, that they

10
a See Isa. 13:1 and Rev. 18:2, *notes;* cp. Gen. 11:10, *note*
11
b See Nah. 1:1, *note*
22
c Gen. 11:10–26; 1 Chr. 1:17–28
d v. 24; Lk. 3:36
CHAPTER 11
4
e Dt. 1:28
7
f Miracles (OT): vv. 7–9; Gen. 12:17. (Gen. 5:24; Jon. 1:17, *note*)

*
10:23 Called *Meshech* in Septuagint and 1 Chronicles 1:17 **10:24** Following Masoretic Text, Vulgate, and Targum; Septuagint reads *Arphaxad begot Cainan, and Cainan begot Salah* (compare Luke 3:35-36). **10:28** Spelled *Ebal* in 1 Chronicles 1:22

[1](10:15) Sidon, sometimes called "Zidon," once was the capital of ancient Phoenicia.
[2](10:15) Ancestor of the Hittites.
[3](10:16) A tribe in the neighborhood of Jerusalem, which was also called Jebus (Jud. 19:10).
[4](10:22) A people east of Babylon and the Persian Gulf.
[5](10:22) Assyria.
[6](10:23) A place in northern Arabia, where Job lived (Job 1:1).
[7](10:29) Ophir, at the southern end of the Red Sea, was famous for its gold (1 Ki. 9:28; 10:11); almug trees were evidently plentiful there also. See 1 Ki. 10:11, *note*.
[8](11:1) In judgment upon sinful man's first attempt to establish a world state in opposition to the divine rule, God struck at the very thing which binds men together, namely, a common language (vv. 7–9).
[9](11:4) Among the discoveries of archaeology in Mesopotamia are the ziggurats, terrace towers built for worship of pagan deities.

may not understand one another's
speech."
8 So the LORD scattered them
abroad from there over the face of all
the earth, and they ceased building
the city.
9 Therefore its name is called [a]Ba-
bel, because there the LORD confused
the language of all the earth; and from
there the LORD scattered them abroad
over the face of all the earth.

V. From the Call of Abram to the Death of Joseph, 11:10—50:26

Ancestry of Abram

10 This *is* the [1]genealogy of Shem:
Shem *was* one hundred years old, and
begot [b]Arphaxad two years after the
[2]flood.
11 After he begot Arphaxad, Shem
lived five hundred years, and begot
sons and daughters.
12 Arphaxad lived thirty-five
years, and begot Salah.
13 After he begot Salah, Arphaxad
lived four hundred and three years,
and begot sons and daughters.
14 Salah lived thirty years, and begot Eber.
15 After he begot Eber, Salah lived
four hundred and three years, and begot sons and daughters.
16 Eber lived thirty-four years, and
begot Peleg.
17 After he begot Peleg, Eber lived
four hundred and thirty years, and begot sons and daughters.
18 Peleg lived thirty years, and begot Reu.
19 After he begot Reu, Peleg lived
two hundred and nine years, and begot sons and daughters.
20 Reu lived thirty-two years, and
begot Serug.
21 After he begot Serug, Reu lived
two hundred and seven years, and begot sons and daughters.
22 Serug lived thirty years, and begot Nahor.
23 After he begot Nahor, Serug
lived two hundred years, and begot
sons and daughters.

9
[a] As an interesting play on words, Babel is compared with *balal* the Heb. word meaning *to confuse.* See v. 1 and Isa. 13:1, *notes;* cp. Rev. 18:2, *note*

10
[b] Gen. 10:22,24; 1 Chr. 1:17,18; Lk. 3:36

---

[1](11:10) Genesis 11 and 12 mark an important turning point in the divine dealing. Up to this point the history has been that of the whole Adamic race. There has been neither Jew nor Gentile; all have been one in "the first man Adam." Henceforth, in the Scripture record, humanity must be thought of as a vast stream from which God, in the call of Abram and the creation of the nation of Israel, has but drawn off a rivulet through which He may at last purify the great river itself. Israel was called to be a witness to the unity of God in the midst of universal idolatry (Dt. 6:4; Isa. 43:10–12); to illustrate the blessedness of serving the true God (Dt. 33:26–29); to receive and preserve the divine revelations (Dt. 4:5–8; Rom. 3:1–2); and to be the human channel for the Messiah (Gen. 21:12; 28:10,14; 49:10; 2 Sam. 7:16–17; Isa. 7:13–14; Mt. 1:1).

The reader of Scripture should hold firmly in mind: (1) From Gen. 12 to Mt. 12:45 the Scriptures have primarily in view Israel, the rivulet, not the great Gentile river; though again and again the universality of the ultimate divine intent breaks into view (e.g. Gen. 12:3; Isa. 2:2,4; 5:26; 9:1–2; 11:10–12; 42:1–6; 49:6,12; 52:15; 54:3; 55:5; 60:3,5,11–16; 61:6,9; 62:2; 66:12,18–19; Jer. 16:19; Joel 3:9–10; Mal. 1:11; Rom. 9; 10; and 11; Gal. 3:8–14). (2) The human race, Gentile and Jew, goes on under the Adamic and Noahic Covenants, continuing under the dispensations (stewardship responsibilities) of Conscience (Moral Responsibility) and Human Government. Israel, in addition, received the light and added responsibility of, first the Abrahamic, and then the Mosaic and Palestinian Covenants. (3) The moral history of the Gentile world beginning with Babel, as it descended into the sin of idolatry and its resulting perversion of morals, is described by the Holy Spirit in Rom. 1:18–32, along with its moral accountability (Rom. 2:1–16). Conscience never acquits: it either *accuses* or *excuses.* (4) Where the law later became known to the Gentiles, it was to them, as to Israel, "the ministry of death," a "curse" (Rom. 3:19–20; 7:9–10; 2 Cor. 3:7; Gal. 3:10). And (5) a wholly new responsibility arises when either Jew or Gentile knows the gospel (Jn. 3:18–19,36; 15:22–24; 16:9; 1 Jn. 5:9–12).

[2](11:10) Scripture does not provide data by which the date of the flood can be discovered. (See *notes* on Gen. 1:1; 5:3.) The Hebrew word rendered "begot" does not necessarily mean *only* that, but often means *became an ancestor of;* and the Biblical word "son," though often indicating an immediate child, may also be the equivalent of our English word "descendant." Thus Mt. 1:1 calls Jesus Christ "the Son of David, the Son of Abraham." See also Mt. 22:42. The genealogy in Mt. 1:8 says that Joram was the father of Uzziah, thus omitting three links: Ahaziah, Joash, and Amaziah, all kings of Judah whose names would have been known to every Jew. Also compare Ezra 7:3 with 1 Chr. 6:7–11. In view of all these facts we see that Gen. 11:10 means that, when Shem was 100 years old, his wife bore a child who was either Arphaxad or an ancestor of Arphaxad. Many links in the chain of ancestry may have been left unmentioned.

24 Nahor lived twenty-nine years,
and begot Terah.
25 After he begot Terah, Nahor
lived one hundred and nineteen years,
and begot sons and daughters.
26 Now Terah lived seventy years,
and begot Abram, Nahor, and Haran.
27 This *is* the genealogy of Terah:
Terah begot [1a]Abram, Nahor, and Haran. Haran begot Lot.
28 And Haran died before his father Terah in his native land, in [2]Ur of
the Chaldeans.
29 Then Abram and Nahor took
wives: the name of Abram's wife *was*
[b]Sarai, and the name of Nahor's wife,
[c]Milcah, the daughter of Haran the
father of Milcah and the father of Iscah.
30 But Sarai was barren; she had
no child.

Wasted years at Haran

31 And Terah took his son Abram
and his grandson Lot, the son of [d]Haran, and his daughter-in-law Sarai, his
son Abram's wife, and they went out
with them from Ur of the Chaldeans to
go to the land of Canaan; and they
came to Haran and dwelt there.
32 So the days of Terah were two
hundred and five years, and Terah
died in Haran.

Fourth Dispensation: Promise (Gen. 12:1—Ex. 18:27).

Fourth or Abrahamic Covenant. (See Gen. 12:2, note; cp. 13:14–18; 15:1–21; 17:4–8; 22:15–24; 26:1–5; 28:10–15)

12 [3]NOW the LORD had said to
[4]Abram:

"Get [e]out of your country,
From your family
And from your father's house,
To a land that I will show you.

27 *a* c. 1950 B.C. Later called *Abraham,* Gen. 17:5

29 *b* Later called *Sarah,* Gen. 17:15 *c* Ancestress of Rebekah; cp. Gen. 22:20; 24:15

31 *d* A city in northwestern Mesopotamia, about 600 miles from Ur, is named after this man. See latter part of this verse.

12:1 *e Separation:* vv. 1–5; Gen. 13:9. (Gen.12:1; 2 Cor. 6:17, *note*)

[1](11:27) Evidence is not yet available for setting a precise date for the life of Abram. Some conservative scholars place him as early as 2200 B.C.; others, as late as 1650. In this edition of the Bible, an estimate of approximately 2100 B.C. for the birth of Abram is used.

[2](11:28) This city was located in southern Mesopotamia. Excavations have shown that its material civilization was far advanced, even long before the time of Abram; its houses show a level of material welfare in Abram's day equal to that of Babylon in Nebuchadnezzar's time, more than 1000 years later.

[3](12:1) *The Fourth Dispensation: Promise.* This dispensation extended from the call of Abram to the giving of the law at Sinai (Ex. 19:3ff.). Its stewardship was based upon God's covenant with Abram, first cited here, Gen. 12:1–3, and confirmed and enlarged in Gen. 13:14–17; 15:1–7; 17:1–8,15–19; 22:16–18; 26:2–5,24; 28:13–15; 31:13; 35:9–12.

Observe (1) the specific provisions affecting Abram himself (Gen. 15:15) and his son and grandson, Isaac and Jacob (Gen. 26:1–5; 28:10–16), under which individual blessing depended on individual obedience (Gen. 12:1; cp. 22:18; 26:5).

(2) God made an unconditional promise of blessings through Abram's seed (a) to the nation Israel to inherit a specific territory forever (Gen. 12:2; 15:18–21; 17:7–8); (b) to the Church as in Christ (Gal. 3:16,28–29); and (c) to the Gentile nations (Gen. 12:3).

(3) There was a promise of blessing on those individuals and nations who bless Abram's descendants, and a curse laid on those who persecute the Jews (Gen. 12:3; Mt. 25:31–46). Consequently this dispensation had varied emphases. To the Gentiles of that period, there was little direct application other than the test implied by Gen. 12:3 and illustrated by God's blessing or judgment upon individuals (Pharaoh, Gen. 12:17; Abimelech, Gen. 20:3,17, etc.), or nations (e.g. Egypt, Gen. 47—50; Ex. 1—15) who treated Abram or his descendants well or ill.

In the continuance through the centuries of this stewardship of truth, believers of the Church age are called upon to trust God as Abram did (Rom. 4:11,16,23–25; Gal. 3:6–9), and thus enter into the blessings of the covenant which inaugurated the dispensation of Promise.

God's promises to Abram and his seed certainly did not terminate at Sinai with the giving of the law (Gal. 3:17). Both OT and NT are full of post-Sinaitic promises concerning Israel and the land which is to be Israel's everlasting possession (e.g. Ex. 32:13; 33:1–3; Lev. 23:10; 25:2; 26:6; Dt. 6:1–23; 8:1–18; Josh. 1:2,11; 24:13; Acts 7:17; Rom. 9:4). But as a specific test of Israel's stewardship of divine truth, the dispensation of Promise was superseded, though not annulled, by the law that was given at Sinai (Ex. 19:3ff.).

Other dispensational *notes:* Innocence (Gen. 1:28); Conscience or Moral Responsibility (Gen. 3:7); Human Government (Gen. 8:15); Law (Ex. 19:1); Church (Acts 2:1); Kingdom (Rev. 20:4).

[4](12:1) The events of this sentence are referred to in chapter 11:27–32.

2 [1][a]I will make you a great
[b]nation;
I will bless you
And make your name great;
And you shall be a blessing.
3 I will bless those who bless
you,
And I will curse him who
curses you;
And in [c]you all the families of
the earth shall be [d]blessed."

Abram in the land: worship, communion, and promise

4 So Abram departed as the LORD
had spoken to him, and Lot went with
him. And Abram *was* seventy-five
years old when he departed from Haran.
5 Then Abram took Sarai his wife
and Lot his brother's son, and all their
possessions that they had gathered,
and the people whom they had acquired in Haran, and they [e]departed
to go to the land of Canaan. So they
came to the land of Canaan.
6 Abram passed through the land
to the place of [f]Shechem, as far as the
terebinth tree of Moreh.* And the Canaanites *were* then in the land.
7 Then the LORD [2]appeared to
Abram and said, "To your descendants I will [3]give this land." And there
he built an [g]altar to the LORD, who had
[h]appeared to him.
8 And he moved from there to the
mountain east of [4]Bethel, and he

2
a *Eight Covenants:* vv. 1–3,7; Ex. 19:5. (Gen. 2:16; Heb. 8:8)
b *Israel* (origin): vv. 1–3; Gen. 13:15. (Gen. 12:2; Rom. 11:26, *note*)

3
c *Christ* (first advent): v. 3; Gen. 17:19. (Gen. 3:15; Acts 1:11, *note*)
d *Gospel:* v. 3; Isa. 41:27. (Gen. 12:3; Rev. 14:6)

12:5 *e Faith:* vv. 1–5; Gen. 13:18. (Gen. 3:20; Heb. 11:39, *note*) **12:6** *f* Ps. 60:6, *note* **12:7** *g Sacrifice* (typical): vv. 7–8; Gen. 13:18. (Gen. 3:15; Heb. 10:18, *note*) *h Theophanies:* v. 7; Gen. 17:1. (Gen. 12:7, *note;* Dan. 10:5)

*12:6 Hebrew *Alon Moreh*

[1](12:2) The Abrahamic Covenant as formed (Gen. 12:1–4) and confirmed (Gen. 13:14–17; 15:1–7,18–21; 17:1–8) is in three aspects:

(1) The promise of a great nation: "I will make you a great nation" (Gen. 12:2). This had primary reference to Israel, the descendants of Jacob, to whom the everlasting possession of the land is promised (Gen. 17:8), to whom the everlasting covenant is given (Gen. 17:7), and to whom God said, "I will be their God" (Gen. 17:8). Abraham was also promised that he would father other nations (cp. Gen. 17:6,20), principally fulfilled through Ishmael and Esau.

(2) Four personal promises are given to Abraham: (a) To be the father of numerous descendants (Gen. 17:16). (b) To receive personal blessing, "I will bless you," fulfilled in two ways: temporally (Gen. 13:14–15,17; 15:18; 24:34–35); and spiritually (Gen. 15:6; Jn. 8:56). (c) To receive personal honor, "and make your name great" (Gen. 12:2), fulfilled in recognition by all who honor the Bible. And (d) to be the channel of blessing, "And you shall be a blessing" (Gen. 12:2), fulfilled: in blessings to others through his seed, Israel, who became the instruments of divine revelation; through Abraham as an example of pious faith (Rom. 4:1–22); and preeminently through Christ, Abraham's Seed (Gal. 3:16).

(3) Promises to the Gentiles. (a) "I will bless those who bless you" (Gen. 12:3). Those who honor Abraham will be blessed. (b) "And I will curse him who curses you" (Gen. 12:3). This was a warning literally fulfilled in the history of Israel's persecutions. It has invariably fared ill with the people who have persecuted the Jew—well with those who have protected him. For a nation to commit the sin of anti-Semitism brings inevitable judgment. The future will still more remarkably prove this principle (Dt. 30:7; Isa. 14:1–2; Joel 3:1–8; Mic. 5:7–9; Hag. 2:22; Zech. 14:1–3; Mt. 25:40,45). (c) "And in you all the families of the earth shall be blessed" (Gen. 12:3). This is the great evangelic promise fulfilled in Abraham's Seed, Christ, and in all the spiritual seed of Abraham who, like Abraham, are justified by faith (Rom. 4:3; Gal. 3:6–9,16,29; cp. Jn. 8:56–58). It gives added revelation and confirmation of the promise of the Adamic Covenant concerning the Seed of the woman (Gen. 3:15).

The Abrahamic Covenant reveals the sovereign purpose of God to fulfill through Abraham His program for Israel, and to provide in Christ the Savior for all who believe. The ultimate fulfillment is made to rest upon the divine promise and the power of God rather than upon human faithfulness.

For *notes* on the other major covenants, see: Edenic (Gen. 2:16); Adamic (Gen. 3:15); Noahic (Gen. 9:16); Mosaic (Ex. 19:5); Palestinian (Dt. 30:3); Davidic (2 Sam. 7:16); New (Heb. 8:8).

[2](12:7) Theophanies are preincarnate appearances of God the Son either in angelic or human form, by manifested glory (Ezek. 1), or in a manner not described (Gen. 17:1). See marginal note *h* also.

[3](12:7) The verb "give" appears over 1000 times in the Bible, with greatest frequency in relation to God's giving the land of Palestine to His people Israel, a truth here announced for the first time but repeated in nearly 150 passages in the OT from the days of the patriarchs to the return from the exile (Neh. 9:35,36) and even incorporated in the Decalogue (Ex. 20:12).

[4](12:8) Bethel, one of the sacred places of Canaan, means *house of God* (Gen. 28:1–22; see 35:7, *note*). It was at this place that Jeroboam chose to practice his idolatry (1 Ki. 12:28—13:6), whereupon God's judgment decreed the destruction of Bethel despite its sacred memories

pitched his tent *with* Bethel on the
west and Ai on the east; there he built
an altar to the LORD and called on the
name of the LORD.
9 So Abram journeyed, going on
still toward the [1]South.

Under trial Abram fails, forsaking the place of blessing

10 Now there was a famine in the
land, and Abram went down to Egypt
to dwell there, for the famine *was* severe in the land.
11 And it came to pass, when he
was close to entering Egypt, that he
said to Sarai his wife, "Indeed I know
that you *are* a woman of beautiful
countenance.
12 "Therefore it will happen, when
the Egyptians see you, that they will
say, 'This *is* his wife'; and they will kill
me, but they will let you live.
13 [a]"Please say you *are* my [2]sister,
that it may be well with me for your
sake, and that I* may live because of
you."
14 So it was, when Abram came
into Egypt, that the Egyptians saw the
woman, that she *was* very beautiful.
15 The princes of Pharaoh also saw
her and commended her to Pharaoh.
And the woman was taken to Pharaoh's house.
16 He [b]treated Abram well for her
sake. He [c]had sheep, oxen, male donkeys, male and female servants, female donkeys, and camels.
17 But the LORD [d]plagued Pharaoh
and his house with great plagues because of Sarai, Abram's wife.
18 And Pharaoh called Abram and

13 *a* Cp. Gen. 20:1–18; 26:6–11
16 *b* Gen. 20:14 *c* Gen. 13:2
17 *d Miracles* (OT): v. 17; Gen. 15:17. (Gen. 5:24; Jon. 1:17, *note*)

*12:13 Literally *my soul*

(1 Ki. 13:1–5; 2 Ki. 23:15–17; Amos 3:14–15). Although God must act ultimately in judgment against that which is contrary to His character, whatever its former associations, such action is accompanied by the sorrow of His divine compassion (Ex. 34:6–7).

[1](12:9) "The South" translates the Hebrew word Negev, which is based on a word meaning "to be dry." It is a geographical term which refers to a specific section of Palestine (e.g. Gen. 13:1) located between Debir and the Arabian Desert. It is an arid region most of the year. Since this area was south of the larger part of Israel, the word also came to be used to denote that direction (cp. Gen. 13:14; Dan. 8:4,9; 11:5, etc.).

[2](12:13) Abram's proposal was partial truth, for Sarai was his half sister (Gen. 20:12), but what was told was with intent of deception. Cp. Gen. 26:7.

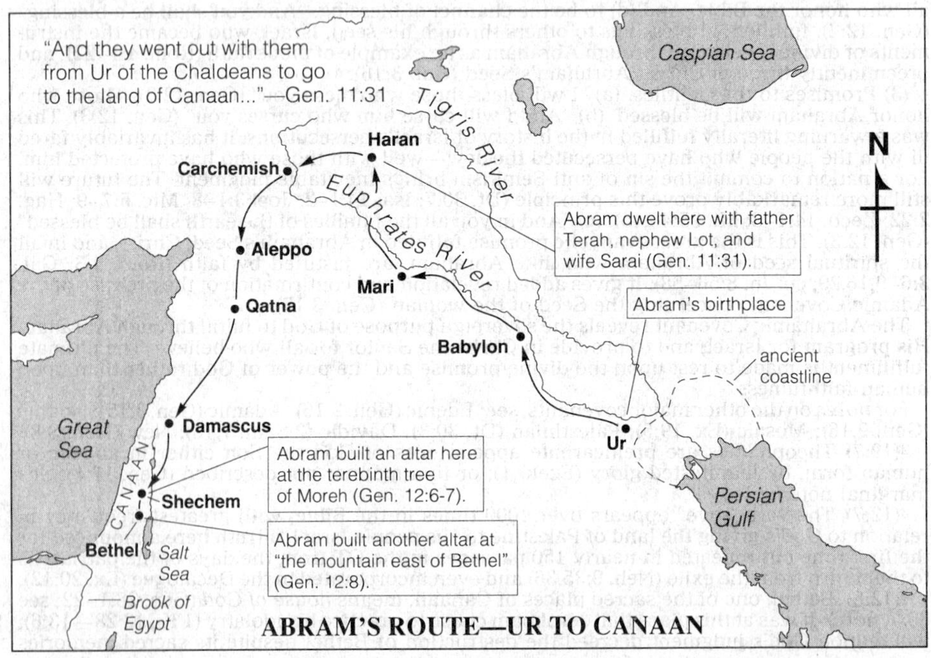
"And they went out with them from Ur of the Chaldeans to go to the land of Canaan..."—Gen. 11:31
Caspian Sea
Tigris River
Euphrates River
Haran
Carchemish
Aleppo
Qatna
Mari
Babylon
Ur
N
Abram dwelt here with father Terah, nephew Lot, and wife Sarai (Gen. 11:31).
Abram's birthplace
ancient coastline
Persian Gulf
Great Sea
Damascus
CANAAN
Shechem
Bethel
Salt Sea
Brook of Egypt
Abram built an altar here at the terebinth tree of Moreh (Gen. 12:6-7).
Abram built another altar at "the mountain east of Bethel" (Gen. 12:8).

ABRAM'S ROUTE—UR TO CANAAN

said, "What *is* this you have done to me? Why did you not tell me that she *was* your wife?

19 "Why did you say, 'She *is* my sister'? I might have taken her as my wife. Now therefore, here is your wife; take *her* and go your way."

20 So Pharaoh commanded *his* men concerning him; and they sent him away, with his wife and all that he had.

Abram's return

13 THEN Abram went up from Egypt, he and his wife and all that he had, and [a]Lot with him, to the [b]South.*

2 Abram *was* very [c]rich in livestock, in silver, and in gold.

3 And he went on his journey from the [b]South as far as Bethel, to the place where his tent had been at the beginning, between Bethel and Ai,

4 to the place of the altar which he had made there at first. And there Abram [d]called on the name of the LORD.

Abram's separation from Lot

5 Lot also, who went with Abram, had flocks and herds and tents.

6 Now the land was not able to support them, that they might dwell together, for their possessions were so great that they could not dwell together.

7 And there was strife between the herdsmen of Abram's livestock and the herdsmen of Lot's livestock. The Canaanites and the Perizzites then dwelt in the land.

8 So Abram said to Lot, "Please let there be no strife between you and me, and between my herdsmen and your herdsmen; for we *are* brethren.

9 "*Is* not the whole land before you? Please [e]separate from me. If *you take* the left, then I will go to the right; or, if *you* go to the right, then I will go to the left."

Lot's first step in backsliding
(see Gen. 13:12; 19:1,33)

10 And Lot lifted his eyes and saw all the plain of Jordan, that it *was* well watered [1]everywhere (before the LORD destroyed Sodom and Gomorrah) like the garden of the LORD, like the land of Egypt as you go toward Zoar.

11 Then Lot chose for himself all the plain of Jordan, and Lot journeyed east. And they separated from each other.

Lot's second step in backsliding
(see Gen. 13:10; 19:1,33)

12 Abram dwelt in the land of Canaan, and Lot dwelt in the cities of the plain and pitched *his* tent even as far as Sodom.

13 But the [f]men of Sodom *were* exceedingly wicked and sinful against the LORD.

Under Abrahamic Covenant
the land is given;
natural posterity promised (v. 16)

14 And the LORD said to Abram, after Lot had separated from him: "Lift your eyes now and look from the place where you are—northward, southward, eastward, and westward;

15 "for all the land which you see I give to you and your [g]descendants* forever.

16 "And I will make your descendants [h]as the dust of the earth; so that if a man could number the dust of the earth, *then* your descendants also could be numbered.

17 "Arise, walk in the land through its length and its width, for I give it to you."

18 [i]Then Abram moved *his* tent, and went and dwelt by the terebinth trees of Mamre,* which *are* in Hebron, and built an [j]altar there to the LORD.

Abram delivers Lot

14 AND it came to pass in the days of Amraphel king of Shinar, Arioch king of Ellasar, Chedorlaomer king of Elam, and Tidal king of nations,*

2 *that* they made war with Bera king of Sodom, Birsha king of Gomorrah, Shinab king of Admah, Shemeber king of Zeboiim, and the king of Bela (that is, Zoar).

3 All these joined together in the

CHAPTER 13

1
a Gen. 12:4; 14:12,16
b See Gen. 12:9, *note*

2
c Gen. 24:35

4
d Gen. 12:8; 21:33

9
e Separation: vv. 7–11, 14–17; Ex. 6:6. (Gen. 12:1; 2 Cor. 6:17, *note*)

13
f Gen. 18:20–21

15
g Israel (covenant): vv. 15–17; Gen. 15:5. (Gen. 12:2; Rom. 11:26, *note*)

16
h Gen. 15:5; 28:14

18
i Faith: vv. 14–18; Gen. 14:22. (Gen. 3:20; Heb. 11:39, *note*)
j Sacrifice (typical): v. 18; Gen. 22:8. (Gen. 3:15; Heb. 10:18, *note*)

*
13:1 Hebrew *Negev* throughout the book
14:1 Hebrew *goyim*
13:15 Literally *seed,* and so
13:18 Hebrew *Alon Mamre*

[1](13:10) At least as early as the time of Joshua, most of the Jordan valley was desolate, utterly unlike the description in this verse. Yet the destructive critics have thought that this story originated in the time of the later Israelite kingdom. Archaeological research has now proved that the Jordan valley was filled with populous cities for many centuries, but that most of these had disappeared by the time of Joshua. The spade of the archaeologist has served again and again to confirm the Scriptures, not to deny them.

Valley of Siddim (that is, the Salt Sea).
4 Twelve years they served Chedorlaomer, and in the thirteenth year
they rebelled.
5 In the fourteenth year Chedorlaomer and the kings that *were* with him
came and attacked the Rephaim in
Ashteroth Karnaim, the Zuzim in
Ham, the Emim in Shaveh Kiriathaim,
6 and the Horites in their mountain of Seir, as far as El Paran, which
is by the wilderness.
7 Then they turned back and came
to En Mishpat (that *is*, Kadesh), and
attacked all the country of the Amalekites, and also the Amorites who
dwelt in Hazezon Tamar.
8 And the king of Sodom, the king
of Gomorrah, the king of Admah, the
king of Zeboiim, and the king of Bela
(that *is*, Zoar) went out and joined together in battle in the Valley of Siddim
9 against Chedorlaomer king of
Elam, Tidal king of nations,* Amraphel king of Shinar, and Arioch king
of Ellasar—four kings against [1]five.
10 Now the Valley of Siddim *was*
full of asphalt pits; and the kings of
Sodom and Gomorrah fled; *some* fell
there, and the remainder fled to the
mountains.
11 Then they took all the goods of
Sodom and Gomorrah, and all their
provisions, and went their way.
12 They also took Lot, Abram's
brother's son who dwelt in Sodom,
and his goods, and departed.
13 Then one who had escaped
came and told Abram the [2a]Hebrew,
for he dwelt by the terebinth trees of
Mamre* the Amorite, brother of Eshcol and brother of Aner; and they
were allies with Abram.
14 Now [b]when Abram heard that
his brother was taken captive, he
armed his three hundred and eighteen
[3]trained *servants* who were born in
his own house, and went in pursuit as
far as Dan.
15 He divided his forces against
them by night, and he and his servants
attacked them and pursued them as
far as Hobah, which *is* north of Damascus.
16 So he brought back all the
goods, and also brought back his
brother Lot and his goods, as well as
the women and the people.

God reveals Himself as El Elyon (v. 18)

17 And the king of Sodom went out
to meet him at the Valley of Shaveh
(that *is*, the King's Valley), after his
return from the defeat of Chedorlaomer and the kings who *were* with him.
18 Then [4c]Melchizedek king of
[5]Salem brought out bread and wine;

CHAPTER 14

13
a Gen. 39:14

14
b Abram, the separated man, had power to help. Cp. Gen. 19:29; 2 Tim. 2:20–21

18
c Meaning *king of righteousness*. Salem means *peace*. Cp. Heb. 7:2

*
14:9 Hebrew *goyim* 14:13 Hebrew *Alon Mamre*

[1](14:9) It was formerly doubted that kings from distant Mesopotamia could conduct a powerful expedition so far from their own land at this early time, but there is now much evidence of similar expeditions. One reason that some have questioned the historicity of this chapter is the description of the kings as following a route near the extreme eastern edge of Palestine (v. 5). Archaeologists, however, have discovered the towns mentioned in v. 5 and have found that they were heavily fortified at the time of Abram. Regarding Sodom and Gomorrah, see Gen. 19:28, *note*.

[2](14:13) This is the first time that the word "Hebrew" is used in the Bible. It may be derived from "Eber," Abram's ancestor (Gen. 10:25).

[3](14:14) The Hebrew word used here occurs nowhere else in the Hebrew Bible; it is employed in early Egyptian documents to indicate the hired soldiers of Palestinian chiefs at this period.

[4](14:18) Melchizedek, a type of Christ the King-Priest. The type strictly applies to the priestly work of Christ in resurrection, since Melchizedek presents only the memorials of sacrifice, bread and wine. "According to the order of Melchizedek" (Ps. 110:4; Heb.5:5–6; 6:20) refers to the royal authority and unending duration of Christ's high priesthood (Heb. 7:23–24). The Aaronic priesthood was often interrupted by death. Christ is a priest according to the order of Melchizedek, as King of righteousness, King of peace (Isa. 11:4–9; Heb.7:2), and in the endlessness of His priesthood; but the Aaronic priesthood typifies His priestly work.

[5](14:18) This is the first mention of Jerusalem in the Bible. Its existence as early as this is evidenced by the Tell el Amarna Tablets, discovered at Tell el Amarna in Egypt. These tablets are letters between the kings of Egypt in the 15th century B.C.and various rulers in Palestine and elsewhere. They throw much light on conditions in Palestine at that early time and corroborate the general picture of Canaan given in Genesis.

Archaeology has demonstrated the existence, as early as the time of Abram, of numerous Palestinian cities mentioned in Genesis. Many cities referred to in later books of the Bible, but not in Genesis, were not founded until a much later period, as excavation proves.

he *was* the [a]priest of [1b]God Most
High.
19 And he blessed him and said:

"Blessed be Abram of God Most
High,
Possessor of heaven and earth;
20 And blessed be God Most
High,
Who has delivered your
enemies into your hand."

And he [c]gave him a [d]tithe of all.
21 Now the king of Sodom said to
Abram, "Give me the persons, and
take the goods for yourself."
22 But Abram [e]said to the king of
Sodom, "I have raised my hand to the
LORD, God Most High, the Possessor of
heaven and earth,
23 "that I *will take* nothing, from a
thread to a sandal strap, and that I will

18
a First mention of priest
b Deity (names of): v. 18; 15:2; Gen. 17:1. (Gen. 1:1; Mal. 3:18)

20
c Heb. 7:4
d Gen. 28:22; Lev. 27:30

22
e Faith: vv. 22–24; Gen. 15:6. (Gen. 3:20; Heb. 11:39, *note*)

CHAPTER 15

2
f Bible

not take anything that *is* yours, lest
you should say, 'I have made Abram
rich'—
24 "except only what the young
men have eaten, and the portion of the
men who went with me: Aner, Eshcol,
and Mamre; let them take their portion."

Abrahamic Covenant confirmed: a spiritual seed promised (v. 5)

15 AFTER these things the word
of the LORD came to Abram in a
vision, saying, "Do not be afraid,
Abram. I *am* your shield, your exceedingly great reward."
2 [f]But Abram said, [2]"Lord [3]GOD,
what will You give me, seeing I go

prayers (OT): vv. 2–3; Gen. 17:18. (Gen. 15:2; Hab. 3:1)

[1](14:18) "Most High," or "God Most High" (Heb. *El Elyon*). *"Elyon"* means simply *highest; El Elyon* is "God the highest."

(1) The first revelation of this name (v. 18) indicates its distinctive meanings. Abram, returning from his victory over the confederated kings (Gen. 14:1–17), is met by Melchizedek, king of Salem . . . the "priest of God Most High" *(El Elyon)*, who blesses Abram in the name of *El Elyon*, "Possessor of heaven and earth." This revelation produced a remarkable impression upon the patriarch. Not only did he at once give Melchizedek "a tithe of" the spoil of the battle, but when the king of Sodom offered some of that spoil to Abram, his answer was: "I have raised my hand to the LORD [Jehovah], God Most High [*El Elyon*], the Possessor of heaven and earth, that I will take nothing, from a thread to a sandal strap," etc. (Gen. 14:22–23).

(a) The LORD (Jehovah) is known to a Gentile king (Melchizedek) by the name "God Most High" *(El Elyon);* (b) a Gentile is the priest of *El Elyon* and (c) His distinctive character as Most High God is "Possessor of heaven and earth."

Appropriately to this Gentile knowledge of God by His name "Most High," it is written that "the Most High divided their inheritance to the nations [i.e. Gentiles], When He separated the sons of Adam," etc. (Dt. 32:8). As "Possessor of heaven and earth," it was the prerogative of the Most High to distribute the earth among the nations according to whatever principle He chose. That principle is declared in Dt. 32:8. The same thing is taught by the use of the name in Daniel, the book of Gentile prophecy (Dan. 3:26; 4:17,24,25,32,34; 5:18,21).

(2) As "Possessor of heaven and earth," the Most High God has and exercises authority in both spheres: (a) the heavenly authority of *El Elyon* (e.g. Dan. 4:35,37; Isa. 14:13–14; Mt. 28:18); (b) the earthly authority of *El Elyon* (e.g. Dt. 32:8; 2 Sam. 22:14–15; Ps. 9:2–5; 21:7; 47:2–4; 56:2–3; 82:6,8; 83:16–18; 91:9–12; Dan. 5:18). For other names of Deity, see *notes* on: Gen. 1:1; 15:2 (2); 17:1; 21:33; Ex. 34:6; 1 Sam. 1:3; Mal. 3:18.

[2](15:2) "Lord" (Heb. *Adon, Adonai*).

(1) The primary meaning of *"Adon," "Adonai,"* is *Master*, and it is applied in the OT Scriptures both to Deity and to man. The latter instances are distinguished by the omission of the capital. As applied to man, the word is used of two relationships: master and husband (Gen. 24:9,10,12: "master," may illustrate the former; Gen. 18:12, "lord," the latter). Both these relationships exist between Christ and the believer (Jn. 13:13, Teacher; 2 Cor. 11:2, husband).

(2) Two principles inhere in the relation of master and servant: (a) the master's right to implicit obedience (Lk. 6:46; Jn. 13:13–14); (b) the servant's right to direction in service (Isa. 6:8–11). Clear distinction in the use of the divine names is illustrated in Ex. 4:10–12. Moses feels his weakness and incompetence, and "Moses said to the LORD [Jehovah], O my Lord, [*Adonai*], I am not eloquent," etc. Since service is in question, Moses appropriately addresses Jehovah as Lord. But now power is in question, and it is not the Lord *(Adonai)* but Jehovah (LORD) who answers (referring to creation power)—"The LORD said to him, Who has made man's mouth? . . . Now therefore, go, and I will be with your mouth." The same distinction appears in Josh. 7:8–11. For other names of Deity, see *notes* on: Gen. 1:1; 14:18; 17:1; 21:33; Ex. 34:6; 1 Sam. 1:3; Mal. 3:18; also next *note*.

[3](15:2) "Lord GOD" (Heb. *Adonai Jehovah*). When used distinctively this compound name, while gathering into one the special meanings of each (see Gen. 15:2, *note 2*; Ex. 34:6, *note*), will be found to emphasize the *Adonai* rather than the *Jehovah* character of Deity. (The

childless, and the heir of my house *is* Eliezer of Damascus?"

3 Then Abram said, "Look, You have given me no offspring; indeed one born in my house is my heir!"

4 And behold, the word of the LORD *came* to him, saying, "This one shall not be your heir, but one who will come from your own body shall be your heir."

5 Then He brought him outside and said, "Look now toward heaven, and count the stars if you are able to number them." And He said to him, [a]"So shall your [b]descendants be."

6 And he [c]believed in the LORD, and He [1d]accounted it to him for [e]righteousness.

Israel's captivity predicted by God

7 Then He said to him, "I *am* the LORD, who brought you out of Ur of the Chaldeans, to give you this land to inherit it."

8 And he said, "Lord GOD, how shall I know that I will inherit it?"

9 So He said to him, "Bring Me a three-year-old heifer, a three-year-old female goat, a three-year-old ram, a turtledove, and a young pigeon."

10 Then he brought all these to Him and cut them in two, down the middle, and placed each piece opposite the other; but he did not cut the birds in two.

11 And when the vultures came down on the carcasses, Abram drove them away.

12 Now when the sun was going down, a deep sleep fell upon Abram; and behold, horror *and* great darkness fell upon him.

13 Then He said to Abram: "Know certainly that your descendants will be strangers in a land *that is* not theirs, and will serve them, and they will afflict them four hundred years.

14 "And also the nation whom they serve I will judge; afterward they shall come out with great possessions.

15 "Now as for you, you shall go to your fathers in peace; you shall be buried at a good old age.

16 "But in the fourth generation they shall return here, for the [f]iniquity of the Amorites *is* not yet complete."

17 And it came to pass, when the sun went down and it was dark, that behold, there appeared a smoking [g]oven and a burning torch that [h]passed between those pieces.

Boundaries of the land

18 On the same day the LORD made a covenant with Abram, saying:

"To your descendants I have given this [2]land, from the [i]river of Egypt to the great river, the River Euphrates—

19 "the [3]Kenites, the Kenezzites, the Kadmonites,

20 "the [j]Hittites, the Perizzites, the Rephaim,

21 "the Amorites, the Canaanites, the Girgashites, and the Jebusites."

Sarai's scheme fails

16 NOW Sarai, Abram's wife, had borne him no *children*. And she had an Egyptian maidservant whose name was Hagar.

2 So Sarai said to Abram, "See now, the LORD has restrained me from bearing *children*. Please, go in to my maid; perhaps I shall [k]obtain children by her." And Abram [l]heeded the voice of Sarai.

3 Then Sarai, Abram's wife, took

5 *a* Rom. 4:18; cp. Heb. 11:12 *b Israel* (covenant): vv. 1–5, 18–21; Gen. 17:19. (Gen. 12:2; Rom. 11:26, *note*)
6 *c Faith:* v. 6; Gen. 21:1. (Gen. 3:20; Heb. 11:39, *note*) *d Imputation:* v. 6; Ps. 32:2. (Gen. 15:6; Jas. 2:23) *e Righteousness* (OT): v. 6; Prov. 21:15. (Gen. 6:9; Lk. 2:25, *note*)
16 *f* See Lev. 18:24, *note*
17 *g* Heb. denotes *a portable firepot* *h Miracles* (OT): v. 17; Gen. 19:11. (Gen. 5:24; Jon. 1:17, *note*)
18 *i* Not the Nile but a small stream south of Gaza, known as *Wadi el Arish*
15:20 *j* See 2 Ki. 7:6, *note* 16:2 *k* Cp. Gen. 30:3 *l* Gen. 3:17

following passages may suffice to illustrate this: Gen. 15:2,8; Dt. 3:24; 9:26; Josh. 7:7; Jud. 6:22; 16:28; 2 Sam. 7:18–20,28–29; 1 Ki. 2:26; Ps. 69:6; 71:5; Isa. 7:7). For other names of Deity, see *notes* on: Gen. 1:1; 14:18; 17:1; 21:33; Ex. 34:6; 1 Sam. 1:3; Mal. 3:18; also preceding *note*.

[1](15:6) "Accounted it to him for righteousness." This is the first occurrence of the vital and sole condition of salvation. Man is without righteousness (Ps. 51:5; Rom. 3:23); if he is to be just in God's sight, God must reckon His own righteousness to man's account through man's trust in Him. The quotation of this passage in Rom. 4:3 indicates that the method of salvation in OT and NT is the same. Galatians 3:3,6 affirms that the Christian life is one of faith, because it was entered by this way. In Jas. 2:21 the teaching is that saving faith manifests itself in works as in Abraham's offering of Isaac (Gen. 22).

[2](15:18) The gift of the land is modified by prophecies of three dispossessions and restorations (vv. 13–14,16; Dt. 28:62–65; 30:1–3; Jer. 25:11–12). Two dispossessions and restorations have been accomplished. Israel is now in the third dispersion, from which she will be restored at the return of the Lord as King under the Davidic Covenant (see 2 Sam. 7:16, *note;* cp. Dt. 30:3; Jer. 23:5–8; Ezek. 37:21–25; Lk. 1:30–33; Acts 15:14–17).

[3](15:19) These ten nations (vv. 19–21) are sometimes summarized by three, as in Ex. 23:28; or by six, Ex. 3:17; or by seven, Josh. 24:11; cp. Acts 13:19.

[1]Hagar her maid, the Egyptian, and
gave her to her husband Abram to be
his wife, after Abram had dwelt ten
years in the land of Canaan.
4 So he went in to Hagar, and she
conceived. And when she saw that she
had conceived, her mistress became
[a]despised in her eyes.
5 Then Sarai said to Abram, "My
wrong *be* upon you! I gave my maid
into your embrace; and when she saw
that she had conceived, I became despised in her eyes. The LORD judge between you and me."
6 So Abram said to Sarai, "Indeed
your maid *is* in your hand; do to her as
you please." And when Sarai dealt
harshly with her, she fled from her
presence.
7 Now the [b]Angel of the LORD
found her by a spring of water in the
wilderness, by the spring on the way
to Shur.
8 And He said, "Hagar, Sarai's
maid, where have you come from, and
where are you going?" She said, "I am
fleeing from the presence of my mistress Sarai."
9 The Angel of the LORD said to
her, "Return to your mistress, and
submit yourself under her hand."
10 Then the Angel of the LORD said
to her, "I will [c]multiply your descendants exceedingly, so that they shall
not be counted for multitude."
11 And the Angel of the LORD said
to her:

"Behold, you *are* with child,
And you shall bear a son.
You shall call his name
[2][d]Ishmael,
Because the LORD has heard
your affliction.
12 He shall be a wild man;
His hand *shall be* against every
man,
And every man's hand against
him.
And he shall dwell in the
presence of all his brethren."

13 Then she called the name of the
LORD who spoke to her, You-Are-the-
God-Who-Sees; for she said, "Have I
also here seen Him who sees me?"
14 Therefore the well was called
[e]Beer Lahai Roi; observe, *it is* between Kadesh and Bered.
15 So Hagar bore Abram a son; and
Abram named his son, whom Hagar
bore, Ishmael.
16 Abram *was* eighty-six years old
when Hagar bore Ishmael to Abram.

Revelation of God as El Shaddai, Almighty God

17 WHEN Abram was ninety-
nine years old, the LORD [f]ap-
peared to Abram and said to him, "I
am [3]Almighty [g]God; walk before Me
and be [h]blameless.
2 "And I will make My covenant

CHAPTER 16
4
a 1 Sam. 1:6–7
7
b Angel (of the LORD): vv. 7–12; Gen. 21:17. (Gen. 16:7; Jud. 2:1, *note*)
10
c Gen. 17:20
11
d Lit. *God shall hear*
14
e Lit. *the well of Him who lives and sees me.* Gen. 24:62; 25:11
CHAPTER 17
1
f Theophanies: vv. 1–22; Gen. 18:1. (Gen. 12:7, *note;* Dan. 10:5)
g Deity (names of): v. 1; Gen. 21:33. (Gen. 1:1; Mal. 3:18)
h Lit. *upright* or *sincere*

[1](16:3) Hagar is a type of the law which, as Paul says, "gives birth to bondage." Cp. Gal. 4:24–25.

[2](16:11) Ishmael, the child of Sarai's and Abram's lapse into unbelief, was the progenitor of the Arabs, the traditional enemies of the Jewish people. Moreover Muhammed, the founder of Islam, whose adherents form Christianity's most difficult missionary problem, came from the line of Ishmael. Islam is the world religion which is, perhaps, closest to Christianity; thus it is the hardest to penetrate with the Gospel of Christ.

[3](17:1) "Almighty God." *Shaddai* is the name of God characteristically used by the patriarchs prior to the giving of the law at Sinai. Its most frequent occurrence is in the Book of Job, where *Shaddai* occurs thirty-one times. The name *Jehovah* largely replaces it from Ex. 6 onward, where attention is centered more particularly on Israel as God's covenant people.

(1) *El Shaddai* is the name of God which sets Him forth primarily as the strengthener and satisfier of His people. It is to be regretted that *Shaddai* was translated "Almighty." The primary name, *El* or *Elohim,* sufficiently signifies almightiness. "All-sufficient" would far better express the characteristic use of the name in Scripture.

(2) Almighty God *(El Shaddai)* not only enriches but makes fruitful. This is nowhere better illustrated than in the first occurrence of the name (Gen. 17:1–8). To a man ninety-nine years of age, and "as good as dead" (Heb. 11:12), He said: "I am Almighty God . . . I will make My covenant between Me and you, and will multiply you exceedingly." The same thing is taught by the use of the name in Gen. 28:3–4.

(3) As bestower of fruitfulness, Almighty God *(El Shaddai)* chastens His people. For the moral connection of chastening with fruit-bearing, see Jn. 15:2; cp. Ruth 1:20; Heb. 12:10. Hence, Almighty is the characteristic name of God in Job. The hand of *Shaddai* falls upon Job, the best man of his time, not in judgment but in purifying unto greater fruitfulness (Job 5:17–25). For other names of Deity, see *notes* on: Gen. 1:1; 14:18; 15:2 (2); 21:33; Ex. 34:6; 1 Sam. 1:3; Mal. 3:18.

between Me and you, and will [a]multi-
ply you exceedingly."
3 Then Abram fell on his face, and
God talked with him, saying:

Abram becomes Abraham

4 "As for Me, behold, My covenant
is with you, and you shall be a father
of many nations.
5 "No longer shall your name be
called [b]Abram, but your name shall
be [c]Abraham; for I have made you a
[d]father of many nations.

Abrahamic Covenant confirmed again and made everlasting

6 "I will make you exceedingly
fruitful; and I will make [e]nations of
you, and [f]kings shall come from you.
7 "And I will establish My covenant between Me and you and your
descendants after you in their generations, for an everlasting covenant, to
be God to you and your descendants
after you.
8 "Also I [g]give to you and your descendants after you the land in which
you are a stranger, all the land of Canaan, as an everlasting possession;
and I will be their God."

Circumcision instituted as sign of Abrahamic Covenant

9 And God said to Abraham: "As
for you, you shall keep My covenant,
you and your descendants after you
throughout their generations.
10 "This *is* My covenant which you
shall keep, between Me and you and
your descendants after you: Every
male child among you shall be [1]cir-
cumcised;
11 "and you shall be circumcised in
the flesh of your foreskins, and it shall
be a [h]sign of the covenant between
Me and you.
12 "He who is eight days old among
you shall be [i]circumcised, every male
child in your generations, he who is
born in your house or bought with
money from any foreigner who is not
your descendant.

2 *a* Gen. 12:2; 18:18
5 *b* Lit. *exalted father* *c* Lit. *father of a multitude* *d* Rom. 4:17
6 *e* Gen. 35:11 *f* Gen. 36:31; 1 Sam. 8:22
8 *g* Gen. 12:7; 13:15; Acts 7:5
11 *h* Rom. 4:9–12
12 *i* Lk. 2:21; Rom. 2:25–29; 4:9–12; 1 Cor. 7:18–19; Gal. 5:2–3; cp. Col. 2:11
15 *j* Lit. *princess*
16 *k* Gen. 36:31; 1 Sam. 8:22
17 *l* v. 3 *m* Gen. 18:12
18 *n Bible prayers* (OT): vv. 17–18; Gen. 18:23. (Gen. 15:2; Hab. 3:1)
19 *o* Lit. *he laughs* *p Israel* (covenant): vv. 15–21; Gen. 22:16. (Gen. 12:2;

13 "He who is born in your house
and he who is bought with your
money must be circumcised, and My
covenant shall be in your flesh for an
everlasting covenant.
14 "And the uncircumcised male
child, who is not circumcised in the
flesh of his foreskin, that person shall
be cut off from his people; he has broken My covenant."

Promise concerning Isaac, in whom the line of Christ runs

15 Then God said to Abraham, "As
for Sarai your wife, you shall not call
her name Sarai, but [j]Sarah *shall be*
her name.
16 "And I will bless her and also
give you a son by her; then I will bless
her, and she shall be *a mother of* nations; [k]kings of peoples shall be from
her."
17 Then Abraham [l]fell on his face
and [m]laughed, and said in his heart,
"Shall *a child* be born to a man who is
one hundred years old? And shall
Sarah, who is ninety years old, bear *a*
child?"
18 And Abraham [n]said to God,
"Oh, that Ishmael might live before
You!"
19 Then God said: "No, Sarah your
wife shall bear you a son, and you
shall call his name [o]Isaac; I will establish My [p]covenant with him for an
everlasting covenant, *and* with his
[q]descendants after him.

Ishmael to be a nation

20 "And as for Ishmael, I have
heard you. Behold, I have blessed him,
and will make him fruitful, and will
multiply him exceedingly. He shall beget [r]twelve princes, and I will make
him a great [s]nation.
21 "But My [t]covenant I will establish with Isaac, whom Sarah shall

Rom. 11:26, *note*) *q Christ* (first advent): v. 19; Gen. 24:60. (Gen. 3:15; Acts 1:11, *note*) **17:20** *r* Gen. 16:10; 25:12–16 *s* Gen. 21:13,18 **17:21** *t* Gen. 26:2–5

[1](17:10) The rite of circumcision first appears in the Biblical record after the announcement of the Abrahamic Covenant (Gen. 12:1). The sign of the covenant between the LORD and Noah was the rainbow (Gen. 9:13; cp. 8:20–22), in regard to which man himself had no responsibility. But this token of God's covenant with Abraham, circumcision, becomes effective only by the voluntary obedience of man, especially of parent toward child, and thus indicates (1) man's responsibility; (2) his faith in God's Word (Rom. 4:11–12); and (3) his assent to the condition of divine mercy. The circumcised man was to identify himself as a member of Israel.

Circumcision was practiced in Egypt at a very early time, but not among the Babylonians or the Hurrians (Horites) who made up a large part of the population of Palestine in Abraham's day. Genesis 17 does not describe its origin but tells how God prescribed it for Abraham and his descendants, and gave it a spiritual meaning.

bear to you at this set [a]time next
year."
22 Then He finished talking with
him, and God went up from Abraham.
23 So Abraham took Ishmael his
son, all who were born in his house
and all who were bought with his
money, every male among the men of
Abraham's house, and circumcised
the flesh of their foreskins that very
same day, as God had said to him.
24 Abraham *was* ninety-nine years
old when he was circumcised in the
flesh of his foreskin.
25 And Ishmael his son *was* thirteen years old when he was circumcised in the flesh of his foreskin.
26 That very same day Abraham
was circumcised, and his son Ishmael;
27 and all the men of his house,
born in the house or bought with
money from a foreigner, were circumcised with him.

Abraham, "the Friend of God"
(cp. Jn. 3:29; 15:13–15)

18 THEN the LORD [b]appeared to
him by the terebinth trees of
Mamre,* as he was sitting in the tent
door in the heat of the day.
2 So he lifted his eyes and looked,
and behold, three men were standing
by him; and when he saw *them,* he ran
from the tent door to meet them, and
bowed himself to the ground,
3 and said, "My Lord, if I have now
found favor in Your sight, do not pass
on by Your servant.
4 "Please let a little water be
brought, and wash your feet, and rest
yourselves under the tree.
5 "And I will bring a morsel of
bread, that you may refresh your
hearts. After that you may pass by,
inasmuch as you have come to your
servant." They said, "Do as you have
said."
6 So Abraham hurried into the
tent to Sarah and said, "Quickly, make
ready three measures of fine meal;
knead *it* and make cakes."
7 And Abraham ran to the herd,
took a tender and good calf, gave *it* to
a young man, and he hastened to prepare it.
8 So he took butter and milk and
the calf which he had prepared, and
set *it* before them; and he stood by
them under the tree as they ate.
9 Then they said to him, "Where *is*
Sarah your wife?" So he said, "Here,
in the tent."
10 And He said, "I will certainly re-

21
a Gen. 18:14
CHAPTER 18
1
b Theophanies: vv. 1,17,22, 33; Gen. 26:2. (Gen. 12:7, *note;* Dan. 10:5). The three men in v. 2 apparently are the Second Person of the Godhead and two angels (see Heb. 1:4, *note*). The two angels appear again in Gen. 19:1
10
c Rom. 9:9
11
d Cp. Lk. 1:18
12
e Gen. 17:17
14
f Num. 11:23; Mt. 19:26; Mk. 10:27
18
g Gen. 12:3; 22:18
20
h Gen. 19:13
i Gen. 13:13
23
j vv. 1–8: communion and intercession go together
k Bible prayers (OT): vv. 23–33; Gen. 24:12. (Gen. 15:2; Hab. 3:1)
l Job 9:22
m Gen. 20:4

turn to you according to the time of
life, and behold, [c]Sarah your wife
shall have a son." (Sarah was listening
in the tent door which *was* behind
him.)
11 Now Abraham and Sarah were
[d]old, well advanced in age; *and* Sarah
had passed the age of childbearing.*
12 Therefore Sarah [e]laughed
within herself, saying, "After I have
grown old, shall I have pleasure, my
lord being old also?"
13 And the LORD said to Abraham,
"Why did Sarah laugh, saying, 'Shall
I surely bear *a child,* since I am old?'
14 "Is [f]anything too hard for the
LORD? At the appointed time I will return to you, according to the time of
life, and Sarah shall have a son."
15 But Sarah denied *it,* saying, "I
did not laugh," for she was afraid. And
He said, "No, but you did laugh!"
16 Then the men rose from there
and looked toward Sodom, and Abraham went with them to send them on
the way.
17 And the LORD said, "Shall I hide
from Abraham what I am doing,
18 "since Abraham shall surely become a great and mighty nation, and
all the nations of the earth shall be
[g]blessed in him?
19 "For I have known him, in order
that he may command his children
and his household after him, that they
keep the way of the LORD, to do righteousness and justice, that the LORD
may bring to Abraham what He has
spoken to him."
20 And the LORD said, "Because the
[h]outcry against Sodom and Gomorrah is great, and because their [i]sin is
very grave,
21 "I will go down now and see
whether they have done altogether according to the outcry against it that
has come to Me; and if not, I will
know."
22 Then the men turned away from
there and went toward Sodom, but
Abraham still stood before the LORD.

Abraham, the intercessor

23 And Abraham came [j]near and
said, [k]"Would You also [l]destroy the
[m]righteous with the wicked?
24 "Suppose there were fifty righteous within the city; would You also
destroy the place and not spare *it* for
the fifty righteous that were in it?

*
18:1 Hebrew *Alon Mamre* **18:11** Literally *the manner of women had ceased to be with Sarah*

25 "Far be it from You to do such a thing as this, to slay the righteous with the wicked, so that the righteous should be as the wicked; far be it from You! Shall not the Judge of all the earth [a]do right?"

26 So the LORD said, [b]"If I find in Sodom fifty righteous within the city, then I will spare all the place for their sakes."

27 Then Abraham answered and said, "Indeed now, I who *am but* dust and ashes have taken it upon myself to speak to the Lord:

28 "Suppose there were five less than the fifty righteous; would You destroy all of the city for *lack of* five?" So He said, "If I find there forty-five, I will not destroy *it*."

29 And he spoke to Him yet again and said, "Suppose there should be forty found there?" So He said, "I will not do *it* for the sake of forty."

30 Then he said, "Let not the Lord be angry, and I will speak: Suppose thirty should be found there?" So He said, "I will not do *it* if I find thirty there."

31 And he said, "Indeed now, I have taken it upon myself to speak to the Lord: Suppose twenty should be found there?" So He said, "I will not destroy *it* for the sake of twenty."

32 Then he said, "Let not the Lord be angry, and I will speak but once more: Suppose ten should be found there?" And He said, "I will not destroy *it* for the sake of ten."

33 So the LORD went His way as soon as He had finished speaking with Abraham; and Abraham returned to his place.

Lot's third step in backsliding: a great man in Sodom (v. 1; cp. Gen. 13:10,12; 19:33)

19 NOW the two [c]angels [d]came to Sodom in the evening, and Lot [1]was sitting in the gate of Sodom. When Lot saw *them*, he rose to meet them, and he bowed himself with his face toward the ground.

2 And he said, "Here now, my lords, please turn in to your servant's house and spend the night, and [e]wash your feet; then you may rise early and go on your way." And they said, "No, but we will spend the night in the open square."

3 But he insisted strongly; so they turned in to him and entered his house. Then he made them a feast, and baked [f]unleavened bread, and they ate.

4 Now before they lay down, the men of the city, the men of Sodom, both old and young, all the people from every quarter, surrounded the house.

5 And they called to Lot and said to him, "Where are the men who came to you tonight? Bring them out to us that we may know them *carnally*."

6 So Lot went out to them through the doorway, shut the door behind him,

7 and said, "Please, my brethren, do not do so wickedly!

8 "See now, I have two daughters who have not known a man; please, let me bring them out to you, and you may do to them as you wish; only do nothing to these men, since this is the reason they have come under the shadow of my roof."

9 And they said, "Stand back!" Then they [g]said, "This one came in to stay *here*, and he keeps acting as a [h]judge; now we will deal worse with you than with them." So they pressed hard against the man Lot, and came near to break down the door.

10 But the men reached out their hands and pulled Lot into the house with them, and shut the door.

11 And they [i]struck the men who *were* at the doorway of the house with blindness, both small and great, so that they became weary *trying* to find the door.

12 Then the men said to Lot, "Have you anyone else here? Son-in-law, your sons, your daughters, and whomever you have in the city—take *them* out of this place!

13 "For we will destroy this place, because the [j]outcry against them has grown great before the face of the LORD, and the LORD has sent us to destroy it."

14 So [2]Lot went out and spoke to his sons-in-law, who had married his daughters, and said, "Get up, get out of this place; for the LORD will destroy this city!" But to his sons-in-law he seemed to be joking.

25
a Dt. 32:4
26
b Jer. 5:1
CHAPTER 19
1
c See Heb. 1:4, *note*
d Cp. Gen. 18:2,16,22
2
e Gen. 18:4; 24:32
3
f *Leaven:* v. 3; Ex. 12:8. (Gen. 19:3; Mt. 13:33, *note*)
9
g The world's contempt for a worldly believer
h Cp. Ex. 2:14
11
i *Miracles* (OT): vv. 11, 24–26; Gen. 20:17. (Gen. 5:24; Jon. 1:17, *note*)
13
j Gen. 18:20

[1](19:1) Lot held a position of authority in Sodom (cp. Dt. 21:19–21).
[2](19:14) Lot had utterly lost his testimony. In gaining influence (Gen. 19:1) he had lost power even in his own family.

Destruction of Sodom

15 When the morning dawned, the
[a]angels urged Lot to hurry, saying,
"Arise, take your wife and your two
daughters who are here, lest you be
consumed in the punishment of the
city."
16 And while he lingered, the men
took hold of his hand, his wife's hand,
and the hands of his two daughters,
the LORD being merciful to him, and
they brought him out and set him outside the city.
17 So it came to pass, when they
had brought them outside, that he*
said, "Escape for your life! Do not
[b]look behind you nor stay anywhere
in the plain. Escape [c]to the mountains, lest you be destroyed."
18 Then Lot said to them, "Please,
no, my lords!
19 "Indeed now, your servant has
found favor in your sight, and you
have increased your mercy which you
have shown me by saving my life; but
I cannot escape to the mountains, lest
some evil overtake me and I die.
20 "See now, this city *is* near
enough to flee to, and it *is* a little one;
please let me escape there (*is* it not a
little one?) and my soul shall live."
21 And he said to him, "See, I have
favored you concerning this thing
also, in that I will not overthrow this
city for which you have spoken.
22 "Hurry, escape there. For I cannot do anything until you arrive
there." Therefore the name of the city
was called [d]Zoar.
23 The sun had risen upon the earth
when Lot entered Zoar.
24 Then the LORD rained brimstone
and [e]fire on [f]Sodom and Gomorrah,
from the LORD out of the heavens.
25 So He overthrew those cities, all
the plain, all the inhabitants of the cities, and what grew on the ground.
26 But his [g]wife looked back behind him, and she became a pillar of
salt.

15
a See Heb. 1:4, *note*
17
b Cp. Mt. 24:16–18
c Gen. 14:10
22
d i.e. *Little*
24
e Lev. 10:2
f Dt. 29:23; Isa. 9–10; 3:9; 13:19; Jer. 23:14; 49:18; 50:40; Lam. 4:6; Ezek. 16:48,56; Amos 4:11; Zeph. 2:9; Mt. 10:15; Mk. 6:11; Rom. 9:29; 2 Pet. 2:6; Jude 7; Rev. 11:8; Cp. Mt. 11:23–24; Lk. 10:12; 17:29
26
g Lk. 17:32
27
h Gen. 18:22
29
i See v. 36, *note*

27 And Abraham went early in the
morning to the place where he had
[h]stood before the LORD.
28 Then he looked toward [1]Sodom
and Gomorrah, and toward all the
land of the plain; and he saw, and behold, the smoke of the land which
went up like the smoke of a furnace.
29 And it came to pass, [i]when God
destroyed the cities of the plain, that
God remembered Abraham, and sent
Lot out of the midst of the overthrow,
when He overthrew the cities in which
Lot had dwelt.

Lot's final step in backsliding
(cp. Gen. 13:10,12; 19:1; cp. Lk. 22:31–62)

30 Then Lot went up out of Zoar
and dwelt in the mountains, and his
two daughters were with him; for he
was afraid to dwell in Zoar. And he
and his two daughters dwelt in a cave.
31 Now the firstborn said to the
younger, "Our father *is* old, and *there
is* no man on the earth to come in to us
as is the custom of all the earth.
32 [2]"Come, let us make our father
drink wine, and we will lie with him,
that we may preserve the lineage of
our father."
33 So they made their father drink
wine that night. And the firstborn
went in and lay with her father, and he
did not know when she lay down or
when she arose.
34 It happened on the next day that
the firstborn said to the younger, "Indeed I lay with my father last night; let
us make him drink wine tonight also,
and you go in *and* lie with him, that we
may preserve the lineage of our father."
35 Then they made their father
drink wine that night also. And the
younger arose and lay with him, and
he did not know when she lay down or
when she arose.
36 [3]Thus both the daughters of Lot
were with child by their father.

* 19:17 Septuagint, Syriac, and Vulgate read *they*.

[1](19:28) The ruins of Sodom and Gomorrah are probably hidden beneath the waters of the shallow southern end of the Dead Sea, which has risen greatly in recent years and now covers a much larger area than formerly. Ruins of a festival center on a neighboring plateau, where inhabitants of these cities may have gathered, have been discovered. Archaeological examination proves that the center was used for centuries but abandoned after Abraham's time.

[2](19:32) Lot "pitched his tent even as far as Sodom" (Gen. 13:12) for worldly gain; then he became an important man in Sodom (Gen. 19:1) at the cost of his daughters' accepting the morals of Sodom.

[3](19:36) Abraham and Lot are contrasted characters. Of the same stock (Gen. 11:31), subjected to the same environment, and both justified men (Gen. 15:6; 2 Pet. 2:7–8), the contrast in character and career is shown to be the result of their respective choices at a crisis in their lives. Lot "chose for himself all the plain of Jordan" for present advantage; Abraham, waiting

37 The firstborn bore a son and
called his name Moab; he *is* the father
of the [a]Moabites to this day.
38 And the younger, she also bore a
son and called his name Ben-Ammi;
he *is* the father of the people of [b]Am-
mon to this day.

Abraham's lapse at Gerar
(cp. Gen. 26:6–32)

20 AND Abraham journeyed
from there to the [c]South, and
dwelt between [d]Kadesh and Shur,
and stayed in [e]Gerar.
2 Now Abraham said of Sarah his
wife, "She *is* my [f]sister." And Abimelech king of Gerar sent and took
Sarah.
3 But God came to Abimelech in a
dream by night, and said to him, "Indeed you *are* a dead man because of
the woman whom you have taken, for
she *is* a man's wife."
4 But Abimelech had not come
near her; and he said, "Lord, [g]will
You slay a righteous nation also?
5 "Did he not say to me, 'She *is* my
sister'? And she, even she herself said,
'He *is* my brother.' In the integrity of
my heart and innocence of my hands
I have done this."
6 And God said to him in a dream,
"Yes, I know that you did this in the
integrity of your heart. For I also
[h]withheld you from sinning [i]against
Me; therefore I did not let you touch
her.
7 "Now therefore, restore the
man's wife; for he *is* a prophet, and he
will pray for you and you shall live.
But if you do not restore *her,* know
that you shall surely die, you and all
who *are* yours."
8 So Abimelech rose early in the
morning, called all his servants, and
told all these things in their hearing;
and the men were very much afraid.
9 And Abimelech called Abraham
and said to him, "What have you done
to us? How have I offended you, that
you have brought on me and on my
kingdom a great sin? You have done
deeds to me that ought not to be done."
10 Then Abimelech said to Abraham, "What did you have in view, that
you have done this thing?"
11 And Abraham said, "Because I
thought, surely the [j]fear of God *is* not
in this place; and they will [k]kill me on
account of my wife.
12 "But indeed *she is* truly my sister. She *is* the daughter of my father,
but not the daughter of my mother;
and she became my wife.
13 "And it came to pass, when God
caused me to wander from my father's
house, that I said to her, 'This *is* your
kindness that you should do for me: in
every place, wherever we go, say of
me, "He *is* my brother." ' "
14 Then Abimelech took sheep,
oxen, and male and female servants,
and gave *them* to Abraham; and he
restored Sarah his wife to him.
15 And Abimelech said, "See, my
land *is* before you; dwell where it
pleases you."
16 Then to Sarah he said, "Behold,
I have given your brother a thousand
pieces of silver; indeed this vindicates
you* before all who *are* with you and
before everybody." Thus she was rebuked.
17 So Abraham prayed to God; and
God [l]healed Abimelech, his wife, and
his female servants. Then they bore
children;
18 for the LORD had closed up all the
wombs of the house of Abimelech
[m]because of Sarah, Abraham's wife.

Birth of Isaac

21 AND the LORD visited Sarah as
He had [n]said, and the LORD did
for Sarah as He had [o]spoken.
2 For Sarah [l]conceived and bore
Abraham a son in his [p]old age, at the
[q]set time of which God had spoken to
him.
3 And Abraham called the name
of his son who was born to him—
whom [1]Sarah bore to him—[2r]Isaac.

37 *a* Dt. 2:9,19
38 *b* Num. 21:24
CHAPTER 20
1 *c* See Gen. 12:9, *note* *d* Gen. 16:14; Num. 13:26 *e* Gen. 26:1, 6
2 *f* Gen. 12:13; 26:7
4 *g* Gen. 18:23; Num. 16:22
6 *h* Cp. 1 Sam. 25:26,34 *i* Cp. Gen. 39:9; 2Sam. 12:13
11 *j* See Ps. 19:9, *note* *k* Cp. Gen. 12:12
17 *l* *Miracles* (OT): vv. 17–18; 21:2; Ex. 4:3. (Gen. 5:24; Jon. 1:17, *note*)
18 *m* Cp. Gen. 12:17
CHAPTER 21
1 *n* *Faith:* vv. 1–6; Gen. 22:3. (Gen. 3:20; Heb. 11:39, *note*) *o* Gen. 18:10
2 *p* Heb. 11:11–12 *q* Gen. 18:14; cp. Gal. 4:4

21:3 *r* Cp. Gen. 17:19

*

20:16 Literally *it is a covering of the eyes for you*

"for the city which has foundations" (Heb. 11:10), "went and dwelt by the terebinth trees of Mamre [fatness], which are in Hebron [communion]" (Gen. 13:18). The men are representative of the worldly and the spiritual believer.

[1](21:3) Sarah, a type of grace, the "freewoman," and of "the Jerusalem above." Cp. Gen. 17:15–19; Gal. 4:22–31.

[2](21:3) Isaac is typical in a fourfold way: (1) of the Church as composed of the spiritual children of Abraham (Gal. 4:28); (2) of Christ as the Son "obedient to the point of death" (Gen. 22:1–10; Phil. 2:5–8); (3) of Christ as the Bridegroom of a called-out bride (cp. Gen. 24; see Church, Mt. 16:18, *note*); and (4) of the new nature of the believer as "born according to the Spirit" (Gal. 4:29).

4 Then Abraham [1]circumcised his son Isaac when he was [a]eight days old, as God had commanded him.

5 Now Abraham was [b]one hundred years old when his son Isaac was born to him.

6 And Sarah said, "God has made me laugh, *and* all who hear will laugh with me."

7 She also said, "Who would have said to Abraham that Sarah would nurse children? For I have borne *him* a son in his old age."

8 So the child grew and was weaned. And Abraham made a great feast on the same day that Isaac was weaned.

Bondwoman and her son cast out
(Gal. 4:21–31)

9 And Sarah saw the [c]son of Hagar the Egyptian, whom she had borne to Abraham, scoffing.

10 Therefore she said to Abraham, [d]"Cast out this bondwoman and her son; for the son of this bondwoman shall not be heir with my son, *namely* with Isaac."

11 And the matter was very displeasing in Abraham's sight because of his son.

12 But God said to Abraham, "Do not let it be displeasing in your sight because of the lad or because of your bondwoman. Whatever Sarah has said to you, listen to her voice; for [e]in Isaac your seed shall be called.

13 "Yet I will also make a [f]nation of the son of the [2]bondwoman, because he *is* your seed."

14 So Abraham rose early in the morning, and took bread and a skin of water; and putting *it* on her shoulder, he gave *it* and the [3]boy to Hagar, and sent her away. Then she departed and wandered in the Wilderness of Beersheba.

15 And the water in the skin was used up, and she placed the boy under one of the shrubs.

16 Then she went and sat down across from *him* at a distance of about a bowshot; for she said to herself, "Let me not see the death of the boy." So she sat opposite *him,* and lifted her voice and wept.

17 And God heard the voice of the lad. Then the [g]angel of God called to Hagar out of heaven, and said to her, "What ails you, Hagar? Fear not, for God has heard the voice of the lad where he *is.*

18 "Arise, lift up the lad and hold him with your hand, for I will make him a great nation."

19 Then God [4h]opened her eyes, and she saw a well of water. And she went and filled the skin with water, and gave the lad a drink.

20 So God was with the lad; and he grew and dwelt in the wilderness, and became an archer.

21 He dwelt in the Wilderness of Paran; and his mother took a wife for him from the land of Egypt.

Abraham at Beersheba

22 And it came to pass at that time that Abimelech and Phichol, the commander of his army, spoke to Abraham, saying, "God *is* with you in all that you do.

23 "Now therefore, swear to me by God that you will not deal falsely with me, with my offspring, or with my posterity; but that according to the kindness that I have done to you, you will do to me and to the land in which you have dwelt."

4 *a* Gen. 17:12; Lev. 12:3
5 *b* Gen. 17:1, 17
9 *c* Gen. 16:1, 15; Gal. 4:22–23
10 *d* Gal. 3:18; 4:30
12 *e* Rom. 9:7
13 *f* v. 18; Gen. 17:20
17 *g* *Angel* (of the LORD): v. 17; Gen. 22:11. (Gen. 16:7; Jud. 2:1, *note*)
19 *h* Gen. 3:7; Num. 22:31; 2 Ki. 6:17; Lk. 24:31

[1](21:4) By this rite Isaac became, as a child, identified with the nation Israel. See Gen. 17:10, *note.*

[2](21:13) Many features of Abraham's treatment of Hagar seem strange to a modern reader, but they are exactly in accord with the provisions of the Code of Hammurabi, the great Babylonian law code of Mesopotamia, the region from which he had come. Before the discovery of this code many critics had questioned whether so complex a code as that of Moses could have been written at so early a time. However, the Code of Hammurabi is more complex than that of Moses and comes from a much earlier period. The Mosaic Code was not derived from it, but many of the customs of the Book of Genesis show that its prescriptions were familiar in Abraham's day.

[3](21:14) The Hebrew word for "boy" *(yeled),* meaning *one begotten* or *one born,* was used for anyone up to young manhood (cp. same word translated "young man" in Gen. 4:23). Ishmael was now about fifteen years old (cp. Gen. 16:16; 21:5), and Hagar abandoned the exhausted child in the shade of a shrub.

[4](21:19) Here is a touching scene: the bondwoman, seemingly alone and without help; and the God of grace, calling to her from heaven. "Then God opened her eyes, and she saw a well of water." So the Holy Spirit opens the eyes of believing sinners and directs them to the water of life (cp. Jn. 4:14).

24 And Abraham said, "I will swear."

25 Then Abraham rebuked Abimelech because of a well of water which Abimelech's servants had [a]seized.

26 And Abimelech said, "I do not know who has done this thing; you did not tell me, nor had I heard *of it* until today."

27 So Abraham took sheep and oxen and gave them to Abimelech, and the two of them made a covenant.

28 And Abraham set seven ewe lambs of the flock by themselves.

29 Then Abimelech asked Abraham, "What *is the meaning of* these seven ewe lambs which you have set by themselves?"

30 And he said, "You will take *these* seven ewe lambs from my hand, that they may be my witness that I have dug this well."

31 Therefore he called that place Beersheba,* because the two of them swore an oath there.

32 Thus they made a covenant at Beersheba. So Abimelech rose with Phichol, the commander of his army, and they returned to the land of the Philistines.

25
a Cp. Gen. 26:20

33
b Gen. 13:4; 26:25
c *Deity* (names of): v. 33; Gen. 35:11. (Gen. 1:1; Mal. 3:18)

CHAPTER 22

1
d *Test/tempt:* v. 1; Ex. 15:25. (Gen. 3:1; Jas. 1:14, *note*)

2
e First use of word *love.* Cp. Jn. 5:20

3
f *Faith:* vv. 1–14; Gen. 50:24. (Gen. 3:20; Heb. 11:39, *note*)

33 Then *Abraham* planted a tamarisk tree in Beersheba, and there [b]called on the name of the LORD, the [c]Everlasting [1]God.

34 And Abraham stayed in the land of the [2]Philistines many days.

Offering of Isaac (Heb. 11:17–19)

22 [3]NOW it came to pass after these things that God [4d]tested Abraham, and said to him, "Abraham!" And he said, "Here I am."

2 Then He said, "Take now your son, your only *son* Isaac, whom you [e]love, and go to the land of [5]Moriah, and offer him there as a burnt offering on one of the mountains of which I shall tell you."

3 [f]So Abraham rose early in the morning and saddled his donkey, and took two of his young men with him, and Isaac his son; and he split the wood for the burnt offering, and arose and went to the place of which God had told him.

4 Then on the third day Abraham lifted his eyes and saw the place afar off.

5 And Abraham said to his young men, "Stay here with the donkey; the

*
21:31 Literally *Well of the Oath* or *Well of the Seven*

[1](21:33) "Everlasting God" (Heb. *El Olam*).

(1) The Hebrew *Olam* is used in Scripture: (a) of secret or hidden things (2 Ki. 4:27, "hidden"; Ps. 10:1, "hide"); (b) of an indefinite time or age (Lev. 25:32, "at any time"; Josh. 24:2, "in old times"). Hence the word is used to express the eternal duration of the Being of God (Ps. 90:2, "from everlasting to everlasting"); it is also the Hebrew synonym of the Greek *aion,* age. See Gen. 1:28, *note 4.*

(2) The ideas, therefore, of things kept secret and of indefinite duration combine in this word. Both ideas inhere in the doctrine of the dispensations or ages. They are among the "mysteries" of God (Mt. 13:11; Eph. 1:9–10; 3:2–6). The "Everlasting God" *(El Olam)* is, therefore, that name of Deity in virtue of which He is the God whose wisdom has divided all time and eternity into the mystery of successive ages or dispensations. It is not merely that He is eternal, but that He is God over eternal things. For other names of Deity see *notes* on: Gen. 1:1; 14:18; 15:2 (2); 17:1; Ex. 34:6; 1 Sam. 1:3; Mal. 3:18.

[2](21:34) The presence of Philistines in Palestine at this period has sometimes been called an inaccuracy in the narrative, since the great invasion of the Philistines did not occur until about 1200 B.C.However, as Genesis declares (21:32,34; 26:15,18; etc.) there were smaller groups of the Philistines in Palestine at an earlier time. See also Jud. 13:1, *note.*

[3](22:1) The spiritual experience of Abraham was marked by four great crises, each of which involved a surrender of something naturally most dear. These were: (1) country and relatives (Gen. 12:1. Cp. Mt. 10:34–39; 2 Cor. 6:14–18). (2) His nephew, Lot; especially dear to Abraham by nature, as a possible heir and as a fellow believer (Gen. 13:1–18; 2 Pet. 2:7–8). The completeness of Abraham's separation from one who, though a believer, was a vessel "for dishonor," is shown by Gen. 15:1–3. Cp. Acts 15:36–40; 2 Tim. 2:20–21. (3) His own plan about Ishmael (Gen. 17:17–18. Cp. 1 Chr. 13:1–14; 15:1–2). And (4) Isaac, "your son, your only son Isaac, whom you love" (Gen. 22:1–19. Cp. Heb. 11:17–19).

[4](22:1) God tested Abraham's sincerity, loyalty, and faith. The NT categorically says that God does not solicit any man to do evil (tempt). See Jas. 1:2,13–14, with *note.* Compare other OT references where this word is used: Ex. 17:2,7; Num. 14:22; Dt. 6:16; Ps. 78:18,41,56; 95:9; 106:14; Isa. 7:12; and another word, Mal. 3:15.

[5](22:2) The offering of Isaac may have occurred near the place where the temple of Solomon was built. Cp. 2 Chr. 3:1.

lad* and I will go yonder and worship, and we will [a]come back to you."

6 So Abraham took the wood of the burnt offering and [1]laid *it* on Isaac his son; and he took the [b]fire in his hand, and a knife, and the two of them went together.

7 But Isaac spoke to Abraham his father and said, "My father!" And he said, "Here I am, my son." Then he said, "Look, the fire and the wood, but where *is* the lamb for a burnt offering?"

8 And Abraham said, "My son, God will provide for Himself the [c]lamb for a [d]burnt offering." So the two of them went together.

9 Then they came to the place of which God had told him. And Abraham built an altar there and placed the wood in order; and he bound Isaac his son and [2]laid him on the altar, upon the wood.

10 And Abraham stretched out his hand and took the knife to slay his son.

11 But the [e]Angel of the LORD called to him from heaven and said, "Abraham, Abraham!" So he said, "Here I am."

12 And He said, "Do not lay your hand on the lad, or do anything to him; for now I know that you [f]fear God, since you have not [g]withheld your son, your only *son,* from Me."

13 Then Abraham lifted his eyes and looked, and there behind *him was* a ram caught in a thicket by its horns. So Abraham went and took the ram, and offered it up for a burnt offering instead of his son.

14 And Abraham called the name of the place, [h]The-LORD-Will-Provide;* as it is said *to* this day, "In the Mount of the LORD it shall be provided."

Abrahamic Covenant confirmed again

15 Then the [e]Angel of the LORD called to Abraham a second time out of heaven,

16 and [i]said: "By Myself I have sworn, says the LORD, because you have done this thing, and have not withheld your son, your only *son—*

17 "blessing I will [j]bless you, and multiplying I will multiply your descendants as the [k]stars of the heaven and as the [l]sand which *is* on the seashore; and your descendants shall possess the [m]gate of their enemies.

18 "In your seed [n]all the nations of the earth shall be blessed, because you have [o]obeyed My voice."

19 So Abraham returned to his young men, and they rose and went together to Beersheba; and Abraham dwelt at Beersheba.

20 Now it came to pass after these things that it was told Abraham, saying, "Indeed [p]Milcah also has borne children to your brother Nahor:

21 "Huz his firstborn, Buz his brother, Kemuel the father of Aram,

22 "Chesed, Hazo, Pildash, Jidlaph, and Bethuel."

23 And Bethuel begot [q]Rebekah.* These eight Milcah bore to Nahor, Abraham's brother.

24 His concubine, whose name was Reumah, also bore Tebah, Gaham, Thahash, and Maachah.

Death and burial of Sarah

23 SARAH lived one hundred and twenty-seven years; *these were* the years of the life of Sarah.

2 So Sarah died in [r]Kirjath Arba (that *is,* Hebron) in the land of Canaan, and Abraham came to mourn for Sarah and to weep for her.

3 Then Abraham stood up from before his dead, and spoke to the sons of [s]Heth, saying,

4 "I *am* a foreigner and a visitor among you. Give me property for a [t]burial place among you, that I may bury my dead out of my sight."

5 And the sons of Heth answered Abraham, saying to him,

6 "Hear us, my lord: You *are* a [u]mighty prince among us; bury your

5
a Heb. 11:19
6
b Perhaps a lighted bundle of twigs or pan of embers
8
c Jn. 1:29,36
d *Sacrifice* (typical): vv. 8,13; Ex. 12:3. (Gen. 3:15; Heb. 10:18, *note*)
11
e *Angel* (of the LORD): vv. 11,15; Gen. 31:11. (Gen. 16:7; Jud. 2:1, *note*)
12
f See Ps. 19:9, *note*
g Cp. Jn. 3:16
14
h Lit. *Jehovah Jireh.* See Ex. 34:6, *note*
16
i *Israel* (covenant): vv. 16–18; Gen. 26:3. (Gen. 12:2; Rom. 11:26, *note*)
17
j Gen. 17:16; 26:3,24
k Gen. 15:5; 26:4
l Gen. 32:12
m Gen. 24:60
18
n Gen. 18:18; 26:4
o Gen. 26:5
20
p Gen. 11:29; 24:15
23
q Gen.

24:15 **23:2** r Gen. 35:27 **23:3** s i.e. *the Hittites.* See 2 Ki. 7:6, *note* **23:4** t v. 17; see Acts 7:16, *note* **23:6** u Lit. *prince with God*

*
22:5 Or *young man* **22:14** Hebrew *YHWH Yireh*
22:23 Spelled *Rebecca* in Romans 9:10

[1](22:6) Abraham "laid it on Isaac his son." Isaac was not a child, but a young man (cp. Gen. 21:14, *note*). Observe his loving submission to his father (cp. Christ, Heb. 5:7–8).

[2](22:9) The typical lessons are: (1) Isaac, a type of Christ "obedient to the point of death" (Phil. 2:5–8); (2) Abraham, a type of the Father who "did not spare His own Son, but delivered Him up for us all" (Rom. 8:32; Jn. 3:16); (3) the ram, a type of substitution—Christ offered as a burnt offering in our stead (Heb. 10:5–10); and (4) cp. resurrection (Heb. 11:17–19), where the statement "from the dead . . . he also received him in a figurative sense" (v. 19) confirms the typology. Cp. Jas. 2:21–23.

dead in the choicest of our burial places. None of us will withhold from you his burial place, that you may bury your dead."

7 Then Abraham stood up and bowed himself to the people of the land, the sons of Heth.

8 And he spoke with them, saying, "If it is your wish that I bury my dead out of my sight, hear me, and meet with Ephron the son of Zohar for me,

9 "that he may give me the cave of [a]Machpelah which he has, which *is* at the end of his field. Let him give it to me at the full price, as property for a burial place among you."

10 Now Ephron dwelt among the sons of Heth; and Ephron the [b]Hittite answered Abraham in the presence of the sons of Heth, all who entered at the gate of his city, saying,

11 "No, my lord, hear me: I give you the field and the cave that *is* in it; I give it to you in the presence of the sons of my people. I give it to you. Bury your dead!"

12 Then Abraham bowed himself down before the people of the land;

13 and he spoke to Ephron in the hearing of the people of the land, saying, "If you *will give it,* please hear me. I will give you money for the field; take *it* from me and I will bury my dead there."

14 And Ephron answered Abraham, saying to him,

15 "My lord, listen to me; the land *is worth* four hundred [c]shekels of silver. What *is* that between you and me? So bury your dead."

16 And Abraham listened to Ephron; and Abraham weighed out the silver for Ephron which he had named in the hearing of the sons of Heth, four hundred shekels of silver, currency of the merchants.

17 So the field of Ephron which *was* in Machpelah, which *was* before Mamre, the field and the cave which *was* in it, and all the trees that *were* in the field, which *were* within all the surrounding borders, were deeded

18 to Abraham as a possession in the presence of the sons of Heth, before all who went in at the gate of his city.

19 And after this, Abraham [d]buried Sarah his wife in the cave of the field of Machpelah, before Mamre (that *is,* Hebron) in the land of Canaan.

20 So the field and the cave that *is* in it were deeded to Abraham by the sons of Heth as property for a burial place.

A bride sought for Isaac

24 [1]NOW Abraham was old, well advanced in age; and the LORD [e]had blessed Abraham in all things.

2 So Abraham said to the oldest [f]servant of his house, who ruled over all that he had, "Please, [g]put your hand under my thigh,

3 "and I will make you swear by the LORD, the God of heaven and the God of the earth, that you will not take a wife for my son from the daughters of the Canaanites, among whom I dwell;

4 "but you shall go to [h]my country and to my family, and take a wife for my son Isaac."

5 And the servant said to him, "Perhaps the woman will not be willing to follow me to this land. Must I take your son back to the land from which you came?"

6 But Abraham said to him, "Beware that you do not take my son back there.

7 "The LORD God of heaven, who took me from my father's house and from the land of my family, and who spoke to me and swore to me, saying, 'To your descendants* I give this land,' He will send His [i]angel before you, and you shall take a wife for my son from there.

8 "And if the woman is not willing to follow you, then you will be [j]re-

CHAPTER 23
9 *a* Gen. 25:9
10 *b* i.e. *the Hittites.* See 2 Ki. 7:6, *note*
15 *c* See Coinage (OT), Ex. 30:13, *note*
19 *d* v. 4; see Acts 7:16, *note*

CHAPTER 24
1 *e* Gen. 17:20; 25:11
2 *f* Gen. 15:2 *g* Gen. 47:29
4 *h* Cp. Gen. 28:2
7 *i* See Heb. 1:4, *note*
8 *j* Cp. Josh. 2:17–20

* 24:7 Literally *seed*

[1](24:1) The entire chapter is highly typical: (1) Abraham, a type of a certain king who arranged a marriage for his son (Mt. 22:2); (2) the unnamed servant, a type of the Holy Spirit, who does not "speak on His own authority" but takes of the things of the Bridegroom with which to win the bride (Jn. 16:13–14); (3) the servant, a type of the Spirit as enriching the bride with the Bridegroom's gifts (1 Cor. 12:7–11; Gal. 5:22–23); (4) the servant, a type of the Spirit as bringing the bride to the meeting with the Bridegroom (Acts 13:4; 16:6–7; Rom. 8:11; 1 Th. 4:14–17); (5) Rebekah, a type of the Church, the *ecclesia,* the "called out" virgin bride of Christ (Gen. 24:16; 2 Cor. 11:2; Eph. 5:25–32); (6) Isaac, a type of the Bridegroom "not seen" as yet, whom the bride nevertheless loves through the testimony of the unnamed Servant (1 Pet. 1:8); and (7) Isaac, a type of the Bridegroom who goes out to meet and receive His bride (Gen. 24:63; 1 Th. 4:14–17).

leased from this oath; only do not take
my son back there."
9 So the servant put his hand under the thigh of Abraham his master,
and swore to him concerning this matter.
10 Then the servant took ten of his
master's camels and departed, for all
his master's goods *were in* his hand.
And he arose and went to Mesopotamia, to the city of [1a]Nahor.
11 And he made his camels kneel
down outside the city by a well of water at evening time, the time when
[b]women go out to draw *water*.
12 Then he [c]said, "O LORD God of
my master Abraham, please give me
success this day, and show kindness
to my master Abraham.
13 "Behold, *here* I stand by the well
of water, and the daughters of the men
of the city are coming out to draw water.
14 "Now let it be that the young
woman to whom I say, 'Please let
down your pitcher that I may drink,'
and she says, 'Drink, and I will also
give your camels a drink'—*let* her *be
the one* You have appointed for Your
servant Isaac. And [d]by this I will
know that You have shown kindness
to my master."

The servant's prayer answered

15 And it happened, [e]before he had
finished speaking, that behold, Rebekah, who was born to [f]Bethuel, son
of Milcah, the wife of Nahor, Abraham's brother, came out with her
pitcher on her shoulder.
16 Now the young woman *was* very
beautiful to behold, a virgin; no man
had known her. And she went down to
the well, filled her pitcher, and came
up.
17 And the servant ran to meet her
and said, "Please let me drink a little
water from your pitcher."
18 So she said, "Drink, my lord."
Then she quickly let her pitcher down
to her hand, and gave him a drink.
19 And when she had finished giving him a drink, she said, "I will draw
water for your camels also, until they
have finished drinking."
20 Then she quickly emptied her
pitcher into the trough, ran back to the
well to draw *water*, and drew for all
his camels.

10
a Gen. 22:20; 29:5
11
b 1 Sam. 9:11
12
c Bible prayers (OT): vv. 12–14; Gen. 32:9. (Gen. 15:2; Hab. 3:1)
14
d Jud. 6:17, 37; 2 Ki. 20:9; Prov. 16:33; Acts 1:26; cp. Mt. 12:39. Signs are given to faith, not to doubt
15
e Isa. 65:24
f Gen. 22:20–23
22
g See Coinage (OT), Ex. 30:13, *note*
32
h Gen. 19:2; 43:24; cp. Jn. 13:5, 13–15

21 And the man, wondering at her,
remained silent so as to know whether
the LORD had made his journey prosperous or not.
22 So it was, when the camels had
finished drinking, that the man took a
golden nose ring weighing half a
[g]shekel, and two bracelets for her
wrists weighing ten *shekels* of gold,
23 and said, "Whose daughter *are*
you? Tell me, please, is there room *in*
your father's house for us to lodge?"
24 So she said to him, "I *am* the
daughter of Bethuel, Milcah's son,
whom she bore to Nahor."
25 Moreover she said to him, "We
have both straw and feed enough, and
room to lodge."
26 Then the man bowed down his
head and worshiped the LORD.
27 And he said, "Blessed *be* the
LORD God of my master Abraham,
who has not forsaken His mercy and
His truth toward my master. As for
me, being on the way, the LORD led me
to the house of my master's brethren."
28 So the young woman ran and
told her mother's household these
things.
29 Now Rebekah had a brother
whose name *was* Laban, and Laban
ran out to the man by the well.
30 So it came to pass, when he saw
the nose ring, and the bracelets on his
sister's wrists, and when he heard the
words of his sister Rebekah, saying,
"Thus the man spoke to me," that he
went to the man. And there he stood
by the camels at the well.
31 And he said, "Come in, O blessed
of the LORD! Why do you stand outside? For I have prepared the house,
and a place for the camels."
32 Then the man came to the house.
And he unloaded the camels, and provided straw and feed for the camels,
and water to [h]wash his feet and the
feet of the men who *were* with him.
33 *Food* was set before him to eat,
but he said, "I will not eat until I have
told about my errand." And he said,
"Speak on."

The servant announces his mission

34 So he said, "I *am* Abraham's servant.
35 "The LORD has blessed my master greatly, and he has become great;
and He has given him flocks and

[1](24:10) The existence of this city in Abraham's time has been evidenced by the finding of many references to it in clay tablets from this period, discovered at Mari in northern Mesopotamia.

herds, silver and gold, male and female servants, and camels and donkeys.
36 "And Sarah my master's wife
bore a son to my master when she was
old; and [a]to him he has given all that
he has.
37 "Now my master [b]made me
swear, saying, 'You shall not take a
wife for my son from the daughters of
the Canaanites, in whose land I dwell;
38 'but you shall go to my father's
house and to my family, and take a
wife for my son.'
39 "And I said to my master, 'Perhaps the woman will not follow me.'
40 "But he said to me, 'The LORD,
[c]before whom I walk, will send His
[d]angel with you and prosper your
way; and you shall take a wife for my
son from my family and from my father's house.
41 'You will be clear from this oath
when you arrive among my family; for
if they will not give *her* to you, then
you will be released from my oath.'
42 "And this day I came to the well
and said, 'O [e]LORD God of my master
Abraham, if You will now prosper the
way in which I go,
43 'behold, I stand by the well of
water; and it shall come to pass that
when the virgin comes out to draw
water, and I say to her, "Please give
me a little water from your pitcher to
drink,"
44 'and she says to me, "Drink, and
I will draw for your camels also,"—*let*
her *be* the woman whom the LORD has
appointed for my master's son.'
45 "But before I had finished speaking in my [f]heart, there was Rebekah,
coming out with her pitcher on her
shoulder; and she went down to the
well and drew *water.* And I said to
her, 'Please let me drink.'
46 "And she made haste and let her
pitcher down from her *shoulder,* and
said, 'Drink, and I will give your camels a drink also.' So I drank, and she
gave the camels a drink also.
47 "Then I asked her, and said,
'Whose daughter *are* you?' And she
said, 'The daughter of Bethuel, Nahor's son, whom Milcah bore to him.'
So I put the nose ring on her nose and
the bracelets on her wrists.
48 "And I bowed my head and worshiped the LORD, and blessed the LORD
God of my master Abraham, who had
led me in the way of truth to take the
daughter of my master's brother for
his son.

36
a Gen. 25:5
37
b Gen. 24:3
40
c 1 Ki. 8:23
d See Heb. 1:4, *note*
42
e Gen. 24:12
45
f 1 Sam. 1:13
50
g Gen. 31:24
59
h Gen. 35:8
60
i *Christ* (first advent): v. 60; Gen. 28:14. (Gen. 3:15; Acts 1:11, *note*)
j Gen. 22:17
62
k Lit. *the well of Him who lives and sees me.* Gen. 16:14; 25:11
l See Gen. 12:9, *note*

49 "Now if you will deal kindly and
truly with my master, tell me. And if
not, tell me, that I may turn to the right
hand or to the left."
50 Then Laban and Bethuel answered and said, "The thing comes
from the LORD; we cannot speak to you
either [g]bad or good.
51 "Here *is* Rebekah before you;
take *her* and go, and let her be your
master's son's wife, as the LORD has
spoken."
52 And it came to pass, when Abraham's servant heard their words, that
he worshiped the LORD, *bowing him-*
self to the earth.
53 Then the servant brought out
jewelry of silver, jewelry of gold, and
clothing, and gave *them* to Rebekah.
He also gave precious things to her
brother and to her mother.
54 And he and the men who *were*
with him ate and drank and stayed all
night. Then they arose in the morning,
and he said, "Send me away to my
master."
55 But her brother and her mother
said, "Let the young woman stay with
us *a few* days, at least ten; after that
she may go."
56 And he said to them, "Do not
hinder me, since the LORD has prospered my way; send me away so that
I may go to my master."

A bride brought to Isaac

57 So they said, "We will call the
young woman and ask her personally."
58 Then they called Rebekah and
said to her, "Will you go with this
man?" And she said, "I will go."
59 So they sent away Rebekah their
sister and her [h]nurse, and Abraham's
servant and his men.
60 And they blessed Rebekah and
said to her:

"Our sister, *may* you *become*
The mother of thousands of
ten thousands;
And may your [i]descendants
possess
The [j]gates of those who hate
them."

61 Then Rebekah and her maids
arose, and they rode on the camels
and followed the man. So the servant
took Rebekah and departed.
62 Now Isaac came from the way of
[k]Beer Lahai Roi, for he dwelt in the
[l]South.
63 And Isaac went out to meditate

in the field in the evening; and he lifted his eyes and looked, and there, the camels *were* coming.

64 Then Rebekah lifted her eyes, and when she saw Isaac she dismounted from her camel;

65 for she had said to the servant, "Who *is* this man walking in the field to meet us?" The servant said, "It *is* my master." So she took a veil and covered herself.

66 And the [1]servant told Isaac all the things that he had done.

67 Then Isaac brought her into his mother Sarah's tent; and he took Rebekah and she became his wife, and he loved her. So Isaac was comforted after his mother's *death*.

Abraham weds Keturah

25 ABRAHAM again took a wife, and her name *was* [a]Keturah.

2 And she bore him Zimran, Jokshan, Medan, Midian, Ishbak, and Shuah.

3 Jokshan begot Sheba and Dedan. And the sons of Dedan were Asshurim, Letushim, and Leummim.

4 And the sons of Midian *were* Ephah, Epher, Hanoch, Abidah, and Eldaah. All these *were* the children of Keturah.

Isaac heir of all things (Heb. 1:2)

5 And Abraham gave all that he had to Isaac.

6 But Abraham gave gifts to the sons of the concubines which Abraham had; and while he was still living he sent them eastward, away from Isaac his son, to the country of the east.

Death of Abraham

7 This *is* the sum of the [2]years of Abraham's life which he lived: one hundred and seventy-five years.

8 Then [3]Abraham breathed his last and died in a [b]good old age, an old man and full *of years*, and was [4]gathered to his people.

9 And his sons Isaac and Ishmael buried him in the cave of [c]Machpelah, which *is* before Mamre, in the field of Ephron the son of Zohar the Hittite,

10 the field which Abraham purchased from the sons of Heth. There Abraham was buried, and [d]Sarah his wife.

11 And it came to pass, after the death of Abraham, that God blessed his son Isaac. And Isaac dwelt at Beer Lahai Roi.

Genealogy of Ishmael

12 Now this *is* the [e]genealogy of Ishmael, Abraham's [5]son, whom Hagar the Egyptian, Sarah's maidservant, bore to Abraham.

13 And these *were* the names of the sons of Ishmael, by their names, according to their generations: The firstborn of Ishmael, Nebajoth; then Kedar, Adbeel, Mibsam,

14 Mishma, Dumah, Massa,

15 Hadar,* Tema, Jetur, Naphish, and Kedemah.

16 These *were* the sons of Ishmael and these *were* their names, by their towns and their settlements, twelve princes according to their nations.

17 These *were* the years of the life of Ishmael: one hundred and thirty-seven years; and he breathed his last and died, and was gathered to his people.

18 (They dwelt from Havilah as far as Shur, which *is* east of Egypt as you go toward Assyria.) He died in the presence of all his brethren.

Genealogy of Isaac

19 This *is* the [f]genealogy of Isaac,

CHAPTER 25
1 a 1 Chr. 1:32–33
8 b Gen. 15:15; cp. Jud. 8:32
9 c Gen. 23:9, 17; 49:30
10 d Gen. 23:19
12 e Cp. v. 19; Gen. 11:10,27
19 f Cp. v. 12; Gen. 36:1, 9

*25:15 Masoretic Text reads *Hadad*.

[1](24:66) This is the model servant: he (1) does not run unsent, vv. 2–9; (2) goes where he is sent, vv. 4,10; (3) does nothing else; (4) is prayerful and thankful, vv. 12–14,26–27; (5) is wise to win, vv. 17–18,21. Cp. Jn. 4:7; (6) speaks not of himself but of his master's riches and Isaac's heirship, vv. 22,34–36; Acts 1:8; and (7) presents the true issue, and requires clear decision, v. 49.

[2](25:7) Thus Abraham lived thirty-eight years after Sarah's death. The children of Keturah evidence the supernatural renewing of the body of Abraham (Gen. 17:5–6,15–17; Rom. 4:17–22).

[3](25:8) The NT gives great significance to the history of Abraham: he is called "the friend of God" (Jas. 2:23); he is referred to as "Abraham our father" (Jas. 2:21; cp. Mt. 3:9); he is an illustration of justification (Rom. 4; Gal. 3; Jas. 2:21); and an illustration of faith (Heb. 11:8–19).

[4](25:8) This implies life after death and not physical burial.

[5](25:12) It was told Abraham that he would be the father of many nations (Gen. 17:4,6,16) and not of Israel only. Of Ishmael, Abraham's son, God said that he would "multiply him exceedingly" (Gen. 17:20). Keturah also bore sons to Abraham (Gen. 25:1–4) who were neither Israelites (Isaac's descendants) nor Arabs (Ishmael's descendants), but another nation.

Abraham's son. Abraham begot Isaac.
20 Isaac was forty years old when
he took [a]Rebekah as wife, the daughter of Bethuel the Syrian of Padan
Aram, the sister of Laban the Syrian.
21 Now Isaac pleaded with the
LORD for his wife, because she *was*
barren, and the LORD granted his plea,
and Rebekah his wife [b]conceived.
22 But the children struggled together within her, and she said, "If *all*
is well, why *am I like* this?" So she
went to inquire of the LORD.
23 And the LORD said to her:

> [c]"Two nations *are* in your womb,
> Two peoples shall be separated
> from your body;
> *One* people shall be stronger
> than the other,
> And the [d]older shall serve the
> younger."

Birth of Esau and Jacob

24 So when her days were fulfilled
for her to give birth, indeed *there were*
twins in her womb.
25 And the first came out red. *He*
was like a [e]hairy garment all over; so
they called his name [1f]Esau.
26 Afterward his brother came out,
and his [g]hand took hold of Esau's
heel; so his name was called [h]Jacob.
Isaac *was* sixty years old when she
bore them.

Sale of the birthright

27 So the boys grew. And Esau was
a skillful hunter, a man of the field; but
Jacob was a mild man, dwelling in
tents.
28 And Isaac loved Esau because
he [i]ate *of his* game, but Rebekah
loved Jacob.
29 Now Jacob cooked a stew; and
Esau came in from the field, and he
was weary.
30 And Esau said to Jacob, "Please
feed me with that same red *stew*, for
I *am* weary." Therefore his name was
called [j]Edom.
31 But Jacob said, "Sell me your
[2]birthright as of this day."
32 And Esau said, "Look, I *am*
about to die; so [k]what *is* this birthright
to me?"
33 Then Jacob said, "Swear to me
as of this day." So he swore to him,
and sold his birthright to Jacob.
34 And Jacob gave Esau bread and
stew of lentils; then he ate and drank,
arose, and went his way. Thus Esau
[l]despised *his* birthright.

Abrahamic Covenant confirmed to Isaac

26 THERE was a [m]famine in the
land, besides the first famine
that was in the days of Abraham. And
Isaac went to [n]Abimelech king of the
Philistines, in Gerar.
2 Then the LORD [o]appeared to him
and said: [p]"Do not go down to Egypt;
live in the land of which I shall tell
you.
3 [q]"Dwell in this land, and I will
be with you and bless you; for to you
and your descendants I give all these
lands, and I will perform the [3r]oath
which I swore to Abraham your father.
4 "And I will make your descendants multiply as the stars of heaven;
I will give to your descendants all
these lands; and in your seed all the
nations of the earth shall be blessed;
5 "because Abraham obeyed My
voice and kept My charge, My commandments, My statutes, and My
laws."

Lapse of Isaac (cp. Gen. 20)

6 So Isaac dwelt in Gerar.
7 And the men of the place asked
about his wife. And he said, "She *is* my
[s]sister"; for he was [t]afraid to say,
"*She is* my wife," *because he thought,*

20 *a* Gen. 24:15
21 *b* Rom. 9:10–13
23 *c* Gen. 17:16; 24:60 *d* Rom. 9:12
25 *e* Gen. 27:11 *f* Lit. *hairy,* or *thick-haired*
26 *g* Hos. 12:3, c. 1790 B.C. *h* Lit. *sup-planter*
28 *i* Gen. 27:4, 31
30 *j* Lit. *red*
32 *k* Cp. Mt. 16:26; Mk. 8:36–37
34 *l* Heb. 12:16–17
CHAPTER 26
1 *m* Gen. 12:10 *n* Cp. Gen. 20
2 *o Theophanies:* v. 2; Gen. 26:24. (Gen. 12:7, *note;* Dan. 10:5) *p* Cp. Gen. 46:3
3 *q Israel* (cov-enant): vv. 2–5; Gen. 28:13. (Gen. 12:2; Rom. 11:26, *note*) *r* Gen. 22:15–18
26:7 *s* Gen. 12:13 *t* Cp. Gen. 31:31

[1](25:25) Esau stands for the mere man of the earth (Heb. 12:16–17). Destitute of faith, he despised the birthright—a spiritual thing, of value only as there was faith to apprehend it.

[2](25:31) The birthright had three elements: (1) until the establishment of the Aaronic priesthood the head of the family exercised priestly rights. (2) The Abrahamic family held the Edenic promise of the Satan-Bruiser (Gen. 3:15)—Abel, Seth, Shem, Abraham, Isaac, Esau. And (3) Esau, as the firstborn, was in the direct line of the Abrahamic promise of the Earth-Blesser (Gen. 12:3). He sold this birthright for a momentary fleshly gratification. Esau had only natural priority in the birthright, and God never meant that the line of blessing should come through him (Rom. 9:11–13; cp. Gen. 25:23). Jacob's conception of the birthright at that time was, doubtless, carnal and inadequate, but his desire for it evidenced faith.

[3](26:3) Here the LORD confirmed to Isaac the covenant He had made with Abraham. The principal promises to the patriarchs are written in the following Scriptures: (1) to Abraham, Gen. 12:1–3,7; 13:14–18; 15; 17:1–8,15–22; 22:15–18; (2) to Isaac, Gen. 26:1–5; 28:13–15; and (3) to Jacob, Gen. 28:13–15; 35:11–12.

"lest the men of the place kill me for Rebekah, because she *is* beautiful to behold."

8 Now it came to pass, when he had been there a long time, that Abimelech king of the Philistines looked through a window, and saw, and there was Isaac, showing endearment to Rebekah his wife.

9 Then Abimelech called Isaac and said, "Quite obviously she *is* your wife; so how could you say, 'She *is* my sister'?" Isaac said to him, "Because I said, 'Lest I die on account of her.' "

10 And Abimelech said, "What *is* this you have done to us? One of the people might soon have lain with your wife, and you would have brought [a]guilt on us."

11 So Abimelech charged all *his* people, saying, "He who touches this man or his wife shall surely be put to death."

12 Then Isaac sowed in that land, and reaped in the same year a [b]hundredfold; and the LORD [c]blessed him.

13 The man began to prosper, and continued prospering until he became very prosperous;

14 for he had possessions of flocks and possessions of herds and a great number of servants. So the Philistines envied him.

15 Now the Philistines had stopped up all the wells which his father's servants had dug in the days of Abraham his father, and they had filled them with earth.

16 And Abimelech said to Isaac, "Go away from us, for you are much [d]mightier than we."

Isaac, the well-digger

17 Then Isaac departed from there and pitched his tent in the Valley of Gerar, and dwelt there.

18 And Isaac dug again the wells of water which they had dug in the days of Abraham his father, for the Philistines had stopped them up after the death of Abraham. He called them by the names which his father had called them.

19 Also Isaac's servants dug in the valley, and found a well of running water there.

10
a Cp. Ex. 32:21

12
b Mt. 13:8, 23
c Gen. 25:11

16
d Ex. 1:9

24
e Theophanies: v. 24; Gen. 35:9. (Gen. 12:7, *note;* Dan. 10:5)

25
f Gen. 22:9; 33:20
g Gen. 21:33; cp. 1 Ki. 18:24

33
h Or *Shibah,* lit. *oath*

20 But the herdsmen of Gerar quarreled with Isaac's herdsmen, saying, "The water *is* ours." So he called the [1]name of the well Esek, because they quarreled with him.

21 Then they dug another well, and they quarreled over that *one* also. So he called its name Sitnah.

22 And he moved from there and dug another well, and they did not quarrel over it. So he called its name Rehoboth, because he said, "For now the LORD has made room for us, and we shall be fruitful in the land."

23 Then he went up from there to Beersheba.

24 And the LORD [e]appeared to him the same night and said, "I *am* the God of your father Abraham; do not fear, for I *am* with you. I will bless you and multiply your descendants for My servant Abraham's sake."

25 So he [f]built an altar there and [g]called on the name of the LORD, and he pitched his tent there; and there Isaac's servants dug a well.

26 Then Abimelech came to him from Gerar with Ahuzzath, one of his friends, and Phichol the commander of his army.

27 And Isaac said to them, "Why have you come to me, since you hate me and have sent me away from you?"

28 But they said, "We have certainly seen that the LORD is with you. So we said, 'Let there now be an oath between us, between you and us; and let us make a covenant with you,

29 'that you will do us no harm, since we have not touched you, and since we have done nothing to you but good and have sent you away in peace. You *are* now the blessed of the LORD.' "

30 So he made them a feast, and they ate and drank.

31 Then they arose early in the morning and swore an oath with one another; and Isaac sent them away, and they departed from him in peace.

32 It came to pass the same day that Isaac's servants came and told him about the well which they had dug, and said to him, "We have found water."

33 So he called it [h]Shebah. There-

[1](26:20) The wells of Genesis have significant names and are associated with significant events: (1) Beer Lahai Roi, *well of the Living One who sees me* (Gen. 16:14; 24:62; 25:11). (2) Beersheba, *the well of the oath* or *covenant* (Gen. 21:25–33; 22:19; 26:23–25; 46:1–5). (3) Esek, *dispute* (Gen. 26:20). (4) Sitnah, *opposition* (Gen. 26:21). Esek and Sitnah were Isaac's own attempts at well-digging. Afterward he dwelt by the old wells of his father. And (5) Rehoboth, *room* (Gen. 26:22). Upon Isaac's return to Beersheba, the LORD made Himself known.

fore the name of the city *is* [a]Beer-
sheba to this day.
34 When Esau was forty years old,
he took as wives Judith the daughter
of Beeri the [b]Hittite, and Basemath
the daughter of Elon the Hittite.
35 And they were a grief of mind to
Isaac and Rebekah.

The stolen blessing

27 NOW it came to pass, when
Isaac was [c]old and his [d]eyes
were so dim that he could not see, that
he called Esau his older son and said
to him, "My son." And he answered
him, "Here I am."
2 Then he said, "Behold now, I am
old. I do not know the day of my death.
3 "Now therefore, please take
your weapons, your quiver and your
bow, and go out to the field and hunt
game for me.
4 "And make me savory food,
such as I love, and bring *it* to me that
I may eat, that my soul may bless you
before I die."
5 Now Rebekah was listening
when Isaac spoke to Esau his son. And
Esau went to the field to hunt game
and to bring *it*.
6 So Rebekah spoke to Jacob her
son, saying, "Indeed I heard your father speak to Esau your brother, saying,
7 'Bring me game and make savory food for me, that I may eat it and
bless you in the presence of the LORD
before my death.'
8 "Now therefore, my son, obey
my voice according to what I command you.
9 "Go now to the flock and bring
me from there two choice kids of the
goats, and I will make savory food
from them for your father, such as he
loves.
10 "Then you shall take *it* to your
father, that he may eat *it*, and that he
may bless you before his death."
11 And Jacob said to Rebekah his
mother, "Look, Esau my brother *is* a
hairy man, and I *am* a smooth-*skinned*
man.
12 "Perhaps my father will feel me,
and I shall seem to be a deceiver to
him; and I shall bring a curse on myself and not a blessing."
13 But his mother said to him, "*Let*
your curse *be* on me, my son; only
obey my voice, and go, get *them* for
me."
14 And he went and got *them* and
brought *them* to his mother, and his
mother made savory food, such as his
father loved.
15 Then Rebekah took the choice
clothes of her elder son Esau, which
were with her in the house, and put
them on Jacob her younger son.
16 And she put the skins of the kids
of the goats on his hands and on the
smooth part of his neck.
17 Then she gave the savory food
and the bread, which she had prepared, into the hand of her son Jacob.
18 So he went to his father and said,
"My father." And he said, "Here I am.
Who *are* you, my son?"
19 Jacob said to his father, "I *am*
Esau your firstborn; I have done just
as you told me; please arise, sit and eat
of my game, that your soul may bless
me."
20 But Isaac said to his son, "How *is*
it that you have found *it* so quickly,
my son?" And he said, "Because the
LORD your God brought *it* to me."
21 Then Isaac said to Jacob,
"Please come near, that I may feel you,
my son, whether you *are* really my
son Esau or not."
22 So Jacob went near to Isaac his
father, and he felt him and said, "The
voice *is* Jacob's voice, but the hands
are the hands of Esau."
23 And he did not recognize him,
because his hands were hairy like his
brother Esau's hands; so he blessed
him.
24 Then he said, "*Are* you really my
son Esau?" He said, "I *am*."
25 He said, "Bring *it* near to me,
and I will eat of my son's game, so that
my soul may bless you." So he brought
it near to him, and he ate; and he
brought him wine, and he drank.
26 Then his father Isaac said to
him, "Come near now and kiss me, my
son."
27 And he came near and [e]kissed
him; and he smelled the smell of his
clothing, and blessed him and said:

"Surely, the smell of my son
Is like the smell of a field
Which the LORD has blessed.
28 Therefore may God give you
Of the dew of heaven,
Of the fatness of the earth,
And plenty of [f]grain and wine.
29 Let peoples serve you,
And nations bow down to you.
Be [g]master over your brethren,
And let your mother's sons
bow down to you.

33 [a] Lit. *the well of the oath.* Cp. Gen. 21:31
34 [b] Gen. 36:2; see 2 Ki. 7:6, *note*
CHAPTER 27
1 [c] Gen. 35:28 [d] Gen. 48:10
27 [e] Gen. 29:13
28 [f] Dt. 7:13
29 [g] Gen. 25:23

[a]Cursed *be* everyone who
curses you,
And blessed *be* those who
bless you!"

30 Now it happened, as soon as
Isaac had finished blessing Jacob, and
Jacob had scarcely gone out from the
presence of Isaac his father, that Esau
his brother came in from his hunting.
31 He also had made savory food,
and brought it to his father, and said
to his father, "Let my father arise and
eat of his son's game, that your soul
may bless me."
32 And his father Isaac said to him,
"Who *are* you?" So he said, "I *am* your
son, your firstborn, Esau."
33 Then Isaac [b]trembled exceedingly, and said, "Who? Where *is* the
one who hunted game and brought *it*
to me? I ate all *of it* before you came,
and I have blessed him—*and* [1]indeed
he shall be blessed."

Esau's unavailing remorse
(cp. Heb. 12:16–17)

34 When Esau heard the words of
his father, he cried with an exceedingly great and bitter cry, and said to
his father, "Bless me—me also, O my
father!"
35 But he said, "Your brother came
with deceit and has taken away your
blessing."
36 And *Esau* said, "Is he not rightly
named Jacob? For he has supplanted
me these two times. He [c]took away
my birthright, and now look, he has
taken away my blessing!" And he
said, "Have you not reserved a blessing for me?"
37 Then Isaac answered and said to
Esau, "Indeed I have made him your
master, and all his brethren I have
given to him as servants; with grain
and wine I have sustained him. What
shall I do now for you, my son?"
38 And Esau said to his father,
"Have you only one blessing, my father? Bless me—me also, O my father!" And Esau lifted up his voice and
wept.
39 Then Isaac his father answered
and said to him:

"Behold, your dwelling shall be
of the fatness of the earth,
And of the dew of heaven from
above.
40 By your sword you shall live,
And you shall serve your
brother;
And it shall come to pass,
when you become restless,
That you shall [d]break his yoke
from your neck."

41 So Esau [e]hated Jacob because
of the blessing with which his father
blessed him, and Esau said in his
heart, "The days of mourning for my
father are at hand; then I will kill my
brother Jacob."
42 And the words of Esau her older
son were told to Rebekah. So she sent
and called Jacob her younger son, and
said to him, "Surely your brother Esau
comforts himself concerning you *by
intending* to kill you.
43 "Now therefore, my son, obey
my voice: arise, flee to my brother
[f]Laban in Haran.
44 "And stay with him a [g]few days,
until your brother's fury turns away,
45 "until your brother's anger turns
away from you, and he forgets what
you have done to him; then I will send
and [h]bring you from there. Why
should I be bereaved also of you both
in one day?"
46 And Rebekah said to Isaac, "I
am weary of my life because of the
daughters of Heth; if Jacob takes a
wife of the daughters of [i]Heth, like
these *who are* the daughters of the
land, what good will my life be to me?"

Jacob at Bethel: Abrahamic Covenant
confirmed to him

28 THEN Isaac called Jacob and
blessed him, and charged him,
and said to him: "You shall not take a
wife from the daughters of Canaan.
2 [j]"Arise, go to Padan Aram, to
the house of [k]Bethuel your mother's
father; and take yourself a wife from
there of the daughters of [l]Laban your
mother's brother.

3 "May God [m]Almighty bless you,
And make you [n]fruitful and
multiply you,
That you may be an assembly
of peoples;
4 And give you the [o]blessing of
Abraham,
To you and your descendants
with you,
That you may inherit the land
In which you are a [p]stranger,
Which God gave to Abraham."

5 So Isaac sent Jacob away, and

29
a See Gen. 12:2, *note*, par. (3). Cp. Num. 24:9
33
b Lit. *trembled with a great trembling*: or *trembled greatly*
36
c Gen. 25:31–34
40
d 2 Ki. 8:20–22
41
e Cp. Gen. 26:27; 37:4–5
43
f Gen. 25:20; 28:2,5
44
g Cp. Gen. 31:41
45
h Rebekah never saw Jacob again
46
i Gen. 26:34–35; see 2 Ki. 7:6, *note*
CHAPTER 28
2
j Jacob was now 77 years old
k Gen. 25:20
l Gen. 27:43; 29:5
3
m See Gen. 17:1, *note*
n Gen. 26:24
4
o Gen. 12:2–3
p Gen. 23:4; 36:7

[1](27:33) Isaac recognizes that God's will for his sons is better than his own will for them.

he went to Padan Aram, to Laban the
son of Bethuel the Syrian, the brother
of Rebekah, the mother of Jacob and
Esau.
6 Esau saw that Isaac had blessed
Jacob and sent him away to Padan
Aram to take himself a wife from
there, *and that* as he blessed him he
gave him a charge, saying, "You shall
not take a wife from the daughters of
Canaan,"
7 and that Jacob had obeyed his
father and his mother and had gone to
Padan Aram.
8 Also Esau saw that the daughters of Canaan did not please his father Isaac.
9 So Esau went to Ishmael and
[a]took [b]Mahalath the daughter of Ishmael, Abraham's son, the sister of Nebajoth, to be his wife in addition to the
wives he had.
10 Now Jacob went out from Beersheba and went toward [c]Haran.
11 So he came to a certain place
and stayed there all night, because the
sun had set. And he took one of the
stones of that place and put it at his
head, and he lay down in that place to
sleep.
12 Then he [d]dreamed, and behold,
a ladder *was* set up on the earth, and
its top reached to heaven; and there
the [e]angels of God were [f]ascending
and descending on it.
13 And behold, the LORD stood
above it and said: "I *am* the LORD God
of Abraham your father and the God
of Isaac; the [g]land on which you lie I
will [h]give to you and your descendants.
14 "Also your descendants shall be
[i]as the dust of the earth; you shall
spread abroad to the [j]west and the
east, to the north and the south; and in
you and in your [k]seed [l]all the families
of the earth shall be blessed.
15 "Behold, I *am* [m]with you and will
keep you wherever you go, and will
bring you [n]back to this land; for I
will not [o]leave you until I have done
what I have spoken to you."
16 Then Jacob awoke from his
sleep and said, "Surely the LORD is in
this [p]place, and I did not know *it.*"
17 And he was afraid and said,
"How awesome *is* this place! This *is*
none other than the house of God, and
this *is* the gate of heaven!"
18 Then Jacob rose early in the
morning, and took the stone that he
had put at his head, set it up as a [q]pil-
lar, and poured oil on top of it.
19 And he called the name of [r]that
place [1][s]Bethel; but the name of that
city had been Luz previously.
20 Then Jacob [t]made a vow, saying, [u]"If God will be with me, and keep
me in this way that I am going, and
give me bread to eat and clothing to
put on,
21 "so that I come back to my father's house in peace, then the LORD
shall be my God.
22 "And this stone which I have set
as a pillar shall be God's house, and of
all that You give me I will surely give
a [v]tenth to You."

Jacob reaches Haran and marries Leah and Rachel

29 SO Jacob went on his journey
and [2]came to the land of the
people of the [w]East.
2 And he looked, and saw a [x]well
in the field; and behold, there *were*
three flocks of sheep lying by it; for
out of that well they watered the
flocks. A large stone *was* on the well's
mouth.
3 Now all the flocks would be
gathered there; and they would roll
the stone from the well's mouth, water
the sheep, and put the stone back in its
place on the well's mouth.
4 And Jacob said to them, "My
brethren, where *are* you from?" And
they said, "We *are* from [y]Haran."
5 Then he said to them, "Do you
know [z]Laban the son of Nahor?" And
they said, "We know him."
6 So he said to them, "Is he well?"
And they said, "*He is* well. And look,

9 *a* Gen. 26:34–35 *b* Called *Basemath* in Gen. 36:3
10 *c* Gen. 27:43; 29:4
12 *d* Cp. Gen. 31:10 *e* See Heb. 1:4, *note* *f* Jn. 1:51
13 *g Israel* (covenant): vv. 13–15; Gen. 35:11. (Gen. 12:2; Rom. 11:26, *note*) *h* Gen. 26:3; 35:12
14 *i* Gen. 13:16; Num. 23:10 *j* Gen. 13:14 *k Christ* (first advent): v. 14; Gen. 49:10. (Gen. 3:15; Acts 1:11, *note*) *l* Gen. 26:4
15 *m* Gen. 26:3 *n* Gen. 31:3, 13 *o* Lev. 26:44; Dt. 31:6; Heb. 13:5
16 *p* Cp. Ex. 3:5
18 *q* Gen. 31:45
19 *r* Gen. 13:3; 31:13 *s* Lit. *the house of God.* Cp. Gen. 35:7
20 *t* Gen. 28:15 *u* Or *Since*

28:22 *v* Gen. 14:20; Lev. 27:30 **29:1** *w* Gen. 25:6; Num. 23:7 **29:2** *x* Gen. 24:11; Ex. 2:15 **29:4** *y* Gen. 28:10 **29:5** *z* Gen. 28:2

[1](28:19) Bethel becomes, because of Jacob's night vision there, one of the significant places of Scripture. To the Christian it stands for a realization, however imperfect, of the heavenly and spiritual contents of faith, answering to Paul's prayer in Eph. 1:17–23.

[2](29:1) Jacob at Haran is a striking illustration of the nation descended from him in its present long dispersion. Like Israel, he (1) was out of the place of blessing (Gen. 26:3); (2) was without an altar (Hos. 3:4–5); (3) gained an evil name (Gen. 31:1; Rom. 2:17–24); but (4) was under the covenant care of the LORD (Gen. 28:13–15; Rom. 11:1,25–31); and (5) was ultimately brought back (Gen. 31:3; 35:1–4; Ezek. 37:21–23). The personal lesson is obvious: while Jacob was not forsaken, he was permitted to reap the shame and sorrow of his self-chosen way.

his daughter Rachel is [a]coming with the sheep."

7 Then he said, "Look, *it is* still high day; *it is* not time for the cattle to be gathered together. Water the sheep, and go and feed *them*."

8 But they said, "We cannot until all the flocks are gathered together, and they have rolled the stone from the well's mouth; then we water the sheep."

9 Now while he was still speaking with them, Rachel came with her father's sheep, for she was a shepherdess.

10 And it came to pass, when Jacob saw Rachel the daughter of Laban his mother's brother, and the sheep of Laban his mother's brother, that Jacob went near and rolled the stone from the well's mouth, and watered the flock of Laban his mother's brother.

11 Then Jacob kissed Rachel, and lifted up his voice and wept.

12 And Jacob told Rachel that he *was* her father's relative and that he *was* Rebekah's [b]son. So she ran and told her father.

13 Then it came to pass, when Laban heard the report about Jacob his sister's son, that he [c]ran to meet him, and embraced him and kissed him, and brought him to his house. So he told Laban all these things.

14 And Laban said to him, "Surely you *are* my [d]bone and my flesh." And he stayed with him for a month.

15 Then Laban said to Jacob, "Because you *are* my relative, should you therefore serve me for nothing? Tell me, [e]what *should* your wages *be*?"

16 Now Laban had two daughters: the name of the elder *was* Leah, and the name of the younger *was* Rachel.

17 Leah's [f]eyes *were* delicate, but Rachel was [g]beautiful of form and appearance.

18 Now Jacob loved Rachel; so he said, "I will serve you seven years for Rachel your younger daughter."

19 And Laban said, "*It is* better that I give her to you than that I should give her to another man. Stay with me."

20 So Jacob served seven years for Rachel, and they seemed *only* a few days to him because of the love he had for her.

21 Then Jacob said to Laban, "Give *me* my wife, for my days are fulfilled, that I may go in to her."

22 And Laban gathered together all the men of the place and made a [h]feast.

23 Now it came to pass in the evening, that he took Leah his daughter and brought her to Jacob; and he went in to her.

24 And Laban gave his maid [i]Zilpah to his daughter Leah *as* a maid.

25 So it came to pass in the morning, that behold, it *was* Leah. And he said to Laban, "What is this you have done to me? Was it not for Rachel that I served you? Why then have you [j]deceived me?"

26 And Laban said, "It must not be done so in our country, to give the younger before the firstborn.

27 "Fulfill her [k]week, and we will give you this one also for the service which you will serve with me still another seven years."

28 Then Jacob did so and fulfilled her week. So he [1]gave him his daughter Rachel as wife also.

29 And Laban gave his maid [l]Bilhah to his daughter Rachel as a maid.

30 Then *Jacob* also went in to Rachel, and he also [m]loved Rachel more than Leah. And he served with Laban still another seven years.

31 When the LORD saw that Leah *was* unloved, He opened her womb; but Rachel *was* barren.

32 So Leah conceived and bore a son, and she called his name [n]Reuben; for she said, "The LORD has surely [o]looked on my affliction. Now therefore, my husband will love me."

33 Then she conceived again and bore a son, and said, "Because the LORD has heard that I *am* unloved, He has therefore given me this *son* also." And she called his name [p]Simeon.

34 She conceived again and bore a son, and said, "Now this time my husband will become attached to me, because I have borne him three sons." Therefore his name was called [q]Levi.

35 And she conceived again and bore a son, and said, "Now I will praise the LORD." Therefore she called his name [r]Judah. Then she stopped bearing.

Jacob's family grows

30 NOW when Rachel saw that she bore Jacob [s]no children,

CHAPTER 29

6 a Gen. 24:11; Ex. 2:16–17

12 b Gen. 28:5

13 c Cp. Lk. 15:20

14 d Gen. 2:23; 37:27

15 e Gen. 30:28

17 f Lit. *weak-eyed* g Gen. 26:7

22 h Jud. 14:10; cp. Lk. 15:23

24 i Gen. 30:9–10

25 j Gen. 31:7; cp. 27:35

27 k See Dan. 9:24, *note*

29 l Gen. 30:3–5

30 m Gen. 29:20; cp. Dt. 21:15–17

32 n Lit. *see, a son* o Gen. 16:11; 31:42

33 p Lit. *hearing*

34 q Lit. *joined, attached.* Num. 18:2–4

35 r Lit. *praise*

CHAPTER 30

1 s Cp. Gen. 16:1–2

[1](29:28) Jacob did not have to *wait* seven more years for Rachel, who was given to him immediately. But Jacob had to *work* seven more years without wages (v. 30).

Rachel envied her sister, and said to
Jacob, "Give me children, or else I
die!"
2 And Jacob's anger was aroused
against Rachel, and he said, "*Am* I in
the [a]place of God, who has withheld
from you the fruit of the womb?"
3 So she said, "Here is my maid
Bilhah; go in to her, and she will bear
a child on my knees, that I also may
have children by her."
4 Then she gave him Bilhah her
maid as wife, and Jacob went in to her.
5 And Bilhah conceived and bore
Jacob a son.
6 Then Rachel said, "God has
judged my case; and He has also
heard my voice and given me a son."
Therefore she called his name [b]Dan.
7 And Rachel's maid Bilhah conceived again and bore Jacob a second
son.
8 Then Rachel said, "With great
wrestlings I have wrestled with my
sister, *and* indeed I have prevailed."
So she called his name [c]Naphtali.
9 When Leah saw that she had
stopped bearing, she took Zilpah her
maid and gave her to Jacob as wife.
10 And Leah's maid Zilpah bore Jacob a son.
11 Then Leah said, "A troop
comes!"* So she called his name
[d]Gad.
12 And Leah's maid Zilpah bore Jacob a second son.
13 Then Leah said, "I am happy, for
the daughters will call me blessed." So
she called his name [e]Asher.
14 Now Reuben went in the days of
wheat harvest and found mandrakes
in the field, and brought them to his
mother Leah. Then Rachel said to
Leah, "Please give me *some* of your
son's mandrakes."
15 But she said to her, "*Is it* a small
matter that you have taken away my
husband? Would you take away my
son's mandrakes also?" And Rachel
said, "Therefore he will lie with you
tonight for your son's mandrakes."
16 When Jacob came out of the
field in the evening, Leah went out to
meet him and said, "You must come in
to me, for I have surely hired you with
my son's mandrakes." And he lay with
her that night.
17 And God listened to Leah, and
she conceived and bore Jacob a fifth
son.
18 Leah said, "God has given me
my wages, because I have given my
maid to my husband." So she called
his name [f]Issachar.
19 Then Leah conceived again and
bore Jacob a sixth son.
20 And Leah said, "God has endowed me *with* a good endowment;
now my husband will dwell with me,
because I have borne him six sons." So
she called his name [g]Zebulun.
21 Afterward she bore a [h]daughter,
and called her name [i]Dinah.
22 Then God [j]remembered Rachel,
and God listened to her and opened
her womb.
23 And she conceived and bore a
son, and said, "God has taken away
my [k]reproach."
24 So she called his name [l]Joseph,
and said, "The LORD shall [m]add to me
another son."

God multiplies Jacob's cattle

25 And it came to pass, when Rachel had borne Joseph, that Jacob said
to Laban, "Send me away, that I may
go to my own place and to my country.
26 "Give *me* my wives and my children for whom I have [n]served you,
and let me go; for you know my service which I have done for you."
27 And Laban said to him, "Please
stay, if I have found favor in your
eyes, *for* I have [o]learned by experience that the LORD has blessed me for
your [p]sake."
28 Then he said, "Name me your
wages, and I will give *it.*"
29 So *Jacob* said to him, "You know
how I have served you and how your
livestock has been with me.
30 "For what you had before I *came*
was little, and it has increased to a
great amount; the LORD has blessed
you since my coming. And now, when
shall I also [q]provide for my own
house?"
31 So he said, "What shall I give
you?" And Jacob said, "You shall not
give me anything. If you will do this
thing for me, I will again feed and
keep your flocks:
32 "Let me pass through all your
flock today, [1]removing from there all

2
a Gen. 50:19
6
b Lit. *judging*
8
c Lit. *wrestling*
11
d Lit. *a troop*
13
e Lit. *happy*
18
f Lit. *hire*
20
g Lit. *dwelling*
21
h Gen. 34:1
i Lit. *judgment*
22
j Gen. 19:29; 1 Sam. 1:19
23
k Lk. 1:25; cp. 1 Sam. 1:6
24
l Lit. *adding*
m Gen. 35:16–18
26
n Gen. 29:18–20
27
o Lit. *I have divined*
p Gen. 26:24; 39:5
30
q 1 Tim. 5:8

*30:11 Following Qere, Syriac, and Targum; Kethib, Septuagint, and Vulgate read *in fortune.*

[1](30:32) It was God's control over the breeding process operating through the laws of heredity, not Jacob's highly dubious scheme of prenatal influence, that produced the increase in the colored animal progeny. Cp. Gen. 31:11–12, where the Angel of God showed Jacob what

the speckled and spotted sheep, and all the brown ones among the lambs, and the spotted and speckled among the goats; and *these* shall be my [a]wages.

33 "So my righteousness will answer for me in time to come, when the subject of my wages comes before you: every one that *is* not speckled and spotted among the goats, and brown among the lambs, will be considered stolen, if *it is* with me."

34 And Laban said, "Oh, that it were according to your word!"

35 So he removed that day the male goats that were [b]speckled and spotted, all the female goats that were speckled and spotted, every one that had *some* white in it, and all the brown ones among the lambs, and gave *them* into the hand of his sons.

36 Then he put three days' journey between himself and Jacob, and Jacob fed the rest of Laban's flocks.

37 Now Jacob took for himself rods of green poplar and of the almond and chestnut trees, peeled white strips in them, and exposed the white which *was* in the rods.

38 And the rods which he had peeled, he set before the flocks in the gutters, in the watering troughs where the flocks came to drink, so that they should conceive when they came to drink.

39 So the flocks conceived before the rods, and the flocks brought forth streaked, speckled, and spotted.

40 Then Jacob separated the lambs, and made the flocks face toward the streaked and all the brown in the flock of Laban; but he put his own flocks by themselves and did not put them with Laban's flock.

41 And it came to pass, whenever the stronger livestock conceived, that Jacob placed the rods before the eyes of the livestock in the gutters, that they might conceive among the rods.

42 But when the flocks were feeble, he did not put *them* in; so the feebler were Laban's and the stronger Jacob's.

43 Thus the man became exceedingly [c]prosperous, and had [d]large flocks, female and male servants, and camels and donkeys.

32 *a* Gen. 31:8
35 *b* Gen. 31:9–12
43 *c* v. 30 *d* Cp. Gen. 26:14; 32:5

God orders Jacob back to Bethel

31 NOW *Jacob* heard the words of Laban's sons, saying, "Jacob has taken away all that was our fa-

was really happening: "Lift your eyes now and see, all the rams which leap on the flocks are streaked, speckled and grey-spotted." This is recognized by Jacob's own testimony: "So God has taken away the livestock of your father" (31:9).

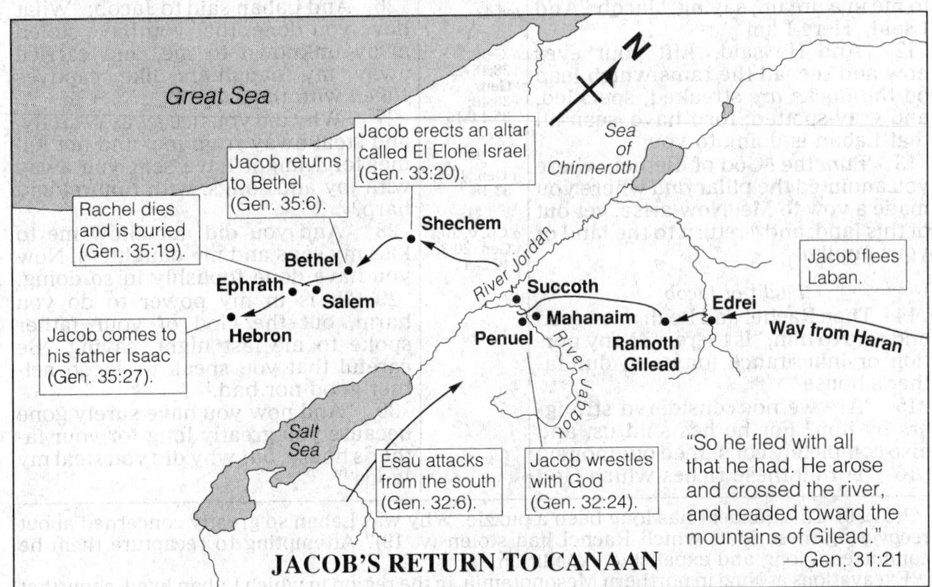

JACOB'S RETURN TO CANAAN

ther's, and from what was our father's
he has acquired all this wealth."
2 And Jacob saw the countenance
of Laban, and indeed it *was* not *favor-*
able toward him as before.
3 Then the LORD said to Jacob,
[a]"Return to the land of your fathers
and to your family, and I will [b]be with
you."
4 So Jacob sent and called Rachel
and Leah to the field, to his flock,
5 and said to them, "I see your father's countenance, that it *is* not *favor-*
able toward me as before; but the God
of my father [c]has been with me.
6 "And you [d]know that with all
my might I have [e]served your father.
7 "Yet your father has deceived
me and changed my wages ten times,
but God did not allow him to hurt me.
8 "If he said thus: 'The [f]speckled
shall be your wages,' then all the
flocks bore speckled. And if he said
thus: 'The streaked shall be your
wages,' then all the flocks bore
streaked.
9 [g]"So God has taken away the
livestock of your father and given
them to me.
10 "And it happened, at the time
when the flocks conceived, that I lifted
my eyes and saw in a [h]dream, and
behold, the rams which leaped upon
the flocks *were* streaked, speckled,
and gray-spotted.
11 "Then the [i]Angel of God spoke
to me in a dream, saying, 'Jacob.' And
I said, 'Here I am.'
12 "And He said, 'Lift your eyes
now and see, all the rams which leap
on the flocks *are* streaked, speckled,
and gray-spotted; for I have [j]seen all
that Laban is doing to you.
13 'I *am* the [k]God of [l]Bethel, where
you anointed the pillar *and* where you
made a vow to Me. Now arise, get out
of this land, and [m]return to the land of
your family.' "

Flight of Jacob

14 Then Rachel and Leah answered
and said to him, "Is there still any portion or inheritance for us in our father's house?
15 "Are we not considered strangers by him? For he has sold us, and
also completely consumed our money.
16 "For all these riches which God
has taken from our father are *really*
ours and our children's; now then,
whatever God has said to you, do it."
17 Then Jacob rose and set his sons
and his wives on camels.
18 And he carried away all his livestock and all his possessions which he
had gained, his acquired livestock
which he had gained in Padan Aram,
to go to his father Isaac in the land of
[n]Canaan.
19 Now Laban had gone to shear
his sheep, and Rachel had stolen the
household idols that were her father's.
20 And Jacob stole away, unknown
to Laban the Syrian, in that he did not
tell him that he intended to flee.
21 So he fled with all that he had.
He arose and crossed the river, and
headed toward the mountains of Gilead.
22 And Laban was told on the third
day that Jacob had fled.
23 Then he took his brethren with
him and pursued him for seven days'
journey, and he overtook him in the
mountains of Gilead.
24 But God had come to Laban the
Syrian in a [o]dream by night, and said
to him, "Be careful that you speak to
Jacob neither good nor bad."
25 So Laban overtook Jacob. Now
Jacob had pitched his tent in the
mountains, and Laban with his brethren pitched in the mountains of Gilead.
26 And Laban said to Jacob: "What
have you done, that you have stolen
away unknown to me, and carried
away my daughters like captives
taken with the sword?
27 "Why did you flee away secretly,
and steal away from me, and not tell
me; for I might have sent you away
with joy and songs, with timbrel and
harp?
28 "And you did not allow me to
kiss my sons and my daughters. Now
you have done foolishly in *so* doing.
29 "It is in my power to do you
harm, but the God of your father
spoke to me last night, saying, 'Be
careful that you speak to Jacob neither good nor bad.'
30 "And now you have surely gone
because you greatly long for your father's house, *but* why did you steal my
[1]gods?"

CHAPTER 31

3
a Gen. 28:15; 32:9
b Gen. 46:4

5
c vv. 2–3

6
d Gen. 30:29
e vv. 38–41; cp. Gen. 30:29

8
f Gen. 30:32

9
g v. 16

10
h Cp. v. 24; Gen. 28:12–13; 37:5–7, 10–11

11
i *Angel* (of the LORD): vv. 11–13; Gen. 48:16. (Gen. 16:7; Jud. 2:1, *note*)

12
j v. 42

13
k Gen. 28:16–22
l Gen. 28:19; 35:1,6,15
m v. 3

18
n Gen. 17:8; 33:18

24
o Cp. v. 10; Gen. 20:3; 46:2–4

[1](31:30) This incident has long been a puzzle. Why was Laban so greatly concerned about recovering these idols which Rachel had stolen (v. 19)? Attempting to recapture them he conducted a long and expensive expedition.

Excavations at Nuzi in northern Mesopotamia, in the region in which Laban lived, show that

31 Then Jacob answered and said
to Laban, "Because I was [a]afraid, for
I said, 'Perhaps you would take your
daughters from me by force.'
32 [b]"With whomever you find your
gods, do not let him live. In the presence of our brethren, identify what I
have of yours and take *it* with you."
For Jacob did not know that Rachel
had stolen them.
33 And Laban went into Jacob's
tent, into Leah's tent, and into the two
maids' tents, but he did not find *them.*
Then he went out of Leah's tent and
entered Rachel's tent.
34 Now Rachel had taken the
household idols, put them in the
camel's saddle, and sat on them. And
Laban searched all about the tent but
did not find *them.*
35 And she said to her father, "Let
it not displease my lord that I cannot
rise before you, for the manner of
women *is* with me." And he searched
but did not find the household idols.
36 Then Jacob was angry and rebuked Laban, and Jacob answered
and said to Laban: "What *is* my trespass? What *is* my sin, that you have so
hotly pursued me?
37 "Although you have searched all
my things, what part of your household things have you found? Set *it*
here before my brethren and your
brethren, that they may judge between us both!
38 "These twenty years I *have been*
with you; your ewes and your female
goats have not miscarried their
young, and I have not eaten the rams
of your flock.
39 "That which was torn *by beasts*
I did not bring to you; I bore the [c]loss
of it. You required it from my hand,
whether stolen by day or stolen by
night.
40 "*There* I was! In the day the
drought consumed me, and the frost
by night, and my sleep departed from
my eyes.

31
a Gen. 32:7, 11; cp. 26:7
32
b Gen. 44:9
39
c Ex. 22:10–13
41
d Gen. 29:20,28
42
e Gen. 29:32
44
f Gen. 26:28
45
g Gen. 28:22; 35:14
47
h Lit. (Aram.) *the heap of witness*
i Lit. (Heb.) *the heap of witness*
49
j Lit. *watch-tower*

41 "Thus I have been in your house
[d]twenty years; I served you fourteen
years for your two daughters, and six
years for your flock, and you have
changed my wages ten times.
42 "Unless the God of my father,
the God of Abraham and the Fear of
Isaac, had been with me, surely now
you would have sent me away empty-
handed. God has [e]seen my affliction
and the labor of my hands, and rebuked *you* last night."
43 And Laban answered and said to
Jacob, "*These* daughters *are* my
daughters, and *these* children *are* my
children, and *this* flock *is* my flock; all
that you see *is* mine. But what can I do
this day to these my daughters or to
their children whom they have borne?
44 "Now therefore, come, let us
make a [f]covenant, you and I, and let
it be a witness between you and me."
45 So Jacob took a [g]stone and set it
up *as* a pillar.
46 Then Jacob said to his brethren,
"Gather stones." And they took stones
and made a heap, and they ate there
on the heap.
47 Laban called it [h]Jegar Sahadu-
tha, but Jacob called it [i]Galeed.
48 And Laban said, "This heap *is* a
witness between you and me this
day." Therefore its name was called
Galeed,
49 also [j]Mizpah, because he said,
"May the LORD watch between you
and me when we are absent one from
[1]another.
50 "If you afflict my daughters, or if
you take *other* wives besides my
daughters, *although* no man *is* with
us—see, God *is* witness between you
and me!"
51 Then Laban said to Jacob, "Here
is this heap and here is *this* pillar,
which I have placed between you and
me.
52 "This heap *is* a witness, and *this*
pillar *is* a witness, that I will not pass
beyond this heap to you, and you will

---

the possession of the household gods of a father-in-law by a son-in-law was legally acceptable as proof of the designation of that son-in-law as principal heir. This not only explains the story but also proves that it was written at a time when the facts were so well-known that no explanation was needed. It is no wonder that Jacob was very angry that he should be accused of such a deed (v. 36), and that the two men set up a boundary and promised not to cross it to injure one another (vv. 45–52). Jacob never made evil use of these idols which Rachel had stolen, but ordered that they should be buried at Shechem (Gen. 35:2–4).

[1](31:49) Often used incorrectly as a benediction, in their original context these words were, rather, a malediction. Laban and Jacob distrusted one another. At their parting Jacob had a heap of stones erected as a witness of his covenant with Laban, and Laban said that the stones would serve as a reminder that God was watching the way in which Jacob would treat Leah and Rachel in the future.

not pass beyond this heap and this pillar to me, for harm.
53 "The God of Abraham, the God
of Nahor, and the God of their father
judge between us." And Jacob swore
by the [a]Fear of his father Isaac.
54 Then Jacob offered a sacrifice
on the mountain, and called his brethren to eat bread. And they ate bread
and stayed all night on the mountain.
55 And early in the morning Laban
arose, and [b]kissed his sons and
daughters and blessed them. Then Laban departed and returned to his
place.

Jacob renamed Israel

32 SO Jacob went on his way, and
the [c]angels of God met him.
2 When Jacob saw them, he said,
"This *is* God's camp." And he called
the name of that place [d]Mahanaim.
3 Then Jacob sent messengers before him to Esau his brother in the
land of Seir, the country of [e]Edom.
4 And he commanded them, saying, "Speak thus to my lord Esau,
'Thus your servant Jacob says: "I have
dwelt with Laban and stayed there until now.
5 "I have oxen, donkeys, flocks,
and male and female servants; and I
have sent to tell my lord, that I may
find favor in your sight." ' "
6 Then the messengers returned
to Jacob, saying, "We came to your
brother Esau, and he also is coming to
meet you, and four hundred men *are*
with him."
7 So Jacob was greatly [f]afraid
and distressed; and he divided the
people that *were* with him, and the
flocks and herds and camels, into two
companies.
8 And he said, "If Esau comes to
the one company and attacks it, then
the other company which is left will
escape."
9 Then Jacob [g]said, "O God of my
father Abraham and God of my father
Isaac, the LORD who said to me, [h]'Return to your country and to your family, and I will deal well with you':
10 "I am not worthy of the least of
all the [i]mercies and of all the truth
which You have shown Your servant;
for I crossed over this Jordan with my
staff, and now I have become two
companies.
11 "Deliver me, I pray, from the
hand of my brother, from the hand of
Esau; for I fear him, lest he come and
attack me *and* the mother with the
children.
12 "For You [j]said, 'I will surely
treat you well, and make your descendants as the [k]sand of the sea, which
cannot be numbered for multitude.' "
13 So he lodged there that same
night, and took what came to his hand
as a present for Esau his brother:
14 two hundred female goats and
twenty male goats, two hundred ewes
and twenty rams,
15 thirty milk camels with their
colts, forty cows and ten bulls, twenty
female donkeys and ten foals.
16 Then he delivered *them* to the
hand of his servants, every drove by
itself, and said to his servants, "Pass
over before me, and put some distance
between successive droves."
17 And he commanded the first
one, saying, "When Esau my brother
meets you and asks you, saying, 'To
whom do you belong, and where are
you going? Whose *are* these in front of
you?'
18 "then you shall say, 'They *are*
your servant Jacob's. It *is* a present
sent to my lord Esau; and behold, he
also *is* behind us.' "
19 So he commanded the second,
the third, and all who followed the
droves, saying, "In this manner you
shall speak to Esau when you find
him;
20 "and also say, 'Behold, your servant Jacob *is* behind us.' " For he said,
"I will appease him with the present
that goes before me, and afterward I
will see his face; perhaps he will accept me."
21 So the present went on over before him, but he himself lodged that
night in the camp.
22 And he arose that night and took
his two wives, his two female servants, and his eleven sons, and
crossed over the ford of [l]Jabbok.
23 He took them, sent them over
the brook, and sent over what he had.
24 Then Jacob was left alone; [m]and
a Man [n]wrestled with him until the
breaking of day.
25 Now when He saw that He did
not prevail against him, He touched
the socket of his hip; and the socket of
Jacob's hip was out of joint as He
wrestled with him.
26 And He said, "Let Me go, for the
day breaks." But he said, "I will not let
You go unless You bless me!"
27 So He said to him, "What *is* your
name?" He said, "Jacob."

53
a v. 42
55
b Cp. Gen. 29:11,13
CHAPTER 32
1
c See Heb. 1:4, *note*
2
d Lit. *two hosts* or *bands*—the visible band, Jacob and his servants; the invisible band, God's angels. Cp. 2 Ki. 6:13–17
3
e Esau's country. Gen. 25:30. See Gen. 36:1, *note*
7
f Gen. 31:31; 35:3
9
g Bible prayers (OT): vv. 9–12; Ex. 32:11. (Gen. 15:2; Hab. 3:1)
h Gen. 31:3, 13; 35:6
10
i Gen. 24:7
12
j Gen. 28:13–15
k Gen. 22:17
22
l Num. 21:24
24
m Jacob's crisis. Cp. Josh. 5:13–15; Job 42:5–6; Isa. 6:1–8; Jer. 1:4–9; Ezek. 1:28; 2:1–7; Dan. 10:1–12; Acts 9:1–6; Rev. 1:13–18
n Hos. 12:2–4

28 And He said, "Your name shall no longer be called [a]Jacob, but [b]Israel; for you have struggled with God and with men, and have prevailed."

29 Then Jacob asked, saying, "Tell *me* Your name, I pray." And He said, "Why *is* it *that* you ask about My name?" And He [c]blessed him there.

30 So Jacob called the name of the place [d]Peniel: "For I have [e]seen God [1]face to face, and my life is preserved."

31 Just as he crossed over [f]Penuel the sun rose on him, and he limped on his hip.

32 Therefore to this day the children of Israel do not eat the muscle that shrank, which *is* on the hip socket, because He touched the socket of Jacob's hip in the muscle that shrank.

Jacob humbles himself and is forgiven by Esau

33 NOW Jacob lifted his eyes and looked, and there, Esau was coming, and with him were four hundred men. So he divided the children among Leah, Rachel, and the two maidservants.

2 And he put the maidservants and their children in front, Leah and her children behind, and Rachel and Joseph last.

3 Then he crossed over before them and bowed himself to the ground seven times, until he came near to his brother.

4 But Esau ran to meet him, and embraced him, and fell on his neck and kissed him, and they wept.

5 And he lifted his eyes and saw the women and children, and said, "Who *are* these with you?" So he said, "The children whom God has graciously given your servant."

6 Then the maidservants came near, they and their children, and bowed down.

7 And Leah also came near with her children, and they bowed down. Afterward Joseph and Rachel came near, and they bowed down.

8 Then Esau said, "What *do* you *mean by* all this company which I met?" And he said, "*These are* to [g]find favor in the sight of my lord."

9 But Esau said, "I have enough, my brother; keep what you have for yourself."

10 And Jacob said, "No, please, if I have now found favor in your sight, then receive my present from my hand, inasmuch as I have seen your face as though I had seen the face of God, and you were pleased with me.

11 "Please, take my blessing that is brought to you, because God has dealt [h]graciously with me, and because I have enough." So he urged him, and he took *it*.

12 Then Esau said, "Let us take our journey; let us go, and I will go before you."

13 But Jacob said to him, "My lord knows that the children *are* weak, and the flocks and herds which are nursing *are* with me. And if the men should drive them hard one day, all the flock will die.

14 "Please let my lord go on ahead before his servant. I will lead on slowly at a pace which the livestock that go before me, and the children, are able to endure, [2]until I come to my lord in [i]Seir."

15 And Esau said, "Now let me leave with you *some* of the people who *are* with me." But he said, "What need is there? Let me find favor in the sight of my lord."

16 So Esau returned that day on his way to Seir.

Jacob worships

17 And Jacob journeyed to Succoth, built himself a house, and made booths for his livestock. Therefore the name of the place is called [j]Succoth.

18 Then Jacob came safely to the city of [k]Shechem, which *is* in the land of Canaan, when he came from Padan Aram; and he pitched his tent before the city.

19 And he [l]bought the parcel of land, where he had pitched his tent, from the children of Hamor, She-

28
a Both names, *Jacob* and *Israel*, are applied to the nation descended from Jacob
b Lit. *he who strives with God;* or *God strives;* or *God rules*

29
c Gen. 35:9

30
d Lit. *the face of God*
e Isa. 6:5; see Jn. 1:18, *note*; cp. Gen. 12:7, *note*

31
f Another form of *Peniel.* Cp. v. 30

CHAPTER 33

8
g Gen. 32:5

11
h Ex. 33:19

14
i Gen. 32:3; 36:8

17
j Lit. *booths* (of branches)

18
k Gen. 12:6; 35:4. See Ps. 60:6, *note*

19
l Josh. 24:32. See Acts 7:16, *note*

---

[1](32:30) The concept of seeing the face of God is not always the same in Scripture. In Ex. 33:20 God said to Moses, "You cannot see My face; for no man shall see Me, and live," but at that time God did reveal Himself to Moses by a manifestation of His glory. When Jacob said that he had seen the LORD face to face, he simply meant that he had looked upon a divine Being, the Angel of the LORD, not that he had beheld God in all of His resplendent glory, which no man could look upon, even as we cannot look upon the sun without being blinded. All that these passages imply culminates in man's beholding the glory of God in the face of Jesus Christ (cp. Ps. 27:8; 2 Cor. 4:6; see Gen. 12:7 and Jn. 1:18, *notes*).

[2](33:14) Not all at once does "Jacob" cease to dominate the walk of "Israel." Compare Gen. 35:1–10, where the walk becomes according to the new name.

chem's father, for one hundred pieces
of money.
20 Then he erected an altar there
and called it [1][a]El Elohe Israel.

Sin in Jacob's family

34 NOW [b]Dinah the daughter of
Leah, whom she had borne to
Jacob, went out to see the daughters
of the land.
2 And when Shechem the son of
Hamor the Hivite, prince of the country, saw her, he took her and lay with
her, and violated her.
3 His soul was strongly attracted
to Dinah the daughter of Jacob, and
he loved the young woman and spoke
kindly to the young woman.
4 So Shechem spoke to his father
Hamor, saying, "Get me this young
woman as a wife."
5 And Jacob heard that he had defiled Dinah his daughter. Now his
sons were with his livestock in the
field; so Jacob held his peace until
they came.
6 Then Hamor the father of Shechem went out to Jacob to speak with
him.
7 And the sons of Jacob came in
from the field when they heard *it;* and
the men were grieved and very angry,
because he had [c]done a disgraceful
thing in Israel by lying with Jacob's
daughter, a thing which ought not to
be done.
8 But Hamor spoke with them,
saying, "The soul of my son Shechem
longs for your daughter. Please give
her to him as a wife.
9 "And make marriages with us;
give your daughters to us, and take
our daughters to yourselves.
10 "So you shall dwell with us, and
the land shall be before you. Dwell
and trade in it, and acquire possessions for yourselves in it."
11 Then Shechem said to her father
and her brothers, "Let me find favor in
your eyes, and whatever you say to
me I will give.
12 "Ask me ever so much dowry
and gift, and I will give according to
what you say to me; but give me the
young woman as a wife."
13 But the sons of Jacob answered
Shechem and Hamor his father, and
spoke [d]deceitfully, because he had defiled Dinah their sister.
14 And they said to them, "We cannot do this thing, to give our sister to
one who is [e]uncircumcised, for that
would be a [f]reproach to us.
15 "But on this *condition* we will
consent to you: If you will become as
we *are,* if every male of you is circumcised,
16 "then we will give our daughters
to you, and we will take your daughters to us; and we will dwell with you,
and we will become one people.
17 "But if you will not heed us and
be circumcised, then we will take our
daughter and be gone."
18 And their words pleased Hamor
and Shechem, Hamor's son.
19 So the young man did not delay
to do the thing, because he delighted
in Jacob's daughter. He *was* more
honorable than all the household of
his father.
20 And Hamor and Shechem his
son came to the [g]gate of their city, and
spoke with the men of their city, saying:
21 "These men *are* at peace with us.
Therefore let them dwell in the land
and trade in it. For indeed the land *is*
large enough for them. Let us take
their daughters to us as wives, and let
us give them our daughters.
22 "Only on this *condition* will the
men consent to dwell with us, to be
one people: if every male among us is
circumcised as they *are* circumcised.
23 "*Will* not their livestock, their
property, and every animal of theirs
be ours? Only let us consent to them,
and they will dwell with us."
24 And all who went out of the gate
of his city heeded Hamor and Shechem his son; every male was circumcised, all who went out of the gate of
his city.
25 Now it came to pass on the third
day, when they were in pain, that two
of the sons of Jacob, [h]Simeon and
[i]Levi, Dinah's brothers, each took his
sword and came boldly upon the city
and killed all the males.
26 And they [j]killed Hamor and
Shechem his son with the edge of the
sword, and took Dinah from Shechem's house, and went out.
27 The sons of Jacob came upon the

20
a Lit. *God, the God of Israel*

CHAPTER 34

1
b Gen. 30:21

7
c Dt. 22:21

13
d Ex. 8:29; cp. Gen. 31:7

14
e Ex. 12:48
f Josh. 5:2–9

20
g Gen. 19:1; 23:10; Ruth 4:1, 11

25
h Gen. 29:33; 42:24
i Gen. 29:34

26
j Gen. 49:5–6

[1](33:20) This was an act of faith on Jacob's part. In calling the altar *El-Elohe-Israel,* not only did he appropriate his new name but also claimed *Elohim* in a new sense, as the God through whom alone he could walk according to this new name. See Gen. 14:18–23 (with *note 1* at v. 18) for a similar appropriation by Abraham.

slain, and plundered the city, because
their sister had been defiled.
28 They took their sheep, their
oxen, and their donkeys, what *was* in
the city and what *was* in the field,
29 and all their wealth. All their little ones and their wives they took captive; and they plundered even all that
was in the houses.
30 Then Jacob said to Simeon and
Levi, "You have troubled me by making me obnoxious among the inhabitants of the land, among the Canaanites and the Perizzites; and since I *am*
few in number, they will gather themselves together against me and kill
me. I shall be destroyed, my household and I."
31 But they said, "Should he treat
our sister like a harlot?"

Jacob, the wanderer, returns to Bethel: communion restored

35 [1]THEN God said to Jacob,
"Arise, go up to [a]Bethel and
dwell there; and make an altar there
to God, who appeared to you when
you fled from the face of Esau your
brother."
2 And Jacob said to his household
and to all who *were* with him, [b]"Put
away the foreign gods that *are* among
you, purify yourselves, and change
your garments.
3 "Then let us arise and go up to
Bethel; and I will make an altar there
to God, who answered me in the day
of my distress and has been [c]with me
in the way which I have gone."
4 So they gave Jacob all the foreign gods which *were* in their hands,
and the earrings which *were* in their
ears; and Jacob hid them under the
terebinth tree which *was* by Shechem.
5 And they journeyed, and the terror of God was upon the cities that
were all around them, and they did not
pursue the sons of Jacob.
6 So Jacob came to [d]Luz (that *is*,
Bethel), which *is* in the land of Canaan, he and all the people who *were*
with him.
7 And he built an [e]altar there and
called the place [2]El Bethel, because
there God appeared to him when he
fled from the face of his brother.
8 Now Deborah, Rebekah's nurse,
died, and she was buried below Bethel
under the terebinth tree. So the name
of it was called [f]Allon Bachuth.
9 Then God [g]appeared to Jacob
again, when he came from Padan
Aram, and [h]blessed him.
10 And God said to him, "Your
name *is* Jacob; [i]your name shall not
be called Jacob anymore, but Israel
shall be your name." So He called his
name Israel.
11 Also God said to him: "I *am*
[j]God Almighty. [k]Be fruitful and multiply; a [l]nation and a [m]company of
nations shall proceed from you, and
kings shall come from your body.
12 "The [n]land which I gave Abraham and Isaac I give to you; and to
your descendants after you I give this
land."
13 Then God went up from him in
the place where He talked with him.
14 So Jacob set up a [o]pillar in the

CHAPTER 35
1 *a* Gen. 28:19; 31:13
2 *b* Ex. 23:24
3 *c* Gen. 28:20
6 *d* Gen. 28:19; 48:3
7 *e* Gen. 33:20
8 *f* Lit. *the oak of weeping*
9 *g Theophanies:* vv. 9–13; Josh. 5:13. (Gen. 12:7, *note;* Dan. 10:5) *h* Gen. 32:29
10 *i* Gen. 32:28
11 *j Deity* (names of): v. 11; Ex. 3:14. (Gen. 1:1; Mal. 3:18) *k* Gen. 9:1,7 *l Israel* (covenant): vv. 11–12; Gen. 37:13. (Gen. 12:2; Rom. 11:26, *note*) *m* Gen. 17:6

35:12 *n* Gen. 28:13; 48:4 **35:14** *o* Gen. 31:13,45

[1](35:1) This is the first revival recorded in the Bible and it has nearly all the salient features of the many subsequent revivals described in the OT. They are: (1) revival is often, as here, preceded by a period of gross iniquity, disgrace, and consequent fear (34:30–31); (2) it is initiated by a word from God, direct or through a consecrated leader—"God said"; (3) there must be a forsaking of all that is displeasing to God—"Put away the foreign gods . . . purify yourselves" (v. 2); (4) there is a corresponding return to obedience to God's revealed will—"go up to Bethel," "make an altar"; (5) past blessings are remembered—"who appeared to you when you fled," "answered me in the day of my distress"; (6) those who genuinely seek to serve the Lord are assured of divine protection from their enemies—"they did not pursue" (v. 5); (7) revival is accompanied by a new revelation of the character of God (v. 11); (8) the promises of God are renewed and a revelation of the possibility of a higher spiritual life is given (vv. 10–11); (9) revival may prove to have been God's preparation for meeting a coming test or bereavement, as here in the death of Rachel (vv. 16–20); and (10) later OT revivals almost always are marked by a resumption of the offering of blood sacrifices. For other revivals of the OT see the following: under King Asa (2 Chr. 15:1–15); under King Jehoash (2 Ki. 11—12; 2 Chr. 23—24); under King Hezekiah (2 Ki. 18:4–7; and especially 2 Chr. 29—31); under Josiah (2 Ki. 22—23; 2 Chr. 34—35); in Nineveh (Jon. 3); at the time of Zerubbabel (Ezra 5—6); and under Nehemiah (Neh. 8—9; 13:1–6).

[2](35:7) Compare Gen. 28:19, where it was the place, as the scene of the ladder-vision, which impressed Jacob. He called the place "Bethel," i.e. *the house of God.* Now it is the God of the place, rather than the place, and he calls it "El Bethel," i.e. *the God of the house of God.* See Gen. 33:20, *note.*

place where He talked with him, a pillar of stone; and he poured a [1]drink
offering on it, and he poured oil on it.
15 And Jacob called the name of
the place where God spoke with him,
Bethel.

Death of Rachel; birth of Benjamin

16 Then they journeyed from
Bethel. And when there was but a little
distance to go to Ephrath, Rachel labored *in childbirth,* and she had hard
labor.
17 Now it came to pass, when she
was in hard labor, that the midwife
said to her, "Do not fear; you will have
this son [a]also."
18 And so it was, as her soul was
departing (for she died), that she
called his name [b]Ben-Oni; but his father called him [2]Benjamin.
19 So Rachel died and was buried
on the way to Ephrath (that *is,* [3c]Beth-
lehem).
20 And Jacob set a [d]pillar on her
grave, which *is* the pillar of Rachel's
grave to this day.
21 Then Israel journeyed and
pitched his tent beyond the tower of
Eder.
22 And it happened, when Israel
dwelt in that land, that [e]Reuben went
and lay with Bilhah his father's concubine; and Israel heard *about it.*
Now the [4]sons of Jacob were
twelve:
23 the sons of Leah *were* Reuben,
Jacob's firstborn, and Simeon, Levi,
Judah, Issachar, and Zebulun;
24 the sons of Rachel *were* Joseph
and Benjamin;
25 the sons of Bilhah, Rachel's
maidservant, *were* Dan and Naphtali;
26 and the sons of Zilpah, Leah's
maidservant, *were* Gad and Asher.
These *were* the sons of Jacob who
were born to him in Padan Aram.

Jacob restored to Isaac; Isaac dies

27 Then Jacob came to his father
Isaac at Mamre, or Kirjath Arba*
(that *is,* Hebron), where Abraham and
Isaac had dwelt.
28 Now the days of Isaac were one
hundred and eighty years.
29 So Isaac [5]breathed his last and
died, and was gathered to his people,
being old and full of days. And his
sons Esau and Jacob buried him.

Genealogy of Esau (Edom)

36 NOW this *is* the [f]genealogy of
Esau, who is [6]Edom.

17 *a* Cp. Gen. 30:24
18 *b* Lit. *the son of my sorrow*
19 *c* Gen. 48:7
20 *d* Gen. 31:13,45
22 *e* Gen. 49:3–4
CHAPTER 36
1 *f* v. 9; Gen. 25:19; 37:2

* **35:27** Literally *Town of Arbah*

[1](35:14) The first mention of the drink offering. It is not found among the Levitical offerings of Lev. 1—7, though included in the instructions for sacrifice in the land (Num. 15:5–7). It was always "poured," never drunk, and may be considered a type of Christ in the sense of Ps. 22:14; Isa. 53:12.

[2](35:18) Benjamin, *the son of my sorrow* (Ben-Oni) to his mother, but *son of my right hand* to his father, illustrates two aspects of Christ. As Ben-Oni, He was the suffering One because of whom a sword pierced His mother's heart (Lk. 2:35); as Benjamin, head of the warrior tribe (Gen. 49:27), firmly joined to Judah the kingly tribe (Gen. 49:8–12; 1 Ki. 12:21), He pictures the victorious One.

[3](35:19) This is the first reference in the Bible to Bethlehem. The word itself means *house of bread.* In this city our Lord was born, appearing in the flesh which He was to give for the life of the world. It is the city of motherhood, but motherhood in relation to death as here (Mt. 2:16–18; Lk. 2:34–35). Bethlehem is never mentioned in the NT as the site of any event in the ministry of our Lord or in the church of the first century. There has never been any question as to the site of Bethlehem, which is located about five miles south of Jerusalem.

[4](35:22) Here is the first complete list of the twelve sons of Jacob, whose births have been described in the preceding chapters. From them came the twelve tribes of Israel, the tribal blessings being given each of them respectively at the time of Jacob's death (Gen. 49). The names reappear in the genealogies of 1 Chr. 2:1–2. As tribal names, they are listed on seven different occasions in the Book of Numbers, and appear again in the blessing of Moses (Dt. 33), in the division of the land in Josh. 15, elsewhere in the OT, and finally as the twelve sealed tribes of Rev. 7:4–8. The order in which the names are given varies.

[5](35:29) How wrong Isaac had been about the time of his death! See Gen. 27:2. He lived for forty-three years after the incident of chapter 27, and twenty-five years after Jacob returned from Padan Aram (35:27). Jacob was away twenty years (31:41).

[6](36:1) Edom (called "Seir," Gen. 32:3; 36:8) is the name of the country lying south of the ancient kingdom of Judah and extending from the Dead Sea to the Gulf of Aqaba. It includes the ruins of Petra, and is bounded on the north by Moab. Peopled by descendants of Esau (Gen. 36:1–19), Edom has a remarkable prominence in the prophetic Word as (together with Moab) the scene of the final destruction of Gentile world-power in the Day of the LORD. See Armageddon (Rev. 16:13–16; 19:17–21) and Times of the Gentiles (Lk. 21:24; Rev. 16:19). Cp. Ps. 137:7;

2 Esau took his wives from the daughters of Canaan: Adah the daughter of Elon the [a]Hittite; Aholibamah the daughter of Anah, the daughter of Zibeon the Hivite;

3 and Basemath, Ishmael's daughter, sister of Nebajoth.

4 Now Adah bore Eliphaz to Esau, and Basemath bore Reuel.

5 And Aholibamah bore Jeush, Jaalam, and Korah. These *were* the sons of Esau who were born to him in the land of Canaan.

6 Then Esau took his wives, his sons, his daughters, and all the persons of his household, his cattle and all his animals, and all his goods which he had gained in the land of Canaan, and went to a country away from the presence of his brother Jacob.

7 For their possessions were too great for them to dwell together, and the land where they were strangers could not support them because of their livestock.

8 So Esau dwelt in Mount Seir. Esau *is* Edom.

9 And this *is* the genealogy of Esau the father of the Edomites in Mount Seir.

10 These *were* the names of Esau's sons: Eliphaz the son of Adah the wife of Esau, and Reuel the son of Basemath the wife of Esau.

11 And the sons of Eliphaz were Teman, Omar, Zepho,* Gatam, and Kenaz.

12 Now Timna was the concubine of Eliphaz, Esau's son, and she bore [b]Amalek to Eliphaz. These *were* the sons of Adah, Esau's wife.

13 These *were* the sons of Reuel: Nahath, Zerah, Shammah, and Mizzah. These were the sons of Basemath, Esau's wife.

14 These were the sons of Aholibamah, Esau's wife, the daughter of Anah, the daughter of Zibeon. And she bore to Esau: Jeush, Jaalam, and Korah.

15 These *were* the chiefs of the sons of Esau. The sons of Eliphaz, the firstborn *son* of Esau, were Chief Teman, Chief Omar, Chief Zepho, Chief Kenaz,

16 Chief Korah,* Chief Gatam, *and* Chief Amalek. These *were* the chiefs of Eliphaz in the land of Edom. They *were* the sons of Adah.

17 These *were* the sons of Reuel, Esau's son: Chief Nahath, Chief Zerah, Chief Shammah, and Chief Mizzah. These *were* the chiefs of Reuel in the land of Edom. These *were* the sons of Basemath, Esau's wife.

18 And these *were* the sons of Aholibamah, Esau's wife: Chief Jeush, Chief Jaalam, and Chief Korah. These *were* the chiefs *who descended* from Aholibamah, Esau's wife, the daughter of Anah.

19 These *were* the sons of Esau, who is Edom, and these *were* their chiefs.

20 These *were* the sons of Seir the [1]Horite who inhabited the land: Lotan, Shobal, Zibeon, Anah,

21 Dishon, Ezer, and Dishan. These *were* the chiefs of the Horites, the sons of Seir, in the land of Edom.

22 And the sons of Lotan were Hori and Hemam.* Lotan's sister *was* Timna.

23 These *were* the sons of Shobal: Alvan,* Manahath, Ebal, Shepho,* and Onam.

24 These *were* the sons of Zibeon: both Ajah and Anah. This *was the* Anah who found the water* in the wilderness as he pastured the donkeys of his father Zibeon.

25 These *were* the children of Anah: Dishon and Aholibamah the daughter of Anah.

26 These *were* the sons of Dishon:* Hemdan,* Eshban, Ithran, and Cheran.

27 These *were* the sons of Ezer: Bilhan, Zaavan, and Akan.*

28 These *were* the sons of Dishan: [c]Uz and Aran.

29 These *were* the chiefs of the Horites: Chief Lotan, Chief Shobal, Chief Zibeon, Chief Anah,

30 Chief Dishon, Chief Ezer, and

2 [a] See 2 Ki. 7:6, *note*

12 [b] Ex. 17:8–14; 1 Sam. 15:1–33

28 [c] Job 1:1

*

36:11 Spelled *Zephi* in 1 Chronicles 1:36
36:16 Samaritan Pentateuch omits *Chief Korah.*
36:22 Spelled *Homam* in 1 Chronicles 1:39
36:23 Spelled *Alian* in 1 Chronicles 1:40 • Spelled *Shephi* in 1 Chronicles 1:40 **36:24** Following Masoretic Text and Vulgate (*hot springs*); Septuagint reads *Jamin;* Targum reads *mighty men;* Talmud interprets as *mules.* **36:26** Hebrew *Dishan* • Spelled *Hamran* in 1 Chronicles 1:41
36:27 Spelled *Jaakan* in 1 Chronicles 1:42

Isa. 34:1–8; 63:1–6; Jer. 49:17–22; Ezek. 25:12–14; Obad. 1–21.

[1](36:20) The Horites, or Hurrians, were completely forgotten for thousands of years. It has now been discovered that they were a large group of people who settled in northern Mesopotamia, in Syria, and in Palestine before 2000 B.C. Thousands of tablets containing their business documents and other records have been recovered by excavation.

Chief Dishan. These *were* the chiefs of the Horites, according to their chiefs in the land of Seir.

31 [1]Now these *were* the [a]kings who reigned in the land of Edom before any king reigned over the children of Israel:

32 Bela the son of Beor reigned in Edom, and the name of his city *was* Dinhabah.

33 And when Bela died, Jobab the son of Zerah of Bozrah reigned in his place.

34 When Jobab died, Husham of the land of the Temanites reigned in his place.

35 And when Husham died, Hadad the son of Bedad, who attacked Midian in the field of Moab, reigned in his place. And the name of his city *was* Avith.

36 When Hadad died, Samlah of Masrekah reigned in his place.

37 And when Samlah died, Saul of Rehoboth-*by*-the-River reigned in his place.

38 When Saul died, Baal-Hanan the son of Achbor reigned in his place.

39 And when Baal-Hanan the son of Achbor died, Hadar* reigned in his place; and the name of his city *was* Pau.* His wife's name *was* Mehetabel, the daughter of Matred, the daughter of Mezahab.

40 And these *were* the names of the chiefs of Esau, according to their families and their places, by their names: Chief Timnah, Chief Alvah,* Chief Jetheth,

41 Chief Aholibamah, Chief Elah, Chief Pinon,

42 Chief Kenaz, Chief Teman, Chief Mibzar,

43 Chief Magdiel, and Chief Iram. These *were* the chiefs of Edom, according to their dwelling places in the land of their possession. Esau *was* the father of the Edomites.

History of Jacob resumed

37 NOW Jacob dwelt in the land where his father was a stranger, in the land of Canaan.

Joseph, the beloved of his father

2 This *is* the history of Jacob. [2]Joseph, *being* seventeen years old, was feeding the flock with his brothers. And the lad *was* with the sons of Bilhah and the sons of Zilpah, his father's wives; and Joseph brought a bad report of them to his father.

3 Now Israel loved Joseph more than all his children, because he *was* the [b]son of his old age. Also he [c]made him a [d]tunic of *many* colors.

4 But when his brothers saw that their father loved him more than all his brothers, they [e]hated him and could not speak peaceably to him.

5 Now Joseph had a dream, and he told *it* to his brothers; and they hated him even more.

6 So he said to them, "Please hear this dream which I have [f]dreamed:

7 "There we were, binding sheaves in the field. Then behold, my sheaf arose and also stood upright; and indeed your sheaves stood all around and [g]bowed down to my sheaf."

Joseph hated and rejected by his brothers

8 And his brothers said to him, "Shall you indeed reign over us? Or shall you indeed have [h]dominion over

31
a Gen. 17:6

CHAPTER 37
3
b Gen. 44:20
c 1 Sam. 2:19
d Or a long-sleeved robe, a mark of special honor.
4
e Gen. 27:41; cp. Jn. 15:18–20
6
f vv. 9–10; cp. Gen. 40:5–23
7
g Gen. 42:6; 44:14; cp. Phil. 2:10
8
h Cp. Jn. 19:15

*

36:39 Spelled *Hadad* in Samaritan Pentateuch, Syriac, and 1 Chronicles 1:50 • Spelled *Pai* in 1 Chronicles 1:50 **36:40** Spelled *Aliah* in 1 Chronicles 1:51

[1](36:31) It is characteristic of Scripture that the kings of Edom should be named before the kings of Israel. The principle is stated in 1 Cor. 15:46. First things are "natural," man's best, and always fail; second things are "spiritual," God's things, and succeed. Adam—Christ; Cain—Abel; Cain's posterity—Seth's posterity; Saul—David, etc.

The mention of kings at this point, when Israel actually had no kings until the time of Saul (1 Sam. 10), has been used by some as an argument against Mosaic authorship. The answer to the objection is found in Gen. 17:6,16, where already Abraham and Sarah were promised kings among their descendants.

[2](37:2) While it is nowhere asserted that Joseph was a type of Christ, the many analogies are significant. They are: (1) both were special objects of a father's love (Gen. 37:3; Mt. 3:17; Jn. 3:35; 5:20); (2) both were hated by their brothers (Gen. 37:4; Jn. 15:25); (3) the superior claims of both were rejected by their brothers (Gen. 37:8; Mt. 21:37–39; Jn. 15:24–25); (4) the brothers of both conspired against them to slay them (Gen. 37:18; Mt. 26:3–4); (5) Joseph was, in intent and figure, slain by his brothers, as was Christ (Gen. 37:24; Mt. 27:35–37); (6) each became a blessing among the Gentiles and gained a bride (Gen. 41:1–45; Acts 15:14; Eph. 5:25–32); and (7) as Joseph reconciled his brothers to himself and afterward exalted them, so will it be with Christ and His Jewish brethren (Gen. 45:1–15; Dt. 30:1–10; Hos. 2:14–18; Rom. 11:1,15,25–26).

us?" So they hated him even more for
his dreams and for his words.
9 Then he dreamed still another
dream and told it to his brothers, and
said, "Look, I have dreamed another
dream. And this time, the sun, the
moon, and the eleven stars bowed
down to me."
10 So he told *it* to his father and his
brothers; and his father rebuked him
and said to him, "What *is* this dream
that you have dreamed? Shall your
mother and I and your brothers indeed come to bow down to the earth
before you?"
11 And his brothers [a]envied him,
but his father kept the matter *in mind.*
12 Then his brothers went to feed
their father's flock in Shechem.
13 [b]And Israel said to Joseph, "Are
not your brothers feeding *the flock* in
Shechem? Come, I will send you to
them." So he said to him, "Here I am."
14 Then he said to him, "Please go
and see if it is well with your brothers
and well with the flocks, and bring
back word to me." So he [c]sent him out
of the Valley of Hebron, and he went
to Shechem.
15 Now a certain man found him,
and there he was, wandering in the
field. And the man asked him, saying,
"What are you seeking?"
16 So he said, "I am seeking my
brothers. Please tell me where they
are feeding *their flocks.*"
17 And the man said, "They have
departed from here, for I heard them
say, 'Let us go to [d]Dothan.'" So Joseph went after his brothers and
found them in Dothan.
18 Now when they saw him afar
off, even before he came near them,
they [e]conspired against him to kill
him.
19 Then they said to one another,
"Look, this dreamer is coming!

Joseph cast into pit

20 "Come therefore, let us now kill
him and cast him into some pit; and
we shall say, 'Some wild beast has devoured him.' We shall see what will
become of his dreams!"
21 But Reuben heard *it,* and he delivered him out of their hands, and
said, "Let us not kill him."
22 And Reuben said to them, "Shed
no blood, *but* cast him into this pit
which *is* in the wilderness, and do not
lay a hand on him"—that he might deliver him out of their hands, and bring
him back to his father.
23 So it came to pass, when Joseph
had come to his brothers, that they
[f]stripped Joseph *of* his tunic, the [g]tu-
nic of *many* colors that *was* on him.
24 Then they took him and cast him
into a pit. And the pit *was* empty;
there was no water in it.
25 And they sat down to eat a meal.
Then they lifted their eyes and looked,
and there was a company of Ishmaelites, coming from Gilead with their
camels, bearing spices, balm, and
myrrh, on their way to carry *them*
down to Egypt.
26 So Judah said to his brothers,
"What profit *is there* if we kill our
brother and conceal his blood?
27 "Come and let us sell him to the
Ishmaelites, and let not our hand be
upon him, for he *is* our brother *and*
our flesh." And his brothers listened.

Joseph pulled up from pit and sold into Egypt

28 Then Midianite traders passed
by; so *the brothers* pulled Joseph up
and lifted him out of the pit, and [h]sold
him to the [1]Ishmaelites for twenty
shekels of silver. And they took Joseph to Egypt.
29 Then Reuben returned to the pit,
and indeed Joseph *was* not in the pit;
and he [i]tore his clothes.
30 And he returned to his brothers
and said, "The lad *is* no *more;* and I,
where shall I go?"
31 So they took Joseph's tunic,
killed a kid of the goats, and dipped
the tunic in the blood.
32 Then they sent the tunic of *many*
colors, and they brought *it* to their father and said, "We have found this. Do
you know whether it *is* your son's tunic or not?"
33 And he recognized it and said,
"*It is* my son's tunic. A wild beast has
devoured him. Without doubt Joseph
is torn to pieces."
34 Then Jacob [i]tore his clothes,
put [j]sackcloth on his waist, and
[k]mourned for his son many days.
35 And all his sons and all his
daughters arose to comfort him; but

11
a Mt. 27:17–18; Acts 7:9
13
b Israel (history): vv. 13–28; Gen. 46:1. (Gen. 12:2; Rom. 11:26, *note*)
14
c Cp. 1 Sam. 17:17–18; Lk. 20:13–15; Jn. 3:16
17
d 2 Ki. 6:13
18
e Cp. Mt. 21:38; 26:3–4
23
f Mt. 27:28
g v. 3
28
h Cp. Mt. 26:15; 27:9
29
i Gen. 44:13
34
j 2 Sam. 3:31
k Gen. 50:10; cp. 27:41

[1](37:28) A contradiction has been imagined between the reference to the traders who carried Joseph into Egypt as Ishmaelites, in vv. 25,27,28 (and 39:1), and as Midianites in vv. 28 and 36. Actually, the precise meaning of these terms is not known and there is no reason to doubt that they overlapped.

he refused to be comforted, and he said, "For I shall go down into the [a]grave to my son in mourning." Thus his father wept for him.

36 Now the Midianites* had sold him in Egypt to [b]Potiphar, an officer of Pharaoh *and* captain of the guard.

Judah's shameful sin

38 IT came to pass at that time that [c]Judah departed from his brothers, and visited a certain Adullamite whose name *was* Hirah.

2 And Judah saw there a daughter of a certain Canaanite whose name *was* [d]Shua, and he married her and went in to her.

3 So she conceived and bore a son, and he called his name [e]Er.

4 She conceived again and bore a son, and she called his name [e]Onan.

5 And she conceived yet again and bore a son, and called his name [e]Shelah. He was at Chezib when she bore him.

6 Then Judah took a wife for Er his firstborn, and her name *was* [f]Tamar.

7 But Er, Judah's firstborn, was wicked in the sight of the LORD, and the LORD [g]killed him.

8 And Judah said to Onan, "Go in to your brother's wife and marry her, and [1]raise up an heir to your brother."

9 But Onan knew that the heir would not be his; and it came to pass, when he went in to his brother's wife, that he emitted on the ground, lest he should give an heir to his brother.

10 And the thing which he did [h]displeased the LORD; therefore He killed him also.

11 Then Judah said to Tamar his daughter-in-law, [i]"Remain a widow in your father's house till my son Shelah is grown." For he said, "Lest he also die like his brothers." And Tamar went and dwelt in her father's house.

12 Now in the process of time the daughter of Shua, Judah's wife, died; and Judah was comforted, and went up to his sheepshearers at Timnah, he and his friend Hirah the Adullamite.

13 And it was told Tamar, saying, "Look, your father-in-law is going up to Timnah to shear his sheep."

14 So she took off her widow's garments, covered *herself* with a veil and wrapped herself, and [j]sat in an open place which *was* on the way to Timnah; for she saw that Shelah was grown, and she was not given to him as a wife.

15 When Judah saw her, he thought she *was* a harlot, because she had covered her face.

16 Then he turned to her by the way, and said, "Please let me come in to you"; for he did not know that she *was* his daughter-in-law. So she said, "What will you give me, that you may come in to me?"

17 And he said, "I will send a [k]young goat from the flock." So she said, "Will you give *me* a pledge till you send *it*?"

18 Then he said, "What pledge shall I give you?" So she said, "Your [l]signet and cord, and your staff that *is* in your hand." Then he gave *them* to her, and went in to her, and she conceived by him.

19 So she arose and went away, and laid aside her veil and put on the garments of her widowhood.

20 And Judah sent the young goat by the hand of his friend the Adullamite, to receive *his* pledge from the woman's hand, but he did not find her.

21 Then he asked the men of that place, saying, "Where is the harlot who *was* openly by the roadside?" And they said, "There was no harlot in this *place*."

22 So he returned to Judah and said, "I cannot find her. Also, the men of the place said there was no harlot in this *place*."

23 Then Judah said, "Let her take [m]*them* for herself, lest we [n]be shamed; for I sent this young goat and you have not found her."

24 And it came to pass, about three months after, that Judah was told, saying, "Tamar your daughter-in-law has played the harlot; furthermore she *is* with child by harlotry." So Judah said, "Bring her out and let her be [o]burned!"

25 When she *was* brought out, she sent to her father-in-law, saying, "By the man to whom these belong, I *am* with child." And she said, "Please determine whose these *are*—the signet and cord, and staff."

26 So Judah acknowledged *them*

35
a See Hab. 2:5, *note*
36
b Gen. 39:1
CHAPTER 38
1
c Gen. 37:26; 43:3,8
2
d 1 Chr. 2:3
3
e Gen. 46:12
6
f Ruth 4:12
7
g 1 Chr. 2:3; Job 8:3–4
10
h Lit. *was evil in the eyes of the LORD*
11
i Cp. Ruth 1:12–13
14
j Prov. 7:12
17
k Jud. 15:1
18
l v. 25; cp. 41:42
23
m i.e., *the signet, the cord, and the staff*
n Lit. *become a contempt*
24
o Lev. 20:14

*
37:36 Masoretic Text reads *Medanites.*

[1](38:8) This custom later became part of the Mosaic law (Dt. 25:5–6); each man would generally have his line of descent carried on by this provision. Compare Mt. 22:23–33, where the Sadducees presented a hypothetical case in their attempt to confute Jesus.

and said, "She has been [a]more righteous than I, because I did not give her to Shelah my son." And he never knew her again.

27 Now it came to pass, at the time for giving birth, that behold, twins *were* in her womb.

28 And so it was, when she was giving birth, that *the one* put out *his* hand; and the midwife took a scarlet *thread* and bound it on his hand, saying, "This one came out first."

29 Then it happened, as he drew back his hand, that his brother came out unexpectedly; and she said, "How did you break through? *This* breach *be* upon you!" Therefore his name was called [b]Perez.*

30 Afterward his brother came out who had the scarlet *thread* on his hand. And his name was called [b]Zerah.

Joseph resists temptation

39

NOW Joseph had been taken [c]down to Egypt. And [d]Potiphar, an officer of Pharaoh, captain of the guard, an Egyptian, [e]bought him from the Ishmaelites who had taken him down there.

2 The LORD was [f]with Joseph, and he was a successful man; and he was in the house of his master the Egyptian.

3 And his master saw that the LORD *was* with him and that the LORD made all he did to prosper in his hand.

4 So Joseph found favor in his sight, and served him. Then he made him [g]overseer of his house, and all *that* he had he put under his authority.

5 So it was, from the time *that* he had made him overseer of his house and all that he had, that the LORD [h]blessed the Egyptian's house for Joseph's sake; and the blessing of the LORD was on all that he had in the house and in the field.

6 Thus he left all that he had in Joseph's hand, and he did not know what he had except for the bread which he ate. Now Joseph was handsome in form and appearance.

7 And it came to pass after these things that his master's wife cast longing eyes on Joseph, and she said, "Lie with me."

8 But he refused and said to his master's wife, "Look, my master does not know what *is* with me in the house, and he has committed all that he has to my hand.

9 "*There is* no one greater in this house than I, nor has he kept back anything from me but you, because you *are* his wife. How then can I do this great [i]wickedness, and [j]sin [k]against God?"

10 So it was, as she spoke to Joseph day by day, that he did not [l]heed her, to lie with her *or* to be with her.

11 But it happened about this time, when Joseph went into the house to do his work, and none of the men of the house *was* inside,

12 that she [m]caught him by his garment, saying, "Lie with me." But he left his garment in her hand, and fled and ran outside.

Joseph falsely accused

13 And so it was, when she saw that he had left his garment in her hand and fled outside,

14 that she called to the men of her house and spoke to them, saying, "See, he has brought in to us a [n]Hebrew to mock us. He came in to me to lie with me, and I cried out with a loud voice.

15 "And it happened, when he heard that I lifted my voice and cried out, that he left his garment with me, and fled and went outside."

16 So she kept his garment with her until his master came home.

17 Then she spoke to him with words like these, saying, "The Hebrew servant whom you brought to us came in to me to mock me;

18 "so it happened, as I lifted my voice and cried out, that he left his garment with me and fled outside."

19 So it was, when his master heard the words which his wife spoke to him, saying, "Your servant did to me after this manner," that his anger was aroused.

20 Then Joseph's master took him and put him into the [o]prison, a place where the king's prisoners *were* confined. And he was there in the prison.

21 But the LORD was with Joseph and showed him mercy, and He gave him [p]favor in the sight of the keeper of the prison.

22 And the keeper of the prison committed to Joseph's hand all the prisoners who *were* in the prison; whatever they did there, it was his doing.

23 The keeper of the prison did not look into anything *that was* under Jo-

26
a 1 Sam. 24:17
29
b Gen. 46:12; Mt. 1:3
CHAPTER 39
1
c Gen. 12:10; 43:15
d Gen. 37:36
e Gen. 37:28; 45:4; Ps. 105:17
2
f Cp. Gen. 35:3
4
g Gen. 41:40; cp. 24:10
5
h Gen. 18:26; 30:27; 2 Sam. 6:11
9
i Lev. 20:10
j Gen. 20:6
k Ps. 51:4
10
l Prov. 1:10
12
m Prov. 7:13
14
n Gen. 14:13; 41:12
20
o Ps. 105:18
21
p Dan. 1:9; Acts 7:9–10

* 38:29 Literally *Breach* or *Breakthrough*

seph's authority,* because the LORD was with him; and whatever he did, the LORD made *it* prosper.

Joseph forgotten in prison

40 IT came to pass after these things *that* the butler and the baker of the king of Egypt offended their lord, the king of Egypt.

2 And Pharaoh was angry with his two officers, the chief butler and the chief baker.

3 So he put them in custody in the house of the [a]captain of the guard, in the [b]prison, the place where Joseph *was* confined.

4 And the captain of the guard charged Joseph with them, and he served them; so they were in custody for a while.

5 Then the butler and the baker of the king of Egypt, who *were* confined in the prison, [c]had a dream, both of them, each man's dream in one night *and* each man's dream with its *own* interpretation.

6 And Joseph came in to them in the morning and looked at them, and saw that they *were* sad.

7 So he asked Pharaoh's officers who *were* with him in the custody of his lord's house, saying, [d]"Why do you look *so* sad today?"

8 And they said to him, "We each have had a dream, and *there is* no interpreter of it." So Joseph said to them, "Do not [e]interpretations belong to God? Tell *them* to me, please."

9 Then the chief butler told his dream to Joseph, and said to him, "Behold, in my dream a vine *was* before me,

10 "and in the vine *were* three branches; it *was* as though it budded, its blossoms shot forth, and its clusters brought forth ripe grapes.

11 "Then Pharaoh's cup *was* in my hand; and I took the grapes and pressed them into Pharaoh's cup, and placed the cup in Pharaoh's hand."

12 And Joseph said to him, "This *is* the [f]interpretation of it: The three branches *are* [g]three days.

13 "Now within three days Pharaoh will lift up your [h]head and restore you to your place, and you will put Pharaoh's cup in his hand according to the former manner, when you were his butler.

14 "But [i]remember me when it is well with you, and please [j]show kindness to me; make mention of me to Pharaoh, and get me out of this house.

15 "For indeed I was [k]stolen away from the land of the Hebrews; and also I have done nothing here that they should put me into the dungeon."

16 When the chief baker saw that the interpretation was good, he said to Joseph, "I also *was* in my dream, and there *were* three white baskets on my head.

17 "In the uppermost basket *were* all kinds of baked goods for Pharaoh, and the birds ate them out of the basket on my head."

18 So Joseph answered and said, "This *is* the interpretation of it: The three baskets *are* three days.

19 "Within three days Pharaoh will lift off your head from you and [l]hang you on a tree; and the birds will eat your flesh from you."

20 Now it came to pass on the third day, *which was* Pharaoh's [m]birthday, that he made a feast for all his servants; and he lifted up the head of the chief butler and of the chief baker among his servants.

21 Then he restored the chief butler to his butlership again, and he placed the [n]cup in Pharaoh's hand.

22 But he hanged the chief baker, as Joseph had interpreted to them.

23 Yet the chief butler did not remember Joseph, but [o]forgot him.

Pharaoh's prophetic dream

41 THEN it came to pass, at the end of two full years, that Pharaoh [p]had a dream; and behold, he stood by the river.

2 Suddenly there came up out of the river seven cows, fine looking and fat; and they fed in the meadow.

3 Then behold, seven other cows came up after them out of the river, ugly and gaunt, and stood by the *other* cows on the bank of the river.

4 And the ugly and gaunt cows ate up the seven fine looking and fat cows. So Pharaoh awoke.

5 He slept and dreamed a second time; and suddenly seven heads of grain came up on one stalk, plump and good.

6 Then behold, seven thin heads, blighted by the [q]east wind, sprang up after them.

7 And the seven thin heads devoured the seven plump and full heads. So Pharaoh awoke, and indeed, *it was* a dream.

8 Now it came to pass in the morn-

CHAPTER 40

3 *a* Gen. 39:1; 41:10 *b* Gen. 39:20,23

5 *c* Gen. 37:5; 41:1

7 *d* Cp. Neh. 2:2

8 *e* Dan. 2:20–22

12 *f* Dan. 2:36 *g* v. 18; Gen. 42:17

13 *h* 2 Ki. 25:27; Jer. 52:31

14 *i* Cp. 1 Sam. 25:31; Lk. 23:42 *j* Cp. Gen. 24:49; 47:29

15 *k* Gen. 37:28

19 *l* Dt. 21:22

20 *m* Cp. Mt. 14:6–10

21 *n* Cp. Neh. 2:1

23 *o* v. 9; cp. Isa. 49:15

CHAPTER 41

1 *p* Gen. 40:5; Jud. 7:13

6 *q* Ex. 10:13; Ezek. 17:10

* 39:23 Literally *his hand*

ing that his [a]spirit was troubled, and he sent and called for all the [b]magicians of Egypt and all its wise men. And Pharaoh told them his dreams, but *there was* no one who could interpret them for Pharaoh.

9 Then the [c]chief butler spoke to Pharaoh, saying: "I remember my faults this day.

10 "When Pharaoh was angry with his servants, and put me in custody in the house of the captain of the guard, *both* me and the chief baker,

11 "we each [d]had a dream in one night, he and I. Each of us dreamed according to the [e]interpretation of his *own* dream.

12 "Now there *was* a young [f]Hebrew man with us there, a servant of the captain of the guard. And we told him, and he interpreted our dreams for us; to each man he interpreted according to his *own* dream.

13 "And it came to pass, just as he interpreted for us, so it happened. He restored me to my office, and he hanged him."

Joseph's exaltation in Egypt

14 Then Pharaoh [g]sent and called Joseph, and they [h]brought him quickly [i]out of the dungeon; and he shaved, [j]changed his clothing, and came to Pharaoh.

15 And Pharaoh said to Joseph, "I have had a dream, and *there is* no one who can interpret it. But I have [k]heard it said of you *that* you can understand a dream, to interpret it."

16 So Joseph answered Pharaoh, saying, "*It is* not in me; [l]God will give Pharaoh an answer of peace."

17 Then Pharaoh said to Joseph: "Behold, in my dream I stood on the bank of the river.

18 "Suddenly seven cows came up out of the river, fine looking and fat; and they fed in the meadow.

19 "Then behold, seven other cows came up after them, poor and very ugly and gaunt, such ugliness as I have never seen in all the land of Egypt.

20 "And the gaunt and ugly cows ate up the first seven, the fat cows.

21 "When they had eaten them up, no one would have known that they had eaten them, for they *were* just as ugly as at the beginning. So I awoke.

22 "Also I saw in my dream, and suddenly seven heads came up on one stalk, full and good.

23 "Then behold, seven heads, withered, thin, *and* blighted by the east wind, sprang up after them.

24 "And the thin heads devoured the seven good heads. So I [m]told *this* to the magicians, but *there was* no one who could explain *it* to me."

25 Then Joseph said to Pharaoh, "The dreams of Pharaoh *are* one; God has shown Pharaoh what He *is* [n]about to do:

26 "The seven good cows *are* seven years, and the seven good heads *are* seven years; the dreams *are* one.

27 "And the seven thin and ugly cows which came up after them *are* [o]seven years, and the seven empty heads blighted by the east wind are seven years of famine.

28 "This *is* the thing which I have spoken to Pharaoh. God has shown Pharaoh what He *is* about to do.

29 "Indeed seven years of great plenty will come throughout all the land of Egypt;

30 "but after them seven years of famine will arise, and all the plenty will be forgotten in the land of Egypt; and the famine will deplete the land.

31 "So the plenty will not be known in the land because of the famine following, for it *will be* very severe.

32 "And the dream was repeated to Pharaoh twice because the thing *is* established by God, and God will shortly bring it to pass.

33 "Now therefore, let Pharaoh select a discerning and wise man, and set him over the land of Egypt.

34 "Let Pharaoh do *this,* and let him appoint officers over the land, to collect one-fifth *of the produce* of the land of Egypt in the seven plentiful years.

35 "And let them gather all the food of those good years that are coming, and store up grain under the authority of Pharaoh, and let them keep food in the cities.

36 "Then that food shall be as a reserve for the land for the seven years of famine which shall be in the land of Egypt, that the land may not perish during the famine."

37 So the advice was good in the eyes of Pharaoh and in the eyes of all his servants.

38 And Pharaoh said to his servants, "Can we find *such a one* as this, a man in whom *is* the [p]Spirit of God?"

39 Then Pharaoh said to Joseph, "Inasmuch as God has shown you all this, *there is* no one as discerning and wise as you.

8
a Dan. 2:1,3
b Ex. 7:11, 22
9
c Gen. 40:1
11
d Gen. 40:5; Jud. 7:13
e Gen. 40:5; Jud. 7:15
12
f Gen. 39:14; 43:32
14
g Ps. 105:20–21
h Cp. Dan. 2:25
i Cp. 1 Sam. 2:8
j Cp. 2 Ki. 25:27–29
15
k Dan. 5:16
16
l Gen. 40:8; Dan. 2:28
24
m Dan. 4:7
25
n Cp. Dan. 2:29,45
27
o 2 Ki. 8:1
38
p *Holy Spirit* (OT): v. 38; Ex. 28:3. (Gen. 1:2; Zech. 12:10). Cp. Ex. 31:3

40 "You shall be over my house, and all my people shall be ruled according to your word; only in regard to the throne will I be greater than you."

41 And Pharaoh said to Joseph, "See, I have [a]set you over all the land of Egypt."

42 Then Pharaoh [b]took his signet ring off his hand and put it on Joseph's hand; and he [c]clothed him in garments of fine linen and put a gold chain around his neck.

43 And he had him ride in the second [d]chariot which he had; and they [e]cried out before him, "Bow the knee!" So he set him over all the land of [1]Egypt.

44 Pharaoh also said to Joseph, "I *am* Pharaoh, and without your consent no man may lift his hand or foot in all the land of Egypt."

Joseph, rejected by his brothers, receives a bride

45 And Pharaoh called Joseph's name Zaphnath-Paaneah. And he gave him as a wife [2f]Asenath, the daughter of Poti-Pherah priest of On. So Joseph went out over *all* the land of Egypt.

46 Joseph was thirty years old when he stood before Pharaoh king of Egypt. And Joseph went out from the presence of Pharaoh, and went throughout all the land of Egypt.

47 Now in the seven plentiful years the ground brought forth abundantly.

48 So he gathered up all the food of the seven years which were in the land of Egypt, and laid up the food in the cities; he laid up in every city the food of the fields which surrounded them.

49 Joseph gathered very much grain, as the sand of the sea, until he stopped counting, for *it was* immeasurable.

50 And to Joseph were born two sons before the years of famine came, whom Asenath, the daughter of Poti-Pherah priest of On, bore to him.

51 Joseph called the name of the firstborn [g]Manasseh: "For God has made me forget all my toil and all my [h]father's house."

52 And the name of the second he called [i]Ephraim: "For God has caused me to be fruitful in the land of my affliction."

53 Then the seven years of plenty which were in the land of Egypt ended,

54 and the seven years of famine began to come, as Joseph had said. The famine was in all lands, but in all the land of Egypt there was bread.

55 So when all the land of Egypt was famished, the people cried to Pharaoh for bread. Then Pharaoh said to all the Egyptians, "Go to Joseph; [j]whatever he says to you, do."

56 The famine was over all the face of the earth, and Joseph opened all the storehouses* and sold to the Egyptians. And the famine became severe in the land of Egypt.

57 So all countries came to Joseph in Egypt to [k]buy *grain,* because the famine was severe in all lands.

Joseph's brothers, except Benjamin, come to Egypt for food

42

WHEN Jacob [l]saw that there was grain in Egypt, Jacob said to his sons, "Why do you look at one another?"

2 And he said, "Indeed I have heard that there is grain in Egypt; go down to that place and buy for us there, that we may [m]live and not die."

3 So Joseph's ten brothers went down to buy grain in Egypt.

4 But Jacob did not send Joseph's brother Benjamin with his brothers, for he said, "Lest some calamity befall him."

5 And the sons of Israel went to buy *grain* among those who journeyed, for the [n]famine was in the land of Canaan.

Joseph tests his ten brothers

6 Now Joseph *was* governor over the land; and it was he who sold to all the people of the land. And Joseph's brothers came and [o]bowed down before him with *their* faces to the earth.

7 Joseph saw his brothers and recognized them, but he acted as a

41
a Gen. 42:6; Dan. 6:3
42
b Est. 3:10
c Cp. Est. 8:15
43
d Gen. 46:29
e Cp. Est. 6:9
45
f Gen. 46:20
51
g Lit. *forgetting.* Gen. 46:20
h Ps. 45:10
52
i Lit. *fruitful.* Gen. 48:5
55
j Cp. Jn. 2:5
57
k Gen. 42:3; cp. Gen. 27:28,37
CHAPTER 42
1
l Acts 7:12
2
m Gen. 43:8
5
n Gen. 12:10
6
o Gen. 37:8

*41:56 Literally *all that was in them*

[1](41:43) The possibility of the elevation of a foreigner to a high office in Egypt has been doubted, but Egyptian records show that such an occurrence, while rare, was by no means unique.

[2](41:45) Asenath, the bride espoused by Joseph the rejected one (Jn. 19:15), portrays the Church, called out from the world to be the bride of Christ during the time of His rejection by His brethren, Israel (Jn. 1:10–12; Acts 15:14; Eph. 5:31–32). Israel, like Joseph's brothers, will be preserved (Ezek. 11:16). See Gen. 37:2, *note.*

[a]stranger to them and spoke roughly
to them. Then he said to them, "Where
do you come from?" And they said,
"From the land of Canaan to buy
food."
8 So Joseph recognized his brothers, but they did not recognize him.
9 Then Joseph [b]remembered the
dreams which he had dreamed about
them, and said to them, "You *are*
spies! You have come to see the nakedness of the land!"
10 And they said to him, "No, my
lord, but your servants have come to
buy food.
11 "We *are* all one man's sons; we
are honest *men;* your servants are not
spies."
12 But he said to them, "No, but you
have come to see the nakedness of the
land."
13 And they said, "Your servants
are twelve brothers, the sons of one
man in the land of Canaan; and in fact,
the youngest *is* with our father today,
and one *is* no more."
14 But Joseph said to them, "It *is* as
I spoke to you, saying, 'You *are* spies!'
15 "In this *manner* you shall be
tested: By the life of Pharaoh, you
shall not leave this place unless your
youngest brother comes here.
16 "Send one of you, and let him
bring your brother; and you shall be
kept in prison, that your words may be
tested to see whether *there is* any
truth in you; or else, by the life of
Pharaoh, surely you *are* spies!"
17 So he put them all together in
prison [c]three days.
18 Then Joseph said to them the
third day, "Do this and live, *for* I [d]fear
God:
19 "If you *are* honest *men,* let one of
your brothers be confined to your
prison house; but you, go and carry
grain for the famine of your houses.
20 "And bring your [e]youngest
brother to me; so your words will be
verified, and you shall not die." And
they did so.

Simeon kept as hostage
while other brothers go home

21 Then they said to one another,
"We *are* truly [f]guilty concerning our
brother, for we saw the anguish of his
soul when he pleaded with us, and we
would not hear; therefore this distress
has come upon us."
22 And [g]Reuben answered them,
saying, "Did I not speak to you, saying, 'Do not sin against the boy'; and

7 *a* Cp. Gen. 45:1–2
9 *b* Gen. 37:5, 9
17 *c* Cp. Gen. 40:12
18 *d* Gen. 22:12; Ex. 1:17; Prov 1:7; 9:10; see Ps. 19:9, *note*
20 *e* v. 34
21 *f* Gen. 44:16
22 *g* Gen. 37:21–22, 29
h Gen. 9:5–6; Ps. 9:12
24 *i* Gen. 43:30
j Gen. 34:25,30; 43:23
25 *k* Gen. 44:1
l Gen. 43:12
34 *m* Gen. 42:20; 43:3,5
36 *n* Gen. 43:14

you would not listen? Therefore behold, his blood is now [h]required of
us."
23 But they did not know that Joseph understood *them,* for he spoke to
them through an interpreter.
24 And he turned himself away
from them and [i]wept. Then he returned to them again, and talked with
them. And he took [j]Simeon from
them and bound him before their eyes.
25 Then Joseph gave a [k]command
to fill their sacks with grain, to [l]re-
store every man's money to his sack,
and to give them provisions for the
journey. Thus he did for them.
26 So they loaded their donkeys
with the grain and departed from
there.
27 But as one *of them* opened his
sack to give his donkey feed at the
encampment, he saw his money; and
there it was, in the mouth of his sack.
28 So he said to his brothers, "My
money has been restored, and there it
is, in my sack!" Then their hearts
failed *them* and they were afraid, saying to one another, "What *is* this *that*
God has done to us?"
29 Then they went to Jacob their
father in the land of Canaan and told
him all that had happened to them,
saying:
30 "The man *who is* lord of the land
spoke roughly to us, and took us for
spies of the country.
31 "But we said to him, 'We *are*
honest *men;* we are not spies.
32 'We *are* twelve brothers, sons of
our father; one *is* no *more,* and the
youngest *is* with our father this day in
the land of Canaan.'
33 "Then the man, the lord of the
country, said to us, 'By this I will know
that you *are* honest *men:* Leave one of
your brothers *here* with me, take *food*
for the famine of your households, and
be gone.
34 'And bring your [m]youngest
brother to me; so I shall know that you
are not spies, but *that* you *are* honest
men. I will grant your brother to you,
and you may trade in the land.'"
35 Then it happened as they emptied their sacks, that surprisingly each
man's bundle of money *was* in his
sack; and when they and their father
saw the bundles of money, they were
afraid.
36 And Jacob their father said to
them, "You have [n]bereaved me: Joseph is no *more,* Simeon is no *more,*

and you want to take [a]Benjamin. All these things are against me."

37 Then Reuben spoke to his father, saying, "Kill my two sons if I do not bring him *back* to you; put him in my hands, and I will bring him back to you."

38 But he said, "My son shall not go down with you, for his brother is [b]dead, and he is left alone. If any calamity should befall him along the way in which you go, then you would bring down my gray hair with sorrow to the [c]grave."

Judah becomes surety for Benjamin
(cp. Gen. 37:26–28)

43 NOW the [d]famine *was* severe in the land.

2 And it came to pass, when they had eaten up the grain which they had brought from Egypt, that their father said to them, "Go back, [e]buy us a little food."

3 But Judah spoke to him, saying, "The man solemnly warned us, saying, 'You shall not [f]see my face unless your brother *is* with you.'

4 "If you send our brother with us, we will go down and buy you food.

5 "But if you will not send *him*, we will not go down; for the man said to us, 'You shall not see my face unless your brother *is* with you.' "

6 And Israel said, "Why did you deal *so* wrongfully with me *as* to tell the man whether you had still *another* brother?"

7 But they said, "The man asked us pointedly about ourselves and our family, saying, '*Is* your father still alive? Have you *another* brother?' And we told him according to these words. Could we possibly have known that he would say, 'Bring your brother down'?"

8 Then Judah said to Israel his father, "Send the lad with me, and we will arise and go, that we may [g]live and not die, both we and you *and* also our little ones.

9 "I myself will be [h]surety for him; from my hand you shall require him. If I do not bring him *back* to you and set him before you, then [i]let me bear the blame forever.

10 "For if we had not lingered, surely by now we would have returned this second time."

11 And their father Israel said to them, "If *it must be* so, then do this: Take some of the best fruits of the land in your vessels and carry down a [j]present for the man—a little [k]balm and a little honey, spices and myrrh, pistachio nuts and almonds.

12 "Take double money in your hand, and take back in your hand the money that was [l]returned in the mouth of your sacks; perhaps it was an oversight.

13 "Take your brother also, and arise, go back to the man.

14 "And may God [m]Almighty [n]give you mercy before the man, that he may release your other brother and Benjamin. If I am bereaved, I am bereaved!"

15 So the men took that present and Benjamin, and they took double money in their hand, and arose and went [o]down to Egypt; and they stood before Joseph.

Joseph entertains his eleven brothers

16 When Joseph saw Benjamin with them, he said to the [p]steward of his house, "Take *these* men to my home, and slaughter an animal and make ready; for *these* men will dine with me at noon."

17 Then the man did as Joseph ordered, and the man brought the men into Joseph's house.

18 Now the men were [q]afraid because they were brought into Joseph's house; and they said, "*It is* because of the money, which was returned in our sacks the first time, that we are brought in, so that he may [r]make a case against us and seize us, to take us as [s]slaves with our donkeys."

19 When they drew near to the steward of Joseph's house, they talked with him at the door of the house,

20 and said, "O sir, we indeed came down the first time to buy food;

21 "but it happened, when we came to the encampment, that we [t]opened our sacks, and there, *each* man's money *was* in the mouth of his sack, our money in full weight; so we have brought it back in our hand.

22 "And we have brought down other money in our hands to buy food. We do not know who put our money in our sacks."

23 But he said, "Peace *be* with you, do not be afraid. Your God and the God of your father has given you treasure in your sacks; I had your money." Then he brought [u]Simeon out to them.

24 So the man brought the men into Joseph's house and gave *them* water,

36
[a] Gen. 35:18; 43:14; cp. Rom. 8:28, 31
38
[b] Gen. 37:33; 44:20,28
[c] See Hab. 2:5, *note*. Cp. Gen. 37:35; 44:29,31
CHAPTER 43
1
[d] Gen. 42:5; 45:6,11
2
[e] Gen. 42:2; 44:25
3
[f] Gen. 44:23
8
[g] Gen. 42:2; 47:19
9
[h] Gen. 44:32
[i] Cp. Gen. 27:13; 1 Sam. 25:24; cp. Phile. 18
11
[j] Gen. 33:10
[k] Gen. 37:25
12
[l] Gen. 42:25
14
[m] Gen. 35:11; 48:3
[n] Cp. Gen. 39:21
15
[o] Gen. 39:1; 46:3,6
16
[p] Gen. 44:1
18
[q] Gen. 42:28
[r] Jud. 14:4
[s] Gen. 44:9, 33
21
[t] Gen. 42:27,35
23
[u] Gen. 42:24

and they washed their feet; and he
gave their donkeys feed.
25 Then they made the present
ready for Joseph's coming at noon, for
they heard that they would eat bread
there.
26 And when Joseph came home,
they brought him the present which
was in their hand into the house, and
[1a]bowed down before him to the
earth.
27 Then he asked them about *their*
well-being, and said, [b]"*Is* your father
well, the old man of whom you spoke?
Is he still alive?"
28 And they answered, "Your ser-
vant our father *is* in good health; he *is*
still alive." And they bowed their
heads down and prostrated themselves.
29 Then he lifted his eyes and saw
his brother Benjamin, his mother's
son, and said, "*Is* this your younger
brother of whom you spoke to me?"
And he said, "God be gracious to you,
my son."
30 Now his [c]heart yearned for his
brother; so Joseph made haste and
sought *somewhere* to weep. And he
went into *his* chamber and [d]wept
there.
31 Then he washed his face and
came out; and he restrained himself,
and said, "Serve the bread."
32 So they set him a place by himself, and them by themselves, and the
Egyptians who ate with him by themselves; because the Egyptians could
not eat food with the [e]Hebrews, for
that *is* an [f]abomination to the Egyptians.
33 And they sat before him, the
firstborn according to his [g]birthright
and the youngest according to his
youth; and the men looked in astonishment at one another.
34 Then he took servings to them
from before him, [2]but [h]Benjamin's
serving was five times as much as any
of theirs. So they drank and were
merry with him.

Judah fulfills promise (Gen. 43:9)

44 AND he commanded the
[i]steward of his house, saying,
[j]"Fill the men's sacks with food, as
much as they can carry, and put each
man's money in the mouth of his sack.

26
a Gen. 42:6; 44:14
27
b Gen. 29:6; 2 Ki. 4:26
30
c 1 Ki. 3:26
d Gen. 42:24; 45:2,14
32
e Gen. 41:12; Ex. 1:15
f Gen. 46:34; Ex. 8:26
33
g Gen. 27:36; Dt. 21:16–17
34
h Gen. 45:22
CHAPTER 44
1
i Gen. 43:16
j Gen. 42:25
4
k 1 Sam. 25:21
9
l Gen. 31:32
m Gen. 43:18; Ex. 22:2–3
13
n Gen. 37:29; Num. 14:6
16
o Num. 32:23

2 "Also put my cup, the silver cup,
in the mouth of the sack of the youngest, and his grain money." So he did
according to the word that Joseph had
spoken.
3 As soon as the morning dawned,
the men were sent away, they and
their donkeys.
4 When they had gone out of the
city, *and* were not *yet* far off, Joseph
said to his steward, "Get up, follow the
men; and when you overtake them,
say to them, 'Why have you [k]repaid
evil for good?
5 '*Is* not this *the one* from which
my lord drinks, and with which he indeed practices divination? You have
done evil in so doing.' "
6 So he overtook them, and he
spoke to them these same words.
7 And they said to him, "Why does
my lord say these words? Far be it
from us that your servants should do
such a thing.
8 "Look, we brought back to you
from the land of Canaan the money
which we found in the mouth of our
sacks. How then could we steal silver
or gold from your lord's house?
9 [l]"With whomever of your servants it is found, let him die, and we
also will be my lord's [m]slaves."
10 And he said, "Now also *let* it *be*
according to your words; he with
whom it is found shall be my slave,
and you shall be blameless."
11 Then each man speedily let
down his sack to the ground, and each
opened his sack.
12 So he searched. He began with
the oldest and left off with the youngest; and the cup was found in Benjamin's sack.
13 Then they [n]tore their clothes,
and each man loaded his donkey and
returned to the city.
14 So Judah and his brothers came
to Joseph's house, and he *was* still
there; and they fell before him on the
ground.
15 And Joseph said to them, "What
deed *is* this you have done? Did you
not know that such a man as I can
certainly practice divination?"
16 Then Judah said, "What shall we
say to my lord? What shall we speak?
Or how shall we clear ourselves? God
has [o]found out the iniquity of your

[1](43:26) Joseph's brothers had thought that they would never do this. Cp. Gen. 37:8–11,19–20.

[2](43:34) Cp. Gen. 35:18, *note.* Benjamin now becomes prominent. He foreshadows Christ as His power is to be revealed in the kingdom. See *notes* at Gen. 1:26; 1 Sam. 8:7; Zech. 12:8.

servants; here we are, my lord's
slaves, both we and *he* also with
whom the cup was found."
17 But he said, "Far be it from me
that I should do so; the man in whose
hand the cup was found, he shall be
my slave. And as for you, go up in
peace to your father."
18 Then Judah came near to him
and said: "O my lord, please let your
servant speak a word in my lord's
hearing, and do not let your anger
burn against your servant; for you *are*
even like Pharaoh.
19 "My lord asked his servants,
saying, 'Have you a father or a
brother?'
20 "And we said to my lord, 'We
have a father, an old man, and a child
of *his* old age, *who is* young; his
brother is [a]dead, and he [b]alone is left
of his mother's children, and his [c]fa-
ther loves him.'
21 "Then you said to your servants,
'Bring him down to me, that I may set
my eyes on him.'
22 "And we said to my lord, 'The
lad cannot leave his father, for *if* he
should leave his father, *his father*
would die.'
23 "But you said to your servants,
[d]'Unless your youngest brother
comes down with you, you shall see
my face no more.'
24 "So it was, when we went up to
your servant my father, that we told
him the words of my lord.
25 "And our father said, 'Go back
and [e]buy us a little food.'
26 "But we said, 'We cannot go
down; if our youngest brother is with
us, then we will go down; for we may
not see the man's face unless our
youngest brother *is* with us.'
27 "Then your servant my father
said to us, 'You know that my wife
bore me [f]two sons;
28 'and the one went out from me,
and I said, [g]"Surely he is torn to
pieces"; and I have not seen him since.
29 'But if you take this one also
from me, and [a]calamity befalls him,
you shall bring down my gray hair
with sorrow to the [h]grave.'
30 "Now therefore, when I come to
your servant my father, and the lad *is*
not with us, since his life is [i]bound up
in the lad's life,
31 "it will happen, when he sees
that the lad *is* not *with us,* that he will
die. So your servants will bring down
the gray hair of your servant our father with sorrow to the [h]grave.

20
a Gen. 42:38
b Gen. 46:19
c Gen. 37:3; 42:4
23
d Gen. 43:3, 5
25
e Gen. 43:2
27
f Gen. 30:22–24; 35:16–18; 46:19
28
g Gen. 37:33
29
h See Hab. 2:5, *note*
30
i Cp. 1 Sam. 18:1, 25:29
CHAPTER 45
1
j Gen. 43:31
k Cp. Hos. 2:14–23
2
l Gen. 43:30; 46:29
3
m Acts 7:13
n Cp. Zech. 12:10–14
4
o Gen. 37:28; 39:1; Ps. 105:17
5
p Gen. 50:20
6
q Gen. 43:1; 47:4,13
7
r Gen. 50:20; cp. Acts 2:23–24
s Lit. *to make a remnant for you.* See Isa. 1:9 and Rom. 11:5, *notes*
8
t Rom. 8:28
u Isa. 22:21
v Gen. 42:6
10
w Gen. 47:6; Ex. 9:26
11
x Gen. 47:12

32 "For your servant became surety
for the lad to my father, saying, 'If I do
not bring him *back* to you, then I shall
bear the blame before my father forever.'
33 "Now therefore, please let your
servant remain instead of the lad as a
slave to my lord, and let the lad go up
with his brothers.
34 "For how shall I go up to my father if the lad *is* not with me, lest perhaps I see the evil that would come
upon my father?"

Joseph reveals himself to his brothers

45 THEN Joseph could not [j]re-
strain himself before all those
who stood by him, and he cried out,
"Make everyone go out from me!" So
no one stood with him [k]while Joseph
made himself known to his brothers.
2 And he [l]wept aloud, and the
Egyptians and the house of Pharaoh
heard *it.*
3 Then Joseph said to his broth-
ers, [m]"I *am* Joseph; does my father still
live?" But his brothers could not answer him, for they were [n]dismayed in
his presence.
4 And Joseph said to his brothers,
"Please come near to me." So they
came near. Then he said: "I *am* Joseph
your brother, whom you [o]sold into
Egypt.
5 "But now, do not therefore be
grieved or angry with yourselves because you sold me here; for [p]God sent
me before you to preserve life.
6 "For these two years the [q]fam-
ine *has been* in the land, and *there are*
still five years in which *there will be*
neither plowing nor harvesting.
7 "And God [r]sent me before you
to [s]preserve a posterity for you in the
earth, and to save your lives by a great
deliverance.
8 "So now *it was* not you *who* sent
me here, but [t]God; and He has made
me a [u]father to Pharaoh, and lord of
all his house, and a [v]ruler throughout
all the land of Egypt.
9 "Hurry and go up to my father,
and say to him, 'Thus says your son
Joseph: "God has made me lord of all
Egypt; come down to me, do not tarry.
10 "You shall dwell in the land of
[w]Goshen, and you shall be near to me,
you and your children, your children's
children, your flocks and your herds,
and all that you have.
11 "There I will [x]provide for you,
lest you and your household, and all
that you have, come to poverty; for

there are still five years of famine." '
12 "And behold, your eyes and the
eyes of my brother Benjamin see that
it is my mouth that speaks to you.
13 "So you shall tell my father of all
my glory in Egypt, and of all that you
have seen; and you shall hurry and
[a]bring my father down here."
14 Then he fell on his brother Benjamin's neck and wept, and Benjamin
wept on his neck.
15 Moreover he [b]kissed all his
brothers and wept over them, and after that his brothers talked with him.

Joseph's brothers blessed and sent to bring Jacob

16 Now the report of it was heard in
Pharaoh's house, saying, "Joseph's
brothers have come." So it pleased
Pharaoh and his servants well.
17 And Pharaoh said to Joseph,
"Say to your brothers, 'Do this: Load
your animals and depart; go to the
land of Canaan.
18 'Bring your father and your
households and come to me; I will give
you the best of the land of Egypt, and
you will [c]eat the fat of the land.
19 'Now you are commanded—do
this: Take carts out of the land of
Egypt for your little ones and your
wives; bring your father and come.
20 'Also do not be concerned about
your goods, for the best of all the land
of Egypt *is* yours.' "
21 Then the sons of Israel did so;
and Joseph gave them [d]carts, according to the command of Pharaoh, and
he gave them provisions for the journey.
22 He gave to all of them, to each
man, [e]changes of garments; but to
Benjamin he gave three hundred
pieces of silver and five changes of
garments.
23 And he sent to his father these
things: ten donkeys loaded with the
good things of Egypt, and ten female
donkeys loaded with grain, bread, and
food for his father for the journey.
24 So he sent his brothers away,
and they departed; and he said to
them, "See that you do not become
troubled along the way."
25 Then they went up out of Egypt,
and came to the land of Canaan to
Jacob their father.
26 And they told him, saying, "Joseph *is* still alive, and he *is* governor
over all the land of Egypt." And Jacob's heart stood still, because he did
not believe them.
27 But when they told him all the
words which Joseph had said to them,
and when he saw the carts which Joseph had sent to carry him, the [f]spirit
of Jacob their father revived.
28 Then Israel said, "*It is* enough.
Joseph my son *is* still alive. I will go
and see him before I die."

Jacob journeys to Egypt

46 SO [g]Israel took his journey
with all that he had, and came
to [h]Beersheba, and offered sacrifices
to the [i]God of his father Isaac.
2 Then God spoke to Israel in the
[j]visions of the night, and said, "Jacob,
Jacob!" And he said, "Here I am."
3 So He said, "I *am* God, the God
of your father; do not fear to go down
to Egypt, for I will [k]make of you a
great nation there.
4 "I will go down [l]with you to
Egypt, and I will also surely [m]bring
you up *again;* and Joseph will put his
hand on your eyes."
5 Then Jacob arose from Beersheba; and the sons of Israel carried
their father Jacob, their little ones,
and their wives, in the [n]carts which
Pharaoh had sent to carry him.
6 So they took their livestock and
their goods, which they had acquired
in the land of Canaan, and went to
[o]Egypt, Jacob and all his descendants
with him.
7 His sons and his sons' sons, his
daughters and his sons' daughters,
and all his descendants he brought
with him to Egypt.

Register of those who came to Egypt

8 Now these *were* the names of the
children of Israel, Jacob and his sons,
who went to Egypt: Reuben *was* Jacob's firstborn.
9 The [p]sons of Reuben *were* Hanoch, Pallu, Hezron, and Carmi.
10 The [q]sons of Simeon *were* Jemuel,* Jamin, Ohad, Jachin,* Zohar,* and Shaul, the son of a Canaanite woman.
11 The [r]sons of Levi *were* Gershon,
Kohath, and Merari.
12 The [s]sons of Judah *were* Er,
Onan, Shelah, Perez, and Zerah (but
Er and Onan died in the land of Canaan). The sons of Perez were Hezron
and Hamul.

13
a Gen. 46:6–28; Acts 7:14
15
b Gen. 48:10
18
c Gen. 47:6; Dt. 32:9–14
21
d Gen. 46:5
22
e Jud. 14:12; 2 Ki. 5:5
27
f Jud. 15:19; Isa. 40:29
CHAPTER 46
1
g Israel (history): vv. 1–6; Ex. 3:15. (Gen. 12:2; Rom. 11:26, *note*)
h Gen. 21:33; 26:32–33; 28:10
i Gen. 32:9
2
j Gen. 31:11; cp. 22:11
3
k Ex. 12:37; Dt. 26:5; cp. Gen. 35:11; 48:4
4
l Gen. 31:3; Ex. 3:12
m Gen. 15:16; 50;13,25; Ex. 3:8
5
n Gen. 45:19–21
6
o c. 1660 B.C.
9
p Ex. 6:14
10
q Ex. 6:15
11
r Ex. 6:16–17
12
s Num. 26:19–20

*
46:10 Spelled *Nemuel* in 1 Chronicles 4:24 • Called *Jarib* in 1 Chronicles 4:24 • Called *Zerah* in 1 Chronicles 4:24

13 The [a]sons of Issachar *were* Tola, Puvah,* Job,* and Shimron.

14 The [b]sons of Zebulun *were* Sered, Elon, and Jahleel.

15 These *were* the [c]sons of Leah, whom she bore to Jacob in Padan Aram, with his daughter Dinah. All the persons, his sons and his daughters, *were* thirty-three.

16 The [d]sons of Gad *were* Ziphion,* Haggi, Shuni, Ezbon,* Eri, Arodi,* and Areli.

17 The [e]sons of Asher *were* Jimnah, Ishuah, Isui, Beriah, and Serah, their sister. And the sons of Beriah *were* Heber and Malchiel.

18 These *were* the [f]sons of Zilpah, whom Laban gave to Leah his daughter; and these she bore to Jacob: sixteen persons.

19 The [g]sons of Rachel, Jacob's wife, *were* Joseph and Benjamin.

20 And to Joseph in the land of Egypt were born [h]Manasseh and [h]Ephraim, whom [i]Asenath, the daughter of Poti-Pherah priest of On, bore to him.

21 The [j]sons of Benjamin *were* Belah, Becher, Ashbel, Gera, Naaman, Ehi, Rosh, Muppim, Huppim,* and Ard.

22 These *were* the sons of Rachel, who were born to Jacob: fourteen persons in all.

23 The [k]son of Dan *was* Hushim.*

24 The [l]sons of Naphtali *were* Jahzeel,* Guni, Jezer, and Shillem.*

25 These *were* the [m]sons of Bilhah, whom Laban gave to Rachel his daughter, and she bore these to Jacob: seven persons in all.

26 All the [1]persons who went with Jacob to Egypt, who came from his body, besides Jacob's sons' wives, *were* sixty-six persons in all.

27 And the sons of Joseph who were born to him in Egypt *were* two persons. All the persons of the house of Jacob who went to Egypt were seventy.

28 Then he sent Judah before him to Joseph, to point out before him *the way* to Goshen. And they came to the land of Goshen.

29 So Joseph made ready his [n]chariot and went up to Goshen to meet his father Israel; and he presented himself to him, and fell on his neck and wept on his neck a good while.

30 And Israel said to Joseph, "Now [o]let me die, since I have seen your face, because you *are* still alive."

31 Then Joseph said to his brothers and to his father's household, "I will go up and tell Pharaoh, and say to him, 'My brothers and those of my father's house, who *were* in the land of Canaan, have come to me.

32 'And the men *are* [p]shepherds, for their occupation has been to feed livestock; and they have brought their flocks, their herds, and all that they have.'

33 "So it shall be, when Pharaoh calls you and says, 'What is your occupation?'

34 "that you shall say, 'Your servants' occupation has been with livestock from our youth even till now, both we *and* also our fathers,' that you may dwell in the land of Goshen; for every shepherd *is* an [q]abomination to the Egyptians."

Jacob's family honored

47 THEN Joseph went and told Pharaoh, and said, "My father and my brothers, their flocks and their herds and all that they possess, have come from the land of Canaan; and indeed they *are* in the land of [r]Goshen."

2 And he took five men from among his brothers and [s]presented them to Pharaoh.

3 Then Pharaoh said to his brothers, [t]"What *is* your occupation?" And they said to Pharaoh, "Your servants *are* [u]shepherds, both we *and* also our fathers."

4 And they said to Pharaoh, "We have come to [v]dwell in the land, because your servants have no pasture for their flocks, for the [w]famine *is* se-

13 [a] Num. 26:23
14 [b] Num. 26:26
15 [c] Gen. 35:23; 49:31
16 [d] Num. 26:15–18
17 [e] Num. 26:44–47
18 [f] Gen. 37:2
19 [g] Gen. 35:24
20 [h] Gen. 41:51–52; 48:1 [i] Gen. 41:45
21 [j] Num. 26:38
23 [k] Num. 26:42
24 [l] Num. 26:48
25 [m] 1 Chr. 7:13
29 [n] Gen. 41:43
30 [o] Cp. Lk. 2:29,30
32 [p] Gen. 47:3
34 [q] Gen. 43:32

CHAPTER 47

1 [r] Gen. 50:8
2 [s] Acts 7:13
3 [t] Gen. 46:33; Jon. 1:8 [u] Gen. 46:32; Ex. 2:17,19
4 [v] Gen. 15:13; Dt. 26:5 [w] Gen. 45:6; Ps. 105:16

*

46:13 Spelled *Puah* in 1 Chronicles 7:1 • Same as *Jashub* in Numbers 26:24 and 1 Chronicles 7:1
46:16 Spelled *Zephon* in Samaritan Pentateuch, Septuagint, and Numbers 26:15 • Called *Ozni* in Numbers 26:16 • Spelled *Arod* in Numbers 26:17
46:21 Called *Hupham* in Numbers 26:39
46:23 Called *Shuham* in Numbers 26:42
46:24 Spelled *Jahziel* in 1 Chronicles 7:13 • Spelled *Shallum* in 1 Chronicles 7:13

[1](46:26) A discrepancy has been imagined between vv. 26 and 27. "All the persons who went with Jacob to Egypt" were sixty-six (v. 26). The "persons of the house of Jacob" (v. 27, i.e. the *entire* Jacobean family) were seventy, i.e. the sixty-six who came with Jacob, plus Joseph and Joseph's two sons, who were already in Egypt, which equals sixty-nine, plus Jacob himself, which equals seventy. See Acts 7:14, *note.*

vere in the land of Canaan. Now therefore, please let your servants dwell in the land of Goshen."

5 Then Pharaoh spoke to Joseph, saying, "Your father and your brothers have come to you.

6 "The land of Egypt *is* before you. Have your father and brothers dwell in the [a]best of the land; let them dwell in the land of Goshen. And if you know *any* competent men among them, then make them chief herdsmen over my livestock."

7 Then Joseph brought in his father Jacob and set him before Pharaoh; and Jacob [b]blessed Pharaoh.

8 Pharaoh said to Jacob, "How old *are* you?"

9 And Jacob said to Pharaoh, "The days of the years of my pilgrimage *are* [c]one hundred and thirty years; few and evil have been the days of the years of my life, and they have not [d]attained to the days of the years of the life of my fathers in the days of their pilgrimage."

10 So Jacob blessed Pharaoh, and went out from before Pharaoh.

11 And Joseph situated his father and his brothers, and gave them a possession in the land of Egypt, in the best of the land, in the land of [e]Rameses, as Pharaoh had commanded.

12 Then Joseph [f]provided his father, his brothers, and all his father's household with bread, according to the number in *their* families.

13 Now *there was* no bread in all the land; for the famine *was* very severe, so that the land of Egypt and the land of Canaan languished because of the famine.

14 And Joseph [g]gathered up all the money that was found in the land of Egypt and in the land of Canaan, for the grain which they bought; and Joseph brought the money into Pharaoh's house.

15 So when the money failed in the land of Egypt and in the land of Canaan, all the Egyptians came to Joseph and said, "Give us bread, for why should we die in your presence? For the money has failed."

16 Then Joseph said, "Give your livestock, and I will give you *bread* for your livestock, if the money is gone."

17 So they brought their livestock to Joseph, and Joseph gave them bread *in exchange* for the horses, the flocks, the cattle of the herds, and for the donkeys. Thus he fed them with bread *in exchange* for all their livestock that year.

18 When that year had ended, they came to him the next year and said to him, "We will not hide from my lord that our money is gone; my lord also has our herds of livestock. There is nothing left in the sight of my lord but our bodies and our lands.

19 "Why should we die before your eyes, both we and our land? [h]Buy us and our land for bread, and we and our land will be servants of Pharaoh; give *us* seed, that we may [i]live and not die, that the land may not be desolate."

20 Then Joseph [j]bought all the land of Egypt for Pharaoh; for every man of the Egyptians sold his field, because the famine was severe upon them. So the land became Pharaoh's.

21 And as for the people, he moved them into the cities,* from *one* end of the borders of Egypt to the *other* end.

22 [k]Only the land of the priests he did not buy; for the priests had rations *allotted to them* by Pharaoh, and they ate their rations which Pharaoh gave them; therefore they did not sell their lands.

23 Then Joseph said to the people, "Indeed I have [l]bought you and your land this day for Pharaoh. Look, *here is* seed for you, and you shall sow the land.

24 "And it shall come to pass in the harvest that you shall give one-fifth to Pharaoh. Four-fifths shall be your own, as seed for the field and for your food, for those of your households and as food for your little ones."

25 So they said, "You have saved our lives; let us find favor in the sight of my lord, and we will be Pharaoh's servants."

26 And Joseph made it a law over the land of Egypt to this day, *that* Pharaoh should have one-fifth, except for the land of the priests only, *which* did not become Pharaoh's.

Joseph promises to bury Jacob in Canaan

27 So Israel dwelt in the land of Egypt, in the country of Goshen; and they had possessions there and grew and [m]multiplied exceedingly.

28 And Jacob lived in the land of Egypt seventeen years. So the [n]length

6 [a] Gen. 45:18
7 [b] Gen. 48:15,20; cp. Heb. 7:7
9 [c] Cp. Gen. 46:6 [d] Gen. 5:5; 11:10–11; 25:7–8
11 [e] Ex. 12:37
12 [f] Gen. 45:11; 50:21
14 [g] Gen. 42:6
19 [h] v. 23 [i] Gen. 43:8
20 [j] Cp. Rev. 5:5–10; 11:15
22 [k] Cp. Lev. 25:34
23 [l] v. 19; cp. 1 Cor. 6:20
27 [m] Gen. 15:13–16; Ex. 1:7–12; 12:37; Heb. 11:12
28 [n] Lit. *days of the years of his life.* Gen. 47:9

*47:21 Following Masoretic Text and Targum; Samaritan Pentateuch, Septuagint, and Vulgate read *made the people virtual slaves.*

of Jacob's life was one hundred and
forty-seven years.
29 When the time drew near that
Israel must die, he called his son Joseph and said to him, "Now if I have
found favor in your sight, please [a]put
your hand under my thigh, and [b]deal
kindly and truly with me. Please do
not bury me in Egypt,
30 "but let me [c]lie with my fathers;
you shall carry me out of Egypt and
bury me in their burial place." And he
said, "I will do as you have said."
31 Then he said, "Swear to me."
And he swore to him. So Israel bowed
himself on the head of the bed.

Jacob blesses Joseph's sons

48 NOW it came to pass after
these things that Joseph was
told, "Indeed your father *is* sick"; and
he took with him his two sons, [d]Ma-
nasseh and Ephraim.
2 And Jacob was told, "Look, your
son Joseph is coming to you"; and Israel strengthened himself and sat up
on the bed.
3 Then Jacob said to Joseph: "God
[e]Almighty appeared to me at [f]Luz in
the land of Canaan and blessed me,
4 "and said to me, 'Behold, I will
[g]make you fruitful and multiply you,
and I will make of you a multitude of
people, and [h]give this land to your descendants after you *as* an [i]everlasting
possession.'
5 "And now your two sons,
Ephraim and Manasseh, who were
born to you in the land of Egypt before
I came to you in Egypt, *are* mine; as
Reuben and Simeon, they shall be
mine.
6 "Your offspring whom you beget
after them shall be yours; they will be
called by the name of their brothers in
their inheritance.
7 "But as for me, when I came
from Padan, Rachel died beside me in
the land of Canaan on the way, when
there was but a little distance to go to
Ephrath; and I buried her there on the
way to Ephrath (that is, [j]Bethlehem)."
8 Then Israel saw Joseph's sons,
and said, "Who *are* these?"
9 And Joseph said to his father,
"They *are* my sons, [k]whom God has
given me in this *place*." And he said,
"Please bring them to me, and I will
[l]bless them."
10 Now the [m]eyes of Israel were
dim with age, *so that* he could not see.
Then Joseph brought them near him,
and he [n]kissed them and embraced
them.
11 And Israel said to Joseph, "I had
not thought to see your face; but in
fact, God has also shown me your offspring!"
12 So Joseph brought them from
beside his knees, and he bowed down
with his face to the earth.
13 And Joseph took them both,
Ephraim with his right hand toward
Israel's left hand, and Manasseh with
his left hand toward Israel's right
hand, and brought *them* near him.
14 Then Israel stretched out his
right hand and [o]laid *it* on Ephraim's
head, who *was* the younger, and his
left hand on Manasseh's head, guiding
his hands knowingly, for Manasseh
was the [p]firstborn.
15 And he [q]blessed Joseph, and
said:

"God, before whom my fathers
Abraham and Isaac
[r]walked,
The God who has fed me all
my life long to this day,
16 [s]The Angel who has [t]redeemed
me from all evil,
Bless the lads;
Let my name be named upon
them,
And the name of my fathers
Abraham and Isaac;
And let them [u]grow into a
multitude in the midst of the
earth."

17 Now when Joseph saw that his
father laid his right hand on the head
of Ephraim, it displeased him; so he
took hold of his father's hand to remove it from Ephraim's head to Manasseh's head.
18 And Joseph said to his father,
"Not so, my father, for this *one is* the
firstborn; put your right hand on his
head."
19 But his father refused and said,
"I know, my son, I know. He also shall
become a people, and he also shall be
great; but truly his younger brother
shall be greater than he, and his descendants shall become a multitude of
nations."
20 So he blessed them that day,
saying, "By you Israel will bless, saying, 'May God make you as Ephraim
and as Manasseh!' " And thus he set
Ephraim before Manasseh.
21 Then Israel said to Joseph, "Behold, I am dying, but God will be [v]with

29
a Gen. 24:2–4
b Josh. 2:14
30
c Gen. 50:5–13; Heb. 11:21
CHAPTER 48
1
d Gen. 46:20; 50:23
3
e Gen. 43:14; 49:25
f Gen. 35:6
4
g Gen. 46:3
h Gen. 35:12; Ex. 6:8
i Gen. 17:8
7
j Gen. 35:19
9
k Gen. 33:5
l v. 15
10
m Gen. 27:1; 1 Sam. 3:2
n Gen. 45:15; 50:1
14
o Cp. Mt. 19:15; Mk. 10:16
p Josh. 17:1
15
q Gen. 47:7, 10
r Gen. 24:40; cp. 2 Ki. 20:8
16
s Angel (of the LORD): v. 16; Ex. 3:2. (Gen. 16:7; Jud. 2:1, *note*)
t Redemption (redeeming relative type): v. 16; Ex. 6:6. (Gen. 48:16; Isa. 59:20, *note*)
u Num. 26:34,37
21
v Gen. 46:4

you and bring you back to the land of
your fathers.
22 "Moreover I have given to you
one portion above your brothers,
[a]which I took from the hand of the
Amorite with my sword and my bow."

Jacob's prophetic blessing

49 [b]AND Jacob called his sons
and said, "Gather together,
that I may tell you what shall befall
you [c]in the [1]last days:

2 "Gather together and hear, you
sons of Jacob,
And listen to Israel your
father.

3 "Reuben, you are my firstborn,
My might and the beginning of
my strength,
The excellency of dignity and
the excellency of power.
4 Unstable as water, you shall
not excel,
[d]Because you went up to your
father's bed;
Then you defiled *it*—
He went up to my couch.

5 "Simeon and Levi *are* brothers;
Instruments of cruelty *are in*
their dwelling place.
6 Let not my soul enter their
council;
Let not my honor be united to
their assembly;
For in their anger they [e]slew a
man,
And in their self-will they
hamstrung an ox.
7 Cursed *be* their anger, for *it is*
fierce;
And their wrath, for it is cruel!
I will [f]divide them in Jacob
And scatter them in Israel.

8 [g]"Judah, you *are he* whom your
brothers shall praise;
Your hand *shall be* on the
neck of your enemies;
Your father's children shall
[h]bow down before you.
9 Judah *is* a [i]lion's whelp;
From the prey, my son, you
have gone up.
He bows down, he lies down
as a lion;
And as a lion, who shall rouse
him?
10 The [j]scepter shall not depart
from Judah,
Nor a lawgiver from between
his feet,
Until [2k]Shiloh comes;
And [l]to Him *shall be* the
obedience of the people.
11 Binding his donkey to the
vine,
And his donkey's colt to the
choice vine,
He washed his garments in
wine,
And his clothes in the blood of
grapes.
12 His eyes *are* darker than wine,
And his teeth whiter than
milk.

22
a Gen. 14:7

CHAPTER 49

1
b vv. 1–27; cp. Dt. 33:6–25
c Isa. 2:2

4
d Gen. 35:22; 1 Chr. 5:1

6
e Gen. 34:26

7
f Num. 18:24; Josh. 19:1, 9; 1 Chr. 4:24–27

8
g vv. 8–10; Rev. 5:5
h 1 Chr. 5:2

9
i Cp. Dt. 33:22

10
j Num. 24:17
k *Christ* (first advent): v. 10; 2 Sam 7:16. (Gen. 3:15; Acts 1:11, *note*)
l Ps. 2:8

---

[1](49:1) This is the first occurrence of the term "the last days," a most important concept in Biblical prophecy. (The Hebrew word for "last" here is *acharith.*) In general, the expression (as also "latter days," "last time(s)") refers to that terminal period in the history of a particular group of people or nations when God's announced purposes for them are about to be consummated. (1) In Dan. 2:28—10:14, it refers to the end of the rule of the Gentile nations. (2) Most frequently in the OT, the term relates to Israel's final rebellion against God (Dt. 31:29), accompanied by a season of great trouble (Dt. 4:30; Ezek. 38:16), to be followed by her return to the LORD (Hos. 3:5), this being succeeded, in turn, by the establishment in Jerusalem of the center of divine sovereignty on earth, to which the nations of the world will come up to learn the law of the LORD (Mic. 4:1). This is no doubt contemporary with the universal outpouring of the Holy Spirit predicted by Joel (Joel 2:28–29; Acts 2:17). (3) In the NT the expression is twice used for that period of history introduced by the advent of Christ (Heb. 1:2; 1 Pet. 1:20); but (4) more frequently of the end of the Church age, when departure from the faith, iniquity, and consequent peril will attain their greatest intensity (2 Tim. 3:1; Jas. 5:3; 1 Pet. 1:5; 2 Pet. 3:3). And (5) our Lord's use of the expression "the last day" is found only in John's Gospel, where it relates to the resurrection (6:39,40,44,54; 12:48; cp. 11:24). Chapter 49 would seem to combine the second and third of these definitions. Cp. Acts 2:17, *note;* also Joel 2:28, *note.*

[2](49:10) Several suggestions have been offered to explain the word "Shiloh." The oldest translations render it "whose it is" or "to whom it belongs" with reference to the Messiah's reign and the prophecy of Ezek. 21:27. The view that refers it to the city of Shiloh is notably weak, for Judah experienced no epochal crisis at Shiloh. The suggestion of a few that the passage is fulfilled in David empties the passage of its force. Actually there was no manifest rule of Judah until David; therefore, the text indicates rule in Judah before Shiloh comes. *The reference is to Messiah.* Rule in Judah will not depart until He comes, when that sovereignty will be heightened to include the world.

13 "Zebulun shall dwell by the
haven of the sea;
He *shall become* a haven for
ships,
And his border shall adjoin
[a]Sidon.

14 [b]"Issachar is a strong donkey,
Lying down between two
burdens;
15 He saw that rest *was* good,
And that the land *was*
pleasant;
He bowed his shoulder to bear
a burden,
And became a band of slaves.

16 [c]"Dan shall judge his people
As one of the tribes of Israel.
17 Dan shall be a serpent by the
way,
A viper by the path,
That bites the horse's heels
So that its rider shall fall
backward.
18 I have waited for your
salvation, O LORD!

19 [d]"Gad, a troop shall tramp upon
him,
But he shall triumph at last.

20 "Bread from [e]Asher *shall be*
rich,
And he shall yield royal
dainties.

21 "Naphtali *is* a deer let loose;
He uses beautiful words.

22 "Joseph *is* a fruitful bough,
A fruitful bough by a well;
His branches run over the
wall.
23 The archers have bitterly
grieved him,
Shot *at him* and hated him.
24 But his bow remained in
strength,
And the arms of his hands
were made strong
By the hands of the [f]Mighty
God of Jacob
(From there *is* the [g]Shepherd,
the [h]Stone of Israel),
25 By the [i]God of your father
who will help you,
And by the Almighty who will
bless you
With blessings of heaven
above,
Blessings of the [j]deep that lies
beneath,
Blessings of the breasts and of
the womb.
26 The blessings of your father
Have excelled the blessings of
my ancestors,
Up to the utmost bound of the
[k]everlasting hills.
They shall be on the head of
Joseph,
And on the crown of the head
of him who was separate
from his brothers.

27 "Benjamin is a ravenous wolf;
In the morning he shall devour
the prey,
And at night he shall divide
the spoil."

28 All these *are* the twelve tribes of
Israel, and this *is* what their father
spoke to them. And he [1]blessed them;
he blessed each one according to his
own blessing.
29 Then he charged them and said
to them: "I am to be [l]gathered to my
people; bury me with my fathers in the
cave that *is* in the field of Ephron the
[m]Hittite,
30 "in the cave that *is* in the field of
Machpelah, which *is* before Mamre in
the land of Canaan, which Abraham
bought with the field of Ephron the
Hittite as a possession for a [n]burial
place.
31 [o]"There they buried Abraham
and Sarah his wife, there they buried
Isaac and Rebekah his wife, and there
I buried Leah.
32 "The field and the cave that *is*
there *were* purchased from the sons of
Heth."
33 And when Jacob had finished
commanding his sons, he drew his
feet up into the bed and breathed his
last, and was gathered to his people.

Burial of Jacob

50 THEN [p]Joseph fell on his father's face, and [q]wept over
him, and kissed him.
2 And Joseph commanded his servants the physicians to [r]embalm his

13 [a] Gen. 10:19; Josh. 11:8
14 [b] 1 Chr. 12:32
16 [c] Gen. 30:6
19 [d] Gen. 30:11
20 [e] Josh. 19:24–31
24 [f] Ps. 132:2,5 [g] Ps. 23 [h] *Christ* (Stone): v. 24; Ex. 17:6. (Gen. 49:24; 1 Pet. 2:8)
25 [i] Gen. 50:17 [j] Dt. 33:13
26 [k] Dt. 33:15
29 [l] Gen. 35:29 [m] See 2 Ki. 7:6, *note*
30 [n] See Acts 7:16, *note*
31 [o] Cp. Gen. 23:19–20; 25:9; 35:29; 50:13
CHAPTER 50
1 [p] Gen. 46:4 [q] Gen. 46:29
2 [r] Gen. 50:26

[1](49:28) Jacob's life, ending in serenity and blessing, testifies to God's power to transform character. Jacob's spiritual life has six notable phases: (1) the first exercise of faith, as shown in the purchase of the birthright (Gen. 25:28–34; 27:9–29); (2) the vision at Bethel (Gen. 28:10–19); (3) walking in the flesh (Gen. 29:1—31:55); (4) the transforming experience (Gen. 32:24–31); (5) the return to Bethel: idols put away (Gen. 35:1–7); and (6) the walk of faith in God (Gen. 37:1—49:33).

father. So the physicians [1]embalmed
Israel.
3 Forty days were required for
him, for such are the days required for
those who are embalmed; and the
Egyptians [a]mourned for him seventy
days.
4 Now when the days of his
mourning were past, Joseph spoke to
the household of Pharaoh, saying, "If
now I have found favor in your eyes,
please speak in the hearing of Pharaoh, saying,
5 'My father made me [b]swear,
saying, "Behold, I am dying; in my
grave which I dug for myself in the
land of Canaan, there you shall bury
me." Now therefore, please let me go
up and bury my father, and I will come
back.'"
6 And Pharaoh said, "Go up and
bury your father, as he made you
swear."
7 So Joseph went up to bury his
father; and with him went up all the
servants of Pharaoh, the elders of his
house, and all the elders of the land of
Egypt,
8 as well as all the house of Joseph, his brothers, and his father's
house. Only their little ones, their
flocks, and their herds they left in the
land of Goshen.
9 And there went up with him both
chariots and horsemen, and it was a
very great gathering.
10 Then they came to the threshing
floor of Atad, which *is* beyond the Jordan, and they mourned there with a
great and very solemn lamentation.
He observed seven days of mourning
for his father.
11 And when the inhabitants of the
land, the Canaanites, saw the
[c]mourning at the threshing floor of
Atad, they said, "This *is* a deep mourning of the Egyptians." Therefore its
name was called [d]Abel Mizraim,
which *is* beyond the Jordan.
12 So his sons did for him just as he
had commanded them.
13 For his sons carried him to the
land of Canaan, and [e]buried him in
the cave of the field of Machpelah, before Mamre, which Abraham bought
with the field from Ephron the [f]Hittite
as property for a burial place.
14 And after he had buried his father, Joseph returned to Egypt, he and
his brothers and all who went up with
him to bury his father.

Joseph's brothers afraid

15 When Joseph's brothers saw
that their father was dead, they said,
"Perhaps Joseph will hate us, and may
actually repay us for all the evil which
we did to him."
16 So they sent *messengers* to Joseph, saying, "Before your father died
he commanded, saying,
17 'Thus you shall say to Joseph: "I
beg you, please forgive the trespass of
your brothers and their sin; for they
did evil to you."' Now, please, forgive
the trespass of the servants of the
[g]God of your father." And Joseph
wept when they spoke to him.
18 Then his brothers also went and
[h]fell down before his face, and they
said, "Behold, we *are* your servants."
19 Joseph said to them, "Do not be
afraid, for [i]*am* I in the place of God?
20 "But as for you, you meant evil
against me; *but* [j]God meant it for
[k]good, in order to bring it about as *it
is* this day, to save many people alive.
21 "Now therefore, do not be
afraid; I will provide for you and your
little ones." And he comforted them
and spoke [l]kindly to them.

Joseph's last days, and his death

22 So Joseph dwelt in Egypt, he and
his father's household. And Joseph
lived one hundred and ten years.
23 Joseph saw [m]Ephraim's children
to the third *generation.* The children
of [n]Machir, the son of Manasseh,
were also brought up on Joseph's
knees.
24 And Joseph [o]said to his brethren, "I am dying; but God will surely
[p]visit you, and bring you out of this
land [q]to the land of which He swore to
Abraham, to Isaac, and to Jacob."
25 Then Joseph took an [r]oath from
the children of Israel, saying, "God
will surely visit [s]you, and you shall
carry up my [t]bones from here."
26 So Joseph died, *being* one hundred and ten years old; and they [u]em-
balmed him, and he was put in a coffin
in Egypt.

3 *a* Gen. 37:34; Num. 20:29; Dt. 34:8
5 *b* Gen. 47:29–31
11 *c* i.e. *of Egypt* *d* Lit. *mourning of the Egyptians*
13 *e* Gen. 49:30–31. See Acts 7:16, *note* *f* See 2 Ki. 7:6, *note*
17 *g* Gen. 49:25
18 *h* Gen. 44:14
19 *i* Gen. 30:2; 2 Ki. 5:7
20 *j* Gen. 45:5, 7 *k* An OT counter-part of Rom. 8:28
21 *l* Lit. *to their hearts*
23 *m* Gen. 48:1 *n* Num. 26:29
24 *o Faith:* vv. 24–25; Ex. 1:17. (Gen. 3:20; Heb. 11:39, *note*) *p* Ex. 3:16 *q* Gen. 48:4; Ex. 6:8
25 *r* Ex. 13:19; Josh. 24:32; Acts 7:15–16; Heb. 11:22 *s* Gen. 17:8; 28:13; 35:12; Dt. 1:8; 30:1–8 *t* Ex. 13:19
26 *u* v. 2

[1](50:2) It was regular procedure in ancient Egypt to embalm people of prominence. Many mummies have been found, often in an excellent state of preservation. How elaborate the process was can be seen by the fact that it required forty days (v. 3).

The Second Book of Moses Called

EXODUS

Author: Moses *Theme:* Deliverance *Date of writing:* c. 1450–1410 B.C.

EXODUS, like Genesis, is a title that is not of Hebrew but Greek origin. The Septuagint, a Greek translation of the OT, calls the book *Exodos*, a word meaning *exit, departure*—a fitting title for that which describes the going out of the chosen people from the land where they had suffered helplessly as slaves for generations. The word *exodos* is found in the Greek version of Ex. 19:1 and significantly in the Greek NT in Lk. 9:31, Heb. 11:22, and 2 Pet. 1:15.

This redemption from Egypt was accomplished by divine, miraculous intervention and required, on the part of the Israelites, only faith in the efficacy of shed blood (12:1–13). As in the NT, redemption is for the purpose of making possible fellowship of a redeemed people with God. After the accomplishment of redemption from Egypt the law was given, followed by a revelation of the great truths of worship acceptable to God as set forth in the tabernacle, with its accompanying sacrifices and attending priesthood.

In Exodus, God, up to then connected with the Israelite people only through His covenant with Abraham (see Gen. 12:2, *note*), brings them to Himself nationally through redemption, puts them under the Mosaic Covenant (19:5, *note*), and dwells among them in the cloud of glory. Galatians explains the relation of the law to the Abrahamic Covenant. In the commandments God taught Israel His just demands. Experience under the commandments convicted Israel of sin; and the provision of priesthood and sacrifice (filled with precious types of Christ) gave a guilty people a way of forgiveness, cleansing, restoration to fellowship, and worship.

Exodus presents many types of rich meaning. See *notes* on the following passages for the typical significance of Moses (2:2); the Passover (12:11); manna (16:35); the rock (17:6); the tabernacle (25:9); also *notes* on oil (27:20); and the priesthood (29:4–5).

Exodus may be divided into three major sections:

I. Israel in Egypt: Oppression and Conflict with Pharaoh, 1:1—12:36.
II. The Exodus from Egypt and Journey to Sinai, 12:37—18:27.
III. At Sinai: the Giving of the Law and the Construction of the Tabernacle, 19:1—40:38.

I. Israel in Egypt: Oppression and Conflict with Pharaoh, 1:1—12:36

Events following Joseph's death

1 NOW these *are* the [a]names of the children of Israel who came to Egypt; each man and his household came with Jacob:

2 Reuben, Simeon, Levi, and Judah;

3 Issachar, Zebulun, and Benjamin;

4 Dan, Naphtali, Gad, and Asher.

5 All those who were descendants* of Jacob were [b]seventy* persons (for Joseph was in Egypt *already*).

6 And [c]Joseph died, all his brothers, and all that generation.

7 But the children of Israel were [d]fruitful and increased abundantly, multiplied and grew exceedingly mighty; and the land was filled with them.

CHAPTER 1

1 *a* Cp. Gen. 46:8–27; Ex. 6:14–16

5 *b* Gen. 46:27; Dt. 10:22

6 *c* Gen. 50:26; cp. Gen. 37:1–50:26

7 *d* Gen. 28:3; 35:11; 46:3; 47:27; 48:4; Num. 22:3; Dt. 1:10–11; Acts 7:17

8 *e* Acts 7:18–19

The Egyptian bondage

8 [1]Now there arose a new king over Egypt, [e]who did not know Joseph.

9 And he said to his people, "Look, the people of the children of Israel *are* more and [f]mightier than we;

10 "come, let us [g]deal shrewdly with them, lest they multiply, and it happen, in the event of war, that they also join our enemies and fight against us, and *so* go up out of the land."

11 Therefore they set [h]taskmasters over them to afflict them with their burdens. And they built for Pharaoh [i]supply cities, Pithom and Raamses.

1:9 *f* Gen. 26:16 1:10 *g* Ps. 105:25 1:11 *h* Ex. 3:7; 5:6 *i* Cp. 1 Ki. 9:19; 2 Chr. 8:4

*

1:5 Literally *who came from the loins of* • Dead Sea Scrolls and Septuagint read *seventy-five* (compare Acts 7:14).

---

[1](1:8) Since Scripture does not give the personal name of any Egyptian king in this period but calls them all by their official title, Pharaoh, the time of the events from Exodus to Ruth is uncertain. The date of 1447 B.C. has been suggested for the Exodus and is used in this edition of the Bible; the beginning of the oppression would then be about 1550 B.C. However, some conservative scholars place the dates as much as two centuries later.

12 But the more they afflicted them, the more they multiplied and grew. And they were in dread of the children of Israel.

13 So the Egyptians made the children of Israel [a]serve with rigor.

14 And they made their lives bitter with hard bondage—in mortar, in brick, and in all manner of service in the field. All their service in which they made them serve *was* with rigor.

15 Then the king of Egypt spoke to the [b]Hebrew [c]midwives, of whom the name of one *was* Shiphrah and the name of the other Puah;

16 and he said, "When you do the duties of a midwife for the Hebrew women, and see *them* on the birthstools, if it *is* a [d]son, then you shall kill him; but if it *is* a daughter, then she shall live."

17 But the midwives [e]feared God, and did [f]not do as the king of Egypt commanded them, but [g]saved the male children alive.

18 So the king of Egypt called for the midwives and said to them, "Why have you done this thing, and saved the male children alive?"

19 And the midwives said to Pharaoh, "Because the Hebrew women *are* not like the Egyptian women; for they *are* lively and give birth before the midwives come to them."

20 Therefore God [h]dealt well with the midwives, and the people [i]multiplied and grew very mighty.

21 And so it was, because the midwives feared God, that He provided households for them.

22 So Pharaoh commanded all his people, saying, "Every [d]son who is born* you shall cast into the [j]river, and every daughter you shall save alive."

13
a Gen. 15:13; Ex. 5:7–19
15
b Ex. 2:6
c Evidently the two leaders *among* the midwives
16
d Acts 7:19
17
e See Ps. 19:9, *note*
f Cp. Dan. 3:16–18
g *Faith:* v. 17; Ex. 12:28. (Gen. 3:20; Heb. 11:39, *note*)
20
h Cp. Gen. 15:1; Ruth 2:12
i v. 17
22
j i.e., *the Nile*
CHAPTER 2
1
k Ex. 6:16–19
l Ex. 6:20
2
m Heb. 11:23
n Acts 7:20; Heb. 11:23
3
o Isa. 18:2
p Gen. 14:10
q Gen. 6:14; Isa. 34:9
r Isa. 19:6
4
s Ex. 15:20; Num. 26:59
6
t vv. 1–2
10
u Heb. *Mosheh.* Cp. Heb.

Birth of Moses: God prepares a deliverer (Ex. 2:1—4:28)

2 AND a [k]man of the house of Levi went and took *as wife* a [l]daughter of Levi.

2 So the woman conceived and bore a [1]son. And when she saw that he *was* a [m]beautiful *child,* she [n]hid him three months.

3 But when she could no longer hide him, she took an ark of [o]bulrushes for him, daubed it with [p]asphalt and [q]pitch, put the child in it, and laid *it* in the [r]reeds by the river's bank.

4 And his [s]sister stood afar off, to know what would be done to him.

5 Then the daughter of Pharaoh came down to bathe at the river. And her maidens walked along the riverside; and when she saw the ark among the reeds, she sent her maid to get it.

6 And when she opened *it,* she saw the child, and behold, the baby wept. So she had compassion on him, and said, "This is one of the [t]Hebrews' children."

7 Then his sister said to Pharaoh's daughter, "Shall I go and call a nurse for you from the Hebrew women, that she may nurse the child for you?"

8 And Pharaoh's daughter said to her, "Go." So the maiden went and called the child's mother.

9 Then Pharaoh's daughter said to her, "Take this child away and nurse him for me, and I will give *you* your wages." So the woman took the child and nursed him.

10 And the child grew, and she brought him to Pharaoh's daughter, and he became her son. So she called his name [2][u]Moses, saying, "Because I drew him out of the water."

Mashah, to draw out

*1:22 Samaritan Pentateuch, Septuagint, and Targum add *to the Hebrews.*

[1](2:2) Moses, a type of Christ the Deliverer (Isa. 61:1–2; Lk. 4:18–19; 2 Cor. 1:10; 1 Th. 1:10): (1) A divinely chosen deliverer (Ex. 3:7–10; Acts 7:25; Jn. 3:16). (2) Rejected by Israel he turns to the Gentiles (Ex. 2:11–15; Acts 7:23–29; 18:5–6; cp. Acts 28:17–28). (3) During his rejection he gains a bride (Ex. 2:16–21; Mt. 12:14–21; 2 Cor. 11:2; Eph. 5:30–32). (4) Afterward he again appears as Israel's deliverer, and is accepted (Ex. 4:29–31; Rom. 11:24–26; cp. Acts 15:14–17). And (5) officially, Moses typifies Christ as Prophet (Acts 3:22–23), Advocate (Ex. 32:31–35; 1 Jn. 2:1–2), Intercessor (Ex. 17:1–6; Heb. 7:25), and Leader, or King (Dt. 33:4–5; Isa. 55:4; Heb. 2:10); whereas in relation to the house of God, he is in contrast with Christ. Moses was faithful as a servant over another's house; Christ, as a Son over His own house (Heb. 3:5–6).

[2](2:10) The name Moses was already familiar in the Egyptian court. Several Pharaohs had borne names compounded from the element "Moses," as Ramose (or Rameses) and Thutmose (or Thothmes). The fact that this Hebrew woman's child was given such a name corroborates the Egyptian background of the story. Verse 10 points out that the name seemed to her to be especially appropriate because of its similarity to a Hebrew word meaning *draw out.*

Moses identifies himself with Israel; rejected, he flees to Midian (Heb. 11:23–27)

11 Now it came to pass in those days, when Moses was grown, that he went out to his brethren and looked at their burdens. And he saw an Egyptian beating a Hebrew, one of his brethren.

12 So he looked this way and that way, and when he saw no one, he killed the Egyptian and hid him in the sand.

13 And when he went out the second day, behold, two Hebrew men were [a]fighting, and he said to the one who did the wrong, "Why are you striking your companion?"

14 Then he said, "Who made you a prince and a judge over us? Do you intend to kill me as you killed the Egyptian?" So Moses [b]feared and said, "Surely this thing is known!"

15 When Pharaoh heard of this matter, he sought to kill Moses. But Moses [c]fled from the face of Pharaoh and dwelt in the land of [d]Midian; and he sat down by a [e]well.

16 Now the priest of Midian had seven daughters. And they [f]came and drew water, and they filled the [g]troughs to water their father's flock.

17 Then the [h]shepherds came and [i]drove them away; but Moses stood up and helped them, and [j]watered their flock.

18 When they came to [k]Reuel their father, he said, "How *is it that* you have come so soon today?"

19 And they said, "An Egyptian delivered us from the hand of the shepherds, and he also drew enough water for us and watered the flock."

20 So he said to his daughters, "And where *is* he? Why *is* it *that* you have left the man? Call him, that he may [l]eat bread."

21 Then Moses was content to live with the man, and he gave Zipporah his daughter to Moses.

22 And she bore *him* a son. He called his name Gershom,* for he said, "I have been a stranger in a foreign land."

God's pity upon Israel

23 Now it happened in the process of time that the king of Egypt died. Then the children of Israel groaned because of the bondage, and they cried out; and their cry came up to God because of the bondage.

24 So God heard their groaning,

13
a Prov. 25:8
14
b Cp. Gen. 32:7; Jud. 6:27; Heb. 11:27
15
c Acts 7:29; cp. Heb. 11:27
d Ex. 3:1
e Gen. 24:11; 29:2; Ex. 15:27
16
f Cp. Gen. 29:6–9
g Gen. 30:38
17
h Gen. 47:3; 1 Sam. 25:7
i Cp. Gen. 26:19–21
j Gen. 29:3, 10
18
k Or *Raguel,* Num. 10:29
20
l Gen. 43:25
24
m Gen. 12:1–3; 15:18–21; 17:1–14; 22:15–18; 26:1–5; 28:13–15
CHAPTER 3
1
n Kingdom (OT): vv. 1–10; Ex. 19:9. (Gen. 1:26; Zech. 12:8, *note*)
o Ex. 4:18
p Ex. 2:15; 4:19
q Ex. 17:6
2
r Angel (of the LORD): 3:2–4:17; Ex. 14:19. (Gen. 16:7; Jud. 2:1, *note*)
s c. 1450 B.C. See Ex. 1:8, *note*
6
t Mt. 22:32; Mk. 12:26; Acts 7:32
8
u Gen. 15:21; Ex. 13:5; Josh. 24:11
v See 2 Ki. 7:6, *note*

and God remembered His [m]covenant with Abraham, with Isaac, and with Jacob.

25 And God looked upon the children of Israel, and God acknowledged *them.*

The burning bush: Moses called

3 [n]NOW Moses was tending the flock of [o]Jethro his father-in-law, the priest of [p]Midian. And he led the flock to the back of the desert, and came to [q]Horeb, the mountain of God.

2 And the [r]Angel of the LORD [s]appeared to him in a flame of fire from the midst of a bush. So he looked, and behold, the bush was burning with fire, but the bush *was* not consumed.

3 Then Moses said, "I will now turn aside and see this great sight, why the bush does not burn."

4 So when the LORD saw that he turned aside to look, God called to him from the midst of the bush and said, "Moses, Moses!" And he said, "Here I am."

5 Then He said, "Do not draw near this place. Take your sandals off your feet, for the place where you stand *is* holy ground."

6 Moreover He said, "I *am* the God of your father—the [t]God of Abraham, the God of Isaac, and the God of Jacob." And Moses hid his face, for he was afraid to look upon God.

7 And the LORD said: "I have surely seen the oppression of My people who *are* in Egypt, and have heard their cry because of their taskmasters, for I know their sorrows.

8 "So I have come down to deliver them out of the hand of the Egyptians, and to bring them up from that land to a good and large land, to a land flowing with milk and honey, to the place of the [u]Canaanites and the [v]Hittites and the Amorites and the Perizzites and the Hivites and the Jebusites.

9 "Now therefore, behold, the cry of the children of Israel has come to Me, and I have also seen the oppression with which the Egyptians oppress them.

10 "Come now, therefore, and I will send you to Pharaoh that you may bring My people, the children of Israel, out of Egypt."

11 But Moses said to God, [w]"Who *am* I that I should go to Pharaoh, and

3:11 *w* Ex. 4:10

* 2:22 Literally *Stranger There*

that I should bring the children of Israel out of Egypt?"
12 So He said, "I will certainly be
with you. And this *shall be* a [a]sign to
you that I have sent you: When you
have brought the people out of Egypt,
you shall serve God on this mountain."

God reveals Himself as the L*ORD*:
Moses commissioned

13 Then Moses said to God, "Indeed, *when* I come to the children of
Israel and say to them, 'The God of
your fathers has sent me to you,' and
they say to me, 'What *is* His name?'
what shall I say to them?"
14 And God said to Moses, [1b]"I AM
WHO I AM." And He said, "Thus you
shall say to the children of Israel, 'I
AM has sent me to you.' "
15 Moreover God said to Moses,
"Thus you shall say to the children of
[c]Israel: 'The LORD God of your fathers,
the God of Abraham, the God of Isaac,
and the God of Jacob, has sent me to
you. This *is* My name forever, and this
is My memorial to all generations.'
16 "Go and [d]gather the elders of Israel together, and say to them, 'The
LORD God of your fathers, the God of
Abraham, of Isaac, and of Jacob, appeared to me, saying, "I have surely
[e]visited you and *seen* what is done to
you in Egypt;
17 "and I have said I will bring you
up out of the affliction of Egypt to the
land of the Canaanites and the [f]Hit-
tites and the Amorites and the Perizzites and the Hivites and the Jebusites, to a land flowing with milk and
honey." '
18 "Then they will heed your voice;
and you shall come, you and the elders of Israel, to the king of Egypt; and
you shall say to him, 'The [g]LORD God
of the Hebrews has [h]met with us; and
now, please, let us go three days' journey into the wilderness, that we may
[i]sacrifice to the LORD our God.'
19 "But I am sure that the king of

12
a Ex. 4:8
14
b Deity (names of): vv. 13–15; Ex. 34:6. (Gen. 1:1; Mal. 3:18)
15
c Israel (history): vv. 15–17; Ex. 12:1. (Gen. 12:2; Rom. 11:26, *note*)
16
d Ex. 4:29
e Gen. 50:24; Ex. 4:31
17
f See 2 Ki. 7:6, *note*
18
g Ex. 5:3
h Cp. Ex. 4:24
i Ex. 5:1
19
j Ex. 5:2
20
k Ex. 6:6
l Ex. 4:21
m Cp. Ex. 12:31–37
21
n Ex. 11:3
22
o Ex. 11:2
p Ex. 33:6
q Ex. 12:36
CHAPTER 4
2
r The use of little things. Cp. Jud. 3:31; 1 Ki. 17:12–16; Jn. 6:9; 1 Cor. 1:25–31
3
s Miracles (OT): vv. 3–4, 6–7; Ex. 7:10. (Gen. 5:24; Jon. 1:17, *note*)
4:5 *t* Ex. 19:9
4:6 *u* Num. 12:10

Egypt will [j]not let you go, no, not
even by a mighty hand.
20 "So I will [k]stretch out My hand
and strike Egypt with all My [l]won-
ders which I will do in its midst; and
after that he will [m]let you go.
21 "And I will [n]give this people favor in the sight of the Egyptians; and
it shall be, when you go, that you shall
not go empty-handed.
22 "But every [o]woman shall ask of
her neighbor, namely, of her who
dwells near her house, [p]articles of silver, articles of gold, and clothing; and
you shall put *them* on your sons and
on your daughters. So you shall
[q]plunder the Egyptians."

Moses' first objection: unbelief
of the people

4 THEN Moses answered and said,
"But suppose they will not believe
me or listen to my voice; suppose they
say, 'The LORD has not appeared to
you.' "
2 So the LORD said to him, "What *is*
that in your [r]hand?" He said, "A [2]rod."
3 And He said, "Cast it on the
ground." So he cast it on the ground,
and it [s]became a serpent; and Moses
fled from it.
4 Then the LORD said to Moses,
"Reach out your hand and take *it* by
the tail" (and he reached out his hand
and caught it, and it became a rod in
his hand),
5 "that they may [t]believe that the
LORD God of their fathers, the God of
Abraham, the God of Isaac, and the
God of Jacob, has appeared to you."
6 Furthermore the LORD said to
him, "Now [3]put your hand in your bosom." And he put his hand in his bosom, and when he took it out, behold,
his hand *was* [u]leprous, like snow.
7 And He said, "Put your hand in
your bosom again." So he put his hand
in his bosom again, and drew it out of

[1](3:14) In this initial self-identification of God it is significant that the verb is in the first person; the Speaker names Himself, thus emphasizing His personal identification. It is the announcement of a present God, who has come to fulfill His covenant and keep His promise to the afflicted posterity of Abraham, Isaac, and Jacob. Cp. 34:6, *note;* Mal. 3:18, *note.*

[2](4:2) The sign of the rod=power (Ps. 2:9; 110:2; Rev. 2:27). It was Moses' shepherd's crook, the tool of his calling. Cast down, it became a serpent; taken up in faith it became "the rod of God" (4:20; see 7:12, *note*).

[3](4:6) The sign of leprosy. Inside his cloak, Moses' hand covered his heart. The heart stands for what we are, the hand for what we do. What we are, that ultimately we do. It is a sign of Lk. 6:43–45. The two signs, rod and hand, speak of preparation for service: (1) consecration—our capacity taken up for God; (2) the hand that holds the rod of God's power must be a cleansed hand swayed by a new heart (Isa. 52:11).

his bosom, and behold, it was restored
like his *other* flesh.
8 "Then it will be, if they do not
believe you, nor heed the message of
the [a]first sign, that they may believe
the message of the latter sign.
9 "And it shall be, if they do not
believe even these [b]two signs, or listen to your voice, that you shall take
water from the river* and pour *it* on
the dry *land.* The water which you
take from the river will become blood
on the dry *land.*"

Moses' second objection: his lack of eloquence

10 Then Moses [c]said to the LORD,
"O my Lord, I *am* not eloquent, neither
before nor since You have spoken to
Your servant; but I *am* slow of speech
and slow of tongue."
11 So the LORD said to him, [d]"Who
has made man's mouth? Or who
makes the mute, the deaf, the seeing,
or the blind? *Have* not I, the LORD?
12 "Now therefore, go, and I will be
[e]with your mouth and teach you what
you shall say."
13 But he said, "O my Lord, please
send by the hand of whomever *else*
You may send."

God appoints Aaron spokesman

14 So the [f]anger of the LORD was
kindled against Moses, and He said:
"Is not Aaron [1]the Levite your
[g]brother? I know that he can speak
well. And look, he is also coming out
to meet you. When he sees you, he will
be glad in his heart.
15 "Now you shall [h]speak to him
and [i]put the words in his [j]mouth.
And I will be with your mouth and
with his mouth, and I will teach you
what you shall do.
16 "So he shall be your spokesman
to the people. And he himself shall be
[k]as a mouth for you, and you shall be
to him as God.
17 "And you shall take this [l]rod in
your hand, with which you shall do
the signs."

Moses returns to Egypt

18 So Moses went and returned to
[m]Jethro his father-in-law, and said to
him, "Please let me go and return to
my brethren who *are* in Egypt, and see
whether they are still alive." And
Jethro said to Moses, [n]"Go in peace."
19 Now the LORD said to Moses in
[o]Midian, "Go, return to [p]Egypt; for
[q]all the men who sought your life are
dead."
20 Then Moses [r]took his wife and
his sons and set them on a donkey,
and he returned to the land of Egypt.
And Moses took the [s]rod of God in his
hand.
21 And the LORD said to Moses,
"When you go back to Egypt, see that
you do all those [t]wonders before
Pharaoh which I have put in your
hand. But I will [2u]harden his heart, so
that he will not let the people go.
22 "Then you shall [v]say to Pharaoh, 'Thus says the LORD: [w]"Israel *is*
My son, My firstborn.
23 "So I say to you, let My son go
that he may serve Me. But if you refuse to let him go, indeed I will [x]kill
your son, your firstborn."'"
24 And it came to pass on the way,
at the [y]encampment, that the LORD
[z]met him and sought to [3]kill him.
25 Then [aa]Zipporah took a [bb]sharp
stone and cut off the foreskin of her
son and cast *it* at *Moses'** feet, and

8 *a* Ex. 7:6–13
9 *b* vv. 1–8,21
10 *c* Ex. 3:11; 6:12
11 *d* Ps. 94:9
12 *e* Cp. Num. 22:38
14 *f* Num. 11:1, 33
g Num. 26:59
15 *h* Ex. 7:1–2
i 2 Sam. 14:3,19
j *Inspiration:* vv. 15,28, 30; Ex. 17:14. (Ex. 4:15; 2 Tim. 3:16, *note*)
16 *k* v. 30; 7:1–2
17 *l* Ex. 7:15
18 *m* Ex. 3:1
n Jud. 18:6; cp. Gen. 43:23
19 *o* Ex. 3:1; 18:1
p Gen. 46:3, 6
q Ex. 2:15, 23
20 *r* Ex. 18:2–5
s Ex. 17:9
21 *t* Ex. 3:20; 11:9–10
u Ex. 11:9
22 *v* Cp. Ex. 5:1

w Hos. 11:1 **4:23** *x* Ex. 11:5 **4:24** *y* Gen. 42:27 *z* Ex. 3:18; 5:3 **4:25** *aa* Ex. 2:21; 18:2 *bb* Josh. 5:2–3

* 4:9 That is, the Nile 4:25 Literally *his*

[1](4:14) See Ex. 28:1, *note.*

[2](4:21) Compare Ex. 7:3,13,14,22; 8:15,19,32; 9:7,12,34–35; 10:1,20,27; 11:10; 14:4,8. There are two aspects of the hardening of Pharaoh's heart: (1) the judicial; and (2) the personal. The first expresses the sovereignty of God; the second reflects the responsibility of man. In the course of the narrative of the contest with Pharaoh, the LORD is spoken of in nine instances as hardening Pharaoh's heart, whereas Pharaoh himself is in three instances said to have hardened his own heart. In five references it is stated, without indicating the cause, that Pharaoh's heart was hardened.

The Hebrew uses three different words to tell the condition of Pharaoh's heart. These words indicate obstinacy. God permitted the wicked nature of Pharaoh to be manifested and then, in subduing Pharaoh's opposition, God revealed His sovereign majesty. Light rejected, rightful obedience refused, inevitably hardens conscience and heart. Cp. Rom. 9:17–24.

[3](4:24) Compare Gen. 17:14. The context (v. 25) interprets v. 24. Moses was forgetful of the foundation sign of Israel's covenant relation to God. On the eve of delivering Israel he was reminded that without circumcision an Israelite was cut off from the covenant. See Josh. 5:2–9.

said, "Surely you *are* a husband of blood to me!"

26 So He let him go. Then she said, "*You are* a husband of blood!"—because of the circumcision.

Aaron meets Moses: deliverance announced to Israel

27 And the LORD said to Aaron, "Go into the wilderness to meet Moses." So he went and met him on the mountain of God, and kissed him.

28 So Moses told Aaron all the words of the LORD who had sent him, and all the signs which He had commanded him.

29 Then Moses and Aaron went and gathered together [a]all the elders of the children of Israel.

30 And Aaron spoke all the words which the LORD had spoken to Moses. Then he did the signs in the sight of the people.

31 So the people believed; and when they heard that the LORD had [b]visited the children of Israel and that He had [c]looked on their affliction, then they [d]bowed their heads and worshiped.

The contest with Pharaoh (Ex. 5—14)

5 AFTERWARD Moses and Aaron went in and told Pharaoh, "Thus says the [e]LORD God of Israel: 'Let My people go, that they may [f]hold a feast to Me in the wilderness.'"

2 And Pharaoh said, [g]"Who *is* the LORD, that I should obey His voice to let Israel go? I do not know the LORD, [h]nor will I let Israel go."

3 So they said, [f]"The God of the Hebrews has [i]met with us. Please, let us go three days' journey into the desert and sacrifice to the LORD our God, lest He fall upon us with [j]pestilence or with the sword."

4 Then the king of Egypt said to them, "Moses and Aaron, why do you take the people from their work? Get *back* to your [k]labor."

5 And Pharaoh said, "Look, the people of the land *are* many now, and you make them rest from their labor!"

6 So the same day Pharaoh commanded the [l]taskmasters of the people and their officers, saying,

7 "You shall no longer give the people straw to make [m]brick as before. Let them go and gather straw for themselves.

8 "And you shall lay on them the quota of bricks which they made before. You shall not reduce it. For they are [n]idle; therefore they cry out, saying, 'Let us go *and* sacrifice to our God.'

9 "Let more work be laid on the men, that they may labor in it, and let them not regard false words."

10 And the taskmasters of the people and their officers went out and spoke to the people, saying, "Thus says Pharaoh: 'I will not give you straw.

11 'Go, get yourselves straw where you can find it; yet [o]none of your work will be reduced.'"

12 So the people were scattered abroad throughout all the land of Egypt to gather stubble instead of straw.

13 And the taskmasters forced *them* to hurry, saying, "Fulfill your work, *your* daily quota, as when there was straw."

14 Also the [p]officers of the children of Israel, whom Pharaoh's taskmasters had set over them, were [q]beaten *and* were asked, "Why have you not fulfilled your task in making brick both yesterday and today, as before?"

15 Then the officers of the children of Israel came and cried out to Pharaoh, saying, "Why are you dealing thus with your servants?

16 "There is no straw given to your servants, and they say to us, 'Make brick!' And indeed your servants *are* beaten, but the fault *is* in your *own* people."

17 But he said, "You *are* idle! Idle! Therefore you say, 'Let us go *and* sacrifice to the LORD.'

18 "Therefore go now *and* work; for no straw shall be given you, yet you shall deliver the quota of bricks."

19 And the officers of the children of Israel saw *that* they *were* in trouble after it was said, "You shall not reduce *any* bricks from your daily quota."

20 Then, as they came out from Pharaoh, they met Moses and Aaron who stood there to meet them.

21 And they said to them, "Let the LORD look on you and judge, because you have made us abhorrent in the sight of Pharaoh and in the sight of his servants, to put a sword in their hand to kill us."

22 So Moses returned to the LORD and said, "Lord, why have You brought trouble on this people? Why *is* it You have sent me?

23 "For since I came to Pharaoh to speak in Your name, he has done evil

29
a Ex. 3:16; 12:21
31
b Ex. 3:16; 13:19
c Ex. 3:7; Dt. 26:7
d Gen. 24:26; Ex. 12:27
CHAPTER 5
1
e The first time this name, the LORD God of Israel, is used in OT
f Ex. 3:18; 7:16
2
g 2 Ki. 18:35
h Ex. 3:19; 7:14
3
i Ex. 4:24; Num. 23:3
j Ex. 9:15
4
k Ex. 2:11; 6:6
6
l Ex. 3:7
7
m Ex. 1:14
8
n v. 17
11
o v. 19
14
p Ex. 5:6
q Isa. 10:24

to this people; neither have You delivered Your people at all."

The God of Abraham, Isaac,
and Jacob encourages Moses

6 THEN the LORD said to Moses,
"Now you shall see what I will do
to Pharaoh. For with a strong hand he
will let them go, and with a [a]strong
hand he will drive them out of his
land."
2 And God spoke to Moses and
said to him: "I *am* the LORD.
3 "I [b]appeared to Abraham, to
Isaac, and to Jacob, as [c]God Almighty, but *by* My name [1d]LORD I was
not known to them.
4 "I have also established My
[e]covenant with them, to give them the
land of Canaan, the land of their [f]pil-
grimage, in which they were strangers.
5 "And I have also [g]heard the
groaning of the children of Israel
whom the Egyptians keep in bondage,
and I have remembered My covenant.
6 "Therefore say to the children of
Israel: [h]'I *am* the LORD; I will [i]bring
you [j]out from under the burdens of
the Egyptians, I will rescue you from
their bondage, and I will [2k]redeem
you with an outstretched arm and
with great judgments.
7 'I will take you as My [l]people,
and I will be your God. Then you shall
know that I *am* the LORD your God
who brings you out from under the
burdens of the Egyptians.
8 'And I will bring you into the

CHAPTER 6
1
a Cp. Ex. 3:19
3
b Gen. 17:1
c Gen. 49:25; Num. 24:4
d Ex. 3:15; 15:3
4
e Gen. 12:7; 15:18; 17:8; 26:3; 28:4,13
f Gen. 47:9; Lev. 25:23
5
g Ex. 2:24; Acts 7:34
6
h Ex. 13:3, 14; 20:2; Dt. 6:12
i Ex. 3:8; 7:5; 12:51; 16:6; 18:1
j Separation: vv. 6–7; Ex. 8:26. (Gen. 12:1; 2 Cor. 6:17, *note*)
k Redemption (redeeming relative type): vv. 6–7; Ex. 15:13. (Gen. 48:16; Isa. 59:20, *note*)
7
l Lev. 26:12
8
m v. 4; Gen.

land which I [m]swore to give to Abraham, Isaac, and Jacob; and I will give
it to you *as* a heritage: I *am* the LORD.'"
9 So Moses spoke thus to the children of Israel; but they did not heed
Moses, because of [n]anguish of spirit
and cruel bondage.
10 And the LORD spoke to Moses,
saying,
11 "Go in, tell Pharaoh king of
Egypt to let the children of Israel go
out of his land."
12 And Moses spoke before the
LORD, saying, "The children of Israel
have not heeded me. How then shall
Pharaoh heed me, for I *am* of uncircumcised lips?"
13 Then the LORD spoke to Moses
and Aaron, and gave them a [o]com-
mand for the children of Israel and for
Pharaoh king of Egypt, to bring the
children of Israel out of the land of
Egypt.

The heads of the children of Israel:
sons of Reuben, Simeon, Levi

14 These *are* the heads of their fathers' houses: The [p]sons of Reuben,
the firstborn of Israel, *were* Hanoch,
Pallu, Hezron, and Carmi. These are
the families of Reuben.
15 And the [q]sons of Simeon *were*
Jemuel,* Jamin, Ohad, Jachin, Zohar,
and Shaul the son of a Canaanite

15:18; 26:3; 35:12 **6:9** *n* Ex. 2:23; cp. Num. 21:4 **6:13** *o* Num. 27:19,23; Dt. 31:14 **6:14** *p* Gen. 46:9; Num. 26:5–11 **6:15** *q* Gen. 46:10; Num. 26:12–14

* **6:15** Spelled *Nemuel* in Numbers 26:12

[1](6:3) On the basis of this verse many critics have claimed that two of the sources of the books of Moses are a document using *Elohim* for the name of God, and one employing *Jehovah;* and that this passage reveals that the writer was ignorant of the many sections of Genesis in which *Jehovah* (usually written LORD) is used (see Preface, p. xvi). It is further assumed that the writer of Ex. 6:3 believed that the name *Jehovah* was first made known in Moses' time. The answer to these assumptions is as follows: (1) The statement, "by My name LORD [JEHOVAH] I was not known to them" can also be translated as a rhetorical question, "By My name LORD [JEHOVAH] was I not known to them?" (2) In the OT the verb "to know" generally means far more than to have an intellectual knowledge. There are many instances of this, such as Amos 3:2: "You only have I known of all the families of the earth." (3) The patriarchs were familiar with the name *Jehovah,* but their experience of God was largely that of Him as *El-Shaddai* (cp. Gen. 17:1, *note*), the One who provided for all their needs. Here in Ex. 6:3 God tells Moses that He is now about to be revealed in that aspect of His character signified by *Jehovah*—i.e. His covenant-relation to Israel as the One who redeems her from sin and delivers her from Egypt (cp. vv. 6–8). (4) Actually there is no contrast in Ex. 6:3 between *Elohim* and *Jehovah,* the names in this text being *El-Shaddai* and *Jehovah.* And (5) the Genesis record over and over reveals knowledge of the name *Jehovah;* for an outstanding example, cp. Gen. 49:18.

[2](6:6) Redemption: (Exodus) Summary. Exodus is the book of redemption and teaches: (1) redemption is wholly from God (Ex. 3:7–8; Jn. 3:16); (2) redemption is through a person (Ex. 2:2, *note;* Jn. 3:16–17); (3) redemption is by blood (Ex. 12:13,23,27; 1 Pet. 1:18–19); and (4) redemption is by power (Ex. 6:6; 13:14; Rom. 8:2. See Isa. 59:20 and Rom. 3:24, *notes*).

The blood of Christ redeems the believer from the guilt and penalty of sin (1 Pet. 1:18–19) and the power of the Holy Spirit delivers from the dominion of sin on the basis of Calvary (Rom. 8:2; Gal. 5:16).

woman. These *are* the families of Simeon.

16 These *are* the names of the [a]sons of Levi according to their generations: Gershon, Kohath, and Merari. And the years of the life of Levi *were* one hundred and thirty-seven.

17 The sons of Gershon *were* Libni and Shimi according to their families.

18 And the sons of Kohath *were* Amram, Izhar, Hebron, and Uzziel. And the years of the life of Kohath *were* one hundred and thirty-three.

19 The sons of Merari *were* Mahli and Mushi. These *are* the families of Levi according to their generations.

20 Now [b]Amram took for himself [c]Jochebed, his father's sister, as wife; and she bore him [c]Aaron and Moses. And the years of the life of Amram *were* one hundred and thirty-seven.

21 The sons of Izhar *were* Korah, Nepheg, and Zichri.

22 And the sons of Uzziel *were* Mishael, Elzaphan, and Zithri.

23 Aaron took to himself Elisheba, daughter of Amminadab, sister of Nahshon, as wife; and she bore him [d]Nadab, Abihu, [e]Eleazar, and Ithamar.

24 And the sons of Korah *were* Assir, Elkanah, and Abiasaph. These are the families of the Korahites.

25 Eleazar, Aaron's son, took for himself one of the daughters of Putiel as wife; and she bore him [f]Phinehas. These *are* the heads of the fathers' houses of the Levites according to their families.

26 These *are the same* Aaron and Moses to whom the LORD said, [g]"Bring out the children of Israel from the land of Egypt according to their armies."

27 These *are* the ones who spoke to Pharaoh king of Egypt, to bring out the children of Israel from Egypt. These *are the same* Moses and Aaron.

Despite God's encouragement (v. 1), Moses pleads his lack of eloquence

28 And it came to pass, on the day the LORD spoke to Moses in the land of Egypt,

29 that the LORD spoke to Moses, saying, "I *am* the LORD. Speak to Pharaoh king of Egypt all that I say to you."

30 But Moses said before the LORD, "Behold, I *am* of uncircumcised lips, and how shall Pharaoh heed me?"

Moses' commission renewed

7 SO the LORD said to Moses: "See, I have made you *as* [h]God to Pharaoh, and [i]Aaron your brother shall be your prophet.

2 [j]"You shall speak all that I command you. And Aaron your brother shall tell Pharaoh to send the children of Israel out of his land.

3 "And I will [k]harden Pharaoh's heart, and multiply My [l]signs and My wonders in the land of Egypt.

4 "But [m]Pharaoh will not heed you, so that I may [n]lay My hand on Egypt and bring My armies *and* My people, the children of Israel, out of the land of Egypt by great [o]judgments.

5 "And the Egyptians shall [p]know that I *am* the LORD, [1]when I [q]stretch out My hand on Egypt and [r]bring out the children of Israel from among them."

6 Then Moses and Aaron did *so;* just as the LORD commanded them, so they did.

7 And [s]Moses *was* eighty years old and [t]Aaron eighty-three years old when they spoke to Pharaoh.

Aaron's rod becomes a serpent; Egypt's magicians also do enchantments

8 Then the LORD spoke to Moses and Aaron, saying,

9 "When Pharaoh speaks to you, saying, [u]'Show a miracle for yourselves,' then you shall say to Aaron, 'Take your rod and cast *it* before Pharaoh, *and* let it become a [v]serpent.'"

10 So Moses and Aaron went in to Pharaoh, and they did so, just as the LORD commanded. And Aaron cast down his rod before Pharaoh and before his servants, and it [w]became a serpent.

11 But Pharaoh also called the wise men and the sorcerers; so the [x]magicians of Egypt, they also did in like manner with their enchantments.

12 For every man threw down his rod, and they [2]became serpents. But

16 *a* Gen. 46:11; 1 Chr. 6:16–30
20 *b* Num. 3:19 *c* Num. 26:59
23 *d* Num. 3:2; Lev. 10:1 *e* Ex. 28:1
25 *f* Num. 25:7, 11
26 *g* Ex. 5:1; 7:4
CHAPTER 7
1 *h* Ex. 4:16 *i* Ex. 4:15–16
2 *j* Dt. 18:18
3 *k* Ex. 4:21; 9:12 *l* Dt. 4:34
4 *m* Ex. 3:19–20; 11:9 *n* Ex. 9:14 *o* Ex. 6:6; 12:12
5 *p* Ex. 6:7; 8:19,22 *q* Ex. 9:15 *r* Ex. 6:6; 12:51
7 *s* Cp. Dt. 31:2 *t* Cp. Num. 33:39
9 *u* Ex. 10:1 *v* Ex. 4:3
10 *w Miracles* (OT): vv. 10–12, 20–25; Ex. 8:6. (Gen. 5:24; Jon. 1:17, *note*)
11 *x* Gen. 41:8; Ex. 8:7, 18–19

[1](7:5) A prophetic sign also. The nations will know the LORD when He restores and blesses Israel in the kingdom (Isa. 2:1–3; 11:10–12; 14:1; 60:4–5; Ezek. 37:28).

[2](7:12) The rods of the magicians are said to have become serpents just as in Moses' act. Some believe that this can be explained only by assuming that either (1) the magicians themselves had power to create life; or (2) on this occasion God gave them such power. Preferably it would seem that (3) the rods of the magicians were actually rigid snakes which,

Aaron's [1]rod swallowed up their rods.
13 And Pharaoh's heart grew hard,
and he did not heed them, as the LORD
had said.

Water turned to blood

14 So the LORD said to Moses:
"Pharaoh's heart *is* hard; he refuses to
let the people go.
15 "Go to Pharaoh in the morning,
when he goes out to the [a]water, and
you shall stand by the river's bank to
meet him; and the [b]rod which was
turned to a serpent you shall take in
your hand.
16 "And you shall say to him, 'The
LORD God of the Hebrews has sent me
to you, saying, "Let My people go, that
they may [c]serve Me in the wilderness"; but indeed, until now you
would not hear!
17 'Thus says the LORD: "By this you
shall know that I *am* the LORD. Behold,
I will strike the waters which *are* in
the river with the rod that *is* in my
hand, and they shall be turned to
[d]blood.
18 "And the fish that *are* in the river
shall die, the river shall stink, and the
Egyptians will loathe to drink the water of the river." ' "
19 Then the LORD spoke to Moses,
"Say to Aaron, 'Take your rod and
stretch out your hand over the waters
of Egypt, over their streams, over
their rivers, over their ponds, and over
all their pools of water, that they may
become blood. And there shall be
blood throughout all the land of
Egypt, both in *buckets of* wood and
pitchers of stone.' "
20 And Moses and Aaron did so,
just as the LORD commanded. So he
lifted up the rod and struck the waters
that *were* in the river, in the sight of
Pharaoh and in the sight of his ser-

15
[a] Ex. 2:5
[b] Ex. 7:10
16
[c] Ex. 5:1; 8:1
17
[d] Ex. 4:9; Rev. 16:4
20
[e] Ps. 78:44; 105:29
22
[f] Ex. 7:11
[g] Ex. 8:7
[h] Ex. 3:19
CHAPTER 8
1
[i] Ex. 7:16; 9:1
2
[j] Rev. 16:13

vants. And [e]all the waters that *were* in
the river were turned to [2]blood.
21 The fish that *were* in the river
died, the river stank, and the Egyptians could not drink the water of the
river. So there was blood throughout
all the land of Egypt.
22 Then the [f]magicians of Egypt
did [g]so with their enchantments; and
Pharaoh's heart grew hard, and he did
not heed them, [h]as the LORD had said.
23 And Pharaoh turned and went
into his house. Neither was his heart
moved by this.
24 So all the Egyptians dug all
around the river for water to drink,
because they could not drink the water of the river.
25 And seven days passed after the
LORD had struck the river.

Frogs cover land

8 AND the LORD spoke to Moses,
"Go to Pharaoh and say to him,
'Thus says the LORD: "Let My people
go, that they may [i]serve Me.
2 "But if you refuse to let *them* go,
behold, I will smite all your territory
with [3j]frogs.
3 "So the river shall bring forth
frogs abundantly, which shall go up
and come into your house, into your
bedroom, on your bed, into the houses
of your servants, on your people, into
your ovens, and into your kneading
bowls.
4 "And the frogs shall come up on
you, on your people, and on all your
servants." ' "
5 Then the LORD spoke to Moses,
"Say to Aaron, 'Stretch out your hand
with your rod over the streams, over
the rivers, and over the ponds, and
cause frogs to come up on the land of
Egypt.' "
6 So Aaron stretched out his hand

---

when cast upon the ground, were seen to be what they really were—snakes. Snakes were, and still are, a common element in the paraphernalia of Egyptian magicians.

[1](7:12) Compare Ex. 4:2. As here the serpents, symbols of Satan, who had the power of death (Heb. 2:14; Rev. 12:9), are swallowed up, so in resurrection death will be "swallowed up in victory" (1 Cor. 15:54). Cp. Num. 17:8. Victory was won by our Lord Jesus Christ through His death at Calvary for sin, and by His resurrection.

[2](7:20) A helpful classification of these plagues has been suggested: (1) loathsome—water turned to blood, frogs, lice; (2) painful—stinging flies, cattle plague, boils; (3) appalling—hail, locusts, darkness; and (4) the overwhelming plague—death of the firstborn. Not even the first nine plagues, as frightful as they were, could move the unregenerate and hardened heart of Pharaoh.

[3](8:2) The gods of the Egyptians were numerous indeed, supposedly inhabiting the heavens, the earth, and the subterranean regions. It would be impossible to bring judgment in any one of these three spheres without touching one or more deities of Egypt. The ten plagues were designed as visitations on the Egyptians and their gods at the same time. Thus the plague of darkness (10:21–23) was directed against the sun-god *Ra*, the most prominent of the Egyptian deities.

over the waters of Egypt, [a]and the
[b]frogs came up and covered the land
of Egypt.
7 And the [c]magicians did so with
their enchantments, and brought up
frogs on the land of Egypt.
8 Then Pharaoh called for Moses
and Aaron, and said, [d]"Entreat the
LORD that He may take away the frogs
from me and from my people; and I
will let the people [e]go, that they may
sacrifice to the LORD."
9 And Moses said to Pharaoh,
"Accept the honor of saying when I
shall intercede for you, for your servants, and for your people, to destroy
the frogs from you and your houses,
that they may remain in the river
only."
10 So he said, "Tomorrow." And he
said, "*Let it be* according to your
word, that you may know that *there is*
[f]no one like the LORD our God.
11 "And the frogs shall depart from
you, from your houses, from your servants, and from your people. They
shall remain in the river only."

Frogs destroyed

12 Then Moses and Aaron went out
from Pharaoh. And Moses cried out to
the LORD concerning the frogs which
He had brought against Pharaoh.
13 So the LORD did according to the
word of Moses. And the frogs died out
of the houses, out of the courtyards,
and out of the fields.
14 They gathered them together in
heaps, and the land stank.
15 But when Pharaoh saw that
there was [g]relief, he [h]hardened his
heart and did not heed them, as the
LORD had said.

Plague of lice

16 So the LORD said to Moses, "Say
to Aaron, 'Stretch out your rod, and
strike the dust of the land, so that it
may become lice throughout all the
land of Egypt.' "
17 And they did so. For Aaron
stretched out his hand with his rod
and struck the dust of the earth, and it
became [i]lice on man and beast. All
the dust of the land became lice
throughout all the land of Egypt.
18 Now the magicians so worked
with their enchantments to bring forth
lice, but they [j]could not. So there
were lice on man and beast.
19 Then the magicians said to Pharaoh, [k]"This *is* the finger of God." But
Pharaoh's heart grew hard, and he did
not heed them, just as the LORD had
said.

Swarms of flies

20 And the LORD said to Moses,
"Rise early in the morning and stand
before Pharaoh as he comes out to the
water. Then say to him, 'Thus says the
LORD: "Let My people go, that they
may serve Me.
21 "Or else, if you will not let My
people go, behold, I will send swarms
of flies on you and your servants, on
your people and into your houses. The
houses of the Egyptians shall be full of
swarms *of flies,* and also the ground
on which they *stand.*
22 "And in that day I will set apart
the land of [l]Goshen, in which My people dwell, that no swarms *of flies* shall
be there, in order that you may [m]know
that I *am* the LORD in the midst of the
[n]land.
23 "I will make a [o]difference between My people and your people. Tomorrow this [p]sign shall be." ' "
24 And the LORD did so. Thick
swarms *of flies* came into the house of
Pharaoh, *into* his servants' houses,
and into all the land of Egypt. The land
was corrupted because of the swarms
of flies.

Pharaoh's compromise refused

25 Then Pharaoh called for Moses
and Aaron, and said, "Go, sacrifice to
your God [1q]in the land."
26 And Moses [r]said, "It is not right
to do so, for we would be sacrificing
the [s]abomination of the Egyptians
to the LORD our God. If we sacrifice
the abomination of the Egyptians before their eyes, then will they not
stone us?

6
a Miracles (OT): vv. 5–14, 16–18, 20–24; Ex. 9:3. (Gen. 5:24; Jon. 1:17, *note*)
b Ps. 78:45; 105:30

7
c Ex. 7:11, 22

8
d Ex. 8:28; 9:28; 10:17
e Ex. 10:8, 24

10
f Ex. 9:14; 15:11; Dt. 33:26

15
g Eccl. 8:11
h Ex. 7:14, 22; 9:34; 1 Sam. 6:6

17
i Ps. 105:31

18
j Cp. Ex. 7:11; 8:7

19
k Ex. 7:5; 10:7

22
l Gen. 50:8
m Ex. 7:5, 17; 10:2; 14:4
n Ex. 9:29

23
o Heb. *peduth,* trans. *redemption.* Ps. 111:9; 130:7. It is, in type, Gal. 6:14
p Ex. 4:8

25
q Ex. 8:28; 10:8–11, 24; 12:31

26
r Separation: vv. 25–27; Ex. 10:8. (Gen. 12:1; 2 Cor. 6:17, *note*)
s Gen. 46:34

[1](8:25) Three compromises proposed by Pharaoh are similar to those urged upon Christians today: (1) Here he says in effect: "Be a Christian if you will, but not a narrow one—stay in Egypt." This invariably ends in conformity with the world. Cp. Ps. 50:9–17; 2 Cor. 6:14–18; Gal. 1:4. (2) Pharaoh, in suggesting that the Israelites should "not go very far away" (v. 28) simply modifies the former proposal, as if to say: "Do not be too unworldly." Cp. 1 Sam. 15:3,9,13–15,19–23. And (3) Pharaoh then makes the most subtle proposal of the three, saying (10:8–11) that the Israelites might go out to offer sacrifices to their God, but their children should remain in Egypt. Even some of the most godly parents are inclined to desire prosperity and worldly position for their children. Cp. Mt. 20:20–21.

27 "We will go [a]three days' journey into the wilderness and sacrifice to the LORD our God as He will command us."

28 So Pharaoh said, "I will let you go, that you may sacrifice to the LORD your God in the wilderness; only you shall not go [b]very far away. Intercede for me."

29 Then Moses said, "Indeed I am going out from you, and I will entreat the LORD, that the swarms *of flies* may depart tomorrow from Pharaoh, from his servants, and from his people. But let Pharaoh not deal [c]deceitfully anymore in not letting the people go to sacrifice to the LORD."

Flies destroyed

30 So Moses went out from Pharaoh and entreated the LORD.

31 And the LORD did according to the word of Moses; He removed the swarms *of flies* from Pharaoh, from his servants, and from his people. Not one remained.

32 But Pharaoh [d]hardened his heart at this time also; neither would he let the people go.

Livestock stricken

9 THEN the LORD said to Moses, "Go in to Pharaoh and tell him, 'Thus says the LORD God of the Hebrews: "Let My people go, that they may [e]serve Me.

2 "For if you refuse to let *them* go, and still hold them,

3 "behold, the hand of the LORD will be on your cattle in the field, on the horses, on the donkeys, on the camels, on the oxen, and on the sheep—a very severe [f]pestilence.

4 "And the LORD will [g]make a difference between the livestock of Israel and the livestock of Egypt. So nothing shall die of all *that* belongs to the children of Israel." ' "

5 Then the LORD appointed a set time, saying, "Tomorrow the LORD will do this thing in the land."

6 So the LORD did this thing on the next day, and all the livestock of Egypt died; but of the livestock of the children of Israel, not one died.

7 Then Pharaoh sent, and indeed, not even one of the livestock of the Israelites was dead. But the heart of Pharaoh became hard, and he did not let the people go.

Boils afflict man and beast

8 So the LORD said to Moses and Aaron, "Take for yourselves handfuls of ashes from a furnace, and let Moses scatter it toward the heavens in the sight of Pharaoh.

9 "And it will become fine dust in all the land of Egypt, and it will cause boils that break out in sores on man and beast throughout all the land of Egypt."

10 Then they took ashes from the furnace and stood before Pharaoh, and Moses scattered *them* toward heaven. And *they* caused boils that break out in sores on man and beast.

11 And the [h]magicians could not stand before Moses because of the [i]boils, for the boils were on the magicians and on all the Egyptians.

12 But the LORD [d]hardened the heart of Pharaoh; and he did not [j]heed them, just as the LORD had spoken to Moses.

Judgment of hail and fire

13 Then the LORD said to Moses, [k]"Rise early in the morning and stand before Pharaoh, and say to him, 'Thus says the LORD God of the Hebrews: "Let My people go, that they may [l]serve Me,

14 "for at this time I will send all My plagues to your very heart, and on your servants and on your people, that you may know that *there is* [m]none like Me in all the earth.

15 "Now if I had [n]stretched out My hand and struck you and your people with [o]pestilence, then you would have been cut off from the earth.

16 "But indeed for [p]this *purpose* I have raised you up, that I may [q]show My power *in* you, and that My [r]name may be declared in all the earth.

17 "As yet you exalt yourself against My people in that you will not let them go.

18 "Behold, tomorrow about this time I will cause very heavy hail to rain down, such as has not been in Egypt since its founding until now.

19 "Therefore send now *and* gather your [s]livestock and all that you have in the field, for the hail shall come down on every man and every animal which is found in the field and is not brought home; and they shall die." ' "

20 He who [t]feared the word of the LORD among the [u]servants of Pharaoh made his servants and his livestock flee to the houses.

21 But he who did not regard the word of the LORD left his servants and his livestock in the field.

22 Then the LORD said to Moses, "Stretch out your hand toward

27
a Ex. 3:18; 5:3
28
b See Ex. 8:25, *note*
29
c Ex. 8:15
32
d Ps. 52:2
CHAPTER 9
1
e Ex. 7:16
3
f *Miracles* (OT): vv. 3–6, 8–11, 22–26, 33–35; Ex. 10:13. (Gen. 5:24; Jon. 1:17, *note*)
4
g Ex. 8:22
11
h Ex. 8:18
i Dt. 28:27; Job 2:7; Rev. 16:1,2
12
j Ex. 7:13
13
k Ex. 8:20
l Ex. 9:1
14
m Ex. 8:10
15
n Ex. 7:5
o Ex. 5:3
16
p Rom. 9:17; cp. 2 Cor. 2:16; 1 Pet. 2:8
q Ex. 7:4–5; 10:1; 11:9; 14:17
r 1 Ki. 8:43
19
s v. 6
20
t Ex. 1:17; 14:31; Prov. 13:13
u Ex. 8:19; 10:7

heaven, that there may be hail in all
the land of Egypt—on man, on beast,
and on every herb of the field,
throughout the land of Egypt."
23 And Moses stretched out his rod
toward heaven; and the LORD sent
thunder and hail, and fire darted to the
ground. And the LORD rained hail on
the land of Egypt.
24 So there was hail, and fire mingled with the hail, so very heavy that
there was none like it in all the land of
Egypt since it became a nation.
25 And the [a]hail struck throughout
the whole land of Egypt, all that *was*
in the field, both man and beast; and
the hail struck every herb of the field
and broke every tree of the field.
26 [b]Only in the land of Goshen,
[c]where the children of Israel *were,*
there was no hail.

Pharaoh consents; then retracts

27 And Pharaoh sent and [d]called
for Moses and Aaron, and said to
them, "I have [e]sinned this time. The
LORD *is* righteous, and my people and
I *are* wicked.
28 [d]"Entreat the LORD, that there
may be no *more* mighty thundering
and hail, for *it is* enough. I will let you
[f]go, and you shall stay no longer."
29 So Moses said to him, "As soon
as I have gone out of the city, I will
spread out my hands to the LORD; the
thunder will cease, and there will be
no more hail, that you may know that
the [g]earth *is* the LORD's.
30 [h]"But as for you and your servants, I know that you will not yet fear
the LORD God."
31 Now the flax and the barley
were struck, for the barley *was* in the
head and the flax *was* in bud.
32 But the wheat and the spelt were
not struck, for they *are* late crops.
33 So Moses went out of the city
from Pharaoh and spread out his
hands to the LORD; then the thunder
and the hail ceased, and the rain was
not poured on the earth.
34 And when Pharaoh saw that the
rain, the hail, and the thunder had
ceased, he sinned yet more; and he
hardened his heart, he and his servants.
35 So the heart of Pharaoh was
hard; neither would he let the children
of Israel go, as the LORD had spoken by
Moses.

25
a Ps. 78:47–48; 105:32
26
b Ex. 8:22
c Ex. 8:23
27
d Ex. 8:8
e Ex. 9:34; 10:16,17
28
f Ex. 8:25
29
g Ex. 8:22; 19:5; 20:11; Ps. 24:1
30
h Ex. 8:29; Isa. 26:10
CHAPTER 10
1
i Ex. 4:21; 9:12; 10:27; 11:10; 14:4
j Ex. 9:16
2
k Ex. 12:26; 13:8,14; Dt. 4:9; 6:7; 11:19
3
l Ex. 8:1; 9:1
4
m Prov. 30:27; Rev. 9:3
5
n Ex. 9:32
6
o Ex. 8:3,21
7
p Ex. 8:19; 9:20; 12:33
8
q *Separation:* vv. 8–11, 24–26; Ex. 11:7. (Gen. 12:1; 2 Cor. 6:17, *note*)
9
r Ex. 5:1; 7:16
11
s See Ex. 8:25, *note*
t Ex. 10:28

Plague of locusts

10 NOW the LORD said to Moses,
"Go in to Pharaoh; for I have
[i]hardened his heart and the hearts of
his servants, that I may [j]show these
signs of Mine before him,
2 "and that you may [k]tell in the
hearing of your son and your son's
son the mighty things I have done in
Egypt, and My signs which I have
done among them, that you may
[b]know that I *am* the LORD."
3 So Moses and Aaron came in to
Pharaoh and said to him, "Thus says
the LORD God of the Hebrews: 'How
long will you refuse to humble yourself before Me? Let My people go, that
they may [l]serve Me.
4 'Or else, if you refuse to let My
people go, behold, tomorrow I will
bring [m]locusts into your territory.
5 'And they shall cover the face of
the earth, so that no one will be able to
see the earth; and they shall eat the
[n]residue of what is left, which remains to you from the hail, and they
shall eat every tree which grows up
for you out of the field.
6 'They shall [o]fill your houses, the
houses of all your servants, and the
houses of all the Egyptians—which
neither your fathers nor your fathers'
fathers have seen, since the day that
they were on the earth to this day.'"
And he turned and went out from
Pharaoh.
7 Then Pharaoh's [p]servants said
to him, "How long shall this man be a
snare to us? Let the men go, that they
may serve the LORD their God. Do you
not yet know that Egypt is destroyed?"
8 So Moses and Aaron were
brought again to Pharaoh, and he said
to them, [q]"Go, serve the LORD your
God. Who *are* the ones that are going?"
9 And Moses said, "We will go
with our young and our old; with our
sons and our daughters, with our
flocks and our herds we will go, for we
must hold a [r]feast to the LORD."
10 Then he said to them, "The LORD
had better be with you when I let you
and your little ones go! Beware, for
evil is ahead of you.
11 "Not so! Go now, [s]you *who are*
men, and serve the LORD, for that is
what you desired." And they were
[t]driven out from Pharaoh's presence.
12 Then the LORD said to Moses,
"Stretch out your hand over the land
of Egypt for the locusts, that they may
come upon the land of Egypt, and eat

every herb of the land—all that the
hail has left."
13 So Moses stretched out his rod
over the land of Egypt, and the LORD
brought an east wind on the land all
that day and all *that* night. When it
was morning, the east wind brought
the [a]locusts.
14 And the locusts went up over all
the land of Egypt and rested on all the
territory of Egypt. *They were* very severe; previously there had been no
such locusts as they, [b]nor shall there
be such after them.
15 For they covered the face of the
whole earth, so that the land was
darkened; and they ate every herb of
the land and all the fruit of the trees
which the hail had left. So there remained nothing green on the trees or
on the plants of the field throughout
all the land of Egypt.
16 Then Pharaoh [c]called for Moses
and Aaron in haste, and said, "I have
[d]sinned against the LORD your God
and against you.
17 "Now therefore, please forgive
my sin only this once, and [e]entreat the
LORD your God, that He may take
away from me this death only."
18 So he went out from Pharaoh
and entreated the LORD.
19 And the LORD turned a very
strong west wind, which took the locusts away and blew them into the
Red Sea. There remained not one locust in all the territory of Egypt.
20 But the LORD [f]hardened Pharaoh's heart, and he did not let the
children of Israel go.

Judgment of darkness and light

21 Then the LORD said to Moses,
"Stretch out your hand toward
heaven, that there may be darkness
over the land of Egypt, darkness
which may even be felt."
22 So Moses stretched out his hand
toward heaven, and there was thick
[g]darkness in all the land of Egypt
[h]three days.
23 They did not see one another;
nor did anyone rise from his place for
three days. [i]But all the children of Israel had light in their dwellings.

Final compromise refused

24 Then Pharaoh called to Moses
and said, [j]"Go, serve the LORD; only
let your flocks and your herds be kept
back. Let your little ones also go with
you."
25 But Moses said, "You must also

13
a Miracles (OT): vv. 12–19, 21–23; Ex. 12:29. (Gen. 5:24; Jon. 1:17, *note*)
14
b Joel 2:2
16
c Ex. 8:8; 9:27
d Ex. 9:27
17
e Ex. 8:8
20
f Ex. 10:1
22
g Ps. 105:28
h Ex. 3:18
23
i Cp. Ex. 8:23
24
j Ex. 8:25
26
k Ex. 10:9
28
l Ex. 10:11
29
m Heb. 11:27
CHAPTER 11
1
n Ex. 12:33
o Ex. 6:1; 12:39
3
p Ex. 3:21; 12:36
q Dt. 34:10–12; cp. Num. 12:3
4
r Ex. 12:29
5
s Ex. 4:23
t Ps. 78:51; 105:36; 135:8; 136:10
6
u Ex. 12:30
v Ex. 10:14
7
w Separation: v. 7; Ex. 19:4. (Gen. 12:1; 2 Cor. 6:17, *note*)
8
x Ex. 12:31–33

give us sacrifices and burnt offerings,
that we may sacrifice to the LORD our
God.
26 "Our [k]livestock also shall go
with us; not a hoof shall be left behind.
For we must take some of them to
serve the LORD our God, and even we
do not know with what we must serve
the LORD until we arrive there."
27 But the LORD [f]hardened Pharaoh's heart, and he would not let
them go.
28 Then Pharaoh said to him, [l]"Get
away from me! Take heed to yourself
and see my face no more! For in the
day you see my face you shall die!"
29 So Moses said, "You have spoken well. I will never [m]see your face
again."

Pharaoh warned of judgment upon firstborn

11 AND the LORD said to Moses, "I
will bring one more plague on
Pharaoh and on Egypt. [n]Afterward he
will let you go from here. When he lets
you go, he will surely [o]drive you out of
here altogether.
2 "Speak now in the hearing of the
people, and let every man ask from his
neighbor and every woman from her
neighbor, articles of silver and articles
of gold."
3 And the LORD gave the people
[p]favor in the sight of the Egyptians.
Moreover the [q]man Moses *was* very
great in the land of Egypt, in the sight
of Pharaoh's servants and in the sight
of the people.
4 Then Moses said, "Thus says the
LORD: 'About [r]midnight I will go out
into the midst of Egypt;
5 'and all the firstborn in the land
of Egypt shall [s]die, from the [t]first-
born of Pharaoh who sits on his
throne, even to the firstborn of the female servant who *is* behind the hand-
mill, and all the firstborn of the animals.
6 'Then there shall be a great [u]cry
throughout all the land of Egypt,
[v]such as was not like it *before,* nor
shall be like it again.
7 'But against none of the children
of Israel shall a dog move its tongue,
against man or beast, that you may
know that the LORD does make a [w]dif-
ference between the Egyptians and Israel.'
8 "And all these your servants
shall [x]come down to me and bow
down to me, saying, 'Get out, and all
the people who follow you!' After that

I will go out." Then he [a]went out from Pharaoh in great anger.

9 But the LORD said to Moses, "Pharaoh will not heed you, so that My [b]wonders may be multiplied in the land of Egypt."

10 So Moses and Aaron did all these wonders before Pharaoh; and the LORD [c]hardened Pharaoh's heart, and he did not let the children of Israel go out of his land.

God commands sacrifice of Passover lamb

12 NOW the LORD spoke to Moses and Aaron in the land of Egypt, [d]saying,

2 "This [e]month *shall be* your beginning of months; it *shall be* the [f]first month of the year to you.

3 "Speak to all the congregation of Israel, saying: 'On the [g]tenth of this month every man shall take for himself a [h]lamb, according to the house of *his* father, a lamb for a household.

4 'And if the household is too small for the lamb, let him and his neighbor next to his house take *it* according to the number of the persons; according to each man's need you shall make your count for the lamb.

5 'Your lamb shall be without [i]blemish, a male of the first year. You may take *it* from the sheep or from the goats.

6 'Now you shall keep it until the [j]fourteenth day of the same month. Then the whole assembly of the congregation of Israel shall kill it at [k]twilight.

7 'And they shall take *some* of the blood and put *it* on the two doorposts and on the lintel of the houses where they eat it.

8 'Then they shall eat the flesh on that [l]night; [m]roasted in fire, with [n]unleavened bread *and* with bitter *herbs* they shall eat it.

9 'Do not eat it raw, nor boiled at all with water, but roasted in fire—its head with its legs and its entrails.

10 'You shall let none of it remain until morning, and what remains of it until morning you shall burn with fire.

11 'And thus you shall eat it: *with* a belt on your waist, your sandals on your feet, and your staff in your hand. So you shall eat it in haste. It *is* the LORD's [1]Passover.

Redemption: (1) by blood

12 'For I will pass through the land of Egypt on that night, and will strike all the firstborn in the land of Egypt, both man and beast; and against all the gods of Egypt I will execute judgment: I *am* the LORD.

13 'Now the blood shall be a sign for you on the houses where you *are*. And when I see the blood, I will pass over you; and the plague shall not be on you to destroy *you* when I strike the land of Egypt.

The Passover: a memorial of redemption

14 'So this day shall be to you a memorial; and you shall keep it as a feast to the LORD throughout your generations. You shall keep it as a feast by an everlasting ordinance.

15 [o]'Seven days you shall eat unleavened bread. On the first day you shall remove leaven from your houses. For whoever eats leavened bread from the first day until the seventh day, that person shall be cut off from Israel.

16 'On the first day *there shall be* a holy [p]convocation, and on the seventh day there shall be a holy convocation for you. No manner of work shall be done on them; but *that* which everyone must eat—that only may be prepared by you.

17 'So you shall observe *the Feast of* Unleavened Bread, for on this same day I will have brought your [q]armies out of the land of Egypt. Therefore

8
a Ex. 10:29; Heb. 11:27
9
b Ex. 9:16
10
c Ex. 10:1
CHAPTER 12
1
d Israel (history): vv. 1–13; Ex. 13:22. (Gen. 12:2; Rom. 11:26, *note*)
2
e Ex. 13:4; 23:15; 34:18; Dt. 16:1
f See Lev. 23:2, *note*
3
g Josh. 4:19
h Sacrifice (typical): vv. 3–11, 27; Ex. 17:15. (Gen. 3:15; Heb. 10:18, *note*)
5
i Lev. 22:18–20
6
j vv. 14–28; Lev. 23:5; Num. 9:1–5,11
k Lit. *between the evenings*. See Num. 28:4, *note;* cp. Dt. 16:4,6
8
l Ex. 34:25; Num. 9:12
m Dt. 16:7
n Leaven: vv. 8, 15–20,34, 39; Ex. 13:3. (Gen. 19:3; Mt. 13:33, *note*)
15
o Ex. 13:6

12:16 *p* Lev. 23:2 12:17 *q* Num. 33:1

[1](12:11) The Passover, a type of Christ our Redeemer (Ex. 12:1–28; Jn. 1:29; 1 Cor. 5:6–7; 1 Pet. 1:18–19): (1) The lamb must be without blemish, and to test this it was kept for four days (Ex. 12:5–6). So our Lord's public life, under hostile scrutiny, was the testing which proved His holiness (Lk. 11:53–54; Jn. 8:46; 18:38). (2) The lamb thus tested must be killed (Ex. 12:6; Jn. 12:24; Heb. 9:22). (3) The blood must be applied (Ex. 12:7). This answers to appropriation by personal faith, and refutes universalism (Jn. 3:36). (4) The blood thus applied of itself, without anything in addition, constituted a perfect protection from judgment (Ex. 12:13; Heb. 10:10,14; 1 Jn. 1:7). And (5) the feast typified Christ the Bread of life, answering to the memorial supper (Mt. 26:26–28; 1 Cor. 11:23–26). To observe the feast was a duty and privilege but not a condition of safety. The believer in Christ is saved by the blood of "the Lamb slain from the foundation of the world" (Rev. 13:8), and is strengthened daily by feasting on the Word—the living Word, Christ, and the written Word, the Scriptures.

you shall observe this day throughout
your generations as an everlasting ordinance.
18 'In the first [a]*month,* on the fourteenth day of the month at evening,
you shall eat unleavened bread, until
the twenty-first day of the month at
evening.
19 'For seven days no leaven shall
be found in your houses, since whoever eats what is leavened, that same
person shall be cut off from the congregation of Israel, whether *he is* a
[b]stranger or a native of the land.
20 'You shall eat nothing leavened;
in all your dwellings you shall eat unleavened bread.' "
21 Then [c]Moses called for all the
[d]elders of Israel and said to them,
"Pick out and take lambs for yourselves according to your families, and
kill the Passover *lamb.*
22 "And you shall take a bunch of
hyssop, dip *it* in the blood that *is* in the
basin, and [e]strike the lintel and the
two doorposts with the blood that *is* in
the basin. And none of you shall go
out of the door of his house until
morning.
23 "For the LORD will [f]pass through
to strike the Egyptians; and when He
sees the [g]blood on the lintel, and on
the two doorposts, the LORD will pass
over the door and not [h]allow the destroyer to come into your houses to
strike *you.*
24 "And you shall [i]observe this
thing as an ordinance for you and
your sons forever.
25 "It will come to pass when you
come to the land which the LORD will
give you, just as He promised, that you
shall keep this service.
26 "And it shall be, when your
[j]children say to you, 'What do you
mean by this service?'
27 "that you shall say, 'It *is* the
Passover sacrifice of the [k]LORD, who
passed over the houses of the children
of Israel in Egypt when He struck the
Egyptians and delivered our households.' " So the people bowed their
heads and [l]worshiped.
28 Then the children of Israel went
away and [m]did *so;* just as the LORD had
commanded Moses and Aaron, so
they did.

18
a Ex. 12:2; Lev. 23:5–8; Num. 28:16–25
19
b Ex. 12:43–49
21
c Heb. 11:28
d Ex. 3:16
22
e Ex. 12:7
23
f Ex. 12:12–13
g Ex. 24:8
h Cp. 2 Sam. 24:16; Heb. 12:24
24
i Ex. 13:5,10
26
j Ex. 10:2
27
k Ex. 12:11
l Ex. 4:31
28
m Faith: vv. 21–28; Ex. 14:22. (Gen. 3:20; Heb. 11:39, *note*)
29
n Ex. 11:4–5
o Miracles (OT): vv. 29–30; Ex. 14:21. (Gen. 5:24; Jon. 1:17, *note*)
p Ex. 9:6
31
q Ex. 10:28–29
r Ex. 8:25; 11:1
s Ex. 10:9
32
t Ex. 10:26
33
u Ex. 10:7
v Ps. 105:38
37
w c. 1447 B.C. See Ex. 1:8, *note*
x Gen. 47:11; Ex. 1:11; Num. 33:3–4
y Ex. 38:26; Num. 1:46; 2:32; 11:21; 26:51

Death of the firstborn

29 And it came to pass at [n]midnight
that the LORD [o]struck all the firstborn
in the land of Egypt, from the firstborn
of Pharaoh who sat on his throne to
the firstborn of the captive who *was* in
the dungeon, and all the firstborn of
[p]livestock.
30 So Pharaoh rose in the night, he,
all his servants, and all the Egyptians;
and there was a great cry in Egypt, for
there was not a house where *there
was* not one dead.

Children of Israel commanded to depart from Egypt hastily

31 Then he [q]called for Moses and
Aaron by night, and said, "Rise, [r]go
out from among my people, both you
and the children of Israel. And go,
serve the LORD as you have [s]said.
32 "Also take your flocks and your
herds, as you have [t]said, and be gone;
and bless me also."
33 And the [u]Egyptians [v]urged the
people, that they might send them out
of the land in haste. For they said, "We
shall all *be* dead."
34 So the people took their dough
before it was leavened, having their
kneading bowls bound up in their
clothes on their shoulders.
35 Now the children of Israel had
done according to the word of Moses,
and they had asked from the Egyptians articles of silver, articles of gold,
and clothing.
36 And the LORD had given the people favor in the sight of the Egyptians,
so that they granted them *what they
requested.* Thus they plundered the
Egyptians.

II. The Exodus of the Children of Israel from Egypt, and the Journey to Sinai, 12:37—18:27

Redemption: (2) by power (to 15:21); first stage of journey

37 Then the children of Israel
[w]journeyed from [x]Rameses to Succoth, [y]about six hundred thousand
men on foot, besides children.
38 A [1z]mixed multitude went up
with them also, and flocks and
herds—a great deal of [aa]livestock.
39 And they baked unleavened

12:38 *z* Num. 11:4 *aa* Num. 32:1; Dt. 3:19

[1](12:38) This "mixed multitude," similar to unconverted church members in the present age, was a source of weakness and division then as now (cp. Num. 11:4–6). There had been a manifestation of divine power, and men were drawn to it without a change of heart. Cp. Lk. 14:25–27.

cakes of the dough which they had
brought out of Egypt; for it was not
leavened, because they were driven
out of Egypt and could not wait, nor
had they prepared provisions for
themselves.
40 Now the sojourn of the children
of Israel who lived in Egypt* *was* four
hundred and thirty [a]years.
41 And it came to pass at the end of
the four hundred and thirty [1]years—
on that very same day—it came to
pass that all the armies of the LORD
[b]went out from the land of Egypt.
42 It *is* a night of solemn observance to the LORD for bringing them
out of the land of Egypt. This *is* that
night of the LORD, a solemn observance for all the children of Israel
throughout their generations.
43 And the LORD said to Moses and
Aaron, "This *is* the ordinance of the
Passover: No [c]foreigner shall eat it.
44 "But every man's servant who is
bought for money, when you have
[d]circumcised him, then he may eat it.
45 "A sojourner and a hired servant
shall not eat it.
46 "In one house it shall be eaten;
you shall not carry any of the flesh
outside the house, nor shall you
[e]break one of its [f]bones.
47 "All the congregation of Israel
shall [g]keep it.
48 "And when a stranger dwells
with you *and wants* to keep the Passover to the LORD, let all his males be
circumcised, and then let him come
near and keep it; and he shall be as a
native of the land. For no uncircumcised person shall eat it.
49 [h]"One law shall be for the
native-born and for the stranger who
dwells among you."
50 Thus all the children of Israel
did; as the LORD commanded Moses
and Aaron, so they did.
51 And it came to pass, on that very
same day, that the LORD [i]brought the
children of Israel out of the land of
Egypt according to their armies.

Firstborn set apart for the LORD

13 THEN the LORD spoke to Moses, saying,
2 [j]"Consecrate to Me all the firstborn, whatever opens the womb
among the children of Israel, *both* of
man and beast; it is Mine."
3 And Moses said to the people:
[k]"Remember this day in which you
went out of Egypt, out of the house of
bondage; for by strength of hand the
LORD brought you out of this *place.*
[l]No leavened bread shall be eaten.
4 "On this day you are going out,
in the month [m]Abib.
5 "And it shall be, when the LORD
[n]brings you into the [o]land of the Canaanites and the [p]Hittites and the
Amorites and the Hivites and the Jebusites, which He swore to your fathers
to give you, a land flowing with milk
and honey, that you shall [q]keep this
service in this month.
6 [r]"Seven days you shall eat unleavened bread, and on the seventh
day *there shall be* a feast to the LORD.
7 "Unleavened bread shall be
eaten seven days. And no leavened
bread shall be seen among you, nor
shall leaven be seen among you in all
your quarters.
8 "And you shall [s]tell your son in
that day, saying, '*This is done* because
of what the LORD did for me when I
came up from Egypt.'
9 "It shall be as a [t]sign to you on
your hand and as a memorial between
your eyes, that the LORD's law may be
in your mouth; for with a strong hand
the LORD has brought you out of Egypt.
10 "You shall therefore [u]keep this
ordinance in its season from year to
year.
11 "And it shall be, when the LORD
[v]brings you into the land of the [w]Ca-
naanites, as He swore to you and your
fathers, and gives it to you,
12 "that you shall [x]set apart to the
LORD all that open the womb, that is,
every firstborn that comes from an animal which you have; the males *shall*
be the LORD's.
13 "But every [2y]firstborn of a donkey you shall [z]redeem with a lamb;
and if you will not redeem *it,* then you
shall break its neck. And all the firstborn of man among your sons you
shall redeem.
14 "So it shall [aa]be, when your son
asks you in time to come, saying,

40 *a* Gen. 15:13,16; Acts 7:6; Gal. 3:17
41 *b* Ex. 3:8; 6:6
43 *c* Ex. 12:19, 48
44 *d* Gen. 17:12–13
46 *e* Num. 9:12 *f* See Jn. 19:36
47 *g* Num. 9:13–14
49 *h* Lev. 24:22; Num. 15:15–16
51 *i* Ex. 20:2
CHAPTER 13
2 *j* Ex. 13:12–15; 22:29; Lk. 2:22–23
3 *k* Dt. 16:3 *l Leaven:* vv. 3,6–7; Ex. 23:15. (Gen. 19:3; Mt. 13:33, *note*)
4 *m* See Lev. 23:2, *note* 2
5 *n* Ex. 3:8,17; 6:8; Josh. 24:11 *o* Gen. 17:8; Dt. 30:5 *p* See 2 Ki. 7:6, *note* *q* Ex. 12:25
6 *r* Ex. 12:15–20
8 *s* Ex. 10:2; 13:14
9 *t* Ex. 12:14; 31:13; Dt. 6:8; 11:18
10 *u* Ex. 12:14
11 *v* Ex. 13:5 *w* Num. 21:3

13:12 *x* v. 2; Lk. 2:23 **13:13** *y* Ex. 34:20 *z* Num. 18:15 **13:14** *aa* Ex. 10:2; 13:8

* **12:40** Samaritan Pentateuch and Septuagint read *Egypt and Canaan.*

[1](12:41) This period of time probably began with the descent of Abraham into Egypt. Cp. Gen. 12:10; also 1 Ki. 6:1.
[2](13:13) The redemption of the firstborn was a memorial to Israel of their own redemption.

'What *is* this?' that you shall say to
him, 'By strength of hand the LORD
brought us out of Egypt, out of the
house of bondage.
15 'And it came to pass, when Pharaoh was stubborn about letting us go,
that the LORD [a]killed all the firstborn
in the land of Egypt, both the firstborn
of man and the firstborn of beast.
Therefore I sacrifice to the LORD all
males that open the womb, but all the
firstborn of my sons I redeem.'
16 "It shall be as a [b]sign on your
hand and as frontlets between your
eyes, for by strength of hand the LORD
brought us out of Egypt."

Journey resumed

17 Then it came to pass, when
Pharaoh had let the people go, that
God did not lead them *by* way of the
land of the Philistines, although that
was near; for God said, "Lest perhaps
the people [c]change their minds when
they see war, and return to Egypt."
18 So God led the people around *by*
way of the wilderness of the Red Sea.
And the children of Israel went up in
orderly ranks out of the land of Egypt.
19 And Moses took the [d]bones of
[e]Joseph with him, for he had placed
the children of Israel under solemn
oath, saying, "God will surely [f]visit
you, and you shall carry up my bones
from here with you."
20 So they took their [g]journey from
[h]Succoth and camped in Etham at the
edge of the wilderness.

Guidance by cloud and fire

21 And the LORD [i]went before them
by day in a pillar of cloud to lead the
way, and by night in a pillar of fire to
give them light, so as to go by day and
night.
22 He did not take away the pillar
of cloud by day or the pillar of fire by
night *from* before the [j]people.

Pharaoh pursues Israel

14 NOW the LORD spoke to Moses,
saying:
2 "Speak to the children of Israel,
that they turn and camp before [k]Pi
Hahiroth, between Migdol and the
sea, opposite Baal Zephon; you shall
camp before it by the sea.
3 "For Pharaoh will say of the children of Israel, 'They *are* bewildered
by the land; the wilderness has closed
them in.'
4 "Then I will [l]harden Pharaoh's
heart, so that he will pursue them; and
I will gain honor over Pharaoh and
over all his army, that the Egyptians
may [m]know that I *am* the LORD." And
they did so.
5 Now it was told the king of
Egypt that the people had fled, and the
heart of Pharaoh and his servants was
turned against the people; and they
said, "Why have we done this, that we
have let Israel go from serving us?"
6 So he made ready his chariot
and took his people with him.
7 Also, he took six hundred choice
chariots, and all the chariots of Egypt
with captains over every one of them.
8 And the LORD hardened the heart
of Pharaoh king of Egypt, and he pursued the children of Israel; and the
children of Israel went out with [n]bold-
ness.
9 So the Egyptians [o]pursued
them, all the horses *and* chariots of

15
a Ex. 12:29
16
b Ex. 13:9
17
c Zech. 8:14, *note*
19
d Gen. 50:24–25; Josh. 24:32
e Ex. 1:6,8; Dt. 33:13–17
f Ex. 4:31
20
g Num. 33:6–8
h Ex. 12:37
21
i Ex. 14:19; 33:9; Dt. 1:33; Ps. 78:14; 99:7; 105:39
22
j *Israel* (history): vv. 17–22; Ex. 14:19. (Gen. 12:2; Rom. 11:26, *note*)
CHAPTER 14
2
k Num. 33:7
4
l Ex. 10:1
m Ex. 10:2
8
n Num. 33:3; Acts 13:17
9
o Josh. 24:6

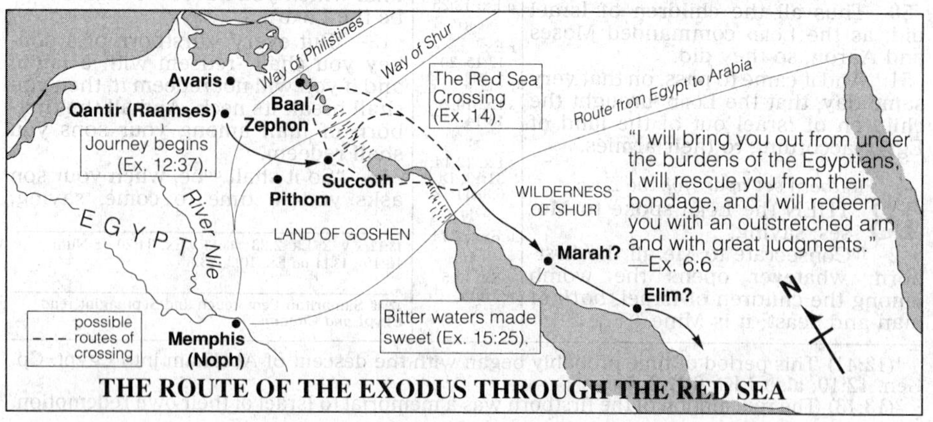

THE ROUTE OF THE EXODUS THROUGH THE RED SEA

Pharaoh, his horsemen and his army,
and overtook them camping by the
sea beside Pi Hahiroth, before Baal
Zephon.
10 And when Pharaoh drew near,
the children of Israel lifted their eyes,
and behold, the Egyptians marched
after them. So they were very afraid,
and the children of Israel [a]cried out to
the LORD.
11 Then they [b]said to Moses, "Because *there were* no graves in Egypt,
have you taken us away to die in the
wilderness? Why have you so dealt
with us, to bring us up out of Egypt?
12 "*Is* this not the word that we
[c]told you in Egypt, saying, 'Let us
alone that we may serve the Egyptians?' For *it would have been* better
for us to serve the Egyptians than that
we should die in the wilderness."

God miraculously makes way of deliverance through Red Sea

13 And Moses said to the people,
[d]"Do not be afraid. [e]Stand still, and
see the [f]salvation of the LORD, which
He will accomplish for you today. For
the Egyptians whom you see today,
you shall [g]see again no more forever.
14 "The LORD will [h]fight for you,
and you shall hold your peace."
15 And the LORD said to Moses,
"Why do you cry to Me? Tell the children of Israel to go forward.
16 "But lift up your [i]rod, and
stretch out your hand over the sea and
divide it. And the children of Israel
shall go on dry *ground* through the
midst of the sea.
17 "And I indeed will [j]harden the
hearts of the Egyptians, and they shall
follow them. So I will gain [k]honor
over Pharaoh and over all his army,
his chariots, and his horsemen.
18 "Then the Egyptians shall know
that I *am* the LORD, when I have gained
honor for Myself over Pharaoh, his
chariots, and his horsemen."
19 And the [l]Angel of God, who
went before the camp of [m]Israel,
moved and went [n]behind them; and
the pillar of cloud went from before
them and stood behind them.
20 So it came between the camp of
the Egyptians and the camp of Israel.
Thus it was a cloud and darkness *to
the one*, and it gave light by night *to
the other*, so that the one did not come
near the other all that night.
21 Then Moses stretched out his
hand over the sea; and the LORD
[o]caused the sea to go *back* by a strong
east wind all that night, and made the
sea into dry [p]*land*, and the waters
were [q]divided.
22 So the children of Israel [r]went
into the midst of the sea on the dry
ground, and the waters *were* a wall to
them on their right hand and on their
left.
23 And the Egyptians pursued and
went after them into the midst of the
sea, all Pharaoh's horses, his chariots,
and his horsemen.
24 Now it came to pass, in the
morning [s]watch, that the [t]LORD
looked down upon the army of the
Egyptians through the pillar of fire
and cloud, and He troubled the army
of the Egyptians.
25 And He took off* their chariot
wheels, so that they drove them with
difficulty; and the Egyptians said, "Let
us flee from the face of Israel, for the
LORD [u]fights for them against the
Egyptians."
26 Then the LORD said to Moses,
"Stretch out your hand over the sea,
that the waters may come back upon
the Egyptians, on their chariots, and
on their horsemen."
27 And Moses stretched out his
hand over the sea; and when the
morning appeared, the sea returned to
its full depth, while the Egyptians
were fleeing into it. So the LORD overthrew the Egyptians in the midst of the
sea.
28 Then the waters returned and
covered the chariots, the horsemen,
and all the army of Pharaoh that came
into the sea after them. Not so much as
one of them remained.
29 But the [v]children of Israel had
walked on dry [w]*land* in the midst of
the sea, and the waters *were* a wall to
them on their right hand and on their
left.
30 [x]So the LORD [1]saved Israel that
day out of the hand of the Egyptians,

10 *a* Neh. 9:9
11 *b* Ex. 5:21; 15:24; 16:2; 17:3; Num. 14:2–3; 20:3
12 *c* Ex. 5:21; 6:9
13 *d* Ex. 20:20 *e* 2 Chr. 20:17; Ps. 46:10–11; Isa. 30:15 *f* Ex. 14:30; 15:2 *g* Cp. Dt. 28:68
14 *h* Ex. 14:25; 15:3; Dt. 1:30
16 *i* Ex. 4:17, 20; Isa. 10:26
17 *j* Ex. 10:1 *k* Ex. 9:16
19 *l* *Angel* (of the LORD): v. 19; Ex. 23:20. (Gen. 16:7; Jud. 2:1, *note*) *m* *Israel* (history): vv. 19–31; Ex. 19:1. (Gen. 12:2; Rom. 11:26, *note*) *n* Isa. 52:12; 58:8
21 *o* *Miracles* (OT): vv. 21–31; Ex. 15:25. (Gen. 5:24; Jon. 1:17, *note*) *p* Ps. 106:9; 136:13,14 *q* Ps. 78:13; 114:1–8; Isa. 63:12–13
22 *r* *Faith:* vv. 21–22; Josh. 6:20. (Gen. 3:20; Heb. 11:39, *note*)
24 *s* Jud. 7:19

t Ex. 13:21 **14:25** *u* Ex. 7:5; 14:4,14 **14:29** *v* v. 22 *w* Ps. 66:6; cp. Isa. 11:15 **14:30** *x* See Ps. 19:9, *note*

* **14:25** Samaritan Pentateuch, Septuagint, and Syriac read *bound*.

[1](14:30) The word "saved" is a translation of the Hebrew word *yasha*, the root of the name Joshua which, in turn, is an abbreviation of *Jehoshua* meaning *Jehovah saves*. Joshua is the Hebrew form of Jesus, and Christ was named Jesus, because "He will save His people from

and Israel saw the Egyptians dead on
the seashore.
31 Thus Israel saw the great work
which the LORD had done in Egypt; so
the people feared the LORD, and believed the LORD and His servant Moses.

Song of the redeemed

15 THEN Moses and the children of Israel [a]sang this song to the LORD, and spoke, saying:

"I will [b]sing to the LORD,
For He has triumphed gloriously!
The horse and its rider
He has thrown into the sea!
2 The LORD *is* my strength and song,
And He has become my salvation;
He *is* my God, and I will praise Him;
My father's [c]God, and I will exalt Him.
3 The LORD *is* a man of [d]war;
The LORD *is* His name.
4 Pharaoh's chariots and his army He has cast into the sea;
His chosen captains also are drowned in the Red Sea.
5 The depths have covered them;
They sank to the bottom like a stone.
6 "Your right [e]hand, O LORD, has become glorious in power;
Your right hand, O LORD, has dashed the enemy in pieces.
7 And in the greatness of Your excellence
You have overthrown those who rose against You;
You sent forth Your [f]wrath;
It [g]consumed them like stubble.
8 And with the blast of Your [h]nostrils
The waters were gathered together;
The floods stood upright like a heap;
The depths congealed in the heart of the sea.
9 The enemy said, 'I will pursue,
I will overtake,
I will divide the spoil;
My desire shall be satisfied on them.
I will draw my sword,
My hand shall destroy them.'
10 You blew with Your wind,
The sea covered them;
They sank like lead in the mighty waters.
11 "Who *is* like You, O LORD, among the gods?
Who *is* like You, glorious in [i]holiness,
Fearful in [j]praises, doing [k]wonders?
12 You stretched out Your right hand;
The earth swallowed them.
13 You in Your mercy have led forth
The people whom You have [l]redeemed;
You have guided *them* in Your strength
To Your holy [m]habitation.
14 "The people will hear *and* be afraid;
Sorrow will take hold of the inhabitants of Philistia.
15 Then the chiefs of [n]Edom will be dismayed;
The mighty men of [o]Moab,
Trembling will take hold of them;
All the inhabitants of Canaan will [p]melt away.
16 [q]Fear and dread will fall on them;
By the greatness of Your arm
They will be *as* still as a stone,
Till Your people pass over, O LORD,
Till the people pass over
Whom You have purchased.
17 You will bring them in and [r]plant them
In the [s]mountain of Your inheritance,
In the place, O LORD, *which* You have made
For Your own [t]dwelling,
The sanctuary, O LORD, *which* Your hands have established.

18 "The LORD shall [u]reign forever and ever."

19 For the horses of Pharaoh went

CHAPTER 15
1 [a] Ps. 106:12 [b] Cp. Isa. 12:1–6
2 [c] Ex. 3:6,15
3 [d] Ex. 14:14
6 [e] Ex. 3:20; Ps. 17:7
7 [f] Ps. 78:49–50 [g] Isa. 5:24
8 [h] Ex. 14:21–22
11 [i] Ps. 68:35; Isa. 6:3 [j] 1 Chr. 16:25 [k] Ex. 3:20; Ps. 77:11
13 [l] *Redemption* (redeeming relative type): v. 13; Lev. 25:25. (Gen. 48:16; Isa. 59:20, *note*) [m] Dt. 12:5; Ps. 78:54
15 [n] Gen. 36:15 [o] Gen. 19:37; Num. 22:3 [p] Josh. 2:9–11,24
16 [q] vv. 5–6,13
17 [r] Ps. 80:8,15 [s] Ps. 2:6; 78:54 [t] Ps. 68:16; 76:2; 132:14
18 [u] 2 Sam. 7:16

their sins" (Mt. 1:21). The divine deliverance to which this verse refers is a remarkable illustration of redemption provided by Christ.

with his chariots and his horsemen into the sea, and the LORD brought back the waters of the sea upon them. But the children of Israel went on dry *land* in the midst of the sea.

20 [a]Then [b]Miriam the prophetess, the sister of Aaron, took the timbrel in her hand; and all the women went out after her with timbrels and with [c]dances.

21 And Miriam answered them:

"Sing to the LORD,
For He has triumphed
gloriously!
The horse and its rider
He has thrown into the sea!"

Redemption: (3) experience (to 19:25); God satisfies hunger and thirst, and provides rest

22 So Moses brought Israel from the Red Sea; then they went out into the [d]Wilderness of Shur. And they went three days in the wilderness and found no [e]water.

23 Now when they came to Marah, they could not drink the waters of [f]Marah, for they *were* bitter. Therefore the name of it was called Marah.

24 And the people complained against Moses, saying, "What shall we drink?"

25 So he cried out to the LORD, and the LORD showed him a tree. [1]When he cast *it* into the waters, the waters were made [g]sweet. There He made a statute and an ordinance for them, and there He [h]tested them,

26 and said, "If you diligently heed the voice of the LORD your God and do what is right in His sight, give ear to His commandments and keep all His statutes, I will put none of the diseases on you which I have brought on the Egyptians. For I *am* the LORD who heals you."

27 Then they came to Elim, where there *were* twelve wells of water and seventy palm trees; so they camped there by the waters.

Manna provided

16 AND they journeyed from Elim, and all the congregation of the children of Israel came to the Wilderness of [i]Sin, which is between Elim and [j]Sinai, on the fifteenth day of the [k]second month after they departed from the land of Egypt.

2 Then the whole congregation of the children of Israel [l]complained against Moses and Aaron in the wilderness.

3 And the children of Israel said to them, "Oh, that we had died by the hand of the LORD in the land of Egypt, when we sat by the pots of meat *and* when we ate bread to the full! For you have brought us out into this wilderness to kill this whole assembly with hunger."

4 Then the LORD said to Moses, "Behold, I will rain [m]bread from heaven for you. And the people shall go out and gather a certain quota every day, that I may [h]test them, whether they will [n]walk in My law or not.

5 "And it shall be on the sixth day that they shall prepare what they bring in, and it shall be twice as much as they gather [o]daily."

6 Then Moses and Aaron said to all the children of Israel, "At evening you shall [p]know that the LORD has brought you out of the land of Egypt.

7 "And in the morning you shall see the glory of the LORD; for He [q]hears your complaints against the LORD. But what *are* we, that you complain against [r]us?"

8 Also Moses said, "*This shall be seen* when the LORD gives you meat to eat in the evening, and in the morning bread to the full; for the LORD hears your complaints which you make against Him. And what *are* we? Your complaints *are* not against us but against the LORD."

9 Then Moses spoke to Aaron, "Say to all the congregation of the children of Israel, 'Come near before the LORD, for He has heard your complaints.'"

10 Now it came to pass, as Aaron spoke to the whole congregation of the children of Israel, that they looked toward the wilderness, and behold, the [s]glory of the LORD appeared in the cloud.

20
a Cp. 2 Sam. 6:5
b Ex. 2:4; Num. 12:1; 20:1
c Ps. 150:4
22
d Num. 33:8
e Ex. 17:1; Num. 20:2
23
f i.e. *bitter.* Cp. Ruth 1:20
25
g Miracles (OT): vv. 23–25; Ex. 16:15. (Gen. 5:24; Jon. 1:17, *note*)
h Test/tempt: vv. 25; 16:4; Ex. 17:2. (Gen. 3:1; Jas. 1:14, *note*)
CHAPTER 16
1
i Num. 33:11–12
j Ex. 19:1
k See Lev. 23:2, *note* 2
2
l Ex. 14:11
4
m Ps. 78:23–25; Jn. 6:31–32
n Jud. 2:22
5
o Cp. Lev. 25:20,21
6
p Ex. 6:7
7
q Num. 14:27; 17:5
r Num. 16:11
10
s Ex. 24:16–17

[1](15:25) Israel came to this bitter water while walking in the very path of the LORD's leading, thus indicating that difficult experiences for God's people are educative rather than punitive. The piece of wood which healed the water should remind the Christian that the cross of Christ can take all the bitterness out of all such experiences (cp. Rom. 15:3–4; Gal. 3:13). See v. 27 and observe that after trial which is accepted as the Father's will, blessing and growth will follow (cp. Ps. 1:3; 92:12).

11 And the LORD spoke to Moses, saying,

12 "I have heard the complaints of the children of Israel. Speak to them, saying, 'At twilight you shall eat meat, and in the morning you shall be filled with bread. And you shall know that I *am* the LORD your God.' "

13 So it was that [a]quails came up at evening and covered the camp, and in the morning the [b]dew lay all around the camp.

Manna described and gathered

14 And when the layer of dew lifted, there, on the surface of the wilderness, was a [c]small round [d]substance *as* fine as [e]frost on the ground.

15 So when the children of Israel saw *it,* they said to one another, [f]"What is it?" For they did not know what it *was.* And Moses said to them, "This *is* the [g]bread which the LORD has [h]given you to eat.

16 "This is the thing which the LORD has commanded: 'Let every man gather it [1][i]according to each one's need, one [j]omer for each person, *according to the* number of persons; let every man take for *those* who *are* in his tent.' "

17 Then the children of Israel did so and gathered, some more, some less.

18 So when they measured *it* by [j]omers, he who gathered much had nothing left over, and he who gathered little had no [k]lack. Every man had gathered according to each one's need.

19 And Moses said, "Let no one [l]leave any of it till morning."

20 Notwithstanding they did not heed Moses. But some of them [2]left part of it until morning, and it bred worms and stank. And Moses was angry with them.

21 So they gathered it every morning, every man according to his need. And when the sun became hot, it melted.

22 And so it was, on the sixth day, *that* they gathered twice as much bread, two omers for each one. And all the rulers of the congregation came and told Moses.

Sabbath invested with special covenant significance to Israel (cp. Ex. 31:13; Neh. 9:13–14; see Mt. 12:1, note)

23 Then he said to them, "This *is what* the LORD has said: 'Tomorrow *is* a Sabbath rest, a holy Sabbath to the LORD. Bake what you will bake *today,* and boil what you will boil; and lay up for yourselves all that remains, to be kept until morning.' "

24 So they laid it up till morning, as Moses commanded; and it did not stink, nor were there any worms in it.

25 Then Moses said, "Eat that today, for today *is* a [m]Sabbath to the LORD; today you will not find it in the field.

26 "Six days you shall gather it, but on the seventh day, the Sabbath, there will be none."

27 Now it happened *that some* of the people went out on the seventh day to gather, but they found none.

28 And the LORD said to Moses, "How long do you refuse to keep My commandments and My laws?

29 "See! For the LORD has given you the Sabbath; therefore He gives you on the sixth day bread for two days. Let every man remain in his place; let no man go out of his place on the seventh day."

30 So the people rested on the seventh day.

31 And the house of Israel called its name Manna. And it *was* like white [n]coriander seed, and the taste of it *was* like wafers *made* with honey.

32 Then Moses said, "This *is* the thing which the LORD has commanded: 'Fill an omer with it, to be kept for your generations, that they may see the bread with which I fed you in the wilderness, when I brought you out of the land of Egypt.' "

33 And Moses said to Aaron, "Take a pot and put an omer of manna in it, and lay it up before the LORD, to be kept for your generations."

34 As the LORD commanded Moses, so Aaron laid it up before the [o]Testimony, to be kept.

35 And the children of Israel [p]ate

13
a Num. 11:31
b Num. 11:9
14
c Cp. Isa. 53:2; Mk. 6:3
d Ex. 16:31; Num. 11:7–8
e Ps. 147:16
15
f See Ex. 16:35, *note*
g v. 4
h *Miracles* (OT): vv. 14–35; Ex. 17:6. (Gen. 5:24; Jon. 1:17, *note*)
16
i Ex. 12:4
j See Weights and Measures (OT), 2 Chr. 2:10, *note*
18
k 2 Cor. 8:15
19
l Ex. 12:10
25
m *Sabbath:* vv. 22–25; Ex. 20:8. (Gen. 2:3; Mt. 12:1, *note*)
31
n The coriander plant, which grows wild in Palestine and Egypt, produces small, spicy gray-white seeds.
34
o Ex. 25:16
35
p Dt. 8:3,16

[1](16:16) Compare Jn. 6:33 with Jn. 6:41,42,52. Christ gives Himself unreservedly, but we have no more of Him experientially than faith appropriates (v. 18). In Josh. 1 cp. v. 2 with v. 3. Verse 2 is the title; v. 3, the law of possession.

[2](16:20) As man is not nourished by the memory of food, so the Christian cannot be spiritually sustained on past appropriations of Christ.

[1]manna [2][a]forty years, until they came
to an inhabited land; they ate manna
until they [b]came to the border of the
land of Canaan.
36 Now an [c]omer *is* one-tenth of an
[c]ephah.

Water from the rock

17 THEN all the congregation of
the children of Israel set out on
their journey from the Wilderness of
[d]Sin, according to the commandment
of the LORD, and camped in [e]Rephi-
dim; but *there was* no water for the
people to [f]drink.
2 Therefore the people [g]con-
tended with Moses, and said, "Give us
water, that we may drink." So Moses
said to them, "Why do you contend
with me? Why do you [h]tempt the
LORD?"
3 And the people thirsted there for
water, and the people complained
against Moses, and said, "Why *is* it
you have brought us up out of Egypt,
to kill us and our children and our
[i]livestock with thirst?"
4 So Moses cried out to the LORD,
saying, "What shall I do with this people? They are almost ready to stone
me!"
5 And the LORD said to Moses, "Go
on before the people, and take with
you some of the elders of Israel. Also
take in your hand your rod with which
you struck the river, and go.
6 "Behold, I will stand before you
there on the [3][j]rock in Horeb; and you
shall strike the rock, and [k]water will
come out of it, that the people may
drink." And Moses did so in the sight
of the elders of Israel.
7 So he called the name of the
place Massah* and Meribah,* because of the contention of the children
of Israel, and because they [l]tempted
the LORD, saying, "Is the LORD among
us or not?"

Conflict with Amalek

8 Now Amalek came and fought
with Israel in Rephidim.
9 And Moses said to Joshua,
"Choose us some men and go out,
fight with Amalek. Tomorrow I will
stand on the top of the hill with the rod
of God in my hand."
10 So Joshua did as Moses said to
him, and fought with Amalek. And
Moses, Aaron, and Hur went up to the
top of the hill.
11 And so it was, when Moses held
up his hand, that Israel prevailed; and
when he let down his hand, Amalek
prevailed.
12 But Moses' hands *became*
heavy; so they took a stone and put *it*
under him, and he sat on it. And
Aaron and Hur supported his hands,
one on one side, and the other on the

35
a Num. 14:33
b Josh. 5:12; Neh. 9:20–21

36
c See Weights and Measures (OT), 2 Chr. 2:10, *note*

CHAPTER 17

1
d Ex. 16:1
e Num. 33:11–15
f Ex. 15:22; Num. 20:2

2
g Ex. 14:11
h *Test/tempt:* vv. 2,7; Ex. 20:20. (Gen. 3:1; Jas. 1:14, *note*)

3
i Ex. 12:38

6
j *Christ (Rock):* v. 6; Ex. 33:22. (Gen. 49:24; 1 Pet. 2:8)
k *Miracles (OT):* vv. 5–7; Lev. 10:2. (Gen. 5:24; Jon. 1:17, *note*)

17:7 *l* Ex. 17:2

* 17:7 Literally *Tempted* • Literally *Contention*

[1](16:35) The word "manna" is a transliteration of two Hebrew words meaning *What is it?* (cp. v. 15), the question the Israelites asked on first seeing it. Referred to as "bread" (Ex. 16:4), "the bread of heaven" and "angels' food" (Ps. 78:24–25), it was preserved in a pot in the tabernacle (Heb. 9:4). Manna is compared to coriander seed with the resin-like color of bdellium, resembling hoarfrost as it lay on the ground and tasting like pastry prepared with oil (Num. 11:7–8). It fell throughout the forty years of wilderness wanderings and ceased to fall when Israel began eating grain at Gilgal (Josh. 5:10–12). Although organic in nature, manna is called "spiritual food" (1 Cor. 10:3) in reference to its supernatural origin.

Manna is a type of Christ in humiliation giving His flesh that the believer might have life (Jn. 6:49–51). To meditate upon the Lord Jesus as He lived among men, doing not His own will but the will of the Father (Jn. 6:38–40), is to feed on the manna.

[2](16:35) Moses' life divides into three equal periods of forty years—in Egypt (Ex. 2:1–14); in Midian (2:15—12:36); and in the wilderness (12:37—Dt. 34:8). The Scriptures often refer to the forty-year period of wandering in the wilderness (Ex. 16:35; Acts 7:36–40); Stephen informs us that the length of time Moses spent as a shepherd in Midian was forty years (Acts 7:30); and once we are told that Moses lived to the age of 120 (Dt. 34:7), making his residence in Pharaoh's court to be forty years in length also.

The period spent by Moses at Mount Sinai was forty days (Ex. 24:18; 34:28), which was the length of time that our Lord was in the wilderness at the beginning of His ministry (Mt. 4:2) and also the time intervening between His resurrection and ascension (Acts 1:3).

[3](17:6) The rock, a type of life through the Holy Spirit by grace: (1) Christ the Rock (1 Cor. 10:4); (2) the people utterly unworthy (v. 2; Eph. 2:1–6); and (3) characteristics of life through grace: (a) free (Jn. 4:10; Rom. 6:23; Eph. 2:8); (b) abundant (Rom. 5:20; cp. Ps. 105:41); (c) near (Rom. 10:8); and (d) the people had only to take (Isa. 55:1). The struck rock aspect of the death of Christ looks toward the outpouring of the Holy Spirit (Jn. 7:37–39) as a result of accomplished redemption, rather than toward our guilt. It is the affirmative side of Jn. 3:16. "Not perish" speaks of atoning blood; "but have" alludes to life bestowed (Rom. 8:2,10–11).

other side; and his hands were steady
until the going down of the sun.
13 So Joshua defeated Amalek and
his people with the edge of the sword.
14 Then the LORD said to Moses,
[1]"Write this *for* a memorial in the
[a]book and recount *it* in the hearing of
Joshua, that I will utterly blot out the
remembrance of Amalek from under
heaven."
15 And Moses built an [b]altar and
called its name, [c]The-LORD-Is-My-
Banner;*
16 for he said, "Because the LORD
has [d]sworn: the LORD *will have* war
with Amalek from generation to generation."

Visit of Jethro, Moses' father-in-law

18 AND [e]Jethro, the priest of
Midian, Moses' father-in-law,
heard of all that God had done for Moses and for Israel His people—that the
LORD had brought Israel out of Egypt.
2 Then Jethro, Moses' father-in-
law, took [f]Zipporah, Moses' wife, after he had sent her [g]back,
3 with her two sons, of whom the
name of one *was* [h]Gershom (for he
said, "I have been a stranger in a foreign land")
4 and the name of the other *was*
[i]Eliezer (for *he said,* "The God of my
father *was* my [j]help, and delivered
me from the sword of Pharaoh");
5 and Jethro, Moses' father-in-
law, came with his sons and his wife to
Moses in the wilderness, where he
was encamped at the [k]mountain of
God.
6 Now he had said to Moses, "I,
your father-in-law Jethro, am coming
to you with your wife and her two sons
with her."
7 So Moses went out to meet his
father-in-law, bowed down, and
[l]kissed him. And they asked each
other about *their* well-being, and they
went into the tent.
8 And Moses told his father-in-law
all that the LORD had done to Pharaoh
and to the Egyptians for Israel's sake,
all the hardship that had come upon
them on the way, and *how* the LORD
had [m]delivered them.
9 Then Jethro rejoiced for all the
[n]good which the LORD had done for

14
a Inspiration: v. 14; Ex. 19:6. (Ex. 4:15; 2 Tim. 3:16, *note*)
15
b Sacrifice (typical): v. 15; Lev. 1:3. (Gen. 3:15; Heb. 10:18, *note*)
c See Gen. 2:3 and 4, *notes*
16
d Cp. Gen. 22:14–16
CHAPTER 18
1
e Ex. 3:1
2
f Ex. 2:21
g Ex. 4:20–26
3
h i.e. *a stranger is there*
4
i i.e. *my God is my help*
j Gen. 49:25

18:5 *k* Ex. 3:1,12; 4:27; 24:13 **18:7** *l* Ex. 4:27
18:8 *m* Ex. 15:6,16 **18:9** *n* Isa. 63:7–14

* **17:15** Hebrew *YHWH Nissi*

[1](17:14) This passage and others in the Pentateuch clearly teach that Moses could write. Cp. Dt. 28:58; 31:24. Ancient writing has been found in Mesopotamia and Egypt from dates long before the time of Moses.

Until the rise of higher criticism, within the last two centuries, it was the belief of the entire Christian world that Moses wrote the Pentateuch. In 1753 a French physician named Jean Astruc advanced the theory that the change from the word "God," in Gen. 1:1—2:4 to the word, "LORD," in the next few chapters indicates that these come from two distinct sources and give a hint as to the sources which Moses used in writing the Pentateuch. After a long process, during which many views were suggested, there developed from this start the Graf-Wellhausen hypothesis, which was presented in 1878 by Julius Wellhausen and came to be accepted by most higher critics.

This theory divides the Pentateuch into a patchwork of various documents, all of them said to have been written many years after the time of Moses and to have been eventually combined into one work by a long procedure, in which a series of redactors (editors) took part. Four main arguments were advanced for this theory: (1) the use of various names for God in different passages; (2) the proposal that each of four principal documents could be read as a complete unit by itself; (3) the claim that there were many repetitions of parallel statements, events, laws, and even individual stories; and (4) the charge that the style of the documents differs widely.

Not one of these claims has been substantiated by careful investigation: (1) Similar alterations of divine names are found in other books whose unity is unquestioned. (2) The alleged continuity of each document proves on careful examination not to be a fact. (3) The so-called parallel passages often record different events. When the same account is repeated twice, there is generally a clear reason why the repetition should occur. And (4) the style of the different alleged documents does not usually vary greatly in the Hebrew. Where there is a striking difference, it is due to the dissimilarity of subject matter.

Archaeology has brought numerous evidences to support a Mosaic authorship, all of which fit with the Bible as it stands, many of them in sharp contradiction to the critical theory of the origin of the documents. Our Lord Jesus Christ personally referred to the Pentateuch as the work of Moses. Christians should follow their Lord in taking these five books as actually the work of this great prophet (Mk. 10:3–5; 12:26; Jn. 5:45–46; cp. Mt. 8:4; 19:8; Mk. 1:44; 7:10; Lk. 5:14; 24:44; Jn. 7:19,22–23). For a related *note*, see Ex. 6:3. Cp. also *notes* at Dt. 31:24; 34:12.

Israel, whom He had delivered out of
the hand of the Egyptians.
10 And Jethro said, "Blessed *be* the
LORD, who has delivered you out of the
hand of the Egyptians and out of the
hand of Pharaoh, *and* who has delivered the people from under the hand
of the Egyptians.
11 "Now I know that the LORD *is*
greater than all the [a]gods; for in the
very thing in which they behaved
proudly, *He was* above them."
12 Then Jethro, Moses' father-in-
law, took* a burnt [b]offering and
other sacrifices *to offer* to God. And
Aaron came with all the elders of Israel to [c]eat bread with Moses' father-
in-law before God.
13 And so it was, on the next day,
that Moses [d]sat to judge the people;
and the people stood before Moses
from morning until evening.
14 So when Moses' father-in-law
saw all that he did for the people, he
said, "What *is* this thing that you are
doing for the people? Why do you
alone sit, and all the people stand before you from morning until evening?"
15 And Moses said to his father-in-
law, "Because the people come to me
to [e]inquire of God.
16 "When they have a [f]difficulty,
they come to me, and I judge between
one and another; and I make known
the statutes of God and His laws."
17 So Moses' father-in-law said to
him, "The thing that you do *is* not
good.
18 "Both you and these people who
are with you will surely wear yourselves out. For this thing *is* too much
for you; you are [g]not able to perform
it by yourself.
19 "Listen now to my voice; I will
give you counsel, and God will be with
you: Stand [h]before God for the people, so that you may [i]bring the difficulties to God.
20 "And you shall [j]teach them the

11
a Ex. 12:12; 15:11
12
b Ex. 24:5
c Gen. 31:54; Dt. 12:7
13
d Dt. 33:4–5; Mt. 23:2
15
e Cp. Dt. 17:8–13
16
f Dt. 19:17
18
g Num. 11:14,17; Dt. 1:12
19
h Ex. 4:16; 20:19
i Num. 9:8; 27:5
20
j Dt. 1:18
21
k Cp. Acts 6:3
l Dt. 1;13, 15; Ps. 15:1–5
m 2 Sam. 23:3; see Ps. 19:9, *note*
22
n Dt. 1:17–18
o Num. 11:17
CHAPTER 19
1
p See Lev. 23:2, *note*
2
q Israel (history): vv. 1–8; Ex. 20:1. (Gen. 12:2; Rom. 11:26, *note*)
r Law (of Moses): vv. 1–25; Ex. 20:1. (Ex. 19:1; Gal. 3:24, *note*)

statutes and the laws, and show them
the way in which they must walk and
the work they must do.
21 "Moreover you shall [k]select
from all the people [l]able men, such as
[m]fear God, men of truth, hating covetousness; and place *such* over them *to*
be rulers of thousands, rulers of hundreds, rulers of fifties, and rulers of
tens.
22 "And let them judge the people
at all times. Then it will be *that* every
great matter they shall [n]bring to you,
but every small matter they themselves shall judge. So it will be easier
for you, for they will [o]bear *the burden*
with you.
23 "If you do this thing, and God *so*
commands you, then you will be able
to endure, and all this people will also
go to their place in peace."
24 So Moses heeded the voice of his
father-in-law and did all that he had
said.
25 And Moses chose able men out
of all Israel, and made them heads
over the people: rulers of thousands,
rulers of hundreds, rulers of fifties,
and rulers of tens.
26 So they judged the people at all
times; the hard cases they brought to
Moses, but they judged every small
case themselves.
27 Then Moses let his father-in-law
depart, and he went his way to his
own land.

III. At Sinai: the Giving of the Law and the Construction of the Tabernacle, 19:1—40:38

Israel arrives at Sinai

19 IN the [p]third month after the
children of [q]Israel had gone
out of the land of Egypt, on the same
day, they [1]came *to* the Wilderness of
[r]Sinai.
2 For they had departed from

*18:12 Following Masoretic Text and Septuagint; Syriac, Targum, and Vulgate read *offered*.

[1](19:1) *The Fifth Dispensation: the Law.* This dispensation began with the giving of the law at Sinai and was brought to its close as a time-era in the sacrificial death of Christ, who fulfilled all its provisions and types. In the previous dispensation, Abraham, Isaac, and Jacob, as well as multitudes of other individuals, failed in the tests of faith and obedience which were made man's responsibility (e.g. Gen. 16:1–4; 26:6–10; 27:1–25). Egypt also failed to heed God's warning (Gen. 12:3) and was judged. God nevertheless provided a deliverer (Moses), a sacrifice (Passover lamb), and miraculous power to bring the Israelites out of Egypt (judgments on Egypt; Red Sea deliverance).

As a result of their transgressions (Gal. 3:19) the Israelites were now placed under the precise discipline of the law. The law teaches: (1) the awesome holiness of God (Ex. 19:10–25); (2) the exceeding sinfulness of sin (Rom. 7:13; 1 Tim. 1:8–10); (3) the necessity of obedience (Jer. 7:23–24); (4) the universality of man's failure (Rom. 3:19–20); and (5) the marvel of God's

[a]Rephidim, had come *to* the Wilderness of Sinai, and camped in the wilderness. So Israel [b]camped there before the mountain.

The Fifth Dispensation: the Law
(Ex. 19:3—Acts 1:26).
The children of Israel tested
at Sinai

3 And Moses went up to God, and
the LORD called to him from the mountain, saying, [1]“Thus you shall say to
the house of Jacob, and tell the children of Israel:

2
a Ex. 17:1
b Cp. Ex. 3:12
4
c Separation: v. 4; Ex. 33:16. (Gen. 12:1; 2 Cor. 6:17, *note*)
5
d Ex. 15:26; 23:22
e Ps. 78:10
f Eight

4 ‘You have seen what I did to the
Egyptians, and *how* I bore you on eagles’ wings and brought you to [c]My-
self.

Fifth, or Mosaic Covenant
(Ex. 19:5, note 3)

5 ‘Now therefore, [2]if you will indeed [d]obey My voice and [e]keep My
[3][f]covenant, then you shall be a [g]spe-

Covenants: vv. 3–8; Dt. 30:3. (Gen. 2:16; Heb. 8:8)
g Lit. *a people for His own possession.* Dt. 7:6; 14:2; 26:18; cp. Ti. 2:14; 1 Pet. 2:9

grace in providing a way of approach to Himself through typical blood sacrifice, looking forward to a Savior who would become the Lamb of God to bear away the sin of the world (Jn. 1:29), “being witnessed by the Law and the Prophets” (Rom. 3:21).

The law did not change the provisions or abrogate the promise of God as given in the Abrahamic Covenant. It was not given as a way to life (i.e. a means of justification, Acts 15:10–11; Gal. 2:16,21; 3:3–9,14,17,21,24–25), but as a rule of living for a people already in the covenant of Abraham and covered by blood sacrifice, e.g. Passover lamb, etc. One of its purposes was to make clear the purity and holiness which should characterize the life of a people with whom the law of the nation was at the same time the law of God (Ex. 19:5–6).

Hence, the law's function in relation to Israel was one of disciplinary restriction and correction (Gal. 3:24), like that exercised over Greek and Roman children by the trusted household slave or tutor, to hold Israel in check for their own good (Dt. 6:24): (1) until Christ should come (Christ is actually our Tutor, for the grace which saves us also teaches us, Gal. 3:24; Ti. 2:11–12); and (2) until the Father's appointed time that the heirs (children of promise) should be removed from a condition of legal minority into the privileges of heirs who have come of age (Gal. 4:1–3). This God did in sending His Son, and believers are now in the position of sons in the Father's house (Gal. 3:26; 4:4–7).

But Israel misinterpreted the purpose of the law (1 Tim. 1:8–10), sought righteousness by good deeds and ceremonial ordinances (Acts 15:1; Rom. 9:31—10:3), and rejected their own Messiah (Jn. 1:10–11). The history of Israel in the wilderness, in the land, and scattered among the nations has been one long record of the violation of the law. For *notes* on the other dispensations, see Innocence (Gen. 1:28); Conscience or Moral Responsibility (Gen. 3:7); Human Government (Gen. 8:15); Promise (Gen. 12:1); Church (Acts 2:1); Kingdom (Rev. 20:4); see also Gen. 1:26 and 11:10, *notes.*

[1](19:3) It is exceedingly important to observe that: (1) the LORD reminded the people that up to then they had been the objects of His free grace; (2) the law is not here proposed as a means of salvation but as a means by which Israel, already redeemed as a nation, might through obedience fulfill her proper destiny as a people for God's possession, a holy nation, and a kingdom of priests; and (3) the law was not imposed until it had been proposed and voluntarily accepted.

[2](19:5) Compare 1 Pet. 2:9; Rev. 1:6; 5:10. What under law was conditional is, under grace, freely given to every believer. The “if” of v. 5 is the essence of law as a method of divine dealing, and the fundamental reason why “the law made nothing perfect” (Heb. 7:18–19; cp. Rom. 8:3). To Abraham the promise preceded the requirement; at Sinai the requirement preceded the promise. In the New Covenant the Abrahamic order is followed (see Heb. 8:8–12, *note*).

[3](19:5) The Mosaic Covenant, given to Israel in three divisions, each essential to the others and together forming the Mosaic Covenant, i.e. the commandments, expressing the righteous will of God (Ex. 20:1–26); the judgments, governing the social life of Israel (Ex. 21:1—24:11); and the ordinances, governing the religious life of Israel (Ex. 24:12—31:18). These three elements form “the law,” as that expression is generically used in the NT (e.g. Mt. 5:17,18). The commandments and the ordinances formed one religious system. The commandments were a “ministry of condemnation” and “death” (2 Cor. 3:7–9); the ordinances gave, in the high priest, a representative of the people with the LORD; and, in the sacrifices, a cover (see Atonement, Lev. 16:6, *note*) for their sins in anticipation of the cross (Heb. 5:1–3; 9:6–9; cp. Rom. 3:25–26). The Christian is not under the conditional Mosaic Covenant of works, the law, but under the unconditional New Covenant of grace (Rom. 3:21–27; 6:14–15; Gal. 2:16; 3:10–14,16–18,24–26; 4:21–31; Heb. 10:11–17). The law did not change the provision of the Abrahamic Covenant but was an added thing for a limited time only—till the Seed should come (Gal. 3:17–19).

For *notes* on other major covenants, see: Edenic (Gen. 2:16); Adamic (Gen. 3:15); Noahic cial treasure to Me above all people; for all the earth *is* [a]Mine.

6 'And you shall be to Me a [1]kingdom of [b]priests and a holy [c]nation.' These *are* the [d]words which you shall speak to the children of Israel."

7 So Moses came and called for the [e]elders of the people, and laid before them all these words which the LORD commanded him.

8 Then all the people answered together and said, [2]"All that the LORD has spoken we will [f]do." So Moses brought back the words of the people to the LORD.

Sinful man made aware of God's unapproachable holiness (vv. 9–24; cp. Rom. 7:7–24)

9 And the LORD said to Moses, "Behold, I come to you in the thick [g]cloud, that the people may hear when I [h]speak with you, and [i]believe you forever." So Moses told the words of the people to the LORD.

10 Then the LORD said to Moses, "Go to the people and consecrate them today and tomorrow, and let them wash their clothes.

11 "And let them be ready for the third day. For on the third day the LORD will come down upon Mount Sinai in the sight of all the people.

12 "You shall set bounds for the people all around, saying, 'Take heed to yourselves *that* you do *not* go up to the mountain or touch its base. Whoever touches the mountain shall surely be put to [j]death.

13 'Not a hand shall touch him, but he shall surely be stoned or shot *with an arrow;* whether man or beast, he shall not live.' When the trumpet sounds long, they shall come near the mountain."

14 So Moses went down from the mountain to the people and sanctified the people, and they washed their clothes.

15 And he said to the people, "Be ready for the third day; do not come near *your* wives."

16 Then it came to pass on the third day, in the morning, that there were thunderings and lightnings, and a thick cloud on the mountain; and the sound of the trumpet was very loud, so that all the people who *were* in the camp trembled.

17 And Moses brought the people out of the camp to meet with God, and they stood at the foot of the mountain.

18 Now Mount Sinai *was* completely in [k]smoke, because the LORD descended upon it in [l]fire. Its smoke ascended like the smoke of a furnace, and the whole mountain* [m]quaked greatly.

19 And when the blast of the trumpet sounded long and became louder and louder, Moses spoke, and God answered him by voice.

20 Then the LORD came down upon Mount Sinai, on the top of the mountain. And the LORD called Moses to the top of the mountain, and Moses went up.

21 And the LORD said to Moses, "Go down and warn the people, lest they break through to gaze at the LORD, and many of them perish.

22 "Also let the [n]priests who come near the LORD [o]consecrate themselves, lest the LORD break out [p]against them."

23 But Moses said to the LORD, "The people cannot come up to Mount Sinai; for You warned us, saying, 'Set [q]bounds around the mountain and [r]consecrate it.' "

24 Then the LORD said to him, "Away! Get down and then come up, you and Aaron with you. But do not let the priests and the people break through to come up to the LORD, lest He break out against them."

25 So Moses went down to the people and spoke to them.

5
a Ex. 9:29
6
b Cp. 1 Pet. 2:5,9; Rev. 1:6; 5:10
c Dt. 26:19
d *Inspiration:* vv. 6–7; Ex. 20:1. (Ex. 4:15; 2 Tim. 3:16, *note*)
7
e Ex. 4:29–30
8
f Ex. 24:3,7; Dt. 5:27
9
g Ex. 19:16; 20:21
h Cp. Jn. 12:29
i *Kingdom* (OT): v. 9; Ex. 24:12. (Gen. 1:26; Zech. 12:8, *note*)
12
j Ex. 34:3; cp. 3:5
18
k Ps. 104:32; 144:5
l Ex. 3:2; Dt. 5:4
m Ps. 68:8; cp. 1 Ki. 19:12
22
n Ex. 24:5
o Lev. 21:6–8
p Lev. 10:1–3
23
q Ex. 19:12
r *Sanctification* (OT): v. 23; Ex. 28:1. (Gen. 2:3; Zech. 8:3)

*19:18 Septuagint reads *all the people.*

(Gen. 9:16); Abrahamic (Gen. 12:2); Palestinian (Dt. 30:3); Davidic (2 Sam. 7:16); New (Heb. 8:8).

[1](19:6) This is the first Biblical occurrence of the word "kingdom" as referring to the divine rule, and marks the beginning of the theocratic kingdom. See *notes* at 1 Sam. 8:7; Zech. 12:8.

[2](19:8) This oral response of the people is commended by the LORD in Dt. 5:27–28: "They are right in all that they have spoken." Their subsequent history, however, shows that they had failed to realize their own spiritual and moral weakness and the infinite perfection of the divine law which they so easily were engaging themselves to obey. See God's lament in Dt. 5:29: "Oh, that they had such a heart in them that they would fear Me and always keep all My commandments."

The [1]*Law: (1) the Ten Commandments*

20 AND God [a]spoke all these [b]words, [2c]saying:

2 "I *am* the LORD your God, who brought you out of the land of Egypt, out of the house of bondage.

3 "You shall have no other gods before Me.

4 "You shall not make for yourself a carved image—any likeness *of anything* that *is* in heaven above, or that *is* in the earth beneath, or that *is* in the water under the earth;

5 you shall not bow down to them nor serve them. For I, the LORD your God, *am* a jealous God, visiting the iniquity of the fathers upon the children to the third and fourth *generations* of those who hate Me,

6 but showing mercy to thousands, to those who love Me and keep My commandments.

7 "You shall not take the name of the LORD your God in vain, for the LORD will not hold *him* guiltless who takes His name in vain.

8 "Remember the [d]Sabbath day, to keep it holy.

9 Six days you shall labor and do all your work,

10 but the seventh day *is* the Sabbath of the LORD your God. *In it* you shall do no work: you, nor your son, nor your daughter, nor your male servant, nor your female servant, nor your cattle, nor your stranger who *is* within your gates.

11 For *in* six days the LORD made the heavens and the earth, the sea, and all that *is* in them, and rested the seventh day. Therefore the LORD blessed the Sabbath day and hallowed it.

12 [e]"Honor your father and your mother, that your days may be [f]long upon the land which the LORD your God is giving you.

13 [g]"You shall not [3]murder.

14 [h]"You shall not commit [i]adultery.

15 "You shall not [j]steal.

16 "You shall not bear false witness against your [k]neighbor.

17 "You shall not [l]covet your neighbor's house; you shall not covet your neighbor's [m]wife, nor his male servant, nor his female servant, nor his ox, nor his donkey, nor anything that *is* your neighbor's."

CHAPTER 20

1

a Law (of Moses): vv. 1–17; Ex. 31:18. (Ex. 19:1; Gal. 3:24, *note*)

b Inspiration: v. 1; Ex. 24:3. (Ex. 4:15; 2 Tim. 3:16, *note*)

c Israel (history): vv. 1–17; Ex. 40:1. (Gen. 12:2; Rom. 11:26, *note*)

8

d Sabbath: vv. 8–11; Ex. 31:13. (Gen. 2:3; Mt. 12:1, *note*)

12

e Mt. 15:4; 19:19; Mk. 7:10; Eph. 6:2,3

f Dt. 5:33

13

g Mt. 5:21; 19:18; Mk. 10:19; Lk. 18:20

14

h Mt. 5:27; Mk. 10:19; Lk. 18:20; Rom. 13:9; Jas. 2:11

i Lev. 20:10

20:15 *j* Mt. 19:18; Mk. 10:19; Lk. 18:20; Rom. 13:9 **20:16** *k* Lev. 19:18 **20:17** *l* Cp. Rom. 7:7; 13:9 *m* Cp. 2 Sam. 11:2

[1](20:1, heading) There are six important factors that should be borne in mind about the law: (1) the origin and source of the law—God (Ex. 31:18; Acts 7:53); (2) the avenue of the bestowal of the law—Moses and angels (Jn. 1:17; Gal. 3:19; Heb. 2:2); (3) the nature of the law—(a) not grace (Rom. 10:5; Gal. 3:10; Heb. 10:28), (b) holy, just, good, and spiritual (Rom. 7:12,14), and (c) a unit (Jas. 2:10–11); (4) the effects of the law—(a) declares all men guilty (Rom. 3:19), (b) justifies no one (Rom. 3:20), (c) cannot impart righteousness or life (Gal. 3:21), (d) makes offenses abound (Rom. 5:20; 7:7–13; 1 Cor. 15:56), and (e) served as a tutor until Christ (Gal. 3:24); (5) the relation of the believer to the law—(a) is not saved by law (Gal. 2:21), (b) does not live under law (Rom. 6:14; 8:4), but (c) stands and grows in grace (Rom. 5:2; 2 Pet. 3:18); and (6) the recipients of the law—Israel alone (Ex. 20:2). Some of the laws of the Decalogue are written in the hearts of men everywhere, are found in legal codes of other ancient nations, and are of universal application.

[2](20:1) There is a threefold giving of the law: (1) Orally. In 20:1–17 ten commandments are given. They are followed by judgments concerning the relations of Hebrew with Hebrew (21:1—23:13), to which are added directions for keeping three annual feasts (23:14–19), and instructions for the conquest of Canaan (23:20–33). These words Moses communicates to the people (24:3–8). Immediately, in the persons of their elders, they are admitted to the fellowship of God (24:9–11). (2) Moses is then called up to receive the tablets of stone (24:12–18). The story then divides. Moses, on the mount, receives the gracious instructions concerning the tabernacle, priesthood, and sacrifice (chs. 25—31). Meantime the people, led by Aaron, break the first commandment (ch. 32). Moses, returning, breaks the tablets "written with the finger of God" (31:18; 32:16–19). And (3) the second tablets are made by Moses and the law is again written by the hand of the LORD (34:1,28–29; Dt. 10:4).

[3](20:13) The Hebrew language employs several words to express the idea, *to kill.* The verb used here is a special word which can only mean *murder* and always indicates intentional slaying.

The effect on the people

18 Now all the people witnessed the
thunderings, the lightning flashes, the
sound of the trumpet, and the mountain smoking; and when the people
saw *it,* they trembled and stood [a]afar
[b]off.
19 Then they said to Moses, "You
speak with us, and we will hear; but let
not God speak with us, lest we [c]die."
20 And Moses said to the people,
"Do not fear; for God has come to
[d]test you, and that His [e]fear may be
before you, so that you may not sin."
21 So the people stood afar off, but
Moses drew near the thick darkness
where God *was.*
22 Then the LORD said to Moses,
"Thus you shall say to the children of
Israel: 'You have seen that I have
[f]talked with you from heaven.
23 'You shall not make *anything to
be* with Me—gods of silver or gods of
gold you shall not make for yourselves.

Gracious provision for sacrifices

24 'An altar of [g]earth you shall
make for Me, and you shall sacrifice
on it your burnt offerings and your
peace offerings, your sheep and your
oxen. In every place where I [h]record
My name I will come to you, and I will
bless you.
25 'And if you make Me an altar of
stone, you shall not build it of [i]hewn
stone; for if you [j]use your tool on it,
you have profaned it.
26 'Nor shall you go up by steps to
My altar, that your [k]nakedness may
not be exposed on it.'

The Law: (2) the judgments:
master and servant relationship

21 "NOW these *are* the [l]judg-
ments which you shall set before them:
2 "If you buy a [m]Hebrew servant,
he shall serve six years; and in the
seventh he shall go out free and pay
nothing.
3 "If he comes in by himself, he
shall go out by himself; if he *comes in*
married, then his wife shall go out
with him.
4 "If his master has given him a
wife, and she has borne him sons or
daughters, the wife and her children
shall be her master's, and he shall go
out by himself.
5 "But if the servant plainly says, 'I
love my master, my wife, and my children; I will not go out free,'
6 "then his master shall bring him
to the [n]judges. He shall also bring him
to the door, or to the doorpost, and his
master shall pierce his [o]ear with an
awl; and he shall serve him forever.
7 "And if a man sells his daughter
to be a female slave, she shall not go
out as the male slaves do.
8 "If she does not please her master, who has betrothed her to himself,
then he shall let her be redeemed. He
shall have no right to sell her to a foreign people, since he has dealt deceitfully with her.
9 "And if he has betrothed her to
his son, he shall deal with her according to the custom of daughters.
10 "If he takes another *wife,* he
shall not diminish her food, her clothing, and her marriage rights.
11 "And if he does not do these
three for her, then she shall go out
free, without *paying* money.

The judgments: personal injuries

12 "He who strikes a man so that he
dies shall surely be put to [p]death.
13 "However, if he did not lie in
wait, but God delivered *him* into his
hand, then I will appoint for you a
[q]place where he may flee.
14 "But if a man acts with premedi-
tation against his neighbor, to kill him
by treachery, you shall [r]take him
from My altar, that he may die.
15 "And he who strikes his father or
his mother shall surely be put to
death.
16 "He who [s]kidnaps a man and
sells him, or if he is found in his hand,
shall surely be put to death.
17 "And he who curses his father or
his mother shall surely be put to
death.
18 "If men contend with each other,
and one strikes the other with a stone
or with *his* fist, and he does not die but
is confined to *his* bed,
19 "if he rises again and walks
about outside with his staff, then he
who struck *him* shall be acquitted. He
shall only pay *for* the loss of his time,
and shall provide *for him* to be thoroughly healed.
20 "And if a man beats his male or
female servant with a rod, so that he
dies under his hand, he shall surely be
punished.
21 "Notwithstanding, if he remains
alive a day or two, he shall not be punished; for he *is* his [t]property.
22 "If men fight, and hurt a woman
with child, so that she gives birth pre-

18
a For contrast between law and grace cp. Lk. 1:10; Eph. 2:13; with Heb. 10:19–22
b Ex. 19:16
19
c Dt. 5:5, 23–27; 18:16; Heb. 12:19
20
d *Test/tempt:* v. 20; Num. 14:22. (Gen. 3:1; Jas. 1:14, *note*)
e See Ps. 19:9, *note*
22
f Dt. 5:24; 18:18
24
g Ex. 27:1–8
h Dt. 12:5
25
i Dt. 27:5–6
j Josh. 8:30–31; cp. Eph. 2:8–9
26
k Ex. 28:42–43
CHAPTER 21
1
l Ex. 24:3
2
m Lev. 25:39–43; Dt. 15:12–18; Jer. 34:8–14
6
n Ex. 22:8–9
o Cp. Ps. 40:6–8; Heb. 10:5–7
12
p Gen. 9:6
13
q See Num. 35:6, *note*
14
r 1 Ki. 2:29
16
s Dt. 24:7
21
t Lev. 25:44–46

maturely, yet no harm follows, he
shall surely be punished accordingly
as the woman's husband imposes on
him; and he shall pay as the [a]judges
determine.
23 "But if *any* harm follows, then
you shall give life for life,
24 [b]"eye for eye, tooth for tooth,
hand for hand, foot for foot,
25 "burn for burn, wound for
wound, stripe for stripe.
26 "If a man strikes the eye of his
male or female servant, and destroys
it, he shall let him go free for the sake
of his eye.
27 "And if he knocks out the tooth
of his male or female servant, he shall
let him go free for the sake of his
tooth.
28 "If an [c]ox gores a man or a
woman to death, then the ox shall
surely be stoned, and its flesh shall not
be eaten; but the owner of the ox *shall
be* acquitted.
29 "But if the ox tended to thrust
with its horn in times past, and it has
been made known to his owner, and
he has not kept it confined, so that it
has killed a man or a woman, the ox
shall be stoned and its owner also
shall be put to death.
30 "If there is imposed on him a
sum of money, then he shall pay to
redeem his life, whatever is imposed
on him.
31 "Whether it has gored a son or
gored a daughter, according to this
judgment it shall be done to him.
32 "If the ox gores a male or female
servant, he shall give to their master
[d]thirty [e]shekels of silver, and the ox
shall be stoned.
33 "And if a man opens a pit, or if a
man digs a pit and does not cover it,
and an ox or a donkey falls in it,
34 "the owner of the pit shall make
it good; he shall give money to their
owner, but the dead *animal* shall be
his.
35 "If one man's ox hurts another's,
so that it dies, then they shall sell the
live ox and divide the money from it;
and the dead *ox* they shall also divide.
36 "Or if it was known that the ox
tended to thrust in time past, and its
owner has not kept it confined, he
shall surely pay ox for ox, and the
dead animal shall be his own.

The judgments: property rights

22 "IF a man steals an ox or a
sheep, and slaughters it or sells

22
a Ex. 18:21–22
24
b Lev. 24:20; Dt. 19:21; cp. Mt. 5:38–44; 1 Pet. 2:19–21
28
c Gen. 9:5
32
d Cp. Zech. 11:12; Mt. 26:15
e See Coinage (OT), Ex. 30:13, *note;* cp. 2 Chr. 2:10, *note*
CHAPTER 22
1
f Lk. 19:8
g 2 Sam. 12:6
2
h Job 24:16
7
i Lev. 6:1–7
8
j Ex. 21:6, 22; Dt. 17:8–9; 19:17
11
k Heb. 6:16
13
l Cp. Gen. 31:39

it, he shall [f]restore five oxen for an ox
and [g]four sheep for a sheep.
2 "If the thief is found [h]breaking
in, and he is struck so that he dies,
there shall be no guilt for his bloodshed.
3 "If the sun has risen on him,
there shall be guilt for his bloodshed.
He should make full restitution; if he
has nothing, then he shall be sold for
his theft.
4 "If the theft is certainly found
alive in his hand, whether it is an ox or
donkey or sheep, he shall restore double.
5 "If a man causes a field or vineyard to be grazed, and lets loose his
animal, and it feeds in another man's
field, he shall make restitution from
the best of his own field and the best
of his own vineyard.
6 "If fire breaks out and catches in
thorns, so that stacked grain, standing
grain, or the field is consumed, he who
kindled the fire shall surely make restitution.
7 "If a man [i]delivers to his neighbor money or articles to keep, and it is
stolen out of the man's house, if the
thief is found, he shall pay double.
8 "If the thief is not found, then the
master of the house shall be brought
to the [j]judges *to see* whether he has
put his hand into his neighbor's
goods.
9 "For any kind of trespass,
whether it concerns an ox, a donkey,
a sheep, or clothing, *or* for any kind of
lost thing which *another* claims to be
his, the cause of both parties shall
come before the judges; *and* whomever the judges condemn shall pay
double to his neighbor.
10 "If a man delivers to his neighbor a donkey, an ox, a sheep, or any
animal to keep, and it dies, is hurt, or
driven away, no one seeing *it,*
11 "*then* an [k]oath of the LORD shall
be between them both, that he has not
put his hand into his neighbor's
goods; and the owner of it shall accept
that, and he shall not make *it* good.
12 "But if, in fact, it is stolen from
him, he shall make restitution to the
owner of it.
13 "If it is [l]torn to pieces *by a beast,
then* he shall bring it as evidence, *and*
he shall not make good what was torn.
14 "And if a man borrows *anything*
from his neighbor, and it becomes injured or dies, the owner of it not *being*
with it, he shall surely make *it* good.
15 "If its owner *was* with it, he shall

not make *it* good; if it *was* hired, it came for its hire.

The judgments: crimes against humanity

16 "If a man entices a virgin who is not betrothed, and lies with her, he shall surely pay the bride-price for her *to be* his wife.

17 "If her father utterly refuses to give her to him, he shall pay money according to the [a]bride-price of virgins.

18 "You shall not permit a [b]sorceress to live.

19 "Whoever lies with an [c]animal shall surely be put to death.

20 "He who [d]sacrifices to *any* [e]god, except to the LORD only, he shall be utterly destroyed.

21 "You shall neither mistreat a [f]stranger nor oppress him, for you were strangers in the land of Egypt.

22 "You shall not [g]afflict any widow or fatherless child.

23 "If you afflict them in any way, *and* they cry at all to Me, I will surely [h]hear their cry;

24 "and My wrath will become hot, and I will [i]kill you with the sword; your wives shall be widows, and your children fatherless.

25 "If you lend money to *any of* My people *who are* poor among you, you shall not be like a moneylender to him; you shall not charge him [j]interest.

26 "If you ever take your neighbor's garment as a [k]pledge, you shall return it to him before the sun goes down.

27 "For that *is* his only covering, it *is* his garment for his skin. What will he sleep in? And it will be that when he cries to Me, I will hear, for I *am* [l]gracious.

28 "You shall not revile [m]God, nor [n]curse a [o]ruler of your people.

29 "You shall not delay *to offer* the first of your ripe [p]produce and your juices. The [q]firstborn of your sons you shall give to Me.

30 "Likewise you shall do with your oxen *and* your sheep. It shall be with its mother seven days; on the eighth day you shall give it to Me.

31 "And you shall be [r]holy men to Me: you shall not eat meat torn *by* [s]*beasts* in the field; you shall throw it to the dogs.

23

"YOU shall not circulate a false report. Do not put your hand with the wicked to be an unrighteous [t]witness.

2 "You shall not follow a crowd to do evil; nor shall you testify in a dispute so as to turn aside after many to pervert *justice*.

3 "You shall not show partiality to a [u]poor man in his dispute.

4 "If you meet your enemy's ox or his donkey going astray, you shall surely bring it back to him again.

5 "If you see the donkey of one who hates you lying under its burden, and you would refrain from helping it, you shall surely help him with it.

6 "You shall not pervert the judgment of your poor in his dispute.

7 "Keep yourself far from a false matter; do not kill the innocent and righteous. For I will not justify the wicked.

8 "And you shall take no bribe, for a bribe blinds the discerning and perverts the words of the righteous.

9 "Also you shall not oppress a [f]stranger, for you know the heart of a stranger, because you were strangers in the land of Egypt.

The judgments: the land and the Sabbath

10 "Six years you shall sow your land and gather in its produce,

11 "but the seventh *year* you shall let it rest and lie fallow, that the poor of your people may eat; and what they leave, the beasts of the field may eat. In like manner you shall do with your vineyard *and* your olive grove.

12 "Six days you shall do your work, and on the seventh day you shall rest, that your ox and your donkey may rest, and the son of your female servant and the stranger may be refreshed.

13 "And in all that I have said to you, be circumspect and make no mention of the name of other [v]gods, nor let it be heard from your mouth.

Three national feasts: Unleavened Bread; Firstfruits; Ingathering

14 [w]"Three times you shall keep a feast to Me in the year:

15 "You shall keep the Feast of [x]Unleavened Bread (you shall eat unleavened bread seven days, as I commanded you, at the time appointed in the month of [y]Abib, for in it you came out of Egypt; none shall appear before Me empty);

16 "and the Feast of [z]Harvest, the

---

17 *a* Cp. Gen. 34:12; 1 Sam.18:25
18 *b* Lev. 20:27; Dt. 18:10–11; cp. 1 Sam. 28:3–10
19 *c* Lev. 20:15–16; Dt. 27:21
20 *d* Ex. 32:8; 34:15; Lev. 17:7 *e* Dt. 13:6–16
21 *f* Dt. 14:29
22 *g* Dt. 24:17–18
23 *h* Dt. 10:17–18; Prov. 23:10–11; Jer. 7:6
24 *i* Ps. 10:14, 18; 68:5
25 *j* Lev. 25:35–37; Dt. 23:19–20; Neh. 5:1–13
26 *k* Dt. 24:6, 10–13
27 *l* Ex. 34:6–7
28 *m* Heb. *Elohim.* Lev. 24:15–16 *n* Eccl.10:20 *o* Acts 23:5
29 *p* Ex. 23:16, 19; Dt. 26:2–11 *q* Ex. 13:12, 15
31 *r* Ex. 19:6; Lev. 11:44–47 *s* Lev. 17:15
CHAPTER 23
1 *t* Ex. 20:16; Dt. 19:16–21
3 *u* v. 6; Dt. 1:17
13 *v* Josh. 23:7; Ps. 16:4
14 *w* Cp. Lev.

23:4–44, where provision for feasts in promised land is made **23:15** *x Leaven:* vv. 15,18; Ex. 29:2. (Gen. 19:3; Mt. 13:33, *note*) *y* See Lev. 23:2, *note*
23:16 *z* Ex. 34:22

firstfruits of your labors which you have sown in the field; and the Feast of Ingathering at the end of the year, when you have gathered in *the fruit of* your labors from the field.

17 [a]"Three times in the year all your males shall appear before the Lord GOD.*

18 "You shall not offer the blood of My sacrifice with leavened [b]bread; nor shall the fat of My sacrifice remain until morning.

19 "The first of the firstfruits of your land you shall bring into the house of the LORD your God. You shall not boil a young goat in its mother's milk.

Instructions and promises concerning conquest of the land

20 "Behold, I send an [c]Angel before you to keep you in the way and to bring you into the place which I have [d]prepared.

21 "Beware of Him and obey His voice; do not provoke Him, for He will not pardon your transgressions; for My name *is* in Him.

22 "But if you indeed obey His voice and do all that I speak, then I will be an enemy to your enemies and an adversary to your adversaries.

23 "For My Angel will go before you and bring you in to the Amorites and the [e]Hittites and the Perizzites and the Canaanites and the Hivites and the Jebusites; and I will cut them off.

24 "You shall not [f]bow down to their gods, nor serve them, nor do according to their works; but you shall utterly [g]overthrow them and completely break down their *sacred* pillars.

25 "So you shall [h]serve the LORD your God, and He will [i]bless your bread and your water. And I will take [j]sickness away from the midst of you.

26 "No one shall suffer miscarriage or be barren in your land; I will fulfill the number of your days.

27 "I will send My [k]fear before you, I will [l]cause confusion among all the people to whom you come, and will make all your enemies turn *their* backs to you.

28 "And I will send [m]hornets before you, which shall drive out the Hivite, the Canaanite, and the Hittite from before you.

29 "I will not drive them out from before you in one year, lest the land become desolate and the beasts of the field become too numerous for you.

30 "Little by little I will drive them out from before you, until you have increased, and you inherit the land.

31 "And I will set your bounds from the Red Sea to the sea, Philistia, and from the desert to the [n]River. For I will deliver the inhabitants of the land into your hand, and you shall drive them out before you.

32 "You shall make no covenant with them, nor with their gods.

33 "They shall not dwell in your land, lest they make you sin against Me. For *if* you serve their gods, it will surely be a snare to you."

Order of worship before building the tabernacle

24

NOW He said to Moses, "Come up to the LORD, you and Aaron, [o]Nadab and Abihu, and [p]seventy of the elders of Israel, and worship from afar.

2 "And Moses alone shall come near the LORD, but they shall not come near; nor shall the people go up with him."

People acknowledge the covenant: their worship

3 So Moses came and told the people all the [q]words of the LORD and all the judgments. And all the people answered with one voice and said, "All the words which the LORD has said we will do."

4 And Moses wrote all the words of the LORD. And he rose early in the morning, and [r]built an altar at the foot of the mountain, and twelve pillars according to the twelve tribes of Israel.

5 Then he sent young men of the children of Israel, who offered [s]burnt offerings and sacrificed peace offerings of oxen to the LORD.

6 And Moses took half the blood and put *it* in basins, and half the blood he sprinkled on the [t]altar.

7 Then he took the [u]Book of the Covenant and read in the hearing of the people. And they said, "All that the LORD has said we will do, and be obedient."

8 And Moses took the blood, sprinkled *it* on the people, and said, "This is the [v]blood of the covenant

17
a Cp. Lev. 23:4–44, where provision for feasts in promised land is made
18
b Ex. 34:25–26
20
c *Angel* (of the LORD): vv. 20–23; Ex. 32:34. (Gen. 16:7; Jud. 2:1, *note*)
d Ex. 13:5
23
e See 2 Ki. 7:6, *note*
24
f Ex. 20:5
g Ex. 34:13; Num. 33:52
25
h Dt. 6:13; Mt. 4:10
i Dt. 7:13–16
j Ex. 15:26
27
k Ex. 15:16
l Dt. 7:23
28
m Dt. 7:20; Josh. 24:12
31
n i.e. *the Euphrates*
CHAPTER 24
1
o Ex. 6:23; Lev. 10:1–2
p Num. 11:16
3
q *Inspiration:* vv. 3–4, 7–8,12; Ex. 32:16. (Ex. 4:15; 2 Tim. 3:16, *note*)
4
r Cp. Ex. 33:7–11. This arrangement for worship was temporarily called the "tabernacle"
5
s Ex. 18:12; 20:24
6
t Ex. 29:16, 20
7
u v. 4

24:8 *v* Heb. 9:20; cp. Mt. 26:28; Mk. 14:24; Lk. 22:20; 1 Cor. 11:25

*
23:17 Hebrew *YHWH*, usually translated LORD

which the LORD has made with you according to all these words."

Moses ascends Mount Sinai

9 Then Moses went up, also Aaron, Nadab, and Abihu, and seventy of the elders of Israel,

10 and they [a]saw the God of Israel. And *there was* under His feet as it were a paved work of sapphire stone, and it was like the very heavens in *its* clarity.

11 But on the nobles of the children of Israel He did not lay His hand. So they saw God, and they [b]ate and drank.

12 Then the LORD said to Moses, "Come up to Me on the mountain and be there; and I will give you tablets of stone, and the law and commandments which I have written, that [c]you may teach them."

13 So Moses arose with his assistant Joshua, and Moses went up to the mountain of God.

14 And he said to the elders, "Wait here for us until we come back to you. Indeed, Aaron and [d]Hur *are* with you. If any man has a difficulty, let him go to them."

15 Then Moses went up into the mountain, and a [e]cloud covered the mountain.

16 Now the [f]glory of the LORD rested on Mount Sinai, and the cloud covered it six days. And on the seventh day He called to Moses out of the midst of the cloud.

17 The sight of the glory of the LORD *was* like a consuming [g]fire on the top of the mountain in the eyes of the children of Israel.

18 So Moses went into the midst of the cloud and went up into the mountain. And Moses was on the mountain forty days and forty nights.

Moses on the mount.
The tabernacle

25 THEN [1]the LORD spoke to Moses, saying:

2 "Speak to the children of Israel, that they bring Me an offering. From everyone who gives it [h]willingly with his heart you shall take My offering.

Materials for the tabernacle

3 "And this *is* the offering which you shall take from them: gold, silver, and bronze;

4 "blue, purple, and scarlet *thread,* fine linen, and goats' *hair;*

5 "ram skins dyed red, badger skins, and acacia wood;

6 "oil for the light, and spices for the anointing oil and for the sweet incense;

7 "onyx stones, and stones to be set in the [i]ephod and in the breastplate.

8 "And let them make Me a sanctuary, that I may [j]dwell among them.

9 "According to all that I show you, *that is,* the pattern of the [2]tabernacle and the pattern of all its furnishings, just so you shall make *it.*

Ark of the Testimony

10 "And they shall [k]make an [3]ark

10
a See Jn. 1:18, *note*
11
b Symbol of fellowship on the basis of blood sacrifice. Cp. v. 8; Heb. 9:19–22; 1 Jn. 1:7
12
c *Kingdom (OT):* v. 12; Num. 24:17. (Gen. 1:26; Zech. 12:8, *note*)
14
d Ex. 17:10, 12
15
e Ex. 19:9, 16
16
f Ex. 33:18
17
g Dt. 4:24; 9:3; Heb. 12:29
CHAPTER 25
2
h See 2 Cor. 8:1, *note*
7
i See Ex. 29:5, *note*
8
j Ex. 29:45–46
10
k vv. 10–20; cp. Ex. 37:1–9

[1](25:1) The general authority for the types of Exodus is found: (1) as to the persons and events, in 1 Cor. 10:1–11; and (2) as to the tabernacle, in Heb. 9:1–24. Having the assurance that the tabernacle and its furnishings are typical, the details of necessity must be received as typical also. But since there is no explicit NT reference for the meaning of some of them, the significance in such instances is based on spiritual analogy. See Gen. 2:23, *note.* The typical meanings of the materials and colors of the tabernacle are believed to be as follows: gold, Deity in manifestation—divine glory; silver, redemption (see Ex. 26:19, *note;* 30:11–16; 38:27); bronze, symbol of judgment, as in the bronze altar and in the bronze serpent (Num. 21:6–9); blue, heavenly in nature or origin; purple, royalty; scarlet, sacrifice.

[2](25:9) The tabernacle, speaking comprehensively, is explained in the NT as typical in three ways: (1) of the Church as a habitation of God through the Spirit (v. 8; Eph. 2:19–22); (2) of the believer (2 Cor. 6:16); and (3) as a figure of things in the heavens (Heb. 9:23–24). In detail, all speak of Christ: (1) The ark, in its materials, acacia wood and gold, is a type of the humanity and Deity of Christ (see Ex. 26:15, *note*). (2) In its contents, the ark is a type of Christ, as: (a) having God's law in His heart (Ex. 25:16); (b) the wilderness food (or portion) of His people (Ex. 16:33); and (c) Himself the resurrection, of which Aaron's rod is the symbol (Num. 17:10; Heb. 9:4). And (3) in its use the ark, especially the mercy seat, is a type of God's throne. That it was, to the sinning Israelite, a throne of grace and not of judgment was due to the mercy seat formed of gold and sprinkled with the blood of atonement, which vindicated the law, and the divine holiness guarded by the cherubim (Gen. 3:24; Ezek. 1:5, *note*). See Sacrifice of Atonement, Rom. 3:25, *note.*

[3](25:10) The long history of the ark of the Testimony begins at Mount Sinai where the ark was built. Throughout its history the ark contained the tablets of the Law (1 Ki. 8:9) and for

of acacia wood; two and a half [a]cubits *shall be* its length, a cubit and a half its width, and a cubit and a half its height.

11 "And you shall overlay it with pure gold, inside and out you shall overlay it, and shall make on it a molding of [b]gold all around.

12 "You shall cast four rings of gold for it, and put *them* in its four corners; two rings *shall be* on one side, and two rings on the other side.

13 "And you shall make poles *of* acacia wood, and overlay them with gold.

14 "You shall put the poles into the rings on the sides of the ark, that the ark may be carried by them.

15 "The poles shall be in the rings of the ark; they shall not be [c]taken from it.

16 "And you shall put into the ark the [d]Testimony which I will give you.

17 "You shall make a [e]mercy seat of pure gold; two and a half cubits *shall be* its length and a cubit and a half its width.

18 "And you shall make two [f]cherubim of gold; of hammered work you shall make them at the two ends of the mercy seat.

19 "Make one cherub at one end, and the other cherub at the other end; you shall make the cherubim at the two ends of it *of one piece* with the mercy seat.

20 "And the cherubim shall [g]stretch out *their* wings above, covering the mercy seat with their wings, and they shall face one another; the faces of the cherubim *shall be* toward the mercy seat.

21 "You shall put the mercy seat on top of the ark, and in the ark you shall put the Testimony that I will give you.

22 "And there I will [h]meet with you, and I will speak with you from above the mercy seat, from [i]between the two cherubim which *are* on the ark of the Testimony, about everything which I will give you in commandment to the children of Israel.

Table of showbread

23 "You shall also [j]make a [k]table of acacia wood; two cubits *shall be* its length, a cubit its width, and a cubit and a half its height.

24 "And you shall overlay it with pure gold, and make a molding of gold all around.

25 "You shall make for it a frame of a handbreadth all around, and you shall make a gold molding for the frame all around.

26 "And you shall make for it four rings of gold, and put the rings on the four corners that *are* at its four legs.

27 "The rings shall be close to the frame, as holders for the poles to bear the table.

28 "And you shall make the poles of acacia wood, and overlay them with gold, that the table may be carried with them.

29 "You shall make its dishes, its pans, its pitchers, and its bowls for pouring. You shall make them of pure gold.

30 "And you shall [l]set the [1]showbread on the table before Me always.

10 [a] See Weights and Measures (OT), 2 Chr. 2:10, *note*
11 [b] Ex. 37:2
15 [c] Num. 4:6
16 [d] Heb. 9:4
17 [e] See Rom. 3:25, *note*
18 [f] See Ezek. 1:5, *note*
20 [g] 1 Ki. 8:6–7; Heb. 9:5
22 [h] Ex. 29:42–43; [i] Num. 7:89
23 [j] Ex. 37:10–16; [k] Ex. 26:35
30 [l] Lev. 24:5–9

---

a time also the golden pot containing manna and Aaron's rod (Heb. 9:4). The ark ordinarily was kept in the Most Holy of the tabernacle. During the journeys of the Israelites it was carried by the priests or the Kohathites of the tribe of Levi (Num. 3:30–31). After Solomon built the temple, it was kept there (1 Ki. 8:6–9). The ark accompanied the children of Israel on their journeys through the wilderness; at Jericho it preceded their army (Josh. 6). The ark's frequent mention in Scripture testifies to its prominence in Israel (Num. 3:31; 10:33; Josh. 3:3–17; 6:4; Jud. 20:27; 1 Sam. 3:3; 4:1–11; 5:1–11; 6:1–21; 7:1–2; 2 Sam. 6:2–17; 7:2; 15:24–29; 1 Ki. 8:1–21).

The description of the furnishings of the tabernacle begins with the ark which, as already stated, was placed in the Most Holy; because in revelation God begins from Himself, working outward toward man, as in approach the worshiper begins from himself, moving toward God in the Most Holy. The same order is followed in the Levitical offerings (Lev. 1—5). In approach man begins at the bronze altar, a type of the cross where, in the fire of judgment, atonement is made.

[1](25:30) "The showbread," a type of Christ, the Bread of God, nourisher of the Christian's life as a believer-priest (1 Pet. 2:9; Rev. 1:6). In Jn. 6:33–58 our Lord has more in mind the manna, that food which "comes down from heaven"; but all typical meanings of bread are there gathered into His words. The manna is the life-giving Christ; the showbread, the life-sustaining Christ. The showbread typifies Christ as the "grain of wheat" (Jn. 12:24) ground in the mill of suffering (Jn. 12:27) and brought into the fire of judgment (Jn. 12:31–33). We, as priests, by faith feed upon Him as having undergone that in our stead and for our sakes. We are fed by meditation upon Christ, as in Heb. 12:2–3.

Golden lampstand

31 "You shall also [a]make a [1b]lamp-
stand of pure gold; the lampstand
shall be of hammered work. Its shaft,
its branches, its bowls, its *ornamental*
knobs, and flowers shall be *of one*
piece.
32 "And six branches shall come
out of its sides: three branches of the
lampstand out of one side, and three
branches of the lampstand out of the
other side.
33 "Three bowls *shall be* made like
almond *blossoms* on one branch, *with*
an *ornamental* knob and a flower, and
three bowls made like almond *blos-*
soms on the other branch, *with* an *or-*
namental knob and a flower—and so
for the six branches that come out of
the lampstand.
34 "On the lampstand itself four
bowls *shall be* made like almond *blos-*
soms, each with its *ornamental* knob
and flower.
35 "And *there shall be* a knob under
the *first* two branches of the same, a
knob under the *second* two branches
of the same, and a knob under the
third two branches of the same, according to the six branches that extend from the lampstand.
36 "Their knobs and their branches
shall be of one piece; all of it *shall be*
one hammered piece of pure gold.
37 "You shall make seven lamps for
it, and they shall arrange its lamps so
that they give light in front of it.
38 "And its wick-trimmers and
their trays *shall be* of pure gold.
39 "It shall be made of a [c]talent of
pure gold, with all these utensils.
40 "And see to it that you make
them according to the [d]pattern which
was shown you on the mountain.

Curtains of linen

26 "MOREOVER you shall [e]make
the tabernacle *with* ten curtains *of* [2]fine woven linen, and blue,
purple, and scarlet *thread;* with artistic designs of [f]cherubim you shall
weave them.
2 "The length of each curtain *shall*
be twenty-eight [g]cubits, and the width
of each curtain four cubits. And every
one of the curtains shall have the
same measurements.
3 "Five curtains shall be coupled
to one another, and *the other* five curtains *shall be* coupled to one another.
4 "And you shall make loops of
blue *yarn* on the edge of the curtain on
the selvedge of *one* set, and likewise
you shall do on the outer edge of *the*
other curtain of the second set.
5 "Fifty loops you shall make in
the one curtain, and fifty loops you
shall make on the edge of the curtain
that *is* on the end of the second set,
that the loops may be clasped to one
another.
6 "And you shall make fifty clasps
of gold, and couple the curtains together with the clasps, so that it may
be one tabernacle.

Curtains of goats' hair

7 "You shall also make curtains of
goats' *hair,* to be a tent over the tabernacle. You shall make eleven curtains.
8 "The length of each curtain *shall*
be thirty cubits, and the width of each
curtain four cubits; and the eleven
curtains shall all have the same measurements.
9 "And you shall couple five curtains by themselves and six curtains
by themselves, and you shall double
over the sixth curtain at the forefront
of the tent.
10 "You shall make fifty loops on
the edge of the curtain that is outermost in *one* set, and fifty loops on the
edge of the curtain of the second set.
11 "And you shall make fifty
bronze clasps, put the clasps into the
loops, and couple the tent together,
that it may be one.
12 "The remnant that remains of
the curtains of the tent, the half curtain that remains, shall hang over the
back of the tabernacle.
13 "And a cubit on one side and a
cubit on the other side, of what remains of the length of the curtains of
the tent, shall hang over the sides of
the tabernacle, on this side and on that
side, to cover it.

Covering of ram skins

14 "You shall also make a covering

31
a vv. 31–39; cp. Ex. 37:17–24
b Cp. Rev. 1:12,13,20
39
c See Coinage (OT), Ex. 30:13, *note;* cp. 2 Chr. 2:10, *note*
40
d Ex. 25:9; 26:30; Heb. 8:5
CHAPTER 26
1
e vv. 1–37; cp. Ex. 36:8–38
f See Ezek. 1:5, *note*
2
g See Weights and Measures (OT), 2 Chr. 2:10, *note*

[1](25:31) Lampstand, a type of Christ our Light (Jn. 1:4,9; 8:12; 9:5) shining in the fullness of the power of the sevenfold Spirit (Isa. 11:2; Heb. 1:9; Rev. 1:4). Natural light was excluded from the tabernacle. Cp. 1 Cor. 2:14–15.

[2](26:1) Fine linen typifies personal righteousness (Rev. 19:8). Here it speaks of the sinless life of Christ. Observe the three colors: (1) blue, signifying Christ's heavenly origin; (2) purple, suggesting His royalty as David's Son; and (3) scarlet, indicative of His sacrificial blood shed for mankind.

DIAGRAM OF THE TABERNACLE

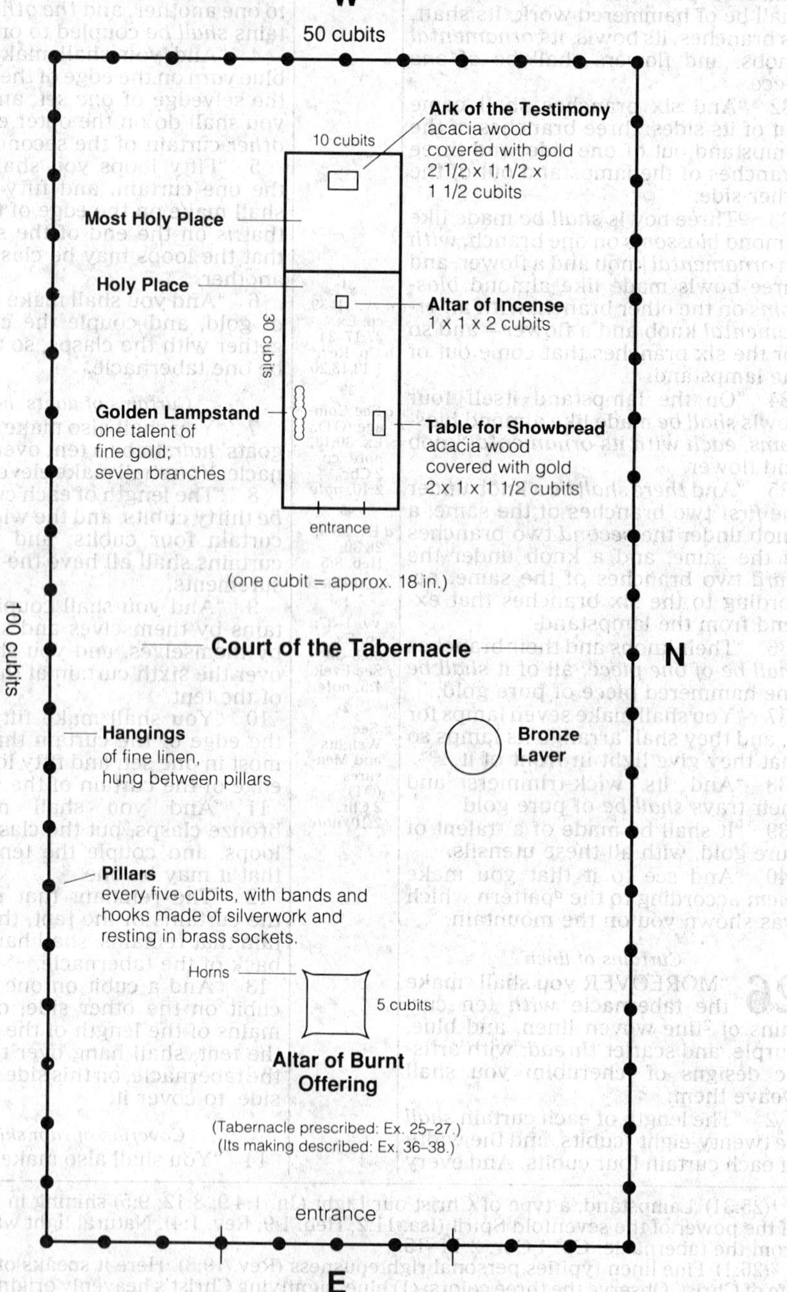
W
50 cubits
Ark of the Testimony
acacia wood
covered with gold
2 1/2 x 1 1/2 x
1 1/2 cubits
10 cubits
Most Holy Place
Holy Place
Altar of Incense
1 x 1 x 2 cubits
30 cubits
Golden Lampstand
one talent of
fine gold;
seven branches
Table for Showbread
acacia wood
covered with gold
2 x 1 x 1 1/2 cubits
entrance
(one cubit = approx. 18 in.)
S
100 cubits
Court of the Tabernacle
N
Hangings
of fine linen,
hung between pillars
Bronze
Laver
Pillars
every five cubits, with bands and
hooks made of silverwork and
resting in brass sockets.
Horns
5 cubits
Altar of Burnt
Offering
(Tabernacle prescribed: Ex. 25–27.)
(Its making described: Ex. 36–38.)
entrance
E

of [a]ram skins dyed red for the tent,
and a covering of badger skins above
that.

Boards and sockets

15 "And for the tabernacle you
shall [b]make the [1]boards of acacia
wood, standing upright.
16 "Ten cubits *shall be* the length of
a board, and a cubit and a half *shall be*
the width of each board.
17 "Two tenons *shall be* in each
board for binding one to another.
Thus you shall make for all the boards
of the tabernacle.
18 "And you shall make the boards
for the tabernacle, twenty boards for
the south side.
19 "You shall make forty sockets of
[2]silver under the twenty boards: two
sockets under each of the boards for
its two tenons.
20 "And for the second side of the
tabernacle, the north side, *there shall
be* twenty boards
21 "and their forty sockets of silver:
two sockets under each of the boards.
22 "For the far side of the tabernacle, westward, you shall make six
boards.
23 "And you shall also make two
boards for the two back corners of the
tabernacle.
24 "They shall be coupled together
at the bottom and they shall be coupled together at the top by one ring.
Thus it shall be for both of them. They
shall be for the two corners.
25 "So there shall be eight boards
with their sockets of silver—sixteen
sockets—two sockets under each of
the boards.
26 "And you shall make bars of
acacia wood: five for the boards on
one side of the tabernacle,
27 "five bars for the boards on the
other side of the tabernacle, and five
bars for the boards of the side of the
tabernacle, for the far side westward.
28 "The [c]middle bar shall pass
through the midst of the boards from
end to end.

Overlay of gold

29 "You shall overlay the boards
with gold, make their rings of gold *as*
holders for the bars, and overlay the
bars with gold.
30 "And you shall raise up the tabernacle according to its [d]pattern
which you were shown on the mountain.

Veil

31 "You shall [e]make a [3f]veil woven of blue, purple, and scarlet *thread,*
and fine woven linen. It shall be woven with an artistic design of cherubim.
32 "You shall hang it upon the four
pillars of acacia *wood* overlaid with

14
a Ex. 35:7, 23; 36:19; 39:34
15
b Ex. 36:20–34
28
c Ex. 36:33
30
d Ex. 25:9, 40; 27:8; 39:32; Num. 8:4; Acts 7:44; Heb. 8:2,5
31
e Ex. 36:35–38
f Ex. 27:21; Mt. 27:51; Heb. 9:3; 10:20

[1](26:15) The typical meaning of the boards is clear as to Christ. Acacia wood, a desert growth, is a fitting symbol of Christ in His humanity as "a root out of dry ground" (Isa. 53:2). The covering, gold, typifying Deity in manifestation, speaks of His divine glory. As applied to the individual believer, the meaning of the boards is less clear. The connection may be found in Jn. 17:21–23; Eph. 1:4,6; 1 Jn. 4:13. Only as seen in Him could the boards be taken as representing the believer. So viewed the type is beautiful. In the world, and yet separated from it by the silver of redemption (Ex. 30:11–16; 38:25–27; Gal. 1:4) as the boards of the tabernacle were separated from the earth by the sockets of silver, and united by the middle bar (v. 28), representing both one life (Gal. 2:20) and one Spirit (Eph. 4:3), "the whole building, being fitted together, grows into a holy temple in the Lord" (Eph. 2:21).

[2](26:19) In Bible times, silver was variously used for money, jewelry, and idols. In the construction of the tabernacle God told Moses to collect from every Israelite a redemption price in silver of half a shekel (Ex. 30:11–16), which is described as "atonement money" to be used "to make atonement for yourselves" (Ex. 30:16). The silver collected in this way was used for the sockets of the sanctuary, and for the bands and hooks (see Ex. 25:1, *note;* cp. 26:15, *note*). Thus the tabernacle rested upon silver sockets; the curtains of the door, the way of access, were suspended from silver bands and hooks (see Ex. 27:17, *note*). The silver paid as atonement money was only a token payment; ultimately, the price of redemption had to be paid by Christ with the shedding of His own blood (1 Pet. 1:18–19).

[3](26:31) The inner veil, a type of Christ's human body (Mt. 26:26; 27:50; Heb. 10:20). This veil, barring entrance into the Most Holy, was the most expressive symbol of the truth that "by the deeds of the law no flesh will be justified in His sight" (Rom. 3:20; Heb. 9:8). Torn by an unseen hand when Christ died (Mt. 27:51), thus giving instant access to God to all who come by faith in His Son, it was the end of all legality; the way to God was open. It is deeply significant that the priests must have replaced the veil that God had rent, for the temple services went on for nearly forty years. That substitute veil is Galatianism—the attempt to put the believer back under law (cp. Gal. 1:6–9). Anything but "the grace of Christ" is "a different gospel," and under anathema.

gold. Their hooks *shall be* gold, upon four sockets of silver.

33 "And you shall hang the veil from the clasps. Then you shall bring the ark of the [a]Testimony in there, behind the veil. The veil shall be a divider for you between the holy *place* and the Most Holy.

34 "You shall put the [b]mercy seat upon the ark of the Testimony in the Most Holy.

35 "You shall set the table [c]outside the veil, and the lampstand across from the table on the side of the tabernacle toward the south; and you shall put the table on the north side.

Screen

36 "You shall make a screen for the door of the tabernacle, *woven of* blue, purple, and scarlet *thread,* and fine woven linen, made by a weaver.

37 "And you shall make for the screen five pillars of acacia *wood,* and overlay them with gold; their hooks *shall be* gold, and you shall cast five sockets of bronze for them.

Bronze altar

27 "YOU shall [d]make an [1]altar of acacia [2]wood, five cubits long and five cubits wide—the altar shall be square—and its [3]height *shall be* three [e]cubits.

2 "You shall make its horns on its four corners; its horns shall be of one piece with it. And you shall overlay it with [4]bronze.

3 "Also you shall make its pans to receive its ashes, and its shovels and its basins and its forks and its firepans; you shall make all its utensils of bronze.

4 "You shall make a grate for it, a network of bronze; and on the network you shall make four bronze rings at its four corners.

5 "You shall put it under the rim of the altar beneath, that the network may be midway up the altar.

6 "And you shall make poles for the altar, poles of acacia wood, and overlay them with bronze.

7 "The poles shall be put in the rings, and the poles shall be on the two sides of the altar to bear it.

8 "You shall make it hollow with boards; as it was shown you on the mountain, [f]so shall they make *it.*

Court of the tabernacle

9 "You shall also [g]make the court of the tabernacle. For the south side *there shall be* hangings for the court *made of* [5]fine woven linen, one hundred [e]cubits long for one side.

10 "And its twenty pillars and their twenty sockets *shall be* bronze. The hooks of the pillars and their bands *shall be* silver.

11 "Likewise along the length of the north side *there shall be* hangings one hundred *cubits* long, with its twenty pillars and their twenty sockets of [h]bronze, and the hooks of the pillars and their bands of silver.

12 "And along the width of the court on the west side *shall be* hangings of fifty cubits, with their ten pillars and their ten sockets.

13 "The width of the court on the east side *shall be* fifty cubits.

14 "The hangings on *one* side *of the gate shall be* fifteen cubits, *with* their three pillars and their three sockets.

15 "And on the other side *shall be* hangings of fifteen *cubits, with* their three pillars and their three sockets.

Gate of the court

16 "For [6]the gate of the court *there shall be* a screen twenty cubits long, *woven of* blue, purple, and scarlet *thread,* and fine woven linen, made by

33 [a] Ex. 25:10–16
34 [b] Ex. 25:17–22
35 [c] Ex. 25:23–30
CHAPTER 27
1 [d] vv. 1–8; cp. Ex. 38:1–7
[e] vv. 11–16, 18. See Weights and Measures (OT), 2 Chr. 2:10, *note*
8 [f] Ex. 26:30
9 [g] vv. 9–19; cp. Ex. 38:9–20
11 [h] See Num. 21:9, *note*

[1](27:1) Bronze altar, a type of the cross upon which Christ, our whole burnt offering, "offered Himself without spot to God" (Heb. 9:14).

[2](27:1) The wood, as a symbol of Christ's humanity (see Ex. 26:15, *note*) and enclosed here in bronze, must have become completely charred by the sacrificial fires. Cp. Heb. 10:5–7.

[3](27:1) Compare Ex. 25:10. The altar of burnt offering is double the height of the mercy seat. The atonement more than saves us; it glorifies God (Jn. 17:4).

[4](27:2) Compare Num. 21:9; where see *note,* and Jn. 3:14 with Jn. 12:31–33, thus fixing the symbolic meaning of bronze as *divine manifestation in judgment.*

[5](27:9) The fine linen commonly typifies personal righteousness (see Ex. 26:1, *note*), and in the hangings of the court suggests that measure of righteousness which God demands of any who would, in his own righteousness, approach Him. Christ, figuratively speaking, put up the hangings of the court in Lk. 10:25–28. The only way of approach was the "gate of the court" (v. 16, and *note;* Jn. 10:9). The hangings of the court exclude equally the self-righteous man and the open sinner, for the height was above seven feet (v. 18).

[6](27:16) In the hangings of the court (see v. 9, *note*), representing that practical righteousness which God demands in the law and which, therefore, excludes all men (Rom. 3:19–20;

a weaver. It *shall have* four pillars and
four sockets.
17 "All the [1]pillars around the court
shall have bands of silver; their
[a]hooks *shall be* of silver and their
sockets of [b]bronze.
18 "The length of the court *shall be*
one hundred cubits, the width fifty
throughout, and the height five cubits,
made of fine woven linen, and its
sockets of bronze.
19 "All the utensils of the tabernacle for all its service, all its pegs, and
all the pegs of the court, *shall be* of
bronze.

Oil for the lamp

20 "And you shall command the
children of Israel that they bring you
pure [2c]oil of pressed olives for the
light, to cause the lamp to burn continually.
21 "In the tabernacle of meeting,
outside the veil which *is* before the
[d]Testimony, Aaron and his sons shall
tend it from evening until morning before the LORD. *It shall be* a [e]statute
forever to their generations on behalf
of the children of Israel.

The Law: (3) the priesthood

28 "NOW take [3f]Aaron your
brother, and his sons with him,
from [g]among the children of Israel,
that he may minister to Me as [h]priest,
Aaron *and* Aaron's sons: [i]Nadab,
Abihu, [j]Eleazar, and Ithamar.
2 "And you shall make holy [k]gar-
ments for Aaron your brother, for
glory and for beauty.
3 "So you shall speak to all *who
are* gifted artisans, whom I have filled
with the [l]spirit of wisdom, that they
may make Aaron's garments, to consecrate him, that he may minister to
Me as priest.
4 "And these *are* the garments
which they shall make: a breastplate,
an [k]ephod, a [m]robe, a skillfully woven
[n]tunic, a [k]turban, and a [o]sash. So
they shall make holy garments for
Aaron your brother and his sons, that
he may minister to Me as priest.
5 "They shall [p]take the gold, blue,
purple, and scarlet *thread*, and the
fine linen,

The ephod

6 "and they shall [q]make the ephod
of gold, blue, purple, *and* scarlet
thread, and fine woven linen, artistically worked.
7 "It shall have two shoulder
straps joined at its two edges, and *so*
it shall be joined together.
8 "And the intricately woven band
of the ephod, which *is* on it, shall be of
the same workmanship, *made of* gold,

17
a Ex. 38:19
b See Num. 21:9, *note*
20
c Ex. 35:8, 28; Lev. 24:1–4
21
d Ex. 16:34; 25:16; 30:6,36
e Ex. 12:14–17; 29:42
CHAPTER 28
1
f Num. 3:10
g Sanctification (OT): vv. 1–3; Ex. 29:37. (Gen. 2:3; Zech. 8:3)
h Ps. 99:6; Heb. 5:4
i Ex. 24:1,9; Lev. 10:1
j Ex. 6:23; Lev. 10:6, 16
2
k See Ex. 29:5, *note*
3
l Holy Spirit (OT): v. 3; Ex. 31:3. (Gen. 1:2; Zech. 12:10)
4
m Ex. 28:31–34 *n* Ex. 28:39–40 *o* Lev. 8:7 **28:5** *p* See Ex. 26:1, *note* **28:6** *q* vv. 6–14, cp. Ex. 39:2–7

10:3–5), there are no colors. But the "gate" is Christ (Jn. 10:9), and so the colors reappear, as in the veil (Ex. 26:31).

[1](27:17) The bands and hooks upholding the linen hangings were of silver (see 26:19, *note*), for it is in virtue of Christ's redemptive work that He is our way of access, and not by virtue of His righteous life (symbolized by the fine linen); but the pillars of the court rested upon bronze sockets, not silver as in the case of the boards; and bronze symbolizes divine manifestation in judgment (v. 2; see Num. 21:9, *note*). Redemption not only displays God's mercy but vindicates His righteousness in showing that mercy (Rom. 3:21–26).

[2](27:20) Oil is a symbol of the Holy Spirit (cp. Zech. 4:2–6 [v. 2, *note*] and Jn. 3:34 with Heb. 1:9. See Acts 2:4, *note*). In Christ the oil-fed light ever burns, the Light of the world (Jn. 8:12). But here there is not the world but the sanctuary. It is a question not of testimony in and to the world, but of our communion and worship as believer-priests in the Holiest (Heb. 10:19–20). In the tabernacle there were two compartments, two lights: (1) the holy place with the lampstand (see Ex. 25:31, *note*); and (2) the Most Holy with the Shekinah, or manifested glory of God. These two places are now one (Mt. 27:50–51; Heb. 9:6–8; 10:19–22), but it is important to see that there are still two lights: (1) Christ, the Light of life (Jn. 1:4), through the Spirit giving light upon the holy things of God, the showbread and altar of incense; and (2) the Shekinah, now, on the face of Jesus Christ (2 Cor. 4:6). Into this twofold light we, as believer-priests, are brought (1 Pet. 2:9). We "walk in the light," not merely which He gives but in which He lives (1 Jn. 1:7). But what of the command here to bring pure oil? It is because our access, apprehension, communion, and transformation are by the Spirit (Eph. 2:18; cp. 1 Cor. 2:14–15; 2 Cor. 3:18; 13:14; Phil. 2:1). Our title to His presence is the blood (Eph. 2:13), but only as we are filled with the Spirit (Eph. 5:18) do we really walk in the light.

[3](28:1) Aaron and his sons typify Christ and believers of the Church age. Aaron is a type of Christ as our High Priest. Christ is a priest after the order of Melchizedek (Heb. 7) but He executes His priestly office after the pattern of Aaron (Heb. 9). See Gen. 14:18–20 (see v. 18, *note 4*). Aaron's sons are a type of believer-priests of the Church age (Rev. 1:6; cp. 1 Pet. 2:9, where see *note*).

blue, purple, and scarlet *thread,* and fine woven linen.

9 "Then you shall take two onyx [a]stones and engrave on them the names of the sons of Israel:

10 "six of their names on one stone and six names on the other stone, in order of their [b]birth.

11 "With the work of an [c]engraver in stone, *like* the engravings of a signet, you shall engrave the two stones with the names of the sons of Israel. You shall set them in settings of gold.

12 "And you shall put the two stones on the shoulders of the ephod *as* memorial stones for the sons of Israel. So Aaron shall [d]bear their names before the LORD on his two [e]shoulders as a memorial.

13 "You shall also make settings of gold,

14 "and you shall make two chains of pure gold like braided cords, and fasten the braided chains to the settings.

The breastplate

15 "You shall [f]make the breastplate of judgment. Artistically woven according to the workmanship of the ephod you shall make it: of gold, blue, purple, and scarlet *thread,* and fine woven linen, you shall make it.

16 "It shall be doubled into a square: a [g]span *shall be* its length, and a span *shall be* its width.

17 "And you shall put settings of stones in it, four rows of stones: *The first* row *shall be* a sardius, a topaz, and an emerald; *this shall be* the first row;

18 "the second row *shall be* a turquoise, a sapphire, and a diamond;

19 "the third row, a jacinth, an agate, and an amethyst;

20 "and the fourth row, a beryl, an onyx, and a jasper. They shall be set in gold settings.

21 "And the stones shall have the names of the sons of Israel, twelve according to their names, *like* the engravings of a signet, each one with its own name; they shall be according to the twelve tribes.

22 "You shall make chains for the breastplate at the end, like braided cords of pure gold.

23 "And you shall make two rings of gold for the breastplate, and put the two rings on the two ends of the breastplate.

24 "Then you shall put the two braided *chains* of gold in the two rings which are on the ends of the breastplate;

25 "and the *other* two ends of the two braided *chains* you shall fasten to the two settings, and put them on the shoulder straps of the ephod in the front.

26 "You shall make two rings of gold, and put them on the two ends of the breastplate, on the edge of it, which is on the inner side of the ephod.

27 "And two *other* rings of gold you shall make, and put them on the two shoulder straps, underneath the ephod toward its front, right at the seam above the intricately woven band of the ephod.

28 "They shall bind the breastplate by means of its rings to the rings of the ephod, using a blue cord, so that it is above the intricately woven band of the ephod, and so that the breastplate does not come loose from the ephod.

29 "So Aaron shall [h]bear the names of the sons of Israel on the breastplate of judgment over his [i]heart, when he goes into the holy *place,* as a memorial before the LORD continually.

Urim and Thummim

30 "And you shall put in the breastplate of judgment the [1]Urim and the Thummim, and they shall be over Aaron's heart when he goes in before the LORD. So Aaron shall bear the judgment of the children of Israel over his heart before the LORD continually.

Robe of the ephod

31 "You shall [j]make the [k]robe of the ephod all of blue.

32 "There shall be an opening for his head in the middle of it; it shall have a woven binding all around its opening, like the opening in a coat of mail, so that it does not tear.

33 "And upon its hem you shall

9 *a* Ex. 35:27
10 *b* Gen. 29:31; 30:13, 16–24; 35:16–18
11 *c* Ex. 35:35
12 *d* Ex. 28:29–30 *e* i.e. *the place of strength.* Isa. 9:6; Lk. 15:4–5
15 *f* vv. 15–28, cp. Ex. 39:8–21
16 *g* See Weights and Measures (OT), 2 Chr. 2:10, *note*
29 *h* Ex. 28:12 *i* i.e. *the place of affection.* Cp. vv. 9–12
31 *j* vv. 15–28, cp. Ex. 39:22–26 *k* See Ex. 29:5, *note*

[1](28:30) Urim and Thummim mean *lights and perfections.* Some make these to be simply a collective name for the stones of the breastplate, so that the total effect of the twelve stones is to manifest the lights and the perfections of Him who is the antitype of the Aaronic high priest. Cp. Lev. 8:8. It would seem to be conclusive that the Urim and the Thummim are additional to the stones of the breastplate. In use the Urim and the Thummim were connected, in some way not clearly expressed, with the ascertainment of the divine will in particular cases (Num. 27:21; Dt. 33:8; 1 Sam. 28:6; Ezra 2:63).

make pomegranates of blue, purple,
and scarlet, all around its hem, and
bells of gold between them all around:
34 "a golden bell and a pomegranate, a golden bell and a pomegranate,
upon the hem of the robe all around.
35 "And it shall be upon Aaron
when he ministers, and its sound will
be heard when he goes into the holy
place before the LORD and when he
comes out, that he may not die.

The holy turban

36 "You shall also [a]make a plate of
pure gold and engrave on it, *like* the
engraving of a signet:

HOLINESS TO THE LORD.

37 "And you shall put it on a blue
cord, that it may be on the turban; it
shall be on the front of the turban.
38 "So it shall be on Aaron's forehead, that Aaron may [b]bear the iniquity of the holy things which the children of Israel hallow in all their holy
gifts; and it shall always be on his
forehead, that they may be accepted
before the LORD.

Priestly garments

39 "You shall skillfully [c]weave the
tunic of fine linen *thread,* you shall
make the turban of fine linen, and you
shall make the sash of woven work.
40 "For Aaron's sons you shall
make tunics, and you shall make
sashes for them. And you shall make
hats for them, for glory and [d]beauty.

36
[a] vv. 36–38, cp. Ex. 39:30–31
38
[b] i.e. *be responsible for every neglect or offense respecting "the holy things"*
39
[c] Ex. 35:35; 39:27–29
40
[d] Ex. 28:2
41
[e] Ex. 29:8–9
[f] Ex. 19:22; 29:21,44
42
[g] Ex. 39:28
43
[h] Ex. 20:26
CHAPTER 29
1
[i] Cp. Heb. 7:26–28
[j] See Lev. 1:3, *note*
2
[k] *Leaven:* vv. 2,23; Ex. 34:18. (Gen. 19:3; Mt. 13:33, *note*)
[l] Lev. 6:19–23
[m] See Ex. 25:30 and Lev. 2:1, *notes*

41 "So you shall put them on Aaron
your brother and on his [e]sons with
him. You shall anoint them, consecrate them, and [f]sanctify them, that
they may minister to Me as priests.
42 "And you shall make for them
linen [g]trousers to cover their nakedness; they shall reach from the waist
to the thighs.
43 "They shall be on Aaron and on
his sons when they come into the tabernacle of meeting, or when they
[h]come near the altar to minister in the
holy *place,* that they do not incur iniquity and die. *It shall be* a statute forever to him and his descendants after
him.

Consecration of priests

29 "AND this is what you shall do
to them to hallow them for ministering to Me as priests: [i]Take one
young [j]bull and two rams without
blemish,
2 "and [k]unleavened [l]bread, unleavened [m]cakes mixed with oil, and
unleavened wafers anointed with oil
(you shall make them of wheat flour).
3 "You shall put them in one basket and bring them in the basket, with
the bull and the two rams.
4 "And [1]Aaron and his sons you
shall bring to the door of the tabernacle of meeting, and you shall [2n]wash
them with water.
5 "Then you shall take the [3]gar-

29:4 [n] Ex. 40:12

[1](29:4) Aaron shares in the washing (i.e. symbol of regeneration, Ti. 3:5; Jn. 3:5–6): (1) as needing it, being in this in contrast with Christ (Heb. 7:26–28); and (2) to typify Christ's action, who received the baptism of John, not as needing it but as thus identifying Himself with sinners, and as fulfilling the Aaronic type. As in Aaron's case, His anointing followed the washing (vv. 4,7; Mt. 3:14–16).

[2](29:4) Distinguish this washing from the use of the laver (Ex. 30:18–21). The washing here typifies regeneration (Ti. 3:5); the laver, daily cleansing (1 Jn. 1:9). See both in Jn. 13:10.

[3](29:5) The high priest's garments were put on in reverse order of the instructions for making them:

(1) The tunic (Ex. 28:39), an oriental long garment worn next to the person, made of fine linen (see Ex. 27:9, *note*).

(2) The robe of the ephod (Ex. 28:31–35), a long seamless garment of blue linen with an opening for the head, worn over the tunic. Pomegranates, symbol of fruitfulness, were embroidered on the skirt of the robe in blue, purple, and scarlet, alternated with golden bells, a symbol of testimony, which gave a sound as the high priest went in and out of the sanctuary. The robe was secured by an embroidered sash.

(3) The ephod (Ex. 28:6–30; 39:1–21; Lev. 8:7–8), a short outer garment. It was "of gold, blue, purple, and scarlet thread, and fine woven linen" (Ex. 28:6). It consisted of two pieces, front and back, united by two shoulder straps and by a band about the bottom. Two onyx stones, set in gold and engraved with the names of the twelve tribes of Israel, were on the shoulders (Ex. 28:7,12,27).

(4) The breastplate, fastened by golden chains to the shoulder pieces of the ephod. It was composed of a square pouch that held the Urim and the Thummim, and an oblong gold setting containing twelve precious stones (four rows, three stones in each row) upon which were engraved the names of the tribes of Israel, one on each stone (Ex. 28:15–21,29–30). As the Urim and the Thummim were in certain cases connected in some way with discovering the

ments, put the tunic on Aaron, and the
robe of the ephod, the ephod, and the
breastplate, and gird him with the intricately woven band of the ephod.
6 "You shall put the turban on his
head, and put the holy crown on the
turban.
7 "And you shall take the anointing [a]oil, pour *it* on his head, and
anoint him.
8 "Then you shall bring his [b]sons
and put tunics on them.
9 "And you shall [c]gird them with
sashes, Aaron and his sons, and put
the hats on them. The priesthood shall
be theirs for a perpetual [d]statute. So
you shall [e]consecrate Aaron and his
sons.

Sacrifices of consecration

10 "You shall also have the bull
brought before the tabernacle of
meeting, and Aaron and his sons shall
[f]put their hands on the head of the
bull.
11 "Then you shall kill the bull before the LORD, *by* the door of the tabernacle of meeting.
12 "You shall take *some* of the
blood of the bull and put *it* on the
horns of the altar with your finger,
and [g]pour all the blood beside the
base of the altar.
13 "And you shall take all the [h]fat
that covers the entrails, the fatty lobe
attached to the liver, and the two kidneys and the fat that *is* on them, and
burn *them* on the altar.
14 "But the flesh of the bull, with its
skin and its offal, you shall burn with
fire [i]outside the camp. It *is* a sin offering.
15 "You shall also take one ram,
and Aaron and his sons shall put their
hands on the head of the ram;
16 "and you shall kill the ram, and
you shall take its blood and [j]sprinkle
it all around on the altar.
17 "Then you shall cut the ram in

7 *a* Ex. 25:6; 30:25–31; Ps. 133:2
8 *b* Ex. 28:40
9 *c* A symbol of service. Lk. 12:37; 17:8; Jn. 13:4; Rev. 1:13
d Num. 3:10
e Ex. 28:41
10 *f* See Lev. 1:4, *note*
12 *g* Lev. 4:7
13 *h* Lev. 1:8
14 *i* See Lev. 4:12, *note*
16 *j* Ex. 24:6; Lev. 1:5,11
18 *k* Ex. 20:24
21 *l* Cp. Lev. 8:23–24
24 *m* Cp. Lev. 8:27

pieces, wash its entrails and its legs,
and put *them* with its pieces and with
its head.
18 "And you shall burn the whole
ram on the altar. It *is* a [k]burnt offering
to the LORD; it *is* a sweet aroma, an
offering made by fire to the LORD.
19 "You shall also take the other
ram, and Aaron and his sons shall put
their hands on the head of the ram.
20 "Then you shall kill the ram, and
take some of its blood and put *it* on the
tip of the right ear of Aaron and on the
tip of the right ear of his sons, on
the thumb of their right hand and on
the big toe of their right foot, and sprinkle the blood all around on the altar.
21 "And you shall take some of the
blood that is on the altar, and some of
the anointing oil, and [l]sprinkle *it* on
Aaron and on his garments, on his
sons and on the garments of his sons
with him; and he and his garments
shall be [e]hallowed, and his sons and
his sons' garments with him.
22 "Also you shall take the fat of the
ram, the fat tail, the fat that covers the
entrails, the fatty lobe *attached to* the
liver, the two kidneys and the fat on
them, the right thigh (for it *is* a ram of
consecration),
23 "one loaf of bread, one cake
made with oil, and one wafer from the
basket of the unleavened bread that *is*
before the LORD;
24 "and you shall put all these in the
[m]hands of Aaron and in the hands of
his sons, and you shall wave them *as*
a wave offering before the LORD.
25 "You shall receive them back
from their hands and burn *them* on
the altar as a burnt offering, as a sweet
aroma before the LORD. It *is* an offering made by fire to the LORD.

Food of the priests

26 "Then you shall take the breast
of the ram of Aaron's consecration
and wave it *as* a wave offering before

---

will of God (see Ex. 28:30, *note*), so the ephod, with its attachments, was apparently employed for the same purpose (1 Sam. 23:9–12; 30:7–8).

Although they would hardly have been precisely like the high priest's ephod, it is recorded that linen ephods were worn by Samuel (1 Sam. 2:18), the priests at Nob (1 Sam. 22:18), and David (2 Sam. 6:14).

Our Lord, as our great High Priest (Heb. 3:1; 5:10; 7:26; 9:11), now represents us before God (Rom. 8:33–34; Heb. 7:25; 9:24; 1 Jn. 2:1–2; cp. Isa. 49:16), bearing our names before Him as the high priest of old carried the names of the tribes of Israel upon his shoulders and on the breastplate.

(5) The turban of fine linen (Ex. 28:37) to cover the head, bearing upon the front a gold plate engraved: HOLINESS TO THE LORD (v. 36).

(6) Linen trousers, "from the waist to the thighs" (Ex. 28:42). The tunic and trousers were made for the priests also, and were the ordinary garments of high priest and priests as distinguished from other garments, which were "for glory and for beauty" (Ex. 28:2).

the LORD; and it shall be your [a]portion.

27 "And from the ram of the consecration you shall consecrate the breast of the wave offering which is waved, and the thigh of the heave offering which is raised, of *that* which *is* for Aaron and of *that* which is for his sons.

28 "It shall be from the children of Israel *for* Aaron and his sons by a statute forever. For it is a heave offering; it shall be a heave offering from the children of Israel from the sacrifices of their [b]peace offerings, *that is*, their heave offering to the LORD.

29 "And the [c]holy garments of Aaron shall [d]be his sons' after him, to be [e]anointed in them and to be consecrated in them.

30 "That son who becomes priest in his place shall put them on for seven days, when he enters the tabernacle of meeting to minister in the holy *place*.

31 "And you shall take the ram of the consecration and boil its flesh in the holy place.

32 "Then Aaron and his sons shall eat the flesh of the ram, and the bread that *is* in the basket, *by* the door of the tabernacle of meeting.

33 "They shall eat those things with which the [1]atonement was made, to consecrate *and* to sanctify them; but an [f]outsider shall not eat *them*, because they *are* holy.

34 "And if any of the flesh of the consecration offerings, or of the bread, remains until the morning, then you shall burn the [g]remainder with fire. It shall not be eaten, because it *is* holy.

35 "Thus you shall do to Aaron and his sons, according to all that I have commanded you. Seven days you shall consecrate them.

36 "And you shall offer a bull every day *as* a sin offering for [h]atonement. You shall cleanse the altar when you make atonement for it, and you shall [i]anoint it to [j]sanctify it.

37 "Seven days you shall make atonement for the altar and [k]sanctify it. And the altar shall be most holy. Whatever touches the altar must be holy.*

The continual burnt offering

38 "Now this *is* what you shall offer on the altar: two lambs of the first year, day by day [l]continually.

39 "One lamb you shall offer in the morning, and the other lamb you shall offer at twilight.

40 "With the one lamb shall be one-tenth *of an ephah* of flour mixed with one-fourth of a [m]hin of pressed oil, and one-fourth of a hin of wine *as* a drink offering.

41 "And the other lamb you shall offer at twilight; and you shall offer with it the grain offering and the drink offering, as in the morning, for a sweet aroma, an offering made by fire to the LORD.

42 "*This shall be* a continual burnt offering throughout your generations *at* the door of the tabernacle of meeting before the LORD, where I will [n]meet you to speak with you.

43 "And there I will meet with the children of Israel, and *the tabernacle* shall be sanctified by My [o]glory.

44 "So I will consecrate the tabernacle of meeting and the altar. I will also consecrate both Aaron and his sons to minister to Me as priests.

45 "I will [p]dwell among the children of Israel and will [q]be their God.

46 "And they shall [r]know that I *am* the LORD their God, who [s]brought them up out of the land of Egypt, that I may dwell among them. I *am* the LORD their God.

The Law: (4) the tabernacle: its use; altar of incense

30 "YOU shall [t]make an altar to burn [2]incense on; you shall make it of acacia wood.

2 "A [m]cubit *shall be* its length and a cubit its width—it shall be square—

---

26 [a] Lev. 7:31–34; 8:29
28 [b] Lev. 3:1
29 [c] Ex. 28:2 [d] Num. 20:28 [e] Ex. 28:41; 30:30
33 [f] Ex. 12:43; Lev. 22:10
34 [g] Ex. 12:10; 23:18; 34:25
36 [h] See v. 33, *note* [i] Ex. 30:26–29 [j] Ex. 40:10–11
37 [k] *Sanctification* (OT): vv. 37,44; Ex. 30:30. (Gen. 2:3; Zech. 8:3)
38 [l] Num. 28:3–31; 29:6–38
40 [m] See Weights and Measures (OT), 2 Chr. 2:10, *note*
42 [n] Ex. 25:22; 33:7,9
43 [o] Ex. 40:34
45 [p] Ex. 25:8; Dt. 12:11 [q] Gen. 17:8; Lev. 11:45
46 [r] Ex. 16:12; Dt. 4:35 [s] Lev. 11:45
CHAPTER 30
1 [t] vv. 1–5, cp. Ex. 37:25–29

*
29:37 Compare Numbers 4:15 and Haggai 2:11–13

---

[1](29:33) Hebrew *kaphar, to propitiate, to atone for sin.* According to Scripture the sacrifice of the law only covered the offerer's sin and secured the divine forgiveness. The OT sacrifices never *removed* man's sin; it was "not possible that the blood of bulls and goats could take away sins" (Heb. 10:4). The Israelite's offering implied confession of sin and recognized its due penalty as death; and God passed over his sin in anticipation of Christ's sacrifice which did, finally, put away those "sins that were previously committed" [in OT times] (Heb. 9:15,26; Rom. 3:25, *note*). See Gen. 4:4; with marginal ref., Sacrifice, and Lev. 16:6, *note.*

[2](30:1) Altar of incense, a type of Christ our Intercessor (Jn. 17:1–26; Heb. 7:25) through whom our prayers and praises ascend to God, and of the believer-priest's sacrifice of praise and worship (Heb. 13:15; Rev. 8:3–4).

and two cubits *shall be* its height. Its horns *shall be* of one piece with it.

3 "And you shall overlay its top, its sides all around, and its horns with pure gold; and you shall make for it a molding of gold all around.

4 "Two gold rings you shall make for it, under the molding on both its sides. You shall place *them* on its two sides, and they will be holders for the poles with which to bear it.

5 "You shall make the poles of acacia wood, and overlay them with gold.

6 "And you shall put it before the [a]veil that *is* before the [b]ark of the Testimony, before the mercy seat that *is* over the Testimony, where I will meet with you.

7 "Aaron shall burn on it sweet incense every morning; when he tends the [c]lamps, he shall burn incense on it.

8 "And when Aaron lights the lamps at twilight, he shall burn incense on it, a perpetual incense before the LORD throughout your generations.

9 "You shall not offer [1]strange incense on it, or a burnt offering, or a grain offering; nor shall you pour a drink offering on it.

10 "And Aaron shall make [d]atonement upon its horns once a year with the blood of the sin offering of [e]atonement; once a year he shall make atonement upon it throughout your generations. It *is* most holy to the LORD."

Who may worship? (1) the redeemed (Ex. 15:1–21; Ps. 107:1–2)

11 Then the LORD spoke to Moses, saying:

12 "When you take the [f]census of the children of Israel for their number, then every man shall give a ransom for himself to the LORD, when you number them, that there may be no [g]plague among them when *you* [h]number them.

13 [i]"This is what everyone among those who are numbered shall give: half a [2]shekel according to the shekel of the sanctuary (a shekel *is* twenty [j]gerahs). The half-shekel *shall be* an offering to the LORD.

14 "Everyone included among those who are numbered, from twenty years old and above, shall give an offering to the LORD.

15 "The rich shall not [k]give more and the poor shall not give less than half a shekel, when *you* give an offering to the LORD, to make atonement for yourselves.

16 "And you shall take the atonement money of the children of Israel, and shall [l]appoint it for the service of the tabernacle of meeting, that it may be a memorial for the children of Israel before the LORD, to make atonement for yourselves."

Who may worship? (2) the cleansed (Jn. 13:3–10; Heb. 10:22; 1 Jn. 1:9)

17 Then the LORD spoke to Moses, saying:

18 "You shall also make a [3m]laver of bronze, with its base also of bronze, for washing. You shall put it between the tabernacle of meeting and the altar. And you shall put water in it,

19 "for Aaron and his sons shall [n]wash their hands and their feet in water from it.

20 "When they go into the tabernacle of meeting, or when they come near the altar to minister, to burn an offering made by fire to the LORD, they

6
a Ex. 26:31–35
b Ex. 25:10–22
7
c Ex. 25:31–40; 27:20–21
10
d See Ex. 29:33, *note*
e Lev. 16:3–34
12
f Num. 1:2; 26:2
g Cp. 2 Sam. 24:15
h Num. 1:2
13
i i.e. *silver.* See Ex. 26:19, *note*
j See Weights and Measures (OT), 2 Chr. 2:10, *note*
15
k Cp. Job 34:19
16
l Ex. 38:25–31
18
m Ex. 38:8
19
n Ex. 40:31–32; Jn. 13:8

[1](30:9) Compare Lev. 10:1–3. Two prohibitions are given concerning worship: (1) No "strange" incense is to be offered. This speaks of simulated or purely formal worship. And (2) no "profane" fire is permitted. This may refer to the substitution for devotion to the LORD of any other devotion, as to religious causes or sects. Cp. 1 Cor. 1:11–13; Col. 2:8,16–19. See Ex. 30:38, *note.*

[2](30:13) Coinage (OT). The shekel here is a piece of silver, not a coin. Minted coins before 700 B.C. have not been found in Bible lands. Financial transactions were carried on by a system of barter using cattle, grain, spices, and precious metal as a means of exchange. The Hebrews did not use coins until about 500 B.C. (cp. Ezra 1:4). Mention of shekels and talents in earlier Hebrew history refers to weights, not coins (cp. Gen. 23:15–16; Ex. 21:32; 1 Chr. 21:25). The exact worth of gold and silver is difficult to ascertain because of the fluctuation in purchasing power in different periods. Coins, except for the Persian drachma (daric), differed in weight and varied in value from light to heavy coins, light coins being half the value of heavy ones, though designated by the same name. For Coinage (NT) see Mt. 5:26, *note.*

[3](30:18) Laver, a type of Christ's cleansing us from defilement and from every "spot or wrinkle or any such thing" (Eph. 5:25–27; cp. Jn. 13:2–10). It is significant that the priests could not enter the holy place after serving at the bronze altar until their hands and feet were cleansed.

shall wash with water, lest they die.

21 "So they shall wash their hands and their feet, lest they die. And it shall be a statute forever to them—to him and his descendants throughout their generations."

Who may worship? (3) the anointed (Jn. 4:23; Eph. 2:18; 5:18–19)

22 Moreover the LORD spoke to Moses, saying:

23 "Also take for yourself quality spices—five hundred *shekels* of liquid [a]myrrh, half as much sweet-smelling cinnamon (two hundred and fifty *shekels*), two hundred and fifty *shekels* of sweet-smelling cane,

24 "five hundred *shekels* of [b]cassia, according to the shekel of the sanctuary, and a hin of olive oil.

25 "And you shall make from these a holy anointing oil, an ointment compounded according to the art of the perfumer. It shall be a holy [c]anointing oil.

26 "With it you shall [d]anoint the tabernacle of meeting and the ark of the Testimony;

27 "the table and all its utensils, the lampstand and its utensils, and the altar of incense;

28 "the altar of burnt offering with all its utensils, and the laver and its base.

29 "You shall consecrate them, that they may be most holy; whatever touches them must be holy.*

30 "And you shall anoint Aaron and his sons, and [e]consecrate them, that *they* may minister to Me as priests.

31 "And you shall speak to the children of Israel, saying: 'This shall be a holy anointing [1]oil to Me throughout your generations.

32 'It shall not be poured on man's flesh; nor shall you make *any other* like it, according to its composition. It *is* holy, *and* it shall be holy to you.

33 'Whoever compounds *any* like it, or whoever puts *any* of it on an outsider, shall be cut off from his people.' "

Incense: type of prayer and praise

34 And the LORD said to Moses: "Take sweet spices, [f]stacte and [g]onycha and [h]galbanum, and pure [2i]frankincense with *these* sweet spices; there shall be equal amounts of each.

35 "You shall make of these an incense, a compound according to the art of the perfumer, salted, pure, *and* holy.

36 "And you shall beat *some* of it very fine, and put some of it before the Testimony in the tabernacle of meeting where I will meet with you. It shall be most holy to you.

37 "But *as for* the incense which you shall make, you shall not make any for yourselves, according to its composition. It shall be to you holy for the LORD.

38 "Whoever makes *any* like it, to [3]smell it, he shall be cut off from his people."

Spirit-filled craftsmen

31 THEN the LORD [j]spoke to Moses, saying:

2 "See, I have called by name Bezalel the son of Uri, the son of Hur, of the tribe of Judah.

3 "And I have filled him with the [k]Spirit of God, in [l]wisdom, in understanding, in knowledge, and in all *manner of* [4]workmanship,

4 "to design artistic works, to work in gold, in silver, in bronze,

5 "in cutting jewels for setting, in carving wood, and to work in all *manner of* workmanship.

6 "And I, indeed I, have appointed with him Aholiab the son of Ahisamach, of the tribe of Dan; and I have put wisdom in the hearts of all the gifted artisans, that they may make all that I have commanded you:

23 *a* Song 4:14
24 *b* Ps. 45:8
25 *c* Ex. 37:29; Lev. 8:10
26 *d* Ex. 40:9–16
30 *e Sanctification* (OT): vv. 30,37; Lev. 8:15. (Gen. 2:3; Zech. 8:3)
34 *f* Gum of the storax tree; sweet spice
g Lid of a shell mollusc, which gave forth perfume when burned
h Gum from the milky sap of the Syrian fennel, fragrant spice
i Fragrant gum, white in color, of a tree in S. Arabia
CHAPTER 31
1 *j* vv. 1–11, cp. Ex. 35:30–35
3 *k Holy Spirit* (OT): v. 3; Ex. 35:31. (Gen. 1:2; Zech. 12:10)
l Ex. 28:3

* **30:29** Compare Numbers 4:15 and Haggai 2:11–13

[1](30:31) Anointing oil, a type of the Holy Spirit for service (Acts 1:8). See Ex. 27:20, *note.*

[2](30:34) Frankincense is not to be confused with incense (to which it was to be added), as it is often used apart from incense. It is told what composed the incense, but never in Scripture what the frankincense was. All speak of Christ—the sweet spices of those perfections which we may apprehend, the frankincense of that which God saw in Jesus as ineffable.

[3](30:38) What is condemned here is making worship a mere pleasure to the natural man. Cp. Jn. 4:23–24.

[4](31:3) This unique ability of Bezalel, given by the Spirit, included not only manual skill but also the intellectual wisdom and understanding essential to all art. Artistic talent of every kind is a divine gift (Jas. 1:17). The God who by His Spirit "adorned the heavens" (Job 26:13) also created man with aesthetic faculties which, like all the human faculties, were corrupted in the fall.

7 "the tabernacle of meeting, the ark of the Testimony and the mercy seat that *is* on it, and all the furniture of the tabernacle—

8 "the table and its utensils, the pure *gold* lampstand with all its utensils, the altar of incense,

9 "the altar of burnt offering with all its utensils, and the laver and its base—

10 "the garments of ministry,* the holy garments for Aaron the priest and the garments of his sons, to minister as priests,

11 "and the anointing oil and sweet incense for the holy *place*. According to all that I have commanded you they shall do."

The Sabbath a sign between the LORD *and Israel*

12 And the LORD spoke to Moses, saying,

13 "Speak also to the children of Israel, saying: 'Surely My [a]Sabbaths you shall keep, for it *is* a [b]sign between Me and you throughout your generations, that *you* may know that I *am* the LORD who [c]sanctifies you.

14 'You shall keep the Sabbath, therefore, for *it is* holy to you. Everyone who profanes it shall surely be put to [d]death; for whoever does *any* work on it, that person shall be cut off from among his people.

15 'Work shall be done for six days, but the seventh *is* the Sabbath of rest, holy to the LORD. Whoever does *any* work on the Sabbath day, he shall surely be put to death.

16 'Therefore the children of Israel shall keep the Sabbath, to observe the Sabbath throughout their generations *as* a perpetual covenant.

17 'It *is* a sign between Me and the children of Israel forever; for *in* six days the LORD made the heavens and the earth, and on the seventh day He [e]rested and was refreshed.' "

18 And when He had made an end of speaking with him on Mount Sinai, He gave Moses two tablets of the [f]Testimony, [g]tablets of stone, [h]written with the [i]finger of God.

13
a Sabbath: vv. 13–16; Ex. 35:2. (Gen. 2:3; Mt. 12:1, *note*)
b Ezek. 20:12,20
c Lev. 20:8
14
d Cp. Num. 15:32–36
17
e Gen. 2:2–3
18
f See Ex. 20:1, *notes*
g Law (of Moses): v. 18; Ex. 34:18. (Ex. 19:1; Gal. 3:24, *note*)
h Ex. 24:12; 32:15–16
i Cp. Jn. 8:6
CHAPTER 32
1
j Ex. 24:18; Dt. 9:11–12
k Ex. 17:1–3
l Acts 7:40
m Ex. 32:8
2
n Ex. 11:2; 35:22
4
o Acts 7:41
p Ex. 20:3,4, 23
q Cp. Ex. 29:45–46
6
r Ex. 32:17–19; Num. 25:2
7
s Dt. 9:8–21
t Cp. v. 11
9
u Ex. 33:3,5; 34:9; Dt. 9:6; Acts 7:51

The broken law: the golden calf

32 NOW when the people saw that Moses [j]delayed coming down from the mountain, the people [k]gathered together to Aaron, and said to him, "Come, [l]make us gods that shall go before us; for *as for* this Moses, the man who [m]brought us up out of the land of Egypt, we do not know what has become of him."

2 And Aaron said to them, "Break off the golden [n]earrings which *are* in the ears of your wives, your sons, and your daughters, and bring *them* to me."

3 So all the people broke off the golden earrings which *were* in their ears, and brought *them* to Aaron.

4 And he received *the gold* from their hand, and he fashioned it with an engraving tool, and made a molded [o]calf. Then they said, "This *is* your [p]god, O Israel, that [q]brought you out of the land of Egypt!"

5 So when Aaron saw *it*, he built an altar before it. And Aaron made a proclamation and said, "Tomorrow *is* a feast to the LORD."

6 Then they rose early on the next day, offered burnt offerings, and brought peace offerings; and the people sat down to eat and drink, and rose up to [r]play.

The LORD *condemns Israel's apostasy*

7 [s]And the LORD said to Moses, "Go, get down! For [t]your people whom you brought out of the land of Egypt have corrupted *themselves*.

8 "They have turned aside quickly out of the way which I commanded them. They have made themselves a molded calf, and worshiped it and sacrificed to it, and said, 'This *is* your god, O Israel, that brought you out of the land of Egypt!' "

9 And the LORD said to Moses, "I have seen this people, and indeed it *is* a [u]stiff-necked people!

10 [1]"Now therefore, let Me alone, that My wrath may burn hot against them and I may consume them. And I will make of you a great nation."

*
31:10 Or *woven garments*

[1](32:10) God was testing Moses by offering to replace Israel with a new nation descending from Moses. Theologically, a test of this kind must be considered in the light of the sovereign will of God that underlies all human decision. For Moses this test was real, even though the proposed destruction of Israel was not in God's plan, as shown by the Abrahamic Covenant and such promises as Gen. 49:10 to Judah. Likewise Christ in the Gospels offered Himself as King to Israel even though His rejection and His death on the cross, according to "the determined purpose and foreknowledge of God" (Acts 2:23), had to precede the glorious kingdom.

Moses' advocacy

11 Then Moses pleaded with the LORD his God, and [a]said: "LORD, why does Your wrath burn hot against Your people whom You have brought out of the land of Egypt with great power and with a mighty hand?

12 "Why should the Egyptians speak, and say, 'He brought them out to harm them, to kill them in the mountains, and to consume them from the face of the earth'? Turn from Your fierce wrath, and [b]relent from this harm to Your people.

13 "Remember Abraham, Isaac, and Israel, Your servants, to whom You swore by Your own self, and said to them, 'I will multiply your descendants as the stars of heaven; and all this land that I have spoken of I give to your descendants, and they shall inherit *it* forever.' "*

14 So the LORD relented from the harm which He said He would do to His people.

Disciplinary judgment

15 And Moses turned and went down from the mountain, and the two tablets of the Testimony *were* in his hand. The tablets *were* written on both sides; on the one *side* and on the other they were written.

16 Now the [c]tablets *were* the work of God, and the [d]writing *was* the writing of God engraved on the tablets.

17 And when Joshua heard the noise of the people as they shouted, he said to Moses, "*There is* a noise of war in the camp."

18 But he said:

"*It is* not the noise of the shout
of victory,
Nor the noise of the cry of
defeat,
But the sound of singing I
hear."

19 So it was, as soon as he came near the camp, that he saw the calf *and* the dancing. So Moses' anger became hot, and he [e]cast the tablets out of his hands and broke them at the foot of the mountain.

20 Then he took the calf which they had made, burned *it* in the fire, and ground *it* to powder; and he scattered *it* on the water and made the children of Israel [f]drink *it*.

21 And Moses said to Aaron, "What did this people do to you that you have brought *so* great a sin upon them?"

22 So Aaron said, "Do not let the anger of my lord become hot. You know the people, that they *are* [g]*set* on evil.

23 "For they said to me, 'Make us gods that shall go before us; *as for* this Moses, the man who brought us out of the land of Egypt, we do not know what has become of him.'

24 "And I said to them, 'Whoever has any gold, let them break *it* off.' So they gave *it* to me, and I cast it into the fire, and this calf [h]came out."

25 Now when Moses saw that the people *were* unrestrained (for Aaron had not restrained them, to *their* shame among their enemies),

26 then Moses stood in the entrance of the camp, and said, "Whoever *is* on the LORD's side—*come* to me!" And all the sons of Levi gathered themselves together to him.

27 And he said to them, "Thus says the LORD God of Israel: 'Let every man put his sword on his side, and go in and out from entrance to entrance throughout the camp, and let every man [i]kill his brother, every man his companion, and every man his neighbor.' "

28 So the sons of Levi did according to the word of Moses. And about three thousand men of the people fell that day.

29 Then Moses said, [j]"Consecrate yourselves today to the LORD, that He may bestow on you a blessing this day, for every man has opposed his son and his brother."

Moses' intercession

30 Now it came to pass on the next day that Moses said to the people, "You have committed a great sin. So now I will go up to the LORD; perhaps I can make [k]atonement for your sin."

31 Then Moses returned to the LORD and said, "Oh, these people have committed a great sin, and have made for themselves a god of [l]gold!

32 "Yet now, if You will forgive their sin—but if not, I pray, blot me out of Your [m]book which You have written."

33 And the LORD said to Moses, [n]"Whoever has sinned against Me, I will [o]blot him out of My book.

34 "Now therefore, go, lead the people to *the place* of which I have [p]spoken to you. Behold, My [q]Angel shall go before you. Nevertheless, in the day when I visit for punishment, I

11 *a Bible prayers* (OT): vv. 11–14; Ex. 33:12. (Gen. 15:2; Hab. 3:1)
12 *b* Zech. 8:14, *note*
16 *c* See Ex. 20:1, *note*; *d Inspiration*: v. 16; Ex. 34:1. (Ex. 4:15; 2 Tim. 3:16, *note*)
19 *e* Dt. 9:17
20 *f* Cp. Num. 5:17,24
22 *g* Dt. 9:24
24 *h* v. 4
27 *i* Cp. Num. 25:7–13; Dt. 33:9
29 *j* Ex. 28:41
30 *k* See Ex. 29:33, *note*
31 *l* Ex. 20:23
32 *m* Ps. 69:28; Dan. 12:1
33 *n* Ezek. 18:4,20; *o* Cp. Ex. 17:14
34 *p* Ex. 3:17; *q Angel* (of the LORD): 32:34–33:1; Ex. 33:2. (Gen. 16:7; Jud. 2:1, *note*)

*32:13 Genesis 13:15 and 22:17

will [a]visit punishment upon them for
their sin."
35 So the LORD plagued the people
because of what they did with the calf
which Aaron made.

Moses ordered to resume journey

33 THEN the LORD said to Moses,
"Depart *and* go up from here,
you and the people whom you [b]have
brought out of the land of Egypt, to the
land of which I [c]swore to Abraham,
Isaac, and Jacob, saying, 'To your descendants I will give it.'
2 "And I will send *My* [d]Angel before you, and I will [e]drive out the Canaanite and the Amorite and the [f]Hit-
tite and the Perizzite and the Hivite
and the Jebusite.
3 "*Go up* to a land flowing with
milk and honey; for I will not go up in
your midst, lest I consume you on the
way, for you *are* a [g]stiff-necked people."
4 And when the people heard this
bad news, they mourned, and no one
put on his ornaments.
5 For the LORD had said to Moses,
"Say to the children of Israel, 'You *are*
a stiff-necked people. I could come up
into your midst in one moment and
consume you. Now therefore, take off
your ornaments, that I may know
what to do to you.' "
6 So the children of Israel stripped
themselves of their ornaments by
Mount Horeb.

The tabernacle of meeting outside the camp

7 Moses took his [1]tent and pitched
it outside the camp, far from the camp,
and called it the tabernacle of meeting. And it came to pass *that* everyone
who sought the LORD went out to the
tabernacle of meeting which *was* outside the camp.
8 So it was, whenever Moses went
out to the tabernacle, *that* all the people rose, and each man stood *at* his
tent door and watched Moses until he
had gone into the tabernacle.
9 And it came to pass, when Moses entered the tabernacle, that the
pillar of cloud descended and stood *at*
the door of the tabernacle, and *the*
LORD [h]talked with Moses.
10 All the people saw the pillar of
cloud standing *at* the tabernacle door,
and all the people rose and worshiped,
each man *in* his tent door.
11 So the LORD spoke to Moses face
to [i]face, as a man speaks to his friend.
And he would return to the camp, but
his servant Joshua the son of Nun, a
young man, did not depart from the
tabernacle.

Moses' prayer; the LORD's answer

12 Then Moses [j]said to the LORD,
"See, You say to me, [k]'Bring up this
people.' But You have not let me know
whom You will send with me. Yet You
have said, 'I know you by name, and
you have also found [l]grace in My
sight.'
13 "Now therefore, I pray, if I have
found grace in Your sight, show me
now [m]Your way, that I may know You
and that I may find grace in Your
sight. And [n]consider that this nation
is Your people."
14 And He said, "My Presence will
[o]go *with you,* and I will give you
[p]rest."
15 Then he said to Him, "If Your
Presence does not go *with us,* do not
bring us up from here.
16 "For how then will it be known
that Your people and I have found
grace in Your sight, except You [q]go
with us? So we shall be [r]separate,
Your people and I, from all the people
who *are* upon the face of the earth."
17 So the LORD said to Moses, "I will
also do this thing that you have spoken; for you have found grace in My
sight, and I know you by name."

Moses seeks a new vision for the new task

18 And he said, "Please, show me
Your [s]glory."
19 Then He said, "I will make all My
[t]goodness pass before you, and I will
proclaim the name of the LORD before
you. I will be gracious to whom I [u]will
be gracious, and I will have compassion on whom I will have compassion."
20 But He said, "You cannot see My
[v]face; for no man shall see Me, and
live."
21 And the LORD said, "Here is a
place by Me, and you shall stand on
the rock.
22 "So it shall be, while My glory
passes by, that I will put you in the

34
a Cp. Ps. 99:8

CHAPTER 33

1
b Ex. 32:1,7
c Ex. 32:13

2
d Angel (of the LORD): 32:34–33:2; Num. 22:22. (Gen. 16:7; Jud. 2:1, *note*)
e Ex. 23:27–31
f See 2 Ki. 7:6, *note*

3
g Ex. 34:9

9
h Ps. 99:7

11
i Num. 12:8; Dt. 34:10

12
j Bible prayers (OT): vv. 12–23; Num. 6:23. (Gen. 15:2; Hab. 3:1)
k Ex. 32:34
l vv. 13–17

13
m Ps. 25:4
n Ex. 3:7,10

14
o Ex. 3:12
p Dt. 12:10

16
q Num. 14:14
r Separation: v. 16; Lev. 20:24. (Gen. 12:1; 2 Cor. 6:17, *note*)

18
s Ex. 24:16–17

19
t Ex. 34:6–7
u Rom. 9:15

20
v See Jn. 1:18, *note*. Cp. 2 Cor. 4:6

---

[1](33:7) This tabernacle of meeting was a temporary place of worship and is not to be confused with the tabernacle and its appointments which are described in 25:1—31:11. The account of the erection of the latter, whose architecture and furnishings had been so minutely defined by the LORD to Moses, begins in ch. 36. Chapter 40:33 tells of its completion.

[a]cleft of the [b]rock, and will cover you
with My [c]hand while I pass by.
23 "Then I will take away My hand,
and you shall see My back; but My
face shall not be seen."

The second tablets of the law

34 AND the LORD said to Moses,
[d]"Cut two tablets of stone [e]like
the first *ones*, and I will write on *these*
tablets the [f]words that were on the
first tablets which you broke.
2 "So be ready in the morning, and
come up in the morning to Mount [g]Si-
nai, and present yourself to Me there
on the top of the mountain.
3 "And [h]no man shall come up
with you, and let no man be seen
throughout all the mountain; let neither flocks nor herds feed before that
mountain."
4 So he cut two tablets of stone
like the first *ones*. Then Moses rose
early in the morning and went up
Mount Sinai, as the LORD had commanded him; and he took in his hand
the two tablets of stone.

The new vision (cp. Ex. 33:18–23)

5 Now the LORD descended in the
[i]cloud and stood with him there, and
proclaimed the [j]name of the LORD.
6 And the LORD passed before him
and proclaimed, "The [1]LORD, the

22
a Cp. Song 2:14
b Christ (Rock): vv. 21–22; Num. 20:11. (Gen. 49:24; 1 Pet. 2:8)
c Isa. 49:2; cp. Jn. 10:28–29

CHAPTER 34
1
d See Ex. 20:1, *note* 2
e Ex. 32:15–16; Dt. 4:13
f Inspiration: vv. 1, 27–28; Ex.

35:1. (Ex. 4:15; 2 Tim. 3:16, *note*) 34:2 *g* Ex. 19:11, 18,20 34:3 *h* Ex. 19:12–13; cp. Ex. 24:9–11
34:5 *i* Ex. 19:9 *j* Ex. 33:19

[1](34:6) LORD (Heb. *YHWH*).

(1) The primary meaning of the name "LORD" (perhaps pronounced Yahweh, in English *Jehovah*) is the *self-existent One;* literally (as in Ex. 3:14), *He that is who He is*, therefore, *the eternal I AM.*

(2) It is significant that the first appearance of the name *Jehovah* in Scripture follows the creation of man. It was God *(Elohim)* who said, "Let Us make man in Our image" (Gen. 1:26); but when man, as in Gen. 2, is to fill the scene and become dominant over creation, it is the LORD God *(Jehovah Elohim)* who acts (Gen. 2:4ff.). This clearly indicates a special relation of Deity, in His *Jehovah* character, to man, and all Scripture emphasizes this.

(3) *Jehovah* is distinctly the redemption name of Deity. When sin entered the world and man's redemption became necessary, it was *Jehovah Elohim* who sought the sinning ones (Gen. 3:9–13) and clothed them with coats of skins (Gen. 3:21), a beautiful type of the righteousness provided by the LORD God through sacrifice (Rom. 3:21–25). The first distinctive revelation of Himself by His name *Jehovah* was in connection with the redemption of the covenant people out of Egypt (Ex. 3:13–17).

As Redeemer, emphasis is laid upon those attributes of *Jehovah* which the sin and salvation of man bring into exercise. These are (a) His holiness (Lev. 11:44–45; 19:1–2; 20:26; Hab. 1:12–13); (b) His hatred and judgment of sin (Dt. 32:35–42; cp. Gen. 6:5–7; Ex. 34:6–7; Ps. 11:4–6; 66:18); and (c) His love for and redemption of sinners, which he always carries out righteously. (Gen. 3:21; 8:20–21; Ex. 12:12–13; Lev. 16:2–3; Isa. 53:5–6,10). Salvation by *Jehovah* apart from sacrifice is unknown in Scripture.

(4) LORD is also the distinctive name of Deity as in covenant with Israel (Ex. 19:3; 20:1–2; Jer. 31:31–34).

(5) LORD God (Heb. *Jehovah Elohim*) is the first of the compound names of God. LORD God is used distinctively: (1) Of the relation of Deity to man (a) as Creator (Gen. 2:7–15); (b) as morally in authority over man (Gen. 2:16–17); (c) as creating and governing the earthly relationships of man (Gen. 2:18–24; 3:16–19,22–24); and (d) as redeeming man (Gen. 3:8–15,21). (2) Of the relation of Deity to Israel (Gen. 24:7; 28:13; Ex. 3:15,18; 4:5; 5:1; 7:5; etc.; Dt. 1:11,21; 4:1; 6:3; 12:1; etc.; Josh. 7:13,19–20; 10:40,42; Jud. 2:12; 1 Sam. 2:30; 1 Ki. 1:48; 2 Ki. 9:6; 10:31; 1 Chr. 22:19; 2 Chr. 1:9; Ezra 1:3; Isa. 21:17).

(6) In God's redemptive relation to man, various compound names of *Jehovah* are found which reveal Him as meeting every need of man from his lost state to the end. These compound names are: (a) *Jehovah-jireh,* "The-LORD-Will-Provide" (Gen. 22:13–14), i.e. will provide a sacrifice. (b) *Jehovah-rapha,* "the LORD who heals you" (Ex. 15:26). That this refers to physical healing the context shows, but the deeper healing of soul malady is implied. (c) *Jehovah-nissi,* "The-LORD-Is-My-Banner" (Ex. 17:8–15). The name is interpreted by the context. The enemy was Amalek, a figure for the flesh, and the conflict that day illustrates the conflict of Gal. 5:17—the war of the Spirit against the flesh. Victory was wholly due to divine help. (d) *Jehovah-shalom,* "The-LORD-Is-Peace," or "The-LORD-Send-Peace" (Jud. 6:24). Almost the whole ministry of *Jehovah* finds expression and illustration in that chapter. *Jehovah* hates and judges sin (vv. 1–5); *Jehovah* loves and saves sinners (vv. 7–18), but only through sacrifice (vv. 19–21; cp. Rom. 5:1; Eph. 2:14; Col. 1:20). (e) *Jehovah-tsidkenu,* "The LORD Our Righteousness" (Jer. 23:6). This name of *Jehovah* occurs in a prophecy concerning the future restoration and conversion of Israel. Then Israel will hail Him as *Jehovah-tsidkenu*—"The LORD Our Righteousness." And (f) *Jehovah-shammah,* "The LORD Is There" (Ezek. 48:35). This name signifies *Jehovah's* abiding presence with His people (Ex. 33:14–15; 1 Chr. 16:27,33; Ps. 16:11;

[a]LORD God, merciful and gracious, longsuffering, and abounding in goodness and truth,

7 "keeping mercy for thousands, forgiving iniquity and transgression and sin, by no means clearing *the guilty*, visiting the iniquity of the fathers upon the children and the children's children to the third and the fourth [b]generation."

8 So Moses made haste and bowed his head toward the earth, and worshiped.

9 Then he said, "If now I have found [c]grace in Your sight, O Lord, let my Lord, I pray, go among us, even though we *are* a [d]stiff-necked people; and pardon our iniquity and our sin, and take us as Your inheritance."

The renewed commission

10 And He said: "Behold, I make a [e]covenant. Before all your people I will do marvels such as have not been done in all the earth, nor in any nation; and all the people among whom you *are* shall see the work of the LORD. For it *is* an awesome thing that I will do with you.

11 "Observe what I command you this day. Behold, I am [f]driving out from before you the Amorite and the Canaanite and the [g]Hittite and the Perizzite and the Hivite and the Jebusite.

12 "Take heed to yourself, lest you make a [h]covenant with the inhabitants of the land where you are going, lest it be a snare in your midst.

13 "But you shall destroy their altars, break their *sacred* pillars, and cut down their [i]wooden images

14 "(for you shall worship no other [j]god, for the LORD, whose name *is* Jealous, *is* a [k]jealous God),

15 "lest you make a covenant with the inhabitants of the land, and they play the harlot with their gods and make sacrifice to their gods, and *one of them* [l]invites you and you eat of his sacrifice,

16 "and you [m]take of his daughters for your sons, and his daughters play the harlot with their gods and make your sons play the harlot with their gods.

17 "You shall make no molded [n]gods for yourselves.

Feasts and Sabbaths again enjoined (cp. Lev. 23:4–44)

18 "The Feast of [o]Unleavened Bread you shall keep. Seven days you shall eat unleavened bread, as I commanded you, in the appointed time of the month of Abib; for in the month of [p]Abib you came out from [q]Egypt.

19 "All that open the womb *are* Mine, and every male firstborn among your livestock, *whether* ox or sheep.

20 "But the firstborn of a donkey you shall redeem with a lamb. And if you will not redeem *him*, then you shall break his neck. All the firstborn of your sons you shall redeem. And none shall appear before Me empty-handed.

21 "Six days you shall work, but on the seventh day you shall rest; in plowing time and in harvest you shall rest.

22 "And you shall observe the Feast of Weeks, of the firstfruits of wheat harvest, and the Feast of Ingathering at the year's end.

23 "Three times in the year all your men shall appear before the Lord, the LORD God of Israel.

24 "For I will cast out the nations before you and enlarge your borders; neither will any man covet your land when you go up to appear before the LORD your God three times in the year.

25 "You shall not offer the blood of My sacrifice with leaven, nor shall the sacrifice of the Feast of the Passover be [r]left until morning.

26 "The first of the firstfruits of your land you shall bring to the house of the LORD your God. You shall not boil a young goat in its mother's milk."

27 Then the LORD said to Moses, [s]"Write these words, for according to the tenor of these words I have made a covenant with you and with Israel."

28 So he was there with the LORD forty days and forty nights; he neither ate bread nor drank water. And He wrote on the tablets the words of the

6
a Deity (names of): vv. 5–7; 1 Sam. 1:3. (Gen. 1:1; Mal. 3:18)
7
b Ex. 20:5–6
9
c Ex. 33:12–13
d Ex. 33:3
10
e Ex. 34:27
11
f Ex. 23:20–33; 33:2
g See 2 Ki. 7:6, *note*
12
h Josh. 23:12,13; Ps. 106:34–38; 2 Cor. 6:14; 2 Tim. 2:20–21; Jas. 4:4
13
i Heb. *Asherim*, images of the heathen goddess, *Asherah*. See Dt. 16:21, *note*
14
j Ex. 20:3–5
k Dt. 4:24
15
l Cp. Num. 25:1–2
16
m Cp. Gen. 28:1; Josh. 23:12–13
17
n Ex. 20:23
18
o Leaven: vv. 18,25; Lev. 2:4. (Gen. 19:3; Mt. 13:33, *note*)
p See Lev. 23:2, *note*
q Law (of Moses): vv. 18–28; Lev. 1:1. (Ex. 19:1; Gal. 3:24, *note*)

34:25 *r* Ex. 12:10 **34:27** *s* Ex. 24:4

97:5; Mt. 28:20; Heb. 13:5). There are also descriptions in the OT of the activities of the LORD which are in some cases similar to compound names of *Jehovah*, but are not properly so (e.g. Ps. 23:1; 27:1; 28:1; cp. Ps. 61:3–4; 62:6–7).

See other names of Deity, Gen. 1:1, *note;* 2:3, *note;* 14:18, *note;* 15:2, *notes;* 17:1, *note;* 21:33, *note;* 1 Sam. 1:3, *note;* Mal. 3:18, *note.*

covenant, the Ten Commandments.*

Moses' face shines

29 Now it was so, when Moses
came down from Mount Sinai (and the
two tablets of the Testimony *were* in
Moses' hand when he came down
from the mountain), that Moses did
not know that the skin of his face
[a]shone while he talked with Him.
30 So when Aaron and all the children of Israel saw Moses, behold, the
skin of his face shone, and they were
afraid to come near him.
31 Then Moses called to them, and
Aaron and all the rulers of the congregation returned to him; and Moses
talked with them.
32 Afterward all the children of Israel came near, and he gave them as
commandments all that the LORD had
spoken with him on Mount Sinai.
33 And when Moses had finished
speaking with them, he put a veil on
his face.
34 But whenever Moses went in before the LORD to speak with Him, he
would take the [b]veil off until he came
out; and he would come out and speak
to the children of Israel whatever he
had been commanded.
35 And whenever the children of Israel saw the face of Moses, that the
skin of Moses' face shone, then Moses
would put the veil on his face again,
until he went in to speak with Him.

The Sabbath re-emphasized

35 THEN Moses gathered all the
congregation of the children of
Israel together, and said to them,
[c]"These *are* the [d]words which the
LORD has commanded *you* to do:
2 "Work shall be done for six
days, but the seventh day shall be a
holy day for you, a [e]Sabbath of rest to
the LORD. Whoever does any work on
it shall be put to [f]death.
3 "You shall [g]kindle no fire
throughout your dwellings on the
Sabbath day."

Gifts for the tabernacle
(cp. Ex. 25:1–8)

4 And Moses spoke to all the congregation of the children of Israel,
saying, "This *is* the thing which the
LORD commanded, saying:
5 'Take from among you an offer-
ing to the LORD. Whoever *is* of a [h]will-
ing heart, let him bring it as an offering to the LORD: [i]gold, silver, and
bronze;
6 [j]'blue, purple, and scarlet
thread, fine linen, and [k]goats' *hair;*
7 'ram skins dyed red, badger
skins, and acacia wood;
8 'oil for the light, and [l]spices for
the anointing oil and for the sweet incense;
9 'onyx stones, and stones to be
set in the ephod and in the breastplate.
10 'All *who are* [m]gifted artisans
among you shall come and make all
that the LORD has commanded:
11 'the tabernacle, its [k]tent, its covering, its clasps, its boards, its bars, its
pillars, and its sockets;
12 'the ark and its poles, *with* the
mercy seat, and the veil of the covering;
13 'the table and its poles, all its
utensils, and the [n]showbread;
14 'also the lampstand for the light,
its utensils, its lamps, and the oil for
the light;
15 'the incense altar, its poles, the
anointing oil, the sweet incense, and
the screen for the door at the entrance
of the tabernacle;
16 'the altar of burnt offering with
its bronze grating, its poles, all its
utensils, *and* the laver and its base;
17 'the hangings of the court, its pillars, their sockets, and the screen for
the gate of the court;
18 'the pegs of the tabernacle, the
pegs of the court, and their cords;
19 'the garments of ministry,* for
ministering in the holy *place*—the
holy garments for Aaron the priest
and the garments of his sons, to minister as priests.' "
20 And all the congregation of the
children of Israel departed from the
presence of Moses.
21 Then [o]everyone came whose
heart was stirred, and everyone
whose spirit was willing, *and* they
[p]brought the LORD's offering for the
work of the tabernacle of meeting, for
all its service, and for the holy garments.
22 They came, both men and
women, as many as had a willing
heart, *and* brought [q]earrings and nose
rings, rings and necklaces, all [r]jew-
elry of gold, that is, every man who
made an offering of gold to the LORD.
23 And every man, with whom was
found blue, purple, and scarlet *thread*,
fine linen, and goats' *hair*, red skins of

29
a 2 Cor. 3:7
34
b Cp. 2 Cor. 3:13–16
CHAPTER 35
1
c Ex. 34:32
d Inspiration: v. 1; Num. 11:24. (Ex. 4:15; 2 Tim. 3:16, *note*)
2
e Sabbath: vv. 2–3; Lev. 19:3. (Gen. 2:3; Mt. 12:1, *note*)
f Num. 15:32–36
3
g Ex. 12:16
5
h vv. 21,22, 26,29; Ex. 36:3–6; 1 Chr. 29:14; Mk. 12:41–44; 2 Cor. 8:10–12; 9:7
i Ex. 38:24
6
j Ex. 36:8
k Ex. 36:14
8
l Ex. 30:23–25
10
m Ex. 31:2–6; 36:1–2
13
n See Ex. 25:30, *note*
21
o Ex. 25:2
p Ex. 36:2
22
q Ex. 32:2–3
r Ex. 11:2

*34:28 Literally *Ten Words* 35:19 Or *woven garments*

rams, and badger skins, brought *them.*

24 Everyone who offered an offering of silver or bronze brought the LORD's offering. And everyone with whom was found acacia wood for any work of the service, brought *it.*

25 All the women *who were* gifted artisans spun yarn with their hands, and brought what they had spun, of blue, purple, *and* scarlet, and fine linen.

26 And all the women whose hearts stirred with wisdom spun yarn of goats' *hair.*

27 The rulers brought onyx stones, and the stones to be set in the ephod and in the breastplate,

28 and spices and oil for the light, for the anointing oil, and for the sweet incense.

29 The children of Israel brought a [a]freewill offering to the LORD, all the men and women whose hearts were willing to bring *material* for all kinds of work which the LORD, by the hand of Moses, had commanded to be done.

Bezalel and Aholiab to design and teach

30 And Moses said to the children of Israel, "See, the LORD has called by [b]name Bezalel the son of Uri, the son of Hur, of the tribe of Judah;

31 "and He has filled him with the [c]Spirit of God, in wisdom and understanding, in knowledge and all manner of workmanship,

32 "to design artistic works, to work in gold and silver and bronze,

33 "in cutting jewels for setting, in carving wood, and to work in all manner of artistic workmanship.

34 "And He has put in his heart the ability to teach, *in* him and Aholiab the son of Ahisamach, of the tribe of Dan.

35 "He has filled them with skill to do all manner of work of the engraver and the designer and the tapestry maker, in blue, purple, and scarlet *thread,* and fine linen, and of the weaver—those who do every work and those who design artistic works.

Construction of the tabernacle
(Ex. 36—39)

36 "AND Bezalel and Aholiab, and every [d]gifted artisan in whom the LORD has put [e]wisdom and understanding, to know how to do all manner of work for the service of the sanctuary, shall do according to all that the LORD has commanded."

2 Then Moses called Bezalel and Aholiab, and every gifted artisan in whose [f]heart the LORD had put wisdom, everyone whose heart was stirred, to come and do the work.

3 And they received from Moses all the [g]offering which the children of Israel had brought for the work of the service of making the sanctuary. So they continued bringing to him [h]freewill offerings every morning.

4 Then all the craftsmen who were doing all the work of the sanctuary came, each from the work he was doing,

5 and they spoke to Moses, saying, "The people bring much more than [i]enough for the service of the work which the LORD commanded *us* to do."

6 So Moses gave a commandment, and they caused it to be proclaimed throughout the camp, saying, "Let neither man nor woman do any more work for the offering of the sanctuary." And the people were restrained from bringing,

7 for the material they had was sufficient for all the work to be done—indeed too [j]much.

Linen curtains

8 Then all the gifted artisans among them who [k]worked on the tabernacle made ten curtains woven of fine linen, and of blue, purple, and scarlet *thread; with* artistic designs of cherubim they made them.

9 The length of each curtain *was* twenty-eight [l]cubits, and the width of each curtain four cubits; the curtains *were* all the same size.

10 And he coupled five curtains to one another, and *the other* five curtains he coupled to one another.

11 He made loops of blue *yarn* on the edge of the curtain on the selvedge of one set; likewise he did on the outer edge of *the other* curtain of the second set.

12 Fifty loops he made on one curtain, and fifty loops he made on the edge of the curtain on the end of the second set; the loops held one *curtain* to another.

13 And he made fifty clasps of gold, and coupled the curtains to one another with the clasps, that it might be one tabernacle.

Curtains of goats' hair

14 He made curtains of goats' *hair*

29
a v. 5; 36:3
30
b Ex. 31:1–6
31
c Holy Spirit (OT): v. 31; Num. 11:17. (Gen. 1:2; Zech. 12:10)
CHAPTER 36
1
d Ex. 28:3; 31:6; 35:10,35
e Ex. 35:30–31
2
f Ex. 35:25, 26; 1 Chr. 29:5,9,17
3
g Ex. 35:5
h See 2 Cor. 8:1, *note*
5
i Cp. 2 Chr. 24:14; 31:6–10; 2 Cor. 8:2–3
7
j Cp. 1 Ki. 8:64
8
k vv. 8–19; cp. Ex. 26:1–14
9
l See Weights and Measures (OT), 2 Chr. 2:10, *note*

for the [a]tent over the tabernacle; he made eleven curtains.

15 The length of each curtain *was* thirty cubits, and the width of each curtain four cubits; the eleven curtains *were* the same size.

16 He coupled five curtains by themselves and six curtains by themselves.

17 And he made fifty loops on the edge of the curtain that is outermost in one set, and fifty loops he made on the edge of the curtain of the second set.

18 He also made fifty bronze clasps to couple the tent together, that it might be one.

Ram skin covering

19 Then he made a [b]covering for the tent of ram skins dyed red, and a covering of badger skins above *that*.

Boards and sockets

20 For the tabernacle he [c]made boards of acacia wood, standing upright.

21 The length of each board *was* ten cubits, and the width of each board a cubit and a half.

22 Each board had two tenons [d]for binding one to another. Thus he made for all the boards of the tabernacle.

23 And he made boards for the tabernacle, twenty boards for the south side.

24 Forty sockets of silver he made to go under the twenty boards: two sockets under each of the boards for its two tenons.

25 And for the other side of the tabernacle, the north side, he made twenty boards

26 and their forty sockets of silver: two sockets under each of the boards.

27 For the west side of the tabernacle he made six boards.

28 He also made two boards for the two back corners of the tabernacle.

29 And they were coupled at the bottom and coupled together at the top by one ring. Thus he made both of them for the two corners.

30 So there were eight boards and their sockets—sixteen sockets of silver—two sockets under each of the boards.

31 And he made bars of acacia wood: five for the boards on one side of the tabernacle,

32 five [e]bars for the boards on the other side of the tabernacle, and five bars for the boards of the tabernacle on the far side westward.

33 And he made the middle bar to pass through the boards from one end to the other.

Overlay of gold

34 He overlaid the boards with gold, made their rings of gold *to be* holders for the bars, and overlaid the bars with gold.

Veil

35 And he [f]made a [g]veil of blue, purple, and scarlet *thread,* and fine woven linen; it was worked *with* an artistic design of cherubim.

36 He made for it four pillars of acacia *wood,* and overlaid them with gold, with their hooks of gold; and he cast four sockets of silver for them.

Screen

37 He also made a [h]screen for the tabernacle door, of blue, purple, and scarlet *thread,* and fine woven linen, made by a weaver,

38 and its five pillars with their hooks. And he overlaid their capitals and their rings with gold, but their five sockets *were* bronze.

The ark of the Testimony

37 THEN [i]Bezalel [j]made the ark of acacia wood; two and a half [k]cubits *was* its length, a cubit and a half its width, and a cubit and a half its height.

2 He overlaid it with pure gold inside and outside, and made a molding of gold all around it.

3 And he cast for it four rings of gold *to be set* in its four corners: two rings on one side, and two rings on the other side of it.

4 He made poles of acacia wood, and overlaid them with gold.

5 And he put the poles into the rings at the sides of the ark, to bear the ark.

The mercy seat

6 He also made the mercy seat of pure gold; two and a half cubits *was* its length and a cubit and a half its width.

7 He made two [l]cherubim of beaten gold; he made them of one piece at the two ends of the mercy seat:

8 one cherub at one end on this side, and the other cherub at the *other* end on that side. He made the cherubim at the two ends *of one piece* with the mercy seat.

9 The cherubim spread out *their* wings above, *and* covered the mercy

14 *a* Ex. 35:11; 40:19
19 *b* Ex. 26:14
20 *c* vv. 20–34; Ex. 26:15–29
22 *d* Ex. 26:17
32 *e* Ex. 26:26
35 *f* vv. 35–38, cp. Ex. 26:31–37 *g* Ex. 26:31; 30:6; Heb. 10:20
37 *h* Ex. 26:36
CHAPTER 37
1 *i* Ex. 35:30; 36:1 *j* vv. 1–9, cp. Ex. 25:10–20 *k* See Weights and Measures (OT), 2 Chr. 2:10, *note*
7 *l* 1 Ki. 6:23; see Ezek. 1:5, *note*

seat with their wings. They faced one another; the faces of the cherubim were toward the [a]mercy seat.

Table of showbread

10 He [b]made the [c]table of acacia wood; two cubits *was* its length, a cubit its width, and a cubit and a half its height.

11 And he overlaid it with pure gold, and made a molding of gold all around it.

12 Also he made a frame of a handbreadth all around it, and made a molding of gold for the frame all around it.

13 And he cast for it four rings of gold, and put the rings on the four corners that *were* at its four legs.

14 The rings were close to the frame, as holders for the poles to bear the table.

15 And he made the poles of acacia wood to bear the table, and overlaid them with gold.

16 He made of pure gold the utensils which were on the table: its dishes, its cups, its bowls, and its pitchers for pouring.

Golden lampstand

17 He also [d]made the lampstand of pure gold; of hammered work he made the lampstand. Its shaft, its branches, its bowls, its *ornamental* knobs, and its flowers were of the same piece.

18 And six branches came out of its sides: three branches of the lampstand out of one side, and three branches of the lampstand out of the other side.

19 There were three bowls made like almond *blossoms* on one branch, with an *ornamental* knob and a flower, and three bowls made like almond *blossoms* on the other branch, with an *ornamental* knob and a flower—and so for the six branches coming out of the lampstand.

20 And on the lampstand itself *were* four bowls made like almond *blossoms, each with* its *ornamental* knob and flower.

21 *There was* a knob under the *first* two branches of the same, a knob under the *second* two branches of the same, and a knob under the *third* two branches of the same, according to the six branches extending from it.

22 Their knobs and their branches were of one piece; all of it *was* one hammered piece of pure gold.

23 And he made its seven lamps, its [e]wick-trimmers, and its trays of pure gold.

24 Of a [f]talent of pure gold he made it, with all its utensils.

Altar of incense

25 He [g]made the incense altar of acacia wood. Its length *was* a cubit and its width a cubit—*it was* square—and two cubits *was* its height. Its horns were *of one piece* with it.

26 And he overlaid it with pure gold: its top, its sides all around, and its horns. He also made for it a molding of gold all around it.

27 He made two rings of gold for it under its molding, by its two corners on both sides, as holders for the poles with which to bear it.

28 And he [h]made the poles of acacia wood, and overlaid them with gold.

Anointing oil

29 He also made the [i]holy anointing oil and the pure incense of sweet spices, according to the work of the [j]perfumer.

Altar of burnt offering

38 THE [k]made the altar of burnt offering of acacia wood; five [l]cubits *was* its length and five cubits its width—*it was* square—and its height *was* three cubits.

2 He made its horns on its four corners; the horns were *of one piece* with it. And he overlaid it with bronze.

3 He made all the utensils for the altar: the pans, the shovels, the basins, the forks, and the firepans; all its utensils he made of bronze.

4 And he made a grate of bronze network for the altar, under its rim, midway from the bottom.

5 He cast four rings for the four corners of the bronze grating, *as* holders for the poles.

6 And he made the poles of acacia wood, and overlaid them with bronze.

7 Then he put the poles into the rings on the sides of the altar, with which to bear it. He made the altar hollow with boards.

Laver of bronze

8 He made the laver of bronze and its base of bronze, from the bronze mirrors of the serving women who assembled at the door of the tabernacle of meeting.

The court

9 Then he [m]made the court on the

9 [a] Ex. 25:20
10 [b] vv. 10–16, cp. Ex. 25:23–29 [c] Ex. 25:23; 35:13; 40:4,22
17 [d] vv. 17–24, cp. Ex. 25:31–39
23 [e] Num. 4:9
24 [f] See Coinage (OT), Ex. 30:13, *note;* cp. 2 Chr. 2:10, *note*
25 [g] vv. 25–28, cp. Ex. 30:1–5
28 [h] Ex. 30:5
29 [i] Ex. 30:23–24, 31–33 [j] Ex. 30:35
CHAPTER 38
1 [k] vv. 1–7, cp. Ex. 27:1–8 [l] See Weights and Measures (OT), 2 Chr. 2:10, *note*
9 [m] vv. 9–20, cp. Ex. 27:9–19

south side; the hangings of the court
were of fine woven linen, one hundred
cubits long.
10 There *were* twenty pillars for
them, with twenty bronze sockets.
The hooks of the pillars and their
bands *were* silver.
11 On the north side *the hangings*
were one hundred cubits *long,* with
twenty pillars and their twenty bronze
sockets. The hooks of the pillars and
their bands *were* silver.
12 And on the west side *there were*
hangings of fifty cubits, with ten pillars and their ten sockets. The hooks
of the pillars and their bands *were* silver.
13 For the east side *the hangings*
were fifty cubits.
14 The hangings of one side *of the*
gate were fifteen cubits *long, with*
their three pillars and their three sockets,
15 and the same for the other side
of the court gate; on this side and that
were hangings of fifteen cubits, *with*
their three pillars and their three sockets.
16 All the hangings of the court all
around *were of* fine woven linen.
17 The sockets for the pillars *were*
bronze, the hooks of the pillars and
their bands *were* silver, and the overlay of their capitals *was* silver; and all
the pillars of the court had bands of
silver.

Gate of the court

18 The screen for the gate of the
court *was* woven of blue, purple, and
scarlet *thread,* and of fine woven
linen. The length *was* twenty cubits,
and the height along its width *was* five
cubits, corresponding to the hangings
of the court.
19 And *there were* four pillars *with*
their four sockets of bronze; their
hooks *were* silver, and the overlay of
their capitals and their bands *was* silver.
20 All the pegs of the tabernacle,
and of the court all around, *were*
bronze.

Cost of tabernacle

21 This is the inventory of the [a]tab-
ernacle, the tabernacle of the Testimony, which was counted according
to the commandment of Moses, for the
service of the [b]Levites, by the hand of
[c]Ithamar, son of Aaron the priest.
22 [d]Bezalel the son of Uri, the son
of Hur, of the tribe of Judah, made all
that the LORD had commanded Moses.
23 And with him *was* [e]Aholiab the
son of Ahisamach, of the tribe of Dan,
an engraver and designer, a weaver of
blue, purple, and scarlet *thread,* and
of fine linen.
24 All the gold that was used in all
the work of the holy *place,* that is, the
gold of the [f]offering, was twenty-nine
[g]talents and seven hundred and thirty
[g]shekels, according to the shekel of
the sanctuary.
25 And the silver from those who
were [h]numbered of the congregation
was one hundred talents and one
thousand seven hundred and seventy-
five shekels, according to the shekel
of the sanctuary:
26 a [g]bekah for each man (*that is,*
[i]half a shekel, according to the shekel
of the sanctuary), for everyone included in the numbering from twenty
years old and above, for six hundred
and three thousand, five hundred and
fifty [j]*men.*
27 And from the hundred talents of
silver were cast the [k]sockets of the
sanctuary and the bases of the veil:
one hundred sockets from the hundred talents, one talent for each
socket.
28 Then from the one thousand
seven hundred and seventy-five *shek-*
els he made hooks for the pillars, overlaid their capitals, and made bands for
them.
29 The offering of bronze *was* seventy talents and two thousand four
hundred shekels.
30 And with it he made the sockets
for the door of the tabernacle of meeting, the bronze altar, the bronze grating for it, and all the utensils for the
altar,
31 the sockets for the court all
around, the bases for the court gate,
all the pegs for the tabernacle, and all
the pegs for the court all around.

Aaron's holy garments

39 OF the [l]blue, purple, and scarlet *thread* they made [m]gar-
ments of ministry,* for ministering in
the holy *place,* and made the holy garments for Aaron, as the LORD had commanded Moses.
2 He [n]made the [o]ephod of gold,
blue, purple, and scarlet *thread,* and
of fine woven linen.
3 And they beat the gold into thin
sheets and cut *it into* threads, to work

21
a Ex. 36:13; 39:32
b Num. 1:50–53
c Ex. 28:1; Lev. 10:6, 16

22
d Ex. 31:2; 1 Chr. 2:18–20

23
e Ex. 36:1

24
f Ex. 35:5,22
g See Coinage (OT), Ex. 30:13, *note;* cp. 2 Chr. 2:10, *note*

25
h Ex. 30:11–16; Num. 1:2

26
i Ex. 30:15
j Ex. 12:37; Num. 1:46

27
k See Ex. 26:19, *note*

CHAPTER 39
1
l Ex. 25:4; 35:23
m Ex. 31:10; 35:19

2
n vv. 2–7; cp. Ex. 28:6–14
o Lev. 8:7

*
39:1 Or *woven garments*

it in *with* the blue, purple, and scarlet
thread, and the fine linen, *into* artistic
designs.
4 They made shoulder straps for it
to couple *it* together; it was coupled
together at its two edges.
5 And the intricately woven band
of his ephod that *was* on it *was* of the
same workmanship, *woven of* gold,
blue, purple, and scarlet *thread,* and
of fine woven linen, as the LORD had
commanded Moses.
6 And they set onyx stones, enclosed in settings of gold; they were
engraved, as signets are engraved,
with the names of the sons of Israel.
7 He put them on the shoulders of
the ephod *as* [a]memorial stones for the
sons of Israel, as the LORD had commanded Moses.
8 And he [b]made the breastplate,
artistically woven like the workmanship of the ephod, of gold, blue, purple, and scarlet *thread,* and of fine woven linen.
9 They made the breastplate
square by doubling it; a [c]span *was* its
length and a span its width when doubled.
10 And they set in it four rows of
stones: a row with a sardius, a topaz,
and an emerald was the first row;
11 the second row, a turquoise, a
sapphire, and a diamond;
12 the third row, a jacinth, an agate,
and an amethyst;
13 the fourth row, a beryl, an onyx,
and a jasper. *They were* enclosed in
settings of gold in their mountings.
14 *There were* [d]twelve stones according to the names of the sons of
Israel: according to their names, *engraved like* a signet, each one with its
own name according to the twelve
tribes.
15 And they made chains for the
breastplate at the ends, like braided
cords of pure gold.
16 They also made two settings of
gold and two gold rings, and put the
two rings on the two ends of the
breastplate.
17 And they put the two braided
chains of gold in the two rings on the
ends of the breastplate.
18 The two ends of the two braided
chains they fastened in the two settings, and put them on the shoulder
straps of the ephod in the front.
19 And they made two rings of gold
and put *them* on the two ends of the
breastplate, on the edge of it, which
was on the inward side of the ephod.
20 They made two *other* gold rings
and put them on the two shoulder
straps, underneath the ephod toward
its front, right at the seam above the
intricately woven band of the ephod.
21 And they bound the breastplate
by means of its rings to the rings of the
ephod with a blue cord, so that it
would be above the intricately woven
band of the ephod, and that the breastplate would not come loose from the
ephod, as the LORD had commanded
Moses.
22 He [e]made the [f]robe of the
ephod of woven work, all of blue.
23 And *there was* an opening in the
middle of the robe, like the opening in
a coat of mail, *with* a woven binding
all around the opening, so that it
would not tear.
24 They made on the hem of the
robe pomegranates of blue, purple,
and scarlet, and of fine woven *linen.*
25 And they made [g]bells of pure
gold, and put the bells between the
pomegranates on the hem of the robe
all around between the pomegranates:
26 a bell and a pomegranate, a bell
and a pomegranate, all around the
hem of the robe to minister in, as the
LORD had commanded Moses.
27 They made [h]tunics, artistically
woven of fine linen, for Aaron and his
sons,
28 a [i]turban of fine linen, exquisite
hats of fine linen, short [j]trousers of
fine woven linen,
29 and a [k]sash of fine woven linen
with blue, purple, and scarlet *thread,*
made by a weaver, as the LORD had
commanded Moses.
30 Then they made the [l]plate of the
holy crown of pure gold, and wrote on
it an inscription *like* the engraving of
a signet:

[m]HOLINESS TO THE LORD.

31 And they tied to it a blue cord, to
fasten *it* above on the turban, as the
LORD had commanded Moses.
32 Thus all the work of the tabernacle of the tent of meeting was [n]fin-
ished. And the children of Israel did
[o]according to all that the LORD had
commanded Moses; so they did.
33 And they brought the tabernacle
to Moses, the tent and all its furnishings: its clasps, its boards, its bars, its
pillars, and its sockets;
34 the covering of ram skins dyed
red, the covering of badger skins, and
the veil of the covering;

7 *a* Ex. 28:29; Josh. 4:7
8 *b* vv. 8–21, Ex. 28:15–29
9 *c* See Weights and Measures (OT), 2 Chr. 2:10, *note*
14 *d* Rev. 21:12
22 *e* vv. 22–31, cp. Ex. 28:31–37 *f* Ex. 29:5; Lev. 8:7
25 *g* Ex. 28:33
27 *h* Ex. 28:40
28 *i* Ex. 28:4, 39; Lev. 8:9 *j* Ex. 28:42; Lev. 6:10
29 *k* Ex. 28:39
30 *l* Ex. 28:36–37 *m* Zech. 14:20
32 *n* Ex. 40:17 *o* Ex. 25:40; 26:30

35 the ark of the Testimony with its poles, and the mercy seat;

36 the table, all its utensils, and the [a]showbread;

37 the pure *gold* lampstand with its lamps (the lamps set in order), all its utensils, and the oil for light;

38 the gold altar, the anointing oil, and the sweet incense; the screen for the tabernacle door;

39 the bronze altar, its grate of bronze, its poles, and all its utensils; the laver with its base;

40 the hangings of the court, its pillars and its sockets, the screen for the court gate, its cords, and its pegs; all the utensils for the service of the tabernacle, for the tent of meeting;

41 and the garments of ministry,* to minister in the holy *place:* the holy garments for Aaron the priest, and his sons' garments, to minister as priests.

42 According to all that the LORD had commanded Moses, so the children of Israel did all the work.

43 Then Moses looked over all the work, and indeed they had done it; as the LORD had commanded, just so they had done it. And Moses [b]blessed them.

Tabernacle erected

40 THEN the LORD [c]spoke to Moses, [d]saying:

2 "On the [e]first day of the [f]first month you shall [g]set up the tabernacle of the tent of meeting.

3 "You shall put in it the ark of the Testimony, and [h]partition off the ark with the veil.

4 "You shall bring in the table and arrange the [i]things that are to be set in order on it; and you shall bring in the lampstand and light its lamps.

5 "You shall also set the altar of gold for the incense before the ark of the Testimony, and put up the screen for the door of the tabernacle.

6 "Then you shall set the [j]altar of the burnt offering before the door of the tabernacle of the tent of meeting.

7 "And you shall set the laver between the tabernacle of meeting and the altar, and put water in it.

8 "You shall set up the court all around, and hang up the screen at the court gate.

9 "And you shall take the anointing oil, and anoint the tabernacle and all that *is* in it; and you shall hallow it and all its utensils, and it shall be holy.

10 "You shall [k]anoint the altar of the burnt offering and all its utensils, and consecrate the altar. The altar shall be most holy.

11 "And you shall anoint the laver and its base, and consecrate it.

12 "Then you shall [l]bring Aaron and his sons to the door of the tabernacle of meeting and wash them with water.

13 "You shall put the holy [m]garments on Aaron, and anoint him and consecrate him, that he may minister to Me as priest.

14 "And you shall bring his sons and clothe them with tunics.

15 "You shall anoint them, as you anointed their father, that they may minister to Me as priests; for their anointing shall surely be an [n]everlasting priesthood throughout their generations."

16 Thus Moses did; according to all that the LORD had commanded him, so he did.

17 And it came to pass in the first month of the second year, on the first *day* of the month, *that* the tabernacle was [o]raised up.

18 So Moses raised up the tabernacle, fastened its sockets, set up its boards, put in its bars, and raised up its pillars.

19 And he spread out the tent over the tabernacle and put the covering of the tent on top of it, as the LORD had commanded Moses.

20 He took the [p]Testimony and put *it* into the ark, inserted the poles through the rings of the ark, and put the mercy seat on top of the ark.

21 And he brought the ark into the tabernacle, hung up the veil of the covering, and partitioned off the ark of the Testimony, as the LORD had commanded Moses.

22 He put the table in the tabernacle of meeting, on the north side of the tabernacle, outside the veil;

23 and he set the [q]bread in order upon it before the LORD, as the LORD had commanded Moses.

24 He put the lampstand in the tabernacle of meeting, across from the table, on the south side of the tabernacle;

25 and he [r]lit the lamps before the LORD, as the LORD had commanded Moses.

26 He put the gold altar in the tabernacle of meeting in front of the veil;

27 and he burned sweet incense on it, as the LORD had commanded Moses.

36
a Ex. 25:23–30
43
b Lev. 9:22–23
CHAPTER 40
1
c Cp. Ex. 25:1–31:18
d *Israel* (history): vv. 1–38; Lev. 16:1. (Gen. 12:2; Rom. 11:26, *note*)
2
e Cp. Ex. 19:1; Num. 1:1
f See Lev. 23:2, *note*
g Ex. 40:17
3
h Lev. 16:2
4
i Ex. 39:36; Lev. 24:6
6
j Ex. 39:39
10
k Ex. 30:26–30
12
l Ex. 29:4–9
13
m Ex. 29:5; 39:1,41
15
n Ex. 29:9; Num. 25:13
17
o Ex. 40:2; cp. Num. 7:1–89
20
p Ex. 25:16; Dt. 10:2,5; Heb. 9:4
23
q Lev. 24:5–6
25
r Ex. 30:7–8; Lev. 24:3–4

* 39:41 Or *woven garments*

28 He hung up the screen *at* the
door of the tabernacle.
29 And he put the altar of burnt offering *before* the door of the tabernacle of the tent of meeting, and offered
upon it the burnt offering and the
grain offering, as the LORD had commanded Moses.
30 He set the laver between the tabernacle of meeting and the altar, and
put water there for washing;
31 and Moses, Aaron, and his sons
would [a]wash their hands and their
feet *with water* from it.
32 Whenever they went into the
tabernacle of meeting, and when they
came near the altar, they washed, as
the LORD had commanded Moses.
33 And he raised up the court all
around the tabernacle and the altar,
and hung up the screen of the court
gate. So Moses [b]finished the work.

31
a Ex. 30:19–20; cp. Jn. 13:8
33
b Heb. 3:2–5
34
c Cp. 1 Ki. 8:10,11
d Lev. 16:2; Num. 9:15–22; 1 Ki. 8:10; 2 Chr. 5:13
e Lev. 9:6, 23
36
f Ex. 13:21–22
38
g Neh. 9:12; Ps. 78:14; Isa. 4:5

Shekinah glory fills tabernacle

34 [c]Then the [d]cloud covered the
tabernacle of meeting, and the [1e]glory
of the LORD filled the tabernacle.
35 And Moses was not able to enter the tabernacle of meeting, because the cloud rested above it, and
the glory of the LORD filled the tabernacle.
36 Whenever the [f]cloud was taken
up from above the tabernacle, the children of Israel would go onward in all
their journeys.
37 But if the cloud was not taken
up, then they did not journey till the
day that it was taken up.
38 For the [g]cloud of the LORD *was*
above the tabernacle by day, and fire
was over it by night, in the sight of all
the house of Israel, throughout all
their journeys.

[1](40:34) Compare Eph. 2:19–22. What the Shekinah glory was to the tabernacle and temple, the Spirit is to the "holy temple" (Eph. 2:21), the church, and to the temple which is the believer's body (1 Cor. 3:16; 6:19).

The Third Book of Moses Called

LEVITICUS

Author: Moses *Theme:* Holiness *Date of writing:* c. 1450–1410 B.C.

LEVITICUS is devoted to the worship of the redeemed people of God, as is shown by the frequent occurrence of words relating to holiness and sacrifice. In the Hebrew Bible this book is called by its first word, *wayyiqra,* meaning *and He called.* The English title Leviticus, from the Septuagint, is based on the name of Levi, who was one of the twelve sons of Jacob (Israel), Gen. 46:1–27.

The vocabulary of sacrifice pervades the book: the words "priest," "sacrifice," "blood," and "offering" occur very frequently; and "*qodesh,*" rendered "holiness" or "holy," appears more than 150 times. Observe also the repeated command: "Be holy, for I the LORD your God am holy" (11:44,45; 19:2; 20:7,26).

Leviticus may be divided as follows:

I. The Offerings, 1—7.
II. Consecration of Aaron and His Sons, 8—10.
III. Laws of Cleanliness and Holiness, 11—15; 17—22.
IV. The Day of Atonement, 16.
V. Laws Regulating the Personal Relationships of the Redeemed People, 18—20.
VI. Laws Regulating the Priesthood and the Seven Great Feasts of the Hebrew Calendar, 21—23.
VII. Additional Laws, Promises and Warnings, 24—27.

I. The Offerings, 1—7

Sweet aroma offerings: (1) the burnt offering (v. 4). (See Lev. 6:8–13)

1 NOW the LORD [a]called to [b]Moses, and spoke to him from the tabernacle of meeting, saying,
2 "Speak to the children of Israel, and say to them: 'When any one of you brings an offering to the LORD, you shall bring your offering of the livestock—of the herd and of the flock.
3 'If his offering *is* a [1][c]burnt sacrifice of the herd, let him offer a male without [d]blemish; he shall offer it of his own free will at the door of the tabernacle of meeting before the LORD.
4 'Then he shall put his [2]hand on

CHAPTER 1
1
a c. 1445 B.C. See Ex. 1:8, *note*
b Law (of Moses): vv. 1–16; Lev. 16:34. (Ex. 19:1; Gal. 3:24, *note*)

1:3 *c Sacrifice* (typical): vv. 3–17; Lev. 2:2. (Gen. 3:15; Heb. 10:18, *note*) *d* Lev. 22:20–24

---

[1](1:3) The burnt offering (1) typifies Christ offering Himself without spot to God in delight to do His Father's will even in death; (2) is atoning because the believer has not had this delight in the will of God; and (3) is substitutionary (v. 4) because Christ did it in the sinner's stead. But the thought of penalty is not prominent (Heb. 9:11–14; 10:5–7; cp. Ps. 40:6–8; Phil. 2:8). The emphatic words (Lev. 1:3–5) are "burnt sacrifice," "own free will," "it will be accepted on his behalf," and "atonement."

The creatures acceptable for sacrifice are five:

(1) The young bull, or ox, typifies Christ as the patient and enduring Servant (Heb. 12:2–3), "obedient to the point of death" (Isa. 52:13–15; Phil. 2:5–8). His offering in this character is substitutionary, for we have been disobedient.

(2) The sheep, or lamb, typifies Christ in unresisting self-surrender to the death of the cross (Isa. 53:7; Acts 8:32–35).

(3) The goat typifies the sinner (Mt. 25:33,41–46) and, when used sacrificially, Christ as "numbered with the transgressors" (Isa. 53:12; Lk. 23:33). God "made Him who knew no sin to be sin for us" (2 Cor. 5:21). The holy Son of God became "a curse for us" (Gal. 3:13) when He hung upon the cross.

(4–5) The turtledove and pigeon, naturally symbols of mourning innocence (Isa. 38:14; 59:11; Mt. 23:37; Heb. 7:26), are associated with poverty in Lev. 5:7; 12:8 and speak of Him who for our sakes became poor (Lk. 9:58), whose pathway of poverty began with His emptying Himself of His preincarnate glory and ended in the sacrifice through which we became rich (2 Cor. 8:9; Phil. 2:6–8; cp. Jn. 17:5). The sacrifice of the poor Man, Christ Jesus, becomes the poor man's sacrifice (Lk. 2:24; 1 Tim. 2:5–6; cp. Heb. 9:26; 13:15).

These grades of typical sacrifice test the measure of our understanding of the varied aspects of Christ's one sacrifice on the cross. The mature Christian should see the crucified Christ in all these aspects.

[2](1:4) The laying on of the offerer's hand signified acceptance and identification of himself with his offering. In figure it answers to the Christian's faith accepting and identifying himself with Christ (Rom. 4:5; 6:3–11). The believer is justified by faith, and his faith is reckoned for

the head of the burnt offering, and it
will be accepted on his behalf to make
[a]atonement for him.
5 'He shall kill the bull before the
LORD; and the priests, Aaron's sons,
shall bring the blood and sprinkle the
[b]blood all around on the altar that *is*
by the door of the tabernacle of meeting.
6 'And he shall [c]skin the burnt offering and cut it into its pieces.
7 'The sons of Aaron the priest
shall put [d]fire on the altar, and lay the
wood in order on the fire.
8 'Then the priests, Aaron's sons,
shall lay the parts, the head, and the
[e]fat in order on the wood that *is* on the
[1]fire upon the altar;
9 'but he shall wash its entrails
and its legs with water. And the priest
shall burn all on the altar as a burnt
sacrifice, an [f]offering made by fire, a
[2][g]sweet [h]aroma to the LORD.
10 'If his offering *is* of the flocks—
of the sheep or of the goats—as a
burnt sacrifice, he shall bring a male
without blemish.
11 'He shall kill it on the north side
of the altar before the LORD; and the
priests, Aaron's sons, shall sprinkle
its blood all around on the altar.
12 'And he shall cut it into its
pieces, with its head and its fat; and
the priest shall lay them in order on
the wood that *is* on the fire upon the
altar;
13 'but he shall wash the entrails
and the legs with water. Then the
priest shall bring *it* all and burn *it* on
the altar; it *is* a burnt sacrifice, an [i]of-

4
a See Ex. 29:33, *note*
5
b Lev. 17:11
6
c Lev. 7:8
7
d Cp. Mal. 1:10
8
e i.e. *that which burns most quickly—devotedness, zeal.* Lev. 3:3–4; 7:23–24
9
f Num. 15:3, 8–10
g Ex. 29:18; cp. Eph. 5:2
h i.e. *aroma of satisfaction*
13
i Num. 15:4–7; 28:12–14
14
j Gen. 15:9; Lev. 5:7,11
16
k Lev. 6:10
17
l Gen. 15:10; Lev. 5:8
CHAPTER 2
1
m Cp. Lev. 5:11

fering made by fire, a sweet aroma to
the LORD.
14 'And if the burnt sacrifice of his
offering to the LORD *is* of birds, then he
shall bring his offering of [j]turtledoves
or young pigeons.
15 'The priest shall bring it to the
altar, wring off its head, and burn *it* on
the altar; its blood shall be drained out
at the side of the altar.
16 'And he shall remove its crop
with its feathers and cast it beside the
altar on the east side, into the place for
[k]ashes.
17 'Then he shall split it at its
wings, *but* shall not divide *it* [l]com-
pletely; and the priest shall burn it on
the altar, on the wood that *is* on the
fire. It *is* a burnt sacrifice, an offering
made by fire, a sweet aroma to the
LORD.

Sweet aroma offerings: (2) the grain offering (v. 1). (See Lev. 6:14–23)

2 'WHEN anyone offers a grain offering to the LORD, his offering
shall be *of* [3]fine flour. And he shall
pour oil on it, and put [m]frankincense
on it.
2 'He shall bring it to Aaron's
sons, the priests, one of whom shall
take from it his handful of fine flour
and oil with all the frankincense. And
the priest shall burn *it as* a [n]memorial
on the altar, an [o]offering made by fire,
a sweet aroma to the LORD.
3 'The rest of the grain offering

2:2 *n* Lev. 2:9,16 *o Sacrifice* (typical): vv. 1–16; Lev. 3:1. (Gen. 3:15; Heb. 10:18, *note*)

righteousness because his faith identifies him with Christ, who died as his sin offering (2 Cor. 5:21; 1 Pet. 2:24).

[1](1:8) Fire. Essentially this is a symbol of God's holiness (Heb. 12:29). As such it expresses God in three ways: (1) in judgment upon that which His holiness utterly condemns (e.g. Gen. 19:24; Mk. 9:43–48; Rev. 20:15); (2) in the manifestation of Himself and of that which He approves (e.g. Ex. 3:2; 13:21; 1 Pet. 1:7); and (3) in purification (e.g. Mal. 3:2–3; 1 Cor. 3:12–14). So, in Leviticus, the fire which only manifests the sweet aroma of the burnt, grain, and peace offerings wholly consumes the sin offering.

[2](1:9) The "sweet aroma" offerings are so called because they typify Christ in His own perfections and in His affectionate devotion to the Father's will. The offerings which are not "sweet aroma" offerings typify Christ as bearing the whole demerit of the sinner. Both are substitutional. In our place Christ, in the burnt offering, makes good our lack of devotedness and, in the sin offering and trespass offering, suffers because of our disobedience.

[3](2:1) The grain offering: (1) fine flour speaks of the evenness and balance of the character of Christ, of that perfection in which no quality was in excess, none lacking; (2) fire, of His testing by suffering, even to the point of death; (3) frankincense, of the fragrance of His life before God (see Ex. 30:34, *note*); (4) absence of leaven, of His character as "the Truth" (Jn. 14:6, cp. Ex. 12:8, *marg.*); (5) absence of honey—His was not that mere natural sweetness which may exist quite apart from grace; (6) oil mixed, of Christ as born of the Holy Spirit (Mt. 1:18–23); (7) oil on, of Christ as baptized with the Spirit (Jn. 1:32; 6:27); (8) the oven, of the unseen sufferings of Christ—His inner agonies (Mt. 27:45–46; Heb. 2:18); (9) the pan, of His more evident sufferings (e.g. Mt. 27:27–31); and (10) salt, of the pungency of the truth of God—that which arrests the action of leaven.

shall be Aaron's and his [a]sons'. *It is*
most holy of the offerings to the LORD
made by fire.
4 'And if you bring as an offering
a grain offering baked in the oven, *it*
shall be unleavened cakes of fine flour
mixed with oil, or [b]unleavened wafers
anointed with oil.
5 'But if your offering *is* a grain
offering *baked* in a pan, *it shall be of*
fine flour, unleavened, mixed with oil.
6 'You shall break it in pieces and
pour oil on it; it *is* a grain offering.
7 'If your offering *is* a grain offering *baked* in a [c]covered pan, it shall
be made *of* fine flour with oil.
8 'You shall bring the grain offering that is made of these things to the
LORD. And when it is presented to the
priest, he shall bring it to the altar.
9 'Then the priest shall take from
the grain offering a [d]memorial portion, and burn *it* on the altar. *It is* an
offering made by fire, a sweet aroma
to the LORD.
10 'And what is left of the grain offering *shall be* Aaron's and his sons'.
It is most holy of the offerings to the
LORD made by fire.
11 'No grain offering which you
bring to the LORD shall be made with
[1]leaven, for you shall burn no leaven
nor any [2]honey in any offering to the
LORD made by fire.

(Offering of firstfruits)

12 'As for the offering of the [e]first-
fruits, you shall offer them to the LORD,
but they shall not be burned on the
altar for a sweet aroma.
13 'And every offering of your
grain offering you shall season with
[3]salt; you shall not allow the salt of the
covenant of your God to be lacking
from your grain offering. With all
your offerings you shall offer salt.
14 'If you offer a grain offering of
your [f]firstfruits to the LORD, you shall
offer for the grain offering of your
firstfruits green heads of grain
roasted on the fire, grain beaten from
full heads.
15 'And you shall put oil on it, and
lay frankincense on it. It *is* a grain offering.
16 'Then the priest shall burn the
memorial portion: *part* of its beaten
grain and *part* of its oil, with all the
frankincense, as an offering made by
fire to the LORD.

Sweet aroma offerings: (3) the peace offering (v. 1). (See Lev. 7:11–21)

3 'WHEN his offering *is* a [g]sacrifice
of a [4]peace offering, if he offers *it*
of the herd, whether male or female,
he shall offer it without [h]blemish before the LORD.
2 'And he shall [i]lay his hand on
the head of his offering, and kill it *at*
the door of the tabernacle of meeting;
and Aaron's sons, the priests, shall
[j]sprinkle the blood all around on the
altar.
3 'Then he shall offer from the sacrifice of the peace offering an offering
made by fire to the LORD. The fat that
covers the entrails and all the [k]fat that
is on the entrails,
4 'the two kidneys and the fat that
is on them by the flanks, and the fatty
lobe *attached* to the liver above the
kidneys, he shall remove;
5 'and Aaron's [l]sons shall [m]burn
it on the altar upon the [n]burnt sacrifice, which *is* on the wood that *is* on
the fire, *as* an [o]offering made by fire,
a [p]sweet aroma to the LORD.
6 'If his offering as a sacrifice of a
peace offering to the LORD *is* of the
flock, *whether* male or female, he
shall offer it without blemish.
7 'If he offers a [q]lamb as his offering, then he shall [r]offer it [s]before the
LORD.
8 'And he shall lay his hand on the
head of his offering, and kill it before
the tabernacle of meeting; and
Aaron's sons shall sprinkle its blood
all around on the altar.

3
a Lev. 6:16; 10:12–13
4
b Leaven: vv. 4–5,11; Lev. 6:16. (Gen. 19:3; Mt. 13:33, *note*)
7
c Lev. 7:9
9
d v. 2
12
e Ex. 34:22; Lev. 23:10, 17
14
f Lev. 23:14
CHAPTER 3
1
g Sacrifice (typical): vv. 1–17; Lev. 4:3. (Gen. 3:15; Heb. 10:18, *note*)
h Lev. 22:20–24
2
i Lev. 1:4; 16:21; cp. Isa. 53:6
j Lev. 1:5
3
k Lev. 1:8; 3:16
5
l Ex. 29:27–28; Lev. 7:28–34
m 2 Chr. 35:14
n Num. 28:3–10
o Num. 15:8–10
p Lev. 1:9
7
q Num. 15:4–5
r 1 Ki. 8:62
s Lev. 17:8–9

[1](2:11) For meanings of leaven, see Mt. 13:33, *note;* also Lev. 7:13, *note.*

[2](2:11) Honey is mere natural sweetness and could not symbolize the divine graciousness of the Lord Jesus.

[3](2:13) Compare Num. 18:19; 2 Chr. 13:5; Ezek. 43:24; Mk. 9:49–50; Col. 4:6.

[4](3:1) The peace offering. The whole work of Christ in relation to the believer's peace is here in type. Christ (1) made peace, Col. 1:20; (2) preached peace, Eph. 2:17; and (3) is our peace, Eph. 2:14. In Christ, God and the sinner meet in peace: God is propitiated, the sinner reconciled; both are alike satisfied with what Christ has done. But all this was at the cost of blood and fire. The details speak of fellowship. This brings in prominently the thought of fellowship with God through Christ. Hence the peace offering is set forth as affording food for the priests (Lev. 7:31–34). Observe that it is the breast (affections) and thighs (strength) on which we, as priests (1 Pet. 2:9), feed in fellowship with the Father. This it is which makes the peace offering especially a thank offering (Lev. 7:11–13).

THE LEVITICAL SACRIFICES

Sacrifice	*Method*	*Purpose*	***New Testament Typology***
1. Burnt Offering (Hebrew *olah*): A sweet aroma and a freewill offering. A male sheep, goat, bull, turtledoves, or young pigeons. (Lev. 1:3–17; 6:8–13)	All except skin burned on the altar of burnt offering (Lev. 1:8; 7:8) morning and evening (Ex. 29:38–39). The skin was given to the priests (Lev. 7:8).	Denoted total surrender to God as well as substitutionary atonement for offerer.	Christ's total surrender to God on behalf of the believer (Heb. 12:2–3) and His emptying of Himself to become sin for the sinner (2 Cor. 5:21; Phil. 2:6–8). Cp. Lev. 1:3, *note*.
2. Grain Offering (Hebrew *minchah*): A sweet aroma and a freewill offering. Either: a. Fine flour, oil, and frankincense. b. Unleavened cakes or wafers of fine flour and oil. c. Green heads of grain. (Lev. 2:1–16; 6:14–23)	Memorial portions of either of the following were burned on the altar of burnt offering: a. Fine flour, oil, and frankincense mixed (Lev. 2:1–2). b. Cakes or wafers baked in oven, pan, or covered pan (Lev. 2:4–5,7). c. Green grain roasted, mixed with oil and frankincense (Lev. 2:14–15). Remaining portions eaten by priests (Lev. 2:3,10; 6:16–18).	Grain offerings were made together with burnt offerings as sacrifices of thanksgiving and devotion to God.	Christ's sinless humanity is denoted by absence of leaven (Heb. 4:15). Oil signifies Christ born of and baptized with the Holy Spirit (Jn. 1:32). Cp. Lev. 2:1, *note*.
3. Peace Offering (Hebrew *shelem*): A sweet aroma and a freewill offering. An unblemished male or female from cattle, sheep, or goats. A bull or lamb could have a limb too short. (Lev. 3:1–17; 22:23)	Fat on entrails, on breast, and on right thigh burned with kidneys on the altar of burnt offering (Lev. 3:3–4). Priests were given right thigh and breast (Lev. 7:31–32). Offerer and family ate remaining portions (Lev. 7:15–17). Only peace offerings were eaten by offerer.	Right relationship and friendship with God were represented by peace offerings and celebrated at a fellowship meal. Peace offerings were rendered as thanksgiving for divine help and blessing.	Believers enjoy peace with God through Jesus Christ, their eternal Peace Offering (Rom. 5:1). Cp. Lev. 3:1, *note*.
4. Sin Offering (Hebrew *chattath*): Was not a sweet aroma and was a required offering. Four classes: a. A young bull for the high priest. b. A young bull for the congregation. c. A male goat for a ruler. d. A female goat or female lamb for the common people. (Lev. 4:1–35; 6:24–30)	Fat on entrails, along with kidneys, was burned on the altar of burnt offering (Lev. 4:8–10,19,26,31,35). For the high priest or the congregation, what remained of the young bull was burned outside the camp (Lev. 4:11–12,20–21). For a ruler or member of the common people, remaining portions of the lamb or goat were eaten by the priests in the court of the tabernacle (Lev. 6:26).	The sin offering was required for unintentional sin (Lev. 4:2).	In His death Christ bore the believer's sin in His own body in place of the sinner (2 Cor. 5:21; 1 Pet. 2:24). Cp. Lev. 4:3, *note*.
5. Trespass Offering (Hebrew *asham*): Was not a sweet aroma and was a required offering. Unintentional sins against holy things or against a neighbor: An unblemished ram and restitution of value plus one fifth. Other sins against God: An unblemished ram. Poor persons could bring two turtledoves or two young pigeons, and even poorer persons could bring fine flour. (Lev. 5:1—6:7; 7:1–7)	Fat and kidneys of the unblemished ram were burned on the altar of burnt offering (Lev. 7:3–5). Remaining portions of the ram were eaten by priests in a holy place (Lev. 7:6–7). Restitution plus one fifth was made for trespasses against holy things and neighbors (Lev. 5:16; 6:5). Birds were drained of blood. Birds or flour were then burned on the altar (Lev. 5:7–12).	The trespass offering was required for unintentional sin against the Lord, against holy things, and against neighbors (Lev. 5:15,17; 6:2–3).	Christ is the only remaining sacrifice for all sin and trespasses (Rom. 8:3–4; 1 Jn. 1:7). Cp. Lev. 5:6, *note*.

9 'Then he shall offer from the sacrifice of the peace offering, as an offering made by fire to the LORD, its fat *and* the whole fat tail which he shall remove close to the backbone. And the fat that covers the entrails and all the fat that *is* on the entrails,

10 'the two kidneys and the [a]fat that *is* on them by the flanks, and the fatty lobe *attached* to the liver above the kidneys, he shall remove;

11 'and the priest shall burn *them* on the altar *as* [b]food, an offering made by fire to the LORD.

12 'And if his [c]offering *is* a goat, then he shall offer it before the LORD.

13 'He shall lay his hand on its head and kill it before the tabernacle of meeting; and the sons of Aaron shall sprinkle its blood all around on the altar.

14 'Then he shall offer from it his offering, as an offering made by fire to the LORD. The fat that covers the entrails and all the fat that *is* on the entrails,

15 'the two kidneys and the fat that *is* on them by the flanks, and the fatty lobe *attached* to the liver above the kidneys, he shall remove;

16 'and the priest shall burn them on the altar *as* [d]food, an offering made by fire for a sweet aroma; [e]all the fat *is* the LORD's.

17 '*This shall be* a perpetual statute throughout your generations in all your dwellings: you shall eat neither fat nor [f]blood.' "

Non-sweet aroma offerings: (1) the sin offering (v. 3). (See Lev. 6:25–30)

4 NOW the LORD spoke to Moses, saying,

2 "Speak to the children of Israel, saying: 'If a person sins [g]unintentionally against any of the commandments of the LORD *in anything* which ought not to be done, and does any of them,

3 'if the [h]anointed priest sins, bringing guilt on the people, then let him [i]offer to the LORD for his sin which he has sinned a young bull without [j]blemish as a [1k]sin offering.

4 'He shall bring the bull to the door of the tabernacle of meeting before the LORD, [l]lay his hand on the bull's head, and kill the bull before the LORD.

5 'Then the anointed priest shall take some of the bull's blood and bring it to the tabernacle of meeting.

6 'The priest shall dip his finger in the blood and sprinkle some of the blood seven times before the LORD, in front of the [m]veil of the sanctuary.

7 'And the priest shall put some of the blood on the horns of the [n]altar of sweet incense before the LORD, which is in the tabernacle of meeting; and he shall pour the remaining blood of the bull at the base of the [o]altar of the burnt offering, which is at the door of the tabernacle of meeting.

8 'He shall take from it all the fat of the bull as the sin offering. The fat that covers the entrails and all the fat which *is* on the entrails,

9 'the two kidneys and the fat that *is* on them by the flanks, and the fatty lobe *attached* to the liver above the kidneys, he shall remove,

10 'as it was taken from the bull of the sacrifice of the [p]peace offering; and the priest shall burn them on the altar of the burnt offering.

11 'But the bull's [q]hide and all its flesh, with its head and legs, its entrails and offal—

12 'the whole bull he shall carry [2]outside the camp to a clean place, where the ashes are poured out, and burn it on wood with fire; where the

10
a v. 4
11
b Num. 28:2; Lev. 21:6,8,17
12
c Num. 15:6–11
16
d v. 11
e Lev. 7:23–25
17
f Lev. 7:26; 17:10–16
CHAPTER 4
2
g Lev. 5:15–18; cp. Acts 3:17
3
h Ex. 40:15
i Sacrifice (typical): vv. 3–35; Lev. 5:1. (Gen. 3:15; Heb. 10:18, *note*)
j Lev. 3:1
k Lev. 9:7
4
l Lev. 1:4
6
m Ex. 40:21, 26
7
n Cp. Lev. 4:18,25,30, 34
o Ex. 40:5–6
10
p Lev. 3:3–4
11
q Ex. 29:14; Lev. 9:11

[1](4:3) The sin offering symbolizes Christ laden with the believer's sin, absolutely in the sinner's place and stead and not, as in the "sweet aroma" offerings, in His own perfections. It is Christ's death as viewed in Isa. 53; Ps. 22; Mt. 26:28; 1 Pet. 2:24; 3:18. But observe how the essential holiness of Him who was "made sin for us" is guarded (Lev. 6:24–30; 2 Cor. 5:21). The sin offerings are expiatory, substitutional, and efficacious (vv. 12,29,35), and have in view the vindication of the law through substitutional sacrifice.

[2](4:12) Compare Ex. 29:14; Lev. 16:27; Num. 19:3; Heb. 13:10–13. The last passage is the interpretative one. The "camp" was Judaism—a religion of forms and ceremonies. "Therefore Jesus also, that He might sanctify [separate, or set apart for God] the people with His own blood, suffered outside the gate [temple gate, i.e. Judaism civil and religious]" (Heb. 13:12). But how does this sanctify, or set apart a people? "Therefore let us go forth to Him, outside the camp [Judaism then, legalistic Christianity now—anything religious which denies Christ as our sin offering], bearing His reproach" (Heb. 13:13). The sin offering, burned outside the camp, typifies this aspect of the death of Christ. The cross becomes a new altar in a new place where, without the smallest merit in themselves, the redeemed gather to offer, as believer-priests, spiritual sacrifices (Heb. 13:15; 1 Pet. 2:5). The bodies of the sin-offering beasts were

ashes are poured out it shall be burned.

13 'Now if the [a]whole congregation of Israel sins unintentionally, and the thing is hidden from the eyes of the assembly, and they have done *something against* any of the commandments of the LORD *in anything* which should not be done, and are guilty;

14 'when the sin which they have committed becomes known, then the assembly shall offer a young [b]bull for the sin, and bring it before the tabernacle of meeting.

15 'And the elders of the congregation shall lay their hands on the head of the bull [c]before the LORD. Then the bull shall be killed before the LORD.

16 'The anointed priest shall bring some of the bull's blood to the tabernacle of meeting.

17 'Then the priest shall dip his finger in the blood and sprinkle *it* seven times before the LORD, in front of the veil.

18 'And he shall put *some* of the blood on the horns of the [d]altar which *is* before the LORD, which *is* in the tabernacle of meeting; and he shall pour the remaining blood at the base of the altar of burnt offering, which is at the door of the tabernacle of meeting.

19 'He shall take all the fat from it and burn *it* on the altar.

20 'And he shall do with the bull as he did with the bull as a [e]sin offering; thus he shall do with it. So the priest shall make [f]atonement for them, and it shall be [g]forgiven them.

21 'Then he shall [h]carry the bull outside the camp, and burn it as he burned the first bull. It *is* a sin offering for the assembly.

22 'When a ruler has sinned, and done *something* unintentionally *against* any of the commandments of the LORD his God *in anything* which should not be done, and is guilty,

23 'or if his sin which he has committed comes to his knowledge, he shall bring as his offering a kid of the goats, a male without blemish.

24 'And he shall lay his hand on the head of the goat, and kill it at the place where they kill the burnt offering before the LORD. It *is* a sin offering.

25 'The priest shall take some of the blood of the sin offering with his finger, put *it* on the horns of the altar of burnt offering, and pour its blood at the base of the altar of burnt offering.

26 'And he shall burn all its fat on the altar, like the fat of the sacrifice of the [i]peace offering. So the priest shall make [j]atonement for him concerning his sin, and it shall be forgiven him.

27 'If anyone of the common people sins unintentionally by doing *something against* any of the commandments of the LORD *in anything* which ought not to be done, and is guilty,

28 'or if his sin which he has committed comes to his knowledge, then he shall bring as his offering a kid of the goats, a female without blemish, for his sin which he has committed.

29 'And he shall lay his hand on the head of the sin offering, and kill the sin offering at the place of the burnt offering.

30 'Then the priest shall take *some* of its blood with his finger, put *it* on the horns of the altar of burnt offering, and pour all *the remaining* blood at the base of the altar.

31 'He shall remove all its fat, as fat is removed from the sacrifice of the [i]peace offering; and the priest shall burn it on the altar for a [k]sweet aroma to the LORD. So the priest shall make [j]atonement for him, and it shall be forgiven him.

32 'If he brings a lamb as his sin offering, he shall bring a female without blemish.

33 'Then he shall [l]lay his hand on the head of the sin offering, and kill it as a sin offering at the place where they kill the burnt offering.

34 'The priest shall take *some* of the blood of the sin offering with his finger, put *it* on the horns of the altar of burnt offering, and pour all *the remaining* blood at the base of the altar.

35 'He shall remove all its fat, as the fat of the lamb is removed from the sacrifice of the [i]peace offering. Then the priest shall burn it on the altar, according to the offerings made by fire to the LORD. So the priest shall make [m]atonement for his sin that he has committed, and it shall be forgiven him.

Non-sweet aroma offerings: (2) the trespass offering (v. 6). (See Lev. 7:1–7)

5 'IF a person [n]sins in [o]hearing the utterance of an oath, and *is* a witness, whether he has seen or known *of*

13 *a* Num. 15:24–26
14 *b* v. 3; cp. vv. 23,28
15 *c* Lev. 1:3–5
18 *d* v. 7
20 *e* vv. 3–12 *f* Lev. 1:4. See Ex. 29:33, *note* *g Forgiveness:* vv. 20,26, 31,35; Lev. 5:10. (Lev. 4:20; Mt. 26:28, *note*)
21 *h* See v. 12, *note*
26 *i* Lev. 3:3–4 *j* See Lev. 16:6, *note*
31 *k* Lev. 1:9
33 *l* Num. 8:12
35 *m* See Ex. 29:33, *note*
CHAPTER 5
1 *n Sacrifice* (typical): vv. 1–19; Lev. 6:2. (Gen. 3:15; Heb. 10:18, *note*) *o* Cp. Jud. 17:12; Prov. 29:24

---

burned outside the camp, not because they were unfit for a holy camp but, rather, because an unholy camp was an unfit place for a holy sin offering.

the matter—if he does not tell *it*, he bears guilt.

2 'Or if a person touches any unclean thing, whether *it is* the carcass of an unclean beast, or the carcass of unclean livestock, or the carcass of unclean creeping things, and he is unaware of it, he also shall be unclean and guilty.

3 'Or if he touches human uncleanness—whatever uncleanness with which a man may be defiled, and he is unaware of it—when he realizes *it*, then he shall be guilty.

4 'Or if a person swears, speaking thoughtlessly with *his* lips to do evil or to do good, whatever *it is* that a man may pronounce by an [a]oath, and he is unaware of it—when he realizes *it*, then he shall be guilty in any of these *matters*.

5 'And it shall be, when he is guilty in any of these *matters*, that he shall [b]confess that he has sinned in that *thing;*

6 'and he shall bring his [1]trespass offering to the LORD for his sin which he has committed, a female from the flock, a lamb or a kid of the goats as a sin offering. So the priest shall make [c]atonement for him concerning his sin.

7 'If he is [d]not able to bring a lamb, then he shall bring to the LORD, for his trespass which he has committed, two turtledoves or two young pigeons: one as a sin offering and the other as a burnt offering.

8 'And he shall bring them to the priest, who shall offer *that* which *is* for the sin offering first, and wring off its head from its neck, but shall not divide *it* [e]completely.

9 'Then he shall sprinkle *some* of the blood of the sin offering on the side of the altar, and the rest of the blood shall be [f]drained out at the base of the altar. It *is* a sin offering.

10 'And he shall offer the second *as* a burnt offering according to the prescribed [g]manner. So the priest shall make [c]atonement on his behalf for his sin which he has committed, and it shall be [h]forgiven him.

11 'But if he is [i]not able to bring two turtledoves or two young pigeons, then he who sinned shall bring for his offering one-tenth of an [j]ephah of fine flour as a sin offering. He shall put no oil on it, nor shall he put frankincense [k]on it, for it *is* a sin offering.

12 'Then he shall bring it to the priest, and the priest shall take his handful of it as a memorial portion, and burn *it* on the altar according to the offerings made by fire to the LORD. It *is* a sin offering.

13 'The priest shall make atonement for him, for his sin that he has committed in any of these matters; and it shall be forgiven him. *The rest* shall be the [l]priest's as a grain offering.' "

14 Then the LORD spoke to Moses, saying:

15 "If a person commits a [m]trespass, and sins [n]unintentionally in regard to the holy things of the LORD, then he shall bring to the LORD as his trespass offering a ram without blemish from the flocks, with your valuation in [j]shekels of silver according to the [o]shekel of the sanctuary, as a [p]trespass offering.

16 "And he shall make restitution for the harm that he has done in regard to the holy thing, and shall add [q]one-fifth to it and give it to the priest. So the priest shall make [c]atonement for him with the ram of the trespass offering, and it shall be forgiven him.

17 "If a person sins, and commits any of these things which are forbidden to be done by the commandments of the LORD, though he does not know *it*, yet he is guilty and shall bear his iniquity.

18 "And he shall bring to the priest a ram without blemish from the flock, with your valuation, as a trespass offering. So the priest shall make [c]atonement for him regarding his ignorance in which he erred and did not know *it*, and it shall be forgiven him.

19 "It is a trespass offering; he has certainly trespassed against the LORD."

The trespass offering and restitution
(v. 5; see Lev. 7:1–7)

6

AND the LORD spoke to Moses, saying:

2 [r]"If a person sins and commits a [s]trespass [t]against the LORD by lying to his neighbor about what was delivered to him for [u]safekeeping, or about

4 [a] Cp. Mt. 5:33–37; Jas. 5:12
5 [b] Num. 5:7; Ps. 32:5; 1 Jn. 1:9; cp. Lev. 16:21; Josh. 7:19
6 [c] See Ex. 29:33, *note*
7 [d] Lev. 12:8; 14:21
8 [e] Lev. 1:17
9 [f] Lev. 4:7
10 [g] Lev. 1:14–17 [h] *Forgiveness:* vv. 10,13, 16,18; Lev. 6:7. (Lev. 4:20; Mt. 26:28, *note*)
11 [i] Cp. Lev. 14:21–32 [j] See Weights and Measures (OT), 2 Chr. 2:10, *note* [k] Cp. Lev. 2:1–2; 6:15
13 [l] Lev. 2:3; 6:17,26
15 [m] Num. 5:5–8 [n] Lev. 4:2 [o] See Ex. 30:13, *note* [p] Ezra 10:19
16 [q] Lev. 6:5
CHAPTER 6
2 [r] *Sacrifice (typical):* vv. 1–7; Lev. 16:5. (Gen. 3:15; Heb. 10:18, *note*) [s] Num. 5:6 [t] Cp. Ps. 51:4 [u] Ex. 22:7–15

[1](5:6) The trespass offerings (5:1—6:7 and 7:1–10) have in view the injury which sin does rather than its guilt, which is the aspect of the sin offering. What is due to God's rights in every human being is here meant. Ps. 51:4 is a perfect expression of this.

a pledge, or about a robbery, or if he has extorted from his neighbor,

3 "or if he has found what was [a]lost and lies concerning it, and swears falsely—in any one of these things that a man may do in which he sins:

4 "then it shall be, because he has sinned and is guilty, that he shall [b]restore what he has stolen, or the thing which he has extorted, or what was delivered to him for safekeeping, or the lost thing which he found,

5 "or all that about which he has sworn falsely. He shall restore its full value, add [c]one-fifth more to it, *and* give it to whomever it belongs, on the day of his [d]trespass offering.

6 "And he shall bring his trespass offering to the LORD, a ram without [e]blemish from the flock, with your valuation, as a trespass offering, to the priest.

7 "So the [f]priest shall make [g]atonement for him before the LORD, and he shall be [h]forgiven for any one of these things that he may have done in which he trespasses."

Law of the offerings: (1) the burnt offering (Lev. 1:1–17)

8 Then the LORD spoke to Moses, saying,

9 "Command Aaron and his sons, saying, 'This *is* the [i]law of the burnt offering: The burnt offering *shall be* on the hearth upon the altar all night until morning, and the fire of the altar shall be kept burning on it.

10 'And the priest shall put on his linen [j]garment, and his linen [k]trousers he shall put on his body, and take up the ashes of the burnt offering which the fire has consumed on the [l]altar, and he shall put them beside the altar.

11 'Then he shall take off his garments, put on other garments, and carry the ashes [m]outside the camp to a clean place.

12 'And the fire on the altar shall be kept burning on it; it shall not be put out. And the priest shall burn wood on it every morning, and lay the burnt offering in order on it; and he shall burn [n]on it the fat of the peace offerings.

13 'A fire shall always be burning on the [o]altar; it shall never go out.

Law of the offerings: (2) the grain offering (Lev. 2:1–16)

14 'This *is* the law of the grain offering: The sons of Aaron shall offer it on the altar before the LORD.

15 'He shall take from it his handful of the fine flour of the grain offering, with its oil, and all the frankincense which *is* on the grain offering, and shall burn *it* on the altar *for* a sweet aroma, as a memorial to the LORD.

16 'And the remainder of it Aaron and his sons shall eat; with [p]unleavened bread it shall be eaten in a holy place; in the [q]court of the tabernacle of meeting they shall eat it.

17 'It shall not be baked with leaven. I have given it *as* their portion of My offerings made by fire; it *is* most holy, like the sin offering and the [r]trespass offering.

18 'All the males among the children of Aaron may eat it. *It shall be* a statute forever in your generations concerning the offerings made by fire to the LORD. Everyone who touches them must be holy.' "*

19 And the LORD spoke to Moses, saying,

20 "This *is* the offering of Aaron and his sons, which they shall offer to the LORD, *beginning* on the day when he is [s]anointed: one-tenth of an [t]ephah of fine flour as a [u]daily grain offering, half of it in the morning and half of it at night.

21 "It shall be made in a [v]pan with oil. *When it is* mixed, you shall bring it in. The baked pieces of the grain offering you shall offer *for* a sweet aroma to the LORD.

22 "The priest from among his sons, who is anointed in his place, shall offer it. *It is* a statute forever to the LORD. It shall be wholly burned.

23 "For every grain offering for the priest shall be wholly burned. It shall not be eaten."

Law of the offerings: (3) the sin offering (Lev. 4:1–35)

24 Also the LORD spoke to Moses, saying,

25 "Speak to Aaron and to his sons, saying, 'This *is* the law of the sin offering: In the [w]place where the burnt offering is killed, the sin offering shall be killed before the LORD. It *is* most holy.

26 'The priest who offers it for sin shall eat it. In a holy place it shall be eaten, in the court of the tabernacle of meeting.

27 'Everyone who touches its flesh

3 *a* Ex. 23:4; Dt. 22:1–4
4 *b* Lev. 24:18,21
5 *c* Lev. 5:16 *d* Num. 5:7–8
6 *e* Lev. 1:3
7 *f* Lev. 4:26 *g* See Ex. 29:33, *note* *h Forgiveness:* v. 7; Lev. 19:22. (Lev. 4:20; Mt. 26:28, *note*)
9 *i* Num. 28:3–10
10 *j* Ex. 28:39 *k* Ex. 28:42 *l* v. 9
11 *m* Lev. 4:12
12 *n* Lev. 3:5
13 *o* Lev. 6:25; 7:2
16 *p Leaven:* vv. 16–17; Lev. 7:12. (Gen. 19:3; Mt. 13:33, *note*) *q* Ex. 40:8
17 *r* Lev. 7:7
20 *s* Lev. 8:1–36 *t* See Weights and Measures (OT), 2 Chr. 2:10, *note* *u* Num. 4:16
21 *v* Ex. 29:2
25 *w* vv. 9–13; cp. Lev. 10:16–20

* 6:18 Compare Numbers 4:15 and Haggai 2:11–13

must be holy.* And when its blood is
sprinkled on any garment, you shall
wash that on which it was sprinkled,
in a holy place.
28 'But the earthen vessel in which
it is boiled shall be [a]broken. And if it
is boiled in a bronze pot, it shall be
both scoured and rinsed in water.
29 'All the males among the priests
may eat it. It *is* most holy.
30 'But no sin offering from which
any of the blood is brought into the
tabernacle of meeting, to [b]make
atonement in the holy [c]*place,** shall
be [d]eaten. It shall be [e]burned in the
fire.

Law of the offerings: (4) the trespass offering (Lev. 5:1—6:7)

7 'LIKEWISE this *is* the law of the
trespass offering (it *is* most holy):
2 'In the [f]place where they kill the
burnt offering they shall kill the trespass offering. And its blood he shall
sprinkle all around on the altar.
3 'And he shall offer from it all its
fat. The fat tail and the fat that covers
the entrails,
4 'the two kidneys and the fat that
is on them by the flanks, and the fatty
lobe *attached* to the liver above the
kidneys, he shall remove;
5 'and the priest shall burn them
on the altar *as* an offering made by
fire to the LORD. It *is* a trespass offering.
6 'Every male among the priests
may eat [g]it. It shall be eaten in a holy
place. It *is* most holy.
7 'The trespass offering *is* like the
sin offering; *there is* one [h]law for
them both: the priest who makes
[i]atonement with it shall have *it*.
8 'And the priest who offers anyone's burnt offering, that priest shall

28
[a] Lev. 11:33
30
[b] See Lev. 16:6, *note;* cp. Ex. 29:33, *note*
[c] Ex. 26:33
[d] Lev. 4:1–21; 16:2–7
[e] Lev. 16:27
CHAPTER 7
2
[f] vv. 9–13; cp. Lev. 10:16–20
6
[g] Lev. 6:18
7
[h] Lev. 6:24–30
[i] See Ex. 29:33, *note*
12
[j] *Leaven:* vv. 12–13; Lev. 8:2. (Gen. 19:3; Mt. 13:33, *note*)
15
[k] Lev. 22:29–30
16
[l] Lev. 22:18–23; 27:2–33

have for himself the skin of the burnt
offering which he has offered.
9 'Also every grain offering that is
baked in the oven and all that is prepared in the covered pan, or in a pan,
shall be the priest's who offers it.
10 'Every grain offering, *whether*
mixed with oil, or dry, shall belong to
all the sons of Aaron, to one *as much*
as the other.

Law of the offerings: (5) the peace offering (Lev. 3:1–17)

11 'This *is* the law of the sacrifice of
[1]peace offerings which he shall offer
to the LORD:
12 'If he offers it for a thanksgiving,
then he shall offer, with the sacrifice
of thanksgiving, unleavened cakes
mixed with oil, [j]unleavened wafers
anointed with oil, or cakes of blended
flour mixed with oil.
13 'Besides the cakes, *as* his offering he shall offer [2j]leavened bread
with the sacrifice of thanksgiving of
his peace offering.
14 'And from it he shall offer one
cake from each offering *as* a heave
offering to the LORD. It shall belong to
the priest who sprinkles the blood of
the peace offering.
15 'The flesh of the sacrifice of his
peace offering for thanksgiving shall
be eaten the same day it is offered. He
shall not leave any of it until [k]morn-
ing.
16 'But if the sacrifice of his offering *is* a [l]vow or a voluntary offering,
it shall be eaten the same day that he
offers his sacrifice; but on the next
day the remainder of it also may be
eaten;

*
6:27 Compare Numbers 4:15 and Haggai 2:11–13
6:30 The Most Holy Place when capitalized

[1](7:11) In the regulations of the offerings, the peace offering is taken out of its place as third of the "sweet aroma" offerings and placed alone, and after all the "non-sweet aroma" offerings (Lev. 1:9, *note*). The explanation is as simple as the fact is beautiful. In revealing the offerings the LORD works from Himself out to the sinner (see Ex. 25:10, *note*). The whole burnt offering comes first as meeting what is due to the divine affections, and the trespass offering last as meeting the simplest aspect of sin—its injuriousness. But the sinner begins of necessity with that which lies nearest to a newly awakened conscience—a sense, namely, that because of sin he is at enmity with God. His first need, therefore, is peace with God. And that is precisely the Gospel order. Following His resurrection Christ's first message was "Peace" (Jn. 20:19); afterward He showed His hands and His side (v. 20). It is the order of 2 Cor. 5:18–21: first, "the word of reconciliation" (v. 19); then, the trespass offerings (v. 21). Experience thus reverses the order of revelation.

[2](7:13) The use of leaven here is significant. Peace with God is something which the believer shares with God. Christ is our peace offering (Eph. 2:13–18). Any thanksgiving for peace must, first of all, present Him. In v. 12 this is seen, in type, and so leaven is excluded. In v. 13 it is the offerer who gives thanks for his participation in the peace; so leaven fitly signifies that, although he has peace with God through the work of another, the offerer still has evil in him. This is illustrated in Amos 4:5, where the evil in Israel is before God.

17 'the remainder of the flesh of the
sacrifice on the third day must be
burned with fire.
18 'And if *any* of the flesh of the
sacrifice of his peace offering is eaten
at all on the third day, it shall not be
accepted, nor shall it be imputed to
him; it shall be an abomination *to* him
who offers it, and the person who eats
of it shall bear guilt.
19 'The flesh that touches any unclean thing shall not be eaten. It shall
be burned with fire. And as for the
clean flesh, all who are clean may eat
of it.
20 'But the person who eats the
flesh of the sacrifice of the peace offering that *belongs* to the [a]LORD, while he
is [b]unclean, that person shall be [c]cut
off from his people.
21 'Moreover the [d]person who
touches any unclean thing, *such as*
human uncleanness, *an* unclean animal, or any abominable unclean
thing,* and who eats the flesh of the
sacrifice of the peace offering that *belongs* to the LORD, that person shall be
cut off from his people.' "
22 And the LORD spoke to Moses,
saying,
23 "Speak to the children of Israel,
saying: 'You shall not eat any [e]fat, of
ox or sheep or goat.
24 'And the fat of an animal that
dies *naturally*, and the fat of what is
torn by wild beasts, may be used in
any other way; but you shall by no
[f]means eat it.
25 'For whoever eats the fat of the
animal of which men offer an offering
made by fire to the LORD, the person
who eats *it* shall be cut off from his
people.
26 'Moreover you shall not eat any
[g]blood in any of your dwellings,
whether of bird or beast.
27 'Whoever eats any blood, that
person shall be [h]cut off from his people.' "
28 Then the LORD spoke to Moses,
saying,
29 "Speak to the children of Israel,
saying: 'He who offers the sacrifice of
his peace offering to the LORD shall
bring his offering to the LORD from the
sacrifice of his peace offering.
30 'His own hands shall bring the
offerings made by fire to the LORD. The
fat with the breast he shall bring, that

20
a Cp. Heb. 2:17
b Lev. 5:3; 22:3–7; Num. 19:13
c Ex. 31:14
21
d Lev. 11:24,28
23
e Lev. 3:17
24
f Ex. 22:31; Lev. 22:8
26
g Lev. 17:10–16
27
h v. 20
30
i Ex. 29:24–27; Lev. 8:27; 9:21
31
j Num. 18:11; Dt. 18:3
32
k Num. 6:20
35
l Num. 18:8
36
m Ex. 40:13, 15; Lev. 8:12,30
37
n Lev. 6:9, 14,25; 7:1
o Ex. 29:22–34; Lev. 8:22–33
38
p Lev. 1:1
CHAPTER 8
1
q Ex. 29:1–46
2
r Lev. 6:10
s Ex. 30:25
t Ex. 29:10
u Ex. 29:15, 19
v Leaven: vv. 2,26; Lev. 10:12. (Gen. 19:3; Mt. 13:33, *note*)

the breast may be waved *as* a [i]wave
offering before the LORD.
31 'And the priest shall burn the fat
on the altar, but the breast shall be
Aaron's and his [j]sons'.
32 'Also the right thigh you shall
give to the [k]priest *as* a heave offering
from the sacrifices of your peace offerings.
33 'He among the sons of Aaron,
who offers the blood of the peace offering and the fat, shall have the right
thigh for *his* part.
34 'For the breast of the wave offering and the thigh of the heave offering
I have taken from the children of Israel, from the sacrifices of their peace
offerings, and I have given them to
Aaron the priest and to his sons from
the children of Israel by a statute forever.' "
35 This *is* the [l]consecrated portion
for Aaron and his sons, from the offerings made by fire to the LORD, on the
day when *Moses* presented them to
minister to the LORD as priests.
36 The LORD commanded this to be
given to them by the children of Israel,
on the day that [m]He anointed them, *by*
a statute forever throughout their generations.
37 This *is* the [n]law of the burnt offering, the grain offering, the sin offering, the trespass offering, the [o]conse-
crations, and the sacrifice of the peace
offering,
38 which the LORD commanded Moses on Mount Sinai, on the day when
He [p]commanded the children of Israel
to offer their offerings to the LORD in
the Wilderness of Sinai.

II. Consecration of Aaron and His Sons, 8—10

8 AND the LORD spoke to Moses,
[q]saying:
2 "Take [1]Aaron and his sons with
him, and the [r]garments, [s]the anointing oil, a [t]bull as the sin offering, two
[u]rams, and a basket of [v]unleavened
bread;
3 "and gather all the congregation
together at the door of the tabernacle
of meeting."
4 So Moses did as the LORD commanded him. And the congregation

*
7:21 Following Masoretic Text, Septuagint, and Vulgate; Samaritan Pentateuch, Syriac, and Targum read *swarming thing* (compare 5:2).

[1](8:2) The priests did not consecrate themselves, but all was done by another, in this instance Moses acting for the LORD. The priests simply presented their bodies in the sense of Rom. 12:1.

was gathered together at the door of
the tabernacle of meeting.
5 And Moses said to the congregation, "This *is* what the LORD commanded to be done."

Consecration: (1) cleansing
(Eph. 5:25–27; Jn. 13:3–10)

6 Then Moses brought Aaron and
his sons and [a]washed them with water.

Consecration: (2) the high
priest clothed

7 And he [b]put the tunic on him,
girded him with the sash, clothed him
with the robe, and put the ephod on
him; and he girded him with the intricately woven band of the ephod, and
with it tied *the ephod* on him.
8 Then he put the breastplate on
him, and he put the [c]Urim and the
Thummim in the breastplate.
9 And he put the turban on his
head. Also on the [d]turban, on its front,
he put the golden plate, the holy
crown, as the LORD had commanded
Moses.

Consecration: (3) the high
priest's anointing

10 Also Moses took the anointing
oil, and anointed the tabernacle and
all that *was* in it, and [e]consecrated
them.
11 He sprinkled some of it on the
altar seven times, anointed the altar
and all its utensils, and the laver and
its base, to consecrate them.
12 And he [1]poured some of the
anointing oil on Aaron's [f]head and
anointed him, to [g]consecrate him.

Consecration: (4) the priests
clothed (cp. Rom. 13:14)

13 Then Moses brought Aaron's
sons and put tunics on them, girded
them with sashes, and put hats on
them, as the LORD had commanded
Moses.

Consecration: (5) the offerings

14 And he brought the bull for the
sin offering. Then Aaron and his sons
laid their hands on the head of the bull
for the sin offering,
15 and Moses killed *it*. Then he
took the blood, and put *some* on the
horns of the altar all around with his
finger, and purified the altar. And he
poured the blood at the base of the
[h]altar, and [i]consecrated it, to make
[j]atonement for it.
16 Then he took all the fat that *was*
on the entrails, the fatty lobe *attached*
to the liver, and the two kidneys with
their fat, and Moses burned *them* on
the altar.
17 But the bull, its hide, its flesh,
and its offal, he [k]burned with fire
[l]outside the camp, as the LORD had
commanded Moses.
18 Then he brought the ram as the
burnt offering. And Aaron and his
sons laid their hands on the head of
the ram,
19 and Moses killed *it*. Then he
sprinkled the blood all around on the
altar.
20 And he cut the ram into pieces;
and Moses [m]burned the head, the
pieces, and the fat.
21 Then he washed the entrails and
the legs in water. And Moses burned
the whole ram on the altar. It *was* a
burnt sacrifice for a sweet aroma, an
offering made by fire to the LORD, as
the LORD had commanded Moses.

Consecration: (6) the blood applied

22 And he brought the [n]second
ram, the ram of consecration. Then
Aaron and his sons laid their hands on
the head of the ram,
23 and Moses killed *it*. Also he took
some of its [o]blood and put it on the tip
of Aaron's right ear, on the thumb of
his right hand, and on the big toe of his
right foot.
24 Then he brought Aaron's sons.
And Moses put *some* of the [p]blood on
the tips of their right ears, on the
thumbs of their right hands, and on
the big toes of their right feet. And
Moses [q]sprinkled the blood all around
on the altar.
25 Then he [r]took the fat and the fat
tail, all the fat that *was* on the entrails,
the fatty lobe *attached to* the liver, the
two kidneys and their fat, and the
right thigh;
26 and from the basket of unleav-

6
a Cp. Heb. 10:22
7
b Ex. 39:1–31
8
c Urim, *lights;* Thummim, *perfections.* See Ex. 28:30, *note*
9
d Ex. 28:37; 29:6
10
e Ex. 40:10–11
12
f Ps. 133:2
g Ex. 40:13
15
h Lev. 5:9
i Sanctification (OT): v. 15; Lev. 27:14. (Gen. 2:3; Zech. 8:3)
j Heb. *kaphar, to cover.* See Lev. 16:6, *note;* cp. Ex. 29:33, *note*
17
k See Lev. 4:12, *note*
l Lev. 4:11–12
20
m Lev. 1:8
22
n Ex. 29:19, 31
23
o Lev. 14:14
24
p Ex. 29:20; cp. Heb. 9:13–14, 22–23
q v. 19
25
r Ex. 29:22

[1](8:12) Two important distinctions are made in the case of the high priest, thus confirming his typical relation to Christ, the antitype: (1) Aaron is anointed before the sacrifices are slain, whereas in the case of the priests the application of blood precedes the anointing. Christ the sinless One required no preparation for receiving the anointing oil, a symbol of the Holy Spirit. And (2) upon the high priest only was the anointing oil poured. "God does not give the Spirit by measure" (Jn. 3:34). "God, Your God, has anointed You with the oil of gladness more than Your companions" (Heb. 1:9).

ened bread that was before the LORD
he took one unleavened cake, a cake
of bread *anointed with* oil, and one
wafer, and put *them* on the fat and on
the right thigh;

Consecration: (7) the hands filled

27 and he put all *these* in Aaron's
[a]hands and in his sons' hands, and
[b]waved them *as* a wave offering before the LORD.
28 Then Moses took them from
their hands and burned *them* on the
altar, on the burnt offering. They *were*
consecration offerings for a sweet
aroma. That *was* an offering made by
fire to the LORD.
29 And [c]Moses took the [d]breast
and waved it *as* a wave offering before
the LORD. It was Moses' part of the ram
of consecration, as the LORD had commanded Moses.

Consecration: (8) the anointing of the priests

30 Then Moses took some of the
anointing oil and some of the blood
which *was* on the altar, and sprinkled
it on Aaron, on his garments, on his
sons, and on the garments of his sons
with him; and he consecrated Aaron,
his garments, his sons, and the garments of his sons with him.

Consecration: (9) the food of the priests (see Ex. 29:26 and refs.)

31 And Moses said to Aaron and his
sons, "Boil the flesh *at* the door of the
tabernacle of meeting, and eat it there
with the bread that *is* in the basket of
consecration offerings, as I [e]com-
manded, saying, 'Aaron and his sons
shall eat it.'
32 "What remains of the flesh and
of the bread you shall burn with fire.

Consecration: (10) the priests separated to God

33 "And you shall not go outside
the door of the tabernacle of meeting
for seven days, until the days of your
consecration are ended. For seven
days he shall consecrate [f]you.
34 "As he has done this day, *so* the
LORD has commanded to do, to make
[g]atonement for you.
35 "Therefore you shall stay *at* the
door of the tabernacle of meeting day
and night for seven days, and keep the
[h]charge of the LORD, so that you may
not die; for so I have been commanded."
36 So Aaron and his sons did all the
things that the LORD had commanded
by the hand of Moses.

Priests begin their ministry

9 IT came to pass on the [i]eighth
day that Moses called Aaron and
his sons and the elders of Israel.
2 And he said to Aaron, "Take for
yourself a young [j]bull as a sin offering and a ram as a burnt offering,
without blemish, and offer *them* before the LORD.
3 "And to the children of Israel
you shall speak, saying, 'Take a [k]kid
of the goats as a sin offering, and a calf
and a lamb, *both* of the first year,
without blemish, as a burnt offering,
4 'also a bull and a ram as peace
offerings, to sacrifice before the LORD,
and a grain offering mixed with oil;
for today the LORD will appear to
you.' "
5 So they brought what Moses
commanded before the tabernacle of
meeting. And all the congregation
drew near and stood before the LORD.
6 Then Moses said, "This *is* the
thing which the LORD commanded you
to do, and the glory of the LORD will
appear to you."
7 And Moses said to Aaron, "Go to
the altar, offer your sin offering and
your burnt offering, and make [g]atone-
ment for yourself and for the people.
Offer the offering of the people, and
make atonement for them, as the LORD
commanded."
8 Aaron therefore went to the altar and killed the calf of the sin offering, which *was* for [l]himself.
9 Then the sons of Aaron brought
the [m]blood to him. And he dipped his
finger in the blood, put *it* on the horns
of the altar, and poured the blood at
the base of the altar.
10 But the fat, the kidneys, and the
fatty lobe from the liver of the sin offering he burned on the altar, as the
LORD had commanded Moses.
11 The flesh and the hide he burned
with fire outside the camp.
12 And he killed the burnt offering;
and Aaron's sons presented to him the
blood, which he sprinkled all around
on the altar.
13 Then they presented the burnt
offering to him, with its pieces and
head, and he burned *them* on the altar.
14 And he washed the entrails and
the legs, and burned *them* with the
burnt offering on the altar.
15 Then he brought the people's of-

27
a Cp. Ex. 29:24
b Lev. 7:30, 34
29
c Ps. 99:6
d Ex. 29:27
31
e Lev. 7:31–36
33
f Lev. 10:7
34
g See Ex. 29:33, *note*
35
h Num. 1:53
CHAPTER 9
1
i Cp. Ezek. 43:27
2
j Lev. 4:1–12
3
k Lev. 4:23, 28
8
l vv. 8–11; cp. Lev. 4:1–12
9
m Ex. 29:20; cp. Heb. 9:13–14, 22–23

fering, and took the goat, which *was*
the sin offering for the people, and
killed it and offered it for sin, like the
first one.
16 And he brought the burnt offering and offered it according to the prescribed [a]manner.
17 Then he brought the grain offering, took a handful of it, and burned *it*
on the altar, besides the burnt sacrifice of the morning.
18 He also killed the bull and the
ram *as* sacrifices of peace offerings,
which *were* for the people. And
Aaron's sons presented to him the
blood, which he sprinkled all around
on the altar,
19 and the fat from the bull and the
ram—the fatty tail, what covers *the
entrails* and the kidneys, and the fatty
lobe *attached to* the liver;
20 and they put the fat on the
breasts. Then he burned the fat on the
altar;
21 but the breasts and the right
thigh Aaron waved *as* a wave offering
before the LORD, as Moses had commanded.
22 Then Aaron [b]lifted his hand toward the people, blessed them, and
came down from offering the sin offering, the burnt offering, and peace
offerings.
23 And Moses and Aaron went into
the tabernacle of meeting, and came
out and blessed the people. Then the
glory of the LORD appeared to all the
people,
24 and fire came out from before
the [c]LORD and consumed the burnt offering and the fat on the altar. When
all the people saw *it*, they [d]shouted
and fell on their [e]faces.

Profane fire of Nadab and Abihu

10 THEN [f]Nadab and [g]Abihu,
the sons of Aaron, each took
his censer and put fire in it, put incense on it, and offered [1h]profane fire
before the LORD, which He had not
commanded them.
2 So [i]fire went out from the LORD
and devoured them, and they [j]died
before the LORD.
3 And Moses said to Aaron, "This
is what the LORD spoke, saying:
'By those who come near Me
I must be regarded as [k]holy;
And before all the people
I must be glorified.'"
So Aaron held his peace.
4 Then Moses called [l]Mishael and
[m]Elzaphan, the sons of [n]Uzziel the uncle of Aaron, and said to them, "Come
near, [o]carry your brethren from before the sanctuary out of the camp."
5 So they went near and carried
them by their tunics out of the camp,
as Moses had said.

*Three prohibitions (vv. 6,7,9)
and further instructions*

6 And Moses said to Aaron, and to
[p]Eleazar and [q]Ithamar, his sons, "Do
not uncover your heads nor tear your
clothes, lest you die, and [r]wrath come
upon all the people. But let your brethren, the whole house of Israel, bewail
the burning which the LORD has kindled.
7 "You shall [s]not go out from the
door of the tabernacle of meeting, lest
you die, for the anointing oil of the
LORD *is* upon you." And they did according to the word of Moses.
8 Then the LORD spoke to Aaron,
saying:
9 "Do not drink wine or intoxicating [t]drink, you, nor your sons with
you, when you go into the tabernacle
of meeting, lest you die. *It shall be* a
statute forever throughout your generations,
10 "that you may [u]distinguish between holy and unholy, and between
unclean and clean,
11 "and that you may teach the children of Israel all the statutes which
the LORD has spoken to them by the
hand of Moses."
12 And Moses spoke to Aaron, and
to Eleazar and Ithamar, his sons who
were left: "Take the grain offering that
remains of the offerings made by fire
to the LORD, and eat it without [v]leaven
beside the altar; for it *is* most holy.
13 "You shall eat it in a [w]holy place,
because it *is* your due and your sons'
due, of the sacrifices made by fire to
the LORD; for so I have been commanded.

16
a Lev. 1:1–13
22
b Cp. Lk. 24:50
24
c Cp. Jud. 6:21
d Cp. Ezra 3:11
e 1 Ki. 18:38–39
CHAPTER 10
1
f Lit. *liberal*
g Lit. *he is my father*
h Cp. Ex. 30:9
2
i Gen. 19:24; Num. 11:1; Rev. 20:9
j Miracles (OT): vv. 1–2; Num. 11:1. (Gen. 5:24; Jon. 1:17, *note*)
3
k Ex. 19:22
4
l Lit. *who belongs to God*
m Lit. *God has protected*
n Lit. *my strength is God*
o Cp. Acts 5:6,10
6
p Lit. *God has helped*
q Perhaps *isle of palms*
r Num. 16:46; Josh. 7:1; 22:18,20; 2 Sam. 24:1,15
7
s Lev. 8:33
9
t Cp. Gen. 9:21; Ezek. 44:21
10
u Lev. 11:47; Ezek. 22:26
12
v Leaven: v. 12; Lev. 23:6. (Gen. 19:3; Mt. 13:33, *note*) **10:13** *w* Num. 18:10

[1](10:1) Profane fire. Fire "from before the LORD" (Lev. 9:24) had kindled upon the altar of burnt offering the flame which the priests were to keep alive (Lev. 6:12–13). No commandment had yet been given how the incense should be kindled (cp. Lev. 16:12–13). The sin of Nadab and Abihu was in acting in the things of God without seeking the mind of God. It was "self-imposed religion" which often has "an appearance of wisdom" (Col. 2:23).

14 "The breast of the wave offering and the thigh of the heave offering you shall eat in a clean place, you, your sons, and your [a]daughters with you; for *they are* your due and your sons' [b]due, *which* are given from the sacrifices of peace offerings of the children of Israel.

15 "The thigh of the heave offering and the breast of the wave offering they shall bring with the offerings of fat made by fire, to offer *as* a wave offering before the LORD. And it shall be yours and your sons' with you, by a statute forever, as the LORD has commanded."

16 Then Moses made careful inquiry about the goat of the sin offering, and there it was—burned up. And he was angry with Eleazar and Ithamar, the sons of Aaron *who were* left, saying,

17 "Why have you not [c]eaten the sin offering in a holy place, since it *is* most holy, and *God* has given it to you to [d]bear the guilt of the congregation, to make [e]atonement for them before the LORD?

18 "See! Its blood was not brought inside the [f]holy *place;** indeed you should have eaten it in a holy *place,* as I commanded."

19 And Aaron said to Moses, "Look, this day they have offered their sin offering and their burnt offering before the LORD, and such things have befallen me! *If* I had eaten the sin offering today, would it have been [g]accepted in the sight of the LORD?"

20 So when Moses heard *that,* he was content.

III. Laws of Cleanliness and Holiness, 11—15; 17—22

A holy God—a holy people:

(1) their food

11 NOW the LORD [h]spoke to Moses and Aaron, saying to them,

2 "Speak to the children of Israel, saying, [1]'These *are* the animals which you may eat among all the animals that *are* on the earth:

3 'Among the animals, whatever divides the hoof, having cloven hooves *and* chewing the cud—that you may eat.

4 'Nevertheless these you shall [i]not eat among those that chew the cud or those that have cloven hooves: the camel, because it chews the cud but does not have cloven hooves, is unclean to you;

5 'the rock hyrax, because it chews the cud but does not have cloven hooves, *is* unclean to you;

6 'the [2]hare, because it chews the cud but does not have cloven hooves, *is* unclean to you;

7 'and the [j]swine, though it divides the hoof, having cloven hooves, yet does not chew the cud, *is* unclean to you.

8 'Their flesh you shall not eat, and their carcasses you shall not touch. They *are* unclean to you.

9 'These you may eat of all that *are* in the water: whatever in the water has fins and scales, whether in the seas or in the rivers—that you may eat.

10 'But all in the seas or in the rivers that do not have fins and scales, all that move in the water or any living thing which *is* in the water, they *are* an [k]abomination to you.

11 'They shall be an abomination to you; you shall not eat their flesh, but you shall regard their carcasses as an abomination.

12 'Whatever in the water does not have fins or scales—that *shall be* an abomination to you.

13 'And these you shall regard as an abomination among the birds; they shall not be eaten, they *are* an [l]abomination: the eagle, the vulture, the buzzard,

14 'the kite, and the falcon after its kind;

15 'every raven after its kind,

16 'the ostrich, the short-eared owl, the sea gull, and the hawk after its kind;

17 'the little owl, the fisher owl, and the screech owl;

14
a Cp. Lev. 22:13
b Lev. 7:30–34
17
c Lev. 6:24–30
d Ex. 28:38; Lev. 22:16; Num. 18:1
e See Lev. 16:6, *note*
18
f Lev. 6:26, 30
19
g Isa. 1:11, 15; Jer. 6:20; 14:12; Hos. 9:4; Mal. 1:10, 13
CHAPTER 11
1
h vv. 1–47, cp. Dt. 14:3–20
4
i Cp. Acts 10:14
7
j Cp. Mk. 5:1–17
10
k Lev. 7:21
13
l Isa. 66:17

* **10:18** The Most Holy Place when capitalized

[1](11:2) The dietary regulations of the covenant people must be regarded primarily as sanitary. Israel, it must be remembered, was a nation living on the earth under a theocratic government. Of necessity the divine legislation concerned itself with the social as well as the religious life of that people. To force upon every word of that legislation a typical meaning is to strain 1 Cor. 10:1–11 and Heb. 9:23–24 beyond all reasonable interpretation.

[2](11:6) Heb. *arnebeth* is an unidentified animal, apparently not equivalent to the English *hare.* The supposed error in the text is due entirely to the translators' assumption that the English hare and the ancient *arnebeth* were identical.

18 ‘the white owl, the jackdaw, and the carrion vulture;

19 ‘the stork, the heron after its kind, the hoopoe, and the bat.

20 ‘All flying insects that creep on *all* fours *shall be* an abomination to you.

21 ‘Yet these you may eat of every flying insect that creeps on *all* fours: those which have jointed legs above their feet with which to leap on the earth.

22 ‘These you may eat: the [a]locust after its kind, the destroying locust after its kind, the cricket after its kind, and the grasshopper after its kind.

23 ‘But all *other* flying insects which have [b]four feet *shall be* an abomination to you.

24 ‘By these you shall become unclean; whoever [c]touches the carcass of any of them shall be unclean until evening;

25 ‘whoever carries part of the carcass of any of them shall [d]wash his clothes and be unclean until evening:

26 ‘*The carcass* of any animal which divides the foot, but is not cloven-hoofed or does not chew the cud, *is* unclean to you. Everyone who touches it shall be unclean.

27 ‘And whatever goes on its paws, among all kinds of animals that go on *all* fours, those *are* unclean to you. Whoever touches any such carcass shall be unclean until evening.

28 ‘Whoever carries *any such* carcass shall [e]wash his clothes and be unclean until evening. It *is* unclean to you.

29 ‘These also *shall be* unclean to you among the creeping things that creep on the earth: the mole, the [f]mouse, and the large lizard after its kind;

30 ‘the gecko, the monitor lizard, the sand reptile, the sand lizard, and the chameleon.

31 ‘These *are* unclean to you among all that creep. Whoever [g]touches them when they are dead shall be unclean until evening.

32 ‘Anything on which *any* of them falls, when they are dead shall be unclean, whether *it is* any [h]item of wood or clothing or skin or sack, whatever item *it is*, in which *any* work is done, it must be put in water. And it shall be unclean until evening; then it shall be clean.

33 ‘Any [i]earthen vessel into which *any* of them falls you shall [j]break; and whatever *is* in it shall be unclean:

34 ‘in such a vessel, any edible food upon which water falls becomes unclean, and any drink that may be drunk from it becomes unclean.

35 ‘And everything on which *a part* of *any such* carcass falls shall be unclean; *whether it is* an oven or cooking stove, it shall be broken down; *for* they *are* unclean, and shall be unclean to you.

36 ‘Nevertheless a spring or a cistern, *in which there is* plenty of water, shall be clean, but whatever touches any such carcass becomes unclean.

37 ‘And if a part of *any such* carcass falls on any planting seed which is to be sown, it *remains* clean.

38 ‘But if water is put on the seed, and if *a part* of *any such* carcass falls on it, it *becomes* unclean to you.

39 ‘And if any animal which you may eat dies, he who touches its carcass shall be [k]unclean until evening.

40 ‘He who [l]eats of its carcass shall wash his clothes and be unclean until evening. He also who carries its carcass shall wash his clothes and be unclean until evening.

41 ‘And every creeping thing that creeps on the earth *shall be* an abomination. It shall not be eaten.

42 ‘Whatever crawls on its belly, whatever goes on *all* fours, or whatever has many feet among all creeping things that creep on the earth—these you shall not eat, for they *are* an abomination.

43 ‘You shall not make yourselves abominable with any creeping thing that creeps; nor shall you make yourselves unclean with them, lest you be defiled by them.

44 ‘For I *am* the LORD your [m]God. You shall therefore consecrate yourselves, and you shall be holy; for I *am* [n]holy. Neither shall you defile yourselves with any creeping thing that creeps on the earth.

45 ‘For I *am* the LORD who brings you up out of the land of Egypt, to be your [o]God. You shall therefore be holy, for I *am* holy.

46 ‘This *is* the law of the animals and the birds and every living creature that moves in the waters, and of every creature that creeps on the earth,

47 ‘to [p]distinguish between the unclean and the clean, and between the animal that may be eaten and the animal that may not be eaten.’ ”

22 *a* Cp. Mt. 3:4
23 *b* vv. 20,42
24 *c* v. 8
25 *d* Num. 19:10,21; 31:24; cp. Zech. 13:1; Heb. 9:10; 10:22
28 *e* vv. 24–25
29 *f* Isa. 66:17
31 *g* v. 8; Hag. 2:13
32 *h* Lev. 15:12
33 *i* Lev. 6:28 *j* Lev. 6:28; 15:12
39 *k* Hag. 2:11–13
40 *l* Cp. Ex. 22:31; Lev. 17:15; 22:8
44 *m* Ex. 6:7 *n* Lev. 19:2; 1 Pet. 1:16
45 *o* Lev. 22:33; 25:38; 26:45
47 *p* Lev. 10:10; cp. Ex. 11:7

A holy God—a holy people: (2) the law of motherhood (Ps. 51:5; Jn. 3:6)

12 THEN the LORD spoke to Moses, saying,

2 "Speak to the children of Israel, saying: 'If a woman has conceived, and borne a male child, then she shall be unclean [a]seven days; as in the days of her [b]customary impurity she shall be unclean.

3 'And on the [1]eighth day the flesh of his foreskin shall be [c]circumcised.

4 'She shall then continue in the blood of *her* purification thirty-three days. She shall not touch any hallowed thing, nor come into the sanctuary until the days of her purification are fulfilled.

5 'But if she bears a female child, then she shall be unclean two weeks, as in her customary impurity, and she shall continue in the blood of *her* purification sixty-six days.

6 'When the days of her purification are fulfilled, whether for a son or a daughter, she shall bring to the priest a [d]lamb of the first year as a burnt offering, and a young pigeon or a turtledove as a [e]sin offering, to the door of the tabernacle of meeting.

7 'Then he shall offer it before the LORD, and make [f]atonement for her. And she shall be clean from the flow of her blood. This *is* the law for her who has borne a male or a female.

8 'And if she is not [e]able to bring a lamb, then she may bring two [g]turtledoves or two young [h]pigeons—one as a burnt offering and the other as a sin offering. So the priest shall make [f]atonement for her, and she will be clean.' "

A holy God—a holy people: (3) leprosy—type of sin as in Rom. 6:12–14; 1 Jn. 1:8

13 AND the LORD spoke to Moses and Aaron, saying:

2 "When a man has on the skin of his body a [i]swelling, a scab, or a bright spot, and it becomes on the skin of his body *like* a [2]leprous* sore, then he shall be brought to Aaron the [j]priest or to one of his sons the priests.

3 "The priest shall examine the sore on the skin of the body; and if the hair on the sore has turned white, and the sore appears *to be* deeper than the skin of his body, it *is* a leprous sore. Then the priest shall examine him, and pronounce him unclean.

4 "But if the bright spot *is* white on the skin of his body, and does not appear *to be* deeper than the skin, and its hair has not turned white, then the priest shall isolate *the one who has* the sore [k]seven days.

5 "And the priest shall examine him on the seventh day; and indeed *if* the sore appears to be as it was, *and* the sore has not spread on the skin, then the priest shall isolate him another seven days.

6 "Then the priest shall examine him again on the seventh day; and indeed *if* the sore has faded, *and* the sore has not spread on the skin, then the priest shall pronounce him clean; it *is only* a scab, and he shall [l]wash his clothes and be clean.

7 "But if the scab should at all spread over the skin, after he has been seen by the priest for his cleansing, he shall be seen by the priest again.

8 "And *if* the priest sees that the scab has indeed spread on the skin, then the priest shall pronounce him unclean. It *is* leprosy.

9 "When the leprous sore is on a person, then he shall be brought to the priest.

10 [m]"And the priest shall examine *him;* and indeed *if* the swelling on the skin *is* white, and it has turned the hair white, and *there is* a spot of raw flesh in the swelling,

11 "it *is* an old leprosy on the skin of his body. The priest shall pronounce him unclean, and shall not isolate him, for he *is* unclean.

12 "And if leprosy breaks out all over the skin, and the leprosy covers all the skin of *the one who has* the

CHAPTER 12

2 *a* Ex. 22:30; Lev. 8:33; 13:4 *b* Lev. 15:19; 18:19

3 *c* Gen. 17:12; cp. Lk. 1:59; 2:21

6 *d* Cp. Jn. 1:29; 1 Pet. 1:18–19 *e* Lev. 5:7

7 *f* See Lev. 16:6, *note*

8 *g* See Lev. 12:3, *note* *h* Lk. 2:22–24

CHAPTER 13

2 *i* vv. 1–28; cp. 14:56 *j* Dt. 17:8–9; 24:8; Mal. 2:7; Lk. 17:14

4 *k* Lev. 14:8

6 *l* Lev. 11:25; cp. Jn. 13:8,10

10 *m* vv. 1–28; cp. Num. 12:10,12; 2 Ki. 5:27; 2 Chr. 26:20

* **13:2** Hebrew *saraath,* disfiguring skin diseases, including leprosy, and so in verses 2–46 and 14:1–32

[1](12:3) Lk. 2:21–24, with vv. 3–4 shows that our Lord was presented at the temple after forty days (7 plus 33). The poverty of Joseph and Mary is emphasized by the offering of turtledoves (v. 8).

[2](13:2) Medically considered, the symptoms described in chs. 13—14 are not those of the disease known today as leprosy, more accurately called "Hansen's disease," a malady now amenable to treatment. Leprosy in the Bible, as in Num. 12:10–15; 2 Ki. 5; Lk. 5:12–14; and in parts of these two chapters in Leviticus, was something much worse.

Leprosy in the Bible speaks of sin as (1) becoming overt in loathsome ways; and (2) as incurable by human means. The antitype as applied to the people of God is "sin," demanding self-judgment (1 Cor. 11:31); and "sins," demanding confession and cleansing (1 Jn. 1:9).

sore, from his head to his foot, wherever the priest looks,
13 "then the priest shall consider;
and indeed *if* the leprosy has covered
all his body, he shall pronounce *him*
clean *who has* the sore. It has all
turned [a]white. He *is* clean.
14 "But when raw flesh appears on
him, he shall be unclean.
15 "And the priest shall examine
the raw flesh and pronounce him to be
unclean; *for* the raw flesh *is* unclean.
It *is* leprosy.
16 "Or if the raw flesh changes and
turns white again, he shall come to the
priest.
17 "And the priest shall examine
him; and indeed *if* the sore has turned
white, then the priest shall pronounce
him clean *who has* the sore. He *is*
clean.
18 "If the body develops a boil in
the skin, and it is healed,
19 "and in the place of the boil there
comes a white swelling or a bright
spot, reddish-white, then it shall be
shown to the priest;
20 "and *if*, when the priest sees it, it
indeed *appears* deeper than the skin,
and its hair has turned white, the
priest shall pronounce him unclean. It
is a leprous sore which has broken out
of the boil.
21 "But if the priest examines it,
and indeed *there are* no white hairs in
it, and it *is* not deeper than the skin,
but has faded, then the priest shall isolate him seven days;
22 "and if it should at all spread
over the skin, then the priest shall pronounce him unclean. It *is* a leprous
sore.
23 "But if the bright spot stays in
one place, *and* has not spread, it *is* the
scar of the boil; and the priest shall
pronounce him clean.
24 "Or if the body receives a [b]burn
on its skin by fire, and the raw *flesh* of
the burn becomes a bright spot,
reddish-white or white,
25 "then the priest shall examine it;
and indeed *if* the hair of the bright spot
has turned white, and it appears
deeper than the skin, it *is* leprosy broken out in the burn. Therefore the
priest shall pronounce him unclean. It
is a leprous sore.
26 "But if the priest examines it,
and indeed *there are* no white hairs in
the bright spot, and it *is* not deeper
than the skin, but has faded, then the
priest shall isolate him seven days.
27 "And the priest shall examine
him on the seventh day. If it has at all
spread over the skin, then the priest
shall pronounce him unclean. It *is* a
leprous sore.
28 "But if the bright spot stays in
one place, *and* has not spread on the
skin, but has faded, it *is* a swelling
from the burn. The priest shall pronounce him clean, for it *is* the scar
from the burn.
29 "If a man or woman has a [c]sore
on the head or the beard,
30 "then the priest shall examine
the sore; and indeed if it appears
deeper than the skin, *and there is* in it
thin yellow hair, then the priest shall
pronounce him unclean. It *is* a scaly
leprosy of the head or beard.
31 "But if the priest examines the
scaly sore, and indeed it does not appear deeper than the skin, and *there is*
no black hair in it, then the priest shall
isolate *the one who has* the scale
[d]seven days.
32 "And on the seventh day the
priest shall examine the sore; and indeed *if* the scale has not spread, and
there is no yellow hair in it, and the
scale does not appear deeper than the
skin,
33 "he shall shave himself, but the
scale he shall not shave. And the
priest shall isolate *the one who has* the
scale another seven days.
34 "On the seventh day the priest
shall examine the scale; and indeed *if*
the scale has not spread over the skin,
and does not appear deeper than the
skin, then the priest shall pronounce
him clean. He shall wash his clothes
and be clean.
35 "But if the scale should at all
[e]spread over the skin after his cleansing,
36 "then the priest shall examine
him; and indeed *if* the scale has spread
over the skin, the priest need not seek
for yellow hair. He *is* unclean.
37 "But if the scale appears to be at
a standstill, and there is black hair
grown up in it, the scale has healed.
He *is* clean, and the priest shall pronounce him clean.
38 "If a man or a woman has bright
spots on the skin of the body, *specifically* white bright spots,
39 "then the priest shall look; and
indeed *if* the bright spots on the skin of
the body *are* dull white, it *is* a white
spot *that* grows on the skin. He *is*
clean.
40 "As for the man whose hair has

13 *a* Cp. Ex. 4:6
24 *b* Isa. 3:24
29 *c* vv. 29–46; cp. 14:54
31 *d* vv. 4,6
35 *e* vv. 7,27

fallen from his head, he *is* bald, *but* he *is* clean.

41 "He whose hair has fallen from his forehead, he *is* bald on the forehead, *but* he *is* clean.

42 "And if there is on the bald head or bald [a]forehead a reddish-white sore, it *is* leprosy breaking out on his bald head or his bald forehead.

43 "Then the priest shall examine it; and indeed *if* the swelling of the sore *is* reddish-white on his bald head or on his bald forehead, as the appearance of leprosy on the skin of the body,

44 "he is a leprous man. He *is* unclean. The priest shall surely pronounce him unclean; his sore *is* on his [b]head.

45 "Now the leper on whom the sore *is*, his clothes shall be torn and his head [c]bare; and he shall cover his [d]mustache, and cry, [e]'Unclean! Unclean!'

46 "He shall be unclean. All the days he has the sore he shall be unclean. He *is* unclean, and he shall dwell [f]alone; his dwelling *shall be* [g]outside the camp.

47 "Also, if a garment has a [1]leprous plague in it, *whether it is* a woolen garment or a linen garment,

48 "whether *it is* in the warp or woof of linen or wool, whether in leather or in anything made of leather,

49 "and if the plague is greenish or reddish in the garment or in the leather, whether in the warp or in the woof, or in anything made of leather, it *is* a leprous plague and shall be shown to the priest.

50 "The priest shall examine the plague and isolate *that which has* the plague seven days.

51 "And he shall examine the plague on the seventh day. If the plague has spread in the garment, either in the warp or in the woof, in the leather *or* in anything made of leather, the plague *is* an [h]active leprosy. It *is* unclean.

52 "He shall therefore burn that garment in which is the plague, whether warp or woof, in wool or in linen, or anything of leather, for it *is* an active leprosy; *the garment* shall be burned in the fire.

53 "But if the priest examines *it*, and indeed the plague has not spread in the garment, either in the warp or in the woof, or in anything made of leather,

54 "then the priest shall command that they wash *the thing* in which *is* the plague; and he shall isolate it another seven days.

55 "Then the priest shall examine the plague after it has been washed; and indeed *if* the plague has not changed its color, though the plague has not spread, it *is* unclean, and you shall burn it in the fire; it continues eating away, *whether* the damage *is* outside or inside.

56 "If the priest examines *it*, and indeed the plague has faded after washing it, then he shall tear it out of the garment, whether out of the warp or out of the woof, or out of the leather.

57 "But if it appears again in the garment, either in the warp or in the woof, or in anything made of leather, it *is* a spreading *plague;* you shall burn with fire that in which is the plague.

58 "And if you wash the garment, either warp or woof, or whatever is made of leather, if the plague has disappeared from it, then it shall be washed a second time, and shall be clean.

59 "This *is* the law of the leprous plague in a garment of wool or linen, either in the warp or woof, or in anything made of leather, to pronounce it clean or to pronounce it unclean."

A holy God—a holy people: (4) the law of the leper's cleansing

14 THEN the LORD spoke to Moses, saying,

2 "This shall be the [i]law of the leper for the day of his cleansing: He shall be brought to the [j]priest.

3 "And the priest shall [2]go out of the camp, and the priest shall examine *him;* and indeed, *if* the leprosy is healed in the leper,

4 "then the priest shall command to take for him who is to be cleansed two living *and* clean [3]birds, [k]cedar wood, [l]scarlet, and [m]hyssop.

42
a Cp. 2 Chr. 26:19
44
b Isa. 1:5
45
c Cp. Lev. 10:6; 21:10
d Cp. Ezek. 24:17,22
e Cp. Job 40:4; Ps. 51:3,5; Isa. 6:5; 64:6; Lk. 5:8
46
f 2 Chr. 26:21; Ps. 38:11
g Num. 5:1–4; 12:14
51
h vv. 47–59; cp. 14:55
CHAPTER 14
2
i vv. 2–32; Dt. 24:8
j Mt. 8:4; Mk. 1:44; Lk. 5:14; 17:14
4
k vv. 49–52; Num. 19:6; Heb. 9:19
l Ex. 25:4
m Ex. 12:22

[1](13:47) This may also refer to other kinds of mold or fungus. See also Lev. 13:2, *note.*

[2](14:3) As a type of Gospel salvation the points are: (1) the leper does nothing (Rom. 4:4–5); (2) the priest seeks the leper, not the leper the priest (Lk. 19:10); (3) "without shedding of blood there is no remission" (Heb. 9:22); and (4) "if Christ is not risen, your faith is futile; you are still in your sins!" (1 Cor. 15:17).

[3](14:4) The killed bird and the live bird, dipped in blood and released, present the two

5 "And the priest shall command that one of the birds be killed in an earthen [1]vessel over running water.

6 "As for the living bird, he shall take it, the cedar wood and the scarlet and the hyssop, and dip them and the living bird in the blood of the bird *that was* killed over the running water.

7 "And he shall sprinkle it seven times on him who is to be cleansed from the leprosy, and shall pronounce him clean, and shall let the living bird loose in the open field.

8 "He who is to be [a]cleansed shall [b]wash his clothes, shave off all his hair, and wash himself in water, that he may be clean. After that he shall come into the camp, and shall stay outside his tent [c]seven days.

9 "But on the [d]seventh day he shall shave all the hair off his head and his beard and his eyebrows—all his hair he shall shave off. He shall wash his clothes and wash his body in water, and he shall be clean.

10 "And on the eighth day he shall take two male lambs without blemish, one ewe lamb of the first year without blemish, three-tenths *of an ephah* of fine flour mixed with oil as a grain offering, and one [e]log of oil.

11 "Then the priest who makes *him* clean shall present the man who is to be made clean, and those things, before the LORD, *at* the door of the tabernacle of meeting.

12 "And the priest shall take one male lamb and offer it as a trespass offering, and the log of oil, and wave them *as* a wave offering before the LORD.

13 "Then he shall kill the lamb in the [f]place where he kills the sin offering and the burnt offering, in a holy place; for as the sin offering *is* the [g]priest's, so *is* the trespass offering. It *is* most holy.

14 "The priest shall take *some* of the blood of the trespass offering, and the priest shall [h]put *it* on the tip of the right ear of him who is to be cleansed, on the thumb of his right hand, and on the big toe of his right foot.

15 "And the priest shall take *some* of the log of oil, and pour *it* into the palm of his own left hand.

16 "Then the priest shall dip his right finger in the oil that *is* in his left hand, and shall [i]sprinkle some of the oil with his finger seven times before the LORD.

17 "And of the rest of the oil in his hand, the priest shall put *some* on the tip of the right ear of him who is to be cleansed, on the thumb of his right hand, and on the big toe of his right foot, on the blood of the trespass offering.

18 "The rest of the oil that *is* in the priest's hand he shall put on the head of him who is to be cleansed. So the priest shall make [j]atonement for him before the LORD.

19 "Then the priest shall offer the [k]sin offering, and make [j]atonement for him who is to be cleansed from his uncleanness. Afterward he shall kill the burnt offering.

20 "And the priest shall offer the burnt offering and the grain offering on the altar. So the priest shall make [j]atonement for him, and he shall be [l]clean.

21 "But if he *is* [m]poor and cannot afford it, then he shall take one male lamb *as* a trespass offering to be waved, to make [j]atonement for him, one-tenth *of an ephah* of fine flour mixed with oil as a grain offering, a log of oil,

22 "and two turtledoves or two young pigeons, such as he is able to afford: one shall be a sin offering and the other a burnt offering.

23 "He shall bring them to the priest on the eighth day for his cleansing, to the door of the tabernacle of meeting, before the LORD.

24 "And the priest shall take the lamb of the trespass offering and the log of oil, and the priest shall wave them *as* a wave offering before the LORD.

25 "Then he shall kill the lamb of the trespass offering, and the priest shall take *some* of the blood of the trespass offering and put *it* on the tip of the right ear of him who is to be cleansed, on the thumb of his right hand, and on the big toe of his right foot.

26 "And the priest shall pour some of the oil into the palm of his own left hand.

8 *a* Cp. Num. 8:7 *b* Lev. 13:6 *c* Lev. 13:5
9 *d* Cp. Num. 19:19
10 *e* See Weights and Measures (OT), 2 Chr. 2:10, *note*
13 *f* Lev. 1:11 *g* Lev. 6:24–30
14 *h* Lev. 8:23–24
16 *i* Cp. Lev. 4:6
18 *j* See Lev. 16:6, *note*
19 *k* Cp. 2 Cor. 5:21
20 *l* Lev. 14:8,9
21 *m* Lev. 5:11; 12:8; 27:8

---

aspects of salvation in Rom. 4:25. Christ "was delivered up because of our offenses, and was raised because of our justification."

[1](14:5) The earthen vessel typifies the humanity of Christ and the running water typifies the Holy Spirit as the "Spirit of life" (Rom. 8:2). Christ was "put to death in the flesh but made alive by the Spirit" (1 Pet. 3:18).

27 "Then the priest shall sprinkle with his right finger *some* of the oil that *is* in his left hand seven times before the LORD.

28 "And the priest shall put *some* of the oil that *is* in his hand on the tip of the right ear of him who is to be cleansed, on the thumb of the right hand, and on the big toe of his right foot, on the place of the blood of the trespass offering.

29 "The rest of the oil that *is* in the priest's hand he shall put on the head of him who is to be cleansed, to make [a]atonement for him before the LORD.

30 "And he shall offer one of the turtledoves or young pigeons, such as he can afford—

31 "such as he is able to afford, the one *as* a sin offering and the other *as* a burnt offering, with the grain offering. So the priest shall make [a]atonement for him who is to be cleansed before the LORD.

32 "This *is* the law *for one* who had a leprous sore, who cannot [b]afford the usual cleansing."

(Cleansing a leprous house)

33 And the LORD spoke to Moses and Aaron, saying:

34 "When you have come into the land of Canaan, which I give [c]you as a possession, and [d]I put the [1]leprous plague in a house in the land of your possession,

35 "and he who owns the house comes and tells the priest, saying, 'It seems to me that *there is* some [e]plague in the house,'

36 "then the priest shall command that they [f]empty the house, before the priest goes *into it* to examine the plague, that all that *is* in the house may not be made unclean; and afterward the priest shall go in to examine the house.

37 "And he shall examine the plague; and indeed *if* the plague *is* on the walls of the house with ingrained streaks, greenish or reddish, which appear to be deep in the wall,

38 "then the priest shall go out of the house, to the door of the house, and shut up the house seven days.

39 "And the priest shall come again on the seventh day and look; and indeed *if* the plague has spread on the walls of the house,

40 "then the priest shall command that they take away the stones in which *is* the plague, and they shall cast them into an unclean place outside the city.

41 "And he shall cause the house to be scraped inside, all around, and the dust that they scrape off they shall pour out in an unclean place outside the city.

42 "Then they shall take other stones and put *them* in the place of *those* stones, and he shall take other mortar and plaster the house.

43 "Now if the plague comes back and breaks out in the house, after he has taken away the stones, after he has scraped the house, and after it is plastered,

44 "then the priest shall come and look; and indeed *if* the plague has spread in the house, it *is* an [g]active leprosy in the house. It *is* unclean.

45 "And he shall break down the house, its stones, its timber, and all the plaster of the house, and he shall carry *them* outside the city to an unclean place.

46 "Moreover he who goes into the house at all while it is shut up shall be [h]unclean until evening.

47 "And he who lies down in the house shall [i]wash his clothes, and he who eats in the house shall wash his clothes.

48 "But if the priest comes in and examines *it*, and indeed the plague has not spread in the house after the house was plastered, then the priest shall pronounce the house clean, because the plague is healed.

49 "And he shall [j]take, to cleanse the house, two birds, cedar wood, scarlet, and hyssop.

50 "Then he shall kill one of the birds in an earthen vessel over running water;

51 "and he shall take the cedar wood, the hyssop, the scarlet, and the living bird, and dip them in the blood of the slain bird and in the running water, and sprinkle the house seven times.

52 "And he shall cleanse the house with the blood of the bird and the running water and the living bird, with the cedar wood, the hyssop, and the scarlet.

53 "Then he shall let the living bird loose outside the city in the open field,

29 *a* See Lev. 16:6, *note*
32 *b* vv. 21–32
34 *c* Gen. 12:7; 13:17; 17:8; Dt. 32:49 *d* Prov. 3:33
35 *e* Ps. 91:10
36 *f* Or *prepare*
44 *g* Lev. 13:51; Zech. 5:4
46 *h* Lev. 11:24; 15:5
47 *i* Lev. 14:8
49 *j* vv. 49–53, cp. Lev. 14:4–8

[1](14:34) As in the case of mildew (leprous plague) in relation to garments (13:47ff.), this passage probably refers also to some mold or fungus. See also Lev. 13:2, *note*.

and make [a]atonement for the house,
and it shall be clean.
54 "This *is* the law for any leprous
[b]sore and scale,
55 "for the leprosy of a [c]garment
and of a house,
56 "for a swelling and a scab and a
bright spot,
57 "to [d]teach when *it is* unclean
and when *it is* clean. This *is* the law of
leprosy."

A holy God—a holy people:
(5) cleansing necessary (Jn. 13:3–10;
Eph. 5:24–27; 1 Jn. 1:9)

15 AND the LORD spoke to Moses
and Aaron, saying,
2 "Speak to the children of Israel,
and say to them: 'When any man has
a [e]discharge from his body, his discharge *is* unclean.
3 'And this shall be his uncleanness in regard to his discharge—
whether his body runs with his discharge, or his body is stopped up by
his discharge, it *is* his uncleanness.
4 'Every bed is unclean on which
he who has the discharge lies, and everything on which he sits shall be unclean.
5 'And whoever [f]touches his bed
shall [g]wash his clothes and bathe in
water, and be unclean until evening.
6 'He who sits on anything on
which he who has the [h]discharge sat
shall wash his clothes and bathe in
water, and be unclean until evening.
7 'And he who touches the body of
him who has the discharge shall wash
his clothes and bathe in water, and be
unclean until evening.
8 'If he who has the discharge
[i]spits on him who is clean, then he
shall wash his clothes and bathe in
water, and be unclean until evening.
9 'Any saddle on which he who
has the discharge rides shall be unclean.
10 'Whoever touches anything that
was under him shall be unclean until
evening. He who carries *any of* those
things shall wash his clothes and
bathe in water, and be unclean until
evening.
11 'And whomever the one who has
the discharge touches, and has not
rinsed his hands in water, he shall
wash his clothes and bathe in water,
and be unclean until evening.
12 'The [j]vessel of earth that he who
has the discharge touches shall be
broken, and every vessel of wood
shall be rinsed in water.

53
[a] See Lev. 16:6, *note*
54
[b] Lev. 13:30
55
[c] Lev. 13:47
57
[d] Lev. 10:10; 11:47; 20:25
CHAPTER 15
2
[e] Lev. 22:4; Num. 5:2; 2 Sam. 3:29
5
[f] Lev. 14:46
[g] Lev. 14:8, 47
6
[h] Lev. 15:10; Dt. 23:10
8
[i] Num. 12:14
12
[j] Lev. 6:28; 11:33
13
[k] v. 28; Lev. 14:8; Num. 19:11–12
14
[l] Lev. 14:22, 30–31
15
[m] Lev. 5:7
16
[n] Lev. 22:4; Dt. 23:10–11
18
[o] Cp. 1 Sam. 21:4
19
[p] Lev. 12:2
24
[q] Lev. 18:19; 20:18
25
[r] Mt. 9:20

13 'And when he who has a discharge is cleansed of his discharge,
then he shall count for [k]himself seven
days for his cleansing, wash his
clothes, and bathe his body in running
water; then he shall be clean.
14 'On the eighth day he shall take
for himself [l]two turtledoves or two
young pigeons, and come before the
LORD, to the door of the tabernacle of
meeting, and give them to the priest.
15 'Then the priest shall offer them,
the one *as* a sin offering and the other
as a [m]burnt offering. So the priest
shall make [a]atonement for him before
the LORD because of his discharge.
16 'If any man has an emission of
[n]semen, then he shall wash all his
body in water, and be unclean until
evening.
17 'And any garment and any
leather on which there is semen, it
shall be washed with water, and be
unclean until evening.
18 'Also, when a woman lies with a
man, and *there is* an emission of semen, they shall bathe in water, and be
[o]unclean until evening.
19 'If a [p]woman has a discharge,
and the discharge from her body is
blood, she shall be set apart seven
days; and whoever touches her shall
be unclean until evening.
20 'Everything that she lies on during her impurity shall be unclean; also
everything that she sits on shall be unclean.
21 'Whoever touches her bed shall
wash his clothes and bathe in water,
and be unclean until evening.
22 'And whoever touches anything
that she sat on shall wash his clothes
and bathe in water, and be unclean
until evening.
23 'If *anything* is on *her* bed or on
anything on which she sits, when he
touches it, he shall be unclean until
evening.
24 'And if any man [q]lies with her at
all, so that her impurity is on him, he
shall be unclean seven days; and every bed on which he lies shall be unclean.
25 'If a woman has a [r]discharge of
blood for many days, other than at the
time of her *customary* impurity, or if
it runs beyond her *usual time of* impurity, all the days of her unclean discharge shall be as the days of her *customary* impurity. She *shall be*
unclean.
26 'Every bed on which she lies all
the days of her discharge shall be to

her as the bed of her impurity; and
whatever she sits on shall be unclean,
as the uncleanness of her impurity.
27 'Whoever touches those things
shall be unclean; he shall wash his
clothes and bathe in water, and be unclean until evening.
28 'But if she is cleansed of her discharge, then she shall count for herself seven days, and after that she
shall be clean.
29 'And on the eighth day she shall
take for herself two turtledoves or two
young pigeons, and bring them to the
priest, to the door of the tabernacle of
meeting.
30 'Then the priest shall offer the
one *as* a sin offering and the other *as*
a [a]burnt offering, and the priest shall
make [b]atonement for her before the
LORD for the discharge of her uncleanness.
31 'Thus you shall [c]separate the
children of Israel from their uncleanness, lest they die in their uncleanness
when they [d]defile My tabernacle that
is among them.
32 'This *is* the law for one who has
a discharge, and *for him* who emits
semen and is unclean thereby,
33 'and for her who is indisposed
because of her *customary* impurity,
and for one who has a discharge, either man or woman, and for him who
lies with her who is unclean.' "

30
a Lev. 5:7
b See Lev. 16:6, *note*
31
c Lev. 14:57; 22:2
d Lev. 20:3; Num. 19:13,20; Ezek. 36:17
CHAPTER 16
1
e *Israel* (history): vv. 1–34; Num. 3:1. (Gen. 12:2; Rom. 11:26, *note*)
f Lev. 10:1–2
2
g Ex. 30:10; Lev. 16:34; Heb. 9:7–8; cp. Heb. 4:16; 10:19
h Ex. 25:21–22
3
i Lev. 4:1–12
4
j v. 24
5
k Lev. 4:14
l *Sacrifice* (typical): vv. 2–34; Lev. 17:11. (Gen. 3:15; Heb. 10:18, *note*)
16:6 *m* Heb. 5:3

IV. The Day of Atonement, 16

The Day of Atonement: Christ as high priest and sacrifice (Heb. 9:1–14)

16 NOW the LORD spoke to [e]Mo-
ses after the death of the [f]two
sons of Aaron, when they offered *pro-*
fane fire before the LORD, and died;
2 and the LORD said to Moses: "Tell
Aaron your brother not to come at *just*
any [g]time into the Holy *Place* inside
the veil, before the mercy seat which
is on the ark, lest he die; for I will
[h]appear in the cloud above the mercy
seat.
3 "Thus Aaron shall come into the
Holy *Place*: with *the blood of* a young
bull as a [i]sin offering, and *of* a ram as
a burnt offering.
4 "He shall put the holy linen tunic
and the linen trousers on his body; he
shall be girded with a linen sash, and
with the linen turban he shall be at-
tired. These *are* holy garments. Therefore he shall [j]wash his body in water,
and put them on.
5 "And he shall take from the
[k]congregation of the children of Israel
two kids of the [1]goats as a [l]sin offering, and one ram as a burnt offering.
6 "Aaron shall offer the bull as a
sin offering, which *is* for [m]himself, and
make [2]atonement for himself and for
his house.

[1](16:5) The two goats. The offering of the high priest for himself has no antitype in Christ (Heb. 7:26–27). The typical interest centers upon the two goats and the high priest. Typically (1) all is done by the high priest (Heb. 1:3); the people only bring the sacrifice (Mt. 26:47,50; 27:24–25). (2) The killed goat (the LORD's lot) is that aspect of Christ's death which vindicates the holiness and righteousness of God as expressed in the law (Rom. 3:24–26), and is expiatory. (3) The living goat typifies that aspect of Christ's work which puts away our sins from before God (Heb. 9:26; Rom. 8:33–34). (4) The high priest, entering the Holy Place, typifies Christ entering "heaven itself" with "His own blood" for us (Heb. 9:11–12,24). His blood makes that to be a "throne of grace" and "mercy seat" which otherwise must have been a throne of judgment (Heb. 4:16). And (5) for us, the priests of the New Covenant, there is what Israel never had, a torn veil (Mt. 27:51; Heb. 10:19–20). So that for worship and blessing we enter, in virtue of Christ's blood, where He is, into the Holiest (Heb. 4:14–16; 10:19–22).

The atonement of Christ, as foreshadowed by the OT sacrificial types, has these necessary elements: (1) It is substitutionary—the offering takes the offerer's place in death. (2) The law is not evaded but honored—every sacrificial death was an execution of the sentence of the law. (3) The sinlessness of Him who bore our sins is expressed in every animal sacrifice—it must be without blemish. And (4) the effect of the atoning work of Christ is typified (a) in the promise, "he shall be forgiven" (Lev. 6:7); and (b) in the peace offering, the expression of fellowship—the highest privilege of the believer. See Ex. 29:33, *note*.

[2](16:6) Atonement. The Biblical use and meaning of the word must be sharply distinguished from its use in theology. In theology it is a term which covers the whole sacrificial and redemptive work of Christ. In the OT, atonement is the English word used to translate the Hebrew words which mean *cover, coverings,* or *to cover.* Atonement is, therefore, not a translation of the Hebrew but a purely theological concept. The Levitical offerings "covered" the sins of Israel until and in anticipation of the cross, but did not "take away" (Heb. 10:4) those sins. These were the sins done in OT times ("covered" meantime by the Levitical sacrifices), which God "passed over" (Rom. 3:25), for which passing over God's righteousness was never vindicated until, in the cross, Jesus Christ was "set forth as a propitiation." See Propitiation,

7 "He shall take the two goats and present them before the LORD *at* the door of the tabernacle of meeting.

8 "Then Aaron shall cast lots for the two goats: one lot for the LORD and the other lot for the scapegoat.

9 "And Aaron shall bring the goat on which the LORD's lot fell, and offer it *as* a sin offering.

10 "But the goat on which the lot fell to be the scapegoat shall be presented alive before the LORD, to make [a]atonement upon it, *and* to let it go as the scapegoat into the wilderness.

11 "And Aaron shall bring the bull of the sin offering, which is for [b]himself, and make [c]atonement for himself and for his house, and shall kill the bull as the sin offering which *is* for himself.

12 "Then he shall take a censer full of burning coals of fire from the [d]altar before the LORD, with his hands full of sweet [e]incense beaten fine, and bring *it* inside the veil.

13 "And he shall put the incense on the fire before the LORD, that the cloud of incense may cover the mercy seat that *is* on the Testimony, [f]lest he die.

14 "He shall [g]take some of the blood of the bull and sprinkle *it* with his finger on the mercy seat on the east *side;* and before the mercy seat he shall sprinkle some of the blood with his finger seven times.

15 "Then he shall kill the goat of the sin offering, which *is* for the [h]people, bring its blood inside the veil, do with that blood as he did with the blood of the bull, and sprinkle it on the mercy seat and before the mercy seat.

16 "So he shall make [c]atonement for the Holy [i]*Place,* because of the uncleanness of the children of Israel, and because of their transgressions, for all their sins; and so he shall do for the tabernacle of meeting which remains among them in the midst of their uncleanness.

17 "There shall be [j]no man in the tabernacle of meeting when he goes in to make atonement in the Holy *Place,* until he comes out, that he may make atonement for himself, for his household, and for all the assembly of Israel.

18 "And he shall go [1]out to the altar that *is* before the LORD, and make [c]atonement for [k]it, and shall take some of the blood of the bull and some of the blood of the goat, and put it on the horns of the altar all around.

19 "Then he shall sprinkle some of the blood on it with his finger seven times, cleanse it, and consecrate it from the uncleanness of the children of Israel.

The scapegoat (2 Cor. 5:21)

20 "And when he has made an end of [l]atoning for the Holy *Place,* the tabernacle of meeting, and the altar, he shall bring the live goat.

21 "Aaron shall lay both his hands on the head of the live goat, [m]confess over it all the iniquities of the children of Israel, and all their transgressions, concerning all their sins, putting them on the head of the goat, and shall send *it* away into the wilderness by the hand of a suitable man.

22 "The goat shall [n]bear on itself all their iniquities to an uninhabited land; and he shall [o]release the goat in the wilderness.

23 "Then Aaron shall come into the tabernacle of meeting, shall [p]take off the linen garments which he put on when he went into the Holy *Place,* and shall leave them there.

24 "And he shall wash his body with water in a holy place, put on his garments, come out and offer his burnt offering and the burnt offering of the people, and make [c]atonement for himself and for the people.

25 "The [q]fat of the sin offering he shall burn on the altar.

26 "And he who released the goat as the scapegoat shall wash his clothes and bathe his body in water, and afterward he may come into the camp.

27 "The bull *for* the sin offering and the goat *for* the sin offering, whose blood was brought in to make [c]atonement in the Holy *Place,* shall be car-

10
a Cp. Isa. 53:5–6; Heb. 7:27; 9:23–24
11
b Heb. 9:7
c See v. 6, *note;* Lev. 17:11
12
d Cp. Isa. 6:6–7
e Ex. 30:34–38
13
f Ex. 28:43; Num. 4:15, 20
14
g Heb. 9:25
15
h Heb. 7:27
16
i Ex. 30:10
17
j Cp. Ex. 34:3; Lk. 1:10
18
k Ex. 29:36
20
l Heb. *kaphar, to cover.* See 16:6, *note;* cp. Ex. 29:33, *note*
21
m Lev. 5:5; 26:40
22
n Lev. 8:14; cp. Isa. 53:6
o Cp. Lev. 14:7
23
p Lev. 6:11
25
q Lev. 1:8

Rom. 3:25, *note.* It was the cross, not the Levitical sacrifices, which made full and complete redemption. The OT sacrifices enabled God to go on with a guilty people because those sacrifices typified the cross. To the offerer they were the confession of his deserving death and the expression of his faith; to God they were the "shadows" of good things that were to come, of which Christ was the reality (cp. Heb. 10:1). See Ex. 29:33, *note.*

[1](16:18) Dispensationally, for Israel this is yet future; Christ the High Priest is still in the Holiest. When He comes out to His ancient people they will be converted and restored (Rom. 11:23–27; cp. Zech. 12:10–12; 13:1; Rev. 1:7). Meantime, believers of the Church Age, as a holy priesthood, enter into the Holiest where He is (1 Pet. 2:9; Heb. 10:19–22).

ried outside the camp. And they shall
[a]burn in the fire their skins, their
flesh, and their offal.
28 "Then he who burns them shall
wash his clothes and bathe his body in
water, and afterward he may come
into the camp.
29 "*This* shall be a statute forever
for you: In the [b]seventh month, on the
tenth *day* of the [c]month, you shall afflict your souls, and do no work at all,
whether a native of your own country
or a stranger who dwells among
you.
30 "For on [1]that day *the priest* shall
make [d]atonement for you, to cleanse
you, *that* you may be clean from all
your sins before the LORD.
31 "It *is* a sabbath of solemn rest for
you, and you shall [e]afflict your souls.
It is a statute forever.
32 "And the priest, who is
[f]anointed and consecrated to minister as priest in his father's place, shall
make [d]atonement, and put on the
linen clothes, the holy garments;
33 "then he shall make [d]atonement
for the Holy Sanctuary,* and he shall
make [d]atonement for the tabernacle
of meeting and for the altar, and he
shall make atonement for the priests
and for all the people of the assembly.
34 "This shall be an everlasting
statute for you, to make [d]atonement
for the children of Israel, for all their
sins, once a year." And he did as the
LORD commanded [g]Moses.

The one acceptable place of sacrifice (yet to be revealed)

17 AND the LORD spoke to Moses,
saying,
2 "Speak to Aaron, to his sons,
and to all the children of Israel, and
say to them, 'This *is* the thing which
the LORD has commanded, saying:
3 "Whatever man of the house of
Israel who kills an ox or lamb or goat
in the camp, or who kills *it* outside the
camp,
4 "and does not bring it to the door
of the tabernacle of [h]meeting to offer
an offering to the LORD before the tabernacle of the LORD, the guilt of bloodshed shall be imputed to that man. He
has shed blood; and that man shall be
cut off from among his people,
5 "to the [i]end that the children of
Israel may bring their sacrifices which
they offer in the open field, that they
may bring them to the LORD at the door
of the tabernacle of meeting, to the
priest, and offer them *as* peace offerings to the LORD.
6 "And the priest shall sprinkle
the blood on the altar of the LORD *at*
the door of the tabernacle of meeting,
and [j]burn the fat for a sweet aroma to
the LORD.
7 "They shall no more offer their
sacrifices to [k]demons, after whom
they have played the harlot. This shall
be a statute forever for them throughout their generations." '
8 "Also you shall say to them:
'Whatever man of the house of Israel,
or of the [l]strangers who dwell among
you, who offers a burnt offering or
sacrifice,
9 'and does not [m]bring it to the
door of the tabernacle of [n]meeting, to
offer it to the LORD, that man shall be
cut off from among his people.

Significance of the blood

10 'And whatever man of the house
of Israel, or of the strangers who dwell
among you, who eats any [o]blood, I
will [p]set My face against that person
who eats blood, and will cut him off
from among his people.
11 'For the [q]life of the flesh *is* in the
blood, and I have given it to you upon
the [2]altar to make [r]atonement for

27 *a* Lev. 6:30; Heb. 13:11
29 *b* See Lev. 23:2, *note* *c* Lev. 23:27–32
30 *d* See v. 6, *note;* Lev. 17:11
31 *e* Lev. 23:27, 32; cp. Isa. 58:3–5
32 *f* Lev. 21:10
34 *g Law* (of Moses): v. 34; Lev. 26:3. (Ex. 19:1; Gal. 3:24, *note*)
CHAPTER 17
4 *h* Cp. Dt. 5:5–21
5 *i* Ezek. 20:28; cp. Dt. 12:1–27
6 *j* Ex. 29:13
7 *k* Dt. 32:17. Lit. *hairy ones.* Ex. 34:16
8 *l* Lev. 18:26
9 *m* v. 4 *n* Lev. 14:23
10 *o* Lev. 3:17; 7:26–27; Dt. 12:16, 23–25 *p* Lev. 20:3, 6
11 *q* Gen. 9:4 *r* See Lev. 16:6, *note*

* 16:33 That is, the Most Holy Place

[1](16:30) The Day of Atonement was the most important single day in the Hebrew calendar. It is often called simply, "the Day," in modern usage "*Yom Kippur.*"

In v. 31 it is referred to as "a sabbath of solemn rest," or "a sabbath of sabbaths." Only on this day did the high priest enter into the Holy Place (Ex. 30:10; cp. Heb. 9:7–8), and only on this day were the people told to "afflict your souls" (v. 29). That the high priest entered three times into the Holy Place and that the blood of the sin offering was sprinkled seven times before the mercy seat, emphasize the importance of this sacrifice. On this day the dual typology for the putting away of sin was manifested in killing the one goat and in driving the other goat (the scapegoat) into the wilderness. See also Num. 29:7–11.

[2](17:11) Two especially important truths are pertinent here: (1) The value of the "life" is the measure of the value of the "blood." This gives the blood of Christ its inconceivable worth. When it was shed the sinless God-man gave His life. "For it is not possible that the blood of bulls and goats could take away sins" (Heb. 10:4). And (2) it is not the blood in the veins of the sacrifice, but the blood *upon the altar* which is efficacious. The Scripture knows nothing

your [a]souls; for it *is* the [1]blood *that*
makes atonement for the soul.'
12 "Therefore I said to the children
of Israel, 'No one among you shall eat
blood, nor shall any stranger who
dwells among you eat blood.'
13 "Whatever man of the children
of Israel, or of the strangers who dwell
among you, who hunts and catches
any animal or bird that may be eaten,
he shall pour out its blood and [b]cover
it with dust;
14 "for *it is* the life of all flesh. Its
blood sustains its life. Therefore I said
to the children of Israel, 'You shall not
eat the blood of any flesh, for the life
of all flesh is its blood. Whoever eats
it shall be cut off.'
15 "And every person who eats
what died *naturally* or what was torn
by beasts, whether he is a native of
your own country or a stranger, he
shall both wash his clothes and bathe
in water, and be unclean until evening. Then he shall be clean.
16 "But if he does not wash *them* or
bathe his body, then he shall bear his
guilt."

V. Laws Regulating the Personal Relationships of the Redeemed People, 18—20

Relationships and walk of God's earthly people: (1) unlawful marriages

18 THEN the LORD spoke to Moses, saying,
2 "Speak to the children of Israel,
and say to them: [c]'I am the LORD your
God.
3 [d]'According to the doings of the
land of Egypt, where you dwelt, you
shall not do; and [e]according to the doings of the land of Canaan, where I am
bringing you, you shall not do; nor
shall you walk in their ordinances.
4 'You shall observe My judgments and keep My ordinances, to
walk in them: I *am* the LORD your God.
5 'You shall therefore keep My
statutes and My judgments, which if a
man does, he shall live by them: I *am*
the LORD.
6 'None of you shall approach
anyone who is near of kin to him, to
uncover his nakedness: I *am* the LORD.
7 [f]'The nakedness of your father
or the nakedness of your mother you
shall not uncover. She *is* your mother;
you shall not uncover her nakedness.
8 'The nakedness of your [g]fa-
ther's wife you shall not uncover; it *is*
your father's nakedness.
9 'The nakedness of your [h]sister,
the daughter of your father, or the
daughter of your mother, *whether*
born at home or elsewhere, their nakedness you shall not uncover.
10 'The nakedness of your son's
daughter or your daughter's daughter,
their nakedness you shall not uncover; for theirs *is* your own nakedness.
11 'The nakedness of your father's
wife's daughter, begotten by your
father—she *is* your sister—you shall
not uncover her nakedness.
12 'You shall not uncover the nakedness of your father's sister; she *is*
near of kin to your father.
13 'You shall not uncover the nakedness of your mother's sister, for
she *is* near of kin to your mother.
14 'You shall not uncover the nakedness of your father's brother. You
shall not approach his wife; she *is*
your aunt.
15 'You shall not uncover the nakedness of your daughter-in-law—
she *is* your son's wife—you shall not
uncover her nakedness.
16 'You shall not uncover the nakedness of your brother's wife; it *is*
your brother's nakedness.
17 'You shall not uncover the nakedness of a woman and her [i]daugh-
ter, nor shall you take her son's
daughter or her daughter's daughter,
to uncover her nakedness. They *are*
near of kin to her. It *is* wickedness.
18 'Nor shall you take a woman as
a rival to her sister, to uncover her
nakedness while the other is alive.

(2) Unlawful lust

19 'Also you shall not approach a
woman to uncover her nakedness as
[j]long as she is in her *customary* [k]im-
purity.
20 [l]'Moreover you shall not lie

11 *a Sacrifice* (typical, prophetic): v. 11; Ps. 22:1. (Gen. 3:15; Heb. 10:18, *note*)
13 *b* Cp. Ezek. 24:7
CHAPTER 18
2 *c* Lev. 11:44–45; 19:3
3 *d* Josh. 24:14; Ezek. 20:7–8
e Lev. 18:24–30; Dt. 12:30–31
7 *f* vv. 7–16; cp. Lev. 20:11–21
8 *g* Cp. Gen. 35:22
9 *h* Dt. 27:22
17 *i* Lev. 20:14
19 *j* Ezek. 18:6
k Lev. 15:24
20 *l* Prov. 6:25–33

---

of salvation by the imitation or influence of Christ's life, but only by that life yielded up on the cross.

[1](17:11) The meaning of sacrifice for sin is here explained. Every such offering was an execution of the sentence of the law upon a substitute for the offender, and pointed forward to that substitutionary death of Christ which alone vindicated the righteousness of God in passing over the sins of those who offered the typical sacrifices (Rom. 3:24–25; see Ex. 29:33, *note*).

THE LAWS OF THE BIBLE

I. FORMS OF GOVERNMENT

A. Theocracy. God was absolute ruler (Ex. 19:3–8; 20:2–3).

B. Patriarchy. Family, with father or head, was basic unit of society (Gen. 22:1–12; Jud. 11:29–40).

C. Judges. Later military rulers raised up to save erring and penitent Israel from enemies (Jud. 2:13–18).

D. Monarchy. Established when Israel demanded a king (1 Sam. 8:19; 10:1) and ended with Babylonian captivity (2 Ki. 25:5–9).

E. Persian province. Following Babylonian captivity Zerubbabel, Ezra, and Nehemiah were permitted to govern.

F. Greek province. During period between Old and New Testaments high priests were permitted to rule.

G. Roman province. During New Testament era the Herods ruled as puppet kings.

II. THEOCRATIC CITIZENSHIP

A. Israelites (Ex. 19:5–8).

B. Edomites and Egyptians in their third generation (Dt. 23:7–8).

III. THEOCRATIC ADMINISTRATION

A. Citizens and strangers (Gen. 34:14; Lev. 24:22).

B. Slaves:

1. How obtained (Ex. 21:2; 22:3; Lev. 25:45–46).
2. Treatment (Ex. 21:2,20–21; Lev. 25:39–41; Dt. 23:15–16).

C. Taxation:

1. Purpose (Ex. 30:11–16).
2. Exemption (Ezra 7:24).
3. Continued (Mt. 22:15–21; Rom. 13:6–7).

D. Military:

1. Eligibility (Num. 1:2–3).
2. Exemption (Num. 1:49; Dt. 20:5–8).
3. Hygiene (Dt. 23:9–14).
4. Battle regulations (Num. 21:2–3,35; 31:17–18; Dt. 20:14–18).

IV. CRIMINAL LAW

A. Crimes against society:

1. Bribery (Ex. 23:8).
2. Contempt for law (Num. 15:31).
3. Perjury (Ex. 20:16).
4. Perverting justice (Ex. 23:1–2,6).

B. Crimes of immorality:

1. Adultery (Ex. 20:14).
2. Rape (Dt. 22:25–26).
3. Prostitution (Dt. 23:17).
4. Seduction (Ex. 22:16–17).
5. Incest (Lev. 18:6–18).
6. Sodomy (Lev. 18:22).

C. Crimes against persons:

1. Murder (Ex. 20:13).
2. Manslaughter (Ex. 21:12–14; Josh. 20:3–6).
3. Assault (Ex. 21:18–26).
4. Kidnapping (Ex. 21:16; Dt. 24:7).
5. Slander (Ex. 20:16; Lev. 19:16).

D. Crimes against property:

1. Stealing (Ex. 20:15).
2. Arson (Ex. 22:6).
3. Moving a landmark (Dt. 19:14).
4. Envy (Ex. 20:17).

V. DOMESTIC RELATIONS

A. Marriage:

1. Ordained by God (Gen. 1:27–28; 2:18,24).
2. Within tribe (Num. 36:6).
3. Polygamy forbidden (1 Cor. 7:2; 1 Tim. 3:2).
4. Kinds of marriage forbidden (Lev. 18:8,10,15,17; Dt. 7:3).
5. Divorce (Lev. 21:7; 22:13; Dt. 24:1–4; Jer. 3:8; Mt. 19:3–9; Mk. 10:2–12; Lk. 16:18; 1 Cor. 7:10–16).

B. Parents and children:

1. Father's authority (Num. 30:3–5).
2. Marriages arranged (Gen. 24:2–4).
3. Education (Ex. 12:26–27; Dt. 4:9; Prov. 22:6; Eph. 6:4).
4. Discipline (Dt. 21:18–21; Prov. 22:15).
5. Honor parents (Ex. 20:12; 21:15; Eph. 6:1–3).

VI. ESTATES—DESCENT AND DISTRIBUTION

A. Inheritance:

1. Sons inherit fathers' estates (Gen. 21:10–13; 1 Chr. 5:1).
2. Double portion to firstborn (Dt. 21:15–17).
3. Wife not heir, but descends with property to next of kin (Ruth 4:1–12).
4. Daughters heirs when no sons (Num. 27:8–9).
5. Nearest relative when no sons or daughters (Num. 27:9–11).

B. Real estate:

1. Land divided among tribes (Num. 26:52–56).
2. Not transferable (Num. 36:6–9).
3. Not permanently sold (Lev. 25:23–28).
4. Value of land according to years after jubilee (Lev. 25:15–16).
5. Release of land (Lev. 25:8–34).
6. Mode of transfer:
   a. Deed made (Jer. 32:9–14).
   b. Taking off sandal (Ruth 4:3–11).
   c. Deed delivered in presence of witnesses (Jer. 32:10,12).
   d. Deed recorded (Jer. 32:14).

C. Personal property:
1. Sale recognized (Lev. 25:14).
2. Pledges (Ex. 22:26–27; Dt. 24:6,10–11,13; 2 Ki. 4:1–7).

VII. SOCIAL SECURITY AND WELFARE

A. Widows and orphans (Ex. 22:22–23; Dt. 14:28–29; Acts 6:1–4; 1 Tim. 5:3–16):
1. Marriage of widows (Dt. 25:5–10).
2. Oppression forbidden (Zech. 7:9–12).

B. Neighbors (Lev. 19:13).

C. The poor (Dt. 15:7–11; 24:14–15; Gal. 2:10).

D. The handicapped (Lev. 19:14; Dt. 27:18; Lk. 14:12–14).

VIII. CONTRACTS

A. Debts (Dt. 15:1–5; Neh. 5:10–11).

B. Neighbors and foreigners (Dt. 15:1–3).

C. Loans and interest (Ex. 22:25; Lev. 25:35–37; Dt. 23:19–20; Neh. 5:11–13).

D. Mortgages (Neh. 5:2–6).

E. Sales (Lev. 25:14,23–28; Ruth 4:3–11; Jer. 32:9–14).

F. Terms of service (Ex. 21:2–4).

G. Surety (Prov. 17:18).

H. Weights and measures (Dt. 25:13–16).

IX. RELIGIOUS LAWS

A. Clean and unclean meat (Lev. 11:2–40; Dt. 14:3–21).

B. Forbidden foods (Ex. 22:31; Lev. 17:10–14; Lev. 19:23–25).

C. Sacred obligations:
1. Firstborn (Ex. 34:19–20).
2. Firstfruits (Ex. 34:26).
3. Tithes (Lev. 27:30–33; Mal. 3:8–12; Mt. 23:23).
4. Atonement money (Ex. 30:12–16).
5. Freewill offering (Lev. 22:17–20; Num. 15:1–7).

D. Sacred calendar:
1. Sabbath (Gen. 2:1–3; Ex. 16:23; Dt. 5:12–15; Mk. 2:23–28; Lk. 13:14–17).
2. Passover (Ex. 12:1–14; Dt. 16:1–8).
3. Feast of Unleavened Bread (Ex. 34:18).
4. Feast of Weeks (Dt. 16:9–11).
5. Feast of Tabernacles (Dt. 16:13–17).
6. Sabbatical Year (Ex. 23:10–11).
7. Day of Atonement (Lev. 23:26–32).
8. Year of Jubilee (Lev. 25:8–55).

E. Offenses against God:
1. Idolatry (Ex. 20:1–5).
2. Spiritualism (Lev. 20:27).
3. Blasphemy (Dt. 5:11).

X. LEGAL PROCEDURES

A. Judges appointed (Ex. 18:13–26; 2 Chr. 19:4–11):
1. Moses, first judge (Ex. 18:13–27).
2. Elders judge in small matters (Ex. 18:22).
3. King as judge (1 Ki. 7:7).

B. Courts held:
1. At city gate (Dt. 21:19).
2. In Hall of Judgment (1 Ki. 7:7).

C. Judgments:
1. Regarded as from God (Dt. 1:17).
2. Righteous justified, wicked condemned (Dt. 25:1).
3. Sentence was executed (Dt. 25:2–3).

D. Damages:
1. Disfigurement (Lev. 24:19–20).
2. Theft (Ex. 22:4–5).
3. Fire damage (Ex. 22:6).
4. Breach of trust (Lev. 6:1–5).
5. Killing an animal (Ex. 21:35–36; Lev. 24:18,21).
6. Animal fallen in pit (Ex. 21:33–34).
7. Loss of borrowed property (Ex. 22:14).

E. Penalties:
1. Infliction in kind (Gen. 9:6; Lev. 24:18–20).
2. Burning (Lev. 20:14).
3. Mutilation (Dt. 25:11–12).
4. Hanging (Dt. 21:22–23).
5. Stoning (Lev. 24:16).
6. Beating (Dt. 25:2–3).
7. Excommunication (Ezra 10:8).
8. Prison (Ezra 7:26).
9. Restitution (Ex. 22:12,14–15).

F. Methods of protection:
1. Cities of refuge (Num. 35:6–15).
2. Protection until trial (Num. 35:12).
3. Murderer unprotected (Num. 35:30–31).
4. Unintentional manslaughter (Josh. 20:1–6).

XI. TORTS

A. Assault (Ex. 21:18–19).

B. Compensation (Ex. 21:18–19,32,36).

C. Injury to animals (Ex. 21:33–36; Lev. 24:18,21).

D. Personal injury (Lev. 24:19–20).

E. Rights of strangers (Lev. 24:22).

XII. SANITATION AND HYGIENE

A. Cleansing of mother following childbirth (Lev. 12:1–8).

B. Test for leprosy (Lev. 13:1–59).

C. Cleansing the leper's house (Lev. 14:33–53).

D. Cleansing for male discharges (Lev. 15:1–18).

E. Cleansing for female discharges (Lev. 15:19–33).

carnally with your [a]neighbor's wife, to defile yourself with her.

21 'And you shall not let any of your descendants [b]pass through *the* [c]fire to [d]Molech, nor shall you profane the name of your God: I *am* the LORD.

22 'You shall not lie with a [e]male as with a woman. It *is* an abomination.

23 'Nor shall you mate with any [f]animal, to defile yourself with it. Nor shall any woman stand before an animal to mate with it. It *is* perversion.

24 'Do not defile yourselves with any of these things; for by all these the nations are defiled, which I am [g]casting out before [1]you.

25 'For the [h]land is defiled; [i]therefore I visit the punishment of its iniquity upon it, and the land [j]vomits out its inhabitants.

26 'You shall therefore keep My statutes and My judgments, and shall not commit *any* of these abominations, *either* any of your own nation or any stranger who dwells among you

27 '(for all these abominations the men of the land have done, who *were* before you, and thus the land is defiled),

28 'lest the land vomit you out also when you defile it, as it vomited out the nations that *were* before you.

29 'For whoever commits any of these abominations, the persons who commit *them* shall be cut off from among their people.

30 'Therefore you shall [k]keep My ordinance, so that *you* do not commit *any* of these abominable customs which were committed before you, and that you do not defile yourselves by them: [l]I *am* the LORD your God.' "

(3) Idolatry forbidden

19 AND the LORD spoke to Moses, saying,

2 "Speak to all the congregation of the children of Israel, and say to them: 'You shall be [m]holy, for I the LORD your God *am* holy.

3 'Every one of you shall revere his [n]mother and his father, and [o]keep My [p]Sabbaths: I *am* the LORD your God.

4 'Do not turn to [q]idols, nor make for yourselves molded gods: I *am* the LORD your God.

(4) Peace offering not to be profaned

5 'And if you offer a sacrifice of a peace offering to the LORD, you shall offer it of your own free will.

6 'It shall be eaten the same day you offer *it*, and on the next day. And if any remains until the third day, it shall be burned in the fire.

7 'And if it is eaten at all on the third day, it *is* an abomination. It shall not be accepted.

8 'Therefore *everyone* who eats it shall bear his iniquity, because he has profaned the hallowed *offering* of the LORD; and that person shall be cut off from his people.

(5) Provision for unfortunate

9 'When you reap the harvest of your land, you shall not wholly reap the corners of your field, nor shall you gather the gleanings of your harvest.

10 'And you shall not glean your vineyard, nor shall you gather *every* grape of your vineyard; you shall leave them for the poor and the [r]stranger: I *am* the LORD your God.

11 'You shall not steal, nor deal falsely, nor lie to one another.

12 'And you shall not [s]swear by My name [t]falsely, nor shall you profane the name of your God: I *am* the LORD.

13 'You shall not [u]cheat your neighbor, nor rob *him*. The [v]wages of him who is hired shall not remain with you all night until morning.

14 'You shall not curse the deaf, nor put a stumbling block before the blind, but shall [w]fear your God: I *am* the LORD.

(6) Righteous actions demanded

15 'You shall do no injustice in [x]judgment. You shall not be [y]partial to the poor, nor honor the person of the mighty. In righteousness you shall judge your neighbor.

16 'You shall not go about *as* a [z]talebearer among your people; nor shall you take a stand against the life of your neighbor: I *am* the LORD.

20 *a* Ex. 20:14; Lev. 20:10
21 *b* Lev. 20:2–5; Dt. 12:31 *c* 2 Ki. 16:3 *d* Called *Moloch,* Acts 7:43
22 *e* Lev. 20:13; Rom. 1:27
23 *f* Ex. 22:19
24 *g* Lev. 20:23
25 *h* Num. 35:33–34 *i* Dt. 9:5 *j* Lev. 20:22
30 *k* Lev. 22:9 *l* Lev. 18:2
CHAPTER 19
2 *m* Lev. 11:44–45; 1 Pet. 1:16
3 *n* Ex. 20:12; Mt. 15:4; Eph. 6:2 *o* Ex. 16:23; 20:8 *p Sabbath:* vv. 3,30; Lev. 23:3. (Gen. 2:3; Mt. 12:1, *note*)
4 *q* Ex. 20:4; Ps. 96:5; 115:4–7; 1 Cor. 10:14; Col. 3:5
10 *r* Ex. 23:9; Dt. 24:19–21
12 *s* Ex. 20:7; Dt. 5:11 *t* Mt. 5:33
13 *u* Ex. 22:7–15, 21–27 *v* Dt. 24:15
14 *w* Lev. 25:17; see Ps. 19:9, *note*
19:15 *x* Dt. 16:19 *y* Ex. 23:3,6; Dt. 1:17; cp. 10:17
19:16 *z* Prov. 11:13; 18:8; 20:19

[1](18:24) This list of abominable practices which the Hebrews were to avoid vividly points out the utter degradation of Canaanite morality. Archaeological discoveries have brought many illustrations of this condition, which was so bad that a holy God had to order the complete extermination of the Canaanites. Several centuries earlier God had predicted that by this time "the iniquity of the Amorites" would be complete (Gen. 15:16). Archaeology illustrates the increasing moral degeneracy of Canaanite civilization during this period.

17 'You shall not [a]hate your brother in your heart. You shall [b]surely rebuke your neighbor, and not bear sin because of him.

18 'You shall not take [c]vengeance, nor bear any grudge against the children of your people, but you shall [d]love your neighbor as yourself: I *am* the LORD.

19 'You shall keep My statutes. You shall not let your livestock breed with another kind. You shall not sow your field with mixed seed. Nor shall a garment of mixed linen and wool come upon you.

20 'Whoever lies carnally with a woman who *is* betrothed to a man as a [e]concubine, and who has not at all been redeemed nor given her freedom, for this there shall be scourging; *but* they shall not be put to death, because she was not free.

21 'And he shall bring his trespass offering to the LORD, to the door of the tabernacle of meeting, a ram as a trespass offering.

22 'The priest shall make atonement for him with the ram of the trespass offering before the LORD for his sin which he has committed. And the sin which he has committed shall be [f]forgiven him.

23 'When you come into the land, and have planted all kinds of trees for food, then you shall count their fruit as uncircumcised. Three years it shall be as uncircumcised to you. *It* shall not be eaten.

24 'But in the fourth year all its fruit shall be holy, a praise to the LORD.

25 'And in the fifth year you may eat its fruit, that it may yield to you its increase: I *am* the LORD your God.

26 'You shall not eat *anything* with the blood, nor shall you practice divination or soothsaying.

27 'You shall not shave around the sides of your head, nor shall you disfigure the edges of your beard.

28 'You shall not make any [g]cuttings in your flesh for the dead, nor tattoo any marks on you: I *am* the LORD.

29 'Do not [h]prostitute your daughter, to cause her to be a harlot, lest the land fall into harlotry, and the land become full of wickedness.

30 'You shall keep My Sabbaths and reverence My sanctuary: I *am* the LORD.

31 'Give no regard to [i]mediums and familiar spirits; do not seek after them, to be defiled by them: I *am* the LORD your God.

32 'You shall rise before the gray headed and honor the presence of an old man, and [j]fear your God: I *am* the LORD.

33 'And if a stranger dwells with you in your land, you shall not mistreat him.

34 'The stranger who dwells among you shall be to you as one born among you, and you shall love him as yourself; for you were strangers in the land of Egypt: I *am* the LORD your God.

35 'You shall do no injustice in judgment, in measurement of length, weight, or volume.

36 'You shall have honest scales, honest weights, an honest [k]ephah, and an honest [k]hin: I *am* the LORD your God, who brought you out of the land of Egypt.

37 'Therefore you shall observe all My statutes and all My judgments, and perform them: I *am* the LORD.' "

(7) Regulations about human sacrifices, spiritism, and various immoralities

20 THEN the LORD spoke to Moses, saying,

2 "Again, you shall say to the children of Israel: 'Whoever of the children of Israel, or of the strangers who dwell in Israel, who gives *any* of his descendants to Molech, he shall surely be put to death. The people of the land shall [l]stone him with stones.

3 'I will set My face against that man, and will cut him off from his people, because he has given *some* of his descendants to Molech, to defile My sanctuary and profane My holy name.

4 'And if the people of the land should in any way hide their eyes from the man, when he gives *some* of his descendants to Molech, and they do not [l]kill him,

5 'then I will set My face against that man and against his family; and I will cut him off from his people, and all who prostitute themselves with him to commit harlotry with Molech.

6 [m]'And the person who turns to mediums and familiar spirits, to prostitute himself with them, I will set My face against that person and cut him off from his people.

7 [n]'Consecrate yourselves therefore, and be holy, for I *am* the LORD your God.

8 'And you shall [o]keep My statutes, and perform them: [p]I *am* the LORD who sanctifies you.

17
a 1 Jn. 2:9, 11; 3:15
b Ps. 141:5; Mt. 18:15
18
c Dt. 32:35; cp. 1 Sam. 24:12
d Mt. 5:43; 19:19; 22:39; Mk. 12:31; Lk. 10:27; Gal. 5:14; Jas. 2:8
20
e Cp. Dt. 22:23–27
22
f *Forgiveness:* v. 22; Num. 15:25. (Lev. 4:20; Mt. 26:28, *note*)
28
g Cp. 1 Ki. 18:28
29
h Dt. 23:17
31
i Lev. 20:6, 27
32
j Lev. 25:17; see Ps. 19:9, *note*
36
k See Weights and Measures (OT), 2 Chr. 2:10, *note*
CHAPTER 20
2
l Dt. 17:2–5
6
m Lev. 19:31; 1 Sam. 28:7–25
7
n Heb. 12:14
8
o Lev. 19:19,37
p Ex. 31:13; Dt. 14:2; Ezek. 37:28

9 'For [a]everyone who curses his father or his mother shall surely be put to death. He has cursed his father or his mother. His [b]blood *shall be* upon him.

10 'The man who commits [c]adultery with *another* man's wife, *he* who commits adultery with his neighbor's wife, the adulterer and the adulteress, shall surely be put to death.

11 'The man who lies with his [d]father's wife has uncovered his father's nakedness; both of them shall surely be put to death. Their blood *shall be* upon them.

12 'If a man lies with his [e]daughter-in-law, both of them shall surely be put to death. They have committed perversion. Their blood *shall be* upon them.

13 'If a man lies with a [f]male as he lies with a woman, both of them have committed an abomination. They shall surely be put to death. Their blood *shall be* upon them.

14 'If a man marries a woman and her [g]mother, it *is* wickedness. They shall be burned with fire, both he and they, that there may be no wickedness among you.

15 'If a man mates with an [h]animal, he shall surely be put to death, and you shall kill the animal.

16 'If a woman approaches any animal and mates with it, you shall kill the woman and the animal. They shall surely be put to death. Their blood *is* upon them.

17 'If a man takes his [i]sister, his father's daughter or his mother's daughter, and sees her nakedness and she sees his nakedness, it *is* a wicked thing. And they shall be cut off in the sight of their people. He has uncovered his sister's nakedness. He shall bear his guilt.

18 'If a man lies with a woman during her [j]sickness and uncovers her nakedness, he has exposed her flow, and she has uncovered the flow of her blood. Both of them shall be cut off from their people.

19 'You shall not uncover the nakedness of your [k]mother's sister nor of your [l]father's sister, for that would uncover his near of kin. They shall bear their guilt.

20 'If a man lies with his [m]uncle's wife, he has uncovered his uncle's nakedness. They shall bear their sin; they shall die childless.

21 'If a man takes his [n]brother's wife, it *is* an unclean thing. He has

9
a Ex. 21:17; Prov. 20:20; Mt. 15:4
b vv. 11,13, 16,17
10
c Ex. 20:14; Lev. 18:20; Jn. 8:5
11
d Lev. 18:8
12
e Lev. 18:15
13
f Lev. 18:22; cp. Jud. 19:22
14
g Lev. 18:17; Dt. 27:22
15
h Lev. 18:23
17
i Lev. 18:9
18
j Lev. 18:19; Ezek. 18:6
19
k Lev. 18:13
l Lev. 18:12
20
m Lev. 18:14
21
n Lev. 18:16; cp. Mt. 14:3–4
22
o Lev. 18:25,28
23
p 1 Ki. 14:24
24
q Ex. 13:5
r *Separation:* vv. 24–26; Num. 6:2. (Gen. 12:1; 2 Cor. 6:17, *note*)
25
s Lev. 10:10; 11:1–47
27
t Lev. 19:31; 1 Sam. 28:9
CHAPTER 21
1
u Ezek. 44:25
v Lev. 19:28
5
w Dt. 14:1; Ezek. 44:20
6
x Ex. 22:31

uncovered his brother's nakedness. They shall be childless.

22 'You shall therefore keep all My statutes and all My judgments, and perform them, that the land where I am bringing you to dwell may not [o]vomit you out.

23 'And you shall not walk in the statutes of the nation which I am casting out before you; for they commit all these [p]things, and therefore I abhor them.

24 'But I have said to you, "You shall inherit their land, and [q]I will give it to you to possess, a land flowing with milk and honey." I *am* the LORD your God, who has [r]separated you from the peoples.

25 'You shall therefore [s]distinguish between clean animals and unclean, between unclean birds and clean, and you shall not make yourselves abominable by beast or by bird, or by any kind of living thing that creeps on the ground, which I have separated from you as unclean.

26 'And you shall be holy to Me, for I the LORD *am* holy, and have separated you from the peoples, that you should be Mine.

27 'A man or a woman who is a medium, or who has familiar [t]spirits, shall surely be put to death; they shall stone them with stones. Their blood *shall be* upon them.' "

VI. Laws Regulating the Priesthood and the Seven Great Feasts of the Hebrew Calendar, 21—23

(8) Regulations concerning priests

21 AND the LORD said to Moses, "Speak to the priests, the sons of Aaron, and say to them: [u]'None shall [v]defile himself for the dead among his people,

2 'except for his relatives who are nearest to him: his mother, his father, his son, his daughter, and his brother;

3 'also his virgin sister who is near to him, who has had no husband, for her he may defile himself.

4 '*Otherwise* he shall not defile himself, *being* a chief man among his people, to profane himself.

5 'They shall [w]not make any bald *place* on their heads, nor shall they shave the edges of their beards nor make any cuttings in their flesh.

6 'They shall be [x]holy to their God and not profane the name of their God, for they offer the offerings of the

LORD made by fire, *and* the [a]bread of their God; [b]therefore they shall be holy.

7 'They shall not take a wife *who is* a harlot or a defiled woman, nor shall they take a woman [c]divorced from her husband; for *the priest** is holy to his God.

8 [1]'Therefore you shall [d]consecrate him, for he offers the bread of your God. He shall be [d]holy to you, for [e]I the LORD, who [f]sanctify you, *am* holy.

9 'The daughter of any priest, if she profanes herself by playing the harlot, she profanes her father. She shall be [g]burned with fire.

10 '*He who is* the high priest among his brethren, on whose head the anointing oil was [h]poured and who is consecrated to wear the garments, shall not [i]uncover his head nor tear his clothes;

11 'nor shall he go [j]near any dead body, nor defile himself for his father or his mother;

12 [k]'nor shall he go out of the sanctuary, nor profane the sanctuary of his God; for the [l]consecration of the anointing oil of his God *is* upon him: I *am* the LORD.

13 'And he shall take a wife in her virginity.

14 'A widow or a divorced woman or a [m]defiled woman *or* a harlot—these he shall not marry; but he shall take a virgin of his own people as wife.

15 'Nor shall he profane his posterity among his people, for I the LORD sanctify him.' "

16 And the LORD spoke to Moses, saying,

17 "Speak to Aaron, saying: 'No man of your descendants in *succeeding* generations, who has *any* defect, may approach to offer the bread of his God.

18 'For any man who has a [n]defect shall not approach: a man blind or lame, who has a marred *face* or any *limb* [o]too long,

19 'a man who has a broken foot or broken hand,

20 'or is a hunchback or a dwarf, or *a man* who has a defect in his eye, or eczema or scab, or is a [p]eunuch.

21 'No man of the descendants of Aaron the priest, who has a defect, shall come near to offer the offerings made by fire to the LORD. He has a defect; he shall not come near to offer the bread of his God.

22 'He may eat the bread of his God, *both* the most holy and the holy;

23 'only he shall not go near the [q]veil or approach the altar, because he has a defect, lest he profane My sanctuaries; for I the LORD sanctify them.' "

24 And Moses told *it* to Aaron and his sons, and to all the children of Israel.

Separation of the priests

22 THEN the LORD spoke to Moses, saying,

2 "Speak to Aaron and his sons, that they [r]separate themselves from the holy things of the children of Israel, and [s]that they do not profane My holy name *by* what they [t]dedicate to Me: I *am* the LORD.

3 "Say to them: 'Whoever of all your descendants throughout your generations, who goes near the holy things which the children of Israel dedicate to the LORD, [u]while he has uncleanness upon him, that person shall be cut off from My presence: I *am* the LORD.

4 'Whatever man of the descendants of Aaron, who *is* a [v]leper or has a [w]discharge, shall not eat the holy offerings until he is [x]clean. And [y]whoever touches anything made unclean *by* a corpse, or a man who has had an emission of [z]semen,

5 'or whoever touches any [aa]creeping thing by which he would be made unclean, or any person by whom he would become unclean, whatever his uncleanness may be—

6 'the person who has touched any such thing shall be unclean until evening, and shall not eat the holy *offerings* unless he [bb]washes his body with water.

7 'And when the sun goes down he shall be clean; and afterward he may eat the holy *offerings*, [cc]because it *is* his food.

8 'Whatever dies [dd]*naturally* or is torn *by beasts* he shall not eat, to defile himself with it: I *am* the LORD.

9 'They shall therefore [ee]keep My

---

6 *a* Lev. 3:11 *b* Isa. 52:11
7 *c* Ezek. 44:22; cp. Dt. 24:2
8 *d* Heb. *qodesh.* See Gen. 2:3, *note* *e* Lev. 11:44–45 *f* Lev. 8:12, 30
9 *g* Cp. Dt. 22:21
10 *h* Lev. 8:12 *i* Lev. 10:6,7
11 *j* Num. 19:14
12 *k* Lev. 10:7 *l* Ex. 29:7
14 *m* v. 7
18 *n* Cp. Lev. 22:19–22 *o* Lev. 22:23
20 *p* Dt. 23:1; cp. Isa. 56:3–5
23 *q* Lev. 16:2
CHAPTER 22
2 *r* Num. 6:3 *s* Lev. 18:21 *t* Lev. 16:19; 25:10
3 *u* Lev. 7:20
4 *v* Num. 5:2 *w* Lev. 15:2 *x* Lev. 15:13 *y* Lev. 11:24–28, 39–40; Num. 19:11 *z* Lev. 15:16–17
5 *aa* Lev. 11:23–24
6 *bb* Lev. 15:5; cp. Heb. 10:22
7 *cc* Lev. 21:22; Num. 18:11,13

22:8 *dd* Lev. 7:24; 17:15 **22:9** *ee* Lev. 18:30

* **21:7** Literally *he*

[1](21:8) Here is an illustration of OT holiness or sanctification—a person set apart for the service of God.

ordinance, [a]lest they bear sin for it
and die thereby, if they profane it: I
the LORD sanctify them.
10 'No [b]outsider shall eat the holy
offering; one who dwells with the
priest, or a hired servant, shall not eat
the holy thing.
11 'But if the priest [c]buys a person
with his money, he may eat it; and one
who is born in his house may eat his
food.
12 'If the priest's daughter is married to an outsider, she may not eat of
the holy offerings.
13 'But if the priest's daughter is a
widow or divorced, and has no child,
and has returned to her father's house
as in her youth, she may eat her father's food; but no outsider shall eat it.
14 'And if a man eats the holy *offering* unintentionally, then he shall restore a holy *offering* to the priest, and
add one-fifth to it.
15 'They shall not profane the
[d]holy *offerings* of the children of Israel, which they offer to the LORD,
16 'or allow them to bear the guilt
of trespass when they eat their holy
offerings; for I the LORD sanctify
them.' "

Sacrifices must be physically perfect—type of the moral perfections of Christ (Heb. 9:14)

17 And the LORD spoke to Moses,
saying,
18 "Speak to Aaron and his sons,
and to all the children of Israel, and
say to them: 'Whatever man of the
house of Israel, or of the strangers in
Israel, who offers his sacrifice for any
of his vows or for any of his freewill
offerings, which they offer to the LORD
as a burnt offering—
19 '*you shall offer* of your own free
will a male without blemish from the
cattle, from the sheep, or from the
goats.
20 'Whatever has a [e]defect, you
shall not offer, for it shall not be acceptable on your behalf.
21 'And whoever offers a sacrifice
of a peace offering to the LORD, to fulfill *his* vow, or a freewill offering from
the cattle or the sheep, it must be perfect to be accepted; there shall be no
defect in it.
22 'Those *that are* blind or broken
or maimed, or have an ulcer or eczema or scabs, you shall not offer to
the LORD, nor make an offering by fire
of them on the altar to the LORD.
23 'Either a bull or a lamb that has
any limb too long or too short you may
offer *as* a freewill offering, but for a
vow it shall not be accepted.
24 'You shall not offer to the LORD
what is bruised or crushed, or torn or
cut; nor shall you make *any offering of
them* in your land.
25 'Nor from a [f]foreigner's hand
shall you offer any of these as the
[g]bread of your God, because their corruption *is* in them, *and* defects *are* in
them. They shall not be accepted on
your behalf.' "
26 And the LORD spoke to Moses,
saying:
27 "When a bull or a sheep or a goat
is born, it shall be [h]seven days with its
mother; and from the eighth day and
thereafter it shall be accepted as an
offering made by fire to the LORD.
28 "*Whether it is* a cow or ewe, do
not [i]kill both her and her young on
the same day.
29 "And when you offer a sacrifice
of [j]thanksgiving to the LORD, offer *it*
of your own free will.
30 "On the same day it shall be
eaten; you shall leave none of it until
[k]morning: I *am* the LORD.
31 [l]"Therefore you shall keep My
commandments, and perform them: I
am the LORD.
32 "You shall not profane My holy
name, but [m]I will be hallowed among
the children of Israel. I *am* the LORD
who sanctifies you,
33 "who [n]brought you out of the
land of Egypt, to be your God: I *am* the
LORD."

Feasts of the LORD: the Sabbath and the feasts

23 AND the LORD spoke to Moses,
saying,
2 "Speak to the children of Israel,
and say to them: 'The [1]feasts of the
LORD, which you shall proclaim *to be*
[o]holy [2]convocations, these *are* My
feasts.
3 'Six days shall work be done, but
the seventh day *is* a Sabbath of sol-

9 *a* Ex. 28:43
10 *b* Ex. 29:33
11 *c* Ex. 12:44
15 *d* Num. 18:32
20 *e* Dt. 15:21
25 *f* Num. 16:40 *g* Lev. 22:7
27 *h* Ex. 22:30
28 *i* Dt. 22:6–7
29 *j* Lev. 7:12
30 *k* Lev. 7:15
31 *l* Lev. 19:37; Num. 15:40; Dt. 4:40
32 *m* Lev. 10:3
33 *n* Lev. 19:36
CHAPTER 23
2 *o* Ex. 12:16

[1](23:2) The feasts of the LORD. These were seven great religious festivals which were to be observed by Israel every year. The first three verses of this chapter do not relate to the feasts, but separate the Sabbath from the feasts.

[2](23:2) Israel's religious calendar began in Nisan (in the spring); their civil year, in Tishri (in the autumn). The seven festivals of the Hebrews were included within the first seven

emn rest, a holy convocation. You
shall do no work *on it;* it *is* the [a]Sab-
bath of the LORD in all your dwellings.

The feasts of the LORD:
(1) Passover; Christ our Redeemer

4 'These *are* the feasts of the LORD,
holy convocations which you shall
proclaim at their appointed times.
5 'On the fourteenth *day* of the
[b]first month at twilight *is* the LORD's
[1c]Passover.

The feasts of the LORD:
(2) Unleavened Bread. Memorial
feast (cp. 1 Cor. 11:23–26)

6 'And on the fifteenth day of the
same month *is* the Feast of [2d]Unleav-
ened Bread to the LORD; seven days
you must eat unleavened bread.
7 'On the first day you shall have
a holy convocation; you shall do no
customary work on it.
8 'But you shall offer an offering
made by fire to the LORD for seven
days. The seventh day *shall be* a holy
convocation; you shall do no customary work *on it.*' "

The feasts of the LORD: (3) Firstfruits;
Christ risen (1 Cor. 15:23)

9 And the LORD spoke to Moses,
saying,
10 "Speak to the children of Israel,
and say to them: 'When you come into
the land which I give to you, and reap

3
a Sabbath: v. 3; Num. 15:32. (Gen. 2:3; Mt. 12:1, *note*)
5
b See v. 2, *note 2*
c Ex. 12:1–28; Num. 9:1–5; 28:16–25
6
d Leaven: vv. 6–17; Num. 6:15. (Gen. 19:3; Mt. 13:33, *note*)
13
e See Weights and Measures (OT), 2 Chr. 2:10, *note*
14
f Ex. 34:26; Num. 15:20–21
15
g Ex. 34:22; Dt. 16:9–12

its harvest, then you shall bring a
sheaf of the [3]firstfruits of your harvest
to the priest.
11 'He shall wave the sheaf before
the LORD, to be accepted on your behalf; on the day after the Sabbath the
priest shall wave it.
12 'And you shall offer on that day,
when you wave the sheaf, a male lamb
of the first year, without blemish, as a
burnt offering to the LORD.
13 'Its grain offering *shall be* two-
tenths *of an ephah* of fine flour mixed
with oil, an offering made by fire to
the LORD, for a sweet aroma; and its
drink offering *shall be* of wine, one-
fourth of a [e]hin.
14 'You shall eat neither bread nor
parched grain nor fresh grain until the
same day that you have [f]brought an
offering to your God; *it shall be* a statute forever throughout your generations in all your dwellings.

The feasts of the LORD: (4) Wave
Loaves (Feast of Weeks);
the Church at Pentecost, fifty days
after the resurrection of Christ

15 'And you shall [g]count for yourselves from the day after the Sabbath,
from the day that you brought the
sheaf of the wave offering: seven Sabbaths shall be completed.
16 'Count [4]fifty days to the day after the seventh Sabbath; then you

---

months of the religious calendar: the first three feasts (Passover, Unleavened Bread, and Firstfruits) took place in the first month, Nisan; the last three (Trumpets, Day of Atonement, and Tabernacles), in the seventh month, Tishri. Between the first and last three was the Feast of Weeks (Pentecost) which followed fifty days after the offering of the firstfruits.

The following table correlates the Hebrew religious calendar with the one generally accepted by Christians:

Nisan (or Abib)	= March–April	Tishri (or Ethanim)	= September–October
Iyyar (or Ziv)	= April–May	Marchesvan (or Bul)	= October–November
Sivan	= May–June	Chislev	= November–December
Tammuz	= June–July	Tebeth	= December–January
Ab	= July–August	Shebet	= January–February
Elul	= August–September	Adar	= February–March

About every six years an extra month (Second Adar, or leap-year month) was added because the calendar was based on the moon instead of the sun.

[1](23:5) The Passover, vv. 4–5. This feast is memorial and brings into view redemption upon which all blessing rests. Typically, it stands for "Christ, our Passover, was sacrificed" (1 Cor. 5:7; cp. 1 Pet. 1:19). The Passover was the initial Jewish festival and took place on the fourteenth day of the first month, Nisan.

[2](23:6) The Feast of Unleavened Bread, vv. 6–8. This feast speaks of communion with Christ, the unleavened wave loaf, in the full blessing of His redemption and of a holy walk. The divine order is beautiful; first, redemption; then, holy living. Cp. 1 Cor. 5:6–8; 2 Cor. 7:1; Gal. 5:7–9. The festival began on the fifteenth day of the first month, Nisan, and continued for a week.

[3](23:10) The Feast of Firstfruits, vv. 10–14. This festival is typical of resurrection—first, of Christ, then of those who are His at His coming (1 Cor. 15:23; 1 Th. 4:13–18). The feast, observed in the same week as the Feast of Unleavened Bread, was held on the sixteenth day of the first month, Nisan, being the beginning of the barley harvest.

[4](23:16) The Feast of Weeks, a harvest feast known as Pentecost, vv. 15–22. The antitype is the descent of the Holy Spirit to form the Church. For this reason leaven is present, because

shall offer a new grain offering to the
LORD.
17 'You shall bring from your
dwellings two [1]wave *loaves* of two-
tenths *of an ephah.* They shall be of
fine flour; they shall be baked [a]with
leaven. *They are* the firstfruits to the
LORD.
18 'And you shall offer with the
bread seven lambs of the first year,
without blemish, one young bull, and
two rams. They shall be *as* a burnt
offering to the LORD, with their grain
offering and their drink offerings, an
offering made by fire for a sweet
aroma to the LORD.
19 'Then you shall sacrifice one kid
of the goats as a [b]sin offering, and two
male lambs of the first year as a sacrifice of a peace offering.
20 'The priest shall wave them with
the bread of the firstfruits *as* a wave
offering before the LORD, with the two
lambs. They shall be holy to the LORD
[c]for the priest.
21 'And you shall proclaim on the
same day *that* it is a holy convocation
to you. You shall do no customary
work *on it. It shall be* a statute forever
in all your dwellings throughout your
generations.
22 'When you [d]reap the harvest of
your land, you shall not wholly reap
the corners of your field when you
reap, nor shall you gather any gleaning from your harvest. You shall leave
them for the poor and for the stranger:
I *am* the LORD your God.' "

The feasts of the LORD: (5) Trumpets; prophetic of the future regathering of Israel

23 Then the LORD spoke to Moses,
saying,
24 "Speak to the children of Israel,
saying: 'In the [e]seventh month, on the
first *day* of the month, you shall have
a sabbath-*rest,* a memorial of blowing
of [2f]trumpets, a holy convocation.
25 'You shall do no customary
work *on it;* and you shall offer an offering made by fire to the LORD.' "

The feasts of the LORD: (6) Day of Atonement (Heb. 9:1–16)

26 And the LORD spoke to Moses,
saying:
27 "Also the tenth *day* of this seventh month *shall be* the Day of
[3g]Atonement. It shall be a holy convocation for you; you shall afflict your
souls, and offer an offering made by
fire to the LORD.
28 "And you shall do no work on
that same day, for it *is* the Day of
Atonement, [h]to make [i]atonement for
you before the LORD your God.
29 "For any person who is not [j]af-

17
a See Lev. 7:13, *note*
19
b Num. 28:30; cp. 2 Cor. 5:21
20
c Lev. 14:13
22
d Lev. 19:9; Dt. 24:19–22
24
e See v. 2, *note 2*
f Num. 29:1–6
27
g Lev. 16:1–34; 25:9; Num. 29:7
28
h Lev. 16:34
i See Lev. 16:6, *note*
29
j Cp. Isa. 22:12; Jer. 31:9; Ezek. 7:16

---

there is evil in the Church (Mt. 13:33; Acts 5:1–10; 15:1). Observe, it is now loaves; not a sheaf of separate growths loosely bound together, but a real union of particles making one homogeneous body. The descent of the Holy Spirit at Pentecost united the separate disciples into one organism (1 Cor. 10:16–17; 12:12–13,20). Pentecost took place fifty days after the offering of the firstfruits, coming at about the beginning of summer.

[1](23:17) The wave loaves were offered fifty days after the wave sheaf. This is precisely the period between the resurrection of Christ and the formation of the Church at Pentecost by the baptism of the Holy Spirit (Acts 2:1–4; 1 Cor. 12:12–13). See Church (Mt. 16:18, *note 2*; Heb. 12:23, *note*). With the wave sheaf no leaven was offered, for there was no evil in Christ; but the wave loaves, typifying the Church, are "baked with leaven," for in the Church there is still evil.

[2](23:24) The Feast of Trumpets, vv. 23–25. This feast is a prophetic type and refers to the future regathering of long-dispersed Israel. A great interval elapsed between Pentecost and the Feast of Trumpets, answering to the period occupied in the work of the Holy Spirit in the Church Age. Study carefully Isa. 18:3; 27:13 (with contexts), and Joel 2:1—3:21 in connection with the trumpets, and it will be seen that these trumpets, always symbols of testimony, are connected with the regathering and repentance of Israel after the Church Age is ended. This feast, which was held on the first day of the seventh month, Tishri, was immediately followed by the Day of Atonement.

[3](23:27) The Day of Atonement, vv. 26–32. The day is the same as that described in Lev. 16, but here the stress is laid upon the sorrow and repentance of Israel. That is, the prophetic feature is made prominent, looking forward to the repentance of Israel after their regathering under the Palestinian Covenant (Dt. 30:1–10) preparatory to the second advent of Messiah and the establishment of the kingdom. See the connection between the trumpet in Joel 2:1 and the mourning which follows in vv. 11–15; also Zech. 12:10–14 in connection with the atonement of Zech. 13:1. Historically, the fountain of Zech. 13:1 was opened at the crucifixion but rejected by most Jews of that and the succeeding centuries. After the regathering of Israel the fountain will be efficaciously opened to Israel. The Day of Atonement was the tenth day of the seventh month, Tishri.

flicted *in soul* on that same day shall be cut off from his people.

30 "And any person who does any work on that same day, that person I will [a]destroy from among his people.

31 "You shall do no manner of work; *it shall be* a statute forever throughout your generations in all your dwellings.

32 "It *shall be* to you a sabbath of *solemn* rest, and you shall afflict your souls; on the ninth *day* of the month at evening, from evening to evening, you shall celebrate your sabbath."

The feasts of the LORD*:*
(7) Tabernacles (Ezra 3:4)

33 Then the LORD spoke to Moses, saying,

34 "Speak to the children of Israel, saying: 'The fifteenth day of this seventh month *shall be* the [b]Feast of [1c]Tabernacles *for* seven days to the LORD.

35 'On the first day *there shall be* a holy convocation. You shall do no customary work *on it.*

36 '*For* seven days you shall offer an [d]offering made by fire to the LORD. On the eighth day you shall have a holy convocation, and you shall offer an [e]offering made by fire to the LORD. It *is* a sacred assembly, *and* you [f]shall do no customary work *on it.*

37 'These *are* the feasts of the LORD which you shall proclaim *to be* holy convocations, to offer an offering made by fire to the LORD, a burnt offering and a grain offering, a sacrifice and drink offerings, everything on its day—

38 'besides the Sabbaths of the LORD, besides your gifts, besides all your vows, and [g]besides all your freewill offerings which you give to the LORD.

39 'Also on the fifteenth day of the seventh month, when you have gathered in the fruit of the land, you shall keep the feast of the LORD *for* seven days; on the first day *there shall be* a sabbath-*rest,* and on the eighth day a sabbath-*rest.*

40 'And you shall take for yourselves on the first day the fruit of beautiful trees, branches of palm trees, the boughs of leafy trees, and willows of the brook; and you shall [h]rejoice before the LORD your God for seven days.

41 'You shall keep it as a feast to the LORD for seven days in the year. *It shall be* a statute forever in your generations. You shall celebrate it in the seventh month.

42 'You shall [i]dwell in booths for seven days. [j]All who are native Israelites shall dwell in booths,

43 'that your [k]generations may [l]know that I made the children of Israel dwell in booths when [m]I brought them out of the land of Egypt: I *am* the LORD your God.'"

44 So Moses declared to the children of Israel the feasts of the LORD.

VII. Additional Laws, Promises, and Warnings, 24—27

Oil for the light in the holy place (Ex. 25:6)

24 THEN the LORD spoke to Moses, saying:

2 [n]"Command the children of Israel that they bring to you pure oil of pressed olives for the light, to make the lamps burn continually.

3 "Outside the veil of the Testimony, in the tabernacle of meeting, Aaron shall be in charge of it from evening until morning before the LORD continually; *it shall be* a statute forever in your generations.

4 "He shall be in charge of the lamps on the pure *gold* lampstand before the LORD continually.

Showbread (Ex. 25:23–30)

5 "And you shall take fine flour and bake [o]twelve cakes with it. Two-tenths *of an ephah* shall be in each cake.

6 "You shall set them in two rows, six in a row, on the [p]pure *gold* table before the LORD.

7 "And you shall put pure frankincense on *each* row, that it may be on the bread for a [q]memorial, an offering made by fire to the LORD.

8 [r]"Every Sabbath he shall set it in order before the LORD [s]continually,

30 a Lev. 20:3–6
34 b Dt. 16:13; cp. Zech. 14:16–19
c Num. 29:12; Dt. 16:16
36 d Num. 29:12–34
e Num. 29:35–38
f Continued at v. 39
38 g Num. 29:39
40 h Cp. Dt. 12:7
42 i Cp. Heb. 11:13,16
j Neh. 8:14–18
43 k Ex. 13:14
l Ex. 10:2
m Lev. 22:33
CHAPTER 24
2 n Ex. 27:20
5 o Ex 25:30
6 p Ex. 25:24
7 q Lev. 2:2
8 r 1 Chr. 9:32; cp. Mt. 12:4–5
s Ex. 25:30

[1](23:34) The Feast of Tabernacles, or Ingathering, vv. 34–44, is, like the Lord's Supper for the Church, both memorial and prophetic—memorial as to redemption out of Egypt (v. 43); prophetic as to the kingdom-rest of Israel after her regathering and restoration, when the feast again becomes memorial, not for Israel alone, but also for all nations (Ezra 3:4; Zech. 14:16–21; cp. Rev. 21:3). This festival, its name derived from the fact that during its observance the Israelites dwelt in booths or tabernacles (vv. 42–43), began on the fifteenth day of the seventh month, Tishri, and lasted for one week.

being taken from the children of Israel by an everlasting covenant.

9 "And it shall be for Aaron and his sons, and they shall eat it in a holy place; for it *is* most holy to him from the offerings of the LORD made by fire, by a perpetual statute."

Penalty of blasphemy (Jn. 8:59; 10:31)

10 Now the son of an Israelite woman, whose father *was* an Egyptian, went out among the children of Israel; and this Israelite *woman's* son and a man of Israel fought each other in the camp.

11 And the Israelite woman's son [a]blasphemed the name *of the LORD* and cursed; and so they [b]brought him to Moses. (His mother's name *was* Shelomith the daughter of Dibri, of the tribe of Dan.)

12 Then they put him in custody, that the [c]mind of the LORD might be shown to them.

13 And the LORD spoke to Moses, saying,

14 "Take outside the camp him who has cursed; then let all who heard *him* lay their hands on his head, and let all the congregation stone him.

15 "Then you shall speak to the children of Israel, saying: 'Whoever curses his God shall bear his sin.

16 'And [d]whoever blasphemes the name of the LORD shall surely be put to death. All the congregation shall certainly stone him, the stranger as well as him who is born in the land. When he blasphemes the name *of the LORD*, he shall be put to death.

Penalty for killing and injuring

17 'Whoever kills any man shall surely be put to death.

18 'Whoever kills an animal shall make it good, animal for animal.

19 'If a man causes disfigurement of his neighbor, as he has done, so shall it be done to him—

20 'fracture for [e]fracture, [f]eye for eye, tooth for tooth; as he has caused disfigurement of a man, so shall it be done to him.

21 'And whoever kills an animal shall restore it; but whoever kills a man shall be put to death.

22 'You shall have the [g]same law for the stranger and for one from your own country; for I *am* the LORD your God.' "

Penalty for blasphemy executed

23 Then Moses spoke to the children of Israel; and they took outside the camp him who had cursed, and stoned him with stones. So the children of Israel did as the LORD commanded Moses.

Law of the land: (1) sabbatic year

25 AND the LORD spoke to Moses on Mount [h]Sinai, saying,

2 "Speak to the children of Israel, and say to them: 'When you come into the land which I give you, then the land shall [i]keep a sabbath to the LORD.

3 'Six years you shall sow your field, and six years you shall prune your vineyard, and gather its fruit;

4 'but in the [j]seventh year there shall be a sabbath of solemn [k]rest for the land, a sabbath to the LORD. You shall neither sow your field nor prune your vineyard.

5 [l]'What grows of its own accord of your harvest you shall not reap, nor gather the grapes of your untended vine, *for* it is a year of rest for the land.

6 'And the sabbath *produce* of the land shall be food for you: for you, your male and female servants, your hired man, and the stranger who dwells with you,

7 'for your livestock and the beasts that *are* in your land—all its produce shall be for food.

Law of the land: (2) year of Jubilee

8 'And you shall count seven sabbaths of years for yourself, seven times seven years; and the time of the seven sabbaths of years shall be to you forty-nine years.

9 'Then you shall cause the trumpet of the Jubilee to sound on the tenth *day* of the [m]seventh month; on the Day of [n]Atonement you shall make the trumpet to sound throughout all your land.

10 'And you shall consecrate the fiftieth year, and proclaim [o]liberty throughout *all* the land to all its inhabitants. It shall be a Jubilee for you; and each of you shall [p]return to his possession, and each of you shall return to his family.

11 'That fiftieth year shall be a Jubilee to you; in it you shall neither sow nor reap what grows of its own accord, nor gather *the grapes* of your untended vine.

12 'For it *is* the Jubilee; it shall be holy to you; you shall eat its produce from the field.

13 'In this Year of Jubilee, each of you shall return to his [q]possession.

11
a Ex. 22:28
b Ex. 18:26
12
c Num. 27:5
16
d Ex. 20:7
20
e Ex. 21:23
f Mt. 5:38
22
g Ex. 12:49; Lev. 19:33–37
CHAPTER 25
1
h Lev. 26:46
2
i Lev. 26:34–35
4
j Dt. 15:1; Neh. 10:31
k Cp. Heb. 4:9
5
l 2 Ki. 19:29
9
m See Lev. 23:2, *note*
n See Lev. 16:6, *note*
10
o Cp. Isa. 61:1
p Lev. 25:13,28,54
13
q Lev. 27:24

14 'And if you sell anything to your neighbor or buy from your neighbor's hand, you shall not [a]oppress one another.

15 'According to the number of years after the Jubilee you shall buy from your neighbor, and [b]according to the number of years of crops he shall sell to you.

16 'According to the multitude of years you shall increase its price, and according to the fewer number of years you shall diminish its price; for he sells to you *according* to the number *of the years* of the crops.

17 'Therefore you shall not oppress one another, but you shall [c]fear your God; for I *am* the LORD your God.

18 'So you shall observe My statutes and keep My judgments, and perform them; and you will dwell in the land in safety.

19 'Then the land will yield its fruit, and you will eat your fill, and dwell there in safety.

20 'And if you say, "What shall we [d]eat in the seventh year, since we shall not sow nor gather in our produce?"

21 'Then I will [e]command My blessing on you in the [f]sixth year, and it will bring forth produce enough for three years.

22 'And you shall sow in the eighth year, and eat old produce until the ninth year; until its produce comes in, you shall eat *of* the old *harvest*.

23 'The land shall not be sold permanently, for the land *is* [g]Mine; for you *are* [h]strangers and sojourners with Me.

24 'And in all the land of your possession you shall grant redemption of the land.

Law of the land: (3) redemption of the inheritance

25 'If one of your brethren becomes poor, and has sold *some* of his possession, [i]and if his redeeming relative comes to [j]redeem it, then he may redeem what his brother sold.

26 'Or if the man has no one to redeem it, but he himself becomes able to redeem it,

27 'then let him count the years since its sale, and restore the remainder to the man to whom he sold it, that he may return to his possession.

28 'But if he is not able to have *it* restored to himself, then what was sold shall remain in the hand of him who bought it until the Year of Jubilee; and in the Jubilee it shall be released, and he shall return to his possession.

29 'If a man sells a house in a walled city, then he may redeem it within a whole year after it is sold; *within* a full year he may redeem it.

30 'But if it is not [k]redeemed within the space of a full year, then the house in the walled city shall belong permanently to him who bought it, throughout his generations. It shall not be released in the Jubilee.

31 'However the houses of villages which have no wall around them shall be counted as the fields of the country. They may be redeemed, and they shall be released in the Jubilee.

32 'Nevertheless the [l]cities of the Levites, *and* the houses in the cities of their possession, the Levites may redeem at any time.

33 'And if a man purchases a house from the Levites, then the house that was sold in the city of his possession shall be released in the Jubilee; for the houses in the cities of the Levites *are* their possession among the children of Israel.

34 'But the field of the commonland of their cities may [m]not be [n]sold, for it *is* their perpetual possession.

Law of the land: (4) poor brother

35 'If one of your brethren becomes poor, and falls into poverty among you, then you shall [o]help him, like a stranger or a sojourner, that he may live with you.

36 'Take no [p]usury or interest from him; but [q]fear your God, that your brother may live with you.

37 'You shall not lend him your money for usury, nor lend him your food at a profit.

38 'I *am* the LORD your God, who brought you out of the land of Egypt, to give you the land of Canaan *and* to be your God.

39 'And if *one of* your brethren *who dwells* by you becomes poor, and sells himself to you, you shall not compel him to serve as a slave.

40 'As a hired servant *and* a sojourner he shall be with you, *and* shall serve you until the Year of Jubilee.

41 'And *then* he shall depart from you—he and his children with him—and shall return to his own family. He shall return to the possession of his fathers.

42 'For they *are* My servants, whom

14
a Lev. 19:13
15
b Lev. 27:18,23
17
c Lev. 19:14; see Ps. 19:9, *note*
20
d Cp. Mt. 6:25,31
21
e Dt. 28:8
f Cp. Ex. 16:29
23
g Ex. 19:5; Dt. 11:12; 2 Chr. 7:20
h Ex. 6:4; Ps. 39:12; Heb. 11:13
25
i Num. 5:8; Job 19:25; Jer. 32:7,8
j *Redemption* (redeeming relative type): vv. 25–27, 48–49; Lev. 25:54. (Gen. 48:16; Isa. 59:20, *note*)
30
k *Redemption* (redeeming relative type), see Isa. 59:20, *note*
32
l Num. 35:1–8
34
m Cp. Gen. 47:22; Ezra 7:24
n Cp. Acts 4:36–37
35
o Dt. 15:7–11
36
p Ex. 22:25; Dt. 23:19–20
q See Ps. 19:9, *note*

I brought out of the land of Egypt; they
shall not be sold as slaves.
43 'You shall not rule over him with
rigor, but you shall [a]fear your God.
44 'And as for your male and female slaves whom you may have—
from the nations that are around you,
from them you may buy male and female slaves.
45 'Moreover you may buy the children of the strangers who dwell
among you, and their families who are
with you, which they beget in your
land; and they shall become your
property.
46 'And you may take them as an
inheritance for your children after
you, to inherit *them as* a possession;
they shall be your permanent slaves.
But regarding your brethren, the children of Israel, you shall not rule over
one another with rigor.

Law of the land: (5) redemption of the poor brother—Christ our Redeeming Relative

47 'Now if a sojourner or stranger
close to you becomes rich, and *one of*
your brethren *who dwells* by him becomes poor, and sells himself to the
stranger *or* sojourner close to you, or
to a member of the stranger's family,
48 'after he is sold he may be redeemed again. One of his brothers
may redeem him;
49 'or his uncle or his uncle's son
may redeem him; or *anyone* who is
near of [1]kin to him in his family may
redeem him; or if he is able he may
redeem himself.
50 'Thus he shall reckon with him
who bought him: The price of his release shall be according to the number
of years, from the year that he was
sold to him until the Year of Jubilee; *it*
shall be according to the time of a
hired servant for him.
51 'If *there are* still many years *re-*
maining, according to them he shall
repay the price of his redemption from
the money with which he was bought.
52 'And if there remain but a few
years until the Year of Jubilee, then he
shall reckon with him, *and* according
to his years he shall repay him the
price of his redemption.
53 'He shall be with him as a yearly
hired servant, and he shall not rule
with rigor over him in your sight.
54 'And if he is not [b]redeemed in
these *years,* then he shall be released
in the Year of Jubilee—he and his
children with him.
55 'For the children of Israel *are*
servants to Me; they *are* My servants
whom I brought out of the land of
Egypt: I *am* the LORD your God.

Law of the land: (6) conditions of blessing; warnings of chastisement

26 [2]YOU shall not make [c]idols
for yourselves;
neither a [d]carved image nor a
sacred pillar shall you rear
up for yourselves;
nor shall you set up an engraved stone in your land,
to bow down to it;
for I *am* the LORD your God.
2 You shall keep My Sabbaths
and [e]reverence My sanc-
tuary:
I *am* the LORD.

Conditions of blessing

3 [f]'If you walk in My statutes
and keep My [g]command-
ments, and perform them,
4 then I will give you rain in its
season, the land shall
yield its produce, and the
trees of the field shall yield
their fruit.
5 Your threshing shall last till
the time of vintage, and
the vintage shall [h]last till
the time of sowing;
you shall eat your bread to
the full, and dwell in your
land safely.
6 I will give peace in the land,
and you shall [i]lie down,
and none will make *you*
[j]afraid;
I will rid the land of evil
[k]beasts,
and the sword will not go
through your land.
7 You will chase your enemies,
and they shall fall by the
sword before you.
8 [l]Five of you shall chase a
hundred, and a hundred of
you shall put ten thousand
to flight;

43
a See Ps. 19:9, *note*
54
b Redemp-tion (re-deeming relative type): v. 54; Lev. 27:13. (Gen. 48:16; Isa. 59:20, *note*)
CHAPTER 26
1
c Dt. 4:15–18
d Ex. 20:4
2
e Lev. 19:30
3
f vv. 3–13, cp. Dt. 7:12–26; 28:1–14
g Law (of Moses): v. 3; Lev. 27:1. (Ex. 19:1; Gal. 3:24, *note*)
5
h Cp. Amos 9:13
6
i Ps. 4:8
j Job 11:19
k Cp. Hos. 2:18
8
l Dt. 32:30; cp. Jud. 7:7–12

[1](25:49) The redeeming relative. The word *goel* is used to indicate the redeemer—the one who pays. The case of Ruth and Boaz (Ruth 2:1; 3:10–18; 4:1–10) perfectly illustrates this beautiful type of Christ. See Redemption, Isa. 59:20, *note.*

[2](26:1) Chapter 26 should be read in connection with Dt. 28—30, referring to the Palestinian Covenant. Be sure to read also Dt. 30:3, *note.*

your enemies shall fall by the sword before you.

9 'For I will look on you [a]favorably and make you fruitful, multiply you and confirm My [b]covenant with you.
10 You shall eat the [c]old harvest, and clear out the old because of the new.
11 I will [d]set My tabernacle among you, and My soul shall not abhor you.
12 I will walk among you and be your [e]God, and you shall be My people.
13 I *am* the LORD your God, who brought you out of the land of Egypt, that *you* should not be their [f]slaves;
I have broken the bands of your [g]yoke and made you walk upright.

Warnings of chastisement

14 'But if you do not obey Me, and do not observe all these commandments,
15 and if you despise My statutes, or if your soul abhors My judgments, so that you do not perform all My commandments, *but* break My covenant,

First chastisement: distress

16 I also will do this to you:
I will even appoint terror over you, wasting disease and fever which shall consume the eyes and [h]cause sorrow of heart.
And you shall sow your seed in [i]vain, for your enemies shall eat it.
17 I will [j]set My face against you, and you shall be [k]defeated by your enemies.
Those who hate you shall [l]reign over you, and you shall [m]flee when no one pursues you.

Second chastisement: drought

18 'And after all this, if you do not obey Me, then I will punish you seven times more for your sins.
19 I will break the pride of your power;
I will make your [n]heavens like iron and your earth like bronze.
20 And your strength shall be spent [o]in vain;
for your land shall not yield its produce, nor shall the trees of the land [p]yield their fruit.

Third chastisement: beasts

21 'Then, if you walk contrary to Me, and are not willing to obey Me, I will bring on you seven times more plagues, according to your sins.
22 I will also send [q]wild beasts among you, which shall rob you of your children, destroy your livestock, and make you few in number;
and your highways shall be [r]desolate.

Fourth chastisement: disease

23 'And if by these things you are not reformed by Me, but walk contrary to Me,
24 then I also will walk contrary to you, and I will punish you yet seven times for your sins.
25 And I will bring a sword against you that will execute the vengeance of the covenant;
when you are gathered together within your cities I will send [s]pestilence among you;
and you shall be delivered into the hand of the enemy.
26 When I have cut off your supply of [t]bread, ten women shall bake your bread in one oven, and they shall bring back your bread by weight, and you shall eat and not be [u]satisfied.

Fifth chastisement: famine

27 'And after all this, if you do not obey Me, but walk contrary to Me,
28 then I also will walk contrary to you in fury;
and I, even I, will chastise you seven times for your sins.
29 You shall [v]eat the flesh of your sons, and you shall eat the flesh of your daughters.

9
a 2 Ki. 13:23
b Gen. 17:1–7
10
c Lev. 25:22
11
d Ex. 29:45–46
12
e Jer. 7:23; 2 Cor. 6:16
13
f Ex. 20:2
g Cp. Gen. 27:40
16
h Ezek. 24:23
i Jud. 6:3–6
17
j Ps. 34:16
k 1 Sam. 4:10; 31:1
l Ps. 106:41
m Prov. 28:1
19
n Dt. 28:23; cp. 1 Ki. 17:1
20
o Ps. 127:1
p Gen. 4:12
22
q Dt. 32:24; Ezek. 14:21
r Jud. 5:6
25
s Num. 16:49; 2 Sam. 24:15
26
t Ps. 105:16; Ezek. 4:16–17
u Hag. 1:6
29
v 2 Ki. 6:28–29

30 I will destroy your [a]high places, cut down your incense altars, and [b]cast your carcasses on the lifeless forms of your idols;
and My soul shall abhor you.
31 I will lay your [c]cities waste and bring your [d]sanctuaries to desolation, and I will not [e]smell the fragrance of your sweet aromas.

Sixth chastisement: dispersion (cp. Dt. 28:58–67)

32 I will bring the land to desolation, and your enemies who dwell in it shall be [f]astonished at it.
33 I will [g]scatter you among the nations and draw out a sword after you;
your land shall be desolate and your cities waste.
34 Then the land shall enjoy its [h]sabbaths as long as it lies desolate and you *are* in your enemies' land;
then the land shall rest and enjoy its sabbaths.
35 As long as *it* lies desolate it shall rest—
for the time it did not rest on your sabbaths when you dwelt in it.

36 'And as for those of you who are left, I will send [i]faintness into their hearts in the lands of their enemies;
the sound of a shaken leaf shall cause them to flee;
they shall flee as though fleeing from a sword, and they shall fall when no one pursues.
37 They shall stumble over one another, as it were before a sword, when no one pursues;
and you shall have no *power* to [j]stand before your enemies.
38 You shall [k]perish among the nations, and the land of your enemies shall eat you up.
39 And those of you who are left shall [l]waste away in their iniquity in your enemies' lands;
also in their [m]fathers' iniquities, which are with them, they shall waste away.

30
a 2 Ki. 23:8, 20; see Jud. 3:7 and 1 Ki. 3:2, *notes*
b 1 Ki. 13:2
31
c 2 Ki. 25:4, 10
d 2 Chr. 36:19
e Isa. 1:11–15
32
f Jer. 18:16
33
g Ps. 44:11
34
h 2 Chr. 36:21
36
i Ezek. 21:7, 12,15
37
j Josh. 7:12–13
38
k Dt. 4:26
39
l Ezek. 33:10
m Ex. 34:7
40
n 1 Ki. 8:33–34; Neh. 9:2; 1 Jn. 1:9
41
o 2 Chr. 12:6,7,12; 1 Pet. 5:5–6
p Ps. 39:9; 51:3,4; Dan. 9:7
42
q Ex. 6:5; Ps. 106:45
44
r Dt. 4:31; Jer. 30:11; Rom. 11:1–36
CHAPTER 27
1
s *Law* (of Moses): vv. 1–34; Dt. 5:1. (Ex. 19:1; Gal. 3:24, *note*)
2
t Lev. 7:16; Num. 30:2–16

Abrahamic Covenant remains despite the disobedience and dispersion

40 '*But* if they [n]confess their iniquity and the iniquity of their fathers, with their unfaithfulness in which they were unfaithful to Me, and that they also have walked contrary to Me,
41 and *that* I also have walked contrary to them and have brought them into the land of their enemies;
if their uncircumcised hearts are [o]humbled, and they [p]accept their guilt—
42 then I will [q]remember My covenant with Jacob, and My covenant with Isaac and My covenant with Abraham I will remember;
I will remember the land.
43 The land also shall be left empty by them, and will enjoy its sabbaths while it lies desolate without them;
they will accept their guilt, because they despised My judgments and because their soul abhorred My statutes.
44 Yet for all that, when they are in the land of their enemies, I will not [r]cast them away, nor shall I abhor them, to utterly destroy them and break My covenant with them;
for I *am* the LORD their God.
45 But for their sake I will remember the covenant of their ancestors, whom I brought out of the land of Egypt in the sight of the nations, that I might be their God:
I *am* the LORD.' "

46 These *are* the statutes and judgments and laws which the LORD made between Himself and the children of Israel on Mount Sinai by the hand of Moses.

About dedicated persons and things

27 NOW the LORD spoke to [s]Moses, saying,
2 "Speak to the children of Israel, and say to them: 'When a man consecrates by a [t]vow certain persons to the LORD, according to your valuation,

3 'if your valuation is of a male from twenty years old up to sixty years old, then your valuation shall be fifty [a]shekels of silver, according to the shekel of the sanctuary.

4 'If it *is* a female, then your valuation shall be thirty shekels;

5 'and if from five years old up to twenty years old, then your valuation for a male shall be twenty shekels, and for a female ten shekels;

6 'and if from a month old up to five years old, then your valuation for a male shall be five shekels of silver, and for a female your valuation shall be three shekels of silver;

7 'and if from sixty years old and above, if *it is* a male, then your valuation shall be fifteen shekels, and for a female ten shekels.

8 'But if he is too poor to pay your valuation, then he shall present himself before the priest, and the priest shall set a value for [b]him; according to the ability of him who vowed, the priest shall value him.

9 'If *it is* an animal that men may bring as an offering to the LORD, all that *anyone* gives to the LORD shall be holy.

10 'He shall not substitute it or exchange it, good for bad or bad for good; and if he at all exchanges animal for animal, then both it and the one exchanged for it shall be [c]holy.

11 'If *it is* an unclean animal which they do not offer as a sacrifice to the LORD, then he shall present the animal before the priest;

12 'and the priest shall set a value for it, whether it is good or bad; as you, the priest, value it, so it shall be.

13 'But if he *wants* at all *to* [d]redeem it, then he must add [e]one-fifth to your valuation.

14 'And when a man [f]dedicates his house *to be* holy to the LORD, then the priest shall set a value for it, whether it is good or bad; as the priest values it, so it shall stand.

15 'If he who dedicated it *wants to* [d]redeem his house, then he must add one-fifth of the money of your valuation to it, and it shall be his.

16 'If a man dedicates to the LORD *part* of a field of his possession, then your valuation shall be according to the seed for it. A [a]homer of barley seed *shall be valued* at fifty [a]shekels of silver.

17 'If he dedicates his field from the Year of Jubilee, according to your valuation it shall stand.

18 'But if he dedicates his field after the Jubilee, then the priest shall [g]reckon to him the money due according to the years that [h]remain till the Year of Jubilee, and it shall be deducted from your valuation.

19 'And if he who dedicates the field ever wishes to [d]redeem it, then he must add one-fifth of the money of your valuation to it, and it shall belong to him.

20 'But if he does not want to [d]redeem the field, or if he has sold the field to another man, it shall not be redeemed anymore;

21 'but the field, when it is [h]released in the [i]Jubilee, shall be holy to the LORD, as a [j]devoted field; it shall be the possession of the priest.

22 'And if a man dedicates to the LORD a field which he has bought, which is not the field of his possession,

23 'then the priest shall reckon to him the worth of your valuation, up to the Year of Jubilee, and he shall give your valuation on that day *as* a holy *offering* to the LORD.

24 'In the Year of Jubilee the field shall [k]return to him from whom it was bought, to the one who *owned* the land as a possession.

25 'And all your valuations shall be according to the shekel of the sanctuary: twenty [a]gerahs to the shekel.

Three things that are the LORD's absolutely: (1) firstborn of the animals

26 'But the firstborn of the animals, which should be the [l]LORD's firstborn, no man shall dedicate; whether *it is* an ox or sheep, it *is* the LORD's.

27 'And if *it is* an unclean animal, then he shall [d]redeem *it* according to your valuation, and shall add one-fifth to it; or if it is not redeemed, then it shall be sold according to your valuation.

(2) Any dedicated thing

28 'Nevertheless no devoted *offering* that a man may devote to the LORD of all that he has, *both* man and beast, or the field of his possession, shall be sold or [d]redeemed; every devoted *offering is* most holy to the LORD.

29 'No person under the ban, who may become doomed to destruction among men, shall be redeemed, *but* shall surely be put to death.

3
[a] See Coinage (OT), Ex. 30:13, *note;* cp. 2 Chr. 2:10, *note*

8
[b] Lev. 14:21–24

10
[c] Lev. 27:33

13
[d] *Redemption* (redeeming relative type): vv. 13–15, 19–20, 27–28; Lev. 27:33. (Gen. 48:16; Isa. 59:20, *note*)
[e] Lev. 6:5; 22:14

14
[f] *Sanctification* (OT): vv. 14–22; Josh. 5:15. (Gen. 2:3; Zech. 8:3)

18
[g] For divine imputation, see Jas. 2:23, *note*
[h] Lev. 25:28

21
[i] Lev. 25:8–10
[j] Num. 18:14

24
[k] Lev. 25:10–13

26
[l] Ex. 13:2

(3) All tithes of land, trees, and animals

30 'And [a]all the [b]tithe of the land, *whether* of the seed of the land *or* of the fruit of the tree, *is* the LORD's. It *is* holy to the LORD.
31 'If a man wants at all to redeem *any* of his tithes, he shall add one-fifth to it.
32 'And concerning the tithe of the herd or the flock, of whatever [c]passes under the rod, the tenth one shall be holy to the LORD.
33 'He shall not inquire whether it is good or bad, nor shall he exchange it; and if he exchanges it at all, then both it and the one exchanged for it shall be holy; it shall not be [d]redeemed.' "
34 [e]These *are* the commandments which the LORD commanded Moses for the children of Israel on Mount [f]Sinai.

30 *a* Gen. 28:22; Num. 18:21,24 *b* See 2 Cor. 8:1, *note*
32 *c* Cp. Jer. 33:13; Ezek. 20:37; Mic. 7:14
33 *d* Redemption (redeeming relative type): v. 33; Num. 5:8. (Gen. 48:16; Isa. 59:20, *note*) 27:34 *e* Mal. 4:4 *f* Ex. 19:1–6,25; cp. Heb. 12:18–29

The Fourth Book of Moses Called

NUMBERS

Author: Moses *Theme:* Wilderness Wanderings *Date of writing:* c. 1450–1410 B.C.

NUMBERS derives its name from the record of the two numberings of the Israelite host (chs. 1 and 26), being called in the Greek version *Arithmoi*, and in the Vulgate, *Numeri*. More accurate is the Hebrew title, *Bemidbar* ("In the Wilderness").

The first part of the book concludes the divine record of the experiences at Sinai and thus points back to Exodus. The major part of Numbers recounts the years of wandering, from the time that Israel departed from Sinai until, as a new generation, they reached the Jordan River. The first year and a half (approximately) of Israel's forty years' wandering is recorded in Ex. 12:37—Num. 14:45; and the last few months, in Num. 20:14 to the end of the book. Between 14:45 and 20:14 there is a period of about thirty-eight years (cp. Dt. 2:14).

Redeemed from Egypt, possessing the law, led by Moses, daily looking upon the tabernacle, and supernaturally guided by cloud and pillar of fire, Israel should have walked triumphantly in the perfect will of God. Instead they failed repeatedly, as this book records.

As in Israel each person had his definitely assigned place and task for the welfare of the whole nation, so in the Church each member of the body of Christ has his particular place and function "for the edifying of the body of Christ" (1 Cor. 12; Eph. 4:1–16).

Numbers may be divided into four major sections:

I. Preparations for Departure from Sinai, 1:1—10:10.
II. From Sinai to the Plains of Moab, 10:11—21:35.
III. The Prophecies of Balaam, 22:1—25:18.
IV. Instructions and Preparations for Entering the Promised Land, 26:1—36:13.

I. Preparations for Departure from Sinai, 1:1—10:10

Order of the army: (1) Moses numbers able men of war

1 NOW the LORD [a]spoke to Moses in the Wilderness of [b]Sinai, in the tabernacle of meeting, on the [c]first *day* of the [d]second month, in the second year after they had come out of the land of Egypt, saying:

2 [e]"Take a census of all the congregation of the children of Israel, by their families, by their fathers' houses, according to the number of names, every male [f]individually,

3 "from [g]twenty years old and above—all who *are able to* go to war in Israel. You and Aaron shall number them by their armies.

4 "And with you there shall be a man from every tribe, each one the head of his father's house.

5 "These are the names of the men who shall stand with you: from Reuben, Elizur the son of Shedeur;

6 "from Simeon, Shelumiel the son of Zurishaddai;

7 "from Judah, Nahshon the son of Amminadab;

8 "from Issachar, Nethanel the son of Zuar;

9 "from Zebulun, Eliab the son of Helon;

10 "from the sons of Joseph: from Ephraim, Elishama the son of Ammihud; from Manasseh, Gamaliel the son of Pedahzur;

11 "from Benjamin, Abidan the son of Gideoni;

12 "from Dan, Ahiezer the son of Ammishaddai;

13 "from Asher, Pagiel the son of Ocran;

14 "from Gad, Eliasaph the son of Deuel;*

15 "from Naphtali, Ahira the son of Enan."

16 [h]These *were* [i]chosen from the congregation, leaders of their fathers' tribes, [j]heads of the divisions in Israel.

17 Then Moses and Aaron took these men who had been mentioned by name,

18 and they assembled all the congregation together on the first *day* of the [d]second month; and they recited their ancestry by families, by their fathers' houses, according to the number of names, from twenty years old and above, each one individually.

19 [k]As the LORD commanded Moses, so he numbered them in the Wilderness of Sinai.

20 Now the children of [l]Reuben, Israel's oldest son, their genealogies

CHAPTER 1

1
a c. 1445 B.C. See Ex. 1:8, *note*
b Ex. 19:1; Num. 10:12; cp. Heb. 12:18
c Cp. Ex. 40:2,17; Num. 9:1; 10:11
d v. 18; see Lev. 23:2, *note*

2
e vv. 2–46; cp. Ex. 30:12; Num. 26:1–63; 2 Sam. 24:2; 1 Chr. 21:2
f Ex. 30:12–13; 38:26

3
g Ex. 30:14

16
h Num. 7:2; 1 Chr. 27:16–22
i Num. 16:2
j Ex. 18:21, 25; Jer. 5:5; Mic. 3:1,9; 5:2

19
k v. 2

20
l Cp. Num.

26:5–11

*

1:14 Spelled *Reuel* in 2:14

by their families, by their fathers' house, according to the number of names, every male individually, from twenty years old and above, all who *were able to* go to war:

21 those who were numbered of the tribe of Reuben *were* forty-six thousand five hundred.

22 From the children of [a]Simeon, their genealogies by their families, by their fathers' house, of those who were numbered, according to the number of names, every male individually, from twenty years old and above, all who *were able to* go to war:

23 those who were numbered of the tribe of Simeon *were* fifty-nine thousand three hundred.

24 From the children of [b]Gad, their genealogies by their families, by their fathers' house, according to the number of names, from twenty years old and above, all who *were able to* go to war:

25 those who were numbered of the tribe of Gad *were* forty-five thousand six hundred and fifty.

26 From the children of [c]Judah, their genealogies by their families, by their fathers' house, according to the number of names, from twenty years old and above, all who *were able to* go to war:

27 those who were numbered of the tribe of Judah *were* seventy-four thousand six hundred.

28 From the children of [d]Issachar, their genealogies by their families, by their fathers' house, according to the number of names, from twenty years old and above, all who *were able to* go to war:

29 those who were numbered of the tribe of Issachar *were* fifty-four thousand four hundred.

30 From the children of [e]Zebulun, their genealogies by their families, by their fathers' house, according to the number of names, from twenty years old and above, all who *were able to* go to war:

31 those who were numbered of the tribe of Zebulun *were* fifty-seven thousand four hundred.

32 From the sons of [f]Joseph, the children of Ephraim, their genealogies by their families, by their fathers' house, according to the number of names, from twenty years old and above, all who *were able to* go to war:

33 those who were numbered of the tribe of [g]Ephraim *were* forty thousand five hundred.

34 From the children of [h]Manasseh, their genealogies by their families, by their fathers' house, according to the number of names, from twenty years old and above, all who *were able to* go to war:

35 those who were numbered of the tribe of Manasseh *were* thirty-two thousand two hundred.

36 From the children of [i]Benjamin, their genealogies by their families, by their fathers' house, according to the number of names, from twenty years old and above, all who *were able to* go to war:

37 those who were numbered of the tribe of Benjamin *were* thirty-five thousand four hundred.

38 From the children of [j]Dan, their genealogies by their families, by their fathers' house, according to the number of names, from twenty years old and above, all who *were able to* go to war:

39 those who were numbered of the tribe of Dan *were* sixty-two thousand seven hundred.

40 From the children of [k]Asher, their genealogies by their families, by their fathers' house, according to the number of names, from twenty years old and above, all who *were able to* go to war:

41 those who were numbered of the tribe of Asher *were* forty-one thousand five hundred.

42 From the children of [l]Naphtali, their genealogies by their families, by their fathers' house, according to the number of names, from twenty years old and above, all who *were able to* go to war:

43 those who were numbered of the tribe of Naphtali *were* fifty-three thousand four hundred.

44 These are the ones who were numbered, whom Moses and Aaron numbered, with the leaders of Israel, twelve men, each one representing his father's house.

45 So all who were numbered of the children of Israel, by their fathers' houses, from twenty years old and above, all who *were able to* go to war in Israel—

46 [m]all who were numbered were [1]six hundred and three thousand five hundred and fifty.

22 *a* Cp. Num. 26:12–14
24 *b* Cp. Num. 26:15–18
26 *c* Cp. Num. 26:19–22
28 *d* Cp. Num. 26:23–25
30 *e* Cp. Num. 26:26–27
32 *f* Cp. Gen. 48:1–22; Num. 26:28–37
33 *g* Cp. Num. 26:35–37
34 *h* Cp. Num. 26:29–34
36 *i* Cp. Num. 26:38–41
38 *j* Cp. Num. 26:42–43
40 *k* Cp. Num. 26:44–47
42 *l* Cp. Num. 26:48–50
46 *m* Ex. 38:26; Num. 2:32; 26:63; cp. Ex. 12:37; Num. 14:22–38; 26:51, 64–65; Heb. 11:12; Rev. 7:4–8; see Num. 3:43, *note*

[1](1:46) 603,550 here (cp. Num. 26:51—601,730, a decrease of 1820). Of those in the first

Levites exempted for other service

47 [a]But the [1]Levites were not numbered among them by their fathers' tribe;

48 for the LORD had spoken to Moses, saying:

49 "Only the tribe of Levi you shall not number, nor take a census of them among the children of Israel;

50 "but you shall [b]appoint the Levites over the tabernacle of the Testimony, over all its furnishings, and over all things that belong to it; they shall carry the tabernacle and all its furnishings; they shall attend to it and camp around the tabernacle.

51 "And when the tabernacle is to go forward, the [c]Levites shall take it down; and when the tabernacle is to be set up, the Levites shall set it [d]up. The outsider who comes near shall be put to death.

52 "The children of Israel shall pitch their tents, [e]everyone by his own camp, everyone by his own standard, according to their armies;

53 "but the Levites shall [f]camp around the tabernacle of the Testimony, that there may be no [g]wrath on the congregation of the children of Israel; and the Levites shall [h]keep charge of the tabernacle of the Testimony."

54 Thus the children of Israel did; according to all that the LORD commanded Moses, so they did.

Order of the army: (2) arrangement of the camp

2 AND the LORD spoke to Moses and Aaron, saying:

2 "Everyone of the children of Israel shall camp by his own standard, beside the emblems of his father's house; they shall camp some distance from the tabernacle of meeting.

3 "On the [i]east side, toward the rising of the sun, those of the standard of the forces with Judah shall camp according to their armies; and [j]Nahshon the son of Amminadab *shall be* the leader of the children of Judah."

4 And his army was numbered at seventy-four thousand six hundred.

5 "Those who camp next to him *shall be* the tribe of Issachar, and Nethanel the son of Zuar *shall be* the leader of the children of Issachar."

6 And his army was numbered at fifty-four thousand four hundred.

7 "Then *comes* the tribe of Zebulun, and Eliab the son of Helon *shall be* the leader of the children of Zebulun."

8 And his army was numbered at fifty-seven thousand four hundred.

9 "All who were numbered according to their armies of the forces with Judah, one hundred and eighty-six thousand four hundred—these shall break camp [k]first.

10 "On the [l]south side *shall be* the standard of the forces with Reuben according to their armies, and the leader of the children of Reuben *shall be* Elizur the son of Shedeur."

11 And his army was numbered at forty-six thousand five hundred.

12 "Those who camp next to him *shall be* the tribe of Simeon, and the leader of the children of Simeon *shall be* Shelumiel the son of Zurishaddai."

13 And his army was numbered at fifty-nine thousand three hundred.

14 "Then *comes* the tribe of Gad, and the leader of the children of Gad *shall be* Eliasaph the son of Reuel."*

15 And his army was numbered at forty-five thousand six hundred and fifty.

16 "All who were numbered according to their armies of the forces with Reuben, one hundred and fifty-one thousand four hundred and

* 2:14 Spelled *Deuel* in 1:14 and 7:42

47 [a] Num. 2:33; cp. 3:14–22; 26:57–62; 1 Chr. 6:1–47; 21:6
50 [b] Num. 3:7–8, 25–38
51 [c] Num. 4:5–15; 10:17 [d] Num. 10:21
52 [e] Num. 2:2; 24:2
53 [f] Cp. Num. 3:23,29,35 [g] Lev. 10:6; Num. 8:19 [h] 1 Chr. 23:32
CHAPTER 2
3 [i] Num. 10:5 [j] Num. 1:7; 7:12; 10:14; 1 Chr. 2:10
9 [k] Num. 10:14
10 [l] Num. 10:6

numbering, all but two (Caleb and Joshua) perished in the wilderness.

[1](1:47) The Levites derive their name from the fact that they were of the tribe of Levi. Levi had three sons: Gershon, Kohath, and Merari (Gen. 46:11). Kohath's grandsons were Moses and Aaron through Amram (see Ex. 6:16–20; Num. 3:14–24; 1 Chr. 6:1–48). All true priests in Israel were descendants of Aaron; hence they are known as the Aaronic priesthood (Ex. 28:1ff.; 31:10; Lev. 8:2ff.; 9:1ff.; Num. 3:1–4).

The transportation and maintenance of the tabernacle of meeting, and, later, the care of the temple required the labor of many more men than the descendants of Aaron. Those who so ministered were Levites. They did not, as other tribes, have a definite portion of the land assigned them, but lived in various towns and cities (Josh. 21). Originally the age of those who served was between thirty and fifty; later the age limit was lowered to twenty (2 Chr. 31:17).

In ch. 18 the distinctive tasks of the three major divisions of the Levites are described. They served in the place of the firstborn of all the families of Israel who originally had been declared set apart to the service of God (Ex. 13:1–2,12–16). All priests were also, as the descendants of Levi, true Levites, but the priesthood is more accurately called Aaronic than Levitical.

fifty—they shall be the [a]second to break camp.

17 [b]"And the tabernacle of meeting shall move out with the camp of the Levites [c]in the middle of the camps; as they camp, so they shall move out, everyone in his place, by their standards.

18 "On the west side *shall be* the standard of the forces with Ephraim according to their armies, and the leader of the children of Ephraim *shall be* Elishama the son of Ammihud."

19 And his army was numbered at forty thousand five hundred.

20 "Next to him *comes* the tribe of Manasseh, and the leader of the children of Manasseh *shall be* Gamaliel the son of Pedahzur."

21 And his army was numbered at thirty-two thousand two hundred.

22 "Then *comes* the tribe of Benjamin, and the leader of the children of Benjamin *shall be* Abidan the son of Gideoni."

23 And his army was numbered at thirty-five thousand four hundred.

24 "All who were numbered according to their armies of the forces with Ephraim, one hundred and eight thousand one hundred—[d]they shall be the [e]third to break camp.

25 "The standard of the forces with Dan *shall be* on the north side according to their armies, and the leader of the children of Dan *shall be* Ahiezer the son of Ammishaddai."

26 And his army was numbered at sixty-two thousand seven hundred.

27 "Those who camp next to him *shall be* the tribe of Asher, and the leader of the children of Asher *shall be* Pagiel the son of Ocran."

28 And his army was numbered at forty-one thousand five hundred.

29 "Then *comes* the tribe of Naphtali, and the leader of the children of Naphtali *shall be* Ahira the son of Enan."

30 And his army was numbered at fifty-three thousand four hundred.

31 "All who were numbered of the forces with Dan, one hundred and fifty-seven thousand six hundred—they shall break camp [f]last, with their standards."

32 These *are* the ones who were numbered of the children of Israel by their fathers' houses. [g]All who were numbered according to their armies of the forces *were* six hundred and three thousand five hundred and fifty.

33 But the Levites were [h]not numbered among the children of Israel, just as the LORD commanded Moses.

34 Thus the children of Israel [i]did according to all that the LORD commanded Moses; so they [j]camped by their standards and so they broke camp, each one by his family, according to their fathers' houses.

Order of the army: (3) the priests

3 NOW these *are* the [k]records of Aaron and Moses when the LORD spoke with Moses on Mount [l]Sinai.

2 And these *are* the names of the sons of Aaron: Nadab, the firstborn, and [m]Abihu, Eleazar, and Ithamar.

3 These *are* the names of the sons of Aaron, the anointed priests, whom he consecrated to minister as priests.

4 Nadab and Abihu had died before the LORD when they offered profane fire before the LORD in the Wilderness of Sinai; and they had no children. So Eleazar and Ithamar ministered as priests in the presence of Aaron their father.

Order of the army: (4) the tribe of Levi

5 And the LORD spoke to Moses, saying:

6 [n]"Bring the tribe of Levi near, and present them before Aaron the priest, that they may serve him.

7 "And they shall attend to his needs and the needs of the whole congregation before the tabernacle of meeting, to do the work of the tabernacle.

8 "Also they shall attend to all the furnishings of the tabernacle of meeting, and to the needs of the children of Israel, to do the work of the tabernacle.

9 "And you shall [o]give the Levites to Aaron and his sons; they *are* given entirely to him* from among the children of Israel.

10 "So you shall appoint Aaron and his sons, and they shall attend to their [p]priesthood; but the outsider who comes near shall be put to death."

11 Then the LORD spoke to Moses, saying:

12 "Now behold, I Myself have taken the Levites from among the children of Israel [q]instead of every firstborn who opens the womb among the children of Israel. Therefore the Levites shall be [r]Mine,

16
a Num. 10:18
17
b Num. 10:17,21
c Num. 1:53
24
d Cp. Ps. 80:2
e Num. 10:22
31
f Num. 10:25
32
g Ex. 38:26; Num. 1:46
33
h Num. 1:47
34
i Num. 1:54
j Num. 24:2, 5
CHAPTER 3
1
k Ex. 6:16–27
l *Israel* (history): vv. 1–10; Dt. 1:1. (Gen. 12:2; Rom. 11:26, *note*)
2
m Lev. 10:1–2; Num. 26:61; 1 Chr. 24:2
6
n Num. 8:6–19; 18:2–4; cp. Ex. 32:26–28; Dt. 33:8–11
9
o Num. 18:6–7
10
p Ex. 29:9
12
q Ex. 13:2
r Num. 8:14

*3:9 Samaritan Pentateuch and Septuagint read *Me*.

13 “because all the firstborn *are*
[a]Mine. On the day that I struck all the
firstborn in the land of Egypt, I sanctified to Myself all the firstborn in Israel, both man and beast. They shall
be Mine: I *am* the LORD.”

Order of the army: (5) the
families of Levi

14 Then the LORD spoke to Moses in
the Wilderness of Sinai, saying:
15 “Number the children of [b]Levi
by their fathers’ houses, by their families; you shall number every male
from a month old and above.”
16 So Moses numbered them according to the word of the LORD, as he
was commanded.
17 These were the sons of Levi by
their names: Gershon, Kohath, and
Merari.
18 And these *are* the names of the
sons of [c]Gershon by their families:
Libni and Shimei.
19 And the sons of [d]Kohath by
their families: [e]Amram, Izehar, Hebron, and Uzziel.
20 And the sons of [f]Merari by their
families: Mahli and Mushi. These *are*
the families of the Levites by their fathers’ houses.
21 From Gershon *came* the family
of the Libnites and the family of the
Shimites; these *were* the families of
the Gershonites.
22 Those who were numbered, according to the number of all the males
from a month old and above—of those
who were numbered *there were* seven
thousand five hundred.
23 The families of the Gershonites
were to camp behind the tabernacle
westward.
24 And the leader of the father’s
house of the Gershonites *was* Eliasaph the son of Lael.

Order of the army: (6) the
duties of the sons of Levi

25 The duties of the children of Gershon in the tabernacle of meeting *in-*
cluded the tabernacle, the tent with its
covering, the screen for the door of the
tabernacle of meeting,
26 the screen for the door of the
court, the hangings of the court which
are around the tabernacle and the altar, and their [g]cords, according to all
the work relating to them.
27 From [h]Kohath *came* the family
of the Amramites, the family of the
Izharites, the family of the Hebronites, and the family of the Uzzielites;
these *were* the families of the Kohathites.
28 According to the number of all
the males, from a month old and
above, *there were* eight thousand six★
hundred keeping charge of the sanctuary.
29 The families of the [i]children of
Kohath were to camp on the south
side of the tabernacle.
30 And the leader of the fathers’
house of the families of the Kohathites
was Elizaphan the son of [j]Uzziel.
31 Their duty *included* the ark, the
table, the lampstand, the altars, the
utensils of the sanctuary with which
they ministered, the screen, and all
the work relating to them.
32 And Eleazar the son of Aaron
the priest *was to be* chief over the
leaders of the Levites, *with* oversight
of those who kept charge of the sanctuary.
33 From Merari *came* the family of
the Mahlites and the family of the Mushites; these *were* the families of Merari.
34 And those who were numbered,
according to the number of all the
males from a month old and above,
were six thousand two hundred.
35 The leader of the fathers’ house
of the families of Merari *was* Zuriel
the son of Abihail. These *were* to
camp on the north side of the tabernacle.
36 And the appointed [k]duty of the
children of Merari *included* the boards
of the tabernacle, its bars, its pillars,
its sockets, its utensils, all the work
relating to them,
37 and the pillars of the court all
around, with their sockets, their pegs,
and their cords.
38 Moreover those who were to
camp before the tabernacle on the
east, before the tabernacle of meeting,
were Moses, Aaron, and his sons,
keeping charge of the sanctuary, to
meet the needs of the children of Israel; but the outsider who came near
was to be put to [l]death.
39 [m]All who were numbered of the
Levites, whom Moses and Aaron
numbered at the commandment of the
LORD, by their families, all the males
from a month old and above, *were*
twenty-two thousand.

13 [a] Lev. 27:26; Num. 8:16–17
15 [b] v. 22; 4:46–49; cp. 1:47–49; 26:57–62
18 [c] Num. 4:38–41
19 [d] Num. 4:34–37 [e] v. 27; 26:58–59
20 [f] Num. 4:42–45
26 [g] Ex. 35:18
27 [h] 1 Chr. 26:23
29 [i] Ex. 6:18
30 [j] Lev. 10:4
36 [k] Num. 4:31–32
38 [l] Num. 1:51
39 [m] v. 34; 4:46–49; cp. 26:57–63

★ 3:28 Some manuscripts of the Septuagint read *three.*

Order of the army: (7) firstborn redeemed

40 Then the LORD said to Moses: [a]"Number all the firstborn males of the children of Israel from a month old and above, and take the number of their names.

41 [b]"And you shall take the Levites for Me—I *am* the LORD—instead of all the firstborn among the children of Israel, and the livestock of the Levites instead of all the firstborn among the livestock of the children of Israel."

42 So Moses numbered all the firstborn among the children of Israel, as the LORD commanded him.

43 And [c]all the firstborn males, according to the number of names from a month old and above, of those who were [1]numbered of them, were twenty-two thousand two hundred and seventy-three.

44 Then the LORD spoke to Moses, saying:

45 [d]"Take the Levites instead of all the firstborn among the children of Israel, and the livestock of the Levites instead of their livestock. The Levites shall be Mine: I *am* the LORD.

46 "And for the redemption of the two hundred and seventy-three of the firstborn of the children of Israel, who are more than the number of the Levites,

47 "you shall take [e]five [f]shekels for each one [g]individually; you shall take *them* in the currency of the shekel of the sanctuary, the shekel of twenty [f]gerahs.

48 "And you shall give the money, with which the excess number of them is redeemed, to Aaron and his sons."

49 So Moses took the redemption money from those who were over and above those who were redeemed by the Levites.

50 From the firstborn of the children of Israel he took the money, one thousand three hundred and sixty-five *shekels,* according to the shekel of the sanctuary.

51 And Moses gave their redemption money to Aaron and his sons, according to the word of the LORD, as the LORD commanded Moses.

40 *a* Num. 3:15
41 *b* Num. 3:12,45
43 *c* Cp. v. 39
45 *d* v. 41
47 *e* Num. 18:16 *f* See Coinage (OT), Ex. 30:13, *note;* cp. 2 Chr. 2:10, *note* *g* Num. 1:2, 18,20
CHAPTER 4
2 *h* Num. 3:27–32
3 *i* vv. 23,30, 35,39,43, 47; cp. 8:24
5 *j* Ex. 26:31; Heb. 9:3; 10:20 *k* Ex. 25:10, 16
6 *l* Ex. 39:1 *m* 1 Ki. 8:7,8
7 *n* See Ex. 25:30, *note* *o* Lev. 24:5–9
11 *p* Ex. 30:1–5
12 *q* Ex. 25:9; 1 Chr. 9:29

Order of the army: (8) the service of the Kohathites

4

THEN the LORD spoke to Moses and Aaron, saying:

2 "Take a census of the sons of [h]Kohath from among the children of Levi, by their families, by their fathers' house,

3 "from [i]thirty years old and above, even to fifty years old, all who enter the service to do the work in the tabernacle of meeting.

4 "This *is* the service of the sons of Kohath in the tabernacle of meeting, *relating to* the most holy things:

5 "When the camp prepares to journey, Aaron and his sons shall come, and they shall take down the covering [j]veil and cover the [k]ark of the Testimony with it.

6 "Then they shall put on it a covering of badger skins, and spread over *that* a cloth entirely of [l]blue; and they shall insert its [m]poles.

7 "On the table of [n]showbread they shall spread a blue cloth, and put on it the dishes, the pans, the bowls, and the pitchers for pouring; and the [o]showbread* shall be on it.

8 "They shall spread over them a scarlet cloth, and cover the same with a covering of badger skins; and they shall insert its poles.

9 "And they shall take a blue cloth and cover the lampstand of the light, with its lamps, its wick-trimmers, its trays, and all its oil vessels, with which they service it.

10 "Then they shall put it with all its utensils in a covering of badger skins, and put *it* on a carrying beam.

11 "Over the [p]golden altar they shall spread a blue cloth, and cover it with a covering of badger skins; and they shall insert its poles.

12 "Then they shall take all the [q]utensils of service with which they minister in the sanctuary, put *them* in a blue cloth, cover them with a cover-

*4:7 Literally *the continual bread*

[1](3:43) Inasmuch as Num. 1:45–46 states that at the time of the Exodus there were 603,550 men "able to go to war in Israel," and here it is said that there were 22,273 firstborn males "a month old and above" in Israel, there would appear to be a contradiction; otherwise it must be assumed that in Israel each family had at least fifty males, which is hardly conceivable. The problem is solved in that the law of the firstborn did not go into effect until the time of the Exodus (Ex. 13:1–2). The 600,000 or more males were those who had been born in the years preceding the Exodus, whereas the 22,273 firstborn were born after the Exodus from the land of Egypt.

ing of badger skins, and put *them* on a carrying beam.

13 "Also they shall take away the ashes from the altar, and spread a purple cloth over it.

14 "They shall put on it all its implements with which they minister there—the firepans, the forks, the shovels, the basins, and all the utensils of the altar—and they shall spread on it a covering of badger skins, and insert its poles.

15 "And when Aaron and his sons have finished covering the sanctuary and all the furnishings of the sanctuary, when the camp is set to go, then the sons of [a]Kohath shall come to carry *them;* but they shall not touch any holy thing, lest they [b]die. These *are* the things in the tabernacle of meeting which the sons of Kohath are to carry.

Order of the army: (9) the office of Eleazar

16 "The appointed duty of Eleazar the son of Aaron the priest *is* the [c]oil for the light, the [d]sweet incense, the daily grain offering, the [e]anointing oil, the oversight of all the tabernacle, of all that *is* in it, with the sanctuary and its furnishings."

17 Then the LORD spoke to Moses and Aaron, saying:

18 "Do not cut off the tribe of the families of the Kohathites from among the Levites;

19 "but do this in regard to them, that they may live and not die when they approach the most [f]holy things: Aaron and his sons shall go in and appoint each of them to his service and his task.

20 "But they shall not go in to [g]watch while the holy things are being covered, lest they die."

Order of the army: (10) the service of the Gershonites

21 Then the LORD spoke to Moses, saying:

22 "Also take a census of the sons of [h]Gershon, by their fathers' house, by their families.

23 "From [i]thirty years old and above, even to fifty years old, you shall number them, all who enter to perform the service, to do the work in the tabernacle of meeting.

24 "This *is* the [j]service of the families of the Gershonites, in serving and carrying:

25 [k]"They shall carry the [l]curtains of the tabernacle and the tabernacle of meeting *with* its covering, the covering of [m]badger skins that *is* on it, the screen for the door of the tabernacle of meeting,

26 "the screen for the door of the gate of the court, the hangings of the court which *are* around the tabernacle and altar, and their cords, all the furnishings for their service and all that is made for these things: so shall they serve.

27 "Aaron and his sons shall assign all the service of the sons of the Gershonites, all their tasks and all their service. And you shall appoint to them all their tasks as their duty.

28 "This *is* the service of the families of the sons of Gershon in the tabernacle of meeting. And their duties *shall be* under the authority* of [n]Ithamar the son of Aaron the priest.

Order of the army: (11) the service of the Merarites

29 "*As for* the sons of [o]Merari, you shall number them by their families and by their fathers' house.

30 "From [i]thirty years old and above, even to fifty years old, you shall number them, everyone who enters the service to do the work of the tabernacle of meeting.

31 "And [p]this *is* what they must [q]carry as all their service for the tabernacle of meeting: the [r]boards of the tabernacle, its bars, its pillars, its sockets,

32 "and the pillars around the court with their sockets, pegs, and cords, with all their [s]furnishings and all their service; and you shall assign *to each man* by name the items he must carry.

33 "This *is* the service of the families of the sons of Merari, as all their service for the tabernacle of [t]meeting, under the authority* of Ithamar the son of Aaron the priest."

34 And Moses, Aaron, and the leaders of the congregation numbered the sons of the Kohathites by their families and by their fathers' house,

35 from [u]thirty years old and above, even to fifty years old, everyone who entered the service for work in the tabernacle of meeting;

36 and those who were numbered by their families were two thousand seven hundred and fifty.

37 These *were* the ones who were

15 a Num. 7:9; 10:21; Dt. 31:9; Josh. 4:10; 2 Sam. 6:13; 1 Chr. 15:2,15 b Cp. 2 Sam. 6:6–7
16 c Ex. 25:6; Lev. 24:2 d Ex. 30:34 e Ex. 30:23–25
19 f Num. 4:4
20 g Cp. 1 Sam. 6:19
22 h Num. 3:22
23 i Num. 4:3
24 j Num. 7:7
25 k Num. 3:25,26 l Ex. 36:8 m Ex. 26:14
28 n v. 33
29 o Num. 3:33–37
31 p Num. 3:36,37 q Num. 7:8 r Ex. 26:15
32 s Ex. 25:9
33 t v. 28
35 u v. 47

* 4:28 Literally *hand* 4:33 Literally *hand*

numbered of the families of the Kohathites, all who might serve in the
tabernacle of meeting, whom Moses
and Aaron numbered according to the
commandment of the LORD by the
hand of Moses.
38 And those who were numbered
of the sons of Gershon, by their families and by their fathers' house,
39 from thirty years old and above,
even to fifty years old, everyone who
entered the service for work in the
tabernacle of meeting—
40 those who were numbered by
their families, by their fathers' house,
were two thousand six hundred and
thirty.
41 [a]These *are* the ones who were
numbered of the families of the sons
of Gershon, of all who might serve in
the tabernacle of meeting, whom Moses and Aaron numbered according to
the commandment of the LORD.
42 Those of the families of the sons
of Merari who were numbered, by
their families, by their fathers' house,
43 from thirty years old and above,
even to fifty years old, everyone who
entered the service for work in the
tabernacle of meeting—
44 those who were numbered by
their families were three thousand
two hundred.
45 These *are* the ones who were
numbered of the families of the sons
of Merari, whom Moses and Aaron
numbered according to the word of
the LORD by the hand of Moses.
46 All who were [b]numbered of the
Levites, whom Moses, Aaron, and the
leaders of Israel numbered, by their
families and by their fathers' houses,
47 [c]from thirty years old and
above, even to fifty years old, everyone who came to do the work of service and the work of bearing burdens
in the tabernacle of meeting—
48 those who were numbered were
eight thousand five hundred and
eighty.
49 According to the commandment
of the LORD they were numbered by
the hand of Moses, each according to
his [d]service and according to his task;
thus were they numbered by him, as
the LORD commanded Moses.

Order of the army: (12) purity required; defilement banished

5 AND the LORD spoke to Moses,
saying:
2 "Command the children of Israel
that they [e]put out of the camp every
leper, everyone who has a [f]discharge,
and whoever becomes [g]defiled by a
corpse.
3 "You shall put out both male and
female; you shall put them outside the
camp, that they may not defile their
camps [h]in the midst of which I dwell."
4 And the children of Israel did so,
and put them outside the camp; as the
LORD spoke to Moses, so the children
of Israel did.
5 Then the LORD spoke to Moses,
saying,
6 "Speak to the children of Israel:
'When a man or woman commits any
sin that men commit in unfaithfulness
against the LORD, and that person is
guilty,
7 'then he shall [i]confess the sin
which he has committed. He shall
make [j]restitution for his trespass in
full, plus one-fifth of it, and give *it* to
the one he has wronged.
8 'But if the man has no [k]relative
to whom restitution may be made for
the wrong, the restitution for the
wrong *must go* to the LORD for the
priest, in addition to the [l]ram of the
[m]atonement with which atonement is
made for him.
9 'Every offering of all the holy
things of the children of Israel, which
they bring to the priest, shall be [n]his.
10 'And every man's holy things
shall be his; whatever any man gives
the priest shall be his.' "
11 And the LORD spoke to Moses,
saying,
12 "Speak to the children of Israel,
and say to them: 'If any man's wife
goes astray and behaves unfaithfully
toward him,
13 'and a man [o]lies with her carnally, and it is hidden from the eyes of
her husband, and it is concealed that
she has defiled herself, and *there was*
no witness against her, nor was she
[p]caught—
14 'if the spirit of jealousy comes
upon him and he becomes [q]jealous of
his wife, who has defiled herself; or if
the spirit of jealousy comes upon him
and he becomes jealous of his wife,
although she has not defiled herself—
15 'then the man shall bring his
wife to the priest. He shall bring the
[r]offering required for her, one-tenth
of an [s]ephah of barley meal; he shall
pour no oil on it and put no frankincense on it, because it *is* a grain offering of jealousy, an offering for remembering, for [t]bringing iniquity to
remembrance.

41
a v. 22
46
b Num. 3:39; cp. 26:57–62; 1 Chr. 23:3–23
47
c vv. 3,23, 30; cp. 1 Chr. 23:3
49
d vv. 15,24, 31
CHAPTER 5
2
e Lev. 13:46
f Lev. 15:2
g Num. 19:11
3
h Lev. 26:12; Num. 35:34
7
i Lev. 5:5; Ps. 32:5; 1 Jn. 1:9
j Lev. 6:4–5
8
k *Redemption* (redeeming relative type): v. 8; Num. 35:12. (Gen. 48:16; Isa. 59:20, *note*)
l Lev. 5:15
m See Ex. 29:33, *note*
9
n Lev. 7:32–34; 10:14–15
13
o Lev. 20:10
p Cp. Jn. 8:4
14
q Prov. 6:34
15
r Lev. 5:11
s See Weights and Measures (OT), 2 Chr. 2:10, *note*
t 1 Ki. 17:18; Ezek. 29:16; Heb. 10:3

16 'And the priest shall bring her
near, and set her before the LORD.
17 'The priest shall take holy water
in an earthen vessel, and take some of
the dust that is on the floor of the tabernacle and put *it* into the water.
18 'Then the priest shall stand the
woman before the [a]LORD, uncover the
woman's head, and put the offering
for remembering in her hands, which
is the grain offering of jealousy. And
the priest shall have in his hand the
[b]bitter water that brings a curse.
19 'And the priest shall put her under oath, and say to the woman, "If no
man has lain with you, and if you have
not gone astray to uncleanness *while*
under your husband's *authority*, be
free from this bitter water that brings
a curse.
20 "But if you have gone astray
while under your husband's *authority*, and if you have defiled yourself
and some man other than your husband has lain with you"—
21 'then the priest shall [c]put the
woman under the oath of the curse,
and he shall say to the woman—"the
LORD make you a curse and an oath
among your people, when the LORD
makes your thigh rot and your belly
swell;
22 "and may this water that causes
the curse [d]go into your stomach, and
make *your* belly swell and *your* thigh
rot." Then the woman shall say,
[e]"Amen, so be it."
23 'Then the priest shall write these
curses in a book, and he shall scrape
them off into the bitter water.
24 'And he shall make the woman
drink the bitter water that brings a
curse, and the water that brings the
curse shall enter her *to become* bitter.
25 'Then the priest shall take the
grain offering of jealousy from the
woman's hand, shall [f]wave the offering before the LORD, and bring it to the
altar;
26 'and the priest shall take a handful of the offering, [g]as its memorial
portion, burn *it* on the altar, and after-

18
a Heb. 13:4
b vv. 17,22, 24
21
c Josh. 6:26; 1 Sam. 14:24; Neh. 10:29
22
d Ps. 109:18
e Dt. 27:15–26
25
f Lev. 8:27
26
g Lev. 2:2,9
27
h Dt. 28:37; Isa. 65:15; Jer. 24:9; 29:18,22; 42:18
CHAPTER 6
2
i Jud. 13:5; Lam. 4:7; Amos 2:11–12
j *Separation:* vv. 1–8; Num. 16:21. (Gen. 12:1; 2 Cor. 6:17, *note*)
3
k Lev. 10:9
5
l 1 Sam. 1:11
m Ezek. 44:20; cp. Jud. 16:17–22; 1 Cor. 11:14

ward make the woman drink the water.
27 'When he has made her drink
the water, then it shall be, if she has
defiled herself and behaved unfaithfully toward her husband, that the water that brings a [h]curse will enter her
and become bitter, and her belly will
swell, her thigh will rot, and the
woman will become a curse among
her people.
28 'But if the woman has not defiled
herself, and is clean, then she shall be
free and may conceive children.
29 'This *is* the law of jealousy, when
a wife, *while* under her husband's *authority*, goes astray and defiles herself,
30 'or when the spirit of jealousy
comes upon a man, and he becomes
jealous of his wife; then he shall stand
the woman before the LORD, and the
priest shall execute all this law upon
her.
31 'Then the man shall be free from
iniquity, but that woman shall bear
her guilt.'"

Order of the army:
(13) the Nazirites

6 THEN the LORD spoke to Moses,
[1]saying,
2 "Speak to the children of Israel,
and say to them: 'When either a man
or woman consecrates an offering to
take the vow of a [2i]Nazirite, to [j]sepa-
rate himself to the LORD,
3 'he shall separate himself from
[k]wine and *similar* drink; he shall
drink neither vinegar made from wine
nor vinegar made from *similar* drink;
neither shall he drink any grape juice,
nor eat fresh grapes or raisins.
4 'All the days of his separation he
shall eat nothing that is produced by
the grapevine, from seed to skin.
5 'All the days of the vow of his
separation no razor shall come upon
his [l]head; until the days are fulfilled
for which he separated himself to the
LORD, he shall be holy. *Then* he shall
let the [m]locks of the hair of his head
grow.

[1](6:1) There is a stimulating moral order in chs. 6—7: (1) separation, 6:1–12; (2) worship, 6:13–21; (3) blessing, 6:22–27; and (4) service, 7:1–89. Cp. Heb. 13:12–16.

[2](6:2) The Nazirite, sometimes spelled Nazarite (meaning *one separated*), was a person who was separated completely to the LORD. Abstention from wine, the symbol of natural joy (Ps. 104:15), was the expression of a devotedness which found all its joy in the LORD (cp. Ps. 97:12; Hab. 3:18; Phil. 3:1; 4:4,10). The long hair, naturally a reproach to a man (1 Cor. 11:14), was at once the visible sign of the Nazirite's separation and willingness to bear reproach for the LORD's sake. The type found its perfect fulfillment in Jesus who was "holy, harmless, undefiled, separate from sinners" (Heb. 7:26), was utterly set apart to the Father (Jn. 1:18; 6:38), and allowed no mere natural claim to hinder or divert Him (Mt. 12:46–50).

6 'All the days that he separates
himself to the LORD he shall not go
near a dead [a]body.
7 'He shall not make himself unclean even for his father or his mother,
for his brother or his sister, when they
die, because his separation to God *is*
on his head.
8 'All the days of his separation he
shall be holy to the LORD.
9 'And if anyone dies very suddenly beside him, and he defiles his
consecrated head, then he shall
[b]shave his head on the day of his
cleansing; on the seventh day he shall
shave it.
10 'Then on the eighth day he shall
[c]bring [d]two turtledoves or two young
pigeons to the priest, to the door of the
tabernacle of meeting;
11 'and the priest shall offer one as
a sin offering and *the* other as a burnt
offering, and make [e]atonement for
him, because he sinned in regard to
the corpse; and he shall sanctify his
head that same day.
12 'He shall consecrate to the LORD
the days of his separation, and bring a
male lamb in its first year as a trespass
offering; but the former days shall be
lost, because his separation was defiled.
13 'Now this *is* the law of the Nazirite: When the days of his separation
are [f]fulfilled, he shall be brought to
the door of the tabernacle of meeting.
14 'And he shall present his offering to the LORD: one male lamb in its
first year without blemish as a burnt
offering, one ewe lamb in its first year
without blemish as a sin offering, one
ram without blemish as a peace offering,
15 'a basket of [g]unleavened bread,
cakes of fine flour mixed with oil, unleavened wafers anointed with oil,
and their [h]grain offering with their
drink offerings.
16 'Then the priest shall bring *them*
before the LORD and offer his sin offering and his burnt offering;
17 'and he shall offer the ram as a
sacrifice of a peace offering to the
LORD, with the basket of unleavened
bread; the priest shall also offer its
grain offering and its drink offering.
18 'Then the Nazirite shall shave
his consecrated head *at* the door of
the tabernacle of meeting, and shall
take the hair from his consecrated
head and put *it* on the fire which is
under the sacrifice of the peace offering.
19 'And the priest shall [i]take the
[j]boiled shoulder of the ram, one [k]un-
leavened cake from the basket, and
one unleavened wafer, and put *them*
upon the hands of the Nazirite after he
has shaved his consecrated *hair*,
20 'and the priest shall wave them
as a wave offering before the LORD;
they *are* holy for the priest, together
with the breast of the wave offering
and the thigh of the heave offering.
[l]After that the Nazirite may drink
wine.'
21 "This is the law of the Nazirite
who vows to the LORD the offering for
his separation, and besides that, whatever else his hand is able to provide;
according to the vow which he takes,
so he must do according to the law of
his separation."

The Aaronic benediction

22 And the LORD spoke to Moses,
saying:
23 "Speak to Aaron and his sons,
saying, 'This is the way you shall
[m]bless the children of Israel. [n]Say to
them:

24 "The LORD [o]bless you and
[p]keep you;
25 The LORD make His [q]face shine
upon you,
And be gracious to you;
26 The LORD [r]lift up His
countenance upon you,
And give you [s]peace." '

27 "So they shall [t]put My name on
the children of Israel, and I will [u]bless
them."

Order of the army: (14) the gifts of the leaders (see vv. 12,18,24,30,36, 42,48,54,60,66,72,78)

7 NOW it came to pass, [v]when Moses had finished setting up the
tabernacle, that he [w]anointed it and
consecrated it and all its furnishings,
and the altar and all its utensils; so he
anointed them and consecrated them.
2 Then the [x]leaders of Israel, the
heads of their fathers' houses, who
were the leaders of the tribes and over
those who were numbered, made an
offering.
3 And they [1]brought their offering

6 *a* Num. 19:11–22
9 *b* Lev. 14:8–9
10 *c* Lev. 15:14,29 *d* Lev. 5:7
11 *e* See Ex. 29:33, *note*
13 *f* Acts 21:26
15 *g* *Leaven:* vv. 15,17, 19; Num. 9:11. (Gen. 19:3; Mt. 13:33, *note*) *h* Num. 15:1–7
19 *i* Lev. 7:28–34 *j* 1 Sam. 2:15 *k* Ex. 29:23, 28
20 *l* v. 13
23 *m* 1 Chr. 23:13 *n* *Bible prayers (OT):* vv. 22–26; Num. 10:35. (Gen. 15:2; Hab. 3:1)
24 *o* Dt. 28:3–6 *p* Ex. 23:20; 1 Sam. 2:9; 1 Chr. 4:10
25 *q* Ps. 31:16; 80:3,7,19; Dan. 9:17
26 *r* Ps. 89:15 *s* Lev. 26:6; Isa. 26:3, 12
27 *t* 2 Sam. 7:23 *u* Ex. 20:24
CHAPTER 7
1 *v* Ex. 40:17–34 *w* Lev. 8:10–11
2 *x* Num. 1:4

[1](7:3) It is heart-warming to observe that, although the offerings of the leaders were identical, each is separately recorded by inspiration. Cp. Mk. 12:41–44.

before the LORD, six [a]covered carts
and twelve oxen, a cart for *every* two
of the leaders, and for each one an ox;
and they presented them before the
tabernacle.
4 Then the LORD spoke to Moses,
saying,
5 "Accept *these* from them, that
they may be used in doing the work of
the tabernacle of meeting; and you
shall give them to the Levites, *to* every
man according to his service."
6 So Moses took the carts and the
oxen, and gave them to the Levites.
7 Two carts and four oxen he gave
to the sons of [b]Gershon, according to
their service;
8 and four carts and eight oxen he
gave to the sons of [c]Merari, according
to their service, under the authority*
of Ithamar the son of Aaron the priest.
9 But to the sons of Kohath he
gave none, because theirs *was* the
[d]service of the holy things, *which* they
carried on their shoulders.
10 Now the leaders offered the
[e]dedication *offering* for the altar
when it was anointed; so the leaders
offered their offering before the altar.
11 For the LORD said to Moses,
"They shall offer their offering, one
leader each day, for the dedication of
the altar."
12 And the one who offered his offering on the first day *was* [f]Nahshon
the son of Amminadab, from the tribe
of Judah.
13 His offering *was* one silver platter, the weight of which *was* one hundred and thirty [g]*shekels,* and one silver bowl of seventy shekels,
according to the shekel of the sanctuary, both of them full of fine flour
mixed with oil as a grain offering;
14 one gold pan of ten *shekels,* full
of incense;
15 one young bull, one ram, and
one male lamb in its first year, as a
[h]burnt offering;
16 one kid of the goats as a [i]sin
offering;
17 and for the sacrifice of [j]peace
offerings: two oxen, five rams, five
male goats, and five male lambs in
their first year. This *was* the offering
of Nahshon the son of Amminadab.
18 On the second day Nethanel the
son of Zuar, leader of Issachar, presented *an offering.*
19 *For* his offering he [k]offered one
silver platter, the weight of which *was*
one hundred and thirty [g]*shekels,* and
one silver bowl of seventy shekels, according to the shekel of the sanctuary,
both of them full of fine flour mixed
with oil as a grain offering;
20 one gold pan of ten *shekels,* full
of incense;
21 one young bull, one ram, and
one male lamb in its first year, as a
burnt offering;
22 one kid of the goats as a sin offering;
23 and as the sacrifice of peace offerings: two oxen, five rams, five male
goats, and five male lambs in their
first year. This *was* the offering of Nethanel the son of Zuar.
24 On the third day Eliab the son of
Helon, leader of the children of Zebulun, *presented an offering.*
25 His offering *was* one silver
[l]platter, the weight of which *was* one
hundred and thirty *shekels,* and one
silver bowl of seventy shekels, according to the shekel of the sanctuary,
both of them full of fine flour mixed
with oil as a grain offering;
26 one gold pan of ten *shekels,* full
of incense;
27 one young bull, one ram, and
one male lamb in its first year, as a
burnt offering;
28 one kid of the goats as a sin offering;
29 and for the sacrifice of peace offerings: two oxen, five rams, five male
goats, and five male lambs in their
first year. This *was* the offering of
Eliab the son of Helon.
30 On the fourth day [m]Elizur the
son of Shedeur, leader of the children
of Reuben, *presented an offering.*
31 His offering *was* one silver platter, the weight of which *was* one hundred and thirty *shekels,* and one silver
bowl of seventy shekels, according to
the shekel of the sanctuary, both of
them full of fine flour mixed with oil as
a grain offering;
32 one gold pan of ten *shekels,* full
of incense;
33 one young bull, one ram, and
one male lamb in its first year, as a
burnt offering;
34 one kid of the goats as a sin offering;
35 and as the sacrifice of peace offerings: two oxen, five rams, five male
goats, and five male lambs in their
first year. This *was* the offering of Elizur the son of Shedeur.
36 On the fifth day Shelumiel the
son of Zurishaddai, leader of the chil-

3 *a* Cp. Isa. 66:20
7 *b* Num. 4:24–28
8 *c* Num. 4:29–33
9 *d* Num. 4:4–15
10 *e* 2 Chr. 7:9
12 *f* Num. 2:3
13 *g* See Coinage (OT), Ex. 30:13, *note;* cp. 2 Chr. 2:10, *note*
15 *h* Lev. 1:2,3
16 *i* Lev. 4:23
17 *j* Lev. 3:1
19 *k* v. 13
25 *l* Cp. Mt. 14:1–12
30 *m* Num. 1:5; 2:10

*7:8 Literally *hand*

dren of Simeon, *presented an offering.*
37 His [a]offering *was* one silver
platter, the weight of which *was* one
hundred and thirty *shekels,* and one
silver bowl of seventy shekels, according to the shekel of the sanctuary,
both of them full of fine flour mixed
with oil as a grain offering;
38 one gold pan of ten *shekels,* full
of incense;
39 one young bull, one ram, and
one male lamb in its first year, as a
burnt offering;
40 one kid of the goats as a sin offering;
41 and as the sacrifice of peace offerings: two oxen, five rams, five male
goats, and five male lambs in their
first year. This *was* the offering of
Shelumiel the son of Zurishaddai.
42 On the sixth day [b]Eliasaph the
son of [c]Deuel, leader of the children
of Gad, *presented an offering.*
43 His offering *was* one silver platter, the weight of which *was* one hundred and thirty *shekels,* and one silver
bowl of seventy shekels, according to
the shekel of the sanctuary, both of
them full of fine flour mixed with oil as
a grain [a]offering;
44 one gold pan of ten *shekels,* full
of incense;
45 one young bull, one ram, and
one male lamb in its first year, as a
burnt offering;
46 one kid of the goats as a sin offering;
47 and as the sacrifice of peace offerings: two oxen, five rams, five male
goats, and five male lambs in their
first year. This *was* the offering of Eliasaph the son of Deuel.
48 On the seventh day Elishama the
son of Ammihud, leader of the children of Ephraim, *presented an offering.*
49 His [a]offering *was* one silver
platter, the weight of which *was* one
hundred and thirty *shekels,* and one
silver bowl of seventy shekels, according to the shekel of the sanctuary,
both of them full of fine flour mixed
with oil as a grain offering;
50 one gold pan of ten *shekels,* full
of incense;
51 one young bull, one ram, and
one male lamb in its first year, as a
burnt offering;
52 one kid of the goats as a sin offering;
53 and as the sacrifice of peace offerings: two oxen, five rams, five male
goats, and five male lambs in their

37
a Num. 1:5; 2:10
42
b Num. 1:14; 2:14
c Called *Reuel,* Num. 2:14
54
d Num. 1:10; 2:20
55
e v. 13

first year. This *was* the offering of
Elishama the son of Ammihud.
54 On the eighth day Gamaliel the
son of Pedahzur, leader of the children of Manasseh, [d]*presented an offering.*
55 His [e]offering *was* one silver
platter, the weight of which *was* one
hundred and thirty *shekels,* and one
silver bowl of seventy shekels, according to the shekel of the sanctuary,
both of them full of fine flour mixed
with oil as a grain offering;
56 one gold pan of ten *shekels,* full
of incense;
57 one young bull, one ram, and
one male lamb in its first year, as a
burnt offering;
58 one kid of the goats as a sin offering;
59 and as the sacrifice of peace offerings: two oxen, five rams, five male
goats, and five male lambs in their
first year. This *was* the offering of Gamaliel the son of Pedahzur.
60 On the ninth day Abidan the son
of Gideoni, leader of the children of
Benjamin, *presented an offering.*
61 His offering *was* one silver platter, the weight of which *was* one hundred and thirty *shekels,* and one silver
bowl of seventy shekels, according to
the shekel of the sanctuary, both of
them full of fine flour mixed with oil as
a grain offering;
62 one gold pan of ten *shekels,* full
of incense;
63 one young bull, one ram, and
one male lamb in its first year, as a
burnt offering;
64 one kid of the goats as a sin offering;
65 and as the sacrifice of peace offerings: two oxen, five rams, five male
goats, and five male lambs in their
first year. This *was* the offering of
Abidan the son of Gideoni.
66 On the tenth day Ahiezer the son
of Ammishaddai, leader of the children of Dan, *presented an offering.*
67 His offering *was* one silver platter, the weight of which *was* one hundred and thirty *shekels,* and one silver
bowl of seventy shekels, according to
the shekel of the sanctuary, both of
them full of fine flour mixed with oil as
a grain offering;
68 one gold pan of ten *shekels,* full
of incense;
69 one young bull, one ram, and
one male lamb in its first year, as a
burnt offering;

70 one kid of the goats as a sin offering;

71 and as the sacrifice of peace offerings: two oxen, five rams, five male goats, and five male lambs in their first year. This *was* the offering of Ahiezer the son of Ammishaddai.

72 On the eleventh day [a]Pagiel the son of Ocran, leader of the children of Asher, *presented an offering*.

73 His offering *was* one silver platter, the weight of which *was* one hundred and thirty *shekels,* and one silver bowl of seventy shekels, according to the shekel of the sanctuary, both of them full of fine flour mixed with oil as a grain offering;

74 one gold pan of ten *shekels,* full of incense;

75 one young bull, one ram, and one male lamb in its first year, as a burnt offering;

76 one kid of the goats as a sin offering;

77 and as the sacrifice of peace offerings: two oxen, five rams, five male goats, and five male lambs in their first year. This *was* the offering of Pagiel the son of Ocran.

78 On the twelfth day Ahira the son of Enan, leader of the children of Naphtali, *presented an offering*.

79 His offering *was* one silver platter, the weight of which *was* one hundred and thirty *shekels,* and one silver bowl of seventy shekels, according to the shekel of the sanctuary, both of them full of fine flour mixed with oil as a grain offering;

80 one gold pan of ten *shekels,* full of incense;

81 one young bull, one ram, and one male lamb in its first year, as a burnt offering;

82 one kid of the goats as a sin offering;

83 and as the sacrifice of peace offerings: two oxen, five rams, five male goats, and five male lambs in their first year. This *was* the offering of Ahira the son of Enan.

Summary of leaders' gifts

84 This *was* the [b]dedication *offering* for the altar from the leaders of Israel, when it was anointed: twelve silver platters, twelve silver bowls, and twelve gold pans.

85 Each silver platter *weighed* one hundred and thirty *shekels* and each bowl seventy *shekels.* All the silver of the vessels *weighed* two thousand four hundred *shekels,* according to the shekel of the sanctuary.

86 The twelve gold pans full of incense *weighed* ten *shekels* apiece, according to the shekel of the sanctuary; all the gold of the pans *weighed* one hundred and twenty *shekels.*

87 All the oxen for the burnt offering *were* twelve young bulls, the rams twelve, the male lambs in their first year twelve, with their grain offering, and the kids of the goats as a sin offering twelve.

88 And all the oxen for the sacrifice of peace offerings were twenty-four bulls, the rams sixty, the male goats sixty, and the lambs in their first year sixty. This *was* the dedication *offering* for the altar after it was [c]anointed.

89 Now when Moses went into the tabernacle of meeting to [d]speak with Him, he heard the voice of One speaking to him from above the [e]mercy seat that *was* on the ark of the Testimony, from [f]between the two cherubim; thus He spoke to him.

Order of the army: (15) the lamps and lampstand

8 AND the LORD spoke to Moses, saying:

2 "Speak to Aaron, and say to him, 'When you [g]arrange the lamps, the seven [h]lamps shall give light in front of the [i]lampstand.' "

3 And Aaron did so; he arranged the lamps to face toward the front of the lampstand, as the LORD commanded Moses.

4 Now this workmanship of the lampstand *was* hammered gold; from its shaft to its flowers it *was* hammered work. According to the [j]pattern which the LORD had shown Moses, so he made the lampstand.

Order of the army: (16) cleansing the Levites

5 Then the LORD spoke to Moses, saying:

6 "Take the Levites from among the children of Israel and [k]cleanse them *ceremonially.*

7 "Thus you shall do to them to cleanse them: Sprinkle [l]water of purification on them, and let them [m]shave all their body, and let them wash their clothes, and *so* make themselves clean.

8 "Then let them take a young bull with [n]its grain offering of fine flour mixed with oil, and you shall take another young bull as a sin offering.

72
a Num. 1:13; 2:27
84
b Num. 7:10
88
c Num. 7:1
89
d Ex. 33:9, 11; Num. 12:8
e Ps. 80:1; 99:1
f Ex. 25:22
CHAPTER 8
2
g Lev. 24:3–4
h Ex. 25:37; 40:25
i Ex. 25:31
4
j Ex. 25:40; Acts 7:44
6
k v. 15; cp. 2 Cor. 7:1
7
l Num. 19:9, 17; cp. Ps. 51:2,7; Heb. 9:13–14
m Lev. 14:8–9
8
n Num. 15:8–10

9 "And you shall bring the Levites before the tabernacle of meeting, and you shall gather together the whole congregation of the children of Israel.

10 "So you shall bring the Levites before the LORD, and the children of Israel shall lay their hands on the Levites;

11 "and Aaron shall [a]offer the Levites before the LORD, *like* a wave [b]offering from the children of Israel, that they may perform the work of the LORD.

12 "Then the Levites shall lay their hands on the heads of the young bulls, and you shall offer one as a sin offering and the other as a burnt offering to the LORD, to make [c]atonement for the Levites.

13 "And you shall stand the Levites before Aaron and his sons, and then offer them *like* a wave offering to the LORD.

14 "Thus you shall [d]separate the Levites from among the children of Israel, and the Levites shall be [e]Mine.

15 "After that the Levites shall go in to service the tabernacle of meeting. So you shall cleanse them and offer them, *like* a wave offering.

16 "For they *are* [f]wholly given to Me from among the children of Israel; I have taken them for Myself [g]instead of all who open the womb, the firstborn of all the children of Israel.

17 "For all the firstborn among the children of Israel *are* Mine, *both* man and beast; on the day that I struck all the firstborn in the land of Egypt I sanctified them to Myself.

18 "I have taken the Levites instead of all the firstborn of the children of Israel.

19 "And I have given the Levites as a [f]gift to Aaron and his sons from among the children of Israel, to do the work for the children of Israel in the tabernacle of meeting, and to make [c]atonement for the children of Israel, that there be no [h]plague among the children of Israel when the children of Israel come near the sanctuary."

20 Thus Moses and Aaron and all the congregation of the children of Israel did to the Levites; according to all that the LORD commanded Moses concerning the Levites, so the children of Israel did to them.

21 And the Levites purified themselves and washed their clothes; then Aaron presented them, *like* a wave offering before the LORD, and Aaron made [c]atonement for them to cleanse them.

22 After that the Levites went in to do their work in the tabernacle of meeting before Aaron and his sons; as the LORD commanded Moses concerning the Levites, so they did to them.

23 Then the LORD spoke to Moses, saying,

24 "This *is* what *pertains* to the Levites: From [i]twenty-five years old and above one may enter to perform service in the work of the tabernacle of meeting;

25 "and at the age of fifty years they must cease performing this work, and shall work no more.

26 "They may minister with their brethren in the tabernacle of meeting, to attend to needs, but they *themselves* shall do no work. Thus you shall do to the Levites regarding their duties."

Order of the army: (17) the Passover

9 NOW the LORD spoke to Moses in the Wilderness of Sinai, in the [j]first month of the second year after they had come out of the land of Egypt, saying:

2 "Let the children of Israel keep the [k]Passover at its appointed [l]time.

3 "On the fourteenth day of this month, at twilight, you shall keep it at its appointed time. According to all its rites and ceremonies you shall keep it."

4 So Moses told the children of Israel that they should keep the Passover.

5 And they kept the Passover on the fourteenth day of the first month, at twilight, in the Wilderness of Sinai; according to all that the LORD commanded Moses, so the children of Israel did.

6 Now there were *certain* men who were [m]defiled by a human corpse, so that they could not keep the Passover on that day; and they came before Moses and Aaron that day.

7 And those men said to him, "We *became* defiled by a human corpse. Why are we kept from presenting the offering of the LORD at its appointed time among the children of Israel?"

8 And Moses said to them, "Stand still, that I may [n]hear what the LORD will command concerning you."

9 Then the LORD spoke to Moses, saying,

10 "Speak to the children of Israel, saying: 'If anyone of you or your pos-

11
a vv. 11–22; cp. Rom. 15:16
b Lev. 7:30–34; Num. 18:6
12
c See Ex. 29:33, *note*
14
d Num. 16:9
e Num. 3:12
16
f Num. 3:9
g Num. 3:45; cp. Ex. 13:2
19
h Num. 1:53
24
i Cp. Num. 4:3; 1 Chr. 23:3
CHAPTER 9
1
j See Lev. 23:2, *note;* cp. Ex. 40:2,17; Num. 1:1
2
k Lev. 23:5; Num. 28:16
l Ex. 12:3; Dt. 16:1; 2 Chr. 30:1–15; Lk. 22:7; cp. 1 Cor. 5:7–8
6
m Num. 19:11–22
8
n Ex. 18:22

terity is unclean because of a corpse, or *is* far away on a journey, he may still keep the LORD's Passover.

11 'On the fourteenth day of the [a]second month, at twilight, they may [b]keep it. They shall eat it with [c]unleavened bread and bitter herbs.

12 'They shall leave none of it until morning, nor break one of its [d]bones. According to all the ordinances of the Passover they shall keep it.

13 'But the man who *is* clean and is not on a journey, and ceases to keep the Passover, that same [e]person shall be cut off from among his people, because he did not bring the offering of the LORD at its appointed time; that man shall bear his sin.

14 'And if a stranger dwells among you, and would keep the LORD's Passover, he must do so according to the rite of the Passover and according to its ceremony; you shall have one ordinance, both for the stranger and the native of the land.' "

Order of the army: (18) the guiding cloud

15 Now on the day that the tabernacle was raised up, the [f]cloud [g]covered the tabernacle, the tent of the Testimony; from evening until morning it was above the tabernacle like the appearance of [h]fire.

16 So it was always: the cloud covered it *by day*, and the appearance of fire by night.

17 Whenever the [i]cloud was taken up from above the tabernacle, after that the children of Israel would journey; and in the place where the cloud settled, there the children of Israel would pitch their tents.

18 At the command of the LORD the children of Israel would journey, and at the command of the LORD they would camp; as long as the cloud stayed above the tabernacle they remained encamped.

19 Even when the cloud continued long, many days above the tabernacle, the children of Israel kept the charge of the LORD and did not journey.

20 So it was, when the cloud was above the tabernacle a few days: according to the command of the LORD they would remain encamped, and according to the command of the LORD they would journey.

21 So it was, when the cloud remained only from evening until morning: when the cloud was taken up in the morning, then they would journey; whether by day or by night, whenever the cloud was taken up, they would journey.

22 *Whether it was* two days, a month, or a year that the cloud remained above the tabernacle, the children of Israel would [j]remain encamped and not journey; but when it was taken up, they would journey.

23 At the command of the LORD they remained encamped, and at the command of the LORD they journeyed; they kept the charge of the LORD, at the command of the LORD by the hand of Moses.

Order of the army: (19) the silver assembly trumpets

10 AND the LORD spoke to Moses, saying:

2 "Make two silver trumpets for yourself; you shall make them of hammered work; you shall use them for calling the congregation and for directing the movement of the camps.

3 "When they blow both of them, all the congregation shall gather before you at the door of the tabernacle of meeting.

4 "But if they blow *only* one, then the leaders, the [k]heads of the divisions of Israel, shall gather to you.

5 "When you sound the [l]advance, the camps that lie on the [m]east side shall then begin their journey.

6 "When you sound the advance the second time, then the camps that lie on the [n]south side shall begin their journey; they shall sound the call for them to begin their journeys.

7 "And when the assembly is to be gathered together, you shall blow, but not sound the advance.

8 "The sons of Aaron, the [o]priests, shall blow the trumpets; and these shall be to you as an ordinance forever throughout your generations.

9 "When you go to war in your land against the enemy who oppresses you, then you shall sound an alarm with the trumpets, and you will be [p]remembered before the LORD your God, and you will be saved from your enemies.

10 [q]"Also in the day of your gladness, in your appointed feasts, and at the beginning of your months, you shall blow the trumpets over your burnt offerings and over the sacrifices of your peace offerings; and they shall be a [r]memorial for you before your God: I *am* the LORD your God."

11
a See Lev. 23:2, *note;* cp. Ex. 40:2,17; Num. 1:1
b v. 2
c *Leaven:* v. 11; Num. 28:17. (Gen. 19:3; Mt. 13:33, *note*)

12
d Ex. 12:46; cp. Jn. 19:36

13
e Cp. Heb. 10:29; 12:25

15
f Ex. 40:34
g Isa. 4:5
h Ex. 13:21–22

17
i Ex. 40:36–38; Num. 10:11–12, 33–34; cp. Ex. 33:14–15

22
j Ex. 40:37

CHAPTER 10

4
k Ex. 18:21; Num. 1:16

5
l Joel 2:1
m Num. 2:3

6
n Num. 2:10

8
o Num. 31:6; 1 Chr. 15:24; 2 Chr. 13:12

9
p Cp. Josh. 6:5

10
q Lev. 23:24; Num. 29:1; 2 Chr. 5:12; Ps. 81:3; Isa. 18:3–7; 27:13
r Lev. 23:24

II. From Sinai to the Plains of Moab, 10:11—21:35

From Sinai to Kadesh Barnea: (1) the first march and halt

11 Now it came to pass on the [a]twentieth *day* of the [b]second month, in the second year, that the cloud was taken up from above the tabernacle of the Testimony.

12 And the children of Israel set out from the Wilderness of Sinai on their journeys; then the cloud settled down in the Wilderness of [c]Paran.

13 So they started out for the first time according to the command of the LORD by the hand of Moses.

14 The standard of the camp of the children of Judah set out [d]first according to their armies; over their army was Nahshon the son of Amminadab.

15 Over the army of the tribe of the children of Issachar *was* Nethanel the son of Zuar.

16 And over the army of the tribe of the children of Zebulun *was* Eliab the son of Helon.

17 Then the tabernacle was [e]taken down; and the sons of Gershon and the sons of Merari [f]set out, carrying the tabernacle.

18 And the standard of the camp of Reuben [g]set out according to their armies; over their army *was* Elizur the son of Shedeur.

19 Over the army of the tribe of the children of Simeon *was* Shelumiel the son of Zurishaddai.

20 And over the army of the tribe of the children of Gad *was* Eliasaph the son of Deuel.

21 Then the [h]Kohathites set out, [i]carrying the holy things. (The tabernacle would be prepared for their arrival.)

22 And the standard of the camp of the children of Ephraim [j]set out according to their armies; over their army *was* Elishama the son of Ammihud.

11 [a] Cp. Ex. 19:1; 40:17; Dt. 1:6 [b] See Lev. 23:2, *note*
12 [c] Gen. 21:21; Num. 12:16
14 [d] Num. 2:3–9
17 [e] Num. 1:51 [f] Num. 4:21–32; 7:7–9
18 [g] Num. 2:10–16
21 [h] Num. 4:4–20 [i] v. 17
22 [j] Num. 2:18–24

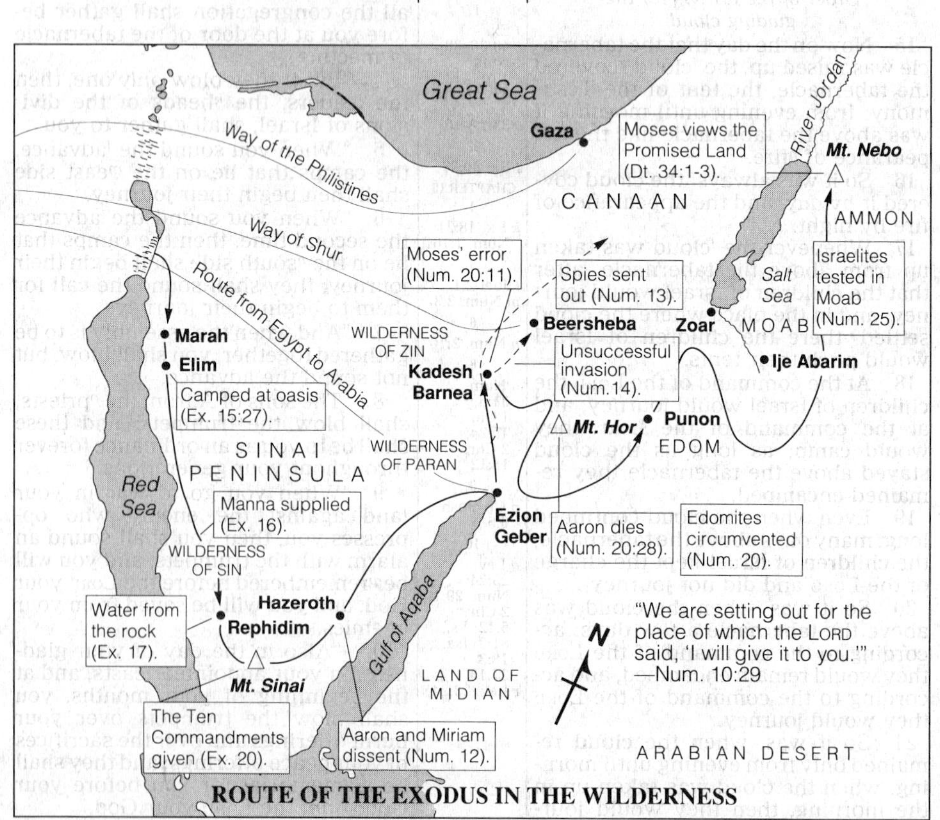
Great Sea
Gaza
Moses views the Promised Land (Dt. 34:1-3).
River Jordan
Mt. Nebo
Way of the Philistines
CANAAN
AMMON
Way of Shur
Route from Egypt to Arabia
Moses' error (Num. 20:11).
Spies sent out (Num. 13).
Israelites tested in Moab (Num. 25).
Salt Sea
Beersheba
Zoar
MOAB
Marah
Elim
WILDERNESS OF ZIN
Kadesh Barnea
Unsuccessful invasion (Num.14).
Ije Abarim
Camped at oasis (Ex. 15:27).
Mt. Hor
Punon
EDOM
SINAI PENINSULA
WILDERNESS OF PARAN
Red Sea
Manna supplied (Ex. 16).
Ezion Geber
Aaron dies (Num. 20:28).
Edomites circumvented (Num. 20).
WILDERNESS OF SIN
Water from the rock (Ex. 17).
Hazeroth
Rephidim
Gulf of Aqaba
"We are setting out for the place of which the LORD said, 'I will give it to you.'" —Num. 10:29
N
Mt. Sinai
LAND OF MIDIAN
The Ten Commandments given (Ex. 20).
Aaron and Miriam dissent (Num. 12).
ARABIAN DESERT
ROUTE OF THE EXODUS IN THE WILDERNESS

23 Over the army of the tribe of the children of Manasseh *was* Gamaliel the son of Pedahzur.

24 And over the army of the tribe of the children of Benjamin *was* Abidan the son of Gideoni.

25 Then the standard of the camp of the children of Dan (the rear guard of all the camps) [a]set out according to their armies; over their army *was* Ahiezer the son of Ammishaddai.

26 Over the army of the tribe of the children of Asher *was* Pagiel the son of Ocran.

27 And over the army of the tribe of the children of Naphtali *was* Ahira the son of Enan.

28 Thus *was* the order of march of the children of Israel, according to their armies, when they began their journey.

29 Now Moses said to [b]Hobab the son of Reuel* the [c]Midianite, Moses' father-in-law, "We are setting out for the [d]place of which the LORD said, 'I will give it to you.' [e]Come with us, and we will treat you well; for the LORD has promised good things to Israel."

30 And he said to him, "I will not go, but I will depart to my *own* land and to my relatives."

31 So *Moses* said, "Please do not leave, inasmuch as you know how we are to camp in the wilderness, and you can be our eyes.

32 "And it shall be, if you go with us—indeed it shall be—that whatever [f]good the LORD will do to us, the [g]same we will do to you."

33 So they departed from the [h]mountain of the LORD on a journey of three days; and the ark of the covenant of the LORD went before them for the three days' journey, to [i]search out a [j]resting place for them.

34 And the cloud of the LORD *was* above them by day when they went out from the camp.

35 So it was, whenever the ark set out, that Moses [k]said:

> [l]"Rise up, O LORD!
> Let Your enemies be scattered,
> And let those who hate You
> flee before You."

36 And when it rested, he said:

> "Return, O LORD,
> *To* the many thousands of
> Israel."

From Sinai to Kadesh Barnea:
(2) God judges complainers

11 NOW *when* the people [m]complained, it displeased the LORD; for the LORD heard *it*, and His anger was aroused. So the fire of the LORD burned among them, and [n]consumed *some* in the outskirts of the camp.

2 Then the people [o]cried out to Moses, and when Moses prayed to the LORD, the fire was quenched.

3 So he called the name of the place [p]Taberah, because the fire of the LORD had burned among them.

From Sinai to Kadesh Barnea:
(3) the fleshpots of Egypt

4 Now the mixed multitude who were among them yielded to intense [q]craving; so the children of Israel also wept again and said: "Who will give us meat to eat?

5 "We [r]remember the fish which we ate freely in Egypt, the cucumbers, the melons, the leeks, the onions, and the garlic;

6 "but now our whole being *is* dried up; *there is* nothing at all except this [s]manna *before* our eyes!"

7 Now the [t]manna *was* like coriander seed, and its color like the color of bdellium.

8 The people went about and gathered *it*, ground *it* on millstones or beat *it* in the mortar, cooked *it* in pans, and made cakes of it; and its taste was like the taste of pastry prepared with oil.

9 And when the dew fell on the camp in the night, the manna fell on it.

From Sinai to Kadesh Barnea:
(4) the complaint of Moses

10 Then Moses heard the people weeping throughout their families, everyone at the door of his tent; and the anger of the LORD was greatly aroused; Moses also was displeased.

11 So Moses [k]said to the LORD, "Why have You afflicted Your servant? And why have I not found favor in Your sight, that You have laid the burden of all these people on me?

12 "Did I conceive all these people? Did I beget them, that You should say to me, [u]'Carry them in your bosom, as a [v]guardian carries a nursing child,' to the land which You swore to their fathers?

13 "Where am I to get meat to give to [w]all these people? For they weep all

25
a Num. 2:25–31
29
b Jud. 4:11
c Cp. Ex. 18:14–27
d Cp. Ex. 18:27; Jud. 1:16
e Cp. Jer. 32:42
32
f Lev. 19:34
g Ex. 18:9
33
h Dt. 1:6
i Dt. 1:33
j Cp. Isa. 11:10
35
k Bible prayers (OT): vv. 35–36; 11:11–15; Num. 12:13. (Gen. 15:2; Hab. 3:1)
l Ps. 68:1–2
CHAPTER 11
1
m Num. 14:2
n Miracles (OT): vv. 1–3; Num. 16:31. (Gen. 5:24; Jon. 1:17, *note*)
2
o Num. 21:7
3
p Lit. *a burning.* Dt. 9:22
4
q 1 Cor. 10:6
5
r Ex. 16:3
6
s See Ex. 16:35, *note 1*
7
t Ex. 16:14, 31
12
u Cp. Isa. 40:11; Acts 13:18
v Isa. 49:23
13
w Cp. Jn. 6:5–14

*10:29 Septuagint reads *Raguel* (compare Exodus 2:18).

over me, saying, 'Give us meat, that
we may eat.'
14 "I am not able to bear all these
people alone, because the burden *is*
too heavy for me.
15 "If You treat me like this, please
[a]kill me here and now—if I have
found favor in Your sight—and do not
let me see my wretchedness!"

From Sinai to Kadesh Barnea:
(5) the seventy elders (cp. Ex. 18:19)

16 So the LORD said to Moses:
"Gather to Me seventy men of the elders of Israel, whom you [b]know to be
the elders of the people and officers
over them; bring them to the tabernacle of meeting, that they may stand
there with you.
17 "Then I will come down and talk
with you there. I will take of the
[c]Spirit that *is* upon you and will put
the same upon them; and they shall
bear the burden of the people with
you, that you may not bear *it* yourself
alone.
18 "Then you shall say to the people, 'Consecrate yourselves for tomorrow, and you shall eat meat; for you
have wept in the hearing of the LORD,
saying, "Who will give us meat to eat?
For *it was* well with us in Egypt."
Therefore the LORD will give you meat,
and you shall eat.
19 'You shall eat, not one day, nor
two days, nor five days, nor ten days,
nor twenty days,
20 'but *for* a whole month, until it
comes out of your nostrils and becomes loathsome to you, because you
have [d]despised the LORD who is
among you, and have wept before
Him, saying, "Why did we ever come
up out of Egypt?" ' "
21 And Moses said, "The people
whom I *am* among *are* [e]six hundred
thousand men on foot; yet You have
said, 'I will give them meat, that they
may eat *for* a whole month.'
22 "Shall flocks and herds be
slaughtered for them, to provide
enough for them? Or shall all the fish
of the sea be gathered together for
them, to provide enough for them?"
23 And the LORD said to Moses,
"Has the LORD's arm been [f]shortened?
Now you shall see whether [g]what I
say will happen to you or not."
24 So Moses went out and told the

15
a Cp. 1 Ki. 19:4
16
b Ex. 18:25
17
c *Holy Spirit* (OT): vv. 17, 25–26,29; Num. 24:2. (Gen. 1:2; Zech. 12:10)
20
d 1 Sam. 10:19
21
e Num. 2:32
23
f Isa. 50:2; 59:1
g Num. 23:19
24
h *Inspiration:* v. 24; Num. 22:38. (Ex. 4:15; 2 Tim. 3:16, *note*)
28
i Cp. Mk. 9:38–40
29
j Cp. 1 Cor. 12:1–31; 14:5
31
k Ps. 78:26–31
l Ex. 16:13
m See Weights and Measures (OT), 2 Chr. 2:10, *note*

people the [h]words of the LORD, and he
gathered the seventy men of the elders
of the people and placed them around
the tabernacle.
25 Then the LORD came down in the
cloud, and spoke to him, and took of
the [c]Spirit that *was* upon him, and
placed *the same* upon the seventy elders; and it happened, when the Spirit
rested upon them, that they prophesied, although they never did *so*
again.*

From Sinai to Kadesh Barnea:
(6) Eldad and Medad prophesy

26 But two men had remained in
the camp: the name of one *was* Eldad,
and the name of the other Medad. And
the [c]Spirit rested upon them. Now
they *were* among those listed, but who
had not gone out to the tabernacle; yet
they prophesied in the camp.
27 And a young man ran and told
Moses, and said, "Eldad and Medad
are prophesying in the camp."
28 So Joshua the son of Nun, Moses' assistant, *one* of his choice men,
answered and said, "Moses my lord,
[i]forbid them!"
29 Then Moses said to him, "Are
you [j]zealous for my sake? Oh, that all
the LORD's people were prophets *and*
that the LORD would put His [c]Spirit
upon them!"
30 And Moses returned to the
camp, *both* he and the elders of Israel.

From Sinai to Kadesh Barnea:
(7) the quail and the plague

31 Now a [k]wind went out from the
LORD, and it brought [l]quail from the
sea and left *them* fluttering near the
camp, about a day's journey on this
side and about a day's journey on the
other side, all around the camp, and
about two [m]cubits [1]above the surface
of the ground.
32 And the people stayed up all that
day, all night, and all the next day, and
gathered the quail (he who gathered
least gathered ten [m]homers); and they
spread *them* out for themselves all
around the camp.
33 But while the meat *was* still between their teeth, before it was
chewed, the wrath of the LORD was
aroused against the people, and the

*11:25 Targum and Vulgate read *did not cease.*

[1](11:31) "Two cubits above the surface of the ground" was within reach of the people, that they might kill them for food. The statement is not that the quails were piled up from the face of the earth two cubits deep; the level of their flight was two cubits above the earth.

LORD struck the people with a very great plague.

34 So he called the name of that place [a]Kibroth Hattaavah, because there they buried the people who had yielded to craving.

35 From Kibroth Hattaavah the people [b]moved to Hazeroth, and camped at Hazeroth.

From Sinai to Kadesh Barnea: (8) the criticism of Miriam and Aaron

12 THEN [c]Miriam and Aaron spoke [d]against Moses because of the Ethiopian woman whom he had married; for he had married an Ethiopian woman.

2 So they said, "Has the LORD indeed spoken [e]only through [f]Moses? Has He not spoken through us also?" And the LORD heard *it.*

3 (Now the man Moses *was* very [1g]humble, more than all men who *were* on the face of the earth.)

4 Suddenly the LORD said to Moses, Aaron, and Miriam, "Come out, you three, to the tabernacle of meeting!" So the three came out.

5 Then the LORD came down in the pillar of [h]cloud and stood *in* the door of the tabernacle, and called Aaron and Miriam. And they both went forward.

6 Then He said, "Hear now My words:

If there is a [i]prophet among
you,
I, the LORD, make Myself
known to him in a vision;
I speak to him in a [j]dream.

7 Not so with My [k]servant
Moses;
[l]He *is* faithful in all My house.

8 I speak with him face to [m]face,
Even plainly, and not in dark
sayings;
And he sees the [n]form of the
LORD.
Why then were you not
[o]afraid
To speak against My servant
Moses?"

9 So the anger of the LORD was aroused against them, and He departed.

10 And when the cloud departed from above the tabernacle, suddenly Miriam [p]*became* [q]leprous, as *white as* snow. Then Aaron turned toward Miriam, and there she was, a leper.

11 So Aaron said to Moses, "Oh, my lord! Please do not lay *this* sin on us, in which we have done foolishly and in which we have sinned.

12 "Please do not let her be as one dead, whose flesh is half consumed when he comes out of his mother's womb!"

13 So Moses cried out to the LORD, saying, "Please [r]heal her, O God, I [s]pray!"

14 Then the LORD said to Moses, "If her father had but [t]spit in her face, would she not be shamed seven days? Let her be [u]shut out of the camp seven days, and afterward she may be received *again.*"

15 So Miriam was shut out of the camp seven days, and the people did not journey till Miriam was brought in *again.*

16 And afterward the people moved from [v]Hazeroth and [w]camped in the Wilderness of Paran.

At Kadesh Barnea: (1) the spies sent to appraise the land

13 AND the [x]LORD spoke to Moses, saying,

2 [y]"Send men to spy out the land of Canaan, which I am giving to the children of Israel; from each tribe of their fathers you shall send a man, every one a leader among them."

3 So Moses sent them from the Wilderness of Paran according to the command of the LORD, all of them men who *were* heads of the children of Israel.

4 Now these *were* their names: from the tribe of Reuben, Shammua the son of Zaccur;

5 from the tribe of Simeon, Shaphat the son of Hori;

6 from the tribe of Judah, Caleb the son of Jephunneh;

7 from the tribe of Issachar, Igal the son of Joseph;

34
a i.e. *graves of craving*
35
b Num. 33:17
CHAPTER 12
1
c Ex. 15:20, 21; Num. 20:1
d Num. 11:1
2
e Cp. Lk. 9:33–36
f Num. 16:3
3
g Cp. Num. 20:10
5
h Ex. 34:5
6
i Cp. Num. 11:25
j Gen. 31:10–11; 1 Ki. 3:5
7
k Josh. 1:1
l Heb. 3:2,5
8
m Cp. Ex. 33:11; Dt. 34:10
n Ex. 33:20–23
o Ps. 105:15
10
p Dt. 24:9
q Cp. 2 Ki. 5:27; 2 Chr. 26:19
13
r Ps. 103:3
s *Bible prayers (OT):* v. 13; Num. 14:13. (Gen. 15:2; Hab. 3:1)
14
t Dt. 25:9
u Lev. 13:4, 46
16
v Num. 33:17–18
w Num. 33:18
CHAPTER 13
1
x Cp. Dt. 1:22–23
2
y vv. 2–25; Num. 32:8

[1](12:3) It is sometimes questioned whether this statement could have been written by Moses. As a divinely inspired book the Bible never conceals the weaknesses and faults of its characters; so it speaks plainly about their virtues. Despite baseless criticism against his family, Moses said nothing and made no attempt to defend himself until the LORD intervened on his behalf (v. 4). If the account is to be fully understood, this statement of Moses' humility is necessary. Its presence here is therefore no argument against his authorship.

8 from the tribe of Ephraim, [a]Hoshea* the son of Nun;

9 from the tribe of Benjamin, Palti the son of Raphu;

10 from the tribe of Zebulun, Gaddiel the son of Sodi;

11 from the tribe of Joseph, *that is,* from the tribe of Manasseh, Gaddi the son of Susi;

12 from the tribe of Dan, Ammiel the son of Gemalli;

13 from the tribe of Asher, Sethur the son of Michael;

14 from the tribe of Naphtali, Nahbi the son of Vophsi;

15 from the tribe of Gad, Geuel the son of Machi.

16 These *are* the names of the men whom Moses sent to spy out the land. And Moses called Hoshea* the son of Nun, [b]Joshua.

17 Then Moses sent them to spy out the land of Canaan, and said to them, "Go up this *way* [c]into the South, and go up to the mountains,

18 "and see what the land is like: whether the people who dwell in it *are* strong or weak, few or many;

19 "whether the land they dwell in *is* good or bad; whether the cities they inhabit *are* like camps or strongholds;

20 "whether the land *is* rich or poor; and whether there are forests there or not. Be of good [d]courage. And bring some of the fruit of the land." Now the time *was* the season of the first ripe grapes.

21 So they went up and spied out the land from the Wilderness of [e]Zin as far as Rehob, near the entrance of [f]Hamath.

22 And they went up through the [c]South and came to [g]Hebron; Ahiman, Sheshai, and Talmai, the descendants of [h]Anak, *were* there. (Now Hebron was built seven years before Zoan in Egypt.)

23 Then they came to the Valley of [i]Eshcol, and there cut down a branch with one cluster of grapes; they carried it between two of them on a pole. *They* also *brought* some of the pomegranates and figs.

24 The place was called the Valley of Eshcol, because of the cluster which the men of Israel cut down there.

25 And they returned from spying out the land after forty days.

At Kadesh Barnea: (2) the contradictory reports of the spies

26 Now they departed and came back to Moses and Aaron and all the congregation of the children of Israel in the [j]Wilderness of Paran, at [k]Kadesh; they brought back word to them and to all the congregation, and showed them the fruit of the land.

27 Then they told him, and said: "We went to the land where you sent us. It truly [l]flows with milk and honey, and this *is* its fruit.

28 "Nevertheless the [m]people who dwell in the land *are* strong; the cities *are* fortified *and* very large; moreover we saw the descendants of [h]Anak there.

29 "The [n]Amalekites dwell in the land of the [c]South; the [o]Hittites, the Jebusites, and the Amorites dwell in the mountains; and the Canaanites dwell by the sea and along the banks of the Jordan."

30 Then Caleb quieted the people before Moses, and said, "Let us go up at once and take possession, for we are well able to overcome it."

31 But the men who had gone up with him said, "We are not able to go up against the people, for they *are* stronger than we."

32 And they gave the children of Israel a [p]bad report of the land which they had spied out, saying, "The land through which we have gone as spies *is* a land that [1]devours its inhabitants, and [q]all the people whom we saw in it *are* men of *great* stature.

33 "There we saw the giants* (the descendants of [h]Anak came from the giants); and we were like grasshoppers in our own sight, and so we were in their sight."

At Kadesh Barnea: (3) the rebellious unbelief of Israel (1 Cor. 10:1–5; Heb. 3:7–19)

14 [2]SO all the congregation lifted up their voices and cried, and the people [r]wept that night.

8 a i.e. *Joshua,* v. 16; Dt. 32:44
16 b i.e. *savior,* or *deliverer*
17 c See Gen. 12:9, *note*
20 d Dt. 31:6, 23
21 e Num. 20:1; 27:14; 33:36 f Num. 34:8; Josh. 13:5
22 g Jud. 1:10; cp. Josh. 15:14 h Josh. 11:21,22
23 i Meaning *cluster.* Num. 32:9
26 j v. 3 k Num. 20:1,16; 32:8; 33:36; Dt. 1:19; Josh. 14:6
27 l Ex. 3:8; 33:3
28 m Dt. 1:28; 9:1–2
29 n Ex. 17:8–16; Num. 14:25,45 o See 2 Ki. 7:6, *note*
32 p Num. 14:36–37 q Amos 2:9
CHAPTER 14
1 r Num. 11:4; Dt. 1:45

*13:8 Septuagint and Vulgate read *Oshea.*
13:16 Septuagint and Vulgate read *Oshea.*
13:33 Hebrew *nephilim*

[1](13:32) This is a reference to the strength of the warring factions in Canaan, which made life insecure, and not in any sense a denial of the great productivity of the land.

[2](14:1) Because of certain repetitions, there are some who claim that chs. 13 and 14 are a composite of conflicting accounts. But repetition for emphasis is common in the OT, and each of the alleged discrepancies may be explained in full accord with the unity of the narrative.

2 And all the children of Israel [a]complained against Moses and Aaron, and the whole congregation said to them, "If only we had died in the land of Egypt! Or if only we had died in this wilderness!

3 "Why has the LORD brought us to this land to fall by the sword, that our wives and [b]children should become victims? Would it not be better for us to return to Egypt?"

4 So they said to one another, "Let us select a leader and [c]return to Egypt."

5 Then Moses and Aaron fell on their faces before all the assembly of the congregation of the children of Israel.

6 But Joshua the son of Nun and Caleb the son of Jephunneh, *who were* among those who had spied out the land, tore their clothes;

7 and they spoke to all the congregation of the children of Israel, saying: "The land we passed through to spy out *is* an exceedingly good land.

8 "If the LORD delights in us, then He will bring us into this land and give it to us, 'a land which flows with milk and honey.'*

9 "Only do not [d]rebel against the LORD, nor fear the people of the land, for they *are* our bread; their protection has departed from them, [e]and the LORD *is* with us. Do not fear them."

10 And all the congregation said to stone them with [f]stones. Now the glory of the LORD appeared in the tabernacle of meeting before all the children of Israel.

At Kadesh Barnea: (4) Moses pleads for pardon for the people

11 Then the LORD said to Moses: "How long will these people [g]reject Me? And how long will they not believe Me, with all the signs which I have performed among them?

12 "I will strike them with the pestilence and disinherit them, and I will [h]make of you a nation greater and mightier than they."

13 [i]And [j]Moses said to the LORD: [k]"Then the Egyptians will hear *it*, for by Your might You brought these people up from among them,

14 "and they will tell *it* to the inhabitants of this land. They have [l]heard that You, LORD, *are* among these people; that You, LORD, are seen face to face and Your cloud stands above them, and You go before them in a pillar of cloud by day and in a pillar of fire by night.

15 "Now *if* You kill these people as one man, then the nations which have heard of Your fame will speak, saying,

16 'Because the LORD was not [m]able to bring this people to the land which He swore to give them, therefore He killed them in the wilderness.'

17 "And now, I pray, let the power of my Lord be great, just as You have spoken, saying,

18 'The [n]LORD is longsuffering and abundant in mercy, forgiving iniquity and transgression; but He by no means clears *the guilty*, visiting the iniquity of the fathers on the children to the third and fourth *generation*.'

19 [o]"Pardon the iniquity of this people, I pray, [p]according to the greatness of Your mercy, just as You have forgiven this people, from Egypt even until now."

At Kadesh Barnea: (5) the LORD pardons but rebukes the people

20 Then the LORD said: "I have [q]pardoned, according to your word;

21 "but truly, as I live, all the earth shall be [r]filled with the glory of the LORD—

22 "because [s]all these men who have seen My glory and the signs which I did in Egypt and in the wilderness, and have put Me to the [t]test now these ten times, and have not heeded My voice,

23 [1]"they certainly shall not [u]see the land of which I swore to their fathers, nor shall any of those who rejected Me see it.

24 "But My servant Caleb, because he has a different spirit in him and has followed Me fully, I will bring into the land where he went, and his descendants shall inherit it.

25 "Now the Amalekites and the

2 a Ex. 16:2; 17:3; Num. 16:41; Ps. 106:25; 1 Cor. 10:10
3 b Dt. 1:39
4 c Acts 7:39
9 d 1 Sam. 15:23 e Gen. 48:21; Ex. 33:16; Dt. 20:1,3–4; 31:6–8; Josh. 1:5; Jud. 1:22; 2 Chr. 13:12; Ps. 46:7,11; Zech. 8:23; Mt. 28:20; Heb. 13:5
10 f Ex. 17:4
11 g v. 23; Dt. 9:7,8,22; Heb. 3:8, 16
12 h Ex. 32:10
13 i *Bible prayers (OT):* vv. 13–19; Num. 27:15. (Gen. 15:2; Hab. 3:1) j Ps. 106:23 k Ex. 32:12; Dt. 9:26–28; 32:27
14 l Dt. 2:25
16 m Cp. Josh. 7:9
18 n Ex. 34:6–7
19 o Ps. 51:1 p Ex. 34:9
20 q 2 Sam. 12:13; Mic. 7:18–20
21 r Ps. 72:19; Isa. 6:3; 11:9; 66:18–19; Hab. 2:14; Mt. 6:10 **14:22** s Dt. 1:35; 1 Cor. 10:5 t *Test/tempt:* v. 22; Dt. 6:16. (Gen. 3:1; Jas. 1:14, *note*) **14:23** u Num. 26:65; 32:11

*
14:8 Exodus 3:8

[1](14:23) Kadesh Barnea is, by the unbelief of Israel there and the divine comment on that unbelief (vv. 22–38; Dt. 1:19–40; 1 Cor. 10:1–5; Heb. 3:12–19), invested with immense spiritual significance. The people had obeyed God in sprinkling the blood (Ex. 12:28) and coming out of Egypt, but did not enter the Canaan rest because of unbelief (Heb. 3:18–19). Therefore, although members of a redeemed nation, they were a forty-years' grief to the LORD.

Canaanites dwell in the valley; tomorrow turn and move out into the wilderness by the Way of the [a]Red Sea."
26 And the LORD spoke to Moses
and Aaron, saying,
27 "How long *shall I bear with* this
evil congregation who complain
against Me? I have heard the complaints which the children of Israel
make against Me.
28 "Say to them, 'As I live,' says the
LORD, 'just as you have spoken in My
hearing, so I will [b]do to you:
29 'The carcasses of you who have
complained against Me shall fall in
this wilderness, all of you who were
[c]numbered, according to your entire
number, from twenty years old and
above.
30 [d]'Except for Caleb the son of Jephunneh and Joshua the son of Nun,
you shall by no means enter the land
which I swore I would make you dwell
in.
31 'But your little ones, whom you
said would be victims, I will bring in,
and they shall know the land which
you have despised.
32 'But *as for* you, your carcasses
shall fall in this wilderness.
33 'And your sons shall be shepherds in the wilderness forty years,
and bear the brunt of your infidelity,
until your carcasses are consumed in
the wilderness.
34 'According to the number of the
days in which you spied out the land,
forty days, for each day you shall bear
your guilt one year, *namely* forty
years, and you shall know My rejection.
35 'I the LORD have spoken this. I
will surely do so to all this evil congregation who are gathered together
against Me. In this wilderness they
shall be consumed, and there they
shall die.' "
36 Now the men whom Moses sent
to spy out the land, who returned and
made all the congregation complain
against him by bringing a bad report
of the land,
37 those very men who brought the
evil report about the land, [e]died by the
plague before the LORD.
38 But Joshua the son of Nun and
Caleb the son of Jephunneh remained
alive, of the men who went to spy out
the land.

At Kadesh Barnea: (6) a wrong reaction; Israel defeated

39 Then Moses told these words to
all the children of Israel, and the people [f]mourned greatly.
40 And they rose early in the morning and went up to the top of the
mountain, saying, "Here we are, and
we [g]will go up to the place which the
LORD has promised, for we have
sinned!"
41 And Moses said, "Now why do
you transgress the command of the
LORD? For this will not succeed.
42 "Do [h]not go up, lest you be defeated by your enemies, for the LORD *is*
not among you.
43 "For the Amalekites and the Canaanites *are* there before you, and you
shall fall by the sword; because you
have turned away from the LORD, the
LORD will not be with you."
44 But they [i]presumed to go up to
the mountaintop. Nevertheless, neither the ark of the covenant of the
LORD nor Moses departed from the
camp.
45 Then the Amalekites and the Canaanites who dwelt in that mountain
came down and attacked them, and
drove them back as far as [j]Hormah.

Years of wandering: (1) rules for Israel on entering Canaan

15 [1]AND the LORD spoke to Moses,
saying,
2 "Speak to the children of Israel,
and say to them: [2]'When you have

25 *a* Num. 21:4
28 *b* Heb. 3:16–19
29 *c* Num. 1:46
30 *d* v. 38; Num. 26:65; 32:12; Dt. 1:36–38; Josh. 14:6–15
37 *e* Num. 16:49
39 *f* Ex. 33:4
40 *g* Dt. 1:41–44
42 *h* Dt. 31:17
44 *i* Cp. Josh. 7:1–8
45 *j* Num. 21:3

[1](15:1) The wilderness was part of the necessary discipline of the redeemed people, but not the years of wandering. The latter were due wholly to the unbelief of the people at Kadesh Barnea. The Red Sea, Marah, Elim, and Sinai were God's ways in development and discipline and have, of necessity, their counterpart in Christian experience: (1) the Red Sea suggests the cross as that which (death to Christ but life for us) separates us from Egypt, the world (Gal. 6:14); (2) Marah, God's power to turn vexatious things into blessing; (3) Elim, God's power to give rest and refreshment along the way; and (4) Sinai, God's holiness and our deep inherent evil, the experience of Rom. 7:7–25. So far the path was and is of God. But from Kadesh Barnea to Jordan all (except the grace of God toward an unbelieving people) is for warning, not imitation (1 Cor. 10:1–11; Heb. 3:17–19). There is a present rest of God, of which the Sabbath and Canaan were types, into which believers may and, therefore, should enter by faith (Heb. 3—4).

[2](15:2) It is remarkable that just when the people are turning in unbelief from the land, God

come into the land you are to inhabit, which I am giving to you,

3 'and you make an offering by fire to the LORD, a burnt offering or a sacrifice, to fulfill a vow or as a freewill offering or in your appointed feasts, to make a [a]sweet aroma to the LORD, from the herd or the flock,

4 'then he who presents his offering to the LORD shall [b]bring a grain offering of one-tenth *of an ephah* of fine flour mixed with one-fourth of a [c]hin of oil;

5 'and one-fourth of a [c]hin of wine as a drink offering you shall prepare with the burnt offering or the sacrifice, for each [d]lamb.

6 'Or for a [e]ram you shall prepare as a grain offering two-tenths *of an ephah* of fine flour mixed with one-third of a [c]hin of oil;

7 'and as a drink offering you shall offer one-third of a [c]hin of wine as a sweet aroma to the LORD.

8 'And when you prepare a young bull as a burnt offering, or as a sacrifice to fulfill a vow, or as a peace offering to the LORD,

9 'then shall be offered with the young bull a grain offering of three-tenths *of an ephah* of fine flour mixed with half a [c]hin of oil;

10 'and you shall bring as the drink offering half a [c]hin of wine as an offering made by fire, a sweet aroma to the LORD.

11 'Thus it shall be done for each young bull, for each ram, or for each lamb or young goat.

12 'According to the number that you prepare, so you shall do with everyone according to their number.

13 'All who are native-born shall do these things in this manner, in presenting an offering made by fire, a sweet aroma to the LORD.

Law of the stranger dwelling in the land (vv. 14–16)

14 'And if a stranger dwells with you, or whoever *is* among you throughout your generations, and would present an offering made by fire, a sweet aroma to the LORD, just as you do, so shall he do.

15 'One ordinance *shall be* for you of the assembly and for the stranger who dwells *with you,* an ordinance forever throughout your generations; as you are, so shall the stranger be before the LORD.

16 'One law and one custom shall be for you and for the stranger who dwells with you.' "*

17 Again the LORD spoke to Moses, saying,

18 "Speak to the children of Israel, and say to them: 'When you come into the land to which I bring you,

19 'then it will be, when you [f]eat of the bread of the land, that you shall offer up a heave offering to the LORD.

20 'You shall offer up a cake of the [g]first of your ground meal *as* a heave offering; as a heave offering of the threshing floor, so shall you offer it up.

21 'Of the first of your ground meal you shall give to the LORD a heave offering throughout your generations.

22 'If you sin unintentionally, and do not observe all these commandments which the LORD has spoken to Moses—

23 'all that the LORD has commanded you by the hand of Moses, from the day the LORD gave commandment and onward throughout your generations—

24 'then it will be, if it is [h]unintentionally committed, without the knowledge of the congregation, that the whole congregation shall offer one young bull as a burnt offering, as a sweet aroma to the LORD, with its grain offering and its drink offering, according to the ordinance, and one kid of the goats as a sin offering.

25 'So the priest shall make [i]atonement for the whole congregation of the children of Israel, and it shall be [j]forgiven them, for it was unintentional; they shall bring their offering, an offering made by fire to the LORD, and their sin offering before the LORD, for their unintended sin.

26 'It shall be forgiven the whole congregation of the children of Israel and the stranger who dwells among them, because all the people *did it* unintentionally.

27 'And if [k]a person sins unintentionally, then he shall bring a female goat in its first year as a sin offering.

28 'So the priest shall make [i]atonement for the person who sins unintentionally, when he sins unintentionally before the LORD, to make atonement for him; and it shall be forgiven him.

29 'You shall have one law for him

CHAPTER 15

3 *a* Lev. 1:9

4 *b* Num. 28:1–29:40
c See Weights and Measures (OT), 2 Chr. 2:10, *note*

5 *d* Lev. 1:10; 3:6; Num. 28:4–5

6 *e* Num. 28:12,14

19 *f* Josh. 5:11–12

20 *g* Lev. 23:10,14,17

24 *h* Lev. 4:13

25 *i* See Ex. 29:33, *note*
j *Forgiveness:* vv. 25–26, 28; Ps. 32:5. (Lev. 4:20; Mt. 26:28, *note*)

27 *k* Lev. 4:27

*15:16 Compare Exodus 12:49

gives directions for conduct when they shall have entered it. Cp. Rom. 11:29; Phil. 1:6.

who sins unintentionally, *for* him who is native-born among the children of Israel and for the stranger who dwells among them.

30 'But the person who does *anything* [a]presumptuously, *whether he is* native-born or a stranger, that one brings reproach on the LORD, and he shall be cut off from among his people.

31 'Because he has despised the word of the LORD, and has broken His commandment, that person shall be completely cut off; his guilt *shall be* upon him.' "

The law's condemnation (Rom. 3:19; 7:7–11; 2 Cor. 3:7,9; Gal. 3:10)

32 Now while the children of Israel were in the wilderness, they found a man gathering [b]sticks on the [c]Sabbath day.

33 And those who found him gathering sticks brought him to Moses and Aaron, and to all the congregation.

34 They put him under guard, because it had not been explained what should be done to him.

35 Then the LORD said to Moses, "The man must surely be put to death; all the congregation shall stone him with stones outside the camp."

36 So, as the LORD commanded Moses, all the congregation brought him outside the camp and stoned him with stones, and he died.

The blue thread—reminder of separated walk

37 Again the LORD spoke to Moses, saying,

38 "Speak to the children of Israel: Tell them to make [d]tassels on the corners of their garments throughout their generations, and to put a [1]blue thread in the tassels of the corners.

39 "And you shall have the tassel, that you may look upon it and [e]remember all the commandments of the LORD and do them, and that you *may* not follow the harlotry to which your own heart and your own eyes are inclined,

40 "and that you may remember and do all My commandments, and be [f]holy for your God.

41 "I *am* the LORD your God, who brought you out of the land of Egypt, to be your God: I *am* the LORD your God."

Years of wandering: (2) Korah's rebellion (vv. 8–10; Jude 11)

16 NOW [g]Korah the son of Izhar, the son of Kohath, the son of Levi, with [h]Dathan and Abiram the sons of Eliab, and On the son of Peleth, sons of Reuben, took *men;*

2 and they rose up before Moses with some of the children of Israel, two hundred and fifty leaders of the congregation, [i]representatives of the congregation, men of renown.

3 They gathered together [j]against Moses and Aaron, and said to them, "*You take* too much upon yourselves, for all the congregation *is* holy, every one of them, and the LORD *is* among them. Why then do you exalt yourselves above the assembly of the LORD?"

4 So when Moses heard *it,* he [k]fell on his face;

5 and he spoke to Korah and all his company, saying, "Tomorrow morning the LORD will show who *is* [l]His and *who is* holy, and will cause *him* to come near to Him. That one whom He chooses He will cause to come near to Him.

6 "Do this: Take censers, Korah and all your company;

7 "put fire in them and put incense in them before the LORD tomorrow, and it shall be *that* the man whom the LORD chooses *is* the holy one. *You take* too much upon yourselves, you sons of Levi!"

8 Then Moses said to Korah, "Hear now, you sons of Levi:

9 "*Is it* a small thing to you that the God of Israel has separated you from the congregation of Israel, to bring you near to Himself, to [m]do the work of the tabernacle of the LORD, and to stand before the congregation to serve them;

10 "and that He has brought you near *to Himself,* you and all your brethren, the sons of Levi, with you? And are you [2]seeking the priesthood also?

11 "Therefore you and all your

30 *a* Dt. 1:43; 17:12–13
32 *b* Ex. 35:3 *c* *Sabbath:* vv. 32–36; Neh. 9:14. (Gen. 2:3; Mt. 12:1, *note*)
38 *d* Dt. 22:12; Mt. 23:5
39 *e* Ps. 103:18
40 *f* Lev. 11:44–45
CHAPTER 16
1 *g* Ex. 6:21; Jude 11 *h* Num. 26:9; Dt. 11:6
2 *i* Num. 1:16
3 *j* Num. 12:2; 14:2
4 *k* Num. 14:5; 20:6
5 *l* 2 Tim. 2:19
9 *m* Num. 3:41–45; 8:13–16; Dt. 10:8

[1](15:38) The blue thread. Blue, the heavenly color, used on the corners of the priests' garments, signified that the servants of God were to be heavenly in obedience and character, and separate from earthly ambitions and desires.

[2](16:10) "The rebellion of Korah" (Jude 11) was intrusion into the priest's office, for "no man takes the honor to himself" (Heb. 5:4). It was a rebellion against the divine order in the theocratic kingdom.

company *are* gathered together
against the LORD. And [a]what *is* Aaron
that you complain against him?"
12 And Moses sent to call Dathan
and Abiram the sons of Eliab, but they
said, "We will not come up!
13 "*Is it* a small thing that you have
brought us up out of a [b]land flowing
with milk and honey, to kill us in the
wilderness, that you should keep acting like a [c]prince over us?
14 "Moreover [d]you have not
brought us into a land flowing with
milk and honey, nor given us inheritance of fields and vineyards. Will you
put out the eyes of these men? We will
not come up!"
15 Then Moses was very angry, and
said to the LORD, "Do not [e]respect
their offering. I have [f]not taken one
donkey from them, nor have I hurt one
of them."
16 And Moses said to Korah, "Tomorrow, you and all your company be
present before the LORD—you and
they, as well as Aaron.
17 "Let each take his censer and put
incense in it, and each of you bring his
censer before the LORD, two hundred
and fifty censers; both you and Aaron,
each *with* his censer."
18 So every man took his censer,
put fire in it, laid incense on it, and
stood at the door of the tabernacle of
meeting with Moses and Aaron.
19 And Korah gathered all the congregation against them at the door of
the tabernacle of meeting. Then the
glory of the LORD appeared to all the
congregation.
20 And the LORD spoke to Moses
and Aaron, saying,
21 [g]"Separate yourselves from
among this congregation, that I may
[h]consume them in a moment."
22 Then they fell on their faces, and
said, "O God, the [i]God of the spirits of
all flesh, shall one man sin, and You
be angry with all the [j]congregation?"
23 So the LORD spoke to Moses, saying,
24 "Speak to the congregation, saying, 'Get away from the tents of Korah, Dathan, and Abiram.' "
25 Then Moses rose and went to
Dathan and Abiram, and the elders of
Israel followed him.
26 And he spoke to the congregation, saying, "Depart now from the
tents of these wicked men! Touch
nothing of theirs, [k]lest you be consumed in all their sins."
27 So they got away from around

11
a Ex. 16:7–8
13
b Num. 11:4–6
c Ex. 2:14
14
d Num. 14:1–4
15
e Gen. 4:4–5
f 1 Sam. 12:3
21
g *Separation:* vv. 20–26; Dt. 22:10. (Gen. 12:1; 2 Cor. 6:17, *note*)
h Ex. 32:10
22
i Num. 27:16
j Gen. 18:23–32; 20:4
26
k Gen. 19:15,17
27
l Num. 26:11
30
m Ps. 55:15
n See Hab. 2:5, *note*
31
o *Miracles (OT):* vv. 31–35; Num. 17:8. (Gen. 5:24; Jon. 1:17, *note*)
32
p 1 Chr. 6:22–28; cp. Num. 26:11
35
q Num. 11:1–3
37
r Lev. 27:28
38
s Num. 17:10
40
t Cp. 1 Sam. 13:9; Heb. 5:4; Jude 11
u Num. 3:10

the tents of Korah, Dathan, and Abiram; and Dathan and Abiram came
out and stood at the door of their tents,
with their wives, their sons, and their
little [l]children.
28 And Moses said: "By this you
shall know that the LORD has sent me
to do all these works, for *I have* not
done them of my own will.
29 "If these men die naturally like
all men, or if they are visited by the
common fate of all men, *then* the LORD
has not sent me.
30 "But if the LORD creates a new
thing, and the earth opens its mouth
and swallows them up with all that
belongs to them, and they [m]go down
alive into the [n]pit, then you will understand that these men have rejected
the LORD."
31 Now it came to pass, as he finished speaking all these words, that
the ground [o]split apart under them,
32 and the earth opened its mouth
and swallowed them up, with their
households and [p]all the men with Korah, with all *their* goods.
33 So they and all those with them
went down alive into the [n]pit; the
earth closed over them, and they perished from among the assembly.
34 Then all Israel who *were* around
them fled at their cry, for they said,
"Lest the earth swallow us up *also!*"
35 And a [q]fire came out from the
LORD and consumed the two hundred
and fifty men who were offering incense.

Plague falls on complainers

36 Then the LORD spoke to Moses,
saying:
37 "Tell Eleazar, the son of Aaron
the priest, to pick up the censers out of
the blaze, for they are [r]holy, and scatter the fire some distance away.
38 "The censers of these men who
sinned against their own souls, let
them be made into hammered plates
as a covering for the altar. Because
they presented them before the LORD,
therefore they are holy; and they shall
be a [s]sign to the children of Israel."
39 So Eleazar the priest took the
bronze censers, which those who
were burned up had presented, and
they were hammered out as a covering on the altar,
40 *to be* a memorial to the children
of Israel [t]that no outsider, who *is* not
a descendant of Aaron, should come
near [u]to offer incense before the LORD,
that he might not become like Korah

and his companions, just as the LORD
had said to him through Moses.
41 On the next day all the congregation of the children of Israel complained against Moses and Aaron,
saying, "You have killed the people of
the LORD."
42 Now it happened, when the congregation had gathered against Moses
and Aaron, that they turned toward
the tabernacle of meeting; and suddenly the cloud covered it, and the
glory of the LORD appeared.
43 Then Moses and Aaron came before the tabernacle of meeting.
44 And the LORD spoke to Moses,
saying,
45 "Get away from among this congregation, that I may consume them in
a moment." And they [a]fell on their
faces.
46 So Moses said to Aaron, "Take a
censer and put fire in it from the altar,
put incense *on it*, and take it quickly to
the congregation and make [b]atone-
ment for them; for [c]wrath has gone
out from the LORD. The plague has begun."
47 Then Aaron took *it* as Moses
commanded, and ran into the midst of
the assembly; and already the plague
had begun among the people. So he
put in the incense and made [b]atone-
ment for the people.
48 And he [d]stood between the dead
and the living; so the plague was
stopped.
49 Now those who died in the
plague were [e]fourteen thousand
seven hundred, [f]besides those who
died in the Korah incident.
50 So Aaron returned to Moses at
the door of the tabernacle of meeting,
for the plague had stopped.

Years of wandering: (3) Aaron's rod that budded

17 AND the LORD spoke to Moses,
saying:
2 "Speak to the children of Israel,
and get from them a rod from each
father's house, all their leaders according to their fathers' houses—
twelve rods. Write each man's name
on his rod.
3 "And you shall write Aaron's
name on the rod of Levi. For there
shall be one rod for the head of *each*
father's house.
4 "Then you shall place them in
the tabernacle of meeting before the
[g]Testimony, [h]where I meet with you.
5 "And it shall be *that* the rod of
the man whom I [i]choose will blossom; thus I will rid Myself of the complaints of the children of Israel, which
they make against you."
6 So Moses spoke to the children
of Israel, and each of their leaders
gave him a rod apiece, for each leader
according to their fathers' houses,
twelve rods; and the rod of Aaron *was*
among their rods.
7 And Moses placed the rods before the LORD in the [j]tabernacle of witness.
8 Now it came to pass on the next
day that Moses went into the tabernacle of witness, and behold, the [1][k]rod of
Aaron, of the house of Levi, had
[l]sprouted and put forth buds, had
produced blossoms and yielded ripe
almonds.
9 Then Moses brought out all the
rods from before the LORD to all the
children of Israel; and they looked,
and each man took his rod.
10 And the LORD said to Moses,
"Bring Aaron's rod back before the
Testimony, to be kept as a [m]sign
against the [n]rebels, that you may put
their complaints away from Me, lest
they die."
11 Thus did Moses; just as the LORD
had commanded him, so he did.
12 So the children of Israel spoke to
Moses, saying, "Surely we die, we
[o]perish, we all perish!
13 "Whoever even comes near the
tabernacle of the LORD must die. Shall
we all utterly die?"

Years of wandering: (4) duties and privileges of Aaron and Levites confirmed

18 THEN the LORD said to Aaron:
"You and your sons and your
father's house with you shall [p]bear
the iniquity *related to* the sanctuary,
and you and your sons with you shall
bear the iniquity *associated with* your
priesthood.
2 "Also bring with you your brethren of the [q]tribe of Levi, the tribe of
your father, that they may be [r]joined

45 *a* Num. 16:4
46 *b* Num. 25:13; see Ex. 29:33, *note* *c* Num. 18:5
48 *d* Cp. 2 Cor. 2:15–16
49 *e* Cp. Num. 25:9 *f* v. 35
CHAPTER 17
4 *g* Ex. 25:16 *h* Ex. 25:22; 29:42,43; 30:36
5 *i* Num. 16:5
7 *j* Num. 9:15
8 *k* Heb. 9:4 *l Miracles* (OT): v. 8; Num. 20:11. (Gen. 5:24; Jon. 1:17, *note*)
10 *m* Num. 16:38 *n* Dt. 9:7,24
12 *o* Cp. Isa. 6:5
CHAPTER 18
1 *p* i.e. *be responsible for every neglect or offense relating to.* Cp. Ex. 28:38
2 *q* Num. 1:47 *r* Num. 3:5–10

[1](17:8) Aaron's rod that budded: a type of Christ in resurrection, acknowledged by God as high priest. Aaron's priesthood had been questioned in the rebellion of Korah; so God Himself would confirm it (v. 5). The head of each tribe brought a dead rod; God put life into Aaron's only.

with you and serve you while you and your sons *are* with you before the tabernacle of witness.

3 "They shall attend to your needs and all the needs of the tabernacle; but they shall [a]not come near the articles of the sanctuary and the altar, lest they die—they and you also.

4 "They shall be joined with you and attend to the needs of the tabernacle of meeting, for all the work of the tabernacle; but an outsider shall not come near you.

5 "And you shall attend to the [b]duties of the sanctuary and the duties of the altar, that there *may* be no more [c]wrath on the children of Israel.

6 "Behold, I Myself have taken your brethren the Levites from among the children of Israel; *they are* a gift to you, given by the LORD, to do the work of the tabernacle of meeting.

7 "Therefore you and your sons with you shall attend to your priesthood for everything at the altar and behind the veil; and you shall serve. I give your priesthood *to you* as a gift for [d]service, but the outsider who comes near shall be put to death."

8 And the LORD spoke to Aaron: "Here, I Myself have also given you charge of My [e]heave offerings, all the holy gifts of the children of Israel; I have given them as a portion to you and your sons, as an ordinance forever.

9 "This shall be yours of the most holy things *reserved* from the fire: every offering of theirs, every grain offering and every sin offering and every trespass offering which they render to Me, *shall be* most holy [f]for you and your sons.

10 "In a most holy *place* you shall eat it; every male shall eat it. It shall be holy to you.

11 "This also *is* [g]yours: the heave offering of their gift, with all the wave offerings of the children of Israel; I have given them to you, and your sons and daughters with you, as an ordinance forever. Everyone who is clean in your house may eat it.

12 "All the best of the oil, all the best of the new wine and the grain, their [h]firstfruits which they offer to the LORD, I have given them to you.

13 "Whatever first ripe fruit is in their land, which they bring to the LORD, shall be yours. Everyone who is clean in your house may eat it.

14 "Every [i]devoted thing in Israel shall be yours.

15 "Everything that first opens the womb of all flesh, which they bring to the LORD, whether man or beast, shall be yours; nevertheless the [j]firstborn of man you shall surely redeem, and the firstborn of unclean animals you shall redeem.

16 "And those redeemed of the devoted things you shall redeem when one month old, according to your valuation, for five [k]shekels of silver, according to the shekel of the sanctuary, which *is* twenty [k]gerahs.

17 "But the firstborn of a cow, the firstborn of a sheep, or the firstborn of a goat you shall not redeem; they *are* holy. You shall sprinkle their blood on the altar, and burn their fat *as* an offering made by fire for a sweet aroma to the LORD.

18 "And their flesh shall be yours, [l]just as the wave breast and the right thigh are yours.

19 "All the heave offerings of the holy things, which the children of Israel offer to the LORD, I have given to you and your sons and daughters with you as an ordinance forever; it *is* a covenant of [m]salt forever before the LORD with you and your descendants with you."

20 Then the LORD said to Aaron: "You shall have [n]no inheritance in their land, nor shall you have any portion among them; [o]I *am* your portion and your inheritance among the children of Israel.

21 "Behold, I have given the children of Levi all the [p]tithes in Israel as an inheritance in return for the work which they perform, the work of the tabernacle of meeting.

22 "Hereafter the children of Israel shall not come near the tabernacle of meeting, lest they bear sin and die.

23 "But the Levites shall perform the work of the tabernacle of meeting, and they shall [q]bear their iniquity; *it shall be* a statute forever, throughout your generations, that among the children of Israel they shall have no inheritance.

24 "For the tithes of the children of Israel, which they offer up *as* a heave offering to the LORD, I have given to the Levites as an inheritance; therefore I have said to them, 'Among the children of Israel they shall have no inheritance.' "

25 Then the LORD spoke to Moses, saying,

26 "Speak thus to the Levites, and say to them: 'When you take from the

3
a Num. 4:15–20; cp. 2 Sam. 6:6
5
b Num. 3:31,38
c Num. 8:19
7
d Num. 3:9; 8:19; cp. 1 Pet. 5:2–3
8
e Lev. 7:28–34
9
f Num. 5:8–10
11
g Dt. 18:3–5
12
h Lev. 23:20
14
i Lev. 27:1–33
15
j Ex. 13:2, 12–15; 34:20; cp. Lk. 2:22–24
16
k See Coinage (OT), Ex. 30:13, *note;* cp. 2 Chr. 2:10, *note*
18
l Ex. 29:26–28; Lev. 7:31–36
19
m Lev. 2:13; 2 Chr. 13:5; Mk. 9:49–50; Col. 4:6
20
n Dt. 10:8–9; 12:12; 14:27–29; 18:1–2; Josh. 13:14,33; 14:3; 18:7
o Ps. 16:5; Ezek. 44:28
21
p vv. 24,26; Lev. 27:30, 32; Neh. 10:37; 12:44; Mal. 3:8–10; Heb. 7:4–10
23
q v. 1

children of Israel the tithes which I
have given you from them as your inheritance, then you shall offer up a
heave offering of it to the LORD, a
[a]tenth of the tithe.
27 'And your heave offering shall
be reckoned to you [b]as though *it were*
the grain of the [c]threshing floor and
as the fullness of the winepress.
28 'Thus you shall also offer a
heave offering to the LORD from all
your tithes which you receive from the
children of Israel, and you shall give
the LORD's heave offering from it to
Aaron the priest.
29 'Of all your gifts you shall offer
up every heave offering due to the
LORD, from all the best of them, the
consecrated part of them.'
30 "Therefore you shall say to
them: 'When you have lifted up the
best of it, then *the rest* shall be accounted to the Levites as the produce
of the threshing floor and as the produce of the winepress.
31 'You may eat it in any place, you
and your households, for it *is* your reward for your work in the tabernacle
of meeting.
32 'And you shall bear no sin because of it, when you have lifted up the
best of it. But you shall not [d]profane
the holy gifts of the children of Israel,
lest you die.' "

Years of wandering: (5) the ordinance of the red heifer

19 NOW the LORD spoke to Moses
and Aaron, saying,
2 "This *is* the ordinance of the law
which the LORD has commanded, saying: 'Speak to the children of Israel,
that they bring you a [1]red heifer without blemish, in which there *is* no [e]de-
fect *and* [f]on which a yoke has never
come.
3 'You shall give it to [g]Eleazar the
priest, that he may take it [h]outside the

26
a Neh. 10:38
27
b Cp. 2 Cor. 8:12
c Num. 15:20
32
d Lev. 19:8; 22:2, 15–16; Ezek. 22:26
CHAPTER 19
2
e Lev. 22:20–25
f Dt. 21:3; 1 Sam. 6:7
3
g Num. 3:4
h See Lev. 4:12, *note*
4
i Lev. 4:6; 16:14–19
5
j Lev. 9:11
6
k Lev. 14:4, 6,49
l Ex. 12:22; 1 Ki. 4:33
7
m Lev. 16:26,28
9
n Heb. 9:13–14
o vv. 13,20, 21; Num. 31:23; cp. Num. 8:7
11
p Num. 5:2; 6:6
12
q Lit. *purge himself from sin*
13
r Lev. 22:3–7

camp, and it shall be slaughtered before him;
4 'and Eleazar the priest shall take
some of its blood with his finger, and
[i]sprinkle some of its blood seven
times directly in front of the tabernacle of meeting.
5 'Then the heifer shall be burned
in his sight: its [j]hide, its flesh, its
blood, and its offal shall be burned.
6 'And the priest shall take [k]cedar
wood and [l]hyssop and scarlet, and
cast *them* into the midst of the fire
burning the heifer.
7 'Then the priest shall [m]wash his
clothes, he shall bathe in water, and
afterward he shall come into the
camp; the priest shall be unclean until
evening.
8 'And the one who burns it shall
wash his clothes in water, bathe in water, and shall be unclean until evening.
9 'Then a man *who is* clean shall
gather up the [n]ashes of the heifer, and
store *them* [h]outside the camp in a
clean place; and they shall be kept for
the congregation of the children of Israel for the [o]water of purification;* it
is for purifying from sin.
10 'And the one who gathers the
ashes of the heifer shall wash his
clothes, and be unclean until evening.
It shall be a statute forever to the children of Israel and to the stranger who
dwells among them.
11 'He who [p]touches the dead body
of anyone shall be unclean seven
days.
12 'He shall [q]purify himself with
the water on the third day and on the
seventh day; *then* he will be clean. But
if he does not purify himself on the
third day and on the seventh day, he
will not be clean.
13 'Whoever touches the body of
anyone who has died, and does [r]not

*
19:9 Literally *impurity*

[1](19:2) The red heifer: a type of the sacrifice of Christ as the ground of the cleansing of the believer from the defilement contracted in his pilgrim walk through this world, and an illustration of the method of his cleansing. The order is: (1) the killing of the sacrifice; (2) the sevenfold sprinkling of the blood, typical public testimony before the eyes of all of the complete and never-to-be repeated putting away of all of the believer's sins as before God (Heb. 9:12–14; 10:10–12); (3) the reduction of the sacrifice to ashes which are preserved and become a memorial of the sacrifice; and (4) the cleansing from defilement (sin has two aspects—guilt and uncleanness) by sprinkling with the ashes mixed with water. Water is a type of both the Spirit and the Word (Jn. 7:37–39; Eph. 5:26). The operation typified is this: the Holy Spirit uses the Word to convict the believer of some evil allowed in his life that hinders his joy, growth, and service. Thus convicted, he remembers that the guilt of his sin has been met by the sacrifice of Christ (1 Jn. 1:7). Instead, therefore, of despairing, the convicted believer judges and confesses the defiling thing as unworthy of a Christian, and is forgiven and cleansed (Jn. 13:3–10; 1 Jn. 1:7–10).

purify himself, [a]defiles the tabernacle of the LORD. That person shall be cut off from Israel. He shall be unclean, because the water of purification was not sprinkled on him; his uncleanness *is* still on him.

14 'This *is* the law when a man dies in a tent: All who come into the tent and all who *are* in the tent shall be unclean seven days;

15 'and every open vessel, which has no cover fastened on it, *is* unclean.

16 'Whoever in the open field [b]touches one who is slain by a sword or who has died, or a bone of a man, or a grave, shall be unclean seven days.

17 'And [c]for an unclean *person* they shall take some of the ashes of the heifer burnt for purification from sin, and running water shall be put on them in a vessel.

18 'A clean person shall take hyssop and dip *it* in the water, sprinkle *it* on the tent, on all the vessels, on the persons who were there, or on the one who touched a bone, the slain, the dead, or a grave.

19 'The clean *person* shall sprinkle the unclean on the third day and on the seventh day; and on the seventh day he shall purify himself, wash his clothes, and bathe in water; and at evening he shall be clean.

20 'But the man who is unclean and does not purify himself, that person shall be cut off from among the assembly, because he has defiled the sanctuary of the LORD. The water of purification has not been sprinkled on him; he *is* unclean.

21 'It shall be a perpetual statute for them. He who sprinkles the water of purification shall wash his clothes; and he who touches the water of purification shall be unclean until evening.

22 'Whatever the unclean *person* touches shall be [d]unclean; and the person who touches *it* shall be unclean until evening.' "

Years of wandering: (6) death of Miriam

20 THEN the children of Israel, the whole congregation, came into the Wilderness of [e]Zin in the [f]first month, and the people stayed in [g]Kadesh; and [h]Miriam died there and was buried there.

Years of wandering: (7) thirst in Meribah Kadesh (Dt. 32:51; cp. Ex. 17:1–7)

2 Now there was [i]no water for the congregation; so they gathered together [j]against Moses and Aaron.

3 And the people [k]contended with Moses and spoke, saying: "If only we had died [l]when our brethren died before the LORD!

4 "Why have you brought up the assembly of the LORD into this wilderness, that we and our animals should die here?

5 "And why have you made us come up out of Egypt, to bring us to this evil place? It *is* not a place of grain or figs or vines or pomegranates; nor *is* there any [m]water to drink."

6 So Moses and Aaron went from the presence of the assembly to the door of the tabernacle of meeting, and they [n]fell on their faces. And the glory of the LORD appeared to them.

Sin of Moses in striking the rock

7 Then the LORD spoke to Moses, saying,

8 "Take the [o]rod; you and your brother Aaron gather the congregation together. [1]Speak to the rock before their eyes, and it will yield its water; thus you shall bring water for them out of the [p]rock, and give drink to the congregation and their animals."

9 So Moses took the rod from before the LORD as He commanded him.

10 And Moses and Aaron gathered the assembly together before the rock; and he said to them, [q]"Hear now, you rebels! Must we bring water for you out of this rock?"

11 Then Moses lifted his hand and struck the [r]rock twice with his rod;

13
a Lev. 15:31
16
b Num. 31:19
17
c See Num. 19:2 and Jn. 13:10, *notes*
22
d Hag. 2:11–13
CHAPTER 20
1
e See Lev. 23:2, *note*
f Num. 13:21
g Num. 13:26
h Ex. 15:20; Num. 26:59
2
i Ex. 17:1
j Num. 16:19,42
3
k Cp. Ex. 17:2; Num. 14:2
l Num. 16:31–35
5
m v. 8, *note*
6
n Num. 16:4
8
o Ex. 17:5–6; cp. Num. 17:9–10
p Neh. 9:15; Ps. 78:15–16; 105:41; 1 Cor. 10:4
10
q Ps. 106:33
11
r *Christ* (Rock): vv. 8–11; Dt. 32:4. (Gen. 49:24; 1 Pet. 2:8)

[1](20:8) The gravity of the offense may be seen from these features: Moses (1) took credit to himself for what God had done ("must we"), v. 10; (2) disobeyed God in not speaking to the rock, v. 11; (3) lost his temper (he struck the rock twice when told to speak to it), v. 11; (4) used a harsh expression in addressing the people ("rebels," cp. Ps. 106:33), v. 10; (5) was provoked about their need and resented them ("must we"), v. 10; (6) was guilty of unbelief, because he did not trust the power of God, as though the power of God needed his help ("did not believe Me"), v. 12; (7) failed to glorify God before His people ("to hallow Me in the eyes of the children of Israel"), v. 12; and (8) rebelled against God, v. 24. Aaron was with him in this offense, so he suffered the same punishment.

and [a]water came out abundantly, and
the congregation and their animals
drank.
12 Then the LORD spoke to Moses
and Aaron, "Because you [b]did not believe Me, to hallow Me in the eyes of
the children of Israel, therefore you
shall [c]not bring this assembly into the
land which I have given them."
13 This *was* the water of [d]Meribah,
because the children of Israel contended with the LORD, and He was hallowed among them.

Years of wandering: (8) the never-forgiven sin of Edom (Gen. 25:30; Obad. 10)

14 [1e]Now Moses sent messengers
from Kadesh [f]to the king of [g]Edom.
"Thus says your brother Israel: 'You
[h]know all the hardship that has befallen us,
15 'how our fathers went down to
Egypt, and we dwelt in Egypt a [i]long
time, and the Egyptians afflicted us
and our fathers.
16 'When we cried out to the LORD,
He heard our voice and sent the [j]An-
gel and brought us up out of Egypt;
now here we are in Kadesh, a city on
the edge of your border.
17 'Please let us pass through your
country. We will not pass through
fields or vineyards, nor will we drink
water from wells; we will go along the
King's Highway; we will not turn
aside to the right hand or to the left
until we have passed through your territory.' "
18 Then [k]Edom said to him, "You
shall not pass through my *land,* lest I
come out against you with the sword."
19 So the children of Israel said to
him, "We will go by the Highway, and
if I or my livestock drink any of your
water, then I will pay for it; let me only
pass through on foot, nothing *more.*"
20 Then he said, "You shall not
pass through." So Edom came out
against them with many men and with
a strong hand.
21 Thus Edom refused to give Israel
passage through his territory; so Israel turned away from him.
22 Now the children of Israel, the
whole congregation, journeyed from
Kadesh and came to Mount Hor.

11
a Miracles (OT): vv. 7–11; Num. 21:9. (Gen. 5:24; Jon. 1:17, *note*)
12
b Num. 27:14; Dt. 3:26–27
c vv. 24,28; Dt. 3:23–26
13
d Ex. 17:7
14
e c. 1408 B.C. See Ex. 1:8, *note*
f Jud. 11:16–17
g Gen. 36:31–39; Dt. 2:4–8
h Cp. Dt. 31:17–21
15
i Gen. 15:13
16
j See Jud. 2:1 and Heb. 1:4, *notes*
18
k Num. 24:18; Ps. 137:7; Ezek. 25:12–13; Obad. 10–15
24
l Cp. Dt. 32:48–52
28
m Ex. 29:29–30; Dt. 10:6
n Num. 33:38
CHAPTER 21
1
o Num. 33:40
p See Gen. 12:9, *note*
2
q Cp. Gen. 28:20; Jud. 11:30
3
r Num. 14:45
5
s Ps. 78:19
t Cp. Ex. 16:3; 17:3

Death of Aaron

23 And the LORD spoke to Moses
and Aaron in Mount Hor by the border
of the land of Edom, saying:
24 "Aaron shall be gathered to his
people, for he shall not enter the land
which I have given to the children of
Israel, [l]because you rebelled against
My word at the water of Meribah.
25 "Take Aaron and Eleazar his
son, and bring them up to Mount Hor;
26 "and strip Aaron of his garments
and put them on Eleazar his son; for
Aaron shall be gathered *to his people*
and die there."
27 So Moses did just as the LORD
commanded, and they went up to
Mount Hor in the sight of all the congregation.
28 Moses stripped Aaron of his garments and [m]put them on Eleazar his
son; and Aaron [2n]died there on the top
of the mountain. Then Moses and Eleazar came down from the mountain.
29 Now when all the congregation
saw that Aaron was dead, all the
house of Israel mourned for Aaron
thirty days.

March of Israel: (1) victory

21 THE king of [o]Arad, the Canaanite, who dwelt in the
[p]South, heard that Israel was coming
on the road to Atharim. Then he
fought against Israel and took *some* of
them prisoners.
2 So Israel made a vow to the
LORD, and said, [q]"If You will indeed
deliver this people into my hand, then
I will utterly destroy their cities."
3 And the LORD listened to the
voice of Israel and delivered up the
Canaanites, and they utterly destroyed them and their cities. So the
name of that place was called [r]Hor-
mah.
4 Then they journeyed from
Mount Hor by the Way of the Red Sea,
to go around the land of Edom; and
the soul of the people became very discouraged on the way.

March of Israel: (2) the bronze serpent (Gen. 3:1, note; Jn. 3:14–15; 2 Cor. 5:21)

5 And the people [s]spoke against
God and against Moses: [t]"Why have

[1](20:14) Between Num. 14:45 and 20:14 there is a period of about thirty-eight years (cp. Dt. 2:14).
[2](20:28) The death of Aaron marks the end of the wanderings. Henceforth Israel marches or halts but does not wander (see Num. 15:1, *note*).

you brought us up out of Egypt to die
in the wilderness? For *there is* no food
and no water, [a]and our soul loathes
[b]this worthless bread."
6 So the LORD [c]sent fiery serpents
among the people, and they bit the
people; and many of the people of Israel died.
7 Therefore the people [d]came to
Moses, and said, "We have [e]sinned,
for we have spoken against the LORD
and against you; pray to the LORD that
He take away the serpents from us."
So Moses prayed for the people.
8 Then the LORD said to Moses,
[f]"Make a [g]fiery *serpent,* and set it on
a pole; and it shall be that everyone
who is bitten, when he looks at it, shall
live."
9 So Moses made a bronze serpent, and put it on a [1]pole; and so it
was, if a serpent had bitten anyone,
when he looked at the bronze serpent,
he [h]lived.
10 Now the children of Israel
moved on and camped in [i]Oboth.
11 And they journeyed from Oboth
and camped at [j]Ije Abarim, in the wilderness which *is* east of Moab, toward
the sunrise.
12 From there they moved and
camped in the Valley of Zered.
13 From there they moved and
camped on the other side of the [k]Ar-
non, which *is* in the wilderness that
extends from the border of the Amorites; for the Arnon *is* the border of
Moab, between Moab and the Amorites.
14 Therefore it is said in the Book
of the Wars of the LORD:

"Waheb in Suphah,*
The brooks of the Arnon,
15 And the slope of the brooks
That reaches to the dwelling of
[l]Ar,
And lies on the border of
Moab."

16 From there *they went* to Beer,
which *is* the well where the LORD said
to Moses, "Gather the people together,
and I will give them water."
17 [2]Then Israel sang this song:

5
a Cp. Num. 11:4–6
b Cp. Jn. 6:48–52, 60–64
6
c Dt. 8:15; 1 Cor. 10:9
7
d Num. 11:2
e Lev. 26:40
8
f Jn. 3:14–15
g Isa. 30:6
9
h Miracles (OT): vv. 8–9; Josh. 3:16. (Gen. 5:24; Jon. 1:17, *note*)
10
i Num. 33:43–44
11
j i.e. *ruins of Abarim*
13
k Num. 22:36
15
l Dt. 2:9
20
m Meaning *the division*
21
n Num. 32:33; Dt. 2:26–37
22
o Num. 20:17
25
p Amos 2:10

"Spring up, O well!
All of you sing to it—
18 The well the leaders sank,
Dug by the nation's nobles,
By the lawgiver, with their
staves."

And from the wilderness *they went* to
Mattanah,
19 from Mattanah to Nahaliel, from
Nahaliel to Bamoth,
20 and from Bamoth, *in* the valley
that *is* in the country of Moab, to the
top of [m]Pisgah which looks down on
the wasteland.*

March of Israel: (3) two victories

21 Then Israel sent messengers to
[n]Sihon king of the Amorites, saying,
22 [o]"Let me pass through your
land. We will not turn aside into fields
or vineyards; we will not drink water
from wells. We will go by the King's
Highway until we have passed
through your territory."
23 But Sihon would not allow Israel
to pass through his territory. So Sihon
gathered all his people together and
went out against Israel in the wilderness, and he came to Jahaz and fought
against Israel.
24 Then Israel defeated him with
the edge of the sword, and took possession of his land from the Arnon to
the Jabbok, as far as the people of Ammon; for the border of the people of
Ammon *was* fortified.
25 So Israel took all these cities,
and Israel [p]dwelt in all the cities of the
Amorites, in Heshbon and in all its villages.
26 For Heshbon *was* the city of Sihon king of the Amorites, who had
fought against the former king of
Moab, and had taken all his land from
his hand as far as the Arnon.
27 Therefore those who speak in
proverbs say:

"Come to Heshbon, let it be
built;
Let the city of Sihon be
repaired.

*
21:14 Ancient unknown places; Vulgate reads *what He did in the Red Sea.* 21:20 Hebrew *Jeshimon*

[1](21:9) See Gen. 3:15, *note 3.* The serpent here is a symbol of sin judged; bronze speaks of the divine judgment, as in the bronze altar (see Ex. 27:1–2, *notes*), and of self-judgment as in the laver of bronze. The bronze serpent is a type of Christ "made . . . to be sin for us" (Jn. 3:14–15; 2 Cor. 5:21) in bearing our judgment. Historically, the moment is indicated in the cry: "My God, My God, why have You forsaken Me?" (Mt. 27:46).

[2](21:17) The spiritual order here is beautiful: (1) atonement (vv. 8–9; Jn. 3:14–15); (2) water, symbol of the Spirit bestowed (v. 16; Jn. 7:37–39); (3) joy (vv. 17–18; Rom. 14:17); and (4) power (vv. 21–24).

28 "For fire went out from
[a]Heshbon,
A flame from the city of Sihon;
It consumed Ar of Moab,
The lords of the [b]heights of
the Arnon.
29 Woe to you, [c]Moab!
You have perished, O people
of [d]Chemosh!
He has given his [e]sons as
fugitives,
And his [f]daughters into
captivity,
To Sihon king of the Amorites.
30 "But we have shot at them;
Heshbon has perished as far as
[g]Dibon.
Then we laid waste as far as
Nophah,
Which *reaches* to Medeba."
31 Thus Israel dwelt in the land of
the Amorites.
32 Then Moses sent to spy out [h]Ja-
zer; and they took its villages and
drove out the Amorites who *were*
there.
33 [i]And they turned and went up
by the way to [j]Bashan. So Og king of
Bashan went out against them, he and
all his people, to battle at Edrei.
34 Then the LORD [k]said to Moses,
"Do not fear him, for I have delivered
him into your hand, with all his people
and his land; and you shall do to him
as you did to Sihon king of the Amorites, who dwelt at Heshbon."
35 So they defeated him, his sons,
and all his people, until there was no
survivor left him; and they took possession of his land.

III. The Prophecies of Balaam, 22:1—25:18

March of Israel: (4) Balaam (2 Pet. 2:15; Jude 11; Rev. 2:14)

22 THEN the children of Israel
moved, and camped in the
[l]plains of Moab on the side of the Jordan *across from* Jericho.
2 Now [m]Balak the son of Zippor
saw all that Israel had done to the Amorites.

28
a Jer. 48:45
b Num. 22:41; 33:52
29
c Jer. 48:46
d Jud. 11:24; 1 Ki. 11:33
e Isa. 15:2
f Isa. 16:2
30
g Num. 32:3,34
32
h Num. 32:1
33
i Dt. 29:7
j Dt. 3:1,3–7
34
k Dt. 3:2
CHAPTER 22
1
l Num. 33:48–49
2
m Josh. 24:9; Jud. 11:25; Mic. 6:5; Rev. 2:14
3
n Ex. 15:15
4
o Num. 25:15–18; 31:1–3
5
p Num. 31:8,16; Josh. 13:22; Neh. 13:2; 2 Pet. 2:15; Jude 11; Rev. 2:14
6
q Num. 23:7
r Num. 24:9
12
s Cp. v. 20
t Num. 23:20

3 And Moab was exceedingly
[n]afraid of the people because they
were many, and Moab was sick with
dread because of the children of Israel.
4 So Moab said to the elders of
[o]Midian, "Now this company will lick
up everything around us, as an ox
licks up the grass of the field." And
Balak the son of Zippor *was* king of
the Moabites at that time.
5 Then he sent messengers to
[1][p]Balaam the son of Beor at Pethor,
which *is* near the River* in the land of
the sons of his people,* to call him,
saying: "Look, a people has come
from Egypt. See, they cover the face of
the earth, and are settling next to me!
6 "Therefore please [q]come at
once, [r]curse this people for me, for
they *are* too mighty for me. Perhaps I
shall be able to defeat them and drive
them out of the land, for I know that he
whom you bless *is* blessed, and he
whom you curse is cursed."
7 So the elders of Moab and the
elders of Midian departed with the diviner's fee in their hand, and they
came to Balaam and spoke to him the
words of Balak.
8 And he said to them, "Lodge
here tonight, and I will bring back
word to you, as the LORD speaks to
me." So the princes of Moab stayed
with Balaam.
9 Then God came to Balaam and
said, "Who *are* these men with you?"
10 So Balaam said to God, "Balak
the son of Zippor, king of Moab, has
sent to me, *saying,*
11 'Look, a people has come out of
Egypt, and they cover the face of the
earth. Come now, curse them for me;
perhaps I shall be able to overpower
them and drive them out.'"
12 And God said to Balaam, "You
shall [s]not go with them; you shall not
curse the people, for they *are*
[t]blessed."
13 So Balaam rose in the morning
and said to the princes of Balak, "Go

* 22:5 That is, the Euphrates • Or *the people of Amau*

[1](22:5) Balaam was a typical hireling prophet, seeking only to make a market of his gift. This is the *way* of Balaam (2 Pet. 2:15) and characterizes false teachers. The *error* of Balaam (Jude 11) was that he could see only the natural morality. A holy God, he reasoned, must curse such a people as Israel. Like all false teachers he was ignorant of the higher morality of vicarious atonement, by which God could be just and yet the justifier of believing sinners (Rom. 3:26). The *doctrine* of Balaam (Rev. 2:14) refers to his teaching Balak to corrupt the people whom he could not curse (cp. Num. 31:16 with Num. 25:1–3 and Jas. 4:4). Spiritually, Balaamism in teaching never rises above natural reasonings; in practice, it is easy world-conformity. See Rev. 2:14, *note.*

back to your land, for the LORD has
refused to give me permission to go
with you."
14 And the princes of Moab rose
and went to Balak, and said, "Balaam
refuses to come with us."
15 Then Balak again sent princes,
more numerous and more honorable
than they.
16 And they came to Balaam and
said to him, "Thus says Balak the son
of Zippor: 'Please let nothing hinder
you from coming to me;
17 'for I will certainly [a]honor you
greatly, and I will do whatever you say
to me. Therefore please come, curse
this people for me.' "
18 Then Balaam answered and said
to the servants of Balak, "Though Balak were to give me his house full of
silver and gold, I [b]could not go beyond the word of the LORD my God, to
do less or more.
19 "Now therefore, please, you also
stay here tonight, that I may know
what more the LORD will say to me."
20 And God came to Balaam at
night and said to him, [c]"If the men
come to call you, rise *and* go with
them; but [d]only the word which I
speak to you—that you shall do."
21 So Balaam rose in the morning,
saddled his donkey, and went with the
princes of Moab.
22 Then God's [1]anger was aroused
because he went, and the [e]Angel of
the LORD took His stand in the way as
an adversary against him. And he was
riding on his donkey, and his two servants *were* with him.
23 Now the donkey saw the Angel
of the LORD standing in the way with
His drawn sword in His [f]hand, and
the donkey turned aside out of the
way and went into the field. So Balaam struck the donkey to turn her
back onto the road.
24 Then the Angel of the LORD stood
in a narrow path between the vineyards, *with* a wall on this side and a
wall on that side.
25 And when the donkey saw the
Angel of the LORD, she pushed herself
against the wall and crushed Balaam's
foot against the wall; so he struck her
again.
26 Then the Angel of the LORD went
further, and stood in a narrow place
where there *was* no way to turn either
to the right hand or to the left.
27 And when the donkey saw the
Angel of the LORD, she lay down under
Balaam; so Balaam's anger was
aroused, and he struck the donkey
with his staff.
28 Then the LORD [g]opened the
mouth of the donkey, and she [2]said to
Balaam, "What have I done to you,
that you have struck me these three
times?"
29 And Balaam said to the donkey,
"Because you have abused me. I wish
there were a sword in my hand, for
now I would kill you!"
30 So the donkey said to Balaam,
"*Am* I not your donkey on which you
have ridden, ever since *I became*
yours, to this day? Was I ever disposed to do this to you?" And he said,
"No."
31 Then the LORD [h]opened Balaam's eyes, and he saw the Angel of
the LORD standing in the way with His
drawn sword in His hand; and he
bowed his head and fell flat on his
face.
32 And the Angel of the LORD said
to him, "Why have you struck your
donkey these three times? Behold, I
have come out to stand against you,
because *your* way is [i]perverse before
Me.
33 "The donkey saw Me and turned
aside from Me these three times. If she
had not turned aside from Me, surely
I would also have killed you by now,
and let her live."
34 And Balaam said to the Angel of
the LORD, "I have [j]sinned, for I did not
know You stood in the way against
me. Now therefore, if it [k]displeases
You, I will turn back."
35 Then the [l]Angel of the LORD said
to Balaam, "Go with the men, but only

17
a Num. 24:11
18
b Num. 24:13
20
c v. 12
d Num. 23:5,16; 24:13
22
e Angel (of the LORD): vv. 22–35; Jud. 2:1. (Gen. 16:7; Jud. 2:1, *note*)
23
f Josh. 5:13
28
g 2 Pet. 2:16
31
h Gen. 21:19; 2 Ki. 6:17; Lk. 24:16
32
i Cp. 2 Pet. 2:15–16
34
j Cp. Num. 14:40
k i.e. *be evil in Your eyes*
35
l See Jud. 2:1, *note*

[1](22:22) In v. 12 the directive will of the LORD was made known to Balaam; in v. 20, the LORD's permissive will. The prophet was now free to go but knew the true mind of the LORD about it. The matter was wholly one between the LORD and His servant. The permission of v. 20 really constituted a testing of Balaam. He chose the path of self-will and self-advantage, and the LORD could not but gravely disapprove. The whole scene (vv. 22–35) prepared Balaam for what was to follow.

[2](22:28) Aside from the serpent in the Garden of Eden, this is the only instance in Scripture where an animal is described as speaking. God, who created the vocal organs of man and beast, used the animal, in this one case, to rebuke the weakness of the prophet and to insure that he would carry out the intention he had expressed in v. 18 (cp. v. 20).

the word that I speak to you, that you
shall speak." So Balaam went with the
princes of Balak.
36 Now when Balak heard that Balaam was coming, he went out to meet
him at the city of Moab, [a]which *is* on
the border at the Arnon, the boundary
of the territory.
37 Then Balak said to Balaam, "Did
I not earnestly send to you, calling for
you? Why did you not come to me?
Am I not able to honor you?"
38 And Balaam said to Balak,
"Look, I have come to you! Now, have
I any power at all to say anything? The
[b]word that God puts in my mouth,
that I must [c]speak."
39 So Balaam went with Balak, and
they came to [d]Kirjath Huzoth.
40 Then Balak offered oxen and
sheep, and he sent *some* to Balaam
and to the princes who *were* with him.
41 So it was, the next day, that Balak took Balaam and brought him up
to the [e]high places of Baal, that from
there he might observe the [1]extent of
the people.

Balaam blesses Israel from high places of Baal

23 THEN Balaam said to Balak,
"Build [f]seven altars for me
here, and prepare for me here seven
bulls and seven rams."
2 And Balak did just as Balaam
had spoken, and Balak and Balaam
offered a bull and a ram on *each* altar.
3 Then Balaam said to Balak,
"Stand by your burnt offering, and I
will go; perhaps the LORD will come to
meet me, and whatever He shows me
I will tell you." So he went to a desolate height.
4 And God met Balaam, and he
said to Him, "I have prepared the
seven altars, and I have offered on
each altar a bull and a ram."
5 Then the LORD [g]put a [b]word in
Balaam's mouth, and said, "Return to
Balak, and thus you shall speak."

36 *a* Num. 21:13
38 *b Inspiration:* vv. 38; 23:5, 12–16; Dt. 4:2. (Ex. 4:15; 2 Tim. 3:16, *note*) *c* Num. 23:26; 24:13; 1 Ki. 22:14; 2 Chr. 18:13
39 *d* Meaning *a city of streets*
41 *e* Num. 21:28
CHAPTER 23
1 *f* vv. 14,30; cp. 1 Chr. 15:26
5 *g* Num. 22:20,38; Dt. 18:18
7 *h* Num. 22:5; Dt. 23:4 *i* Num. 22:6
8 *j* Num. 22:12
9 *k* Dt. 32:8; 33:28
10 *l* Gen. 28:14
12 *m* v. 5
13 *n* Better you *see only the outer part of them, and do not see them all*

6 So he returned to him, and there
he was, standing by his burnt offering,
he and all the princes of Moab.
7 And he took up his oracle and
said:

"Balak the king of Moab has
[2]brought me from [h]Aram,
From the mountains of the
east.
[i]'Come, curse Jacob for me,
And come, denounce Israel!'

8 "How shall I curse whom God
has not [j]cursed?
And how shall I denounce
whom the LORD has not
denounced?
9 For from the top of the rocks I
see him,
And from the hills I behold
him;
There! A people dwelling
[k]alone,
Not reckoning itself among the
nations.

10 "Who can count the [l]dust* of
Jacob,
Or number one-fourth of
Israel?
Let me die the death of the
righteous,
And let my end be like his!"

11 Then Balak said to Balaam,
"What have you done to me? I took
you to curse my enemies, and look,
you have blessed *them* bountifully!"
12 So he answered and said, "Must
I not take heed to speak what the LORD
has [m]put in my mouth?"

Balaam: the prophecy from Pisgah: the justification and power of Israel

13 Then Balak said to him, "Please
come with me to another place from
which you may see them; [n]you shall
see only the outer part of them, and

* 23:10 Or *dust cloud*

[1](22:41) The expression, "the extent of the people," refers to the end of the encampment, "one-fourth of Israel" (Num. 23:10). Balak's thought was not at all to permit Balaam to see the whole of the Hebrew host. In bringing Balaam to Pisgah, Balak corrects what, evidently, he thought was a blunder (Num. 23:13–14). But when the hireling sees the whole camp he must utter a grander word than before, "He has not observed iniquity in Jacob," and that with the nation in full view. Here is a superb illustration of the truth of Rom. 4:5–8.

[2](23:7) In the prophecies of Balaam, God testifies *on behalf of* His people rather than *to* them. It is the divine testimony to their standing as a redeemed people in view of the serpent "lifted up", and of the water from the struck rock (Num. 21:5–9; 20:11). Their state was morally bad, but this was a matter concerning the discipline of God, not His judgment. Through Christ "lifted up" (Jn. 3:14–15) the Christian's standing is eternally secure and perfect, though his state may require the Father's discipline (1 Cor. 11:30–32; Heb. 12:4–10); meantime, against all enemies God is "for us" (Rom. 8:31).

shall not see them all; curse them for
me from there."
14 So he brought him to the field of
Zophim, to the top of Pisgah, and built
seven altars, and offered a bull and a
ram on *each* altar.
15 And he said to Balak, "Stand
here by your burnt offering while I
meet* *the* LORD over there."
16 Then the LORD met Balaam, and
put a word in his mouth, and said, "Go
back to Balak, and thus you shall
speak."
17 So he came to him, and there he
was, standing by his burnt offering,
and the princes of Moab were with
him. And Balak said to him, "What
has the LORD spoken?"
18 Then he took up his oracle and
said:

"Rise up, Balak, and hear!
Listen to me, son of Zippor!

19 "God *is* not a man, that He
should lie,
Nor a son of man, that He
should [a]repent.
Has He [b]said, and will He not
do?
Or has He spoken, and will He
not make it good?
20 Behold, I have received *a*
command to bless;
He has blessed, and I cannot
reverse it.

21 "He has not observed iniquity in
Jacob,
Nor has He seen wickedness in
Israel.
The LORD his God *is* [c]with him,
And the shout of a King *is*
among them.
22 God brings them out of Egypt;
He has strength like a wild ox.

23 "For *there is* no sorcery
[d]against Jacob,
Nor any divination [d]against
Israel.
It now must be said of Jacob
And of Israel, 'Oh, [e]what God
has done!'
24 Look, a people rises like a
[f]lioness,
And lifts itself up like a lion;
It shall not lie down until it
devours the prey,
And drinks the blood of the
slain."

25 Then Balak said to Balaam,
"Neither curse them at all, nor bless
them at all!"
26 So Balaam answered and said to
Balak, "Did I not tell you, saying, 'All
that the LORD speaks, that I must do'?"

Balaam: the prophecy from Peor:
(1) the beauty and order of Israel

27 Then Balak said to Balaam,
"Please come, I will take you to another place; perhaps it will please God
that you may curse them for me from
there."
28 So Balak took Balaam to the top
of Peor, that [g]overlooks the wasteland.*
29 Then Balaam said to Balak,
"Build for me here seven altars, and
prepare for me here seven bulls and
seven rams."
30 And Balak did as Balaam had
said, and offered a bull and a ram on
every altar.

The prophecy from Peor (continued)

24 NOW when Balaam saw that it
pleased the LORD to bless Israel,
he did not go as at other times, to seek
to use [h]sorcery, but he set his face
toward the wilderness.
2 And Balaam raised his eyes, and
saw Israel [i]encamped according to
their tribes; and [j]the [k]Spirit of God
came upon him.
3 [l]Then he took up his oracle and
said:

"The utterance of Balaam the
son of Beor,
The utterance of the man
whose eyes are opened,
4 The utterance of him who
hears the words of God,
Who sees the vision of the
Almighty,
Who [m]falls down, with eyes
wide open:

5 "How lovely are your tents, O
Jacob!
Your dwellings, O Israel!
6 Like valleys that stretch out,
Like gardens by the riverside,
Like aloes planted by the LORD,
Like cedars beside the waters.
7 He shall pour water from his
buckets,
And his seed *shall be* [n]in
many waters.

"His king shall be higher than
[o]Agag,
And his [p]kingdom shall be
exalted.

19
a See Zech. 8:14, *note*
b Num. 11:23; 1 Ki. 8:56

21
c v. 23; Ex. 29:45–46

23
d Or *in*
e Ps. 31:19; 44:1

24
f Cp. Gen. 49:8–12

28
g Num. 21:20

CHAPTER 24

1
h Or *to the meeting of sorceries*

2
i Num. 2:2, 34
j Num. 11:25; 1 Sam. 10:10; 19:20,23; 2 Chr. 15:1
k *Holy Spirit* (OT): v. 2; Num. 27:18. (Gen. 1:2; Zech. 12:10)

3
l Num. 23:7, 18

4
m i.e. *prostrated by the prophetic impulse.* Cp. 1 Sam. 19:24; Ezek. 1:28; Dan. 8:18; 10:15–16; 2 Cor. 12:2–4; Rev. 1:10, 17

7
n Cp. Jer. 51:13; Rev. 17:1, 15
o King of the Amalekites, ancestor of the Agag of 1 Sam. 15:9
p 2 Sam. 5:12; 1 Chr. 14:2

***23:15** Following Masoretic Text, Targum, and Vulgate; Syriac reads *call;* Septuagint reads *go and ask God.* **23:28** Hebrew *Jeshimon*

8 "God brings him out of Egypt;
He has strength like a wild ox;
He shall [a]consume the nations,
his enemies;
He shall [b]break their bones
And pierce *them* with his
arrows.
9 'He bows down, he lies down
as a lion;
And as a lion, who shall rouse
him?'*

[c]"Blessed *is* he who blesses you,
And cursed *is* he who curses
you."

10 Then Balak's anger was aroused
against Balaam, and he struck his
hands together; and Balak said to Balaam, "I called you to curse my enemies, and look, you have bountifully
blessed *them* these three times!
11 "Now therefore, flee to your
place. [d]I said I would greatly honor
you, but in fact, the LORD has kept you
back from honor."
12 So Balaam said to Balak, "Did I
not also speak to your messengers
whom you sent to me, saying,
13 'If Balak were to give me his
house full of silver and gold, I could
not go beyond the word of the LORD, to
do good or bad of my own will. What
the LORD says, that I must speak'?
14 "And now, indeed, I am going to
my people. Come, I will advise you
what this people will do to your people
in the [e]latter days."

Balaam: the prophecy from Peor:
(2) the Messianic kingdom

15 So he took up his oracle and
said:

"The utterance of Balaam the
son of Beor,
And the utterance of the man
whose eyes are opened;
16 The utterance of him who
hears the words of God,
And has the knowledge of the
Most High,
Who sees the vision of the
Almighty,
Who falls down, with eyes
wide open:

17 "I see Him, but not now;
I behold Him, but not near;
A Star shall come out of
Jacob;
A [f]Scepter shall rise out of
Israel,
And batter the brow of Moab,
And destroy all the sons of
tumult.*

18 "And Edom shall be a
possession;
Seir also, his enemies, shall be
a possession,
While Israel does valiantly.
19 Out of Jacob One shall have
[g]dominion,
And destroy the remains of the
city."

20 Then he looked on Amalek, and
he took up his oracle and said:

"Amalek *was* first among the
[h]nations,
But *shall be* last until he
perishes."

21 Then he looked on the Kenites,
and he took up his oracle and said:

"Firm is your dwelling place,
And your nest is set in the
rock;
22 Nevertheless Kain shall be
burned.
How long until Asshur carries
you away captive?"

23 Then he took up his oracle and
said:

"Alas! Who shall live when God
does this?
24 But ships *shall come* from the
coasts of [i]Cyprus,*
And they shall afflict Asshur
and afflict Eber,
And so shall *Amalek*,* until he
perishes."

25 So Balaam rose and departed
and [j]returned to his place; Balak also
went his way.

The doctrine of Balaam (Num. 31:16;
Jas. 4:4; Rev. 2:14)

25 NOW Israel remained in Acacia Grove,* and the [k]people
began to commit harlotry with the
women of Moab.
2 They invited the people to the
sacrifices of their gods, and the [l]peo-
ple ate and [m]bowed down to their
gods.
3 So Israel was joined to [n]Baal of
Peor, and the anger of the LORD was
aroused against Israel.
4 Then the LORD said to Moses,
"Take all the leaders of the people and
hang the offenders before the LORD,

8
a Num. 14:9; 23:24
b Ps. 2:9
9
c Gen. 12:3; 27:29
11
d Num. 22:17,37
14
e Gen. 49:1; Dt. 4:30
17
f Kingdom (OT): v. 17; Dt. 30:1. (Gen. 1:26; Zech. 12:8, *note*). See Gen. 49:10, *note*
19
g Amos 9:11–12
20
h Or *the first of the nations that warred against Israel.* Ex. 17:8
24
i Gen. 10:4; Dan. 11:30
25
j v. 14; 31:8
CHAPTER 25
1
k Num. 31:16; 1 Cor. 10:8
2
l Ex. 34:15–16; cp. 1 Cor. 10:20
m Ex. 20:5
3
n Num. 23:28; Ps. 106:28–29; Hos. 9:10

*
24:9 Genesis 49:9 24:17 Hebrew *Sheth* (compare Jeremiah 48:45) 24:24 Hebrew *Kittim*
• Literally *he* or *that one* 25:1 Hebrew *Shittim*

out in the sun, that the fierce anger of the LORD may turn away from Israel."

5 So Moses said to the judges of Israel, "Every one of you [a]kill his men who were joined to Baal of Peor."

6 And indeed, one of the children of Israel came and presented to his brethren a Midianite woman in the sight of Moses and in the sight of all the congregation of the children of Israel, who *were* weeping at the door of the tabernacle of meeting.

7 Now when Phinehas the son of Eleazar, the son of Aaron the priest, saw *it*, he rose from among the congregation and took a javelin in his hand;

8 and he went after the man of Israel into the tent and thrust both of them through, the man of Israel, and the woman through her body. [b]So the plague was [c]stopped among the children of Israel.

9 And those who [d]died in the plague were twenty-four thousand.

10 Then the LORD spoke to Moses, saying:

11 "Phinehas the son of Eleazar, the son of Aaron the priest, has turned back My wrath from the children of Israel, because he was zealous with My zeal among them, so that I did not consume the children of Israel in My [e]zeal.

12 "Therefore say, [f]'Behold, I give to him My [g]covenant of peace;

13 'and it shall be to him and his [h]descendants after him a covenant of an [i]everlasting priesthood, because he was zealous for his God, and made [j]atonement for the children of Israel.'"

14 Now the name of the Israelite who was killed, who was killed with the Midianite woman, *was* Zimri the son of Salu, a leader of a father's house among the Simeonites.

15 And the name of the Midianite woman who was killed *was* Cozbi the daughter of [k]Zur; he *was* head of the people of a father's house in Midian.

16 Then the LORD spoke to Moses, saying:

17 [l]"Harass the Midianites, and attack them;

18 "for they harassed you with their schemes by which they seduced you in the matter of Peor and in the matter of Cozbi, the daughter of a leader of Midian, their sister, who was killed in the day of the plague because of Peor."

5
a Cp. Ex. 32:27
8
b Ps. 106:30
c Num. 16:48
9
d Dt. 4:3; see 1 Cor. 10:8, *note*
11
e Ex. 20:5; Dt. 32:16, 21; 1 Ki. 14:22
12
f Mal. 2:4; 3:1
g Isa. 54:10; Ezek. 34:25; Mal. 2:5
13
h 1 Chr. 6:4–15
i Ex. 40:15
j See Ex. 29:33, *note*
15
k Num. 31:8
17
l Num. 31:1–3
CHAPTER 26
1
m Num. 25:9
2
n Num. 1:2; 14:29
4
o Num. 1:1
5
p Gen. 46:8; Ex. 6:14; 1 Chr. 5:1–3
7
q Cp. Num. 1:20–21
10
r Num. 16:32–35
s Num. 16:36–40; cp. 1 Cor. 10:6; 2 Pet. 2:6
11
t Ex. 6:24; 1 Chr. 6:22–23
12
u Gen. 46:10; 1 Chr. 4:24

IV. Instructions and Preparations for Entering the Promised Land, 26:1—36:13

Moses numbers new generation of men able to go to war (vv. 64–65)

26 AND it came to pass, after the [m]plague, that the LORD spoke to Moses and Eleazar the son of Aaron the priest, saying:

2 "Take a [n]census of all the congregation of the children of Israel from twenty years old and above, by their fathers' houses, all who are able to go to war in Israel."

3 So Moses and Eleazar the priest spoke with them in the plains of Moab by the Jordan, *across from* Jericho, saying:

4 "*Take a census of the people* from twenty years old and above, just as the LORD [o]commanded Moses and the children of Israel who came out of the land of Egypt."

5 Reuben *was* the firstborn of Israel. The children of [p]Reuben *were: of* Hanoch, the family of the Hanochites; *of* Pallu, the family of the Palluites;

6 *of* Hezron, the family of the Hezronites; *of* Carmi, the family of the Carmites.

7 These *are* the families of the Reubenites: those who were numbered of them were [q]forty-three thousand seven hundred and thirty.

8 And the son of Pallu *was* Eliab.

9 The sons of Eliab *were* Nemuel, Dathan, and Abiram. These *are* the Dathan and Abiram, representatives of the congregation, who contended against Moses and Aaron in the company of Korah, when they contended against the LORD;

10 [r]and the earth opened its mouth and swallowed them up together with Korah when that company died, when the fire devoured two hundred and fifty men; [s]and they became a sign.

11 Nevertheless the children of [t]Korah did not die.

12 The sons of [u]Simeon according to their families *were: of* Nemuel,* the family of the Nemuelites; *of* Jamin, the family of the Jaminites; *of* Jachin,* the family of the Jachinites;

13 *of* Zerah,* the family of the Zarhites; *of* Shaul, the family of the Shaulites.

14 These *are* the families of the

*
26:12 Spelled *Jemuel* in Genesis 46:10 and Exodus 6:15 • Called *Jarib* in 1 Chronicles 4:24
26:13 Called *Zohar* in Genesis 46:10

Simeonites: [a]twenty-two thousand two hundred.

15 The sons of [b]Gad according to their families *were: of* Zephon,* the family of the Zephonites; *of* Haggi, the family of the Haggites; *of* Shuni, the family of the Shunites;

16 *of* Ozni,* the family of the Oznites; *of* Eri, the family of the Erites;

17 *of* Arod,* the family of the Arodites; *of* Areli, the family of the Arelites.

18 These *are* the families of the sons of Gad according to those who were numbered of them: forty thousand five hundred.

19 The sons of [c]Judah *were* Er and Onan; and Er and Onan died in the land of Canaan.

20 And the sons of Judah according to their families were: *of* Shelah, the family of the Shelanites; *of* Perez, the family of the Parzites; *of* Zerah, the family of the Zarhites.

21 And the sons of Perez were: *of* Hezron, the family of the Hezronites; *of* Hamul, the family of the Hamulites.

22 These *are* the families of Judah according to those who were numbered of them: [d]seventy-six thousand five hundred.

23 The sons of [e]Issachar according to their families *were: of* Tola, the family of the Tolaites; of Puah,* the family of the Punites;*

24 of Jashub, the family of the Jashubites; of Shimron, the family of the Shimronites.

25 These *are* the families of Issachar according to those who were numbered of them: [f]sixty-four thousand three hundred.

26 The sons of [g]Zebulun according to their families *were:* of Sered, the family of the Sardites; of Elon, the family of the Elonites; of Jahleel, the family of the Jahleelites.

27 These *are* the families of the Zebulunites according to those who were numbered of them: [h]sixty thousand five hundred.

28 The sons of [i]Joseph according to their families, by Manasseh and Ephraim, *were:*

29 The sons of [j]Manasseh: of Machir, the family of the Machirites; and Machir begot Gilead; of Gilead, the family of the Gileadites.

30 These *are* the sons of Gilead: *of* Jeezer,* the family of the Jeezerites; of Helek, the family of the Helekites;

31 *of* Asriel, the family of the Asrielites; *of* Shechem, the family of the Shechemites;

14 *a* Cp. Num. 1:22–23
15 *b* Gen. 46:16; cp. Num. 1:24–25
19 *c* Gen. 38:3–5; 46:12; 1 Chr. 2:3
22 *d* Cp. Num. 1:26–27
23 *e* Gen. 46:13; 1 Chr. 7:1
25 *f* Cp. Num. 1:28–29
26 *g* Gen. 46:14
27 *h* Cp. Num. 1:30–31
28 *i* Gen. 46:20
29 *j* 1 Chr. 7:14–20
33 *k* Num. 27:1
34 *l* Cp. Num. 1:34–35
37 *m* Cp. Num. 1:32–33
38 *n* Gen. 46:21; 1 Chr. 7:6; 8:1–2
41 *o* Cp. Num. 1:36–37; 1 Chr. 7:9
42 *p* Gen. 46:23
43 *q* Cp. Num. 1:38–39

32 *of* Shemida, the family of the Shemidaites; *of* Hepher, the family of the Hepherites.

33 Now Zelophehad the son of Hepher had no sons, but [k]daughters; and the names of the daughters of Zelophehad *were* Mahlah, Noah, Hoglah, Milcah, and Tirzah.

34 These *are* the families of Manasseh; and those who were numbered of them *were* [l]fifty-two thousand seven hundred.

35 These *are* the sons of Ephraim according to their families: of Shuthelah, the family of the Shuthalhites; of Becher,* the family of the Bachrites; of Tahan, the family of the Tahanites.

36 And these *are* the sons of Shuthelah: of Eran, the family of the Eranites.

37 These *are* the families of the sons of Ephraim according to those who were numbered of them: [m]thirty-two thousand five hundred. These *are* the sons of Joseph according to their families.

38 The sons of [n]Benjamin according to their families were: of Bela, the family of the Belaites; of Ashbel, the family of the Ashbelites; of Ahiram, the family of the Ahiramites;

39 of Shupham,* the family of the Shuphamites; of Hupham,* the family of the Huphamites.

40 And the sons of Bela were Ard* and Naaman: *of Ard,* the family of the Ardites; of Naaman, the family of the Naamites.

41 These *are* the sons of Benjamin according to their families; and those who were numbered of them *were* [o]forty-five thousand six hundred.

42 These *are* the sons of [p]Dan according to their families: of Shuham,* the family of the Shuhamites. These *are* the families of Dan according to their families.

43 All the families of the Shuhamites, according to those who were numbered of them, *were* [q]sixty-four thousand four hundred.

*

26:15 Called *Ziphion* in Genesis 46:16 **26:16** Called *Ezbon* in Genesis 46:16 **26:17** Spelled *Arodi* in Samaritan Pentateuch, Syriac, and Genesis 46:16 **26:23** Hebrew *Puvah* (compare Genesis 46:13 and 1 Chronicles 7:1); Samaritan Pentateuch, Septuagint, Syriac, and Vulgate read *Puah.* • Samaritan Pentateuch, Septuagint, Syriac, and Vulgate read *Puaites.* **26:30** Called *Abiezer* in Joshua 17:2 **26:35** Called *Bered* in 1 Chronicles 7:20 **26:39** Masoretic Text reads *Shephupham,* spelled *Shephuphan* in 1 Chronicles 8:5. • Called *Huppim* in Genesis 46:21 **26:40** Called *Addar* in 1 Chronicles 8:3 **26:42** Called *Hushim* in Genesis 46:23

44 The sons of [a]Asher according to their families *were:* of Jimna, the family of the Jimnites; of Jesui, the family of the Jesuites; of Beriah, the family of the Beriites.

45 Of the sons of Beriah: of Heber, the family of the Heberites; of Malchiel, the family of the Malchielites.

46 And the name of the daughter of Asher *was* Serah.

47 These *are* the families of the sons of Asher according to those who were numbered of them: [b]fifty-three thousand four hundred.

48 The sons of [c]Naphtali according to their families *were:* of Jahzeel,* the family of the Jahzeelites; of Guni, the family of the Gunites;

49 of Jezer, the family of the Jezerites; of Shillem, the family of the Shillemites.

50 These *are* the families of Naphtali according to their families; and those who were numbered of them *were* [d]forty-five thousand four hundred.

51 These *are* those who were [e]numbered of the children of [f]Israel: [1]six hundred and one thousand seven hundred and thirty.

52 Then the LORD spoke to Moses, saying:

53 [g]"To these the land shall be [h]divided as an inheritance, according to the number of names.

54 "To a [h]large *tribe* you shall give a larger inheritance, and to a small *tribe* you shall give a smaller inheritance. Each shall be given its inheritance according to those who were numbered of them.

55 "But the land shall be divided by lot; they shall inherit according to the names of the tribes of their fathers.

56 "According to the lot their inheritance shall be divided between the larger and the smaller."

57 And these *are* those who were numbered of the [i]Levites according to their families: of Gershon, the family of the Gershonites; of Kohath, the family of the Kohathites; of Merari, the family of the Merarites.

58 These *are* the families of the Levites: the family of the Libnites, the family of the Hebronites, the family of the Mahlites, the family of the Mushites, and the family of the Korathites. And Kohath begot Amram.

59 The name of Amram's wife *was* [j]Jochebed the daughter of Levi, who was born to Levi in Egypt; and to Amram she bore Aaron and Moses and their sister Miriam.

60 To Aaron were born [k]Nadab and Abihu, Eleazar and Ithamar.

61 And Nadab and Abihu died when they offered profane fire before the LORD.

62 Now those who were numbered of them were [l]twenty-three thousand, every male from a month old and above; for they were not numbered among the other children of Israel, because there was no [m]inheritance given to them among the children of Israel.

63 These *are* those who were numbered by Moses and Eleazar the priest, who numbered the children of Israel in the plains of Moab by the Jordan, *across from* Jericho.

64 But among these there was not a man of those who were numbered by Moses and Aaron the priest when they numbered the children of Israel in the [n]Wilderness of Sinai.

65 For the LORD had said of them, [o]"They shall surely die in the wilderness." So there was not left a man of them, [p]except Caleb the son of Jephunneh and Joshua the son of Nun.

Law of inheritance

27 THEN came the [q]daughters of Zelophehad the son of Hepher, the son of Gilead, the son of Machir, the son of Manasseh, from the families of Manasseh the son of Joseph; and these *were* the names of his daughters: Mahlah, Noah, Hoglah, Milcah, and Tirzah.

2 And they stood before Moses, before Eleazar the priest, and before the leaders and all the congregation, *by* the doorway of the tabernacle of meeting, saying:

3 "Our father died in the wilderness; but he was not in the company of those who gathered together against the LORD, in company with Korah, but he died in his own [r]sin; and he had no sons.

4 "Why should the name of our father be [s]removed from among his family because he had no son? [t]Give us a possession among our father's brothers."

44
a Gen. 46:17; 1 Chr. 7:30
47
b Cp. Num. 1:40–41
48
c Gen. 46:24; 1 Chr. 7:13
50
d Cp. Num. 1:42–43
51
e Cp. Ex. 12:37; 38:26; Num. 1:46; 11:21
f See Num. 1:46, *note*
53
g Josh. 11:23; 14:1
h Num. 33:54
57
i Gen. 46:11; Num. 3:15; 1 Chr. 6:1
59
j Ex. 6:20
60
k Lev. 10:1–2; Num. 3:4; 1 Chr. 24:2
62
l Cp. Num. 3:15–39; 1 Chr. 6:2–53
m Num. 18:23–24
64
n Num. 1:1–46
65
o Num. 14:28–29; 1 Cor. 10:5
p Num. 14:30
CHAPTER 27
1
q Num. 26:33; 36:1–12
3
r Num. 26:64–65
4
s Dt. 25:6
t vv. 7–11

* 26:48 Spelled *Jahziel* in 1 Chronicles 7:13

[1](26:51) Compare Num. 1:46. Of the 603,550 mentioned there, all the adults except Caleb and Joshua perished in the wilderness. Yet the figure here, 601,730, is only 1820 less.

5 So Moses [a]brought their case before the LORD.

6 And the LORD spoke to Moses, saying:

7 "The daughters of Zelophehad speak *what is* [b]right; you shall surely give them a possession of inheritance among their father's brothers, and cause the inheritance of their father to pass to them.

8 "And you shall speak to the children of Israel, saying: 'If a man dies and has no son, then you shall cause his inheritance to pass to his daughter.

9 'If he has no daughter, then you shall give his inheritance to his brothers.

10 'If he has no brothers, then you shall give his inheritance to his father's brothers.

11 'And if his father has no brothers, then you shall give his inheritance to the relative closest to him in his family, and he shall possess it.'" And it shall be to the children of Israel a statute of judgment, just as the LORD commanded Moses.

Moses to prepare for death

12 Now the LORD said to Moses: [c]"Go up into this Mount Abarim, and see the land which I have given to the children of Israel.

13 "And when you have seen it, you also [d]shall be gathered to your people, as Aaron your brother was gathered.

14 "For in the Wilderness of Zin, during the strife of the congregation, you [e]rebelled against My command to hallow Me at the waters before their eyes." (These *are* the waters of Meribah, at Kadesh in the Wilderness of Zin.)

Joshua to succeed Moses

15 Then Moses spoke to the LORD, [f]saying:

16 "Let the LORD, the [g]God of the spirits of all flesh, set a man over the congregation,

17 "who may go out before them and go in before them, who may lead them out and bring them in, that the congregation of the LORD may not be like [h]sheep which have no shepherd."

18 And the LORD said to Moses: "Take Joshua the son of Nun with you, a man in whom *is* the [i]Spirit, and lay your hand on him;

19 "set him before Eleazar the priest and before all the congregation, and [j]inaugurate him in their sight.

20 "And you shall give *some* of your authority to him, that all the congregation of the children of Israel may be [k]obedient.

21 "He shall stand before Eleazar the priest, who shall inquire before the LORD for him [l]by the judgment of the Urim. [m]At his word they shall go out, and at his word they shall come in, he and all the children of Israel with him—all the congregation."

22 So Moses did as the LORD commanded him. He took Joshua and set him before Eleazar the priest and before all the congregation.

23 And he laid his hands on him and [n]inaugurated him, just as the LORD commanded by the hand of Moses.

The order of the offerings
(vv. 1,9,11,16,17,26)

28 NOW the LORD spoke to Moses, saying,

2 "Command the children of Israel, and say to them, 'My offering, My food for My offerings made by fire as a sweet [o]aroma to Me, you shall be careful to offer to Me at their appointed time.'

3 "And you shall say to them, 'This *is* the offering made by fire which you shall offer to the LORD: two male lambs in their first year without blemish, day by day, as a [p]regular burnt offering.

4 'The one lamb you shall offer in the morning, the other lamb you shall offer in the [1]evening,

5 'and one-tenth of an [q]ephah of fine flour as a grain offering mixed with one-fourth of a [q]hin of pressed oil.

6 '*It is* a regular burnt offering which was ordained at Mount Sinai for a sweet aroma, an offering made by fire to the LORD.

7 'And its drink offering *shall be* one-fourth of a [q]hin for each lamb; in a holy *place* you shall pour out the drink to the LORD as an offering.

5 *a* Ex. 18:13–26
7 *b* Josh. 17:3–7
12 *c* Dt. 32:48–52; 34:1–4
13 *d* Num. 20:12,24, 28; 31:2; Dt. 10:6; 34:5–6
14 *e* Dt. 1:37; 32:51; Ps. 106:33
15 *f* *Bible prayers* (OT): vv. 15–17; Dt. 3:23. (Gen. 15:2; Hab. 3:1)
16 *g* Num. 16:22; Heb. 12:9
17 *h* 1 Ki. 22:17; Zech. 10:2; Mt. 9:36; Mk. 6:34
18 *i* *Holy Spirit* (OT): v. 18; Dt. 34:9. (Gen. 1:2; Zech. 12:10)
19 *j* Dt. 3:28; 31:7
20 *k* Josh. 1:16–18
21 *l* See Ex. 28:30, *note*
m Jud. 20:18,23,26
23 *n* Dt. 31:7–8
CHAPTER 28
2 *o* Or *an aroma of satisfaction.* See Lev. 1:9, *note*
3 *p* Ex. 29:38–42

28:5 *q* See Weights and Measures (OT), 2 Chr. 2:10, *note*

[1](28:4) Literally "between the two evenings," taken by the Jews to mean after noon and until nightfall, the time during which the second of the two daily sacrifices was offered. According to Josephus the Passover lamb was slain between the ninth and eleventh hours, 3–5 p.m. (cp. Ex. 12:6, "at twilight"). Thus the death of our Lord at the ninth hour (Mt. 27:45) agrees with the time of the offering of the Passover lamb as well as the second daily sacrifice.

8 'The other lamb you shall offer
in the evening; as the morning grain
offering and its drink offering, you
shall offer *it* as an offering made by
fire, a sweet aroma to the LORD.
9 'And on the Sabbath day two
lambs in their first year, without blemish, and two-tenths *of an ephah* of fine
flour as a grain offering, mixed with
oil, with its drink offering—
10 '*this is* the burnt offering for every Sabbath, besides the regular burnt
offering with its drink offering.
11 'At the [a]beginnings of your
months you shall present a burnt offering to the LORD: two young bulls,
one ram, and seven lambs in their first
year, without blemish;
12 'three-tenths *of an ephah* of fine
flour as a [b]grain offering, mixed with
oil, for each bull; two-tenths *of an
ephah* of fine flour as a grain offering,
mixed with oil, for the one ram;
13 'and one-tenth *of an ephah* of
fine flour, mixed with oil, as a grain
offering for each lamb, as a burnt offering of sweet aroma, an offering
made by fire to the LORD.
14 'Their drink offering shall be
half a [c]hin of wine for a bull, one-third
of a hin for a ram, and one-fourth of a
hin for a lamb; this *is* the burnt offering for each month throughout the
months of the year.
15 'Also one kid of the goats as a sin
offering to the LORD shall be offered,
besides the regular burnt offering and
its drink offering.
16 'On the fourteenth day of the
[d]first month *is* the [e]Passover of the
LORD.
17 'And on the fifteenth day of this
month *is* the feast; [f]unleavened bread
shall be eaten for seven days.
18 'On the first day *you shall have* a
holy convocation. You shall do no customary work.
19 'And you shall present an offering made by fire as a burnt offering to
the LORD: two young bulls, one ram,
and seven lambs in their first year. Be
sure they are without blemish.
20 'Their grain offering shall be of
fine flour mixed with oil: three-tenths
of an ephah you shall offer for a bull,
and two-tenths for a ram;
21 'you shall offer one-tenth *of an
ephah* for each of the seven lambs;
22 'also one goat *as* a sin offering,
to make [g]atonement for you.
23 'You shall offer these besides the
burnt offering of the morning, which
is for a regular burnt offering.

11
a Num. 10:10; Ezek. 46:6–7
12
b Num. 15:4–12
14
c See Weights and Measures (OT), 2 Chr. 2:10, *note*
16
d See Lev. 23:2, *note*
e Ex. 12:3–18; Lev. 23:5; Num. 9:2–5; Dt. 16:1; Ezek. 45:21
17
f Leaven: v. 17; Dt. 16:3. (Gen. 19:3; Mt. 13:33, *note*)
22
g See Ex. 29:33, *note*
25
h Ex. 12:16; 13:6; Lev. 23:8
26
i Ex. 23:16; 34:22; Lev. 23:10–21; Dt. 16:10; Acts 2:1
CHAPTER 29
1
j See Lev. 23:24, *note;* cp. Neh. 8:1–12
6
k Num. 28:11–15
l Num. 28:3
7
m Lev. 16:29–34; 23:26–32
n Cp. Isa. 58:3–7

24 'In this manner you shall offer
the food of the offering made by fire
daily for seven days, as a sweet aroma
to the LORD; it shall be offered besides
the regular burnt offering and its
drink offering.
25 'And [h]on the seventh day you
shall have a holy convocation. You
shall do no customary work.
26 'Also [i]on the day of the firstfruits, when you bring a new grain offering to the LORD at your *Feast of*
Weeks, you shall have a holy convocation. You shall do no customary
work.
27 'You shall present a burnt offering as a sweet aroma to the LORD: two
young bulls, one ram, and seven
lambs in their first year,
28 'with their grain offering of fine
flour mixed with oil: three-tenths *of an
ephah* for each bull, two-tenths for the
one ram,
29 'and one-tenth for each of the
seven lambs;
30 '*also* one kid of the goats, to
make [g]atonement for you.
31 'Be sure they are without blemish. You shall present *them* with their
drink offerings, besides the regular
burnt offering with its grain offering.

Order of the offerings (vv. 1,7,12)

29 'AND in the [d]seventh month,
on the first *day* of the month,
you shall have a holy convocation.
You shall do no customary work. [j]For
you it is a day of blowing the trumpets.
2 'You shall offer a burnt offering
as a sweet aroma to the LORD: one
young bull, one ram, *and* seven lambs
in their first year, without blemish.
3 'Their grain offering *shall be*
fine flour mixed with oil: three-tenths
of an ephah for the bull, two-tenths for
the ram,
4 'and one-tenth for each of the
seven lambs;
5 'also one kid of the goats *as* a sin
offering, to make [g]atonement for you;
6 'besides the burnt offering with
its grain offering for the [k]New Moon,
the [l]regular burnt offering with its
grain offering, and their drink offerings, according to their ordinance, as
a sweet aroma, an offering made by
fire to the LORD.
7 'On the [m]tenth *day* of this [d]sev-
enth month you shall have a holy convocation. You shall [n]afflict your
souls; you shall not do any work.
8 'You shall present a burnt offering to the LORD *as* a sweet aroma: one

young bull, one ram, *and* seven lambs in their first year. Be sure they are without blemish.

9 'Their grain offering *shall be of* fine flour mixed with oil: three-tenths *of an ephah* for the bull, two-tenths for the one ram,

10 'and one-tenth for each of the seven lambs;

11 'also one kid of the goats *as* a [a]sin offering, besides the sin offering for [b]atonement, the regular burnt offering with its grain offering, and their drink offerings.

12 [c]'On the fifteenth day of the [d]seventh month you shall have a holy convocation. You shall do no customary work, and you shall keep a feast to the LORD seven days.

13 [e]'You shall present a burnt offering, an offering made by fire as a sweet aroma to the LORD: thirteen young bulls, two rams, *and* fourteen lambs in their first year. They shall be without blemish.

14 'Their grain offering *shall be of* fine flour mixed with oil: three-tenths *of an ephah* for each of the thirteen bulls, two-tenths for each of the two rams,

15 'and one-tenth for each of the fourteen lambs;

16 'also one kid of the goats *as* a sin offering, besides the regular burnt offering, its grain offering, and its drink offering.

17 'On the [f]second day *present* twelve young bulls, two rams, fourteen lambs in their first year without blemish,

18 'and their grain offering and their drink offerings for the bulls, for the rams, and for the lambs, by their number, [g]according to the ordinance;

19 'also one kid of the goats *as* a sin offering, besides the regular burnt offering with its grain offering, and their drink offerings.

20 'On the third day *present* eleven bulls, two rams, fourteen lambs in their first year without blemish,

21 'and their grain offering and their drink offerings for the bulls, for the rams, and for the lambs, by their number, according to the ordinance;

22 'also one goat *as* a sin offering, besides the regular burnt offering, its grain offering, and its drink offering.

23 'On the fourth day *present* ten bulls, two rams, *and* fourteen lambs in their first year, without blemish,

24 'and their grain offering and their drink offerings for the bulls, for the rams, and for the lambs, by their number, according to the ordinance;

25 'also one kid of the goats *as* a sin offering, besides the regular burnt offering, its grain offering, and its drink offering.

26 'On the fifth day *present* nine bulls, two rams, *and* fourteen lambs in their first year without blemish,

27 'and their grain offering and their drink offerings for the bulls, for the rams, and for the lambs, by their number, according to the ordinance;

28 'also one goat *as* a sin offering, besides the regular burnt offering, its grain offering, and its drink offering.

29 'On the sixth day *present* eight bulls, two rams, *and* fourteen lambs in their first year without blemish,

30 'and their grain offering and their drink offerings for the bulls, for the rams, and for the lambs, by their number, according to the ordinance;

31 'also one goat *as* a sin offering, besides the regular burnt offering, its grain offering, and its drink offering.

32 'On the seventh day *present* seven bulls, two rams, *and* fourteen lambs in their first year without blemish,

33 'and their grain offering and their drink offerings for the bulls, for the rams, and for the lambs, by their number, according to the ordinance;

34 'also one goat *as* a sin offering, besides the regular burnt offering, its grain offering, and its drink offering.

35 'On the eighth day you shall have a [h]sacred assembly. You shall do no customary work.

36 'You shall present a burnt offering, an offering made by fire as a sweet aroma to the LORD: one bull, one ram, seven lambs in their first year without blemish,

37 'and their grain offering and their drink offerings for the bull, for the ram, and for the lambs, by their number, according to the ordinance;

38 'also one goat *as* a sin offering, besides the regular burnt offering, its grain offering, and its drink offering.

39 'These you shall present to the LORD at your [i]appointed feasts (besides your [j]vowed offerings and your freewill offerings) as your burnt offerings and your grain offerings, as your drink offerings and your peace offerings.' "

40 So Moses told the children of Israel everything, just as the LORD commanded Moses.

11
a Lev. 16:3, 5
b See Ex. 29:33, *note*

12
c Lev. 23:34; Dt. 16:13; Ezek. 45:25
d See Lev. 23:2, *note*

13
e Ezra 3:4

17
f Lev. 23:36

18
g vv. 3,4,9, 10; Num. 15:12; 28:7,14

35
h Lev. 23:36; Neh. 8:18

39
i Lev. 23:1–44; 1 Chr. 23:31; 2 Chr. 31:3; Ezra 3:5; Neh. 10:33; Isa. 1:14
j Lev. 7:16; 22:18; 23:38

Law of vows

30 THEN Moses spoke [a]to the heads of the tribes concerning the children of Israel, saying, "This *is* the thing which the LORD has commanded:

2 "If a man makes a [b]vow to the LORD, or [c]swears an oath to bind himself by some agreement, he shall not break his word; he shall do according to all that proceeds out of his mouth.

3 "Or if a woman makes a vow to the LORD, and binds *herself* by some agreement while in her father's house in her youth,

4 "and her father hears her vow and the agreement by which she has bound herself, and her father holds his peace, then all her vows shall stand, and every agreement with which she has bound herself shall stand.

5 "But if her father overrules her on the day that he hears, then none of her vows nor her agreements by which she has bound herself shall stand; and the LORD will release her, because her father overruled her.

6 "If indeed she takes a husband, while bound by her vows or by a rash utterance from her lips by which she bound herself,

7 "and her husband hears *it,* and makes no response to her on the day that he hears, then her vows shall stand, and her agreements by which she bound herself shall stand.

8 "But if her husband [d]overrules her on the day that he hears *it,* he shall make void her vow which she took and what she uttered with her lips, by which she bound herself, and the LORD will release her.

9 "Also any vow of a widow or a divorced woman, by which she has bound herself, shall stand against her.

10 "If she vowed in her husband's house, or bound herself by an agreement with an oath,

11 "and her husband heard *it,* and made no response to her *and* did not overrule her, then all her vows shall stand, and every agreement by which she bound herself shall stand.

12 "But if her husband truly made them void on the day he heard *them,* then whatever proceeded from her lips concerning her vows or concerning the agreement binding her, it shall not stand; her husband has made them void, and the LORD will release her.

13 "Every vow and every binding oath to afflict her soul, her husband may confirm it, or her husband may make it void.

14 "Now if her husband makes no response whatever to her from day to day, then he confirms all her vows or all the agreements that bind her; he confirms them, because he made no response to her on the day that he heard *them.*

15 "But if he does make them void after he has heard *them,* then he shall bear her guilt."

16 These *are* the statutes which the LORD commanded Moses, between a man and his wife, and between a father and his daughter in her youth in her father's house.

Midian judged (Num. 25:6–18)

31 AND the LORD spoke to Moses, saying:

2 [e]"Take vengeance on the Midianites for the children of Israel. Afterward you shall [f]be gathered to your people."

3 So Moses spoke to the people, saying, "Arm some of yourselves for war, and let them go against the Midianites to [g]take vengeance for the LORD on [h]Midian.

4 "A thousand from each tribe of all the tribes of Israel you shall send to the war."

5 So there were recruited from the divisions of Israel one thousand from *each* tribe, twelve thousand armed for war.

6 Then Moses sent them to the war, one thousand from *each* tribe; he sent them to the war with Phinehas the son of Eleazar the priest, with the [i]holy articles and [j]the [k]signal trumpets in his hand.

7 And they warred against the Midianites, just as the LORD commanded Moses, and they killed all the [l]males.

8 They killed the kings of Midian with *the rest of* those who were killed—Evi, Rekem, [m]Zur, Hur, and Reba, the five kings of Midian. [n]Balaam the son of Beor they also killed with the sword.

9 And the children of Israel took the women of Midian captive, with their little ones, and took as spoil all their cattle, all their flocks, and all their goods.

10 They also burned with fire all the cities where they dwelt, and all their forts.

CHAPTER 30

1 *a* Num. 1:4, 16; 7:2

2 *b* Lev. 27:2; Dt. 23:21–23; Jud. 11:30–31, 35; Eccl. 5:4; cp. Jud. 11:30–40 *c* Lev. 5:4; Mt. 14:9; Acts 23:14; cp. Mt. 5:33–37

8 *d* vv. 5,11; cp. Gen. 3:16

CHAPTER 31

2 *e* Num. 25:17 *f* Num. 27:12–13

3 *g* vv. 7–12 *h* Josh. 13:21

6 *i* Cp. Num. 14:44 *j* Num. 10:9 *k* i.e. *alarm clarions*

7 *l* Gen. 34:25; Dt. 20:13

8 *m* Num. 25:15 *n* Josh. 13:22

11 And [a]they took all the spoil and
all the booty—of man and beast.
12 Then they brought the captives,
the booty, and the spoil to Moses, to
Eleazar the priest, and to the congregation of the children of Israel, to the
camp in the plains of Moab by the Jordan, *across from* Jericho.
13 And Moses, Eleazar the priest,
and all the leaders of the congregation, went to meet them [b]outside the
camp.
14 But Moses was angry with the
officers of the army, *with* the captains
over thousands and captains over
hundreds, who had come from the
battle.
15 And Moses said to them: "Have
you [c]kept all the women alive?
16 "Look, [d]these *women* caused
the children of Israel, through the
[e]counsel of Balaam, to trespass
against the LORD in the incident of
Peor, and there was a plague among
the congregation of the LORD.
17 "Now therefore, [f]kill every male
among the little ones, and kill every
woman who has known a man intimately.
18 "But keep alive [g]for yourselves
all the young girls who have not
known a man intimately.
19 "And as for you, remain [b]out-
side the camp seven days; whoever
has killed any person, and whoever
has touched any slain, purify yourselves and your captives on the third
day and on the seventh day.
20 "Purify every garment, everything made of leather, everything woven of goats' *hair*, and everything
made of wood."
21 Then Eleazar the priest said to
the men of war who had gone to the
battle, "This *is* the ordinance of the
law which the LORD commanded Moses:
22 "Only the gold, the silver, the
bronze, the iron, the tin, and the lead,
23 "everything that can endure fire,
you shall put through the fire, and it
shall be clean; and it shall be purified
with the water of purification. But all
that cannot endure fire you shall put
through water.
24 "And you shall wash your
clothes on the seventh day and be
clean, and afterward you may come
into the camp."

Plunder distributed

25 Now the LORD spoke to Moses,
saying:

11
a Dt. 20:14
13
b Dt. 23:10, 12; cp. Num. 19:11–22
15
c Cp. 1 Sam. 15:3
16
d Num. 25:2
e 2 Pet. 2:15; Rev. 2:14
17
f Dt. 7:2; 20:16–18
18
g Dt. 21:10–14
28
h vv. 37–41, 51,54; cp. 18:26–27
29
i Dt. 18:1–5
30
j vv. 42–47
k Num. 3:7, 8,25,31,36; 18:3,4
41
l Cp. Num. 18:8–19

26 "Count up the plunder that was
taken—of man and beast—you and
Eleazar the priest and the chief fathers of the congregation;
27 "and divide the plunder into two
parts, between those who took part in
the war, who went out to battle, and
all the congregation.
28 "And levy a [h]tribute for the LORD
on the men of war who went out to
battle: one of every five hundred of the
persons, the cattle, the donkeys, and
the sheep;
29 "take *it* from their half, and
[i]give *it* to Eleazar the priest as a
heave offering to the LORD.
30 "And from the children of Israel's half you shall take [j]one of every
fifty, drawn from the persons, the cattle, the donkeys, and the sheep, from
all the livestock, and give them to the
Levites [k]who keep charge of the tabernacle of the LORD."
31 So Moses and Eleazar the priest
did as the LORD commanded Moses.
32 The booty remaining from the
plunder, which the men of war had
taken, was six hundred and seventy-
five thousand sheep,
33 seventy-two thousand cattle,
34 sixty-one thousand donkeys,
35 and thirty-two thousand persons
in all, of women who had not known
a man intimately.
36 And the half, the portion for
those who had gone out to war, was in
number three hundred and thirty-
seven thousand five hundred sheep;
37 and the LORD's tribute of the
sheep was six hundred and seventy-
five.
38 The cattle *were* thirty-six thousand, of which the LORD's tribute *was*
seventy-two.
39 The donkeys *were* thirty thousand five hundred, of which the LORD's
tribute *was* sixty-one.
40 The persons *were* sixteen thousand, of which the LORD's tribute *was*
thirty-two persons.
41 So Moses gave the tribute *which*
was the LORD's heave offering to Eleazar the priest, [l]as the LORD commanded Moses.
42 And from the children of Israel's
half, which Moses separated from the
men who fought—
43 now the half belonging to the
congregation was three hundred and
thirty-seven thousand five hundred
sheep,
44 thirty-six thousand cattle,

45 thirty thousand five hundred
donkeys,
46 and sixteen thousand persons—
47 and from the children [a]of Israel's half Moses took one of every
fifty, drawn from man and beast, and
gave them to the Levites, who kept
charge of the tabernacle of the LORD,
as the LORD commanded Moses.
48 Then the officers who *were* over
thousands of the army, the captains of
thousands and captains of hundreds,
came near to Moses;
49 and they said to Moses, "Your
servants have taken a count of the
men of war who *are* under our command, and not a man of us is missing.
50 "Therefore we have [b]brought an
offering for the LORD, what every man
found of ornaments of gold: armlets
and bracelets and signet rings and
earrings and necklaces, to make
[c]atonement for [d]ourselves before the
LORD."
51 So Moses and Eleazar the priest
received the gold from them, all the
fashioned ornaments.
52 And all the gold of the offering
that they offered to the LORD, from the
captains of thousands and captains of
hundreds, was sixteen thousand
seven hundred and fifty [e]shekels.
53 (The [f]men of war had taken
spoil, every man for himself.)
54 And Moses and Eleazar the
priest received the gold from the captains of thousands and of hundreds,
and brought it into the tabernacle of
meeting as a memorial [g]for the children of Israel before the LORD.

Reuben and Gad settle in Gilead

32 NOW the children of [1]Reuben
and the children of Gad had a
very great multitude of livestock; and
when they saw the land of [h]Jazer and
the land of [i]Gilead, that indeed the
region *was* a place for livestock,
2 the children of Gad and the children of Reuben came and spoke to
Moses, to Eleazar the priest, and to the
leaders of the congregation, saying,
3 "Ataroth, Dibon, Jazer, Nimrah,
[j]Heshbon, Elealeh, Shebam, Nebo,
and Beon,
4 "the country which the LORD
[k]defeated before the congregation of
Israel, *is* a land for livestock, and your
servants have livestock."
5 Therefore they said, "If we have
found favor in your sight, let this land
be given to your servants as a possession. Do not take us over the Jordan."
6 And Moses said to the children
of Gad and to the children of Reuben:
"Shall your brethren go to war while
you sit here?
7 "Now why will you [l]discourage
the heart of the children of Israel from
going over into the land which the
LORD has given them?
8 "Thus your fathers did [m]when I
sent them away from [n]Kadesh Barnea
to see the land.
9 "For [o]when they went up to the
Valley of Eshcol and saw the land,
they discouraged the heart of the children of Israel, so that they did not go
into the land which the LORD had given
them.
10 "So the LORD's anger was
aroused on that day, and He swore an
oath, [p]saying,
11 'Surely [q]none of the men who
came up from Egypt, from twenty
years old and above, shall see the land
of which I swore to Abraham, Isaac,
and Jacob, because they have not
wholly followed Me,
12 'except Caleb the son of Jephunneh, the Kenizzite, and Joshua the son
of Nun, [r]for they have wholly followed the LORD.'
13 "So the LORD's anger was
aroused against Israel, and He made
them wander in the wilderness forty
years, until all the generation that had
done evil in the sight of the LORD was
gone.
14 "And look! You have risen in
your fathers' place, a brood of sinful
men, to increase still more the [s]fierce
anger of the LORD against Israel.
15 "For if you [t]turn away from following Him, He will once again leave
them in the wilderness, and you will
destroy all these people."
16 Then they came near to him and
said: "We will build sheepfolds here
for our livestock, and cities for our little ones,
17 "but [u]we ourselves will be
armed, ready *to go* before the children
of Israel until we have brought them
to their place; and our little ones will
dwell in the fortified cities because of
the inhabitants of the land.
18 [v]"We will not return to our

47
a v. 30
50
b Cp. Jud. 8:24–26
c See Ex. 29:33, *note*
d Ex. 30:12–16
52
e See Coinage (OT), Ex. 30:13, *note;* cp. 2 Chr. 2:10, *note*
53
f Dt. 20:14
54
g Ex. 30:16
CHAPTER 32
1
h Num. 21:32; Josh. 13:25; 2 Sam. 24:5
i Dt. 3:13
3
j Josh. 13:17,26
4
k Num. 21:24,35
7
l Num. 13:27–14:4
8
m Num. 13:3–26
n Dt. 1:19–22
9
o Dt. 1:24, 28
10
p Dt. 1:34–36
11
q Num. 26:63–65
12
r Num. 14:6–9,24, 30; Dt. 1:36; Josh. 14:8–9
14
s Num. 11:1
15
t Dt. 30:17; Josh. 22:16–18; 2 Chr. 7:19; 15:2
17
u Josh. 4:12–13

32:18 *v* Josh. 22:3–4

[1](32:1) The Reubenites and the Gadites, who chose their inheritance just outside the land, symbolize world-borderers—carnal Christians (2 Tim. 4:10; cp. Gen. 11:31).

homes until every one of the children
of Israel has received his inheritance.
19 "For we will not inherit with
them on the other side of the Jordan
and beyond, because our inheritance
has fallen to us on this eastern side of
the Jordan."
20 Then [a]Moses said to them: "If
you do this thing, if you arm yourselves before the LORD for the war,
21 "and all your armed men cross
over the Jordan before the LORD until
He has driven out His enemies from
before Him,
22 "and the land is subdued before
the LORD, then afterward you may return and be blameless before the LORD
and before Israel; and this land shall
be your possession before the LORD.
23 "But if you do not do so, then
take note, you have sinned against the
LORD; and be sure [b]your sin will find
you out.
24 "Build cities for your little ones
and folds for your sheep, and [c]do
what has proceeded out of your
mouth."
25 And the children of Gad and the
children of Reuben spoke to Moses,
saying: "Your servants will do as my
lord commands.
26 "Our little ones, our wives, our
flocks, and all our livestock will be
there in the cities of Gilead;
27 "but your servants will cross
over, every man armed for war, before
the LORD to battle, just as my lord
says."
28 So Moses gave command concerning them to Eleazar the priest, to
Joshua the son of Nun, and to the chief
fathers of the tribes of the children of
Israel.
29 And Moses said to them: "If the
children of Gad and the children of
Reuben cross over the Jordan with
you, every man armed for battle before the LORD, and the land is subdued
before you, then you shall give them
the land of Gilead as a possession.
30 "But if they do not cross over
armed with you, they shall have possessions among you in the land of Canaan."
31 Then the children of Gad and the
children of Reuben answered, saying:
"As the LORD has said to your servants,
so we will do.
32 "We will cross over armed before the LORD into the land of Canaan,
but the possession of our inheritance
shall remain with us on this side of the
Jordan."

20
[a] v. 33; Dt. 3:18–20; Josh. 1:12–15
23
[b] Gen. 4:7; 44:16; Isa. 59:12; Josh. 7:1–26
24
[c] Cp. Num. 30:2
33
[d] Dt. 3:8–17; Josh. 12:1–6; 13:8–31
39
[e] Num. 27:1; 36:1
41
[f] Or *the towns of Jair.* Dt. 3:14; Jud. 10:4
CHAPTER 33
1
[g] Ps. 77:20
3
[h] Ex. 12:37
[i] Variously known as *Tanis, Avaris, Zoan;* located in the Delta
[j] See Lev. 23:3, *note*
4
[k] Ex. 12:12; 18:11; Isa. 19:1
6
[l] Ex. 13:20

33 So Moses [d]gave to the children
of Gad, to the children of Reuben, and
to half the tribe of Manasseh the son
of Joseph, the kingdom of Sihon king
of the Amorites and the kingdom of
Og king of Bashan, the land with its
cities within the borders, the cities of
the surrounding country.
34 And the children of Gad built Dibon and Ataroth and Aroer,
35 Atroth and Shophan and Jazer
and Jogbehah,
36 Beth Nimrah and Beth Haran,
fortified cities, and folds for sheep.
37 And the children of Reuben built
Heshbon and Elealeh and Kirjathaim,
38 Nebo and Baal Meon (*their*
names being changed) and Shibmah;
and they gave *other* names to the cities which they built.
39 And the children of [e]Machir the
son of Manasseh went to Gilead and
took it, and dispossessed the Amorites
who *were* in it.
40 So Moses gave Gilead to Machir
the son of Manasseh, and he dwelt in
it.
41 Also Jair the son of Manasseh
went and took its small towns, and
called them [f]Havoth Jair.
42 Then Nobah went and took Kenath and its villages, and he called it
Nobah, after his own name.

Summary of the journeys from Egypt to Jordan

33 THESE *are* the journeys of the
children of Israel, who went
out of the land of Egypt by their armies under the [g]hand of Moses and
Aaron.
2 Now Moses wrote down the
starting points of their journeys at the
command of the LORD. And these *are*
their journeys according to their starting points:
3 They [h]departed from [i]Rameses
in the [j]first month, on the fifteenth
day of the first month; on the day after
the Passover the children of Israel
went out with boldness in the sight of
all the Egyptians.
4 For the Egyptians were burying
all *their* firstborn, whom the LORD had
killed among them. Also [k]on their
gods the LORD had executed judgments.
5 [h]Then the children of Israel
moved from Rameses and camped at
Succoth.
6 They departed from [l]Succoth
and camped at Etham, which *is* on the
edge of the wilderness.

7 They [a]moved from Etham and
turned back to Pi Hahiroth, which *is*
east of Baal Zephon; and they camped
near Migdol.
8 They departed from before Hahiroth* and [b]passed through the
midst of the sea into the wilderness,
went three days' journey in the Wilderness of Etham, and camped at Marah.
9 They moved from [1]Marah and
came to Elim. At Elim *were* twelve
springs of water and seventy palm
trees; so they camped there.
10 They moved from Elim and
camped by the [c]Red Sea.
11 They moved from the Red Sea
and camped in the [d]Wilderness of Sin.
12 They journeyed from the Wilderness of Sin and camped at [e]Doph-
kah.
13 They departed from Dophkah
and camped at Alush.
14 They moved from Alush and
camped at [f]Rephidim, where there
was no water for the people to drink.
15 They departed from Rephidim
and camped in the [g]Wilderness of Sinai.
16 They moved from the Wilderness of Sinai and camped [h]at [i]Kib-
roth Hattaavah.
17 They departed from Kibroth
Hattaavah and camped at [j]Hazeroth.
18 They departed from Hazeroth
and camped at Rithmah.
19 They departed from Rithmah
and camped at Rimmon Perez.
20 They departed from Rimmon
Perez and camped at Libnah.
21 They moved from Libnah and
camped at Rissah.
22 They journeyed from Rissah and
camped at Kehelathah.
23 They went from Kehelathah and
camped at Mount Shepher.
24 They moved from Mount Shepher and camped at Haradah.
25 They moved from Haradah and
camped at Makheloth.
26 They moved from Makheloth
and camped at Tahath.
27 They departed from Tahath and
camped at Terah.
28 They moved from Terah and
camped at Mithkah.
29 They went from Mithkah and
camped at Hashmonah.

7 *a* Ex. 14:2,9
8 *b* Ex. 14:22; 15:22–23
10 *c* Heb. *Yam Suph*. Lit. *Reed* or *Marsh Sea*
11 *d* Ex. 16:1
12 *e* Word suggests smelting operations; perhaps *Serâbît–el-Khâdim*
14 *f* Perhaps *Wâdî Refâyed*. Ex. 17:1; 19:2
15 *g* Ex. 19:1
16 *h* Num. 11:34 *i* Meaning *the graves of craving*
17 *j* Num. 11:35
30 *k* Or *Moserah*, Dt. 10:6
32 *l* Or *Gudgodah*, Dt. 10:7
35 *m* 1 Ki. 9:26 speaks of it as beside *Elath;* at northern end of the Gulf of Akabah
37 *n* Num. 20:22
38 *o* See Lev. 23:3, *note*
39 *p* Cp. Ex. 7:7
40 *q* Num. 21:1 *r* See Gen. 12:9, *note*
43 *s* Num. 21:10–11

30 They departed from Hashmonah and [k]camped at Moseroth.
31 They departed from Moseroth
and camped at Bene Jaakan.
32 They moved from Bene Jaakan
and [l]camped at Hor Hagidgad.
33 They went from Hor Hagidgad
and camped at Jotbathah.
34 They moved from Jotbathah and
camped at Abronah.
35 They departed from Abronah
and camped at [m]Ezion Geber.
36 They moved from Ezion Geber
and camped in the Wilderness of Zin,
which *is* Kadesh.
37 They moved from Kadesh and
camped at [n]Mount Hor, on the boundary of the land of Edom.
38 Then Aaron the priest went up to
Mount Hor at the command of the
LORD, and died there in the fortieth
year after the children of Israel had
come out of the land of Egypt, on the
first *day* of the [o]fifth month.
39 Aaron *was* [p]one hundred and
twenty-three years old when he died
on Mount Hor.
40 Now the king of [q]Arad, the Canaanite, who dwelt in the [r]South in
the land of Canaan, heard of the coming of the children of Israel.
41 So they departed from Mount
Hor and camped at Zalmonah.
42 They departed from Zalmonah
and camped at Punon.
43 They departed from Punon and
camped at [s]Oboth.
44 They departed from Oboth and
camped at [t]Ije Abarim, at the border
of Moab.
45 They departed from [u]Ijim and
camped at Dibon Gad.
46 They moved from Dibon Gad
and camped at Almon Diblathaim.
47 They moved from Almon Diblathaim and camped in the [v]mountains
of Abarim, before Nebo.
48 They departed from the mountains of Abarim and camped in the

33:44 *t* i.e. *the ruins of Abarim*. Dt. 32:49
33:45 *u* Shortened form of *Ije Abarim*, v. 44
33:47 *v* The mountains to the east of the Jordan River and the Dead Sea

*
33:8 Many Hebrew manuscripts, Samaritan Pentateuch, Syriac, Targum, and Vulgate read *from Pi Hahiroth* (compare verse 7).

[1](33:9) While the exact location of a number of the fifty-six geographical names recorded in this chapter is known, many are not. It should be kept in mind that many of the places mentioned were only stations at which the children of Israel encamped.

[a]plains of Moab by the Jordan, *across*
from Jericho.
49 They camped by the Jordan,
from Beth Jesimoth as far as the
[b]Abel Acacia Grove* in the plains of
Moab.

Law of the possession of the land

50 Now the LORD spoke to Moses in
the plains of Moab by the Jordan,
across from Jericho, saying,
51 "Speak to the children of Israel,
and say to them: [c]'When you have
crossed the Jordan into the land of Canaan,
52 [d]'then you shall drive out all the
inhabitants of the land from before
you, destroy all their engraved stones,
destroy all their molded images, and
[e]demolish all their high places;
53 'you shall dispossess *the inhab-*
itants of the land and dwell in it, for I
have given you the land to [f]possess.
54 'And you shall [g]divide the land
by lot as an inheritance among your
families; to the larger you shall give a
larger inheritance, and to the smaller
you shall give a smaller inheritance;
there everyone's *inheritance* shall be
whatever falls to him by lot. You shall
inherit according to the tribes of your
fathers.
55 'But if you do not drive out the
inhabitants of the land from before
you, then it shall be that those whom
you let remain *shall be* [h]irritants in
your eyes and thorns in your sides,
and they shall harass you in the land
where you dwell.
56 'Moreover it shall be *that* I will
do to you as I thought to do to them.' "

Preparations to enter the land

34 THEN the LORD spoke to Moses, saying,
2 "Command the children of Israel, and say to them: 'When you
come into the land of [i]Canaan, this *is*
the land that shall fall to you as an
inheritance—the land of Canaan to its
boundaries.
3 'Your southern border shall be
from the Wilderness of Zin along the
border of Edom; then [j]your southern
border shall extend eastward to the
end of [k]the Salt Sea;
4 'your border shall turn from the
southern side of the Ascent of Akrabbim, continue to Zin, and be on the
south of Kadesh Barnea; then it shall
go on to Hazar Addar, and continue to
Azmon;
5 'the border shall turn from Azmon [l]to the Brook of Egypt, and it
shall end at the Sea.
6 'As for the [m]western border, you
shall have the Great Sea for a border;
this shall be your western border.
7 'And this shall be your [n]north-
ern border: From the Great Sea you
shall mark out your *border* line to
Mount Hor;
8 'from Mount Hor you shall mark
out *your border* to the [o]entrance of
Hamath; then the direction of the border shall be toward [p]Zedad;
9 'the border shall proceed to
Ziphron, and it shall end at [q]Hazar
Enan. This shall be your northern border.
10 'You shall mark out your [r]east-
ern border from Hazar Enan to Shepham;
11 'the border shall go down from
Shepham to [s]Riblah on the east side
of Ain; the border shall go down and
reach to the eastern side of the Sea of
[t]Chinnereth;
12 'the border shall go down along
the Jordan, and it shall end at the Salt
Sea. This shall be your land with its
surrounding boundaries.' "
13 Then Moses commanded the
children of Israel, saying: "This *is* the
land which you shall inherit by lot,
which the LORD has commanded to
give to the nine tribes and to the half-
tribe.
14 [u]"For the tribe of the children of
Reuben according to the house of
their fathers, and the tribe of the children of Gad according to the house of
their fathers, have received *their in-*
heritance; and the half-tribe of Manasseh has received its inheritance.
15 "The two tribes and the half-
tribe have received their inheritance
on this side of the Jordan, *across from*
Jericho eastward, toward the sunrise."
16 And the LORD spoke to Moses,
saying,
17 "These *are* the [v]names of the
men who shall divide the land among
you as an inheritance: Eleazar the
priest and Joshua the son of Nun.
18 "And you shall take one leader
of every tribe to divide the land for the
inheritance.
19 "These *are* the names of the

48 a Num. 22:1; 31:12; 35:1
49 b Meaning *Acacia Grove Plains*
51 c Dt. 7:1,2; 9:1; Josh. 3:17
52 d Ex. 23:24, 33; 34:13; Dt. 7:2,5; 12:3; Josh. 11:12; Jud. 2:2
e See Jud. 3:7 and 1 Ki. 3:2, *notes*
53 f Dt. 11:31; Josh. 21:43
54 g Num. 26:53–56
55 h Josh. 23:13; Jud. 2:3; Ps. 106:34–36; cp. Ex. 23:33; Ezek. 28:24
CHAPTER 34
2 i Gen. 17:8; Dt. 1:7–8; Ps. 78:55; 105:11; cp. Ezek. 47:14
3 j Josh. 15:1; cp. Ezek. 47:19
k Gen. 14:3; Josh. 15:2
5 l Gen. 15:18; Josh. 15:4, 47; 1 Ki. 8:65; Isa. 27:12
6 m Ex. 23:31; Josh. 15:12; cp. Ezek. 47:20
7 n Cp. Ezek. 47:15–17
8 o Josh. 13:5
p Ezek. 47:15
9 q Ezek. 47:17
10 r Josh. 15:5; cp. Ezek. 47:18
34:11 s 2 Ki. 23:33; Jer. 39:5,6 t Dt. 3:17; Josh. 12:3; 13:27; Lk. 5:1; Jn. 6:1 **34:14** u Num. 32:33 **34:17** v Josh. 14:1–2

*33:49 Hebrew *Abel Shittim*

men: from the tribe of Judah, Caleb
the son of Jephunneh;
20 "from the tribe of the children of
Simeon, Shemuel the son of Ammihud;
21 "from the tribe of Benjamin, Eli-
dad the son of Chislon;
22 "a leader from the tribe of the
children of Dan, Bukki the son of
Jogli;
23 "from the sons of Joseph: a
leader from the tribe of the children of
Manasseh, Hanniel the son of Ephod,
24 "and a leader from the tribe of
the children of Ephraim, Kemuel the
son of Shiphtan;
25 "a leader from the tribe of the
children of Zebulun, Elizaphan the
son of Parnach;
26 "a leader from the tribe of the
children of Issachar, Paltiel the son of
Azzan;
27 "a leader from the tribe of the
children of Asher, Ahihud the son of
Shelomi;
28 "and a leader from the tribe of
the children of Naphtali, Pedahel the
son of Ammihud."
29 These *are* the ones the LORD
commanded to divide the inheritance
among the children of Israel in the
land of Canaan.

The Levites' forty-eight cities

35 AND the LORD spoke to Moses
in the plains of Moab by the
Jordan *across from* Jericho, saying:
2 [a]"Command the children of Israel that they give the Levites cities to
dwell in from the inheritance of their
possession, and you shall *also* give the
Levites common-land around the cities.
3 "They shall have the cities to
dwell in; and their common-land shall
be for their cattle, for their herds, and
for all their animals.
4 "The common-land of the cities
which you will give the Levites *shall
extend* from the wall of the city outward a thousand [b]cubits all around.
5 "And you shall measure outside
the city on the east side two thousand
[b]cubits, on the south side two thousand cubits, on the west side two thousand cubits, and on the north side two
thousand cubits. The city *shall be* in
the middle. This shall belong to them
as common-land for the cities.

The six cities of refuge

6 "Now among the cities which
you will give to the Levites *you shall
appoint* six cities of [1]refuge, to which
a manslayer may flee. And to these
you shall add forty-two cities.
7 "So all the cities you will give to
the Levites *shall be* forty-eight; these
you shall give with their common-
land.
8 "And the cities which you will
give *shall be* from the possession of
the children of Israel; from the larger
tribe you shall give many, from the
smaller you shall give few. Each shall
give some of its cities to the Levites, in
proportion to the inheritance that
each receives."
9 Then the LORD spoke to Moses,
saying,
10 "Speak to the children of Israel,
and say to them: 'When you cross the
Jordan into the land of Canaan,
11 'then you shall appoint cities to
be [c]cities of refuge for you, that the
manslayer who kills any person accidentally may flee there.
12 'They shall be cities of refuge for
you from the [d]avenger, [e]that the manslayer may not die until he stands before the congregation in judgment.
13 'And of the cities which you
give, you shall have six cities of refuge.
14 [f]'You shall appoint three cities
on this side of the Jordan, and three
cities you shall appoint in the land of
Canaan, *which* will be cities of refuge.
15 'These six cities shall be for refuge for the children of Israel, for the
stranger, and for the sojourner among
them, that anyone who kills a person
accidentally may flee there.
16 'But if he [g]strikes him with an
iron implement, so that he dies, he *is*
a murderer; the murderer shall surely
be put to death.
17 'And if he strikes him with a

CHAPTER 35

2 — *a* Josh. 21:2–3; cp. Lev. 25:32–34; Josh. 14:3–4; Ezek. 48:10–20

4 — *b* See Weights and Measures (OT), 2 Chr. 2:10, *note*

11 — *c* Dt. 19:1–13

12 — *d Redemption* (redeeming relative type): v. 12; Num. 35:19. (Gen. 48:16; Isa. 59:20, *note*) *e* Dt. 19:6; Josh. 20:3, 5,6

14 — *f* Dt. 4:41; Josh. 20:8

16 — *g* Ex. 21:12, 14; Lev. 24:17; Dt. 19:11,12

[1](35:6) Here in vv. 6,9–28 the general command is given to set aside six cities of refuge, three on each side of the Jordan River (v. 14). In Dt. 4:41–43, Moses sets aside three cities east of the Jordan (Bezer, Ramoth, and Golan, v. 43) prior to the conquest of Canaan. Joshua 20 records the law of the cities of refuge and tells of the assignment by Joshua of three cities west of the river (Kedesh, Shechem, and Kirjath Arba, v. 7). Here, too, reassignment of the three cities on the other side of the Jordan is recorded (v. 8). The law of the cities of refuge is recounted in detail in Dt. 19:1–13, and they are alluded to in Ex. 21:13.

The cities of refuge are illustrative of Christ sheltering the sinner from judgment (Rom. 8:1,33–34; Heb. 6:17–20; cp. Ps. 46:1; 142:5).

stone in the hand, by which one could
die, and he does die, he *is* a murderer;
the murderer shall surely be put to
death.
18 'Or *if* he strikes him with a
wooden hand weapon, by which one
could die, and he does die, he *is* a murderer; the murderer shall surely be put
to death.
19 'The [a]avenger of blood himself
shall put the murderer to death; when
he meets him, he shall put him to
death.
20 'If he pushes him out of hatred
or, [b]while lying in wait, hurls something at him so that he dies,
21 'or in enmity he strikes him with
his hand so that he dies, the one who
struck *him* shall surely be put to death.
He *is* a murderer. The avenger of
blood shall put the murderer to death
when he meets him.
22 'However, if he pushes him suddenly without enmity, or throws anything at him without lying in wait,
23 'or uses a stone, by which a man
could die, throwing *it* at him without
seeing *him,* so that he dies, while he
was not his enemy or seeking his
harm,
24 'then the congregation shall
judge between the manslayer and the
avenger of blood according to these
judgments.
25 'So the congregation shall deliver the manslayer from the hand of
the avenger of blood, and the congregation shall return him to the city of
refuge where he had fled, and he shall
remain there until the death of the
high priest who was anointed with the
holy oil.
26 'But if the manslayer at any time
goes outside the limits of the city of
refuge where he fled,
27 'and the avenger of blood finds
him outside the limits of his city of
refuge, and the avenger of blood kills
the manslayer, he shall not be guilty of
blood,
28 'because he should have remained in his city of refuge until the
death of the high priest. But after the
death of the high priest the manslayer
may return to the land of his possession.
29 'And these *things* shall be a statute of judgment to you throughout
your generations in all your dwellings.
30 'Whoever kills a person, the
murderer shall be put to death on the
[c]testimony of witnesses; but one witness is not *sufficient* testimony
against a person for the death *penalty.*
31 'Moreover you shall take no ransom for the life of a murderer who *is*
guilty of death, but he shall surely be
put to death.
32 'And you shall take no ransom
for him who has fled to his city of refuge, that he may return to dwell in the
land before the death of the priest.
33 'So you shall not pollute the land
where you *are;* for blood [d]defiles the
land, and no atonement can be made
for the land, for the blood that is shed
on it, except by the [e]blood of him who
shed it.
34 'Therefore do not [f]defile the
land which you inhabit, in the midst of
which I dwell; for [g]I the LORD dwell
among the children of Israel.' "

As to inheritance

36
NOW the chief fathers of the
families of the children of Gilead the son of Machir, the son of Manasseh, of the families of the sons of
Joseph, came near and [h]spoke before
Moses and before the leaders, the
chief fathers of the children of Israel.
2 And they said: "The LORD commanded my lord *Moses* to give the
land as an inheritance by lot to the
children of Israel, and my lord was
commanded by the LORD to give the
[i]inheritance of our brother Zelophehad to his daughters.
3 "Now if they are married to any
of the sons of the *other* tribes of the
children of Israel, then their inheritance will be taken from the inheritance of our fathers, and it will be
added to the inheritance of the tribe
into which they marry; so it will be
taken from the lot of our inheritance.
4 "And when the [j]Jubilee of the
children of Israel comes, then their inheritance will be added to the inheritance of the tribe into which they
marry; so their inheritance will be
taken away from the inheritance of
the tribe of our fathers."
5 Then Moses commanded the
children of Israel according to the
word of the LORD, saying: "What the
tribe of the sons of Joseph [k]speaks is
right.
6 "This *is* what the LORD commands concerning the daughters of
Zelophehad, saying, 'Let them marry
whom they think best, but they may
marry only within the family of their
father's tribe.'

19
a Redemption (redeeming relative type): vv. 12,19, 21,24–25, 27; Dt. 19:6. (Gen. 48:16; Isa. 59:20, *note*)
20
b Ex. 21:14; Dt. 19:11–12
30
c Dt. 17:6; 19:15; Mt. 18:16; 2 Cor. 13:1; Heb. 10:28
33
d Ps. 106:38; cp. Dt. 21:7–8
e Cp. Gen. 9:6
34
f Lev. 18:24–25
g Ex. 29:45, 46
CHAPTER 36
1
h Num. 27:1–11
2
i Josh. 17:3–4
4
j Lev. 25:10
5
k Num. 27:7

7 "So the inheritance of the children of Israel shall not change hands
from tribe to tribe, for every one of the
children of Israel shall keep the inheritance of the tribe of his fathers.
8 "And [a]every daughter who possesses an inheritance in any tribe of
the children of Israel shall be the wife
of one of the family of her father's
tribe, so that the children of Israel
each may possess the inheritance of
his fathers.
9 "Thus no inheritance shall
change hands from *one* tribe to another, but every tribe of the children of
Israel shall keep its own inheritance."
10 Just as the LORD commanded
Moses, so did the daughters of Zelophehad;
11 for [b]Mahlah, Tirzah, Hoglah,
Milcah, and Noah, the daughters of
Zelophehad, were married to the sons
of their father's brothers.
12 They were married into the families of the children of Manasseh the
son of Joseph, and their inheritance
remained in the tribe of their father's
family.
13 [c]These *are* the commandments
and the judgments which the LORD
commanded the children of Israel by
the hand of Moses [d]in the plains of
Moab by the Jordan, *across from* Jericho.

8
a 1 Chr. 23:22
11
b Num. 26:33
13
c Cp. Lev. 26:46; 27:34
d Num. 26:3; 33:48

The Fifth Book of Moses Called

DEUTERONOMY

Author: Moses *Theme:* Law Restated *Date of writing:* c. 1450–1410 B.C.

DEUTERONOMY begins with a survey of the history of Israel, then enlarges upon some of the basic laws of the preceding books, and concludes with a series of prophecies carrying the history of Israel down to their final return to Palestine.

The title of the book is from the Septuagint and the Vulgate, and means *The Second Law*. The Hebrew title is *Debarim*, literally, *Words*.

The book chiefly consists of the final discourses of Moses given on the plains of Moab, opposite Palestine, shortly before his death. It is referred to over eighty times in the NT and was quoted by Christ more than any other OT book. Prominent in the book are the concepts of God's love and man's obedience.

Deuteronomy may be divided as follows:

I. First Discourse: Review of Israel's History after the Exodus, and Its Lessons, 1—4.
II. Second Discourse: Recounting of the Sinaitic Laws, with Warnings and Exhortations, 5—26.
III. Third Discourse: Blessings and Curses for Obedience and Disobedience, 27—28.
IV. Fourth Discourse: The Palestinian Covenant; Its Warnings and Promised Blessings, 29—30.
V. Conclusion: Final Words and Acts of Moses, and His Death, 31—34.

I. First Discourse: Review of Israel's History after the Exodus, and Its Lessons, 1—4

Moses recounts Israel's failure at Kadesh Barnea (Num. 14)

1 THESE *are* the words which Moses spoke to all [a]Israel on this
[b]side of the Jordan in the wilderness,
in the [1]plain opposite Suph,* between
Paran, Tophel, Laban, Hazeroth, and
Dizahab.
2 *It is* [2]eleven days' *journey* from
Horeb by way of Mount Seir to Kadesh Barnea.
3 Now it came to pass in the fortieth year, in the [c]eleventh month, on
the first *day* of the month, *that* Moses [d]spoke to the children of Israel
according to all that the LORD had
given him as commandments to
them,
4 after he had killed [e]Sihon king
of the Amorites, who dwelt in Heshbon, and Og king of Bashan, who
dwelt at Ashtaroth in* Edrei.
5 On this side of the Jordan in the
land of Moab, Moses began to explain
this law, saying,
6 "The LORD our God spoke to us in
[f]Horeb, saying: 'You have [g]dwelt
long enough at this mountain.
7 'Turn and take your journey,
and go to the mountains of the Amorites, to all the neighboring *places* in
the [h]plain, in the mountains and in the
[3]lowland, in the [i]South and on the
seacoast, to the land of the Canaanites
and to Lebanon, as far as the great
river, the River Euphrates.
8 'See, I have set the land before
you; go in and possess the land which
the LORD swore to your fathers—to
Abraham, Isaac, and Jacob—to give
to them and their descendants after
them.'
9 "And I [j]spoke to you at that

CHAPTER 1
1 *a Israel* (history): vv. 1,6–8, 19–40; Dt. 7:6. (Gen. 12:2; Rom. 11:26, *note*)
b Dt. 4:44–46
3 *c* See Lev. 23:2, *note*
d c. 1407 B.C. See Ex. 1:8, *note*
4 *e* Num. 21:23–24, 33–35
6 *f* Ex. 3:1,12; 19:2
g Cp. Gen. 31:3; Num. 10:11–13
7 *h* See Dt. 1:1, *note*
i See Gen. 12:9, *note*
1:9 *j* Num. 11:14,24; cp. Ex. 18:13–26

*1:1 One manuscript of the Septuagint, also Targum and Vulgate, read *Red Sea*. 1:4 Septuagint, Syriac, and Vulgate read *and* (compare Joshua 12:4).

---

[1](1:1) Arabah in Hebrew. When used with the definite article only, it refers to the valley which runs from the Sea of Galilee to the Gulf of Aqabah. South of the Dead Sea the name is still retained (Wady el-Arabah).

[2](1:2) Because of Israel's unbelief, when they would not enter Canaan after hearing the report of the spies that Moses sent from the wilderness of Paran into the land of promise (Num. 13:1—14:39), a journey which should have required eleven days was prolonged to forty years. See Num. 14:23, *note*.

[3](1:7) The "lowland" or *Shephelah* is a section of the Holy Land bounded on the north by the Valley of Aijalon, on the west by the Maritime Plain, on the east by the Central Plateau, and reaching to Beersheba in the south. It is characterized by low, rounded chalk hills divided by several broad valleys.

time, saying: 'I alone am not able to bear you.

10 'The LORD your God has multiplied you, and here you *are* today, as the stars of heaven in multitude.

11 'May the LORD God of your fathers make you a thousand times more numerous than you are, and bless you as He has promised you!

12 'How can I alone bear your problems and your burdens and your complaints?

13 'Choose wise, understanding, and knowledgeable men from among your tribes, and I will make them heads over you.'

14 "And you answered me and said, 'The thing which you have told *us* to do *is* good.'

15 "So I took the heads of your tribes, wise and knowledgeable men, and made them heads over you, leaders of thousands, leaders of hundreds, leaders of fifties, leaders of tens, and officers for your tribes.

16 "Then I commanded your judges at that time, saying, 'Hear *the cases* between your brethren, and judge righteously between a man and his brother or the stranger who is with him.

17 'You shall not [a]show partiality in judgment; you shall hear the small as well as the great; you shall not be afraid in any man's presence, for the judgment *is* God's. The case that is too hard for you, bring to me, and I will hear it.'

18 "And I commanded you at that time all the things which you should do.

19 "So we departed from Horeb, and went through all that great and terrible wilderness which you saw on the way to the mountains of the Amorites, as the LORD our God had commanded us. Then we [b]came to Kadesh Barnea.

20 "And I said to you, 'You have come to the mountains of the Amorites, which the LORD our God is giving us.

21 'Look, the LORD your God has set the land before you; go up *and* possess *it,* as the LORD God of your fathers has spoken to you; do not fear or be discouraged.'

22 "And [c]every one of you came near to me and said, 'Let us send men before us, and let them search out the land for us, and bring back word to us of the way by which we should go up, and of the cities into which we shall come.'

23 "The plan pleased me well; so I [d]took twelve of your men, one man from *each* tribe.

24 [e]"And they departed and went up into the mountains, and came to the Valley of Eshcol, and spied it out.

25 "They also took *some* of the fruit of the land in their hands and brought *it* down to us; and they brought back word to us, saying, '*It is* a [f]good land which the LORD our God is giving us.'

26 [g]"Nevertheless you would not go up, but rebelled against the command of the LORD your God;

27 "and you [h]complained in your tents, and said, 'Because the LORD hates us, He has brought us out of the land of Egypt to deliver us into the hand of the Amorites, to destroy us.

28 'Where can we go up? Our brethren have discouraged our hearts, saying, [i]"The people *are* greater and taller than we; the cities *are* great and fortified up to heaven; moreover we have seen the sons of the Anakim there." '

29 "Then I said to you, 'Do not be terrified, [j]or afraid of them.

30 'The LORD your God, who goes before you, [k]He will fight for you, according to all He did for you in Egypt before your eyes,

31 'and in the wilderness where you saw how the LORD your God carried you, as a [l]man carries his son, in all the way that you went until you came to this place.'

32 "Yet, for all that, [m]you did not believe the LORD your God,

33 "who went in the way [n]before you to search out a place for you to pitch your tents, to show you the way you should go, in the fire by night and in the cloud by day.

34 "And the LORD heard the sound of your words, and was angry, and took an oath, saying,

35 [o]'Surely not one of these men of this evil generation shall see that good land of which I swore to give to your fathers,

36 [p]'except Caleb the son of Jephunneh; he shall see it, and to him and his children I am giving the land on which he walked, because he [q]wholly followed the LORD.'

37 [r]"The LORD was also angry with me for your sakes, saying, 'Even you shall not go in there.

38 [s]'Joshua the son of Nun, who stands before you, he shall go in there.

17
a Dt. 16:19; Lev. 19:15; Prov. 24:23; Jas. 2:1; cp. 1 Sam. 16:7

19
b Num. 13:26

22
c Cp. Num. 13:1–3

23
d Num. 13:2

24
e Num. 13:22–24

25
f Num. 13:27

26
g Num. 14:1–4; Ps. 106:24

27
h Ps. 106:25

28
i Num. 13:28, 31–33; Dt. 9:1,2

29
j Num. 14:9; Dt. 7:18

30
k Ex. 14:14

31
l Acts 13:18

32
m Num. 20:12; Heb. 3:9–10, 16–19; 4:1–2; Jude 5

33
n Num. 9:15–23

35
o Num. 14:22–23; Ps. 95:10–11

36
p Num. 14:24,30; Josh. 14:9–10
q Num. 32:11–12

37
r Num. 27:14; Dt. 3:26; 4:21; 34:4; Ps. 106:32

38
s Num. 14:30; Dt. 3:28

[a]Encourage him, for he shall cause Israel to inherit it.

39 'Moreover [b]your little ones and your children, who you say will be victims, who today have no knowledge of good and evil, they shall go in there; to them I will give it, and they shall possess it.

40 'But *as for* you, turn and take your journey into the wilderness by the Way of the Red Sea.'

41 "Then you answered and said to me, 'We have [c]sinned against the LORD; we will go up and fight, just as the LORD our God commanded us.' And when everyone of you had girded on his weapons of war, you were ready to go up into the mountain.

42 "And the LORD said to me, 'Tell them, [d]"Do not go up nor fight, for I *am* not among you; lest you be defeated before your enemies." '

43 "So I spoke to you; yet you would not listen, but [e]rebelled against the command of the LORD, and [f]presumptuously went up into the mountain.

44 "And the Amorites who dwelt in that mountain came out against you and chased you as bees do, and [g]drove you back from Seir to Hormah.

45 "Then you returned and wept before the LORD, [h]but the LORD would not listen to your voice nor give ear to you.

46 "So you remained in Kadesh [i]many days, according to the days that you spent *there.*

Wanderings and further conflicts of the wilderness

2 "THEN we turned and [j]journeyed into the wilderness of the Way of the Red Sea, as the LORD spoke to me, and we skirted Mount Seir for [i]many days.

2 "And the LORD spoke to me, saying:

3 'You have skirted this mountain [k]long enough; turn northward.

4 'And command the people, saying, "You *are about to* [l]pass through the territory of [m]your brethren, the descendants of Esau, who live in Seir; and they will be afraid of you. Therefore watch yourselves carefully.

5 "Do not meddle with them, for I will not give you *any* of their land, no, not so much as one footstep, because I have [n]given Mount Seir to Esau *as* a possession.

6 "You shall buy food from them with money, that you may eat; and you shall also buy water from them with money, that you may drink.

7 "For the LORD your God has blessed you in all the work of your hand. He [o]knows your trudging through this great wilderness. These forty years the LORD your God *has been* with you; you have lacked nothing." '

8 "And when we passed beyond our brethren, the descendants of Esau who dwell in Seir, away from the road of the [p]plain, away from [q]Elath and Ezion Geber, we [r]turned and passed by way of the [s]Wilderness of Moab.

9 "Then the LORD said to me, 'Do not harass Moab, nor contend with them in battle, for I will not give you *any* of their land *as* a possession, because I have [t]given Ar to the descendants of Lot *as* a possession.' "

10 (The [u]Emim had dwelt there in times past, a people as great and numerous and tall as the [v]Anakim.

11 They were also regarded as giants,* like the Anakim, but the Moabites call them Emim.

12 The [w]Horites formerly dwelt in Seir, but the descendants of Esau dispossessed them and destroyed them from before them, and dwelt in their place, just as Israel did to the land of their possession which the LORD gave them.)

13 " 'Now rise and cross over the Valley of the [x]Zered.' So we crossed over the Valley of the Zered.

14 "And the time we took to come from [y]Kadesh Barnea until we crossed over the Valley of the Zered *was* thirty-eight years, [z]until all the generation of the men of war was consumed from the midst of the camp, [aa]just as the LORD had sworn to them.

15 "For indeed the hand of the LORD was against them, to destroy them from the midst of the camp until they were consumed.

16 "So it was, when all the men of war had finally perished from among the people,

17 "that the LORD spoke to me, saying:

18 'This day you are to cross over at Ar, the boundary of Moab.

19 'And *when* you come near the people of [bb]Ammon, do not harass

38
a Dt. 31:7, 23
39
b Num. 14:3,31; 32:17
41
c Num. 14:40
42
d Num. 14:41–43
43
e Num. 14:44
f Dt. 17:12–13
44
g Num. 14:45
45
h Cp. Zech. 7:11–13
46
i i.e. *the 38 years of waiting and wandering.* Dt. 2:14
CHAPTER 2
1
j Dt. 1:40
3
k Cp. Dt. 1:6,7
4
l Num. 20:14–21
m Dt. 23:7
5
n Gen. 36:8; Josh. 24:4
7
o Ps. 1:6; 37:18; 44:21; 69:5; 94:11; 103:14; Mt. 6:8,32; 2 Pet. 2:9
8
p See Dt. 1:1, *note*
q 1 Ki. 9:26
r Num. 21:4
s A region east of the Dead Sea
9
t Gen. 19:36–38
10
u Gen. 14:5
v Num. 13:22,33; Dt. 9:2
12
w v. 22; Gen. 14:6; 36:20
13
x Num. 21:12

2:14 *y* Num. 13:26 *z* Num. 26:64; Dt. 1:34–35
aa Ezek. 20:15; Heb. 3:17–18 2:19 *bb* Num. 21:24

*

2:11 Hebrew *rephaim*

them or meddle with them, for I will
not give you *any* of the land of the
people of Ammon *as* a possession, because I have given it to the descendants of Lot *as* a possession.' "
20 (That was also regarded as a
land of giants;* giants formerly dwelt
there. But the Ammonites call them
[a]Zamzummim,
21 a people as great and numerous
and tall as the Anakim. But the LORD
destroyed them before them, and they
dispossessed them and dwelt in their
place,
22 just as He had done for the descendants of Esau, who dwelt in Seir,
when He destroyed the Horites from
before them. They dispossessed them
and dwelt in their place, even to this
day.
23 And the [b]Avim, who dwelt in villages as far as Gaza—the Caphtorim,
who came from [c]Caphtor, destroyed
them and dwelt in their place.)
24 " 'Rise, take your journey, and
cross over the River Arnon. Look, I
have given into your hand [d]Sihon the
Amorite, king of Heshbon, and his
land. Begin to possess *it,* and engage
him in battle.
25 'This day I will begin to put the
[e]dread and fear of you upon the nations under the whole heaven, who
shall hear the report of you, and shall
[f]tremble and be in anguish because of
you.'
26 "And I [g]sent messengers from
the Wilderness of Kedemoth to Sihon
king of Heshbon, with [h]words of
peace, saying,
27 'Let me pass through your land;
I will keep strictly to the road, and I
will turn neither to the right nor to the
left.
28 'You shall sell me food for
money, that I may eat, and give me
water for money, that I may drink;
only let me pass through on foot,
29 'just as the descendants of Esau
who dwell in Seir and the Moabites
who dwell in Ar did for me, until I
cross the Jordan to the land which the
LORD our God is giving us.'
30 "But Sihon king of Heshbon
would not let us pass through, for the
LORD your God [i]hardened his spirit
and made his heart obstinate, that He
might deliver him into your hand, as *it*
is this day.
31 "And the LORD said to me, 'See, I
have begun to give Sihon and his land
over to you. Begin to [j]possess *it,* that
you may inherit his land.'

20 [a] Or *Zuzim,* Gen. 14:5
23 [b] Josh. 13:3 [c] Gen. 10:14
24 [d] Dt. 1:4
25 [e] Ex. 23:27; Dt. 11:25 [f] Ex. 15:14–16
26 [g] Num. 21:21–32 [h] Dt. 20:10
30 [i] Cp. Ex. 4:21
31 [j] Josh. 1:3
36 [k] Dt. 3:12; 4:48; Josh. 13:9 [l] Josh. 13:9, 16
CHAPTER 3
1 [m] Num. 21:33–35; Dt. 29:7
2 [n] Josh. 13:21
6 [o] Dt. 2:34–35
8 [p] Num. 32:33; Josh. 12:6; 13:8–12 [q] Dt. 4:48; 1 Chr. 5:23; Ps. 29:6

32 "Then Sihon and all his people
came out against us to fight at Jahaz.
33 "And the LORD our God delivered
him over to us; so we defeated him, his
sons, and all his people.
34 "We took all his cities at that
time, and we utterly destroyed the
men, women, and little ones of every
city; we left none remaining.
35 "We took only the livestock as
plunder for ourselves, with the spoil of
the cities which we took.
36 "From [k]Aroer, which *is* on the
bank of the River Arnon, and *from* the
[l]city that *is* in the ravine, as far as
Gilead, there was not one city too
strong for us; the LORD our God delivered all to us.
37 "Only you did not go near the
land of the people of Ammon—
anywhere along the River Jabbok, or
to the cities of the mountains, or wherever the LORD our God had forbidden
us.

Defeat of Og king of Bashan

3 "THEN we turned and went up
the road to Bashan; and [m]Og king
of Bashan came out against us, he and
all his people, to battle at [d]Edrei.
2 "And the LORD said to me, 'Do
not fear him, for I have delivered him
and all his people and his land into
your hand; you shall do to him as you
did to [n]Sihon king of the Amorites,
who dwelt at Heshbon.'
3 "So the LORD our God also delivered into our hands Og king of Bashan, with all his people, and we attacked him until he had no survivors
remaining.
4 "And we took all his cities at that
time; there was not a city which we
did not take from them: sixty cities, all
the region of Argob, the kingdom of
Og in Bashan.
5 "All these cities *were* fortified
with high walls, gates, and bars, besides a great many rural towns.
6 "And we utterly destroyed them,
as we did to Sihon king of Heshbon,
[o]utterly destroying the men, women,
and children of every city.
7 "But all the livestock and the
spoil of the cities we took as booty for
ourselves.
8 "And at that time we took the
[p]land from the hand of the two kings
of the Amorites who *were* on this side
of the Jordan, from the River Arnon to
Mount [q]Hermon

*
2:20 Hebrew *rephaim*

9 "(the Sidonians call Hermon Sirion, and the Amorites call it Senir),

10 "all the cities of the plain, all Gilead, and all Bashan, as far as Salcah and Edrei, cities of the kingdom of Og in Bashan.

11 "For only Og king of Bashan remained of the remnant of the [a]giants.* Indeed his bedstead *was* an iron bedstead. (*Is* it not in Rabbah of the people of Ammon?) Nine [b]cubits *is* its length and four cubits its width, according to the standard cubit.

Og's land given to the 2½ tribes

12 "And this [c]land, *which* we possessed at that time, from [d]Aroer, which *is* by the River Arnon, and half the mountains of Gilead and its cities, I [e]gave to the Reubenites and the Gadites.

13 [f]"The rest of Gilead, and all Bashan, the kingdom of Og, I gave to half the tribe of Manasseh. (All the region of Argob, with all Bashan, was called the land of the giants.*

14 [g]"Jair the son of Manasseh took all the region of Argob, as far as the border of the Geshurites and the Maachathites, and called Bashan after his own name, Havoth Jair,* to this day.)

15 "Also I gave [h]Gilead to Machir.

16 "And to the Reubenites and the Gadites I gave from Gilead as far as the River Arnon, the middle of the river as *the* border, as far as the River Jabbok, the border of the people of Ammon;

17 "the [i]plain also, with the Jordan as *the* border, from Chinnereth as far as the east side of the Sea of the Arabah (the Salt Sea), below the slopes of Pisgah.

18 "Then I commanded you at that time, saying: 'The LORD your God has given you this land to possess. All you men of valor [j]shall cross over armed before your brethren, the children of Israel.

19 'But your wives, your little ones, and your livestock (I know that you have much livestock) shall stay in your cities which I have given you,

20 'until the LORD has given [k]rest to your brethren as to you, and they also possess the land which the LORD your God is giving them beyond the Jordan. Then each of you may [l]return to his possession which I have given you.'

21 "And [m]I commanded Joshua at that time, saying, 'Your eyes have seen all that the LORD your God has done to these two kings; so will the LORD do to all the kingdoms through which you pass.

22 'You must not fear them, for [n]the LORD your God Himself fights for you.'

Moses may see but not enter land

23 "Then I [o]pleaded with the LORD at that time, saying:

24 'O Lord GOD, You have begun to show Your servant Your greatness and [p]Your mighty hand, for what god *is there* in heaven or on earth who can do *anything* like Your works and Your mighty *deeds?*

25 'I pray, let me cross over and see the good land beyond the Jordan, those pleasant mountains, and Lebanon.'

26 "But the LORD [q]was angry with me on your account, and would not listen to me. So the LORD said to me: 'Enough of that! Speak no more to Me of this matter.

27 'Go up to the top of Pisgah, and lift your eyes toward the west, the north, the south, and the east; behold *it* with your eyes, for you shall not cross over this Jordan.

28 'But command Joshua, and encourage him and strengthen him; for he shall go over before this people, and he shall cause them to inherit the land which you will see.'

29 "So we stayed in the [r]valley opposite [s]Beth Peor.

New generation taught greatness of the law

4 "NOW, O Israel, listen to the [t]statutes and the judgments which I teach you to observe, that you may live, and go in and possess the land which the LORD God of your fathers is giving you.

2 [u]"You shall not add to the [v]word which I command you, nor take from it, that you may keep the commandments of the LORD your God which I command you.

3 "Your eyes have seen what the LORD did at [w]Baal Peor; for the LORD your God has destroyed from among you all the men who followed Baal of Peor.

11 *a* Dt. 2:11, 20 *b* See Weights and Measures (OT), 2 Chr. 2:10, *note*
12 *c* Num. 32:33; Josh. 12:6; 13:8–12 *d* Dt. 2:36 *e* Num. 34:14
13 *f* Josh. 13:29–31; 17:1
14 *g* 1 Chr. 2:22
15 *h* Num. 32:39–40
17 *i* See Dt. 1:1, *note*
18 *j* Josh. 4:12–13; cp. Num. 32:1–32
20 *k* Dt. 12:9–10 *l* Josh. 22:4
21 *m* Num. 27:22–23
22 *n* Ex. 14:14; Dt. 1:30; 20:4
23 *o Bible prayers* (OT): vv. 23–25; Dt. 9:26. (Gen. 15:2; Hab. 3:1)
24 *p* Dt. 5:24
26 *q* Num. 20:12; 27:14; Dt. 1:37; 31:2; 32:51,52; 34:4; Ps. 106:32,33
29 *r* Or *ravine* *s* Dt. 34:6
CHAPTER 4
1 *t* Lev. 19:37; 20:8; 22:31; Dt. 5:1; 8:1; Ezek. 20:11; Rom. 10:5

4:2 *u* Dt. 12:32; Prov. 30:6; Rev. 22:18–19
v *Inspiration:* vv. 2,13; Dt. 5:22. (Ex. 4:15; 2 Tim. 3:16, *note*) 4:3 *w* Num. 25:4–9

*

3:11 Hebrew *rephaim* 3:13 Hebrew *rephaim*
3:14 Literally *Towns of Jair*

4 "But you who held fast to the LORD your God *are* alive today, every one of you.

5 "Surely I have taught you statutes and judgments, just as the LORD my God commanded me, that you should act according *to them* in the land which you go to possess.

6 "Therefore be careful to observe *them;* for this *is* your wisdom and your understanding in the sight of the peoples who will hear all these statutes, and say, 'Surely this great nation *is* a wise and understanding people.'

7 "For what great nation *is there* that has God *so* [a]near to it, as the LORD our God *is* to us, for whatever *reason* we may call upon Him?

8 "And what great nation *is there* that has *such* statutes and righteous judgments as are in all this law which I set before you this day?

9 "Only take heed to yourself, and diligently [b]keep yourself, lest you [c]forget the things your eyes have seen, and lest they depart from your heart all the days of your life. And [d]teach them to your children and your grandchildren,

10 "*especially concerning* the day you stood before the LORD your God in [e]Horeb, when the LORD said to me, 'Gather the people to Me, and I will let them hear My words, that they may learn to [f]fear Me all the days they live on the earth, and *that* they may teach their children.'

11 "Then you came near and stood at the foot of the mountain, and the mountain burned with fire to the midst of heaven, with darkness, cloud, and thick darkness.

12 "And the LORD spoke to you out of the midst of the fire. You heard the sound of the words, but saw no form; *you* [g]only *heard* a voice.

13 "So He declared to you His covenant which He commanded you to perform, the [h]Ten Commandments; and He wrote them on two tablets of stone.

14 "And the LORD commanded me at that time to teach you statutes and judgments, that you might observe them in the land which you cross over to possess.

15 "Take careful heed to yourselves, for you [i]saw no form when the LORD spoke to you at Horeb out of the midst of the fire,

16 "lest you act [j]corruptly and make for yourselves a carved image in the form of any figure: the [k]likeness of male or female,

17 "the likeness of any animal that *is* on the earth or the likeness of any winged bird that flies in the air,

18 "the likeness of anything that creeps on the ground or the likeness of any fish that *is* in the water beneath the earth.

19 "And *take heed,* lest you lift your eyes to heaven, and *when* you see the sun, the moon, and the stars, all the host of heaven, you feel [l]driven to worship them and serve them, [1]which the LORD your God has given to all the peoples under the whole heaven as a heritage.

20 "But the LORD has taken you and [m]brought you out of the iron furnace, out of Egypt, to be His [n]people, an inheritance, as you are this day.

21 "Furthermore the [o]LORD was angry with me for your sakes, and swore that [p]I would not cross over the Jordan, and that I would not enter the good land which the LORD your God is giving you as an inheritance.

22 "But I must die in this land, I must not cross over the Jordan; but you shall cross over and possess that good land.

23 "Take heed to yourselves, lest you forget the covenant of the LORD your God which He made with you, and make for yourselves a carved image in the form of anything which the LORD your God has forbidden you.

24 "For the LORD your God *is* a [q]consuming fire, a [r]jealous God.

25 "When you beget children and grandchildren and have grown old in the land, and act corruptly and make a carved image in the form of anything, and do evil in the sight of the LORD your God to provoke Him to anger,

26 [s]"I call heaven and earth to witness against you this day, that you will soon utterly perish from the land which you cross over the Jordan to possess; you will not prolong *your* days in it, but will be utterly destroyed.

27 "And the LORD will [t]scatter you among the peoples, and you will be

7
a Ps. 46:1; 145:18; 148:14; Isa. 55:6
9
b Prov. 4:23
c Dt. 29:2–8
d Dt. 6:7, 20–25
10
e Ex. 19:17
f Dt. 14:23; 17:19; 31:12,13; see Ps. 19:9, *note*
12
g Ex. 19:17–19; 20:22; 1 Ki. 19:11–18
13
h Ex. 34:28
15
i See Jn. 1:18, *note*
16
j Dt. 9:12; 31:29
k Rom. 1:23
19
l Or *drawn away.* Dt. 13:5,10
20
m 1 Ki. 8:51; Jer. 11:4
n Dt. 27:9
21
o Dt. 1:37; 3:26
p Num. 27:13–14
24
q Dt. 9:3; Heb. 12:29
r Ex. 34:14
26
s Dt. 30:18, 19; Isa. 1:2; Mic. 6:2
27
t Lev. 26:33; Dt. 28:62,64; Neh. 1:8

[1](4:19) The last clause does not mean that the worship of the heavenly bodies was assigned by God to "all the peoples," but that the purpose of these bodies is the same for all peoples, for the regulation of seasons, signs, etc., as in Gen. 1:14–19.

left few in number among the nations where the LORD will drive you.

28 "And there you will serve gods, the work of men's hands, wood and stone, [a]which neither see nor hear nor eat nor smell.

29 "But from there you will [b]seek the LORD your God, and you will find *Him* if you seek Him with all your heart and with all your soul.

30 "When you are in distress, and all these things come upon you [c]in the latter days, when you turn to the LORD your God and obey His voice

31 "(for the LORD your God *is* a merciful God), He will not forsake you nor [d]destroy you, nor forget the covenant of your fathers which He swore to them.

32 "For ask now concerning the days that are past, which were before you, since the day that God created man on the earth, and *ask* from one end of heaven to the other, whether *any* great *thing* like this has happened, or *anything* like it has been heard.

33 "Did *any* people *ever* [e]hear the voice of God speaking out of the midst of the fire, as you have heard, and live?

34 "Or did God *ever* try to go *and* take for Himself a nation from the midst of *another* [f]nation, by trials, by signs, by wonders, by war, by a mighty hand and [g]an outstretched arm, and by [h]great terrors, according to all that the LORD your God did for you in Egypt before your eyes?

35 "To you it was shown, that you might [i]know that the LORD Himself *is* God; *there is* none other besides Him.

36 [j]"Out of heaven He let you hear His voice, that He might instruct you; on earth He showed you His great fire, and you heard His words out of the midst of the fire.

37 "And because He [k]loved your fathers, therefore He chose their descendants after them; and He brought you out of Egypt with His Presence, with His mighty power,

38 "driving out from before you nations [l]greater and mightier than you, to bring you in, to give you their land *as* an inheritance, as *it is* this day.

39 "Therefore know this day, and consider *it* in your heart, that the LORD Himself *is* God in heaven above and on the earth beneath; *there is* no other.

40 "You shall therefore keep His [m]statutes and His commandments

28
a Ps. 115:4–7; 135:15–17; Isa. 44:9; 46:7
29
b Dt. 30:1–3; Jer. 50:4
30
c Gen. 49:1; Dt. 31:29; Jer. 23:20; Hos. 3:5
31
d Lev. 26:44; Jer. 30:11
33
e Ex. 20:22; Dt. 5:24–26
34
f Ex. 14:30
g Dt. 7:19; Ps. 136:12
h Dt. 26:8
35
i Ex. 8:10; 9:14
36
j Ex. 19:9, 19; 20:18–22; 24:16; Heb. 12:19
37
k Dt. 7:7–8; 10:15; 33:3
38
l Dt. 7:1
40
m Dt. 4:1; 6:1; see Ex. 20:1, *note*
n Dt. 5:16; 32:46–47
42
o Dt. 19:4
43
p Josh. 20:8
46
q Num. 21:24; Dt. 1:4
48
r Dt. 2:36; 3:12
49
s See Dt. 1:1, *note*
CHAPTER 5
1
t Law (of Moses): vv. 1–22; Dt. 6:1. (Ex. 19:1; Gal. 3:24, *note*)
2
u Ex. 19:5; Dt. 4:23; Mal. 4:4

which I command you today, that it may go well with [n]you and with your children after you, and that you may prolong *your* days in the land which the LORD your God is giving you for all time."

Three cities of refuge east of the Jordan

41 Then Moses set apart three cities on this side of the Jordan, toward the rising of the sun,

42 [o]that the manslayer might flee there, who kills his neighbor unintentionally, without having hated him in time past, and that by fleeing to one of these cities he might live:

43 [p]Bezer in the wilderness on the plateau for the Reubenites, Ramoth in Gilead for the Gadites, and Golan in Bashan for the Manassites.

Setting for recounting the law

44 Now this *is* the law which Moses set before the children of Israel.

45 These *are* the testimonies, the statutes, and the judgments which Moses spoke to the children of Israel after they came out of Egypt,

46 on this side of the Jordan, in the valley opposite Beth Peor, in the land of Sihon king of the Amorites, who dwelt at Heshbon, whom Moses and the children of Israel [q]defeated after they came out of Egypt.

47 And they took possession of his land and the land of Og king of Bashan, two kings of the Amorites, who *were* on this side of the Jordan, toward the rising of the sun,

48 from [r]Aroer, which *is* on the bank of the River Arnon, even to Mount Sion* (that is, Hermon),

49 and all the [s]plain on the east side of the Jordan as far as the Sea of the Arabah, below the slopes of Pisgah.

II. Second Discourse: Recounting of the Sinaitic Laws, with Warnings and Exhortations, 5—26

The new generation taught fundamentals of the law

5 AND Moses called all Israel, and said to them: "Hear, O Israel, the [m]statutes and judgments which I speak in your hearing today, that you may learn them and be careful to [t]observe them.

2 "The LORD our God made a [u]covenant with us in Horeb.

* 4:48 Syriac reads *Sirion* (compare 3:9).

3 "The LORD [a]did not make this
covenant with our fathers, but with us,
those who *are* here today, all of us
who *are* alive.
4 "The LORD talked with you face
to face on the mountain from the
midst of the fire.
5 [b]"I stood between the LORD and
you at that time, to declare to you the
word of the LORD; for you were afraid
because of the fire, and you did not go
up the mountain. *He* said:
6 [c]'I *am* the LORD your God who
brought you out of the land of
Egypt, out of the house of
bondage.
7 'You shall have [d]no other gods
before Me.
8 'You shall not make for yourself
a [e]carved image—any likeness *of anything* that *is* in
heaven above, or that *is* in the
earth beneath, or that *is* in the
water under the earth;
9 you shall not [f]bow down to
them nor serve them. For I,
the LORD your God, *am* a jealous God, visiting the iniquity
of the fathers upon the children to the third and fourth
generations of those who
hate Me,
10 but showing [g]mercy to thousands, to those who love Me
and keep My command-
ments.
11 'You shall not take the name of
the LORD your God [h]in vain,
for the LORD will not hold *him*
guiltless who takes His name
in vain.
12 'Observe the Sabbath day, to
keep it [i]holy, as the LORD
your God commanded you.
13 [j]Six days you shall labor and
do all your work,
14 but the seventh day *is* the
Sabbath of the LORD your
God. *In it* you shall do no
work: you, nor your son, nor
your daughter, nor your male
servant, nor your female servant, nor your ox, nor your
donkey, nor any of your cattle, nor your stranger who *is*
within your gates, that your
male servant and your female
servant may rest as well as
you.
15 And [k]remember that you
were a slave in the land of
Egypt, and the LORD your God
brought you out from there
by a mighty hand and by an
outstretched arm; therefore
the LORD your God com-
manded you to keep the Sabbath day.
16 'Honor your father and your
[l]mother, as the LORD your
God has commanded you,
that your days may be [m]long,
and that it may be well with
[n]you in the land which the
LORD your God is giving you.
17 'You shall not [o]murder.
18 'You shall not commit adultery.
19 'You shall not steal.
20 'You shall not bear false witness
against your neighbor.
21 'You shall not covet your neighbor's wife; and you shall not
desire your neighbor's house,
his field, his male servant, his
female servant, his ox, his
donkey, or anything that *is*
your neighbor's.'

Mediatorship of Moses

22 "These [p]words the LORD spoke
to all your assembly, in the mountain
from the midst of the fire, the cloud,
and the thick darkness, with a loud
voice; and He added no more. And He
[q]wrote them on two tablets of stone
and gave them to me.
23 "So it was, when you heard the
voice from the midst of the darkness,
while the mountain was burning with
fire, that you came near to me, all the
heads of your tribes and your elders.
24 "And you said: 'Surely the LORD
our God has shown us His glory and
His greatness, and we have heard His
voice from the midst of the fire. We
have seen this day that God speaks
with man; yet he *still* [r]lives.
25 'Now therefore, why should we
[s]die? For this great fire will consume
us; if we hear the voice of the LORD our
God anymore, then we shall die.
26 'For who *is there* of all flesh who
has heard the voice of the living God
speaking from the midst of the fire, as
we *have*, and lived?
27 'You go near and hear all that
the LORD our God may say, and [t]tell us
all that the LORD our God says to you,
and we will hear and do *it*.'
28 "Then the LORD heard the voice
of your words when you spoke to me,
and the LORD said to me: 'I have heard
the voice of the words of this people
which they have spoken to you. They
are right *in* all that they have [u]spoken.
29 [v]'Oh, that they had such a heart

3 *a* Cp. Num. 26:63–65; Heb. 8:9
5 *b* Ex. 20:19–21; Gal. 3:19
6 *c* vv. 6–21; cp. Ex. 20:2–17
7 *d* Ex. 23:13; Hos. 13:4
8 *e* Dt. 4:15–18
9 *f* Ex. 34:14–16
10 *g* Jer. 32:18; Dan. 9:4
11 *h* Dt. 6:13; 10:20
12 *i* Ezek. 20:12
13 *j* Ex. 23:12; 35:2
15 *k* Dt. 15:15
16 *l* Lev. 19:3; Mt. 15:4; Eph. 6:2,3; Col. 3:20
m Dt. 6:2
n Dt. 4:40
17 *o* See Ex. 20:13, *note*
22 *p* *Inspiration:* v. 22; Dt. 10:1. (Ex. 4:15; 2 Tim. 3:16, *note*)
q Ex. 31:18; Dt. 4:13
24 *r* Dt. 4:33; cp. Jud. 13:21–23
25 *s* Dt. 18:16
27 *t* Ex. 20:19; Heb. 12:19
28 *u* Dt. 18:17
29 *v* Dt. 32:29; Ps. 81:13; Isa. 48:18; Mt. 23:37; Lk. 19:42

in [a]them that they would [b]fear Me
and always keep all My commandments, that it might be well with them
and with their children forever!
30 'Go and say to them, "Return to
your tents."
31 'But as for you, stand here by
Me, and I will speak to you all the
commandments, the statutes, and the
judgments which you shall teach
them, that they may observe *them* in
the land which I am giving them to
possess.'
32 "Therefore you shall be careful
to do as the LORD your God has commanded you; you shall not turn aside
to the right hand or to the left.
33 "You shall walk in [c]all the ways
which the LORD your God has commanded you, that you may live and
that it may be well with you, and *that*
you may prolong *your* days in the land
which you shall possess.

Essence of the law (vv. 4–5)

6

"NOW this *is* the commandment,
and these are the statutes and
judgments which the LORD your God
has commanded to teach you, that you
may [d]observe *them* in the land which
you are crossing over to possess,
2 "that you may [e]fear the LORD
your God, to keep all His statutes and
His commandments which I command you, you and your son and your
grandson, all the days of your life, and
that your days may be prolonged.
3 "Therefore hear, O Israel, and be
careful to observe *it*, that it may be
well with you, and that you may [f]mul-
tiply greatly as the LORD God of your
fathers has promised you—'a [g]land
flowing with milk and honey.'
4 [1]"Hear, O Israel: The LORD our
God, the [h]LORD *is* [i]one!*
5 "You shall [2]love the LORD your
God with all your heart, with all your
soul, and with all your strength.

Parents to instruct children

6 "And these words which I command you today shall be in your
[j]heart.
7 "You shall [k]teach them diligently to your children, and shall talk
of them when you sit in your house,
when you walk by the way, when you
lie down, and when you rise up.
8 "You shall bind them as a sign
on your hand, and they shall be as
frontlets between your eyes.
9 "You shall write them on the
doorposts of your house and on your
gates.
10 "So it shall be, when the LORD
your God brings you into the land of
which He swore to your fathers, to
Abraham, Isaac, and Jacob, to give
you large and beautiful cities which
you did [l]not build,
11 "houses full of all good things,
which you did not fill, hewn-out wells
which you did not dig, vineyards and
olive trees which you did not plant—
when you have eaten and are full—
12 "*then* beware, lest you forget the
[m]LORD who brought you out of the land
of Egypt, from the house of bondage.
13 "You shall [e]fear the LORD your
God and serve [n]Him, and shall take
oaths in His [o]name.
14 "You shall not go after other
gods, the gods of the peoples who *are*
all around you
15 "(for the LORD your God *is* a
[p]jealous God [q]among you), lest the
anger of the LORD your God be
aroused against you and destroy you
from the face of the earth.
16 "You shall not [r]tempt the LORD
your [s]God as you tempted *Him* in
[t]Massah.
17 "You shall diligently keep the

29
a Cp. Jer. 31:31–34
b See Ps. 19:9, *note*
33
c Dt. 10:12; Ps. 119:3; Jer. 7:23; Lk. 1:6
CHAPTER 6
1
d *Law* (of Moses): vv. 1–5; Ps. 1:2. (Ex. 19:1; Gal. 3:24, *note*)
2
e Dt. 10:20; see Ps. 19:9, *note*
3
f Dt. 7:13
g Ex. 3:8,17
4
h Mk. 12:29
i Dt. 4:35
6
j Dt. 11:18–20
7
k Dt. 4:9
10
l Josh. 24:13
12
m Dt. 8:11–18
13
n Mt. 4:10; Lk. 4:8
o Dt. 5:11
15
p Dt. 4:24
q Ex. 33:3
16
r *Test/tempt:* v. 16; Dt. 7:25. (Gen. 3:1; Jas. 1:14, *note*)
s Mt. 4:7; Lk. 4:12
t Ex. 17:7

* 6:4 Or *The LORD is our God, the LORD alone* (that is, the only one)

[1](6:4) *"Shema"* (pronounced Sh'mah) is the initial Hebrew word of this verse; the entire verse is recited as the Jewish confession of faith. In Hebrew liturgy the *Shema* includes Dt. 6:4–9; 11:13–21; and Num. 15:37–41. The *Shema* is understood to emphasize the monotheistic belief of Judaism. Moses is credited with the commandment to read the *Shema* twice daily ("when you lie down, and when you rise up"), and the Jews have always regarded it as divinely prescribed. At the end of the first and last word of the sentence in the Hebrew text, large letters are used. They were meant to emphasize, according to Jewish tradition, the need for pronouncing these important words distinctly and without slur.

[2](6:5) The concept of love is one of the great themes of Deuteronomy. There is first the declaration of God's love for His people (7:7; 10:15; 23:5); then the exhortation that God's people should always love Him with their whole being (6:5; 10:12; 11:1,13,22; 19:9; 30:6,16,20); and finally the exhortation that they love even the stranger among them (10:19). Our Lord sums up all these earlier commands in His address to the Pharisees on "the first and great commandment" (Mt. 22:34–40; Mk. 12:28–34, where He refers also to Lev. 19:18. Cp. Lk. 10:27).

commandments of the LORD your God,
His testimonies, and His statutes
which He has commanded you.
18 "And you shall do *what is* right
and good in the sight of the LORD, that
it may be well with you, and that you
may go in and possess the [a]good land
of which the LORD swore to your fathers,
19 [b]"to cast out all your enemies
from before you, as the LORD has spoken.
20 "When your son asks you in time
to come, saying, 'What *is the meaning
of* the testimonies, the statutes, and
the judgments which the LORD our
God has commanded you?'
21 "then you shall say to your son:
'We were [c]slaves of Pharaoh in
Egypt, and the LORD brought us out of
Egypt with a mighty hand;
22 'and the LORD showed signs and
wonders before our eyes, great and
severe, against Egypt, Pharaoh, and
all his household.
23 'Then He brought us out from
there, that He might [1]bring us in, to
give us the land of which He swore to
our fathers.
24 'And the LORD commanded us to
observe all these statutes, to [d]fear the
LORD our God, [e]for our good always,
that He might preserve us alive, as *it
is* this day.
25 'Then [f]it will be righteousness
for us, if we are careful to observe all
these commandments before the LORD
our God, as He has commanded us.'

*Results of obedience and disobedience
(Dt. 7—12). The command to be separate*

7 "WHEN the LORD your God brings
you into the land [g]which you go
to possess, and has cast out many [h]na-
tions before you, the [i]Hittites and the
Girgashites and the Amorites and the
Canaanites and the Perizzites and the
Hivites and the Jebusites, seven nations greater and mightier than you,
2 "and when the LORD your God
delivers [j]them over to you, you shall
conquer them *and* utterly destroy
them. You shall make no covenant
with them nor show mercy to them.
3 [k]"Nor shall you make marriages
with them. You shall not give your
daughter to their son, nor take their
daughter for your son.
4 "For they will turn your sons
away from following Me, to serve

18
a Dt. 8:7–10
19
b Num. 33:52–53
21
c Ex. 13:3
24
d See Ps. 19:9, *note*
e Dt. 10:13; Job 35:7,8; Jer. 32:39
25
f Lev. 18:5; Dt. 24:13; Rom. 10:3, 5
CHAPTER 7
1
g Dt. 6:10
h Gen. 15:19–21; Ex. 33:2
i See 2 Ki. 7:6, *note*
2
j Ex. 23:32–33; Num. 31:17; Dt. 20:16–18
3
k Josh. 23:12–13; 1 Ki. 11:2; cp. Ezra 9:2
4
l Dt. 6:15
5
m See Dt. 16:21, *note*
6
n Ex. 19:6
o *Israel* (history): vv. 6–8; Dt. 28:58. (Gen. 12:2; Rom. 11:26, *note*)
p *Election* (corporate): vv. 6–7; Dt. 10:15. (Dt. 7:6; 1 Pet. 5:13, *note*)
q Lit. *a people for His own possession.* Ex. 19:5; Dt. 14:2; 26:18; cp. Ti. 2:14; 1 Pet. 2:9
7
r Dt. 4:37
8
s See Ex. 6:6, *note*

other gods; so the anger of the LORD
will be aroused against you and [l]de-
stroy you suddenly.
5 "But thus you shall deal with
them: you shall destroy their altars,
and break down their *sacred* pillars,
and cut down their [m]wooden images,
and burn their carved images with
fire.
6 "For you *are* a [n]holy [o]people to
the LORD your God; the LORD your God
has [p]chosen you to be [q]a people for
Himself, a special treasure above all
the peoples on the face of the earth.
7 "The LORD did not set His [r]love
on you nor choose you because you
were more in number than any other
people, for you were the least of all
peoples;
8 "but because the LORD loves you,
and because He would keep the oath
which He swore to your fathers, the
LORD has brought you out with a
mighty hand, and redeemed you from
the house of [s]bondage, from the hand
of Pharaoh king of Egypt.
9 "Therefore know that the LORD
your God, He *is* God, the faithful God
[t]who keeps covenant and mercy for a
thousand generations with those who
love Him and keep His commandments;
10 "and He repays those who hate
Him to their face, to destroy them. He
will not be [u]slack with him who hates
Him; He will repay him to his face.
11 "Therefore you shall keep the
commandment, the statutes, and the
judgments which I command you today, to observe them.

Promise of victory

12 "Then [v]it shall come to pass, because you listen to these judgments,
and keep and do them, that the LORD
your God will keep with you the covenant and the mercy which He swore
to your fathers.
13 "And He will [w]love you and bless
you and multiply you; He will also
bless the fruit of your womb and the
fruit of your land, your [x]grain and
your new wine and your oil, the increase of your cattle and the offspring
of your flock, in the land of which He
swore to your fathers to give you.
14 "You shall be blessed above all

7:9 t Ex. 20:6; Dt. 5:10; Neh. 1:5; Dan. 9:4
7:10 u 2 Pet. 3:9 7:12 v vv. 12–26, cp. Lev. 26:3–13; Dt. 28:1–14 7:13 w Jn. 14:21 x Gen. 27:28

[1](6:23) Redemption must always be followed by sanctification and growth in grace. God has not "brought us out" in order to leave us wandering in the wilderness.

peoples; there shall not be a male or
female [a]barren among you or among
your livestock.
15 "And the LORD will take away
from you all sickness, and will afflict
you with none of the [b]terrible diseases of Egypt which you have
known, but will lay *them* on all those
who hate you.
16 "Also you shall destroy all the
peoples whom the LORD your God delivers over to you; your eye shall have
no pity on them; nor shall you serve
their gods, for that *will be* a [c]snare to
you.
17 "If you should say in your heart,
'These nations are greater than I; how
can I dispossess them?'—
18 "you shall not be afraid of them,
but you shall remember well what the
LORD your God did to Pharaoh and to
all Egypt:
19 "the great trials which your eyes
saw, the signs and the wonders, the
mighty hand and the outstretched
arm, by which the LORD your God
brought you out. So shall the LORD
your God do to all the peoples of
whom you are afraid.
20 "Moreover the LORD your God
will send the hornet among them until
those who are left, who hide themselves from you, are destroyed.
21 "You shall not be terrified of
them; for the LORD your God, the great
and [d]awesome God, *is* among you.
22 "And the LORD your God will
drive out those nations before you
[e]little by little; you will be unable to
destroy them at once, lest the beasts of
the field become *too* numerous for
you.
23 "But the LORD your God will deliver them over to you, and will inflict
defeat upon them until they are destroyed.
24 "And He [f]will deliver their
kings into your hand, and you will destroy their name from under heaven;
no one shall be able to stand against
[g]you until you have destroyed them.
25 "You shall burn the carved images of their gods with fire; you shall
not [h]covet the silver or gold *that is* on
them, nor take *it* for yourselves, lest
you be [i]snared by it; for it *is* an abomination to the LORD your God.
26 "Nor shall you bring an abomination into your house, lest you be

14
a Ex. 23:26
15
b Ex. 9:14; 15:26; Dt. 28:27,60
16
c Ex. 23:33; Jud. 8:27; Ps. 106:36
21
d Dt. 10:17
22
e Ex. 23:30
24
f Josh. 10:24,42; 12:1–24
g Josh. 23:9
25
h Prov. 23:6
i *Test/tempt:* v. 25; 8:2; Dt. 8:16. (Gen. 3:1; Jas. 1:14, *note*)
CHAPTER 8
1
j Dt. 4:1; 6:24
k Dt. 30:16
2
l Dt. 2:7; 29:5; Ps. 136:16; Amos 2:10
m Ex. 15:25; 20:20
n Cp. 2 Chr. 32:31
3
o Mt. 4:4; Lk. 4:4
4
p Dt. 29:5; Neh. 9:21
5
q Ps. 89:30–33; Prov. 3:11–12; Heb. 12:5–11; Rev. 3:19; cp. 2 Sam. 7:14–15
6
r Dt. 10:12; see Ps. 19:9, *note*
7
s Dt. 11:9–12
10
t Dt. 6:11

doomed to destruction like it. You
shall utterly detest it and utterly abhor
it, for it *is* an accursed thing.

Moses looks backward and onward

8 "EVERY commandment which I
command you today you must be
careful to observe, that you may [j]live
and [k]multiply, and go in and possess
the land of which the LORD swore to
your fathers.
2 "And you shall remember that
the LORD your God [l]led you all the
way these forty years in the wilderness, to humble you *and* [m]test you, to
[1]know what *was* in your [n]heart,
whether you would keep His commandments or not.
3 "So He humbled you, allowed
you to hunger, and fed you with
manna which you did not know nor
did your fathers know, that He might
make you know that man shall not
live by bread [o]alone; but man lives by
every *word* that proceeds from the
mouth of the LORD.
4 "Your [p]garments did not wear
out on you, nor did your foot swell
these forty years.
5 [q]"You should know in your
heart that as a man chastens his son,
so the LORD your God chastens you.
6 "Therefore you shall keep the
commandments of the LORD your God,
to walk in His ways and to [r]fear Him.
7 "For the LORD your God is bringing you into a [s]good land, a land of
brooks of water, of fountains and
springs, that flow out of valleys and
hills;
8 "a land of wheat and barley, of
vines and fig trees and pomegranates,
a land of olive oil and honey;
9 "a land in which you will eat
bread without scarcity, in which you
will lack nothing; a land whose stones
are iron and out of whose hills you can
dig copper.
10 "When you have eaten and are
[t]full, then you shall bless the LORD
your God for the good land which He
has given you.
11 "Beware that you do not forget
the LORD your God by not keeping His
commandments, His judgments, and
His statutes which I command you today,

[1](8:2) This does not mean that God did not "know" what was in the hearts of men. The knowledge here is something that is to be demonstrated by testing men in moral experience. See the connection between the two verbs: "to . . . *test* you, to *know* . . ."

12 [a]"lest—*when* you have eaten
and are full, and have built beautiful
houses and dwell *in them;*
13 "and *when* your herds and your
flocks multiply, and your silver and
your gold are multiplied, and all that
you have is multiplied;
14 [b]"when your heart is lifted up,
and you [c]forget the LORD your God
who brought you out of the land of
Egypt, from the house of bondage;
15 "who led you through that great
and terrible wilderness, *in which were*
[d]fiery serpents and scorpions and
thirsty land where there was no water;
who brought water for you out of the
flinty [e]rock;
16 "who fed you in the wilderness
with manna, which your fathers did
not know, that He might humble you
and that He might [f]test you, [g]to do
you good in the end—
17 "then you say in your heart,
[h]'My power and the might of my hand
have gained me this wealth.'
18 "And you shall remember the
LORD your God, for *it is* [i]He who gives
you power to get wealth, that He may
establish His covenant which He
swore to your fathers, as *it is* this day.
19 "Then it shall be, if you by any
means forget the LORD your God, and
follow other gods, and serve them and
worship them, I testify against you
this day that you shall surely perish.
20 "As the nations which the LORD
destroys before you, so you shall perish, because you would not be obedient to the voice of the LORD your God.

Sad recollections

9 "HEAR, O Israel: You *are* to cross
over the Jordan today, and go in
to dispossess nations greater and
mightier than yourself, cities great
and fortified up to heaven,
2 "a people great and tall, the [j]de-
scendants of the Anakim, whom you
know, and *of whom* you heard *it said,*
'Who can stand before the descendants of Anak?'
3 "Therefore understand today
that the LORD your God *is* He who
[k]goes over before you *as* a [l]consum-
ing fire. He will destroy them and
bring them down before you; so you
shall drive them out and destroy them
quickly, as the LORD has said to you.
4 [m]"Do not think in your heart, after the LORD your God has cast them
out before you, saying, 'Because of my
righteousness the LORD has brought
me in to possess this land'; but *it is*
[n]because of the [o]wickedness of these
nations *that* the LORD is driving them
out from before you.
5 "*It is* not because of your righteousness or the uprightness of your
heart *that* you go in to possess their
land, but because of the wickedness of
these nations *that* the LORD your God
drives them out from before you, and
that He may fulfill the [p]word which
the LORD swore to your fathers, to
Abraham, Isaac, and Jacob.
6 "Therefore understand that the
LORD your God is not giving you this
good land to possess because of your
righteousness, for you *are* a [q]stiff-
necked people.
7 "Remember! Do not forget how
you [r]provoked the LORD your God to
wrath in the wilderness. From the day
that you departed from the land of
Egypt until you came to this place, you
have been rebellious against the LORD.
8 "Also in [s]Horeb you provoked
the LORD to wrath, so that the LORD was
angry *enough* with you to have destroyed you.
9 "When I went up into the mountain to receive the tablets of stone, the
[t]tablets of the covenant which the
LORD made with you, then I stayed on
the mountain [u]forty days and forty
nights. I neither ate bread nor drank
water.
10 [v]"Then the LORD delivered to me
two tablets of stone [w]written with the
finger of God, and on them *were* all
the words which the LORD had spoken
to you on the mountain from the midst
of the fire in the day of the assembly.
11 "And it came to pass, at the end
of forty days and forty nights, *that* the
LORD gave me the two tablets of stone,
the tablets of the covenant.
12 [x]"Then the LORD said to me,
'Arise, go down quickly from here, for
your people whom you brought out of
Egypt have acted corruptly; they have
quickly turned aside from the way
which I commanded them; they have
made themselves a molded image.'
13 "Furthermore the LORD spoke to
me, saying, 'I have seen this people,
and indeed they are a stiff-necked
people.
14 'Let Me alone, that I may destroy
them and [y]blot out their name from
under heaven; and I will [z]make of you
a nation mightier and greater than
they.'
15 "So I turned and came down

12 *a* Dt. 28:47; Prov. 30:9; Hos. 13:6; cp. Dt. 32:15
14 *b* 1 Cor. 4:7; cp. Ezek. 28:17 *c* Ps. 106:21
15 *d* Num. 21:6 *e* Ex. 17:6; Num. 20:11
16 *f Test/tempt:* vv. 15–16; Dt. 13:3. (Gen. 3:1; Jas. 1:14, *note*) *g* Jer. 24:5, 6; Heb. 12:11
17 *h* Dt. 9:4; cp. Dan. 4:30
18 *i* Hos. 2:8
CHAPTER 9
2 *j* Num. 13:22,28, 32,33
3 *k* Dt. 1:33; 31:3; Josh. 3:11; cp. Jn. 10:4 *l* Dt. 4:24
4 *m* Dt. 8:17; cp. Rom. 11:6,20; 1 Cor. 4:4, 7 *n* Gen. 15:16 *o* Lev. 18:3, 24–30; Dt. 12:31; 18:9–14
5 *p* Gen. 50:24
6 *q* Ex. 34:9; Dt. 31:27
7 *r* Num. 14:22
8 *s* Ex. 32:4; Ps. 106:19
9 *t* Dt. 5:2–22 *u* Ex. 24:18
10 *v* See Ex. 20:1, *note* *w* Dt. 4:13
12 *x* vv. 12–14; cp. Ex. 32:7–10

9:14 *y* Ex. 32:33 *z* Num. 14:12

from the mountain, and the mountain burned with fire; and the two tablets of the covenant *were* in my two hands.

16 "And I looked, and behold, you had sinned against the LORD your God—had made for yourselves a molded calf! You had turned aside quickly from the way which the LORD had commanded you.

17 "Then I took the two tablets and threw them out of my two hands and [a]broke them before your eyes.

18 "And I [b]fell down before the LORD, as at the [c]first, forty days and forty nights; I neither ate bread nor drank water, because of all your sin which you committed in doing wickedly in the sight of the LORD, to provoke Him to anger.

19 "For I was afraid of the anger and hot displeasure with which the LORD was angry with you, to destroy you. But the LORD listened to me at that time also.

20 "And the LORD was very angry with Aaron *and* would have destroyed him; so I prayed for Aaron also at the same time.

21 "Then I took your sin, the calf which you had made, and burned it with fire and crushed it *and* ground *it* very small, until it was as fine as dust; and I [d]threw its dust into the brook that descended from the mountain.

22 "Also at [e]Taberah and [f]Massah and [g]Kibroth Hattaavah you provoked the LORD to wrath.

23 "Likewise, when the LORD sent you from [h]Kadesh Barnea, saying, 'Go up and possess the land which I have given you,' then you rebelled against the commandment of the LORD your God, and you did not believe Him nor obey His voice.

24 "You have been rebellious against the LORD from the day that I knew you.

25 "Thus I prostrated myself before the LORD; forty days and forty nights I kept prostrating myself, because the LORD had said He would destroy you.

26 "Therefore I [i]prayed to the LORD, and said: 'O Lord GOD, do not destroy Your people and [j]Your inheritance whom You have [k]redeemed through Your greatness, whom You have brought out of Egypt with a mighty hand.

27 'Remember Your servants, Abraham, Isaac, and Jacob; do not look on the stubbornness of this people, or on their wickedness or their sin,

28 'lest the land from which You brought us should say, "Because the LORD was not able to bring them to the land which He promised them, and because He hated them, He has brought them out to kill them in the wilderness."

29 'Yet they *are* Your people and Your inheritance, whom You brought out by Your mighty power and by Your outstretched arm.'

God's mercy in replacing broken tablets of the law

10 "AT that time the LORD [l]said to me, 'Hew for yourself two tablets of stone like the first, and come up to Me on the mountain and make yourself an [m]ark of wood.

2 'And I will write on the tablets the words that were on the first tablets, which you broke; and you shall put them in the ark.'

3 "So I [n]made an ark of acacia wood, hewed two tablets of stone like the first, and went up the mountain, having the two tablets in my hand.

4 "And He wrote on the tablets according to the first writing, the [o]Ten Commandments, which the LORD had spoken to you in the mountain from the midst of the fire in the day of the assembly; and the LORD gave them to me.

5 "Then I turned and came down from the mountain, and put the tablets in the ark which I had made; and there they [p]are, just as the LORD commanded me."

6 (Now the children of Israel journeyed from the wells of Bene Jaakan to Moserah, where Aaron [q]died, and where he was buried; and Eleazar his son ministered as priest in his stead.

7 From there they journeyed to Gudgodah, and from Gudgodah to [r]Jotbathah, a land of rivers of water.

8 At that time the LORD [s]separated the tribe of Levi to [t]bear the ark of the covenant of the LORD, to stand before the LORD to minister to Him and to bless in His name, to this day.

9 Therefore Levi has [u]no portion nor inheritance with his brethren; the LORD *is* his inheritance, just as the LORD your God promised him.)

10 "As at the first time, I stayed in the mountain [v]forty days and forty nights; the LORD also heard me at that time, *and* the LORD chose not to destroy you.

11 "Then the LORD said to me, 'Arise, begin *your* journey before the

17
a Ex. 32:19
18
b Ex. 34:28; Ps. 106:23
c v. 9; cp. 10:10
21
d Ex. 32:20
22
e Num. 11:3
f Ex. 17:7
g Num. 11:34
23
h Num. 14:11
26
i *Bible prayers (OT):* vv. 26–29; Dt. 21:8. (Gen. 15:2; Hab. 3:1)
j Dt. 32:9
k See Ex. 6:6, *note*

CHAPTER 10
1
l *Inspiration:* vv. 1–4; Dt. 29:29. (Ex. 4:15; 2 Tim. 3:16, *note*)
m Ex. 25:10
3
n Cp. Ex. 37:1–9
4
o Ex. 34:28; Dt. 4:13
5
p 1 Ki. 8:9
6
q Num. 20:25–28; 33:38
7
r Num. 33:33,34
8
s Num. 3:6
t Num. 10:21
9
u Num. 18:20,24
10
v Dt. 9:18, 25

people, that they may go in and possess the land which I swore to their fathers to give them.'

12 "And now, Israel, [a]what does the LORD your God require of you, but to [b]fear the LORD your God, to walk in all His ways and to [c]love Him, to serve the LORD your God with all your heart and with all your soul,

13 "*and* to keep the commandments of the LORD and His statutes which I command you today [d]for your good?

14 "Indeed heaven and the highest heavens belong to the [e]LORD your God, *also* the earth with all that *is* in it.

15 "The LORD delighted only in your fathers, to love them; and He [f]chose their descendants after them, you above all peoples, as *it is* this day.

16 "Therefore circumcise the foreskin of your [g]heart, and be stiff-necked no longer.

17 "For the LORD your God *is* [h]God of gods and Lord of lords, the great God, mighty and awesome, who shows no partiality nor takes a bribe.

18 "He administers [i]justice for the fatherless and the widow, and loves the [j]stranger, giving him food and clothing.

19 "Therefore love the stranger, for you were strangers in the land of Egypt.

20 "You shall fear the LORD your God; you shall serve Him, and to Him you shall hold fast, and take oaths in His name.

21 "He *is* your praise, and He *is* your God, who has done for you these great and awesome things which your eyes have seen.

22 "Your fathers went down to Egypt with seventy persons, and now the LORD [k]your God has made you as the stars of heaven in multitude.

Importance of heeding God's Word

11 "THEREFORE you shall love the LORD your God, and keep His charge, His statutes, His [l]judgments, and His commandments always.

2 "Know today that *I do* not *speak* with your children, who have not known and who have not seen the chastening of the LORD your God, His greatness and His mighty hand and His outstretched arm—

3 "His signs and His acts which He did in the midst of Egypt, to Pharaoh king of Egypt, and to all his land;

4 "what He did to the army of Egypt, to their horses and their chariots: how He made the waters of the Red Sea overflow them as they pursued [m]you, and *how* the LORD has destroyed them to this day;

5 "what He did for you in the wilderness until you came to this place;

6 "and [n]what He did to Dathan and Abiram the sons of Eliab, the son of Reuben: how the earth opened its mouth and swallowed them up, their households, their tents, and all the substance that *was* in their possession, in the midst of all Israel—

7 "but your eyes have [o]seen every great act of the LORD which He did.

8 "Therefore you shall keep every commandment which I command you today, that you may be strong, and go in and possess the land which you cross over to possess,

9 "and that you may [p]prolong *your* days in the land which the LORD swore to give your fathers, to them and their descendants, 'a land flowing with milk and honey.'*

10 "For the land which you go to possess *is* not like the land of [q]Egypt from which you have come, where you sowed your seed and watered *it* by foot, as a vegetable garden;

11 "but the [r]land which you cross over to possess *is* a land of hills and valleys, which drinks water from the rain of heaven,

12 "a land for which the LORD your God cares; the eyes of the LORD your God *are* always on it, from the beginning of the year to the very end of the year.

13 'And it shall be that if you earnestly obey My commandments which I command you today, to love the LORD your God and serve Him with all your heart and with all your soul,

14 'then I* will give *you* the [s]rain for your land in its season, the [t]early rain and the latter rain, that you may gather in your grain, your new wine, and your oil.

15 'And I will send grass in your fields for your livestock, that you may eat and be [u]filled.'

16 "Take heed to yourselves, lest your heart be deceived, and you turn aside and serve other gods and worship them,

17 "lest the LORD's anger be aroused against you, and He shut up the heavens so that there be [v]no rain, and the

---

12
a Mic. 6:8
b See Ps. 19:9, *note*
c Dt. 6:5

13
d Dt. 6:24

14
e Neh. 9:6

15
f Election (corporate): v. 15; Dt. 14:2. (Dt. 7:6; 1 Pet. 5:13, *note*)

16
g Dt. 30:6; Jer. 4:4; Rom. 2:28–29

17
h Dt. 4:35, 39; Isa. 44:8; 45:5; 46:9; 1 Cor. 8:5–6

18
i Ex. 22:22–24
j Lev. 19:34

22
k Ex. 1:1–5; see Gen. 46:26 and Acts 7:14, *notes*

CHAPTER 11

1
l Dt. 6:5; 10:12

4
m Ex. 14:28

6
n Num. 16:1–33; 26:9–10; 27:3; Ps. 106:17

7
o Dt. 10:21; 29:2

9
p Dt. 6:2

10
q Cp. Zech. 14:17–18

11
r Dt. 8:7

14
s Dt. 28:12
t Cp. Jer. 5:24; Joel 2:23; Jas. 5:7

15
u Dt. 6:11

17
v Dt. 28:24

---

*11:9 Exodus 3:8 11:14 Following Masoretic Text and Targum; Samaritan Pentateuch, Septuagint, and Vulgate read *He*.

land yield no produce, and you perish
quickly from the good land which the
LORD is giving you.
18 "Therefore you shall lay up
these words of mine in your [a]heart
and in your [b]soul, and bind them as a
sign on your hand, and they shall be
as frontlets between your eyes.
19 "You shall teach them to your
children, speaking of them when you
sit in your house, when you walk by
the way, when you lie down, and
when you rise up.
20 "And you shall write them on the
doorposts of your house and on your
gates,
21 "that your days and the days of
your children may be multiplied in the
land of which the LORD swore to your
fathers to give them, [c]like the days of
the heavens above the earth.
22 "For if you carefully keep all
these commandments which I command you to do—to love the LORD
your God, to walk in all His ways, and
to [d]hold fast to Him—
23 "then the LORD will drive out all
these nations from before you, and
you will dispossess greater and mightier nations than yourselves.
24 [e]"Every place on which the sole
of your foot treads shall be yours:
from the wilderness and Lebanon,
from the river, the River Euphrates,
even to the [f]Western Sea,* shall be
your territory.
25 "No man shall be able to [g]stand
against you; the LORD your God will
put the [h]dread of you and the fear of
you upon all the land where you tread,
just as He has said to you.
26 [i]"Behold, I set before you today
a blessing and a curse:
27 "the [j]blessing, if you obey the
commandments of the LORD your God
which I command you today;
28 "and the [k]curse, if you do not
obey the commandments of the LORD
your God, but turn aside from the way
which I command you today, to go after other gods which you have not
known.
29 "Now it shall be, when the LORD
your God has brought you into the
land which you go to possess, that you
shall put the [l]blessing on Mount Gerizim and the [m]curse on Mount Ebal.
30 "*Are* they not on the other side of
the Jordan, toward the setting sun, in
the land of the Canaanites who dwell
in the [n]plain opposite Gilgal, beside
the terebinth trees of Moreh?
31 "For you will cross over the Jordan and go in to possess the land
which the LORD your God is giving
you, and you will possess it and dwell
in it.
32 "And you shall be careful to observe all the statutes and judgments
which I set before you today.

Law of the central sanctuary

12 "THESE *are* the statutes and
judgments which you shall be
careful to observe in the land which
the LORD God of your fathers is giving
you to possess, all the days that you
live on the earth.
2 "You shall utterly destroy all the
places where the nations which you
shall dispossess served their gods, on
the high mountains and on the hills
and under every green tree.
3 "And you shall destroy their altars, break their *sacred* pillars, and
burn their [o]wooden images with fire;
you shall cut down the carved images
of their gods and destroy their names
from that place.
4 "You shall not worship the LORD
your God *with* [p]such *things.*
5 "But you shall seek the [1q]place
where the LORD your God chooses, out
of all your tribes, to put His name for
His [r]dwelling place; and there you
shall go.
6 [s]"There you shall take your
burnt offerings, your sacrifices, your
tithes, the heave offerings of your
hand, your vowed offerings, your
freewill offerings, and the [t]firstborn
of your herds and flocks.
7 "And there you shall eat before
the LORD your God, and you shall [u]re-
joice in all to which you have put your
hand, you and your households, in
which the LORD your God has blessed
you.
8 "You shall not at all do as we are
doing here today—[v]every man doing
whatever *is* right in his own eyes—
9 "for as yet you have not come to
the [w]rest and the inheritance which
the LORD your God is giving you.
10 "But *when* you cross over the
Jordan and dwell in the land which
the LORD your God is giving you to
inherit, and He gives you rest from all

18
a Dt. 6:6–9
b Ps. 119:2, 34
21
c Ps. 72:5; 89:29
22
d Dt. 10:20
24
e Josh. 1:3; 14:9
f Dt. 34:2
25
g Dt. 7:24
h Ex. 23:27; Dt. 2:25; Josh. 2:9–11
26
i Dt. 30:1, 15,19
27
j Dt. 28:2–14
28
k Dt. 28:15–45
29
l Dt. 27:12–13; Josh. 8:33
m Dt. 27:13–26
30
n See Dt. 1:1, *note*
CHAPTER 12
3
o See Dt. 16:21, *note*
4
p Dt. 12:31
5
q Ex. 20:24
r Ex. 15:13; 1 Sam. 2:29
6
s Lev. 17:3–4
t Dt. 14:23
7
u Dt. 14:26
8
v Jud. 17:6; 21:25
9
w Dt. 3:20

* 11:24 That is, the Mediterranean

[1](12:5) Jerusalem was the place where God ultimately put His name (v. 11; 26:2; Josh. 9:27; 1 Ki. 8:29; 2 Chr. 7:12; Ps. 78:68).

your enemies round [a]about, so that
you dwell in safety,
11 "then there will be the place
where the LORD your God chooses to
make His name abide. There you shall
bring all that I command you: your
burnt offerings, your sacrifices, your
tithes, the heave offerings of your
hand, and all your choice offerings
which you vow to the LORD.
12 "And [b]you shall rejoice before
the LORD your God, you and your sons
and your daughters, your male and female servants, and the [c]Levite who *is*
within your gates, since he has no portion nor inheritance with you.
13 "Take heed to yourself that you
do not offer your burnt offerings in
every place that you see;
14 "but in the place which the LORD
chooses, in one of your tribes, there
you shall offer your burnt offerings,
and there you shall do all that I command you.
15 "However, you may slaughter
and eat meat within all your gates,
whatever your heart desires, according to the blessing of the LORD your
God which He has given you; the unclean and the clean may eat of it, of the
[d]gazelle and the deer alike.
16 [e]"Only you shall not eat the
blood; you shall pour it on the earth
like water.
17 "You may not eat within your
gates the tithe of your grain or your
new wine or your oil, of the firstborn
of your herd or your flock, of any of
your offerings which you vow, of your
freewill offerings, or of the heave offering of your hand.
18 "But you must eat them before
the LORD your God in the place which
the LORD your God chooses, you and
your son and your daughter, your
male servant and your female servant,
and the Levite who *is* within your
gates; and you shall rejoice before the
LORD your God in all to which you put
your hands.
19 "Take heed to yourself that you
do not forsake the Levite as long as
you live in your land.
20 "When the LORD your God [f]en-
larges your border as He has promised you, and you say, 'Let me eat
meat,' because you long to eat meat,
you may eat as much meat as your
heart desires.
21 "If the place where the LORD your
God chooses to put His name is too far
from [g]you, then you may slaughter
from your herd and from your flock

10
a Josh. 11:23
12
b v. 18; Dt. 26:11
c Dt. 14:27
15
d Dt. 14:5
16
e vv. 23–24; Gen. 9:4; Lev. 7:26; 17:10; Dt. 15:23
20
f Ex. 34:24; Dt. 19:8
21
g Dt. 14:24
23
h Dt. 12:16; Lev. 17:11–14
25
i Dt. 6:18
27
j Lev. 1:5,9, 13,17
29
k Ex. 23:23; Dt. 19:1; Josh. 23:4
31
l Lev. 20:1–2; Dt. 18:10
32
m Dt. 4:2; 13:18; Josh. 1:7; Prov. 30:6; Rev. 22:18–19
CHAPTER 13
1
n Num. 12:6; Jer. 23:28; Zech. 10:2
o Mt. 24:24; Mk. 13:22; 2 Th. 2:9; cp. Heb. 2:4

which the LORD has given you, just as
I have commanded you, and you may
eat within your gates as much as your
heart desires.
22 "Just as the [d]gazelle and the
deer are eaten, so you may eat them;
the unclean and the clean alike may
eat them.
23 "Only be sure that you do not eat
the [h]blood, for the blood *is* the life;
you may not eat the life with the meat.
24 "You shall not eat it; you shall
pour it on the earth like water.
25 "You shall not eat it, that it may
go well with [i]you and your children
after you, when you do *what is* right in
the sight of the LORD.
26 "Only the holy things which you
have, and your vowed offerings, you
shall take and go to the place which
the LORD chooses.
27 "And [j]you shall offer your burnt
offerings, the meat and the blood, on
the altar of the LORD your God; and the
blood of your sacrifices shall be
poured out on the altar of the LORD
your God, and you shall eat the meat.
28 "Observe and obey all these
words which I command you, that it
may go well with you and your children after you forever, when you do
what is good and right in the sight of
the LORD your God.
29 "When the [k]LORD your God cuts
off from before you the nations which
you go to dispossess, and you displace
them and dwell in their land,
30 "take heed to yourself that you
are not ensnared to follow them, after
they are destroyed from before you,
and that you do not inquire after their
gods, saying, 'How did these nations
serve their gods? I also will do likewise.'
31 "You shall not worship the LORD
your God in that way; for every abomination to the LORD which He hates
they have done to their [l]gods; for they
burn even their sons and daughters in
the fire to their gods.
32 "Whatever I command you, be
careful to observe it; [m]you shall not
add to it nor take away from it.

Test of false prophets

13 "IF there arises among you a
prophet or a [n]dreamer of
dreams, [o]and he gives you a sign or a
wonder,
2 "and the sign or the wonder
comes to pass, of which he spoke to
you, saying, 'Let us go after other

gods'—which you have not known—
'and let us serve them,'
3 "you shall not listen to the words
of that prophet or that dreamer of
dreams, for the LORD your God is
[a]testing you to know whether you
love the LORD your God with all your
heart and with all your soul.
4 "You shall walk after the LORD
your God and [b]fear [c]Him, and keep
His commandments and [1]obey His
voice; you shall serve Him and hold
fast to Him.
5 "But that prophet or that
dreamer of dreams shall be put to
[d]death, because he has spoken in order to turn *you* away from the LORD
your God, who brought you out of the
land of Egypt and [e]redeemed you
from the house of bondage, to entice
you from the way in which the LORD
your God commanded you to walk. So
you shall put away the evil from [f]your
midst.
6 "If your brother, the son of your
mother, your son or your daughter,
the [g]wife of your bosom, or your
friend who is as your own soul, secretly entices you, saying, 'Let us go
and serve other gods,' which you have
not known, neither you nor your fathers,
7 "of the gods of the people which
are all around you, near to you or far
off from you, from *one* end of the earth
to the *other* end of the earth,
8 "you shall not consent to him or
listen to him, nor shall your eye [h]pity
him, nor shall you spare him or conceal him;
9 "but you shall surely kill him;
your hand shall be first against him to
put him to [i]death, and afterward the
hand of all the people.
10 "And you shall stone him with
stones until he dies, because he sought
to entice you away from the LORD your
God, who brought you out of the land
of Egypt, from the house of bondage.
11 "So all Israel shall hear and
[j]fear, and not again do such wickedness as this among you.

Idolatrous cities to be judged

12 "If you hear someone in one of
your cities, which the LORD your God
gives you to dwell in, saying,
13 'Corrupt men have gone out
from among you and enticed the inhabitants of their city, saying, "Let us
go and serve other gods"'—which
you have not known—
14 "then you shall inquire, search
out, and ask diligently. And *if it is* indeed true *and* certain *that* such an
abomination was committed among
you,
15 "you shall surely strike the inhabitants of that city with the edge of
the sword, utterly destroying it, all
that is in it and its livestock—with the
edge of the sword.
16 "And you shall gather all its
plunder into the middle of the street,
and completely burn with fire the city
and all its plunder, for the LORD your
God. It shall be a heap forever; it shall
not be built again.
17 "So none of the accursed things
shall remain in your hand, that the
LORD may turn from the fierceness of
His [k]anger and show you mercy, have
compassion on you and multiply you,
just as He swore to your fathers,
18 "because you have listened to
the voice of the LORD your God, to
keep all His commandments which I
command you today, to do *what is*
right in the eyes of the LORD your God.

Pagan mourning customs forbidden

14 "YOU *are* the [l]children of the
LORD your God; you shall not
cut yourselves nor shave the front of
your head for the [m]dead.
2 [n]"For you *are* a [o]holy people to
the LORD your God, and the LORD has
[p]chosen you to be [q]a people for Himself, a special treasure above all the
peoples who *are* on the face of the
earth.

Dietary laws

3 "You shall not eat any detestable
thing.
4 [r]"These *are* the animals which
you may eat: the ox, the sheep, the
goat,
5 "the deer, the gazelle, the roe
deer, the wild goat, the mountain
goat,* the antelope, and the mountain
sheep.
6 "And you may eat every animal
with cloven hooves, having the hoof
split into two parts, *and that* chews
the cud, among the animals.
7 "Nevertheless, of those that

3
a Test/tempt: v. 3; Dt. 33:8. (Gen. 3:1; Jas. 1:14, *note*). Cp. Dt. 8:1
4
b See Ps. 19:9, *note*
c Dt. 10:12, 20
5
d Dt. 18:20
e See Ex. 6:6, *note*
f Dt. 17:5; cp. 1 Cor. 5:13
6
g Cp. Lk. 14:26
8
h Dt. 7:16
9
i Dt. 17:7
11
j Dt. 17:13
17
k Cp. Josh. 7:26
CHAPTER 14
1
l Gal. 3:26
m Lev. 21:1–5
2
n Dt. 7:6; cp. 1 Pet. 2:9
o Dt. 7:6
p Election (corporate): vv. 1–2; Dt. 26:18. (Dt. 7:6; 1 Pet. 5:13, *note*)
q Lit. *a people for His own possession.* Ex. 19:5; Dt. 7:6; 26:18; cp. Ti. 2:14; 1 Pet. 2:9
4
r vv. 4–19; Lev. 11:1–20; cp. Acts 10:13–14

* 14:5 Or *addax*

[1](13:4) The chief credential of the true prophet is not to be found merely in his ability to perform "a sign or a wonder" (v. 1), but rather in the harmony of his message and works with the objective Word of God.

chew the cud or have cloven hooves, you shall not eat, *such as* these: the camel, the [a]hare, and the rock hyrax; for they chew the cud but do not have cloven hooves; they *are* unclean for you.

8 "Also the swine is unclean for you, because it has cloven hooves, yet *does* not *chew* the cud; you shall not eat their flesh or touch their dead carcasses.

9 "These you may eat of all that *are* in the waters: you may eat all that have fins and scales.

10 "And whatever does not have fins and scales you shall not eat; it *is* unclean for you.

11 "All clean birds you may eat.

12 "But these you shall not eat: the eagle, the vulture, the buzzard,

13 "the red kite, the falcon, and the kite after their kinds;

14 "every raven after its kind;

15 "the ostrich, the short-eared owl, the sea gull, and the hawk after their kinds;

16 "the little owl, the screech owl, the white owl,

17 "the jackdaw, the carrion vulture, the fisher owl,

18 "the stork, the heron after its kind, and the hoopoe and the bat.

19 "Also every creeping thing that flies is unclean for you; they shall not be eaten.

20 "You may eat all clean birds.

21 "You shall not eat anything that dies *of itself;* you may give it to the alien who *is* within your gates, that he may eat it, or you may sell it to a foreigner; for you *are* a holy people to the LORD your God. You shall not boil a young goat in its mother's milk.

22 [b]"You shall truly tithe all the increase of your grain that the field produces year by year.

23 "And you shall eat before the LORD your God, in the [c]place where He chooses to make His name abide, the tithe of your grain and your new wine and your oil, of the firstborn of your herds and your flocks, that you may [d]learn to [e]fear the LORD your God always.

24 "But if the journey is too long for you, so that you are not able to carry *the tithe, or* if the place where the LORD your God chooses to put His name is too far from [f]you, when the LORD your God has blessed you,

25 "then you shall exchange *it* for money, take the money in your hand, and go to the place which the LORD your God chooses.

26 "And you shall spend that money for whatever your heart desires: for oxen or sheep, for wine or similar drink, for whatever your heart desires; you shall eat there before the LORD your God, and you shall [g]rejoice, you and your household.

27 "You shall not forsake the [h]Levite who *is* within your gates, for he has no part nor inheritance with you.

28 [i]"At the end of *every* third year you shall bring out the [j]tithe of your produce of that year and store *it* up within your gates.

29 "And the Levite, because he has no portion nor inheritance with you, and the stranger and the fatherless and the widow who *are* within your gates, may come and eat and be satisfied, that the [k]LORD your God may bless you in all the work of your hand which you do.

Sabbatic year

15 "AT the end of [l]*every* seven years you shall grant a release *of debts.*

2 "And this *is* the form of the release: Every creditor who has lent *anything* to his neighbor shall release *it;* he shall not require *it* of his neighbor or his brother, because it is called the LORD's release.

3 "Of a foreigner you may require [m]*it;* but you shall give up your claim to what is owed by your brother,

4 "except when there may be no poor among you; for the LORD will greatly [n]bless you in the land which the LORD your God is giving you to possess *as* an inheritance—

5 "only if you carefully obey the voice of the LORD your God, to observe with care all these commandments which I command you today.

6 "For the LORD your God will bless you just as He promised you; you shall lend to many nations, but you shall not borrow; you shall reign over many nations, but they shall not reign over [o]you.

7 "If there is among you a poor man of your brethren, within any of the gates in your land which the LORD your God is giving you, you shall not harden your heart nor shut your hand from your [p]poor brother,

8 "but [q]you shall open your hand wide to him and willingly lend him sufficient for his need, whatever he needs.

7
a See Lev. 11:6, *note*
22
b Lev. 27:30; Dt. 12:6,17; Neh. 10:37
23
c Dt. 12:5
d Dt. 4:10
e See Ps. 19:9, *note*
24
f Dt. 12:21
26
g Dt. 12:7
27
h Dt. 12:12
28
i Dt. 26:12; Amos 4:4
j Num. 18:21–24
29
k Cp. Mal. 3:10
CHAPTER 15
1
l Ex. 21:2; 23:10–11; Lev. 25:4; Jer. 34:14
3
m Cp. Dt. 23:20
4
n Dt. 7:13
6
o Dt. 28:12–13
7
p Ex. 23:6; Lev. 25:35–37; Dt. 24:12–14
8
q 1 Jn. 3:17

9 "Beware lest there be a wicked
thought in your heart, saying, 'The
seventh year, the year of release, is at
hand,' and your eye be evil against
your poor brother and you give him
nothing, and he [a]cry out to the LORD
against you, and it become sin among
you.
10 "You shall surely give to him,
and your heart should not be grieved
when you [b]give to him, because for
this thing the LORD your God will bless
you in all your works and in all to
which you put your hand.
11 "For the [c]poor will never cease
from the land; therefore I command
you, saying, 'You shall open your
hand wide to your brother, to your
poor and your needy, in your land.'
12 [d]"If your brother, a Hebrew
man, or a Hebrew woman, is [e]sold to
you and serves you six years, then in
the seventh year you shall let him go
free from you.
13 "And when you send him away
free from you, you shall not let him go
away empty-handed;
14 "you shall supply him liberally
from your flock, from your threshing
floor, and from your winepress. *From
what* the LORD has blessed you with,
you shall give to him.
15 "You shall remember that you
were a slave in the land of Egypt, and
the LORD your God [f]redeemed you;
therefore I command you this thing
today.

The perpetual servant (Ps. 40:6–8)

16 "And if it happens that he says to
you, 'I will not go away from you,' because he loves you and your house,
since he prospers with you,
17 "then you shall take an awl and
thrust *it* through his [g]ear to the door,
and he shall be your servant forever.
Also to your [h]female servant you shall
do likewise.
18 "It shall not seem hard to you
when you send him away free from
you; for he has been worth a double
hired servant in serving you six years.
Then the LORD your God will bless you
in all that you do.
19 "All the firstborn males that
come from your herd and your flock

9
a Ex. 22:23; Jas. 5:4
10
b 2 Cor. 9:7
11
c Mt. 26:11; Mk. 14:7; Jn. 12:8
12
d Ex. 21:2–6; Jer. 34:14
e Lev. 25:39–46
15
f See Ex. 6:6, *note*
17
g See Heb. 10:5, *note*
h Cp. Ex. 21:7–11
19
i Ex. 13:2
20
j Dt. 14:23
21
k Lev. 22:19–25
CHAPTER 16
1
l vv. 1–8; cp. Ex. 12:2–39
m See Lev. 23:2, *note*
2
n Dt. 15:20
3
o *Leaven:* vv. 3–4,8, 16; Amos 4:5. (Gen. 19:3; Mt. 13:33, *note*)
p Num. 29:12
q Ex. 13:3
4
r Ex. 13:7
s Num. 9:12

you shall [i]sanctify to the LORD your
God; you shall do no work with the
firstborn of your herd, nor shear the
firstborn of your flock.
20 "You and your household shall
eat *it* before the LORD your God year
by year in the [j]place which the LORD
chooses.
21 "But if there is a [k]defect in it, *if
it is* lame or blind *or has* any serious
defect, you shall not sacrifice it to the
LORD your God.
22 "You may eat it within your
gates; the unclean and the clean *person* alike *may eat it,* as *if it were* a
gazelle or a deer.
23 "Only you shall not eat its blood;
you shall pour it on the ground like
water.

The Passover

16 [l]"OBSERVE the month of
Abib, and [1]keep the Passover
to the LORD your God, for in the month
of [m]Abib the LORD your God brought
you out of Egypt by night.
2 "Therefore you shall sacrifice
the Passover to the LORD your God,
from the flock and the herd, in the
[n]place where the LORD chooses to put
His name.
3 "You shall eat no [o]leavened
bread with it; [p]seven days you shall
eat unleavened bread with it, *that is,*
the bread of affliction (for you came
out of the land of Egypt in haste), that
you may [q]remember the day in which
you came out of the land of Egypt all
the days of your life.
4 "And [r]no leaven shall be seen
among you in all your territory for
seven days, nor shall *any* of the meat
which you sacrifice the first day at
twilight remain overnight until
[s]morning.
5 "You may not sacrifice the Passover within any of your gates which
the LORD your God gives you;
6 "but at the place where the LORD
your God chooses to make His name
abide, there you shall sacrifice the
Passover at twilight, at the going
down of the sun, at the time you came
out of Egypt.
7 "And you shall roast and eat *it* in
the place which the LORD your God

[1](16:1) Compare the order of the feasts in Lev. 23. Here the Passover and the Feast of Tabernacles are given special emphasis as marking the beginning and the consummation of God's ways with Israel: the former speaking of redemption, the foundation of all; the latter, of regathered Israel blessed in the kingdom. Between, in Dt. 16:9–12, comes the Feast of Weeks—the joy of a redeemed people anticipating greater blessing yet to come. Cp. Rom. 5:1–2.

chooses, and in the morning you shall
turn and go to your tents.
8 "Six days you shall eat unleavened bread, and on the seventh day
there *shall be* a sacred assembly to the
LORD your God. You shall do no work
on it.

The Feast of Weeks

9 "You shall count seven weeks
for yourself; begin to count the seven
weeks from *the time* you begin *to put*
the sickle to the grain.
10 "Then you shall keep the [a]Feast
of Weeks to the LORD your God with
the tribute of a freewill offering from
your hand, which you shall give [b]as
the LORD your God blesses you.
11 "You shall rejoice before the
LORD your God, you and your son and
your daughter, your male servant and
your female servant, the Levite who *is*
within your gates, the stranger and
the fatherless and the widow who *are*
among you, at the place where the
LORD your God chooses to make His
name abide.
12 "And you shall remember that
you were a slave in Egypt, and you
shall be careful to observe these statutes.

The Feast of Tabernacles

13 "You shall observe the Feast of
Tabernacles seven days, when you
have gathered from your threshing
floor and from your winepress.
14 "And you shall rejoice in your
feast, you and your son and your
daughter, your male servant and your
female servant and the Levite, the
stranger and the fatherless and the
widow, who *are* within your gates.
15 [c]"Seven days you shall keep a
sacred feast to the LORD your God in
the place which the LORD chooses, because the LORD your God will bless
you in all your produce and in all the
work of your hands, so that you surely
rejoice.

The gifts of the males

16 [d]"Three times a year all your
males shall appear before the LORD
your God in the place which He
chooses: at the Feast of Unleavened
Bread, at the Feast of Weeks, and at
the Feast of Tabernacles; and they
shall not appear before the LORD
empty-handed.

10
a Ex. 34:22; Lev. 23:15–16; Num. 28:26
b v. 17; cp. 1 Cor. 16:2; 2 Cor. 8:12
15
c Lev. 23:39–41
16
d Ex. 23:14–17; 34:22–24
18
e Ex. 23:1–8; Dt. 1:16–17; Jn. 7:24
CHAPTER 17
1
f Dt. 15:21
5
g Lev. 24:14,16; Josh. 7:25
h Dt. 13:6–18
6
i Num. 35:30; Dt. 19:15

17 "Every man *shall give* as he is
able, according to the blessing of the
LORD your God which He has given
you.

Judges in the gates

18 "You shall appoint judges and
officers in all your gates, which the
LORD your God gives you, according to
your tribes, and they shall judge the
people with [e]just judgment.
19 "You shall not pervert justice;
you shall not show partiality, nor take
a bribe, for a bribe blinds the eyes of
the wise and twists the words of the
righteous.
20 "You shall follow what is altogether just, that you may live and inherit the land which the LORD your
God is giving you.
21 "You shall not plant for yourself
any tree, as a [1]wooden image, near the
altar which you build for yourself to
the LORD your God.
22 "You shall not set up a sacred
pillar, which the LORD your God hates.

Offerings must be unblemished

17 "YOU shall not sacrifice to the
LORD your God a bull or sheep
which has any [f]blemish *or* defect, for
that *is* an abomination to the LORD
your God.

Idolators to be stoned

2 "If there is found among you,
within any of your gates which the
LORD your God gives you, a man or a
woman who has been wicked in the
sight of the LORD your God, in transgressing His covenant,
3 "who has gone and served other
gods and worshiped them, either the
sun or moon or any of the host of
heaven, which I have not commanded,
4 "and it is told you, and you hear
of it, then you shall inquire diligently.
And if *it is* indeed true *and* certain that
such an abomination has been committed in Israel,
5 "then you shall bring out to your
gates that man or woman who has
committed that wicked thing, and
shall [g]stone to [h]death that man or
woman with stones.
6 "Whoever is deserving of death
shall be put to death on the testimony
of two or three [i]witnesses; he shall
not be put to death on the testimony of
one witness.

[1](16:21) These were "groves" (Heb. *asherim*) devoted to the worship of Asherah, who was the Babylonian goddess Ishtar, the Aphrodite of the Greeks, the Venus of the Romans. See Jud. 2:13, *note.*

7 "The hands of the witnesses shall be the first against him to put him to death, and afterward the hands of all the people. So you shall put away the evil from among [a]you.

Obedience to authority

8 "If a matter arises which is [b]too hard for you to judge, between degrees of guilt for bloodshed, between one judgment or another, or between one punishment or another, matters of controversy within your gates, then you shall arise and go up to the [c]place which the LORD your God chooses.

9 "And [d]you shall come to the [e]priests, the Levites, and to the judge *there* in those days, and inquire *of them;* they shall pronounce upon you the sentence of judgment.

10 "You shall do according to the sentence which they pronounce upon you in that place which the LORD chooses. And you shall be careful to do according to all that they order you.

11 "According to the sentence of the law in which they instruct you, according to the judgment which they tell you, you shall do; you shall not turn aside *to* the right hand or *to* the left from the sentence which they pronounce upon you.

12 "Now [f]the man who acts presumptuously and will not heed the priest who stands to minister there before the LORD your God, or the judge, that man shall die. So you shall put away the evil from Israel.

13 "And all the people shall hear and fear, and no longer act presumptuously.

Concerning a king

14 "When you come to the land which the LORD your God is giving you, and possess it and dwell in it, and say, [g]'I will set a king over me like all the nations that *are* around me,'

15 "you shall surely set a king over you [h]whom the LORD your God chooses; *one* from among your brethren you shall set as king over you; you may not set a foreigner over you, who *is* not your brother.

16 "But he shall not multiply horses for himself, nor cause the people to return to Egypt to multiply horses, for the LORD has said to you, 'You shall not return that way again.'

17 "Neither shall he multiply wives for himself, lest [i]his heart turn away; nor shall he greatly multiply silver and [j]gold for himself.

18 [k]"Also it shall be, when he sits on the throne of his kingdom, that he shall [l]write for himself a copy of this law in a book, from *the one* [m]before the priests, the Levites.

19 "And it shall be with him, and he shall [n]read it all the days of his life, that he may learn to [o]fear the LORD his God and be careful to observe all the words of this law and these statutes,

20 "that his heart may not be lifted above his brethren, that he may not turn aside from the commandment *to* the right hand or *to* the left, and that he may [p]prolong *his* days in his kingdom, he and his children in the midst of Israel.

Portion for Levites and priests

18 "THE priests, the Levites—all the tribe of Levi—shall have no part nor [q]inheritance with Israel; they shall eat the offerings of the LORD made by fire, and His portion.

2 "Therefore they shall have no inheritance among their brethren; the LORD is their inheritance, as He said to them.

3 "And this shall be the priest's [r]due from the people, from those who offer a sacrifice, whether *it is* bull or sheep: they shall give to the priest the shoulder, the cheeks, and the stomach.

4 "The firstfruits of your grain and your new wine and your oil, and the first of the fleece of your sheep, you shall give him.

5 "For the LORD your God has chosen him out of all your tribes to stand to minister in the name of the LORD, him and his sons forever.

6 "So if a Levite comes from any of your gates, from where he dwells among all Israel, and comes with all the desire of his mind to the [s]place which the LORD chooses,

7 "then he may serve in the name of the LORD his God as all his brethren the Levites *do,* who stand there before the LORD.

8 "They shall have equal portions to eat, besides what comes from the sale of his inheritance.

Spiritism forbidden

9 "When you come into the land which the LORD your God is giving you, you shall not learn to follow the [t]abominations of those nations.

7
a Dt. 13:5; 19:19
8
b Dt. 1:17
c Dt. 12:5; 16:2
9
d Dt. 19:17; cp. Jer. 18:18
e Dt. 19:17–19
12
f Num. 15:30; Dt. 1:43; Hos. 4:4; cp. Ezra 10:8
14
g 1 Sam. 8:5,19–20
15
h 1 Sam. 9:15–16; 10:24; 16:12–13; 1 Chr. 22:8–10; cp. Hos. 8:4
17
i Cp. 2 Sam. 5:13; 1 Ki. 11:1–8
j 1 Ki. 10:14
18
k Cp. 2 Ki. 11:12
l See Ex. 17:14, *note*
m Dt. 31:24–26
19
n Cp. Josh. 1:7–8
o See Ps. 19:9, *note*
20
p Dt. 11:9
CHAPTER 18
1
q Dt. 10:9; 1 Cor. 9:13
3
r Lev. 7:32–34; Num. 18:11–12; cp. 1 Sam. 2:13–16,29
6
s Dt. 14:23
9
t Dt. 20:16–18

10 [1]"There shall not be found
among you *anyone* who makes his son
or his daughter pass through the fire,
or one who practices witchcraft, *or* a
soothsayer, or one who interprets
omens, or a sorcerer,
11 "or one who conjures spells, or a
medium, or a spiritist, or one who
calls up the dead.
12 "For all who do these things *are*
an abomination to the LORD, and because of these abominations the LORD
your God drives them out from before
you.
13 "You shall be [a]blameless before
the LORD your God.
14 "For these nations which you
will dispossess listened to soothsayers
and diviners; but as for you, the LORD
your God has not appointed such for
you.

The Great Prophet: Christ

15 "The LORD your God will raise up
for you a [2]Prophet like me from your
midst, from your brethren. Him you
shall [b]hear,
16 [c]"according to all you desired of
the LORD your God in Horeb in the day
of the assembly, saying, 'Let me not
hear again the voice of the LORD my
God, nor let me see this great fire anymore, lest I die.'
17 "And the LORD said to me: 'What
they have [d]spoken is good.
18 'I will raise up for them a
Prophet like [e]you from among their
brethren, and will [f]put My words in
His mouth, and He shall speak to them
all that I command Him.
19 [g]'And it shall be *that* whoever
will not hear My words, which He
speaks in My name, I will require *it* of
him.

Test of the prophets

20 'But the [h]prophet who presumes
to speak a word in My name, which I
have not commanded him to speak, or
[i]who speaks in the name of other
[j]gods, that prophet shall die.'
21 "And if you say in your heart,
'How shall we know the word which
the LORD has not spoken?'—
22 "when a [k]prophet speaks in the
name of the LORD, if the thing does not
happen or come to pass, that *is* the
thing which the LORD has not spoken;
the prophet has spoken it presumptuously; you shall not be afraid of him.

Cities of refuge (Num. 35:1–34)

19 "WHEN the LORD your God has
cut off the nations whose land
the LORD your God is giving you, and
you dispossess them and dwell in their
cities and in their houses,
2 [l]"you shall separate three [m]cit-
ies for yourself in the midst of your
land which the LORD your God is giving you to possess.
3 "You shall prepare roads for
yourself, and divide into three parts
the territory of your land which the
LORD your God is giving you to inherit,
that any manslayer may flee there.
4 "And this *is* the case of the manslayer who flees there, that he may
live: Whoever kills his neighbor unintentionally, not having hated him in
time past—
5 "as when *a man* goes to the
woods with his neighbor to cut timber,
and his hand swings a stroke with the
ax to cut down the tree, and the head
slips from the handle and strikes his
neighbor so that he dies—he shall flee
to one of these cities and live;
6 "lest the [n]avenger of blood,
while his anger is hot, pursue the manslayer and overtake him, because the
way is long, and kill him, though he
was not deserving of death, since he
had not hated the victim in time past.
7 "Therefore I command you, say-

13
a i.e. *up-right*, or *sincere*. Cp. Gen. 17:1; Mt. 5:48
15
b Cp. Mt. 21:33–44
16
c Ex. 20:18–19; Dt. 5:23–27
17
d Dt. 5:28
18
e Dt. 34:10
f Num. 23:5; Isa. 49:2
19
g Acts 3:23; Heb. 12:25
20
h Dt. 13:5; Jer. 14:14–15; cp. Zech. 13:2–5
i Dt. 13:1–3; Jer. 2:8
j Cp. Josh. 23:7
22
k Cp. Jer. 28:9
CHAPTER 19
2
l Ex. 21:13; Josh. 20:2
m See Num. 35:6, *note*
6
n Redemption (redeeming relative type): vv. 6,12; Josh. 20:3. (Gen. 48:16; Isa. 59:20, *note*)

[1](18:10) This is an important passage concerning proscribed practices of sacrifice, and of inquiry concerning the future, which were followed by the heathen nations. The item of sacrifice that is condemned had to do with the worship of Molech (cp. Lev. 18:21; 20:2–5; Dt. 12:31; Jer. 19:5; Ezek. 16:21; 23:37).

The eight banned practices for determining future actions are those of (1) witchcraft; (2) a soothsayer—possibly referring to conjuring or astrology; (3) one who interprets omens; (4) a sorcerer—one who makes use of magic formulas or incantation; (5) one who conjures spells; (6) a medium—see (7); (7) a spiritist, often used with (6)—Isa. 8:19 describes the practice; and (8) one who calls up the dead.

Two things should be kept in mind: (1) this commandment had specific application to Israel's entering the land; it was made to preserve them from the abominations of their predecessors (vv. 9,12,14); and (2) the contrast between these false prophets and the Prophet like Moses is clearly intended (vv. 15–19).

[2](18:15) That the allusion in vv. 15–19 is to the Lord Jesus Christ is made clear by the NT (Jn. 1:21,45; 6:14; Acts 3:22–23; 7:37).

ing, 'You shall separate three cities for yourself.'

8 "Now if the LORD your God [a]enlarges your territory, as He swore to your [b]fathers, and gives you the land which He promised to give to your fathers,

9 "and if you keep all these commandments and do them, which I command you today, to love the LORD your God and to walk always in His ways, then you shall add three more cities for yourself besides these [c]three,

10 "lest [d]innocent blood be shed in the midst of your land which the LORD your God is giving you *as* an inheritance, and *thus* guilt of bloodshed be upon you.

11 "But if anyone [e]hates his neighbor, lies in wait for him, rises against him and strikes him mortally, so that he dies, and he flees to one of these cities,

12 "then the elders of his city shall send and bring him from there, and deliver him over to the hand of the avenger of blood, that he may die.

13 "Your eye shall not [f]pity him, but you shall put away *the guilt of* innocent blood from Israel, that it may go well with you.

The sacred landmark

14 "You shall not remove your neighbor's [g]landmark, which the men of old have set, in your inheritance which you will inherit in the land that the LORD your God is giving you to possess.

Terror of the law

15 "One witness shall not rise against a man concerning any iniquity or any sin that he commits; by the mouth of two or three [h]witnesses the matter shall be established.

16 "If a [i]false witness rises against any man to testify against him of wrongdoing,

17 "then both men in the controversy shall stand before the LORD, before the priests and the [j]judges who serve in those days.

18 "And the judges shall make careful inquiry, and indeed, *if* the witness *is* a false witness, who has testified falsely against his brother,

19 "then you shall do to him as he thought to have done to his brother; so you shall put away the evil from among you.

20 "And those who remain shall hear and [k]fear, and hereafter they shall not again commit such evil among you.

21 "Your eye shall not pity: [l]life *shall be* for life, eye for eye, tooth for tooth, hand for hand, foot for foot.

Law of warfare

20 "WHEN you go out to battle against your enemies, and see horses and [m]chariots *and* people more numerous than you, do not be [n]afraid of them; for the LORD your God *is* with you, who brought [o]you up from the land of Egypt.

2 "So it shall be, when you are on the verge of battle, that the priest shall approach and speak to the people.

3 "And he shall say to them, 'Hear, O Israel: Today you are on the verge of battle with your enemies. Do not let your heart faint, do not be afraid, and do not tremble or be terrified because of them;

4 'for the LORD your God *is* He who goes with you, [p]to fight for you against your enemies, to save you.'

5 "Then the officers shall speak to the people, saying: 'What man *is there* who has built a new house and has not dedicated it? Let him go and return to his house, lest he die in the battle and another man dedicate it.

6 'Also what man *is there* who has planted a vineyard and has not eaten of it? Let him go and return to his house, lest he die in the battle and another man eat of it.

7 'And what man *is there* who is betrothed to a [q]woman and has not married her? Let him go and return to his house, lest he die in the battle and another man marry her.'

8 "The officers shall speak further to the people, and say, 'What man *is there who is* fearful and fainthearted? Let him go and return to his house, lest the heart of his brethren faint* like his heart.'

9 "And so it shall be, when the officers have finished speaking to the people, that they shall make captains of the armies to lead the people.

10 "When you go near a city to fight against it, [r]then [s]proclaim an offer of peace to it.

11 "And it shall be that if they accept your offer of peace, and open to you, then all the people *who are* found

8 *a* Dt. 12:20 *b* Gen. 15:18–21
9 *c* Josh. 20:7–9
10 *d* Dt. 21:1–9
11 *e* Lev. 19:17; cp. 1 Jn. 2:9, 11
13 *f* Dt. 13:8
14 *g* Dt. 27:17
15 *h* Dt. 17:6; Mt. 18:16; Jn. 8:17; 2 Cor. 13:1
16 *i* Ex. 23:1
17 *j* Dt. 17:8–11
20 *k* Dt. 17:13
21 *l* Ex. 21:23–25; Lev. 24:20; cp. Mt. 5:38–39
CHAPTER 20
1 *m* Ps. 20:7 *n* Dt. 7:18 *o* Dt. 5:6
4 *p* Dt. 1:30; 3:22; Josh. 23:10
7 *q* Dt. 24:5
10 *r* Cp. 2 Sam. 20:18–22 *s* Cp. Dt. 2:26–29

*
20:8 Following Masoretic Text and Targum; Samaritan Pentateuch, Septuagint, Syriac, and Vulgate read *lest he make his brother's heart faint.*

in it shall be placed under tribute to you, and serve you.

12 "Now if *the city* will not make peace with you, but makes war against you, then you shall besiege it.

13 "And when the LORD your God delivers it into your hands, [a]you shall strike every male in it with the edge of the sword.

14 "But the women, the little ones, the [b]livestock, and all that is in the city, all its spoil, you shall plunder for yourself; and you shall eat the enemies' plunder which the LORD your God gives you.

15 "Thus you shall do to all the cities *which are* very far from you, which *are* not of the cities of these nations.

16 "But of the cities of [c]these peoples which the LORD your God gives you *as* an inheritance, you shall let nothing that breathes remain alive,

17 "but you shall utterly destroy them: the [d]Hittite and the Amorite and the Canaanite and the Perizzite and the Hivite and the Jebusite, just as the LORD your God has commanded you,

18 "lest they teach you to do according to all their [e]abominations which they have done for their gods, and you [f]sin against the LORD your God.

19 "When you besiege a city for a long time, while making war against it to take it, you shall not destroy its [g]trees by wielding an ax against them; if you can eat of them, do not cut them down to use in the siege, for the tree of the field *is* man's *food*.

20 "Only the trees which you know *are* not trees for food you may destroy and cut down, to build siegeworks against the city that makes war with you, until it is subdued.

Inquest for the slain

21 "IF *anyone* is found slain, lying in the field in the land which the LORD your God is giving you to possess, *and* it is not known who killed him,

2 "then your elders and your judges shall go out and measure *the distance* from the slain man to the surrounding cities.

3 "And it shall be *that* the elders of the city nearest to the slain man will take a heifer which has not been worked *and* which has not pulled with a [h]yoke.

4 "The elders of that city shall bring the heifer down to a valley with flowing water, which is neither plowed nor sown, and they shall break the heifer's neck there in the valley.

5 "Then the priests, the sons of Levi, shall come near, for the LORD your God has chosen them to minister to Him and to bless in the name of the LORD; by their word every controversy and every assault shall be *settled*.

6 "And all the elders of that city nearest to the slain *man* shall wash their hands over the heifer whose neck was broken in the valley.

7 "Then they shall answer and say, 'Our hands have not shed this blood, nor have our eyes seen *it*.

8 'Provide [i]atonement, O LORD, for Your people Israel, whom You have [j]redeemed, and do not lay [k]innocent blood to the charge of Your people Israel.' And atonement shall be provided on their behalf for the blood.

9 "So you shall put away the *guilt of* innocent blood from among you when you do *what is* right in the sight of the LORD.

Domestic regulations

10 "When you go out to war against your enemies, and the LORD your God delivers them into your hand, and you take them captive,

11 "and you see among the captives a beautiful woman, and desire her and would take her for your [l]wife,

12 "then you shall bring her home to your house, and she shall [m]shave her head and trim her nails.

13 "She shall put off the clothes of her captivity, remain in your house, and mourn her father and her mother a full month; after that you may go in to her and be her husband, and she shall be your wife.

14 "And it shall be, if you have no delight in her, then you shall set her [n]free, but you certainly shall not sell her for money; you shall not treat her brutally, because you have humbled her.

15 "If a man has two wives, one loved and the other [o]unloved, and they have borne him children, *both* the loved and the unloved, and *if* the firstborn son is of her who is unloved,

16 "then it shall be, on the day he bequeaths his possessions to his sons, *that* he must not bestow firstborn status on the son of the loved wife in preference to the son of the unloved, the *true* firstborn.

17 "But he shall [p]acknowledge the

13 *a* Num. 31:7
14 *b* Josh. 8:2
16 *c* Dt. 7:1–5
17 *d* See 2 Ki. 7:6, *note*
18 *e* Dt. 18:9 *f* Ex. 23:33
19 *g* Cp. 2 Ki. 3:19,25
CHAPTER 21
3 *h* Num. 19:2
8 *i* *Bible prayers* (OT): vv. 6–8; Dt. 26:5. (Gen. 15:2; Hab. 3:1) *j* See Ex. 6:6, *note* *k* Num. 35:33–34; Dt. 19:10, 13
11 *l* Num. 31:18
12 *m* Lev. 14:8–9
14 *n* Cp. Jer. 34:16
15 *o* Gen. 29:33
17 *p* 1 Chr. 5:1

son of the unloved wife *as* the firstborn by giving him a double portion of
all that he has, for he *is* the beginning
of his [a]strength; the [b]right of the firstborn *is* his.

A disobedient son under law
(cp. Lk. 15:11–23)

18 "If a man has a stubborn and rebellious son who will not obey the
voice of his father or the voice of his
mother, and *who,* when they have
chastened him, will not heed them,
19 "then his father and his mother
shall take hold of him and bring him
out to the elders of his city, to the gate
of his city.
20 "And they shall say to the elders
of his city, 'This son of ours is stubborn and rebellious; he will not obey
our voice; he is a glutton and a drunkard.'
21 "Then all the men of his city
shall stone him to death with [c]stones;
so you shall put away the evil from
among you, and all Israel shall hear
and [d]fear.
22 "If a man has committed a sin
deserving of [e]death, and he is put to
death, and you hang him on a tree,
23 [f]"his body shall not remain
overnight on the tree, but you shall
surely bury him that day, so that you
do not defile the land which the LORD
your God is giving you *as* an inheritance; for he who is hanged *is* [g]ac-
cursed of God.

Law of brotherhood

22 "YOU [h]shall not see your
brother's ox or his sheep going
astray, and hide yourself from them;
you shall certainly bring them back to
your brother.
2 "And if your brother *is* not near
you, or if you do not know him, then
you shall bring it to your own house,
and it shall remain with you until your
brother seeks it; then you shall restore
it to him.
3 "You shall do the same with his
donkey, and so shall you do with his
garment; with any lost thing of your
brother's, which he has lost and you
have found, you shall do likewise; you
must not hide yourself.
4 "You [i]shall not see your
brother's donkey or his ox fall down
along the road, and hide yourself from
them; you shall surely help him lift
them up again.
5 "A woman shall not wear anything that pertains to a man, nor shall
a man put on a woman's garment, for
all who do so *are* an abomination to
the LORD your God.
6 "If a bird's nest happens to be
before you along the way, in any tree
or on the ground, with young ones or
eggs, with the mother sitting on the
young or on the eggs, [j]you shall not
take the mother with the young;
7 "you shall surely let the mother
go, and take the young for yourself,
that it may be well with you and *that*
you may prolong *your* days.
8 "When you build a new house,
then you shall make a parapet for
your roof, that you may not bring guilt
of bloodshed on your household if
anyone falls from it.

Law of separation

9 [k]"You shall not sow your vineyard with different kinds of seed, lest
the yield of the seed which you have
sown and the fruit of your vineyard be
defiled.
10 [l]"You shall not plow with an ox
and a donkey [m]together.
11 [k]"You shall not wear a garment
of different sorts, *such as* wool and
linen mixed together.
12 "You shall make [n]tassels on the
four corners of the clothing with
which you cover *yourself.*

Innocent wife

13 "If any man takes a wife, and
goes in to her, and [o]detests her,
14 "and charges her with shameful
conduct, and brings a bad name on
her, and says, 'I took this woman, and
when I came to her I found she *was*
not a virgin,'
15 "then the father and mother of
the young woman shall take and bring
out *the evidence of* the young
woman's virginity to the elders of the
city at the gate.
16 "And the young woman's father
shall say to the elders, 'I gave my
daughter to this man as wife, and he
detests her.
17 'Now he has charged her with
shameful conduct, saying, "I found
your daughter *was* not a virgin," and
yet these *are the evidences of* my
daughter's virginity.' And they shall
spread the cloth before the elders of
the city.
18 "Then the elders of that city shall
take that man and punish him;
19 "and they shall fine him one
hundred [p]*shekels* of silver and give
them to the father of the young

17
a Gen. 49:3
b Cp. Gen. 25:31–33
21
c Dt. 17:5,7; 22:21,24
d Dt. 19:20
22
e Mt. 26:66
23
f Josh. 8:29; 10:26–27; Jn. 19:31
g Gal. 3:13
CHAPTER 22
1
h Ex. 23:4
4
i Ex. 23:5
6
j Lev. 22:28
9
k Lev. 19:19
10
l Cp. 2 Cor. 6:14–16
m *Separation:* v. 10; 1 Ki. 8:53. (Gen. 12:1; 2 Cor. 6:17, *note*)
12
n Num. 15:37–40; cp. Mt. 23:5
13
o Dt. 21:15; 24:3
19
p See Coinage (OT), Ex. 30:13, *note;* cp. 2 Chr. 2:10, *note*

woman, because he has brought a bad name on a virgin of Israel. And she shall be his wife; he cannot [a]divorce her all his days.

20 "But if the thing is true, *and evidences of* virginity are not found for the young woman,

21 "then they shall bring out the young woman to the door of her father's house, and the men of her city shall stone her to death with [b]stones, because she has [c]done a disgraceful thing in Israel, to play the [d]harlot in her father's house. So you shall put away the evil from among you.

22 "If a man is found lying with a woman married to a [e]husband, then both of them shall [f]die—the man that lay with the woman, and the woman; so you shall put away the evil from Israel.

23 "If a young woman *who is* a virgin is betrothed to a husband, and a man finds her in the city and lies with her,

24 "then you shall bring them both out to the gate of that city, and you shall stone them to [g]death with stones, the young woman because she did not cry out in the city, and the man because he humbled his neighbor's wife; so you shall put away the evil from among you.

25 "But if a man finds a betrothed young woman in the countryside, and the man forces her and lies with her, then only the man who lay with her shall die.

26 "But you shall do nothing to the young woman; *there is* in the young woman no sin *deserving* of death, for just as when a man rises against his neighbor and kills him, even so *is* this matter.

27 "For he found her in the countryside, *and* the betrothed young woman cried out, but *there was* no one to save her.

28 "If a man finds a young woman *who is* a virgin, who is not betrothed, and he seizes her and lies with her, and they are found out,

29 "then the man who lay with her shall give to the young woman's father [h]fifty [i]*shekels* of silver, and she shall be his wife because he has humbled her; he shall not be permitted to divorce her all his days.

30 "A man shall not take his father's [j]wife, nor uncover his father's bed.

Regulations about certain people

23 "HE who is emasculated by crushing or mutilation shall [k]not enter the assembly of the LORD.

2 "One of illegitimate birth shall not enter the assembly of the LORD; even to the tenth generation none of his *descendants* shall enter the assembly of the LORD.

3 "An [l]Ammonite or Moabite shall not enter the assembly of the LORD; even to the tenth generation none of his *descendants* shall enter the assembly of the LORD forever,

4 [m]"because they did not meet you with bread and water on the road when you came out of Egypt, and [n]because they hired against you Balaam the son of Beor from Pethor of Mesopotamia,* to curse you.

5 "Nevertheless the LORD your God would not listen to Balaam, but the LORD your God turned the curse into a blessing for you, because the LORD your God [o]loves you.

6 [p]"You shall not seek their peace nor their prosperity all your days forever.

7 "You shall not abhor an Edomite, for he *is* your [q]brother. You shall not abhor an Egyptian, because you were an alien in his land.

8 "The children of the third generation born to them may enter the assembly of the LORD.

Uncleanness forbidden

9 "When the army goes out against your enemies, then keep yourself from every wicked thing.

10 "If there is any man among you who becomes unclean by some occurrence in the night, then he shall go outside the camp; he shall not come inside the camp.

11 "But it shall be, when evening comes, that he shall wash with water; and when the sun sets, he may come into the camp.

12 "Also you shall have a place outside the camp, where you may go out;

13 "and you shall have an implement among your equipment, and when you sit down outside, you shall dig with it and turn and cover your refuse.

14 "For the LORD your God [r]walks in the midst of your camp, to deliver you and give your enemies over to you; therefore your camp shall be holy, that He may see no unclean

*23:4 Hebrew *Aram Naharaim*

19
a Cp. Dt. 24:2

21
b Dt. 21:21
c Cp. Gen. 34:7; Jud. 20:6,10; 2 Sam. 13:12
d Cp. Lev. 21:9

22
e Lev. 20:10
f Cp. Ezek. 16:38

24
g Cp. Lev. 19:20–22

29
h Ex. 22:16–17
i See Coinage (OT), Ex. 30:13, *note;* cp. 2 Chr. 2:10, *note*

30
j Lev. 20:11; Dt. 27:20

CHAPTER 23

1
k Lev. 21:20

3
l Neh. 13:1–2

4
m See Dt. 2:27–30
n Num. 22:5–6

5
o Dt. 4:37

6
p Ezra 9:12

7
q Gen. 25:24–26; Dt. 2:4,8; Amos 1:11; Obad. 10, 12

14
r Lev. 26:12; Dt. 7:21

thing among you, and turn away from
you.
15 "You shall not [a]give back to his
master the slave who has escaped
from his master to you.
16 "He may dwell with you in your
midst, in the place which he chooses
within one of your gates, where it
seems best to him; you shall not [b]op-
press him.
17 "There shall be no *ritual* [c]har-
lot* of the daughters of Israel, or a
perverted* one of the sons of Israel.
18 "You shall not bring the wages
of a harlot or the price of a [d]dog to the
house of the LORD your God for any
vowed offering, for both of these *are*
an abomination to the LORD your God.
19 "You shall not charge [e]interest
to your brother—interest on money *or*
food *or* anything that is lent out at interest.
20 "To a foreigner you may charge
interest, but to your brother you shall
not charge interest, that the LORD your
God may bless you in all to which you
set your hand in the land which you
are entering to possess.

Instructions about vows

21 "When you make a vow to the
LORD your God, you shall not delay to
pay it; for the LORD your God will
surely require it of you, and it would
be sin to you.
22 "But if you abstain from vowing,
it shall not be sin to you.
23 [f]"That which has gone from
your lips you shall keep and perform,
for you voluntarily vowed to the LORD
your God what you have promised
with your mouth.
24 "When you come into your
neighbor's vineyard, you may eat
your fill of grapes at your pleasure,
but you shall not put *any* in your container.
25 "When you come into your
neighbor's standing grain, [g]you may
pluck the heads with your hand, but
you shall not use a sickle on your
neighbor's standing grain.

Mosaic law of divorce

24 "WHEN a man takes a wife and
marries her, and it happens
that she finds no favor in his eyes because he has found some uncleanness
in her, and he writes her a [h]certificate
of [i]divorce, puts *it* in her hand, and
sends her out of his [j]house,
2 "when she has departed from his
house, and [k]goes and becomes another man's *wife,*
3 "*if* the latter husband detests her
and writes her a certificate of divorce,
puts *it* in her hand, and sends her out
of his house, or if the latter husband
dies who took her as his wife,
4 "*then* her former husband who
divorced her must not take her back to
be his [l]wife after she has been defiled;
for that *is* an abomination before the
LORD, and you shall not bring sin on
the land which the LORD your God is
giving you *as* an inheritance.

Further regulations of holiness and mercy

5 "When a man has taken a new
wife, he shall not go out to war or be
charged with any business; he shall be
free at home [m]one year, and bring
happiness to his wife whom he has
taken.
6 "No man shall take the lower or
the upper millstone in [n]pledge, for he
takes *one's* living in pledge.
7 [o]"If a man is found kidnapping
any of his brethren of the children of
Israel, and mistreats him or sells him,
then that kidnapper shall die; and you
shall put away the evil from among
you.
8 "Take heed in an [p]outbreak of
leprosy, that you carefully observe
and do according to all that the
priests, the Levites, shall teach you;
just as I commanded them, *so* you
shall be careful to do.
9 [q]"Remember what the LORD
your God did [r]to Miriam on the way
when you came out of Egypt!
10 "When you [s]lend your brother
anything, you shall not go into his
house to get his pledge.
11 "You shall stand outside, and the
man to whom you lend shall bring the
pledge out to you.
12 "And if the man *is* poor, you
shall not keep his pledge overnight.
13 "You shall in any case [t]return
the pledge to him again when the sun
goes down, that he may sleep in his
own garment and bless you; and it
shall be [u]righteousness to you before
the LORD your God.
14 "You shall not [v]oppress a hired
servant *who is* poor and needy,
whether one of your brethren or one

15
a 1 Sam. 30:15
16
b Ex. 22:21
17
c Lev. 19:29; Dt. 22:21
18
d A term used for a male prostitute, sodomite, or catamite. Lev. 18:22; 20:13
19
e Ex. 22:25; Lev. 25:35–37
23
f Num. 30:2; Ps. 66:13, 14
25
g Mt. 12:1; Mk. 2:23; Lk. 6:1
CHAPTER 24
1
h Mt. 5:31; cp. Jer. 3:8
i Mk. 10:4
j Mt. 19:7–8; cp. Mt. 5:32; 19:9
2
k Cp. Lev. 21:7; Dt. 21:14
4
l Cp. Jer. 3:1
5
m Dt. 20:7
6
n vv. 10–13; Ex. 22:26
7
o Ex. 21:16
8
p Lev. 13:2; 14:2
9
q Lk. 17:32; 1 Cor. 10:6
r Num. 12:10
10
s Mt. 5:42
13
t Ezek. 18:7
u Dt. 6:25
14
v Lev. 25:35–43; Dt. 15:7–18; 1 Tim. 5:18

*
23:17 Hebrew *qedeshah,* feminine of *qadesh* (see following note) • Hebrew *qadesh,* that is, one practicing sodomy and prostitution in religious ritual

of the aliens who *is* in your land within
your gates.
15 "Each day you shall give *him* his
wages, and not let the sun go down on
it, for he *is* poor and has set his heart
on it; lest he cry out against you to the
LORD, and it be sin to you.
16 "Fathers shall not be put to death
for *their* children, nor shall children
be put to death for *their* [a]fathers; a
person shall be put to death for his
own sin.
17 "You shall not pervert justice
due the stranger or the fatherless, nor
take a widow's garment as a pledge.
18 "But you shall remember that
you were a slave in Egypt, and the
LORD your God redeemed you from
there; therefore I command you to do
this thing.
19 "When you [b]reap your harvest
in your field, and forget a sheaf in the
field, you shall not go back to get it; it
shall be for the stranger, the fatherless, and the widow, that the LORD
your God may [c]bless you in all the
work of your hands.
20 "When you beat your olive trees,
you shall not go over the boughs
again; it shall be for the stranger, the
fatherless, and the widow.
21 "When you gather the grapes of
your vineyard, you shall not glean *it*
afterward; it shall be for the stranger,
the fatherless, and the widow.
22 "And you shall remember that
you were a slave in the land of Egypt;
therefore I command you to do this
thing.

Forty stripes

25 "IF there is a dispute between
men, and they come to court,
that *the* [d]*judges* may judge them, and
they justify the righteous and condemn the wicked,
2 "then it shall be, if the wicked
man [e]deserves to be beaten, that the
judge will cause him to lie down and
be beaten in his presence, according
to his guilt, with a certain number of
blows.
3 [f]"Forty blows he may give him
and no more, lest he should exceed
this and beat him with many blows
above these, and your brother be humiliated in your sight.
4 "You shall not muzzle an ox
while it treads out *the* [g]*grain.*

Perpetuating a brother's name

5 "If brothers dwell together, and
one of them dies and has no [h]son, the
widow of the dead man shall not be
married to a stranger [i]outside *the*
family; her husband's brother shall go
in to her, take her as his wife, and
perform the duty of a husband's
brother to her.
6 "And it shall be *that* the firstborn son which she bears will succeed
to the name of his dead brother, that
his name may not be blotted out of
Israel.
7 "But if the man does not want to
take his brother's wife, then let his
brother's wife go up to the [j]gate to the
elders, and say, 'My husband's
brother refuses to raise up a name to
his brother in Israel; he will not perform the duty of my husband's
brother.'
8 "Then the elders of his city shall
call him and speak to him. But *if* he
stands firm and says, [k]'I do not want
to take her,'
9 "then his brother's wife shall
come to him in the presence of the
elders, [l]remove his sandal from his
foot, spit in his face, and answer and
say, 'So shall it be done to the man
who will not [m]build up his brother's
house.'
10 "And his name shall be called in
Israel, 'The house of him who had his
sandal removed.'

Severe punishments

11 "If *two* men fight together, and
the wife of one draws near to rescue
her husband from the hand of the one
attacking him, and puts out her hand
and seizes him by the genitals,
12 "then you shall cut off her hand;
your eye shall not pity *her.*
13 "You shall not have in your bag
[n]differing weights, a heavy and a
light.
14 "You shall not have in your
house [n]differing measures, a large
and a small.
15 "You shall have a perfect and
just weight, a perfect and just measure, [o]that your days may be lengthened in the land which the LORD your
God is giving you.
16 "For [p]all who do such things, all
who behave unrighteously, *are* an
abomination to the LORD your God.

Amalek to be judged

17 [q]"Remember what Amalek did
to you on the way as you were coming
out of Egypt,

16
a 2 Ki. 14:6; 2 Chr. 25:4; Ezek. 18:20
19
b Lev. 19:9–10
c Dt. 15:10; Ps. 41:1; Prov. 19:17
CHAPTER 25
1
d Dt. 17:8–13
2
e Lk. 12:48
3
f 2 Cor. 11:24
4
g 1 Cor. 9:9; 1 Tim. 5:18
5
h Mt. 22:24; Mk. 12:19; Lk. 20:28
i Gen. 38:9
7
j Cp. Ruth 4:1–2
8
k Cp. Ruth 4:6
9
l Cp. Ruth 4:7
m Cp. Ruth 4:11
13
n Lev. 19:35–37
15
o Ex. 20:12
16
p Prov. 11:1; 1 Th. 4:6
17
q Ex. 17:8; 1 Sam. 15:1–3

18 "how he met you on the way and
attacked your rear ranks, all the strag-
glers at your rear, when you *were*
tired and weary; and he did not fear
God.
19 "Therefore it shall be, when the
LORD your God has given you rest
from your enemies all around, in the
land which the LORD your God is giving you to possess *as* an inheritance,
that you will blot out the remembrance of Amalek from under heaven.
You shall not forget.

Law of the offering of firstfruits
(cp. Ex. 23:16–19)

26 "AND it shall be, when you
come into the land which the
LORD your God is giving you *as* an inheritance, and you possess it and
dwell in it,
2 "that you shall take some of the
[a]first of all the produce of the ground,
which you shall bring from your land
that the LORD your God is giving you,
and put *it* in a basket and go to the
place where the LORD your God
chooses to make His name abide.
3 "And you shall go to the one who
is priest in those days, and say to him,
'I declare today to the LORD your* God
that I have come to the country which
the LORD swore to our fathers to give
us.'
4 "Then the priest shall take the
basket out of your hand and set it
down before the altar of the LORD your
God.
5 "And you shall answer and [b]say
before the LORD your God: 'My father
was a [c]Syrian,* [d]about to perish, and
he went down to Egypt and dwelt
there, [e]few in number; and there he
became a nation, [f]great, mighty, and
populous.
6 'But the [g]Egyptians mistreated
us, afflicted us, and laid hard bondage
on us.
7 [h]'Then we cried out to the LORD
God of our fathers, and the LORD heard
our voice and looked on our affliction
and our labor and our oppression.
8 'So the [i]LORD brought us out of
Egypt with a mighty hand and with an
outstretched arm, with great terror
and with signs and wonders.
9 'He has brought us to this place
and has given us this land, "a [j]land
flowing with milk and honey";
10 'and now, behold, I have brought
the firstfruits of the land which you, O

CHAPTER 26
2
a Ex. 22:29; 23:16,19
5
b *Bible prayers* (OT): vv. 5–10, 13–15; Josh. 7:7. (Gen. 15:2; Hab. 3:1)
c Gen. 25:20; Hos. 12:12
d Gen. 13:1–2; 45:7,11
e Gen. 46:27; Dt. 10:22
f Dt. 1:10
6
g Ex. 1:11, 14
7
h Ex. 2:23–25; 3:9; 4:31
8
i Ex. 12:42, 51; 13:3, 14,16; Dt. 5:15
9
j Ex. 3:8
12
k Dt. 14:28–29
14
l Lev. 7:20; Jer. 16:7; Hos. 9:4
17
m Dt. 15:5
18
n *Election* (corporate): vv. 18–19; 27:9; 1 Chr. 16:13. (Dt. 7:6; 1 Pet. 5:13, *note*)
o Lit. *a people for His own possession.* Ex. 19:5; Dt. 7:6; 14:2; cp. Ti. 2:14; 1 Pet. 2:9
19
p Dt. 28:1

LORD, have given me.' Then you shall
set it before the LORD your God, and
worship before the LORD your God.
11 "So you shall rejoice in every
good *thing* which the LORD your God
has given to you and your house, you
and the Levite and the stranger who *is*
among you.
12 "When you have [k]finished laying aside all the tithe of your increase
in the third year—the year of tithing—
and have given *it* to the Levite, the
stranger, the fatherless, and the
widow, so that they may eat within
your gates and be filled,
13 "then you shall say before the
LORD your God: 'I have removed the
holy *tithe* from *my* house, and also
have given them to the Levite, the
stranger, the fatherless, and the
widow, according to all Your commandments which You have commanded me; I have not transgressed
Your commandments, nor have I forgotten *them*.
14 [l]'I have not eaten any of it when
in mourning, nor have I removed *any*
of it for an unclean *use*, nor given *any*
of it for the dead. I have obeyed the
voice of the LORD my God, and have
done according to all that You have
commanded me.
15 'Look down from Your holy habitation, from heaven, and bless Your
people Israel and the land which You
have given us, just as You swore to
our fathers, "a land flowing with milk
and honey." '*
16 "This day the LORD your God
commands you to observe these statutes and judgments; therefore you
shall be careful to observe them with
all your heart and with all your
soul.
17 "Today you have proclaimed the
LORD to be your God, and that you will
walk in His ways and keep His statutes, His commandments, and His
judgments, and that you will [m]obey
His voice.
18 "Also today the LORD has [n]pro-
claimed you to be [o]His special people,
just as He promised you, that *you*
should keep all His commandments,
19 "and that He will set you [p]high
above all nations which He has made,
in praise, in name, and in honor, and
that you may be a holy people to the
LORD your God, just as He has spoken."

*
26:3 Septuagint reads *my*. **26:5** Or *Aramean*
26:15 Exodus 3:8

III. Third Discourse: Blessings and Curses for Obedience and Disobedience, 27—28

The stones of the law in Mount Ebal

27 NOW Moses, with the elders of Israel, commanded the people, saying: "Keep all the commandments which I command you today.

2 "And it shall be, on the [a]day when you cross over the Jordan to the land which the LORD your God is giving you, that you shall [b]set up for yourselves large stones, and whitewash them with lime.

3 "You shall write on them all the words of this law, when you have crossed over, that you may enter the land which the LORD your God is giving you, 'a land flowing with milk and honey,'* just as the LORD God of your fathers promised you.

4 "Therefore it shall be, when you have crossed over the Jordan, *that* on Mount [c]Ebal you shall set up these stones, which I command you today, and you shall whitewash them with lime.

5 [d]"And there you shall build an altar to the LORD your God, an altar of stones; you shall not use an iron *tool* on them.

6 "You shall build with whole stones the altar of the LORD your God, and offer burnt offerings on it to the LORD your God.

7 "You shall offer peace offerings, and shall eat there, and [e]rejoice before the LORD your God.

8 "And you shall [b]write very plainly on the stones all the words of this law."

Blessings and curses from Ebal and Gerizim

9 Then Moses and the priests, the Levites, spoke to all Israel, saying, "Take heed and listen, O Israel: This day [f]you have become the people of the LORD your God.

10 "Therefore you shall obey the voice of the LORD your God, and observe His commandments and His statutes which I command you today."

11 And Moses commanded the people on the same day, saying,

12 "These shall stand [g]on Mount Gerizim to bless the people, when you have crossed over the Jordan: Simeon, Levi, Judah, Issachar, Joseph, and Benjamin;

13 "and these shall stand [h]on Mount Ebal to curse: Reuben, Gad, Asher, Zebulun, Dan, and Naphtali.

CHAPTER 27
2 a Josh. 4:1 b Josh. 8:32
4 c Dt. 11:29; Josh. 8:30
5 d Ex. 20:25; Josh. 8:31
7 e Dt. 26:11
9 f Dt. 26:18
12 g Dt. 11:29; Josh. 8:33; Jud. 9:7
13 h Dt. 11:29
14 i Dt. 33:10; Dan. 9:11
15 j Ex. 20:4, 23; Ex. 34:17; Lev 19:4; 26:1
16 k Lev. 20:9; Ezek. 22:7
17 l Dt. 19:14
19 m Lev. 19:14 n Dt. 24:17
21 o Lev. 18:23
22 p Lev. 18:9
23 q Lev. 20:14
24 r Ex. 21:12
25 s Ex. 23:7
26 t Gal. 3:10

14 "And the [i]Levites shall speak with a loud voice and say to all the men of Israel:

15 [j]'Cursed *is* the one who makes a carved or molded image, an abomination to the LORD, the work of the hands of the craftsman, and sets *it* up in secret.'

And all the people shall answer and say, 'Amen!'

16 [k]'Cursed *is* the one who treats his father or his mother with contempt.'

And all the people shall say, 'Amen!'

17 [l]'Cursed *is* the one who moves his neighbor's landmark.'

And all the people shall say, 'Amen!'

18 'Cursed *is* the one who makes the blind to wander off the road.'

And all the people shall say, 'Amen!'

19 [m]'Cursed *is* the one who perverts the [n]justice due the stranger, the fatherless, and widow.'

And all the people shall say, 'Amen!'

20 'Cursed *is* the one who lies with his father's wife, because he has uncovered his father's bed.'

And all the people shall say, 'Amen!'

21 [o]'Cursed *is* the one who lies with any kind of animal.'

And all the people shall say, 'Amen!'

22 [p]'Cursed *is* the one who lies with his sister, the daughter of his father or the daughter of his mother.'

And all the people shall say, 'Amen!'

23 [q]'Cursed *is* the one who lies with his mother-in-law.'

And all the people shall say, 'Amen!'

24 [r]'Cursed *is* the one who attacks his neighbor secretly.'

And all the people shall say, 'Amen!'

25 [s]'Cursed *is* the one who takes a bribe to slay an innocent person.'

And all the people shall say, 'Amen!'

26 'Cursed *is* the one who does not confirm *all* the words of this [t]law.'

And all the people shall say, 'Amen!'

*
27:3 Exodus 3:8

Those things that bring blessing

28 [1a]"NOW it shall come to pass,
if you diligently [b]obey the
voice of the LORD your God, to observe
carefully all His commandments
which I command you today, that the
LORD your God will set you [c]high
above all nations of the earth.
2 "And all these blessings shall
come upon you and [d]overtake you,
because you obey the voice of the
LORD your God:
3 "Blessed *shall* you *be* in the city,
and blessed *shall* you *be* in the country.
4 "Blessed *shall be* the fruit of
your body, the produce of your
ground and the increase of your
herds, the increase of your cattle and
the offspring of your flocks.
5 "Blessed *shall be* your basket
and your kneading bowl.
6 "Blessed *shall* you *be* when you
come in, and blessed *shall* you *be*
when you go out.
7 "The LORD will cause your enemies who rise against you to be defeated before your face; they shall
come out against you one way and flee
before you seven ways.
8 "The LORD will [e]command the
blessing on you in your storehouses
and in all to which you set your hand,
and He will bless you in the land
which the LORD your God is giving
you.
9 "The LORD will establish you as a
holy people to Himself, just as He has
sworn to you, if you keep the commandments of the LORD your God and
walk in His ways.
10 "Then all peoples of the earth
shall see that you are [f]called by the
name of the LORD, and they shall be
[g]afraid of you.
11 "And the LORD will grant you
plenty of goods, in the fruit of your
body, in the increase of your livestock,
and in the produce of your ground, in
the land of which the LORD swore to
your fathers to give you.
12 "The LORD will open to you His
good treasure, the heavens, to give the
[h]rain to your land in its season, and to
bless all the work of your hand. You
shall lend to many nations, but you
shall not [i]borrow.
13 "And the LORD will make you the
[j]head and not the tail; you shall be
above only, and not be beneath, if you
heed the commandments of the LORD
your God, which I command you today, and are careful to observe *them*.
14 "So you shall not turn aside from
any of the words which I command
you this day, *to* the right or the left, to
go after other gods to serve them.

Those things that bring a curse

15 [k]"But it shall come to pass, [l]if
you do not obey the voice of the LORD
your God, to observe carefully all His
commandments and His statutes
which I command you today, that all
these curses will come upon you and
overtake you:
16 "Cursed *shall* you *be* in the city,
and cursed *shall* you *be* in the country.
17 "Cursed *shall be* your basket
and your kneading bowl.
18 "Cursed *shall be* the fruit of your
body and the produce of your land, the
increase of your cattle and the offspring of your flocks.
19 "Cursed *shall* you *be* when you
come in, and cursed *shall* you *be* when
you go out.
20 "The LORD will send on you
[m]cursing, [n]confusion, and [o]rebuke in
all that you set your hand to do, until
you are destroyed and until you perish
quickly, because of the wickedness of
your doings in which you have forsaken Me.
21 "The LORD will make the plague
cling to you until He has consumed
you from the land which you are going
to possess.
22 "The LORD will strike you with
consumption, with fever, with inflammation, with severe burning fever,
with the sword, with scorching, and
with [p]mildew; they shall pursue you
until you perish.
23 "And your heavens which *are*
over your head shall be bronze, and
the earth which is under you *shall be*
iron.
24 "The LORD will change the rain of
your land to powder and dust; from
the heaven it shall come down on you
until you are destroyed.
25 "The LORD will cause you to be
defeated before your enemies; you
shall go out one way against them and
flee seven ways before them; and you
shall become [q]troublesome to all the
kingdoms of the earth.
26 "Your carcasses shall be food for
all the [r]birds of the air and the beasts

CHAPTER 28

1
a vv. 1–14; cp. Ex. 23:22–27; Lev. 26:3–13; Dt. 7:12–26
b Ex. 15:26; Isa. 55:2
c Dt. 26:19

2
d Cp. v. 15

8
e Lev. 25:21

10
f Num. 6:27; 2 Chr. 7:14; Isa. 63:19; Dan. 9:18–19
g Dt. 11:25

12
h Dt. 11:14
i Dt. 15:6

13
j Cp. v. 44; Isa. 9:14–15

15
k vv. 15–68; cp. Lev. 26:14–43
l Dan. 9:10–14; Mal. 2:2

20
m Mal. 2:2
n Isa. 65:14; Zech. 14:13; cp. 1 Sam. 14:20
o Ps. 80:16; Isa. 30:17; 51:20

22
p Amos 4:9

25
q v. 49

26
r Ps. 79:2

[1](28:1) Chapters 28—29 are an integral part of the Palestinian Covenant that is announced in 30:1–9. See 30:3, *note*.

of the earth, and no one shall frighten
them away.
27 "The LORD will strike you with
the [a]boils of Egypt, with tumors, with
the scab, and with the itch, from
which you cannot be healed.
28 "The LORD will strike you with
madness and blindness and confusion
of heart.
29 "And you shall grope at noonday, as a blind man gropes in darkness; you shall not prosper in your
ways; you shall be only oppressed and
plundered continually, and no one
shall save *you.*
30 "You shall betroth a wife, but another man shall lie with [b]her; you
shall build a house, but you shall not
dwell [c]in it; you shall plant a vineyard, but shall not gather its grapes.
31 "Your ox *shall be* slaughtered
before your eyes, but you shall not eat
of it; your donkey *shall be* violently
taken away from before you, and shall
not be restored to you; your sheep
shall be given to your enemies, and
you shall have no one to rescue *them.*
32 "Your sons and your daughters
shall be given to [d]another people, and
your eyes shall look and fail *with
longing* for them all day long; and
there shall be no strength in your
[e]hand.
33 "A nation whom you have not
known shall eat the fruit of your land
and the produce of your labor, and
you shall be only oppressed and
crushed continually.
34 "So you shall be driven mad because of the sight which your eyes see.
35 "The LORD will strike you in the
knees and on the legs with severe
[a]boils which cannot be healed, and
from the sole of your foot to the top of
your head.
36 "The LORD will [f]bring you and
the king whom you set over you to a
nation which neither you nor your fathers have known, and there you shall
serve other [g]gods—wood and stone.
37 "And you shall become [h]an astonishment, a proverb, and a byword
among all nations where the LORD will
drive you.
38 "You shall carry much seed out
to the field but gather little [i]in, for the
[j]locust shall consume it.
39 "You shall plant vineyards and
tend *them,* but you shall neither drink
of the [k]wine nor gather the *grapes;* for
the worms shall eat them.
40 "You shall have olive trees
throughout all your territory, but you
shall not anoint *yourself* with the oil;
for your olives shall drop off.
41 "You shall beget sons and
daughters, but they shall not be yours;
for they shall go into captivity.
42 "Locusts shall consume all your
trees and the produce of your land.
43 "The alien who *is* among you
shall rise higher and higher above
you, and you shall come down lower
and lower.
44 "He shall lend to you, but you
shall not lend to him; he shall be the
[l]head, and you shall be the tail.
45 "Moreover all these curses shall
come upon you and pursue and overtake you, until you are destroyed, because you did not obey the voice of the
LORD your God, to keep His commandments and His statutes which He commanded you.
46 "And they shall be upon [m]you for
a sign and a wonder, and on your descendants forever.
47 "Because you [n]did not serve the
LORD your God with joy and gladness
of heart, for the abundance of everything,
48 "therefore you shall serve your
enemies, whom the LORD will send
against you, in [o]hunger, in thirst, in
nakedness, and in need of everything;
and He [p]will put a yoke of iron on
your neck until He has destroyed you.

Invasion

49 "The LORD will bring a [q]nation
against you from afar, from the end of
the [r]earth, *as swift* as the eagle flies,
a nation whose language you will not
understand,
50 "a nation of fierce countenance,
which does not respect the elderly nor
show favor to the [s]young.
51 "And they shall eat the increase
of your livestock and the produce of
your land, until you are destroyed;
they shall not leave you grain or new
wine or oil, *or* the increase of your
cattle or the offspring of your flocks,
until they have destroyed you.
52 "They shall besiege you at all
your gates until your high and fortified walls, in which you trust, come
down throughout all your land; and
they shall besiege you at all your gates
throughout all your land which the
LORD your God has given you.
53 "You shall eat the [t]fruit of your
own body, the flesh of your sons and
your daughters whom the LORD your
God has given you, in the siege and

27 a Ex. 9:9; Dt. 7:15
30 b 2 Sam. 12:11; Jer. 8:10 c Amos 5:11
32 d 2 Chr. 29:9 e Neh. 5:5
36 f v. 49; 2 Ki. 17:6; 24:12,14; 25:7,11; 2 Chr. 33:11; 36:6,20 g Jer. 16:13
37 h 1 Ki. 9:7–8; Jer. 24:9; 25:9; Zech. 8:13
38 i Isa. 5:10; Mic. 6:15 j Joel 1:4
39 k Zeph. 1:13
44 l v. 13
46 m Isa. 8:18; Ezek. 14:8
47 n Dt. 31:20
48 o Lam. 4:4–6 p Cp. Jer. 28:14
49 q *Times of the Gentiles:* vv. 49–68; cp. 25–29; 2 Ki. 18:11. (Dt. 28:49; Rev. 16:19) r Lam. 4:19; cp. Ezek. 17:3,12
50 s 2 Chr. 36:17
53 t Lev. 26:29; cp. 2 Ki. 6:28–29

desperate straits in which your enemy
shall distress you.
54 "The sensitive and very refined
man among you will be hostile toward
his brother, toward the wife of his bosom, and toward the rest of his children whom he leaves behind,
55 "so that he will not give any of
them the flesh of his children whom
he will eat, because he has nothing left
in the siege and desperate straits in
which your enemy shall distress you
at all your gates.
56 "The tender and delicate woman
among you, who would not venture to
set the sole of her foot on the ground
because of her delicateness and sensi-
tivity, will refuse* to the husband of
her bosom, and to her son and her
daughter,
57 "her placenta which comes out
from between her feet and her children whom she bears; for she will eat
them secretly for lack of everything in
the siege and desperate straits in
which your enemy shall distress you
at all your gates.
58 "If [a]you do not carefully observe
all the words of this law that are written in this book, that you may [b]fear
this [c]glorious and awesome name,
THE LORD YOUR GOD,
59 "then the LORD will bring upon
you and your descendants extraordi-
nary plagues—great and prolonged
plagues—and serious and prolonged
sicknesses.
60 "Moreover He will bring back on
you all the diseases of Egypt, of which
you were afraid, and they shall cling
to you.
61 "Also every sickness and every
plague, which *is* not written in this
Book of the Law, will the LORD bring
upon you until you are destroyed.
62 "You shall be left few in number,
whereas you were [d]as the stars of
heaven in multitude, because you
would not obey the voice of the LORD
your God.

World-wide dispersion

63 "And it shall be, *that* just as the
LORD rejoiced over you to do you good
and multiply you, so the LORD [e]will
rejoice over you to destroy you and
bring you to nothing; and you shall be
[f]plucked from off the land which you
go to possess.
64 "Then the LORD will [g]scatter you
among all peoples, from one end of
the earth to the other, and there you
shall serve other gods, which neither

58
a *Israel* (history): vv. 58–68; Dt. 30:1. (Gen. 12:2; Rom. 11:26, *note*)
b See Ps. 19:9, *note*
c Ex. 6:3; see Ex. 34:6, *note*

62
d Dt. 10:22; Neh. 9:23

63
e Isa. 1:24
f Jer. 12:14

64
g Dt. 4:27; Jer. 16:13; Amos 9:9

65
h Lam. 1:3; Amos 9:4

68
i Dt. 17:16

CHAPTER 29

1
j Lev. 26:46; 27:34; Dt. 5:2–3

2
k Ex. 19:4; Dt. 11:7

4
l Isa. 6:9–10; Acts 28:26–27; Rom. 11:8; 2 Cor. 3:14–16; cp. Jn. 8:43; Eph. 4:18

5
m Dt. 8:4

6
n Dt. 8:3

7
o Num. 21:21–24, 33–35

you nor your fathers have known—
wood and stone.
65 "And [h]among those nations you
shall find no rest, nor shall the sole of
your foot have a resting place; but
there the LORD will give you a trembling heart, failing eyes, and anguish
of soul.
66 "Your life shall hang in doubt
before you; you shall fear day and
night, and have no assurance of life.
67 "In the morning you shall say,
'Oh, that it were evening!' And at evening you shall say, 'Oh, that it were
morning!' because of the fear which
terrifies your heart, and because of
the sight which your eyes see.
68 "And the LORD will take you back
to Egypt in ships, by the way of which
I said to you, 'You shall never see it
[i]again.' And there you shall be offered for sale to your enemies as male
and female slaves, but no one will buy
you."

IV. Fourth Discourse: The Palestinian Covenant; Its Warnings and Promised Blessings, 29—30

Review of the past

29 THESE *are* the words of the
covenant which the LORD commanded Moses to make with the children of Israel in the land of Moab, besides the [j]covenant which He made
with them in Horeb.
2 Now Moses called all Israel and
said to them: [k]"You have seen all that
the LORD did before your eyes in the
land of Egypt, to Pharaoh and to all
his servants and to all his land—
3 "the great trials which your eyes
have seen, the signs, and those great
wonders.
4 "Yet the [l]LORD has not given you
a heart to perceive and eyes to see and
ears to hear, to this *very* day.
5 "And I have led you forty years
in the wilderness. Your clothes have
not worn out on you, and your sandals
have not worn out on your [m]feet.
6 "You have not eaten [n]bread, nor
have you drunk wine or *similar* drink,
that you may know that I *am* the LORD
your God.
7 "And when you came to this
place, Sihon king of Heshbon and Og
king of Bashan came out against us to
battle, and we [o]conquered them.
8 "We took their land and gave it
as an inheritance to the Reubenites, to

*28:56 Literally *her eye shall be evil toward*

the Gadites, and to half the tribe of Manasseh.

Obedience will bring blessing

9 "Therefore keep the words of this covenant, and do them, that you may prosper in all that you do.

10 "All of you stand today before the LORD your God: your leaders and your tribes and your elders and your officers, all the men of Israel,

11 "your little ones and your wives—also the stranger who *is* in your camp, from the one who cuts your wood to the one who draws your water—

12 "that you may enter into covenant with the LORD your God, and into His oath, which the LORD your God makes with you today,

13 "that He may establish you today as a people for Himself, and *that* He may be [a]God to you, just as He has spoken to you, and just as He has sworn to your fathers, to Abraham, Isaac, and Jacob.

Warning against disobedience

14 "I make this covenant and this oath, not with you [b]alone,

15 "but with *him* who stands here with us today before the LORD our God, as well as with *him* who *is* not here with us today

16 (for you know that we dwelt in the land of Egypt and that we came through the nations which you passed by,

17 and you saw their abominations and their idols which *were* among them—wood and stone and silver and gold);

18 "so that there may not be among you man or woman or family or tribe, whose heart turns away today from the LORD our God, to go *and* serve the gods of these nations, and [c]that there may not be among you a root bearing [d]bitterness or wormwood;

19 "and so it may not happen, when he hears the words of this curse, that he blesses himself in his heart, saying, 'I shall have peace, even though I follow the dictates* of my heart'—as though the drunkard could be included with the sober.

20 "The LORD would not spare him; for then the anger of the LORD and His jealousy would burn against that man, and every curse that is written in this book would settle on him, and the LORD would blot out his name from under heaven.

21 "And the LORD would separate him from all the tribes of Israel for adversity, according to all the curses of the covenant that are written in this Book of the [e]Law,

22 "so that the coming generation of your children who rise up after you, and the foreigner who comes from a far land, would say, when they [f]see the plagues of that land and the sicknesses which the LORD has laid on it:

23 'The [g]whole land *is* brimstone, salt, and burning; it is not sown, nor does it bear, nor does any grass grow there, [h]like the overthrow of Sodom and Gomorrah, Admah, and Zeboiim, which the LORD overthrew in His anger and His wrath.'

24 "All nations would say, 'Why has the LORD done so to this land? What does the heat of this great [i]anger mean?'

25 "Then *people* would say: 'Because they have forsaken the covenant of the LORD God of their fathers, which He made with them when He brought them out of the land of Egypt;

26 'for they went and served other gods and worshiped them, gods that they did not know and that He had not given to them.

27 'Then the anger of the LORD was aroused against this land, to bring on it every curse that is written in this book.

28 'And the LORD [j]uprooted them from their land in anger, in wrath, and in great indignation, and cast them into another land, as *it is* this day.'

29 "The secret *things belong* to the LORD our God, but those *things which are* [k]revealed *belong* to us and to our children forever, that *we* may do all the words of this law.

Restoration dependent on repentance

30 "NOW it shall come to pass, when all these things come upon [l]you, the [m]blessing and the [n]curse which I have set before you, and you call *them* to mind among all the nations where the [o]LORD your God drives you,

2 "and you [p]return to the LORD your God and obey His voice, according to all that I command you today, you and your children, with all your heart and with all your soul,

13 *a* Gen. 17:7–8; Ex. 6:7
14 *b* Jer. 31:31–33; Heb. 8:7–10
18 *c* Heb. 12:15; cp. Acts 8:23
d Dt. 32:32
21 *e* Dt. 30:10
22 *f* Jer. 19:8
23 *g* Dt. 28:52
h Gen. 19:24–25; Isa. 1:9; Hos. 11:8
24 *i* 1 Ki. 9:8–9
28 *j* 1 Ki. 14:15; Ezek. 19:12–13
29 *k Inspiration:* v. 29; Dt. 31:24. (Ex. 4:15; 2 Tim. 3:16, *note*)
CHAPTER 30
1 *l Israel (history):* vv. 1–7; Dt. 31:19. (Gen. 12:2; Rom. 11:26, *note*)
m Dt. 28:2
n Dt. 28:15
o Kingdom (OT): vv. 1–9; Dt. 33:5. (Gen. 1:26; Zech. 12:8, *note*)
2 *p* Dt. 4:29–30

*29:19 Or *stubbornness*

Sixth, or Palestinian Covenant
(v. 3, note; read also chs. 29—30)

3 [a]"that the LORD your God will
[1]bring you back from captivity, and
have compassion on you, and [b]gath-
er you again from all the nations
where the LORD your God has scattered you.
4 "If *any* of you are driven out to
the farthest *parts* under heaven, from
there the LORD your God will gather
you, and [c]from there He will bring
you.
5 [2]"Then the LORD your God will
bring you to the land which your fathers possessed, and you shall possess
it. He will prosper you and multiply
you more than your fathers.
6 "And the [d]LORD your God will
circumcise your heart and the heart of
your descendants, to love the LORD
your God with all your heart and with
all your soul, that you may live.
7 "Also the LORD your God will put
all these [e]curses on your enemies and
on those who hate you, who persecuted you.
8 "And you will [f]again obey the
voice of the LORD and do all His commandments which I command you today.
9 "The LORD your God will make
you abound in all the work of your
hand, in the fruit of your body, in the
increase of your livestock, and in the
produce of your land for good. For
the LORD will again [g]rejoice over you
for good as He rejoiced over your fathers,
10 "if you obey the voice of the LORD
your God, to keep His commandments
and His statutes which are written in
this Book of the Law, *and* if you turn
to the LORD your God with all your
heart and with all your soul.

3
a Eight Covenants: vv. 1–9 (cp. Dt. 28:63–68); 2 Sam. 7:8. (Gen. 2:16; Heb. 8:8)
b Christ (second advent): v. 3; Ps. 2:9. (Dt. 30:3; Acts 1:11, *note*)
4
c Isa. 62:11–12
6
d Jer. 32:39; Ezek. 11:19; 36:26
7
e Isa. 54:15–17; Jer. 30:16, 20; see Gen. 12:2, *note*
8
f Zeph. 3:20; see v. 3, *note*
9
g Jer. 32:41
12
h Cp. Rom. 10:6–7
14
i Rom. 10:8
19
j Dt. 30:15; cp. Dt. 4:26
20
k Dt. 10:20
l Jn. 11:25; 14:6; Col. 3:4

The crucial choice before them

11 "For this commandment which I
command you today *is* not *too* mysterious for you, nor *is* it far off.
12 "It *is* not in heaven, that you
should say, 'Who will ascend into
[h]heaven for us and bring it to us, that
we may hear it and do it?'
13 "Nor *is* it beyond the sea, that
you should say, 'Who will go over the
sea for us and bring it to us, that we
may hear it and do it?'
14 "But the word *is* very near you,
in your [i]mouth and in your heart, that
you may do it.
15 "See, I have set before you today
life and good, death and evil,
16 "in that I command you today to
love the LORD your God, to walk in His
ways, and to keep His commandments, His statutes, and His judgments, that you may live and multiply;
and the LORD your God will bless you
in the land which you go to possess.
17 "But if your heart turns away so
that you do not hear, and are drawn
away, and worship other gods and
serve them,
18 "I announce to you today that
you shall surely perish; you shall not
prolong *your* days in the land which
you cross over the Jordan to go in and
possess.
19 "I call heaven and earth as [j]wit-
nesses today against you, *that* I have
set before you life and death, blessing
and cursing; therefore choose life,
that both you and your descendants
may live;
20 "that you may love the LORD your
God, that you may obey His voice, and
that you may [k]cling to Him, for He *is*
your [l]life and the length of your days;
and that you may dwell in the land
which the LORD swore to your fathers,

[1](30:3) The Palestinian Covenant gives the conditions under which Israel entered the land of promise. It is important to see that the nation has never as yet taken the land under the unconditional Abrahamic Covenant (see Gen. 12:2, *note*), nor has it ever possessed the whole land (cp. Gen. 15:18 with Num. 34:1–12). The Palestinian Covenant is in seven parts: (1) dispersion for disobedience, v. 1 (Dt. 28:63–68; see Gen. 15:18, *note*); (2) the future repentance of Israel while in the dispersion, v. 2; (3) the return of the LORD, v. 3 (Amos 9:9–15; Acts 15:14–17); (4) restoration to the land, v. 5 (Isa. 11:11–12; Jer. 23:3–8; Ezek. 37:21–25); (5) national conversion, v. 6 (Hos. 2:14–16; Rom. 11:26–27); (6) the judgment of Israel's oppressors, v. 7 (Isa. 14:1–2; Joel 3:1–8; Mt. 25:31–46); and (7) national prosperity, v. 9 (Amos 9:11–15).

For *notes* on other major covenants, see: Edenic (Gen. 2:16); Adamic (Gen. 3:15); Noahic (Gen. 9:16); Abrahamic (Gen. 12:2); Mosaic (Ex. 19:5); Davidic (2 Sam. 7:16); New (Heb. 8:8).

[2](30:5) No passage of Scripture has found fuller confirmation in the events of history than Dt. 28–30. In A.D. 70 the Jewish nation was scattered throughout the world because of disobedience and rejection of Christ. In world-wide dispersion they experienced exactly the punishments foretold by Moses. On the other hand, when the nation walked in conformity with the will of God, it enjoyed the blessing and protection of God. In the twentieth century the exiled people began to be restored to their homeland.

to Abraham, Isaac, and Jacob, to give
them."

V. Conclusion: Final Words and Acts of Moses, and His Death, 31—34

Moses' last counsels to nations, Joshua, and priests

31 THEN Moses went and spoke
these words to all Israel.
2 And he said to them: "I *am* one
[a]hundred and twenty years old today.
I can no longer [b]go out and come in.
Also the LORD has said to me, 'You
shall not cross over this Jordan.'
3 "The LORD your God Himself
crosses over before you; He will destroy these nations from before you,
and you shall dispossess them.
[c]Joshua himself crosses over before
you, just as the LORD has said.
4 "And the LORD will do to them as
He did to Sihon and Og, the kings of
the Amorites and their land, when He
destroyed them.
5 "The LORD will give them over to
you, that you may do to them [d]accord-
ing to every commandment which I
have commanded you.
6 [e]"Be strong and of good courage, do not fear nor be afraid of them;
for the LORD your God, He *is* the One
who goes with you. [f]He will not leave
you nor forsake you."
7 Then Moses called Joshua and
said to him in the sight of all [g]Israel,
"Be strong and of good courage, for
you must go with this people to the
land which the LORD has sworn to their
fathers to give them, and you shall
cause them to inherit it.
8 "And the LORD, He *is* the One
who goes before you. [h]He will be with
you, He will not leave you nor forsake
you; do not fear nor be dismayed."
9 So Moses wrote this law and
[i]delivered it to the priests, the sons of
Levi, who [j]bore the ark of the covenant of the LORD, and to all the elders
of Israel.
10 And Moses commanded them,
saying: "At the end of *every* seven
years, at the appointed time in the
[k]year of release, at the Feast of Tabernacles,
11 "when all Israel comes to [l]ap-
pear before the LORD your God in the
[m]place which He chooses, you shall
[n]read this law before all Israel in their
hearing.
12 "Gather the people together,
men and women and little ones, and
the stranger who *is* within your gates,
that they may hear and that they may
learn to [o]fear the LORD your God and
carefully observe all the words of this
law,
13 "and *that* their children, who
have not known it, may hear and learn
to fear the LORD your God as long as
you live in the [p]land which you cross
the Jordan to possess."

The LORD warns Moses of Israel's [q]apostasy

14 Then the LORD said to Moses,
"Behold, the days approach when you
must die; call Joshua, and present
yourselves in the tabernacle of meeting, that I may [r]inaugurate him." So
Moses and Joshua went and presented themselves in the tabernacle of
meeting.
15 Now the LORD appeared at the
tabernacle in a [s]pillar of cloud, and
the pillar of cloud stood above the
door of the tabernacle.
16 And the LORD said to Moses: "Behold, you will rest with your fathers;
and this people will rise and play the
harlot with the gods of the foreigners
of the land, where they go *to be*
among them, and they will forsake Me
and break My covenant which I have
made with them.
17 "Then My anger shall be
[t]aroused against them in that day,
and I will forsake them, and I will hide
My face from them, and they shall be
devoured. And many evils and troubles shall befall them, so that they will
say in that day, 'Have not these evils
come upon us because our God *is* not
among us?'
18 "And I will surely hide My face
in that day because of all the evil
which they have done, in that they
have turned to other gods.
19 "Now therefore, write down this
song for yourselves, and teach it to the
children of [u]Israel; put it in their
mouths, that this song may be a witness for Me against the children of Israel.
20 "When I have brought them to
the land flowing with milk and honey,
of which I swore to their fathers, and
they have eaten and filled themselves
and [v]grown fat, then they will turn to
other gods and serve them; and they
will provoke Me and break my covenant.
21 "Then it shall be, when many
evils and troubles have come upon
them, that this song will testify
against them as a witness; for it will

CHAPTER 31
2
a Dt. 34:7; cp. Ex. 7:7
b Cp. Num. 27:17; Josh. 14:11
3
c Num. 27:18
5
d Dt. 7:2; 20:10–20
6
e Josh. 10:25; 1 Chr. 22:13
f Heb. 13:5
7
g Num. 27:19
8
h Josh. 1:5, 9; 1 Chr. 28:20
9
i Dt. 17:18
j Dt. 10:8
10
k Dt. 15:1–2
11
l Dt. 16:16
m Dt. 12:5
n Josh. 8:34–35
12
o See Ps. 19:9, *note*
13
p Dt. 12:1
14
q Cp. 1 Tim. 4:1–3; 2 Tim. 3:1–8; Jude 4–19
r v. 23; Num. 27:19; Dt. 3:28
15
s Ex. 33:9
17
t Jud. 2:14
19
u *Israel* (history): vv. 16–23; Dt. 32:8. (Gen. 12:2; Rom. 11:26, *note*)
20
v Dt. 32:15, 17

not be forgotten in the mouths of their
descendants, for I know the inclina-
tion of their behavior today, even before I have brought them to the land of
which I swore *to give them*."
22 Therefore Moses wrote this
[a]song the same day, and taught it to
the children of Israel.
23 Then He inaugurated Joshua the
son of Nun, and said, "Be strong and
of good courage; for you shall bring
the children of Israel into the land of
which I swore to them, and I will be
with you."
24 So it was, when Moses had completed writing the [b]words of this law
in a [1c]book, when they were finished,
25 that Moses commanded the Levites, who bore the ark of the covenant of the LORD, saying:
26 "Take this Book of the Law, and
put it beside the ark of the covenant of
the LORD your God, that it may be
there as a witness against you;
27 "for I know your [d]rebellion and
your [e]stiff neck. *If* today, while I am
yet alive with you, you have been rebellious against the LORD, then how
much more after my death?
28 "Gather to me all the elders of
your tribes, and your officers, that I
may speak these words in their hearing and [f]call heaven and earth to witness against them.
29 "For I [g]know that after my death
you will become utterly corrupt, and
[h]turn aside from the way which I have
commanded you. And evil will befall
you in the [i]latter days, because you
will do evil in the sight of the LORD, to
provoke Him to anger through the
work of your hands."
30 Then Moses spoke in the hearing of all the assembly of Israel the
words of this song until they were
ended:

22
a vv. 19,21; 32:1–44
24
b Inspiration: v. 24; 2 Sam. 23:2. (Ex. 4:15; 2 Tim. 3:16, *note*)
c See 2 Ki. 22:8, *note*
27
d Dt. 9:7; Neh. 9:26
e Dt. 10:16; 2 Ki. 17:14
28
f Dt. 30:19
29
g Cp. Jud. 2:19; Acts 20:29
h Jud. 2:17
i Dt. 4:30; cp. Isa. 2:2; see Acts 2:17, *note*
CHAPTER 32
1
j Dt. 4:26; Isa. 1:2
2
k Isa. 55:10–11; 1 Cor. 3:6–8
3
l Ex. 33:19
m Dt. 28:58
4
n Christ (Rock): vv. 4,15, 30–31; 2 Sam. 23:3. (Gen. 49:24; 1 Pet. 2:8)
o Dan. 4:37; Rev. 15:3
p Dt. 7:9
5
q Dt. 31:29
r Cp. 2 Pet. 2:13

Song of Moses

32 "GIVE ear, O heavens, and I
will speak;
And hear, O [j]earth, the words
of my mouth.
2 Let [k]my teaching drop as the
rain,
My speech distill as the dew,
As raindrops on the tender
herb,
And as showers on the grass.
3 For I [l]proclaim the [m]name of
the LORD:
Ascribe greatness to our God.
4 *He is* the [n]Rock, His work *is*
perfect;
For all His ways *are* [o]justice,
A God of [p]truth and without
injustice;
Righteous and upright *is* He.

5 "They have [q]corrupted
themselves;
They are not His children,
Because of their [r]blemish:
A perverse and crooked
generation.

God's selection and protection

6 Do you thus deal with the
LORD,
O foolish and unwise people?
Is He not your [s]Father, *who*
bought you?
Has He not made you and
established you?

7 [t]"Remember the days of old,
Consider the years of many
generations.
[u]Ask your father, and he will
show you;
Your elders, and they will tell
you:
8 When the Most High [v]divided

32:6 *s* Ex. 4:22; Dt. 1:31 **32:7** *t* Ps. 44:1 *u* Ps. 78:5–8
32:8 *v* Gen. 11:8; Acts 17:26

[1](31:24) Certain critics have denied the Mosaic authorship of Deuteronomy. (1) They point out its difference of style from the preceding books. (2) They declare that it must be the book found by Josiah which led to his great reform (2 Ki. 22:8—23:27), alleging that Josiah's destruction of the high places, centralizing worship at Jerusalem, was entirely new and was based on Dt. 12. And (3) they say that the laws of Deuteronomy differ at certain points from those of the first four books of the Pentateuch.

There are answers to these objections. (1) The difference of style is easily explained by the fact that Deuteronomy consists of formal addresses and exhortations orally delivered by Moses, and these would naturally be in a style dissimilar to written narrative and technical law. (2) Josiah's centralization of worship was not new. Hezekiah had instituted a similar reform a century earlier, and Josh. 22 shows knowledge of the same law at the time of Joshua. And (3) as for differences in laws between the earlier parts of the Pentateuch and Deuteronomy, these divergences may be explained by the fact that it was necessary for Moses, not only to reiterate the general law applicable to the people under all situations, but also to restate certain laws to fit the changed conditions of settled life scattered over the entire land of Palestine. See *notes* at Ex. 17:14; Dt. 34:12.

their [a]inheritance to the nations,
When He separated the sons of Adam,
He set the boundaries of the peoples
According to the number of the children of Israel.
9 For the LORD's portion *is* His people;
Jacob *is* the place of His inheritance.

10 "He found him [b]in a desert land
And in the wasteland, a howling wilderness;
He encircled him, He instructed him,
He kept him as the [c]apple of His eye.
11 As an eagle stirs up its nest,
Hovers over its young,
Spreading out its wings, taking them up,
Carrying them on its wings,
12 *So* the LORD alone led him,
And *there was* no foreign god with him.

13 "He made him ride in the heights of the earth,
That he might eat the produce of the fields;
He made him draw honey from the rock,
And oil from the flinty rock;
14 Curds from the cattle, and milk of the flock,
With fat of lambs;
And rams of the breed of Bashan, and goats,
With the choicest wheat;
And you drank wine, the blood of the grapes.

Danger of apostasy and judgment

15 "But [d]Jeshurun grew fat and kicked;
You grew fat, you grew thick,
You are obese!
Then he forsook God *who* made him,
And scornfully esteemed the Rock of his salvation.
16 They provoked Him to jealousy with foreign *gods;*
With abominations they provoked Him to anger.
17 They sacrificed to [e]demons, not to God,
To gods they did not know,
To new *gods,* new arrivals
That your fathers did not fear.

8
a Israel (history): vv. 8–9; Dt. 34:1. (Gen. 12:2; Rom. 11:26, *note*)
10
b Jer. 2:6; Hos. 13:5
c Zech. 2:8
15
d Lit. *upright one.* A poetical name for Israel, designating it under its ideal character
17
e Ps. 106:37; 1 Cor. 10:20
18
f Isa. 17:10
19
g Jud. 2:14
21
h Rom. 10:19
22
i See Hab. 2:5, *note*
23
j Dt. 29:24
24
k Lev. 26:22
26
l Ezek. 20:23

18 [f]Of the Rock *who* begot you, you are unmindful,
And have forgotten the God who fathered you.

19 [g]"And when the LORD saw *it,* He spurned *them,*
Because of the provocation of His sons and His daughters.
20 And He said: 'I will hide My face from them,
I will see what their end *will be,*
For they *are* a perverse generation,
Children in whom *is* no faith.
21 They have provoked Me to [h]jealousy by *what* is not God;
They have moved Me to anger by their foolish idols.
But I will provoke them to jealousy by *those who are* not a nation;
I will move them to anger by a foolish nation.
22 For a fire is kindled in My anger,
And shall burn to the lowest [i]hell;
It shall consume the earth with her increase,
And set on fire the foundations of the mountains.

23 'I will [j]heap disasters on them;
I will spend My arrows on them.
24 *They shall be* wasted with hunger,
Devoured by pestilence and bitter destruction;
I will also send against them the [k]teeth of beasts,
With the poison of serpents of the dust.
25 The sword shall destroy outside;
There shall be terror within
For the young man and virgin,
The nursing child with the man of gray hairs.

Mercy and judgment

26 [l]I would have said, "I will dash them in pieces,
I will make the memory of them to cease from among men,"
27 Had I not feared the wrath of the enemy,
Lest their adversaries should misunderstand,

Lest they should say, [a]"Our
hand *is* high;
And it is not the LORD who has
done all this." '

28 "For they *are* a nation void of
counsel,
Nor *is there any* understanding
in them.
29 [b]Oh, that they were wise, *that*
they understood this,
That they would consider their
[c]latter end!
30 How could one chase a
thousand,
And two put ten thousand to
flight,
Unless their Rock had [d]sold
them,
And the LORD had surrendered
them?
31 For their rock *is* not like our
Rock,
[e]Even our enemies themselves
being judges.
32 For their vine *is* of the vine of
Sodom
And of the fields of Gomorrah;
Their grapes *are* grapes of gall,
Their clusters *are* bitter.
33 Their wine *is* the poison of
serpents,
And the cruel venom of
cobras.

34 '*Is* this not laid up in store
with Me,
Sealed up among My
treasures?
35 Vengeance is Mine, and
[f]recompense;
Their foot shall slip in *due*
time;
For the day of their calamity *is*
at hand,
And the things to come hasten
upon them.'

36 "For the LORD will judge His
[g]people
And [h]have compassion on His
servants,
When He sees that *their* power
is gone,
And *there is* no one *remaining*,
bond or free.
37 He will say: 'Where *are* their
[i]gods,
The rock in which they
[j]sought refuge?
38 Who ate the fat of their
sacrifices,
And drank the wine of their
drink offering?

27
a Isa. 10:12–15
29
b Ps. 81:13
c Dt. 31:29
30
d Jud. 2:14; Ps. 44:12; cp. Josh. 23:10
31
e 1 Sam. 4:7–8; Jer. 40:2–3; cp. 1 Sam. 2:2
35
f Rom. 12:19; Heb. 10:30
36
g Ps. 106:45
h Lit. *repent*. See Zech. 8:14, *note*
37
i Jer. 2:28
j See Ps. 2:12, *note*
39
k Isa. 41:4
l 1 Sam. 2:6
41
m Isa. 1:24; Jer. 50:28–32
44
n Cp. Num. 13:8,16
46
o Dt. 11:19
47
p Dt. 30:15–20
49
q Num. 27:12–14

Let them rise and help you,
And be your refuge.
39 'Now see that I, *even* [k]I, *am*
He,
And *there is* no God besides
Me;
[l]I kill and I make alive;
I wound and I heal;
Nor *is there any* who can
deliver from My hand.
40 For I raise My hand to heaven,
And say, "*As* I live forever,
41 If I whet My glittering sword,
And My hand takes hold on
judgment,
I will render vengeance to My
[m]enemies,
And repay those who hate Me.
42 I will make My arrows drunk
with blood,
And My sword shall devour
flesh,
With the blood of the slain and
the captives,
From the heads of the leaders
of the enemy." '

43 "Rejoice, O Gentiles, *with* His
people;*
For He will avenge the blood
of His servants,
And render vengeance to His
adversaries;
He will provide atonement for
His land *and* His people."

44 So Moses came with [n]Joshua*
the son of Nun and spoke all the words
of this song in the hearing of the people.
45 Moses finished speaking all
these words to all Israel,
46 and he said to them: "Set your
hearts on all the words which I testify
among you today, which you shall
command your [o]children to be careful
to observe—all the words of this law.
47 "For it *is* not a futile thing for
you, because it *is* your [p]life, and by
this word you shall prolong *your* days
in the land which you cross over the
Jordan to possess."

Moses ordered up Mount Nebo

48 Then the LORD spoke to Moses
that very same day, saying:
49 [q]"Go up this mountain of the
Abarim, Mount Nebo, which *is* in the
land of Moab, across from Jericho;
view the land of Canaan, which I give

*32:43 A Dead Sea Scroll fragment adds *And let all the gods (angels) worship Him* (compare Septuagint and Hebrews 1:6). 32:44 Hebrew *Hoshea* (compare Numbers 13:8, 16)

to the children of Israel as a possession;
50 "and die on the mountain which
you ascend, and be gathered to your
people, just [a]as Aaron your brother
died on Mount Hor and was gathered
to his people;
51 "because [b]you trespassed
against Me among the children of Israel at the waters of Meribah Kadesh,
in the Wilderness of Zin, because you
did not hallow Me in the midst of the
children of Israel.
52 "Yet you shall [c]see the land before *you,* though you shall not go
there, into the land which I am giving
to the children of Israel."

Moses blesses the tribes

33 NOW this *is* the [d]blessing with
which Moses the man of God
blessed the children of Israel before
his death.
2 And he said:

"The LORD came from [e]Sinai,
And dawned on them from [f]Seir;
He shone forth from [g]Mount Paran,
And He came with [h]ten thousands of saints;
From His right hand
Came a fiery law for them.
3 Yes, He loves the people;
All His saints *are* in Your hand;
They [i]sit down at Your feet;
Everyone receives Your words.
4 [j]Moses commanded a law for us,
A heritage of the congregation of Jacob.
5 And He was [k]King in Jeshurun,
When the leaders of the people were gathered,
All the tribes of Israel together.

6 "Let [l]Reuben live, and not die,
Nor let his men be few."

7 And this he said of [m]Judah:

"Hear, LORD, the voice of Judah,
And bring him to his people;
Let his hands be sufficient for him,
And may You be a help against his enemies."

8 And of [n]Levi he said:

"*Let* Your [o]Thummim and Your Urim *be* with Your [1]holy one,
[p]Whom You [q]tested at Massah,
And with whom You contended at the waters of Meribah,
9 [r]Who says of his father and mother,
'I have not seen them';
Nor did he acknowledge his brothers,
Or know his own children;
For they have observed Your word
And kept Your covenant.
10 They shall teach Jacob Your judgments,
And Israel Your law.
They shall put incense before You,
And a whole burnt sacrifice on Your altar.
11 Bless his substance, LORD,
And accept the work of his hands;
Strike the loins of those who rise against him,
And of those who hate him, that they rise not again."

12 Of Benjamin he said:

"The beloved of the LORD shall dwell in safety by Him,
Who shelters him all the day long;
And he shall dwell between His shoulders."

13 And of [s]Joseph he said:

"Blessed of the LORD *is* his land,
With the precious things of heaven, with the dew,
And the deep lying beneath,
14 With the precious fruits of the sun,
With the precious produce of the months,
15 With the best things of the ancient mountains,
With the precious things of the everlasting hills,
16 With the precious things of the earth and its fullness,
And the favor of [t]Him who dwelt in the bush.
Let *the blessing* come 'on the head of Joseph,
And on the crown of the head

50 [a] Num. 33:38
51 [b] Num. 20:12
52 [c] Dt. 34:1–5
CHAPTER 33
1 [d] Cp. Gen. 49:28
2 [e] Ex. 19:18, 20 [f] Dt. 2:1,4 [g] Num. 10:12 [h] Cp. Dan. 7:10
3 [i] Lk. 10:39; cp. Acts 22:3
4 [j] Jn. 1:17; 7:19
5 [k] *Kingdom* (OT): vv. 4–5; Josh. 1:1. (Gen. 1:26; Zech. 12:8, *note*)
6 [l] Gen. 49:3
7 [m] Gen. 49:8–12
8 [n] Gen. 49:5 [o] See Ex. 28:30, *note* [p] Ex. 17:1–7; 28:30; Num. 20:2–13; Ps. 106:14 [q] *Test/tempt:* vv. 8–9; Jud. 6:39. (Gen. 3:1; Jas. 1:14, *note*)
9 [r] Ex. 32:26–29; Num. 25:5–8
13 [s] Gen. 49:22–26
16 [t] Ex. 3:2–4; Acts 7:30–35

[1](33:8) The usual Hebrew words rendered "holy" are *qadosh* and *qodesh,* meaning *set apart.* Here, and in Ps. 16:10; 86:2; 89:19; and 145:17, the Heb. *chasid* is employed, denoting *kind, gracious* or *favored.* See *notes* at Zech. 8:3; Mt. 4:5; and Rev. 22:11.

of him *who was* separate
from his brothers.'
17 His glory *is like* a firstborn
bull,
And his [1]horns *like* the horns
of the wild ox;
Together with them
He shall push the peoples
To the ends of the earth;
They *are* the ten thousands of
Ephraim,
And they *are* the thousands of
Manasseh."

18 And of [a]Zebulun he said:

"Rejoice, Zebulun, in your
going out,
And Issachar in your tents!
19 They shall [b]call the peoples *to*
the mountain;
There they shall offer
sacrifices of righteousness;
For they shall partake *of* the
abundance of the seas
And *of* treasures hidden in the
sand."

20 And of Gad he said:

"Blessed *is* he who enlarges
Gad;
He dwells as a lion,
And tears the arm and the
crown of his head.
21 He provided the first *part* for
himself,
Because a lawgiver's portion
was reserved there.
He came *with* the heads of the
people;
He administered the [c]justice of
the LORD,
And His judgments with
Israel."

22 And of [d]Dan he said:

"Dan *is* a lion's whelp;
He shall leap from Bashan."

23 And of [e]Naphtali he said:

"O Naphtali, satisfied with
favor,
And full of the blessing of the
LORD,
Possess the west and the
south."

24 And of [f]Asher he said:

"Asher *is* most blessed of sons;
Let him be favored by his
brothers,
And let him dip his foot in oil.
25 Your sandals *shall be* iron and
bronze;
As your days, *so shall* your
strength *be*.

26 "*There is* no one like the God of
Jeshurun,
Who [g]rides the heavens to
help you,
And in His excellency on the
clouds.
27 The eternal God *is your*
[h]refuge,
And underneath *are* the
everlasting arms;
He will thrust out the enemy
from before you,
And will say, 'Destroy!'
28 Then [i]Israel shall dwell in
safety,
The fountain of Jacob [j]alone,
In a land of grain and new
wine;
His heavens shall also drop
dew.
29 Happy *are* you, O Israel!
Who *is* like [k]you, a people
saved by the LORD,
The shield of your help
And the sword of your
majesty!
Your enemies shall submit to
you,
And you shall tread down their
high places."

Moses views the land

34 THEN Moses [l]went up from
the plains of Moab to Mount
Nebo, to the top of Pisgah, which is
across from Jericho. And the LORD
[m]showed him all the land of Gilead as
far as Dan,
2 all Naphtali and the land of
Ephraim and Manasseh, all the land of
Judah as far as the [n]Western Sea,*
3 the [o]South, and the plain of the
Valley of Jericho, the city of palm
trees, as far as Zoar.
4 Then the LORD said to him, "This
is the land of which I swore to give
Abraham, Isaac, and Jacob, saying, 'I
will give it to your descendants.' I
have caused you to see *it* with your

* 34:2 That is, the Mediterranean

18
a Gen. 49:13–15
19
b Cp. Isa. 2:3
21
c Josh. 4:12
22
d Gen. 49:16–17
23
e Gen. 49:21
24
f Gen. 49:20
26
g Ps. 68:33–34
27
h Ps. 91:2,9
28
i Jer. 23:6; 33:16
j Num. 23:9
29
k Dt. 4:32–34
CHAPTER 34
1
l Dt. 32:49
m Israel (history): vv. 1–5; Josh. 3:9. (Gen. 12:2; Rom. 11:26, *note*)
2
n Num. 34:6; Dt. 11:24
3
o See Gen. 12:9, *note*

[1](33:17) The words "horn" and "horns" (OT, *qeren;* NT *keras*) are used in Scripture both literally and figuratively. In the latter sense at least three meanings appear: (1) strength in general (Dt. 33:17); (2) arrogant pride (Ps. 75:4–5); and (3) political and military power (Dan. 8:20–21).

eyes, but you shall not cross over
there."

Death of Moses

5 So Moses the [a]servant of the
LORD died there in the land of Moab,
according to the word of the LORD.
6 And He buried him in a valley in
the land of Moab, opposite Beth Peor;
but [b]no one knows his grave to this
day.
7 Moses *was* one [c]hundred and
twenty years old when he died. His
eyes were not dim nor his natural
vigor diminished.
8 And the children of Israel wept
for Moses in the plains of Moab
[d]thirty days. So the [e]days of weeping
and mourning for Moses ended.

5
a Num. 12:7
6
b Jude 9
7
c Dt. 31:2
8
d Gen. 50:3
e Cp. Num. 20:29
9
f Num. 27:18; cp. Acts 6:5
g *Holy Spirit* (OT): v. 9; Jud. 3:10. (Gen. 1:2; Zech. 12:10)
h Num. 27:23; cp. 1 Tim. 4:14

Joshua succeeds Moses

9 Now Joshua the son of Nun was
[f]full of the [g]spirit of wisdom, for Moses had [h]laid his hands on him; so the
children of Israel heeded him, and did
as the LORD had commanded Moses.

Moses extolled

10 But since then there has not
arisen in Israel a prophet [i]like Moses,
[j]whom the LORD knew face to face,
11 in all the signs and wonders
which the LORD sent him to do in the
land of Egypt, before Pharaoh, before
all his servants, and in all his land,
12 [1]and by all that mighty power
and all the great terror which Moses
performed in the sight of all [2]Israel.

34:10 *i* Dt. 18:15,18 *j* Ex. 33:11; Num. 12:6,8

[1](34:12) In some printed texts of the Hebrew Bible the Pentateuch is concluded after this verse with these words: "Be strong! The five-fifths of the Law are completed. Praise to God, great and fearful!"

[2](34:12) The question has been raised whether Moses wrote the account of his own death. Although it is entirely possible that the LORD directed Joshua to add this account to what Moses had written, it is equally possible that He may have led Moses to write it in advance, since He had already revealed to him the manner and time of his approaching death. See *notes* at Ex. 17:14; Dt. 31:24.

The Historical Books

THE TWELVE historical books of the Old Testament (Josh.—Est.) are designated history in contrast with the rest of the OT described as law (Gen.—Dt.), as poetry (Job—Song), and as prophecy (Isa.—Mal.). Divine laws, history, and prophecy as well as exhortation are found, of course, throughout the OT. The accuracy of the historical books, though questioned by some critics, has been confirmed repeatedly in modern times by discoveries of extra-Biblical evidences.

The historical books relate the rise and fall of the theocracy, the captivities of Israel and Judah, the return to the promised land (Gen. 15:18–21; Ezra 2:1), and the restoration of the temple and the city of Jerusalem. Chronologically, the historical books reach to the time of Malachi. By contrast, the prophetic books foretell God's judgment on sin, exhort the people of each generation to faith and righteousness, and hold before even the disobedient nation Israel the bright picture of future national restoration, glory, honor, and peace under the reign of their Messiah.

The historical and prophetic program of Israel may be separated into eight divisions:

I. From the call of Abraham to the Exodus (Gen. 12:1—Ex. 12:51; cp. Acts 7). In this period the Abrahamic Covenant was given, partially fulfilled in the formation of Israel as a great nation. (It is believed that the events of the Book of Job occurred in this period and that the book documents the divine revelation and the profound philosophic and religious thought of that day.)

II. From the Exodus to the death of Joshua. In this period, in which the law was given to Israel, the history of Israel's deliverance from Egypt, her wilderness wanderings and the possession of the promised land are set forth in Exodus, Numbers, Deuteronomy, Joshua, as well as in portions of Leviticus. Moses, Aaron, and Joshua are the principal historical characters.

III. The period of the judges, from the death of Joshua to the choice of Saul, is unfolded in Judges, Ruth, and 1 Sam. 1:1—10:24. Cycles of apostasy, divine judgment, repentance, and restoration characterize this span of time. A godly remnant continued, however, as seen in Ruth. Israel was rescued from moral, spiritual, and political chaos by the prophet Samuel who, as the last of the early prophets, inducted into office the first of the kings, Saul.

IV. The period of the kings, from Saul to the captivities, is described in 1 Sam. 10:25—31:13, 2 Samuel, 1 and 2 Kings, and 1 and 2 Chronicles. The glory and power of the kingdom under David and Solomon declined during the divided kingdoms of Israel and Judah, and was accompanied by almost complete spiritual failure.

V. The period of the captivities. This time of divine chastisement, predicted by Moses and the prophets, is unfolded in Jeremiah, Lamentations, Ezekiel, Daniel, and Esther. The captivity of Judah (586 B.C.) began the prophetically important "times of the Gentiles" (Lk.21:24) during which Jerusalem has been under Gentile control.

VI. The period from the partial restoration of the nation of Israel to the death, resurrection, and ascension of Christ. The inspired history of this period is found in Ezra, Nehemiah, and the prophetic writings of Haggai, Zechariah, and Malachi in the OT, and in the Gospels in the NT. Toward the end of this period Christ, the promised King of the Davidic Covenant, and the Seed of the Adamic and Abrahamic Covenants, appeared, was rejected as King and Savior, was crucified, rose again from the dead, and ascended into heaven. These tremendous events also marked the close of the sixty-nine prophetic weeks of Dan. 9:24–27.

VII. The period of the Church, from Pentecost to the rapture, during which Israel's national program is set aside. Historically this is presented in The Acts and theologically in portions of the Gospels and in the Epistles. In the early part of the period Jerusalem was destroyed (A.D. 70) and Israel began its third and final dispersion. During the Church period, all national priorities and distinctions are in abeyance in the Church, both Jewish and Gentile believers being joined together with equal standing in the one body of Christ (1 Cor. 12:13; Eph. 3:6).

VIII. Israel's later history is given prophetically as beginning with the fulfillment of the seventieth week of Dan. 9:27, the latter half of which is the great tribulation (Dan. 12:1; Mt. 24:21). The tribulation will end at the second coming of Christ in power and glory to judge the earth and reign over it for 1000 years, an epoch in which Israel will be restored to a place of privilege and glory. At the close of the millennium, Israel will likewise have her part in the eternal state, and will continue to illustrate the faithfulness and righteousness of God throughout eternity.

The Book of

JOSHUA

Author: Joshua *Theme:* Conquering Canaan *Date of writing:* 14th Cent. B.C.

JOSHUA records in part the military campaigns waged by Joshua in conquering the promised land and concludes with detailed instructions for the division of the land among the tribes. It is the first Bible book to bear the name of its principal character. As a young man Joshua served in the tabernacle (Ex. 33:11). He and Caleb were the two among the twelve spies who brought back a favorable report (Num. 14:6–9,30). Toward the end of the wanderings Moses was divinely led to appoint Joshua as his successor as "a man in whom is the Spirit" (Num. 27:18–23; Dt. 1:38) who had with Caleb "wholly followed the LORD" (Num. 32:12).

Israel entered Palestine with a promise of the land, the presence of the LORD, the law of the LORD, and the leadership of Joshua. With all this they should have been everywhere successful, but disobedience led to defeat. The events here recorded may cover as many as thirty years. The book illustrates the principle that the child of God will be involved in conflict with evil powers and with Satan himself if he earnestly undertakes to possess all that God has promised to him on this earth (Eph. 1:3; 6:10–18).

Joshua may be divided as follows:

I. Preparation for Entering Palestine, 1—5.
II. The Conquest of the Land, 6—12.
III. The Allocation of Territories to the Tribes, 13—22.
IV. Joshua's Final Message and Death, 23—24.

I. Preparation for Entering Palestine, 1—5

Joshua succeeds Moses as Israel's leader (Dt. 34:9)

1 AFTER the [a]death of [b]Moses the
servant of the LORD, it came to
pass that the LORD [1]spoke to [2c]Joshua
the [d]son of Nun, Moses' assistant,
saying:
2 "Moses My [e]servant is dead.
Now therefore, arise, go over this Jordan, you and all this people, to the
land which I am giving to them—the
children of Israel.
3 [f]"Every place that the sole of
your foot will tread upon I have given
you, [g]as I said to Moses.
4 "From the wilderness and this
Lebanon as far as the great river, the
River Euphrates, all the land of the
[h]Hittites, and to the Great Sea toward
the going down of the sun, shall be
your territory.
5 "No man shall *be able to* stand
before you all the days of your life; as
I was with Moses, *so* [i]I will be with
you. I will not leave you nor forsake
you.
6 "Be [j]strong and of good courage, for to this people you shall divide
as an inheritance the [3]land which I
swore to their fathers to give them.
7 "Only be strong and very courageous, that you may observe to do according to all the law which Moses My
servant [k]commanded you; do not
[l]turn from it to the right hand or to the
left, that you may prosper wherever
you go.
8 "This [m]Book of the Law shall not
depart from your mouth, but you shall
[n]meditate in it day and night, that you
may observe to do according to all
that is written in it. For then you will
make your way prosperous, and then
you will have good success.
9 "Have I not commanded you? Be
strong and of good courage; do not be
afraid, nor be dismayed, for the LORD
your God *is* with you wherever you
go."

Joshua assumes command

10 Then Joshua commanded the officers of the people, saying,
11 "Pass through the camp and
command the people, saying, 'Prepare

CHAPTER 1

1
a c. 1407 B.C.
b Dt. 34:5; cp. Rev. 1:18
c *Kingdom* (OT): vv. 1–5; Jud. 2:16. (Gen. 1:26; Zech. 12:8, *note*)
d Num. 13:16; 14:6,29–30, 37–38; Acts 7:45

2
e Num. 12:7

3
f The law of appropriation. God gives, but we must take
g Dt. 11:24

4
h See 2 Ki. 7:6, *note*

5
i Dt. 31:6–7; Heb. 13:5

6
j Eph. 6:10; cp. Phil.

4:13 **1:7** *k* Josh 11:15 *l* Dt. 5:32; cp. 1 Cor. 9:26–27 **1:8** *m* Dt. 31:26; Josh. 8:34 *n* Ps. 1:2–3; cp. Dt. 17:18–20

[1](1:1) It is not certain just when the conquest of Palestine occurred. Some Bible scholars think it began about 1407 B.C. Others state that it was much later.

[2](1:1) Joshua (meaning *Jehovah-Savior;* see *note 4* at Gen. 2:3) is a type of Christ, the Captain of our salvation (Heb. 2:10). The more important points are: (1) He comes after Moses (Jn. 1:17; Rom. 8:3–4; 10:4–5; Gal. 3:23–25). (2) He leads to victory (Rom. 8:37; 2 Cor. 1:10; 2:14). (3) He is our Advocate when we have suffered defeat (1 Jn. 2:1–2; cp. Josh. 7:5–9). And (4) He allots our inheritance (Eph. 1:11,14; 4:7–11).

[3](1:6) The land had been promised to Abraham and his seed (Gen. 12:6–7; 13:14–15; 15:18–21), and Moses had been reminded of this. The promise was now to be fulfilled.

provisions for yourselves, for within three days you will cross over this Jordan, to go in to possess the land which the LORD your God is giving you to possess.' "

12 And to the Reubenites, the Gadites, and half the tribe of Manasseh Joshua spoke, saying,

13 "Remember the [a]word which Moses the servant of the LORD commanded you, saying, 'The LORD your God is giving you rest and is giving you this land.'

14 "Your wives, your little ones, and your livestock shall remain in the land which Moses gave you on this side of the Jordan. But you shall pass before your brethren armed, all your mighty men of valor, and help them,

15 "until the LORD has given your brethren rest, as He *gave* you, and they also have taken possession of the land which the LORD your God is giving them. Then you shall [b]return to the land of your possession and enjoy it, which Moses the LORD's servant gave you on this side of the Jordan toward the sunrise."

16 So they answered Joshua, saying, "All that you command us we will do, and wherever you send us we will go.

17 "Just as we heeded Moses in all things, so we will [c]heed you. Only the LORD your God be with you, as He was with Moses.

18 "Whoever rebels against your command and does not heed your words, in all that you command him, shall be put to death. Only be strong and of good courage."

Rahab shelters spies

2 NOW Joshua the son of Nun sent out two men from [d]Acacia Grove* to spy secretly, saying, "Go, view the land, especially Jericho." So they went, and came to the house of a harlot named [1e]Rahab, and lodged there.

2 And it was told the king of Jericho, saying, "Behold, men have come here tonight from the children of Israel to search out the country."

3 So the king of Jericho sent to Rahab, saying, "Bring out the men who have come to you, who have entered your house, for they have come to search out all the country."

4 Then the woman took the two men and [f]hid them. So she said, "Yes, the men came to me, but I did not know where they *were* from.

5 "And it happened as the gate was being shut, when it was dark, that the men went out. Where the men went I do not know; pursue them quickly, for you may overtake them."

6 (But she had brought them up to the roof and hidden them with the stalks of flax, which she had laid in order on the roof.)

7 Then the men pursued them by the road to the Jordan, to the fords. And as soon as those who pursued them had gone out, they shut the gate.

8 Now before they lay down, she came up to them on the roof,

9 and said to the men: [g]"I know that the LORD has given you the land, that the [h]terror of you has fallen on us, and that all the inhabitants of the land are [i]fainthearted because of you.

10 "For we have heard how the LORD [j]dried up the water of the Red Sea for you when you came out of Egypt, and what you [k]did to the two kings of the Amorites who *were* on the other side of the Jordan, Sihon and Og, whom you [l]utterly destroyed.

11 "And as soon as we heard *these things*, our hearts melted; neither did there remain any more courage in anyone because of you, for the LORD your God, He *is* God in heaven above and on earth beneath.

12 "Now therefore, I beg you, swear to me by the LORD, since I have shown you kindness, that you also will show kindness to my father's house, and give me a true [m]token,

13 "and [n]spare my father, my

*

2:1 Hebrew *Shittim*

13
a Dt. 3:18–20
15
b Josh. 22:1–4
17
c Cp. Num. 27:20
CHAPTER 2
1
d Num. 25:1; Josh. 3:1
e Jas. 2:25
4
f Josh. 6:17; cp. 2 Sam. 17:19
9
g Dt. 1:8
h Dt. 2:25; Josh. 9:9–10
i Ex. 15:15; Josh. 5:1
10
j Ex. 14:21; Num. 23:22
k Num. 21:23–24, 33–35
l Dt. 20:17; Josh. 6:21
12
m v. 18; cp. Ex. 12:13
13
n Josh. 6:23–25

[1](2:1) No more unlikely character than Rahab could have been divinely chosen for deliverance from ungodly Jericho. The salvation of Rahab, the harlot, illustrates that even in a doomed city a wicked individual could find grace by turning to God in faith. Those who charge Israel with barbaric cruelty in exterminating the inhabitants of Jericho fail to comprehend that Israel was God's instrument of divine judgment. The people of Jericho, hopelessly depraved (cp. Lev. 18:24–26), had chosen to fight Israel instead of seeking mercy as did Rahab. Those who perished did not believe (Heb. 11:31). Even Rahab's lie (vv. 4–5), not to be taken as an example, was evidently motivated by her belief that God would destroy Jericho as had been predicted (vv. 9–11; cp. Josh. 1:1–11). Rahab, as an ancestress of David, is thus in the Messianic line (Ruth 4:21–22; Mt. 1:5–6; Lk. 3:31–32).

mother, my brothers, my sisters, and
all that they have, and deliver our
lives from death."
14 So the men answered her, "Our
lives for yours, if none of you tell this
business of ours. And it shall be, when
the LORD has given us the land, that we
will [a]deal kindly and truly with you."

Spies escape and report to Joshua

15 Then she let them down by a
rope through the window, for her
house *was* on the city wall; she dwelt
on the wall.
16 And she said to them, "Get to the
mountain, lest the pursuers meet you.
Hide there three days, until the pursuers have returned. Afterward you may
go your way."
17 So the men said to her: "We *will*
be blameless of this oath of yours
which you have made us swear,
18 "unless, *when* we come into the
land, you bind this [b]line of scarlet
cord in the window through which
you let us down, and unless you
[c]bring your father, your mother, your
brothers, and all your father's household to your own home.
19 "So it shall be *that* whoever goes
outside the doors of your house into
the street, his blood *shall be* on his
own head, and we *will be* guiltless.
And whoever is with you in the house,
his blood *shall be* on our head if a
hand is laid on him.
20 "And if you tell this business of
ours, then we will be free from your
oath which you made us swear."
21 Then she said, "According to
your words, so *be* it." And she sent
them away, and they departed. And
she bound the scarlet [1]cord in the window.
22 They departed and went to the
mountain, and stayed there three days
until the pursuers returned. The pursuers sought *them* all along the way,
but did not find *them.*
23 So the two men returned, descended from the mountain, and
crossed over; and they came to Joshua
the son of Nun, and told him all that
had befallen them.
24 And they said to Joshua, "Truly
the LORD has delivered all the land into
our hands, for indeed all the inhabitants of the country are fainthearted
because of us."

Israel crosses Jordan dry-shod

3 THEN Joshua rose early in the
morning; and they set out from
[d]Acacia Grove* and came to the [2]Jor-
dan, he and all the children of Israel,
and lodged there before they crossed
over.
2 So it was, after [e]three days, that
the officers went through the camp;
3 and they commanded the people, saying, "When you see the ark of
the covenant of the LORD your God,
and the priests, the Levites, bearing it,
then you shall set out from your place
and go after it.
4 "Yet there shall be a [f]space between you and it, about two thousand
[g]cubits by measure. Do not come near
it, that you may know the way by
which you must go, for you have not
passed *this* way before."
5 And Joshua said to the people,
[h]"Sanctify yourselves, for tomorrow
the LORD will do wonders among you."
6 Then Joshua spoke to the
priests, saying, "Take up the ark of the
covenant and cross over before the
people." So they took up the ark of the
covenant and went before the people.
7 And the LORD said to Joshua,
"This day I will begin to [i]exalt you in
the sight of all Israel, that they may
know that, as I was with Moses, [j]*so* I
will be with you.
8 "You shall command the priests
who bear the ark of the covenant, saying, 'When you have come to the edge
of the water of the Jordan, you shall
stand in the Jordan.'"
9 So Joshua said to the children of
[k]Israel, "Come here, and hear the
words of the LORD your God."
10 And Joshua said, "By this you
shall know that the living God *is*
[l]among you, and *that* [m]He will without fail drive out from before you the
[n]Canaanites and the [o]Hittites and the
Hivites and the Perizzites and the Girgashites and the Amorites and the
Jebusites:
11 "Behold, the ark of the covenant
of the Lord of all the earth is crossing
over [p]before you into the Jordan.

* 3:1 Hebrew *Shittim*

14 *a* Gen. 47:29
18 *b* v. 21 *c* Josh. 6:23
CHAPTER 3
1 *d* Josh. 2:1
2 *e* Josh. 1:10–11
4 *f* Ex. 19:12, 23; cp. Heb. 10:19–22 *g* See Weights and Measures (OT), 2 Chr. 2:10, *note*
5 *h* Ex. 19:10–11; Josh. 7:13; Job 1:5; Joel 2:16
7 *i* Josh. 4:14 *j* Josh. 1:5,9
9 *k* *Israel* (history): vv. 9–17; Josh. 24:9. (Gen. 12:2; Rom. 11:26, *note*)
10 *l* Dt. 31:8; cp. Dt. 31:17 *m* Dt. 18:12 *n* Acts 13:19 *o* See 2 Ki. 7:6, *note*
11 *p* Ex. 13:21–22; Dt. 31:3; cp. Jn. 10:4

[1](2:21) The scarlet cord of Rahab may speak, by its color, of safety through sacrifice (Heb. 9:19–22).
[2](3:1) The passage of the Jordan is a figure of our death with Christ (Rom. 6:3–4,6–11; Eph. 2:5–6; Col. 3:1–3).

12 "Now therefore, take for yourselves [a]twelve men from the tribes of Israel, one man from every tribe.

13 "And it shall come to pass, as soon as the soles of the feet of the priests who bear the ark of the LORD, the Lord of all the earth, shall rest in the waters of the Jordan, *that* the waters of the Jordan shall be cut off, the waters that come down from upstream, and they shall stand as a [b]heap."

14 So it was, when the people set out from their camp to cross over the Jordan, with the priests bearing the ark of the covenant before the people,

15 and as those who bore the ark came to the Jordan, and the feet of the priests who bore the ark dipped in the edge of the water (for the Jordan overflows all its banks during the whole time of [c]harvest),

16 that the [d]waters which came down from upstream stood *still, and* rose in a heap very far away at Adam, the city that *is* beside Zaretan. So the waters that went down into the Sea of the [e]Arabah, the [f]Salt Sea, failed, *and* were cut off; and the people crossed over opposite Jericho.

17 Then the priests who bore the ark of the covenant of the LORD stood firm on [g]dry ground in the midst of the Jordan; and all Israel crossed over on dry ground, until all the people had crossed completely over the Jordan.

The two sets of stones (vv. 9,20)

4 AND it came to pass, when all the people had completely crossed over the Jordan, that the LORD spoke to Joshua, saying:

2 "Take for yourselves [h]twelve men from the people, one man from every tribe,

3 "and command them, saying, 'Take for yourselves twelve stones from here, out of the midst of the Jordan, from the place where the priests' feet stood firm. You shall carry them over with you and leave them in the [i]lodging place where you lodge tonight.' "

4 Then Joshua called the twelve men whom he had appointed from the children of Israel, one man from every tribe;

5 and Joshua said to them: "Cross over before the ark of the LORD your God into the midst of the Jordan, and each one of you take up a stone on his shoulder, according to the number of the tribes of the children of Israel,

6 "that this may be a [j]sign among you when your [k]children ask in time to come, saying, 'What do these stones *mean* to you?'

7 "Then you shall answer them that the waters of the Jordan were cut off before the ark of the covenant of the LORD; when it crossed over the Jordan, the waters of the Jordan were cut off. And these stones shall be for a memorial to the children of Israel forever."

8 And the children of Israel did so, just as Joshua commanded, and took up twelve stones from the midst of the Jordan, as the LORD had spoken to Joshua, according to the number of the tribes of the children of Israel, and carried them over with them to the place where they lodged, and laid them down there.

9 Then Joshua set up twelve [1]stones in the midst of the Jordan, in the place where the feet of the priests who bore the ark of the covenant stood; and they are there to this day.

10 So the priests who bore the ark stood in the midst of the Jordan until everything was finished that the LORD had commanded Joshua to speak to the people, according to all that Moses had commanded Joshua; and the people hurried and crossed over.

11 Then it came to pass, when all the people had completely crossed over, that the [l]ark of the LORD and the priests crossed over in the presence of the people.

12 And the men of Reuben, the men of Gad, and half the tribe of Manasseh crossed over [m]armed before the children of Israel, as Moses had spoken to them.

13 About forty thousand prepared for war crossed over before the LORD for battle, to the plains of Jericho.

14 On that day the LORD [n]exalted Joshua in the sight of all Israel; and they feared him, as they had feared Moses, all the days of his life.

15 Then the LORD spoke to Joshua, saying,

16 "Command the priests who bear the ark of the Testimony to come up from the Jordan."

3:12 *a* Josh. 4:2,4
13 *b* Ps. 66:6; 74:15; 114:3; cp. Ex. 15:8
15 *c* Cp. Josh. 5:12
16 *d* *Miracles* (OT): vv. 15–17; 4:15–16; Josh. 4:18. (Gen. 5:24; Jon. 1:17, *note*) *e* See Dt. 1:1, *note* *f* Dt. 3:17
17 *g* Ex. 14:29
CHAPTER 4
2 *h* Josh. 3:12
3 *i* Josh. 4:20
6 *j* Dt. 27:2; Ps. 103:2 *k* Ex. 12:26; 13:14; Dt. 6:20
11 *l* Josh. 3:11; 6:11
12 *m* Num. 32:17; Josh. 1:14
14 *n* Josh. 3:7; 1 Chr. 29:25

---

[1](4:9) The erection of both of these memorials was probably done in obedience to a direct command from God, but only the commandment concerning the memorial on the far side of the Jordan is actually recorded (vv. 1–8).

17 Joshua therefore commanded the priests, saying, "Come up from the Jordan."

18 And it came to pass, when the priests who bore the ark of the covenant of the LORD had come from the midst of the Jordan, *and* the soles of the priests' feet touched the dry land, that the waters of the [a]Jordan returned to their place and [b]overflowed all its banks as before.

19 Now the people came up from the Jordan on the [c]tenth *day* of the [d]first month, and they camped in Gilgal on the east border of Jericho.

20 And those twelve stones which they took out of the Jordan, Joshua set up in [e]Gilgal.

21 Then he spoke to the children of Israel, saying: "When your children ask their fathers in time to come, saying, 'What *are* these stones?'

22 "then [f]you shall let your children know, saying, 'Israel crossed over this Jordan on [g]dry land';

23 "for the LORD your God dried up the waters of the Jordan before you until you had crossed over, as the LORD your God did to the Red Sea, which He dried up before us until we had crossed over,

24 "that all the peoples of the earth may know the hand of the LORD, that it *is* mighty, that you may fear the LORD your God forever."

Fear falls on Amorites

5 SO it was, when all the kings of the Amorites who *were* on the west side of the Jordan, and all the kings of the Canaanites who *were* [h]by the sea, heard that the LORD had dried up the waters of the Jordan from before the children of Israel until we* had crossed over, that their heart [i]melted; and there was no spirit in them any longer because of the children of Israel.

New generation circumcised

2 At that time the LORD said to Joshua, "Make flint knives for yourself, and [1]circumcise the sons of Israel again the second time."

3 So Joshua made flint knives for himself, and [j]circumcised the sons of Israel at the hill of the foreskins.*

4 And this *is* the reason why Joshua circumcised them: All the people who came out of Egypt *who were* males, all the men of war, had [k]died in the wilderness on the way, after they had come out of Egypt.

5 For all the people who came out had been circumcised, but all the people born in the wilderness, on the way as they came out of Egypt, had not been circumcised.

6 For the children of Israel walked [l]forty years in the wilderness, till all the people *who were* men of war, who came out of Egypt, were consumed, because they did not obey the voice of the LORD—to whom the LORD swore that He would not show them the [m]land which the LORD had sworn to their fathers that He would give us, "a land flowing with milk and honey."*

7 Then Joshua circumcised their sons *whom* He raised up in their place; for they were uncircumcised, because they had not been circumcised on the way.

8 So it was, when they had finished circumcising all the people, that they stayed in their places in the camp till they were healed.

9 Then the LORD said to Joshua, "This day I have rolled away the [n]reproach of Egypt from you." Therefore the name of the place is called [o]Gilgal to this day.

10 Now the children of Israel camped in Gilgal, and kept the Passover on the fourteenth day of the [p]month at twilight on the plains of Jericho.

11 And they ate of the produce of the land on the day after the Passover, unleavened bread and parched grain, on the very same day.

12 Then the manna ceased on the day after they had eaten the produce of the land; and the children of Israel no longer had [q]manna, but they ate

18
a *Miracles* (OT): vv. 15–18; Josh. 6:20. (Gen. 5:24; Jon. 1:17, *note*)
b Josh. 3:15; 1 Chr. 12:15
19
c Ex. 12:1–3; cp. Dt. 1:3; 34:8
d See Lev. 23:2, *note*
20
e Dt. 11:30; Josh. 5:9–10
22
f Ex. 12:26–27; 13:8–14; Dt. 26:5–9; cp. 1 Cor. 11:23–26
g Josh. 3:17
CHAPTER 5
1
h Num. 13:29
i Josh. 2:10–11; 9:9
3
j Cp. Dt. 30:6; Jer. 9:25–26
4
k Dt. 2:14–16
6
l Dt. 29:5
m Num. 14:29–35; 26:63–65
9
n Gen. 34:14
o Lit. *a rolling*
10
p Cp. Josh. 4:19; see Ex. 12:11, *note*
12
q Ex. 16:35

*5:1 Following Kethib; Qere, some Hebrew manuscripts and editions, Septuagint, Syriac, Targum, and Vulgate read *they*. 5:3 Hebrew *Gibeath Haaraloth* 5:6 Exodus 3:8

[1](5:2) Circumcision was the sign of the Abrahamic Covenant (Gen. 17:10–14; see Gen. 12:2, *note;* Rom. 4:11). "The reproach of Egypt" (v. 9) was that, during the later years of the Egyptian bondage, this separating sign had been neglected (cp. Ex. 4:24–26), and this neglect had continued during the wilderness wanderings. The NT analogy is world conformity—the failure openly to take a believer's place with Christ in death and resurrection (Rom. 6:2–11; Gal. 6:14–16). Spiritually, circumcision is putting to death the deeds of the body through the Spirit (Rom. 8:13; Gal. 5:16–17; Col. 2:11–12; 3:5–10).

the food of the land of Canaan that year.

The divine Commander

13 And it came to pass, when Joshua was by Jericho, that he lifted his eyes and looked, and behold, a [a]Man stood opposite him with His [b]sword drawn in His hand. And Joshua went to Him and said to Him, "*Are* You for us or for our adversaries?"

14 So He said, "No, but *as* Commander of the army of the LORD I have now come." And Joshua [c]fell on his face to the earth and [d]worshiped, and said to Him, "What does my Lord say to His servant?"

15 Then the Commander of the LORD's army said to Joshua, [e]"Take your sandal off your foot, for the place where you stand *is* [f]holy." And Joshua did so.

II. The Conquest of the Land, 6—12

Conquest of Jericho

6 NOW [g]Jericho was securely shut up because of the children of Israel; none went out, and none came in.

2 And the LORD said to Joshua: "See! [h]I have given Jericho into your hand, its king, *and* the mighty men of valor.

3 "You shall march around the city, all *you* men of war; you shall go all around the city once. This you shall do six days.

4 "And seven priests shall bear seven [i]trumpets of rams' horns before the ark. But the seventh day you shall march around the city [j]seven times, and the priests shall blow the trumpets.

5 [1]"It shall come to pass, when they make a long *blast* with the ram's horn, *and* when you hear the sound of the trumpet, that all the people shall shout with a great shout; then the wall of the city will fall down flat. And the people shall go up every man straight before him."

6 Then Joshua the son of Nun called the priests and said to them, "Take up the ark of the covenant, and let seven priests bear seven trumpets of rams' horns before the ark of the LORD."

7 And he said to the people, "Proceed, and march around the city, and let him who is armed advance before the ark of the LORD."

8 So it was, when Joshua had spoken to the people, that the seven priests bearing the seven trumpets of rams' horns before the LORD advanced and blew the trumpets, and the ark of the covenant of the LORD followed them.

9 The armed men went before the priests who blew the trumpets, and the [k]rear guard came after the ark, while *the priests* continued blowing the trumpets.

10 Now Joshua had commanded the people, saying, "You shall not shout or make any noise with your voice, nor shall a word proceed out of your mouth, until the day I say to you, 'Shout!' Then you shall shout."

11 So he had the [l]ark of the LORD circle the city, going around *it* once. Then they came into the camp and lodged in the camp.

12 And Joshua rose early in the morning, and the priests took up the ark of the LORD.

13 Then seven priests bearing seven trumpets of rams' horns before the ark of the LORD went on continually and blew with the trumpets. And the armed men went before them. But the [k]rear guard came after the ark of the LORD, while *the priests* continued blowing the trumpets.

14 And the second day they marched around the city once and returned to the camp. So they did six days.

15 But it came to pass on the seventh day that they rose early, about the dawning of the day, and marched around the city seven times in the same manner. On that day only they marched around the city seven times.

16 And the seventh time it happened, when the priests blew the trumpets, that Joshua said to the people: "Shout, for the LORD has given you the city!

17 "Now the city shall be [2m]doomed by the LORD to destruction, it and all who *are* in it. Only [n]Rahab the harlot shall live, she and all who *are* with her

13
a Theophanies: vv. 13–15; Ezek. 40:3. (Gen. 12:7, *note;* Dan. 10:5). Cp. Isa. 6:1,5; Ezek. 1:28; Acts 9:3–6; Rev. 1:17
b Num. 22:23; 1 Chr. 21:16
14
c Gen. 17:3; Num. 20:6
d Ex. 34:8
15
e Cp. Ex. 3:5
f Sanctification (OT): v. 15; Josh. 6:19. (Gen. 2:3; Zech. 8:3)
CHAPTER 6
1
g Josh. 2:1
2
h Dt. 7:24; Josh. 8:1
4
i Lev. 25:9
j 1 Ki. 18:43; 2 Ki. 4:35; 5:10
9
k Isa. 52:12
11
l Josh. 4:11
17
m Dt. 13:17; Josh. 7:1
n Josh. 2:1; Mt. 1:5

[1](6:5) Spiritual victories are won by means and upon principles utterly foolish and inadequate in the view of the wisdom of sinful men (1 Cor. 1:17–29; 2 Cor. 10:3–5).

[2](6:17) Joshua meant that it was the will of God that the whole city be put to the sword and its riches devoted to Him. To take anything for oneself, as Achan did, was to bring a curse. Compare the similar severity with which God judged the sin of Ananias and Sapphira (Acts 5:1–11).

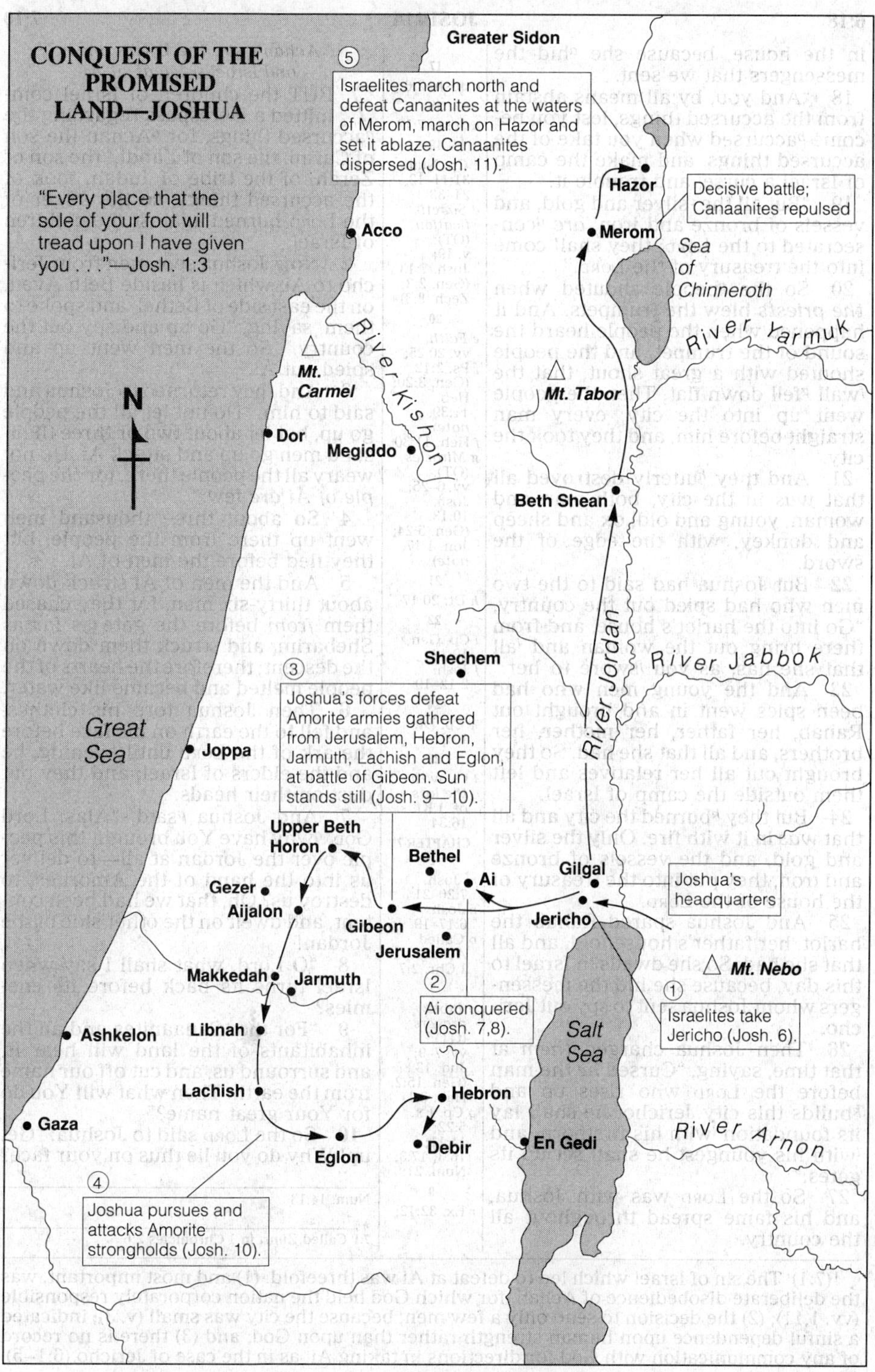

CONQUEST OF THE PROMISED LAND—JOSHUA
"Every place that the sole of your foot will tread upon I have given you . . ."—Josh. 1:3
N
Greater Sidon
5
Israelites march north and defeat Canaanites at the waters of Merom, march on Hazor and set it ablaze. Canaanites dispersed (Josh. 11).
Hazor
Decisive battle; Canaanites repulsed
Merom
Sea of Chinneroth
Acco
River Kishon
Mt. Carmel
Mt. Tabor
River Yarmuk
Dor
Megiddo
Beth Shean
River Jordan
River Jabbok
Shechem
3
Joshua's forces defeat Amorite armies gathered from Jerusalem, Hebron, Jarmuth, Lachish and Eglon, at battle of Gibeon. Sun stands still (Josh. 9—10).
Great Sea
Joppa
Upper Beth Horon
Bethel
Ai
Gilgal
Joshua's headquarters
Gezer
Aijalon
Gibeon
Jericho
Jerusalem
Mt. Nebo
Makkedah
Jarmuth
2
Ai conquered (Josh. 7,8).
1
Israelites take Jericho (Josh. 6).
Ashkelon
Libnah
Salt Sea
Lachish
Hebron
Gaza
Eglon
Debir
En Gedi
River Arnon
4
Joshua pursues and attacks Amorite strongholds (Josh. 10).

in the house, because she [a]hid the
messengers that we sent.
18 "And you, by all means abstain
from the accursed things, lest you become [b]accursed when you take of the
accursed things, and make the camp
of Israel a curse, and trouble it.
19 "But all the [c]silver and gold, and
vessels of bronze and iron, *are* [d]con-
secrated to the LORD; they shall come
into the treasury of the LORD."
20 So the [e]people shouted when
the priests blew the trumpets. And it
happened when the people heard the
sound of the trumpet, and the people
shouted with a great shout, that the
[f]wall [g]fell down flat. Then the people
went up into the city, every man
straight before him, and they took the
city.
21 And they [h]utterly destroyed all
that *was* in the city, both man and
woman, young and old, ox and sheep
and donkey, with the edge of the
sword.
22 But Joshua had said to the two
men who had spied out the country,
"Go into the harlot's house, and from
there bring out the woman and [i]all
that she has, as you [j]swore to her."
23 And the young men who had
been spies went in and brought out
Rahab, her father, her mother, her
brothers, and all that she had. So they
brought out all her relatives and left
them outside the camp of Israel.
24 But they [k]burned the city and all
that *was* in it with fire. Only the silver
and gold, and the vessels of bronze
and iron, they put into the treasury of
the house of the LORD.
25 And Joshua spared Rahab the
harlot, her father's household, and all
that she had. So she dwells in Israel to
this day, because she hid the messengers whom Joshua sent to spy out Jericho.
26 Then Joshua charged *them* at
that time, saying, "Cursed *be* the man
before the LORD who rises up and
[k]builds this city Jericho; he shall lay
its foundation [l]with his firstborn, and
[l]with his youngest he shall set up its
gates."
27 So the LORD was with Joshua,
and his fame spread throughout all
the country.

17
a Josh. 2:6
18
b Josh. 7:12
19
c Cp. Num. 31:11–12, 21–33
d *Sanctification* (OT): v. 19; Josh. 7:13. (Gen. 2:3; Zech. 8:3)
20
e *Faith:* vv. 20,25; Ps. 2:12. (Gen. 3:20; Heb. 11:39, *note*)
f Heb. 11:30
g *Miracles* (OT): vv. 6–25; Josh. 10:13. (Gen. 5:24; Jon. 1:17, *note*)
21
h Dt. 20:17
22
i Cp. Gen. 19:12
j Josh. 2:12–19
24
k Cp. Dt. 13:16
26
l i.e. *with the loss of.* 1 Ki. 16:34
CHAPTER 7
1
m Josh. 7:20–21
n Josh. 6:17–19
o Called *Achar,* 1 Chr. 2:7
7
p *Bible prayers* (OT): vv. 7–9; Jud. 13:8. (Gen. 15:2; Hab. 3:1)
q Cp. Ex. 5:22; 14:11; 16:3; 17:3; Num. 21:5
9
r Ex. 32:12; Num. 14:13

Achan's sin; the LORD's anger and Israel's defeat at Ai

7 BUT the children of Israel committed a [1m]trespass regarding the
[n]accursed things, for [o]Achan the son
of Carmi, the son of Zabdi,* the son of
Zerah, of the tribe of Judah, took of
the accursed things; so the anger of
the LORD burned against the children
of Israel.
2 Now Joshua sent men from Jericho to Ai, which *is* beside Beth Aven,
on the east side of Bethel, and spoke to
them, saying, "Go up and spy out the
country." So the men went up and
spied out Ai.
3 And they returned to Joshua and
said to him, "Do not let all the people
go up, but let about two or three thousand men go up and attack Ai. Do not
weary all the people there, for *the people of Ai are* few."
4 So about three thousand men
went up there from the people, but
they fled before the men of Ai.
5 And the men of Ai struck down
about thirty-six men, for they chased
them *from* before the gate as far as
Shebarim, and struck them down on
the descent; therefore the hearts of the
people melted and became like water.
6 Then Joshua tore his clothes,
and fell to the earth on his face before
the ark of the LORD until evening, he
and the elders of Israel; and they put
dust on their heads.
7 And Joshua [p]said, "Alas, Lord
GOD, [q]why have You brought this people over the Jordan at all—to deliver
us into the hand of the Amorites, to
destroy us? Oh, that we had been content, and dwelt on the other side of the
Jordan!
8 "O Lord, what shall I say when
Israel turns its back before its enemies?
9 "For the [r]Canaanites and all the
inhabitants of the land will hear *it,*
and surround us, and cut off our name
from the earth. Then what will You do
for Your great name?"
10 So the LORD said to Joshua: "Get
up! Why do you lie thus on your face?

*
7:1 Called *Zimri* in 1 Chronicles 2:6

[1](7:1) The sin of Israel which led to defeat at Ai was threefold: (1) and most important, was the deliberate disobedience of Achan, for which God held the nation corporately responsible (vv. 1,11); (2) the decision to send only a few men, because the city was small (v. 3), indicated a sinful dependence upon human strength rather than upon God; and (3) there is no record of any communication with God for directions in taking Ai, as in the case of Jericho (6:1–5).

11 [1]"Israel has sinned, and they
have also [a]transgressed My covenant
which I [b]commanded them. For they
have even [c]taken some of the accursed things, and have both stolen
and [d]deceived; and they have also put
it among their own stuff.
12 "Therefore the children of Israel
could not stand before their enemies,
but turned *their* backs before their enemies, because they have become
doomed to destruction. Neither will I
be with you anymore, unless you destroy the accursed from among you.
13 "Get up, [e]sanctify the people,
and say, [f]'Sanctify yourselves for tomorrow, because thus says the LORD
God of Israel: "*There is* an accursed
thing in your midst, O Israel; you cannot stand before your enemies until
you take away the accursed thing
from among you."
14 'In the morning therefore you
shall be brought [g]according to your
tribes. And it shall be *that* the tribe
which the LORD takes shall come according to families; and the family
which the LORD takes shall come by
households; and the household which
the LORD takes shall come man by
man.
15 'Then it shall be *that* he who is
taken with the accursed thing shall be
burned with fire, he and all that he
has, because he has transgressed the
covenant of the LORD, and because he
has done a disgraceful thing in Israel.' "
16 So Joshua rose early in the
morning and brought Israel by their
tribes, and the tribe of Judah was
taken.
17 He brought the clan of Judah,
and he took the family of the Zarhites;
and he brought the family of the Zarhites man by man, and Zabdi was
taken.
18 Then he brought his household
man by man, and Achan the son of
Carmi, the son of Zabdi, the son of
Zerah, of the tribe of Judah, was
taken.
19 Now Joshua said to Achan, "My
son, I beg you, give glory to the LORD
God of Israel, and make [h]confession
to Him, and tell me now what you
have done; do not hide *it* from me."
20 And Achan answered Joshua
and said, "Indeed [i]I have sinned
against the LORD God of Israel, and
this is what I have done:
21 "When I saw among the spoils a
beautiful Babylonian garment, two
hundred [j]shekels of silver, and a
wedge of gold weighing fifty shekels,
I coveted them and took them. And
there they are, hidden in the earth in
the midst of my tent, with the silver
under it."
22 So Joshua sent messengers, and
they ran to the tent; and there it was,
hidden in his tent, with the silver under it.
23 And they took them from the
midst of the tent, brought them to
Joshua and to all the children of Israel, and laid them out before the
LORD.
24 Then Joshua, and all Israel with
him, took Achan the son of Zerah, the
silver, the garment, the wedge of gold,
his sons, his daughters, his oxen, his
donkeys, his sheep, his tent, and [k]all
that he had, and they brought them to
the Valley of Achor.
25 And Joshua said, "Why have
you [l]troubled us? The LORD will trouble you this day." So all Israel stoned
him with stones; and they burned
them with fire after they had stoned
them with stones.
26 Then they raised over him a
[m]great heap of stones, still there to this
day. So the LORD turned from the
fierceness of His anger. Therefore the
name of that place has been called the
[n]Valley of [o]Achor to this day.

Ai taken by ambush

8 NOW the LORD said to Joshua:
[p]"Do not be afraid, nor be dismayed; take [q]all the people of war
with you, and arise, go up to Ai. See,
I have [r]given into your hand the king
of Ai, his people, his city, and his land.
2 "And you shall do to Ai and its
king [s]as you did to Jericho and its
king. Only its [t]spoil and its cattle you
shall take as booty for yourselves. Lay
an ambush for the city behind it."
3 So Joshua arose, and all the people of war, to go up against Ai; and
Joshua chose thirty thousand mighty
men of valor and sent them away by
night.
4 And he commanded them, saying: "Behold, you shall lie in ambush
against the city, behind the city. Do

11
a v. 15
b Josh. 6:17–19
c v. 21
d Acts 5:1–2; cp. Heb. 4:13
13
e Josh. 3:5
f *Sanctification* (OT): v. 13; 1 Ki. 7:51. (Gen. 2:3; Zech. 8:3)
14
g Cp. 1 Sam. 10:19
19
h Num. 5:6–7; Ps. 32:5; Prov. 28:13; Jer. 3:12–13
20
i Num. 22:34; 1 Sam. 15:24
21
j See Coinage (OT), Ex. 30:13, *note*
24
k Num. 16:32–33; Dan. 6:24
25
l Josh. 6:18
26
m Cp. Josh. 8:29
n Isa. 65:10; Hos. 2:15
o i.e. *trouble;* cp. v. 25
CHAPTER 8
1
p Josh. 1:9; 10:8
q Cp. Josh. 7:4
r Josh. 6:2
2
s Josh. 6:21
t Cp. Dt. 20:14

[1](7:11) The sin of Achan and its results teach the great truth of the oneness of the people of God: "Israel has sinned." See in illustration 1 Cor. 5:1–7; 12:12–14,26. The whole cause of Christ is injured by the sin, neglect, or unspirituality of even one believer.

not go very far from the city, but all of
you be ready.
5 "Then I and all the people who
are with me will approach the city;
and it will come about, when they
come out against us [a]as at the first,
that we shall flee before them.
6 "For they will come out after us
till we have drawn them from the city,
for they will say, '*They are* fleeing before us as at the first.' Therefore we
will flee before them.
7 "Then you shall rise from the
ambush and seize the city, for the
LORD your God will deliver it into your
hand.
8 "And it will be, when you have
taken the city, *that* you shall set the
city on fire. [b]According to the commandment of the LORD you shall do.
See, I have commanded you."
9 Joshua therefore sent them out;
and they went to lie in ambush, and
stayed between Bethel and Ai, on the
west side of Ai; but Joshua [c]lodged
that night among the people.
10 Then Joshua rose up early in the
morning and mustered the people,
and went up, he and the elders of Israel, before the people to Ai.
11 And all the people of war who
were with him went up and drew near;
and they came before the city and
camped on the north side of Ai. Now
a valley *lay* between them and Ai.
12 So he took about five thousand
men and set them in ambush between
Bethel and Ai, on the west side of the
city.
13 And when they had set the people, all the army that *was* on the north
of the city, and its rear guard on the
west of the city, Joshua went that
night into the midst of the valley.
14 Now it happened, when the king
of Ai saw *it*, that the men of the city
hurried and rose early and went out
against Israel to battle, he and all his
people, at an appointed place before
the [d]plain. But he did not know that
there was an ambush against him behind the city.
15 And Joshua and all Israel [e]made
as if they were beaten before them,
and fled by the way of the wilderness.
16 So all the people who *were* in Ai
were called together to pursue them.
And they pursued Joshua and were
drawn away from the city.

5
a Josh. 7:5
8
b Josh. 8:2; Dt. 20:16–18
9
c Cp. 2 Sam. 17:8
14
d See Dt. 1:1, *note*
15
e Cp. Jud. 20:36
18
f v. 26; Ps. 44:3; cp. Ex. 14:16
26
g Cp. Ex. 17:11–12
h Josh. 6:21

17 There was not a man left in Ai or
[1]Bethel who did not go out after Israel.
So they left the city open and pursued
Israel.
18 Then the LORD said to Joshua,
[f]"Stretch out the spear that *is* in your
hand toward Ai, for I will give it into
your hand." And Joshua stretched out
the spear that *was* in his hand toward
the city.
19 So *those in* ambush arose
quickly out of their place; they ran as
soon as he had stretched out his hand,
and they entered the city and took it,
and hurried to set the city on fire.
20 And when the men of Ai looked
behind them, they saw, and behold,
the smoke of the city ascended to
heaven. So they had no power to flee
this way or that way, and the people
who had fled to the wilderness turned
back on the pursuers.
21 Now when Joshua and all Israel
saw that the ambush had taken the
city and that the smoke of the city ascended, they turned back and struck
down the men of Ai.
22 Then the others came out of the
city against them; so they were *caught*
in the midst of Israel, some on this side
and some on that side. And they
struck them down, so that they let
none of them remain or escape.
23 But the king of Ai they took
alive, and brought him to Joshua.
24 And it came to pass when Israel
had made an end of slaying all the
inhabitants of Ai in the field, in the
wilderness where they pursued them,
and when they all had fallen by the
edge of the sword until they were consumed, that all the Israelites returned
to Ai and struck it with the edge of the
sword.
25 So it was *that* all who fell that
day, both men and women, *were*
twelve thousand—all the people of Ai.
26 For Joshua did not draw back
his hand, with which he [g]stretched
out the spear, until he had [h]utterly destroyed all the inhabitants of Ai.
27 Only the livestock and the spoil
of that city Israel took as booty for
themselves, according to the word of
the LORD which He had commanded
Joshua.
28 So Joshua burned Ai and made
it a heap forever, a desolation to this
day.

[1](8:17) Here it is seen that Bethel and Ai were associated in the fight against Joshua. Joshua 12:16 lists Bethel as one of the cities that had been conquered, but there is no mention of its conquest except in connection with that of Ai.

29 And the king of Ai he [a]hanged on a tree until evening. And as soon as the sun was down, Joshua commanded that they should take his corpse down from the tree, cast it at the entrance of the gate of the city, and raise over it a great heap of stones *that remains* to this day.

Blessings and curses read

30 Now Joshua built an [b]altar to the LORD God of Israel in Mount Ebal,

31 as Moses the servant of the LORD had commanded the children of Israel, as it is written in the Book of the Law of Moses: "an [c]altar of whole stones over which no man has wielded an iron *tool.*" And they offered on it burnt offerings to the LORD, and sacrificed peace offerings.

32 And there, in the presence of the children of Israel, he [d]wrote on the stones a copy of the law of Moses, which he had written.

33 Then all Israel, with their elders and officers and judges, stood on either side of the ark before the priests, the Levites, who bore the ark of the covenant of the LORD, the [e]stranger as well as he who was born among them. [f]Half of them *were* in front of Mount Gerizim and half of them in front of Mount Ebal, as Moses the servant of the LORD had commanded before, that they should bless the people of Israel.

34 And afterward he [g]read all the words of the law, the blessings and the cursings, according to all that is written in the [h]Book of the Law.

35 There was not a word of all that Moses had commanded which Joshua did not read before all the assembly of Israel, with the [i]women, the little ones, and the strangers who were living among them.

Joshua deceived by the trickery of the Gibeonites

9 AND it came to pass when [j]all the kings who *were* on this side of the Jordan, in the hills and in the [k]lowland and in all the coasts of the Great Sea toward Lebanon—the [l]Hittite, the Amorite, the Canaanite, the Perizzite, the Hivite, and the Jebusite—heard *about it,*

2 that they [m]gathered together to fight with Joshua and Israel with one accord.

3 But when the inhabitants of Gibeon heard what Joshua had done to Jericho and Ai,

4 they worked craftily, and went and pretended to be ambassadors. And they took old sacks on their donkeys, old wineskins torn and mended,

5 old and patched sandals on their feet, and old garments on themselves; and all the bread of their provision was dry *and* moldy.

6 And they went to Joshua, to the [n]camp at Gilgal, and said to him and to the men of Israel, "We have come from a [o]far country; now therefore, make a covenant with us."

7 Then the men of Israel said to the [p]Hivites, "Perhaps you dwell among us; so how can we make a covenant with you?"

8 But they said to Joshua, "We *are* your servants." And Joshua said to them, "Who *are* you, and where do you come from?"

9 So they said to him: "From a very far country your servants have come, because of the name of the LORD your God; for we have [q]heard of His fame, and all that He did in Egypt,

10 "and all that He did to the two kings of the Amorites who *were* beyond the Jordan—to Sihon king of Heshbon, and Og king of Bashan, who was at Ashtaroth.

11 "Therefore our elders and all the inhabitants of our country spoke to us, saying, 'Take provisions with you for the journey, and go to meet them, and say to them, "We *are* your servants; now therefore, make a covenant with us."'

12 "This bread of ours we took hot *for* our provision from our houses on the day we departed to come to you. But now look, it is dry and moldy.

13 "And these wineskins which we filled *were* new, and see, they are torn; and these our garments and our sandals have become old because of the very long journey."

14 Then the men of Israel took some of their provisions; but they [1r]did not ask counsel [s]of the LORD.

15 So Joshua made peace with

29 [a] Dt. 21:22–23
30 [b] Dt. 27:4–6
31 [c] Ex. 20:25
32 [d] Dt. 27:2–3,8; cp. Dt. 17:18; Josh. 24:26
33 [e] Dt. 31:12 [f] Dt. 11:29; 27:12,13
34 [g] Dt. 31:11; 28:1–30:20 [h] Josh. 1:8
35 [i] Cp. Dt. 29:11
CHAPTER 9
1 [j] Josh. 3:10 [k] See Dt. 1:7, *note* [l] See 2 Ki. 7:6, *note*
2 [m] Josh. 10:5
6 [n] Josh. 5:10 [o] Cp. Dt. 20:15
7 [p] Josh. 11:19; cp. Ex. 23:32
9 [q] Josh. 2:9–10; 5:1
14 [r] Isa. 30:1; cp. Num. 27:21 [s] 1 Sam. 23:11; 30:8; 2 Sam. 2:1; 5:19

[1](9:14) Though Israel had found that obedience was necessary for victory at Jericho and Ai, they had yet to learn their need of divine guidance at every step. The Gibeonites brought only trouble to Israel (Josh. 10:4–15; 2 Sam. 21:1–14). Furthermore, the presence of the Gibeonites across the center of Canaan tended to isolate the tribes in the north from those in the south, led to sectional feeling, and ultimately had its share in the dividing of the kingdom in Rehoboam's day (1 Ki. 12).

them, and made a covenant with them
to let them live; and the rulers of the
congregation swore to them.

Gibeonites made slaves

16 And it happened at the end of
three days, after they had made a covenant with them, that they heard that
they *were* their neighbors who dwelt
near them.
17 Then the children of Israel journeyed and came to their cities on the
third day. Now their cities *were* Gibeon, Chephirah, Beeroth, and Kirjath
Jearim.
18 But the children of Israel did not
attack them, because the rulers of the
congregation had sworn to them by
the LORD God of Israel. And all the
congregation complained against the
rulers.
19 Then all the rulers said to all the
congregation, "We have sworn to
them by the LORD God of Israel; now
therefore, we may not touch them.
20 "This we will do to them: We will
let them live, lest wrath be upon us
[a]because of the oath which we swore
to them."
21 And the rulers said to them, "Let
them live, but let them be woodcutters
and water carriers for all the congregation, as the rulers had promised
them."
22 Then Joshua called for them,
and he spoke to them, saying, "Why
have you deceived us, saying, 'We *are*
very far from you,' when you dwell
near us?
23 "Now therefore, you *are* cursed,
and none of you shall be freed from
being [b]slaves—woodcutters and water carriers for the house of my God."
24 So they answered Joshua and
said, "Because your servants were
clearly told that the LORD your God
commanded His servant Moses to give
you all the land, and to destroy all the
inhabitants of the land from before
you; therefore we were very much
[c]afraid for our lives because of you,
and have done this thing.
25 "And now, here we are, in your
hands; do with us as it seems good and
right to do to us."
26 So he did to them, and delivered
them out of the hand of the children of
Israel, so that they did not kill them.
27 And that day Joshua made them
woodcutters and water carriers for
the congregation and for the altar of
the LORD, in the [d]place which He
would choose, even to this day.

Gibeon miraculously defended

10 NOW it came to pass when
Adoni-Zedek king of [e]Jerusa-
lem [f]heard how Joshua had taken [g]Ai
and had utterly destroyed it—as he
had done to Jericho and its king, so he
had done to Ai and its king—and how
the inhabitants of [h]Gibeon had made
peace with Israel and were among
them,
2 that they feared [i]greatly, because Gibeon *was* a great city, like
one of the royal cities, and because it
was greater than Ai, and all its men
were mighty.
3 Therefore Adoni-Zedek king of
Jerusalem sent to Hoham king of Hebron, Piram king of Jarmuth, Japhia
king of Lachish, and Debir king of Eglon, saying,
4 "Come up to me and help me,
that we may attack Gibeon, for it has
made peace with Joshua and with the
children of Israel."
5 Therefore the five kings of the
[j]Amorites, the king of Jerusalem, the
king of Hebron, the king of Jarmuth,
the king of Lachish, *and* the king of
Eglon, [k]gathered together and went
up, they and all their armies, and
camped before Gibeon and made war
against it.
6 And the men of Gibeon sent to
Joshua at the camp at Gilgal, saying,
"Do not forsake your servants; come
up to us quickly, save us and [l]help us,
for all the kings of the Amorites who
dwell in the mountains have gathered
together against us."
7 So Joshua ascended from Gilgal,
he and all the people of war with him,
and all the mighty men of valor.
8 And the LORD said to Joshua,
[m]"Do not fear them, for I have delivered them into your hand; not a man
of them shall [n]stand before you."
9 Joshua therefore came upon
them suddenly, having marched all
night from Gilgal.
10 So the LORD [o]routed them before
Israel, killed them with a great slaughter at Gibeon, chased them along the
road that goes to Beth Horon, and
struck them down as far as Azekah
and Makkedah.
11 And it happened, as they fled before Israel *and* were on the descent of
Beth Horon, that the LORD cast down
large hailstones from heaven on them
as far as Azekah, and they died. *There
were* more who died from the [p]hail-
stones than the children of Israel
killed with the sword.

20
a 2 Sam. 21:2
23
b Cp. Gen. 9:25–27; see Neh. 3:26, *note*
24
c Josh. 9:3; 10:2
27
d Dt. 12:5
CHAPTER 10
1
e See Gen. 14:18, *note*
f Josh. 9:1
g Josh. 8:1
h Josh. 9:15
2
i Ex. 15:14; Dt. 11:25; 1 Chr. 14:17; cp. Heb. 10:27
5
j Num. 13:29
k Josh. 9:2
6
l See Josh. 9:14, *note*
8
m Josh. 1:5, 9
n Josh. 21:44
10
o Dt. 7:23
11
p Cp. Ex. 9:23

12 Then Joshua spoke to the LORD
in the day when the LORD delivered up
the Amorites before the children of Israel, and he said in the sight of Israel:

"Sun, stand [a]still over Gibeon;
And Moon, in the Valley of
Aijalon."
13 So the sun [b]stood still,
And the moon stopped,
Till the people had revenge
Upon their enemies.

Is this not written in the [c]Book of [d]Ja-
sher? So the sun stood still in the midst
of heaven, and did not hasten to go
down for about a whole day.
14 And there has been [e]no day like
that, before it or after it, that the LORD
heeded the voice of a man; for the
[f]LORD fought for Israel.

Victory at Makkedah

15 Then Joshua [g]returned, and all
Israel with him, to the camp at Gilgal.
16 But these five kings had fled and
hidden themselves in a cave at Makkedah.
17 And it was told Joshua, saying,
"The five kings have been found hidden in the cave at Makkedah."
18 So Joshua said, "Roll large
stones against the mouth of the cave,
and set men by it to guard them.
19 "And do not stay *there* yourselves, *but* pursue your enemies, and
attack their [h]rear *guard.* Do not allow
them to enter their cities, for the LORD
your God has delivered them into your
hand."
20 Then it happened, while Joshua
and the children of Israel made an end
of slaying them with a very great
slaughter, till they had finished, that
those who escaped entered fortified
cities.
21 And all the people returned to
the camp, to Joshua at Makkedah, in
peace. No one moved his tongue
against any of the children of Israel.
22 Then Joshua said, "Open the
mouth of the cave, and bring out those
five kings to me from the cave."
23 And they did so, and brought out
those five kings to him from the cave:
the king of Jerusalem, the king of Hebron, the king of Jarmuth, the king of
Lachish, *and* the king of Eglon.
24 So it was, when they brought out
those kings to Joshua, that Joshua
called for all the men of Israel, and
said to the captains of the men of war
who went with him, "Come near, put
your feet on the necks of these kings."

12
a Cp. Isa. 28:21; Hab. 3:11
13
b *Miracles* (OT): vv. 12–14; Jud. 14:6. (Gen. 5:24; Jon. 1:17, *note*)
c See 1 Chr. 29:29, *note*
d 2 Sam. 1:18
14
e Cp. 2 Ki. 20:11; Isa. 38:7–8
f Dt. 1:30; 20:4
15
g Josh. 10:43
19
h Cp. Dt. 29:18
25
i Dt. 31:6–8; cp. 2 Tim. 4:17–18
j Dt. 7:19
26
k Josh. 8:29
27
l Dt. 21:22–23
28
m Dt. 7:2, 16; cp. 1 Cor. 15:25
n Josh. 6:21
29
o Josh. 15:42; 21:13; 2 Ki. 8:22; 19:8
34
p v. 3

And they drew near and put their feet
on their necks.
25 Then Joshua said to them, [i]"Do
not be afraid, nor be dismayed; be
strong and of good courage, for thus
the LORD will [j]do to all your enemies
against whom you fight."
26 And afterward Joshua struck
them and killed them, and [k]hanged
them on five trees; and they were
hanging on the trees until evening.
27 So it was at the time of the going
down of the [l]sun *that* Joshua commanded, and they took them down
from the trees, cast them into the cave
where they had been hidden, and laid
large stones against the cave's mouth,
which remain until this very day.
28 On that day Joshua took Makkedah, and struck it and its king with the
edge of the sword. He utterly [m]de-
stroyed them*—all the people who
were in it. He let none remain. He also
did to the king of Makkedah [n]as he
had done to the king of Jericho.

Southern Palestine campaign completed

29 Then Joshua passed from Makkedah, and all Israel with him, to
[o]Libnah; and they fought against Libnah.
30 And the LORD also delivered it
and its king into the hand of Israel; he
struck it and all the people who *were*
in it with the edge of the sword. He let
none remain in it, but did to its king as
he had done to the king of Jericho.
31 Then Joshua passed from Libnah, and all Israel with him, to Lachish; and they encamped against it
and fought against it.
32 And the LORD delivered Lachish
into the hand of Israel, who took it on
the second day, and struck it and all
the people who *were* in it with the
edge of the sword, according to all
that he had done to Libnah.
33 Then Horam king of Gezer came
up to help Lachish; and Joshua struck
him and his people, until he left him
none remaining.
34 From Lachish Joshua passed to
[p]Eglon, and all Israel with him; and
they encamped against it and fought
against it.
35 They took it on that day and
struck it with the edge of the sword; all
the people who *were* in it he utterly

*10:28 Following Masoretic Text and most authorities; many Hebrew manuscripts, some manuscripts of the Septuagint, and some manuscripts of the Targum read *it.*

destroyed that day, according to all
that he had done to Lachish.
36 So Joshua went up from Eglon,
and all Israel with him, to [a]Hebron;
and they fought against it.
37 And they took it and struck it
with the edge of the sword—its king,
all its cities, and all the people who
were in it; he left none remaining, according to all that he had done to Eglon, but utterly destroyed it and all the
people who *were* in it.
38 Then Joshua returned, and all
Israel with him, to [b]Debir; and they
fought against it.
39 And he took it and its king and
all its cities; they struck them with the
edge of the sword and utterly destroyed all the people who *were* in it.
He left none remaining; as he had
done to Hebron, so he did to Debir and
its king, as he had done also to Libnah
and its king.
40 So Joshua conquered all the
land: the [c]mountain country and the
[d]South and the [e]lowland and the wilderness slopes, and [f]all their kings;
he left none remaining, but [g]utterly
destroyed all that breathed, as the
LORD God of Israel had commanded.
41 And Joshua [1]conquered them
from [h]Kadesh Barnea as far as [i]Gaza,
and all the country of Goshen, even as
far as Gibeon.
42 All these kings and their land
Joshua took at one [2]time, because the
[j]LORD God of Israel fought for Israel.
43 Then Joshua [k]returned, and all
Israel with him, to the camp at Gilgal.

Northern Palestine campaign

11 AND it came to pass, when Jabin king of Hazor heard *these*
things, that he [l]sent to Jobab king of
Madon, to the king of Shimron, to the
king of Achshaph,
2 and to the kings who *were* from
the north, in the mountains, in the
[m]plain south of Chinneroth, in the
[e]lowland, and in the heights of Dor on
the west,
3 to the Canaanites in the east and
in the west, the [n]Amorite, the [o]Hittite,
the Perizzite, the Jebusite in the
mountains, and the Hivite below Hermon in the land of Mizpah.

36 [a] Num. 13:22; Josh. 14:13–15
38 [b] Josh. 11:21; 15:15; Jud. 1:11
40 [c] Dt. 1:7 [d] See Gen. 12:9, *note* [e] See Dt. 1:7, *note* [f] Dt. 7:24 [g] Dt. 20:16
41 [h] Num. 13:26; Dt. 9:23 [i] Josh. 11:22
42 [j] v. 14
43 [k] v. 15
CHAPTER 11
1 [l] Cp. Josh. 10:3
2 [m] See Dt. 1:1, *note*
3 [n] Josh. 9:1 [o] See 2 Ki. 7:6, *note*
4 [p] Jud. 7:12; 1 Sam. 13:5
6 [q] Josh. 10:8 [r] 2 Sam. 8:4
8 [s] Gen. 49:13 [t] Josh. 13:6
11 [u] Josh. 10:40
13 [v] Cp. Josh. 24:13
14 [w] Dt. 20:14–18

4 So they went out, they and all
their armies with them, *as* many people *as* the [p]sand that *is* on the seashore in multitude, with very many
horses and chariots.
5 And when all these kings had
met together, they came and camped
together at the waters of Merom to
fight against Israel.
6 But the LORD said to Joshua,
[q]"Do not be afraid because of them,
for tomorrow about this time I will deliver all of them slain before Israel.
You shall [r]hamstring their horses and
burn their chariots with fire."
7 So Joshua and all the people of
war with him came against them suddenly by the waters of Merom, and
they attacked them.
8 And the LORD delivered them
into the hand of Israel, who defeated
them and chased them to Greater [s]Si-
don, to the [t]Brook Misrephoth,* and
to the Valley of Mizpah eastward;
they attacked them until they left none
of them remaining.
9 So Joshua did to them as the
LORD had told him: he hamstrung their
horses and burned their chariots with
fire.
10 Joshua turned back at that time
and took Hazor, and struck its king
with the sword; for Hazor was formerly the head of all those kingdoms.
11 And they struck all the people
who *were* in it with the edge of the
sword, [g]utterly destroying *them*.
There was none left [u]breathing. Then
he burned Hazor with fire.
12 So all the cities of those kings,
and all their kings, Joshua took and
struck with the edge of the sword. He
utterly destroyed them, as Moses the
servant of the LORD had commanded.
13 But *as for* the cities that stood on
their mounds,* Israel burned none of
them, [v]except Hazor only, *which*
Joshua burned.
14 And all the [w]spoil of these cities
and the livestock, the children of Israel took as booty for themselves; but
they struck every man with the edge

*11:8 Hebrew *Misrephoth Maim* 11:13 Hebrew *tel*, a heap of successive city ruins

[1](10:41) With Jericho destroyed, the heart of Palestine was exposed to assault. By swift marches and decisive battles in the open country, first in the southern campaign (ch. 10) and then in the northern campaign (ch. 11), Joshua defeated major coalitions of Canaanites.

[2](10:42) Compare Josh. 11:18. As the context shows, the verses refer to different parts of Palestine and different kings. These chapters emphasize a faith that is expressed in works, whereas the Ai defeat illustrates work without faith.

of the sword until they had destroyed them, and they left none breathing.

15 As the LORD had commanded Moses his servant, so Moses commanded [a]Joshua, and so Joshua did. He left nothing undone of all that the LORD had commanded [b]Moses.

Summary of conquests (v. 18)

16 Thus Joshua took all this land: the [c]mountain country, all the [d]South, all the land of Goshen, the [e]lowland, and the Jordan [f]plain—the mountains of Israel and its lowlands,

17 from Mount Halak and the ascent to Seir, even as far as Baal Gad in the Valley of Lebanon below Mount Hermon. He captured [g]all their kings, and struck them down and killed them.

18 Joshua made war a [h]long time with all those kings.

19 There was not a city that made peace with the children of Israel, except the Hivites, the inhabitants of Gibeon. All *the others* they took in battle.

20 For it was of the LORD to [i]harden their hearts, that they should come against Israel in battle, that He might utterly destroy them, *and* that they might receive no mercy, but that He might destroy them, as the LORD had commanded Moses.

21 And at that time Joshua came and cut off the [j]Anakim from the mountains: from Hebron, from Debir, from Anab, from all the mountains of Judah, and from all the mountains of Israel; Joshua utterly destroyed them with their cities.

22 None of the Anakim were left in the land of the children of Israel; they remained only in Gaza, in Gath, and in Ashdod.

23 So Joshua took the whole land, according to all that the LORD had [k]said to Moses; and Joshua gave it as an inheritance to Israel according to their divisions by their tribes. Then the land [l]rested from war.

Roster of the kings conquered by Moses and Joshua

12 THESE *are* the [m]kings of the [n]land whom the children of Israel defeated, and whose land they possessed on the other side of the Jordan toward the rising of the sun, from the River Arnon to Mount Hermon, and all the eastern Jordan [f]plain:

2 *One king was* [o]Sihon king of the Amorites, who dwelt in Heshbon *and* ruled half of Gilead, from Aroer, which is on the bank of the River Arnon, from the middle of that river, even as far as the River Jabbok, *which is* the border of the Ammonites,

3 and the eastern Jordan [f]plain from the Sea of Chinneroth as far as the Sea of the [f]Arabah (the Salt Sea), the road to Beth Jeshimoth, and southward below the slopes of Pisgah.

4 *The other king was* Og king of Bashan and his territory, *who was* of the remnant of the giants, who dwelt at Ashtaroth and at Edrei,

5 and reigned over Mount [p]Hermon, over Salcah, over all Bashan, as far as the border of the Geshurites and the Maachathites, and over half of Gilead *to* the border of Sihon king of Heshbon.

6 These Moses the servant of the LORD and the children of Israel had conquered; and Moses the servant of the LORD had given [q]it *as* a possession to the Reubenites, the Gadites, and half the tribe of Manasseh.

7 And these *are* the kings of the country which Joshua and the children of Israel conquered on this side of the Jordan, on the west, from [r]Baal Gad in the Valley of Lebanon as far as Mount Halak and the ascent to Seir, which Joshua gave to the tribes of Israel *as* a possession according to their divisions,

8 in the mountain country, in the [e]lowlands, in the *Jordan* [f]plain, in the slopes, in the wilderness, and in the [d]South—the [s]Hittites, the Amorites, the Canaanites, the Perizzites, the Hivites, and the Jebusites:

9 the king of [t]Jericho, one; the king of Ai, which *is* beside Bethel, one;

10 the king of [u]Jerusalem, one; the king of Hebron, one;

11 the king of Jarmuth, one; the king of Lachish, one;

12 the king of Eglon, one; the king of Gezer, one;

13 the king of Debir, one; the king of Geder, one;

14 the king of Hormah, one; the king of Arad, one;

15 the king of Libnah, one; the king of Adullam, one;

16 the king of Makkedah, one; the king of [v]Bethel, one;

17 the king of Tappuah, one; the king of [w]Hepher, one;

18 the king of Aphek, one; the king of Lasharon, one;

19 the king of Madon, one; the king of Hazor, one;

15
a Josh. 1:7
b Ex. 34:10–17

16
c Josh. 10:40–41
d See Gen. 12:9, *note*
e See Dt. 1:7, *note*
f See Dt. 1:1, *note*

17
g Dt. 7:24

18
h See Josh. 10:42, *note*

20
i See Ex. 4:21, *note*

21
j Num. 13:22; Dt. 9:2

23
k Ex. 33:2; Num. 34:2
l Dt. 12:9–10; cp. Heb. 4:1–16

CHAPTER 12

1
m Kings of vv. 1–6 defeated by Moses; vv. 7–24, by Joshua
n Dt. 3:8–17

2
o Dt. 2:24–27

5
p Dt. 3:8,14; Josh. 13:11–12

6
q Num. 32:29–33

7
r Josh. 11:17

8
s Ex. 23:23; Josh. 11:3; see 2 Ki. 7:6, *note*

9
t Josh. 6:2

10
u Josh. 10:23

16
v Jud. 1:22

17
w 1 Ki. 4:10

20 the king of Shimron Meron, one;
the king of Achshaph, one;
21 the king of Taanach, one; the
king of Megiddo, one;
22 the king of Kedesh, one; the king
of Jokneam in Carmel, one;
23 the king of Dor in the heights of
Dor, one; the king of the people of Gilgal, one;
24 the king of Tirzah, one—[a]all the
kings, thirty-one.

III. The Allocation of Territories to the Tribes, 13—22

Allotment of two and one-half tribes

13 NOW Joshua was old, advanced in [b]years. And the LORD
said to him: "You are old, advanced in
years, and there remains very much
land yet to be possessed.
2 [1]"This is the land that yet [c]re-
mains: all the [d]territory of the Philistines and all *that of* the Geshurites,
3 "from [e]Sihor, which *is* east of
Egypt, as far as the border of Ekron
northward (*which* is counted as Canaanite); the five lords of the
Philistines—the Gazites, the Ashdodites, the Ashkelonites, the Gittites,
and the Ekronites; also the Avites;
4 "from the south, all the land of
the Canaanites, and Mearah that belongs to the Sidonians as far as
[f]Aphek, to the border of the Amorites;
5 "the land of the Gebalites,* and
all Lebanon, toward the sunrise, from
[g]Baal Gad below Mount Hermon as
far as the [h]entrance to Hamath;
6 "all the inhabitants of the mountains from Lebanon as far as the
[i]Brook Misrephoth,* *and* all the
Sidonians—them I will drive out from
before the children of Israel; only divide it by lot to Israel as an [j]inheri-
tance, as I have commanded you.
7 "Now therefore, divide this land
as an inheritance to the nine tribes
and half the tribe of Manasseh."
8 With the other half tribe the
Reubenites and the Gadites received
their inheritance, which [k]Moses had
given them, [l]beyond the Jordan eastward, as Moses the servant of the LORD
had given them:
9 from Aroer which *is* on the bank
of the River Arnon, and the town that

24
a Dt. 7:24
CHAPTER 13
1
b Josh. 14:10; 23:1–2
2
c Jud. 3:1–3; cp. Num. 34:2–15; Dt. 34:1–4
d Cp. Joel 3:4
3
e 1 Chr. 13:5
4
f Josh. 12:18
5
g Josh. 12:7
h Num. 34:8
6
i Josh. 11:8
j Josh. 12:7; 14:2
8
k Num. 32:33
l Josh. 12:1–6
11
m Num. 32:1
12
n Num. 21:34
13
o Cp. Num. 33:55; Josh. 23:12–13; Jud. 2:2–3
14
p v. 33; Dt. 18:1; Josh. 14:3–4
15
q vv. 15–23; Num. 34:14
16
r Josh. 12:2
17
s Num. 21:28,30
18
t Num. 21:23
21
u Num. 31:8
22
v Num. 31:8; cp. Num. 22–25

is in the midst of the ravine, and all the
plain of Medeba as far as Dibon;
10 all the cities of Sihon king of the
Amorites, who reigned in Heshbon, as
far as the border of the children of
Ammon;
11 [m]Gilead, and the border of the
Geshurites and Maachathites, all
Mount Hermon, and all Bashan as far
as Salcah;
12 all the kingdom of Og in Bashan,
who reigned in Ashtaroth and Edrei,
who remained of the remnant of the
giants; for Moses had defeated and
cast out [n]these.
13 Nevertheless the children of Israel [o]did not drive out the Geshurites
or the Maachathites, but the Geshurites and the Maachathites dwell
among the Israelites until this day.
14 Only to the tribe of Levi he had
given [p]no inheritance; the sacrifices
of the LORD God of Israel made by fire
are their inheritance, as He said to
them.
15 [q]And Moses had given to the
tribe of the children of Reuben *an inheritance* according to their families.
16 Their territory was from [r]Aroer,
which *is* on the bank of the River Arnon, and the city that *is* in the midst of
the ravine, and all the plain by Medeba;
17 [s]Heshbon and all its cities that
are in the plain: Dibon, Bamoth Baal,
Beth Baal Meon,
18 [t]Jahaza, Kedemoth, Mephaath,
19 Kirjathaim, Sibmah, Zereth
Shahar on the mountain of the valley,
20 Beth Peor, the slopes of Pisgah,
and Beth Jeshimoth—
21 all the cities of the plain and all
the kingdom of Sihon king of the Amorites, who reigned in Heshbon,
whom Moses had struck with the
princes of [u]Midian: Evi, Rekem, Zur,
Hur, and Reba, who *were* princes of
Sihon dwelling in the country.
22 The children of Israel also killed
with the sword [v]Balaam the son of
Beor, the soothsayer, among those
who were killed by them.
23 And the border of the children of
Reuben was the bank of the Jordan.
This *was* the inheritance of the chil-

*13:5 Or *Giblites* 13:6 Hebrew *Misrephoth Maim*

[1](13:2) Joshua 13—19 is devoted to a geographical description of the areas of Canaan allocated to the twelve tribes of Israel. This list is of great help in locating places forgotten with the lapse of years. As archaeological research proceeds, many such places are being rediscovered.

dren of Reuben according to their
families, the cities and their villages.
24 [a]Moses also had given *an inheritance* to the tribe of Gad, to the children of Gad according to their families.
25 Their territory was Jazer, and all
the cities of Gilead, and half the land
of the Ammonites as far as Aroer,
which *is* before [b]Rabbah,
26 and from Heshbon to Ramath
Mizpah and Betonim, and from Mahanaim to the border of Debir,
27 and in the valley [c]Beth Haram,
Beth Nimrah, Succoth, and Zaphon,
the rest of the kingdom of Sihon king
of Heshbon, with the Jordan as *its*
border, as far as the edge of the Sea of
Chinnereth, on the other side of the
Jordan eastward.
28 This *is* the inheritance of the
children of Gad according to their
families, the cities and their villages.
29 [d]Moses also had given *an inheritance* to half the tribe of Manasseh; it
was for half the tribe of the children of
Manasseh according to their families:
30 Their territory was from Mahanaim, all Bashan, all the kingdom of
Og king of Bashan, and all the [e]towns
of Jair which are in Bashan, sixty cities;
31 half of Gilead, and Ashtaroth
and Edrei, cities of the kingdom of Og
in Bashan, *were* for the children of
[f]Machir the son of Manasseh, for half
of the children of Machir according to
their families.
32 These *are the areas* which Moses had distributed as an inheritance
in the plains of Moab on the other side
of the Jordan, by Jericho eastward.
33 But to the tribe of Levi Moses
had given no inheritance; the LORD
God of Israel *was* their inheritance, as
He had said to them.

Caleb's request granted

14 THESE *are the areas* which the
children of Israel inherited in
the land of Canaan, which [g]Eleazar
the priest, Joshua the son of Nun, and
the heads of the fathers of the tribes of
the children of Israel distributed as an
inheritance to them.
2 Their inheritance *was* by [h]lot, as
the LORD had commanded by the hand
of Moses, for the nine tribes and the
half-tribe.
3 For Moses had given the inheritance of the two tribes and the half-
tribe on the other side of the Jordan;
but to the Levites he had given no inheritance among them.
4 For the children of Joseph [i]were
two tribes: Manasseh and Ephraim.
And they gave no part to the Levites in
the land, except [j]cities to dwell *in*,
with their common-lands for their
livestock and their property.
5 As the LORD had commanded
Moses, so the children of Israel did;
and they divided the land.
6 Then the children of Judah came
to Joshua in Gilgal. And [k]Caleb the
son of Jephunneh the Kenizzite said to
him: "You know the word which the
LORD said to Moses the man of God
concerning you and me in Kadesh
Barnea.
7 "I *was* forty years old when Moses the servant of the LORD [l]sent me
from Kadesh Barnea to spy out the
land, and I brought back word to him
as *it was* in my heart.
8 "Nevertheless my [m]brethren
who went up with me made the heart
of the people melt, but I [n]wholly followed the LORD my God.
9 "So Moses swore on that day,
saying, 'Surely the land where your
foot has [o]trodden shall be your inheritance and your children's forever, because you have wholly followed the
LORD my God.'
10 "And now, behold, the LORD has
kept me [p]alive, as He said, these
[q]forty-five years, ever since the LORD
spoke this word to Moses while Israel
wandered in the wilderness; and now,
here I am this day, eighty-five years
old.
11 "As yet I *am as* [r]strong this day
as on the day that Moses sent me; just
as my strength *was* then, so now *is* my
strength for war, both [s]for going out
and for coming in.
12 "Now therefore, give me this
mountain of which the LORD spoke in
that day; for you heard in that day
[t]how the Anakim *were* there, and
that the cities *were* great *and* fortified.
It may be that the LORD *will be* with
me, and I shall be able to drive them
out as the LORD said."
13 And Joshua blessed him, and
gave Hebron to Caleb the son of Jephunneh as an inheritance.
14 Hebron therefore became the inheritance of Caleb the son of Jephunneh the Kenizzite to this day, because
he wholly followed the LORD God of
Israel.

24 *a* vv. 24–28; Num. 32:1; 34:14; 1 Chr. 5:11
25 *b* Dt. 3:11
27 *c* Num. 32:36
29 *d* vv. 29–33; Num. 34:14; Josh. 13:8; 17:11; Jud. 1:27; 1 Chr. 5:23
30 *e* Num. 32:41
31 *f* Josh. 17:1
CHAPTER 14
1 *g* Num. 34:16–29
2 *h* Num. 26:55; 33:54; 34:13; cp. Ps. 16:5–6; 47:4
4 *i* Gen. 48:5; 1 Chr. 5:1–2 *j* Num. 35:2–8; Josh. 21:1–42
6 *k* Num. 14:24,30; 32:11–12
7 *l* Num. 13:6, 26
8 *m* Dt. 1:28 *n* Num. 14:24
9 *o* Dt. 1:36
10 *p* Num. 14:24,30,38 *q* Josh. 5:6; Neh. 9:21
11 *r* Cp. Dt. 34:7 *s* Cp. Dt. 31:2
12 *t* Num. 13:28,33

15 And the name of [1]Hebron formerly was Kirjath Arba (*Arba was* the
greatest man among the Anakim).
Then the land had rest from war.

Allotment of Judah

15 SO [a]*this* was the lot of the tribe
of the children of Judah ac-
cording to their families: The border
of Edom at the Wilderness of Zin
southward *was* the extreme southern
boundary.
2 And their [b]southern border began at the shore of the Salt Sea, from
the bay that faces southward.
3 Then it went out to the southern
side of the Ascent of Akrabbim,
passed along to Zin, ascended on the
south side of Kadesh Barnea, passed
along to Hezron, went up to Adar, and
went around to Karkaa.
4 *From there* it passed toward Azmon and went out to the Brook of
Egypt; and the border ended at the
sea. This shall be your southern border.
5 The east border *was* the Salt Sea
as far as the mouth of the Jordan. And
the [c]border on the northern quarter
began at the bay of the sea at the
mouth of the Jordan.
6 The border went up to [d]Beth
Hoglah and passed north of Beth Arabah; and the border went up to the
stone of Bohan the son of Reuben.
7 Then the border went up toward
[e]Debir from the [f]Valley of Achor, and
it turned northward toward Gilgal,
which *is* before the Ascent of Adummim, which *is* on the south side of the
valley. The border continued toward
the waters of En Shemesh and ended
at En Rogel.
8 And the border went up by the
Valley of the Son of Hinnom to the
southern slope of the [g]Jebusite *city*
(which *is* Jerusalem). The border went
up to the top of the mountain that *lies*
before the Valley of Hinnom westward, which *is* at the end of the Valley
of Rephaim* northward.
9 Then the border went around
from the top of the hill to the [h]fountain
of the water of Nephtoah, and extended to the cities of Mount Ephron.
And the border went around to [i]Ba-
alah (which *is* Kirjath Jearim).
10 Then the border turned westward from Baalah to Mount Seir,
passed along to the side of Mount Jearim on the north (which *is* Chesalon),
went down to [j]Beth Shemesh, and
passed on to [k]Timnah.
11 And the border went out to the
side of Ekron northward. Then the
border went around to Shicron,
passed along to Mount Baalah, and
extended to Jabneel; and the border
ended at the sea.
12 The [l]west border *was* the coastline of the Great Sea. This *is* the
boundary of the children of Judah all
around according to their families.
13 [m]Now to Caleb the son of Jephunneh he [n]gave a share among the
children of [o]Judah, according to the
commandment of the LORD to Joshua,
namely, Kirjath Arba, which *is* Hebron (*Arba was* the father of Anak).
14 Caleb drove out the three [p]sons
of Anak from there: Sheshai, Ahiman,
and Talmai, the children of Anak.
15 Then he went up from there to
the inhabitants of Debir (formerly the
name of Debir *was* [q]Kirjath Sepher).
16 And Caleb said, "He who attacks
[q]Kirjath Sepher and takes it, to him I
will give Achsah my daughter as
wife."
17 So [r]Othniel the [s]son of Kenaz,
the brother of Caleb, took it; and he
gave him [t]Achsah his daughter as
wife.
18 Now it was so, when she came *to
him,* that she persuaded him to ask her
father for a field. So she dismounted
from *her* donkey, and Caleb said to
her, "What do you wish?"
19 She answered, "Give me a blessing; since you have given me land in
the [u]South, give me also [2]springs of
water." So he gave her the upper
springs and the lower springs.
20 This *was* the inheritance of the
tribe of the children of Judah according to their families:
21 The cities at the limits of the
tribe of the children of Judah, toward
the border of Edom in the [u]South,
were Kabzeel, [v]Eder, Jagur,
22 Kinah, Dimonah, Adadah,
23 Kedesh, Hazor, Ithnan,
24 [w]Ziph, Telem, Bealoth,

CHAPTER 15
1 a vv. 1–62
2 b Num. 34:3–4
5 c Josh. 18:15–19
6 d Josh. 18:19,21
7 e Josh. 13:26 f Josh. 7:26
8 g Josh. 15:63
9 h Josh. 18:15 i 2 Sam. 6:2; 1 Chr. 13:6
10 j Josh. 19:22,38 k Gen. 38:13; Jud. 14:1
12 l Num. 34:6
13 m vv. 13–19; cp. Jud. 1:10–15 n Josh. 14:13–15 o Num. 13:6
14 p Num. 13:22; Jud. 1:10,20
15 q Or *Kirjath Sannah,* v. 49
17 r Jud. 3:9 s Jud. 1:13 t Jud. 1:12
19 u See Gen. 12:9, *note*
21 v Gen. 35:21
24 w 1 Sam. 23:14

* 15:8 Literally *Giants*

[1](14:15) Hebron (Gen. 23:2; 35:27; Josh. 15:13; 21:11) was where Abraham and Sarah were buried (Gen. 23:19; 25:10).
[2](15:19) Water was of the utmost importance in the hot and arid climate of the East; thus Achsah's request. Of how much more value spiritual refreshment! Cp. Ps. 87:7; Jn. 4:14.

25 Hazor, Hadattah, Kerioth, Hezron (which *is* Hazor),
26 [a]Amam, Shema, Moladah,
27 Hazar Gaddah, Heshmon, Beth
Pelet,
28 Hazar Shual, [b]Beersheba, Biz-
jothjah,
29 Baalah, Ijim, Ezem,
30 Eltolad, Chesil, [c]Hormah,
31 [d]Ziklag, Madmannah, Sansan-
nah,
32 Lebaoth, Shilhim, Ain, and
[e]Rimmon: all the cities *are* twenty-
nine, with their villages.
33 In the [f]lowland: [g]Eshtaol, Zorah, Ashnah,
34 Zanoah, En Gannim, Tappuah,
Enam,
35 Jarmuth, [h]Adullam, Socoh,
Azekah,
36 Sharaim, Adithaim, Gederah,
and Gederothaim: fourteen cities with
their villages;
37 Zenan, Hadashah, Migdal Gad,
38 Dilean, Mizpah, Joktheel,
39 [i]Lachish, Bozkath, [j]Eglon,
40 Cabbon, Lahmas,* Kithlish,
41 Gederoth, Beth Dagon, Naamah, and Makkedah: sixteen cities
with their villages;
42 [k]Libnah, Ether, Ashan,
43 Jiphtah, Ashnah, Nezib,
44 Keilah, Achzib, and Mareshah:
nine cities with their villages;
45 Ekron, with its towns and villages;
46 from Ekron to the sea, all that
lay near [l]Ashdod, with their villages;
47 Ashdod with its towns and villages, [l]Gaza with its towns and
villages—as far as the [m]Brook of
Egypt and the Great Sea with *its*
coastline.
48 And in the mountain country:
Shamir, Jattir, Sochoh,
49 Dannah, [n]Kirjath Sannah
(which *is* Debir),
50 Anab, Eshtemoh, Anim,
51 Goshen, Holon, and Giloh:
eleven cities with their villages;
52 Arab, Dumah, Eshean,
53 Janum, Beth Tappuah, Aphe-
kah,
54 Humtah, Kirjath Arba (which *is*
Hebron), and Zior: nine cities with
their villages;
55 [o]Maon, Carmel, Ziph, Juttah,
56 Jezreel, Jokdeam, Zanoah,
57 Kain, Gibeah, and Timnah: ten
cities with their villages;
58 Halhul, Beth Zur, Gedor,
59 Maarath, Beth Anoth, and Elte-
kon: six cities with their villages;
60 [p]Kirjath Baal (which *is* Kirjath
Jearim) and Rabbah: two cities with
their villages.
61 In the wilderness: Beth Arabah,
Middin, Secacah,
62 Nibshan, the City of Salt, and
[q]En Gedi: six cities with their villages.
63 As for the [r]Jebusites, the inhabitants of Jerusalem, the children of Judah could not drive them out; but the
Jebusites dwell with the children of
Judah at Jerusalem to this day.

Allotment of Ephraim

16 [s]THE lot fell to the children of
Joseph from the Jordan, by
Jericho, to the waters of Jericho on the
east, to the [t]wilderness that goes up
from Jericho through the mountains
to Bethel,
2 then went out from [u]Bethel to
Luz,* passed along to the border of
the Archites at Ataroth,
3 and went down westward to the
boundary of the Japhletites, as far as
the boundary of [v]Lower Beth Horon
to [w]Gezer; and it ended at the sea.
4 So the children of Joseph, Manasseh and Ephraim, took their inheritance.
5 [x]The border of the children of
Ephraim, according to their families,
was *thus:* The border of their inheritance on the east side was [u]Ataroth
Addar as far as Upper Beth Horon.
6 And the border went out toward
the sea on the north side of [y]Michme-
thath; then the border went around
eastward to Taanath Shiloh, and
passed by it on the east of Janohah.
7 Then it went down from Janohah to Ataroth and [z]Naarah, reached
to Jericho, and came out at the Jordan.
8 The border went out from [aa]Tap-
puah westward to the Brook [bb]Kanah,
and it ended at the sea. This *was* the
inheritance of the tribe of the children
of Ephraim according to their families.
9 The separate cities for the children of Ephraim *were* among the inheritance of the children of Manasseh,
all the cities with their villages.
10 And they [cc]did not drive out the
Canaanites who dwelt in Gezer; but
the Canaanites dwell among the

26 *a* vv. 26–32, cp. Josh. 19:1–7
28 *b* Gen. 21:31; Josh. 19:2
30 *c* Josh. 19:4
31 *d* Josh. 19:5; 1 Sam. 27:6
32 *e* Jud. 20:45,47
33 *f* See Dt. 1:7, *note* *g* Jud. 13:25; 16:31
35 *h* 1 Sam. 22:1
39 *i* 2 Ki. 14:19 *j* Josh. 10:3
42 *k* Josh. 21:13
46 *l* Josh. 11:22
47 *m* Num. 34:5
49 *n* Or *Kirjath Sepher,* Josh. 15:15,16
55 *o* 1 Sam. 23:24,25
60 *p* Josh. 18:14
62 *q* 1 Sam. 23:29; Ezek. 47:10
63 *r* Jud. 1:8, 21; 2 Sam. 5:6
CHAPTER 16
1 *s* vv. 1–4; cp. Josh. 17:14–18 *t* Josh. 8:15; 18:12
2 *u* Josh. 18:13
3 *v* 2 Chr. 8:5 *w* Josh. 21:21
5 *x* vv. 5–9; Jud. 1:29; 1 Chr. 7:28–29 **16:6** *y* Josh. 17:7 **16:7** *z* Or *Naaran,* 1 Chr. 7:28 **16:8** *aa* Josh. 17:8 *bb* Josh. 17:9 **16:10** *cc* Josh. 15:63; 17:12–13; 1 Ki. 9:16

* **15:40** Or *Lahmam* **16:2** Septuagint reads *Bethel* (that is, Luz).

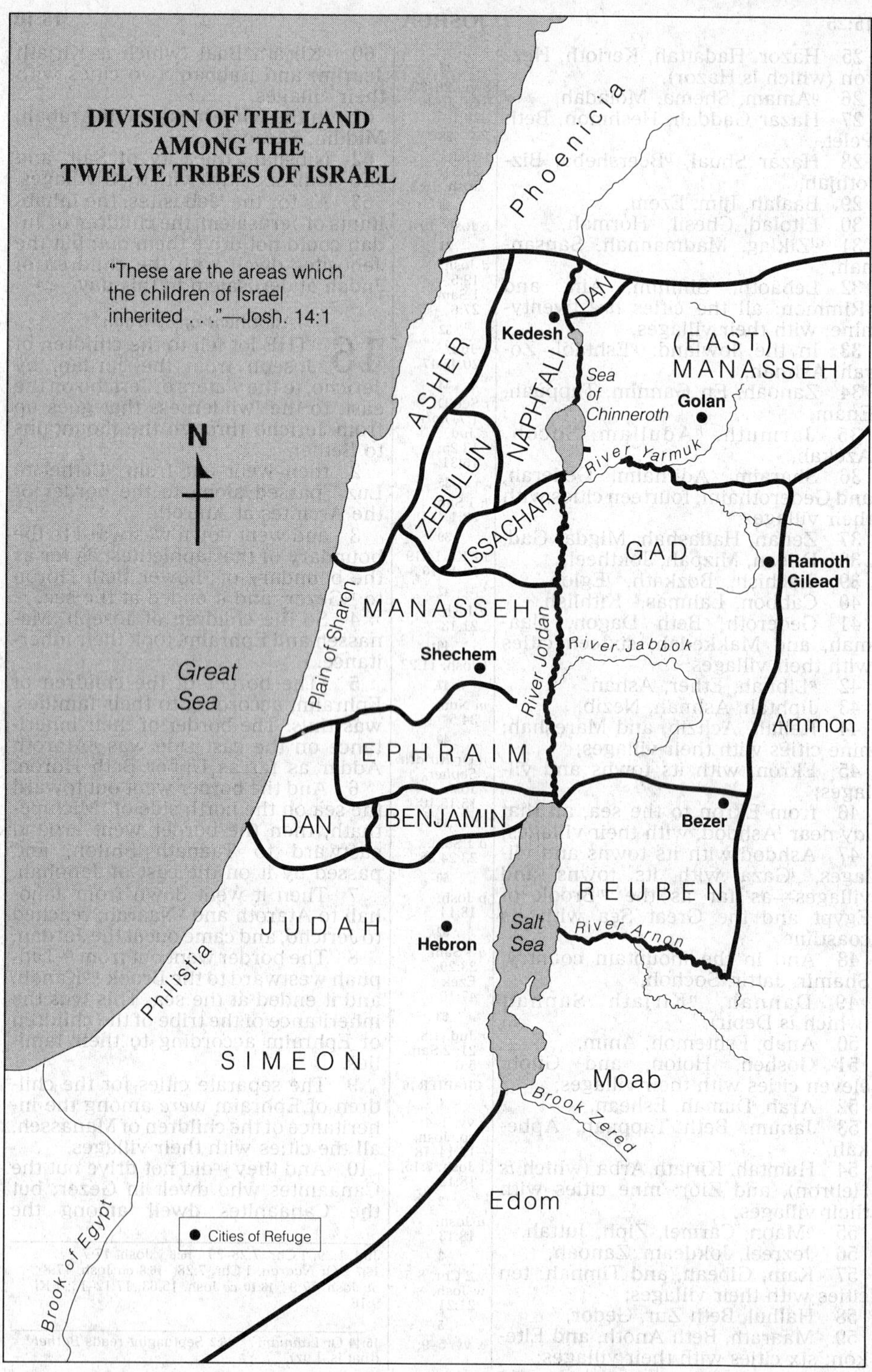

DIVISION OF THE LAND AMONG THE TWELVE TRIBES OF ISRAEL
"These are the areas which the children of Israel inherited . . ."—Josh. 14:1
N
Phoenicia
DAN
Kedesh
ASHER
NAPHTALI
Sea of Chinneroth
(EAST) MANASSEH
Golan
ZEBULUN
River Yarmuk
ISSACHAR
GAD
Ramoth Gilead
MANASSEH
Plain of Sharon
River Jabbok
Shechem
River Jordan
Great Sea
Ammon
EPHRAIM
DAN
BENJAMIN
Bezer
REUBEN
JUDAH
Salt Sea
River Arnon
Hebron
Philistia
SIMEON
Moab
Brook Zered
Edom
Cities of Refuge
Brook of Egypt

Ephraimites to this day and have become forced laborers.

Allotment of Manasseh

17 [a]THERE was also a lot for the tribe of Manasseh, for he *was* the firstborn of Joseph: *namely* for [b]Machir the firstborn of Manasseh, the father of Gilead, because he was a man of war; therefore he was given Gilead and Bashan.

2 And there was *a lot* for the rest of the [c]children of Manasseh according to their families: for the children of Abiezer,* the children of Helek, the children of Asriel, the children of Shechem, the children of Hepher, and the children of Shemida; these *were* the male children of Manasseh the son of Joseph according to their families.

3 But [d]Zelophehad the son of Hepher, the son of Gilead, the son of Machir, the son of Manasseh, had no sons, but only daughters. And these *are* the names of his daughters: Mahlah, Noah, Hoglah, Milcah, and Tirzah.

4 And they came near before [e]Eleazar the priest, before Joshua the son of Nun, and before the rulers, saying, "The LORD commanded Moses to give us an inheritance among our brothers." Therefore, [f]according to the commandment of the LORD, he gave them an inheritance among their father's brothers.

5 Ten shares fell to [g]Manasseh, besides the land of Gilead and Bashan, which *were* on the other side of the Jordan,

6 because the daughters of Manasseh received an inheritance among his sons; and the rest of Manasseh's sons had the land of Gilead.

7 And the territory of Manasseh was from Asher to [h]Michmethath, that *lies* east of Shechem; and the border went along south to the inhabitants of En Tappuah.

8 Manasseh had the land of Tappuah, but Tappuah on the border of Manasseh *belonged* to the children of Ephraim.

9 And the border descended to the Brook Kanah, southward to the brook. [i]These cities of Ephraim *are* among the cities of Manasseh. The border of Manasseh *was* on the north side of the brook; and it ended at the sea.

10 Southward *it was* Ephraim's, northward *it was* Manasseh's, and the sea was its border. Manasseh's territory was adjoining Asher on the north and Issachar on the east.

11 And in Issachar and in Asher, [j]Manasseh had [k]Beth Shean and its towns, Ibleam and its towns, the inhabitants of Dor and its towns, the inhabitants of En Dor and its towns, the inhabitants of Taanach and its towns, and the inhabitants of Megiddo and its towns—three hilly regions.

12 Yet the children of Manasseh could [l]not drive out *the inhabitants of* those cities, but the Canaanites were determined to dwell in that land.

13 And it happened, when the children of Israel grew strong, that they put the Canaanites to [m]forced labor, but did not utterly drive them out.

14 Then the children of Joseph spoke to Joshua, saying, "Why have you given us *only* one lot and one share to inherit, since we *are* a [n]great people, inasmuch as the LORD has blessed us until now?"

15 So Joshua answered them, "If you *are* a great people, *then* go up to the forest *country* and clear a place for yourself there in the land of the Perizzites and the [o]giants, since the mountains of Ephraim are too confined for you."

16 But the children of Joseph said, "The mountain country is not enough for us; and all the Canaanites who dwell in the land of the valley have chariots of iron, *both those* who *are* of Beth Shean and its towns and *those* who *are* of the Valley of Jezreel."

17 And Joshua spoke to the house of Joseph—to Ephraim and Manasseh—saying, "You *are* a great people and have great power; you shall not have *only* one lot,

18 "but the mountain country shall be yours. Although it *is* wooded, you shall cut it down, and its farthest extent shall be yours; for you shall drive out the Canaanites, though they have iron [p]chariots *and* are strong."

Tabernacle set up at Shiloh

18 NOW the whole congregation of the children of Israel assembled together at [1q]Shiloh, and set up

CHAPTER 17
1
a vv. 1–11; Num. 32:33, 39–40; Josh. 13:29–33; 1 Chr. 5:23
b Jud. 5:14
2
c Num. 26:29–33
3
d Num. 26:33; 27:1
4
e Josh. 14:1
f Num. 27:2–11
5
g Josh. 22:7
7
h Josh. 16:6
9
i Josh. 16:9
11
j 1 Chr. 7:29
k Jud. 1:27; 1 Ki. 4:12
12
l Jud. 1:19, 28
13
m Josh. 16:10
14
n Gen. 48:19–20; Num. 26:34,37
15
o Heb. *Rephaim.* Gen. 15:20
18
p Dt. 20:1
CHAPTER 18
1
q Cp. Dt. 12:5

* 17:2 Called *Jeezer* in Numbers 26:30

[1](18:1) Shiloh was situated in the tribal allotment of Ephraim. Built on a hill about nine miles north of Bethel (cp. Jud. 21:19), it had a commanding and somewhat central location. The

the tabernacle of meeting there. And the land was subdued before them.

Division of remaining land

2 But there remained among the children of Israel seven tribes which had not yet received their inheritance.

3 Then Joshua said to the children of Israel: "How long will you [a]neglect to go and possess the land which the LORD God of your fathers has given you?

4 "Pick out from among you three men for *each* tribe, and I will send them; they shall rise and go through the land, survey it according to their inheritance, and come *back* to me.

5 "And they shall divide it into seven parts. [b]Judah shall remain in their territory on the south, and the [c]house of Joseph shall remain in their territory on the north.

6 "You shall therefore survey the land in seven parts and bring *the survey* here to me, that I may cast lots for you here before the LORD our God.

7 "But the [d]Levites have no part among you, for the priesthood of the LORD *is* their inheritance. And Gad, Reuben, and half the tribe of Manasseh have received their inheritance beyond the Jordan on the east, which Moses the servant of the LORD gave them."

8 Then the men arose to go away; and Joshua charged those who went to survey the land, saying, "Go, walk [e]through the land, survey it, and come back to me, that I may cast lots for you here before the LORD in Shiloh."

9 So the men went, passed through the land, and wrote the survey in a book in seven parts by cities; and they came to Joshua at the camp in Shiloh.

10 Then Joshua cast [f]lots for them in Shiloh before the LORD, and there [g]Joshua divided the land to the children of Israel according to their divisions.

Allotment of Benjamin

11 [h]Now the lot of the tribe of the children of Benjamin came up according to their families, and the territory of their lot came out between the children of Judah and the children of Joseph.

3
a Jud. 18:9; cp. Eccl. 9:10
5
b Josh. 15:1–63
c Josh. 16:1–17:18
7
d Num. 18:20
8
e Gen. 13:17
10
f Acts 13:19
g Num. 34:16–29
11
h vv. 11–28; Jud. 1:21
13
i Gen. 28:19; Josh. 16:2; Jud. 1:23
j Josh. 16:3
15
k 1 Chr. 13:5–6
l Josh. 15:9
17
m Josh. 15:6
18
n See Dt. 1:1, *note*
19
o Josh. 15:2, 5

12 Their border on the north side began at the Jordan, and the border went up to the side of Jericho on the north, and went up through the mountains westward; it ended at the Wilderness of Beth Aven.

13 The border went over from there toward Luz, to the side of [i]Luz (which *is* Bethel) southward; and the border descended to Ataroth Addar, near the hill that *lies* on the south side of [j]Lower Beth Horon.

14 Then the border extended around the west side to the south, from the hill that *lies* before Beth Horon southward; and it ended at Kirjath Baal (which *is* Kirjath Jearim), a city of the children of Judah. This *was* the west side.

15 The south side *began* at the end of [k]Kirjath Jearim, and the border extended on the west and went out to the spring of the [l]waters of Nephtoah.

16 Then the border came down to the end of the mountain that *lies* before the Valley of the Son of Hinnom, which *is* in the Valley of the Rephaim* on the north, descended to the Valley of Hinnom, to the side of the Jebusite *city* on the south, and descended to En Rogel.

17 And it went around from the north, went out to En Shemesh, and extended toward Geliloth, which is before the Ascent of Adummim, and descended to the [m]stone of Bohan the son of Reuben.

18 Then it passed along toward the north side of [n]Arabah,* and went down to Arabah.

19 And the border passed along to the north side of Beth Hoglah; then the border ended at the north bay at the [o]Salt Sea, at the south end of the Jordan. This *was* the southern boundary.

20 The Jordan was its border on the east side. This *was* the inheritance of the children of Benjamin, according to its boundaries all around, according to their families.

21 Now the cities of the tribe of the children of Benjamin, according to

*

18:16 Literally *Giants* 18:18 Or *Beth Arabah* (compare 15:6 and 18:22)

---

tabernacle of meeting was temporarily located there (Josh. 18:1; 19:51; Jud. 18:31), and at that time the meeting place had doorposts and doors and was called a "tabernacle" (1 Sam. 1:9; 3:3). Although the destruction of Shiloh is not described in the records of this period (1 Sam. 4), it must have been overwhelming, on account of the wickedness of the children of Israel (Ps. 78:60; Jer. 7:12,14; 26:6).

their families, were Jericho, Beth Hoglah, Emek Keziz,
22 Beth Arabah, Zemaraim, Bethel,
23 Avim, Parah, Ophrah,
24 Chephar Haammoni, Ophni, and Gaba: twelve cities with their villages;
25 [a]Gibeon, [b]Ramah, Beeroth,
26 Mizpah, Chephirah, Mozah,
27 Rekem, Irpeel, Taralah,
28 Zelah, Eleph, Jebus (which *is* [c]Jerusalem), Gibeath, *and* Kirjath: fourteen cities with their villages. This was the inheritance of the children of Benjamin according to their families.

Allotments of Simeon (v. 1), Zebulun (v. 10), Issachar (v. 17), Asher (v. 24), Naphtali (v. 32), Dan (v. 40)

19 [d]THE second lot came out for Simeon, for the tribe of the children of Simeon according to their families. And their inheritance was within the inheritance of the children of Judah.
2 They had in their inheritance [e]Beersheba (Sheba), Moladah,
3 Hazar Shual, Balah, Ezem,
4 Eltolad, Bethul, Hormah,
5 Ziklag, Beth Marcaboth, [f]Hazar Susah,
6 Beth Lebaoth, and Sharuhen: thirteen cities and their villages;
7 Ain, Rimmon, Ether, and Ashan: four cities and their villages;
8 and all the villages that *were* all around these cities as far as Baalath Beer, [g]Ramah of the [h]South. This *was* the inheritance of the tribe of the children of Simeon according to their families.
9 [1]The inheritance of the children of Simeon *was included* in the share of the children of Judah, for the share of the children of Judah was too much for them. Therefore the children of Simeon had *their* inheritance within the inheritance of that people.
10 [i]The third lot came out for the children of Zebulun according to their families, and the border of their inheritance was as far as Sarid.
11 Their [j]border went toward the west and to Maralah, went to Dabbasheth, and extended along the brook that is east of [k]Jokneam.
12 Then from Sarid it went eastward toward the sunrise along the border of Chisloth Tabor, and went out toward [l]Daberath, bypassing Japhia.
13 And from there it passed along on the east of [m]Gath Hepher, toward Eth Kazin, and extended to Rimmon, which borders on Neah.
14 Then the border went around it on the north side of Hannathon, and it ended in the Valley of Jiphthah El.
15 Included were Kattath, Nahallal, Shimron, Idalah, and Bethlehem: twelve cities with their villages.
16 This *was* the inheritance of the children of Zebulun according to their families, these cities with their villages.
17 [n]The fourth lot came out to Issachar, for the children of Issachar according to their families.
18 And their territory went to Jezreel, and *included* Chesulloth, Shunem,
19 Haphraim, Shion, Anaharath,
20 Rabbith, Kishion, Abez,
21 Remeth, En Gannim, En Haddah, and Beth Pazzez.
22 And the border reached to Tabor, Shahazimah, and [o]Beth Shemesh; their border ended at the Jordan: sixteen cities with their villages.
23 This *was* the inheritance of the tribe of the children of Issachar according to their families, the cities and their villages.
24 [p]The fifth lot came out for the tribe of the children of Asher according to their families.
25 And their territory included Helkath, Hali, Beten, Achshaph,
26 Alammelech, Amad, and Mishal; it reached to [q]Mount Carmel westward, along *the Brook* Shihor Libnath.
27 It turned toward the sunrise to Beth Dagon; and it reached to Zebulun and to the Valley of Jiphthah El, then northward beyond Beth Emek and Neiel, bypassing [r]Cabul *which was* on the left,
28 including Ebron,* Rehob, Hammon, and Kanah, as far as Greater Sidon.
29 And the border turned to Ramah and to the fortified city of Tyre; then the border turned to Hosah, and

25
a Josh. 11:19; 21:17; 1 Ki. 3:4,5
b Jer. 31:15
28
c Josh. 15:8, 63
CHAPTER 19
1
d vv. 1–9; Jud. 1:3; 1 Chr. 4:28–33
2
e Gen. 21:31; 1 Chr. 4:28
5
f Or *Hazar Susim,* 1 Chr. 4:31
8
g 1 Sam. 30:27
h See Gen. 12:9, *note*
10
i vv. 10–16; Gen. 49:13; Jud. 1:30; cp. Dt. 33:18–19
11
j Gen. 49:13
k Josh. 21:34
12
l 1 Chr. 6:72
13
m 2 Ki. 14:25
17
n vv. 17–23; cp. Gen. 49:14–15; Dt. 33:18–19
22
o Josh. 15:10; Jud. 1:33
24
p vv. 24–31; Jud. 1:31–32
26
q 1 Sam. 15:12; 1 Ki. 18:20; Isa. 33:9; 35:2; Jer. 46:18
27
r 1 Ki. 9:13

*19:28 Following Masoretic Text, Targum, and Vulgate; a few Hebrew manuscripts read *Abdon* (compare 21:30 and 1 Chronicles 6:74).

[1](19:9) Inasmuch as Simeon had no definite portion allotted to it (Gen. 49:5–7), its inheritance was "included in the share of the children of Judah."

ended at the sea by the region of Achzib.

30 Also Ummah, Aphek, and Rehob *were included:* twenty-two cities with their villages.

31 This *was* the inheritance of the tribe of the children of Asher according to their families, these cities with their villages.

32 [a]The sixth lot came out to the children of Naphtali, for the children of Naphtali according to their families.

33 And their border began at Heleph, enclosing the territory from the terebinth tree in Zaanannim, Adami Nekeb, and Jabneel, as far as Lakkum; it ended at the Jordan.

34 From Heleph the border extended westward to Aznoth Tabor, and went out from there toward Hukkok; it adjoined Zebulun on the south side and Asher on the west side, and ended at Judah by the Jordan toward the sunrise.

35 And the fortified cities *are* Ziddim, Zer, Hammath, Rakkath, Chinnereth,

36 Adamah, Ramah, Hazor,

37 [b]Kedesh, Edrei, En Hazor,

38 Iron, Migdal El, Horem, Beth Anath, and Beth Shemesh: nineteen cities with their villages.

39 This *was* the inheritance of the tribe of the children of Naphtali according to their families, the cities and their villages.

40 [c]The seventh lot came out for the tribe of the children of Dan according to their families.

41 And the territory of their inheritance was Zorah, [d]Eshtaol, Ir Shemesh,

42 [e]Shaalabbin, [f]Aijalon, Jethlah,

43 Elon, Timnah, [g]Ekron,

44 Eltekeh, Gibbethon, Baalath,

45 Jehud, Bene Berak, Gath Rimmon,

46 Me Jarkon, and Rakkon, with the region near Joppa.

47 And the border of the children of Dan went beyond these, because the children of Dan went up to fight against Leshem and took it; and they struck it with the edge of the sword, took possession of it, and dwelt in it. They called Leshem, Dan, after the name of Dan their father.

48 This *is* the inheritance of the tribe of the children of Dan according to their families, these cities with their villages.

Joshua's special portion

49 When they had made an end of dividing the land as an inheritance according to their borders, the children of Israel gave an inheritance among them to Joshua the son of Nun.

50 According to the word of the LORD they gave him the city which he asked for, [h]Timnath Serah in the mountains of Ephraim; and he built the city and dwelt in it.

51 These *were* the inheritances [1]which Eleazar the priest, Joshua the son of Nun, and the heads of the fathers of the tribes of the children of Israel divided as an inheritance by lot in [i]Shiloh before the LORD, at the door of the tabernacle of meeting. So they made an end of dividing the country.

Six cities appointed as places of refuge (Num. 35)

20 THE LORD also spoke to Joshua, saying,

2 "Speak to the children of Israel, saying: 'Appoint for yourselves cities of [j]refuge, of which I spoke to you through Moses,

3 'that the slayer who kills a person accidentally *or* unintentionally may flee there; and they shall be your refuge from the [k]avenger of blood.

4 'And when he flees to one of those cities, and stands at the [l]entrance of the gate of the city, and declares his case in the hearing of the elders of that city, they shall take him into the city as one of them, and give him a place, that he may [m]dwell among them.

5 'Then if the [n]avenger of blood pursues him, they shall not deliver the slayer into his hand, because he struck his neighbor unintentionally, but did not hate him beforehand.

6 'And he shall dwell in that city until he stands before the congregation for [o]judgment, *and* until the death of the one who is high priest in those days. Then the slayer may return and come to his own city and his own house, to the city from which he fled.' "

7 So they appointed [p]Kedesh in Galilee, in the mountains of Naphtali, Shechem in the mountains of Ephraim, and Kirjath Arba (which *is* Hebron) in the mountains of Judah.

32 *a* vv. 32–39; Jud. 1:33
37 *b* Josh. 20:7
40 *c* vv. 40–48; Jud. 1:34–36
41 *d* Josh. 15:33
42 *e* Or *Shaalbim,* Jud. 1:35; 1 Ki. 4:9 *f* Josh. 10:12; 21:24
43 *g* Josh. 15:11; Jud. 1:18
50 *h* Josh. 24:30
51 *i* Josh. 18:1, 10
CHAPTER 20
2 *j* See Num. 35:6, *note*
3 *k Redemption* (redeeming relative type): vv. 2–6; Ruth 2:20. (Gen. 48:16; Isa. 59:20, *note*)
4 *l* Cp. Ruth 4:1,2 *m* Cp. Heb. 6:18
5 *n* Cp. Num. 35:26–28
6 *o* Num. 35:12,24
7 *p* Josh. 21:32; 1 Chr. 6:76

[1](19:51) God had told Moses whom he should appoint to divide the land (Num. 34:17–29).

8 And on the other side of the Jordan, by Jericho eastward, they assigned [a]Bezer in the wilderness on the
plain, from the tribe of Reuben, [b]Ra-
moth in Gilead, from the tribe of Gad,
and [b]Golan in Bashan, from the tribe
of Manasseh.
9 These were the cities appointed
for all the children of Israel and for the
stranger who dwelt among them, that
whoever killed a person accidentally
might flee there, and not die by the
hand of the avenger of blood until he
stood before the congregation.

Levites' forty-eight cities

21 THEN the heads of the fathers'
houses of the [c]Levites came
near to [d]Eleazar the priest, to Joshua
the son of Nun, and to the heads of the
fathers' *houses* of the tribes of the children of Israel.
2 And they spoke to them at [e]Shi-
loh in the land of Canaan, saying,
"The [f]LORD commanded through Moses to give us cities to dwell in, with
their common-lands for our livestock."
3 So the children of Israel gave to
the Levites from their inheritance, at
the commandment of the LORD, these
cities and their common-lands:
4 Now the [g]lot came out for the
families of the Kohathites. And the
children of [h]Aaron the priest, *who
were* of the Levites, had thirteen cities
by lot from the tribe of Judah, from the
tribe of Simeon, and from the tribe of
Benjamin.
5 The rest of the children of Kohath had ten cities by lot from the families of the tribe of Ephraim, from the
tribe of Dan, and from the half-tribe of
Manasseh.
6 And the children of Gershon had
thirteen cities by lot from the families
of the tribe of Issachar, from the tribe
of Asher, from the tribe of Naphtali,
and from the half-tribe of Manasseh in
Bashan.
7 The children of Merari according to their families had twelve cities
from the tribe of Reuben, from the
tribe of Gad, and from the tribe of Zebulun.
8 And the children of Israel gave
these cities with their common-lands
by lot to the Levites, as the LORD had
commanded by the hand of Moses.
9 So they gave from the tribe of
the children of Judah and from the
tribe of the children of Simeon these
cities which are designated by name,
10 which were for the children of
Aaron, one of the families of the Kohathites, *who were* of the children of
Levi; for the lot was theirs first.
11 [i]And they gave them Kirjath
Arba ([j]*Arba was* the father of Anak),
which *is* Hebron, in the mountains of
Judah, with the common-land surrounding it.
12 But the fields of the city and its
villages they gave to [k]Caleb the son of
Jephunneh as his possession.
13 Thus to the children of Aaron
the priest they gave Hebron with its
common-land (a [l]city of refuge for the
slayer), [m]Libnah with its common-
land,
14 Jattir with its common-land,
Eshtemoa with its common-land,
15 [n]Holon with its common-land,
Debir with its common-land,
16 [o]Ain with its common-land, Juttah with its common-land, and Beth
Shemesh with its common-land: nine
cities from those two tribes;
17 and from the tribe of Benjamin,
Gibeon with its common-land, Geba
with its common-land,
18 Anathoth with its common-land,
and Almon with its common-land:
four cities.
19 All the cities of the children of
Aaron, the priests, *were* thirteen cities
with their common-lands.
20 [p]And the families of the children
of Kohath, the Levites, the rest of the
children of Kohath, even they had the
cities of their lot from the tribe of
Ephraim.
21 For they gave them [q]Shechem
with its common-land in the mountains of Ephraim (a city of refuge for
the slayer), [r]Gezer with its common-
land,
22 Kibzaim with its common-land,
and Beth Horon with its common-
land: four cities;
23 and from the tribe of Dan, Eltekeh with its common-land, Gibbethon
with its common-land,
24 [s]Aijalon with its common-land,
and Gath Rimmon with its common-
land: four cities;
25 and from the half-tribe of Manasseh, Tanach with its common-land
and Gath Rimmon with its common-
land: two cities.
26 All the ten cities with their
common-lands were for the rest of the
families of the children of Kohath.
27 [t]Also to the children of Gershon, of the families of the Levites,
from the *other* half-tribe of Manasseh,

8
[a] Dt. 4:43; Josh. 21:36; 1 Chr. 6:78
[b] Dt. 4:43

CHAPTER 21

1
[c] Num. 35:1–8
[d] Num. 34:16–29; Josh. 14:1; 17:4

2
[e] Josh. 18:1
[f] Num. 35:2; cp. 1 Cor. 9:14

4
[g] Cp. Num. 26:55
[h] vv. 8,19; Josh. 24:33

11
[i] vv. 11–19; cp. 1 Chr. 6:54–60
[j] Josh. 15:13

12
[k] Josh. 14:14

13
[l] Josh. 20:2, 7
[m] 2 Ki. 8:22

15
[n] Josh. 15:51; or *Hilen*, 1 Chr. 6:58

16
[o] Or *Ashan*, Josh. 15:42; 1 Chr. 6:59

20
[p] vv. 20–26; cp. 1 Chr. 6:66–70

21
[q] Josh. 20:7
[r] Jud. 1:29

24
[s] Josh. 10:12

27
[t] vv. 27–33; cp. 1 Chr. 6:71–76

they gave [a]Golan in Bashan with its common-land (a city of refuge for the slayer), and Be Eshterah with its common-land: two cities;

28 and from the tribe of Issachar, Kishion with its common-land, Daberath with its common-land,

29 Jarmuth with its common-land, *and* En Gannim with its common-land: four cities;

30 and from the tribe of Asher, Mishal with its common-land, Abdon with its common-land,

31 Helkath with its common-land, and Rehob with its common-land: four cities;

32 and from the tribe of Naphtali, [b]Kedesh in Galilee with its common-land (a city of refuge for the slayer), Hammoth Dor with its common-land, and Kartan with its common-land: three cities.

33 All the cities of the Gershonites according to their families *were* thirteen cities with their common-lands.

34 [c]And to the families of the children of [d]Merari, the rest of the Levites, from the tribe of Zebulun, Jokneam with its common-land, Kartah with its common-land,

35 Dimnah with its common-land, *and* Nahalal with its common-land: four cities;

36 and from the tribe of [a]Reuben, Bezer with its common-land, Jahaz with its common-land,

37 Kedemoth with its common-land, and Mephaath with its common-land: four cities;*

38 and from the tribe of Gad, [a]Ramoth in Gilead with its common-land (a city of refuge for the slayer), Mahanaim with its common-land,

39 Heshbon with its common-land, *and* Jazer with its common-land: four cities in all.

40 So all the cities for the children of Merari according to their families, the rest of the families of the Levites, were *by* their lot twelve cities.

41 All the cities of the Levites within the possession of the children of Israel *were* [e]forty-eight cities with their common-lands.

42 Every one of these cities had its common-land surrounding it; thus *were* all these cities.

God's promise fulfilled

43 So the LORD gave to Israel all the land of which He had [f]sworn to give to their fathers, and they took [g]possession of it and dwelt in it.

44 [h]The LORD gave them [i]rest all around, according to all that He had sworn to their fathers. And not a man of all their enemies stood against them; the LORD delivered all their enemies into their hand.

45 [j]Not a word failed of any good thing which the LORD had spoken to the house of Israel. All came to pass.

The two and one-half tribes sent home

22 THEN Joshua called the Reubenites, the Gadites, and half the tribe of Manasseh,

2 and said to them: "You have kept all that [k]Moses the servant of the LORD commanded you, and have obeyed my voice in all that [l]I commanded you.

3 "You have not left your brethren these many days, up to this day, but have kept the charge of the commandment of the LORD your God.

4 "And now the LORD your God has given [m]rest to your brethren, as He promised them; now therefore, return and go to your tents *and* to the land of your possession, which Moses the servant of the LORD gave you on the other side of the Jordan.

5 "But take careful heed to do the commandment and the law which Moses the servant of the LORD commanded [n]you, to love the LORD your God, to walk in all His ways, to keep His commandments, to hold fast to Him, and to serve Him with all your heart and with all your soul."

6 So Joshua blessed them and sent them away, and they went to their tents.

7 Now to half the tribe of Manasseh Moses had given a possession in Bashan, but to the [o]*other* half of it Joshua gave *a possession* among their brethren on this side of the Jordan, westward. And indeed, when Joshua sent them away to their tents, he blessed them,

8 and spoke to them, saying, "Return with much riches to your tents, with very much livestock, with silver, with gold, with bronze, with iron, and with very much clothing. Divide the spoil of your enemies with your brethren."

9 So the children of Reuben, the children of Gad, and half the tribe of Manasseh returned, and departed from the children of Israel at Shiloh,

27
a Josh. 20:8
32
b Josh. 20:7
34
c vv. 34–40; cp. 1 Chr. 6:77–81
d Josh. 21:7; 1 Chr. 6:77–81
41
e Num. 35:7
43
f Gen. 12:7; 26:3–4; 28:4,13–14
g Num. 33:53; Josh. 1:11
44
h Dt. 7:23–24; Josh. 11:23; 22:4
i Josh. 1:13, 15; 11:23
45
j Num. 23:19; Josh. 23:14; 1 Ki. 8:56; cp. 1 Cor. 1:9; 1 Th. 5:24; Ti. 1:2
CHAPTER 22
2
k Num. 32:20–22
l Josh. 1:12–18
4
m Josh. 21:44
5
n Dt. 10:12; 11:13,22
7
o Josh. 17:1–13

*21:37 Following Septuagint and Vulgate (compare 1 Chronicles 6:78–79); Masoretic Text, Bomberg, and Targum omit verses 36 and 37.

which *is* in the land of Canaan, to go to the country of Gilead, to the land of their possession, which they had obtained according to the word of the LORD by the hand of Moses.

The misunderstood altar built by the two and one-half tribes

10 And when they came to the region of the Jordan which *is* in the land of Canaan, the children of Reuben, the children of Gad, and half the tribe of Manasseh built an [1]altar there by the Jordan—a great, impressive altar.

11 Now the children of Israel [a]heard *someone* say, "Behold, the children of Reuben, the children of Gad, and half the tribe of Manasseh have built an [b]altar on the frontier of the land of Canaan, in the region of the Jordan—on the children of Israel's side."

12 And when the children of Israel heard *of it,* the whole congregation of the children of Israel gathered together at [c]Shiloh to go to war against them.

13 Then the children of Israel sent [d]Phinehas the son of Eleazar the priest to the children of Reuben, to the children of Gad, and to half the tribe of Manasseh, into the land of Gilead,

14 and with him ten rulers, one ruler each from the chief house of every tribe of Israel; and each one *was* the head of the house of his father among the divisions* of Israel.

15 Then they came to the children of Reuben, to the children of Gad, and to half the tribe of Manasseh, to the land of Gilead, and they spoke with them, saying,

16 "Thus says the whole congregation of the LORD: 'What [e]treachery *is* this that you have committed against the God of Israel, to turn away this day from following the LORD, in that you have built for yourselves an altar, that you might [f]rebel this day against the LORD?

17 '*Is* the iniquity of [g]Peor not enough for us, from which we are not cleansed till this day, although there was a plague in the congregation of the LORD,

18 'but that you must turn away this day from following the LORD? And it shall be, if you rebel today against the LORD, that tomorrow He will be angry with the [h]whole congregation of Israel.

19 'Nevertheless, if the land of your possession *is* unclean, *then* cross over to the land of the possession of the LORD, where the LORD's tabernacle stands, and take possession among us; but do not rebel against the LORD, nor rebel against us, by building yourselves an altar besides the altar of the LORD our God.

20 'Did not [i]Achan the son of Zerah commit a trespass in the accursed thing, and wrath fell on all the congregation of Israel? And that man did not perish alone in his iniquity.'"

21 Then the children of Reuben, the children of Gad, and half the tribe of Manasseh answered and said to the heads of the divisions* of Israel:

22 "The [j]LORD God of gods, the LORD God of gods, He knows, and let Israel itself know—if *it is* in rebellion, or if in treachery against the LORD, do not save us this day.

23 "If we have built ourselves an altar to turn from following the LORD, or if to offer on it [k]burnt offerings or grain offerings, or if to offer peace offerings on it, let the LORD Himself require *an account.*

24 "But in fact we have done it for fear, for a reason, saying, 'In time to come your descendants may speak to our [l]descendants, saying, "What have you to do with the LORD God of Israel?

25 "For the LORD has made the Jordan a border between you and us, *you* children of Reuben and children of Gad. You have no part in the LORD." So your descendants would make our descendants cease fearing the LORD.'

26 "Therefore we said, 'Let us now prepare to build ourselves an altar, not for burnt offering nor for sacrifice,

27 'but *that* it *may be* a [m]witness between you and us and our generations after us, that we may perform the service of the [n]LORD before Him with our burnt offerings, with our sacrifices, and with our peace offerings; that your descendants may not say to our descendants in time to come, "You have no part in the LORD."'

28 "Therefore we said that it will

11
a vv. 11–34; cp. Dt. 13:12–18
b Cp. Dt. 12:1–14
12
c Josh. 18:1
13
d Ex. 6:25; Num. 25:7
16
e Dt. 12:5–14
f Lev. 17:8–9
17
g Num. 25:1–9
18
h Num. 16:22
20
i Josh. 7:1–26
22
j Dt. 4:35, 39; Isa. 44:8; 45:5; 46:9; 1 Cor. 8:5–6
23
k v. 27; cp. Lev. 17:3–4
24
l Cp. Josh. 4:6
27
m v. 34, Dt. 31:19
n Dt. 12:18

* 22:14 Literally *thousands* 22:21 Literally *thousands*

[1](22:10) The fact that only one altar was used by the whole nation as early as this time is strong evidence against the erroneous contention of certain critics that centralization of worship (in Jerusalem) did not take place until the reformation of Josiah (2 Ki. 22:8–20).

be, when they say *this* to us or to our generations in time to come, that we may say, 'Here is the replica of the altar of the LORD which our fathers made, though not for burnt offerings nor for sacrifices; but it *is* a [a]witness between you and us.'

29 "Far be it from us that we should rebel against the LORD, and turn from following the LORD this day, to build an altar for burnt offerings, for grain offerings, or for sacrifices, besides the altar of the LORD our God which *is* before His tabernacle."

30 Now when Phinehas the priest and the rulers of the congregation, the heads of the divisions* of Israel who *were* with him, heard the words that the children of Reuben, the children of Gad, and the children of Manasseh spoke, it pleased them.

31 Then Phinehas the son of Eleazar the priest said to the children of Reuben, the children of Gad, and the children of Manasseh, "This day we perceive that the [b]LORD *is* among us, because you have not committed this treachery against the LORD. Now you have delivered the children of Israel out of the hand of the LORD."

32 And Phinehas the son of Eleazar the priest, and the rulers, returned from the children of Reuben and the children of Gad, from the land of Gilead to the land of Canaan, to the children of Israel, and brought back word to them.

33 So the thing pleased the children of Israel, and the children of Israel [c]blessed God; they spoke no more of going against them in battle, to destroy the land where the children of Reuben and Gad dwelt.

34 The children of Reuben and the children of Gad* called the altar, [d]*Witness*, "For *it is* a witness between us that the LORD *is* God."

IV. Joshua's Final Message and Death, 23—24

Joshua's appeal

23 NOW it came to pass, a long time after the LORD had given [e]rest to Israel from all their enemies round about, that Joshua was [f]old, advanced in age.

2 And Joshua [g]called for all Israel, for their elders, for their heads, for their judges, and for their officers, and [1]said to them: "I am old, advanced in age.

3 "You have seen all that the [h]LORD your God has done to all these nations because of you, [i]for the LORD your God *is* He who has fought for you.

4 "See, [j]I have divided to you by lot these nations that remain, to be an inheritance for your tribes, from the Jordan, with all the nations that I have cut off, as far as the Great Sea westward.

5 "And the LORD your God will expel them from before you and drive them out of your sight. So you shall possess their land, as the LORD your God [k]promised you.

6 "Therefore be very courageous to keep and to do all that is written in the Book of the Law of Moses, lest you turn aside from it to the right hand or to the [l]left,

7 "*and* lest you go among these nations, these who remain among you. You shall not make [m]mention of the name of their gods, nor cause *anyone* to [n]swear *by them;* you shall not [o]serve them nor bow down to them,

8 "but you shall [p]hold fast to the LORD your God, as you have done to this day.

9 "For the LORD has driven out from before you great and strong nations; but *as for* [q]you, no one has been able to stand against you to this day.

10 "One man of you shall chase a [r]thousand, for the LORD your God *is* He who fights for you, as He promised you.

11 "Therefore take careful heed to yourselves, that you love the LORD your God.

12 "Or else, if indeed you do go back, and cling to the remnant of

28 *a* Cp. Gen. 31:44–49
31 *b* Lev. 26:11–12; Zech. 8:23
33 *c* 1 Chr. 29:20
34 *d* Josh. 24:27
CHAPTER 23
1 *e* Josh. 22:4 *f* Josh. 13:1; 24:29
2 *g* Josh. 24:1; cp. Dt. 31:28; 1 Chr. 28:1
3 *h* Ps. 44:3 *i* Dt. 1:30; Josh. 10:14,42
4 *j* Josh. 18:10
5 *k* Num. 33:53
6 *l* Josh. 1:7
7 *m* Ex. 23:13; Ps. 16:4; Hos. 2:17 *n* Dt. 6:13; 10:20 *o* Ex. 20:5
8 *p* Josh. 22:5
9 *q* Dt. 7:24
10 *r* Isa. 30:17; cp. Lev. 26:28; Dt. 28:7

*22:30 Literally *thousands* 22:34 Septuagint adds *and half the tribe of Manasseh*

[1](23:2) The last counsels of Joshua should be compared with those of Moses in Deuteronomy, especially chs. 31—33. Like Moses, Joshua reminded Israel of God's past blessings upon them, the necessity of continued obedience, and urged them to further conquest. He warned of the dangers of worshiping heathen gods and of worldly alliance with heathen nations. Departure from God would lead inevitably to Israel's judgment. Joshua's last counsels concluded with a stirring challenge to choose the LORD, to serve Him, and were highlighted by the exhortation to put away foreign gods (24:23), shocking evidence of incipient apostasy which was already invading Israel. To Joshua's plea Israel readily responded, but this pledge was tragically forsaken after the death of Joshua and the elders associated with him.

these nations—these that remain
among you—and make marriages
with them, and go in to them and they
to you,
13 "know for certain that the LORD
your God will [a]no longer drive out
these nations from before you. But
they shall be snares and [b]traps to you,
and scourges on your sides and thorns
in your eyes, until you perish from this
good land which the LORD your God
has given you.
14 "Behold, this day I *am* going the
way of all the [c]earth. And you know
in all your hearts and in all your souls
that not one thing has [d]failed of all the
good things which the LORD your God
spoke concerning you. All have come
to pass for you; not one word of them
has failed.
15 "Therefore it shall come to pass,
that as all the good things have come
upon you which the LORD your God
promised you, so the LORD will bring
upon you [e]all harmful things, until He
has destroyed you from this good land
which the LORD your God has given
you.
16 "When you have transgressed
the covenant of the LORD your God,
which He commanded you, and have
gone and served other gods, and
bowed down to them, then the [f]anger
of the LORD will burn against you, and
you shall perish quickly from the good
land which He has given you."

Joshua reviews Israel's history

24 THEN Joshua gathered all the
tribes of Israel to Shechem and
[g]called for the elders of Israel, for
their heads, for their judges, and for
their officers; and they presented
themselves before God.
2 And Joshua said to all the people, "Thus says the LORD God of Israel:
[h]'Your fathers, *including* Terah, the
father of Abraham and the father of
Nahor, dwelt on the other side of the
[i]River in old times; and they served
other gods.
3 'Then I took your father Abraham from the other side of the [i]River,
led him throughout all the land of Canaan, and multiplied his descendants
and gave him [j]Isaac.
4 'To Isaac I gave Jacob and Esau.
To Esau I gave the [k]mountains of Seir
to possess, but Jacob and his children
went down to [l]Egypt.
5 'Also I sent Moses and Aaron,
and I plagued Egypt, according to
what I did among them. Afterward I
brought you out.
6 'Then I brought your fathers out
of Egypt, and you came to the [m]sea;
and the Egyptians pursued your fathers with chariots and horsemen to
the Red Sea.
7 'So they cried out to the LORD;
and He put [n]darkness between you
and the Egyptians, brought the sea
upon them, and covered them. And
your eyes saw what I did in Egypt.
Then you dwelt in the wilderness a
long time.
8 'And I brought you into the land
of the [o]Amorites, who dwelt on the
other side of the Jordan, and they
fought with you. But I gave them into
your hand, that you might possess
their land, and I destroyed them from
before you.
9 'Then [p]Balak the son of Zippor,
king of Moab, arose to make war
against [q]Israel, and sent and called
Balaam the son of Beor to curse you.
10 'But I would not listen to Balaam; therefore he continued to [r]bless
you. So I delivered you out of his
hand.
11 'Then you went over the Jordan
and came to Jericho. And the men of
Jericho fought against you—*also* the
Amorites, the Perizzites, the Canaanites, the [s]Hittites, the Girgashites, the
Hivites, and the Jebusites. But I delivered them into your hand.
12 'I sent the [t]hornet before you
which drove them out from before
you, *also* the two kings of the Amorites, *but* not with your sword or with
your bow.
13 'I have given you a land for
which you did not labor, and cities
which you did not build, and you
dwell in them; you [u]eat of the vineyards and olive groves which you did
not plant.'

"Choose for yourselves this day"

14 "Now therefore, [v]fear the LORD,
serve Him in sincerity and in truth,
and put away the gods which your fathers served on the other side of the
[i]River and in Egypt. Serve the LORD!
15 "And if it seems evil to you to
serve the LORD, [w]choose for yourselves this day whom you will serve,
[x]whether the gods which your fathers
served that *were* on the other side of
the [i]River, or the gods of the Amorites, in whose land you dwell. [y]But as

13
a Jud. 2:3
b Ex. 23:33
14
c 1 Ki. 2:2
d Josh. 21:45
15
e Lev. 26:14–39; Dt. 28:15–68
16
f Dt. 4:24–28
CHAPTER 24
1
g Josh. 23:2
2
h Gen. 11:7–32
i i.e. *the Euphrates*
3
j Gen. 12:3; 21:1–8
4
k Dt. 2:5
l Gen. 46:3
6
m Ex. 14:2–31
7
n Ex. 14:20
8
o Num. 21:21–35
9
p Num. 22:2–14
q *Israel* (history): vv. 1–33; Jud. 2:8. (Gen. 12:2; Rom. 11:26, *note*)
10
r Num. 24:10
11
s See 2 Ki. 7:6, *note*
12
t Ex. 23:28; Dt. 7:20
13
u Dt. 6:10–11
14
v See Ps. 19:9, *note*
15
w 1 Ki. 18:21
x Ezek. 20:39; cp. Jn. 6:66–69
y Gen. 18:19; Ps. 101:2; 1 Tim. 3:4–5

for me and my house, we will serve the
LORD."
16 So the people answered and
said: "Far be it from us that we should
forsake the LORD to serve other gods;
17 "for the LORD our God *is* He who
brought us and our fathers up out of
the land of Egypt, from the house of
bondage, who did those great signs in
our sight, and preserved us in all the
way that we went and among all the
people through whom we passed.
18 "And the LORD drove out from
before us all the people, including the
Amorites who dwelt in the land. [a]We
also will serve the LORD, for He *is* our
God."
19 But Joshua said to the people,
"You cannot serve the LORD, for He *is*
a [b]holy God. He *is* a [c]jealous God; He
will [d]not forgive your transgressions
nor your sins.
20 [e]"If you forsake the LORD and
serve [f]foreign gods, then He will turn
and do you harm and consume you,
after He has done you good."
21 And the people said to Joshua,
"No, but we will serve the LORD!"
22 So Joshua said to the people,
"You *are* witnesses against yourselves
that you have chosen the LORD for
yourselves, to serve Him." And they
said, "*We are* witnesses!"
23 "Now therefore," *he said,* [g]"put
away the [f]foreign gods which *are*
among you, and [h]incline your heart to
the LORD God of Israel."
24 And the people [i]said to Joshua,
"The LORD our God we will serve, and
His voice we will obey!"
25 So Joshua made a covenant with
the people that day, and made for
them a statute and an ordinance in
Shechem.
26 Then Joshua wrote these words
in the Book of the Law of God. And he
took a large stone, and set it up [j]there
under the oak that *was* by the sanctuary of the LORD.
27 And Joshua said to all the people, "Behold, this stone shall be a witness to us, for it has heard all the
words of the LORD which He spoke to
us. It shall therefore be a witness to
you, lest you deny your God."
28 So Joshua let the people [k]de-
part, each to his own inheritance.

Death of Joshua and Eleazar; Joseph's bones buried

29 Now it came to pass after these
things that Joshua the son of Nun, the
servant of the LORD, [l]died, *being* one
hundred and ten years old.
30 And they [m]buried him within the
border of his inheritance at Timnath
Serah, which *is* in the mountains of
Ephraim, on the north side of Mount
Gaash.
31 Israel served the LORD all the
days of Joshua, and all the days of the
elders who outlived Joshua, who had
known all the works of the LORD which
He had done for Israel.
32 The [n]bones of Joseph, which the
children of Israel had brought up out
of Egypt, they [o]buried at Shechem, in
the [p]plot of ground which Jacob had
bought from the sons of Hamor the
father of Shechem for one hundred
pieces of silver, and which had become an inheritance of the children of
Joseph.
33 And [q]Eleazar the son of Aaron
died. They buried him in a hill *belonging to* Phinehas his son, which was
given to him in the mountains of
Ephraim.

18
a Ps. 116:16
19
b Lev. 11:44–45
c Ex. 20:5
d Ex. 23:21
20
e 1 Chr. 28:9; Ezra 8:22; Isa. 63:10; 65:11–12
f See Josh. 23:2, *note*
23
g Gen. 35:2; Jud. 10:15–16; 1 Sam. 7:3; cp. 2 Cor. 6:16–18
h 1 Ki. 8:58; cp. Jer. 25:4
24
i Dt. 5:24–27
26
j Jud. 9:6
28
k Jud. 2:6–7
29
l Jud. 2:8
30
m Josh. 19:50; Jud. 2:9
32
n Gen. 50:25; Ex. 13:19; Heb. 11:22
o See Acts 7:16, *note*
p Gen. 33:19
33
q Ex. 7:23; 28:1; Num. 20:28; Josh. 14:1

The Book of

JUDGES

Author: Unknown *Theme:* Defeat and Deliverance *Date of writing:* 11th Cent. B.C.

JUDGES takes its title from the fact that it records the activities of twelve men and one woman, designated as judges and raised up by God to deliver Israel in times of declension and disunion after Joshua's death. No one was capable of such leadership as Joshua had exercised. The fourfold cycle so common in Israel's history (rebellion, retribution, repentance, and restoration) occurs repeatedly. Joshua is a book of victory; Judges is a book of defeat. Joshua, the leader, had died but God remained. There was no necessity for defeat.

The judges were chosen from different tribes. Not all of them exercised jurisdiction over the entire territory of Israel; the influence of some was local. In a number of cases their periods of administration probably overlapped. See also 2:18, *note*.

The book may be divided into six major parts:

I. Review of the Past, and Institution of the Office of Judge, 1:1—3:4.
II. Five Judges, 3:5—5:31.
III. Gideon, 6:1—9:57.
IV. Six Judges, 10:1—12:15.
V. Samson, 13:1—16:31.
VI. Confusion in Israel, 17:1—21:25.

I. View of the Past, and Institution of the Office of Judge, 1:1—3:4

State of things at the death of Joshua (1:1—2:10)

1 NOW after the [a]death of Joshua
[b]it came to pass that the children
of Israel [c]asked the LORD, [1]saying,
"Who shall be first to go up for us
against the [d]Canaanites to fight
against them?"
2 And the LORD said, [e]"Judah shall
go up. Indeed I have delivered the land
into his hand."
3 So Judah said to [f]Simeon his
brother, "Come up with me to my allotted territory, that we may fight
against the Canaanites; and I will likewise go with you to your allotted territory." And Simeon went with him.

Judah's victories

4 Then Judah went up, and the
LORD delivered the Canaanites and the
Perizzites into their hand; and they
killed ten thousand men at Bezek.
5 And they found Adoni-Bezek in
Bezek, and fought against him; and
they defeated the Canaanites and the
Perizzites.
6 Then Adoni-Bezek fled, and
they pursued him and caught him and
[2]cut off his thumbs and big toes.
7 And Adoni-Bezek said, "Seventy kings with their thumbs and big
toes cut off used to gather *scraps* under my [g]table; as I have done, so God
has repaid me." Then they brought
him to Jerusalem, and there he died.
8 Now the children of Judah
fought against [h]Jerusalem and took it;
they struck it with the edge of the
sword and set the city on fire.
9 And afterward the children of
Judah went down to fight against the
Canaanites who dwelt in the mountains, in the [i]South, and in the [j]low-
land.
10 [k]Then Judah went against the
Canaanites who dwelt in [l]Hebron.
(Now the name of Hebron *was* formerly Kirjath Arba.) And they killed
Sheshai, Ahiman, and Talmai.
11 From there they went against
the inhabitants of Debir. (The name of
Debir *was* formerly Kirjath Sepher.)
12 Then [m]Caleb said, "Whoever attacks Kirjath Sepher and takes it, to
him I will give my daughter Achsah
as wife."
13 And [n]Othniel the son of Kenaz,
Caleb's younger brother, took it; so he
gave him his daughter Achsah as wife.
14 Now it happened, when she
came *to him,* that she urged him* to
ask her father for a field. And she dismounted from *her* donkey, and Caleb
said to her, "What do you wish?"
15 So she said to him, "Give me a

CHAPTER 1
1
a Josh. 24:29
b 1400–1100 B.C. See *note 1*
c Num. 27:21
d Josh. 17:12
2
e Gen. 49:8–9; Rev. 5:5
3
f Josh. 19:1
7
g Cp. Lk. 16:21
8
h Josh. 15:63; Jud. 1:21
9
i See Gen. 12:9, *note*
j See Dt. 1:7, *note*
10
k vv. 10–15, cp. Josh. 15:13–19
l Josh. 15:13
12
m Josh. 15:16
13
n Jud. 3:9

*1:14 Septuagint and Vulgate read *he urged her.*

---

[1](1:1) Most of the events recorded in Judges occurred between 1400 and 1100 B.C. There is little indication in the Bible for precise chronology of this book, so most of the dates are in round figures. Some of the judges were contemporaries, serving in different parts of the country.

[2](1:6) "Eye for eye . . . hand for hand, foot for foot" (Ex. 21:24). As Adoni-Bezek had done to seventy kings (v. 7), so divine retribution fell upon him (Lev. 24:19; cp. Mt. 5:38–45).

[a]blessing; since you have given me
land in the [b]South, give me also
springs of water." And Caleb gave her
the upper springs and the lower
springs.
16 Now the children of the [c]Kenite,
Moses' father-in-law, went up from
the City of [d]Palms with the children of
Judah into the Wilderness of Judah,
which *lies* in the South *near* [e]Arad;
and they went and dwelt among the
people.
17 And Judah went with his
brother Simeon, and they attacked the
Canaanites who inhabited Zephath,
and utterly destroyed it. So the name
of the city was called [f]Hormah.
18 Also Judah took Gaza with its
territory, Ashkelon with its territory,
and Ekron with its territory.
19 So the LORD was with Judah.
And they drove out the mountaineers,
but they could not drive out the inhabitants of the lowland, because they
had [g]chariots of iron.
20 And they gave [h]Hebron to Caleb, as Moses had said. Then he expelled from there the [i]three sons of
Anak.

Incomplete victories of Benjamin and Manasseh

21 But the children of Benjamin did
not drive out the Jebusites who inhabited [j]Jerusalem; so the Jebusites
dwell with the children of Benjamin in
Jerusalem to this day.
22 And the house of Joseph also
went up against Bethel, and the LORD
was with them.
23 So the house of Joseph sent men
to spy out Bethel. (The name of the
city *was* formerly [k]Luz.)
24 And when the spies saw a man
coming out of the city, they said to
him, "Please show us the entrance to
the city, and [l]we will show you
mercy."
25 So he showed them the entrance
to the city, and they struck the city
with the edge of the sword; but they let
the man and all his family go.
26 And the man went to the land of
the [m]Hittites, built a city, and called its
name Luz, which *is* its name to this
day.

27 However, [n]Manasseh did not
drive out *the inhabitants of* Beth
Shean and its villages, or [o]Taanach
and its villages, or the inhabitants of
[p]Dor and its villages, or the inhabitants of Ibleam and its villages, or the
inhabitants of Megiddo and its villages; for the Canaanites were determined to dwell in that land.
28 And it came to pass, when Israel
was strong, that they put the Canaanites under [q]tribute, but did not completely drive them out.
29 Nor did [r]Ephraim drive out the
Canaanites who dwelt in Gezer; so the
Canaanites dwelt in Gezer among
them.
30 Nor did [s]Zebulun drive out the
inhabitants of Kitron or the inhabitants of Nahalol; so the Canaanites
dwelt among them, and were put under tribute.
31 Nor did [t]Asher drive out the inhabitants of Acco or the inhabitants of
Sidon, or of Ahlab, Achzib, Helbah,
Aphik, or Rehob.
32 So the Asherites dwelt among
the Canaanites, the inhabitants of the
land; for they did not drive them out.
33 Nor did [u]Naphtali drive out the
inhabitants of Beth Shemesh or the
inhabitants of Beth Anath; but they
dwelt among the Canaanites, the inhabitants of the land. Nevertheless the
inhabitants of Beth Shemesh and Beth
Anath were put under tribute to them.
34 And the Amorites forced the
children of [v]Dan into the mountains,
for they would not allow them to come
down to the valley;
35 and the Amorites were determined to dwell in Mount Heres, in Aijalon, and in Shaalbim;* yet when the
strength of the house of Joseph became greater, they were put under
tribute.
36 Now the boundary of the Amorites *was* from the Ascent of Akrabbim, from Sela, and upward.

Israel rebuked for disobedience

2 THEN the [1w]Angel of the LORD
came up from Gilgal to Bochim,

15
a Cp. 1 Ki. 9:16
b See Gen. 12:9, *note*
16
c Num. 10:29–32
d Dt. 34:3
e Num. 21:1
17
f Num. 21:3
19
g Josh. 17:18
20
h Josh. 14:9,14
i Josh. 15:14
21
j Josh. 15:63
23
k Gen. 28:19
24
l Cp. Josh. 2:12; 1 Sam. 30:15
26
m See 2 Ki. 7:6, *note*
27
n Josh. 17:11–13
o Josh. 21:25
p Josh. 17:11
28
q Josh. 17:13
29
r Josh. 16:10
30
s Josh. 19:10–16
31
t Josh. 19:24–30
33
u Josh. 19:32–39
34
v Cp. Josh. 19:47–48
CHAPTER 2
1
w *Angel* (of the LORD): vv. 1–4; Jud. 5:23. (Gen. 16:7; Jud. 2:1, *note*)

* 1:35 Spelled *Shaalabbin* in Joshua 19:42

[1](2:1) This particular Angel, as distinguished in Scripture from all others, is often referred to in the OT (cp. Gen. 16:9; 22:11; 48:16; Ex. 3:2; 14:19; Num. 22:22; Jud. 2:4; 6:11; 13:3; 2 Ki. 19:35; Isa. 63:9; Zech. 1:12; 12:8).

(1) He is named "the Angel of the LORD [*Jehovah*]" (Gen. 16:7), "the angel of God" (Gen. 21:17), "The Angel of His [God's] Presence" (Isa. 63:9), and probably "the Messenger [Angel] of the covenant" (Mal. 3:1).

and said: [a]"I led you up from Egypt and [b]brought you to the land of which I swore to your fathers; and I [c]said, 'I will never break My covenant with you.

2 'And you shall make [d]no covenant with the inhabitants of this land; you shall tear down their [e]altars.' [f]But you have not obeyed My voice. Why have you done this?

3 "Therefore I also said, 'I will not drive them out before you; but they shall be *thorns* in your side,* and their gods shall be a snare to [g]you.' "

4 So it was, when the Angel of the LORD spoke these words to all the children of Israel, that the people lifted up their voices and wept.

5 Then they called the name of that place [h]Bochim; and they sacrificed there to the LORD.

6 And when Joshua had [i]dismissed the people, the children of Israel went each to his own inheritance to possess the land.

7 So the people served the LORD all the days of Joshua, and all the days of the elders who outlived Joshua, who had seen all the great works of the LORD which He had done for Israel.

8 Now [j]Joshua the son of Nun, the servant of the LORD, died *when he was* one hundred and ten years old.

9 And they buried him within the border of his inheritance at [k]Timnath Heres, in the mountains of Ephraim, on the north side of Mount Gaash.

Wicked new generation

10 When all that generation had been gathered to their fathers, another generation arose after them who [l]did not know the LORD nor the work which He had done for Israel.

11 Then the children of Israel did [m]evil in the sight of the LORD, and served the Baals;

12 and they [n]forsook the LORD God of their fathers, who had brought them out of the land of Egypt; and they followed other gods from *among* the gods of the people who *were* all around them, and they bowed down to them; and they provoked the LORD to anger.

13 They forsook the LORD and served Baal and the [1]Ashtoreths.

14 And the anger of the LORD was [o]hot against Israel. So He [p]delivered them into the hands of plunderers who despoiled them; and He sold them into the hands of their enemies all around, so that they could no longer stand before their enemies.

15 Wherever they went out, the hand of the LORD was against them for calamity, as the LORD had said, and as the LORD had [q]sworn to them. And they were greatly distressed.

God raises up deliverers

16 Nevertheless, the LORD raised up

1
a Ex. 20:2; Jud. 6:8–9
b Dt. 11:29
c Gen. 17:7; Ex. 23:20; Ps. 89:34
2
d Ex. 23:32
e Ex. 34:12–13
f Ps. 106:34
3
g Num. 33:55; Josh. 23:13
5
h Lit. *weepers*
6
i Josh. 24:28
8
j Israel (history): vv. 8–18; 1 Sam. 8:1. (Gen. 12:2; Rom. 11:26, *note*)
9
k Or *Timnath Serah,* Josh. 19:50
10
l Cp. Dt. 6:6–25; 1 Sam. 2:12
11
m Jud. 3:7, 12; 4:1; 6:1
12
n Dt. 13:6; Jud. 8:33; 10:6

2:14 *o* Dt. 31:17 *p* 2 Ki. 17:20 **2:15** *q* Lev. 26:14–26; Dt. 28:15–68

* 2:3 Septuagint, Targum, and Vulgate read *enemies to you.*

(2) He is clearly identified with the LORD Himself in His self-manifestation to men. In Gen. 31:11–13 the Angel said to Jacob, "I am the God of Bethel." In Ex. 3:2–6 the same Angel said to Moses, "I am the God of your father—the God of Abraham."

(3) Divine attributes and prerogatives are ascribed to this Angel. He said to Hagar, "I will multiply your descendants exceedingly, so that they shall not be counted for multitude" (Gen. 16:10), and Hagar spoke of Him as the all-seeing God (v. 13). Jacob referred to Him as "the Angel who has redeemed me from all evil" (Gen. 48:16). The place where this Angel appeared was holy ground and He was to be worshiped (Ex. 3:5–6), whereas worship is sternly forbidden in the case of ordinary angels (Rev. 22:8–9). "The Angel of the LORD" was the keeper of Israel, and His voice had to be obeyed, for the name of God was in Him (Ex. 23:20–23).

(4) In the light of NT revelation, this OT Angel may properly be identified with the preincarnate Son of God. In Jud. 13:18 the angel referred to His name as "wonderful," and Isa. 9:6 gives this name to the predicted Messiah of Israel. Malachi affirmed that "the Lord" who would "suddenly come to His temple" would also be "the Messenger [Angel] of the covenant" (3:1). The identification of this Angel with our Lord harmonizes with His distinctive function in relation to the Godhead, for He is the eternal Word through whom the invisible God speaks and manifests Himself (Jn. 1:1,18).

It is significant that in the NT there is no further reference to the Angel of the LORD. The Greek definite article is used only to identify some ordinary angel previously mentioned in the context. See Mt. 1:20, where the article is absent in the Greek, and 1:24, where it properly occurs as referring back to v. 20.

[1](2:13) These were figures of Ashtoreth (see 1 Ki. 11:5), the equivalent of the Phoenician goddess of fertility, Astarte (see Dt. 16:21, *note*), which were worshiped as idols during times of spiritual declension in Israel (Jud. 10:6; 1 Sam. 7:3–4; 12:10; 31:10; 1 Ki. 11:5,33; 2 Ki. 23:13).

[a]judges who [b]delivered them out of
the hand of those who plundered
them.
17 Yet they would not listen to their
judges, but they played the harlot with
other gods, and bowed down to them.
They turned quickly from the way in
which their fathers walked, in obeying the commandments of the LORD;
they did not do so.
18 And when the LORD raised up
[1]judges for them, the LORD was with
the judge and delivered them out of
the hand of their enemies all the days
of the judge; for the LORD was [c]moved
to pity by their groaning because of
those who oppressed them and harassed them.
19 And it came to pass, when the
judge was dead, that they reverted
and behaved more corruptly than
their fathers, by following other gods,
to serve them and bow down to them.
They did not cease from their own doings nor from their stubborn way.

Canaanites left to test Israel

20 Then the anger of the LORD was
hot against Israel; and He said, "Because this nation has [d]transgressed
My covenant which I commanded
their fathers, and has not heeded My
voice,
21 "I also will no longer drive out
before them any of the nations which
Joshua [e]left when he died,
22 "so that through them I may
[f]test Israel, whether they will keep
the ways of the LORD, to walk in them
as their fathers kept *them,* or not."
23 Therefore the LORD left those nations, without driving them out immediately; nor did He deliver them into
the hand of Joshua.

Idolatry brings servitude

3 NOW these *are* the nations which
the LORD left, that He might [f]test
Israel by them, *that is,* all who had
[g]not known any of the wars in Canaan
2 (*this was* only so that the gener-

16
a Kingdom (OT): vv. 16–18; 1 Sam. 8:1. (Gen. 1:26; Zech. 12:8, *note*)
b Ps. 106:43–45
18
c Lit. *re-lented.* See Zech. 8:14, *note*
20
d Josh. 23:16
21
e Josh. 23:4, 13
22
f See Dt. 8:2, *note*
CHAPTER 3
1
g Cp. Ex. 13:17
3
h Josh. 13:3
i Josh. 13:5
5
j See 2 Ki. 7:6, *note*
6
k Ex. 34:15–16; Dt. 7:3–4; Josh. 23:12
7
l Jud. 2:11
m Dt. 32:18
n See Dt. 16:21, *note*
8
o Dt. 32:30; Jud. 2:14
9
p Jud. 2:16
q Lit. *savior*
r Jud. 1:13
10
s Holy Spirit (OT): v. 10; Jud. 6:34. (Gen. 1:2; Zech. 12:10)
11
t Cp. Josh. 14:15

ations of the children of Israel might
be taught to know war, at least those
who had not formerly known it),
3 *namely,* [h]five lords of the Philistines, all the Canaanites, the Sidonians, and the Hivites who dwelt in
Mount Lebanon, from Mount Baal
Hermon [i]to the entrance of Hamath.
4 And they were *left, that He
might* [f]test Israel by them, to know
whether they would obey the commandments of the LORD, which He had
commanded their fathers by the hand
of Moses.

II. Five Judges, 3:5—5:31

5 Thus the children of Israel dwelt
among the Canaanites, the [j]Hittites,
the Amorites, the Perizzites, the Hivites, and the Jebusites.
6 [k]And they took their daughters
to be their wives, and gave their
daughters to their sons; and they
served their gods.
7 So the children of Israel did
[l]evil in the sight of the LORD. They
[m]forgot the LORD their God, and served
the Baals and [2n]Asherahs.

*Othniel, the first judge,
defeats Mesopotamia*

8 Therefore the anger of the LORD
was hot against Israel, and He [o]sold
them into the hand of Cushan-
Rishathaim king of Mesopotamia; and
the children of Israel served Cushan-
Rishathaim eight years.
9 When the children of Israel cried
out to the LORD, the LORD [p]raised up a
[q]deliverer for the children of Israel,
who delivered them: [r]Othniel the son
of Kenaz, Caleb's younger brother.
10 The [s]Spirit of the LORD came
upon him, and he judged Israel. He
went out to war, and the LORD delivered Cushan-Rishathaim king of Mesopotamia into his hand; and his hand
prevailed over Cushan-Rishathaim.
11 So the land had [t]rest for forty
years. Then Othniel the son of Kenaz
died.

---

[1](2:18) The judges were tribesmen in Israel upon whom the LORD laid the burden of Israel's apostate and oppressed state. They were people raised up by God, the theocratic King, to represent Him in the nation. They were patriots and religious reformers because national security and prosperity were inseparably connected with loyalty and obedience to the LORD.

[2](3:7) Asherahs, like high places, have been associated with idolatrous worship from time immemorial. The Hebrew *asherah,* sometimes rendered "wooden images" in the NKJV, means also the idol enshrined there (Dt. 16:21). This idol seems often to have been a sacred tree, the figure of which is constantly found on Assyrian monuments. In apostate Israel, however, such places were associated with every form of idolatry (e.g., 2 Ki. 17:16–17). See also "high places" (1 Ki. 3:2, *note*), and "Ashtoreths" (Jud. 2:13, *note*).

Ehud, the second judge,
delivers from Moab

12 And the children of Israel again
did [a]evil in the sight of the LORD. So
the LORD strengthened Eglon king of
Moab against Israel, because they had
done evil in the sight of the [b]LORD.
13 Then he gathered to himself the
people of [c]Ammon and [d]Amalek,
went and defeated Israel, and took
possession of the [e]City of Palms.
14 So the children of Israel served
Eglon king of Moab [f]eighteen years.
15 But when the children of Israel
cried out to the LORD, the LORD raised
up a deliverer for them: Ehud the son
of Gera, the Benjamite, a [g]left-handed
man. By him the children of Israel sent
tribute to Eglon king of Moab.
16 Now Ehud made himself a dagger (it was double-edged and a [h]cubit
in length) and fastened it under his
clothes on his right thigh.
17 So he brought the tribute to Eglon king of Moab. (Now Eglon *was* a
very fat man.)
18 And when he had finished presenting the tribute, he sent away the
people who had carried the tribute.
19 But he himself turned back from
the stone images that *were* at Gilgal,
and said, "I have a secret message for
you, O king." He said, "Keep silence!"
And all who attended him went out
from him.
20 So Ehud came to him (now he
was sitting upstairs in his cool private
chamber). Then Ehud said, "I have a
message from God for you." So he
arose from *his* seat.
21 Then Ehud reached with his left
hand, took the dagger from his right
thigh, and thrust it into his belly.
22 Even the hilt went in after the
blade, and the fat closed over the
blade, for he did not draw the dagger
out of his belly; and his entrails came
out.
23 Then Ehud went out through the
porch and shut the doors of the upper
room behind him and locked them.
24 When he had gone out, *Eglon's**
servants came to look, and *to their*
surprise, the doors of the upper room
were locked. So they said, "He is probably [i]attending to his needs in the
cool chamber."
25 So they waited till they were
[j]embarrassed, and still he had not
opened the doors of the upper room.
Therefore they took the key and
opened *them*. And there was their
master, fallen dead on the floor.
26 But Ehud had escaped while
they delayed, and passed beyond the
stone images and escaped to Seirah.
27 And it happened, when he arrived, that he [k]blew the trumpet in the
mountains of Ephraim, and the children of Israel went down with him
from the mountains; and he led them.
28 Then he said to them, "Follow
me, for the LORD has delivered your
enemies the Moabites into your
hand." So they went down after him,
seized the [l]fords of the Jordan leading to Moab, and did not allow anyone
to cross over.
29 And at that time they killed
about ten thousand men of Moab, all
stout men of valor; not a man escaped.
30 So Moab was subdued that day
under the hand of Israel. And the land
had rest for eighty years.

Shamgar, the third judge,
delivers from Philistines

31 After him was [m]Shamgar the
son of Anath, who killed six hundred
men of the Philistines with an [1]ox
goad; and he also delivered Israel.

Deborah, Barak, the fourth and
fifth judges, deliver from Canaanites

4 WHEN Ehud was dead, the children of Israel [n]again did [o]evil in
the sight of the LORD.
2 So the LORD [p]sold them into the
hand of [q]Jabin king of Canaan, who
reigned in Hazor. The commander of
his army *was* Sisera, who dwelt in
[r]Harosheth Hagoyim.
3 And the children of Israel cried
out to the LORD; for Jabin had nine
hundred [s]chariots of iron, and for
[t]twenty years he had harshly oppressed the children of Israel.
4 Now Deborah, a prophetess, the
wife of Lapidoth, was judging Israel at
that time.
5 And she would sit under the
palm tree of [u]Deborah between Ramah and Bethel in the mountains of
Ephraim. And the children of Israel
came up to her for judgment.
6 Then she sent and called for
[v]Barak the son of Abinoam from [w]Ke-
desh in Naphtali, and said to him,
"Has not the LORD God of Israel com-

12
a Cp. v. 7
b Cp. 2 Ki. 5:1; Isa. 10:5,6; 45:1–6
13
c Descendants of Lot
d Descendants of Esau. Dt. 25:17,19
e Dt. 34:3; 2 Chr. 28:15
14
f Cp. v. 8; 4:3
15
g Jud. 20:16
16
h See Weights and Measures (OT), 2 Chr. 2:10, *note*
24
i 1 Sam. 24:3
25
j 2 Ki. 2:17; 8:11
27
k Jud. 6:34
28
l Jud. 2:7
31
m Jud. 5:6
CHAPTER 4
1
n Jud. 2:19
o Jud. 2:11
2
p Jud. 2:14; cp. Jud. 3:8; 1 Sam. 12:9. It seems to concern only north Israel
q Cp. Josh. 11:1,12
r vv. 13,16
3
s Dt. 20:1; Jud. 1:19
t Cp. Jud. 3:8,14
5
u Gen. 35:8
6
v Heb. 11:32
w Josh. 21:32

*3:24 Literally *his*

[1](3:31) Observe seven illustrations of 1 Cor. 1:27: (1) ox goad (v. 31); (2) tent peg (4:21); (3) trumpets; (4) pitchers; (5) torches (7:20); (6) millstone (9:53); (7) jawbone of a donkey (15:15).

manded, 'Go and deploy *troops* at
Mount [a]Tabor; take with you ten
thousand men of the sons of Naphtali
and of the sons of Zebulun;
7 'and against you [b]I will deploy
Sisera, the commander of Jabin's
army, with his chariots and his multitude at the River Kishon; and I will
deliver him into your hand'?"
8 And Barak said to her, "If you
will go with me, then I will go; but if
you will not go with me, I will not go!"
9 So she said, "I will surely go with
you; nevertheless there will be no
glory for you in the journey you are
taking, for the LORD will sell Sisera
into the hand of a [c]woman." Then
Deborah arose and went with Barak
to Kedesh.
10 And Barak called [d]Zebulun and
Naphtali to Kedesh; he went up with
ten thousand men under his command,* [e]and Deborah went up with
him.
11 Now Heber the [f]Kenite, of the
children of Hobab the father-in-law of
Moses, had separated himself from
the Kenites and pitched his tent near
the terebinth tree at Zaanaim, which
is beside Kedesh.

Sisera's defeat and death

12 And they reported to Sisera that
Barak the son of Abinoam had gone
up to Mount Tabor.
13 So Sisera [g]gathered together all
his chariots, nine hundred chariots of
iron, and all the people who *were* with
him, from Harosheth Hagoyim to the
River Kishon.
14 Then Deborah said to Barak,
"Up! For this *is* the day in which the
LORD has delivered Sisera into your
hand. Has not the LORD gone out [h]be-
fore you?" So Barak went down from
Mount Tabor with ten thousand men
following him.
15 And the [i]LORD [1]routed Sisera
and all *his* chariots and all *his* army
with the edge of the sword before
Barak; and Sisera alighted from *his*
chariot and fled away on foot.
16 But Barak pursued the chariots
and the army as far as Harosheth Hagoyim, and all the army of Sisera fell
by the edge of the sword; not a man
was [j]left.
17 However, Sisera had fled away
on foot to the tent of [k]Jael, the wife of
Heber the Kenite; for *there was* peace
between Jabin king of Hazor and the
house of Heber the Kenite.
18 And Jael went out to meet Sisera, and said to him, "Turn aside, my
lord, turn aside to me; do not fear."
And when he had turned aside with
her into the tent, she covered him with
a blanket.
19 Then he said to her, "Please give
me a little water to drink, for I am
thirsty." So she opened a jug of milk,
gave him a drink, and covered him.
20 And he said to her, "Stand at the
door of the tent, and if any man comes
and inquires of you, and says, 'Is there
any man here?' you shall say, 'No.'"
21 Then Jael, Heber's wife, took a
tent peg and took a hammer in her
hand, and went softly to him and
drove the peg into his temple, and it
went down into the ground; for he was
fast asleep and weary. So he [l]died.
22 And then, as Barak pursued Sisera, Jael came out to meet him, and
said to him, "Come, I will show you
the man whom you seek." And when
he went into her *tent*, there lay Sisera,
dead with the peg in his temple.
23 So on that day God subdued Jabin king of Canaan in the presence of
the children of Israel.
24 And the hand of the children of
Israel grew stronger and stronger
against Jabin king of Canaan, until
they had destroyed Jabin king of Canaan.

Song of Deborah and Barak

5 [m]THEN [n]Deborah and Barak the
son of Abinoam sang on that day,
saying:

2 "When leaders lead in Israel,
When the people [o]willingly
offer themselves,
Bless the LORD!

3 "Hear, O kings! Give ear, O
princes!
I, *even* [p]I, will sing to the
LORD;
I will sing praise to the LORD
God of Israel.

4 [q]"LORD, when You went out from
[r]Seir,
When You marched from the
field of Edom,

6 *a* Jud. 8:18
7 *b* Ps. 83:9; cp. Ex. 14:4
9 *c* vv. 18,21
10 *d* Jud. 5:18 *e* v. 14; cp. Dt. 20:1
11 *f* Jud. 1:16
13 *g* Lit. *gathered by cry*, or *proclamation*
14 *h* Dt. 31:3
15 *i* Dt. 7:23; cp. Josh. 10:10
16 *j* Ex. 14:28
17 *k* Jud. 5:6
21 *l* Jud. 5:24–27
CHAPTER 5
1 *m* vv. 1–31; cp. Ex. 15:1–19; Ps. 18, *title;* Rev. 15:3–4 *n* Jud. 4:4
2 *o* Cp. 2 Chr. 17:16
3 *p* Ps. 27:6
4 *q* vv. 4–5; cp. Ps. 68:7–8 *r* Dt. 33:2

* 4:10 Literally *at his feet*

[1](4:15) A hint of what led to Sisera's defeat is given in 5:21–22. God sent heavy cloudbursts; the Kishon rose, overflowing the plain. Sisera's horses and chariots became mired in the mud, so he fled on foot (v. 17).

The earth trembled and the heavens poured,
The clouds also poured water;
5 The mountains [a]gushed before the LORD,
This Sinai, before the LORD God of Israel.

6 "In the days of [b]Shamgar, son of Anath,
In the days of [c]Jael,
The highways were deserted,
And the travelers walked along the byways.
7 Village life ceased, it ceased in Israel,
Until I, Deborah, arose,
Arose a mother in Israel.
8 They chose [d]new gods;
Then *there was* war in the gates;
Not a shield or spear was seen among forty thousand in Israel.
9 My heart *is* with the rulers of Israel
Who offered themselves [e]willingly with the people.
Bless the LORD!

10 "Speak, you who ride on white [f]donkeys,
Who sit in judges' attire,
And who walk along the road.
11 Far from the noise of the archers, among the watering places,
There they shall recount the [g]righteous acts of the LORD,
The righteous acts *for* His villagers in Israel;
Then the people of the LORD shall go down to the gates.

12 [h]"Awake, awake, Deborah!
Awake, awake, sing a song!
Arise, Barak, and [i]lead your captives away,
O son of Abinoam!

13 "Then the survivors came down, the people against the nobles;
The LORD came down for me against the mighty.
14 From Ephraim *were* those whose roots were in [j]Amalek.
After you, Benjamin, with your peoples,
From Machir rulers came down,
And from Zebulun those who bear the recruiter's staff.
15 And the princes of Issachar* *were* with Deborah;
As Issachar, so *was* Barak
Sent into the valley under his command;*
Among the divisions of Reuben
There were great resolves of heart.
16 Why did you sit among the sheepfolds,
To hear the pipings for the flocks?
The divisions of Reuben have great searchings of heart.
17 [k]Gilead stayed beyond the Jordan,
And why did Dan remain on ships?*
[l]Asher continued at the seashore,
And stayed by his inlets.
18 [m]Zebulun *is* a people *who* jeopardized their lives to the point of death,
Naphtali also, on the heights of the battlefield.

19 "The kings came *and* fought,
Then the kings of Canaan fought
In [n]Taanach, by the waters of [1]Megiddo;
They took no spoils of silver.
20 They fought from the heavens;

5 [a] Lit. *flowed.* Ps. 97:5
6 [b] Jud. 3:31 [c] Jud. 4:17
8 [d] Dt. 32:17
9 [e] v. 2
10 [f] Jud. 10:4; 12:14
11 [g] Lit. *righteousnesses.* 1 Sam. 12:7
12 [h] Ps. 57:8 [i] Ps. 68:18; Eph. 4:8
14 [j] Jud. 3:13
17 [k] Josh. 22:9 [l] Josh. 19:29,31
18 [m] Jud. 4:6, 10
19 [n] Jud. 1:27

* 5:15 Following Septuagint, Syriac, Targum, and Vulgate; Masoretic Text reads *And my princes in Issachar.* • Literally *at his feet* 5:17 Or *at ease*

[1](5:19) This strongly fortified elevation, on the northern side of the great plains of Jezreel, was one of a chain of cities that remained unconquered during the period of the judges (e.g. Josh. 17:11; Jud. 1:27). Later Solomon's huge stables were built here. The famous battle between the Syrian states and the Egyptians under Thutmose III (c. 1500 B.C.) took place at Megiddo. This is recorded in ancient literature in such detail as to provide the starting point for the history of military science.

Megiddo commanded the pass between the plains of Jezreel and Sharon, and for this reason was the scene of several battles recorded in the Scriptures: (1) Deborah's victory (Jud. 4:10–24); (2) Gideon's victory (Jud. 6:33; cp. 7:1–25); (3) Saul's defeat (1 Sam. 31:1; cp. 29:1); and (4) the death of King Josiah in battle with Pharaoh Necho (2 Ki. 23:28–30; 2 Chr. 35:20–24).

The last great battle of this age will be fought here at Armageddon (Rev. 16:12–16; 17:14; see Rev. 19:17, *note*).

The [a]stars from their courses
fought against Sisera.
21 The torrent of Kishon swept
them away,
That ancient torrent, the
torrent of Kishon.
O my soul, march on in
strength!
22 Then the horses' hooves
pounded,
The galloping, galloping of his
steeds.
23 'Curse Meroz,' said the [b]angel
of the LORD,
'Curse its inhabitants bitterly,
Because they did not come to
the help of the LORD,
To the help of the LORD against
the mighty.'

24 "Most blessed among women is
Jael,
The wife of Heber the Kenite;
Blessed is she among women
in tents.
25 He asked for water, she gave
milk;
She brought out cream in a
lordly bowl.
26 She stretched her hand to the
tent peg,
Her right hand to the
workmen's hammer;
She pounded Sisera, she
pierced his head,
She split and struck through
his temple.
27 At her feet he sank, he fell, he
lay still;
At her feet he sank, he fell;
Where he sank, there he fell
[c]dead.

28 "The mother of Sisera looked
through the window,
And cried out through the
lattice,
'Why is his chariot *so* long in
coming?
Why tarries the clatter of his
chariots?'
29 Her wisest ladies answered
her,
Yes, she answered herself,
30 'Are they not finding and
dividing the [d]spoil:
To every man a girl *or* two;
For Sisera, plunder of dyed
garments,
Plunder of garments
embroidered and dyed,
Two pieces of dyed embroidery
for the neck of the looter?'

31 "Thus let all Your enemies
[e]perish, O LORD!
But *let* those who love Him *be*
[f]like the [g]sun
When it comes out in full
[h]strength."

So the land had rest for forty years.

III. Gideon, 6:1—9:57

Israel sins; Midian oppresses

6 THEN the children of Israel did
[i]evil in the sight of the LORD. So
the LORD delivered them into the hand
of [j]Midian for seven years,
2 and the hand of Midian prevailed against Israel. Because of the
Midianites, the children of Israel
made for themselves the dens, the
[k]caves, and the strongholds which *are*
in the mountains.
3 So it was, whenever Israel had
sown, Midianites would come up; also
Amalekites and the [l]people of the
East would come up against them.
4 Then they would encamp
against them and [m]destroy the produce of the earth as far as Gaza, and
leave no sustenance for Israel, neither
sheep nor ox nor [n]donkey.
5 For they would come up with
their livestock and their tents, coming
in as numerous as locusts; both they
and their camels were without number; and they would enter the land to
destroy it.
6 So Israel was greatly impoverished because of the Midianites, and
the children of Israel [o]cried out to the
LORD.
7 And it came to pass, when the
children of Israel cried out to the LORD
because of the Midianites,
8 that the LORD sent a [p]prophet to
the children of Israel, who said to
them, "Thus says the LORD God of Israel: 'I brought you up from Egypt and
brought you out of the [q]house of
bondage;
9 'and I delivered you out of the
hand of the Egyptians and out of the
hand of all who oppressed you, and
drove them out before you and gave
you their land.
10 'Also I said to you, "I *am* the
LORD your God; do not fear the gods of
the Amorites, in whose land you
dwell." But you have not obeyed My
[r]voice.' "

Gideon appointed the sixth judge

11 Now the [b]Angel of the LORD
came and sat under the terebinth tree
which *was* in Ophrah, which *belonged*

20
a Cp. Josh. 10:11–12
23
b Angel (of the LORD): vv. 23–31; 6:11–24; Jud. 13:3. (Gen. 16:7; Jud. 2:1, *note*)
27
c Jud. 4:18–21
30
d Ex. 15:9
31
e Ps. 92:9
f 2 Sam. 23:4
g Ps. 37:6; 89:36–37
h Ps. 19:5
CHAPTER 6
1
i Jud. 2:11
j Num. 22:4; 31:1–3
2
k 1 Sam. 13:6
3
l Jud. 7:12
4
m Lev. 26:16
n Dt. 28:31
6
o Ps. 50:15; Hos. 5:15
8
p Cp. 1 Sam. 2:27
q Josh. 24:17
10
r Jud. 2:1–2

to Joash the [a]Abiezrite, while his son
[b]Gideon threshed wheat in the winepress, in order to hide *it* from the Midianites.
12 And the Angel of the LORD appeared to him, and said to him, "The
LORD *is* with you, you mighty man of
valor!"
13 Gideon said to Him, "O my
lord,* [c]if the LORD is with us, why then
has all this happened to us? And
where *are* all His miracles which our
fathers [d]told us about, saying, 'Did
not the LORD bring us up from Egypt?'
But now the LORD [e]has forsaken us
and delivered us into the hands of the
Midianites."
14 Then the LORD turned to him and
said, "Go in this might of yours, and
you shall save Israel from the hand of
the Midianites. Have I not sent [f]you?"
15 So he said to Him, "O my Lord,*
how can [g]I save Israel? Indeed my
clan *is* the weakest in Manasseh, and
I *am* the [h]least in my father's house."
16 And the LORD said to him,
"Surely I will be with [i]you, and you
shall defeat the Midianites as one
man."
17 Then he said to Him, "If now I
have found favor in Your sight, then
show me a [j]sign that it is You who
talk with me.
18 [k]"Do not depart from here, I
pray, until I come to You and bring out
my offering and set *it* before You."
And He said, "I will wait until you
come back."
19 So Gideon went in and [l]pre-
pared a young goat, and unleavened
bread from an [m]ephah of flour. The
meat he put in a basket, and he put the
broth in a pot; and he brought *them*
out to Him under the terebinth tree
and presented *them*.
20 The Angel of God said to him,
"Take the meat and the unleavened
bread and lay *them* on this [n]rock, and
[o]pour out the broth." And he did so.
21 Then the Angel of the LORD put
out the end of the [p]staff that *was* in
His hand, and touched the meat and
the unleavened bread; and [q]fire rose
out of the rock and consumed the
meat and the unleavened bread. And
the Angel of the LORD departed out of
his sight.
22 Now Gideon [r]perceived that He
was the Angel of the LORD. So Gideon
said, "Alas, O Lord GOD! For I have
seen the Angel of the LORD [s]face to
face."
23 Then the LORD said to him,

11
a Josh. 17:2
b Jud. 7:1; Heb. 11:32
13
c Cp. Gen. 25:22; Ps. 44:9–25
d Josh. 4:6, 21
e Dt. 31:17; Ps. 44:9
14
f Josh. 1:9
15
g Cp. Ex. 3:11
h Cp. 1 Sam. 9:21
16
i Ex. 3:12; Josh. 1:5
17
j Cp. Isa. 38:7–8
18
k Cp. Gen. 19:1–3; Jud. 13:15
19
l Gen. 18:6–8
m See Weights and Measures (OT), 2 Chr. 2:10, *note*
20
n Jud. 13:19
o Cp. 1 Ki. 18:33–34
21
p Cp. Mk. 6:8
q Lev. 9:24
22
r Jud. 13:21
s Cp. Gen. 32:30; Ex. 33:20; Jud. 13:22
24
t See Ex. 34:6, *note*
25
u Jud. 2:2
v Jud. 3:7
w See Dt. 16:21 and Jud. 3:7, *notes*
30
x Cp. Dt. 13:6–9
31
y Cp. 1 Ki. 18:27
32
z Lit. *let Baal plead*

"Peace *be* with you; do not fear, you
shall not die."
24 So Gideon built an altar there to
the LORD, and called it [t]The-LORD-*Is*-
Peace.* To this day it *is* still in Ophrah
of the Abiezrites.

Gideon repudiates Baal;
calls Israel to arms

25 Now it came to pass the same
night that the LORD said to him, "Take
your father's young bull, the second
bull of seven years old, and [u]tear
down the altar of [v]Baal that your father has, and cut down the [w]wooden
image that *is* beside it;
26 "and build an altar to the LORD
your God on top of this rock in the
proper arrangement, and take the second bull and offer a burnt sacrifice
with the wood of the [w]image which
you shall cut down."
27 So Gideon took ten men from
among his servants and did as the
LORD had said to him. But because he
feared his father's household and the
men of the city too much to do *it* by
day, he did *it* by night.
28 And when the men of the city
arose early in the morning, there was
the altar of Baal, torn down; and the
[w]wooden image that *was* beside it was
cut down, and the second bull was being offered on the altar *which had*
been built.
29 So they said to one another,
"Who has done this thing?" And when
they had inquired and asked, they
said, "Gideon the son of Joash has
done this thing."
30 Then the men of the city said to
Joash, "Bring out your son, that he
may [x]die, because he has torn down
the altar of Baal, and because he has
cut down the [w]wooden image that *was*
beside it."
31 But Joash said to all who stood
against him, "Would you plead for
Baal? Would you save him? Let the
one who would plead for him be put to
death by morning! [y]If he *is* a god, let
him plead for himself, because his altar has been torn down!"
32 Therefore on that day he called
him [z]Jerubbaal, saying, "Let Baal
plead against him, because he has
torn down his altar."
33 Then all the Midianites and Amalekites, the people of the East, gathered together; and they crossed over

*
6:13 Hebrew *adoni*, used of man **6:15** Hebrew *Adonai*, used of God **6:24** Hebrew *YHWH Shalom*

and encamped in the [a]Valley of Jezreel.
34 But the [b]Spirit of the LORD came
upon Gideon; then he [c]blew the trumpet, and the Abiezrites gathered behind him.
35 And he sent messengers
throughout all Manasseh, who also
gathered behind him. He also sent
messengers to [d]Asher, [e]Zebulun, and
Naphtali; and they came up to meet
them.
36 So Gideon said to God, [f]"If You
will save Israel by my hand as You
have said—
37 "look, I shall put a fleece of wool
on the threshing floor; if there is dew
on the [1]fleece only, and *it is* dry on all
the ground, then I shall know that You
will save Israel by my hand, as You
have said."
38 And it was so. When he rose
early the next morning and squeezed
the fleece together, he wrung the dew
out of the fleece, a bowlful of water.
39 Then Gideon said to God, "Do
not be angry with me, but let me speak
just [g]once more: Let me [h]test, I pray,
just once more with the fleece; let it
now be dry only on the fleece, but on
all the ground let there be dew."
40 And God did so that night. It was
dry on the fleece only, but there was
dew on all the ground.

Three hundred alert warriors chosen

7 THEN [i]Jerubbaal (that *is*, Gideon) and all the people who *were*
with him rose early and encamped beside the well of Harod, so that the
camp of the Midianites was on the
north side of them by the hill of Moreh
in the valley.
2 And the LORD said to Gideon,
"The people who *are* with you *are* too
many for Me to give the Midianites
into their hands, lest Israel [j]claim
glory for itself against Me, saying, 'My
own hand has saved me.'
3 "Now therefore, proclaim in the
[k]hearing of the people, saying, 'Whoever *is* fearful and afraid, let him turn
and depart at once from Mount Gilead.'" And twenty-two thousand of
the people returned, and ten thousand
remained.
4 But the LORD said to Gideon,

33
a Josh. 17:16; Hos. 1:5
34
b Holy Spirit (OT): v. 34; Jud. 11:29. (Gen. 1:2; Zech. 12:10)
c Jud. 3:27
35
d Jud. 5:17; 7:23
e Jud. 4:6, 10; 5:18
36
f vv. 14–16
39
g Cp. Gen. 18:32
h Test/tempt: v. 39; 2 Sam. 24:1. (Gen. 3:1; Jas. 1:14, *note*)
CHAPTER 7
1
i Jud. 6:32
2
j Dt. 8:17; 1 Cor. 1:29; 2 Cor. 4:7; cp. Isa. 10:13; Rom. 11:18; Jas. 4:6
3
k Dt. 20:8
4
l Cp. 1 Sam. 14:6
8
m Josh. 9:11
9
n Jud. 6:25
11
o Lit. *ranks by five.* Ex. 13:18
12
p Jud. 6:3, 33
q Jud. 8:10

"The people *are* still [l]*too* many; bring
them down to the water, and I will test
them for you there. Then it will be,
that of whom I say to you, 'This one
shall go with you,' the same shall go
with you; and of whomever I say to
you, 'This one shall not go with you,'
the same shall not go."
5 So he brought the people down
to the water. And the LORD said to Gideon, "Everyone who laps from the water with his tongue, as a dog laps, you
shall set apart by himself; likewise everyone who gets down on his knees to
drink."
6 And the number of those who
lapped, *putting* their hand to their
mouth, was three hundred men; but
all the rest of the people got down on
their knees to drink water.
7 Then the LORD said to Gideon,
"By the three hundred men who
lapped I will save you, and deliver the
Midianites into your hand. Let all the
other people go, every man to his
place."
8 So the people took [m]provisions
and their trumpets in their hands. And
he sent away all *the rest of* Israel, every man to his tent, and retained those
three hundred men. Now the camp of
Midian was below him in the valley.

Decisive victory over Midian

9 It happened on the [n]same night
that the LORD said to him, "Arise, go
down against the camp, for I have delivered it into your hand.
10 "But if you are afraid to go down,
go down to the camp with Purah your
servant,
11 "and you shall hear what they
say; and afterward your hands shall
be strengthened to go down against
the camp." Then he went down with
Purah his servant to the outpost of the
[o]armed men who *were* in the camp.
12 Now the Midianites and Amalekites, all the [p]people of the East,
were lying in the valley as [q]numerous
as locusts; and their camels *were*
without number, as the sand by the
seashore in multitude.
13 And when Gideon had come,
there was a man telling a dream to his
companion. He said, "I have had a
dream: *To my* surprise, a loaf of bar-

[1](6:37) Gideon was not here seeking to learn God's will, because that had already been clearly revealed to him (vv. 14,16). He put out the fleece for two reasons: (1) to strengthen the weakness of his own faith; and (2) to give him evidence that would convince the people that he was really God's instrument. This is not to be taken as the usual method for discovering God's will. See Prov. 3:5–6; Jas. 1:5–8.

ley bread tumbled into the camp of
Midian; it came to a tent and struck it
so that it fell and overturned, and the
tent collapsed."
14 Then his companion answered
and said, "This *is* nothing else but the
sword of Gideon the son of Joash, a
man of Israel! Into his hand [a]God has
delivered Midian and the whole
camp."
15 And so it was, when Gideon
heard the telling of the dream and its
interpretation, that he worshiped. He
returned to the camp of Israel, and
said, "Arise, for the LORD has delivered
the camp of Midian into your hand."
16 Then he divided the three hundred men *into* three companies, and
he put a trumpet into every man's
hand, with empty pitchers, and
torches inside the pitchers.
17 And he said to them, "Look at
me and do likewise; watch, and when
I come to the edge of the camp you
shall do as I do:
18 "When I blow the trumpet, I and
all who *are* with me, then you also
blow the trumpets on every side of the
whole camp, and say, '*The sword of*
the LORD and of Gideon!' "
19 So Gideon and the hundred men
who *were* with him came to the outpost of the camp at the beginning of
the middle watch, just as they had
posted the watch; and they blew the
trumpets and broke the pitchers that
were in their hands.
20 Then the three companies blew
the trumpets and broke the pitchers—
they held the torches in their left
hands and the trumpets in their right
hands for blowing—and they cried,
"The sword of the LORD and of Gideon!"
21 And every man [b]stood in his
place all around the camp; and the
whole army ran and cried out and
[c]fled.
22 When the three hundred [d]blew
the trumpets, the LORD set every man's
sword against his companion
throughout the whole camp; and the
army fled to Beth Acacia,* toward
Zererah, as far as the border of [e]Abel
Meholah, by Tabbath.

Other Israelites join pursuit

23 And the men of Israel gathered
together from [f]Naphtali, Asher, and
all Manasseh, and pursued the Midianites.
24 Then Gideon sent messengers
throughout all the mountains of
Ephraim, saying, "Come down
against the Midianites, and seize from
them the watering places as far as
[g]Beth Barah and the [h]Jordan." Then
all the men of Ephraim gathered together and seized the watering places
as far as Beth Barah and the Jordan.
25 And they captured two princes
of the [i]Midianites, [j]Oreb and Zeeb.
They killed Oreb at the rock of Oreb,
and Zeeb they killed at the winepress
of Zeeb. They pursued Midian and
brought the heads of Oreb and Zeeb to
Gideon on the other side of the Jordan.

Zebah and Zalmunna slain

8 NOW the men of [1]Ephraim said to
him, "Why have you done this to
us by not calling us when you went to
fight with the Midianites?" And they
reprimanded him sharply.
2 So he said to them, "What have
I done now in comparison with you? *Is*
not the gleaning *of the grapes* of
Ephraim better than the vintage of
[k]Abiezer?
3 "God has delivered into your
hands the princes of Midian, Oreb and
Zeeb. And what was I able to do in
comparison with you?" Then their anger toward him subsided when he said
that.
4 When Gideon came [l]to the Jordan, he and [m]the three hundred men
who *were* with him crossed over, exhausted but still in pursuit.
5 Then he said to the men of Succoth, "Please give loaves of bread to
the people who follow me, for they are
exhausted, and I am pursuing Zebah
and Zalmunna, kings of Midian."
6 And the leaders of Succoth said,
"*Are* the hands of Zebah and Zalmunna now in your hand, that we
should give bread to your [n]army?"
7 So Gideon said, "For this cause,
when the LORD has delivered Zebah
and Zalmunna into my hand, then I
will tear your flesh with the thorns of
the wilderness and with [o]briers!"
8 Then he went up from there to
Penuel and spoke to them in the same

14
a Jud. 6:14, 16
21
b Cp. Ex. 14:13–14; 2 Chr. 20:17
c Cp. 2 Ki. 7:7
22
d Cp. Josh. 6:16,20
e 1 Ki. 4:12
23
f Jud. 6:35
24
g Or *Beth Arabah*, Josh. 15:6, 61; 18:22
h Jud. 3:28
25
i Ps. 83:9
j Ps. 83:11; Isa. 10:26
CHAPTER 8
2
k Jud. 6:11
4
l Jud. 7:25
m Jud. 7:6
6
n Cp. 1 Sam. 25:11
7
o v. 16

*7:22 Hebrew *Beth Shittah*

[1](8:1) Compare Jud. 12:1; 1 Ki. 12:16–17. Here begins the deep-rooted severance in Israel which culminated in the division of Solomon's kingdom into Israel under Jeroboam, and Judah under Rehoboam.

way. And the men of Penuel answered him as the men of Succoth had answered.

9 So he also spoke to the men of Penuel, saying, "When I come back in peace, I will tear down this [a]tower!"

10 Now Zebah and Zalmunna *were* at Karkor, and their armies with them, about fifteen thousand, all who were left of all the army of the people of the East; for [b]one hundred and twenty thousand men who drew the sword had fallen.

11 Then Gideon went up by the road of those who dwell in tents on the east of [c]Nobah and Jogbehah; and he attacked the army while the camp felt secure.

12 When Zebah and Zalmunna fled, he pursued them; and he took the two kings of Midian, Zebah and Zalmunna, and routed the whole army.

13 Then Gideon the son of Joash returned from battle, from the Ascent of Heres.

14 And he caught a young man of the men of Succoth and interrogated him; and he [d]wrote down for him the leaders of Succoth and its elders, seventy-seven men.

15 Then he came to the men of Succoth and said, "Here are Zebah and Zalmunna, about whom you ridiculed me, saying, '*Are* the hands of Zebah and Zalmunna now in your hand, that we should give bread to your weary men?' "

16 And he took the elders of the city, and thorns of the wilderness and [e]briers, and with them he taught the men of Succoth.

17 Then he tore down the [f]tower of Penuel and killed the men of the city.

18 And he said to Zebah and Zalmunna, "What kind of men *were they* whom you killed at [g]Tabor?" So they answered, "As you *are,* so *were* they; each one resembled the son of a king."

19 Then he said, "They *were* my brothers, the sons of my mother. *As* the LORD lives, if you had let them live, I would not kill you."

20 And he said to Jether his firstborn, "Rise, kill them!" But the youth would not draw his sword; for he was afraid, because he *was* still a youth.

21 So Zebah and Zalmunna said, "Rise yourself, and kill us; for as a man *is, so is* his strength." So Gideon arose and killed [h]Zebah and Zalmunna, and took the crescent ornaments that *were* on their camels' necks.

9
a v. 17
10
b Jud. 6:5; 7:12; Isa. 9:4
11
c Num. 32:42
14
d See Ex. 17:14, *note*
16
e v. 7
17
f v. 9
18
g Ps. 89:12
21
h Ps. 83:11
22
i Jud. 9:8
j Jud. 3:9; 9:17
24
k Ex. 15:9
26
l See Weights and Measures (OT), 2 Chr. 2:10, *note*
27
m See Ex. 29:5, *note*
n Jud. 6:11, 24
o Jud. 2:17
p Ps. 106:36
28
q Jud. 5:31
29
r Jud. 6:32; 7:1
30
s Jud. 9:2,5
31
t Jud. 9:1
33
u Jud. 2:19
v Jud. 6:25
w Jud. 9:4
34
x Dt. 4:9; Jud. 3:7
35
y Jud. 9:16, 18

Forty years' rest under Gideon

22 Then the men of Israel said to Gideon, [i]"Rule over us, both you and your son, and your grandson also; for you have [j]delivered us from the hand of Midian."

23 But Gideon said to them, "I will not rule over you, nor shall my son rule over you; the LORD shall rule over you."

24 Then Gideon said to them, "I would like to make a request of you, that each of you would give me the earrings from his [k]plunder." For they had golden earrings, because they *were* Ishmaelites.

25 So they answered, "We will gladly give *them.*" And they spread out a garment, and each man threw into it the earrings from his plunder.

26 Now the weight of the gold earrings that he requested was one thousand seven hundred [l]*shekels* of gold, besides the crescent ornaments, pendants, and purple robes which *were* on the kings of Midian, and besides the chains that *were* around their camels' necks.

27 Then Gideon made it into an [m]ephod and set it up in his city, [n]Ophrah. And all Israel [o]played the harlot with it there. It became a [p]snare to Gideon and to his house.

28 Thus Midian was subdued before the children of Israel, so that they lifted their heads no more. And the country was [q]quiet for forty years in the days of Gideon.

29 Then [r]Jerubbaal the son of Joash went and dwelt in his own house.

30 Gideon had seventy [s]sons who were his own offspring, for he had many wives.

31 And his concubine who *was* in Shechem also bore him a son, whose name he called [t]Abimelech.

32 Now Gideon the son of Joash died at a good old age, and was buried in the tomb of Joash his father, in Ophrah of the Abiezrites.

Confusion after Gideon's death

33 So it was, [u]as soon as Gideon was dead, that the children of Israel again played the harlot with the [v]Baals, and made [w]Baal-Berith their god.

34 Thus the children of Israel [x]did not remember the LORD their God, who had delivered them from the hands of all their enemies on every side;

35 nor did they show kindness to the [y]house of Jerubbaal (Gideon) in

accordance with the good he had done for Israel.

Career of Gideon's son, Abimelech

9 THEN Abimelech the son of Jerubbaal went to Shechem, to his mother's brothers, and spoke with them and with all the family of the house of his mother's father, saying,

2 "Please speak in the [a]hearing of all the men of Shechem: 'Which is better for you, that all seventy of the sons of Jerubbaal reign over you, or that one reign over you?' Remember that I *am* your own flesh and bone."

3 And his mother's brothers spoke all these words concerning him in the hearing of all the men of Shechem; and their heart was inclined to follow Abimelech, for they said, "He is our brother."

4 So they gave him seventy *shekels* of silver from the temple of [b]Baal-Berith, with which Abimelech hired [c]worthless and reckless men; and they followed him.

5 Then he went to his father's house at Ophrah and [d]killed his brothers, the seventy sons of Jerubbaal, on one stone. But Jotham the youngest son of Jerubbaal was left, because he hid himself.

6 And all the men of Shechem gathered together, all of Beth Millo, and they went and made Abimelech king beside the [e]terebinth tree at the pillar that *was* in Shechem.

7 Now when they told Jotham, he went and stood on top of Mount Gerizim, and lifted his voice and cried out. And he said to them:

"Listen to me, you men of
Shechem,
That God may listen to you!

8 "The [f]trees once went forth to
anoint a king over them.
And they said to the olive tree,
[g]'Reign over us!'

9 But the olive tree said to them,
'Should I cease giving my oil,
With which they honor God
and men,
And go to sway over trees?'

10 "Then the trees said to the fig
tree,
'You come *and* reign over us!'

11 But the fig tree said to them,
'Should I cease my sweetness
and my good fruit,
And go to sway over trees?'

12 "Then the trees said to the vine,
'You come *and* reign over us!'

13 But the vine said to them,
'Should I cease my new wine,
Which cheers *both* God and
men,
And go to sway over trees?'

14 "Then all the trees said to the
bramble,
'You come *and* reign over us!'

15 And the bramble said to the
trees,
'If in truth you anoint me as
king over you,
Then come *and* [h]take shelter
in my shade;
But if not, let fire come out of
the bramble
And devour the cedars of
Lebanon!'

16 "Now therefore, if you have acted in truth and sincerity in making Abimelech king, and if you have dealt well with Jerubbaal and his house, and have done to him as he deserves—

17 "for my [i]father fought for you, risked his life, and [j]delivered you out of the hand of Midian;

18 "but [k]you have risen up against my father's house this day, and killed his seventy sons on one stone, and made Abimelech, the son of his [l]female servant, king over the men of Shechem, because he is your brother—

19 "if then you have acted in truth and sincerity with Jerubbaal and with his house this day, *then* rejoice in Abimelech, and let him also rejoice in you.

20 "But if not, let fire come from [m]Abimelech and devour the men of Shechem and Beth Millo; and let fire come from the men of Shechem and from Beth Millo and devour Abimelech!"

21 And Jotham ran away and fled; and he went to Beer and dwelt there, for fear of Abimelech his brother.

Abimelech and Shechem punished

22 After Abimelech had reigned over Israel three years,

23 God [n]sent a [o]spirit of ill will between Abimelech and the men of Shechem; and the men of Shechem dealt treacherously with Abimelech,

24 that the crime *done* to the seventy sons of Jerubbaal might be [p]settled and their [q]blood be laid on Abimelech their brother, who killed them, and on the men of Shechem, who

CHAPTER 9

2
a Cp. Josh. 20:4

4
b Jud. 8:33
c Jud. 11:3

5
d Cp. 2 Ki. 10:7; 11:1–2

6
e Gen. 35:4; Josh. 24:26

8
f *Parables* (OT): vv. 7–15; 2 Sam. 12:1. (Jud. 9:8; Zech. 11:7)
g Jud. 8:22–23

15
h See Ps. 2:12, *note*

17
i Jud. 7
j Jud. 8:22

18
k Jud. 8:35
l Jud. 8:31

20
m Jud. 9:45

23
n 1 Ki. 12:15; Isa. 19:14
o 1 Sam. 16:14

24
p vv. 55–56; cp. Jud. 1:7
q Num. 35:33

aided him in the killing of his brothers.
25 And the men of Shechem set
men in ambush against him on the
tops of the mountains, and they
robbed all who passed by them along
that way; and it was told Abimelech.
26 Now Gaal the son of Ebed came
with his brothers and went over to
Shechem; and the men of Shechem
put their confidence in him.
27 So they went out into the fields,
and gathered *grapes* from their vineyards and trod *them,* and made merry.
And they went into the house of their
god, and ate and drank, and cursed
Abimelech.
28 Then Gaal the son of Ebed said,
"Who [a]*is* Abimelech, and who *is* Shechem, that we should serve him? *Is he*
not the son of Jerubbaal, and *is not*
Zebul his officer? Serve the men of
[b]Hamor the father of Shechem; but
why should we serve him?
29 [c]"If only this people were under
my authority!* Then I would remove
Abimelech." So he* said to Abimelech, "Increase your army and come
out!"
30 When Zebul, the ruler of the
city, heard the words of Gaal the son
of Ebed, his anger was aroused.
31 And he sent messengers to
Abimelech secretly, saying, "Take
note! Gaal the son of Ebed and his
brothers have come to Shechem; and
here they are, fortifying the city
against you.
32 "Now therefore, get up by night,
you and the people who *are* with you,
and lie in wait in the field.
33 "And it shall be, as soon as the
sun is up in the morning, *that* you
shall rise early and rush upon the city;
and *when* he and the people who are
with him come out against you, you
may then do to them as you find opportunity."
34 So Abimelech and all the people
who *were* with him rose by night, and
lay in wait against Shechem in four
companies.
35 When Gaal the son of Ebed went
out and stood in the entrance to the
city gate, Abimelech and the people
who *were* with him rose from lying in
wait.
36 And when Gaal saw the people,
he said to Zebul, "Look, people are
coming down from the tops of the
mountains!" But Zebul said to him,
"You see the shadows of the mountains as *if they were* men."

28
[a] Cp. 1 Sam. 25:10; 1 Ki. 12:16
[b] Josh. 24:32
29
[c] Ps. 10:3; cp. 2 Sam. 15:4
45
[d] v. 20
[e] 2 Ki. 3:25
46
[f] Jud. 8:33

37 So Gaal spoke again and said,
"See, people are coming down from
the center of the land, and another
company is coming from the Diviners'* Terebinth Tree."
38 Then Zebul said to him, "Where
indeed *is* your mouth now, with which
you said, 'Who is Abimelech, that we
should serve him?' *Are* not these the
people whom you despised? Go out, if
you will, and fight with them now."
39 So Gaal went out, leading the
men of Shechem, and fought with
Abimelech.
40 And Abimelech chased him, and
he fled from him; and many fell
wounded, to the *very* entrance of the
gate.
41 Then Abimelech dwelt at Aru-
mah, and Zebul drove out Gaal and
his brothers, so that they would not
dwell in Shechem.
42 And it came about on the next
day that the people went out into the
field, and they told Abimelech.
43 So he took his people, divided
them into three companies, and lay in
wait in the field. And he looked, and
there were the people, coming out of
the city; and he rose against them and
attacked them.
44 Then Abimelech and the company that *was* with him rushed forward and stood at the entrance of the
gate of the city; and the *other* two
companies rushed upon all who *were*
in the fields and killed them.
45 So Abimelech fought against the
city all that day; [d]he took the city and
killed the people who *were* in it; and
he [e]demolished the city and sowed it
with salt.
46 Now when all the men of the
tower of Shechem had heard *that,*
they entered the stronghold of the
[f]temple of the god Berith.
47 And it was told Abimelech that
all the men of the tower of Shechem
were gathered together.
48 Then Abimelech went up to
Mount Zalmon, he and all the people
who *were* with him. And Abimelech
took an ax in his hand and cut down
a bough from the trees, and took it and
laid *it* on his shoulder; then he said to
the people who were with him, "What
you have seen me do, make haste *and*
do as I *have done.*"
49 So each of the people likewise

*

9:29 Literally *hand* • Following Masoretic Text and Targum; Dead Sea Scrolls read *they;* Septuagint reads *I.* 9:37 Hebrew *Meonenim*

cut down his own bough and followed
Abimelech, put *them* against the
stronghold, and set the stronghold on
fire above them, so that all the people
of the tower of Shechem died, about a
thousand men and women.
50 Then Abimelech went to Thebez, and he encamped against Thebez
and took it.
51 But there was a strong tower in
the city, and all the men and women—
all the people of the city—fled there
and shut themselves in; then they
went up to the top of the tower.
52 So Abimelech came as far as the
tower and fought against it; and he
drew near the door of the tower to
burn it with fire.
53 But a certain woman [a]dropped
an upper millstone on Abimelech's
head and crushed his skull.
54 Then he called quickly to the
young man, his [b]armorbearer, and
said to him, "Draw your sword and
kill me, lest men say of me, 'A woman
killed him.' " So his young man thrust
him through, and he died.
55 And when the men of Israel saw
that Abimelech was dead, they departed, every man to his place.
56 Thus God [c]repaid the wickedness of Abimelech, which he had done
to his father by killing his seventy
brothers.
57 And all the evil of the men of
Shechem God returned on their own
heads, and on them came the [d]curse
of Jotham the son of Jerubbaal.

IV. Six Judges, 10:1—12:15

Tola, the seventh judge (23 years)

10 AFTER Abimelech there arose
to save Israel Tola the son of
Puah, the son of Dodo, a man of Issachar; and he dwelt in Shamir in the
mountains of Ephraim.
2 He judged Israel twenty-three
years; and he died and was buried in
Shamir.

Jair, the eighth judge (22 years)

3 After him arose Jair, a Gileadite;
and he judged Israel twenty-two
years.
4 Now he had [e]thirty sons who
rode on thirty [f]donkeys; they also had
thirty towns, which are called [g]"Havoth Jair" to this day, which *are* in the
land of Gilead.
5 And Jair died and was buried in
Camon.

53
[a] 2 Sam. 11:21
54
[b] Cp. 1 Sam. 31:4
56
[c] v. 24
57
[d] vv. 20,45. Cp. Gen. 27:12
CHAPTER 10
4
[e] Cp. Jud. 12:9
[f] Jud. 5:10; 12:14
[g] Lit. *towns of Jair.* Num. 32:41
6
[h] Jud. 6:1; 13:1
[i] Jud. 2:13
[j] Heb. *Aram*
7
[k] Jud. 4:2
[l] Jud. 13:1
[m] Jud. 3:13
8
[n] Num. 32:33
10
[o] Jud. 6:6
[p] Num. 21:7
11
[q] Jud. 3:31
12
[r] Jud. 7:12
13
[s] Cp. Dt. 31:17; 1 Ki. 9:9
14
[t] Dt. 32:37–38

*Servitude under Philistines
and Ammonites (18 years)*

6 Then the children of Israel again
did [h]evil in the sight of the LORD, and
[i]served the Baals and the Ashtoreths,
the gods of [j]Syria, the gods of Sidon,
the gods of Moab, the gods of the people of Ammon, and the gods of the
Philistines; and they forsook the LORD
and did not serve Him.
7 So the anger of the LORD was hot
against Israel; and He [k]sold them into
the hands of the [l]Philistines and into
the hands of the people of [1][m]Ammon.
8 From that year they harassed
and oppressed the children of Israel
for eighteen years—all the children of
Israel who *were* on the other side of
the Jordan in the [n]land of the Amorites, in Gilead.
9 Moreover the people of Ammon
crossed over the Jordan to fight
against Judah also, against Benjamin,
and against the house of Ephraim, so
that Israel was severely distressed.
10 And the children of Israel [o]cried
out to the LORD, saying, "We have
[p]sinned against You, because we
have both forsaken our God and
served the Baals!"
11 So the LORD said to the children
of Israel, *"Did I* not *deliver you* from
the Egyptians and from the Amorites
and from the [m]people of Ammon and
from the [q]Philistines?
12 "Also the Sidonians and [r]Ama-
lekites and Maonites* oppressed you;
and you cried out to Me, and I delivered you from their hand.
13 "Yet you have forsaken Me and
served other gods. Therefore I will deliver you [s]no more.
14 "Go and cry out to the gods
which you have chosen; let them deliver you in your time of [t]distress."
15 And the children of Israel said to
the LORD, "We have sinned! Do to us
whatever seems best to You; only deliver us this day, we pray."
16 So they put away the foreign
gods from among them and served the
LORD. And His soul could no longer
endure the misery of Israel.
17 Then the people of Ammon
gathered together and encamped in
Gilead. And the children of Israel assembled together and encamped in
Mizpah.
18 And the people, the leaders of

*10:12 Some Septuagint manuscripts read *Midianites.*

[1](10:7) The Ammonites were descendants of Lot, Abraham's nephew (Gen. 19:38).

Gilead, said to one another, "Who *is*
the man who will begin the fight
against the people of Ammon? He
shall be [a]head over all the inhabitants
of Gilead."

Jephthah, the ninth judge

11 NOW [b]Jephthah the Gileadite
was a mighty man of valor, but
he *was* the son of a harlot; and Gilead
begot Jephthah.
2 Gilead's wife bore sons; and
when his wife's sons grew up, they
drove Jephthah out, and said to him,
"You shall have [c]no inheritance in our
father's house, for you *are* the son of
another woman."
3 Then Jephthah fled from his
brothers and dwelt in the land of
[d]Tob; and [e]worthless men banded together with Jephthah and went out
raiding with him.
4 It came to pass [f]after a time that
the [g]people of Ammon made war
against Israel.
5 And so it was, when the people
of Ammon made war against Israel,
that the elders of Gilead went to get
Jephthah from the land of Tob.
6 Then they said to Jephthah,
"Come and be our commander, that
we may fight against the people of
Ammon."
7 So Jephthah said to the elders of
Gilead, "Did you not [h]hate me, and
expel me from my father's house?
Why have you come to me now when
you are in distress?"
8 And the elders of Gilead said to
Jephthah, "That is why we have
turned again to you now, that you may
go with us and fight against the people
of Ammon, and be our [i]head over all
the inhabitants of Gilead."
9 So Jephthah said to the elders of
Gilead, "If you take me back home to
fight against the people of Ammon,
and the LORD delivers them to me,
shall I be your head?"
10 And the elders of Gilead said to
Jephthah, "The LORD will be a [j]wit-
ness between us, if we do not do according to your words."
11 Then Jephthah went with the elders of Gilead, and the people made
him head and commander over them;
and Jephthah spoke all his words before the LORD in [j]Mizpah.
12 Now Jephthah sent messengers
to the king of the people of Ammon,
saying, [k]"What do you have against
me, that you have come to fight
against me in my land?"

18
[a] Jud. 11:8–9
CHAPTER 11
1
[b] Heb. 11:32
2
[c] Gen. 21:10; Dt. 23:2
3
[d] 2 Sam. 10:6,8
[e] Jud. 9:4
4
[f] Lit. *after days*
[g] Jud. 10:9, 17
7
[h] Cp. Gen. 37:4; 2 Sam. 13:22
8
[i] Jud. 10:18
10
[j] Gen. 31:49–50
12
[k] Dt. 20:10, 12
13
[l] Num. 21:24
[m] Josh. 13:9
15
[n] Dt. 2:9,19
16
[o] Num. 20:1,14–21
17
[p] Josh. 24:9
18
[q] Dt. 2:9, 18–19
[r] Num. 21:4
19
[s] Num. 21:21; Dt. 2:26–36
21
[t] Josh. 24:8
24
[u] 1 Ki. 11:7

13 And the king of the people of
Ammon answered the messengers of
Jephthah, "Because [l]Israel took away
my land when they came up out of
Egypt, from the [m]Arnon as far as the
Jabbok, and to the Jordan. Now therefore, restore those *lands* peaceably."
14 So Jephthah again sent messengers to the king of the people of Ammon,
15 and said to him, "Thus says
Jephthah: 'Israel [n]did not take away
the land of Moab, nor the land of the
people of Ammon;
16 'for when Israel came up from
Egypt, they walked through the wilderness as far as the Red Sea and
came to [o]Kadesh.
17 'Then Israel sent messengers to
the king of Edom, saying, "Please let
me pass through your land." But the
king of Edom would not heed. And in
like manner they sent to the [p]king of
Moab, but he would not *consent*. So
Israel remained in Kadesh.
18 'And they [q]went along through
the wilderness and [r]bypassed the
land of Edom and the land of Moab,
came to the east side of the land of
Moab, and encamped on the other
side of the Arnon. But they did not
enter the border of Moab, for the Arnon *was* the border of Moab.
19 'Then Israel [s]sent messengers to
Sihon king of the Amorites, king of
Heshbon; and Israel said to him,
"Please let us pass through your land
into our place."
20 'But Sihon did not trust Israel to
pass through his territory. So Sihon
gathered all his people together, encamped in Jahaz, and fought against
Israel.
21 'And the LORD God of Israel [t]de-
livered Sihon and all his people into
the hand of Israel, and they defeated
them. Thus Israel gained possession
of all the land of the Amorites, who
inhabited that country.
22 'They took possession of all the
territory of the Amorites, from the Arnon to the Jabbok and from the wilderness to the Jordan.
23 'And now the LORD God of Israel
has dispossessed the Amorites from
before His people Israel; should you
then possess it?
24 'Will you not possess whatever
[u]Chemosh your god gives you to possess? So whatever the LORD our God
takes possession of before us, we will
possess.
25 'And now, *are* you any better

than [a]Balak the son of Zippor, king of Moab? Did he ever strive against Israel? Did he ever fight against them?

26 'While Israel [b]dwelt in Heshbon and its villages, in Aroer and its villages, and in all the cities along the banks of the Arnon, for three hundred years, why did you not recover *them* within that time?

27 'Therefore I have not sinned against you, but you wronged me by fighting against me. May the LORD, the [c]Judge, render judgment this day between the children of Israel and the people of Ammon.' "

28 However, the king of the people of Ammon did not heed the words which Jephthah sent him.

Jephthah's tragic vow

29 Then the [d]Spirit of the LORD came upon [1]Jephthah, and he passed through Gilead and Manasseh, and passed through Mizpah of Gilead; and from Mizpah of Gilead he advanced *toward* the people of Ammon.

30 And Jephthah [e]made a vow to the LORD, and said, "If You will indeed deliver the people of Ammon into my hands,

31 "then it will be that whatever comes out of the doors of my house to meet me, when I return in peace from the people of Ammon, [f]shall surely be the LORD's, and I will offer it up as a burnt offering."

32 So Jephthah advanced toward the people of Ammon to fight against them, and the LORD delivered them into his hands.

33 And he defeated them from Aroer as far as Minnith—twenty cities—and to Abel Keramim,* with a very great slaughter. Thus the people of Ammon were subdued before the children of Israel.

34 When Jephthah came to his house at [g]Mizpah, there was his daughter, coming out to meet him with timbrels and dancing; and she *was his* only child. Besides her he had neither son nor daughter.

35 And it came to pass, when he saw her, that he tore his clothes, and said, "Alas, my daughter! You have brought me very low! You are among those who trouble me! For I have given my word to the LORD, and I [h]cannot go [i]back on it."

36 So she said to him, "My father, *if* you have given your word to the LORD, do to me according to what has gone out of your mouth, because the LORD has avenged you of your enemies, the people of Ammon."

37 Then she said to her father, "Let this thing be done for me: let me alone for two months, that I may go and wander on the mountains and bewail my virginity, my friends and I."

38 So he said, "Go." And he sent her away *for* two months; and she went with her friends, and bewailed her virginity on the mountains.

39 And it was so at the end of two months that she returned to her father, and he carried out his vow with her which he had [2]vowed. She knew no man. And it became a custom in Israel

40 *that* the daughters of Israel went four days each year to [j]lament the daughter of Jephthah the Gileadite.

Petulant Ephraim punished. Jephthah rules six years

12 THEN the men of [k]Ephraim gathered together, crossed over toward Zaphon, and said to Jephthah, "Why did you cross over to fight against the people of Ammon, and did not call us to go with you? We will burn your house down on you with fire!"

2 And Jephthah said to them, "My people and I were in a great struggle with the people of Ammon; and when

25
a Num. 22:2
26
b Num. 21:25–26
27
c Gen. 16:5; 18:25; 31:53; 1 Sam. 24:12,15
29
d Holy Spirit (OT): v. 29; Jud. 13:25. (Gen. 1:2; Zech. 12:10)
30
e Gen. 28:20; Num. 30:2; 1 Sam. 1:11
31
f Lev. 27:2–3,28
34
g v. 11
35
h Num. 30:2
i Eccl. 5:4–5
40
j Lit. *celebrate*
CHAPTER 12
1
k Jud. 10:9; see 8:1, *note*

*
11:33 Literally *Plain of Vineyards*

[1](11:29) Jephthah appears to have been a judge of northeastern Israel only.

[2](11:39) In view of the divine commands in the Mosaic law against human sacrifice (Lev. 18:21; 20:2–5; Dt. 12:31; 18:10), a question has been raised about Jephthah's action here. There is considerable doubt as to what he actually did. Those who think that he killed his daughter see no divine approval of the act, but rather attribute it to his rash vow. Passages like 2 Ki. 3:27; 16:3; 17:17; 2 Chr. 33:6; Jer. 7:31; 19:5; 32:35 show how widespread this evil and cruel practice was even in later days. Others do not believe that Jephthah sacrificed his daughter, but that he set her apart to perpetual virginity. The latter view emphasizes the unusual expression (in such a context) in v. 31: "shall surely be the LORD's," and the stress upon virginity instead of death in vv. 37,39: "my virginity," "she knew no man." Jephthah's vow (vv. 30–31) was hasty and seemingly improvident. Our Lord expressed Himself about vows in the Sermon on the Mount (Mt. 5:33–37).

I called you, you did not deliver me out of their hands.

3 "So when I saw that you would not deliver *me,* I took my life in my hands and crossed over against the people of Ammon; and the LORD delivered them into my hand. Why then have you come up to me this day to fight against me?"

4 Now Jephthah gathered together all the men of Gilead and fought against Ephraim. And the men of Gilead defeated Ephraim, because they said, "You Gileadites *are* fugitives of Ephraim among the Ephraimites *and* among the Manassites."

5 The Gileadites seized the [a]fords of the Jordan before the Ephraimites *arrived.* And when *any* Ephraimite who escaped said, "Let me cross over," the men of Gilead would say to him, "*Are* you an Ephraimite?" If he said, "No,"

6 then they would say to him, "Then say, [b]'Shibboleth'!" And he would say, "Sibboleth," for he could not pronounce *it* right. Then they would take him and kill him at the fords of the Jordan. There fell at that time forty-two thousand Ephraimites.

7 And Jephthah judged Israel six years. Then Jephthah the Gileadite died and was buried in among the cities of Gilead.

8 After him, [1]Ibzan of Bethlehem judged Israel.

9 He had [c]thirty sons. And he gave away thirty daughters in marriage, and brought in thirty daughters from elsewhere for his sons. He judged Israel seven years.

10 Then Ibzan died and was buried at Bethlehem.

Elon, the eleventh judge (10 years)

11 After him, Elon the Zebulunite judged Israel. He judged Israel ten years.

12 And Elon the Zebulunite died and was buried at Aijalon in the country of Zebulun.

Abdon, the twelfth judge (8 years)

13 After him, Abdon the son of Hillel the Pirathonite judged Israel.

14 He had forty sons and thirty grandsons, who rode on seventy [c]young donkeys. He judged Israel eight years.

15 Then Abdon the son of Hillel the Pirathonite died and was buried in Pirathon in the land of Ephraim, in the mountains of the Amalekites.

V. Samson, 13:1—16:31

Servitude under the Philistines (40 years)

13 AGAIN the children of Israel did [d]evil in the sight of the LORD, and the LORD delivered them into the hand of the [2e]Philistines for forty years.

Samson, the thirteenth judge, born

2 Now there was a certain man from [f]Zorah, of the family of the Danites, whose name *was* Manoah; and his wife *was* barren and had no children.

3 And the [g]Angel of the LORD appeared to the woman and [h]said to her, "Indeed now, you are barren and have borne no children, but you shall conceive and bear a son.

4 "Now therefore, please be careful not to drink wine or *similar* [i]drink, and not to eat anything unclean.

5 "For behold, you shall conceive and bear a son. And no razor shall come upon his head, for the child shall be a [j]Nazirite to God from the womb; and he shall begin to deliver Israel out of the hand of the Philistines."

6 So the woman came and told her husband, saying, "A [k]Man of God came to me, and His countenance *was* like the countenance of the Angel of God, very awesome; but I did not ask Him where He *was* from, and He did not tell me His name.

7 "And He said to me, 'Behold, you shall conceive and bear a son. Now drink no wine or *similar* drink, nor eat anything unclean, for the child shall

5
a Jud. 3:28
6
b Lit. *stream.* Ps. 69:2, 15; Isa. 27:12
9
c Cp. Jud. 10:4
CHAPTER 13
1
d Jud. 2:11
e Jud. 10:7
2
f Josh. 19:41
3
g *Angel* (of the LORD): vv. 3–14; Jud. 13:15. (Gen. 16:7; Jud. 2:1, *note*)
h Cp. Lk. 1:13,30–31
4
i Num. 6:3, 20; Lk. 1:15
5
j Num. 6:2
6
k Cp. 1 Sam. 2:27

[1](12:8) Ibzan appears to have been only a civil judge in northeastern Israel.

[2](13:1) The Philistines were a non-semitic people, sometimes referred to in the Scriptures as "the uncircumcised" (Jud. 14:3; 15:18; 1 Sam. 14:6; 31:4; 2 Sam. 1:20; 1 Chr. 10:4). They settled in the plain and low hill country of southwestern Palestine, being part of the great invasion of the sea peoples referred to by Rameses III of Egypt about 1200 B.C. Their knowledge of metallurgy and access to sources of iron gave them a great advantage over other nations and enabled a comparatively small number to conquer far larger groups and to extend their sway for a time over most of Palestine. They were the leading enemy of Israel from the time of Samson to the middle of the reign of David. See 1 Sam. 13:19, *note.* Eventually the Philistines gave their name to the whole land, in the form "Palestine." Cp. Isa. 14:29,31; see Gen. 21:34, *note.*

be a Nazirite to God from the womb to the day of his death.' "

Manoah prays

8 Then Manoah [a]prayed to the LORD, and said, "O my Lord, please let the Man of God whom You sent come to us again and teach us what we shall do for the child who will be born."

9 And God listened to the voice of Manoah, and the Angel of God came to the woman again as she was sitting in the field; but Manoah her husband *was* not with her.

10 Then the woman ran in haste and told her husband, and said to him, "Look, the Man who came to me the *other* day has just now appeared to me!"

11 So Manoah arose and followed his wife. When he came to the Man, he said to Him, "Are You the Man who spoke to this woman?" And He said, "I *am*."

12 Manoah said, "Now let Your words come *to pass!* What will be the boy's rule of life, and his work?"

13 So the Angel of the LORD said to Manoah, "Of all that I said to the woman let her be careful.

14 "She may not eat anything that comes from the [b]vine, nor may she drink wine or *similar* drink, nor eat anything unclean. All that I commanded her let her observe."

15 Then Manoah said to the [c]Angel of the LORD, "Please let us [d]detain You, and we will prepare a young goat for You."

16 And the Angel of the LORD said to Manoah, "Though you detain Me, I will not eat your food. But if you offer a [e]burnt offering, you must offer it to the LORD." (For Manoah did not know He *was* the Angel of the LORD.)

17 Then Manoah said to the Angel of the LORD, "What *is* Your name, that when Your words come *to pass* we may honor You?"

18 And the Angel of the LORD said to him, "Why do you ask My name, seeing it *is* [f]wonderful?"

19 So Manoah took the young goat with the grain offering, and offered it upon the rock to the LORD. And He did a wondrous thing while Manoah and his wife looked on—

20 it happened as the [g]flame went up toward heaven from the altar—the Angel of the LORD ascended in the flame of the altar! When Manoah and his wife saw *this,* they fell on their faces to the ground.

21 When the Angel of the LORD appeared no more to Manoah and his wife, then Manoah knew that He *was* the Angel of the LORD.

22 And Manoah said to his wife, "We shall surely [h]die, because we have seen [i]God!"

23 But his wife said to him, "If the LORD had desired to kill us, He would not have accepted a burnt offering and a grain offering from our hands, nor would He have shown us all these *things,* nor would He have told us *such things* as these at this time."

24 So the woman bore a son and called his name Samson; and the child grew, and the LORD blessed him.

25 And the [j]Spirit of the LORD began to move upon him at [k]Mahaneh Dan* between Zorah and [l]Eshtaol.

Samson promised a wife

14 NOW Samson went down to [m]Timnah, and saw a woman in Timnah of the daughters of the Philistines.

2 So he went up and told his father and mother, saying, "I have seen a woman in Timnah of the daughters of the Philistines; now therefore, get her for me [n]as a wife."

3 Then his father and mother said to him, "*Is there* no woman among the daughters of your brethren, or among all my [o]people, that you must go and get a wife from the uncircumcised Philistines?" And Samson said to his father, "Get her for me, for she pleases me well."

4 But his father and mother did not know that it was of the [p]LORD—that He was seeking an occasion to move against the Philistines. For at that time the Philistines had dominion over Israel.

Samson kills a lion; his riddle

5 So Samson went down to Timnah with his father and mother, and came to the vineyards of Timnah.

Now *to his* surprise, a young [q]lion *came* roaring against him.

6 And the [j]Spirit of the LORD came mightily upon him, and he tore the lion apart as one would have torn apart a young goat, though *he had* [r]nothing in his hand. But he did not tell his father or his mother what he had done.

7 Then he went down and talked

---

* 13:25 Literally *Camp of Dan* (compare 18:12)

---

8 *a Bible prayers* (OT): vv. 8–9; Jud. 16:28. (Gen. 15:2; Hab. 3:1)
14 *b* Num. 6:4
15 *c Angel* (of the LORD): vv. 3–21; 2 Sam. 24:16. (Gen. 16:7; Jud. 2:1, *note*)
d Cp. Jud. 6:18
16 *e* Cp. Jud. 6:20–22
18 *f* Cp. Isa. 9:6
20 *g* Cp. 1 Ki. 18:38
22 *h* Cp. Jud. 6:22–23
i See Jn. 1:18, *note*
25 *j Holy Spirit* (OT): v. 25; 14:6; Jud. 14:19. (Gen. 1:2; Zech. 12:10)
k Jud. 18:12
l Jud. 16:31
CHAPTER 14
1 *m* Josh. 15:10,57
2 *n* Dt. 7:3–4
3 *o* Cp. Gen. 24:3–4
4 *p* Josh. 11:20; 1 Sam. 2:25
5 *q* Cp. 1 Sam. 17:34–35
6 *r Miracles* (OT): vv. 5–6,19; Jud. 15:14. (Gen. 5:24; Jon. 1:17, *note*)

with the woman; and she pleased Samson well.

8 After some time, when he returned to get her, he turned aside to see the carcass of the lion. And behold, a swarm of bees and honey *were* in the carcass of the lion.

9 [a]He took some of it in his hands and went along, eating. When he came to his father and mother, he gave *some* to them, and they also ate. But he did not tell them that he had taken the honey out of the [b]carcass of the lion.

10 So his father went down to the woman. And Samson gave a [c]feast there, for young men used to do so.

11 And it happened, when they saw him, that they brought thirty companions to be with him.

12 Then Samson said to them, "Let me pose a riddle to you. If you can correctly solve and explain it to me within the [d]seven days of the feast, then I will give you thirty linen garments and thirty [e]changes of clothing.

13 "But if you cannot explain *it* to me, then you shall give me thirty linen garments and thirty changes of clothing." And they said to him, [f]"Pose your riddle, that we may hear it."

14 So he said to them:

"Out of the eater came
  something to eat,
And out of the strong came
  something sweet."

Now for three days they could not explain the riddle.

Samson deceived; kills thirty

15 But it came to pass on the seventh* day that they said to Samson's wife, [g]"Entice your husband, that he may explain the riddle to us, [h]or else we will burn you and your father's house with fire. Have you invited us in order to take what is ours? *Is that* not *so?*"

16 Then Samson's wife wept on him, and said, [i]"You only hate me! You do not love me! You have posed a riddle to the sons of my people, but you have not explained *it* to me." And he said to her, "Look, I have not explained *it* to my father or my mother; so should I explain *it* to you?"

17 Now she had wept on him the seven days while their feast lasted. And it happened on the seventh day that he told her, because she [j]pressed him so much. Then she explained the riddle to the sons of her people.

18 So the men of the city said to him on the seventh day before the sun went down:

"What *is* sweeter than honey?
And what *is* stronger than a
  lion?"

And he said to them:

"If you had not plowed with my
  heifer,
You would not have solved my
  riddle!"

19 Then the [k]Spirit of the LORD came upon him mightily, and he went down to Ashkelon and killed thirty of their men, took their apparel, and gave the changes *of clothing* to those who had explained the riddle. So his anger was aroused, and he went back up to his father's house.

20 And Samson's wife was [l]*given* to his companion, who had been his best man.

Samson burns Philistines' crops

15 AFTER a while, in the time of wheat harvest, it happened that Samson visited his wife with a [m]young goat. And he said, [n]"Let me go in to my wife, into *her* room." But her father would not permit him to go in.

2 Her father said, "I really thought that you thoroughly hated her; [o]therefore I gave her to your companion. *Is* not her younger sister better than she? Please, take her instead."

3 And Samson said to them, "This time I shall be blameless regarding the Philistines if I harm them!"

4 Then Samson went and caught three hundred foxes; and he took torches, turned *the foxes* tail to tail, and put a torch between each pair of tails.

5 When he had set the torches on fire, he let *the foxes* go into the standing grain of the Philistines, and [p]burned up both the shocks and the standing grain, as well as the vineyards *and* olive groves.

6 Then the Philistines said, "Who has done this?" And they answered, "Samson, the son-in-law of the Timnite, because he has taken his wife and given her to his companion." So the Philistines came up and [q]burned her and her father with fire.

9
a Cp. 1 Sam. 14:25–26
b Lev. 11:27
10
c Cp. Gen. 29:22
12
d Cp. Gen. 29:27
e Gen. 45:22; 2 Ki. 5:5
13
f Ezek. 17:2
15
g Jud. 16:5
h Jud. 15:6
16
i Cp. Jud. 16:15
17
j Jud. 16:16
19
k *Holy Spirit* (OT): v. 19; Jud. 15:14. (Gen. 1:2; Zech. 12:10)
20
l Jud. 15:2
CHAPTER 15
1
m Gen. 38:17
n Jud. 14:1; cp. 16:1
2
o 14:20
5
p Cp. Ex. 22:6; 2 Sam. 14:30
6
q Jud. 14:15

*14:15 Following Masoretic Text, Targum, and Vulgate; Septuagint and Syriac read *fourth.*

7 Samson said to them, "Since you would do a thing like this, I will surely take revenge on you, and after that I will cease."

8 So he attacked them hip and thigh with a great slaughter; then he went down and dwelt in the cleft of the rock of [a]Etam.

Samson kills a thousand Philistines

9 Now the Philistines went up, encamped in Judah, and deployed themselves against Lehi.

10 And the men of Judah said, "Why have you come up against us?" So they answered, "We have come up to arrest Samson, to do to him as he has done to us."

11 Then three thousand men of Judah went down to the cleft of the rock of Etam, and said to Samson, "Do you not know that the Philistines [b]rule over us? What *is* this you have done to us?" And he said to them, "As they did to me, so I have done to them."

12 But they said to him, "We have come down to arrest you, that we may deliver you into the hand of the Philistines." Then Samson said to them, "Swear to me that you will not kill me yourselves."

13 So they spoke to him, saying, "No, but we will tie you securely and deliver you into their hand; but we will surely not kill you." And they bound him with two [c]new ropes and brought him up from the rock.

14 When he came to [d]Lehi, the Philistines came shouting against him. Then the [e]Spirit of the LORD came mightily upon him; and the ropes that *were* on his arms became like flax that is burned with fire, and his bonds [f]broke loose from his hands.

15 He found a fresh [g]jawbone of a donkey, reached out his hand and took it, and killed a thousand men with it.

16 Then Samson said:

> "With the jawbone of a donkey,
> Heaps upon heaps,
> With the jawbone of a donkey
> I have slain a thousand men!"

17 And so it was, when he had finished speaking, that he threw the jawbone from his hand, and called that place [h]Ramath Lehi.

18 Then he became very thirsty; so he cried out to the LORD and said, "You have given this great deliverance by the hand of Your servant; and now shall I die of thirst and fall into the hand of the uncircumcised?"

19 So God split the hollow place that *is* in [1]Lehi,* and water came out, and he drank; and his spirit returned, and he revived. Therefore he called its name [i]En Hakkore, which is in Lehi to this day.

20 And [j]he judged Israel [k]twenty years in the [l]days of the Philistines.

Samson's moral weakness

16 NOW Samson went to [m]Gaza and saw a harlot there, and went in to her.

2 *When* the Gazites *were told,* "Samson has come here!" they surrounded *the place* and lay in wait for him all night at the gate of the city. They were quiet all night, saying, "In the morning, when it is daylight, we will kill him."

3 And Samson lay *low* till midnight; then he arose at midnight, took hold of the doors of the gate of the city and the two gateposts, pulled them up, bar and all, put *them* on his shoulders, and carried them to the top of the hill that faces Hebron.

4 Afterward it happened that he loved a [n]woman in the Valley of Sorek, whose name *was* Delilah.

5 And the [o]lords of the Philistines came up to her and said to her, [p]"Entice him, and find out where his great strength *lies,* and by what *means* we may overpower him, that we may bind him to afflict him; and every one of us will give you eleven hundred *pieces* of silver."

6 So Delilah said to Samson, "Please tell me where your great strength *lies,* and with what you may be bound to afflict you."

7 And Samson said to her, "If they bind me with seven fresh bowstrings, not yet dried, then I shall become weak, and be like any *other* man."

8 So the lords of the Philistines brought up to her seven fresh bowstrings, not yet dried, and she bound him with them.

9 Now *men were* lying in wait, staying with her in the room. And she

* 15:19 Literally *Jawbone* (compare verse 14)

8
a 2 Chr. 11:6
11
b Jud. 13:1; 14:4
13
c Jud. 16:11–12
14
d Meaning *jawbone*
e Holy Spirit (OT): v. 14; 1 Sam. 10:6. (Gen. 1:2; Zech. 12:10)
f Miracles (OT): vv. 14–19; Jud. 16:30. (Gen. 5:24; Jon. 1:17, *note*)
15
g Cp. 1 Cor. 1:27–28
17
h Meaning *the hill of the jawbone*
19
i Meaning *the well of him who cried*
20
j Heb. 11:32
k Jud. 16:31
l Jud. 13:1
CHAPTER 16
1
m Josh. 15:47
4
n Cp. 1 Ki. 11:1
5
o Josh. 13:3
p Jud. 14:15

[1](15:19) Verse 17 states that this place received this name because Samson had killed so many people there with a jawbone. At that place God caused a spring suddenly to gush out of the ground to give water to Samson.

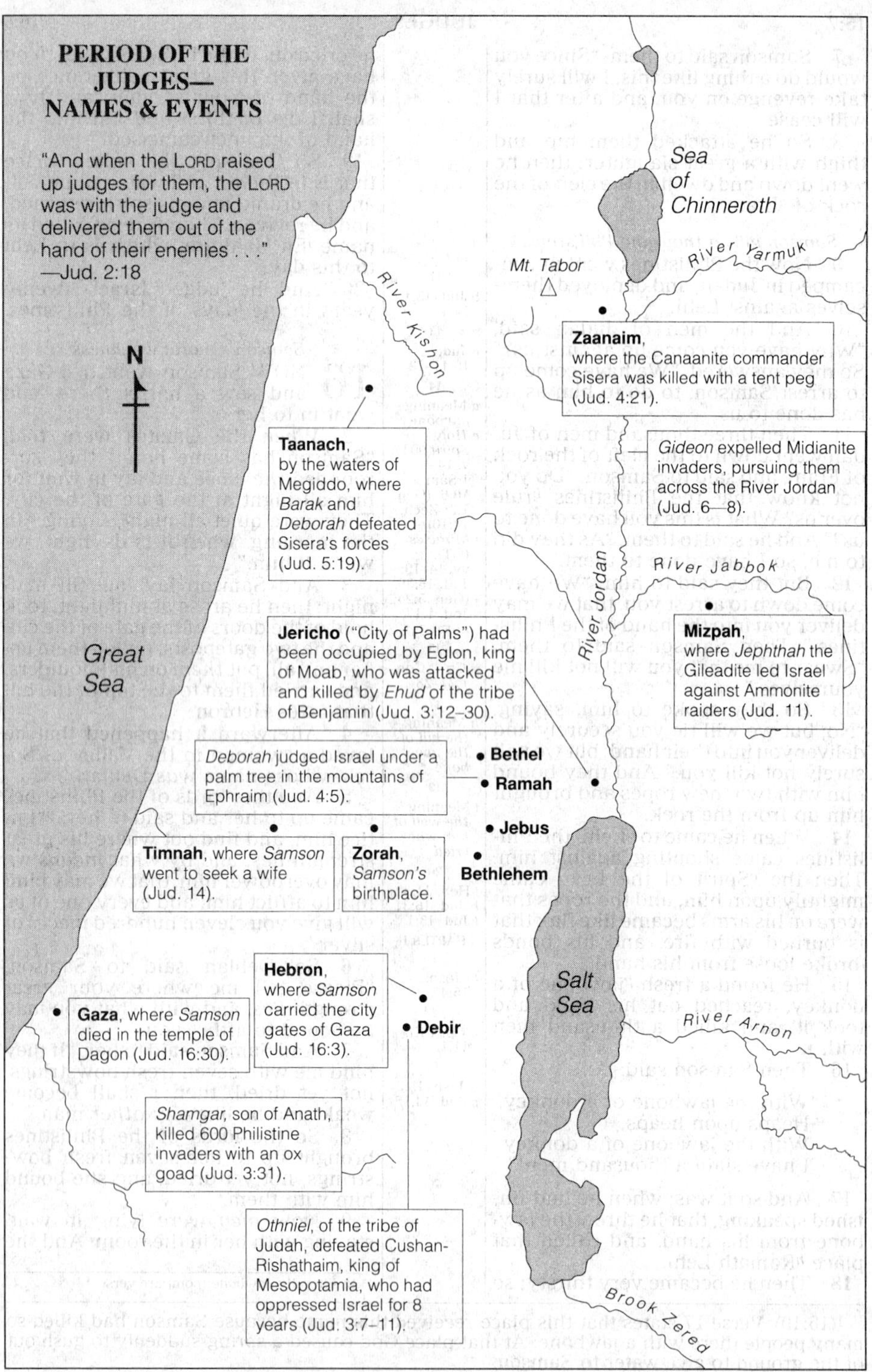

PERIOD OF THE JUDGES— NAMES & EVENTS
"And when the LORD raised up judges for them, the LORD was with the judge and delivered them out of the hand of their enemies . . ." —Jud. 2:18
N
Sea of Chinneroth
River Yarmuk
Mt. Tabor
River Kishon
Zaanaim, where the Canaanite commander Sisera was killed with a tent peg (Jud. 4:21).
Taanach, by the waters of Megiddo, where Barak and Deborah defeated Sisera's forces (Jud. 5:19).
Gideon expelled Midianite invaders, pursuing them across the River Jordan (Jud. 6—8).
River Jabbok
River Jordan
Mizpah, where Jephthah the Gileadite led Israel against Ammonite raiders (Jud. 11).
Great Sea
Jericho ("City of Palms") had been occupied by Eglon, king of Moab, who was attacked and killed by Ehud of the tribe of Benjamin (Jud. 3:12–30).
Deborah judged Israel under a palm tree in the mountains of Ephraim (Jud. 4:5).
Bethel
Ramah
Jebus
Bethlehem
Timnah, where Samson went to seek a wife (Jud. 14).
Zorah, Samson's birthplace.
Salt Sea
Hebron, where Samson carried the city gates of Gaza (Jud. 16:3).
Gaza, where Samson died in the temple of Dagon (Jud. 16:30).
Debir
River Arnon
Shamgar, son of Anath, killed 600 Philistine invaders with an ox goad (Jud. 3:31).
Othniel, of the tribe of Judah, defeated Cushan-Rishathaim, king of Mesopotamia, who had oppressed Israel for 8 years (Jud. 3:7–11).
Brook Zered

said to him, "The Philistines *are* upon
you, Samson!" But he broke the bowstrings as a strand of yarn breaks
when it touches fire. So the secret of
his strength was not known.
10 Then Delilah said to Samson,
"Look, you have mocked me and told
me lies. Now, please tell me what you
may be bound with."
11 So he said to her, "If they bind
me securely with [a]new ropes that
have never been used, then I shall become weak, and be like any *other*
man."
12 Therefore Delilah took new
ropes and bound him with them, and
said to him, "The Philistines *are* upon
you, Samson!" And *men were* lying in
wait, staying in the room. But he
broke them off his arms like a thread.
13 Delilah said to Samson, "Until
now you have mocked me and told me
lies. Tell me what you may be bound
with." And he said to her, "If you
weave the seven locks of my head into
the web of the loom"—
14 So she wove *it* tightly with the
batten of the loom, and said to him,
"The Philistines *are* upon you, Samson!" But he awoke from his sleep,
and pulled out the batten and the web
from the loom.

Samson, tormented by Delilah, reveals his secret

15 Then she said to him, [b]"How can
you say, 'I love you,' when your heart
is not with me? You have mocked me
these three times, and have not told
me where your great strength *lies.*"
16 [c]And it came to pass, when she
pestered him daily with her words and
pressed him, *so* that his soul was
[d]vexed to death,
17 that he [e]told her all his heart,
and said to her, "No [f]razor has ever
come upon my head, for I *have been* a
Nazirite to God from my mother's
womb. If I am shaven, then my
strength will leave me, and I shall become weak, and be like any *other*
man."
18 When Delilah saw that he had
told her all his heart, she sent and
called for the lords of the Philistines,
saying, "Come up once more, for he
has told me all his heart." So the lords
of the Philistines came up to her and
brought the money in their hand.
19 Then she lulled him to sleep on
her knees, and called for a man and
had him shave off the seven locks of
his head. Then she began to torment
him,* and his strength left him.
20 And she said, "The Philistines
are upon you, Samson!" So he awoke
from his sleep, and said, "I will go out
as before, at other times, and shake
myself free!" But he [g]did not know
that the LORD had [h]departed from him.
21 Then the Philistines took him
and [i]put out his [j]eyes, and brought
him down to Gaza. They bound him
with bronze fetters, and he became a
[1]grinder in the prison.
22 However, the hair of his head
began to grow again after it had been
shaven.

Samson avenged in his death

23 Now the lords of the Philistines
gathered together to offer a great sacrifice to [k]Dagon their god, and to rejoice. And they said:

"Our [l]god has delivered into
our hands
Samson our enemy!"

24 When the people saw him, they
[m]praised their god; for they said:

"Our god has delivered into our
hands our enemy,
The destroyer of our land,
And the one who multiplied
our dead."

25 So it happened, when their
hearts were merry, that they said,
"Call for Samson, that he may perform for us." So they called for Samson from the prison, and he performed
for them. And they stationed him between the pillars.
26 Then Samson said to the lad
who held him by the hand, "Let me
feel the pillars which support the temple, so that I can lean on them."
27 Now the temple was full of men
and women. All the lords of the Philistines *were* there—about three thousand men and women on the roof
watching while Samson performed.
28 Then Samson [n]called to the
LORD, saying, "O Lord GOD, remember
me, I pray! Strengthen me, I pray, just
this once, O God, that I may with one
blow take vengeance on the Philistines for my two eyes!"
29 And Samson took hold of the
two middle pillars which supported

11 a Jud. 15:13
15 b Cp. Jud. 14:16
16 c Cp. Gen. 39:10; d Cp. Jud. 14:17
17 e Cp. Mic. 7:5; f Jud. 13:5
20 g Cp. Ex. 34:29; h 1 Sam. 16:14
21 i Lit. *bored out*; j 2 Ki. 25:7
23 k 1 Sam. 5:2; l Cp. 1 Sam. 31:9
24 m Dan. 5:4–5
28 n *Bible prayers* (OT): v. 28; 1 Sam. 1:11. (Gen. 15:2; Hab. 3:1)

* 16:19 Following Masoretic Text, Targum, and Vulgate; Septuagint reads *he began to be weak.*

[1](16:21) Grinding grain between millstones was the task of a beast or a slave.

the temple, and he braced himself
against them, one on his right and the
other on his left.
30 Then Samson said, "Let me die
with the Philistines!" And he pushed
with *all his* might, and the temple [a]fell
on the lords and all the people who
were in it. So the dead that he killed at
his death were more than he had
killed in his life.
31 And his brothers and all his father's household came down and took
him, and brought *him* up and buried
him between Zorah and Eshtaol in the
tomb of his father Manoah. He had
[1]judged Israel [b]twenty years.

VI. Confusion in Israel, 17:1—21:25

Religious confusion

17 [2]NOW there was a man from
the mountains of Ephraim,
whose name *was* [c]Micah.
2 And he said to his mother, "The
eleven hundred [d]*shekels* of silver that
were taken from you, and on which
you put a [e]curse, even saying it in my
ears—here *is* the silver with me; I took
it." And his mother said, "*May you be*
blessed by the LORD, my son!"
3 So when he had returned the
eleven hundred [f]*shekels* of silver to
his mother, his mother said, "I had
wholly dedicated the silver from my
hand to the LORD for my son, to make
a carved image and a molded [g]image;
now therefore, I will return it to you."
4 Thus he returned the silver to his
mother. Then his mother took two
hundred [f]*shekels* of silver and gave
them to the [h]silversmith, and he made
it into a carved image and a molded
image; and they were in the house of
Micah.
5 The man Micah had a [i]shrine,
and made an [j]ephod and [k]household
idols;* and he consecrated one of his
sons, who became his [l]priest.
6 In those days *there was* no [m]king
in Israel; everyone did *what was* right
in his own [n]eyes.
7 Now there was a young man
from Bethlehem in Judah, of the family of Judah; he *was* a Levite, and
[o]was staying there.
8 The man departed from the city
of Bethlehem in Judah to stay wherever he could find *a place*. Then he
came to the mountains of Ephraim, to
the house of Micah, as he journeyed.
9 And Micah said to him, "Where
do you come from?" So he said to him,
"I *am* a Levite from Bethlehem in Judah, and I am on my way to find *a*
place to stay."
10 Micah said to him, "Dwell with
me, and be a father and a priest to me,
and I will give you ten [f]*shekels* of silver per year, a suit of clothes, and your
sustenance." So the Levite went in.
11 Then the Levite was content to
dwell with the man; and the young
man became like one of his sons to
him.
12 So Micah consecrated the Levite, and the young man became his
priest, and lived in the house of Micah.
13 Then Micah said, "Now I [3]know

30
a *Miracles* (OT): vv. 28–30; 1 Sam. 5:6. (Gen. 5:24; Jon. 1:17, *note*)
31
b Jud. 15:20
CHAPTER 17
1
c Jud. 18:2
2
d See Coinage (OT), Ex. 30:13, *note;* cp. 2 Chr. 2:10, *note*
e Lev. 5:1
3
f See Weights and Measures (OT), 2 Chr. 2:10, *note;* cp. Ex. 30:13, *note*
g Ex. 20:4, 23; 34:17
4
h Cp. Isa. 46:6
5
i Jud. 18:24
j Jud. 8:27
k See Gen. 31:30, *note*
l Cp. Num. 3:10
6
m Jud. 18:1; 19:1
n Dt. 12:8; Jud. 21:25

17:7 *o* Dt. 18:6

* 17:5 Hebrew *teraphim*

[1](16:31) The character and work of Samson are both enigmatic. Announced by an Angel (13:2–21), he was a Nazirite (Num. 6; Jud. 13:5) who constantly defiled his Nazirite separation through fleshly appetites. Called by God to judge Israel, and endued wonderfully with the Spirit, he accomplished no abiding work for Israel and perished in captivity to his enemies, the Philistines. What was real in the man was his mighty faith in the LORD in a time of doubt and spiritual declension, and this faith God honored (Heb. 11:32).

[2](17:1) After the death of Samson, chronological sequence in Judges ends. It is not possible to assign the events in the last five chapters to any particular period. They may, however, be considered an appendix which shows the utter apostasy of Israel in their religious, civil, and moral life. These chapters picture the climax of the downward path of Israel resulting from departure from the Word of God. Samson, the last judge in the book, partook of the same sins for which Israel as a whole had suffered. The Levite consecrated by Micah was a man-made priest for the divine order of Aaron (chs. 17—18; see 17:13, *note*). The horrible story of ch. 19, issuing in civil war and practical destruction of Benjamin in ch. 20, pictures Israel at its lowest moral state in the entire OT. Written in complete honesty to the facts, characteristic of biblical history, the account reveals the moral degradation of Israel caused by departure from the law. However, a godly remnant existed during this period, as seen in the Book of Ruth. Samuel was the last of the judges, as well as an important prophet. His ministry restored civil and moral order in Israel.

[3](17:13) A striking illustration of all apostasy. With Micah's entire departure from the revealed will of God concerning worship and priesthood, there is yet an exaltation of false priesthood. Saying, "May you be blessed by the LORD, my son!" Micah's mother makes an idol;

that the LORD will be good to me, since
I have a Levite as [a]priest!"

Danites seek further territory

18 IN those days *there was* no
[b]king in Israel. And in those
days the [c]tribe of the Danites was
seeking an inheritance for itself to
dwell in; for until that day *their* inheritance among the tribes of Israel had
not fallen to them.
2 So the children of Dan sent five
men of their family from their territory, men of valor from [d]Zorah and
Eshtaol, to spy out the land and search
it. They said to them, "Go, search the
land." So they went to the mountains
of Ephraim, to the house of Micah,
and lodged there.
3 While they *were* at the house of
[e]Micah, they recognized the voice of
the young Levite. They turned aside
and said to him, "Who brought you
here? What are you doing in this
place? What do you have here?"
4 He said to them, "Thus and so
Micah did for me. He has hired me,
and I have become his priest."
5 So they said to him, [f]"Please inquire of God, that we may know
whether the journey on which we go
will be prosperous."
6 And the priest said to them, "Go
in peace. The presence of the LORD *be*
with you on your way."
7 So the five men departed and
went to [g]Laish. They saw the people
who *were* there, how they dwelt
safely, in the manner of the [h]Sidoni-
ans, quiet and secure. *There were* no
rulers in the land who might put *them*
to shame for anything. They *were* far
from the Sidonians, and they had no
ties with anyone.*
8 Then *the spies* came back to
their brethren at [i]Zorah and Eshtaol,
and their brethren said to them,
"What *is* your *report?*"
9 So they said, [j]"Arise, let us go
up against them. For we have seen the
land, and indeed it *is* very good.
Would you *do* nothing? [k]Do not hesitate to go, *and* enter to possess the
land.
10 "When you go, you will come to
a secure people and a large land. For
[l]God has given it into your hands, a
place where *there is* no lack of anything that *is* on the earth."
11 And six hundred men of the family of the Danites went from there,
from Zorah and Eshtaol, armed with
weapons of war.
12 Then they went up and encamped in Kirjath Jearim in Judah.
(Therefore they call that place [m]Maha-
neh Dan to this day. There *it is,* west
of Kirjath Jearim.)
13 And they passed from there to
the mountains of Ephraim, and came
to the house of Micah.

Danites take Micah's idols and his priest, Jonathan

14 Then the five men who had gone
to spy out the country of Laish answered and said to their brethren, "Do
you know that there are in these
houses an [n]ephod, household idols, a
carved image, and a molded image?
Now therefore, consider what you
should [o]do."
15 So they turned aside there, and
came to the house of the young Levite
man—to the house of Micah—and
greeted him.
16 The six hundred men armed
with their weapons of war, who *were*
of the children of Dan, stood by the
entrance of the gate.
17 Then the five men who had gone
to spy out the land went up. Entering
there, they took the carved image, the
ephod, the household idols, and the
molded image. The priest stood at the
entrance of the gate with the six hundred men *who were* armed with weapons of war.
18 When these went into Micah's
house and took the carved image, the
ephod, the household idols, and the
molded image, the priest said to them,
"What are you doing?"
19 And they said to him, "Be quiet,
put your hand over your mouth, and
come with us; be a father and a priest
to us. *Is it* better for you to be a priest
to the household of one man, or that
you be a priest to a tribe and a family
in Israel?"
20 So the priest's heart was glad;
and he took the ephod, the household
idols, and the carved image, and took
his place among the people.
21 Then they turned and departed,
and put the little ones, the livestock,
and the goods in front of them.
22 When they were a good way

17:13 *a* Dt. 10:8–9
CHAPTER 18
1 *b* Jud. 17:6 *c* Josh. 19:40–48
2 *d* Jud. 13:25
3 *e* Jud. 17:1
5 *f* Jud. 1:1; 20:18; Hos. 4:12
7 *g* Jud. 18:29; or *Leshem,* Josh. 19:47 *h* Jud. 10:12
8 *i* v. 2
9 *j* Cp. Num. 13:30 *k* Cp. Josh. 18:3
10 *l* Josh. 2:23–24
12 *m* Meaning *the camp of Dan,* Jud. 13:25
14 *n* Jud. 17:5 *o* Cp. Dt. 13:6–18

*18:7 Following Masoretic Text, Targum, and Vulgate; Septuagint reads *with Syria.*

and Micah expects the blessing of the LORD because he has linked his idolatry to the ancient Levitical order.

from the house of Micah, the men who
were in the houses near Micah's house
gathered together and overtook the
children of Dan.
23 And they called out to the children of Dan. So they turned around
and said to Micah, [a]"What ails you,
that you have gathered such a company?"
24 So he said, "You have [b]taken
away my gods which I made, and the
priest, and you have gone away. Now
what more do I have? How can you
say to me, 'What ails you?' "
25 And the children of Dan said to
him, "Do not let your voice be heard
among us, lest angry men fall upon
you, and you lose your life, with the
lives of your household!"
26 Then the children of Dan went
their way. And when Micah saw that
they *were* too strong for him, he
turned and went back to his house.

Danites attack unsuspecting Laish; dwell there

27 So they took *the things* Micah
had made, and the priest who had belonged to him, and went to [c]Laish, to
a people quiet and secure; and they
struck them with the edge of the
sword and burned the city with fire.
28 *There was* no deliverer, because
it *was* far from Sidon, and they had no
ties with anyone. It was in the valley
that belongs to [d]Beth Rehob. So they
rebuilt the city and dwelt there.
29 And they called the name of the
city [e]Dan, after the name of Dan their
father, who was born to Israel. However, the name of the city formerly
was Laish.
30 Then the children of Dan set up
for themselves the carved image; and
Jonathan the son of Gershom, the son
of Manasseh,* and his sons were
[f]priests to the tribe of Dan until the
day of the [g]captivity of the land.
31 So they set up for themselves
Micah's carved image which he made,
all the time that the house of God was
in [h]Shiloh.

Moral degradation—Levite's concubine

19 AND it came to pass in those
days, when *there was* no [i]king
in Israel, that there was a certain [j]Le-
vite staying in the remote mountains
of Ephraim. He took for himself a concubine from [k]Bethlehem in Judah.
2 But his concubine played the
harlot against him, and went away
from him to her father's house at Bethlehem in Judah, and was there four
whole months.
3 Then her husband arose and
went after her, to [l]speak kindly to her
and bring her back, having his [m]ser-
vant and a couple of donkeys with
him. So she brought him into her father's house; and when the father of
the young woman saw him, he was
glad to meet him.
4 Now his father-in-law, the
young woman's father, detained him;
and he stayed with him three days. So
they ate and drank and lodged there.
5 Then it came to pass on the
fourth day that they arose early in the
morning, and he stood to depart; but
the young woman's father said to his
son-in-law, "Refresh your [n]heart with
a morsel of bread, and afterward go
your way."
6 So they sat down, and the two of
them ate and drank together. Then the
young woman's father said to the
man, "Please be content to stay all
night, and let your heart be merry."
7 And when the man stood to depart, his father-in-law urged him; so
he lodged there again.
8 Then he arose early in the morning on the fifth day to depart, but the
young woman's father said, "Please
refresh your heart." So they delayed
until afternoon; and both of them ate.
9 And when the man stood to
depart—he and his concubine and his
servant—his father-in-law, the young
woman's father, said to him, "Look,
the day is now drawing toward evening; please spend the night. See, the
day is coming to an end; lodge here,
that your heart may be merry. Tomorrow go your way early, so that you
may get home."
10 However, the man was not willing to spend that night; so he rose and
departed, and came to opposite [o]Je-
bus (that *is*, Jerusalem). With him
were the two saddled donkeys; his
concubine *was* also with him.
11 They *were* near Jebus, and the
day was far spent; and the servant
said to his master, "Come, please, and
let us turn aside into this city of the
[p]Jebusites and lodge in it."
12 But his master said to him, "We
will not turn aside here into a city of
foreigners, who *are* not of the children
of Israel; we will go on to Gibeah."
13 So he said to his servant, "Come,
let us draw near to one of these places,

23
a 2 Ki. 6:28
24
b Gen. 31:30
27
c v. 7
28
d 2 Sam. 10:6
29
e Gen. 14:14; Josh. 19:47; 1 Ki. 12:29–30; 15:20
30
f Cp. Num. 16:1–40
g 2 Ki. 17:6
31
h Dt. 12:1–32; Josh. 18:1, 8
CHAPTER 19
1
i Jud. 18:1; 21:25
j Cp. Jud. 17:7
k Jud. 17:7; Ruth 1:1
3
l Gen. 34:3
m vv. 9,11, 13
5
n Ps. 104:15
10
o 1 Chr. 11:4–5
11
p Jud. 1:21; 2 Sam. 5:6

* **18:30** Septuagint and Vulgate read *Moses*.

and spend the night in Gibeah or in Ramah."

14 And they passed by and went their way; and the sun went down on them near Gibeah, which belongs to Benjamin.

15 They turned aside there to go in to lodge in Gibeah. And when he went in, he sat down in the open square of the city, for no one would take them into *his* house to [a]spend the night.

16 Just then an old man came in from his work in the field at evening, who also *was* from the mountains of Ephraim; he was staying in Gibeah, whereas the men of the place *were* Benjamites.

17 And when he raised his eyes, he saw the traveler in the open square of the city; and the old man said, "Where are you going, and where do you come from?"

18 So he said to him, "We *are* passing from Bethlehem in Judah toward the remote mountains of Ephraim; I *am* from there. I went to Bethlehem in Judah; *now* I am going to the [b]house of the LORD. But there *is* no one who will take me into his house,

19 "although we have both straw and fodder for our donkeys, and bread and wine for myself, for your female servant, and for the young man *who is* with your servant; *there is* no lack of anything."

20 And the old man said, [c]"Peace *be* with you! However, *let* all your needs *be* my responsibility; only do not spend the night in the open square."

21 So he brought him into his house, and gave fodder to the donkeys. And they washed their feet, and ate and drank.

22 As they were [d]enjoying themselves, suddenly certain [e]men of the city, [f]perverted men,* surrounded the house *and* beat on the door. They spoke to the master of the house, the old man, saying, "Bring out the man who came to your house, that we may know him *carnally!*"

23 But the man, the master of the house, went out to them and said to them, "No, my brethren! I beg you, do not act *so* wickedly! Seeing this man has come into my house, do not commit this [g]outrage.

24 "Look, *here is* my virgin [h]daughter and *the man's** concubine; let me bring them out now. Humble them, and do with them as you please; but to this man do not do such a vile thing!"

25 But the men would not heed him. So the man took his concubine and brought *her* out to them. And they knew her and abused her all night until morning; and when the day began to break, they let her go.

26 Then the woman came as the day was dawning, and fell down at the door of the man's house where her master *was,* till it was light.

27 When her master arose in the morning, and opened the doors of the house and went out to go his way, there was his concubine, fallen *at* the door of the house with her hands on the threshold.

28 And he said to her, "Get up and let us be going." But [i]there was no answer. So the man lifted her onto the donkey; and the man got up and went to his place.

Levite's concubine dismembered; anger of the tribes aroused

29 When he entered his house he took a knife, laid hold of his concubine, and [j]divided her into twelve pieces, limb by limb,* and sent her throughout all the territory of Israel.

30 And so it was that all who saw it said, [k]"No such deed has been done or seen from the day that the children of Israel came up from the land of Egypt until this day. Consider it, [l]confer, and speak up!"

Israel before the LORD at Mizpah; Benjamin warned

20 SO all the children of Israel came out, from [m]Dan to [n]Beersheba, as well as from the land of Gilead, and the congregation gathered together as one man before the LORD at [o]Mizpah.

2 And the leaders of all the people, all the tribes of Israel, presented themselves in the assembly of the people of God, four hundred thousand foot soldiers who drew the sword.

3 (Now the children of Benjamin heard that the children of Israel had gone up to Mizpah.) Then the children of Israel said, "Tell *us,* how did this wicked deed happen?"

4 So the Levite, the husband of the woman who was murdered, answered and said, "My concubine and I [p]went into Gibeah, which belongs to Benjamin, to spend the night.

5 "And the [q]men of Gibeah rose against me, and surrounded the house

15
a Cp. Lev. 25:35
18
b Josh. 18:1; 1 Sam. 1:3, 7
20
c Jud. 6:23; 1 Sam. 25:6
22
d Jud. 16:25; 19:6,9
e Gen. 19:4
f Dt. 13:13; 1 Sam. 2:12
23
g Jud. 20:6, 10
24
h Cp. Gen. 19:8
28
i Jud. 20:5
29
j Jud. 20:6; cp. 1 Sam. 11:7
30
k Cp. Hos. 9:9; 10:9
l Jud. 20:7
CHAPTER 20
1
m 1 Sam. 3:20; 2 Sam. 3:10; 24:2
n Josh. 19:2
o 1 Sam. 7:5
4
p Jud. 19:15
5
q Cp. Rom. 1:24–27

*
19:22 Literally *sons of Belial* **19:24** Literally *his*
19:29 Literally *with her bones*

at night because of me. They intended
to kill me, but instead they ravished
my concubine so that she died.
6 "So I took hold of my concubine,
[a]cut her in pieces, and sent her
throughout all the territory of the inheritance of Israel, because they committed lewdness and [b]outrage in Israel.
7 "Look! All of you *are* children of
Israel; give your advice and counsel
here and now!"
8 So all the people arose as one
man, saying, "None *of us* will go to his
tent, nor will any turn back to his
house;
9 "but now this *is* the thing which
we will do to Gibeah: *We will go up*
against it by [c]lot.
10 "We will take ten men out of *ev-*
ery hundred throughout all the tribes
of Israel, a hundred out of *every* thousand, and a thousand out of *every* ten
thousand, to make [d]provisions for the
people, that when they come to Gibeah in Benjamin, they may repay all
the vileness that they have done in Israel."
11 So all the men of Israel were
gathered against the city, united together as one man.
12 Then the tribes of Israel sent
men through all the tribe of Benjamin,
saying, "What *is* this wickedness that
has occurred among you?
13 "Now therefore, deliver up the
men, the [e]perverted men* who *are* in
Gibeah, that we may put them to death
and remove the evil from Israel!" But
the children of Benjamin would not
listen to the voice of their brethren,
the children of Israel.
14 Instead, the children of Benjamin gathered together from their cities to Gibeah, to go to battle against
the children of Israel.
15 And from their cities at that time
the [f]children of Benjamin numbered
twenty-six thousand men who drew
the sword, besides the inhabitants of
Gibeah, who numbered seven hundred select men.
16 Among all this people *were*
seven hundred select men *who were*
[g]left-handed; every one could sling a
stone at a hair's *breadth* and not miss.
17 Now besides Benjamin, the men
of Israel numbered four hundred
thousand men who drew the sword;
all of these *were* men of war.

Civil war with Benjamin

18 Then the children of Israel arose
and went up to the house of God* to
[h]inquire of God. They said, "Which of
us shall go up first to battle against the
children of Benjamin?" The LORD said,
[i]"Judah first!"
19 So the children of Israel rose in
the morning and encamped against
Gibeah.
20 And the men of Israel went out
to battle against Benjamin, and the
men of Israel put themselves in battle
array to fight against them at Gibeah.
21 Then the children of Benjamin
came out of Gibeah, and on that day
cut down to the ground twenty-two
thousand men of the Israelites.
22 And the people, that is, the men
of Israel, encouraged themselves and
again formed the battle line at the
place where they had put themselves
in array on the first day.
23 Then the children of Israel went
up and wept before the LORD until evening, and asked counsel of the LORD,
saying, "Shall I again draw near for
battle against the children of my
brother Benjamin?" And the LORD
said, "Go up against him."
24 So the children of Israel approached the children of Benjamin on
the second day.
25 And Benjamin went out against
them from Gibeah on the second day,
and cut down to the ground eighteen
thousand more of the children of Israel; all these drew the sword.
26 [j]Then all the children of Israel,
that is, all the people, went up and
came to the house of God* and [k]wept.
They sat there before the LORD and
fasted that day until evening; and they
offered burnt offerings and peace offerings before the LORD.
27 So the children of Israel inquired
of the LORD (the ark of the covenant of
God *was* [l]there in those days,
28 and [m]Phinehas the son of Eleazar, the son of Aaron, stood before it
in those days), saying, "Shall I yet
again go out to battle against the children of my brother Benjamin, or shall
I cease?" And the LORD said, "Go up,
for tomorrow I will deliver them into
your hand."
29 Then Israel set [n]men in ambush
all around Gibeah.
30 And the children of Israel went
up against the children of Benjamin
on the third day, and put themselves

6
a Jud. 19:29
b Josh. 7:15
9
c Jud. 1:3
10
d Josh. 1:11
13
e Jud. 19:22
15
f Num. 1:36–37; 2:23; 26:41
16
g Jud. 3:15; 1 Chr. 12:2
18
h Num. 27:21
i Jud. 1:1–2
26
j Jud. 20:18, 23
k Jud. 21:2
27
l 1 Sam. 1:3; 3:3
28
m Num. 25:7,13; Josh. 24:33
29
n Cp. Josh. 8:4

*
20:13 Literally *sons of Belial* **20:18** Hebrew *Bethel*
20:26 Hebrew *Bethel*

in battle array against Gibeah as at the
other times.
31 So the children of Benjamin
went out against the people, *and* were
drawn away from the city. They began
to strike down *and* kill some of the
people, as at the other times, in the
highways ([a]one of which goes up to
Bethel and the other to Gibeah) and in
the field, about thirty men of Israel.
32 And the children of Benjamin
said, "They *are* defeated before us, as
at first." But the children of Israel said,
"Let us flee and draw them away from
the city to the highways."
33 So all the men of Israel rose from
their place and put themselves in battle array at Baal Tamar. Then Israel's
men in ambush burst forth from their
position in the plain of Geba.
34 And ten thousand select men
from all Israel came against Gibeah,
and the battle was fierce. [b]But *the
Benjamites** did not know that disaster *was* upon them.
35 The LORD defeated Benjamin before Israel. And the children of Israel
destroyed that day [c]twenty-five thousand one hundred Benjamites; all
these drew the sword.
36 So the children of Benjamin saw
that they were defeated. The men of
[d]Israel had given ground to the Benjamites, because they relied on the men
in ambush whom they had set against
Gibeah.
37 And the men in ambush quickly
rushed upon Gibeah; the men in ambush spread out and struck the whole
city with the edge of the sword.
38 Now the appointed signal between the men of Israel and the men in
ambush was that they would make a
great cloud of [e]smoke rise up from the
city,
39 whereupon the men of Israel
would turn in battle. Now Benjamin
had begun to strike *and* kill about
thirty of the men of Israel. For they
said, "Surely they are defeated before
us, as *in* the first battle."
40 But when the cloud began to rise
from the city in a column of smoke,
the Benjamites looked behind them,
and there was the whole city going up
in smoke to heaven.
41 And when the men of Israel
turned back, the men of Benjamin
panicked, for they saw that disaster
had come upon them.
42 Therefore they turned *their
backs* before the men of Israel in the
direction of the wilderness; but the
battle overtook them, and whoever
came out of the cities they destroyed
in their midst.
43 They surrounded the Benjamites, chased them, *and* easily trampled them down as far as the front of
Gibeah toward the east.
44 And [f]eighteen thousand men of
Benjamin fell; all these *were* men of
valor.
45 Then they* turned and fled toward the wilderness to the rock of
[g]Rimmon; and they cut down five
thousand of them on the highways.
Then they pursued them relentlessly
up to Gidom, and killed two thousand
of them.
46 So all who fell of Benjamin that
day were twenty-five thousand men
who drew the sword; all these *were*
men of valor.
47 [h]But six hundred men turned
and fled toward the wilderness to the
rock of Rimmon, and they stayed at
the rock of Rimmon for four months.
48 And the men of Israel turned
back against the children of Benjamin, and struck them down with the
edge of the sword—from *every* city,
men and beasts, all who were found.
They also set fire to [i]all the cities they
came to.

Mourning for lost tribe

21 NOW the men of Israel had
[j]sworn an oath at [k]Mizpah,
saying, "None of us shall give his
daughter to Benjamin as a wife."
2 Then the people came to the
house of God,* and remained there
before God till evening. They lifted up
their voices and [l]wept bitterly,
3 and said, "O LORD God of Israel,
why has this come to pass in Israel,
that today there should be one [1]tribe
missing in Israel?"
4 So it was, on the next morning,
that the people rose early and built an
altar there, and offered burnt offerings and peace offerings.
5 The children of Israel said,
"Who *is there* among all the tribes of

31 a Jud. 21:19
34 b Cp. Josh. 8:14
35 c v. 15
36 d Josh. 8:15
38 e Josh. 8:20
44 f Cp. vv. 35, 46
45 g Josh. 15:32; 1 Chr. 6:77; Zech. 14:10
47 h Jud. 21:13
48 i Cp. Jud. 1:8
CHAPTER 21
1 j vv. 7–8 k Jud. 20:1
2 l Jud. 20:26

*20:34 Literally *they* 20:45 Septuagint reads *the rest.* 21:2 Hebrew *Bethel*

[1](21:3) There is here no mourning for sin, no humbling because of national transgression, no return to the LORD. Accordingly no word from the LORD comes to them. They act wholly in self-will (v. 10). Cp. Dan. 9:3–13.

Israel who did not come up with the assembly to the LORD?" For they had made a great oath concerning anyone who [a]had not come up to the LORD at Mizpah, saying, "He shall surely be put to death."

6 And the children of Israel [b]grieved for Benjamin their brother, and said, "One tribe is cut off from Israel today.

7 "What shall we do for wives for those who remain, seeing we have sworn by the LORD that we will not give them our daughters as wives?"

Provision for tribe's future

8 And they said, "What one *is there* from the tribes of Israel who did not come up to Mizpah to the LORD?" And, in fact, no one had come to the camp from Jabesh Gilead to the assembly.

9 For when the people were counted, indeed, not one of the inhabitants of [c]Jabesh Gilead *was* there.

10 So the congregation sent out there twelve thousand of their most valiant men, and commanded them, saying, [d]"Go and strike the inhabitants of Jabesh Gilead with the edge of the sword, including the women and children.

11 "And this *is* the thing that you shall do: [e]You shall utterly destroy every male, and every woman who has known a man intimately."

12 So they found among the inhabitants of Jabesh Gilead four hundred young virgins who had not known a man intimately; and they brought them to the camp at [f]Shiloh, which is in the land of Canaan.

13 Then the whole congregation sent *word* to the children of Benjamin who *were* at the rock of Rimmon, and announced peace to them.

14 So Benjamin came back at that time, and they gave them the women whom they had saved alive of the women of Jabesh Gilead; and yet they had not found enough for them.

15 And the people [b]grieved for Benjamin, because the LORD had made a void in the tribes of Israel.

16 Then the elders of the congregation said, "What shall we do for wives for those who remain, since the women of Benjamin have been destroyed?"

17 And they said, "*There must be* an inheritance for the survivors of Benjamin, that a tribe may not be destroyed from Israel.

18 "However, we cannot give them wives from our daughters, for the children of Israel have sworn an oath, saying, [g]'Cursed *be* the one who gives a wife to Benjamin.'"

19 Then they said, "In fact, *there is* a yearly [h]feast of the LORD in [i]Shiloh, which *is* north of Bethel, on the east side of the [j]highway that goes up from Bethel to Shechem, and south of Lebonah."

20 Therefore they instructed the children of Benjamin, saying, "Go, lie in wait in the vineyards,

21 "and watch; and just when the daughters of Shiloh come out to [k]perform their dances, then come out from the vineyards, and every man catch a wife for himself from the daughters of Shiloh; then go to the land of Benjamin.

22 "Then it shall be, when their fathers or their brothers come to us to complain, that we will say to them, 'Be kind to them for our sakes, because we did not take a wife for any of them in the war; for *it is* not *as though* you have given the *women* to them at this time, making yourselves [l]guilty of your oath.'"

23 And the children of Benjamin did so; they took enough wives for their number from those who danced, whom they caught. Then they went and returned to their inheritance, and they rebuilt the [m]cities and dwelt in them.

24 So the children of Israel departed from there at that time, every man to his tribe and family; they went out from there, every man to his inheritance.

25 In those days *there was* no [n]king in Israel; [1]everyone did *what was* right in his own [o]eyes.

5
a Cp. Jud. 5:23
6
b Lit. *repented.* See Zech. 8:14, *note*
9
c 1 Sam. 11:1
10
d v. 5; cp. 1 Sam. 11:7
11
e Num. 31:17; Dt. 20:13–14
12
f Jud. 18:31
18
g v. 1; cp. 1 Sam. 14:24
19
h Lev. 23:2
i Dt. 12:5; Josh. 18:1; 1 Sam. 1:3
j Jud. 20:31
21
k Jud. 11:34
22
l vv. 1,18
23
m Jud. 20:48
25
n Jud. 19:1
o Jud. 17:6

[1](21:25) The final clause of Judges does not necessarily mean that conditions were totally bad under the judges, for the beautiful story of Ruth is set in this historical context. Nor does v. 25 teach that all the evil of the times was caused by the lack of a king; later, under some of the kings, conditions were no better. The verse does raise the perennial problem of striking a proper balance between strong central government and personal liberty. Cp. 17:6; 18:1; 19:1.

The Book of

RUTH

Author: Unknown *Theme:* Redeeming Relative *Date of writing:* c. 10th Cent. B.C.

IN RUTH the events set forth are contemporary with the first half of Judges. In contrast with that period of strife and bloodshed is this lovely idyll, renowned in world literature as a masterpiece of narration. The book, however, is more than a beautiful picture of pastoral life; for behind the story of Ruth's fidelity there are clear implications of our Lord's redeeming work. Boaz, the redeeming relative, points to Christ; Ruth portrays those who enter into a new life through trust in Him. It is significant that both Boaz and Ruth are mentioned in the Messianic genealogy (Mt. 1:5).

The book may be divided according to chapters, as follows:

I. Ruth Deciding, 1.
II. Ruth Serving, 2.
III. Ruth Resting, 3.
IV. Ruth's Reward, 4.

I. Ruth Deciding, 1

Famine in Judah

1 NOW it came to pass, in the days
when the [a]judges ruled, that there
was a [b]famine in the land. And a certain man of [c]Bethlehem, Judah, went
to dwell in the country of [d]Moab, he
and his wife and his two sons.

Residing in Moab

2 The name of the man *was* [e]Elim-
elech, the name of his wife *was*
[f]Naomi, and the names of his two sons
were [g]Mahlon and [h]Chilion—
[i]Ephrathites of Bethlehem, Judah.
And they went to the country of Moab
and remained there.
3 Then Elimelech, Naomi's husband, died; and she was left, and her
two sons.
4 Now they took wives of the
women of Moab: the name of the one
was Orpah, and the name of the other
[j]Ruth. And they dwelt there about ten
years.
5 Then both Mahlon and Chilion
also died; so the woman survived her
two sons and her husband.

Return to Judah

6 Then she arose with her
daughters-in-law that she might return from the country of Moab, for she
had heard in the country of Moab that
the LORD had [k]visited His people by
giving them bread.
7 Therefore she went [l]out from
the place where she was, and her two
daughters-in-law with her; and they
went on the way to return to the land
of Judah.
8 And Naomi said to her two
daughters-in-law, "Go, return each to
her mother's house. The LORD deal
kindly with you, as you have dealt
with the dead and with me.
9 "The LORD grant that you may
find [m]rest, each in the house of her
husband." So she kissed them, and
they lifted up their voices and wept.
10 And they said to her, "Surely we
will return with you to your people."

Ruth's loyal decision

11 But Naomi said, "Turn back, my
daughters; why will you go with me?
Are there still sons in my womb, that
they may be your [n]husbands?
12 "Turn back, my daughters, go—
for I am too old to have a husband. If
I should say I have hope, *if* I should
have a husband tonight and should
also bear sons,
13 "would you wait for them till
they were grown? Would you restrain
yourselves from having husbands?
No, my daughters; for it grieves me
very much for your sakes that the
[o]hand of the LORD has gone out against
me!"
14 Then they lifted up their voices
and wept again; and Orpah kissed her
mother-in-law, but Ruth clung to her.
15 And she said, "Look, your sister-
in-law has gone back to her people
and to her [p]gods; return after your
sister-in-law."
16 But Ruth said:

"Entreat me not to leave you,
Or to turn back from following
after you;
For wherever you go, I will go;
And wherever you lodge, I will
lodge;
[q]Your people *shall be* my
people,
And your God, my God.
17 Where you die, I will die,
And there will I be buried.
The LORD do so to me, and
more also,

CHAPTER 1

1
[a] Jud. 2:16, 18
[b] Gen. 12:10
[c] Or *Bethlehem Judah,* lit. *house of bread and praise.* Jud. 17:7; 19:1
[d] Gen. 19:37

2
[e] Lit. *my God is King*
[f] Lit. *pleasant*
[g] Lit. *sick*
[h] Lit. *pining*
[i] Gen. 35:19; 1 Sam. 1:1; 1 Ki. 11:26

4
[j] Lit. *friendship*

6
[k] Ex. 3:16; 4:31; cp. Isa. 29:6

7
[l] Probably about 1100 B.C. Cp. Ruth 4:17

9
[m] Ruth 3:1

11
[n] Cp. Dt. 25:5

13
[o] Jud. 2:15; Ps. 38:2

15
[p] Josh. 24:15

16
[q] Ruth 2:11–12

If *anything but* death parts you
and me."

18 When she saw that she was determined to go with her, she stopped
speaking to her.

Back to Bethlehem

19 Now the two of them went until
they came to Bethlehem. And it happened, when they had come to Bethlehem, that all the city was excited because of them; and the women said,
"*Is* this Naomi?"
20 But she said to them, "Do not call
me Naomi; call me [a]Mara, for the
[b]Almighty has dealt very bitterly
with me.
21 "I went out full, and the LORD has
brought me home again empty. Why
do you call me Naomi, since the LORD
has testified against me, and the Almighty has afflicted me?"
22 So Naomi returned, and Ruth
the Moabitess her daughter-in-law
with her, who returned from the country of Moab. Now they came to Bethlehem at the beginning of barley harvest.

II. Ruth Serving, 2

Boaz compliments Ruth's unselfish care of Naomi

2 THERE was a [c]relative of Naomi's husband, a man of great
wealth, of the family of [d]Elimelech.
His name *was* Boaz.
2 So Ruth the Moabitess said to
Naomi, "Please let me go to the [e]field,
and [f]glean [g]heads of grain after *him*
in whose sight I may find [h]favor." And
she said to her, "Go, my daughter."
3 Then she left, and went and
gleaned in the field after the reapers.
And she happened to come to the part
of the field *belonging* to Boaz, who
was of the family of Elimelech.
4 Now behold, Boaz came from
[i]Bethlehem, and said to the reapers,
"The LORD *be* with you!" And they answered him, "The LORD bless [j]you!"
5 Then Boaz said to his servant
who was in charge of the reapers,
"Whose young woman *is* this?"
6 So the servant who was in
charge of the reapers answered and
said, "It *is* the young Moabite woman
who came back with Naomi from the
country of Moab.
7 "And she said, 'Please let me
glean and gather after the reapers
among the sheaves.' So she came and
has continued from morning until
now, though she rested a little in the
house."
8 Then Boaz said to Ruth, "You
will listen, my daughter, will you not?
Do not go to glean in another field, nor
go from here, but stay close by my
young women.

20
a Lit. *bitter*
b See Gen. 17:1, *note*

CHAPTER 2

1
c Ruth 3:2, 12; see 4:5, *note*
d Ruth 1:2

2
e Lev. 19:9–10; 23:22
f v. 15
g Dt. 23:25
h Cp. v. 10

4
i Ruth 1:1
j Ps. 129:7–8

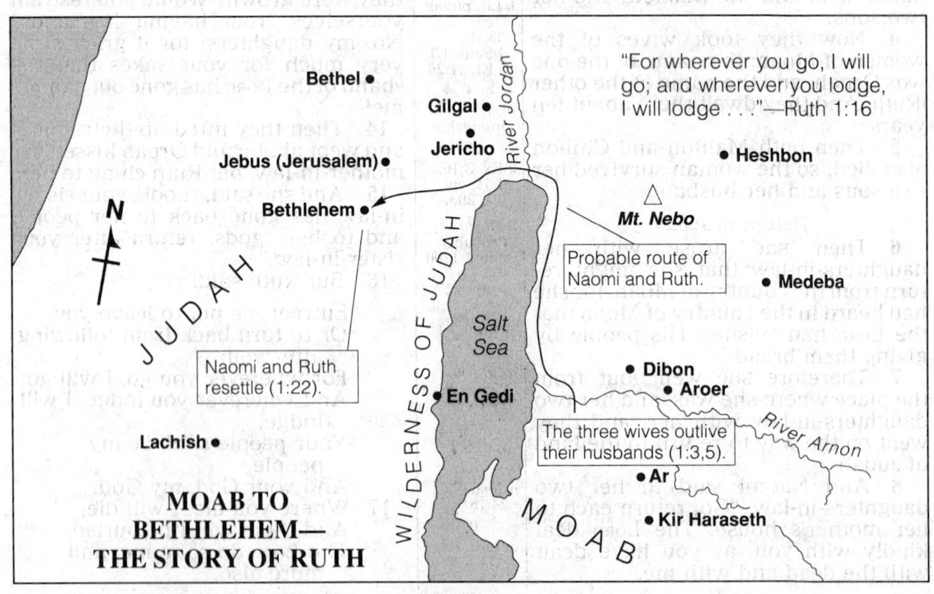

9 "*Let* your eyes *be* on the field which they reap, and go after them. Have I not commanded the young men not to touch you? And when you are thirsty, go to the vessels and drink from what the young men have drawn."

10 So she [a]fell on her face, bowed down to the ground, and said to him, "Why have I found [b]favor in your eyes, that you should take notice of me, since I *am* a foreigner?"

11 And Boaz answered and said to her, "It has been fully reported to me, [c]all that you have done for your mother-in-law since the death of your husband, and *how* you have left your father and your mother and the land of your birth, and have come to a people whom you did not know before.

12 "The LORD repay your work, and a full [d]reward be given you by the LORD God of Israel, under whose wings you have come [e]for refuge."

13 Then she said, "Let me find favor in your sight, my lord; for you have comforted me, and have spoken kindly to your maidservant, though I am not like one of your maidservants."

14 Now Boaz said to her at mealtime, "Come here, and eat of the bread, and dip your piece of bread in the vinegar." So she sat beside the reapers, and he passed parched *grain* to her; and she ate and was satisfied, and kept some back.

15 And when she rose up to glean, Boaz commanded his young men, saying, "Let her glean even among the sheaves, and do not reproach her.

16 "Also let *grain* from the bundles fall purposely for her; leave *it* that she may glean, and do not rebuke her."

17 So she gleaned in the field until evening, and beat out what she had gleaned, and it was about an [f]ephah of [g]barley.

18 Then she took *it* up and went into the city, and her mother-in-law saw what she had gleaned. So she brought out and gave to her what she had kept back after she had been satisfied.

19 And her mother-in-law said to her, "Where have you gleaned today? And where did you work? [h]Blessed be the one who took notice of you." So she told her mother-in-law with whom she had worked, and said, "The man's name with whom I worked today *is* Boaz."

20 Then Naomi said to her daughter-in-law, "Blessed *be* he of the LORD, who has not forsaken His kindness to the living and the dead!" And Naomi said to her, "This man *is* a relation of ours, one of our close [i]relatives."

21 Ruth the Moabitess said, "He also said to me, 'You shall stay close by my young men until they have finished all my harvest.' "

22 And Naomi said to Ruth her daughter-in-law, "*It is* good, my daughter, that you go out with his young women, and that people do not meet you in any other field."

23 So she stayed close by the young women of Boaz, to glean until the [j]end of barley harvest and wheat harvest; and she dwelt with her mother-in-law.

III. Ruth Resting, 3

Ruth's obedient faith (v. 18)

3 THEN Naomi her mother-in-law said to her, "My daughter, shall I not seek [k]security for you, that it may be well with you?

2 "Now Boaz, whose young women you were with, *is he* not our [l]relative? In fact, he is winnowing barley tonight at the threshing floor.

3 "Therefore wash yourself and anoint yourself, put on your *best* garment and go down to the threshing floor; *but* do not make yourself known to the man until he has finished eating and drinking.

4 "Then it shall be, when he lies down, that you shall notice the place where he lies; and you shall go in, uncover his feet, and lie down; and he will tell you what you should do."

5 And she said to her, "All that you say to me I will do."

6 So she went down to the threshing floor and did according to all that her mother-in-law instructed her.

7 And after Boaz had eaten and drunk, and his heart was [m]cheerful, he went to lie down at the end of the heap of grain; and she came softly, uncovered his feet, and lay down.

8 Now it happened at midnight that the man was startled, and turned himself; and there, a woman was lying at his feet.

9 And he said, "Who *are* you?" So she answered, "I *am* Ruth, your [1]maid-

10
a 1 Sam. 25:23,41
b v. 2; 1 Sam. 1:18
11
c Ruth 1:14–18
12
d 1 Sam. 24:19; cp. Gen. 15:1
e Ps. 91:2; see Ps. 2:12, *note*
17
f See Weights and Measures (OT), 2 Chr. 2:10, *note;* cp. Jud. 6:19
g Ruth 1:22
19
h Ps. 41:1
20
i Redemption (redeeming relative type): v. 20; Ruth 3:9. (Gen. 48:16; Isa. 59:20, *note*)
23
j Cp. Dt. 16:9
CHAPTER 3
1
k Ruth 1:9
2
l Ruth 2:3
7
m Jud. 19:22

[1](3:9) This action of Ruth should be interpreted in the light of the customs of that day. It

servant. [a]Take your maidservant under your wing,* for you are a close
[b]relative."
10 Then he said, "Blessed *are* you
of the LORD, my daughter! For you
have shown more kindness at the end
than at the beginning, in that you did
not go after young men, whether poor
or rich.
11 "And now, my daughter, do not
fear. I will do for you all that you
request, for all the people of my
town know that you *are* a [c]virtuous
woman.
12 "Now it is true that I *am* a close
[b]relative; [d]however, there is a relative
closer than I.
13 "Stay this night, and in the
morning it shall be *that* if he will [e]per-
form the duty of a close [b]relative for
you—good; let him do it. But if he does
not want to perform the duty for you,
then I will perform the duty for you,
as the LORD lives! Lie down until morning."
14 So she lay at his feet until morning, and she arose before one could
recognize another. Then he said, "Do
not let it be known that the woman
came to the threshing floor."
15 Also he said, "Bring the shawl
that *is* on you and hold it." And when
she held it, he measured six *ephahs* of
barley, and laid *it* on her. Then she*
went into the city.
16 When she came to her mother-
in-law, she said, "*Is* that you, my
daughter?" Then she told her all that
the man had done for her.
17 And she said, "These six *ephahs*
of barley he gave me; for he said to
me, 'Do not go empty-handed to your
mother-in-law.' "
18 Then she said, "Sit still, my
daughter, until you know how the
matter will turn out; for the man will
not rest until he has concluded the
matter this day."

9
a Cp. Ezek. 16:8
b Redemption (redeeming relative type): vv. 9, 12–13; 4:4–13; Ruth 4:14. (Gen. 48:16; Isa. 59:20, *note*)
11
c Prov. 31:10–31
12
d Ruth 4:1
13
e Dt. 25:5–10; Ruth 4:5, 10
CHAPTER 4
1
f Ruth 3:12
3
g Lev. 25:25
5
h Ruth 3:13
6
i Job 19:14
7
j Dt. 25:7–9

IV. Ruth's Reward, 4

Ruth requited with marriage

4 NOW Boaz went up to the gate
and sat down there; and behold,
the close relative of whom Boaz had
[f]spoken came by. So Boaz said,
"Come aside, friend,* sit down here."
So he came aside and sat down.
2 And he took ten men of the elders of the city, and said, "Sit down
here." So they sat down.
3 Then he said to the close relative, "Naomi, who has come back
from the country of Moab, sold the
piece of land [g]which *belonged* to our
brother Elimelech.
4 "And I thought to inform you,
saying, 'Buy *it* back in the presence of
the inhabitants and the elders of my
people. If you will redeem *it*, [b]redeem
it; but if you* will not redeem *it, then*
tell me, that I may know; for *there is*
no one but you to redeem *it*, and I *am*
next after you.' " And he said, "I will
redeem *it*."
5 Then Boaz said, "On the day you
buy the field from the hand of Naomi,
you must also buy *it* from Ruth the
Moabitess, the wife of the dead, [h]to
perpetuate* the name of the dead
through his [1]inheritance."
6 And the close relative said, "I
cannot [b]redeem *it* for myself, lest I
ruin my own inheritance. You redeem
my right of redemption for yourself,
for I [i]cannot redeem *it*."
7 Now [j]this *was the custom* in
former times in Israel concerning redeeming and exchanging, to confirm
anything: one man took off his sandal
and gave *it* to the other, and this *was*
a confirmation in Israel.
8 Therefore the close [b]relative

*
3:9 Or *Spread the corner of your garment over your maidservant* **3:15** Many Hebrew manuscripts, Syriac, and Vulgate read *she;* Masoretic Text, Septuagint, and Targum read *he.* **4:1** Hebrew *peloni almoni;* literally *so and so* **4:4** Following many Hebrew manuscripts, Septuagint, Syriac, Targum, and Vulgate; Masoretic Text reads *he.* **4:5** Literally *raise up*

---

was clearly a way of letting a close relative *(goel)* know that he had not only the right but also the request to proceed with the legal steps necessary to the exercise of his responsibility. That Ruth's conduct was above reproach is indicated in Boaz's reception, protection, and tacit agreement with the general evaluation of her character (vv. 10–11).

[1](4:5) Two OT laws are involved in this story (vv. 3–5). The law regulating redemption of property ("the piece of land which belonged to our brother Elimelech," v. 3) is given in Lev. 25:25–34. The law concerning a brother's duty to raise up seed to the deceased, the levirate law, is given in Dt. 25:5–10. The word "brother" is capable of extended interpretation (cp. Lev. 25:48–49; Jud. 9:3).

The story pictures most beautifully one aspect of our redemption. Boaz represents our Lord. Ruth stands for the believer. On our Lord's part (Heb. 2:14–15), He paid the price with His own blood, for He was both able and willing to redeem. See *notes* at Ex. 6:6; Isa. 59:20; Rom. 3:24.

said to Boaz, "Buy *it* for yourself." So
he took off his sandal.

9 And Boaz said to the elders and
all the people, "You *are* witnesses this
day that I have bought all that was
Elimelech's, and all that *was* Chilion's
and Mahlon's, from the hand of Naomi.

10 "Moreover, Ruth the Moabitess,
the widow of Mahlon, I have acquired
as my wife, to perpetuate the name of
the dead through his inheritance, that
the name of the dead may not be cut
off from among his brethren and from
his position at the gate.* You *are* witnesses this day."

11 And all the people who *were* at
the gate, and the elders, said, "*We are*
witnesses. The LORD make the woman
who is coming to your house like Rachel and Leah, the [a]two who built the
house of Israel; and may you prosper
in [b]Ephrathah and be famous in
[c]Bethlehem.

12 "May your house be like the
house of [d]Perez, whom [e]Tamar bore
to Judah, because of the offspring
which the LORD will give you from this
young woman."

13 So Boaz took Ruth and she became his wife; and when he went in to
her, the [f]LORD gave her conception,
and she bore a son.

14 Then the [g]women said to Naomi, "Blessed *be* the LORD, who has
not left you this day without a close
[h]relative; and may his name be famous in Israel!

15 "And may he be to you a restorer
of life and a nourisher of your old age;
for your daughter-in-law, who loves
you, who is [i]better to you than seven
sons, has borne him."

16 Then Naomi took the child and
laid him on her bosom, and became a
nurse to him.

Ruth's son to be David's grandfather

17 Also the neighbor [j]women gave
him a name, saying, "There is a son
born to Naomi." And they called his
name [k]Obed. He *is* the father of Jesse,
the father of [l]David.

18 [m]Now this *is* the genealogy of
[n]Perez: Perez begot Hezron;

19 Hezron begot Ram, and Ram begot Amminadab;

20 Amminadab begot Nahshon,
and Nahshon begot [o]Salmon;

21 Salmon begot Boaz, and Boaz
begot Obed;

22 Obed begot Jesse, and Jesse begot [1]David.

11 *a* Gen. 29:30 *b* Gen. 35:16–18 *c* 1 Sam. 16:4–13; Mic. 5:2; Mt. 2:1–8
12 *d* Mt. 1:3 *e* Gen. 38:6–29
13 *f* Gen. 29:31; 33:5; cp. Gen. 30:2
14 *g* Lk. 1:58; Rom. 12:15 *h* *Redemption* (redeeming relative type): vv. 4–14; 2 Sam. 14:11. (Gen. 48:16; Isa. 59:20, *note*)
15 *i* Cp. 1 Sam. 1:8
17 *j* v. 14 *k* Lit. *worshiped* *l* Lit. *beloved*

4:18 *m* vv. 18–22; 1 Chr. 2:4–15; Mt. 1:1–7 *n* Num. 26:20–21 **4:20** *o* Heb. *Salmah*

* **4:10** Probably his civic office

[1](4:22) In this book may be seen the majestic fulfillment of God's purpose. Even in the dark days of the judges He was watching over the line through which Christ would come into the world. The genealogy in vv. 18–22 discloses that Ruth, the Moabitess, was rewarded for her devotion and loyalty by becoming the great-grandmother of David. The birth of her son was probably not less than forty nor more than 100 years before the birth of David.

The First Book of

SAMUEL

Author: Unknown *Theme:* Samuel, Saul, and David *Date of writing:* 10th Cent. B.C.

FIRST and SECOND SAMUEL are counted as one book in the Hebrew Bible. Although 1 Samuel begins with the life of Samuel, it tells more about David than about Samuel. The book records Samuel's life, Saul's life, and David's anointing and early years.

Samuel, descended from Levi, was a priest and also a prophet. Sometimes he is referred to as initiating the prophetic order, as in Acts 3:24: "all the prophets, from Samuel and those who follow" (cp. Acts 13:20; Heb. 11:32). Samuel's career forms the bridge connecting the judges with the establishment of the Davidic kingdom.

First Samuel may be divided as follows:

I. The Youth and Judgeship of Samuel, 1—8.
II. The Anointing and Rejection of Saul as King of Israel, 9—15.
III. The Parallel Lives of Saul and David to the Death of Saul, 16—31.

I. The Youth and Judgeship of Samuel, 1—8

The mother of Samuel

1 NOW there was a certain man of
[a]Ramathaim Zophim, of the
[b]mountains of Ephraim, and his name
was [c]Elkanah the son of Jeroham, the
son of Elihu,* the son of Tohu,* the son
of Zuph, an Ephraimite.
2 And he had [d]two wives: the
name of one *was* Hannah, and the
name of the other Peninnah. Peninnah had children, but Hannah had no
children.
3 This man went up from his city
[e]yearly to [f]worship and sacrifice to the
[1][g]LORD of hosts in [h]Shiloh. Also the
two sons of Eli, Hophni and Phinehas, the priests of the LORD, *were*
there.
4 And whenever the time came for
Elkanah to make an offering, he
would give [i]portions to Peninnah his
wife and to all her sons and daughters.
5 But to Hannah he would give a
double portion, for he loved Hannah,
although the [j]LORD had closed her
womb.
6 And her rival also provoked her
severely, to make her miserable, because the LORD had closed her womb.
7 So it was, year by year, when
she went up to the house of the LORD,
that she [2]provoked her; therefore she
wept and did not eat.
8 Then Elkanah her husband said
to her, "Hannah, why do you weep?
Why do you not eat? And why is your
heart grieved? *Am* I not better to you
than ten sons?"

CHAPTER 1
1 [a] Cp. 1 Sam. 1:19 [b] Josh. 17:17–18 [c] 1 Chr. 6:22–28
2 [d] Dt. 21:15–17
3 [e] Ex. 34:23; Jud. 21:19; Lk. 2:41 [f] Dt. 12:5–7 [g] *Deity* (names of): v. 3; Ps. 110:1. (Gen. 1:1; Mal. 3:18) [h] Josh. 18:1
4 [i] Dt. 12:17–18
1:5 [j] Cp. Ruth 4:13

*
1:1 Spelled *Eliel* in 1 Chronicles 6:34 • Spelled *Toah* in 1 Chronicles 6:34

---

[1](1:3) LORD of hosts (Heb. *Jehovah Sabaoth*). For the distinctive meanings of LORD *(Jehovah)* see Ex. 34:6, *note. Sabaoth* means simply *hosts*, but with special reference to warfare or service. In use the two ideas are united; *Jehovah* is LORD of (warrior) hosts. It is the name, therefore, of the LORD in manifestation of power. "The LORD of hosts, He is the King of glory" (Ps. 24:10), and accordingly in the OT this name is revealed in the time of Israel's need. It is never found in the Pentateuch, or directly in Joshua or Judges, and occurs but rarely in the Psalms; but Jeremiah, the prophet of approaching national judgment, uses the name about 80 times; Haggai employs it 14 times; Zechariah calls upon the LORD of hosts about 50 times; and in Malachi the name occurs about 25 times. The meanings and uses of this name may be thus summarized: (1) The word "hosts" is related to (a) heavenly bodies (Gen. 2:1; Neh. 9:6; Isa. 40:26); (b) angels (Lk. 2:13); (c) saints (Josh. 5:15); and (d) sinners (Jud. 4:2; 2 Sam. 10:16; 2 Ki. 5:1). As LORD of hosts, God is able to marshal all these hosts to fulfill His purposes and to help His people (Gen. 32:1–2; Jud. 5:20; 1 Sam. 11:8–11; 1 Ki. 22:19; 2 Ki. 6:16–17; Isa. 10:16; 14:24–27; Jer. 27:6–8; 43:10–13; Acts 4:27–28). No wonder the Psalmist derives such confidence from this name (Ps. 46:7,11). And (2), this is the distinctive name of Deity for Israel's help and comfort in the time of her division and failure (1 Ki. 18:15; 19:14; Isa. 1:9; 8:11–14; 9:13–19; 10:24–27; 31:4–5; Hag. 2:4; Mal. 3:16–17; Jas. 5:4). For other names of Deity see *notes* on Gen. 1:1; 14:18; 15:2; 17:1; 21:33; Ex. 34:6; Mal. 3:18.

[2](1:7) Monogamy was ordained by God from the beginning for the highest happiness of men and women (Gen. 2:21–24; Mt. 19:3–6; Eph. 5:21–33). Polygamy, though not expressly forbidden in the OT (Dt. 21:15–17), falls short of God's ideal in marriage. The OT significantly shows the unhappiness of much of polygamous family life.

Hannah's vow

9 So Hannah arose after they had finished eating and drinking in Shiloh. Now Eli the priest was sitting on the seat by the doorpost of the tabernacle* of the LORD.

10 And she *was* in bitterness of soul, and prayed to the LORD and wept in anguish.

11 Then she made a [a]vow and [b]said, "O LORD of hosts, if You will indeed look on the affliction of Your maidservant and remember me, and not forget Your maidservant, but will give Your maidservant a male child, then I will give him to the LORD all the days of his life, and no [c]razor shall come upon his head."

12 And it happened, as she continued praying before the LORD, that Eli watched her mouth.

13 Now Hannah spoke in her [d]heart; only her lips moved, but her voice was not heard. Therefore Eli thought she was drunk.

14 So Eli said to her, "How long will you be [e]drunk? Put your wine away from you!"

15 But Hannah answered and said, "No, my lord, I *am* a woman of sorrowful spirit. I have drunk neither wine nor intoxicating drink, but have [f]poured out my soul before the LORD.

16 "Do not consider your maidservant a wicked woman,* for out of the abundance of my complaint and grief I have spoken until now."

17 Then Eli answered and said, "Go in peace, and the God of Israel grant your petition which you have asked of Him."

18 And she said, "Let your maidservant find favor in your sight." So the woman went her way and ate, and her [g]face was no longer *sad.*

Prayer answered; Samuel born

19 Then they rose early in the morning and worshiped before the LORD, and returned and came to their house at Ramah. And Elkanah knew Hannah his wife, and the LORD [h]remembered her.

20 So it came to pass in the process of time that Hannah conceived and [i]bore a son, and called his name Samuel,* *saying,* "Because I have asked for him from the LORD."

21 Now the man Elkanah and all his house [j]went up to offer to the LORD the yearly sacrifice and his vow.

22 But Hannah did not go up, for she said to her husband, "*Not* until the child is weaned; then I will take him, that he may appear before the LORD and remain there forever."

23 So Elkanah her [k]husband said to her, "Do what seems best to you; wait until you have weaned him. Only let the LORD establish His* word." Then the woman stayed and nursed her son until she had weaned him.

Samuel brought to Eli

24 Now when she had weaned him, she took him up with her, [l]with three bulls,* one [m]ephah of flour, and a skin of wine, and brought him to the house of the LORD in Shiloh. And the child *was* young.

25 Then they slaughtered a bull, and brought the child to Eli.

26 And she said, "O my lord! As your soul lives, my lord, I *am* the woman who stood by you here, praying to the LORD.

27 "For this child I prayed, and the LORD has granted me my petition which I asked of Him.

28 "Therefore I also have lent him to the LORD; as long as he lives he shall be lent to the LORD." So they worshiped the LORD there.

Hannah's prophetic prayer

2 [n]AND Hannah [b]prayed and [1]said:

"My heart [o]rejoices in the LORD;
My [p]horn is exalted in the LORD.
I smile at my enemies,
Because I rejoice in Your salvation.

2 [q]"No one is holy like the LORD,
For *there is* none besides You,
Nor *is there* any [r]rock like our God.

3 "Talk no more so very proudly;
Let no arrogance come from your mouth,
For the LORD *is* the God of [s]knowledge;

11
a Num. 30:6–11
b *Bible prayers* (OT): v. 11; 2:1; 2 Sam. 7:18. (Gen. 15:2; Hab. 3:1)
c Num. 6:5
13
d Cp. Gen. 24:42–45
14
e Cp. Acts 2:13
15
f Ps. 42:4; 62:8
18
g Prov. 15:13; cp. Rom. 15:13
19
h Gen. 30:22
20
i Probably 1100 B.C.
21
j 1 Sam. 1:3
23
k Num. 30:7
24
l Num. 15:9–10
m See Weights and Measures (OT), 2 Chr. 2:10, *note*
CHAPTER 2
1
n vv. 1–10
o Ps. 97:11–12
p See Dt. 33:17, *note*
2
q Rev. 15:4
r Dt. 32:4, 30–31; 2 Sam. 22:32; Ps. 18:2
3
s 1 Sam. 16:7

*

1:9 Hebrew *heykal,* palace or temple **1:16** Literally *daughter of Belial* **1:20** Literally *Heard by God* **1:23** Following Masoretic Text, Targum, and Vulgate; Dead Sea Scrolls, Septuagint, and Syriac read *your.* **1:24** Dead Sea Scrolls, Septuagint, and Syriac read *a three-year-old bull.*

[1](2:1) Compare Mary's song, the Magnificat (Lk. 1:46–55), where Mary echoes the words of Hannah.

And by Him actions are
weighed.
4 "The bows of the mighty men
are broken,
And those who stumbled are
girded with strength.
5 *Those who were* full have
hired themselves out for
bread,
And the hungry have ceased *to*
hunger.
Even the [a]barren has borne
seven,
And she who has many
children has become feeble.
6 "The LORD [b]kills and makes
alive;
He brings down to the [c]grave
and brings up.
7 The LORD makes poor and
makes rich;
He brings low and lifts up.
8 He raises the poor from the
dust
And [d]lifts the beggar from the
[e]ash heap,
To set *them* among princes
And make them inherit the
[f]throne of glory.

"For the pillars of the earth *are*
the LORD's,
And He has set the world upon
them.
9 He will [g]guard the feet of His
saints,
But the [h]wicked shall be silent
in darkness.

"For by strength no man shall
prevail.
10 The adversaries of the LORD
shall be broken in pieces;
From heaven He will thunder
against them.
The LORD will [i]judge the ends
of the earth.

[j]"He will give [k]strength to His
king,
And [l]exalt the [m]horn of His
[n]anointed."

11 Then Elkanah went to his house
at Ramah. But the child ministered to
the LORD before Eli the priest.

The evil sons of Eli

12 Now the sons of Eli *were* [o]cor-
rupt;* they did not know the LORD.
13 And the priests' custom with the
people *was that* when any man offered a sacrifice, the priest's servant
would come with a three-pronged
fleshhook in his hand while the meat
was boiling.
14 Then he would thrust *it* into the
pan, or kettle, or caldron, or pot; and
the priest would take for [p]himself all
that the fleshhook brought up. So they
did in [q]Shiloh to all the Israelites who
came there.
15 Also, before they burned the
[r]fat, the priest's servant would come
and say to the man who sacrificed,
"Give meat for roasting to the priest,
for he will not take boiled meat from
you, but raw."
16 And *if* the man said to him,
"They should really burn the fat first;
then you may take *as much* as your
heart desires," he would then answer
him, "*No,* but you must give *it* now;
and if not, I will take *it* by force."
17 Therefore the sin of the young
men was very great before the LORD,
for men [s]abhorred the offering of the
LORD.

The child Samuel before the LORD

18 But Samuel ministered before
the LORD, *even as* a child, wearing a
linen ephod.
19 Moreover his mother used to
make him a little [t]robe, and bring *it* to
him year by year when she came up
with her husband to offer the yearly
sacrifice.
20 And Eli would [u]bless Elkanah
and his wife, and say, "The LORD give
you descendants from this woman for
the [v]loan that was given to the LORD."
Then they would go to their own
home.
21 And the LORD visited Hannah, so
that she conceived and bore three
sons and two daughters. Meanwhile
the child Samuel [w]grew before the
LORD.

Eli rebukes his sons

22 Now Eli was very old; and he
heard everything his sons did to all
Israel,* and how they lay with the
women who [x]assembled at the door of
the tabernacle of meeting.
23 So he said to them, "Why do you
do such things? For I hear of your evil
dealings from all the people.
24 "No, my sons! For *it is* not a good
[y]report that I hear. You make the
LORD's people transgress.
25 "If one man sins against another,
God will [z]judge him. But if a man sins

5
a Ps. 113:9
6
b Dt. 32:39; 2 Ki. 5:7; Ps. 116:3
c See Hab. 2:5, *note;* cp. Lk. 16:23, *note*
8
d Ps. 75:7
e Ps. 113:7–8
f Cp. Gen. 41:41
9
g Ps. 37:23–24; 91:11–12; 94:18; 121:3; 1 Pet. 1:5
h Rom. 3:19
10
i Ps. 96:13; Mt. 25:31–32
j Mt. 28:18
k Ps. 21:1,7
l Ps. 89:24
m See Dt. 33:17, *note*
n A prophecy of Christ as King; cp. Ps. 2:1–9
12
o Cp. Jer. 2:8
14
p Cp. Lev. 7:29–34; Dt. 18:1–5
q 1 Sam. 1:3
15
r Lev. 3:3–5, 16
17
s Mal. 2:7–9
19
t Cp. Ex. 28:31
20
u Lk. 2:34
v 1 Sam. 1:28
21
w 1 Sam. 3:19–21
22
x Ex. 38:8
24
y vv. 13–17
25
z Dt. 25:1–2

*

2:12 Literally *sons of Belial* 2:22 Following Masoretic Text, Targum, and Vulgate; Dead Sea Scrolls and Septuagint omit the rest of this verse.

against the [a]LORD, who will intercede for him?" Nevertheless they did not heed the voice of their father, because the LORD desired to kill them.

26 And the child Samuel grew in stature, and in favor both with the LORD and [b]men.

God warns of judgment upon Eli's sons

27 Then a [c]man of God came to Eli and said to him, "Thus says the LORD: 'Did I not clearly reveal Myself to the [d]house of your father when they were in Egypt in Pharaoh's house?

28 'Did I not [e]choose him out of all the tribes of Israel *to be* My priest, to offer upon My altar, to burn incense, and to wear an ephod before Me? And did I not give to the house of your father all the offerings of the children of Israel made by fire?

29 'Why do you kick at My sacrifice and My offering which I have commanded *in My* [f]dwelling place, and honor your sons more than [g]Me, to make yourselves fat with the best of all the offerings of Israel My people?'

30 "Therefore the LORD God of Israel says: 'I [h]said indeed *that* your house and the house of your father would walk before Me forever.' [i]But now the LORD says: 'Far be it from Me; for those who honor Me I will honor, and those who despise Me shall be lightly esteemed.

31 [j]'Behold, the days are coming that I will cut off your arm and the arm of your father's house, so that there will not be an old man in your house.

32 'And you will see an enemy *in My* dwelling place, *despite* all the good which God does for Israel. And there shall not be an old man in your house forever.

33 'But any of your men *whom* I do not cut off from My altar shall consume your eyes and grieve your heart. And all the descendants of your house shall die in the flower of their age.

34 'Now this *shall be* a [k]sign to you that will come upon your two sons, on Hophni and Phinehas: in one day they shall [l]die, both of them.

35 'Then I will [m]raise up for Myself a faithful priest *who* shall do according to what *is* in My heart and in My mind. I will build him a sure house, and he shall walk [n]before My anointed forever.

36 'And it shall come to pass that everyone who is left in your house will come *and* bow down to him for a piece of silver and a morsel of bread, and say, "Please, put me in one of the priestly positions, that I may eat a piece of bread." ' "

God rebukes Eli; Samuel is called

3 NOW the boy Samuel [o]ministered to the LORD before Eli. And the word of the LORD was [p]rare in those days; *there was* no widespread revelation.

2 And it came to pass at that time, while Eli *was* lying down in his place, and when his eyes had begun to grow so [q]dim that he could not see,

3 and before the [r]lamp of God went out in the tabernacle* of the LORD where the ark of God *was*, and while Samuel was lying down,

4 that the LORD called Samuel. And he answered, "Here [s]I am!"

5 So he ran to Eli and said, "Here I am, for you called me." And he said, "I did not call; lie down again." And he went and lay down.

6 Then the LORD called yet again, "Samuel!" So Samuel arose and went to Eli, and said, "Here I am, for you called me." He answered, "I did not call, my son; lie down again."

7 (Now Samuel did not yet know the [t]LORD, nor was the word of the LORD yet revealed to him.)

8 And the LORD called Samuel again the third time. So he arose and went to Eli, and said, "Here I am, for you did call me." Then Eli perceived that the LORD had called the boy.

9 Therefore Eli said to Samuel, "Go, lie down; and it shall be, if He calls you, that you must say, [u]'Speak, LORD, for Your servant hears.' " So Samuel went and lay down in his place.

10 Now the LORD came and stood and called as at other times, "Samuel! Samuel!" And Samuel answered, "Speak, for Your servant hears."

Samuel becomes a prophet-priest

11 Then the LORD said to Samuel: "Behold, I will do something in Israel at which both ears of everyone who hears it will [v]tingle.

12 "In that day I will perform against Eli all that I have [w]spoken concerning his house, from beginning to end.

13 "For I have told him that I will judge his house forever for the iniquity which he [x]knows, because his

* 3:3 Hebrew *heykal*, palace or temple

25
a Num. 15:30; Ps. 51:4,16
26
b Cp. Lk. 2:52
27
c Dt. 33:1; Jud. 13:6; 1 Sam. 9:6
d Ex. 4:14–16
28
e Ex. 28:1–4
29
f Ps. 26:8
g Mt. 10:37
30
h Ex. 29:9
i Cp. Jer. 18:8–10
31
j vv. 31–35; 1 Ki. 2:27, 35; 1 Sam. 4:11–18; 22:18–19
34
k 1 Ki. 13:3
l 1 Sam. 4:11
35
m Heb. 2:17; 7:26–28
n Cp. 1 Sam. 12:3; 16:13
CHAPTER 3
1
o 1 Sam. 2:11,18
p Cp. 2 Chr. 15:3; Amos 8:11
2
q 1 Sam. 4:15
3
r Ex. 27:20–21
4
s Cp. Isa. 6:8
7
t 1 Sam. 2:12
9
u v. 10; Ps. 85:8
11
v 2 Ki. 21:12; Jer. 19:3
12
w 1 Sam. 2:29–36
13
x 1 Sam. 2:22

[a]sons made themselves vile, and he [b]did not restrain them.

14 "And therefore I have sworn to the house of Eli that the iniquity of Eli's house shall [c]not be atoned for by sacrifice or offering forever."

15 So Samuel lay down until morning,* and opened the [d]doors of the house of the LORD. And Samuel was afraid to tell Eli the vision.

16 Then Eli called Samuel and said, "Samuel, my son!" He answered, "Here I am."

17 And he said, "What *is* the word that *the* LORD spoke to you? Please do not hide *it* from me. God do so to you, and more also, if you hide anything from me of all the things that He said to you."

18 Then Samuel told him everything, and hid nothing from him. And he said, "It *is* the [e]LORD. Let Him do what seems good to Him."

The LORD is with Samuel

19 So Samuel [f]grew, and the LORD was with him and let none of his words fall to the [g]ground.

20 And all Israel [h]from Dan to Beersheba knew that Samuel *had been* established as a prophet of the LORD.

21 Then the LORD appeared again in Shiloh. For the LORD revealed Himself to Samuel in Shiloh by the word of the LORD.

Philistines capture ark of God; Eli's two sons die

4 [i]AND the word of Samuel came to all Israel.*

Now Israel went out to battle against the Philistines, and encamped beside [j]Ebenezer; and the Philistines encamped in Aphek.

2 Then the [k]Philistines put themselves in battle array against Israel. And when they joined battle, Israel was defeated by the Philistines, who killed about four thousand men of the army in the field.

3 And when the people had come into the camp, the elders of Israel said, [l]"Why has the LORD defeated us today before the Philistines? [m]Let us bring the ark of the covenant of the LORD from Shiloh to us, that when it comes among us it may save us from the hand of our enemies."

4 So the people sent to Shiloh, that they might bring from there the ark of the covenant of the LORD of hosts, who [n]dwells *between* the cherubim. And the [o]two sons of Eli, Hophni and Phinehas, *were* there with the ark of the covenant of God.

5 And when the ark of the covenant of the LORD came into the camp, all Israel shouted so loudly that the earth shook.

6 Now when the Philistines heard the noise of the shout, they said, "What *does* the sound of this great shout in the camp of the Hebrews *mean?*" Then they understood that the ark of the LORD had come into the camp.

7 So the Philistines were afraid, for they said, "God has come into the camp!" And they said, [p]"Woe to us! For such a thing has never happened before.

8 "Woe to us! Who will deliver us from the hand of these mighty gods? These *are* the gods who struck the Egyptians with all the plagues in the wilderness.

9 "Be strong and conduct yourselves like men, you Philistines, that you do not become servants of the Hebrews, as they have been to [q]you. Conduct yourselves like [r]men, and fight!"

10 So the Philistines fought, and Israel was defeated, and every man fled to his [s]tent. There was a very great slaughter, and there fell of Israel thirty thousand foot soldiers.

11 Also the ark of God was [t]captured; and the two sons of Eli, Hophni and Phinehas, [u]died.

Eli dies; God's glory departs from Israel

12 Then a man of Benjamin ran from the battle line the same day, and came to Shiloh with his clothes torn and dirt on his head.

13 Now when he came, there was Eli, [v]sitting on a seat by the wayside watching,* for his heart trembled for the ark of God. And when the man came into the city and told *it*, all the city cried out.

14 When Eli heard the noise of the outcry, he said, "What *does* the sound of this tumult *mean?*" And the man came quickly and told Eli.

15 Eli was ninety-eight years old,

13 *a* 1 Sam. 2:12–17 *b* Dt. 17:12; 21:18
14 *c* Num. 15:30; Isa. 22:14; Heb. 10:4, 26–31
15 *d* Cp. 1 Chr. 15:23
18 *e* Gen. 24:50; Acts 5:39
19 *f* 1 Sam. 2:21 *g* 1 Sam. 9:6
20 *h* Jud. 20:1
CHAPTER 4
1 *i* First sentence relates to 1 Sam. 3:21 *j* 1 Sam. 7:12
2 *k* 1 Sam. 12:9
3 *l* Josh. 7:7–8; Prov. 19:3 *m* Josh. 6:6–21
4 *n* Ex. 25:18–22 *o* 1 Sam. 2:12
7 *p* Ex. 15:14
9 *q* Jud. 10:7 *r* 1 Cor. 16:13
10 *s* 2 Sam. 18:17
11 *t* Ps. 78:60–61 *u* 1 Sam. 2:34
13 *v* Cp. 1 Sam. 1:9

*

3:15 Following Masoretic Text, Targum, and Vulgate; Septuagint adds *and he arose in the morning.* **4:1** Following Masoretic Text and Targum; Septuagint and Vulgate add *And it came to pass in those days that the Philistines gathered themselves together to fight;* Septuagint adds further *against Israel.* **4:13** Following Masoretic Text and Vulgate; Septuagint reads *beside the gate watching the road.*

and his eyes were so [a]dim that he
could not see.
16 Then the man said to Eli, "I *am*
he who came from the battle. And I
fled today from the battle line." And
he said, "What happened, my son?"
17 So the messenger answered and
said, "Israel has fled before the Philistines, and there has been a great
slaughter among the people. Also
your two sons, Hophni and Phinehas,
are dead; and the ark of God has been
captured."
18 Then it happened, when he
made mention of the ark of God, that
Eli fell off the seat backward by the
side of the gate; and his neck was broken and he died, for the man was old
and heavy. And he had judged Israel
forty years.
19 Now his daughter-in-law, Phinehas' wife, was with child, *due* to be
delivered; and when she heard the
news that the ark of God was captured, and that her father-in-law and
her husband were dead, she bowed
herself and gave birth, for her labor
pains came upon her.
20 And about the time of her death
the women who stood by her said to
her, [b]"Do not fear, for you have borne
a son." But she did not answer, nor did
she regard *it*.
21 Then she named the child [c]Icha-
bod,* saying, "The glory has departed
from Israel!" because the ark of God
had been captured and because of her
father-in-law and her husband.
22 And she said, "The glory has departed from Israel, for the ark of God
has been captured."

God provoked with Philistines because of the ark

5 THEN the Philistines took the ark
of God and brought it from [d]Eb-
enezer to [e]Ashdod.
2 When the Philistines took the
ark of God, they brought it into the
house of Dagon* and set it by [f]Da-
gon.
3 And when the people of Ashdod
arose early in the morning, there was
Dagon, fallen on its face to the earth
before the ark of the LORD. So they
took Dagon and [g]set it in its place
again.
4 And when they arose early the
next morning, there was Dagon, fallen
on its face to the ground before the ark
of the LORD. The head of Dagon and
both the palms of its hands *were* broken off on the threshold; only Dagon's
torso* was left of it.
5 Therefore neither the priests of
Dagon nor any who come into Dagon's house tread on the threshold of
Dagon in Ashdod to this day.
6 But the [h]hand of the LORD was
heavy on the people of Ashdod, and
He ravaged them and [i]struck them
with [j]tumors,* *both* Ashdod and its
territory.
7 And when the men of Ashdod
saw how *it was,* they said, "The ark of
the [k]God of Israel must not remain
with us, for His hand is harsh toward
us and Dagon our god."
8 Therefore they sent and gathered to themselves all the [l]lords of the
Philistines, and said, "What shall we
do with the ark of the God of Israel?"
And they answered, "Let the ark of the
God of Israel be carried away to
[m]Gath." So they carried the ark of the
God of Israel away.
9 So it was, after they had carried
it away, that the [h]hand of the LORD
was against the city with a very great
destruction; and He struck the men of
the city, both small and great, and tumors broke out on them.
10 Therefore they sent the ark of
God to Ekron. So it was, as the ark of
God came to Ekron, that the Ekronites
cried out, saying, "They have brought
the ark of the God of Israel to us, to kill
us and our people!"
11 So they sent and gathered together all the lords of the Philistines,
and said, "Send away the ark of the
God of Israel, and let it go back to its
own place, so that it does not kill us
and our people." For there was a
deadly destruction throughout all the
city; the [h]hand of God was very heavy
there.
12 And the men who did not die
were stricken with the tumors, and the
[n]cry of the city went up to heaven.

Ark returned to Israel

6 NOW the ark of the LORD was in
the country of the Philistines
seven months.
2 And the Philistines called for the
priests and the [o]diviners, saying,
"What shall we do with the ark of the

15
a 1 Sam. 3:2
20
b Gen. 35:17
21
c 1 Sam. 14:3
CHAPTER 5
1
d 1 Sam. 4:1; 7:12
e Or *Azotus,* Acts 8:40
2
f Jud. 16:23–30; 1 Chr. 10:10
3
g Isa. 46:7
6
h vv. 7,9,11; Ex. 9:3; Dt. 2:15; 1 Sam. 7:13; 12:15
i *Miracles* (OT): vv. 3–12; 2 Sam. 6:7. (Gen. 5:24; Jon. 1:17, *note*)
j Dt. 28:27
7
k 1 Sam. 6:5
8
l 1 Sam. 6:4
m Josh. 11:22
12
n 1 Sam. 9:16; Jer. 14:2
CHAPTER 6
2
o Gen. 41:8; Ex. 7:11; Isa. 47:13

*4:21 Literally *Inglorious* 5:2 A Philistine idol
5:4 Following Septuagint, Syriac, Targum, and Vulgate; Masoretic Text reads *Dagon.*
5:6 Probably bubonic plague. Septuagint and Vulgate add here *And in the midst of their land rats sprang up, and there was a great death panic in the city.*

LORD? Tell us how we should send it to its place."

3 So they said, "If you send away the ark of the God of Israel, do not send it [a]empty; but by all means return *it* to Him *with* a [b]trespass offering. [c]Then you will be healed, and it will be known to you why His hand is not removed from you."

4 Then they said, "What *is* the trespass offering which we shall return to Him?" They answered, [d]"Five golden tumors and five golden rats, *according to* the number of the lords of the Philistines. For the same plague *was* on all of you and on your lords.

5 "Therefore you shall make images of your tumors and images of your rats that ravage the land, and you shall give [e]glory to the God of Israel; perhaps He will [f]lighten His hand from you, from your gods, and from your land.

6 "Why then do you harden your hearts as the Egyptians and Pharaoh [g]hardened their hearts? When He did mighty things among them, did they not let the people [h]go, that they might depart?

7 "Now therefore, make a new [i]cart, take two milk cows which have never been yoked, and hitch the cows to the cart; and take their calves home, away from them.

8 "Then take the ark of the LORD and set it on the cart; and put the articles of gold which you are returning to Him *as* a trespass offering in a chest by its side. Then send it away, and let it go.

9 "And watch: if it goes up the road to its own territory, to Beth Shemesh, *then* He has done us this great evil. But if not, then we shall know that *it is* not His hand *that* struck us—it happened to us by chance."

10 Then the men did so; they took two milk cows and hitched them to the cart, and shut up their calves at home.

11 And they set the ark of the LORD on the cart, and the chest with the gold rats and the images of their tumors.

12 Then the cows headed straight for the road to Beth Shemesh, *and* went along the [j]highway, lowing as they went, and did not turn aside to the right hand or the left. And the lords of the Philistines went after them to the border of Beth Shemesh.

13 Now *the people of* Beth Shemesh *were* reaping their [k]wheat harvest in the valley; and they lifted their eyes and saw the ark, and rejoiced to see *it*.

14 Then the cart came into the field of Joshua of Beth Shemesh, and stood there; a large stone *was* there. So they split the wood of the cart and offered the cows as a burnt offering to the LORD.

15 The Levites took down the ark of the LORD and the chest that *was* with it, in which *were* the articles of gold, and put *them* on the large stone. Then the men of Beth Shemesh offered burnt offerings and made sacrifices the same day to the LORD.

16 So when the five lords of the Philistines had seen *it*, they returned to Ekron the same day.

17 These *are* the golden tumors which the Philistines returned *as* a trespass offering to the LORD: one for Ashdod, one for Gaza, one for Ashkelon, one for [l]Gath, one for Ekron;

18 and the golden rats, *according to* the number of all the cities of the Philistines *belonging* to the five lords, *both* fortified cities and country villages, even as far as the large *stone of* Abel on which they set the ark of the LORD, *which stone remains* to this day in the field of Joshua of Beth Shemesh.

19 Then He struck the men of Beth Shemesh, [m]because they had looked into the ark of the LORD. He [n]struck [1]fifty thousand and seventy men* of the people, and the people lamented because the LORD had struck the people with a great slaughter.

20 And the men of Beth Shemesh said, [o]"Who is able to stand before this holy LORD God? And [p]to whom shall it go up from us?"

21 So they sent messengers to the inhabitants of [q]Kirjath Jearim, saying, "The Philistines have brought back the ark of the LORD; come down *and* take it up with you."

Twenty years waiting; revival begins

7 THEN the men of Kirjath Jearim came and took the ark of the LORD,

3
a Dt. 16:16
b Cp. Lev. 5:15–16
c Cp. Heb. 9:22
4
d 1 Sam. 6:17
5
e Josh. 7:19; Jer. 13:16
f Cp. 1 Sam. 5:6,11
6
g Ex. 9:34
h Ex. 12:31
7
i Cp. 2 Sam. 6:3
12
j Num. 20:19
13
k 1 Sam. 12:17
17
l 1 Sam. 5:8
19
m Num. 4:15–16; cp. 1 Chr. 13:9–10
n 2 Sam. 6:7
20
o Ps. 24:3–4
p Cp. 2 Sam. 6:9
21
q Josh. 15:9,60; Jud. 18:12

* **6:19** Or *He struck seventy men of the people and fifty oxen of a man*

[1](6:19) This number is generally considered to be a scribal error. Some discrepant statements concerning numbers are found in the extant Hebrew manuscripts. Error by scribes in transcription of Hebrew numbers was easy, whereas preservation of numerical accuracy was difficult. Inspiration extends only to the inerrancy of the original autographs.

and brought it into the house of [a]Abinadab on the hill, and [b]consecrated Eleazar his son to keep the ark of the LORD.

2 So it was that the ark remained in Kirjath Jearim a long time; it was there twenty years. And all the house of Israel [c]lamented after the LORD.

3 Then Samuel spoke to all the house of Israel, saying, "If you [d]return to the LORD with all your hearts, *then* put away the [e]foreign gods and the [f]Ashtoreths from among you, and [g]prepare your hearts for the LORD, and serve Him [h]only; and He will deliver you from the hand of the Philistines."

4 So the children of Israel [i]put away the Baals and the Ashtoreths, and served the LORD only.

5 And Samuel said, "Gather all Israel to [j]Mizpah, and [k]I will pray to the LORD for you."

6 So they gathered together at Mizpah, drew water, and poured *it* out before the LORD. And they [l]fasted that day, and said there, "We have [m]sinned against the LORD." And Samuel judged the children of Israel at Mizpah.

7 Now when the Philistines heard that the children of Israel had gathered together at Mizpah, the lords of the Philistines went up against Israel. And when the children of Israel heard *of it,* they were afraid of the Philistines.

8 So the children of Israel said to Samuel, [n]"Do not cease to cry out to the LORD our God for us, that He may save us from the hand of the Philistines."

Israelites victorious at Ebenezer

9 And Samuel took a [o]suckling lamb and offered *it as* a whole burnt offering to the LORD. Then Samuel cried out to the LORD for Israel, and the LORD [p]answered him.

10 Now as Samuel was offering up the burnt offering, the Philistines drew near to battle against Israel. But the LORD thundered with a loud [q]thunder upon the Philistines that day, and so [r]confused them that they were overcome before Israel.

11 And the men of Israel went out of Mizpah and pursued the Philistines, and drove them back as far as below Beth Car.

12 Then Samuel took a [s]stone and set *it* up between Mizpah and Shen, and called its name [t]Ebenezer, saying, "Thus far the LORD has helped us."

13 So the Philistines were subdued, and they did not come anymore into the territory of Israel. And the hand of the LORD was against the Philistines all the days of Samuel.

14 Then the cities which the Philistines had taken from Israel were restored to Israel, from Ekron to Gath; and Israel recovered its territory from the hands of the Philistines. Also there was peace between Israel and the Amorites.

Summary of Samuel's ministry

15 And Samuel judged Israel all the days of his life.

16 He went from year to year on a circuit to Bethel, Gilgal, and Mizpah, and judged Israel in all those places.

17 But he always returned to Ramah, for his home *was* there. There he judged Israel, and there he built an altar to the LORD.

Israel demands a king

8 NOW it [u]came to pass when Samuel was [v]old that he made his sons [w]judges over Israel.

2 The name of his firstborn was [x]Joel, and the name of his second, Abijah; *they were* judges in Beersheba.

3 But his sons did not walk in his ways; they turned aside after dishonest gain, took [y]bribes, and perverted [z]justice.

4 Then all the elders of Israel gathered together and came to Samuel at Ramah,

5 and said to him, "Look, you are old, and your sons do not walk in your ways. Now [aa]make us a king to judge us like all the nations."

God protests Israel's demand

6 But the thing [bb]displeased Samuel when they said, "Give us a king to judge us." So Samuel [cc]prayed to the LORD.

7 And the LORD said to Samuel, "Heed the voice of the people in all that they say to you; [dd]for they have not rejected you, but they have [1][ee]re-

CHAPTER 7
1
a 2 Sam. 6:3–4
b Lev. 21:8
2
c Cp. Zech. 12:10–11
3
d Dt. 30:2, 10; Joel 2:13; cp. 2 Chr. 30:6–9
e Josh. 24:14–23; Jud. 10:16
f See Jud. 2:13, *note*
g Cp. 2 Chr. 19:3
h Mt. 4:10
4
i Jud. 10:16
5
j Jud. 10:17; 20:1; 1 Sam. 10:17
k 1 Sam. 12:17–19
6
l Jud. 20:26; Neh. 9:1
m 1 Sam. 12:10
8
n 1 Sam. 12:19–24
9
o Lev. 22:27
p 1 Sam. 12:18; Ps. 99:6; Jer. 15:1
10
q 2 Sam. 22:14–15
r Ps. 18:14
12
s Josh. 4:9; 24:26
t Lit. *the stone of help*
CHAPTER 8
1
u Israel (history): vv. 1–8; 2 Sam. 7:8. (Gen. 12:2; Rom. 11:26, *note*)
v 1 Sam. 12:2
w Kingdom (OT): vv. 1–7; 1 Sam. 9:17. (Gen. 1:26; Zech. 12:8, *note*). Dt.16:18–19

8:2 *x* Or *Vashni,* 1 Chr. 6:28 8:3 *y* Ex. 23:6–8; cp. 1 Sam. 12:3 *z* Dt. 27:25 8:5 *aa* Dt. 17:14–15; Hos. 13:10–11 8:6 *bb* 1 Sam. 12:17 *cc* 1 Sam. 7:9 8:7 *dd* Cp. Ex. 16:8 *ee* 1 Sam. 10:19; cp. Lk. 10:16

[1](8:7) The demand of Israel, as recorded in this chapter (vv. 5,19–20), did not mean the end of the theocratic kingdom. Although it implied a rejection of God (v. 7), the people's demand was granted only in part. They were given a king, but certainly not "like all the nations." God

jected Me, that I should not reign over
them.
8 "According to all the works
which they have done since the day
that I brought them up out of Egypt,
even to this day—with which they
have forsaken Me and served other
gods—so they are doing to you also.
9 "Now therefore, heed their
voice. However, you shall solemnly
[a]forewarn them, and show them the
behavior of the king who will reign
over them."

Samuel warns about a king

10 So Samuel told all the words of
the LORD to the people who asked him
for a king.
11 And he said, "This will be the
[b]behavior of the king who will reign
over you: He will take your [c]sons and
appoint *them* for his own [d]chariots
and *to be* his horsemen, and *some* will
run before his chariots.
12 "He will [e]appoint captains over
his thousands and captains over his
fifties, *will set some* to plow his
ground and reap his harvest, and
some to make his weapons of war and
equipment for his chariots.
13 "He will take your daughters *to
be* perfumers, cooks, and bakers.
14 "And he will take the best of
your [f]fields, your vineyards, and your
olive groves, and give *them* to his servants.
15 "He will take a tenth of your
grain and your vintage, and give it to
his officers and servants.

9
a Cp. Ezek. 3:18
11
b Dt. 17:14–20; 1 Sam. 10:25
c 1 Sam. 14:52
d 2 Sam. 15:1
12
e 1 Sam. 22:7
14
f 1 Ki. 21:7; Ezek. 46:18
18
g Prov. 1:25–28
h Isa. 1:15; Mic. 3:4
22
i Hos. 13:11
CHAPTER 9
1
j 1 Chr. 9:36–39

16 "And he will take your male servants, your female servants, your finest young men,* and your donkeys,
and put *them* to his work.
17 "He will take a tenth of your
sheep. And you will be his servants.
18 "And you will cry out in that day
because of your king whom you have
chosen for yourselves, and the LORD
will [g]not [h]hear you in that day."

God agrees to a king

19 Nevertheless the people refused
to obey the voice of Samuel; and they
said, "No, but we will have a king over
us,
20 that we also may be like all the
nations, and that our king may judge
us and go out before us and fight our
battles."
21 And Samuel heard all the words
of the people, and he repeated them in
the hearing of the LORD.
22 So the LORD said to Samuel,
"Heed their voice, and make them a
[i]king." And Samuel said to the men of
Israel, "Every man go to his city."

II. The Anointing and Rejection of Saul as King of Israel, 9—15

God chooses Saul as king

9 THERE was a man of Benjamin
whose name *was* [j]Kish the son of
Abiel, the son of Zeror, the son of Be-
chorath, the son of Aphiah, a Benjamite, a mighty man of power.
2 And he had a choice and handsome son whose name *was* Saul.

* 8:16 Septuagint reads *cattle.*

is always sovereign over the nations in providential control (Acts 17:26), but in this instance He reserved for Himself the right to choose the king by direct control (9:17; Hos. 13:11), and the king was made personally responsible to God for his actions (13:13–14), thus clearly indicating an unbroken continuance of the LORD's particular sovereignty over the nation.

The theocratic kingdom established at Sinai over the nation of Israel, through which God purposed to bless all other nations (Ex. 19:5–6), was a rule of God administered mediatorially, i.e. through divinely chosen persons who spoke and acted for God in governing functions, and who were directly responsible to God for what they did. These mediatorial rulers could be great leaders like Moses and Joshua, military judges, or even kings; but God is always the real sovereign down to the end of the kingdom in history (1 Chr. 29:25). The visible symbol of God's presence as the divine Ruler was the Shekinah glory. This glory entered and filled the tabernacle at the establishment of the kingdom at Sinai (Ex. 40:34–38), led the nation into the land, was manifested in the temple of Solomon (2 Chr. 7:1–2), and departed spectacularly from Jerusalem as the kingdom came to an end at the Babylonian captivity, when governmental sovereignty was transferred to the Gentiles (cp. Ezek. 11:23 with Dan. 2:31–38). When the times of the Gentiles are fulfilled, this mediatorial kingdom of God on earth will be restored at the coming of God's Messiah in great power and glory to reign over the nations as the perfect mediatorial King (Mic. 4:1–8).

This mediatorial kingdom on earth should not be confused with that original and universal kingdom of God which always exists efficaciously and embraces all objects, persons, and events, all doings of individuals and nations, all operations and changes of nature and history absolutely without exception (Ps. 103:19; Dan. 4:17). However, the mediatorial earthly kingdom may properly be regarded as a phase of the universal kingdom of God (1 Cor. 15:24). For a Summary of the Kingdom in OT, see Zech. 12:8, *note.*

There was not a more handsome person than he among the children of Israel. From his shoulders upward *he* [a]*was* taller than any of the people.

3 Now the donkeys of Kish, Saul's father, were lost. And Kish said to his son Saul, "Please take one of the servants with you, and arise, go and look for the donkeys."

4 So he passed through the mountains of Ephraim and through the land of [b]Shalisha, but they did not find *them.* Then they passed through the land of Shaalim, and *they were* not *there.* Then he passed through the land of the Benjamites, but they did not find *them.*

5 When they had come to the land of [c]Zuph, Saul said to his servant who *was* with him, "Come, let [d]us return, lest my father cease *caring* about the donkeys and become worried about us."

6 And he said to him, "Look now, *there is* in this city a [e]man of God, and *he is* an honorable man; all that he says surely comes to [f]pass. So let us go there; perhaps he can show us the way that we should go."

7 Then Saul said to his servant, "But look, *if* we go, what shall we [g]bring the man? For the bread in our vessels is all gone, and *there is* no present to bring to the man of God. What do we have?"

8 And the servant answered Saul again and said, "Look, I have here at hand one-fourth of a [h]shekel of silver. I will give *that* to the man of God, to tell us our way."

9 (Formerly in Israel, when a man went to inquire of God, he spoke thus: "Come, let us go to the seer"; for *he who is* now *called* a prophet was formerly called a [i]seer.)

10 Then Saul said to his servant, "Well said; come, let us go." So they went to the city where the man of God *was.*

11 As they went up the hill to the city, they met some young [j]women going out to draw water, and said to them, "Is the seer here?"

12 And they answered them and said, "Yes, there he is, just ahead of you. Hurry now; for today he came to this city, because there is a sacrifice of the people today on the [k]high place.

13 "As soon as you come into the city, you will surely find him before he goes up to the high place to eat. For the people will not eat until he comes, because he must bless the sacrifice; afterward those who are invited will eat. Now therefore, go up, for about this time you will find him."

14 So they went up to the city. As they were coming into the city, there was Samuel, coming out toward them on his way up to the high place.

15 Now the LORD had told Samuel in his ear the day before Saul came, saying,

16 "Tomorrow about this time [l]I will send you a man from the land of Benjamin, and you shall [m]anoint him commander over My people Israel, that he may save My people from the hand of the Philistines; for I have [n]looked upon My people, because their cry has come to Me."

17 So when Samuel saw Saul, the LORD said to him, [o]"There he is, the man of whom I spoke to you. This one shall [p]reign over My people."

18 Then Saul drew near to Samuel in the gate, and said, "Please tell me, where *is* the seer's house?"

19 Samuel answered Saul and said, "I *am* the seer. Go up before me to the high place, for you shall eat with me today; and tomorrow I will let you go and will tell you all that *is* in your heart.

20 "But as for your donkeys that were lost three days ago, do not be anxious about them, for they have been found. And on whom *is* all the desire of Israel? *Is it* not on you and on all your father's house?"

21 And Saul answered and said, "*Am* I not a Benjamite, of the [q]smallest of the tribes of Israel, and [r]my family the least of all the families of the tribe* of Benjamin? [s]Why then do you speak like this to me?"

22 Now Samuel took Saul and his servant and brought them into the hall, and had them sit in the place of honor among those who were invited; there *were* about thirty persons.

23 And Samuel said to the cook, "Bring the portion which I gave you, of which I said to you, 'Set it apart.' "

24 So the cook took up the [t]thigh with its upper part and set *it* before Saul. And *Samuel* said, "Here it is, what was kept back. *It* was set apart for you. Eat; for until this time it has been kept for you, since I said I invited the people." So Saul ate with Samuel that day.

25 When they had come down from the high place into the city, *Samuel*

2
a 1 Sam. 10:23
4
b 2 Ki. 4:42
5
c 1 Sam. 1:1
d 1 Sam. 10:2
6
e Dt. 33:1; 2 Ki. 5:8
f 1 Sam. 3:19
7
g Cp. 1 Ki. 14:3; 2 Ki. 5:15; 8:8–9
8
h See Coinage (OT), Ex. 30:13, *note*
9
i vv. 11,19; 1 Chr. 9:22; cp. Isa. 30:10
11
j Gen. 24:11; Ex. 2:16
12
k 1 Sam. 7:17; 10:5; 1 Ki. 3:2
16
l Dt. 17:15; 1 Sam. 10:24
m 1 Sam. 10:1
n Ex. 2:23–25
17
o 1 Sam. 16:12
p *Kingdom* (OT): vv. 15–17; 1 Sam. 10:25. (Gen. 1:26; Zech. 12:8, *note*)
21
q Ps. 68:27; cp. Jud. 20:46
r Cp. Jud. 6:15
s Cp. 1 Sam. 15:17
24
t Cp. Lev. 7:32–33

*
9:21 Literally *tribes*

spoke with Saul on the top of the house.*

26 They arose early; and it was about the dawning of the day that Samuel called to Saul on the top of the house, saying, "Get up, that I may send you on your way." And Saul arose, and both of them went outside, he and Samuel.

27 As they were going down to the outskirts of the city, Samuel said to Saul, "Tell the servant to go on ahead of us." And he went on. "But you stand here awhile, that I may announce to you the word of God."

Saul privately anointed king

10 THEN [a]Samuel took a flask of oil and poured *it* on his head, and [b]kissed him and said: "*Is it* not because the LORD has anointed you [c]commander over His [d]inheritance?*

2 "When you have departed from me today, you will find two men by Rachel's [e]tomb in the territory of Benjamin at Zelzah; and they will say to you, 'The donkeys which you went to look for have been found. And now your father has ceased caring about the donkeys and is worrying about [f]you, saying, "What shall I do about my son?" '

3 "Then you shall go on forward from there and come to the terebinth tree of Tabor. There three men going up to God [g]at Bethel will meet you, one carrying three young goats, another carrying three loaves of bread, and another carrying a skin of wine.

4 "And they will greet you and give you two *loaves* of bread, which you shall receive from their hands.

5 "After that you shall come to the [h]hill of God where the Philistine garrison *is*. And it will happen, when you have come there to the city, that you will meet a [i]group of prophets coming down from the high place with a stringed instrument, a tambourine, a flute, and a harp before them; and they will be prophesying.

6 "Then the [j]Spirit of the LORD will come upon you, and you will prophesy with them and be turned into another man.

7 "And let it be, when these signs come to you, *that* you do as the occasion demands; for God *is* with [k]you.

8 "You shall go down before me to [l]Gilgal; and surely I will come down to you to offer burnt offerings *and* make sacrifices of peace offerings. [m]Seven days you shall wait, till I come to you and show you what you should do."

9 So it was, when he had turned his back to go from Samuel, that God gave him another heart; and all those signs came to pass that day.

10 When they came there to the hill, there was a group of prophets to meet him; then the [j]Spirit of God came upon [n]him, and he prophesied among them.

11 And it happened, when all who knew him formerly saw that he indeed prophesied among the [o]prophets, that the people said to one another, "What *is* this *that* has come upon the son of Kish? *Is* Saul also among the prophets?"

12 Then a man from there answered and said, "But who *is* their father?" Therefore it became a proverb: "*Is* Saul also among the prophets?"

13 And when he had finished prophesying, he went to the high place.

14 Then Saul's [p]uncle said to him and his servant, "Where did you go?" So he said, "To look for the donkeys. When we saw that *they were* nowhere *to be found*, we went to Samuel."

15 And Saul's uncle said, "Tell me, please, what Samuel said to you."

16 So Saul said to his uncle, "He told us plainly that the donkeys had been [q]found." But about the matter of the kingdom, he did not tell him what Samuel had said.

Saul publicly installed as king of Israel

17 Then Samuel called the people together to the LORD at [r]Mizpah,

18 and said to the children of Israel, "Thus says the LORD God of Israel: 'I brought up Israel out of [s]Egypt, and delivered you from the hand of the Egyptians *and* from the hand of all kingdoms and from those who oppressed you.'

19 "But you have today [t]rejected your God, who Himself saved you from all your adversities and your tribulations; and you have said to Him, 'No, set a king over us!' Now therefore, present yourselves before

CHAPTER 10

1 a 1 Sam. 9:16; cp. 16:13; 2 Ki. 9:3,6 b Cp. Ps. 2:12 c 2 Sam. 5:2 d Ex. 34:9; Dt. 32:9

2 e Gen. 35:19–20 f 1 Sam. 9:5

3 g Gen. 35:1

5 h 1 Sam. 13:2–3 i 1 Sam. 19:20

6 j *Holy Spirit* (OT): vv. 6–10; 1 Sam. 11:6. (Gen. 1:2; Zech. 12:10)

7 k Josh. 1:5; 1 Sam. 3:19

8 l 1 Sam. 11:14 m 1 Sam. 13:8–10

10 n Cp. 1 Sam. 18:10

11 o 1 Sam. 19:24; cp. Amos 7:14–15; Mt. 13:54–57

14 p 1 Sam. 14:50

16 q 1 Sam. 9:20

17 r 1 Sam. 7:5

18 s Jud. 6:8–9; 1 Sam. 8:8; 12:6,8

19 t 1 Sam. 8:7; 12:12

*

9:25 Following Masoretic Text and Targum; Septuagint omits *He spoke with Saul on top of the house;* Septuagint and Vulgate add *And he prepared a bed for Saul on top of the house, and he slept.* **10:1** Following Masoretic Text, Targum, and Vulgate; Septuagint reads *His people Israel; and you shall rule the people of the Lord;* Septuagint and Vulgate add *And you shall deliver His people from the hands of their enemies all around them. And this shall be a sign to you, that God has anointed you to be prince.*

the LORD by your [a]tribes and by your clans."*

20 And when Samuel had caused all the tribes of Israel to come near, the tribe of Benjamin was chosen.

21 When he had caused the tribe of Benjamin to come near by their families, the family of Matri was chosen. And Saul the son of Kish was chosen. But when they sought him, he could not be found.

22 Therefore they [b]inquired of the LORD further, "Has the man come here yet?" And the LORD answered, "There he is, hidden among the equipment."

23 So they ran and brought him from there; and when he stood among the people, he was [c]taller than any of the people from his shoulders upward.

24 And Samuel said to all the people, "Do you see him whom the LORD has [d]chosen, that *there is* no one like him among all the people?" So all the people shouted and said, "Long live the king!"

25 Then Samuel explained to the people the [e]behavior of [f]royalty, and wrote *it* in a book and [g]laid *it* up before the LORD. And Samuel sent all the people away, every man to his house.

26 And Saul also went home to Gibeah; and valiant *men* went with him, whose hearts God had touched.

27 But some rebels said, "How can this man save us?" So they despised him, and brought him no [h]presents. But he held his peace.

Saul defeats the Ammonites

11 THEN [i]Nahash the Ammonite came up and encamped against [j]Jabesh Gilead; and all the men of Jabesh said to Nahash, "Make a [k]covenant with us, and we will serve you."

2 And Nahash the Ammonite answered them, "On this *condition* I will make *a covenant* with you, that I may put out all your right eyes, and bring [l]reproach on all Israel."

3 Then the elders of Jabesh said to him, "Hold off for seven days, that we may send messengers to all the territory of Israel. And then, if *there is* no one to save us, we will come out to you."

4 So the messengers came to [m]Gibeah of Saul and told the news in the hearing of the people. And all the people lifted up their voices and wept.

5 Now there was Saul, coming behind the herd from the field; and Saul said, "What *troubles* the people, that they weep?" And they told him the words of the men of Jabesh.

6 Then the [n]Spirit of God came upon Saul when he heard this news, and his anger was greatly aroused.

7 So he took a yoke of oxen and [o]cut them in pieces, and sent *them* throughout all the territory of Israel by the hands of messengers, saying, "Whoever does not go out with Saul and Samuel to battle, so it shall be done to his oxen." And the fear of the LORD fell on the people, and they came out with one [p]consent.

8 When he numbered them in Bezek, the children of Israel were [q]three hundred thousand, and the men of Judah thirty thousand.

9 And they said to the messengers who came, "Thus you shall say to the men of Jabesh Gilead: 'Tomorrow, by *the time* the sun is hot, you shall have help.'" Then the messengers came and reported *it* to the men of Jabesh, and they were glad.

10 Therefore the men of Jabesh said, "Tomorrow we will come out to you, and you may do with us whatever seems good to you."

11 So it was, on the next day, that Saul put the people in three companies; and they came into the midst of the camp in the morning watch, and killed Ammonites until the heat of the day. And it happened that those who survived were scattered, so that no two of them were left together.

Saul confirmed in kingship

12 Then the people said to Samuel, [r]"Who *is* he who said, 'Shall Saul reign over us?' Bring the men, that we may put them to [s]death."

13 But Saul said, [t]"Not a man shall be put to death this day, for today the LORD has accomplished salvation in Israel."

14 Then Samuel said to the people, "Come, let us go to [u]Gilgal and renew the kingdom there."

15 So all the people went to Gilgal, and there they [v]made Saul king before the LORD in Gilgal. There they made sacrifices of peace offerings [w]before the LORD, and there Saul and all the men of Israel rejoiced greatly.

Integrity of Samuel's judgeship

12 NOW Samuel said to all Israel: "Indeed I have [x]heeded your

19 *a* Cp. Josh. 7:14–17
22 *b* Cp. 1 Sam. 9:9; 14:37
23 *c* 1 Sam. 9:2
24 *d* 1 Sam. 9:16
25 *e* 1 Sam. 8:11
f *Kingdom* (OT): v. 25; 1 Sam. 15:1. (Gen. 1:26; Zech. 12:8, *note*)
g Cp. Dt. 31:26
27 *h* 1 Ki. 10:25; 2 Chr. 17:5
CHAPTER 11
1 *i* 1 Sam. 12:12
j Jud. 21:8; 1 Sam. 31:11
k Cp. Ex. 23:31–33
2 *l* Ps. 44:13
4 *m* 1 Sam. 10:26
6 *n* *Holy Spirit* (OT): v. 6; 1 Sam. 16:13. (Gen. 1:2; Zech. 12:10)
7 *o* Cp. Jud. 19:29
p Cp. Jud. 20:1
8 *q* Cp. Jud. 20:15–17; 2 Sam. 24:9
12 *r* 1 Sam. 10:27
s Cp. Lk. 19:27
13 *t* Cp. 2 Sam. 19:22
14 *u* 1 Sam. 10:8
15 *v* 1051 B.C.
w Josh. 8:31
CHAPTER 12
1 *x* 1 Sam. 8:7

* **10:19** Literally *thousands*

voice in all that you said to me, and
have made a king over you.
2 "And now here is the king, walking before you; and I am [a]old and
grayheaded, and look, my sons *are*
with you. I have walked before you
from my childhood to this day.
3 "Here I am. Witness against me
before the LORD and before His
[b]anointed: Whose ox have I taken, or
whose donkey have I [c]taken, or
whom have I cheated? Whom have I
oppressed, or from whose hand have
I received *any* [d]bribe with which to
[e]blind my eyes? I will restore *it* to
you."
4 And they said, [f]"You have not
cheated us or oppressed us, nor have
you taken anything from any man's
hand."
5 Then he said to them, "The LORD
is witness against you, and His
anointed *is* witness this day, that you
have not found anything [g]in my
hand." And they answered, "*He is* witness."

Samuel recounts the LORD's past deliverances of Israel

6 Then Samuel said to the people,
"*It is* the LORD who raised up Moses
and Aaron, and who brought your fathers up from the land of Egypt.
7 "Now therefore, stand still, that I
may [h]reason with you [i]before the
LORD concerning all the [j]righteous
acts of the LORD which He did to you
and your fathers:
8 "When Jacob had gone into
[k]Egypt,* and your fathers cried out to
the LORD, then the LORD [l]sent Moses
and Aaron, who brought your fathers
out of Egypt and made them dwell in
this place.
9 "And when they [m]forgot the
LORD their God, He sold them into
the hand of [n]Sisera, commander of the
army of Hazor, into the hand of the
[o]Philistines, and into the hand of
the king of [p]Moab; and they fought
against them.
10 "Then they cried out to the LORD,
and [q]said, 'We have sinned, because
we have forsaken the LORD and served
the Baals and [r]Ashtoreths; but now
[s]deliver us from the hand of our enemies, and we will serve You.'
11 "And the LORD sent [t]Jerub-
baal,* Bedan,* [u]Jephthah, and
[v]Samuel,* and delivered you out of
the hand of your enemies on every
side; and you dwell in safety.

God confirms kingship

12 "And [w]when you saw that Nahash king of the Ammonites came
against you, you said to me, 'No, but a
[x]king shall reign over us,' when the
LORD your God *was* your [y]king.
13 "Now therefore, here is the king
whom you have chosen *and* whom
you have desired. And take note, the
LORD has set a king over you.
14 "If you [z]fear the LORD and serve
Him and obey His voice, and do not
rebel against the commandment of the
LORD, then both you and the king who
reigns over you will continue following the LORD your God.
15 "However, if you do [aa]not obey
the voice of the LORD, but [bb]rebel
against the commandment of the
LORD, then the hand of the LORD will be
against you, as *it was* against your fathers.
16 "Now therefore, [cc]stand and see
this great thing which the LORD will do
before your eyes:
17 "*Is* today not the wheat harvest?
I will call to the LORD, and He will send
[dd]thunder and [ee]rain, that you may perceive and see that your [ff]wickedness *is*
great, which you have done in the
sight of the LORD, in asking a king for
yourselves."
18 So Samuel called to the LORD,
and the LORD sent thunder and rain
that day; and all the people greatly
[gg]feared the LORD and Samuel.
19 And all the people said to Samuel, [hh]"Pray for your servants to the
LORD your God, that we may not die;
for we have added to all our sins the
evil of asking a king for ourselves."
20 Then Samuel said to the people,
"Do not fear. You have done all this
wickedness; yet [ii]do not turn aside
from following the LORD, but serve the
LORD with all your heart.
21 "And do not turn aside; for *then
you would go* after [jj]empty things
which cannot profit or deliver, for
they *are* nothing.
22 "For the LORD will [kk]not forsake
[ll]His people, for His great name's
sake, because it has pleased the LORD
to make you His people.
23 "Moreover, as for me, far be it

2 *a* 1 Sam. 8:1,5
3 *b* 1 Sam. 10:1; 24:6 *c* Num. 16:15; cp. Acts 20:33 *d* Ex. 23:8 *e* Dt. 16:19
4 *f* Lev. 19:13; cp. 2 Cor. 7:2
5 *g* Ex. 22:4
7 *h* Cp. Isa. 1:18; Mic. 6:2–3 *i* 1 Sam. 11:15 *j* Jud. 5:11; cp. Ps. 103:6
8 *k* Ps. 105:23 *l* Ex. 3:10
9 *m* Jud. 3:7 *n* Jud. 4:2 *o* Jud. 10:7 *p* Jud. 3:12
10 *q* Jud. 10:10 *r* See Jud. 2:13, *note* *s* Cp. Jud. 10:15–16
11 *t* Jud. 7:1 *u* Jud. 11:1 *v* 1 Sam. 7:13
12 *w* 1 Sam. 11:1–2 *x* 1 Sam. 8:5,19–20 *y* Jud. 8:23; Ps. 59:13
14 *z* Josh. 24:14; see Ps. 19:9, *note*
15 *aa* Dt. 28:15 *bb* Isa. 1:20
16 *cc* Ex. 14:13
17 *dd* 1 Sam. 7:10 *ee* Ezra 10:9 *ff* 1 Sam. 8:7
18 *gg* Ex. 14:31
19 *hh* 1 Sam. 7:8
20 *ii* Dt. 11:16
21 *jj* Ps. 60:11; 108:12; Isa. 41:29 **12:22** *kk* Dt. 31:6 *ll* Dt. 7:6–11; Isa. 43:21

*

12:8 Following Masoretic Text, Targum, and Vulgate; Septuagint adds *and the Egyptians afflicted them.* **12:11** Syriac reads *Deborah*; Targum reads *Gideon.* • Septuagint and Syriac read *Barak;* Targum reads *Simson.* • Syriac reads *Simson.*

from me that I should sin against the
LORD in [a]ceasing to pray for you; but
I will teach you the good and the right
way.
24 "Only [b]fear the LORD, and serve
Him in truth with all your heart; for
consider what great things He has
done for you.
25 "But if you still do wickedly, you
shall be swept away, both you and
your king."

Saul's self-seeking and cowardice

13 SAUL reigned one year; and
when he had reigned two years
over Israel,*
2 Saul chose for himself three
thousand *men* of Israel. Two thousand
were with Saul in [c]Michmash and in
the mountains of Bethel, and a thousand were with [d]Jonathan in [e]Gibeah
of Benjamin. The rest of the people he
sent away, every man to his tent.
3 And Jonathan attacked the
[f]garrison of the Philistines that *was* in
[g]Geba, and the Philistines heard *of it*.
Then Saul blew the trumpet throughout all the land, saying, "Let the Hebrews hear!"
4 Now all Israel heard it said *that*
Saul had attacked a garrison of the
Philistines, and *that* Israel had also
become an abomination to the Philistines. And the people were called together to Saul at Gilgal.
5 Then the Philistines gathered together to fight with Israel, thirty*
thousand chariots and six thousand
horsemen, and people [h]as the sand
which *is* on the seashore in multitude.
And they came up and encamped in
Michmash, to the east of [i]Beth Aven.
6 When the men of Israel saw that
they were in danger (for the people
were distressed), then the people [j]hid
in caves, in thickets, in rocks, in holes,
and in pits.
7 And *some of* the Hebrews
crossed over the Jordan to the [k]land
of Gad and Gilead. As for Saul, he *was*
still in Gilgal, and all the people followed him trembling.

Saul intrudes into priest's office and is rejected by God

8 Then he waited seven days, according to the time set by Samuel. But
Samuel did not come to Gilgal; and
the people were scattered from him.
9 So Saul said, "Bring a burnt offering and peace offerings here to
me." And [l]he offered the burnt offering.
10 Now it happened, as soon as he
had finished presenting the burnt offering, that Samuel came; and Saul
went out to meet him, that he might
[m]greet him.
11 And Samuel said, "What have
you done?" Saul said, "When I saw
that the people were scattered from
me, and *that* you did not come within
the days appointed, and *that* the Philistines gathered together at Michmash,
12 "then I said, 'The Philistines will
now come down on me at Gilgal, and
I have not made supplication to the
LORD.' Therefore I felt compelled, and
offered a burnt offering."
13 And Samuel said to Saul, [n]"You
have done [o]foolishly. You have not
kept the commandment of the LORD
your God, which He [p]commanded
you. For now the LORD would have established your kingdom over Israel
forever.
14 "But now your kingdom shall
[q]not continue. The LORD has [r]sought
for Himself a man [s]after His own
heart, and the LORD has commanded
him *to be* commander over His people, because you have [t]not kept what
the LORD commanded you."

Israel helpless before Philistines

15 Then Samuel arose and went up
from Gilgal to Gibeah of Benjamin.*
And Saul numbered the people present with him, about six hundred men.
16 Saul, Jonathan his son, and the
people present with them remained in
Gibeah of Benjamin. But the Philistines encamped in Michmash.
17 Then raiders came out of the
camp of the Philistines in three companies. One company turned onto the
road to [u]Ophrah, to the land of Shual,
18 another company turned to the
road *to* [v]Beth Horon, and another
company turned *to* the road of the
border that overlooks the Valley of
[w]Zeboim toward the wilderness.
19 Now there was no [1x]blacksmith
to be found throughout all the land of

23 *a* Cp. Rom. 1:9
24 *b* Josh. 24:14; see Ps. 19:9, *note*
CHAPTER 13
2 *c* 1 Sam. 14:5,31 *d* 1 Sam. 14:1 *e* 1 Sam. 10:26
3 *f* 1 Sam. 10:5 *g* 1 Sam. 14:5
5 *h* Jud. 7:12 *i* Josh. 7:2
6 *j* 1 Sam. 14:11; cp. Jud. 6:2
7 *k* Num. 32:1–42
9 *l* Cp. Num. 16:1–3
10 *m* 1 Sam. 15:13
13 *n* 2 Chr. 16:9 *o* Cp. 1 Sam. 26:21 *p* 1 Sam. 15:11
14 *q* 1 Sam. 15:28 *r* 1 Sam. 16:1 *s* Ps. 89:20; Acts 13:22 *t* 1 Sam. 15:11,19
17 *u* Josh. 18:23
18 *v* Josh. 16:3 *w* Neh. 11:34
19 *x* Cp. 2 Ki. 24:14

*
13:1 The Hebrew is difficult (compare 2 Samuel 5:4; 2 Kings 14:2; see also 2 Samuel 2:10; Acts 13:21). **13:5** Following Masoretic Text, Septuagint, Targum, and Vulgate; Syriac and some manuscripts of the Septuagint read *three*. **13:15** Following Masoretic Text and Targum; Septuagint and Vulgate add *And the rest of the people went up after Saul to meet the people who fought against them, going from Gilgal to Gibeah in the hill of Benjamin.*

[1](13:19) One reason for the great power of the Philistines, despite their relatively small

Israel, for the Philistines said, "Lest
the Hebrews make swords or spears."
20 But all the Israelites would go
down to the Philistines to sharpen
each man's plowshare, his mattock,
his ax, and his sickle;
21 and the charge for a sharpening
was a [1]pim for the plowshares, the
mattocks, the forks, and the axes, and
to set the points of the goads.
22 So it came about, on the day of
battle, that [a]there was neither sword
nor spear found in the hand of any of
the people who *were* with Saul and
Jonathan. But they were found with
Saul and Jonathan his son.
23 And the garrison of the Philistines went out to the [b]pass of Michmash.

Jonathan's bold assault

14 NOW it happened one day that
Jonathan the son of Saul said
to the young man who bore his armor,
"Come, let us go over to the Philistines' garrison that *is* on the other
side." But he did not tell his father.
2 And Saul was sitting in the outskirts of [c]Gibeah under a pomegranate tree which *is* in Migron. The people who *were* with him *were* about six
hundred men.
3 [d]Ahijah the son of Ahitub, [e]Ich-
abod's brother, the son of Phinehas,
the son of Eli, the LORD's priest in Shiloh, was [f]wearing an ephod. But the
people did not know that Jonathan
had gone.
4 Between the [g]passes, by which
Jonathan sought to go over to the Philistines' garrison, *there was* a sharp
rock on one side and a sharp rock on
the other side. And the name of one
was Bozez, and the name of the other
Seneh.
5 The front of one faced northward opposite Michmash, and the
other southward opposite Gibeah.
6 Then Jonathan said to the young
man who bore his armor, "Come, let
us go over to the garrison of these
[h]uncircumcised; it may be that the
LORD will work for us. For nothing restrains the LORD from [i]saving by
many or by few."
7 So his armorbearer said to him,
"Do all that is in your heart. Go then;
here I am with you, according to your
heart."
8 Then Jonathan said, "Very well,
let us cross over to *these* men, and we
will show ourselves to them.
9 "If they say thus to us, 'Wait until
we come to you,' then we will stand
still in our place and not go up to them.
10 "But if they say thus, 'Come up
to us,' then we will go up. For the LORD
has delivered them into our hand, and
this *will be* a [j]sign to us."
11 So both of them showed themselves to the garrison of the Philistines. And the Philistines said, "Look,
the Hebrews are coming out of the
holes where they have [k]hidden."
12 Then the men of the garrison
called to Jonathan and his armorbearer, and said, "Come up to us, and
we will show you something." Jonathan said to his armorbearer, "Come
up after me, for the LORD has delivered
them into the hand of Israel."
13 And Jonathan climbed up on his
hands and knees with his armorbearer after him; and they [l]fell before
Jonathan. And as he came after him,
his armorbearer killed them.
14 That first slaughter which Jonathan and his armorbearer made was
about twenty men within about half
an acre of land.*
15 And there was [m]trembling in the
camp, in the field, and among all the
people. The garrison and the [n]raiders
also trembled; and the earth quaked,
so that it was a very great trembling.

Subsequent victory of Israel

16 Now the watchmen of Saul in
Gibeah of Benjamin looked, and *there*
was the multitude, melting away; and
they went here and there.
17 Then Saul said to the people
who *were* with him, "Now call the roll
and see who has gone from us." And
when they had called the roll, surprisingly, Jonathan and his armorbearer
were not *there*.
18 And Saul said to Ahijah, [o]"Bring
the ark* of God here" (for at that time

22
a Cp. Jud. 3:31; 5:8
23
b 1 Sam. 14:4–5
CHAPTER 14
2
c 1 Sam. 13:15–16
3
d Called *Ahimelech,* 1 Sam. 22:9,14,20
e 1 Sam. 4:21
f Cp. Num. 16:1–3; 1 Sam. 2:27–33; Jude 11
4
g 1 Sam. 13:23
6
h 1 Sam. 17:26
i Dt. 32:36; Jud. 7:4,7; 2 Chr. 14:11; Rom. 8:31
10
j Cp. 1 Sam. 6:9
11
k 1 Sam. 13:6
13
l Lev. 26:8; Josh. 23:10
15
m Dt. 28:7; Job 18:11; cp. 2 Ki. 7:6–7
n 1 Sam. 13:17
18
o Cp. 1 Sam. 23:9; 30:7

*

14:14 Literally *half the area plowed by a yoke* (of oxen in a day) 14:18 Following Masoretic Text, Targum, and Vulgate; Septuagint reads *ephod.*

number among the peoples of Palestine, was the fact that at this time they alone knew how to make iron implements and weapons. See Jud. 13:1, *note.*

[1](13:21) The word *pim* has now been found marked on a weight (two-thirds of a shekel) which has been turned up in excavations from this period. For Weights and Measures (OT), see 2 Chr. 2:10, *note.*

the ark* of God was with the children
of Israel).
19 Now it happened, while Saul
[a]talked to the priest, that the noise
which *was* in the camp of the Philistines continued to increase; so Saul
said to the priest, "Withdraw your
hand."
20 Then Saul and all the people
who *were* with him assembled, and
they went to the battle; and indeed every man's sword was against his
[b]neighbor, *and there was* very great
confusion.
21 Moreover the [c]Hebrews *who*
were with the Philistines before that
time, who went up with them into the
camp *from the* surrounding *country*,
they also joined the Israelites who
were with Saul and Jonathan.
22 Likewise all the men of Israel
who had hidden in the mountains of
Ephraim, *when* they heard that the
Philistines fled, they also followed
hard after them in the battle.
23 So the LORD [d]saved Israel that
day, and the battle shifted to [e]Beth
Aven.

Saul's rash order overridden

24 And the men of Israel were distressed that day, for Saul had [f]placed
the people under oath, saying,
"Cursed *is* the man who eats *any* food
until evening, before I have taken vengeance on my enemies." So none of
the people tasted food.
25 Now all *the people* of the land
came to a forest; and there was honey
on the ground.
26 And when the people had come
into the woods, there was the honey,
dripping; but no one put his hand to
his mouth, for the people feared the
oath.
27 But Jonathan had not heard his
father charge the people with the
oath; therefore he stretched out the
end of the rod that *was* in his hand and
dipped it in a honeycomb, and put his
hand to his mouth; and his countenance [g]brightened.
28 Then one of the people said,
"Your father strictly charged the people with an oath, saying, 'Cursed *is* the
man who eats food this day.' " And the
people were faint.
29 But Jonathan said, "My father
has troubled the land. Look now, how
my countenance has brightened because I tasted a little of this honey.
30 "How much better if the people
had eaten freely today of the spoil of
their enemies which they found! For
now would there not have been a
much greater slaughter among the
Philistines?"
31 Now they had driven back the
Philistines that day from Michmash to
Aijalon. So the people were very faint.
32 And the people rushed on the
spoil, and took sheep, oxen, and
calves, and slaughtered *them* on the
ground; and the people ate *them* with
the [h]blood.
33 Then they told Saul, saying,
"Look, the people are sinning against
the LORD by eating with the blood!" So
he said, "You have dealt treacherously; roll a large stone to me this
day."
34 Then Saul said, "Disperse yourselves among the people, and say to
them, 'Bring me here every man's ox
and every man's sheep, slaughter
them here, and eat; and do not sin
against the LORD by eating with the
blood.' " So every one of the people
brought his ox with him that night,
and slaughtered *it* there.
35 Then Saul [i]built an altar to the
LORD. This was the first altar that he
built to the LORD.
36 Now Saul said, "Let us go down
after the Philistines by night, and
plunder them until the morning light;
and let us not leave a man of them."
And they said, "Do whatever seems
good to you." Then the priest said,
"Let us draw near to God here."
37 So Saul [j]asked counsel of God,
"Shall I go down after the Philistines?
Will You deliver them into the hand of
Israel?" But He [k]did not answer him
that day.
38 And Saul said, "Come over here,
all you chiefs of the people, and know
and see what this sin was today.
39 "For *as* the LORD lives, who saves
Israel, [l]though it be in Jonathan my
son, he shall surely die." But not a man
among all the people answered him.
40 Then he said to all Israel, "You
be on one side, and my son Jonathan
and I will be on the other side." And
the people said to Saul, "Do what
seems good to you."
41 Therefore Saul said to the LORD
God of Israel, [m]"Give a perfect [n]*lot*."*

19 *a* Num. 27:21
20 *b* Jud. 7:22
21 *c* Cp. 1 Sam. 29:4
23 *d* Ex. 14:30; 2 Chr. 32:22 *e* 1 Sam. 13:5
24 *f* Cp. Josh. 6:26
27 *g* Cp. 1 Sam. 30:12
32 *h* Cp. Lev. 3:17; 17:10; Dt. 12:23–24; Ezek. 33:25; Acts 15:19–20
35 *i* 1 Sam. 7:17
37 *j* Jud. 20:18 *k* 1 Sam. 28:6
39 *l* v. 44
41 *m* Cp. Josh. 7:14–18 *n* Acts 1:24–26

*

14:18 Following Masoretic Text, Targum, and Vulgate; Septuagint reads *ephod.* **14:41** Following Masoretic Text and Targum; Septuagint and Vulgate read *Why do You not answer Your servant today? If the injustice is with me or Jonathan my son, O LORD God of Israel, give proof; and if You say it is with Your people Israel, give holiness.*

So Saul and Jonathan were taken, but
the people escaped.
42 And Saul said, "Cast *lots* between my son Jonathan and me." So
Jonathan was taken.
43 Then Saul said to Jonathan,
[a]"Tell me what you have done." And
Jonathan told him, and said, "I only
tasted a little honey with the end of the
rod that *was* in my hand. So now I
must die!"
44 Saul answered, "God do so and
more also; [b]for you shall surely die,
Jonathan."
45 But the people said to Saul,
"Shall Jonathan die, who has accomplished this great deliverance in Israel? Certainly not! *As* the LORD lives,
not one hair of his head shall fall to the
ground, for he has worked [c]with God
this day." So the people rescued Jonathan, and he did not die.
46 Then Saul returned from pursuing the Philistines, and the Philistines
went to their own place.

Summary of Saul's reign: constant warfare on every side

47 So Saul established his sovereignty over Israel, and fought against
all his enemies on every side, against
Moab, against the people of [d]Ammon,
against Edom, against the kings of
[e]Zobah, and against the Philistines.
Wherever he turned, he harassed
*them.**
48 And he gathered an army and
attacked the [f]Amalekites, and delivered Israel from the hands of those
who plundered them.
49 The [g]sons of Saul were Jonathan, Jishui,* and Malchishua. And
the names of his two daughters *were*
these: the name of the firstborn Merab, and the name of the younger [h]Mi-
chal.
50 The name of Saul's wife *was*
Ahinoam the daughter of Ahimaaz.
And the name of the commander of
his army *was* Abner the son of Ner,
Saul's [i]uncle.
51 Kish *was* the father of Saul, and
Ner the father of Abner *was* the son of
Abiel.
52 Now there was fierce war with
the Philistines all the days of Saul.
And when Saul saw any strong man
or any valiant man, he [j]took him for
himself.

Saul's incomplete obedience

15 SAMUEL also [k]said to Saul,
"The LORD sent me to anoint
you [l]king over His people, over Israel.
Now therefore, heed the voice of the
words of the LORD.
2 "Thus says the LORD of hosts: 'I
will punish [m]Amalek *for* what he did
to Israel, how he ambushed him on the
way when he came up from Egypt.
3 'Now go and [n]attack Amalek,
and utterly [o]destroy all that they
have, and do not spare them. But kill
both man and woman, infant and
nursing child, ox and sheep, camel
and donkey.' "
4 So Saul gathered the people together and numbered them in Telaim,
two hundred thousand foot soldiers
and ten thousand men of Judah.
5 And Saul came to a city of Amalek, and lay in wait in the valley.
6 Then Saul said to the [p]Kenites,
"Go, depart, get down from among the
Amalekites, lest I destroy you with
them. For you showed kindness to all
the children of Israel when they came
up out of Egypt." So the Kenites departed from among the Amalekites.
7 And Saul attacked the Amalekites, from [q]Havilah all the way to
[r]Shur, which is east of Egypt.
8 He also took Agag king of the
Amalekites alive, and [s]utterly destroyed all the people with the edge of
the sword.
9 [t]But Saul and the people spared
Agag and the best of the sheep, the
oxen, the fatlings, the lambs, and all
that was good, and were unwilling to
utterly destroy them. But everything
despised and worthless, that they utterly destroyed.
10 Now the word of the LORD came
to Samuel, saying,
11 "I greatly [u]regret that I have set
up Saul *as* king, for he has turned
back from following Me, and has not
performed My commandments." And
it grieved Samuel, and he [v]cried out to
the LORD all night.

Samuel rebukes Saul

12 So when Samuel rose early in
the morning to meet Saul, it was told
Samuel, saying, "Saul went to Carmel,
and indeed, he set up a monument for
himself; and he has gone on around,
passed by, and gone down to Gilgal."
13 Then Samuel went to Saul, and
Saul said to him, "Blessed *are* you of
the LORD! I have performed the commandment of the LORD."

43
a Josh. 7:19
44
b v. 39
45
c Cp. 2 Chr. 19:11; Isa. 13:3; 2 Cor. 6:1; Phil. 2:12–13
47
d 1 Sam. 11:1–13
e Cp. 2 Sam. 8:3–10
48
f Ex. 17:16; 1 Sam. 15:3–7
49
g 1 Sam. 31:2
h 1 Sam. 18:17–20, 27; 19:12
50
i 1 Sam. 10:14
52
j Cp. 1 Sam. 8:11–22
CHAPTER 15
1
k 1 Sam. 9:16
l *Kingdom* (OT): vv. 1–26; 1 Sam. 16:1. (Gen. 1:26; Zech. 12:8, *note*)
2
m Ex. 17:8–14; Dt. 25:17–19
3
n Dt. 25:19
o Num. 24:20
6
p Num. 24:21; Jud. 1:16; 4:11–22; 1 Chr. 2:55
7
q Gen. 25:17–18
r Ex. 15:22; 1 Sam. 27:8
8
s 1 Sam. 27:8–9
9
t Cp. vv. 3, 18
11
u See Zech. 8:14, *note*
v Cp. Ex. 32:11–13; Lk. 6:12

*
14:47 Septuagint and Vulgate read *prospered.*
14:49 Called *Abinadab* in 1 Chronicles 8:33 and 9:39

14 But Samuel said, "What then *is* this bleating of the sheep in my ears, and the lowing of the oxen which I hear?"

15 And Saul said, "They have brought them from the Amalekites; for the [a]people spared the best of the sheep and the oxen, to sacrifice to the LORD your God; and the rest we have utterly destroyed."

16 Then Samuel said to Saul, "Be quiet! And I will tell you what the LORD said to me last night." And he said to him, "Speak on."

17 So Samuel said, [b]"When you *were* little in your own eyes, *were* you not head of the tribes of Israel? And did not the LORD anoint you king over Israel?

18 "Now the LORD sent you on a mission, and said, 'Go, and utterly destroy the sinners, the Amalekites, and fight against them until they are consumed.'

19 [c]"Why then did you not obey the voice of the LORD? Why did you swoop down on the spoil, and do evil in the sight of the LORD?"

20 And Saul said to Samuel, "But I have [d]obeyed the voice of the LORD, and gone on the mission on which the LORD sent me, and brought back Agag king of Amalek; I have utterly destroyed the Amalekites.

21 "But the people took of the plunder, sheep and oxen, the best of the things which should have been utterly destroyed, to sacrifice to the LORD your God in Gilgal."

22 So Samuel said:

[e]"Has the LORD *as great* delight
in burnt offerings and
sacrifices,
As in obeying the voice of the
LORD?
Behold, to obey is better than
sacrifice,
And to heed than the fat of
rams.

23 For rebellion *is as* the sin of
witchcraft,
And stubbornness *is as*
iniquity and idolatry.
[f]Because you have rejected the
word of the LORD,
He also has [g]rejected you from
being king."

24 Then Saul said to Samuel, [h]"I have sinned, for I have transgressed the commandment of the LORD and your words, because I feared the [i]people and obeyed their voice.

25 "Now therefore, please pardon my sin, and return with me, that I may worship the LORD."

26 But Samuel said to Saul, "I will not return with you, for you have rejected the word of the LORD, and the LORD has rejected you from being king over Israel."

27 And as Samuel turned around to go away, *Saul* seized the edge of his robe, and it [j]tore.

28 So Samuel said to him, "The LORD has [k]torn the kingdom of Israel from you today, and has given it to a neighbor of yours, *who is* better than you.

29 "And also the Strength of Israel will not [l]lie nor [m]relent. For He *is* not a man, that He should relent."

30 Then he said, "I have sinned; *yet* [n]honor me now, please, before the elders of my people and before Israel, and return with me, that I may worship the LORD your God."

31 So Samuel turned back after Saul, and Saul worshiped the LORD.

32 Then Samuel said, "Bring Agag king of the Amalekites here to me." So Agag came to him cautiously. And Agag said, "Surely the bitterness of death is past."

33 But Samuel said, [o]"As your sword has made women childless, so shall your mother be childless among women." And Samuel hacked Agag in pieces before the LORD in Gilgal.

34 Then Samuel went to [p]Ramah, and Saul went up to his house at [q]Gibeah of Saul.

35 And Samuel went no more to see Saul until the day of his [r]death. Nevertheless Samuel mourned for Saul, and the LORD [m]regretted that He had made Saul king over Israel.

III. The Parallel Lives of Saul and David to the Death of Saul, 16—31

Samuel sent to Bethlehem

16 NOW the LORD said to Samuel, "How long will you mourn for Saul, seeing I have [s]rejected him from reigning over Israel? Fill your horn with [t]oil, and go; I am sending you to [u]Jesse the Bethlehemite. For I have provided Myself a [v]king among his sons."

2 And Samuel said, "How can I go? If Saul hears *it*, he will kill me." But the LORD said, "Take a heifer with

15 *a* vv. 9,21
17 *b* 1 Sam. 9:21
19 *c* 1 Sam. 14:32
20 *d* Prov. 28:13
22 *e* Ps. 50:8–9; 51:16–17; Prov. 21:3; Isa. 1:11–17; Jer. 7:22–23; Mic. 6:6–8; Heb. 10:4–10
23 *f* Cp. Jn. 8:47; 10:26; 12:48; 15:22
g 1 Sam. 13:14; 16:1
24 *h* Josh. 7:20; 1 Sam. 26:21
i Prov. 29:25; cp. Isa. 51:12–13
27 *j* Cp. 1 Ki. 11:31
28 *k* 1 Sam. 28:17
29 *l* Num. 23:19
m See Zech. 8:14, *note*
30 *n* Cp. Jn. 5:44; 12:43
33 *o* Gen. 9:6; Mt. 7:2; cp. Jud. 1:7
34 *p* 1 Sam. 7:17
q 1 Sam. 11:4
35 *r* Cp. 1 Sam. 19:24
CHAPTER 16
1 *s* 1 Sam. 15:23
t 1 Sam. 10:1
u Ruth 4:18–22; 1 Sam. 17:12
v Kingdom (OT): vv. 1–13; 2 Sam.2:1. (Gen. 1:26; Zech. 12:8, *note*)

you, and say, 'I have come to sacrifice to the LORD.'

3 "Then invite Jesse to the sacrifice, and I will show you what you shall do; you shall anoint for Me the one I name to you."

4 So Samuel did what the LORD said, and went to Bethlehem. And the elders of the town trembled at his coming, and said, "Do you come peaceably?"

5 And he said, "Peaceably; I have come to sacrifice to the LORD. [a]Sanctify yourselves, and come with me to the sacrifice." Then he consecrated Jesse and his sons, and invited them to the sacrifice.

6 So it was, when they came, that he looked at [b]Eliab and said, "Surely the LORD's anointed *is* before Him!"

7 But the LORD said to Samuel, [c]"Do not look at his appearance or at his physical stature, because I have refused him. [d]For *the LORD does* not *see* as man sees;* for man looks at the [e]outward appearance, but the LORD looks at the [f]heart."

8 So Jesse called Abinadab, and made him pass before Samuel. And he said, "Neither has the LORD chosen this one."

9 Then Jesse made Shammah pass by. And he said, "Neither has the LORD chosen this one."

10 Thus Jesse made seven of his sons pass before Samuel. And Samuel said to Jesse, "The LORD has not chosen these."

11 And Samuel said to Jesse, "Are all the young men here?" Then he said, "There remains yet the youngest, and there he is, keeping the [g]sheep." And Samuel said to Jesse, "Send and bring him. For we will not sit down* till he comes here."

12 So he sent and brought him in. Now he *was* [h]ruddy, with bright eyes, and [i]good-looking. And the LORD said, [j]"Arise, anoint him; for this *is* the one!"

13 Then Samuel took the horn of oil and anointed him in the midst of his brothers; and the [k]Spirit of the LORD came upon David from that day forward. So Samuel arose and went to Ramah.

David in Saul's court

14 But the Spirit of the LORD [l]departed from Saul, and a [m]distressing spirit from the LORD troubled him.

15 And Saul's servants said to him, "Surely, a distressing spirit from God is troubling you.

16 "Let our master now command your servants, *who are* before you, to seek out a man *who is* a skillful player on the harp. And it shall be that he will [n]play it with his hand when the distressing spirit from God is upon you, and you shall be well."

17 So Saul said to his servants, "Provide me now a man who can play well, and bring *him* to me."

18 Then one of the servants answered and said, "Look, I have seen a son of Jesse the Bethlehemite, *who is* skillful in playing, a mighty man of valor, a man of war, prudent in speech, and a handsome person; and the [o]LORD *is* with him."

19 Therefore Saul sent messengers to Jesse, and said, "Send me your son David, who *is* with the sheep."

20 And Jesse took a donkey *loaded with* bread, a skin of wine, and a young goat, and sent *them* by his son David to Saul.

21 So David [1]came to Saul and [p]stood before him. And he loved him greatly, and he became his armorbearer.

22 Then Saul sent to Jesse, saying, "Please let David stand before me, for he has found favor in my sight."

23 And so it was, whenever the spirit from God was upon Saul, that David would take a harp and play *it* with his hand. Then Saul would become refreshed and well, and the distressing spirit would depart from him.

Goliath defies Israel

17 NOW the Philistines gathered their armies together to battle, and were gathered at [q]Sochoh, which *belongs* to Judah; they encamped be-

5 *a* Gen. 35:2; Ex. 19:10
6 *b* 1 Sam. 17:13,28
7 *c* Ps. 147:10 *d* Isa. 55:8–9 *e* 2 Cor. 10:7; cp. 1 Pet. 2:4 *f* 1 Ki. 8:39
11 *g* 2 Sam. 7:8; Ps. 78:70–72
12 *h* 1 Sam. 17:42; cp. Song 5:10 *i* Gen. 39:6; Ex. 2:2 *j* 1 Sam. 9:17
13 *k* *Holy Spirit* (OT): vv. 13–14; 1 Sam. 19:20. (Gen. 1:2; Zech. 12:10)
14 *l* Jud. 16:20 *m* 1 Sam. 18:10
16 *n* 1 Sam. 19:9
18 *o* 1 Sam. 18:12,14
21 *p* Prov. 22:29; cp. Gen. 41:46
CHAPTER 17
1 *q* Josh. 15:35

*

16:7 Septuagint reads *For God does not see as man sees;* Targum reads *It is not by the appearance of a man;* Vulgate reads *Nor do I judge according to the looks of a man.* 16:11 Following Septuagint and Vulgate; Masoretic Text reads *turn around;* Targum and Syriac read *turn away.*

[1](16:21) Compare 1 Sam. 17:55–56. The order of events is: (1) David, whose skill on the harp and whose valor in the combat with the lion or the bear (1 Sam. 17:34–36) were known to one of the servants of Saul, was brought to play before the king (1 Sam. 16:17–23). (2) David returned to Bethlehem (1 Sam. 17:15). (3) David was sent to Saul's camp (1 Sam. 17:17–18) and performed his great exploit. And (4) Saul's question (1 Sam. 17:55–56) implied only that he had forgotten the name of David's father—certainly not remarkable in an oriental king.

tween Sochoh and Azekah, in [a]Ephes
Dammim.
2 And Saul and the men of Israel
were gathered together, and they encamped in the Valley of Elah, and
drew up in battle array against the
Philistines.
3 The Philistines stood on a mountain on one side, and Israel stood on a
mountain on the other side, with a valley between them.
4 And a champion went out from
the camp of the Philistines, named
[b]Goliath, from [c]Gath, whose height
was six [d]cubits and a [d]span.
5 *He had* a bronze helmet on his
head, and he *was* armed with a coat of
mail, and the weight of the coat *was*
five thousand shekels of bronze.
6 And *he had* bronze armor on his
legs and a bronze javelin between his
shoulders.
7 Now the staff of his spear *was*
like a [e]weaver's beam, and his iron
spearhead *weighed* six hundred shekels; and a shield-bearer went before
him.
8 Then he stood and cried out to
the armies of Israel, and said to them,
"Why have you come out to line up for
battle? *Am* I not a Philistine, and you
the [f]servants of Saul? Choose a man
for yourselves, and let him come down
to me.
9 "If he is able to fight with me and
kill me, then we will be your servants.
But if I prevail against him and kill
him, then you shall be our servants
and serve [g]us."
10 And the Philistine said, "I defy
the armies of Israel this day; give me
a man, that we may fight together."
11 When Saul and all Israel heard
these words of the Philistine, they
were dismayed and greatly afraid.
12 Now David *was* the [h]son of that
[i]Ephrathite of Bethlehem Judah,
whose name *was* Jesse, and who had
[j]eight sons. And the man was old, advanced *in years,* in the days of Saul.
13 The three oldest sons of Jesse
had gone to follow Saul to the battle.
The names of his three sons who went
to the battle *were* [k]Eliab the firstborn,
next to him Abinadab, and the third
Shammah.
14 David *was* the youngest. And
the three oldest followed Saul.
15 But David occasionally went
and returned from Saul to [l]feed his
father's sheep at Bethlehem.
16 And the Philistine drew near
and presented himself forty days,
morning and evening.

David visits brothers and hears the boasting of the Philistines

17 Then Jesse said to his son David,
"Take now for your brothers an
[d]ephah of this dried *grain* and these
ten loaves, and run to your brothers at
the camp.
18 "And [m]carry these ten cheeses to
the captain of *their* thousand, and
[n]see how your brothers fare, and
bring back news of them."
19 Now Saul and they and all the
men of Israel *were* in the Valley of
Elah, fighting with the Philistines.
20 So David rose early in the morning, left the sheep with a keeper, and
took *the things* and went as Jesse had
commanded him. And he came to the
camp as the army was going out to the
fight and shouting for the battle.
21 For Israel and the Philistines
had drawn up in battle array, army
against army.
22 And David left his [o]supplies in
the hand of the supply keeper, ran to
the army, and came and greeted his
brothers.
23 Then as he talked with them,
there was the champion, the Philistine
of Gath, Goliath by name, coming up
from the armies of the Philistines; and
he spoke according to the same
words. So David heard *them.*
24 And all the men of Israel, when
they saw the man, fled from him and
were dreadfully afraid.
25 So the men of Israel said, "Have
you seen this man who has come up?
Surely he has come up to defy Israel;
and it shall be *that* the man who kills
him the king will enrich with great
riches, will [p]give him his daughter,
and give his father's house exemption
from taxes in Israel."
26 Then David spoke to the men
who stood by him, saying, "What shall
be done for the man who kills this Philistine and takes away the [q]reproach
from Israel? For who *is* this [r]uncir-
cumcised Philistine, that he should
defy the armies of the [s]living God?"
27 And the people answered him in
this manner, saying, "So shall it be
done for the man who kills him."
28 Now Eliab his oldest brother
heard when he spoke to the men; and
Eliab's [t]anger was aroused against
David, and he said, "Why did you
come down here? And with whom
have you left those few sheep in the

1
a Or *Pas Dammim,* 1 Chr. 11:13
4
b Cp. 2 Sam. 21:19
c Josh. 11:21–22
d See Weights and Measures (OT), 2 Chr. 2:10, *note*
7
e Cp. 1 Chr. 11:23
8
f 1 Sam. 8:17
9
g Cp. 2 Sam. 2:12–16
12
h Ruth 4:22
i Gen. 35:19
j 1 Sam. 16:10–11
13
k 1 Chr. 2:13
15
l 2 Sam. 7:8
18
m Cp. 1 Sam. 16:20
n Gen. 37:14
22
o Jud. 18:21
25
p Josh. 15:16
26
q v. 10; 1 Sam. 11:2
r 1 Sam. 14:6
s Dt. 5:26; Josh. 3:10
28
t Gen. 37:4, 8

wilderness? I know your pride and the insolence of your heart, for you have come down to see the battle."

29 And David said, "What have I done now? *Is there* not a cause?"

30 Then he turned from him toward another and said the same thing; and these people answered him as the first ones *did*.

David kills Goliath

31 Now when the words which David spoke were heard, they reported *them* to Saul; and he sent for him.

32 Then David said to Saul, "Let no man's heart [a]fail because of him; [b]your servant will go and fight with this Philistine."

33 And Saul said to David, "You are not able to go against this Philistine to fight with him; for you *are* a youth, and he a man of war from his youth."

34 But David said to Saul, "Your servant used to keep his father's sheep, and when a [c]lion or a bear came and took a lamb out of the flock,

35 I went out after it and struck it, and [d]delivered *the lamb* from its mouth; and when it arose against me, I caught *it* by its beard, and struck and killed it.

36 "Your servant has killed both lion and bear; and this uncircumcised Philistine will be like one of them, seeing he has defied the armies of the living God."

37 Moreover David said, "The LORD, who [e]delivered me from the paw of the lion and from the paw of the bear, He will deliver me from the hand of this Philistine." And Saul said to David, "Go, and the [f]LORD be with you!"

38 So Saul clothed David with his armor, and he put a bronze helmet on his head; he also clothed him with a coat of mail.

39 David fastened his sword to his armor and tried to walk, for he had not tested *them*. And David said to Saul, "I cannot walk with these, for I have not tested *them*." So David took them off.

40 Then he took his staff in his hand; and he chose for himself five smooth stones from the brook, and put them in a shepherd's bag, in a pouch which he had, and his [g]sling was in his hand. And he drew near to the Philistine.

41 So the Philistine came, and began drawing near to David, and the man who bore the shield *went* before him.

42 And when the Philistine looked about and saw David, he [h]disdained him; for he was *only* a youth, [i]ruddy and good-looking.

43 So the Philistine said to David, "*Am* I a [j]dog, that you come to me with sticks?" And the Philistine [k]cursed David by his gods.

44 And the Philistine [l]said to David, "Come to me, and I will give your flesh to the birds of the air and the beasts of the [m]field!"

45 Then David said to the Philistine, "You come to me with a sword, with a spear, and with a javelin. But [n]I come to you in the name of the LORD of hosts, the God of the armies of Israel, whom you have [o]defied.

46 "This day the LORD will deliver you into my hand, and I will strike you and [p]take your head from you. And this day I will give the carcasses of the camp of the Philistines to the birds of the air and the wild beasts of the earth, that all the earth may [q]know that there is a God in Israel.

47 "Then all this assembly shall know that the LORD [r]does not save with sword and spear; for the battle *is* the [s]LORD's, and He will give you into our hands."

48 So it was, when the Philistine arose and came and drew near to meet David, that David hurried and [t]ran toward the army to meet the Philistine.

49 Then David put his hand in his bag and took out a stone; and he slung *it* and struck the Philistine in his forehead, so that the stone sank into his forehead, and he fell on his face to the earth.

50 So David prevailed over the Philistine with a [u]sling and a stone, and struck the Philistine and killed him. But *there was* no sword in the hand of David.

51 Therefore David ran and stood over the Philistine, took his [v]sword and drew it out of its sheath and killed him, and cut off his head with it. And when the Philistines saw that their champion was dead, they [w]fled.

52 Now the men of Israel and Judah arose and shouted, and pursued the Philistines as far as the entrance of the valley* and to the gates of Ekron. And the wounded of the Philistines fell along the road to Shaaraim, even as far as Gath and Ekron.

32
a Cp. Dt. 20:2–3
b 1 Sam. 16:18
34
c Jud. 14:5
35
d Cp. Amos 3:12
37
e Cp. Dan. 3:28; 6:22; 2 Tim. 4:17
f 1 Sam. 20:13; 1 Chr. 22:11
40
g Cp. Jud. 20:16
42
h Prov. 16:18
i 1 Sam. 16:12
43
j 2 Ki. 8:13
k Cp. Jud. 16:23
44
l Cp. 1 Ki. 20:10–11
m Cp. Dt. 28:26
45
n 2 Sam. 22:23; Ps. 124:8; Heb. 11:32–34
o 1 Sam. 17:10
46
p v. 51
q Josh. 4:24; 1 Ki. 8:43; 18:36; 2 Ki. 19:19; Ps. 46:10; Isa. 52:10
47
r Ps. 44:6–7; Hos. 1:7; Zech. 4:6
s Cp. 2 Chr. 20:15
48
t Ps. 27:3
50
u v. 40; Jud. 3:31; 15:15
51
v 1 Sam. 21:9
w Heb. 11:34

*17:52 Following Masoretic Text, Syriac, Targum, and Vulgate; Septuagint reads *Gath*.

53 Then the children of Israel returned from chasing the Philistines,
and they plundered their tents.
54 And David took the head of the
Philistine and brought it to Jerusalem,
but he put his armor in his tent.
55 When Saul saw David going out
against the Philistine, he said to [a]Ab-
ner, the commander of the army,
"Abner, whose son *is* this youth?"
And Abner said, "As your soul lives,
O king, I do not know."
56 So the king said, "Inquire whose
[b]son this young man *is*."
57 Then, as David returned from
the slaughter of the Philistine, Abner
took him and brought him before Saul
with the head of the Philistine in his
hand.
58 And Saul said to him, "Whose
son *are* you, young man?" So David
answered, "*I am* the son of your servant Jesse the Bethlehemite."

David beloved by Jonathan

18 NOW when he had finished
speaking to Saul, the soul of
Jonathan was knit to the soul of David, and Jonathan loved him [c]as his
own soul.
2 Saul took him that day, and
[d]would not let him go home to his father's house anymore.
3 Then Jonathan and David made
a [e]covenant, because he loved him as
his own soul.
4 And Jonathan took off the robe
that *was* on him and [f]gave it to David,
with his armor, even to his sword and
his bow and his belt.

Jealous Saul attempts to kill David

5 So David went out wherever
Saul sent him, *and* behaved wisely.
And Saul set him over the men of war,
and he was accepted in the sight of all
the people and also in the sight of
Saul's servants.
6 Now it had happened as they
were coming *home,* when David was
returning from the slaughter of the
Philistine, that the women had come
out of all the cities of Israel, singing
and dancing, to meet King Saul, with
tambourines, with joy, and with musical instruments.
7 So the women sang as they
danced, and said:

"Saul has [g]slain his thousands,
And David his [h]ten
thousands."

8 Then Saul was very angry, and
the saying displeased him; and he
said, "They have ascribed to David ten
thousands, and to me they have ascribed *only* thousands. Now *what*
more can he have but the [i]kingdom?"
9 So Saul eyed David from that
day forward.
10 And it happened on the next day
that the [j]distressing spirit from God
came upon Saul, and he [k]prophesied
inside the house. So David [l]played
music with his hand, as at other times;
but *there was* a [m]spear in Saul's hand.
11 And Saul cast the spear, for he
said, "I will pin David to the wall!" But
David escaped his presence twice.
12 Now Saul was [n]afraid of David,
because the LORD was with [o]him, but
had departed from Saul.
13 Therefore Saul removed him
from his presence, and made him his
captain over a thousand; and he
[p]went out and came in before the people.
14 And David behaved wisely in all
his ways, and the LORD *was* with him.
15 Therefore, when Saul saw that
he behaved very wisely, he was afraid
of him.
16 But all Israel and Judah loved
David, [q]because he went out and
came in before them.

David marries Saul's daughter

17 Then Saul said to David, "Here is
my older daughter [r]Merab; I will give
her to you as a wife. Only be valiant
for me, and [s]fight the LORD's battles."
For Saul thought, "Let my hand not be
against him, but let the [t]hand of the
Philistines be against him."
18 So David [u]said to Saul, "Who
am I, and what *is* my life *or* my father's
family in Israel, that I should be son-
in-law to the king?"
19 But it happened at the time when
Merab, Saul's daughter, should have
been given to David, that she was
given to [v]Adriel the [w]Meholathite as a
wife.
20 Now Michal, Saul's daughter,
loved David. And they told Saul, and
the thing pleased him.
21 So Saul said, "I will give her to
him, that she may be a snare to him,
and that the [t]hand of the Philistines
may be against him." Therefore Saul
said to David a second time, "You
shall be my son-in-law today."
22 And Saul commanded his servants, "Communicate with David secretly, and say, 'Look, the king has
delight in you, and all his servants

55
a 1 Sam. 14:50
56
b See 1 Sam. 16:21, *note*
CHAPTER 18
1
c Dt. 13:6; cp. Gen. 44:30
2
d Cp. 1 Sam. 17:15
3
e 1 Sam. 20:16
4
f Cp. Gen. 41:42
7
g 1 Sam. 21:11
h Cp. 2 Sam. 18:3
8
i Cp. 1 Sam. 15:28
10
j 1 Sam. 16:14
k 1 Sam. 19:24
l 1 Sam. 16:23
m 1 Sam. 19:9–10
12
n Cp. v. 29; 1 Sam. 15:28
o 1 Sam. 16:13,18
13
p 1 Sam. 29:6
16
q Num. 27:16–17; 2 Sam. 5:2; 1 Ki. 3:7
17
r 1 Sam. 14:49; 17:25
s 1 Sam. 25:28
t vv. 21,25; cp. 2 Sam. 12:9
18
u v. 23; 1 Sam. 9:21; 2 Sam. 7:18
19
v 2 Sam. 21:8
w Jud. 7:22; 2 Sam. 21:8

love you. Now therefore, become the king's son-in-law.' "

23 So Saul's servants spoke those words in the hearing of David. And David said, "Does it seem to you *a* light *thing* to be a king's son-in-law, seeing I *am* a [a]poor and lightly esteemed man?"

24 And the servants of Saul told him, saying, "In this manner David spoke."

25 Then Saul said, "Thus you shall say to David: 'The king does not desire any [b]dowry but one hundred foreskins of the Philistines, to take [c]vengeance on the king's enemies.' " But Saul thought to make David fall by the hand of the Philistines.

26 So when his servants told David these words, it pleased David well to become the king's son-in-law. Now the days had not expired;

27 therefore David arose and went, he and his men, and killed two hundred men of the Philistines. And David brought their [d]foreskins, and they gave them in full count to the king, that he might become the king's son-in-law. Then Saul gave him Michal his daughter as a wife.

28 Thus Saul saw and knew that the LORD *was* with David, and *that* Michal, Saul's daughter, loved him;

29 and Saul was still more afraid of David. So Saul became David's enemy continually.

30 Then the princes of the Philistines went out *to war.* And so it was, whenever they went out, *that* David behaved more [e]wisely than all the servants of Saul, so that his name became highly esteemed.

David is protected from Saul three times

19 NOW Saul spoke to Jonathan his son and to all his servants, that they should kill [f]David; but Jonathan, Saul's son, delighted [g]greatly in David.

2 So Jonathan told David, saying, "My father Saul seeks to kill you. Therefore please be on your guard until morning, and stay in a secret *place* and hide.

3 "And I will go out and stand beside my father in the field where you *are,* and I will speak with my father about you. Then what I observe, I will tell [h]you."

4 Thus Jonathan spoke well of David to Saul his father, and said to him, "Let not the king sin against his servant, against David, because he has not sinned against you, and because his works *have been* very [i]good toward you.

5 "For he [j]took his life in his hands and [k]killed the Philistine, and the LORD brought about a great deliverance for all Israel. You saw *it* and rejoiced. Why then will you sin against [l]innocent blood, to kill David without a cause?"

6 So Saul heeded the voice of Jonathan, and Saul swore, "*As* the LORD lives, he shall not be killed."

7 Then Jonathan called David, and Jonathan told him all these things. So Jonathan brought David to Saul, and he was in his presence [m]as in times past.

8 And there was war again; and David went out and fought with the Philistines, and [n]struck them with a mighty blow, and they fled from him.

9 Now the [o]distressing spirit from the LORD came upon Saul as he sat in his house with his spear in his hand. And David was playing *music* with *his* hand.

10 Then Saul sought to pin David to the wall with the spear, but he slipped away from Saul's presence; and he drove the spear into the wall. So David fled and escaped that night.

11 Saul also sent messengers to David's house to [p]watch him and to kill him in the morning. And Michal, David's wife, told him, saying, "If you do not save your life tonight, tomorrow you will be killed."

12 So Michal [q]let David down through a window. And he went and fled and escaped.

13 And Michal took an image and laid *it* in the bed, put a cover of goats' *hair* for his head, and covered *it* with clothes.

14 So when Saul sent messengers to take David, she said, "He *is* sick."

15 Then Saul sent the messengers *back* to see David, saying, "Bring him up to me in the bed, that I may kill him."

16 And when the messengers had come in, there was the image in the bed, with a cover of goats' *hair* for his head.

17 Then Saul said to Michal, "Why have you deceived me like this, and sent my enemy away, so that he has escaped?" And Michal answered Saul, "He said to me, 'Let me go! Why should I kill you?' "

18 So David fled and escaped, and

23
a Cp. Gen. 34:11–12
25
b Cp. Ex. 22:17
c 1 Sam. 14:24
27
d 2 Sam. 3:14
30
e 1 Sam. 18:5
CHAPTER 19
1
f 1 Sam. 18:8–9
g 1 Sam. 18:1
3
h 1 Sam. 20:8–13
4
i 1 Sam. 24:17
5
j Jud. 12:3
k 1 Sam. 17:49–50
l Dt. 19:10–13
7
m 1 Sam. 18:2,10,13
8
n 1 Sam. 18:27; 23:5
9
o 1 Sam. 16:14; 18:10–11
11
p Ps. 59
12
q Cp. Josh. 2:15; 2 Cor. 11:33

went to [a]Samuel at [b]Ramah, and told him all that Saul had done to him. And he and Samuel went and stayed in [c]Naioth.

19 Now it was told Saul, saying, "Take note, David *is* at Naioth in Ramah!"

20 Then Saul sent messengers to take David. And when they saw the [d]group of prophets prophesying, and Samuel standing *as* leader over them, the [e]Spirit of God came upon the messengers of Saul, and they also prophesied.

21 And when Saul was told, he sent other messengers, and they prophesied likewise. Then Saul sent messengers again the third time, and they prophesied also.

22 Then he also went to Ramah, and came to the great well that *is* at Sechu. So he asked, and said, "Where *are* Samuel and David?" And *someone* said, "Indeed *they are* at Naioth in Ramah."

23 So he went there to Naioth in Ramah. Then the Spirit of God was upon him also, and he went on and prophesied until he came to Naioth in Ramah.

24 And he also stripped off his clothes and prophesied [f]before Samuel in like manner, and lay down [g]naked all that day and all that night. Therefore they say, "*Is* [h]Saul also among the prophets?"

David and Jonathan renew covenant

20 THEN David fled from Naioth in Ramah, and went and [i]said to Jonathan, "What have I done? What *is* my iniquity, and what *is* my sin before your father, that he seeks my life?"

2 So Jonathan said to him, "By no means! You shall not die! Indeed, my father will do nothing either great or small without first [j]telling me. And why should my father hide this thing from me? It *is* not *so!*"

3 Then David took an oath again, and said, "Your father certainly knows that I have found favor in your eyes, and he has said, 'Do not let Jonathan know this, lest he be grieved.' But [k]truly, *as* the LORD lives and *as* your soul lives, *there is* but a step between me and death."

4 So Jonathan said to David, "Whatever you yourself desire, I will do *it* for you."

5 And David said to Jonathan, "Indeed tomorrow *is* the [l]New Moon, and I should not fail to sit with the king to eat. But let me go, that I may hide in the [m]field until the third *day* at evening.

6 "If your father misses me at all, then say, 'David earnestly asked *permission* of me that he might run over to [n]Bethlehem, his city, for *there is* a yearly sacrifice there for all the family.'

7 "If he says thus: '*It is* well,' your servant will be safe. But if he is very angry, be sure that [o]evil is determined by him.

8 "Therefore you shall deal kindly with your servant, for you have brought your servant into a [p]covenant of the LORD with you. Nevertheless, if there is iniquity in me, kill me yourself, for why should you bring me to your father?"

9 But Jonathan said, "Far be it from you! For if I knew certainly that evil was determined by my father to come upon you, then would I not tell you?"

10 Then David said to Jonathan, "Who will tell me, or what *if* your father answers you roughly?"

11 And Jonathan said to David, "Come, let us go out into the field." So both of them went out into the field.

12 Then Jonathan said to David: "The LORD God of Israel *is witness!* When I have sounded out my father sometime tomorrow, *or* the third *day*, and indeed *there is* good toward David, and I do not send to you and tell you,

13 [q]"may the LORD do so and much more to Jonathan. But if it pleases my father *to do* you evil, then I will report it to you and send you away, that you may go in safety. And the LORD be with [r]you as He has [s]been with my father.

14 "And you shall not only show me the kindness of the LORD while I still live, that I may not die;

15 "but you shall [t]not cut off your kindness from my house forever, no, not when the LORD has cut off every one of the enemies of David from the face of the earth."

16 So Jonathan made *a* [p]*covenant* with the house of David, *saying,* "Let the LORD [u]require *it* at the hand of David's enemies."

17 Now Jonathan again caused David to vow, because he loved him; for he loved him [v]as he loved his own soul.

18 Then Jonathan said to David, "Tomorrow *is* the New Moon; and you

18
a 1 Sam. 16:13
b 1 Sam. 7:17
c v. 22
20
d 1 Sam. 10:5–6
e *Holy Spirit* (OT): vv. 20–23; 2 Sam. 23:2. (Gen. 1:2; Zech. 12:10)
24
f Cp. 1 Sam. 15:35
g Cp. Isa. 20:2
h 1 Sam. 10:10–12
CHAPTER 20
1
i Cp. 1 Sam. 24:9
2
j 1 Sam. 19:1; cp. 22:8
3
k 1 Sam. 27:1
5
l Num. 10:10; 28:11–15
m 1 Sam. 19:2–3
6
n 1 Sam. 17:12; Jn. 7:42
7
o 1 Sam. 25:17
8
p 1 Sam. 18:3; 23:18
13
q Ruth 1:17; 1 Sam. 3:17
r 1 Sam. 18:12
s 1 Sam. 10:7; cp. 2 Sam. 7:15
15
t 1 Sam. 24:21; cp. 2 Sam. 9:1–7
16
u 2 Sam. 4:7
17
v 1 Sam. 18:1

will be missed, because your seat will be empty.

19 "And *when* you have stayed three days, go down quickly and come to the place where you hid on the day of the deed; and remain by the stone Ezel.

20 "Then I will shoot three arrows to the side, as though I shot at a target;

21 "and there I will send a lad, *saying,* 'Go, find the arrows.' If I expressly say to the lad, 'Look, the arrows *are* on this side of you; get them and come'—then, as the LORD lives, *there is* safety for you and no harm.

22 "But if I say thus to the young man, 'Look, the arrows *are* beyond you'—go your way, for the LORD has sent you away.

23 "And as for the [a]matter which you and I have spoken of, indeed the [b]LORD *be* between you and me forever."

Saul angry with Jonathan

24 Then David hid in the field. And when the New Moon had come, the king sat down to eat the feast.

25 Now the king sat on his seat, as at other times, on a seat by the wall. And Jonathan arose,* and Abner sat by Saul's side, but David's place was empty.

26 Nevertheless Saul did not say anything that day, for he thought, "Something has happened to him; he *is* [c]unclean, surely he *is* unclean."

27 And it happened the next day, the second *day* of the month, that David's place was empty. And Saul said to Jonathan his son, "Why has the son of Jesse not come to eat, either yesterday or today?"

28 So Jonathan answered Saul, "David earnestly asked *permission* of me *to* go to Bethlehem.

29 "And he said, 'Please let me go, for our family has a sacrifice in the city, and my brother has commanded me *to be there.* And now, if I have found favor in your eyes, please let me get away and see my brothers.' Therefore he has not come to the king's table."

30 Then Saul's anger was aroused against Jonathan, and he said to him, "You son of a perverse, rebellious *woman!* Do I not know that you have chosen the son of Jesse to your own shame and to the shame of your mother's nakedness?

31 "For as long as the son of Jesse lives on the earth, you shall not be established, nor your [d]kingdom. Now therefore, send and bring him to [e]me, for he shall surely die."

32 And Jonathan answered Saul his father, and said to him, "Why should he be killed? [f]What has he done?"

33 Then Saul cast a [g]spear at him to kill him, by which Jonathan knew that it was determined by his father to kill David.

34 So Jonathan arose from the table in fierce anger, and ate no food the second day of the month, for he was grieved for David, because his father had treated him shamefully.

35 And so it was, in the morning, that Jonathan went out into the field at the time appointed with David, and a little lad *was* with him.

36 Then he said to his lad, "Now run, find the arrows which I shoot." As the lad ran, he shot an arrow beyond him.

37 When the lad had come to the place where the arrow was which Jonathan had shot, Jonathan cried out after the lad and said, "*Is* not the arrow [h]beyond you?"

38 And Jonathan cried out after the lad, "Make haste, hurry, do not delay!" So Jonathan's lad gathered up the arrows and came back to his master.

39 But the lad did not know anything. Only Jonathan and David knew of the matter.

40 Then Jonathan gave his weapons to his lad, and said to him, "Go, carry *them* to the city."

41 As soon as the lad had gone, David arose from *a place* toward the south, fell on his face to the ground, and bowed down three times. And they kissed one another; and they wept together, but David more so.

42 Then Jonathan said to David, "Go in peace, since we have both sworn in the name of the LORD, saying, 'May the LORD be between you and me, and between your descendants and my descendants, forever.'" So he arose and departed, and Jonathan went into the city.

David flees

21 NOW David came to Nob, to [i]Ahimelech the priest. And Ahimelech was afraid when he met David, and said to him, "Why *are* you alone, and no one is with you?"

23
a vv. 14–15
b Cp. Gen. 31:49–53
26
c Lev. 15:5
31
d Cp. 1 Sam. 15:28
e Cp. 1 Sam. 19:6–11
32
f Cp. 1 Sam. 19:4–5
33
g 1 Sam. 18:11
37
h 1 Sam. 20:21–22
CHAPTER 21
1
i Called *Ahijah,* 1 Sam. 14:3; also *Abiathar,* Mk. 2:26

*
20:25 Following Masoretic Text, Syriac, Targum, and Vulgate; Septuagint reads *he sat across from Jonathan.*

2 So David said to Ahimelech the
priest, "The king has ordered me on
some business, and said to me, 'Do not
let anyone know anything about the
business on which I send you, or what
I have commanded you.' And I have
directed *my* young men to such and
such a place.
3 "Now therefore, what have you
on hand? Give *me* five *loaves of* bread
in my hand, or whatever can be
found."
4 And the priest answered David
and said, "*There is* no common bread
on hand; but there is [a]holy bread, if
the young men have at least kept
themselves from [b]women."
5 Then David answered the priest,
and said to him, "Truly, women *have*
been kept from us about three days
since I came out. And the vessels of
the young men are holy, and *the bread*
is in effect common, even though it
was consecrated in the vessel this
day."
6 So the priest gave him holy
bread; for there was no bread there
but the [c]showbread which had been
taken from before the [d]LORD, in order
to put hot bread *in its place* on the day
when it was taken away.
7 Now a certain man of the servants of Saul *was* there that day, detained before the LORD. And his name
was [e]Doeg, an Edomite, the chief of
the herdsmen who *belonged* to Saul.
8 And David said to Ahimelech,
"Is there not here on hand a spear or
a sword? For I have brought neither
my sword nor my weapons with me,
because the king's business required
haste."
9 So the priest said, "The [f]sword
of Goliath the Philistine, whom you
killed in the Valley of Elah, there it is,
wrapped in a cloth behind the ephod.
If you will take that, take *it*. For *there*
is no other [g]except that one here."
And David said, "*There is* none like it;
give it to me."

David, for fear of Saul, seeks safety at Gath

10 Then David arose and fled that
day from before Saul, and went to
Achish the king of Gath.
11 And the [h]servants of Achish
said to him, "*Is* this not David the king
of the land? Did they not sing of him
to one another in dances, saying:

'Saul has slain his thousands,
And David his [i]ten
thousands'?"

12 Now David took these words to
heart, and was [j]very much afraid of
Achish the king of Gath.
13 So he [k]changed his behavior before them, pretended madness in their
hands, scratched on the doors of the
gate, and let his saliva fall down on his
beard.
14 Then Achish said to his servants, "Look, you see the man is insane. Why have you brought him to
me?
15 "Have I need of madmen, that
you have brought this *fellow* to play
the madman in my presence? Shall
this *fellow* come into my house?"

David and his mighty men at Adullam (cp. 1 Chr. 12:16–18)

22 DAVID therefore departed
from there and escaped to the
[l]cave of Adullam. So when his brothers and all his father's house heard *it*,
they went down there to him.
2 And everyone *who was* in distress, everyone who *was* in debt, and
everyone *who was* discontented gathered to him. So he became [m]captain
over them. And there were about
[n]four hundred men with him.
3 Then David went from there to
Mizpah of [o]Moab; and he said to the
king of Moab, "Please let my father
and mother come here with you, till I
know what God will do for me."
4 So he brought them before the
king of Moab, and they dwelt with him
all the time that David was in the
stronghold.
5 Now the prophet [p]Gad said to
David, "Do not stay in the stronghold;
depart, and go to the land of Judah."
So David departed and went into the
forest of Hereth.

Saul kills priests

6 When Saul heard that David and
the men who *were* with him had been
discovered—now Saul was staying in
[q]Gibeah under a tamarisk tree in Ramah, with his spear in his hand, and
all his servants standing about him—
7 then Saul said to his servants
who stood about him, "Hear now, you
Benjamites! Will the [r]son of Jesse
give every one of you fields and vineyards, *and* make you all captains of
thousands and captains of hundreds?
8 "All of you have conspired
against me, and *there is* no one who
reveals to me that my son has made a

4
a Ex. 25:30; Lev. 24:5–9; Mt. 12:4
b Cp. Ex. 19:14–15
6
c See Ex. 25:30, *note*
d Lev. 24:8–9
7
e 1 Sam. 22:9; Ps. 52, *title*
9
f 1 Sam. 17:1–51
g 1 Sam. 22:10
11
h Ps. 56, *title*
i 1 Sam. 18:6–8
12
j Ps. 34:4; 56:3
13
k Cp. Ps. 34, *title*
CHAPTER 22
1
l Ps. 57, *title;* 142, *title*
2
m Cp. Jud. 11:13; Heb. 2:10
n 1 Sam. 25:13; cp. 23:13
3
o 2 Sam. 8:2
5
p 2 Sam. 24:11
6
q 1 Sam. 15:34
7
r Cp. 1 Sam. 8:14

[a]covenant with the son of Jesse; and *there is* not one of you who is [b]sorry for me or reveals to me that my son has stirred up my servant against me, to lie in wait, as *it is* this day."

9 Then answered [c]Doeg the Edomite, who was set over the servants of Saul, and said, "I saw the son of Jesse going to [d]Nob, to Ahimelech the son of [e]Ahitub.

10 "And he inquired of the LORD for him, gave him provisions, and gave him the sword of Goliath the Philistine."

11 So the king sent to call Ahimelech the priest, the son of Ahitub, and all his father's house, the priests who *were* in Nob. And they all came to the king.

12 And Saul said, "Hear now, son of Ahitub!" He answered, "Here I am, my lord."

13 Then Saul said to him, "Why have you conspired against me, you and the son of Jesse, in that you have given him bread and a sword, and have inquired of God for him, that he should rise against me, to lie in wait, as it is this day?"

14 So Ahimelech answered the king and said, "And who among all your servants *is as* [f]faithful as David, who is the king's son-in-law, who goes at your bidding, and is honorable in your house?

15 "Did I then begin to inquire of God for him? Far be it from me! Let not the king [g]impute anything to his servant, *or* to any in the house of my father. For your servant knew nothing of all this, little or much."

16 And the king said, "You shall surely die, Ahimelech, you and all [h]your father's house!"

17 Then the king said to the guards who stood about him, "Turn and kill the priests of the LORD, because their hand also *is* with David, and because they knew when he fled and did not tell it to me." But the servants of the king would not [i]lift their hands to strike the priests of the LORD.

18 And the king said to Doeg, "You turn and kill the priests!" So Doeg the Edomite turned and struck the priests, and [j]killed on that day eighty-five men who wore a linen ephod.

19 Also [k]Nob, the [l]city of the priests, he struck with the edge of the sword, both men and women, children and nursing infants, oxen and donkeys and sheep—with the edge of the sword.

8 [a] 1 Sam. 18:3; 20:16 [b] Cp. 1 Sam. 23:21
9 [c] 1 Sam. 21:7; 22:22; Ps. 52, *title* [d] 1 Sam. 21:1 [e] 1 Sam. 14:3
14 [f] 1 Sam. 19:4–5; 24:11
15 [g] For divine imputation, see Jas. 2:23, *note;* cp. 2 Sam. 19:19
16 [h] Dt. 24:16
17 [i] Cp. Ex. 1:17
18 [j] 1 Sam. 2:31
19 [k] vv. 9,11 [l] Josh. 21:1–45
20 [m] 1 Sam. 23:6; 1 Ki. 2:26,27 [n] 1 Sam. 2:33
CHAPTER 23
1 [o] Josh. 15:44
2 [p] 1 Sam. 22:10; 28:6
5 [q] 1 Sam. 19:8; 2 Sam. 5:20
6 [r] 1 Sam. 22:20
9 [s] 1 Sam. 30:7; cp. Num. 27:21

20 Now one of the sons of Ahimelech the son of Ahitub, named [m]Abiathar, [n]escaped and fled after David.

21 And Abiathar told David that Saul had killed the LORD's priests.

22 So David said to Abiathar, "I knew that day, when Doeg the Edomite *was* there, that he would surely tell Saul. I have caused *the death* of all the persons of your father's house.

23 "Stay with me; do not fear. For he who seeks my life seeks your life, but with me you *shall be* safe."

David saves Keilah from the Philistines

23 THEN they told David, saying, "Look, the Philistines are fighting against [o]Keilah, and they are robbing the threshing floors."

2 Therefore David [p]inquired of the LORD, saying, "Shall I go and attack these Philistines?" And the LORD said to David, "Go and attack the Philistines, and save Keilah."

3 But David's men said to him, "Look, we are afraid here in Judah. How much more then if we go to Keilah against the armies of the Philistines?"

4 Then David inquired of the LORD once again. And the LORD answered him and said, "Arise, go down to Keilah. For I will deliver the Philistines into your hand."

5 And David and his men went to Keilah and [q]fought with the Philistines, struck them with a mighty blow, and took away their livestock. So David saved the inhabitants of Keilah.

6 Now it happened, when Abiathar the son of Ahimelech [r]fled to David at Keilah, *that* he went down *with* an ephod in his hand.

7 And Saul was told that David had gone to Keilah. So Saul said, "God has delivered him into my hand, for he has shut himself in by entering a town that has gates and bars."

8 Then Saul called all the people together for war, to go down to Keilah to besiege David and his men.

9 When David knew that Saul plotted evil against him, he [s]said to Abiathar the priest, "Bring the ephod here."

10 Then David said, "O LORD God of Israel, Your servant has certainly heard that Saul seeks to come to Keilah to destroy the city for my sake.

11 "Will the men of Keilah deliver me into his hand? Will Saul come down, as Your servant has heard? O LORD God of Israel, I pray, tell Your

servant." And the LORD said, "He will
come down."
12 Then David said, "Will the men
of Keilah deliver me and my men into
the hand of Saul?" And the LORD said,
"They will deliver [a]*you*."

God protects David again; David goes to En Gedi

13 So David and his men, about
[b]six hundred, arose and departed
from Keilah and went [c]wherever they
could go. Then it was told Saul that
David had escaped from Keilah; so he
halted the expedition.
14 And David stayed in strongholds in the [d]wilderness, and remained in the mountains in the Wilderness of Ziph. Saul sought him
every day, but [e]God did not deliver
him into his hand.
15 So David saw that Saul had
come out to seek his life. And David
was in the Wilderness of Ziph in [f]a
forest.
16 Then Jonathan, Saul's son,
arose and went to David in [f]the
woods and strengthened his hand in
God.
17 And he said to him, [g]"Do not
fear, for the hand of Saul my father
shall not find you. You shall be [h]king
over Israel, and I shall be next to you.
Even my father Saul knows that."
18 So the two of them made a [i]cov-
enant before the LORD. And David
stayed in [f]the woods, and Jonathan
went to his own house.
19 [j]Then the Ziphites came up to
Saul at Gibeah, saying, "Is David not
hiding with us in strongholds in [k]the
woods, in the hill of Hachilah, which
is on the south of Jeshimon?
20 "Now therefore, O king, come
down according to all the desire of
your soul to come down; and [l]our
part *shall be* to deliver him into the
king's hand."
21 And Saul said, "Blessed *are* you
of the LORD, for you have [m]compassion
on me.
22 "Please go and find out for sure,
and see the place where his hideout is,
and who has seen him there. For I am
told he is very crafty.
23 "See therefore, and take knowledge of all the lurking places where he
hides; and come back to me with certainty, and I will go with you. And it
shall be, if he is in the land, that I will
[n]search for him throughout all the
clans* of Judah."
24 So they arose and went to Ziph
before Saul. But David and his men
were in the Wilderness of [o]Maon, in
the [p]plain on the south of Jeshimon.
25 When Saul and his men went to
seek *him*, they told David. Therefore
he went down to the rock, and stayed
in the Wilderness of Maon. And when
Saul heard *that*, he pursued David in
the Wilderness of Maon.
26 Then Saul went on one side of
the mountain, and David and his men
on the other side of the mountain. So
David made haste to get away from
Saul, for Saul and his men were [q]en-
circling David and his men to take
them.
27 But a [r]messenger came to Saul,
saying, "Hurry and come, for the Philistines have invaded the land!"
28 Therefore Saul returned from
pursuing David, and went against the
Philistines; so they called that place
the Rock of Escape.*
29 Then David went up from there
and dwelt in strongholds at [s]En Gedi.

David's mercy to Saul in En Gedi

24 NOW it happened, when Saul
had returned from following
the Philistines, that it was [t]told him,
saying, "Take note! David *is* in the
Wilderness of En Gedi."
2 Then Saul took [u]three thousand
chosen men from all Israel, and went
to seek David and his men on the
Rocks of the Wild Goats.
3 So he came to the sheepfolds by
the road, where there *was* a [v]cave;
and Saul went in to [w]attend to his
needs. (David and his men were staying in the recesses of the cave.)
4 Then the men of David said to
him, [x]"This is the day of which the
LORD said to you, 'Behold, I will deliver
your enemy into your hand, that you
may do to him as it seems good to
you.'" And David arose and secretly
cut off a corner of Saul's robe.
5 Now it happened afterward that
David's heart [y]troubled him because
he had cut Saul's *robe*.
6 And he said to his men, "The
[z]LORD forbid that I should do this
thing to my master, the LORD's
anointed, to stretch out my hand
against him, seeing he *is* the anointed
of the LORD."
7 So David restrained his servants

12
a Cp. Jud. 15:10–13
13
b Cp. 1 Sam. 22:2
c 2 Sam. 15:20
14
d 1 Sam. 26:2; Ps. 63, *title*
e Ps. 32:7
15
f Or *Horesh.*
17
g Ps. 27:1–3; Isa. 54:17; Heb. 13:6
h 1 Sam. 24:20
18
i 1 Sam. 18:3; 20:12–17; 2 Sam. 21:7
19
j 1 Sam. 26:1; Ps. 54, *title*
k Or *Horesh.*
20
l Cp. v. 12
21
m Cp. 1 Sam. 22:8
23
n Cp. 1 Ki. 18:10
24
o 1 Sam. 25:2
p See Dt. 1:1, *note*
26
q Ps. 17:9
27
r Cp. 2 Ki. 19:9
29
s Josh. 15:62; 2 Chr. 20:2
CHAPTER 24
1
t 1 Sam. 23:19
2
u 1 Sam. 26:2
3
v Ps. 54, *title;* 57, *title*
w Jud. 3:24
4
x 1 Sam. 26:8–11
5
y 2 Sam. 24:10

24:6 *z* 1 Sam. 26:11

*

23:23 Literally *thousands* **23:28** Hebrew *Sela Hammahlekoth*

with *these* words, and did not allow
them to rise against Saul. And Saul
got up from the cave and went on *his*
way.
8 David also arose afterward,
went out of the cave, and called out to
Saul, saying, "My lord the king!" And
when Saul looked behind him, David
stooped with his face to the earth, and
bowed down.
9 And David said to Saul: "Why do
you listen to the words of men who
say, 'Indeed David seeks your harm'?
10 "Look, this day your eyes have
seen that the LORD delivered you today
into my hand in the cave, and *someone* urged *me* to kill you. But *my eye*
spared you, and I said, 'I will not
stretch out my hand against my lord,
for he *is* the LORD's anointed.'
11 "Moreover, my father, see! Yes,
see the corner of your robe in my
hand! For in that I cut off the corner of
your robe, and did not kill you, know
and see that *there is* neither evil nor
rebellion in my hand, and I have [a]not
sinned against you. Yet you [b]hunt my
life to take it.
12 "Let the LORD [c]judge between
you and me, and let the LORD avenge
me on you. But my hand shall not be
against you.
13 "As the proverb of the ancients
says, [d]'Wickedness proceeds from the
wicked.' But my hand shall not be
against you.
14 "After whom has the king of Israel come out? Whom do you pursue?
A dead dog? A flea?
15 "Therefore let the LORD be judge,
and judge between you and me, and
see and [e]plead my case, and deliver
me out of your hand."
16 So it was, when David had finished speaking these words to Saul,
that Saul said, "*Is* this your [f]voice, my
son David?" And Saul lifted up his
voice and wept.
17 Then he said to David: "You *are*
more righteous than [g]I; for you have
rewarded me with good, whereas I
have rewarded you with evil.
18 "And you have shown this day
how you have dealt well with me; for
when the LORD delivered me into your
hand, you did not kill me.
19 "For if a man finds his enemy,
will he let him get away safely? Therefore may the LORD reward you with
good for what you have done to me
this day.
20 "And now [h]I know indeed that
you shall surely be king, and that the

11
a Jud. 11:27
b 1 Sam. 26:20
12
c 1 Sam. 26:10–23
13
d Mt. 7:16–20
15
e Ps. 35:1; cp. 1 Sam. 25:39
16
f 1 Sam. 26:17
17
g 1 Sam. 26:21
20
h 1 Sam. 23:17
21
i 2 Sam. 21:1–9
22
j 1 Sam. 23:29
CHAPTER 25
1
k 1 Sam. 28:3
l Num. 20:29; Dt. 34:8
m Gen. 21:21; Num. 10:12
2
n 1 Sam. 23:24
o Josh. 15:55
3
p Lit. *fool.* v. 25
q vv. 10–11, 17
r Josh. 15:13
4
s Gen. 38:13; cp. 2 Sam. 13:23
6
t Jud. 19:20; 1 Chr. 12:18
8
u Lit. *good day.* Cp. Est. 8:17

kingdom of Israel shall be established
in your hand.
21 "Therefore swear now to me by
the LORD [i]that you will not cut off my
descendants after me, and that you
will not destroy my name from my father's house."
22 So David swore to Saul. And
Saul went home, but David and his
men went up to the [j]stronghold.

Samuel dies and is mourned

25 THEN Samuel [k]died; and the
Israelites gathered together
and [l]lamented for him, and buried
him at his home in Ramah. And David
arose and went down to the Wilderness of [m]Paran.*

Nabal's ingratitude; Abigail's wisdom

2 Now *there was* a man in [n]Maon
whose business *was* in [o]Carmel, and
the man *was* very rich. He had three
thousand sheep and a thousand goats.
And he was shearing his sheep in Carmel.
3 The name of the man *was* [p]Na-
bal, and the name of his wife Abigail.
And *she was* a woman of good understanding and beautiful appearance;
but the man *was* [q]harsh and evil in *his*
doings. He *was of the house of* [r]Caleb.
4 When David heard in the wilderness that Nabal was [s]shearing his
sheep,
5 David sent ten young men; and
David said to the young men, "Go up
to Carmel, go to Nabal, and greet him
in my name.
6 "And thus you shall say to him
who lives *in prosperity:* [t]'Peace *be* to
you, peace to your house, and peace to
all that you have!
7 'Now I have heard that you have
shearers. Your shepherds were with
us, and we did not hurt them, nor was
there anything missing from them all
the while they were in Carmel.
8 'Ask your young men, and they
will tell you. Therefore let *my* young
men find favor in your eyes, for we
come on a [u]feast day. Please give
whatever comes to your hand to your
servants and to your son David.' "
9 So when David's young men
came, they spoke to Nabal according
to all these words in the name of David, and waited.
10 Then Nabal answered David's
servants, and said, "Who *is* David, and
who *is* the son of Jesse? There are

*
25:1 Following Masoretic Text, Syriac, Targum, and Vulgate; Septuagint reads *Maon.*

many servants nowadays who break away each one from his master.

11 [a]"Shall I then take my bread and my water and my meat that I have killed for my shearers, and give *it* to men when I do not know where they *are* from?"

12 So David's young men turned on their heels and went back; and they came and told him all these words.

13 Then David said to his men, "Every man gird on his sword." So every man girded on his sword, and David also girded on his sword. And about four hundred men went with David, and two hundred stayed with the [b]supplies.

14 Now one of the young men told Abigail, Nabal's wife, saying, "Look, David sent messengers from the wilderness to greet our master; and he reviled them.

15 "But the men *were* very good to us, and [c]we were not hurt, nor did we miss anything as long as we accompanied them, when we were in the fields.

16 "They were a wall to us both by night and day, all the time we were with them keeping the sheep.

17 "Now therefore, know and consider what you will do, for harm is determined against our master and against all his household. For he *is such* a [d]scoundrel* that *one* cannot speak to him."

18 Then Abigail made haste and [e]took two hundred *loaves* of bread, two skins of wine, five sheep already dressed, five [f]seahs of roasted *grain*, one hundred clusters of raisins, and two hundred cakes of figs, and loaded *them* on donkeys.

19 And she said to her servants, "Go on before me; see, I am coming after you." But she did not tell her husband Nabal.

20 So it was, *as* she rode on the donkey, that she went down under cover of the hill; and there were David and his men, coming down toward her, and she met them.

21 Now David had said, "Surely in vain I have protected all that this *fellow* has in the wilderness, so that nothing was missed of all that *belongs* to him. And he has repaid me evil for [g]good.

22 "May God do so, and more also, to the enemies of David, if I leave one male of all who *belong* to him by morning light."

23 Now when Abigail saw David, she [h]dismounted quickly from the donkey, [i]fell on her face before David, and bowed down to the ground.

24 So she fell at his feet and said: "On me, my lord, *on* me *let* this iniquity *be!* And please let your maidservant speak in your ears, and hear the words of your maidservant.

25 "Please, let not my lord regard this scoundrel Nabal. For as his name *is*, so *is* he: Nabal* *is* his name, and folly *is* with him! But I, your maidservant, did not see the young men of my lord whom you sent.

26 "Now therefore, my lord, *as* the LORD lives and *as* your soul lives, since the LORD has held you back from coming to bloodshed and from [j]avenging yourself with your own hand, now then, [k]let your enemies and those who seek harm for my lord be as Nabal.

27 "And now this [l]present which your maidservant has brought to my lord, let it be given to the young men who follow my lord.

28 "Please forgive the trespass of your maidservant. For the LORD will certainly make for my lord an [m]enduring house, because my lord [n]fights the battles of the LORD, and [o]evil is not found in you throughout your days.

29 "Yet a man has risen to pursue you and seek your life, but the life of my lord shall be [p]bound in the bundle of the living with the LORD your God; and the lives of your enemies He shall [q]sling out, *as from* the pocket of a sling.

30 "And it shall come to pass, when the LORD has done for my lord according to all the good that He has spoken concerning you, and has appointed you [r]ruler over Israel,

31 "that this will be no grief to you, nor offense of heart to my lord, either that you have shed blood without cause, or that my lord has avenged himself. But when the LORD has dealt well with my lord, then remember your maidservant."

32 Then David said to Abigail: "Blessed *is* the LORD God of Israel, who sent you this day to meet me!

33 "And blessed *is* your advice and blessed *are* you, because you have kept me this day from coming to bloodshed and from avenging myself with my own hand.

34 "For indeed, *as* the LORD God of Israel lives, who has kept me back from hurting you, unless you had hurried and come to meet me, surely by

11 *a* Jud. 8:6
13 *b* 1 Sam. 30:24
15 *c* v. 7
17 *d* 2 Sam. 23:6–7
18 *e* Cp. 2 Sam. 16:1; 1 Chr. 12:40
f See Weights and Measures (OT), 2 Chr. 2:10, *note*
21 *g* 1 Sam. 24:17
23 *h* Josh. 15:18
i Cp. Ruth 2:10
26 *j* Cp. Heb. 10:30
k Cp. 2 Sam. 18:32
27 *l* Cp. 1 Sam. 30:26
28 *m* 2 Sam. 7:11–16
n 1 Sam. 18:17
o 1 Sam. 24:11
29 *p* Ps. 66:9; Mal. 3:17; Col. 3:3
q Jer. 10:18
30 *r* 1 Sam. 13:14; 15:28

*

25:17 Literally *son of Belial* **25:25** Literally *Fool*

morning light no males would have
been left to Nabal!"
35 So David received from her
hand what she had brought him, and
said to her, "Go up in peace to your
house. See, I have heeded your voice
and respected your person."

Nabal dies

36 Now Abigail went to Nabal, and
there he was, holding a feast in his
house, like the feast of a king. And
Nabal's heart *was* [a]merry within him,
for he *was* very drunk; therefore she
told him nothing, little or much, until
morning light.
37 So it was, in the morning, when
the wine had gone from Nabal, and his
wife had told him these things, that his
heart died within him, and he became
like a stone.
38 Then it happened, *after* about
ten days, that the LORD [b]struck Nabal,
and he died.
39 So when David heard that Nabal
was dead, he said, [c]"Blessed *be* the
LORD, who has [d]pleaded the cause of
my reproach from the hand of Nabal,
and has kept His servant from evil!
For the LORD has returned the wickedness of Nabal on his own head." And
David sent and proposed to Abigail, to
take her as his wife.
40 When the servants of David had
come to Abigail at Carmel, they spoke
to her saying, "David sent us to you, to
ask you to become his wife."
41 Then she arose, bowed her face
to the earth, and said, "Here is your
maidservant, a servant to [e]wash the
feet of the servants of my lord."
42 So Abigail rose in haste and
rode on a donkey, attended by five of
her maidens; and she followed the
messengers of David, and became his
wife.
43 David also took [f]Ahinoam of
[g]Jezreel, and so both of them were his
wives.
44 But Saul had given [h]Michal his
daughter, David's wife, to Palti* the
son of Laish, who *was* from Gallim.

David again spares Saul

26 NOW the Ziphites came to
Saul at Gibeah, saying, "Is David not hiding in the hill of Hachilah,
opposite [i]Jeshimon?"
2 Then Saul arose and went down
to the Wilderness of Ziph, having
[j]three thousand chosen men of Israel
with him, to seek David in the Wilderness of Ziph.

36
a 2 Sam. 13:28; Prov. 20:1
38
b 1 Sam. 26:10; 2 Ki. 15:5
39
c v. 32
d 1 Sam. 24:15; Prov. 22:23
41
e Lk. 7:38, 44
43
f 1 Sam. 27:3
g Josh. 15:56
44
h 1 Sam. 18:20
CHAPTER 26
1
i 1 Sam. 23:19; Ps. 54, *title*
2
j 1 Sam. 24:2
5
k 1 Sam. 14:50
6
l See 2 Ki. 7:6, *note*
m 2 Sam. 2:13
n 2 Sam. 2:18,24
8
o 1 Sam. 24:4
9
p 1 Sam. 24:6; 2 Sam. 1:16
10
q 1 Sam. 25:38
r Dt. 31:14
s 1 Sam. 31:6
11
t 1 Sam. 24:6–12
12
u Gen. 2:21; 15:12

3 And Saul encamped in the hill of
Hachilah, which *is* opposite Jeshimon, by the road. But David stayed in
the wilderness, and he saw that Saul
came after him into the wilderness.
4 David therefore sent out spies,
and understood that Saul had indeed
come.
5 So David arose and came to the
place where Saul had encamped. And
David saw the place where Saul lay,
and [k]Abner the son of Ner, the commander of his army. Now Saul lay
within the camp, with the people encamped all around him.
6 Then David answered, and said
to Ahimelech the [l]Hittite and to
Abishai the son of Zeruiah, brother of
[m]Joab, saying, "Who will go down
with me to Saul in the camp?" And
[n]Abishai said, "I will go down with
you."
7 So David and Abishai came to
the people by night; and there Saul lay
sleeping within the camp, with his
spear stuck in the ground by his head.
And Abner and the people lay all
around him.
8 Then Abishai said to David,
[o]"God has delivered your enemy into
your hand this day. Now therefore,
please, let me strike him at once with
the spear, right to the earth; and I will
not *have to strike* him a second time!"
9 But David said to Abishai, "Do
not destroy him; for [p]who can stretch
out his hand against the LORD's
anointed, and be guiltless?"
10 David said furthermore, "*As* the
LORD lives, the [q]LORD shall strike him,
or his day shall come to [r]die, or he
shall go out to battle and [s]perish.
11 "The LORD [t]forbid that I should
stretch out my hand against the LORD's
anointed. But please, take now the
spear and the jug of water that *are* by
his head, and let us go."
12 So David took the spear and the
jug of water *by* Saul's head, and they
got away; and no man saw or knew *it*
or awoke. For they *were* all asleep,
because a [u]deep sleep from the LORD
had fallen on them.
13 Now David went over to the
other side, and stood on the top of a
hill afar off, a great distance *being* between them.
14 And David called out to the people and to Abner the son of Ner, saying, "Do you not answer, Abner?"

*25:44 Spelled *Paltiel* in 2 Samuel 3:15

Then Abner answered and said, "Who *are* you, calling out to the king?"

15 So David said to Abner, "*Are* you not a man? And who *is* like you in Israel? Why then have you not guarded your lord the king? For one of the people came in to destroy your lord the king.

16 "This thing that you have done *is* not good. *As* the LORD lives, you deserve to die, because you have not guarded your master, the LORD's anointed. And now see where the king's spear *is*, and the jug of water that *was* by his head."

17 Then Saul knew David's voice, and said, "*Is* that your voice, my son David?" David said, "*It is* my voice, my lord, O king."

18 And he said, "Why does my lord thus pursue his servant? For what have I done, or what evil *is* in my hand?

19 "Now therefore, please, let my lord the king hear the words of his servant: If the [a]LORD has stirred you up against me, let Him accept an offering. But if *it is* the children of men, *may* they *be* [b]cursed before the LORD, for they have driven me out this day from sharing in the [c]inheritance of the LORD, saying, 'Go, serve other gods.'

20 "So now, do not let my blood fall to the earth before the face of the [d]LORD. For the king of Israel has come out to seek a [e]flea, as when one hunts a partridge in the mountains."

Saul admits his guilt

21 Then Saul said, [f]"I have sinned. Return, my son David. For I will harm you no more, because my [g]life was precious in your eyes this day. Indeed I have played the [h]fool and erred exceedingly."

22 And David answered and said, "Here is the king's spear. Let one of the young men come over and get it.

23 "May the [i]LORD [j]repay every man *for* his righteousness and his faithfulness; for the LORD delivered you into *my* hand today, but I would not stretch out my hand against the LORD's anointed.

24 "And indeed, as your life was [k]valued much this day in my eyes, so let my life be valued much in the eyes of the LORD, and let Him deliver me out of all tribulation."

25 Then Saul said to David, "*May* you *be* blessed, my son David! You shall both do great things and also still [l]prevail." So David went on his way, and Saul returned to his place.

David seeks shelter

27 AND David [m]said in his heart, "Now I shall perish someday by the hand of Saul. *There is* nothing better for me than that I should speedily escape to the land of the Philistines; and Saul will despair of me, to seek me anymore in any part of Israel. So I shall escape out of his hand."

2 Then David arose and went over with the six hundred [n]men who *were* with him to [o]Achish the son of Maoch, king of Gath.

3 So David dwelt with Achish at Gath, he and his men, each man with his household, *and* David with his two wives, [p]Ahinoam the Jezreelitess, and [q]Abigail the Carmelitess, Nabal's widow.

4 And it was told Saul that David had fled to Gath; so he sought him no more.

5 Then David said to Achish, "If I have now found favor in your eyes, let them give me a place in some town in the country, that I may dwell there. For why should your servant dwell in the royal city with you?"

6 So Achish gave him [r]Ziklag that day. Therefore Ziklag has belonged to the kings of Judah to this day.

7 Now the time that David [s]dwelt in the country of the Philistines was one full year and four months.

8 And David and his men went up and raided the [t]Geshurites, the [u]Girzites,* and the [v]Amalekites. For those nations were the inhabitants of the land from of old, as you go to Shur, even as far as the land of Egypt.

9 Whenever David attacked the land, he left neither man nor woman alive, but took away the sheep, the oxen, the donkeys, the camels, and the apparel, and returned and came to Achish.

10 Then Achish would say, "Where have you made a raid today?" And David would say, "Against the southern *area* of Judah, or against the southern *area* of the [w]Jerahmeelites, or against the southern *area* of the [x]Kenites."

11 David would save neither man nor woman alive, to bring *news* to Gath, saying, "Lest they should inform on us, saying, 'Thus David did.' " And thus *was* his behavior all the time

* 27:8 Or *Gezrites*

19 *a* Cp. 2 Sam. 16:11 *b* 1 Sam. 14:24 *c* Cp. Josh. 22:25–27; 2 Sam. 14:16
20 *d* Cp. Gen. 4:11 *e* 1 Sam. 24:14
21 *f* 1 Sam. 15:24; 24:17; 2 Sam. 12:13 *g* v. 24 *h* Cp. 2 Sam. 24:10
23 *i* Ps. 7:8 *j* 2 Sam. 22:21
24 *k* 1 Sam. 18:30
25 *l* 1 Sam. 24:20
CHAPTER 27
1 *m* Cp. 1 Chr. 29:28
2 *n* 1 Sam. 25:13 *o* 1 Sam. 21:10; 1 Ki. 2:39
3 *p* 1 Sam. 25:43; 30:5 *q* 1 Sam. 25:3
6 *r* Josh. 19:5; 1 Chr. 12:1
7 *s* 1 Sam. 29:3
8 *t* Josh. 13:13 *u* Jud. 1:29 *v* 1 Sam. 15:7–8
10 *w* 1 Sam. 30:29; 1 Chr. 2:9, 25 *x* Jud. 1:16; 4:11

he dwelt in the country of the Philistines.

12 So Achish believed David, saying, "He has made his people Israel utterly abhor him; therefore he will be my servant forever."

Philistines plan attack

28 NOW it happened in those days that the Philistines gathered their armies together for war, to fight with Israel. And Achish said to David, "You assuredly know that you will go out with me to battle, you and your [a]men."

2 So David said to Achish, "Surely you know what your servant can do." And Achish said to David, "Therefore I will make you one of my chief guardians forever."

3 Now [b]Samuel had died, and all Israel had lamented for him and buried him in Ramah, in his own city. And Saul had put the [c]mediums and the spiritists out of the land.

4 Then the Philistines gathered together, and came and encamped at [d]Shunem. So Saul gathered all Israel together, and they encamped at [e]Gilboa.

5 When Saul saw the army of the Philistines, he was afraid, and his heart trembled greatly.

6 And when Saul inquired of the LORD, the LORD did [f]not answer him, either by dreams or by [g]Urim or by the prophets.

Saul consults witch of En Dor

7 Then Saul said to his servants, [h]"Find me a woman who is a medium, [i]that I may go to her and inquire of her." And his servants said to him, "In fact, *there is* a woman who is a [1]medium at En Dor."

8 So Saul [j]disguised himself and put on other clothes, and he went, and two men with him; and they came to the woman by night. And he said, "Please conduct a séance for me, and bring up for me the one I shall name to you."

9 Then the woman said to him, "Look, you know what Saul has done, how he has [k]cut off the mediums and the spiritists from the land. Why then do you lay a snare for my life, to cause me to die?"

10 And Saul swore to her by the LORD, saying, "*As* the LORD lives, no punishment shall come upon you for this thing."

11 Then the woman said, "Whom shall I bring up for you?" And he said, "Bring up Samuel for me."

12 When the woman saw Samuel, she cried out with a loud voice. And the woman spoke to Saul, saying, "Why have you deceived me? For you *are* Saul!"

13 And the king said to her, "Do not be afraid. What did you see?" And the woman said to Saul, "I saw a spirit* ascending out of the earth."

14 So he said to her, "What *is* his form?" And she said, "An old man is coming up, and he *is* covered with a mantle." And Saul perceived that it *was* Samuel, and he stooped with *his* face to the ground and bowed down.

15 Now Samuel said to Saul, "Why have you disturbed me by bringing me up?" And Saul answered, "I am deeply distressed; for the Philistines make war against me, and God has departed from me and does not answer me anymore, neither by prophets nor by dreams. Therefore I have called you, that you may reveal to me what I should do."

16 Then Samuel said: "So why do you ask me, seeing the LORD has departed from you and has become your enemy?

17 "And the LORD has done for Himself* as He spoke by me. For the LORD has [l]torn the kingdom out of your

CHAPTER 28

1 [a] 1 Sam. 29:1–2

3 [b] 1 Sam. 25:1 [c] Cp. Ex. 22:18; Lev. 19:31; Dt. 18:10

4 [d] Josh. 19:18; 2 Ki. 4:8 [e] 1 Sam. 31:1

6 [f] 1 Sam. 14:37 [g] See Ex. 28:30, *note*

7 [h] Cp. Isa. 8:19 [i] 1 Chr. 10:13

8 [j] Cp. 2 Chr. 18:29; 35:22

9 [k] v. 3

17 [l] 1 Sam. 15:28

* 28:13 Hebrew *elohim* 28:17 Or *him*, that is, David

[1](28:7) The Bible gives strict instructions against delving into the realm of spirits (Lev. 19:31; 20:6–7,27; Dt. 18:10–12). Some who claim to have contact with spirits are frauds, but certainly there are genuine cases. God is against any form of spiritism, fraudulent or real. See 1 Chr. 10:13–14.

The most likely explanation is that the woman expected contact with a demon (posing as Samuel, v. 11) but, to her amazement and terror (v. 12), God actually permitted Samuel to appear to her and give a message of doom to Saul. The text clearly states that it was Samuel (vv. 15–16,20). No agent of Satan could have given a message so clearly from the LORD as v. 17.

The passage does not say that the woman "brought up" Samuel from the dead. The incident gives no support to the false contention of spiritists that they can speak with the dead. Mediums do not have access to the dead but communicate with spirits posing as persons who have died; thus these spirits are called lying spirits (1 Ki. 22:22).

hand and given it to your neighbor, David.

18 [a]"Because you did not obey the voice of the LORD nor execute His fierce wrath upon [b]Amalek, therefore the LORD has done this thing to you this day.

19 "Moreover the LORD will also deliver Israel with you into the hand of the Philistines. And tomorrow you and your sons *will be* with [c]me. The LORD will also deliver the army of Israel into the hand of the Philistines."

20 Immediately Saul fell full length on the ground, and was dreadfully afraid because of the words of Samuel. And there was no strength in him, for he had eaten no food all day or all night.

21 And the woman came to Saul and saw that he was severely troubled, and said to him, "Look, your maidservant has obeyed your voice, and I have put my life in my hands and heeded the words which you spoke to me.

22 "Now therefore, please, heed also the voice of your maidservant, and let me set a piece of bread before you; and eat, that you may have strength when you go on *your* way."

23 But he refused and said, "I will not eat." So his servants, together with the woman, urged him; and he heeded their voice. Then he arose from the ground and sat on the bed.

24 Now the woman had a fatted calf in the house, and she hastened to kill it. And she took flour and kneaded *it*, and baked unleavened bread from it.

25 So she brought *it* before Saul and his servants, and they ate. Then they rose and went away that night.

David kept from fighting Israel

29 THEN the Philistines gathered together all their [d]armies at [e]Aphek, and the Israelites encamped by a fountain which *is* in Jezreel.

2 And the [f]lords of the Philistines passed in review by hundreds and by thousands, but [d]David and his men passed in review at the rear with Achish.

3 Then the princes of the Philistines said, "What *are* these Hebrews *doing here?*" And Achish said to the princes of the Philistines, "*Is* this not David, the servant of Saul king of Israel, who has been with me these days, or these [g]years? And to this day I have found no fault in him since he defected *to me*."

4 But the princes of the Philistines were angry with him; so the princes of the Philistines said to him, "Make this fellow return, that he may go back to the [h]place which you have appointed for him, and do not let him go down with us to [i]battle, lest in the battle he become [i]our adversary. For with what could he [j]reconcile himself to his master, if not with the heads of these [k]men?

5 "*Is* this not David, [l]of whom [m]they sang to one another in dances, saying:

'Saul has slain his thousands,
And David his ten
thousands'?"

6 Then Achish called David and said to him, "Surely, [n]*as* the LORD lives, you have been upright, and your going out and your coming in with me in the army *is* good in my sight. [o]For to this day I have not found evil in you since the day of your coming to me. Nevertheless the lords do not favor you.

7 "Therefore return now, and go in peace, that you may not displease the lords of the Philistines."

8 So David said to Achish, "But what have I [p]done? And to this day what have you found in your servant as long as I have been with you, that I may not go and fight against the enemies of my lord the king?"

9 Then Achish answered and said to David, "I know that you *are* as good in my sight [q]as an [r]angel of God; nevertheless the princes of the Philistines have said, 'He shall not go up with us to the battle.'

10 "Now therefore, rise early in the morning with your master's servants [s]who have come with you.* And as soon as you are up early in the morning and have light, depart."

11 So David and his men rose early to [1]depart in the morning, to return to the land of the Philistines. And the Philistines went up to Jezreel.

18
a 1 Sam. 13:9–13; 15:1–26; 1 Chr. 10:13
b 1 Sam. 15:3–9
19
c 1 Sam. 31:1–6; cp. Job. 3:17–19
CHAPTER 29
1
d 1 Sam. 28:1
e 1 Sam. 4:1
2
f 1 Sam. 6:4; 7:7
3
g 1 Sam. 27:7
4
h 1 Sam. 27:6
i 1 Sam. 14:21
j Lit. *make himself pleasing*
k 1 Chr. 12:19–20
5
l 1 Sam. 21:11
m 1 Sam. 18:7
6
n 1 Sam. 26:10,16
o v. 3
8
p Cp. 1 Sam. 27:10–12
9
q 2 Sam. 14:17,20
r See Heb. 1:4, *note*
10
s 1 Chr. 12:1–22

*29:10 Following Masoretic Text, Targum, and Vulgate; Septuagint adds *and go to the place which I have selected for you there; and set no bothersome word in your heart, for you are good before me. And rise on your way.*

[1](29:11) See a list of men who joined David on his way to Ziklag, in 1 Chr. 12:20–22.

David rescues Ziklag captives

30 NOW it happened, when David and his men came to [a]Ziklag, on the third day, that the [b]Amalekites had invaded the South and Ziklag, attacked Ziklag and burned it with fire,

2 and had taken captive the [c]women and those who *were* there, from small to great; they did not kill anyone, but carried *them* away and went their way.

3 So David and his men came to the city, and there it was, burned with fire; and their wives, their sons, and their daughters had been taken captive.

4 Then David and the people who *were* with him lifted up their voices and wept, until they had no more power to weep.

5 And David's two [d]wives, Ahinoam the Jezreelitess, and Abigail the widow of Nabal the Carmelite, had been taken captive.

6 Now David was greatly distressed, for the people spoke of stoning him, because the soul of all the people was grieved, every man for his sons and his daughters. But David [e]strengthened himself in the LORD his God.

7 Then David said to Abiathar the priest, Ahimelech's son, "Please [f]bring the ephod here to me." And [g]Abiathar brought the ephod to David.

8 So David inquired of the LORD, saying, "Shall I pursue this troop? Shall I overtake them?" And He answered him, "Pursue, for you shall surely overtake *them* and without fail recover *all*."

9 So David went, he and the six hundred men who *were* with him, and came to the Brook Besor, where those stayed who were left behind.

10 But David pursued, he and four hundred men; for two hundred stayed *behind*, who were so weary that they could not cross the Brook Besor.

11 Then they found an Egyptian in the field, and brought him to David; and they gave him bread and he ate, and they let him drink water.

12 And they gave him a piece of a cake of figs and two clusters of raisins. So when he had eaten, his [h]strength came back to him; for he had eaten no bread nor drunk water for three days and three nights.

13 Then David said to him, "To whom do you *belong*, and where *are* you from?" And he said, "I *am* a young man from Egypt, servant of an Amalekite; and my master left me behind, because three days ago I fell sick.

14 "We made an invasion of the southern *area* of the [i]Cherethites, in the *territory* which *belongs* to Judah, and of the southern *area* of Caleb; and we burned Ziklag with fire."

15 And David said to him, "Can you take me down to this troop?" So he said, "Swear to me by God that you will neither kill me nor deliver me into the hands of my [j]master, and I will take you down to this troop."

16 And when he had brought him down, there they were, spread out over all the land, eating and drinking and dancing, because of all the great spoil which they had taken from the land of the Philistines and from the land of Judah.

17 Then David attacked them from twilight until the evening of the next day. Not a man of them escaped, except four hundred young men who rode on camels and fled.

18 So David recovered all that the Amalekites had carried away, and David rescued his two wives.

19 And nothing of theirs was lacking, either small or great, sons or daughters, spoil or anything which they had taken from them; David [k]recovered all.

20 Then David took all the flocks and herds they had driven before those *other* livestock, and said, "This *is* David's [l]spoil."

David divides booty

21 Now David came to the two hundred men who had been so weary that they could not follow David, whom they also had made to stay at the Brook Besor. So they went out to meet David and to meet the people who *were* with him. And when David came near the people, he greeted them.

22 Then all the wicked and worthless men* of those who went with David answered and said, "Because they did not go with us, we will not give them *any* of the spoil that we have recovered, except for every man's wife and children, that they may lead *them* away and depart."

23 But David said, "My brethren, you shall not do so with what the LORD has given us, who has preserved us and delivered into our hand the troop that came against us.

CHAPTER 30

1
a 1 Sam. 27:6; 29:4
b 1 Sam. 27:8

2
c 1 Sam. 27:2–3

5
d 1 Sam. 25:42–43

6
e Ps. 18:6; 25:1–2; 34:1–8; 40:1–2; 42:5–11; 56:1–4; Isa. 25:4; Hab. 3:17–19

7
f 1 Sam. 23:2–9
g 1 Sam. 23:6

12
h Jud. 15:19; 1 Sam. 14:27

14
i 2 Sam. 8:18; 1 Ki. 1:38

15
j Dt. 23:15

19
k v. 8

20
l vv. 26–31

*30:22 Literally *men of Belial*

24 "For who will heed you in this matter? But as his part *is* who goes down to the battle, so *shall* his part *be* who stays by the [a]supplies; they shall share alike."

25 So it was, from that day forward; he made it a statute and an ordinance for Israel to this day.

26 Now when David came to Ziklag, he sent *some* of the spoil to the elders of Judah, to his friends, saying, "Here is a [b]present for you from the spoil of the [c]enemies of the LORD"—

27 to *those* who *were* in [d]Bethel, *those* who *were* in [e]Ramoth of the South, *those* who *were* in [f]Jattir,

28 *those* who *were* in [g]Aroer, *those* who *were* in [h]Siphmoth, *those* who *were* in [i]Eshtemoa,

29 *those* who *were* in Rachal, *those* who *were* in the cities of the [j]Jerahmeelites, *those* who *were* in the cities of the [k]Kenites,

30 *those* who *were* in [l]Hormah, *those* who *were* in [m]Chorashan, *those* who *were* in Athach,

31 *those* who *were* in [n]Hebron, and to all the places where David himself and his men were accustomed to [o]rove.

Israel defeated on Gilboa.
Saul and Jonathan killed
(cp. 1 Chr. 10:1–14)

31 [p]NOW the Philistines fought against Israel; and the men of Israel fled from before the Philistines, and fell slain on Mount [q]Gilboa.

2 Then the Philistines followed hard after Saul and his sons. And the Philistines killed Jonathan, Abinadab, and Malchishua, [r]Saul's sons.

3 [s]The battle became fierce against Saul. The archers [t]hit him, and he was severely wounded by the archers.

4 [u]Then Saul said to his armorbearer, "Draw your sword, and thrust me through with it, lest these [v]uncircumcised men come and thrust me through and abuse me." But his armorbearer would not, for he was greatly afraid. Therefore Saul took a sword and fell on it.

5 And when his armorbearer saw that Saul was dead, he also fell on his sword, and died with him.

6 So Saul, his three sons, his armorbearer, and all his men died together that same day.

7 And when the men of Israel who *were* on the other side of the valley, and *those* who *were* on the other side of the Jordan, saw that the men of Israel had fled and that Saul and his sons were dead, they forsook the cities and fled; and the Philistines came and dwelt in them.

8 So it happened the next day, when the Philistines came to strip the slain, that they found Saul and his three sons fallen on Mount Gilboa.

9 And they cut off his head and stripped off his armor, and sent *word* throughout the land of the Philistines, to [w]proclaim *it in* the temple of their [x]idols and among the people.

10 Then they put his [y]armor in the temple of the [z]Ashtoreths, and they fastened his body to the wall of [aa]Beth Shan.

11 Now when the inhabitants of [bb]Jabesh Gilead heard what the Philistines had done to Saul,

12 all the valiant men arose and traveled all night, and took the body of Saul and the bodies of his sons from the wall of Beth Shan; and they came to Jabesh and [cc]burned them there.

13 Then they took their bones and [dd]buried *them* under the tamarisk tree at Jabesh, and fasted seven days.

24
a Cp. Num. 31:27; Josh. 22:8
26
b Cp. 1 Sam. 25:27
c Cp. 1 Sam. 18:17; 25:28
27
d Or *Bethul,* Josh. 19:4
e Or *Ramah,* Josh. 19:8
f Josh. 21:14
28
g Josh. 13:16
h 1 Chr. 27:27
i Or *Eshtemoh,* Josh. 15:50
29
j 1 Sam. 27:10
k Jud. 1:16; 1 Sam. 27:10
30
l Jud. 1:17
m Or *Borashan.* Cp. Josh. 15:42
31
n Josh. 14:13; 2 Sam. 2:1
o 1 Sam. 23:22
CHAPTER 31
1
p vv. 1–13; 1 Chr. 10:1–2
q 1 Sam. 28:4
2
r 1 Sam. 14:49; 1 Chr. 8:33
3
s v. 3–4; cp. 2 Sam. 1:1–10

t See 2 Sam. 1:10, *note* **31:4** *u* Jud. 9:54 *v* 1 Sam. 17:26 **31:9** *w* 2 Sam. 1:20 *x* Cp. Jud. 16:23–24 **31:10** *y* Cp. 1 Sam. 21:9 *z* Jud. 2:13 *aa* Or *Beth Shean,* Josh. 17:11 **31:11** *bb* 1 Sam. 11:1–3 **31:12** *cc* Cp. 2 Chr. 16:14 **31:13** *dd* 2 Sam. 2:4–5; 2 Sam. 21:12–14

The Second Book of

SAMUEL

Author: Unknown *Theme:* David's Reign *Date of writing:* 10th Cent. B.C.

FIRST and SECOND SAMUEL are counted as one book in the Hebrew Bible. Second Samuel is occupied with the reign of David; the full record of his life extends from 1 Sam. 16:12—1 Ki. 2:11.

First Samuel closes with the tragic death of Israel's first king, Saul; 2 Samuel begins with an account of the strife that preceded the establishment of the Davidic throne at Jerusalem. The book records David's military victories, his great sin, his flight at the time of Absalom's revolt, his return to Jerusalem, and his sin in numbering the people. The Davidic Covenant is set forth in 7:8–17.

Whereas the duration of the events in 1 Samuel is not known precisely, 2 Samuel covers a period of forty years.

The book may be divided as follows:

I. From the Death of Saul to the Beginning of David's Reign, 1—4.
II. From the Anointing of David as King of Israel to the Revolt of Absalom, 5—14.
III. From the Revolt of Absalom to the Numbering of the People, 15—24.

I. From the Death of Saul to the Beginning of David's Reign, 1—4

David hears of Saul's death

1 NOW it came to pass after the
[a]death of Saul, when David had
returned from the [b]slaughter of the
Amalekites, and David had stayed
two days in Ziklag,
2 on the third day, behold, it happened that a man came from Saul's
camp with his clothes torn and dust on
his [c]head. So it was, when he came to
David, that he [d]fell to the ground and
prostrated himself.
3 And David said to him, "Where
have you come from?" So he said to
him, "I have escaped from the camp of
Israel."
4 Then David said to him, [e]"How
did the matter go? Please tell me." And
he answered, "The people have fled
from the battle, many of the people
are fallen and dead, and Saul and
[f]Jonathan his son are dead also."
5 So David said to the young man
who told him, "How do you know that
Saul and Jonathan his son are dead?"
6 Then the young man who told
him said, "As I happened by chance *to
be* on Mount Gilboa, there was Saul,
leaning on his spear; and indeed the
chariots and horsemen followed hard
after him.
7 "Now when he looked behind
him, he saw me and called to me. And
I answered, 'Here I am.'
8 "And he said to me, 'Who *are*
you?' So I answered him, 'I *am* an
[g]Amalekite.'
9 "He said to me again, 'Please
stand over me and kill me, for anguish
has come upon me, but my life still
remains in me.'
10 "So I stood over him and [1]killed
him, because I was sure that he could
not live after he had fallen. And I took
the [h]crown that *was* on his head and
the bracelet that *was* on his arm, and
have brought them here to my lord."
11 Therefore David took hold of his
own clothes and tore them, and [i]*so
did* all the men who *were* with him.
12 And they [j]mourned and wept
and [k]fasted until evening for Saul and
for Jonathan his son, for the [l]people
of the LORD and for the house of Israel,
because they had fallen by the sword.
13 Then David said to the young
man who told him, "Where *are* you
from?" And he answered, "I *am* the
son of an alien, an Amalekite."
14 So David said to him, "How was
it you were not afraid to put forth
your hand to destroy the [m]LORD'S
anointed?"
15 Then David called one of the
young men and said, "Go near, *and*
execute him!" And he struck him so
that he [n]died.
16 So David said to him, "Your
[o]blood *is* on your own head, for your
own mouth has testified against you,
saying, 'I have killed the LORD'S
anointed.'"

CHAPTER 1

1 *a* 1 Sam. 31:6 *b* 1 Sam. 30:17–26
2 *c* 1 Sam. 4:12 *d* 1 Sam. 25:23
4 *e* 1 Sam. 31:3; cp. 1 Sam. 4:16 *f* 1 Sam. 31:2
8 *g* Cp. 1 Sam. 15:1–23
10 *h* 2 Ki. 11:12
11 *i* 2 Sam. 13:31
12 *j* 2 Sam. 3:31 *k* 1 Sam. 31:13 *l* 2 Sam. 6:21
14 *m* 1 Sam. 26:9
15 *n* 2 Sam. 4:10–12
16 *o* 1 Ki. 2:32, 33–37

---

[1](1:10) The seeming discrepancy in the two accounts (1 Sam. 31:3–5; 2 Sam. 1:6–10) may be explained by the supposition that the Amalekite was lying to ingratiate himself with David (cp. 2 Sam. 4:9–11).

David's elegy

17 Then David lamented with this lamentation over Saul and over Jonathan his son,

18 and he told *them* to teach the children of Judah *the Song of* the Bow; indeed *it is* written in the [a]Book of Jasher:

19 "The beauty of Israel is slain on
your high places!
How the mighty have fallen!
20 Tell *it* not in [b]Gath,
Proclaim *it* not in the streets of
[c]Ashkelon—
Lest the [d]daughters of the
Philistines [e]rejoice,
Lest the daughters of the
uncircumcised triumph.

21 "O [f]mountains of Gilboa,
Let there be no dew nor rain
upon you,
Nor fields of offerings.
For the shield of the mighty is
cast away there!
The shield of Saul, not
anointed with oil.
22 [g]From the blood of the slain,
From the fat of the mighty,
The bow of Jonathan did not
turn back,
And the sword of Saul did not
return empty.

23 "Saul and Jonathan *were*
beloved and pleasant in their
lives,
And in their [h]death they were
not divided;
They were swifter than eagles,
They were stronger than lions.

24 "O daughters of Israel, weep
over Saul,
Who clothed you in scarlet,
with luxury;
Who put ornaments of gold on
your apparel.

Special tribute to Jonathan

25 "How the mighty have fallen in
the midst of the battle!
Jonathan *was* slain in your
high places.
26 I am distressed for you, my
brother Jonathan;
You have been very pleasant
to me;
[i]Your love to me was
wonderful,
Surpassing the love of women.

27 "How the mighty have fallen,
And the weapons of war
perished!"

18
a Josh. 10:13; see 1 Chr. 29:29, *note*
20
b 1 Sam. 27:2; Mic. 1:10
c 1 Sam. 6:17; Jer. 25:20
d Cp. 1 Sam. 18:6
e Jud. 16:23
21
f 1 Sam. 31:1
22
g Dt. 32:42; cp. Isa. 34:6
23
h 1 Sam. 31:2–4
26
i 1 Sam. 18:1–4
CHAPTER 2
1
j *Kingdom* (OT): vv. 1–4; 2 Sam. 5:1. (Gen. 1:26; Zech. 12:8, *note*)
k 1 Sam. 30:31; 2 Sam. 5:1–3
2
l 1 Sam. 25:42–43
3
m 1011 B.C.
n 1 Sam. 27:2–3; 1 Chr. 12:1
4
o 1 Sam. 30:26; 2 Sam. 19:14, 41–43
p 1 Sam. 16:13
q 1 Sam. 31:11–13
8
r 1 Sam. 14:50; 2 Sam. 3:6; see Jud. 8:1, *note*
s Or *Esh-Baal,* 1 Chr. 8:33; 9:39
t Josh. 21:38; 2 Sam. 17:24
9
u Josh. 22:9
v Jud. 1:32
w 1 Sam. 29:1

David received as king by Judah

2 IT happened after this that [j]David inquired of the LORD, saying, "Shall I go up to any of the cities of Judah?" And the LORD said to him, "Go up." David said, "Where shall I go up?" And He said, "To [k]Hebron."

2 So David went up there, and his [l]two wives also, Ahinoam the Jezreelitess, and Abigail the widow of Nabal the Carmelite.

3 And [m]David brought up the [n]men who *were* with him, every man with his household. So they dwelt in the cities of Hebron.

4 Then the men of [o]Judah came, and there they [p]anointed David king over the house of Judah. And they told David, saying, "The men of [q]Jabesh Gilead *were the ones* who buried Saul."

David commends Jabesh Gilead

5 So David sent messengers to the men of Jabesh Gilead, and said to them, "You *are* blessed of the LORD, for you have shown this kindness to your lord, to Saul, and have buried him.

6 "And now may the LORD show kindness and truth to you. I also will repay you this kindness, because you have done this thing.

7 "Now therefore, let your hands be strengthened, and be valiant; for your master Saul is dead, and also the house of Judah has anointed me king over them."

Ishbosheth made king over northern tribes

8 But [r]Abner the son of Ner, commander of Saul's army, took [s]Ishbosheth the son of Saul and brought him over to [t]Mahanaim;

9 and he made him king over [u]Gilead, over the [v]Ashurites, over [w]Jezreel, over Ephraim, over Benjamin, and over all Israel.

10 Ishbosheth, Saul's son, *was* forty years old when he began to reign over Israel, and he reigned two years. Only the house of Judah followed David.

11 And the time that David was king in Hebron over the house of Judah was [x]seven years and six months.

Civil war

12 Now Abner the son of Ner, and the servants of Ishbosheth the son of Saul, went out from Mahanaim to [y]Gibeon.

2:11 *x* 2 Sam. 5:5 **2:12** *y* Josh. 10:2–12

13 And [a]Joab the son of Zeruiah, and the servants of David, went out and met them by the [b]pool of Gibeon. So they sat down, one on one side of the pool and the other on the other side of the pool.

14 Then Abner said to Joab, "Let the young men now arise and compete before us." And Joab said, "Let them arise."

15 So they arose and went over by number, twelve from Benjamin, *followers* of Ishbosheth the son of Saul, and twelve from the servants of David.

16 And each one grasped his opponent by the head and *thrust* his sword in his opponent's side; so they fell down together. Therefore that place was called the Field of Sharp Swords,* which *is* in Gibeon.

17 So there was a very fierce battle that day, and Abner and the men of Israel were beaten before the servants of David.

18 Now the three sons of [1]Zeruiah were there: Joab and Abishai and Asahel. And Asahel *was as* fleet of foot as a wild gazelle.

19 So Asahel pursued Abner, and in going he did not turn to the right hand or to the left from following Abner.

20 Then Abner looked behind him and said, "*Are* you Asahel?" He answered, "I *am*."

21 And Abner said to him, "Turn aside to your right hand or to your left, and lay hold on one of the young men and take his armor for yourself." But Asahel would not turn aside from following him.

22 So Abner said again to Asahel, "Turn aside from following me. Why should I strike you to the ground? How then could I face your brother Joab?"

23 However, he refused to turn aside. Therefore Abner [c]struck him in the stomach with the blunt end of the spear, so that the spear came out of his back; and he fell down there and died on the spot. So it was *that* as many as came to the place where Asahel fell down and died, stood [d]still.

24 Joab and Abishai also pursued Abner. And the sun was going down when they came to the hill of Ammah, which *is* before Giah by the road to the Wilderness of Gibeon.

25 Now the children of Benjamin gathered together behind Abner and became a unit, and took their stand on top of a hill.

26 Then Abner called to Joab and said, "Shall the sword devour forever? Do you not know that it will be bitter in the latter end? How long will it be then until you tell the people to return from pursuing their brethren?"

27 And Joab said, "*As* God lives, unless you had spoken, surely then by morning all the people would have given up pursuing their brethren."

28 So Joab [e]blew a trumpet; and all the people stood still and did not pursue Israel [f]anymore, nor did they fight anymore.

29 Then Abner and his men went on all that night through the [g]plain, crossed over the Jordan, and went through all Bithron; and they came to [h]Mahanaim.

30 So Joab returned from pursuing Abner. And when he had gathered all the people together, there were missing of David's servants nineteen men and Asahel.

31 But the servants of David had struck down, of Benjamin and Abner's men, three hundred and sixty men who died.

32 Then they took up Asahel and buried him in his father's tomb, which *was in* [i]Bethlehem. And Joab and his men went all night, and they came to Hebron at daybreak.

David's strength increases
(1 Chr. 3:1–4)

3 NOW there was a long [j]war between the house of Saul and the house of David. But David grew stronger and stronger, and the house of Saul grew weaker and weaker.

2 Sons were born to David in [k]Hebron: His firstborn was Amnon by Ahinoam the Jezreelitess;

3 his second, Chileab, by Abigail the widow of Nabal the Carmelite; the third, [l]Absalom the son of Maacah, the daughter of Talmai, king of [m]Geshur;

4 the fourth, [n]Adonijah the son of

* 2:16 Hebrew *Helkath Hazzurim*

13
a 1 Sam. 26:6; 1 Chr. 2:16
b Cp. Jer. 41:12
23
c 2 Sam. 3:27; 4:6; 20:10
d 2 Sam. 20:12
28
e 1 Sam. 13:3
f Cp. 2 Sam. 3:1
29
g See Dt. 1:1, *note*
h 2 Sam. 2:12
32
i 1 Sam. 20:6
CHAPTER 3
1
j 1 Ki. 14:30
2
k Cp. 2 Sam. 5:13–16
3
l 2 Sam. 15:1–18
m Josh. 13:13; 1 Sam. 27:8; 2 Sam. 13:37; 14:32; 15:8
4
n 1 Ki. 1:5

[1](2:18) Zeruiah was David's sister; these three men were therefore David's relatives, his nephews (1 Chr. 2:16). Another sister had a son, Amasa (1 Chr. 2:16–17), whom Absalom made captain instead of Joab (2 Sam. 17:25; cp. 18:2).

Haggith; the fifth, Shephatiah the son of Abital;

5 and the sixth, Ithream, by David's wife Eglah. These were born to David in Hebron.

Abner deserts to David

6 Now it was so, while there was war between the house of Saul and the house of David, that Abner was strengthening *his hold* on the house of Saul.

7 And Saul had a concubine, whose name *was* [a]Rizpah, the daughter of Aiah. So *Ishbosheth* said to Abner, "Why have you gone in to my father's concubine?"

8 Then Abner became very angry at the words of Ishbosheth, and said, "*Am* I a dog's head that belongs to Judah? Today I show loyalty to the house of Saul your father, to his brothers, and to his friends, and have not delivered you into the hand of David; and you charge me today with a fault concerning this woman?

9 "May God do so to [b]Abner, and more also, if I do not do for David [c]as the LORD has sworn to him—

10 "to transfer the kingdom from the house of Saul, and set up the throne of David over Israel and over Judah, [d]from Dan to Beersheba."

11 And he could not answer Abner another word, because he feared him.

12 Then Abner sent messengers on his behalf to David, saying, "Whose *is* the land?" saying *also*, "Make your covenant with me, and indeed my hand *shall be* with you to bring all Israel to you."

13 And *David* said, "Good, I will make a covenant with you. But one thing I require of you: you shall not see my face unless you first bring [e]Michal, Saul's daughter, when you come to see my face."

14 So David sent messengers to [f]Ishbosheth, Saul's son, saying, "Give *me* my wife Michal, whom I betrothed to myself [g]for a hundred foreskins of the Philistines."

15 And Ishbosheth sent and took her from *her* husband, from [h]Paltiel the son of Laish.

16 Then her husband went along with her to [i]Bahurim, weeping behind her. So Abner said to him, "Go, return!" And he returned.

17 Now Abner had communicated with the elders of Israel, saying, "In time past you were seeking for David *to be* king over you.

18 "Now then, do *it!* For the LORD has spoken of David, saying, 'By the hand of My servant David, I* will save My people Israel from the hand of the [j]Philistines and the hand of all their enemies.' "

19 And Abner also spoke in the hearing of Benjamin. Then Abner also went to speak in the hearing of David in Hebron all that seemed good to Israel and the whole house of Benjamin.

20 So Abner and twenty men with him came to David at Hebron. And David made a feast for Abner and the men who *were* with him.

21 Then Abner said to David, "I will arise and go, [k]and gather all Israel to my lord the king, that they may make a covenant with you, and that you may reign over all that your heart [l]desires." So David sent Abner away, and he went in peace.

22 At that moment the servants of David and Joab came from a raid and brought much spoil with them. But Abner *was* not with David in Hebron, for he had sent him away, and he had gone in peace.

23 When Joab and all the troops that *were* with him had come, they told Joab, saying, "Abner the son of Ner came to the king, and he sent him away, and he has gone in peace."

24 Then Joab came to the king and said, "What have you done? Look, Abner came to you; why *is* it *that* you sent him away, and he has already gone?

25 "Surely you realize that Abner the son of Ner came to deceive you, to know your [m]going out and your coming in, and to know all that you are doing."

26 And when Joab had gone from David's presence, he sent messengers after Abner, who brought him back from the well of Sirah. But David did not know *it*.

Joab murders Abner

27 Now when Abner had returned to Hebron, Joab took him [n]aside in the gate to speak with him privately, and there stabbed him in the stomach, so that he died for the blood of [o]Asahel his brother.

28 Afterward, when David heard *it*, he said, "My kingdom and I *are* guiltless before the LORD forever of the blood of Abner the son of Ner.

7 *a* 2 Sam. 21:8
9 *b* v. 21; cp. v. 27 *c* 1 Sam. 15:28
10 *d* 1 Sam. 3:20
13 *e* 1 Sam. 18:20; 19:11; 25:44; 2 Sam. 6:16
14 *f* 2 Sam. 2:10 *g* 1 Sam. 18:25–27
15 *h* Or *Palti,* 1 Sam. 25:44
16 *i* 2 Sam. 16:5; 19:16
18 *j* 1 Sam. 9:16; 2 Sam. 19:9
21 *k* vv. 10,12 *l* 1 Ki. 11:37
25 *m* 1 Sam. 29:6
27 *n* 1 Ki. 2:5; cp. 2 Sam. 20:9–10 *o* 2 Sam. 2:23

*3:18 Following many Hebrew manuscripts, Septuagint, Syriac, and Targum; Masoretic Text reads *he*.

29 "Let it [a]rest on the head of Joab
and on all his father's house; and let
there never fail to be in the house of
Joab one who has a discharge or is a
leper, who leans on a staff or falls by
the sword, or who lacks bread."
30 So Joab and Abishai his brother
killed Abner, because he had killed
their brother Asahel at Gibeon in the
battle.
31 Then David said to Joab and to
all the people who were with him,
[b]"Tear your clothes, gird yourselves
with sackcloth, and mourn for Abner." And King David followed the
coffin.
32 So they buried Abner in Hebron;
and the king lifted up his voice and
wept at the grave of Abner, and all the
people wept.
33 And the king [c]sang *a lament*
over Abner and said:

"Should Abner die as a fool
dies?
34 Your hands were not bound
Nor your feet put into fetters;
As a man falls before wicked
men, *so* you fell."

Then all the people wept over him
again.
35 And when all the people came to
persuade David to eat food while it
was still day, David took an oath, saying, "God do so to me, and more also,
if I taste bread or anything else [d]till
the sun goes down!"
36 Now all the people took note *of*
it, and it pleased them, since whatever
the king did [e]pleased all the people.
37 For all the people and all Israel
understood that day that it had not
been the king's *intent* to kill Abner the
son of Ner.
38 Then the king said to his servants, "Do you not know that a prince
and a great man has fallen this day in
Israel?
39 "And I *am* weak today, though
anointed king; and these men, the
sons of Zeruiah, *are* [f]too harsh for
me. The LORD shall [g]repay the evildoer according to his wickedness."

Ishbosheth is murdered

4 WHEN Saul's son* heard that
Abner had died in [h]Hebron, he
lost heart, and all Israel was troubled.
2 Now Saul's son *had* two men
who were captains of troops. The
name of one *was* Baanah and the
name of the other Rechab, the sons of
Rimmon the [i]Beerothite, of the children of Benjamin. (For Beeroth also
was *part* of Benjamin,
3 because the Beerothites fled to
[j]Gittaim and have been sojourners
there until this day.)
4 Jonathan, Saul's son, had a son
who was lame in *his* feet. He was five
years old when the news about Saul
and Jonathan came from [k]Jezreel;
and his nurse took him up and fled.
And it happened, as she made haste to
flee, that he fell and became lame. His
name *was* [l]Mephibosheth.*
5 Then the sons of Rimmon the
Beerothite, Rechab and Baanah, set
out and came at about the heat of the
day to the [m]house of Ishbosheth, who
was lying on his bed at noon.
6 And they came there, all the way
into the house, *as though* to get wheat,
and they stabbed him in the stomach.
Then Rechab and Baanah his brother
escaped.
7 For when they came into the
house, he was lying on his bed in his
bedroom; then they struck him and
killed him, beheaded him and took his
head, and were all night escaping
through the [n]plain.
8 And they brought the head of
Ishbosheth to David at Hebron, and
said to the king, "Here is the head of
Ishbosheth, the son of Saul your enemy, [o]who sought your life; and the
LORD has avenged my lord the king
this day of Saul and his [p]descen-
dants."
9 But David answered Rechab and
Baanah his brother, the sons of Rimmon the Beerothite, and said to them,
"*As* the LORD lives, who has [q]re-
deemed my life from all adversity,
10 [r]"when someone told me, saying, 'Look, Saul is dead,' thinking to
have brought good news, I arrested
him and had him executed in Ziklag—
the one who *thought* I would give him
a reward for *his* news.
11 "How much more, when wicked
men have killed a righteous person in
his own house on his bed? Therefore,
shall I not now [s]require his blood at
your hand and remove you from the
earth?"
12 So David commanded his young
men, and they executed them, cut off
their hands and feet, and hanged *them*
by the pool in Hebron. But they took
the head of Ishbosheth and buried *it* in
the [h]tomb of Abner in Hebron.

29 *a* Dt. 21:6–9; 1 Ki. 2:32–33
31 *b* 2 Sam. 1:11; cp. Joel 2:12–13
33 *c* 2 Sam. 1:17
35 *d* Jud. 20:26; 2 Sam. 1:12
36 *e* Lit. *was good in their eyes*
39 *f* Cp. 2 Sam. 19:5–7 *g* 1 Ki. 2:32–34
CHAPTER 4
1 *h* 2 Sam. 3:32
2 *i* Josh. 18:25
3 *j* Neh. 11:33
4 *k* 1 Sam. 29:1,11 *l* 2 Sam. 9:6
5 *m* 2 Sam. 2:8–9
7 *n* See Dt. 1:1, *note*
8 *o* 1 Sam. 19:2; 23:15; 25:29 *p* Cp. Jer. 29:32; 36:31
9 *q* See Ex. 14:30 and Isa. 59:20, *notes*
10 *r* 2 Sam. 1:2–16
11 *s* Gen. 9:5–6

*4:1 That is, Ishbosheth 4:4 Called *Merib-Baal* in 1 Chronicles 8:34 and 9:40

II. From the Anointing of David as King of Israel to the Revolt of Absalom, 5—14

David becomes king over all Israel (cp. 1 Chr. 11:1–3)

5 THEN all the tribes of Israel came to [a]David at Hebron and spoke, saying, "Indeed we *are* your bone and your [b]flesh.

2 "Also, in time past, when Saul was king over us, you were the one who led Israel out and [c]brought them in; and the LORD said to you, 'You shall shepherd My people Israel, and be ruler over Israel.' "

3 Therefore all the [d]elders of Israel came to the king at Hebron, and King David made a [e]covenant with them at Hebron [f]before the LORD. And they [g]anointed David king over Israel.

4 David *was* [h]thirty years old when he began to reign, *and* he [i]reigned forty years.

5 In Hebron he reigned over Judah seven years and six months, and in Jerusalem he reigned thirty-three years over all Israel and Judah.

Jerusalem becomes capital (1 Chr. 11:4–9)

6 And the king and his men went to [j]Jerusalem against the Jebusites, the inhabitants of the land, who spoke to David, saying, "You shall not come in here; but the [1]blind and the lame will repel you," thinking, "David cannot come in here."

7 Nevertheless David took the stronghold of Zion (that *is,* the City of David).

8 Now David said on that day, "Whoever climbs up by way of the water shaft and defeats the Jebusites (the lame and the blind, *who are* hated by David's soul), *he shall be chief and captain.*"* Therefore they say, "The blind and the lame shall not come into the house."

9 Then David dwelt in the stronghold, and called it the City of David. And David built all around from the [k]Millo* and inward.

10 So David went on and became great, and the [l]LORD God of hosts *was* with [m]him.

David's alliance with Hiram

11 [n]Then [o]Hiram [p]king of Tyre sent messengers to David, and cedar trees, and carpenters and masons. And they built David a [q]house.

12 So David knew that the LORD had established him as king over Israel, and that He had [r]exalted His kingdom for the [s]sake of His people Israel.

David's sons born in Jerusalem (cp. 2 Sam. 3:2–5; 1 Chr. 3:1–4)

13 And David took more concubines and [t]wives from Jerusalem, after he had come from Hebron. Also more sons and daughters were born to David.

14 Now these *are* the names of those who were born to him in Jerusalem: Shammua,* Shobab, Nathan, [u]Solomon,

15 Ibhar, Elishua,* Nepheg, Japhia,

16 Elishama, Eliada, and Eliphelet.

Wars against Philistines (cp. 2 Sam. 23:13–17; 1 Chr. 14:8–17; 11:15–19; 12:8–15)

17 Now when the Philistines heard that they had anointed David king over Israel, all the Philistines [2]went up to search for David. And David heard *of it* and went down to the [v]stronghold.

18 The [w]Philistines also went and deployed themselves in the Valley of Rephaim.

19 So David [x]inquired of the LORD, saying, "Shall I go up against the Philistines? Will You deliver them into my hand?" And the LORD said to David, "Go up, for I will doubtless deliver the Philistines into your hand."

20 So David went to Baal Perazim, and David [y]defeated them there; and he said, "The LORD has broken through my enemies before me, like a breakthrough of water." Therefore he called the name of that place [z]Baal Perazim.

CHAPTER 5
1 *a* Kingdom (OT): vv. 1–3; 2 Sam. 7:16. (Gen. 1:26; Zech. 12:8, *note*) *b* Jud. 9:2; 2 Sam. 19:12
2 *c* 1 Sam. 18:5,13,16
3 *d* 2 Sam. 3:17–21; cp. 1 Chr. 12:23–40 *e* 2 Sam. 3:21 *f* 1 Sam. 23:18 *g* 1003 B.C. 2 Sam. 2:4
4 *h* Gen. 41:46; Num. 4:3; Lk. 3:23 *i* 1 Ki. 2:11
6 *j* Josh. 15:63
9 *k* 1 Ki. 9:15, 24
10 *l* 1 Sam. 17:45 *m* 1 Sam. 18:12,28
11 *n* vv. 11–25; cp. 1 Chr. 14:1–16 *o* 1 Ki. 5:1–18; 2 Chr. 2:3–12. See 1 Ki. 7:13, *note* *p* 1 Chr. 14:1 *q* Ps. 30, *title*
12 *r* Num. 24:7 *s* Isa. 45:4
13 *t* Dt. 17:17
14 *u* 2 Sam. 12:24
17 *v* 2 Sam. 23:14
18 *w* 1 Chr. 11:15

5:19 *x* 2 Sam. 2:1; cp. Jas. 4:15 **5:20** *y* 1 Sam. 23:5; 2 Sam. 8:1 *z* Lit. master of breakthroughs. Isa. 28:21

*
5:8 Compare 1 Chronicles 11:6 **5:9** Literally *The Landfill* **5:14** Spelled *Shimea* in 1 Chronicles 3:5 **5:15** Spelled *Elishama* in 1 Chronicles 3:6

[1](5:6) The city was so strong that the Jebusites claimed that the blind and the lame could defend Jerusalem, but David saw that the water shaft could be climbed and the city taken (v. 8).

[2](5:17) Two campaigns against the Philistines are recorded here: the first in vv. 17–21; the second, vv. 22–25. Cp. 2 Sam. 8:1; 21:15–22 for later campaigns.

21 And they left their images there,
and David and his men carried them
away.
22 Then the Philistines went up
once again and deployed themselves
in the Valley of Rephaim.
23 Therefore David inquired of the
LORD, and He said, "You shall not go
up; circle around behind them, and
come upon them in front of the mulberry trees.
24 "And it shall be, when you [a]hear
the sound of marching in the tops of
the mulberry trees, then you shall advance quickly. For then the LORD will
go out before you to strike the camp of
the Philistines."
25 And David did so, as the LORD
commanded him; and he drove back
the Philistines from [b]Geba* as far as
Gezer.

Doing a right thing in a wrong way
(cp. 1 Chr. 13:1–14)

6 [c]AGAIN David gathered all *the*
choice *men* of Israel, thirty thousand.
2 And David arose and went with
all the people who *were* with him from
[d]Baale Judah to bring up from there
the ark of God, whose name is called
by the Name,* the LORD of Hosts, who
dwells *between* the [e]cherubim.
3 So they set the ark of God on a
new [1]cart, and brought it out of the
house of Abinadab, which *was* on the
hill; and Uzzah and Ahio, the sons of
Abinadab, drove the new cart.*
4 And they brought it out of the
house of Abinadab, which *was* on the
hill, accompanying the ark of God;
and Ahio went before the ark.
5 Then David and all the house of
Israel [f]played *music* before the LORD
on all kinds of *instruments of* fir
wood, on harps, on stringed instruments, on tambourines, on sistrums,
and on cymbals.
6 And when they came to [g]Na-
chon's threshing floor, Uzzah put out
his [h]*hand* to the ark of God and took
hold of it, for the oxen stumbled.
7 Then the anger of the LORD was
aroused against Uzzah, and God
[i]struck him there for *his* error; and he
died there by the ark of God.
8 And David became angry because of the LORD's [j]outbreak against
Uzzah; and he called the name of the
place Perez Uzzah* to this day.
9 David was [k]afraid of the LORD
that day; and he said, "How can the
ark of the LORD come to me?"
10 So David would not move the
ark of the LORD with him into the [l]City
of David; but David took it aside into
the house of [m]Obed-Edom the Gittite.
11 The ark of the LORD remained in
the house of Obed-Edom the Gittite
three months. And the LORD blessed
Obed-Edom and all his household.

David brings ark to Jerusalem
(1 Chr. 15:1—16:3; esp. 15:26—16:1)

12 [n]Now it was told King David,
saying, "The LORD has blessed the
house of Obed-Edom and all that *be-*
longs to him, because of the ark of
God." So David went and brought up
the ark of God from the house of
Obed-Edom [o]to the City of David with
gladness.
13 And so it was, when [p]those
bearing the ark of the LORD had gone
six [q]paces, that he sacrificed oxen and
fatted sheep.
14 Then David [r]danced before the
LORD with all *his* might; and David
was wearing a [s]linen ephod.
15 So David and all the house of
Israel brought up the ark of the LORD
with shouting and with the sound of
the trumpet.
16 Now as the ark of the LORD came
into the City of David, [t]Michal, Saul's
daughter, looked through a window
and saw King David leaping and
whirling before the LORD; and she despised him in her heart.
17 [u]So they brought the ark of the
LORD, and set it in its place [v]in the
midst of the tabernacle that David had
erected for it. Then David offered
burnt offerings and peace offerings
before the LORD.
18 And when David had finished
offering burnt offerings and peace offerings, he [w]blessed the people in the
name of the LORD of hosts.

24 *a* Cp. 2 Ki. 7:6
25 *b* 1 Chr. 14:16
CHAPTER 6
1 *c* vv. 1–11
2 *d* Or *Kirjath Jearim,* Josh. 15:9, 60; 1 Sam. 7:1 *e* Ex. 25:22
5 *f* 1 Sam. 18:6–7
6 *g* Or *Kidon,* 1 Chr. 13:9 *h* Num. 4:15
7 *i Miracles* (OT): v. 7; 1 Ki. 13:4. (Gen. 5:24; Jon. 1:17, *note*). 1 Sam. 6:19
8 *j* 2 Sam. 5:20
9 *k* Dt. 9:19
10 *l* 2 Sam. 5:7 *m* 1 Chr. 26:4–8
12 *n* vv. 12–19 *o* Cp. 1 Ki. 8:1
13 *p* 1 Sam. 6:15; 2 Sam. 15:24 *q* See Weights and Measures (OT), 2 Chr. 2:10, *note*
14 *r* v. 21; Ps. 149:3 *s* 1 Sam. 2:18,28; cp. Ex. 19:6
16 *t* 2 Sam. 3:14
17 *u* Cp. 1 Ki. 8:1–11 *v* 2 Chr. 1:4

6:18 *w* 1 Ki. 8:14

*

5:25 Following Masoretic Text, Targum, and Vulgate; Septuagint reads *Gibeon.* 6:2 Septuagint, Targum, and Vulgate omit *by the Name*; many Hebrew manuscripts and Syriac read *there.* 6:3 Septuagint adds *with the ark.* 6:8 Literally *Outburst Against Uzzah*

[1](6:3) The story of David's new cart and its results is a striking illustration of the spiritual truth that blessing does not follow even the best intentions in the service of God, except as that service is rendered in God's way. God had given explicit directions how the ark should be carried (Num. 4:1–15), but David adopted a Philistine expedient (1 Sam. 6:7–8).

19 Then he distributed among all
the people, among the whole multitude of Israel, both the women and the
men, to everyone a loaf of bread, a
[a]piece *of meat,* and a cake of raisins.
So all the people departed, everyone
to his house.
20 Then David returned to bless his
household. And Michal the daughter
of Saul came out to meet David, and
said, "How glorious was the king of
Israel today, uncovering himself today in the eyes of the maids of his
servants, as one of the base fellows
shamelessly uncovers himself!"
21 So David said to Michal, "*It was*
before the LORD, [b]who chose me instead of your father and all his house,
to appoint me ruler over the [c]people
of the LORD, over Israel. Therefore I
will play *music* before the LORD.
22 "And I will be even more undignified than this, and will be humble in
my own sight. But as for the maidservants of whom you have spoken, by
them I will be held in honor."
23 Therefore Michal the daughter
of Saul had no [d]children to the day of
her death.

David's desire to build the LORD a house (1 Chr. 17:1–2)

7 [e]NOW it came to pass when the
king was dwelling in his house,
and the LORD had given him rest from
all his enemies all around,
2 that the king said to Nathan the
prophet, "See now, I dwell in a house
of cedar, but the ark of God dwells
inside tent curtains."
3 Then Nathan said to the king,
"Go, do all that *is* in your [f]heart, for
the LORD *is* with you."

The Davidic Covenant (1 Chr. 17:3–15)

4 But it happened that night that
the word of the LORD came to Nathan,
saying,
5 "Go and tell My servant David,
'Thus says the LORD: "Would you build
a house for Me to dwell in?
6 "For I have not dwelt in a house
since the time that I brought the children of Israel up from Egypt, even to
this day, but have moved about in a
tent and in a tabernacle.
7 "Wherever I have [g]moved about
with all the children of Israel, have I
ever spoken a word to anyone from
the tribes of Israel, whom I commanded to [h]shepherd My people Israel, saying, 'Why have you not built
Me a house of cedar?' " '
8 "Now therefore, [i]thus shall you
say to My servant [j]David, 'Thus says
the LORD of hosts: "I took you from the
sheepfold, from following the sheep,
to be ruler over My people, over Israel.
9 "And I have been with you wherever you have gone, and have cut off
all your enemies from before you, and
have made you a great name, like the
name of the great men who *are* on the
earth.
10 "Moreover I will appoint a place
for My people Israel, and will plant
them, that they may dwell in a place of
their own and move no more; nor shall
the sons of wickedness oppress them
anymore, as previously,
11 "since the time that I commanded judges *to be* over My people
Israel, and have caused you to rest
from all your enemies. Also the LORD
tells you that He will make you a
house.*
12 "When your days are fulfilled
and you rest with your fathers, I will
set up your seed after you, who will
come from your body, and I will establish his kingdom.
13 "He shall build a house for My
name, and [k]I will establish the throne
of his kingdom forever.
14 [l]"I will be his Father, and he
shall be [m]My son. If he commits iniquity, I will [n]chasten him with the rod
of men and with the blows of the sons
of men.
15 "But [1]My mercy shall not depart
from him, as I took *it* from Saul, whom
I removed from before you.
16 "And your [o]house and your
kingdom [2]shall be established forever

19
a Perhaps *a portion of wine.* Heb. uncertain
21
b 1 Sam. 13:14; 15:28
c 2 Ki. 11:17
23
d Cp. 2 Sam. 21:8
CHAPTER 7
1
e vv. 1–29
3
f 1 Ki. 8:17–18
7
g Lev. 26:11–12
h 2 Sam. 5:2
8
i *Eight Covenants:* vv. 4–17; Heb. 8:8. (Gen. 2:16; Heb. 8:8)
j *Israel* (history): vv. 8–17; 2 Ki. 17:6. (Gen. 12:2; Rom. 11:26, *note*)
13
k Isa. 9:7; 49:8
14
l Heb. 1:5
m Ps. 2:7; 89:26–27
n *Judgments* (the seven): vv. 14–15; 2 Sam. 12:14. (2 Sam. 7:14; Rev. 20:12, *note*)
16
o *Christ* (first advent): v. 16; Ps. 2:2. (Gen. 3:15; Acts 1:11, *note*)

* 7:11 That is, a royal dynasty

[1](7:15) Verses 14–15 state the principle of judgment within the family of God (see 1 Cor. 11:31, *note*). It is always remedial, not penal (Heb. 12:5–11). Judgment of the wicked is penal, not remedial.

[2](7:16) The Davidic Covenant (vv. 8–17), upon which the future kingdom of Christ, "who was born of the seed of David according to the flesh" (Rom. 1:3), was to be founded, provided for David: (1) the promise of posterity in the Davidic house; (2) a throne symbolic of royal authority; (3) a kingdom, or rule on earth; and (4) certainty of fulfillment, for the promises to David "shall be established forever."

Solomon, whose birth God predicted (v. 12), was not promised a perpetual seed, but only

before you.* Your [a]throne shall be established [b]forever." ' "
17 According to all these words and
according to all this vision, so Nathan
spoke to David.

David's prayer (1 Chr. 17:16–27)

18 Then King David went in and sat
before the LORD; and he [c]said: "Who
am [d]I, O Lord GOD? And what is my
house, that You have brought me this
far?
19 "And yet this was a small thing
in Your sight, O Lord GOD; and You
have also spoken of Your servant's
house for a great while to come. *Is* this
the manner of man, O Lord GOD?
20 "Now what more can David say
to You? For You, Lord GOD, [e]know
Your servant.
21 "For Your word's sake, and according to Your own heart, You have
done all these great things, to make
Your servant know *them.*
22 "Therefore You are [f]great, O
Lord GOD.* For *there is* none [g]like
You, nor *is there any* God besides
You, according to all that we have
heard with our [h]ears.
23 "And who *is* like Your [i]people,
like Israel, the one nation on the earth
whom God went to [j]redeem for Himself as a people, to make for Himself a
name—and to do for Yourself great
and [k]awesome deeds for Your land—
before Your people whom You redeemed for Yourself from Egypt, the
nations, and their gods?
24 "For You have made Your people Israel Your very own people [l]for-
ever; and You, LORD, have become
their God.
25 "Now, O LORD God, the word
which You have spoken concerning
Your servant and concerning his
house, establish *it* forever and do as
You have said.
26 "So let Your name be magnified
forever, saying, 'The LORD of hosts *is*
the God over Israel.' And let the house
of Your servant David be established
before You.
27 "For You, O LORD of hosts, God
of Israel, have revealed *this* to Your
servant, saying, 'I will build you a
house.' Therefore Your servant has
found it in his heart to pray this prayer
to You.
28 "And now, O Lord GOD, You are
God, and Your words are [m]true, and
You have promised this goodness to
Your servant.
29 "Now therefore, let it please You
to bless the house of Your servant,
that it may continue before You forever; for You, O Lord GOD, have spoken *it,* and with Your blessing let the
house of Your servant be blessed forever."

Extension of David's kingdom
(1 Chr. 18:1–17)

8 AFTER this it came to pass that
David attacked the Philistines
and subdued them. And David took
Metheg Ammah from the hand of the
Philistines.

16
a Kingdom (OT): vv. 8–16; 2 Sam. 23:1. (Gen. 1:26; Zech. 12:8, *note*)
b Ps. 89:36–37

18
c Bible prayers (OT): vv. 18–29; 2 Sam. 24:17. (Gen. 15:2; Hab. 3:1)
d Ex. 3:11; Jud. 6:15; 1 Sam. 18:18

20
e 1 Sam. 16:7; Jn. 21:17

22
f Dt. 10:17; Ps. 86:10
g Ex. 15:11
h Ex. 10:2; Ps. 44:1

23
i Dt. 33:29
j Dt. 15:15; see Ex. 6:6, *note*
k Dt. 10:21; Ps. 65:5

24
l Gen. 17:7; Dt. 30:1–10

28
m Josh. 21:45; Jn. 17:17

*
7:16 Septuagint reads *Me.* **7:22** Targum and Syriac read *O LORD God.*

assured that (1) he would "build a house for My name" (v. 13); (2) his kingdom would be established (v. 12); (3) his throne, i.e. royal authority, would endure forever; and (4) if Solomon sinned, he would be chastised but not deposed.

The continuance of Solomon's throne, but not Solomon's seed, shows the accuracy of the prediction. Israel had nine dynasties; Judah had one. Christ was born of Mary, who was not of Solomon's line (Jer. 22:28–30); He was a descendant of Nathan, another son of David (cp. see Lk. 3:23–31 and *note* at Lk. 3:23). Joseph, the husband of Mary, was descended from Solomon and through him the throne legally passed to Christ (cp. Mt. 1:6,16). Thus the throne, but not the seed, came through Solomon, which is in precise fulfillment of the LORD's promise to David.

In contrast with the irrevocable promise of perpetual fulfillment made to David, Solomon illustrates the conditional character of the Davidic Covenant as applied to the kings who followed him. Disobedience on the part of David's descendants would result in chastisement, but not in annulment of the covenant (2 Sam. 7:15; Ps. 89:20–37; Isa. 54:3,8,10). So chastisement fell, first in the division of the kingdom under Rehoboam, and finally in the captivities (2 Ki. 25:1–21). Since that time but one king of the Davidic family has been crowned at Jerusalem, and He was crowned with thorns. But the Davidic Covenant, given to David by the oath of the LORD and confirmed to Mary by the Angel Gabriel, is immutable (Ps. 89:20–37); and the LORD will yet give to that thorn-crowned One "the throne of His father David" (Lk. 1:31–33; Acts 2:29–32; 15:14–17). Both David and Solomon understood the promise to refer to a literal earthly kingdom (2 Sam. 7:18–29; 2 Chr. 6:14–16).

For *notes* on other major covenants, see: Edenic (Gen. 2:16); Adamic (Gen. 3:15); Noahic (Gen. 9:16); Abrahamic (Gen. 12:2); Mosaic (Ex. 19:5); Palestinian (Dt. 30:3); New (Heb. 8:8).

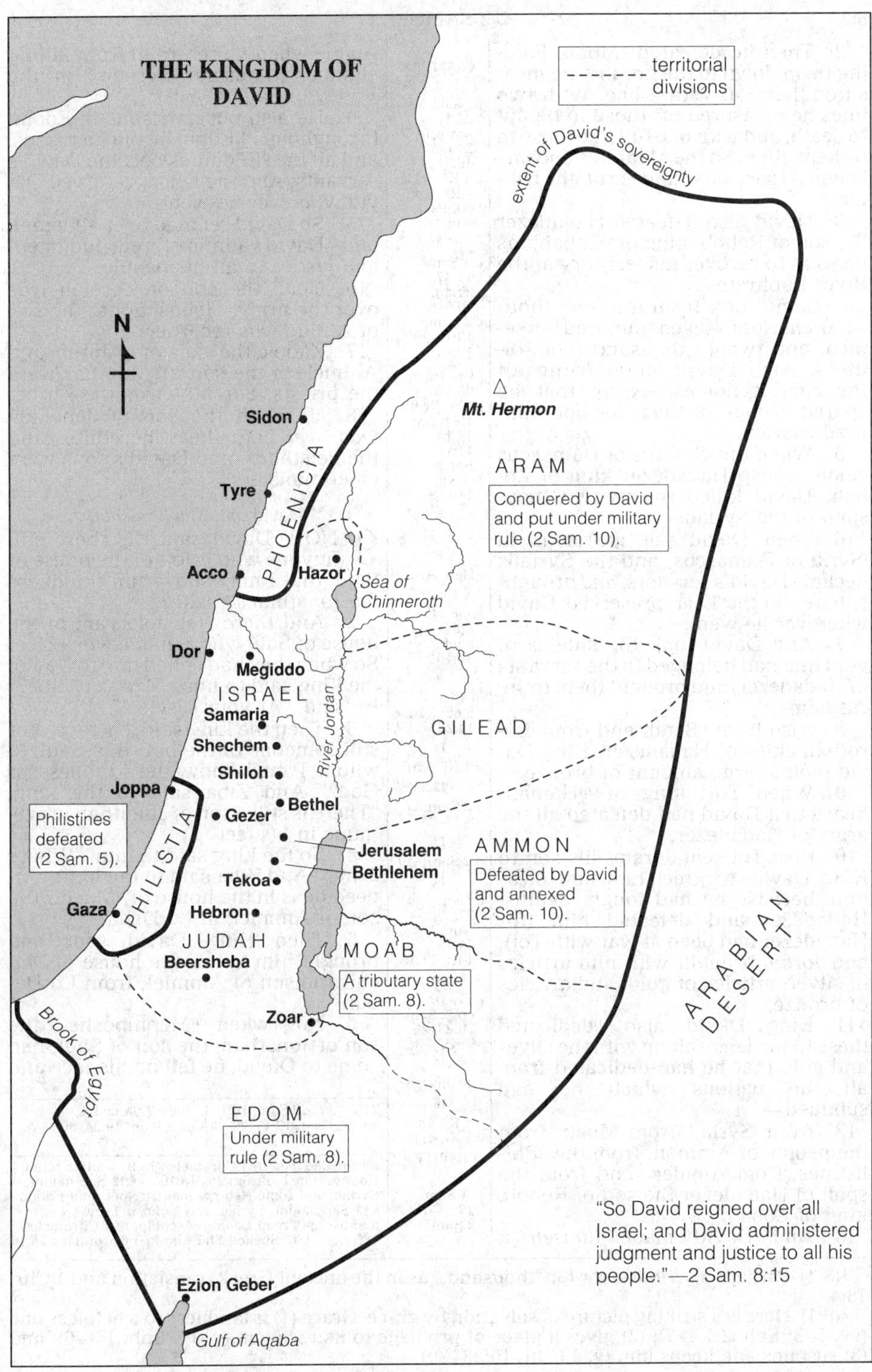
THE KINGDOM OF DAVID
territorial divisions
extent of David's sovereignty
N
Sidon
Mt. Hermon
PHOENICIA
ARAM
Conquered by David and put under military rule (2 Sam. 10).
Tyre
Acco
Hazor
Sea of Chinnereth
Dor
Megiddo
ISRAEL
Samaria
Shechem
River Jordan
GILEAD
Shiloh
Joppa
Bethel
Philistines defeated (2 Sam. 5).
Gezer
PHILISTIA
Jerusalem
Bethlehem
AMMON
Defeated by David and annexed (2 Sam. 10).
Tekoa
Gaza
Hebron
JUDAH
MOAB
ARABIAN DESERT
Beersheba
A tributary state (2 Sam. 8).
Zoar
Brook of Egypt
EDOM
Under military rule (2 Sam. 8).
"So David reigned over all Israel; and David administered judgment and justice to all his people."—2 Sam. 8:15
Ezion Geber
Gulf of Aqaba

2 Then he defeated [a]Moab. Forcing them down to the ground, he measured them off with a line. With two
lines he measured off those to be put
to death, and with one full line those to
be kept alive. So the Moabites became
David's [b]servants, *and* [c]brought tribute.
3 David also defeated Hadadezer
the son of Rehob, king of [d]Zobah, [e]as
he went to recover his territory at the
River Euphrates.
4 David took from him one thou-
sand [f]*chariots,* [g]seven [1]hundred horsemen, and twenty thousand foot soldiers. Also David [h]hamstrung all
the chariot horses, except that he
spared *enough* of them for one hundred chariots.
5 When the [i]Syrians of Damascus
came to help Hadadezer king of Zobah, David killed twenty-two thousand of the Syrians.
6 Then David put garrisons in
[j]Syria of Damascus; and the Syrians
became David's servants, *and* brought
tribute. So the LORD preserved David
wherever he went.
7 And David took the shields of
gold that had belonged to the servants
of Hadadezer, and brought them to Jerusalem.
8 Also from [k]Betah and from [l]Be-
rothai, cities of Hadadezer, King David took a large amount of bronze.
9 When Toi* king of [m]Hamath
heard that David had defeated all the
army of Hadadezer,
10 then Toi sent Joram* his son to
King David, to greet him and bless
him, because he had fought against
Hadadezer and defeated him (for
Hadadezer had been at war with Toi);
and *Joram* brought with him articles
of silver, articles of gold, and articles
of bronze.
11 King David also [n]dedicated
these to the LORD, along with the silver
and gold that he had dedicated from
all the nations which he had
subdued—
12 from [j]Syria,* from Moab, from
the people of Ammon, from the [o]Phi-
listines, from Amalek, and from the
spoil of Hadadezer the son of Rehob,
king of Zobah.
13 And David made *himself* a
[p]name when he returned from killing
eighteen thousand Syrians* in the
Valley of Salt.
14 He also put garrisons in Edom;
throughout all Edom he put garrisons,
and all the [q]Edomites became David's
servants. And the LORD preserved David wherever he went.
15 So David reigned over all Israel;
and David administered judgment
and justice to all his people.
16 [r]Joab the son of Zeruiah *was*
over the army; [s]Jehoshaphat the son
of Ahilud *was* recorder;
17 Zadok the son of [t]Ahitub and
Ahimelech the son of Abiathar *were*
the priests; Seraiah* *was* the scribe;
18 [u]Benaiah the son of Jehoiada
was over both the [v]Cherethites and
the Pelethites; and David's sons were
chief ministers.

David and Mephibosheth

9 NOW David said, "Is there still
anyone who is left of the house of
Saul, that I may show him [2]kindness
for Jonathan's [w]sake?"
2 And *there was* a servant of the
house of Saul whose name *was* [x]Ziba.
So when they had called him to David,
the king said to him, "*Are* you Ziba?"
He said, "At your service!"
3 Then the king said, "*Is* there not
still someone of the house of Saul, to
whom I may show the kindness of
God?" And Ziba said to the king,
"There is still a son of Jonathan *who is*
[y]lame in *his* feet."
4 So the king said to him, "Where
is he?" And Ziba said to the king, "Indeed he *is* in the house of [z]Machir the
son of Ammiel, in Lo Debar."
5 Then King David sent and
brought him out of the house of Machir the son of Ammiel, from Lo Debar.
6 Now when [aa]Mephibosheth the
son of Jonathan, the son of Saul, had
come to David, he fell on his face and

CHAPTER 8
2
a Num. 24:17
b vv. 6,14; 2 Sam. 12:31
c 1 Ki. 4:21; 2 Ki. 3:4; cp. Ps. 60:8
3
d 1 Sam. 14:47; 2 Sam. 10:6–8
e 2 Sam. 10:15–19
4
f Cp. Ps. 68:17
g Cp. 1 Chr. 18:4; see 1 Chr. 11:11, *note*
h Josh. 11:6–9
5
i 1 Ki. 11:24
6
j Heb. *Aram*
8
k Or *Tibhath*
l Ezek. 47:16
9
m 1 Ki. 8:65; 2 Ki. 14:28
11
n 1 Ki. 7:51
12
o 2 Sam. 5:17–25
13
p 2 Sam. 7:9
14
q Gen. 27:29; Num. 24:18; 1 Ki. 11:15
16
r vv. 16–18; cp. 2 Sam. 20:23–26
s 1 Ki. 4:3
17
t 1 Chr. 6:8
18
u 1 Ki. 1:8
v 1 Ki. 1:38
CHAPTER 9
1
w 1 Sam. 20:14–16; 2 Sam. 21:7 **9:2** *x* 2 Sam. 16:1–4 **9:3** *y* 2 Sam. 4:4 **9:4** *z* 2 Sam. 17:17–29 **9:6** *aa* 2 Sam. 19:24–30

* **8:9** Spelled *Tou* in 1 Chronicles 18:9 **8:10** Spelled *Hadoram* in 1 Chronicles 18:10 **8:12** Septuagint, Syriac, and some Hebrew manuscripts read *Edom.* **8:13** Septuagint, Syriac, and some Hebrew manuscripts read *Edomites* (compare 1 Chronicles 18:12). **8:17** Spelled *Shavsha* in 1 Chronicles 18:16

[1](8:4) Perhaps a scribal error for "thousand," as in the ancient Greek translation and 1 Chr. 18:4.
[2](9:1) Here is a striking picture of salvation by grace. Grace (1) is kindness to a helpless one (vv. 1–3; Eph. 2:1,4–7); (2) gives a place of privilege to its recipient (v. 11; Eph. 1:3–6); and (3) sustains and keeps him (v. 13; Jn. 10:28–29).

prostrated himself. Then David said,
"Mephibosheth?" And he answered,
"Here is your servant!"
7 So David said to him, [a]"Do not
fear, for I will surely show you kindness for Jonathan your father's sake,
and will restore to you all the land of
Saul your grandfather; and you shall
eat bread at my table continually."
8 Then he bowed himself, and
said, "What *is* your servant, that you
should look upon such a dead [b]dog as
I?"
9 And the king called to Ziba,
Saul's servant, and said to him, "I have
[c]given to your master's son all that
belonged to Saul and to all his house.
10 "You therefore, and your sons
and your servants, shall work the land
for him, and you shall bring in *the*
harvest, that your master's son may
have food to eat. But Mephibosheth
your master's son shall eat bread at
my table [d]always." Now Ziba had fifteen sons and twenty servants.
11 Then Ziba said to the king, "According to all that my lord the king has
commanded his servant, so will your
servant do." "As for Mephibosheth,"
said the king, "he shall eat at my table* like one of the king's sons."
12 Mephibosheth had a young son
whose name *was* [e]Micha. And all who
dwelt in the house of Ziba *were* servants of Mephibosheth.
13 So Mephibosheth dwelt in Jerusalem, for he ate continually at the
king's [f]table. And he was lame in
both his feet.

The Ammonite-Syrian campaigns
under Joab (v. 7) and David (v. 15)
(1 Chr. 19)

10 IT happened after this that the
king of the [g]people of Ammon
died, and Hanun his son reigned in his
place.
2 Then David said, "I will show
[h]kindness to Hanun the son of [i]Na-
hash, as his father showed kindness to
me." So David sent by the hand of his
servants to comfort him concerning
his father. And David's servants came
into the land of the people of Ammon.
3 And the princes of the people of
Ammon said to Hanun their lord, "Do
you think that David really honors
your father because he has sent comforters to you? Has David not *rather*
sent his servants to you to search the
city, to spy it out, and to overthrow it?"
4 Therefore Hanun took David's
servants, [j]shaved off half of their

7
a Cp. 1 Sam. 23:17
8
b 2 Sam. 16:9
9
c 2 Sam. 9:7
10
d v. 13
12
e 1 Chr. 8:34
13
f vv. 7,10, 11; 1 Ki. 2:7
CHAPTER 10
1
g 2 Sam. 11:1
2
h 2 Sam. 9:1; 1 Ki. 2:7
i 1 Sam. 11:1
4
j Cp. Isa. 15:2
k Cp. Isa. 20:4
6
l 2 Sam. 8:5–6
m Jud. 18:28
n Dt. 3:14; Josh. 13:11,13
o Jud. 11:3, 5
10
p 1 Sam. 26:6; 2 Sam. 3:30
12
q Dt. 31:6; Josh. 1:6, 7,9; Neh. 4:14
r 1 Cor. 16:13
s 1 Sam. 3:18
13
t Cp. 1 Ki. 20:13–21

beards, cut off their garments in the
middle, at their [k]buttocks, and sent
them away.
5 When they told David, he sent to
meet them, because the men were
greatly ashamed. And the king said,
"Wait at Jericho until your beards
have grown, and *then* return."
6 When the people of Ammon saw
that they had made themselves repulsive to David, the people of Ammon
sent and hired the [l]Syrians of [m]Beth
Rehob and the Syrians of Zoba,
twenty thousand foot soldiers; and
from the king of [n]Maacah one thousand men, and from [o]Ish-Tob twelve
thousand men.
7 Now when David heard *of it,* he
sent Joab and all the army of the
mighty men.
8 Then the people of Ammon
came out and put themselves in battle
array at the entrance of the gate. And
the Syrians of Zoba, Beth Rehob, Ish-
Tob, and Maacah *were* by themselves
in the field.
9 When Joab saw that the battle
line was against him before and behind, he chose some of Israel's best
and put *them* in battle array against
the Syrians.
10 And the rest of the people he put
under the command of [p]Abishai his
brother, that he might set *them* in battle array against the people of Ammon.
11 Then he said, "If the Syrians are
too strong for me, then you shall help
me; but if the people of Ammon are
too strong for you, then I will come
and help you.
12 "Be of good [q]courage, and [r]let
us be strong for our people and for the
cities of our God. And may the LORD do
what is [s]good in His sight."
13 So Joab and the people who
were with him drew near for the battle
against the Syrians, and they [t]fled before him.
14 When the people of Ammon saw
that the Syrians were fleeing, they
also fled before Abishai, and entered
the city. So Joab returned from the
people of Ammon and went to [g]Jeru-
salem.
15 When the Syrians saw that they
had been defeated by Israel, they
gathered together.
16 Then Hadadezer* sent and
brought out the Syrians who *were* be-

*

9:11 Septuagint reads *David's table.* **10:16** Hebrew *Hadarezer*

yond the River,* and they came to Helam. And [a]Shobach the commander
of Hadadezer's army *went* before
them.
17 When it was told David, he gathered all Israel, crossed over the Jordan, and came to Helam. And the Syrians set themselves in battle array
against David and fought with him.
18 Then the Syrians fled before Israel; and David killed [b]seven [1]hun-
dred charioteers and forty thousand
horsemen of the Syrians, and struck
Shobach the commander of their
army, who died there.
19 And when all the kings *who
were* servants to Hadadezer* saw that
they were defeated by Israel, they
made peace with Israel and served
them. So the Syrians were afraid to
help the people of Ammon anymore.

David's great sin

11 IT happened in the spring of
the year, at the [c]time when
kings go out *to battle*, that David sent
[d]Joab and his servants with him, and
all Israel; and they destroyed the people of Ammon and besieged [e]Rabbah.
But David remained at Jerusalem.
2 Then it happened one evening
that David arose from his bed and
walked on the roof of the king's house.
And from the roof he [f]saw a woman
bathing, and the woman *was* very
beautiful to behold.
3 So David sent and inquired
about the woman. And *someone* said,
"*Is* this not [g]Bathsheba, the daughter
of Eliam, the wife of [h]Uriah the [i]Hit-
tite?"
4 Then David sent messengers,
and took her; and she came to him,
and he [j]lay with her, for she was
cleansed from her [k]impurity; and she
returned to her house.
5 And the woman conceived; so
she sent and told David, and said, "I
am with child."
6 Then David sent to Joab, *saying*,
"Send me Uriah the Hittite." And Joab
sent Uriah to David.
7 When Uriah had come to him,
David asked how Joab was doing, and
how the people were doing, and how
the war prospered.
8 And David said to Uriah, "Go
down to your house and [l]wash your
feet." So Uriah departed from the
king's house, and a gift *of food* from
the king followed him.

16
a Or *Shophach*, 1 Chr. 19:16,18
18
b Cp. 1 Chr. 19:18; see 1 Chr. 11:11, *note*
CHAPTER 11
1
c 1 Ki. 20:22–26
d 1 Chr. 20:1
e 2 Sam. 12:26; Jer. 49:2,3; Amos 1:14
2
f Ex. 20:17
3
g Or *Bathshua*, 1 Chr. 3:5
h 2 Sam. 23:39
i 1 Sam. 26:6; see 2 Ki. 7:6, *note*
4
j Lev. 20:10; Dt. 22:22; Jas. 1:14–15
k Lev. 15:19–28; 18:19
8
l Gen. 19:2
9
m 1 Ki. 14:27
11
n Cp. 2 Sam. 7:2, 6
15
o 2 Sam. 12:9
21
p Or *Jerubbaal*, Jud. 6:32
q Jud. 9:50–54

9 But Uriah slept at the [m]door of
the king's house with all the servants
of his lord, and did not go down to his
house.
10 So when they told David, saying,
"Uriah did not go down to his house,"
David said to Uriah, "Did you not
come from a journey? Why did you
not go down to your house?"
11 And Uriah [n]said to David, "The
ark and Israel and Judah are dwelling
in tents, and my lord Joab and the servants of my lord are encamped in the
open fields. Shall I then go to my
house to eat and drink, and to lie with
my wife? *As* you live, and *as* your soul
lives, I will not do this thing."
12 Then David said to Uriah, "Wait
here today also, and tomorrow I will
let you depart." So Uriah remained in
Jerusalem that day and the next.
13 Now when David called him,
he ate and drank before him; and he
made him drunk. And at evening he
went out to lie on his bed with the
servants of his lord, but he did not go
down to his house.
14 In the morning it happened that
David wrote a letter to Joab and sent
it by the hand of Uriah.
15 And he wrote in the letter, saying, "Set Uriah in the forefront of the
hottest battle, and retreat from him,
that he may be [o]struck down and die."
16 So it was, while Joab besieged
the city, that he assigned Uriah to a
place where he knew there *were* valiant men.
17 Then the men of the city came
out and fought with Joab. And *some* of
the people of the servants of David
fell; and Uriah the Hittite died also.
18 Then Joab sent and told David
all the things concerning the war,
19 and charged the messenger, saying, "When you have finished telling
the matters of the war to the king,
20 if it happens that the king's
wrath rises, and he says to you: 'Why
did you approach so near to the city
when you fought? Did you not know
that they would shoot from the wall?
21 'Who struck Abimelech the son
of [p]Jerubbesheth? Was it not a
woman who cast a piece of a millstone
on him from the [q]wall, so that he died
in Thebez? Why did you go near the
wall?'—then you shall say, 'Your servant Uriah the Hittite is dead also.'"

*
10:16 That is, the Euphrates **10:19** Hebrew *Hadarezer*

[1](10:18) Perhaps a scribal error for "thousand"; cp. 2 Sam. 8:4.

22 So the messenger went, and came and told David all that Joab had sent by him.

23 And the messenger said to David, "Surely the men prevailed against us and came out to us in the field; then we drove them back as far as the entrance of the gate.

24 "The archers shot from the wall at your servants; and *some* of the king's servants are dead, and your servant Uriah the Hittite is dead also."

25 Then David said to the messenger, "Thus you shall say to Joab: 'Do not let this thing displease you, for the sword devours one as well as another. Strengthen your attack against the city, and overthrow it.' So encourage him."

26 When the wife of Uriah heard that Uriah her husband was dead, she mourned for her husband.

27 And when her mourning was [a]over, David sent and brought her to his house, and she became his wife and bore him a son. But the thing that David had done [b]displeased the LORD.

Nathan rebukes David

12 THEN the LORD sent [c]Nathan to David. And he [d]came to him, and said to him: "There were two men in one city, one rich and the other poor.

2 "The rich *man* had exceedingly many flocks and herds.

3 "But the poor *man* had nothing, except [e]one little ewe lamb which he had bought and nourished; and it grew up together with him and with his children. It ate of his own food and drank from his own cup and lay in his bosom; and it was like a daughter to him.

4 "And a traveler came to the rich man, who refused to take from his own flock and from his own herd to prepare one for the wayfaring man who had come to him; but he [f]took the poor man's lamb and prepared it for the man who had come to him."

5 So David's anger was greatly aroused against the man, and he said to Nathan, "*As* the LORD lives, the man who has done this shall surely [g]die!

6 "And he shall restore [h]fourfold for the lamb, because he did this thing and because he had no pity."

7 Then Nathan said to David, "You *are* the man! Thus says the LORD God of Israel: [i]'I anointed you king over Israel, and I delivered you from the hand of Saul.

8 'I gave you your master's house and your master's wives into your keeping, and gave you the house of Israel and Judah. And if *that had been* too little, I also would have given you much more!

9 [j]'Why have you despised the commandment of the LORD, to do evil in His [k]sight? [l]You have killed Uriah the [m]Hittite with the sword; you have taken his wife *to be* your wife, and have killed him with the sword of the people of Ammon.

10 'Now therefore, the sword shall never depart from your [n]house, because you have despised Me, and have taken the wife of Uriah the Hittite to be your wife.'

11 "Thus says the LORD: 'Behold, I will raise up adversity against you from your own house; and I will take your wives before your eyes and give *them* to your neighbor, and he shall lie with your wives in the sight of this [o]sun.

12 'For you did *it* secretly, but I will do this thing before all Israel, before the sun.' "

David repents of his sin with Bathsheba

13 So David said to Nathan, [p]"I have [q]sinned against the LORD." And Nathan said to David, "The LORD also has [r]put away your sin; you shall not die.

14 "However, because by this deed you have given great occasion to the enemies of the LORD to [s]blaspheme, the child also *who is* born to you shall surely [t]die."

15 Then Nathan departed to his house.

And the [u]LORD struck the child that Uriah's wife bore to David, and it became ill.

16 David therefore pleaded with God for the child, and David fasted and went in and [v]lay all night on the ground.

17 So the elders of his house arose *and went* to him, to raise him up from the ground. But he would not, nor did he eat food with them.

18 Then on the seventh day it came to pass that the child died. And the servants of David were afraid to tell him that the child was dead. For they said, "Indeed, while the child was alive, we spoke to him, and he would not heed our voice. How can we tell

27
a Cp. Gen. 50:10; 1 Sam. 31:13
b 1 Chr. 21:7; Heb. 13:4

CHAPTER 12

1
c *Parables* (OT): vv. 1–4; 2 Sam. 14:3. (Jud. 9:8; Zech. 11:7). Cp. 2 Sam. 7:2; 1 Ki. 1:18
d Ps. 51, *title*

3
e Cp. 2 Sam. 11:3

4
f Cp. 2 Sam. 11:4

5
g Cp. 1 Ki. 20:38–40

6
h Ex. 22:1; Lk. 19:8

7
i 1 Sam. 16:3–13; 2 Sam. 5:3

9
j Num. 15:30–31
k Cp. 1 Sam. 15:19–23
l 2 Sam. 11:14–17, 27
m See 2 Ki. 7:6, *note*

10
n 2 Sam. 13:28; 18:14; 1 Ki. 2:25

11
o 2 Sam. 16:21–22

13
p 2 Sam. 24:10; Lk. 18:13
q Ps. 51; cp. Ps. 32
r Ps. 32:1–5; Prov. 28:13; Mic. 7:18

14
s Isa. 52:5; Rom. 2:24
t *Judgments* (the seven): vv. 13–14; Ps. 50:3. (2 Sam. 7:14; Rev. 20:12, *note*)

12:15 *u* 1 Sam. 25:38 **12:16** *v* 2 Sam. 13:31

him that the child is dead? He may do some harm!"

19 When David saw that his servants were whispering, David perceived that the child was dead. Therefore David said to his servants, "Is the child dead?" And they said, "He is dead."

20 So David arose from the ground, washed and [a]anointed himself, and changed his clothes; and he went into the house of the LORD and worshiped. Then he went to his own house; and when he requested, they set food before him, and he ate.

21 Then his servants said to him, "What *is* this that you have done? You fasted and wept for the child *while he was* alive, but when the child died, you arose and ate food."

22 And he said, "While the child was alive, I fasted and wept; for I said, [b]'Who can tell *whether* the LORD[*] will be gracious to me, that the child may live?'

23 "But now he is dead; why should I fast? Can I bring him back again? I shall go [c]to him, but he shall [d]not return to me."

Birth of Solomon

24 Then David comforted Bathsheba his wife, and went in to her and lay with her. So she bore a son, and [e]he[*] called his name Solomon. Now the LORD loved him,

25 and He sent *word* by the hand of Nathan the prophet: So he[*] called his name [f]Jedidiah, because of the LORD.

David and Joab take Rabbah
(1 Chr. 20:1–3)

26 Now Joab fought against [g]Rabbah of the people of Ammon, and took the royal city.

27 And Joab sent messengers to David, and said, "I have fought against Rabbah, and I have taken the city's water *supply.*

28 "Now therefore, gather the rest of the people together and encamp against the city and take it, lest I take the city and it be called after my name."

29 So David gathered all the people together and went to Rabbah, fought against it, and took it.

30 Then he took their king's crown from his head. Its weight *was* a [h]talent of gold, with precious stones. And it was *set* on David's head. Also he brought out the spoil of the city in great abundance.

31 And he brought out the people who *were* in it, and put *them to work* with saws and iron picks and iron axes, and made them cross over to the brick works. So he did to all the cities of the people of Ammon. Then David and all the people returned to Jerusalem.

Consequences of David's sin
(chs. 13—20): Amnon's crime

13 AFTER this [i]Absalom the son of David had a lovely sister, whose name *was* [j]Tamar; and [k]Amnon the son of David loved her.

2 Amnon was so [l]distressed over his sister Tamar that he became sick; for she *was* a virgin. And it was improper for Amnon to do anything to her.

3 But Amnon had a friend whose name *was* Jonadab the son of [m]Shimeah, David's brother. Now Jonadab *was* a very crafty man.

4 And he said to him, "Why *are* you, the king's son, becoming thinner day after day? Will you not tell me?" Amnon said to him, "I love Tamar, my brother Absalom's sister."

5 So Jonadab said to him, "Lie down on your bed and pretend to be ill. And when your father comes to see you, say to him, 'Please let my sister Tamar come and give me food, and prepare the food in my sight, that I may see *it* and eat it from her hand.'"

6 Then Amnon lay down and pretended to be ill; and when the king came to see him, Amnon said to the king, "Please let Tamar my sister come and make a couple of [n]cakes for me in my sight, that I may eat from her hand."

7 And David sent home to Tamar, saying, "Now go to your brother Amnon's house, and prepare food for him."

8 So Tamar went to her brother Amnon's house; and he was lying down. Then she took flour and kneaded *it,* made cakes in his sight, and baked the cakes.

9 And she took the pan and placed *them* out before him, but he refused to eat. Then Amnon said, "Have everyone go out from [o]me." And they all went out from him.

10 Then Amnon said to Tamar,

20 *a* Ruth. 3:3
22 *b* Isa. 38:2–3; Joel 2:14; Jon. 3:9
23 *c* Gen. 37:35 *d* Job 7:10
24 *e* Cp. 1 Chr. 22:9
25 *f* Lit. *beloved of the* LORD. Neh. 13:26; cp. Mt. 3:17
26 *g* 2 Sam. 11:1
30 *h* See Weights and Measures (OT), 2 Chr. 2:10, *note*

CHAPTER 13
1 *i* 2 Sam. 3:3; 1 Chr. 3:1–2 *j* 1 Chr. 3:9 *k* 2 Sam. 3:2
2 *l* i.e. *frustrated in his desire.* Cp. Gen. 39:2–12; Mt. 5:27–30
3 *m* Or *Shammah,* 1 Sam. 16:9
6 *n* Gen. 18:6
9 *o* Cp. Gen. 45:1

*12:22 A few Hebrew manuscripts and Syriac read *God.* 12:24 Following Kethib, Septuagint, and Vulgate; Qere, a few Hebrew manuscripts, Syriac, and Targum read *she.* 12:25 Qere, some Hebrew manuscripts, Syriac, and Targum read *she.*

"Bring the food into the bedroom, that I may eat from your hand." And Tamar took the cakes which she had made, and brought *them* to Amnon her brother in the bedroom.

11 Now when she had brought *them* to him to eat, he took hold of her and said to her, "Come, [a]lie with me, my sister."

12 But she answered him, "No, my brother, do not force me, for no such thing should be done in [b]Israel. Do not do this [c]disgraceful thing!

13 "And I, where could I take my shame? And as for you, you would be like one of the fools in Israel. Now therefore, please speak to the king; for he will not withhold me from you."

14 However, he would not heed her voice; and being stronger than she, he forced her and lay with her.

15 Then Amnon hated her exceedingly, so that the hatred with which he hated her *was* greater than the love with which he had loved her. And Amnon said to her, "Arise, be gone!"

16 So she said to him, "No, indeed! This evil of sending me away *is* worse than the other that you did to me." But he would not listen to her.

17 Then he called his servant who attended him, and said, "Here! Put this *woman* out, away from me, and bolt the door behind her."

18 Now she had on a [d]robe of many colors, [e]for the king's virgin daughters wore such apparel. And his servant put her out and bolted the door behind her.

19 Then Tamar put [f]ashes on her head, and [g]tore her robe of many colors that *was* on her, and [h]laid her hand on her head and went away crying bitterly.

20 And Absalom her brother said to her, "Has Amnon your brother been with you? But now hold your peace, my sister. He *is* your brother; do not take this thing to heart." So Tamar remained desolate in her brother Absalom's house.

21 But when King David heard of all these things, he was very angry.

22 And Absalom spoke to his brother Amnon neither good nor bad. For Absalom hated Amnon, because he had forced his sister Tamar.

Absalom avenges Tamar and flees to Geshur

23 And it came to pass, after two full years, that Absalom had sheepshearers in Baal Hazor, which *is* near Ephraim; so Absalom invited all the king's sons.

24 Then Absalom came to the king and said, "Kindly note, your servant has sheepshearers; please, let the king and his servants go with your servant."

25 But the king said to Absalom, "No, my son, let us not all go now, lest we be a burden to you." Then he urged him, but he would not go; and he blessed him.

26 Then Absalom said, "If not, please let my brother Amnon go with us." And the king said to him, "Why should he go with you?"

27 But Absalom urged him; so he let Amnon and all the king's sons go with him.

28 Now Absalom had commanded his servants, saying, "Watch now, when Amnon's heart is [i]merry with wine, and when I say to you, 'Strike Amnon!' then kill him. Do not be afraid. Have I not commanded you? Be courageous and valiant."

29 So the servants of Absalom [j]did to Amnon as Absalom had commanded. Then all the king's sons arose, and each one got on [k]his mule and fled.

30 And it came to pass, while they were on the way, that news came to David, saying, "Absalom has killed all the king's sons, and not one of them is left!"

31 So the king arose and tore his garments and [l]lay on the ground, and all his servants stood by with their clothes torn.

32 Then [m]Jonadab the son of Shimeah, David's brother, answered and said, "Let not my lord suppose they have killed all the young men, the king's sons, for only Amnon is dead. For by the command of Absalom this has been determined from the day that he forced his sister Tamar.

33 "Now therefore, let not my lord the king take the thing to his [n]heart, to think that all the king's sons are dead. For only Amnon is dead."

34 Then Absalom fled. And the young man who was keeping watch lifted his eyes and looked, and there, many people were coming from the road on the hillside behind him.*

35 And Jonadab said to the king,

---

11 a Dt. 27:22; Ezek. 22:11
12 b Lev. 18:9–11; 20:17
c Gen. 34:7; Jud. 19:23; 20:6
18 d Lit. *a long-sleeved robe.* Cp. Gen. 37:3
e Ps. 45:13–14
19 f Job 42:6
g Cp. v. 31
h Jer. 2:37
28 i 1 Sam. 25:36
29 j 2 Sam. 12:10
k 2 Sam. 18:9
31 l 2 Sam. 12:16
32 m 2 Sam. 13:5
33 n 2 Sam. 19:19

---

* 13:34 Septuagint adds *And the watchman went and told the king, and said, "I see men from the way of Horonaim, from the regions of the mountains."*

"Look, the king's sons are coming; as your servant said, so it is."

36 So it was, as soon as he had finished speaking, that the king's sons indeed came, and they lifted up their voice and wept. Also the king and all his servants wept very bitterly.

Absalom's flight to Geshur

37 But Absalom fled and went to [a]Talmai the son of Ammihud, king of Geshur. And *David* mourned for his son every day.

38 So Absalom fled and went to Geshur, and was there three years.

39 And King David* longed to go to* Absalom. For he had been [b]comforted concerning Amnon, because he was dead.

Joab's stratagem to effect the return of Absalom

14 SO Joab the son of Zeruiah perceived that the king's heart *was* concerned about Absalom.

2 And Joab sent to [c]Tekoa and brought from there a wise woman, and said to her, "Please pretend to be a mourner, and [d]put on mourning apparel; do not anoint yourself with oil, but act like a woman who has been mourning a long time for the dead.

3 "Go to the king and [e]speak to him in this manner." So [f]Joab put the words in her mouth.

4 And when the woman of Tekoa spoke* to the king, she [g]fell on her face to the ground and prostrated herself, and said, "Help, O king!"

5 Then the king said to her, "What troubles you?" And she answered, "Indeed I *am* a widow, my husband is dead.

6 "Now your maidservant had two sons; and the two fought with each other in the field, and *there was* no one to part them, but the one struck the other and killed him.

7 "And now the whole family has risen up against your maidservant, and they said, 'Deliver him who struck his brother, that we may execute him [h]for the life of his brother whom he killed; and we will destroy the heir also.' So they would extinguish my ember that is left, and leave to my husband *neither* name nor remnant on the earth."

8 Then the king said to the woman, "Go to your house, and I will give orders concerning you."

9 And the woman of Tekoa said to the king, "My lord, O king, *let* the [i]iniquity *be* on me and on my father's house, and the king and his throne *be* [j]guiltless."

10 So the king said, "Whoever says *anything* to you, bring him to me, and he shall not touch you anymore."

11 Then she said, "Please let the king remember the LORD your God, and do not permit the [k]avenger of blood to destroy anymore, lest they destroy my son." And he said, "*As* the LORD lives, not one hair of your son shall fall to the [l]ground."

12 Therefore the woman said, "Please, let your maidservant speak *another* word to my lord the king." And he said, "Say on."

13 So the woman said: "Why then have you schemed such a thing against the people of God? For the king speaks this thing as one who is guilty, *in that* the king does not bring [m]his banished one home again.

14 "For we will surely [n]die and *become* like water spilled on the ground, which cannot be gathered up again. Yet God does not take away a life; but He [o]devises means, so that His banished ones are not expelled from Him.

15 "Now therefore, I have come to speak of this thing to my lord the king because the people have made me afraid. And your maidservant said, 'I will now speak to the king; it may be that the king will perform the request of his maidservant.

16 'For the king will hear and deliver his maidservant from the hand of the man *who would* destroy me and my son together from the [p]inheritance of God.'

17 "Your maidservant said, 'The word of my lord the king will now be comforting; for [q]as the [r]angel of God, so *is* my lord the king in [s]discerning good and evil. And may the LORD your God be with you.' "

18 Then the king answered and said to the woman, "Please do not hide from me anything that I ask you." And the woman said, "Please, let my lord the king speak."

19 So the king said, "*Is* the hand of Joab with you in all this?" And the woman answered and said, "*As* you live, my lord the king, no one can turn

37
a 2 Sam. 3:3; 1 Chr. 3:2
39
b Gen. 38:12; 2 Sam. 12:19–23
CHAPTER 14
2
c 2 Chr. 11:6
d Cp. Ruth 3:3
3
e Parables (OT): vv. 1–14; 1 Ki. 20:35. (Jud. 9:8; Zech. 11:7)
f v. 19; cp. Ex. 4:15
4
g 1 Sam. 25:23
7
h Num. 35:19; Dt. 19:12–13
9
i 1 Sam. 25:24; cp. Mt. 27:25
j 1 Ki. 2:33
11
k Redemption (redeeming relative type): v. 11; Neh. 5:8. (Gen. 48:16; Isa. 59:20, *note*)
l Cp. 1 Sam. 14:45; 1 Ki. 1:52
13
m 2 Sam. 13:37–38
14
n Job 30:23; 34:15; Heb. 9:27
o Num. 35:15
16
p Dt. 32:9; 1 Sam. 26:19; 2 Sam. 20:19
17
q 1 Sam. 29:9; 2 Sam. 19:27
r See Heb. 1:4, *note*
s 1 Ki. 3:9

*

13:39 Following Masoretic Text, Syriac, and Vulgate; Septuagint reads *the spirit of the king;* Targum reads *the soul of King David.* • Following Masoretic Text and Targum; Septuagint and Vulgate read *ceased to pursue after.* **14:4** Many Hebrew manuscripts, Septuagint, Syriac, and Vulgate read *came.*

to the right hand or to the left from
anything that my lord the king has
spoken. For your servant Joab commanded me, and [a]he put all these
words in the mouth of your maidservant.
20 "To bring about this change of
affairs your servant Joab has done
this thing; but my lord *is* wise, according to the wisdom of the [b]angel of
God, to [c]know everything that *is* in
the earth."

David forgives Absalom

21 And the king said to Joab, "All
right, I have granted this thing. Go
therefore, bring back the young man
Absalom."
22 Then Joab fell to the ground on
his face and bowed himself, and
thanked the king. And Joab said, "Today your servant knows that I have
found favor in your sight, my lord, O
king, in that the king has fulfilled the
request of his servant."
23 So Joab arose and went to [d]Ge-
shur, and brought Absalom to Jerusalem.
24 And the king said, "Let him return to his own house, but do not let
him see my face." So Absalom returned to his own house, but did not
see the king's face.
25 Now in all Israel there was no
one who was praised as much as Absalom for his good looks. From the
sole of his foot to the crown of his
head there was no blemish in him.
26 And when he cut the hair of his
head—at the end of every year he [e]cut
it because it was heavy on him—when
he cut it, he weighed the hair of his
head at two hundred shekels according to the king's standard.
27 To Absalom were born three
sons, and one daughter whose name
was [f]Tamar. She was a woman of
beautiful appearance.
28 And Absalom dwelt two full
years in Jerusalem, but did not see the
king's face.
29 Therefore Absalom sent for
Joab, to send him to the king, but he
would not come to him. And when he
sent again the second time, he would
not come.
30 So he said to his servants, "See,
Joab's field is near mine, and he has
barley there; go and set it on fire." And
Absalom's servants set the field on
fire.
31 Then Joab arose and came to
Absalom's house, and said to him,
"Why have your servants set my field
on fire?"
32 And Absalom answered Joab,
"Look, I sent to you, saying, 'Come
here, so that I may send you to the
king, to say, "Why have I come from
Geshur? *It would be* better for me *to
be* there still." ' Now therefore, let me
see the king's face; but [g]if there is iniquity in me, let him execute me."
33 So Joab went to the king and
told him. And when he had called for
Absalom, he came to the king and
bowed himself on his face to the
ground before the king. Then the king
[h]kissed Absalom.

III. From the Revolt of Absalom to the Numbering of the People, 15—24

15 AFTER this it happened that
Absalom [i]provided himself
with chariots and horses, and fifty
men to run before him.
2 Now Absalom would rise early
and [j]stand beside the way to the gate.
So it was, whenever anyone who had
a [k]lawsuit came to the king for a decision, that Absalom would call to him
and say, "What city *are* you from?"
And he would say, "Your servant *is*
from such and such a tribe of Israel."
3 Then Absalom would say to him,
"Look, your case *is* good and right; but
there is no deputy of the king to hear
you."
4 Moreover Absalom would [l]say,
"Oh, that I were made judge in the
land, and everyone who has any suit
or cause would come to me; then I
would give him justice."
5 And so it was, whenever anyone
came near to bow down to him, that he
would put out his hand and take him
and [m]kiss him.
6 In this manner Absalom acted
toward all Israel who came to the king
for judgment. So Absalom stole the
hearts of the men of Israel.

Absalom's rebellion

7 Now it came to pass after [n]forty
years that Absalom said to the king,
"Please, let me go to [o]Hebron and pay
the [p]vow which I made to the LORD.
8 "For your servant took a vow
while I dwelt at Geshur in [q]Syria, saying, 'If the LORD indeed brings me back
to Jerusalem, [r]then I will serve the
LORD.' "
9 And the king said to him, "Go in
peace." So he arose and went to Hebron.
10 Then Absalom sent spies

19 a 2 Sam. 14:3
20 b See Heb. 1:4, *note* c 2 Sam. 18:13
23 d 2 Sam. 13:37
26 e Ezek. 44:20
27 f 2 Sam. 13:1
32 g 1 Sam. 20:8
33 h Gen. 33:4; Lk. 15:20
CHAPTER 15
1 i 1 Ki. 1:5
2 j Cp. 2 Sam. 19:8 k Dt. 19:17
4 l Cp. Jud. 9:29
5 m 2 Sam. 14:33; cp. 20:9
7 n Some authorities read *four.* See 1 Chr. 11:11, *note* o 2 Sam. 3:2–3 p Dt. 23:21
8 q Heb. *Aram.* 2 Sam. 13:37 r Gen. 28:20–21

throughout all the tribes of Israel, saying, "As soon as you hear the [a]sound of the trumpet, then you shall say, 'Absalom [b]reigns in [c]Hebron!' "
11 And with Absalom went two hundred men invited from Jerusalem, and they went along innocently and did not know anything.
12 Then Absalom sent for [d]Ahithophel the Gilonite, David's counselor, from his city—from [e]Giloh—while he offered sacrifices. And the conspiracy grew strong, for the people with Absalom continually [f]increased in number.

David flees

13 Now a messenger came to David, saying, "The hearts of the men of Israel are with Absalom."
14 So David said to all his servants who *were* with him at Jerusalem, [g]"Arise, and let us flee, or we shall not escape from Absalom. Make haste to depart, lest he overtake us suddenly and bring disaster upon us, and strike the city with the edge of the sword."
15 And the king's servants said to the king, "We *are* your servants, *ready to do* whatever my lord the king commands."
16 Then the king went out with all his household after him. But the king left ten women, [h]concubines, to keep the house.
17 And the king went out with all the people after him, and stopped at the outskirts.
18 Then all his servants passed before him; and all the [i]Cherethites, all the Pelethites, and all the Gittites, [j]six hundred men who had followed him from Gath, passed before the king.
19 Then the king said to Ittai the Gittite, "Why are you also going with us? Return and remain with the king. For you *are* a foreigner and also an exile from your own place.
20 "In fact, you came *only* yesterday. Should I make you wander up and down with us today, since I go I know not where? Return, and take your brethren back. Mercy and truth *be* with you."
21 But Ittai answered the king and said, "*As* the LORD lives, and *as* my lord the king lives, surely in whatever place my lord the king shall [k]be, whether in death or life, even there also your servant will be."
22 So David said to Ittai, "Go, and cross over." Then Ittai the Gittite and all his men and all the little ones who *were* with him crossed over.
23 And all the country wept with a loud voice, and all the people crossed over. The king himself also crossed over the Brook Kidron, and all the

10
a Cp. 2 Sam. 18:16
b 1 Ki. 1:34; 2 Ki. 9:13
c Cp. 2 Sam. 2:3–4
12
d 2 Sam. 16:15; 1 Chr. 27:33
e Josh. 15:51
f Ps. 3:1
14
g 2 Sam. 12:11; Ps. 3, *title*
16
h 2 Sam. 12:11; 16:21–22
18
i 2 Sam. 8:18
j 1 Sam. 23:13; 30:9
21
k Cp. Ruth 1:16–17

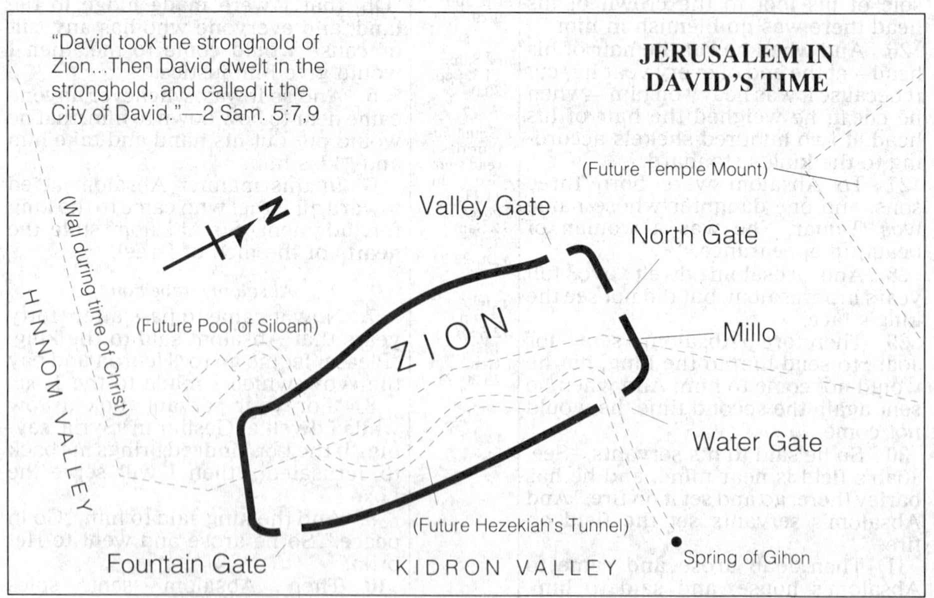

people crossed over toward the way of the [a]wilderness.

Ark returned to Jerusalem

24 There was [b]Zadok also, and all the Levites with him, bearing the [c]ark of the covenant of God. And they set down the ark of God, and [d]Abiathar went up until all the people had finished crossing over from the city.

25 Then the king said to Zadok, "Carry the ark of God back into the city. If I find favor in the eyes of the LORD, He will [e]bring me back and show me *both* it and [f]His dwelling place.

26 "But if He says thus: 'I have no [g]delight in you,' here I am, [h]let Him do to me as seems good to Him."

27 The king also said to Zadok the priest, "*Are* you *not* a [i]seer? Return to the city in peace, and your two sons with you, [j]Ahimaaz your son, and Jonathan the son of Abiathar.

28 "See, I will wait in the plains of the [k]wilderness until word comes from you to inform me."

29 Therefore Zadok and Abiathar carried the ark of God back to Jerusalem. And they remained there.

30 So David went up by the Ascent of the *Mount of* Olives, and wept as he went up; and he had his [l]head covered and went [m]barefoot. And all the people who *were* with him covered their heads and went up, weeping as they went up.

31 Then *someone* told David, saying, [n]"Ahithophel *is* among the conspirators with Absalom." And David said, "O LORD, I pray, [o]turn the counsel of Ahithophel into foolishness!"

Hushai sent back

32 Now it happened when David had come to the top *of the mountain,* where he worshiped God—there was Hushai the [p]Archite coming to meet him with his robe torn and dust on his head.

33 David said to him, "If you go on with me, then you will become a burden to me.

34 "But if you return to the city, and say to Absalom, 'I will be your [q]servant, O king; *as* I *was* your father's servant previously, so I *will* now also *be* your servant,' then you may defeat the counsel of Ahithophel for me.

35 "And *do* you not *have* [r]Zadok and Abiathar the priests with you there? Therefore it will be *that* whatever you hear from the king's house, you shall tell to Zadok and Abiathar the priests.

36 "Indeed *they have* there with them their two sons, Ahimaaz, Zadok's *son,* and Jonathan, Abiathar's *son;* and by them you shall send me everything you hear."

37 So Hushai, David's [s]friend, went into the city. And Absalom came into [t]Jerusalem.

Ziba, the false servant of Mephibosheth

16 WHEN David was a little [u]past the top *of the mountain,* there was [v]Ziba the servant of Mephibosheth, who met him [w]with a couple of saddled donkeys, and on them two hundred *loaves* of bread, one hundred clusters of raisins, one hundred summer fruits, and a skin of wine.

2 And the king said to Ziba, "What do you mean to do with these?" So Ziba said, "The donkeys *are* for the king's household to ride on, the bread and summer fruit for the young men to eat, and the wine for those who are faint in the [k]wilderness to drink."

3 Then the king said, "And where *is* your [x]master's son?" And Ziba said to the [y]king, "Indeed he is staying in Jerusalem, for he said, 'Today the house of Israel will restore the kingdom of my father to me.' "

4 So the king said to Ziba, "Here, all that *belongs* to Mephibosheth *is* yours." And Ziba said, "I humbly bow before you, *that* I may find favor in your sight, my lord, O king!"

Shimei curses David

5 Now when King David came to [z]Bahurim, there was a man from the family of the house of Saul, whose name *was* Shimei the son of Gera, coming from there. He came out, [aa]cursing continuously as he came.

6 And he threw stones at David and at all the servants of King David. And all the people and all the mighty men *were* on his right hand and on his left.

7 Also Shimei said thus when he cursed: "Come out! Come out! You bloodthirsty man, you [bb]rogue!

8 "The LORD has brought upon you all the [cc]blood of the house of Saul, in whose place you have reigned; and the LORD has delivered the kingdom into the hand of Absalom your son. So now you *are caught* in your own evil,

23 *a* 2 Sam. 16:2
24 *b* 2 Sam. 8:17 *c* Num. 4:15 *d* 1 Sam. 22:20
25 *e* Ps. 43:3 *f* Ex. 15:13
26 *g* Cp. Num. 14:8; 1 Ki. 10:9 *h* 1 Sam. 3:18
27 *i* 1 Sam. 9:9 *j* 2 Sam. 17:17–20
28 *k* 2 Sam. 15:23
30 *l* Est. 6:12; cp. 2 Sam. 19:4 *m* Isa. 20:2–4
31 *n* 2 Sam. 15:12 *o* 2 Sam. 17:14–23; cp. 16:23
32 *p* Josh. 16:2
34 *q* 2 Sam. 16:19
35 *r* 2 Sam. 17:15–16
37 *s* 1 Chr. 27:33 *t* 2 Sam. 16:15
CHAPTER 16
1 *u* 2 Sam. 15:30,32 *v* 2 Sam. 9:2; 19:17, 29 *w* Cp. 1 Sam. 25:18; 2 Sam. 17:17–29
3 *x* 2 Sam. 9:9–10 *y* 2 Sam. 19:27
5 *z* 2 Sam. 3:16 *aa* 2 Sam. 19:21; 1 Ki. 2:8–9, 44–46
7 *bb* 1 Sam. 2:12

16:8 *cc* 2 Sam. 1:16; 3:28–29; 4:8,12; cp. 21:1–9

because you are a bloodthirsty man!"

9 Then Abishai the son of Zeruiah said to the king, "Why should this dead [a]dog curse my lord the king? Please, let me go over and [b]take off his head!"

10 But the king said, [c]"What have I to do with you, you [d]sons of Zeruiah? So let him curse, because the LORD has said to him, 'Curse David.' Who then shall say, 'Why have you done so?' "

11 And David said to Abishai and all his servants, "See how my son who came from my own body seeks my life. How much more now *may this* Benjamite? Let him alone, and let him curse; [e]for so the LORD has ordered him.

12 "It may be that the LORD will look on my affliction,* and that the LORD will [f]repay me with [g]good for his cursing this day."

13 And as David and his men went along the road, Shimei went along the hillside opposite him and cursed as he went, threw stones at him and kicked up dust.

14 Now the king and all the people who *were* with him became weary; so they refreshed themselves there.

Absalom enters Jerusalem

15 Meanwhile Absalom and all the people, the men of Israel, came to [h]Jerusalem; and Ahithophel *was* with him.

16 And so it was, [i]when Hushai the Archite, David's friend, came to Absalom, that [j]Hushai said to Absalom, "*Long* live the king! *Long* live the king!"

17 So Absalom said to Hushai, "*Is* this your loyalty to your friend? [k]Why did you not go with your [l]friend?"

18 And Hushai said to Absalom, "No, but whom the LORD and this people and all the men of Israel choose, his I will be, and with him I will remain.

19 "Furthermore, whom should I serve? *Should I* not *serve* in the presence of his son? As I have served in your father's presence, so will I be in your presence."

20 Then Absalom said to [m]Ahithophel, "Give advice as to what we should do."

21 And Ahithophel said to Absalom, "Go in to your father's [n]concubines, whom he has left to keep the house; and all Israel will hear that you are abhorred by your father. Then the

9
a 2 Sam. 9:8
b Cp. 1 Sam. 26:8; 2 Sam. 19:21; Lk. 9:54
10
c i.e. *What have we in common?*
d 2 Sam. 3:39; 19:22
11
e Cp. 1 Sam. 26:19
12
f Dt. 23:5; Neh. 13:2; Prov. 20:22
g Rom. 8:28; Heb. 12:10–11
15
h Cp. 2 Sam. 15:14,17
16
i 2 Sam. 15:37
j 2 Sam. 15:34
17
k Cp. 2 Sam. 19:25
l 1 Chr. 27:33
20
m 2 Sam. 15:12
21
n 2 Sam. 15:16; 20:3
o 2 Sam. 2:7
22
p 2 Sam. 12:11–12
q Cp. Gen. 49:4; 1 Chr. 5:1
CHAPTER 17
2
r 2 Sam. 16:14; cp. Dt. 25:18
s Cp. 1 Ki. 22:31
4
t 2 Sam. 5:3; 19:11
5
u 2 Sam. 15:32–34
8
v Hos. 13:8
10
w Josh. 2:11
11
x 2 Sam. 3:10

[o]hands of all who are with you will be strong."

22 So they pitched a tent for Absalom on the top of the house, and Absalom went [p]in [q]to his father's concubines in the sight of all Israel.

23 Now the advice of Ahithophel, which he gave in those days, *was* as if one had inquired at the oracle of God. So *was* all the advice of Ahithophel both with David and with Absalom.

Hushai thwarts Ahithophel

17 MOREOVER Ahithophel said to Absalom, "Now let me choose twelve thousand men, and I will arise and pursue David tonight.

2 "I will come upon him while he *is* [r]weary and weak, and make him afraid. And all the people who *are* with him will flee, and I will strike [s]only the king.

3 "Then I will bring back all the people to you. When all return except the man whom you seek, all the people will be at peace."

4 And the saying pleased Absalom and all the [t]elders of Israel.

5 Then Absalom said, "Now call Hushai the Archite also, and let us hear what he [u]says too."

6 And when Hushai came to Absalom, Absalom spoke to him, saying, "Ahithophel has spoken in this manner. Shall we do as he says? If not, speak up."

7 So Hushai said to Absalom: "The advice that Ahithophel has given *is* not good at this time.

8 "For," said Hushai, "you know your father and his men, that they *are* mighty men, and they *are* enraged in their minds, [v]like a bear robbed of her cubs in the field; and your father *is* a man of war, and will not camp with the people.

9 "Surely by now he is hidden in some pit, or in some *other* place. And it will be, when some of them are overthrown at the first, that whoever hears *it* will say, 'There is a slaughter among the people who follow Absalom.'

10 "And even he *who is* valiant, whose heart *is* like the heart of a lion, will [w]melt completely. For all Israel knows that your father *is* a mighty man, and *those* who *are* with him *are* valiant men.

11 "Therefore I advise that all Israel be fully gathered to you, [x]from Dan to

*
16:12 Following Kethib, Septuagint, Syriac, and Vulgate; Qere reads *my eyes;* Targum reads *tears of my eyes.*

Beersheba, [a]like the sand that *is* by the sea for multitude, and that you go to battle in person.

12 "So we will come upon him in some place where he may be found, and we will fall on him as the dew falls on the ground. And of him and all the men who *are* with him there shall not be left so much as one.

13 "Moreover, if he has withdrawn into a city, then all Israel shall bring ropes to that city; and we will [b]pull it into the river, until there is not one small stone found there."

14 So Absalom and all the men of Israel said, "The advice of Hushai the Archite *is* better than the advice of Ahithophel." For the [c]LORD had purposed to defeat the good advice of Ahithophel, to the intent that the LORD might bring disaster on Absalom.

Hushai's warning saves David

15 Then Hushai said to Zadok and Abiathar the priests, "Thus and so Ahithophel advised Absalom and the elders of Israel, and thus and so I have advised.

16 "Now therefore, send quickly and tell David, saying, 'Do not spend this night in the [d]plains of the wilderness, but speedily cross over, lest the king and all the people who *are* with him be swallowed up.' "

17 Now [e]Jonathan and Ahimaaz stayed at [f]En Rogel, for they dared not be seen coming into the city; so a female servant would come and tell them, and they would go and tell King David.

18 Nevertheless a lad saw them, and told Absalom. But both of them went away quickly and came to a man's house in [g]Bahurim, who had a well in his court; and they went down into it.

19 Then the woman took and spread a covering over the well's mouth, and spread ground grain on it; and the thing was not [h]known.

20 And when Absalom's servants came to the woman at the house, they said, "Where *are* Ahimaaz and Jonathan?" So the woman [i]said to them, "They have gone over the water brook." And when they had searched and could not find *them,* they returned to Jerusalem.

21 Now it came to pass, after they had departed, that they came up out of the well and went and told King David, and said to David, "Arise and cross over the water quickly. For thus has Ahithophel advised against you."

22 So David and all the people who *were* with him arose and crossed over the Jordan. By morning light not one of them was left who had not gone over the Jordan.

23 Now when Ahithophel saw that his advice was not followed, he saddled a donkey, and arose and went home to his house, to [j]his city. Then he put his [k]household in order, and [l]hanged himself, and died; and he was buried in his father's tomb.

Absalom pursues David

24 Then David went to [m]Mahanaim. And Absalom crossed over the Jordan, he and all the men of Israel with him.

25 And Absalom made [n]Amasa captain of the army instead of Joab. This Amasa *was* the son of a man whose name *was* Jithra,* an Israelite,* who had gone in to Abigail the daughter of Nahash, sister of Zeruiah, Joab's mother.

26 So Israel and Absalom encamped in the land of Gilead.

David befriended

27 Now it happened, when David had come to Mahanaim, that Shobi the son of [o]Nahash from Rabbah of the people of Ammon, [p]Machir the son of Ammiel from Lo Debar, and [q]Barzillai the Gileadite from Rogelim,

28 brought beds and basins, earthen vessels and wheat, barley and flour, parched *grain* and beans, lentils and parched *seeds,*

29 honey and curds, sheep and cheese of the herd, for David and the people who *were* with him to eat. For they said, "The [r]people are hungry and weary and thirsty in the wilderness."

Battle in woods of Ephraim

18 AND David numbered the people who *were* with him, and [s]set captains of thousands and captains of hundreds over them.

2 Then David sent out one [t]third of the people under the hand of Joab, one third under the hand of Abishai the son of Zeruiah, Joab's brother, and one third under the hand of [u]Ittai the Gittite. And the king said to the

11
a Josh. 11:4; 1 Ki. 20:10
13
b Mic. 1:6
14
c 2 Sam. 15:31
16
d 2 Sam. 15:28
17
e 2 Sam. 15:27,36; 1 Ki. 1:42, 43
f Josh. 15:7
18
g 2 Sam. 16:5
19
h Cp. Josh. 2:4–6
20
i Cp. Lev. 19:11; 1 Sam. 19:12–17
23
j 2 Sam. 15:12
k 2 Ki. 20:1
l Mt. 27:5; cp. Est. 7:1–10
24
m Gen. 32:2; 2 Sam. 2:8; 19:32
25
n 2 Sam. 19:13; 1 Ki. 2:5
27
o 1 Sam. 11:1; cp. 2 Sam. 10:1
p 2 Sam. 9:4
q 2 Sam. 19:31,32; 1 Ki. 2:7
29
r 2 Sam. 16:2,14
CHAPTER 18
1
s Ex. 18:25
2
t Jud. 7:16; 1 Sam. 11:11
u 2 Sam. 15:19–22

*

17:25 Spelled *Jether* in 1 Chronicles 2:17 and elsewhere • Following Masoretic Text, some manuscripts of the Septuagint, and Targum; some manuscripts of the Septuagint read *Ishmaelite* (compare 1 Chronicles 2:17); Vulgate reads of *Jezrael.*

people, "I also will surely go out with you myself."

3 But the people answered, "You shall not go out! For if we flee away, they will not care about us; nor if half of us die, will they care about us. But *you are* worth ten thousand of us now. For you are now more help to us in the city."

4 Then the king said to them, "Whatever seems best to you I will do." So the king stood beside the gate, and all the people went out by hundreds and by thousands.

5 Now the king had commanded Joab, Abishai, and Ittai, saying, "*Deal* gently for my sake with the young man Absalom." And all the people heard when the king gave all the captains [a]orders concerning Absalom.

6 So the people went out into the field of battle against Israel. And the battle was in the [b]woods of Ephraim.

7 The people of Israel were overthrown there before the servants of David, and a great slaughter of twenty thousand took place there that day.

8 For the battle there was scattered over the face of the whole countryside, and the woods devoured more people that day than the sword devoured.

Joab kills Absalom

9 Then Absalom met the servants of David. Absalom rode on a mule. The mule went under the thick boughs of a great terebinth tree, and [c]his head caught in the terebinth; so he was left hanging between heaven and earth. And the mule which *was* under him went on.

10 Now a certain man saw *it* and told Joab, and said, "I just saw Absalom hanging in a terebinth tree!"

11 So Joab said to the man who told him, "You just saw *him!* And why did you not strike him there to the ground? I would have given you ten [d]*shekels* of silver and a belt."

12 But the man said to Joab, "Though I were to receive a thousand [d]*shekels* of silver in my hand, I would not raise my hand against the king's son. For in our hearing the king commanded you and Abishai and Ittai, saying, 'Beware lest anyone *touch* the young man Absalom!'*

13 "Otherwise I would have dealt falsely against my own life. For there is nothing hidden from the king, and you yourself would have set yourself against *me.*"

5
a v. 12
6
b Cp. Josh. 17:15–18
9
c 2 Sam. 14:26
11
d See Coinage (OT), Ex. 30:13, *note*
16
e Cp. 2 Sam. 15:10
17
f 2 Sam. 19:8
19
g 2 Sam. 17:17,20
24
h Jud. 5:11
i 2 Ki. 9:17

14 Then Joab said, "I cannot linger with you." And he took three spears in his hand and thrust them through Absalom's heart, while he was *still* alive in the midst of the terebinth tree.

15 And ten young men who bore Joab's armor surrounded Absalom, and struck and killed him.

16 So Joab [e]blew the trumpet, and the people returned from pursuing Israel. For Joab held back the people.

17 And they took Absalom and cast him into a large pit in the woods, and laid a very large heap of stones over him. Then all Israel [f]fled, everyone to his tent.

18 Now Absalom in his lifetime had taken and set up a pillar for himself, which *is* in the King's Valley. For he said, "I have no son to keep my name in remembrance." He called the pillar after his own name. And to this day it is called Absalom's Monument.

David's grief

19 Then [g]Ahimaaz the son of Zadok said, "Let me run now and take the news to the king, how the LORD has avenged him of his enemies."

20 And Joab said to him, "You shall not take the news this day, for you shall take the news another day. But today you shall take no news, because the king's son is dead."

21 Then Joab said to the Cushite, "Go, tell the king what you have seen." So the Cushite bowed himself to Joab and ran.

22 And Ahimaaz the son of Zadok said again to Joab, "But whatever happens, please let me also run after the Cushite." So Joab said, "Why will you run, my son, since you have no news ready?"

23 "But whatever happens," *he said,* "let me run." So he said to him, "Run." Then Ahimaaz ran by way of the plain, and outran the Cushite.

24 Now David was sitting between the two [h]gates. And the [i]watchman went up to the roof over the gate, to the wall, lifted his eyes and looked, and there was a man, running alone.

25 Then the watchman cried out and told the king. And the king said, "If he *is* alone, *there is* news in his mouth." And he came rapidly and drew near.

26 Then the watchman saw *another* man running, and the watch-

*

18:12 The ancient versions read '*Protect the young man Absalom for me!*'

man called to the gatekeeper and said,
"There is *another* man, running
alone!" And the king said, "He also
brings news."
27 So the watchman said, "I think
the running of the first is like the running of Ahimaaz the son of Zadok."
And the king said, "He *is* a good man,
and comes with [a]good news."
28 So Ahimaaz called out and said
to the king, "All is well!" Then he
bowed down with his face to the earth
before the king, and said, [b]"Blessed
be the LORD your God, who has delivered up the men who raised their hand
against my lord the king!"
29 The king said, "Is the young man
Absalom safe?" Ahimaaz answered,
"When [c]Joab sent the king's servant
and *me* your servant, I saw a great
tumult, but I did not know what *it was
about*."
30 And the king said, "Turn aside
and stand here." So he turned aside
and stood still.
31 Just then the Cushite came, and
the Cushite said, "There is good news,
my lord the king! For the LORD has
avenged you this day of all those who
rose against you."
32 And the king said to the Cushite,
"Is the young man Absalom safe?" So
the Cushite answered, "May the enemies of my lord the king, and all who
rise against you to do harm, be like
that young man!"
33 Then the king was deeply
moved, and went up to the chamber
over the gate, and wept. And as he
went, he said thus: "O my son [d]Ab-
salom—my son, my son Absalom—if
only I had died in [e]your place! O Absalom my son, [f]my son!"

Joab reproves David

19 AND Joab was told, "Behold,
the king is weeping and
[g]mourning for Absalom."
2 So the victory that day was
turned into [h]mourning for all the people. For the people heard it said that
day, "The king is grieved for his son."
3 And the people stole back into
the city that day, as people who are
ashamed steal away when they flee in
battle.
4 But the king covered his face,
and the king cried out with a loud
voice, "O my son Absalom! O Absalom, my son, [i]my son!"
5 Then [j]Joab came into the house
to the king, and said, "Today you have
disgraced all your servants who today
have saved your life, the lives of your
sons and daughters, the lives of your
wives and the lives of your concubines,
6 "in that you love your enemies
and hate your friends. For you have
declared today that you regard neither princes nor servants; for today I
perceive that if Absalom had lived and
all of us had died today, then it would
have pleased you well.
7 "Now therefore, arise, go out
and speak comfort to your servants.
For I swear by the LORD, if you do not
go out, not one will stay with you this
night. And that will be worse for you
than all the evil that has befallen you
from your youth until now."

David restored to his kingdom

8 Then the king arose and sat in
the [k]gate. And they told all the people,
saying, "There is the king, sitting in
the gate." So all the people came before the king. For everyone of Israel
had [l]fled to his tent.
9 Now all the people were in a dispute throughout all the tribes of Israel,
saying, "The king saved us from the
hand of our [m]enemies, he delivered us
from the hand of the [n]Philistines, and
now [o]he has fled from the land because of Absalom.
10 "But Absalom, whom [p]we
anointed over us, has died in battle.
Now therefore, why do you say nothing about bringing back the king?"
11 So King David sent to [q]Zadok
and Abiathar the priests, saying,
"Speak to the elders of Judah, saying,
'Why are you the last to bring the king
back to his house, since the words of
all Israel have come to the king, to his
very house?
12 'You *are* my brethren, you *are*
my [r]bone and my flesh. Why then are
you the last to bring back the king?'
13 "And say to [s]Amasa, '*Are* you
not my bone and my flesh? God do so
to me, and more also, if you are not
commander of the army before me
continually in place of [t]Joab.'"
14 So he swayed the hearts of all
the [u]men of Judah, just as *the heart of*
one man, so that they sent *this word* to
the king: "Return, you and all your
servants!"
15 Then the king returned and
came to the Jordan. And Judah came
to [v]Gilgal, to go to meet the king, to
escort the king [w]across the Jordan.
16 And [x]Shimei the son of Gera, a
Benjamite, who *was* from Bahurim,

27
a 1 Ki. 1:42
28
b 2 Sam. 16:12
29
c vv. 14–17
33
d 2 Sam. 12:10
e Cp. Ex. 32:32; Rom. 9:3
f 2 Sam. 19:4
CHAPTER 19
1
g Jer. 14:2
2
h Est. 4:3
4
i 2 Sam. 18:33
5
j 2 Sam. 18:14
8
k 2 Sam. 18:24
l 2 Sam. 18:17
9
m 2 Sam. 8:1–14
n 2 Sam. 3:18
o 2 Sam. 15:14
10
p Cp. 2 Sam. 12:7
11
q 2 Sam. 15:24
12
r 2 Sam. 5:1; 1 Chr. 11:1
13
s 2 Sam. 17:25; 1 Chr. 2:17
t 2 Sam. 3:37–39
14
u 2 Sam. 2:4; 20:2
15
v Josh. 5:9
w 2 Sam. 17:22
16
x 2 Sam. 16:5; 1 Ki. 2:8

hurried and came down with the men of Judah to meet King David.

17 *There were* a thousand men of [a]Benjamin with him, and [b]Ziba the servant of the house of Saul, and his fifteen sons and his twenty servants with him; and they went over the Jordan before the king.

18 Then a ferryboat went across to carry over the king's household, and to do what he thought good.

Now Shimei the son of Gera fell down before the king when he had crossed the Jordan.

19 Then he said to the king, "Do not let my lord [c]impute iniquity to me, or remember what [d]wrong your servant did on the day that my lord the king left Jerusalem, that the king should take *it* to [e]heart.

20 "For I, your servant, know that I have sinned. Therefore here I am, the first to come today of all the [f]house of Joseph to go down to meet my lord the king."

21 But Abishai the son of Zeruiah answered and said, "Shall not Shimei be put to death for this, [g]because he [h]cursed the LORD's anointed?"

22 And David said, [i]"What have I to do with you, you sons of [j]Zeruiah, that you should be adversaries to me today? Shall any [k]man be put to death today in Israel? For do I not know that today I *am* king over Israel?"

23 Therefore the king said to Shimei, "You shall not die." And the king swore to him.

24 Now [l]Mephibosheth the son of Saul came down to meet the king. And he had not cared for his feet, nor trimmed his mustache, nor washed his clothes, from the day the king departed until the day he returned in peace.

25 So it was, when he had come to Jerusalem to meet the king, that the king said to him, "Why did you not go with me, Mephibosheth?"

26 And he answered, "My lord, O king, my servant deceived me. For your servant said, 'I will saddle a donkey for myself, that I may ride on it and go to the king,' because your servant *is* lame.

27 "And he [m]has slandered your servant to my lord the king, but my lord the king *is* [n]like the [o]angel of God. Therefore do *what is* good in your eyes.

28 "For all my father's house were but dead men before my lord the king. Yet you [p]set your servant among those who eat at your own table. Therefore what right have I still to cry out anymore to the king?"

29 So the king said to him, "Why do you speak anymore of your matters? I have said, 'You and Ziba divide the land.' "

30 Then Mephibosheth said to the king, "Rather, let him take it all, inasmuch as my lord the king has come back in peace to his own house."

31 And [q]Barzillai the Gileadite came down from Rogelim and went across the Jordan with the king, to escort him across the Jordan.

32 Now Barzillai was a very aged man, eighty years old. And he had provided the king with supplies while he stayed at Mahanaim, for he *was* a very rich man.

33 And the king said to Barzillai, "Come across with me, and I will provide for you while you are with me in Jerusalem."

34 But Barzillai said to the king, "How long have I to live, that I should go up with the king to Jerusalem?

35 "I *am* today eighty years old. Can I discern between the good and bad? Can your servant taste what I eat or what I drink? Can I hear any longer the voice of singing men and singing women? Why then should your servant be a further burden to my lord the king?

36 "Your servant will go a little way across the Jordan with the king. And why should the king repay me *with* such a reward?

37 "Please let your servant turn back again, that I may die in my own city, near the grave of my father and mother. But here is your servant [r]Chimham; let him cross over with my lord the king, and do for him what seems good to you."

38 And the king answered, "Chimham shall cross over with me, and I will do for him what seems good to you. Now whatever you request of me, I will do for you."

39 Then all the people went over the Jordan. And when the king had crossed over, the king kissed Barzillai and blessed him, and he returned to his own place.

40 Now the king went on to Gilgal, and Chimham* went on with him. And all the people of Judah escorted the king, and also half the people of Israel.

17
a 2 Sam. 3:19; 1 Ki. 12:21
b 2 Sam. 9:2–10
19
c For divine imputation, see Jas. 2:23, *note;* cp. 1 Sam. 22:15
d 2 Sam. 16:5
e 2 Sam. 13:33
20
f Jud. 1:22; 1 Ki. 11:28
21
g Ex. 22:28
h 1 Sam. 26:9
22
i i.e. *What have we in common?*
j 2 Sam. 3:39; 16:10
k 1 Sam. 11:13
24
l 2 Sam. 9:6; 21:7
27
m 2 Sam. 16:3
n 2 Sam. 14:17
o See Heb. 1:4, *note*
28
p 2 Sam. 9:7–13
31
q 2 Sam. 17:27; 1 Ki. 2:7
37
r Cp. Jer. 41:17

*
19:40 Masoretic Text reads *Chimhan.*

Strife between Judah and Israel about their part in David, the king

41 Just then all the men of Israel came to the king, and said to the king, [a]"Why have our brethren, the men of Judah, stolen you away and [b]brought the king, his household, and all David's men with him across the Jordan?"

42 So all the men of Judah answered the men of Israel, "Because the king *is* a close relative of ours. Why then are you angry over this matter? Have we ever eaten at the king's *expense?* Or has he given us any gift?"

43 And the men of Israel answered the men of Judah, and said, "We have [c]ten shares in the king; therefore we also have more *right* to David than you. Why then do you despise us—were we not the first to advise bringing back our king?" Yet the words of the men of Judah were fiercer than the words of the men of Israel.

Revolt under Sheba mars David's return to Jerusalem

20 AND there happened to be there a rebel,* whose name *was* Sheba the son of Bichri, a Benjamite. And he blew a trumpet, and said:

"We have no [d]share in David,
Nor do we have inheritance in
the son of Jesse;
Every man to his [e]tents, O
Israel!"

2 So every man of Israel deserted David, *and* followed Sheba the son of Bichri. But the [f]men of Judah, from the Jordan as far as Jerusalem, remained loyal to their king.

3 Now David came to his house at Jerusalem. And the king took the ten women, his [g]concubines whom he had left to keep the house, and put them in seclusion and supported them, but did not go in to them. So they were shut up to the day of their death, living in widowhood.

Joab murders Amasa

4 And the king said to Amasa, [h]"Assemble the men of Judah for me within three days, and be present here yourself."

5 So Amasa went to assemble *the men of* Judah. But he delayed longer than the set time which David had appointed him.

6 And David said to [i]Abishai, "Now Sheba the son of Bichri will do us more harm than Absalom. Take your lord's servants and pursue him, lest he find for himself fortified cities, and escape us."

7 So Joab's men, with the [j]Cherethites, the Pelethites, and [k]all the mighty men, went out after him. And they went out of Jerusalem to pursue Sheba the son of Bichri.

8 When they *were* at the large stone which *is* in Gibeon, Amasa came before them. Now Joab was dressed in battle armor; on it was a belt *with* a sword fastened in its sheath at his hips; and as he was going forward, it fell out.

9 Then Joab said to Amasa, "*Are* you in health, my brother?" And Joab took Amasa by the beard with his right hand to kiss him.

10 But Amasa did not notice the sword that *was* in Joab's hand. And he [l]struck him with it in the stomach, and his entrails poured out on the ground; and he did not *strike* him again. Thus he died. Then Joab and Abishai his brother pursued Sheba the son of Bichri.

11 Meanwhile one of Joab's men stood near Amasa, and said, "Whoever favors Joab and whoever *is* for David—follow Joab!"

12 But Amasa wallowed in *his* blood in the middle of the highway. And when the man saw that all the people stood still, he moved Amasa from the highway to the field and threw a garment over him, when he saw that everyone who came upon him halted.

13 When he was removed from the highway, all the people went on after Joab to pursue Sheba the son of Bichri.

Sheba's revolt is suppressed

14 And he went through all the tribes of Israel to [m]Abel and Beth Maachah and all the Berites. So they were gathered together and also went after *Sheba.**

15 Then they came and besieged him in Abel of Beth Maachah; and they cast up a siege [n]mound against the city, and it stood by the rampart. And all the people who *were* with Joab battered the wall to throw it down.

16 Then a wise woman cried out from the city, "Hear, hear! Please say to Joab, 'Come nearby, that I may speak with you.' "

41
a Cp. Jud. 8:1; 12:1
b vv. 11–15
43
c 2 Sam. 5:1; 1 Ki. 11:30–31
CHAPTER 20
1
d 1 Ki. 12:16
e 2 Sam. 18:17
2
f 2 Sam. 19:14
3
g 2 Sam. 15:16; 16:21,22
4
h 2 Sam. 19:13
6
i 2 Sam. 21:17
7
j 2 Sam. 8:18; 1 Ki. 1:38,44
k 2 Sam. 15:18
10
l 2 Sam. 3:27; 1 Ki. 2:5
14
m 1 Ki. 15:20; 2 Ki. 15:29
15
n 2 Ki. 19:32

*
20:1 Literally *man of Belial* **20:14** Literally *him*

17 When he had come near to her, the woman said, "*Are* you Joab?" He answered, "I *am*." Then she said to him, "Hear the words of your maidservant." And he answered, "I am listening."

18 So she spoke, saying, "They used to talk in former times, saying, 'They shall surely seek *guidance* at Abel,' and so they would end *disputes*.

19 "I *am among the* peaceable *and* faithful in Israel. You [a]seek to destroy a city and a mother in Israel. Why would you swallow up the [b]inheritance of the LORD?"

20 And Joab answered and said, "Far be it, far be it from me, that I should swallow up or destroy!

21 "That *is* not so. But a man from the mountains of Ephraim, Sheba the son of Bichri by name, has raised his hand against the king, against David. Deliver him only, and I will depart from the city." So the woman said to Joab, "Watch, his head will be thrown to you over the wall."

22 Then the woman in her [c]wisdom went to all the people. And they cut off the head of Sheba the son of Bichri, and threw *it* out to Joab. Then he blew a trumpet, and they withdrew from the city, every man to his tent. So Joab returned to the king at Jerusalem.

23 [d]And [e]Joab *was* over all the army of Israel; Benaiah the son of Jehoiada *was* over the Cherethites and the Pelethites;

24 Adoram *was* in charge of [f]revenue; Jehoshaphat the son of Ahilud *was* recorder;

25 Sheva *was* scribe; Zadok and Abiathar *were* the priests;

26 and [g]Ira the Jairite was a chief minister under David.

Restitution to Gibeonites

21 NOW there was a famine in the days of David for three years, year after year; and David [h]inquired of the LORD. And the LORD answered, "*It is* because of Saul and *his* bloodthirsty house, because he killed the Gibeonites."

2 So the king called the Gibeonites and spoke to them. Now the Gibeonites *were* [i]not of the children of Israel, but of the remnant of the Amorites; the children of Israel had sworn protection to them, but Saul had sought to kill them [j]in his zeal for the children of Israel and Judah.

3 Therefore David said to the Gibeonites, "What shall I do for you? And with what shall I make [k]atonement, that you may bless the [l]inheritance of the LORD?"

4 And the Gibeonites said to him, "We will have [m]no silver or gold from Saul or from his house, nor shall you kill any man in Israel for us." So he said, "Whatever you say, I will do for you."

5 Then they answered the king, "As for the man who consumed us and plotted against us, *that* we should be destroyed from remaining in any of the territories of Israel,

6 "let [n]seven men of his descendants be delivered [o]to us, and we will hang them before the LORD in [p]Gibeah of Saul, *whom* the LORD [q]chose." And the king said, "I will give *them*."

7 But the king spared [r]Mephibosheth the son of Jonathan, the son of Saul, because of the [s]LORD's oath that *was* between them, between David and Jonathan the son of Saul.

8 So the king took Armoni and Mephibosheth, the two sons of [t]Rizpah the daughter of Aiah, whom she bore to Saul, and the five [1]sons of Michal the daughter of Saul, whom she brought up for Adriel the son of Barzillai the Meholathite;

9 and he delivered them into the hands of the Gibeonites, and they hanged them on the hill before the LORD. So they fell, *all* seven together, and were put to death in the days of harvest, in the first *days*, in the beginning of barley harvest.

10 Now Rizpah the daughter of Aiah took sackcloth and spread it for herself on the rock, from the beginning of harvest until the late rains poured on them from heaven. And she [u]did not allow the birds of the air to rest on them by day nor the beasts of the field by [v]night.

11 And David was told what Rizpah the daughter of Aiah, the concubine of Saul, had done.

12 Then David went and [w]took the bones of Saul, and the bones of Jonathan his son, from the men of Jabesh Gilead who had stolen them from the

19
a Cp. Dt. 20:10
b 1 Sam. 26:19; 2 Sam. 14:16
22
c Cp. Eccl. 9:13–16
23
d For vv. 23–26, cp. 1 Ki. 4:3–6; 1 Chr. 18:14–17
e 2 Sam. 8:16–18
24
f 1 Ki. 12:18
26
g Cp. 2 Sam. 23:38
CHAPTER 21
1
h Num. 27:21; 2 Sam. 5:19
2
i Josh. 9:3–27
j Ex. 34:11–16
3
k See Ex. 29:33, *note*
l 1 Sam. 26:19; 2 Sam. 20:19
4
m Cp. Num. 35:31,32
6
n Cp. Gen. 4:15,24; Ps. 79:12
o Num. 25:4
p 1 Sam. 10:26
q 1 Sam. 10:24; Hos. 13:11
7
r 2 Sam. 4:4; 9:10; 19:24
s 1 Sam. 20:15–16
8
t 2 Sam. 3:7
10
u Cp. Dt. 21:23
v Cp. 1 Sam. 17:44–46
12
w 1 Sam. 31:11–13

[1](21:8) Compare 2 Sam. 6:23. The five sons of Michal were her sister Merab's, wife of Adriel (1 Sam. 18:19), "whom she brought up for Adriel."

street of Beth Shan,* where the [a]Philistines had hung them up, after the Philistines had struck down Saul in Gilboa.

13 So he brought up the bones of Saul and the bones of Jonathan his son from there; and they gathered the bones of those who had been hanged.

14 They buried the bones of Saul and Jonathan his son in the country of Benjamin in [b]Zelah, in the tomb of Kish his father. So they performed all that the king commanded. And after that God [c]heeded the prayer for the land.

Final campaigns against Philistines

15 When the Philistines were at war again with Israel, David and his servants with him went down and fought against the Philistines; and David grew faint.

16 Then Ishbi-Benob, who *was* one of the sons of the [d]giant, the weight of whose bronze spear *was* three hundred *shekels,* who was bearing a new *sword,* thought he could kill David.

17 But [e]Abishai the son of Zeruiah came to his aid, and struck the Philistine and killed him. Then the men of David swore to him, saying, [f]"You shall go out no more with us to battle, lest you quench the [g]lamp of Israel."

18 Now it happened afterward that there was again a battle with the Philistines at Gob. Then [h]Sibbechai the Hushathite killed Saph,* who *was* one of the sons of the giant.

19 Again there was war at Gob with the Philistines, where [i]Elhanan the son of Jaare-Oregim* the Bethlehemite killed *the brother of* [j]Goliath the Gittite, the shaft of whose spear *was* like a weaver's beam.

20 Yet again there was war at Gath, where there was a man of *great* stature, who had six fingers on each hand and six toes on each foot, twenty-four in number; and he also was born to the giant.

21 So when he [k]defied Israel, Jonathan the son of [l]Shimea, David's brother, killed him.

22 These four were born to the giant in Gath, and fell by the hand of David and by the hand of his [m]servants.

David's song of deliverance

22 [n]THEN David spoke to the LORD the words of this song, on the day when the LORD had [o]delivered him from the hand of all his enemies, and from the hand of Saul.

2 And he said:

"The LORD *is* my [p]rock and my
[q]fortress and my deliverer;
3 The God of my strength, [r]in
whom I will [s]trust;
My [t]shield and the [u]horn of
my salvation,
My stronghold and my
[v]refuge;
My Savior, You save me from
violence.
4 I will call upon the LORD, *who
is worthy* to be praised;
So shall I be saved from my
enemies.

5 "When the waves of death
surrounded me,
The floods of ungodliness
made me afraid.
6 The sorrows of [w]Sheol
surrounded me;
The snares of death confronted
me.
7 [x]In my distress I called upon
the LORD,
And cried out to my God;
He [y]heard my voice from His
temple,
And my cry *entered* His ears.

8 "Then the earth shook and
[z]trembled;
The foundations of heaven*
quaked and were shaken,
Because He was angry.
9 Smoke went up from His
nostrils,
And devouring [aa]fire from His
mouth;
Coals were kindled by it.
10 He bowed the heavens also,
and [bb]came down
With darkness under His feet.
11 He rode upon a cherub, and
flew;
And He was seen* upon the
wings of the [cc]wind.
12 He made darkness [dd]canopies
around Him,

12 *a* 1 Sam. 13:10 **14** *b* Josh. 18:28 *c* 2 Sam. 24:25 **16** *d* Num. 13:22,28; Josh. 15:14 **17** *e* 2 Sam. 20:6,10 *f* 2 Sam. 18:3 *g* 1 Ki. 11:36 **18** *h* 1 Chr. 20:4 **19** *i* 2 Sam. 23:24 *j* 1 Sam. 17:4 **21** *k* 1 Sam. 17:10 *l* Or *Shammah,* 1 Sam. 16:9; *Shimeah,* 2 Sam. 13:3 **22** *m* 1 Chr. 20:8 **CHAPTER 22** **1** *n* This chapter is almost identical with Ps. 18 *o* Ps. 34:19 **2** *p* Dt. 32:4; 1 Sam. 2:2 *q* Ps. 91:2 **3** *r* Ps. 7:1; Heb. 2:13 *s* See Ps. 2:12, *note* *t* Gen. 15:1; Ps. 84:11 *u* See Dt. 33:17, *note* *v* Ps. 46:1,7, 11 **6** *w* See Hab. 2:5, *note;* cp. Lk. 16:23, *note* **7** *x* Ps. 116:4; 120:1 *y* Ps. 34:6,15 **8** *z* Jud. 5:4 **9** *aa* Dt. 32:22; Ps. 97:3–4; Heb. 12:29 **22:10** *bb* Ex. 19:16–20 **22:11** *cc* Ps. 104:3 **22:12** *dd* Job 36:29

*

21:12 Spelled *Beth Shean* in Joshua 17:11 and elsewhere **21:18** Spelled *Sippai* in 1 Chronicles 20:4 **21:19** Spelled *Jair* in 1 Chronicles 20:5 **22:8** Following Masoretic Text, Septuagint, and Targum; Syriac and Vulgate read *hills* (compare Psalm 18:7). **22:11** Following Masoretic Text and Septuagint; many Hebrew manuscripts, Syriac, and Vulgate read *He flew* (compare Psalm 18:10); Targum reads *He spoke with power.*

Dark waters *and* thick clouds
of the skies.
13 From the brightness before
Him
Coals of fire were kindled.
14 "The LORD [a]thundered from
heaven,
And the Most High uttered His
voice.
15 He sent out [b]arrows and
scattered them;
Lightning bolts, and He
vanquished them.
16 Then the channels of the sea
[c]were seen,
The foundations of the world
were uncovered,
At the rebuke of the LORD,
At the blast of the breath of
His nostrils.
17 "He sent from above, He took
me,
He drew me out of many
[d]waters.
18 He delivered me from my
strong enemy,
From those who hated me;
For they were too strong for
me.
19 They confronted me in the day
of my calamity,
But the LORD was my [e]support.
20 He also brought me out into a
[f]broad place;
He delivered me because He
delighted in me.
21 "The LORD rewarded me
[g]according to my
righteousness;
According to the [h]cleanness of
my hands
He has recompensed me.
22 For I have kept the ways of the
LORD,
And [i]have not wickedly
departed from my God.
23 For all His judgments *were*
before me;
And *as for* His statutes, I did
not depart from them.
24 I was also [j]blameless before
Him,
And I kept myself from my
iniquity.
25 Therefore the LORD has
recompensed me according
to my righteousness,
According to my cleanness in
His eyes.*
26 "With the merciful You will
show Yourself [k]merciful;

14
a Ps. 29:3
15
b Dt. 32:23
16
c Nah. 1:4
17
d Isa. 43:2
19
e Isa. 10:20
20
f Ps. 118:5
21
g 1 Sam. 26:23
h Job 17:9
22
i 2 Chr. 34:33
24
j Gen. 6:9; Eph. 1:4
26
k Mt. 5:7
27
l Mt. 5:8
28
m Ps. 72:12–13
29
n Ps. 132:17; cp. 119:105
30
o 2 Sam. 5:6–8
31
p Mt. 5:48
q Ps. 12:6
34
r Hab. 3:19

With a blameless man You will
show Yourself blameless;
27 With the pure You will show
Yourself [l]pure;
And with the devious You will
show Yourself shrewd.
28 You will [m]save the humble
people;
But Your eyes *are* on the
haughty, *that* You may
bring *them* down.

29 "For You *are* my [n]lamp, O
LORD;
The LORD shall enlighten my
darkness.
30 For by You I can run against a
troop;
By my God I can leap over a
[o]wall.
31 *As for* God, His way *is*
[p]perfect;
The word of the LORD *is*
[q]proven;
He *is* a shield to all who trust
in Him.

32 "For who *is* God, except the
LORD?
And who *is* a rock, except our
God?
33 God *is* my strength *and*
power,*
And He makes my* way
perfect.
34 He makes my* [r]feet like the
feet of deer,
And sets me on my high
places.
35 He teaches my hands to make
war,
So that my arms can bend a
bow of bronze.

36 "You have also given me the
shield of Your salvation;
Your gentleness has made me
great.
37 You enlarged my path under
me;
So my feet did not slip.

38 "I have pursued my enemies
and destroyed them;

22:25 Septuagint, Syriac, and Vulgate read *the cleanness of my hands in His sight* (compare Psalm 18:24); Targum reads *my cleanness before His word.* **22:33** Dead Sea Scrolls, Septuagint, Syriac, and Vulgate read *It is God who arms me with strength* (compare Psalm 18:32); Targum reads *It is God who sustains me with strength.* • Following Qere, Septuagint, Syriac, Targum, and Vulgate (compare Psalm 18:32); Kethib reads *His.*
22:34 Following Qere, Septuagint, Syriac, Targum, and Vulgate (compare Psalm 18:33); Kethib reads *His.*

Neither did I turn back again
till they were destroyed.
39 And I have destroyed them
and wounded them,
So that they could not rise;
They have fallen under my
feet.
40 For You have armed me with
strength for the battle;
You have subdued under me
those who rose against me.
41 You have also given me the
necks of my enemies,
So that I destroyed those who
hated me.
42 They looked, but *there was*
none to save;
Even to the LORD, but He did
[a]not answer them.
43 Then I beat them as fine as the
[b]dust of the earth;
I trod them like dirt in the
streets,
And I spread them out.

44 "You have also delivered me
from the [c]strivings of my
people;
You have kept me as the head
of the [d]nations.
A people I have not known
shall serve me.
45 The foreigners submit to me;
As soon as they hear, they
obey me.
46 The foreigners fade away,
And [e]come frightened* from
their hideouts.

47 "The LORD lives!
Blessed *be* my Rock!
Let God be exalted,
The Rock of my salvation!
48 *It is* God who [f]avenges me,
And subdues the peoples under
me;
49 He delivers me from my
enemies.
You also lift me up above
those who rise against me;
You have delivered me from
the violent man.
50 Therefore I will give thanks to
You, O LORD, among the
Gentiles,
And [g]sing praises to Your
[h]name.

51 *He is* the tower of salvation to
His king,
And shows mercy to His
anointed,
To David and his descendants
[i]forevermore."

42
a 1 Sam. 28:6
43
b 2 Ki. 13:7
44
c 2 Sam. 3:1
d 2 Sam. 8:1–14
46
e Mic. 7:17
48
f 1 Sam. 24:12
50
g Ps. 57:7
h Rom. 15:9
51
i 2 Sam. 7:12–16
CHAPTER 23
1
j Kingdom (OT): vv. 1–5; 1 Ki. 8:20. (Gen. 1:26; Zech. 12:8, *note*)
k 2 Sam. 7:8–9
2
l Holy Spirit (OT): v. 2; 1 Ki. 18:12. (Gen. 1:2; Zech. 12:10)
m Inspiration: v. 2; Job 6:10. (Ex. 4:15; 2 Tim. 3:16, *note*)
3
n Christ (Rock): v. 3; Ps. 62:2. (Gen. 49:24; 1 Pet. 2:8). 2 Sam. 22:2–3
o Isa. 11:1–5
p See Ps. 19:9, *note*
4
q Isa. 60:1
5
r 2 Sam. 7:12; Ps. 89:29; Isa. 55:3

David's last prophetic words

23 NOW these *are* the last words
of David.

Thus says [j]David the son of
Jesse;
Thus says the man [k]raised up
on high,
The anointed of the God of
Jacob,
And the sweet psalmist of
Israel:
2 "The [l]Spirit of the LORD spoke
by me,
And His [m]word *was* on my
tongue.
3 The God of Israel said,
The [n]Rock of Israel spoke to
me:
'He who rules over men *must*
be [o]just,
Ruling in the [p]fear of God.
4 And [q]*he shall be* like the light
of the morning *when* the sun
rises,
A morning without clouds,
Like the tender grass *springing*
out of the earth,
By clear shining after rain.'

5 "Although my house *is* not so
with God,
Yet He has made with me an
[r]everlasting covenant,
Ordered in all *things* and
secure.
For *this is* all my salvation and
all *my* desire;
Will He not make *it* increase?
6 But *the sons* of rebellion *shall*
all *be* as thorns thrust away,
Because they cannot be taken
with hands.
7 But the man *who* touches them
Must be armed with iron and
the shaft of a spear,
And they shall be utterly
burned with fire in *their*
place."

Roll of David's mighty men
(cp. 1 Chr. 11:10–47)

8 These *are* the names of the
mighty men whom David had:
Josheb-Basshebeth* the Tachmonite,
chief among the captains.* He was
called Adino the Eznite, because he

*

22:46 Following Septuagint, Targum, and Vulgate (compare Psalm 18:45); Masoretic Text reads *gird themselves.* **23:8** Literally *One Who Sits in the Seat* (compare 1 Chronicles 11:11) • Following Masoretic Text and Targum; Septuagint and Vulgate read *the three.*

had killed [a]eight hundred men at one time.

9 And after him *was* Eleazar the son of [b]Dodo, the Ahohite, *one* of the three mighty men with David when they defied the Philistines *who* were gathered there for battle, and the men of Israel had retreated.

10 He arose and attacked the Philistines until his hand was [c]weary, and his hand stuck to the sword. The LORD brought about a great victory that day; and the people returned after him only to [d]plunder.

11 And after him *was* Shammah the son of Agee the Hararite. The Philistines had gathered together into a troop where there was a piece of ground full of lentils. So the people fled from the Philistines.

12 But he stationed himself in the middle of the field, defended it, and killed the Philistines. So the LORD brought about a great victory.

13 Then three of the thirty chief men went down at harvest time and came to David at the [e]cave of Adullam. And the troop of Philistines encamped in the [f]Valley of Rephaim.

14 David *was* then in the stronghold, and the garrison of the Philistines *was* then *in* Bethlehem.

15 And David said with longing, "Oh, that someone would give me a drink of the water from the well of Bethlehem, which *is* by the gate!"

16 So the three mighty men broke through the camp of the Philistines, drew water from the well of Bethlehem that *was* by the gate, and took it and brought *it* to David. Nevertheless he would not drink it, but poured it out to the LORD.

17 And he said, "Far be it from me, O LORD, that I should do this! Is *this not* the blood of the men who went in *jeopardy of* their lives?" Therefore he would not drink it. These things were done by the three mighty men.

18 Now [g]Abishai the brother of Joab, the son of Zeruiah, was chief of *another* three.* He lifted his spear against three hundred *men*, killed *them*, and won a name among *these* three.

19 Was he not the most honored of three? Therefore he became their captain. However, he did not attain to the *first* three.

20 Benaiah *was* the son of Jehoiada, the son of a valiant man from [h]Kabzeel, who had done many deeds. He had killed two lion-like heroes of Moab. He also had gone down and killed a lion in the midst of a pit on a snowy day.

21 And he killed an Egyptian, a spectacular man. The Egyptian *had* a spear in his hand; so he went down to him with a staff, wrested the spear out of the Egyptian's hand, and killed him with his own spear.

22 These *things* Benaiah the son of Jehoiada did, and won a name among three mighty men.

23 He was more honored than the thirty, but he did not attain to the *first* three. And David appointed him [i]over his guard.

24 [j]Asahel the brother of Joab *was* one of the thirty; Elhanan the son of Dodo of Bethlehem,

25 Shammah the Harodite, Elika the Harodite,

26 Helez the Paltite, Ira the son of Ikkesh the Tekoite,

27 Abiezer the Anathothite, Mebunnai the Hushathite,

28 Zalmon the Ahohite, Maharai the Netophathite,

29 Heleb the son of Baanah (the Netophathite), Ittai the son of Ribai from Gibeah of the children of Benjamin,

30 Benaiah a Pirathonite, Hiddai from the brooks of [k]Gaash,

31 Abi-Albon the Arbathite, Azmaveth the Barhumite,

32 Eliahba the Shaalbonite (of the sons of Jashen), Jonathan,

33 [l]Shammah the Hararite, Ahiam the son of Sharar the Hararite,

34 Eliphelet the son of Ahasbai, the son of the Maachathite, [m]Eliam the son of Ahithophel the Gilonite,

35 Hezrai* the Carmelite, Paarai the Arbite,

36 Igal the son of Nathan of [n]Zobah, Bani the Gadite,

37 Zelek the Ammonite, Naharai the Beerothite (armorbearer of Joab the son of Zeruiah),

38 [o]Ira the Ithrite, Gareb the Ithrite,

39 *and* [p]Uriah the [q]Hittite: thirty-seven in all.

Three days' plague
(1 Chr. 21:1–17)

24 [r]AGAIN the anger of the LORD was aroused against Israel,

8
a See 1 Chr. 11:11, *note*
9
b Or *Dodai*, 1 Chr. 27:4
10
c Jud. 8:4
d 1 Sam. 30:24–25
13
e 1 Sam. 22:1
f 2 Sam. 5:18
18
g 2 Sam. 21:17
20
h Josh. 15:21
23
i 2 Sam. 8:18; 20:23
24
j 2 Sam. 2:18
30
k Jud. 2:9
33
l 2 Sam. 23:11
34
m 2 Sam. 11:3
36
n 2 Sam. 8:3
38
o 2 Sam. 20:26
39
p 2 Sam. 11:3,6
q See 2 Ki. 7:6, *note*
CHAPTER 24
1
r 2 Sam. 21:1

*

23:18 Following Masoretic Text, Septuagint, and Vulgate; some Hebrew manuscripts and Syriac read *thirty*; Targum reads *the mighty men*.
23:35 Spelled *Hezro* in 1 Chronicles 11:37

and [1][a]He [b]moved David against them
to say, "Go, [c]number Israel and Judah."
2 So the king said to Joab the commander of the army who *was* with
him, "Now [d]go throughout all the
tribes of Israel, [e]from Dan to Beersheba, and count the people, that [f]I
may know the number of the people."
3 And Joab said to the king, "Now
may the LORD your God [g]add to the
people a hundred times more than
there are, and may the eyes of my lord
the king see *it*. But why does my lord
the king desire this thing?"
4 Nevertheless the king's word
prevailed against Joab and against the
captains of the army. Therefore Joab
and the captains of the army went out
from the presence of the king to count
the people of Israel.
5 And they crossed over the Jordan and camped in [h]Aroer, on the
right side of the town which *is* in the
midst of the ravine of Gad, and toward
[i]Jazer.
6 Then they came to Gilead and to
the land of Tahtim Hodshi; they came
to Dan Jaan and around to [j]Sidon;
7 and they came to the stronghold
of [k]Tyre and to all the cities of the
[l]Hivites and the Canaanites. Then
they went out to South Judah *as far as*
Beersheba.
8 So when they had gone through
all the land, they came to Jerusalem at
the end of nine months and twenty
days.
9 Then Joab gave the [m]sum of the
number of the people to the king. And
there were in Israel [n]eight hundred
thousand valiant men who drew the
sword, and the men of Judah were
[n]five hundred thousand men.
10 And David's heart [o]condemned
him after he had numbered the people. So [p]David said to the LORD, [q]"I
have sinned greatly in what I have
done; but now, I pray, O LORD, take
away the iniquity of Your servant, for
I have done very foolishly."
11 Now when David arose in the
morning, the word of the LORD came to
the prophet Gad, David's seer, saying,
12 "Go and tell David, 'Thus says
the LORD: "I offer you three *things;*
choose one of them for yourself, that
I may do *it* to you." ' "
13 So Gad came to David and told
him; and he said to him, "Shall
[r]seven* years of [s]famine come to you
in your land? Or shall you flee three
months before your enemies, while
they pursue you? Or shall there be
three days' plague in your land? Now
consider and see what answer I
should take back to Him who sent
me."
14 And David said to Gad, "I am in
great distress. Please let us fall into
the hand of the LORD, for His [t]mercies
are great; but do not let me fall into the
hand of man."
15 So the LORD sent a plague upon
Israel from the morning till the appointed time. From Dan to Beersheba
seventy thousand men of the people
died.
16 And when the [u]angel stretched
out His hand over Jerusalem to destroy it, the LORD [v]relented from the
destruction, and said to the angel who
was destroying the people, "It is
enough; now restrain your hand."
And the angel of the LORD was by the
threshing floor of Araunah the Jebusite.
17 Then David [w]spoke to the LORD
when he saw the angel who was striking the people, and said, "Surely I
have sinned, and I have done wickedly; but these [x]sheep, what have
they done? Let Your hand, I pray, be
against me and against my father's
house."

Plague averted by David's offering
(1 Chr. 21:18–30)

18 And Gad came that day to David
and said to him, "Go up, erect an altar
to the LORD on the threshing floor of
[y]Araunah the Jebusite."
19 So David, according to the word
of Gad, went up as the LORD commanded.
20 Now Araunah looked, and saw
the king and his servants coming toward him. So Araunah went out and
bowed before the king with his face to
the ground.
21 Then Araunah said, "Why has
my lord the king come to his servant?"
And David said, "To buy the threshing

1 *a* Cp. Jas. 1:13–14 *b Test/tempt:* v. 1; 1 Chr. 21:1. (Gen. 3:1; Jas. 1:14, *note*) *c* Num. 26:2
2 *d* Cp. 1 Chr. 27:23–24 *e* Jud. 20:1 *f* Cp. Jer. 17:5
3 *g* Dt. 1:11
5 *h* Dt. 2:36; Josh. 13:9 *i* Num. 32:1, 3
6 *j* Josh. 19:28; Jud. 18:28
7 *k* Josh. 19:29 *l* Josh. 11:3; Jud. 3:3
9 *m* Cp. Num. 1:44–46; 1 Sam. 11:8 *n* Cp. 1 Chr. 21:5; see 1 Chr. 11:11, *note*
10 *o* 1 Sam. 24:5 *p* 2 Sam. 23:1 *q* 2 Sam. 12:13
13 *r* Cp. 1 Chr. 21:12; see 1 Chr. 11:11, *note* *s* See Gen. 12:10, *note*
14 *t* Ps. 51:1
16 *u Angel* (of the LORD): vv. 16–17; 1 Ki. 19:5. (Gen. 16:7; Jud. 2:1, *note*) *v* See Zech. 8:14, *note*
17 *w Bible prayers* (OT): v. 17; 1 Ki. 3:5. (Gen. 15:2; Hab. 3:1) *x* Ps. 74:1 **24:18** *y* Or *Ornan*, 2 Chr. 3:1; cp. 1 Chr. 21:20

* **24:13** Following Masoretic Text, Syriac, Targum, and Vulgate; Septuagint reads *three* (compare 1 Chronicles 21:12).

[1](24:1) It is stated in 1 Chr. 21:1 that Satan moved David to do this. Evidently God permitted the devil to influence His servant in order that His own purposes might be carried out.

floor from you, to build an altar to the LORD, that the plague may be withdrawn from the people."

22 Now Araunah said to David, "Let my lord the king take and offer up whatever *seems* good to him. Look, *here are* oxen for burnt sacrifice, and threshing implements and the yokes of the oxen for wood.

23 "All these, O king, Araunah has given to the king." And Araunah said to the king, "May the LORD your God [a]accept you."

24 Then the king said to Araunah, "No, but I will surely buy *it* from you for a price; nor will I [b]offer burnt offerings to the LORD my God with that which costs me nothing." So David bought the [c]threshing floor and the oxen for [d]fifty [e]shekels of silver.

25 And David built there an altar to the LORD, and offered burnt offerings and peace offerings. So the LORD [f]heeded the prayers for the land, and the [g]plague was withdrawn from Israel.

23 *a* Ezek. 20:40,41

24 *b* See 2 Cor. 8:1, *note* *c* See 1 Chr. 21:25, *note* *d* Cp. 1 Chr. 21:25; see 1 Chr. 11:11, *note* *e* See Coinage (OT), Ex. 30:13, *note*

24:25 *f* 2 Sam. 21:14 *g* Cp. Num. 16:44–50

The First Book of the

KINGS

Author: Unknown *Theme:* Kingdom United; Divided *Date of writing:* 6th Cent. B.C.

FIRST and SECOND KINGS were originally one book. They are appropriately called the Books of the Kings because they record the principal events and characteristics of the reigns of the kings of Judah and Israel from the death of David to the end of the kingdom of Judah and the fall of Jerusalem.

The three major narratives of 1 Kings cover the reign of Solomon, including an extended account of the building of the temple; the ministry of Elijah; and the reign of Ahab.

Judah's nineteen kings were all descendants of David and reigned 345 years. Israel had nineteen kings of nine dynasties, reigning 210 years, eight of whom were either slain or committed suicide. Judah had frequent revivals; the divided Israel, none.

The book may be divided as follows:

I. David's Last Days, 1:1—2:11.
II. The Reign of Solomon, 2:12—11:43.
III. The Division of the Kingdom under Rehoboam and Jeroboam, 12:1—14:31.
IV. The Kings of Judah and Israel to the Accession of Ahab, 15:1—16:27.
V. The Reign of Ahab, 16:28—22:39.
VI. The Reigns of Jehoshaphat and Ahaziah, 22:40–53.

I. David's Last Days, 1:1—2:11

David's strength declines

1 NOW King David was [a]old, advanced in years; and they put covers on him, but he could not get warm.
2 Therefore his servants said to
him, "Let a young woman, a virgin, be
sought for our lord the king, and let
her stand before the king, and let her
care for him; and let her lie in your
bosom, that our lord the king may be
warm."
3 So they sought for a lovely
young woman throughout all the territory of Israel, and found [b]Abishag the
[c]Shunammite, and brought her to the
king.
4 The young woman *was* very
lovely; and she cared for the king, and
served him; but the king did not know
her.

Plot of Adonijah

5 Then Adonijah the [d]son of Haggith exalted himself, saying, "I will be
[1]king"; and [e]he prepared for himself
chariots and horsemen, and fifty men
to run before him.
6 (And his father had not rebuked
him at any time by saying, "Why have
you done so?" He *was* also very good-
looking. [f]*His mother* had borne him
after Absalom.)
7 Then he conferred with [g]Joab
the son of Zeruiah and with [h]Abiathar
the priest, and [i]they followed and
helped Adonijah.
8 But [j]Zadok the priest, [k]Benaiah
the son of Jehoiada, [l]Nathan the
prophet, [m]Shimei, Rei, and the
[n]mighty men who *belonged* to David
were not with Adonijah.
9 And Adonijah sacrificed sheep
and oxen and fattened cattle by the
stone of Zoheleth, which *is* by [o]En Rogel; he also invited all his brothers, the
king's sons, and all the men of Judah,
the king's servants.
10 But he did not invite Nathan the
prophet, Benaiah, the mighty men, or
[p]Solomon his brother.

Plan of Nathan and Bathsheba

11 So Nathan spoke to Bathsheba
the mother of Solomon, saying, "Have
you not heard that Adonijah the son of
Haggith has become king, and David
our lord does not know *it?*
12 "Come, please, let me now give
you advice, that you may save your
own life and the life of your son Solomon.
13 "Go immediately to King David
and say to him, 'Did you not, my lord,
O king, swear to your maidservant,
saying, [q]"Assuredly your son Solomon

CHAPTER 1
1 *a* 1 Chr. 23:1
3 *b* 1 Ki. 2:17 *c* Josh. 19:18
5 *d* 2 Sam. 3:4 *e* 2 Sam. 15:1
6 *f* 2 Sam. 3:3–4
7 *g* 1 Chr. 11:6 *h* 1 Sam. 22:20–23; 2 Sam. 20:25 *i* Cp. 1 Ki. 2:22–34
8 *j* 1 Ki. 2:35 *k* 1 Ki. 2:25; 2 Sam. 8:18 *l* 2 Sam. 12:1 *m* 1 Ki. 4:18 *n* 2 Sam. 23:8
9 *o* Josh. 15:7
10 *p* 2 Sam. 12:24
13 *q* 1 Chr. 22:9–10

---

[1](1:5) Adonijah was Solomon's older brother (2:22; cp. 1 Chr. 3:1–5), the oldest of David's living sons. Because he knew that David had previously proclaimed publicly that Solomon would succeed him (1 Chr. 22:1–19; 28:1–8), Adonijah plotted to seize the throne by a coup d'état. The plot failed. Nothing could thwart God's sovereign purpose for Solomon (1 Chr. 22:9–10; 28:5–7).

shall reign after me, and he shall sit
on my throne"? Why then has Adonijah become king?'
14 "Then, while you are still talking
there with the king, I also will come in
after you and confirm your words."
15 So Bathsheba went into the
chamber to the king. (Now the king
was very old, and Abishag the Shunammite was serving the king.)
16 And Bathsheba bowed and did
homage to the king. Then the king
said, "What is your wish?"
17 Then she said to him, "My lord,
you swore by the LORD your God to
your maidservant, *saying*, 'Assuredly
Solomon your son shall reign after
me, and he shall sit on my throne.'
18 "So now, look! Adonijah has become king; and now, my lord the king,
you do not know about *it*.
19 "He has sacrificed oxen and fattened cattle and sheep in abundance,
and has invited all the sons of the
king, Abiathar the priest, and Joab the
commander of the army; but Solomon
your servant he has not invited.
20 "And as for you, my lord, O king,
the eyes of all Israel *are* on you, that
you should tell them who will sit on
the throne of my lord the king after
him.
21 "Otherwise it will happen, when
my lord the king [a]rests with his fathers, that I and my son Solomon will
be counted as offenders."
22 And just then, while she was still
talking with the king, Nathan the
prophet also came in.
23 So they told the king, saying,
"Here is Nathan the prophet." And
when he came in before the king, he
bowed down before the king with his
face to the ground.
24 And Nathan said, "My lord, O
king, have you said, 'Adonijah shall
reign after me, and he shall sit on my
throne'?
25 "For he has gone down today,
and has sacrificed oxen and fattened
cattle and sheep in abundance, and
has invited all the king's sons, and the
commanders of the army, and Abiathar the priest; and look! They are eating and drinking before him; and they
say, '*Long* live King Adonijah!'
26 "But he has not invited me—me
your servant—nor Zadok the priest,
nor Benaiah the son of Jehoiada, nor
your servant Solomon.
27 "Has this thing been done by my
lord the king, and you have not told
your servant who should sit on the
throne of my lord the king after him?"
28 Then King David answered and
said, "Call Bathsheba to me." So she
came into the king's presence and
stood before the king.
29 And the king took an oath and
said, [b]"*As* the LORD lives, who has [c]re-
deemed my life from every distress,
30 "just as I swore to you by the
LORD God of Israel, saying, 'Assuredly
Solomon your son shall be king after
me, and he shall sit on my throne in
my place,' so I certainly will do this
day."
31 Then Bathsheba bowed with *her*
face to the earth, and paid [d]homage to
the king, and said, "Let my lord King
David live forever!"
32 And King David said, "Call to
me Zadok the priest, Nathan the
prophet, and Benaiah the son of Jehoiada." So they came before the king.
33 The king also said to them,
[e]"Take with you the servants of your
lord, and have Solomon my son ride
on my own [f]mule, and take him down
to Gihon.
34 "There let Zadok the priest and
Nathan the prophet [g]anoint him king
over Israel; and [h]blow the horn, and
say, '*Long* live King Solomon!'
35 "Then you shall come up after
him, and he shall come and sit on my
throne, and he shall be king in my
place. For I have appointed him to be
ruler over Israel and Judah."
36 Benaiah the son of Jehoiada answered the king and said, [i]"Amen!
May the LORD God of my lord the king
say so *too*.
37 [j]"As the LORD has been with my
lord the king, even so may He be with
Solomon, and make his throne greater
than the throne of my lord King David."

Solomon's second anointing as king (1 Chr. 29:22b)

38 So Zadok the priest, Nathan the
prophet, [k]Benaiah the son of Jehoiada, the [l]Cherethites, and the Pelethites went down and had Solomon
ride on King David's mule, and took
him to Gihon.
39 Then Zadok the priest took a
horn of oil from the [m]tabernacle and
[g]anointed Solomon. And they blew
the horn, and [n]all the people said,
"*Long* live King Solomon!"
40 And all the people went up after
him; and the people played the flutes
and rejoiced with great joy, so that the
earth *seemed to* split with their sound.

21
a Dt. 31:16; 1 Ki. 2:10
29
b 2 Sam. 4:9
c See Isa. 59:20, *note 1*, cp. Ex. 14:30, *note*
31
d 2 Sam. 9:6
33
e 2 Sam. 20:6
f Est. 6:8
34
g 1 Sam. 10:1; 16:13; 1 Chr. 29:22
h 2 Sam. 15:10; 2 Ki. 9:13; 11:14
36
i Jer. 28:6
37
j 1 Sam. 20:13; cp. Josh. 1:5
38
k 2 Sam. 8:18
l 2 Sam. 20:7,23; 1 Chr. 18:17
39
m Ex. 30:23–32; Ps. 89:20
n 1 Sam. 10:24

Adonijah's submission

41 Now Adonijah and all the guests who *were* with him heard *it* as they finished eating. And when Joab heard the sound of the horn, he said, "Why *is* the city in such a noisy uproar?"

42 While he was still speaking, there came [a]Jonathan, the son of Abiathar the priest. And Adonijah said to him, "Come in, for [b]you *are* a prominent man, and bring good news."

43 Then Jonathan answered and said to Adonijah, "No! Our lord King David has made Solomon king.

44 "The king has sent with him Zadok the priest, Nathan the prophet, Benaiah the son of Jehoiada, the Cherethites, and the Pelethites; and they have made him ride on the king's mule.

45 "So Zadok the priest and Nathan the prophet have anointed him king at Gihon; and they have gone up from there rejoicing, so that the city is in an uproar. This *is* the noise that you have heard.

46 "Also Solomon [c]sits on the throne of the kingdom.

47 "And moreover the king's servants have gone to bless our lord King David, saying, 'May God make the name of Solomon better than your name, and may He make his throne greater than your throne.' Then the king [d]bowed himself on the bed.

48 "Also the king said thus, 'Blessed *be* the LORD God of Israel, who has [e]given *one* to sit on my throne this day, while my eyes see [f]*it!*' "

49 So all the guests who were with Adonijah were afraid, and arose, and each one went his way.

50 Now Adonijah was afraid of Solomon; so he arose, and went and took hold of the [g]horns of the altar.

51 And it was told Solomon, saying, "Indeed Adonijah is afraid of King Solomon; for look, he has taken hold of the horns of the altar, saying, 'Let King Solomon swear to me today that he will not put his servant to death with the sword.' "

52 Then Solomon said, "If he proves himself a worthy man, [h]not one hair of him shall fall to the earth; but if wickedness is found in him, he shall die."

53 So King Solomon sent them to bring him down from the altar. And he came and fell down before King Solomon; and Solomon said to him, "Go to your house."

42 [a] 2 Sam. 17:17,20 [b] 2 Sam. 18:27
46 [c] 1 Ki. 2:12
47 [d] Gen. 47:31
48 [e] 1 Ki. 3:6; Ps. 132:11–12 [f] 2 Sam. 7:12
50 [g] 1 Ki. 2:28
52 [h] 1 Sam. 14:45; Acts 27:34

CHAPTER 2
1 [i] Cp. Gen. 47:29; Dt. 31:14
2 [j] Josh. 23:14 [k] 1 Chr. 22:13
3 [l] Dt. 29:9; Josh. 1:7; 1 Chr. 22:12–13
4 [m] 2 Sam. 7:25 [n] 2 Ki. 20:3 [o] 2 Sam. 7:12–13; 1 Ki. 8:25 [p] Ps. 132:12
5 [q] 2 Sam. 18:9–14 [r] 2 Sam. 3:27–39; 20:4–10
6 [s] See Hab. 2:5, *note;* cp. Lk. 16:23, *note*
7 [t] 2 Sam. 19:31–39 [u] 2 Sam. 17:27
8 [v] 2 Sam. 16:5–13 [w] 2 Sam. 19:18–23
9 [x] Ex. 20:7; Job 9:28
10 [y] Acts 2:29; 13:36
11 [z] 2 Sam. 5:4

David's charge to Solomon

2 NOW the [i]days of David drew near that he should die, and he charged Solomon his son, saying:

2 [j]"I go the way of all the earth; [k]be strong, therefore, and prove yourself a man.

3 "And keep the charge of the LORD your God: to walk in His ways, to keep His statutes, His commandments, His judgments, and His testimonies, as it is written in the Law of Moses, that you may [l]prosper in all that you do and wherever you turn;

4 "that the LORD may [m]fulfill His word which He spoke concerning me, saying, 'If your sons take heed to their way, to [n]walk before Me in truth with all their heart and with all their soul,' He said, [o]'you shall not lack a man on the throne of [p]Israel.'

5 "Moreover you know also what Joab the son of Zeruiah [q]did to me, *and* what he [r]did to the two commanders of the armies of Israel, to Abner the son of Ner and Amasa the son of Jether, whom he killed. And he shed the blood of war in peacetime, and put the blood of war on his belt that *was* around his waist, and on his sandals that *were* on his feet.

6 "Therefore do according to your wisdom, and do not let his gray hair go down to the [s]grave in peace.

7 "But show kindness to the sons of [t]Barzillai the Gileadite, and let them be among those who eat at your table, for so [u]they came to me when I fled from Absalom your brother.

8 "And see, *you have* with you [v]Shimei the son of Gera, a Benjamite from Bahurim, who cursed me with a malicious curse in the day when I went to Mahanaim. But [w]he came down to meet me at the Jordan, and I swore to him by the LORD, saying, 'I will not put you to death with the sword.'

9 "Now therefore, [x]do not hold him guiltless, for you *are* a wise man and know what you ought to do to him; but bring his gray hair down to the [s]grave with blood."

David dies (1 Chr. 29:26–30)

10 So David rested with his fathers, and was [y]buried in the City of David.

11 The period that David reigned over Israel *was* [z]forty years; seven years he reigned in Hebron, and in Jerusalem he reigned thirty-three years.

II. The Reign of Solomon, 2:12—11:43

Solomon's accession (1 Chr. 29:23–25)

12 Then Solomon [a]sat on the
throne of his father David; and his
kingdom was firmly [b]established.

Adonijah's execution

13 Now Adonijah the son of Haggith came to Bathsheba the mother of
Solomon. So she said, "Do you come
[c]peaceably?" And he said, "Peaceably."
14 Moreover he said, "I have something *to say* to you." And she said,
"Say it."
15 Then he said, "You know that
the kingdom was [d]mine, and all Israel
had set their expectations on me, that
I should reign. However, the kingdom
has been turned over, and has become
my brother's; for [e]it was his from the
LORD.
16 "Now I ask one petition of you;
do not deny me." And she said to him,
"Say it."
17 Then he said, "Please speak to
King Solomon, for he will not refuse
you, that he may give me [f]Abishag
the Shunammite as wife."
18 So Bathsheba said, "Very well, I
will speak for you to the king."
19 Bathsheba therefore went to
King Solomon, to speak to him for Adonijah. And the king rose up to meet
her and bowed down to her, and sat
down on his throne and had a throne
set for the king's mother; so she sat at
his [g]right hand.
20 Then she said, "I desire one
small petition of you; do not refuse
me." And the king said to her, "Ask it,
my mother, for I will not refuse you."
21 So she said, "Let Abishag the
Shunammite be given to Adonijah
your brother as wife."
22 And King Solomon answered
and said to his mother, "Now why do
you ask Abishag the Shunammite for
Adonijah? Ask for him the kingdom
[h]also—for he *is* my [i]older brother—
for him, and for [j]Abiathar the priest,
and for Joab the son of Zeruiah."
23 Then King Solomon swore by
the LORD, saying, "May God do so to
me, and more also, if Adonijah has not
spoken this word against his own
[k]life!
24 "Now therefore, *as* the LORD
lives, who has confirmed me and set
me on the throne of David my father,
and who has established a house* for
me, as He [l]promised, Adonijah shall
be put to death today!"
25 So King Solomon sent by the
hand of [m]Benaiah the son of Jehoiada;
and he struck him down, and he died.

Abiathar is removed from the priesthood

26 And to Abiathar the priest the
king said, "Go to [n]Anathoth, to your
own fields, for you *are* deserving of
death; but I will not put you to death
at this time, because you carried the
ark of the Lord GOD before my father
David, and [o]because you were afflicted every time my father was afflicted."
27 So Solomon removed Abiathar
from being priest to the LORD, that he
might [p]fulfill the word of the LORD
which He spoke concerning the house
of Eli at Shiloh.

Innocent blood finally avenged; Joab's execution

28 Then news came to Joab, for
Joab [j]had defected to Adonijah,
though he had not defected to Absalom. So Joab fled to the tabernacle of
the LORD, and [q]took hold of the horns
of the altar.
29 And King Solomon was told,
"Joab has fled to the tabernacle of the
LORD; there *he is*, by the altar." Then
Solomon sent Benaiah the son of Jehoiada, saying, "Go, [r]strike him
down."
30 So Benaiah went to the tabernacle of the LORD, and said to him, "Thus
says the king, [s]'Come out!' " And he
said, "No, but I will die here." And Benaiah brought back word to the king,
saying, "Thus said Joab, and thus he
answered me."
31 Then the king said to him, "Do as
he has said, and strike him down and
bury him, [t]that you may take away
from me and from the house of my
father the innocent blood which Joab
shed.
32 "So the LORD will [u]return his
blood on his head, because he struck
down two men more righteous and
better than he, and killed them with
the sword—[v]Abner the son of Ner,
the commander of the army of Israel,
and [w]Amasa the son of Jether, the
commander of the army of Judah—
though my father David did not know
it.
33 "Their blood shall therefore return upon the head of Joab and [x]upon
the head of his descendants forever.

12 *a* 1 Ki. 1:46 *b* 971 B.C. 1 Ki. 2:46; 2 Chr. 1:1
13 *c* 1 Sam. 16:4–5
15 *d* 1 Ki. 1:11, 18 *e* 1 Chr. 22:9–10; 28:5–7; Dan. 2:21
17 *f* 1 Ki. 1:3–4
19 *g* Cp. Ps. 45:9
22 *h* Cp. 2 Sam. 12:8 *i* 1 Chr. 3:2–5 *j* 1 Ki. 1:7
23 *k* Cp. 1 Ki. 1:52
24 *l* 2 Sam. 7:11–13; 1 Chr. 22:10
25 *m* 2 Sam. 8:18; 1 Ki. 4:4
26 *n* Josh. 21:18 *o* 1 Sam. 22:23; 23:6; 2 Sam. 15:24,29
27 *p* 1 Sam. 2:31–35
28 *q* 1 Ki. 1:50
29 *r* 1 Ki. 2:5–6
30 *s* Ex. 21:14
31 *t* Num. 35:33; Dt. 19:13; 21:8–9
32 *u* Gen. 9:6; Jud. 9:24, 57 *v* 2 Sam. 3:27 *w* 2 Sam. 20:9–10
33 *x* 2 Sam. 3:29

*
2:24 That is, a royal dynasty

But upon David and his descendants, upon his house and his throne, there shall be peace forever from the [a]LORD."

34 So Benaiah the son of Jehoiada went up and struck and killed him; and he was buried in his own house in the wilderness.

Benaiah made chief captain, and Zadok high priest

35 The king put Benaiah the son of Jehoiada in his place over the army, and the king put [b]Zadok the priest in the place of Abiathar.

Shimei is executed

36 Then the king sent and called for [c]Shimei, and said to him, "Build yourself a house in Jerusalem and dwell there, and do not go out from there anywhere.

37 "For it shall be, on the day you go out and cross the Brook [d]Kidron, know for certain you shall surely die; your blood shall be on your own head."

38 And Shimei said to the king, "The saying *is* good. As my lord the king has said, so your servant will do." So Shimei dwelt in Jerusalem many days.

39 Now it happened at the end of three years, that two slaves of Shimei ran away to [e]Achish the son of Maachah, king of Gath. And they told Shimei, saying, "Look, your slaves *are* in Gath!"

40 So Shimei arose, saddled his donkey, and went to Achish at Gath to seek his slaves. And Shimei went and brought his slaves from Gath.

41 And Solomon was told that Shimei had gone from Jerusalem to Gath and had come back.

42 Then the king sent and called for Shimei, and said to him, "Did I not make you swear by the LORD, and warn you, saying, 'Know for certain that on the day you go out and travel anywhere, you shall surely die'? And you said to me, 'The word I have heard *is* good.'

43 "Why then have you not kept the oath of the LORD and the commandment that I gave you?"

44 The king said moreover to [c]Shimei, "You know, as your heart acknowledges, all the wickedness that you did to my father David; therefore the LORD will return your wickedness on your own [f]head.

45 "But King Solomon *shall be* blessed, and the throne of David shall be established before the LORD forever."

46 So the king commanded Benaiah the son of Jehoiada; and he went out and struck him down, and he died. Thus the kingdom was [g]established in the hand of Solomon.

Solomon's treaty with Pharaoh

3 NOW [h]Solomon made a treaty with Pharaoh king of Egypt, and married Pharaoh's daughter; then he brought her to the [i]City of David until he had finished building his own [j]house, and the [k]house of the LORD, and the [l]wall all around Jerusalem.

2 Meanwhile the people sacrificed [1]at the [m]high places, because there was no house built for the name of the LORD until those days.

Solomon's sacrifice and prayer for wisdom (2 Chr. 1:2–10)

3 And Solomon loved the LORD, walking in the statutes of his father David, [n]except that he sacrificed and burned incense at the high places.

4 Now the king went to [o]Gibeon to sacrifice there, for that *was* the great [p]high place: Solomon offered a thousand burnt offerings on that altar.

5 At Gibeon the LORD appeared to Solomon in a dream by night; and God said, [q]"Ask! What shall I give you?"

6 [r]And Solomon said: "You have shown great mercy to Your servant David my father, because he [s]walked before You in truth, in righteousness, and in uprightness of heart with You; You have continued this great [t]kindness for him, and You have given him a son to sit on his throne, as *it is* this day.

7 "Now, O LORD my God, You have made Your servant king instead of my

33
a Prov. 25:5
35
b 1 Ki. 4:4; 1 Chr. 29:22
36
c v. 8; 2 Sam. 16:5–13
37
d 2 Sam. 15:23
39
e 1 Sam. 27:2
44
f 1 Sam. 25:39
46
g 1 Ki. 2:12; 2 Chr. 1:1
CHAPTER 3
1
h 1 Ki. 7:8; 9:24
i 2 Sam. 5:7
j 1 Ki. 7:1
k 1 Ki. 6
l 1 Ki. 9:15
2
m Lev. 17:3–5; Dt. 12:13–14; 1 Ki. 11:7
3
n Cp. 1 Ki. 11:4,6,38
4
o 1 Ki. 9:2
p 1 Chr. 16:39; 21:29
5
q *Bible prayers* (OT): vv. 5–14; 1 Ki. 8:23. (Gen. 15:2; Hab. 3:1)
6
r 2 Chr. 1:8
s 1 Ki. 2:4; 9:4
t 2 Sam. 7:8–17

[1](3:2) Compare Lev. 26:30; Dt. 12:1–4. The use of commanding elevations for altars seems to have been immemorial and universal. In itself the practice was not evil (Gen. 12:7–8; 22:2–4; 31:54). After the establishment of Mount Moriah and the temple as the center of divine worship (cp. Dt. 12:5 with 2 Chr. 7:12) the Mosaic prohibition of the use of high places (Dt. 12:1–4), which had looked forward to the setting up of such a center, came into effect, and high places became identified with idolatrous practices. The constant reference to the use of high places after the temple was built, even for the worship of the LORD, proves how entrenched the custom was. See Jud. 3:7, *note;* cp. 2 Ki. 18:4,22; 23:4–20; 2 Chr. 33:3,17,19.

father David, but I *am* a [a]little child; I
do not know *how* to go out or come
[b]in.
8 "And Your servant *is* in the
midst of Your people whom You
[c]have chosen, a great people, [d]too numerous to be numbered or counted.
9 "Therefore give to Your servant
an [e]understanding heart to judge
Your people, that I may [f]discern between good and evil. For who is able
to judge this great people of Yours?"

Solomon's prayer answered
(2 Chr. 1:11–13)

10 The speech pleased the LORD,
that Solomon had asked this thing.
11 Then God said to him: "Because
you have asked this thing, and have
not asked long life for yourself, nor
have asked riches for yourself, nor
have asked the life of your enemies,
but have asked for yourself understanding to discern justice,
12 "behold, I have done according
to your words; [g]see, I have given you
a wise and understanding heart, so
that there has not been anyone like
you before you, nor shall any like you
arise after you.
13 "And I have also given you what
you have not asked: both [h]riches and
[i]honor, so that there shall not be anyone like you among the kings all your
[j]days.
14 "So [k]if you walk in My ways, to
keep My statutes and My commandments, [l]as your father David walked,
then I will lengthen your days."
15 Then Solomon awoke; and indeed it had been a dream. And he
came to Jerusalem and stood before
the ark of the covenant of the LORD,
offered up burnt offerings, offered
peace offerings, and made a feast for
all his servants.
16 Now two women *who were* harlots came to the king, and [m]stood before him.
17 And one woman said, "O my
lord, this woman and I dwell in the
same house; and I gave birth while she
was in the house.
18 "Then it happened, the third day
after I had given birth, that this
woman also gave birth. And we *were*
together; no one *was* with us in the
house, except the two of us in the
house.
19 "And this woman's son died in
the night, because she lay on him.
20 "So she arose in the middle of
the night and took my son from my
side, while your maidservant slept,
and laid him in her bosom, and laid
her dead child in my bosom.
21 "And when I rose in the morning
to nurse my son, there he was, dead.
But when I had examined him in the
morning, indeed, he was not my son
whom I had borne."
22 Then the other woman said,
"No! But the living one *is* my son, and
the dead one *is* your son." And the first
woman said, "No! But the dead one *is*
your son, and the living one *is* my
son." Thus they spoke before the king.
23 And the king said, "The one
says, 'This *is* my son, who lives, and
your son *is* the dead one'; and the
other says, 'No! But your son *is* the
dead one, and my son *is* the living
one.' "
24 Then the king said, "Bring me a
sword." So they brought a sword before the king.
25 And the king said, "Divide the
living child in two, and give half to
one, and half to the other."
26 Then the [n]woman whose son
was living spoke to the king, for she
yearned with compassion for her son;
and she said, "O my lord, give her the
living child, and by no means kill
him!" But the other said, "Let him be
neither mine nor yours, *but* divide
him."
27 So the king answered and said,
"Give the first woman the living child,
and by no means kill him; she *is* his
mother."
28 And all Israel heard of the judgment which the king had rendered;
and they feared the king, for they saw
that the wisdom of God *was* in him to
administer justice.

Solomon's eleven officials

4 SO King Solomon was king over
all Israel.
2 And these *were* his officials: Azariah the [o]son of Zadok, the priest;
3 Elihoreph and Ahijah, the sons
of Shisha, scribes; [p]Jehoshaphat the
son of Ahilud, the recorder;
4 [q]Benaiah the son of Jehoiada,
over the army; Zadok and [r]Abiathar,
the priests;
5 Azariah the son of Nathan, over
the officers; Zabud the son of Nathan,
a [s]priest *and* the [t]king's friend;
6 Ahishar, over the household;
and Adoniram the son of Abda, over
the [u]labor force.

7
a 1 Chr. 22:5; Jer. 1:6–7
b Num. 27:17; 2 Sam. 5:2
8
c Dt. 7:6
d Gen. 13:16; 15:5
9
e Lit. *hearing.* Ps. 72:1–2; Prov. 2:3–9; Jas. 1:5
f 2 Sam. 14:17; Isa. 7:15; Heb. 5:14
12
g 1 Ki. 4:29–31; 5:12; 10:24; Eccl. 1:16
13
h 1 Chr. 29:12
i Cp. Prov. 3:16
j Cp. Mt. 6:29
14
k 1 Ki. 6:12
l 1 Ki. 15:5
16
m Num. 27:2
26
n Cp. Isa. 49:15; Jer. 31:20; Hos. 11:8
CHAPTER 4
2
o Cp. 1 Chr. 6:8–10
3
p 2 Sam. 8:16; 20:24
4
q 1 Ki. 2:35
r 1 Ki. 2:27
5
s Or *chief minister,* 2 Sam. 8:18; 20:26
t 2 Sam. 15:37; 16:16; 1 Chr. 27:33
6
u 1 Ki. 5:14

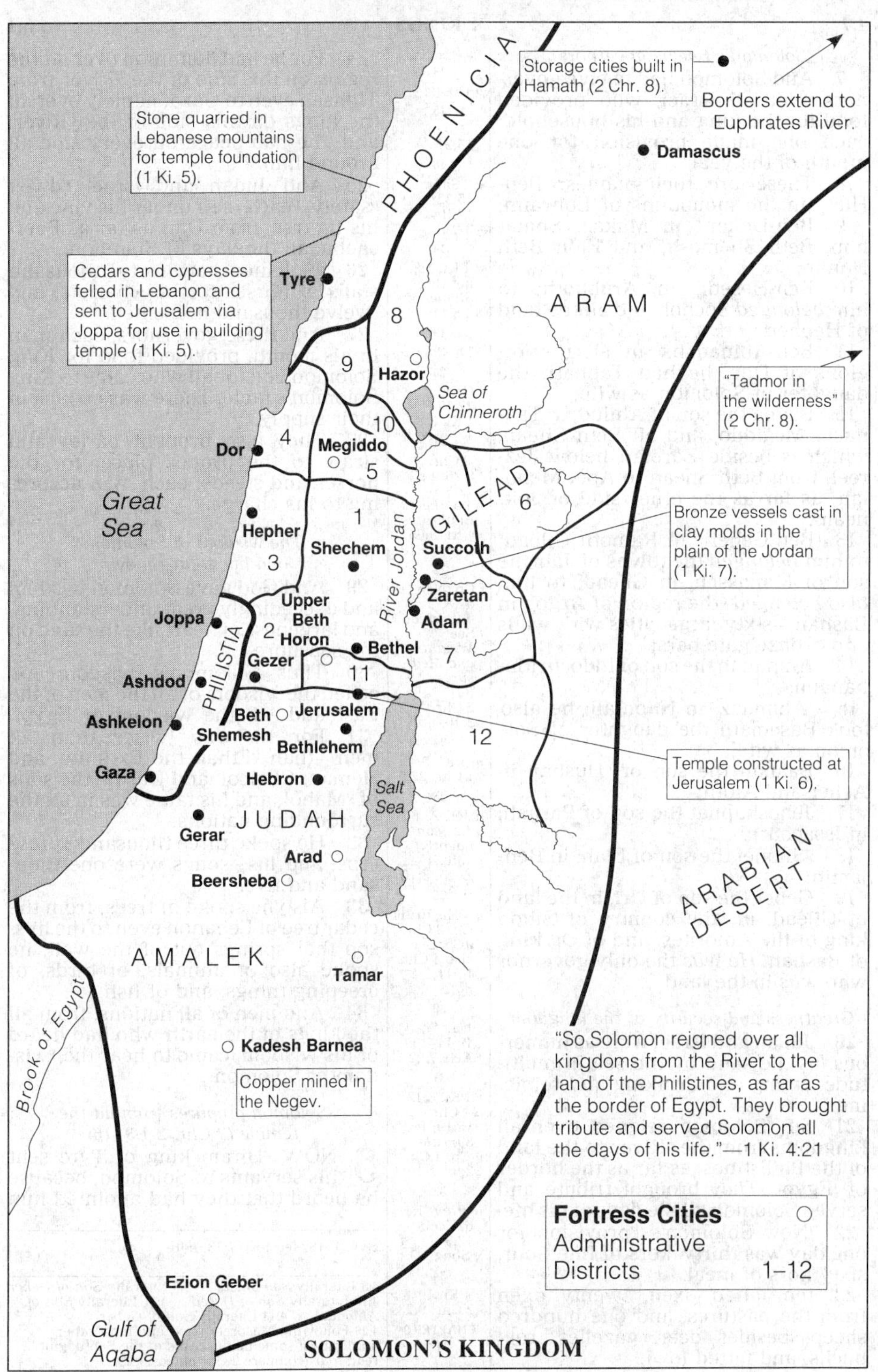

Storage cities built in Hamath (2 Chr. 8).
Borders extend to Euphrates River.
PHOENICIA
Stone quarried in Lebanese mountains for temple foundation (1 Ki. 5).
Damascus
Cedars and cypresses felled in Lebanon and sent to Jerusalem via Joppa for use in building temple (1 Ki. 5).
Tyre
ARAM
8
9
Hazor
"Tadmor in the wilderness" (2 Chr. 8).
Sea of Chinneroth
10
4
Dor
Megiddo
5
GILEAD
6
Great Sea
1
Hepher
Bronze vessels cast in clay molds in the plain of the Jordan (1 Ki. 7).
Shechem
River Jordan
Succoth
3
Zaretan
Upper Beth Horon
Joppa
Adam
2
PHILISTIA
Bethel
7
Gezer
11
Ashdod
Jerusalem
Beth Shemesh
Ashkelon
12
Bethlehem
Temple constructed at Jerusalem (1 Ki. 6).
Gaza
Hebron
Salt Sea
JUDAH
Gerar
Arad
Beersheba
ARABIAN DESERT
AMALEK
Tamar
Brook of Egypt
Kadesh Barnea
Copper mined in the Negev.
"So Solomon reigned over all kingdoms from the River to the land of the Philistines, as far as the border of Egypt. They brought tribute and served Solomon all the days of his life."—1 Ki. 4:21
Fortress Cities
Administrative Districts 1–12
Ezion Geber
Gulf of Aqaba

SOLOMON'S KINGDOM

Solomon's twelve governors

7 And Solomon had twelve governors over all Israel, who provided
food for the king and his household;
each one made provision for one
month of the year.
8 These *are* their names: Ben-
Hur,* in the mountains of Ephraim;
9 Ben-Deker,* in Makaz, Shaalbim, Beth Shemesh, and Elon Beth
Hanan;
10 Ben-Hesed,* in Arubboth; to
him *belonged* Sochoh and all the land
of Hepher;
11 Ben-Abinadab,* *in* all the regions of Dor; he had Taphath the
daughter of Solomon as wife;
12 Baana the son of Ahilud, *in* Taanach, Megiddo, and all Beth Shean,
which *is* beside Zaretan below Jezreel, from Beth Shean to Abel Meholah, as far as the other side of Jokneam;
13 Ben-Geber,* in Ramoth Gilead;
to him *belonged* the towns of Jair the
son of Manasseh, in Gilead; to him
also belonged [a]the region of Argob in
Bashan—sixty large cities with walls
and bronze gate-bars;
14 Ahinadab the son of Iddo, *in* Mahanaim;
15 [b]Ahimaaz, in Naphtali; he also
took Basemath the daughter of Solomon as wife;
16 Baanah the son of [c]Hushai, in
Asher and Aloth;
17 Jehoshaphat the son of Paruah,
in Issachar;
18 [d]Shimei the son of Elah, in Benjamin;
19 Geber the son of Uri, in the land
of Gilead, *in* [e]the country of Sihon
king of the Amorites, and of Og king
of Bashan. *He was* the only governor
who *was* in the land.

Greatness and security of the kingdom

20 Judah and Israel *were* as numerous [f]as the sand by the sea in multitude, eating and drinking and rejoicing.
21 So [g]Solomon reigned over all
kingdoms from the [h]River *to* the land
of the Philistines, as far as the border
of [i]Egypt. *They* brought tribute and
served Solomon all the days of his life.
22 [j]Now Solomon's [k]provision for
one day was thirty [l]kors of fine flour,
sixty kors of meal,
23 ten fatted oxen, twenty oxen
from the pastures, and one hundred
sheep, besides deer, gazelles, roe-
bucks, and fatted fowl.
24 For he had dominion over all *the
region* on this side of the [h]River from
Tiphsah even to Gaza, namely over all
the kings on this side of the [h]River;
and [m]he had peace on every side all
around him.
25 And Judah and Israel [n]dwelt
[o]safely, [p]each man under his vine and
his fig tree, from Dan as far as Beersheba, all the days of Solomon.
26 [q]Solomon had [r]forty* thousand
stalls of horses for his chariots, and
twelve thousand horsemen.
27 And these governors, each man
in his month, provided food for King
Solomon and for all who came to King
Solomon's table. There was no lack in
their supply.
28 They also brought barley and
straw to the proper place, for the
horses and steeds, each man according to his charge.

The wisdom of Solomon, and his great renown

29 And God gave Solomon wisdom
and exceedingly great understanding,
and largeness of heart like the sand on
the seashore.
30 Thus Solomon's wisdom excelled the wisdom of all the men of the
East and [s]all the wisdom of Egypt.
31 For he was [t]wiser than all
men—than [u]Ethan the Ezrahite, and
Heman, Chalcol, and Darda, the sons
of [v]Mahol; and his fame was in all the
surrounding nations.
32 He spoke three thousand [w]prov-
erbs, and his [x]songs were one thousand and five.
33 Also he spoke of trees, from the
cedar tree of Lebanon even to the hyssop that springs out of the wall; he
spoke also of animals, of birds, of
creeping things, and of fish.
34 And men of all nations, from all
the kings of the earth who had heard
of his wisdom, came to hear the [y]wis-
dom of Solomon.

Solomon prepares to build the temple (2 Chr. 2:1,3–16)

5 NOW [z]Hiram king of Tyre sent
his servants to Solomon, because
he heard that they had anointed him

13
a Dt. 3:4
15
b 2 Sam. 15:27
16
c 2 Sam. 15:32; 1 Chr. 27:33
18
d 1 Ki. 1:8; not the *Shimei* of 2:8,44
19
e Dt. 3:8
20
f Gen. 22:17; 1 Ki. 3:8
21
g 2 Chr. 9:26; Ps. 72:8
h i.e. *the Euphrates.* 1 Ki. 8:65
i Gen. 15:18
22
j Cp. Neh. 5:18
k Lit. *bread*
l See *Weights and Measures* (OT), 2 Chr. 2:10, *note*
24
m 1 Ki. 5:4; 1 Chr. 22:9
25
n Jer. 23:6
o Lit. *confidently*
p Mic. 4:4; Zech. 3:10
26
q 1 Ki. 10:26
r Cp. 2 Chr. 9:25. See also 1 Chr. 11:11, *note*
30
s Isa. 19:11–12; Acts 7:22
31
t 1 Ki. 3:12
u 1 Chr. 15:19; Ps. 89, *title*
v Cp. 1 Chr. 2:6
32
w Prov. 1:1, 6; Eccl. 12:9
x Song 1:1
34
y 1 Ki. 10:1; 2 Chr. 9:23
CHAPTER 5
1
z vv. 1–18; see 1 Ki. 7:13, *note*

*

4:8 Literally *Son of Hur* 4:9 Literally *Son of Deker* 4:10 Literally *Son of Hesed* 4:11 Literally *Son of Abinadab* 4:13 Literally *Son of Geber* 4:26 Following Masoretic Text and most other authorities; some manuscripts of the Septuagint read *four* (compare 2 Chronicles 9:25).

king in place of his father, for Hiram
had always loved David.
2 Then Solomon sent to Hiram,
saying:

3 [a]You know how my father
David could not build a house
for the name of the LORD his
God [b]because of the wars
which were fought against him
on every side, until the LORD
put *his foes** under the soles of
his feet.
4 But now the LORD my God has
given me [c]rest on every side;
there is neither adversary nor
evil occurrence.
5 And behold, I propose to build
a house for the name of the
LORD my God, as the LORD
spoke to my father David,
saying, "Your son, whom I will
set on your throne in your
place, he shall build the house
for My [d]name."
6 Now therefore, command that
they cut down cedars for me
from Lebanon; and my
servants will be with your
servants, and I will pay you
wages for your servants
according to whatever you say.
For you know *there is* none
among us who has skill to cut
timber like the Sidonians.

7 So it was, when Hiram heard the
words of Solomon, that he rejoiced
greatly and said,

Blessed *be* the LORD this day,
for He has given David a wise
son over this great people!

8 Then Hiram sent to Solomon,
saying:

I have considered *the message*
which you sent me, *and* I will
do all you desire concerning
the cedar and cypress logs.
9 My servants shall bring *them*
down [e]from Lebanon to the
sea; I will float them in rafts
by sea to the place you
indicate to me, and will have
them broken apart there; then
you can take *them* away. And
you shall fulfill my desire [f]by
giving food for my household.

10 Then Hiram gave Solomon ce-

3
a 1 Chr. 28:2–3
b 1 Chr. 22:8; 28:3
4
c 1 Ki. 4:24
5
d 2 Sam. 7:12–13; 1 Chr. 17:12; 22:10; 28:6
9
e Ezra 3:7
f v. 11
11
g See Weights and Measures (OT), 2 Chr. 2:10, *note*
12
h 1 Ki. 3:12
13
i 1 Ki. 9:15, 20–22
14
j 1 Ki. 4:6; 12:18
16
k 1 Ki. 9:23
17
l 1 Ki. 6:7; 1 Chr. 22:2
CHAPTER 6
1
m See Lev. 23:2, *note*
2
n Cp. Ezek. 40:1–42:20

dar and cypress logs *according to* all
his desire.
11 And Solomon gave Hiram
twenty thousand [g]kors of wheat *as*
food for his household, and twenty*
[g]kors of pressed oil. Thus Solomon
gave to Hiram year by year.
12 So the LORD gave Solomon wisdom, as He had [h]promised him; and
there was peace between Hiram and
Solomon, and the two of them made a
treaty together.

Labor force raised up (2 Chr. 2:2,17–18)

13 Then King Solomon [i]raised up a
labor force out of all Israel; and the
labor force was thirty thousand men.
14 And he sent them to Lebanon,
ten thousand a month in shifts: they
were one month in Lebanon *and* two
months at home; Adoniram *was* in
charge of the [j]labor force.
15 Solomon had seventy thousand
who carried burdens, and eighty thousand who quarried *stone* in the mountains,
16 besides three thousand three
hundred* from the [k]chiefs of Solomon's deputies, who supervised the
people who labored in the work.
17 And the king commanded them
to quarry large stones, costly stones,
and [l]hewn stones, to lay the foundation of the temple.*
18 So Solomon's builders, Hiram's
builders, and the Gebalites quarried
them; and they prepared timber and
stones to build the temple.

Temple begun (2 Chr. 3:1–2)

6 AND it came to pass in the four
hundred and eightieth* year after
the children of Israel had come out of
the land of Egypt, in the fourth year of
Solomon's reign over Israel, in the
month of [m]Ziv, which *is* the second
month, that he began to build the
[1]house of the LORD.

Materials and details of structure (2 Chr. 3:3–14)

2 [n]Now the [2]house which King
Solomon built for the LORD, its length

*5:3 Literally *them* 5:11 Following Masoretic Text, Targum, and Vulgate; Septuagint and Syriac read *twenty thousand.* 5:16 Following Masoretic Text, Targum, and Vulgate; Septuagint reads *three thousand six hundred.* 5:17 Literally *house*, and so frequently throughout this book 6:1 Following Masoretic Text, Targum, and Vulgate; Septuagint reads *fortieth.*

[1](6:1) The NT invariably expands the typology of the tabernacle, not the temple. No reference to the structure of the temple, as in the case of the tabernacle (Heb. 9—10), is traceable.
[2](6:2) The details pertaining to the temple may be summarized from this chapter and 2 Chr.

was sixty [a]cubits, its width twenty,
and its height [1]thirty cubits.
3 The vestibule in front of the
sanctuary* of the house *was* twenty
cubits long across the width of the
house, *and* the width of *the vestibule**
extended ten cubits from the front of
the house.
4 And he made for the house windows with beveled frames.
5 Against the wall of the temple he
built chambers all around, *against* the
walls of the temple, all around the
sanctuary and the inner sanctuary.*
Thus he made side chambers all
around it.
6 The lowest chamber *was* five cubits wide, the middle *was* six cubits
wide, and the third *was* seven cubits
wide; for he made narrow ledges
around the outside of the temple, so
that *the support beams* would not be
fastened into the walls of the temple.
7 And the temple, when it was being built, was built with stone finished
at the quarry, so that no hammer or
chisel *or* any iron tool was heard in the
temple while it was being built.
8 The doorway for the middle
story* *was* on the right [b]side of the
temple. They went up by stairs to the
middle *story,* and from the middle to
the third.
9 [c]So he built the temple and finished it, and he paneled the temple
with beams and boards of cedar.
10 And he built side chambers
against the entire temple, each five cubits high; they were attached to the
temple with cedar beams.
11 Then the word of the LORD came
to Solomon, [2]saying:
12 "*Concerning* this temple which
you are building, if you walk in My
statutes, execute My [d]judgments,
keep all My commandments, and
walk in them, then I will perform My
word with you, [e]which I spoke to your
father David.
13 "And [f]I will dwell among the
children of Israel, and will not [g]for-
sake My people Israel."
14 So Solomon built the temple and
finished it.
15 And he built the inside walls of
the temple with cedar boards; from
the floor of the temple to the ceiling he
paneled the inside with wood; and he
covered the floor of the temple with
planks of cypress.
16 Then he built the twenty-cubit
room at the rear of the temple, from
floor to ceiling, with cedar boards; he
built *it* inside as the inner sanctuary,
as the [h]Most Holy *Place.*
17 And in front of it the temple
sanctuary was forty cubits *long.*
18 The inside of the temple was cedar, carved with ornamental buds and
open flowers. All *was* cedar; there
was no stone *to be* seen.
19 And he prepared the inner sanctuary inside the temple, to set the ark
of the covenant of the LORD there.
20 The inner sanctuary *was* twenty
cubits long, twenty cubits wide, and
twenty cubits high. He overlaid it with
pure gold, and overlaid the altar of cedar.
21 So Solomon overlaid the inside
of the temple with pure gold. He
stretched gold chains across the front
of the inner sanctuary, and overlaid it
with gold.
22 The [i]whole temple he overlaid
with gold, until he had finished all the
temple; also he overlaid with gold the
entire altar that *was* by the inner sanctuary.
23 [j]Inside the inner sanctuary he
made two [k]cherubim *of* olive wood,
each ten cubits high.
24 One wing of the cherub *was* five
cubits, and the other wing of the

2
a See Weights and Measures (OT), 2 Chr. 2:10, *note*
8
b Lit. *shoulder*
9
c vv. 14,38
12
d 1 Ki. 9:4
e 2 Sam. 7:13; 1 Chr. 22:10
13
f Ex. 25:8; Lev. 26:11; 2 Cor. 6:16; Rev. 21:3
g Dt. 31:6
16
h Ex. 26:33–34; 1 Ki. 8:6
22
i Ex. 30:1–6
23
j vv. 23–28; cp. Ex. 25:18–22
k Ex. 37:7–9

*

6:3 Hebrew *heykal;* here the main room of the temple, elsewhere called the holy place (compare Exodus 26:33 and Ezekiel 41:1) • Literally *it*
6:5 Hebrew *debir;* here the inner room of the temple, elsewhere called the Most Holy Place (compare verse 16) 6:8 Following Masoretic Text and Vulgate; Septuagint reads *upper story;* Targum reads *ground story.*

3, as follows: (1) its dimensions (v. 2; 2 Chr. 3:3); (2) its materials (vv. 7,9,22; 2 Chr. 3:5–7); (3) its vestibule (v. 3; 2 Chr. 3:4); (4) its windows (v. 4); (5) its stories (vv. 5–6,8,10; 2 Chr. 3:9); (6) the Most Holy Place (vv. 16–22; 2 Chr. 3:8–9); (7) the cherubim (vv. 23–28; 2 Chr. 3:10–13); (8) the center veil (2 Chr. 3:14); (9) its walls (vv. 15,29; 2 Chr. 3:7); (10) its floor (vv. 15,30); (11) its doors (vv. 31–35); (12) the courts (v. 36; 2 Chr. 4:9); and (13) its completion (vv. 9,14,37–38). See 1 Ki. 7:14, *note.*

[1](6:2) The height of the house itself; cp. 2 Chr. 3:4 which states that the height of the vestibule was 120 cubits. The latter may possibly be a scribal error. See *notes* at 1 Sam. 6:19; 1 Chr. 11:11.

[2](6:11) Solomon is reminded (vv. 12–13) that God's favor is found not in earthly gifts but in obedience.

cherub five cubits: ten cubits from the tip of one wing to the tip of the other.

25 And the other cherub *was* ten cubits; both cherubim *were* of the same size and shape.

26 The height of one cherub *was* ten cubits, and so *was* the other cherub.

27 Then he set the cherubim inside the inner room;* and [a]they stretched out the wings of the cherubim so that the wing of the one touched *one* wall, and the wing of the other cherub touched the other wall. And their wings touched [b]each other in the middle of the room.

28 Also he overlaid the cherubim with gold.

29 Then he carved all the walls of the temple all around, both the inner and outer *sanctuaries,* with carved [c]figures of cherubim, palm trees, and open flowers.

30 And the floor of the temple he overlaid with gold, both the inner and outer *sanctuaries.*

31 For the entrance of the inner sanctuary he made doors *of* olive wood; the lintel *and* doorposts *were* one-fifth *of the wall.*

32 The two doors *were of* olive wood; and he carved on them figures of cherubim, palm trees, and open flowers, and overlaid *them* with gold; and he spread gold on the [d]cherubim and on the palm trees.

33 So for the door of the sanctuary he also made doorposts *of* olive wood, one-fourth *of the wall.*

34 And the two doors *were of* cypress wood; two [e]panels *comprised* one folding door, and two [e]panels *comprised* the other folding door.

35 Then he carved cherubim, palm trees, and open flowers *on them,* and overlaid *them* with gold applied evenly on the carved work.

36 And he built the [f]inner court with three rows of hewn stone and a row of cedar beams.

The house of the LORD *was seven years in building*

37 In the fourth year the foundation of the house of the LORD was laid, in the month of [g]Ziv.

38 And in the eleventh year, in the month of [g]Bul, which is the eighth month, the house was finished in all its details and according to all its plans. So he was [h]seven years in building it.

Solomon's palace

7 BUT Solomon took thirteen years to build his own house; so he finished all his [i]house.

2 He also built the [j]House of the Forest of Lebanon; its length *was* one hundred [k]cubits, its width fifty cubits, and its height thirty cubits, with four rows of cedar pillars, and cedar beams on the pillars.

3 And *it was* paneled with cedar above the [l]beams that *were* on forty-five pillars, fifteen *to* a row.

4 *There were* windows *with beveled frames in* three rows, and window *was* opposite window *in* three tiers.

5 And all the doorways and doorposts *had* rectangular frames; and window *was* opposite window *in* three tiers.

6 He also made the Hall of Pillars: its length *was* fifty cubits, and its width thirty cubits; and in front of them *was* a portico with pillars, and a canopy *was* in front of them.

7 Then he made a hall for the throne, the Hall of Judgment, where he might judge; and *it was* paneled with cedar from floor to ceiling.*

8 And the house where he dwelt *had* another court inside the hall, of like workmanship. Solomon also made a house like this hall for Pharaoh's daughter, [m]whom he had taken *as wife.*

9 All these *were of* costly stones cut to size, trimmed with saws, inside and out, from the foundation to the eaves, and also on the outside to the great court.

10 The foundation *was of* costly stones, large stones, some ten cubits and some eight cubits.

11 And above *were* costly stones, hewn to size, and cedar wood.

12 The great court *was* enclosed with three rows of hewn stones and a row of cedar beams. So were the [n]inner court of the house of the LORD and [o]the vestibule of the temple.

Huram, the artisan

13 Now King Solomon sent and brought [1p]Huram from Tyre.

14 He *was* the son of a widow from

27 *a* Or *the cherubim stretched out their wings* *b* Ex. 25:20
29 *c* Ex. 36:8, 35
32 *d* Cp. Ex. 25:18
34 *e* Cp. Ezek. 41:24
36 *f* 1 Ki. 7:12
37 *g* See Lev. 23:2, *note*
38 *h* Cp. v. 1
CHAPTER 7
1 *i* 1 Ki. 9:10; 2 Chr. 8:1
2 *j* 1 Ki. 10:17, 21; 2 Chr. 9:16 *k* See Weights and Measures (OT), 2 Chr. 2:10, *note*
3 *l* Lit. *ribs*
8 *m* 1 Ki. 3:1; 9:24; 11:1; 2 Chr. 8:11
12 *n* 1 Ki. 6:36 *o* Jn. 10:23; Acts 3:11
13 *p* vv. 13–46; 2 Chr. 2:13–14; 4:11–16. Contra. 1 Ki. 5:1–18; 2 Chr. 2:3–12. See note below

*6:27 Literally *house* 7:7 Literally *floor,* that is, of the upper level

[1](7:13) The Huram of this passage (vv. 13–14; 2 Chr. 2:13–14; 4:11–17) was an artisan of Tyre, whereas the Hiram of 5:1–18 (also 2 Chr. 2:3–12) was a king of Tyre.

the tribe of Naphtali, and [a]his father
was a man of Tyre, a [1]bronze worker;
[b]he was filled with wisdom and understanding and skill in working with
all kinds of bronze work. So he came
to King Solomon and did all his work.
15 And he cast two pillars of
bronze, each one [c]eighteen cubits
high, and a line of twelve cubits measured the circumference of each.
16 Then he made two capitals *of*
cast bronze, to set on the tops of the
pillars. The height of one capital *was*
five cubits, and the height of the other
capital *was* five cubits.
17 *He made* a lattice network, with
wreaths of chainwork, for the capitals
which *were* on top of the pillars: seven
chains for one capital and seven for
the other capital.
18 So he made the pillars, and two
rows of pomegranates above the network all around to cover the capitals
that *were* on top; and thus he did for
the other capital.
19 The capitals which *were* on top
of the pillars in the hall *were* in the
shape of lilies, four cubits.
20 The capitals on the two pillars
also *had pomegranates* above, by the
convex surface which *was* next to the
network; and there *were* two hundred
such pomegranates in rows on each of
the capitals all around.
21 Then he set up the pillars by the
vestibule of the temple; he set up the
pillar on the right and called its name
[d]Jachin, and he set up the pillar on the
left and called its name [e]Boaz.
22 The tops of the pillars were in
the shape of lilies. So the work of the
pillars was finished.
23 [f]And he made the [g]Sea of cast
bronze, ten cubits from one brim to
the other; *it was* completely round. Its
height *was* five cubits, and a line of
thirty cubits measured its circumference.
24 Below its brim *were* ornamental
buds encircling it all around, ten to a
cubit, all the way around the Sea. The
ornamental buds *were* cast in two
rows when it was cast.
25 It stood on twelve oxen: three
looking toward the north, three looking toward the west, three looking toward the south, and three looking toward the east; the Sea *was set* upon
them, and all their back parts *pointed*
inward.
26 It *was* a handbreadth thick; and
its brim was shaped like the brim of a
cup, *like* a lily blossom. It contained
[h]two thousand* [i]baths.
27 He also made ten carts of
bronze; four cubits *was* the length of
each cart, four cubits its width, and
three cubits its height.
28 And this *was* the design of the
carts: They had [j]panels, and the panels *were* between frames;
29 on the panels that *were* between
the frames *were* lions, oxen, and cherubim. And on the frames *was* a pedestal on top. Below the lions and oxen
were wreaths of plaited work.
30 Every cart had four bronze
wheels and axles of bronze, and its
four feet had supports. Under the laver *were* supports of cast *bronze* beside each wreath.
31 Its opening inside the crown at
the top *was* one cubit in diameter; and
the opening *was* round, shaped *like* a
pedestal, one and a half cubits in outside diameter; and also on the opening
were engravings, but the panels were
square, not round.
32 Under the panels *were* the four
wheels, and the axles of the wheels
were [k]*joined* to the cart. The height of
a wheel *was* one and a half cubits.
33 The workmanship of the wheels
was like the workmanship of a chariot
wheel; their axle pins, their rims, their
spokes, and their hubs *were* all of cast
bronze.
34 And *there were* four supports at
the four corners of each cart; its supports *were* part of the cart itself.
35 On the top of the cart, at the
height of half a cubit, *it was* perfectly
round. And on the top of the cart, its
flanges and its [j]panels *were* of the
same casting.
36 On the plates of its flanges and
on its panels he engraved cherubim,
lions, and palm trees, wherever there
was a clear space on each, with
wreaths all around.

14
a 2 Chr. 4:16
b Cp. Ex. 31:3; 36:1
15
c Cp. 2 Chr. 3:15; see 1 Chr. 11:11, *note*
21
d Meaning, *He shall establish*
e Meaning, *in Him [is] strength*
23
f vv. 23–26; 2 Chr. 4:2–5
g 2 Ki. 25:13; 2 Chr. 4:2; Jer. 52:17; cp. Ex. 30:18
26
h Cp. 2 Chr. 4:5; see 1 Chr. 11:11, *note*
i See Weights and Measures (OT), 2 Chr. 2:10, *note*
28
j 2 Ki. 16:17
32
k Lit. *in the cart*

*7:26 Or *three thousand* (compare 2 Chronicles 4:5)

[1](7:14) Further detail in this chapter and 2 Chr. 3–4 on the temple, particularly Huram's work in bronze, may be itemized: (1) the two pillars (vv. 15–22; 2 Chr. 3:15–17); (2) the bronze altar (2 Chr. 4:1); (3) the Sea of cast bronze (vv. 23–26,39; 2 Chr. 4:2–5,10); (4) the ten carts (vv. 27–37); (5) the ten lavers (vv. 38–39; 2 Chr. 4:6); (6) summary of Huram's work in bronze (vv. 40–45; 2 Chr. 4:11–16); (7) summary of Huram's work on golden vessels (vv. 48–50; 2 Chr. 4:7–8,19–22); and (8) completion of work (v. 51; 2 Chr. 5:1). See 1 Ki. 6:2, *note*.

37 Thus he made the ten carts. All of them were of the same mold, one measure, *and* one shape.

38 Then he [a]made ten lavers of bronze; each laver contained forty baths, *and* each laver *was* four cubits. On each of the ten carts *was* a laver.

39 And he put five carts on the right side of the house, and five on the left side of the house. He set the Sea on the right side of the house, toward the southeast.

40 [b]Huram [c]made the lavers and the shovels and the bowls. So Huram finished doing all the work that he was to do for King Solomon *for* the house of the LORD:

41 the two pillars, the *two* bowl-shaped capitals that *were* on top of the two pillars; the two networks covering the two bowl-shaped capitals which *were* on top of the pillars;

42 [d]four hundred pomegranates for the two networks (two rows of pomegranates for each network, to cover the two bowl-shaped capitals that *were* on top of the pillars);

43 the ten carts, and ten lavers on the carts;

44 one Sea, and twelve oxen under the Sea;

45 the pots, the shovels, and the bowls. All these articles which Huram made for King Solomon *for* the house of the LORD *were of* burnished bronze.

46 In the plain of Jordan the king had them cast in clay molds, between Succoth and [e]Zaretan.

47 And Solomon did not weigh all the articles, [f]because *there were* so many; the weight of the bronze was not [g]determined.

48 Thus Solomon had all the furnishings made for the house of the LORD: the [h]altar of gold, and the [i]table of gold on which *was* the [j]showbread;

49 the lampstands of pure gold, five on the right *side* and five on the left in front of the [k]inner sanctuary, with the flowers and the lamps and the wick-trimmers of gold;

50 the basins, the trimmers, the bowls, the ladles, and the censers of pure gold; and the hinges of gold, *both* for the doors of the inner room (the Most Holy *Place*) *and* for the doors of the main hall of the temple.

51 So all the work that King Solomon had done for the house of the LORD was finished; and Solomon brought in the things which his father David had [l]dedicated: the silver and the gold and the furnishings. He put them in the treasuries of the house of the LORD.

Ark brought in: the Shekinah glory fills the house (2 Chr. 5:2–14)

8

NOW Solomon assembled the elders of Israel and all the [m]heads of the tribes, the chief fathers of the children of Israel, to King Solomon in Jerusalem, that they might bring up the ark of the covenant of the LORD from the City of David, which *is* Zion.

2 Therefore all the men of Israel assembled with King Solomon at the [n]feast in the month of [o]Ethanim, which *is* the seventh month.

3 So all the elders of Israel came, and the [p]priests took up the ark.

4 Then they brought up the ark of the LORD, the [q]tabernacle of meeting, and all the holy furnishings that *were* in the tabernacle. The priests and the Levites brought them up.

5 Also King Solomon, and all the congregation of Israel who were assembled with him, *were* with him before the ark, [r]sacrificing sheep and oxen that could not be counted or numbered for multitude.

6 Then the priests brought in the ark of the covenant of the LORD to its [s]place, into the [k]inner sanctuary of the temple, to the Most Holy *Place*, under the wings of the cherubim.

7 For the cherubim spread *their* two wings over the place of the ark, and the cherubim overshadowed the ark and its poles.

8 The poles extended so that the ends of the poles could be seen from the holy *place*, in front of the [k]inner sanctuary; but they could not be seen from outside. And they are there to this day.

9 [t]Nothing *was* in the ark except the [u]two tablets of stone which Moses put there at Horeb, when the LORD made *a covenant* with the children of Israel, when they came out of the land of Egypt.

10 And it came to pass, when the priests came out of the holy *place*, that the [v]cloud filled the house of the LORD,

11 so that the priests could not continue ministering because of the cloud; for the [w]glory of the LORD filled the house of the LORD.

Solomon's sermon (2 Chr. 6:1–11)

12 Then Solomon spoke:

"The LORD said He would dwell
in the dark [x]cloud.

38 [a] 2 Chr. 4:6
40 [b] v. 13 [c] vv. 40–51; 2 Chr. 4:11—5:1
42 [d] 1 Ki. 7:20
46 [e] Cp. 2 Chr. 4:17
47 [f] Lit. *for the very great multitude* [g] 1 Chr. 22:3,14
48 [h] Ex. 37:25–26 [i] Ex. 37:10–11 [j] See Ex. 25:30, *note*
49 [k] 1 Ki. 6:5
51 [l] *Sanctification* (OT): v. 51; 2 Chr. 2:4. (Gen. 2:3; Zech. 8:3)
CHAPTER 8
1 [m] Num. 1:4; 7:2
2 [n] Lev. 23:34; 2 Chr. 7:8–10 [o] See Lev. 23:2, *note*
3 [p] Num. 7:9
4 [q] 1 Ki. 3:4; 2 Chr. 1:3
5 [r] Cp. 2 Sam. 6:13
6 [s] 1 Ki. 6:19
9 [t] Cp. Heb. 9:4 [u] Ex. 25:16, 21; Dt. 10:2–5
10 [v] vv. 10,11; see Ex. 40:34, *note*
11 [w] 2 Chr. 7:1–2
12 [x] Ps. 97:2

13 I have surely built You an
exalted house,
And a place for You to dwell
in forever."

14 Then the king turned around
and blessed the whole assembly of Israel, while all the assembly of Israel
was standing.
15 And he said: [a]"Blessed *be* the
LORD God of Israel, who spoke with
His mouth to my father David, and
with His hand has fulfilled *it*, [b]saying,
16 'Since the day that I brought My
people Israel out of Egypt, I have chosen no city from any tribe of Israel *in*
which to build a house, that My name
might be [c]there; but [d]I chose David to
be over My people Israel.'
17 "Now it was in the heart of my
father David to build a temple* for the
name of the LORD God of [e]Israel.
18 "But the LORD said to my father
David, 'Whereas it was in your heart
to build a temple for My name, you did
well that it was in your heart.
19 'Nevertheless you shall not build
the temple, but your son who will
come from your body, he shall build
the temple for My [f]name.'
20 "So the LORD has fulfilled His
word which He spoke; and I have
filled the position of my father [g]Da-
vid, and sit on the throne of Israel, as
the LORD promised; and I have built a
temple for the name of the LORD God
of Israel.
21 "And there I have made a place
for the ark, in which *is* the covenant of
the LORD which He made with our fathers, when He brought them out of
the land of Egypt."

Solomon's prayer of dedication
(2 Chr. 6:12–42)

22 Then Solomon stood before the
altar of the LORD in the presence of all
the assembly of Israel, and spread out
his hands toward heaven;
23 and he [h]said: "LORD God of Israel, *there is* no God in heaven above
or on earth below like You, who keep
Your covenant and mercy with Your
servants who walk before You with all
their [i]hearts.
24 "You have kept what You promised Your servant David my father;
You have both spoken with Your
mouth and fulfilled *it* with Your hand,
as *it is* this day.
25 "Therefore, LORD God of Israel,
now keep what You promised Your
servant David my father, saying, 'You
shall not fail to have a man sit before
Me on the throne of Israel, only if your
sons take heed to their way, that they
walk before Me as you have walked
before [j]Me.'
26 "And now I pray, O God of Israel, let Your word come true, [k]which
You have spoken to Your servant David my father.
27 "But [l]will God indeed dwell on
the earth? Behold, heaven and the
heaven of heavens cannot contain
You. How much less this temple
which I have built!
28 "Yet regard the prayer of Your
servant and his supplication, O LORD
my God, and listen to the cry and the
prayer which Your servant is praying
before You today:
29 "that Your eyes may be open toward this temple night and day, toward the place of which You said,
[m]'My name shall be [n]there,' that You
may hear the prayer which Your servant makes toward this place.
30 "And may You hear the supplication of Your servant and of Your
people Israel, when they pray [o]to-
ward this place. Hear in heaven Your
dwelling place; and when You hear,
forgive.
31 "When anyone sins against his
neighbor, and is forced to take [p]an
oath, and comes *and* takes an [q]oath
before Your altar in this temple,
32 "then hear in heaven, and act,
and judge Your servants, condemning
the [r]wicked, bringing his way on his
head, and justifying the righteous by
giving him according to his righteousness.
33 "When Your people Israel are
defeated before an enemy because
they have sinned against [s]You, and
when they turn back to You and confess Your name, and pray and make
supplication to You in this temple,
34 "then hear in heaven, and forgive the sin of Your people Israel, and
bring them back to the land which
You gave to their [t]fathers.
35 "When the heavens are shut up
and there is no rain because they have
sinned against [u]You, when they pray
toward this place and confess Your
name, and turn from their sin because
You afflict them,
36 "then hear in heaven, and forgive the sin of Your servants, Your
people Israel, that You may teach
them [v]the good way in which they

15
a 1 Chr. 29:10,20
b 2 Sam. 7:12–13
16
c Dt. 12:5
d 2 Sam. 7:8
17
e 2 Sam. 7:3; 1 Chr. 17:2
19
f 1 Chr. 22:8–10
20
g *Kingdom* (OT): v. 20; 1 Ki. 11:31. (Gen. 1:26; Zech. 12:8, *note*)
23
h *Bible prayers* (OT): vv. 22–53; 1 Ki. 17:20. (Gen. 15:2; Hab. 3:1)
i Dt. 7:9; Neh. 1:5
25
j 1 Ki. 2:4; 9:5
26
k 2 Sam. 7:25
27
l 2 Chr. 2:6; Isa. 66:1; Jer. 23:24; Acts 7:49; 17:24
29
m Dt. 12:11
n 1 Ki. 9:3; 2 Chr. 7:15
30
o Dan. 6:10
31
p Cp. Lev. 5:1
q Ex. 22:8–11
32
r Dt. 25:1
33
s Lev. 26:17,25; Dt. 28:25
34
t Lev. 26:40–42; Dt. 30:1–3
35
u Dt. 28:23
36
v 1 Sam. 12:23

*8:17 Literally *house*, and so in verses 18–20

should walk; and [a]send rain on Your
land which You have given to Your
people as an inheritance.
37 [b]"When there is famine in the
land, pestilence *or* blight *or* mildew,
locusts *or* grasshoppers; when their
enemy besieges them in the land of
their cities; whatever plague or whatever sickness *there is;*
38 "whatever prayer, whatever
supplication is made by anyone, *or* by
all Your people Israel, when each one
knows the plague of his own heart,
and spreads out his hands toward this
temple:
39 "then hear in heaven Your
dwelling place, and forgive, and act,
and give to everyone according to all
his ways, whose heart You know (for
You alone know the hearts of all the
sons of [c]men),
40 "that they may [d]fear You all the
days that they live in the land which
You gave to our fathers.
41 "Moreover, concerning a foreigner, who *is* not of Your people Israel, but has come from a far country
for Your name's sake
42 "(for they will hear of Your great
name and Your strong hand and Your
outstretched arm), when he comes
and prays toward this temple,
43 "hear in heaven Your dwelling
place, and do according to all for
which the foreigner calls to You, [e]that
all peoples of the earth may know
Your [f]name and [d]fear You, as *do*
Your people Israel, and that they may
know that this temple which I have
built is called by Your name.
44 "When Your people go out to
battle against their enemy, wherever
You send them, and when they pray to
the LORD toward the city which You
have chosen and the temple which I
have built for Your name,
45 "then hear in heaven their
prayer and their supplication, and
maintain their [g]cause.
46 "When they sin against You (for
there is no one who does [h]not sin),
and You become angry with them and
deliver them to the enemy, and they
take them captive [i]to the land of the
enemy, far or near;
47 "*yet* when they come to themselves in the land where they were
carried captive, and repent, and make
supplication to You in the land of
those who took them captive, [j]saying,
'We have sinned and done wrong, we
have committed wickedness';
48 "and *when* they return to You

36
a Cp. Jer. 14:22
37
b Lev. 26:16, 25–26; Dt. 28:21–22, 27,38,42, 52; 2 Chr. 20:9
39
c 1 Sam. 16:7; 1 Chr. 28:9
40
d See Ps. 19:9, *note*
43
e 1 Sam. 17:46; 2 Ki. 19:19; Ps. 67:2
f Ex. 9:16
45
g Lit. *right*
46
h Ps. 130:3; Prov. 20:9; Rom. 3:23
i Lev. 26:34, 44; Dt. 28:36,64; 2 Ki. 17:6, 18; 25:21
47
j Ezra 9:6–7; Neh. 1:6; Ps. 106:6; Dan. 9:5
48
k Dan. 6:10; Jon. 2:4
50
l 2 Chr. 30:9
51
m Dt. 9:26–29; Rom. 11:28–29
n Dt. 4:20; Jer. 11:4
52
o vv. 28,30, 33,54,59; 9:3
53
p *Separation:* v. 53; Ezra 6:21. (Gen. 12:1; 2 Cor. 6:17, *note*)
q Cp. Ex. 19:5–6
54
r 2 Chr. 7:1
56
s 1 Chr. 22:18
t Josh. 23:14–15
57
u Gen. 48:21; Rom. 8:35–37

with all their heart and with all their
soul in the land of their enemies who
led them away captive, and pray to
You [k]toward their land which You
gave to their fathers, the city which
You have chosen and the temple
which I have built for Your name:
49 "then hear in heaven Your
dwelling place their prayer and their
supplication, and maintain their
cause,
50 "and forgive Your people who
have sinned against You, and all their
transgressions which they have transgressed against You; and grant them
compassion before those who took
them captive, that they may have
[l]compassion on them
51 "(for they *are* Your people and
Your [m]inheritance, whom You
brought out of Egypt, [n]out of the iron
furnace),
52 [o]"that Your eyes may be open to
the supplication of Your servant and
the supplication of Your people Israel,
to listen to them whenever they call to
You.
53 "For You [p]separated them from
among all the peoples of the earth *to*
be Your inheritance, [q]as You spoke
by Your servant Moses, when You
brought our fathers out of Egypt, O
Lord GOD."

Solomon's benediction

54 [r]And so it was, when Solomon
had finished praying all this prayer
and supplication to the LORD, that he
arose from before the altar of the
LORD, from kneeling on his knees with
his hands spread up to heaven.
55 Then he stood and blessed all
the assembly of Israel with a loud
voice, saying:
56 "Blessed *be* the LORD, who has
given [s]rest to His people Israel, according to all that He promised. There
has not failed one word of all His good
[t]promise, which He promised
through His servant Moses.
57 "May the LORD our God be with
us, as He was with our fathers. May
He not leave us nor forsake [u]us,
58 "that He may [v]incline our hearts
to Himself, to walk in all His ways,
and to keep His commandments and
His statutes and His judgments, which
He commanded our fathers.
59 "And may these words of mine,
with which I have made supplication
before the LORD, be near the LORD our

8:58 *v* Ps. 119:36

God day and night, that He may maintain the cause of His servant and the
cause of His people Israel, as each day
may require,
60 "that all the peoples of the earth
may know that the LORD *is* God; *there*
is no other.
61 "Let your heart therefore be
loyal to the LORD our God, to walk in
His statutes and keep His [a]command-
ments, as at this day."

Sacrifice and rejoicing (2 Chr. 7:4–10)

62 Then the king and all Israel with
him offered sacrifices before the LORD.
63 And Solomon offered a sacrifice
of peace offerings, which he offered to
the LORD, twenty-two thousand bulls
and one hundred and twenty thousand sheep. So the king and all the
children of Israel [b]dedicated the
house of the LORD.
64 On the same day the king consecrated the middle of the court that *was*
in front of the house of the LORD; for
there he offered burnt offerings, grain
offerings, and the fat of the peace offerings, because the [c]bronze altar that
was before the LORD *was* too small to
receive the burnt offerings, the grain
offerings, and the fat of the peace offerings.
65 At that time Solomon held a
[d]feast, and all Israel with him, a great
assembly [e]from the entrance of Ha-

61
a Dt. 18:13; 1 Ki. 9:4
63
b Cp. Ezra 6:15–18; Neh. 12:27
64
c 2 Chr. 4:1
65
d Lev. 23:34–42; cp. 1 Ki. 8:2
e 1 Ki. 4:21, 24; 2 Ki. 14:25
f Cp. 2 Chr. 30:23
CHAPTER 9
1
g 1 Ki. 7:1
h 2 Chr. 8:6
2
i Cp. 1 Ki. 11:9–13
j 1 Ki. 3:5
3
k 2 Ki. 20:5; Ps. 10:17
l 1 Ki. 8:29
m Dt. 11:12
4
n Gen. 17:1
o 1 Ki. 11:4, 6
p 1 Ki. 8:61

math to the Brook of Egypt, before the
LORD our God, seven days and seven
more [f]days—fourteen days.
66 On the eighth day he sent the
people away; and they blessed the
king, and went to their tents joyful and
glad of heart for all the good that the
LORD had done for His servant David,
and for Israel His people.

God's second appearance to
Solomon (2 Chr. 7:11–22)

9 AND it came to pass, when Solomon had finished building the
house of the LORD [g]and the king's
house, and [h]all Solomon's desire
which he wanted to do,
2 that the LORD appeared to Solomon the [i]second time, [j]as He had appeared to him at Gibeon.
3 And the LORD said to him: [k]"I
have heard your prayer and your supplication that you have made before
Me; I have consecrated this house
which you have built [l]to put My name
there forever, and [m]My eyes and My
heart will be there perpetually.
4 "Now if you [n]walk before Me
[o]as your father David walked, in integrity of heart and in uprightness, to
do according to all that I have commanded you, *and* if you [p]keep My
statutes and My judgments,
5 "then I will establish the throne
of your kingdom over Israel forever,

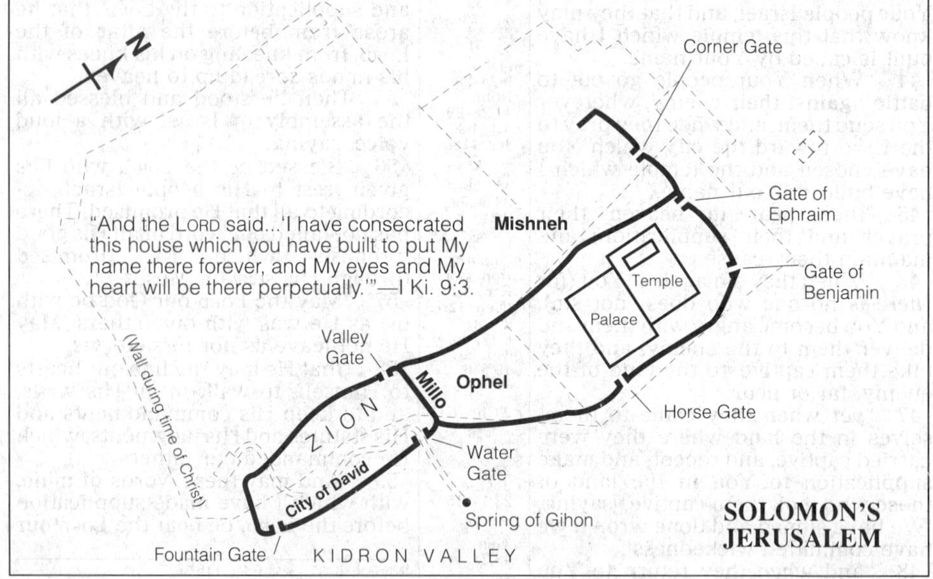

SOLOMON'S JERUSALEM

as I promised David your father, saying, 'You shall not fail to have a man on the throne of [a]Israel.'

6 "*But* if you or your sons at all turn from following Me, and do not keep My commandments *and* My statutes which I have set before you, but go and serve other gods and worship them,

7 [b]"then I will cut off Israel from the land which I have given them; and this house which I have consecrated [c]for My name I will cast out of My sight. [d]Israel will be a proverb and a byword among all peoples.

8 "And as for this house, *which* is exalted, everyone who passes by it will be astonished and will hiss, and say, [e]'Why has the LORD done thus to this land and to this house?'

9 "Then they will answer, 'Because they forsook the LORD their God, who brought their fathers out of the land of Egypt, and have embraced other gods, and worshiped them and served them; therefore the LORD has brought all this [f]calamity on them.' "

King Hiram and Solomon exchange gifts (2 Chr. 8:1–2)

10 Now it happened at the end of twenty years, when Solomon had built the two houses, the house of the LORD and the king's house

11 [g](Hiram the king of Tyre had supplied Solomon with cedar and cypress and gold, as much as he desired), *that* King Solomon then gave Hiram twenty cities in the land of Galilee.

12 Then Hiram went from Tyre to see the cities which Solomon had given him, but they did not please him.

13 So he said, "What *kind of* cities *are* these which you have given me, my brother?" And he called them the land of [h]Cabul,* as they are to this day.

14 Then Hiram sent the king one hundred and twenty [i]talents of gold.

Fame of Solomon (2 Chr. 8:3–18)

15 And this *is* the reason for the [j]labor force which King Solomon raised: to build the house of the LORD, his own house, the [k]Millo,* the wall of Jerusalem, [l]Hazor, [m]Megiddo, and [n]Gezer.

16 (Pharaoh king of Egypt had gone up and taken Gezer and burned it with fire, had killed the [o]Canaanites who dwelt in the city, and had given it *as* a dowry to his daughter, Solomon's [p]wife.)

17 And Solomon built Gezer, Lower Beth Horon,

18 Baalath, and Tadmor in the wilderness, in the land *of Judah*,

19 all the storage cities that Solomon had, cities for his [q]chariots and cities for his [r]cavalry, and whatever Solomon desired to build in Jerusalem, in Lebanon, and in all the land of his dominion.

20 All the people *who were* left of the Amorites, [s]Hittites, Perizzites, Hivites, and Jebusites, who *were* not of the children of Israel—

21 that is, their descendants who were left in the land after them, whom the children of Israel had not been able to [t]destroy completely—from these Solomon raised forced labor, as it is to this day.

22 But of the children of Israel Solomon made no [u]forced laborers, because they *were* men of war and his servants: his officers, his captains, commanders of his chariots, and his cavalry.

23 Others *were* chiefs of the officials who *were* over Solomon's work: [v]five hundred and fifty, who ruled over the people who did the work.

24 But [w]Pharaoh's daughter came up from the City of David to her house which *Solomon** had built for her. [x]Then he built the Millo.

25 Now [y]three times a year Solomon offered burnt offerings and peace offerings on the altar which he had built for the LORD, and he burned incense with them *on the altar* that *was* before the LORD. So he finished the temple.

26 King Solomon also built a fleet of ships at Ezion Geber, which *is* near Elath* on the shore of the Red Sea, in the land of Edom.

27 Then Hiram sent his servants with the fleet, seamen who knew the sea, to work with the servants of Solomon.

28 And they went to Ophir, and acquired four hundred and [z]twenty talents of gold from there, and brought *it* to King Solomon.

5
a 2 Sam. 7:12,16; 1 Ki. 2:4; 6:12; 8:25
7
b Dt. 4:26; 2 Ki. 17:23; 25:21
c Jer. 7:14
d Dt. 28:37; Ps. 44:14
8
e Dt. 29:24–26; Jer. 22:8–9
9
f Dt. 29:25–28
11
g 1 Ki. 5:1
13
h Josh. 19:27
14
i See Coinage (OT) Ex. 30:13, *note*
15
j 1 Ki. 5:13
k v. 24; 2 Sam. 5:9
l Josh. 19:36
m Josh. 17:11
n Josh. 16:10; Jud. 1:29
16
o Josh. 16:10
p 1 Ki. 3:1; 7:8
19
q 1 Ki. 10:26
r 1 Ki. 4:26
20
s See 2 Ki. 7:6, *note*
21
t Jud. 1:21–29; 3:1
22
u Lev. 25:39
23
v Cp. 2 Chr. 8:10; see 1 Chr. 11:11, *note*
24
w 1 Ki. 3:1; 2 Chr. 8:11
x 2 Sam. 5:9; 1 Ki. 11:27; 2 Chr. 32:5
25
y Ex. 23:14–17
28
z Cp. 2 Chr. 8:18; see 1 Chr. 11:11, *note*

*

9:13 Literally *Good for Nothing* **9:15** Literally *The Landfill* **9:24** Literally *he* (compare 2 Chronicles 8:11) **9:26** Hebrew *Eloth* (compare 2 Kings 14:22)

Queen of Sheba visits Solomon (2 Chr. 9:1–12)

10 NOW when the [a]queen of
Sheba heard of the fame of Solomon concerning the name of the
LORD, she came to test him with hard
questions.
2 She came to Jerusalem with a
very great retinue, with camels that
bore spices, very much gold, and precious stones; and when she came to
Solomon, she spoke with him about
all that was in her heart.
3 So Solomon answered all her
questions; there was nothing so difficult for the king that he could not explain *it* to her.
4 And when the queen of Sheba
had seen all the wisdom of Solomon,
the house that he had built,
5 the food on his table, the seating
of his servants, the service of his waiters and their apparel, his cupbearers,
[b]and [c]his entryway by which he went
up to the house of the LORD, there was
no more spirit in her.
6 Then she said to the king: "It was
a true report which I heard in my own
land about your words and your wisdom.
7 "However I did not believe the
words until I came and saw with my
own eyes; and indeed the half was not
told me. Your wisdom and prosperity
exceed the fame of which I heard.
8 "Happy *are* your men and happy
are these your servants, who stand
continually before you *and* hear your
wisdom!
9 [d]"Blessed be the LORD your God,
who [e]delighted in you, setting you on
the throne of Israel! Because the LORD
has loved Israel forever, therefore He
made you [f]king, to do justice and
righteousness."
10 Then she gave the king one hundred and twenty [g]talents of gold,
spices in great quantity, and precious
stones. There never again came such
abundance of spices as the queen of
Sheba gave to King Solomon.
11 Also, the ships of Hiram, which
brought gold from [h]Ophir, brought
great *quantities* of [1]almug wood and
precious stones from Ophir.
12 And the king made steps of the
almug wood for the house of the LORD
and for the king's house, also harps
and stringed instruments for singers.
There never again came such almug
wood, nor has the like been seen to
this day.
13 Now King Solomon gave the
queen of Sheba all she desired, whatever she asked, besides what Solomon
had given her according to the royal
generosity. So she turned and went to
her own country, she and her servants.

Solomon's splendor (2 Chr. 9:13–28)

14 The weight of [i]gold that came to
Solomon yearly was six hundred and
sixty-six talents of gold,
15 besides *that* from the traveling
[j]merchants, from the income of traders, [k]from all the kings of Arabia, and
from the governors of the country.
16 And King Solomon made two
hundred large shields *of* hammered
gold; six hundred *shekels* of gold went
into each shield.
17 He also *made* three hundred
[l]shields *of* hammered gold; three
[g]minas of gold went into each shield.
The king put them in the [m]House of
the Forest of Lebanon.
18 Moreover the king made a great
throne of ivory, and overlaid it with
pure gold.
19 The throne had six steps, and the
top of the throne *was* round at the
back; *there were* armrests on either
side of the place of the seat, and two
lions stood beside the armrests.
20 Twelve lions stood there, one on
each side of the six steps; nothing like
this had been made for any *other*
kingdom.
21 [n]All King Solomon's drinking
vessels *were* gold, and all the vessels
of the House of the Forest of Lebanon
were pure gold. Not *one was* silver, for
this was accounted as nothing in the
days of Solomon.
22 For the king had [o]merchant
ships at sea with the fleet of Hiram.
Once every three years the [p]merchant
ships came bringing gold, silver,
ivory, apes, and monkeys.*
23 [q]So King Solomon surpassed all
the kings of the earth in riches and
wisdom.
24 Now all the earth sought the
presence of Solomon to hear his wis-

CHAPTER 10

1
a 2 Chr. 9:1; Mt. 12:42; Lk. 11:31

5
b 2 Chr. 9:4
c Or *his burnt offerings which he offered in*

9
d 1 Ki. 5:7
e 2 Sam. 22:20
f 2 Chr. 2:11

10
g See Weights and Measures (OT), 2 Chr. 2:10, *note*

11
h 1 Ki. 9:27–28

14
i Cp. Dt. 17:17

15
j 2 Chr. 1:16
k 2 Chr. 9:24; Ps. 72:10

17
l Cp. 1 Ki. 14:26–28
m 1 Ki. 7:2

21
n 2 Chr. 9:20

22
o Lit. *ships of Tarshish;* cp. Gen. 10:4; 2 Chr. 20:36
p 1 Ki. 9:26–28; 22:48

23
q 1 Ki. 3:12–13; 4:30

*

10:22 Or *peacocks*

[1](10:11) The almug tree is traditionally the sandalwood tree *(Santalum album).* Close-grained and fragrant, the wood is employed for ornamental work and was thus particularly suited for the purpose for which Solomon used it.

dom, which God had put in his heart.
25 Each man brought his present:
articles of silver and gold, garments,
armor, spices, horses, and mules, at a
set rate year by year.
26 [a]And Solomon gathered chariots and horsemen; he had one thousand four hundred chariots and
twelve thousand horsemen, whom he
stationed* in the [b]chariot cities and
with the king at Jerusalem.
27 [c]The king made silver *as common* in Jerusalem as stones, and he
made cedar trees as abundant as the
sycamores which *are* in the [d]lowland.
28 Also Solomon had horses imported from [e]Egypt and Keveh; the
king's merchants bought them in Keveh at the *current* price.
29 Now a chariot that was imported
from Egypt cost six hundred *shekels*
of silver, and a horse one hundred and
fifty; and thus, through their agents,*
they exported *them* to all the kings of
the [f]Hittites [g]and the kings of Syria.

Solomon forsakes God

11 BUT King Solomon loved
many [h]foreign women, as well
as the [i]daughter of Pharaoh: women
of the Moabites, Ammonites, Edomites, Sidonians, *and* [f]Hittites—
2 from the nations of whom the
LORD had said to the children of Israel,
"You shall not intermarry with them,
nor they with you. Surely they will
turn away your hearts after their
[j]gods." Solomon clung to these in
love.
3 And he had seven hundred
wives, princesses, and three hundred
concubines; and his wives turned
away his heart.
4 For it was so, when Solomon
was old, that his wives turned his
heart after other gods; and his heart
was not loyal to the LORD his God, as
was the heart of his [k]father David.
5 For Solomon went after [l]Ashto-
reth the goddess of the Sidonians, and
after [m]Milcom the abomination of the
[n]Ammonites.
6 Solomon did evil in the sight of
the LORD, and did not fully follow the
LORD, as *did* his father David.
7 Then Solomon built a high place
for Chemosh the abomination of
Moab, on the hill that *is* east of Jerusalem, and for Molech the abomination
of the people of Ammon.
8 And he did likewise for all his
foreign wives, who burned incense
and sacrificed to their gods.

26
a 1 Ki. 4:26; 2 Chr. 1:14; 9:25
b 1 Ki. 9:19
27
c 2 Chr. 1:15–17
d See Dt. 1:7, *note*
28
e Dt. 17:16; 2 Chr. 9:28
29
f See 2 Ki. 7:6, *note*
g Josh. 1:4; 2 Ki. 7:6
CHAPTER 11
1
h Dt. 17:17; Neh. 13:23–27
i 1 Ki. 3:1
2
j Ex. 34:12–16; Dt. 7:3–4
4
k 1 Ki. 9:4
5
l v. 33. See Jud. 2:13, *note*
m Called *Molech*, v. 7; Lev. 20:2–5
n 2 Ki. 23:13; see Jud. 3:7 and 1 Ki. 3:2, *notes*
9
o 1 Ki. 3:5; 9:2
10
p 1 Ki. 6:12; 9:6–7
11
q v. 31; 1 Ki. 12:15–16
r Cp. 1 Sam. 15:28
s 1 Ki. 11:31,37
13
t 1 Ki. 12:20
u 2 Sam. 7:15–16
v 1 Ki. 9:3; 14:21
15
w 2 Sam. 8:14; 1 Chr. 18:12–13
x Num. 24:19; Dt. 20:13

God sternly rebukes Solomon and tells him that the kingdom will be taken away

9 So the LORD became angry with
Solomon, because his heart had
turned from the LORD God of Israel,
who had appeared to him [o]twice,
10 and [p]had commanded him concerning this thing, that he should not
go after other gods; but he did not
keep what the LORD had commanded.
11 Therefore the LORD said to Solomon, "Because you have done this,
and have not kept My covenant and
My statutes, which I have commanded
you, [q]I will surely [r]tear the kingdom
away from you and give it to your
[s]servant.
12 "Nevertheless I will not do it in
your days, for the sake of your father
David; I will tear it out of the hand of
your son.
13 "However I will not tear away
the whole kingdom; I will give [t]one
tribe to your son [u]for the sake of my
servant David, and for the sake of Jerusalem which I have [v]chosen."

Solomon chastened by Hadad, Rezon, and Jeroboam

14 Now the LORD raised up an adversary against Solomon, Hadad the
Edomite; he *was* a descendant of the
king in Edom.
15 For it happened, when David
was in [w]Edom, and Joab the commander of the army had gone up to
bury the slain, [x]after he had killed every male in Edom
16 (because for six months Joab remained there with all Israel, until he
had cut down every male in Edom),
17 that Hadad fled to go to Egypt,
he and certain Edomites of his father's
servants with him. Hadad *was* still a
little child.
18 Then they arose from Midian
and came to Paran; and they took men
with them from Paran and came to
Egypt, to Pharaoh king of Egypt, who
gave him a house, apportioned food
for him, and gave him land.
19 And Hadad found great favor in
the sight of Pharaoh, so that he gave
him as wife the sister of his own wife,
that is, the sister of Queen Tahpenes.
20 Then the sister of Tahpenes bore
him Genubath his son, whom Tahpenes weaned in Pharaoh's house. And
Genubath was in Pharaoh's household among the sons of Pharaoh.

*
10:26 Following Septuagint, Syriac, Targum, and Vulgate (compare 2 Chronicles 9:25); Masoretic Text reads *led.* **10:29** Literally *by their hands*

21 [a]So when Hadad heard in Egypt that David rested with his fathers, and that Joab the commander of the army was dead, Hadad said to Pharaoh, "Let me depart, that I may go to my own country."

22 Then Pharaoh said to him, "But what have you lacked with me, that suddenly you seek to go to your own country?" So he answered, "Nothing, but do let me go anyway."

23 And God raised up *another* adversary against him, Rezon the son of Eliadah, who had fled from his lord, [b]Hadadezer king of Zobah.

24 So he gathered men to him and became captain over a band *of raiders,* [c]when David killed those *of Zobah.* And they went to Damascus and dwelt there, and reigned in [d]Damascus.

25 He was an adversary of Israel all the days of Solomon (besides the trouble that Hadad *caused*); and he abhorred Israel, and reigned over Syria.

26 Then Solomon's servant, [e]Jeroboam the son of Nebat, an Ephraimite from Zereda, whose mother's name *was* Zeruah, a widow, [f]also [g]rebelled against the king.

27 And this *is* what caused him to rebel against the king: [h]Solomon had built the Millo *and* repaired the damages to the City of David his father.

28 The man Jeroboam *was* a mighty man of valor; and Solomon, seeing that the young man was [i]industrious, made him the officer over all the labor force of the house of Joseph.

29 Now it happened at that time, when Jeroboam went out of Jerusalem, that the prophet [j]Ahijah the Shilonite met him on the way; and he had clothed himself with a new garment, and the two *were* alone in the field.

30 Then Ahijah took hold of the new garment that *was* on him, and [k]tore it *into* twelve pieces.

31 And he said to Jeroboam, "Take for yourself ten pieces, for [l]thus says the LORD, the God of Israel: 'Behold, I will tear the [m]kingdom out of the hand of Solomon and will give ten tribes to you

32 '(but he shall have one tribe for the sake of My servant David, and for the sake of Jerusalem, the city which I have chosen out of all the tribes of Israel),

33 'because they have* forsaken Me, and worshiped Ashtoreth the goddess of the Sidonians, Chemosh the god of the Moabites, and Milcom the god of the people of Ammon, and have not walked in My ways to do *what is* right in My eyes and *keep* My statutes and My judgments, as *did* his father David.

34 'However I will not take the whole kingdom out of his hand, because I have made him ruler all the days of his life for the sake of My servant David, whom I chose because he kept My commandments and My statutes.

35 'But I will take the kingdom out of his son's hand and give it to you—[n]ten tribes.

36 'And to his son I will give one tribe, that My servant David may always have a [o]lamp before Me in Jerusalem, the city which I have chosen for Myself, to put My name there.

37 'So I will take you, and you shall reign over all your heart desires, and you shall be king over Israel.

38 'Then it shall be, if you heed all that I command you, walk in My ways, and do *what is* right in My sight, to keep My statutes and My commandments, as My servant David did, then I will be with [p]you and [q]build for you an enduring house, as I built for David, and will give Israel to [r]you.

39 'And I will afflict the descendants of David because of this, but not forever.' "

40 Solomon therefore sought to kill Jeroboam. But Jeroboam arose and fled to Egypt, to [s]Shishak king of Egypt, and was in Egypt until the death of Solomon.

Solomon dies (2 Chr. 9:29–31)

41 Now the [t]rest of the acts of Solomon, all that he did, and his wisdom, *are* they not written in the [u]book of the acts of Solomon?

42 And the period that Solomon reigned in Jerusalem over all Israel *was* forty years.

43 Then [v]Solomon rested with his fathers, and was buried in the City of David his father. And [w]Rehoboam his son [x]reigned in his [y]place.

III. The Division of the Kingdom under Rehoboam and Jeroboam, 12:1—14:31

Accession and folly of Rehoboam (2 Chr. 12:1; cp. Eccl. 2:18–19)

12 AND [w]Rehoboam went to [z]Shechem, for all Israel had gone to Shechem to make him king.

---

21 a 1 Ki. 2:10, 34
23 b 2 Sam. 8:3; 10:16
24 c 2 Sam. 10:8–18 d Cp. 1 Ki. 15:18
26 e 1 Ki. 12:2; 2 Chr. 13:6 f 1 Ki. 11:11 g 2 Sam. 20:21
27 h 1 Ki. 9:24
28 i Prov. 22:29
29 j 1 Ki. 12:15; 14:2; 2 Chr. 9:29
30 k 1 Sam. 15:27–28
31 l vv. 11–13 m *Kingdom* (OT): vv. 9,13, 30–37; 2 Ki. 25:7. (Gen. 1:26; Zech. 12:8, *note*)
35 n 1 Ki. 12:16–17
36 o 1 Ki. 15:4; 2 Ki. 8:19
38 p Dt. 31:8; Josh. 1:5 q 2 Sam. 7:11,27 r Cp. 1 Ki. 14:7–10
40 s 1 Ki. 11:17; 2 Chr. 12:2–9
41 t 2 Chr. 9:29 u See 1 Chr. 29:29, *note*
43 v 2 Chr. 9:31 w 2 Chr. 10:1 x 931 B.C. y 1 Ki. 14:21
CHAPTER 12
1 z Jud. 9:6; see Ps. 60:6, *note*

---

*11:33 Following Masoretic Text and Targum; Septuagint, Syriac, and Vulgate read *he has.*

2 So it happened, when [a]Jeroboam the son of Nebat heard *it* (he was still in [b]Egypt, for he had fled from the presence of King Solomon and had been dwelling in Egypt),

3 that they sent and called him. Then Jeroboam and the whole assembly of Israel came and spoke to Rehoboam, saying,

4 "Your father made our [c]yoke heavy; now therefore, lighten the burdensome service of your father, and his heavy yoke which he put on us, and we will serve you."

5 So he said to them, "Depart *for* three days, then come back to me." And the people departed.

6 Then King Rehoboam consulted the elders who stood before his father Solomon while he still lived, and he said, "How do you advise *me* to answer these people?"

7 And they spoke to him, saying, [d]"If you will be a servant to these people today, and serve them, and answer them, and speak good words to them, then they will be your servants forever."

8 But he rejected the advice which the elders had given him, and consulted the young men who had grown up with him, who stood before him.

9 And he said to them, "What advice do you give? How should we answer this people who have spoken to me, saying, 'Lighten the yoke which your father put on us'?"

10 Then the young men who had grown up with him spoke to him, saying, "Thus you should speak to this people who have spoken to you, saying, 'Your father made our yoke heavy, but you make *it* lighter on us'—thus you shall say to them: 'My little *finger* shall be thicker than my father's waist!

11 'And now, whereas my father put a heavy yoke on you, I will add to your yoke; my father chastised you with whips, but I will chastise you with scourges!' "*

12 So Jeroboam and all the people came to Rehoboam the third day, as the king had directed, saying, "Come back to me the third day."

13 Then the king answered the people [e]roughly, and rejected the advice which the elders had given him;

14 and he spoke to them according to the advice of the young men, saying, "My father made your yoke heavy, but I will [f]add to your yoke; my father chastised you with whips, but I will chastise you with scourges!"*

15 So the king did not listen to the people; for the [g]turn *of events* was from the LORD, that He might fulfill His word, which the LORD had spoken by [h]Ahijah the Shilonite to Jeroboam the son of Nebat.

Kingdom divided; Jeroboam becomes king over Israel (2 Chr. 10:12–19; 11:1–4)

16 Now when all Israel saw that the king did not listen to them, the people answered the king, [i]saying:

[j]"What share have we in David?
We have no inheritance in the son of Jesse.
To your tents, O Israel!
Now, see to your own house, O David!"

So Israel departed to their tents.

17 But Rehoboam reigned over [k]the children of Israel who dwelt in the cities of Judah.

18 Then King Rehoboam [l]sent [m]Adoram, who *was* in charge of the revenue; but all Israel stoned him with stones, and he died. Therefore King Rehoboam mounted his chariot in haste to flee to Jerusalem.

19 So [1]Israel has been in rebellion

2
a 1 Ki. 11:26
b 1 Ki. 11:40
4
c 1 Sam. 8:11–18; 1 Ki. 4:7; 5:13–15
7
d 2 Chr. 10:7; Prov. 15:1
13
e Lit. *harshly*
14
f Cp. Ex. 5:5–9
15
g v. 24; Jud. 14:4; 2 Chr. 10:15; 22:7; 25:20
h 1 Ki. 11:29
16
i See Jud. 8:1, *note*
j 2 Sam. 2:1–17; 5:1–3; 20:1
17
k 1 Ki. 11:13,36; 2 Chr. 11:14–17
18
l 1 Ki. 4:6; 5:14
m Or *Adoniram,* 1 Ki. 4:6; or *Hadoram,* 2 Chr. 10:18

* 12:11 Literally *scorpions* 12:14 Literally *scorpions*

[1](12:19) Difficulties arise in comparing the chronology of the two kingdoms, Israel and Judah. Before the modern system of numbering years was adopted in the fifth century A.D., events were usually dated by the reigns of kings, beginning a new series with each new king. In some instances the remaining months of the year of a king's death were counted as the first year of his successor; in others the new series of numbers did not begin until the next full year. Frequently a king associated his son with him on the throne, so that the year could be designated by either king; in such cases one writer might begin the new king's reign when this occurred, whereas another writer might not begin the enumeration until after the father's death. Interest in precise chronology is comparatively recent. Until modern times the year was commenced at different dates in various countries. When these facts are recognized, most of the chronological discrepancies in the narratives of the two kingdoms can be resolved.

The total length of the kingdoms of Israel and Judah can be learned from events mentioned in the history of other countries. A much larger sum is reached by adding together the number

against the house of David to this day.
20 Now it came to pass when all Israel heard that Jeroboam had come
back, they sent for him and called him
to the congregation, and made him
king over all [a]Israel. There was none
who followed the house of David, but
the tribe of Judah only.
21 [b]And when Rehoboam came to
Jerusalem, he assembled all the house
of Judah with the tribe of [c]Benjamin,
one hundred and eighty thousand
chosen *men* who were warriors, to
fight against the house of Israel, that
he might restore the kingdom to Rehoboam the son of Solomon.
22 But the word of God came to
[d]Shemaiah the man of God, saying,
23 "Speak to Rehoboam the son of
Solomon, king of Judah, to all the
house of Judah and Benjamin, and to
the rest of the people, saying,
24 'Thus says the LORD: [e]"You shall
not go up nor fight against your brethren the children of Israel. Let every
man return to his house, for this thing
is from Me." ' " Therefore they obeyed
the word of the LORD, and turned back,
according to the word of the LORD.

Jeroboam's idolatry divides the nation

25 Then Jeroboam built [f]Shechem
in the mountains of Ephraim, and
dwelt there. Also he went out from
there and built [g]Penuel.
26 And Jeroboam said in his heart,
"Now the kingdom may return to the
house of David:
27 "If these people [h]go up to offer
sacrifices in the house of the LORD at
Jerusalem, then the heart of this people will turn back to their lord, Rehoboam king of Judah, and they will kill
me and go back to Rehoboam king of
Judah."
28 Therefore the king asked advice,
made [i]two calves of gold, and said to
the people, "It is too much for you to
go up to Jerusalem. Here are your
gods, O Israel, which brought you up
from the land of [j]Egypt!"
29 And he set up one in Bethel, and
the other he put in Dan.
30 Now this thing [k]became a sin,
for the people went *to worship* before
the one as far as Dan.
31 He made shrines* on the high

20 *a* 2 Ki. 17:21
21 *b* vv. 21–24; 2 Chr. 11:1–4 *c* 2 Sam. 19:17
22 *d* 2 Chr. 12:5–7
24 *e* Cp. 2 Ki. 17:12
25 *f* 1 Ki. 12:1 *g* Jud. 8:17
27 *h* Dt. 12:5–7
28 *i* 2 Ki. 10:29 *j* Ex. 32:4–8
30 *k* 1 Ki. 13:34

* 12:31 Literally *a house*

of years of each king's reign, because fractions of a year would appear as full years in each reign.

From 1050–931 B.C. the united kingdom was ruled by Saul, David, and Solomon. The approximate dates of the reigns of the kings of Israel and Judah are shown in the table below:

Israel	*Reign*	*Co-Regency*	*Judah*	*Reign*	*Co-Regency*
Jeroboam I	931–910 B.C.		Rehoboam	931–913 B.C.	
			Abijah	913–911	
Nadab	910–909		Asa	911–870	
Baasha	909–886				
Elah	886–885				
Zimri	885				
Omri	885–874	885–880 B.C.			
Ahab	874–853		Jehoshaphat	870–848	873–870 B.C.
Ahaziah	853–852		Jehoram	848–841	853–848
Joram	852–841		Ahaziah	841	
Jehu	841–814		Athaliah	841–835	
Jehoahaz	814–798		Joash	835–796	
Jehoash	798–782		Amaziah	796–767	
Jeroboam II	782–753	793–782	Azariah	767–740	791–767
Zechariah	753–752				
Shallum	752				
Menahem	752–742		Jotham	740–732	750–740
Pekahiah	742–740				
Pekah	740–732	752–740	Ahaz	732–716	
Hoshea	732–721				
			Hezekiah	716–687	
			Manasseh	687–642	696–687
			Amon	642–640	
			Josiah	640–608	
			Jehoahaz	608	
			Jehoiakim	608–597	
			Jehoiachin	597	
			Zedekiah	597–586	

[a]places, and made priests from every
class of people, who were not of the
sons of [b]Levi.
32 Jeroboam ordained a feast on
the fifteenth day of the [c]eighth month,
[d]like the feast that *was* in Judah, and
offered sacrifices on the [e]altar. So he
did at Bethel, sacrificing to the calves
that he had made. And at Bethel he
installed the [f]priests of the high
places which he had made.
33 So he made offerings on the altar which he had made at Bethel on
the fifteenth day of the eighth month,
in the month which he had devised in
his own heart. And he ordained a feast
for the children of Israel, and offered
sacrifices on the altar and burned incense.

Prophecy against Jeroboam's false altar

13 AND behold, [g]a man of God
went from Judah to Bethel by
the word of the LORD, [h]and Jeroboam
stood by the altar to burn incense.
2 Then he cried out against the altar by the word of the LORD, and said,
"O altar, altar! Thus says the LORD:
'Behold, a child, Josiah by name, shall
be born to the house of David; and on
you he shall sacrifice the priests of the
[i]high places who burn incense on
you, and men's bones shall be
[j]burned on you.' "
3 And he gave a [k]sign the same
day, saying, "This *is* the sign which
the LORD has spoken: Surely the altar
shall split apart, and the ashes on it
shall be poured out."

Jeroboam's hand becomes paralyzed in judgment; it is then restored

4 So it came to pass when King
Jeroboam heard the saying of the man
of God, who cried out against the altar
in Bethel, that he stretched out his
hand from the altar, saying, "Arrest
him!" Then his hand, which he
stretched out toward him, [l]withered,
so that he could not pull it back to
himself.
5 The altar also was split apart,
and the ashes poured out from the altar, according to the sign which the
man of God had given by the word of
the LORD.
6 Then the king answered and
said to the man of God, "Please [m]en-
treat the favor of the LORD your God,
and pray for me, that my hand may be
restored to me." So the man of God
[n]entreated the LORD, and the king's
hand was restored to him, and became
as before.
7 Then the king said to the man of
God, "Come home with me and refresh yourself, and I will give you a
[o]reward."
8 But the man of God said to the
king, [p]"If you were to give me half
your house, I would not go in with
you; nor would I eat bread nor drink
water in this place.
9 "For so it was commanded me by
the word of the LORD, saying, 'You
shall not eat bread, nor drink water,
nor return by the same way you
came.' "
10 So he went another way and did
not return by the way he came to
Bethel.

Man of God disobeys

11 Now an [q]old prophet dwelt in
Bethel, and his sons came and told
him all the works that the man of God
had done that day in Bethel; they also
told their father the words which he
had spoken to the king.
12 And their father said to them,
"Which way did he go?" For his sons
had seen* which way the man of God
went who came from Judah.
13 Then he said to his sons, "Saddle
the donkey for me." So they saddled
the donkey for him; and he rode on it,
14 and went after the man of God,
and found him sitting under an oak.
Then he said to him, "*Are* you the man
of God who came from Judah?" And
he said, "I *am.*"
15 Then he said to him, "Come
home with me and eat bread."
16 And he said, [r]"I cannot return
with you nor go in with you; neither
can I eat bread nor drink water with
you in this place.
17 "For I have been told [s]by the
word of the LORD, 'You shall not eat
bread nor drink water there, nor return by going the way you came.' "
18 He said to him, "I too *am* a
prophet as you *are,* [1]and an [t]angel
spoke to me by the word of the LORD,
saying, 'Bring him back with you to
your house, that he may eat bread and
drink water.' " (He was lying to him.)
19 So he went back with him, and

31
a Cp. 2 Chr. 11:15
b Num. 17:1–11; Jud. 17:5; 1 Ki. 13:33; 2 Ki. 17:32
32
c See Lev. 23:2, *note*
d Lev. 23:33–34; cp. Isa. 14:12–15
e vv. 26–33; cp. Dt. 12:4–14; see Amos 4:4, *note*
f Amos 7:10–13
CHAPTER 13
1
g 2 Ki. 23:17
h 1 Ki. 12:32–33
2
i See Jud. 3:7 and 1 Ki. 3:2, *notes*
j Lev. 26:30
3
k Isa. 7:14; Jn. 2:18; 1 Cor. 1:22
4
l Miracles (OT): vv. 4–6; 1 Ki. 17:16. (Gen. 5:24; Jon. 1:17, *note*)
6
m Ex. 8:8; Jer. 37:3; Acts 8:24
n Cp. Lk. 6:27–28
7
o 1 Sam. 9:7; 2 Ki. 5:15
8
p Num. 22:18; 24:13
11
q v. 31; 2 Ki. 23:18
16
r vv. 8–9
17
s 1 Ki. 20:35
18
t See Heb. 1:4, *note*

*13:12 Septuagint, Syriac, Targum, and Vulgate read *showed him.*

[1](13:18) Here is an impressive illustration of Gal. 1:8–9.

ate bread in his house, and drank water.

Man of God killed

20 Now it happened, as they sat at the table, that the word of the LORD came to the prophet who had brought him back;

21 and he cried out to the man of God who came from Judah, saying, "Thus says the LORD: 'Because you have disobeyed the word of the LORD, and have not kept the commandment which the LORD your God commanded you,

22 'but you came back, ate bread, and drank water in the [a]place of which *the LORD* said to you, "Eat no bread and drink no water," your corpse shall not come to the tomb of your fathers.' "

23 So it was, after he had eaten bread and after he had drunk, that he saddled the donkey for him, the prophet whom he had brought back.

24 When he was gone, a [b]lion met him on the road and killed him. And his corpse was thrown on the road, and the donkey stood by it. The lion also stood by the corpse.

25 And there, men passed by and saw the corpse thrown on the road, and the lion standing by the corpse. Then they went and told *it* in the city where the old prophet dwelt.

26 Now when the prophet who had brought him back from the way heard *it*, he said, "It *is* the man of God who was disobedient to the word of the LORD. Therefore the LORD has delivered him to the lion, which has torn him and killed him, according to the word of the LORD which He spoke to him."

27 And he spoke to his sons, saying, "Saddle the donkey for me." So they saddled *it*.

28 Then he went and found his corpse thrown on the road, and the donkey and the lion standing by the corpse. The lion had not eaten the corpse nor torn the donkey.

29 And the prophet took up the corpse of the man of God, laid it on the donkey, and brought it back. So the old prophet came to the city to mourn, and to bury him.

30 Then he laid the corpse in his own tomb; and they mourned over him, *saying*, [c]"Alas, my brother!"

31 So it was, after he had buried him, that he spoke to his sons, saying, "When I am dead, then bury me in the tomb where the man of God *is* buried; [d]lay my bones beside his bones.

32 [e]"For the saying which he cried out by the word of the LORD against the altar in Bethel, and against all the shrines* on the [f]high places which *are* in the cities of Samaria, will surely come to pass."

Persistence in false worship

33 After this event Jeroboam did not turn from his evil way, but again he made priests from [g]every class of people for the high places; whoever wished, he consecrated him, and he became *one* of the [h]priests of the high places.

34 And this thing was the sin of the house of Jeroboam, so as [i]to exterminate and destroy *it* from the face of the earth.

Jeroboam's son dies

14 AT that time Abijah the son of Jeroboam became sick.

2 And Jeroboam said to his wife, "Please arise, and disguise yourself, that they may not recognize you as the wife of Jeroboam, and go to Shiloh. Indeed, Ahijah the prophet *is* there, who told me that [j]*I would be* king over this people.

3 [k]"Also take with you ten loaves, *some* cakes, and a jar of honey, and go to him; he will tell you what will become of the child."

4 And Jeroboam's wife did so; she arose and went to Shiloh, and came to the house of Ahijah. But Ahijah could not see, for his eyes were glazed by reason of his age.

5 Now the LORD had said to Ahijah, "Here is the wife of Jeroboam, coming to ask you something about her son, for he *is* sick. Thus and thus you shall say to her; for it will be, when she comes in, that she will pretend *to be* another *woman*."

6 And so it was, when Ahijah heard the sound of her footsteps as she came through the door, he said, "Come in, wife of Jeroboam. Why do you pretend *to be* another *person?* For I *have been* sent to you *with* [l]bad *news*.

7 "Go, tell Jeroboam, 'Thus says the LORD God of Israel: [m]"Because I exalted you from among the people, and made you ruler over My people Israel,

8 "and [j]tore the kingdom away

22
a v. 9
24
b 1 Ki. 20:36
30
c Cp. Jer. 22:18
31
d 2 Ki. 23:17–18
32
e v. 2; 2 Ki. 23:16
f See Jud. 3:7 and 1 Ki. 3:2, *notes*
33
g Cp. Lev. 21:1–24
h 1 Ki. 12:31
34
i 1 Ki. 14:10; cp. 14:16
CHAPTER 14
2
j 1 Ki. 11:31
3
k Cp. 1 Sam. 9:7–8; 2 Ki. 4:42
6
l Lit. *hard*
7
m 1 Ki. 16:2; cp. 2 Sam. 12:7–8

*
13:32 Literally *houses*

from the house of David, and gave it to you; and *yet* you have not been as My servant David, [a]who kept My commandments and who followed Me with all his heart, to do only *what was* right in My eyes;

9 "but you have done more evil than all who were before you, [b]for you have gone and made for yourself other gods and [c]molded images to provoke Me to anger, and have [d]cast Me behind your back—

10 "therefore behold! I will [e]bring disaster on the house of Jeroboam, and will cut off from Jeroboam every male in Israel, bond and free; I will [f]take away the remnant of the house of Jeroboam, as one takes away refuse until it is all [g]gone.

11 "The dogs shall eat whoever belongs to Jeroboam and dies in the city, and the birds of the air shall [h]eat whoever dies in the field; for the LORD has spoken!" '

12 "Arise therefore, go to your own house. When your feet enter the city, the child shall die.

13 "And all Israel shall mourn for him and bury him, for he is the only one of Jeroboam who shall come to the grave, because in him there is found something good toward the LORD God of Israel in the house of Jeroboam.

14 "Moreover the LORD will raise up for Himself a king over Israel who shall [i]cut off the house of Jeroboam; this is the day. What? Even now!

15 "For the LORD will strike Israel, as a reed is shaken in the water. He will [j]uproot Israel from this good land which He gave to their fathers, and will scatter them beyond the [k]River, because they have made their wooden [l]images, provoking the LORD to anger.

16 "And He will give Israel up because of the sins of Jeroboam, who sinned and who made Israel sin."

17 Then Jeroboam's wife arose and departed, and came to [m]Tirzah. When she came to the threshold of the house, the child died.

18 And they buried him; and all Israel mourned for him, according to the word of the LORD which He spoke through His servant Ahijah the prophet.

Nadab succeeds Jeroboam (2 Chr. 13:20)

19 Now the rest of the acts of Jeroboam, how he [n]made war and how he reigned, indeed they *are* written in the book of the chronicles of the kings of Israel.

20 The period that Jeroboam reigned *was* twenty-two years. So he rested with his fathers. Then [o]Nadab his son reigned in his [p]place.

Judah's apostasy under Rehoboam
(2 Chr. 12:1)

21 And Rehoboam the son of Solomon reigned in Judah. Rehoboam *was* forty-one years old when he [q]became king. He reigned seventeen years in Jerusalem, the city which the LORD had chosen out of all the tribes of Israel, to put His name [r]there. His mother's name *was* Naamah, an Ammonitess.

22 Now Judah did evil in the sight of the LORD, and they provoked Him to jealousy with their sins which they committed, more than all that their fathers had done.

23 For they [s]also built for themselves [t]high places, [u]*sacred* pillars, and wooden [l]images on every high hill and under every green tree.

24 And there were also [v]perverted persons* in the land. They did according to all the [w]abominations of the nations which the LORD had cast out before the children of [x]Israel.

Invasion by Shishak
(2 Chr. 2:2–12)

25 It happened in the fifth year of King Rehoboam *that* Shishak king of Egypt came up against Jerusalem.

26 And he took away the treasures of the house of the LORD and the treasures of the king's house; he took away [y]everything. He also took away all the gold shields which Solomon had [z]made.

27 Then King Rehoboam made bronze shields in their place, and committed *them* to the hands of the captains of the guard, who guarded the doorway of the king's house.

28 And whenever the king entered the house of the LORD, the guards carried them, then brought them back into the guardroom.

Rehoboam dies (2 Chr. 12:13–16)

29 [aa]Now the rest of the acts of Rehoboam, and all that he did, *are* they not written in the book of the chronicles of the kings of Judah?

30 And there was [bb]war between

8 a 1 Ki. 11:33–38; 15:5
9 b 1 Ki. 12:28; 2 Chr. 11:15 c Ex. 34:17 d 2 Chr. 29:6; Ps. 50:17
10 e 1 Ki. 15:27–30 f Cp. 1 Ki. 11:11; 16:3; 21:21–22 g 1 Ki. 15:29
11 h 1 Ki. 16:4; 21:24
14 i 1 Ki. 15:27–29
15 j Dt. 29:28; 2 Ki. 17:6 k i.e. *the Euphrates* l See Dt. 16:21, *note*
17 m 1 Ki. 15:21,33
19 n 2 Chr. 13:2–20
20 o 1 Ki. 15:25 p 910 B.C.
21 q 931 B.C. r 1 Ki. 11:32
23 s 2 Ki. 17:9–10 t Cp. Dt. 12:2 u Dt. 16:22
24 v Dt. 23:17 w Dt. 20:18 x Dt. 9:4–5
26 y Cp. 1 Ki. 15:18 z 1 Ki. 10:17
29 aa vv. 29–31
30 bb 1 Ki. 12:21–24

* 14:24 Hebrew *qadesh*, that is, one practicing sodomy and prostitution in religious rituals

Rehoboam and Jeroboam all *their*
days.
31 So Rehoboam rested with his fathers, and was buried with his fathers
in the City of David. His mother's
name *was* Naamah, an Ammonitess.
Then [a]Abijam* his son reigned in his
place.

IV. The Kings of Judah and Israel to the Accession of Ahab, 15:1—16:27

Abijam (or Abijah) succeeds Rehoboam (2 Chr. 13:1–2)

15 IN the eighteenth year of King
Jeroboam the son of Nebat,
Abijam [b]became king over Judah.
2 He reigned three years in Jerusalem. His mother's name *was* Maachah the granddaughter of [c]Abisha-
lom.
3 And he walked in all the sins of
his father, which he had done before
him; his heart was not [d]loyal to the
LORD his God, as was the heart of his
father David.
4 Nevertheless for David's sake
the LORD his God gave him a [e]lamp in
Jerusalem, by setting up his son after
him and by establishing Jerusalem;
5 because David did *what was*
right in the eyes of the LORD, and had
not turned aside from anything that
He commanded him all the days of his
life, [f]except in the matter of Uriah the
[g]Hittite.
6 And there was [h]war between
Rehoboam* and Jeroboam all the
days of his life.

Asa succeeds Abijam (or Abijah) (2 Chr. 14:1–5; 15:1–19)

7 [i]Now the rest of the acts of Abijam, and all that he did, *are* they not
written in the book of the chronicles of
the kings of Judah? And there was
war between Abijam and Jeroboam.
8 So [j]Abijam rested with his fathers, and they buried him in the City
of David. Then Asa his son reigned in
his place.
9 In the twentieth year of Jeroboam king of Israel, Asa [k]became
king over Judah.
10 And he reigned forty-one years
in Jerusalem. His grandmother's
name *was* Maachah the granddaughter of [l]Abishalom.
11 [m]Asa did *what was* right in the
eyes of the LORD, as *did* his father David.
12 And he banished the [n]perverted
persons* from the land, and removed
all the idols that his fathers had made.
13 Also he [o]removed Maachah his
grandmother from *being* queen
mother, because she had made an obscene [p]image of Asherah. And Asa
cut down her obscene image and
burned *it* by the Brook Kidron.
14 But the [q]high places were [r]not
removed. Nevertheless Asa's [s]heart
was [d]loyal to the LORD all his days.
15 He also brought into the house
of the LORD the things which his father
[t]had dedicated, and the things which
he himself had dedicated: silver and
gold and utensils.

Asa's league with Syria; war with Baasha (2 Chr. 14:6–15; 16:1–10)

16 Now there was [u]war between
Asa and Baasha king of Israel all their
days.
17 And [v]Baasha king of Israel
came up against Judah, and built [w]Ra-
mah, that he might let none go out or
come in to Asa king of Judah.
18 Then Asa took all the silver and
gold *that was* left in the treasuries of
the house of the LORD and the treasuries of the king's house, and [x]delivered
them into the hand of his servants.
And King Asa sent them to Ben-
Hadad the son of Tabrimmon, the son
of Hezion, king of Syria, who dwelt in
[y]Damascus, saying,
19 "*Let there be* a treaty between
you and me, as there was between my
father and your father. See, I have
sent you a present of silver and gold.
Come and break your treaty with Baasha king of Israel, so that he will withdraw from me."
20 So Ben-Hadad heeded King Asa,
and [z]sent the captains of his armies
against the cities of Israel. He attacked [aa]Ijon, [bb]Dan, [cc]Abel Beth Maachah, and all Chinneroth, with all the
land of Naphtali.
21 Now it happened, when Baasha
heard *it*, that he stopped building Ramah, and remained in [dd]Tirzah.
22 Then King Asa made a proclamation throughout all Judah; none
was exempted. And they took away
the stones and timber of Ramah,
which Baasha had used for building;

31 *a* 2 Chr. 13:1
CHAPTER 15
1 *b* 913 B.C.
2 *c* Cp. 2 Chr. 11:20–22
3 *d* 1 Ki. 8:61; see Phil. 3:12, *note*
4 *e* 2 Sam. 21:17; 1 Ki. 11:36
5 *f* 2 Sam. 11:4, 15–17; 12:9–10 *g* See 2 Ki. 7:6, *note*
6 *h* 1 Ki. 14:30
7 *i* 2 Chr. 13:2–22
8 *j* 2 Chr. 14:1
9 *k* 911 B.C.
10 *l* Cp. v. 2
11 *m* 2 Chr. 14:2
12 *n* 1 Ki. 14:24; 22:46
13 *o* 2 Chr. 15:16–18 *p* See Dt. 16:21, *note*
14 *q* 2 Chr. 14:3; see 1 Ki. 3:2, *note* *r* 1 Ki. 3:2; 22:43 *s* 1 Sam. 16:7
15 *t* 1 Ki. 7:51
16 *u* v. 32
17 *v* 2 Chr. 16:1 *w* Josh. 18:25
18 *x* Cp. 2 Ki. 12:8 *y* 1 Ki. 11:23–24
20 *z* 1 Ki. 20:1 *aa* 2 Ki.

15:29 *bb* Jud. 18:29 *cc* 2 Sam. 20:14 **15:21** *dd* 1 Ki. 14:17

*

14:31 Spelled *Abijah* in 2 Chronicles 12:16ff
15:6 Following Masoretic Text, Septuagint, Targum, and Vulgate; some Hebrew manuscripts and Syriac read *Abijam*. **15:12** Hebrew *qedeshim*, that is, those practicing sodomy and prostitution in religious rituals

and with them King Asa built Geba of
Benjamin, and Mizpah.

Jehoshaphat succeeds Asa
(2 Chr. 16:11—17:1)

23 The rest of all the acts of Asa, all
his might, all that he did, and the cities
which he built, *are* they not written in
the book of the chronicles of the kings
of Judah? But in the time of his old age
he was diseased in his feet.
24 So Asa rested with his fathers,
and was buried with his fathers in the
City of David his father. [a]Then [b]Je-
hoshaphat his son reigned in his
place.

Baasha slays and succeeds Nadab

25 Now [c]Nadab the son of Jeroboam [d]became king over Israel in the
second year of Asa king of Judah, and
he reigned over Israel two years.
26 And he did evil in the sight of the
LORD, and walked in the way of his
father, and in his [e]sin by which he had
made Israel sin.
27 Then Baasha the son of [f]Ahijah,
of the house of Issachar, conspired
against him. And Baasha killed him at
Gibbethon, which *belonged* to the Philistines, while Nadab and all Israel
laid siege to Gibbethon.
28 Baasha killed him in the third
year of Asa king of Judah, and reigned
in his place.
29 And it was so, when he became
king, *that* he killed all the house of
Jeroboam. He did not leave to Jeroboam anyone that breathed, until he
had destroyed him, according to the
[g]word of the LORD which He had spoken by His servant Ahijah the Shilonite,
30 because of the sins of Jeroboam,
which he had sinned and by which he
had made Israel sin, because of his
provocation with which he had provoked the LORD God of Israel to anger.
31 Now the rest of the acts of Nadab, and all that he did, *are* they not
written in the book of the chronicles of
the kings of Israel?

Baasha wars with Asa of Judah

32 And there was [h]war between
Asa and Baasha king of Israel all their
days.
33 In the third year of Asa king of
Judah, Baasha the son of Ahijah [i]be-
came king over all Israel in Tirzah,
and *reigned* twenty-four years.
34 He did evil in the sight of the
LORD, and walked in the way of Jeroboam, and in his sin by which he had
made Israel [j]sin.

Prophecy against Baasha; his death

16 THEN the word of the LORD
came to [k]Jehu the son of [l]Ha-
nani, against [m]Baasha, saying:
2 [n]"Inasmuch as I lifted you out of
the dust and made you ruler over My
people Israel, and you have walked in
the [o]way of Jeroboam, and have made
My people Israel sin, to provoke Me to
anger with their sins,
3 "surely I will [p]take away the
posterity of Baasha and the posterity
of his house, and I will make your
house like the [q]house of Jeroboam the
son of Nebat.
4 [r]"The dogs shall eat whoever
belongs to Baasha and dies in the city,
and the birds of the air shall eat whoever dies in the fields."
5 Now the rest of the acts of Baasha, what he did, and his might, [s]*are*
they not written in the book of the
chronicles of the kings of Israel?
6 So Baasha rested with his fathers and was buried in [t]Tirzah. Then
Elah his son reigned in his place.
7 And also the word of the LORD
came by the prophet Jehu the son of
Hanani against Baasha and his house,
because of all the evil that he did in the
sight of the LORD in provoking Him to
anger with the work of his hands, in
being like the house of Jeroboam, and
because [u]he killed them.

Reigns of Elah and Zimri

8 In the twenty-sixth year of Asa
king of Judah, Elah the son of Baasha
[v]became king over Israel, *and reigned*
two years in Tirzah.
9 [w]Now his servant Zimri, commander of half *his* chariots, conspired
against him as he was in Tirzah drinking himself drunk in the house of
Arza, [x]steward of *his* house in Tirzah.
10 And Zimri went in and struck
him and killed him in the twenty-
seventh year of Asa king of Judah,
and [y]reigned in his place.
11 Then it came to pass, when he
began to reign, as soon as he was
seated on his throne, *that* he killed all
the household of Baasha; he did [z]not
leave him one male, neither of his relatives nor of his friends.
12 Thus Zimri destroyed all the
household of Baasha, [aa]according to
the word of the LORD, which He spoke
against Baasha by Jehu the prophet,
13 for all the sins of Baasha and the

24
a 2 Chr. 17:1
b 1 Ki. 22:41–44; Mt. 1:8
25
c 1 Ki. 14:20
d 910 B.C.
26
e 1 Ki. 12:28–33
27
f Not the *Abijah* of vv. 1–8
29
g 1 Ki. 14:10–14
32
h 1 Ki. 15:16
33
i 909 B.C.
34
j v. 26
CHAPTER 16
1
k v. 7; 2 Chr. 19:2; 20:34
l 2 Chr. 16:7–10
m 1 Ki. 15:27
2
n 1 Ki. 14:7
o 1 Ki. 12:25–33
3
p v. 11; 1 Ki. 21:21
q 1 Ki. 14:10; 15:29
4
r 1 Ki. 14:11
5
s 2 Chr. 16:1
6
t 1 Ki. 14:17; 15:21
7
u 1 Ki. 15:27–29; Hos. 1:4
8
v 886 B.C.
9
w 2 Ki. 9:31
x 1 Ki. 18:3
10
y 885 B.C.
11
z 1 Sam. 25:22
12
aa v. 3

sins of Elah his son, by which they had
sinned and by which they had made
Israel sin, in provoking the LORD God
of Israel to anger with their idols.
14 Now the rest of the acts of Elah,
and all that he did, *are* they not written
in the book of the chronicles of the
kings of Israel?
15 In the twenty-seventh year of
Asa king of Judah, Zimri had reigned
in Tirzah seven days. And the people
were encamped against Gibbethon,
which *belonged* to the Philistines.
16 Now the people *who were* encamped heard it said, "Zimri has conspired and also has killed the king."
So all Israel made Omri, the commander of the army, king over Israel
that day in the camp.
17 Then Omri and all Israel with
him went up from Gibbethon, and
they besieged Tirzah.
18 And it happened, when Zimri
saw that the city was taken, that he
went into the citadel of the king's
house and burned the king's house
down upon himself with fire, and died,
19 because of the sins which he had
committed in doing evil in the sight of
the LORD, [a]in walking in the [b]way of
Jeroboam, and in his sin which he had
committed to make Israel sin.
20 Now the rest of the acts of Zimri,
and the treason he committed, *are*
they not written in the book of the
chronicles of the kings of Israel?

Tibni and Omri are rival kings of Israel; Tibni dies

21 Then the people of Israel were
divided into two parts: half of the people followed Tibni the son of Ginath,
to make him king, and half followed
Omri.
22 But the people who followed
Omri prevailed over the people who
followed Tibni the son of Ginath. So
Tibni died and Omri reigned.

Omri reigns over Israel; he makes Samaria the capital

23 In the [c]thirty-first year of Asa
king of Judah, Omri became king over
Israel, *and reigned* twelve years. Six
years he reigned in [d]Tirzah.
24 And he bought the hill of Samaria from Shemer for two [e]talents of
silver; then he built on the hill, and
called the name of the city which he
built, Samaria, after the name of Shemer, owner of the hill.

19
a 1 Ki. 12:28; 15:26,34
b 1 Ki. 12:25–33
23
c Cp. 1 Ki. 16:15
d 1 Ki. 15:21
24
e See Coinage (OT), Ex. 30:13, *note*
25
f Mic. 6:16
29
g 874 B.C.
30
h v. 25; cp. 1 Ki. 14:9
31
i 1 Ki. 18:4
j Gen. 10:19; 1 Ki. 11:1
k Dt. 7:1–5
32
l 2 Ki. 10:18–28
33
m See Dt. 16:21, *note*
34
n i.e. *with the loss of, by sudden death*
o Josh. 6:26
CHAPTER 17
1
p Jud. 12:4
q 1 Ki. 18:1; Jas. 5:17

25 Omri did evil in the eyes of the
LORD, and did worse than all who *were*
before [f]him.
26 For he walked in all the ways of
Jeroboam the son of Nebat, and in his
sin by which he had made Israel sin,
provoking the LORD God of Israel to
anger with their idols.
27 Now the rest of the acts of Omri
which he did, and the might that he
showed, *are* they not written in the
book of the chronicles of the kings of
Israel?

V. The Reign of Ahab, 16:28—22:39

Ahab becomes king; marries Jezebel

28 So Omri rested with his fathers
and was buried in Samaria. Then
Ahab his son reigned in his place.
29 In the thirty-eighth year of Asa
king of Judah, Ahab the son of Omri
[g]became king over Israel; and Ahab
the son of Omri reigned over Israel in
Samaria twenty-two years.
30 Now Ahab the son of Omri did
evil in the sight of the LORD, more than
all who *were* before [h]him.
31 And it came to pass, as though it
had been a trivial thing for him to
walk in the sins of Jeroboam the son
of Nebat, that he took as wife [i]Jezebel
the daughter of Ethbaal, king of the
[j]Sidonians; and he went and served
Baal and worshiped [k]him.
32 Then he set up an altar for Baal
in the [l]temple of Baal, which he had
built in Samaria.
33 And Ahab made a wooden [m]im-
age. Ahab did more to provoke the
LORD God of Israel to anger than all
the kings of Israel who were before
him.
34 In his days Hiel of Bethel built
Jericho. He laid its foundation [n]with
Abiram his firstborn, and [n]with his
youngest *son* Segub he set up its gates,
according to the [o]word of the LORD,
which He had spoken through Joshua
the son of Nun.

Elijah's ministry (1 Ki. 17—2 Ki. 1); predicts three-year drought

17 AND Elijah the Tishbite, of the
[p]inhabitants of Gilead, said to
[1]Ahab, "*As* the LORD God of Israel
lives, before whom I stand, there shall
not be dew nor rain these [q]years, except at my word."

[1](17:1) It was a small thing for a man whose life was lived in the presence of the LORD to stand before Ahab.

God feeds Elijah at Cherith

2 Then the word of the LORD came
to him, saying,
3 "Get away from here and turn
eastward, and hide by the Brook Cherith, which flows into the Jordan.
4 "And it will be *that* you shall
drink from the brook, and I have commanded the [a]ravens to feed you
there."
5 So he went and did according to
the word of the LORD, for he went and
stayed by the Brook Cherith, which
flows into the Jordan.
6 The ravens brought him bread
and meat in the morning, and bread
and meat in the evening; and he drank
from the brook.
7 And it happened after a while
that the brook dried up, because there
had been no rain in the land.

God feeds Elijah at Zarephath

8 Then the word of the LORD came
to him, saying,
9 "Arise, go to [b]Zarephath, which
belongs to [c]Sidon, and dwell there.
See, I have commanded a widow there
to provide for you."
10 So he arose and went to Zarephath. And when he came to the gate
of the city, indeed a widow *was* there
gathering sticks. And he called to her
and said, "Please bring me a little water in a cup, that I may [d]drink."
11 And as she was going to get *it*,
he called to her and said, "Please bring
me a morsel of bread in your hand."
12 So she said, "As the LORD your
God lives, I do not have bread, only a
handful of flour in a bin, and a [e]little
oil in a jar; and see, I *am* gathering a
couple of sticks that I may go in and
prepare it for myself and my son, that
we may eat it, and [f]die."
13 And Elijah said to her, "Do not
fear; go *and* do as you have said, but
make me a small cake from it first, and
bring *it* to me; and afterward make
some for yourself and your son.
14 "For thus says the LORD God of
Israel: 'The bin of flour shall not be
used up, nor shall the jar of oil run dry,
until the day the LORD sends rain on
the earth.' "
15 So she went away and did according to the word of Elijah; and she
and he and her household ate for
many days.
16 The bin of flour was not used up,
nor did the jar of oil run dry, [g]accord-
ing to the word of the LORD which He
spoke by Elijah.

Elijah raises a widow's son

17 Now it happened after these
things *that* the son of the woman who
owned the house became sick. And his
sickness was so serious that there was
no breath left in him.
18 So she said to Elijah, [h]"What
have I to do with you, O man of [i]God?
Have you come to me to bring my sin
to remembrance, and to kill [j]my
son?"
19 And he said to her, "Give me
your son." So he took him out of her
arms and carried him to the upper
room where he was staying, and laid
him on his own bed.
20 Then he [k]cried out to the LORD
and said, "O LORD my God, have You
also brought tragedy on the widow
with whom I lodge, by killing her
son?"
21 And he stretched himself out on
the child three times, and cried out to
the LORD and said, "O LORD my God, I
pray, let this child's soul come back to
him."
22 Then the LORD heard the voice of
Elijah; and the soul of the child came
back to him, and he revived.
23 And Elijah took the child and
brought him down from the upper
room into the house, and gave him to
his mother. And Elijah said, "See,
your son lives!"
24 Then the woman said to Elijah,
"Now by this I [l]know that you *are* a
man of God, *and* that the word of the
LORD in your mouth *is* the truth."

Elijah and Obadiah

18 AND it came to pass *after*
many days that the word of the
LORD came to Elijah, in the third [m]year,
saying, "Go, present yourself to Ahab,
and I will send rain on the earth."
2 So Elijah went to present himself to Ahab; and *there was* a severe
famine in Samaria.
3 And Ahab had called Obadiah,
who *was* in charge of *his* house. (Now
Obadiah [n]feared the LORD greatly.
4 For so it was, while Jezebel mas-
sacred the prophets of the LORD, that
Obadiah had taken one hundred
prophets and hidden them, fifty to a
cave, and had fed them with bread and
water.)
5 And Ahab had said to Obadiah,
"Go into the land to all the springs of
water and to all the brooks; perhaps
we may find grass to keep the horses
and mules alive, so that we will not
have to kill any livestock."

4
a Job 38:41
9
b Obad. 20; Lk. 4:25–26
c 2 Sam. 24:6
10
d Cp. Gen. 24:17; Jn. 4:7
12
e Cp. 2 Ki. 4:2–7
f Dt. 28:23–24
16
g *Miracles* (OT): vv. 14–16; 17–24; 1 Ki. 18:38. (Gen. 5:24; Jon. 1:17, *note*)
18
h i.e. *What have we in common?*
i Cp. Lk. 5:8
j Cp. Jn. 4:16–19
20
k *Bible prayers* (OT): vv. 20–24; 1 Ki. 18:36. (Gen. 15:2; Hab. 3:1)
24
l Cp. Jn. 3:2; 11:45
CHAPTER 18
1
m 1 Ki. 17:1
3
n See Ps. 19:9, *note*

6 So they divided the land between them to explore it; Ahab went one way by himself, and Obadiah went another way by himself.

7 Now as Obadiah was on his way, suddenly Elijah met him; and he [a]recognized him, and fell on his face, and said, "*Is* that you, my lord Elijah?"

8 And he answered him, "*It is* I. Go, tell your master, 'Elijah *is here.*' "

9 So he said, "How have I sinned, that you are delivering your servant into the hand of Ahab, to kill me?

10 "*As* the LORD your God lives, there is no nation or kingdom where my master has not sent someone to hunt for you; and when they said, '*He is* not *here,*' he took an oath from the kingdom or nation that they could not find you.

11 "And now you say, 'Go, tell your master, "Elijah *is here*" '!

12 "And it shall come to pass, *as soon as* I am gone from you, that the [b]Spirit of the LORD will carry you to a place I do not know; so when I go and tell Ahab, and he cannot find you, he will kill me. But I your servant have [c]feared the LORD from my youth.

13 "Was it not reported to my lord what I did when Jezebel killed the prophets of the LORD, how I hid one hundred men of the LORD's prophets, fifty to a cave, and fed them with bread and water?

14 "And now you say, 'Go, tell your master, "Elijah *is here.*" ' He will kill me!"

15 Then Elijah said, "*As* the LORD of hosts lives, before whom I stand, I will surely present myself to him today."

16 So Obadiah went to meet Ahab, and told him; and Ahab went to meet Elijah.

Elijah challenges Ahab

17 Then it happened, when Ahab saw Elijah, that Ahab said to him, "*Is that* you, O troubler of Israel?"

18 And he answered, "I have not troubled Israel, but you and your father's house *have,* in that you have forsaken the commandments of the LORD and have [d]followed the Baals.

19 "Now therefore, send *and* gather all Israel to me on Mount [e]Carmel, the four hundred and fifty prophets of Baal, and the four hundred prophets of [f]Asherah, who eat at Jezebel's table."

Mount Carmel; the LORD versus Baal

20 So Ahab sent for all the children of Israel, and gathered the prophets together on Mount Carmel.

21 And Elijah came to all the people, and said, [g]"How long will you falter between two opinions? If the LORD *is* God, follow Him; but if Baal, follow him." But the people answered him not a word.

22 Then Elijah said to the people, [h]"I alone am left a prophet of the LORD; but Baal's prophets *are* four hundred and fifty men.

23 "Therefore let them give us two bulls; and let them choose one bull for themselves, cut it in pieces, and lay *it* on the wood, but put no fire *under it;* and I will prepare the other bull, and lay *it* on the wood, but put no fire *under it.*

24 "Then you call on the name of your gods, and I will call on the name of the LORD; and the God who [i]answers by fire, He is God." So all the people answered and said, "It is well spoken."

25 Now Elijah said to the prophets of Baal, "Choose one bull for yourselves and prepare *it* first, for you *are* many; and call on the name of your god, but put no fire *under it.*"

26 So they took the bull which was given them, and they prepared *it,* and called on the name of Baal from morning even till noon, saying, "O Baal, hear us!" But *there was* no voice; no one answered. Then they leaped about the altar which they had made.

27 And so it was, at noon, that Elijah mocked them and said, "Cry aloud, for he *is* a god; either he is meditating, or he is busy, or he is on a journey, *or* perhaps he is sleeping and must be [j]awakened."

28 So they cried aloud, and cut themselves, as was their custom, with [k]knives and lances, until the blood gushed out on them.

29 And when midday was past, they prophesied until the *time* of the offering of the [l]*evening* sacrifice. But *there was* no voice; no one answered, no one paid attention.

30 Then Elijah said to all the people, "Come near to me." So all the people came near to him. And he repaired the altar of the LORD *that was* [h]broken down.

31 And Elijah took twelve stones, according to the number of the tribes of the sons of Jacob, to whom the word of the LORD had come, saying, "Israel shall be your [m]name."

32 Then with the [n]stones he built

7 *a* 2 Ki. 1:6–8
12 *b Holy Spirit* (OT): v. 12; 2 Ki. 2:16. (Gen. 1:2; Zech. 12:10)
c See Ps. 19:9, *note*
18 *d* 1 Ki. 16:30–33
19 *e* Josh. 19:26
f See Dt. 16:21, *note*
21 *g* 2 Ki. 17:41; Mt. 6:24
22 *h* 1 Ki. 19:10,14
24 *i* v. 38; 1 Chr. 21:26
27 *j* Cp. Jud. 6:31
28 *k* Cp. Lev. 19:28; Dt. 14:1
29 *l* Ex. 29:39, 41
31 *m* Gen. 32:28; 35:10; 2 Ki. 17:34
32 *n* Ex. 20:25

an altar in the name of the LORD; and he made a trench around the altar large enough to hold two [a]seahs of seed.

33 And he put the wood [b]in order, cut the bull in pieces, and laid *it* on the wood, and said, "Fill four waterpots with water, and [c]pour *it* on the burnt sacrifice and on the wood."

34 Then he said, "Do *it* a second time," and they did *it* a second time; and he said, "Do *it* a third time," and they did *it* a third time.

35 So the water ran all around the altar; and he also filled the trench with water.

36 And it came to pass, at *the time of* the offering of the *evening* sacrifice, that Elijah the prophet came near and [d]said, "LORD God of Abraham, Isaac, and Israel, let it be known this day that You *are* God in Israel and I *am* Your servant, and *that* I have done all these things at Your word.

37 "Hear me, O LORD, hear me, that this people may know that You *are* the LORD God, and *that* You have turned their hearts back *to You* again."

38 Then the fire of the LORD [e]fell and consumed the burnt sacrifice, and the wood and the stones and the dust, and it licked up the water that *was* in the trench.

39 Now when all the people saw *it*, they fell on their faces; and they said, "The LORD, He *is* God! The LORD, He *is* God!"

40 And Elijah said to them, "Seize the prophets of Baal! Do not let one of them escape!" So they seized them; and Elijah brought them down to the Brook [f]Kishon and [g]executed them there.

Elijah's prophecy and prayer for rain (Jas. 5:17–18)

41 Then Elijah said to Ahab, "Go up, eat and drink; for *there is* the sound of abundance of rain."

42 So Ahab went up to eat and drink. And Elijah went up to the top of Carmel; then he bowed down on the ground, and put his face between his knees,

43 and said to his servant, "Go up now, look toward the sea." So he went up and looked, and said, "*There is* nothing." And seven times he said, "Go again."

44 Then it came to pass the seventh *time*, that he said, "There is a cloud, as small as a man's hand, rising out of the sea!" So he said, "Go up, say to Ahab, 'Prepare *your chariot*, and go down before the rain stops you.' "

45 Now it happened in the meantime that the sky became black with clouds and wind, and there was a heavy rain. So Ahab rode away and went to Jezreel.

46 Then the [h]hand of the LORD came upon Elijah; and he girded up his loins and ran ahead of Ahab to the entrance of Jezreel.

Elijah flees from Jezebel; the angel of the LORD ministers to him

19 AND Ahab told Jezebel all that Elijah had done, also how he had executed all the prophets with the [i]sword.

2 Then Jezebel sent a messenger to Elijah, saying, "So let the gods do *to me*, and more also, if I do not make your life as the life of one of them by tomorrow about this time."

3 And when he saw *that*, he arose and ran for his life, and went to Beersheba, which *belongs* to Judah, and left his servant there.

God encourages Elijah

4 But he himself went a day's journey into the wilderness, and came and sat down under a broom tree. And he [d]prayed that he might [j]die, and said, "It is enough! Now, LORD, take my life, for I *am* no better than my fathers!"

5 Then as he lay and slept under a broom tree, suddenly an [k]angel touched him, and said to him, "Arise *and* eat."

6 Then he looked, and there by his head *was* a cake baked on coals, and a jar of water. So he ate and drank, and lay down again.

7 And the [k]angel of the LORD came back the second time, and touched him, and said, "Arise *and* eat, because the journey *is* too great for you."

Elijah at Horeb

8 So he arose, and ate and drank; and he went in the strength of that food [l]forty days and forty nights as far as Horeb, the mountain of God.

9 And there he went into a cave, and spent the night in that place; and behold, the word of the LORD *came* to him, and He said to him, "What are you doing here, Elijah?"

10 So he said, "I have been very zealous for the LORD God of hosts; for the children of Israel have forsaken Your covenant, torn down Your altars, and killed Your [m]prophets with

32
a See Weights and Measures (OT), 2 Chr. 2:10, *note*
33
b Lev. 1:7
c Cp. Jud. 6:20–21
36
d Bible prayers (OT): vv. 36–37; 19:4; 2 Ki. 6:17. (Gen. 15:2; Hab. 3:1)
38
e Miracles (OT): vv. 30–38; 2 Ki. 1:10. (Gen. 5:24; Jon. 1:17, *note*). Lev. 10:1–2; Jud. 13:19–20; 2 Ki. 1:12; 1 Chr. 21:26
40
f Jud. 4:7; 5:21
g Dt. 13:5; 2 Ki. 10:24
46
h 2 Ki. 3:15
CHAPTER 19
1
i 1 Ki. 18:40
4
j Num. 11:15; Jer. 20:14–18; Jon. 4:3,8
5
k Angel (of the LORD): vv. 5,7; 2 Ki. 1:3. (Gen. 16:7; Jud. 2:1, *note*)
8
l Ex. 34:28; Mt. 4:2
10
m v. 14; Rom. 11:3

the sword. I alone am left; and they
seek to take my life."
11 Then He said, "Go out, and stand
on the mountain before the LORD."
And behold, the LORD [a]passed by, and
a [b]great and strong wind tore into the
mountains and broke the rocks in
pieces before the LORD, *but* the LORD
was not in the wind; and after the
wind an earthquake, *but* the LORD *was*
not in the earthquake;
12 and after the earthquake a fire,
but the LORD *was* not in the fire; and
after the fire a still small voice.
13 So it was, when Elijah heard *it*,
that he wrapped his face in his mantle
and went out and stood in the entrance of the cave. Suddenly a voice
came to him, and said, "What are you
doing here, Elijah?"
14 And he said, "I have been very
zealous for the LORD God of hosts; because the children of Israel have forsaken Your covenant, torn down Your
altars, and killed Your prophets with
the sword. I alone am left; and they
seek to take my life."
15 Then the LORD said to him: "Go,
return on your way to the Wilderness
of Damascus; [c]and when you arrive,
anoint Hazael *as* king over Syria.
16 "Also you shall anoint [d]Jehu the
son of Nimshi *as* king over Israel. And
[e]Elisha the son of Shaphat of Abel
Meholah you shall anoint *as* prophet
in your place.
17 "It shall be *that* whoever escapes the [f]sword of Hazael, Jehu will
[g]kill; and whoever escapes the sword
of Jehu, Elisha will kill.
18 "Yet [h]I have [i]reserved seven
thousand in Israel, all whose knees
have not bowed to Baal, and every
mouth that has not [j]kissed him."

Call of Elisha

19 So he departed from there, and
found Elisha the son of Shaphat, who
was plowing *with* twelve yoke *of oxen*
before him, and he was with the
twelfth. Then Elijah passed by him
and threw his [k]mantle on him.
20 And he left the oxen and ran after Elijah, and said, "Please let me kiss
my father and my mother, and *then* I
will follow you." And he said to him,
"Go back again, for what have I done
to [l]you?"
21 So *Elisha* turned back from him,
and took a yoke of oxen and slaughtered them and boiled their flesh, using the oxen's [m]equipment, and gave it
to the people, and they ate. Then he

11
a Ex. 33:21–22
b Ezek. 1:4
15
c 2 Ki. 8:12–13
16
d 2 Ki. 9:1–3
e 2 Ki. 2:9–15
17
f 2 Ki. 8:12; 13:3,22
g 2 Ki. 9:14-10:28
18
h Rom. 11:4
i Cp. Isa. 1:9; see Rom. 11:5, *note*
j Hos. 13:2
19
k 2 Ki. 2:8, 13–14
20
l Cp. Mt. 8:21–22
21
m 2 Sam. 24:22
CHAPTER 20
1
n 1 Ki. 15:18–20; 2 Ki. 6:24
o 1 Ki. 16:24
7
p Cp. 2 Ki. 5:7
10
q 1 Ki. 19:2
r Lit. *[are] at my feet*
11
s Prov. 27:1

arose and followed Elijah, and became his servant.

Ahab's first Syrian campaign

20 NOW [n]Ben-Hadad the king of
Syria gathered all his forces together; thirty-two kings *were* with
him, with horses and chariots. And he
went up and besieged [o]Samaria, and
made war against it.
2 Then he sent messengers into
the city to Ahab king of Israel, and
said to him, "Thus says Ben-Hadad:
3 'Your silver and your gold *are*
mine; your loveliest wives and children are mine.' "
4 And the king of Israel answered
and said, "My lord, O king, just as you
say, I and all that I have *are* yours."
5 Then the messengers came back
and said, "Thus speaks Ben-Hadad,
saying, 'Indeed I have sent to you, saying, "You shall deliver to me your silver and your gold, your wives and
your children";
6 'but I will send my servants to
you tomorrow about this time, and
they shall search your house and the
houses of your servants. And it shall
be, *that* whatever is pleasant in your
eyes, they will put *it* in their hands and
take *it*.' "
7 So the king of Israel called all
the elders of the land, and said, "Notice, please, and see how this *man*
seeks [p]trouble, for he sent to me for
my wives, my children, my silver, and
my gold; and I did not deny him."
8 And all the elders and all the
people said to him, "Do not listen or
consent."
9 Therefore he said to the messengers of Ben-Hadad, "Tell my lord the
king, 'All that you sent for to your servant the first time I will do, but this
thing I cannot do.' " And the messengers departed and brought back word
to him.
10 Then Ben-Hadad sent to him
and said, "The [q]gods do so to me, and
more also, if enough dust is left of Samaria for a handful for each of the
people who [r]follow me."
11 So the king of Israel answered
and said, "Tell *him*, 'Let not the one
who puts on *his armor* [s]boast like the
one who takes *it off*.' "
12 And it happened when *Ben-
Hadad* heard this message, as he and
the kings *were* drinking at the command post, that he said to his servants, "Get ready." And they got ready
to attack the city.

Victory of Ahab

13 Suddenly a prophet approached Ahab king of Israel, saying, "Thus says the LORD: 'Have you seen all this great multitude? Behold, [a]I will deliver it into your hand today, and you shall [b]know that I *am* the LORD.' "

14 So Ahab said, "By whom?" And he said, "Thus says the LORD: 'By the young leaders of the provinces.' " Then he said, "Who will set the battle in order?" And he answered, "You."

15 Then he mustered the young leaders of the provinces, and there were two hundred and thirty-two; and after them he mustered all the people, all the children of Israel—seven thousand.

16 So they went out at noon. Meanwhile Ben-Hadad and the thirty-two kings helping him were getting drunk at the command post.

17 The young leaders of the provinces went out first. And Ben-Hadad sent out *a patrol*, and they told him, saying, "Men are coming out of Samaria!"

18 So he said, "If they have come out for peace, take them alive; and if they have come out for war, take them alive."

19 Then these young leaders of the provinces went out of the city with the army which followed them.

20 And each one killed his man; so the Syrians fled, and Israel pursued them; and Ben-Hadad the king of Syria escaped on a horse with the cavalry.

21 Then the king of Israel went out and attacked the horses and chariots, and killed the Syrians with a great slaughter.

Ahab's second Syrian campaign

22 And the prophet came to the king of Israel and said to him, "Go, strengthen yourself; take note, and see what you should do, [c]for in the spring of the year the king of Syria will come up against you."

23 Then the servants of the king of Syria said to him, "Their gods *are* gods of the hills. Therefore they were stronger than we; but if we fight against them in the plain, surely we will be stronger than they.

24 "So do this thing: Dismiss the kings, each from his position, and put captains in their places;

25 "and you shall muster an army like the army that you have lost, horse for horse and chariot for chariot. Then we will fight against them in the plain; surely we will be stronger than they." And he listened to their voice and did so.

26 So it was, in the spring of the year, that Ben-Hadad mustered the Syrians and went up to [d]Aphek to fight against Israel.

27 And the children of Israel were mustered and given provisions, and they went against them. Now the children of Israel encamped before them like two little flocks of goats, while the Syrians filled the [e]countryside.

28 Then a [f]man of God came and spoke to the king of Israel, and said, "Thus says the LORD: 'Because the Syrians have said, "The LORD *is* God of the hills, but He *is* not God of the valleys," therefore I [g]will deliver all this great multitude into your hand, and you shall [h]know that I *am* the LORD.' "

29 And they encamped opposite each other for seven days. So it was that on the seventh day the battle was joined; and the children of Israel killed one hundred thousand foot soldiers *of* the Syrians in one day.

30 But the rest fled to Aphek, into the city; then a wall fell on [1]twenty-seven thousand of the men *who were* left. And Ben-Hadad fled and went into the city, into an inner chamber.

Ahab rebuked for sparing Ben-Hadad

31 Then his servants said to him, "Look now, we have heard that the kings of the house of Israel *are* merciful kings. Please, let us [i]put sackcloth around our waists and ropes around our heads, and go out to the king of Israel; perhaps he will spare your [j]life."

32 So they wore sackcloth around their waists and *put* ropes around their heads, and came to the king of Israel and said, "Your servant Ben-Hadad says, 'Please let me live.' " And he said, "*Is* he still alive? He *is* my brother."

33 Now the men were watching closely to see whether *any sign of mercy would come* from him; and they quickly grasped *at this word* and said, "Your brother Ben-Hadad." So he said, "Go, bring him." Then Ben-Hadad came out to him; and he had him come up into the chariot.

34 So *Ben-Hadad* said to him, "The

13
a v. 28
b 1 Ki. 18:36
22
c v. 26; 2 Sam. 11:1
26
d Josh. 13:4; 2 Ki. 13:17
27
e Jud. 6:3–5; 1 Sam. 13:5–8
28
f 1 Ki. 17:18
g v. 13
h 1 Ki. 20:13
31
i Gen. 37:34
j Cp. Josh. 9:3–15

[1](20:30) The number is possibly a scribal error. See *notes* at 1 Sam. 6:19; 1 Chr. 11:11.

[a]cities which my father took from
your father I will restore; and you may
set up marketplaces for yourself in
Damascus, as my father did in Samaria." Then *Ahab said,* "I will send
you away with this treaty." So he
made a treaty with him and sent him
away.
35 [b]Now a certain man of the [c]sons
of the prophets said to his neighbor
[d]by the word of the LORD, "Strike me,
please." And the man refused to strike
him.
36 Then he said to him, "Because
you have not obeyed the voice of the
LORD, surely, as soon as you depart
from me, a [e]lion shall kill you." And
as soon as he left him, a lion found him
and killed him.
37 And he found another man, and
said, "Strike me, please." So the man
struck him, inflicting a wound.
38 Then the prophet departed and
waited for the king by the road, and
disguised himself with a bandage over
his eyes.
39 Now as the king passed by, he
cried out to the king and said, "Your
servant went out into the midst of the
battle; and there, a man came over
and brought a man to me, and said,
'Guard this man; if by any means he is
missing, your life shall be for his [f]life,
or else you shall pay a [g]talent of silver.'
40 "While your servant was busy
here and there, [h]he was gone." Then
the king of Israel said to him, "So *shall*
your judgment *be;* you yourself have
decided *it.*"
41 And he hastened to take the bandage away from his eyes; and the king
of Israel recognized him as one of the
prophets.
42 Then he said to him, "Thus says
the LORD: [i]'Because you have let slip
out of *your* hand a man whom I appointed to utter destruction, therefore
your life shall go for his life, and your
people for his [j]people.'"
43 So the king of Israel [k]went to his
house sullen and displeased, and
came to Samaria.

Ahab covets Naboth's vineyard

21 AND it came to pass after these
things *that* Naboth the Jezreelite had a vineyard which *was* in [l]Jez-
reel, next to the palace of Ahab king of
Samaria.
2 So Ahab spoke to Naboth, saying, "Give me your [m]vineyard, that I
may have it for a vegetable garden,
because it *is* near, next to my house;
and for it I will give you a vineyard
better than it. *Or,* if it seems good to
you, I will give you its worth in
money."
3 But Naboth said to Ahab, "The
LORD forbid [n]that I should give the inheritance of my fathers to you!"
4 So Ahab went into his house sullen and displeased because of the
word which Naboth the Jezreelite had
spoken to him; for he had said, "I will
not give you the inheritance of my fathers." And he lay down on his bed,
and turned away his face, and would
[o]eat no food.

Jezebel's murderous plot

5 But [p]Jezebel his wife came to
him, and said to him, "Why is your
spirit so sullen that you eat no food?"
6 He said to her, "Because I spoke
to Naboth the Jezreelite, and said to
him, 'Give me your vineyard for
money; or else, if it pleases you, I will
give you *another* vineyard for it.' And
he answered, 'I will not give you my
vineyard.'"
7 Then Jezebel his wife said to
him, "You now exercise authority
over Israel! Arise, eat food, and let
your heart be cheerful; I will give you
the vineyard of Naboth the Jezreelite."
8 And she wrote letters in Ahab's
name, sealed *them* with his seal, and
sent the letters to the elders and the
nobles who *were* dwelling in the city
with Naboth.
9 She wrote in the letters, saying,

> Proclaim a fast, and seat
> Naboth with high honor
> among the people;
> 10 and seat two men, scoundrels,
> before him to bear witness
> against him, saying, "You have
> [q]blasphemed God and the
> king." *Then* take him out, and
> [r]stone him, that he may die.

11 So the men of his city, the elders
and nobles who were inhabitants of
his city, did as Jezebel had sent to
them, as it *was* written in the letters
which she had sent to them.
12 [s]They proclaimed a fast, and
seated Naboth with high honor
among the people.
13 And two men, scoundrels, came
in and sat before him; and the scoundrels [t]witnessed against him, against
Naboth, in the presence of the people,

34
a 1 Ki. 15:20
35
b Parables (OT): vv. 35–40; 1 Ki. 22:19. (Jud. 9:8; Zech. 11:7)
c 2 Ki. 2:3–7
d 1 Ki. 13:17
36
e Cp. 1 Ki. 13:24
39
f 2 Ki. 10:24
g See Coinage (OT), Ex. 30:13, *note*
40
h Lit. *he [was] not*
42
i 1 Ki. 22:31–37
j Cp. 1 Sam. 15:9–23
43
k 1 Ki. 21:4
CHAPTER 21
1
l 1 Ki. 18:45, 46
2
m 1 Sam. 8:14
3
n Lev. 25:23; Num. 36:7; Ezek. 46:18
4
o Cp. 1 Sam. 28:20–25
5
p 1 Ki. 19:1, 2
10
q Ex. 22:28; Lev. 24:15–16; Acts 6:11
r Lev. 24:14
12
s Isa. 58:4
13
t Ex. 20:16; 23:1,7

saying, "Naboth has blasphemed God
and the king!" Then they took him outside the city and stoned him with
[a]stones, so that he died.
14 Then they sent to Jezebel, saying, "Naboth has been stoned and is
dead."
15 And it came to pass, when Jezebel heard that Naboth had been
stoned and was dead, that Jezebel
said to Ahab, "Arise, take possession
of the vineyard of Naboth the Jezreelite, which he refused to give you for
money; for Naboth is not alive, but
dead."
16 So it was, when Ahab heard that
Naboth was dead, that Ahab got up
and went down to take possession of
the vineyard of Naboth the Jezreelite.

Doom of Ahab and Jezebel predicted; Ahab repents

17 [b]Then the word of the LORD
came to [c]Elijah the Tishbite, saying,
18 "Arise, go down to meet Ahab
king of Israel, [d]who *lives* in Samaria.
There *he is*, in the vineyard of Naboth,
where he has gone down to take possession of it.
19 "You shall speak to him, saying,
'Thus says the LORD: "Have you murdered and also taken possession?" '
And you shall speak to him, saying,
'Thus says the LORD: [e]"In the place
where dogs licked the blood of Naboth, dogs shall lick your blood, even
yours." ' "
20 So Ahab said to Elijah, [f]"Have
you found me, O my enemy?" And he
answered, "I have found *you*, because
[g]you have sold yourself to do evil in
the sight of the LORD:
21 'Behold, [h]I will bring calamity
on you. I will take away your [i]poster-
ity, and will cut off from Ahab every
male in Israel, both bond and free.
22 'I will make your house [j]like the
house of Jeroboam the son of Nebat,
and [k]like the house of Baasha the son
of Ahijah, because of the provocation
with which you have provoked *Me* to
anger, and made Israel sin.'
23 "And [l]concerning Jezebel the
LORD also spoke, saying, 'The dogs
shall eat Jezebel by the wall* of Jezreel.'
24 [m]"The dogs shall eat whoever
belongs to Ahab and dies in the city,
and the birds of the air shall eat whoever dies in the field."
25 But there was [n]no one like Ahab
who sold himself to do wickedness in

13
a 2 Ki. 9:26
17
b Ps. 9:12
c 1 Ki. 19:1
18
d 1 Ki. 13:32; 2 Chr. 22:9
19
e 1 Ki. 22:38
20
f Cp. 1 Ki. 18:17
g 2 Ki. 17:17; Rom. 7:14
21
h 1 Ki. 14:10; 2 Ki. 9:8
i 2 Ki. 10:10
22
j 1 Ki. 15:29
k 1 Ki. 16:3, 11
23
l 2 Ki. 9:36
24
m 1 Ki. 14:11; 16:4
25
n 1 Ki. 16:30–33
26
o Gen. 15:16; Lev. 18:25–30; 2 Ki. 21:11
27
p Gen. 37:34
29
q 2 Ki. 22:19
r 2 Ki. 9:25
CHAPTER 22
2
s 1 Ki. 15:24; 2 Chr. 18:2
3
t Dt. 4:43; Josh. 21:38
4
u 2 Ki. 3:7
5
v 2 Ki. 3:11
6
w 1 Ki. 18:19; cp. Dt. 18:20

the sight of the LORD, because Jezebel
his wife stirred him up.
26 And he behaved very abomina-
bly in following idols, according to all
that the [o]Amorites had done, whom
the LORD had cast out before the children of Israel.
27 So it was, when Ahab heard
those words, that he tore his clothes
and put [p]sackcloth on his body, and
fasted and lay in sackcloth, and went
about mourning.
28 And the word of the LORD came
to Elijah the Tishbite, saying,
29 "See how Ahab has [q]humbled
himself before Me? Because he has
humbled himself before Me, I will not
bring the calamity in his days. [r]In the
days of his son I will bring the calamity on his house."

Ahab's third Syrian campaign; Jehoshaphat aids him

22 NOW three years passed without war between Syria and Israel.
2 Then it came to pass, in the third
year, that [s]Jehoshaphat the king of
Judah went down to *visit* the king of
Israel.
3 And the king of Israel said to his
servants, "Do you know that [t]Ramoth
in Gilead *is* ours, but we hesitate to
take it out of the hand of the king of
Syria?"
4 So he said to Jehoshaphat, "Will
you go with me to fight at Ramoth Gilead?" Jehoshaphat said to the king of
Israel, [u]"I *am* as you *are*, my people as
your people, my horses as your
horses."

Ahab's lying prophets promise victory (2 Chr. 18:4–5,9–11)

5 Also Jehoshaphat said to the
king of Israel, "Please [v]inquire for the
word of the LORD today."
6 Then the king of Israel gathered
the [w]prophets together, about four
hundred men, and said to them, "Shall
I go against Ramoth Gilead to fight, or
shall I refrain?" So they said, "Go up,
for the Lord will deliver *it* into the
hand of the king."
7 And Jehoshaphat said, "*Is there*
not still a prophet of the LORD here,
that we may inquire of Him?"*
8 So the king of Israel said to Jehoshaphat, "*There is* still one man, Mi-

*

21:23 Following Masoretic Text and Septuagint; some Hebrew manuscripts, Syriac, Targum, and Vulgate read *plot of ground* (compare 2 Kings 9:36).
22:7 Or *him*

caiah the son of Imlah, by whom we may inquire of the LORD; but I hate him, because he does not prophesy good concerning me, but evil." And Jehoshaphat said, "Let not the king say such things!"

9 Then the king of Israel called an officer and said, "Bring Micaiah the son of Imlah quickly!"

10 The king of Israel and Jehoshaphat the king of Judah, having put on *their* robes, sat each on his throne, at a threshing floor at the entrance of the gate of Samaria; and all the prophets prophesied before them.

11 Now Zedekiah the son of Chenaanah had made [a]horns of iron for himself; and he said, "Thus says the LORD: 'With these you shall [b]gore the Syrians until they are destroyed.' "

12 And all the prophets prophesied so, saying, "Go up to Ramoth Gilead and prosper, for the LORD will deliver *it* into the king's hand."

Micaiah prophesies defeat
(2 Chr. 18:6–8,12–27)

13 Then the [c]messenger who had gone to call Micaiah spoke to him, saying, "Now listen, the words of the prophets with one accord encourage the king. Please, let your word be like the word of one of them, and speak encouragement."

14 And Micaiah said, "*As* the LORD lives, whatever the LORD says to me, that I will [d]speak."

15 Then he came to the king; and the king said to him, "Micaiah, shall we go to war against Ramoth Gilead, or shall we refrain?" And he answered him, "Go and prosper, for the LORD will deliver *it* into the hand of the king!"

16 So the king said to him, "How many times shall I make you swear that you tell me nothing but the truth in the name of the LORD?"

17 Then he said, "I saw all Israel scattered on the mountains, as sheep that have no shepherd. And the LORD said, 'These have no master. Let each return to his house in peace.' "

18 And the king of Israel said to Jehoshaphat, "Did I not tell you he would not prophesy good concerning me, but evil?"

19 Then *Micaiah* said, [e]"Therefore hear the word of the LORD: [f]I saw the LORD sitting on His throne, [g]and all the host of heaven standing by, on His right hand and on His left.

20 "And the LORD said, 'Who will [h]persuade Ahab to go up, that he may fall at Ramoth Gilead?' So one spoke in this manner, and another spoke in that manner.

21 "Then a spirit came forward and stood before the LORD, and said, 'I will persuade him.'

22 "The LORD said to him, 'In what way?' So he said, 'I will go out and be a lying spirit in the mouth of all his prophets.' And the LORD said, [i]'You shall persuade *him*, and also prevail. Go out and do so.'

23 "Therefore look! The LORD has put a lying spirit in the mouth of all these prophets of yours, and the LORD has declared disaster against you."

24 Now Zedekiah the son of Chenaanah went near and [j]struck Micaiah on the cheek, and said, [k]"Which way did the spirit from the LORD go from me to speak to you?"

25 And Micaiah said, "Indeed, you shall see on that day when you go into an [l]inner chamber to hide!"

26 So the king of Israel said, "Take Micaiah, and return him to Amon the governor of the city and to Joash the king's son;

27 "and say, 'Thus says the king: "Put this *fellow* in [m]prison, and feed him with bread of affliction and water of affliction, until I come in peace." ' "

28 But Micaiah said, "If you ever return in peace, [n]the LORD has not spoken by me." And he said, "Take heed, all you people!"

Defeat and death of Ahab
(2 Chr. 18:28–34)

29 So the king of Israel and Jehoshaphat the king of Judah went up to Ramoth Gilead.

30 And the king of Israel said to Jehoshaphat, "I will [o]disguise myself and go into battle; but you put on your robes." So the king of Israel disguised himself and went into battle.

31 Now the [p]king of Syria had commanded the thirty-two [q]captains of his chariots, saying, "Fight with no one small or great, [r]but only with the king of Israel."

32 So it was, when the captains of the chariots saw Jehoshaphat, that they said, "Surely it *is* the king of Israel!" Therefore they turned aside to fight against him, and Jehoshaphat cried out.

33 And it happened, when the captains of the chariots saw that it *was* not the king of Israel, that they turned back from pursuing him.

11
a Zech. 1:18–21
b Dt. 33:17

13
c vv. 7–9

14
d Cp. Num. 22:18; 24:13

19
e *Parables* (OT): vv. 19–23; 2 Ki. 14:9. (Jud. 9:8; Zech. 11:7)
f Isa. 6:1; Dan. 7:9; Ezek. 1:26–28
g Job. 1:6; 2:1; Ps. 103:20; Dan. 7:10

20
h Lit. *entice*

22
i Jud. 9:23; Job 12:16; Ezek. 14:9

24
j Jer. 20:2
k 2 Chr. 18:23

25
l 1 Ki. 20:30

27
m 2 Chr. 16:10; 18:25–27

28
n Num. 16:29; Dt. 18:20–22

30
o Cp. 2 Chr. 35:22

31
p 1 Ki. 20:1
q 1 Ki. 20:24
r Cp. 2 Sam. 17:2

34 Now a *certain* man drew a bow at random, and struck the king of Israel between the joints of his armor. So he said to the driver of his chariot, "Turn around and take me out of the battle, for I am wounded."

35 The battle increased that day; and the king was propped up in his chariot, facing the Syrians, and died at evening. The blood ran out from the wound onto the floor of the chariot.

36 Then, as the sun was going down, a shout went throughout the army, saying, "Every man to his city, and every man to his own country!"

37 So the king died, and was brought to Samaria. And they buried the king in Samaria.

38 Then *someone* washed the chariot at a pool in Samaria, and the dogs licked up his blood while the harlots bathed,* according [a]to the word of the LORD which He had spoken.

39 Now the rest of the acts of Ahab, and all that he did, the ivory house which he built and all the cities that he built, *are* they not written in the book of the chronicles of the kings of Israel?

VI. The Reigns of Jehoshaphat and Ahaziah, 22:40–53

Ahaziah succeeds Ahab as king of Israel

40 So Ahab rested with his fathers. Then [b]Ahaziah his son reigned in his place.

Summary of Jehoshaphat's reign over Judah (2 Chr. 17:19–20)

41 [c]Jehoshaphat the son of Asa had [d]become king over Judah in the fourth year of Ahab king of Israel.

42 Jehoshaphat *was* thirty-five years old when he became king, and he reigned twenty-five years in Jerusalem. His mother's name *was* Azubah the daughter of Shilhi.

43 And he [e]walked in all the ways of his father Asa. He did not turn aside from them, doing *what was* right in the eyes of the LORD. Nevertheless the [f]high places were not taken away, *for* the people offered sacrifices and burned incense on the high places.

44 Also [g]Jehoshaphat made [h]peace with the king of Israel.

45 Now the rest of the acts of Jehoshaphat, the might that he showed, and how he made war, *are* they not written [i]in the book of the chronicles of the kings of Judah?

46 And the rest of the [j]perverted persons,* who remained in the days of his father Asa, he banished from the land.

47 *There was* then no king in Edom, only a deputy of the king.

48 Jehoshaphat made [k]merchant ships* to go to [l]Ophir for gold; but they never sailed, for the ships were wrecked at [m]Ezion Geber.

49 Then Ahaziah the son of Ahab said to Jehoshaphat, "Let my servants go with your servants in the ships." But Jehoshaphat would not.

Jehoram succeeds Jehoshaphat (2 Chr. 21:1)

50 And [n]Jehoshaphat rested with his fathers, and was buried with his fathers in the City of David his father. Then Jehoram his son reigned in his place.

Ahaziah, Ahab's wicked son, reigns over Israel

51 [o]Ahaziah the son of Ahab [p]became king over Israel in Samaria in the seventeenth year of Jehoshaphat king of Judah, and reigned two years over Israel.

52 He did evil in the sight of the LORD, and [q]walked in the way of his father and in the way of his mother and in the way of Jeroboam the son of Nebat, who had made Israel sin;

53 for [r]he served Baal and worshiped him, and provoked the LORD God of Israel to anger, [s]according to all that his father had done.

38 *a* 1 Ki. 21:19
40 *b* 2 Ki. 1:2, 18
41 *c* 2 Chr. 20:31 *d* 870 B.C.
43 *e* 2 Chr. 17:3; 2 Chr. 20:32–33 *f* 1 Ki. 14:23; 15:14; 2 Ki. 12:3; see Jud. 3:7 and 1 Ki. 3:2, *notes*
44 *g* 2 Chr. 19:1–2 *h* 2 Chr. 18:1
45 *i* 2 Chr. 20:34
46 *j* 1 Ki. 14:24; 15:12; 2 Ki. 23:7
48 *k* 1 Ki. 10:22; 2 Chr. 20:35–37 *l* 1 Ki. 9:28 *m* 1 Ki. 9:26
50 *n* 2 Chr. 21:1
51 *o* v. 40 *p* 853 B.C
52 *q* 1 Ki. 15:26
53 *r* Jud. 2:11 *s* 1 Ki. 16:30–32

*

22:38 Syriac and Targum read *they washed his armor.* 22:46 Hebrew *qadesh*, that is, one practicing sodomy and prostitution in religious rituals 22:48 Or *ships of Tarshish*

The Second Book of the

KINGS

Author: Unknown *Theme:* Israel and Judah *Date of writing:* 6th Cent. B.C.

FIRST and SECOND KINGS were originally one book. Second Kings contains the record of two great national tragedies—the fall of the northern kingdom, Israel, in 721 B.C.; and the fall of Judah, with the destruction of Jerusalem, in 586 B.C.—as well as an account of the mighty ministry of Elisha. During the period recorded in this book, Israel received warnings and exhortations from Amos and Hosea, and a number of prophets arose in Judah, including Isaiah and Jeremiah. The Books of Kings conclude with the people of Judah in captivity in Babylon.

Second Kings may be divided as follows:

I. The Last Ministry and Translation of Elijah, 1:1—2:12.
II. The Ministry of Elisha, 2:13—8:15.
III. The Kings of Israel and Judah to the Fall of Samaria, 8:16—17:41.
IV. From the Accession of Hezekiah to the Captivity of Judah, 18:1—25:30.

I. The Last Ministry and Translation of Elijah, 1:1—2:11

Rebellion of Moab: illness of Ahaziah, king of Israel

1 [a]MOAB rebelled against Israel after the death of Ahab.

2 Now [b]Ahaziah fell through the lattice of his upper room in Samaria, and was injured; so he sent messengers and said to them, "Go, inquire of [c]Baal-Zebub, the god of [d]Ekron, whether I shall recover from this [e]injury."

3 But the [f]angel of the LORD said to Elijah the Tishbite, "Arise, go up to meet the messengers of the king of Samaria, and say to them, '*Is it* because *there is* no God in Israel *that* you are going to inquire of Baal-Zebub, the god of Ekron?'

4 "Now therefore, thus says the LORD: 'You shall not come down from the bed to which you have gone up, but you shall surely die.'" So Elijah departed.

God protects Elijah

5 And when the messengers returned to him, he said to them, "Why have you come back?"

6 So they said to him, "A man came up to meet us, and said to us, 'Go, return to the king who sent you, and say to him, "Thus says the LORD: '*Is it* because *there is* no God in Israel *that* you are sending to inquire of Baal-Zebub, the god of Ekron? Therefore you shall not come down from the bed to which you have gone up, but you shall surely die.'"'"

7 Then he said to them, "What kind of man *was it* who came up to meet you and told you these words?"

8 So they answered him, [g]"A hairy man wearing a leather belt around his waist." And he said, [h]"It *is* Elijah the Tishbite."

9 Then the king sent to him a captain of fifty with his fifty men. So he went up to him; and there he was, sitting on the top of a hill. And he spoke to him: "Man of God, the king has said, 'Come down!'"

10 So Elijah answered and said to the captain of fifty, "If I *am* a man of God, then [i]let fire come down from heaven and consume you and your fifty men." And fire came down from heaven and [j]consumed him and his fifty.

11 Then he sent to him another captain of fifty with his fifty men. And he answered and said to him: "Man of God, thus has the king said, 'Come down quickly!'"

12 So Elijah answered and said to them, "If I *am* a man of God, let fire come down from heaven and consume you and your fifty men." And the fire of God came down from heaven and consumed him and his fifty.

Jehoram becomes king of Israel

13 Again, he sent a third captain of fifty with his fifty men. And the third captain of fifty went up, and came and fell on his knees before Elijah, and pleaded with him, and said to him: "Man of God, please let my life and the life of these fifty servants of yours be [k]precious in your sight.

14 "Look, fire has come down from heaven and burned up the first two captains of fifties with their fifties. But let my life now be precious in your sight."

15 And the [f]angel of the LORD said

CHAPTER 1

1 [a] 2 Sam. 8:2; 2 Ki. 3:5

2 [b] 1 Ki. 22:40 [c] Mt. 10:25 [d] 1 Sam. 5:10 [e] Cp. 2 Ki. 8:7–10

3 [f] *Angel* (of the LORD): vv. 3–4, 15–16; 2 Ki. 19:35. (Gen. 16:7; Jud. 2:1, *note*)

8 [g] Cp. Mt. 3:4 [h] 1 Ki. 18:7

10 [i] Lk. 9:54 [j] *Miracles* (OT): vv. 10–12; 2 Ki. 2:8. (Gen. 5:24; Jon. 1:17, *note*). Cp. Num. 16:35

13 [k] 1 Sam. 26:21; Ps. 72:14

to Elijah, "Go down with him; do not
be afraid of him." So he arose and
went down with him to the king.
16 Then he said to him, "Thus says
the LORD: 'Because you have sent messengers to inquire of Baal-Zebub, the
god of Ekron, *is it* because *there is* no
God in Israel to inquire of His word?
Therefore you shall not come down
from the bed to which you have gone
up, but you shall surely die.' "
17 So *Ahaziah* died according to
the word of the LORD which Elijah had
spoken. Because he had no son, [a]Je-
horam [b]became king in his place, in
the second year of [c]Jehoram the son
of Jehoshaphat, king of Judah.
18 Now the rest of the acts of Ahaziah which he did, *are* they not written
in the book of the chronicles of the
kings of Israel?

The LORD takes Elijah into heaven by a whirlwind

2 AND it came to pass, when the
LORD was about to [d]take up Elijah
into heaven by a whirlwind, that Elijah went with [e]Elisha from Gilgal.
2 Then Elijah said to Elisha,
[f]"Stay here, please, for the LORD has
sent me on to Bethel." But Elisha said,
"*As* the LORD lives, and [g]*as* your soul
lives, I will not leave [h]you!" So they
went down to Bethel.
3 Now the [i]sons of the prophets
who *were* at Bethel came out to Elisha,
and said to him, "Do you know that
the LORD will take away your master
from over you today?" And he said,
"Yes, I know; keep silent!"
4 Then Elijah said to him, "Elisha,
stay here, please, for the LORD has sent
me on to Jericho." But he said, "*As* the
LORD lives, and *as* your soul lives, I will
not leave you!" So they came to Jericho.
5 Now the sons of the prophets
who *were* at Jericho came to Elisha
and said to him, "Do you know that
the LORD will take away your master
from over you today?" So he answered, "Yes, I know; keep silent!"
6 Then Elijah said to him, "Stay
here, please, for the LORD has sent me
on to the Jordan." But he said, "*As* the
LORD lives, and *as* your soul lives, I will
not leave you!" So the two of them
went on.
7 And fifty men of the sons of the
prophets went and stood facing *them*
at a distance, while the two of them
stood by the Jordan.
8 Now Elijah took his [j]mantle,
rolled *it* up, and [k]struck the water;
and it was [l]divided this way and that,
so that the two of them crossed over
on dry [m]ground.
9 And so it was, when they had
crossed over, that Elijah said to Elisha, "Ask! What may I do for you, before I am taken away from you?" Elisha said, "Please let a [n]double portion
of your spirit be upon me."
10 So he said, "You have asked a
[o]hard thing. *Nevertheless,* if you see
me *when I am* taken from you, it shall
be so for you; but if not, it shall not be
so."
11 Then it happened, as they continued on and talked, that suddenly a
[p]chariot of fire *appeared* with horses
of fire, and separated the two of them;
and Elijah [q]went up by a whirlwind
into heaven.

II. The Ministry of Elisha, 2:12—8:15

Elisha receives double portion of Elijah's spirit (v. 9)

12 And Elisha saw *it,* and he cried
out, "My father, my father, the chariot
of Israel and [r]its horsemen!" So he
saw him no more. And he took hold of
his own clothes and tore them into two
pieces.
13 He also took up the mantle of
Elijah that had fallen from him, and
went back and stood by the bank of
the Jordan.
14 Then he took the mantle of Elijah that had fallen from him, and
struck the water, and said, "Where *is*
the LORD God of Elijah?" And when he
also had struck the water, it was divided this way and that; and Elisha
crossed over.

Elisha succeeds Elijah

15 Now when the sons of the prophets who *were* from Jericho saw him,
they said, "The spirit of Elijah rests on
Elisha." And they came to meet him,
and bowed to the ground before him.
16 Then they said to him, "Look
now, there are fifty strong men with
your servants. Please let them go and
search for your master, lest perhaps
the [s]Spirit of the LORD [t]has taken him
up and cast him upon some mountain
or into some valley." And he said,
"You shall not send anyone."
17 But when they urged him till he
was [u]ashamed, he said, "Send *them!*"
Therefore they sent fifty men, and
they searched for three days but did
not find him.
18 And when they came back to

17
a Or *Joram,* the son of *Ahab.* 2 Ki. 8:16; cp. 2 Ki. 3:1; 1 Ki. 12:19, *note*
b 852 B.C.
c 1 Ki. 22:50; Mt. 1:8

CHAPTER 2

1
d Gen. 5:24
e 1 Ki. 19–21

2
f v. 6
g vv. 4,6; 1 Sam. 1:26; 2 Ki. 4:30
h Cp. 2 Sam. 15:21

3
i vv. 5,7,15; 1 Ki. 20:35; 2 Ki. 4:1, 38

8
j v. 13
k v. 14; Ex. 14:21–22
l *Miracles* (OT): vv. 7–14; 2 Ki. 2:22. (Gen. 5:24; Jon. 1:17, *note*)
m Josh. 3:17

9
n Cp. Dt. 21:17

10
o Cp. Gen. 18:14

11
p 2 Ki. 6:17
q Gen. 5:24; Heb. 11:5; cp. 1 Th. 4:13–17

12
r 2 Ki. 13:14

16
s *Holy Spirit* (OT): v. 16; 1 Chr. 12:18. (Gen. 1:2; Zech. 12:10)
t 1 Ki. 18:12; Acts 8:39

17
u 2 Ki. 8:11

him, for he had stayed in Jericho, he
said to them, "Did I not say to you, 'Do
not go'?"
19 Then the men of the city said to
Elisha, "Please notice, the situation of
this city *is* pleasant, as my lord sees;
but the water *is* bad, and the ground
barren."
20 And he said, "Bring me a new
bowl, and put salt in it." So they
brought *it* to him.
21 Then he went out to the source
of the water, and [a]cast in the salt
there, and said, "Thus says the LORD: 'I
have healed this water; from it there
shall be no more death or barrenness.' "
22 [b]So the water remains [c]healed
to this day, according to the word of
Elisha which he spoke.

Irreverence judged

23 Then he went up from there to
Bethel; and as he was going up the
road, some youths came from the city
and mocked him, and said to him, "Go
up, you baldhead! Go up, you baldhead!"
24 So he turned around and looked
at them, and [d]pronounced a curse on
them in the name of the LORD. And two
female bears came out of the woods
and mauled forty-two of the [1]youths.
25 Then he went from there to
[e]Mount Carmel, and from there he returned to Samaria.

Jehoram's reign over Israel

3 NOW [f]Jehoram the son of Ahab
[g]became king over Israel at Samaria in the eighteenth year of Jehoshaphat king of Judah, and reigned
twelve years.
2 And he did evil in the sight of the
LORD, but not like his father and
mother; for he put away the *sacred*
pillar of Baal [h]that his father had
made.
3 Nevertheless he persisted in the
[i]sins of Jeroboam the son of Nebat,
who had made Israel sin; he did not
depart from them.
4 Now Mesha king of Moab was a
sheepbreeder, and he regularly [j]paid
the king of Israel one hundred thousand lambs and the wool of one hundred thousand rams.
5 But it happened, when Ahab
died, that the king of Moab rebelled
against the king of Israel.
6 So King Jehoram went out of Samaria at that time and mustered all
Israel.
7 Then he went and sent to Jehoshaphat king of Judah, saying, "The
king of Moab has rebelled against me.
Will you go with me to fight against
Moab?" And he said, "I will go up; [k]I
am as you *are*, my people as your people, my horses as your horses."
8 Then he said, "Which way shall
we go up?" And he answered, "By way
of the Wilderness of Edom."

Elisha reproves Jehoram

9 So the king of Israel went with
the king of Judah and the [l]king of
Edom, and they marched on that
roundabout route seven days; and
there was no water for the army, nor
for the animals that followed them.
10 And the king of Israel said,
"Alas! For the LORD has called these
three kings together to deliver them
into the hand of Moab."
11 But [m]Jehoshaphat said, "*Is there*
no prophet of the LORD here, that we
may inquire of the LORD by him?" So
one of the servants of the king of Israel answered and said, "Elisha the
son of Shaphat *is* here, who [n]poured
water on the hands of Elijah."
12 And Jehoshaphat said, "The
word of the LORD is with him." So the
king of Israel and Jehoshaphat and
the king of Edom [o]went down to him.
13 Then Elisha said to the king of
Israel, [p]"What have I to do with [q]you?
[r]Go to the [s]prophets of your father
and the [t]prophets of your mother."
But the king of Israel said to him, "No,
for the LORD has called these three
kings *together* to deliver them into the
hand of Moab."
14 And Elisha said, [u]"*As* the LORD
of hosts lives, before whom I stand,
surely were it not that I regard the
presence of Jehoshaphat king of Ju-

21
a Ex. 15:25; 2 Ki. 4:41
22
b *Miracles* (OT): vv. 19–24; 2 Ki. 3:20. (Gen. 5:24; Jon. 1:17, *note*)
c Ezek. 47:8–9
24
d Dt. 27:13–26
25
e 1 Ki. 18:19; 2 Ki. 4:25
CHAPTER 3
1
f 2 Ki. 1:17
g 852 B.C.
2
h 1 Ki. 16:31–32
3
i 1 Ki. 12:28–32
4
j 2 Sam. 8:2
7
k 1 Ki. 22:4
9
l Cp. 1 Ki. 22:47; 2 Ki. 8:20
11
m 1 Ki. 22:7
n 1 Ki. 19:21
12
o 2 Ki. 2:25
13
p i.e. *What do we have in common?*
q Cp. Ezek. 14:3–5
r Jud. 10:14
s 1 Ki. 22:6–11
t 1 Ki. 18:19
14
u 1 Ki. 17:1; 2 Ki. 5:16

[1](2:24) The word *na'ar* ("youth") specifies no definite age. It is used of Joseph at seventeen (Gen. 37:2), and of Benjamin (Gen. 43:8) and Absalom (2 Sam. 18:5). The word *bq'* (translated "mauled") indicates the infliction of serious wounds but does not mean *kill* or *destroy*. The gravity of the offense is seen from these factors: (1) the young men mocked the features of Elisha, the man of God; (2) by saying, "Go up, you baldhead!" they were scoffing at Elijah's translation (v. 11), the offense in itself implying that the offenders were above the age of childhood; and (3) in ridiculing the man of God, they were guilty of blaspheming the God he represented.

dah, I would not look at you, nor see you.

15 "But now bring me a [a]musician." Then it happened, when the musician [b]played, that the [c]hand of the LORD came upon him.

Moab defeated

16 And he said, "Thus says the LORD: 'Make this valley full of ditches.'

17 "For thus says the LORD: 'You shall not see wind, nor shall you see rain; yet that valley shall be filled with water, so that you, your cattle, and your animals may drink.'

18 "And this is a simple matter in the sight of the LORD; He will also deliver the Moabites into your hand.

19 "Also you shall attack every fortified city and every choice city, and shall [d]cut down every good tree, and stop up every spring of water, and ruin every good piece of land with stones."

20 Now it happened in the morning, when the grain offering was offered, that suddenly [e]water came by way of Edom, and the land was filled with water.

21 And when all the Moabites heard that the kings had come up to fight against them, all who were able to bear arms and older were gathered; and they stood at the border.

22 Then they rose up early in the morning, and the sun was shining on the water; and the Moabites saw the water on the other side *as* red as blood.

23 And they said, "This is blood; the kings have surely struck swords and have killed one another; now therefore, Moab, to the spoil!"

24 So when they came to the camp of Israel, Israel rose up and attacked the Moabites, so that they fled before them; and they entered *their* land, killing the Moabites.

25 Then they destroyed the cities, and each man threw a stone on every good piece of land and filled it; and they stopped up all the springs of water and cut down all the good trees. But they left the stones of Kir Haraseth *intact*. However the slingers surrounded and attacked it.

26 And when the king of Moab saw that the battle was too fierce for him, he took with him seven hundred men who drew swords, to break through to the king of Edom, but they could not.

27 Then he took his eldest son who would have reigned in his place, and [f]offered him *as* a burnt offering upon the wall; and there was great indignation against Israel. So they departed from him and returned to *their own* land.

Increase of widow's oil

4 A CERTAIN woman of the wives of the [g]sons of the prophets cried out to Elisha, saying, "Your servant my husband is dead, and you know that your servant [h]feared the LORD. And the creditor is coming to [i]take my two sons to be his slaves."

2 So Elisha said to her, "What shall I do for you? Tell me, what do you have in the house?" And she said, "Your maidservant has nothing in the house but a jar of oil."

3 Then he said, "Go, borrow vessels from everywhere, from all your neighbors—empty vessels; do not gather just a few.

4 "And when you have come in, you shall shut the door behind you and your sons; then [j]pour it into all those vessels, and set aside the full ones."

5 So she went from him and shut the door behind her and her sons, who brought *the vessels* to her; and she poured *it* out.

6 Now it came to pass, when the vessels were full, that she said to her son, "Bring me another vessel." And he said to her, "*There is* not another vessel." [e]So the oil ceased.

7 Then she came and told the man of God. And he said, "Go, sell the oil and pay your debt; and you *and* your sons live on the rest."

Shunammite rewarded

8 Now it happened one day that Elisha went to [k]Shunem, where there *was* a notable woman, and she persuaded him to eat some food. So it was, as often as he passed by, he would turn in there to eat some food.

9 And she said to her husband, "Look now, I know that this *is* a holy man of God, who passes by us regularly.

10 "Please, let us make a small upper room on the wall; and let us put a bed for him there, and a table and a chair and a lampstand; so it will be, whenever he comes to us, he can turn in there."

11 And it happened one day that he came there, and he turned in to the upper room and lay down there.

12 Then he said to [l]Gehazi his ser-

15
a 1 Sam. 10:5
b 1 Sam. 16:16,23; 1 Chr. 25:1
c Ezek. 1:3; 3:14,22; 8:1

19
d Cp. Dt. 20:19–20

20
e *Miracles* (OT): vv. 16–20; 4:2–7, 32–44; 2 Ki. 5:14. (Gen. 5:24; Jon. 1:17, *note*)

27
f Dt. 18:10; Amos 2:1

CHAPTER 4

1
g 2 Ki. 2:3
h See Ps. 19:9, *note*
i Cp. Lev. 25:39; Neh. 5:2–5

4
j Cp. Jn. 2:6–10

8
k Josh. 19:18

12
l 2 Ki. 5:20–27; 8:4–5

vant, "Call this Shunammite woman."
When he had called her, she stood before him.
13 And he said to him, "Say now to
her, 'Look, you have been concerned
for us with all this care. What *can I* do
for you? Do you want me to speak on
your behalf to the king or to the commander of the army?' " She answered,
"I dwell among my own people."
14 So he said, "What then *is* to be
done for her?" And Gehazi answered,
"Actually, she has no son, and her
husband is old."
15 So he said, "Call her." When he
had called her, she stood in the doorway.
16 Then he said, "About this time
next year you shall embrace a son."
And she said, "No, my lord. Man of
God, [a]do not lie to your maidservant!"
17 But the woman conceived, and
bore a son when the appointed time
had come, of which Elisha had told
her.

Shunammite's son raised

18 And the child grew. Now it happened one day that he went out to his
father, to the reapers.
19 And he said to his father, "My
head, my head!" So he said to a servant, "Carry him to his mother."
20 When he had taken him and
brought him to his mother, he sat on
her knees till noon, and *then* died.
21 And she went up and laid him on
the bed of the man of God, shut *the
door* upon him, and went out.
22 Then she called to her husband,
and said, "Please send me one of the
young men and one of the donkeys,
that I may run to the man of God and
come back."
23 So he said, "Why are you going
to him today? *It is* neither the [b]New
Moon nor the Sabbath." And she said,
[c]"*It is* well."
24 Then she saddled a donkey, and
said to her servant, "Drive, and go forward; do not slacken the pace for me
unless I tell you."
25 And so she departed, and went
to the man of God at Mount [d]Carmel.
So it was, when the man of God
saw her afar off, that he said to his
servant Gehazi, "Look, the Shunammite woman!
26 "Please run now to meet her, and
say to her, '*Is it* well with you? *Is it*
well with your husband? *Is it* well with
the child?' " And she answered, "*It is*
well."

16
a v. 28
23
b Num. 10:10; 28:11; 1 Chr. 23:31
c Lit. *Peace*
25
d 2 Ki. 2:25
27
e 1 Sam. 1:10
28
f 2 Ki. 4:16
29
g 1 Ki. 18:46; 2 Ki. 9:1
h Lk. 10:4
30
i 2 Ki. 2:2
j 2 Ki. 2:4
33
k Cp. Mt. 9:25; Acts 9:40
35
l *Resurrection:* vv. 33–35; 2 Ki. 13:21. (2 Ki. 4:35; 1 Cor. 15:52, *note*)
37
m 1 Ki. 17:23; Heb. 11:35
38
n 2 Ki. 2:1
o 2 Ki. 8:1

27 Now when she came to the man
of God at the hill, she caught him by
the feet, but Gehazi came near to push
her away. But the man of God said,
"Let her alone; for her soul *is* in deep
[e]distress, and the LORD has hidden *it*
from me, and has not told me."
28 So she said, "Did I ask a son of
my lord? [f]Did I not say, 'Do not deceive me'?"
29 Then he said to Gehazi, [g]"Get
yourself ready, and take my staff in
your hand, and be on your way. If you
meet anyone, [h]do not greet him; and
if anyone greets you, do not answer
him; but lay my staff on the face of the
child."
30 And the mother of the child said,
[i]"*As* the LORD lives, and *as* your soul
lives, I will not [j]leave you." So he
arose and followed her.
31 Now Gehazi went on ahead of
them, and laid the staff on the face of
the child; but *there was* neither voice
nor hearing. Therefore he went back
to meet him, and told him, saying,
"The child has not awakened."
32 When Elisha came into the
house, there was the child, lying dead
on his bed.
33 He went in therefore, [k]shut the
door behind the two of them, and
prayed to the LORD.
34 And he went up and lay on the
child, and put his mouth on his mouth,
his eyes on his eyes, and his hands on
his hands; and he stretched himself
out on the child, and the flesh of the
child became warm.
35 He returned and walked back
and forth in the house, and again went
up and stretched himself out on him;
then the child sneezed seven times,
and the child [l]opened his eyes.
36 And he called Gehazi and said,
"Call this Shunammite woman." So he
called her. And when she came in to
him, he said, "Pick up your son."
37 So she went in, fell at his feet,
and bowed to the ground; then she
[m]picked up her son and went out.

Two further miracles

38 And Elisha returned to [n]Gilgal,
and *there was* a [o]famine in the land.
Now the sons of the prophets *were* sitting before him; and he said to his servant, "Put on the large pot, and boil
stew for the sons of the prophets."
39 So one went out into the field to
gather herbs, and found a wild vine,
and gathered from it a lapful of wild
gourds, and came and sliced *them* into

the pot of stew, though they did not
know *what they were.*
40 Then they served it to the men to
eat. Now it happened, as they were
eating the stew, that they cried out
and said, "Man of God, *there is* [a]death
in the pot!" And they could not eat *it.*
41 So [b]he said, "Then bring some
flour." And [b]he put *it* into the pot, and
said, "Serve *it* to the people, that they
may eat." And there was nothing
[c]harmful in the pot.
42 Then a man came from [d]Baal
Shalisha, and brought the man of God
bread of the firstfruits, twenty loaves
of barley bread, and newly ripened
grain in his knapsack. And he said,
"Give *it* to the people, that they may
eat."
43 But his servant said, [e]"What?
Shall I set this before one hundred
men?" He said again, "Give it to the
people, that they may eat; for thus
says the LORD: [f]'They shall eat and
have *some* left over.' "
44 So he [g]set *it* before them; and
they ate and had *some* [h]left over, according to the word of the LORD.

Naaman, the Syrian, is healed

5 NOW [i]Naaman, commander of
the army of the king of Syria, was
a great and honorable man in the eyes
of his master, because by him the LORD
had given victory to Syria. He was
also a mighty man of valor, *but* a
leper.
2 And the Syrians had gone out
[j]on raids, and had brought back captive a young girl from the land of Israel. She waited on Naaman's wife.
3 Then she said to her mistress, "If
only my master *were* with the prophet
who *is* in Samaria! For he would heal
him of his leprosy."
4 And *Naaman* went in and told
his master, saying, "Thus and thus
said the girl who *is* from the land of
Israel."
5 Then the king of Syria said, "Go
now, and I will send a letter to the king
of Israel." So he departed and [k]took
with him ten [l]talents of silver, six
thousand *shekels* of gold, and ten
changes of clothing.
6 Then he brought the letter to the
king of Israel, which said,

> Now be advised, when this
> letter comes to you, that I have
> sent Naaman my servant to
> you, that you may heal him of
> his leprosy.

7 And it happened, when the king
of Israel read the letter, that he tore his
clothes and said, "*Am* I [m]God, to kill
and make alive, that this man sends a
man to me to heal him of his leprosy?
Therefore please consider, and see
how he seeks a quarrel with me."
8 So it was, when Elisha the man
of God heard that the king of Israel
had torn his clothes, that he sent to the
king, saying, "Why have you torn
your clothes? Please let him come to
me, and he shall know that there is a
prophet in Israel."
9 Then Naaman went with his
horses and chariot, and he stood at the
door of Elisha's house.
10 And Elisha sent a messenger to
him, saying, "Go and [n]wash in the Jordan seven times, and your flesh shall
be restored to you, and *you shall* be
clean."
11 But Naaman became furious,
and went away and said, "Indeed, I
said to myself, 'He will surely come
out *to me,* and stand and call on the
name of the LORD his God, and wave
his hand over the place, and heal the
leprosy.'
12 "*Are* not the Abanah* and the
Pharpar, the rivers of Damascus, better than all the waters of Israel? Could
I not wash in them and be clean?"
So he turned and went away in a
rage.
13 And his [o]servants came near
and spoke to him, and said, "My father, *if* the prophet had told you *to do*
something great, would you not have
done *it?* How much more then, when
he says to you, 'Wash, and be clean'?"
14 So he went down and [p]dipped
seven times in the Jordan, according
to the saying of the man of God; and
his [q]flesh was restored like the flesh
of a little child, and he was [r]clean.

Gehazi's sin and its penalty

15 And he returned to the man of
God, he and all his aides, and came
and stood before him; and he said, "Indeed, now I know that *there is* [s]no
God in all the earth, except in Israel;
now therefore, please take a gift from
your servant."
16 But he said, [t]"*As* the LORD lives,
before whom I stand, I will receive
[u]nothing." And he urged him to take
it, but he refused.
17 So Naaman said, "Then, if not,

40
a Ex. 10:17
41
b Ex. 15:25; 2 Ki. 2:21
c Lit. *evil thing*
42
d 1 Sam. 9:4
43
e Cp. Mt. 15:33; Jn. 6:9
f Cp. Jn. 6:12
44
g Cp. Mk. 8:6
h Cp. Mt. 14:20; 15:37; Jn. 6:13
CHAPTER 5
1
i Lk. 4:27
2
j 2 Ki. 6:23
5
k 1 Sam. 9:8; 2 Ki. 8:8
l See Coinage (OT), Ex. 30:13, *note*
7
m Gen. 30:2; Dt. 32:39; 1 Sam. 2:6
10
n Cp. Jn. 9:7
13
o 1 Sam. 28:23
14
p *Miracles* (OT): vv. 10–14, 27; 2 Ki. 6:6. (Gen. 5:24; Jon. 1:17, *note*)
q Job 33:25
r Lk. 5:13
15
s Ezra 1:3; Dan. 2:47; 3:29; 6:26–27
16
t 2 Ki. 3:14
u Cp. Gen. 14:23

*5:12 Following Kethib, Septuagint, and Vulgate; Qere, Syriac, and Targum read *Amanah.*

please let your servant be given two
mule-loads of [a]earth; for your servant
will no longer offer either burnt offering or sacrifice to other gods, but to
the LORD.
18 "Yet in this thing may the LORD
pardon your servant: when my master
goes into the temple of Rimmon to
worship there, and he [b]leans on my
hand, and I bow down in the temple of
Rimmon—when I bow down in the
temple of Rimmon, may the LORD
please pardon your servant in this
thing."
19 Then he said to him, "Go in
peace." So he departed from him a
short distance.
20 But [c]Gehazi, the servant of Elisha the man of God, said, "Look, my
master has spared Naaman this Syrian, while not receiving from his
hands what he brought; but *as* the
LORD lives, I will run after him and
take something from him."
21 So Gehazi pursued Naaman.
When Naaman saw *him* running after
him, he got down from the chariot to
meet him, and said, "*Is* all well?"
22 And he said, "All *is* [d]well. My
master has sent me, saying, 'Indeed,
just now two young men of the sons of
the prophets have come to me from
the mountains of Ephraim. Please
give them a talent of silver and two
changes of garments.' "
23 So Naaman said, "Please, take
two talents." And he urged him, and
bound two talents of silver in two
bags, with two changes of garments,
and handed *them* to two of his servants; and they carried *them* on ahead
of him.
24 When he came to the citadel, he
took *them* from their hand, and stored
them away in the house; then he let
the men go, and they departed.
25 Now he went in and stood before
his master. Elisha said to him, "Where
did you go, Gehazi?" And he said,
"Your servant did not go anywhere."
26 Then he said to him, "Did not my
heart go *with you* when the man
turned back from his chariot to meet
you? *Is it* [e]time to receive money and
to receive clothing, olive groves and
vineyards, sheep and oxen, male and
female servants?
27 "Therefore the leprosy of Naaman shall [f]cling to you and your descendants forever." And he went out
from his presence [g]leprous, *as white*
as snow.

17
[a] Cp. Ex. 20:24
18
[b] 2 Ki. 7:2, 17
20
[c] 2 Ki. 4:12; 8:4–5
22
[d] 2 Ki. 4:26
26
[e] Eccl. 3:1,6
27
[f] Cp. 1 Tim. 6:10
[g] Ex. 4:6; Num. 12:10; 2 Ki. 15:5
CHAPTER 6
1
[h] 2 Ki. 4:38
3
[i] 2 Ki. 5:23
5
[j] Ex. 22:14
6
[k] *Miracles* (OT): vv. 5–7, 18–20; 2 Ki. 13:21. (Gen. 5:24; Jon. 1:17, *note*)
8
[l] 2 Ki. 8:28–29
13
[m] Gen. 37:17

Elisha recovers lost ax head

6 AND the [h]sons of the prophets
said to Elisha, "See now, the place
where we dwell with you is too small
for us.
2 "Please, let us go to the Jordan,
and let every man take a beam from
there, and let us make there a place
where we may dwell." So he answered, "Go."
3 Then one said, [i]"Please consent
to go with your servants." And he answered, "I will go."
4 So he went with them. And
when they came to the Jordan, they
cut down trees.
5 But as one was cutting down a
tree, the iron *ax head* fell into the water; and he cried out and said, "Alas,
master! For it was [j]borrowed."
6 So the man of God said, "Where
did it fall?" And he showed him the
place. So he cut off a stick, and threw
it in there; and he made the iron
[k]float.
7 Therefore he said, "Pick *it* up for
yourself." So he reached out his hand
and took it.

Elisha reveals Syria's war plans

8 Now the [l]king of Syria was
making war against Israel; and he
consulted with his servants, saying,
"My camp *will be* in such and such a
place."
9 And the man of God sent to the
king of Israel, saying, "Beware that
you do not pass this place, for the Syrians are coming down there."
10 Then the king of Israel sent
someone to the place of which the
man of God had told him. Thus he
warned him, and he was watchful
there, not just once or twice.
11 Therefore the heart of the king
of Syria was greatly troubled by this
thing; and he called his servants and
said to them, "Will you not show me
which of us *is* for the king of Israel?"
12 And one of his servants said,
"None, my lord, O king; but Elisha, the
prophet who *is* in Israel, tells the king
of Israel the words that you speak in
your bedroom."
13 So he said, "Go and see where he
is, that I may send and get him." And
it was told him, saying, "Surely *he is* in
[m]Dothan."
14 Therefore he sent horses and
chariots and a great army there, and
they came by night and surrounded
the city.
15 And when the servant of the

man of God arose early and went out,
there was an army, surrounding the
city with horses and chariots. And his
servant said to him, "Alas, my master!
What shall we do?"
16 So he answered, [a]"Do not fear,
for [b]those who *are* with us *are* more
than those who *are* with them."
17 And Elisha prayed, and [c]said,
"LORD, I pray, open his eyes that he
may see." Then the LORD [d]opened the
eyes of the young man, and he saw.
And behold, the mountain *was* full of
[e]horses and chariots of fire all around
Elisha.

Syrian soldiers blinded

18 So when *the Syrians* came down
to him, Elisha prayed to the LORD, and
said, "Strike this people, I pray, with
blindness." And He [f]struck them with
blindness according to the word of
Elisha.
19 Now Elisha said to them, "This *is*
not the way, nor *is* this the city. Follow
me, and I will bring you to the man
whom you seek." But he led them to
Samaria.
20 So it was, when they had come
to Samaria, that Elisha said, "LORD,
open the eyes of these *men,* that they
may see." And the LORD opened their
eyes, and they saw; and there *they
were,* inside Samaria!
21 Now when the king of Israel saw
them, he said to Elisha, [g]"My father,
shall I kill *them?* Shall I kill *them?*"
22 But he answered, "You shall not
kill *them.* Would you kill those whom
you have taken captive with your
sword and your bow? Set food and
water before them, that they may eat
and drink and go to their master."
23 Then he [h]prepared a great feast
for them; and after they ate and drank,
he sent them away and they went to
their master. So the bands of Syrian
raiders came no more into the land of
Israel.

Ben-Hadad besieges Samaria

24 And it happened after this that
[i]Ben-Hadad king of Syria gathered
all his army, and went up and besieged Samaria.
25 And there was a great [j]famine
in Samaria; and indeed they besieged
it until a donkey's head was *sold* for
eighty *shekels* of silver, and one-
fourth of a [k]kab of dove droppings for
five *shekels* of silver.
26 Then, as the king of Israel was
passing by on the wall, a woman cried
out to him, saying, "Help, my lord, O
king!"
27 And he said, "If the LORD does
not help you, where can I find help for
you? From the threshing floor or from
the winepress?"
28 Then the king said to her, "What
is troubling you?" And she answered,
"This woman said to me, 'Give your
son, that we may eat him today, and
we will eat my son tomorrow.'
29 "So we [l]boiled my son, and ate
him. And I said to her on the next day,
'Give your son, that we may eat him';
but she has hidden her son."
30 Now it happened, when the king
heard the words of the woman, that he
[m]tore his clothes; and as he passed by
on the wall, the people looked, and
there underneath *he had* sackcloth on
his body.
31 Then he said, [n]"God do so to me
and more also, if the head of Elisha the
son of Shaphat remains on him today!"
32 But Elisha was sitting in his
house, and the [o]elders were sitting
with him. And *the king* sent a man
ahead of him, but before the messenger came to him, he said to the elders,
"Do you see how this son of a [p]mur-
derer has sent someone to take away
my head? Look, when the messenger
comes, shut the door, and hold him
fast at the door. *Is* not the sound of his
master's feet behind him?"
33 And while he was still talking
with them, there was the messenger,
coming down to him; and then *the
king* said, "Surely this calamity *is*
from the [q]LORD; [r]why should I wait
for the LORD any longer?"

Elisha promises abundant food

7 THEN Elisha said, "Hear the
word of the LORD. Thus says the
LORD: 'Tomorrow about this time a
[k]seah of fine flour *shall be sold* for a
[s]shekel, and two seahs of barley for a
shekel, at the gate of Samaria.' "
2 So an officer on whose hand the
king [t]leaned answered the man of
God and said, "Look, *if* the LORD would
make windows in heaven, could this
thing be?" And he said, "In fact, you
shall see *it* with your eyes, but you
shall not eat of it."
3 Now there were four [u]leprous
men at the entrance of the gate; and
they said to one another, "Why are we
sitting here until we die?
4 "If we say, 'We will enter the
city,' the famine *is* in the city, and we

16
a Ex. 14:13; 1 Ki. 17:13
b 2 Chr. 32:7; Ps. 55:18; Rom. 8:31
17
c *Bible prayers (OT):* vv. 17–18; 2 Ki. 19:15. (Gen. 15:2; Hab. 3:1)
d Num. 22:31; Lk. 24:31
e 2 Ki. 2:11; Ps. 34:7; 68:17
18
f Gen. 19:11; Acts 13:11
21
g 2 Ki. 2:12; 5:13
23
h Cp. 2 Chr. 28:8–15
24
i 1 Ki. 20:1
25
j 2 Ki. 4:38; 8:1
k See Weights and Measures (OT), 2 Chr. 2:10, *note*
29
l Lev. 26:29; Dt. 28:53–57
30
m 1 Ki. 21:27
31
n Ruth 1:17; 1 Ki. 19:2
32
o Ezek. 8:1
p 1 Ki. 18:4
33
q Cp. Amos 3:6
r Job 2:9
CHAPTER 7
1
s See Coinage (OT), Ex. 30:13, *note*
2
t 2 Ki. 5:18
3
u Lev. 13:46; Num. 5:2–4; 12:10–14

shall die there. And if we sit here, we die also. Now therefore, come, let us surrender to the [a]army of the Syrians. If they keep us alive, we shall live; and if they kill us, we shall only die."

5 And they rose at twilight to go to the camp of the Syrians; and when they had come to the outskirts of the Syrian camp, to their surprise no one *was* there.

6 For the LORD had caused the army of the Syrians to [b]hear the noise of chariots and the noise of horses—the noise of a great army; so they said to one another, "Look, the king of Israel has hired against us the [c]kings of the [1]Hittites and the kings of the Egyptians to attack us!"

7 Therefore they arose and fled at twilight, and left the camp intact—their tents, their horses, and their donkeys—and they fled for their lives.

8 And when these lepers came to the outskirts of the camp, they went into one tent and ate and drank, and carried from it silver and gold and clothing, and went and hid *them;* then they came back and entered another tent, and carried *some* from there *also,* and went and hid *it.*

9 Then they said to one another, "We are not doing right. This day *is* a day of good news, and we remain [d]silent. If we wait until morning light, some punishment will come upon us. Now therefore, come, let us go and tell the king's household."

10 So they went and called to the gatekeepers of the city, and told them, saying, "We went to the Syrian camp, and surprisingly no one *was* there, not a human sound—only horses and donkeys tied, and the tents intact."

11 And the gatekeepers called out, and they told *it* to the king's household inside.

Elisha's promise is fulfilled

12 So the king arose in the night and said to his servants, "Let me now tell you what the Syrians have done to us. They know that we *are* [e]hungry; therefore they have gone out of the camp to [f]hide themselves in the field, saying, 'When they come out of the city, we shall catch them alive, and get into the city.'"

13 And one of his servants answered and said, "Please, let several *men* take five of the remaining horses which are left in the city. Look, they *may either become* like all the multitude of Israel that are left in it; or indeed, *I say,* they *may become* like all the multitude of Israel left from those who are consumed; so let us send them and see."

14 Therefore they took two chariots with horses; and the king sent them in the direction of the Syrian army, saying, "Go and see."

15 And they went after them to the Jordan; and indeed all the road *was* full of garments and weapons which the Syrians had thrown away in their haste. So the messengers returned and told the king.

16 Then the people went out and plundered the tents of the Syrians. So a seah of fine flour was *sold* for a shekel, and two seahs of barley for a shekel, [g]according to the word of the LORD.

17 Now the king had appointed the officer on whose hand he leaned to have charge of the gate. But the people trampled him in the gate, and he died, just [h]as the man of God had said, who spoke when the king came down to him.

18 So it happened just as the man of God had spoken to the king, saying, [g]"Two seahs of barley for a shekel, and a seah of fine flour for a shekel, shall be *sold* tomorrow about this time in the gate of Samaria."

19 Then that officer had answered the man of God, and said, "Now look, *if* the LORD would make windows in heaven, could such a thing be?" And he had said, "In fact, you shall see *it* with your eyes, but you shall not eat of it."

20 And so it happened to him, for the people trampled him in the gate, and he died.

Elisha predicts seven years of famine

8 THEN Elisha spoke to the woman [i]whose son he had restored to life, saying, "Arise and go, you and

4
a 2 Ki. 6:24
6
b 2 Sam. 5:24; 2 Ki. 19:7; Job 15:21
c 1 Ki. 10:29
9
d Cp. Rom. 1:14; 1 Cor. 9:16; 2 Cor. 6:1–2
12
e 2 Ki. 6:24–29
f Cp. Josh. 8:4–12
16
g v. 1
17
h 2 Ki. 7:2; 6:32
CHAPTER 8
1
i 2 Ki. 4:35

[1](7:6) Until the twentieth century the Hittites were unknown apart from the Bible. This once puzzling reference to them has, however, been illuminated by the findings of archaeology. From Egyptian monuments (Tell el-Amarna Tablets) and the Assyrian texts, it has been shown that these were the Kheta or Hatti. Expeditions in the first dozen years of this century have revealed that Boghaz-koi in Asia Minor (east of Ankara, Turkey) was the capital of the Hittite Empire. Periods of Hittite prominence: about 2000–1800 B.C. and about 1400–1200 B.C.

your household, and stay wherever you can; for the LORD [a]has called for a [b]famine, and furthermore, it will come upon the land for [c]seven years."

2 So the woman arose and did according to the saying of the man of God, and she went with her household and dwelt in the land of the Philistines seven years.

Jehoram restores the Shunammite's land

3 It came to pass, at the end of seven years, that the woman returned from the land of the Philistines; and she went to make an appeal to the king for her house and for her land.

4 Then the king talked with [d]Gehazi, the servant of the man of God, saying, "Tell me, please, all the great things Elisha has done."

5 Now it happened, as he was telling the king how he had restored the dead to life, that there was the woman whose son he had restored to life, appealing to the king for her house and for her land. And Gehazi said, "My lord, O king, this *is* the woman, and this *is* her son whom Elisha restored to life."

6 And when the king asked the woman, she told him. So the king appointed a certain officer for her, saying, "Restore all that *was* hers, and all the proceeds of the field from the day that she left the land until now."

Elisha predicts Hazael's reign over Syria

7 Then Elisha went to Damascus, and [e]Ben-Hadad king of Syria was sick; and it was told him, saying, "The man of God has come here."

8 And the king said to Hazael, "Take a [f]present in your hand, and go to meet the man of God, and inquire of the LORD by him, saying, 'Shall I recover from this disease?' "

9 So [g]Hazael went to meet him and took a present with him, of every good thing of Damascus, forty camel-loads; and he came and stood before him, and said, "Your son Ben-Hadad king of Syria has sent me to you, saying, 'Shall I recover from this disease?' "

10 And Elisha said to him, "Go, say to him, 'You shall certainly recover.' However the LORD has shown me that he will really [h]die."

11 Then he set his countenance in a stare until he was [i]ashamed; and the man of God wept.

12 And Hazael said, "Why is my lord weeping?" He answered, "Because I know the [j]evil that you will do to the children of Israel: Their strongholds you will set on fire, and their young men you will kill with the sword; and you [k]will dash their children, and rip open their women with child."

13 So Hazael said, "But what [l]*is* your servant—a dog, that he should do this gross thing?" And Elisha answered, "The LORD has shown me that you *will become* king over Syria."

14 Then he departed from Elisha, and came to his master, who said to him, "What did Elisha say to you?" And he answered, "He told me you would surely [m]recover."

15 But it happened on the next day that he took a thick cloth and dipped *it* in water, and spread *it* over his face so that he died; and Hazael reigned in his place.

III. The Kings of Israel and Judah to the Fall of Samaria, 8:16—17:41

Jehoram reigns with his father over Judah (2 Chr. 21:5)

16 Now [n]in the fifth year of Joram the son of Ahab, king of Israel, Jehoshaphat *having been* king of Judah, [o]Jehoram the son of Jehoshaphat [p]began to reign as king of Judah.

17 He was [q]thirty-two years old when he became king, and he reigned eight years in Jerusalem.

18 And he walked in the way of the kings of Israel, just as the house of Ahab had done, for the [r]daughter of Ahab was his [1]wife; and he did evil in the sight of the LORD.

19 Yet the LORD would not destroy Judah, for the sake of his servant David, [s]as He promised him to give a lamp to him *and* his sons forever.

Edom and Libnah revolt against Judah (2 Chr. 21:8–10)

20 In his days [t]Edom revolted against Judah's authority, and made a king over themselves.

21 So Joram* went to Zair, and all his chariots with him. Then he rose by

1
[a] Ps. 105:16; Hag. 1:11
[b] 2 Sam. 21:1; 1 Ki. 18:2; 2 Ki. 4:38; 6:25
[c] Cp. Gen. 41:27
4
[d] 2 Ki. 5:20
7
[e] 2 Ki. 6:24
8
[f] 1 Ki. 14:3; 2 Ki. 5:5
9
[g] 1 Ki. 19:15
10
[h] v. 15
11
[i] 2 Ki. 2:17
12
[j] 2 Ki. 10:32; 12:17; 13:3,7; Amos 1:3–4
[k] 2 Ki. 15:16; Hos. 13:16; Amos 1:13; Nah. 3:10
13
[l] 1 Sam. 17:43
14
[m] v. 10
16
[n] 2 Ki. 1:17; 3:1
[o] Called *Joram*, vv. 21,23–24
[p] 848 B.C. He reigned in consort with his father
17
[q] vv. 17–22; cp. 2 Chr. 21:5–10
18
[r] Cp. 2 Ki. 8:26–27
19
[s] 2 Sam. 7:13; 1 Ki. 11:36; 15:4; 2 Chr. 21:7
20
[t] Gen. 27:40; 2 Ki. 3:27; 2 Chr. 21:8–10

*8:21 Spelled *Jehoram* in verse 16

[1](8:18) The marriage of Jehoshaphat's son, Jehoram, to Ahab's daughter, Athaliah, was a great mistake. The union was supposed to foster peace and cooperation between the two kingdoms, but it only degraded Judah.

night and attacked the Edomites who
had surrounded him and the captains
of the chariots; and the troops fled to
their tents.
22 Thus Edom has been in revolt
against Judah's authority to this day.
And [a]Libnah revolted at that time.

Ahaziah succeeds Joram
(2 Chr. 21:18—22:4)

23 Now the rest of the acts of Joram, and all that he did, *are* they not
written in the book of the chronicles of
the kings of Judah?
24 So Joram rested with his fathers,
and was buried with his fathers in the
City of David. Then [b]Ahaziah his son
reigned in his place.
25 [c]In the twelfth year of Joram the
son of Ahab, king of Israel, Ahaziah
the son of Jehoram, king of Judah,
[d]began to reign.
26 Ahaziah *was* [e]twenty-two years
old when he became king, and he
reigned one year in Jerusalem. His
mother's name *was* Athaliah the
granddaughter of Omri, king of Israel.
27 And he walked in the way of the
house of Ahab, and did evil in the
sight of the LORD, like the house of
Ahab, for he *was* the son-in-law of the
house of Ahab.

Defense of Ramoth Gilead (2 Chr. 22:5)

28 Now he went with Joram the son
of Ahab to war against Hazael king of
Syria at [f]Ramoth Gilead; and the Syrians wounded Joram.
29 Then King Joram went back to
Jezreel to recover from the wounds
which the Syrians had inflicted on
him at Ramah, when he fought
against Hazael king of Syria. And
[g]Ahaziah the son of Jehoram, king of
Judah, went down to see Joram the
son of Ahab in Jezreel, because he
was sick.

Jehu anointed king over Israel

9 AND Elisha the prophet called
[h]one of the sons of the prophets,
and said to him, [i]"Get yourself ready,
take this [j]flask of oil in your hand,
and go to [k]Ramoth Gilead.
2 "Now when you arrive at that
place, look there for Jehu the son of
Jehoshaphat, the son of Nimshi, and
go in and make him rise up from
among his associates, and take him to
an inner room.
3 "Then take the flask of oil, and
pour *it* on his head, and say, 'Thus
says the LORD: "I have anointed you
king over Israel." ' Then open the door
and flee, and do not delay."
4 So the young man, the servant of
the prophet, went to Ramoth Gilead.
5 And when he arrived, there *were*
the captains of the army sitting; and
he said, "I have a message for you,
Commander." Jehu said, "For which
one of us?" And he said, "For you,
Commander."
6 Then he arose and went into the
house. And he poured the oil on his
head, and said to him, [l]"Thus says the
LORD God of Israel: 'I have anointed
you king over the people of the LORD,
over Israel.
7 'You shall strike down the house
of Ahab your master, that I may
[m]avenge the blood of My servants the
prophets, and the blood of all the servants of the LORD, [n]at the hand of Jezebel.
8 'For the whole house of Ahab
shall perish; and [o]I will cut off from
Ahab all the males in Israel, both bond
and free.
9 'So I will make the house of
Ahab like the house of [p]Jeroboam the
son of Nebat, and like the house of
[q]Baasha the son of Ahijah.
10 [r]'The dogs shall eat Jezebel on
the plot *of ground* at Jezreel, and *there
shall be* none to bury *her.*' " And he
opened the door and fled.
11 Then Jehu came out to the servants of his master, and *one* said to
him, "*Is* all well? Why did this madman come to you?" And he said to
them, "You know the man and his
babble."
12 And they said, "A lie! Tell us
now." So he said, "Thus and thus he
spoke to me, saying, 'Thus says the
LORD: "I have anointed you king over
Israel." ' "
13 Then each man hastened to take
his garment and [s]put *it* under him on
the top of the steps; and they blew
trumpets, saying, "Jehu is [d]king!"

Jehu executes Joram (Jehoram)

14 So Jehu the son of Jehoshaphat,
the son of Nimshi, conspired against
Joram. (Now [t]Joram had been defending Ramoth Gilead, he and all Israel, against Hazael king of Syria.
15 But King Joram had returned to
Jezreel to [u]recover from the wounds
which the Syrians had inflicted on
him when he fought with Hazael king
of Syria.) And Jehu said, "If you are so
minded, let no one leave *or* escape

22 *a* Josh. 21:13; 2 Ki. 19:8
24 *b* Cp. 2 Chr. 21:17; 22:6
25 *c* Cp. 2 Ki. 9:29; see 1 Chr. 11:11, *note* *d* 841 B.C.
26 *e* Cp. 2 Chr. 22:2; see 1 Chr. 11:11, *note*
28 *f* 1 Ki. 22:3, 29
29 *g* 2 Ki. 9:16; 2 Chr. 22:6–7
CHAPTER 9
1 *h* vv. 4–10 *i* 2 Ki. 4:29; Jer. 1:17 *j* 1 Ki. 1:39 *k* 2 Ki. 8:28–29
6 *l* 1 Ki. 19:16; 2 Chr. 22:7
7 *m* Dt. 32:35, 41 *n* 1 Ki. 18:4; 21:15
8 *o* 1 Ki. 14:10; 21:21; 2 Ki. 10:17
9 *p* 1 Ki. 15:29; 21:22 *q* 1 Ki. 16:3, 11
10 *r* vv. 35–36; 1 Ki. 21:23
13 *s* Cp. Mt. 21:8
14 *t* 2 Ki. 8:28
15 *u* 2 Ki. 8:29

from the city to go and tell *it* in Jezreel."

16 So Jehu rode in a chariot and went to Jezreel, for Joram was laid up there; and Ahaziah king of Judah had come down to see Joram.

17 Now a watchman stood on the tower in Jezreel, and he saw the company of Jehu as he came, and said, "I see a company of men." And Joram said, "Get a horseman and send him to meet them, and let him say, '*Is it* peace?' "

18 So the horseman went to meet him, and said, "Thus says the king: '*Is it* peace?' " And Jehu said, "What have you to do with peace? Turn around and follow me." So the watchman reported, saying, "The messenger went to them, but is not coming back."

19 Then he sent out a second horseman who came to them, and said, "Thus says the king: '*Is it* peace?' " And Jehu answered, "What have you to do with peace? Turn around and follow me."

20 So the watchman reported, saying, "He went up to them and is not coming back; and the driving *is* [a]like the driving of Jehu the son of Nimshi, for he drives furiously!"

21 Then Joram said, "Make ready." And his chariot was made ready. Then [b]Joram king of Israel and Ahaziah king of Judah went out, each in his chariot; and they went out to meet Jehu, and met him [c]on the property of Naboth the Jezreelite.

22 Now it happened, when Joram saw Jehu, that he said, "*Is it* peace, Jehu?" So he answered, "What peace, as long as the [d]harlotries of your mother Jezebel and her witchcraft *are* so many?"

23 Then Joram turned around and fled, and said to Ahaziah, [e]"Treachery, Ahaziah!"

24 Now Jehu drew his bow with full strength and [b]shot Jehoram between his arms; and the arrow came out at his heart, and he sank down in his chariot.

25 Then *Jehu* said to Bidkar his captain, "Pick *him* up, *and* throw him into the tract of the field of Naboth the Jezreelite; for remember, when you and I were riding together behind Ahab his father, that the [f]LORD laid this [g]burden upon him:

26 'Surely I saw yesterday the blood of Naboth and the blood of his sons,' says the LORD, [h]'and I will repay you in this plot,' says the LORD. Now therefore, take *and* throw him on the plot *of ground,* according to the word of the LORD."

Jehu executes Ahaziah (2 Chr. 22:7,9)

27 But when Ahaziah king of Judah saw *this,* he fled by the road to Beth Haggan.* So Jehu pursued him, and said, "Shoot him also in the chariot." *And they shot him* at the Ascent of Gur, which is by Ibleam. Then he fled to [i]Megiddo, and died there.

28 And his servants carried him in the chariot to Jerusalem, and [j]buried him in his tomb with his fathers in the City of David.

29 [k]In the eleventh year of Joram the son of Ahab, Ahaziah had become king over Judah.

Jehu executes Jezebel

30 Now when Jehu had come to Jezreel, Jezebel heard *of it;* and she put [l]paint on her eyes and adorned her head, and looked through a window.

31 Then, as Jehu entered at the gate, she said, "*Is it* peace, Zimri, [m]murderer of your master?"

32 And he looked up at the window, and said, "Who *is* on my side? Who?" So two *or* three eunuchs looked out at him.

33 Then he said, "Throw her down." So they threw her down, and *some* of her blood spattered on the wall and on the horses; and he trampled her underfoot.

34 And when he had gone in, he ate and drank. Then he said, "Go now, see to this accursed *woman,* and bury her, for [n]she was a king's daughter."

35 So they went to bury her, but they found no more of her than the skull and the feet and the palms of *her* hands.

36 Therefore they came back and told him. And he said, "This *is* the word of the LORD, which He spoke by His servant Elijah the Tishbite, saying, [o]'On the plot *of ground* at Jezreel dogs shall eat the flesh of Jezebel;

37 'and the corpse of Jezebel shall be [p]as [q]refuse on the surface of the field, in the plot at Jezreel, so that they shall not say, "Here *lies* Jezebel." ' "

Judgment on the house of Ahab

10 NOW Ahab had [r]seventy sons in Samaria. And Jehu wrote and sent letters to Samaria, to the rul-

20 [a] Cp. 2 Sam. 18:27
21 [b] 1 Ki. 19:17; 2 Chr. 22:7 [c] 1 Ki. 21:1–14
22 [d] Rev. 2:20
23 [e] Cp. 2 Ki. 11:13–16
25 [f] 1 Ki. 21:29 [g] Isa. 13:1
26 [h] 1 Ki. 21:19
27 [i] 2 Chr. 22:9
28 [j] Cp. 2 Ki. 23:30
29 [k] Cp. 2 Ki. 8:25; see 1 Chr. 11:11, *note*
30 [l] Jer. 4:30; Ezek. 23:40
31 [m] 1 Ki. 16:9–10
34 [n] 1 Ki. 16:31
36 [o] 1 Ki. 21:23
37 [p] Ps. 83:10 [q] Cp. Jer. 8:1–3
CHAPTER 10
1 [r] vv. 6–7; cp. 1 Ki. 16:29

* 9:27 Literally *The Garden House*

ers of Jezreel,* to the elders, and to
[a]those who reared Ahab's *sons,* saying:

> 2 Now as soon as this letter
> comes to you, since your
> master's sons *are* with you,
> and you have chariots and
> horses, a fortified city also,
> and weapons,
> 3 choose the best qualified of
> your master's sons, set *him* on
> his father's throne, and fight
> for your master's house.

4 But they were exceedingly
afraid, and said, "Look, [b]two kings
could not stand up to him; how then
can we stand?"
5 And he who *was* in charge of the
house, and he who *was* in charge of
the city, the elders also, and those who
reared *the sons,* sent to Jehu, saying,
"We *are* your servants, we will do all
you tell us; but we will not make anyone king. Do *what is* good in your
sight."
6 Then he wrote a second letter to
them, saying:

> If you *are* for me and will obey
> my voice, take the heads of the
> men, your master's sons, and
> come to me at Jezreel by this
> time tomorrow.

Now the king's sons, seventy persons,
were with the great men of the city,
who were rearing them.
7 So it was, when the letter came
to them, that they took the king's sons
and [c]slaughtered seventy persons,
put their heads in baskets and sent
them to him at Jezreel.
8 Then a messenger came and told
him, saying, "They have brought the
heads of the king's sons." And he said,
"Lay them in two heaps at the entrance of the gate until morning."
9 So it was, in the morning, that he
went out and stood, and said to all the
people, "You *are* righteous. Indeed [d]I
conspired against my master and
killed him; but who killed all these?
10 "Know now that [e]nothing shall
fall to the earth of the word of the LORD
which the LORD spoke concerning the
house of Ahab; for the LORD has done
what He [f]spoke by His servant Elijah."
11 So Jehu killed all who remained
of the house of Ahab in Jezreel, and all
his great men and his close acquaintances and his [g]priests, until he left
him none remaining.

Jehu massacres the royal princes of Judah (2 Chr. 22:8)

12 And he arose and departed and
went to Samaria. On the way, at Beth
Eked* of the Shepherds,
13 Jehu met with the brothers of
Ahaziah king of Judah, and said,
"Who *are* you?" So they answered,
"We *are* the brothers of Ahaziah; we
have come down to greet the sons of
the king and the sons of the queen
mother."
14 And he said, "Take them alive!"
So they took them alive, and [h]killed
them at the well of Beth Eked, forty-
two men; and he left none of them.
15 Now when he departed from
there, he met [i]Jehonadab the son of
[j]Rechab, *coming* to meet him; and he
greeted him and said to him, "Is your
heart right, as my heart *is* toward your
heart?" And Jehonadab answered, "It
is." *Jehu said,* "If it is, give *me* your
hand." So he gave *him* his hand, and
he took him up to him into the chariot.
16 Then he said, "Come with me,
and see my [k]zeal for the LORD." So
they had him ride in his chariot.
17 And when he came to Samaria,
he killed all who remained to Ahab in
Samaria, till he had destroyed them,
according to the word of the LORD
which He spoke to [l]Elijah.

Jehu exterminates Baal worshipers

18 Then Jehu gathered all the people together, and said to them, [m]"Ahab
served Baal a little, Jehu will serve
him much.
19 "Now therefore, call to me all the
[n]prophets of Baal, all his servants,
and all his priests. Let no one be missing, for I have a great sacrifice for
Baal. Whoever is missing shall not
live." But Jehu acted deceptively, with
the intent of destroying the worshipers of Baal.
20 And Jehu said, "Proclaim a solemn assembly for Baal." So they proclaimed *it.*
21 Then Jehu sent throughout all
Israel; and all the worshipers of Baal
came, so that there was not a man left
who did not come. So they came into
the temple* of Baal, and the [o]temple
of Baal was full from one end to the
other.
22 And he said to the one in charge
of the wardrobe, "Bring out vestments

1 [a] Lit. *the nourishers*
4 [b] 2 Ki. 9:24, 27
7 [c] 1 Ki. 21:21; cp. Jud. 9:5
9 [d] 2 Ki. 9:14–24
10 [e] 1 Ki. 8:56 [f] 1 Ki. 21:19–24, 29; 2 Ki. 9:7–10
11 [g] v. 17; 11:18
14 [h] 2 Chr. 22:8
15 [i] Called *Jonadab,* Jer. 35:6,8, 10,14,16, 18,19 [j] 2 Sam. 4:2; 1 Chr. 2:55
16 [k] 1 Ki. 19:10
17 [l] v. 10
18 [m] 1 Ki. 16:31–32
19 [n] 1 Ki. 18:19; 22:6
21 [o] vv. 22–27

*
10:1 Following Masoretic Text, Syriac, and Targum; Septuagint reads *Samaria;* Vulgate reads *city.* **10:12** Or *The Shearing House* **10:21** Literally *house,* and so elsewhere in this chapter

for all the worshipers of Baal." So he
brought out vestments for them.
23 Then Jehu and Jehonadab the
son of Rechab went into the temple of
Baal, and said to the worshipers of
Baal, "Search and see that no servants
of the LORD are here with you, but only
the worshipers of Baal."
24 So they went in to offer sacrifices and burnt offerings. Now Jehu
had appointed for himself eighty men
on the outside, and had said, "*If* any of
the men whom I have brought into
your hands escapes, *whoever lets him
escape, it shall be* [a]his life for the life
of the other."
25 Now it happened, as soon as he
had made an end of offering the burnt
offering, that Jehu said to the guard
and to the captains, "Go in *and* kill
them; let no one come out!" And they
killed them with the edge of the
sword; then the guards and the officers threw *them* out, and went into the
inner room of the temple of Baal.
26 And they brought the *sacred* pillars out of the temple of Baal and
[b]burned them.
27 Then they broke down the *sacred* pillar of Baal, and tore down the
temple of Baal [c]and made it a refuse
dump to this day.
28 Thus Jehu destroyed Baal from
Israel.

But Jehu follows Jeroboam's sins

29 However Jehu did not turn away
from the sins of Jeroboam the son of
Nebat, who had made Israel sin, *that
is,* from the [d]golden calves that *were*
at Bethel and Dan.
30 And the LORD [e]said to Jehu, "Because you have done well in doing
what is right in My sight, *and* have
done to the house of Ahab all that *was*
in My heart, [f]your sons shall sit on the
throne of Israel to the [1]fourth *generation.*"
31 But Jehu took no heed to walk in
the law of the LORD God of Israel with
all his heart; for he did not depart from
the [g]sins of Jeroboam, who had made
Israel sin.

Hazael of Syria smites Israel

32 In those days the LORD began to
cut off *parts* of Israel; and [h]Hazael
conquered them in all the territory of
Israel
33 from the Jordan eastward: all
the land of Gilead—Gad, Reuben, and

24
a 1 Ki. 20:39
26
b Dt. 7:5,25
27
c Ezra 6:11; Dan. 2:5; 3:29
29
d 1 Ki. 12:28–29
30
e 2 Ki. 9:6–7
f v. 35; 2 Ki. 13:1,10; 14:23; 15:8,12
31
g 1 Ki. 14:16
32
h 1 Ki. 19:17; 2 Ki. 8:12; 13:22
33
i Dt. 2:36
j Amos 1:3–5
35
k 2 Ki. 13:1
l 814 B.C.
CHAPTER 11
1
m 2 Chr. 22:10
n 2 Ki. 8:26
o 2 Ki. 9:27
p 841 B.C.
q Cp. Rev. 12:1–5
2
r 2 Ki. 8:25
s Or *Jehoash,* 2 Ki. 12:1
4
t vv. 4–20; cp. 2 Chr. 23:1–21
u 2 Ki. 12:2
5
v 1 Chr. 9:25

Manasseh—from [i]Aroer, which *is* by
the River Arnon, including [j]Gilead
and Bashan.

Jehoahaz succeeds Jehu

34 Now the rest of the acts of Jehu,
all that he did, and all his might, *are*
they not written in the book of the
chronicles of the kings of Israel?
35 So Jehu rested with his fathers,
and they buried him in Samaria. Then
[k]Jehoahaz his son [l]reigned in his
place.
36 And the period that Jehu
reigned over Israel in Samaria *was*
twenty-eight years.

*Queen Athaliah murders royal
seed of Judah (2 Chr. 22:9–12)*

11 WHEN [m]Athaliah the [n]mother
of Ahaziah saw that her son
was [o]dead, she [p]arose and [q]de-
stroyed all the royal heirs.
2 But Jehosheba, the daughter of
King Joram, [r]sister of Ahaziah, took
[s]Joash the son of Ahaziah, and stole
him away from among the king's sons
who were being murdered; and they
hid him and his nurse in the bedroom,
from Athaliah, so that he was not
killed.
3 So he was hidden with her in the
house of the LORD for six years, while
Athaliah reigned over the land.

*Joash (Jehoash) elevated to throne
of Judah (2 Chr. 23:1–11)*

4 [t]In the seventh year [u]Jehoiada
sent and brought the captains of
hundreds—of the bodyguards and the
escorts—and brought them into the
house of the LORD to him. And he made
a covenant with them and took an
oath from them in the house of the
LORD, and showed them the king's son.
5 Then he commanded them, saying, "This *is* what you shall do: One-
third of you who come on duty [v]on the
Sabbath shall be keeping watch over
the king's house,
6 "one-third *shall be* at the gate of
Sur, and one-third at the gate behind
the escorts. You shall keep the watch
of the house, lest it be broken down.
7 "The two contingents of you
who go off duty on the Sabbath shall
keep the watch of the house of the
LORD for the king.
8 "But you shall surround the king
on all sides, every man with his weapons in his hand; and whoever comes

[1](10:30) The four: Jehoahaz, Joash, Jeroboam II, and Zechariah. Jehu's dynasty was the longest of the northern kingdom.

within range, let him be put to death. You are to be with the king as he goes out and as he comes [a]in."

9 So the [b]captains of the hundreds did according to all that Jehoiada the priest commanded. Each of them took his men who were to be on duty on the Sabbath, with those who were going off duty on the Sabbath, and came to Jehoiada the priest.

10 And the priest gave the captains of hundreds the spears and [c]shields which *had belonged* to King David, that were in the temple of the LORD.

11 Then the escorts stood, every man with his weapons in his hand, all around the king, from the right side of the temple to the left side of the temple, by the altar and the house.

12 And he brought out the king's son, put the crown on him, and *gave him* the [d]Testimony;* they made him king and anointed him, and they clapped their hands and said, [e]"Long live the king!"

Athaliah is killed
(2 Chr. 23:12–15; 23:21)

13 Now when [f]Athaliah heard the noise of the escorts *and* the people, she came to the people *in* the temple of the LORD.

14 When she looked, there was the king standing by a pillar according to custom; and the leaders and the trumpeters were by the king. All the people of the land were rejoicing and blowing trumpets. So Athaliah tore her clothes and cried out, "Treason! Treason!"

15 And Jehoiada the priest commanded the captains of the hundreds, the officers of the army, and said to them, "Take her outside under guard, and slay with the sword whoever follows her." For the priest had said, "Do not let her be killed in the house of the LORD."

16 So they seized her; and she went by way of the horses' entrance *into* the king's house, and there she was killed.

Revival through Jehoiada
(2 Chr. 23:16–21)

17 [g]Then Jehoiada [h]made a covenant [i]between the LORD, the king, and the people, that they should be the LORD's people, and *also* between the king and the people.

18 And all the people of the land went to the [j]temple of Baal, and tore it down. They thoroughly [k]broke in pieces its altars and images, and [l]killed Mattan the priest of Baal before the altars. And the priest appointed officers over the house of the LORD.

19 Then he took the captains of hundreds, the bodyguards, the escorts, and all the people of the land; and they brought the king down from the house of the LORD, and went by way of the gate of the escorts to the king's house. Then he sat on the throne of the kings.

20 So all the people of the land rejoiced; and the city was quiet, for they had slain Athaliah with the sword *in* the king's house.

21 [m]Jehoash *was* seven years old when he became king.

Reign of Joash (Jehoash)
(2 Ki. 11:4; 2 Chr. 24:2)

12 IN the seventh year of Jehu, Jehoash* [n]became king, and he reigned forty years in Jerusalem. His mother's name *was* Zibiah of Beersheba.

2 Jehoash did *what was* right in the sight of the LORD all the days in which [o]Jehoiada the priest instructed him.

3 But the [p]high places were not taken away; the people still sacrificed and burned incense on the high places.

Temple repairs delayed twenty-three years (2 Chr. 24:4–5)

4 And Jehoash said to the priests, "All the money of the [q]dedicated gifts that are [r]brought into the house of the LORD—each man's census money, each man's assessment money*—*and* all the money that a man purposes in his [s]heart to bring into the house of the LORD,

5 "let the priests take *it* themselves, each from his constituency; and let them repair the damages of the temple, wherever any dilapidation is found."

6 Now it was so, by the twenty-third year of King Jehoash, *that* the priests had not [t]repaired the damages of the temple.

7 So [u]King Jehoash called Jehoiada the priest and the *other* priests, and said to them, "Why have you not repaired the damages of the temple? Now therefore, do not take *more* money from your constituency, but

8
a Cp. Num. 27:16–17
9
b Cp. 1 Sam. 8:12
10
c 2 Sam. 8:7
12
d Ex. 31:18
e 1 Sam. 10:24
13
f 2 Ki. 8:26
17
g v. 1; 2 Chr. 24:15–16
h Josh. 24:24–25; 2 Chr. 15:12–15
i Cp. Gen. 9:16; 2 Sam. 5:3
18
j 2 Ki. 10:26, 27
k Dt. 12:3
l 1 Ki. 18:40; 2 Ki. 10:11
21
m 11:21-12:15; cp. 2 Chr. 24:1–14
CHAPTER 12
1
n 835 B.C.
2
o 2 Ki. 11:4
3
p 1 Ki. 15:14; 22:43; 2 Ki. 14:4; see Jud. 3:7 and 1 Ki. 3:2, *notes*
4
q Lit. *holy things*
r 2 Ki. 22:4
s Ex. 35:5; 1 Chr. 29:3–9; cp. 2 Cor. 9:6–15
6
t Cp. Ezra 9:9
7
u 2 Chr. 24:6

*

11:12 That is, the Law (compare Exodus 25:16,21 and Deuteronomy 31:9) **12:1** Spelled *Joash* in 11:2ff **12:4** Compare Leviticus 27:2ff

deliver it for repairing the damages of
the temple."
8 And the priests agreed that they
would neither receive *more* money
from the people, nor repair the damages of the temple.

Temple repairs completed by freewill offerings (2 Chr. 24:8–14)

9 Then [a]Jehoiada the priest took a
chest, bored a hole in its lid, and set it
beside the altar, on the right side as
one comes into the house of the LORD;
and the priests who kept the door put
[b]there all the money brought into the
house of the LORD.
10 So it was, whenever they saw
that *there was* much money in the
chest, that the king's [c]scribe and the
high priest came up and put it in bags,
and counted the money that was
found in the house of the LORD.
11 Then they gave the money,
which had been apportioned, into the
hands of those who did the work, who
had the oversight of the house of the
LORD; and they paid it out to the carpenters and builders who worked on
the house of the LORD,
12 and to masons and stonecutters,
and for buying timber and hewn
stone, to [d]repair the damage of the
house of the LORD, and for all that was
paid out to repair the temple.
13 However [e]there were not made
for the house of the LORD basins of
silver, trimmers, sprinkling-bowls,
trumpets, any articles of gold or articles of silver, from the money brought
into the house of the LORD.
14 But they gave that to the workmen, and they repaired the house of
the LORD with it.
15 Moreover [f]they did not require
an account from the men into whose
hand they delivered the money to be
paid to workmen, for they dealt faithfully.
16 The [g]money from the trespass
offerings and the money from the sin
offerings was not brought into the
house of the LORD. [h]It belonged to the
priests.

Hazael of Syria bribed with temple treasures

17 [1][i]Hazael king of Syria went up
and fought against Gath, and took it;
then Hazael set his face to go up to
Jerusalem.
18 And Jehoash king of Judah
[j]took all the sacred things that his fathers, Jehoshaphat and Jehoram and
Ahaziah, kings of Judah, had dedicated, and his own sacred things, and
all the gold found in the treasuries of
the house of the LORD and in the king's
house, and sent *them* to Hazael king
of Syria. Then he went away from Jerusalem.

Joash (Jehoash) dies; Amaziah reigns over Judah (2 Chr. 24:25–27)

19 Now the rest of the acts of Joash,* and all that he did, *are* they not
written in the book of the chronicles of
the kings of Judah?
20 And [k]his servants arose and
formed a conspiracy, and killed Joash
in the [l]house of the Millo,* which
goes down to Silla.
21 For [m]Jozachar the son of Shimeath and Jehozabad the son of [n]Sho-
mer, his [o]servants, struck him. So he
died, and they buried him with his fathers in the City of David. Then [p]Am-
aziah his son reigned in his place.

Jehoahaz reigns over Israel

13 IN the twenty-third year of
[q]Joash* the son of Ahaziah,
king of Judah, [r]Jehoahaz the son of
Jehu [s]became king over Israel in Samaria, *and reigned* seventeen years.
2 And he did evil in the sight of the
LORD, and followed the [t]sins of Jeroboam the son of Nebat, who had made
Israel sin. He did not depart from
them.

Jehoahaz repents; idols not abolished

3 Then the [u]anger of the LORD was
aroused against Israel, and He delivered them into the hand of [v]Hazael
king of Syria, and into the hand of
[v]Ben-Hadad the son of Hazael, all
their days.
4 So Jehoahaz [w]pleaded with the
LORD, and the LORD listened to him; for
He [x]saw the oppression of Israel, because the king of Syria oppressed
them.
5 [y]Then the LORD gave Israel a
[z]deliverer, so that they escaped from
under the hand of the Syrians; and the
children of Israel dwelt in their tents
as before.
6 Nevertheless they did not depart
from the sins of the house of Jero-

9
a 2 Chr. 23:1
b Mk. 12:41; Lk. 21:1
10
c 2 Sam. 8:17; 2 Ki. 19:2; 22:3–4
12
d 2 Ki. 22:5–6
13
e Cp. 2 Ki. 7:48,50
15
f 2 Ki. 22:7
16
g Lev. 5:15–18
h Lev. 7:7; Num. 18:9
17
i 2 Ki. 8:12
18
j 1 Ki. 15:18; 2 Ki. 18:15–16
20
k Cp. 2 Ki. 14:5
l Or *Beth Millo*
21
m Or *Zabad,* 2 Chr. 24:26
n Or *Shimrith,* 2 Chr. 24:26
o 2 Ki. 14:5
p 2 Ki. 14:1
CHAPTER 13
1
q 2 Ki. 12:1
r 2 Ki. 10:35
s 814 B.C.
2
t 1 Ki. 12:26–33
3
u Jud. 2:14
v Amos 1:4
4
w Ps. 78:34
x Ex. 3:7; Jud. 2:18
5
y v. 25; 2 Ki. 14:25–27
z Evidently *Jehoash,* vv. 19,25; later *Jeroboam II,* v. 13; Neh. 9:27

*

12:19 Spelled *Jehoash* in 12:1ff **12:20** Literally *The Landfill* **13:1** Spelled *Jehoash* in 12:1ff

[1](12:17) Hazael invaded Judah twice. This was the first invasion; for the second, refer to 2 Chr. 24:23.

boam, who had made Israel sin, *but* walked in them; and the [a]wooden image also [b]remained in Samaria.

7 For He left of the army of Jehoahaz only fifty horsemen, ten chariots, and ten thousand foot soldiers; for the king of Syria [c]had destroyed them and made them [d]like the dust at threshing.

Jehoahaz dies; Jehoash (Joash) reigns over Israel

8 Now the rest of the acts of Jehoahaz, all that he did, and his might, *are* they not written in the book of the chronicles of the kings of Israel?

9 So Jehoahaz rested with his fathers, and they buried him in Samaria. Then Joash his son reigned in his place.

10 In the thirty-seventh year of Joash king of Judah, Jehoash* the son of Jehoahaz [e]became king over Israel in Samaria, *and reigned* sixteen years.

11 And he did evil in the sight of the LORD. He did not depart from all the sins of Jeroboam the son of Nebat, who made Israel sin, *but* walked in them.

Parenthesis: Jehoash's (Joash's) death

12 Now the [f]rest of the acts of Joash, all that he did, and his might with which he fought against Amaziah king of Judah, *are* they not written in the book of the chronicles of the kings of Israel?

13 So Joash [g]rested with his fathers. Then Jeroboam sat on his throne. And Joash was buried in Samaria with the kings of Israel.

Jehoash's (Joash's) scant faith

14 Elisha had become sick with the illness of which he would die. Then Joash the king of Israel came down to him, and wept over his face, and said, "O my father, my father, the [h]chariots of Israel and their horsemen!"

15 And Elisha said to him, "Take a bow and some arrows." So he took himself a bow and some arrows.

16 Then he said to the king of Israel, "Put your hand on the bow." So he put his hand *on it,* and Elisha put his hands on the king's hands.

17 And he said, "Open the east window"; and he opened *it.* Then Elisha said, "Shoot"; and he shot. And he said, "The arrow of the LORD's deliverance and the arrow of deliverance from Syria; for you must strike the Syrians at [i]Aphek till you have destroyed *them.*"

18 Then he said, "Take the arrows"; so he took *them.* And he said to the king of Israel, "Strike the ground"; so he struck three times, and stopped.

19 And the man of God was angry with him, and said, "You should have struck five or six times; then you would have struck Syria till you had destroyed *it!* [j]But now you will strike Syria *only* three times."

Elisha dies; his prophecy fulfilled; miracle at his tomb

20 Then Elisha died, and they buried him. And the *raiding* [k]bands from Moab invaded the land in the spring of the year.

21 So it was, as they were burying a man, that suddenly they spied a band *of raiders;* and they put the man in the tomb of Elisha; and when the man was let down and touched the bones of Elisha, he [l]revived and [m]stood on his feet.

22 And [n]Hazael king of Syria oppressed Israel all the days of Jehoahaz.

23 But the LORD was [o]gracious to them, had compassion on them, and [p]regarded them, [q]because of His covenant with Abraham, Isaac, and Jacob, and would not yet destroy them or cast them from His presence.

24 Now Hazael king of Syria died. Then Ben-Hadad his son reigned in his place.

25 And Jehoash* the son of Jehoahaz recaptured from the hand of Ben-Hadad, the son of Hazael, the cities which he had taken out of the hand of Jehoahaz his father by [r]war. [s]Three times Joash defeated him and recaptured the cities of Israel.

Amaziah reigns over Judah (2 Ki. 12:21; 2 Chr. 25:1–4)

14

IN the second year of Joash the son of [t]Jehoahaz, king of Israel, [u]Amaziah the son of Joash, king of Judah, [v]became king.

2 He was twenty-five years old when he became king, and he reigned twenty-nine years in Jerusalem. His mother's name was Jehoaddan of Jerusalem.

3 And he did *what was* right in the sight of the LORD, yet not like his father David; he did everything [w]as his father Joash had done.

4 [x]However the high places were not taken away, and the people still

---

6 *a* See Dt. 16:21, *note* · *b* 1 Ki. 16:33
7 *c* 2 Ki. 10:32 · *d* Amos 1:3
10 *e* 798 B.C.
12 *f* 2 Ki. 14:8–15
13 *g* 2 Ki. 14:16
14 *h* 2 Ki. 2:12
17 *i* 1 Ki. 20:26
19 *j* v. 25
20 *k* 2 Ki. 3:5; 24:2
21 *l* *Resurrection:* v. 21; Job 19:25. (2 Ki. 4:35; 1 Cor. 15:52, *note*) · *m* *Miracles* (OT): v. 21; 2 Ki. 19:35. (Gen. 5:24; Jon. 1:17, *note*)
22 *n* 2 Ki. 8:12
23 *o* 2 Ki. 14:27 · *p* Ex. 2:24–25 · *q* Gen. 17:2–7; Ex. 32:13
25 *r* 2 Ki. 10:32–33; 12:17; 14:25 · *s* vv. 18–19
CHAPTER 14
1 *t* 2 Ki. 13:10 · *u* 2 Chr. 25:1 · *v* 796 B.C.
3 *w* 2 Ki. 12:2
4 *x* 2 Ki. 12:3; see Jud. 3:7 and 1 Ki. 3:2, *notes*

---

*13:10 Spelled *Joash* in verse 9   13:25 Spelled *Joash* in verses 12-14,25

sacrificed and burned incense on the
high places.
5 Now it happened, as soon as the
kingdom was established in his hand,
that he executed his servants [a]who
had murdered his father the king.
6 But the children of the murderers he did not execute, according to
what is written in the Book of the Law
of Moses, in which the LORD commanded, saying, [b]"Fathers shall not
be put to death for their children, nor
shall children be put to death for their
fathers; but a person shall be put to
death for his own sin."
7 He killed ten thousand [c]Edom-
ites in the [d]Valley of Salt, and took
Sela by war, and called its name Joktheel to this day.

Amaziah defeated (2 Chr. 25:14–24)

8 Then Amaziah sent messengers
to Jehoash* the son of Jehoahaz, the
son of Jehu, king of Israel, saying,
"Come, let us face one another *in battle.*"
9 And Jehoash king of Israel sent
to Amaziah king of Judah, saying,
[e]"The thistle that *was* in Lebanon sent
to the cedar that *was* in Lebanon, saying, 'Give your daughter to my son as
wife'; and a wild beast that *was* in
Lebanon passed by and trampled the
thistle.
10 "You have indeed defeated
Edom, and your heart has [f]lifted you
up. Glory *in that,* and stay at home;
for why should you meddle with trouble so that you fall—you and Judah
with you?"
11 But Amaziah would not heed.
Therefore Jehoash king of Israel went
out; so he and Amaziah king of Judah
faced one another at Beth Shemesh,
which *belongs* to Judah.
12 And Judah was defeated by Israel, and every man fled to his tent.
13 Then Jehoash king of Israel captured Amaziah king of Judah, the son
of Jehoash, the son of Ahaziah, at
Beth Shemesh; and he went to Jerusalem, and broke down the wall of Jerusalem from the Gate of Ephraim to the
Corner Gate—four hundred [g]cubits.
14 And he [h]took all the gold and
silver, all the articles that were found
in the house of the LORD and in the
treasuries of the king's house, and
hostages, and returned to Samaria.

Jehoash (Joash) dies; Jeroboam II reigns over Israel (cp. 2 Ki. 13:12–15)

15 Now the rest of the acts of Jehoash which he did—his might, and how
he fought with Amaziah king of
Judah—*are* they not written in the
book of the chronicles of the kings of
Israel?
16 So Jehoash rested with his fathers, and was buried in Samaria with
the kings of Israel. Then Jeroboam his
son reigned in his place.

Amaziah dies; Azariah (Uzziah) reigns over Judah (2 Chr. 25:26–28)

17 Amaziah the son of Joash, king
of Judah, lived fifteen years after the
death of Jehoash the son of Jehoahaz,
king of Israel.
18 Now the rest of the acts of Amaziah, *are* they not written in the book
of the chronicles of the kings of Judah?
19 And they formed a conspiracy
against him in Jerusalem, and he fled
to Lachish; but they sent after him to
Lachish and killed him there.
20 Then they brought him on
horses, and he was buried at Jerusalem with his fathers in the City of David.
21 And all the people of Judah took
[i]Azariah, who *was* sixteen years old,
and made him king instead of his father Amaziah.
22 He built [j]Elath and restored it to
Judah, after the king rested with his
fathers.

Jeroboam II reigns over Israel, doing evil before the LORD; he restores territory according to Jonah's prophecy

23 In the fifteenth year of Amaziah
the son of Joash, king of Judah, Jeroboam the son of Joash, king of Israel,
[k]became king in Samaria, *and reigned*
forty-one years.
24 And he did evil in the sight of the
LORD; he did not depart from all the
[l]sins of Jeroboam the son of Nebat,
who had made Israel sin.
25 He [m]restored the territory of Israel [n]from the entrance of Hamath to
the [o]Sea of the [p]Arabah, according to
the word of the LORD God of Israel,
which He had spoken through His servant [q]Jonah the son of Amittai, the
prophet who *was* from [r]Gath Hepher.
26 For the LORD [s]saw *that* the affliction of Israel *was* very bitter; and
[t]whether bond or free, there was no
helper for Israel.
27 And the LORD [u]did not say that
He would blot out the name of Israel

5
a 2 Ki. 12:20
6
b Dt. 24:16; Ezek. 18:4, 20
7
c 2 Chr. 25:5–16
d 2 Sam. 8:13; 1 Chr. 18:12
9
e *Parables* (OT): vv. 9–10; 2 Chr. 25:18. (Jud. 9:8; Zech. 11:7)
10
f Cp. 2 Chr. 26:16; Prov. 16:18
13
g See Weights and Measures (OT), 2 Chr. 2:10, *note*
14
h 2 Ki. 12:18; 16:8
21
i Called *Uzziah,* 15:13
22
j 2 Ki. 16:6
23
k 782 B.C.
24
l 1 Ki. 12:26–33
25
m Fulfills prophecy of 2 Ki. 13:5. Cp. 2 Ki. 13:25
n 1 Ki. 8:65
o Dt. 3:17
p See Dt. 1:1, *note*
q Jon. 1:1
r Josh. 19:13
26
s Ex. 3:7; 2 Ki. 13:4; Ps. 106:44
t Dt. 32:36
27
u 2 Ki. 13:23

*14:8 Spelled *Joash* in 13:12ff and 2 Chronicles 25:17ff

from under heaven; but He saved
them by the hand of Jeroboam the son
of Joash.

Jeroboam II dies; Zechariah reigns over Israel

28 Now the rest of the acts of Jeroboam, and all that he did—his might,
how he made war, and how he recaptured for Israel, from [a]Damascus and
Hamath, [b]*what had belonged* to
Judah—*are* they not written in the
book of the chronicles of the kings of
Israel?
29 So Jeroboam rested with his fathers, the kings of Israel. Then Zechariah his son reigned in his place.

Azariah (Uzziah) reigns over Judah (2 Ki. 14:21–22; 2 Chr. 26:1–15)

15 IN the twenty-seventh year of
Jeroboam king of Israel, [c]Aza-
riah the son of Amaziah, king of Judah, became king.
2 He was sixteen years old when
he became king, and he reigned fifty-
two years in Jerusalem. His mother's
name *was* Jecholiah of Jerusalem.
3 And he did *what was* right in the
sight of the LORD, according to all that
his father Amaziah had done,
4 [d]except that the high places
were not removed; the people still sacrificed and burned incense on the high
places.

Azariah (Uzziah) struck with leprosy (2 Chr. 26:16–21); his death: Jotham reigns over Judah

5 Then the LORD [e]struck the king,
so that he was a leper until the day of
his [f]death; so he dwelt in an isolated
house. And Jotham the king's son *was*
over the *royal* house, judging the people of the land.
6 Now the rest of the acts of Azariah, and all that he did, *are* they not
written in the book of the chronicles of
the kings of Judah?
7 So Azariah rested with his fathers, and they [g]buried him with his
fathers in the City of David. Then Jotham his son reigned in his place.

Zechariah reigns over Israel; Shallum assassinates him

8 In the thirty-eighth year of Azariah king of Judah, [h]Zechariah the
son of Jeroboam [i]reigned over Israel
in Samaria six months.
9 And he did evil in the sight of the
LORD, [j]as his fathers had done; he did
not depart from the sins of Jeroboam
the son of Nebat, who had made Israel
sin.
10 Then Shallum the son of Jabesh
conspired against him, and [k]struck
and killed him in front of the people;
and he reigned in his place.
11 Now the rest of the acts of Zechariah, indeed they *are* written in the
book of the chronicles of the kings of
Israel.
12 This *was* the [l]word of the LORD
which He spoke to Jehu, saying,
"Your sons shall sit on the throne of
Israel to the fourth *generation*." And
so it was.

Shallum reigns over Israel; is murdered

13 Shallum the son of Jabesh [m]be-
came king in the thirty-ninth year of
[n]Uzziah king of Judah; and he
reigned a full month in Samaria.
14 For Menahem the son of Gadi
went up from [o]Tirzah, came to Samaria, and struck Shallum the son of
Jabesh in Samaria and killed him; and
he reigned in his place.
15 Now the rest of the acts of Shallum, and the conspiracy which he led,
indeed they *are* written in the book of
the chronicles of the kings of Israel.

Menahem reigns over Israel

16 Then from Tirzah, Menahem attacked Tiphsah, all who *were* there,
and its territory. Because they did not
surrender, therefore he attacked *it*.
All the women there who were with
child he [p]ripped open.
17 In the thirty-ninth year of Azariah king of Judah, Menahem the son
of Gadi [m]became king over Israel, *and*
reigned ten years in Samaria.
18 And he did evil in the sight of the
LORD; he did not depart all his days
from the sins of Jeroboam the son of
Nebat, who had made Israel sin.

Pul invades Israel (1 Chr. 5:26)

19 [q]Pul* king of Assyria came
against the land; and Menahem gave
Pul a thousand [r]talents of silver, that
his hand might be with him to
strengthen the kingdom under his
control.
20 And Menahem [s]exacted the
money from Israel, from all the very
wealthy, from each man fifty [r]shekels
of silver, to give to the king of Assyria.
So the king of Assyria turned back,
and did not stay there in the land.

28
a 1 Ki. 11:24
b 2 Sam. 8:6; 1 Ki. 11:24; 2 Chr. 8:3
CHAPTER 15
1
c Called *Uzziah*, v. 13
4
d v. 35; 2 Ki. 12:3; 14:4; see Jud. 3:7 and 1 Ki. 3:2, *notes*
5
e Ps. 78:31
f Isa. 6:1
7
g 2 Chr. 26:23
8
h 2 Ki. 14:29
i 753 B.C.
9
j 2 Ki. 14:24
10
k Amos 7:9
12
l 2 Ki. 10:30
13
m 752 B.C.
n Called *Azariah*, v. 1
14
o 1 Ki. 14:17; Song 6:4
16
p Cp. 2 Ki. 8:12
19
q 1 Chr. 5:25; Isa. 9:1; Hos. 8:9
r See Coinage (OT), Ex. 30:13, *note*
20
s 2 Ki. 23:35

* **15:19** That is, Tiglath-Pileser III (compare verse 29)

Menahem dies; Pekahiah reigns over Israel

21 Now the rest of the acts of Menahem, and all that he did, *are* they not
written in the book of the chronicles of
the kings of Israel?
22 So Menahem rested with his fathers. Then Pekahiah his son reigned
in his place.
23 In the fiftieth year of Azariah
king of Judah, Pekahiah the son of
Menahem [a]became king over Israel in
Samaria, *and reigned* two years.
24 And he did evil in the sight of the
LORD; he did not depart from the sins
of Jeroboam the son of Nebat, who
had made Israel sin.

Pekah assassinates Pekahiah and usurps the throne of Israel

25 Then Pekah the son of Remaliah, an officer of his, conspired
against him and killed him in Samaria, in the [b]citadel of the king's
house, along with Argob and Arieh;
and with him were fifty men of Gilead.
He killed him and reigned in his place.
26 Now the rest of the acts of Pekahiah, and all that he did, indeed they
are written in the book of the chronicles of the kings of Israel.
27 In the fifty-second year of Azariah king of Judah, [c]Pekah the son of
Remaliah [d]became king over Israel in
Samaria, *and reigned* twenty years.
28 And he did evil in the sight of the
LORD; he did not depart from the sins
of Jeroboam the son of Nebat, who
had made Israel sin.

Tiglath-Pileser invades Israel; Pekah is assassinated by Hoshea

29 In the days of Pekah king of Israel, [e]Tiglath-Pileser king of Assyria
came and took [f]Ijon, Abel Beth Maachah, Janoah, Kedesh, Hazor, Gilead,
and Galilee, all the land of Naphtali;
and he [g]carried them captive to Assyria.
30 Then Hoshea the son of Elah led
a conspiracy against Pekah the son of
Remaliah, and struck and killed him;
so he [h]reigned in his [i]place in the
twentieth year of Jotham the son of
Uzziah.
31 Now the rest of the acts of Pekah, and all that he did, indeed they
are written in the book of the chronicles of the kings of Israel.

Jotham reigns over Judah (v. 7; 2 Chr. 26:23; 27:1–9)

32 In the second year of Pekah the
son of Remaliah, king of Israel, [j]Jo-
tham the son of Uzziah, king of Judah,
began to reign.
33 He was twenty-five years old
when he became king, and he reigned
sixteen years in Jerusalem. His
mother's name *was* Jerusha* the
daughter of Zadok.
34 And he did *what was* right in the
sight of the LORD; he did according to
all that his father Uzziah had done.
35 [k]However the high places were
not removed; the people still sacrificed and burned incense on the high
places. He built the Upper Gate of the
house of the LORD.
36 Now the rest of the acts of Jotham, and all that he did, *are* they not
written in the book of the chronicles of
the kings of Judah?
37 In those days the LORD began to
send [l]Rezin king of Syria and Pekah
the son of Remaliah against Judah.
38 So Jotham rested with his fathers, and was buried with his fathers
in the City of David his father. Then
Ahaz his son reigned in his place.

Ahaz reigns over Judah (2 Ki. 15:38; 2 Chr. 28:1–4)

16 IN the seventeenth year of [m]Pe-
kah the son of Remaliah,
[n]Ahaz the son of Jotham, king of Judah, began to reign.
2 Ahaz *was* twenty years old
when he became king, and he reigned
sixteen years in Jerusalem; and he did
not do *what was* right in the sight of
the LORD his God, as his father David
had done.
3 But he walked in the way of the
kings of Israel; indeed [o]he made his
son pass through the fire, according to
the [p]abominations of the nations
whom the LORD had cast out from before the children of Israel.
4 And he sacrificed and burned incense on the [q]high places, on the hills,
and under every green tree.

Rezin, king of Syria, and Pekah, king of Israel invade Judah (2 Chr. 28:5–19)

5 Then Rezin king of Syria and Pekah the son of Remaliah, king of Israel, came up to Jerusalem to *make*
war; and they besieged Ahaz but
could [c]not overcome *him.*
6 At that time Rezin king of Syria
captured [r]Elath for Syria, and drove
the men of Judah from Elath. Then the

23 *a* 742 B.C. **25** *b* 1 Ki. 16:18 **27** *c* Isa. 7:1 *d* 740 B.C. **29** *e* 2 Ki. 16:7, 10 *f* 1 Ki. 15:20 *g* 2 Ki. 17:6 **30** *h* 2 Ki. 17:1 *i* 732 B.C. **32** *j* 1 Chr. 5:17 **35** *k* 2 Ki. 15:4 **37** *l* 2 Ki. 16:5–9; Isa. 7:1–17 **CHAPTER 16** **1** *m* 2 Ki. 15:26 *n* Isa. 1:1 **3** *o* Lev. 18:21; 2 Ki. 17:17; Ps. 106:37–38 *p* Dt. 12:31 **4** *q* 2 Ki. 15:34–35; see Jud. 3:7 and 1 Ki. 3:2, *notes* **6** *r* Heb. *Eloth.* 2 Ki. 14:22

*15:33 Spelled *Jerushah* in 2 Chronicles 27:1

Edomites* went to Elath, and dwell there to this day.

Ahaz seeks help from Assyria (2 Chr. 28:16–25)

7 So Ahaz sent messengers to [a]Tiglath-Pileser king of Assyria, saying, "I *am* your servant and your son. Come up and save me from the hand of the king of Syria and from the hand of the king of Israel, who rise up against me."

8 And Ahaz [b]took the silver and gold that was found in the house of the LORD, and in the treasuries of the king's house, and sent *it as* a present to the king of Assyria.

Assyrians take Damascus

9 So the king of Assyria heeded him; for the king of Assyria went up against [c]Damascus and [d]took it, carried *its people* captive to [e]Kir, and killed Rezin.

10 Now King Ahaz went to Damascus to meet Tiglath-Pileser king of Assyria, and saw an altar that *was* at Damascus; and King Ahaz sent to Urijah the priest the design of the altar and its pattern, according to all its workmanship.

11 Then [f]Urijah the priest built an altar according to all that King Ahaz had sent from Damascus. So Urijah the priest made *it* before King Ahaz came back from Damascus.

12 And when the king came back from Damascus, the king saw the altar; and the king approached the altar and made offerings on it.

13 So he burned his burnt offering and his grain offering; and he poured his drink offering and sprinkled the blood of his peace offerings on the altar.

14 He also brought the bronze altar which *was* before the LORD, [g]from the front of the temple—from between the *new* altar and the house of the LORD—and put it on the north side of the *new* altar.

15 Then King Ahaz commanded Urijah the priest, saying, "On the great *new* altar burn the [h]morning burnt offering, the evening grain offering, the king's burnt sacrifice, and his grain offering, with the burnt offering of all the people of the land, their grain offering, and their drink offerings; and sprinkle on it all the blood of the burnt offering and all the blood of the sacrifice. And the bronze altar shall be for me to inquire *by*."

16 Thus did Urijah the priest, according to all that King Ahaz commanded.

17 And King Ahaz cut off the [i]panels of the carts, and removed the lavers from them; and he took down the [j]Sea from the bronze oxen that *were* under it, and put it on a pavement of stones.

18 Also he removed the Sabbath pavilion which they had built in the temple, and he removed the king's outer entrance from the house of the LORD, on account of the king of Assyria.

Ahaz dies; Hezekiah reigns over Judah (2 Chr. 28:26–27)

19 Now the rest of the acts of Ahaz which he did, *are* they not written in the book of the chronicles of the kings of Judah?

20 So Ahaz rested with his fathers, and was buried with his fathers in the City of David. Then Hezekiah his son reigned in his place.

Hoshea reigns over Israel

17 IN the twelfth year of Ahaz king of Judah, [k]Hoshea the son of Elah [l]became king of Israel in Samaria, *and he reigned* nine years.

2 And he did evil in the sight of the LORD, but not as the kings of Israel who were before him.

Israel becomes subservient to Assyria

3 Shalmaneser king of Assyria came up against him; and Hoshea [m]became his vassal, and paid him tribute money.

Israel (ten tribes) taken away to Assyria (cp. 2 Ki. 18:9–12)

4 And the king of Assyria uncovered a conspiracy by Hoshea; for he had sent messengers to So, king of Egypt, and brought no tribute to the king of Assyria, as *he had done* year by year. Therefore the king of Assyria shut him up, and bound him in prison.

5 Now the king of Assyria went throughout all the land, and went up to [n]Samaria and besieged it for three years.

Sins for which Israel was carried into captivity

6 In the ninth year of Hoshea, the king of Assyria [o]took Samaria and carried [p]Israel away to Assyria, and placed them in Halah and by the Ha-

7
a 2 Ki. 15:29; 1 Chr. 5:26; 2 Chr. 28:20
8
b 2 Ki. 12:18
9
c 2 Ki. 14:28
d Amos 1:5
e Amos 9:7
11
f Or *Uriah*, Isa. 8:2
14
g Ex. 40:6, 29
15
h Ex. 29:39–41
17
i 1 Ki. 7:28–29
j 1 Ki. 7:23–25
CHAPTER 17
1
k 2 Ki. 15:30
l 732 B.C.
3
m 2 Ki. 24:1
5
n Hos. 13:16
6
o 722–721 B.C.
p *Israel* (history): vv. 6–23; 2 Ki. 24:10. (Gen. 12:2; Rom. 11:26, *note*). Dt. 28:64; 2 Ki. 15:29

*
16:6 Some ancient authorities read *Syrians*.

bor, the River of Gozan, and in the
cities of the Medes.
7 For [a]so it was that the children
of Israel had sinned against the LORD
their God, who had brought them up
out of the land of Egypt, from under
the hand of Pharaoh king of Egypt;
and they had [b]feared other gods,
8 and had [c]walked in the statutes
of the nations whom the LORD had cast
out from before the children of Israel,
and of the kings of Israel, which they
had made.
9 Also the children of Israel secretly did against the LORD their God
things that *were* not right, and they
built for themselves [d]high places in all
their cities, from watchtower to fortified city.
10 They [e]set up for themselves *sacred* pillars and [f]wooden images on
every high hill and under every green
tree.
11 There they burned incense on all
the high places, like the nations whom
the LORD had carried away before
them; and they did wicked things to
provoke the LORD to anger,
12 for they served idols, of which
the LORD had [g]said to them, "You shall
not do this thing."
13 Yet the LORD testified against Israel and against Judah, by all of His
[h]prophets, every [i]seer, saying,
[j]"Turn from your evil ways, and keep
My commandments *and* My statutes,
according to all the law which I commanded your fathers, and which I sent
to you by My servants the [h]prophets."
14 Nevertheless they would not
hear, but [k]stiffened their necks, like
the necks of their fathers, who [l]did
not believe in the LORD their God.
15 And they [m]rejected His statutes
and His [n]covenant that He had made
with their fathers, and His testimonies

7 *a* Josh. 23:16 *b* Jud. 6:10
8 *c* Lev. 18:3; Dt. 18:9
9 *d* vv. 10,11, 29; see Jud. 3:7 and 1 Ki. 3:2, *notes*
10 *e* Ex. 34:12–14 *f* See Dt. 16:21, *note*
12 *g* Ex. 20:4–5
13 *h* Neh. 9:29–30 *i* 1 Sam. 9:9 *j* Jer. 18:11; 25:5; 35:15
14 *k* Ex. 32:9; 33:3; Dt. 31:27; Prov. 29:1; Acts 7:51 *l* Dt. 9:23; Ps. 78:22
15 *m* Jer. 44:3 *n* Ex. 24:6–8; Dt. 29:25 *o* 2 Chr. 13:7; cp. Rom. 12:1–3
16 *p* 1 Ki. 12:28 *q* See Dt. 16:21, *note;* 1 Ki. 14:15,23 *r* Dt. 4:19 *s* 1 Ki. 16:31
17 *t* 2 Ki. 16:3 *u* Dt. 18:10

which He had testified against them;
they followed idols, [o]became idolaters, and *went* after the nations who
were all around them, *concerning*
whom the LORD had charged them that
they should not do like them.
16 So they left all the commandments of the LORD their God, [p]made
for themselves a molded image *and*
two calves, made a [q]wooden image
and worshiped all the [r]host of
heaven, and served [s]Baal.
17 And they caused their sons and
daughters to pass through the [t]fire,
[u]practiced witchcraft and soothsaying, and sold themselves to do evil in
the sight of the LORD, to provoke Him
to anger.
18 Therefore the LORD was very angry with Israel, and removed them
from His sight; there was none left
[v]but the tribe of Judah alone.
19 [w]Also Judah did not keep the
commandments of the LORD their God,
but walked in the statutes of Israel
which they made.
20 And the LORD rejected all the descendants of Israel, afflicted them,
and [x]delivered them into the hand of
plunderers, until He had cast them
from His [y]sight.
21 For He [z]tore Israel from the
house of David, and [aa]they made Jeroboam the son of Nebat king. Then Jeroboam drove Israel from following
the LORD, and made them commit a
great sin.
22 For the children of Israel walked
in all the sins of Jeroboam which he
did; they did not depart from them,
23 until the LORD [1]removed Israel
out of His sight, [bb]as He had said by all

17:18 *v* 1 Ki. 11:13,32 **17:19** *w* Jer. 3:8 **17:20** *x* Jud. 2:14; 2 Ki. 13:3; 15:29 *y* 2 Ki. 24:20 **17:21** *z* 1 Ki. 11:11,31 *aa* 1 Ki. 12:20 **17:23** *bb* 1 Ki. 14:16

[1](17:23) There are not, as some assert, "ten lost tribes," known only to God and later to be found by Him, variously conjectured to be the Anglo-Saxon people, the gypsies, or certain peoples of Central Asia or Africa. These misconceptions arise from a misreading of passages such as vv. 7–23 (cp. 2 Chr. 6:6–11), and especially v. 18.

(1) The expression "tribe of Judah" (v. 18) is here used idiomatically for the southern kingdom (Judah) in contrast with the northern kingdom (Israel), as vv. 21–23 compared with 1 Ki. 11:13,32 make clear. In these contexts everyone out of all the tribes who remained loyal to the house of David is included, as well as the two tribes of Benjamin and Judah who unitedly and officially stood by the Davidic house.

(2) The removal of the bulk of the people composing the northern kingdom does not mean that only two tribes of Israel continued in the land. Verses 7–23 (see v. 20, "cast . . . from"), implying that the portion of the nation taken into captivity by Assyria is excluded from any promised future return to the land, are in harmony with the principle of Rom. 9:4–7, which explains that the total physical descendants of Abraham were not the "children" to whom the promises were made.

(3) Before the Assyrian captivity, substantial numbers from the ten tribes had identified themselves with the house of David. This began at the time of the rebellion of Jeroboam I (1 Ki.

His servants the prophets. [a]So Israel
was carried away from their own land
to Assyria, *as it is* to this day.

Cities of Israel repopulated with foreigners

24 Then the king of Assyria
brought [b]*people* from [c]Babylon, Cu-
thah, Ava, Hamath, and from Sepharvaim, and placed *them* in the cities of
Samaria instead of the children of Israel; and they took possession of Samaria and dwelt in its cities.
25 And it was so, at the beginning
of their dwelling there, *that* they did
not [d]fear the LORD; therefore the LORD
sent lions among them, which killed
some of them.
26 So they spoke to the king of Assyria, saying, "The nations whom you
have removed and placed in the cities
of Samaria do not know the rituals of
the God of the land; therefore He has
sent lions among them, and indeed,
they are killing them because they do
not know the rituals of the God of the
land."
27 Then the king of Assyria commanded, saying, "Send there one of
the priests whom you brought from
there; let him go and dwell there, and
let him teach them the rituals of the
God of the land."
28 Then one of the priests whom
they had carried away from Samaria
came and dwelt in Bethel, and taught
them how they should [d]fear the LORD.
29 However every nation continued to make gods of its own, and put
them [e]in the shrines on the high
places which the Samaritans had
made, *every* nation in the cities where
they dwelt.
30 The men of Babylon made Succoth Benoth, the men of Cuth made
Nergal, the men of Hamath made
Ashima,
31 and the Avites made Nibhaz and
Tartak; and the Sepharvites burned
their children in fire to [f]Adramme-
lech and Anammelech, the gods of
Sepharvaim.
32 So they [d]feared the LORD, and
from [g]every class they appointed for
themselves priests of the high places,
who sacrificed for them in the shrines
of the high places.
33 They [d]feared the LORD, [h]yet
served their own gods—according to
the rituals of the nations from among
whom they were carried away.
34 To this day they continue practicing the former rituals; they do not
[d]fear the LORD, nor do they follow
their statutes or their ordinances, or
the law and commandment which the
LORD had commanded the children of
Jacob, whom He named [i]Israel,
35 with whom the LORD had made a
covenant and charged them, saying:
"You shall not fear other gods, nor
bow down to them nor serve [j]them
nor sacrifice to them;
36 "but the LORD, who [k]brought you
up from the land of Egypt with great
power and an [l]outstretched arm, Him
you shall [d]fear, Him you shall worship, and to Him you shall offer sacrifice.
37 "And the statutes, the ordinances, the law, and the commandment which He wrote for you, you
shall [m]be careful to observe forever;
you shall not fear other gods.
38 "And the covenant that I have
made with you, you shall [n]not forget,
nor shall you fear other gods.
39 "But the LORD your God you shall

23
a 2 Ki. 17:6
24
b Ezra 4:2, 10
c v. 30
25
d See Ps. 19:9, *note*
29
e 1 Ki. 12:31; 13:32
31
f 2 Ki. 19:37
32
g 1 Ki. 13:33
33
h Cp. Zeph. 1:5
34
i Gen. 32:28; 35:10
35
j Ex. 20:5
36
k Ex. 14:15–30
l Ex. 6:6; 9:15
37
m Dt. 5:32
38
n Dt. 4:23; 6:12

12:16–20; 2 Chr. 11:16–17) and continued when reformations, invasions, and other crises led many to repudiate the northern kingdom and unite with the southern kingdom in a common allegiance to the house of David and the worship of the LORD (2 Chr. 19:4; 30:1,10–11,25–26; 34:5–7,33; 35:17–18; etc.). Thus in God's view all the tribes were represented in the kingdom of Judah and constituted His continuing Israel.

(4) These facts show the correctness of this view: (a) the remnant who returned from Babylon is represented as the nation, not simply two tribes; (b) our Lord is said to have offered Himself, not merely to two tribes (Judah) but to the nation, "the lost sheep of the house of Israel" (Mt. 10:5–6); and (c) other tribes than Judah are mentioned specifically in the NT as being represented in the land (Mt. 4:13,15; Lk. 2:36; Acts 4:36; Phil. 3:5; cp. "twelve tribes," Acts 26:7; Jas. 1:1).

(5) Although Israel is now in age-long dispersion because of their rejection of their Messiah, nevertheless they still continue as a people, preserved distinct from other peoples, known to God though not knowing Him (Dt. 28:62; Isa. 11:11–13; Hos. 3:4–5; Rom. 11:1–2,11–12). A partial restoration of Israel to the land in unbelief has already taken place in accordance with prophecy. The Scriptures clearly state that there will yet be a spiritual restoration, through the salvation of substantial numbers, which will heal the ancient political division (Ezek. 37:15–28). These will be God's Israel (Amos 9:13–15; Zech. 12:9–14; Rom. 11:25–27). See Palestinian Covenant, Dt. 30:3, *note;* 2 Sam. 7:8–17.

[a]fear; and He will deliver you from
the hand of all your enemies."
40 However they did not obey, but
they followed their former rituals.
41 So these nations [a]feared the
LORD, yet served their carved images;
also their children and their children's
children have continued doing as their
fathers did, even to this day.

IV. From the Accession of Hezekiah to the Captivity of Judah, 18:1—25:30

Hezekiah reigns over Judah (2 Ki. 16:20; 2 Chr. 29:1—31:21)

18 NOW it came to pass in the
third year of [b]Hoshea the son
of Elah, king of Israel, *that* Hezekiah
the son of Ahaz, king of Judah, began
to reign.
2 He was twenty-five years old
when he became king, and he reigned
twenty-nine years in Jerusalem. His
mother's name *was* Abi* the daughter
of Zechariah.
3 And he did *what was* right in the
sight of the LORD, according to all that
his father David had done.

Revival under Hezekiah (2 Chr. 29:3—31:21)

4 He removed the [c]high places
and broke the *sacred* pillars, cut down
the [d]wooden image and broke in
pieces the [e]bronze serpent that Moses
had made; for until those days the
children of Israel burned incense to it,
and called it Nehushtan.*
5 He [f]trusted in the LORD God of
Israel, so that after him was [g]none
like him among all the kings of Judah,
nor who were before him.
6 For he held fast to the LORD; he
did not depart from following Him,
but kept His commandments, which
the LORD had commanded Moses.

39
a See Ps. 19:9, *note*
CHAPTER 18
1
b 2 Ki. 17:1
4
c v. 22; see Jud. 3:7 and 1 Ki. 3:2, *notes*
d See Dt. 16:21, *note*
e Num. 21:5–9
5
f See Ps. 2:12, *note;* 2 Ki. 19:10
g 2 Ki. 23:25
7
h 2 Ki. 16:7
8
i 2 Chr. 28:18; Isa. 14:29
9
j Mt. 1:9
11
k *Times of the Gentiles:* vv. 9–12; 2 Ki. 25:4. (Dt. 28:49; Rev. 16:19)
12
l 2 Ki. 17:7–18
13
m For parallel accounts, see vv. 7 and 13, *notes;* Isa. 36:1, *note*

Hezekiah rebels against Assyria; defeats the Philistines

7 The LORD was with him; he prospered wherever he went. And he [1]re-
belled against the king of [h]Assyria
and did not serve him.
8 He subdued the [i]Philistines, as
far as Gaza and its territory, from
watchtower to fortified city.

Israel's captivity reviewed (cp. 2 Ki. 17:4–6); first invasion of Judah (Isa. 36:1)

9 Now it came to pass in the fourth
year of King [j]Hezekiah, which *was*
the seventh year of Hoshea the son of
Elah, king of Israel, *that* Shalmaneser
king of Assyria came up against Samaria and besieged it.
10 And at the end of three years
they took it. In the sixth year of Hezekiah, that *is*, the ninth year of Hoshea
king of Israel, Samaria was taken.
11 Then the king of Assyria [k]car-
ried Israel away captive to Assyria,
and put them in Halah and by the Habor, the River of Gozan, and in the
cities of the Medes,
12 because they did [l]not obey the
voice of the LORD their God, but transgressed His covenant *and* all that Moses the servant of the LORD had commanded; and they would neither hear
nor do *them*.
13 [m]And in the fourteenth year of
King Hezekiah, [2]Sennacherib king of
Assyria came up against all the fortified cities of Judah and took them.
14 Then Hezekiah king of Judah
sent to the king of Assyria at Lachish,
saying, "I have done wrong; turn
away from me; whatever you impose
on me I will pay." And the king of Assyria assessed Hezekiah king of Ju-

*18:2 Called *Abijah* in 2 Chronicles 29:1ff
18:4 Literally *Bronze Thing*

[1](18:7) The sequence of events in the story of the kingdom of Judah after the fall of the kingdom of Israel—the last twenty-three years of Hezekiah's reign—was as follows: (1) Hezekiah's throwing off the Assyrian yoke (2 Ki. 18:7); (2) Hezekiah's successful Philistine campaign (2 Ki. 18:8); (3) Sennacherib's first invasion of Judah (2 Ki. 18:13–16; see Isa. 36:1, *note*); (4) Hezekiah's illness and recovery (2 Ki. 20:1–11; 2 Chr. 32:24; Isa. 38); (5) Hezekiah's imprudent exposure of his defenses and wealth to the Babylonian embassy (2 Ki. 20:12–19; 2 Chr. 32:25–26,31; Isa. 39); (6) Hezekiah's wealth and building (2 Chr. 32:27–29); (7) Sennacherib's second invasion of Judah and God's miraculous deliverance in answer to prayer (2 Ki. 18:17—19:37; 2 Chr. 32:1–23,30; Isa. 36:2—37:38); and (8) Hezekiah's death (2 Ki. 20:20–21; 2 Chr. 32:32–33).

[2](18:13) Of all the kings of Judah, none is given higher praise than Hezekiah (vv. 3–7). Moreover, the fact that the record of his encounter with Sennacherib and the subsequent events of his reign is the only narrative occurring three times in the OT (2 Ki. 18:13—20:21; 2 Chr. 32:1–33; Isa. 36:1—39:8) points to the peculiar significance of the LORD's dealing with this godly king.

dah three hundred [a]talents of silver
and thirty [a]talents of gold.
15 So Hezekiah [b]gave *him* all the
silver that was found in the house of
the LORD and in the treasuries of the
king's house.
16 At that time Hezekiah stripped
the gold from the doors of the temple
of the LORD, and *from* the pillars which
Hezekiah king of Judah had overlaid,
and gave it to the king of Assyria.

Sennacherib's second invasion of Judah; he seeks to terrify Jerusalem (2 Chr. 32:1–15,30; Isa. 36:2–10)

17 Then the king of Assyria sent
the Tartan,* *the* Rabsaris,* *and the*
Rabshakeh* from Lachish, with a
great army against Jerusalem, to King
Hezekiah. And they went up and came
to Jerusalem. When they had come
up, they went and stood by the [c]aque-
duct from the upper pool, [d]which *was*
on the highway to the Fuller's Field.
18 And when they had called to the
king, [e]Eliakim the son of Hilkiah, who
was over the household, Shebna the
scribe, and Joah the son of Asaph, the
recorder, came out to them.
19 Then *the* Rabshakeh said to
them, "Say now to Hezekiah, 'Thus
says the great king, the king of Assyria: "What [f]confidence *is* this in
which you [g]trust?
20 "You speak of *having* plans and
power for war; but *they are* [h]mere
words. And in whom do you trust, that
you rebel against me?
21 [i]"Now look! You are trusting in
the staff of this broken reed, Egypt, on
which if a man leans, it will go into his
hand and pierce it. So *is* Pharaoh king
of Egypt to all who trust in him.
22 "But if you say to me, 'We trust
in the LORD our God,' *is* it not He
whose high places and [j]whose altars
Hezekiah has taken away, and said to
Judah and Jerusalem, 'You shall worship before this altar in Jerusalem'?" '
23 "Now therefore, I urge you, give
a [k]pledge to my master the king of
Assyria, and I will give you two thousand horses—if you are able on your
part to put riders on them!
24 "How then will you repel one
captain of the least of my master's servants, and put your trust in Egypt for
chariots and horsemen?
25 "Have I now come up without
the LORD against this place to destroy
it? The LORD said to me, 'Go up against
this land, and destroy it.' "

14
a See Coinage (OT), Ex. 30:13, *note*
15
b 2 Ki. 16:8
17
c 2 Ki. 20:20
d Isa. 7:3
18
e 2 Ki. 19:2; Isa. 22:20
19
f Ps. 118:8–9
g 2 Ki. 18:5
20
h Lit. *word of the lips*
21
i Isa. 30:2–7; Ezek. 29:6–7
22
j 2 Ki. 18:4; 2 Chr. 31:1; see Jud. 3:7 and 1 Ki. 3:2, *notes*
23
k Lit. *hostage*
26
l 2 Ki. 18:26–20:21 is virtually identical with Isa. 36:11–39:8. See also v. 13, *note*
m Ezra 4:7; see Dan. 2:4, *note*
n Cp. Neh. 13:24
29
o 2 Chr. 32:15
31
p Lit. *Make a blessing*
q 1 Ki. 4:25
32
r Dt. 8:7–8
33
s 2 Ki. 19:12; cp. Isa. 10:9–11
34
t 2 Ki. 19:13
u Or *Ava*, 2 Ki. 17:24
35
v Dan. 3:15

The Rabshakeh's further threats (2 Chr. 32:16,18–19; Isa. 36:11–21)

26 [l]Then Eliakim the son of Hilkiah, Shebna, and Joah said to *the*
Rabshakeh, "Please speak to your servants in [m]Aramaic, for we understand
it; and do not speak to us in Hebrew*
in the [n]hearing of the people who *are*
on the wall."
27 But *the* Rabshakeh said to them,
"Has my master sent me to your master and to you to speak these words,
and not to the men who sit on the wall,
who will eat and drink their own
waste with you?"
28 Then *the* Rabshakeh stood and
called out with a loud voice in Hebrew, and spoke, saying, "Hear the
word of the great king, the king of Assyria!
29 "Thus says the king: [o]'Do not let
Hezekiah deceive you, for he shall not
be able to deliver you from his hand;
30 'nor let Hezekiah make you trust
in the LORD, saying, "The LORD will
surely deliver us; this city shall not be
given into the hand of the king of Assyria." '
31 "Do not listen to Hezekiah; for
thus says the king of Assyria: [p]'Make
peace with me by a present and come
out to me; and every one of you eat
from his own [q]vine and every one
from his own fig tree, and every one of
you drink the waters of his own cistern;
32 'until I come and take you away
to a land like your own land, a [r]land
of grain and new wine, a land of bread
and vineyards, a land of olive groves
and honey, that you may live and not
die. But do not listen to Hezekiah, lest
he persuade you, saying, "The LORD
will deliver us."
33 [s]'Has any of the gods of the nations at all delivered its land from the
hand of the king of Assyria?
34 [t]'Where *are* the gods of Hamath
and Arpad? Where *are* the gods of
Sepharvaim and Hena and [u]Ivah? Indeed, have they delivered Samaria
from my hand?
35 'Who among all the gods of the
lands have delivered their countries
from my hand, that the LORD should
[v]deliver Jerusalem from my hand?' "
36 But the people held their peace
and answered him not a word; for the

*
18:17 A title, probably *Commander in Chief* • A title, probably *Chief Officer* • A title, probably *Chief of Staff* or *Governor* **18:26** Literally *Judean*

king's commandment was, "Do not
answer him."
37 Then Eliakim the son of Hilkiah,
who *was* over the household, Shebna
the scribe, and Joah the son of Asaph,
the recorder, came to Hezekiah [a]with
their clothes torn, and told him the
words of *the* Rabshakeh.

Hezekiah requests Isaiah's intercession (2 Chr. 32:2–22; Isa. 36:22—37:5)

19 [b]AND so it was, when King
Hezekiah heard *it*, that he tore
his clothes, covered himself with
[c]sackcloth, and went into the house of
the LORD.
2 Then he sent Eliakim, who *was*
over the household, Shebna the
scribe, and the elders of the priests,
covered with sackcloth, to Isaiah the
prophet, the son of Amoz.
3 And they said to him, "Thus says
Hezekiah: 'This day *is* a day of trouble, and rebuke, and blasphemy; for
the children have come to birth, but
there is no strength [d]to bring them
forth.
4 [e]'It may be that the LORD your
God will hear all the words of *the* Rabshakeh, whom his master the king of
Assyria has sent to reproach the living
God, and will rebuke the words which
the LORD your God has heard. There-

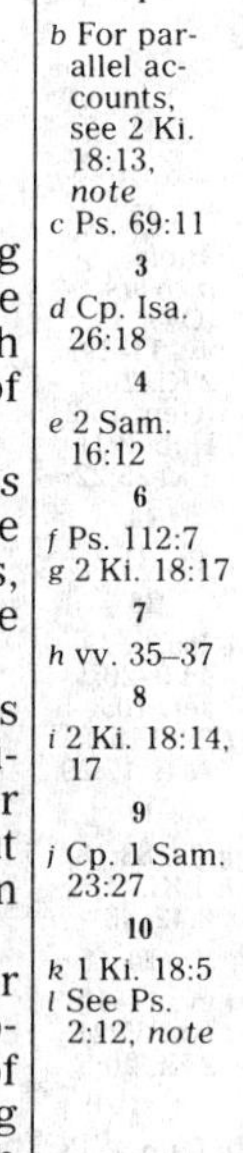
37
a Isa. 33:7
CHAPTER 19
1
b For parallel accounts, see 2 Ki. 18:13, *note*
c Ps. 69:11
3
d Cp. Isa. 26:18
4
e 2 Sam. 16:12
6
f Ps. 112:7
g 2 Ki. 18:17
7
h vv. 35–37
8
i 2 Ki. 18:14, 17
9
j Cp. 1 Sam. 23:27
10
k 1 Ki. 18:5
l See Ps. 2:12, *note*

fore lift up *your* prayer for the remnant that is left.' "
5 So the servants of King Hezekiah came to Isaiah.

The LORD's answer through Isaiah (Isa. 37:6–7)

6 And Isaiah said to them, "Thus
you shall say to your master, 'Thus
says the LORD: "Do not be [f]afraid of
the words which you have heard, with
which the [g]servants of the king of Assyria have blasphemed Me.
7 "Surely I will send a [h]spirit upon
him, and he shall hear a rumor and
return to his own land; and I will cause
him to fall by the sword in his own
land." ' "

Sennacherib defies God (2 Chr. 32:17; Isa. 37:8–13)

8 Then *the* Rabshakeh returned
and found the king of Assyria warring
against Libnah, for he heard that he
had departed from [i]Lachish.
9 And [j]the king heard concerning
Tirhakah king of Ethiopia, "Look, he
has come out to make war with you."
So he again sent messengers to Hezekiah, saying,
10 "Thus you shall speak to Hezekiah king of Judah, saying: 'Do not let
your God [k]in whom you [l]trust deceive you, saying, "Jerusalem shall

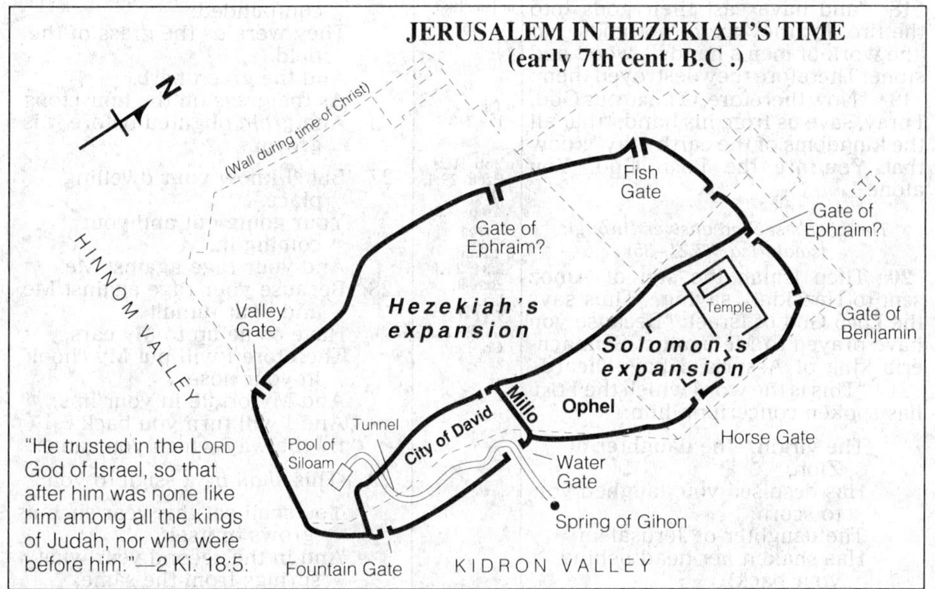

"He trusted in the LORD God of Israel, so that after him was none like him among all the kings of Judah, nor who were before him."—2 Ki. 18:5.

not be given into the hand of the king
of Assyria."'
11 'Look! You have heard what the
kings of Assyria have done to all lands
by utterly destroying them; and shall
you be delivered?
12 'Have the gods of the nations
[a]delivered those whom my fathers
have destroyed, Gozan and Haran and
Rezeph, and the people of Eden who
were in Telassar?
13 'Where *is* the king of Hamath,
the king of Arpad, and the king of the
city of Sepharvaim, Hena, and Ivah?' "

Hezekiah's prayer in the temple (2 Chr. 32:20; Isa. 37:14–20)

14 And Hezekiah received the letter from the hand of the messengers,
and read it; and Hezekiah went up to
the house of the LORD, and spread it
before the LORD.
15 Then Hezekiah prayed before
the LORD, and [b]said: "O LORD God of
Israel, *the One* who dwells *between*
the [c]cherubim, You are God, You
alone, of all the kingdoms of the earth.
You have made heaven and earth.
16 [d]"Incline Your ear, O LORD, and
hear; open Your eyes, O LORD, and
see; and hear the words of Sennacherib, which he has sent to reproach the
living God.
17 "Truly, LORD, the kings of Assyria have laid waste the nations and
their lands,
18 "and have cast their gods into
the fire; for they *were* [e]not gods, but
[f]the work of men's hands—wood and
stone. Therefore they destroyed them.
19 "Now therefore, O LORD our God,
I pray, save us from his hand, [g]that all
the kingdoms of the earth may [h]know
that You *are* the LORD God, You
alone."

The LORD's second answer through Isaiah (Isa. 37:21–35)

20 Then Isaiah the son of Amoz
sent to Hezekiah, saying, "Thus says
the LORD God of Israel: [i]'Because you
have prayed to Me against Sennacherib king of Assyria, I have [j]heard.'
21 "This *is* the word which the LORD
has spoken concerning him:

'The virgin, [k]the daughter of
Zion,
Has despised you, laughed you
to scorn;
The daughter of Jerusalem
Has shaken *her* head behind
your back!

12
a 2 Ki. 18:33
15
b Bible prayers (OT): vv. 14–19; 2 Ki. 20:3. (Gen. 15:2; Hab. 3:1)
c Ex. 25:22
16
d Ps. 31:2
18
e Isa. 44:9–20; Jer. 10:3–5
f Ps. 115:4; Acts 17:29
19
g Ps. 83:18
h 1 Ki. 8:42–43
20
i vv. 14–19; Isa. 37:21
j 2 Ki. 20:5
21
k Lam. 2:13
23
l 2 Ki. 18:17
24
m Isa. 19:6
25
n Isa. 10:5–6
27
o Ps. 139:2–3
28
p Job 41:2; Ezek. 29:4; 38:4; Amos 4:2
29
q 1 Sam. 2:34; 2 Ki. 20:8–9; Isa. 7:11–14; Lk. 2:12
r Cp. Lev. 25:5

22 'Whom have you reproached
and blasphemed?
Against whom have you raised
your voice,
And lifted up your eyes on
high?
Against the Holy *One* of Israel.
23 [l]By your messengers you have
reproached the Lord,
And said: "By the multitude of
my chariots
I have come up to the height of
the mountains,
To the limits of Lebanon;
I will cut down its tall cedars
And its choice cypress trees;
I will enter the extremity of its
borders,
To its fruitful forest.
24 I have dug and drunk strange
water,
And with the soles of my feet I
have [m]dried up
All the brooks of defense."
25 'Did you not hear long ago
How I made it,
From ancient times that I
formed it?
Now [n]I have brought it to
pass,
That you should be
For crushing fortified cities
into heaps of ruins.
26 Therefore their inhabitants had
little power;
They were dismayed and
confounded;
They were *as* the grass of the
field
And the green herb,
As the grass on the housetops
And *grain* blighted before it is
grown.

27 'But [o]I know your dwelling
place,
Your going out and your
coming in,
And your rage against Me.
28 Because your rage against Me
and your tumult
Have come up to My ears,
Therefore I will put My [p]hook
in your nose
And My bridle in your lips,
And I will turn you back
By the way which you came.

29 'This *shall be* a [q]sign to you:

You shall eat this year such as
[r]grows of itself,
And in the second year what
springs from the same;

Also in the third year sow and
reap,
Plant vineyards and eat the
fruit of them.
30 And the [a]remnant who have
escaped of the house of
Judah
Shall again take root
downward,
And bear fruit upward.
31 For out of Jerusalem shall go a
remnant,
And those who escape from
Mount Zion.
The zeal of the LORD of hosts*
will do this.'

32 "Therefore thus says the LORD
concerning the king of Assyria:

'He shall [b]not come into this
city,
Nor shoot an arrow there,
Nor come before it with shield,
Nor build a siege mound
against it.
33 By the way that he came,
By the same shall he return;
And he shall not come into this
city,'
Says the LORD.
34 'For [c]I will [d]defend this city, to
save it
[e]For My own sake and for My
servant David's sake.'"

The LORD kills 185,000 Assyrians
(2 Chr. 32:21a; Isa. 37:36)

35 And [f]it came to pass on a certain
night that the [g]angel of the LORD went
out, and [h]killed in the camp of the Assyrians one hundred and eighty-five
thousand; and when *people* arose
early in the morning, there were the
corpses—all dead.

Sennacherib's sons assassinate him
(2 Chr. 32:21b; Isa. 37:37–38)

36 So Sennacherib king of Assyria
departed and went away, returned
home, and remained at Nineveh.
37 Now it came to pass, as he was
worshiping in the temple of Nisroch
his god, that his sons [i]Adrammelech
and Sharezer struck him down with
the sword; and they escaped into the
land of Ararat. Then Esarhaddon his
son reigned in his place.

Hezekiah's illness and recovery
(2 Chr. 32:24–29; Isa. 38)

20 IN those days [j]Hezekiah was
sick and near death. And Isaiah the prophet, the son of Amoz, went
to him and said to him, "Thus says the
LORD: 'Set your house in order, for you
shall die, and not live.'"
2 Then he turned his face toward
the wall, and prayed to the LORD, saying,
3 "Remember now, O LORD, I
[k]pray, how I have walked before You
in truth and with a [l]loyal heart, and
have done *what was* [m]good in Your
sight." And Hezekiah wept bitterly.
4 And it happened, before Isaiah
had gone out into the middle court,
that the word of the LORD came to him,
saying,
5 "Return and tell Hezekiah the
[n]leader of My people, 'Thus says the
LORD, the God of David your father:
[o]"I have heard your prayer, I have
seen [p]your tears; surely I will heal
you. On the third day you shall go up
to the house of the LORD.
6 "And I will add to your days fifteen years. I will deliver you and this
city from the hand of the king of Assyria; and [q]I will defend this city for
My own sake, and for the sake of My
servant David."'"
7 Then Isaiah said, "Take a lump
of figs." So they took and laid *it* on the
boil, and he recovered.
8 And Hezekiah said to Isaiah,
[r]"What *is* the sign that the LORD will
heal me, and that I shall go up to the
house of the LORD the third day?"
9 Then Isaiah said, "This is the
sign to you from the LORD, that the
LORD will do the thing which He has
[s]spoken: *shall* the shadow go forward
ten degrees or go backward ten degrees?"
10 And Hezekiah answered, "It is
an easy thing for the shadow to go
down ten degrees; no, but let the
shadow go backward ten degrees."
11 So Isaiah the prophet cried out
to the LORD, and [t]He brought the
shadow ten degrees [h]backward, by
which it had gone down on the sundial
of Ahaz.

Hezekiah exposes his wealth and
defenses to Babylonian embassy
(2 Chr. 32:25–31; Isa. 39)

12 At that time Berodach-Baladan*
the son of Baladan, king of Babylon,
sent letters and a [u]present to Hezekiah, for he heard that Hezekiah had
been sick.

30 a 2 Chr. 32:22–23
32 b Isa. 8:7–10
34 c 2 Ki. 20:6 d Isa. 31:5 e 1 Ki. 11:12–13
35 f Ex. 12:29 g *Angel* (of the LORD): v. 35; 1 Chr. 21:12. (Gen. 16:7; Jud. 2:1, *note*) h *Miracles* (OT): v. 35; 20:11; 2 Chr. 26:19. (Gen. 5:24; Jon. 1:17, *note*)
37 i 2 Ki. 17:31
CHAPTER 20
1 j For parallel accounts, see 2 Ki. 18:13, *note*
3 k *Bible prayers* (OT): vv. 2–3; 1 Chr. 4:10. (Gen. 15:2; Hab. 3:1) l 1 Ki. 8:61; see Phil. 3:12, *note* m 2 Ki. 18:3–6
5 n 1 Sam. 9:16; 10:1 o 2 Ki. 19:20; Ps. 65:2 p Ps. 39:12; 56:8
6 q 2 Ki. 19:34
8 r Jud. 6:17–39; Isa. 7:11–14
9 s Num. 23:19; cp. Isa. 7:10–14
11 t Cp. Josh. 10:12–14
12 u 2 Ki. 8:8–9

*
19:31 Following many Hebrew manuscripts and ancient versions (compare Isaiah 37:32); Masoretic Text omits *of hosts*. **20:12** Spelled *Merodach-Baladan* in Isaiah 39:1

13 And Hezekiah [a]was attentive to
them, and showed them all the house
of his treasures—the silver and gold,
the spices and precious ointment, and
all* his [b]armory—all that was found
among his treasures. There was nothing in his house or in all his dominion
that Hezekiah did not show them.
14 Then Isaiah the prophet went to
King Hezekiah, and said to him,
"What did these men say, and from
where did they come to you?" So Hezekiah said, "They came from a far
country, from Babylon."
15 And he said, "What have they
seen in your house?" So Hezekiah answered, "They have seen all that *is* in
my house; there is nothing among my
treasures that I have not shown them."
16 Then Isaiah said to Hezekiah,
"Hear the word of the LORD:
17 'Behold, the days are coming
when all that *is* in your house, and
what your fathers have accumulated
until this day, [c]shall be carried to Babylon; nothing shall be left,' says the
LORD.
18 'And [d]they shall take away
some of your sons who will descend
from you, whom you will beget; [e]and
they shall be [f]eunuchs in the palace of
the king of Babylon.' "
19 So Hezekiah said to Isaiah,
[g]"The word of the LORD which you
have spoken *is* good!" For he said,
"Will there not be peace and truth at
least in my days?"

Hezekiah's death (2 Chr. 32:32–33)

20 Now the rest of the acts of
Hezekiah—all his might, and how he
[h]made a [i]pool and a tunnel and
brought [j]water into the city—*are* they
not written in the book of the chronicles of the kings of Judah?
21 So Hezekiah [k]rested with his fathers. Then Manasseh his son reigned
in his place.

Manasseh's reign; his flagrant idolatries (2 Chr. 33:1–9)

21 MANASSEH *was* twelve years
old when he became king, and
he reigned fifty-five years in Jerusalem. His mother's name *was* Hephzibah.
2 And he did evil in the sight of the
LORD, according to the abominations
of the nations whom the LORD had cast
out before the children of Israel.
3 For he rebuilt the [l]high places
which Hezekiah his father had [m]de-
stroyed; he raised up altars for Baal,
and made a [n]wooden image, [o]as Ahab
king of Israel had done; and he worshiped all the host of heaven* and
served them.
4 He also built altars [p]in the house
of the LORD, of which the LORD had
said, "In [q]Jerusalem I will put My
name."
5 And he built altars for all the
host of heaven in the [r]two courts of
the house of the LORD.
6 [s]Also he made his son pass
through the fire, practiced [t]soothsay-
ing, used witchcraft, and consulted
spiritists and mediums. He did much
evil in the sight of the LORD, to provoke
Him to anger.
7 He even set a carved image of
[n]Asherah that he had made, in the
house of which the LORD had said to
David and to Solomon his son, "In this
house and in Jerusalem, which I have
chosen out of all the tribes of Israel, I
will put My name [u]forever;
8 "and I will not make the feet of
Israel wander anymore from the land
which I gave their fathers—only if
they are careful to do according to all
that I have commanded them, and according to all the law that My servant
[v]Moses commanded them."
9 But they paid no attention, and
Manasseh seduced them to do more
evil than the nations whom the LORD
had destroyed before the children of
Israel.

Manasseh rebuked (2 Chr. 33:10)

10 And the LORD spoke [w]by His servants the prophets, saying,
11 [x]"Because Manasseh king of Judah has done these abominations
([y]he has acted more wickedly than all
the [z]Amorites who *were* before him,
and has also made Judah sin with his
idols),
12 "therefore thus says the LORD
God of Israel: 'Behold, *I* am bringing
such calamity upon Jerusalem and Judah, that whoever hears of it, both
[aa]his ears will tingle.
13 'And I will stretch over Jerusalem the measuring [bb]line of Samaria
and the plummet of the house of
Ahab; [cc]I will wipe Jerusalem as *one*
wipes a dish, wiping *it* and turning *it*
upside down.

13
a 2 Ki. 16:9
b Isa. 22:8
17
c 2 Ki. 24:13; 25:13; Jer. 27:21–22; 52:17
18
d 2 Ki. 24:12; 2 Chr. 33:11
e Fulfilled, Dan. 1:3–7
f Dan. 1:11, 18
19
g 1 Sam. 3:18
20
h Neh. 3:16
i 2 Ki. 18:17; Isa. 7:3
j 2 Chr. 32:3
21
k 2 Ki. 16:20
CHAPTER 21
3
l See Jud. 3:7 and 1 Ki. 3:2, *notes*
m 2 Ki. 18:4, 22
n See Dt. 16:21, *note*
o 1 Ki. 16:31–33
4
p Jer. 7:30
q 2 Sam. 7:13; 1 Ki. 8:29; 9:3
5
r 1 Ki. 6:36; 7:12
6
s Lev. 18:21; 20:2; 2 Ki. 16:3; 17:17
t Lev. 19:26; Dt. 18:10
7
u 1 Ki. 8:29; 9:3
8
v 2 Ki. 18:12
10
w 2 Ki. 17:13
11
x 2 Ki. 23:26–27; 24:3–4; Jer. 15:4
y 1 Ki. 21:26
z Gen. 15:16
12
aa 1 Sam. 3:11; Jer. 19:3

21:13 *bb* Isa. 34:11; Lam. 2:8; Amos 7:7–8 *cc* 2 Ki. 22:16–19

* **20:13** Following many Hebrew manuscripts, Syriac, and Targum; Masoretic Text omits *all*. **21:3** The gods of the Assyrians

14 'So I will forsake the [a]remnant
of My inheritance and deliver them
into the hand of their enemies; and
they shall become victims of plunder
to all their enemies,
15 'because they have done evil in
My sight, and have provoked Me to
anger since the day their fathers came
out of Egypt, even to this day.' "

Manasseh's further sins;
his death (2 Chr. 33:11–20)

16 [b]Moreover Manasseh shed very
much innocent blood, till he had filled
Jerusalem from one end to another,
besides his sin by which he made Judah sin, in doing evil in the sight of the
LORD.
17 Now the [c]rest of the acts of
[d]Manasseh—all that he did, and the
sin that he committed—*are* they not
written in the book of the chronicles of
the kings of Judah?
18 So Manasseh rested with his fathers, and was buried in the garden of
his own house, in the garden of Uzza.
Then his son Amon reigned in his
place.

Amon reigns over Judah
(2 Chr. 33:20–23)

19 [e]Amon *was* twenty-two years
old when he [f]became king, and he
reigned two years in Jerusalem. His
mother's name *was* Meshullemeth the
daughter of Haruz of Jotbah.
20 And he did evil in the sight of the
LORD, as his father Manasseh had
done.
21 So he walked in all the ways that
his father had walked; and he served
the idols that his father had served,
and worshiped them.
22 He [g]forsook the LORD God of his
fathers, and did not walk in the way of
the LORD.

Amon assassinated by his servants;
Josiah reigns over Judah
(2 Chr. 33:24–25)

23 Then the servants of [h]Amon
[i]conspired against him, and killed the
king in his own house.
24 But the people of the land [j]exe-
cuted all those who had conspired
against King Amon. Then the people
of the land made his son Josiah king
in his place.
25 Now the rest of the acts of Amon
which he did, *are* they not written in
the book of the chronicles of the kings
of Judah?
26 And he was buried in his tomb in
the garden of Uzza. Then Josiah his
son reigned in his place.

14
a Jer. 6:9
16
b 2 Ki. 24:4
17
c 2 Chr. 33:11–19
d 2 Chr. 33:20
19
e 2 Chr. 33:21–23
f 642 B.C.
22
g Jud. 2:12–13; 1 Ki. 11:33; 1 Chr. 28:9
23
h 1 Chr. 3:14; Mt. 1:10
i 2 Ki. 12:20; 14:19
24
j 2 Ki. 14:5
CHAPTER 22
1
k 1 Ki. 13:2
l 640 B.C.
m Josh. 15:39
2
n Dt. 5:32
3
o vv. 3–20; cp. 2 Chr. 34:8–28
4
p 2 Ki. 12:4
5
q 2 Ki. 12:11–14
7
r 2 Ki. 12:15
8
s Dt. 31:24–26; cp. Dt. 17:18

Josiah's upright life (2 Chr. 34:1–7)

22 [k]JOSIAH *was* eight years old
when he [l]became king, and he
reigned thirty-one years in Jerusalem.
His mother's name *was* Jedidah the
daughter of Adaiah of [m]Bozkath.
2 And he did *what was* right in the
sight of the LORD, and walked in all the
ways of his father David; he [n]did not
turn aside to the right hand or to the
left.

Josiah repairs the temple
(2 Chr. 34:8–13)

3 [o]Now it came to pass, in the
eighteenth year of King Josiah, *that*
the king sent Shaphan the scribe, the
son of Azaliah, the son of Meshullam,
to the house of the LORD, saying:
4 "Go up to Hilkiah the high priest,
that he may count the money [p]which
has been brought into the house of the
LORD, which the doorkeepers have
gathered from the people.
5 "And let them [q]deliver it into the
hand of those doing the work, who are
the overseers in the house of the LORD;
let them give it to those who *are* in the
house of the LORD doing the work, to
repair the damages of the house—
6 "to carpenters and builders and
masons—and to buy timber and hewn
stone to repair the house.
7 "However there need be [r]no accounting made with them of the
money delivered into their hand, because they deal faithfully."

Hilkiah discovers the Book
of the Law (2 Chr. 34:14–21)

8 Then Hilkiah the high priest said
to Shaphan the scribe, [s]"I have [1]found
the Book of the Law in the house of the

[1](22:8) This passage (vv. 8–10) has been used to teach that Deuteronomy was the book found, and that it was composed as a "pious fraud" in the time of Josiah (621 B.C.) to bring about centralization of worship in Jerusalem. From the distinctive use of the names of Deity, the laws peculiar to Deuteronomy, the nature of the commands which presuppose the wilderness wanderings and the prospective entrance into Canaan, the minutely accurate geographical data employed, and the evident anachronism of emphasizing centralization of worship in Jerusalem in 621 B.C. after the deportation of the northern kingdom, conservative scholars have consistently held to the Mosaic authorship (15th Cent. B.C.) of the book. Furthermore, not

LORD." And Hilkiah gave the book to
Shaphan, and he read it.
9 So Shaphan the scribe went to
the king, bringing the king word, saying, "Your servants have gathered the
money that was found in the house,
and have delivered it into the hand of
those who do the work, who oversee
the house of the LORD."
10 Then Shaphan the scribe
showed the king, saying, "Hilkiah the
priest has given me a book." And Shaphan read it before the king.

"By the law is the knowledge of sin"

11 Now it happened, when the king
heard the words of the Book of the
Law, that he tore his clothes.
12 Then the king commanded Hilkiah the priest, [a]Ahikam the son of
Shaphan, [b]Achbor the son of Michaiah, Shaphan the scribe, and Asaiah a
servant of the king, saying,
13 "Go, inquire of the LORD for me,
for the people and for all Judah, concerning the words of this book that
has been found; for great *is* the wrath
of the LORD that is aroused against us,
because our fathers have not obeyed
the words of this book, to do according to all that is written concerning
us."
14 So Hilkiah the priest, Ahikam,
Achbor, Shaphan, and Asaiah went to
[1]Huldah the prophetess, the wife of
Shallum the son of [c]Tikvah, the son of
Harhas, keeper of the wardrobe. (She
dwelt in Jerusalem in the Second
Quarter.) And they spoke with her.

Huldah the prophetess speaks (2 Chr. 34:22–28)

15 Then she said to them, "Thus
says the LORD God of Israel, 'Tell the
man who sent you to Me,
16 "Thus says the LORD: 'Behold, [d]I
will bring calamity on this place and
on its inhabitants—all the words of
the book which the king of Judah has
read—
17 [e]'because they have forsaken
Me and burned incense to other gods,
that they might provoke Me to anger
with all the works of their hands.
Therefore My wrath shall be aroused
against this place and shall not be
quenched.'"'
18 "But as for the [f]king of Judah,
who sent you to inquire of the LORD, in
this manner you shall speak to him,
'Thus says the LORD God of Israel:
"*Concerning* the words which you
have heard—
19 [g]"because your heart was tender, and you [h]humbled yourself before the LORD when you heard what I
spoke against this place and against
its inhabitants, that they would become a [i]desolation and a curse, and
you tore your clothes and wept before
Me, I also have heard *you*," says the
LORD.
20 "Surely, therefore, I will gather
you to your fathers, and you shall be
gathered to your grave in peace; and
your eyes shall not see all the calamity
which I will bring on this place."'" So
they brought back word to the king.

Josiah reads the Law to the people (2 Chr. 34:29–30)

23 NOW the king sent them to
gather all the [j]elders of Judah
and Jerusalem to him.
2 The king went up to the house of
the LORD with all the men of Judah,
and with him all the inhabitants of
Jerusalem—the priests and the prophets and all the people, both small and
great. And he [k]read in their hearing
all the words of the Book of the Covenant [l]which had been found in the
house of the LORD.

Josiah's covenant (2 Chr. 34:31–32)

3 Then the king [m]stood by a pillar
and made a [n]covenant before the
LORD, to follow the LORD and to keep
His commandments and His testimonies and His statutes, with all *his* heart
and all *his* soul, to perform the words
of this covenant that were written in
this book. And all the people took a
stand for the covenant.

Josiah's further reformations (2 Chr. 34:33)

4 And the king commanded Hil-
kiah the high priest, the [o]priests of the
second order, and the doorkeepers, to
[p]bring out of the temple of the LORD all
the articles that were made for Baal,
for [q]Asherah, and for all the host of
heaven;* and he burned them outside
Jerusalem in the fields of Kidron, and
carried their ashes to Bethel.

* 23:4 The gods of the Assyrians

12
a 2 Ki. 25:22; Jer. 26:24
b Or *Abdon*, the son of Micah, 2 Chr. 34:20
14
c Or *Tokhath*, 2 Chr. 34:22
16
d Dt. 29:27; Dan. 9:11–14
17
e Dt. 29:25–26
18
f v. 1
19
g Ps. 51:17; Isa. 57:15
h 1 Ki. 21:29; 2 Chr. 7:14
i Lev. 26:31
CHAPTER 23
1
j 2 Sam. 19:11
2
k Dt. 31:10–13
l 2 Ki. 22:8
3
m 2 Ki. 11:14
n 2 Ki. 11:17
4
o 2 Ki. 25:18
p 2 Ki. 21:3–7
q See Dt. 16:21, *note*

only Deuteronomy but the entire Pentateuch was doubtless indicated by the term, "the Book of the Law."

[1](22:14) There were other women who had the gift of prophecy, e.g. Miriam, the sister of Moses (Ex. 15:20), and Deborah (Jud. 4:4).

5 Then he removed the idolatrous priests whom the kings of Judah had ordained to burn incense on the [a]high places in the cities of Judah and in the places all around Jerusalem, and those who burned incense to Baal, to the sun, to the moon, to the constellations, and to all the host of heaven.

6 And he brought out the [b]wooden image from the house of the LORD, to the Brook Kidron outside Jerusalem, burned it at the Brook Kidron and ground *it* to [c]ashes, and threw its ashes on the [d]graves of the common people.

7 Then he tore down the *ritual* booths of the [e]perverted persons* that *were* in the house of the LORD, [f]where the [g]women wove hangings for the [b]wooden image.

8 And he brought all the priests from the cities of Judah, and defiled the high places where the priests had burned incense, from Geba to Beersheba; also he broke down the high places at the gates which *were* at the entrance of the Gate of Joshua the governor of the city, which *were* to the left of the city gate.

9 [h]Nevertheless the priests of the high places did not come up to the altar of the LORD in Jerusalem, [i]but they ate unleavened bread among their brethren.

10 And he defiled [j]Topheth, which *is* in the [k]Valley of the Son* of Hinnom, [l]that no man might make his son or his daughter [m]pass through the fire to Molech.

11 Then he removed the horses that the kings of Judah had dedicated to the sun, at the entrance to the house of the LORD, by the chamber of Nathan-Melech, the officer who *was* in the court; and he burned the chariots of the sun with fire.

12 The altars that *were* [n]on the roof, the upper chamber of Ahaz, which the kings of Judah had made, and the altars which [o]Manasseh had made in the two courts of the house of the LORD, the king broke down and pulverized there, and threw their dust into the Brook Kidron.

13 Then the king defiled the high places that *were* east of Jerusalem, which *were* on the south of the Mount of Corruption, which [p]Solomon king of Israel had built for [q]Ashtoreth the abomination of the Sidonians, for Chemosh the abomination of the Moabites, and for Milcom the abomination of the people of Ammon.

14 And he [r]broke in pieces the *sacred* pillars and cut down the wooden images, and filled their places with the [s]bones of men.

15 Moreover the altar that *was* at Bethel, *and* the high place [t]which Jeroboam the son of Nebat, who made Israel sin, had made, both that altar and the high place he broke down; and he burned the high place *and* crushed *it* to powder, and burned the wooden image.

16 As Josiah turned, he saw the tombs that *were* there on the mountain. And he sent and took the bones out of the tombs and burned *them* on the altar, and defiled it according to the [u]word of the LORD which the man of God proclaimed, who proclaimed these words.

17 Then he said, "What gravestone *is* this that I see?" So the men of the city told him, "*It is* the tomb of the man of God who came from Judah and proclaimed these things which you have done against the altar of Bethel."

18 And he said, "Let him alone; let no one move his bones." So they let his bones alone, with the bones of the [v]prophet who came from Samaria.

19 Now Josiah also took away all the shrines of the high places that *were* [w]in the cities of Samaria, which the kings of Israel had made to provoke the LORD* to anger; and he did to them according to all the deeds he had done in Bethel.

20 He [x]executed all the priests of the high places who *were* there, on the altars, and burned men's bones on them; and he returned to Jerusalem.

Passover reinstituted (2 Chr. 35:1–19)

21 Then the king commanded all the people, saying, [y]"Keep the Passover to the LORD your God, [z]as *it is* written in this Book of the Covenant."

22 Such a Passover surely had never been held since the days of the judges who judged Israel, nor in all the days of the kings of Israel and the kings of Judah.

23 But in the eighteenth year of King Josiah this Passover was held before the LORD in Jerusalem.

24 Moreover Josiah put away those who consulted mediums and spiritists, the household gods and idols, all the

5 *a* vv. 8,9,13, 20; see Jud. 3:7 and 1 Ki. 3:2, *notes*
6 *b* See Dt. 16:21, *note* *c* Ex. 32:20 *d* 2 Chr. 34:4
7 *e* 1 Ki. 14:24; 15:12 *f* Ezek. 16:16 *g* Ex. 38:8
9 *h* Ezek. 44:10–14 *i* 1 Sam. 2:36
10 *j* Isa. 30:33; Jer. 7:31–32 *k* Josh. 15:8 *l* Lev. 18:21; Dt. 18:10; Ezek. 23:37–39 *m* 2 Ki. 21:6
12 *n* Jer. 19:13; Zeph. 1:5 *o* 2 Ki. 21:5
13 *p* 1 Ki. 11:5–7 *q* See Jud. 2:13, *note*
14 *r* Ex. 23:24; Dt. 7:5–25 *s* Cp. Jer. 8:1–2
15 *t* 1 Ki. 12:28–33; see Jud. 3:7 and 1 Ki. 3:2, *notes*
16 *u* 1 Ki. 13:2
18 *v* 1 Ki. 13:31
19 *w* 2 Chr. 34:6–7
20 *x* 2 Ki. 10:25; 11:18
21 *y* Num. 9:5; Josh. 5:10 *z* Ex. 12:3; Lev. 23:5; Num. 9:2; Dt. 16:2

*

23:7 Hebrew *qedeshim*, that is, those practicing sodomy and prostitution in religious rituals **23:10** Kethib reads *Sons*. **23:19** Following Septuagint, Syriac, and Vulgate; Masoretic Text and Targum omit *the LORD*.

abominations that were seen in the land of Judah and in Jerusalem, that he might perform the words of the law [a]which were written in the book [b]that Hilkiah the priest found in the house of the LORD.

25 Now before him there was no king [c]like him, who turned to the LORD with all his heart, with all his soul, and with all his might, according to all the Law of Moses; nor after him did *any* arise like him.

26 Nevertheless the LORD did not turn from the fierceness of His great wrath, with which His anger was aroused against Judah, [d]because of all the provocations with which Manasseh had provoked Him.

27 And the LORD said, "I will also remove Judah from My sight, as [e]I have removed Israel, and will cast off this city Jerusalem which I have chosen, and the house of which I said, [f]'My name shall be there.' "

28 Now the rest of the acts of Josiah, and all that he did, *are* they not written in the book of the chronicles of the kings of Judah?

Josiah dies (2 Chr. 35:20–27)

29 [g]In his days Pharaoh Necho king of Egypt went to the aid of the king of Assyria, to the River Euphrates; and King Josiah went against him. And *Pharaoh Necho* killed him at [h]Megiddo when he [i]confronted him.

30 Then his servants moved his body in a chariot from Megiddo, brought him to Jerusalem, and buried him in his own tomb. [j]And the people of the land took Jehoahaz the son of Josiah, anointed him, and made him king in his father's place.

Jehoahaz reigns; he is dethroned (2 Chr. 36:1–3)

31 [k]Jehoahaz *was* twenty-three years old when he [l]became king, and he reigned three months in Jerusalem. His mother's name *was* [m]Hamutal the daughter of Jeremiah of Libnah.

32 And he did evil in the sight of the LORD, according to all that his fathers had done.

33 Now Pharaoh Necho put him in prison at [n]Riblah in the land of Hamath, that he might not reign in Jerusalem; and he imposed on the land a tribute of one hundred [o]talents of silver and a talent of gold.

Jehoiakim is made king by Pharaoh Necho (2 Chr. 36:4–5)

34 Then Pharaoh Necho made [p]Eliakim the son of Josiah king in place of his father Josiah, and [q]changed his name to [r]Jehoiakim. And *Pharaoh* took Jehoahaz [s]and went to Egypt, and he* died there.

35 So Jehoiakim gave the silver and gold to Pharaoh; but he [t]taxed the land to give money according to the command of Pharaoh; he exacted the silver and gold from the people of the land, from every one according to his assessment, to give *it* to Pharaoh Necho.

36 Jehoiakim *was* twenty-five years old when he became king, and he reigned eleven years in Jerusalem. His mother's name *was* Zebudah the daughter of Pedaiah of Rumah.

37 And he did evil in the sight of the LORD, according to all that his fathers had done.

Jehoiakim becomes subservient to Nebuchadnezzar, king of Babylon (2 Chr. 36:6–7)

24

IN [u]his days Nebuchadnezzar king of [v]Babylon came up, and Jehoiakim became his vassal *for* three years. Then he turned and rebelled against him.

2 And the LORD sent against him *raiding* [w]bands of Chaldeans, bands of Syrians, bands of Moabites, and bands of the people of Ammon; He sent them against Judah to destroy it, [x]according to the word of the LORD which He had spoken by His servants the prophets.

3 Surely at the commandment of the LORD *this* came upon Judah, to remove *them* from His sight because of the sins of Manasseh, according to all that he had done,

4 and also because of the [y]innocent blood that he had shed; for he had filled Jerusalem with innocent blood, which the LORD would not pardon.

Jehoiakim dies; Jehoiachin reigns (2 Chr. 36:8–9)

5 Now the rest of the acts of Jehoiakim, and all that he did, *are* they not written in the book of the chronicles of the kings of Judah?

6 So Jehoiakim [z]rested with his fathers. Then Jehoiachin his son reigned in his place.

7 And the king of [aa]Egypt did not come out of his land anymore, for the king of Babylon had taken all that belonged to the king of Egypt from the

---

24 *a* Lev. 19:31; Dt. 18:11 *b* 2 Ki. 22:8
25 *c* 2 Ki. 18:5
26 *d* 2 Ki. 21:11–13; Jer. 15:4
27 *e* 2 Ki. 17:18–20; 18:11; 21:13 *f* 1 Ki. 8:29; 9:3; 2 Ki. 21:4,7
29 *g* Jer. 46:2 *h* Jud. 5:19; Zech. 12:11 *i* 2 Ki. 14:8
30 *j* vv. 30–34
31 *k* Or *Shallum*, Jer. 22:11 *l* 608 B.C. *m* 2 Ki. 24:18
33 *n* 2 Ki. 25:6–21 *o* See Coinage (OT), Ex. 30:13, *note*
34 *p* 2 Chr. 36:4 *q* 2 Ki. 24:17 *r* 1 Chr. 3:15 *s* Jer. 22:11–12; Ezek. 19:3–4
35 *t* Cp. 2 Ki. 15:20
CHAPTER 24
1 *u* Jer. 25:1–9; Dan. 1:1 *v* Dt. 29:22–29
2 *w* Jer. 35:11 *x* 2 Ki. 20:17; 21:12–14
4 *y* 2 Ki. 21:16
6 *z* Jer. 22:18–19
7 *aa* Jer. 37:5–7

---

* 23:34 That is, Jehoahaz

Brook of Egypt to the River Euphrates.

8 Jehoiachin *was* [a]eighteen years old when he [b]became king, and he reigned in Jerusalem three months. His mother's name *was* Nehushta the daughter of Elnathan of Jerusalem.

9 And he did evil in the sight of the LORD, according to all that his father had done.

The first deportation to Babylon; Jehoiachin is taken captive (2 Chr. 36:10)

10 At that time the servants of Nebuchadnezzar king of Babylon came up against [c]Jerusalem, and the city was besieged.

11 And Nebuchadnezzar king of Babylon came against the city, as his servants were besieging it.

12 Then [d]Jehoiachin king of Judah, his mother, his servants, his princes, and his officers went out to the king of Babylon; and [e]the king of Babylon, in the eighth year of his reign, took him prisoner.

13 And he carried out from there all the treasures of the house of the LORD and the treasures of the king's house, and he [f]cut in pieces all the articles of gold which Solomon king of Israel had made in the temple of the LORD, [g]as the LORD had said.

14 Also [h]he carried into captivity all Jerusalem: all the captains and all the mighty men of valor, ten thousand captives, and all the craftsmen and smiths. None remained except the poorest people of the land.

15 And he [i]carried Jehoiachin captive to Babylon. The king's mother, the king's wives, his officers, and the mighty of the land he carried into captivity from Jerusalem to Babylon.

16 All the valiant men, seven thousand, and craftsmen and smiths, one thousand, all *who were* strong *and* fit for war, these the king of Babylon brought captive to Babylon.

Nebuchadnezzar makes Zedekiah (Mattaniah) king (2 Chr. 36:10–12)

17 Then the [j]king of Babylon made Mattaniah, *Jehoiachin's** uncle, king in his place, and changed his name to [k]Zedekiah.

18 [l]Zedekiah *was* twenty-one years old when he [b]became king, and he reigned eleven years in Jerusalem. His mother's name *was* Hamutal the daughter of Jeremiah of Libnah.

19 He also did evil in the sight of the LORD, according to all that Jehoiakim had done.

Zedekiah rebels (2 Chr. 36:13–16)

20 For because of the anger of the LORD *this* happened in Jerusalem and Judah, that He finally cast them out from His presence. Then Zedekiah rebelled against the king of Babylon.

Nebuchadnezzar besieges Jerusalem (2 Chr. 36:1–4; Jer. 39:8–10)

25

NOW it came to pass in the ninth year of his reign, in the [m]tenth month, on the tenth *day* of the month, *that* Nebuchadnezzar king of Babylon and all his army came against [c]Jerusalem and encamped against it; and they built a [n]siege wall against it all around.

2 So the city was besieged until the eleventh year of King Zedekiah.

3 By the ninth *day* of the [m]*fourth* month the [o]famine had become so severe in the city that there was no food for the people of the land.

Zedekiah is taken captive

4 Then the city wall was [p]broken through, and all the men of war *fled* at night by way of the gate between two walls, which was by the king's garden, even though the Chaldeans *were* still encamped all around against the city. And *the king** went by way of the [q]plain.

5 But the army of the Chaldeans pursued the king, and they overtook him in the plains of Jericho. All his army was scattered from him.

6 So they took the king and [r]brought him up to the king of Babylon at Riblah, and they pronounced judgment on him.

7 [s]Then they killed the sons of [t]Zedekiah before his eyes, put out the eyes of Zedekiah, bound him with bronze fetters, and took him to Babylon.

Jerusalem burned; temple plundered, nobles put to death (2 Chr. 36:17–21)

8 [u]And in the [m]fifth month, on the seventh *day* of the month (which *was* the [v]nineteenth year of King Nebuchadnezzar king of Babylon), Nebuzaradan the captain of the guard, a servant of the king of Babylon, [w]came to Jerusalem.

9 He [x]burned the house of the

8 *a* Cp. 2 Chr. 36:9; see 1 Chr. 11:11, *note* *b* 597 B.C.
10 *c Israel* (history): vv. 10–16; 25:1–7; Ezra 1:3. (Gen. 12:2; Rom. 11:26, *note*)
12 *d* Or *Jeconiah*, Jer. 29:1–2 *e* In Nebuchadnezzar's eighth year. Cp. Jer. 25:1
13 *f* Dan. 5:2–3 *g* Jer. 20:5
14 *h* Jer. 24:1
15 *i* Est. 2:6
17 *j* Jer. 37:1 *k* Ezek. 17:11–15
18 *l* Jer. 37:1; 52:1
CHAPTER 25
1 *m* See Lev. 23:2, *note* *n* Ezek. 4:2
3 *o* Lam. 4:9–10
4 *p Times of the Gentiles:* vv. 1–21; 2 Chr. 36:20. (Dt. 28:49; Rev. 16:19) *q* See Dt. 1:1, *note*
6 *r* Jer. 32:4
7 *s Kingdom* (OT): vv. 1–7; Ps. 2:6. (Gen. 1:26; Zech. 12:8, *note*) *t* Ezek. 17:16
8 *u* vv. 8–12; cp. Jer. 39:8–12; 52:12–16

v Cp. 2 Ki. 24:12 *w* 586 B.C. **25:9** *x* Ps. 79:1

*

24:17 Literally *his* **25:4** Literally *he*

LORD and the king's house; all the houses of Jerusalem, that is, all the houses of the great, he [a]burned with fire.

10 And all the army of the Chaldeans who *were with* the captain of the guard [b]broke down the walls of Jerusalem all around.

11 Then Nebuzaradan the captain of the guard carried away captive the rest of the people *who* remained in the city and the defectors who had deserted to the king of Babylon, with the rest of the multitude.

12 But the captain of the guard [c]left *some* of the poor of the land as vinedressers and farmers.

13 [d]The bronze pillars that *were* in the house of the LORD, and the carts and the bronze Sea that *were* in the house of the LORD, the Chaldeans broke in pieces, and [e]carried their bronze to Babylon.

14 They also took away the pots, the shovels, the trimmers, the spoons, and all the bronze utensils with which the priests ministered.

15 The firepans and the basins, the things of solid gold and solid silver, the captain of the guard took away.

16 The two pillars, one Sea, and the carts, which Solomon had made for the house of the LORD, the bronze of all these articles was [f]beyond measure.

17 The height of one pillar *was* eighteen [g]cubits, and the capital on it *was* of bronze. The height of the capital was three cubits, and the network and pomegranates all around the capital were all of bronze. The second pillar was the same, with a network.

18 And the [h]captain of the guard took [i]Seraiah the chief priest, [j]Zephaniah the second priest, and the three doorkeepers.

19 He also [k]took out of the city an officer who had charge of the men of war, five men of the king's close associates who were found in the city, the chief recruiting officer of the army, who mustered the people of the land, and sixty men of the people of the land *who were* found in the city.

20 So Nebuzaradan, captain of the guard, took these and brought them to the king of Babylon at Riblah.

21 Then the king of Babylon struck them and put them to death at Riblah in the land of Hamath. Thus Judah was carried away captive from its own land.

9
[a] Jer. 17:27
10
[b] Neh. 1:3
12
[c] 2 Ki. 24:14; Jer. 39:10; 40:7; 52:16
13
[d] vv. 13–17; cp. Jer. 52:17–23
[e] Jer. 27:19–22
16
[f] 1 Ki. 7:47
17
[g] See Weights and Measures (OT), 2 Chr. 2:10, *note*
18
[h] Jer. 39:9–13; cp. 52:12–16
[i] 1 Chr. 6:14; Ezra 7:1
[j] Jer. 29:25, 29
19
[k] Jer. 52:25
22
[l] Jer. 40:5
[m] 2 Ki. 22:12
23
[n] Jer. 40:7–9
25
[o] See Lev. 23:2, *note*
[p] Jer. 41:1–3
26
[q] Jer. 43:4–7
27
[r] vv. 27–30; cp. Jer. 52:31–34
[s] 2 Ki. 24:12,15
[t] 561 B.C.
[u] Gen. 40:13,20
29
[v] 2 Sam. 9:7

Gedaliah appointed governor

22 [l]Then he made Gedaliah the son of [m]Ahikam, the son of Shaphan, governor over the people who remained in the land of Judah, whom Nebuchadnezzar king of Babylon had left.

23 Now when all the captains of the armies, they and *their* men, heard that the king of Babylon had made Gedaliah governor, they [n]came to Gedaliah at Mizpah—Ishmael the son of Nethaniah, Johanan the son of Careah, Seraiah the son of Tanhumeth the Netophathite, and Jaazaniah* the son of a Maachathite, they and their men.

24 And Gedaliah took an oath before them and their men, and said to them, "Do not be afraid of the servants of the Chaldeans. Dwell in the land and serve the king of Babylon, and it shall be well with you."

Gedaliah assassinated; people flee to Egypt

25 But it happened in the [o]seventh month that Ishmael the son of Nethaniah, the son of Elishama, of the royal family, came with ten men and [p]struck and killed Gedaliah, the Jews, as well as the Chaldeans who were with him at Mizpah.

26 And all the people, small and great, and the captains of the armies, arose and [q]went to Egypt; for they were afraid of the Chaldeans.

Jehoiachin, king of Judah, freed from prison

27 [r]Now it came to pass in the thirty-seventh year of the [s]captivity of Jehoiachin king of Judah, in the [o]twelfth month, on the twenty-seventh *day* of the month, *that* Evil-Merodach* king of Babylon, in the year that he began to [t]reign, [u]released Jehoiachin king of Judah from prison.

28 He spoke kindly to him, and gave him a more prominent seat than those of the kings who *were* with him in Babylon.

29 So Jehoiachin changed from his prison garments, and he [v]ate bread regularly before the king all the days of his life.

30 And as for his provisions, *there was* a regular ration given him by the king, a portion for each day, all the days of his life.

*

25:23 Spelled *Jezaniah* in Jeremiah 40:8
25:27 Literally *Man of Marduk*

The First Book of the

CHRONICLES

Author: Unknown *Theme:* Genealogy and History *Date of writing:* 5th Cent. B.C.

FIRST AND SECOND CHRONICLES formed one book in the old Hebrew canon. The two books embody many of the events recorded in 1 and 2 Kings, being devoted to the history of Judah from the time of Saul's death to the Babylonian captivity. They were composed much later than the Books of the Kings, possibly after the captivity, and were written, for the most part, from the priestly point of view. For this reason, 1 Chronicles begins with the most extensive collection of genealogical records in the Bible, the purpose of which is to draw all lines of redemptive history to their focal point in David. Much emphasis is placed upon the dedication and services of the temple and the ministry of the Levites.

The account in 1 Chronicles of Judah under David and Solomon omits certain of the darker incidents included in 1 and 2 Kings. The northern kingdom (Israel) is not in view in the Books of the Chronicles, except as it relates to Judah.

Some portions of this book are unique in the historical records, e.g. David's preparation of material for building the temple (22:1–5), the divisions of personnel ministering in the temple (chs. 23—27), and David's final exhortation to Israel and Solomon (chs. 28—29).

First Chronicles may be divided as follows:

I. Genealogies of the Patriarchs and the Twelve Sons of Israel, 1—9.
II. The Last Days and Death of King Saul, 10.
III. The Reign of David, 11—29.

I. Genealogies of the Patriarchs and the Twelve Sons of Israel, 1—9

Adam to Noah (Gen. 5:1–32)

1 [a]ADAM, [b]Seth, Enosh,
2 Cainan,* Mahalalel, Jared,
3 Enoch, Methuselah, Lamech,
4 [c]Noah,* Shem, Ham, and Japheth.

Sons of Japheth (Gen. 10:2–5)

5 The [d]sons of Japheth *were* Gomer, [e]Magog, Madai, Javan, Tubal,
Meshech, and Tiras.
6 The sons of Gomer *were* Ashkenaz, [f]Diphath, and Togarmah.
7 The sons of Javan *were* Elishah,
Tarshishah,* Kittim, and [g]Rodanim.

Sons of Ham (Gen. 10:6–21)

8 The [h]sons of Ham *were* Cush,
Mizraim, Put, and Canaan.
9 The sons of Cush *were* Seba,
Havilah, Sabta,* Raama,* and Sabte-
cha. The sons of Raama *were* Sheba
and Dedan.
10 Cush begot [i]Nimrod; he began
to be a mighty one on the earth.
11 Mizraim begot Ludim, Anamim,
Lehabim, Naphtuhim,
12 Pathrusim, Casluhim (from
whom came the Philistines and the
Caphtorim).
13 [j]Canaan begot Sidon, his firstborn, and Heth;
14 the Jebusite, the Amorite, and
the Girgashite;
15 the Hivite, the Arkite, and the Si-
nite;

CHAPTER 1

1
a vv. 1–4; Gen. 1:27; 2:7; 5:1–2, 5
b Gen. 4:25–26; 5:3–4,6–8

4
c Gen. 5:28–10:1

5
d vv. 5–7
e Cp. Ezek. 39:6; Rev. 20:8; see Gen. 10:2 and Ezek. 38:2, *notes*

6
f Or *Riphath*, Gen. 10:3

7
g Or *Dodanim*, Gen. 10:4

8
h vv. 8–16

10
i Gen. 10:8–10; cp. Mic. 5:6

13
j Gen. 9:18, 25–27

17
k vv. 17–23
l Gen. 11:10–13; Lk. 3:36
m Or *Mash*, Gen. 10:23

16 the Arvadite, the Zemarite, and
the Hamathite.

Sons of Shem (Gen. 10:22–31)

17 The [k]sons of Shem *were* Elam,
Asshur, [l]Arphaxad, Lud, Aram, Uz,
Hul, Gether, and [m]Meshech.
18 Arphaxad begot Shelah, and
Shelah begot Eber.
19 To Eber were born two sons: the
name of one *was* [n]Peleg, for in his
days the earth was divided; and his
brother's name *was* Joktan.
20 Joktan begot Almodad, Sheleph,
Hazarmaveth, Jerah,
21 Hadoram, Uzal, Diklah,
22 [o]Ebal, Abimael, Sheba,
23 Ophir, Havilah, and Jobab. All
these *were* the sons of Joktan.

Shem to Abraham (Gen. 11:10–26)

24 [p]Shem, Arphaxad, Shelah,
25 Eber, Peleg, Reu,
26 Serug, Nahor, Terah,
27 and [q]Abram, who *is* Abraham.
28 The [r]sons of Abraham *were*
Isaac and Ishmael.

Ishmael's sons (Gen. 25:12–19)

29 [s]These *are* their genealogies:

1:19 *n* Lit. *division* **1:22** *o* Or *Obal*, Gen. 10:28
1:24 *p* vv. 24–27; Lk. 3:36 **1:27** *q* Gen. 17:5
1:28 *r* Gen. 16:11,15; 21:2–3 **1:29** *s* vv. 29–31

*

1:2 Hebrew *Qenan* 1:4 Following Masoretic Text and Vulgate; Septuagint adds *the sons of Noah.* 1:7 Spelled *Tarshish* in Genesis 10:4 1:9 Spelled *Sabtah* in Genesis 10:7 • Spelled *Raamah* in Genesis 10:7

The firstborn of Ishmael *was* Nebajoth; then Kedar, Adbeel, Mibsam,
30 Mishma, Dumah, Massa, Hadad,* Tema,
31 Jetur, Naphish, and Kedemah.
These *were* the sons of Ishmael.

Keturah's sons (Gen. 25:1–4)

32 Now the [a]sons born to Keturah,
Abraham's concubine, *were* Zimran,
Jokshan, Medan, Midian, Ishbak, and
Shuah. The sons of Jokshan *were*
Sheba and Dedan.
33 The sons of Midian *were* Ephah,
Epher, Hanoch, Abida, and Eldaah.
All these were the children of Ketu-
rah.

Sons of Isaac (Gen. 25:19–26)

34 And Abraham begot Isaac. The
[b]sons of Isaac *were* Esau and Israel.

Esau's sons and grandsons (Gen. 36:1–14)

35 The [c]sons of Esau *were* Eliphaz,
Reuel, Jeush, Jaalam, and Korah.
36 And the sons of Eliphaz *were* Teman, Omar, [d]Zephi, Gatam, *and* Kenaz; and *by* Timna,* Amalek.
37 The sons of Reuel *were* Nahath,
Zerah, Shammah, and Mizzah.
38 The [e]sons of Seir *were* Lotan,
Shobal, Zibeon, Anah, Dishon, Ezer,
and Dishan.
39 And the sons of Lotan *were* Hori
and [f]Homam; Lotan's sister *was*
Timna.
40 The sons of Shobal *were* [g]Alian,
Manahath, Ebal, [h]Shephi, and Onam.
The sons of Zibeon *were* Ajah and
Anah.
41 The son of Anah *was* Dishon.
The sons of Dishon *were* [i]Hamran,
Eshban, Ithran, and Cheran.
42 The sons of Ezer *were* Bilhan,
Zaavan, *and* [j]Jaakan. The sons of Di-
shan *were* Uz and Aran.

Early kings and leaders of Edom (Gen. 36:15–19,25–43)

43 Now these *were* the [k]kings who
reigned in the land of Edom before a
king reigned over the children of Israel: Bela the son of Beor, and the
name of his city was Dinhabah.
44 And when Bela died, Jobab the
son of Zerah of Bozrah reigned in his
place.
45 When Jobab died, Husham of
the land of the Temanites reigned in
his place.
46 And when Husham died, Hadad
the son of Bedad, who attacked Midian in the field of Moab, reigned in his
place. The name of his city *was* Avith.
47 When Hadad died, Samlah of
Masrekah reigned in his place.
48 And when Samlah died, Saul of
Rehoboth-by-the-River reigned in his
place.
49 When Saul died, Baal-Hanan the
son of Achbor reigned in his place.
50 And when Baal-Hanan died,
[l]Hadad reigned in his place; and the
name of his city was [m]Pai. His wife's
name was Mehetabel the daughter of
Matred, the daughter of Mezahab.
51 Hadad died also. And the chiefs
of Edom were Chief Timnah, Chief
[n]Aliah, Chief Jetheth,
52 Chief Aholibamah, Chief Elah,
Chief Pinon,
53 Chief Kenaz, Chief Teman,
Chief Mibzar,
54 Chief Magdiel, and Chief Iram.
These *were* the chiefs of Edom.

Twelve sons of Jacob (Israel) (Gen. 29:31—30:24; 35:16–18)

2 THESE *were* the [o]sons of [p]Israel:
Reuben, Simeon, Levi, Judah, Issachar, Zebulun,
2 Dan, Joseph, Benjamin, Naphtali, Gad, and Asher.

Judah's sons and line to Hezron (Gen. 46:12; Num. 26:19–22)

3 The [q]sons of Judah *were* [r]Er,
Onan, and Shelah. *These* three were
born to him by the daughter of [s]Shua,
the Canaanitess. Er, the firstborn of
Judah, was wicked in the sight of the
LORD; so He killed him.
4 And Tamar, his daughter-in-
law, [t]bore him Perez and Zerah. All
the sons of Judah *were* five.
5 The sons of [u]Perez *were* [1]Hez-
ron and Hamul.
6 The sons of Zerah *were* [v]Zimri,
Ethan, Heman, Calcol, and [w]Dara—
five of them in all.
7 The son of Carmi *was* [x]Achar,

32 *a* vv. 32–33 **34** *b* Gen. 25:9; 35:29 **35** *c* vv. 35–37 **36** *d* Or *Zepho,* Gen. 36:11 **38** *e* vv. 38–42; Gen. 36:20–28 **39** *f* Or *Hemam,* Gen. 36:22 **40** *g* Or *Alvan,* Gen. 36:23 *h* Or *Shepho,* Gen. 36:23 **41** *i* Or *Hemdan,* Gen. 36:26 **42** *j* Or *Akan,* Gen. 36:27 **43** *k* vv. 43–54; Gen. 36:31–39 **50** *l* Or *Hadar,* Gen. 36:39 *m* Or *Pau,* Gen. 36:39 **51** *n* Or *Alvah,* Gen. 36:40 **CHAPTER 2** **1** *o* Gen. 29:32–35; 35:23–26; 46:8–27 *p* Gen. 32:24–28; 35:9–10 **3** *q* vv. 3–8; Gen. 38:12–30; cp. Num. 26:19–22 *r* Gen. 38:3–10 *s* Or *Shuhah,* 1 Chr. 4:11 **4** *t* Mt. 1:3 **5** *u* Ruth 4:18 **6** *v* Or *Zabdi,* Josh. 7:1 *w* Or *Darda,* 1 Ki. 4:31 **2:7** *x* Or *Achan,* Josh. 7:1–26; 22:20

* **1:30** Spelled *Hadar* in Genesis 25:15 **1:36** Compare Genesis 36:12

[1](2:5) Hezron is a key figure in the genealogies of ch. 2. Through Hezron's son, Ram, the line of promise passes from Judah to Boaz to Jesse to David (vv. 10–15). From King David the line leads to Him who was the fulfillment of the promise, the Lord Jesus Christ.

the troubler of Israel, who transgressed in the accursed thing.
8 The son of Ethan *was* Azariah.
9 Also the sons of Hezron who
were born to him *were* Jerahmeel,
Ram, and [a]Chelubai.

Ram's line to David
(v. 9; Ruth 4:17–22)

10 Ram [b]begot Amminadab, and
Amminadab begot Nahshon, [c]leader
of the children of Judah;
11 Nahshon begot [d]Salma, and
Salma begot Boaz;
12 Boaz begot Obed, and Obed begot Jesse;
13 [e]Jesse begot Eliab his firstborn,
Abinadab the second, [f]Shimea the
third,
14 Nethanel the fourth, Raddai the
fifth,
15 Ozem the sixth, *and* David the
[g]seventh.
16 Now their sisters *were* Zeruiah
and Abigail. And the [h]sons of Zeruiah
were Abishai, Joab, and Asahel—
three.
17 [i]Abigail bore Amasa; and the
father of Amasa *was* Jether the Ishmaelite.

Sons of Caleb, the son of Hezron,
by Azubah and Ephrath (v. 50)

18 [j]Caleb the son of Hezron had
children by Azubah, *his* wife, and by
Jerioth. Now these were her sons: Je-
sher, Shobab, and Ardon.
19 When Azubah died, Caleb took
Ephrath* as his wife, who bore him
Hur.
20 And Hur begot Uri, and Uri begot [k]Bezalel.

Hezron's later children
(cp. v. 9) by Abijah,
Machir's daughter

21 Now afterward Hezron went in
to the daughter of [l]Machir the father
of Gilead, whom he married when he
was sixty years old; and she bore him
Segub.
22 Segub begot [m]Jair, who had
twenty-three cities in the land of Gilead.
23 (Geshur and Syria took from
them the [n]towns of Jair, with Kenath
and its [o]towns—sixty towns.) All
these *belonged to* the sons of Machir
the father of Gilead.
24 After Hezron died in Caleb Ephrathah, Hezron's wife Abijah bore
him [p]Ashhur the father of Tekoa.

9
a Called *Caleb*, vv. 18,42
10
b Mt. 1:4
c Num. 1:7
11
d Or *Salmon*, Ruth 4:21; Mt. 1:5
13
e 1 Sam. 16:6
f Or *Shammah*, 1 Sam. 16:9
15
g 1 Sam. 16:10–11; 17:12
16
h 2 Sam. 2:18
17
i 2 Sam. 17:25
18
j Cp. v. 9
20
k Ex. 38:22
21
l Jud. 5:14; 1 Chr. 7:14
22
m Jud. 10:3; 1 Ki. 4:13
23
n Or *Havoth Jair*, Num. 32:41; Jud. 10:4; Dt. 3:14
o Lit. *daughters*
24
p 1 Chr. 4:5
31
q vv. 34–41
36
r 1 Chr. 11:41
37
s 2 Chr. 23:1

Jerahmeel's (v. 9) line through
Sheshan (vv. 31,34–35)

25 The sons of Jerahmeel, the firstborn of Hezron, *were* Ram, the firstborn, and Bunah, Oren, Ozem, *and*
Ahijah.
26 Jerahmeel had another wife,
whose name was Atarah; she was the
mother of Onam.
27 The sons of Ram, the firstborn of
Jerahmeel, were Maaz, Jamin, and
Eker.
28 The sons of Onam were Shammai and Jada. The sons of Shammai
were Nadab and Abishur.
29 And the name of the wife of Abishur *was* Abihail, and she bore him
Ahban and Molid.
30 The sons of Nadab *were* Seled
and Appaim; Seled died without children.
31 The son of Appaim *was* Ishi, the
son of Ishi *was* Sheshan, and [q]She-
shan's son *was* Ahlai.
32 The sons of Jada, the brother of
Shammai, *were* Jether and Jonathan;
Jether died without children.
33 The sons of Jonathan *were* Peleth and Zaza. These were the sons of
Jerahmeel.
34 Now Sheshan had no sons, only
daughters. And Sheshan had an Egyptian servant whose name *was* Jarha.
35 Sheshan gave his daughter to
Jarha his servant as wife, and she bore
him Attai.
36 Attai begot Nathan, and Nathan
begot [r]Zabad;
37 Zabad begot Ephlal, and Ephlal
begot [s]Obed;
38 Obed begot Jehu, and Jehu begot Azariah;
39 Azariah begot Helez, and Helez
begot Eleasah;
40 Eleasah begot Sismai, and Sismai begot Shallum;
41 Shallum begot Jekamiah, and
Jekamiah begot Elishama.

Further sons of Caleb (cp. v. 18)

42 The descendants of [j]Caleb the
brother of Jerahmeel *were* Mesha, his
firstborn, who was the father of Ziph,
and the sons of Mareshah the father of
Hebron.
43 The sons of Hebron *were* Korah,
Tappuah, Rekem, and Shema.
44 Shema begot Raham the father
of Jorkoam, and Rekem begot Shammai.
45 And the son of Shammai *was*

* 2:19 Spelled *Ephrathah* elsewhere

Maon, and Maon *was* the father of
Beth Zur.
46 Ephah, Caleb's concubine, bore
Haran, Moza, and Gazez; and Haran
begot Gazez.
47 And the sons of Jahdai *were* Re-
gem, Jotham, Geshan, Pelet, Ephah,
and Shaaph.
48 Maachah, Caleb's concubine,
bore Sheber and Tirhanah.
49 She also bore Shaaph the father
of Madmannah, Sheva the father of
Machbenah and the father of Gibea.
And the daughter of Caleb *was* [a]Ach-
sah.

Line of Hur, the son of Caleb
(v. 19; cp. 1 Chr. 4:1)

50 These were the descendants of
Caleb: The sons of [b]Hur, the firstborn
of [c]Ephrathah, *were* Shobal the father
of [d]Kirjath Jearim,
51 [e]Salma the father of Bethlehem,
and Hareph the father of Beth Gader.
52 And Shobal the father of Kirjath
Jearim had descendants: [f]Haroeh,
and half of the families of Manuhoth.*
53 The families of Kirjath Jearim
were the Ithrites, the Puthites, the
Shumathites, and the Mishraites.
From these came the Zorathites and
the Eshtaolites.
54 The sons of Salma *were* Bethlehem, the Netophathites, Atroth Beth
Joab, half of the Manahethites, and
the Zorites.
55 And the families of the scribes
who dwelt at Jabez *were* the Tirath-
ites, the Shimeathites, *and* the Su-
chathites. These *were* the [g]Kenites
who came from Hammath, the father
of the house of [h]Rechab.

Family of David, born in Hebron
(2 Sam. 3:2–5; 5:13–16)

3 NOW these were the sons of David who were [i]born to him in Hebron: The firstborn *was* [j]Amnon, by
[k]Ahinoam the Jezreelitess; the second, [l]Daniel, by [m]Abigail the Carmelitess;
2 the third, [n]Absalom the son of
Maacah, the daughter of Talmai, king
of Geshur; the fourth, [o]Adonijah the
son of Haggith;
3 the fifth, Shephatiah, by Abital;
the sixth, Ithream, by his wife Eglah.
4 *These* six were born to him in
Hebron. There he reigned seven years
and six months, and in Jerusalem he
reigned thirty-three [p]years.
5 And these were born to him in
[q]Jerusalem: Shimea,* Shobab, Nathan, and [r]Solomon—four by [s]Bath-
shua the daughter of Ammiel.*
6 Also *there* were Ibhar, Elishama,* Eliphelet,*
7 Nogah, Nepheg, Japhia,
8 Elishama, Eliada,* and
Eliphelet—nine *in all.*
9 *These were* all the sons of David,
besides the sons of the [t]concubines,
and [u]Tamar their sister.

David's line to Zedekiah

10 [v]Solomon's son *was* Rehoboam;
Abijah* *was* his son, Asa his son, Jehoshaphat his son,
11 Joram* his son, Ahaziah his
son, Joash* his son,
12 Amaziah his son, Azariah* his
son, Jotham his son,
13 Ahaz his son, Hezekiah his son,
Manasseh his son,
14 Amon his son, *and* Josiah his
son.
15 The sons of Josiah *were* Johanan the firstborn, the second [w]Jehoia-
kim, the third Zedekiah, and the
fourth [x]Shallum.
16 The sons of Jehoiakim *were* Jeconiah his son *and* Zedekiah* his son.

Jeconiah's sons

17 And the sons of Jeconiah* *were*
Assir,* [y]Shealtiel his son,
18 *and* Malchiram, Pedaiah, She-
nazzar, Jecamiah, Hoshama, and
Nedabiah.
19 The sons of Pedaiah *were* [1]Ze-
rubbabel and Shimei. The sons of Zerubbabel *were* Meshullam, Hananiah,
Shelomith their sister,

49 *a* Josh. 15:17
50 *b* 1 Chr. 4:4 *c* Called *Ephrath,* v. 19 *d* Josh. 9:17; 18:14
51 *e* Not to be confused with *Salma* in *Ram's* line, vv. 10–11
52 *f* Or *Reaiah,* 1 Chr. 4:2
55 *g* Jud. 1:16 *h* 2 Ki. 10:15; Jer. 35:2
CHAPTER 3
1 *i* vv. 1–4 *j* 2 Sam. 13:1 *k* 1 Sam. 25:43 *l* Or *Chileab,* 2 Sam. 3:3 *m* 1 Sam. 25:39–42
2 *n* 2 Sam. 13:37; 15:1 *o* 1 Ki. 1:5
4 *p* 2 Sam. 2:11; 5:4–5
5 *q* 1 Chr. 14:4–7 *r* Or *Jedidiah,* 2 Sam. 12:24–25 *s* Or *Bath-sheba,* 2 Sam. 11:2–27
9 *t* Cp. 1 Ki. 11:3 *u* 2 Sam. 13:1–20
10 *v* vv. 10–14; Mt. 1:7–10
15 *w* Or *Eliakim,* 2 Ki. 23:34 *x* Or *Jehoahaz,* 2 Ki. 23:30 **3:17** *y* Mt. 1:12

*
2:52 Same as *the Manahethites,* verse 54
3:5 Spelled *Shammua* in 14:4 and 2 Samuel 5:14 • Spelled *Eliam* in 2 Samuel 11:3 **3:6** Spelled *Elishua* in 14:5 and 2 Samuel 5:15 • Spelled *Elpelet* in 14:5 **3:8** Spelled *Beeliada* in 14:7
3:10 Spelled *Abijam* in 1 Kings 15:1 **3:11** Spelled *Jehoram* in 2 Kings 1:17 and 8:16 • Spelled *Jehoash* in 2 Kings 12:1 **3:12** Called *Uzziah* in Isaiah 6:1 **3:16** Compare 2 Kings 24:17
3:17 Also called *Coniah* in Jeremiah 22:24 and *Jehoiachin* in 2 Kings 24:8 • Or *the captive* were

[1](3:19) To Zerubbabel is assigned a greater importance in Israel's later history than is generally recognized. It was he who led the first expedition of Jews back to Jerusalem, following the decree of Cyrus. Zerubbabel probably acted as governor of the city until at least 515 B.C. (Ezra 3:2,8; Neh. 12:1; Hag. 1:1,12,14; 2:2,21). As a grandson of Jehoiachin, he was the representative of the Davidic monarchy (Hag. 2:20–23). In the NT Messianic genealogy Zerubbabel's is the last name mentioned from the OT (Mt. 1:13; Lk. 3:27).

20 and Hashubah, Ohel, Berechiah,
Hasadiah, and Jushab-Hesed—five *in*
all.
21 The sons of Hananiah *were* Pelatiah and Jeshaiah, the sons of Rephaiah, the sons of Arnan, the sons of
Obadiah, and the sons of Shechaniah.
22 The son of Shechaniah was Shemaiah. The sons of Shemaiah *were*
[a]Hattush, Igal, Bariah, Neariah, and
Shaphat—six *in all.*
23 The sons of Neariah *were* Elioenai, Hezekiah, and Azrikam—three *in*
all.
24 The sons of Elioenai *were* Hodaviah, Eliashib, Pelaiah, Akkub, Johanan, Delaiah, and Anani—seven *in all.*

Further line of Hur
(cp. 1 Chr. 2:50)

4 THE [b]sons of Judah *were* [c]Perez,
Hezron, Carmi, Hur, and Shobal.
2 And Reaiah the son of Shobal
begot Jahath, and Jahath begot Ahu-
mai and Lahad. These *were* the families of the Zorathites.
3 These *were* the sons *of the fa-*
ther of Etam: Jezreel, Ishma, and Id-
bash; and the name of their sister *was*
Hazelelponi;
4 and Penuel *was* the father of Gedor, and Ezer *was the* father of Hu-
shah. These *were* the sons of [d]Hur, the
firstborn of Ephrathah the father of
Bethlehem.

Family of Ashhur,
Hezron's posthumous son
(1 Chr. 2:24)

5 And [e]Ashhur the father of Tekoa had two wives, Helah and Naarah.
6 Naarah bore him Ahuzzam, Hepher, Temeni, and Haahashtari. These
were the sons of Naarah.
7 The sons of Helah *were* Zereth,
Zohar, and Ethnan;
8 and Koz begot Anub, Zobebah,
and the families of Aharhel the son of
Harum.

Jabez's prayer to God,
and His answer

9 Now Jabez was [f]more honorable than his brothers, and his mother
called his name Jabez,* saying, "Because I bore *him* in pain."
10 And Jabez [g]called on the God of
Israel saying, "Oh, that You would
bless me indeed, and enlarge my territory, that Your hand would be with
me, and that You would keep *me* from
evil, that I may not cause pain!" So
God [h]granted him what he requested.

Other men of Judah, including
Caleb, the son of Jephunneh

11 Chelub the brother of [i]Shuhah
begot Mehir, who *was* the father of
Eshton.
12 And Eshton begot Beth-Rapha,
Paseah, and Tehinnah the father of Ir-
Nahash. These *were* the men of Re-
chah.
13 The sons of Kenaz *were* [j]Oth-
niel and Seraiah. The sons of Othniel
were Hathath,*
14 and Meonothai *who* begot Ophrah. Seraiah begot Joab the father of
[k]Ge Harashim,* for they were craftsmen.
15 The sons of [l]Caleb the son of
Jephunneh *were* Iru, Elah, and Naam.
The son of Elah *was* Kenaz.
16 The sons of Jehallelel *were* Ziph,
Ziphah, Tiria, and Asarel.
17 The sons of Ezrah *were* Jether,
Mered, Epher, and Jalon. And *Me-*
*red's wife** *bore* Miriam, Shammai,
and Ishbah the father of Eshtemoa.
18 (His wife [m]Jehudijah bore Jered
the father of Gedor, Heber the father
of Sochoh, and Jekuthiel the father of
Zanoah.) And these were the sons of
Bithiah the daughter of Pharaoh,
whom Mered took.
19 The sons of Hodiah's wife, the
sister of Naham, *were* the fathers of
Keilah the Garmite and of Eshtemoa
the [n]Maachathite.
20 And the sons of Shimon *were*
Amnon, Rinnah, Ben-Hanan, and Ti-
lon. And the sons of Ishi *were* Zoheth
and Ben-Zoheth.

Judah's posterity through
Shelah (1 Chr. 2:3)

21 The sons of [o]Shelah the [p]son of
Judah *were* Er the father of Lecah, La-
adah the father of Mareshah, and the
families of the house of the linen
workers of the house of Ashbea;
22 also Jokim, the men of Chozeba,
and Joash; Saraph, who ruled in
Moab, and Jashubi-Lehem. Now the
[q]records are ancient.
23 These *were* the potters and those
who dwell at Netaim* and Gederah;*
there they dwelt with the king for his
work.

Simeon's posterity; their
cities and conquests

24 The [r]sons of Simeon *were*

22 *a* Ezra 8:2
CHAPTER 4
1 *b* Cp. 1 Chr. 2:3–4 *c* Gen. 38:29; 46:12
4 *d* Ex. 31:2
5 *e* 1 Chr. 2:24
9 *f* Gen. 34:19
10 *g Bible prayers* (OT): v. 10; 1 Chr. 29:10. (Gen. 15:2; Hab. 3:1) *h* Cp. 1 Chr. 26:5
11 *i* Gen. 38:1–5; cp. 1 Chr. 2:3
13 *j* Called *Caleb's brother.* Josh. 15:17; Jud. 3:9,11
14 *k* Neh. 11:35
15 *l* 1 Chr. 6:56; Josh. 14:6,14; 15:13,17
18 *m* Or *the Jewess*
19 *n* 2 Ki. 25:23
21 *o* Gen. 38:11,14 *p* Gen. 38:1–5; 46:12
22 *q* Lit. *words*
24 *r* Num. 26:12–14

*
4:9 Literally *He Will Cause Pain* 4:13 Septuagint and Vulgate add *and Meonothai.* 4:14 Literally *Valley of Craftsmen* 4:17 Literally *she* 4:23 Literally *Plants* • Literally *Hedges*

[a]Nemuel, Jamin, [b]Jarib, [c]Zerah, *and*
Shaul,
25 Shallum his son, Mibsam his
son, and Mishma his son.
26 And the sons of Mishma *were*
Hamuel his son, Zacchur his son, and
Shimei his son.
27 Shimei had sixteen sons and six
daughters; but his brothers did not
have many children, [d]nor did any of
their families multiply as much as the
children of Judah.
28 They [e]dwelt at [f]Beersheba,
Moladah, Hazar Shual,
29 [g]Bilhah, Ezem, [h]Tolad,
30 Bethuel, Hormah, Ziklag,
31 Beth Marcaboth, Hazar Susim,
Beth Biri, and at Shaaraim. These
were their cities until the reign of David.
32 And their villages *were* [i]Etam,
Ain, Rimmon, Tochen, and Ashan—
five cities—
33 and all the villages that *were*
around these cities as far as Baal.*
These *were* their dwelling places, and
they maintained their genealogy:
34 Meshobab, Jamlech, and Joshah
the son of Amaziah;
35 Joel, and Jehu the son of Joshi-
biah, the son of Seraiah, the son of
Asiel;
36 Elioenai, Jaakobah, Jeshohaiah,
Asaiah, Adiel, Jesimiel, and Benaiah;
37 Ziza the son of Shiphi, the son of
Allon, the son of Jedaiah, the son of
Shimri, the son of Shemaiah—
38 these mentioned by name *were*
leaders in their families, and their father's house increased [j]greatly.
39 So they went to the entrance of
Gedor, as far as the east side of the
valley, to seek pasture for their flocks.
40 And they found rich, good pasture, and the land *was* broad, quiet,
and peaceful; for some Hamites formerly lived there.
41 These recorded by name came in
the days of Hezekiah king of Judah;
and they [k]attacked their tents and the
Meunites who were found there, and
utterly [l]destroyed them, as it is to this
day. So they dwelt in their place, because *there was* pasture for their
flocks there.
42 Now *some* of them, five hundred
men of the sons of Simeon, went to
Mount Seir, having as their captains
Pelatiah, Neariah, Rephaiah, and Uzziel, the sons of Ishi.
43 And they defeated the rest of the
[m]Amalekites who had escaped. They
have dwelt there to this day.

Reuben's line to the captivity

5 NOW the [n]sons of Reuben the
firstborn of Israel—[o]he *was* indeed the firstborn, but because he
[p]defiled his father's bed, his birthright
was given to the sons of Joseph, the
son of Israel, so that the genealogy is
not listed according to the [q]birthright;
2 yet [r]Judah prevailed over his
brothers, and from him *came* a [s]ruler,
although the birthright was
Joseph's—
3 the sons of [t]Reuben the firstborn of Israel were Hanoch, Pallu,
Hezron, and Carmi.
4 The sons of Joel *were* Shemaiah
his son, Gog his son, Shimei his son,
5 Micah his son, Reaiah his son,
Baal his son,
6 and Beerah his son, whom
[u]Tiglath-Pileser* king of Assyria
[v]carried into captivity. He *was* leader
of the Reubenites.
7 And his brethren by their families, when the [w]genealogy of their
generations was registered: the chief,
Jeiel, and Zechariah,
8 and Bela the son of Azaz, the son
of Shema, the son of Joel, who dwelt
in [x]Aroer, as far as Nebo and Baal
Meon.

Reuben's conquests

9 Eastward they settled as far as
the entrance of the wilderness this
side of the River Euphrates, [y]because
their cattle had multiplied in the land
of Gilead.
10 Now in the days of Saul they
made war with the [1]Hagrites, who fell
by their hand; and they dwelt in their
tents throughout the entire *area* east
of Gilead.

Gad's descendants and habitation

11 And the [z]children of Gad dwelt
next to them in the land of [aa]Bashan as
far as [bb]Salcah:
12 Joel *was* the chief, Shapham the
next, then Jaanai and Shaphat in Bashan,
13 and their brethren of their father's house: Michael, Meshullam,

24 *a* Num. 26:12; or *Jemuel,* Gen. 46:10; Ex. 6:15 *b* Or *Jachin,* Gen. 46:10 *c* Or *Zohar,* Gen. 46:10
27 *d* Cp. Gen. 49:7; Num. 2:9,12–13
28 *e* vv. 28–33; cp. Josh. 19:1,8 *f* Josh. 19:2
29 *g* Or *Balah,* Josh. 19:3 *h* Or *Eltolad,* Josh. 19:4
32 *i* Or *Ether,* Josh. 19:7
38 *j* Cp. v. 27
41 *k* 2 Ki. 18:8 *l* 2 Ki. 19:11
43 *m* 1 Sam. 15:8; 30:17
CHAPTER 5
1 *n* v. 3; cp. 1 Chr. 2:1 *o* Gen. 29:32; 49:3 *p* Gen. 35:22; 49:4 *q* Gen. 48:15–22
2 *r* Gen. 49:8–10; Ps. 60:7; 108:8 *s* Cp. Mt. 2:6
3 *t* Gen. 46:9; Ex. 6:14; Num. 26:5
6 *u* 2 Ki. 15:29; 16:7 *v* 2 Ki. 18:11
7 *w* 1 Chr. 5:17
8 *x* Num. 32:34
9 *y* Josh. 22:8–9
11 *z* Num. 26:15–18 *aa* Josh. 13:11,24–28 *bb* Dt. 3:10

*

4:33 Or *Baalath Beer* (compare Joshua 19:8)
5:6 Hebrew *Tilgath-Pilneser*

[1](5:10) The descendants of Ishmael, the son of Hagar (Gen. 25:12; cp. Ps. 83:6).

Sheba, Jorai, Jachan, Zia, and Eber—
seven *in all.*
14 These *were* the children of Abihail the son of Huri, the son of Jaroah,
the son of Gilead, the son of Michael,
the son of Jeshishai, the son of Jahdo,
the son of Buz;
15 Ahi the son of Abdiel, the son of
Guni, *was* chief of their father's house.
16 And *the Gadites* dwelt in Gilead,
in Bashan and in its villages, and in all
the common-lands of [a]Sharon within
their borders.
17 All these were registered by genealogies in the days of [b]Jotham king
of Judah, and in the days of [c]Jero-
boam king of Israel.

Conquests of Reuben, Gad, and half-tribe of Manasseh; their sin and captivity

18 The sons of Reuben, the Gadites,
and half the tribe of Manasseh *had*
forty-four thousand seven hundred
and sixty valiant men, men able to
bear [d]shield and sword, to shoot with
the bow, and skillful in war, who went
to war.
19 They made war with the Hagrites, [e]Jetur, Naphish, and Nodab.
20 And they were helped against
them, and the Hagrites were delivered
into their hand, and all who *were* with
them, for they [f]cried out to God in the
battle. He heeded their prayer, because they put their [g]trust in Him.
21 Then they took away their
livestock—fifty thousand of their
camels, two hundred and fifty thousand of their sheep, and two thousand
of their donkeys—also one hundred
thousand of their men;
22 for many fell dead, because the
war [h]*was* God's. And they dwelt in
their place until the captivity.
23 So the children of the half-tribe
of Manasseh dwelt in the land. Their
numbers increased from Bashan to
Baal Hermon, that is, to [i]Senir, or
Mount Hermon.
24 These *were* the heads of their fathers' houses: Epher, Ishi, Eliel, Azriel, Jeremiah, Hodaviah, and Jahdiel.
They were mighty men of valor, famous men, *and* heads of their fathers'
houses.
25 And they were unfaithful to the
God of their fathers, and played the
harlot after the gods of the peoples of
the land, whom God had destroyed
before them.
26 So the God of Israel stirred up
the spirit of Pul king of [j]Assyria, that
is, Tiglath-Pileser* king of Assyria.
He carried the Reubenites, the Gadites, and the half-tribe of Manasseh
into captivity. He [k]took them to Halah, Habor, Hara, and the river of Gozan to this day.

Levi's sons through Kohath to Aaron and Moses; Eleazar to the captivity (cp. vv. 49–53)

6 THE [l]sons of Levi *were* Gershon,
Kohath, and Merari.
2 The sons of Kohath *were* Amram, Izhar, Hebron, and Uzziel.
3 The children of Amram *were*
Aaron, Moses, and Miriam. And the
sons of Aaron *were* [m]Nadab, Abihu,
Eleazar, and Ithamar.
4 [n]Eleazar begot Phinehas, *and*
Phinehas begot Abishua;
5 Abishua begot Bukki, and Bukki
begot Uzzi;
6 Uzzi begot Zerahiah, and Zerahiah begot Meraioth;
7 Meraioth begot Amariah, and
Amariah begot Ahitub;
8 [o]Ahitub begot [p]Zadok, and Zadok begot Ahimaaz;
9 Ahimaaz begot Azariah, and
Azariah begot Johanan;
10 Johanan begot [q]Azariah (it was
he who ministered as priest in the temple that Solomon built in Jerusalem);
11 Azariah begot [r]Amariah, and
Amariah begot Ahitub;
12 Ahitub begot Zadok, and Zadok
begot [s]Shallum;
13 Shallum begot Hilkiah, and Hilkiah begot Azariah;
14 Azariah begot [t]Seraiah, and Seraiah begot Jehozadak.
15 [u]Jehozadak went *into captivity*
when the LORD carried Judah and Jerusalem into captivity by the hand of
Nebuchadnezzar.

Sons of Gershon, Merari, and Kohath

16 The sons of Levi *were* [v]Ger-
shon,* Kohath, and Merari.
17 These are the names of the sons
of Gershon: Libni and Shimei.
18 The sons of Kohath *were* Amram, Izhar, Hebron, and Uzziel.
19 The sons of Merari *were* Mahli
and Mushi. Now these *are* the families
of the Levites according to their fathers:
20 Of Gershon *were* Libni his son,
Jahath his son, Zimmah his son,

16
a 1 Chr. 27:29
17
b 2 Ki. 15:5, 32
c 2 Ki. 14:16,28
18
d Cp. Num. 1:3
19
e Gen. 25:15; 1 Chr. 1:31
20
f 2 Chr. 14:11–13
g 2 Ki. 18:5; Ps. 9:10; 20:7–8; see Ps. 2:12, *note*
22
h Josh. 23:10; 2 Chr. 32:8
23
i Dt. 3:9
26
j Cp. 2 Ki. 15:19
k 2 Ki. 17:6
CHAPTER 6
1
l Ex. 6:16–25; Num. 26:57–62
3
m Lev. 10:1–2
4
n vv. 4–14; cp. Ezra 7:1–5
8
o 2 Sam. 8:17
p 2 Sam. 15:27
10
q 2 Chr. 26:17–18
11
r 2 Chr. 19:11
12
s Or *Meshullam,* 1 Chr. 9:11
14
t 2 Ki. 25:18–21
15
u Or *Jozadak,* Ezra 3:2
16
v Ex. 6:16

*
5:26 Hebrew *Tilgath-Pilneser* **6:16** Hebrew *Gershom* (alternate spelling of *Gershon,* as in verses 1,17,20,43,62,71)

21 [a]Joah his son, [b]Iddo his son, Zerah his son, *and* [c]Jeatherai his son.
22 The sons of Kohath *were* [d]Am-
minadab his son, [e]Korah his son, Assir his son,
23 Elkanah his son, Ebiasaph his
son, Assir his son,
24 Tahath his son, [f]Uriel his son,
[g]Uzziah his son, and [h]Shaul his son.
25 The sons of Elkanah *were*
[i]Amasai and Ahimoth.
26 *As for* Elkanah, the sons of Elkanah *were* [j]Zophai his son, [k]Nahath
his son,
27 [l]Eliab his son, Jeroham his son,
and Elkanah his son.
28 The sons of Samuel *were Joel**
the firstborn, and Abijah the second.*
29 The sons of Merari *were* Mahli,
Libni his son, Shimei his son, Uzzah
his son,
30 Shimea his son, Haggiah his
son, *and* Asaiah his son.

Ancestry of choir leaders,
Heman, Asaph, and Ethan

31 Now [m]these are the men whom
David appointed over the service of
song in the house of the LORD, after the
ark came to [n]rest.
32 They were ministering with music before the dwelling place of the
tabernacle of meeting, until Solomon
had built the house of the LORD in Jerusalem, and they served in their office
according to their order.
33 And these *are* the ones who
[o]ministered with their sons: Of the
sons of the [p]Kohathites *were* Heman
the singer, the son of Joel, the son of
Samuel,
34 the son of Elkanah, the son of
Jeroham, the son of Eliel,* the son of
Toah,*
35 the son of Zuph, the son of Elkanah, the son of Mahath, the son of
Amasai,
36 the son of Elkanah, the son of
Joel, the son of Azariah, the son of
Zephaniah,
37 the son of Tahath, the son of Assir, the son of [q]Ebiasaph, the son of
Korah,
38 the son of Izhar, the son of Kohath, the son of Levi, the son of Israel.
39 And his brother [r]Asaph, who
stood at his right hand, *was* Asaph the
son of Berachiah, the son of Shimea,
40 the son of Michael, the son of
Baaseiah, the son of Malchijah,
41 the son of Ethni, the son of Zerah, the son of Adaiah,

21 *a* Or *Ethan,* v. 42 *b* Or *Adaiah,* v. 41 *c* Or *Ethni,* v. 41
22 *d* Or *Izhar,* vv. 2,18,38 *e* Num. 16:1
24 *f* Or *Zephaniah,* v. 36 *g* Or *Azariah,* v. 36 *h* Or *Joel,* v. 36
25 *i* v. 35
26 *j* Or *Zuph,* v. 35 *k* Or *Toah,* v. 34
27 *l* Or *Eliel,* v. 34
31 *m* 1 Chr. 15:16–22, 27; 16:4–6 *n* 2 Sam. 6:17; 1 Chr. 15:25–16:1
33 *o* Lit. *stood* *p* Num. 26:57
37 *q* Ex. 6:24
39 *r* 2 Chr. 5:12
44 *s* Or *Jeduthun,* 1 Chr. 9:16; 25:1, 3,6 *t* Or *Kushaiah,* 1 Chr. 15:17
48 *u* 1 Chr. 9:14–34
49 *v* Ex. 28:1–29:44; Num. 18:1–8 *w* Lev. 1:8–9 *x* See Ex. 29:33, *note*
50 *y* vv. 50–53; 1 Chr. 6:4–8
54 *z* vv. 54–60; cp. Josh. 21:1–42

42 the son of Ethan, the son of Zimmah, the son of Shimei,
43 the son of Jahath, the son of Gershon, the son of Levi.
44 Their brethren, the sons of Merari, on the left hand, *were* [s]Ethan the
son of [t]Kishi, the son of Abdi, the son
of Malluch,
45 the son of Hashabiah, the son of
Amaziah, the son of Hilkiah,
46 the son of Amzi, the son of Bani,
the son of Shamer,
47 the son of Mahli, the son of Mushi, the son of Merari, the son of Levi.
48 And their brethren, the Levites,
were appointed to every [u]kind of service of the tabernacle of the house of
God.

Aaron's priesthood to Ahimaaz

49 [v]But Aaron and his sons offered
sacrifices [w]on the altar of burnt offering and on the altar of incense, for all
the work of the Most Holy *Place,* and
to make [x]atonement for Israel, according to all that Moses the servant
of God had commanded.
50 Now these *are* the [y]sons of
Aaron: Eleazar his son, Phinehas his
son, Abishua his son,
51 Bukki his son, Uzzi his son, Zerahiah his son,
52 Meraioth his son, Amariah his
son, Ahitub his son,
53 Zadok his son, *and* Ahimaaz his
son.

Cities of priests and Levites

54 Now [z]these *are* their dwelling
places throughout their settlements in
their territory, for they were *given* by
lot to the sons of Aaron, of the family
of the Kohathites:
55 They gave them Hebron in the
land of Judah, with its surrounding
common-lands.
56 But the fields of the city and its
villages they gave to [aa]Caleb the son of
Jephunneh.
57 And to the sons of Aaron they
[bb]gave *one of* the cities of refuge, Hebron; also Libnah with its common-
lands, Jattir, Eshtemoa with its
common-lands,
58 [cc]Hilen with its common-lands,
Debir with its common-lands,

6:56 *aa* Josh. 14:13; 15:13 **6:57** *bb* vv. 57–60; Josh. 21:13–19 **6:58** *cc* Or *Holon,* Josh. 15:51; 21:15

*
6:28 Following Septuagint, Syriac, and Arabic (compare verse 33 and 1 Samuel 8:2) • Hebrew *Vasheni* **6:34** Spelled *Elihu* in 1 Samuel 1:1 • Spelled *Tohu* in 1 Samuel 1:1

59 [a]Ashan with its common-lands, and Beth Shemesh with its common-lands.

60 And from the tribe of Benjamin: Geba with its common-lands, [b]Alemeth with its common-lands, and Anathoth with its common-lands. All their cities among their families *were* thirteen.

61 To the [c]rest of the family of the tribe of the Kohathites *they gave* by lot ten cities from half the tribe of Manasseh.

62 And to the sons of Gershon, throughout their families, *they gave* thirteen cities from the tribe of Issachar, from the tribe of Asher, from the tribe of Naphtali, and from the tribe of Manasseh in Bashan.

63 [d]To the sons of Merari, throughout their families, *they gave* twelve cities from the tribe of Reuben, from the tribe of Gad, and from the tribe of Zebulun.

64 So the children of Israel gave *these* cities with their common-lands to the Levites.

65 And they gave by lot from the tribe of the children of Judah, from the tribe of the children of Simeon, and from the tribe of the children of Benjamin these cities which are called by *their* names.

66 Now [e]some of the families of the sons of Kohath *were given* cities as their territory from the tribe of Ephraim.

67 And they gave them *one of* the cities of refuge, Shechem with its common-lands, in the mountains of Ephraim, also Gezer with its common-lands,

68 [f]Jokmeam with its common-lands, Beth Horon with its common-lands,

69 Aijalon with its common-lands, and Gath Rimmon with its common-lands.

70 And from the half-tribe of Manasseh: Aner with its common-lands and Bileam with its common-lands, for the rest of the family of the sons of Kohath.

71 From the family of the half-tribe of Manasseh [g]the sons of Gershon *were given* Golan in Bashan with its common-lands and Ashtaroth with its common-lands.

72 And from the tribe of Issachar: Kedesh with its common-lands, Daberath with its common-lands,

73 Ramoth with its common-lands, and Anem with its common-lands.

74 And from the tribe of Asher: Mashal with its common-lands, Abdon with its common-lands,

75 Hukok with its common-lands, and Rehob with its common-lands.

76 And from the tribe of Naphtali: Kedesh in Galilee with its common-lands, Hammon with its common-lands, and Kirjathaim with its common-lands.

77 From the tribe of Zebulun [h]the rest of the children of Merari *were given* Rimmon* with its common-lands and Tabor with its common-lands.

78 And on the other side of the Jordan, across from Jericho, on the east side of the Jordan, *they were given* from the tribe of Reuben: Bezer in the wilderness with its common-lands, Jahzah with its common-lands,

79 Kedemoth with its common-lands, and Mephaath with its common-lands.

80 And from the tribe of Gad: Ramoth in Gilead with its common-lands, Mahanaim with its common-lands,

81 Heshbon with its common-lands, and Jazer with its common-lands.

Sons of Issachar

7 THE sons of Issachar *were* [i]Tola, [j]Puah, [k]Jashub, and Shimron—four *in all.*

2 The sons of Tola *were* Uzzi, Rephaiah, Jeriel, Jahmai, Jibsam, and Shemuel, heads of their father's house. *The sons* of Tola *were* mighty men of valor in their generations; [l]their number in the days of David *was* twenty-two thousand six hundred.

3 The son of Uzzi *was* Izrahiah, and the sons of Izrahiah *were* Michael, Obadiah, Joel, and Ishiah. All five of them *were* chief men.

4 And with them, by their generations, according to their fathers' houses, *were* thirty-six thousand troops ready for war; for they had many wives and sons.

5 Now their brethren among all the families of Issachar *were* mighty men of valor, listed by their genealogies, eighty-seven thousand in all.

Sons of Benjamin

6 *The sons* of [m]Benjamin *were*

59 [a] Or *Ain,* Josh. 15:32; 21:16
60 [b] Or *Almon,* Josh. 21:18
61 [c] v. 66; Josh. 21:5
63 [d] Josh. 21:7, 34–40
66 [e] vv. 66–70; cp. Josh. 21:20–26
68 [f] Some names written differently in Josh. 21:22–39
71 [g] vv. 71–76; cp. Josh. 21:27–33
77 [h] vv. 77–81; cp. Josh. 21:34–39
CHAPTER 7
1 [i] Gen. 46:13; Num. 26:23
[j] Or *Puvah,* Gen. 46:13
[k] Or *Job,* Gen. 46:13
2 [l] Cp. 2 Sam. 24:1–9; 1 Chr. 27:1
6 [m] Gen. 46:21; Num. 26:38; 1 Chr. 8:1

*6:77 Hebrew *Rimmono,* alternate spelling of *Rimmon;* see 4:32

Bela, Becher, and Jediael—[1]three *in all.*

7 The sons of Bela were Ezbon, Uzzi, Uzziel, Jerimoth, and [a]Iri—five *in all.* They *were* heads of *their* fathers' houses, and they were listed by their genealogies, twenty-two thousand and thirty-four mighty men of valor.

8 The sons of Becher *were* Zemirah, Joash, Eliezer, Elioenai, Omri, Jerimoth, Abijah, Anathoth, and Alemeth. All these *are* the sons of Becher.

9 And they were recorded by genealogy according to their generations, heads of their fathers' houses, twenty thousand two hundred mighty men of valor.

10 The son of Jediael *was* Bilhan, and the sons of Bilhan *were* Jeush, Benjamin, Ehud, Chenaanah, Zethan, Tharshish, and Ahishahar.

11 All these sons of Jediael *were* heads of their fathers' houses; *there were* seventeen thousand two hundred mighty men of valor fit to go out for war *and* battle.

12 [b]Shuppim and [c]Huppim *were* the sons of Ir, *and* Hushim *was* the son of [d]Aher.

Sons of Naphtali

13 The [e]sons of Naphtali *were* [f]Jahziel, Guni, Jezer, and [g]Shallum, the sons of Bilhah.

Descendants of Manasseh

14 The [h]descendants of Manasseh: his Syrian concubine bore him [i]Machir the father of Gilead, the father of Asriel.*

15 Machir took as his wife *the sister* of Huppim and Shuppim,* whose name *was* Maachah. The name of *Gilead's* grandson* *was* [j]Zelophehad,* but Zelophehad begot only daughters.

16 (Maachah the wife of Machir bore a son, and she called his name Peresh. The name of his brother *was* Sheresh, and his sons *were* Ulam and Rakem.

17 The son of Ulam *was* [k]Bedan.) These *were* the descendants of Gilead the son of Machir, the son of Manasseh.

18 His sister Hammoleketh bore Ishhod, [l]Abiezer, and Mahlah.

19 And the sons of Shemida were Ahian, Shechem, Likhi, and Aniam.

Sons of Ephraim and their habitations

20 The [m]sons of Ephraim *were* Shuthelah, Bered his son, Tahath his son, Eladah his son, Tahath his son,

21 Zabad his son, Shuthelah his son, and Ezer and Elead. The men of Gath who were born in *that* land killed *them* because they came down to take away their cattle.

22 Then Ephraim their father mourned many days, and his brethren came to comfort him.

23 And when he went in to his wife, she conceived and bore a son; and he called his name Beriah,* because tragedy had come upon his house.

24 Now his daughter *was* Sheerah, who built Lower and Upper [n]Beth Horon and Uzzen Sheerah;

25 and Rephah *was* his son, *as well* as Resheph, and Telah his son, Tahan his son,

26 Laadan his son, Ammihud his son, [o]Elishama his son,

27 [p]Nun his son, and [q]Joshua his son.

28 Now their [r]possessions and dwelling places *were* Bethel and its towns: to the east [s]Naaran, to the west Gezer and its towns, and Shechem and its towns, as far as Ayyah* and its towns;

29 and by the borders of the children of [t]Manasseh *were* Beth Shean and its towns, Taanach and its towns, [u]Megiddo and its towns, Dor and its towns. In these dwelt the children of Joseph, the son of Israel.

Sons of Asher

30 The [v]sons of Asher *were* Imnah, Ishvah, Ishvi, Beriah, and their sister Serah.

31 The sons of Beriah *were* Heber and Malchiel, who was the father of Birzaith.*

32 And Heber begot Japhlet, [w]Shomer, Hotham,* and their sister Shua.

33 The sons of Japhlet *were* Pasach, Bimhal, and Ashvath. These *were* the children of Japhlet.

7 [a] Or *Ir*, v. 12
12 [b] Or *Shupham*, Num. 26:39 [c] Or *Hupham*, Num. 26:39 [d] Or *Ahiram*, Num. 26:38
13 [e] Num. 26:48–50 [f] Or *Jahzeel*, Gen. 46:24 [g] Or *Shillem*, Gen. 46:24
14 [h] Num. 26:29–34 [i] 1 Chr. 2:21
15 [j] Num. 27:1
17 [k] 1 Sam. 12:11
18 [l] Or *Iezer*, Num. 26:30
20 [m] Num. 26:35–37
24 [n] Josh. 16:3,5
26 [o] Num. 10:22
27 [p] Heb. *Non*. Num. 13:8, 16 [q] Ex. 17:9, 14; 24:13; 33:11
28 [r] Josh. 16:1–10 [s] Or *Naarah*, Josh. 16:7
29 [t] Josh. 17:7 [u] Josh. 17:11
30 [v] Gen. 46:17; Num. 26:44–47
32 [w] Or *Shemer*, v. 34

*
7:14 The son of Gilead (compare Numbers 26:30,31) **7:15** Compare verse 12 • Literally *the second* • Compare Numbers 26:30-33 **7:23** Literally *In Tragedy* **7:28** Many Hebrew manuscripts, Bomberg, Septuagint, Targum, and Vulgate read *Gazza*. **7:31** Or *Birzavith* or *Birzoth* **7:32** Spelled *Helem* in verse 35

[1](7:6) Benjamin had other sons than these three. Cp. Gen. 46:21; Num. 26:38–41; 1 Chr. 8:1–2.

34 The sons of Shemer *were* Ahi,
Rohgah, Jehubbah, and Aram.
35 And the sons of his brother Helem
were Zophah, Imna, Shelesh, and
Amal.
36 The sons of Zophah *were* Suah,
Harnepher, Shual, Beri, Imrah,
37 Bezer, Hod, Shamma, Shilshah,
Jithran,* and Beera.
38 The sons of Jether *were* Jephunneh,
Pispah, and Ara.
39 The sons of Ulla *were* Arah,
Haniel, and Rizia.
40 All these *were* the children of
Asher, heads of *their* fathers' houses,
choice men, mighty men of valor,
chief leaders. And they were recorded
by genealogies among the army fit for
battle; their number *was* twenty-six
thousand.

Sons and chief men of Benjamin

8 NOW Benjamin begot [a]Bela his
firstborn, Ashbel the second,
[b]Aharah the third,
2 Nohah the fourth, and Rapha the
fifth.
3 The sons of Bela *were* [c]Addar,
Gera, Abihud,
4 Abishua, Naaman, Ahoah,
5 Gera, [d]Shephuphan, and Huram.
6 These *are* the sons of Ehud, who
were the heads of the fathers' *houses*
of the inhabitants of [e]Geba, and who
forced them to move to [f]Manahath:
7 Naaman, Ahijah, and Gera who
forced them to move. He begot Uzza
and Ahihud.
8 Also Shaharaim had children in
the country of Moab, after he had sent
away Hushim and Baara his wives.
9 By Hodesh his wife he begot Jobab,
Zibia, Mesha, Malcam,
10 Jeuz, Sachiah, and Mirmah.
These *were* his sons, heads of their
fathers' *houses*.
11 And by Hushim he begot Abitub
and Elpaal.
12 The sons of Elpaal *were* Eber,
Misham, and Shemed, who built Ono
and Lod with its towns;
13 and Beriah and [g]Shema, who
were heads of their fathers' *houses* of
the inhabitants of Aijalon, who drove
out the inhabitants of Gath.
14 Ahio, Shashak, Jeremoth,
15 Zebadiah, Arad, Eder,
16 Michael, Ispah, and Joha *were*
the sons of Beriah.
17 Zebadiah, Meshullam, Hizki,
Heber,

CHAPTER 8

1
a Gen. 46:21; Num. 26:38; 1 Chr. 7:6
b Or *Ahiram*, Num. 26:38

3
c Or *Ard*, Gen. 46:21; Num. 26:40

5
d Or *Shuppim*, 1 Chr. 7:12

6
e 1 Chr. 6:60
f Or *Menuhoth*, 1 Chr. 2:52

13
g Or *Shimei*, v. 21

29
h 1 Chr. 9:35

31
i Or *Zechariah*, 1 Chr. 9:37

32
j Or *Shimeam*, 1 Chr. 9:38

33
k 1 Sam. 14:51
l vv. 33–39; cp. 1 Chr. 9:39–44
m Or *Jishui*, 1 Sam. 14:49
n Or *Ishbosheth*, 2 Sam. 2:8

34
o Or *Mephibosheth*, 2 Sam. 4:4; 9:6,10

35
p Or *Tahrea*, 1 Chr. 9:41

36
q Or *Jarah*, 1 Chr. 9:42

37
r Or *Rephaiah*, 1 Chr. 9:43

18 Ishmerai, Jizliah, and Jobab
were the sons of Elpaal.
19 Jakim, Zichri, Zabdi,
20 Elienai, Zillethai, Eliel,
21 Adaiah, Beraiah, and Shimrath
were the sons of Shimei.
22 Ishpan, Eber, Eliel,
23 Abdon, Zichri, Hanan,
24 Hananiah, Elam, Antothijah,
25 Iphdeiah, and Penuel *were* the
sons of Shashak.
26 Shamsherai, Shehariah, Athaliah,
27 Jaareshiah, Elijah, and Zichri
were the sons of Jeroham.
28 These *were* heads of the fathers'
houses by their generations, chief
men. These dwelt in Jerusalem.

Ancestry of King Saul,
the son of Kish

29 Now the [h]father of Gibeon,
whose wife's name *was* Maacah,
dwelt at Gibeon.
30 And his firstborn son *was* Abdon,
then Zur, Kish, Baal, Nadab,
31 Gedor, Ahio, [i]Zecher,
32 and Mikloth, *who* begot [j]Shimeah.
They also dwelt alongside their
relatives in Jerusalem, with their
brethren.
33 [k]Ner* [l]begot Kish, Kish begot
Saul, and Saul begot Jonathan, Malchishua,
[m]Abinadab, and [n]Esh-Baal.
34 The son of Jonathan *was*
[o]Merib-Baal, and Merib-Baal begot
Micah.
35 The sons of Micah *were* Pithon,
Melech, [p]Tarea, and Ahaz.
36 And Ahaz begot [q]Jehoaddah;
Jehoaddah begot Alemeth, Azmaveth,
and Zimri; and Zimri begot
Moza.
37 Moza begot Binea, [r]Raphah his
son, Eleasah his son, *and* Azel his son.
38 Azel had six sons whose names
were these: Azrikam, Bocheru, Ishmael,
Sheariah, Obadiah, and Hanan.
All these *were* the sons of Azel.
39 And the sons of Eshek his
brother *were* Ulam his firstborn, Jeush
the second, and Eliphelet the
third.
40 The sons of Ulam were mighty
men of valor—archers. *They* had
many sons and grandsons, one hundred
and fifty *in all*. These *were* all
sons of Benjamin.

*

7:37 Spelled *Jether* in verse 38 8:33 Also the son of Gibeon (compare 9:36,39)

Inhabitants of Jerusalem

9 [a]SO all Israel was recorded by genealogies, and indeed, they *were* inscribed in the book of the kings of Israel. But [b]Judah was carried away captive to Babylon because of their unfaithfulness.

2 And the [c]first inhabitants who *dwelt* in their possessions in their cities *were* Israelites, [d]priests, Levites, and the [e]Nethinim.

3 Now in Jerusalem the children of Judah [f]dwelt, and some of the children of Benjamin, and of the children of Ephraim and Manasseh:

4 Uthai the son of Ammihud, the son of Omri, the son of Imri, the son of Bani, of the descendants of Perez, the son of Judah.

5 Of the Shilonites: Asaiah the firstborn and his sons.

6 Of the sons of Zerah: Jeuel, and their brethren—six hundred and ninety.

7 Of the sons of Benjamin: Sallu the son of Meshullam, the son of Hodaviah, the son of Hassenuah;

8 Ibneiah the son of Jeroham; Elah the son of Uzzi, the son of Michri; Meshullam the son of Shephatiah, the son of Reuel, the son of Ibnijah;

9 and their brethren, according to their generations—[g]nine hundred and fifty-six. All these men *were* heads of a father's *house* in their fathers' houses.

10 Of the [h]priests: Jedaiah, Jehoiarib, and Jachin;

11 [i]Azariah the son of Hilkiah, the son of Meshullam, the son of Zadok, the son of Meraioth, the son of Ahitub, the [j]officer over the house of God;

12 Adaiah the son of Jeroham, the son of Pashur, the son of Malchijah; Maasai the son of Adiel, the son of Jahzerah, the son of Meshullam, the son of Meshillemith, the son of Immer;

13 and their brethren, heads of their fathers' *houses*—one thousand seven hundred and sixty. *They were* very [k]able men for the work of the service of the house of God.

14 Of the [l]Levites: Shemaiah the son of Hasshub, the son of Azrikam, the son of Hashabiah, of the sons of Merari;

15 Bakbakkar, Heresh, Galal, and Mattaniah the son of Micah, the son of [m]Zichri, the son of Asaph;

16 [n]Obadiah the son of [o]Shemaiah, the son of Galal, the son of Jeduthun; and Berechiah the son of Asa, the son of Elkanah, who lived in the villages of the Netophathites.

17 And the gatekeepers *were* Shallum, Akkub, Talmon, Ahiman, and their brethren. Shallum *was* the chief.

18 Until then *they had been* gatekeepers for the camps of the children of Levi at the King's Gate on the east.

19 Shallum the son of Kore, the son of Ebiasaph, the son of Korah, and his brethren, from his father's house, the Korahites, *were* in charge of the work of the service, gatekeepers of the tabernacle. Their fathers had been keepers of the entrance to the camp of the LORD.

20 And [p]Phinehas the son of Eleazar had been the officer over them in time past; the LORD *was* with him.

21 [q]Zechariah the son of Meshelemiah *was* keeper of the door of the tabernacle of meeting.

22 All those chosen as [r]gatekeepers *were* two hundred and twelve. They were recorded by their genealogy, in their villages. David and Samuel the seer had appointed them to their trusted office.

23 So they and their children *were* in charge of the gates of the house of the LORD, the house of the tabernacle, by assignment.

24 The gatekeepers were assigned to the four directions: the east, west, north, and south.

25 And their brethren in their villages *had* to come with them from time to time for [s]seven days.

26 For in this trusted office *were* four chief gatekeepers; they were Levites. And they had charge over the chambers and treasuries of the house of God.

27 And they lodged *all* around the house of God [t]because they *had* the responsibility, and they *were* in charge of opening *it* every morning.

28 Now *some* of them were in charge of the serving vessels, for they brought them in and took them out by count.

29 *Some* of them *were* appointed over the furnishings and over all the implements of the sanctuary, and over the [u]fine flour and the wine and the oil and the incense and the spices.

30 And *some* of the sons of the priests made the [v]ointment of the spices.

31 Mattithiah of the Levites, the firstborn of Shallum the Korahite, had the [w]trusted office over the things that were baked in the pans.

CHAPTER 9

1 a Cp. Ezra 2:59,62 b Cp. 1 Chr. 5:25–26

2 c Ezra 2:70; Neh. 7:73 d vv. 2–22; cp. Neh. 11:3–22 e See Neh. 3:26, *note*

3 f Neh. 11:1–2

9 g Cp. Neh. 11:8

10 h Neh. 11:10–14

11 i Or *Seraiah,* Neh. 11:11 j 2 Chr. 31:13; Jer. 20:1

13 k Lit. *men of courage*

14 l vv. 14–17; cp. Neh. 11:15–19

15 m Or *Zabdi,* Neh. 11:17

16 n Or *Abda,* Neh. 11:17 o Or *Shammua,* Neh. 11:17

20 p Num. 25:6–13; 31:6

21 q 1 Chr. 26:2,14

22 r 1 Chr. 26:1

25 s 2 Ki. 11:4–7; 2 Chr. 23:8

27 t 1 Chr. 23:30–32

29 u 1 Chr. 23:29

30 v Ex. 30:22–25

31 w Lev. 2:5; 6:21

32 And some of their brethren of the sons of the [a]Kohathites *were* in charge of preparing the [b]showbread for every Sabbath.

33 These are the [c]singers, heads of the fathers' *houses* of the Levites, *who lodged* in the chambers, *and were* free *from other duties;* for they were employed in *that* work day and night.

34 These heads of the fathers' *houses* of the Levites *were* heads throughout their generations. They dwelt at Jerusalem.

Ancestry and descendants of Saul and Jonathan

35 Jeiel the father of [d]Gibeon, whose wife's name *was* [e]Maacah, dwelt at Gibeon.

36 His firstborn son *was* Abdon, then Zur, Kish, Baal, Ner, Nadab,

37 Gedor, Ahio, Zechariah,* and Mikloth.

38 And Mikloth begot [f]Shimeam. They also dwelt alongside their relatives in Jerusalem, with their brethren.

39 [g]Ner begot Kish, Kish begot Saul, and Saul begot Jonathan, Malchishua, Abinadab, and Esh-Baal.

40 The son of Jonathan *was* Merib-Baal, and Merib-Baal begot Micah.

41 The sons of Micah *were* Pithon, Melech, [h]Tahrea, *and* [i]*Ahaz.**

42 And Ahaz begot [j]Jarah; Jarah begot Alemeth, Azmaveth, and Zimri; and Zimri begot Moza;

43 Moza begot Binea, Rephaiah* his son, Eleasah his son, and Azel his son.

44 And Azel had six sons whose names *were* these: Azrikam, Bocheru, Ishmael, Sheariah, Obadiah, and Hanan; these *were* the sons of Azel.

(For history prior to 1 Chr. 10 —see 1 Sam. 1–30)

II. The Last Days and Death of King Saul, 10

Saul defeated by Philistines; the death of Saul

(1 Sam. 31:1–10; 2 Sam. 1)

10 [k]NOW the Philistines fought against Israel; and the men of Israel fled from before the Philistines, and fell slain on Mount Gilboa.

2 Then the Philistines followed hard after Saul and his sons. And the Philistines killed Jonathan, [l]Abinadab, and Malchishua, Saul's sons.

3 The battle became fierce against Saul. The archers hit him, and he was wounded by the archers.

4 [m]Then Saul said to his armorbearer, "Draw your sword, and thrust me through with it, lest these uncircumcised men come and abuse me." But his armorbearer would not, for he was greatly afraid. Therefore Saul took a sword and fell on it.

5 And when his armorbearer saw that Saul was dead, he also fell on his sword and died.

6 So Saul and his three sons died, and all his house died together.

7 And when all the men of Israel who *were* in the valley saw that they had fled and that Saul and his sons were dead, they forsook their cities and fled; then the Philistines came and dwelt in them.

8 So it happened the next day, when the Philistines came to strip the slain, that they found Saul and his sons fallen on Mount Gilboa.

9 And they stripped him and [n]took his head and his armor, and sent word *throughout* the land of the Philistines to proclaim the news *in the temple* of their idols and among the people.

10 Then they put his armor in the temple of their gods, and fastened his head in the temple of Dagon.

Loyalty of Jabesh Gilead to Saul

(1 Sam. 31:11–13; 2 Sam. 2:5–7)

11 And when all Jabesh Gilead heard all that the Philistines had done to Saul,

12 all the [o]valiant men arose and took the body of Saul and the bodies of his sons; and they brought them to [p]Jabesh, and buried their bones under the tamarisk tree at Jabesh, and fasted seven days.

Saul's sin which cost the throne

13 So Saul [q]died for his [r]unfaithfulness which he had committed against the LORD, because he did not keep the word of the LORD, and [s]also because he consulted a medium for guidance.

14 But *he* did not inquire of the LORD; therefore He killed him, and [t]turned the kingdom over to David the son of Jesse.

32
a Lev. 24:8
b See Ex. 25:30, *note*
33
c 1 Chr. 6:31–32; see 15:16, *note*
35
d vv. 35–44; cp. 1 Chr. 8:29–38
e 1 Chr. 8:29
38
f Or *Shimeah,* 1 Chr. 8:32
39
g 1 Chr. 8:33
41
h Or *Tarea,* 1 Chr. 8:35
i 1 Chr. 8:35
42
j Or *Jehoaddah,* 1 Chr. 8:36
CHAPTER 10
1
k vv. 1–12; cp. 1 Sam. 31:1–13
2
l Or *Jishui,* 1 Sam. 14:49
4
m Cp. 2 Sam. 1:1–16
9
n Cp. 1 Sam. 31:9–10
12
o 1 Sam. 14:52
p 2 Sam. 21:12
13
q 1011 B.C.
r 1 Sam. 13:13–14; 15:22–26
s 1 Sam. 28:7–8
14
t 1 Sam. 15:28; 1 Chr. 12:23

*

9:37 Called *Zecher* in 8:31 9:41 Following Arabic, Syriac, Targum, and Vulgate (compare 8:35); Masoretic Text and Septuagint omit *and Ahaz.*
9:43 Spelled *Raphah* in 8:37

III. The Reign of David, 11—29

David anointed king over all Israel (2 Sam. 5:1–3; review 2 Sam. 2—4)

11 THEN all Israel [a]came together to David at Hebron, saying, "Indeed we *are* your bone and
your flesh.
2 "Also, in time past, even when
Saul was king, you *were* the one who
led Israel out and brought them in;
and the LORD your [b]God said to you,
'You shall [c]shepherd My people Israel, and be ruler over My people Israel.' "
3 Therefore all the elders of Israel
came to the king at Hebron, and David
made a covenant with them at Hebron
before the LORD. And they [d]anointed
David king over Israel, according to
the word of the LORD by Samuel.

Jerusalem becomes capital of united kingdom (2 Sam. 5:6–10)

4 And David and all Israel went to
Jerusalem, which is [e]Jebus, where the
Jebusites *were,* the inhabitants of the
land.
5 But the inhabitants of Jebus said
to David, "You shall not come in
here!" Nevertheless David took the
stronghold of [1]Zion (that is, the City of
David).
6 Now David said, "Whoever at-
tacks the Jebusites first shall be [f]chief
and captain." And Joab the son of Zeruiah went up first, and became chief.
7 Then David dwelt in the stronghold; therefore they called it the City
of David.
8 And he built the city around it,
from the Millo* to the surrounding
area. Joab repaired the rest of the city.
9 So David went on and [g]became
great, and the LORD of hosts *was* with
[h]him.

Roll of David's mighty men (cp. 2 Sam. 23:8–39)

10 [i]Now these *were* the heads of
the mighty men whom David had,
who strengthened themselves with
him in his kingdom, with all Israel, to
make him king, according to the word
of the LORD concerning Israel.
11 And this *is* the number of the
mighty men whom David had: [j]Ja-
shobeam the son of a Hachmonite,
[k]chief of the captains;* he had lifted
up his spear against [2]three hundred,
killed *by him* at one time.
12 After him *was* Eleazar the son of
[l]Dodo, the Ahohite, who *was one* of
the three mighty men.
13 He was with David at Pasdam-
mim. Now there the Philistines were

CHAPTER 11
1
a 1003 B.C.
2
b 1 Sam. 16:1–3; Ps. 78:70–72
c 2 Sam. 7:7
3
d 1 Sam. 16:4–13
4
e Jud. 1:21; 19:10,11
6
f 2 Sam. 8:16
9
g 2 Sam. 3:1
h 1 Sam. 16:18
10
i vv. 11–47
11
j 1 Chr. 27:2
k 1 Chr. 12:18
12
l Or *Dodai,* 1 Chr. 27:4

*
11:8 Literally *The Landfill* 11:11 Following Qere; Kethib, Septuagint, and Vulgate read *the thirty* (compare 2 Samuel 23:8).

---

[1](11:5) Zion, the ancient Jebusite stronghold, was on the south part of the eastern hill of Jerusalem. It is called "the City of David" and is associated with the Davidic royalty both historically and prophetically (vv. 5,7; Ps. 2:6). The name "Zion" is often used of the whole city of Jerusalem, considered as the city of God (Ps. 48:2–3), especially in passages referring to the future kingdom age (Isa. 1:27; 2:3; 4:1–6; Joel 3:16; Zech. 1:16–17; 8:3–8; Rom. 11:26). In Heb. 12:22 the word is used symbolically of heaven. "Sion" (Dt. 4:48) refers to Mount Hermon.

[2](11:11) In copying manuscripts, mistakes in numbers sometimes occur. Many disagreements between numbers in Samuel and Kings, and those in Chronicles, are alleged. Actually, out of the approximately 150 instances of parallel numbers in these books, fewer than one-sixth disagree. In two cases a different number is given for the age of a king at his accession (cp. 2 Chr. 22:2, *text note* with 2 Ki. 8:26; and 2 Chr. 36:9, *text note* with 2 Ki. 24:8); in the other thirteen cases of this type, numbers agree. Certain disagreements are very small (cp. 1 Chr. 21:5, as to Judah, with 2 Sam. 24:9; 2 Chr. 2:2,17–18 with 1 Ki. 5:15–16; and 2 Chr. 8:18 with 1 Ki. 9:28). Sometimes the apparent discrepancy disappears on careful study (cp. 1 Chr. 21:25 with 2 Sam. 24:24; 2 Chr. 3:4 with 1 Ki. 6:2).

When numbers seem clearly to disagree, it is generally best to keep an open mind unless evidence is available on which to make a decision.

God gave us a Bible free from error in the original manuscripts. In its preservation through many generations of recopying, He providentially kept it from serious error, although He permitted a few scribal mistakes.

The small proportion of numbers where there is disagreement testifies to the scrupulous care with which Bible manuscripts were copied. That there are some divergences should warn us to compare Scripture with Scripture and always to recognize the danger of overemphasizing any isolated passage.

Some say that Chronicles, written much later than Samuel and Kings, has exaggerated numbers so as to enhance the reputation of ancient Israel. Whereas a few numbers in Chronicles are much larger than in Samuel or Kings (1 Chr. 18:4; 19:18; 21:5, as to Israel: 2 Chr. 3:15; 4:5), yet there are almost as many instances where numbers in Samuel or Kings are much larger than in Chronicles (1 Chr. 11:11; 21:12; 2 Chr. 8:10; 9:25).

gathered for battle, and there was a
piece of ground full of barley. So the
people fled from the Philistines.
14 But they stationed themselves in
the middle of *that* field, defended it,
and killed the Philistines. So the LORD
brought about a great victory.
15 Now three of the thirty chief
men went down to the rock to David,
into the cave of Adullam; and the
army of the Philistines [a]encamped in
the Valley of Rephaim.
16 David *was* then in the stronghold, and the garrison of the Philistines *was* then in Bethlehem.
17 And David said with longing,
"Oh, that someone would give me a
drink of water from the well of Bethlehem, which is by the gate!"
18 So the three broke through the
camp of the Philistines, drew water
from the well of Bethlehem that *was*
by the gate, and took *it* and brought *it*
to David. Nevertheless David would
not drink it, but poured it out to the
LORD.
19 And he said, "Far be it from me,
O my God, that I should do this! Shall
I drink the blood of these men *who*
have put their lives *in jeopardy*? For at
the risk of their lives they brought it."
Therefore he would not drink it. These
things were done by the three mighty
men.
20 [b]Abishai the brother of Joab
was chief of *another* three.* He had
lifted up his spear against three hundred *men*, killed *them*, and won a
name among *these* three.
21 Of the three he was more honored than the other two men. Therefore he became their captain. However he did not attain to the *first* three.
22 Benaiah was the son of Jehoiada, the son of a valiant man from
Kabzeel, who had done many deeds.
He had killed two [c]lion-like heroes of
Moab. He also had gone down and
killed a lion in the midst of a pit on a
snowy day.
23 And he killed an Egyptian, a
man of *great* height, five [d]cubits tall.
In the Egyptian's hand *there was* a
spear like a weaver's beam; and he
went down to him with a staff,
wrested the spear out of the Egyptian's hand, and killed him with his
own spear.
24 These *things* Benaiah the son of
Jehoiada did, and won a name among
three mighty men.
25 Indeed he was more honored
than the thirty, but he did not attain to
the *first* three. And David appointed
him over his guard.
26 Also the mighty warriors *were*
Asahel the brother of Joab, Elhanan
the son of Dodo of Bethlehem,
27 [e]Shammoth the Harorite, [f]He-
lez the [g]Pelonite,
28 [h]Ira the son of Ikkesh the Tekoite, [i]Abiezer the Anathothite,
29 [j]Sibbechai the Hushathite, [k]Ilai
the Ahohite,
30 [l]Maharai the Netophathite,
[m]Heled the son of Baanah the Netophathite,
31 Ithai* the son of Ribai of Gibeah, of the sons of Benjamin, [n]Bena-
iah the Pirathonite,
32 [o]Hurai of the brooks of Gaash,
[p]Abiel the Arbathite,
33 Azmaveth the Baharumite,* Eliahba the Shaalbonite,
34 the sons of [q]Hashem the Gizo-
nite, Jonathan the son of Shageh the
Hararite,
35 Ahiam the son of [r]Sacar the Hararite, [s]Eliphal the son of [t]Ur,
36 Hepher the Mecherathite, Ahijah the Pelonite,
37 Hezro the Carmelite, [u]Naarai
the son of Ezbai,
38 Joel the brother of Nathan, Mib-
har the son of Hagri,
39 Zelek the Ammonite, Naharai
the Berothite* (the armorbearer of
Joab the son of Zeruiah),
40 Ira the Ithrite, Gareb the Ithrite,
41 [v]Uriah the [w]Hittite, Zabad the
son of Ahlai,
42 Adina the son of Shiza the Reu-
benite (a chief of the Reubenites) and
thirty with him,
43 Hanan the son of Maachah,
Joshaphat the Mithnite,
44 Uzzia the Ashterathite, Shama
and Jeiel the sons of Hotham the Aro-
erite,
45 Jediael the son of Shimri, and
Joha his brother, the Tizite,
46 Eliel the Mahavite, Jeribai and
Joshaviah the sons of Elnaam, Ithmah
the Moabite,
47 Eliel, Obed, and Jaasiel the Me-
zobaite.

15 *a* 2 Sam. 5:18
20 *b* 1 Chr. 18:12
22 *c* Heb. uncertain. Other English versions read *Ariels*, and *sons of Ariel*
23 *d* See Weights and Measures (OT), 2 Chr. 2:10, *note*
27 *e* Or *Shammah the Harodite*, 2 Sam. 23:25 *f* 1 Chr. 27:10 *g* Or *Paltite*, 2 Sam. 23:26
28 *h* 1 Chr. 27:9 *i* 1 Chr. 27:12
29 *j* Or *Mebunnai*, 2 Sam. 23:27 *k* Or *Zalmon*, 2 Sam. 23:28
30 *l* 1 Chr. 27:13 *m* Or *Heleb*, 2 Sam. 23:29
31 *n* 1 Chr. 27:14
32 *o* Or *Hiddai*, 2 Sam. 23:30 *p* Or *Abi-Albon*, 2 Sam. 23:31
34 *q* Or *Jashen*, 2 Sam. 23:32
35 *r* Or *Sharar*, 2 Sam. 23:33 *s* Or *Eliphelet*, 2 Sam. 23:34 *t* Or *Ahasbai*, 2 Sam. 23:34 **11:37** *u* Or *Paarai, the Arbite*, 2 Sam. 23:35 **11:41** *v* 2 Sam. 11:1–27 *w* See 2 Ki. 7:6, *note*

*

11:20 Following Masoretic Text, Septuagint, and Vulgate; Syriac reads *thirty*. **11:31** Spelled *Ittai* in 2 Samuel 23:29 **11:33** Spelled *Barhumite* in 2 Samuel 23:31 **11:39** Spelled *Beerothite* in 2 Samuel 23:37

Companies that came to David at Ziklag

12 NOW these *were* the men who came to David at [a]Ziklag while he was still a fugitive from Saul the son of Kish; and they *were* among the mighty men, helpers in the war,

2 armed with bows, using both the right hand and the left in [b]*hurling* stones and *shooting* arrows with the bow. *They were* of Benjamin, Saul's brethren.

3 The chief *was* Ahiezer, then Joash, the sons of Shemaah the Gibeathite; Jeziel and Pelet the sons of Azmaveth; Berachah, and Jehu the Anathothite;

4 Ishmaiah the Gibeonite, a mighty man among the thirty, and over the thirty; Jeremiah, Jahaziel, Johanan, and Jozabad the Gederathite;

5 Eluzai, Jerimoth, Bealiah, Shemariah, and Shephatiah the Haruphite;

6 Elkanah, Jisshiah, Azarel, Joezer, and Jashobeam, the Korahites;

7 and Joelah and Zebadiah the sons of Jeroham of Gedor.

(In the order of events 1 Chr. 12:8–15 follows 2 Sam. 5:17; 1 Chr. 14:8)

8 *Some* Gadites joined David at the stronghold in the wilderness, mighty men of valor, men trained for battle, who could handle shield and spear, whose faces *were like* the faces of lions, and *were* as swift as gazelles on the mountains:

9 Ezer the first, Obadiah the second, Eliab the third,

10 Mishmannah the fourth, Jeremiah the fifth,

11 Attai the sixth, Eliel the seventh,

12 Johanan the eighth, Elzabad the ninth,

13 Jeremiah the tenth, and Machbanai the eleventh.

14 These *were* from the sons of Gad, captains of the army; the least was over a hundred, and the greatest was over a [c]thousand.

15 These *are* the ones who crossed the Jordan in the [d]first month, when it had [e]overflowed all its banks; and they put to flight all *those* in the valleys, to the east and to the west.

16 Then some of the sons of Benjamin and Judah came to David at the stronghold.

17 And David went out to meet them, and answered and said to them, "If you have come peaceably to me to help me, my heart will be united with you; but if to betray me to my enemies, since *there is* no wrong in my hands, may the God of our fathers look and bring judgment."

18 Then the [f]Spirit came upon [g]Amasai, chief of the captains, *and he said:*

"*We are* yours, O David;
We *are* on your side, O son of Jesse!
Peace, peace to you,
And peace to your helpers!
For your God helps you."

So David received them, and made them captains of the troop.

19 And *some* from [h]Manasseh defected to David when he was going with the Philistines to battle against Saul; but they did not help them, for the lords of the Philistines sent him away by agreement, [i]saying, "He may defect to his master Saul *and endanger* our heads."

20 When he went to Ziklag, those of Manasseh who defected to him were Adnah, Jozabad, Jediael, Michael, Jozabad, Elihu, and Zillethai, captains of the thousands who *were* from Manasseh.

21 And they [j]helped David against the bands *of raiders,* for they *were* all mighty men of valor, and they were captains in the army.

22 For at *that* time they came to David day by day to help him, until *it was* a great army, [k]like the army of God.

Men of Israel who made David king (cp. 2 Sam. 5:1–3)

23 Now these *were* the numbers of the divisions *that were* equipped for war, *and* came [l]to David at [m]Hebron to [n]turn *over* the kingdom of Saul to him, [o]according to the word of the LORD:

24 of the sons of Judah bearing shield and spear, six thousand eight hundred armed for war;

25 of the sons of Simeon, mighty men of valor fit for war, seven thousand one hundred;

26 of the sons of Levi four thousand six hundred;

27 Jehoiada, the leader of the Aaronites, and with him three thousand seven hundred;

28 [p]Zadok, a young man, a valiant warrior, and from his father's house twenty-two captains;

29 of the sons of Benjamin, relatives of Saul, three thousand (until

CHAPTER 12

1 *a* 1 Sam. 27:6
2 *b* Jud. 20:16
14 *c* 1 Sam. 18:13
15 *d* See Lev. 23:2, *note* *e* Josh. 3:15; 4:18–19
18 *f Holy Spirit* (OT): v. 18; 1 Chr. 28:12. (Gen. 1:2; Zech. 12:10) *g* Or *Amasa,* 2 Sam. 17:25
19 *h* vv. 20–21 *i* 1 Sam. 29:4
21 *j* 1 Sam. 30:1–20
22 *k* Josh. 5:13–15
23 *l* 2 Sam. 2:1–4 *m* 1 Chr. 11:1 *n* 1 Chr. 10:14 *o* 1 Sam. 16:1–4
28 *p* 2 Sam. 8:17; 1 Chr. 6:8, 53

then the greatest part of them had remained loyal to the house of Saul);
30 of the sons of Ephraim twenty
thousand eight hundred, mighty men
of valor, famous men throughout their
father's house;
31 of the half-tribe of Manasseh
eighteen thousand, who were designated by name to come and make David king;
32 of the sons of Issachar who had
understanding of the [a]times, to know
what Israel ought to do, their chiefs
were two hundred; and all their brethren were at their command;
33 of Zebulun there were fifty thousand who went out to battle, expert in
war with all weapons of war, [b]stout-
hearted men who could keep ranks;
34 of Naphtali one thousand captains, and with them thirty-seven
thousand with shield and spear;
35 of the Danites who could keep
battle formation, twenty-eight thousand six hundred;
36 of Asher, those who could go out
to war, able to keep battle formation,
forty thousand;
37 of the Reubenites and the Gadites and the half-tribe of Manasseh,
from the other side of the Jordan, one
hundred and twenty thousand armed
for battle with every *kind* of weapon of
war.
38 All these men of war, who could
keep ranks, came to Hebron with a
[c]loyal heart, to make David king over
all Israel; and all the rest of Israel *were*
of [d]one mind to make David king.
39 And they were there with David
three days, eating and drinking, for
their brethren had prepared for them.
40 Moreover those who were near
to them, from as far away as Issachar
and Zebulun and Naphtali, were
bringing food on donkeys and camels,
on mules and oxen—provisions of
flour and cakes of figs and cakes of
raisins, wine and oil and oxen and
sheep abundantly, for *there was* joy in
Israel.

Doing a right thing in a wrong way
(2 Sam. 6:1–11)

13 THEN David consulted with
the [e]captains of thousands and
hundreds, *and* with every leader.
2 And David said to all the assembly of Israel, "If *it seems* good to you,
and if it is of the LORD our God, let us
send out to our brethren everywhere
who are left in all the land of Israel,
and with them to the priests and Levites *who are* in their [f]cities *and* their
common-lands, that they may gather
together to us;
3 "and let us bring the ark of our
God back to us, for we have not inquired at it since the days of Saul."
4 Then all the assembly said that
they would do so, for the thing was
right in the eyes of all the people.
5 So David gathered all Israel together, from Shihor in Egypt to as far
as the entrance of Hamath, to bring
the ark of God from [g]Kirjath Jearim.
6 And David and all Israel went up
to [h]Baalah,* to Kirjath Jearim, which
belonged to Judah, to bring up from
there the ark of God the LORD, who
[i]dwells *between* the cherubim, where
His name is proclaimed.
7 So they [j]carried the ark of God
on a new cart from the house of Abinadab, and Uzza and Ahio drove the
cart.
8 Then David and all Israel played
music before God with all *their* might,
with singing, on harps, on stringed instruments, on tambourines, on cymbals, and with trumpets.

Uzza struck for touching the ark

9 And when they came to [k]Chi-
don's threshing floor, Uzza put out his
hand to hold the ark, for the oxen
stumbled.
10 Then the anger of the LORD was
aroused against Uzza, and He struck
him [l]because he put his hand to the
ark; and he died there before God.
11 And David became angry because of the LORD's outbreak against
Uzza; therefore that place is called
[m]Perez Uzza to this day.
12 David was afraid of God that
day, saying, "How can I bring the ark
of God to me?"
13 So David would not move the
ark with him into the City of David,
but took it aside into the house of
Obed-Edom the Gittite.
14 The ark of God [n]remained with
the family of Obed-Edom in his house
three months. And the LORD [o]blessed
the house of Obed-Edom and all that
he had.

The prosperity of David's reign
(2 Sam. 5:11–25; 23:13–17;
1 Chr. 3:5–9; 11:15–19; 12:8–15)

14 NOW [p]Hiram king of Tyre sent
messengers to David, and ce-

32 a Est. 1:13
33 b Lit. *not of double heart;* cp. Ps. 12:2; Jas. 1:8
38 c 1 Ki. 8:61; see Phil. 3:12, *note*
d 2 Chr. 30:12
CHAPTER 13
1 e 1 Chr. 11:15; 12:34
2 f 1 Chr. 6:64
5 g 1 Sam. 6:21; 7:1–2
6 h Josh. 15:9
i Ex. 25:22
7 j Cp. Num. 4:15; 1 Chr. 15:2,15
9 k Or *Nachon,* 2 Sam. 6:6
10 l Num. 4:15, 19–20; cp. 1 Chr. 15:12–15
11 m Lit. *the outburst against Uzza*
14 n 2 Sam. 6:11
o 1 Chr. 26:4–8
CHAPTER 14
1 p 1 Ki. 5:1

* 13:6 Called *Baale Judah* in 2 Samuel 6:2

dar trees, with masons and carpenters, to build him a house.
2 So David knew that the LORD
had established him as king over Israel, for his kingdom was [a]highly exalted for the sake of His people Israel.
3 Then David took more wives in
Jerusalem, and David begot more
sons and daughters.
4 And these are the [b]names of his
children whom he had in Jerusalem:
Shammua,* Shobab, Nathan, Solomon,
5 Ibhar, Elishua,* Elpelet,*
6 Nogah, Nepheg, Japhia,
7 Elishama, [c]Beeliada,* and Eliphelet.
8 Now [d]when the Philistines
heard that David had been anointed
king over all Israel, all the Philistines
went up to search for David. And David heard *of it* and went out against
them.
9 Then the Philistines went and
made a raid on the [e]Valley of Rephaim.
10 And David [f]inquired of God,
saying, "Shall I go up against the Philistines? Will You deliver them into
my hand?" The LORD said to him, "Go
up, for I will deliver them into your
hand."
11 So they went up to Baal Perazim, and David defeated them there.
Then David said, "God has broken
through my enemies by my hand like
a breakthrough of water." Therefore
they called the name of that place Baal
Perazim.*
12 And when they left their gods
there, David gave a commandment,
and they were burned with fire.
13 Then the Philistines once [g]again
made a raid on the valley.
14 Therefore David inquired again
of God, and God said to him, "You
shall not go up after them; circle
around them, and come upon them in
front of the mulberry trees.
15 "And it shall be, when you hear
a sound of marching in the tops of the
mulberry trees, then you shall go out
to battle, for God has gone out [h]before
you to strike the camp of the Philistines."
16 So David did as God commanded him, and they drove back the
army of the Philistines from [i]Gibeon
as far as Gezer.
17 Then the fame of David went out
into all lands, and the LORD brought
the [j]fear of him upon all nations.

2
a Num. 24:7
4
b 1 Chr. 3:5–8
7
c Or *Eliada,* 2 Sam. 5:16
8
d 2 Sam. 5:17–21
9
e Lit. *valley of the giants.* Josh. 17:15; 18:16
10
f 1 Sam. 23:2,4; 30:8; 2 Sam. 2:1; 5:19,23; 21:1
13
g 2 Sam. 5:22–25
15
h Cp. Josh. 5:13–15
16
i Or *Geba,* 2 Sam. 5:25
17
j Dt. 2:25; 11:25; 2 Chr. 20:29
CHAPTER 15
1
k 1 Chr. 16:1
2
l Num. 4:15; cp. 2 Sam. 6:1–11
m Num. 4:2–15; Dt. 10:8; 31:9
3
n Cp. 2 Chr. 5:3–14
o Cp. 1 Chr. 13
p 2 Sam. 6:12,17
11
q 2 Sam. 8:17; 15:24–29, 35–36; 18:19,22, 27; 19:11; 20:25; 1 Chr. 12:28
r 1 Sam. 22:20–23; 23:6; 30:7; 1 Ki. 2:22, 26–27; Mk. 2:6
13
s 1 Chr. 13:7–11

David prepares to bring the ark to Jerusalem (2 Sam. 6:12a)

15 *DAVID* built houses for himself in the City of David; and he
[k]prepared a place for the ark of God,
and pitched a tent for it.
2 Then David said, [l]"No one may
carry the ark of God but the Levites,
for the LORD has chosen [m]them to
carry the ark of God and to minister
before Him forever."
3 And David [n]gathered all Israel
together at Jerusalem, to [o]bring up
the ark of the LORD to its [p]place, which
he had prepared for it.
4 Then David assembled the children of Aaron and the Levites:
5 of the sons of Kohath, Uriel the
chief, and one hundred and twenty of
his brethren;
6 of the sons of Merari, Asaiah the
chief, and two hundred and twenty of
his brethren;
7 of the sons of Gershom, Joel the
chief, and one hundred and thirty of
his brethren;
8 of the sons of Elizaphan, Shemaiah the chief, and two hundred of his
brethren;
9 of the sons of Hebron, Eliel the
chief, and eighty of his brethren;
10 of the sons of Uzziel, Amminadab the chief, and one hundred and
twelve of his brethren.
11 And David called for [q]Zadok
and [r]Abiathar the priests, and for the
Levites: for Uriel, Asaiah, Joel, Shemaiah, Eliel, and Amminadab.
12 He said to them, "You *are* the
heads of the fathers' *houses* of the Levites; sanctify yourselves, you and
your brethren, that you may bring up
the ark of the LORD God of Israel to *the
place* I have prepared for it.
13 "For [s]because you *did* not *do it*
the first *time,* the LORD our God broke
out against us, because we did
not consult Him about the proper
order."
14 So the priests and the Levites
sanctified themselves to bring up the
ark of the LORD God of Israel.
15 And the children of the Levites
bore the ark of God on their shoulders,
by its poles, as Moses had commanded according to the word of the
LORD.
16 Then David spoke to the leaders

*
14:4 Spelled *Shimea* in 3:5 • **14:5** Spelled *Elishama* in 3:6 • Spelled *Eliphelet* in 3:6 **14:7** Spelled *Eliada* in 3:8 **14:11** Literally *Master of Breakthroughs*

of the Levites to appoint their brethren *to be* the [1]singers accompanied by
instruments of music, stringed instruments, harps, and cymbals, by raising
the voice with resounding joy.
17 So the Levites [a]appointed Heman the son of Joel; and of his brethren, Asaph the son of Berechiah; and
of their brethren, the sons of Merari,
Ethan the son of Kushaiah;
18 and with them their [b]brethren of
the second *rank:* Zechariah, Ben,* Jaaziel, Shemiramoth, Jehiel, Unni,
Eliab, Benaiah, Maaseiah, Mattithiah,
Elipheleh, Mikneiah, Obed-Edom,
and Jeiel, the gatekeepers;
19 the singers, Heman, Asaph, and
Ethan, *were* to sound the cymbals of
bronze;
20 Zechariah, [c]Aziel, Shemiramoth, Jehiel, Unni, Eliab, Maaseiah,
and Benaiah, with strings according
to [d]Alamoth;
21 Mattithiah, Elipheleh, Mikneiah, Obed-Edom, Jeiel, and Azaziah,
to direct with harps on the [e]Shemi-
nith;
22 Chenaniah, leader of the Levites, was instructor *in charge of* the
music, because he *was* skillful;
23 Berechiah and Elkanah *were*
doorkeepers for the ark;
24 Shebaniah, Joshaphat, Nethanel, Amasai, Zechariah, Benaiah,
and Eliezer, the priests, were to blow
the trumpets before the ark of God;
and [f]Obed-Edom and Jehiah, doorkeepers for the ark.

The joyful procession with the ark (2 Sam. 6:12b–16,20–23)

25 So David, the elders of Israel,
and the captains over thousands went
to [g]bring up the ark of the covenant of
the LORD from the house of Obed-
Edom with joy.
26 And so it was, when God helped
the Levites who bore the ark of the
covenant of the LORD, that they offered
seven bulls and seven rams.
27 David was clothed with a robe of
fine [h]linen, as were all the Levites
who bore the ark, the singers, and
Chenaniah the music master *with* the
singers. David also wore a linen
[i]ephod.
28 Thus all Israel brought up the
ark of the covenant of the LORD with
[j]shouting and with the sound of the
horn, with trumpets and with cymbals, making music with stringed instruments and harps.
29 And it happened, *as* the ark of
the covenant of the LORD came to the
City of David, that [k]Michal, Saul's
daughter, looked through a window
and saw King David whirling and
playing music; and she despised him
in her heart.

17
a 1 Chr. 25:1
18
b i.e. *helpers*
20
c Or *Jaaziel,* v. 18
d Ps. 46, *title*
21
e Ps. 6, *title*
24
f v. 25; 1 Chr. 13:13,14
25
g 1 Ki. 8:1
27
h 1 Sam. 2:18,28
i See Ex. 25:9, *note*
28
j Num. 23:21; Josh. 6:5, 20; Zech. 4:7; 1 Th. 4:16
29
k 1 Sam. 18:20,27; 19:11–17; 2 Sam. 3:13–14; 6:20–23
CHAPTER 16
1
l 1 Chr. 15:1
2
m 1 Ki. 8:14
3
n Perhaps *a portion of wine.* Heb. uncertain
4
o See Ps. 38 and 70, *titles*
5
p Or *Jaaziel,* 1 Chr. 15:18
7
q 2 Sam. 23:1
r vv. 8–22; Ps. 105:1–15
8
s 1 Chr. 17:19–20

The ark placed in the tabernacle at Jerusalem (2 Sam. 6:17–19)

16 SO they brought the ark of
God, and set it in the midst of
the [l]tabernacle that David had
erected for it. Then they offered burnt
offerings and peace offerings before
God.
2 And when David had finished
offering the burnt offerings and the
peace offerings, he [m]blessed the people in the name of the LORD.
3 Then he distributed to everyone
of Israel, both man and woman, to everyone a loaf of bread, a [n]piece *of
meat,* and a cake of raisins.

Psalm of thanksgiving

4 And he appointed some of the
Levites to minister before the ark of
the LORD, to [o]commemorate, to thank,
and to praise the LORD God of Israel:
5 Asaph the chief, and next to him
Zechariah, *then* [p]Jeiel, Shemiramoth,
Jehiel, Mattithiah, Eliab, Benaiah, and
Obed-Edom: Jeiel with stringed instruments and harps, but Asaph made
music with cymbals;
6 Benaiah and Jahaziel the priests
regularly *blew* the trumpets before the
ark of the covenant of God.
7 On that day [q]David first delivered *this* [r]psalm into the hand of
Asaph and his brethren, to thank the
LORD:

8 Oh, give thanks to the LORD!
Call upon His name;
[s]Make known His deeds among
the peoples!
9 Sing to Him, sing psalms to
Him;

* 15:18 Following Masoretic Text and Vulgate; Septuagint omits *Ben.*

[1](15:16) Music is a vital factor in the worship in both the OT and NT. The new song of praise and joy which God puts in the mouths of His people (Ps. 40:3) is Spirit-born (Eph. 5:18–19). Music also expresses confession (e.g. Ps. 32; 51) and comfort in sorrow (e.g. Ps. 27). For the music of public praise, Scripture stresses a high standard of skill (15:22; cp. 15:16—16:43; 25:1–7).

Talk of all His wondrous works!
10 Glory in His holy name;
Let the hearts of those rejoice who seek the LORD!
11 Seek the LORD and His strength;
Seek His face evermore!
12 Remember His marvelous works which He has done,
His wonders, and the judgments of His mouth,
13 O seed of Israel His servant,
You children of Jacob, His [a]chosen ones!

14 He *is* the LORD our God;
His [b]judgments *are* in all the earth.
15 Remember His covenant forever,
The word which He commanded, for a thousand generations,
16 *The covenant which* He made with [c]Abraham,
And His oath to [d]Isaac,
17 And [e]confirmed it to [f]Jacob for a statute,
To Israel *for* an everlasting covenant,
18 Saying, "To you I will give the land of Canaan
As the [g]allotment of your inheritance,"
19 When you were [h]few in number,
Indeed very few, and strangers in it.
20 When they went from one nation to another,
And from *one* kingdom to another people,
21 He permitted no man to do them wrong;
Yes, He [i]rebuked kings for their sakes,
22 *Saying*, "Do not touch My anointed ones,
And do My [j]prophets no harm."

23 [k]Sing to the LORD, all the earth;
Proclaim the good news of His salvation from day to day.
24 Declare His glory among the nations,
His wonders among all peoples.
25 For the LORD *is* great and greatly to be praised;
He *is* also to be [l]feared above all gods.
26 For all the [m]gods of the peoples *are* idols,
But the LORD made the heavens.
27 Honor and majesty *are* before Him;
Strength and gladness are in His place.

28 Give to the LORD, O families of the peoples,
Give to the LORD glory and strength.
29 Give to the LORD the glory *due* His name;
Bring an offering, and come before Him.
Oh, worship the LORD in the beauty of holiness!
30 Tremble before Him, all the earth.
The world also is firmly established,
It shall not be moved.
31 Let the heavens rejoice, and let the earth be glad;
And let them say among the nations, "The LORD reigns."
32 Let the sea roar, and all its fullness;
Let the field rejoice, and all that *is* in it.
33 Then the [n]trees of the woods shall rejoice before the LORD,
For He is [o]coming to judge the earth.

34 [p]Oh, give thanks to the LORD, for *He is* good!
For His mercy *endures* forever.
35 And say, "Save us, O God of our salvation;
Gather us together, and deliver us from the Gentiles,
To give thanks to Your holy name,
To triumph in Your praise."
36 Blessed *be* the LORD God of Israel
From everlasting to everlasting!

And all the people said, "Amen!" and praised the LORD.

Worship before the ark

37 So he left [q]Asaph and his brothers there before the [1]ark of the covenant of the LORD to minister before

13
a Election (corporate): vv. 13–22; Ps. 33:12. (Dt. 7:6; 1 Pet. 5:13, *note*)
14
b Isa. 26:9
16
c See Gen. 15:18, *note*
d Gen. 26:1–5
17
e Gen. 35:11–12
f Gen. 28:10–15
18
g Lit. *cord*, or *line*
19
h Gen. 34:30
21
i Gen. 20:3
22
j Gen. 20:7
23
k vv. 23–33; cp. Ps. 96
25
l See Ps. 19:9, *note*
26
m 1 Cor. 8:5–6
33
n Isa. 55:12–13
o Joel 3:1–14; Zech. 14:1–14; Mt. 25:31–46
34
p vv. 34–36; Ps. 106:1, 47–48
37
q 1 Chr. 6:39; 15:17; 25:1–9; 2 Chr. 5:12; Ezra 2:41. Asaph was the writer of Ps. 50 and 73–83

[1](16:37) The ancient tabernacle was now divided; the ark was brought into Zion (see 1 Chr.

the ark regularly, as every day's work
[a]required;
38 and [b]Obed-Edom with his sixty-
eight brethren, including Obed-Edom
the son of Jeduthun, and Hosah, *to be*
gatekeepers;
39 and [c]Zadok the priest and his
brethren the priests, before the tabernacle of the LORD at the high place that
was at [d]Gibeon,
40 to offer burnt offerings to the
LORD on the altar of burnt offering regularly morning and evening, and *to do*
according to all that is written in the
Law of the LORD which He [e]com-
manded Israel;
41 and with them Heman and Jeduthun and the rest who were chosen,
who were [f]designated by name, to
give thanks to the LORD, because His
mercy *endures* forever;
42 and with them Heman and Jeduthun, to sound aloud with trumpets
and cymbals and the musical instruments of God. Now the sons of Jeduthun *were* gatekeepers.
43 Then [g]all the people departed,
every man to his house; and David returned to bless his house.

David desires to build the LORD a house (2 Sam. 7:1–3)

17 NOW it came to pass, when
David was dwelling in his
house, that David said to Nathan the
prophet, "See now, I dwell in a house
of [h]cedar, but the ark of the covenant
of the LORD *is* under tent curtains."
2 Then Nathan [1]said to David, "Do
all that *is* in your heart, for God *is* with
you."

The LORD's plan to build David a royal lineage (2 Sam. 7:4–17): The Davidic Covenant

3 But it happened that night that
the word of God came to Nathan, saying,
4 "Go and tell My servant David,
'Thus says the LORD: "You shall [i]not
build Me a house to dwell in.
5 "For I have not dwelt in a house
since the time that I brought up Israel,

37
a Ezra 3:4
38
b 1 Chr. 13:14
39
c 2 Sam. 8:17; 15:24–36; 1 Ki. 2:35; 1 Chr. 29:22; Ezra 7:2; Ezek. 40:46
d 1 Ki. 3:4
40
e Ex. 29:38–42
41
f 1 Chr. 25:1–6
43
g 2 Sam. 6:18–19
CHAPTER 17
1
h 1 Chr. 14:1
4
i 1 Chr. 28:2–3
7
j 1 Sam. 16:11–13
9
k Dt. 30:1–9; Isa. 1:11–13; Jer. 16:14–16; 23:5–8; 24:6; Ezek. 37:21–27; Amos 9:14
l Or *as previously, when I set judges over My people, Israel*
11
m 1 Ki. 2:10; 1 Chr. 29:28
n i.e. *Solomon,* 1 Ki. 5:5; 6:12; 8:19–21; 1 Chr. 22:9–13; 28:20

even to this day, but have gone from
tent to tent, and from *one* tabernacle
to another.
6 "Wherever I have moved about
with all Israel, have I ever spoken a
word to any of the judges of Israel,
whom I commanded to shepherd My
people, saying, 'Why have you not
built Me a house of cedar?' " '
7 "Now therefore, thus shall you
say to My servant David, 'Thus says
the LORD of hosts: "I took you [j]from
the sheepfold, from following the
sheep, to be ruler over My people Israel.
8 "And I have been with you wherever you have gone, and have cut off
all your enemies from before you, and
have made you a name like the name
of the great men who *are* on the earth.
9 "Moreover I will appoint a place
for My people Israel, and will [k]plant
them, that they may dwell in a place of
their own and move no more; nor shall
the sons of wickedness oppress them
anymore, [l]as previously,
10 "since the time that I commanded judges *to be* over My people
Israel. Also I will subdue all your enemies. Furthermore I tell you that the
LORD will build you a house.*
11 "And it shall be, [2]when your
days are [m]fulfilled, when you must go
to be with your fathers, that I will set
up your [n]seed after you, who will be of
your sons; and I will establish his
kingdom.
12 [o]"He shall build Me a house, and
I will establish his throne forever.
13 "I will be his Father, and he shall
be My [p]son; and I will not take My
mercy away from him, [q]as I took *it*
from *him* who was before you.
14 "And I will establish him in My
house and in My kingdom forever;
and his throne shall be established
[r]forever." ' "
15 According to all these words and

17:12 *o* Ps. 89:20–37 **17:13** *p* Heb. 1:5–9 *q* 1 Sam. 15:23–28 **17:14** *r* Ps. 89:3–4; Lk. 1:31–33

*

17:10 That is, a royal dynasty

11:5, *note*), whereas the bronze altar at least, and probably the furnishings of the Holy Place (Ex. 25:23–40; 37:10–28; 40:22–27), were established in the high place at Gibeon. Asaph and the singers (1 Chr. 6:31–47; 15:16–19; 16:5; 25:6) were left before the ark, while the priests ministered in Gibeon before the tabernacle (16:39). All this was confusion (cp. Heb. 9:1–7). With the construction of the temple the divine order seems to have been restored.

[1](17:2) Compare vv. 3–4. It is folly to rely on human judgment in the things that pertain to God.

[2](17:11) Here both the long and short views of prophecy may be seen. The promise of vv. 11–14 was fulfilled first in Solomon (1 Ki. 8:19–20), and will be fulfilled in Christ (Lk. 1:31–33; Acts 15:14–16).

according to all this vision, so Nathan spoke to David.

David's worship, and his prayer that his house might be blessed always (2 Sam. 7:18–29)

16 Then King David went in and sat before the LORD; and he said: "Who *am* I, O LORD God? And what is my house, that You have brought me this far?

17 "And *yet* this was a small thing in Your sight, O God; and You have *also* spoken of Your servant's house for a great while to come, and have regarded me according to the rank of a man of high degree, O LORD God.

18 "What more can David *say* to You for the honor of Your servant? For You know Your servant.

19 "O LORD, for Your servant's sake, and according to Your own heart, You have done all this greatness, in making known all these great things.

20 "O LORD, *there is* none like You, nor *is there any* God besides You, according to all that we have heard with our ears.

21 [a]"And who *is* like Your people Israel, the one nation on the earth whom God went to [b]redeem for Himself *as* a people—to make for Yourself a name by great and awesome deeds, by driving out nations from before Your people whom You redeemed from Egypt?

22 "For You have made Your people Israel Your very own people forever; and You, LORD, have become their God.

23 "And now, O LORD, the word which You have spoken concerning Your servant and concerning his house, *let it* be established forever, and do as You have said.

24 "So let it be established, that Your name may be magnified forever, saying, 'The LORD of hosts, the God of Israel, *is* Israel's God.' And let the house of Your servant David be established before You.

25 "For You, O my God, have revealed to Your servant that You will build him a house. Therefore Your servant has found it *in his heart* to pray before You.

26 "And now, LORD, You are God, and have promised this goodness to Your servant.

27 "Now You have been pleased to bless the house of Your servant, that it may continue before You forever; for

21
a Dt. 4:6–8, 33–38; Ps. 147:20
b See Ex. 14:30, *note*

CHAPTER 18

1
c vv. 1–17

2
d 2 Sam. 8:2; cp. Num. 24:17; Zeph. 2:9
e Ps. 60:8
f Cp. 1 Sam. 10:27

3
g 2 Sam. 8:3

4
h Cp. 2 Sam. 8:4; see 1 Chr. 11:11, *note*

5
i 2 Sam. 8:5–6; cp. 1 Ki. 11:23–25

8
j Or *Betah,* 2 Sam. 8:8
k Or *Berothai,* 2 Sam. 8:8
l 1 Ki. 7:13–51

9
m Or *Toi,* 2 Sam. 8:9

10
n 2 Sam. 8:10–12

11
o 2 Sam. 10:14

You have blessed it, O LORD, and *it shall be* blessed forever."

Full establishment of David's kingdom (2 Sam. 8:1–18)

18 [c]AFTER this it came to pass that David attacked the Philistines, subdued them, and took Gath and its towns from the hand of the Philistines.

2 Then he defeated [d]Moab, and the Moabites became David's [e]servants, *and* [f]brought tribute.

3 And [g]David defeated Hadadezer* king of Zobah *as far as* Hamath, as he went to establish his power by the River Euphrates.

4 David took from him one thousand chariots, [h]seven thousand* horsemen, and twenty thousand foot soldiers. Also David hamstrung all the chariot *horses,* except that he spared enough of them for one hundred chariots.

5 When the [i]Syrians of Damascus came to help Hadadezer king of Zobah, David killed twenty-two thousand of the Syrians.

6 Then David put *garrisons* in Syria of Damascus; and the Syrians became David's servants, *and* brought tribute. So the LORD preserved David wherever he went.

7 And David took the shields of gold that were on the servants of Hadadezer, and brought them to Jerusalem.

8 Also from [j]Tibhath and from [k]Chun, cities of Hadadezer, David brought a large amount of [l]bronze, with which Solomon made the bronze Sea, the pillars, and the articles of bronze.

9 Now when [m]Tou king of Hamath heard that David had defeated all the army of Hadadezer king of Zobah,

10 he sent Hadoram* his son to King David, to greet him and bless him, because he had fought against Hadadezer and defeated him (for Hadadezer had been at war with Tou); and *Hadoram brought with him* all kinds of [n]articles of gold, silver, and bronze.

11 King David also dedicated these to the LORD, along with the silver and gold that he had brought from all *these* nations—from Edom, from Moab, from the [o]people of Ammon,

*

18:3 Hebrew *Hadarezer,* and so throughout chapters 18 and 19 **18:4** Or *seven hundred* (compare 2 Samuel 8:4) **18:10** Spelled *Joram* in 2 Samuel 8:10

from the [a]Philistines, and from [b]Am-
alek.
12 Moreover [c]Abishai the son of
Zeruiah killed eighteen thousand
Edomites* in the Valley of Salt.
13 He also put garrisons in [d]Edom,
and all the Edomites became David's
servants. And the LORD preserved David wherever he went.
14 So David reigned over all Israel,
and administered judgment and justice to all his people.
15 Joab the son of Zeruiah *was*
over the army; Jehoshaphat the son of
Ahilud *was* recorder;
16 Zadok the son of Ahitub and
Abimelech the son of Abiathar *were*
the priests; Shavsha* *was* the scribe;
17 Benaiah the son of Jehoiada *was*
over the Cherethites and the Pelethites; and David's sons *were* chief
ministers at the king's side.

(In chronological order
2 Sam. 9 precedes ch. 19)

The Ammonite-Syrian campaigns under
Joab (v. 8) and David (v. 17);
(2 Sam. 10)

19 IT happened after this that
[e]Nahash the king of the people
of Ammon died, and his son reigned in
his place.
2 Then David said, "I will show
kindness to Hanun the son of Nahash,
because his father showed kindness to
me." So David sent messengers to
comfort him concerning his father.
And David's servants came to Hanun
in the land of the people of Ammon to
comfort him.
3 And the princes of the people of
Ammon said to Hanun, "Do you think
that David really honors your father
because he has sent comforters to
you? Did his servants not come to you
to search and to overthrow and to spy
out the [f]land?"
4 Therefore Hanun took David's
servants, [g]shaved them, and cut off
their garments in the middle, at their
[h]buttocks, and sent them away.
5 Then *some* went and told David
about the men; and he sent to meet
them, because the men were greatly
ashamed. And the king said, "Wait at
Jericho until your beards have grown,
and *then* return."
6 When the people of Ammon saw
that they had made themselves repulsive to David, Hanun and the people of
Ammon sent a thousand [i]talents of
silver to hire for themselves chariots
and horsemen from [j]Mesopotamia,*
from Syrian Maacah, and from Zobah.*
7 So they hired for themselves
thirty-two thousand chariots, with the
king of Maacah and his people, who
came and encamped before Medeba.
Also the people of Ammon gathered
together from their cities, and came to
battle.
8 Now when David heard *of it,* he
sent Joab and all the army of the
mighty men.
9 Then the people of Ammon
came out and put themselves in battle
array before the gate of the city, and
the kings who had come *were* by
themselves in the field.
10 When Joab saw that the battle
line was against him before and behind, he chose some of Israel's best
and put *them* in battle array against
the Syrians.
11 And the rest of the people he put
under the command of Abishai his
brother, and they set *themselves* in
battle array against the people of Ammon.
12 Then he said, "If the Syrians are
too strong for me, then you shall help
me; but if the people of Ammon are
too strong for you, then I will help you.
13 "Be of good courage, and let us
be strong for our people and for the
cities of our God. And may the LORD do
what is good in His sight."
14 So Joab and the people who
were with him drew near for the battle
against the Syrians, and they fled before him.
15 When the people of Ammon saw
that the Syrians were fleeing, they
also fled before Abishai his brother,
and entered the city. So Joab went to
Jerusalem.
16 Now when the Syrians saw that
they had been defeated by Israel, they
sent messengers and brought the Syrians who were beyond the [k]River, and
Shophach* the commander of Hadadezer's army *went* before them.
17 When it was told David, he gathered all Israel, crossed over the Jordan and came upon them, and set up
in battle array against them. So when
David had set up in *battle* array
against the Syrians, they fought with
him.

11
a 2 Sam. 5:17–25
b 2 Sam. 1:1
12
c 2 Sam. 23:18; 1 Chr. 2:16
13
d Gen. 27:29–40; Num. 24:18; 2 Sam. 8:14
CHAPTER 19
1
e 1 Sam. 11:1
3
f Cp. Gen. 42:9–16
4
g Cp. Isa. 15:2
h Isa. 20:4
6
i See Coinage (OT), Ex. 30:13, *note*
j Jud. 3:8,10
16
k i.e. *the Euphrates*

*
18:12 Or *Syrians* (compare 2 Samuel 8:13)
18:16 Spelled *Seraiah* in 2 Samuel 8:17
19:6 Hebrew *Aram Naharaim* • Spelled *Zoba* in 2 Samuel 10:6 **19:16** Spelled *Shobach* in 2 Samuel 10:16

18 Then the Syrians fled before Israel; and David killed [a]seven thousand* charioteers and forty thousand foot soldiers* of the Syrians, and killed Shophach the commander of the army.

19 And when the servants of Hadadezer saw that they were defeated by Israel, they made peace with David and became his servants. So the Syrians were not willing to help the people of Ammon anymore.

Joab and David take Rabbah of Ammon
(2 Sam. 12:26–31; cp. 11:1—12:25)

20 IT happened in the spring of the year, at the time kings go out *to battle,* that Joab led out the armed forces and ravaged the country of the people of Ammon, and came and besieged Rabbah. But [b]David stayed at Jerusalem. And Joab defeated Rabbah and overthrew it.

2 Then David took their king's crown from his head, and found it to weigh a [c]talent of gold, and *there were* precious stones in it. And it was set on David's head. Also he brought out the spoil of the city in great abundance.

3 And he brought out the people who *were* in it, and put *them* to work* with saws, with iron picks, and with axes. So David did to all the cities of the people of Ammon. Then David and all the people returned *to* Jerusalem.

War against Philistines
(2 Sam. 21:15–22)

4 Now it happened afterward that war broke out at [d]Gezer with the Philistines, at which time Sibbechai the Hushathite killed Sippai,* *who was one* of the sons of the giant. And they were subdued.

5 Again there was war with the Philistines, and Elhanan the son of Jair* killed Lahmi the brother of Goliath the Gittite, the shaft of whose spear *was* like a weaver's [e]beam.

6 Yet again there was war at [f]Gath, where there was a man of *great* stature, with twenty-four fingers and toes, six *on each hand* and six *on each foot;* and he also was born to the giant.

7 So when he defied Israel, Jonathan the son of [g]Shimea, David's brother, killed him.

8 These were born to the giant in Gath, and they fell by the hand of David and by the hand of his servants.

(Events of David's family troubles, the revolt of Absalom, etc. in 2 Sam. 13—21, take place prior to ch. 21)

Three days' plague as a result of David's sin of numbering the people
(2 Sam. 24:1–17)

21 NOW [h]Satan stood up [i]against Israel, [j]and [k]moved David to number Israel.

2 So David said to Joab and to the leaders of the people, "Go, number Israel from Beersheba to Dan, and [l]bring the number of them to me that I may know *it.*"

3 And Joab answered, "May the LORD make His people a hundred times more than they are. But, my lord the king, *are* they not all my lord's servants? Why then does my lord require this thing? Why should he be a cause of guilt in Israel?"

4 Nevertheless the king's word prevailed against Joab. Therefore Joab [m]departed and went throughout all Israel and came to Jerusalem.

5 Then Joab gave the sum of the number of the people to David. All Israel *had* one [n]million one hundred thousand men who drew the sword, and Judah *had* [n]four hundred and seventy thousand men who drew the sword.

6 But he did not count Levi and Benjamin among them, for the king's word was abominable to Joab.

7 And God was displeased with this thing; therefore He struck Israel.

8 So David said to God, "I have [o]sinned greatly, because I have done this thing; but now, I pray, take away the iniquity of Your servant, for I have done very foolishly."

9 Then the LORD spoke to Gad, David's [p]seer, saying,

10 "Go and tell David, [q]saying, 'Thus says the LORD: "I offer you three *things;* choose one of them for yourself, that I may do *it* to you." ' "

11 So Gad came to David and said to him, "Thus says the LORD: 'Choose for yourself,

12 'either [r]three* years of famine, or three months to be defeated by your

---

18 *a* Cp. 2 Sam. 10:18; see 1 Chr. 11:11, *note*
CHAPTER 20
1 *b* Here should be read 2 Sam. 11:2–12:25, with Ps. 51
2 *c* See Weights and Measures (OT), 2 Chr. 2:10, *note*
4 *d* Or *Gob,* 2 Sam. 21:18
5 *e* 1 Sam. 17:7
6 *f* 1 Sam. 5:8
7 *g* Or *Shammah,* 1 Sam. 16:9
CHAPTER 21
1 *h Satan:* v. 1; Job 1:6. (Gen. 3:1; Rev. 20:10)
i Cp. Zech. 3:1
j Cp. Mt. 4:1–11
k Test/tempt: v. 1; 2 Chr. 32:31. (Gen. 3:1; Jas. 1:14, *note*)
2 *l* Cp. 1 Chr. 27:23–24
4 *m* Here should be read 2 Sam. 24:4–9
5 *n* Cp. 2 Sam. 24:9; see 1 Chr. 11:11, *note*
8 *o* 2 Sam. 12:13
9 *p* 1 Sam. 9:9; 2 Ki. 17:13; 1 Chr. 29:29; 2 Chr. 16:7,10; Isa. 30:9–10; Amos 7:12–13 **21:10** *q* 2 Sam. 24:12–14 **21:12** *r* Cp. 2 Sam. 24:13; see 1 Chr. 11:11, *note*

★

19:18 Or *seven hundred* (compare 2 Samuel 10:18) • Or *horsemen* (compare 2 Samuel 10:18) **20:3** Septuagint reads *cut them.* **20:4** Spelled *Saph* in 2 Samuel 21:18 **20:5** Spelled *Jaare-Oregim* in 2 Samuel 21:19 **21:12** Or *seven* (compare 2 Samuel 24:13)

foes with the sword of your enemies
overtaking *you*, or else for three days
the sword of the LORD—the plague in
the land, with the [a]angel of the LORD
destroying throughout all the territory
of Israel.' Now consider what answer
I should take back to Him who sent
me."
13 And David said to Gad, "I am in
great distress. Please let me fall into
the hand of the LORD, for His mercies
are very great; but do not let me fall
into the hand of man."
14 So the LORD sent a [b]plague upon
Israel, and seventy thousand men of
Israel fell.
15 [c]And God sent an [a]angel to Jerusalem to destroy it. As he* was destroying, the LORD looked and relented
of the disaster, and said to the angel
who was destroying, "It is enough;
now restrain your* hand." And the
angel of the LORD stood by the
[d]threshing floor of [e]Ornan the Jebusite.
16 Then David lifted his eyes and
saw the [a]angel of the LORD standing
between earth and heaven, having in
his hand a drawn [f]sword stretched
out over Jerusalem. So David and the
elders, clothed in sackcloth, fell on
their faces.
17 And David said to God, "Was it
not I who commanded the people to be
numbered? I am the one who has
sinned and done evil indeed; but these
[g]sheep, what have they done? Let
Your hand, I pray, O LORD my God, be
against me and my father's house, but
not against Your people that they
should be plagued."

Plague stops after David's offering (2 Sam. 24:18–25)

18 Therefore, the [a]angel of the
LORD commanded Gad to say to David
that David should go and erect an altar to the LORD on the [d]threshing floor
of Ornan the Jebusite.
19 So David went up at the word of
Gad, which he had spoken in the name
of the LORD.
20 Now Ornan turned and saw the
[a]angel; and his four sons *who were*
with him hid themselves, but Ornan
continued threshing wheat.
21 So David came to Ornan, and
Ornan looked and saw David. And he
went out from the threshing floor, and
bowed before David with *his* face to
the ground.
22 Then David said to Ornan,
"Grant me the place of *this* threshing
floor, that I may build an altar on it to
the LORD. You shall grant it to me at
the full price, that the plague may be
withdrawn from the people."
23 But Ornan said to David, "Take
it to yourself, and let my lord the king
do *what is* good in his eyes. Look, I
also give *you* the oxen for burnt offerings, the threshing implements for
wood, and the wheat for the grain offering; I give *it* all."
24 Then King David said to Ornan,
"No, but I will surely buy *it* for the full
price, for I will not take what is yours
for the LORD, nor offer burnt offerings
with *that which* costs *me* nothing."
25 So David gave Ornan [1h]six hundred [i]shekels of gold by weight for
the place.
26 And David built there an altar to
the LORD, and offered burnt offerings
and peace offerings, and called on the
LORD; and He answered him from
heaven by [j]fire on the altar of burnt
offering.
27 So the LORD commanded the
[a]angel, and he returned his sword to
its sheath.
28 At that time, when David saw
that the LORD had answered him on
the threshing floor of Ornan the Jebusite, he sacrificed there.
29 [k]For the tabernacle of the LORD
and the altar of the burnt offering,
which Moses had made in the wilderness, *were* at that time at the high
place in [l]Gibeon.
30 But David could not go before it
to inquire of God, for he was afraid of
the sword of the [a]angel of the LORD.

David prepares material for temple

22 THEN David said, [m]"This *is* the
house of the LORD God, and this
is the altar of burnt offering for Israel."
2 So David commanded to gather
the [n]aliens who *were* in the land of
Israel; and he appointed masons to
[o]cut hewn stones to build the house of
God.

12
a *Angel* (of the LORD): vv. 12–20, 27–30; Ps. 34:7. (Gen. 16:7; Jud. 2:1, *note*)
14
b 1 Chr. 27:24
15
c 2 Sam. 24:16
d 2 Chr. 3:1
e Or *Araunah,* 2 Sam. 24:16, 18–24
16
f Josh. 5:13
17
g 2 Sam. 7:8
25
h Cp. 2 Sam. 24:24; see 1 Chr. 11:11, *note*
i See Coinage (OT), Ex. 30:13, *note*
26
j Lev. 9:24; Jud. 6:21; 1 Ki. 18:36–38
29
k 1 Ki. 3:4; 2 Chr. 1:3; see 1 Chr. 16:37, *note*
l 1 Chr. 16:39
CHAPTER 22
1
m Dt. 12:5–7; 2 Sam. 24:18–25; 1 Chr. 21:18–28; 2 Chr. 3:1
2
n 1 Ki. 9:20–21; 2 Chr. 2:17–18
o 1 Ki. 5:17–18

*
21:15 Or *He* • Or *Your*

[1](21:25) A discrepancy has been imagined in the two accounts, 2 Sam. 24:24 and here. The former records the price of the threshing floor (Heb. *goren*); this verse the price of the place (Heb. *maqom*) or area on which afterward the temple, with its spacious courts, was built (2 Chr. 3:1). David gave 50 shekels of silver for the *goren;* 600 shekels of gold for the *maqom.*

3 And David prepared iron in abundance for the nails of the doors of the gates and for the joints, and bronze in abundance [a]beyond measure,

4 and cedar trees in abundance; for the [b]Sidonians and those from Tyre brought much cedar wood to David.

5 Now David [c]said, "Solomon my son *is* young and inexperienced, and the house to be built for the LORD *must be* exceedingly magnificent, famous and glorious throughout all countries. I will now make preparation for it." So David made abundant preparations before his death.

David's charge to Solomon and the leaders

6 Then he called for his son Solomon, and charged him to build a house for the LORD God of Israel.

7 And David said to Solomon: "My son, as for me, [d]it was in my mind to build a house to the name of the LORD my God;

8 "but the word of the LORD came to me, [e]saying, 'You have shed much blood and have made great wars; you shall not build a house for My name, because you have shed much blood on the earth in My sight.

9 'Behold, a son shall be born to you, who shall be a man of rest; and I will give him [f]rest from all his enemies all around. His name shall be [g]Solomon,* for I will give peace and quietness to Israel in his days.

10 [h]'He shall build a house for My name, and he shall be My son, and I *will be* his Father; and I will establish the throne of his kingdom over Israel forever.'

11 "Now, my son, may the LORD be with you; and may you prosper, and build the house of the LORD your God, as He has said to you.

12 "Only may the LORD give you [i]wisdom and understanding, and give you charge concerning Israel, that you may keep the law of the LORD your God.

13 "Then you will prosper, if you take care to fulfill the statutes and judgments with which the LORD charged Moses concerning Israel. Be strong and of good courage; do not fear nor be dismayed.

14 "Indeed I have taken much trouble to prepare for the house of the LORD one hundred thousand talents of gold and one million [j]talents of silver, and bronze and iron beyond measure, for it is so abundant. I have prepared timber and stone also, and you may add to them.

15 "Moreover *there are* workmen with you in abundance: woodsmen and stonecutters, and all types of skillful men for every kind of work.

16 "Of gold and silver and bronze and iron *there is* no limit. Arise and begin working, and the LORD be with you."

17 David also commanded all the [k]leaders of Israel to help Solomon his son, *saying,*

18 "*Is* not the LORD your God with you? And has He *not* given you [l]rest on every side? For He has given the inhabitants of the land into my hand, and the land is subdued before the LORD and before His people.

19 "Now set your heart and your soul to seek the LORD your God. Therefore arise and build the sanctuary of the LORD God, to [m]bring the ark of the covenant of the LORD and the holy articles of God into the house that is to be built for the name of the LORD."

David makes Solomon king and assembles Israel (cp. 1 Chr. 28:1)

23 SO when David was old and full of days, he [n]made his son Solomon king over Israel.

2 And he gathered together all the leaders of Israel, with the priests and the Levites.

The twenty-four houses of the Levites; Gershonites (v. 7); Kohathites (v. 12); Merarites (v. 21). (Cp. Num. 3:25–37)

3 Now the Levites were numbered from the [o]age of thirty years and above; and the [p]number of individual males was thirty-eight thousand.

4 Of these, twenty-four thousand *were* to [q]look after the work of the house of the LORD, six thousand *were* officers and [r]judges,

5 four thousand *were* gatekeepers, and four thousand [s]praised the LORD with *musical* instruments, "which [t]I made," *said David,* "for giving praise."

6 Also David separated them into [u]divisions among the sons of Levi: Gershon, Kohath, and Merari.

7 Of the Gershonites: [v]Laadan and Shimei.

8 The sons of Laadan: the first Je-

3 *a* 1 Ki. 7:47
4 *b* 1 Ki. 5:6
5 *c* 1 Chr. 29:1–2
7 *d* 2 Sam. 7:1–2
8 *e* 1 Chr. 28:3; 2 Sam. 7:5–13
9 *f* 1 Ki. 4:25 *g* 2 Sam. 12:24
10 *h* 1 Chr. 17:12–13
12 *i* 1 Ki. 3:9–12; 2 Chr. 1:10
14 *j* See Coinage (OT), Ex. 30:13, *note*
17 *k* 1 Chr. 28:1–6
18 *l* 1 Ki. 5:4; 8:56
19 *m* 1 Ki. 8:1–11; 2 Chr. 5:2–14
CHAPTER 23
1 *n* 1 Ki. 1:33–40; 1 Chr. 28:4–5
3 *o* Num. 4:1–3 *p* Cp. Num. 4:48
4 *q* 2 Chr. 2:2, 18; cp. Ezra 3:8–9 *r* Dt. 16:18–20
5 *s* 1 Chr. 15:16 *t* 2 Chr. 29:25–27
6 *u* 2 Chr. 8:14
7 *v* Or *Libni,* 1 Chr. 6:17

*22:9 Literally *Peaceful*

hiel, then Zetham and Joel—three *in*
all.
9 The sons of Shimei: Shelomith,
Haziel, and Haran—three *in all.* These
were the heads of the fathers' *houses*
of Laadan.
10 And the sons of Shimei: Jahath,
[a]Zina, Jeush, and Beriah. These *were*
the four sons of Shimei.
11 Jahath was the first and Zizah
the second. But Jeush and Beriah did
not have many sons; therefore they
were assigned as one father's house.
12 The sons of Kohath: Amram, Izhar, Hebron, and Uzziel—four *in all.*
13 The sons of [b]Amram: Aaron and
Moses; and [c]Aaron was set apart, he
and his sons forever, that he should
sanctify the most holy things, to burn
incense before the LORD, to minister to
Him, and to give the blessing in His
name forever.
14 Now the sons of Moses the man
of God were reckoned to the tribe of
Levi.
15 The sons of Moses *were* Gershon* and Eliezer.
16 Of the sons of Gershon, [d]She-
buel *was* the first.
17 Of the descendants of Eliezer,
Rehabiah was the first. And Eliezer
had no other sons, but the sons of Rehabiah were very many.
18 Of the sons of Izhar, [e]Shelomith
was the first.
19 Of the [f]sons of Hebron, Jeriah
was the first, Amariah the second, Jahaziel the third, and Jekameam the
fourth.
20 Of the sons of Uzziel, Michah
was the first and Jesshiah the second.
21 The sons of Merari *were* Mahli
and Mushi. The sons of Mahli *were*
Eleazar and Kish.
22 And Eleazar died, and had no
sons, but only daughters; and their
[g]brethren, the sons of Kish, took them
as wives.
23 The sons of Mushi *were* Mahli,
Eder, and Jeremoth—three *in all.*

Revised duties of Levites
(cp. Num. 3:5–12)

24 These *were* the sons of Levi by
their fathers' houses—the heads of
the fathers' *houses* as they were
counted individually by the number of
their names, who did the work for the
service of the house of the LORD, from
the age of twenty years and above.
25 For David said, "The LORD God
of Israel has given [h]rest to His people,
that they may dwell in Jerusalem forever";
26 and also to the Levites, "They
shall [i]no longer carry the tabernacle,
or any of the articles for its service."
27 For by the [j]last words of David
the Levites *were* numbered from
twenty years old and above;
28 because their [1]duty *was* to help
the sons of Aaron in the service of the
house of the LORD, in the courts and in
the chambers, in the purifying of all
holy things and the work of the service of the house of God,
29 both with the [k]showbread and
the [l]fine flour for the grain offering,
with the unleavened cakes and *what*
is baked in the [m]pan, with what is
mixed and with all kinds of measures
and sizes;
30 to stand every morning to thank
and praise the LORD, and likewise at
evening;
31 and at every presentation of a
burnt offering to the LORD on the Sabbaths and on the New Moons and on
the [n]set feasts, by number according
to the ordinance governing them, regularly before the LORD;
32 and that they should [o]attend to
the [p]needs of the tabernacle of meeting, the needs of the holy *place*, and
the [q]needs of the sons of Aaron their
brethren in the work of the house of
the LORD.

The twenty-four divisions of
the priests (cp. v. 31)

24 NOW *these are* the divisions of
the sons of Aaron. The [r]sons of
Aaron *were* Nadab, Abihu, Eleazar,
and Ithamar.
2 And [s]Nadab and Abihu died before their father, and had no children;
therefore Eleazar and Ithamar ministered as priests.
3 Then David with Zadok of the
sons of Eleazar, and [t]Ahimelech of
the sons of Ithamar, divided them according to the schedule of their service.
4 There were more leaders found
of the sons of Eleazar than of the sons
of Ithamar, and *thus* they were divided. Among the sons of Eleazar
were sixteen heads of *their* fathers'

10 *a* Or *Zizah,* v. 11
13 *b* Ex. 6:18, 20 *c* Ex. 28:1; Heb. 5:4
16 *d* Or *Shubael,* 1 Chr. 24:20
18 *e* Or *Shelomoth,* 1 Chr. 24:22
19 *f* 1 Chr. 24:23
22 *g* i.e. *cousins*
25 *h* 1 Chr. 22:18
26 *i* Num. 4:1–49
27 *j* 2 Sam. 23:1
29 *k* Lev. 24:5–9; see Ex. 25:30, *note* *l* Lev. 2:1 *m* Lev. 2:5; 1 Chr. 9:31
31 *n* Lev. 23:23–44
32 *o* 2 Chr. 13:10–11 *p* Num. 1:53 *q* Num. 3:6–9
CHAPTER 24
1 *r* Lev. 10:1–6; Num. 26:60–61; 1 Chr. 6:3
2 *s* Num. 3:1–4
3 *t* Or *Abimelech,* 1 Chr. 18:16

* 23:15 Hebrew *Gershom* (compare 6:16)

[1](23:28) This was a new duty; their former duty of carrying the tabernacle (Num. 1:50) was ended.

houses, and eight heads of their fathers' houses among the sons of Ithamar.

5 Thus they were divided by lot, one group as another, for there were officials of the sanctuary and officials *of the house* of God, from the sons of Eleazar and from the sons of Ithamar.

6 And the scribe, Shemaiah the son of Nethanel, *one of* the Levites, wrote them down before the king, the leaders, Zadok the priest, Ahimelech the son of Abiathar, and the heads of the fathers' *houses* of the priests and Levites, one father's house taken for Eleazar and *one* for Ithamar.

7 [a]Now the first lot fell to Jehoiarib, the second to Jedaiah,

8 the third to Harim, the fourth to Seorim,

9 the fifth to Malchijah, the sixth to Mijamin,

10 the seventh to Hakkoz, the eighth to [1]Abijah,

11 the ninth to Jeshua, the tenth to Shecaniah,

12 the eleventh to Eliashib, the twelfth to Jakim,

13 the thirteenth to Huppah, the fourteenth to Jeshebeab,

14 the fifteenth to Bilgah, the sixteenth to Immer,

15 the seventeenth to Hezir, the eighteenth to Happizzez,*

16 the nineteenth to Pethahiah, the twentieth to Jehezekel,*

17 the twenty-first to Jachin, the twenty-second to Gamul,

18 the twenty-third to Delaiah, the twenty-fourth to Maaziah.

19 This *was* the schedule of their service for coming into the house of the LORD according to their ordinance by the hand of Aaron their father, as the LORD God of Israel had commanded him.

Kohathites (2 Chr. 23:12) divided

20 And the rest of the sons of Levi: of the sons of Amram, [b]Shubael; of the sons of Shubael, Jehdeiah.

21 Concerning Rehabiah, of the sons of Rehabiah, the first *was* Isshiah.

22 Of the Izharites, [c]Shelomoth; of the sons of Shelomoth, Jahath.

23 Of the [d]sons *of Hebron,** Jeriah *was the first,** Amariah the second, Jahaziel the third, *and* Jekameam the fourth.

24 *Of* the sons of Uzziel, Michah; of the sons of Michah, Shamir.

25 The brother of Michah, Isshiah; of the sons of Isshiah, Zechariah.

Merarites (2 Chr. 23:21) divided

26 The sons of Merari *were* Mahli and Mushi; the son of Jaaziah, Beno.

27 The sons of Merari by Jaaziah *were* Beno, Shoham, Zaccur, and Ibri.

28 Of Mahli: Eleazar, who had [e]no sons.

29 Of Kish: the son of Kish, Jerahmeel.

30 Also the sons of Mushi *were* Mahli, Eder, and Jerimoth. These *were* the sons of the Levites according to their fathers' houses.

31 These also [f]cast lots just as their brothers the sons of Aaron did, in the presence of King David, Zadok, Ahimelech, and the heads of the fathers' *houses* of the priests and Levites. The chief fathers *did* just as their younger brethren.

Number and service of musicians and singers

25 MOREOVER David and the captains of the army separated for the service *some* of the [g]sons of Asaph, of Heman, and of Jeduthun, who *should* prophesy with harps, stringed instruments, and cymbals. And the number of the skilled men performing their service was:

2 Of the sons of Asaph: Zaccur, Joseph, Nethaniah, and [h]Asharelah; the sons of Asaph *were* under the direction of Asaph, who prophesied according to the order of the king.

3 Of [i]Jeduthun, the sons of Jeduthun: Gedaliah, [j]Zeri, Jeshaiah, Shimei, Hashabiah, and Mattithiah, six,* under the direction of their father Jeduthun, who prophesied with a harp to give thanks and to praise the LORD.

4 Of Heman, the sons of Heman: Bukkiah, Mattaniah, [k]Uzziel, [l]Shebuel, Jerimoth,* Hananiah, Hanani, Eliathah, Giddalti, Romamti-Ezer,

7 *a* vv. 7–18; cp. Ezra 2:36–39
20 *b* Or *Shebuel,* 1 Chr. 23:16
22 *c* Or *Shelomith,* 1 Chr. 23:18
23 *d* 1 Chr. 23:19
28 *e* 1 Chr. 23:22
31 *f* vv. 5–6
CHAPTER 25
1 *g* 1 Chr. 6:33,39; 2 Chr. 5:12
2 *h* Or *Jesharelah,* v. 14
3 *i* 1 Chr. 16:41–42 *j* Or *Jizri,* v. 11
4 *k* Or *Azarel,* v. 18 *l* Or *Shubael,* v. 20

*
24:15 Septuagint and Vulgate read *Aphses.*
24:16 Masoretic Text reads *Jehezkel.*
24:23 Supplied from 23:19 (following some Hebrew manuscripts and Septuagint manuscripts)
• Supplied from 23:19 (following some Hebrew manuscripts and Septuagint manuscripts)
25:3 *Shimei,* appearing in one Hebrew and several Septuagint manuscripts, completes the total of six sons (compare verse 17). **25:4** Spelled *Jeremoth* in verse 22

[1](24:10) It was in the division of Abijah that Zechariah, the husband of Elizabeth and the father of John the Baptist, performed his priestly service in the temple in Jerusalem (Lk. 1:5).

Joshbekashah, Mallothi, Hothir, *and* Mahazioth.

5 All these *were* the sons of Heman the king's seer in the words of God, to exalt his [a]horn. For God gave Heman fourteen sons and three daughters.

6 All these *were* under the direction of their father for the music *in* the house of the LORD, with cymbals, stringed instruments, and [b]harps, for the service of the house of God. Asaph, Jeduthun, and Heman *were* under the [c]authority of the king.

7 So the [d]number of them, with their brethren who were instructed in the songs of the LORD, all who were skillful, *was* two hundred and eighty-eight.

Their division into twenty-four orders

8 And they cast lots for their duty, the small as well as the great, the teacher with the student.

9 Now the first lot for Asaph came out for Joseph; the second for Gedaliah, him with his brethren and sons, twelve;

10 the third for Zaccur, his sons and his brethren, twelve;

11 the fourth for [e]Jizri, his sons and his brethren, twelve;

12 the fifth for Nethaniah, his sons and his brethren, twelve;

13 the sixth for Bukkiah, his sons and his brethren, twelve;

14 the seventh for [f]Jesharelah, his sons and his brethren, twelve;

15 the eighth for Jeshaiah, his sons and his brethren, twelve;

16 the ninth for Mattaniah, his sons and his brethren, twelve;

17 the tenth for Shimei, his sons and his brethren, twelve;

18 the eleventh for [g]Azarel, his sons and his brethren, twelve;

19 the twelfth for Hashabiah, his sons and his brethren, twelve;

20 the thirteenth for [h]Shubael, his sons and his brethren, twelve;

21 the fourteenth for Mattithiah, his sons and his brethren, twelve;

22 the fifteenth for Jeremoth,* his sons and his brethren, twelve;

23 the sixteenth for Hananiah, his sons and his brethren, twelve;

24 the seventeenth for Joshbekashah, his sons and his brethren, twelve;

25 the eighteenth for Hanani, his sons and his brethren, twelve;

26 the nineteenth for Mallothi, his sons and his brethren, twelve;

27 the twentieth for Eliathah, his sons and his brethren, twelve;

28 the twenty-first for Hothir, his sons and his brethren, twelve;

29 the twenty-second for Giddalti, his sons and his brethren, twelve;

30 the twenty-third for Mahazioth, his sons and his brethren, twelve;

31 the twenty-fourth for Romamti-Ezer, his sons and his brethren, twelve.

The divisions of the gatekeepers

26 CONCERNING the divisions of the [i]gatekeepers: of the Korahites, [j]Meshelemiah the son of [k]Kore, of the sons of [l]Asaph.

2 And the sons of Meshelemiah *were* [m]Zechariah the firstborn, Jediael the second, Zebadiah the third, Jathniel the fourth,

3 Elam the fifth, Jehohanan the sixth, Eliehoenai the seventh.

4 Moreover the sons of [n]Obed-Edom *were* Shemaiah the firstborn, Jehozabad the second, Joah the third, Sacar the fourth, Nethanel the fifth,

5 Ammiel the sixth, Issachar the seventh, Peulthai the eighth; for God [o]blessed him.

6 Also to Shemaiah his son were sons born who governed their fathers' houses, because they *were* men of great ability.

7 The sons of Shemaiah *were* Othni, Rephael, Obed, and Elzabad, whose brothers Elihu and Semachiah *were* able men.

8 All these *were* of the sons of Obed-Edom, they and their sons and their brethren, [p]able men with strength for the work: sixty-two of Obed-Edom.

9 And Meshelemiah had sons and brethren, eighteen able men.

10 Also [q]Hosah, of the children of Merari, had sons: Shimri the first (for *though* he was not the firstborn, his father [r]made him the first),

11 Hilkiah the second, Tebaliah the third, Zechariah the fourth; all the sons and brethren of Hosah *were* thirteen.

12 Among these *were* the divisions of the gatekeepers, among the chief men, *having* duties just like their brethren, to serve in the house of the LORD.

13 And they [s]cast lots for each gate, the small as well as the great, according to their father's house.

---

5 [a] 1 Chr. 16:42; see Dt. 33:17, *note*
6 [b] 1 Chr. 15:16 [c] 1 Chr. 15:19
7 [d] 1 Chr. 23:5
11 [e] Or *Zeri*, v. 3
14 [f] Or *Asharelah*, v. 2
18 [g] Or *Uzziel*, v. 4
20 [h] Or *Shebuel*, v. 4
CHAPTER 26
1 [i] 2 Chr. 35:15 [j] Or *Shelemiah*, v. 14 [k] Or *Korah*, Ps. 42, *title* [l] Or *Ebiasaph*, 1 Chr. 9:19
2 [m] 1 Chr. 9:21
4 [n] 1 Chr. 15:18,21
5 [o] Cp. 1 Chr. 4:10
8 [p] 1 Chr. 9:13
10 [q] 1 Chr. 16:38 [r] Cp. Gen. 48:19
13 [s] 1 Chr. 24:5,31; 25:8

* **25:22** Spelled *Jerimoth* in verse 4

14 The lot for the East *Gate* fell to [a]Shelemiah. Then they cast lots *for* his son Zechariah, a wise counselor, and his lot came out for the North Gate;

15 to Obed-Edom the South Gate, and to his sons the storehouse.*

16 To Shuppim and Hosah *the lot came out* for the West Gate, with the Shallecheth Gate on the ascending highway—watchman opposite watchman.

17 On the east were *six* Levites, on the north four each day, on the south four each day, and for the storehouse* two by two.

18 As for the Parbar* on the west, *there were* four on the highway *and* two at the Parbar.

19 These were the divisions of the gatekeepers among the sons of Korah and among the sons of Merari.

Levites in charge of the treasuries

20 Of the Levites, Ahijah *was* over the treasuries of the [b]house of God and over the treasuries of the [c]dedicated things.

21 The sons of [d]Laadan, the descendants of the Gershonites of Laadan, heads of their fathers' *houses,* of Laadan the Gershonite: [e]Jehieli.

22 The sons of [e]Jehieli, Zetham and Joel his brother, *were* over the treasuries of the house of the LORD.

23 Of the [f]Amramites, the Izharites, the Hebronites, and the Uzzielites:

24 Shebuel the son of Gershom, the son of Moses, *was* overseer of the treasuries.

25 And his brethren by Eliezer *were* Rehabiah his son, Jeshaiah his son, Joram his son, Zichri his son, and Shelomith his son.

26 This Shelomith and his brethren *were* over all the treasuries of the [c]dedicated things [g]which King David and the heads of fathers' *houses,* the captains over thousands and hundreds, and the captains of the army, had dedicated.

27 Some of the spoils won in battles they dedicated to maintain the house of the LORD.

28 And all that Samuel the seer, Saul the son of Kish, Abner the son of Ner, and Joab the son of Zeruiah had dedicated, every dedicated *thing,* was under the hand of Shelomith and his brethren.

Officials and judges over Israel outside Jerusalem

29 Of the Izharites, Chenaniah and his sons *performed* duties as [h]officials and judges over Israel [i]outside Jerusalem.

30 Of the Hebronites, [j]Hashabiah and his brethren, one thousand seven hundred able men, had the oversight of Israel on the west side of the Jordan for all the business of the LORD, and in the service of the king.

31 Among the Hebronites, [k]Jerijah *was* head of the Hebronites according to his genealogy of the fathers. In the fortieth year of the reign of David they were sought, and there were found among them capable men at Jazer of Gilead.

32 And his brethren *were* two thousand seven hundred able men, heads of fathers' *houses,* whom King David made officials over the Reubenites, the Gadites, and the half-tribe of Manasseh, for every matter pertaining to God and the affairs of the king.

The twelve monthly captains

27 AND the children of Israel, according to their number, the heads of fathers' *houses,* the captains of thousands and hundreds and their officers, served the king in every matter of the *military* divisions. *These divisions* came in and went out month by month throughout all the months of the year, each division *having* twenty-four thousand.

2 Over the first division for the [l]first month *was* [m]Jashobeam the son of Zabdiel, and in his division *were* twenty-four thousand;

3 *he was* of the children of Perez, and the chief of all the captains of the army for the first month.

4 Over the division of the [l]second month *was* [n]Dodai an Ahohite, and of his division Mikloth also *was* the leader; in his division *were* twenty-four thousand.

5 The third captain of the army for the [l]third month *was* [o]Benaiah, the son of Jehoiada the priest, who was chief; in his division *were* twenty-four thousand.

6 This was the [p]Benaiah *who was* mighty *among* the thirty, and was over the thirty; in his division *was* Ammizabad his son.

7 The fourth *captain* for the

14 *a* Or *Meshelemiah,* 1 Chr. 26:1
20 *b* 1 Chr. 9:26 *c* i.e. *holy.* 2 Sam. 8:11
21 *d* Or *Libni,* 1 Chr. 6:17 *e* Or *Jehiel,* 1 Chr. 23:8
23 *f* Num. 3:27
26 *g* 2 Sam. 8:11–12
29 *h* 1 Chr. 23:4 *i* Neh. 11:16
30 *j* 1 Chr. 27:17
31 *k* Or *Jeriah,* 1 Chr. 23:19
CHAPTER 27
2 *l* See Lev. 23:2, *note* *m* 1 Chr. 11:11
4 *n* Or *Dodo,* 1 Chr. 11:12
5 *o* 1 Chr. 18:17
6 *p* 2 Sam. 23:20–23

*
26:15 Hebrew *asuppim* **26:17** Hebrew *asuppim*
26:18 Probably a court or colonnade extending west of the temple

[a]fourth month *was* [b]Asahel the brother of Joab, and Zebadiah his son after him; in his division *were* twenty-four thousand.

8 The fifth *captain* for the [a]fifth month *was* [c]Shamhuth the Izrahite; in his division were twenty-four thousand.

9 The sixth *captain* for the [a]sixth month *was* [d]Ira the son of Ikkesh the Tekoite; in his division *were* twenty-four thousand.

10 The seventh *captain* for the [a]seventh month *was* [e]Helez the Pelonite, of the children of Ephraim; in his division *were* twenty-four thousand.

11 The eighth *captain* for the [a]eighth month *was* [f]Sibbechai the Hushathite, of the Zarhites; in his division *were* twenty-four thousand.

12 The ninth *captain* for the [a]ninth month *was* [d]Abiezer the Anathothite, of the Benjamites; in his division *were* twenty-four thousand.

13 The tenth *captain* for the [a]tenth month *was* [g]Maharai the Netophathite, of the Zarhites; in his division *were* twenty-four thousand.

14 The eleventh *captain* for the [a]eleventh month *was* [h]Benaiah the Pirathonite, of the children of Ephraim; in his division *were* twenty-four thousand.

15 The twelfth *captain* for the [a]twelfth month *was* [i]Heldai the Netophathite, of Othniel; in his division *were* twenty-four thousand.

The chief officers of the twelve tribes

16 Furthermore, over the tribes of Israel: the officer over the Reubenites *was* Eliezer the son of Zichri; over the Simeonites, Shephatiah the son of Maachah;

17 *over* the Levites, Hashabiah the son of Kemuel; over the Aaronites, Zadok;

18 *over* Judah, [j]Elihu, *one* of David's brothers; *over* Issachar, Omri the son of Michael;

19 *over* Zebulun, Ishmaiah the son of Obadiah; *over* Naphtali, Jerimoth the son of Azriel;

20 *over* the children of Ephraim, Hoshea the son of Azaziah; *over* the half-tribe of Manasseh, Joel the son of Pedaiah;

21 *over* the half-*tribe* of Manasseh in Gilead, Iddo the son of Zechariah; *over* Benjamin, Jaasiel the son of Abner;

22 *over* Dan, Azarel the son of Jeroham. These *were* the leaders of the tribes of Israel.

The forbidden numbering (cp. 21:1–7)

23 But David did not take the number of those twenty years old and under, because the LORD had said He would [k]multiply Israel like the [l]stars of the heavens.

24 Joab the son of Zeruiah began a census, but he did not finish, for [m]wrath came upon Israel because of this census; nor was the number recorded in the account of the chronicles of King David.

David's various officials

25 And Azmaveth the son of Adiel *was* over the king's treasuries; and Jehonathan the son of Uzziah was over the storehouses in the field, in the cities, in the villages, and in the fortresses.

26 Ezri the son of Chelub was over those who did the work of the field for tilling the ground.

27 And Shimei the Ramathite *was* over the vineyards, and Zabdi the Shiphmite was over the produce of the vineyards for the supply of wine.

28 Baal-Hanan the Gederite was over the olive trees and the sycamore trees that *were* in the [n]lowlands, and Joash *was* over the store of oil.

29 And Shitrai the Sharonite *was* over the herds that fed in Sharon, and Shaphat the son of Adlai was over the herds *that were* in the valleys.

30 Obil the Ishmaelite *was* over the camels, Jehdeiah the Meronothite *was* over the donkeys,

31 and Jaziz the [o]Hagrite *was* over the flocks. All these *were* the officials over King David's property.

David's special counselors

32 Also Jehonathan, David's uncle, *was* a counselor, a wise man, and a scribe; and Jehiel the son of Hachmoni *was* with the king's sons.

33 [p]Ahithophel *was* the king's counselor, and [q]Hushai the Archite *was* the king's companion.

34 After Ahithophel *was* Jehoiada the son of Benaiah, then [r]Abiathar. And the general of the king's army *was* Joab.

David assembles and addresses a great convocation (cp. 1 Chr. 23:1)

28 NOW David assembled at Jerusalem all the leaders of Israel: the [s]officers of the tribes and the captains of the divisions who served

7
a See Lev. 23:2, *note*
b 1 Chr. 11:26
8
c Or *Shammah,* 2 Sam. 23:25; or *Shammoth,* 1 Chr. 11:27
9
d 1 Chr. 11:28
10
e 1 Chr. 11:27
11
f 1 Chr. 11:29; 20:4
13
g 1 Chr. 11:30
14
h 1 Chr. 11:31
15
i Or *Heled,* 1 Chr. 11:30
18
j Or *Eliab,* 1 Sam. 16:6
23
k Dt. 6:3
l Gen. 22:17; 26:4; Ex. 32:13; Dt. 1:10
24
m 2 Sam. 24:12–15; 1 Chr. 21:7–8
28
n See Dt. 1:7, *note*
31
o 1 Chr. 5:10
33
p 2 Sam. 15:12
q 2 Sam. 15:32–37
34
r 1 Ki. 1:7
CHAPTER 28
1
s 1 Chr. 27:16–22

the king, the [a]captains over thousands and captains over hundreds,
and the [b]stewards over all the substance and possessions of the king
and of his sons, with the officials, the
valiant men, and all the [c]mighty men
of valor.
2 Then King David rose to his feet
and said, "Hear me, my brethren and
my people: I *had* it in my heart to build
a house of rest for the ark of the covenant of the LORD, and for the [d]foot-
stool of our God, and had made preparations to build it.
3 "But God [e]said to me, 'You shall
not build a house for My name, because you *have been* a man of war and
have shed [f]blood.'
4 "However the LORD God of Israel
[g]chose me above all the house of my
father to be king over Israel forever,
for He has chosen [h]Judah *to be* the
ruler. And of the house of Judah, the
house of my father, and among the
sons of my father, He [i]was pleased
with me to make *me* king over all Israel.
5 "And of all my sons (for the LORD
has given me many sons) He has chosen my son [j]Solomon to sit on the
throne of the kingdom of the LORD
over Israel.
6 "Now He said to me, 'It is your
son Solomon *who* shall build My
house and My courts; for I have chosen him *to be* My son, and I will be his
Father.
7 'Moreover I will establish his
kingdom forever, if he is steadfast to
observe My commandments and My
judgments, as it is this day.'
8 "Now therefore, in the sight of
all Israel, the assembly of the LORD,
and in the hearing of our God, be careful to seek out all the commandments
of the LORD your God, that you may
possess this good land, and leave *it* as
an inheritance for your children after
you forever.

David publicly charges Solomon and gives him the divine plans and gold and silver for the temple

9 "As for you, my son Solomon,
know the God of your father, and
[k]serve Him with a [l]loyal heart and
with a willing mind; for the LORD
searches all [m]hearts and understands
all the intent of the thoughts. If you
[n]seek Him, He will be found by you;
but if you forsake Him, He will [o]cast
you off forever.
10 "Consider now, for the LORD has

1
a 1 Chr. 27:1–15
b 1 Chr. 27:25–31
c 2 Sam. 23:8–39; 1 Chr. 11:10–47
2
d Ps. 99:5
3
e 2 Sam. 7:5–13
f 1 Chr. 22:8
4
g 1 Sam. 16:6–13
h Gen. 49:8–10; 1 Chr. 5:2; Ps. 60:7
i 1 Sam. 13:14; Acts 13:22
5
j 1 Chr. 22:9; 29:1
9
k 1 Sam. 12:24
l 1 Ki. 8:61; see Phil. 3:12, *note*
m 1 Sam. 16:7
n Jer. 29:13
o Dt. 31:17
10
p 1 Chr. 22:13
11
q 1 Ki. 6:3
12
r Ex. 25:40; Heb. 8:5
s *Holy Spirit* (OT): v. 12; 2 Chr. 15:1. (Gen. 1:2; Zech. 12:10)
t i.e. *holy*
13
u 1 Chr. 23:6
15
v Ex. 25:31–39; 1 Ki. 7:49
16
w See Ex. 25:30, *note*
x 1 Ki. 7:48
18
y Ex. 30:1–10
19
z Ex. 25:40
20
aa Dt. 31:6–7; Josh. 1:6–9; 1 Chr.

chosen you to build a house for the
sanctuary; [p]be strong, and do it."
11 Then David gave his son Solomon the plans for the [q]vestibule, its
houses, its treasuries, its upper chambers, its inner chambers, and the place
of the mercy seat;
12 and the [r]plans for all that he had
by the [s]Spirit, of the courts of the
house of the LORD, of all the chambers
all around, of the treasuries of the
house of God, and of the treasuries for
the [t]dedicated things;
13 also for the division of the
priests and the [u]Levites, for all the
work of the service of the house of the
LORD, and for all the articles of service
in the house of the LORD.
14 *He gave* gold by weight for
things of gold, for all articles used in
every kind of service; also *silver* for all
articles of silver by weight, for all articles used in every kind of service;
15 the weight for the [v]lampstands
of gold, and their lamps of gold, by
weight for each lampstand and its
lamps; for the lampstands of silver by
weight, for the lampstand and its
lamps, according to the use of each
lampstand.
16 And by weight *he gave* gold for
the tables of the [w]showbread, for each
[x]table, and silver for the tables of silver;
17 also pure gold for the forks, the
basins, the pitchers of pure gold, and
the golden bowls—*he gave gold* by
weight for every bowl; and for the silver bowls, *silver* by weight for every
bowl;
18 and refined gold by weight for
the [y]altar of incense, and for the construction of the chariot, that is, the
gold cherubim that spread *their wings*
and overshadowed the ark of the covenant of the LORD.
19 "All *this*," *said David*, "the LORD
made me understand in writing, by
His hand upon me, all the works of
these [z]plans."

David encourages Solomon to build the temple

20 And David said to his son Solomon, [aa]"Be strong and of good courage, and do *it;* do not fear nor be
dismayed, for the LORD God—my
God—*will be* with you. He [bb]will not
leave you nor forsake you, until you
have finished all the work for the service of the house of the LORD.

22:13 *bb* Josh. 1:5; Heb. 13:5

21 “*Here are* the divisions of the
priests and the Levites for all the service of the house of God; and [a]every
willing craftsman *will be* with you for
all manner of workmanship, for every
kind of service; also the leaders and
all the people *will be* completely at
your command.”

David, by his example, exhorts the people to give willingly

29 FURTHERMORE King David
said to all the assembly: “My
son Solomon, whom alone God has
[b]chosen, *is* [c]young and inexperienced; and the work *is* great, because
the temple* *is* not for man but for the
LORD God.
2 “Now for the house of my God I
have prepared with all my might: gold
for *things to be made of* gold, silver
for *things of* silver, bronze for *things
of* bronze, iron for *things of* iron, wood
for *things of* wood, onyx stones,
stones to be set, glistening stones of
various colors, all kinds of precious
stones, and marble slabs in abundance.
3 “Moreover, because I have set
my affection on the house of my God,
I have given to the house of my God,
over and above all that I have prepared for the holy house, my own special treasure of gold and silver:
4 [d]“three thousand [e]talents of
gold, of the gold of Ophir, and seven
thousand [e]talents of refined silver, to
overlay the walls of the houses;
5 “the gold for *things of* gold and
the silver for *things of* silver, and for
all kinds of work *to be done* by the
hands of craftsmen. Who *then* is
[f]willing to consecrate himself this
day to the LORD?”

The joyous response

6 Then the leaders of the fathers’
houses, leaders of the tribes of Israel,
the captains of thousands and of hundreds, with the [g]officers over the
king’s work, [h]offered willingly.
7 They gave for the work of the
house of God five thousand talents
and ten thousand [e]darics of gold, ten
thousand talents of silver, eighteen
thousand talents of bronze, and one
hundred thousand talents of iron.
8 And whoever had *precious*
stones gave *them* to the treasury of
the house of the LORD, into the hand of
[i]Jehiel* the Gershonite.

21
a Ex. 35:25–35; 36:1–2; 2 Chr. 2:13–14

CHAPTER 29

1
b 1 Chr. 28:5
c 1 Ki. 3:7; 1 Chr. 22:5

4
d Cp. 1 Chr. 22:14
e See Coinage (OT), Ex. 30:13, *note;* cp. 2 Chr. 2:10, *note*

5
f 2 Ki. 12:4; 2 Chr. 29:31; 2 Cor. 8:5, 12

6
g 1 Chr. 27:25–31
h Ex. 35:25–35

8
i 1 Chr. 23:8

9
j Ex. 25:2; 2 Cor. 9:7
k 1 Ki. 8:61; see Phil. 3:12, *note*

10
l Bible prayers (OT): vv. 10–19; 2 Chr. 6:14. (Gen. 15:2; Hab. 3:1)

11
m Mt. 6:13; 1 Tim. 1:17; Rev. 5:13

15
n Lev. 25:23; Ps. 39:12; Heb. 11:13–14; 1 Pet. 2:11

17
o 1 Chr. 28:9

9 Then the people rejoiced, for
they had offered [j]willingly, because
with a [k]loyal heart they had offered
willingly to the LORD; and King David
also rejoiced greatly.

David’s thanksgiving and prayer

10 Therefore David [1]blessed the
LORD before all the assembly; and David [l]said:

“Blessed are You, LORD God of
Israel, our Father, forever
and ever.
11 [m]Yours, O LORD, *is* the
greatness,
The power and the glory,
The victory and the majesty;
For all *that is* in heaven and in
earth *is Yours;*
Yours *is* the kingdom, O LORD,
And You are exalted as head
over all.
12 Both riches and honor *come*
from You,
And You reign over all.
In Your hand *is* power and
might;
In Your hand *it is* to make
great
And to give strength to all.
13 “Now therefore, our God,
We thank You
And praise Your glorious
name.
14 But who *am* I, and who *are* my
people,
That we should be able to offer
so willingly as this?
For all things *come* from You,
And of Your own we have
given You.
15 [n]For we *are* aliens and pilgrims
before You,
As *were* all our fathers;
Our days on earth *are* as a
shadow,
And without hope.

16 “O LORD our God, all this abundance that we have prepared to build
You a house for Your holy name is
from Your hand, and *is* all Your own.
17 “I know also, my God, that You
[o]test the heart and have pleasure in
uprightness. As for me, in the uprightness of my heart I have willingly offered all these *things;* and now with

*
29:1 Literally *palace* **29:8** Possibly the same as *Jehieli* (compare 26:21,22)

[1](29:10) Observe the order: (1) giving (vv. 3–8); (2) joy (v. 9); (3) praising (v. 10); (4) prayer (vv. 11–19); and (5) worship (v. 20).

joy I have seen Your people, who are
present here to offer willingly to You.
18 "O LORD God of Abraham, Isaac,
and Israel, our fathers, keep this forever in the intent of the thoughts of the
heart of Your people, and fix their
heart toward You.
19 "And give my son Solomon a
[a]loyal heart to keep Your commandments and Your testimonies and Your
statutes, to do all *these things*, and to
build the temple* for which I have
made provision."

The people worship; Solomon enthroned (cp. 1 Chr. 23:1; 1 Ki. 2:12; cp. 1 Ki. 1:1—3:1)

20 Then David said to all the assembly, "Now bless the LORD your
God." So all the assembly blessed the
LORD God of their fathers, and bowed
their heads and prostrated themselves
before the LORD and the king.
21 And they made sacrifices to the
LORD and offered burnt offerings to
the LORD on the next day: a thousand
bulls, a thousand rams, a thousand
lambs, with their drink offerings, and
[b]sacrifices in abundance for all Israel.
22 So they ate and drank before the
LORD with great gladness on that day.
And they made Solomon the son of
David king the [c]second time, and
anointed *him* before the LORD *to be* the
leader, and Zadok *to be* priest.
23 Then Solomon sat on the throne
of the LORD as king instead of David
his father, and prospered; and all Israel obeyed him.
24 All the leaders and the mighty
men, and also all the sons of King David, submitted themselves to King Solomon.
25 So the LORD exalted Solomon exceedingly in the sight of all Israel, and
bestowed on him *such* royal majesty
as had not been on any king before
him in Israel.

Reign and death of David (cp. 2 Sam. 5:4,5; 1 Ki. 2:10–12; 1 Chr. 3:4)

26 Thus David the son of Jesse
reigned over all Israel.
27 And the period that he reigned
over Israel *was* forty years; seven
years he reigned in Hebron, and
thirty-three *years* he reigned in Jerusalem.
28 So he [d]died in a good old age,
full of days and riches and honor; and
Solomon his son [e]reigned in his place.
29 Now the acts of King David, first
and last, indeed they *are* written in the
book of Samuel the seer, in the [1]book
of Nathan the prophet, and in the
book of Gad the seer,
30 with all his reign and his might,
and the events that happened to him,
to Israel, and to all the kingdoms of
the lands.

19 *a* 1 Ki. 8:61; see Phil. 3:12, *note*
21 *b* 1 Ki. 8:62–63
22 *c* 1 Ki. 1:32–35; 1 Chr. 23:1
28 *d* Cp. 1 Sam. 27:1 *e* 971 B.C.

*29:19 Literally *palace*

[1](29:29) The OT points to a very extensive literature among the Hebrew people which has not been preserved. Among the uninspired books are the two mentioned here: *The Book of Nathan the Prophet* (also in 2 Chr. 9:29), and *The Book of Gad the Seer*. Among others are: *The Book of Jashar* (Josh. 10:13; 2 Sam. 1:18); *The Book of the Acts of Solomon* (1 Ki. 11:41); *The Prophecy of Ahijah the Shilonite*, and *The Visions of Iddo the Seer* (2 Chr. 9:29; cp. 12:15; 13:22); *The Book of Shemaiah the Prophet* (2 Chr. 12:15); Isaiah's *The Acts of Uzziah* (2 Chr. 26:22); and *The Sayings of Hozai* (2 Chr. 33:19). Some of the facts recorded in these now lost books appear, under the guidance of the Holy Spirit, in the historical records of the OT. The discoveries at and near Qumran included portions of over 200 noncanonical books.

The Second Book of the
CHRONICLES

Author: Unknown *Theme:* Judah's Greatness *Date of writing:* 5th Cent. B.C.

SECOND CHRONICLES begins in the original with the Hebrew connective "*waw*," indicating that it is a continuation of the historical narrative; for 1 and 2 Chronicles formed one book in the old Hebrew Bible (the Masoretic Text of the OT). Second Chronicles records several reformations, including the most extended account of any revival in Bible history—that under Hezekiah, chs. 29—31.

The book may be divided as follows:

I. The Reign of Solomon, with a Detailed Account of the Building and Dedication of the Temple, 1—9.

II. The History of Judah from the Reign of Rehoboam to the Destruction of Jerusalem and the Captivity, 10—36.

I. The Reign of Solomon; the Temple Built and Dedicated, 1—9

The LORD exalts Solomon, who sacrifices and prays for wisdom (1 Ki. 2:12; 3:4–9; 1 Chr. 29:23–25)

1 NOW Solomon the son of David was strengthened in his kingdom, and the LORD his God *was* with him and exalted him exceedingly.

2 And Solomon spoke to all Israel, to the [a]captains of thousands and of hundreds, to the judges, and to every leader in all Israel, the heads of the fathers' *houses.*

3 Then Solomon, and all the assembly with him, went to the [b]high place that *was* at [c]Gibeon; for the [d]tabernacle of meeting with God was there, which Moses the servant of the LORD had [e]made in the wilderness.

4 But David had brought up the [f]ark of God from Kirjath Jearim to *the place* David had prepared for it, for he had pitched a tent for it at Jerusalem.

5 Now the [g]bronze altar that Bezalel the son of Uri, the son of Hur, had [h]made, he put* before the tabernacle of the LORD; Solomon and the assembly sought Him *there.*

6 And Solomon went up there to the bronze altar before the LORD, which *was* at the tabernacle of meeting, and [i]offered a thousand burnt offerings on it.

7 On that night God [j]appeared to Solomon, and said to him, "Ask! What shall I give you?"

8 And Solomon said to God: "You have shown great [k]mercy to David my father, and have made me king in his [l]place.

9 "Now, O LORD God, let Your [m]promise to David my father be established, for You have made me king over a people like the [n]dust of the earth in multitude.

10 "Now give me wisdom and knowledge, that I may go out and come in before this people; for who can judge this great people of Yours?"

God pleased; grants Solomon both wisdom and riches (1 Ki. 3:10–28)

11 Then God said to Solomon: "Because this was in your heart, and you have not asked riches or wealth or honor or the life of your enemies, nor have you asked long life—but have asked wisdom and knowledge for yourself, that you may judge My people over whom I have made you king—

12 "wisdom and knowledge *are* granted to you; and I will give you riches and wealth and honor, such as none of the kings have had who *were* before you, nor shall any after you have the [o]like."

13 So Solomon came to Jerusalem from the [b]high place that *was* at Gibeon, from before the tabernacle of meeting, and reigned over Israel.

14 And [p]Solomon gathered chariots and horsemen; he had one thousand four hundred chariots and twelve thousand horsemen, whom he stationed in the chariot cities and with the king in Jerusalem.

15 Also the king made silver and gold as common in Jerusalem as stones, and he made cedars as abundant as the sycamores which *are* in the [q]lowland.

16 And Solomon had horses imported from [r]Egypt and Keveh; the

CHAPTER 1
2 *a* 1 Chr. 27:1–34
3 *b* See Jud. 3:7 and 1 Ki. 3:2, *notes;* cp. 1 Ki. 15:14 and Amos 4:4, *notes* *c* Cp. 1 Chr. 16:39 *d* See 1 Chr. 16:37, *note* *e* Ex. 25:1–27:21; 35:4–36:38
4 *f* Ex. 25:10–22; 37:1–9; 2 Sam. 6:2–17; 1 Chr. 15:25–16:1
5 *g* Ex. 27:1–2 *h* Ex. 38:1–7
6 *i* Cp. Num. 7:1–89; Lk. 21:1–4
7 *j* 1 Ki. 3:5
8 *k* Ps. 18:50 *l* 1 Chr. 28:5
9 *m* 2 Sam. 7:8–16 *n* Gen. 13:16
12 *o* 2 Chr. 9:22; cp. Mt. 12:42
14 *p* vv. 14–17; 1 Ki. 10:26–29; 2 Chr. 9:25–28 **1:15** *q* See Dt. 1:7, *note* **1:16** *r* Cp. Dt. 17:16

* 1:5 Some authorities read *it was there.*

king's merchants bought them in Keveh at the *current* price.
17 They also acquired and imported from Egypt a chariot for six
hundred *shekels* of silver, and a horse
for one hundred and fifty; thus,
through their agents,* they exported
them to all the kings of the [a]Hittites
and the kings of Syria.

Solomon prepares to build the temple (1 Ki. 5:1–18; 7:12,14)

2 THEN [b]Solomon determined to
build a temple for the name of the
LORD, and a royal house for himself.
2 Solomon selected seventy thousand men to bear burdens, eighty
thousand to quarry *stone* in the mountains, and three thousand six hundred
to oversee them.
3 Then Solomon sent to [c]Hiram*
king of Tyre, saying:

As you have dealt with David
my father, and sent him cedars
to build himself a [d]house to
dwell in, *so deal with me.*
4 Behold, I am building a temple
for the name of the LORD my
God, to [e]dedicate *it* to Him, to
burn before Him sweet
incense, for the continual
[f]showbread, for the [g]burnt
offerings morning and evening,
on the [h]Sabbaths, on the New
Moons, and on the set feasts of
the LORD our God. This *is an*
ordinance forever to Israel.
5 And the temple which I build
will be great, for our God is
greater than all [i]gods.
6 But who is able to build Him a
temple, since heaven and the
heaven of heavens cannot
contain Him? Who *am* I then,
that I should build Him a
temple, except to burn sacrifice
before Him?
7 Therefore send me at once a
man skillful to work in gold
and silver, in bronze and iron,
in purple and crimson and
blue, who has skill to engrave
with the skillful men who are
with me in Judah and
Jerusalem, whom David my
father [j]provided.
8 Also send me cedar and
cypress and [k]algum logs from
Lebanon, for I know that your
servants have skill to cut
timber in Lebanon; and indeed
my servants *will be* with your
servants,
9 to prepare timber for me in
abundance, for the temple
which I am about to build *shall*
be great and wonderful.
10 And indeed I will give to your
servants, the woodsmen who
cut timber, twenty thousand
[1]kors of ground wheat, twenty
thousand kors of barley,

17
a See 2 Ki. 7:6, *note*
CHAPTER 2
1
b 2 Sam. 5:13–14; 1 Chr. 3:5
3
c See 1 Ki. 7:13, *note*
d 1 Chr. 14:1
4
e Sanctification (OT): v. 4; 2 Chr. 5:1. (Gen. 2:3; Zech. 8:3)
f See Ex. 25:30, *note*
g Ex. 29:38–42
h Num. 28:9–10
5
i 1 Cor. 8:5–6
7
j 1 Chr. 22:15
8
k See 1 Ki. 10:11, *note*

*
1:17 Literally *by their hands* 2:3 Hebrew *Huram* (compare 1 Kings 5:1)

[1](2:10) Weights and Measures. The ancient systems of weights and measures were not as precise as the standards known in later years. For example, the cubit measure was based upon the length of the forearm (Babylonian) or six handbreadths (Egyptian and Hebrew). In Babylon and Egypt there were two cubit measures: the common and the royal. They ranged from 20.65–21.26 inches (Babylonian) and 17.70–20.64 inches (Egyptian). The Israelites also had two cubit measures: standard (Dt. 3:11; 2 Chr. 3:3), and another which was one handbreadth longer than the standard cubit (Ezek. 40:5; 43:13).

With weights, too, there were various standards in ancient times. In weighing silver and gold one Hebrew maneh was equal to 50 shekels, but with other commodities 60 shekels to the maneh was standard. In Babylon 60 shekels to the maneh was the scale in both precious metals and grains, etc.

(1) Linear Measures. In Israel the unit was the standard cubit, about 18 inches in length. The table: 4 fingers = 1 handbreadth, about 3 in. (cp. Ex. 37:12); 3 handbreadths (palms) = 1 span, about 9 in. (cp. 1 Sam. 17:4); 2 spans = 1 cubit; 1 cubit + 1 handbreadth = 1 long cubit (about 21 in.); 6 cubits = 1 (measuring) rod (reed); 6 long cubits = 1 rod in Ezek. 40:5, about 10 feet; 400 cubits = 1 stadion (cp. Lk. 24:13), about 600 feet.

(2) Dry Measures. The unit was the ephah, about ½ bushel. The table: 6 kabs (cp. 2 Ki. 6:25—slightly over 1 quart to the kab) = 1 seah, about 7 qts. (cp. 2 Chr. 2:10); 3 seahs or 10 omers (cp. Ex. 16:16) = 1 ephah (Ex. 16:36); 10 ephahs = 1 kor (homer), about 6 bushels (Ezek. 45:11).

(3) Liquid Measures. The unit was the bath, about 6 gallons. The capacity of the bath was equal to that of the ephah (dry measure). The table: 12 logs (cp. Lev. 14:19—about 1/3 qt. to the log) = 1 hin, about 4 qts. (cp. Num. 15:4); 6 hins = 1 bath (cp. Isa. 5:10); 10 baths = 1 kor (homer), about 60 gallons (Ezek. 45:14).

(4) Weights. The Hebrews used scales and weights (Lev. 19:36), weighing money as well as other commodities (Jer. 32:10). The table (except for coinage): 10 gerahs (cp. Lev. 19:36) or

twenty thousand baths of wine,
and twenty thousand baths of
oil.

11 Then [a]Hiram king of Tyre answered in writing, which he sent to
Solomon:

Because the LORD loves His
people, He has made you king
over [b]them.

12 Hiram* also said:

Blessed *be* the LORD God of
Israel, who made heaven and
earth, for He has given King
David a wise son, endowed
with prudence and
understanding, who will build
a temple for the LORD and a
royal house for himself!

13 And now I have sent a skillful
man, endowed with
understanding, [c]Huram my
master* *craftsman*

14 (the son of a woman of the
daughters of Dan, and his
father was a man of Tyre),
skilled to work in gold and
silver, bronze and iron, stone
and wood, purple and blue,
fine linen and crimson, and to
make any engraving and to
accomplish any plan which
may be given to him, with
your skillful men and with the
skillful men of my lord David
your father.

15 Now therefore, the wheat, the
barley, the oil, and the wine
which my lord has spoken of,
let him send to his servants.

16 And we will cut wood from
Lebanon, as much as you
need; we will bring it to you in
rafts by sea to Joppa, and you
will carry it up to Jerusalem.

17 Then [d]Solomon numbered all
the [e]aliens who *were* in the land of
Israel, after the census in which David
his father had numbered them; and
there were found to be one hundred
and fifty-three thousand six hundred.
18 And he made seventy thousand
of them bearers of burdens, eighty
thousand stonecutters in the mountain, and three thousand six hundred
overseers to make the people work.

Solomon begins to build the house of the LORD, the temple in Jerusalem (1 Ki. 6:1)

3 NOW Solomon began to build the
house of the LORD at Jerusalem on
Mount [f]Moriah, where *the LORD** had
appeared to his father David, at the
place that David had prepared on the
[g]threshing floor of Ornan* the Jebusite.
2 And he began to build on the
[h]second *day* of the second month in
the fourth year of his reign.

Dimensions and materials of the temple (1 Ki. 6:2–38; 7:13–22)

3 This is the [i]foundation which
Solomon laid for building the house of
God: The length *was* sixty [j]cubits (by
cubits according to the former measure) and the width twenty cubits.
4 And the [k]vestibule that *was* in
front *of the sanctuary** was twenty
cubits long across the width of the
house, and the height *was* [1]one hundred and* twenty. He overlaid the inside with pure gold.
5 The [l]larger room* he [m]paneled
with cypress which he overlaid with
fine gold, and he carved palm trees
and chainwork on it.
6 And he decorated the house with
precious stones for beauty, and the
gold *was* gold from Parvaim.
7 He also overlaid the house—the
beams and doorposts, its walls and
doors—with gold; and he carved cherubim on the walls.
8 And he made the [n]Most Holy
Place. Its length was according to the
width of the house, twenty cubits, and
its width twenty cubits. He overlaid it
with six hundred [o]talents of fine gold.
9 The weight of the nails *was* fifty

11
a See 1 Ki. 7:13, *note*
b 2 Chr. 9:8
13
c Or *Hiram.* See 1 Ki. 7:13, *note*
17
d Cp. 1 Ki. 5:13–16
e 1 Chr. 22:2
CHAPTER 3
1
f Gen. 22:2–14
g 1 Chr. 21:15–28
2
h See Lev. 23:2, *note*
3
i 1 Chr. 28:11–19
j See Weights and Measures (OT), 2 Chr. 2:10, *note*
4
k 1 Ki. 6:3; 1 Chr. 28:11
5
l 1 Ki. 6:17
m 1 Ki. 6:15; Jer. 22:14
8
n Ex. 26:33
o See Coinage (OT), Ex. 30:13, *note*

*

2:12 Hebrew *Huram* (compare 1 Kings 5:1)
2:13 Literally *father* (compare 1 Kings 7:13,14)
3:1 Literally *He,* following Masoretic Text and Vulgate; Septuagint reads *the LORD;* Targum reads *the Angel of the LORD.* • Spelled *Araunah* in 2 Samuel 24:16ff **3:4** The main room of the temple; elsewhere called the holy place (compare 1 Kings 6:3) • Following Masoretic Text, Septuagint, and Vulgate; Arabic, some manuscripts of the Septuagint, and Syriac omit *one hundred and.*
3:5 Literally *house*

grains = 1 beka or one-half shekel, about 1/5 ounce (cp. Ex. 38:26); 20 gerahs = 1 shekel, about 2/5 ounce (Ex. 30:13; Lev. 27:25); 50 shekels = 1 mina, about 1¼ lb. (Ezek. 45:12); 60 minas = 1 talent, about 75 lbs. (cp. 1 Ki. 9:14).

Prior to 500 B.C. the Hebrews did not deal in coins, financial transactions being carried on by a system of barter. See Coinage (OT), Ex. 30:13, *note.*

[1](3:4) The height of the vestibule. Compare 1 Ki. 6:2, which states that the height of the building itself was thirty cubits. See 1 Chr. 11:11, *note.*

shekels of gold; and he overlaid the
upper [a]area with gold.
10 In the Most Holy Place he made
two cherubim, [b]fashioned by carving,
and [c]overlaid them with gold.
11 The wings of the cherubim *were*
twenty cubits in *overall* length: one
wing *of the one cherub was* five cubits, touching the wall of the room,
and the other wing *was* five cubits,
touching the wing of the other cherub;
12 *one* wing of the other cherub
was five cubits, touching the wall of
the room, and the other wing *also was*
five cubits, touching the wing of the
other cherub.
13 The wings of these cherubim
spanned twenty cubits overall. They
stood on their feet, and they faced inward.
14 And he made the [d]veil of blue,
purple, crimson, and fine linen, and
wove cherubim into it.
15 [e]Also he made in front of the
temple* two pillars [f]thirty-five* cubits high, and the capital that *was* on
the top of each of *them* was five cubits.
16 He made wreaths of chainwork,
as in the inner sanctuary, and put
them on top of the pillars; and he
made one hundred pomegranates,
and put *them* on the wreaths of chainwork.
17 Then he set up the pillars before
the temple, one on the right hand and
the other on the left; he called the
name of the one on the right hand [g]Ja-
chin, and the name of the one on the
left [h]Boaz.

Various furnishings in the temple: bronze altar, Sea of cast bronze, etc. (1 Ki. 7:23–50)

4 MOREOVER he made a bronze
[i]altar: twenty [j]cubits was its
length, twenty cubits its width, and
ten cubits its height.
2 Then he made the [k]Sea of cast
bronze, ten cubits from one brim to
the other; *it was* completely round. Its
height *was* five cubits, and a line of
thirty cubits measured its circumference.
3 And under it *was* the likeness of
oxen encircling it all around, ten to a
cubit, all the way around the Sea. The
oxen *were* cast in two rows, when it
was cast.
4 It stood on twelve [l]oxen: three
looking toward the north, three looking toward the west, three looking toward the south, and three looking toward the east; the Sea *was set* upon
them, and all their back parts *pointed*
inward.
5 It *was* a handbreadth thick; and
its brim was shaped like the brim of a
cup, *like* a lily blossom. It contained
[m]three thousand* [j]baths.
6 He also made ten [n]lavers, and
put five on the right side and five on
the left, to wash in them; such things
as they offered for the burnt offering
they would wash in them, but the Sea
was for the [o]priests to wash in.
7 And he made ten [p]lampstands of
gold according to their design, and set
them in the temple, five on the right
side and five on the left.
8 He also made ten [q]tables, and
placed *them* in the temple, five on the
right side and five on the left. And he
made one hundred [r]bowls of gold.
9 Furthermore he made the
[1][s]court of the priests, and the [t]great
court and doors for the court; and he
overlaid these doors with bronze.
10 He set the Sea on the right side,
toward the southeast.
11 Then [u]Huram made the pots and
the shovels and the bowls. So Huram
finished doing the work that he was to
do for King Solomon for the house of
God:
12 the two pillars and the bowl-
shaped capitals *that were* on top of
the two pillars; the two networks covering the two bowl-shaped capitals
which *were* on top of the pillars;
13 four hundred pomegranates for
the two networks (two rows of pomegranates for each network, to cover
the two bowl-shaped capitals that
were on the pillars);
14 he also made [v]carts and the lavers on the carts;
15 one Sea and twelve oxen under
it;
16 also the pots, the shovels, the
forks—and all their articles Huram
his master* *craftsman* made of burnished bronze for King Solomon for
the house of the LORD.
17 In the plain of Jordan the king

9 a 1 Chr. 28:11
10 b Heb. uncertain c Cp. Ex. 25:18–19
14 d Ex. 26:31; Mt. 27:51; Heb. 9:3
15 e vv. 15–17 f Cp. 1 Ki. 7:15; see 1 Chr. 11:11, *note*
17 g Lit. *He shall establish* h Lit. *In it is strength*
CHAPTER 4
1 i Cp. Ex. 27:1–8 j See Weights and Measures (OT), 2 Chr. 2:10, *note*
2 k 1 Ki. 7:23; Ex. 30:17–21
4 l 1 Ki. 7:25; cp. Jer. 52:20
5 m Cp. 1 Ki. 7:26; see 1 Chr. 11:11, *note*
6 n 1 Ki. 7:38, 40 o Ex. 30:19–21
7 p Cp. Ex. 25:31–40; 1 Ki. 7:49
8 q Cp. Ex. 25:23–30; 1 Ki. 7:48 r 1 Chr. 28:17
9 s 1 Ki. 6:36 t 2 Ki. 21:5
11 u Or *Hiram.* See 1 Ki. 7:13, *note*

4:14 v 1 Ki. 7:27–43

*

3:15 Literally *house* • Or *eighteen* (compare 1 Kings 7:15; 2 Kings 25:17; and Jeremiah 52:21)
4:5 Or *two thousand* (compare 1 Kings 7:26)
4:16 Literally *father*

[1](4:9) There was no court of the priests in the tabernacle of meeting.

had them cast in clay molds, between
Succoth and Zeredah.*
18 And Solomon had all these articles made in such great abundance
that the weight of the bronze was not
determined.
19 Thus Solomon had all the furnishings made for the house of God:
the altar of gold and the tables on
which *was* the [a]showbread;
20 the [b]lampstands with their
lamps of pure gold, to burn in the prescribed manner in front of the inner
sanctuary,
21 with the flowers and the lamps
and the wick-trimmers of gold, of pur-
est gold;
22 the trimmers, the bowls, the ladles, and the censers of pure gold. As
for the entry of the sanctuary, its inner
doors to the Most Holy *Place*, and the
doors of the main hall of the temple,
were gold.

Ark brought in: the Shekinah glory fills the house (1 Ki. 7:51—8:11)

5 SO all the work that Solomon had
done for the house of the LORD
was finished; and Solomon brought in
the things which his father David had
[c]dedicated: the silver and the gold
and all the furnishings. And he put
them in the treasuries of the house of
God.
2 [d]Now Solomon assembled the
elders of Israel and all the heads of the
tribes, the [e]chief fathers of the children of Israel, in Jerusalem, that they
might bring the ark of the covenant of
the LORD up from the City of David,
which *is* Zion.
3 Therefore all the men of Israel
assembled with the king at the [f]feast,
which *was* in the [g]seventh month.
4 So all the elders of Israel came,
and the [h]Levites took up the ark.
5 Then they brought up the ark,
the tabernacle of meeting, and all the
holy furnishings that *were* in the tabernacle. The priests and the Levites
brought them up.
6 Also King Solomon, and all the
congregation of Israel who were assembled with him before the ark, were
sacrificing sheep and oxen that could
not be counted or numbered for multitude.
7 Then the priests brought in the
ark of the covenant of the LORD to its
place, into the [i]inner sanctuary of the
temple,* to the Most Holy *Place*, under the wings of the cherubim.
8 For the cherubim spread *their*
wings over the place of the ark, and
the cherubim overshadowed the ark
and its poles.
9 The [j]poles extended so that the
ends of the poles of the ark could be
seen from *the holy place*, in front of
the inner sanctuary; but they could
not be seen from outside. And they are
there to this day.
10 [k]Nothing was in the ark except
the [l]two tablets which Moses put
there at Horeb, when the LORD made *a*
covenant with the children of Israel,
when they had come out of Egypt.
11 And it came to pass when the
priests came out of the *Most* Holy
Place (for all the priests who *were* present had sanctified themselves, without keeping to their [m]divisions),
12 and the Levites *who were* the
[n]singers, all those of Asaph and Heman and Jeduthun, with their sons
and their brethren, stood at the east
end of the altar, clothed in white linen,
having cymbals, stringed instruments
and harps, and with them one hundred and twenty priests sounding with
trumpets—
13 indeed it came to pass, when the
trumpeters and singers *were* as one, to
make one sound to be heard in praising and thanking the LORD, and when
they lifted up their voice with the
trumpets and cymbals and instruments of music, and praised the LORD,
saying:

"*For He is* good,
For His mercy *endures*
[o]forever,"*

that the house, the house of the LORD,
was filled with a [p]cloud,
14 so that the priests could not continue ministering because of the
cloud; for the [q]glory of the LORD filled
the house of God.

Solomon's sermon (1 Ki. 8:12–21)

6 THEN Solomon spoke:
"The LORD [r]said He would
dwell in the [s]dark cloud.
2 I have surely built You an
exalted house,
And a [t]place for You to dwell
in forever."
3 Then the king turned around
and [u]blessed the whole assembly of
Israel, while all the assembly of Israel
was standing.

19 *a* See Ex. 25:30, *note*
20 *b* Cp. Ex. 25:31–40; 1 Ki. 7:49
CHAPTER 5
1 *c Sanctification* (OT): v. 1; 2 Chr. 29:5. (Gen. 2:3; Zech. 8:3)
2 *d* Cp. 2 Sam. 6:1–2; 1 Chr. 13:1–6
e Ps. 47:9
3 *f* Lev. 23:34; 2 Chr. 7:8–10
g See Lev. 23:2, *note*
4 *h* 1 Chr. 15:2,15
7 *i* 2 Chr. 4:20
9 *j* Ex. 25:13–15
10 *k* Cp. Heb. 9:4
l Ex. 25:16; Dt. 10:2–5
11 *m* 1 Chr. 24:1–5
12 *n* 1 Chr. 25:1–7
13 *o* 1 Chr. 16:34; 2 Chr. 7:3
p vv. 11–14; see Ex. 40:34, *note*
14 *q* Ezek. 43:5
CHAPTER 6
1 *r* Ex. 19:9; 20:21
s Ps. 97:2
2 *t* 2 Chr. 7:12
3 *u* 2 Sam. 6:18

*
4:17 Spelled *Zaretan* in 1 Kings 7:46 **5:7** Literally *house* **5:13** Compare Psalm 106:1

4 And he said: "Blessed *be* the LORD God of Israel, who has fulfilled with His hands *what* He spoke with His mouth to my father David, [a]saying,

5 'Since the day that I brought My people out of the land of Egypt, I have chosen no city from any tribe of Israel *in which* to build a house, that My name might be there, nor did I choose any man to be a ruler over My people Israel.

6 'Yet I have [b]chosen Jerusalem, that My name may be there, and I have chosen [c]David to be over My people Israel.'

7 "Now it was in the heart of my father David to [d]build a temple* for the name of the LORD God of Israel.

8 "But the LORD said to my father David, 'Whereas it was in your heart to build a temple for My name, you did well in that it was in your heart.

9 'Nevertheless you shall not build the temple, but your son who will come from your body, he shall build the temple for My [e]name.'

10 "So the LORD has fulfilled His word which He spoke, and I have filled the position of my father David, and [f]sit on the throne of Israel, as the LORD promised; and I have built the temple for the name of the LORD God of Israel.

11 "And [g]there I have put the ark, in which *is* the covenant of the LORD which He made with the children of Israel."

Solomon's prayer of dedication
(1 Ki. 8:22–61)

12 [h]Then *Solomon** stood [i]before the altar of the LORD in the presence of all the assembly of Israel, and spread out his hands

13 (for Solomon had made a bronze platform five [j]cubits long, five cubits wide, and three cubits high, and had set it in the midst of the court; and he stood on it, knelt down on his knees before all the assembly of Israel, and spread out his hands toward heaven);

14 and he [k]said: "LORD God of Israel, [l]*there is* no God in heaven or on earth like You, who keep *Your* [m]covenant and mercy with Your servants who walk before You with all their hearts.

15 "You have kept what You [n]promised Your servant David my father; You have both spoken with Your mouth and fulfilled *it* with Your hand, as *it is* this day.

16 "Therefore, LORD God of Israel, now keep what You promised Your servant David my father, [o]saying, 'You shall not fail to have a man sit before Me on the throne of Israel, only if your sons take heed to their way, that they walk in My law as you have walked before Me.'

17 "And now, O LORD God of Israel, let Your word come true, which You have spoken to Your servant David.

18 "But will God indeed dwell with men on the earth? [p]Behold, heaven and the heaven of heavens cannot contain You. How much less this temple* which I have built!

19 "Yet regard the prayer of Your servant and his supplication, O LORD my God, and listen to the cry and the prayer which Your servant is praying before You:

20 "that Your eyes may be [q]open toward this temple day and night, toward the place where *You* said *You would* put Your name, that You may hear the prayer which Your servant makes [r]toward this place.

21 "And may You hear the supplications of Your servant and of Your people Israel, when they pray toward this place. Hear from heaven Your dwelling place, and when You hear, [s]forgive.

22 "If anyone sins against his neighbor, and is forced to take an [t]oath, and comes *and* takes an oath before Your altar in this temple,

23 "then hear from heaven, and act, and judge Your servants, bringing retribution on the wicked by bringing his way on his own head, and justifying the righteous by giving him according to his [u]righteousness.

24 [v]"Or if Your people Israel are defeated before an [w]enemy because they have sinned against You, and return and confess Your name, and pray and make supplication before You in this temple,

25 "then hear from heaven and forgive the sin of Your people Israel, and bring them back to the land which You gave to them and their fathers.

26 "When the heavens are [x]shut up and there is no rain because they have sinned against You, when they pray

4 *a* 1 Chr. 17:5
6 *b* Dt. 12:5–7; 2 Chr. 12:13 *c* 1 Sam. 16:7–13
7 *d* 2 Sam. 7:2; 1 Chr. 17:1; Ps. 132:1–5
9 *e* 1 Chr. 28:3–6
10 *f* 1 Ki. 2:12; 10:9
11 *g* 2 Chr. 5:7–10
12 *h* Cp. 1 Ki. 3:15 *i* 2 Chr. 7:7–9
13 *j* See Weights and Measures (OT), 2 Chr. 2:10, *note*
14 *k Bible prayers* (OT): vv. 12–42; 2 Chr. 14:11. (Gen. 15:2; Hab. 3:1) *l* Ex. 15:11; Dt. 4:39 *m* Dt. 7:9
15 *n* 1 Chr. 22:9–10
16 *o* 2 Sam. 7:12–16; 1 Ki. 2:4; 2 Chr. 7:18
18 *p* 2 Chr. 2:6; cp. Isa. 66:1
20 *q* 2 Chr. 7:15 *r* Ps. 5:7; Dan. 6:10
21 *s* Mic. 7:18
22 *t* Ex. 22:8–11
23 *u* Job 34:11
24 *v* vv. 24–42; cp. Lev. 26:14–46; Dt. 28:15–30:10 *w* 2 Ki. 21:14–15
6:26 *x* Dt. 28:23–24; 1 Ki. 17:1; cp. 18:45

*

6:7 Literally *house*, and so in verses 8–10
6:12 Literally *he* (compare 1 Kings 8:22)
6:18 Literally *house*

toward this place and confess Your
name, and turn from their sin because
You afflict them,
27 "then hear *in* heaven, and forgive the sin of Your servants, Your
people Israel, that You may teach
them the good way in which they
should walk; and send rain on Your
land which You have given to Your
people as an inheritance.
28 "When there is famine in the
land, pestilence or blight or mildew,
locusts or grasshoppers; when their
enemies besiege them in the land of
their cities; whatever plague or whatever [a]sickness *there is;*
29 "whatever prayer, whatever
supplication is *made* by anyone, or by
all Your people Israel, when each one
knows his own burden and his own
grief, and spreads out his hands to this
temple:
30 "then hear from heaven Your
dwelling place, and forgive, and give
to everyone according to all his ways,
whose heart You know (for [b]You
alone know the [c]hearts of the sons of
men),
31 "that they may [d]fear You, to
walk in Your ways as long as they live
in the land which You gave to our fathers.
32 "Moreover, concerning a [e]for-
eigner, who is not of Your people Israel, but has come from a far country
for the sake of Your great name and
Your mighty hand and Your outstretched arm, when they come and
pray in this temple;
33 "then hear from heaven Your
dwelling place, and do according to all
for which the foreigner calls to You,
that all peoples of the earth may know
Your name and fear You, as *do* Your
people Israel, and that they may know
that this temple which I have built is
called by Your name.
34 "When Your people go out to
battle against their enemies, wherever
You send them, and when they pray to
You toward this city which You have
chosen and the temple which I have
built for Your name,
35 "then hear from heaven their
prayer and their supplication, and
maintain their cause.
36 "When they sin against You (for
there is [f]no one who does not sin),
and You become angry with them and
deliver them to the enemy, and they
take them [g]captive to a land far or
near;

28
a Mic. 6:13
30
b 1 Chr. 28:9; Prov. 21:2; 24:12
c 1 Sam. 16:7
31
d See Ps. 19:9, *note*
32
e Cp. Est. 8:17
36
f Prov. 20:9; Eccl. 7:20; Rom. 3:9, 19,23; 5:12; Gal. 3:10; Jas. 3:2; 1 Jn. 1:8
g Dt. 28:63–68
38
h Dan. 6:10
40
i v. 20
41
j Ps. 132:8–10, 16
42
k 2 Sam. 7:15; Ps. 89:49; Isa. 55:3
CHAPTER 7
1
l 1 Ki. 8:54
m Lev. 9:24; Jud. 6:21; 1 Ki. 18:38; 1 Chr. 21:26
2
n 2 Chr. 5:14
3
o Ps. 136:1

37 "*yet* when they come to themselves in the land where they were
carried captive, and repent, and make
supplication to You in the land of their
captivity, saying, 'We have sinned, we
have done wrong, and have committed wickedness';
38 "and *when* they return to You
with all their heart and with all their
soul in the land of their captivity,
where they have been carried captive,
and pray toward their land which You
gave to their fathers, the [h]city which
You have chosen, and toward the
temple which I have built for Your
name:
39 "then hear from heaven Your
dwelling place their prayer and their
supplications, and maintain their
cause, and forgive Your people who
have sinned against You.
40 "Now, my God, I pray, let Your
eyes be [i]open and *let* Your ears *be*
attentive to the prayer *made* in this
place.

41 "Now therefore,
[j]Arise, O LORD God, to Your
resting place,
You and the ark of Your
strength.
Let Your priests, O LORD God,
be clothed with salvation,
And let Your saints rejoice in
goodness.

42 "O LORD God, do not turn away
the face of Your Anointed;
Remember the [k]mercies of
Your servant David."

The divine confirmation

7 WHEN Solomon had [l]finished
praying, [m]fire came down from
heaven and consumed the burnt offering and the sacrifices; and the glory of
the LORD filled the temple.*
2 And the priests [n]could not enter
the house of the LORD, because the
glory of the LORD had filled the LORD's
house.
3 When all the children of Israel
saw how the fire came down, and the
glory of the LORD on the temple, they
bowed their faces to the ground on the
pavement, and worshiped and praised
the LORD, *saying:*

"For *He is* [o]good,
For His mercy *endures*
forever."*

*
7:1 Literally *house* 7:3 Compare Psalm 106:1

Sacrifices offered to the LORD;
feasting and rejoicing
(1 Ki. 8:62–66)

4 Then the king and all the people
offered sacrifices before the LORD.
5 King Solomon offered a sacrifice of twenty-two thousand bulls and
one hundred and twenty thousand
sheep. So the king and all the people
dedicated the house of God.
6 And the priests attended to their
services; the [a]Levites also with instruments of the [b]music of the LORD,
which King David had made to praise
the LORD, saying, "For His mercy *en-*
dures forever,"* whenever David offered praise by their ministry. The
priests sounded trumpets opposite
them, while all Israel stood.
7 Furthermore Solomon [c]conse-
crated the middle of the court that *was*
in front of the house of the LORD; for
there he offered burnt offerings and
the fat of the peace offerings, because
the bronze altar which Solomon had
made was not able to receive the burnt
offerings, the grain offerings, and the
fat.
8 At that time Solomon kept the
feast seven days, and all Israel with
him, a very great assembly [d]from the
entrance of Hamath to the Brook of
Egypt.*
9 And on the eighth day they held
a [e]sacred assembly, for they observed
the dedication of the altar seven days,
and the feast seven days.
10 On the twenty-third day of the
[f]seventh month he sent the people
away to their tents, joyful and glad of
heart for the good that the LORD had
done for David, for Solomon, and for
His people Israel.
11 Thus Solomon [g]finished the
house of the LORD and the king's
house; and Solomon successfully accomplished all that came into his
heart to make in the house of the LORD
and in his own house.

The LORD's second appearance
to Solomon (1 Ki. 9:1–9)

12 Then the LORD [h]appeared to Solomon by night, and said to him: "I
have heard your prayer, and have
[i]chosen this [j]place for Myself as a
house of sacrifice.
13 "When I [k]shut up heaven and
there is no rain, or command the locusts to devour the land, or send pestilence among My people,
14 "if My people who are [l]called by
My name will [m]humble themselves,

6
a 1 Chr. 15:16
b 2 Chr. 5:12–13
7
c 1 Ki. 9:3
8
d 1 Ki. 4:21, 24; 2 Ki. 14:25
9
e Lev. 23:36
10
f See Lev. 23:2, *note*
11
g 1 Ki. 9:1
12
h 1 Ki. 3:5; 11:9
i Dt. 12:5
j 2 Chr. 6:20
13
k Dt. 28:23–24; 1 Ki. 17:1; 2 Chr. 6:26
14
l Dt. 28:10; Isa. 43:7
m 2 Chr. 12:6–7
15
n 2 Chr. 6:20,40
18
o 2 Sam. 7:12–16; 1 Ki. 2:4; 2 Chr. 6:16
20
p Dt. 28:63–68; 2 Ki. 25:1–7
q Ps. 44:14
21
r 2 Ki. 25:9
s 2 Chr. 29:8
t Dt. 29:24–25; Jer. 22:8–9
CHAPTER 8
1
u 1 Ki. 9:10–14
v 1 Ki. 6:38–7:1
2
w See 1 Ki. 7:13, *note*

and pray and seek My face, and turn
from their wicked ways, then I will
hear from heaven, and will forgive
their sin and heal their land.
15 "Now My eyes will be [n]open and
My ears attentive to prayer *made* in
this place.
16 "For now I have chosen and
sanctified this house, that My name
may be there forever; and My eyes
and My heart will be there perpetually.
17 "As for you, if you walk before
Me as your father David walked, and
do according to all that I have commanded you, and if you keep My statutes and My judgments,
18 "then I will establish the throne
of your kingdom, as I covenanted with
David your father, saying, [o]'You shall
not fail *to have* a man as ruler in Israel.'
19 "But if you turn away and forsake My statutes and My commandments which I have set before you,
and go and serve other gods, and worship them,
20 [p]"then I will uproot them from
My land which I have given them; and
this house which I have sanctified for
My name I will cast out of My sight,
and will make it a proverb and a [q]by-
word among all peoples.
21 "And *as for* [r]this house, which is
exalted, everyone who passes by it
will be [s]astonished and say, 'Why has
the LORD done thus to this [t]land and
this house?'
22 "Then they will answer, 'Because they forsook the LORD God of
their fathers, who brought them out of
the land of Egypt, and embraced other
gods, and worshiped them and served
them; therefore He has brought all
this calamity on them.' "

Solomon's fame and accomplishments
(1 Ki. 9:15–28; 4:1–34; 10:26–29)

8 [u]IT came to pass at the end of
[v]twenty years, when Solomon
had built the house of the LORD and his
own house,
2 that the cities which [w]Hiram*
had given to Solomon, Solomon built
them; and he settled the children of
Israel there.
3 And Solomon went to Hamath
Zobah and seized it.
4 He also built Tadmor in the wil-

*7:6 Compare Psalm 106:1 7:8 That is, the Shihor (compare 1 Chronicles 13:5) 8:2 Hebrew *Huram* (compare 2 Chronicles 2:3) derness, and all the storage cities which he built in [a]Hamath.

5 He built Upper Beth Horon and Lower [b]Beth Horon, fortified cities *with* walls, gates, and bars,

6 also Baalath and all the storage cities that Solomon had, and all the chariot cities and the cities of the cavalry, and all that Solomon [c]desired to build in Jerusalem, in Lebanon, and in all the land of his dominion.

7 All the people *who were* [d]left of the [e]Hittites, Amorites, Perizzites, Hivites, and Jebusites, who *were* not of Israel—

8 that is, their descendants who were left in the land after them, whom the children of Israel did not destroy—from these Solomon raised forced labor, as it is to this day.

9 But Solomon did not make the children of Israel servants for his work. Some *were* men of war, captains of his officers, captains of his chariots, and his cavalry.

10 And others *were* [f]chiefs of the officials of King Solomon: two hundred and fifty, who ruled over the people.

11 Now Solomon brought the [g]daughter of Pharaoh up from the City of David to the house he had built for her, for he said, "My wife shall not dwell in the house of David king of Israel, because *the places* to which the ark of the LORD has come are holy."

12 Then Solomon offered burnt offerings to the LORD on the altar of the LORD which he had built before the vestibule,

13 according to the daily rate, offering [h]according to the commandment of Moses, for the Sabbaths, the New Moons, and the [i]three appointed yearly [j]feasts—the Feast of Unleavened Bread, the Feast of Weeks, and the Feast of Tabernacles.

14 And, according to the order of David his father, he appointed the [k]divisions of the priests for their service, the [l]Levites for their duties (to praise and serve before the priests) as the duty of each day required, and the [m]gatekeepers by their divisions at each gate; for so David the man of God had commanded.

15 They did not depart from the command of the king to the priests and Levites concerning any matter or concerning the [n]treasuries.

16 Now all the work of Solomon was well-ordered from* the day of the foundation of the house of the LORD until it was finished. So the house of the LORD was completed.

17 Then Solomon went to [1][o]Ezion Geber and [p]Elath* on the seacoast, in the land of Edom.

18 And Hiram sent him ships by the hand of his servants, and servants who knew the sea. They went with the servants of Solomon to [q]Ophir, and acquired four hundred and [r]fifty [s]talents of gold from there, and brought it to King Solomon.

Solomon and the queen of Sheba
(1 Ki. 10:1–13)

9 NOW when the [t]queen of Sheba heard of the fame of Solomon, she [u]came to Jerusalem to test Solomon with hard questions, *having* a very great retinue, camels that bore spices, gold in abundance, and precious stones; and when she came to Solomon, she spoke with him about all that was in her heart.

2 So Solomon answered all her questions; there was nothing so difficult for Solomon that he could not explain it to her.

3 And when the queen of Sheba had seen the wisdom of Solomon, the house that he had built,

4 the food on his table, the seating of his servants, the service of his waiters and their apparel, his [v]cupbearers and their apparel, and his entryway by which he went up to the house of the LORD, there was no more spirit in her.

5 Then she said to the king: "*It was* a true report which I heard in my own land about your words and your wisdom.

6 "However I did not believe their words until I came and saw with my own eyes; and indeed the half of the greatness of your wisdom was not told

4 *a* 1 Chr. 18:3,9
5 *b* 1 Chr. 7:24
6 *c* 2 Chr. 7:11
7 *d* Jud. 1:27–35; 2:1–3; cp. Dt. 20:17; Josh. 3:10 *e* See 2 Ki. 7:6, *note*
10 *f* Cp. 1 Ki. 9:23; see 1 Chr. 11:11, *note*
11 *g* 1 Ki. 3:1; 7:8; 11:1
13 *h* Num. 28:1–29:40 *i* Ex. 23:14–17 *j* Lev. 23:1–44
14 *k* 1 Chr. 24:1–31 *l* Cp. 1 Chr. 25:1–31 *m* Cp. 1 Chr. 26:1–19
15 *n* Cp. 1 Chr. 26:20–28
17 *o* 2 Chr. 20:36 *p* 2 Ki. 14:22
18 *q* 1 Chr. 29:4 *r* Cp. 1 Ki. 9:28; see 1 Chr. 11:11, *note* *s* See Coinage (OT), Ex. 30:13, *note*
CHAPTER 9
1 *t* vv. 9–12; cp. Mt. 12:42 *u* Mt. 12:42; Lk. 11:31
4 *v* Neh. 1:11

*

8:16 Following Septuagint, Syriac, and Vulgate; Masoretic Text reads *as far as*. 8:17 Hebrew *Eloth* (compare 2 Kings 14:22)

[1](8:17) Excavations were carried on at Tell el-Kheleifeh, ancient Ezion Geber on the Gulf of Aqabah, during the years 1937–40. Remains of copper refineries of the tenth century B.C., during Solomon's reign, were found. The refineries, built on principles similar to those of modern smelting, were situated to utilize best the air currents blowing through the Arabah from the north.

me. You exceed the fame of which I
heard.
7 "Happy *are* your men and happy
are these your servants, who stand
continually before you and hear your
wisdom!
8 "Blessed be the LORD your God,
who delighted in you, setting you on
His throne *to be* king for the LORD
your God! Because your God has
[a]loved Israel, to establish them forever, therefore He made you king over
them, to do justice and righteousness."
9 And she gave the king one hundred and twenty [b]talents of gold,
spices in great abundance, and precious stones; there never were any
spices such as those the queen of
Sheba gave to King Solomon.
10 Also, the servants of [c]Hiram
and the servants of Solomon, who
brought gold from Ophir, brought [d]al-
gum wood and precious stones.
11 And the king made walkways *of*
the algum wood for the house of the
LORD and for the king's house, also
harps and stringed instruments for
singers; and there were none such *as*
these seen before in the land of Judah.
12 Now King Solomon gave to the
queen of Sheba all she desired, whatever she asked, *much more* than she
had brought to the king. So she turned
and went to her own country, she and
her servants.

Solomon's revenue and splendor
(cp. 1 Ki. 4:1–34)

13 [e]The weight of gold that came to
Solomon yearly was [f]six hundred
and sixty-six talents of gold,
14 besides *what* the traveling merchants and traders brought. And all
the kings of Arabia and governors of
the country brought gold and silver to
Solomon.
15 And King Solomon made two
hundred large shields of hammered
gold; six hundred *shekels* of hammered gold went into each shield.
16 *He* also *made* three hundred
[g]shields of hammered gold; three
hundred [h]*shekels** of gold went into
each shield. The king put them in the
[i]House of the Forest of Lebanon.
17 Moreover the king made a great
throne of ivory, and overlaid it with
pure gold.
18 The throne *had* six steps, with a
footstool of gold, *which were* fastened
to the throne; there were armrests on
either side of the place of the seat, and
two lions stood beside the armrests.
19 Twelve lions stood there, one on
each side of the six steps; nothing like
this had been made for any *other*
kingdom.
20 All King Solomon's drinking
vessels *were* gold, and all the vessels
of the House of the Forest of Lebanon
were pure gold. Not *one was* silver, for
this was accounted as nothing in the
days of Solomon.
21 For the king's ships went to
[j]Tarshish with the servants of Hiram.* Once every three years the
merchant ships• came, bringing gold,
silver, ivory, apes, and monkeys.•
22 So King Solomon surpassed all
the kings of the earth in riches and
wisdom.
23 And all the kings of the earth
sought the presence of Solomon to
hear his wisdom, which God had put
in his heart.
24 Each man brought his present:
articles of silver and gold, garments,
[k]armor, spices, horses, and mules, at
a set rate year by year.
25 Solomon had [l]four thousand
stalls for [m]horses and chariots, and
twelve thousand horsemen whom he
stationed in the chariot cities and with
the king at Jerusalem.
26 So he [n]reigned over all the kings
from the [o]River to the land of the Philistines, as far as the border of Egypt.
27 The king made [p]silver *as com-*
mon in Jerusalem as stones, and he
made cedar trees as [q]abundant as the
sycamores which *are* in the [r]lowland.
28 And they [s]brought horses to
Solomon from Egypt and from all
lands.

(For Solomon's failure, see
1 Ki. 11:1–40)

Solomon dies (1 Ki. 11:41–43)

29 Now the [t]rest of the acts of Solomon, first and last, *are* they not written in the [u]book of Nathan the
prophet, in the prophecy of Ahijah the
Shilonite, and in the visions of Iddo
the seer concerning Jeroboam the son
of Nebat?
30 Solomon [v]reigned in Jerusalem
over all Israel forty years.
31 Then Solomon rested with his
fathers, and was buried in the City of

8
a Dt. 7:8; 2 Chr. 2:11; Ps. 44:3
9
b See Coinage (OT), Ex. 30:13, *note*
10
c See 1 Ki. 7:13, *note*
d i.e. *almug.* See 1 Ki. 10:11, *note*
13
e vv. 13–28; 1 Ki. 10:14–29
f Cp. Dt. 17:17; Rev. 13:18
16
g Cp. 1 Ki. 14:26–28
h See Weights and Measures (OT), 2 Chr. 2:10, *note;* cp. 1 Ki. 10:17
i 1 Ki. 7:2
21
j 2 Chr. 20:36,37
24
k 1 Ki. 20:11
25
l Cp. 1 Ki. 4:26; see 1 Chr. 11:11, *note*
m Dt. 17:16; 2 Chr. 1:14; Isa. 2:7
26
n 2 Chr. 7:8; Ps. 72:8
o i.e. *the Euphrates*
27
p 1 Ki. 10:27
q 2 Chr. 1:15
r See Dt. 1:7, *note*
28
s 1 Ki. 10:28
29
t Cp. 1 Chr. 29:29
u See 1 Chr. 29:29, *note*
30
v 1 Ki. 4:21; 1 Chr. 29:28

*
9:16 Or *three minas* (compare 1 Kings 10:17)
9:21 Hebrew *Huram* (compare 1 Kings 10:22)
• Literally *ships of Tarshish* (deep-sea vessels)
• Or *peacocks*

David his father. And Rehoboam his
son [a]reigned in his place.

II. The History of Judah from the Reign of Rehoboam to the Destruction of Jerusalem and the Captivity, 10—36

Accession and folly of Rehoboam (1 Ki. 12:1–15)

10 AND Rehoboam went to Shechem, for all Israel had gone to
Shechem to make him king.
2 So it happened, when Jeroboam
the son of Nebat heard *it* (he was in
Egypt, where he had [b]fled from the
presence of King Solomon), that Jeroboam returned from Egypt.
3 Then they sent for him and
called him. And Jeroboam and all Israel came and spoke to Rehoboam,
saying,
4 [c]"Your father made our yoke
heavy; now therefore, lighten the burdensome service of your father and
his heavy yoke which he put on us,
and we will serve you."
5 So he said to them, "Come back
to me after three days." And the people departed.
6 Then King Rehoboam consulted
the elders who stood before his father
Solomon while he still lived, saying,
"How do you advise *me* to answer
these people?"
7 And they spoke to him, saying,
"If you are kind to these people, and
please them, and speak good words to
them, they will be your servants forever."
8 [d]But he rejected the advice
which the elders had given him, and
consulted the young men who had
grown up with him, who stood before
him.
9 And he said to them, "What advice do you give? How should we answer this people who have spoken to
me, saying, 'Lighten the yoke which
your father put on us'?"
10 Then the young men who had
grown up with him spoke to him, saying, "Thus you should speak to the
people who have spoken to you, saying, 'Your father made our yoke
heavy, but you make *it* lighter on us'—
thus you shall say to them: 'My little
finger shall be thicker than my father's waist!
11 'And now, whereas my father
[e]put a heavy yoke on you, I will add to

31
a 931 B.C.
CHAPTER 10
2
b 1 Ki. 11:40
4
c Cp. Ex. 1:14
8
d vv. 8–11; 1 Ki. 12:8–11
11
e Cp. Ex. 5:5–9
12
f 1 Ki. 12:12–14
15
g v. 14; Jud. 14:4; 1 Chr. 5:22; 2 Chr. 11:4; 22:7; 25:20
h 1 Ki. 11:29–39
16
i v. 19; cp. 2 Sam. 19:43–20:2
18
j Or *Adoniram,* 1 Ki. 4:6; 5:14; or *Adoram,* 2 Sam. 20:24; 1 Ki. 12:18

your yoke; my father chastised you
with whips, but I *will chastise you*
with scourges!' "*

Kingdom divided; Jeroboam becomes king over Israel (1 Ki. 12:16–19)

12 So [f]Jeroboam and all the people
came to Rehoboam on the third day,
as the king had directed, saying,
"Come back to me the third day."
13 Then the king answered them
roughly. King Rehoboam rejected the
advice of the elders,
14 and he spoke to them according
to the advice of the young men, saying, "My father* made your yoke
heavy, but I will add to it; my father
chastised you with whips, but I *will*
chastise you with scourges!"*
15 So the king did not listen to the
people; [g]for the turn *of events* was
from God, that the LORD might fulfill
His [h]word, which He had spoken by
the hand of Ahijah the Shilonite to
Jeroboam the son of Nebat.
16 Now when all Israel *saw* that the
king did not listen to them, the people
answered the king, saying:

"What share have we in David?
We have no inheritance in the
son of Jesse.
Every man to your [i]tents, O
[1]Israel!
Now see to your own house, O
David!"

So all Israel departed to their tents.
17 But Rehoboam reigned over the
children of Israel who dwelt in the cities of Judah.
18 Then King Rehoboam sent [j]Ha-
doram, who *was* in charge of revenue;
but the children of Israel stoned him
with stones, and he died. Therefore
King Rehoboam mounted *his* chariot
in haste to flee to Jerusalem.
19 So Israel has been in rebellion
against the house of David to this day.

Rehoboam, forbidden by God to attack Jeroboam, fortifies Judah (cp. 1 Ki. 12:21–24)

11 NOW when Rehoboam came
to Jerusalem, he assembled
from the house of Judah and Benja-

10:11 Literally *scorpions* **10:14** Following many Hebrew manuscripts, Septuagint, Syriac, and Vulgate (compare verse 10 and 1 Kings 12:14); Masoretic Text reads *I.* • Literally *scorpions*

[1](10:16) "Israel," the ten tribes other than Judah and Benjamin, often called Israel in distinction from Judah. This division of the kingdom marks an epoch of great importance in the history of the nation. But see 2 Ki. 17:23, *note.*

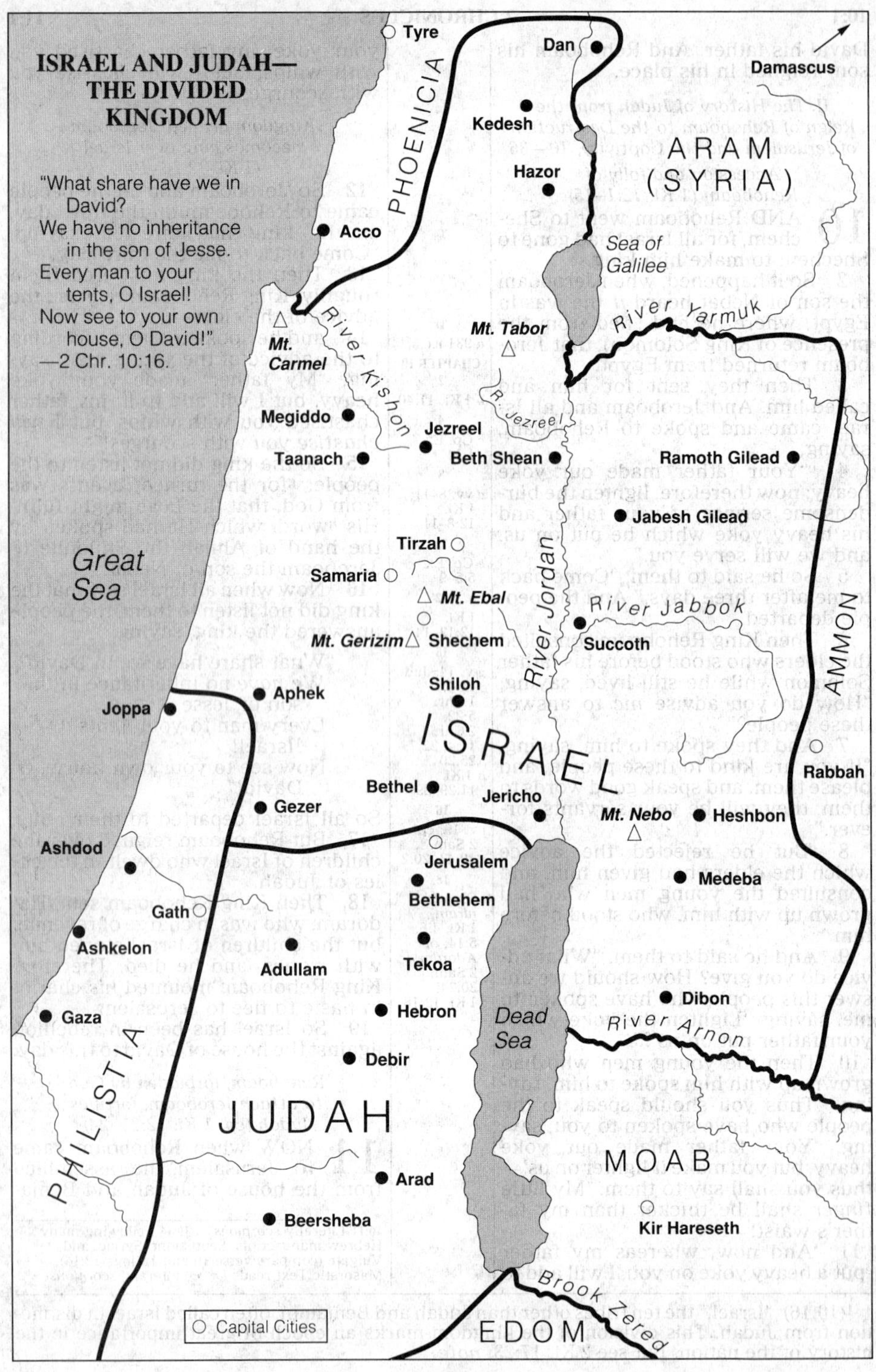
ISRAEL AND JUDAH—
THE DIVIDED
KINGDOM
"What share have we in
David?
We have no inheritance
in the son of Jesse.
Every man to your
tents, O Israel!
Now see to your own
house, O David!"
—2 Chr. 10:16.
Tyre
PHOENICIA
Dan
Damascus
Kedesh
ARAM
(SYRIA)
Hazor
Acco
Sea of
Galilee
River Yarmuk
Mt. Carmel
River Kishon
Mt. Tabor
R. Jezreel
Megiddo
Jezreel
Taanach
Beth Shean
Ramoth Gilead
Jabesh Gilead
Tirzah
Great
Sea
Samaria
Mt. Ebal
River Jabbok
Mt. Gerizim
Shechem
Succoth
River Jordan
AMMON
Aphek
Joppa
Shiloh
ISRAEL
Rabbah
Bethel
Jericho
Gezer
Mt. Nebo
Heshbon
Ashdod
Jerusalem
Medeba
Bethlehem
Gath
Ashkelon
Adullam
Tekoa
Dibon
Gaza
Hebron
Dead
Sea
River Arnon
Debir
PHILISTIA
JUDAH
MOAB
Arad
Beersheba
Kir Hareseth
Brook Zered
Capital Cities
EDOM

min one hundred and eighty thousand
chosen *men* who were warriors, to
[a]fight against Israel, that he might restore the kingdom to Rehoboam.
2 But the word of the LORD came to
[b]Shemaiah the man of God, saying,
3 "Speak to Rehoboam the son of
Solomon, king of Judah, and to all Israel in Judah and Benjamin, saying,
4 'Thus says the LORD: "You shall
not go up or fight against your [c]breth-
ren! Let every man return to his
house, for this thing is from Me."'"
Therefore they obeyed the words of
the LORD, and turned back from attacking Jeroboam.
5 So Rehoboam dwelt in Jerusalem, and built cities for defense in Judah.
6 And he built Bethlehem, Etam,
Tekoa,
7 Beth Zur, Sochoh, Adullam,
8 Gath, Mareshah, Ziph,
9 Adoraim, Lachish, Azekah,
10 Zorah, Aijalon, and Hebron,
which are in Judah and Benjamin, fortified cities.
11 And he fortified the strongholds,
and put captains in them, and stores of
food, oil, and wine.
12 Also in every city *he put* shields
and spears, and made them very
strong, having Judah and Benjamin
on his side.

Rehoboam strengthened by refugee priests and Levites (v. 17)

13 [d]And from all their territories
the priests and the Levites who *were*
in all Israel took their stand with him.
14 For the Levites left their
[e]common-lands and their possessions
and came to Judah and Jerusalem, for
Jeroboam and his sons had [f]rejected
them from serving as priests to the
LORD.

Jeroboam ordains false priests

15 Then [g]he appointed for himself
priests for the [h]high places, for the
[i]demons, and the calf idols which he
had made.
16 And after *the Levites left,**
those from all the tribes of Israel, such
as set their heart to [j]seek the LORD
God of Israel, [k]came to Jerusalem to
sacrifice to the LORD God of their fathers.
17 So they strengthened the kingdom of Judah, and made Rehoboam
the son of Solomon [l]strong for three
years, because they walked in the way
of David and Solomon for three years.

CHAPTER 11
1 *a* Cp. v. 4
2 *b* 2 Chr. 12:5–8,15
4 *c* Cp. 2 Chr. 28:8–11
13 *d* vv. 14–16
14 *e* Num. 35:2–8; Josh. 21:1–41
f 2 Chr. 13:9
15 *g* i.e. *Jeroboam*
h See Jud 3:7 and 1 Ki. 3:2, *notes*
i Lit. *hairy ones,* i.e. *satyrs.* Cp. Isa. 13:21
16 *j* 2 Chr. 14:7
k 2 Chr. 15:9
17 *l* 2 Chr. 12:1,13
18 *m* 1 Sam. 16:6
20 *n* Or *Michaiah the daughter of Uriel,* 2 Chr. 13:2
o Or *Abishalom,* 1 Ki. 15:2
p Or *Abijam,* 1 Ki. 14:31
21 *q* Dt. 17:17
22 *r* Dt. 21:15–17
s 2 Chr. 13:1
23 *t* 2 Chr. 11:5
CHAPTER 12
1 *u* v. 14
2 *v* 1 Ki. 11:40
3 *w* 2 Chr. 16:8
5 *x* 2 Chr. 11:2
y Cp. 2 Chr. 15:2

(For Jeroboam's reign, see 1 Ki. 12:25—14:18)

Rehoboam's family

18 Then Rehoboam took for himself as wife Mahalath the daughter of
Jerimoth the son of David, *and of* Abihail the daughter of [m]Eliah the son of
Jesse.
19 And she bore him children: Jeush, Shamariah, and Zaham.
20 After her he took [n]Maachah the
granddaughter* of [o]Absalom; and
she bore him [p]Abijah, Attai, Ziza, and
Shelomith.
21 Now Rehoboam loved Maachah
the granddaughter of Absalom more
than all his [q]wives and his concubines; for he took eighteen wives and
sixty concubines, and begot twenty-
eight sons and sixty daughters.
22 And Rehoboam [r]appointed
[s]Abijah the son of Maachah as chief,
to be leader among his brothers; for
he *intended* to make him king.
23 He dealt wisely, and dispersed
some of his sons throughout all the
territories of Judah and Benjamin, to
every [t]fortified city; and he gave
them provisions in abundance. He
also sought many wives *for them.*

Rehoboam's apostasy (1 Ki. 14:21–24)

12 NOW it came to pass, when Rehoboam had established the
kingdom and had strengthened himself, that he [u]forsook the law of the
LORD, and all Israel along with him.

God judges Judah through Shishak, king of Egypt (1 Ki. 14:25–28)

2 And it happened in the fifth year
of King Rehoboam *that* [v]Shishak
king of Egypt came up against Jerusalem, because they had transgressed
against the LORD,
3 with twelve hundred chariots,
sixty thousand horsemen, and people
without number who came with him
out of Egypt—the [w]Lubim and the
Sukkiim and the Ethiopians.
4 And he took the fortified cities of
Judah and came to Jerusalem.

Repentance brings respite

5 Then [x]Shemaiah the prophet
came to Rehoboam and the leaders of
Judah, who were gathered together in
Jerusalem because of Shishak, and
said to them, "Thus says the LORD:
[y]'You have forsaken Me, and there-

*11:16 Literally *after them* 11:20 Literally *daughter,* but in the broader sense of granddaughter (compare 2 Chronicles 13:2) fore I also have left you in the hand of Shishak.' "

6 [a]So the leaders of Israel and the king [b]humbled themselves; and they said, "The LORD *is* righteous."

7 Now when the LORD saw that they humbled themselves, the word of the LORD came to Shemaiah, saying, "They have humbled themselves; *therefore* I will not destroy them, but I will grant them some deliverance. My [c]wrath shall not be poured out on Jerusalem by the hand of Shishak.

8 "Nevertheless they will be his servants, that they may distinguish My service from the [d]service of the kingdoms of the nations."

9 So Shishak king of Egypt came up against Jerusalem, and [e]took away the treasures of the house of the LORD and the treasures of the king's house; he took everything. He also carried away the gold [f]shields which Solomon had made.

10 Then King Rehoboam made bronze shields in their place, and committed *them* to the hands of the captains of the guard, who guarded the doorway of the king's house.

11 And whenever the king entered the house of the LORD, the guard would go and bring them out; then they would take them back into the guardroom.

12 When he humbled himself, the wrath of the LORD turned from him, so as not to destroy *him* completely; and things also went well in Judah.

Rehoboam dies (1 Ki. 14:21,29,31)

13 Thus King Rehoboam strengthened himself in Jerusalem and [g]reigned. Now Rehoboam *was* forty-one years old when he became king; and he reigned seventeen years in Jerusalem, the city which the LORD had [h]chosen out of all the tribes of Israel, to put His name there. His mother's name *was* Naamah, an [i]Ammonitess.

14 And he did evil, [j]because he did not prepare his heart to seek the LORD.

15 The acts of Rehoboam, first and last, *are* they not written in the [k]book of Shemaiah the prophet, and of [l]Iddo the seer concerning genealogies? And *there were* [m]wars between Rehoboam and Jeroboam all their days.

16 So Rehoboam rested with his fathers, and was buried in the City of David. Then [n]Abijah his son reigned in his place.

6
a Cp. 2 Chr. 6:24–25
b Cp. 2 Chr. 7:14; 34:27
7
c Cp. 2 Chr. 34:25
8
d Dt. 28:47–48
9
e Cp. 2 Ki. 24:13
f 2 Chr. 9:16
13
g 1 Ki. 14:21
h 2 Chr. 6:6
i 1 Ki. 11:1,5
14
j Cp. 1 Sam. 7:3; 1 Chr. 29:18; 2 Chr. 27:6; 30:19
15
k See 1 Chr. 29:29, *note*
l 2 Chr. 9:29; 13:22
m 1 Ki. 14:30
16
n Or *Abijam*, 1 Ki. 14:31; 2 Chr. 11:20–22
CHAPTER 13
1
o 913 B.C., 1 Ki. 15:1
p 1 Ki. 15:2
2
q Or *Maachah the granddaughter of Absalom*, 2 Chr. 11:20
3
r Cp. 2 Chr. 11:1; 14:8
4
s Josh. 18:22
5
t 2 Sam. 7:8–16
u Num. 18:19
6
v 1 Ki. 11:26
7
w 2 Chr. 12:13
8
x 1 Ki. 12:28; 14:9; Hos. 8:4–6; cp. Ex. 32:1–4

Abijah succeeds Rehoboam; war between Judah and Israel
(1 Ki. 15:1–7)

13 IN the eighteenth year of King Jeroboam, Abijah [o]became king over [p]Judah.

2 He reigned three years in Jerusalem. His mother's name *was* [q]Michaiah the daughter of Uriel of Gibeah. And there was war between Abijah and Jeroboam.

3 Abijah set the battle in order with an army of valiant warriors, [r]four hundred thousand choice men. Jeroboam also drew up in battle formation against him with eight hundred thousand choice men, mighty men of valor.

4 Then Abijah stood on Mount [s]Zemaraim, which *is* in the mountains of Ephraim, and said, "Hear me, Jeroboam and all Israel:

5 "Should you not know that the LORD God of Israel [t]gave the dominion over Israel to David forever, to him and his sons, by a covenant of [u]salt?

6 "Yet Jeroboam the son of Nebat, the servant of Solomon the son of David, rose up and [v]rebelled against his lord.

7 "Then worthless rogues gathered to him, and strengthened themselves against Rehoboam the son of Solomon, when Rehoboam was [w]young and inexperienced and could not withstand them.

8 "And now you think to withstand the kingdom of the LORD, which is in the hand of the sons of David; and you *are* a great multitude, and with you are the gold calves [x]which Jeroboam made for you as gods.

9 "Have you not [y]cast out the priests of the LORD, the sons of Aaron, and the Levites, and made for yourselves priests, like the peoples of *other* lands, so that whoever comes to [z]consecrate himself with a young bull and seven rams may be a priest of [aa]*things that are* not gods?

10 "But as for us, the LORD *is* our [bb]God, and we have not forsaken Him; and the priests who minister to the LORD *are* the sons of Aaron, and the Levites *attend* to *their* duties.

11 "And they burn to the LORD every morning and every evening burnt sacrifices and sweet incense; *they*

13:9 *y* 2 Chr. 11:13–15 *z* Ex. 29:29–33 *aa* Jer. 2:11; 5:7 **13:10** *bb* Josh. 24:15

also *set* the [a]showbread *in order on*
the pure *gold* table, and the lampstand
of gold with its lamps to burn every
evening; for we keep the command of
the LORD our God, but you have forsaken Him.
12 "Now look, God Himself is with
us as *our* [b]head, and His priests with
[c]sounding trumpets to sound the
alarm against you. O children of Israel, do not [d]fight against the LORD
God of your fathers, for you shall not
prosper!"
13 But Jeroboam caused an ambush to go around behind them; so
they were in front of Judah, and the
ambush *was* behind them.
14 And when Judah looked around,
to their surprise the battle line *was* at
both front and rear; and they [e]cried
out to the LORD, and the priests
sounded the trumpets.
15 Then the men of Judah gave a
shout; and as the men of Judah
shouted, it happened that God struck
Jeroboam and all Israel before Abijah
and Judah.
16 And the children of Israel fled
before Judah, and God delivered them
into their hand.
17 Then Abijah and his people
struck them with a great slaughter; so
[f]five hundred thousand choice men of
Israel fell slain.
18 Thus the children of Israel were
subdued at that time; and the children
of Judah prevailed, because they [g]re-
lied on the LORD God of their fathers.
19 And Abijah pursued Jeroboam
and took cities from him: Bethel with
its villages, Jeshanah with its villages,
and [h]Ephrain with its villages.

Jeroboam dies (1 Ki. 14:19–20)

20 So Jeroboam did not recover
strength again in the days of Abijah;
and the LORD [i]struck him, and he died.

(Nadab's reign precedes the record that follows. See 1 Ki. 15:25–31)

The family of Abijah

21 But Abijah grew mighty, married fourteen wives, and begot twenty-
two sons and sixteen daughters.
22 Now the rest of the acts of Abijah, his ways, and his sayings *are* written in the [j]annals of the prophet Iddo.

Abijah dies: Asa succeeds him (1 Ki. 15:7–8)

14 SO Abijah rested with his fathers, and they buried him in
the City of David. Then Asa his son
reigned in his [k]place. In his days the
land was quiet for ten years.

Asa's early reforms (1 Ki. 15:11)

2 Asa did *what was* good and
right in the eyes of the LORD his God,
3 for he removed the altars of the
foreign *gods* and the [l]high places, and
broke down the *sacred* pillars and cut
down the [m]wooden images.
4 He commanded Judah to [n]seek
the LORD God of their fathers, and to
observe the law and the commandment.
5 He also removed the [l]high
places and the [o]incense altars from all
the cities of Judah, and the kingdom
was quiet under [p]him.

Asa defeats Zerah, the Ethiopian (cp. 16:1–10)

6 And he built fortified cities in Judah, for the land had rest; he had no
war in those years, because the LORD
had given him [q]rest.
7 Therefore he said to Judah, "Let
us build these cities and make walls
around *them,* and towers, gates, and
bars, *while* the land *is* yet before us,
because we have sought the LORD our
God; we have sought *Him,* and He has
given us rest on every side." So they
built and prospered.
8 And Asa had an army of three
hundred thousand from Judah who
carried shields and spears, and from
Benjamin two hundred and eighty
thousand men who carried shields
and drew [r]bows; all these *were*
mighty men of [s]valor.
9 Then Zerah the [t]Ethiopian
came out against them with an army
of a million men and three hundred
chariots, and he came to Mareshah.
10 So Asa went out against him,
and they set the troops in battle array
in the Valley of Zephathah at Mareshah.
11 And Asa [u]cried out to the LORD
his God, and said, "LORD, *it is* nothing
for You to help, [v]whether with many
or with those who have no power;
help us, O LORD our God, for we rest on
You, and [w]in Your name we go
against this multitude. O LORD, You
are our God; do not let man prevail
against You!"
12 So the LORD struck the Ethiopians before Asa and Judah, and the
Ethiopians fled.
13 And Asa and the people who

11
a See Ex. 25:30, *note*
12
b Josh. 5:13–15; Heb. 2:10
c Num. 10:8–9
d Cp. Acts 5:39
14
e Josh. 24:7; 2 Chr. 6:34–35; 14:11
17
f Cp. 2 Chr. 13:3; see 1 Chr. 11:11, *note*
18
g 2 Chr. 14:11
19
h Or *Ephron,* Josh. 15:9
20
i 1 Sam. 2:6; 25:38; Acts 12:23
22
j 2 Chr. 9:29; 12:15; see 1 Chr. 29:29, *note*
CHAPTER 14
1
k 911 B.C
3
l See Jud. 3:7 and 1 Ki. 3:2, *notes*
m See Dt. 16:21, *note*
4
n 2 Chr. 7:14
5
o Lit. *sun gods*
p v. 1
6
q 2 Chr. 15:15
8
r 1 Chr. 12:2
s 2 Chr. 13:3
9
t 2 Chr. 12:3; 16:8
11
u Bible prayers (OT): v. 11; 2 Chr. 20:6. (Gen. 15:2; Hab. 3:1)

v 1 Sam. 14:6 *w* 1 Sam. 17:45

were with him pursued them to Gerar.
So the Ethiopians were overthrown,
and they could not recover, for they
were broken before the LORD and His
army. And they carried away very
much spoil.
14 Then they defeated all the cities
around Gerar, for the [a]fear of the
LORD came upon them; and they plundered all the cities, for there was exceedingly much spoil in them.
15 They also attacked the livestock
enclosures, and carried off sheep and
camels in abundance, and returned to
Jerusalem.

The prophet Azariah warns Asa

15 NOW the [b]Spirit of God came
upon Azariah the son of
[c]Oded.
2 And he went out to meet Asa,
and said to him: "Hear me, Asa, and
all Judah and Benjamin. The LORD *is*
with [d]you while you are with Him. If
you seek Him, He will be found by
you; but if you forsake Him, He will
forsake you.
3 "For a long time [e]Israel *has been*
without the true God, without a
[f]teaching priest, and without [g]law;
4 "but when in their trouble they
turned to the LORD God of Israel, and
sought Him, He was found by [h]them.
5 "And in those times *there was* no
peace to the one who went out, nor to
the one who came in, but great turmoil
was on all the inhabitants of the lands.
6 "So nation was destroyed by nation, and city by city, for God troubled
them with every adversity.
7 "But you, be strong and do not
let your hands be weak, for your work
shall be rewarded!"

Asa's response: further and sweeping reforms (1 Ki. 15:12–15)

8 And when Asa heard these
words and the prophecy of Oded* the
prophet, he took courage, and removed the abominable idols from all
the land of Judah and Benjamin and
from the cities which he had taken in
the mountains of [i]Ephraim; and he
restored the altar of the LORD that *was*
before the vestibule of the LORD.
9 Then he gathered all Judah and
Benjamin, and those who dwelt with
them [j]from Ephraim, Manasseh, and
Simeon, for they came over to him in
[k]great numbers from Israel when they
saw that the LORD his God was with
him.
10 So they gathered together at Jerusalem in the [l]third month, in the
fifteenth year of the reign of Asa.
11 And they offered to the LORD at
that time seven hundred bulls and
seven thousand sheep from the [m]spoil
they had brought.
12 Then they entered into a [n]cov-
enant to seek the LORD God of their
fathers with all their heart and with
all their soul;
13 and whoever would not seek the
LORD God of Israel [o]was to be put to
death, whether small or great,
whether man or woman.
14 Then they took an oath before
the LORD with a loud voice, with shouting and trumpets and rams' horns.
15 And all Judah rejoiced at the
oath, for they had sworn with all their
heart and [p]sought Him with all their
soul; and He was found by them, and
the LORD gave them [q]rest all around.
16 Also he removed Maachah, the
[r]mother of Asa the king, from *being*
queen mother, because she had made
an obscene image of [s]Asherah; and
Asa cut down her obscene image, then
crushed and burned *it* by the Brook
Kidron.
17 But the [t]high places were not
removed from [u]Israel. Nevertheless
the heart of Asa was [v]loyal all his
days.
18 He also brought into the house
of God the things that his father had
dedicated and that he himself had
dedicated: silver and gold and utensils.
19 And there was no war until the
thirty-fifth year of the reign of Asa.

Asa, in league with Syria, makes war on Baasha (1 Ki. 15:16–22)

16 IN the thirty-sixth year of the
reign of Asa, Baasha king of
Israel came up against Judah and built
Ramah, that he might let [w]none go out
or come in to Asa king of Judah.
2 Then Asa brought silver and
gold from the treasuries of the house
of the LORD and of the king's house,
and sent to Ben-Hadad king of Syria,
who dwelt in Damascus, saying,
3 "*Let there be* a treaty between
you and me, as there was between my
father and your father. See, I have
sent you silver and gold; come, break

14
a Dt. 11:25; Josh. 2:9; 2 Chr. 17:10
CHAPTER 15
1
b *Holy Spirit* (OT): v. 1; 2 Chr. 20:14. (Gen. 1:2; Zech. 12:10)
c 2 Chr. 15:8
2
d Cp. 2 Chr. 20:14–17
3
e Cp. 1 Ki. 12:28–33
f 2 Ki. 12:2
g 2 Chr. 17:8–9
4
h Dt. 4:29
8
i 2 Chr. 13:19
9
j v. 3
k Cp. 2 Chr. 11:16
10
l See Lev. 23:2, *note*
11
m 2 Chr. 14:13–15
12
n 2 Chr. 23:16
13
o Ex. 22:20; Dt. 13:5–10
15
p v. 2
q 2 Chr. 14:7
16
r i.e. *grandmother.* 1 Ki. 15:2, 10
s See Dt. 16:21, *note*
17
t See Jud. 3:7 and 1 Ki. 3:2, *notes*
u i.e. *the northern or ten-tribe kingdom*
v See Phil. 3:12, *note*
CHAPTER 16
1
w i.e. *none of his subjects.*

vv. 5–6; 2 Chr. 15:9

★
15:8 Following Masoretic Text and Septuagint; Syriac and Vulgate read *Azariah the son of Oded* (compare verse 1).

your treaty with Baasha king of Israel,
so that he will withdraw from me."
4 So Ben-Hadad heeded King Asa,
and sent the captains of his armies
against the cities of Israel. They attacked Ijon, Dan, Abel Maim, and all
the storage cities of Naphtali.
5 Now it happened, when Baasha
heard *it,* that he stopped building Ramah and ceased his work.
6 Then King Asa took all Judah,
and they carried away the stones and
timber of Ramah, which Baasha had
used for building; and with them he
built Geba and Mizpah.

(For a further account about Baasha, see 1 Ki. 15:27—16:7)

Asa, rebuked by Hanani, imprisons the prophet

7 And at that time [a]Hanani the
seer came to Asa king of Judah, and
said to him: "Because you have relied
on the king of [b]Syria, and have not
relied on the LORD your God, therefore
the army of the king of Syria has escaped from your hand.
8 "Were the [c]Ethiopians and the
Lubim not a huge army with very
many chariots and horsemen? Yet, because you relied on the LORD, He delivered them into your [d]hand.
9 "For the [e]eyes of the LORD run to
and fro throughout the whole earth, to
show Himself strong on behalf of
those whose heart *is* [f]loyal to Him. In
this you have done foolishly; therefore from now on you shall have
wars."
10 Then Asa was angry with the
seer, and put him in [g]prison, for *he
was* enraged at him because of this.
And Asa oppressed *some* of the people at that time.

(Reigns of Elah, Zimri, Tibni, Omri, and Ahab's accession precede record that follows. See 1 Ki. 16:6–34)

Asa's illness and death (1 Ki. 15:23–24)

11 Note that the [h]acts of Asa, first
and last, are indeed written in the
book of the kings of Judah and Israel.
12 And in the thirty-ninth year of
his reign, Asa became diseased in his
feet, and his malady was severe; yet in
his disease he did not [i]seek the LORD,
but the physicians.
13 So Asa rested with his fathers;
he died in the forty-first year of his
reign.
14 They buried him in his own
tomb, which he had made for himself
in the City of David; and they laid him
in the bed which was filled with spices
and various ingredients prepared in a
mixture of ointments. They made a
very great [j]burning for him.

Jehoshaphat succeeds Asa (1 Ki. 15:24)

17 THEN [k]Jehoshaphat his son
[l]reigned in his place, and
strengthened himself against Israel.
2 And he placed troops in all the
fortified cities of [m]Judah, and set garrisons in the land of Judah and in the
cities of Ephraim which [n]Asa his father had taken.

Jehoshaphat, walking in the ways of David, institutes reforms

3 Now the LORD was with Jehoshaphat, because he walked in the former
ways of his [1]father David; he did not
seek the Baals,
4 but sought the God* of his father, and walked in His commandments and not according to the acts of
[o]Israel.
5 Therefore the LORD established
the kingdom in his hand; and all Judah [p]gave presents to Jehoshaphat,
and he had riches and honor in [q]abun-
dance.
6 And his heart took delight in the
ways of the LORD; moreover he removed the [r]high places and [s]wooden
images from Judah.
7 Also in the third year of his reign
he sent his leaders, Ben-Hail, Obadiah, Zechariah, Nethanel, and Michaiah, to teach in the cities of Judah.
8 And with them *he sent* Levites:
Shemaiah, Nethaniah, Zebadiah, Asahel, Shemiramoth, Jehonathan, Adonijah, Tobijah, and Tobadonijah—the
Levites; and with them Elishama and
Jehoram, the priests.
9 So they taught in Judah, and *had*
the Book of the Law of the LORD with
them; they went throughout all the cities of Judah and taught the [t]people.

Jehoshaphat's growing power; his men of valor

10 And the [u]fear of the LORD fell on
all the kingdoms of the lands that
were around Judah, so that they did
not make war against Jehoshaphat.
11 Also *some* of the Philistines
brought Jehoshaphat presents and sil-

7
a 2 Chr. 19:2
b vv. 2–4; 2 Chr. 32:8–10; Ps. 118:9; Jer. 17:5
8
c 2 Chr. 14:9
d 2 Chr. 13:16
9
e Job 34:21–22; Prov. 5:21; Jer. 16:17; Zech. 4:10
f See Phil. 3:12, *note*
10
g Cp. Jer. 32:2–3; Dan. 6:16–17; Mt. 14:3
11
h 2 Chr. 14:2
12
i Cp. 2 Ki. 20:1–5
14
j Cp. 2 Chr. 21:18–19

CHAPTER 17
1
k 2 Chr. 20:31
l 870 B.C.
2
m 2 Chr. 11:5
n 2 Chr. 15:8
4
o i.e. *the northern or ten-tribe kingdom*
5
p 1 Ki. 10:25
q 2 Chr. 18:1
6
r Cp. 2 Chr. 15:17; see Jud. 3:7 and 1 Ki. 3:2, *notes*
s See Dt. 16:21, *note*
9
t Dt. 6:4–9; 2 Chr. 35:3; Neh. 8:3; cp. 2 Chr. 15:3
10
u 2 Chr. 14:14

*17:4 Septuagint reads *LORD God*.

[1](17:3) It was a Jewish custom to call a family or tribal head "father" (e.g. Jn. 8:53).

ver as [a]tribute; and the Arabians brought him flocks, seven thousand seven hundred rams and seven thousand seven hundred male goats.

12 So Jehoshaphat became increasingly powerful, and he built fortresses and storage cities in Judah.

13 He had much property in the cities of Judah; and the men of war, mighty men of valor, *were* in Jerusalem.

14 These *are* their numbers, according to their fathers' houses. Of Judah, the captains of thousands: Adnah the captain, and with him [b]three hundred thousand mighty men of valor;

15 and next to him *was* Jehohanan the captain, and with him two hundred and eighty thousand;

16 and next to him *was* Amasiah the son of Zichri, who [c]willingly offered himself to the [d]LORD, and with him two hundred thousand mighty men of valor.

17 Of Benjamin: Eliada a mighty man of valor, and with him two hundred thousand men armed with bow and shield;

18 and next to him *was* Jehozabad, and with him one hundred and eighty thousand prepared for war.

19 These served the king, besides those the king [e]put in the fortified cities throughout all Judah.

(The reign of Ahab and major part of Elijah's ministry precede the record that follows. See 1 Ki. 16:28—21:29)

Jehoshaphat joins Ahab in his third Syrian campaign (1 Ki. 22:2–4)

18 JEHOSHAPHAT had [f]riches and honor in abundance; and [g]by marriage he allied himself with [h]Ahab.

2 After some years he [i]went down to *visit* Ahab in Samaria; and Ahab killed sheep and oxen in abundance for him and the people who were with him, and persuaded him to go up *with him* to Ramoth Gilead.

3 So Ahab king of Israel said to Jehoshaphat king of Judah, "Will you go with me *against* Ramoth Gilead?" And he answered him, "I *am* as you *are,* and my people as your people; *we will be* with you in the [j]war."

Ahab's lying prophets promise victory (1 Ki. 22:5–12)

4 Also Jehoshaphat said to the king of Israel, "Please [k]inquire for the word of the LORD today."

5 Then the king of Israel gathered the prophets [l]together, four hundred men, and said to them, "Shall we go to war against Ramoth Gilead, or shall I refrain?" So they said, "Go up, for God will deliver it into the king's hand."

6 But Jehoshaphat said, "*Is there* not still a prophet of the LORD here, that we may inquire of [m]Him?"*

7 So the king of Israel said to Jehoshaphat, "*There is* still one man by whom we may inquire of the LORD; but I [n]hate him, because he never prophesies good concerning me, but always evil. He *is* Micaiah the son of Imla." And Jehoshaphat said, "Let not the king say such things!"

8 Then the king of Israel called one *of his* officers and said, "Bring Micaiah the son of Imla quickly!"

9 The king of Israel and Jehoshaphat king of Judah, clothed in *their* robes, sat each on his throne; and they sat at a threshing floor at the entrance of the gate of Samaria; and all the prophets prophesied before them.

10 Now Zedekiah the son of Chenaanah had made [o]horns of iron for himself; and he said, "Thus says the LORD: 'With these you shall gore the Syrians until they are destroyed.' "

11 And all the prophets prophesied so, saying, "Go up to Ramoth Gilead and prosper, for the LORD will deliver *it* into the king's hand."

Micaiah truly prophesies defeat (1 Ki. 22:13–28)

12 Then the [p]messenger who had gone to call Micaiah spoke to him, saying, "Now listen, the words of the prophets with one accord encourage the king. Therefore please let your word be like *the word of* one of them, and speak encouragement."

13 And Micaiah said, "*As* the LORD lives, [q]whatever my God says, that I will speak."

14 Then he came to the king; and the king said to him, "Micaiah, shall we go to war against Ramoth Gilead, or shall I refrain?" And he said, "Go and prosper, and they shall be delivered into your hand!"

15 So the king said to him, "How many times shall I make you swear that you tell me nothing but the truth in the name of the LORD?"

16 Then he said, "I saw all Israel [r]scattered on the mountains, as sheep that have no [s]shepherd. And the LORD

11 *a* 2 Chr. 9:14; 26:8
14 *b* See 1 Chr. 11:11, *note*
16 *c* Jud. 5:9 *d* Cp. 1 Chr. 4:10
19 *e* 2 Chr. 17:2
CHAPTER 18
1 *f* 2 Chr. 17:5 *g* 1 Ki. 22:44; cp. 2 Chr. 19:1–3 *h* 1 Ki. 22:40
2 *i* Ex. 23:2
3 *j* Cp. 2 Ki. 3:7
4 *k* Cp. 1 Sam. 23:2–9; 2 Sam. 2:1–2
5 *l* Cp. 1 Ki. 18:19
6 *m* 2 Ki. 3:11
7 *n* Cp. 2 Chr. 16:10
10 *o* Zech. 1:18–21
12 *p* vv. 6–8
13 *q* Num. 22:18,20, 35; 23:12, 26; 24:13
16 *r* Jer. 23:1–8; 31:10 *s* Num. 27:17; Ezek. 34:5–8; Mt. 9:36

* 18:6 Or *him*

said, 'These have no master. Let each
return to his house in peace.' "
17 And the king of Israel said to Jehoshaphat, "Did I not tell you he
would not prophesy good concerning
me, but evil?"
18 Then *Micaiah* said, "Therefore
hear the word of the LORD: I saw the
LORD sitting on His [a]throne, and all
the host of heaven standing on His
right hand and His left.
19 "And the LORD said, 'Who will
persuade Ahab king of Israel to go up,
that he may fall at Ramoth Gilead?' So
one spoke in this manner, and another
spoke in that manner.
20 "Then a spirit came forward and
stood before the LORD, and said, 'I will
persuade him.' The LORD said to him,
'In what way?'
21 "So he said, 'I will go out and be
a lying spirit in the mouth of all his
prophets.' And *the LORD* said, 'You
shall persuade *him* and also prevail;
go out and do so.'
22 "Therefore [b]look! The LORD has
put a [c]lying spirit in the mouth of
these prophets of yours, and the LORD
has declared disaster against you."
23 Then Zedekiah the son of Chenaanah went near and struck Micaiah
on the cheek, and said, "Which way
did the spirit from the LORD go from
me to speak to you?"
24 And Micaiah said, "Indeed you
shall see on that day when you go into
an inner chamber to hide!"
25 Then the king of Israel said,
"Take Micaiah, and return him to
Amon the governor of the city and to
Joash the king's son;
26 "and say, 'Thus says the king:
[d]"Put this *fellow* in prison, and feed
him with bread of affliction and water
of affliction, until I return in peace." ' "
27 But Micaiah said, "If you ever return in peace, the LORD has not spoken
by [e]me." And he said, "Take heed, all
you people!"

Ahab's defeat and death at Ramoth Gilead (1 Ki. 22:29–40)

28 So the king of Israel and Jehoshaphat the king of Judah [f]went up to
Ramoth Gilead.
29 And the king of Israel said to Jehoshaphat, "I will [g]disguise myself
and go into battle; but you put on your
robes." So the king of Israel disguised
himself, and they went into battle.
30 Now the king of Syria had commanded the captains of the chariots
who *were* with him, saying, "Fight
with no one small or great, but only
with the king of Israel."
31 So it was, when the captains of
the chariots saw Jehoshaphat, that
they said, "It *is* the king of Israel!"
Therefore they surrounded him to attack; but Jehoshaphat [h]cried out, and
the LORD helped him, and God di-
verted them from him.
32 For so it was, when the captains
of the chariots saw that it was not the
king of Israel, that they turned back
from pursuing him.
33 Now a certain man drew a bow
at random, and struck the king of Israel between the joints of his armor.
So he said to the driver of his chariot,
"Turn around and take me out of the
battle, for I am wounded."
34 The battle increased that day,
and the king of Israel propped *himself*
up in *his* chariot facing the Syrians
until evening; and about the time of
sunset he [i]died.

(Reigns of Ahaziah and Jehoram over Israel, and ministries of Elijah and Elisha precede the record that follows. See 1 Ki. 22:51—2 Ki. 8:15)

Jehu rebukes Jehoshaphat's alliance with Ahab

19 THEN Jehoshaphat the king of
Judah returned safely to his
house in Jerusalem.
2 And [j]Jehu the son of Hanani the
seer went out to meet him, and [k]said
to King Jehoshaphat, "Should you
help the [l]wicked and love those who
[m]hate the LORD? Therefore the wrath
of the LORD *is* upon you.
3 "Nevertheless good things are
found in you, in that you have removed the [n]wooden images from the
land, and have prepared your heart to
seek God."
4 So Jehoshaphat dwelt at Jerusalem; and he went out again among the
people from Beersheba to the mountains of Ephraim, and brought them
back to the LORD God of their [o]fathers.

Jehoshaphat, trusting in the LORD, makes judicial reforms

5 Then he set [p]judges in the land
throughout all the fortified cities of Judah, city by city,
6 and said to the judges, "Take
heed to what you are doing, [q]for you
do not judge for man but for the LORD,
who *is* with you in the judgment.
7 "Now therefore, let the fear of
the LORD be upon you; take care and
do *it*, for *there is* no iniquity with the

18 *a* Isa. 6:1–5; Dan. 7:9–10
22 *b* Job 12:16–17; Isa. 19:12–14 *c* Cp. Jud. 9:23; 1 Sam. 16:14; 18:10; 19:9
26 *d* 2 Chr. 16:10
27 *e* Dt. 18:22
28 *f* Cp. Dt. 1:43
29 *g* 2 Chr. 35:22
31 *h* 2 Chr. 13:14–15
34 *i* Cp. Ps. 37:35–36, 38
CHAPTER 19
2 *j* 1 Ki. 16:1; 2 Chr. 20:34 *k* Cp. Isa. 7:1–9; 8:12 *l* Ps. 1:6 *m* Ps. 139:21
3 *n* See Dt. 16:21, *note*
4 *o* 2 Chr. 15:8–13
5 *p* Dt. 16:18–20
6 *q* Lev. 19:15; Dt. 1:17; Ps. 58:1; cp. Isa. 11:3–4

LORD our God, no partiality, nor taking
of bribes."
8 Moreover in Jerusalem, for the
judgment of the LORD and for controversies, Jehoshaphat appointed some
of the Levites and priests, and some of
the chief fathers of Israel, when they
returned to Jerusalem.*
9 And he commanded them, say-
ing, "Thus you shall act in the [a]fear of
the LORD, faithfully and with a [b]loyal
heart:
10 "Whatever case comes to you
from your brethren who dwell in their
cities, whether of bloodshed or offenses against law or commandment,
against statutes or ordinances, you
shall warn them, lest they trespass
against the LORD and wrath come
upon you and your brethren. Do this,
and you will not be guilty.
11 "And take notice: [c]Amariah the
chief priest *is* over you in all [d]matters
of the LORD; and Zebadiah the son of
Ishmael, the ruler of the house of Judah, for all the king's matters; also the
Levites *will be* officials before you. Behave courageously, and the [e]LORD will
be with the good."

Judah invaded by Moabites, Ammonites, and Edomites, vv. 10,22

20 IT happened after this *that* the
people of [f]Moab with the people of [g]Ammon, and *others* with them
besides the Ammonites,* came to battle against Jehoshaphat.
2 Then some came and told Jehoshaphat, saying, "A great multitude
is coming against you from beyond
the sea, from Syria;* and they are in
[h]Hazazon Tamar" (which *is* En Gedi).

Jehoshaphat's prayer

3 And Jehoshaphat feared, and set
himself to [i]seek the LORD, and proclaimed a fast throughout all Judah.
4 So Judah gathered together to
ask [j]*help* from the LORD; and from all
the cities of Judah they came to seek
the LORD.
5 Then Jehoshaphat stood in the
assembly of Judah and Jerusalem, in
the house of the LORD, before the new
court,
6 and [k]said: "O LORD God of our
fathers, *are* You not God in [l]heaven,
and do You *not* rule over all the [m]king-
doms of the nations, and in Your hand
is there not power and might, so that
no one is able to withstand [n]You?
7 "*Are* You not our God, *who*
drove out the inhabitants of this land
before Your people Israel, and [o]gave
it to the descendants of Abraham
Your [p]friend forever?
8 "And they dwell in it, and have
built You a sanctuary in it for Your
name, saying,
9 'If disaster comes upon us—
sword, judgment, pestilence, or
famine—we will stand before this
temple and in Your presence (for Your
name *is* in this temple), and cry out to
You in our affliction, and You will
hear and [q]save.'
10 "And now, here are the people of
Ammon, Moab, and Mount Seir—
whom You would [r]not let Israel invade when they came out of the land
of Egypt, but they turned from them
and did not destroy them—
11 "here they are, rewarding us by
coming to [s]throw us out of Your possession which You have given us to
inherit.
12 "O our God, will You not [t]judge
them? For we have no power against
this great multitude that is coming
against us; nor do we know what to
do, but our eyes *are* upon [u]You."
13 Now all Judah, with their little
ones, their wives, and their children,
stood before the LORD.

The LORD answers Jehoshaphat's prayer through Jahaziel

14 Then the [v]Spirit of the LORD
came upon Jahaziel the son of Zechariah, the son of Benaiah, the son of
Jeiel, the son of Mattaniah, a Levite of
the sons of Asaph, in the midst of the
assembly.
15 And he said, "Listen, all you of
Judah and you inhabitants of Jerusalem, and you, King Jehoshaphat! Thus
[w]says the LORD to you: 'Do not be
afraid nor dismayed because of this
great multitude, [x]for the battle *is* not
yours, but God's.
16 'Tomorrow go down against
them. They will surely come up by the
Ascent of Ziz, and you will find them
at the end of the brook before the Wilderness of Jeruel.
17 'You will not *need* to fight in this
battle. Position yourselves, stand
[y]still and see the salvation of the LORD,
who is with you, O Judah and Jerusa-

9 *a* See Ps. 19:9, *note* *b* See Phil. 3:12, *note*
11 *c* Ezra 7:3 *d* 1 Chr. 26:30 *e* 1 Chr. 28:20; 2 Chr. 20:17
CHAPTER 20
1 *f* 1 Chr. 18:2 *g* 1 Chr. 19:15
2 *h* Gen. 14:7
3 *i* 2 Chr. 19:3
4 *j* 2 Chr. 14:11
6 *k* *Bible prayers* (OT): vv. 6–12; 2 Chr. 30:18. (Gen. 15:2; Hab. 3:1) *l* Dt. 4:39 *m* Ps. 22:28; Dan. 4:17, 25,32 *n* 1 Chr. 29:12; 2 Chr. 25:8
7 *o* Gen. 13:14–17 *p* Isa. 41:8
9 *q* 2 Chr. 6:28–30
10 *r* Num. 20:17–21; Dt. 2:4–5
11 *s* Ps. 83:1–18
12 *t* Jud. 11:27 *u* Ps. 25:15
14 *v* *Holy Spirit* (OT): v. 14; 2 Chr. 24:20. (Gen. 1:2; Zech. 12:10)
15 *w* Dt. 1:29–30 *x* vv. 24–25; 1 Sam. 17:47; 2 Chr. 32:8; Zech. 14:3

20:17 *y* Ex. 14:13–14

*
19:8 Septuagint and Vulgate read *for the inhabitants of Jerusalem.* **20:1** Following Masoretic Text and Vulgate; Septuagint reads *Meunites* (compare 26:7). **20:2** Following Masoretic Text, Septuagint, and Vulgate; some Hebrew manuscripts and Old Latin read *Edom.*

lem!' Do not fear or be dismayed; tomorrow go out against them, for the
LORD *is* with you."
18 And Jehoshaphat bowed his
head with *his* face to the ground, and
all Judah and the inhabitants of Jerusalem bowed before the LORD, [a]wor-
shiping the LORD.
19 Then the Levites of the children
of the Kohathites and of the children
of the Korahites stood up to praise the
LORD God of Israel with voices loud
and high.

Jehoshaphat and the people praise the LORD; enemy armies destroy one another

20 So they rose early in the morning and went out into the Wilderness
of Tekoa; and as they went out, Jehoshaphat stood and said, "Hear me,
O Judah and you inhabitants of Jerusalem: [b]Believe in the LORD your God,
and you shall be established; believe
His prophets, and you shall prosper."
21 And when he had consulted with
the people, he appointed those who
should sing to the LORD, and who
should praise the [c]beauty of holiness,
as they went out before the army and
were saying:

> "Praise the LORD,
> [d]For His mercy *endures*
> forever."

22 Now when they began to sing
and to praise, the LORD set ambushes
against the people of Ammon, Moab,
and Mount Seir, who had come
against Judah; and they were defeated.
23 For the people of Ammon and
Moab stood up against the inhabitants
of Mount Seir to utterly kill and destroy *them.* And when they had made
an end of the inhabitants of Seir,
[e]they helped to destroy one another.
24 So when Judah came to a place
overlooking the wilderness, they
looked toward the multitude; and
there *were* their dead bodies, fallen on
the earth. No one had escaped.
25 When Jehoshaphat and his people came to take away their spoil, they
found among them an abundance of
valuables on the dead bodies,* and
precious jewelry, which they stripped
off for themselves, more than they
could carry away; and they were three
days gathering the spoil because there
was so much.

18 *a* 2 Chr. 7:3; 29:28
20 *b* Cp. Isa. 7:9
21 *c* Ps. 29:2; 90:17; 96:9; 110:3 *d* Ps. 136:1–26
23 *e* Jud. 7:22; 1 Sam. 14:20
26 *f* Lit. *blessing.* Cp. 1 Chr. 12:3
28 *g* Cp. v. 21
29 *h* 2 Chr. 14:14; 17:10
30 *i* Job 34:29
31 *j* 1 Ki. 15:24
32 *k* 2 Chr. 14:2
33 *l* See Jud. 3:7 and 1 Ki. 3:2, *notes* *m* 2 Chr. 15:17
34 *n* Cp. 1 Ki. 16:7; see 1 Chr. 29:29, *note*
35 *o* 2 Chr. 18:1 *p* 1 Ki. 22:51–53 *q* 2 Chr. 19:2
36 *r* Cp. 2 Cor. 6:14–18 *s* 1 Ki. 9:26; 10:22

Triumphant return of Jehoshaphat and the people to Jerusalem

26 And on the fourth day they assembled in the Valley of [f]Berachah,
for there they blessed the LORD; therefore the name of that place was called
The Valley of Berachah until this day.
27 Then they returned, every man
of Judah and Jerusalem, with Jehoshaphat in front of them, to go back to
Jerusalem with joy, for the LORD had
made them rejoice over their enemies.
28 So they came to Jerusalem,
[g]with stringed instruments and harps
and trumpets, to the house of the LORD.
29 And the [h]fear of God was on all
the kingdoms of *those* countries when
they heard that the LORD had fought
against the enemies of Israel.
30 Then the realm of Jehoshaphat
was quiet, [i]for his God gave him rest
all around.

Summary of Jehoshaphat's reign (1 Ki. 22:41–49)

31 So Jehoshaphat was [j]king over
Judah. *He was* thirty-five years old
when he became king, and he reigned
twenty-five years in Jerusalem. His
mother's name *was* Azubah the
daughter of Shilhi.
32 And he walked in the way of his
father [k]Asa, and did not turn aside
from it, doing *what was* right in the
sight of the LORD.
33 Nevertheless the [l]high places
were not taken [m]away, for as yet the
people had not directed their hearts to
the God of their fathers.
34 Now the rest of the acts of Jehoshaphat, first and last, indeed they
are written in the [n]book of Jehu the
son of Hanani, which *is* mentioned in
the book of the kings of Israel.

Alliance between the kings of Judah and Israel; the LORD is displeased with Jehoshaphat

35 After this Jehoshaphat king of
Judah [o]allied himself with Ahaziah
king of Israel, [p]who acted very [q]wick-
edly.
36 And he [r]allied himself with him
[s]to make ships to go to Tarshish, and
they made the ships in Ezion Geber.
37 But Eliezer the son of Dodavah
of Mareshah prophesied against Jehoshaphat, saying, "Because you have
allied yourself with Ahaziah, the LORD
has destroyed your works." Then the

*20:25 A few Hebrew manuscripts, Old Latin, and Vulgate read *garments;* Septuagint reads *armor.*

ships were wrecked, so that they were not able to go to Tarshish.

Jehoshaphat dies; Jehoram succeeds him (1 Ki. 22:50; 2 Ki. 8:16–19)

21 AND [a]Jehoshaphat rested with his fathers, and was buried with his fathers in the City of David. Then [b]Jehoram his son reigned in his place.

2 He had brothers, the sons of Jehoshaphat: Azariah, Jehiel, Zechariah, Azaryahu, Michael, and Shephatiah; all these *were* the sons of Jehoshaphat king of Israel.

3 Their father gave them great gifts of silver and gold and precious things, with fortified cities in Judah; but he gave the kingdom to Jehoram, because he *was* the firstborn.

4 Now when Jehoram was established over the kingdom of his father, he strengthened himself and killed all his brothers with the sword, and also *others* of the princes of Israel.

5 Jehoram *was* thirty-two years old when he [1c]became king, and he reigned eight years in Jerusalem.

6 And he walked in the way of the kings of Israel, just as the house of Ahab had done, for he had the daughter of Ahab [d]as a wife; and he did evil in the sight of the LORD.

7 Yet the LORD would not destroy the house of David, because of the [e]covenant that He had made with David, and since He had promised to give a lamp to him and to his sons forever.

Edom and Libnah revolt against Judah (2 Ki. 8:20–23)

8 In his days [f]Edom revolted against Judah's authority, and made a king over themselves.

9 So Jehoram went out with his officers, and all his chariots with him. And he rose by night and attacked the Edomites who had surrounded him and the captains of the chariots.

10 Thus Edom has been in revolt against Judah's authority to this day. At that time Libnah revolted against his rule, because he had forsaken the LORD God of his fathers.

11 Moreover he made [g]high places in the mountains of Judah, and caused the inhabitants of Jerusalem to [h]commit harlotry, and led Judah astray.

Message of Elijah, written before his translation, pronouncing judgment on Jehoram

12 And a letter came to him from [i]Elijah the prophet, saying,

Thus says the LORD God of
your father David:
Because you have not walked
in the ways of Jehoshaphat
your father, or in the ways of
Asa king of Judah,
13 but have walked in the way of
the kings of Israel, and have
[j]made Judah and the
inhabitants of Jerusalem to
play the harlot [k]like the
harlotry of the house of Ahab,
and also have [l]killed your
brothers, those of your father's
household, *who were* [m]better
than yourself,
14 behold, the LORD will strike
your people with a serious
affliction—your children, your
wives, and all your
possessions;
15 and you *will become* very sick
[n]with a disease of your
intestines, until your intestines
come out by [o]reason of the
sickness, day by day.

Judah invaded by Arabians and Philistines

16 Moreover the [p]LORD [q]stirred up against Jehoram the spirit of the Philistines and the [r]Arabians who *were* near the Ethiopians.

17 And they came up into Judah and invaded it, and carried away all the possessions that were found in the king's house, and also his [s]sons and his wives, so that there was not a son left to him except [t]Jehoahaz, the youngest of his sons.

Jehoram becomes ill and dies (2 Ki. 8:23–24)

18 After all this the LORD [u]struck him in his intestines with an incurable [v]disease.

19 Then it happened in the course of time, after the end of two years, that his intestines came out because of his sickness; so he died in severe pain. And his people made no [w]burning for him, like the burning for his fathers.

20 He was thirty-two years old when he became king. He reigned in Jerusalem eight years and, [x]to no

CHAPTER 21

1
a 1 Ki. 15:24
b Or *Joram.* See v. 5, *note*

5
c 848 B.C.

6
d Cp. 2 Chr. 18:1; 22:2

7
e 2 Sam. 7:8–16

8
f 2 Ki. 14:7, 10; 2 Chr. 25:14,19

11
g See Jud. 3:7 and 1 Ki. 3:2, *notes*
h Lev. 20:5

12
i See Elijah's history in 1 Ki. 17:1–2 Ki. 2:12

13
j v. 11
k 1 Ki. 16:31–33; 2 Ki. 9:22
l v. 4
m 1 Ki. 2:32

15
n vv. 18–19
o Gen. 47:13

16
p 2 Chr. 33:11; Jer. 51:11
q 1 Ki. 11:14,23
r 2 Chr. 17:11

17
s 2 Chr. 24:7
t Or *Ahaziah,* 2 Chr. 22:1

18
u v. 15
v 2 Chr. 13:20; Acts 12:23

19
w Cp. 2 Chr. 16:14

20
x Cp. Jer. 22:18,28

[1](21:5) Jehoram (2 Ki. 8:21,23,24; 1 Chr. 3:11) began his reign as co-regent with his father Jehoshaphat (2 Ki. 8:16). Verse 5 marks the beginning of that co-regency.

one's sorrow, departed. However they
buried him in the City of David, but
not in the tombs of the kings.

Ahaziah becomes king of
Judah (2 Ki. 8:24–27)

22 THEN the inhabitants of Jerusalem made [a]Ahaziah his
youngest son king in his [b]place, for
the raiders who came with the [c]Arabi-
ans into the camp had killed all the
older *sons.* So Ahaziah the son of Jehoram, king of Judah, reigned.
2 Ahaziah *was* [d]forty-two* years
old when he became king, and he
reigned one year in Jerusalem. His
mother's name *was* Athaliah the
granddaughter of Omri.
3 He also walked in the ways of
the house of Ahab, for his mother advised him to do wickedly.
4 Therefore he did evil in the sight
of the LORD, like the house of Ahab; for
they were his counselors after the
death of his father, to his destruction.

Ahaziah joins Jehoram
defending Ramoth Gilead
(2 Ki. 8:28)

5 He also followed their advice,
and went with [e]Jehoram the son of
Ahab king of Israel to war against
Hazael king of Syria at Ramoth Gilead; and the Syrians wounded Joram.

Ahaziah visits wounded Jehoram
(Joram) at Jezreel (2 Ki. 8:29; 9:16)

6 Then he returned to Jezreel to
recover from the wounds which he
had received at Ramah, when he
fought against Hazael king of Syria.
And [f]Azariah* the son of Jehoram,
king of Judah, went down to see Jehoram the son of Ahab in Jezreel, because he was sick.
7 His going to Joram was God's
occasion for Ahaziah's [g]downfall; for
when he arrived, he went out with Jehoram against Jehu the son of Nimshi,
whom the LORD had anointed to cut off
the house of Ahab.

(Jehu's anointing and his slaying
of Jehoram precede the record
that follows. See 2 Ki. 9:1–26)

Jehu murders royal princes
of Judah (2 Ki. 10:12–14)

8 And it happened, when Jehu
was executing judgment on the house
of Ahab, and found the princes of Judah and the sons of Ahaziah's brothers who served Ahaziah, that he killed
[h]them.

Jehu executes Ahaziah, king
of Judah (2 Ki. 9:27–29)

9 Then he searched for Ahaziah;
and they caught him (he was hiding in
Samaria), and brought him to Jehu.
When they had killed him, they buried
him, "because," they said, "he is the
son of [i]Jehoshaphat, who [j]sought the
LORD with all his heart." So the house
of Ahaziah had no one to assume
power over the kingdom.

(Cp. 2 Ki. 9:30—10:36: Jehu's reign;
he executes Jezebel, etc.)

Athaliah murders royal seed of
Judah, except Joash (2 Ki. 11:1–3)

10 Now when Athaliah the mother
of Ahaziah saw that her son was dead,
she arose and [k]destroyed all the royal
heirs of the house of Judah.
11 But [l]Jehoshabeath, the daughter of the king, took [m]Joash the son of
Ahaziah, and stole him away from
among the king's sons who were being murdered, and put him and his
nurse in a bedroom. So Jehoshabeath,
the daughter of King Jehoram, the
wife of Jehoiada the priest (for she
was the sister of Ahaziah), hid him
from Athaliah so that she did not kill
him.
12 And he was hidden with them in
the house of God for six years, while
Athaliah reigned over the land.

Jehoiada places Joash on the
throne of Judah (2 Ki. 11:4–12)

23 [n]IN the [o]seventh year [p]Jehoi-
ada strengthened himself, *and*
made a covenant with the captains of
hundreds: Azariah the son of Jeroham, Ishmael the son of Jehohanan,
Azariah the son of [q]Obed, Maaseiah
the son of Adaiah, and Elishaphat the
son of Zichri.
2 And they went throughout Judah and gathered the Levites from all
the cities of Judah, and the [r]chief fathers of Israel, and they came to Jerusalem.
3 Then all the assembly made a
covenant with the king in the house of
God. And he said to them, "Behold, the
king's son shall reign, as the LORD has
[s]said of the sons of David.
4 "This *is* what you shall do: One-
third of you [t]entering on the Sabbath,
of the priests and the Levites, *shall be*
keeping watch over the doors;
5 "one-third *shall be* at the king's

CHAPTER 22

1
[a] Or *Jehoahaz,* 2 Chr. 21:17
[b] 841 B.C
[c] 2 Chr. 21:16

2
[d] Cp. 2 Ki. 8:26; see 1 Chr. 11:11, *note*

5
[e] Or *Joram,* 2 Ki. 8:28

6
[f] Or *Ahaziah,* vv. 1,7–11

7
[g] 2 Ki. 9:22–24

8
[h] Hos. 1:4

9
[i] 1 Ki. 15:24
[j] 2 Chr. 17:4; 20:3–4

10
[k] Cp. Rev. 12:1–5

11
[l] Or *Jehosheba,* 2 Ki. 11:2
[m] Or *Jehoash,* 2 Ki. 12:18

CHAPTER 23

1
[n] vv. 1–21
[o] 2 Ki. 11:4
[p] 2 Ki. 12:2
[q] 1 Chr. 2:37–38

2
[r] Ezra 1:5

3
[s] 2 Sam. 7:12; 1 Ki. 2:4; 9:5; 2 Chr. 6:16; 7:18; 21:7

4
[t] 1 Chr. 9:25

*
22:2 Or *twenty-two* (compare 2 Kings 8:26)
22:6 Some Hebrew manuscripts, Septuagint, Syriac, Vulgate, and 2 Kings 8:29 read *Ahaziah*.

house; and one-third at the Gate of the Foundation. All the people *shall be* in the courts of the house of the LORD.

6 "But let no one come into the house of the LORD except the priests and [a]those of the Levites who serve. They may go in, for they *are* holy; but all the people shall keep the watch of the LORD.

7 "And the Levites shall surround the king on all sides, every man with his weapons in his hand; and whoever comes into the house, let him be put to death. You are to be with the king when he comes in and when he goes out."

8 So the Levites and all Judah did according to all that Jehoiada the priest commanded. And each man took his men who were to be on duty on the Sabbath, with those who were going *off duty* on the Sabbath; for Jehoiada the priest had not dismissed the [b]divisions.

9 And Jehoiada the priest gave to the captains of hundreds the spears and the large and small [c]shields which *had belonged* to King David, that *were* in the temple of God.

10 Then he set all the people, every man with his weapon in his hand, from the right side of the temple to the left side of the temple, along by the altar and by the temple, all around the king.

11 And they brought out the king's son, put the crown on him, [d]*gave him* the [e]Testimony,* and made him king. Then Jehoiada and his sons anointed him, and said, "*Long* live the king!"

Athaliah is executed
(2 Ki. 11:13–16)

12 Now when [f]Athaliah heard the noise of the people running and praising the king, she came to the people *in* the temple of the LORD.

13 When she looked, there was the king standing by his pillar at the entrance; and the leaders and the trumpeters *were* by the king. All the people of the land were rejoicing and blowing trumpets, also the singers with musical instruments, and [g]those who led in praise. So Athaliah tore her clothes and said, [h]"Treason! Treason!"

14 And Jehoiada the priest brought out the captains of hundreds who were set over the army, and said to them, "Take her outside under guard, and slay with the sword whoever follows her." For the priest had said, "Do not kill her in the house of the LORD."

6
a 1 Chr. 23:28–32
8
b 1 Chr. 24:5–31
9
c 2 Sam. 8:7
11
d Dt. 17:18
e Ex. 25:16; 31:18
12
f 2 Chr. 22:10
13
g 1 Chr. 25:8
h 2 Ki. 9:23
15
i Neh. 3:28
j Cp. 2 Chr. 22:10
16
k Josh. 24:24–25; 2 Chr. 15:12–15
17
l Cp. 2 Chr. 24:7
m Dt. 13:9; 1 Ki. 18:40
18
n 1 Chr. 23:6–24:31
o Num. 28:2
19
p 1 Chr. 26:1–9
20
q 1 Ki. 9:22
CHAPTER 24
1
r Or *Jehoash,* 2 Ki. 11:21
s 835 B.C.

15 So they seized her; and she went by way of the entrance of the [i]Horse Gate *into* the king's house, and they [j]killed her there.

Revival through Jehoiada (2 Ki. 11:17–20)

16 Then Jehoiada made a [k]covenant between himself, the people, and the king, that they should be the LORD's people.

17 And all the people went to the [l]temple* of Baal, and tore it down. They broke in pieces its altars and images, and [m]killed Mattan the priest of Baal before the altars.

18 Also Jehoiada appointed the oversight of the house of the LORD to the hand of the priests, the Levites, whom David had [n]assigned in the house of the LORD, to offer the burnt offerings of the LORD, as *it is* written in the [o]Law of Moses, with rejoicing and with singing, *as it was established* by David.

19 And he set the [p]gatekeepers at the gates of the house of the LORD, so that no one *who was* in any way unclean should enter.

20 [q]Then he took the captains of hundreds, the nobles, the governors of the people, and all the people of the land, and brought the king down from the house of the LORD; and they went through the Upper Gate to the king's house, and set the king on the throne of the kingdom.

21 So all the people of the land rejoiced; and the city was quiet, for they had slain Athaliah with the sword.

Joash's reign strongly influenced by Jehoiada, the priest
(2 Ki. 11:21—12:3)

24 [r]JOASH *was* seven years old when he [s]became king, and he reigned forty years in Jerusalem. His mother's name *was* Zibiah of Beersheba.

2 Joash did *what was* right in the sight of the LORD all the days of Jehoiada the priest.

3 And Jehoiada took two wives for him, and he had sons and daughters.

Faithless priests delay temple repairs 23 years (2 Ki. 12:4–8)

4 Now it happened after this *that* Joash set his heart on repairing the house of the LORD.

5 Then he gathered the priests and the Levites, and said to them, "Go out

*
23:11 That is, the Law (compare Exodus 25:16,21; 31:18) **23:17** Literally *house*

to the cities of Judah, and gather from all [a]Israel money to [b]repair the house of your God from year to year, and see that you do it quickly." However the Levites did not do it quickly.

6 So the king called Jehoiada the chief *priest*, and said to him, "Why have you not required the Levites to bring in from Judah and from Jerusalem the [c]collection, *according to the commandment* of [d]Moses the servant of the LORD and of the assembly of Israel, for the [e]tabernacle of witness?"

7 For the [f]sons of Athaliah, that wicked woman, had broken into the house of God, and had also presented all the dedicated things of the house of the LORD to the Baals.

(The "cutting off" of Israel and the reign of Jehoahaz precede the record that follows. See 2 Ki. 10:32–35; 13:1–2)

Temple repairs completed by freewill offerings (2 Ki. 12:9–16)

8 Then at the [g]king's command they made a [h]chest, and set it outside at the gate of the house of the LORD.

9 And they made a proclamation throughout Judah and Jerusalem to bring to the LORD the collection *that* Moses the servant of God *had imposed* on Israel in the wilderness.

10 Then all the leaders and all the people rejoiced, brought their contributions, and put *them* into the chest until all had given.

11 So it was, at that time, when the chest was brought to the king's official by the hand of the Levites, and [i]when they saw that *there was* much money, that the king's scribe and the high priest's officer came and emptied the chest, and took it and returned it to its place. Thus they did day by day, and gathered money in abundance.

12 The king and Jehoiada gave it to those who did the work of the service of the house of the LORD; and they hired masons and carpenters to [j]repair the house of the LORD, and also those who worked in iron and bronze to restore the house of the LORD.

13 So the workmen labored, and the work was completed by them; they restored the house of God to its original condition and reinforced it.

14 When they had finished, they brought the rest of the money before the king and Jehoiada; they made from it articles for the house of the LORD, articles for serving and offering, spoons and vessels of gold and silver. And they offered burnt offerings in the house of the LORD continually all the days of Jehoiada.

Death of Jehoiada; apostasy of the leaders

15 But Jehoiada grew old and was full of days, and he died; *he was* one hundred and thirty years old when he died.

16 And they buried him in the City of David among the [k]kings, because he had done good in Israel, both toward God and His house.

17 Now after the death of Jehoiada the leaders of Judah came and bowed down to the king. And the king listened to them.

18 Therefore they left the house of the LORD God of their fathers, and served [l]wooden images and idols; and wrath came upon Judah and Jerusalem because of their [m]trespass.

19 [n]Yet He sent prophets to them, to bring them back to the LORD; and they testified against them, but they would not listen.

(The repentance of Jehoahaz and Jehoash's co-reign over Israel precede the record that follows. See 2 Ki. 13:4,10)

Joash slays Zechariah, the son of Jehoiada

20 Then the [o]Spirit of God came upon [p]Zechariah the son of Jehoiada the priest, who stood above the people, and said to them, "Thus says God: 'Why do you transgress the commandments of the LORD, so that you cannot [q]prosper? Because you have forsaken the LORD, He also has forsaken [r]you.' "

21 So they conspired against him, and at the command of the king they stoned him with stones in the court of the house of the LORD.

22 Thus Joash the king did [s]not remember the kindness which Jehoiada [t]his father had done to him, but killed his son; and as he died, he said, "The LORD look on *it*, and [u]repay!"

Syria invades and defeats Judah (2 Ki. 12:17–18). Cp. invasion of Israel, 2 Ki. 13:7

23 So it happened in the spring of the year *that* the army of [v]Syria came up against him; and they came to Judah and Jerusalem, and destroyed all the leaders of the people from among the people, and sent all their spoil to the king of Damascus.

24 For the army of the Syrians

5
[a] i.e. *the northern or ten-tribe kingdom*
[b] v. 12

6
[c] Cp. Ex. 30:11–16
[d] Dt. 34:5
[e] Num. 1:50; Acts 7:44

7
[f] 2 Chr. 21:17

8
[g] 2 Chr. 30:12
[h] Cp. Lk. 21:1

11
[i] Cp. Ezra 8:24–30

12
[j] 2 Ki. 22:5–6

16
[k] Cp. 2 Chr. 21:20

18
[l] See Dt. 16:21, *note*
[m] Ex. 34:12–14

19
[n] 2 Ki. 17:13; 21:10–15; 2 Chr. 36:15–16

20
[o] *Holy Spirit* (OT): v. 20; Neh. 9:20. (Gen. 1:2; Zech. 12:10)
[p] Mt. 23:35
[q] Prov. 28:13
[r] 2 Chr. 15:2

22
[s] Cp. Ex. 1:8
[t] i.e. *Zechariah's father*
[u] Gen. 9:5

23
[v] Isa. 7:2

came with a small company of men;
but the LORD delivered a very great
army into their hand, because they
had forsaken the LORD God of their
fathers. So they [a]executed judgment
against Joash.

(For death of Jehoahaz and Elisha
and reign of Jehoash over Israel,
see 2 Ki. 13:8–11,14–20)

Joash dies (2 Ki. 12:19–21)

25 And when they had withdrawn
from him (for they left him severely
wounded), his own [b]servants conspired against him because of the
blood of the sons* of Jehoiada the
priest, and killed him on his bed. So he
died. And they buried him in the City
of David, but they did not bury him in
the tombs of the kings.
26 These are the ones who conspired against him: [c]Zabad the son of
Shimeath the Ammonitess, and Jehozabad the son of [d]Shimrith the Moabitess.
27 Now *concerning* his sons, and
the many oracles about him, and the
repairing of the house of God, indeed
they *are* written in the annals of the
book of the kings. Then Amaziah his
son reigned in his place.

Amaziah becomes king of Judah
(2 Ki. 12:21; 14:1–6)

25

AMAZIAH *was* twenty-five
years old *when* he [e]became
king, and he reigned twenty-nine
years in Jerusalem. His mother's
name *was* Jehoaddan of Jerusalem.
2 And he did *what was* right in the
sight of the LORD, but [f]not with a
[g]loyal heart.
3 Now it happened, as soon as the
kingdom was established for him, that
he executed his [h]servants who had
murdered his father the king.
4 However he did not execute
their children, but *did* as *it is* written
in the Law in the Book of Moses,
where the LORD commanded, saying,
"The fathers shall not be put to death
for their children, nor shall the children be put to death for their fathers;
but a person shall die for his own
[i]sin."

(For miracle at Elisha's tomb;
prophecy fulfilled, see 2 Ki. 13:20–25)

Amaziah defeats Edom without Israelite
mercenaries (2 Ki. 14:7)

5 Moreover Amaziah gathered Judah together and set over them captains of thousands and captains of
hundreds, according to *their* fathers'
houses, throughout all Judah and
Benjamin; and he numbered them
from [j]twenty years old and above,
and found them to be [k]three hundred
thousand choice *men, able* to go to
war, who could handle spear and
shield.
6 He also hired one hundred thousand mighty men of valor from Israel
for one hundred [l]talents of silver.
7 But a [m]man of God came to him,
saying, "O king, do not let the army of
Israel go with you, for the LORD *is* not
with Israel—*not with* any of the children of [1]Ephraim.
8 "But if you go, be gone! Be
strong in battle! *Even so,* God shall
make you fall before the enemy; for
God has power to help and to [n]over-
throw."
9 Then Amaziah said to the man
of God, "But what *shall we* do about
the hundred [l]talents which I have
given to the troops of Israel?" And the
man of God answered, "The LORD is
able to give you much more than this."
10 So Amaziah discharged the
troops that had come to him from
Ephraim, to go back home. Therefore
their anger was greatly aroused
against Judah, and they returned
home in great anger.
11 Then Amaziah strengthened
himself, and leading his people, he
went to the [o]Valley of Salt and killed
ten thousand of the people of Seir.
12 Also the children of Judah took
captive ten thousand alive, brought
them to the top of the rock, and cast
them down from the top of the rock, so
that they all were dashed in [p]pieces.
13 But as for the soldiers of the
army which Amaziah had discharged,
so that they would not go with him to
battle, they raided the cities of Judah
from Samaria to Beth Horon, killed
three thousand in them, and took
much spoil.

Amaziah rebuked for idolatry

14 Now it was so, after Amaziah
came from the slaughter of the Edomites, that he brought the gods of the
people of Seir, set [q]them up *to be* his

24
a 2 Chr. 22:8
25
b 2 Chr. 25:3
26
c Or *Jozabad,* 2 Ki. 12:21
d Or *Shomer,* 2 Ki. 12:21
CHAPTER 25
1
e 796 B.C.
2
f v. 14
g See Phil. 3:12, *note*
3
h 2 Chr. 24:25
4
i Dt. 24:16; Jer. 31:30
5
j Num. 1:3
k Cp. 2 Chr. 17:12–19; 26:12–13
6
l See Coinage (OT), Ex. 30:13, *note*
7
m 2 Chr. 11:2
8
n 2 Chr. 14:11; 20:6
11
o 2 Ki. 14:7
12
p Cp. Obad. 3
14
q Cp. 2 Chr. 28:23

*
24:25 Septuagint and Vulgate read *son* (compare verses 20–22).

[1](25:7) Used in a collective sense for the northern ten-tribe kingdom, called also Israel.

gods, and bowed down before them and burned incense to them.

15 Therefore the anger of the LORD was aroused against Amaziah, and He sent him a prophet who said to him, "Why have you sought the gods of the people, which could not rescue their own people from your [a]hand?"

16 So it was, as he talked with him, that *the king* said to him, "Have we made you the king's counselor? Cease! Why should you be killed?" Then the prophet ceased, and said, "I know that God has determined to destroy you, because you have done this and have not heeded my advice."

Amaziah defeated by Joash (Jehoash), king of Israel (2 Ki. 14:8–14)

17 Now Amaziah king of Judah asked advice and sent to Joash* the son of Jehoahaz, the son of Jehu, king of Israel, saying, "Come, let us face one another *in battle*."

18 And Joash king of Israel sent to Amaziah king of Judah, saying, [b]"The thistle that *was* in Lebanon sent to the cedar that was in Lebanon, saying, 'Give your daughter to my son as wife'; and a wild beast that *was* in Lebanon passed by and trampled the thistle.

19 "Indeed you say that you have defeated the Edomites, and your heart is lifted up to [c]boast. Stay at home now; why should you meddle with trouble, that you should fall—you and Judah with you?"

20 But Amaziah would not heed, for it *came* from God, that He might give them into the hand *of their enemies*, because they sought the gods of Edom.

21 So Joash king of Israel went out; and he and Amaziah king of Judah faced one another at [d]Beth Shemesh, which *belongs* to Judah.

22 And Judah was defeated by Israel, and every man fled to his tent.

23 Then Joash the king of Israel captured Amaziah king of Judah, the son of Joash, the son of [e]Jehoahaz, at Beth Shemesh; and he brought him to Jerusalem, and broke down the wall of Jerusalem from the Gate of Ephraim to the Corner Gate—four hundred [f]cubits.

24 And *he took* all the gold and silver, all the articles that were found in the house of God with [g]Obed-Edom, the treasures of the king's house, and hostages, and returned to Samaria.

15
a vv. 11:12; cp. Jud. 6:31
18
b Parables (OT): vv. 18–19; Isa. 5:1. (Jud. 9:8; Zech. 11:7)
19
c 2 Chr. 26:16; Prov. 16:18
21
d Josh. 19:38
23
e Or *Ahaziah*, 2 Chr. 22:1; cp. 2 Chr. 21:1
f See Weights and Measures (OT), 2 Chr. 2:10, *note*
24
g 1 Chr. 26:15
27
h Cp. 2 Chr. 24:25–26
CHAPTER 26
1
i Or *Azariah*, 2 Ki. 14:21; 15:1
3
j Cp. 2 Ki. 15:32–34
4
k 2 Chr. 24:2
5
l Gen. 41:15; Dan. 1:17
m 2 Chr. 15:2; 20:20; 31:21
7
n 2 Chr. 21:16

(For death of Jehoash of Israel, cp. 2 Ki. 13:12–13; 14:15–16; for reign of Jeroboam II over Israel, see 2 Ki. 13:5,6,13; 14:16,23–27)

Last years and death of Amaziah (2 Ki. 14:17–20)

25 Amaziah the son of Joash, king of Judah, lived fifteen years after the death of Joash the son of Jehoahaz, king of Israel.

26 Now the rest of the acts of Amaziah, from first to last, indeed *are* they not written in the book of the kings of Judah and Israel?

27 After the time that Amaziah turned away from following the LORD, they made a [h]conspiracy against him in Jerusalem, and he fled to Lachish; but they sent after him to Lachish and killed him there.

28 Then they brought him on horses and buried him with his fathers in the City of Judah.

(Interregnum)

Uzziah becomes king of Judah (2 Ki. 14:21—15:4)

26 NOW all the people of Judah took [i]Uzziah, who *was* sixteen years old, and made him king instead of his father Amaziah.

2 He built Elath* and restored it to Judah, after the king rested with his fathers.

3 Uzziah *was* [j]sixteen years old when he became king, and he reigned fifty-two years in Jerusalem. His mother's name was Jecholiah of Jerusalem.

4 And he did *what was* [k]right in the sight of the LORD, according to all that his father Amaziah had done.

5 He sought God in the days of Zechariah, who [l]had understanding in the visions* of God; and as long as he sought the LORD, God made him [m]prosper.

Uzziah's prosperity and prowess in war

6 Now he went out and made war against the Philistines, and broke down the wall of Gath, the wall of Jabneh, and the wall of Ashdod; and he built cities *around* Ashdod and among the Philistines.

7 God helped him against the [n]Philistines, against the Arabians who lived in Gur Baal, and against the Meunites.

*

25:17 Spelled *Jehoash* in 2 Kings 14:8ff
26:2 Hebrew *Eloth* 26:5 Several Hebrew manuscripts, Septuagint, Syriac, Targum, and Arabic read *fear*.

8 Also the Ammonites [a]brought
tribute to Uzziah. His fame spread as
far as the entrance of Egypt, for he
became exceedingly strong.
9 And Uzziah built towers in Jerusalem at the [b]Corner Gate, at the Valley Gate, and at the corner buttress of
the wall; then he fortified them.
10 Also he built towers in the desert. He dug many wells, for he had
much livestock, both in the [c]lowlands
and in the plains; *he also had* farmers
and vinedressers in the mountains
and in Carmel, for he loved the soil.
11 Moreover Uzziah had an army
of fighting men who went out to war
by companies, according to the number on their roll as prepared by Jeiel
the scribe and Maaseiah the officer,
under the hand of Hananiah, *one* of
the king's captains.
12 The total number of chief officers* of the mighty men of valor *was*
two thousand six hundred.
13 And under their authority *was*
an army of three hundred and seven
thousand five hundred, that made war
with mighty power, to help the king
against the enemy.
14 Then Uzziah prepared for them,
for the entire army, shields, spears,
helmets, body armor, bows, and slings
to cast stones.
15 And he made devices in Jerusalem, invented by [d]skillful men, to be
on the towers and the corners, to
shoot arrows and large stones. So his
fame spread far and wide, for he was
marvelously helped till he became
strong.

(Death of Jeroboam II; interregnum and reigns of Zechariah, Shallum, Menahem, precede the record that follows. See 2 Ki. 14:28–29; 15:8–18)

Uzziah's sin and punishment. Jotham succeeds him (2 Ki. 15:5–7,32)

16 But when he was strong his
heart was [e]lifted up, to *his* destruction, for he [f]transgressed against the
LORD his God by [g]entering the temple
of the LORD to burn incense on the altar of incense.
17 So [h]Azariah the priest went in
after him, and with him were eighty
priests of the LORD—valiant men.
18 And they [i]withstood King Uzziah, and said to him, "*It is* [j]not for
you, Uzziah, to burn incense to the
LORD, but for the [k]priests, the sons of
Aaron, who are consecrated to burn
incense. Get out of the sanctuary, for
you have trespassed! You *shall have*
no honor from the LORD God."
19 Then Uzziah became furious;
and he *had* a censer in his hand to
burn incense. And while he was angry
with the priests, [l]leprosy broke out on
his [m]forehead, before the priests in the
house of the LORD, beside the incense
altar.
20 And Azariah the chief priest and
all the priests looked at him, and
there, on his forehead, he *was* leprous;
so they thrust him out of that place.
Indeed he also hurried to get out, because the LORD had struck him.
21 King Uzziah was a [n]leper until
the day of his death. He dwelt in an
[o]isolated house, because he was a
leper; for he was cut off from the
house of the LORD. Then Jotham his
son *was* over the king's house, judging the people of the land.
22 Now the rest of the acts of Uzziah, from first to last, the prophet
[p]Isaiah the son of Amoz [q]wrote.
23 [r]So Uzziah rested with his fathers, and they buried him with his
fathers in the field of burial which *belonged* to the kings, for they said, "He
is a leper." Then Jotham his son
reigned in his place.

(Invasion of Israel by Tiglath-Pileser; reigns of Remaliah and Pekah precede ch. 27. See 2 Ki. 15:22–28)

Jotham of Judah reigns and dies (2 Ki. 15:7,32–38)

27 JOTHAM [s]*was* twenty-five
years old when he became
king, and he reigned sixteen years in
Jerusalem. His mother's name *was* Jerushah* the daughter of Zadok.
2 And he did *what was* right in the
sight of the [t]LORD, according to all
that his father Uzziah had done (although he did not enter the temple of
the LORD). But still the [u]people acted
corruptly.
3 He built the Upper Gate of the
house of the LORD, and he built extensively on the wall of [v]Ophel.
4 Moreover he built cities in the
mountains of Judah, and in the forests
he built fortresses and towers.
5 He also fought with the king of
the [w]Ammonites and defeated them.
And the people of Ammon gave him in
that year one hundred [x]talents of sil-

8 *a* 2 Sam. 8:2; 2 Chr. 17:11
9 *b* 2 Chr. 25:23
10 c See Dt. 1:7, *note*
15 *d* Ex. 39:3,8
16 *e* 2 Chr. 25:19 *f* Cp. 1 Sam. 13:9–14 *g* 1 Ki. 13:1–4; 2 Ki. 16:12–13
17 *h* 1 Chr. 6:10
18 *i* Cp. 2 Chr. 19:2 *j* Num. 16:40 *k* Ex. 30:7–8; Heb. 7:14
19 *l* *Miracles* (OT): vv. 16–21; Isa. 37:36. (Gen. 5:24; Jon. 1:17, *note*) *m* Lev. 13:42
21 *n* Cp. 2 Ki. 5:1–14 *o* Lev. 13:46; Num. 5:2
22 *p* 2 Ki. 20:1; 2 Chr. 32:20,32; Isa. 1:1 *q* See 1 Chr. 29:29, *note*
23 *r* Isa. 6:1
CHAPTER 27
1 *s* 2 Ki. 15:5
2 *t* Cp. 2 Chr. 26:16 *u* Ezek. 20:44
3 *v* 2 Chr. 33:14
5 *w* 2 Chr. 26:8 *x* See Coinage (OT), Ex. 30:13; cp. 2 Chr. 2:10, *note*

*
26:12 Literally *chief fathers* **27:1** Spelled *Jerusha* in 2 Kings 15:33

ver, ten thousand [a]kors of wheat, and ten thousand of barley. The people of Ammon paid this to him in the second and third years also.

6 So Jotham became mighty, [b]because he [c]prepared his ways before the LORD his God.

7 Now the rest of the acts of Jotham, and all his wars and his ways, indeed they *are* written in the book of the kings of Israel and Judah.

8 He was twenty-five years old when he became king, and he reigned sixteen years in Jerusalem.

9 So Jotham rested with his fathers, and they buried him in the City of David. Then [d]Ahaz his son reigned in his place.

(The beginning of northern kingdom's captivity precedes ch. 28. See 1 Chr. 5:25–26)

Ahaz becomes king (2 Ki. 15:38—16:4)

28 [e]AHAZ *was* twenty years old when he became king, and he reigned sixteen years in Jerusalem; and he did not do *what was* right in the sight of the LORD, as his father David *had done.*

2 For he walked in the ways of the kings of Israel, and made [f]molded images for the Baals.

3 He burned incense in the Valley of the Son of [g]Hinnom, and burned [h]his children in the [i]fire, according to the abominations of the nations whom the LORD had [j]cast out before the children of Israel.

4 And he sacrificed and burned incense on the [k]high places, on the hills, and under every green tree.

Syria, Israel, and others invade Judah (2 Ki. 16:5–6)

5 Therefore the LORD his God delivered him into the hand of the king of [l]Syria. They [m]defeated him, and carried away a great multitude of them as captives, and brought *them* to Damascus. Then he was also delivered into the hand of the king of Israel, who defeated him with a great slaughter.

6 For [n]Pekah the son of Remaliah killed one hundred and twenty thousand in Judah in one day, all valiant men, [o]because they had forsaken the LORD God of their fathers.

7 Zichri, a mighty man of Ephraim, killed Maaseiah the king's son, Azrikam the officer over the house, and Elkanah *who was* second to the king.

8 And the children of Israel carried away [p]captive of [q]their brethren two hundred thousand women, sons, and daughters; and they also took away much spoil from them, and brought the spoil to Samaria.

Oded secures release of captives

9 But a [r]prophet of the LORD was there, whose name *was* Oded; and he went out before the army that came to Samaria, and said to them: "Look, [s]because the LORD God of your fathers was angry with Judah, He has delivered them into your hand; but you have killed them in a rage *that* [t]reaches up to heaven.

10 "And now you propose to force the children of Judah and Jerusalem to be your [u]male and female slaves; *but are* you not also guilty before the LORD your God?

11 "Now hear me, therefore, and return the captives, whom you have taken captive from your brethren, for the [v]fierce wrath of the LORD *is* upon you."

12 Then some of the heads of the children of Ephraim, Azariah the son of Johanan, Berechiah the son of Meshillemoth, Jehizkiah the son of Shallum, and Amasa the son of Hadlai, stood up against those who came from the war,

13 and said to them, "You shall not bring the captives here, for we *already* have offended the LORD. You intend to add to our sins and to our guilt; for our guilt is great, and *there is* fierce wrath against Israel."

14 So the armed men left the captives and the spoil before the leaders and all the assembly.

15 Then the men [w]who were designated by name rose up and took the captives, and from the spoil they clothed all who were naked among them, dressed them and gave them sandals, [x]gave them food and drink, and anointed them; and they let all the feeble ones ride on donkeys. So they brought them to their brethren at Jericho, the [y]city of palm trees. Then they returned to Samaria.

Edom and Philistia invade Judah; Ahaz compromises with Assyria (2 Ki. 15:29; 16:7–18)

16 [z]At the same time King Ahaz

5
a See Weights and Measures (OT), 2 Chr. 2:10, *note*
6
b 2 Chr. 26:5
c Lit. *established*
9
d Isa. 1:1; Hos. 1:1; Mic. 1:1
CHAPTER 28
1
e 2 Ki. 16:10–11
2
f Ex. 34:17; Lev. 19:4
3
g Josh. 15:8
h 2 Chr. 33:6
i Lev. 18:21
j Lev. 18:24–30
4
k See Jud. 3:7 and 1 Ki. 3:2, *notes*
5
l Isa. 10:5
m Isa. 7:1, 17
6
n 2 Ki. 15:27
o 2 Chr. 29:8
8
p Dt. 28:25, 41
q Cp. 2 Chr. 11:4
9
r 2 Chr. 25:15
s Ps. 69:26
t Ezra 9:6; Rev. 18:5
10
u Lev. 25:39
11
v Ps. 78:49
15
w v. 12
x 2 Ki. 6:22; Prov. 25:21–22
y Dt. 34:3; Jud. 1:16
16
z Cp. v. 23

sent to the kings* of Assyria to help
him.
17 For again the [a]Edomites had
come, attacked Judah, and carried
away captives.
18 The [b]Philistines also had invaded the cities of the [c]lowland and of
the South of Judah, and had taken
Beth Shemesh, Aijalon, Gederoth, Sochoh with its villages, Timnah with its
villages, and Gimzo with its villages;
and they dwelt there.
19 For the LORD brought Judah low
because of Ahaz king of [d]Israel, for he
had [e]encouraged moral decline in Judah and had been continually unfaithful to the LORD.
20 Also [f]Tiglath-Pileser* king of
Assyria came to him and distressed
him, and did not assist him.
21 For Ahaz took part *of the treasures* from the house of the LORD,
from the house of the king, and from
the leaders, and he gave *it* to the king
of Assyria; but he did [g]not help him.
22 Now in the time of his distress
King Ahaz became increasingly unfaithful to the LORD. This *is that* King
Ahaz.
23 For he sacrificed to the [h]gods of
Damascus which had defeated him,
saying, "Because the gods of the kings
of Syria help them, I will sacrifice to
them that [i]they may help me." But
they were the ruin of him and of all
Israel.
24 So Ahaz gathered the articles of
the house of God, cut in pieces the articles of the house of God, [j]shut up the
doors of the house of the LORD, and
made for himself altars in every corner
of Jerusalem.
25 And in every single city of Judah
he made [k]high places to burn incense
to other gods, and provoked to anger
the LORD God of his fathers.

Ahaz dies;
Hezekiah succeeds him
(2 Ki. 16:19–20)

26 Now the rest of his acts and all
his ways, from first to last, indeed they
are written in the book of the kings of
Judah and Israel.
27 So Ahaz rested with his fathers,
and they buried him in the city, in Jerusalem; but they did [l]not bring him
into the tombs of the kings of Israel.
Then Hezekiah his son reigned in his
place.

17 [a] 2 Chr. 21:10; Obad. 10–14
18 [b] 2 Chr. 21:16–27; Ezek. 16:27,57 [c] See Dt. 1:7, *note*
19 [d] 2 Ki. 16:2 [e] Ex. 32:25
20 [f] 2 Ki. 15:29; 1 Chr. 5:26
21 [g] Cp. 1 Sam. 7:12
23 [h] 2 Chr. 25:14 [i] Jer. 44:17–18
24 [j] 2 Chr. 29:7
25 [k] See Jud. 3:7 and 1 Ki. 3:2, *notes*
27 [l] 2 Chr. 21:20; 24:25
CHAPTER 29
1 [m] 2 Chr. 32:22
3 [n] See Lev. 23:2, *note* [o] Cp. 2 Chr. 28:24
5 [p] *Sanctification* (OT): v. 5; 2 Chr. 29:17. (Gen. 2:3; Zech. 8:3)
6 [q] Isa. 1:4; Ezek. 8:16
8 [r] 2 Chr. 24:18 [s] 2 Chr. 28:5 [t] 1 Ki. 9:8; Jer. 18:16; 19:8; 25:9, 18; 29:18 [u] Dt. 28:32
9 [v] Dt. 28:25; 2 Chr. 28:17
10 [w] 2 Chr. 23:16

(The death of Pekah in Israel,
an interregnum, and Hoshea's
reign over Israel precede ch. 29.
See 2 Ki. 15:30–31; 17:6)

Hezekiah's reign over Judah
(2 Ki. 18:1–7. Cp. Isa. 36—39)

29 [m]HEZEKIAH became king
when he was twenty-five years
old, and he reigned twenty-nine years
in Jerusalem. His mother's name *was*
Abijah* the daughter of Zechariah.
2 And he did *what was* right in the
sight of the LORD, according to all that
his father David had done.

Revival under Hezekiah

3 In the first year of his reign, in
the [n]first month, he [o]opened the
doors of the house of the LORD and repaired them.
4 Then he brought in the priests
and the Levites, and gathered them in
the East Square,
5 and said to them: "Hear me, Levites! Now [p]sanctify yourselves, sanctify the house of the LORD God of your
fathers, and carry out the rubbish
from the holy *place.*
6 "For our fathers have trespassed
and done evil in the eyes of the LORD
our God; they have forsaken Him,
have turned their faces away from the
dwelling place of the LORD, and turned
their [q]backs *on Him.*
7 "They have also shut up the
doors of the vestibule, put out the
lamps, and have not burned incense
or offered burnt offerings in the holy
place to the God of Israel.
8 "Therefore the [r]wrath of the
LORD fell upon Judah and Jerusalem,
and He has [s]given them up to trouble,
to desolation, and to [t]jeering, as you
see with your [u]eyes.
9 "For indeed, because of this our
fathers have fallen by the sword; and
our sons, our daughters, and our wives
are in [v]captivity.
10 "Now *it is* in my heart to make
a [w]covenant with the LORD God of Israel, that His fierce wrath may turn
away from us.
11 "My sons, do not be negligent
now, for the LORD has chosen [x]you to
stand before Him, to serve Him, and
that you should minister to Him and
burn incense."

29:11 [x] Num. 3:6; 8:6; 2 Chr. 30:16–17

*

28:16 Septuagint, Syriac, and Vulgate read *king* (compare verse 20). **28:20** Hebrew *Tilgath-Pilneser* **29:1** Spelled *Abi* in 2 Kings 18:2

12 Then these Levites arose: [a]Mahath the son of Amasai and Joel the son of Azariah, of the sons of the [b]Kohathites; of the sons of Merari, Kish the son of Abdi and Azariah the son of Jehallelel; of the Gershonites, Joah the son of Zimmah and Eden the son of Joah;

13 of the sons of Elizaphan, Shimri and Jeiel; of the sons of Asaph, Zechariah and Mattaniah;

14 of the sons of Heman, Jehiel and Shimei; and of the sons of Jeduthun, Shemaiah and Uzziel.

15 And they gathered their brethren, sanctified themselves, and went according to the commandment of the king, at the words of the LORD, to [c]cleanse the house of the LORD.

16 Then the priests went into the inner part of the house of the LORD to cleanse *it,* and brought out all the debris that they found in the temple of the LORD to the court of the house of the LORD. And the Levites took *it* out and carried *it* to the Brook [d]Kidron.

17 Now they began to sanctify on the first *day* of the [e]first month, and on the eighth day of the month they came to the vestibule of the LORD. So they [f]sanctified the house of the LORD in eight days, and on the sixteenth day of the first month they finished.

18 Then they went in to King Hezekiah and said, "We have cleansed all the house of the LORD, the altar of burnt offerings with all its articles, and the table of the [g]showbread with all its articles.

19 "Moreover all the articles which King Ahaz in his reign had [h]cast aside in his transgression we have prepared and sanctified; and there they *are,* before the altar of the LORD."

Hezekiah restores temple worship

20 Then King Hezekiah rose early, gathered the rulers of the city, and went up to the house of the LORD.

21 And they brought seven bulls, seven rams, seven lambs, and seven male goats for a [i]sin offering for the kingdom, for the sanctuary, and for Judah. Then he commanded the priests, the sons of Aaron, to offer *them* on the altar of the LORD.

22 So they killed the bulls, and the priests received the blood and sprinkled *it* on the altar. Likewise they killed the rams and sprinkled the blood on the altar. They also killed the lambs and sprinkled the blood on the altar.

23 Then they brought out the male goats *for* the sin offering before the king and the assembly, and they [j]laid their hands on them.

24 And the priests killed them; and they presented their blood on the altar as a sin offering to make an [k]atonement for all Israel, for the king commanded *that* the burnt offering and the sin offering *be made* for all Israel.

25 And he [l]stationed the Levites in the house of the LORD with cymbals, with stringed instruments, and with harps, [m]according to the commandment of David, of [n]Gad the king's seer, and of Nathan the prophet; for [o]thus *was* the commandment of the LORD by his prophets.

26 The Levites stood with the instruments of David, and the priests with the [p]trumpets.

27 Then Hezekiah commanded *them* to offer the burnt offering on the altar. And when the burnt offering began, the song of the LORD *also* began, with the trumpets and with the instruments [q]of David king of Israel.

28 So all the assembly worshiped, the singers sang, and the trumpeters sounded; all *this continued* until the burnt offering was finished.

29 And when they had finished offering, the [r]king and all who were present with him bowed and worshiped.

30 Moreover King Hezekiah and the leaders commanded the Levites to sing praise to the LORD with the words of David and of Asaph the seer. So they sang praises with gladness, and they bowed their heads and worshiped.

31 Then Hezekiah answered and said, "Now *that* you have consecrated yourselves to the LORD, come near, and bring sacrifices and thank offerings into the house of the LORD." So the assembly brought in sacrifices and [s]thank offerings, and as many as were of a [t]willing heart *brought* burnt offerings.

32 And the number of the burnt offerings which the assembly brought was seventy bulls, one hundred rams, *and* two hundred lambs; all these *were* for a burnt offering to the LORD.

33 The consecrated things *were* six hundred bulls and three thousand sheep.

34 But the priests were too few, so that they could not skin all the burnt offerings; therefore their brethren the Levites helped them until the work

12 *a* 2 Chr. 31:13 *b* Num. 3:19–20
15 *c* 1 Chr. 23:28
16 *d* 2 Chr. 15:16; 30:14
17 *e* See Lev. 23:2, *note* *f Sanctification* (OT): v. 17; 2 Chr. 29:34. (Gen. 2:3; Zech. 8:3). 2 Chr. 30:15,24
18 *g* See Ex. 25:30, *note*
19 *h* 2 Chr. 28:24
21 *i* Lev. 4:3–26
23 *j* Lev. 8:14
24 *k* See Ex. 29:33, *note*
25 *l* 1 Chr. 16:4; 25:6 *m* 1 Chr. 23:5; 25:1; 2 Chr. 8:14 *n* 2 Sam. 24:11 *o* 2 Chr. 30:12
26 *p* 2 Chr. 5:12
27 *q* 2 Chr. 23:18
29 *r* 2 Chr. 20:18
31 *s* Lev. 7:12 *t* Ex. 35:5, 22

was ended and until the *other* priests had sanctified themselves, [a]for the Levites were more [b]diligent in [c]sanctifying themselves than the priests.

35 Also the burnt offerings *were* in abundance, with the [d]fat of the peace offerings and *with* the [e]drink offerings for *every* burnt offering. So the service of the house of the LORD was set in order.

36 Then Hezekiah and all the people rejoiced that God had prepared the people, since the events took place so suddenly.

Certain Israelites unite with Judah to keep Passover

30 AND Hezekiah sent to all Israel and Judah, and also wrote letters to Ephraim and Manasseh, that they should come to the house of the LORD at Jerusalem, to keep the Passover to the LORD God of Israel.

2 For the king and his leaders and all the assembly in Jerusalem had agreed to keep the Passover in the [1][f]second month.

3 For they could not keep it [g]at the regular time,* [h]because a sufficient number of priests had not consecrated themselves, nor had the people gathered together at Jerusalem.

4 And the matter pleased the king and all the assembly.

5 So they resolved to make a proclamation throughout all Israel, from Beersheba to Dan, that they should come to keep the Passover to the LORD God of Israel at Jerusalem, since they had not done *it* for a long *time* in the *prescribed* manner.

6 Then the [i]runners went throughout all Israel and Judah with the letters from the king and his leaders, and spoke according to the command of the king: "Children of Israel, [j]return to the LORD God of Abraham, Isaac, and Israel; then He will return to the remnant of you who have escaped from the hand of the [k]kings of [l]Assyria.

7 "And do not be [m]like your fathers and your brethren, who trespassed against the LORD God of their fathers, so that He [n]gave them up to [o]desolation, as you see.

8 "Now do not be [p]stiff-necked, as your fathers *were, but* yield yourselves to the LORD; and enter His sanctuary, which He has sanctified forever, and serve the LORD your God, [q]that the fierceness of His wrath may turn away from you.

9 "For if you return to the LORD, your brethren and your children *will be treated* with [r]compassion by those who lead them captive, so that they may come back to this land; for the LORD your God *is* [s]gracious and merciful, and will not turn *His* face from you if you return to Him."

10 So the runners passed from city to city through the country of Ephraim and Manasseh, as far as Zebulun; but they laughed at them and [t]mocked them.

11 Nevertheless some from Asher, Manasseh, and Zebulun humbled themselves and came to Jerusalem.

12 Also the hand of God was on Judah to give them singleness of heart to obey the command of the king and the leaders, [u]at the word of the LORD.

Passover reinstituted; confession is made to the LORD

13 Now many people, a very great assembly, gathered at Jerusalem to keep the Feast of [v]Unleavened Bread in the second month.

14 They arose and took away the [w]altars that *were* in Jerusalem, and they took away all the incense altars and cast *them* into the Brook [x]Kidron.

15 Then they slaughtered the Passover *lambs* on the fourteenth *day* of the second month. The priests and the Levites were [h]ashamed, and sanctified themselves, and brought the burnt offerings to the house of the LORD.

16 They stood in their [y]place according to their custom, according to the Law of Moses the man of God; the priests sprinkled the blood *received* from the hand of the Levites.

17 For *there were* many in the assembly who had not sanctified themselves; therefore the Levites had charge of the slaughter of the Passover *lambs* for everyone *who was* not clean, to sanctify *them* to the LORD.

18 For a multitude of the people, many from Ephraim, Manasseh, Issachar, and Zebulun, had not cleansed themselves, [z]yet they ate the Pass-

34
a 2 Chr. 30:3
b Ps. 7:10
c *Sanctification* (OT): v. 34; 2 Chr. 35:6. (Gen. 2:3; Zech. 8:3). 2 Chr. 30:15,24
35
d Lev. 3:16
e Num. 15:5–10
CHAPTER 30
2
f Num. 9:10–11; see Lev. 23:2, *note*
3
g Ex. 12:6, 18
h 2 Chr. 29:34
6
i Est. 8:14; Job 9:25; Jer. 51:31
j Jer. 4:1; Joel 2:13
k 2 Ki. 15:19,29
l 2 Chr. 28:20
7
m Ezek. 20:18
n Isa. 1:9; cp. Rom. 1:24
o 2 Chr. 29:8
8
p Ex. 32:9; Acts 7:51
q 2 Chr. 29:10
9
r Ps. 106:46
s Ex. 34:6; Mic. 7:18
10
t 2 Chr. 36:16
12
u 2 Chr. 29:25
13
v Lev. 23:6; Num. 9:11
14
w 2 Chr. 28:24
x 2 Chr. 29:16
16
y 2 Chr. 35:10,15
18
z Ex. 12:43–49; Num. 9:10

* 30:3 That is, the first month (compare Leviticus 23:5); literally *at that time*

[1](30:2) Authority for the observance of the Passover in the second month, instead of the first, is given in Num. 9:10–11.

over contrary to what was written. But
Hezekiah [a]prayed for them, saying,
"May the good LORD provide atonement for everyone
19 "*who* [b]prepares his heart to seek
God, the LORD God of his fathers,
though *he is* not *cleansed* according to
the purification of the sanctuary."
20 And the LORD listened to Hezekiah and healed the people.
21 So the children of Israel who
were present at Jerusalem kept the
[c]Feast of Unleavened Bread seven
days with great gladness; and the Levites and the priests praised the LORD
day by day, *singing* to the LORD, accompanied by loud instruments.
22 And Hezekiah [d]gave encouragement to all the Levites [e]who
taught the good knowledge of the
LORD; and they ate throughout the
feast seven days, offering peace offerings and [f]making confession to the
LORD God of their fathers.

"Another seven days" are kept

23 Then the whole assembly
agreed to keep *the feast* [g]another
seven days, and they kept it *another*
seven days with gladness.
24 For Hezekiah king of Judah
gave to the assembly a thousand bulls
and seven thousand [h]sheep, and the
leaders gave to the assembly a thousand bulls and ten thousand sheep;
and a great number of priests [i]sancti-
fied themselves.
25 The whole assembly of Judah rejoiced, also the priests and Levites, all
the assembly that came from Israel,
the sojourners who came from the
land of Israel, and those who dwelt in
Judah.
26 So there was great joy in Jerusalem, for since the time of [j]Solomon
the son of David, king of Israel, *there
had* been nothing like this in Jerusalem.
27 Then the priests, the Levites,
arose and [k]blessed the people, and
their voice was heard; and their
prayer came *up* to [l]His holy dwelling
place, to heaven.

Idols destroyed (2 Ki. 18:4)

31 NOW when all this was finished, all Israel who were present went out to the cities of Judah and
broke the sacred pillars in pieces, cut
down the [m]wooden images, and threw
down the [n]high places and the
altars—from all Judah, Benjamin,
Ephraim, and Manasseh—until they
had utterly destroyed them all. Then
all the children of Israel returned to
their own cities, every man to his possession.

Hezekiah's further reforms

2 And Hezekiah appointed the divisions of the priests and the Levites
according to their divisions, each man
according to his service, the priests
and Levites for [o]burnt offerings and
peace offerings, to serve, to give
thanks, and to praise in the gates of
the camp* of the LORD.
3 The king also *appointed* a portion of his [p]possessions for the burnt
offerings: for the morning and evening burnt offerings, the burnt offerings for the Sabbaths and the New
Moons and the set feasts, as *it is* written in the [q]Law of the LORD.
4 Moreover he commanded the
people who dwelt in Jerusalem to con-
tribute [r]support for the priests and
the Levites, that they might devote
themselves to the Law of the LORD.
5 As soon as the commandment
was circulated, the children of Israel
brought in abundance the [s]firstfruits
of grain and wine, oil and honey, and
of all the produce of the field; and they
brought in abundantly the [t]tithe of
everything.
6 And the children of Israel and
Judah, who dwelt in the cities of Judah, brought the tithe of oxen and
sheep; also the tithe of holy things
which were consecrated to the LORD
their God they laid in heaps.
7 In the [u]third month they began
laying them in heaps, and they finished in the [u]seventh month.
8 And when Hezekiah and the
leaders came and saw the heaps, they
blessed the LORD and His people Israel.
9 Then Hezekiah questioned the
priests and the Levites concerning the
heaps.
10 And Azariah the chief priest,
from the [v]house of Zadok, answered
him and said, "Since *the people* began
to bring the offerings into the house of
the LORD, we have had enough to eat
and have plenty left, for the LORD has
blessed His people; and what is left *is*
this great [w]abundance."
11 Now Hezekiah commanded
them to prepare [x]rooms in the house

18 *a Bible prayers* (OT): vv. 18–20; Ezra 9:6. (Gen. 15:2; Hab. 3:1)
19 *b* Ex. 12:15; 13:6; 2 Chr. 19:3
21 *c* 1 Ki. 8:65
22 *d* Lit. *spoke to the heart of all.* 2 Chr. 32:6 *e* Dt. 33:10; 2 Chr. 17:9; 35:3 *f* Ezra 10:11
23 *g* 2 Chr. 35:17–18
24 *h* Cp. 2 Chr. 35:7–8 *i* 2 Chr. 29:34
26 *j* 2 Chr. 7:8–10
27 *k* Num. 6:23 *l* Dt. 26:15; Ps. 68:5
CHAPTER 31
1 *m* See Dt. 16:21, *note* *n* See Jud. 3:7 and 1 Ki. 3:2, *notes*
2 *o* 1 Chr. 23:30–31
3 *p* 2 Chr. 35:7 *q* Num. 28–29
4 *r* Num. 18:8; 2 Ki. 12:16; Neh. 13:10; Ezek. 44:29
5 *s* Ex. 22:29 *t* Lev. 27:30; Dt. 14:28; 26:12–13
7 *u* See Lev. 23:2, *note*
10 *v* 1 Chr. 6:8–9 *w* Ex. 36:5

31:11 *x* 1 Ki. 6:5–8

*
31:2 That is, the temple

of the LORD, and they prepared them.

12 Then they faithfully brought in the offerings, the tithes, and the dedicated things; [a]Cononiah the Levite had charge of them, and Shimei his brother *was* the next.

13 Jehiel, Azaziah, Nahath, Asahel, Jerimoth, Jozabad, Eliel, Ismachiah, Mahath, and Benaiah *were* overseers under the hand of Cononiah and Shimei his brother, at the commandment of Hezekiah the king and Azariah the [b]ruler of the house of God.

14 Kore the son of Imnah the Levite, the keeper of the East Gate, *was* over the [c]freewill offerings to God, to distribute the offerings of the LORD and the most holy things.

15 And under him *were* [d]Eden, Miniamin, Jeshua, Shemaiah, Amariah, and Shecaniah, *his* [e]faithful assistants [f]in the cities of the priests, to distribute allotments to their brethren by divisions, to the great as well as the small.

16 Besides those males from three years old and up who were written in the genealogy, they distributed to everyone who entered the house of the LORD his daily portion for the work of his service, by his division,

17 and to the priests who were written in the genealogy according to their father's house, and to the Levites from [g]twenty years old and up according to their work, by their divisions,

18 and to all who were written in the genealogy—their little ones and their wives, their sons and daughters, the whole company of them—for in their faithfulness they sanctified themselves in holiness.

19 Also for the sons of Aaron the priests, *who were* [h]in the fields of the common-lands of their cities, in every single city, *there were* men who were designated by name to distribute portions to all the males among the priests and to all who were listed by genealogies among the Levites.

20 Thus Hezekiah did throughout all Judah, and he [i]did what *was* good and right and true before the LORD his God.

21 And in every work that he began in the service of the house of God, in the law and in the commandment, to seek his God, he did *it* with all his heart. So he [1j]prospered.

12 *a* 2 Chr. 35:9
13 *b* 1 Chr. 9:11; Jer. 20:1
14 *c* Dt. 23:23; 2 Chr. 35:8
15 *d* 2 Chr. 29:12 *e* 1 Chr. 9:26 *f* Josh. 21:1–3,9
17 *g* 1 Chr. 23:24
19 *h* Lev. 25:34; Num. 35:1–4
20 *i* 2 Ki. 20:3
21 *j* 2 Chr. 26:5; 32:30; Ps. 1:1–3
CHAPTER 32
1 *k* vv. 1–33; for parallel accounts, cp. 2 Ki. 18:13-20:21; Isa. 36:1-39:8. See 2 Ki. 18:13, *note*
4 *l* 2 Ki. 20:20
5 *m* Cp. Isa. 22:1–13, the divine view at this time *n* Cp. 2 Chr. 25:22–24 *o* 2 Ki. 25:4 *p* 2 Sam. 5:9; 1 Ki. 9:15,24; 11:27; 2 Ki. 12:20; 1 Chr. 11:8
6 *q* 2 Chr. 30:22; Isa. 40:2

(For events of 2 Ki. 17—20, see note below)

Sennacherib's second invasion of Judah. He defies God and intimidates the people (2 Ki. 18:17–37; 19:8–13; Isa. 36:2–20)

32

[k]AFTER these deeds of faithfulness, Sennacherib king of Assyria came and entered Judah; he encamped against the fortified cities, thinking to win them over to himself.

2 And when Hezekiah saw that Sennacherib had come, and that his purpose was to make war against Jerusalem,

3 he consulted with his leaders and commanders* to stop the water from the springs which *were* outside the city; and they helped him.

4 Thus many people gathered together who stopped all the [l]springs and the brook that ran through the land, saying, "Why should the kings* of Assyria come and find much water?"

5 [m]And he strengthened himself, [n]built up all the wall that was broken, raised *it* up to the towers, and *built* another wall [o]outside; also he repaired the [p]Millo* *in* the City of David, and made weapons and shields in abundance.

6 Then he set military captains over the people, gathered them together to him in the open square of the city gate, and gave them [q]encouragement, saying,

7 "Be strong and courageous; do not be afraid nor dismayed before the king of Assyria, nor before all the multitude that *is* with him; [r]for *there are* more with us than with him.

8 "With him *is* an [s]arm of flesh; but with us *is* the LORD our God, to help us and to fight our [t]battles." And the

32:7 *r* 2 Ki. 6:16; Rom. 8:31 **32:8** *s* Jer. 17:5 *t* Ex. 14:13; 1 Sam. 17:45–47; 2 Chr. 20:17

*

32:3 Literally *mighty men* **32:4** Following Masoretic Text and Vulgate; Arabic, Septuagint, and Syriac read *king.* **32:5** Literally *The Landfill*

[1](31:21) In contrast with this revival in Judah, there was deterioration in Israel. The last years of the northern kingdom may be summarized thus: (1) Hoshea's sins and defeat (2 Ki. 17:3–6; 18:9–12); (2) the sins for which Israel was carried captive into Assyria (2 Ki. 17:7–23); and (3) Assyria's movement of people from the north countries into Samaria, followed by the plague of lions and the return of some Israelite priests to teach the new people "how they should fear the LORD" (2 Ki. 17:24–41).

people were strengthened by the words of Hezekiah king of Judah.

9 After this Sennacherib king of Assyria sent his servants to Jerusalem (but he and all the forces with him *laid siege* against [a]Lachish), to Hezekiah king of Judah, and to all Judah who *were* in Jerusalem, saying,

10 "Thus says Sennacherib king of Assyria: 'In what do you trust, that you remain under siege in Jerusalem?

11 'Does not Hezekiah persuade you to give yourselves over to die by famine and by thirst, saying, "The LORD our God will deliver us from the hand of the king of Assyria"?

12 'Has not the same Hezekiah [b]taken away His [c]high places and His altars, and commanded Judah and Jerusalem, saying, "You shall worship before one altar and burn incense on [d]it"?

13 'Do you not know [e]what I and my fathers have done to all the peoples of *other* lands? Were the gods of the nations of those lands in any way able to deliver their lands out of my hand?

14 'Who *was there* among all the gods of those nations that my fathers utterly destroyed that could deliver his people from my hand, that your God should be able to deliver you from my [f]hand?

15 'Now therefore, do not let Hezekiah deceive you or persuade you like this, and do not believe him; for no god of any nation or kingdom was able to deliver his people from my hand or the hand of my fathers. How much less will your God deliver you from my hand?' "

16 Furthermore, his servants spoke against the LORD God and against His servant Hezekiah.

17 He also wrote letters to revile the LORD God of Israel, and to speak against Him, [g]saying, "As the [h]gods of the nations of *other* lands have not delivered their people from my hand, so the God of Hezekiah will not deliver His people from my [i]hand."

18 [j]Then they called out with a loud voice in Hebrew* to the people of Jerusalem who *were* on the wall, to frighten them and trouble them, that they might take the city.

19 And they spoke against the God of Jerusalem, as against the gods of the people of the earth—the work of [k]men's hands.

9 *a* Josh. 10:31
12 *b* 2 Ki. 18:22 *c* See Jud. 3:7; 1 Ki. 3:2, *notes* *d* 2 Chr. 31:1
13 *e* Cp. 1 Sam. 17:43–44
14 *f* Isa. 10:5–11
17 *g* v. 14 *h* 1 Cor. 8:5–6 *i* Dan. 3:15
18 *j* Ps. 59:6
19 *k* Ps. 96:5
20 *l* 2 Ki. 16:20
21 *m* Zech. 14:3 *n* See Heb. 1:4, *note* *o* Ps. 44:7
23 *p* 2 Sam. 8:10; 2 Chr. 17:5; 26:8; Ps. 45:12
24 *q* Isa. 38:1–22
25 *r* 2 Chr. 26:16; Hab. 2:4 *s* 2 Chr. 24:18

Hezekiah's prayer answered; Assyrian army destroyed
(2 Ki. 19:14–37; Isa. 36:21—37:35)

20 Now because of this King [l]Hezekiah and the prophet Isaiah, the son of Amoz, prayed and cried out to heaven.

21 Then the LORD [m]sent an [n]angel who cut down every mighty man of valor, leader, and captain in the camp of the king of Assyria. So he returned [o]shamefaced to his own land. And when he had gone into the temple of his god, some of his own offspring struck him down with the sword there.

22 Thus the LORD saved Hezekiah and the inhabitants of Jerusalem from the hand of Sennacherib the king of Assyria, and from the hand of all *others*, and guided them* on every side.

Hezekiah prospers again

23 And many [p]brought gifts to the LORD at Jerusalem, and presents to Hezekiah king of Judah, so that he was exalted in the sight of all nations thereafter.

Hezekiah's illness and recovery
(2 Ki. 20:1–11. See 2 Ki. 18:7, note)

24 In those days Hezekiah was [q]sick and near death, and he prayed to the LORD; and He spoke to him and gave him a sign.

25 But Hezekiah did not repay according to the favor *shown* him, for his [r]heart was lifted up; therefore [s]wrath was looming over him and over Judah and Jerusalem.

26 Then Hezekiah humbled himself for the pride of his heart, he and the inhabitants of Jerusalem, so that the wrath of the LORD did not come upon them in the days of Hezekiah.

Hezekiah's wealth

27 Hezekiah had very great riches and honor. And he made himself treasuries for silver, for gold, for precious stones, for spices, for shields, and for all kinds of desirable items;

28 storehouses for the harvest of grain, wine, and oil; and stalls for all kinds of livestock, and folds for flocks.*

29 Moreover he provided cities for himself, and possessions of flocks and

*
32:18 Literally *Judean* **32:22** Septuagint reads *gave them rest*; Vulgate reads *gave them treasures.* **32:28** Following Septuagint and Vulgate; Arabic and Syriac omit *folds for flocks*; Masoretic Text reads *flocks for sheepfolds.*

herds in abundance; for God had
given him very much property.
30 This same Hezekiah also
[a]stopped the water outlet of Upper Gihon, and brought the water by tunnel* to the west side of the City of
David. Hezekiah [b]prospered in all his
works.

Hezekiah's folly with embassy from Babylon (2 Ki. 20:12–19; cp. Isa. 39)

31 However, *regarding* the ambassadors of the princes of Babylon,
whom they sent to him to inquire
about the wonder that was *done* in the
land, God withdrew from him, in order to [c]test him, that He might know
all *that was* in his heart.

Hezekiah dies; Manasseh succeeds him (2 Ki. 20:20–21)

32 Now the rest of the acts of Hezekiah, and his goodness, indeed they
are [d]written in the vision of Isaiah the
prophet, the son of Amoz, *and* in the
book of the kings of Judah and Israel.
33 So Hezekiah [e]rested with his fathers, and they buried him in the upper tombs of the sons of David; and all
Judah and the inhabitants of Jerusalem honored him at his death. Then
Manasseh his son reigned in his place.

Manasseh practices idolatry (2 Ki. 21:1–9)

33 [f]MANASSEH *was* twelve
years old when he became
king, and he reigned fifty-five years in
Jerusalem.
2 But he did evil in the sight of the
LORD, according to the [g]abominations
of the nations whom the LORD had cast
out before the children of Israel.
3 For he rebuilt the [h]high places
which Hezekiah his father had [i]bro-
ken down; he raised up altars for the
Baals, and made [j]wooden images;
and he worshiped all the host of
heaven* and served them.
4 He also built altars in the house
of the LORD, of which the LORD had
said, "In [k]Jerusalem shall My name be
forever."
5 And he built altars for all the
host of heaven in the two [l]courts of
the house of the LORD.
6 Also he caused his sons to [m]pass
through the fire in the Valley of the
Son of Hinnom; he practiced soothsaying, used [n]witchcraft and sorcery,
and [o]consulted mediums and spiritists. He did much evil in the sight of
the LORD, to provoke Him to anger.
7 He even [p]set a carved image, the
idol which he had made, [q]in the house
of God, of which God had said to David and to Solomon his son, "In [r]this
house and in Jerusalem, which I have
chosen out of all the tribes of Israel, I
will put My name forever;
8 [s]"and I will not again remove
the foot of Israel from the land which
I have appointed for your fathers—
only if they are careful to do all that I
have commanded them, according to
the whole law and the statutes and the
ordinances by the hand of Moses."
9 So Manasseh seduced Judah
and the inhabitants of Jerusalem to do
more evil than the nations whom the
LORD had destroyed before the children of Israel.

The LORD's prophets rebuke Manasseh (2 Ki. 21:10–16)

10 And the LORD spoke to Manasseh and his people, but they would not
[t]listen.

Manasseh is taken captive by the Assyrians; he repents and is restored, then dies (2 Ki. 21:17–18)

11 [u]Therefore the LORD brought
upon them the captains of the army of
the king of Assyria, who took Manasseh with hooks,* bound him with
bronze *fetters,* and carried him off to
[v]Babylon.
12 Now when he was in affliction,
he implored the LORD his God, and
[w]humbled himself greatly before the
God of his fathers,
13 and prayed to Him; and He received his [x]entreaty, heard his supplication, and brought him back to Jerusalem into his kingdom. Then
Manasseh [y]knew that the LORD *was*
God.
14 After this he built a wall outside
the City of David on the west side of
[z]Gihon, in the valley, as far as the entrance of the Fish Gate; and *it* [aa]en-
closed Ophel, and he raised it to a very
great height. Then he put military captains in all the fortified cities of Judah.
15 He took away the [bb]foreign gods
and the idol from the house of the
LORD, and all the altars that he had
built in the mount of the house of the

30 *a* 2 Ki. 20:20; Isa. 22:9–11 *b* 2 Chr. 31:21
31 *c Test/tempt:* v. 31; Job 7:18. (Gen. 3:1; Jas. 1:14, *note*)
32 *d* Isa. 36–39
33 *e* 1 Ki. 1:21
CHAPTER 33
1 *f* 1 Ki. 24:3–4
2 *g* Dt. 18:9–12; 2 Chr. 28:3
3 *h* See Jud. 3:7 and 1 Ki. 3:2, *notes* *i* 2 Chr. 31:1 *j* See Dt. 16:21, *note*
4 *k* Dt. 12:11; 1 Ki. 8:29; 9:3; 2 Chr. 6:6; 7:16
5 *l* 2 Chr. 4:9
6 *m* Lev. 18:21; Dt. 18:10; 2 Ki. 23:10; 2 Chr. 28:3; Ezek. 23:37 *n* Dt. 18:11; 2 Ki. 17:17 *o* Lev. 19:31; 20:27
7 *p* 2 Chr. 25:14 *q* Cp. Dan. 9:27 *r* Ps. 132:14
8 *s* 2 Sam. 7:10
10 *t* Cp. 1 Ki. 11:9–11
11 *u* Dt. 28:36 *v* 2 Chr. 36:6
12 *w* 2 Chr. 7:14; 32:26
13 *x* 1 Chr. 5:20; Ezra 8:23 *y* 1 Ki. 20:13; Dan. 4:32
33:14 *z* 1 Ki. 1:33 *aa* 2 Chr. 27:3 **33:15** *bb* vv. 3–7

*

32:30 Literally *brought it straight* (compare 2 Kings 20:20) **33:3** The gods of the Assyrians
33:11 That is, nose hooks (compare 2 Kings 19:28)

LORD and in Jerusalem; and he cast *them* out of the city.

16 He also repaired the altar of the LORD, sacrificed peace offerings and [a]thank offerings on it, and commanded Judah to serve the LORD God of Israel.

17 Nevertheless the people still sacrificed on the [b]high places, *but* only to the LORD their God.

18 Now the rest of the acts of Manasseh, his prayer to his God, and the words of the [c]seers who spoke to him in the name of the LORD God of Israel, indeed they *are written* in the book* of the kings of Israel.

19 Also his prayer and *how God* received his entreaty, and all his sin and trespass, and the sites where he built high places and set up [d]wooden images and carved images, before he was humbled, indeed they *are* written among the [e]sayings of Hozai.*

20 So Manasseh [f]rested with his fathers, and they buried him in his own house. Then his son Amon reigned in his place.

Amon reigns over Judah (2 Ki. 21:18–22)

21 [g]Amon *was* twenty-two years old when he [h]became king, and he reigned two years in Jerusalem.

22 But he did evil in the sight of the LORD, as his father Manasseh had done; for Amon sacrificed to all the carved images which his father Manasseh had made, and served them.

23 And he did not humble himself before the LORD, as his father Manasseh had humbled himself; but Amon trespassed more and more.

Amon killed by his servants; Josiah made king (2 Ki. 21:23–26)

24 Then [i]his servants conspired against him, and [j]killed him in his own house.

25 But the people of the land executed all those who had conspired against King Amon. Then the people of the land made his son Josiah king in his place.

Josiah's early reforms (2 Ki. 22:1–2)

34 [k]JOSIAH *was* eight years old when he [l]became king, and he reigned thirty-one years in Jerusalem.

2 And he did *what was* right in the sight of the LORD, and walked in the ways of his father David; *he* did *not* turn aside to the right hand or to the left.

3 For in the eighth year of his reign, while he was still [m]young, he began to [n]seek the God of his father David; and in the twelfth year he began to purge Judah and Jerusalem [o]of the [b]high places, the [d]wooden images, the carved images, and the molded images.

4 They broke down the altars of the Baals in his presence, and the incense altars which *were* above them he cut down; and the [d]wooden images, the carved images, and the molded images he broke in pieces, and made [p]dust of them and [q]scattered *it* on the graves of those who had sacrificed to them.

5 He also [r]burned the bones of the priests on their [s]altars, and cleansed Judah and Jerusalem.

6 And *so he did* in the cities of Manasseh, Ephraim, and Simeon, as far as Naphtali and all around, with axes.*

7 When he had broken down the altars and the [d]wooden images, had [t]beaten the carved images into powder, and cut down all the incense altars throughout all the land of Israel, he returned to Jerusalem.

Josiah repairs the temple (2 Ki. 22:3–7)

8 In the eighteenth year of his reign, when he had purged the land and the temple,* he sent [u]Shaphan the son of Azaliah, Maaseiah the [v]governor of the city, and Joah the son of Joahaz the recorder, to repair the house of the LORD his God.

9 When they came to Hilkiah the high priest, they delivered the [w]money that was brought into the house of God, which the Levites who kept the doors had gathered from the hand of Manasseh and Ephraim, from all the [x]remnant of Israel, from all Judah and Benjamin, and *which* they had brought back to Jerusalem.

10 Then they put *it* in the hand of the foremen who had the oversight of the house of the LORD; and they gave it to the workmen who worked in the house of the LORD, to repair and restore the house.

11 They gave *it* to the craftsmen and builders to buy hewn stone and timber for beams, and to floor the houses which the kings of Judah had destroyed.

12 And the men did the work faithfully. Their overseers *were* Jahath and

16
a Lev. 7:12
17
b See Jud. 3:7 and 1 Ki. 3:2, *notes*
18
c 1 Sam. 9:9
19
d See Dt. 16:21, *note*
e See 1 Chr. 29:29, *note*
20
f 1 Ki. 1:21
21
g 1 Chr. 3:14
h 642 B.C.
24
i 2 Chr. 24:25
j 2 Chr. 25:27
CHAPTER 34
1
k Jer. 2:1
l 640 B.C.
3
m Eccl. 12:1
n 2 Chr. 15:2
o 2 Chr. 33:17–19
4
p Cp. Ex. 32:20
q 2 Ki. 23:6; Ezek. 6:5
5
r 1 Ki. 13:2
s 2 Ki. 23:20
7
t Cp. Dt. 9:21
8
u 2 Ki. 25:22
v 2 Chr. 18:25
9
w 2 Ki. 12:4
x 2 Chr. 30:6

*33:18 Literally *words* 33:19 Septuagint reads *the seers.* 34:6 Literally *swords* 34:8 Literally *house*

Obadiah the Levites, of the sons of
Merari, and Zechariah and Meshullam, of the sons of the Kohathites, to
supervise. *Others of* the Levites, all of
whom were skillful with instruments
of music,
13 *were* [a]over the burden bearers
and *were* overseers of all who did
work in any kind of service. And *some*
of the [b]Levites *were* scribes, officers,
and gatekeepers.

Hilkiah discovers the Book of the Law (2 Ki. 22:8–10)

14 Now when they brought out the
money that was brought into the
house of the LORD, Hilkiah the priest
[c]found the Book of the Law of the
LORD *given* by Moses.
15 Then Hilkiah answered and said
to Shaphan the scribe, "I have found
the [d]Book of the Law in the house of
the LORD." And Hilkiah gave the
[d]book to Shaphan.
16 So Shaphan carried the book to
the king, bringing the king word, saying, "All that was committed to your
servants they are doing.
17 "And they have [e]gathered the
money that was found in the house of
the LORD, and have delivered it into the
hand of the overseers and the workmen."

The solemn effect of its reading (2 Ki. 22:11–13)

18 Then Shaphan the scribe told
the king, saying, "Hilkiah the priest
has given me a book." And Shaphan
[f]read it before the king.
19 Thus it happened, when the king
[g]heard the words of the Law, that he
tore his clothes.
20 Then the king commanded Hilkiah, [h]Ahikam the son of Shaphan,
[i]Abdon the son of Micah, Shaphan
the scribe, and Asaiah a servant of the
king, saying,
21 "Go, inquire of the LORD for me,
and for those who are left in Israel and
Judah, concerning the words of the
book that is found; for great *is* the
wrath of the LORD that is poured out on
us, because our fathers have not [j]kept
the word of the LORD, to do according
to all that is written in this book."

Huldah, the prophetess, speaks (2 Ki. 22:14–20)

22 So Hilkiah and those the king
had appointed went to Huldah the
prophetess, the wife of Shallum the
son of [k]Tokhath, the son of [l]Hasrah,
keeper of the wardrobe. (She dwelt in
Jerusalem in the [m]Second Quarter.)
And they spoke to her to that *effect*.
23 Then she answered them, "Thus
says the LORD God of Israel, 'Tell the
man who sent you to Me,
24 "Thus says the LORD: 'Behold, I
will [n]bring calamity on this place and
on its inhabitants, all the curses that
are written in the [o]book which they
have read before the king of Judah,
25 'because they have forsaken Me
and burned incense to other gods, that
they might provoke Me to anger with
all the works of their hands. Therefore
My wrath will be poured out on this
place, and not be quenched.' " '
26 "But as for the king of Judah,
who sent you to inquire of the LORD, in
this manner you shall speak to him,
'Thus says the LORD God of Israel:
"*Concerning* the words which you
have heard—
27 "because your heart was tender,
and you humbled yourself before God
when you heard His words against
this place and against its inhabitants,
and you humbled yourself before Me,
and you tore your clothes and wept
before Me, I also have heard *you*,"
says the [p]LORD.
28 "Surely I will gather you to your
fathers, and you shall be gathered to
your grave in peace; and your eyes
shall not see all the calamity which I
will bring on this place and its inhabitants." ' " So they brought back word to
the king.

The people hear the Law (2 Ki. 23:1–2)

29 Then the king sent and gathered
all the elders of Judah and Jerusalem.
30 The king went up to the house of
the LORD, with all the men of Judah
and the inhabitants of Jerusalem—the
priests and the Levites, and all the
people, great and small. And he [q]read
in their hearing all the words of the
Book of the Covenant which had been
found in the house of the LORD.

The king's covenant (2 Ki. 23:3)

31 Then the king [r]stood in [s]his
place and made a [t]covenant before
the LORD, to follow the LORD, and to
keep His commandments and His testimonies and His statutes with all his
heart and all his soul, to perform the
words of the covenant that were written in this book.
32 And he made all who were present in Jerusalem and Benjamin take
a stand. So the inhabitants of Jerusa-

13 a 2 Chr. 8:10 b 1 Chr. 23:4–5
14 c See 2 Ki. 22:8, *note*
15 d Dt. 31:24–26
17 e Lit. *poured out* or *melted*
18 f Cp. Neh. 8:1–18
19 g Cp. Neh. 8:9
20 h Jer. 26:24 i Or *Achbor, the son of Micaiah,* 2 Ki. 22:12
21 j 2 Ki. 17:15–19
22 k Or *Tikvah,* 2 Ki. 22:14 l Or *Harhas,* 2 Ki. 22:14 m Heb. *Mishneh*
24 n 2 Chr. 36:14–20 o Dt. 28:15–68
27 p 2 Chr. 12:7; 30:6; 33:12–13
30 q Neh. 8:1–3
31 r 2 Chr. 6:13 s 2 Ki. 11:14 t 2 Chr. 23:16; 29:10

lem did according to the covenant of
God, the God of their fathers.

Josiah's later reforms
(2 Ki. 23:4–14,24)

33 Thus Josiah removed all the
[a]abominations from all the country
that *belonged* to the children of Israel,
and made all who were present in Israel diligently serve the LORD their
God. [b]All his days they did not depart
from following the LORD God of their
fathers.

(Prophecy about Bethel altar is fulfilled;
see 2 Ki. 23:15–20)

Passover reinstituted (2 Ki. 23:21–27)

35 NOW Josiah kept a Passover to
the LORD in Jerusalem, and
they slaughtered the Passover *lambs*
on the [c]fourteenth *day* of the [d]first
month.
2 And he set the priests in their
[e]duties and [f]encouraged them for the
service of the house of the LORD.
3 Then he said to the Levites who
[g]taught all Israel, who were holy to
the LORD: "Put the holy [h]ark in the
house which Solomon the son of David, king of Israel, built. *It shall* no
longer *be* a burden on *your* [i]shoul-
ders. Now serve the LORD your God
and His people Israel.
4 "Prepare *yourselves* according
to your fathers' [j]houses, according to
your divisions, following the [k]written
instruction of David king of Israel and
the written instruction of Solomon his
son.
5 "And stand in the holy *place* according to the divisions of the fathers'
houses of your brethren the *lay* people, and *according to* the division of
the father's house of the Levites.
6 "So [c]slaughter the Passover *offerings*, [l]consecrate yourselves, and
prepare *them* for your brethren, that
they may do according to the word of
the LORD by the hand of Moses."
7 Then Josiah [m]gave the *lay* people lambs and young goats from the
flock, all for Passover *offerings* for all
who were present, to the number of
thirty thousand, as well as three thousand cattle; these *were* from the king's
[n]possessions.
8 And his [o]leaders gave willingly
to the people, to the priests, and to the
Levites. Hilkiah, Zechariah, and Jehiel, rulers of the house of God, gave
to the priests for the Passover *offerings* two thousand six hundred *from
the flock*, and three hundred cattle.

33
a 1 Ki. 11:5; 2 Chr. 33:2
b Cp. Jer. 3:10

CHAPTER 35

1
c Ex. 12:6
d See Lev. 23:2, *note*

2
e 2 Chr. 23:18
f 2 Chr. 29:5–15

3
g Dt. 33:10; 2 Chr. 17:8–9
h Ex. 40:21; 2 Chr. 5:7
i 1 Chr. 23:26

4
j 1 Chr. 9:13
k 1 Chr. 23–26; 2 Chr. 8:14

6
l *Sanctification* (OT): v. 6; Ps. 2:6. (Gen. 2:3; Zech. 8:3). Cp. Ezra 6:20

7
m 2 Chr. 30:24
n 2 Chr. 31:3

8
o Num. 7:2

9
p 2 Chr. 31:12

10
q Heb. 9:6
r 2 Chr. 5:12; 7:6; 8:14–15; 13:10; 29:25–34

11
s Ex. 12:22
t 2 Chr. 29:34

12
u Ezra 6:18

13
v Ex. 12:8–9

15
w 1 Chr. 25:1–6
x 1 Chr. 26:12–19

17
y Ex. 12:15; 2 Chr. 30:21; cp. 1 Cor. 5:8

18
z Cp. 2 Chr. 30:5
aa 2 Ki. 23:22–23

9 Also [p]Conaniah, his brothers
Shemaiah and Nethanel, and Hashabiah and Jeiel and Jozabad, chief of
the Levites, gave to the Levites for
Passover *offerings* five thousand *from
the flock* and five hundred cattle.
10 So the service was prepared,
and the [q]priests stood in their places,
and the [r]Levites in their divisions, according to the king's command.
11 And they [c]slaughtered the Passover *offerings;* and the priests sprinkled *the* [s]*blood* with their hands,
while the Levites skinned *the* [t]*animals.*
12 Then they removed the burnt offerings that *they* might give them to
the divisions of the fathers' houses of
the *lay* people, to offer to the LORD, as
it is [u]written in the Book of Moses.
And so *they did* with the cattle.
13 Also they [v]roasted the Passover
offerings with fire according to the ordinance; but the *other* holy *offerings*
they boiled in pots, in caldrons, and in
pans, and divided *them* quickly
among all the *lay* people.
14 Then afterward they prepared
portions for themselves and for the
priests, because the priests, the sons
of Aaron, *were busy* in offering burnt
offerings and fat until night; therefore
the Levites prepared portions for
themselves and for the priests, the
sons of Aaron.
15 And the singers, the sons of
Asaph, *were* in their places, [w]accord-
ing to the command of David, Asaph,
Heman, and Jeduthun the king's seer.
Also the [x]gatekeepers were at each
gate; they did not have to leave their
position, because their brethren the
Levites prepared portions for them.
16 So all the service of the LORD was
prepared the same day, to keep the
Passover and to offer burnt offerings
on the altar of the LORD, according to
the command of King Josiah.
17 And the children of Israel who
were present kept the Passover at that
time, and the [y]Feast of Unleavened
Bread for seven days.
18 There had been no Passover
[z]kept in Israel [aa]like that since the
days of Samuel the prophet; and none
of the kings of Israel had kept such a
Passover as Josiah kept, with the
priests and the Levites, all Judah and
Israel who were present, and the inhabitants of Jerusalem.
19 In the eighteenth year of the

reign of Josiah this Passover was kept.

Josiah, wounded in battle, dies (2 Ki. 23:28–30)

20 After all this, [a]when Josiah had prepared the temple, Necho king of Egypt came up to fight against [b]Carchemish by the Euphrates; and Josiah went out against him.

21 But he sent messengers to him, saying, "What have I to do with you, king of Judah? *I have* not *come* against you this day, but against the house with which I have war; for God commanded me to make haste. Refrain *from meddling with* God, who *is* with me, [c]lest He destroy you."

22 Nevertheless Josiah would not turn his face from him, but [d]disguised himself so that he might fight with him, and did not heed the words of Necho from the mouth of God. So he came to fight in the Valley of Megiddo.

23 And the archers shot King Josiah; and the king said to his servants, "Take me away, for I am severely wounded."

24 His servants therefore took him out of that chariot and put him in the second chariot that he had, and they brought him to Jerusalem. So he died, and was buried in *one of* the tombs of his fathers. And all Judah and Jerusalem [e]mourned for Josiah.

25 Jeremiah also [f]lamented for [g]Josiah. And to this day all the singing men and the singing women speak of Josiah in their lamentations. They made it a custom in Israel; and indeed they *are* written in the Laments.

26 Now the rest of the acts of Josiah and his goodness, according to *what was* written in the Law of the LORD,

27 and his deeds from first to last, indeed they *are* written in the book of the kings of Israel and Judah.

Reign and dethronement of Jehoahaz (2 Ki. 23:31–33)

36 THEN the people of the land took Jehoahaz the son of Josiah, and made him king in his father's place in Jerusalem.

2 Jehoahaz* *was* twenty-three years old when he [h]became king, and he reigned three months in Jerusalem.

3 Now the king of Egypt deposed him at Jerusalem; and he imposed on the land a tribute of one hundred [i]talents of silver and a [i]talent of gold.

Jehoiakim made king by Pharaoh Necho (2 Ki. 23:34—24:4)

4 Then the king of Egypt made *Jehoahaz's** brother Eliakim king over Judah and Jerusalem, and changed his name to Jehoiakim. And Necho took Jehoahaz* his brother and carried him off to Egypt.

5 [j]Jehoiakim *was* twenty-five years old when he [h]became king, and he reigned eleven years in Jerusalem. And he did [k]evil in the sight of the LORD his God.

6 Nebuchadnezzar king of Babylon [1]came up against him, and bound him in bronze *fetters* to carry him off to [l]Babylon.

7 Nebuchadnezzar also carried off *some* of the articles from the house of the LORD to Babylon, and put them in his temple at Babylon.

Jehoiakim dies; Jehoiachin becomes king (2 Ki. 24:5–9)

8 Now the rest of the acts of Jehoiakim, the abominations which he did, and what was found against him, indeed they *are* written in the book of the kings of Israel and Judah. Then [m]Jehoiachin his son reigned in his place.

9 Jehoiachin *was* [n]eight* years old when he [o]became king, and he reigned in Jerusalem three months and ten days. And he did evil in the sight of the LORD.

First deportation to Babylon; Zedekiah made king (2 Ki. 24:10–20)

10 At the [p]turn of the year King Nebuchadnezzar summoned *him* and took him to Babylon, with the costly articles from the house of the LORD, and made [q]Zedekiah, *Jehoiakim's** [r]brother, king over Judah and Jerusalem.

11 [s]Zedekiah *was* twenty-one years old when he [o]became king, and he reigned eleven years in Jerusalem.

12 He did evil in the sight of the LORD his God, *and* did [t]not humble himself before Jeremiah the prophet, *who spoke* from the mouth of the LORD.

13 And he also [u]rebelled against King Nebuchadnezzar, who had made

20 *a* Jer. 25:11–14; 46:1–12 *b* Jer. 46:2
21 *c* Cp. 2 Chr. 25:19
22 *d* 2 Chr. 18:29
24 *e* 1 Ki. 14:18
25 *f* Lam. 4:20 *g* Jer. 22:10–11
CHAPTER 36
2 *h* 608 B.C.
3 *i* See Coinage (OT), Ex. 30:13, *note;* cp. 2 Chr. 2:10, *note*
5 *j* 1 Chr. 3:15 *k* Jer. 22:13–19
6 *l* Dt. 29:22–29; 2 Chr. 33:11
8 *m* Or *Jeconiah,* 1 Chr. 3:16; or *Coniah,* Jer. 22:24
9 *n* Cp. 2 Ki. 24:8. See also 1 Chr. 11:11, *note* *o* 597 B.C.
10 *p* 2 Sam. 11:1 *q* Jer. 37:1 *r* Cp. 2 Ki. 24:17
11 *s* Jer. 52:1
12 *t* Jer. 21:3–7; 44:10
13 *u* Ezek. 17:15

*
36:2 Masoretic Text reads *Joahaz.* **36:4** Literally *his* • Masoretic Text reads *Joahaz.* **36:9** Some Hebrew manuscripts, Septuagint, Syriac, and 2 Kings 24:8 read *eighteen.* **36:10** Literally *his* (compare 2 Kings 24:17)

[1](36:6) This was the first deportation of Judah (2 Ki. 24:1–4; Jer. 25:1–9; Dan. 1:1; Hab. 1:6). See vv. 15–21 for the final deportation.

him swear *an oath* by God; but he
stiffened his neck and hardened his
heart against turning to the LORD God
of Israel.

The reason for Judah's captivity
(Cp. 2 Ki. 25:1–21; Jer. 39:8–10)

14 Moreover all the leaders of the
priests and the people transgressed
more and more, *according* to all the
abominations of the nations, and defiled the house of the LORD which He
had consecrated in Jerusalem.
15 And the LORD God of their fathers sent *warnings* to them by His
messengers, [a]rising up early and
sending *them*, because He had compassion on His people and on His
dwelling place.
16 But they [b]mocked the messengers of God, despised His words, and
[c]scoffed at His prophets, until the
wrath of the LORD arose against His
people, till *there was* no remedy.
17 Therefore He brought against
them the king of the Chaldeans, who
killed their young men with the sword
in the house of their sanctuary, and
had no compassion on young man or
virgin, on the aged or the weak; He
gave *them* all into his hand.
18 And all the articles from the
house of God, great and small, the
treasures of the house of the LORD, and
the treasures of the king and of his
leaders, all *these* he took to Babylon.
19 Then they burned the house of
God, broke down the wall of Jerusalem, burned all its palaces with fire,
and destroyed all its precious possessions.
20 And those who escaped from the
sword he [d]carried away to Babylon,
where they became servants to him
and his sons until the rule of the kingdom of Persia,
21 to fulfill the word of the LORD by
the [e]mouth of Jeremiah, until the
[f]land had enjoyed her Sabbaths. As
long as she lay desolate she kept Sabbath, to fulfill seventy years.

Cyrus' proclamation: he permits
Jews to return from captivity

22 Now in the [g]first year of Cyrus
king of Persia, that the word of the
LORD by the mouth of Jeremiah might
be fulfilled, the LORD stirred up the
spirit of [h]Cyrus king of Persia, so that
he made a proclamation throughout
all his kingdom, and also *put it* in
writing, saying,

23 Thus [i]says Cyrus king of
Persia: All the kingdoms of the
earth the LORD God of heaven
has given me. And He has
commanded me to build Him a
house at Jerusalem which is in
Judah. Who *is* among you of
all His people? May the LORD
his God *be* with him, and let
him go [1]up!

15
a Jer. 7:13
16
b 2 Chr. 30:10
c Cp. 2 Chr. 24:20–21; Lk. 11:51
20
d Times of the Gentiles: vv. 17–20; Jer. 39:7. (Dt. 28:49; Rev. 16:19). Dt. 28:36–37
21
e Jer. 25:9–12; 27:6–8; 29:10
f Lev. 26:34–43
22
g 538 B.C.
h Ezra 1:1; Isa. 44:28; 45:1; cp. Dan. 9:2
23
i Ezra 1:2–3

[1](36:23) In the order of the books in the Hebrew canon, this is the end of the Old Testament.

The Book of

EZRA

Author: Ezra *Theme:* Return of the Remnant *Date of writing:* 5th Cent. B.C.

EZRA, Nehemiah, and Esther conclude the historical books of the Bible as they are found in the present canonical order. Both Ezra and Nehemiah are devoted to events occurring in the land of Israel at the time of the return from captivity and subsequent years, covering a period of approximately one century, beginning in 538 B.C. The emphasis in Ezra is on the rebuilding of the temple; in Nehemiah, on the rebuilding of the walls of Jerusalem. Both books contain extensive genealogical records, principally for the purpose of establishing the claims to the priesthood on the part of the descendants of Aaron.

Inasmuch as well over half a century elapsed between chs. 6 and 7, the characters of the first part of the book had died by the time Ezra began his ministry in Jerusalem. Ezra is the one person who is prominent in Ezra and Nehemiah. Both books end with prayers of confession (Ezra 9; Neh. 9) and a subsequent separation of the people from the sinful practices into which they had fallen. Some conception of the nature of the encouraging messages of Haggai and Zechariah, who are introduced in this narrative (5:1), may be seen in the prophetic books that bear their names.

The book may be divided as follows:

I. The First Return under Zerubbabel, and the Building of the Second Temple, 1—6.
II. The Ministry of Ezra, 7—10.

I. The First Return under Zerubbabel, and the Building of the Second Temple, 1—6

Decree of Cyrus permitting Jews' return to Jerusalem to rebuild temple

1 [a]NOW in the first year of Cyrus
king of Persia, that the [b]word of
the LORD by the mouth of Jeremiah
might be fulfilled, the LORD stirred up
the spirit of [c]Cyrus king of Persia, so
that he made a proclamation throughout all his kingdom, and also *put it* in
writing, saying,

2 Thus says Cyrus king of
Persia: All the kingdoms of the
earth the LORD God of heaven
has [d]given me. And He has
commanded me to build Him a
house at Jerusalem which *is* in
Judah.
3 Who *is* among you of all His
[e]people? May his God be with
him, and let him go up to
Jerusalem which *is* in Judah,
and build the house of the
LORD God of Israel (He *is* God),
which *is* in Jerusalem.
4 And whoever is left in any
place where he dwells, let the
men of his place help him with
silver and gold, with goods and
livestock, besides the freewill
offerings for the house of God
which *is* in Jerusalem.

Contributions to those returning; Cyrus restores the holy articles

5 Then the heads of the fathers'
houses of Judah and Benjamin, and
the priests and the Levites, with all
whose spirits God had moved, arose
to go up and build the house of the
LORD which *is* in Jerusalem.
6 And all those who *were* around
them encouraged them with articles
of silver and gold, with goods and livestock, and with precious things,
besides all *that* was [f]willingly offered.
7 King Cyrus also brought out the
[g]articles of the house of the LORD,
which Nebuchadnezzar had [h]taken
from Jerusalem and put in the temple
of his gods;
8 and Cyrus king of Persia
brought them out by the hand of Mithredath the treasurer, and counted
them out to [i]Sheshbazzar the prince
of Judah.
9 This *is* the number of them:
thirty gold platters, one thousand silver platters, twenty-nine knives,
10 thirty gold basins, four hundred
and ten silver basins of a similar *kind,*
and one thousand other articles.
11 All the articles of gold and silver
were five thousand four hundred. All
these Sheshbazzar took with the captives who were brought from Babylon
to Jerusalem.

CHAPTER 1

1
a c. 541–515 B.C.
b vv. 1–3; 2 Chr. 36:22–23; cp. Jer. 25:12; 29:10; 33:7–13
c Ezra 5:13–14; Isa. 44:28–45:13

2
d Cp. Dan. 2:37–38

3
e *Israel* (history): vv. 1–5; Ezra 6:15. (Gen. 12:2; Rom. 11:26, *note*)

6
f Ezra 2:68

7
g Ezra 6:5; Dan. 1:2; 5:2–3
h 2 Ki. 24:13; 2 Chr. 36:18

8
i Probably *Zerubbabel.* Ezra 2:2; 5:14, 16

Number of those returning

2 NOW [a]these [1]*are* the people of
the province who came back from
the captivity, of those who had been
carried away, whom [b]Nebuchadnez-
zar the king of Babylon had carried
away to Babylon, and who returned to
Jerusalem and Judah, everyone to his
own city.
2 *Those* who came with Zerubbabel *were* [c]Jeshua, Nehemiah, [d]Sera-
iah, [e]Reelaiah, Mordecai, Bilshan,
[f]Mispar, Bigvai, [g]Rehum, *and* Baanah. The number of the men of the
people of Israel:
3 the people of Parosh, two thousand one hundred and seventy-two;
4 the people of Shephatiah, three
hundred and seventy-two;
5 the people of Arah, seven hundred and seventy-five;
6 the people of Pahath-Moab, of
the people of Jeshua *and* Joab, two
thousand eight hundred and twelve;
7 the people of Elam, one thousand two hundred and fifty-four;
8 the people of Zattu, nine hundred and forty-five;
9 the people of Zaccai, seven hundred and sixty;
10 the people of [h]Bani, six hundred
and forty-two;
11 the people of Bebai, six hundred
and twenty-three;
12 the people of Azgad, one thousand two hundred and twenty-two;
13 the people of Adonikam, six
hundred and sixty-six;
14 the people of Bigvai, two thousand and fifty-six;
15 the people of Adin, four hundred
and fifty-four;
16 the people of Ater of Hezekiah,
ninety-eight;
17 the people of Bezai, three hundred and twenty-three;
18 the people of [i]Jorah, one hundred and twelve;
19 the people of Hashum, two hundred and twenty-three;
20 the people of [j]Gibbar, ninety-
five;
21 the people of Bethlehem, one
hundred and twenty-three;
22 the men of Netophah, fifty-six;
23 the men of Anathoth, one hundred and twenty-eight;
24 the people of [k]Azmaveth, forty-
two;
25 the people of [l]Kirjath Arim,
Chephirah, and Beeroth, seven hundred and forty-three;
26 the people of Ramah and Geba,
six hundred and twenty-one;
27 the men of Michmas, one hundred and twenty-two;
28 the men of Bethel and Ai, two
hundred and twenty-three;
29 the people of Nebo, fifty-two;
30 the people of Magbish, one hundred and fifty-six;
31 the people of the other Elam, one
thousand two hundred and fifty-four;
32 the people of Harim, three hundred and twenty;
33 the people of Lod, Hadid, and
Ono, seven hundred and twenty-five;
34 the people of Jericho, three hundred and forty-five;
35 the people of Senaah, three
thousand six hundred and thirty.

Number of priests returning

36 The [m]priests: the sons of Jedaiah, of the house of Jeshua, nine hundred and seventy-three;
37 the sons of Immer, one thousand
and fifty-two;
38 the sons of [n]Pashhur, one thousand two hundred and forty-seven;
39 the sons of Harim, one thousand
and seventeen.

Number of Levites returning

40 The Levites: the sons of Jeshua
and Kadmiel, of the sons of [o]Hoda-
viah, seventy-four.
41 The singers: the sons of Asaph,
one hundred and twenty-eight.
42 The sons of the gatekeepers: the
sons of Shallum, the sons of Ater, the
sons of Talmon, the sons of Akkub,
the sons of Hatita, and the sons of
Shobai, one hundred and thirty-nine
in all.
43 The [p]Nethinim: the sons of Ziha,
the sons of Hasupha, the sons of Tabbaoth,
44 the sons of Keros, the sons of
[q]Siaha, the sons of Padon,
45 the sons of Lebanah, the sons of
Hagabah, the sons of Akkub,

CHAPTER 2
1
a Cp. Neh. 7:6–67
b 2 Ki. 24:14–16; 2 Chr. 36:20
2
c Or *Joshua*. Not the same man as in Josh. 1:1ff.
d Or *Azariah*, Neh. 7:7
e Or *Raamiah*, Neh. 7:7
f Or *Mispereth*, Neh. 7:7
g Or *Nehum*, Neh. 7:7
10
h Or *Binnui*, Neh. 7:15
18
i Or *Hariph*, Neh. 7:24
20
j Or *Gibeon*, Neh. 7:25
24
k Or *Beth Azmaveth*, Neh. 7:28
25
l Or *Kirjath Jearim*, Neh. 7:29
36
m vv. 36–39; cp. 1 Chr. 24:7–18
38
n 1 Chr. 9:12
40
o Or *Judah*, Ezra 3:9; or *Hodevah*, Neh. 7:43
43
p See Neh. 3:26, *note*
44
q Or *Sia*, Neh. 7:47

[1](2:1) Individuals from all of the tribes are included in this return to Jerusalem. See 2 Ki. 17:23, *note*.

The order of the restoration was as follows: (1) the return of the first detachment under Zerubbabel and Jeshua (538 B.C.), chs. 1—6, and the books of Haggai and Zechariah; (2) the expedition of Ezra (455 B.C.), well over fifty years later (chs. 7—10); and (3) the commission of Nehemiah (445 B.C.), thirteen years after the expedition of Ezra (Neh. 2:1–6).

46 the sons of Hagab, the sons of
[a]Shalmai, the sons of Hanan,
47 the sons of Giddel, the sons of
Gahar, the sons of Reaiah,
48 the sons of Rezin, the sons of Nekoda, the sons of Gazzam,
49 the sons of Uzza, the sons of Paseah, the sons of Besai,
50 the sons of Asnah, the sons of
Meunim, the sons of [b]Nephusim,
51 the sons of Bakbuk, the sons of
Hakupha, the sons of Harhur,
52 the sons of [c]Bazluth, the sons of
Mehida, the sons of Harsha,
53 the sons of Barkos, the sons of
Sisera, the sons of Tamah,
54 the sons of Neziah, and the sons
of Hatipha.

Number of the descendants of Solomon's servants who returned

55 The sons of Solomon's [d]ser-
vants: the sons of Sotai, the sons of
Sophereth, the sons of [e]Peruda,
56 the sons of Jaala, the sons of
Darkon, the sons of Giddel,
57 the sons of Shephatiah, the sons
of Hattil, the sons of Pochereth of Zebaim, and the sons of [f]Ami.
58 All the [g]Nethinim and the children of Solomon's servants were
three hundred and ninety-two.
59 And these *were* the ones who
came up from Tel Melah, Tel Harsha,
Cherub, [h]Addan, and Immer; but they
could not [i]identify their father's
house or their genealogy,* whether
they *were* of Israel:
60 the sons of Delaiah, the sons of
Tobiah, and the sons of Nekoda, six
hundred and fifty-two;

Certain priests removed because of lost genealogy

61 and of the sons of the priests: the
sons of [j]Habaiah, the sons of Koz,*
and the sons of Barzillai, who took a
wife of the daughters of [k]Barzillai the
Gileadite, and was called by their
name.
62 These sought their listing *among*
those who were registered by genealogy, but they were not found; therefore they *were excluded* from the
[l]priesthood as defiled.
63 And the [m]governor* said to
them that they should not eat of the
most holy things till a priest could
consult with the [n]Urim and Thummim.

Total number returning; their substance and offerings to God

64 The whole assembly together
was forty-two thousand three hundred *and* sixty,
65 besides their male and female
servants, of whom *there were* seven
thousand three hundred and thirty-
seven; and they had two hundred men
and women singers.
66 Their horses *were* seven hundred and thirty-six, their mules two
hundred and forty-five,
67 their camels four hundred and
thirty-five, and *their* donkeys six
thousand seven hundred and twenty.
68 *Some* of the heads of the fathers'
houses, when they came to the house
of the LORD which *is* in Jerusalem, [o]of-
fered freely for the house of God, to
erect it in its place:
69 According to their ability, they
gave [p]to the treasury for the work
sixty-one thousand gold [q]drachmas,
five thousand minas of silver, and one
hundred priestly garments.
70 So the priests and the Levites,
some of the people, the singers, the
gatekeepers, and the [g]Nethinim,
dwelt in their cities, and all Israel in
their cities.

The altar set up and ancient sacrifice restored

3 AND when the [r]seventh month
had come, and the children of Israel *were* in the cities, the people gathered together as one man to Jerusalem.
2 Then [s]Jeshua the son of [t]Joza-
dak and his brethren the priests, and
[u]Zerubbabel the son of [v]Shealtiel and
his brethren, arose and built the altar
of the God of Israel, to offer burnt offerings on it, [w]as *it is* written in the
Law of Moses the man of God.
3 Though fear *had come* upon
them because of the people of those
[x]countries, they set the altar on its
bases; and they offered burnt offerings on it to the LORD, *both* the morning and evening burnt offerings.
4 They also kept the Feast of Tabernacles, [y]as *it is* written, and *offered*
the daily burnt offerings in the number required by ordinance for each
day.
5 Afterwards *they* [z]*offered* the
regular burnt offering, and *those* for
New Moons and for all the appointed

46 a Or *Salmai,* Neh. 7:48
50 b Or *Nephishesim,* Neh. 7:52
52 c Or *Bazlith,* Neh. 7:54
55 d Neh. 7:57–60; cp. 1 Ki. 9:21 e Or *Perida,* Neh. 7:57
57 f Or *Amon,* Neh. 7:59
58 g See Neh. 3:26, *note*
59 h Or *Addon,* Neh. 7:61 i Cp. Num. 1:18
61 j Neh. 7:63 k 2 Sam. 17:27; 1 Ki. 2:7
62 l Cp. Num. 3:10; 16:39–40
63 m Neh. 7:65,70 n See Ex. 28:30, *note*
68 o Ezra 1:6; 3:5; Neh. 7:70
69 p Ezra 8:25–30, 33–35 q See Coinage (OT), Ex. 30:13, *note;* cp. Weights and Measures (OT), 2 Chr. 2:10, *note*
CHAPTER 3
1 r v. 6; Neh. 7:73; 8:1–2; see Lev. 23:2, *note*
2 s Ezra 4:3; Neh. 12:1, 8 t Or *Jehozadak,* 1 Chr. 6:14–15 u Ezra 2:2; 4:2–3; 5:2 v 1 Chr. 3:17 w Dt. 12:5–6
3:3 x Cp. Ezra 4:4 **3:4** y Lev. 23:33–43; Neh. 8:14–18
3:5 z Cp. Num. 28:1–29:39

*
2:59 Literally *seed* 2:61 Or *Hakkoz* 2:63 Hebrew *Tirshatha*

feasts of the LORD that were consecrated, and *those* of everyone who
[a]willingly offered a freewill offering
to the LORD.

6 From the first day of the seventh
month they began to offer burnt offerings to the LORD, although the foundation of the temple of the LORD had not
been laid.

7 They also gave money to the masons and the carpenters, and food,
drink, and oil to the people of Sidon
and Tyre to bring cedar logs from Lebanon to the sea, to [b]Joppa, [c]according
to the permission which they had from
Cyrus king of Persia.

Foundations of temple laid with mingled joy and weeping

8 Now in the [d]second month of the
second year of their coming to the
house of God at Jerusalem, [e]Zerubba-
bel the son of Shealtiel, Jeshua the son
of Jozadak,* and the rest of their
brethren the priests and the Levites,
and all those who had come out of the
captivity to Jerusalem, began *work*
and appointed the [f]Levites from
twenty years old and above to [g]over-
see the work of the house of the LORD.

9 Then Jeshua *with* his sons and
brothers, Kadmiel *with* his sons, and
the sons of [h]Judah, arose as one to
oversee those working on the house of
God: the sons of Henadad *with* their
sons and their brethren the Levites.

5
a Ezra 1:4; 2:68; 7:15–16; 8:28
7
b 2 Chr. 2:16
c Ezra 1:2; 6:3
8
d See Lev. 23:2, *note*
e Ezra 4:3
f Cp. 1 Chr. 23:24–27
g v. 9; cp. 1 Chr. 23:4
9
h Or *Hodaviah,* Ezra 2:40
10
i Cp. 1 Chr. 6:31; 16:4; 25:1
11
j Cp. Ex. 15:21; Neh. 12:24,40
k Ps. 136:1; cp. 2 Chr. 7:3
l Cp. Ps. 47:1
12
m Ezra 2:68

10 When the builders laid the foundation of the temple of the LORD, the
priests [i]stood* in their apparel with
trumpets, and the Levites, the sons of
Asaph, with cymbals, to praise the
LORD, according to the ordinance of
David king of Israel.

11 And they [j]sang responsively,
praising and giving thanks to the
LORD:

[k]"For *He is* good,
For His mercy *endures* forever
toward Israel."

Then all the people shouted with a
great [l]shout, when they praised the
LORD, because the foundation of the
house of the LORD was laid.

12 But many of the priests and Levites and [m]heads of the fathers'
houses, old men who had seen the first
temple, wept with a loud voice when
the foundation of this temple was laid
before their eyes. Yet many shouted
aloud for joy,

13 so that the people could not discern the noise of the shout of joy from
the noise of the weeping of the people,
for the people shouted with a loud
shout, and the sound was heard afar
off.

*
3:8 Spelled *Jehozadak* in 1 Chronicles 6:14
3:10 Following Septuagint, Syriac, and Vulgate; Masoretic Text reads *they stationed the priests.*

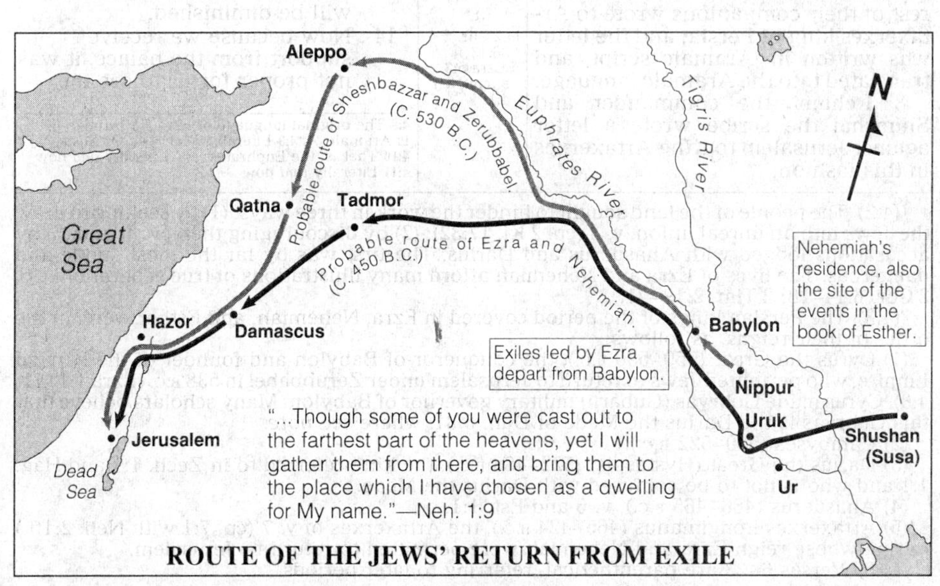

ROUTE OF THE JEWS' RETURN FROM EXILE

Adversaries seek to hinder the work by appeal to Artaxerxes

4 NOW when the [a]adversaries of
Judah and Benjamin heard that
the descendants of the captivity were
building the temple of the LORD God of
Israel,
2 they came to Zerubbabel and the
heads of the fathers' *houses*, and said
to them, "Let us build with you, [1]for
we seek your God as you *do;* and we
have sacrificed to Him since the days
of Esarhaddon king of Assyria, who
[b]brought us here."
3 But Zerubbabel and Jeshua and
the rest of the heads of the fathers'
houses of Israel said to them, [c]"You
may do nothing with us to build a
house for our God; but we alone will
build to the LORD God of Israel, [d]as
King [2]Cyrus the king of Persia has
commanded us."
4 Then the people of the land tried
to discourage the people of Judah.
They [e]troubled them in building,
5 and hired counselors against
them to frustrate their purpose all the
days of Cyrus king of Persia, even until the reign of [f]Darius king of Persia.

Parenthetic explanation

6 [3]In the reign of [g]Ahasuerus, in
the beginning of his reign, they wrote
an accusation against the inhabitants
of Judah and Jerusalem.
7 In the days of [h]Artaxerxes also,
Bishlam, Mithredath, Tabel, and the
rest of their companions wrote to Artaxerxes king of Persia; and the letter
was written in [i]Aramaic script, and
translated into the Aramaic language.
8 Rehum* the commander and
Shimshai the scribe wrote a letter
against Jerusalem to King Artaxerxes
in this fashion:

9 From* Rehum the commander,
Shimshai the scribe, and the
rest of their
companions—*representatives*
of the Dinaites, the
Apharsathchites, the
Tarpelites, the people of Persia
and Erech and Babylon and
Shushan,* the Dehavites, the
Elamites,
10 and the rest of the nations
whom the great and noble
Osnapper took captive and
[j]settled in the cities of
Samaria and the remainder
beyond the River*—and so
forth.*

11 (This *is* a copy of the letter that
they sent him)

To King Artaxerxes from your
servants, the men *of the region*
[k]beyond the River, [l]and so
forth:*
12 Let it be known to the king
that the Jews who came up
from you have come to us at
Jerusalem, and are building
the [m]rebellious and evil city,
and are finishing *its* [n]walls
and repairing the foundations.
13 Let it now be known to the
king that, if this city is built
and the walls completed, they
will not pay tax, tribute, or
custom, and the king's treasury
will be diminished.
14 Now because we receive
support from the palace, it was
not proper for us to see the

CHAPTER 4

1 *a* vv. 7–9; cp. Neh. 4:1–23

2 *b* 2 Ki. 17:24; cp. Ezra 4:10

3 *c* Cp. Neh. 2:20
d Ezra 1:1–4

4 *e* Ezra 3:3; cp. Neh. 4:8

5 *f* Ezra 5:5; 6:1

6 *g* Or *Xerxes.* See v. 3, *note*

7 *h* Ezra 7:1, 7,21; see v. 3, *note*
i 2 Ki. 18:26; see Dan. 2:4, *note*

10 *j* 2 Ki. 17:24

11 *k* Cp. 1 Ki. 4:24
l The date of the letter is not here specified.

12 *m* 2 Chr. 36:13
n Ezra 5:3, 9; cp. Neh. 4:1

*

4:8 The original language of Ezra 4:8 through 6:18 is Aramaic. **4:9** Literally *Then* • Or *Susa*
4:10 That is, the Euphrates • Literally *and now*
4:11 Literally *and now*

[1](4:2) The people of the land sought to hinder the work in three ways: (1) by seeking to draw the Jews into an unreal union, v. 3 (cp. 2 Ki. 17:32); (2) by discouraging them, v. 4; and (3) by accusations lodged with Ahasuerus and Darius. The first was by far the most subtle and dangerous. The lives of Ezra and Nehemiah afford many illustrations of true separation. Cp. 2 Cor. 6:14–18; 2 Tim. 2:19–21.

[2](4:3) The Persian kings of the period covered in Ezra, Nehemiah, and Esther were, in the order of their reigns, as follows:

(1) Cyrus the Great (550–530 B.C.), the conqueror of Babylon and founder of the Persian Empire, who permitted Jews to return to Jerusalem under Zerubbabel in 538 B.C. (Ezra 1:1–11; 4:3). Cyrus made Gobryas (Gubaru) military governor of Babylon. Many scholars believe that this Gobryas is the Darius the Mede of Dan. 5:31, where see *note.*

(2) Cambyses (530–522 B.C.).

(3) Darius the Great (Hystaspis) (522–486 B.C.), the king referred to in Zech. 1:1 and Hag. 1:1 and who is not to be confused with Darius the Mede.

(4) Ahasuerus (486–465 B.C.), v. 6 and Est. 1:1.

(5) Artaxerxes Longimanus (465–424 B.C.), the Artaxerxes of v. 7 (cp. 7:1 with Neh. 2:1ff.) during whose reign Ezra and Nehemiah were permitted to return to Jerusalem.

[3](4:6) Verses 6–23 are parenthetical, referring to later periods.

king's dishonor; therefore we
have sent and informed the
king,
15 that search may be made in
the book of the records of your
fathers. And you will find in
the book of the records and
know that this city *is* a
rebellious city, harmful to
kings and provinces, and that
they have incited sedition
within the city in former times,
for which cause this city was
destroyed.
16 We inform the king that if this
city is rebuilt and its walls are
completed, the result will be
that you will have no dominion
beyond the [a]River.

Artaxerxes orders work on temple suspended

17 The king sent an answer:

To Rehum the commander, *to*
Shimshai the scribe, *to* the rest
of their companions who dwell
in Samaria, and *to* the
remainder beyond the [a]River:

Peace, and so forth.*

18 The letter which you sent to us
has been clearly read before
me.
19 And I gave the command, and
a search has been made, and it
was found that this city in
former times has revolted
against kings, and rebellion
and sedition have been
fostered in it.
20 There have also been mighty
kings over Jerusalem, who
have [b]ruled over all *the region*
[c]beyond the [a]River; and tax,
tribute, and custom were paid
to them.
21 [d]Now give the command to
make these men cease, that
this city may not be built until
the command is given by me.
22 Take heed now that you do not
fail to do this. Why should
damage increase to the hurt of
the kings?

23 Now when the copy of King Artaxerxes' letter *was* read before Rehum, Shimshai the scribe, and their
companions, they went up in haste to
Jerusalem against the Jews, and by
force of arms made them cease.
24 Thus the work of the house of
God which *is* at Jerusalem ceased, and
it was [e]discontinued until the second
year of the reign of Darius king of Persia.

Work on temple resumed through encouragement of prophets

5 THEN the prophet [f]Haggai and
[g]Zechariah the son of Iddo,
prophets, prophesied to the Jews who
were in Judah and Jerusalem, in the
name of the God of Israel, *who was*
over them.
2 So [h]Zerubbabel the son of Shealtiel and Jeshua the son of Jozadak*
rose up and began to build the house
of God which *is* in Jerusalem; and the
prophets of God *were* [i]with them,
helping them.
3 At the same time [j]Tattenai the
governor of *the region* beyond the
[a]River and Shethar-Boznai and their
companions came to them and spoke
thus to them: [k]"Who has commanded
you to build this temple and finish this
wall?"
4 Then, accordingly, we told them
the [l]names of the men who were con-
structing this building.
5 But the [m]eye of their God was
upon the elders of the Jews, so that
they could not make them cease till a
report could go to Darius. Then a written answer was returned concerning
this *matter*.

Adversaries write to Darius

6 This is a copy of the letter that
Tattenai sent:

The governor of *the region*
beyond the [a]River, and
Shethar-Boznai, and his
[n]companions, the Persians
who *were in the region* beyond
the River, to Darius the king.

7 They sent a letter to him, in
which was written thus—

To Darius the king:

All peace.

8 Let it be known to the king
that we went into the province
of Judea, to the temple of the
great God, which is being built
with [o]heavy stones, and timber
is being laid in the walls; and
this work goes on diligently
and prospers in their hands.
9 Then we asked those elders,
and spoke thus to them:

16
a i.e. *the Euphrates*
20
b 1 Ki. 4:21; 1 Chr. 18:3; Ps. 72:8
c Cp. Gen. 15:18; Josh. 1:4
21
d Aram. *Make a new decree*
24
e Cp. Ezra 6:14
CHAPTER 5
1
f Hag. 1:1
g Zech. 1:1
2
h Ezra 3:2
i Ezra 6:14; Hag. 2:4
3
j v. 6; Ezra 6:6
k v. 9
4
l v. 10
5
m 2 Chr. 16:9; Ps. 33:18; cp. Ezra 7:6, 28
6
n Ezra 4:7–10
8
o Aram. *stones of rolling*

*4:17 Literally *and now* 5:2 Spelled *Jehozadak* in 1 Chronicles 6:14

[a]"Who commanded you to build this temple and to finish these walls?"

10 We also asked them their names to inform you, that we might write the names of the men who *were* chief among them.

11 And thus they returned us an answer, saying: "We are the [b]servants of the God of heaven and earth, and we are rebuilding the temple that was built many years ago, which a great king of Israel built and [c]completed.

12 "But because our fathers [d]provoked the God of heaven to wrath, He gave them into the [e]hand of Nebuchadnezzar king of Babylon, the Chaldean, *who* destroyed this temple and [f]carried the people away to Babylon.

13 "However, in the first year of [g]Cyrus king of Babylon, King Cyrus issued a decree to build this house of God.

14 "Also, the gold and silver articles of the house of God, which Nebuchadnezzar had taken from the temple that *was* in Jerusalem and carried into the temple of Babylon—those King Cyrus took from the temple of Babylon, and they were [h]given to one named [i]Sheshbazzar, whom he had made governor.

15 "And he said to him, 'Take these articles; go, carry them to the temple *site* that *is* in Jerusalem, and let the house of God be rebuilt on its former site.'

16 "Then the same [i]Sheshbazzar came *and* [j]laid the foundation of the house of God which *is* in Jerusalem; but from that time even until now it has been under construction, and it is [k]not finished."

17 Now therefore, if *it seems* good to the king, let a [l]search be made in the king's treasure house, which *is* there in Babylon, whether it is *so* that a decree was issued by King Cyrus to build this house of God at Jerusalem, and let the king send us his pleasure concerning this *matter*.

9
a vv. 3–4
11
b Cp. Josh. 24:15; 1 Ki. 18:36; Ps. 119:46; Jon. 1:9
c 1 Ki. 6:1, 38
12
d 2 Chr. 34:25; 36:16
e 2 Chr. 36:17
f 2 Ki. 25:8–11; Jer. 13:19
13
g Ezra 1:1
14
h Ezra 1:7–8; 6:5
i Probably *Zerubbabel.* Hag. 1:14; 2:2, 21
16
j Ezra 3:8–10; Hag. 2:18
k Cp. Ezra 6:15
17
l Ezra 6:1–2
CHAPTER 6
2
m 2 Ki. 17:6
3
n Ezra 1:1; 5:13
o See Weights and Measures (OT), 2 Chr. 2:10, *note*
4
p Cp. 1 Ki. 6:36
q Ezra 3:7
5
r Ezra 1:7–11; 5:14
6
s Ezra 5:3,6
t i.e. *the Euphrates*
7
u Cp. Isa. 44:28
8
v Cp. Ezra 7:12–22

Darius confirms the decree of Cyrus

6 THEN King Darius issued a decree, and a search was made in the archives,* where the treasures were stored in Babylon.

2 And at Achmetha,* in the palace that *is* in the province of [m]Media, a scroll was found, and in it a record *was* written thus:

3 In the first year of King Cyrus, King Cyrus issued a [n]decree *concerning* the house of God at Jerusalem: "Let the house be rebuilt, the place where they offered sacrifices; and let the foundations of it be firmly laid, its height sixty [o]cubits *and* its width sixty cubits,

4 *with* three [p]rows of heavy stones and one row of new timber. Let the [q]expenses be paid from the king's treasury.

5 Also let the gold and silver [r]articles of the house of God, which Nebuchadnezzar took from the temple which *is* in Jerusalem and brought to Babylon, be restored and taken back to the temple which *is* in Jerusalem, *each* to its place; and deposit *them* in the house of God"—

6 Now *therefore,* [s]Tattenai, governor of *the region* beyond the [t]River, and Shethar-Boznai, and your companions the Persians who *are* beyond the [t]River, keep yourselves far from there.

7 Let the work of this house of God alone; let the governor of the Jews and the elders of the Jews [u]build this house of God on its site.

8 Moreover I issue a decree *as to* what you shall do for the elders of these Jews, for the building of this house of God: Let the cost be paid at the king's expense from taxes *on the region* beyond the [t]River; this is to be [v]given immediately to these men, so that they are not hindered.

9 And whatever they need—young bulls, rams, and lambs for the burnt offerings of the God of heaven, wheat, salt, wine, and oil, according to

*
6:1 Literally *house of the scrolls* 6:2 Probably *Ecbatana,* the ancient capital of Media

the request of the priests who
are in Jerusalem—let it be
given them day by day without
fail,
10 that they may offer sacrifices
of sweet aroma to the God of
heaven, and [a]pray for the life
of the king and his sons.
11 Also I issue a decree that
whoever alters this edict, let a
timber be pulled from his
house and erected, and let him
be hanged on it; and let his
house be made a [b]refuse heap
because of this.
12 And may the God who causes
His name to dwell there
destroy any king or people
who put their hand to alter it,
or to destroy this house of God
which is in Jerusalem. I Darius
issue a decree; let it be done
diligently.

Temple completed and dedicated

13 Then Tattenai, governor of *the
region* beyond the [c]River, Shethar-
Boznai, and their companions diligently did according to what King Darius had sent.
14 So the [d]elders of the Jews built,
and they prospered through the
prophesying of Haggai the prophet
and Zechariah the son of Iddo. And
they built and [1]finished *it*, according
to the commandment of the God of
Israel, and according to the command
of [e]Cyrus, [f]Darius, and [g]Artaxerxes
king of Persia.
15 Now the [h]temple was [i]finished
on the third day of the month of
[j]Adar, which was in the sixth year of
the reign of King Darius.
16 Then the children of Israel, the
priests and the Levites and the rest of
the descendants of the captivity, celebrated the [k]dedication of this house of
God with joy.
17 And they offered sacrifices at
the dedication of this house of God,
one hundred bulls, two hundred rams,
four hundred lambs, and as a sin offering for all Israel twelve male goats,
according to the number of the tribes
of Israel.
18 They [l]assigned the priests to
their divisions and the Levites to their
divisions, over the service of God in
Jerusalem, as it is written in the Book
of Moses.

Passover restored

19 And the descendants of the captivity [m]kept the Passover on the fourteenth *day* of the [l]first month.
20 For the priests and the Levites
had [n]purified themselves; all of them
were ritually clean. And they slaughtered the Passover *lambs* for all the
descendants of the captivity, for their
brethren the priests, and for themselves.
21 Then the children of Israel who
had returned from the captivity ate together with all who had [o]separated
themselves from the filth of the nations of the land in order to seek the
LORD God of Israel.
22 And they kept the [p]Feast of Unleavened Bread seven days with joy;
for the LORD made them joyful, and
[q]turned the heart of the [r]king of Assyria toward them, to strengthen their
hands in the work of the house of God,
the God of Israel.

*(More than fifty years elapsed
between chs. 6 and 7; during this period
the events in Esther took place)*

II. The Ministry of Ezra, 7—10

*Ezra's journey from Babylon to
Jerusalem; his ancestry and companions*

7 [s]NOW after these things, in the
reign of Artaxerxes king of Per-
sia, Ezra the [t]son of [u]Seraiah, the son
of Azariah, the son of [v]Hilkiah,
2 the son of Shallum, the son of
Zadok, the son of Ahitub,
3 the son of Amariah, the son of
Azariah, the son of Meraioth,
4 the son of Zerahiah, the son of
Uzzi, the son of Bukki,
5 the son of Abishua, the son of
Phinehas, the son of Eleazar, the son
of Aaron the chief priest—
6 this Ezra came up from Babylon;
and he *was* a [w]skilled scribe in the
Law of Moses, which the LORD God of
Israel had given. The king granted
him all his request, [x]according to the

10
a Cp. Ezra 7:23; Jer. 29:7; 1 Tim. 2:1–2
11
b Dan. 2:5
13
c i.e. *the Euphrates*
14
d Ezra 5:1–2
e v. 3; Ezra 1:1; 5:13
f v. 12; 4:24
g Ezra 7:1, 11; Neh. 2:1
15
h *Israel* (history): vv. 15–18; Neh. 2:3. (Gen. 12:2; Rom. 11:26, *note*)
i Cp. Ezra 5:16
j See Lev. 23:2, *note*
16
k Cp. 2 Chr. 7:5–9
18
l Cp. 1 Chr. 23:6; 1 Chr. 24:1
19
m Ex. 12:6
20
n Cp. 2 Chr. 30:15
21
o *Separation:* v. 21; Ezra 9:12. (Gen. 12:1; 2 Cor. 6:17, *note*)
22
p Ex. 12:15; 13:6–7; cp. 2 Chr. 30:21; 35:17
q Prov. 21:1; cp. Ezra 7:27
r Ezra 1:1
CHAPTER 7
1
s c. 458 B.C.
t v. 6; 1 Chr. 6:14
u Jer. 52:24
v 2 Chr. 35:8

7:6 *w* vv. 11,12,21 *x* v. 9

[1](6:14) The worship of the LORD was thus re-established in Jerusalem, but the theocracy was not restored. The remnant which returned from the Babylonian captivity lived in the land by Gentile sufferance, though doubtless by the providential care of the LORD, until Messiah came and was crucified by soldiers of the fourth Gentile world-empire, Rome (Dan. 2:40; 7:7). Soon after (A.D. 70) Rome destroyed the city and temple. See Times of the Gentiles, Lk. 21:24 and Rev. 16:19, *notes*.

hand of the LORD his God upon him.
7 [a]*Some* of the children of Israel,
the priests, the Levites, the singers,
the gatekeepers, and the [b]Nethinim
came up to Jerusalem in the seventh
year of King Artaxerxes.
8 And Ezra came to Jerusalem in
the [c]fifth month, which *was* in the
seventh year of the king.
9 On the [c]first *day* of the first
month he began *his* journey from Babylon, and on the first *day* of the [c]fifth
month he came to Jerusalem, according to the good hand of his God upon
him.
10 For Ezra had [d]prepared his
heart to seek the Law of the LORD, and
to do *it*, and to [e]teach statutes and
ordinances in Israel.

Decree of Artaxerxes on Ezra's behalf

11 This *is* a copy of the letter that
King Artaxerxes gave Ezra the priest,
the scribe, expert in the words of the
commandments of the LORD, and of
His statutes to Israel:

12 Artaxerxes,* [f]king of kings,
To Ezra the priest, a scribe of
the Law of the God of heaven:
Perfect *peace*, and so forth.*

13 I issue a [g]decree that all those
of the people of Israel and the
priests and Levites in my
realm, who volunteer to go up
to Jerusalem, may go with you.
14 And whereas you are being
sent by the king and his
[h]seven counselors to inquire
concerning Judah and
Jerusalem, with regard to the
Law of your God which *is* in
your hand;
15 and *whereas you are* to carry
the silver and gold which the
king and his counselors have
[i]freely offered to the God of
Israel, whose dwelling *is* in
[j]Jerusalem;
16 [k]and *whereas* all the silver and
gold that you may find in all
the province of Babylon, along
with the freewill offering of the
people and the priests, *are to
be* freely offered for the house
of their God in Jerusalem—
17 now therefore, be careful to
buy with this money bulls,
rams, and lambs, with their
grain offerings and their drink
offerings, and offer them on
the altar of the house of your
God in Jerusalem.
18 And whatever seems good to
you and your brethren to do
with the rest of the silver and
the gold, do it according to the
will of your God.
19 Also the articles that are given
to you for the service of the
house of your God, deliver in
full before the God of
Jerusalem.
20 And whatever more may be
needed for the house of your
God, which you may have
occasion to provide, pay *for it*
from the [l]king's treasury.
21 And I, *even* I, Artaxerxes the
king, issue a decree to all the
treasurers who *are in the
region* beyond the [m]River, that
whatever Ezra the priest, the
scribe of the Law of the God of
heaven, may require of you, let
it be done diligently,
22 up to one hundred [n]talents of
silver, one hundred [o]kors of
wheat, one hundred [o]baths of
wine, one hundred baths of oil,
and salt without prescribed
limit.
23 Whatever is commanded by
the God of heaven, let it
diligently be done for the
house of the God of heaven.
For why should there be wrath
against the realm of the king
and his [p]sons?
24 Also we inform you that it
shall not be lawful to impose
tax, tribute, or custom *on* [q]any
of the priests, Levites, singers,
gatekeepers, Nethinim, or
servants of this house of God.
25 And you, Ezra, according to
your God-given wisdom, [r]set
magistrates and judges who
may judge all the people who
are in the region beyond the
[m]River, all such as know the
laws of your God; and [s]teach
those who do not know *them*.
26 Whoever will not observe the
law of your God and the law of
the king, let judgment be
executed speedily on him,
whether *it be* death, or
banishment, or confiscation of
goods, or imprisonment.

7
a Ezra 8:1–14
b See Neh. 3:26, *note*
8
c See Lev. 23:2, *note*
10
d Cp. 2 Chr. 30:19; Job 11:13–14
e Dt. 33:10; Mal. 2:7; cp. 2 Chr. 35:3; Neh. 8:18
12
f Cp. Ezek. 26:7; Dan. 2:37
13
g Cp. Ezra 1:1; 6:1
14
h Est. 1:14
15
i Cp. Ezra 1:6; cp. 2 Cor. 8:12
j Ezra 6:12
16
k Ezra 8:24–30; cp. 1 Chr. 29:6–9
20
l vv. 21–23
21
m i.e. *the Euphrates*
22
n See Coinage (OT), Ex. 30:13, *note*
o See Weights and Measures (OT), 2 Chr. 2:10, *note*
23
p Cp. Ezra 6:10
24
q Cp. Ezra 4:13
25
r Cp. Ex. 18:21–22; Dt. 16:18
s v. 10; Mal. 2:7; cp. 2 Chr. 17:7

*7:12 The original language of Ezra 7:12–26 is Aramaic. • Literally *and now*

Ezra's thanksgiving

27 [a]Blessed *be* the LORD God of our fathers, who has put *such a thing* as this in the king's [b]heart, to beautify the house of the LORD which *is* in Jerusalem,

28 and has [c]extended mercy to me before the king and his counselors, and before all the king's mighty princes.

So I was encouraged, as the [d]hand of the LORD my God *was* upon me; and I gathered leading men of Israel to go up with me.

Ezra's companions

8 THESE *are* the [e]heads of their fathers' *houses*, and *this is* the genealogy of those who went up with me from Babylon, in the reign of King Artaxerxes:

2 of the sons of Phinehas, Gershom; of the sons of Ithamar, Daniel; of the sons of David, Hattush;

3 of the sons of Shecaniah, of the sons of [f]Parosh, Zechariah; and registered with him *were* one hundred and fifty males;

4 of the sons of [g]Pahath-Moab, Eliehoenai the son of Zerahiah, and with him two hundred males;

5 of the sons of Shechaniah,* Ben-Jahaziel, and with him three hundred males;

6 of the sons of Adin, Ebed the son of Jonathan, and with him fifty males;

7 of the sons of Elam, Jeshaiah the son of Athaliah, and with him seventy males;

8 of the sons of Shephatiah, Zebadiah the son of Michael, and with him eighty males;

9 of the sons of Joab, Obadiah the son of Jehiel, and with him two hundred and eighteen males;

10 of the sons of Shelomith,* Ben-Josiphiah, and with him one hundred and sixty males;

11 of the sons of [h]Bebai, Zechariah the son of Bebai, and with him twenty-eight males;

12 of the sons of Azgad, Johanan the son of Hakkatan, and with him one hundred and ten males;

13 of the last sons of Adonikam, whose names *are* these—Eliphelet, Jeiel, and Shemaiah—and with them sixty males;

14 also of the sons of Bigvai, Uthai and Zabbud, and with them seventy males.

27
a Cp. 1 Chr. 29:10
b Prov. 21:1; cp. Ezra 6:22
28
c Ezra 9:9
d vv. 6,9; 8:18
CHAPTER 8
1
e Ezra 2:68
3
f Ezra 2:3
4
g Ezra 10:30
11
h Ezra 10:28
15
i Cp. Ezra 7:7
16
j Ezra 10:15
17
k See Neh. 3:26, *note*
18
l Cp. Neh. 2:8
m Cp. Neh. 8:7; 9:4–5
19
n Neh. 12:24
21
o Cp. Neh. 9:1–2; 2 Chr. 20:3
p Cp. Lev. 16:29; Isa. 58:3–5
q Cp. Ps. 5:8
22
r Cp. Neh. 5:9
s Cp. Ezra 7:6,9,28
t Ps. 33:18–19; 34:15,22; Rom. 8:28
u Cp. 2 Chr. 15:2; 36:16
23
v Cp. 1 Chr. 5:20; 2 Chr. 33:13; Isa. 19:22

Ezra sends for the Levites and Nethinim

15 Now I gathered them by the river that flows to Ahava, and we camped there three days. And I looked among the people and the priests, and found none of the sons of [i]Levi there.

16 Then I sent for Eliezer, Ariel, Shemaiah, Elnathan, Jarib, Elnathan, Nathan, Zechariah, and [j]Meshullam, leaders; also for Joiarib and Elnathan, men of understanding.

17 And I gave them a command for Iddo the chief man at the place Casiphia, and I told them what they should say to Iddo *and* his brethren* the [k]Nethinim at the place Casiphia—that they should bring us servants for the house of our God.

18 Then, by the [l]good hand of our God upon us, they [m]brought us a man of understanding, of the sons of Mahli the son of Levi, the son of Israel, namely Sherebiah, with his sons and brothers, eighteen men;

19 and [n]Hashabiah, and with him Jeshaiah of the sons of Merari, his brothers and their sons, twenty men;

20 also of the [k]Nethinim, whom David and the leaders had appointed for the service of the Levites, two hundred and twenty Nethinim. All of them were designated by name.

Ezra proclaims a fast for the LORD's protection

21 Then I proclaimed a [o]fast there at the river of Ahava, that we might [p]humble ourselves before our God, to seek from Him the [q]right way for us and our little ones and all our possessions.

22 For I was ashamed to request of the king an escort of soldiers and horsemen to help us against the enemy on the road, [r]because we had spoken to the king, saying, "The [s]hand of our God *is* upon all those for [t]good who seek Him, but His power and His wrath *are* against all those who forsake [u]Him."

23 So we fasted and entreated our God for this, and He [v]answered our prayer.

*
8:5 Following Masoretic Text and Vulgate; Septuagint reads *the sons of Zatho, Shechaniah.*
8:10 Following Masoretic Text and Vulgate; Septuagint reads *the sons of Banni, Shelomith.*
8:17 Following Vulgate; Masoretic Text reads *to Iddo his brother;* Septuagint reads *to their brethren.*

Treasure committed to twelve priests

24 And I separated twelve of the
leaders of the priests—Sherebiah,
Hashabiah, and ten of their brethren
with them—
25 and weighed out to them the silver, the gold, and the articles, the offering for the house of our God which
the king and his counselors and his
princes, and all Israel *who were* present, had [a]offered.
26 I [b]weighed into their hand six
hundred and fifty [c]talents of silver,
silver articles *weighing* one hundred
talents, one hundred talents of gold,
27 twenty gold basins *worth* a
thousand [c]drachmas, and two vessels
of fine polished bronze, precious as
gold.
28 And I said to them, [d]"You *are*
holy to the LORD; the articles *are* holy
also; and the silver and the gold *are* a
freewill offering to the LORD God of
your fathers.
29 "Watch and keep *them* until you
weigh *them* before the leaders of the
priests and the Levites and [e]heads of
the fathers' *houses* of Israel in Jerusalem, *in* the chambers of the house of
the LORD."
30 So the priests and the Levites received the silver and the gold and the
articles by weight, to bring *them* to
Jerusalem to the house of our God.

Ezra arrives in Jerusalem:
treasure placed in temple

31 Then we departed from the river
of Ahava on the twelfth *day* of the
[f]first month, to go to Jerusalem. And
the hand of our God was upon us, and
He delivered us from the hand of the
enemy and from ambush along the
road.
32 So we [g]came to Jerusalem, and
stayed there three days.
33 Now on the fourth day the silver
and the gold and the articles were
[h]weighed in the house of our God by
the hand of Meremoth the son of
Uriah the priest, and with him *was* Eleazar the son of Phinehas; with them
were the Levites, [i]Jozabad the son of
Jeshua and Noadiah the son of Binnui,
34 with the number *and* weight of
everything. All the weight was written
down at that time.
35 The children of those who had
been [j]carried away captive, who had
come from the captivity, [k]offered
burnt offerings to the God of Israel:
twelve bulls for all Israel, ninety-six
rams, seventy-seven lambs, and
twelve male goats *as* a sin offering. All
this was a burnt offering to the LORD.

Governors given king's decree

36 And they delivered the king's orders to the king's [l]satraps and the
governors *in the region* beyond the
[m]River. So they gave support to the
people and the house of God.

God's people fail to separate
from surrounding nations

9 WHEN these things were done,
the leaders came to me, saying,
"The people of Israel and the priests
and the Levites have not [n]separated
themselves from the peoples of the
lands, [o]with respect to the abominations of the Canaanites, the [p]Hittites,
the Perizzites, the Jebusites, the Ammonites, the Moabites, the Egyptians,
and the Amorites.
2 "For they have [q]taken some of
their daughters *as wives* for themselves and their sons, so that the holy
seed is [r]mixed with the peoples of
those lands. Indeed, the hand of the
leaders and rulers has been foremost
in this trespass."
3 So when I heard this thing, I
[s]tore my garment and my robe, and
plucked out some of the hair of my
head and beard, and sat down astonished.
4 Then everyone who [t]trembled
at the words of the God of Israel assembled to me, because of the transgression of those who had been carried away captive, and I sat
astonished until the [u]evening sacrifice.

Ezra's prayer of confession
to the LORD, his God

5 At the evening sacrifice I arose
from my fasting; and having [s]torn my
garment and my robe, I fell on my
knees and [v]spread out my hands to
the LORD my God.
6 And I [w]said: "O my God, I am too
ashamed and humiliated to lift up my
face to You, my God; for our iniquities
have risen higher than *our* heads, and
our guilt has grown up to the heavens.
7 "Since the days of our fathers to
this day we *have been* very [x]guilty,
and for our [y]iniquities we, our kings,
and our priests have been [z]delivered
into the hand of the kings of the lands,
to the [aa]sword, to captivity, to plunder,
and to [bb]humiliation, as *it is* this day.
8 "And now for a little while grace

25 *a* Ezra 7:15
26 *b* Cp. Ezra 1:9–11 *c* See Coinage (OT), Ex. 30:13, *note;* cp. 2 Chr. 2:10, *note*
28 *d* Lev. 21:6–8
29 *e* Ezra 4:3
31 *f* See Lev. 23:2, *note*
32 *g* Ezra 7:9; cp. Neh. 2:11
33 *h* vv. 26–30 *i* Neh. 11:16
35 *j* Ezra 2:1 *k* Cp. Ezra 6:17
36 *l* Cp. Ezra 7:21–24 *m* i.e. *the Euphrates*
CHAPTER 9
1 *n* Cp. Ezra 6:21; Neh. 9:2 *o* Cp. Lev. 18:24–30; Dt. 12:30–31; 2 Chr. 36:14 *p* See 2 Ki. 7:6, *note*
2 *q* Neh. 13:23; cp. Ex. 34:16; Dt. 7:3 *r* Cp. Dt. 7:6; 14:2
3 *s* Cp. 2 Ki. 22:11
4 *t* Ezra 10:3 *u* Ex. 29:39
5 *v* Cp. Ex. 9:29,33
6 *w Bible prayers* (OT): vv. 5–15; Neh. 1:5. (Gen. 15:2; Hab. 3:1)
7 *x* Cp. Neh. 1:6 *y* 2 Chr. 36:14–17

z Dt. 28:36 *aa* Dt. 32:25 *bb* Dan. 9:7–8

has been *shown* from the LORD our God, to leave us a remnant to escape, and to give us a [1a]peg in His holy place, that our God may enlighten our eyes and give us a measure of revival in our bondage.

9 "For we *were* [b]slaves. Yet our God did not [c]forsake us in our bondage; but He extended [d]mercy to us in the sight of the kings of Persia, to revive us, to repair the house of our God, to rebuild its ruins, and to give us a wall in Judah and Jerusalem.

10 "And now, O our God, what shall we say after this? For we have forsaken Your commandments,

11 "which You commanded by Your servants the prophets, saying, 'The land which you are entering to possess is an unclean land, with the [e]uncleanness of the peoples of the lands, with their abominations which have filled it from one end to another with their impurity.

12 'Now therefore, do [f]not [g]give your daughters as wives for their sons, nor take their daughters to your sons; and never seek their [h]peace or prosperity, that you may be strong and eat the good of the land, and leave *it* as an [i]inheritance to your children forever.'

13 "And after all that has come upon us for our evil deeds and for our great guilt, since You our God have punished us less than our iniquities *deserve,* and have given us *such* deliverance as this,

14 "should we again break Your commandments, and join in marriage with the people *committing* these abominations? Would You not be [j]angry with us until You had consumed *us,* so that *there would be* no remnant or survivor?

15 "O LORD God of Israel, You *are* [k]righteous, for we are left as a remnant, as *it is* this day. Here we *are* before You, in our guilt, though no one can [l]stand before You because of this!"

Reconciliation to God through confession and separation

10 NOW while Ezra was [m]praying, and while he was confessing, weeping, and bowing down [n]before the house of God, a very large assembly of men, women, and children gathered to him from Israel; for the people wept very [o]bitterly.

2 And Shechaniah the son of Jehiel, *one* of the sons of Elam, spoke up and said to Ezra, "We have [p]trespassed against our God, and have [q]taken pagan wives from the peoples of the land; yet now there is hope in Israel in spite of this.

3 "Now therefore, let us make a [r]covenant with our God to [s]put away all these wives and those who have been born to them, according to the advice of my master and of those who [t]tremble at the commandment of our God; and let it be done according to the [u]law.

4 "Arise, for *this* matter *is* your *responsibility.* We also *are* with you. [v]Be of good courage, and do *it.*"

5 Then Ezra arose, and made the leaders of the priests, the Levites, and all Israel [w]swear an oath that they would do according to this word. So they swore an oath.

6 Then Ezra rose up from before the house of God, and went into the chamber of Jehohanan the son of Eliashib; and *when* he came there, he [x]ate no bread and drank no water, for he mourned because of the guilt of those from the captivity.

7 And they issued a proclamation throughout Judah and Jerusalem to all the descendants of the captivity, that they must gather at Jerusalem,

8 and that whoever would not come within three days, according to the instructions of the leaders and elders, all his property would be confiscated, and he himself would be separated from the assembly of those from the captivity.

9 So all the men of Judah and Benjamin gathered at Jerusalem within three days. It *was* the [y]ninth month, on the twentieth of the month; and all the people sat in the open square of the house of God, [z]trembling because of *this* matter and because of heavy rain.

10 Then Ezra the priest stood up and said to them, "You have transgressed and have taken pagan wives, adding to the guilt of Israel.

8
a i.e. *a secure hold.* See *note* below; cp. Isa. 22:23
9
b Est. 7:4
c Neh. 9:17; cp. 2 Ki. 13:23
d Ezra 7:28
11
e Ezra 6:21
12
f Dt. 7:3–4
g *Separation:* vv. 10–12; Ezra 10:11. (Gen. 12:1; 2 Cor. 6:17, *note*)
h Dt. 23:6
i Prov. 13:22
14
j Cp. Dt. 9:8
15
k Neh. 9:33; Dan. 9:14
l Cp. Job 9:2
CHAPTER 10
1
m Cp. Dan. 9:20
n 2 Chr. 20:9
o Neh. 8:1–9
2
p Cp. Neh. 13:23–27
q 10:10,13, 14,17,18
3
r Cp. 2 Chr. 34:31
s 10:11
t Cp. Ezra 9:4
u Dt. 24:1–2
4
v 1 Chr. 28:10
5
w vv. 12,19
6
x Cp. Dt. 9:18
9
y See Lev. 23:2, *note*
z Cp. 1 Sam. 12:17–18

[1](9:8) The word *yathed,* here rendered "peg," refers to the remnant returned from exile. In Isa. 22:23,25 ("peg") the reference is to Eliakim of the house of David. In Zech. 10:4 ("tent peg") a Messianic reference is probable. The word conveys the thought of one upon whom authority can be placed, and about whom fixedness of character can be predicated.

11 "Now therefore, make [a]confes-
sion to the LORD God of your fathers,
and do His will; [b]separate yourselves
from the peoples of the land, and from
the pagan wives."
12 Then all the assembly answered
and said with a loud voice, "Yes! As
you have said, so we must do.
13 "But *there are* many people; *it is*
the season for heavy rain, and we are
not able to stand outside. Nor *is this*
the work of one or two days, for *there
are* many of us who have transgressed
in this matter.
14 "Please, let the leaders of our entire assembly stand; and let all those
in our cities who have taken pagan
wives come at appointed times, together with the elders and judges of
their cities, until the fierce wrath of
our God is turned away from us in this
matter."
15 Only Jonathan the son of Asahel
and Jahaziah the son of Tikvah opposed this, and [c]Meshullam and
Shabbethai the Levite gave them support.
16 Then the descendants of the captivity did so. And Ezra the priest, *with*
certain [d]heads of the fathers' *households,* were set apart by the fathers'
households, each of them by name;
and they sat down on the first day of
the [e]tenth month to examine the
[f]matter.
17 By the first day of the [e]first
month they finished *questioning* all
the men who had taken pagan wives.

List of repentant heads of families

18 And among the sons of the
priests who had taken pagan wives
the following were found of the sons
of [g]Jeshua the son of Jozadak,* and
his brothers: Maaseiah, Eliezer, Jarib,
and Gedaliah.
19 And they [h]gave their promise
that they would put away their wives;
and *being* [i]guilty, *they presented* a
ram of the flock as their [j]trespass offering.
20 Also of the sons of Immer: Hanani and Zebadiah;
21 of the sons of Harim: Maaseiah,
Elijah, Shemaiah, Jehiel, and Uzziah;
22 of the sons of Pashhur: Elioenai,
Maaseiah, Ishmael, Nethanel, Jozabad, and Elasah.
23 Also of the Levites: Jozabad,
Shimei, Kelaiah (the same *is* Kelita),
Pethahiah, Judah, and Eliezer.
24 Also of the singers: Eliashib;
and of the gatekeepers: Shallum, Telem, and Uri.
25 And others of Israel: of the
[k]sons of Parosh: Ramiah, Jeziah, Malchiah, Mijamin, Eleazar, Malchijah,
and Benaiah;
26 of the sons of Elam: Mattaniah,
Zechariah, Jehiel, Abdi, Jeremoth,
and Eliah;
27 of the sons of Zattu: Elioenai,
Eliashib, Mattaniah, Jeremoth, Zabad, and Aziza;
28 of the [l]sons of Bebai: Jehohanan, Hananiah, Zabbai, *and* Athlai;
29 of the sons of Bani: Meshullam,
Malluch, Adaiah, Jashub, Sheal, *and*
[m]Ramoth;
30 of the [n]sons of Pahath-Moab:
Adna, Chelal, Benaiah, Maaseiah,
Mattaniah, Bezalel, Binnui, and Manasseh;
31 *of* the sons of Harim: Eliezer,
Ishijah, Malchijah, Shemaiah, Shim-
eon,
32 Benjamin, Malluch, *and* Shemariah;
33 of the sons of Hashum: Mattenai, Mattattah, Zabad, Eliphelet, Jere-
mai, Manasseh, *and* Shimei;
34 of the sons of Bani: Maadai, Amram, Uel,
35 Benaiah, Bedeiah, Cheluh,*
36 Vaniah, Meremoth, Eliashib,
37 Mattaniah, Mattenai, Jaasai,*
38 Bani, Binnui, Shimei,
39 Shelemiah, Nathan, Adaiah,
40 [o]Machnadebai, Shashai, Sharai,
41 Azarel, Shelemiah, Shemariah,
42 Shallum, Amariah, *and* Joseph;
43 of the sons of Nebo: Jeiel, Mattithiah, Zabad, Zebina, Jaddai,* Joel,
and Benaiah.
44 All these had taken pagan wives,
and *some* of them had wives *by whom*
they had children.

11 *a* Lev. 26:40–42; cp. 1 Jn. 1:9 *b Separation:* vv. 10–11, 19; Neh. 9:2. (Gen. 12:1; 2 Cor. 6:17, *note*)
15 *c* Ezra 8:16; Neh. 3:4
16 *d* Ezra 4:3 *e* See Lev. 23:2, *note* *f* v. 14; cp. vv. 10–11 with 1 Cor. 11:28–32
18 *g* Ezra 5:2
19 *h* v. 5; Neh. 13:23–29 *i* Lev. 6:4–6 *j* Lev. 5:6,15
25 *k* Ezra 8:3
28 *l* Ezra 8:11
29 *m* Or *Ramoth*
30 *n* Ezra 8:4
40 *o* Or *Mabnadebai,* according to some mss.

*

10:18 Spelled *Jehozadak* in 1 Chronicles 6:14
10:35 Or *Cheluhi,* or *Cheluhu* **10:37** Or *Jaasu*
10:43 Or *Jaddu*

The Book of
NEHEMIAH

Author: Nehemiah *Theme:* Rebuilding Jerusalem's Walls *Date of writing:* 5th Cent. B.C.

NEHEMIAH records the last historical events in the OT, carrying the history to about 430 B.C. The prophecy of Malachi may have been written a few years later. The principal characters in this book are Ezra and Nehemiah. Though the temple had been rebuilt, as recorded by Ezra, the walls of the city were still in ruins because of the indolence of the people.

Eleven times in the text it is recorded that Nehemiah was engaged in prayer.

The book may be divided as follows:

I. Nehemiah Receives Permission from Artaxerxes to Visit Jerusalem (445 B.C.), 1:1—2:8.
II. The Rebuilding of the Walls of Jerusalem, 2:9—7:73.
III. The Great Revival under Ezra, 8:1—10:39.
IV. Conditions Prevailing in Palestine after a Remnant Had Been Living There for Nearly 100 Years, 11:1—13:31.

I. Nehemiah Receives Permission from Artaxerxes to visit Jerusalem (445 B.C.), 1:1—2:8

Nehemiah learns of distress of the remnant in Jerusalem

1 [a]THE words of [b]Nehemiah the son of Hachaliah.

It came to pass in the month of [c]Chislev, *in* the [d]twentieth year, as I was in [e]Shushan the citadel,

2 that [f]Hanani one of my brethren came with men from Judah; and I asked them concerning the Jews who had escaped, who had survived the captivity, and concerning Jerusalem.

3 And they said to me, "The survivors who are left from the captivity in the [g]province *are* there in great distress and [h]reproach. The wall of Jerusalem *is* also broken down, and its gates *are* burned with fire."

Nehemiah's prayer

4 So it was, when I heard these words, that I sat down and wept, and mourned *for many* days; I was fasting and [i]praying before the God of heaven.

5 And I [j]said: "I pray, LORD God of heaven, O great and [k]awesome God, *You* who [l]keep *Your* covenant and mercy with those who love You* and observe Your* commandments,

6 "please let Your ear be attentive and Your eyes open, that You may hear the prayer of Your servant which I pray before You now, day and night, for the children of Israel Your servants, and [m]confess the sins of the children of Israel which we have sinned against You. Both my father's house and I have sinned.

7 "We have acted very corruptly against You, and have not kept the commandments, the statutes, nor the ordinances which You commanded Your servant Moses.

8 "Remember, I pray, the word that You commanded Your servant Moses, [n]saying, '*If* you are unfaithful, I will scatter you among the nations;*

9 'but *if* you [o]return to Me, and keep My commandments and do them, though some of you were cast out to the farthest part of the heavens, *yet* I will gather them from there, and bring them to the place which I have chosen as a dwelling for My name.'

10 "Now these *are* Your servants and Your people, whom You have [p]redeemed by Your great power, and by Your strong hand.

Nehemiah asks the LORD for favor before the king

11 "O Lord, I pray, please let Your ear be attentive to the prayer of Your servant, and to the prayer of Your servants who desire to [q]fear Your name; and let Your servant prosper this day, I pray, and grant him mercy in the sight of this man." For I was the king's [r]cupbearer.

Nehemiah's prayer answered

2 AND it came to pass in the month of [c]Nisan, in the twentieth year of King [s]Artaxerxes, *when* wine *was* before him, that I took the wine and gave it to the king. Now I had never been sad in his presence before.

2 Therefore the king said to me, "Why *is* your face sad, since you *are*

CHAPTER 1

1 a c. 445 B.C. b Neh. 10:1 c See Lev. 23:2, *note* d Neh. 2:1 e Or *Susa*, ancient capital of Persia. Est. 1:1–2, 5

2 f Neh. 7:2

3 g Neh. 7:6 h Neh. 2:17

4 i Cp. Ezra 9:5–6; 10:6

5 j *Bible prayers (OT):* vv. 5–11; Neh. 4:4. (Gen. 15:2; Hab. 3:1) k Neh. 4:14 l Ex. 34:6–7

6 m Neh. 9:2

8 n Dt. 28:63–67

9 o Dt. 30:1–10

10 p See Ex. 14:30, *note*

11 q See Ps. 19:9, *note* r Neh. 2:1; cp. 2 Chr. 9:4

CHAPTER 2

1 s See Ezra 4:3, *note*

---

*1:5 Literally *Him* • Literally *His* 1:8 Leviticus 26:33

not sick? This *is* nothing but sorrow of [a]heart." So I became dreadfully afraid,

3 and said to the king, "May the king live forever! Why should my face not be sad, [b]when the city, the place of my fathers' tombs, *lies* waste, and its gates are burned with [c]fire?"

4 Then the king said to me, "What do you request?" So I [d]prayed to the God of heaven.

5 And I said to the king, "If it pleases the king, and if your servant has found favor in your sight, I ask that you send me to Judah, to the city of my fathers' tombs, that I may [1]rebuild it."

6 Then the king said to me (the queen also sitting beside him), "How long will your journey be? And when will you return?" So it pleased the king to send me; and I set him a [e]time.

7 Furthermore I said to the king, "If it pleases the king, let letters be given to me for the [f]governors *of the region* beyond the [g]River, that they must permit me to pass through till I come to Judah,

8 "and a letter to Asaph the keeper of the king's forest, that he must give me timber to make beams for the gates of the citadel which *pertains* to the temple,* for the city wall, and for the house that I will occupy." And the king granted *them* to me according to the good [h]hand of my God upon me.

II. The Rebuilding of the Walls of Jerusalem, 2:9—7:73

Nehemiah arrives at Jerusalem; he secretly inspects the ruined walls

9 Then I went to the governors *in the region* beyond the [g]River, and gave them the king's letters. Now the king had sent captains of the army and horsemen with [i]me.

10 When [j]Sanballat the Horonite and [2]Tobiah the Ammonite official* heard *of it,* they were deeply disturbed that a man had come to seek the well-being of the children of Israel.

11 So I came [k]to Jerusalem and was there three days.

12 Then I arose in the night, I and a few men with me; I told no one what my God had put in my heart to do at Jerusalem; nor was there any animal with me, except the one on which I rode.

13 And I went out by night through the [l]Valley Gate to the Serpent Well and the Refuse Gate, and viewed the [m]walls of Jerusalem which were broken down and its gates which were burned with fire.

14 Then I went on to the [n]Fountain Gate and to the [o]King's Pool, but *there was* no room for the animal under me to pass.

15 So I went up in the night by the valley, and viewed the wall; then I turned back and entered by the Valley Gate, and so returned.

16 And the officials did not know where I had gone or what I had done; I had not yet told the Jews, the priests, the nobles, the officials, or the others who did the work.

Nehemiah encourages the people to build the walls

17 Then I said to them, "You see the distress that we *are* in, how Jerusalem *lies* waste, and its gates are burned with fire. Come and let us build the wall of Jerusalem, that we may no longer be a reproach."

18 And I told them of the hand of my God which had been good upon me, and also of the king's words that he had spoken to me. So they said, "Let us rise up and build." Then they [p]set their hands to *this* good *work.*

19 But when Sanballat the Horonite, Tobiah the Ammonite official, and Geshem the Arab heard *of it,* they [q]laughed at us and [r]despised us, and said, "What *is* this thing that you are doing? Will you rebel against the king?"

20 So I answered them, and said to them, "The God of heaven Himself will prosper us; therefore we His servants will arise and build, but you

2
a Prov. 15:13
3
b Israel (history): vv. 1–9; Neh. 8:1. (Gen. 12:2; Rom. 11:26, *note*)
c 2 Ki. 24:10
4
d Neh. 1:4
6
e Neh. 5:14; 13:6
7
f Ezra 7:21; cp. 8:36
g i.e. *the Euphrates*
8
h v. 18; Ezra 7:6,9, 28
9
i Cp. Ezra 8:22
10
j Neh. 4:1
11
k Cp. Ezra 8:32
13
l 2 Chr. 26:9
m Jer. 39:8
14
n Neh. 3:15
o 2 Ki. 20:20
18
p Contrast Ezra 4:4; cp. 2 Sam. 2:7; Ezra 6:22; Heb. 12:12
19
q i.e. *opposition by ridicule*
r Cp. Neh. 4:1–6

*

2:8 Literally *house* 2:10 Literally *servant,* and so elsewhere in this book

[1](2:5) This is the only decree actually recorded in Scripture which relates to the restoring and building of the city of Jerusalem. And since Nehemiah is careful to date the royal decree "in the month of Nisan, in the twentieth year of King Artaxerxes," it is quite certain that here is the starting point of the period of the seventy weeks foretold by Daniel (Dan. 9:24–27). According to competent authorities the year was 445 B.C.

[2](2:10) Two Tobiahs are distinguished: (1) "Tobiah the Ammonite official" (Neh. 2:10,19; 4:3,7; 6:1,12,14); and (2) a Jew whose children were unable to prove his genealogy (Neh. 7:61–62). It is likely that he was already dead at that time. Only one Tobiah, the Ammonite, is active in this book.

have no [a]heritage or right or memorial in Jerusalem."

The builders of the walls

3 THEN [b]Eliashib the high priest
rose up with his brethren the
priests and built the [1c]Sheep Gate;
they consecrated it and hung its doors.
They built as far as the Tower of the
Hundred,* *and* consecrated it, then as
far as the Tower of [d]Hananel.
2 Next to *Eliashib** the [e]men of
Jericho built. And next to them Zaccur
the son of Imri built.
3 Also the sons of Hassenaah built
the [f]Fish Gate; they laid its beams and
hung its doors with its bolts and bars.
4 And next to them [g]Meremoth
the son of Urijah, the son of Koz,*
made repairs. Next to them [h]Meshul-
lam the son of Berechiah, the son of
Meshezabel, made repairs. Next to
them Zadok the son of Baana made
repairs.
5 Next to them the Tekoites made
repairs; but their nobles did not put
their shoulders* to the work of their
[i]Lord.
6 Moreover Jehoiada the son of
Paseah and Meshullam the son of Bes-
odeiah repaired the [j]Old Gate; they
laid its beams and hung its doors, with
its bolts and bars.
7 And next to them Melatiah the
Gibeonite, Jadon the Meronothite, the
[k]men of Gibeon and Mizpah, repaired
the residence* of the [l]governor *of the*
region beyond the [m]River.
8 Next to him Uzziel the son of
Harhaiah, one of the goldsmiths,
made repairs. Also next to him Hananiah, one* of the perfumers, made repairs; and they fortified Jerusalem as
far as the [n]Broad Wall.
9 And next to them Rephaiah the
son of Hur, leader of half the district of
Jerusalem, made repairs.
10 Next to them Jedaiah the son of
Harumaph made repairs in front of his
house. And next to him Hattush the
son of Hashabniah made repairs.
11 Malchijah the son of Harim and
Hashub the son of Pahath-Moab repaired another section, as well as the
Tower of the Ovens.
12 And next to him was Shallum
the son of Hallohesh, leader of half the
district of Jerusalem; he and his
daughters made repairs.
13 Hanun and the inhabitants of
Zanoah repaired the [o]Valley Gate.
They built it, hung its doors with its
bolts and bars, and *repaired* a thousand [p]cubits of the wall as far as the
[q]Refuse Gate.
14 Malchijah the son of Rechab,
leader of the district of [r]Beth Haccerem, repaired the [q]Refuse Gate; he
built it and hung its doors with its
bolts and bars.
15 Shallun the son of Col-Hozeh,
leader of the district of Mizpah, repaired the [s]Fountain Gate; he built it,
covered it, hung its doors with its bolts
and bars, and repaired the wall of the
Pool of [t]Shelah by the [u]King's Garden, as far as the stairs that go down
from the City of David.
16 After him Nehemiah the son of
Azbuk, leader of half the district of
Beth Zur, made repairs as far as *the*
place in front of the tombs* of David,
to the man-made [v]pool, and as far as
the House of the Mighty.
17 After him the Levites, *under* Rehum the son of Bani, made repairs.
Next to him Hashabiah, leader of half
the district of Keilah, made repairs for
his district.
18 After him their brethren, *under*
Bavai* the son of Henadad, leader of
the *other* half of the district of Keilah,
made repairs.
19 And next to him Ezer the son of
Jeshua, the leader of Mizpah, repaired
another section in front of the Ascent
to the Armory at the buttress.
20 After him Baruch the son of Zabbai* carefully repaired the other section, from the buttress to the door of
the house of Eliashib the high priest.
21 After him Meremoth the son of
Urijah, the son of Koz,* repaired another section, from the door of the
house of Eliashib to the end of the
house of Eliashib.
22 And after him the priests, the
men of the [w]plain, made repairs.
23 After him Benjamin and Hasshub made repairs opposite their
house. After them Azariah the son of

20
a Cp. Ezra 4:3
CHAPTER 3
1
b vv. 20–21; Neh. 13:4, 7,28
c v. 32
d Jer. 31:38
2
e Neh. 7:36
3
f Zeph. 1:10
4
g Ezra 8:33
h Ezra 10:15
5
i Or *lord*, or *lords*
6
j Neh. 12:39
7
k Neh. 7:25
l Ezra 8:36; cp. Neh. 2:9
m i.e. *the Euphrates*
8
n Neh. 12:38
13
o Neh. 2:13, 15
p See Weights and Measures (OT), 2 Chr. 2:10, *note*
q Neh. 2:13
14
r Jer. 6:1
15
s Neh. 2:14
t Or *Shiloah*, Isa. 8:6
u 2 Ki. 25:4
16
v 2 Ki. 20:20
22
w Cp. Neh. 12:28

*
3:1 Hebrew *Hammeah*, also at 12:39 **3:2** Literally *On his hand* **3:4** Or *Hakkoz* **3:5** Literally *necks* **3:7** Literally *throne* **3:8** Literally *the son* **3:16** Septuagint, Syriac, and Vulgate read *tomb*. **3:18** Following Masoretic Text and Vulgate; some Hebrew manuscripts, Septuagint, and Syriac read *Binnui* (compare verse 24). **3:20** A few Hebrew manuscripts, Syriac, and Vulgate read *Zaccai*. **3:21** Or *Hakkoz*

[1](3:1) Here the sheep for sacrifice were brought into the city. The towers of the Hundred and Hananel were evidently on either side of the gate.

Maaseiah, the son of Ananiah, made repairs by his house.

24 After him [a]Binnui the son of Henadad repaired another section, from the house of Azariah to the buttress, even as far as the corner.

25 Palal the son of Uzai *made repairs* opposite the buttress, and on the tower which projects from the king's upper house that *was* by the [b]court of the prison. After him Pedaiah the son of Parosh *made repairs.*

26 Moreover the [1]Nethinim who dwelt in Ophel *made repairs* as far as *the place* in front of the [c]Water Gate toward the east, and on the projecting tower.

27 After them the Tekoites repaired another section, next to the great projecting tower, and as far as the wall of [d]Ophel.

28 Beyond the [e]Horse Gate the priests made repairs, each in front of his *own* house.

29 After them Zadok the son of Immer made repairs in front of his *own* house. After him Shemaiah the son of Shechaniah, the keeper of the East Gate, made repairs.

30 After him Hananiah the son of Shelemiah, and Hanun, the sixth son of Zalaph, repaired another section. After him Meshullam the son of Berechiah made repairs in front of his dwelling.

31 After him Malchijah, one of the goldsmiths, made repairs as far as the house of the [f]Nethinim and of the merchants, in front of the Miphkad* Gate, and as far as the upper room at the corner.

32 And between the upper room at the corner, as far as the [g]Sheep Gate, the goldsmiths and the merchants made repairs.

Opposition by ridicule

4 BUT it so happened, when [h]Sanballat heard that we were rebuilding the wall, that he was furious and very indignant, and mocked the Jews.

2 And he spoke before his brethren and the army of [i]Samaria, and said, "What are these feeble Jews doing? Will they fortify themselves? Will they offer sacrifices? Will they complete it in a day? Will they revive the stones from the heaps of rubbish—*stones* that are burned?"

3 Now [j]Tobiah the Ammonite *was* beside him, and he said, "Whatever they build, if even a fox goes up *on it,* he will break down their stone wall."

Nehemiah answers by prayer

4 [k]Hear, O our God, for we are despised; turn their [l]reproach on their own heads, and give them as plunder to a land of captivity!

5 Do [m]not cover their iniquity, and do not let their sin be blotted out from before You; for they have provoked *You* to anger before the builders.

6 So we built the wall, and the entire wall was joined together up to half its *height,* for the people had a mind to work.

7 Now it happened, when Sanballat, Tobiah, the [j]Arabs, the Ammonites, and the Ashdodites heard that the walls of Jerusalem were being restored and the gaps were beginning to be closed, that they became very angry,

8 and all of them [n]conspired together to come *and* attack Jerusalem and create confusion.

9 Nevertheless we made our prayer to our God, and because of them we set a watch against them day and night.

Opposition by discouraged brethren: the resource of faith

10 Then Judah said, "The strength of the laborers is failing, and *there is* so much rubbish that we are not able to build the wall."

11 And our adversaries said, "They will neither know nor see anything, till we come into their midst and kill them and cause the work to cease."

12 So it was, when the Jews who dwelt near them came, that they told us [o]ten times, "From whatever place you turn, *they will be* upon us."

13 Therefore I positioned *men* behind the lower parts of the wall, at the openings; and I set the people according to their families, with their swords, their spears, and their bows.

14 And I looked, and arose and said

24 *a* Ezra 8:33
25 *b* Jer. 32:2
26 *c* Neh. 8:1
27 *d* Cp. 2 Chr. 27:3; 33:14. Perhaps part of the fort called *Millo,* 2 Chr. 32:5
28 *e* 2 Chr. 23:15
31 *f* See v. 26, *note*
32 *g* Neh. 3:1
CHAPTER 4
1 *h* Neh. 2:10, 19
2 *i* Cp. Ezra 4:9–10
3 *j* Neh. 2:19
4 *k Bible prayers* (OT): vv. 4–5; Neh. 9:5. (Gen. 15:2; Hab. 3:1) *l* Cp. Ps. 79:12; Prov. 3:34
5 *m* Cp. Ps. 69:27; Jer. 18:23
8 *n* Cp. Ps. 83:5
12 *o* Cp. Num. 14:22

* 3:31 Literally *Inspection* or *Recruiting*

[1](3:26) *Nethinim* means *given.* Probably this is another name for the Gibeonites who were assigned by Joshua to be perpetual slaves as "woodcutters and water carriers" for the house of God (Josh. 9:23). As water carriers it is appropriate that they dwelt at the Water Gate. The Nethinim are mentioned: 1 Chr. 9:2; Ezra 2:43,58,70; 7:7,24; 8:17,20; Neh. 3:31; 7:46,60,73; 10:28; 11:3,21.

to the nobles, to the leaders, and to the rest of the people, "Do not be [a]afraid of them. Remember the Lord, great and [b]awesome, and fight for your brethren, your sons, your daughters, your wives, and your houses."

15 And it happened, when our enemies heard that it was known to us, and *that* God had brought their [c]plot to nothing, that all of us returned to the wall, everyone to his work.

16 So it was, from that time on, *that* half of my servants worked at construction, while the other half held the spears, the shields, the bows, and *wore* armor; and the leaders *were* behind all the house of Judah.

17 Those who built on the wall, and those who carried burdens, loaded themselves so that with one hand they worked at construction, and with the other held a weapon.

18 Every one of the builders had his sword girded at his side as he built. And the one who sounded the trumpet *was* beside me.

19 Then I said to the nobles, the rulers, and the rest of the people, "The work *is* great and extensive, and we are separated far from one another on the wall.

20 "Wherever you hear the sound of the trumpet, rally to us there. Our God will [d]fight for us."

21 So we labored in the work, and half of *the men** held the spears from daybreak until the stars appeared.

22 At the same time I also said to the people, "Let each man and his servant stay at night in Jerusalem, that they may be our guard by night and a working party by day."

23 So neither I, my brethren, my servants, nor the men of the guard who followed me took off our clothes, *except* that everyone took them off for washing.

Opposition of unbrotherly greed: the resource of restitution

5 AND there was a great outcry of the people and their wives [e]against their Jewish brethren.

2 For there were those who said, "We, our sons, and our daughters *are* many; therefore let us get grain, that we may eat and live."

3 There were also *some* who said, "We have mortgaged our lands and vineyards and houses, that we might buy grain because of the famine."

4 There were also those who said, "We have borrowed money for the king's [f]tax *on* our lands and vineyards.

5 "Yet now our flesh *is* as the flesh of our brethren, our children as their children; and indeed we are forcing our sons and our [g]daughters to be slaves, and *some* of our daughters have been brought into slavery. *It is* not in our power *to redeem* [h]*them*, for other men have our lands and vineyards."

6 And I became very angry when I heard their outcry and these words.

7 After serious thought, I rebuked the nobles and rulers, and said to them, "Each of you is exacting [i]usury from his brother." So I called a great assembly against them.

8 And I said to them, "According to our ability we have [j]redeemed our Jewish brethren who were sold to the nations. Now indeed, will you even sell your brethren? Or should they be sold to us?" Then they were silenced and found nothing *to say*.

9 Then I said, "What you are doing *is* not good. Should you not walk in the [k]fear of our God because of the reproach of the nations, our enemies?"

10 "I also, *with* my brethren and my servants, am lending them money and grain. Please, let us stop this usury!

11 "Restore now to them, even this day, their lands, their vineyards, their olive groves, and their houses, also a hundredth of the money and the grain, the new wine and the oil, that you have charged them."

12 So they said, "We will [l]restore *it*, and will require nothing from them; we will do as you say." Then I called the priests, and required an oath from them that they would do according to this [m]promise.

13 Then I shook out [n]the fold of my garment* and said, "So may God shake out each man from his house, and from his property, who does not perform this promise. Even thus may he be shaken out and emptied." And all the assembly said, [o]"Amen!" and praised the LORD. Then the people did according to this promise.

Nehemiah's unselfish example

14 Moreover, from the time that I was appointed to be their governor in the land of Judah, from the [p]twentieth year until the thirty-second year of King Artaxerxes, twelve years, nei-

14 *a* Cp. Num. 14:9; Dt. 1:29–30 *b* Neh. 1:5
15 *c* Cp. 2 Sam. 17:14
20 *d* Ex. 14:14; Dt. 1:30; 2 Chr. 20:29
CHAPTER 5
1 *e* vv. 2–5; Isa. 5:7–8; cp. Lev. 25:35; Dt. 15:7–8
4 *f* Cp. Ezra 4:13,20; 7:24
5 *g* Ex. 21:7 *h* Cp. Lev. 25:48
7 *i* Ex. 22:25; Lev. 25:36
8 *j* *Redemption* (redeeming relative type): v. 8; Job 19:25. (Gen. 48:16; Isa. 59:20, *note*)
9 *k* See Ps. 19:9, *note*
12 *l* v. 13; cp. 2 Chr. 28:15; Prov. 6:31 *m* Cp. Ezra 10:1–5
13 *n* Cp. Acts 18:6 *o* Cp. Neh. 8:6
14 *p* Neh. 2:1

* 4:21 Literally *them* 5:13 Literally *my lap*

ther I nor my brothers [a]ate the governor's provisions.
15 But the former governors who
were before me laid burdens on the
people, and took from them bread and
wine, besides forty [b]shekels of silver.
Yes, even their servants bore rule over
the people, but I did not do so, because
of the [c]fear of God.
16 Indeed, I also continued the
[d]work on this wall, and we* did not
buy any land. All my servants *were*
gathered there for the work.
17 And at my table *were* one hundred and fifty Jews and rulers, besides
those who came to us from the nations
around us.
18 Now *that* which was [e]prepared
daily *was* one ox *and* six choice sheep.
Also fowl were prepared for me, and
once every ten days an abundance of
all kinds of wine. Yet in spite of this I
did [f]not demand the governor's provisions, because the bondage was
heavy on this people.
19 Remember me, my God, for
[g]good, *according to* all that I have
done for this people.

Opposition by craftiness:
the resource of manly firmness

6 NOW it happened when [h]Sanbal-
lat, Tobiah, Geshem the Arab,
and the rest of our enemies heard that
I had rebuilt the wall, and *that* there
were no breaks left in it (though at
that time I had not hung the doors in
the gates),
2 that Sanballat and Geshem sent
to me, saying, "Come, let us meet together among the villages in the plain
of Ono." But they thought to do me
harm.
3 So I sent messengers to them,
saying, "I *am* doing a great work, so
that I cannot come down. Why should
the work cease while I leave it and go
down to you?"
4 But they sent me this message
four times, and I answered them in the
same manner.
5 Then Sanballat sent his servant
to me as before, the fifth time, with an
open letter in his hand.
6 In it *was* written:

It is reported among the
nations, and Geshem* says,
that you and the Jews plan to
[i]rebel; therefore, according to
these rumors, you are
rebuilding the wall, that you
may be their king.

7 And you have also appointed
prophets to proclaim
concerning you at Jerusalem,
saying, "*There is* a king in
Judah!" Now these matters will
be reported to the king. So
come, therefore, and let us
consult together.

8 Then I sent to him, saying, "No
such things as you say are being done,
but you invent them in your own
heart."
9 For they all *were trying to* make
us afraid, saying, "Their [j]hands will
be weakened in the work, and it will
not be done."
Now therefore, *O God*, strengthen my hands.
10 Afterward I came to the house of
Shemaiah the son of Delaiah, the son
of Mehetabel, who *was* a secret in-
former; and he said, "Let us meet together in the house of God, within the
temple, and let us close the doors of
the temple, for they are coming to kill
you; indeed, at night they will come to
kill you."
11 And I said, "Should such a man
as I flee? And who *is there* such as I
who would go into the temple to save
his life? I will not go in!"
12 Then I perceived that God had
not sent him at all, but that he pronounced *this* prophecy against me because Tobiah and Sanballat had hired
him.
13 For this reason he *was* hired,
that I should be [k]afraid and act that
way and sin, so *that* they might have
cause for an evil report, that they
might reproach me.
14 My God, remember Tobiah and
Sanballat, according to these their
[l]works, and the prophetess Noadiah
and the rest of the prophets who
would have made me afraid.

The wall finished in fifty-two days

15 So the wall was finished on the
twenty-fifth *day* of [m]Elul, in fifty-two
days.
16 And it happened, when all our
enemies heard *of it*, and all the nations
around us saw *these things*, that they
were very [n]disheartened in their own
eyes; for they perceived that this work
was [o]done by our God.
17 Also in those days the nobles of
Judah sent many letters to [p]Tobiah,

14
a Cp. 1 Sam. 12:3; Acts 20:33–35; 1 Th. 2:9
15
b See Coinage (OT), Ex. 30:13, *note*
c See Ps. 19:9, *note*
16
d Neh. 4:1; 6:1
18
e Cp. 1 Ki. 4:22–23
f Cp. 2 Th. 3:8
19
g Cp. 2 Ki. 20:3; Neh. 13:14
CHAPTER 6
1
h Neh. 2:10, 19; 4:1,7; 13:28
6
i Neh. 2:19
9
j Cp. Ezra 4:4
13
k Cp. 2 Cor. 11:26
14
l Cp. Neh. 13:29
15
m See Lev. 23:2, *note*
16
n Cp. Neh. 2:10; 4:1,7
o Ps. 31:19; cp. Ps. 126:2
17
p See Neh. 2:10, *note*

*
5:16 Following Masoretic Text; Septuagint, Syriac, and Vulgate read *I*. **6:6** Hebrew *Gashmu*

and *the letters of* Tobiah came to
them.
18 For many in Judah were pledged
to him, because he was the [a]son-in-
law of Shechaniah the son of Arah,
and his son Jehohanan had married
the daughter of [b]Meshullam the son
of Berechiah.
19 Also they reported his good
deeds before me, and reported my
words to him. Tobiah sent letters to
frighten me.

Hanani and Hananiah put in charge of Jerusalem

7 THEN it was, when the wall was
built and I had hung the [c]doors,
when the gatekeepers, the singers,
and the Levites had been appointed,
2 that I gave the charge of Jerusalem to my brother [d]Hanani, and
[e]Hananiah the leader of the [f]citadel,
for he *was* a faithful man and [g]feared
God more than many.
3 And I said to them, "Do not let
the gates of Jerusalem be opened until
the sun is hot; and while they stand
guard, let them shut and bar the doors;
and appoint guards from among the
inhabitants of Jerusalem, one at his
watch station and another in front of
his own house."
4 Now the city *was* large and spacious, but the people in it *were* [h]few,
and the houses *were* not rebuilt.

Register of genealogy of people first returning from Babylon

5 Then my God put it into my
heart to gather the nobles, the rulers,
and the people, that they might be registered by genealogy. And I found a
register of the genealogy of those who
had come up in the first *return,* and
found written in it:

6 [i]These *are* the people of the
province who came back from
the captivity, of those who had
been carried away, whom
Nebuchadnezzar the king of
Babylon had carried away, and
who returned to Jerusalem and
Judah, everyone to his city.
7 Those who came with
[j]Zerubbabel *were* [k]Jeshua,
Nehemiah, Azariah, Raamiah,
Nahamani, Mordecai, Bilshan,
Mispereth,* Bigvai, Nehum,
and Baanah.
The number of the men of
the people of Israel:
8 the sons of Parosh, two
thousand one hundred and
seventy-two;
9 the sons of Shephatiah, three
hundred and seventy-two;
10 the sons of Arah, six hundred
and fifty-two;
11 the sons of Pahath-Moab, of
the sons of Jeshua and Joab,
two thousand eight hundred
and eighteen;
12 the sons of Elam, one thousand
two hundred and fifty-four;
13 the sons of Zattu, eight
hundred and forty-five;
14 the sons of Zaccai, seven
hundred and sixty;
15 the sons of Binnui,* six
hundred and forty-eight;
16 the sons of Bebai, six hundred
and twenty-eight;
17 the sons of Azgad, two
thousand three hundred and
twenty-two;
18 the sons of Adonikam, six
hundred and sixty-seven;
19 the sons of Bigvai, two
thousand and sixty-seven;
20 the sons of Adin, six hundred
and fifty-five;
21 the sons of Ater of Hezekiah,
ninety-eight;
22 the sons of Hashum, three
hundred and twenty-eight;
23 the sons of Bezai, three
hundred and twenty-four;
24 the sons of Hariph,* one
hundred and twelve;
25 the sons of Gibeon,*
ninety-five;
26 the men of Bethlehem and
Netophah, one hundred and
eighty-eight;
27 the men of Anathoth, one
hundred and twenty-eight;
28 the men of Beth Azmaveth,*
forty-two;
29 the men of Kirjath Jearim,
Chephirah, and Beeroth, seven
hundred and forty-three;
30 the men of Ramah and Geba,
six hundred and twenty-one;
31 the men of Michmas, one
hundred and twenty-two;
32 the men of Bethel and Ai, one
hundred and twenty-three;
33 the men of the other Nebo,
fifty-two;
34 the sons of the other Elam, one

18
[a] Neh. 13:4, 28
[b] Ezra 10:15; Neh. 3:4

CHAPTER 7

1
[c] Cp. Neh. 6:1

2
[d] Neh. 1:2
[e] Neh. 10:23
[f] Cp. Neh. 2:8
[g] See Ps. 19:9, *note*

4
[h] Dt. 4:27

6
[i] Cp. Ezra 2:1–64; 2 Chr. 36:20

7
[j] Ezra 5:2; Neh. 12:1, 47; Mt. 1:12,13
[k] Or *Joshua.* Not the same man as in Josh. 1:1ff.

*7:7 Spelled *Mispar* in Ezra 2:2 7:15 Spelled *Bani* in Ezra 2:10 7:24 Called *Jorah* in Ezra 2:18 7:25 Called *Gibbar* in Ezra 2:20 7:28 Called *Azmaveth* in Ezra 2:24

thousand two hundred and
fifty-four;
35 the sons of Harim, three
hundred and twenty;
36 the sons of Jericho, three
hundred and forty-five;
37 the sons of Lod, Hadid, and
Ono, seven hundred and
twenty-one;
38 the sons of Senaah, three
thousand nine hundred and
thirty.
39 The priests: the sons of
Jedaiah, of the house of
Jeshua, nine hundred and
seventy-three;
40 the sons of [a]Immer, one
thousand and fifty-two;
41 the sons of Pashhur, one
thousand two hundred and
forty-seven;
42 the sons of Harim, one
thousand and seventeen.

Register of returning Levites

43 The Levites: the sons of
Jeshua, of Kadmiel, *and* of the
sons of [b]Hodevah,
seventy-four.
44 The singers: the sons of Asaph,
one hundred and forty-eight.
45 The gatekeepers: the sons of
Shallum, the sons of Ater, the
sons of Talmon, the sons of
Akkub, the sons of Hatita, the
sons of Shobai, one hundred
and thirty-eight.

Register of returning Nethinim

46 The [c]Nethinim: the sons of
Ziha, the sons of Hasupha, the
sons of Tabbaoth,
47 the sons of Keros, the sons of
Sia,* the sons of Padon,
48 the sons of Lebana,* the sons
of Hagaba,* the sons of
Salmai,*
49 the sons of Hanan, the sons of
Giddel, the sons of Gahar,
50 the sons of Reaiah, the sons of
Rezin, the sons of Nekoda,
51 the sons of Gazzam, the sons
of Uzza, the sons of Paseah,
52 the sons of Besai, the sons of
Meunim, the sons of
[d]Nephishesim,*
53 the sons of Bakbuk, the sons
of Hakupha, the sons of
Harhur,
54 the sons of Bazlith,* the sons
of Mehida, the sons of Harsha,
55 the sons of Barkos, the sons of
Sisera, the sons of Tamah,

40
a 1 Chr. 9:12
43
b Or *Hodeiah*
46
c See Neh. 3:26, *note*
52
d Or *Nephphishesim*
57
e Cp. 1 Ki. 9:21; Ezra 2:55,58
61
f i.e. *prove*
62
g See Neh. 2:10, *note*
65
h See Ex. 28:30, *note*
i Cp. Ezra 2:61–63

56 the sons of Neziah, and the
sons of Hatipha.

Register of descendants of Solomon's servants

57 The [e]sons of Solomon's
servants: the sons of Sotai, the
sons of Sophereth, the sons of
Perida,*
58 the sons of Jaala, the sons of
Darkon, the sons of Giddel,
59 the sons of Shephatiah, the
sons of Hattil, the sons of
Pochereth of Zebaim, and the
children of Amon.*
60 All the Nethinim, and the sons
of Solomon's servants, *were*
three hundred and ninety-two.
61 And these *were* the ones who
came up from Tel Melah, Tel
Harsha, Cherub, Addon,* and
Immer, but they could not
[f]identify their father's house
nor their lineage, whether they
were of Israel:
62 the sons of Delaiah, the sons
of [g]Tobiah, the sons of
Nekoda, six hundred and
forty-two;

Priests without genealogy disqualified

63 and of the priests: the sons of
Habaiah, the sons of Koz,* the
sons of Barzillai, who took a
wife of the daughters of
Barzillai the Gileadite, and was
called by their name.
64 These sought their listing
among those who were
registered by genealogy, but it
was not found; therefore they
were excluded from the
priesthood as defiled.
65 And the governor* said to
them that they should not eat
of the most holy things till a
priest could consult with the
[h]Urim and [i]Thummim.

Total number of the remnant

66 Altogether the whole assembly
was forty-two thousand three
hundred and sixty,
67 besides their male and female
servants, of whom *there were*
seven thousand three hundred
and thirty-seven; and they had

*
7:47 Spelled *Siaha* in Ezra 2:44 **7:48** Masoretic Text reads *Lebanah*. • Masoretic Text reads *Hogabah*. • Or *Shalmai*, or *Shamlai*
7:52 Spelled *Nephusim* in Ezra 2:50 **7:54** Spelled *Bazluth* in Ezra 2:52 **7:57** Spelled *Peruda* in Ezra 2:55 **7:59** Spelled *Ami* in Ezra 2:57 **7:61** Spelled *Addan* in Ezra 2:59 **7:63** Or *Hakkoz*
7:65 Hebrew *Tirshatha*

two hundred and forty-five
men and women singers.

Their substance and gifts

68 Their horses were seven
hundred and thirty-six, their
mules two hundred and
forty-five,
69 *their* camels four hundred and
thirty-five, *and* donkeys six
thousand seven hundred and
twenty.
70 And some of the [a]heads of the
fathers' houses gave to the
work. The governor* gave to
the treasury one thousand gold
[b]drachmas, fifty basins, and
five hundred and thirty priestly
garments.
71 Some of the [c]heads of the
fathers' *houses* gave to the
treasury of the work twenty
thousand gold [b]drachmas, and
two thousand two hundred
silver minas.
72 And that which the rest of the
people gave *was* twenty
thousand gold [b]drachmas, two
thousand silver minas, and
sixty-seven priestly garments.

73 So the priests, the Levites, the
gatekeepers, the singers, *some* of the
people, the Nethinim, and all Israel
dwelt in their cities.
When the [d]seventh month came,
the children of Israel *were* in their cities.

III. The Great Revival under Ezra,
8:1—10:39

The Law read and explained

8 NOW all the people gathered together as one man in the open
square that *was* in front of the Water
Gate; and they told [e]Ezra the scribe to
bring the [f]Book of the Law of Moses,
which the LORD had commanded Israel.
2 So Ezra the priest [g]brought the
Law before the assembly of men and
women and all who *could* hear with
understanding [h]on the first day of the
[d]seventh month.
3 Then he [i]read from it in the
open square that *was* in front of the
Water Gate from morning until midday, before the men and women and
those who could understand; and the
ears of all the people *were attentive* to
the Book of the Law.
4 So Ezra the [j]scribe stood on a
platform of wood which they had
made for the purpose; and beside him,

70
a v. 71; 8:13; 11:13; 12:12,22,23
b See Coinage (OT), Ex. 30:13, *note*
71
c v. 70; 8:13; 11:13; 12:12,22,23
73
d The time of the Feast of Trumpets; see Lev. 23:2, *note*
CHAPTER 8
1
e Israel (history): vv. 1–8; Ps. 78:1. (Gen. 12:2; Rom. 11:26, *note*)
f Cp. 2 Chr. 34:14–16
2
g Cp. Ezra 7:10; Jer. 2:8
h Lev. 23:24; Num. 29:1–6
3
i Dt. 31:9–11; 2 Ki. 23:2
4
j Cp. v. 2
6
k Neh. 5:13
l Ps. 28:2; cp. Gen. 14:22
7
m Dt. 33:10; Mal. 2:7
n Neh. 9:3
9
o Neh. 7:65, 70
p Cp. Dt. 12:7,12
10
q Dt. 26:11–13; Est. 9:19, 22; cp. Rev. 11:10
12
r vv. 7,8,13

at his right hand, stood Mattithiah,
Shema, Anaiah, Urijah, Hilkiah, and
Maaseiah; and at his left hand Pedaiah, Mishael, Malchijah, Hashum,
Hashbadana, Zechariah, *and* Meshullam.
5 And Ezra opened the book in the
sight of all the people, for he was
standing above all the people; and
when he opened it, all the people
stood up.
6 And Ezra blessed the LORD, the
great God. Then all the people answered, [k]"Amen, Amen!" while lifting
up their [l]hands. And they bowed their
heads and worshiped the LORD with
their faces to the ground.
7 Also Jeshua, Bani, Sherebiah,
Jamin, Akkub, Shabbethai, Hodijah,
Maaseiah, Kelita, Azariah, Jozabad,
Hanan, Pelaiah, and the Levites,
[m]helped the people to understand the
Law; and the people [n]*stood* in their
place.
8 So they read distinctly from the
book, in the Law of God; and they
gave the sense, and helped *them* to
understand the reading.
9 And Nehemiah, who *was* the
[o]governor,* Ezra the priest *and*
scribe, and the Levites who taught the
people said to all the people, "This
[j]day *is* holy to the LORD your God; do
not [p]mourn nor weep." For all the people wept, when they heard the words
of the Law.
10 Then he said to them, "Go your
way, eat the fat, drink the sweet, and
send [q]portions to those for whom
nothing is prepared; for *this* day *is*
holy to our LORD. Do not sorrow, for
the joy of the LORD is your strength."
11 So the Levites quieted all the
people, saying, "Be still, for the day *is*
holy; do not be grieved."
12 And all the people went their
way to eat and drink, to send portions
and rejoice greatly, [r]because they understood the words that were declared
to them.

Feast of Tabernacles restored

13 Now on the second day the
heads of the fathers' *houses* of all the
people, with the priests and Levites,
were gathered to Ezra the scribe, in
order to understand the words of the
Law.
14 And they found written in the
Law, which the LORD had commanded
by Moses, that the children of Israel

*7:70 Hebrew *Tirshatha* 8:9 Hebrew *Tirshatha*

should dwell in booths during the
feast of the seventh month,
15 and that they should announce
and proclaim in all their cities and in
Jerusalem, saying, "Go out to the
mountain, and bring olive branches,
branches of oil trees, myrtle branches,
palm branches, and branches of leafy
trees, to make booths, as *it is* [a]writ-
ten."
16 Then the people went out and
brought *them* and made themselves
booths, each one on the roof of his
house, or in their courtyards or the
courts of the house of God, and in the
open square of the Water Gate and in
the open square of the Gate of
Ephraim.
17 So the whole assembly of those
who had returned from the captivity
made booths and sat under the
booths; [1]for since the days of Joshua
the son of Nun until that day the children of Israel had [b]not done so. And
there was very [c]great gladness.
18 Also day by day, from the first
day until the last day, he read from the
Book of the Law of God. And they
kept the feast [d]seven days; and on the
[e]eighth day *there was* a sacred assembly, according to the *prescribed*
manner.

People fast and repent

9 NOW on the twenty-fourth day of
this [f]month the children of Israel
were assembled with fasting, in sackcloth, and with dust on their heads.*
2 Then those of Israelite lineage
[g]separated themselves from all foreigners; and they stood and [h]con-
fessed their sins and the iniquities of
their fathers.
3 And they stood up in their place
and [i]read from the Book of the Law of
the LORD their God *for one*-fourth of
the day; and *for another* fourth they
confessed and worshiped the LORD
their God.

Praise and confession of the Levites

4 Then Jeshua, Bani, Kadmiel,
Shebaniah, Bunni, Sherebiah, Bani,
and Chenani stood on the stairs of the
Levites and cried out with a loud voice
to the LORD their God.
5 And the Levites, Jeshua, Kadmiel, Bani, Hashabniah, Sherebiah,
Hodijah, Shebaniah, *and* Pethahiah,
said:

15
a Lev. 23:40
17
b Cp. Ezra 3:4; 2 Chr. 8:13
c 2 Chr. 30:21
18
d Lev. 23:36
e Num. 29:35
CHAPTER 9
1
f Cp. Neh. 8:2
2
g Separation: v. 2; Neh. 13:3. (Gen. 12:1; 2 Cor. 6:17, *note*)
h Neh. 1:6
3
i Neh. 8:7–8
5
j Bible prayers (OT): vv. 5–38; Ps. 51:1. (Gen. 15:2; Hab. 3:1)
6
k Ps. 36:6; cp. Col. 1:17
7
l Gen. 11:31; 12:1–3; 17:5
8
m Gen. 22:1–3; Jas. 2:21–23
n See Gen. 12:2 and 15:18, *notes*
o See 2 Ki. 7:6, *note*
p Cp. Josh. 23:14
9
q Ex. 2:25; 3:7
10
r Ex. 7–14
11
s Ex. 14:20–28

"Stand up *and* [j]bless the LORD
your God
Forever and ever!

"Blessed be Your glorious
name,
Which is exalted above all
blessing and praise!
6 You alone *are* the LORD;
You have made heaven,
The heaven of heavens, with
all their host,
The earth and everything on it,
The seas and all that is in
them,
And You [k]preserve them all.
The host of heaven worships
You.

7 "You *are* the LORD God,
Who [l]chose Abram,
And brought him out of Ur of
the Chaldeans,
And gave him the name
Abraham;
8 You found his heart [m]faithful
before You,
And made a [n]covenant with
him
To give the land of the
Canaanites,
The [o]Hittites, the Amorites,
The Perizzites, the Jebusites,
And the Girgashites—
To give *it* to his descendants.
You have [p]performed Your
words,
For You *are* righteous.

9 "You [q]saw the affliction of our
fathers in Egypt,
And heard their cry by the Red
Sea.
10 You showed [r]signs and
wonders against Pharaoh,
Against all his servants,
And against all the people of
his land.
For You knew that they acted
proudly against them.
So You made a name for
Yourself, as *it is* this day.
11 And You [s]divided the sea
before them,
So that they went through the
midst of the sea on the dry
land;

* 9:1 Literally *earth on them*

[1](8:17) It is not meant that there had not been some formal observance of the Feast of Tabernacles (cp. 2 Chr. 8:13; Ezra 3:4), but that the people had not dwelt in booths since Joshua's days.

And their persecutors You
threw into the deep,
As a stone into the mighty
waters.
12 Moreover You [a]led them by
day with a cloudy pillar,
And by night with a pillar of
fire,
To give them light on the road
Which they should travel.

13 "You came down also on Mount
Sinai,
And spoke with them from
heaven,
And gave them just
[b]ordinances and true laws,
Good statutes and
commandments.
14 You [1]made known to them
Your holy [c]Sabbath,
And commanded them
precepts, statutes and laws,
By the hand of Moses Your
servant.
15 You [d]gave them bread from
heaven for their hunger,
And brought them [e]water out
of the rock for their thirst,
And [f]told them to go in to
possess the land
Which You had sworn to give
them.

16 "But they and our fathers acted
proudly,
Hardened their necks,
And did not heed Your
commandments.
17 They refused to obey,
And they were not [g]mindful of
Your wonders
That You did among them.
But they hardened their necks,
And in their rebellion*
They [h]appointed a leader
To return to their bondage.
But You *are* God,
Ready to pardon,
Gracious and merciful,
Slow to anger,
Abundant in [i]kindness,
And did not forsake them.

18 "Even [j]when they made a
molded calf for themselves,
And said, 'This *is* your god
That brought you up out of
Egypt,'
And worked great
provocations,
19 Yet in Your manifold mercies
You did not forsake them in
the wilderness.
The [k]pillar of the cloud did not
depart from them by day,
To lead them on the road;
Nor the pillar of fire by night,
To show them light,
And the way they should go.
20 You also [l]gave Your good
[m]Spirit to instruct them,
And did not withhold Your
[n]manna from their mouth,
And gave them water for their
thirst.
21 Forty years You sustained
them in the wilderness;
They lacked [o]nothing;
Their [p]clothes did not wear
out
And their feet did not swell.

22 "Moreover You gave them
kingdoms and nations,
And divided them into
districts.*
So they took [q]possession of
the land of Sihon,
The land of* the king of
Heshbon,
And the land of Og king of
Bashan.
23 You also multiplied their
children as the [r]stars of
heaven,
And brought them into the
land
Which You had told their
fathers
To go in and possess.
24 So the people [s]went in
And possessed the land;
You [t]subdued before them the
inhabitants of the land,
The Canaanites,
And gave them into their
hands,
With their kings
And the people of the land,
That they might do with them
as they wished.
25 And they took strong [u]cities
and a rich land,

12 *a* Ex. 13:21
13 *b* Ex. 19–24
14 *c* *Sabbath:* vv. 13–14; Mt. 12:1. (Gen. 2:3; Mt. 12:1, *note*)
15 *d* Ex. 16:14–17; Jn. 6:31 *e* Num. 20:8; 1 Cor. 10:4 *f* Dt. 1:8
17 *g* Ps. 78:11, 42–45 *h* Num. 14:4; Acts 7:39 *i* Ex. 34:6–7; Mic. 7:18
18 *j* Ex. 32:1–14
19 *k* Ex. 13:20–22; 1 Cor. 10:1
20 *l* Num. 11:17 *m* *Holy Spirit* (OT): v. 20; Neh. 9:30. (Gen. 1:2; Zech. 12:10) *n* Ex. 16:14–16; cp. Jn. 6:22–60
21 *o* Dt. 2:7 *p* Dt. 29:5
22 *q* Num. 21:21–35
23 *r* Gen. 22:17; Heb. 11:12
24 *s* Josh. 1:2–4 *t* Josh. 18:1
25 *u* Cp. Dt. 3:5

*
9:17 Following Masoretic Text and Vulgate; Septuagint reads *in Egypt.* 9:22 Literally *corners* • Following Masoretic Text and Vulgate; Septuagint omits *The land of.*

[1](9:14) This important passage fixes beyond all cavil the time when the Sabbath, God's rest (Gen. 2:1–3), was given to man. Cp. Ex. 20:8–11. In Ex. 31:13–17 the Sabbath is invested with the character of a sign between the LORD and Israel. See Mt. 12:1, *note.*

And possessed houses full of
all goods,
Cisterns *already* dug,
vineyards, olive groves,
And fruit trees in [a]abundance.
So they ate and were filled and
grew fat,
And delighted themselves in
Your great goodness.

26 "Nevertheless they were
[b]disobedient
And rebelled against You,
Cast Your law behind their
[c]backs
And [d]killed Your prophets,
who testified against them
To turn them to Yourself;
And they worked great
provocations.
27 Therefore You delivered them
into the hand of their
enemies,
Who oppressed them;
And in the time of their
trouble,
[e]When they cried to You,
You heard from heaven;
And according to Your
abundant mercies
You gave them deliverers who
saved them
From the hand of their
enemies.
28 "But after they had rest,
They again did evil before
You.
Therefore You left them in the
hand of their enemies,
So that they had dominion
over them;
Yet when they returned and
cried out to You,
You heard from heaven;
And [f]many times You
delivered them according to
Your mercies,
29 And testified against them,
That You might bring them
back to Your law.
Yet they acted proudly,
And did not heed Your
commandments,
But sinned against Your
[g]judgments,
'Which if a man does, he shall
live by them.'
And they [h]shrugged their
shoulders,
Stiffened their necks,
And would not hear.
30 Yet for many years You had
patience with them,
And testified against them by
Your [i]Spirit in Your
prophets.
Yet they would not [j]listen;
Therefore You gave them into
the hand of the peoples of
the lands.
31 Nevertheless in Your great
mercy
You did not [k]utterly consume
them nor forsake them;
For You *are* God, gracious and
merciful.

32 "Now therefore, our God,
The great, the mighty, and
awesome God,
Who keeps covenant and
mercy:
Do not let all the trouble seem
small before You
That has come upon us,
Our kings and our princes,
Our priests and our prophets,
Our fathers and on all Your
people,
[l]From the days of the kings of
Assyria until this day.
33 However You *are* just in all
that has befallen us;
For You have dealt faithfully,
But we have done wickedly.
34 Neither our kings nor our
princes,
Our priests nor our fathers,
Have kept Your law,
Nor heeded Your
commandments and Your
testimonies,
With which You testified
against them.
35 For they have not served You
in their kingdom,
Or in the many good *things*
that You gave them,
Or in the large and rich land
which You set before them;
Nor did they turn from their
wicked works.

36 "Here we *are*, [m]servants today!
And the land that You gave to
our fathers,
To eat its fruit and its bounty,
Here we *are*, servants in it!
37 And it yields much increase to
the kings
You have set over us,
Because of our sins;
Also they have dominion over
our bodies and our cattle
At their pleasure;
And we *are* in great distress.

25
a Dt. 6:11; Josh. 24:13
26
b Jud. 2:11
c 1 Ki. 14:9
d 1 Ki. 18:4; 19:10; Mt. 23:37; Acts 7:52
27
e Jud. 2:18
28
f Ps. 106:43
29
g Lev. 18:5
h Lit. *gave a stubborn shoulder*
30
i Holy Spirit (OT): v. 30; Job 26:13. (Gen. 1:2; Zech. 12:10)
j 2 Ki. 17:13–18; 2 Chr. 36:11–20
31
k Rom. 11:2
32
l 2 Ki. 15:19
36
m Dt. 28:48; Ezra 9:9

A covenant made and signed

38 "And because of all this,
We make a sure *covenant* and
write *it;*
Our leaders, our Levites, *and*
our priests [a]seal *it.*"

Signers and terms of the covenant

10 NOW those who [b]placed *their*
seal on *the document were:*
Nehemiah the governor, the son
of Hacaliah, and Zedekiah,
2 [c]Seraiah, Azariah, Jeremiah,
3 Pashhur, Amariah, Malchijah,
4 Hattush, Shebaniah, Malluch,
5 Harim, Meremoth, Obadiah,
6 Daniel, Ginnethon, Baruch,
7 Meshullam, Abijah, Mijamin,
8 Maaziah, Bilgai, *and* Shemaiah.
These *were* the priests.
9 The Levites: Jeshua the son of
Azaniah, Binnui of the sons of Henadad, *and* Kadmiel.
10 Their brethren: Shebaniah, Hodijah, Kelita, Pelaiah, Hanan,
11 Micha, Rehob, Hashabiah,
12 Zaccur, Sherebiah, Shebaniah,
13 Hodijah, Bani, *and* Beninu.
14 The leaders of the people: Parosh, Pahath-Moab, Elam, Zattu,
Bani,
15 Bunni, Azgad, Bebai,
16 Adonijah, Bigvai, Adin,
17 Ater, Hezekiah, Azzur,
18 Hodijah, Hashum, Bezai,
19 Hariph, Anathoth, Nebai,
20 Magpiash, Meshullam, Hezir,
21 Meshezabel, Zadok, Jaddua,
22 Pelatiah, Hanan, Anaiah,
23 Hoshea, Hananiah, Hasshub,
24 Hallohesh, Pilha, Shobek,
25 Rehum, Hashabnah, Maaseiah,
26 Ahijah, Hanan, Anan,
27 Malluch, Harim, *and* Baanah.
28 Now the rest of the people—the
priests, the Levites, the gatekeepers,
the singers, the [d]Nethinim, and all
those who had [e]separated themselves
from the peoples of the lands to
the Law of God, their wives, their
sons, and their daughters, everyone
who had knowledge and understanding—
29 these joined with their brethren,
their nobles, and entered into a curse
and an oath to walk in God's Law,
which was given by Moses the servant
of God, and to observe and do all
the commandments of the LORD our
Lord, and His [f]ordinances and His
statutes:
30 We would not give our daughters as wives to the peoples of the
land, nor take their daughters for our
sons;
31 *if* the peoples of the land brought
wares or any grain to sell on the [g]Sab-
bath day, we would not buy it from
them on the Sabbath, or on a holy day;
and we would forego the [h]seventh
year's *produce* and the exacting of every [i]debt.
32 Also we made ordinances for
ourselves, to exact from ourselves
yearly [j]one-third of a [k]shekel for the
service of the house of our God:
33 for the [l]showbread, for the regular grain offering, for the regular
burnt offering of the Sabbaths, the
New Moons, and the set feasts; for
the holy things, for the sin offerings to make [m]atonement for Israel,
and all the work of the house of our
God.
34 We cast lots among the priests,
the Levites, and the people, for *bringing* the [n]wood offering into the house
of our God, according to our fathers'
houses, at the appointed times year
by year, to burn on the altar of the
LORD our God as *it is* written in the
Law.
35 And *we made ordinances* to
bring the [o]firstfruits of our ground
and the firstfruits of all fruit of all
trees, year by year, to the house of the
LORD;
36 to bring the [p]firstborn of our
sons and our cattle, as *it is* written in
the Law, and the firstborn of our herds
and our flocks, to the house of our
God, to the priests who minister in the
house of our God;
37 to bring the firstfruits of our
dough, our offerings, the fruit from all
kinds of trees, *the* new wine and oil, to
the priests, to the storerooms of the
house of our God; and to bring the
[q]tithes of our land to the Levites, for
the Levites should receive the tithes in
all our farming communities.
38 And the priest, the descendant
of Aaron, shall be with the Levites
when the Levites receive tithes; and
the Levites shall bring up a [r]tenth of
the tithes to the house of our God, to
the rooms of the storehouse.
39 For the children of Israel and the
children of Levi shall bring the offering of the grain, of the new wine and
the oil, to the storerooms where the
articles of the sanctuary *are, where*
the priests who minister and the gatekeepers and the singers *are;* and
we will not [s]neglect the house of our
God.

38
a Neh. 10:1
CHAPTER 10
1
b Neh. 9:38
2
c vv. 2–27; cp. Neh. 12:2–21
28
d See Neh. 3:26, *note*
e Neh. 9:2; 13:3
29
f Cp. Ex. 34:16; Dt. 7:2–3; Ezra 10:2
31
g Ex. 20:9–10
h Lev. 25:4; Jer. 34:14
i Dt. 15:1–2
32
j Ex. 30:11–16; 38:25–26; 2 Chr. 24:6,9; Mt. 17:24
k See Coinage (OT), Ex. 30:13, *note*
33
l See Ex. 25:30, *note*
m See Ex. 29:33, *note*
34
n Neh. 13:31
35
o Ex. 23:19; 34:26; Dt. 26:1–2
36
p Ex. 13:1–15; Lev. 27:26–27
37
q Lev. 27:30; Mal. 3:10
38
r Num. 18:26
39
s Heb. 10:25

IV. Conditions Prevailing in Palestine after a Remnant Had Been Living There for Nearly 100 Years, 11:1—13:31

Those dwelling at Jerusalem

11 NOW the leaders of the people dwelt at Jerusalem; the rest of the people cast lots to bring one out of ten to dwell in [a]Jerusalem, the [b]holy city, and nine-tenths *were to dwell* in *other* cities.

2 And the people blessed all the men who [c]willingly offered themselves to dwell at Jerusalem.

3 [d]These *are* the heads of the province who dwelt in Jerusalem. (But in the cities of Judah everyone dwelt in his own possession in their cities—Israelites, priests, Levites, [e]Nethinim, and descendants of Solomon's servants.)

4 Also in Jerusalem dwelt *some* of the children of Judah and of the children of Benjamin.

The children of Judah: Athaiah the son of Uzziah, the son of Zechariah, the son of Amariah, the son of Shephatiah, the son of Mahalalel, of the children of Perez;

5 and Maaseiah the son of Baruch, the son of Col-Hozeh, the son of Hazaiah, the son of Adaiah, the son of Joiarib, the son of Zechariah, the son of Shiloni.

6 All the sons of Perez who dwelt at Jerusalem *were* four hundred and sixty-eight valiant men.

7 And these are the sons of Benjamin: Sallu the son of Meshullam, the son of Joed, the son of Pedaiah, the son of Kolaiah, the son of Maaseiah, the son of Ithiel, the son of Jeshaiah;

8 and after him Gabbai *and* Sallai, nine hundred and twenty-eight.

9 Joel the son of Zichri *was* their overseer, and Judah the son of Senuah* *was* second over the city.

10 Of the priests: Jedaiah the son of Joiarib, and Jachin;

11 Seraiah the son of Hilkiah, the son of Meshullam, the son of Zadok, the son of Meraioth, the son of Ahitub, *was* the leader of the house of God.

12 Their brethren who did the work of the house *were* eight hundred and twenty-two; and Adaiah the son of Jeroham, the son of Pelaliah, the son of Amzi, the son of Zechariah, the son of Pashhur, the son of Malchijah,

13 and his brethren, [f]heads of the fathers' *houses, were* two hundred and forty-two; and Amashai the son of Azarel, the son of Ahzai, the son of Meshillemoth, the son of Immer,

14 and their brethren, mighty men of valor, *were* one hundred and twenty-eight. Their overseer *was* Zabdiel the son of *one of* the great men.*

15 Also of the Levites: Shemaiah the son of Hasshub, the son of Azrikam, the son of Hashabiah, the son of Bunni;

16 [g]Shabbethai and [h]Jozabad, of the heads of the Levites, *had* the oversight of the business [i]outside of the house of God;

17 Mattaniah the son of Micha,* the son of Zabdi, the son of Asaph, the leader *who* began the thanksgiving with prayer; Bakbukiah, the second among his brethren; and Abda the son of Shammua, the son of Galal, the son of Jeduthun.

18 All the Levites in the holy city *were* two hundred and eighty-four.

19 Moreover the gatekeepers, Akkub, Talmon, and their brethren who kept the gates, *were* one hundred and seventy-two.

Those dwelling in other cities

20 And the rest of Israel, of the priests *and* Levites, *were* in all the cities of Judah, everyone in his inheritance.

21 But the [e]Nethinim dwelt in Ophel. And Ziha and Gishpa *were* over the Nethinim.

22 Also the overseer of the Levites at Jerusalem *was* Uzzi the son of Bani, the son of Hashabiah, the son of Mattaniah, the son of Micha, of the sons of Asaph, the singers in charge of the service of the house of God.

23 For *it was* the king's [j]command concerning them that a certain portion should be for the singers, [k]a quota day by day.

24 Pethahiah the son of Meshezabel, of the children of Zerah the son of Judah, *was* the king's deputy* in all matters concerning the people.

25 And as for the villages with their fields, *some* of the children of Judah dwelt in [l]Kirjath Arba and its villages, Dibon and its villages, Jekabzeel and its villages;

26 in Jeshua, Moladah, Beth Pelet,

27 Hazar Shual, and Beersheba and its villages;

28 in Ziklag and Meconah and its villages;

CHAPTER 11

1
a Cp. 1 Chr. 9:3
b v. 18; Mt. 4:5; 5:35; cp. Rev. 21:2

2
c Jud. 5:9; 2 Chr. 17:16

3
d vv. 3–22; cp. 1 Chr. 9:2–22
e See Neh. 3:26, *note*

13
f Neh. 7:70, 71; 8:13; 12:12,22,23

16
g Ezra 10:15
h Ezra 8:33
i 1 Chr. 26:29

23
j Cp. Ezra 6:8; 7:20
k Neh. 12:47

25
l Josh. 14:15

*11:9 Or *Hassenuah* 11:14 Or *the son of Haggedolim* 11:17 Or *Michah* 11:24 Literally *at the king's hand*

29 in En Rimmon, Zorah, Jarmuth,
30 Zanoah, Adullam, and their villages; in Lachish and its fields; in Azekah and its villages. They dwelt from Beersheba to the Valley of Hinnom.
31 Also the children of Benjamin from Geba *dwelt* in Michmash, Aija, and Bethel, and their villages;
32 in Anathoth, Nob, Ananiah;
33 in Hazor, Ramah, Gittaim;
34 in Hadid, Zeboim, Neballat;
35 in Lod, Ono, *and* the Valley of Craftsmen.
36 Some of the Judean divisions of Levites *were* in Benjamin.

Priests and Levites who returned to Jerusalem with Zerubbabel

12 NOW [a]these *are* the priests
and the Levites who came up
with [b]Zerubbabel the son of Shealtiel,
and Jeshua: [c]Seraiah, Jeremiah,
Ezra,
2 Amariah, Malluch, Hattush,
3 Shechaniah, Rehum, Meremoth,
4 Iddo, Ginnethoi,* Abijah,
5 Mijamin, Maadiah, Bilgah,
6 Shemaiah, Joiarib, Jedaiah,
7 Sallu, Amok, Hilkiah, *and* Jedaiah.
These *were* the heads of the priests and their brethren in the days of Jeshua.
8 Moreover the Levites *were* Jeshua, Binnui, Kadmiel, Sherebiah, Judah, *and* [d]Mattaniah *who led* the thanksgiving *psalms,* he and his brethren.
9 Also Bakbukiah and Unni, their brethren, *stood* across from them in *their* duties.

Genealogy of the priests

10 Jeshua begot Joiakim, Joiakim begot Eliashib, Eliashib begot Joiada,
11 Joiada begot Jonathan, and Jonathan begot Jaddua.
12 Now in the days of Joiakim, the priests, the [e]heads of the fathers' *houses were:* of Seraiah, Meraiah; of Jeremiah, Hananiah;
13 of Ezra, Meshullam; of Amariah, Jehohanan;
14 of Melichu,* Jonathan; of Shebaniah,* Joseph;
15 of Harim,* Adna; of Meraioth,* Helkai;
16 of Iddo, Zechariah; of Ginnethon, Meshullam;
17 of Abijah, Zichri; *the son* of Minjamin;* of Moadiah,* Piltai;
18 of Bilgah, Shammua; of Shemaiah, Jehonathan;

CHAPTER 12
1
a Cp. Ezra 2:36–54, 61–63
b Neh. 7:7; Mt. 1:12–13
c vv. 1–21; cp. Neh. 10:2–27
8
d Neh. 11:17
12
e Neh. 7:70, 71; 8:13; 11:13

*12:4 Or *Ginnethon* (compare verse 16) 12:14 Or *Malluch* (compare verse 2) • Or *Shechaniah* (compare verse 3) 12:15 Or *Rehum* (compare verse 3) • Or *Meremoth* (compare verse 3) 12:17 Or *Mijamin* (compare verse 5) • Or *Maadiah* (compare verse 5)

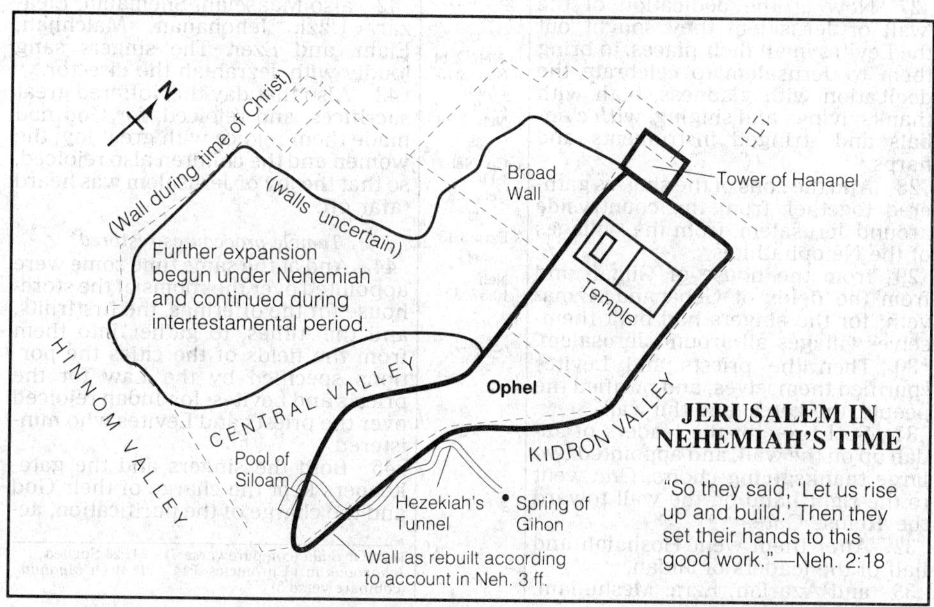

JERUSALEM IN NEHEMIAH'S TIME

"So they said, 'Let us rise up and build.' Then they set their hands to this good work."—Neh. 2:18

19 of Joiarib, Mattenai; of Jedaiah, Uzzi;

20 of Sallai,* Kallai; of Amok, Eber;

21 of Hilkiah, Hashabiah; *and* of Jedaiah, Nethanel.

The chief Levites

22 During the reign of Darius the Persian, a [a]record *was also kept* of the Levites and priests *who had been* [b]heads of their fathers' *houses* in the days of Eliashib, Joiada, Johanan, and Jaddua.

23 The sons of Levi, the [b]heads of the fathers' *houses* until the days of Johanan the son of Eliashib, *were* [c]written in the book of the chronicles.

24 And the heads of the Levites *were* Hashabiah, Sherebiah, and Jeshua the son of Kadmiel, with their brothers across from them, to [d]praise *and* give thanks, group alternating with group, [e]according to the command of David the man of God.

25 Mattaniah, Bakbukiah, Obadiah, Meshullam, Talmon, and Akkub *were* gatekeepers keeping the watch at the storerooms of the gates.

26 These *lived* in the days of Joiakim the son of Jeshua, the son of Jozadak,* and in the days of Nehemiah the governor, and of Ezra the priest, the scribe.

Dedication of the wall

27 Now at the dedication of the [f]wall of Jerusalem they sought out the Levites in all their places, to bring them to Jerusalem to celebrate the dedication with gladness, both with thanksgivings and singing, *with* cymbals and stringed instruments and harps.

28 And the sons of the singers gathered together from the countryside around Jerusalem, from the [g]villages of the Netophathites,

29 from the house of Gilgal, and from the fields of Geba and Azmaveth; for the singers had built themselves villages all around Jerusalem.

30 Then the priests and Levites [h]purified themselves, and purified the people, the gates, and the wall.

31 So I brought the leaders of Judah up on the wall, and appointed two large thanksgiving choirs. *One* went to the right hand on the wall toward the [i]Refuse Gate.

32 After them went Hoshaiah and half of the leaders of Judah,

33 and Azariah, Ezra, Meshullam,

34 Judah, Benjamin, Shemaiah, Jeremiah,

35 and some of the priests' sons with trumpets—Zechariah the son of Jonathan, the son of Shemaiah, the son of Mattaniah, the son of Michaiah, the son of Zaccur, the son of Asaph,

36 and his brethren, Shemaiah, Azarel, Milalai, Gilalai, Maai, Nethanel, Judah, *and* Hanani, [j]with the musical [k]instruments of David the man of God. Ezra the [l]scribe *went* before them.

37 By the [m]Fountain Gate, in front of them, they went up the [n]stairs of the [o]City of David, on the stairway of the wall, beyond the house of David, as far as the [p]Water Gate eastward.

38 The other thanksgiving choir went the opposite *way*, and I *was* behind them with half of the people on the wall, going past the [q]Tower of the Ovens as far as the [r]Broad Wall,

39 and above the Gate of Ephraim, above the Old Gate, above the Fish Gate, the Tower of Hananel, the Tower of the Hundred, as far as the Sheep Gate; and they stopped by the Gate of the Prison.

40 So the two thanksgiving choirs stood in the house of God, likewise I and the half of the rulers with me;

41 and the priests, Eliakim, Maaseiah, Minjamin,* Michaiah, Elioenai, Zechariah, *and* Hananiah, with trumpets;

42 also Maaseiah, Shemaiah, Eleazar, Uzzi, Jehohanan, Malchijah, Elam, and Ezer. The singers sang loudly with Jezrahiah the director.

43 Also that day they offered great sacrifices, and rejoiced, for God had made them rejoice with great joy; the women and the children also rejoiced, so that the joy of Jerusalem was heard [s]afar off.

Temple procedures restored

44 And at the same time some were appointed over the rooms of the storehouse for the offerings, the firstfruits, and the [t]tithes, to gather into them from the fields of the cities the portions specified by the Law for the priests and Levites; for Judah rejoiced over the priests and Levites who ministered.

45 Both the singers and the gatekeepers kept the charge of their God and the charge of the purification, ac-

22 *a* 1 Chr. 24:6 *b* Neh. 7:70, 71; 8:13; 11:13
23 *c* 1 Chr. 9:14–22
24 *d* Neh. 11:17 *e* 1 Chr. 23–25
27 *f* Neh. 7:1
28 *g* 1 Chr. 9:16
30 *h* Ezra 6:20; Neh. 13:22
31 *i* Neh. 2:13
36 *j* 1 Chr. 23:5 *k* 2 Chr. 29:26–27 *l* v. 26
37 *m* Neh. 2:14 *n* Neh. 3:15 *o* 2 Sam. 5:7–9 *p* Neh. 3:26
38 *q* Cp. Neh. 3:11 *r* Neh. 3:8
43 *s* Ezra 3:13
44 *t* Neh. 10:37–39

*

12:20 Or *Sallu* (compare verse 7) **12:26** Spelled *Jehozadak* in 1 Chronicles 6:14 **12:41** Or *Mijamin* (compare verse 5)

cording to the [a]command of David
and Solomon his son.
46 For in the days of David and
[b]Asaph of old *there were* chiefs of the
singers, and songs of praise and
thanksgiving to God.
47 In the days of Zerubbabel and in
the days of Nehemiah all Israel gave
the portions for the singers and the
gatekeepers, a portion for [c]each day.
They also [d]consecrated *holy things*
for the Levites, and the Levites consecrated *them* for the children of Aaron.

The Book of Moses read;
separation from mixed multitude

13 ON that day they [e]read from
the [f]Book of Moses in the
hearing of the people, and in it was
found written that no Ammonite or
Moabite should ever come into the assembly of God,
2 because they had not met the
children of Israel with bread and water, but hired [g]Balaam against them to
curse them. However, our God turned
the curse into a blessing.
3 So it was, when they had heard
the Law, that they [h]separated all the
[i]mixed multitude from Israel.

Tobiah repudiated and the
temple cleansed

4 Now before this, [j]Eliashib the
priest, having authority over the
[k]storerooms of the house of our God,
was allied with [l]Tobiah.
5 And he had prepared for him a
large room, where previously they
had stored the grain offerings, the
frankincense, the articles, the tithes of
grain, the new wine and oil, which
were commanded *to be given* to the
Levites and singers and gatekeepers,
and the offerings for the priests.
6 But during all this I was not in
Jerusalem, for in the [m]thirty-second
year of Artaxerxes king of Babylon I
had returned to the king. Then after
certain days I obtained leave from the
king,
7 and I came to Jerusalem and discovered the evil that Eliashib had
done for [n]Tobiah, in preparing a room
for him in the courts of the house of
God.
8 And it grieved me bitterly; therefore I threw all the household goods of
Tobiah out of the room.
9 Then I commanded them to
cleanse the rooms; and I brought back
into them the articles of the house of
God, with the grain offering and the
frankincense.

Proper provision made for
Levites and singers

10 I also realized that the [o]portions
for the Levites had [p]not been given
them; for each of the Levites and the
singers who did the work had gone
back to his field.
11 So I [q]contended with the rulers,
and said, "Why is the house of God
[r]forsaken?" And I gathered them together and set them in their place.
12 Then all Judah brought the tithe
of the grain and the new wine and the
oil to the storehouse.
13 And I appointed as treasurers
over the storehouse Shelemiah the
priest and Zadok the scribe, and of the
Levites, Pedaiah; and next to them
was Hanan the son of Zaccur, the son
of Mattaniah; for they were considered [s]faithful, and their task *was* to
distribute to their brethren.
14 [t]Remember me, O my God, concerning this, and do not wipe out my
good deeds that I have done for the
house of my God, and for its services!

Sabbath rest restored

15 In those days I saw *people* in Judah treading wine presses on the
[u]Sabbath, and bringing in sheaves,
and loading donkeys with wine,
grapes, figs, and all *kinds of* burdens,
which they brought into Jerusalem on
the [v]Sabbath day. And I warned *them*
about the day on which they were selling provisions.
16 Men of Tyre dwelt there also,
who brought in fish and all kinds of
goods, and sold *them* on the Sabbath
to the children of Judah, and in Jerusalem.
17 Then I contended with the nobles of Judah, and said to them, "What
evil thing *is* this that you do, by which
you profane the Sabbath day?
18 "Did not your fathers do thus,
and did not our God bring all this disaster on us and on this city? Yet you
bring [w]added wrath on Israel by profaning the Sabbath."
19 So it was, at the gates of Jerusalem, as it began to be dark before the
Sabbath, that I commanded the gates
to be [x]shut, and charged that they
must not be opened till after the Sabbath. Then I posted *some* of my servants at the gates, *so that* no burdens
would be brought in on the Sabbath
day.

45
a 1 Chr. 25–26
46
b 2 Chr. 29:30
47
c Neh. 11:23
d Num. 18:21, 24–26
CHAPTER 13
1
e Neh. 9:3
f Dt. 23:3–4
2
g Num. 22–24
3
h Separation: v. 3; Jn. 15:19. (Gen. 12:1; 2 Cor. 6:17, *note*). Neh. 9:2; 10:28
i Cp. Ex. 12:38; 2 Cor. 6:14–18
4
j Neh. 12:10
k Cp. Neh. 12:44
l Neh. 2:10; 4:3; 6:1
6
m Neh. 5:14–16
7
n See Neh. 2:10, *note*
10
o Neh. 10:37
p Cp. Mal. 3:7–10
11
q vv. 17,25
r Cp. Neh. 10:39
13
s Cp. Neh. 7:2
14
t Neh. 5:19
15
u Ex. 20:10
v Neh. 10:31
18
w Cp. Ezra 9:13–14
19
x Jer. 17:21–22

20 Now the merchants and sellers of all kinds of wares lodged outside Jerusalem once or twice.

21 Then I warned them, and said to them, "Why do you spend the night around the wall? If you do *so* again, I will lay hands on you!" From that time on they came no *more* on the Sabbath.

22 And I commanded the Levites [a]that they should cleanse themselves, and that they should go and guard the gates, to sanctify the Sabbath day.

[b]Remember me, O my God, *concerning* this also, and spare me according to the greatness of Your mercy!

Law against intermarriage with other peoples enforced

23 In those days I also saw Jews *who* had [c]married women of [d]Ashdod, Ammon, *and* Moab.

24 And half of their children spoke the language of Ashdod, and could not speak the language of Judah, but spoke according to the language of one or the other people.

25 So I [e]contended with them and cursed them, struck some of them and pulled out their hair, and made them swear by God, *saying*, "You shall not give your daughters as wives to their sons, nor take their daughters for your sons or yourselves.

26 "Did not [f]Solomon king of Israel sin by these things? Yet among many nations there was no king like him, who was beloved of his God; and God made him king over all Israel. Nevertheless pagan women caused [g]even him to sin.

27 "Should we then hear of your doing all this great evil, transgressing against our God by marrying pagan women?"

28 And *one* of the [h]sons of Joiada, the son of Eliashib the high priest, *was* a son-in-law of [i]Sanballat the Horonite; therefore I drove him from me.

29 Remember them, O my God, [j]because they have defiled the priesthood and the covenant of the priesthood and the Levites.

30 Thus I cleansed them of everything pagan. I also assigned duties to the priests and the Levites, each to his service,

31 and *to bringing* the [k]wood offering and the firstfruits at appointed times.

Remember me, O my God, for good!

22
a Neh. 12:30
b vv. 14,31
23
c Ex. 34:16; Dt. 7:3–4; Ezra 9:2; Neh. 10:30
d Neh. 4:7
25
e vv. 11,17
26
f 1 Ki. 11:1–2
g 1 Ki. 11:4–8
28
h Neh. 12:10
i Neh. 4:1,7; 6:1–2
29
j Mal. 2:1–9
31
k Neh. 10:34

The Book of

ESTHER

Author: Unknown *Theme:* God's Providential Care *Date of writing:* 5th Cent. B.C.

ESTHER, which closes the historical section of the OT, records events that occurred when the Jews were captives in Persia. Esther (the name means *star*) was a Jewish maiden who, as queen of Persia, was used to deliver her people from massacre. The king, called Ahasuerus in this book, was Xerxes, who reigned 486–465 B.C. (cp. Ezra 4:3–6, and *note* at v. 3).

The name of God is never mentioned in Esther, nor is there any allusion to the book in the NT, but in no other portion of the Bible is God's providential care of His people more evident.

The book may be divided as follows:

I. Esther Chosen Queen, 1:1—2:18.
II. Esther's Deliverance of Her People, the Jews, 2:19—7:10.
III. The Jews' Revenge on Their Enemies, 8:1—10:3.

I. Esther Chosen Queen, 1:1—2:18

The feasts of King Ahasuerus in Shushan the citadel

1 [a]NOW it came to pass in the days
of [b]Ahasuerus (this *was* the
Ahasuerus who reigned [c]over one
hundred and twenty-seven provinces,
from [d]India to Ethiopia),
2 in those days when King Ahasuerus [e]sat on the throne of his kingdom, which *was* in [f]Shushan* the citadel,
3 *that* in the third year of his reign
he [g]made a feast for all his officials
and servants—the powers of Persia
and Media, the nobles, and the princes
of the provinces *being* before him—
4 when he showed the riches of his
glorious kingdom and the splendor of
his excellent majesty for many days,
one hundred and eighty days *in all.*
5 And when these days were completed, the king made a feast lasting
seven days for all the people who were
present in Shushan the citadel, from
great to small, in the court of the [h]gar-
den of the king's palace.
6 *There were* white and blue linen
curtains fastened with cords of fine
linen and purple on silver rods and
marble pillars; *and the* [i]couches *were*
of gold and silver on a *mosaic* pavement of alabaster, turquoise, and
white and black marble.
7 And they served drinks in
golden vessels, each vessel being different from the other, with royal wine
in abundance, [j]according to the [k]gen-
erosity of the king.
8 In accordance with the law, the
drinking was not compulsory; for so
the king had ordered all the officers of
his household, that they should do according to each man's pleasure.
9 Queen Vashti also made a feast
for the women *in* the royal palace
which *belonged* to King Ahasuerus.

Vashti deposed

10 On the seventh day, when the
heart of the king was [l]merry with
wine, he commanded Mehuman, Biz-
tha, [m]Harbona, Bigtha, Abagtha, Ze-
thar, and Carcas, seven eunuchs who
served in the presence of King Ahasuerus,
11 to bring Queen Vashti before the
king, *wearing* her royal crown, in order to show her beauty to the people
and the officials, for she *was* beautiful
to behold.
12 But Queen Vashti refused to
come at the king's command *brought*
by *his* eunuchs; therefore the king was
furious, and his anger burned within
him.
13 Then the king said to the wise
men who [n]understood the times (for
this *was* the king's manner toward all
who knew law and justice,
14 those closest to him *being* Car-
shena, Shethar, Admatha, Tarshish,
Meres, Marsena, and Memucan, the
[o]seven princes of Persia and Media,
[p]who had access to the king's presence, *and* who ranked highest in the
kingdom):
15 "What *shall we* do to Queen
Vashti, according to law, because she
did not obey the command of King
Ahasuerus *brought to her* by the eunuchs?"
16 And Memucan answered before
the king and the princes: "Queen

CHAPTER 1

1
a c. 485 B.C.
b Xerxes. Ezra 4:6; see Ezra 4:3, *note*
c Cp. Dan. 6:1
d Est. 8:9

2
e Cp. 1 Ki. 1:46
f Neh. 1:1

3
g Cp. Gen. 40:20

5
h Cp. Est. 7:7,8

6
i Cp. Ezek. 23:41; Amos 6:4

7
j Est. 2:18
k Lit. *hand*

10
l Cp. 2 Sam. 13:28
m Est. 7:9

13
n Cp. 1 Chr. 12:32

14
o Cp. Ezra 7:14
p Cp. 2 Ki. 25:19; Mt. 18:10

*1:2 Or *Susa,* and so throughout this book

Vashti has not only wronged the king, but also all the princes, and all the people who *are* in all the provinces of King Ahasuerus.

17 "For the queen's behavior will become known to all women, so that they will despise their husbands in their eyes, when they report, 'King Ahasuerus commanded Queen Vashti to be brought in before him, but she did not come.'

18 "This very day the *noble* ladies of Persia and Media will say to all the king's officials that they have heard of the behavior of the queen. Thus *there will be* excessive contempt and wrath.

19 "If it pleases the king, let a royal decree go out from him, and let it be recorded in the laws of the Persians and the Medes, so that it will [a]not be altered, that Vashti shall come no more before King Ahasuerus; and let the king give her royal position to another who is better than she.

20 "When the king's decree which he will make is proclaimed throughout all his empire (for it is great), all wives will [b]honor their husbands, both great and small."

21 And the reply pleased the king and the princes, and the king did according to the word of Memucan.

22 Then he sent letters to all the king's provinces, [c]to each province in its own script, and to every people in their own language, that each man should be master in his own house, and speak in the language of his own people.

Vashti's successor sought

2 AFTER these things, when the wrath of King Ahasuerus [d]subsided, he remembered Vashti, what she had done, and [e]what had been decreed against her.

2 Then the king's servants who attended him said: "Let beautiful young virgins be sought for the king;

3 "and let the king appoint officers in all the provinces of his kingdom, that they may gather all the beautiful young virgins to Shushan the citadel, into the women's quarters, under the custody of Hegai* the king's eunuch, custodian of the women. And let [f]beauty preparations be given *them.*

4 "Then let the young woman who pleases the king be queen instead of Vashti." This thing pleased the king, and he did so.

5 In Shushan the citadel there was a certain Jew whose name *was* Mordecai the son of Jair, the son of Shimei, the son of [g]Kish, a Benjamite.

6 [h]*Kish** had been carried away from Jerusalem with the captives who had been captured with [i]Jeconiah king of Judah, whom Nebuchadnezzar the king of Babylon had carried away.

7 And *Mordecai* had [j]brought up Hadassah, that *is,* Esther, his uncle's [k]daughter, for she had neither father nor mother. The young woman *was* lovely and beautiful. When her father and mother died, Mordecai took her as his own daughter.

8 So it was, when the king's command and decree were heard, and when many young women were [l]gathered at Shushan the citadel, *under* the custody of Hegai, that Esther also was taken to the king's palace, into the care of Hegai the custodian of the women.

9 Now the young woman pleased him, and she obtained his favor; so he readily gave [f]beauty preparations to her, besides her allowance. Then seven choice maidservants were provided for her from the king's palace, and he moved her and her maidservants to the best *place* in the house of the women.

10 [m]Esther had not revealed her people or family, for Mordecai had charged her not to reveal *it.*

11 And every day Mordecai paced in front of the court of the women's quarters, to learn of Esther's welfare and what was happening to her.

12 Each young woman's turn came [n]to go in to King Ahasuerus after she had completed twelve months' preparation, according to the regulations for the women, for thus were the days of their preparation apportioned: six months with oil of myrrh, and six months with perfumes and preparations for beautifying women.

13 Thus *prepared, each* young woman went to the king, and she was given whatever she desired to take with her from the women's quarters to the king's palace.

14 In the evening she went, and in the morning she returned to the second house of the women, to the custody of Shaashgaz, the king's eunuch who kept the concubines. She would not go in to the king again unless the king delighted in her and [o]called for her by name.

19
a Est. 8:8; Cp. Dan. 6:8
20
b Cp. Eph. 5:22; Col. 3:18
22
c Cp. Est. 3:12; 8:9
CHAPTER 2
1
d Cp. Est. 7:10
e Est. 1:19–20
3
f v. 12
5
g 1 Sam. 9:1
6
h 2 Ki. 24:14–15; 2 Chr. 36:10,20; Jer. 24:1
i Or *Jehoiachin,* 2 Ki. 24:6
7
j Cp. Lev. 25:25; Dt. 25:5
k v. 15
8
l v. 3
10
m v. 20
12
n Cp. 1 Th. 4:4–5
14
o Cp. Isa. 43:1

*2:3 Hebrew *Hege* 2:6 Literally *Who*

Esther becomes queen

15 Now when the turn came for Esther the [a]daughter of Abihail the uncle of Mordecai, who had taken her as
his daughter, to go in to the king, she
requested nothing but what Hegai the
king's eunuch, the custodian of the
women, advised. And Esther [b]ob-
tained favor in the sight of all who saw
her.
16 So Esther was taken to King
Ahasuerus, into his royal palace, in
the [c]tenth month, which *is* the month
of Tebeth, in the seventh year of his
reign.
17 The king loved Esther more than
all the *other* women, and she obtained
grace and favor in his sight more than
all the virgins; so he set the royal
[d]crown upon her head and made her
queen instead of Vashti.
18 Then the king [e]made a great
feast, the Feast of Esther, for all his
officials and servants; and he proclaimed a holiday in the provinces and
gave gifts [f]according to the [g]generos-
ity of a king.

II. Esther's Deliverance of Her People, the Jews, 2:19—7:10

19 When virgins were gathered together a second time, Mordecai sat
within the [h]king's gate.
20 *Now* Esther had not revealed
her family and her people, just as Mordecai had [i]charged her, for Esther
obeyed the command of Mordecai as
when she was brought up by him.

Mordecai saves the king's life

21 In those days, while Mordecai
sat within the king's gate, two of the
king's eunuchs, [j]Bigthan and Teresh,
doorkeepers, became furious and
sought to lay hands on King Ahasuerus.
22 So the matter became known to
Mordecai, [k]who told Queen Esther,
and Esther informed the king in Mordecai's name.
23 And when an inquiry was made
into the matter, it was confirmed, and
both were hanged on a gallows; and it
was written in the [l]book of the chronicles in the presence of the king.

Haman's conspiracy against the Jews

3 AFTER these things King Ahasuerus [m]promoted Haman, the son
of Hammedatha the [n]Agagite, and advanced him and set his seat above all
the princes who *were* with him.
2 And all the king's servants who
were within the [o]king's gate bowed
and paid homage to Haman, for so the
king had commanded concerning
him. But Mordecai would not [p]bow or
pay homage.
3 Then the king's servants who
were within the king's gate said to
Mordecai, "Why do you transgress the
king's command?"
4 Now it happened, when they
spoke to him daily and he would not
listen to them, that they told *it* to Haman, to see whether Mordecai's
words would stand; for *Mordecai* had
told them that he *was* a Jew.
5 When Haman saw that Mordecai did not bow or pay him homage,
Haman was filled with wrath.
6 But he disdained to lay hands on
Mordecai alone, for they had told him
of the people of Mordecai. Instead,
Haman [q]sought to destroy all the
Jews who *were* throughout the whole
kingdom of Ahasuerus—the people of
Mordecai.
7 In the [c]first month, which is the
month of Nisan, in the twelfth year of
King Ahasuerus, they cast [r]Pur (that
is, the lot), before Haman to determine
the day and the month,* until *it fell on
the* [c]twelfth *month*,* which *is* the
month of Adar.
8 Then Haman said to King Ahasuerus, "There is a certain people scattered and [s]dispersed among the people in all the provinces of your
kingdom; their laws *are* different from
all *other* people's, and they do not
keep the king's laws. Therefore it *is*
not fitting for the king to let them remain.
9 "If it pleases the king, [t]let *a decree* be written that they be destroyed,
and I will pay ten thousand [u]talents of
silver into the hands of those who do
the work, to bring *it* into the king's
treasuries."
10 So the king took his signet [v]ring
from his hand and gave it to Haman,
the son of Hammedatha the Agagite,
the [w]enemy of the Jews.
11 And the king said to Haman,
"The money and the people *are* given
to you, to do with them as seems good
to you."
12 Then the king's scribes were
called on the thirteenth day of the
first month, and *a decree* was written
[x]according to all that Haman

15 a v. 7 b Est. 5:2,8
16 c See Lev. 23:2, *note*
17 d Est. 1:11
18 e Cp. Est. 1:3,5 f Cp. Est. 1:7 g Lit. *hand*
19 h Cp. Est. 3:2,3
20 i Prov. 22:6; cp. Eph. 6:1–3
21 j Or *Bigthana*, Est. 6:2
22 k Est. 6:2
23 l Est. 6:1
CHAPTER 3
1 m Est. 5:11 n Cp. Num. 24:7; 1 Sam. 15:8
2 o Est. 2:21 p v. 5; cp. Dt. 25:19; Ps. 15:4
6 q Cp. Ps. 83:4; Rev. 12:1–17
7 r Est. 9:24–26
8 s Lev. 26:33; Dt. 4:27
9 t Cp. Ezra 4:12–15; Acts 16:20–21 u See Coinage (OT), Ex. 30:13, *note*
10 v Cp. Est. 8:2,8 w Lit. *oppression*. Est. 7:6
12 x Est. 1:22; cp. Est. 8:9

*
3:7 Septuagint adds *to destroy the people of Mordecai in one day;* Vulgate adds *the nation of the Jews should be destroyed.* • Following Masoretic Text and Vulgate; Septuagint reads *and the lot fell on the fourteenth of the month.*

commanded—to the king's satraps, to the governors who *were* over each province, to the officials of all people, to every province according to its script, and to every people in their language. In the [a]name of King Ahasuerus it was written, and sealed with the king's signet ring.

13 And the letters were [b]sent by couriers into all the king's provinces, to destroy, to kill, and to annihilate all the Jews, [c]both young and old, little children and women, in one day, on the thirteenth *day* of the twelfth *month,* which *is* the month of Adar, and [d]to plunder their possessions.*

14 A copy of the document was to be issued as law in every province, being published for all people, that they should be ready for that day.

15 The couriers went out, [e]hastened by the king's command; and the decree was proclaimed in Shushan the citadel. So the king and Haman sat down to [f]drink, but the [g]city of Shushan was perplexed.

Mourning among the Jews; Esther learns of the conspiracy

4 WHEN Mordecai learned all that had happened, he [h]tore his clothes and put on sackcloth and ashes, and went out into the midst of the city. He cried out with a loud and bitter cry.

2 He went as far as the front of the king's gate, for no one *might* enter the king's gate clothed with sackcloth.

3 And in every province where the king's command and decree arrived, *there was* great mourning among the Jews, with fasting, weeping, and wailing; and many lay in [i]sackcloth and [j]ashes.

4 So Esther's maids and eunuchs came and told her, and the queen was deeply distressed. Then she sent garments to clothe Mordecai and take his sackcloth away from him, but he would [k]not accept *them.*

5 Then Esther called Hathach, *one* of the king's eunuchs whom he had appointed to attend her, and she gave him a command concerning Mordecai, to learn what and why this *was.*

6 So Hathach went out to Mordecai in the city square that *was* in front of the king's gate.

7 And Mordecai told him all that had happened to him, and the [l]sum of money that Haman had promised to pay into the king's treasuries to destroy the Jews.

8 He also gave him a copy of the written decree for their destruction, which was given at Shushan, that he might show it to Esther and explain it to her, and that he might command her to go in to the king to make supplication to him and [m]plead before him for her people.

9 So Hathach returned and told Esther the words of Mordecai.

Esther sends message to Mordecai; he calls upon her to risk her life for her people

10 Then Esther spoke to Hathach, and gave him a command for Mordecai:

11 "All the king's servants and the people of the king's provinces know that any man or woman who goes into the [n]inner court to the king, who has not been called, [o]*he has* but one law: put *all* to death, except the one to whom the king holds out the [p]golden scepter, that he may live. Yet I myself have not been [q]called to go in to the king these thirty days."

12 So they told Mordecai Esther's words.

13 And Mordecai told *them* to answer Esther: [r]"Do not think in your heart that you will escape in the king's palace any more than all the other Jews.

14 "For if you remain completely silent at this time, relief and deliverance will arise for the Jews from another place, but you and your father's house will perish. Yet who knows whether you have come to the kingdom for *such* a time as this?"

15 Then Esther told *them* to reply to Mordecai:

16 "Go, gather all the Jews who are present in Shushan, and [s]fast for me; neither eat nor drink for [u]three days, night or day. My maids and I will fast likewise. And so I will go to the king, which *is* against the law; and if I [t]perish, I perish!"

17 So Mordecai went his way and did according to all that Esther commanded him.*

Esther's courage; her request

5 NOW it happened on the [u]third day that Esther put on *her* royal *robes* and stood in the [v]inner court of the king's palace, across from the king's house, while the king sat on his

12
a Est. 8:8–10; cp. 1 Ki. 21:8
13
b Cp. Est. 1:1
c Cp. 1 Sam. 15:3
d Cp. Est. 8:11
15
e Cp. Prov. 1:16
f Cp. Amos 6:6
g Cp. Est. 8:15
CHAPTER 4
1
h Cp. 2 Sam. 1:11
3
i Cp. Isa. 58:5; Dan. 9:3
j Cp. Neh. 9:1
4
k Cp. Gen. 37:35; Ps. 77:2
7
l Est. 3:9
8
m Cp. Prov. 21:1
11
n Est. 5:1
o Cp. Dan. 2:9
p Est. 5:2; 8:4
q Est. 2:14
13
r Cp. Prov. 24:10–12
16
s Cp. 2 Chr. 20:3; Neh. 1:11
t Cp. 1 Sam. 19:5; Acts 20:24
CHAPTER 5
1
u Est. 4:16
v Est. 4:11

*
3:13 Septuagint adds the text of the letter here.
4:17 Septuagint adds a prayer of Mordecai here.

royal throne in the royal house, facing
the entrance of the house.*
2 So it was, when the king saw
Queen Esther standing in the court,
that [a]she found favor in his sight, and
the king held out to Esther the
[b]golden scepter that *was* in his hand.
Then Esther went near and touched
the top of the scepter.
3 And the king said to her, "What
do you wish, Queen Esther? What *is*
your request? It shall be given to
you—up to half the [c]kingdom!"
4 So Esther answered, "If it
pleases the king, let the king and Haman come today to the banquet that I
have prepared for him."
5 Then the king said, "Bring Haman quickly, that he may do as Esther
has said." So the king and Haman
went to the banquet that Esther had
prepared.
6 At the banquet of wine the king
said to Esther, [d]"What *is* your petition? It shall be granted you. What *is*
your request, up to half the kingdom?
It shall be done!"
7 Then Esther answered and said,
"My petition and request *is this:*
8 "If I have found favor in the sight
of the king, and if it pleases the king
to grant my petition and fulfill my request, then let the king and Haman
come to the [e]banquet which I will prepare for them, and tomorrow I will do
as the king has said."
9 So Haman went out that day
[f]joyful and with a glad heart; but
when Haman saw Mordecai in the
king's gate, and [g]that he did not stand
or tremble before him, he was filled
with indignation against Mordecai.
10 Nevertheless Haman restrained
himself and went home, and he sent
and called for his friends and his wife
Zeresh.
11 Then Haman told them of his
great riches, the multitude of his [h]chil-
dren, everything in which the king
had promoted him, and how he had
[i]advanced him above the officials
and servants of the king.
12 Moreover Haman said, "Besides,
Queen Esther invited no one but me to
come in with the king to the banquet
that she prepared; and tomorrow I am
again invited by her, along with the
king.
13 "Yet all this avails me nothing,
so long as I see Mordecai the Jew sitting at the king's gate."
14 Then his wife Zeresh and all his
friends said to him, "Let a gallows be
made, fifty [j]cubits high, and in the
morning [k]suggest to the king that
Mordecai be hanged on it; then go
merrily with the king to the banquet."
And the thing pleased Haman; so he
had the [l]gallows made.

The king's insomnia

6 THAT night the king [m]could not
[1]sleep. So one was commanded to
bring the [n]book of the records of the
chronicles; and they were read before
the king.
2 And it was found written that
Mordecai had told of [o]Bigthana and
Teresh, two of the king's eunuchs, the
doorkeepers who had sought to lay
hands on King Ahasuerus.
3 Then the king said, "What honor
or dignity has been bestowed on Mordecai for this?" And the king's servants who attended him said, "Nothing has been done for him."

Haman forced to honor Mordecai

4 So the king said, "Who *is* in the
court?" Now Haman had *just* entered
the [p]outer court of the king's palace to
[q]suggest that the king hang Mordecai
on the gallows that he had prepared
for him.
5 The king's servants said to him,
"Haman is there, standing in the
court." And the king said, "Let him
come in."
6 So Haman came in, and the king
asked him, "What shall be done for
the man whom the king delights to
honor?" Now Haman thought in his
heart, "Whom would the king delight
to honor more than [r]me?"
7 And Haman answered the king,
"*For* the man whom the king delights
to honor,
8 "let a royal robe be brought
which the king has worn, and a horse
on which the king has ridden, which
has a royal crest placed [s]on its head.

2
a Cp. Prov. 21:1
b Est. 4:11; 8:4
3
c Cp. Ps. 116:1
6
d Est. 9:12
8
e Est. 6:14
9
f Job 20:5; cp. Lk. 6:25
g Est. 3:5
11
h Est. 9:7–10
i Est. 3:1
14
j See Weights and Measures (OT), 2 Chr. 2:10, *note*
k Est. 7:9
l Est. 7:10
CHAPTER 6
1
m Lit. *the king's sleep fled away*
n Cp. Mal. 3:16
2
o Or *Bigthan,* Est. 2:21
4
p Cp. Est. 5:1
q Est. 5:14
6
r Prov. 16:18; 18:12
8
s Cp. 1 Ki. 1:33

*
5:1 Septuagint adds many extra details in verses 1 and 2.

[1](6:1) Here is a remarkable instance of the veiled providential control of God over circumstances of human history. Upon the king's insomnia, humanly speaking, hinged the survival of the chosen nation, the fulfillment of prophecy, the coming of the Redeemer, and therefore the whole work of redemption. Yet the outcome was never in doubt; for God was in control, making the most trivial of events work together for Haman's defeat and Israel's preservation.

9 "Then let this robe and horse be
delivered to the hand of one of the
king's most noble princes, that he may
array the man whom the king delights
to honor. Then parade him on horseback through the city square, and
[a]proclaim before him: 'Thus shall it
be done to the man whom the king
delights to honor!' "
10 Then the king said to Haman,
"Hurry, take the robe and the horse, as
you have suggested, and do so for
Mordecai the Jew who sits within the
king's gate! Leave nothing undone of
all that you have spoken."
11 So Haman took the robe and the
horse, arrayed Mordecai and led him
on horseback through the city square,
and proclaimed before him, "Thus
shall it be done to the man whom the
king delights to honor!"
12 Afterward Mordecai went back
to the king's gate. But Haman [b]hur-
ried to his house, mourning and with
his head [c]covered.
13 When Haman told his wife Zeresh and all his friends everything
that had happened to him, his wise
men and his wife Zeresh said to him,
"If Mordecai, before whom you have
begun to fall, is of Jewish descent, you
will not prevail against [d]him but will
surely fall before him."
14 While they *were* still talking
with him, the king's eunuchs came,
and hastened to bring Haman to the
[e]banquet which Esther had prepared.

Esther pleads for herself
and her people

7 SO the king and Haman went to
dine with Queen Esther.
2 And on the second day, at the
banquet of wine, the king again said to
Esther, "What *is* your petition, Queen
Esther? It shall be granted you. And
what *is* your request, up to half the
kingdom? It shall be done!"
3 Then Queen Esther answered
and said, "If I have found favor in your
sight, O king, and if it pleases the king,
let my life be given me at my petition,
and my people at my request.
4 "For we have been [f]sold, my
people and I, to be destroyed, to be
killed, and to be annihilated. Had we
been sold as [g]male and female slaves,
I would have held my tongue, although the enemy could never com-
pensate for the king's loss."
5 So King Ahasuerus answered
and said to Queen Esther, "Who is he,
and where is he, who would dare presume in his heart to do such a thing?"
6 And Esther said, "The adversary
and [h]enemy *is* this wicked Haman!"
So Haman was terrified before the
king and queen.

Haman hanged on his own gallows

7 Then the king arose in his wrath
from the banquet of wine *and went*
into the palace [i]garden; but Haman
stood before Queen Esther, pleading
for his life, for he saw that evil was
determined against him by the king.
8 When the king returned from
the palace garden to the place of the
banquet of wine, Haman had fallen
across the [j]couch where Esther *was*.
Then the king said, "Will he also assault the queen while I *am* in the
house?" As the word left the king's
mouth, they covered Haman's face.
9 Now [k]Harbonah, one of the eunuchs, said to the king, "Look! The
[l]gallows, fifty [m]cubits high, which
Haman made for Mordecai, who
spoke [n]good on the king's behalf, is
standing at the house of Haman."
Then the king said, "Hang him on it!"
10 [o]So they [p]hanged Haman on the
gallows that he had prepared for Mordecai. Then the king's wrath subsided.

III. The Jews' Revenge on Their
Enemies, 8:1—10:3

Haman's conspiracy defeated
through the king's decree

8 ON that day King Ahasuerus gave
Queen Esther the house of Haman, the [q]enemy of the Jews. And
Mordecai came before the king, for
Esther had told [r]how he *was related*
to her.
2 So the king took off his signet
[s]ring, which he had taken from Haman, and gave it to Mordecai; and Esther [t]appointed Mordecai over the
house of Haman.
3 Now Esther spoke again to the
king, fell down at his feet, and implored him with tears to counteract
the evil of Haman the Agagite, and the
scheme which he had devised against
the Jews.
4 And the king held out the
[u]golden scepter toward Esther. So Esther arose and stood before the king,
5 and said, "If it pleases the king,
and if I have found favor in his sight
and the thing *seems* right to the king
and I am pleasing in his eyes, let it be
written to revoke the [v]letters devised
by Haman, the son of Hammedatha
the Agagite, which he wrote to annihi-

9
a Cp. Gen. 41:43
12
b Cp. 2 Chr. 26:20
c Cp. 2 Sam. 15:30; Jer. 14:3,4
13
d Gen. 12:3; Zech. 2:8
14
e Est. 5:8
CHAPTER 7
4
f Est. 3:9; 4:7; cp. Gen. 37:26–28
g Dt. 28:68
6
h Est. 3:10
7
i Est. 1:5–6
8
j Est. 1:6
9
k Est. 1:10
l Est. 5:14
m See Weights and Measures (OT), 2 Chr. 2:10, *note*
n Est. 6:2
10
o Ps. 7:16; Prov. 11:5–6
p Ps. 37:35–36; cp. Dan. 6:24
CHAPTER 8
1
q Est. 7:6
r Est. 2:7
2
s Cp. Est. 3:10
t Cp. Ps. 37:34
4
u Est. 4:11; 5:2
5
v Est. 3:13

late the Jews who *are* in all the king's
provinces.
6 "For how can I endure to see the
[a]evil that will come to my people? Or
how can I endure to see the destruction of my countrymen?"
7 Then King Ahasuerus said to
Queen Esther and Mordecai the Jew,
"Indeed, [b]I have given Esther the
house of Haman, and they have
hanged him on the gallows because he
tried to lay his hand on the Jews.
8 "You yourselves write *a decree*
concerning the Jews, as you please, in
the king's name, and seal *it* with the
king's signet ring; for whatever is
written in the king's name and sealed
with the king's signet ring [c]no one can
revoke."
9 So the king's scribes were called
at that time, in the [d]third month,
which *is* the month of Sivan, on the
twenty-third *day;* and it was written,
according to all that Mordecai commanded, to the Jews, the satraps, the
governors, and the princes of the
provinces from [e]India to Ethiopia,
one hundred and twenty-seven provinces *in all,* to every province [f]in its
own script, to every people in their
own language, and to the Jews in their
own script and language.
10 And he [g]wrote in the name of
King Ahasuerus, sealed *it* with the
king's signet ring, and sent letters by
couriers on horseback, riding on royal
horses bred from swift steeds.*
11 By these letters the king permitted the Jews who *were* in every city to
[h]gather together and protect their
lives—to [i]destroy, kill, and annihilate
all the forces of any people or province that would assault them, *both* little children and women, and to [j]plun-
der their possessions,
12 [k]on one day in all the provinces
of King Ahasuerus, on the thirteenth
day of the [d]twelfth month, which *is*
the month of Adar.*
13 A copy of the document was to
be issued as a decree in every province and published for all people, so
that the Jews would be ready on that
day to avenge themselves on their enemies.
14 The couriers who rode on royal
horses went out, hastened and
pressed on by the king's command.
And the decree was issued in Shushan
the citadel.

Mordecai exalted; Jews rejoice

15 So Mordecai went out from the

6
a Neh. 2:3; Est. 7:4
7
b v. 1; Prov. 13:22
8
c Est. 1:19; Dan. 6:8, 12,15
9
d See Lev. 23:2, *note*
e Est. 1:1
f Cp. Est. 1:22; 3:12
10
g Cp. Est. 3:12–13; cp. 1 Ki. 21:8
11
h Est. 9:2
i Est. 9:10, 15,16
j Cp. 2 Chr. 15:11–15
12
k Est. 3:13; 9:1
15
l Est. 3:15; Prov. 29:2
16
m Ps. 97:11
17
n Est. 9:19
o Gen. 35:5; Ex. 15:16; Dt. 2:25; 11:25; 1 Chr. 14:17
CHAPTER 9
1
p Est. 3:13
2
q Cp. Ps. 41:7
r Est. 8:17
4
s Cp. 2 Sam. 3:1
6
t Est. 1:2; 3:15; 4:16
10
u vv. 7–10; Est. 5:11
v vv. 15–16; cp. Gen. 14:23; Est. 8:11

presence of the king in royal apparel
of blue and white, with a great crown
of gold and a garment of fine linen and
purple; and the [l]city of Shushan rejoiced and was glad.
16 The Jews had [m]light and gladness, joy and honor.
17 And in every province and city,
wherever the king's command and decree came, the Jews had joy and gladness, a feast and a [n]holiday. Then
many of the people of the land became
Jews, because [o]fear of the Jews fell
upon them.

Jews destroy their enemies;
they rest and are glad

9 NOW in the [d]twelfth month, that
is, the month of Adar, on the thirteenth day, [p]*the time* came for the
king's command and his decree to be
executed. On the day that the enemies
of the Jews had hoped to overpower
them, the opposite occurred, in that
the Jews themselves overpowered
those who hated them.
2 The Jews gathered together in
their cities throughout all the provinces of King Ahasuerus to lay hands
on those who sought their [q]harm. And
no one could withstand them, because
[r]fear of them fell upon all people.
3 And all the officials of the provinces, the satraps, the governors, and
all those doing the king's work,
helped the Jews, because the fear of
Mordecai fell upon them.
4 For Mordecai *was* great in the
king's palace, and his fame spread
throughout all the provinces; for this
man Mordecai [s]became increasingly
prominent.
5 Thus the Jews defeated all their
enemies with the stroke of the sword,
with slaughter and destruction, and
did what they pleased with those who
hated them.
6 And in [t]Shushan the citadel the
Jews killed and destroyed five hundred men.
7 Also Parshandatha, Dalphon,
Aspatha,
8 Poratha, Adalia, Aridatha,
9 Parmashta, Arisai, Aridai, and
Vajezatha—
10 the [u]ten sons of Haman the son
of Hammedatha, the enemy of the
Jews—they killed; [v]but they did not
lay a hand on the plunder.
11 On that day the number of those

*
8:10 Literally *sons of the swift horses*
8:12 Septuagint adds the text of the letter here.

who were killed in Shushan the citadel was brought to the king.

12 And the king said to Queen Esther, "The Jews have killed and destroyed five hundred men in Shushan the citadel, and the ten sons of Haman. What have they done in the rest of the king's provinces? [a]Now what *is* your petition? It shall be granted to you. Or what *is* your further request? It shall be done."

13 Then Esther said, "If it pleases the king, let it be granted to the Jews who *are* in Shushan to do again tomorrow [b]according to today's decree, and let Haman's ten sons be hanged on the gallows."

14 So the king commanded this to be done; the decree was issued in Shushan, and they hanged Haman's ten sons.

15 And the Jews who *were* in Shushan [c]gathered together again on the fourteenth day of the month of [d]Adar and killed three hundred men at Shushan; but they did not lay a hand on the [e]plunder.

16 The remainder of the Jews in the king's provinces gathered together and protected their lives, had rest from their enemies, and killed seventy-five thousand of their enemies; but they did not lay a hand on the [e]plunder.

17 *This was* on the thirteenth day of the month of Adar. And on the fourteenth of *the month** they rested and made it a day of feasting and gladness.

18 But the Jews who *were* at Shushan assembled together on the thirteenth *day*, as well as on the fourteenth; and on the fifteenth of *the month** they rested, and made it a day of feasting and gladness.

19 Therefore the Jews of the villages who dwelt in the unwalled towns celebrated the fourteenth day of the month of Adar *with* [f]gladness and feasting, as a holiday, and for [g]sending presents to one another.

The Feast of Purim instituted

20 And Mordecai wrote these things and sent letters to all the Jews, near and far, who *were* in all the provinces of King Ahasuerus,

21 to establish among them that they should celebrate yearly the fourteenth and fifteenth days of the month of Adar,

22 as the days on which the Jews had rest from their enemies, as the month which was [h]turned from sorrow to joy for them, and from mourning to a holiday; that they should make them days of feasting and joy, of sending presents to one another and gifts to the [i]poor.

23 So the Jews accepted the custom which they had begun, as Mordecai had written to them,

24 because Haman, the son of Hammedatha the Agagite, the enemy of all the Jews, had plotted against the Jews to annihilate them, and had cast [j]Pur (that *is*, the lot), to consume them and destroy them;

25 but when *Esther** came before the king, he commanded by letter that this* wicked plot which *Haman* had devised against the Jews should [k]return on his own head, and that he and his sons should be hanged on the gallows.

26 So they called these days Purim, after the name Pur. Therefore, because of all the words of this letter, what they had seen concerning this matter, and what had happened to them,

27 the Jews established and imposed it upon themselves and their descendants and all who would [l]join them, that without fail they should celebrate these two days every year, according to the written *instructions* and according to the *prescribed* time,

28 *that* these days *should be* remembered and kept throughout every generation, every family, every province, and every city, that these days of Purim should not fail *to be observed* among the Jews, and *that* the memory of them should not perish among their descendants.

29 Then Queen Esther, the [m]daughter of Abihail, with Mordecai the Jew, [n]wrote with full authority to confirm this second letter about Purim.

30 And *Mordecai* sent letters to all the Jews, [o]to the one hundred and twenty-seven provinces of the kingdom of Ahasuerus, *with* words of peace and truth,

31 to confirm these days of Purim at their *appointed* time, as Mordecai the Jew and Queen Esther had prescribed for them, and as they had decreed for themselves and their descendants concerning matters of their [p]fasting and lamenting.

32 So the decree of Esther con-

12 a Cp. Est. 5:6; 7:2
13 b Est. 8:11
15 c Cp. v. 2 d vv. 17,19, 21; see Lev. 23:2, *note* e v. 10
19 f Est. 8:16–17 g v. 22; cp. Neh. 8:10, 12; Rev. 11:10
22 h Cp. Ps. 30:11 i Dt. 15:7–11; cp. Job 29:16
24 j v. 26; Est. 3:7
25 k Est. 7:10; cp. Ps. 7:16
27 l Est. 8:17; cp. Isa. 56:3,6; Zech. 2:11
29 m Est. 2:15 n v. 20; cp. Est. 8:10
30 o Cp. Est. 1:1
31 p Est. 4:3,16

*

9:17 Literally *it* 9:18 Literally *it* 9:25 Literally *she* or *it* • Literally *his*

firmed these matters of Purim, and it
was written in the book.

Mordecai's further advancement

10 AND King Ahasuerus imposed
tribute on the land and *on* the
[a]islands of the sea.
2 Now all the acts of his power and
his might, and the account of the
[b]greatness of Mordecai, to which the
king advanced him, *are* they not written in the book of the [c]chronicles
of the kings of Media and Persia?
3 For Mordecai the Jew *was* [d]sec-
ond to King Ahasuerus, and was great
among the Jews and well received by
the multitude of his brethren, [e]seek-
ing the good of his people and speaking peace to all his countrymen.*

CHAPTER 10

1
a Cp. Gen. 10:5

2
b Est. 8:15; 9:4
c Est. 6:1

3
d Cp. Gen. 41:43–44; Neh. 1:11; Dan. 2:48
e Cp. Neh. 2:10; Ps. 122:8–9

*10:3 Literally *seed.* Septuagint and Vulgate add a dream of Mordecai here; Vulgate adds six more chapters.

The Poetical and Wisdom Books

THE books classed as poetical are Job, Psalms, Proverbs, Ecclesiastes, Song of Solomon, and also Lamentations. Poetical passages are found still elsewhere in the OT (cp. Ex. 15:1–21; Jud. 5; and extensive portions of the prophetic writings, e.g. Mic.). Because these books portray the experiences of the people of God, their range is as wide as that of life itself. In them inspiration clothes human experience with a universal quality that has brought comfort, strength, and guidance to countless believers down through the ages.

The basis of Hebrew poetry is parallelism of thought. Rhythm is not achieved by similarity of sound, as in rhymed verse, or by metrical accent, as in blank verse (although Hebrew poetry is not entirely without accent), but chiefly by the repetition, contrast, and elaboration of ideas.

Thus, when the thoughts are essentially the same, the parallelism is called *synonymous;* e.g.

> Show me Your ways, O LORD;
> Teach me Your paths. (Ps. 25:4).

When the thoughts are contrasting, the parallelism is called *antithetic;* e.g.

> For the LORD knows the way of the righteous,
> But the way of the ungodly shall perish (Ps. 1:6).

When the primary thought is developed and enriched, the parallelism is called *synthetic;* e.g.

> And you would be secure, because there is hope;
> Yes, you would dig around you, and take your rest in safety (Job 11:18).

By no means, however, does all Hebrew poetry fit precisely into these three categories; the matching and development of thought show wide and subtle variety through such means as triple and quadruple parallels, inversions, alternating lines, and refrains. The Hebrew vocabulary is powerfully vivid, and OT poetry is studded with figures of speech like personification, hyperbole, metaphor, simile, and alliteration. There are also certain structural devices, including stanzas and, as in the whole of Psalm 119 and in Lamentations, acrostic patterns. Finally, Hebrew poetry may be classed under the broader heads of lyric, dramatic, and didactic expression.

Three of the poetical books—Job, Proverbs, Ecclesiastes—together with certain of the Psalms, such as Ps. 1, 10, 14, 19, 37, 90, stand among the foremost examples of wisdom literature. By this term is meant the form of Hebrew literature that struggles not only with practical problems of life as in Proverbs, but also with great moral and spiritual questions like the prosperity of the wicked (cp. Ps. 37), materialism, fatalism, and pessimism (cp. Eccl.), and the suffering of the righteous (cp. Job). In their clear-sighted practicality the wisdom books are far removed from speculative philosophy. Reflecting everyday living, they at the same time look up to the one true God. Their emphasis upon God's wisdom (e.g. Prov. 8:22ff.) helped prepare for the advent of the Lord Jesus Christ, "who became for us wisdom" (1 Cor. 1:30), "in whom are hidden all the treasures of wisdom and knowledge" (Col. 2:3), and who said of Himself, "I am the way, the truth, and the life. No one comes to the Father except through Me" (Jn. 14:6).

The Book of

JOB

Author: Unknown *Theme:* Problem of Suffering *Date of writing:* Uncertain

JOB is the first of the Wisdom Books in the OT canon, the others being Proverbs and Ecclesiastes. Wisdom literature, of which the Epistle of James is the NT example, deals with the broad realm of human experience, and is set forth in short, pithy sayings (proverbs), essays, monologues, and, as in Job, in drama.

Although the book does not name its author, Ezek. 14:14,20 and James 5:11 refer to Job as an historical person. That he may have lived in the patriarchal period is inferred from his great age, various geographical references in the book, and the absence of mention of the law and the tabernacle or temple. The presence in this book of lofty Biblical concepts of God, man, Satan, righteousness, redemption, and resurrection may show, in view of its probable early date, the wide extent of revelation even before the writing of Scripture.

The subject of Job is God's providential and ethical government considered in the light of the age-old problem of the suffering of a righteous man. To this problem, neither Job who justified himself, nor his three counselors who charged him with sin, had the solution. Elihu, who explained Job's suffering as God's chastening with a view to experiential purification, reached higher ground, yet also fell short of the answer.

It was not until God revealed Himself in His majesty and power (chs. 38—41) that Job, "blameless and upright" though he was, turned from his own goodness and confessed: "I abhor myself, and repent in dust and ashes" (42:6). Then it was that, having seen himself to be worse than anything he had ever done, Job emerged from suffering into blessing and restoration. Notable Messianic passages in the book are: 9:33; 16:19; 19:25; 33:23–24; 36:18. Chapter 28 contains a beautiful discussion of wisdom, and chs. 38—41 are surpassingly great poetry.

The book may be divided into six parts:

I. Prologue, 1—2.
II. Job's Dialogues with His Counselors, 3—31.
III. Elihu's Monologue, 32—37.
IV. The LORD Speaks, 38—41.
V. Job's Confession, 42:1–6.
VI. Epilogue, 42:7–17.

I. The Prologue, 1—2

Job's character

1 THERE was a man in the land of [1][a]Uz, whose name *was* Job; and that man was [b]blameless and upright, and one who [c]feared God and shunned evil.

Job's family and prosperity

2 And [d]seven sons and three daughters were born to him.
3 Also, his [e]possessions were seven thousand sheep, three thousand camels, five hundred yoke of oxen, five hundred female donkeys, and a very large household, so that this man was the greatest of all the people of the East.
4 And his sons would go and feast *in their* houses, each on his *appointed* day, and would send and invite their three sisters to eat and drink with them.

Job's piety

5 So it was, when the days of feasting had run their course, that Job would send and sanctify them, and he would rise early in the morning and offer burnt offerings *according to* the number of them all. For Job said, "It may be that my sons have sinned and [f]cursed* God in their hearts." Thus Job did regularly.

Job accused by Satan in heaven (cp. Rev. 12:10). Mystery of God's permissive will

6 Now there was a day when the [g]sons of God came to present themselves [h]before the LORD, and [i]Satan also came among them.

CHAPTER 1

1
[a] Gen. 36:28; Jer. 25:20
[b] See Phil. 3:12, *note*
[c] See Ps. 19:9, *note*

2
[d] Cp. Job 42:13

3
[e] Cp. Job 42:12

5
[f] Cp. 1 Ki. 21:10,13

6
[g] Job 2:1; see Gen. 6:4, *note*
[h] This scene is in heaven. Cp. Job 2:1–7
[i] *Satan:* vv. 6–9,12; Job 2:1. (Gen. 3:1; Rev. 20:10)

*1:5 Literally *blessed*, but used here in the evil sense, and so in verse 11 and 2:5,9

---

[1](1:1) The name "Uz" is connected with Edom (Lam. 4:21). The residence of Eliphaz was Teman, generally agreed as the place of that name in Edom. Uz was the object of raids from Chaldea and Sabea (vv. 15,17). It is probable, therefore, that Uz included eastern Edom and northern Arabia.

7 And the LORD said to [a]Satan, "From where do you come?" So Satan answered the LORD and said, "From going to and fro on the earth, and from walking back and forth on it."

8 Then the LORD said to Satan, [b]"Have you considered My servant Job, that *there is* none like him on the earth, a [c]blameless and upright man, one who [d]fears God and shuns evil?"

9 So Satan answered the LORD and said, "Does Job [d]fear God for nothing?

10 "Have You not made a hedge around him, around his household, and around all that he has on every side? You have [e]blessed the work of his hands, and his possessions have increased in the land.

11 "But now, stretch out Your hand and touch all that he has, and he will surely curse You to Your face!"

12 And the LORD said to Satan, "Behold, all that he has *is* in your power; only do not lay a hand on his *person*." So Satan went out from the presence of the LORD.

Satan's first assault: Job's wealth and children taken

13 Now there was a [f]day when his sons and daughters *were* eating and drinking wine in their oldest brother's house;

14 and a messenger came to Job and said, "The oxen were plowing and the donkeys feeding beside them,

15 "when the Sabeans* raided *them* and took them away—indeed they have killed the servants with the edge of the sword; and I alone have escaped to tell you!"

16 While he *was* still speaking, another also came and said, "The fire of God fell from heaven and burned up the sheep and the servants, and [g]consumed them; and I alone have escaped to tell you!"

17 While he *was* still speaking, another also came and said, "The [h]Chaldeans formed three bands, raided the camels and took them away, yes, and killed the servants with the edge of the sword; and I alone have escaped to tell you!"

18 While he *was* still speaking, another also came and said, [i]"Your sons and daughters *were* eating and drinking wine in their oldest brother's house,

19 "and suddenly a great wind came from across* the wilderness and struck the four corners of the house, and it fell on the young people, and they are dead; and I alone have escaped to tell you!"

20 Then Job arose, [j]tore his robe, and shaved his head; and he fell to the ground and worshiped.

21 And he said:

[k]"Naked I came from my
mother's womb,
And naked shall I return there.
The LORD gave, and the [l]LORD
has taken away;
Blessed be the name of the
LORD."

22 In all this Job did not sin nor charge God with wrong.

Satan's second assault: health gone

2 AGAIN [m]there was a day when the sons of God came to present themselves before the LORD, and Satan [n]came also among them to present himself before the LORD.

2 And the LORD said to Satan, "From where do you come?" So [o]Satan answered the LORD and said, "From going to and fro on the earth, and from walking back and forth on it."

3 Then the LORD said to Satan, "Have you considered My servant Job, that *there is* none like him on the earth, a [c]blameless and upright man, one who [d]fears God and shuns evil? And still he [p]holds fast to his integrity, although you incited Me against him, to [q]destroy him without cause."

4 So Satan answered the LORD and said, "Skin for skin! Yes, all that a man has he will give for his life.

5 [r]"But stretch out Your hand now, and touch his [s]bone and his flesh, and he will surely curse You to Your face!"

6 [t]And the LORD said to Satan, "Behold, he *is* in your hand, but spare his life."

7 So Satan went out from the presence of the LORD, and struck Job with painful boils from the sole of his foot to the crown of his head.

8 And he took for himself a [u]potsherd with which to scrape himself while he sat in the midst of the [v]ashes.

Job and his wife speak

9 Then his wife said to him, "Do you still hold fast to your integrity? [w]Curse God and die!"

10 But he said to her, "You speak as

7 *a* Lit. *the adversary.* Rev. 12:9–10
8 *b* Lit. *Have you set your heart on.* Job 2:3 *c* See Phil. 3:12, *note* *d* See Ps. 19:9, *note*
10 *e* Job 29:2–6
13 *f* Eccl. 9:12
16 *g* Cp. 2 Ki. 1:10,12
17 *h* Cp. Gen. 11:28,31
18 *i* vv. 4,13
20 *j* Cp. Est. 4:1; Job 2:12
21 *k* Eccl. 5:15 *l* 1 Sam. 2:6
CHAPTER 2
1 *m* Job 1:6 *n* *Satan:* vv. 1–3, 6–7; Ps. 109:6. (Gen. 3:1; Rev. 20:10)
2 *o* Job 1:7
3 *p* Job 27:5–6 *q* Lit. *to swallow him up.* Cp. Job 9:17
5 *r* Job 1:11 *s* Cp. Job 19:20
6 *t* Job 1:12
8 *u* i.e. *a fragment of a broken pot* *v* Cp. Jer. 6:26; Jon. 3:6
9 *w* Cp. Job 1:5,11

*
1:15 Literally *Sheba* (compare 6:19)
1:19 Septuagint omits *across.*

one of the foolish women speaks. Shall we indeed accept good from God, and shall we not accept adversity?" In all this Job did not [a]sin with his lips.

Job and his three friends: scene, the ash heap outside an oriental village

11 Now when Job's three friends heard of all this adversity that had come upon him, each one came from his own place—Eliphaz the [b]Temanite, Bildad the [c]Shuhite, and Zophar the Naamathite. For they had made an appointment together to come and mourn with him, and to comfort him.

12 And when they raised their eyes from afar, and did not recognize him, they lifted their voices and wept; and each one tore his robe and [d]sprinkled dust on his head toward heaven.

13 So they sat down with him on the ground seven days and seven nights, and no one spoke a word to him, for they saw that *his* grief was very great.

II. Job's Dialogues
with His Counselors, 3—31

His lament

3 AFTER this Job opened his mouth and cursed the day of his *birth.*

2 And Job spoke, and said:

3 [e]"May the day perish on which I
was born,
And the night *in which* it was
said,
'A male child is conceived.'
4 May that day be darkness;
May God above not seek it,
Nor the light shine upon it.
5 May darkness and the
[f]shadow of death claim it;
May a cloud settle on it;
May the blackness of the day
terrify it.
6 *As for* that night, may
darkness seize it;
May it not rejoice* among the
days of the year,
May it not come into the
number of the months.
7 Oh, may that night be barren!
May no joyful shout come into
it!
8 May those curse it who curse
the day,
Those who are ready to arouse
Leviathan.
9 May the stars of its morning
be dark;
May it look for light, but *have*
none,
And not see the [g]dawning of
the day;
10 Because it did not shut up the
doors of my *mother's* womb,
Nor hide sorrow from my eyes.

11 [e]"Why did I not die at birth?
Why did I *not* perish when I
came from the womb?
12 Why did the [h]knees receive
me?
Or why the breasts, that I
should nurse?
13 For now I would have lain still
and been quiet,
I would have been asleep;
Then I would have been at
[i]rest
14 With kings and counselors of
the earth,
Who built [j]ruins for
themselves,
15 Or with princes who had gold,
Who filled their houses *with*
silver;
16 Or *why* was I not hidden like a
[k]stillborn child,
Like infants who never saw
light?
17 There the wicked cease *from*
troubling,
And there the weary are at
[l]rest.
18 *There* the prisoners rest
together;
They do not hear the [m]voice of
the oppressor.
19 The small and great are there,
And the servant *is* free from
his master.

20 [n]"Why is light given to him who
is in misery,
And life to the [o]bitter of soul,
21 Who [p]long for death, but it
does not *come,*
And search for it more than
hidden treasures;
22 Who rejoice exceedingly,
And are glad when they can
find the [q]grave?
23 *Why is light given* to a man
whose way is [r]hidden,
And [s]whom God has hedged
in?
24 For my sighing comes before I
eat,*
And my groanings pour out
like water.
25 For the thing I greatly [t]feared
has come upon me,

10 *a* Job 1:21–22; cp. Jas. 5:10–11
11 *b* 1 Chr. 1:36; Obad. 9 *c* Gen. 25:2; 1 Chr. 1:32
12 *d* Cp. Lam. 2:10
CHAPTER 3
3 *e* Job 10:18–19; cp. Jer. 20:14–18
5 *f* Job 10:21–22
9 *g* Lit. *the eyelids of the morning.* Job 41:18
12 *h* Cp. Gen. 50:23
13 *i* v. 17
14 *j* Cp. Job 15:28
16 *k* Ps. 58:8
17 *l* Job 17:16
18 *m* Cp. Job 39:7
20 *n* Cp. Jer. 20:18 *o* Cp. 1 Sam. 1:10; 2 Ki. 4:27; Prov. 31:6
21 *p* Lit. *wait.* Cp. Rev. 9:6
22 *q* Job 7:15–16
23 *r* Cp. Isa. 40:27 *s* Job 19:8; Lam. 3:7
25 *t* Job 9:28

*3:6 Septuagint, Syriac, Targum, and Vulgate read *be joined.* 3:24 Literally *my bread*

And what I dreaded has
happened to me.
26 I am not at ease, nor am I
quiet;
I have no rest, for trouble
comes."

Eliphaz's first charge: the innocent do not suffer (v. 7)

4 THEN [1]Eliphaz the Temanite answered and said:

2 "*If* one attempts a word with
you, will you become weary?
But who can withhold himself
from speaking?
3 Surely you have instructed
many,
And you [a]have strengthened
weak hands.
4 Your words have upheld him
who was stumbling,
And you [a]have strengthened
the feeble knees;
5 But now it comes upon you,
and you are weary;
It touches you, and you are
troubled.
6 *Is* not your [b]reverence your
confidence?
And the integrity of your ways
your hope?

7 "Remember now, who *ever*
perished being [2]innocent?
Or where were the upright
ever [c]cut off?
8 Even as I have seen,
Those who plow iniquity
And sow trouble reap the
[d]same.
9 By the blast of God they
perish,
And by the [e]breath of His
anger they are consumed.
10 The roaring of the lion,
The voice of the fierce lion,
And the teeth of the young
lions are broken.
11 The old lion perishes for lack
of prey,
And the cubs of the lioness are
scattered.

Eliphaz's night vision

12 "Now a word was [f]secretly
brought to me,
And my ear received a whisper
of it.
13 In disquieting thoughts from
the visions of the night,
When deep sleep falls on men,
14 Fear came upon me, and
trembling,
Which made all my bones
shake.
15 Then a spirit passed before my
face;
The hair on my body stood up.
16 It stood still,
But I could not discern its
appearance.
A form *was* before my eyes;
There was silence;
Then I heard a voice *saying:*
17 'Can a mortal be more
righteous than God?
Can a man be more pure than
his Maker?
18 If He puts no [g]trust in His
servants,
If He charges His [h]angels with
error,
19 How much more those who
dwell in houses of clay,
Whose foundation is in the
dust,
Who are crushed before a
moth?
20 They are broken in pieces
from morning till evening;
They perish forever, with no
one regarding.
21 Does not their own excellence
go away?
They die, even without
wisdom.'

Eliphaz continues: God is faithful

5 "CALL out now;
Is there anyone who will
answer you?
And to which of the [i]holy
ones will you turn?
2 For wrath kills a foolish man,
And envy slays a simple one.
3 [j]I have seen the foolish taking
root,
But suddenly I cursed his
dwelling place.
4 His sons are [k]far from safety,
They are crushed in the gate,
[l]And *there is* no deliverer.

CHAPTER 4

3 *a* Cp. Isa. 35:3

6 *b* Job 1:1

7 *c* Job 8:20; cp. Jn. 9:2

8 *d* Cp. Gal. 6:7

9 *e* Cp. Ex. 15:8; Job 1:19; 15:30; Isa. 11:4; 30:33; 2 Th. 2:8

12 *f* Lit. *by stealth*

18 *g* See Ps. 2:12, *note*
h See Heb. 1:4, *note*

CHAPTER 5

1 *i* Job 15:15

3 *j* Ps. 37:35–36; Jer. 12:1–3

4 *k* Ps. 119:155
l Ps. 109:12

---

[1](4:1) Eliphaz emphasizes the facts of human experience, referring particularly to a mysterious spiritual visitation that had come to him in the night (vv. 12–16). See v. 7, *note.*

[2](4:7) Verses 7–8 state the chief theme that all three of Job's counselors elaborate—namely, the innocent do not suffer. They insist that because suffering comes from sin, Job, who was suffering so acutely, must be a great sinner. Although these counselors speak eloquently and at times truly, they do not really understand Job's problem. Cp. Lk. 13:1–5.

5 Because the hungry eat up his harvest,
Taking it even from the thorns,*
And a snare snatches their substance.*
6 For affliction does not come from the dust,
Nor does trouble spring from the ground;
7 Yet man is [a]born to trouble,
As the sparks fly upward.

8 "But as for me, I would seek God,
And to God I would commit my cause—
9 Who does great things, and unsearchable,
Marvelous things without number.
10 [b]He gives rain on the earth,
And sends waters on the fields.
11 He sets on high those who are lowly,
And those who mourn are lifted to safety.
12 He frustrates the devices of the crafty,
So that their hands cannot carry out their plans.
13 He catches the [c]wise in their own craftiness,
And the counsel of the cunning comes quickly upon them.
14 They meet with darkness in the daytime,
And grope at noontime as in the night.
15 But He [d]saves the needy from the sword,
From the mouth of the mighty,
And from their hand.
16 [e]So the poor have hope,
And injustice shuts her mouth.

17 [f]"Behold, happy *is* the man whom God corrects;
Therefore do not despise the chastening of the Almighty.
18 [g]For He bruises, but He binds up;
He wounds, but His hands make whole.
19 [h]He shall deliver you in six troubles,
Yes, in [i]seven no evil shall touch you.
20 In [j]famine He shall [k]redeem you from death,
And in war from the power of the sword.
21 [l]You shall be hidden from the scourge of the tongue,
And you shall not be afraid of destruction when it comes.
22 You shall laugh at destruction and famine,
And you shall not be [m]afraid of the [n]beasts of the earth.
23 For you shall have a covenant with the stones of the field,
And the beasts of the field shall be at peace with you.
24 You shall know that your tent *is* in peace;
You shall visit your dwelling and find nothing amiss.
25 You shall also know that your descendants *shall be* many,
And your offspring like the [o]grass of the earth.
26 You shall come to the grave at a [p]full age,
As a sheaf of grain ripens in its season.
27 Behold, this we have [q]searched out;
It *is* true.
Hear it, and know for yourself."

Job replies; he pleads for pity (v. 14)

6

THEN Job answered and said:
2 "Oh, that my grief were fully weighed,
And my calamity laid with it on the scales!
3 For then it would be heavier than the sand of the sea—
Therefore my words have been rash.
4 For the arrows of the Almighty *are* within me;
My spirit drinks in their poison;
The [r]terrors of God are arrayed [s]against me.
5 Does the [t]wild donkey bray when it has grass,
Or does the ox low over its fodder?
6 Can flavorless food be eaten without salt?
Or is there *any* taste in the white of an egg?
7 My soul refuses to touch them;
They *are* as loathsome food to me.

8 "Oh, that I might have my request,

7 [a] Gen. 3:17–19
10 [b] Job 28:26
13 [c] 1 Cor 3:19
15 [d] Ps. 35:10
16 [e] 1 Sam. 2:8; Ps. 107:41–42
17 [f] Ps. 94:12; Prov. 3:11–12; Heb. 12:5–6; Jas. 1:12; Rev. 3:19
18 [g] Dt. 32:39; 1 Sam. 2:7; cp. Isa. 30:26; Hos. 6:1
19 [h] Ps. 34:19; 91:3; 1 Cor. 10:13 [i] Ps. 91:10; Prov. 24:16
20 [j] Ps. 33:19; 37:19 [k] v. 22
21 [l] Ps. 31:20
22 [m] Isa. 11:9; 35:9; 65:25; Ezek. 34:25 [n] Hos. 2:18
25 [o] Ps. 72:16
26 [p] Prov. 9:11; 10:27
27 [q] Ps. 111:2
CHAPTER 6
4 [r] Ps. 88:15–16 [s] Job 30:15
5 [t] Job 39:5

*5:5 Septuagint reads *They shall not be taken from evil men;* Vulgate reads *And the armed man shall take him by violence.* • Septuagint reads *The might shall draw them off;* Vulgate reads *And the thirsty shall drink up their riches.*

That God would grant *me* the
thing that I long for!
9 That it would please God to
crush me,
That He would loose His hand
and [a]cut me off!
10 Then I would still have
comfort;
Though in anguish I would
exult,
He will not spare;
For I have not concealed the
[b]words of the Holy One.

11 "What strength do I have, that I
should hope?
And what *is* my end, that I
should prolong my life?
12 *Is* my strength the strength of
stones?
Or is my flesh bronze?
13 *Is* my help not within me?
And is success driven from
me?

14 [c]"To him who is afflicted,
kindness *should be shown*
by his friend,
Even though he forsakes the
[d]fear of the Almighty.
15 [e]My brothers have dealt
deceitfully like a brook,
Like the streams of the brooks
that pass away,
16 Which are dark because of the
ice,
And into which the snow
vanishes.
17 When it is warm, they cease to
flow;
When it is hot, they vanish
from their place.
18 The paths of their way turn
aside,
They go nowhere and perish.
19 The caravans of [f]Tema look,
The travelers of [g]Sheba hope
for them.
20 They are disappointed because
they were confident;
They come there and are
confused.
21 For now you are nothing,
You see terror and are
afraid.
22 Did I ever say, 'Bring
something to me'?
Or, 'Offer a bribe for me from
your wealth'?
23 Or, [h]'Deliver me from the
enemy's hand'?
Or, 'Redeem me from the hand
of oppressors'?

9
[a] Job 7:16; 9:21; 10:1; cp. Num. 11:15; 1 Ki. 19:4; Jon. 4:3,8
10
[b] *Inspiration:* v. 10; Job 32:18. (Ex. 4:15; 2 Tim. 3:16, *note*)
14
[c] Lit. *To him who melts.* Prov. 17:17
[d] See Ps. 19:9, *note*
15
[e] Cp. Ps. 38:11; 41:9
19
[f] Gen. 25:15
[g] 1 Ki. 10:1; Ps. 72:10; Ezek. 27:22,23
23
[h] Cp. Job 6:1–12
29
[i] Job 17:10
[j] Job 27:5–6; 34:5; cp. 23:10; 42:1–6
CHAPTER 7
1
[k] Job 14:5, 13–14; Ps. 39:4
2
[l] Lit. *gapes after*
4
[m] Dt. 28:67
5
[n] Cp. Isa. 14:11
6
[o] Job 9:25; 16:22; 17:11; Ps. 90:5; Isa. 38:12; Jas. 4:14
7
[p] Ps. 78:39; 89:47

24 "Teach me, and I will hold my
tongue;
Cause me to understand
wherein I have erred.
25 How forceful are right words!
But what does your arguing
prove?
26 Do you intend to rebuke *my*
words,
And the speeches of a
desperate one, *which are* as
wind?
27 Yes, you overwhelm the
fatherless,
And you undermine your
friend.
28 Now therefore, be pleased to
look at me;
For I would never lie to your
face.
29 [i]Yield now, let there be no
injustice!
Yes, concede, my
[j]righteousness still stands!
30 Is there injustice on my
tongue?
Cannot my taste discern the
unsavory?

Job continues: all is suffering (v. 4)

7 "*IS there* not a [k]time of hard
service for man on earth?
Are not his days also like the
days of a hired man?
2 Like a servant who [l]earnestly
desires the shade,
And like a hired man who
eagerly looks for his wages,
3 So I have been allotted months
of futility,
And wearisome nights have
been appointed to me.
4 [m]When I lie down, I say, 'When
shall I arise,
And the night be ended?'
For I have had my fill of
tossing till dawn.
5 My flesh is caked with [n]worms
and dust,
My skin is cracked and breaks
out afresh.
6 "My [o]days are swifter than a
weaver's shuttle,
And are spent without hope.
7 Oh, remember that my [p]life *is*
a breath!
My eye will never again see
good.
8 The eye of him who sees me
will see me no *more;*
While your *eyes* are upon me, I
shall no longer *be.*

9 *As* the cloud disappears and vanishes away,
So he who goes down to the [a]grave does not come up.
10 He shall never return to his house,
Nor shall his place know him [b]anymore.

11 "Therefore I will not restrain my mouth;
I will speak in the anguish of my spirit;
I will complain in the bitterness of my soul.
12 *Am* I a sea, or a sea serpent,
That You set a guard over me?
13 When I say, 'My bed will comfort me,
My couch will ease my complaint,'
14 Then You scare me with dreams
And terrify me with visions,
15 So that my soul chooses strangling
And death rather than my body.*
16 I loathe *my life;*
I would not live forever.
Let me alone,
For my days *are but* a breath.

17 [c]"What *is* man, that You should exalt him,
That You should set Your heart on him,
18 That You should visit him every morning,
And [d]test him every moment?
19 How long?
Will You not look away from me,
And let me alone till I swallow my saliva?
20 Have I sinned?
What have I done to You, O watcher of men?
Why have You set me as Your target,
So that I am a burden to myself?*
21 Why then do You not pardon my transgression,
And take away my iniquity?
For now I will lie down in the dust,
And You will seek me diligently,
But I *will* no longer *be*."

9
a See Hab. 2:5, *note;* cp. Lk. 16:23, *note*
10
b Job 10:21; Ps. 103:16
17
c Ps. 8:4; 144:3; Heb. 2:6
18
d *Test/tempt:* v. 18; Job 23:10. (Gen. 3:1; Jas. 1:14, *note*)
CHAPTER 8
3
e 2 Chr. 19:7; Job 34:12; Dan. 9:14
f Cp. Gen. 18:25; Dt. 32:4
5
g Cp. Job 5:17–27
7
h Job 42:12
9
i 1 Chr. 29:15; Job 7:6; Ps. 39:5; 102:11; 144:4; cp. Gen. 47:9
13
j Ps. 9:17
k Job 11:20; 18:14; 27:8; Ps. 112:10; Prov. 10:28

Bildad's first speech: the fathers agree with me (v. 8)

8 THEN [1]Bildad the Shuhite answered and said:

2 "How long will you speak these *things,*
And the words of your mouth *be like* a strong wind?
3 Does God subvert [e]judgment?
Or does the Almighty pervert [f]justice?
4 If your sons have sinned against Him,
He has cast them away for their transgression.
5 If you would earnestly [g]seek God
And make your supplication to the Almighty,
6 If you *were* pure and upright,
Surely now He would awake for you,
And prosper your rightful dwelling place.
7 Though your beginning was small,
Yet your latter end would [h]increase abundantly.

8 "For inquire, please, of the former age,
And consider the things discovered by their fathers;
9 For we *were born* yesterday, and know nothing,
Because our [i]days on earth *are* a shadow.
10 Will they not teach you and tell you,
And utter words from their heart?

11 "Can the papyrus grow up without a marsh?
Can the reeds flourish without water?
12 While it *is* yet green *and* not cut down,
It withers before any *other* plant.
13 So *are* the paths of all who [j]forget God;
And the hope of the [k]hypocrite shall perish,
14 Whose confidence shall be cut off,

*7:15 Literally *my bones* 7:20 Following Masoretic Text, Targum, and Vulgate; Septuagint and Jewish tradition read *to You.*

[1](8:1) Bildad bases his counsel to Job upon tradition (vv. 8–10). His discourses abound in proverbs and pious platitudes which, though true enough, are known to everyone (9:1–3; 13:2). They are superficial and shed no light on Job's problem. See 4:7, *note.*

And whose [a]trust *is* a spider's
web.
15 He leans on his house, but it
does not stand.
He holds it fast, but it does not
endure.
16 He grows green in the sun,
And his branches spread out in
his garden.
17 His roots wrap around the
rock heap,
And look for a place in the
stones.
18 If he is destroyed from his
place,
Then *it* will deny him, *saying,*
'I have not seen you.'

19 "Behold, this is the joy of His
way,
And out of the earth others
will grow.
20 Behold, [b]God will not cast
away the [c]blameless,
Nor will He [d]uphold the
evildoers.
21 He will yet fill your mouth
with laughing,
And your lips with [e]rejoicing.
22 Those who hate you will be
[f]clothed with shame,
And the dwelling place of the
wicked will come to
nothing."*

Job responds: how can a man be righteous before God? (vv. 2,20)

9

THEN Job answered and said:
2 "Truly I know *it is* so,
But how can a [g]man be
[h]righteous before God?
3 If one wished to contend with
Him,
He could not answer Him one
time out of a thousand.
4 [i]*God is* wise in heart and
mighty in strength.
Who has hardened *himself*
against Him and prospered?
5 He removes the mountains,
and they do not know
When He overturns them in
His anger;
6 He [j]shakes the earth out of its
place,
And its pillars tremble;
7 He commands the sun, and it
does not rise;
He seals off the stars;
8 He alone spreads out the
heavens,
And [k]treads on the waves of
the sea;
9 [l]He made the [m]Bear, Orion, and
the Pleiades,
And the chambers of the
south;
10 He does great things past
finding out,
Yes, wonders without
[n]number.
11 If He goes by me, I do [o]not see
Him;
If He moves past, I do not
perceive Him;
12 If He takes away, who can
hinder Him?
Who can say to Him, [p]'What
are You doing?'
13 God will not withdraw His
anger,
The allies of the [q]proud* lie
prostrate beneath Him.

14 "How then can I answer Him,
And choose my words *to
reason* with Him?
15 For though I were righteous, I
could not answer Him;
I would [r]beg mercy of my
Judge.
16 If I called and He answered
me,
I would not believe that He
was listening to my voice.
17 For He crushes me with a
tempest,
And multiplies my wounds
without cause.
18 He will not allow me to catch
my breath,
But fills me with bitterness.
19 If *it is a matter* of strength,
indeed *He is* strong;
And if of justice, who will
appoint my day *in court?*
20 Though I were righteous, my
own mouth would condemn
me;
Though I *were* [c]blameless, it
would prove me perverse.

21 "I am [c]blameless, yet I do not
know myself;
I despise my life.
22 It *is* all one *thing;*
Therefore I say, [s]'He destroys
the [c]blameless and the
wicked.'
23 If the scourge slays suddenly,
He laughs at the plight of the
innocent.

14 *a* See Ps. 2:12, *note*
20 *b* Job 4:7 *c* See Phil. 3:12, *note* *d* Lit. *take the ungodly by the hand*
21 *e* Cp. Ps. 126:2
22 *f* Ps. 35:26; 109:29
CHAPTER 9
2 *g* Job 4:17; 15:14–16; Ps. 143:2; Rom. 3:20 *h* Hab. 2:4; Rom. 1:17; Gal. 3:11; Heb. 10:38
4 *i* Job 36:5
6 *j* Isa. 2:19, 21; Hag. 2:6,21; Heb. 12:26
8 *k* Cp. Mt. 14:25
9 *l* Gen. 1:16; Job 38:31; Amos 5:8 *m* Job 38:32
10 *n* Job 5:9
11 *o* Job 23:8–9; 35:14
12 *p* Isa. 45:9; Dan. 4:35; Rom. 9:19–21
13 *q* Job 26:12; cp. Isa. 30:7
15 *r* Job 23:1–7
22 *s* Eccl. 9:2–3; cp. Ezek. 21:3; Mt. 5:45

* 8:22 Literally *will not be* 9:13 Hebrew *rahab*

24 The earth is given into the
hand of the wicked.
He covers the faces of its
judges.
If it is not *He*, who else could
it be?

25 "Now [a]my days are swifter
than a runner;
They flee away, they see no
good.
26 They pass by like [b]swift ships,
Like an eagle swooping on its
prey.
27 [c]If I say, 'I will forget my
complaint,
I will put off my sad face and
wear a smile,'
28 I am afraid of all my
sufferings;
I know that You will not hold
me [d]innocent.
29 *If* I am condemned,
Why then do I labor in vain?
30 [e]If I wash myself with snow
water,
And cleanse my hands with
soap,
31 Yet You will plunge me into
the pit,
And my own clothes will
abhor me.

32 [f]"For *He is* not a man, as I *am*,
That I may answer Him,
And that we should go to
court together.
33 Nor is there any [1g]mediator
between us,
Who may lay his hand on us
both.
34 Let Him take His rod away
from me,
And do not let dread of Him
terrify me.
35 *Then* I would speak and not
fear Him,
But it is not so with me.

Job continues: he states that both the righteous and the wicked suffer

10 "MY soul [h]loathes my life;
I will give free course to my
complaint,
I will speak in the bitterness of
my soul.

25
a Job 7:6–7
26
b Lit. *ships of Ebeh*
27
c Job 7:13
28
d Cp. Ps. 130:3
30
e Jer. 2:22
32
f Isa. 45:9; Jer. 49:19; Rom. 9:20
33
g v. 19; cp. 1 Sam. 2:25
CHAPTER 10
1
h Job 7:16
3
i Cp. Job 9:22–24; 16:11
4
j Cp. 1 Sam. 16:7
7
k Cp. Ps. 139:1–2
8
l Ps. 119:73
m Job 9:22
12
n Cp. Ps. 8:4
14
o Job 7:20; Ps. 139:1

2 I will say to God, 'Do not
condemn me;
Show me why You contend
with me.
3 *Does it* seem good to You that
You should [i]oppress,
That You should despise the
work of Your hands,
And smile on the counsel of
the wicked?
4 Do You have eyes of flesh?
Or do You [j]see as man sees?
5 *Are* Your days like the days of
a mortal man?
Are Your years like the days
of a mighty man,
6 That You should seek for my
iniquity
And search out my sin,
7 Although You [k]know that I am
not wicked,
And *there is* no one who can
deliver from Your hand?

8 [l]'Your hands have made me and
fashioned me,
An intricate unity;
Yet You would [m]destroy me.
9 Remember, I pray, that You
have made me like clay.
And will You turn me into dust
again?
10 Did You not pour me out like
milk,
And curdle me like cheese,
11 Clothe me with skin and flesh,
And knit me together with
bones and sinews?
12 You have granted me life and
favor,
And Your [n]care has preserved
my spirit.

13 'And these *things* You have
hidden in Your heart;
I know that this *was* with You:
14 If I sin, then You [o]mark me,
And will not acquit me of my
iniquity.
15 If I am wicked, woe to me;
Even *if* I am righteous, I
cannot lift up my head.
I am full of disgrace;
See my misery!
16 If *my head* is exalted,
You hunt me like a fierce lion,

[1](9:33) The Hebrew word for *mediator* is translated in the Septuagint by the same word Paul uses in 1 Tim. 2:5. Job longs for someone who understands both God and man and who will draw them together. Ultimately this is what our Lord Jesus Christ did. But Job desires some man in his own time who has "eyes of flesh" and who can sympathize with his human weakness. This longing increases as the book progresses (9:32–33; 10:4–5,8–10; 13:21–22; 16:21; 23:3). Finally Elihu claims to be the one whom Job seeks, who will be like him and will not make him afraid (33:6–7,23).

And again You show Yourself
awesome against me.
17 You renew Your witnesses
against me,
And increase Your indignation
toward me;
Changes and war are *ever* with
me.
18 'Why then have You brought
me out of the womb?
Oh, that I had perished and no
eye had seen [a]me!
19 I would have been as though I
had not been.
I would have been carried
from the womb to the grave.
20 Are not my days few?
Cease! [b]Leave me alone, that I
may take a little comfort,
21 Before I go *to the place from
which* I shall not return,
[c]To the land of darkness and
the [d]shadow of death,
22 A land as dark as darkness
itself,
As the shadow of death,
without any order,
Where even the light *is* like
darkness.' "

Zophar's first charge: how dares Job claim innocence? (vv. 4–8)

11

THEN [1]Zophar the Naamathite answered and said:

2 "Should not the multitude of
words be answered?
And should a man full of talk
be vindicated?
3 Should your empty talk make
men hold their peace?
And when you mock, should
no one rebuke you?
4 For you have said,
'My doctrine *is* pure,
And I am [e]clean in your eyes.'
5 But oh, that God would speak,
And open His lips against you,
6 That He would show you the
secrets of wisdom!
For *they would* double *your*
prudence.
Know therefore that [f]God
exacts from you
Less than your iniquity
deserves.

7 [g]"Can you search out the deep
things of God?
Can you find out the limits of
the Almighty?

18 *a* Job 3:11–13
20 *b* Job 7:19
21 *c* Job 3:13–19; 7:8–10,21; 14:10–15, 20–22; 16:22; 17:13–16; 19:25–27; 21:13, 23–26; 24:19–20; cp. 2 Sam. 12:23
d Ps. 23:4
CHAPTER 11
4 *e* Job 10:7
6 *f* Ezra 9:13
7 *g* Eccl. 3:11; Rom. 11:33
8 *h* Lit. *as the heights of heaven*
i See Hab. 2:5, *note;* cp. Lk. 16:23, *note*
13 *j* vv. 15–19; cp. Job 5:17–27
14 *k* Job 22:23
CHAPTER 12
2 *l* Cp. Job 16:1–2; 17:10; Prov. 3:7

8 *They are* [h]higher than
heaven—what can you do?
Deeper than [i]Sheol—what can
you know?
9 Their measure *is* longer than
the earth
And broader than the sea.

10 "If He passes by, imprisons, and
gathers *to judgment,*
Then who can hinder Him?
11 For He knows deceitful men;
He sees wickedness also.
Will He not then consider *it?*
12 For an empty-headed man will
be wise,
When a wild donkey's colt is
born a man.

13 [j]"If you would prepare your
heart,
And stretch out your hands
toward Him;
14 If iniquity *were* in your hand,
and you put it far away,
And would not let wickedness
dwell in your [k]tents;
15 Then surely you could lift up
your face without spot;
Yes, you could be steadfast,
and not fear;
16 Because you would forget *your*
misery,
And remember *it* as waters
that have passed away,
17 And *your* life would be
brighter than noonday.
Though you were dark, you
would be like the morning.
18 And you would be secure,
because there is hope;
Yes, you would dig *around
you, and* take your rest in
safety.
19 You would also lie down, and
no one would make *you*
afraid;
Yes, many would court your
favor.
20 But the eyes of the wicked will
fail,
And they shall not escape,
And their hope—loss of life!"

Job's rebuttal: the wicked are not immediately punished

12

THEN Job answered and said:

2 "No doubt [l]you *are* the people,
And wisdom will die with you!

[1](11:1) Zophar in his counsel emphasizes legalism. He presumes to know what God will do in any given case, why He will do it, and what His thoughts about it are. See 4:7, *note.*

3 But I have understanding as
well as you;
I *am* not [a]inferior to you.
Indeed, who does not *know*
such things as these?

4 "I am one mocked by his
friends,
Who [b]called on God, and He
answered him,
The [c]just and blameless *who is*
ridiculed.
5 A lamp* is despised in the
thought of one who is at
ease;
It is made ready for those
whose feet [d]slip.
6 The [e]tents of robbers
[f]prosper,
And those who provoke God
are secure—
In what God [g]provides by His
hand.

7 "But now ask the beasts, and
they will teach you;
And the birds of the air, and
they will tell you;
8 Or speak to the earth, and it
will teach you;
And the fish of the sea will
explain to you.
9 Who among all these does not
know
That the hand of the LORD has
done this,
10 [h]In whose hand *is* the life of
every living thing,
And the [i]breath of all
mankind?
11 Does not the ear test words
And the mouth taste its food?
12 Wisdom *is* with aged men,
And with length of days,
understanding.

13 [j]"With Him *are* [k]wisdom and
strength,
He has counsel and
understanding.
14 If [l]He breaks *a thing* down, it
cannot be rebuilt;
If He imprisons a man, there
can be no release.
15 If [m]He withholds the waters,
they dry up;
[n]*If* He sends them out, they
overwhelm the earth.
16 With Him *are* strength and
prudence.
The deceived and the deceiver
are His.
17 He leads counselors away
plundered,
And makes fools of the judges.
18 He loosens the bonds of kings,
And binds their waist with a
belt.
19 He leads princes* away
plundered,
And overthrows the mighty.
20 He deprives the trusted ones of
speech,
And takes away the
discernment of the elders.
21 [o]He pours contempt on princes,
And disarms the mighty.
22 [p]He uncovers deep things out of
darkness,
And brings the shadow of
death to light.
23 He makes nations great, and
destroys them;
He enlarges nations, and
guides them.
24 He takes away the
understanding* of the chiefs
of the people of the earth,
And makes them wander in a
pathless wilderness.
25 They [q]grope in the dark
without light,
And He makes them stagger
like a drunken *man*.

Job continues his rebuttal

13 "BEHOLD, my eye has seen
all *this*,
My ear has heard and
understood it.
2 What you know, I also know;
I *am* not inferior to you.
3 But I would speak to the
Almighty,
And I desire to [r]reason with
God.
4 But you forgers of lies,
You *are* all worthless
physicians.
5 Oh, that you would be silent,
And it would be your wisdom!
6 Now hear my reasoning,
And heed the pleadings of my
lips.
7 Will you [s]speak wickedly for
God,
And talk deceitfully for Him?
8 Will you show partiality for
Him?
Will you contend for God?
9 Will it be well when He
searches you out?
Or can you mock Him as one
mocks a man?

3
a Job 13:2
4
b Ps. 91:15
c Cp. Job 21:3
5
d Cp. Ps. 38:16; 73:2
6
e Job 15:34
f Job 9:24; 21:6–16; Ps. 73:12
g Cp. Mt. 5:45
10
h Acts 17:28; cp. Num. 16:22; Dan. 5:23
i Job 33:4; cp. Eccl. 12:7
13
j i.e. *With God*
k Job 9:4; 36:5
14
l Job 11:10
15
m Cp. 1 Ki. 8:35; 17:1
n Cp. Gen. 7:11
21
o Ps. 107:40; cp. Dan. 2:21
22
p Dan. 2:22; Mt. 10:26; 1 Cor. 4:5
25
q Job 5:14; 15:30; 18:18
CHAPTER 13
3
r Job 23:4; 31:35
7
s Job 27:4

*
12:5 Or *disaster* **12:19** Literally *priests*, but not in the technical sense **12:24** Literally *heart*

10 He will surely rebuke you
If you secretly show partiality.
11 Will not His excellence make
you afraid,
And the dread of Him fall
upon you?
12 Your platitudes *are* proverbs of
ashes,
Your defenses are defenses of
clay.

13 "Hold your peace with me, and
let me speak,
Then let come on me what
may!
14 Why do I take my flesh in my
teeth,
And put my life in my hands?
15 [a]Though He slay me, yet will I
trust Him.
Even so, I will [b]defend my
own ways before Him.
16 He also *shall* be my salvation,
For a [c]hypocrite could not
come before Him.
17 Listen carefully to my speech,
And to my declaration with
your ears.
18 See now, I have prepared *my*
case,
I know that I shall be
[d]vindicated.
19 Who *is* he *who* will contend
with me?
If now I hold my tongue, I
perish.

20 "Only two *things* do not do to
me,
Then I will not hide myself
from You:
21 [e]Withdraw Your hand far from
me,
And let not the dread of You
make me afraid.
22 Then call, and I will [f]answer;
Or let me speak, then You
respond to me.
23 How many *are* my iniquities
and sins?
Make me know my
transgression and my [g]sin.
24 [h]Why do You hide Your face,
And regard me as Your
enemy?
25 Will You frighten a leaf driven
to and fro?
And will You pursue dry
stubble?
26 For You write bitter things
against me,
And make me inherit the
iniquities of my youth.
27 You put my feet in the stocks,
And watch closely all my
paths.
You set a limit* for the soles
of my feet.

28 "*Man** decays like a rotten
thing,
Like a garment that is
moth-eaten.

15
a Ps. 23:4; Prov. 14:32
b Job 27:5
16
c Job 8:13
18
d Job 6:29
21
e Ps. 39:10
22
f Job 14:15
23
g Cp. Job 22:5–10
24
h Ps. 13:1; 44:24; 88:14; cp. Dt. 32:20; Isa. 8:17
CHAPTER 14
1
i Job 5:7; Eccl. 2:23
2
j Job 8:9; Ps. 90:5,6, 9; 102:11; 103:15; 144:4; Isa. 40:6; Jas. 1:10–11; 1 Pet. 1:24
3
k Cp. Job 7:17–18
5
l Job 21:21; Heb. 9:27
10
m Job 10:21–22
12
n Ps. 102:25–26; Isa. 51:6; 65:17 66:22; 2 Pet. 3:7, 10–11; Rev. 20:11; 21:1
o Cp. Job 19:26

Job continues: he awaits resurrection

14 "MAN *who is* born of woman
Is of few days and [i]full of
trouble.
2 [j]He comes forth like a flower
and fades away;
He flees like a shadow and
does not continue.
3 And do You open Your eyes
on such a [k]one,
And bring me* to judgment
with Yourself?
4 Who can bring a clean *thing*
out of an unclean?
No one!
5 Since his days *are* determined,
The [l]number of his months *is*
with You;
You have appointed his limits,
so that he cannot pass.
6 Look away from him that he
may rest,
Till like a hired man he
finishes his day.
7 "For there is hope for a tree,
If it is cut down, that it will
sprout again,
And that its tender shoots will
not cease.
8 Though its root may grow old
in the earth,
And its stump may die in the
ground,
9 *Yet* at the scent of water it will
bud
And bring forth branches like
a plant.
10 But man dies and is laid away;
Indeed he breathes his last
And where *is* [m]he?
11 *As* water disappears from the
sea,
And a river becomes parched
and dries up,
12 So man lies down and does not
rise.
[n]Till the heavens *are* no more,
They will not awake
Nor be roused from their
[o]sleep.

*
13:27 Literally *inscribe a print* 13:28 Literally *He*
14:3 Septuagint, Syriac, and Vulgate read *him*.

13 "Oh, that You would hide me in the [a]grave,
That You would conceal me until Your wrath is past,
That You would appoint me a set time, and remember me!
14 If a man dies, shall he [1]live *again?*
All the days of my hard service I will wait,
Till my change comes.
15 You shall call, and I will answer You;
You shall desire the work of Your hands.
16 [b]For now You number my steps,
But do not watch over my sin.
17 [c]My transgression *is* sealed up in a bag,
And You cover* my iniquity.

18 "But *as* a mountain falls *and* crumbles away,
And *as* a rock is moved from its place;
19 *As* water wears away stones,
And as torrents wash away the soil of the earth;
So You destroy the hope of man.
20 You prevail forever against him, and he passes on;
You change his countenance and send him away.
21 His sons come to honor, and he does [d]not know *it;*
They are brought low, and he does not perceive *it.*
22 But his flesh will be in pain over it,
And his soul will mourn over it."

Eliphaz's second speech: Job rebuked; the wicked do not prosper

15 THEN [e]Eliphaz the Temanite answered and said:

2 "Should a wise man answer with empty knowledge,
And fill himself with the east wind?
3 Should he reason with unprofitable talk,
Or by speeches with which he can do no good?
4 Yes, you cast off fear,
And restrain prayer before God.
5 For your iniquity teaches your mouth,
And you choose the tongue of the [f]crafty.
6 [g]Your own mouth condemns you, and not I;
Yes, your own lips testify against you.

7 "*Are* you the first man *who* was born?
Or were you [h]made before the hills?
8 Have you heard the counsel of God?
Do you limit wisdom to yourself?
9 What do you know that we do not know?
What do you understand that *is* not in us?
10 Both the gray-haired and the [i]aged *are* among us,
Much older than your father.
11 *Are* the consolations of God too small for you,
And the word *spoken* gently* with you?
12 Why does your heart carry you away,
[j]And what do your eyes wink at,
13 That you turn your spirit against God,
And let *such* words go out of your mouth?

14 "What *is* man, that he could be pure?
And *he who is* born of a woman, that he could be [k]righteous?
15 If *God* puts no [l]trust in His [m]saints,
And the [n]heavens are not pure in His sight,
16 [o]How much less man, *who is* abominable and filthy,
Who drinks iniquity like water!

17 "I will tell you, hear me;

13
a See Hab. 2:5, *note;* cp. Lk. 16:23, *note*
16
b Job 10:6, 14; 13:27; 31:4; 34:21; Ps. 56:8; 139:1–3; Prov. 5:21; Jer. 32:19
17
c Cp. Dt. 32:34; Hos. 13:12
21
d Cp. Eccl. 9:5
CHAPTER 15
1
e Job 4:1
5
f Job 5:12–13
6
g Job 9:20; Lk. 19:22
7
h Job 38:4, 21
10
i Job 8:8–10
12
j Lit. *And why do your eyes flash*
14
k Cp. Job 14:4
15
l See Ps. 2:12, *note*
m Job 5:1; cp. 4:18
n Cp. Col. 1:20; Heb. 9:23
16
o Job 4:19; Ps. 14:3; 53:3

*14:17 Literally *plaster over a secret thing.* 15:11 Septuagint reads *a secret thing.*

[1](14:14) This is one of three great problems raised by the Book of Job, each of which reaches its solution in the Lord Jesus Christ. Considered in logical order, they are: the problems of (1) the invisible God—"Oh, that I knew where I might find Him!" (23:3)—answered by the incarnation of Christ; (2) human sin—"How can a man be righteous before God?" (9:2; 25:4)—answered by the death of Christ; and (3) death and immortality—"If a man dies, shall he live again?" (14:14)—answered by the resurrection of Christ.

What I have seen I will
declare,
18 What wise men have told,
Not hiding *anything received*
from their fathers,
19 To whom alone the land was
given,
And no alien passed among
them:
20 The wicked man writhes with
pain all *his* days,
And the number of years is
hidden from the oppressor.
21 [a]Dreadful sounds *are* in his
ears;
In prosperity the destroyer
comes upon [b]him.
22 He does not believe that he
will [c]return from darkness,
For a sword is waiting for him.
23 He wanders about for bread,
saying, 'Where *is it?*'
He knows that a [d]day of
darkness is ready at his
hand.
24 Trouble and anguish make him
afraid;
They overpower him, like a
king ready for battle.
25 For he stretches out his hand
against God,
And acts defiantly against the
Almighty,
26 Running stubbornly against
Him
With his strong, embossed
shield.

27 [e]"Though he has covered his
face with his fatness,
And made *his* waist heavy
with fat,
28 He dwells in desolate cities,
In houses which no one
inhabits,
Which are destined to become
ruins.
29 He will not be rich,
Nor will his wealth [f]continue,
Nor will his possessions
overspread the earth.
30 He will not depart from
darkness;
The flame will dry out his
branches,
And [g]by the breath of His
mouth he will go away.
31 Let him not trust in futile
things, deceiving himself,
For futility will be his reward.
32 It will be accomplished before
his time,

21
a Lit. *A sound of fears*
b Cp. 1 Th. 5:3
22
c Job 14:10–12
23
d Job 18:12
27
e Ps. 17:10
29
f Job 20:28; 27:16–17
30
g Job 4:9
34
h Cp. Job 12:6
35
i Ps. 7:14; Isa. 59:4; Hos. 10:13
CHAPTER 16
2
j Or *troublesome.* Job 13:4; 21:34
7
k Job 7:3
l Job 19:13–15
8
m Job 10:17
9
n Hos. 6:1
o Job 13:24; 33:10
10
p Ps. 22:13; 35:21

And his branch will not be
green.
33 He will shake off his unripe
grape like a vine,
And cast off his blossom like
an olive tree.
34 For the company of hypocrites
will be barren,
And fire will consume the
[h]tents of bribery.
35 [i]They conceive trouble and
bring forth futility;
Their womb prepares deceit."

Job's reply: his friends are miserable comforters

16 THEN Job answered and said:
2 "I have heard many such
things;
[j]Miserable comforters *are* you
all!
3 Shall words of wind have an
end?
Or what provokes you that you
answer?
4 I also could speak as you *do*,
If your soul were in my soul's
place.
I could heap up words against
you,
And shake my head at you;
5 *But* I would strengthen you
with my mouth,
And the comfort of my lips
would relieve *your grief.*

6 "Though I speak, my grief is
not relieved;
And *if* I remain silent, how am
I eased?
7 But now He has [k]worn me out;
You [l]have made desolate all
my company.
8 You have shriveled me up,
And it is a witness *against me;*
My leanness rises up against
me
And bears [m]witness to my face.
9 He [n]tears *me* in His wrath,
and hates me;
He gnashes at me with His
teeth;
My [o]adversary sharpens His
gaze on me.
10 They [p]gape at me with their
mouth,
They strike me reproachfully
on the cheek,
They gather together against
me.
11 God has delivered me to the
ungodly,

And turned me over to the hands of the wicked.
12 I was at ease, but He has [a]shattered me;
He also has taken *me* by my neck, and shaken me to pieces;
He has set me up for His [b]target,
13 His archers surround me.
He pierces my heart* and does not pity;
He pours out my gall on the ground.
14 He breaks me with wound upon wound;
He runs at me like a warrior.*
15 "I have sewn sackcloth over my skin,
And laid my [c]head* in the dust.
16 My face is flushed from weeping,
And on my eyelids *is* the shadow of death;
17 Although no violence *is* in my hands,
And my prayer *is* pure.
18 "O earth, do not cover my blood,
And let my cry have no *resting* place!
19 Surely even now [d]my witness *is* in heaven,
And my evidence *is* on high.
20 My friends scorn me;
My eyes pour out *tears* to God.
21 [e]Oh, that one might [f]plead for a man with God,
As a man *pleads* for his neighbor!
22 For when a few years are finished,
I shall go the way of no [g]return.

Job continues: will he rest in death? (v. 16)

17 "MY spirit is broken,
My days are extinguished,
The grave *is ready* for me.
2 *Are* not [h]mockers with me?
And does not my eye dwell on their provocation?
3 "Now put down a pledge for me with Yourself.
[i]Who *is* he *who* will shake hands with me?
4 For You have hidden their heart from [j]understanding;
Therefore You will not exalt *them*.

5 He who speaks flattery to *his* friends,
Even the eyes of his children will [k]fail.
6 "But He has made me a byword of the people,
And I have become one in whose face men spit.
7 My eye has also grown dim because of sorrow,
And all my members *are* like shadows.
8 Upright *men* are astonished at this,
And the innocent stirs himself up against the hypocrite.
9 Yet the righteous will hold to his [l]way,
And he who has [m]clean hands will be stronger and stronger.
10 "But please, come back again, all of you,*
For I shall not find *one* wise *man* among you.
11 My days are past,
My purposes are broken off,
Even the thoughts of my heart.
12 They change the night into day;
'The light *is* near,' *they say,* in the face of darkness.
13 If I wait *for* the [n]grave *as* my house,
If I make my bed in the darkness,
14 If I say to corruption, 'You *are* my father,'
And to the worm, 'You *are* my mother and my sister,'
15 Where then *is* my [o]hope?
As for my hope, who can see it?
16 *Will* they go down to the gates of [n]Sheol?
Shall *we have* rest together in the dust?"

Bildad's second speech: a series of proverbs

18 THEN [p]Bildad the Shuhite answered and said:
2 "How long *till* you put an end to words?
Gain understanding, and afterward we will speak.
3 Why are we counted as beasts,

12
a Job 9:17
b Job 7:20
15
c See Dt. 33:17, *note;* Job 30:19; Ps. 7:5
19
d Job 19:25–27; cp. Rom. 1:9
21
e Job 31:35
f Cp. Job 9:33
22
g Job 10:21
CHAPTER 17
2
h Job 12:4; 30:1,9; 34:7
3
i Prov. 6:1; 17:18; 22:26
4
j Job 12:20; 32:9
5
k Job 11:20
9
l Prov. 4:18
m Ps. 24:4
13
n See Hab. 2:5, *note;* cp. Lk. 16:23, *note*
15
o Job 7:6; 13:15; 14:19; 19:10
CHAPTER 18
1
p Job 8:1

*
16:13 Literally *kidneys* **16:14** Vulgate reads *giant.* **16:15** Literally *horn* **17:10** Following some Hebrew manuscripts, Septuagint, Syriac, and Vulgate; Masoretic Text and Targum read *all of them.*

And regarded as stupid in your sight?
4 You who tear yourself in anger,
Shall the earth be forsaken for you?
Or shall the rock be removed from its place?

5 "The light of the wicked indeed goes out,
And the flame of his fire does not shine.
6 The light is dark in his [a]tent,
And his [b]lamp beside him is put out.
7 The steps of his strength are shortened,
And his own counsel [c]casts him down.
8 For he is cast into a net by his own feet,
And he walks into a snare.
9 The net takes *him* by the heel,
And a snare lays hold of him.
10 A noose *is* hidden for him on the ground,
And a trap for him in the road.
11 Terrors frighten him on every side,
And drive him to his feet.
12 His strength is starved,
And [d]destruction *is* ready at his side.
13 It devours patches of his skin;
The firstborn of death devours his limbs.
14 He is uprooted from the shelter of his tent,
And they parade him before the king of terrors.
15 They dwell in his tent *who are* none of his;
Brimstone is scattered on his dwelling.
16 His roots are dried out below,
And his branch withers above.
17 [e]The memory of him perishes from the earth,
And he has no name among the renowned.*
18 He is driven from light into darkness,
And chased out of the world.
19 He has neither son nor posterity among his people,
Nor any remaining in his dwellings.
20 Those in the west are astonished [f]at his day,
As those in the east are frightened.
21 Surely such *are* the dwellings of the wicked,
And this *is* the place *of him* who does not know God."

Job's reply: he knows that his Redeemer lives (vv. 23–27)

19 THEN Job answered and said:
2 "How long will you torment my soul,
And break me in pieces with words?
3 These [g]ten times you have reproached me;
You are not ashamed *that* you have wronged me.*
4 And if indeed I have erred,
My error remains with me.
5 If indeed you exalt *yourselves* against me,
And plead my disgrace against me,
6 Know then that [h]God has wronged me,
And has surrounded me with His net.

7 "If I cry out concerning wrong, I am not heard.
If I cry aloud, *there is* no [i]justice.
8 [j]He has fenced up my way, so that I cannot pass;
And He has set darkness in my paths.
9 [k]He has stripped me of my glory,
And taken the crown *from* my head.
10 He breaks me down on every side,
And I am gone;
My [l]hope He has uprooted like a tree.
11 He has also kindled His wrath against me,
And He counts me as *one of* His [m]enemies.
12 His troops come together
And build up their road against me;
They encamp all around my tent.

13 [n]"He has removed my brothers far from me,
And my acquaintances are completely estranged from me.
14 My relatives have failed,

6 [a] vv. 14,15 [b] Job 21:17
7 [c] Job 5:12–13; 15:6
12 [d] Job 15:23
17 [e] Ps. 34:16
20 [f] Ps. 37:13
CHAPTER 19
3 [g] Cp. Num. 14:22; Neh. 4:12; Dan. 1:20
6 [h] Job 16:11; 27:2
7 [i] Job 6:29
8 [j] Job 3:23; Ps. 88:8
9 [k] Ps. 89:44
10 [l] Job 17:15–16
11 [m] Job 13:24; 33:10
13 [n] Ps. 31:11; 38:11; 69:8; 88:8, 18

*18:17 Literally *before the outside*, meaning distinguished, famous 19:3 A Jewish tradition reads *make yourselves strange to me*.

And my close friends have forgotten me.
15 Those who dwell in my house, and my maidservants,
Count me as a stranger;
I am an alien in their sight.
16 I call my servant, but he gives no answer;
I beg him with my mouth.
17 My breath is offensive to my wife,
And I am repulsive to the children of my own body.
18 Even young children [a]despise me;
I arise, and they speak against me.
19 All my close friends abhor me,
And those whom I love have turned against me.
20 My bone clings to my skin and to my flesh,
And I have escaped by the skin of my teeth.

21 "Have pity on me, have pity on me, O you my friends,
[b]For the hand of God has struck me!
22 Why do you persecute me as God *does*,
And are not satisfied with my flesh?

23 "Oh, that my words were written!
Oh, that they were inscribed in a book!
24 That they were engraved on a [1]rock
With an iron pen and lead, forever!
25 For I know *that* my [c]Redeemer lives,
And He shall [d]stand at last on the earth;
26 And after my skin is destroyed, this *I know,*
That [e]in my [2]flesh I shall [f]see God,
27 Whom I shall see for myself,
And my eyes shall behold, and not another.
How my heart yearns within me!
28 If you should say, 'How shall we persecute him?'—
Since the root of the matter is found in me,
29 Be afraid of the sword for yourselves;
For wrath *brings* the punishment of the sword,
That you may know *there is* a [g]judgment."

Zophar's final speech: the portion of the wicked (v. 29)

20 THEN [h]Zophar the Naamathite answered and said:
2 "Therefore my anxious thoughts make me answer,
Because of the turmoil within me.
3 I have heard the rebuke that reproaches me,
And the spirit of my understanding causes me to answer.

4 "Do you *not* know this of [i]old,
Since man was placed on earth,
5 That the [j]triumphing of the wicked is short,
And the joy of the hypocrite is *but* for a [k]moment?
6 Though his haughtiness mounts up to the heavens,
And his head reaches to the clouds,
7 *Yet* he will perish forever like his own refuse;
Those who have seen him will say, 'Where is he?'
8 He will fly away [l]like a dream, and not be found;
Yes, he [m]will be chased away like a vision of the night.
9 The eye *that* saw him will *see him* no more,
Nor will his place behold him anymore.
10 His children will seek the favor of the poor,
And his hands [n]will restore his wealth.
11 His bones are full of his youthful vigor,
But it will lie down with him in the dust.

12 "Though evil is sweet in his mouth,

18
a Job 17:6
21
b Job 1:11; Ps. 38:2
25
c Redemption (redeeming relative type): vv. 25–27; Ps. 19:14. (Gen. 48:16; Isa. 59:20, *note)*
d Resurrection: vv. 25–27; Ps. 16:9. (2 Ki. 4:35; 1 Cor. 15:52, *note)*
26
e Ps. 17:15; 1 Cor. 13:12; 1 Jn. 3:2
f Cp. Job 14:10–12
29
g Ps. 1:5; Eccl. 12:14
CHAPTER 20
1
h Job 11:1
4
i Job 8:8; 15:10
5
j Ps. 37:35–36
k Job 8:13; 13:16; 15:34; 27:8
8
l Ps. 73:20; 90:5
m Job 18:18; 27:21–23
10
n v. 18

[1](19:24) On a rock for permanence, because papyrus or skin would perish in time.
[2](19:26) This passage contains one of the sublimest expressions in the OT of faith in the living Redeemer, His personal appearance on earth, the personal participation of the godly in the resurrection of bliss because of Him, and the assured vision of God by the righteous. Cp. 14:13–15.

And he hides it under his
tongue,
13 *Though* he spares it and does
not forsake it,
But still keeps it in his mouth,
14 *Yet* his food in his stomach
turns sour;
It becomes cobra venom within
him.
15 He swallows down riches
And vomits them up again;
God casts them out of his
belly.
16 He will suck the poison of
cobras;
The viper's tongue will slay
him.
17 He will not see the streams,
The rivers flowing with honey
and cream.
18 He will restore that for which
he labored,
And will not swallow *it* down;
From the proceeds of business
He will get no enjoyment.
19 For he has [a]oppressed *and*
forsaken the poor,
He has violently seized a
house which he did not
build.

20 "Because he knows no
quietness in his heart,*
He will not save anything he
desires.
21 Nothing is left for him to eat;
Therefore his well-being will
not last.
22 In his self-sufficiency he will
be in distress;
Every hand of misery will
come against him.
23 *When* he is about to fill his
stomach,
God will cast on him the fury
of His wrath,
And will rain *it* on him while
he is eating.
24 He will flee from the iron
weapon;
A [b]bronze bow will pierce him
through.
25 It is drawn, and comes out of
the body;
Yes, the glittering *point comes*
out of his gall.
[c]Terrors *come* upon him;
26 Total darkness *is* reserved for
his treasures.
An unfanned fire will consume
him;
It shall go ill with him who is
left in his [d]tent.

27 The heavens will reveal his
iniquity,
And the earth will rise up
against him.
28 The increase of his house will
[e]depart,
And his goods will flow away
in the day of His [f]wrath.
29 [g]This *is* the portion from God
for a wicked man,
The heritage appointed to him
by God."

Job's answer: the sovereign God will deal with the wicked

21 THEN Job answered and said:
2 "Listen carefully to my speech,
And let this be your
consolation.
3 Bear with me that I may
speak,
And after I have spoken, keep
mocking.

4 "As for me, *is* my complaint
against man?
And if *it were,* why should I
not be impatient?
5 Look at me and be astonished;
Put *your* hand over *your*
mouth.
6 Even when I remember I am
terrified,
And trembling takes hold of
my flesh.
7 [h]Why do the wicked live *and*
become old,
Yes, become mighty in power?
8 Their descendants are
established with them in
their sight,
And their offspring before
their eyes.
9 Their houses *are* safe from
fear,
[i]Neither *is* the rod of God upon
them.
10 Their bull breeds without
failure;
Their cow calves without
miscarriage.
11 They send forth their little
ones like a flock,
And their children dance.
12 They sing to the tambourine
and harp,
And rejoice to the sound of the
flute.
13 They spend their days [j]in
wealth,

19 *a* Lit. *crushed.* Job 24:2–4; 35:9
24 *b* Ps. 18:34
25 *c* Job 18:11
26 *d* Job 18:14, 15
28 *e* Cp. Dt. 28:31 *f* Job 21:30
29 *g* Job 27:13; 31:2–3
CHAPTER 21
7 *h* Job 12:6; Ps. 17:10, 14; 73:3, 12; Jer. 12:1; Hab. 1:16
9 *i* Ps. 73:5
13 *j* Or *in mirth;* or *in good*

* **20:20** Literally *belly*

And in a moment go down to the [a]grave.*
14 Yet they say to God, 'Depart from us,
For we do not desire the knowledge of Your ways.
15 [b]Who *is* the Almighty, that we should serve Him?
And [c]what profit do we have if we pray to Him?'
16 Indeed their prosperity *is* not in their hand;
The [d]counsel of the wicked is far from me.

17 "How often is the lamp of the wicked put out?
How often does their destruction come upon them,
The sorrows [e]*God* distributes in His anger?
18 They are like straw before the wind,
And like chaff that a storm [f]carries away.
19 *They say*, 'God lays up one's* [g]iniquity for his children';
Let Him recompense him, that he may know *it*.
20 Let his eyes see his destruction,
And let him [h]drink of the wrath of the Almighty.
21 For what does he care about his household after him,
When the number of his months is cut in half?

22 "Can *anyone* [i]teach God knowledge,
Since He judges those on high?
23 One dies in his full strength,
Being wholly at ease and secure;
24 His pails* are full of milk,
And the marrow of his bones is moist.
25 Another man dies in the bitterness of his soul,
Never having eaten with pleasure.
26 They lie down alike in the dust,
And worms cover them.

27 "Look, I know your thoughts,
And the schemes *with which* you would wrong me.
28 For you say,
'Where *is* the house of the [j]prince?
And where *is* the tent,*
The dwelling place of the wicked?'

13
a See Hab. 2:5, *note;* cp. Lk. 16:23, *note*
15
b Job 34:9; cp. Ex. 5:2
c Job 35:3; Mal. 3:14
16
d Job 22:18; Ps. 1:1; Prov. 1:10
17
e Lk. 12:46
18
f Lit. *steals away*
19
g i.e. *the punishment of his iniquity*
20
h Ps. 75:8; Isa. 51:17; Jer. 25:15; Rev. 14:10; 19:15
22
i Isa. 40:13; 45:9; Rom. 11:34; 1 Cor. 2:16
28
j Cp. Job 20:6–9
30
k Day (of destruction): v. 30; Isa. 34:2. (Job 21:30; Rev. 20:11)
CHAPTER 22
1
l Job 4:1; 15:1; 42:9
2
m Job 35:7; cp. Lk. 17:10
3
n See Phil. 3:12, *note*
5
o Cp. Job 1:1; 13:23; 31:5–34
6
p Ex. 22:26–27; Dt. 24:10
7
q Dt. 15:7; Job 31:17; Isa. 58:7; Ezek. 18:7; Mt. 25:42

29 Have you not asked those who travel the road?
And do you not know their signs?
30 For the wicked are reserved for the [k]day of doom;
They shall be brought out on the day of wrath.
31 Who condemns his way to his face?
And who repays him *for what* he has done?
32 Yet he shall be brought to the grave,
And a vigil kept over the tomb.
33 The clods of the valley shall be sweet to him;
Everyone shall follow him,
As countless *have gone* before him.
34 How then can you comfort me with empty words,
Since falsehood remains in your answers?"

Eliphaz's final speech: he accuses and exhorts Job

22 THEN [l]Eliphaz the Temanite answered and said:
2 [m]"Can a man be profitable to God,
Though he who is wise may be profitable to himself?
3 *Is it* any pleasure to the Almighty that you are righteous?
Or *is it* gain *to Him* that you make your ways [n]blameless?
4 "Is it because of your fear of Him that He corrects you,
And enters into judgment with you?
5 *Is* not your wickedness great,
And your iniquity [o]without end?
6 For you have [p]taken pledges from your brother for no reason,
And stripped the naked of their clothing.
7 You have not given the weary water to drink,
And [q]you have withheld bread from the hungry.
8 But the mighty man possessed the land,
And the honorable man dwelt in it.

*
21:13 Or *Sheol* **21:19** Literally *his*
21:24 Septuagint and Vulgate read *bowels;* Syriac reads *sides;* Targum reads *breasts.* **21:28** Vulgate omits *the tent.*

9 You have sent widows away
empty,
And the strength of the
fatherless was crushed.
10 Therefore snares *are* all
around you,
And sudden fear troubles you,
11 Or darkness *so that* you
cannot see;
And an abundance of water
covers you.

12 "Is not God in the height of
heaven?
And see the highest stars, how
lofty they are!
13 And you say, 'What does God
know?
Can He judge through the deep
darkness?
14 [a]Thick clouds cover Him, so
that He cannot see,
And He walks above the circle
of heaven.'
15 Will you keep to the old way
Which wicked men have trod,
16 Who were cut down before
their time,
Whose [b]foundations were
swept away by a [c]flood?
17 They said to God, 'Depart from
us!
What can the Almighty do to
[d]them?'*
18 Yet He filled their houses with
good *things;*
But the counsel of the wicked
is far from me.
19 "The righteous see *it* and are
glad,
And the innocent laugh at
them:
20 'Surely our adversaries* are
cut down,
And the fire consumes their
remnant.'

21 "Now acquaint yourself with
Him, and be at peace;
Thereby good will come to
you.
22 Receive, please, [e]instruction
from His mouth,
And [f]lay up His words in your
heart.
23 If you return to the Almighty,
you will be built up;
You will remove iniquity far
from your [g]tents.
24 Then you will lay your gold in
the dust,
And the *gold* of Ophir among
the stones of the brooks.
25 Yes, the Almighty will be your
gold*
And your precious silver;
26 For then you will have your
delight in the Almighty,
And lift up your face to God.
27 You will make your prayer to
Him,
He will hear you,
And you will pay your vows.
28 You will also declare a thing,
And it will be established for
you;
So light will shine on your
ways.
29 When they cast *you* down, and
you say, 'Exaltation *will
come!'*
Then He will save the [h]humble
person.
30 He will *even* deliver one who
is not innocent;
Yes, he will be delivered by
the purity of your hands."

Job replies: he longs for God (v. 3)

23 THEN Job answered and said:
2 "Even today my [i]complaint is
bitter;
My* hand is listless because of
my groaning.
3 [j]Oh, that I knew where I might
find Him,
That I might come to His seat!
4 I would present *my* case before
Him,
And fill my mouth with
arguments.
5 I would know the words *which*
He would answer me,
And understand what He
would say to me.
6 [k]Would He contend with me in
His great power?
No! But He would take *note* of
me.
7 There the upright could reason
with Him,
And I would be delivered
forever from my Judge.

8 [l]"Look, I go forward, but He is
not *there,*
And backward, but I cannot
perceive Him;
9 When He works on the left
hand, I cannot behold *Him;*

14
[a] Ps. 139:11–12
16
[b] Job 14:19; Ps. 90:5; Isa. 28:2; Mt. 7:26–27
[c] Cp. Gen. 7:11
17
[d] 2 Pet. 2:9
22
[e] Job 6:10; 23:12; Prov. 2:6
[f] Ps. 119:11
23
[g] Job 11:14
29
[h] Lit. *him who has low eyes.* Job 5:11; Prov. 29:23; Mt. 23:12; Jas. 4:6; 1 Pet. 5:5
CHAPTER 23
2
[i] Job 7:11
3
[j] Job 13:3, 18; 16:21; 31:35
6
[k] Cp. Isa. 57:15–18
8
[l] Job 9:11

*
22:17 Septuagint and Syriac read *us.*
22:20 Septuagint reads *substance.* **22:25** The ancient versions suggest *defense;* Hebrew reads *gold* as in verse 24. **23:2** Following Masoretic Text, Targum, and Vulgate; Septuagint and Syriac read *His.*

When He turns to the right hand, I cannot see *Him.*
10 But [a]He [b]knows the way that I take;
When He has [c]tested me, I shall come forth [1]as gold.
11 My foot has held fast to His steps;
I have kept His way and not turned aside.
12 I have not departed from the [d]commandment of His lips;
I have treasured the words of His mouth
More than my necessary *food.*

13 "But He *is* unique, and who can [e]make Him change?
And *whatever* His soul desires, *that* He does.
14 For He performs *what is* appointed for me,
And many such *things are* with Him.
15 Therefore I am terrified at His presence;
When I consider *this,* I am afraid of Him.
16 For God made my heart weak,
And the Almighty terrifies me;
17 Because I was not [f]cut off from the presence of darkness,
And He did *not* hide deep darkness from my face.

Job continues: God seems indifferent to the wicked

24 "*SINCE* [g]times are not hidden from the Almighty,
Why do those who know Him see not His [h]days?

2 "*Some* remove [i]landmarks;
They seize flocks violently and feed *on them;*
3 They drive away the donkey of the fatherless;
They take the widow's ox as a [j]pledge.
4 They push the [k]needy off the road;
All the poor of the land are forced to hide.
5 Indeed, *like* wild donkeys in the desert,
They go out to their work, searching for food.
The wilderness *yields* food for them *and* for *their* children.

10
a Ps. 139:1–3
b Ps. 1:6
c *Test/tempt:* v. 10; Job 34:36. (Gen. 3:1; Jas. 1:14, *note*)
12
d Job 6:10; 22:22
13
e Ps. 33:11; 115:3
17
f Job 10:18–19
CHAPTER 24
1
g Acts 1:7
h Isa. 2:12; Jer. 46:10
2
i Dt. 19:14; 27:17
3
j Job 22:9
4
k Job 29:16
7
l Ex. 22:26–27; Jas. 2:15–16
8
m Cp. Lam. 4:5
10
n Job 31:19
12
o Cp. Job 9:23–24; 19:7; 30:20; Eccl. 8:11–13
15
p Prov. 7:9
16
q Cp. Jn. 3:19–20

6 They gather their fodder in the field
And glean in the vineyard of the wicked.
7 They spend the night naked, without clothing,
And have no covering in the [l]cold.
8 They are wet with the showers of the mountains,
And [m]huddle around the rock for want of shelter.

9 "*Some* snatch the fatherless from the breast,
And take a pledge from the poor.
10 They cause *the poor* to go naked, without [n]clothing;
And they take away the sheaves from the hungry.
11 They press out oil within their walls,
And tread winepresses, yet suffer thirst.
12 The dying groan in the city,
And the souls of the wounded cry out;
Yet God does not [o]charge *them* with wrong.

13 "There are those who rebel against the light;
They do not know its ways
Nor abide in its paths.
14 The murderer rises with the light;
He kills the poor and needy;
And in the night he is like a thief.
15 The [p]eye of the adulterer waits for the twilight,
Saying, 'No eye will see me';
And he disguises *his* face.
16 In the [q]dark they break into houses
Which they marked for themselves in the daytime;
They do not know the light.
17 For the morning is the same to them as the shadow of death;
If *someone* recognizes *them,*
They are in the terrors of the shadow of death.

18 "They *should be* swift on the face of the waters,
Their portion *should be* cursed in the earth,
So that no *one would* turn into the way of their vineyards.

[1](23:10) This is probably the high point in Job's search for a solution to his problem.

19 As drought and heat consume
the snow waters,
So the [a]grave* *consumes*
those who have sinned.
20 The womb *should* forget him,
The worm *should* feed sweetly
on him;
[b]He *should* be remembered no
more,
And wickedness *should* be
broken like a tree.
21 For he preys on the barren
who do not bear,
And does no good for the
widow.

22 "But *God* draws the mighty
away with His power;
He rises up, but no *man* is sure
of life.
23 He gives them security, and
they rely *on it;*
[c]Yet His eyes *are* on their ways.
24 They are exalted for a little
while,
Then they are gone.
They are brought low;
They are taken out of the way
like all *others;*
They dry out like the heads of
grain.

25 "Now if *it is* not *so,* who will
prove me a liar,
And make my speech worth
nothing?"

Bildad's final speech: the problem is beyond man

25 THEN [d]Bildad the Shuhite answered and said:

2 "Dominion and fear *belong* to
Him;
He makes peace in His high
places.
3 Is there any number to His
[e]armies?
Upon whom does His light not
rise?
4 [f]How then can man be
righteous before God?
Or how can he be [g]pure *who*
is born of a woman?
5 If even the moon does not
shine,
And the stars are not pure in
His [h]sight,
6 How much less man, *who is* a
maggot,
And a son of man, *who is* a
[i]worm?"

Job replies: Bildad rebuked; the greatness of God affirmed

26 BUT Job answered and said:

2 "How have you helped *him who*
is without power?
How have you saved the arm
that has no strength?
3 How have you counseled *one*
who has no wisdom?
And *how* have you declared
sound advice to many?
4 To whom have you uttered
words?
And whose spirit came from
you?

5 [j]"The dead tremble,
Those under the waters and
those inhabiting them.
6 [k]Sheol *is* naked before Him,
And Destruction has no
covering.
7 He stretches out the north over
empty space;
He hangs the earth on nothing.
8 He binds up the water in His
thick clouds,
Yet the clouds are not broken
under it.
9 He covers the face of *His*
throne,
And spreads His cloud over it.
10 [l]He drew a circular horizon on
the face of the waters,
At the boundary of light and
darkness.
11 The pillars of heaven tremble,
And are astonished at His
rebuke.
12 He stirs up the sea with His
power,
And by His understanding He
breaks up the [m]storm.
13 By His [n]Spirit He adorned the
heavens;
His hand pierced the fleeing
serpent.
14 Indeed these *are* the mere
edges of His ways,
And how small a whisper we
hear of Him!
But the thunder of His power
who can understand?"

Job continues: he maintains his righteousness and deplores wickedness (vv. 6,13)

27 MOREOVER Job continued his discourse, and said:

*24:19 Or *Sheol*

19
a See Hab. 2:5, *note;* cp. Lk. 16:23, *note*
20
b Prov. 10:7
23
c Ps. 11:4; Prov. 15:3
CHAPTER 25
1
d Job 8:1; 18:1
3
e Cp. Mt. 22:7
4
f Job 4:17; 15:14; Ps. 130:3; 143:2
g Job 14:4
5
h Job 15:15
6
i Ps. 22:6
CHAPTER 26
5
j Cp. Isa. 14:9
6
k Cp. vv. 6–14 with Job 9:5–10; Ps. 139:8–11; Prov. 15:11; Heb. 4:13; see Hab. 2:5, *note;* cp. Lk. 16:23, *note*
10
l Job 38:8; Ps. 33:7; 104:9; Prov. 8:29; Jer. 5:22
12
m Job 9:13
13
n *Holy Spirit* (OT): v. 13; Job 33:4. (Gen. 1:2; Zech. 12:10)

2 "*As* God lives, *who* has taken
away my [a]justice,
And the Almighty, *who* has
made my soul bitter,
3 As long as my breath *is* in me,
And the [b]breath of God in my
nostrils,
4 My lips will not speak
[c]wickedness,
Nor my tongue utter deceit.
5 Far be it from me
That I should say you are
right;
Till I die I will not put away
my integrity from me.
6 My [d]righteousness I hold fast,
and will not let it go;
My heart shall not reproach
me as long as I live.

7 "May my enemy be like the
wicked,
And he who rises up against
me like the unrighteous.
8 [e]For what is the hope of the
hypocrite,
Though he may gain *much,*
If God takes away his [f]life?
9 Will God [g]hear his cry
When trouble comes upon
him?
10 Will he delight himself in the
Almighty?
Will he always call on God?

11 "I will teach you about the hand
of God;
What *is* with the Almighty I
will not conceal.
12 Surely all of you have seen *it;*
Why then do you behave with
complete nonsense?

13 "This is the portion of a wicked
man with God,
And the heritage of
oppressors, received from
the Almighty:
14 If his children are multiplied, *it*
is for the sword;
And his offspring shall not be
satisfied with bread.
15 Those who survive him shall
be buried in death,
And their* widows shall not
weep,
16 Though he heaps up silver like
dust,
And piles up clothing like
clay—
17 He may pile *it* up, [h]but the just
will wear *it,*
And the innocent will divide
the silver.
18 He builds his house like a
moth,*
Like a [i]booth *which* a
watchman makes.
19 The rich man will lie down,
But not be gathered *up;**
He opens his eyes,
And he *is* [j]no more.
20 [k]Terrors overtake him like a
flood;
A tempest steals him away in
the night.
21 The east wind carries him
away, and he is gone;
It sweeps him out of his place.
22 It hurls against him and does
not [l]spare;
He flees desperately from its
power.
23 *Men* shall clap their hands at
him,
And shall hiss him out of his
place.

Job continues: the search for wisdom

28 "SURELY there is a mine for
silver,
And a place *where* gold is
refined.
2 Iron is taken from the earth,
And copper *is* smelted *from*
ore.
3 *Man* puts an end to darkness,
And searches every recess
For ore in the darkness and
the shadow of death.
4 He breaks open a shaft away
from people;
In places forgotten by feet
They hang far away from men;
They swing to and fro.
5 *As for* the earth, from it comes
bread,
But underneath it is turned up
as by fire;
6 Its stones *are* the source of
sapphires,
And it contains gold dust.
7 *That* path no bird knows,
Nor has the falcon's eye seen
it.
8 The proud lions* have not
trodden it,
Nor has the fierce lion passed
over it.
9 He puts his hand on the flint;

CHAPTER 27
2 a Job 34:5
3 b Gen. 2:7; cp. Job 32:8; 33:4
4 c Cp. Job 13:7
6 d Job 2:3; 33:9; cp. 23:10; 42:1–6
8 e Mt. 16:26; Lk. 12:20
f Job 12:10
9 g Job 35:12–13; Ps. 18:41; Prov. 1:28; Jer. 14:12; Mic. 3:4
17 h Prov. 28:8; Eccl. 2:26
18 i Cp. Isa. 1:8
19 j Job 20:7
20 k Job 18:11
22 l Jer. 13:14; Ezek. 5:11

*
27:15 Literally *his* **27:18** Following Masoretic Text and Vulgate; Septuagint and Syriac read *spider* (compare 8:14); Targum reads *decay.*
27:19 Following Masoretic Text and Targum; Septuagint and Syriac read *But shall not add* (that is, do it again); Vulgate reads *But take away nothing.* **28:8** Literally *sons of pride,* figurative of the great lions

He overturns the mountains at
the roots.
10 He cuts out channels in the
rocks,
And his eye sees every
precious thing.
11 He dams up the streams [a]from
trickling;
What is hidden he brings forth
to light.

12 "But [b]where can wisdom be
found?
And where *is* the place of
understanding?
13 Man does not know its [c]value,
Nor is it found in the land of
the living.
14 The deep says, '*It is* not in me';
And the sea says, '*It is* not
with me.'
15 It cannot be purchased for
[d]gold,
Nor can silver be weighed *for*
its price.
16 It cannot be valued in the gold
of Ophir,
In precious onyx or sapphire.
17 Neither [e]gold nor crystal can
equal it,
Nor can it be exchanged for
jewelry of fine gold.
18 No mention shall be made of
coral or quartz,
For the price of wisdom *is*
above [f]rubies.
19 The topaz of Ethiopia cannot
equal it,
Nor can it be valued in pure
[g]gold.

20 [h]"From where then does wisdom
come?
And where *is* the place of
understanding?
21 It is hidden from the eyes of
all living,
And concealed from the birds
of the air.
22 [i]Destruction and Death say,
'We have heard a report about
it with our ears.'
23 [j]God understands its way,
And He knows its place.
24 For He looks to the ends of the
earth,
And sees under the whole
heavens,
25 [k]To establish a weight for the
wind,
And apportion the waters by
measure.
26 When He made a law for the
rain,
And a path for the thunderbolt,
27 Then He saw *wisdom** and
declared it;
He prepared it, indeed, He
searched it out.
28 And to man He said,
'Behold, the [l]fear of the Lord,
that *is* wisdom,
And to depart from evil *is*
understanding.' "

The greatness of Job's past

29 JOB further continued his discourse, and said:

2 "Oh, that I were as *in* months
[m]past,
As *in* the days *when* God
[n]watched over me;
3 When His [o]lamp shone upon
my head,
And when by His light I
walked *through* darkness;
4 Just as I was in the days of my
prime,
When the friendly counsel of
God *was* over my [p]tent;
5 When the Almighty *was* yet
with me,
When my children *were*
around me;
6 When my steps were bathed
with cream,*
And the rock poured out rivers
of oil for me!

7 "When I went out to the gate by
the city,
When I took my seat in the
open square,
8 The young men saw me and
hid,
And the aged arose *and* stood;
9 The princes refrained from
talking,
And put *their* hand on their
mouth;
10 The voice of nobles was
hushed,
And their tongue stuck to the
roof of their mouth.
11 When the ear heard, then it
blessed me,
And when the eye saw, then it
approved me;
12 [q]Because I delivered the poor
who cried out,
The fatherless and *the one
who* had no helper.
13 The blessing of a perishing
man came upon me,

CHAPTER 28
11 a Lit. *from weeping*
12 b v. 20; Eccl. 7:24; cp. Prov. 2:1–22
13 c Prov. 3:15
15 d Prov. 3:14
17 e Prov. 8:10; 16:16
18 f Prov. 3:15; 8:11
19 g Prov. 8:19
20 h v. 12; Ps. 111:10; Prov. 1:7; 9:10
22 i Job 28:14
23 j Cp. vv. 23–28 with Prov. 8:22–31
25 k Ps. 135:7
28 l Ps. 111:10; Prov. 1:7; 9:10; see Ps. 19:9, *note*

CHAPTER 29
2 m Job 1:1–5
n Job 1:10
3 o Ps. 27:1
4 p Job 20:26
12 q Job 31:16–23

*28:27 Literally *it* 29:6 Masoretic Text reads *wrath*; ancient versions and some Hebrew manuscripts read *cream* (compare 20:17).

And I caused the widow's
heart to sing for joy.
14 I put on [a]righteousness, and it
clothed me;
My justice *was* like a robe and
a turban.
15 I *was* [b]eyes to the blind,
And I *was* feet to the lame.
16 I *was* a father to the [c]poor,
And I searched out the case
that I did not know.
17 I broke the fangs of the
wicked,
And plucked the victim from
his teeth.

18 "Then I said, 'I shall die in my
nest,
And multiply *my* days as the
sand.
19 My root *is* spread out to the
waters,
And the dew lies all night on
my branch.
20 My glory *is* fresh within me,
And my bow is renewed in my
hand.'

21 "*Men* listened to me and waited,
And kept silence for my
counsel.
22 After my words they did not
speak again,
And my speech settled on
them *as dew.*
23 They waited for me *as* for the
rain,
And they opened their mouth
wide *as* for the spring rain.
24 *If* I mocked at them, they did
not believe *it,*
And the light of my
countenance they did not
cast down.
25 I chose the way for them, and
sat as chief;
So I dwelt as a [d]king in the
army,
As one *who* [e]comforts
mourners.

The humiliation of Job's present state

30 "BUT now they mock at me,
men younger than I,
Whose fathers I disdained to
put with the dogs of my
flock.
2 Indeed, what *profit* is the
strength of their hands to
me?
Their vigor has perished.
3 *They are* gaunt from want and
famine,
Fleeing late to the wilderness,
desolate and waste,
4 Who pluck mallow by the
bushes,
And broom tree roots *for* their
food.
5 They were driven out from
among *men,*
They shouted at them as *at* a
thief.
6 *They had* to live in the clefts of
the valleys,
In caves of the earth and the
rocks.
7 Among the bushes they
brayed,
Under the nettles they nestled.
8 *They were* sons of fools,
Yes, sons of vile men;
They were scourged from the
land.

9 "And now I am their taunting
song;
Yes, [f]I am their byword.
10 They abhor me, they keep far
from me;
They do not hesitate to [g]spit in
my face.
11 Because He has loosed my*
bowstring and afflicted me,
They have [h]cast off restraint
before me.
12 At *my* right *hand* the rabble
arises;
[i]They push away my feet,
And they raise against me
their ways of destruction.
13 They break up my path,
They promote my calamity;
They have no helper.
14 They come as broad breakers;
Under the ruinous storm they
roll along.
15 Terrors are turned upon me;
They pursue my honor as the
wind,
And my prosperity has passed
like a cloud.

16 "And now my [j]soul is [k]poured
out because of my *plight;*
The days of affliction take hold
of me.
17 My bones are pierced in me at
night,
And my gnawing pains take no
rest.
18 By great force my garment is
disfigured;

14 *a Righteousness* (garment): v. 14; Ps. 132:9. (Gen. 3:21; Rev. 19:8)
15 *b* Cp. Lev. 19:14
16 *c* Prov. 29:7
25 *d* Cp. Job 1:3
e Cp. Job 16:2
CHAPTER 30
9 *f* Job 17:6; Ps. 35:15; 69:12; Lam. 3:14, 63
10 *g* Num. 12:14; Dt. 25:9; Isa. 50:6; Mt. 26:67; 27:30
11 *h* Job 12:18
12 *i* Job 19:12
16 *j* Ps. 42:4
k Ps. 22:14

* **30:11** Following Masoretic Text, Syriac, and Targum; Septuagint and Vulgate read *His.*

It binds me about as the collar
of my coat.
19 He has cast me into the mire,
And I have become like dust
and ashes.

20 "I [a]cry out to You, but You do
not answer me;
I stand up, and You regard me.
21 *But* You have become cruel to
me;
With the strength of Your
hand You [b]oppose me.
22 You lift me up to the wind and
cause me to ride *on it;*
You spoil my success.
23 For I know *that* You will bring
me *to* death,
And *to* the house [c]appointed
for all living.

24 "Surely He would not stretch
out *His* hand against a heap
of ruins,
If they cry out when He
destroys *it.*
25 Have I not wept for him who
was in trouble?
Has *not* my soul grieved for
the poor?
26 But [d]when I looked for good,
evil came *to me;*
And when I waited for light,
then came darkness.
27 My heart is in turmoil and
cannot rest;
Days of affliction confront me.
28 [e]I go about mourning, but not
in the sun;
I stand up in the assembly *and*
cry out for help.
29 [f]I am a brother of jackals,
And a companion of ostriches.
30 My [g]skin grows black and
falls from me;
My [h]bones burn with fever.
31 My harp is *turned* to
mourning,
And my flute to the voice of
those who weep.

Job concludes: he justifies himself

31 "I HAVE made a covenant
with my eyes;
Why then should I look upon a
[i]young woman?
2 For what *is* the allotment of
God from above,
And the inheritance of the
Almighty from on high?
3 *Is* it not destruction for the
wicked,
And disaster for the workers
of iniquity?
4 Does He not see my ways,
And count all my steps?

5 "If I have walked with
falsehood,
Or if my foot has hastened to
deceit,
6 [j]Let me be weighed on honest
scales,
That God may know my
[k]integrity.
7 If my step has turned from the
way,
Or my heart walked after my
eyes,
Or if any spot adheres to my
hands,
8 [l]*Then* let me sow, and another
eat;
Yes, let my harvest be rooted
out.

9 "If my heart has been enticed
by a woman,
Or *if* I have lurked at my
neighbor's door,
10 *Then* let my wife grind for
[m]another,
And let others bow down over
her.
11 For that *would be* wickedness;
Yes, [n]it *would be* iniquity
deserving of judgment.
12 For that *would be* a fire *that*
consumes to destruction,
And would root out all my
increase.

13 "If I have [o]despised the cause
of my male or female
servant
When they complained against
me,
14 What then shall I do when God
rises up?
[p]When He punishes, how shall I
answer Him?
15 [q]Did not He who made me in
the womb make them?
Did not the same One fashion
us in the womb?

16 "If I have kept the poor from
their desire,
Or caused the eyes of the
widow to [r]fail,
17 Or eaten my morsel by myself,
So that the fatherless could not
eat of it
18 (But from my youth I reared
him as a father,

---

20 a Job 19:7
21 b Job 10:3; 16:9,14; 19:6,22
23 c Heb. 9:27
26 d Jer. 8:15
28 e Ps. 38:6; 42:9; 43:2
29 f Cp. Ps. 102:6; Mic. 1:8
30 g Ps. 119:83; Lam. 4:8; 5:10
h Ps. 102:3
CHAPTER 31
1 i Mt. 5:28
6 j Lit. *Let Him weigh me in balances of justice*
k Job 6:29; 27:5–6
8 l Lev. 26:16; Dt. 28:30, 38
10 m 2 Sam. 12:11; Jer. 8:10
11 n v. 28; Gen. 38:24; Lev. 20:10; Dt. 22:22
13 o Dt. 24:14
14 p Ps. 44:21
15 q Job 34:19; Prov. 14:31; 22:2; Mal. 2:10
16 r Job 29:12

And from my mother's womb I guided *the widow**);
19 If I have seen anyone perish for lack of clothing,
Or any poor *man* without covering;
20 If his heart* has not [a]blessed me,
And *if* he was *not* warmed with the fleece of my sheep;
21 If I have raised my hand [b]against the fatherless,
When I saw I had help in the gate;
22 *Then* let my arm fall from my shoulder,
Let my arm be torn from the socket.
23 For [c]destruction *from* God *is* a terror to me,
And because of His magnificence I cannot endure.

24 "If I have made [d]gold my hope,
Or said to fine gold, '*You are* my confidence';
25 If I have rejoiced because my wealth *was* great,
And because my hand had gained much;
26 If I have observed the sun* when it shines,
Or the moon moving *in* brightness,
27 So that my heart has been secretly enticed,
And my mouth has kissed my hand;
28 This also *would be* an iniquity *deserving of* judgment,
For I would have denied God *who is* above.

29 "If I have rejoiced at the destruction of him who hated me,
Or lifted myself up when evil found him
30 (Indeed I have not allowed my mouth to sin
By asking for a curse on his soul);
31 If the men of my [e]tent have not said,
'Who is there that has not been satisfied with his meat?'
32 (*But* no sojourner had to lodge in the street,
For I have opened my doors to the traveler*);
33 If I have covered my transgressions as [f]Adam,
By hiding my iniquity in my bosom,
34 Because I feared the great multitude,
And dreaded the contempt of families,
So that I kept silence
And did not go out of the door—
35 [g]Oh, that I had one to hear me!
Here is my mark.
Oh, that the Almighty would answer me,
That my [h]Prosecutor had written a book!
36 Surely I would carry it on my shoulder,
And bind it on me *like* a crown;
37 I would declare to Him the number of my steps;
Like a prince I would approach Him.

38 "If my land cries out against me,
And its furrows weep together;
39 If I have eaten its fruit* without money,
Or [i]caused its owners to lose their lives;
40 *Then* let thistles grow instead of wheat,
And weeds instead of barley."

The words of Job are ended.

III. Elihu's Monologue, 32—37

Though a young man he rebukes Job and others

32 [1]SO these three men ceased answering Job, because he *was* [j]righteous in his own eyes.

20 a Cp. Dt. 24:13
21 b Job 22:9
23 c i.e. *calamity*. v. 3; 21:17
24 d Mt. 6:19–20
31 e Job 20:26
33 f Gen. 3:10; Prov. 28:13
35 g Job 19:7 h Job 13:24; 33:10
39 i Cp. 1 Ki. 21:19
CHAPTER 32
1 j Job 6:29; 31:6; 33:9

*
31:18 Literally *her* (compare verse 16)
31:20 Literally *loins* 31:26 Literally *light*
31:32 Following Septuagint, Syriac, Targum, and Vulgate; Masoretic Text reads *road*.
31:39 Literally *its strength*

[1](32:1) Despite minor differences, Eliphaz, Bildad, and Zophar agree in their explanation of Job's afflictions—namely, that Job is a hypocrite. Otherwise, according to their conception of God, Job's sufferings would be unjust. Job, though himself the sufferer, will not so accuse the justice of God, and his self-defense is complete. Before God he is guilty, helpless, and undone, and there is no mediator (9:33). Later, his faith is rewarded by a revelation of the coming Redeemer, and of the resurrection (19:25–27). But Eliphaz, Bildad, and Zophar are also sinners before God, and yet they are not afflicted. Job refutes the theory of the three that

2 Then the wrath of [1]Elihu, the son
of Barachel the [a]Buzite, of the family
of Ram, was aroused against Job; his
wrath was aroused because he [b]justified [c]himself rather than God.
3 Also against his three friends his
wrath was aroused, because they had
found no answer, and *yet* had condemned Job.
4 Now because they *were* years
older than he, Elihu had waited to
speak to Job.*
5 When Elihu saw that *there was*
no answer in the mouth of these three
men, his wrath was aroused.
6 So Elihu, the son of Barachel the
Buzite, answered and said:

"I *am* [d]young in years, and you
are very old;
Therefore I was afraid,
And dared not declare my
opinion to you.
7 I said, 'Age* should speak,
And multitude of years should
teach wisdom.'
8 But *there is* a [e]spirit in man,
And the [f]breath of the
Almighty gives him
understanding.
9 Great men* are not *always*
wise,
Nor do the aged *always*
understand justice.

10 "Therefore I say, 'Listen to me,
I also will declare my opinion.'
11 Indeed I waited for your
words,
I listened to your reasonings,
while you searched out what
to say.
12 I paid close attention to you;
And surely not one of you
convinced Job,
Or answered his words—
13 [g]Lest you say,
'We have found wisdom';
God will vanquish him, not
man.
14 Now he has not directed *his*
words against me;
So I will not answer him with
your words.

15 "They are dismayed and answer
no more;
Words escape them.
16 And I have waited, because
they did not speak,
Because they stood still *and*
answered no more.
17 I also will answer my part,
I too will declare my opinion.
18 For I am full of words;
The spirit within me [h]compels
me.
19 Indeed my belly *is* like wine
that has no vent;
It is ready to burst like new
wineskins.
20 I will speak, that I may find
relief;
I must open my lips and
answer.
21 Let me not, I pray, show
partiality to anyone;
Nor let me flatter any man.
22 For I do not know how to
flatter,
Else my Maker would soon
take me [i]away.

Elihu continues: he claims to be God's spokesman on behalf of His righteousness

33

"BUT please, Job, hear my
speech,
And listen to all my words.
2 Now, I open my mouth;
My tongue speaks in my
mouth.
3 My words *come* from my
upright heart;
My lips utter pure knowledge.
4 The [j]Spirit of God has made
me,
And the breath of the
Almighty [k]gives me life.
5 If you can answer me,
Set *your words* in order before
me;
Take your stand.
6 [l]Truly I *am* as your
spokesman* before God;

2 *a* Gen. 22:21 *b* Job 27:5–6 *c* Lit. *his soul*
6 *d* Lev. 19:32
8 *e* Cp. Job 27:3; 33:4 *f* 1 Ki. 3:12; 4:29; Job 35:11; 38:36; Prov. 2:6; Eccl. 2:26; Dan. 1:17; 2:21; Mt. 11:25; Jas. 1:5
13 *g* Jer. 9:23; 1 Cor. 1:29
18 *h Inspiration:* v. 18; Ps. 68:11. (Ex. 4:15; 2 Tim. 3:16, *note*)
22 *i* Job 27:8
CHAPTER 33
4 *j Holy Spirit* (OT): v. 4; Ps. 51:11. (Gen. 1:2; Zech. 12:10) *k* Gen. 2:7
6 *l* Cp. Job 9:32–33; see 32:2, *note*

*
32:4 Vulgate reads *till Job had spoken*. **32:7** Literally *Days*, that is, years **32:9** Or *Men of many years* **33:6** Literally *as your mouth*

he is a secret sinner against the common moralities, but the real problem remains: Why are the righteous afflicted?

[1](32:2) Elihu has a more accurate understanding of the problem than Eliphaz, Bildad, and Zophar because he has a higher conception of God. The God of Eliphaz and the others, though mighty in His works, becomes in their thinking petty and exacting in His relations with mankind. By contrast Elihu's account of God is noble and true. Elihu falls short of being a true comforter, however (cp. 34:35–37), and he charges Job with wickedness and folly (34:7–8; 35:16).

I also have been formed out of
clay.
7 Surely no fear of me will
terrify you,
Nor will my hand be heavy on
you.

8 "Surely you have spoken in my
hearing,
And I have heard the sound of
your words, *saying*,
9 [a]'I *am* pure, without
transgression;
I *am* innocent, and *there is* no
iniquity in me.
10 Yet He finds occasions against
me,
He counts me as His [b]enemy;
11 He puts my feet in the [c]stocks,
He watches all my paths.'

12 "Look, *in* this you are not
righteous.
I will answer you,
For God is greater than man.
13 Why do you contend with
Him?
For He does not give an
accounting of any of His
words.
14 For God may speak in one
way, or in another,
Yet man does not perceive it.
15 In a dream, in a vision of the
night,
When deep sleep falls upon
men,
While slumbering on their
beds,
16 Then He opens the ears of
men,
And seals their instruction.
17 In order to turn man *from his*
deed,
And conceal pride from man,
18 He keeps back his soul from
the Pit,
And his life from perishing by
the sword.

19 "*Man* is also chastened with
pain on his [d]bed,
And with strong *pain* in many
of his bones,
20 [e]So that his life abhors [f]bread,
And his soul succulent food.
21 His flesh wastes away from
sight,
And his bones stick out *which*
once were not seen.
22 Yes, his soul draws near the
[g]Pit,
And his life to the
executioners.

9
a Job 6:29; 9:17; 10:7; 11:4; 16:17; 23:10–11; 27:5; 29:14; 31:1
10
b Job 13:24; 31:35
11
c Job 19:8
19
d Job 30:17
20
e Ps. 107:18
f Job 3:24
22
g See Hab. 2:5, *note;* cp. Lk. 16:23, *note*
24
h Or *an atonement.* Mt. 20:28; 1 Tim. 2:6; cp. Job 36:18
27
i 2 Sam. 12:13; Prov. 28:13; Lk. 15:21; 1 Jn. 1:9
j Job 42:6
CHAPTER 34
3
k Job 12:11

23 "If there is a messenger for him,
A mediator, one among a
thousand,
To show man His uprightness,
24 Then He is gracious to him,
and says,
'Deliver him from going down
to the Pit;
I have found a [h]ransom';
25 His flesh shall be young like a
child's,
He shall return to the days of
his youth.
26 He shall pray to God, and He
will delight in him,
He shall see His face with joy,
For He restores to man His
righteousness.
27 Then he looks at men and
[i]says,
'I have [j]sinned, and perverted
what was right,
And it did not profit me.'
28 He will redeem his* soul from
going down to the Pit,
And his* life shall see the
light.

29 "Behold, God works all these
things,
Twice, *in fact,* three *times* with
a man,
30 To bring back his soul from
the Pit,
That he may be enlightened
with the light of life.

31 "Give ear, Job, listen to me;
Hold your peace, and I will
speak.
32 If you have anything to say,
answer me;
Speak, for I desire to justify
you.
33 If not, listen to me;
Hold your peace, and I will
teach you wisdom."

Elihu charges Job with rebellion against sovereign justice

34 ELIHU further answered and
said:

2 "Hear my words, you wise *men;*
Give ear to me, you who have
knowledge.
3 For the ear [k]tests words
As the palate tastes food.
4 Let us choose justice for
ourselves;
Let us know among ourselves
what *is* good.

* 33:28 Or *my* (Kethib) • Or *my* (Kethib)

5 "For Job has said, [a]'I am
righteous,
But God has taken away my
[b]justice;
6 Should I lie concerning my
right?
My wound *is* [c]incurable,
though I am without
transgression.'
7 What man *is* like Job,
Who drinks scorn like [d]water,
8 Who goes in company with the
workers of iniquity,
And walks with wicked men?
9 For he has said, 'It profits a
man nothing
That he should delight in
[e]God.'

10 "Therefore listen to me, you
men of understanding:
[f]Far be it from God *to do*
wickedness,
And *from* the Almighty to
commit iniquity.
11 For He repays man *according
to* his work,
And makes man to find a
reward according to *his* way.
12 Surely God will never do
wickedly,
Nor will the Almighty pervert
justice.
13 Who gave Him charge over the
earth?
Or who appointed *Him over*
the whole world?
14 If He should set His heart on
it,
If He should gather to Himself
His Spirit and His breath,
15 [g]All flesh would perish
together,
And man would return to dust.

16 "If *you have* understanding,
hear this;
Listen to the sound of my
words:
17 Should one who hates justice
govern?
Will you [h]condemn *Him who
is* most just?
18 *Is it fitting* to say to a king,
'*You are* worthless,'
And to nobles, '*You are*
wicked'?
19 Yet He is not partial to
princes,
Nor does He [i]regard the rich
more than the poor;
[j]For they *are* all the work of
His hands.

5 *a* Job 33:9 *b* Job 27:2
6 *c* Job 6:4
7 *d* Job 15:16
9 *e* Job 21:15
10 *f* Gen. 18:25; Dt. 32:4; 2 Chr. 19:7; Job 8:3; 36:23; Ps. 92:15; Rom. 9:14
15 *g* Gen. 3:19; Eccl. 12:7
17 *h* Job 40:8
19 *i* Acts 10:34; Rom. 2:11 *j* Job 31:15
21 *k* 2 Chr. 16:9; Job 31:4; Ps. 34:15; Prov. 5:21; 15:3; Jer. 16:17; 32:19
24 *l* Dan. 2:21
27 *m* Cp. 1 Sam. 15:11
28 *n* Job 35:9; Jas. 5:4 *o* Ex. 22:23

20 In a moment they die, in the
middle of the night;
The people are shaken and
pass away;
The mighty are taken away
without a hand.

21 [k]"For His eyes *are* on the ways
of man,
And He sees all his steps.
22 There is no darkness nor
shadow of death
Where the workers of iniquity
may hide themselves.
23 For He need not further
consider a man,
That he should go before God
in judgment.
24 [l]He breaks in pieces mighty
men without inquiry,
And sets others in their place.
25 Therefore He knows their
works;
He overthrows *them* in the
night,
And they are crushed.
26 He strikes them as wicked *men*
In the open sight of others,
27 [m]Because they turned back from
Him,
And would not consider any of
His ways,
28 So that they [n]caused the cry of
the poor to come to Him;
For He [o]hears the cry of the
afflicted.
29 When He gives quietness, who
then can make trouble?
And when He hides *His* face,
who then can see Him,
Whether *it is* against a nation
or a man alone?—
30 That the hypocrite should not
reign,
Lest the people be ensnared.

31 "For has *anyone* said to God,
'I have borne *chastening;*
I will offend no more;
32 Teach me *what* I do not see;
If I have done iniquity, I will
do no more'?
33 Should He repay *it* according
to your *terms,*
Just because you disavow it?
You must choose, and not I;
Therefore speak what you
know.

34 "Men of understanding say to
me,
Wise men who listen to me:
35 'Job speaks without knowledge,

His words *are* without
wisdom.'
36 [a]Oh, that Job were [b]tried to the
utmost,
Because *his* answers *are like*
those of wicked men!
37 For he adds [c]rebellion to his
sin;
He claps *his hands* among us,
And multiplies his words
against God."

Elihu rebukes Job for speaking rashly

35 MOREOVER Elihu answered
and said:
2 "Do you think this is right?
Do you say,
'My righteousness is more than
God's'?
3 For [d]you say,
'What advantage will it be to
You?
What profit shall I have, more
than *if* I had sinned?'

4 "I will answer you,
And [e]your companions with
you.
5 [f]Look to the heavens and see;
And behold the clouds—
They are higher than you.
6 If you sin, what do you
accomplish against [g]Him?
Or, *if* your transgressions are
multiplied, what do you do
to Him?
7 If you are righteous, what do
you give Him?
Or what does He receive from
your [h]hand?
8 Your wickedness affects a man
such as you,
And your righteousness a son
of man.

9 "Because of the multitude of
oppressions they cry out;
They cry out for help because
of the arm of the mighty.
10 But no one says, [i]'Where *is*
God my Maker,
[j]Who gives songs in the night,
11 Who [k]teaches us more than
the beasts of the earth,
And makes us wiser than the
birds of heaven?'
12 There they cry out, but He
does not answer,
Because of the pride of evil
men.
13 Surely God will not [l]listen to
empty *talk*,
Nor will the Almighty regard
it.
14 Although you say you do not
see Him,
Yet [m]justice *is* before Him, and
you must [n]wait for Him.
15 And now, because He has not
punished in His anger,
Nor taken much notice of folly,
16 Therefore Job opens his mouth
in vain;
He multiplies words without
knowledge."

God in His greatness deals with men according to their works

36 ELIHU also proceeded and
said:
2 "Bear with me a little, and I will
show you
That *there are* yet words to
speak on God's behalf.
3 I will fetch my knowledge
from afar;
I will ascribe righteousness to
my Maker.
4 For truly my words *are* not
false;
One who is perfect in
knowledge *is* with you.

5 "Behold, God *is* mighty, but
despises *no one;*
He is [o]mighty in strength of
understanding.
6 He does not preserve the life of
the wicked,
But gives justice to the
[p]oppressed.
7 He does not withdraw His eyes
from the [q]righteous;
But *they are* on the throne
with kings,
For He has seated them
forever,
And they are exalted.
8 And if *they are* [r]bound in
fetters,
Held in the cords of affliction,
9 Then He tells them their work
and their transgressions—
That they have acted defiantly.
10 [s]He also opens their ear to
instruction,
And commands that they turn
from iniquity.
11 If they obey and serve *Him*,
They shall spend their days in
prosperity,
And their years in pleasures.
12 But if they do not obey,
They shall perish by the
sword,

36
a Or *My father, let Job be tested*
b Test/tempt: v. 36; Ps. 7:9. (Gen. 3:1; Jas. 1:14, *note*)
37
c Job 7:11; 10:1; cp. 1 Sam. 15:23
CHAPTER 35
3
d Job 21:15; 34:9
4
e Job 34:8; cp. 42:7–9
5
f Job 22:12
6
g Cp. Job 7:20; Prov. 8:36
7
h Job 22:2; Prov. 9:12; Lk. 17:10
10
i Cp. Isa. 51:13
j Ps. 42:8; 77:6; 149:5; Acts 16:25
11
k Ps. 94:12; Isa. 48:17; cp. 1 Cor. 2:13
13
l Isa. 1:15; Jer. 11:11; cp. Job 27:8–9
14
m Job 36:17
n See Ps. 2:12, *note*
CHAPTER 36
5
o Job 9:4; 12:13,16; 37:23; Ps. 99:4
6
p Job 5:15
7
q Ps. 33:18; 34:15
8
r Ps. 107:10
10
s Job 33:16

And they shall die without
[a]knowledge.*

13 "But the hypocrites in heart
[b]store up wrath;
They do not cry for help when
He binds them.
14 They die in youth,
And their life *ends* among the
perverted persons.*
15 He delivers the poor in their
affliction,
And opens their ears in
oppression.

16 "Indeed He would have brought
you out of dire distress,
[c]*Into* a broad place where *there*
is no restraint;
And what is set on your table
would be full of richness.
17 But you are filled with the
judgment due the [d]wicked;
Judgment and justice take hold
of you.
18 Because *there is* wrath, *beware*
lest He take you away with
one blow;
For a large ransom would not
help you avoid *it.*
19 Will your riches,
Or all the mighty forces,
Keep you from distress?
20 Do not desire the night,
When people are cut off in
their place.
21 Take heed, do not turn to
iniquity,
For you have chosen [e]this
rather than affliction.

22 "Behold, God is exalted by His
power;
Who teaches like Him?
23 Who has assigned Him His
[f]way,
Or who has said, 'You have
done [g]wrong'?

24 "Remember to magnify His
work,
Of which men have sung.
25 Everyone has seen it;
Man looks on *it* from afar.

26 "Behold, God *is* great, and we
do [h]not [i]know *Him;*
Nor can the number of His
years *be* discovered.
27 For He draws up drops of
water,
Which distill as rain from the
mist,
28 Which the clouds drop down
And pour abundantly on man.
29 Indeed, can *anyone* understand
the spreading of clouds,
The thunder from His canopy?
30 Look, He scatters His light
upon it,
And covers the depths of the
sea.
31 For by these He judges the
peoples;
He gives food in [j]abundance.
32 He [k]covers *His* hands with
lightning,
And commands it to strike.
33 His thunder declares it,
The cattle also, concerning the
rising *storm.*

Elihu concludes: the storm depicts God's greatness

37 "AT this also my heart
trembles,
And leaps from its place.
2 Hear attentively the thunder of
His voice,
And the rumbling *that* comes
from His mouth.
3 He sends it forth under the
whole heaven,
His lightning to the ends of the
earth.
4 After it a voice roars;
He thunders with His majestic
voice,
And He does not restrain them
when His voice is heard.
5 God thunders marvelously
with His voice;
He does [l]great things which
we cannot comprehend.
6 For He says to the [m]snow, 'Fall
on the earth';
Likewise to the gentle rain and
the heavy rain of His
strength.
7 He seals the hand of every
man,
[n]That [o]all men may know His
work.
8 The beasts [p]go into dens,
And remain in their lairs.
9 From the chamber *of the south*
comes the whirlwind,
And cold from the scattering
winds *of the north.*
10 [q]By the breath of God ice is
given,
And the broad waters are
frozen.

12
a Job 4:21
13
b Rom. 2:5
16
c Ps. 18:19; 31:8; 118:5
17
d Job 22:5
21
e Cp. Heb. 11:24–26
23
f Isa. 40:13–14
g Job 8:3
26
h Job 37:5
i Cp. 1 Cor. 13:12
31
j Gen. 9:3; Ps. 104:14–15
32
k Ps. 147:8
CHAPTER 37
5
l Job 5:9; 9:10; 36:26; Rev. 15:3
6
m Ps. 147:16–17
7
n Ps. 109:27
o Ps. 19:4
8
p Ps. 104:22
10
q Job 38:29–30; Ps. 147:17–18

*

36:12 Masoretic Text reads *as one without knowledge.* **36:14** Hebrew *qedeshim*, that is, those practicing sodomy and prostitution in religious rituals

11 Also with moisture He
saturates the thick clouds;
He scatters His bright clouds.
12 And they swirl about, being
turned by His guidance,
[a]That they may do whatever He
commands them
On the face of the whole
earth.*
13 [b]He causes it to come,
Whether for correction,
Or for His land,
Or for mercy.

14 "Listen to this, O Job;
Stand still and [c]consider the
wondrous works of God.
15 Do you know when God
dispatches them,
And causes the light of His
cloud to shine?
16 Do you know how the clouds
are balanced,
Those wondrous works of Him
who is perfect in
knowledge?
17 Why *are* your garments hot,
When He quiets the earth by
the south *wind*?
18 With Him, have you [d]spread
out the [e]skies,
Strong as a cast metal mirror?

19 "Teach us what we should say
to Him,
For we can prepare nothing
because of the darkness.
20 Should He be told that I *wish
to* speak?
If a man were to speak, surely
he would be swallowed up.
21 Even now *men* cannot look at
the light *when it is* bright in
the skies,
When the wind has passed and
cleared them.
22 He comes from the north *as*
golden *splendor;*
With God *is* awesome
majesty.
23 *As for* the Almighty, [f]we
cannot find Him;
He is excellent in power,
In [g]judgment and abundant
justice;
He does not oppress.
24 Therefore men fear Him;
He shows no partiality to any
who are wise of heart."

12
a Ps. 148:8
13
b Cp. Ex. 9:18,23; 1 Sam. 12:18–19; Ezra 10:9; Job 36:27–32
14
c Ps. 111:2
18
d Gen. 1:6; Isa. 44:24
e Ps. 104:2; Isa. 45:12
23
f Job 11:7–8; 1 Tim. 6:16; Rom. 11:33
g Ps. 33:5
CHAPTER 38
1
h Job 40:6
i Cp. Ex. 19:16,18; 1 Ki. 19:11; Ezek. 1:4; Nah. 1:3
2
j Job 34:35; 42:3
4
k Ps. 104:5; Prov. 8:29; 30:4
7
l See Gen. 6:4, *note;* cp. Heb. 1:4, *note*
8
m Gen. 1:9; Ps. 33:7; 104:9; Prov. 8:29; Jer. 5:22
11
n Ps. 89:9; 93:4
12
o Ps. 74:16; 148:5

IV. The LORD *Speaks, 38—41*

The LORD *interrogates Job face to face*

38 THEN the LORD [1h]answered
Job [i]out of the whirlwind, and
said:
2 [j]"Who *is* this who darkens
counsel
By words without knowledge?
3 Now prepare yourself like a
man;
I will question you, and you
shall answer Me.

4 [k]"Where were you when I laid
the foundations of the earth?
Tell *Me,* if you have
understanding.
5 Who determined its
measurements?
Surely you know!
Or who stretched the line upon
it?
6 To what were its foundations
fastened?
Or who laid its cornerstone,
7 When the morning stars sang
together,
And all the [l]sons of God
shouted for joy?

8 [m]"Or *who* shut in the sea with
doors,
When it burst forth *and* issued
from the womb;
9 When I made the clouds its
garment,
And thick darkness its
swaddling band;
10 When I fixed My limit for it,
And set bars and doors;
11 When I said,
'This far you may come, but no
farther,
And here [n]your proud waves
must stop!'

12 "Have you [o]commanded the
morning since your days
began,
And caused the dawn to know
its place,
13 That it might take hold of the
ends of the earth,
And the wicked be shaken out
of it?
14 It takes on form like clay
under a seal,
And stands out like a garment.

*37:12 Literally *the world of the earth*

[1](38:1) The words of the LORD have the effect of bringing Job consciously into His presence (42:5). Up to now the discussions have been about God, but He has been conceived of as absent. Now Job and the LORD are face to face. See 32:2, *note.*

15 From the wicked their light is [a]withheld,
And the upraised arm is broken.

16 [b]"Have you entered the springs of the sea?
Or have you walked in search of the depths?
17 [c]Have the gates of death been revealed to you?
Or have you seen the doors of the shadow of death?
18 Have you comprehended the breadth of the earth?
Tell *Me*, if you know all this.

19 "Where *is* the way *to* the dwelling of light?
And darkness, where *is* its place,
20 That you may take it to its territory,
That you may know the paths *to* its home?
21 Do you know *it*, because you were born then,
Or *because* the number of your days *is* great?

22 "Have you entered the [d]treasury of snow,
Or have you seen the treasury of hail,
23 [e]Which I have reserved for the time of trouble,
For the day of battle and war?
24 By what way is light diffused,
Or the east wind scattered over the earth?

25 "Who has divided a channel for the overflowing *water*,
Or a path for the thunderbolt,
26 To cause it to rain on a land *where there is* no one,
A wilderness in which *there is* no man;
27 To satisfy the desolate waste,
And cause to spring forth the growth of tender grass?
28 [f]Has the rain a father?
Or who has begotten the drops of dew?
29 From whose womb comes the ice?
And the [g]frost of heaven, who gives it birth?
30 The waters harden like stone,
And the surface of the deep is frozen.

31 "Can you bind the cluster of the [h]Pleiades,
Or loose the belt of [h]Orion?
32 Can you bring out [i]Mazzaroth in its season?
Or can you guide the Great Bear with its cubs?
33 Do you know the [j]ordinances of the heavens?
Can you set their dominion over the earth?

34 "Can you lift up your voice to the clouds,
That an abundance of water may cover you?
35 Can you send out lightnings, that they may go,
And say to you, 'Here we *are!*'?
36 Who has put [k]wisdom in the mind?*
Or who has given understanding to the heart?
37 Who can number the clouds by wisdom?
Or who can [l]pour out the bottles of heaven,
38 When the dust hardens in clumps,
And the clods cling together?

39 [m]"Can you hunt the prey for the lion,
Or satisfy the appetite of the young lions,
40 When they crouch in *their* dens,
Or lurk in their lairs to lie in wait?
41 [n]Who provides food for the raven,
When its young ones cry to God,
And wander about for lack of food?

The LORD *asserts His omnipotence*

39 "DO you know the time when the wild mountain [o]goats bear young?
Or can you mark when the [p]deer gives birth?
2 Can you number the months *that* they fulfill?
Or do you know the time when they bear young?
3 They bow down,
They bring forth their young,
They deliver their offspring.*
4 Their young ones are healthy,
They grow strong with grain;
They depart and do not return to them.

15 *a* Prov. 13:9
16 *b* Ps. 77:19
17 c Ps. 9:13
22 *d* Jer. 10:13
23 *e* Ex. 9:18; Josh. 10:11; Isa. 30:30; Ezek. 13:11,13; Rev. 16:21
28 *f* Ps. 147:8; Jer. 14:22
29 *g* Ps. 147:16
31 *h* Job 9:9; Amos 5:8
32 *i* Or *the signs of the Zodiac*
33 *j* Ps. 148:6; Jer. 31:35–36
36 *k* Job 9:4; Ps. 51:6; Eccl. 2:26; Jas. 1:5
37 *l* Lit. *cause to lie down*
39 *m* Ps. 104:21; 145:15
41 *n* Ps. 147:9; Mt. 6:26
CHAPTER 39
1 o Ps. 104:18
p Ps. 29:9

*
38:36 Literally *inward parts*
39:3 Literally *pangs*, figurative of offspring

5 "Who set the wild [a]donkey free?
Who loosed the bonds of the onager,
6 Whose home I have made the wilderness,
And the [b]barren land his dwelling?
7 He scorns the tumult of the city;
He does not heed the shouts of the driver.
8 The range of the mountains *is* his pasture,
And he searches after [c]every green thing.

9 "Will the [d]wild ox be willing to serve you?
Will he bed by your manger?
10 Can you bind the wild ox in the furrow with ropes?
Or will he plow the valleys behind you?
11 Will you trust him because his strength *is* great?
Or will you leave your labor to him?
12 Will you trust him to bring home your grain,
And gather it to your threshing floor?

13 "The wings of the ostrich wave proudly,
But are her wings and pinions *like the* kindly stork's?
14 For she leaves her eggs on the ground,
And warms them in the dust;
15 She forgets that a foot may crush them,
Or that a wild beast may break them.
16 She treats her young [e]harshly, as though *they were* not hers;
Her labor is in vain, without concern,
17 Because God deprived her of wisdom,
And did not endow her with understanding.
18 When she lifts herself on high,
She scorns the horse and its rider.

19 "Have you given the horse strength?
Have you clothed his neck with thunder?*
20 Can you frighten him like a locust?
His majestic snorting strikes terror.
21 He paws in the valley, and rejoices in *his* strength;
He gallops into the clash of arms.
22 He mocks at fear, and is not frightened;
Nor does he turn back from the sword.
23 The quiver rattles against him,
The glittering spear and javelin.
24 He devours the distance with fierceness and rage;
Nor does he come to a halt because the trumpet *has* sounded.
25 At *the blast of* the trumpet he says, 'Aha!'
He smells the battle from afar,
The thunder of captains and shouting.

26 "Does the hawk fly by your wisdom,
And spread its wings toward the south?
27 Does the [f]eagle mount up at your command,
And make its [g]nest on high?
28 On the rock it dwells and resides,
On the crag of the rock and the stronghold.
29 From there it spies out the prey;
Its eyes observe from afar.
30 Its young ones suck up blood;
And where the [h]slain *are*, there it *is*."

A summary question

40 MOREOVER the LORD [i]answered Job, and said:

2 "Shall the one who [j]contends with the Almighty correct Him?
He who [k]rebukes God, let him answer it."

Job answers: he admits his worthlessness

3 Then Job answered the LORD and said:

4 [l]"Behold, I am vile;
What shall I answer You?
I lay my hand over my [m]mouth.
5 Once I have spoken, but I will not answer;

5 *a* Cp. Job 11:12; 24:5; Jer. 2:24
6 *b* Lit. *salt land*
8 *c* Gen. 1:29
9 *d* Num. 23:22; Dt. 33:17
16 *e* Cp. Lam. 4:3
27 *f* Prov. 30:18–19 *g* Jer. 49:16; Obad. 4
30 *h* Mt. 24:28
CHAPTER 40
1 *i* Job 38:1
2 *j* Job 9:3; 10:2; 33:13 *k* Job 13:3; 23:4; 31:35
4 *l* Ezra 9:6; Job 42:6; Ps. 51:4 *m* Job 29:9

* 39:19 Or *a mane*

Yes, twice, but I will proceed
no further."

The Lord *resumes*
His questioning of Job

6 Then the Lord [a]answered Job
out of the whirlwind, and said:

7 "Now prepare yourself like a
man;
I will [b]question you, and you
shall answer Me:

8 "Would you indeed annul My
judgment?
Would you [c]condemn Me that
you may be [d]justified?
9 Have you an arm like God?
Or can you thunder with a
voice like His?
10 Then adorn yourself *with*
majesty and splendor,
And array yourself with glory
and beauty.
11 Disperse the rage of your
wrath;
Look on everyone *who is*
proud, and humble him.
12 Look on everyone *who is*
[e]proud, *and* bring him low;
Tread down the wicked in
their place.
13 Hide them in the dust together,
Bind their faces in hidden
darkness.
14 Then I will also confess to you
That your own right hand can
save you.

15 "Look now at the behemoth,*
which I made *along* with
you;
He eats grass like an ox.
16 See now, his strength *is* in his
hips,
And his power *is* in his
stomach muscles.
17 He moves his tail like a cedar;
The sinews of his thighs are
tightly knit.
18 His bones *are like* beams of
bronze,
His ribs like bars of iron.
19 He *is* the first of the [f]ways of
God;
Only He who made him can
bring near His sword.
20 Surely the mountains [g]yield
food for him,
And all the beasts of the field
play there.
21 He lies under the lotus trees,
In a covert of reeds and marsh.
22 The lotus trees cover him *with*
their shade;
The willows by the brook
surround him.
23 Indeed the river may rage,
Yet he is not disturbed;
He is confident, though the
Jordan gushes into his
mouth,
24 *Though* he takes it in his eyes,
Or one pierces *his* nose with a
snare.

The questioning continued

41 "CAN you draw out
[h]Leviathan* with a hook,
Or *snare* his tongue with a line
which you lower?
2 Can you put a reed through his
nose,
Or pierce his jaw with a hook?
3 Will he make many
supplications to you?
Will he speak softly to you?
4 Will he make a covenant with
you?
Will you take him as a servant
forever?
5 Will you play with him as *with*
a bird,
Or will you leash him for your
maidens?
6 Will *your* companions make a
banquet* of him?
Will they apportion him among
the merchants?
7 Can you fill his skin with
harpoons,
Or his head with fishing
spears?
8 Lay your hand on him;
Remember the battle—
Never do it again!
9 Indeed, *any* hope of
overcoming him is false;
Shall *one not* be overwhelmed
at the sight of him?
10 No one *is so* fierce that he
would dare stir him up.
Who then is able to stand
against Me?
11 Who has preceded Me, that I
should pay *him*?
Everything under heaven is
[i]Mine.

12 "I will not conceal* his limbs,
His mighty power, or his
graceful proportions.
13 Who can remove his outer
coat?

6
a Job 38:1
7
b Job 38:3
8
c Job 16:11; 19:6
d Job 17:9
12
e Isa. 2:12; Dan. 4:37
19
f Job 26:14
20
g Ps. 104:14
CHAPTER 41
1
h Ps. 74:14; 104:26; Isa. 27:1
11
i Dt. 10:14; Ps. 24:1

*
40:15 A large animal, exact identity unknown
41:1 A large sea creature, exact identity unknown
41:6 Or *bargain over him*
41:12 Literally *keep silent about*

Who can approach *him* with a double bridle?
14 Who can open the doors of his face,
With his terrible teeth all around?
15 *His* rows of scales are *his* pride,
Shut up tightly *as with* a seal;
16 One is so near another
That no air can come between them;
17 They are joined one to another,
They stick together and cannot be parted.
18 His sneezings flash forth light,
And his eyes *are* like the eyelids of the morning.
19 Out of his mouth go burning lights;
Sparks of fire shoot out.
20 Smoke goes out of his nostrils,
As *from* a boiling pot and burning rushes.
21 His breath kindles coals,
And a flame goes out of his mouth.
22 Strength dwells in his neck,
And sorrow dances before him.
23 The folds of his flesh are joined together;
They are firm on him and cannot be moved.
24 His heart is as hard as stone,
Even as hard as the lower *millstone.*
25 When he raises himself up, the mighty are afraid;
Because of his crashings they are beside* themselves.
26 *Though* the sword reaches him, it cannot avail;
Nor does spear, dart, or javelin.
27 He regards iron as straw,
And bronze as rotten wood.
28 The arrow cannot make him flee;
Slingstones become like stubble to him.
29 Darts are regarded as straw;
He laughs at the threat of javelins.
30 His undersides *are* like sharp potsherds;
He spreads pointed *marks* in the mire.
31 He makes the deep boil like a pot;
He makes the sea like a pot of ointment.
32 He leaves a shining wake behind him;
One would think the deep had white hair.
33 On earth there is nothing [a]like him,
Which is made without fear.
34 He beholds every high *thing;*
He *is* king over all the children of pride."

V. Job's Confession, 42:1–6

He acknowledges God's sovereignty and humbles himself

42 THEN Job answered the LORD and said:
2 "I know that You [b]can do everything,
And that no purpose *of Yours* can be withheld from You.
3 *You asked,* 'Who *is* this who hides counsel without [c]knowledge?'
Therefore I have uttered what I did not understand,
Things too [d]wonderful for me, which I did not know.
4 Listen, please, and let me speak;
You said, 'I will [e]question you, and you shall answer Me.'
5 "I have [f]heard of You by the hearing of the ear,
But now my eye sees You.
6 [1]Therefore I [g]abhor *myself,*

33 *a* Cp. Job 40:19
CHAPTER 42
2 *b* Mt. 19:26; cp. Gen. 18:14; Ps. 33:6–9; 107:25–29
3 *c* Job 38:2 *d* Ps. 40:5; 139:6
4 *e* Job 38:3; 40:7
5 *f* Job 26:14
6 *g* Job 40:4

*41:25 Or *purify themselves*

[1](42:6) The central problem of the Book of Job, i.e. the sufferings of the LORD's people, is explained at least in part by the divinely beneficent purposes which are served. (1) Job's experiences opened his eyes more fully to the ineffable holiness of God (42:5), leading him thereby to self-knowledge and self-judgment (40:4; 42:6). (2) The sufferings of Job are shown to be corrective rather than penal, being used of God to test and refine his character (23:10). (3) The outcome demonstrates that by God's grace His people trust and serve Him because of what He is, not as a mere return for temporal benefits (13:15). And (4) such experiences, as interpreted here by divine inspiration, reveal the ultimate triumph of a wise and loving God in His unseen contest with Satan over the souls of men (chs. 1—2).

Finally, when all has been said that can be said in relief of the intellectual problem involved, it must be confessed that beyond the revealed purposes of God there still remains much of mystery. And for this there is no answer except the attitude of worship in which we humbly

And [a]repent in dust and
ashes."

VI. Epilogue, 42:7–17

Renewed blessing
and prosperity to Job

7 And so it was, after the LORD had
spoken these words to Job, that the
LORD said to Eliphaz the Temanite,
"My wrath is aroused against you and
your two friends, for you have not
spoken of Me *what is* right, as My servant Job *has*.
8 "Now therefore, take for yourselves [b]seven bulls and seven rams,
go to My servant Job, and offer up for
yourselves a burnt offering; and My
servant Job shall pray for you. For I
will accept him, lest I deal with you
according to your folly; because you
have not spoken of Me *what is* right,
as My servant Job *has*."
9 So Eliphaz the Temanite and Bildad the Shuhite *and* Zophar the Naamathite went and did as the LORD commanded them; for the LORD had
accepted Job.
10 And the LORD [c]restored Job's
losses* when he prayed for his
friends. Indeed the LORD gave Job
[d]twice as much as he had before.
11 Then [e]all his brothers, all his
sisters, and all those who had been his
acquaintances before, came to him
and ate food with him in his house;
and they consoled him and comforted
him for all the adversity that the LORD
had brought upon him. Each one gave
him a piece of silver and each a ring of
gold.
12 Now the LORD blessed the [f]latter
days of Job more than his beginning;
for he had [g]fourteen thousand sheep,
six thousand camels, one thousand
yoke of oxen, and one thousand female donkeys.
13 [h]He also had seven sons and
three daughters.
14 And he called the name of the
first Jemimah, the name of the second
Keziah, and the name of the third
Keren-Happuch.
15 In all the land were found no
women *so* beautiful as the daughters
of Job; and their father gave them an
inheritance among their brothers.
16 After this Job [i]lived one hundred and forty years, and saw his children and grandchildren *for* four generations.
17 So Job died, old and [j]full of
days.

6
a See Zech. 8:14, *note*
8
b Cp. Num. 23:1
10
c Dt. 30:3; Ps. 14:7; 85:1–3; 126:1
d Cp. Isa. 61:7
11
e Job 19:13
12
f Job 8:7; Jas. 5:11
g Cp. Job 1:3
13
h Job 1:2
16
i Job 5:26; Prov. 3:16
17
j Gen. 25:8

*

42:10 Literally *Job's captivity*, that is, what was captured from Job

acknowledge that a sovereign God cannot be required by men to give all the reasons for what He chooses to do (42:1–6; 33:13; Rom. 11:33–36).

The Book of

PSALMS

Author: David and others *Theme:* Praise *Date of writing:* 10th Cent. B.C. and later

PSALMS is a title derived from the Greek *psalmos*, denoting *a poem sung to the accompaniment of musical instruments*. This word occurs in the Greek NT in 1 Cor. 14:26; Eph. 5:19; Col. 3:16. The Hebrew title for the book was *Sepher Tehillim*, meaning *Book of Praises*.

Seventy-three Psalms are assigned to David, twelve to Asaph (50; 73—83), two to Solomon (72; 127), one to Moses (90), one to Ethan (89), and twelve to the sons of Korah, a family of Levitical singers (42—49; 84; 85; 87; 88). These Psalms arise from a consideration of what God has done in the past, what He will do in the future, and the need for God in the immediate present, with a recognition of His sovereignty and goodness.

Whereas a number of Psalms celebrate the creation and other historical events, one particular section is historical throughout: Psalms 104—106, which begin with the creation and end with the captivity. In the historical group should also be included the Psalms which relate exclusively to the glory of the city of Jerusalem and its temple, past and future (especially 48; 84; 122; 132). Seven of the Psalms are called Penitential Psalms (6; 32; 38; 51; 102; 130; 143); fifteen are known as Pilgrim Psalms (120—134). The familiar Psalm of Thanksgiving is Ps. 136, the great Psalm on the Word of God is Ps. 119, and the Hallelujah Psalms, sometimes called Hallel, are Ps. 111—113, and 115—117. Man's frailty and God's glory are contrasted in Ps. 90; God's protecting care is set forth in Ps. 91.

The Psalms include a vast body of Messianic prophecy which describes: (1) Christ's suffering (22; 69); (2) His Kingship (2; 21; 45; 72); (3) His second advent (50; 97; 98); and (4) fundamentally in the 110th Psalm, His position as Son of God and Priest in the order of Melchizedek. This last Psalm is quoted more frequently in the NT than any other single chapter in the OT. There are 186 quotations from the entire Psalter in the NT writings.

The Psalter is generally divided into five books, each concluding with a doxology:

I. Psalms 1—41.
II. Psalms 42—72.
III. Psalms 73—89.
IV. Psalms 90—106.
V. Psalms 107—150.

Book I, Psalms 1—41

Two men, two ways, two destinies

1 [1]BLESSED *is* the man
Who walks not in the counsel
of the ungodly,
Nor stands in the path of
sinners,
Nor sits in the seat of the
scornful;
2 But his delight *is* in the [a]law
of the LORD,
And in His law he meditates
day and night.
3 He shall be like a tree
Planted by the rivers of
water,
That brings forth its fruit in
its season,
Whose leaf also shall not
wither;
And whatever he does shall
prosper.
4 The ungodly *are* not so,
But *are* like the chaff which
the wind drives away.
5 Therefore the ungodly shall
not stand in the judgment,
Nor sinners in the
congregation of the
righteous.
6 For the LORD knows the way of
the righteous,
But the way of the ungodly
shall perish.

PSALM 1
2
a Law (of Moses): v. 2; Ps. 19:7. (Ex. 19:1; Gal. 3:24, *note*)

Christ, the coming King

2 [2]WHY do the nations rage,
And the people plot a vain
thing?
2 The kings of the earth set
themselves,

---

[1](1:1) Whereas about half of the Psalms were written by David in the 10th century B.C., some are known to have been composed by other men. For example, the 90th Psalm is by Moses, who lived several centuries earlier, and the 137th Psalm was written in the 6th century B.C.

[2](2:1) Psalms 2; 8; 16; 22; 23; 24; 40; 41; 45; 68; 69; 72; 89; 102; 110; 118 are generally considered Messianic. These Psalms, either in whole or in part, speak of the Messiah. Undoubtedly many other Psalms also refer to Christ. Though the primary thrust of the Messianic

And the [a]rulers take counsel together,
Against the LORD and against His [b]Anointed, *saying,*
3 "Let us break Their bonds in pieces
And cast away Their cords from us."

4 He who sits in the heavens shall laugh;
The LORD shall hold them in derision.
5 Then He shall speak to them in His wrath,
And [c]distress them in His deep displeasure:
6 "Yet I have set My [1d]King
On My [e]holy hill of Zion."

7 "I will declare the decree:
The LORD has said to Me,
[f]'You *are* My Son,
Today I have begotten You.
8 Ask of Me, and I will give *You*
The nations *for* Your inheritance,
And the ends of the earth *for* Your possession.
9 [g]You shall break* them with a rod of iron;
You shall [h]dash them to pieces like a potter's vessel.' "

10 Now therefore, be wise, O kings;
Be instructed, you judges of the earth.
11 Serve the LORD with [i]fear,
And rejoice with trembling.
12 Kiss the Son,* lest He* be angry,
And you perish *in* the way,
When His wrath is kindled but a little.

PSALM 2
2
a Mt. 12:14; 26:3,4, 59–66; 27:1–2; Mk. 3:6; 11:18
b Christ (first advent): v. 2; Ps. 16:10. (Gen. 3:15; Acts 1:11, *note*)
5
c Tribulation (the great): vv. 1–5; Isa. 24:20. (Ps. 2:5; Rev. 7:14)
6
d Kingdom (OT): vv. 1–9; Ps. 16:9. (Gen. 1:26; Zech. 12:8, *note*)
e Heb. *qodesh. Sanctification* (OT): v. 6; Ps. 20:6. (Gen. 2:3; Zech. 8:3)
7
f Acts 13:33; Heb. 1:5; 5:5
9
g Christ (second advent): vv. 6–9; Ps. 24:10. (Dt. 30:3; Acts 1:11, *note*)
h Day (of the LORD): v. 9; Isa. 2:12. (Ps. 2:9; Rev. 19:19)

Blessed *are* all those who [j]put their [2]trust in Him.

A morning psalm

A Psalm of David when he [k]fled from Absalom his son.

3 LORD, how they have increased who trouble me!
Many *are* they who rise up against me.
2 Many *are* they who say of me,
"There is no help for him in God." [3]Selah.

3 But You, O LORD, *are* a shield for me,
My glory and the One who [l]lifts up my head.
4 I cried to the LORD with my voice,
And He heard me from His holy hill. Selah.

5 I lay down and slept;
I awoke, for the LORD sustained me.
6 I will not be afraid of ten thousands of people
Who have set *themselves* against me all around.

7 Arise, O LORD;
Save me, O my God!
For You have struck all my enemies on the cheekbone;
You have broken the teeth of the ungodly.
8 Salvation *belongs* to the LORD.

2:11 *i* See Ps. 19:9; *note* **2:12** *j Faith:* v. 12; Ps. 28:7. (Gen. 3:20; Heb. 11:39, *note*) **3:title** *k* 2 Sam. 15:14 **3:3** *l* Ps. 27:6

*

2:9 Following Masoretic Text and Targum; Septuagint, Syriac, and Vulgate read *rule* (compare Revelation 2:27). **2:12** Septuagint and Vulgate read *Embrace discipline;* Targum reads *Receive instruction.* • Septuagint reads *the LORD.*

Psalms is Christocentric, there is also much of instruction for the godly in their walk with God. See 118:29, *note.*

[1](2:6) The 2nd Psalm gives the order of the establishment of the kingdom. It is in six parts: (1) The rage and the vain plots of the Jews and Gentiles against the LORD and His Anointed One (vv. 1–3). The inspired interpretation of this is in Acts 4:25–28, which asserts its fulfillment in the crucifixion of Christ. (2) The derision of the LORD (v. 4), that men should suppose it possible to set aside His covenant (2 Sam. 7:8–17) and oath (Ps. 89:34–37). (3) His rebuke (v. 5), fulfilled in the destruction of Jerusalem, A.D. 70, and the dispersion of the Jews at that time; yet to be fulfilled more completely in the tribulation (Mt. 24:29), which immediately precedes the return of the King (Mt. 24:30). (4) The establishment of the rejected King upon Zion (v. 6). (5) The subjection of the earth to the King's rule (vv. 7–9). And (6) the present appeal to the world powers (vv. 10–12). See Ps. 8, next in order of the Messianic Psalms.

[2](2:12) Trust is the characteristic OT word for the NT "faith" and "believe." It occurs 154 times in the OT, and is the rendering of Hebrew words signifying *to take refuge* (Ps. 2:12); *to lean on* (Ps. 56:3); *to roll on* (Ps. 22:8).

[3](3:2) The frequent use in the Psalms of this Hebrew word, *Selah,* possibly marks those places where a musical rest in the chanting or a change of instrumental accompaniment stressed a shift of mood.

Your blessing *is* upon Your
people. Selah.

An evening psalm

To the Chief Musician. With stringed instruments. A Psalm of David.

4 HEAR me when I call, O God
of my righteousness!
You have [1]relieved me in *my*
distress;
Have mercy on me, and hear
my prayer.
2 How long, O you sons of men,
Will you turn my glory to
shame?
How long will you love
worthlessness
And seek falsehood? Selah.
3 But know that the LORD has set
apart* for Himself him who
is godly;
The LORD [a]will hear when I
call to Him.
4 Be angry, and [b]do not sin.
Meditate within your heart on
your bed, and be still. Selah.
5 Offer the [c]sacrifices of
righteousness,
And put your [d]trust in the
LORD.
6 *There are* many who say,
"Who will show us *any* good?"
LORD, [e]lift up the light of Your
countenance upon us.
7 You have put [f]gladness in my
heart,
More than in the season that
their grain and wine
increased.
8 I will both [g]lie down in peace,
and sleep;
For You alone, O LORD, make
me [h]dwell in safety.

A prayer for guidance

To the Chief Musician. With flutes.* A Psalm of David.

5 [i]GIVE ear to my words, O LORD,
Consider my meditation.
2 Give heed to the voice of my
cry,
My King and my God,
For to You I will pray.
3 My voice You shall hear in the
morning, O LORD;
In the [j]morning I will direct *it*
to You,
And I will look up.
4 For You *are* not a God who
takes pleasure in
wickedness,
Nor shall evil dwell with You.
5 The [k]boastful shall not [l]stand
in Your sight;
You hate all workers of
iniquity.
6 You shall destroy those who
speak falsehood;
The LORD abhors the
[m]bloodthirsty and deceitful
man.
7 But as for me, I will come into
Your house in the multitude
of Your mercy;
In [n]fear of You I will worship
toward Your holy temple.
8 [o]Lead me, O LORD, in Your
righteousness because of my
enemies;
Make Your way straight before
my face.
9 For *there is* no faithfulness in
their mouth;
Their inward part *is*
destruction;
[p]Their throat *is* an [q]open tomb;
They flatter with their tongue.
10 Pronounce them guilty, O God!
Let them fall by their own
counsels;
Cast them out in the multitude
of their transgressions,
For they have rebelled against
You.
11 But let all those rejoice who
put their [d]trust in You;
Let them ever shout for joy,
because You defend them;
Let those also who love Your
name
Be joyful in You.
12 For You, O LORD, will bless the
righteous;
With favor You will surround
him as *with* a [r]shield.

A cry for mercy

To the Chief Musician. With stringed instruments. On an eight-stringed harp.* A Psalm of David.

6 O LORD, do not [s]rebuke me
in Your anger,

PSALM 4
3 [a] Cp. Jas. 5:16–18
4 [b] Eph. 4:26
5 [c] Dt. 33:19; Ps. 51:19 [d] See Ps. 2:12, *note*
6 [e] Num. 6:26; Ps. 80:3,7,19; 119:135
7 [f] Cp. Isa. 9:3
8 [g] Job 11:18–19; Ps. 3:5 [h] Lev. 25:18–19; 26:5; Dt. 12:10

PSALM 5
1 [i] Ps. 4:1
3 [j] Ps. 55:17; 88:13
5 [k] Hab. 1:13 [l] Ps. 1:5
6 [m] Ps. 55:23; Rev. 21:8
7 [n] See Ps. 19:9, *note*
8 [o] Ps. 25:4–5; 27:11; 31:3
9 [p] Rom. 3:13 [q] Lit. *a yawning gulf*
12 [r] Cp. Gen. 15:1

PSALM 6
1 [s] Ps. 38:1; Jer. 10:24

* **4:3** Many Hebrew manuscripts, Septuagint, Targum, and Vulgate read *made wonderful.* **5:title** Hebrew *nehiloth* **6:title** Hebrew *sheminith*

[1](4:1) David was in trouble and helpless. The LORD gave him strength and courage (vv. 7–8). He became a greater man for the tasks ahead of him.

Nor chasten me in Your hot
displeasure.
2 Have mercy on me, O LORD, for
I *am* weak;
O LORD, heal me, for my bones
are troubled.
3 My soul also is greatly
[a]troubled;
But You, O LORD—how long?

4 Return, O LORD, deliver me!
Oh, save me for Your mercies'
sake!
5 For in death *there is* [b]no
remembrance of You;
In the [c]grave who will give
You thanks?

6 I am weary with my groaning;
All night I make my bed swim;
I drench my couch with my
tears.
7 My eye wastes away because
of grief;
It grows old because of all my
enemies.

8 Depart from me, all you
workers of [d]iniquity;
For the LORD has heard the
voice of my weeping.
9 The LORD has heard my
supplication;
The LORD will receive my
prayer.
10 Let all my enemies be
ashamed and greatly
troubled;
Let them turn back *and* be
ashamed suddenly.

A prayer for deliverance

A Meditation* of David, which he sang to the LORD concerning the words of Cush, a Benjamite.

7 O LORD my God, in You I put
my [e]trust;
[f]Save me from all those who
persecute me;
And deliver me,
2 Lest they tear me like a lion,
Rending *me* in pieces, while
there is none to deliver.

3 O LORD my God, if I have done
this:
If there is iniquity in my
hands,
4 If I have repaid evil to him
who was at peace with me,
[g]Or have plundered my enemy
without cause,
5 Let the enemy pursue me and
overtake *me;*
Yes, let him trample my life to
the earth,
And lay my honor in the dust.
Selah.

6 Arise, O LORD, in Your anger;
[h]Lift Yourself up because of the
rage of my enemies;
Rise up for me* *to* the
judgment You have
commanded!
7 So the congregation of the
peoples shall surround You;
For their sakes, therefore,
return on high.
8 The LORD shall judge the
peoples;
[i]Judge me, O LORD, [j]according
to my righteousness,
And according to my integrity
within me.

9 Oh, let the wickedness of the
wicked come to an end,
But establish the just;
For the righteous God [k]tests
the hearts and minds.
10 [l]My defense *is* of God,
Who saves the upright in
heart.

11 God *is* a just judge,
And God is angry *with the
wicked* every day.
12 If he does not turn back,
He will [m]sharpen His sword;
He bends His bow and makes
it ready.
13 He also prepares for Himself
instruments of death;
He makes His arrows into fiery
shafts.

14 Behold, *the wicked* brings
forth iniquity;
Yes, he [n]conceives trouble and
brings forth falsehood.
15 He [o]made a pit and dug it out,
And has fallen into the ditch
which he made.
16 His trouble shall [p]return upon
his own head,
And his violent dealing shall
come down on his own
crown.

17 I will praise the LORD
according to His
righteousness,
And will sing praise to the
name of the LORD Most High.

3
a Ps. 88:3; cp. Jn. 12:27
5
b Ps. 30:9; 88:9–11; 115:17; Eccl. 9:10
c See Hab. 2:5, *note;* cp. Lk. 16:23, *note*
8
d Cp. Mt. 7:23
PSALM 7
1
e See Ps. 2:12, *note*
f Ps. 31:15
4
g Cp. 1 Sam. 24:11
6
h Ps. 94:2
8
i Ps. 26:1; 35:24; 43:1
j Ps. 18:20; 35:24
9
k Test/ tempt: v. 9; Ps. 11:4. (Gen. 3:1; Jas. 1:14, *note*). Cp. Prov. 17:3
10
l Lit. *My shield is upon God*
12
m Dt. 32:41
14
n Job 15:35; Isa. 59:4; Jas. 1:15
15
o Ps. 57:6
16
p Cp. Gal. 6:7

*7:title Hebrew *Shiggaion* 7:6 Following Masoretic Text, Targum, and Vulgate; Septuagint reads *O LORD my God.*

God's glory and man's dominion

To the Chief Musician. On the instrument of Gath.* A Psalm of David.

8 O LORD, our Lord,
How excellent *is* Your name in all the earth,
Who have set Your [a]glory above the heavens!

2 [b]Out of the mouth of babes and nursing infants
You have ordained strength,
Because of Your enemies,
That You may silence the enemy and the avenger.

3 When I consider Your heavens, the work of Your fingers,
The moon and the stars, which You have ordained,
4 What is [c]man that You are mindful of him,
And the son of man that You [d]visit him?
5 [1]For You have made him a little lower than the [e]angels,*
And You have crowned him with glory and honor.

6 You have made him to have [f]dominion over the works of Your hands;
You have put [g]all *things* under his feet,
7 All sheep and oxen—
Even the beasts of the field,
8 The birds of the air,
And the fish of the sea
That pass through the paths of the seas.

9 O LORD, our Lord,
How excellent *is* Your name in all the earth!

Praise for victory over enemies

To the Chief Musician. To *the tune of* "Death of the Son."* A Psalm of David.

9 I WILL praise *You,* O LORD, with my whole heart;
I will tell of all Your marvelous works.
2 I will be glad and rejoice in You;
I will sing praise to Your name, O Most High.

3 When my enemies turn back,
They shall fall and perish at Your presence.
4 For You have maintained my right and my cause;
You sat on the throne judging in righteousness.
5 You have rebuked the nations,
You have destroyed the wicked;
You have blotted out their name forever and ever.

6 O enemy, destructions are finished forever!
And you have destroyed cities;
Even their memory has [h]perished.
7 But the LORD shall [i]endure forever;
He has prepared His throne for judgment.
8 He shall [j]judge the world in righteousness,
And He shall administer judgment for the peoples in uprightness.

9 The LORD also will be a [k]refuge for the oppressed,
A refuge in times of trouble.
10 And those who [l]know Your name will put their [m]trust in You;
For You, LORD, have not forsaken those who seek You.

11 Sing praises to the LORD, who dwells in Zion!
Declare His [n]deeds among the people.
12 [o]When He avenges blood, He remembers them;
He does not forget the cry of the [p]humble.

13 Have mercy on me, O LORD!

PSALM 8
1 a Cp. Ps. 19:1
2 b Mt. 21:16; cp. 1 Cor. 1:26–31
4 c Job 7:17–18; Heb. 2:6–8
d Job 10:12
5 e See Heb. 1:4, *note*
6 f Gen. 1:26, 28
g 1 Cor. 15:27
PSALM 9
6 h Ps. 34:16
7 i Ps. 102:12, 26; Heb. 1:11
8 j Ps. 96:13; 98:9; Acts 17:31; see Rev. 20:12, *note*
9 k Ps. 32:7; 46:1; 91:2
10 l Cp. Jn. 10:14
m See Ps. 2:12, *note*
11 n Ps. 66:16
12 o Gen. 9:5; cp. 1 Ki. 21:17–19
p Or *afflicted*

* 8:title Hebrew *Al Gittith* 8:5 Hebrew *Elohim, God;* Septuagint, Syriac, Targum, and Jewish tradition translate as *angels.* 9:title Hebrew *Muth Labben*

[1](8:5) In Ps. 2 Christ is seen as God's Son and King, rejected and crucified but yet to reign in Zion. In Ps. 8, while His Deity is fully recognized (v. 1; Ps. 110 with Mt. 22:41–46), He is seen as Son of Man (vv. 4–6) who, "made . . . [for] a little [while] lower than the angels," is to have dominion over the redeemed creation (Heb. 2:6–11). Thus this Psalm speaks primarily of what God bestowed upon the human race as represented in Adam (Gen. 1:26,28). That which the first man lost, the second Man and "last Adam" more than regained. Hebrews 2:6–11, in connection with Ps. 8 and Rom. 8:17–21, shows that the "many sons" whom He is bringing to glory are joint heirs with Him in both the royal right of Ps. 2 and the human right of Heb. 2. See Ps. 16, next in order of the Messianic Psalms.

Consider my trouble from
those who hate me,
You who lift me up from the
gates of death,
14 That I may tell of all Your
praise
In the gates of the daughter of
Zion.
I will [a]rejoice in Your
salvation.
15 The nations have sunk down
in the pit *which* they made;
In the net which they hid, their
own foot is caught.
16 The LORD is known *by* the
judgment He executes;
The wicked is snared in the
work of his own hands.
Meditation.* Selah.
17 The wicked shall be turned
into [b]hell,
And all the nations that forget
God.
18 For the needy shall not always
be forgotten;
The [c]expectation of the poor
shall *not* perish forever.
19 Arise, O LORD,
Do not let man prevail;
Let the nations be judged in
Your sight.
20 Put them in fear, O LORD,
That the nations may know
themselves *to be but* [d]men.
Selah.

A plea for God's judgment

10 WHY do You stand afar off,
O LORD?
Why do You hide in times of
trouble?
2 The wicked in *his* pride
persecutes the poor;
Let them be caught in the plots
which they have devised.
3 For the wicked boasts of his
heart's desire;
He blesses the greedy *and*
renounces the LORD.
4 The wicked in his proud
countenance does not seek
God;
God *is* in none of his thoughts.
5 His ways are always
prospering;
Your judgments *are* far above,
out of his sight;
As for all his enemies, he
sneers at them.
6 He has said in his heart, "I
shall not be moved;
I shall never be in [e]adversity."
7 His mouth is full of [f]cursing
and deceit and oppression;
Under his tongue *is* trouble
and iniquity.
8 He sits in the lurking places of
the villages;
In the secret places he murders
the [g]innocent;
His eyes are secretly fixed on
the helpless.
9 He lies in wait secretly, as a
lion in his den;
He lies in wait to catch the
poor;
He catches the poor when he
draws him into his net.
10 So he crouches, he lies low,
That the helpless may fall by
his strength.
11 He has said in his heart,
"God has forgotten;
He hides His face;
He will never see."
12 Arise, O LORD!
O God, [h]lift up Your hand!
Do not forget the [i]humble.
13 Why do the wicked renounce
God?
He has said in his heart,
"You will not require *an*
account."
14 But You have [j]seen, for You
observe trouble and grief,
To repay *it* by Your hand.
The helpless commits himself
to You;
[k]You are the helper of the
fatherless.
15 Break the arm of the wicked
and the evil *man;*
Seek out his wickedness *until*
You find none.
16 The LORD *is* King forever and
ever;
The nations have perished out
of His land.
17 LORD, You have heard the
desire of the humble;
You will prepare their heart;
You will cause Your ear to
hear,
18 To do justice to the fatherless
and the oppressed,
That the man of the earth may
[l]oppress no more.

14
a Ps. 13:5; 20:5; 35:9
17
b See Hab. 2:5, *note;* cp. Lk. 16:23, *note;* cp. Job 24:19; Ps. 49:14
18
c Ps. 62:5
20
d Cp. Ps. 62:9
PSALM 10
6
e Cp. Isa. 28:15
7
f Rom. 3:14
8
g Cp. 2 Ki. 24:4
12
h Ps. 94:2
i Ps. 9:12
14
j Ps. 11:4
k Ps. 68:5; Hos. 14:3
18
l Lit. *terrify.* Isa. 29:20–21

*9:16 Hebrew *Higgaion*

Taking refuge in God

To the Chief Musician. A Psalm of David.

11 IN the LORD I put my [a]trust;
How can you say to my soul,
"Flee *as* a bird to your mountain"?
2 For look! The wicked bend *their* bow,
They make ready their arrow on the string,
That they may shoot [b]secretly at the upright in heart.
3 [c]If the foundations are destroyed,
What can the righteous do?
4 The LORD *is* in His holy temple,
The LORD's [d]throne *is* in heaven;
His eyes behold,
His eyelids [e]test the sons of men.
5 The LORD tests the righteous,
But the wicked and the one who loves violence His soul hates.
6 Upon the wicked He will rain coals;
Fire and brimstone and a burning wind
Shall be the [f]portion of their cup.
7 For the LORD *is* righteous,
He loves righteousness;
His countenance beholds the upright.*

The scourge of sinful speech

To the Chief Musician. On an eight-stringed harp.* A Psalm of David.

12 HELP, LORD, for the godly man [g]ceases!
For the faithful disappear from among the sons of men.
2 They speak idly everyone with his neighbor;
With flattering lips *and* a double heart they speak.
3 May the LORD cut off all [h]flattering lips,
And the [i]tongue that speaks proud things,
4 Who have said,
"With our tongue we will prevail;
Our lips *are* our own;
Who *is* lord over us?"
5 "For the oppression of the poor, for the sighing of the needy,
Now I will arise," says the LORD;
"I will set *him* in the safety for which he yearns."
6 The words of the LORD *are* [j]pure words,
Like silver tried in a furnace of earth,
Purified seven times.
7 You shall keep them, O LORD,
You shall preserve them from this generation forever.
8 The wicked prowl on every side,
When vileness is exalted among the sons of men.

The testing of delay

To the Chief Musician. A Psalm of David.

13 HOW long, O LORD? Will You forget me forever?
How long will You hide Your face from me?
2 How long shall I take counsel in my soul,
Having sorrow in my heart daily?
How long will my enemy be exalted over me?
3 Consider *and* hear me, O LORD my God;
[k]Enlighten my eyes,
Lest I sleep the *sleep of* death;
4 Lest my enemy say,
"I have prevailed against him";
Lest those who trouble me rejoice when I am moved.
5 But I have [l]trusted in Your mercy;
My heart shall rejoice in Your salvation.
6 I will sing to the LORD,
Because He has dealt bountifully with me.

A portrait of the godless

To the Chief Musician. A Psalm of David.

14 [m]THE fool has said in his heart,
"*There is* no God."
[n]They are corrupt,
They have done abominable works,
There is none who does good.
2 The LORD looks down from heaven upon the children of men,
To see if there are any who [o]understand, who seek God.
3 [p]They have all turned aside,

PSALM 11
1
a Ps. 7:1; see 2:12, *note*
2
b Lit. *in darkness*
3
c Ps. 82:5
4
d Ps. 2:4; Isa. 66:1; Mt. 5:34; 23:22; Acts 7:49; Rev. 4:2
e *Test/tempt:* vv. 4–5; Ps. 17:3. (Gen. 3:1; Jas. 1:14, *note*). Cp. Gen. 22:1; Jas. 1:12
6
f Ps. 75:8; Ezek. 38:22
PSALM 12
1
g Isa. 57:1
3
h Cp. Job 32:21; Prov. 20:19; Rom. 16:18
i Ps. 17:10; cp. 1 Sam. 2:3; Dan. 7:8,25; Rev. 13:5
6
j Ps. 18:30; 119:140; Prov. 30:5
PSALM 13
3
k Cp. 1 Sam. 14:29; Ezra 9:8
5
l See Ps. 2:12, *note*
PSALM 14
1
m This Psalm is almost identical with Ps. 53
n v. 3; Rom. 3:10
2
o Rom. 3:11
3
p Rom. 3:12

*11:7 Or *The upright beholds His countenance*
12:title Hebrew *sheminith*

They have together become
corrupt;
There is none who does good,
No, not one.

4 Have all the workers of
iniquity no knowledge,
[a]Who eat up my people *as* they
eat bread,
And do not call on the LORD?
5 There they are in great fear,
For God *is* with the generation
of the righteous.
6 You shame the counsel of the
poor,
But the LORD *is* his refuge.

7 [b]Oh, that the salvation of Israel
would come out of Zion!
When the LORD brings back the
[c]captivity of His people,
Let Jacob rejoice *and* Israel be
glad.

The man who abides with God

A Psalm of David.

15 LORD, who may abide in
Your tabernacle?
Who may [d]dwell in Your holy
hill?

2 He who walks uprightly,
And works righteousness,
And speaks the [e]truth in his
heart;
3 He *who* does not [f]backbite
with his tongue,
Nor does evil to his
neighbor,
Nor does he take up a
reproach against his
friend;
4 In whose eyes a vile person is
despised,
But he honors those who
[g]fear the LORD;
He *who* [h]swears to his own
hurt and does not change;
5 He *who* does not put out his
money at [i]usury,
Nor does he take a bribe
against the innocent.

He who does these *things* shall
never be moved.

4
a Jer. 10:25; Amos 8:4; Mic. 3:3
7
b Ps. 53:6; Rom. 11:25–27
c Dt. 30:3
PSALM 15
1
d Ps. 24:3–5
2
e Eph. 4:25
3
f Lev. 19:16–18
4
g See Ps. 19:9, *note*
h Lev. 5:4; cp. Jud. 11:35
5
i Lev. 25:36–37
PSALM 16
1
j Ps. 17:8
k See Ps. 2:12, *note*
3
l Ps. 119:63
4
m Ps. 106:37–38
n Ex. 23:13; Josh. 23:7
8
o vv. 8–11; Acts 2:25–28
9
p Kingdom (OT): vv. 8–11; Ps. 72:1. (Gen. 1:26; Zech. 12:8, *note*)
q Resurrection: vv. 9–11; Isa. 26:19. (2 Ki. 4:35; 1 Cor. 15:52, *note*)
10
r Christ (first advent): v. 10; Ps. 22:1. (Gen. 3:15; Acts 1:11, *note*)
s See Hab. 2:5, *note;* cp. Lk. 16:23, *note*
t Ps. 49:15; Acts 13:35

The path of life and joy

A Michtam of David.

16 [j]PRESERVE me, O God, for in
You I put my [k]trust.

2 O *my soul,* you have said to
the LORD,
"You *are* my Lord,
My goodness is nothing apart
from You."
3 As for the saints who *are* on
the earth,
"They are the excellent ones, in
[l]whom is all my delight."
4 Their sorrows shall be
multiplied who hasten *after*
[1]another *god;*
Their drink offerings of [m]blood
I will not offer,
Nor take up their names on my
[n]lips.

5 O LORD, *You are* the portion of
my inheritance and my cup;
You maintain my lot.
6 The lines have fallen to me in
pleasant *places;*
Yes, I have a good inheritance.

7 I will bless the LORD who has
given me counsel;
My heart also instructs me in
the night seasons.
8 [o]I have set the LORD always
before me;
Because *He is* at my right hand
I shall not be moved.

9 [p]Therefore my heart is glad,
and my glory rejoices;
[2]My flesh also will rest in
[q]hope.
10 For You will not leave [r]my
soul in [s]Sheol,
Nor will You [t]allow Your
Holy One to see corruption.
11 You will show me the path of
life;
In Your presence *is* fullness of
joy;
At Your right hand *are*
pleasures forevermore.

---

[1](16:4) Of course there is only one God (1 Cor. 8:5–6). The pagans had, however, those whom they called "gods", e.g. in David's day, Dagon and Baal. Then and now, whatever preempts the place in one's heart that belongs to the true God may be said to be a god, e.g. self and the pleasures of this world (2 Tim. 3:2,4).

[2](16:9) The 16th Psalm is a prediction of the resurrection of the King. As a prophet, David declared that, not at His first advent but at some time subsequent to His death and resurrection, the Messiah would assume the Davidic throne. Cp. Acts 2:25–31 with Lk. 1:32–33 and Acts 15:13–17. See Davidic Covenant, 2 Sam. 7:16, *note;* Kingdom (OT), Zech. 12:8, *note.* See Ps. 22, next in order of the Messianic Psalms.

Reliance on God

A Prayer of David.

17 HEAR a just cause, O LORD,
Attend to my cry;
Give ear to my prayer *which is*
not from deceitful lips.
2 Let my vindication come from
Your presence;
Let Your eyes look on the
things that are upright.

3 You have tested my heart;
You have visited *me* in the
night;
You have [a]tried me and have
found [b]nothing;
I have purposed that my
mouth shall not [c]transgress.
4 Concerning the works of men,
By the word of Your lips,
I have kept away from the
paths of the destroyer.
5 Uphold my steps in Your
paths,
That my footsteps may not
slip.

6 I have called upon You, for
You will hear me, O God;
Incline Your ear to me, *and*
hear my speech.
7 Show Your marvelous
lovingkindness by Your
right hand,
O You who save those who
trust *in You*
From those who rise up
against them.
8 Keep me as the apple of Your
eye;
Hide me under the shadow of
Your wings,
9 From the wicked who oppress
me,
From my deadly enemies who
surround me.

10 They have closed up their [d]fat
hearts;
With their mouths they speak
proudly.
11 They have now surrounded us
in our steps;
They have set their eyes,
crouching down to the earth,
12 As a lion is eager to tear his
prey,
And like a young lion lurking
in secret places.

13 Arise, O LORD,
Confront him, cast him down;
Deliver my life from the
wicked with Your sword,

PSALM 17

3

a Test/ tempt: v. 3; Ps. 26:2. (Gen. 3:1; Jas. 1:14, *note*)
b Cp. Jer. 50:20
c Ps. 39:1

10

d Ezek. 16:49

14

e Cp. Lk. 16:25
f Cp. Job 21:8,11

15

g Isa. 26:19
h Ps. 16:11

PSALM 18

Title

i vv. 1–50; cp. 2 Sam. 22:1–51

1

j Ps. 144:1

2

k Prov. 2:7
l See Dt. 33:17, *note*

3

m Rev. 5:12

4

n Ps. 116:3
o Heb. *Belial*

5

p See Hab. 2:5, *note;* cp. Lk. 16:23, *note*

7

q Cp. Mt. 27:45–51

14 With Your hand from men, O
LORD,
From men of the world *who
have* their [e]portion in *this*
life,
And whose belly You fill with
Your hidden treasure.
They are satisfied with
[f]children,
And leave the rest of their
possession for their babes.

15 As for me, I will see Your face
in righteousness;
I shall be [g]satisfied when I
[h]awake in Your likeness.

Praise to the God who delivers His own

To the Chief Musician. A Psalm of David the servant of the LORD, who spoke to the LORD the words of this song on the day that the LORD delivered him from the hand of all his enemies and from the hand of Saul. And he [i]said:

18 I WILL love You, O LORD, my
[j]strength.
2 The LORD is my rock and my
fortress and my deliverer;
My God, my strength, in whom
I will trust;
My [k]shield and the [l]horn of
my salvation, my stronghold.
3 I will call upon the LORD, [m]*who
is worthy* to be praised;
So shall I be saved from my
enemies.

4 The [n]pangs of death
surrounded me,
And the floods of [o]ungodliness
made me afraid.
5 The sorrows of [p]Sheol
surrounded me;
The snares of death confronted
me.
6 In my distress I called upon
the LORD,
And cried out to my God;
He heard my voice from His
temple,
And my cry came before Him,
even to His ears.

7 [q]Then the earth shook and
trembled;
The foundations of the hills
also quaked and were
shaken,
Because He was angry.
8 Smoke went up from His
nostrils,
And devouring fire from His
mouth;
Coals were kindled by it.

9 [a]He bowed the heavens also,
and came down
With darkness under His feet.
10 [b]And He rode upon a cherub,
and flew;
He flew upon the wings of the
wind.
11 He made [c]darkness His secret
place;
[d]His canopy around Him *was*
dark waters
And thick clouds of the skies.
12 From the brightness before
Him,
His thick clouds passed with
hailstones and coals of [e]fire.
13 The LORD thundered from
heaven,
And the Most High uttered His
[f]voice,
Hailstones and coals of fire.*
14 He sent out His arrows and
[g]scattered the foe,
Lightnings in abundance, and
He vanquished them.
15 Then the channels of the sea
were seen,
The foundations of the world
were uncovered
At Your rebuke, O LORD,
At the blast of the breath of
Your nostrils.
16 [h]He sent from above, He took
me;
He drew me out of many
waters.
17 He delivered me from my
strong enemy,
From those who hated me,
For they were too strong for
me.
18 They confronted me in the day
of my calamity,
But the LORD was my support.
19 [i]He also brought me out into a
broad place;
He delivered me because He
delighted in me.

20 The LORD rewarded me
according to my
righteousness;
According to the cleanness of
my hands
He has recompensed me.
21 For I have kept the ways of the
LORD,
And have not wickedly
departed from my God.
22 For all His [j]judgments *were*
before me,
And I did not put away His
statutes from me.
23 I was also blameless before
Him,
And I kept myself from my
iniquity.
24 Therefore the LORD has
recompensed me according
to my righteousness,
According to the cleanness of
my hands in His sight.

25 With the [k]merciful You will
show Yourself merciful;
With a blameless man You will
show Yourself blameless;
26 With the pure You will show
Yourself pure;
And with the devious You will
show Yourself shrewd.
27 For You will save the humble
people,
[l]But will bring down haughty
looks.
28 [m]For You will light my [n]lamp;
The LORD my God will
enlighten my darkness.
29 For by You I can run against a
troop,
By my God I can leap over a
wall.
30 *As for* God, His way *is* perfect;
The [o]word of the LORD is
proven;
He *is* a [p]shield to all who
[q]trust in Him.

31 For who *is* God, except the
LORD?
And who *is* a rock, except our
God?
32 *It is* God who arms me with
strength,
And makes my way perfect.
33 He makes my feet like the *feet*
of deer,
And sets me on my high
places.
34 He teaches my hands to make
war,
So that my arms can bend a
bow of [r]bronze.

35 You have also given me the
shield of Your salvation;
Your right hand has held me
up,
Your gentleness has made me
great.

9 a Ps. 144:5
10 b Cp. Ps. 99:1
11 c Cp. Dt. 4:11 d Ps. 97:2
12 e Ps. 97:4
13 f Ps. 29:3–9
14 g Ps. 144:6; cp. Josh. 10:10; Isa. 30:30
16 h Ps. 144:7
19 i Ps. 31:8; 118:5
22 j Ps. 19:9
25 k Mt. 5:7
27 l Prov. 6:17
28 m Ps. 119:105; 132:17; cp. 2 Chr. 21:7 n Prov. 20:27; cp. Prov. 13:9
30 o Ps. 12:6; 119:140; Prov. 30:5 p Ps. 18:2 q See Ps. 2:12, *note*
34 r 2 Sam. 22:35

*18:13 Following Masoretic Text, Targum, and Vulgate; a few Hebrew manuscripts and Septuagint omit *Hailstones and coals of fire.*

36 You enlarged my path under
me,
So my feet did not slip.
37 I have pursued my enemies
and overtaken them;
Neither did I turn back again
till they were destroyed.
38 I have wounded them,
So that they could not rise;
They have fallen under my
feet.
39 For You have armed me with
strength for the battle;
You have [a]subdued under me
those who rose up against
me.
40 You have also given me
the necks of my enemies,
So that I destroyed those who
hated me.
41 They cried out, but *there was*
none to save;
Even to the LORD, [b]but He did
not answer them.
42 Then I beat them as fine as the
dust before the wind;
I [c]cast them out like dirt in the
streets.
43 You have delivered me from
the strivings of the people;
You have made me the head of
the [d]nations;
A [e]people I have not known
shall serve me.
44 As soon as they hear of me
they obey me;
The [f]foreigners submit to me.
45 The foreigners fade away,
And come frightened from
their hideouts.
46 The LORD lives!
Blessed *be* my Rock!
Let the God of my salvation be
exalted.
47 *It is* God who avenges me,
And subdues the peoples under
me;
48 He delivers me from my
enemies.
You also lift me up above
those who rise against me;
You have delivered me from
the violent man.
49 Therefore I will give [g]thanks
to You, O LORD, among the
Gentiles,
And sing praises to Your
name.
50 Great deliverance He gives to
His king,
And shows mercy to His
anointed,
To [h]David and his descendants
forevermore.

39 *a* Lit. *caused to bow*
41 *b* Prov. 1:28; Isa. 1:15; Ezek. 8:18; Zech. 7:13
42 *c* Cp. Zech. 10:5
43 *d* Ps. 2:8 *e* Cp. Isa. 55:5
44 *f* 2 Sam. 22:45–46
49 *g* 2 Sam. 22:50; Rom. 15:9
50 *h* 2 Sam. 7:12
PSALM 19
1 *i* Rom. 1:19–20 *j* Gen. 1:6–7
4 *k* Cp. Eccl. 1:5
7 *l* *Law* (of Moses): vv. 7–8; Ps. 37:31. (Ex. 19:1; Gal. 3:24, *note*) *m* Rom. 7:12 *n* Ps. 119:130
9 *o* Ps. 18:22
10 *p* Ps. 119:72, 127; Prov. 8:10–11,19

The works and Word of God

To the Chief Musician. A Psalm of David.

19 THE heavens [i]declare the
glory of God;
And the [j]firmament shows His
handiwork.
2 Day unto day utters speech,
And night unto night reveals
knowledge.
3 *There is* no speech nor
language
Where their voice is not heard.
4 Their line* has gone out
through all the earth,
And their words to the end of
the world.

In them He has set a
tabernacle for the [k]sun,
5 Which *is* like a bridegroom
coming out of his chamber,
And rejoices like a strong man
to run its race.
6 Its rising *is* from one end of
heaven,
And its circuit to the other
end;
And there is nothing hidden
from its heat.

7 The [1][l]law of the LORD *is*
[m]perfect, converting the soul;
The testimony of the LORD *is*
sure, making [n]wise the
simple;
8 The statutes of the LORD *are*
right, rejoicing the heart;
The commandment of the LORD
is pure, enlightening the
eyes;
9 The [2]fear of the LORD *is* clean,
enduring forever;
The [o]judgments of the LORD
are true *and* righteous
altogether.
10 More to be desired *are they*
than [p]gold,

*19:4 Septuagint, Syriac, and Vulgate read *sound;* Targum reads *business.*

[1](19:7) Whereas the law of the LORD is summarized in the Ten Commandments, it comprises all God's revealed truth—in David's day, the Pentateuch; today the whole Bible.
[2](19:9) "The fear of the LORD" is an OT expression meaning *reverential trust,* including the hatred of evil.

Yea, than much fine gold;
Sweeter also than honey and the honeycomb.
11 Moreover by them Your servant is warned,
And in keeping them *there is* great reward.
12 Who can understand *his* errors?
[a]Cleanse me from secret *faults.*
13 Keep back Your servant also from [b]presumptuous *sins;*
Let them not have [c]dominion over me.
Then I shall be blameless,
And I shall be innocent of great transgression.
14 [d]Let the words of my mouth and the meditation of my heart
Be acceptable in Your sight,
O LORD, my [e]strength and my [f]Redeemer.

A plea for help from the sanctuary

To the Chief Musician. A Psalm of David.

20 MAY the LORD answer you in the day of trouble;
May the name of the God of Jacob [g]defend you;
2 May He send you help from the [h]sanctuary,
And strengthen you out of Zion;
3 May He [i]remember all your offerings,
And accept your burnt sacrifice. Selah.
4 May He grant you according to your heart's *desire,*
And [j]fulfill all your purpose.
5 We will rejoice in your salvation,
And in the name of our God we will set up *our* banners!
May the LORD fulfill all your petitions.
6 Now I know that the LORD saves His anointed;
He will answer him from His [k]holy heaven
With the saving strength of His right hand.
7 Some *trust* in chariots, and some in [l]horses;
[m]But we will remember the name of the LORD our God.
8 They have bowed down and fallen;
But we have risen and stand upright.
9 Save, LORD!
May the King answer us when we call.

God's blessing of the King

To the Chief Musician. A Psalm of David.

21 THE king shall have joy in Your strength, O LORD;
And in Your salvation how greatly shall he rejoice!
2 You have given him his heart's desire,
And have not withheld the [n]request of his lips. Selah.
3 For You meet him with the blessings of goodness;
You set a crown of pure gold upon his head.
4 [o]He asked life from You, *and* You gave *it* to him—
Length of days forever and ever.
5 His glory *is* great in Your salvation;
Honor and majesty You have placed upon him.
6 For You have made him most blessed forever;
[p]You have made him exceedingly glad with Your presence.
7 For the king [q]trusts in the LORD,
And through the mercy of the Most High he shall not be moved.
8 Your hand will [r]find all Your enemies;
Your right hand will find those who hate You.
9 You shall make them as a fiery oven in the time of Your anger;
The LORD shall swallow them up in His wrath,
And the fire shall devour them.
10 Their offspring You shall destroy from the earth,
And their descendants from among the sons of men.
11 For they intended evil against You;
They devised a plot *which* they are not able *to* [s]*perform.*
12 Therefore You will make them turn their back;
You will make ready *Your arrows* on Your string toward their faces.

---

12 *a* Ps. 51:1–2
13 *b* Num. 15:30 *c* Ps. 119:133; Rom. 6:12–14
14 *d* Ps. 51:15 *e* Lit. *rock* *f Redemption* (redeeming relative type): v. 14; Ps. 69:18. (Gen. 48:16; Isa. 59:20, *note*)

PSALM 20
1 *g* Lit. *set you on a high place*
2 *h* Heb. *qodesh,* translated *holy* in v. 6
3 *i* Cp. Acts 10:4
4 *j* Ps. 21:2
6 *k Sanctification* (OT): v. 6; Ps. 89:20. (Gen. 2:3; Zech. 8:3)
7 *l* Dt. 20:1; Ps. 33:16–17; Prov. 21:31; Isa. 31:1 *m* Cp. 2 Chr. 32:8

PSALM 21
2 *n* 2 Sam. 7:26–29
4 *o* Ps. 61:5–6
6 *p* Ps. 16:11; 45:7
7 *q* See Ps. 2:12, *note*
8 *r* Cp. Isa. 10:10
11 *s* Ps. 2:1–4

13 Be exalted, O LORD, in Your
own strength!
We will sing and praise Your
power.

The suffering Savior

To the Chief Musician. Set to "The Deer of the Dawn."* A Psalm of David.

22 [1]MY [a]God, [b]My God, why
have You forsaken Me?
Why are You so far from
helping [c]Me,
And from the words of My
groaning?
2 O My God, I cry in the
daytime, but You do not
hear;
And in the night season, and
am not silent.
3 But You *are* holy,
Enthroned in the praises of
Israel.
4 Our fathers trusted in You;
They [d]trusted, and You
delivered them.
5 They cried to You, and were
delivered;
They trusted in You, and were
not ashamed.
6 But I *am* a worm, and no man;
A reproach of men, and
[e]despised by the people.
7 [2]All those who see Me ridicule
Me;
They shoot out the lip, they
shake the head, *saying*,
8 "He [f]trusted* in the LORD, let
Him rescue Him;
Let Him deliver Him, since He
delights in Him!"
9 But You *are* He who [g]took Me
out of the womb;
You made Me trust *while* on
My mother's breasts.

PSALM 22
1
a Mt. 27:46
b Sacrifice (prophetic): vv. 1–18; Isa. 52:14. (Gen. 3:15; Heb. 10:18, *note*)
c Christ (first advent): vv. 1–18; Isa. 7:14. (Gen. 3:15; Acts 1:11, *note*)
4
d See Ps. 2:12, *note*
6
e vv. 7, 11–13; Ps. 109:25; Mt. 27:39–44
8
f Lit. *rolled.* Cp. Mt. 27:43; see Ps. 2:12, *note*
9
g Ps. 71:6
12
h Dt. 32:14
13
i Job 16:10
16
j Cp. Rev. 22:15
k Isa. 53:7; cp. Jn. 20:20–25
18
l Mt. 27:35

10 I was cast upon You from
birth.
From My mother's womb
You *have been* My God.
11 Be not far from Me,
For trouble *is* near;
For *there is* none to help.
12 Many bulls have surrounded
Me;
Strong *bulls* of [h]Bashan have
encircled Me.
13 They [i]gape at Me *with* their
mouths,
Like a raging and roaring lion.
14 I am poured out like water,
And all My bones are out of
joint;
My heart is like wax;
It has melted within Me.
15 My strength is dried up like a
potsherd,
And My tongue clings to My
jaws;
You have brought Me to the
dust of death.
16 For [j]dogs have surrounded
Me;
The congregation of the
wicked has enclosed Me.
[3]They [k]pierced* My hands and
My feet;
17 I can count all My bones.
They look *and* stare at Me.
18 They divide My garments
among them,
And for My clothing they [l]cast
lots.
19 But You, O LORD, do not be far
from Me;

*

22:title Hebrew *Aijeleth Hashahar* 22:8 Septuagint, Syriac, and Vulgate read *hoped;* Targum reads *praised.* 22:16 Following some Hebrew manuscripts, Septuagint, Syriac, Vulgate; Masoretic Text reads *Like a lion.*

[1](22:1) Psalms 22, 23, and 24 form a trilogy. In Ps. 22 the *good* Shepherd gives His life for the sheep (Jn. 10:11); in Ps. 23 the *great* Shepherd, whom God "brought up . . . from the dead . . . through the blood of the everlasting covenant" (Heb. 13:20), tenderly cares for His sheep; in Ps. 24 the *chief* Shepherd appears as King of glory to reward His sheep (1 Pet. 5:4).

[2](22:7) Psalm 22 is a graphic picture of death by crucifixion. The bones (of the hands, arms, shoulders, and pelvis) out of joint (v. 14); the profuse perspiration caused by intense suffering (v. 14); the action of the heart affected (v. 14); strength exhausted, and extreme thirst (v. 15); the hands and feet pierced (see v. 16, *note*, but cp. Jn. 20:20 also); partial nudity with the hurt to modesty (v. 17), are all associated with that mode of death. The accompanying circumstances are precisely those fulfilled in the crucifixion of Christ. The desolate cry of v. 1 (Mt. 27:46); the periods of light and darkness of v. 2 (Mt. 27:45); the contemptuous and humiliating treatment of vv. 6–8,12–13 (Mt. 27:39–44); the casting lots of v. 18 (Mt. 27:35), were all literally fulfilled. When it is remembered that crucifixion was a Roman, not Jewish, form of execution, the proof of inspiration is irresistible.

[3](22:16) Although the Hebrew text here reads "like the lion," this gives no clear meaning to the passage. Ancient versions and some manuscripts support the translation, "they pierced."

O My Strength, hasten to help
Me!
20 Deliver Me from the sword,
My precious *life* from the
power of the dog.
21 Save Me from the lion's mouth
And from the horns of the wild
oxen!

You have answered Me.

22 [1]I will declare Your name to My
[a]brethren;
In the midst of the assembly I
will praise You.
23 You who [b]fear the LORD, praise
Him!
All you descendants of Jacob,
glorify Him,
And fear Him, all you
offspring of Israel!
24 For He has not despised nor
abhorred the affliction of the
afflicted;
Nor has He hidden His face
from Him;
But when He cried to Him, He
heard.

25 My praise *shall be* of You in
the great assembly;
I will pay My vows before
those who [b]fear Him.
26 [2]The [c]poor shall [d]eat and be
satisfied;
Those who seek Him will
praise the LORD.
Let your heart live forever!

27 All the ends of the world
Shall remember and turn to
the LORD,
And all the families of the
nations
Shall worship before You.*
28 For the kingdom *is* the LORD's,
And He rules over the nations.

29 All the prosperous of the earth
Shall eat and worship;
All those who go down to the
dust
Shall bow before Him,
Even he who cannot keep
himself alive.

30 A [e]posterity shall serve Him.
It will be recounted of the Lord
to the *next* generation,
31 They will come and declare
His righteousness to a
people who will be born,
That He has done *this*.

The divine Shepherd

A Psalm of David.

23 THE LORD *is* my [f]shepherd;
I shall [g]not want.
2 He makes me to lie down in
green [h]pastures;
He leads me beside the [i]still
waters.
3 He restores my soul;
He [j]leads me in the paths of
righteousness
For His name's sake.

4 Yea, though I walk through the
valley of the [k]shadow of
death,
I will [l]fear no evil;
For You *are* [m]with me;
Your rod and Your staff, they
comfort me.

5 You [n]prepare a table before
me in the presence of my
enemies;
You [o]anoint my head with oil;
My cup runs over.
6 Surely goodness and mercy
shall follow me
All the days of my life;
And I will dwell* in the house
of the LORD
Forever.

The ascension of the King of glory

A Psalm of David.

24 THE [p]earth *is* the LORD's, and
all its fullness,
The world and those who
dwell therein.
2 For He has [q]founded it upon
the seas,
And established it upon the
[r]waters.

22
a Heb. 2:12
23
b See Ps. 19:9, *note*
26
c Cp. Mt. 5:5
d Cp. Jn. 6:51–58; 1 Cor. 11:26
30
e Cp. Isa. 53:10–11
PSALM 23
1
f Isa. 40:11; Ezek. 34:11–12; Jn. 10:11; 1 Pet. 2:25
g *Assurance/security:* vv. 1–6; Ps. 91:1. (Ps. 23:1; Jude 1, *note*)
2
h Ezek. 34:14
i Lit. *waters of quietness.* Cp. Rev. 7:17
3
j Ps. 5:8; 31:3; Prov. 8:20
4
k Job 3:5; 10:21–22; 24:17; Ps. 44:19; cp. Rev. 1:18
l Ps. 27:1
m Cp. Isa. 43:2
5
n Ps. 104:15
o Lit. *make fat.* Ps. 92:10; cp. Lk. 7:46
PSALM 24
1
p 1 Cor. 10:26,28
2
q Ps. 89:11
r Lit. *rivers*

*
22:27 Following Masoretic Text, Septuagint, and Targum; Arabic, Syriac, and Vulgate read *Him.*
23:6 Following Septuagint, Syriac, Targum, and Vulgate; Masoretic Text reads *return.*

[1](22:22) At v. 22 the Psalm shifts from crucifixion to resurrection; fulfilled in the "go to My brethren," etc., of Jn. 20:17. The risen Christ declares to His brethren the name, "Father."
[2](22:26) Verses 26–31 relate the results of the suffering and deliverance described in the Psalm and prove its Messianic reference beyond all question. It could not possibly be said of the suffering and subsequent deliverance of any mere human being that it would result in both the meek and the prosperous being fed (vv. 26,29), in all the ends of the earth turning to the LORD (v. 27), in all the dead eventually bowing before Him (v. 29), and in a new people being born (v. 31). See Ps. 23 and 24, next in order of the Messianic Psalms.

3[1][a]Who may ascend into the hill
of the LORD?
Or who may stand in His holy
place?
4 He who has clean hands and a
[b]pure heart,
Who has not lifted up his soul
to an idol,
Nor sworn deceitfully.
5 He shall receive blessing from
the LORD,
And righteousness from the
God of his salvation.
6 This *is* Jacob, the generation of
those who seek Him,
Who seek Your face. Selah.

7 [c]Lift up your heads, O you
gates!
And be lifted up, you
everlasting doors!
And the [d]King of glory shall
come in.
8 Who *is* this King of glory?
The LORD strong and mighty,
The LORD mighty in [e]battle.
9 Lift up your heads, O you
gates!
Lift up, you everlasting doors!
And the King of glory shall
come in.
10 Who is this [f]King of glory?
The LORD of hosts,
He *is* the King of glory. Selah.

A plea for defense, guidance, pardon

A Psalm of David.

25 TO You, O LORD, I lift up my
soul.
2 O my God, I [g]trust in You;
Let me not be ashamed;
[h]Let not my enemies triumph
over me.
3 Indeed, let no one who waits
on You be ashamed;
Let those be ashamed who
deal treacherously without
cause.
4 [i]Show me Your ways, O LORD;
Teach me Your paths.
5 Lead me in Your truth and
teach me,
For You *are* the God of my
salvation;
On You I wait all the day.

6 Remember, O LORD, [j]Your
tender mercies and Your
lovingkindnesses,
For they *are* from of old.
7 Do not remember the [k]sins of
my youth, nor my
transgressions;
[l]According to Your mercy
remember me,
For Your goodness' sake, O
LORD.

8 Good and upright *is* the LORD;
Therefore He teaches sinners
in the way.
9 The humble He guides in
[m]justice,
And the humble He teaches
His way.
10 All the paths of the LORD *are*
mercy and truth,
To such as keep His covenant
and His testimonies.
11 [n]For Your name's sake, O LORD,
Pardon my iniquity, [o]for it *is*
great.

12 Who *is* the man that [p]fears the
LORD?
Him shall He* teach in the
way He* chooses.
13 He himself shall dwell in
prosperity,
And his descendants shall
inherit the earth.
14 The [q]secret of the LORD *is* with
those who fear Him,
And He will show them His
[r]covenant.
15 My eyes *are* ever toward the
LORD,
For He shall [s]pluck my feet
out of the net.

16 Turn Yourself to me, and have
mercy on me,
For I *am* desolate and afflicted.
17 The troubles of my heart have
enlarged;
Bring me out of my distresses!
18 Look on my affliction and my
pain,
And forgive all my sins.
19 Consider my enemies, for they
are many;
And they hate me with cruel
hatred.
20 Keep my soul, and deliver me;
Let me not be ashamed, for I
put my [g]trust in You.

3 *a* Ps. 15:1–5
4 *b* Mt. 5:8
7 *c* Cp. Isa. 26:2; *d* 1 Cor. 2:8
8 *e* Rev. 19:13–16
10 *f Christ* (second advent): vv. 7–10; Ps. 50:3. (Dt. 30:3; Acts 1:11, *note*)
PSALM 25
2 *g* See Ps. 2:12, *note*; *h* Ps. 13:4
4 *i* Ps. 5:8; 27:11; 86:11; 119:27; 143:8; cp. Ex. 33:13
6 *j* Ps. 103:17; 106:1; cp. Isa. 63:15; Jer. 33:11
7 *k* Job 13:26; Jer. 3:25; *l* Ps. 51:1
9 *m* Ps. 9:16
11 *n* Ps. 31:3; 79:9; 109:21; 143:11; *o* Cp. Rom. 5:20
12 *p* See Ps. 19:9, *note*
14 *q* Prov. 3:32; Jn. 7:17; see Jn. 15:15, *note*; *r* Cp. 2 Sam. 7:4–17
15 *s* Lit. *bring forth*

* 25:12 Or *he* • Or *he*

[1](24:3) The order is: (1) the declaration of title, "The earth is the LORD's" (vv. 1–2); (2) who shall rule the earth? (vv. 3–6)—it is a question of worthiness, and no one is worthy but the Lamb (cp. Dan. 7:13–14; Mt. 25:31; Rev. 5:1–10); and (3) the King of glory takes the throne of earth (vv. 7–10). See Ps. 40, next in order of the Messianic Psalms.

21 Let integrity and uprightness
preserve me,
For I wait for You.

22 [a]Redeem Israel, O God,
Out of all their troubles!

David's integrity

A Psalm of David.

26 VINDICATE me, O LORD,
For I have walked in my
integrity.
I have also [b]trusted in the
LORD;
I shall not slip.
2 Examine me, O LORD, and
prove me;
[c]Try my mind and my heart.
3 For Your lovingkindness *is*
before my eyes,
And I have walked in Your
truth.
4 I have not [d]sat with idolatrous
mortals,
Nor will I go in with
hypocrites.
5 I have hated the assembly of
evildoers,
And will not sit with the
wicked.
6 I will wash my hands in
innocence;
So I will go about Your altar,
O LORD,
7 That I may proclaim with the
voice of thanksgiving,
And tell of all Your wondrous
works.
8 LORD, I have [e]loved the
habitation of Your house,
And the place where Your
glory dwells.

9 Do not gather my soul with
sinners,
Nor my life with bloodthirsty
men,
10 In whose hands *is* a sinister
scheme,
And whose right hand is full of
bribes.

11 But as for me, I will walk in
my integrity;
[a]Redeem me and be merciful to
me.
12 My foot stands in an even
place;
In the congregations I will
bless the LORD.

22
[a] See Ex. 14:30 and Isa. 59:20, *notes*

PSALM 26
1
[b] See Ps. 2:12, *note*
2
[c] *Test/tempt*: v. 2; Ps. 66:10. (Gen. 3:1; Jas. 1:14, *note*)
4
[d] Ps. 1:1; Jer. 15:17
8
[e] Ps. 27:4; 84:1–4,10

PSALM 27
1
[f] Ps. 84:11; Isa. 60:19–20; Mic. 7:8
[g] Ps. 62:2,6; 118:14,21; Isa. 12:2
3
[h] Ps. 3:6
4
[i] Ps. 26:8; 65:4; cp. Lk. 2:37
5
[j] Ps. 31:20; 91:1
[k] Ps. 40:2
8
[l] Or *My heart said to You, "Let my face seek Your face"*
9
[m] Ps. 69:17; 143:7
10
[n] Cp. Isa. 63:16
[o] Isa. 49:15

Triumphant faith

A Psalm of David.

27 THE LORD *is* my [f]light and
my salvation;
Whom shall I fear?
The [g]LORD *is* the strength of
my life;
Of whom shall I be afraid?
2 When the wicked came against
me
To eat up my flesh,
My enemies and foes,
They stumbled and fell.
3 [h]Though an army may encamp
against me,
My heart shall not fear;
Though war may rise against
me,
In this I *will be* confident.

4 One *thing* I have desired of the
LORD,
That will I seek:
That I may [i]dwell in the house
of the LORD
All the days of my life,
To behold the beauty of the
LORD,
And to inquire in His temple.
5 For in the time of trouble
He shall [j]hide me in His
pavilion;
In the secret place of His
tabernacle
He shall hide me;
He shall [k]set me high upon a
rock.
6 And now my head shall be
lifted up above my enemies
all around me;
Therefore I will offer sacrifices
of joy in His tabernacle;
I will sing, yes, I will sing
praises to the LORD.

7 Hear, O LORD, *when* I cry with
my voice!
Have mercy also upon me, and
answer me.
8 *When You said*, "Seek My
face,"
[l]My heart said to You, "Your
face, LORD, I will seek."
9 [m]Do not hide Your face from
me;
Do not turn Your servant away
in anger;
You have been my help;
Do not leave me nor forsake
me,
O God of my salvation.
10 When my [n]father and my
[o]mother forsake me,

Then the LORD will take care of
me.
11 [a]Teach me Your way, O LORD,
And lead me in a smooth path,
because of my enemies.
12 Do not deliver me to the will
of my adversaries;
For [b]false witnesses have risen
against me,
And such as breathe out
violence.
13 *I would have lost heart*, unless
I had believed
That I would see the goodness
of the LORD
In the land of the living.
14 [c]Wait on the LORD;
Be of good courage,
And He shall strengthen your
heart;
Wait, I say, on the LORD!

Testimony to answered prayer (v. 6)

A Psalm of David.

28 TO You I will cry, O LORD my
Rock:
Do not be silent to me,
Lest, if You *are* silent to me,
I become like those who go
down to the pit.
2 Hear the voice of my
supplications
When I cry to You,
When I lift up my hands
toward Your [d]holy
sanctuary.
3 Do not take me away with the
wicked
And with the workers of
iniquity,
Who speak peace to their
neighbors,
But evil *is* in their hearts.
4 [e]Give them according to their
deeds,
And according to the
wickedness of their
endeavors;
Give them according to the
work of their hands;
Render to them what they
deserve.
5 Because they do not regard the
works of the LORD,
Nor the operation of His
hands,
He shall destroy them
And not build them up.
6 Blessed *be* the LORD,
Because He has heard the
voice of my supplications!
7 The LORD *is* my strength and
my shield;
My heart [f]trusted in Him, and
I am helped;
Therefore my heart greatly
rejoices,
And with my song I will praise
Him.
8 The LORD *is* their strength,*
And He *is* the saving refuge of
His anointed.
9 Save Your people,
And bless Your inheritance;
Shepherd them also,
And bear them up forever.

God's mighty power

A Psalm of David.

29 GIVE unto the LORD, O you
mighty ones,
Give unto the LORD glory and
strength.
2 Give unto the LORD the glory
due to His name;
Worship the LORD in the
beauty of holiness.
3 The voice of the LORD *is* over
the waters;
The [g]God of glory thunders;
The LORD *is* over many waters.
4 The voice of the LORD *is*
powerful;
The voice of the LORD *is* full of
majesty.
5 The voice of the LORD breaks
the cedars,
Yes, the LORD splinters the
cedars of Lebanon.
6 He makes them also skip like a
calf,
Lebanon and [h]Sirion like a
young wild ox.
7 The voice of the LORD divides
the flames of fire.
8 The voice of the LORD shakes
the wilderness;
The LORD shakes the
Wilderness of Kadesh.
9 The voice of the LORD makes
the [i]deer give birth,
And strips the forests bare;
And in His temple everyone
says, "Glory!"
10 The [j]LORD sat *enthroned* at the
Flood,
And the [k]LORD sits as King
forever.

11
a Ps. 25:4; 86:11; 119:33
12
b Ps. 35:11; cp. 1 Sam. 22:9; 2 Sam. 16:7–8; Mt. 26:60
14
c Ps. 62:1,5; 130:5–6; Isa. 25:9; Hab. 2:3
PSALM 28
2
d Lit. *innermost*
4
e Cp. 2 Tim. 4:14; Rev. 18:6
7
f Faith: v. 7; Ps. 32:10. (Gen. 3:20; Heb. 11:39, *note*)
PSALM 29
3
g Acts 7:2
6
h Dt. 3:9
9
i Job 39:1
10
j Gen. 6:17; Job 38:8, 25
k Ps. 10:16

*28:8 Following Masoretic Text and Targum; Septuagint, Syriac, and Vulgate read *the strength of His people.*

11 The [a]LORD will give strength to
His people;
The LORD will bless His people
with peace.

Praise for deliverance

A Psalm. A Song at the dedication of the house of David.

30 I WILL extol You, O LORD,
for You have lifted me up,
And have not let my foes
rejoice over me.
2 O LORD my God, I cried out to
You,
And You [b]healed me.
3 O LORD, You brought my soul
up from the [c]grave;
You have kept me alive, that I
should not go down to the
pit.*
4 [d]Sing praise to the LORD, you
saints of His,
And give thanks at the
remembrance of His holy
name.*
5 [e]For His anger *is but for* a
moment,
His favor *is for* life;
Weeping may endure [f]for a
night,
But [g]joy *comes* in the
morning.
6 Now in my prosperity I said,
"I shall never be moved."
7 LORD, by Your favor You have
made my mountain stand
strong;
You hid Your face, *and* I was
troubled.
8 I cried out to You, O LORD;
And to the LORD I made
supplication:
9 "What profit *is there* in my
blood,
When I go down to the pit?
Will the [h]dust praise You?
Will it declare Your truth?
10 Hear, O LORD, and have mercy
on me;
LORD, be my helper!"
11 [i]You have turned for me my
mourning into dancing;
You have put off my sackcloth
and clothed me with
gladness,
12 To the end that [j]*my* glory may
sing praise to You and not
be silent.
O LORD my God, I will give
thanks to You forever.

11
a Ps. 28:8

PSALM 30
2
b Ps. 6:2; 103:3
3
c See Hab. 2:5, *note;* cp. Lk. 16:23, *note*
4
d Ps. 97:12; cp. 1 Chr. 16:4
5
e Ps. 103:9; Isa. 54:7–8; cp. 2 Cor. 4:17
f Lit. *in the evening*
g Lit. *singing*
9
h Ps. 6:5
11
i Isa. 61:3; Jer. 31:4; cp. 2 Sam. 6:14
12
j i.e. *my tongue*, or *my soul.* Ps. 16:9; 57:8

PSALM 31
1
k See Ps. 2:12, *note*
4
l Ps. 64:5
5
m Cp. Lk. 23:46
n Dt. 32:4
8
o Ps. 4:1; 18:19
11
p Ps. 38:11; 88:8,18; cp. Job 19:13

A plea for God's protection

To the Chief Musician. A Psalm of David.

31 IN You, O LORD, I put my
[k]trust;
Let me never be ashamed;
Deliver me in Your
righteousness.
2 Bow down Your ear to me,
Deliver me speedily;
Be my rock of refuge,
A fortress of defense to save
me.
3 For You *are* my rock and my
fortress;
Therefore, for Your name's
sake,
Lead me and guide me.
4 Pull me out of the net which
they have [l]secretly laid for
me,
For You *are* my strength.
5 [m]Into Your hand I commit my
spirit;
You have redeemed me, O
LORD God of [n]truth.
6 I have hated those who regard
useless idols;
But I trust in the LORD.
7 I will be glad and rejoice in
Your mercy,
For You have considered my
trouble;
You have known my soul in
adversities,
8 And have not shut me up into
the hand of the enemy;
[o]You have set my feet in a wide
place.
9 Have mercy on me, O LORD, for
I am in trouble;
My eye wastes away with
grief,
Yes, my soul and my body!
10 For my life is spent with grief,
And my years with sighing;
My strength fails because of
my iniquity,
And my bones waste away.
11 I am a reproach among all my
enemies,
But [p]especially among my
neighbors,
And *am* repulsive to my
acquaintances;
Those who see me outside flee
from me.
12 I am forgotten like a dead
man, out of mind;

*
30:3 Following Qere and Targum; Kethib, Septuagint, Syriac, and Vulgate read *from those who descend to the pit.* **30:4** Or *His holiness*

I am like a broken vessel.
13 For I hear the slander of many;
Fear *is* on every side;
While they [a]take counsel together against me,
They scheme to take away my life.

14 But as for me, I trust in You, O LORD;
I say, "You *are* my God."
15 My times *are* in Your [b]hand;
Deliver me from the hand of my enemies,
And from those who persecute me.
16 Make Your face shine upon Your servant;
Save me for Your mercies' sake.
17 Do not let me be ashamed, O LORD, for I have called upon You;
Let the wicked be ashamed;
Let them be silent in the [c]grave.
18 Let the lying lips be put to silence,
Which speak insolent things proudly and contemptuously against the [d]righteous.

19 Oh, how great *is* Your goodness,
Which You have laid up for those who [e]fear You,
Which You have prepared for those who trust in You
In the presence of the sons of men!
20 You shall [f]hide them in the secret place of Your presence
From the plots of man;
You shall keep them secretly in a pavilion
From the strife of tongues.

21 Blessed *be* the LORD,
For He has shown me His marvelous kindness in a strong city!
22 For I said in my haste,
"I am cut off from before Your eyes";
Nevertheless You heard the voice of my supplications
When I cried out to You.

23 Oh, love the LORD, all you His saints!
For the LORD preserves the faithful,
And fully repays the proud person.
24 Be of good courage,
And He shall strengthen your heart,
All you who hope in the LORD.

The blessedness of forgiveness

A Psalm of David. A [g]Contemplation.*

32 BLESSED *is he whose* transgression *is* forgiven,
Whose sin *is* covered.
2 Blessed *is* the man to whom the LORD does not [h]impute [i]iniquity,
And in whose spirit *there is* [j]no deceit.

3 When I kept silent, my bones grew old
Through my groaning all the day long.
4 For day and night Your hand was heavy upon me;
My vitality was turned into the drought of summer. Selah.
5 I acknowledged my sin to You,
And my iniquity I have not hidden.
I said, "I will [k]confess my transgressions to the LORD,"
And You [l]forgave the iniquity of my sin. Selah.

6 For this cause everyone who is godly shall pray to You
In a time when You may be found;
Surely in a flood of great waters
They shall not come near him.
7 You *are* my hiding place;
You shall preserve me from trouble;
You shall surround me with songs of deliverance. Selah.

8 I will instruct you and teach you in the way you should go;
I will guide you with My eye.
9 Do not be like the [m]horse *or* like the mule,
Which have no understanding,
Which must be harnessed with bit and bridle,
Else they will not come near you.

10 Many sorrows *shall be* to the wicked;
But he who [n]trusts in the LORD, mercy shall surround him.
11 Be glad in the LORD and rejoice, you righteous;

13 *a* Cp. Mt. 27:1
15 *b* Job 14:5
17 *c* See Hab. 2:5, *note;* cp. Lk. 16:23, *note*
18 *d* Cp. Jude 15
19 *e* See Ps. 19:9, *note*
20 *f* Ps. 27:5; 32:7
PSALM 32 Title *g* Or *Instruction*
2 *h Imputation:* vv. 1–2; Rom. 4:3. (Gen. 15:6; Jas. 2:23) *i* Rom. 4:7–8 *j* Cp. Jn. 1:47
5 *k* 2 Sam. 12:13; Ps. 38:18; Prov. 28:13; 1 Jn. 1:9 *l Forgiveness:* v. 5; Ps. 99:8. (Lev. 4:20; Mt. 26:28, *note*)
9 *m* Prov. 26:3
10 *n Faith:* v. 10; Ps. 37:3. (Gen. 3:20; Heb. 11:39, *note*)

* **32:title** Hebrew *Maschil*

And shout for joy, all *you*
upright in heart!

A psalm of joy

33 [a]REJOICE in the LORD, O you
righteous!
For praise from the upright is
beautiful.
2 Praise the LORD with the harp;
Make melody to Him with an
instrument of ten strings.
3 Sing to Him a new song;
Play skillfully with a shout of
joy.
4 For the word of the LORD *is*
right,
And all His work *is done* in
truth.
5 He loves righteousness and
[b]justice;
The earth is full of the
goodness of the LORD.
6 [c]By the word of the LORD the
heavens were made,
And all the [d]host of them by
the [e]breath of His mouth.
7 He [f]gathers the waters of the
sea together as a heap;*
He lays up the deep in
storehouses.
8 Let all the earth [g]fear the
LORD;
Let all the inhabitants of the
world stand in awe of Him.
9 For He [h]spoke, and it was
done;
He commanded, and it stood
fast.
10 The LORD brings the counsel of
the nations to [i]nothing;
He makes the plans of the
peoples of no effect.
11 The counsel of the LORD stands
forever,
The plans of His heart to all
generations.
12 [j]Blessed *is* the nation whose
God *is* the LORD,
The people He has [j]chosen as
His own inheritance.
13 The LORD looks from heaven;
He sees all the sons of men.
14 From the place of His dwelling
He looks
On all the inhabitants of the
earth;
15 He fashions their hearts
individually;
He [k]considers all their works.

PSALM 33

1 *a* Ps. 32:11; 97:12

5 *b* Ps. 25:9

6 *c* Gen. 1:6–7; Heb. 11:3; 2 Pet. 3:5 *d* Gen. 2:1 *e* Job 26:13

7 *f* Gen. 1:9; Job 26:10; 38:8

8 *g* See Ps. 19:9, *note*

9 *h* Gen. 1:3; Ps. 148:5

10 *i* Cp. Isa. 8:10; 19:3

12 *j* *Election* (corporate): v. 12; Ps. 105:43. (Dt. 7:6; 1 Pet. 5:13, *note*)

15 *k* 2 Chr. 16:9

16 *l* Jer. 9:23–24

17 *m* Ps. 20:7; Prov. 21:31

19 *n* Cp. Acts 12:11

21 *o* See Ps. 2:21, *note*

PSALM 34

1 *p* Eph. 5:20; 1 Th. 5:18

2 *q* 1 Cor. 1:31

4 *r* Mt. 7:7; Lk. 11:9

7 *s* *Angel* (of the LORD): v. 7; Ps. 35:5. (Gen. 16:7; Jud. 2:1, *note*) *t* Cp. 2 Ki. 6:17; Dan. 6:22

16 No king *is* saved by the
multitude of an army;
A mighty man is [l]not
delivered by great strength.
17 A [m]horse *is* a vain hope for
safety;
Neither shall it deliver *any* by
its great strength.
18 Behold, the eye of the LORD *is*
on those who [g]fear Him,
On those who hope in His
mercy,
19 To [n]deliver their soul from
death,
And to keep them alive in
famine.
20 Our soul waits for the LORD;
He *is* our help and our shield.
21 For our heart shall rejoice in
Him,
Because we have [o]trusted in
His holy name.
22 Let Your mercy, O LORD, be
upon us,
Just as we hope in You.

The LORD delivers His own

A Psalm of David when he pretended madness before Abimelech, who drove him away, and he departed.

34 I WILL bless the LORD at all
[p]times;
His praise *shall* continually *be*
in my mouth.
2 My soul shall make its [q]boast
in the LORD;
The humble shall hear *of it*
and be glad.
3 Oh, magnify the LORD with me,
And let us exalt His name
together.
4 I [r]sought the LORD, and He
heard me,
And delivered me from all my
fears.
5 They looked to Him and were
radiant,
And their faces were not
ashamed.
6 This poor man cried out, and
the LORD heard *him*,
And saved him out of all his
troubles.
7 The [s]angel of the LORD
[t]encamps all around those
who fear Him,
And delivers them.

*33:7 Septuagint, Targum, and Vulgate read *in a vessel.*

8 Oh, [a]taste and see that the
LORD *is* good;
Blessed *is* the man *who* [b]trusts
in Him!
9 Oh, [c]fear the LORD, you His
saints!
There is no want to those who
[c]fear Him.
10 The young lions lack and
suffer hunger;
But those who seek the LORD
shall not lack any good
thing.

11 Come, you children, listen to
me;
I will teach you the [c]fear of
the LORD.
12 Who *is* the man *who* [d]desires
life,
And loves *many* days, that he
may see good?
13 Keep your tongue from evil,
And your lips from speaking
[e]deceit.
14 Depart from evil and do good;
Seek [f]peace and pursue it.

15 The eyes of the LORD *are* on
the righteous,
And His ears *are open* to their
cry.
16 The face of the LORD *is* against
those who do evil,
To cut off the remembrance of
them from the earth.

17 *The righteous* cry out, and the
LORD hears,
And delivers them out of all
their troubles.
18 The LORD *is* near to those who
have a [g]broken heart,
And saves such as have a
contrite spirit.

19 Many *are* the [h]afflictions of
the righteous,
But the LORD delivers him out
of them all.
20 He [i]guards all his bones;
Not one of them is broken.
21 Evil shall slay the wicked,
And those who hate the
righteous shall be
condemned.
22 The LORD [j]redeems the soul of
His servants,
And none of those who trust in
Him shall be condemned.

8
a 1 Pet. 2:3
b See Ps. 2:12, *note*
9
c See Ps. 19:9, *note*
12
d vv. 12–16; 1 Pet. 3:10–12
13
e Eph. 4:25
14
f Rom. 14:19
18
g Ps. 51:17
19
h Cp. 2 Tim. 3:11–12
20
i Cp. Ex. 12:46; Jn. 19:36
22
j See Ex. 14:30 and Isa. 59:20, *notes*
PSALM 35
1
k Cp. Ex. 14:25
2
l Cp. Ps. 44:26; 91:4
4
m v. 26; Ps. 40:14,15
n Ps. 129:5
5
o *Angel* (of the LORD): vv. 5–6; Isa. 37:36. (Gen. 16:7; Jud. 2:1, *note*)
8
p 1 Th. 5:3
10
q Ps. 51:8
r Ex. 15:11; Ps. 71:19; 86:8; Mic. 7:18
11
s Lit. *Witnesses of wrong*
13
t Cp. Job 30:25; Ps. 69:10–11
u Cp. Mt. 10:13; Lk. 10:6

David's prayer against his enemies
A Psalm of David.

35 PLEAD *my cause,* O LORD,
with those who strive with
me;
[k]Fight against those who fight
against me.
2 [l]Take hold of shield and
buckler,
And stand up for my help.
3 Also draw out the spear,
And stop those who pursue
me.
Say to my soul,
"I *am* your salvation."

4 [m]Let those be put to shame and
brought to dishonor
Who seek after my life;
Let those be [n]turned back and
brought to confusion
Who plot my hurt.
5 Let them be like chaff before
the wind,
And let the [o]angel of the LORD
chase *them*.
6 Let their way be dark and
slippery,
And let the [o]angel of the LORD
pursue them.
7 For without cause they have
hidden their net for me *in* a
pit,
Which they have dug without
cause for my life.
8 Let [p]destruction come upon
him unexpectedly,
And let his net that he has
hidden catch himself;
Into that very destruction let
him fall.

9 And my soul shall be joyful in
the LORD;
It shall rejoice in His salvation.
10 [q]All my bones shall say,
"LORD, [r]who *is* like You,
Delivering the poor from him
who is too strong for him,
Yes, the poor and the needy
from him who plunders
him?"
11 [s]Fierce witnesses rise up;
They ask me *things* that I do
not know.
12 They reward me evil for good,
To the sorrow of my soul.
13 But as for me, [t]when they
were sick,
My clothing *was* sackcloth;
I humbled myself with fasting;
And my prayer would [u]return
to my own heart.

14 I [a]paced about as though *he were* my friend *or* brother;
I bowed down heavily, as one who mourns *for his* mother.

15 But in my adversity they rejoiced
And gathered together;
[b]Attackers gathered against me,
And I did not know *it;*
They tore *at me* and did not cease;
16 With ungodly [1]mockers at feasts
They gnashed at me with their teeth.
17 Lord, how long will You [c]look on?
Rescue me from their destructions,
My [d]precious *life* from the lions.
18 I will give You thanks in the great assembly;
I will praise You among many people.

19 [e]Let them not rejoice over me who are wrongfully my enemies;
Nor let them [f]wink with the eye who hate me without a cause.
20 For they do not speak peace,
But they devise deceitful matters
Against *the* quiet ones in the land.
21 They also opened their mouth wide against me,
And said, "Aha, aha!
Our eyes have seen *it.*"

22 *This* You have seen, O LORD;
Do not keep silence.
O Lord, do not be far from me.
23 Stir up Yourself, and awake to my [g]vindication,
To my cause, my God and my Lord.
24 Vindicate me, O LORD my God, according to Your righteousness;
And let them not rejoice over me.
25 Let them not say in their hearts, "Ah, so we would have it!"
Let them not say, "We have swallowed him up."

26 Let them be ashamed and brought to mutual confusion
Who rejoice at my hurt;
Let them be clothed with shame and dishonor
Who exalt themselves against me.

27 [h]Let them shout for joy and be glad,
Who favor my righteous cause;
And let them say continually,
"Let the LORD be magnified,
Who has pleasure in the prosperity of His servant."
28 And my tongue shall speak of Your righteousness
And of Your praise all the day long.

The wicked in contrast to God's mercy

To the Chief Musician. A Psalm of David the servant of the LORD.

36 AN oracle within my heart concerning the transgression of the wicked:
There is [i]no fear of God before his eyes.
2 For he flatters himself in his own eyes,
When he finds out his iniquity *and* when he hates.
3 The words of his mouth *are* wickedness and deceit;
He has ceased to be wise *and* to do good.
4 He devises wickedness on his [j]bed;
He sets himself in a way *that is* not good;
He does not abhor [k]evil.

5 Your mercy, O LORD, *is* in the heavens;
Your faithfulness *reaches* to the clouds.
6 Your righteousness *is* like the great mountains;
Your judgments *are* a great [l]deep;
O LORD, You preserve man and beast.

7 How precious *is* Your lovingkindness, O God!
Therefore the children of men put their [m]trust under the shadow of Your wings.
8 They are abundantly [n]satisfied with the fullness of Your house,

14 [a] Lit. *walked*
15 [b] Cp. Job 30:1
17 [c] Hab. 1:13 [d] Ps. 22:20
19 [e] Ps. 69:4; 109:3; Lam. 3:52; cp. Jn. 15:25 [f] Cp. Prov. 6:13; 10:10
23 [g] Ps. 97:2
27 [h] Cp. Rev. 18:20
PSALM 36
1 [i] Rom. 3:18
4 [j] Prov. 4:16; Mic. 2:1 [k] Rom. 12:9
6 [l] Rom. 11:33
7 [m] See Ps. 2:12, *note*
8 [n] Lit. *watered.* Ps. 65:4

[1](35:16) These were paid jesters who were hired to amuse the guests at a banquet.

And You give them drink from
the [a]river of Your pleasures.
9 For with You *is* the [b]fountain
of life;
In Your light we see light.
10 Oh, [c]continue Your
lovingkindness to those who
know You,
And Your righteousness to the
upright in heart.
11 Let not the foot of pride come
against me,
And let not the hand of the
wicked drive me away.
12 There the workers of iniquity
have fallen;
They have been cast down and
are not able to rise.

Trust in the L*ORD*

A Psalm of David.

37 DO [d]not fret because of
evildoers,
Nor be envious of the workers
of iniquity.
2 For they shall soon be cut
down like the grass,
And wither as the green herb.
3 [e]Trust in the LORD, and do good;
Dwell in the land, and feed on
His faithfulness.
4 [f]Delight yourself also in the
LORD,
And He shall give you the
desires of your [g]heart.
5 [h]Commit your way to the LORD,
Trust also in Him,
And He shall bring *it* to pass.
6 He shall bring forth your
righteousness as the light,
And your [i]justice as the
noonday.
7 [j]Rest in the LORD, and wait
patiently for Him;
[k]Do not fret because of him
who [l]prospers in his way,
Because of the man who
brings wicked schemes to
pass.
8 [m]Cease from anger, and forsake
wrath;
Do not fret—*it* only *causes*
harm.
9 For evildoers shall be cut off;
But those who wait on the
LORD,
They shall inherit the earth.
10 For [n]yet a little while and the
wicked *shall be* no *more;*
Indeed, you will look carefully
for his place,
But it *shall be* no *more.*
11 But the [o]meek shall inherit the
earth,
And shall delight themselves in
the abundance of peace.
12 The wicked plots against the
just,
And gnashes at him with his
teeth.
13 The Lord [p]laughs at him,
For He sees that his day is
coming.
14 The wicked have drawn the
sword
And have bent their bow,
To cast down the poor and
needy,
To slay those who are of
upright conduct.
15 [q]Their sword shall enter their
own heart,
And their bows shall be
broken.
16 A [r]little that a righteous man
has
Is better than the riches of
many wicked.
17 For the arms of the wicked
shall be broken,
But the LORD upholds the
righteous.
18 The LORD knows the days of
the upright,
And their inheritance shall be
forever.
19 They shall not be ashamed in
the evil time,
And in the days of famine they
shall be satisfied.
20 But the wicked shall perish;
And the enemies of the LORD,
Like [s]the splendor of the
meadows, shall vanish.
Into smoke they shall vanish
away.
21 The wicked borrows and does
not repay,
But the righteous shows mercy
and gives.
22 For *those* blessed by Him shall
inherit the earth,
But *those* cursed by Him shall
be cut off.
23 The steps of a *good* man are
ordered by the LORD,
And He delights in his way.
24 Though he fall, he shall not be
utterly cast [t]down;

8 a Ps. 46:4
9 b Jer. 2:13; Jn. 4:10,14
10 c Lit. *draw out at length*
PSALM 37
1 d v. 7; Ps. 73:3; Prov. 23:17; 24:19
3 e *Faith:* vv. 3–5; Ps. 84:12. (Gen. 3:20; Heb. 11:39, *note*)
4 f Isa. 58:14 g Ps. 145:19; Mt. 7:7–8
5 h Lit. *roll your way upon the* L*ORD*
6 i Ps. 106:3
7 j Lit. *Be silent to the* L*ORD.* Ps. 62:1 k vv. 1,8; cp. Jer. 12:1 l Ps. 73:3–12
8 m Eph. 4:26
10 n Cp. Heb. 10:36–37
11 o Mt. 5:5
13 p Ps. 2:4; 59:8
15 q Cp. 1 Sam. 17:50–51
16 r Prov. 15:16; 16:8; 1 Tim. 6:6
20 s Lit. *the preciousness of lambs*
24 t Prov. 24:16

For the LORD upholds *him with*
His hand.
25 I have been young, and *now*
am old;
Yet I have not seen the
righteous forsaken,
Nor his descendants begging
bread.
26 *He is* ever merciful, and lends;
And his descendants *are*
blessed.
27 Depart from evil, and do good;
And dwell forevermore.
28 For the LORD loves [a]justice,
And does not forsake His
saints;
They are preserved forever,
But the descendants of the
wicked shall be cut off.
29 The righteous shall inherit the
land,
And dwell in it forever.
30 The mouth of the righteous
speaks wisdom,
And his tongue talks of justice.
31 The [b]law of his God *is* in his
heart;
None of his steps shall slide.
32 The wicked watches the
righteous,
And seeks to slay him.
33 The LORD will not leave him in
his hand,
Nor condemn him when he is
judged.
34 Wait on the LORD,
And keep His way,
And He shall exalt you to
inherit the land;
When the wicked are cut off,
you shall see *it*.
35 I have seen the wicked in great
power,
And spreading himself like a
native green tree.
36 Yet he passed away,* and
behold, he *was* no *more;*
Indeed I sought him, but he
could not be found.
37 Mark the [c]blameless *man,* and
observe the upright;
For the future of *that* man *is*
peace.
38 But the transgressors shall be
destroyed together;
The future of the wicked shall
be cut off.
39 But the salvation of the
righteous *is* from the LORD;
He is their strength in the time
of trouble.
40 And the LORD shall help them
and deliver them;
He shall deliver them from the
wicked,
And save them,
Because they [d]trust in Him.

Godly sorrow for sin

A Psalm of David. To bring to
remembrance.

38 O LORD, do not [e]rebuke me
in Your wrath,
Nor chasten me in Your hot
displeasure!
2 For Your arrows pierce me
deeply,
And Your hand presses me
down.
3 *There is* no soundness in my
flesh
Because of Your anger,
Nor *any* health in my bones
Because of my sin.
4 For my iniquities have gone
over my head;
Like a heavy burden they are
too heavy for me.
5 My wounds are foul *and*
festering
Because of my foolishness.
6 I am troubled, I am bowed
down greatly;
I go mourning all the day long.
7 For my loins are full of
inflammation,
And *there is* no soundness in
my flesh.
8 I am feeble and severely
broken;
I groan because of the turmoil
of my heart.
9 Lord, all my desire *is* before
You;
And my sighing is not hidden
from You.
10 My heart pants, my strength
fails me;
As for the light of my eyes, it
also has gone from me.
11 My loved ones and my friends
[f]stand aloof from my
plague,
And my relatives stand afar
off.
12 Those also who seek my life
lay snares *for me;*

28
a Ps. 33:5
31
b *Law* (of Moses): v. 31; Ps. 40:8. (Ex. 19:1; Gal. 3:24, *note*)
37
c See Phil. 3:12, *note*
40
d See Ps. 2:12, *note*
PSALM 38
1
e Ps. 6:1
11
f Ps. 31:11; cp. Lk. 23:49

*37:36 Following Masoretic Text, Septuagint, and Targum; Syriac and Vulgate read *I passed by.*

Those who seek my hurt
[a]speak of destruction,
And plan deception all the day
long.

13 But I, like a deaf *man,* do not
hear;
And *I am* like a mute *who*
does not open his mouth.
14 Thus I am like a man who
does not hear,
And in whose mouth *is* no
response.

15 For in You, O LORD, I hope;
You will [b]hear, O Lord my
God.
16 For I said, "*Hear me,* lest they
rejoice over me,
Lest, when my foot slips, they
exalt *themselves* against
me."

17 [c]For I *am* ready to fall,
And my sorrow *is* continually
before me.
18 For I will [d]declare my iniquity;
I will be in [e]anguish over my
sin.
19 But my enemies *are* vigorous,
and they are strong;
And those who hate me
wrongfully have multiplied.
20 Those also who render evil for
good,
They are my adversaries,
[f]because I follow *what is*
good.

21 Do not forsake me, O LORD;
O my God, [g]be not far from
me!
22 Make haste to help me,
O Lord, my salvation!

The frailty of man

To the Chief Musician. To [1]Jeduthun. A Psalm of David.

39 I SAID, "I will guard my
ways,
Lest I sin with my [h]tongue;
I will restrain my mouth with a
muzzle,
While the wicked are before
me."
2 I was mute with silence,
I held my peace *even* from
good;
And my sorrow was stirred up.
3 My heart was hot within me;
While I was musing, the [i]fire
burned.
Then I spoke with my tongue:

4 "LORD, [j]make me to know my
end,
And what *is* the measure of my
days,
That I may know [k]how frail I
am.
5 Indeed, You have made my
days *as* handbreadths,
And my age *is* as nothing
before You;
Certainly every man at his best
state *is* but [l]vapor. Selah.
6 Surely every man walks about
like [m]a shadow;
Surely they busy themselves in
vain;
He heaps up *riches,*
And does not know [n]who will
gather them.

7 "And now, Lord, what do I wait
for?
My [o]hope *is* in You.
8 Deliver me from all my
transgressions;
Do not make me the reproach
of the foolish.
9 I was mute, I did not open my
mouth,
Because it was You who did *it.*
10 [p]Remove Your plague from me;
I am consumed by the blow of
Your hand.
11 When with rebukes You
correct man for iniquity,
You make his beauty melt
away like a moth;
Surely every man *is* vapor.
Selah.

12 "Hear my prayer, O LORD,
And give ear to my cry;
Do not be silent at my tears;
[q]For I *am* a stranger with You,
A sojourner, as all my fathers
were.
13 Remove Your gaze from me,
that I may regain strength,
Before I go away and am no
more."

God's song in our mouths

To the Chief Musician. A Psalm of David.

40 [2]I WAITED patiently for the
LORD;
And He inclined to me,

12 a Cp. 2 Sam. 16:7–8
15 b Or *answer*
17 c Ps. 51:3
18 d Ps. 32:5 e 2 Cor. 7:9–10
20 f Cp. 1 Pet. 3:14; 1 Jn. 3:12
21 g Ps. 35:22
PSALM 39
1 h Jas. 3:5–12
3 i Cp. Jer. 20:9
4 j Ps. 90:12; 119:84 k Or *what time I have here*
5 l Ps. 62:9
6 m Lit. *an image.* Cp. 1 Cor. 7:31; Jas. 4:14 n Cp. Lk. 12:20
7 o Ps. 38:15
10 p Job 9:34; 13:21
12 q Lev. 25:23; 1 Chr. 29:15; Ps. 119:19; Heb. 11:13; 1 Pet. 2:11

[1](39, Title) Jeduthun, a Levite, chief singer and instructor. See 1 Chr. 9:16; 16:38,41,42; 25:1,3,6; 2 Chr. 5:12; 35:15; Neh. 11:17. He is mentioned in the titles of Ps. 39; 62; 77.

[2](40:1) The 40th Psalm speaks of Messiah, the LORD's Servant obedient to the point of death. The Psalm begins with the joy of Christ in resurrection (vv. 1–2). He has been in the horrible

And heard my cry.
2 He also brought me up out of
[a]a horrible pit,
Out of the miry clay,
And set my feet upon a rock,
And established my steps.
3 He has put a new song in my
mouth—
Praise to our God;
Many will see *it* and [b]fear,
And will trust in the LORD.

4 Blessed *is* that man who
makes the LORD his [c]trust,
And does not respect the
proud, nor such as turn
aside to lies.
5 Many, O LORD my God, *are*
Your wonderful works
Which You have done;
And Your thoughts toward us
Cannot be recounted to You in
order;
If I would declare and speak *of*
them,
They are more than can be
numbered.

6 [d]Sacrifice and offering You did
not desire;
My ears You have [e]opened.
Burnt offering and sin offering
You did not require.
7 Then I said, "Behold, I come;
In the scroll of the book *it is*
written of me.
8 I delight to do Your [f]will, O
my God,
And [g]Your law *is* within my
heart."

9 I have proclaimed the good
news of righteousness
In the great assembly;
Indeed, I do not restrain my
lips,
O LORD, You Yourself know.
10 I have not hidden Your
righteousness within my
heart;
I have [h]declared Your
faithfulness and Your
salvation;
I have not concealed Your
lovingkindness and Your
truth
From the great assembly.

11 Do not withhold Your tender
mercies from me, O LORD;
Let Your lovingkindness and
Your truth continually
preserve me.
12 For innumerable evils have
surrounded me;
My iniquities have overtaken
me, so that I am not able to
look up;
They are more than the hairs
of my head;
Therefore my heart fails me.

13 [i]Be pleased, O LORD, to deliver
me;
O LORD, make haste to help
me!
14 Let them be ashamed and
brought to mutual confusion
Who seek to destroy my life;
Let them be driven backward
and brought to dishonor
Who wish me evil.
15 Let them be confounded
because of their shame,
Who say to me, "Aha, aha!"

16 Let all those who seek You
rejoice and be glad in You;
Let such as love Your
salvation say continually,
"The LORD be magnified!"
17 But I *am* poor and needy;
[j]*Yet* the LORD thinks upon me.
You *are* my help and my
deliverer;
[k]Do not delay, O my God.

Help for the charitable

To the Chief Musician. A Psalm of David.

41 BLESSED *is* he who
considers the [l]poor;
The LORD will deliver him in
time of trouble.
2 The LORD will preserve him
and keep him alive,
And he will be blessed on the
earth;
You will not deliver him to the
will of his enemies.
3 The LORD will strengthen him
on his bed of illness;
You will sustain him on his
sickbed.
4 I said, "LORD, be merciful to
me;

PSALM 40
2
a Lit. *a pit of noise*
3
b See Ps. 19:9, *note*
4
c See Ps. 2:12, *note*
6
d vv. 6–8; Heb. 10:5–9
e Cp. Ex. 21:6
8
f vv. 7–8; Mt. 26:39; Jn. 4:34; 6:38; Heb. 10:7
g *Law* (of Moses): v. 8; Ps. 78:10. (Ex. 19:1; Gal. 3:24, *note*)
10
h Cp. Acts 20:20,27
13
i vv. 13–17; cp. Ps. 70:1–5
17
j 1 Pet. 5:7
k Ps. 70:5

PSALM 41
1
l Lit. *the weak* or *sick*. Prov. 14:21

---

pit of the grave but has been brought up. Verses 3–5 are His resurrection testimony, His "new song." Verses 6–8 are retrospective. When sacrifice and offering had become abominable because of the wickedness of the people (Isa. 1:10–15), then the obedient Servant came to make the pure offering (vv. 7–17; Heb. 10:5–17). See Ps. 41, next in order of the Messianic Psalms.

[a]Heal my soul, for I have sinned
against You."
5 My enemies speak evil of me:
"When will he die, and his
name perish?"
6 And if he comes to see *me*, he
speaks lies;
His heart gathers iniquity to
itself;
When he goes out, he tells *it*.

7 All who hate me whisper
together against me;
Against me they devise my
hurt.
8 [b]"An evil disease," *they say*,
"clings to him.
And *now* that he lies down, he
will rise up no more."
9 [1]Even [c]my own familiar friend
in whom I [d]trusted,
Who ate my bread,
Has lifted up *his* heel against
me.
10 But You, O LORD, be merciful
to me, and raise me up,
That I may repay them.
11 By this I know that You are
well pleased with me,
Because my enemy does not
triumph over me.
12 As for me, You uphold me in
my integrity,
And [e]set me before Your face
forever.

13 [f]Blessed *be* the LORD God of
Israel
From everlasting to
everlasting!
Amen and Amen.

Book II, Psalms 42—72

Longing for God

To the Chief Musician. A
[g]Contemplation* of the sons of Korah.

42 AS the deer pants for the
water brooks,
So pants my soul for You, O
God.
2 [h]My soul thirsts for God, for the
[i]living God.
When shall I come and
[j]appear before God?*
3 My [k]tears have been my food
day and night,
While they continually say to
me,
[l]"Where *is* your God?"

4 When I remember these
things,
I pour out my soul within me.
For I used to go with the
multitude;
I went with them to the house
of God,
With the voice of joy and
praise,
With a multitude that kept a
pilgrim feast.

5 Why are you [m]cast down, O
my soul?
And *why* are you disquieted
within me?
[n]Hope in God, for I shall yet
[o]praise Him
For the help of His
countenance.*

6 O my God,* my soul is cast
down within me;
Therefore I will remember You
from the land of the Jordan,
And from the heights of
Hermon,
From the Hill [p]Mizar.
7 Deep calls unto deep at the
noise of Your waterfalls;
All Your waves and billows
have gone over me.
8 The LORD will [q]command His
lovingkindness in the
daytime,
And in the [r]night His song
shall be with me—
A prayer to the God of my life.

9 I will say to God my Rock,
"Why have You forgotten me?
Why do I go mourning because
of the oppression of the
enemy?"
10 *As* with a breaking of my
bones,
My enemies reproach me,
While they say to me all day
long,
[s]"Where *is* your God?"
11 [t]Why are you cast down, O my
soul?

4 *a* Ps. 6:2; 147:3; cp. 2 Chr. 30:20
8 *b* Lit. *A thing of Belial*
9 *c* Ps. 55:12–14; Mt. 26:14–16, 21–25, 47–50; Jn. 13:18, 21–30; Acts 1:16–17 *d* See Ps. 2:12, *note*
12 *e* Job 36:7; Ps. 21:6; 34:15
13 *f* Ps. 106:48
PSALM 42 Title *g* Or *Instruction*
2 *h* Ps. 63:1; 84:2; cp. Jn. 7:37 *i* 1 Th. 1:9 *j* Cp. Ex. 23:17
3 *k* Ps. 80:5; 102:9 *l* v. 10; Ps. 79:10; 115:2
5 *m* Lit. *bowed down* *n* Lam. 3:24 *o* Or *give thanks*
6 *p* Or *the little mountain.* Ps. 133:3
8 *q* Dt. 28:8; cp. Lev. 25:21 *r* Job 35:10; Ps. 149:5
10 *s* v. 3; Joel 2:17; Mic. 7:10
11 *t* v. 5; Ps. 43:5

*

42:title Hebrew *Maschil* **42:2** Following Masoretic Text and Vulgate; some Hebrew manuscripts, Septuagint, Syriac, Targum read *I see the face of God.* **42:5** Following Masoretic Text and Targum; a few Hebrew manuscripts, Septuagint, Syriac, and Vulgate read *The help of my countenance, my God.* **42:6** Following Masoretic Text and Targum; a few Hebrew manuscripts, Septuagint, Syriac, and Vulgate put *my God* at the end of verse 5.

[1](41:9) Here is a reference to the betrayal of the Son of man, as Jesus Himself taught (Jn. 13:18–19). See Ps. 45, next in order of the Messianic Psalms.

And why are you disquieted
within me?
Hope in God;
For I shall yet praise Him,
The help of my countenance
and my God.

Hope in God

43 VINDICATE me, O God,
And plead my cause against
an ungodly nation;
Oh, deliver me from the
deceitful and unjust man!
2 For You *are* the God of my
strength;
Why do You cast me off?
Why do I go mourning because
of the oppression of the
enemy?
3 Oh, send out Your light and
Your truth!
Let them lead me;
Let them bring me to Your
holy hill
And to Your tabernacle.
4 Then I will go to the altar of
God,
To God my [a]exceeding joy;
And on the harp I will praise
You,
O God, my God.
5 [b]Why are you cast down, O my
soul?
And why are you disquieted
within me?
Hope in God;
For I shall yet praise Him,
The help of my countenance
and my God.

A prayer for the distressed

To the Chief Musician. A
Contemplation* of the sons of Korah.

44 WE have heard with our ears,
O God,
Our [c]fathers have told us,
The deeds You did in their
days,
In days of old:
2 You drove out the nations with
Your hand,
But them You planted;
You afflicted the peoples, and
cast them out.
3 [d]For they did not gain
possession of the land by
their own sword,
Nor did their own arm save
them;
But it was Your right hand,
Your arm, and the light of
Your countenance,

PSALM 43

4 [a] Lit. *the gladness of my joy*

5 [b] Ps. 42:5, 11

PSALM 44

1 [c] Ps. 78:3; cp. Ex. 12:26–27

3 [d] Cp. Dt. 8:17; Josh. 24:12
[e] Dt. 4:37; 7:7–8

5 [f] Cp. Dan. 8:4

6 [g] See Ps. 2:12, *note*

8 [h] Ps. 34:2; Jer. 9:24; cp. Rom. 2:17

9 [i] Ps. 43:2; 60:1; 74:1; 89:38; 108:11

10 [j] Lev. 26:17

11 [k] Rom. 8:36
[l] Dt. 28:64

12 [m] Lit. *without riches*

13 [n] Dt. 28:37; Ps. 79:4; 80:6

[e]Because You favored them.
4 You are my King, O God;*
Command* victories for Jacob.
5 Through You [f]we will push
down our enemies;
Through Your name we will
trample those who rise up
against us.
6 For I will not [g]trust in my
bow,
Nor shall my sword save me.
7 But You have saved us from
our enemies,
And have put to shame those
who hated us.
8 [h]In God we boast all day long,
And praise Your name forever.
Selah.
9 But You have [i]cast *us* off and
put us to shame,
And You do not go out with
our armies.
10 You make us [j]turn back from
the enemy,
And those who hate us have
taken spoil for themselves.
11 [k]You have given us up like
sheep *intended* for food,
And have [l]scattered us among
the nations.
12 You sell Your people [m]for *next
to* nothing,
And are not enriched by
selling them.
13 You make us a [n]reproach to
our neighbors,
A scorn and a derision to those
all around us.
14 You make us a byword among
the nations,
A shaking of the head among
the peoples.
15 My dishonor *is* continually
before me,
And the shame of my face has
covered me,
16 Because of the voice of him
who reproaches and reviles,
Because of the enemy and the
avenger.
17 All this has come upon us;
But we have not forgotten You,
Nor have we dealt falsely with
Your covenant.
18 Our heart has not turned back,

*

44:title Hebrew *Maschil* **44:4** Following Masoretic Text and Targum; Septuagint and Vulgate read *and my God.* • Following Masoretic Text and Targum; Septuagint, Syriac, and Vulgate read *who commands.*

Nor have our steps departed
from Your way;
19 But You have severely broken
us in the place of jackals,
And covered us with the
shadow of death.
20 If we had forgotten the name
of our God,
Or stretched out our hands to
a foreign god,
21 [a]Would not God search this
out?
For He knows the secrets of
the heart.
22 Yet [b]for Your sake we are
killed all day long;
We are accounted as sheep for
the slaughter.
23 Awake! Why do You sleep, O
Lord?
Arise! Do not cast *us* off
forever.
24 Why do You hide Your face,
And forget our affliction and
our oppression?
25 For our [c]soul is bowed down
to the dust;
Our body clings to the ground.
26 Arise for our help,
And [d]redeem us for Your
mercies' sake.

The King and His beauty

To the Chief Musician. Set to "The Lilies."* A Contemplation* of the sons of Korah. A Song of Love.

45 MY heart is overflowing with
a good theme;
I recite my composition
concerning the [1]King;
My tongue *is* the pen of a
ready writer.

2 You are fairer than the sons of
men;
[e]Grace is poured upon Your
lips;
Therefore God has blessed You
forever.
3 Gird Your sword upon *Your*
thigh, O [f]Mighty One,
With Your [g]glory and Your
majesty.
4 And in Your majesty ride
prosperously because of
truth, humility, *and*
righteousness;
And Your right hand shall
teach You awesome things.
5 Your arrows *are* sharp in the
heart of the King's enemies;
The peoples fall under You.
6 [h]Your throne, O God, *is* forever
and ever;
A scepter of righteousness *is*
the [i]scepter of Your
kingdom.
7 You love righteousness and
hate wickedness;
Therefore God, Your God, has
[j]anointed You
With the oil of [k]gladness more
than Your companions.
8 All Your garments are
[l]scented with myrrh and
aloes *and* cassia,
Out of the ivory palaces, by
which they have made You
glad.
9 [m]Kings' daughters *are* among
Your honorable women;
At Your [n]right hand stands the
queen in gold from Ophir.
10 Listen, O daughter,
Consider and incline your ear;
[o]Forget your own people also,
and your father's house;
11 So the King will greatly desire
your beauty;
[p]Because He *is* your Lord,
worship Him.
12 And the daughter of Tyre *will*
come with a gift;
The rich among the people will
seek your favor.
13 The royal [q]daughter *is* all
glorious within *the palace;*
Her clothing *is* woven with
gold.
14 [r]She shall be brought to the
King in robes of many
colors;
The virgins, her companions

21
a Job 31:14; Ps. 139:1; Jer. 17:10
22
b Rom. 8:36
25
c Ps. 119:25
26
d See Ex. 14:30 and Isa. 59:20, *notes*
PSALM 45
2
e Lk. 4:22
3
f Isa. 9:6
g Jude 25
6
h Ps. 93:2; Heb. 1:8
i Num. 24:17
7
j Ps. 2:2
k Ps. 21:6; Heb. 1:8–9
8
l Song 1:12–13
9
m Song 6:8
n 1 Ki. 2:19
10
o Cp. Dt. 21:13; Ruth 1:16
11
p Ps. 95:6; Isa. 54:5
13
q Cp. Rev. 19:7–8
14
r Song 1:4

* **45:title** Hebrew *Shoshannim* • Hebrew *Maschil*

[1](45:1) This great Psalm of the King, with Ps. 46—47, obviously looks forward to His advent in glory. The reference in Heb. 1:8–9 is not so much to the anointing as an event (Mt. 3:16–17), as to the permanent state of the King (cp. Isa. 11:1–2). The divisions are: (1) the supreme beauty of the King (vv. 1–2); (2) the coming of the King in glory (vv. 3–5; cp. Rev. 19:11–21); (3) the Deity of the King and the character of His reign (vv. 6–7; Isa. 11:1–5; Heb. 1:8–9); (4) as associated with Him in earthly rule, the bride is presented (vv. 9–13); (5) the virgin companions of the bride, who would seem to be the Jewish remnant (see Rom. 11:5, *note;* Rev. 14:1–4), are next seen (vv. 14–15); and (6) the Psalm closes with a reference to the earthly fame of the King (vv. 16–17). See Ps. 68, next in order of the Messianic Psalms.

who follow her, shall be
brought to You.
15 With gladness and rejoicing
they shall be brought;
They shall enter the King's
palace.
16 Instead of Your fathers shall
be Your sons,
Whom You shall make princes
in all the earth.
17 [a]I will make Your name to be
remembered in all
generations;
Therefore the people shall
praise You forever and ever.

God our refuge and strength

To the Chief Musician. A Psalm of the sons of Korah. A Song for [b]Alamoth.

46 GOD *is* our [c]refuge and
strength,
A very present [d]help in
trouble.
2 Therefore we will not fear,
Even though the earth be
removed,
And though the mountains be
carried into the [e]midst of
the sea;
3 *Though* its waters roar *and* be
troubled,
Though the mountains shake
with its swelling. Selah.
4 *There is* a [f]river whose
streams shall make glad the
[g]city of God,
The holy *place* of the
tabernacle of the Most High.
5 God *is* [h]in the midst of her,
she shall not be moved;
God shall help her, just at the
break of dawn.
6 The nations raged, the
kingdoms were moved;
He uttered His voice, the earth
melted.
7 The [i]LORD of hosts *is* with us;
The God of Jacob *is* [j]our
refuge. Selah.
8 Come, behold the works of the
LORD,
Who has made desolations in
the earth.
9 He [k]makes wars cease to the
end of the earth;
He [l]breaks the bow and cuts
the spear in two;
He [m]burns the chariot in the
fire.
10 Be still, and know that I *am*
God;
I will be exalted among the
nations,
I will be exalted in the earth!
11 The [i]LORD of hosts *is* with us;
The God of Jacob *is* our
refuge. Selah.

God the Sovereign

To the Chief Musician. A Psalm of the sons of Korah.

47 OH, clap your hands, all you
peoples!
Shout to God with the voice of
triumph!
2 For the LORD Most High [n]*is*
awesome;
He is a great [o]King over all
the earth.
3 He will [p]subdue the peoples
under us,
And the nations under our feet.
4 He will choose our
[q]inheritance for us,
The excellence of Jacob whom
He loves. Selah.
5 [r]God has gone up with a shout,
The LORD with the sound of a
trumpet.
6 Sing praises to God, sing
praises!
Sing praises to our King, sing
praises!
7 For [s]God *is* the King of all the
earth;
Sing praises with
understanding.
8 God reigns over the nations;
God [t]sits on His [u]holy throne.
9 The princes of the people have
gathered together,
[v]The people of the God of
Abraham.
[w]For the shields of the earth
belong to God;
He is greatly exalted.

The beauty of Zion

A Song. A Psalm of the sons of Korah.

48 GREAT *is* the LORD, and
greatly to be praised
In the [x]city of our God,
In His holy mountain.
2 Beautiful in elevation,
The joy of the whole earth,
Is Mount Zion *on* the sides of
the north,
The [x]city of the great King.
3 God *is* in her palaces;

17
a Mal. 1:11
PSALM 46
Title
b Soprano, plural of Heb. *almah, a virgin.* Contrast 1 Chr. 15:20
1
c Ps. 62:7–8; 91:2; 142:5
d Dt. 4:7; Ps. 145:18
2
e Lit. *the heart of the seas*
4
f Ezek. 47:1–12
g Ps. 48:1,8; Isa. 60:14
5
h Dt. 23:14; Isa. 12:6; Ezek. 43:7; Hos. 11:9; Joel 2:27; Zeph. 3:15; Zech. 2:5,10–11; 8:3
7
i Num. 14:9; 2 Chr. 13:12
j Lit. *a high place for us.* Ps. 9:9
9
k Isa. 2:4
l Ps. 76:3
m Ezek. 39:9
PSALM 47
2
n Dt. 7:21; Neh. 1:5; Ps. 76:12
o Mal. 1:14
3
p Ps. 18:47
4
q 1 Pet. 1:4
5
r Ps. 68:24–25
7
s Zech. 14:9
8
t Ps. 97:2
u Ps. 48:1
9
v Rom. 4:11–12
w Ps. 89:18
PSALM 48
1
x Ps. 46:4; 87:3; Mt. 5:35

He is known as her refuge.
4 For behold, the kings
[a]assembled,
They passed by together.
5 They saw *it, and* so they
marveled;
They were troubled, they
hastened away.
6 Fear took hold of them there,
And pain, as of a woman in
birth pangs,
7 *As when* You break the [b]ships
of Tarshish
With an east wind.
8 As we have heard,
So we have seen
In the [c]city of the LORD of
hosts,
In the city of our God:
God will [d]establish it forever.
Selah.
9 We have thought, O God, on
Your lovingkindness,
In the midst of Your temple.
10 According to Your [e]name, O
God,
So *is* Your praise to the ends
of the earth;
Your right hand is full of
righteousness.
11 Let Mount Zion rejoice,
Let the daughters of Judah be
glad,
Because of Your judgments.
12 Walk about Zion,
And go all around her.
Count her towers;
13 Mark well her bulwarks;
Consider her palaces;
That you may [f]tell *it* to the
generation following.
14 For this *is* God,
Our God forever and ever;
[g]He will be our guide
Even to death.*

Riches cannot redeem men

To the Chief Musician. A Psalm of the sons of Korah.

49 HEAR this, all peoples;
Give ear, all inhabitants of
the world,
2 Both low and high,
Rich and poor together.
3 My mouth shall speak wisdom,
And the meditation of my
heart *shall give*
understanding.
4 I will incline my ear to a
proverb;
I will disclose my [h]dark saying
on the harp.
5 Why should I fear in the days
of evil,
When the iniquity at my heels
surrounds me?
6 Those who trust in their
wealth
And boast in the multitude of
their riches,
7 None *of them* can by any
means [i]redeem *his* brother,
Nor give to God a ransom for
him—
8 For the [i]redemption of their
souls *is* costly,
And it shall cease forever—
9 That he should continue to live
eternally,
And not see the Pit.
10 For he sees wise men die;
Likewise the fool and the
senseless person perish,
And leave their wealth to
others.
11 Their inner thought *is that*
their houses *will last*
forever,*
Their dwelling places to all
generations;
They call *their* lands after their
own names.
12 Nevertheless man, *though* in
honor, does not remain;*
He is like the beasts *that*
perish.
13 This is the way of those who
are foolish,
And of their posterity who
approve their sayings. Selah.
14 Like sheep they are laid in the
[j]grave;
Death shall feed on them;
The upright shall have
[k]dominion over them in the
morning;
And their beauty shall be
consumed in the [j]grave, far
from their dwelling.
15 But God will [i]redeem my soul
from the power of the
[j]grave,
For He shall [l]receive me.
Selah.

4 *a* Cp. 2 Sam. 10:6–19
7 *b* Ezek. 27:25
8 *c* Ps. 46:4; 87:3; Mt. 5:35 *d* Ps. 87:5; Isa. 2:2; Mic. 4:1
10 *e* Mal. 1:11
13 *f* Ps. 78:5–7
14 *g* Isa. 58:11
PSALM 49
4 *h* i.e. *riddle*
7 *i* See Ex. 14:30 and Isa. 59:20, *notes*
14 *j* See Hab. 2:5, *note;* cp. Lk. 16:23, *note* *k* Dan. 7:18; 1 Cor. 6:2; Rev. 2:26
15 *l* Ps. 73:24

*
48:14 Following Masoretic Text and Syriac; Septuagint and Vulgate read *Forever.*
49:11 Septuagint, Syriac, Targum, and Vulgate read *Their graves shall be their houses forever.*
49:12 Following Masoretic Text and Targum; Septuagint, Syriac, and Vulgate read *understand* (compare verse 20).

16 Do not be afraid when one
becomes rich,
When the glory of his house is
increased;
17 For when he dies he shall
carry nothing away;
His glory shall not descend
after him.
18 Though while he lives he
blesses [a]himself
(For *men* will praise you when
you do well for yourself),
19 He shall go to the generation
of his fathers;
They shall never see light.
20 A man *who is* in honor, yet
does not understand,
Is like the beasts *that* perish.

God, the mighty Judge

A Psalm of Asaph.

50 THE Mighty One, God the
LORD,
Has spoken and called the
earth
From the rising of the sun to
its going down.
2 Out of Zion, the perfection of
beauty,
God will shine forth.
3 Our God shall [b]come, and
shall not keep silent;
A [c]fire shall [d]devour before
Him,
And it shall be very
tempestuous all around Him.
4 He shall [e]call to the heavens
from above,
And to the earth, that He may
judge His people:
5 "Gather My saints together to
Me,
Those who have made a
covenant with Me by
[f]sacrifice."
6 Let the [g]heavens declare His
righteousness,
For God Himself *is* Judge.
Selah.
7 "Hear, O My people, and I will
speak,
O Israel, and I will testify
against you;
[h]I *am* God, your God!
8 I will not rebuke you for your
sacrifices
Or your burnt offerings,
Which are continually before
Me.
9 I will not [i]take a bull from
your house,
Nor goats out of your folds.

18
a Lk. 12:19

PSALM 50
3
b Christ (second advent): vv. 3–6; Ps. 96:13. (Dt. 30:3; Acts 1:11, *note*)
c Judgments (the seven): vv. 3–4,22; Ezek. 20:33. (1 Sam. 7:14; Rev. 20:12, *note*)
d Cp. Lev. 10:2; Num. 16:35; Dan. 7:10
4
e Dt. 32:1; Isa. 1:2
5
f Ex. 24:7–8
6
g Ps. 97:6
7
h Ex. 20:2
9
i vv. 9–15
12
j Ex. 19:5; Dt. 10:14; Job 41:11; Ps. 24:1; 1 Cor. 10:26
13
k Ps. 51:15–17
14
l Hos. 14:2; Heb. 13:15
15
m Job 22:27; Ps. 91:15; 107:6,13; Zech. 13:9
17
n Neh. 9:26
18
o Rom. 1:32
p 1 Tim. 5:22
21
q Rom. 2:4
r Ps. 90:8
22
s vv. 3–4

10 For every beast of the forest *is*
Mine,
And the cattle on a thousand
hills.
11 I know all the birds of the
mountains,
And the wild beasts of the field
are Mine.

12 "If I were hungry, I would not
tell you;
[j]For the world *is* Mine, and all
its fullness.
13 [k]Will I eat the flesh of bulls,
Or drink the blood of goats?
14 [l]Offer to God thanksgiving,
And pay your vows to the
Most High.
15 [m]Call upon Me in the day of
trouble;
I will deliver you, and you
shall glorify Me."

16 But to the wicked God says:
"What *right* have you to declare
My statutes,
Or take My covenant in your
mouth,
17 Seeing you hate instruction
And [n]cast My words behind
you?
18 When you saw a thief, you
[o]consented* with him,
And have been a [p]partaker
with adulterers.
19 You give your mouth to evil,
And your tongue frames
deceit.
20 You sit *and* speak against your
brother;
You slander your own
mother's son.
21 These *things* you have done,
and I kept silent;
[q]You thought that I was
altogether like you;
But I will rebuke you,
And [r]set *them* in order before
your eyes.

22 "Now consider this, you who
forget God,
Lest I [s]tear *you* in pieces,
And *there be* none to deliver:
23 Whoever offers praise glorifies
Me;
And to him who orders *his*
conduct *aright*
I will show the salvation of
God."

*50:18 Septuagint, Syriac, Targum, and Vulgate read *run*.

A psalm of penitence

To the Chief Musician. A Psalm of David when Nathan the prophet went to him, after he had gone in to [a]Bathsheba.

51 [1]HAVE [b]mercy upon me, O God,
According to Your lovingkindness;
According to the multitude of Your tender mercies,
Blot out my transgressions.
2 Wash me thoroughly from my iniquity,
And cleanse me from my sin.
3 For I acknowledge my transgressions,
And my sin *is* always before me.
4 Against You, You only, have I sinned,
And done *this* evil in Your sight—
That You may be found [c]just when You speak,*
And blameless when You judge.
5 [d]Behold, I was brought forth in iniquity,
And in sin my mother conceived me.
6 Behold, You desire truth in the inward parts,
And in the hidden *part* You will make me to know wisdom.
7 [e]Purge me with [2]hyssop, and I shall be clean;
Wash me, and I shall be [f]whiter than snow.
8 Make me hear joy and gladness,
That the [g]bones You have broken may rejoice.
9 Hide Your face from my sins,
And blot out all my iniquities.
10 [h]Create in me a clean heart, O God,
And renew a steadfast spirit within me.
11 Do not cast me away from Your presence,
And do not [3]take Your Holy [i]Spirit from me.
12 Restore to me the joy of Your salvation,
And uphold me *by Your* [j]generous Spirit.
13 *Then* I will [k]teach transgressors Your ways,
And sinners shall be converted to You.
14 Deliver me from the guilt of bloodshed, O God,
The God of my salvation,
And my tongue shall sing aloud of Your righteousness.
15 O Lord, open my lips,
And my mouth shall show forth Your praise.
16 For You do not desire [l]sacrifice, or else I would give *it;*
You do not delight in burnt offering.

PSALM 51
Title
a 2 Sam. 11:1–12:13
1
b Bible prayers (OT): vv. 1–19; Isa. 37:15. (Gen. 15:2; Hab. 3:1)
4
c Rom. 3:4
5
d Job 14:4; Ps. 58:3; Jn. 3:6; Rom. 5:12; Eph. 2:3
7
e Heb. 9:19
f Isa. 1:18
8
g Cp. Ps. 35:9–10
10
h Cp. Acts 15:9; Eph. 2:10
11
i Holy Spirit (OT): vv. 11–12; Ps. 104:30. (Gen. 1:2; Zech. 12:10)
12
j 2 Cor. 3:17
13
k Cp. Ps. 19:7–8; Prov. 11:30; Acts 2:38–41
16
l 1 Sam. 15:22; Ps. 50:8–14; Mic. 6:6–8

* 51:4 Septuagint, Targum, and Vulgate read *in Your words.*

[1](51:1) The 51st Psalm must ever be, in its successive steps, the mold of the experience of a sinning believer who comes back to full communion and service. The steps are: (1) sin thoroughly judged before God (vv. 1–6); (2) forgiveness and cleansing through the blood (v. 7); (3) cleansing (vv. 7–10; cp. Jn. 13:4–10; Eph. 5:26; 1 Jn. 1:9); (4) Spirit-filled for joy and power (vv. 11–12); (5) service (v. 13); (6) worship (vv. 14–17); and (7) the restored believer in fellowship with God. Personally, it was David's pathway to restored communion after his sin with Bathsheba. Prophetically, it will be the pathway of returning Israel (Dt. 30:1–10, marg. and *notes*).

[2](51:7) Hyssop is the little shrub (1 Ki. 4:33) with which the blood and water of purification were applied (Lev. 14:1–7; Num. 19:1–19).

Cleansing in Scripture is twofold: (1) of a sinner from the guilt of sin—the blood (hyssop) aspect; and (2) of a saint from the defilement of sin—the water (wash) aspect. Under grace the sinner is purged by blood when he believes (Mt. 26:28; Heb. 1:3; 9:12; 10:14). Both aspects of cleansing, by blood and by water, are brought out in Jn. 13:10; Eph. 5:25–26: "He who is bathed needs only to wash his feet"; "Christ also loved the church and gave Himself for her [redemption by blood] that He might sanctify and cleanse her with the washing of water by the word": answering to the "wash me" of v. 7.

[3](51:11) No believer of the present Church Age need ever pray, "Do not take Your Holy Spirit from me"; for Christ promised His own that the Spirit would "abide with you forever" (Jn. 14:16; cp. Eph. 4:30). But it is always proper for the Christian to pray that he may be conformed to the conditions essential to the full ministry of the Spirit.

17 The [a]sacrifices of God *are* a
broken spirit,
A broken and a contrite
heart—
These, O God, You will not
despise.

18 Do good in Your good pleasure
to Zion;
Build the walls of Jerusalem.
19 Then You shall be pleased
with the [b]sacrifices of
righteousness,
With burnt offering and whole
burnt offering;
Then they shall offer bulls on
Your altar.

Judgment on the deceitful

To the Chief Musician. A [c]Contemplation* of David when Doeg the Edomite went and told Saul, and said to him, "David has gone to the house of [d]Ahimelech."

52 WHY do you boast in evil, O
mighty man?
The goodness of God *endures*
continually.
2 Your tongue devises
destruction,
Like a sharp razor, working
deceitfully.
3 You love evil more than good,
Lying rather than speaking
righteousness. Selah.
4 You love all devouring words,
You deceitful tongue.

5 God shall likewise [e]destroy
you forever;
He shall take you away, and
pluck you out of *your*
dwelling place,
And uproot you from the land
of the living. Selah.
6 The righteous also shall see
and fear,
And shall laugh at him, *saying*,
7 "Here is the man *who* did not
make God his strength,
But [f]trusted in the abundance
of his riches,
And strengthened himself in
his wickedness."

8 But I *am* like a green olive tree
in the house of God;
I trust in the mercy of God
forever and ever.
9 I will praise You forever,
Because You have done *it;*
And in the presence of Your
saints
I will wait on Your name, for
it is good.

A portrait of the godless

To the Chief Musician. Set to "Mahalath." A [c]Contemplation* of David.

53 [g]THE [h]fool has said in his
heart,
"*There is* no God."
They are corrupt, and have
done abominable iniquity;
[i]*There is* none who does good.

2 God looks down from heaven
upon the children of men,
To see if there are *any* who
understand, who [j]seek God.
3 Every one of them has turned
aside;
They have together become
corrupt;
There is none who does good,
No, not one.

4 Have the workers of iniquity
no knowledge,
Who eat up my people *as* they
eat bread,
And do not call upon God?
5 [k]There they are in great fear
Where no fear was,
For God has scattered the
bones of him who encamps
against you;
You have put *them* to shame,
Because God has despised
them.

6 [l]Oh, that the salvation of Israel
would come out of Zion!
When God brings back the
captivity of His people,
Let Jacob rejoice *and* Israel be
glad.

A cry for deliverance

To the Chief Musician. With stringed instruments.* A [c]Contemplation* of David when the [m]Ziphites went and said to Saul, "Is David not hiding with us?"

54 SAVE me, O God, by Your
name,
And vindicate me by Your
strength.
2 Hear my prayer, O God;
Give ear to the words of my
mouth.
3 For strangers have risen up
against me,
And oppressors have sought
after my life;

17 *a* Ps. 34:18; Isa. 57:15; 66:2
19 *b* Ps. 4:5; cp. Mal. 3:3
PSALM 52 Title *c* Or *Instruction* *d* 1 Sam. 22:9
5 *e* Lit. *beat you down*
7 *f* See Ps. 2:12, *note*
PSALM 53 **1** *g* This Psalm is almost identical with Ps. 14 *h* Ps. 10:4 *i* Rom. 3:10–12
2 *j* Cp. 2 Chr. 15:2; 19:3
5 *k* Lev. 26:17,36; Prov. 28:1
6 *l* Ps. 14:7
PSALM 54 Title *m* 1 Sam. 23:19

* 52:title Hebrew *Maschil* 53:title Hebrew *Maschil*
54:title Hebrew *neginoth* • Hebrew *Maschil*

They have not set God before
them. Selah.
4 Behold, God *is* my helper;
The Lord *is* with those who
uphold my life.
5 He will repay my enemies for
their evil.
Cut them off in Your truth.
6 I will freely sacrifice to You;
I will praise Your name, O
LORD, for *it is* good.
7 For He has delivered me out of
all trouble;
And [a]my eye has seen *its*
desire upon my enemies.

A complaint concerning false friends

To the Chief Musician. With stringed instruments.* A [b]Contemplation* of David.

55 GIVE ear to my prayer, O
God,
And do not hide Yourself from
my supplication.
2 Attend to me, and hear me;
I am restless in my complaint,
and moan noisily,
3 Because of the voice of the
enemy,
Because of the oppression of
the wicked;
For they bring down trouble
upon me,
And in wrath they hate me.
4 My heart is severely pained
within me,
And the terrors of death have
fallen upon me.
5 Fearfulness and trembling
have come upon me,
And horror has [c]overwhelmed
me.
6 So I said, "Oh, that I had
wings like a dove!
I would fly away and be at
rest.
7 Indeed, I would wander far off,
And remain in the wilderness.
Selah.
8 I would hasten my escape
From the windy storm *and*
tempest."
9 Destroy, O Lord, *and* divide
their tongues,
For I have seen violence and
strife in the city.
10 Day and night they go around
it on its walls;
Iniquity and trouble *are* also in
the midst of it.
11 Destruction *is* in its midst;
Oppression and deceit do not
depart from its streets.
12 For *it is* not an enemy *who*
reproaches me;
Then I could bear *it*.
Nor *is it* one *who* hates me
who has [d]exalted *himself*
against me;
Then I could hide from him.
13 But *it was* you, a man my
equal,
My companion and my
[e]acquaintance.
14 We took sweet counsel
together,
And walked to the house of
God in the throng.
15 Let death seize them;
Let them go down [f]alive into
[g]hell,
For wickedness *is* in their
dwellings *and* among them.
16 As for me, I will call upon
God,
And the LORD shall save me.
17 Evening and morning and at
[h]noon
I will pray, and cry aloud,
And He shall hear my voice.
18 He has redeemed my soul in
peace from the battle *that*
was against me,
[i]For there were many against
me.
19 God will hear, and afflict them,
[j]Even He who abides from of
old. Selah.
Because they do not change,
Therefore they do not fear
God.
20 [k]He has put forth his hands
against those who [l]were at
peace with him;
[m]He has broken his covenant.
21 [n]*The words* of his mouth were
smoother than butter,
But war *was* in his heart;
His words were softer than oil,
Yet they *were* drawn swords.
22 [o]Cast your burden on the LORD,
And He shall sustain you;
[p]He shall never permit the
righteous to be moved.
23 But You, O God, shall bring
them down to the pit of
destruction;
Bloodthirsty and deceitful men

7
[a] Ps. 59:10; 92:11
PSALM 55 Title
[b] Or *Instruction*
5
[c] Lit. *covered me*
12
[d] Ps. 35:26; 38:16
13
[e] Ps. 41:9
15
[f] Num. 16:30–33
[g] See Hab. 2:5, *note;* cp. Lk. 16:23, *note*
17
[h] Dan. 6:10
18
[i] 2 Chr. 32:7–8
19
[j] Dt. 33:27
20
[k] Cp. Acts 12:1
[l] Ps. 7:4
[m] Lit. *he has profaned*
21
[n] Ps. 28:3; 57:4; 62:4; 64:3; Prov. 5:3–4; 12:18
22
[o] Ps. 37:5; Mt. 6:25; Lk. 12:22; 1 Pet. 5:7
[p] Ps. 37:24

* 55:title Hebrew *neginoth* • Hebrew *Maschil*

shall not live out half their
days;
But I will trust in You.

Reliance on God

To the Chief Musician. Set to "The Silent Dove in Distant Lands."* A Michtam of David when the Philistines captured him in [a]Gath.

56 [b]BE merciful to me, O God, for
man would swallow me up;
Fighting all day he oppresses
me.
2 My enemies would hound *me*
all day,
For *there are* many who fight
against me, O Most High.
3 Whenever I am afraid,
I will [c]trust in You.
4 In God (I will praise His word),
In God I have put my trust;
[d]I will not fear.
What can flesh do to me?
5 All day they twist my words;
All their thoughts *are* against
me for evil.
6 They gather together,
They hide, they mark my
steps,
When they lie in wait for my
life.
7 Shall they escape by iniquity?
In anger cast down the
peoples, O God!
8 You number my wanderings;
[1]Put my tears into Your bottle;
[e]*Are they* not in Your book?
9 When I cry out *to You,*
Then my enemies will turn
back;
This I know, because [f]God *is*
for me.
10 In God (I will praise *His* word),
In the LORD (I will praise *His*
word),
11 In God I have put my trust;
I will not be afraid.
What can man do to me?
12 Vows *made* to You *are binding*
upon me, O God;
I will render praises to You,
13 [g]For You have delivered my
soul from death.
Have You not *kept* my feet
from falling,
That I may walk before God
In the [h]light of the living?

PSALM 56
Title
a 1 Sam. 21:10–11
1
b Ps. 57:1
3
c Lit. *lean on.* See Ps. 2:12, *note*
4
d Ps. 118:6; Isa. 31:3; Heb. 13:6
8
e Mal. 3:16
9
f Ps. 118:6; Rom. 8:31
13
g Ps. 116:8–9
h Job 33:30
PSALM 57
1
i See Ps. 2:12, *note*
j Ps. 17:8; 63:7
k Isa. 26:20
3
l Ps. 144:5,7

Trust in God amid troubles

To the Chief Musician. Set to "Do Not Destroy."* A Michtam of David when he fled from Saul into the cave.

57 BE merciful to me, O God, be
merciful to me!
For my soul [i]trusts in You;
And in the [j]shadow of Your
wings I will make my refuge,
Until *these* calamities have
[k]passed by.
2 I will cry out to God Most
High,
To God who performs *all
things* for me.
3 [l]He shall send from heaven and
save me;
He reproaches the one who
would swallow me up. Selah.
God shall send forth His mercy
and His truth.
4 My soul *is* among lions;
I lie *among* the sons of men
Who are set on fire,
Whose teeth *are* spears and
arrows,
And their tongue a sharp
sword.
5 Be exalted, O God, above the
heavens;
Let Your glory *be* above all
the earth.
6 They have prepared a net for
my steps;
My soul is bowed down;
They have dug a pit before me;
Into the midst of it they
themselves have fallen.
Selah.
7 My heart is steadfast, O God,
my heart is steadfast;
I will sing and give praise.
8 Awake, my glory!
Awake, lute and harp!
I will awaken the dawn.
9 I will praise You, O Lord,
among the peoples;
I will sing to You among the
nations.
10 For Your mercy reaches unto
the heavens,
And Your truth unto the
clouds.

*
56:title Hebrew *Jonath Elem Rechokim*
57:title Hebrew *Al Tashcheth*

[1](56:8) Sometimes, in the ancient East, mourners would catch their tears in wineskins and place them at the tombs of their loved ones.

11 Be exalted, O God, above the heavens;
Let Your glory be above all the earth.

A cry for God's vengeance
To the Chief Musician. Set to "Do Not Destroy."* A Michtam of David.

58 DO you indeed speak righteousness, you silent ones?
Do you judge uprightly, you sons of men?
2 No, in heart you work wickedness;
You weigh out the violence of your hands in the earth.
3 The wicked are estranged from the womb;
They go [a]astray as soon as they are born, speaking lies.
4 Their poison *is* like the poison of a serpent;
They are like the deaf cobra *that* stops its ear,
5 Which will not [b]heed the voice of charmers,
Charming ever so [c]skillfully.
6 Break their teeth in their mouth, O God!
Break out the fangs of the young lions, O LORD!
7 [d]Let them flow away as waters *which* run continually;
When he bends *his bow*,
Let his arrows be as if cut in pieces.
8 *Let them be* like a snail which melts away as it goes,
Like a stillborn child of a woman, that they may not see the sun.
9 Before your [e]pots can feel *the burning* thorns,
He shall take them away as with a whirlwind,
As in His living and burning wrath.
10 The righteous shall [f]rejoice when he sees the [g]vengeance;
[h]He shall wash his feet in the blood of the [i]wicked,
11 So that men will say,
"Surely *there is* a [j]reward for the righteous;
Surely He is God who [k]judges in the earth."

PSALM 58
3
a Ps. 53:3
5
b Jer. 8:17
c Cp. Mt. 11:16–19
7
d Josh. 7:5; Ps. 112:10
9
e Ps. 118:12; Eccl. 7:6
10
f Cp. Rev. 19:1–5
g Dt. 32:43; Jer. 11:20
h Ps. 68:23
i Cp. Rev. 19:15–21
11
j Prov. 11:18; 2 Cor. 5:10
k Ps. 50:6; 75:7
PSALM 59
Title
l 1 Sam. 19:11
7
m Ps. 10:11; 64:5; 73:11
9
n Lit. *my high place*
10
o Ps. 54:7; 92:11; 112:8

The help of the helpless
To the Chief Musician. Set to "Do Not Destroy."* A Michtam of David when Saul sent men, and they watched the house in order to kill [l]him.

59 DELIVER me from my enemies, O my God;
Defend me from those who rise up against me.
2 Deliver me from the workers of iniquity,
And save me from bloodthirsty men.
3 For look, they lie in wait for my life;
The mighty gather against me,
Not *for* my transgression nor *for* my sin, O LORD.
4 They run and prepare themselves through no fault *of mine.*
Awake to help me, and behold!
5 You therefore, O LORD God of hosts, the God of Israel,
Awake to punish all the nations;
Do not be merciful to any wicked transgressors. Selah.
6 At evening they return,
They growl like a dog,
And go all around the city.
7 Indeed, they belch with their mouth;
Swords *are* in their lips;
For *they say,* "Who [m]hears?"
8 But You, O LORD, shall laugh at them;
You shall have all the nations in derision.
9 I will wait for You, O You his Strength;*
For God *is* [n]my defense.
10 My God of mercy* shall come to meet me;
God shall let [o]me see *my desire* on my enemies.
11 Do not slay them, lest my people forget;
Scatter them by Your power,
And bring them down,
O Lord our shield.

*
58:title Hebrew *Al Tashcheth* **59:title** Hebrew *Al Tashcheth* **59:9** Following Masoretic Text and Syriac; some Hebrew manuscripts, Septuagint, Targum, and Vulgate read *my Strength.* **59:10** Following Qere; some Hebrew manuscripts, Septuagint, and Vulgate read *My God, His mercy;* Kethib, some Hebrew manuscripts and Targum read *O God, my mercy;* Syriac reads *O God, Your mercy.*

12 *For* the sin of their mouth *and*
the words of their lips,
Let them even be taken in
their pride,
And for the cursing and lying
which they speak.
13 [a]Consume *them* in wrath,
consume *them,*
That they *may* not *be;*
And [b]let them know that God
rules in Jacob
To the ends of the earth. Selah.
14 And at evening they return,
They growl like a dog,
And go all around the city.
15 They wander up and down for
food,
And howl* if they are not
satisfied.
16 But I will sing of Your power;
Yes, I will sing aloud of Your
mercy in the morning;
For You have been my defense
And refuge in the day of my
trouble.
17 To You, O my Strength, I will
sing praises;
For God *is* my defense,
My God of mercy.

A prayer for help

To the Chief Musician. Set to "Lily of the Testimony."* A Michtam of David. For teaching. [c]When he fought against Mesopotamia and Syria of Zobah, and Joab returned and killed twelve thousand Edomites in the Valley of Salt.

60 O GOD, You have cast us off;
You have broken us down;
You have been displeased;
Oh, restore us again!
2 You have made the earth
tremble;
You have broken it;
Heal its breaches, for it is
shaking.
3 [d]You have shown Your people
hard things;
You have made us drink the
wine of [e]confusion.

4 You have given a banner to
those who [f]fear You,
That it may be displayed
because of the truth. Selah.
5 [g]That Your beloved may be
delivered,
Save *with* Your right hand,
and hear me.

6 God has [h]spoken in His
holiness:
"I will rejoice;
I will [i]divide [1]Shechem
And measure out the Valley of
[j]Succoth.
7 Gilead *is* Mine, and Manasseh
is Mine;
[k]Ephraim also *is* the helmet for
My head;
[l]Judah *is* My lawgiver.
8 [m]Moab *is* My washpot;
[n]Over Edom I will cast My
shoe;
[o]Philistia, shout in triumph
because of Me."
9 Who will bring me *to* the
strong city?
Who will lead me to Edom?
10 *Is it* not You, O God, *who* cast
us off?
And You, O God, *who* did not
go out with our armies?
11 Give us help from trouble,
[p]For the [q]help of man *is*
useless.
12 Through God we will do
valiantly,
For *it is* He *who* shall tread
down our enemies.

God the Shelter

To the Chief Musician. On a stringed instrument.* A Psalm of David.

61 HEAR my cry, O God;
Attend to my prayer.
2 From the end of the earth I
will cry to You,
When my heart is
overwhelmed;
Lead me to the rock that is
higher than I.
3 For You have been a shelter
for me,
A strong tower from the
enemy.
4 I will abide in Your tabernacle
forever;
I will trust in the [r]shelter of
Your wings. Selah.
5 For You, O God, have heard
my vows;
You have given *me* the

13
a Ps. 104:35
b Ps. 83:18
PSALM 60
Title
c 2 Sam. 8:13; 1 Chr. 18:12; see 1 Chr. 11:11, *note*
3
d Ps. 71:20
e Lit. *staggering.* Cp. Isa. 51:17, 22; Jer. 25:15
4
f See Ps. 19:9, *note*
5
g vv. 5–12 are almost identical with Ps. 108:6–13
6
h Ps. 89:35
i Josh. 1:6
j Josh. 13:27
7
k Dt. 33:17
l Gen. 49:10
8
m 2 Sam. 8:2
n 2 Sam. 8:14; Ps. 108:9
o 2 Sam. 8:1
11
p Ps. 118:8; 146:3
q Lit. *salvation*
PSALM 61
4
r Job 40:21

*
59:15 Following Septuagint and Vulgate; Masoretic Text, Syriac, and Targum read *spend the night.* **60:title** Hebrew *Shushan Eduth* **61:title** Hebrew *neginah*

[1](60:6) Shechem is one of the oldest cities in Palestine (Gen. 12:6; 37:14; 1 Ki. 12:1; etc.). The modern city of Nablus, 30 miles north of Jerusalem, is the ancient Shechem.

heritage of those who fear
Your name.
6 You will prolong the king's
life,
His years as many generations.
7 He shall abide before God
forever.
Oh, prepare mercy and truth,
which may preserve him!
8 So I will sing praise to Your
name forever,
That I may daily perform my
vows.

Waiting for God

To the Chief Musician. To [a]Jeduthun. A Psalm of David.

62 TRULY my soul [b]silently
waits for God;
From Him *comes* my salvation.
2 He only *is* my [c]rock and my
salvation;
He is my [d]defense;
I shall not be greatly [e]moved.
3 How long will you attack a
man?
You shall be slain, all of you,
Like a leaning wall and a
tottering fence.
4 They only consult to cast *him*
down from his high position;
They delight in lies;
[f]They bless with their mouth,
But they curse inwardly. Selah.
5 My soul, wait silently for God
alone,
For my expectation *is* from
Him.
6 He only *is* my rock and my
salvation;
He is my defense;
I shall not be moved.
7 In God *is* my salvation and my
glory;
The rock of my strength,
And my refuge, *is* in God.
8 Trust in Him at all times, you
people;
[g]Pour out your heart before
Him;
God *is* a refuge for us. Selah.
9 Surely men of low degree *are*
a [h]vapor,
Men of high degree *are* a lie;
If they are weighed on the
scales,
They *are* altogether *lighter*
than vapor.
10 Do not trust in oppression,
Nor vainly hope in robbery;

PSALM 62
Title
a See Ps. 39 title, *note*
1
b Lit. *is silent*. Ps. 65:1
2
c Christ (Rock): vv. 2,6–7; Ps. 118:22. (Gen. 49:24; 1 Pet. 2:8)
d Lit. *high place*
e Ps. 55:22
4
f Cp. Jas. 3:8–12
8
g 1 Sam. 1:15; Ps. 42:4; Lam. 2:19
9
h Ps. 39:5; Isa. 40:17
10
i Cp. Lk. 12:15
12
j Rom. 2:6; 1 Cor. 3:8
PSALM 63
Title
k Cp. 1 Sam. 23:14
1
l Ps. 42:2; 84:2; 143:6; Mt. 5:6
2
m Ps. 27:4; cp. Isa. 6:5
3
n Ps. 138:2
4
o Ps. 28:2; 143:6
6
p Ps. 42:8; 119:55; 149:5

If riches increase,
Do not set *your* heart *on*
[i]*them*.
11 God has spoken once,
Twice I have heard this:
That power *belongs* to God.
12 Also to You, O Lord, *belongs*
mercy;
For You render to each one
according to his [j]work.

Thirsting for God

A Psalm of David when he was in the wilderness of [k]Judah.

63 O GOD, You *are* my God;
Early will I seek You;
[l]My soul thirsts for You;
My flesh longs for You
In a dry and thirsty land
Where there is no water.
2 So I have looked for You in
the [m]sanctuary,
To see Your power and Your
glory.
3 [n]Because Your lovingkindness
is better than life,
My lips shall praise You.
4 Thus I will bless You while I
live;
I will [o]lift up my hands in
Your name.
5 My soul shall be satisfied as
with marrow and fatness,
And my mouth shall praise
You with joyful lips.
6 When [p]I remember You on my
bed,
I meditate on You in the *night*
watches.
7 Because You have been my
help,
Therefore in the shadow of
Your wings I will rejoice.
8 My soul follows close behind
You;
Your right hand upholds me.
9 But those *who* seek my life, to
destroy *it*,
Shall go into the lower parts of
the earth.
10 They shall fall by the sword;
They shall be a portion for
jackals.
11 But the king shall rejoice in
God;
Everyone who swears by Him
shall glory;
But the mouth of those who
speak lies shall be stopped.

A cry for God's protection

To the Chief Musician. A Psalm of David.

64 HEAR my voice, O God, in
my meditation;
Preserve my life from fear of
the enemy.
2 Hide me from the secret plots
of the wicked,
From the rebellion of the
workers of iniquity,
3 Who sharpen their tongue like
a sword,
And bend *their bows to shoot*
their arrows—bitter words,
4 That they may shoot in secret
at the [a]blameless;
Suddenly they shoot at him
and do not fear.

5 They encourage themselves *in*
an evil matter;
They talk of laying snares
secretly;
They [b]say, "Who will see
them?"
6 They devise iniquities:
"We have perfected a shrewd
scheme."
Both the inward thought and
the heart of man are deep.

7 But God shall shoot at them
with an arrow;
Suddenly they shall be
wounded.
8 So He will make them stumble
over their own tongue;
All who see them shall flee
away.
9 All men shall fear,
And shall declare the work of
God;
For they shall wisely consider
His doing.

10 [c]The righteous shall be glad in
the LORD, and trust in Him.
And all the upright in heart
shall glory.

God's abundant provision through nature

To the Chief Musician. A Psalm of David.
A Song.

65 PRAISE is awaiting You, O
God, in Zion;
And to You the vow shall be
performed.
2 O You who hear prayer,
[d]To You all flesh will come.
3 Iniquities prevail against me;
As for our transgressions,
You will [e]provide atonement
for them.

4 [f]Blessed *is the man* You
choose,
And cause to approach *You*,
That he may dwell in Your
courts.
[g]We shall be satisfied with the
goodness of Your house,
Of Your holy temple.

5 *By* awesome deeds in
righteousness You will
answer us,
O God of our salvation,
You who are the confidence of
all the ends of the earth,
And of the far-off seas;
6 Who established the mountains
by His strength,
Being clothed with power;
7 You who [h]still the noise of the
seas,
The noise of their waves,
And the tumult of the peoples.
8 They also who dwell in the
farthest parts are afraid of
Your [i]signs;
You make the outgoings of the
morning and evening rejoice.

9 You [j]visit the earth and water
it,
You greatly enrich it;
[k]The river of God is full of
water;
You provide their grain,
For so You have prepared it.
10 You water its ridges
abundantly,
You settle its furrows;
You make it soft with showers,
You bless its growth.

11 You crown the year with Your
goodness,
And Your paths drip *with*
abundance.
12 They drop *on* the pastures of
the wilderness,
And the little hills rejoice on
every side.
13 The pastures are clothed with
flocks;
The valleys also are covered
with grain;
They shout for joy, they also
sing.

Praise for God's many blessings

To the Chief Musician. A Song. A Psalm.

66 MAKE a joyful shout to God,
all the earth!
2 Sing out the honor of His
name;
Make His praise glorious.

PSALM 64
4 *a* See Phil. 3:12, *note*
5 *b* Ps. 59:7
10 *c* Ps. 32:11; 58:10; 68:3
PSALM 65
2 *d* Isa. 66:23
3 *e* Ps. 51:2; 79:9; Isa. 6:7; Heb. 9:14; 1 Jn. 1:7,9
4 *f* Cp. Ps. 32:2; *g* Ps. 36:8
7 *h* Mt. 8:26
8 *i* Ps. 135:9
9 *j* Dt. 11:12; *k* Ps. 104:13; 147:8

3 Say to God,
"How awesome are Your works!
[a]Through the greatness of Your power
Your enemies shall submit themselves to You.
4 [b]All the earth shall worship You
And sing praises to You;
They shall sing praises *to* Your name." Selah.

5 Come and see the works of God;
He is awesome *in His* doing toward the sons of men.
6 [c]He turned the sea into dry *land;*
[d]They went through the river on foot.
There we will rejoice in Him.
7 He rules by His power forever;
His eyes observe the nations;
Do not let the rebellious exalt themselves. Selah.

8 Oh, bless our God, you peoples!
And make the voice of His praise to be heard,
9 Who [e]keeps our soul among the living,
And does not allow our feet to be moved.
10 For You, O God, have [f]tested us;
You have [g]refined us as silver is refined.
11 You brought us into the net;
You laid affliction on our backs.
12 You have caused men to ride over our [h]heads;
We went through fire and through water;
But You brought us out to rich *fulfillment.*

13 [i]I will go into Your house with burnt offerings;
I will pay You my vows,
14 Which my lips have uttered
And my mouth has spoken when I was in trouble.
15 I will offer You burnt sacrifices of fat animals,
With the sweet aroma of rams;
I will offer bulls with goats. Selah.

PSALM 66
3
a Ps. 18:44
4
b Ps. 65:2; 67:7
6
c Ex. 14:21
d Josh. 3:14–16
9
e Lit. *puts*
10
f *Test/tempt:* vv. 10–12; Ps. 78:18. (Gen. 3:1; Jas. 1:14, *note*)
g Cp. Zech. 13:9; 1 Pet. 4:12
12
h Isa. 51:23
13
i Ps. 100:4; 116:14, 17–19
16
j See Ps. 19:9, *note*
18
k Job 27:9; Prov. 15:29; 28:9; Isa. 1:15; Jn. 9:31; Jas. 4:3

PSALM 67
1
l Num. 6:25
2
m Ps. 66:4
4
n Ps. 96:10, 13; 98:9
o Lit. *lead*
6
p Lev. 26:4; Ps. 85:12; Ezek. 34:27

16 Come *and* hear, all you who [j]fear God,
And I will declare what He has done for my soul.
17 I cried to Him with my mouth,
And He was extolled with my tongue.
18 [k]If I regard iniquity in my heart,
The Lord will not hear.
19 *But* certainly God has heard *me;*
He has attended to the voice of my prayer.

20 Blessed *be* God,
Who has not turned away my prayer,
Nor His mercy from me!

God and the nations

To the Chief Musician. On stringed instruments.* A Psalm. A Song.

67 GOD be merciful to us and bless us,
And cause His [l]face to shine upon us, Selah.
2 That Your way may be known on earth,
Your salvation among [m]all nations.

3 Let the peoples praise You, O God;
Let all the peoples praise You.
4 Oh, let the nations be glad and sing for joy!
[n]For You shall judge the people righteously,
And [o]govern the nations on earth. Selah.

5 Let the peoples praise You, O God;
Let all the peoples praise You.
6 [p]*Then* the earth shall yield her increase;
God, our own God, shall bless us.
7 God shall bless us,
And all the ends of the earth shall [j]fear Him.

A song of triumph and glory

To the Chief Musician. A Psalm of David. A Song.

68 [1]LET God arise,
Let His enemies be scattered;
Let those also who hate Him flee before Him.
2 As smoke is driven away,

*67:title Hebrew *neginoth*

[1](68:1) In this Psalm the joy of Israel in the kingdom is prominent. At v. 18 (quoted in Eph. 4:7–16 of Christ's ascension ministry) the Psalm sounds a prophetic note, perhaps looking

So drive *them* away;
[a]As wax melts before the fire,
So let the wicked perish at the presence of God.
3 But [b]let the righteous be glad;
Let them rejoice before God;
Yes, let them rejoice exceedingly.

4 Sing to God, sing praises to His name;
[c]Extol Him who rides on the clouds,*
[d]By His name YAH,
And rejoice before Him.

5 A [e]father of the fatherless, a defender of widows,
Is God in His holy habitation.
6 [f]God sets the solitary in families;
[g]He brings out those who are bound into prosperity;
But the rebellious dwell in a dry *land.*

7 O God, when You went out before Your people,
When You marched through the wilderness, Selah.
8 The earth shook;
The heavens also dropped *rain* at the presence of God;
Sinai itself *was moved* at the presence of God, the God of Israel.
9 You, O God, sent a plentiful rain,
Whereby You confirmed Your inheritance,
When it was weary.
10 Your congregation dwelt in it;
[h]You, O God, provided from Your goodness for the poor.

11 The Lord gave the [i]word;
Great *was* the company of those who proclaimed *it:*
12 "Kings of armies flee, they flee,
And she who remains at home divides the spoil.
13 Though you lie down among the sheepfolds,
You will be like the wings of a dove covered with silver,
And her feathers with yellow gold."
14 When the Almighty scattered kings in it,
It was *white* as snow in Zalmon.

PSALM 68

2
a Ps. 97:5; Mic. 1:4

3
b Ps. 32:11; 58:10; 64:10

4
c v. 33; Dt. 33:26
d Ex. 6:3

5
e Ps. 10:14, 18; 146:9

6
f Ps. 113:9
g Ps. 107:10,14; 146:7; Acts 12:7

10
h Ps. 74:19; cp. Dt. 26:5–9

11
i *Inspiration:* v. 11; Isa. 6:5. (Ex. 4:15; 2 Tim. 3:16, *note*)

18
j Eph. 4:8
k Acts 2:4, 33; 10:44–46; 1 Cor. 12:4–11; Eph. 4:7–12

22
l Dt. 30:1–9

15 A mountain of God *is* the mountain of Bashan;
A mountain *of many* peaks *is* the mountain of Bashan.
16 Why do you fume with envy, you mountains of *many* peaks?
This is the mountain *which* God desires to dwell in;
Yes, the LORD will dwell *in it* forever.

17 The chariots of God *are* twenty thousand,
Even thousands of thousands;
The Lord is among them *as in* Sinai, in the Holy *Place.*
18 You have ascended on high,
You have led captivity [j]captive;
You have received [k]gifts among men,
Even *from* the rebellious,
That the LORD God might dwell *there.*

19 Blessed *be* the Lord,
Who daily loads us *with benefits,*
The God of our salvation! Selah.
20 Our God *is* the God of salvation;
And to GOD the Lord *belong* escapes from death.

21 But God will wound the head of His enemies,
The hairy scalp of the one who still goes on in his trespasses.
22 The Lord said, "I will bring [l]back from Bashan,
I will bring *them* back from the depths of the sea,
23 That your foot may crush *them** in blood,
And the tongues of your dogs *may have* their portion from *your* enemies."

24 They have seen Your procession, O God,
The procession of my God, my King, into the sanctuary.
25 The singers went before, the players on instruments *followed* after;

*68:4 Masoretic Text reads *deserts;* Targum reads *heavens* (compare verse 34 and Isaiah 19:1).
68:23 Septuagint, [Syriac], Targum, and Vulgate read *you may dip your foot.*

forward to the regathering of Israel (vv. 21–23) and the Messianic kingdom. See Ps. 69, the next in order of the Messianic Psalms.

Who desire my hurt.
3 [a]Let them be turned back
because of their shame,
Who say, "Aha, aha!"
4 Let all those who seek You
rejoice and be glad in You;
And let those who love Your
salvation say continually,
"Let God be magnified!"
5 [b]But I *am* poor and needy;
[c]Make haste to me, O God!
You *are* my help and my
deliverer;
O LORD, do not delay.

A prayer for old age

71 [d]IN You, O LORD, I put my
[e]trust;
Let me never be put to shame.
2 Deliver me in Your
righteousness, and cause me
to escape;
Incline Your ear to me, and
save me.
3 [f]Be my strong refuge,
To which I may resort
continually;
You have given the
commandment to save me,
For You *are* my rock and my
fortress.
4 Deliver me, O my God, out of
the hand of the wicked,
Out of the hand of the
unrighteous and cruel man.
5 For You are my hope, O Lord
GOD;
You are my [e]trust from my
youth.
6 By You I have been upheld
from birth;
You are He who [g]took me out
of my mother's womb.
My praise *shall be* continually
of You.
7 [h]I have become as a wonder to
many,
But You *are* my strong refuge.
8 Let my mouth be filled *with*
Your praise
And with Your glory all the
day.
9 Do not cast me off in the time
of old age;
Do not forsake me when my
strength fails.
10 For my enemies speak against
me;
And those who lie in wait for
my life take counsel
together,
11 Saying, "God has forsaken
him;
Pursue and take him, for *there
is* none to deliver *him.*"
12 [i]O God, do not be far from me;
O my God, make haste to
[j]help me!
13 Let them be confounded *and*
consumed
Who are adversaries of my
life;
Let them be covered *with*
reproach and dishonor
Who seek my hurt.
14 But I will hope continually,
And will praise You yet more
and more.
15 My mouth shall tell of Your
righteousness,
And Your salvation all the day,
For I do not know *their* limits.
16 I will go in the strength of the
Lord GOD;
I will make mention of Your
righteousness, of Yours only.
17 O God, You have taught me
from my [k]youth;
And to this *day* I declare Your
wondrous works.
18 Now also [l]when *I am* old and
grayheaded,
O God, do not forsake me,
Until I declare Your strength
to *this* generation,
Your power to everyone *who*
is to come.
19 [m]Also Your righteousness, O
God, *is* very high,
You who have done great
things;
O God, who *is* like You?
20 *You,* who have shown me
great and severe troubles,
Shall revive me again,
And bring me up again from
the depths of the earth.
21 You shall increase my
greatness,
And comfort me on every side.
22 Also with the lute I will praise
You—
And Your faithfulness, O my
God!
To You I will sing with the
harp,
O Holy One of Israel.
23 My lips shall greatly rejoice
when I sing to You,
And my soul, which You have
[n]redeemed.

3
a Ps. 40:15
5
b Ps. 40:17; 72:12–13
c Ps. 141:1
PSALM 71
1
d vv. 1–3; cp. Ps. 31:1–3
e See Ps. 2:12, *note*
3
f Lit. *Be to me a rock of habitation*
6
g Ps. 22:9–10
7
h Isa. 8:18; Zech. 3:8; 1 Cor. 4:9
12
i Ps. 22:11, 19; 35:22; 38:21–22
j Ps. 70:1
17
k Dt. 6:7
18
l Isa. 46:4
19
m Dt. 3:24; Ps. 36:6; cp. Lk. 1:49
23
n Redemption (redeeming relative type): v. 23; Ps. 72:14. (Gen. 48:16; Isa. 59:20, *note*)

24 My tongue also shall talk of
Your righteousness all the
day long;
For they are confounded,
For they are brought to shame
Who seek my hurt.

Messiah's glorious kingdom

A Psalm of Solomon.

72 [1]GIVE the [a]king Your
judgments, O God,
And Your righteousness to the
king's Son.
2 He will judge Your people with
righteousness,
And Your poor with [b]justice.
3 The mountains will bring
peace to the people,
And the little hills, by
righteousness.
4 He will bring justice to the
poor of the people;
He will save the children of the
needy,
And will break in pieces the
oppressor.

5 They shall [c]fear You*
As long as the sun and moon
[d]endure,
Throughout all generations.
6 He shall come down like rain
upon the grass before
mowing,
Like showers *that* water the
earth.
7 In His days the righteous shall
flourish,
And abundance of peace,
Until the moon is no more.

8 He shall have dominion also
from sea to sea,
And from the [e]River to the
ends of the earth.
9 Those who dwell in the
wilderness will bow before
Him,
And His enemies will [f]lick the
dust.
10 The kings of Tarshish and of
the [g]isles
Will bring presents;
The kings of Sheba and Seba
Will offer gifts.
11 Yes, all kings shall fall down
before Him;
All nations shall serve Him.

12 For He will deliver the needy
when he cries,
The poor also, and *him* who
has no helper.
13 He will spare the poor and
needy,
And will save the souls of the
needy.
14 He will [h]redeem their life from
oppression and violence;
And precious shall be their
blood in His sight.

15 And He shall live;
And the gold of [i]Sheba will be
given to Him;
Prayer also will be made for
Him continually,
And daily He shall be praised.

16 There will be an abundance of
grain in the earth,
On the top of the mountains;
Its fruit shall wave like
Lebanon;
[j]And *those* of the city shall
flourish like grass of the
earth.

17 His name [k]shall [d]endure
forever;
His name shall continue as
long as the sun.
And *men* shall be blessed [l]in
Him;
All nations shall call Him
blessed.

18 Blessed *be* the LORD God, the
God of Israel,
Who only does wondrous
things!
19 And blessed *be* His glorious
name forever!
And let the whole [m]earth be
filled *with* His glory.
Amen and Amen.

20 The prayers of David the son
of Jesse are [n]ended.

PSALM 72

1
a Kingdom (OT): vv. 1–20; Ps. 89:4. (Gen. 1:26; Zech. 12:8, *note*)

2
b Ps. 25:9

5
c See Ps. 19:9, *note*
d Ps. 89:36

8
e i.e. *the Euphrates*. Zech. 9:10

9
f Isa. 49:23

10
g i.e. *coasts*

14
h Redemption (redeeming relative type): v. 14; Ps. 74:2. (Gen. 48:16; Isa. 59:20, *note*)

15
i Isa. 60:6

16
j Cp. 1 Ki. 4:20

17
k Lit. *shall be*
l Gen. 12:3

19
m Num. 14:21; Hab. 2:14

20
n Cp. 2 Sam. 23:1–4

*72:5 Following Masoretic Text and Targum; Septuagint and Vulgate read *They shall continue*.

[1](72:1) The 72nd Psalm forms a complete vision of Messiah's kingdom insofar as the OT revelation extended. David's prayers will find their fruition in the kingdom (v. 20; 2 Sam. 23:1–4). Verse 1 refers to the investiture of the King's Son with the kingdom, the formal description of which is given in Dan. 7:13–14; Rev. 5:5–10. Verses 2–7,12–14 give the character of the kingdom (cp. Isa. 11:3–9). The emphatic word is "righteousness." Verses 8–19 speak of the universality of the kingdom. It is through restored Israel that the kingdom is to be extended over the earth (Zech. 8:13,20–23). See Ps. 89, the next in order of the Messianic Psalms.

Book III, Psalms 73—89

Problem of the prosperity of the wicked

A Psalm of Asaph.

73 TRULY God *is* good to Israel,
To such as are pure in heart.
2 But as for me, my feet had almost stumbled;
My steps had nearly [a]slipped.
3 For I *was* envious of the boastful,
When I saw the [b]prosperity of the [c]wicked.
4 For *there are* no pangs in their death,
But their strength *is* firm.
5 They *are* not in trouble *as other* men,
Nor are they plagued like *other* men.
6 Therefore pride serves as their necklace;
Violence covers them *like* a garment.
7 Their eyes bulge* with abundance;
They have more than heart could wish.
8 They scoff and speak wickedly *concerning* oppression;
[d]They speak loftily.
9 They set their mouth [e]against the heavens,
And their tongue walks through the earth.
10 Therefore his people return here,
And waters of a full *cup* are drained by them.
11 And they say, [f]"How does God know?
And is there knowledge in the Most High?"
12 Behold, these *are* the ungodly,
Who are always at ease;
They increase *in* riches.
13 Surely I have cleansed my heart *in* [g]vain,
And washed my hands in innocence.
14 For all day long I have been plagued,
And chastened every morning.
15 If I had said, "I will speak thus,"
Behold, I would have been untrue to the generation of Your children.
16 When I thought *how* to understand this,
It *was* too painful for me—
17 Until I went into the [h]sanctuary of God;
Then I understood their [i]end.
18 Surely You set them in slippery places;
You cast them down to destruction.
19 Oh, how they are *brought* to desolation, as in a [j]moment!
They are utterly consumed with terrors.
20 As a dream when *one* awakes,
So, Lord, when You awake,
You shall despise their image.
21 Thus my heart was grieved,
And I was vexed in my mind.
22 I *was* so foolish and ignorant;
I was *like* a beast before You.
23 Nevertheless I *am* continually with You;
You hold *me* by my right hand.
24 You will guide me with Your counsel,
And afterward receive me *to* [k]glory.
25 Whom have I in heaven *but* [l]*You?*
And *there is* none upon earth *that* I desire besides You.
26 My flesh and my heart fail;
But God *is* the strength of my heart and my [m]portion forever.
27 For indeed, those who are far from You shall perish;
You have destroyed all those who desert You for harlotry.
28 But *it is* good for me to [n]draw near to God;
I have put my [o]trust in the Lord GOD,
That I may [p]declare all Your works.

God's people cry for help

A [q]Contemplation* of Asaph.

74 O GOD, why have You cast *us* off forever?
Why does Your anger smoke against the sheep of Your pasture?
2 Remember Your congregation, *which* You have purchased of old,
The tribe of Your inheritance, *which* You have [r]redeemed—

PSALM 73
2
a Job 12:5
3
b Ps. 37:7
c Job 21:5–16
8
d 2 Pet. 2:18; Jude 16
9
e Rev. 13:6
11
f Job 22:13; Ps. 10:11; 94:7
13
g Job 21:15; 35:3; Mal. 3:14
17
h Cp. Heb. 10:25
i Ps. 37:38; 55:23
19
j Cp. 2 Pet. 3:10
24
k Ps. 49:15
25
l Cp. Jn. 6:67–68
26
m Ps. 16:5
28
n Heb. 10:22; Jas. 4:8
o See Ps. 2:12, *note*
p Ps. 116:10; 2 Cor. 4:13
PSALM 74
Title
q Or *Instruction*
2
r Redemption (redeeming relative type): v. 2; Ps. 77:15. (Gen. 48:16; Isa. 59:20, *note*)

---
*73:7 Targum reads *face bulges;* Septuagint, Syriac, and Vulgate read *iniquity bulges.* 74:title Hebrew *Maschil*

This Mount Zion where You
have dwelt.
3 Lift up Your feet to the
perpetual desolations.
The enemy has damaged
everything in the sanctuary.
4 [a]Your enemies roar in the midst
of Your meeting place;
They set up their banners *for*
signs.
5 They seem like men who lift
up
Axes among the thick trees.
6 And now they break down its
carved work, all at once,
With axes and hammers.
7 They have set fire to Your
sanctuary;
They have defiled the dwelling
place of Your name to the
ground.
8 They said in their hearts,
"Let us destroy them
altogether."
They have burned up all the
meeting places of God in the
land.

9 We do not see our signs;
There is no [b]longer any
prophet;
Nor *is there* any among us
who knows how long.
10 O God, how long will the
adversary reproach?
Will the enemy blaspheme
Your name forever?
11 Why do You withdraw Your
hand, even Your right hand?
Take it out of Your bosom and
destroy *them*.
12 For [c]God *is* my King from of
old,
Working salvation in the midst
of the earth.
13 You [d]divided the sea by Your
strength;
You broke the heads of the sea
serpents in the waters.
14 You broke the heads of
[e]Leviathan in pieces,
And gave him *as* food to the
people inhabiting the
wilderness.
15 [f]You broke open the fountain
and the flood;
[g]You dried up mighty rivers.
16 The day *is* Yours, the night
also *is* [h]Yours;
[i]You have prepared the light
and the sun.
17 You have [j]set all the borders
of the earth;
[k]You have made summer and
winter.

18 Remember this, *that* the
enemy has reproached, O
LORD,
And *that* a foolish people has
blasphemed Your name.
19 Oh, do not deliver the life [l]of
Your turtledove to the wild
beast!
Do not forget the life of Your
poor forever.
20 [m]Have respect to the covenant;
For the dark places of the
earth are full of the haunts
of cruelty.
21 Oh, do not let the oppressed
return ashamed!
Let the poor and needy praise
Your name.
22 Arise, O God, plead Your own
cause;
Remember how the foolish
man reproaches You daily.
23 Do not forget the voice of Your
enemies;
The tumult of those who rise
up against You [n]increases
continually.

Ultimate triumph of the righteous

To the Chief Musician. Set to "Do Not Destroy."* A Psalm of Asaph. A Song.

75 WE give thanks to You, O
God, we give thanks!
For Your wondrous works
declare *that* Your name is
near.

2 "When I choose the proper
time,
I will judge uprightly.
3 The earth and all its
inhabitants are dissolved;
I set up its pillars firmly.
Selah.
4 "I said to the boastful, 'Do not
deal boastfully,'
And to the wicked, 'Do not
[o]lift up the [p]horn.
5 Do not lift up your [p]horn on
high;
Do *not* speak with a stiff
neck.' "
6 For exaltation *comes* neither
from the east
Nor from the west nor from
the south.
7 But God *is* the Judge:

4 *a* Lam. 2:7
9 *b* Cp. 1 Sam. 3:1; Amos 8:11
12 *c* Ps. 44:4
13 *d* Lit. *broke*
14 *e* Perhaps the crocodile
15 *f* Ex. 17:5–6; Num. 20:11; Ps. 105:41; Isa. 48:21 *g* Josh. 3:13
16 *h* Job 38:12 *i* Gen. 1:14
17 *j* Acts 17:26 *k* Gen. 8:22
19 *l* Cp. Song 2:14
20 *m* Gen. 17:7–8; Lev. 26:44–45
23 *n* Lit. *ascends*
PSALM 75
4 *o* 1 Sam. 2:3; Ps. 94:4 *p* See Dt. 33:17, *note*

* **75:title** Hebrew *Al Tashcheth*

He puts down one,
And [a]exalts another.
8 For [b]in the hand of the LORD
there is a cup,
And the wine is red;
It is fully mixed, and He pours
it out;
Surely its dregs shall all the
wicked of the earth
Drain *and* drink down.

9 But I will declare forever,
I will sing praises to the God
of Jacob.

10 [c]"All the [d]horns of the wicked I
will also cut off,
[e]*But* the horns of the righteous
shall be [f]exalted."

The victorious power of God
To the Chief Musician. On stringed instruments.* A Psalm of Asaph. A Song.

76 [g]IN Judah God *is* known;
His name *is* great in Israel.
2 In Salem* also is His
tabernacle,
And His dwelling place in
Zion.
3 There He broke the arrows of
the bow,
The shield and sword of battle.
Selah.
4 You *are* more glorious and
excellent
Than the mountains of prey.
5 The stouthearted were
plundered;
They have sunk into their
sleep;
And none of the mighty men
have found the use of their
hands.
6 [h]At Your rebuke, O God of
Jacob,
Both the chariot and horse
were cast into a dead sleep.

7 You, Yourself, *are* to be
feared;
And who may [i]stand in Your
presence
When once You are angry?
8 You caused judgment to be
heard from heaven;
The earth feared and was still,
9 When God arose to judgment,
To deliver all the oppressed of
the earth. Selah.

10 Surely the wrath of man shall
praise [j]You;

7
a Ps. 147:6; Dan. 2:21
8
b Job 21:20; Ps. 60:3; Jer. 25:15; Rev. 14:10; 16:19
10
c Ps. 101:8; Jer. 48:25
d See Dt. 33:17, *note*
e Ps. 89:17; 148:14
f 1 Sam. 2:1
PSALM 76
1
g Ps. 48:1
6
h Ex. 15:1–21; Ezek. 39:20; Nah. 2:13; Zech. 12:4
7
i Nah. 1:6; Rev. 6:17
10
j Cp. Gen. 50:20; Ex. 9:16; Rom. 9:17
11
k See Ps. 19:9, *note*
12
l Ps. 47:2
PSALM 77
Title
m See Ps. 39 title, *note*
7
n Ps. 44:9; see Rom. 11:1, *note*
8
o 2 Pet. 3:9
9
p Cp. Isa. 49:15

With the remainder of wrath
You shall gird Yourself.
11 Make vows to the LORD your
God, and pay *them;*
Let all who are around Him
bring presents to Him who
ought to be [k]feared.
12 He shall cut off the spirit of
princes;
He is [l]awesome to the kings of
the earth.

Remembrance of God's mighty deeds
To the Chief Musician. To [m]Jeduthun. A Psalm of Asaph.

77 I CRIED out to God with my
voice—
To God with my voice;
And He gave ear to me.
2 In the day of my trouble I
sought the Lord;
My hand was stretched out in
the night without ceasing;
My soul refused to be
comforted.
3 I remembered God, and was
troubled;
I complained, and my spirit
was overwhelmed. Selah.
4 You hold my eyelids *open;*
I am so troubled that I cannot
speak.
5 I have considered the days of
old,
The years of ancient times.
6 I call to remembrance my song
in the night;
I meditate within my heart,
And my spirit makes diligent
search.
7 Will the Lord [n]cast off
forever?
And will He be favorable no
more?
8 Has His mercy ceased forever?
Has *His* [o]promise failed
forevermore?
9 Has God [p]forgotten to be
gracious?
Has He in anger shut up His
tender mercies? Selah.
10 And I said, "This *is* my
anguish;
But I will remember the years
of the right hand of the Most
High."
11 I will remember the works of
the LORD;

*76:title Hebrew *neginoth* 76:2 That is, Jerusalem

Surely I will remember Your
wonders of old.
12 I will also meditate on all Your
work,
And talk of Your deeds.
13 Your way, O God, *is* in the
[a]sanctuary;
Who *is* so great a God as *our*
God?
14 You *are* the God who does
wonders;
You have declared Your
strength among the peoples.
15 You have with *Your* arm
[b]redeemed Your people,
The sons of Jacob and Joseph.
Selah.
16 The waters saw You, O God;
The waters saw You, they
were [c]afraid;
The depths also trembled.
17 The clouds poured out water;
The skies sent out a sound;
Your arrows also flashed
about.
18 The voice of Your thunder *was*
in the whirlwind;
The lightnings lit up the world;
The earth trembled and shook.
19 Your way *was* in the sea,
Your path in the great waters,
And Your footsteps were not
known.
20 You led Your people like a
flock
By the hand of Moses and
Aaron.

God at work in Israel's history

A [d]Contemplation* of Asaph.

78 GIVE ear, O my people, *to*
my law;
Incline your ears to the words
of my [e]mouth.
2 I will open my mouth in a
[f]parable;
I will utter dark sayings of old,
3 Which we have heard and
known,
And our fathers have told us.
4 [g]We will not hide *them* from
their children,
[h]Telling to the generation to
come the praises of the
LORD,
And His strength and His
wonderful works that He has
done.
5 [i]For He established a testimony
in Jacob,
And appointed a law in Israel,
Which He commanded our
fathers,
[j]That they should make them
known to their children;
6 That the generation to come
might know *them*,
The children *who* would be
born,
That they may arise and
declare *them* to their
children,
7 That they may set their hope
in God,
And not forget the works of
God,
But keep His commandments;
8 And may not be like their
fathers,
A stubborn and rebellious
generation,
A generation [k]*that* did not set
its heart aright,
And whose spirit was not
faithful to God.
9 The children of Ephraim, *being*
armed *and* carrying bows,
Turned back in the day of
battle.
10 [l]They did not keep the
covenant of God;
They refused to walk in His
[m]law,
11 And forgot His works
And His wonders that He had
shown them.
12 Marvelous things He did in the
sight of their fathers,
In the land of Egypt, *in* the
field of Zoan.
13 He divided the sea and caused
them to pass through;
And He made the waters stand
up like a heap.
14 In the daytime also He led
them with the cloud,
And all the night with a light
of fire.
15 He split the rocks in the
wilderness,
And gave *them* drink in
abundance like the depths.
16 He also brought streams out of
the rock,
And caused waters to run
down like rivers.
17 But they sinned even more
against Him
By rebelling against the Most
High in the wilderness.

13 *a* Ps. 73:17
15 *b* *Redemption* (redeeming relative type): v. 15; Ps. 103:4. (Gen. 48:16; Isa. 59:20, *note*)
16 *c* Ex. 14:21
PSALM 78 Title *d* Or *Instruction*
1 *e* *Israel* (history): vv. 1–72; Ps. 106:4. (Gen. 12:2; Rom. 11:26, *note*)
2 *f* Mt. 13:34–35
4 *g* Dt. 4:9; 6:7; Joel 1:3 *h* Ex. 12:26–27; Ps. 145:4
5 *i* Ps. 147:19 *j* Dt. 11:19
8 *k* Lit. *that did not prepare its heart*
10 *l* 2 Ki. 17:15 *m* *Law* (of Moses): vv. 9–10; Ps. 119:1. (Ex. 19:1; Gal. 3:24, *note*)

* 78:title Hebrew *Maschil*

18 And they [a]tested God in their
heart
By asking for the food of their
fancy.
19 Yes, they spoke against God:
They said, "Can God prepare a
table in the wilderness?
20 Behold, He struck the rock,
So that the waters gushed out,
And the streams overflowed.
Can He give bread also?
Can He provide meat for His
people?"
21 Therefore the LORD heard *this*
and was furious;
So a fire was kindled against
Jacob,
And anger also came up
against Israel,
22 Because they did not believe in
God,
And did not [b]trust in His
salvation.
23 Yet He had commanded the
clouds above,
And opened the doors of
heaven,
24 Had [c]rained down manna on
them to eat,
And given them of the bread
of [d]heaven.
25 Men ate [e]angels' food;
He sent them food to the full.
26 [f]He caused an east wind to
blow in the heavens;
And by His power He brought
in the south wind.
27 He also rained meat on them
like the dust,
Feathered fowl like the sand of
the seas;
28 And He let *them* fall in the
midst of their camp,
All around their dwellings.
29 [g]So they ate and were well
filled,
For He gave them their own
desire.
30 They were not deprived of
their craving;
[h]But while their food *was* still
in their mouths,
31 The wrath of God came
against them,
And slew the stoutest of them,
And struck down the choice
men of Israel.
32 In spite of this they still
sinned,
And did [i]not believe in His
wondrous works.

18
a *Test/tempt:* v. 18; Ps. 78:41. (Gen. 3:1; Jas. 1;14, *note*)
22
b See Ps. 2:12, *note*
24
c Ex. 16:4
d Jn. 6:31
25
e See Heb. 1:4, *note*
26
f Num. 11:31
29
g Num. 11:20
30
h Num. 11:33
32
i Num. 14:11
34
j Cp. Hos. 5:15
35
k Ex. 15:13; Dt. 7:8; Isa. 41:14; 44:6; 63:9
36
l Ex. 24:7–8; Ezek. 33:31
38
m Num. 14:18–20
n Ex. 34:6
39
o Ps. 103:14–16
p Job 7:7, 16; Jas. 4:14
40
q Eph. 4:30
41
r *Test/tempt:* v. 41; Ps. 78:56. (Gen. 3:1; Jas. 1:14, *note*). Dt. 6:16
45
s Ex. 8:24
t Ex. 8:6
46
u Ex. 10:14
47
v Ex. 9:23

33 Therefore their days He
consumed in futility,
And their years in fear.
34 [j]When He slew them, then they
sought Him;
And they returned and sought
earnestly for God.
35 Then they remembered that
God *was* their rock,
And the Most High God their
[k]Redeemer.
36 Nevertheless they [l]flattered
Him with their mouth,
And they lied to Him with
their tongue;
37 For their heart was not
steadfast with Him,
Nor were they faithful in His
covenant.
38 [m]But He, *being* full of
[n]compassion, forgave *their*
iniquity,
And did not destroy *them*.
Yes, many a time He turned
His anger away,
And did not stir up all His
wrath;
39 [o]For He remembered that they
were but flesh,
A [p]breath that passes away
and does not come again.
40 How often they provoked Him
in the wilderness,
And [q]grieved Him in the
desert!
41 Yes, again and again they
[r]tempted God,
And limited the Holy One of
Israel.
42 They did not remember His
power:
The day when He redeemed
them from the enemy,
43 When He worked His signs in
Egypt,
And His wonders in the field
of Zoan;
44 Turned their rivers into blood,
And their streams, that they
could not drink.
45 He sent swarms of [s]flies
among them, which
devoured them,
And [t]frogs, which destroyed
them.
46 He also gave their crops to the
caterpillar,
And their labor to the [u]locust.
47 He destroyed their vines with
[v]hail,
And their sycamore trees with
frost.

48 He also gave up their [a]cattle to
the hail,
And their flocks to fiery
lightning.
49 He cast on them the fierceness
of His anger,
Wrath, indignation, and
trouble,
By sending angels of
destruction *among them.*
50 He made a path for His anger;
He did not spare their soul
from death,
But gave their life over to the
plague,
51 And destroyed all the
[b]firstborn in Egypt,
The first of *their* strength in
the tents of Ham.
52 But He made His own people
go forth like sheep,
And guided them in the
wilderness like a flock;
53 And He led them on safely, so
that they did not fear;
But the sea [c]overwhelmed
their enemies.
54 And He brought them to His
holy border,
This mountain *which* His right
hand had acquired.
55 He also drove out the nations
before them,
[d]Allotted them an inheritance
by survey,
And made the tribes of Israel
dwell in their tents.
56 Yet they [e]tested and provoked
the Most High God,
And did not keep His
testimonies,
57 But [f]turned back and acted
unfaithfully like their
fathers;
They were turned aside like a
deceitful bow.
58 For they provoked Him to
anger with their [g]high
places,
And moved Him to jealousy
with their carved images.
59 When God heard *this,* He was
furious,
And greatly abhorred Israel,
60 [h]So that He forsook the
tabernacle of Shiloh,
The tent He had placed among
men,
61 And delivered His strength
into captivity,
And His glory into the enemy's
hand.

48 *a* Ex. 9:19
51 *b* Ex. 12:29–30
53 *c* Ex. 14:27–28
55 *d* Josh. 13:7; 19:51
56 *e* *Test/tempt:* v. 56; Ps. 81:7. (Gen. 3:1; Jas. 1:14, *note*)
57 *f* v. 41; Ezek. 20:27–28; Hos. 7:16
58 *g* See Jud. 3:7 and 1 Ki. 3:2, *notes*
60 *h* 1 Sam. 4:11; Jer. 7:12–14; 26:6–9
62 *i* 1 Sam. 4:10
63 *j* Jer. 7:34; 16:9; 25:10
64 *k* 1 Sam. 4:17
68 *l* Ps. 87:2
69 *m* 1 Ki. 6:1–38
70 *n* 1 Sam. 16:11–12; 2 Sam. 7:8
71 *o* 2 Sam. 5:2; 1 Chr. 11:2
72 *p* 1 Ki. 9:4
PSALM 79
1 *q* 2 Ki. 25:9–10; 2 Chr. 36:19; Mic. 3:12

62 [i]He also gave His people over
to the sword,
And was furious with His
inheritance.
63 The fire consumed their young
men,
And [j]their maidens were not
given in marriage.
64 Their [k]priests fell by the
sword,
And their widows made no
lamentation.
65 Then the Lord awoke as *from*
sleep,
Like a mighty man who shouts
because of wine.
66 And He beat back His
enemies;
He put them to a perpetual
reproach.
67 Moreover He rejected the tent
of Joseph,
And did not choose the tribe of
Ephraim,
68 But chose the tribe of Judah,
Mount Zion [l]which He loved.
69 And He built His [m]sanctuary
like the heights,
Like the earth which He has
established forever.
70 [n]He also chose David His
servant,
And took him from the
sheepfolds;
71 From following the ewes that
had young He brought him,
To [o]shepherd Jacob His
people,
And Israel His inheritance.
72 So he shepherded them
according to the [p]integrity
of his heart,
And guided them by the
skillfulness of his hands.

A prayer for God's judgment

A Psalm of Asaph.

79 O GOD, the nations have
come into Your inheritance;
Your holy temple they have
defiled;
[q]They have laid Jerusalem in
heaps.
2 The dead bodies of Your
servants
They have given *as* food for
the birds of the heavens,
The flesh of Your saints to the
beasts of the earth.
3 Their blood they have shed
like water all around
Jerusalem,

And *there was* no one to bury
them.
4 We have become a reproach to
our [a]neighbors,
A scorn and derision to those
who are around us.
5 How long, LORD?
Will You be angry forever?
Will Your jealousy burn like
fire?
6 Pour out Your wrath on the
nations that do [b]not know
You,
And on the kingdoms that do
not call on Your name.
7 For they have devoured Jacob,
And laid waste his dwelling
place.
8 Oh, do not remember former
iniquities against us!
Let Your tender mercies come
speedily to meet us,
For we have been brought very
low.
9 Help us, O God of our
salvation,
For the glory of Your name;
And deliver us, and provide
atonement for our sins,
[c]For Your name's sake!
10 Why should the nations say,
"Where *is* their God?"
Let there be known among the
nations in our sight
The avenging of the blood of
Your servants *which has
been* shed.
11 Let the groaning of the
prisoner come before You;
According to the greatness of
Your power
Preserve those who are
appointed to die;
12 And return to our neighbors
sevenfold into their bosom
Their reproach with which
they have reproached You,
O Lord.
13 So [d]we, Your people and
sheep of Your pasture,
Will give You thanks forever;
We will show forth Your
praise to all generations.

A plea for the return of God's favor

To the Chief Musician. Set to "The Lilies."* A Testimony* of Asaph. A Psalm.

80 GIVE ear, O Shepherd of
Israel,
You who lead Joseph like a
flock;
[e]You who dwell *between* the
cherubim, shine forth!
2 Before [f]Ephraim, Benjamin,
and Manasseh,
Stir up Your strength,
And come *and* save us!
3 Restore us, O God;
[g]Cause Your face to shine,
And we shall be saved!
4 O LORD God of hosts,
[h]How long will You be angry
Against the prayer of Your
people?
5 [i]You have fed them with the
bread of tears,
And given them tears to drink
in great measure.
6 You have made us a strife to
our [a]neighbors,
And our enemies laugh among
themselves.
7 Restore us, O God of hosts;
Cause Your face to shine,
And we shall be saved!
8 You have brought a [j]vine out
of Egypt;
You have cast out the nations,
and planted it.
9 You prepared *room* for it,
And caused it to take deep
root,
And it filled the land.
10 The hills were covered with its
shadow,
And the mighty cedars with its
[k]boughs.
11 She sent out her boughs to the
Sea,*
And her branches to the
[l]River.
12 Why have You [m]broken down
her hedges,
So that all who pass by the
way pluck her *fruit?*
13 The boar out of the woods
uproots it,
And the wild beast of the field
devours it.
14 Return, we beseech You, O
God of hosts;
[n]Look down from heaven and
see,
And visit this vine
15 And the vineyard which Your
right hand has planted,

4 *a* Ps. 44:13
6 *b* Isa. 45:4–5; 2 Th. 1:8
9 *c* Jer. 14:7, 21
13 *d* Ps. 74:1; 95:7; 100:3
PSALM 80
1 *e* Ex. 25:20–22; 1 Sam. 4:4; 2 Sam. 6:2; Ps. 99:1
2 *f* Ps. 78:9,67
3 *g* Num. 6:25; Ps. 4:6; 67:1
4 *h* Ps. 79:5
5 *i* Ps. 42:3; 102:9; Isa. 30:20
8 *j* Isa. 5:1,7; Jer. 2:21; Ezek. 17:6; 19:10; cp. Ezek. 15:1–8
10 *k* Lev. 23:40
11 *l* i.e. *the Euphrates.* Ps. 72:8
12 *m* Isa. 5:5
14 *n* Isa. 63:15

*80:title Hebrew *Shoshannim* • Hebrew *Eduth*
80:11 That is, the Mediterranean

And the branch *that* You
made strong [a]for Yourself.
16 *It is* burned with fire, *it is* cut
down;
They perish at the rebuke of
Your countenance.
17 Let Your [b]hand be upon the
man of Your right hand,
Upon the son of man *whom*
You made strong for
Yourself.
18 Then we will not turn back
from You;
[c]Revive us, and we will call
upon Your name.
19 Restore us, O LORD God of
hosts;
Cause Your face to shine,
And we shall be saved!

A call to proper worship

To the Chief Musician. On an instrument of Gath.* A Psalm of Asaph.

81 SING aloud to God our
strength;
Make a joyful shout to the God
of Jacob.
2 Raise a song and strike the
timbrel,
The pleasant harp with the
lute.
3 Blow the trumpet at the time
of the New Moon,
At the full moon, on our
solemn feast day.
4 For [d]this *is* a statute for Israel,
A law of the God of Jacob.
5 This He established in Joseph
as a testimony,
When He went throughout the
land of Egypt,
Where I heard a language I did
[e]not understand.

6 "I removed his shoulder from
the burden;
His hands were freed from the
baskets.
7 [f]You called in trouble, and I
delivered you;
[g]I answered you in the secret
place of thunder;
I [h]tested you at the waters of
Meribah. Selah.
8 "Hear, O My people, and I will
admonish you!
O Israel, if you will listen to
Me!
9 There shall be no foreign [i]god
among you;
Nor shall you worship any
foreign god.

15
a Isa. 49:5
17
b Ps. 89:21
18
c Ps. 71:20
PSALM 81
4
d Lev. 23:24; Num. 10:10
5
e Cp. Dt. 28:49; Ps. 114:1
7
f Ex. 2:23; 14:10; Ps. 50:15
g Ex. 19:19
h *Test/tempt:* v. 7; Ps. 95:9. (Gen. 3:1; Jas. 1:14, *note*). Ex. 17:6–7; Num. 20:13
9
i See Ps. 16:4, *note*
10
j Ex. 20:2
12
k Acts 7:42; 14:16; Rom. 1:24–26
13
l Dt. 5:29; 10:12–13; 32:29; Isa. 48:18
PSALM 82
1
m 2 Chr. 19:6; Eccl. 5:8
2
n Dt. 1:17
3
o Dt. 24:17
5
p Ps. 11:3
6
q Jn. 10:34
8
r Cp. Gen. 18:25

10 [j]I *am* the LORD your God,
Who brought you out of the
land of Egypt;
Open your mouth wide, and I
will fill it.
11 "But My people would not heed
My voice,
And Israel would *have* none of
Me.
12 [k]So I gave them over to their
own stubborn heart,
To walk in their own counsels.
13 [l]"Oh, that My people would
listen to Me,
That Israel would walk in My
ways!
14 I would soon subdue their
enemies,
And turn My hand against
their adversaries.
15 The haters of the LORD would
pretend submission to Him,
But their fate would endure
forever.
16 He would have fed them also
with the finest of wheat;
And with honey from the rock
I would have satisfied you."

God and the judges

A Psalm of Asaph.

82 GOD [m]stands in the
congregation of the mighty;
He judges among the gods.*
2 How long will you judge
unjustly,
And [n]show partiality to the
wicked? Selah.
3 Defend the poor and
fatherless;
Do justice to the afflicted and
[o]needy.
4 Deliver the poor and needy;
Free *them* from the hand of
the wicked.
5 They do not know, nor do they
understand;
They walk about in darkness;
All the [p]foundations of the
earth are unstable.
6 I said, [q]"You *are* gods,*
And all of you *are* children of
the Most High.
7 But you shall die like men,
And fall like one of the
princes."
8 [r]Arise, O God, judge the earth;

*
81:title Hebrew *Al Gittith* **82:1** Hebrew *elohim, mighty ones;* that is, the judges **82:6** Hebrew *elohim, mighty ones;* that is, the judges

[a]For You shall inherit all
nations.

A prayer against enemies

A Song. A Psalm of Asaph.

83 DO not keep silent, O God!
Do not hold Your peace,
And do not be still, O God!
2 For behold, [b]Your enemies
make a tumult;
And those who hate You have
lifted up their head.
3 They have taken crafty counsel
against Your people,
And consulted together against
Your sheltered ones.
4 They have said, "Come, and
[c]let us cut them off from
being a nation,
That the name of Israel may be
remembered no more."
5 For they have consulted
together with one [d]consent;
They form a confederacy
against You:
6 The tents of Edom and the
Ishmaelites;
Moab and the [e]Hagrites;
7 Gebal, Ammon, and Amalek;
Philistia with the inhabitants of
Tyre;
8 Assyria also has joined with
them;
They have [f]helped the
children of Lot. Selah.
9 Deal with them as *with*
[g]Midian,
As *with* [h]Sisera,
As *with* Jabin at the Brook
Kishon,
10 Who perished at En Dor,
Who became *as* refuse on the
earth.
11 Make their nobles like [i]Oreb
and like Zeeb,
Yes, all their princes like
[j]Zebah and Zalmunna,
12 Who said, "Let us take for
ourselves
The pastures of God for a
possession."
13 O my God, [k]make them like
the whirling dust,
Like the chaff before the wind!
14 As the fire burns the woods,
And as the flame sets the
mountains on fire,
15 So pursue them with Your
tempest,
And frighten them with Your
storm.

8
[a] Ps. 2:8; Rev. 11:15
PSALM 83
2
[b] Ps. 2:1; Acts 4:25
4
[c] Est. 3:6,9; Jer. 11:19; 31:36
5
[d] Lit. *heart*
6
[e] 1 Chr. 5:10
8
[f] Lit. *they have been an arm to the children of Lot*
9
[g] Num. 31:7; Jud. 7:22
[h] Jud. 4:15–24; 5:20–21
11
[i] Jud. 7:25
[j] Jud. 8:12–21
13
[k] Ps. 35:5; cp. Isa. 17:13
18
[l] Ex. 6:3
PSALM 84
1
[m] Ps. 27:4; 46:4–5
2
[n] Ps. 42:1–2; 63:1; 73:26; 119:20
4
[o] Ps. 65:4
6
[p] Lit. *Weeping.* Not a literal valley, but any place of tears. Cp. Ps. 23:4
9
[q] Gen. 15:1

16 Fill their faces with shame,
That they may seek Your
name, O LORD.
17 Let them be confounded and
dismayed forever;
Yes, let them be put to shame
and perish,
18 That they may know that You,
whose [l]name alone *is* the
LORD,
Are the Most High over all the
earth.

Delight in the house of God

To the Chief Musician. On an instrument of Gath.* A Psalm of the sons of Korah.

84 HOW [m]lovely *is* Your
tabernacle,
O LORD of hosts!
2 [n]My soul longs, yes, even faints
For the courts of the LORD;
My heart and my flesh cry out
for the living God.

3 Even the sparrow has found a
home,
And the swallow a nest for
herself,
Where she may lay her
young—
Even Your altars, O LORD of
hosts,
My King and my God.
4 Blessed *are* those who dwell in
Your [o]house;
They will still be praising You.
Selah.

5 Blessed *is* the man whose
strength *is* in You,
Whose heart *is* set on
pilgrimage.
6 *As they* pass through the
Valley of [p]Baca,
They make it a spring;
The rain also covers it with
pools.
7 They go from strength to
strength;
Each one appears before God
in Zion.*
8 O LORD God of hosts, hear my
prayer;
Give ear, O God of Jacob!
Selah.
9 [q]O God, behold our shield,
And look upon the face of
Your anointed.

10 For a day in Your courts *is*
better than a thousand.

*84:title Hebrew *Al Gittith* 84:7 Septuagint, Syriac, and Vulgate read *The God of gods shall be seen.*

[a]I would rather be a doorkeeper
in the house of my God
Than dwell in the tents of
wickedness.
11 For the LORD God *is* a sun and
shield;
The LORD will give grace and
glory;
[b]No good *thing* will He
withhold
From those who walk
uprightly.

12 O LORD of hosts,
Blessed *is* the man who [c]trusts
in You!

A prayer of the returned exiles

To the Chief Musician. A Psalm of the sons of Korah.

85 LORD, You have been
favorable to Your land;
You have [d]brought back the
captivity of Jacob.
2 You have forgiven the iniquity
of Your people;
You have covered all their sin.
Selah.
3 You have taken away all Your
wrath;
You have turned from the
fierceness of Your anger.

4 Restore us, O God of our
salvation,
And cause Your anger toward
us to cease.
5 Will You be angry with us
forever?
Will You prolong Your anger
to all generations?
6 Will You not revive us again,
That Your people may rejoice
in You?
7 Show us Your mercy, LORD,
And grant us Your salvation.

8 I will hear what God the LORD
will speak,
For He will speak peace
To His people and to His
saints;
But let them [e]not turn back to
folly.
9 Surely His salvation *is* near to
those who [f]fear Him,
That glory may dwell in our
land.

10 Mercy and truth have met
together;
[g]Righteousness and peace have
kissed.
11 Truth shall spring out of the
earth,
And righteousness shall look
down from heaven.
12 Yes, the LORD will give *what is*
[h]good;
And our land will yield its
increase.
13 Righteousness will go before
Him,
And shall make His footsteps
our pathway.

Supplication to the compassionate God

A Prayer of David.

86 BOW down Your ear, O LORD,
hear me;
For I *am* poor and needy.
2 Preserve my life, for I *am* holy;
You are my God;
Save Your servant who [i]trusts
in You!
3 Be merciful to me, O Lord,
For I cry to You all day long.
4 Rejoice the soul of Your
servant,
For [j]to You, O Lord, I lift up
my soul.
5 For [k]You, Lord, *are* good, and
ready to forgive,
And abundant in mercy to all
those who call upon You.

6 Give ear, O LORD, to my
prayer;
And attend to the voice of my
supplications.
7 In the day of my [l]trouble I
will call upon You,
For You will answer me.

8 [m]Among the gods *there is* none
like You, O Lord;
Nor *are there any works* like
Your works.
9 All nations whom You have
made
Shall come and worship before
You, O Lord,
And shall glorify Your name.
10 For You *are* great, and do
wondrous things;
You [n]alone *are* God.

11 [o]Teach me Your way, O LORD;
I will walk in Your truth;
Unite my heart to [f]fear Your
name.
12 I will praise You, O Lord my
God, with all my heart,
And I will glorify Your name
forevermore.
13 For great *is* Your mercy
toward me,
And You have delivered my

10 *a* Lit. *I would choose rather to sit at the threshold*
11 *b* Ps. 34:9–10
12 *c Faith:* v. 12; Ps. 125:1. (Gen. 3:20; Heb. 11:39, *note*)

PSALM 85
1 *d* Ezra 1:11–2:1; Ps. 14:7; Jer. 30:18; 31:23; Ezek. 39:25; Joel 3:1
8 *e* Cp. 2 Pet. 2:21
9 *f* See Ps. 19:9, *note*
10 *g* Isa. 32:17; cp. Lk. 2:14
12 *h* Jas. 1:17

PSALM 86
2 *i* See Ps. 2:12, *note*
4 *j* Ps. 25:1; 143:8
5 *k* v. 15; Ps. 130:7; 145:9; Joel 2:13
7 *l* Cp. Ps. 50:15
8 *m* Ex. 15:11; Ps. 89:6; cp. 1 Cor. 8:5–6; see Ps. 16:4, *note*
10 *n* Dt. 6:4
11 *o* Ps. 27:11; 143:8

soul from the depths of
[a]Sheol.
14 O God, the proud have risen
against me,
And a mob of violent *men*
have sought my life,
And have not set You before
them.
15 But [b]You, O Lord, *are* a God
full of compassion, and
gracious,
Longsuffering and abundant in
mercy and truth.
16 Oh, turn to me, and have
mercy on me!
Give Your strength to Your
servant,
And save the son of Your
maidservant.
17 Show me a [c]sign for good,
That those who hate me may
see *it* and be ashamed,
Because You, LORD, have
helped me and comforted
me.

Zion, the city of God

A Psalm of the sons of Korah. A Song.

87 HIS foundation *is* in the holy
mountains.
2 The LORD loves the gates of
Zion
More than all the dwellings of
Jacob.
3 Glorious things are spoken of
you,
O city of God! Selah.
4 "I will make mention of [d]Rahab
and Babylon to those who
know Me;
Behold, O Philistia and Tyre,
with [e]Ethiopia:
'This *one* was born there.' "
5 And of Zion it will be said,
"This *one* and that *one* were
born in her;
And the Most High Himself
shall establish her."
6 The LORD will record,
When He [f]registers the
peoples:
"This *one* was born there."
Selah.
7 Both the singers and the
players on instruments *say*,
"All my springs *are* in you."

13 *a* See Hab. 2:5, *note;* cp. Lk. 16:23, *note*
15 *b* v. 5; Ex. 34:6; Ps. 103:8; 111:4; 130:7
17 *c* Ex. 3:12
PSALM 87
4 *d* Or *Egypt.* Ps. 89:10; Isa. 51:9
e Heb. *Cush.* Isa. 11:11
6 *f* Cp. Ezek. 13:9
PSALM 88
Title *g* Or *Instruction*
1 *h* Lk. 18:7
4 *i* Ps. 28:1
j Ps. 31:12
7 *k* Ps. 42:7
8 *l* Job 19:13, 19; Ps. 31:11; 142:4
m Lam. 3:7
9 *n* Ps. 86:3
10 *o* See Eccl. 9:10, *note*

Lament over affliction

A Song. A Psalm of the sons of Korah. To the Chief Musician. Set to "Mahalath Leannoth." A [g]Contemplation* of Heman the Ezrahite.

88 O LORD, God of my
salvation,
I have [h]cried out day and
night before You.
2 Let my prayer come before
You;
Incline Your ear to my cry.
3 For my soul is full of troubles,
And my life draws near to the
[a]grave.
4 I am counted with those who
[i]go down to the pit;
[j]I am like a man *who has* no
strength,
5 Adrift among the dead,
Like the slain who lie in the
grave,
Whom You remember no
more,
And who are cut off from Your
hand.
6 You have laid me in the lowest
pit,
In darkness, in the depths.
7 Your wrath lies heavy upon
me,
And You have afflicted *me*
with all [k]Your waves. Selah.
8 [l]You have put away my
acquaintances far from me;
You have made me an
abomination to them;
[m]*I am* shut up, and I cannot get
out;
9 My eye wastes away because
of affliction.
[n]LORD, I have called daily upon
You;
I have stretched out my hands
to You.
10 Will You work wonders for the
dead?
Shall the [o]dead arise *and*
praise You? Selah.
11 Shall Your lovingkindness be
declared in the grave?
Or Your faithfulness in the
place of destruction?
12 Shall Your wonders be known
in the dark?
And Your righteousness in the
land of forgetfulness?
13 But to You I have cried out, O
LORD,

* 88:title Hebrew *Maschil*

And in the morning my prayer
comes before You.
14 LORD, why do You cast off my
soul?
[a]*Why* do You hide Your face
from me?
15 I *have been* afflicted and ready
to die from *my* youth;
I suffer Your terrors;
I am distraught.
16 Your fierce wrath has gone
over me;
Your terrors have cut me off.
17 They came around me all day
long like water;
They engulfed me altogether.
18 [b]Loved one and friend You
have put far from me,
And my acquaintances into
darkness.

Psalm of the Davidic Covenant

A [c]Contemplation* of Ethan the Ezrahite.

89 I WILL sing of the mercies of
the LORD forever;
With my mouth will I make
known Your faithfulness to
all generations.
2 For I have said, "Mercy shall
be built up forever;
Your faithfulness You shall
establish in the very
heavens."
3 "I have [1]made a covenant with
My chosen,
I have [d]sworn to My servant
David:
4 'Your seed I will establish
forever,
And build up your [e]throne [f]to
all generations.'" Selah.
5 And the heavens will praise
Your wonders, O LORD;
Your faithfulness also in the
assembly of the saints.
6 [g]For who in the heavens can be
compared to the LORD?
Who among the sons of the
mighty can be likened to the
LORD?
7 God is greatly to be feared in
the assembly of the saints,
And to be held in reverence by
all *those* around Him.
8 O LORD God of hosts,
Who *is* mighty [h]like You, O
LORD?
Your faithfulness also
surrounds You.
9 You [i]rule the raging of the
sea;
When its waves rise, You still
them.
10 You have [j]broken [k]Rahab in
pieces, as one who is slain;
You have scattered Your
enemies with Your mighty
arm.

11 The heavens *are* Yours, the
earth also *is* Yours;
The world and all its fullness,
You have founded them.
12 The north and the south, You
have created them;
[l]Tabor and [m]Hermon rejoice in
Your name.
13 You have [n]a mighty arm;
Strong is Your hand, *and* high
is Your right hand.
14 Righteousness and justice *are*
the foundation of Your
throne;
Mercy and truth go before
Your face.
15 Blessed *are* the people who
know the joyful sound!
They walk, O LORD, in the light
of Your countenance.
16 In Your name they rejoice all
day long,
And in Your righteousness
they are exalted.
17 For You *are* the glory of their
strength,

14
a Cp. Mt. 27:46; Mk. 15:34
18
b Ps. 31:11; 38:11; cp. Job 19:13
PSALM 89 Title
c Or *Instruction*
3
d 2 Sam. 7:11; 1 Chr. 17:10; cp. Jer. 30:9; Ezek. 34:23; Hos. 3:5
4
e *Kingdom* (OT): vv. 3–4, 19–21, 27–29, 34–36; Isa. 1:25. (Gen. 1:26; Zech. 12:8, *note*)
f v. 1; Lk. 1:32–33
6
g Ps. 40:5; 86:8; 113:5
8
h Ex. 15:11; 1 Sam. 2:2; Ps. 35:10; 71:19
9
i Ps. 65:7; 93:3–4; 107:29
10
j Ex. 14:26–28
k Or *Egypt.* Ps. 87:4
12
l Josh. 19:22
m Josh. 12:1
13
n Lit. *an arm with might*

* 89:title Hebrew *Maschil*

[1](89:3) The 89th Psalm is both the confirmation and exposition of the Davidic Covenant (2 Sam. 7:8–16). That the covenant itself looks far beyond David and Solomon is sure from v. 27. "The highest of the kings of the earth" can only refer to Immanuel (Isa. 7:13–15; 9:6–7; Mic. 5:2). The Psalm is in four parts: (1) The covenant, though springing from the loving-kindness of the LORD, yet rests upon His oath (vv. 1–4). (2) The LORD is glorified for His power and goodness in connection with the covenant (vv. 5–18). (3) The LORD responds (vv. 19–37). This is in two parts: (a) it confirms the covenant (vv. 19–29) but (b) warns that disobedience in the royal posterity of David will be punished with chastening (vv. 30–32). This chastening began in the division of the Davidic kingdom (1 Ki. 11:26–40; 12:16–20) and culminated in the captivities. The subsequent history of dispersed Israel bears witness to the continuance of the chastening. See Times of the Gentiles, Lk. 21:24 and Rev. 16:19, *notes*. And (4) there is the plea of the remnant (Isa. 1:9; Rom. 11:5), who urge the severity and long continuance of the chastening (vv. 38–52). See Ps. 102, next in order of the Messianic Psalms.

And in Your favor our [a]horn
is [b]exalted.
18 For our shield *belongs* to the
LORD,
And our king to the Holy One
of Israel.
19 Then You spoke in a vision to
Your holy one,*
And said: "I have given help to
one who is mighty;
I have exalted one [c]chosen
from the people.
20 [d]I have found My servant
David;
With My holy [e]oil I have
anointed him,
21 With whom My hand shall be
established;
Also My arm shall strengthen
him.
22 The enemy shall not [f]outwit
him,
Nor the son of wickedness
afflict him.
23 I will beat down his foes
before his face,
And plague those who hate
him.
24 "But My faithfulness and My
mercy *shall be* with him,
And in My name his [a]horn
shall be exalted.
25 Also I will [g]set his hand over
the sea,
And his right hand over the
rivers.
26 He shall cry to Me, 'You *are*
my [h]Father,
My God, and the rock of my
salvation.'
27 Also I will make him *My*
[i]firstborn,
The [j]highest of the kings of
the earth.
28 My mercy I will keep for him
forever,
And My covenant shall stand
firm with him.
29 His seed also I will make *to*
endure forever,
And his throne as the days of
heaven.
30 "If his sons forsake My law
And do not walk in My
[k]judgments,
31 If they break My statutes
And do not keep My
commandments,
32 Then I will punish their
transgression with the rod,
And their iniquity with stripes.

17
a See Dt. 33:17, *note*
b v. 24; Ps. 75:10; 92:10; 132:17
19
c v. 3; cp. 1 Ki. 11:34
20
d Acts 13:22
e *Sanctification* (OT): v. 20; Jer. 1:5. (Gen. 2:3; Zech. 8:3)
22
f Or *do violence to*
25
g Ps. 72:8; cp. 1 Cor. 15:27
26
h 2 Sam. 7:14; cp. Heb. 1:5
27
i Col. 1:15; cp. Ex. 4:22
j Num. 24:7; Ps. 72:11; Rev. 19:16
30
k Ezek. 20:16
33
l 2 Sam. 7:14–15
34
m Num. 23:19; Jer. 33:20–22
35
n 1 Sam. 15:29; Ti. 1:2
38
o Ps. 44:9; cp. 77:7
39
p Ps. 74:7
q Cp. Lam. 5:16
41
r Ps. 80:12
47
s Ps. 90:9
t Ps. 62:9

33 [l]Nevertheless My
lovingkindness I will not
utterly take from him,
Nor allow My faithfulness to
fail.
34 My covenant I will not break,
Nor [m]alter the word that has
gone out of My lips.
35 Once I have sworn by My
holiness;
I will not [n]lie to David:
36 His seed shall endure forever,
And his throne as the sun
before Me;
37 It shall be established forever
like the moon,
Even *like* the faithful witness
in the sky." Selah.
38 But You have [o]cast off and
abhorred,
You have been furious with
Your anointed.
39 You have renounced the
covenant of Your servant;
You have [p]profaned his
[q]crown *by casting it* to the
ground.
40 You have broken down all his
hedges;
You have brought his
strongholds to ruin.
41 All who pass by the way
[r]plunder him;
He is a reproach to his
neighbors.
42 You have exalted the right
hand of his adversaries;
You have made all his enemies
rejoice.
43 You have also turned back the
edge of his sword,
And have not sustained him in
the battle.
44 You have made his glory
cease,
And cast his throne down to
the ground.
45 The days of his youth You
have shortened;
You have covered him with
shame. Selah.
46 How long, LORD?
Will You hide Yourself
forever?
Will Your wrath burn like fire?
47 Remember how short my time
[s]is;
For what [t]futility have You

*
89:19 Following many Hebrew manuscripts; Masoretic Text, Septuagint, Targum, and Vulgate read *holy ones*.

created all the children of
men?
48 What man can live and not see
[a]death?
Can he deliver his life from the
[b]power of the grave? Selah.

49 Lord, where *are* Your former
lovingkindnesses,
Which You swore to David in
Your truth?
50 Remember, Lord, the reproach
of Your servants—
How I bear in my bosom *the
reproach of* all the many
peoples,
51 With which Your enemies have
reproached, O LORD,
With which they have
reproached the footsteps of
Your anointed.

52 [c]Blessed *be* the LORD
forevermore!
Amen and Amen.

Book IV, Psalms 90—106

The eternal God and mortal men

A Prayer of Moses the man of God.

90 LORD, [d]You have been our
dwelling place* in all
generations.
2 [e]Before the mountains were
brought forth,
Or ever You had formed the
earth and the world,
Even from everlasting to
everlasting, You *are* God.

3 You turn man to destruction,
And say, "Return, O children
of men."
4 For a [f]thousand years in Your
sight
Are like yesterday when it is
past,
And *like* a watch in the night.
5 You carry them away *like* a
flood;
They are like a [g]sleep.
In the morning [h]they are like
grass *which* grows up:
6 In the morning it flourishes
and grows up;
In the evening it is cut down
and withers.

7 For we have been consumed
by Your anger,
And by Your wrath we are
terrified.
8 [i]You have set our iniquities
before You,
Our [j]secret *sins* in the light of
Your countenance.
9 For all our days have passed
away in Your wrath;
We finish our years like a sigh.
10 The days of our lives *are*
seventy years;
And if by reason of strength
they are eighty years,
Yet their boast *is* only labor
and sorrow;
For it is soon cut off, and we
fly away.
11 Who knows the power of Your
anger?
For as the fear of You, *so is*
Your wrath.
12 So [k]teach *us* to number our
days,
That we may gain a heart of
wisdom.

13 Return, O LORD!
How long?
And [l]have compassion on
Your servants.
14 Oh, satisfy us early with Your
mercy,
That we may rejoice and be
glad all our days!
15 Make us glad according to the
days *in which* You have
afflicted us,
The years *in which* we have
seen evil.
16 Let Your work appear to Your
servants,
And Your glory to their
children.
17 And let the [m]beauty of the
LORD our God be upon us,
And [n]establish the work of our
hands for us;
Yes, establish the work of our
hands.

The secret place of security

91 [o]HE who dwells in the secret
place of the Most High
Shall abide under the [p]shadow
of the Almighty.
2 I will say of the LORD, "*He is*
my refuge and my fortress;
My God, in Him I will [q]trust."

3 Surely He shall [r]deliver you
from the snare of the
fowler*
And from the perilous
pestilence.

48
a Eccl. 3:19; see Eccl. 9:10 and Heb. 9:27, *notes*
b See Hab. 2:5, *note;* cp. Lk. 16:23, *note*
52
c Ps. 41:13; 72:19; 106:48
PSALM 90
1
d Dt. 33:27; Ezek. 11:16
2
e Prov. 8:25–26
4
f 2 Pet. 3:8
5
g i.e. *a dream*
h Ps. 103:15; Isa. 40:6
8
i Ps. 50:21; Jer. 16:17
j Ps. 19:12
12
k Ps. 39:4
13
l See Zech. 8:14, *note*
17
m Ps. 27:4
n Isa. 26:12
PSALM 91
1
o Ps. 27:5; 31:20; 32:7
p Assurance/security: v. 1; Isa. 32:17. (Ps. 23:1; Jude 1, *note*)
2
q See Ps. 2:12, *note*
3
r Ps. 124:7

*

90:1 Septuagint, Targum, and Vulgate read *refuge*.
91:3 That is, one who catches birds in a trap or snare

4 [a]He shall cover you with His
feathers,
And under His wings you shall
take refuge;
His truth *shall be your* shield
and buckler.
5 [b]You shall not be afraid of the
terror by night,
Nor of the arrow *that* flies by
day,
6 *Nor* of the pestilence *that*
walks in darkness,
Nor of the destruction *that*
lays waste at noonday.

7 A thousand may fall at your
side,
And ten thousand at your right
hand;
But it shall not come near you.
8 Only [c]with your eyes shall you
look,
And see the reward of the
wicked.

9 Because you have made the
LORD, *who is* my refuge,
Even the Most High, your
[d]dwelling place,
10 [e]No evil shall befall you,
Nor shall any plague come
near your dwelling;
11 [f]For He shall give His [g]angels
charge over you,
To keep you in all your ways.
12 In *their* hands they shall bear
you up,
[h]Lest you dash your foot
against a stone.
13 You shall tread upon the lion
and the cobra,
The young lion and the serpent
you shall trample underfoot.

14 "Because he has set his love
upon Me, therefore I will
deliver him;
I will set him on high, because
he has [i]known My name.
15 He shall [j]call upon Me, and I
will answer him;
I *will be* [k]with him in trouble;
I will deliver him and honor
him.
16 With long life I will satisfy
him,
And show him My salvation."

The propriety of praise

A Psalm. A Song for the Sabbath day.

92 *IT is* [l]good to give thanks to
the LORD,
And to sing praises to Your
name, O Most High;
2 [m]To declare Your
lovingkindness in the
morning,
And Your faithfulness every
night,
3 On an instrument of ten
strings,
On the lute,
And on the harp,
With harmonious sound.
4 For You, LORD, have made me
glad through Your work;
I will triumph in the works of
Your hands.

5 O LORD, how great are Your
works!
Your [n]thoughts are very deep.
6 A senseless man does not
know,
Nor does a fool understand
this.
7 [o]When the wicked spring up
like grass,
And when all the workers of
iniquity flourish,
It is that they may be
[p]destroyed forever.

8 But You, LORD, *are* on high
forevermore.
9 For behold, Your enemies, O
LORD,
For behold, Your enemies shall
perish;
All the workers of iniquity
shall be scattered.

10 But my [q]horn You have
exalted like a wild ox;
I have been [r]anointed with
fresh oil.
11 [s]My eye also has seen *my
desire* on my enemies;
My ears hear *my desire* on the
wicked
Who rise up against me.

12 The [t]righteous shall flourish
like a palm tree,
He shall grow like a cedar in
Lebanon.
13 Those who are planted in the
house of the LORD
Shall flourish in the courts of
our God.
14 They shall still bear [u]fruit in
old age;
They shall be fresh and
[v]flourishing,
15 To declare that the LORD is
upright;
He is my rock, and [w]*there is*
no unrighteousness in Him.

4
a Ps. 17:8; 57:1; 61:4
5
b Job 5:19; Ps. 112:7; 121:7; Prov. 3:23–24; Isa. 43:2
8
c Ps. 37:34; cp. Mal. 1:5
9
d Ps. 71:3; 90:1
10
e Prov. 12:21
11
f Ps. 34:7; Heb. 1:14; cp. Lk. 4:10–11
g See Heb. 1:4, *note*
12
h Mt. 4:6
14
i Ps. 9:10
15
j Ps. 50:15
k Isa. 43:2
PSALM 92
1
l Ps. 147:1
2
m Ps. 89:1
5
n Ps. 139:17–18; Isa. 28:29; Rom. 11:33–34
7
o Job 12:6; Ps. 37:1–2; Jer. 12:1–2; Mal. 3:15
p Ps. 37:38; 73:17
10
q See Dt. 33:17, *note*
r Ps. 23:5
11
s Ps. 54:7; 59:10; 112:8
12
t vv. 13,14; Ps. 1:3; 52:8
14
u Cp. Jn. 15:2
v Lit. *green*
15
w Cp. Rom. 9:14

The majesty of God

93 THE LORD reigns, He is
clothed with majesty;
The LORD is clothed,
He has girded Himself with
strength.
Surely the [a]world is
established, so that it cannot
be moved.
2 Your throne *is* established
from of old;
You *are* from everlasting.

3 The floods have lifted up, O
LORD,
The floods have lifted up their
voice;
The floods lift up their waves.
4 The LORD on high *is* mightier
Than the noise of many
waters,
Than the mighty waves of the
sea.

5 Your testimonies are very sure;
Holiness adorns Your house,
O LORD, forever.

Vengeance belongs to God

94 O LORD God, to whom
[b]vengeance belongs—
O God, to whom vengeance
belongs, shine forth!
2 Rise up, O Judge of the earth;
Render punishment to the
proud.
3 LORD, how long will the
wicked,
How long will the wicked
triumph?

4 They [c]utter speech, *and* speak
insolent things;
All the workers of iniquity
boast in themselves.
5 They break in pieces Your
people, O LORD,
And afflict Your heritage.
6 They slay the widow and the
stranger,
And murder the fatherless.
7 Yet they say, "The LORD does
not see,
Nor does the God of Jacob
understand."

8 Understand, you [d]senseless
among the people;
And *you* fools, when will you
be wise?
9 [e]He who planted the ear, shall
He not hear?
He who formed the eye, shall
He not see?
10 He who instructs the nations,
shall He not correct,
He who teaches man
knowledge?
11 The LORD [f]knows the thoughts
of man,
That they *are* futile.

12 Blessed *is* the man whom You
[g]instruct, O LORD,
And teach out of Your law,
13 That You may give him rest
from the days of adversity,
Until the pit is dug for the
wicked.
14 For the LORD will not cast off
His people,
Nor will He forsake His
inheritance.
15 But judgment will return to
righteousness,
And all the upright in heart
will follow it.

16 Who will rise up for me
against the evildoers?
Who will stand up for me
against the workers of
iniquity?
17 Unless the LORD *had been* my
help,
My soul would soon have
settled in silence.
18 If I say, "My foot slips,"
Your mercy, O LORD, will hold
me up.
19 In the multitude of my
anxieties within me,
Your comforts delight my soul.

20 Shall the throne of iniquity,
which devises evil by [h]law,
Have fellowship with You?
21 They gather together against
the life of the righteous,
And condemn [i]innocent blood.
22 But the LORD has been my
defense,
And my God the rock of my
refuge.
23 He has brought on them their
own iniquity,
And shall cut them off in their
own wickedness;
The LORD our God shall cut
them off.

Exhortation to worship

95 OH come, let us sing to the
LORD!
Let us shout joyfully to the
Rock of our salvation.
2 Let us come before His
presence with thanksgiving;

PSALM 93
1
a Ps. 96:10
PSALM 94
1
b Dt. 32:35; Rom. 12:19
4
c Ps. 31:18; Jude 15
8
d Ps. 92:6
9
e Ex. 4:11; Prov. 20:12
11
f 1 Cor. 3:20
12
g Heb. 12:5–7
20
h Cp. Isa. 10:1
21
i Ex. 23:7; cp. Mt. 27:4

Let us shout joyfully to Him
with [a]psalms.
3 For the LORD *is* the great God,
And the great King above all
[b]gods.
4 In His hand *are* the deep
places of the earth;
The heights of the hills *are* His
also.
5 The sea *is* His, for He made it;
And His hands formed the dry
land.

6 Oh come, let us worship and
bow down;
Let us kneel before the LORD
our Maker.
7 For He *is* our God,
And we *are* the people of His
pasture,
And the sheep of His hand.

[c]Today, if you will hear His
voice:
8 "Do not harden your hearts, as
in the rebellion,*
As *in* the day of trial* in the
wilderness,
9 When your fathers [d]tested Me;
They tried Me, though they
saw My [e]work.
10 For [f]forty years I was grieved
with *that* generation,
And said, 'It *is* a people who
go astray in their hearts,
And they do not know My
ways.'
11 So I [g]swore in My wrath,
'They shall not enter My rest.' "

Praise of God's greatness and glory

96 [h]OH, sing to the LORD a new
song!
Sing to the LORD, all the earth.
2 Sing to the LORD, bless His
name;
Proclaim the good news of His
salvation from day to day.
3 Declare His glory among the
nations,
His wonders among all
peoples.

4 For the LORD *is* great and
greatly to be praised;
He *is* to be [i]feared above all
[j]gods.
5 For all the [j]gods of the
peoples *are* idols,
But the [k]LORD made the
heavens.
6 Honor and majesty *are* before
Him;
Strength and beauty *are* in His
sanctuary.

PSALM 95
2
a Eph. 5:19; Jas. 5:13
3
b 1 Cor. 8:5–6; see Ps. 16:4, *note*
7
c vv. 7–11; Heb. 3:7–11
9
d Test/tempt: v. 9; Ps. 106:14. (Gen. 3:1; Jas. 1:14, *note*)
e Cp. Num. 14:22
10
f Acts 7:36; 13:18; Heb. 3:17
11
g Heb. 4:3
PSALM 96
1
h vv. 1–13; cp. 1 Chr. 16:23–33
4
i See Ps. 19:9, *note*
j Ps. 115:3–7; cp. 1 Cor. 8:5–6; see Ps. 16:4, *note*
5
k Isa. 42:5; Jer. 10:12
10
l Ps. 93:1; 97:1; Rev. 11:15; 19:6
13
m Christ (second advent): vv. 10–13; Ps. 110:1. (Dt. 30:3; Acts 1:11, *note*)
PSALM 97
1
n Ps. 96:10
o i.e. *coasts*
7
p Cp. Heb. 1:6

7 Give to the LORD, O families of
the peoples,
Give to the LORD glory and
strength.
8 Give to the LORD the glory *due*
His name;
Bring an offering, and come
into His courts.
9 Oh, worship the LORD in the
beauty of holiness!
Tremble before Him, all the
earth.

10 Say among the nations, "The
[l]LORD reigns;
The world also is firmly
established,
It shall not be moved;
He shall judge the peoples
righteously."

11 Let the heavens rejoice, and let
the earth be glad;
Let the sea roar, and all its
fullness;
12 Let the field be joyful, and all
that *is* in it.
Then all the trees of the woods
will rejoice before the LORD.
13 For He is [m]coming, for He is
coming to judge the earth.
He shall judge the world with
righteousness,
And the peoples with His truth.

The power of the righteous LORD

97 THE LORD [n]reigns;
Let the earth rejoice;
Let the multitude of [o]isles be
glad!

2 Clouds and darkness surround
Him;
Righteousness and justice *are*
the foundation of His throne.
3 A fire goes before Him,
And burns up His enemies
round about.
4 His lightnings light the world;
The earth sees and trembles.
5 The mountains melt like wax
at the presence of the LORD,
At the presence of the Lord of
the whole earth.
6 The heavens declare His
righteousness,
And all the peoples see His
glory.

7 Let all be put to shame who
serve carved images,
Who boast of idols.
[p]Worship Him, all *you* gods.

---
*95:8 Hebrew *Meribah* • Hebrew *Massah*

8 Zion hears and is glad,
And the daughters of Judah rejoice
Because of Your judgments, O LORD.
9 For You, LORD, *are* most high above all the earth;
[a]You are exalted far above all [b]gods.
10 You who love the LORD, [c]hate evil!
He [d]preserves the souls of His saints;
He delivers them out of the hand of the wicked.
11 Light is sown for the righteous,
And gladness for the upright in heart.
12 Rejoice in the LORD, you righteous,
And give thanks at the remembrance of His holy name.*

Praise to the LORD

A Psalm.

98 OH, [e]sing to the LORD a new song!
For He has [f]done marvelous things;
His right hand and His holy arm have gained Him the victory.
2 The LORD has made [g]known His salvation;
His righteousness He has revealed in the sight of the nations.
3 He has remembered His mercy and His faithfulness to the house of Israel;
[h]All the ends of the earth have seen the salvation of our God.
4 Shout joyfully to the LORD, all the earth;
Break forth in song, rejoice, and sing praises.
5 Sing to the LORD with the harp,
With the harp and the sound of a psalm,
6 With trumpets and the sound of a horn;
Shout joyfully before the LORD, the King.
7 Let the sea roar, and all its fullness,
The world and those who dwell in it;
8 Let the rivers clap *their* hands;
Let the hills be joyful together before the LORD,
9 For He is [i]coming to judge the earth.
With righteousness He shall judge the world,
And the peoples with equity.

Reverence for God's greatness and holiness

99 THE LORD reigns;
Let the peoples tremble!
[j]He dwells *between* the cherubim;
Let the earth be moved!
2 The LORD *is* great in Zion,
And He *is* high above all the peoples.
3 Let them praise Your great and [k]awesome name—
He *is* [l]holy.
4 The King's strength also loves justice;
You have established equity;
You have executed justice and righteousness in Jacob.
5 Exalt the LORD our God,
And worship at His footstool—
He *is* holy.
6 Moses and Aaron were among His priests,
And [m]Samuel was among those who [n]called upon His name;
They called upon the LORD, and He answered them.
7 He spoke to them in the cloudy pillar;
They kept His testimonies and the ordinance He gave them.
8 You answered them, O LORD our God;
You were to them [o]God-Who-Forgives,
Though You took vengeance on their deeds.
9 Exalt the LORD our God,
And worship at His holy hill;
For the LORD our God *is* holy.

Gladness and thanksgiving

A Psalm of Thanksgiving.

100 MAKE a joyful shout to the LORD, all you lands!
2 Serve the LORD with gladness;
Come before His presence with singing.
3 Know that the LORD, He *is* God;

9
a Ex. 18:11; Ps. 95:3; 96:4
b Ps. 115:3–7; cp. 1 Cor. 8:5–6; see Ps. 16:4, *note*
10
c Prov. 8:13; Rom. 12:9
d Ps. 31:23; 37:28; 145:20; Prov. 2:8
PSALM 98
1
e Ps. 33:3; 96:1; Isa. 42:10
f Ex. 15:11; Ps. 77:14; 86:10; 105:5; 136:4; 139:14
2
g Isa. 52:10; Lk. 1:77; 2:30–31
3
h Isa. 49:6; Lk. 3:6; Acts 13:47; 28:28
9
i Ps. 96:10, 13
PSALM 99
1
j Ex. 25:22; Ps. 80:1
3
k Dt. 28:58; cp. Rev. 15:4
l Isa. 6:3; cp. Rev. 4:8
6
m Cp. Jer. 15:1
n 1 Sam. 7:9
8
o *Forgiveness:* v. 8; Ps. 103:12. (Lev. 4:20; Mt. 26:28, *note*)

---

*97:12 Or *His holiness*

It is He *who* has [a]made us,
and not we ourselves;*
[b]*We are* His people and the
sheep of His pasture.

4 [c]Enter into His gates with
thanksgiving,
And into His courts with
praise.
Be thankful to Him, *and* bless
His name.
5 For the LORD *is* good;
His mercy *is* everlasting,
And His truth *endures* to all
generations.

A vow for a holy life

A Psalm of David.

101 I WILL sing of mercy and
[d]justice;
To You, O LORD, I will sing
praises.
2 I will behave wisely in a
[e]perfect way.
Oh, when will You come to
me?
I will walk within my house
with a perfect heart.
3 I will set nothing wicked
before my eyes;
I hate the work of those who
fall away;
It shall not cling to me.
4 A perverse heart shall depart
from me;
I will not know wickedness.
5 Whoever secretly slanders his
neighbor,
Him I will destroy;
The one who has a haughty
look and a proud heart,
Him I will not endure.
6 My eyes *shall be* on the
faithful of the land,
That they may dwell with me;
He who walks in a perfect
way,
He shall serve me.
7 He who works deceit shall not
dwell within my house;
He who tells lies shall not
continue in my presence.
8 Early I will [f]destroy all the
wicked of the land,
That I may cut off all the
evildoers from the [g]city of
the LORD.

PSALM 100
3
a Ps. 119:73; 139:13–14; 149:2
b Ps. 95:7; Ezek. 34:30–31
4
c Ps. 66:13; 116:17–19

PSALM 101
1
d Ps. 94:15
2
e v. 6
8
f Ps. 75:10; cp. Jer. 21:12
g Ps. 48:2,8

PSALM 102
2
h Ps. 27:9; 69:17
3
i Jas. 4:14
13
j Cp. Dan. 8:19

A plea to the unchanging God

A Prayer of the afflicted, when he is
overwhelmed and pours out his
complaint before the LORD.

102 [1]HEAR my prayer, O LORD,
And let my cry come to
You.
2 Do not [h]hide Your face from
me in the day of my trouble;
Incline Your ear to me;
In the day that I call, answer
me speedily.
3 For my days are [i]consumed
like smoke,
And my bones are burned like
a hearth.
4 My heart is stricken and
withered like grass,
So that I forget to eat my
bread.
5 Because of the sound of my
groaning
My bones cling to my skin.
6 I am like a pelican of the
wilderness;
I am like an owl of the desert.
7 I lie awake,
And am like a sparrow alone
on the housetop.
8 My enemies reproach me all
day long;
Those who deride me swear an
oath against me.
9 For I have eaten ashes like
bread,
And mingled my drink with
weeping,
10 Because of Your indignation
and Your wrath;
For You have lifted me up and
cast me away.
11 My days *are* like a shadow
that lengthens,
And I wither away like grass.
12 But You, O LORD, shall endure
forever,
And the remembrance of Your
name to all generations.
13 You will arise *and* have mercy
on Zion;
For the time to favor her,
Yes, the [j]set time, has come.
14 For Your servants take
pleasure in her stones,

*100:3 Following Kethib, Septuagint, and Vulgate; Qere, many Hebrew manuscripts, and Targum read *we are His.*

[1](102:1) The reference of vv. 25–27 to Christ (Heb. 1:10–12) is assurance that, in the preceding verses of this Psalm, there is shown, prophetically, the affliction of His holy soul in the days of His humiliation and rejection. See Ps. 110, next in order of the Messianic Psalms.

And show favor to her dust.
15 So the nations shall [a]fear the name of the LORD,
And all the kings of the earth Your glory.
16 For the LORD shall build up Zion;
He shall appear in His glory.
17 He shall [b]regard the prayer of the destitute,
And shall not despise their prayer.

18 This will be written for the generation to come,
That a people yet to be created may praise the LORD.
19 For He [c]looked down from the height of His sanctuary;
From heaven the LORD viewed the earth,
20 To [d]hear the groaning of the prisoner,
To release [e]those appointed to death,
21 To declare the name of the LORD in Zion,
And His praise in Jerusalem,
22 [f]When the peoples are gathered together,
And the kingdoms, to serve the LORD.

23 He weakened my strength in the way;
He shortened my days.
24 I said, "O my God,
Do not take me away in the midst of my days;
Your years *are* throughout all generations.
25 Of old You laid the [g]foundation of the earth,
And the heavens *are* the work of Your hands.
26 They will [h]perish, but You will endure;
Yes, they will all grow old like a garment;
Like a cloak You will change them,
And they will be changed.
27 But You *are* the [i]same,
And Your years will have no end.
28 The children of Your servants will continue,
And their descendants will be established before You."

A psalm of unmixed praise

A Psalm of David.

103 BLESS the LORD, O my soul;
And all that is within me, *bless* His holy name!
2 Bless the LORD, O my soul,
And [j]forget not all His benefits:
3 Who [k]forgives all your iniquities,
Who [l]heals all your diseases,
4 Who [m]redeems your life from destruction,
Who crowns you with lovingkindness and tender mercies,
5 Who satisfies your mouth with good *things*,
So that your youth is [n]renewed like the eagle's.

6 The LORD executes righteousness
And justice for all who are oppressed.
7 He made known His [o]ways to Moses,
His acts to the children of Israel.
8 [p]The LORD *is* merciful and gracious,
Slow to anger, and abounding in mercy.
9 [q]He will not always strive *with us,*
Nor will He keep *His anger* forever.
10 He has not dealt with us according to our sins,
Nor punished us according to our iniquities.

11 For as the heavens are high above the earth,
So great is His mercy toward those who [r]fear Him;
12 As far as the east is from the west,
So far has He [s]removed our transgressions [t]from us.
13 As a father pities *his* children,
[u]So the LORD pities those who fear Him.
14 For He knows our frame;
He remembers that we *are* dust.

15 *As for* man, his days *are* like [v]grass;
As a flower of the field, so he flourishes.
16 For the wind passes over it, and it is gone,

15 *a* See Ps. 19:9, *note*
17 *b* Cp. Neh. 1:6,11; 2:8
19 *c* Cp. Ex. 3:7
20 *d* Ps. 79:11 *e* Lit. *the children of death*
22 *f* Isa. 2:2–3; 60:3
25 *g* vv. 25–27; Heb. 1:10–12
26 *h* Isa. 34:4; 51:6; Mt. 24:35; 2 Pet. 3:7, 10–12; Rev. 20:11
27 *i* Mal. 3:6; Heb. 13:8; Jas. 1:17
PSALM 103
2 *j* Cp. Dt. 6:11–12
3 *k* Ps. 130:8; Isa. 33:24; cp. Mt. 9:2,6; Mk. 2:5,10–11; Lk. 7:47 *l* Ex. 15:26; Isa. 53:5; Ps. 147:3; Jer. 17:14
4 *m Redemption* (redeeming relative type): v. 4; Ps. 106:10. (Gen. 48:16; Isa. 59:20, *note*)
5 *n* Isa. 40:31
7 *o* Ex. 33:12–17
8 *p* Ex. 34:6–7; Num. 14:18; Dt. 5:10; Neh. 9:17; Ps. 86:15; Jer. 32:18
9 *q* Ps. 30:5; Isa. 57:16; Jer. 3:5; Mic. 7:18

103:11 *r* v. 13; see Ps. 19:9, *note* **103:12** *s* See Ex. 29:33, *note* *t Forgiveness:* v. 12; Isa. 38:17. (Lev. 4:20; Mt. 26:28, *note*) **103:13** *u* Cp. Lk. 11:11–13 **103:15** *v* Isa. 40:6–8; Jas. 1:10–11; 1 Pet. 1:24

And its place remembers it no
more.*
17 But the mercy of the LORD *is*
from everlasting to
everlasting
On those who fear Him,
And His righteousness to
children's children,
18 To such as keep His covenant,
And to those who remember
His commandments to do
them.

19 The LORD has established His
throne in heaven,
And His kingdom rules over
[a]all.
20 Bless the LORD, you His
[b]angels,
Who excel in strength, who do
His word,
Heeding the voice of His word.
21 Bless the LORD, all *you* His
hosts,
You ministers of His, who do
His pleasure.
22 Bless the LORD, all His works,
In all places of His dominion.

Bless the LORD, O my soul!

Praise to the God of creation

104 [c]BLESS the LORD, O my
soul!

O LORD my God, You are very
great:
You are clothed with honor
and majesty,
2 Who cover *Yourself* with light
as *with* a garment,
Who stretch out the heavens
like a curtain.
3 He lays the beams of His
upper chambers in the
waters,
Who makes the clouds His
chariot,
Who walks on the wings of the
wind,
4 Who makes His [b]angels
spirits,
His ministers a flame of fire.
5 *You who* laid the foundations
of the earth,
So *that* it should not be moved
forever,
6 You [d]covered it with the deep
as *with* a garment;
The waters stood above the
mountains.
7 At Your rebuke they fled;
At the voice of Your thunder
they hastened away.
8 They went up over the
mountains;
They went down into the
valleys,
To the place which You
founded for them.
9 You have [e]set a boundary that
they may not pass over,
[f]That they may not return to
cover the earth.

10 He sends the springs into the
valleys;
They flow among the hills.
11 They give drink to every beast
of the field;
The wild donkeys quench their
thirst.
12 By them the birds of the
heavens have their [g]home;
They sing among the branches.
13 He [h]waters the hills from His
upper chambers;
The earth is satisfied with the
fruit of Your works.

14 He causes the grass to grow
for the cattle,
And vegetation for the service
of man,
That he may bring forth food
from the earth,
15 And [i]wine *that* makes glad
the heart of man,
Oil to make *his* face shine,
And bread *which* strengthens
man's heart.
16 The trees of the LORD are full
of sap,
The cedars of Lebanon which
He planted,
17 Where the birds make their
nests;
The stork has her home in the
fir trees.
18 The high hills *are* for the wild
goats;
The cliffs are a refuge for the
rock badgers.*

19 He [j]appointed the moon for
seasons;
The [k]sun knows its going
down.
20 You make [l]darkness, and it is
night,
In which all the beasts of the
forest creep about.
21 The young [m]lions roar after
their prey,

19 *a* Ps. 83:18; Dan. 4:17
20 *b* See Heb. 1:4, *note*
PSALM 104
1 *c* Ps. 103:1
6 *d* Gen. 1:6
9 *e* Job 26:10; Ps. 33:7; Jer. 5:22 *f* Gen. 9:11–15
12 *g* Cp. Mt. 8:20
13 *h* Ps. 147:8
15 *i* Jud. 9:13; Ps. 23:5; Prov. 31:6
19 *j* Gen. 1:14 *k* Job 38:12; Ps. 19:6
20 *l* Isa. 45:7
21 *m* Cp. Job 38:39; Joel 1:20

*
103:16 Compare Job 7:10 **104:18** Or *rock hyrax* (compare Leviticus 11:5)

And seek their food from God.
22 *When* the sun rises, they
gather together
And lie down in their dens.
23 Man goes out to [a]his work
And to his labor until the
evening.
24 O LORD, how [b]manifold are
Your works!
In wisdom You have made
them all.
The earth is full of Your
[c]possessions—
25 This great and wide sea,
In which *are* innumerable
teeming things,
Living things both small and
great.
26 There the ships sail about;
There is that [d]Leviathan
Which You have made to play
there.
27 [e]These all wait for You,
That You may give *them* their
food in due season.
28 *What* You give them they
gather in;
You open Your hand, they are
filled with good.
29 You hide Your face, they are
troubled;
You take away their breath,
they die and [f]return to their
dust.
30 [g]You send forth Your [h]Spirit,
they are created;
And You renew the face of the
earth.
31 May the glory of the LORD
endure forever;
May the LORD [i]rejoice in His
works.
32 He looks on the earth, and it
[j]trembles;
He touches the hills, and they
smoke.
33 I will sing to the LORD as long
as I live;
I will sing praise to my God
while I have my being.
34 May my [k]meditation be sweet
to Him;
I will be glad in the LORD.
35 May sinners be consumed from
the earth,
And the wicked be no more.

Bless the LORD, O my soul!
Praise the LORD!

23
a Gen. 3:19
24
b Ps. 40:5
c Ps. 65:9
26
d Perhaps the crocodile; Job 41:1
27
e Ps. 136:25; 145:15; 147:9; cp. Mt. 6:26–30
29
f Eccl. 12:7
30
g Isa. 32:15; cp. Ezek. 37:9–10
h *Holy Spirit* (OT): v. 30; Ps. 139:7. (Gen. 1:2; Zech. 12:10)
31
i Gen. 1:31; Prov. 8:31
32
j Hab. 3:10
34
k Ps. 19:14
PSALM 105
1
l vv. 1–45; cp. 1 Chr. 16:7–36; Isa. 12:4
m Cp. Ps. 78:3–72; 106:1–48
4
n Ps. 27:8
5
o Ps. 77:11
7
p Isa. 26:9
8
q Lk. 1:72
9
r Gen. 17:2; 22:16–18; 26:3; 28:13; 35:11; Lk. 1:73; Heb. 6:17
11
s Gen. 13:15; 15:18
t Lit. *the cord*
12
u Gen. 34:30; Dt. 7:7; 26:5
v Heb. 11:9

God's faithfulness to Israel

105 OH, [l]give thanks to the
LORD!
Call upon His name;
[m]Make known His deeds among
the peoples!
2 Sing to Him, sing psalms to
Him;
Talk of all His wondrous
works!
3 Glory in His holy name;
Let the hearts of those rejoice
who seek the LORD!
4 Seek the LORD and His
strength;
[n]Seek His face evermore!
5 [o]Remember His marvelous
works which He has done,
His wonders, and the
judgments of His mouth,
6 O seed of Abraham His
servant,
You children of Jacob, His
chosen ones!

7 He *is* the LORD our God;
His [p]judgments *are* in all the
earth.
8 He [q]remembers His covenant
forever,
The word *which* He
commanded, for a thousand
generations,
9 *The* [r]*covenant* which He made
with Abraham,
And His oath to Isaac,
10 And confirmed it to Jacob for
a statute,
To Israel *as* an everlasting
covenant,
11 Saying, [s]"To you I will give
the land of Canaan
As the [t]allotment of your
inheritance,"
12 When they were [u]few in
number,
Indeed very few, and
[v]strangers in it.
13 When they went from one
nation to another,
From *one* kingdom to another
people,
14 He [w]permitted no one to do
them wrong;
Yes, He rebuked kings for
their sakes,
15 *Saying*, "Do not touch My
anointed ones,
And do My [x]prophets no
harm."

105:14 w Gen. 35:5 105:15 x Cp. Gen. 20:7

16 Moreover He called for a
famine in the land;
He destroyed all the provision
of bread.
17 He sent a man before them—
Joseph—*who* was [a]sold as a
slave.
18 They hurt his feet with fetters,
He was laid in irons.
19 Until the time that his word
[b]came to pass,
The word of the LORD tested
him.
20 The king sent and released
him,
The ruler of the people let him
go free.
21 He made him lord of his
house,
And ruler of all his
possessions,
22 To bind his princes at his
pleasure,
And teach his elders wisdom.
23 Israel also came into Egypt,
And Jacob dwelt in the land of
Ham.
24 He [c]increased His people
greatly,
And made them stronger than
their enemies.
25 [d]He turned their heart to hate
His people,
To deal craftily with His
servants.
26 [e]He sent Moses His servant,
And Aaron whom He had
chosen.
27 They [f]performed His signs
among them,
And wonders in the land of
Ham.
28 He sent darkness, and made *it*
dark;
And they did not rebel against
His word.
29 He turned their waters into
[g]blood,
And killed their fish.
30 Their land abounded with
frogs,
Even in the chambers of their
kings.
31 He spoke, and there came
swarms of flies,
And lice in all their territory.
32 He gave them hail for rain,
And flaming fire in their land.
33 He struck their vines also, and
their fig trees,
And splintered the trees of
their territory.

17
a Acts 7:9
19
b Gen. 40:20–21, 23
24
c Ex. 1:7,12
25
d Ex. 1:8–10
26
e Ex. 3:10; 4:12–15; Num. 16:5; 17:5
27
f Ex. 7–12; Ps. 78:43
29
g Ex. 7:20; Ps. 78:44
37
h Ex. 12:35
39
i Ex. 13:21; Neh. 9:12
40
j Ps. 78:24
43
k *Election* (corporate): v. 43; Ps. 106:5. (Dt. 7:6; 1 Pet. 5:13, *note*)
PSALM 106
3
l Lev. 19:15, 35

34 He spoke, and locusts came,
Young locusts without number,
35 And ate up all the vegetation
in their land,
And devoured the fruit of their
ground.
36 He also destroyed all the
firstborn in their land,
The first of all their strength.

37 [h]He also brought them out with
silver and gold,
And *there was* none feeble
among His tribes.
38 Egypt was glad when they
departed,
For the fear of them had fallen
upon them.
39 [i]He spread a cloud for a
covering,
And fire to give light in the
night.
40 *The people* asked, and He
brought quail,
And satisfied them with the
[j]bread of heaven.
41 He opened the rock, and water
gushed out;
It ran in the dry places *like* a
river.
42 For He remembered His holy
promise,
And Abraham His servant.
43 He brought out His people
with joy,
His [k]chosen ones with
gladness.
44 He gave them the lands of the
Gentiles,
And they inherited the labor of
the nations,
45 That they might observe His
statutes
And keep His laws.

Praise the LORD!

Confession of Israel's unfaithfulness

106

PRAISE the LORD!
Oh, give thanks to the LORD,
for *He is* good!
For His mercy *endures* forever.
2 Who can utter the mighty acts
of the LORD?
Who can declare all His
praise?
3 Blessed *are* those who [l]keep
justice,

And he who does*
righteousness at all times!

4 Remember me, O LORD, with
the favor *You have toward*
Your [a]people.
Oh, visit me with Your
salvation,
5 That I may see the benefit of
Your [b]chosen ones,
That I may rejoice in the
gladness of Your nation,
That I may glory with Your
inheritance.

6 [c]We have sinned with our
fathers,
We have committed iniquity,
We have done wickedly.
7 Our fathers in Egypt did not
understand Your wonders;
They did not remember the
multitude of Your mercies,
But [d]rebelled by the sea—the
Red Sea.

8 Nevertheless He saved them
[e]for His name's sake,
[f]That He might make His
mighty power known.
9 [g]He rebuked the Red Sea also,
and it dried up;
So He [h]led them through the
depths,
As through the wilderness.
10 He [i]saved them from the hand
of him who hated *them*,
And [j]redeemed them from the
hand of the enemy.
11 The waters covered their
enemies;
There was not one of them left.
12 Then they believed His words;
They sang His praise.

13 They soon forgot His works;
They did not wait for His
counsel,
14 But lusted exceedingly in the
wilderness,
And [k]tested God in the desert.
15 And He gave them their
request,
But sent leanness into their
soul.

16 When they [l]envied Moses in
the camp,
And Aaron the saint of the
LORD,
17 The [m]earth opened up and
swallowed Dathan,
And covered the faction of
Abiram.

4
a Israel (history): vv. 1–45; Isa. 1:25. (Gen. 12:2; Rom. 11:26, *note*)
5
b Election (corporate): v. 5; Ps. 135:4. (Dt. 7:6; 1 Pet. 5:13, *note*)
6
c Dan. 9:5; cp. Lev. 26:40; 1 Ki. 8:47
7
d Ex. 14:11–12
8
e Cp. Ezek. 20:14
f Ex. 9:16
9
g Ex. 14:21; cp. Ps. 18:15; Nah. 1:4
h Isa. 63:11–14
10
i Ex. 14:30
j Redemption (redeeming relative type): v. 10; Ps. 107:2. (Gen. 48:16; Isa. 59:20, *note*)
14
k Test/tempt: v. 14; Ps. 139:23. (Gen. 3:1; Jas. 1:14, *note*)
16
l Num. 16:2–3
17
m Num. 16:31–33; Dt. 11:6
19
n Ex. 32:1–4
20
o Jer. 2:11; Rom. 1:23
24
p Heb. 3:18
25
q Num. 14:2,27
26
r Num. 14:28–30; Ps. 95:11;

18 A fire was kindled in their
company;
The flame burned up the
wicked.

19 They [n]made a calf in Horeb,
And worshiped the molded
image.
20 Thus they [o]changed their glory
Into the image of an ox that
eats grass.
21 They forgot God their Savior,
Who had done great things in
Egypt,
22 Wondrous works in the land of
Ham,
Awesome things by the Red
Sea.
23 Therefore He said that He
would destroy them,
Had not Moses His chosen one
stood before Him in the
breach,
To turn away His wrath, lest
He destroy *them*.

24 Then they despised the
pleasant land;
They did not [p]believe His
word,
25 But [q]complained in their tents,
And did not heed the voice of
the LORD.
26 [r]Therefore He raised up His
hand *in an oath* against
them,
To overthrow them in the
wilderness,
27 To overthrow their
descendants among the
nations,
And to [s]scatter them in the
lands.
28 They joined themselves also to
Baal of Peor,
And ate sacrifices made to the
dead.
29 Thus they provoked *Him* to
anger with their deeds,
And the plague broke out
among them.
30 [t]Then Phinehas stood up and
intervened,
And the plague was stopped.
31 And that was [u]accounted to
him for righteousness

Ezek. 20:15–16; Heb. 3:11,18 **106:27** *s* Lev. 26:33; Ps. 44:11; Ezek. 20:23 **106:30** *t* Num. 25:7–8 **106:31** *u* Num. 25:11–13

*

106:3 Septuagint, Syriac, Targum, and Vulgate read *those who do.*

To all generations
forevermore.
32 [a]They angered *Him* also at the
waters of strife,*
[b]So that it went ill with Moses
on account of them;
33 Because they rebelled against
His Spirit,
So that he [c]spoke rashly with
his lips.
34 They did not [d]destroy the
peoples,
Concerning whom the LORD
had commanded them,
35 But they mingled with the
Gentiles
And learned their works;
36 They served their idols,
Which became a snare to
them.
37 They even sacrificed their sons
And their daughters to
demons,
38 And shed innocent blood,
The blood of their sons and
daughters,
Whom they sacrificed to the
idols of Canaan;
And the land was polluted with
blood.
39 Thus they were defiled by their
own works,
And played the harlot by their
own deeds.
40 Therefore the wrath of the
LORD was kindled against
His people,
So that He abhorred His own
inheritance.
41 And He gave them into the
hand of the Gentiles,
And those who hated them
ruled over them.
42 Their enemies also oppressed
them,
And they were brought into
subjection under their hand.
43 [e]Many times He delivered them;
But they rebelled in their
counsel,
And were brought low for their
iniquity.
44 Nevertheless He regarded their
affliction,
When He heard their cry;
45 And for their sake He
remembered His covenant,
And [f]relented according to the
multitude of His mercies.
46 He also made them to be
[g]pitied
By all those who carried them
away captive.
47 [h]Save us, O LORD our God,
And gather us from among the
Gentiles,
To give thanks to Your holy
name,
To triumph in Your praise.
48 [i]Blessed *be* the LORD God of
Israel
From everlasting to
everlasting!
And let all the people say,
"Amen!"
Praise the LORD!

Book V, Psalms 107—150

God's provision for the redeemed

107 OH, [j]give thanks to the
LORD, for *He is* good!
For His mercy *endures* forever.
2 Let the [k]redeemed of the LORD
say *so,*
Whom He has redeemed from
the hand of the enemy,
3 And [l]gathered out of the
lands,
From the east and from the
west,
From the north and from the
south.
4 They [m]wandered in the
wilderness in a desolate
way;
They found no city to dwell in.
5 Hungry and thirsty,
Their soul fainted in them.
6 [n]Then they cried out to the LORD
in their trouble,
And He delivered them out of
their distresses.
7 And He led them forth by the
[o]right way,
That they might go to a city
for a dwelling place.
8 Oh, that *men* would give
thanks to the LORD *for* His
goodness,
And *for* His wonderful works
to the children of men!
9 [p]For He satisfies the longing
soul,
And fills the hungry soul with
goodness.
10 Those who sat in [q]darkness
and in the shadow of death,
Bound in affliction and irons—

32
a Num. 20:3–13; Ps. 81:7
b Dt. 1:37; 3:26
33
c Cp. Mt. 26:69–75
34
d Dt. 7:2,16; Jud. 2:2
43
e Jud. 2:16; Neh. 9:27
45
f See Zech. 8:14, *note*
46
g Ezra 9:9; Jer. 42:10–12
47
h 1 Chr. 16:35–36
48
i Ps. 41:13; 72:19; 89:52
PSALM 107
1
j Ps. 106:1
2
k *Redemption* (redeeming relative type): v. 2; Ps. 119:154. (Gen. 48:16; Isa. 59:20, *note*)
3
l Ps. 106:47; Isa. 43:5–6; Jer. 29:14; 31:8–10; Ezek. 39:27–28
4
m v. 40; cp. Dt. 32:10
6
n vv. 13,19, 28; Ps. 50:15; Hos. 5:15
7
o Ezra 8:21
9
p Ps. 34:10; Lk. 1:53
10
q Lk. 1:79

*106:32 Or *Meribah*

11 Because they [a]rebelled against
the words of God,
And despised the counsel of
the Most High,
12 Therefore He brought down
their heart with labor;
They fell down, and *there was*
none to help.
13 Then they cried out to the LORD
in their trouble,
And He saved them out of
their distresses.
14 He brought them out of
darkness and the shadow of
death,
And [b]broke their chains in
pieces.
15 Oh, that *men* would give
thanks to the LORD *for* His
goodness,
And *for* His wonderful works
to the children of men!
16 For He has broken the gates of
bronze,
And cut the bars of iron in
two.
17 Fools, because of their
transgression,
And because of their iniquities,
were afflicted.
18 Their soul abhorred all manner
of food,
And they drew near to the
gates of death.
19 Then they cried out to the LORD
in their trouble,
And He saved them out of
their distresses.
20 [c]He sent His word and healed
them,
And delivered *them* from their
destructions.
21 Oh, that *men* would give
thanks to the LORD *for* His
goodness,
And *for* His wonderful works
to the children of men!
22 Let them [d]sacrifice the
sacrifices of thanksgiving,
And declare His works with
[e]rejoicing.

23 Those who [f]go down to the
sea in ships,
Who do business on great
waters,
24 They see the works of the
LORD,
And His wonders in the deep.
25 For He commands and [g]raises
the stormy wind,
Which lifts up the waves of the
sea.

11
a Lam. 3:42
14
b Ps. 68:6; 146:7; cp. Acts 12:7; 16:26
20
c Ps. 147:15; cp. 2 Ki. 20:1–7; Mt. 8:8
22
d Lev. 7:12; Ps. 50:14; 116:17; Heb. 13:15
e Ps. 9:11
23
f Isa. 42:10; cp. Jon. 1:3–16; Acts 27:9–44
25
g Lit. *makes to stand.* Cp. Jon. 1:4
27
h Lit. *all their wisdom is swallowed up*
29
i Ps. 89:9; cp. Mt. 8:26
33
j Isa. 50:2; cp. 1 Ki. 17:1,7
34
k Cp. Gen. 13:10; 14:3; 19:25
35
l Ps. 114:8; Isa. 41:18
38
m Gen. 12:2; 17:16,20
n Dt. 7:14
40
o Job 12:21, 24
41
p 1 Sam. 2:8; Ps. 113:7–8

26 They mount up to the heavens,
They go down again to the
depths;
Their soul melts because of
trouble.
27 They reel to and fro, and
stagger like a drunken man,
And are [h]at their wits' end.
28 Then they cry out to the LORD
in their trouble,
And He brings them out of
their distresses.
29 [i]He calms the storm,
So that its waves are still.
30 Then they are glad because
they are quiet;
So He guides them to their
desired haven.
31 Oh, that *men* would give
thanks to the LORD *for* His
goodness,
And *for* His wonderful works
to the children of men!
32 Let them exalt Him also in the
assembly of the people,
And praise Him in the
company of the elders.

33 [j]He turns rivers into a
wilderness,
And the watersprings into dry
ground;
34 A fruitful land into
[k]barrenness,
For the wickedness of those
who dwell in it.
35 He [l]turns a wilderness into
pools of water,
And dry land into
watersprings.
36 There He makes the hungry
dwell,
That they may establish a city
for a dwelling place,
37 And sow fields and plant
vineyards,
That they may yield a fruitful
harvest.
38 He also blesses them, and they
[m]multiply greatly;
And He does not let their cattle
[n]decrease.

39 When they are diminished and
brought low
Through oppression, affliction
and sorrow,
40 [o]He pours contempt on princes,
And causes them to wander in
the wilderness *where there
is* no way;
41 [p]Yet He sets the poor on high,
far from affliction,

And makes *their* families like
a flock.
42 The righteous see *it* and
rejoice,
And all iniquity stops its
mouth.
43 [a]Whoever *is* wise will observe
these *things*,
And they will understand the
lovingkindness of the LORD.

Steadfast praise

A Song. A Psalm of David.

108 O GOD, my heart is
steadfast;
I will sing and give praise,
even with my glory.
2 Awake, lute and harp!
I will awaken the dawn.
3 I will praise You, O LORD,
among the peoples,
And I will sing praises to You
among the nations.
4 For Your mercy *is* great above
the heavens,
And Your truth *reaches* to the
clouds.
5 Be exalted, O God, above the
heavens,
And Your glory above all the
earth;
6 [b]That Your beloved may be
delivered,
Save *with* Your right hand,
and hear me.
7 God has spoken in His
holiness:
"I will rejoice;
I will divide Shechem
And measure out the Valley of
Succoth.
8 Gilead *is* Mine; Manasseh *is*
Mine;
Ephraim also *is* the helmet for
My head;
[c]Judah *is* My lawgiver.
9 Moab *is* My washpot;
Over Edom I will cast My
shoe;
Over Philistia I will triumph."
10 Who will bring me *into* the
strong city?
Who will lead me to Edom?
11 *Is it* not *You*, O God, *who* cast
us off?
And *You*, O God, *who* did not
go out with our armies?
12 Give us help from trouble,
For the help of man is useless.
13 [d]Through God we will do
valiantly,
For *it is* He *who* shall tread
down our enemies.

A cry for vengeance and judgment

To the Chief Musician. A Psalm of David.

109 [1]DO not keep silent,
O God of my praise!
2 For the mouth of the wicked
and the mouth of the
deceitful
Have opened against me;
They have spoken against me
with a [e]lying tongue.
3 They have also surrounded me
with words of hatred,
And fought against me
[f]without a cause.
4 In return for my love they are
my accusers,
But I *give myself to* prayer.
5 Thus they have rewarded me
evil for good,
And hatred for my [g]love.
6 [h]Set a [i]wicked man over him,
And let an [j]accuser* stand at
his right hand.
7 When he is judged, let him be
found guilty,
And let his prayer become
[k]sin.
8 Let his days be [l]few,
And [m]let another take his
office.

43
a Ps. 64:9; Jer. 9:12; Hos. 14:9

PSALM 108
6
b vv. 6–13 are almost identical with Ps. 60:5–12
8
c Gen. 49:10
13
d Cp. Phil. 4:13

PSALM 109
2
e Ps. 27:12; cp. Mt. 26:59–62; Lk. 23:1–5
3
f Ps. 35:7; 69:4; Jn. 15:25
5
g Prov. 17:13; cp. Jn. 10:32
6
h vv. 6–15; cp. Ps. 69:22–28
i Cp. Jn. 17:12; 2 Th. 2:3
j *Satan:* v. 6; Isa. 14:12. (Gen. 3:1; Rev. 20:10)
7
k Prov. 28:9
8
l Ps. 55:23; cp. Mt. 27:3–5
m Ps. 69:25; Acts 1:20

*109:6 Hebrew *satan*

[1](109:1) The Imprecatory Psalms (Ps. 35; 52; 55; 58; 59; 79; 109; 137) are cries to God to avenge. Believers in the Word of God explain such invocations of God's vengeance either (1) on the basis of the progressiveness of revelation (in which such prayers were part of Israel's life prior to the giving of God's full and final revelation), or (2) by calling attention to such matters as (a) vengeance is placed in God's hands, not the psalmist's (cp. Dt. 32:35); (b) it is true that unrepentant and unbelieving sinners must face the terrifying punishment of God; (c) ultimately, it is the honor of God which is at stake, the righteousness of God which must be vindicated (cp. Ps. 139:21–22); and (d) the righteous indignation of those who love God is justifiable against injustice, malevolence, lawlessness, and especially against apathy toward or rebellion against Him. God's servants await the day when righteousness will be rewarded and unrighteousness will be punished—in short, the day of the vindication of the moral nature of God (Ps. 72:1–9; Hab. 2:14; Lk. 18:7–8; 1 Cor. 15:25–28; 2 Th. 1:7–10; Rev. 11:17–18; 15:3–4; 19:5–7).

9 Let his children be fatherless,
And his wife a widow.
10 Let his children continually be
[a]vagabonds, and beg;
Let them seek *their bread** also from their desolate places.
11 Let the creditor seize all that he has,
And let strangers plunder his labor.
12 Let there be none to extend mercy to him,
Nor let there be any to favor his fatherless children.
13 Let his posterity be cut off,
And in the generation following let their name be [b]blotted out.
14 Let the iniquity of his fathers be remembered before the LORD,
And let not the sin of his mother be blotted out.
15 Let them be continually before the LORD,
That He may cut off the memory of them from the earth;
16 Because he did not remember to show mercy,
But persecuted the poor and needy man,
That he might even slay the broken in heart.
17 As he loved cursing, so let it come to him;
As he did not delight in blessing, so let it be far from him.
18 As he clothed himself with cursing as with his garment,
So let it enter his body like [c]water,
And like oil into his bones.
19 Let it be to him like the garment which covers him,
And for a belt with which he girds himself continually.
20 *Let* this *be* the LORD's [d]reward to my accusers,
And to those who speak evil against my person.

10
a Cp. Gen. 4:12
13
b Ps. 69:28
18
c Num. 5:22
20
d Cp. 2 Tim. 4:14
25
e Ps. 22:7; Mt. 27:39
30
f Ps. 22:25
PSALM 110
1
g Deity (names of): v. 1; Mal. 2:16. (Gen. 1:1; Mal. 3:18)
h Christ (second advent): vv. 1–7; Isa. 9:7. (Dt. 30:3; Acts 1:11, *note*)
i 1 Cor. 15:25

21 But You, O GOD the Lord,
Deal with me for Your name's sake;
Because Your mercy *is* good, deliver me.
22 For I *am* poor and needy,
And my heart is wounded within me.
23 I am gone like a shadow when it lengthens;
I am shaken off like a locust.
24 My knees are weak through fasting,
And my flesh is feeble from lack of fatness.
25 I also have become a reproach to them;
When they look at me, they [e]shake their heads.
26 Help me, O LORD my God!
Oh, save me according to Your mercy,
27 That they may know that this *is* Your hand—
That You, LORD, have done it!
28 Let them curse, but You bless;
When they arise, let them be ashamed,
But let Your servant rejoice.
29 Let my accusers be clothed with shame,
And let them cover themselves with their own disgrace as with a mantle.
30 I will greatly praise the LORD with my mouth;
Yes, I will praise Him among the [f]multitude.
31 For He shall stand at the right hand of the poor,
To save *him* from those who condemn him.

The psalm of the King-Priest
A Psalm of David.

110 [1]THE [g]LORD said to my [g]Lord,
"Sit at My right hand,
[h]Till I make Your enemies Your [i]footstool."

*109:10 Following Masoretic Text and Targum; Septuagint and Vulgate read *be cast out*.

[1](110:1) The importance of the 110th Psalm is attested by the remarkable prominence given to it in the NT. (1) It affirms the Deity of Jesus, thus answering those who deny the full divine meaning of His NT title of Lord (v. 1; Mt. 22:41–45; Mk. 12:35–37; Lk. 20:41–44; Acts 2:34–35; Heb. 1:13; 10:12–13). (2) It announces the eternal priesthood of Messiah—one of the most important statements of Scripture (v. 4; Gen. 14:18, *note* 4; Jn. 14:6; 1 Tim. 2:5–6; Heb. 5:6, *note;* 7:1–28). (3) Historically, Ps. 110 begins with the ascension of Christ (v. 1; Jn. 20:17; Acts 7:56; Rev. 3:21). And (4) prophetically, it looks forward (a) to the time when Christ will appear as the Rod of the LORD's strength, the Deliverer out of Zion (Rom. 11:25–27), and to the conversion of Israel (v. 3; Joel 2:27; Zech. 13:9; see Dt. 30:1–9, and *note* at v. 3); and (b) to

2 The LORD shall send the rod of
Your strength [a]out of Zion.
[b]Rule in the midst of Your
enemies!
3 Your people *shall be*
volunteers
In the day of Your power;
In the beauties of holiness,
from the womb of the
morning,
You have the dew of Your
youth.
4 The LORD has sworn
And will not [c]relent,
"You *are* a [d]priest forever
According to the order of
[e]Melchizedek."
5 The Lord *is* at Your right
hand;
He shall execute kings in the
day of His wrath.
6 He shall judge among the
nations,
He shall fill *the places* with
dead bodies,
He shall execute the heads of
many countries.
7 He shall drink of the brook by
the wayside;
Therefore He shall lift up the
head.

Praise for God's wonderful works

111 PRAISE the LORD!
I will praise the LORD with *my*
whole heart,
In the assembly of the upright
and *in* the congregation.
2 The works of the LORD *are*
great,
Studied by all who have
pleasure in them.
3 His work *is* honorable and
glorious,
And His righteousness endures
forever.
4 He has made His wonderful
works to be remembered;
The LORD *is* gracious and full
of compassion.
5 He has given food to those
who [f]fear Him;
He will ever be mindful of His
covenant.
6 He has declared to His people
the power of His works,
In giving them the heritage of
the nations.
7 The works of His hands *are*
verity and justice;
All His precepts *are* sure.
8 They stand fast forever and
ever,
And are done in truth and
uprightness.
9 He has sent [g]redemption to
His people;
He has commanded His
covenant forever:
Holy and awesome *is* His
name.
10 The [f]fear of the LORD *is* the
[h]beginning of wisdom;
A good understanding have all
those who do *His
commandments.*
His praise endures forever.

Blessings of the God-fearing man

112 PRAISE the LORD!
[i]Blessed *is* the man *who* fears
the LORD,
Who delights greatly in His
commandments.
2 His [j]descendants will be
mighty on earth;
The generation of the upright
will be blessed.
3 Wealth and riches *will be* in
his house,
And his righteousness endures
forever.
4 [k]Unto the upright there arises
light in the darkness;
He is gracious, and full of
compassion, and righteous.
5 A good man deals graciously
and [l]lends;
He will guide his affairs [m]with
discretion.
6 Surely he will never be
shaken;
The [n]righteous will be in
everlasting remembrance.
7 [o]He will not be afraid of evil
tidings;
His heart is steadfast, [p]trusting
in the LORD.
8 His [q]heart *is* established;
He will not be afraid,
Until he sees *his desire* upon
his enemies.

2
a Rom. 11:26–27
b Ps. 2:9; Dan. 7:13–14
4
c See Zech. 8:14, *note*
d Zech. 6:13
e Heb. 5:6; 6:20; 7:21

PSALM 111
5
f See Ps. 19:9, *note*
9
g See Ex. 6:6, *note*
10
h Prov. 1:7

PSALM 112
1
i Ps. 128:1
2
j Ps. 25:13; 37:26; 102:28
4
k Job 11:17; Ps. 97:11
5
l Ps. 37:26; Lk. 6:35
m Eph. 5:15; Col. 4:5
6
n Prov. 10:7
7
o Prov. 1:33
p See Ps. 2:12, *note*
8
q Heb. 13:9

---

the judgment upon the Gentile powers which precedes the setting up of the kingdom (vv. 5–6; Joel 3:9–17; Zech. 14:1–4; Rev. 19:11–21). See Armageddon (Rev. 16:16; 19:17, *note*); Israel (Gen. 12:2–3; Rom. 11:26, *note*); Kingdom (Zech. 12:8, and 1 Cor. 15:24, *notes*). See Ps. 118, last Messianic Psalm.

9 He has [a]dispersed abroad,
He has given to the poor;
His righteousness endures forever;
His [b]horn will be exalted with honor.
10 The wicked will see *it* and be grieved;
He will gnash his teeth and melt away;
The desire of the wicked shall perish.

God's continual praise

113 [1]PRAISE the LORD!

Praise, O servants of the LORD,
Praise the name of the LORD!
2 [c]Blessed be the name of the LORD
From this time forth and forevermore!
3 [d]From the rising of the sun to its going down
The LORD's name *is* to be praised.
4 The LORD *is* high above all nations,
His [e]glory above the heavens.
5 Who *is* like the LORD our God,
Who dwells on [f]high,
6 Who humbles Himself to behold
The things that are in the heavens and in the earth?
7 He [g]raises the poor out of the dust,
And lifts the [h]needy out of the ash heap,
8 That He may [i]seat *him* with princes—
With the princes of His people.
9 He grants the barren woman a home,
Like a joyful mother of children.

Praise the LORD!

In praise of the Exodus

114 WHEN Israel went out of Egypt,
The house of Jacob from a people of [j]strange language,
2 [k]Judah became His sanctuary,
And Israel His dominion.
3 The sea [l]saw *it* and fled;
[m]Jordan turned back.
4 The mountains skipped like rams,
The little hills like lambs.
5 [n]What ails you, O sea, that you fled?
O Jordan, *that* you turned back?
6 O mountains, *that* you skipped like rams?
O little hills, like lambs?
7 Tremble, O earth, at the presence of the Lord,
At the presence of the God of Jacob,
8 [o]Who turned the rock *into* a pool of water,
The flint into a fountain of waters.

To God alone be the glory

115 [p]NOT unto us, O LORD, not unto us,
But to Your name give glory,
Because of Your mercy,
Because of Your truth.
2 Why should the Gentiles say,
"So where *is* their God?"
3 But our [q]God *is* in heaven;
He does whatever He pleases.
4 [r]Their idols *are* silver and gold,
The work of men's hands.
5 They have mouths, but they do not speak;
Eyes they have, but they do not see;
6 They have ears, but they do not hear;
Noses they have, but they do not smell;
7 They have hands, but they do not handle;
Feet they have, but they do not walk;
Nor do they mutter through their throat.
8 Those who make them are like them;
So is everyone who trusts in them.
9 O Israel, [s]trust in the LORD;

9 *a* 2 Cor. 9:9 *b* See Dt. 33:17, *note*
PSALM 113
2 *c* Dan. 2:20
3 *d* Isa. 59:19; Mal. 1:11
4 *e* Ps. 8:1
5 *f* Ps. 11:4; 138:6; Isa. 57:15
7 *g* 1 Sam. 2:8; Ps. 107:41 *h* Ps. 72:12
8 *i* Job 36:7
PSALM 114
1 *j* Ps. 81:5
2 *k* Ex. 6:7; 19:6; 25:8; 29:45–46; Dt. 27:9
3 *l* Ex. 14:21; Ps. 77:16 *m* v. 5; Josh. 3:13–16
5 *n* Hab. 3:8
8 *o* Ex. 17:6; Num. 20:11; Ps. 107:35
PSALM 115
1 *p* Isa. 48:11; Ezek. 36:32
3 *q* Ps. 103:19; 135:6; Dan. 4:35
4 *r* vv. 4–8; cp. Ps. 135:15–18
9 *s* See Ps. 2:12, *note*

[1](113:1) The Hallelujah Psalms are the following: Ps. 104—106; 111—113; 115—117; 135; 146—150. Of these, Ps. 135—136 and 146—150 were used in daily synagogue worship. Psalms 113—118 were called the Egyptian Hallel and were used in connection with the feasts of Passover, Pentecost, Tabernacles, and Dedication. At the Passover celebration the earlier portion of these Psalms was sung before the feast; Ps. 115—118 (the Great Hallel) were sung after the last cup (cp. Mt. 26:30). *Alleluia*, the Greek form of the Hebrew Hallelujah, is directly transferred to the English text in Rev. 19:1,3,4,6.

He *is* their help and their shield.
10 O house of Aaron, trust in the LORD;
He *is* their help and their shield.
11 You who [a]fear the LORD, [b]trust in the LORD;
He *is* their help and their shield.

12 The LORD has been mindful of *us;*
He will bless us;
He will bless the house of Israel;
He will bless the house of Aaron.
13 He will [c]bless those who [d]fear the LORD,
Both small and great.
14 May the LORD give you increase more and more,
You and your children.
15 *May* you *be* blessed by the LORD,
Who made heaven and earth.

16 The heaven, *even* the heavens, *are* the LORD's;
But the earth He has given to the children of men.
17 The [d]dead do not praise the LORD,
Nor any who go down into silence.
18 But we will bless the LORD
From this time forth and forevermore.

Praise the LORD!

The gratitude of the redeemed

116

I LOVE the LORD, because He has heard
My voice *and* my supplications.
2 Because He has inclined His ear to me,
Therefore I will call *upon Him* as long as I live.

3 The [e]pains of death surrounded me,
And the pangs of [f]Sheol [g]laid hold of me;
I found trouble and sorrow.
4 Then I called upon the name of the LORD:
"O LORD, I implore You, deliver my soul!"

5 Gracious *is* the LORD, and [h]righteous;
Yes, our God *is* merciful.

11 a See Ps. 19:9, *note* b See Ps. 2:12, *note*
13 c Ps. 128:1,4
17 d See Eccl. 9:10, *note*
PSALM 116
3 e Ps. 18:4–6 f See Hab. 2:5, *note;* cp. Lk. 16:23, *note* g Lit. *found me*
5 h Ezra 9:15; Neh. 9:8; Ps. 119:137; 145:17
7 i Cp. Jer. 6:16; Mt. 11:29 j Ps. 13:6; 119:17
8 k Ps. 56:13
10 l 2 Cor. 4:13
15 m Rev. 14:13; cp. Ps. 72:14
17 n Lev. 7:12; Ps. 50:14; 107:22
PSALM 117
1 o Rom. 15:11
PSALM 118
1 p Ps. 136:1–26

6 The LORD preserves the simple;
I was brought low, and He saved me.
7 [i]Return to your rest, O my soul,
For the LORD has [j]dealt bountifully with you.

8 [k]For You have delivered my soul from death,
My eyes from tears,
And my feet from falling.
9 I will walk before the LORD
In the land of the living.
10 [l]I believed, therefore I spoke,
"I am greatly afflicted."
11 I said in my haste,
"All men *are* liars."
12 What shall I render to the LORD
For all His benefits toward me?
13 I will take up the cup of salvation,
And call upon the name of the LORD.
14 I will pay my vows to the LORD
Now in the presence of all His people.

15 [m]Precious in the sight of the LORD
Is the death of His saints.

16 O LORD, truly I *am* Your servant;
I *am* Your servant, the son of Your maidservant;
You have loosed my bonds.
17 I will offer to You the [n]sacrifice of thanksgiving,
And will call upon the name of the LORD.
18 I will pay my vows to the LORD
Now in the presence of all His people,
19 In the courts of the LORD's house,
In the midst of you, O Jerusalem.

Praise the LORD!

The universal praise of God

117

[o]PRAISE, the LORD, all you Gentiles!
Laud Him, all you peoples!
2 For His merciful kindness is great toward us,
And the truth of the LORD *endures* forever.

Praise the LORD!

The lovingkindness of the LORD

118

OH, give thanks to the LORD, for *He is* good!
[p]For His mercy *endures* forever.

2 Let Israel now say,
"His mercy *endures* forever."
3 Let the house of Aaron now say,
"His mercy *endures* forever."
4 Let those who [a]fear the LORD now say,
"His mercy *endures* forever."

5 I called on the LORD in distress;
The LORD answered me *and set me* in a broad place.
6 The [b]LORD *is* on my side;
I will not fear.
What can man do to me?
7 The LORD is for me among those who help me;
Therefore I shall see *my desire* on those who hate me.
8 *It is* better to trust in the LORD
Than to put confidence in [c]man.
9 *It is* better to [d]trust in the LORD
Than to put confidence in princes.

10 All nations surrounded me,
But in the name of the LORD I will destroy them.
11 [e]They surrounded me,
Yes, they surrounded me;
But in the name of the LORD I will destroy them.
12 They surrounded me like [f]bees;
They were quenched [g]like a fire of thorns;
For in the name of the LORD I will destroy them.
13 You pushed me violently, that I might fall,
But the LORD helped me.
14 The [h]LORD *is* my strength and song,
And He has become my salvation.

15 The voice of rejoicing and salvation
Is in the tents of the righteous;
The right hand of the LORD does valiantly.
16 The right hand of the LORD is exalted;
The right hand of the LORD does valiantly.
17 I shall [i]not die, but live,
And declare the works of the LORD.
18 The LORD [j]has chastened me severely,
But He has not given me over to death.

19 [k]Open to me the gates of righteousness;
I will go through them,
And I will praise the LORD.
20 This is the gate of the LORD,
[l]Through which the righteous shall enter.

21 I will praise You,
For You have answered me,
And have become my salvation.

22 The [1][m]stone *which* the builders rejected
Has become the chief cornerstone.
23 [n]This was the LORD's doing;
It *is* marvelous in our eyes.
24 This *is* the day the LORD has made;
We will rejoice and be glad in it.

25 Save now, I pray, O LORD;
O LORD, I pray, send now prosperity.
26 [o]Blessed *is* he who comes in the name of the LORD!
We have blessed you from the house of the LORD.
27 God *is* the LORD,
And He has given us light;
Bind the sacrifice with cords to the horns of the altar.
28 You *are* my God, and I will praise You;
You are my God, I will exalt You.

29 [2]Oh, give thanks to the LORD, for *He is* good!
For His mercy *endures* forever.

4 [a] See Ps. 19:9, *note*
6 [b] Ps. 56:9; Rom. 8:31; Heb. 13:6
8 [c] Cp. 2 Chr. 32:7–8; Isa. 31:1–3
9 [d] See Ps. 2:12, *note*
11 [e] Ps. 88:17
12 [f] Cp. Dt. 1:44
[g] Cp. Nah. 1:10
14 [h] Ex. 15:2; Isa. 12:2
17 [i] Ps. 116:8–9; cp. Ps. 6:5; Hab. 1:12
18 [j] 2 Cor. 6:9
19 [k] Isa. 26:2; cp. Ps. 24:7
20 [l] Isa. 35:8; Rev. 21:27; 22:14–15
22 [m] *Christ* (Stone): v. 22; Isa. 8:14. (Gen. 49:24; 1 Pet. 2:8)
23 [n] Lit. *This is from the LORD*
26 [o] Mt. 21:9; 23:39; Mk. 11:9; Lk. 13:35; 19:38; Jn. 12:13

[1](118:22) See Christ (as Stone or Rock), Gen. 49:24; Ex. 17:6, *note;* 1 Pet. 2:8, *note*. Ps. 118 looks beyond the rejection of the Stone (Christ) to His final exaltation in the kingdom (v. 22).

[2](118:29) The Messianic Psalms: Summary. That the Psalms contain a testimony to Christ, our Lord Himself affirmed (Lk. 24:44, etc.), and the NT quotations from the Psalter point unerringly to those Psalms which have the Messianic character. A similar spiritual and prophetic character identifies others. See Ps. 2:1, *note*.

(1) Christ is seen in the Psalms in two general attitudes: as suffering (e.g. Ps. 22), and as entering into His kingdom glory (e.g. Ps. 2 and 24. Cp. Lk. 24:25–27).

(2) Christ is seen in His Person as (a) Son of God (Ps. 2:7), and very God (Ps. 45:6–7; 102:25; 110:1); (b) Son of man (Ps. 8:4–6); and (c) Son of David (Ps. 89:3–4,27,29).

In praise of God's Word

א [1]ALEPH

119 BLESSED *are* the undefiled in the way,
Who walk in the [2a]law of the LORD!
2 Blessed *are* those who keep His testimonies,
Who seek Him with the [b]whole heart!
3 [c]They also do no iniquity;
They walk in His ways.
4 You have commanded *us*
To keep Your precepts diligently.
5 Oh, that my ways were directed
To keep Your statutes!
6 Then I would not be ashamed,
When I look into all Your commandments.
7 I will praise You with uprightness of heart,
When I learn Your righteous judgments.
8 I will keep Your statutes;
Oh, do not forsake me utterly!

ב BETH

9 How can a young man cleanse his way?
By taking heed according to Your word.
10 [d]With my whole heart I have sought You;
Oh, let me not wander from Your commandments!
11 Your word I have hidden in my heart,
That I might not sin against You.
12 Blessed *are* You, O LORD!
Teach me Your statutes.
13 With my lips I have declared
All the judgments of Your mouth.
14 I have rejoiced in the way of Your testimonies,
As *much as* in all riches.
15 I will meditate on Your precepts,
And contemplate Your ways.
16 I will delight myself in Your statutes;
I will not forget Your word.

ג GIMEL

17 [e]Deal bountifully with Your servant,
That I may live and keep Your word.
18 Open my eyes, that I may see
Wondrous things from Your law.
19 I *am* a [f]stranger in the earth;
Do not hide Your commandments from me.

PSALM 119
1 *a* *Law* (of Moses): vv. 1–176; Isa. 1:10. (Ex. 19:1; Gal. 3:24, *note*)
2 *b* Dt. 6:5; 10:12; 11:13; 13:3
3 *c* 1 Jn. 3:9; 5:18
10 *d* Cp. 2 Chr. 15:15
17 *e* Ps. 116:7
19 *f* 1 Chr. 29:15; Ps. 39:12; Heb. 11:13; cp. 2 Cor. 5:6

(3) Christ is seen in His offices as (a) Prophet (Ps. 22:22,25; 40:9–10); (b) Priest (Ps. 110:4); and (c) King (e.g. Ps. 2 and 24).

(4) Christ is seen in His varied work. As Priest He offers Himself in sacrifice (Ps. 22; 40:6–8, with Heb. 10:5–12), and, in resurrection, as the Priest-Shepherd, ever living to make intercession (Ps. 23, with Heb. 7:21–25; 13:20). As Prophet He proclaims the name of the LORD as Father (Ps. 22:22, with Jn. 20:17). As King He fulfills the Davidic Covenant (Ps. 89) and restores alike the dominion of man over creation (Ps. 8:4–8; Rom. 8:17–21) and of the Father over all (1 Cor. 15:25–28).

(5) The Messianic Psalms give also the inner thoughts, the exercises of soul, of Christ in His earthly experiences (e.g. Ps. 16:8–11; 22:1–21; 40:1–17).

[1](119, Aleph) Psalm 119 is an acrostic poem and is the most elaborate of the alphabetical Psalms (Ps. 9; 10; 25; 34; 37; 111; 112; 119; 145). It is divided into twenty-two sections corresponding to the twenty-two letters of the Hebrew alphabet. The eight verses of each section begin with the same letter, in the proper sequence of the alphabet as designated at the head of each section. For example, each of the first eight verses begins with ALEPH; each of the next eight with BETH; etc. Similar acrostics are found in Prov. 31:10–31; Lam. 1—4.

[2](119:1) This Psalm, born of love for the law of God, extols the beauties and excellences of the written Word of God in a way found nowhere else in the Bible. God's Word is treated under these designations: (1) law, v. 1; (2) testimonies, v. 2; (3) precepts, v. 4; (4) statutes, v. 5; (5) commandments, v. 6; and (6) judgments, v.7; (7) word(s), v. 9; (8) ordinances, v. 43. "Judgments" and "ordinances" are translations of the same Hebrew word. Only vv. 90,121,122, and 132 do not give a synonym for the law.

The shades of meaning in the words employed are as follows: "Law" is primarily instruction or teaching, legal pronouncements, rules of divine administration, then all of God's revelation for life. "Word" is speech or utterance, a general word for the disclosure of God's will. "Ordinances" (also "judgments") refer to legal pronouncements, rules of divine administration. "Commandments" are authoritative orders used as religious principles. "Precepts" relate to man's moral obligations as enjoined by God. "Testimonies" indicate God's own declarations concerning His nature and purpose. "Statutes" refer elsewhere to civil and religious appointments of the Mosaic law. The word "way" is used as a synonym for all of these terms.

20 My soul breaks with longing
For Your judgments at all
times.
21 You rebuke the proud—the
cursed,
Who stray from Your
commandments.
22 [a]Remove from me reproach and
contempt,
For I have kept Your
testimonies.
23 Princes also sit *and* speak
against me,
But Your servant meditates on
Your statutes.
24 Your testimonies also *are* my
delight
And my counselors.

ד DALETH

25 My soul [b]clings to the dust;
[c]Revive me according to Your
word.
26 I have declared my ways, and
You answered me;
Teach me Your statutes.
27 Make me understand the way
of Your precepts;
[d]So shall I meditate on Your
wonderful works.
28 My soul [e]melts from
heaviness;
[f]Strengthen me according to
Your word.
29 Remove from me the way of
lying,
And grant me Your law
graciously.
30 I have chosen the way of truth;
Your judgments I have laid
before me.
31 I cling to Your testimonies;
O LORD, do not put me to
shame!
32 I will run the course of Your
commandments,
For You shall [g]enlarge my
heart.

ה HE

33 Teach me, O LORD, the way of
Your statutes,
And I shall keep it *to* the end.
34 [h]Give me understanding, and I
shall keep Your law;
Indeed, I shall observe it with
my whole heart.
35 Make me walk in the path of
Your commandments,
For I delight in it.
36 Incline my heart to Your
testimonies,
And not to [i]covetousness.

22
a Ps. 39:8
25
b Ps. 44:25
c Ps. 143:11
27
d Ps. 145:5–6
28
e Lit. *drops*
f Cp. 1 Pet. 5:10
32
g Cp. 1 Ki. 4:29; Isa. 60:5; 2 Cor. 6:11
34
h v. 73; Prov. 2:6; Jas. 1:5
36
i Ezek. 33:31; Mk. 7:21–22; 1 Tim. 6:10; Heb. 13:5
38
j Cp. 2 Sam. 7:25
k See Ps. 19:9, *note*
42
l See Ps. 2:12, *note*
45
m Prov. 4:12
46
n Ps. 138:1; cp. Mt. 10:18–19; Acts 26:1–29
50
o v. 40
52
p v. 106

37 Turn away my eyes from
looking at worthless things,
And [c]revive me in Your way.*
38 [j]Establish Your word to Your
servant,
Who *is devoted* to [k]fearing
You.
39 Turn away my reproach which
I dread,
For Your judgments *are* good.
40 Behold, I long for Your
precepts;
Revive me in Your
righteousness.

ו WAW

41 Let Your mercies come also to
me, O LORD—
Your salvation according to
Your word.
42 So shall I have an answer for
him who reproaches me,
For I [l]trust in Your word.
43 And take not the word of truth
utterly out of my mouth,
For I have hoped in Your
ordinances.
44 So shall I keep Your law
continually,
Forever and ever.
45 And I will walk at [m]liberty,
For I seek Your precepts.
46 [n]I will speak of Your
testimonies also before
kings,
And will not be ashamed.
47 And I will delight myself in
Your commandments,
Which I love.
48 My hands also I will lift up to
Your commandments,
Which I love,
And I will meditate on Your
statutes.

ז ZAYIN

49 Remember the word to Your
servant,
Upon which You have caused
me to hope.
50 This *is* my comfort in my
affliction,
For Your word has [o]given me
life.
51 The proud have me in great
derision,
Yet I do not turn aside from
Your law.
52 I remembered Your
[p]judgments of old, O LORD,
And have comforted myself.

*119:37 Following Masoretic Text, Septuagint, and Vulgate; Targum reads *Your words.*

53 [a]Indignation has taken hold of
me
Because of the wicked, who
forsake Your law.
54 Your statutes have been my
songs
In the house of my pilgrimage.
55 I remember Your name in the
night, O LORD,
And I keep Your law.
56 This has become mine,
Because I kept Your precepts.

ח HETH

57 [b]*You are* my portion, O LORD;
I have said that I would keep
Your words.
58 I entreated Your [c]favor with
my whole heart;
Be merciful to me according to
Your word.
59 I [d]thought about my ways,
And turned my feet to Your
testimonies.
60 I made haste, and did not
delay
To keep Your commandments.
61 The cords of the wicked have
bound me,
But I have not forgotten Your
law.
62 At midnight I will rise to give
thanks to You,
Because of Your righteous
[e]judgments.
63 I *am* a companion of all who
[f]fear You,
And of those who keep Your
precepts.
64 The earth, O LORD, is full of
Your mercy;
Teach me Your statutes.

ט TETH

65 You have dealt well with Your
servant,
O LORD, according to Your
word.
66 Teach me good judgment and
[g]knowledge,
For I believe Your
commandments.
67 Before I was [h]afflicted I went
astray,
But now I keep Your word.
68 You *are* good, and do good;
Teach me Your statutes.
69 The proud have forged a lie
against me,
But I will keep Your precepts
with *my* whole heart.
70 Their heart is as fat as grease,
But I delight in Your law.

53
a Cp. Ex. 32:19; Ezra 9:1–4; Neh. 13:25
57
b Num. 18:20; Ps. 16:5; Lam. 3:24
58
c Lit. *face*
59
d Cp. Lk. 15:17–18
62
e v. 106
63
f See Ps. 19:9, *note*
66
g Phil. 1:9
67
h Prov. 3:11; Heb. 12:5–11
73
i Job 10:8; 31:15; Ps. 138:8; 139:15–16
74
j Ps. 107:42; cp. 1 Cor. 13:6
75
k Heb. 12:10
77
l vv. 24,47, 174
81
m Ps. 73:26; 84:2
83
n Cp. Job 30:30
84
o Cp. Rev. 6:10

71 *It is* good for me that I have
been afflicted,
That I may learn Your statutes.
72 The law of Your mouth *is*
better to me
Than thousands of *coins of*
gold and silver.

י YOD

73 Your hands have made me and
[i]fashioned me;
Give me understanding, that I
may learn Your
commandments.
74 Those who [f]fear You will be
[j]glad when they see me,
Because I have hoped in Your
word.
75 I know, O LORD, that Your
judgments *are* right,
And [k]*that* in faithfulness You
have afflicted me.
76 Let, I pray, Your merciful
kindness be for my comfort,
According to Your word to
Your servant.
77 Let Your tender mercies come
to me, that I may live;
For Your law *is* my [l]delight.
78 Let the proud be ashamed,
For they treated me wrongfully
with falsehood;
But I will meditate on Your
precepts.
79 Let those who fear You turn to
me,
Those who know Your
testimonies.
80 Let my heart be blameless
regarding Your statutes,
That I may not be ashamed.

כ KAPH

81 [m]My soul faints for Your
salvation,
But I hope in Your word.
82 My eyes fail *from searching*
Your word,
Saying, "When will You
comfort me?"
83 For I have become like a
[n]wineskin in smoke,
Yet I do not forget Your
statutes.
84 How many *are* the days of
Your servant?
[o]When will You execute
judgment on those who
persecute me?
85 The proud have dug pits for
me,
Which *is* not according to
Your law.

86 All Your commandments *are* faithful;
They [a]persecute me wrongfully;
Help me!
87 They almost made an end of me on earth,
But I did not forsake Your precepts.
88 Revive me according to Your lovingkindness,
So that I may keep the testimony of Your mouth.

ל LAMED

89 [b]Forever, O LORD,
Your word is settled in heaven.
90 Your faithfulness *endures* to all generations;
You established the earth, and it abides.
91 They continue this day according to Your ordinances,
For all *are* Your servants.
92 Unless Your law *had been* my delight,
I would then have perished in my affliction.
93 I will never forget Your precepts,
For by them You have [c]given me life.
94 I *am* Yours, save me;
For I have sought Your precepts.
95 The wicked wait for me to destroy me,
But I will consider Your testimonies.
96 I have seen the consummation of all perfection,
But Your commandment *is* exceedingly broad.

מ MEM

97 Oh, how I love Your law!
[d]It *is* my meditation all the day.
98 You, through Your commandments, make me [e]wiser than my enemies;
For they *are* ever with me.
99 I have more understanding than all my teachers,
For Your [f]testimonies *are* my meditation.
100 I understand more than the [g]ancients,
Because I keep Your precepts.
101 I have [h]restrained my feet from every evil way,
That I may keep Your word.
102 I have not departed from Your [i]judgments,
For You Yourself have taught me.
103 How sweet are Your words to my taste,
Sweeter than honey to my mouth!
104 Through Your precepts I get understanding;
Therefore I hate every false way.

נ NUN

105 Your word *is* a [j]lamp to my feet
And a light to my path.
106 I have [k]sworn and confirmed
That I will keep Your righteous [i]judgments.
107 I am afflicted very much;
Revive me, O LORD, according to Your word.
108 Accept, I pray, the [l]freewill offerings of my mouth, O LORD,
And teach me Your [i]judgments.
109 My life *is* continually in my hand,
Yet I do not forget Your law.
110 The wicked have laid a snare for me,
Yet I have not strayed from Your precepts.
111 [m]Your testimonies I have taken as a heritage forever,
For they *are* the rejoicing of my heart.
112 I have inclined my heart to perform Your statutes
Forever, to the very end.

ס SAMEK

113 I hate the double-minded,
But I love Your law.
114 You *are* my [n]hiding place and my shield;
I hope in Your word.
115 [o]Depart from me, you evildoers,
For I will keep the commandments of my God!
116 Uphold me according to Your word, that I may live;
And do not let me be [p]ashamed of my hope.
117 Hold me up, and I shall be safe,

86 *a* Ps. 38:19; cp. Mt. 5:10
89 *b* Ps. 89:2; Mt. 24:34–35; 1 Pet. 1:25
93 *c* v. 40
97 *d* Ps. 1:2
98 *e* Dt. 4:6
99 *f* Cp. 2 Tim. 3:14–15
100 *g* Job 32:7–9
101 *h* Cp. 1 Ki. 3:14; 8:25; 9:4; 11:38; 2 Chr. 7:17–18
102 *i* vv. 52,56
105 *j* Prov. 6:23
106 *k* Cp. Neh. 10:29
108 *l* Hos. 14:2; Heb. 13:15
111 *m* Dt. 33:4
114 *n* Ps. 32:7; 91:1
115 *o* Ps. 6:8; 139:19; Mt. 7:23
116 *p* Ps. 25:2; Rom. 5:5; 9:33; 10:11

And I shall observe Your
statutes continually.
118 You reject all those who stray
from Your statutes,
For their deceit *is* falsehood.
119 You put away all the wicked
of the earth [a]*like* dross;
Therefore I love Your
testimonies.
120 [b]My flesh trembles for fear of
You,
And I am afraid of Your
judgments.

ע AYIN

121 I have done justice and
righteousness;
Do not leave me to my
oppressors.
122 Be surety for Your servant for
good;
Do not let the proud oppress
me.
123 My eyes fail *from seeking*
Your salvation
And Your righteous word.
124 Deal with Your servant
according to Your mercy,
And [c]teach me Your
statutes.
125 I *am* Your servant;
Give me understanding,
That I may know Your
testimonies.
126 *It is* time for *You* to act, O
LORD,
For they have regarded
Your law as void.
127 Therefore I love Your
commandments
More than gold, yes, than
fine gold!
128 Therefore all *Your* precepts
concerning all *things*
I consider *to be* right;
I hate every false way.

פ PE

129 Your testimonies are
wonderful;
Therefore my soul keeps
them.
130 The entrance of Your words
gives [d]light;
It gives understanding to the
[e]simple.
131 I opened my mouth and
[f]panted,
For I longed for Your
commandments.
132 [g]Look upon me and be
[h]merciful to me,
As Your custom *is* toward
those who love Your
name.
133 Direct my steps by Your
word,
And let no iniquity have
[i]dominion over me.
134 [j]Redeem me from the
oppression of man,
That I may keep Your
precepts.
135 [k]Make Your face shine upon
Your servant,
And teach me Your statutes.
136 Rivers of water run down
from [l]my eyes,
Because *men* do not keep
Your law.

צ TSADDE

137 Righteous *are* You, O LORD,
And upright *are* Your
judgments.
138 Your testimonies, *which* You
have commanded,
Are righteous and very
faithful.
139 My zeal has consumed me,
Because my enemies have
forgotten Your words.
140 Your word *is* very [m]pure;
Therefore Your servant
loves it.
141 I *am* small and despised,
Yet I do not forget Your
precepts.
142 Your righteousness *is* an
everlasting righteousness,
And Your law *is* [n]truth.
143 Trouble and anguish have
overtaken me,
Yet Your commandments
are my delights.
144 The righteousness of Your
testimonies *is* everlasting;
Give me understanding, and
I shall live.

ק QOPH

145 I cry out with *my* whole heart;
Hear me, O LORD!
I will keep Your statutes.
146 I cry out to You;
Save me, and I will keep
Your testimonies.
147 I rise before the dawning of
the [o]morning,
And cry for help;
I hope in Your word.
148 My eyes are awake through
the *night* watches,
That I may meditate on
Your word.

119 *a* Cp. Ezek. 22:18
120 *b* Hab. 3:16
124 *c* v. 12
130 *d* Prov. 6:23 *e* Ps. 19:7; Prov. 1:4
131 *f* Ps. 42:1
132 *g* Ps. 106:4 *h* Ps. 51:1
133 *i* Ps. 19:13; Rom. 6:12, 14
134 *j* Lk. 1:74
135 *k* Ps. 4:6
136 *l* Jer. 9:1; 14:17; cp. Ezek. 9:4
140 *m* Lit. *tried* or *refined*
142 *n* v. 151; Ps. 19:9; Jn. 17:17
147 *o* Ps. 5:3; 88:13; 130:6

149 Hear my voice according to
Your lovingkindness;
O LORD, [a]revive me
according to Your justice.
150 They draw [b]near who
follow after wickedness;
They are far from Your law.
151 You *are* near, O LORD,
And all Your
commandments *are* truth.
152 Concerning Your testimonies,
I have known of old that
You have founded them
forever.

ר RESH

153 [c]Consider my affliction and
deliver me,
For I do not forget Your
law.
154 [d]Plead my cause and [e]redeem
me;
[a]Revive me according to
Your word.
155 Salvation *is* far from the
wicked,
For they do not seek Your
statutes.
156 Great *are* Your tender
mercies, O LORD;
[a]Revive me according to
Your judgments.
157 Many *are* my persecutors
and my enemies,
Yet I do not [f]turn from
Your testimonies.
158 I see the treacherous, and
am disgusted,
Because they do not keep
Your word.
159 Consider how I love Your
precepts;
[a]Revive me, O LORD,
according to Your
lovingkindness.
160 The entirety of Your word *is*
truth,
And every one of Your
righteous judgments
endures forever.

ש SHIN

161 [g]Princes persecute me
without a cause,
But my heart stands in awe
of Your word.
162 I rejoice at Your word
As one who finds great
treasure.
163 I hate and abhor lying,
But I love Your law.
164 Seven times a day I praise
You,
Because of Your righteous
judgments.
165 [h]Great peace have those who
love Your law,
And nothing causes them to
stumble.
166 LORD, I hope for Your
[i]salvation,
And I do Your
commandments.
167 My soul keeps Your
testimonies,
And I love them
exceedingly.
168 I keep Your precepts and
Your testimonies,
For all my ways *are* before
You.

ת TAU

169 Let my cry come before
You, O LORD;
[j]Give me understanding
according to Your word.
170 Let my supplication come
before You;
Deliver me according to
Your word.
171 My lips shall utter praise,
For You teach me Your
statutes.
172 My tongue shall speak of
Your word,
For all Your commandments
are righteousness.
173 Let Your hand become my
help,
For I have chosen Your
precepts.
174 I long for Your salvation, O
LORD,
And Your law *is* my delight.
175 Let my soul live, and it shall
praise You;
And let Your [k]judgments
help me.
176 I have [l]gone astray like a
lost sheep;
Seek Your servant,
For I do not forget Your
commandments.

A cry of distress

A Song of [1]Ascents.

120

IN my distress I cried to
the LORD,
And He heard me.

149 *a* vv. 25,107
150 *b* Cp. Ps. 145:18
153 *c* Lam. 5:1
154 *d* Cp. 1 Sam. 24:15
e Redemption (redeeming relative type): v. 154; Ps. 130:7. (Gen. 48:16; Isa. 59:20, *note*)
157 *f* v. 51; Ps. 44:18
161 *g* v. 23; cp. 1 Sam. 24:11,14; 26:18
165 *h* Prov. 3:2; Isa. 32:17
166 *i* v. 174; Gen. 49:18
169 *j* v. 144
175 *k* Ps. 18:22
176 *l* Isa. 53:6; 1 Pet. 2:25; cp. Lk. 15:4

[1](120—134, titles) Fifteen Psalms (Ps. 120—134) are called "Songs of Ascents." The view most generally accepted is that these Psalms were either sung by pilgrims on the ascending

2 Deliver my soul, O LORD, from lying lips
And from a deceitful tongue.
3 What shall be given to you,
Or what shall be done to you,
You false tongue?
4 Sharp arrows of the warrior,
With coals of the broom tree!

5 Woe is me, that I dwell in [a]Meshech,
That I dwell among the tents of [b]Kedar!
6 My soul has dwelt too long
With one who hates peace.
7 I *am for* peace;
But when I speak, they *are* for war.

The traveler's psalm

A Song of [c]Ascents.

121 I WILL lift up my eyes to the hills—
From whence comes my help?
2 My help [d]*comes* from the LORD,
Who made heaven and earth.

3 He will not allow your [e]foot to be moved;
He who [f]keeps you will not slumber.
4 Behold, He who keeps Israel
Shall neither slumber nor sleep.

5 The LORD *is* your keeper;
The LORD *is* your [g]shade at your [h]right hand.
6 [i]The sun shall not strike you by day,
Nor the moon by night.

7 The LORD shall preserve you from all evil;
He shall [j]preserve your soul.
8 The LORD shall [k]preserve your going out and your coming in
From this time forth, and even forevermore.

Joyful anticipation of Jerusalem

A Song of [c]Ascents. Of David.

122 I WAS glad when they said to me,
[l]"Let us go into the house of the LORD."
2 Our feet have been standing

PSALM 120
5
a Gen. 10:2; Ezek. 27:13
b Gen. 25:13; Jer. 49:28–29

PSALM 121
Title
c See Ps. 120 title, *note*
2
d Jer. 3:23
3
e 1 Sam. 2:9; Prov. 3:23,26
f Ps. 34:19–20; Prov. 24:12
5
g Isa. 25:4
h Ps. 16:8; 109:31
6
i Ps. 91:5; Isa. 49:10; Rev. 7:16
7
j Ps. 41:2; 97:10; 145:20
8
k Dt. 28:6; Prov. 2:8; 3:6

PSALM 122
1
l Cp. Isa. 2:3; Zech. 8:21
3
m Cp. 2 Sam. 5:9
4
n Ex. 23:17; Dt. 16:16
5
o Dt. 17:8; 2 Chr. 19:8

PSALM 123
1
p Ps. 121:1–2; 141:8
2
q Ps. 25:15
4
r Cp. Neh. 2:19; 4:1–5

PSALM 124
1
s Ps. 118:6; Rom. 8:31

Within your gates, O Jerusalem!
3 Jerusalem is built
As a city that is [m]compact together,
4 [n]Where the tribes go up,
The tribes of the LORD,
To the Testimony of Israel,
To give thanks to the name of the LORD.
5 For thrones are [o]set there for judgment,
The thrones of the house of David.

6 Pray for the peace of Jerusalem:
"May they prosper who love you.
7 Peace be within your walls,
Prosperity within your palaces."
8 For the sake of my brethren and companions,
I will now say, "Peace *be* within you."
9 Because of the house of the LORD our God
I will seek your good.

Looking for God's mercy

A Song of [c]Ascents.

123 UNTO You I [p]lift up my eyes,
O You who dwell in the heavens.
2 Behold, as the eyes of servants *look* to the hand of their masters,
As the eyes of a maid to the hand of her mistress,
[q]So our eyes *look* to the LORD our God,
Until He has mercy on us.

3 Have mercy on us, O LORD, have mercy on us!
For we are exceedingly filled with contempt.
4 Our soul is exceedingly filled
With the [r]scorn of those who are at ease,
With the contempt of the proud.

God on the side of His people

A Song of [c]Ascents. Of David.

124 "IF it had not been the LORD who was on our [s]side,"

---

march from the Babylonian captivity to Jerusalem, or that they were sung by worshipers from all parts of Palestine as they went up to Jerusalem for the great festivals (Dt. 16:16). An alternate view is that the headings, "A Song of Ascents," refer to the fifteen steps leading to the Court of Israel in the temple, and that these Psalms were sung on these steps.

Let Israel now say—
2 "If it had not been the LORD
who was on our side,
When men rose up against us,
3 [a]Then they would have
swallowed us alive,
When their wrath was kindled
against us;
4 Then the waters would have
overwhelmed us,
The stream would have gone
over our soul;
5 Then the swollen waters
Would have gone over our
soul."

6 Blessed *be* the LORD,
Who has not given us *as* prey
to their teeth.
7 [b]Our soul has escaped [c]as a
bird from the snare of the
fowlers;*
The snare is broken, and we
have escaped.
8 Our [d]help *is* in the name of the
LORD,
Who made heaven and earth.

The LORD's encompassing protection

A Song of [e]Ascents.

125 THOSE who [f]trust in the
LORD
Are like Mount Zion,
Which cannot be moved, *but*
abides forever.
2 As the mountains surround
Jerusalem,
So the LORD surrounds His
people
From this time forth and
forever.
3 For the [g]scepter of wickedness
shall not rest
On the land allotted to the
righteous,
Lest the righteous reach out
their hands to iniquity.
4 Do good, O LORD, to *those who*
are good,
And to *those who are* upright
in their hearts.
5 As for such as turn aside to
their crooked ways,
The LORD shall lead them away
With the workers of iniquity.

Peace *be* upon Israel!

Remembrance of past blessing

A Song of [e]Ascents.

126 [h]WHEN the LORD brought
back the captivity of Zion,
[i]We were like those who
dream.
2 Then our mouth was filled
with laughter,
And our tongue with singing.
Then they said among the
nations,
"The LORD has done great
things for them."
3 The LORD has done great
things for us,
And we are glad.

4 Bring back our captivity, O
LORD,
As the streams in the [j]South.
5 Those who sow in tears
Shall [k]reap in [l]joy.
6 He who continually goes forth
weeping,
Bearing seed for sowing,
Shall doubtless come again
with [m]rejoicing,
Bringing his sheaves *with him.*

Children are God's heritage

A Song of [e]Ascents. Of Solomon.

127 UNLESS the LORD builds
the house,
They labor in [n]vain who build
it;
[o]Unless the LORD guards the
city,
The watchman stays awake in
vain.
2 *It is* vain for you to rise up
early,
To sit up late,
To [p]eat the bread of sorrows;
For so He gives His beloved
sleep.

3 Behold, [q]children *are* a
heritage from the LORD,
The [r]fruit of the womb *is* a
[s]reward.
4 Like arrows in the hand of a
warrior,
So *are* the children of one's
youth.
5 [t]Happy *is* the man who has his
quiver full of them;
They shall not be ashamed,
But shall speak with their
enemies in the gate.

Blessings on the home of the God-fearing

A Song of [e]Ascents.

128 BLESSED *is* every one
who [u]fears the LORD,
Who walks in His ways.

3
a Ps. 56:1–2; 57:3; Prov. 1:12
7
b Ps. 91:3
c Prov. 6:5
8
d Ps. 121:2
PSALM 125
Title
e See Ps. 120 title, *note*
1
f *Faith:* v. 1; Jon. 3:5. (Gen. 3:20; Heb. 11:39, *note*)
3
g Isa. 14:5
PSALM 126
1
h Ps. 53:6; 85:1; Hos. 6:11; Joel 3:1
i Cp. Acts 12:9
4
j See Gen. 12:9, *note*
5
k Gal. 6:9
l Or *singing.* Cp. Neh. 12:43
6
m Isa. 61:3
PSALM 127
1
n Cp. Lev. 26:20
o Ps. 121:1–5
2
p Cp. Gen. 3:17–19
3
q Gen. 33:5; 48:4; Josh. 24:3–4
r Dt. 28:4
s Ps. 113:9
5
t Ps. 128:2–3
PSALM 128
1
u See Ps. 19:9, *note*

*124:7 That is, persons who catch birds in a trap or snare

2 When you eat the labor of
your hands,
You *shall be* happy, and *it*
shall be [a]well with you.
3 Your wife *shall be* [b]like a
fruitful vine
In the very heart of your
house,
Your [c]children [d]like olive
plants
All around your table.
4 Behold, thus shall the man be
blessed
Who fears the LORD.

5 The LORD bless you out of
Zion,
And may you see the good of
Jerusalem
All the days of your life.
6 Yes, [e]may you see your
children's children.

Peace *be* upon Israel!

A plea from the persecuted
A Song of [f]Ascents.

129 "MANY a time they have
afflicted me [g]from my
youth,"
Let Israel now say—
2 "Many a time they have
afflicted me from my youth;
Yet they have [g]not prevailed
against me.
3 The plowers plowed on my
back;
They made their furrows long."
4 The LORD *is* righteous;
He has cut in pieces the cords
of the wicked.

5 Let all those who hate Zion
Be put to shame and turned
back.
6 Let them be [h]as the grass *on*
the housetops,
Which withers before it grows
up,
7 With which the reaper does
not fill his hand,
Nor he who binds sheaves, his
arms.
8 Neither let those who pass by
them say,
"The blessing of the LORD *be*
upon you;
We [i]bless you in the name of
the LORD!"

Waiting for the morning
A Song of [f]Ascents.

130 OUT of the depths I have
cried to You, O LORD;
2 Lord, hear my voice!
Let Your ears be attentive
To the voice of my
supplications.

3 If You, LORD, should mark
iniquities,
O Lord, who could [j]stand?
4 But *there is* forgiveness with
You,
That You may be [k]feared.

5 I wait for the LORD, my soul
waits,
And in His word I do hope.
6 [l]My soul *waits* for the Lord
More than those who watch
for the morning—
Yes, more than those who
watch for the morning.

7 O Israel, [m]hope in the LORD;
For with the LORD [n]*there is*
mercy,
And with Him *is* abundant
[o]redemption.
8 And He shall redeem Israel
From all his iniquities.

Growing in grace
A Song of [f]Ascents. Of David.

131 LORD, my heart is not
haughty,
Nor my eyes lofty.
Neither do I concern myself
with great matters,
Nor with things too profound
for me.

2 Surely I have calmed and
quieted my soul,
Like a weaned child with his
mother;
Like a weaned child *is* my soul
within me.

3 O Israel, hope in the LORD
From this time forth and
forever.

Trust in the God of David
A Song of [f]Ascents.

132 LORD, remember David
And all his afflictions;
2 How he swore to the LORD,
And vowed to the Mighty One
of Jacob:
3 "Surely I will not go into the
chamber of my house,
Or go up to the comfort of my
bed;
4 I will not give sleep to my eyes
Or slumber to my eyelids,
5 [p]Until I find a place for the
LORD,

2
a Dt. 4:40; Isa. 3:10
3
b Ezek. 19:10
c Ps. 127:3–5
d Ps. 52:8; 144:12
6
e Cp. Gen. 50:23; Job 42:16
PSALM 129
Title
f See Ps. 120 title, *note*
1
g Jer. 1:19; 15:20; Mt. 16:18; 2 Cor. 4:8–9
6
h Ps. 37:2
8
i Cp. Ruth 2:4
PSALM 130
3
j Nah. 1:6
4
k 1 Ki. 8:39–40; see Ps. 19:9, *note*
6
l Ps. 33:20; 40:1; Isa. 8:17
7
m Ps. 131:3
n Ps. 86:5, 15; Isa. 55:7
o Redemption (redeeming relative type): vv. 7–8; Prov. 23:11. (Gen. 48:16; Isa. 59:20, *note*)
PSALM 132
5
p Acts 7:46

A dwelling place for the
Mighty One of Jacob."
6 Behold, we heard of it in
[a]Ephrathah;
We found it in the fields of
[b]the woods.*
7 [c]Let us go into His tabernacle;
Let us worship at His footstool.
8 Arise, O LORD, to Your resting
place,
You and the ark of Your
strength.
9 Let Your priests be clothed
with [d]righteousness,
And let Your saints shout for
joy.
10 For Your servant David's sake,
Do not turn away the face of
Your Anointed.
11 [e]The LORD has sworn *in* truth to
David;
He will not turn from it:
"I will set upon your throne
[f]the fruit of your body.
12 If your sons will keep My
covenant
And My testimony which I
shall teach them,
Their sons also shall sit upon
your throne forevermore."
13 [g]For the LORD has chosen Zion;
He has desired *it* for His
dwelling place:
14 [h]"This *is* My resting place
forever;
Here I will dwell, for I have
desired it.
15 I will abundantly bless her
provision;
I will satisfy her poor with
bread.
16 [i]I will also clothe her priests
with salvation,
And her saints shall [j]shout
aloud for joy.
17 [k]There I will make the [l]horn of
David grow;
I will prepare a [m]lamp for My
Anointed.
18 His enemies I will [n]clothe with
shame,
But upon Himself His crown
shall flourish."

The blessedness of brotherly love

A Song of [o]Ascents. Of David.

133 BEHOLD, how good and
how pleasant *it is*
For [p]brethren to dwell
together in unity!
2 *It is* like the precious oil upon
the head,
Running down on the beard,
The beard of Aaron,
Running down on the edge of
his garments.
3 *It is* like the dew of [q]Hermon,
Descending upon the
mountains of Zion;
For [r]there the LORD
commanded the blessing—
Life forevermore.

Praise by night

A Song of [o]Ascents.

134 BEHOLD, bless the LORD,
All *you* servants of the
LORD,
Who by night stand in the
house of the LORD!
2 Lift up your hands *in* the
sanctuary,
And bless the LORD.
3 The LORD who made heaven
and earth
Bless you from Zion!

The true God contrasted with idols

135 PRAISE the LORD!
Praise the name of the LORD;
Praise *Him*, O you servants of
the LORD!
2 You who stand in the house of
the LORD,
[s]In the courts of the house of
our God,
3 Praise the LORD, [t]for the LORD
is good;
Sing praises to His name, for *it*
is pleasant.
4 For the LORD has chosen Jacob
for Himself,
Israel for His [u]special treasure.
5 For I know that the LORD *is*
great,
And our Lord *is* above all
[v]gods.
6 [w]Whatever the LORD pleases He
does,
In heaven and in earth,
In the seas and in all deep
places.
7 He causes the vapors to ascend
from the ends of the earth;

6
a Or *Ephraim*
b 1 Chr. 13:5
7
c Ps. 122:1–2
9
d *Righteousness* (garment): v. 9; Isa. 11:5. (Gen. 3:21; Rev. 19:8)
11
e Ps. 89:3–4, 33; 110:4
f 2 Sam. 7:12; 1 Ki. 8:25; 2 Chr. 6:16; Lk. 1:69; Acts 2:30
13
g Ps. 48:1–2
14
h Ps. 68:16
16
i 2 Chr. 6:41; Ps. 132:9; 149:4
j 1 Sam. 4:5
17
k Ezek. 29:21; Lk. 1:69
l See Dt. 33:17, *note*
m 1 Ki. 11:36; 15:4; 2 Chr. 21:7
18
n Ps. 35:26; 109:29
PSALM 133
Title
o See Ps. 120 title, *note*
1
p Heb. 13:1; cp. Gen. 13:8
3
q Dt. 4:48
r Lev. 25:21; Dt. 28:8; Ps. 42:8
PSALM 135
2
s Ps. 92:13; 96:8; 116:19
3
t Ps. 119:68
4
u Lit. *own possession. Election* (corporate): v. 4; Isa. 43:20. (Dt. 7:6; 1 Pet. 5:13)
135:5 *v* 135:15–18; 1 Cor. 8:5–6; see Ps. 16:4, *note*
135:6 *w* Ps. 115:3

* 132:6 Hebrew *Jaar*

[a]He makes lightning for the rain;
He brings the wind out of [b]His treasuries.

8 [c]He destroyed the firstborn of Egypt,
Both of man and beast.
9 [d]He sent signs and wonders into the midst of you, O Egypt,
Upon Pharaoh and all his servants.
10 He defeated many nations
And slew [e]mighty kings—
11 Sihon king of the Amorites,
Og king of Bashan,
And all the kingdoms of [f]Canaan—
12 [g]And gave their land *as* a heritage,
A heritage to Israel His people.

13 [h]Your name, O LORD, *endures* forever,
Your fame, O LORD, throughout all generations.
14 For the LORD will judge His people,
And He will [i]have compassion on His servants.

15 [j]The idols of the nations *are* silver and gold,
The work of men's hands.
16 They have mouths, but they do not speak;
Eyes they have, but they do not see;
17 They have ears, but they do not hear;
Nor is there *any* breath in their mouths.
18 Those who make them are like them;
So is everyone who trusts in them.

19 Bless the LORD, O house of Israel!
Bless the LORD, O house of Aaron!
20 Bless the LORD, O house of Levi!
You who [k]fear the LORD, bless the LORD!
21 Blessed be the LORD out of Zion,
Who dwells in Jerusalem!

Praise the LORD!

The LORD's enduring mercy

136

OH, give thanks to the LORD, for *He is* good!
[l]For His mercy *endures* forever.
2 Oh, give thanks to [m]the God of gods!
For His mercy *endures* forever.
3 Oh, give thanks to the Lord of lords!
For His mercy *endures* forever:

4 To Him who alone does great wonders,
For His mercy *endures* forever;
5 [n]To Him who by wisdom made the heavens,
For His mercy *endures* forever;
6 [o]To Him who laid out the earth above the waters,
For His mercy *endures* forever;
7 [p]To Him who made great lights,
For His mercy *endures* forever—
8 [q]The sun to rule by day,
For His mercy *endures* forever;
9 The moon and stars to rule by night,
For His mercy *endures* forever.

10 [r]To Him who struck Egypt in their firstborn,
For His mercy *endures* forever;
11 [s]And brought out Israel from among them,
For His mercy *endures* forever;
12 With a strong hand, and with an outstretched arm,
For His mercy *endures* forever;
13 [t]To Him who divided the Red Sea in two,
For His mercy *endures* forever;
14 And made Israel pass through the midst of it,
For His mercy *endures* forever;
15 [u]But overthrew Pharaoh and his army in the Red Sea,
For His mercy *endures* forever;
16 To Him who led His people through the wilderness,
For His mercy *endures* forever;

7 a Job 28:25–26; 38:24–28; Zech. 10:1 b Jer. 51:16
8 c Ex. 12:12, 29; Ps. 78:51; 136:10
9 d Ex. 7–14
10 e Ps. 136:17–22
11 f Josh. 12:7
12 g Ps. 78:55; 136:21–22
13 h Ex. 3:15; Ps. 102:12
14 i See Zech. 8:14, *note*
15 j vv. 15–18; cp. Ps. 115:4–8
20 k See Ps. 19:9, *note*
PSALM 136
1 l 1 Chr. 16:34,41; 2 Chr. 20:21
2 m Cp. Dt. 4:35,39; Isa. 44:8; 45:5; 46:9; 1 Cor. 8:5–6; see Ps. 16:4, *note*
5 n Gen. 1:1, 6–8; Prov. 3:19; Jer. 51:15
6 o Gen. 1:9; Ps. 24:2; Jer. 10:12
7 p Gen. 1:14
8 q Gen. 1:16
10 r Ex. 12:29; Ps. 135:8
11 s Ex. 12:51; 13:3,16
13 t Ex. 14:21–22; Ps. 78:13
15 u Ex. 14:27;

Ps. 135:9

17 [a]To Him who struck down great kings,
For His mercy *endures* forever;
18 [b]And slew famous kings,
For His mercy *endures* forever—
19 [c]Sihon king of the Amorites,
For His mercy *endures* forever;
20 And [d]Og king of Bashan,
For His mercy *endures* forever—
21 [e]And gave their land as a heritage,
For His mercy *endures* forever;
22 A heritage to Israel His servant,
For His mercy *endures* forever.

23 [f]Who remembered us in our lowly state,
For His mercy *endures* forever;
24 And [g]rescued us from our enemies,
For His mercy *endures* forever;
25 Who gives food to all flesh,
For His mercy *endures* forever.

26 Oh, give thanks to the God of heaven!
For His mercy *endures* forever.

The captive's cry for vengeance

137 BY the rivers of Babylon,
There we sat down, yea, we wept
When we remembered Zion.
2 We hung our harps
Upon the willows in the midst of it.
3 For there those who carried us away captive asked of us a [h]song,
And those who plundered us *requested* mirth,
Saying, "Sing us *one* of the songs of Zion!"

4 How shall we sing the LORD's song
In a foreign land?
5 If I forget you, O Jerusalem,
Let my right hand forget *its skill!*
6 If I do not remember you,
Let my [i]tongue cling to the roof of my mouth—
If I do not exalt Jerusalem
Above my chief joy.

7 Remember, O LORD, against the sons of [j]Edom
The day of Jerusalem,
Who said, "Raze *it,* raze *it,*
To its very foundation!"

8 O daughter of Babylon, [k]who are to be destroyed,
Happy the one who repays you as you have served us!
9 Happy the one who takes and dashes
Your little ones against the rock!

Praise for answered prayer
A Psalm of David.

138 I WILL praise You with my whole heart;
Before the [l]gods I will sing praises to You.
2 I will worship toward Your holy temple,
And praise Your name
For Your lovingkindness and Your truth;
For You have magnified Your word above all Your name.
3 In the day when I cried out,
You answered me,
And made me bold *with* strength in my soul.

4 All the kings of the earth shall praise You, O LORD,
When they hear the words of Your mouth.
5 Yes, they shall sing of the ways of the LORD,
For great *is* the glory of the LORD.
6 Though the LORD *is* on high,
Yet [m]He regards the lowly;
But the proud He knows from afar.

7 [n]Though I walk in the midst of trouble, You will revive me;
You will stretch out Your hand
Against the wrath of my enemies,
And Your right hand will save me.
8 [o]The LORD will perfect *that which* concerns me;
Your mercy, O LORD, *endures* forever;
Do not forsake the works of Your hands.

17 *a* Ps. 135:10–11
18 *b* Dt. 29:7
19 *c* Num. 21:21
20 *d* Num. 21:33
21 *e* Josh. 12:1; Ps. 135:12
23 *f* Gen. 8:1; Dt. 32:36; Ps. 113:7
24 *g* Ps. 44:7
PSALM 137
3 *h* Lit. *the words of a song*
6 *i* Ezek. 3:26
7 *j* Jer. 49:7; Lam. 4:22; Ezek. 25:12; Obad. 10; see Gen. 36:1, *note*
8 *k* Isa. 13:1–6; 47:1; Jer. 25:12; 50:2; 51:24,56
PSALM 138
1 *l* See Ps. 16:4, *note*
6 *m* Prov. 3:34; Jas. 4:6
7 *n* Ps. 23:3–4
8 *o* Ps. 57:2; Phil. 1:6

God's all-seeing eye and inescapable presence

For the Chief Musician. A Psalm of David.

139 O LORD, You have [a]searched me and
known *me.*
2 [b]You know my sitting down
and my rising up;
You [c]understand my thought
afar off.
3 You comprehend my path and
my lying down,
And are acquainted with all
my ways.
4 For *there is* not a word on my
tongue,
But behold, O LORD, [d]You
know it altogether.
5 You have hedged me behind
and before,
And laid Your hand upon me.
6 [e]*Such* knowledge *is* [f]too
wonderful for me;
It is high, I cannot *attain* it.

7 [g]Where can I go from Your
[h]Spirit?
Or where can I flee from Your
presence?
8 If I ascend into heaven, You
are there;
If I make my bed in [i]hell,
behold, You *are* [j]*there.*
9 *If* I take the wings of the
morning,
And dwell in the uttermost
parts of the sea,
10 Even there Your hand shall
lead me,
And Your right hand shall
hold me.
11 If I say, "Surely the darkness
shall fall* on me,"
Even the night shall be light
about me;
12 Indeed, the [k]darkness shall not
hide from You,
But the night shines as the
day;
The darkness and the light *are*
both alike *to You.*
13 For You formed my inward
parts;
You covered me in my
mother's womb.
14 I will praise You, for I am
fearfully *and* wonderfully
made;*
Marvelous are Your works,
And *that* my soul knows very
well.

PSALM 139
1
a Cp. Ps. 139:23
2
b Cp. 2 Ki. 19:27
c Cp. Mt. 9:4; Jn. 2:24–25
4
d Heb. 4:13
6
e Job 42:3; Ps. 40:5
f Cp. Rom. 11:33
7
g Jer. 23:24; Amos 9:2–4; cp. Jon. 1:3
h *Holy Spirit* (OT): v. 7; Ps. 143:10. (Gen. 1:2; Zech. 12:10)
8
i See Hab. 2:5, *note;* cp. Lk. 16:23, *note*
j Amos 9:2–4
12
k Job 26:6; 34:22; Dan. 2:22; Heb. 4:13
15
l Job 10:8–9; Eccl. 11:5
17
m Rom. 11:33
19
n Isa. 11:4
20
o Jude 15
23
p Job 31:6; Ps. 26:2
q *Test/tempt:* vv. 23–24; Prov. 1:10. (Gen. 3:1; Jas. 1:14, *note*)
24
r Ps. 5:8; 143:10

15 [l]My frame was not hidden from
You,
When I was made in secret,
And skillfully wrought in the
lowest parts of the earth.
16 Your eyes saw my substance,
being yet unformed.
And in Your book they all
were written,
The days fashioned for me,
When *as yet there were* none
of them.

17 [m]How precious also are Your
thoughts to me, O God!
How great is the sum of them!
18 *If* I should count them, they
would be more in number
than the sand;
When I awake, I am still with
You.

19 [n]Oh, that You would slay the
wicked, O God!
Depart from me, therefore, you
bloodthirsty men.
20 For they [o]speak against You
wickedly;
Your enemies take *Your name*
in vain.*
21 Do I not hate them, O LORD,
who hate You?
And do I not loathe those who
rise up against You?
22 I hate them with perfect
hatred;
I count them my enemies.

23 [p]Search me, O God, and know
my heart;
[q]Try me, and know my
anxieties;
24 And see if *there is any* wicked
way in me,
And [r]lead me in the way
everlasting.

A prayer for protection against persecutors

To the Chief Musician. A Psalm of David.

140 DELIVER me, O LORD,
from evil men;
Preserve me from violent men,
2 Who plan evil things in *their*
hearts;
They continually gather
together *for* war.
3 They sharpen their tongues
like a serpent;

*139:11 Vulgate and Symmachus read *cover.* 139:14 Following Masoretic Text and Targum; Septuagint, Syriac, and Vulgate read *You are fearfully wonderful.* 139:20 Septuagint and Vulgate read *They take your cities in vain.*

The [a]poison of asps *is* under
their lips. Selah.
4 Keep me, O LORD, from the
hands of the wicked;
Preserve me from violent men,
Who have purposed to make
my steps stumble.
5 The proud have hidden a
[b]snare for me, and cords;
They have spread a net by the
wayside;
They have set traps for me.
Selah.
6 I said to the LORD: "You *are* my
God;
Hear the voice of my
supplications, O LORD.
7 O GOD the Lord, the strength
of my salvation,
You have covered my head in
the day of battle.
8 Do not grant, O LORD, the
desires of the wicked;
Do not further his *wicked*
scheme,
[c]*Lest* they be exalted. Selah.
9 "*As for* the head of those who
surround me,
Let the evil of their lips cover
them;
10 Let burning coals fall upon
them;
Let them be cast into the fire,
Into deep pits, that they rise
not up again.
11 Let not a slanderer be
established in the earth;
Let evil hunt the violent man
to overthrow *him.*"
12 I know that the LORD will
[d]maintain
The cause of the afflicted,
And justice for the poor.
13 Surely the righteous shall give
thanks to Your name;
The upright shall dwell in
Your presence.

A prayer for godliness and for deliverance from sinners

A Psalm of David.

141 LORD, I cry out to You;
Make haste to me!
Give ear to my voice when I
cry out to You.
2 Let my prayer be set before
You [e]*as* incense,
The [f]lifting up of my hands *as*
the evening sacrifice.

PSALM 140
3
a Ps. 58:4; Rom. 3:13
5
b Ps. 35:7; 57:6; 119:110; 141:9; Jer. 18:22
8
c Dt. 32:27
12
d 1 Ki. 8:45; Ps. 9:4
PSALM 141
2
e Rev. 8:3
f Ps. 134:2; 1 Tim. 2:8
3
g Prov. 21:23
4
h Prov. 23:6
5
i Prov. 9:8; 19:25; 25:12; Gal. 6:1
7
j Cp. 2 Cor. 1:9
k See Hab. 2:5, *note;* cp. Lk. 16:23, *note*
8
l 2 Chr. 20:12; Ps. 25:15; 123:1–2
m See Ps. 2:12, *note*
n Lit. *make not my soul bare*
10
o Lit. *pass over*
PSALM 142
Title
p Or *Instruction*
q 1 Sam. 22:1; 24:3; Ps. 57, title
3
r Ps. 77:3
s Ps. 141:9

3 Set a guard, O LORD, over my
[g]mouth;
Keep watch over the door of
my lips.
4 Do not incline my heart to any
evil thing,
To practice wicked works
With men who work iniquity;
And do not let me eat of their
[h]delicacies.
5 [i]Let the righteous strike me;
It shall be a kindness.
And let him rebuke me;
It shall be as excellent oil;
Let my head not refuse it.
For still my prayer *is* against
the deeds of the wicked.
6 Their judges are overthrown
by the sides of the cliff,
And they hear my words, for
they are sweet.
7 Our [j]bones are scattered at
the [k]mouth of the grave,
As when one plows and breaks
up the earth.
8 But my [l]eyes *are* upon You, O
GOD the Lord;
In You I take [m]refuge;
Do not leave my soul
[n]destitute.
9 Keep me from the snares they
have laid for me,
And from the traps of the
workers of iniquity.
10 Let the wicked fall into their
own nets,
While I [o]escape safely.

An experience of deliverance

A [p]Contemplation* of David. A Prayer when he was in the [q]cave.

142 I CRY out to the LORD with
my voice;
With my voice to the LORD I
make my supplication.
2 I pour out my complaint before
Him;
I declare before Him my
trouble.
3 When my spirit was
[r]overwhelmed within me,
Then You knew my path.
In the way in which I walk
They have secretly [s]set a
snare for me.
4 Look on *my* right hand and
see,
For *there is* no one who
acknowledges me;

* 142:title Hebrew *Maschil*

Refuge has failed me;
[a]No one cares for my soul.
5 I cried out to You, O LORD:
I said, "You *are* my refuge,
My portion in the land of the living.
6 Attend to my cry,
For I am brought very low;
Deliver me from my persecutors,
For they are stronger than I.
7 Bring my soul out of prison,
That I may [b]praise Your name;
The righteous shall surround me,
For You shall deal bountifully with me."

An urgent appeal for help
A Psalm of David.

143 HEAR my prayer, O LORD,
Give ear to my supplications!
In Your faithfulness answer me,
And in Your righteousness.
2 Do not enter into judgment with Your servant,
[c]For in Your sight no one living is righteous.
3 For the enemy has persecuted my soul;
He has crushed my life to the ground;
He has made me dwell in darkness,
Like those who have long been dead.
4 Therefore my spirit is [d]overwhelmed within me;
My heart within me is distressed.
5 [e]I remember the days of old;
I meditate on all Your works;
I muse on the work of Your hands.
6 I spread out my hands to You;
My soul *longs* for You like a thirsty land. Selah.
7 Answer me speedily, O LORD;
My spirit fails!
Do not hide Your face from me,
Lest I be like those who go down into the pit.
8 Cause me to hear Your lovingkindness in the morning,
For in You do I trust;
[f]Cause me to know the way in which I should walk,
For I lift up my soul to You.
9 Deliver me, O LORD, from my enemies;
In You I take shelter.*
10 Teach me to do Your will,
For You *are* my God;
Your [g]Spirit *is* good.
Lead me in the land of uprightness.
11 [h]Revive me, O LORD, for Your name's sake!
For Your righteousness' sake bring my soul out of trouble.
12 In Your mercy cut off my enemies,
And destroy all those who afflict my soul;
For I *am* Your servant.

A psalm of trust
A Psalm of David.

144 BLESSED *be* the LORD my Rock,
Who trains my hands for war,
And my fingers for battle—
2 My lovingkindness and my fortress,
My high tower and my deliverer,
My shield and *the One* in whom I take refuge,
Who subdues my people* under me.
3 LORD, [i]what *is* man, that You take knowledge of him?
Or the son of man, that You are mindful of him?
4 Man is like a breath;
[j]His days *are* like a passing shadow.
5 [k]Bow down Your heavens, O LORD, and come down;
Touch the mountains, and they shall smoke.
6 Flash forth lightning and scatter them;
Shoot out Your arrows and destroy them.
7 Stretch out Your hand from above;
Rescue me and deliver me out of great waters,
From the hand of [l]foreigners,
8 Whose mouth speaks lying words,

4 a Lit. *no man sought after my soul*
7 b Ps. 34:2
PSALM 143
2 c Ex. 34:7; Job 4:17; 9:2; 15:14; 25:4; Ps. 130:3; Eccl. 7:20; Rom. 3:20; Gal. 2:16
4 d Ps. 77:3
5 e Ps. 77:5, 10–11
8 f Ps. 5:8
10 g *Holy Spirit* (OT): v. 10; Isa. 11:2. (Gen. 1:2; Zech. 12:10)
11 h Ps. 138:7
PSALM 144
3 i Job 7:17; Ps. 8:4; Heb. 2:6
4 j Job 8:9; 14:2; Ps. 102:11
5 k Ps. 18:9; Isa. 64:1
7 l Hos. 5:7

*143:9 Septuagint and Vulgate read *To You I flee.* 144:2 Following Masoretic Text, Septuagint, and Vulgate; Syriac and Targum read *the peoples* (compare 18:47).

And whose right hand *is* a right hand of falsehood.

9 I will sing a [a]new song to You, O God;
On a harp of ten strings I will sing praises to You,
10 *The One* who gives salvation to kings,
Who delivers David His servant
From the deadly sword.

11 Rescue me and deliver me from the hand of [b]foreigners,
Whose mouth speaks lying words,
And whose right hand *is* a right hand of falsehood—
12 That our sons *may be* as plants grown up in their youth;
That our daughters *may be* as pillars,
Sculptured in palace style;
13 *That* our barns *may be* full,
Supplying all kinds of produce;
That our sheep may bring forth thousands
And ten thousands in our fields;
14 *That* our oxen *may be* well-laden;
That there be no breaking in or going out;
That there be no outcry in our streets.
15 [c]Happy *are* the people who are in such a state;
Happy *are* the people whose God *is* the LORD!

Praise to the gracious God

A Praise of David.

145 I WILL extol You, my God, O King;
And I will bless Your name forever and ever.
2 Every day I will bless You,
And I will praise Your name forever and ever.
3 [d]Great *is* the LORD, and greatly to be praised;
And His [e]greatness *is* unsearchable.
4 One generation shall praise Your works to another,
And shall declare Your mighty acts.
5 I* will meditate on the glorious splendor of Your majesty,
And on Your wondrous works.*
6 *Men* shall speak of the might of Your awesome acts,
And I will declare Your greatness.
7 They shall utter the memory of Your great goodness,
And shall sing of Your righteousness.

8 The LORD *is* [f]gracious and full of compassion,
Slow to anger and great in mercy.
9 The LORD *is* [g]good to all,
And His tender mercies *are* over all His works.

10 All Your works shall praise You, O LORD,
And Your saints shall bless You.
11 They shall speak of the glory of Your kingdom,
And talk of Your power,
12 To make known to the sons of men His mighty acts,
And the glorious majesty of His kingdom.
13 Your [h]kingdom *is* an everlasting kingdom,
And Your dominion *endures* throughout all generations.*
14 The LORD upholds all who fall,
And raises up all *who are* bowed down.
15 The eyes of all look expectantly to You,
And You give them their food in due season.
16 You [i]open Your hand
And satisfy the desire of every living thing.
17 The LORD *is* righteous in all His ways,
Gracious in all His works.
18 The LORD *is* [j]near to all who call upon Him,
To all who call upon Him in [k]truth.
19 He will fulfill the desire of those who [l]fear Him;
He also will hear their cry and save them.
20 The LORD [m]preserves all who love Him,

9 *a* Ps. 33:2–3; 40:3
11 *b* Hos. 5:7
15 *c* Dt. 33:29; Ps. 33:12; 65:4; 146:5; Jer. 17:7
PSALM 145
3 *d* Ps. 96:4 *e* Job 5:9; 9:10; Rom. 11:33
8 *f* Ex. 34:6–7; Num. 14:18; Ps. 86:5,15; 103:8
9 *g* Ps. 100:5; Nah. 1:7
13 *h* Dan. 2:44; 4:3; 1 Tim. 1:17
16 *i* Ps. 104:28
18 *j* Dt. 4:7 *k* Jn. 4:24
19 *l* See Ps. 19:9, *note*
20 *m* Ps. 31:23; 97:10

* 145:5 Following Masoretic Text and Targum; Dead Sea Scrolls, Septuagint, Syriac, and Vulgate read *They.* • Literally *on the words of Your wondrous works* 145:13 Following Masoretic Text and Targum; Dead Sea Scrolls, Septuagint, Syriac, and Vulgate add *The LORD is faithful in all His words, and holy in all His works.*

But all the wicked He will
destroy.
21 My mouth shall speak the
praise of the LORD,
And all flesh shall bless His
holy name
Forever and ever.

God praised for His help

146 [a]PRAISE the LORD!

Praise the LORD, O my soul!
2 While I live I will praise the
LORD;
I will sing praises to my God
while I have my being.

3 Do not put your [b]trust in
princes,
Nor in a son of man, in whom
there is no help.
4 His spirit departs, he returns to
his earth;
In that very day his [c]plans
perish.

5 [d]Happy *is he* who *has* the God
of Jacob for his help,
Whose hope *is* in the LORD his
God,
6 [e]Who made heaven and earth,
The sea, and all that *is* in
them;
Who keeps truth forever,
7 Who executes [f]justice for the
oppressed,
Who gives food to the hungry.
The [g]LORD gives freedom to
the prisoners.
8 [h]The LORD opens *the eyes of* the
blind;
The LORD raises those who are
bowed down;
The LORD loves the righteous.
9 The LORD [i]watches over the
strangers;
He relieves the fatherless and
widow;
But the way of the wicked He
turns upside down.

10 The LORD [j]shall reign
forever—
Your God, O Zion, to all
generations.

Praise the LORD!

God praised for regathering Israel

147 PRAISE the LORD!

For *it is* good to sing
praises to our God;
For *it is* pleasant, *and* praise is
beautiful.
2 The LORD builds up Jerusalem;
He [k]gathers together the
outcasts of Israel.
3 He [l]heals the brokenhearted
And binds up their [m]wounds.
4 He [n]counts the number of the
stars;
He calls them all by name.
5 [o]Great *is* our Lord, and mighty
in power;
His [p]understanding *is* infinite.
6 The LORD lifts up the humble;
He casts the wicked down to
the ground.

7 Sing to the LORD with
thanksgiving;
Sing praises on the harp to our
God,
8 [q]Who covers the heavens with
clouds,
Who prepares rain for the
earth,
Who makes grass to grow on
the mountains.
9 He gives to the beast its food,
And to the young ravens that
cry.

10 He does not delight in the
strength of the horse;
He takes no pleasure in the
legs of a man.
11 The LORD takes pleasure in
those who [r]fear Him,
In those who hope in His
mercy.

12 Praise the LORD, O Jerusalem!
Praise your God, O Zion!
13 For He has strengthened the
bars of your gates;
He has blessed your children
within you.
14 He makes peace *in* your
borders,
And fills you with the finest
wheat.

15 He sends out His command *to
the* earth;
His word runs very swiftly.
16 He gives snow like wool;
He scatters the frost like ashes;
17 He casts out His hail like
morsels;
Who can stand before His
cold?
18 He sends out His word and
melts them;
He causes His wind to blow,
and the waters flow.

19 He [s]declares His word to
Jacob,

PSALM 146
1 *a* Ps. 103:1
3 *b* See Ps. 2:12, *note*
4 *c* Ps. 33:10; cp. 1 Cor. 2:6
5 *d* Dt. 33:29; Ps. 33:12; 65:4; 146:5; Jer. 17:7
6 *e* Gen. 1:1; Ex. 20:11; Acts 4:24; Rev. 14:7
7 *f* Ps. 72:2 *g* Ps. 68:6; 107:10,14
8 *h* Mt. 9:30; Jn. 9:7,32
9 *i* Dt. 10:18; Ps. 68:5
10 *j* Ex. 15:18; Ps. 10:16; Rev. 11:15

PSALM 147
2 *k* Dt. 30:3
3 *l* Ps. 51:17; Isa. 61:1; Lk. 4:18 *m* Lit. *griefs*
4 *n* Gen. 15:5; Isa. 40:26
5 *o* Ps. 96:4 *p* Isa. 40:28
8 *q* Job 38:26–27; Ps. 104:13
11 *r* See Ps. 19:9, *note*
19 *s* Dt. 33:2–4; Ps. 76:1; 78:5; 103:7

His statutes and His
[a]judgments to Israel.
20 He has not [b]dealt thus with
any nation;
And *as for His* judgments, they
have not known them.

Praise the LORD!

God praised by all creation

148 PRAISE the LORD!

Praise the LORD from the
heavens;
Praise Him in the heights!
2 Praise Him, all His [c]angels;
Praise Him, all His hosts!
3 Praise Him, sun and moon;
Praise Him, all you stars of
light!
4 Praise Him, you heavens of
heavens,
And you waters above the
heavens!

5 Let them praise the name of
the LORD,
For He commanded and they
were created.
6 He also established them
forever and ever;
He made a decree which shall
not pass away.

7 Praise the LORD from the earth,
You [d]great sea creatures and
all the depths;
8 Fire and hail, snow and clouds;
Stormy wind, fulfilling His
word;
9 Mountains and all hills;
Fruitful trees and all cedars;
10 Beasts and all cattle;
Creeping things and flying
fowl;
11 Kings of the earth and all
peoples;
Princes and all judges of the
earth;
12 Both young men and maidens;
Old men and children.

13 Let them praise the name of
the LORD,
For His [e]name alone is
exalted;
His glory *is* above the earth
and heaven.
14 And He has [f]exalted the [g]horn
of His people,
The praise of [h]all His saints—
Of the children of Israel,
A [i]people near to Him.

Praise the LORD!

God praised by the children of Zion

149 PRAISE the LORD!

Sing to the LORD a new song,
And His praise in the assembly
of saints.

2 Let Israel rejoice in their
Maker;
Let the children of Zion be
joyful in their [j]King.
3 Let them praise His name with
the dance;
Let them sing praises to Him
with the [k]timbrel and [l]harp.
4 For the LORD takes pleasure in
His people;
He will beautify the humble
with salvation.

5 Let the saints be joyful in
glory;
Let them [m]sing aloud on their
beds.
6 *Let* the high praises of God *be*
[n]in their mouth,
And a [o]two-edged sword in
their hand,
7 To execute vengeance on the
nations,
And punishments on the
peoples;
8 To bind their kings with
chains,
And their nobles with fetters of
iron;
9 To [p]execute on them the
written judgment—
[q]This honor have all His saints.

Praise the LORD!

The summation of God's praise

150 [r]PRAISE the LORD!

Praise God in His sanctuary;
Praise Him in His mighty
firmament!

2 Praise Him for His mighty
acts;
Praise Him according to His
excellent [s]greatness!

3 Praise Him with the sound of
the [t]trumpet;

19
a Ps. 97:8
20
b Dt. 4:32–34; Rom. 3:1–2
PSALM 148
2
c See Heb. 1:4, *note*
7
d Isa. 43:20
13
e Ps. 8:1
14
f Ps. 75:10
g See Dt. 33:17, *note*
h Ps. 149:9
i Cp. Eph. 2:17
PSALM 149
2
j Zech. 9:9; Mt. 21:5
3
k Probably a tambourine
l Probably a zither or lyre
5
m Job 35:10
6
n Lit. *in their throat*
o Heb. 4:12; Rev. 1:16
9
p Dt. 7:1–2
q 1 Cor. 6:2
PSALM 150
1
r Ps. 145:5–6
2
s Dt. 3:24
3
t Heb. *shofar,* the horn of a cow or ram

Praise Him with the lute and
[a]harp!
4 Praise Him with the [b]timbrel
and dance;
Praise Him with stringed
instruments and flutes!
5 Praise Him with loud cymbals;
Praise Him with clashing
cymbals!

6 Let everything that has breath
praise the LORD.

Praise the LORD!

3 a Probably a zither or lyre
4 b Probably a tambourine

The Book of PROVERBS

Author: Solomon and others *Theme:* Wisdom *Date of compilation:* 10th Cent. B.C.

PROVERBS is a collection of pithy sayings in which, by comparison or contrast, some important truth is set forth. Proverbs were common to all nations of the ancient world. This particular collection was made for the most part by Solomon who, in 1 Ki. 4:32, is said to have uttered three thousand proverbs.

Among the virtues commended in this book are the pursuit of wisdom, filial piety, liberality, domestic faithfulness, and honesty in business relationships. Among the vices condemned are intemperance in eating and drinking, lewdness, falsehood, laziness, contentiousness, and the keeping of bad company.

The proverbs collected by Solomon are difficult to classify; the following divisions may be helpful:

I. Fatherly Exhortations Addressed Mainly to the Young, 1—9.
II. Wisdom and the Fear of God Contrasted with Folly and Sin, 10—24.
III. Proverbs of Solomon Selected by the Men of Hezekiah, 25—29.
IV. Supplemental Proverbs by Agur and Lemuel, 30—31.

I. Fatherly Exhortations Addressed Mainly to the Young, 1—9

The purpose of the book, vv. 1–6

1 [1]THE proverbs of Solomon the son of David, king of Israel:

2 To know wisdom and
instruction,
To perceive the words of
understanding,
3 To receive the instruction of
wisdom,
Justice, judgment, and equity;
4 To give prudence to the
[a]simple,
To the young man knowledge
and discretion—
5 A [b]wise *man* will hear and
increase learning,
And a man of understanding
will attain wise counsel,
6 To understand a proverb and
an enigma,
The words of the wise and
their [c]riddles.

Wisdom's foundation: the fear of the LORD

7 The [d]fear of the LORD *is* the
beginning of knowledge,
But [2]fools despise wisdom and
instruction.

8 My son, hear the instruction of
your father,
And do not forsake the law of
your mother;
9 For they *will be* a [e]graceful
ornament on your head,
And [f]chains about your neck.

10 My son, if sinners [g]entice you,
Do not [h]consent.
11 If they say, "Come with us,
Let us lie in wait to *shed*
blood;
Let us lurk secretly for the
innocent without cause;
12 Let us swallow them alive like
[i]Sheol,*
And whole, like those who [j]go
down to the Pit;
13 We shall find all *kinds* of
precious possessions,
We shall fill our houses with
spoil;
14 Cast in your lot among us,
Let us all have one purse"—
15 My son, do not walk in the
way with them,
Keep your foot from their
path;
16 For their [k]feet run to evil,
And they make haste to shed
blood.
17 Surely, in vain the net is
spread

CHAPTER 1
4 *a* Prov. 9:4
5 *b* Prov. 9:9
6 *c* Ps. 78:2
7 *d* See Ps. 19:9, *note*
9 *e* Prov. 3:22
f i.e. *as an adornment*
10 *g* *Test/tempt:* v. 10; Prov. 17:3. (Gen. 3:1; Jas. 1:14, *note*)
h Cp. Gen. 39:7–8; Ps. 1:1; Eph. 5:11
12 *i* See Hab. 2:5, *note;* cp. Lk. 16:23, *note*
j Ps. 28:1; 143:7
16 *k* Isa. 59:7; Rom. 3:15

*1:12 Or *the grave*

---

[1](1:1) Most of the proverbs come from Solomon in the 10th century B.C., though some of them were copied from his other writings later (25:1; cp. 1 Ki. 4:32); others were by Agur (ch. 30) and King Lemuel (ch. 31).

[2](1:7) "Fool" in Scripture refers to one who is arrogant and self-sufficient, one who orders his life as if there were no God. See e.g. Lk. 12:16–21. The rich man was not mentally deficient, but he was a "fool" because he supposed that his soul could live on the things in the barn, giving no thought to his eternal well-being.

In the sight of any bird;
18 But they lie in wait for their *own* blood,
They lurk secretly for their *own* lives.
19 [a]So *are* the ways of everyone who is greedy for gain;
It takes away the life of its owners.

Wisdom's warning

20 [b]Wisdom calls aloud outside;
She raises her voice in the open squares.
21 She cries out in the chief concourses,*
At the openings of the gates in the city
She speaks her words:
22 "How long, you simple ones, will you love simplicity?
For scorners delight in their scorning,
And fools hate knowledge.
23 Turn at my rebuke;
Surely I will pour out my spirit on you;
I will make my words known to you.
24 [c]Because I have called and you refused,
I have stretched out my hand and no one regarded,
25 Because you disdained all my counsel,
And would have none of my rebuke,
26 I also will laugh at your calamity;
I will mock when your terror comes,
27 When your terror comes like a storm,
And your destruction comes like a whirlwind,
When distress and anguish come upon you.

28 [d]"Then they will call on me, but I will not answer;
They will seek me diligently, but they will not find me.
29 Because they hated knowledge
And did not choose the [e]fear of the LORD,
30 They would have none of my counsel
And despised my every rebuke.
31 Therefore they shall eat the fruit of their own way,
And be filled to the full with their own fancies.
32 For the turning away of the simple will slay them,
And the complacency of fools will destroy them;
33 But whoever listens to me will dwell [f]safely,
And [g]will be secure, without fear of evil."

Wisdom delivers from evil

2 MY son, if you receive my words,
And [h]treasure my commands within you,
2 So that you incline your ear to wisdom,
And apply your heart to understanding;
3 Yes, if you cry out for discernment,
And lift up your voice for understanding,
4 If you seek her as silver,
And search for her as *for* hidden treasures;
5 [i]Then you will understand the [e]fear of the LORD,
And find the knowledge of God.
6 For the [j]LORD gives wisdom;
From His mouth *come* knowledge and understanding;
7 He stores up sound wisdom for the upright;
He is a [k]shield to those who walk uprightly;
8 He guards the paths of justice,
And preserves the way of His saints.
9 Then you will understand righteousness and justice,
Equity *and* every good path.

10 When wisdom enters your heart,
And knowledge is pleasant to your soul,
11 Discretion will preserve you;
Understanding will keep you,
12 To deliver you from the way of evil,
From the man who speaks perverse things,
13 From those who leave the paths of uprightness
To walk in the ways of darkness;
14 [l]Who rejoice in doing evil,
And delight in the perversity of the wicked;

19 *a* Prov. 15:27; 1 Tim. 6:10
20 *b* Prov. 8:1; 9:3; cp. Jn. 7:37
24 *c* Isa. 65:12; 66:4; Jer. 7:13; Zech. 7:11
28 *d* Job 27:9; 35:12; Isa. 1:15; Jer. 11:11; 14:12; Ezek. 8:18; Mic. 3:4; Zech. 7:13; Jas. 4:3
29 *e* See Ps. 19:9, *note*
33 *f* Prov. 3:24–26 *g* Ps. 112:7
CHAPTER 2
1 *h* Prov. 4:21; 7:1
5 *i* Jas. 1:5
6 *j* 1 Ki. 3:12; Job 32:8
7 *k* Ps. 84:11; Prov. 30:5
14 *l* Prov. 10:23; Jer. 11:15; Rom. 1:32

*1:21 Septuagint, Syriac, and Targum read *top of the walls;* Vulgate reads *the head of multitudes.*

15 Whose ways *are* crooked,
And *who are* devious in their paths;
16 To deliver you from the [a]immoral woman,
From the seductress *who* flatters with her words,
17 Who forsakes the companion of her youth,
And forgets the covenant of her God.
18 For her house leads down to death,
And her paths to the dead;
19 None who go to her return,
Nor do they regain the paths of life—
20 So you may walk in the way of goodness,
And keep *to* the paths of righteousness.
21 For the upright will dwell in the [b]land,
And the [c]blameless will remain in it;
22 But the wicked will be cut off from the earth,
And the unfaithful will be uprooted from it.

The rewards of wisdom

3 MY son, do not forget my law,
But let your heart keep my commands;
2 For length of days and [d]long life
And peace they will add to you.
3 Let not mercy and truth forsake you;
[e]Bind them around your neck,
[f]Write them on the tablet of your heart,
4 *And* so find favor and high esteem
In the sight of God and [g]man.

5 [h]Trust in the LORD with all your heart,
And [i]lean not on your own understanding;
6 [j]In all your ways acknowledge Him,
And He shall direct* your paths.

7 Do not be wise in your own [k]eyes;
[l]Fear the LORD and depart from evil.
8 It will be [m]health to your flesh,*
And strength* to your bones.

16
a Prov. 6:24; 7:5
21
b Ps. 37:3
c See Phil. 3:12, *note*
CHAPTER 3
2
d Prov. 4:10
3
e Prov. 6:21; cp. Ex. 13:9; Dt. 6:8; Prov. 7:3
f Cp. Jer. 17:1; 2 Cor. 3:3
4
g 1 Sam. 2:26; Lk. 2:52
5
h Ps. 37:3,5; see Ps. 2:12, *note*
i Jer. 9:23
6
j 1 Chr. 28:9
7
k Rom. 12:16
l See Ps. 19:9, *note*
8
m Lit. *medicine*
9
n Ex. 22:29; 23:19; 34:26; Dt. 26:2; Mal. 3:10
10
o Dt. 28:8
11
p Job 5:17; Ps. 94:12; Heb. 12:5–6; Rev. 3:19
15
q Job 28:18
16
r Prov. 8:18; cp. 1 Tim. 4:8
18
s Prov. 11:30; 13:12; 15:4; cp. Gen. 2:9; 3:22,24; Rev. 22:2
19
t Ps. 136:5; Prov. 8:27
20
u Gen. 7:11
23
v Ps. 37:24; 91:11–12; Prov. 10:9

9 [n]Honor the LORD with your possessions,
And with the firstfruits of all your increase;
10 [o]So your barns will be filled with plenty,
And your vats will overflow with new wine.

11 [p]My son, do not despise the chastening of the LORD,
Nor detest His correction;
12 For whom the LORD loves He corrects,
Just as a father the son *in whom* he delights.

13 Happy *is* the man *who* finds wisdom,
And the man *who* gains understanding;
14 For her proceeds *are* better than the profits of silver,
And her gain than fine gold.
15 [q]She *is* more precious than rubies,
And all the things you may desire cannot compare with her.
16 Length of days *is* in her right hand,
[r]In her left hand riches and honor.
17 Her ways *are* ways of pleasantness,
And all her paths *are* peace.
18 She *is* a [s]tree of life to those who take hold of her,
And happy *are all* who retain her.

19 The LORD by [t]wisdom founded the earth;
By understanding He established the heavens;
20 By His knowledge the depths were [u]broken up,
And clouds drop down the dew.

21 My son, let them not depart from your eyes—
Keep sound wisdom and discretion;
22 So they will be life to your soul
And grace to your neck.
23 [v]Then you will walk safely in your way,
And your foot will not stumble.

*

3:6 Or *make smooth* or *straight* 3:8 Literally *navel,* figurative of the body • Literally *drink* or *refreshment*

24 When you lie down, you will
not be [a]afraid;
Yes, you will lie down and
your sleep will be sweet.
25 Do not be afraid of sudden
terror,
Nor of trouble from the wicked
when it comes;
26 For the LORD will be your
confidence,
And will keep your foot from
being caught.

27 [b]Do not withhold good from
those to whom it is due,
When it is in the power of
your hand to do *so.*
28 [c]Do not say to your neighbor,
"Go, and come back,
And tomorrow I will give *it,*"
When *you have* it with you.
29 Do not devise evil against your
neighbor,
For he dwells by you for
safety's sake.
30 [d]Do not strive with a man
without cause,
If he has done you no harm.

31 [e]Do not envy the [f]oppressor,
And choose none of his ways;
32 For the perverse *person is* an
abomination to the LORD,
[g]But His secret counsel *is* with
the upright.
33 The curse of the LORD *is* on the
house of the wicked,
But He blesses the home of the
just.
34 Surely He scorns the scornful,
But gives [h]grace to the
humble.
35 The wise shall inherit [i]glory,
But shame shall be the legacy
of fools.

Fatherly advice

4 HEAR, [j]*my* children, the
instruction of a father,
And give attention to know
understanding;
2 For I give you good doctrine:
Do not forsake my law.
3 When I was my father's son,
[k]Tender and the only one in the
sight of my mother,
4 [l]He also taught me, and said to
me:
"Let your heart retain my
words;
Keep my commands, and live.
5 Get wisdom! Get
understanding!
Do not forget, nor turn away
from the words of my
mouth.
6 Do not forsake her, and she
will preserve you;
[m]Love her, and she will keep
you.
7 [n]Wisdom *is* the principal thing;
Therefore get wisdom.
And in all your getting, get
understanding.
8 [o]Exalt her, and she will
promote you;
She will bring you honor,
when you embrace her.
9 She will place on your head an
ornament of grace;
A crown of glory she will
deliver to you."
10 Hear, my son, and receive my
sayings,
And the years of your life will
be many.
11 I have [p]taught you in the way
of wisdom;
I have led you in right paths.
12 When you walk, your steps
will not be hindered,
And when you run, you will
not stumble.
13 Take firm hold of instruction,
do not let go;
Keep her, for she *is* your [q]life.

14 Do not enter the path of the
wicked,
And do not walk in the way of
evil.
15 Avoid it, do not travel on it;
Turn away from it and pass
on.
16 For they do not sleep unless
they have done evil;
And their sleep is taken away
unless they make *someone*
fall.
17 For they eat the bread of
wickedness,
And drink the wine of
violence.
18 [r]But the path of the just [s]*is* like
the shining sun,*
That shines ever brighter unto
the perfect day.
19 The [t]way of the wicked *is* like
darkness;
They do not know what makes
them stumble.

20 My son, give attention to my
words;
Incline your ear to my sayings.

24 *a* Cp. Prov. 1:33
27 *b* Rom. 13:7; Gal. 6:10
28 *c* Lev. 19:13; Dt. 24:15
30 *d* Rom. 12:18
31 *e* Ps. 37:1; 73:3; Prov. 24:1 *f* Lit. *a man of violence*
32 *g* Ps. 25:14; cp. Gen. 18:17; Dan. 2:19
34 *h* Jas. 4:6; 1 Pet. 5:5
35 *i* Cp. Dan. 12:3
CHAPTER 4
1 *j* Ps. 34:11; Prov. 1:8
3 *k* 1 Chr. 29:1
4 *l* 1 Chr. 28:9; Eph. 6:4
6 *m* 2 Th. 2:10
7 *n* Prov. 3:13–14
8 *o* 1 Sam. 2:30
11 *p* 1 Sam. 12:23
13 *q* Cp. Jn. 6:63
18 *r* Mt. 5:14; Phil. 2:15 *s* 2 Sam. 23:4
19 *t* 1 Sam. 2:9; Job 18:5–6; Isa. 59:9–10; Jer. 23:12; Jn. 12:35

*4:18 Literally *light*

21 Do not let them depart from
your eyes;
Keep them in the midst of your
heart;
22 For they *are* life to those who
find them,
And health to all their flesh.
23 Keep your heart with all
diligence,
For out of it *spring* the issues
of [a]life.
24 Put away from you a deceitful
mouth,
And put perverse lips far from
you.
25 Let your eyes look straight
ahead,
And your eyelids look right
before you.
26 Ponder the path of your [b]feet,
And let all your ways be
established.
27 Do not turn to the right or the
left;
Remove your foot from evil.

Immorality rebuked

5 MY son, pay attention to my
wisdom;
Lend your ear to my
understanding,
2 That you may preserve
discretion,
And your lips [c]may keep
knowledge.
3 For the lips of an [d]immoral
woman drip honey,
And her mouth *is* [e]smoother
than oil;
4 But in the end she is [f]bitter as
wormwood,
Sharp as a two-edged sword.
5 Her feet go down to death,
[g]Her steps lay hold of [h]hell.*
6 Lest you ponder *her* path of
life—
Her ways are unstable;
You do not know *them.*
7 Therefore hear me now, *my*
children,
And do not depart from the
words of my mouth.
8 Remove your way far from
her,
And do not go near the door of
her house,
9 Lest you give your honor to
others,
And your years to the cruel
one;
10 Lest aliens be filled with your
[i]wealth,

23
a Mt. 12:35; 15:18–19
26
b Heb. 12:13
CHAPTER 5
2
c Mal. 2:7
3
d Prov. 2:16
e Ps. 55:21
4
f Cp. Eccl. 7:26
5
g Prov. 7:27
h See Hab. 2:5, *note;* cp. Lk. 16:23, *note*
10
i Lit. *strength*
18
j Dt. 24:5; Eccl. 9:9; Mal. 2:14
19
k Song 2:9; 4:5; 7:3
l Lit. *be filled*
21
m 2 Chr. 16:9; Job 31:4; 34:21; Prov. 15:3; Jer. 16:17; 32:19; Hos. 7:2; Heb. 4:13
22
n Cp. Jn. 8:34; Rom. 6:16; 2 Pet. 2:19
o Num. 32:23; Prov. 1:31; Isa. 3:11
CHAPTER 6
1
p Prov. 11:15

And your labors *go* to the
house of a foreigner;
11 And you mourn at last,
When your flesh and your
body are consumed,
12 And say:
"How I have hated instruction,
And my heart despised
correction!
13 I have not obeyed the voice of
my teachers,
Nor inclined my ear to those
who instructed me!
14 I was on the verge of total
ruin,
In the midst of the assembly
and congregation."
15 Drink water from your own
cistern,
And running water from your
own well.
16 Should your fountains be
dispersed abroad,
Streams of water in the
streets?
17 Let them be only your own,
And not for strangers with
you.
18 Let your fountain be blessed,
And rejoice [j]with the wife of
your youth.
19 [k]*As a* loving deer and a
graceful doe,
Let her breasts satisfy you at
all times;
And always be [l]enraptured
with her love.
20 For why should you, my son,
be enraptured by an
immoral woman,
And be embraced in the arms
of a seductress?
21 [m]For the ways of man *are*
before the eyes of the LORD,
And He ponders all his paths.
22 His own iniquities entrap the
wicked *man,*
And he is [n]caught in the cords
of his [o]sin.
23 He shall die for lack of
instruction,
And in the greatness of his
folly he shall go astray.

Parental warnings

6 MY son, if you become [p]surety
for your friend,
If you have shaken hands in
pledge for a stranger,

*
5:5 Or *Sheol*

2 You are snared by the words
of your mouth;
You are taken by the words of
your mouth.
3 So do this, my son, and deliver
yourself;
For you have come into the
hand of your friend:
Go and humble yourself;
Plead with your friend.
4 Give no sleep to your eyes,
Nor slumber to your eyelids.
5 Deliver yourself like a gazelle
from the hand *of the hunter*,
And like a bird from the hand
of the fowler.*

6 [a]Go to the ant, you sluggard!
Consider her ways and be
wise,
7 Which, having no captain,
Overseer or ruler,
8 Provides her supplies in the
summer,
And gathers her food in the
harvest.
9 [b]How long will you slumber, O
sluggard?
When will you rise from your
sleep?
10 A little sleep, a little slumber,
A little folding of the hands to
sleep—
11 [c]So shall your poverty come on
you like a prowler,
And your need like an armed
man.

12 A worthless person, a wicked
man,
Walks with a perverse mouth;
13 He winks with his eyes,
He shuffles his feet,
He points with his fingers;
14 Perversity *is* in his heart,
He devises evil continually,
He sows discord.
15 Therefore his calamity shall
come [d]suddenly;
Suddenly he shall be broken
without [e]remedy.

16 These six *things* the LORD
hates,
Yes, seven *are* an abomination
to Him:
17 A [f]proud look,
A [g]lying tongue,
[h]Hands that shed innocent
blood,
18 A [i]heart that devises wicked
plans,
[j]Feet that are swift in running
to evil,
19 A [k]false witness *who* speaks
lies,
And one who [l]sows discord
among brethren.

20 My son, keep your father's
command,
And do not forsake the law of
your mother.
21 Bind them continually upon
your heart;
Tie them around your neck.
22 When you roam, they* will
lead you;
When you sleep, they will keep
you;
And *when* you awake, they
will speak with you.
23 [m]For the commandment *is* a
lamp,
And the law a light;
Reproofs of instruction *are* the
way of life,
24 To keep you from the [n]evil
woman,
From the flattering tongue of a
seductress.
25 [o]Do not lust after her beauty in
your heart,
Nor let her allure you with her
[p]eyelids.
26 For by means of a harlot
A man is reduced to a crust of
bread;
And an adulteress* will [q]prey
upon his precious life.
27 Can a man take fire to his
bosom,
And his clothes not be burned?
28 Can one walk on hot coals,
And his feet not be seared?
29 So *is* he who goes in to his
neighbor's wife;
Whoever touches her shall not
be innocent.
30 *People* do not despise a thief
If he steals to satisfy himself
when he is starving.
31 Yet *when* he is found, he must
[r]restore sevenfold;
He may have to give up all the
substance of his house.
32 Whoever commits adultery
with a woman lacks
understanding;
He *who* does so destroys his
own soul.
33 Wounds and dishonor he will
get,

6
a Job 12:7
9
b Prov. 24:33–34
11
c Prov. 10:4; 13:4; 20:4
15
d Prov. 24:22; Isa. 30:13; 1 Th. 5:3
e 2 Chr. 36:16
17
f Ps. 101:5; Prov. 21:4; cp. Ezek. 28:1–19
g Ps. 120:2–3; cp. Acts 5:1–10
h Isa. 1:15; cp. 2 Ki. 21:10–16
18
i Ps. 36:4; cp. Jer. 18:18; Mk. 14:1,43–46
j Isa. 59:7; cp. 2 Ki. 5:20–27
19
k Ps. 27:12; Prov. 19:5, 9; Mt. 26:59–66
l Prov. 6:14; cp. 1 Cor. 1:11–13; Jude 3–4, 16–19
23
m Ps. 19:8; 119:105; 2 Pet. 1:19
24
n Prov. 2:16
25
o Mt. 5:28
p Cp. 2 Ki. 9:30
26
q Ezek. 13:18
31
r Ex. 22:1,4

*
6:5 That is, one who catches birds in a trap or snare
6:22 Literally *it*
6:26 Literally *a man's wife*, that is, of another

And his reproach will not be
wiped away.
34 For [a]jealousy *is* a husband's
fury;
Therefore he will not spare in
the day of vengeance.
35 He will accept no recompense,
Nor will he be appeased
though you give many gifts.

The snare of unchastity

7 MY son, keep my words,
And treasure my commands
within you.
2 [b]Keep my commands and live,
And my law as the apple of
your eye.
3 [c]Bind them on your fingers;
Write them on the tablet of
your heart.
4 Say to wisdom, "You *are* my
sister,"
And call understanding *your*
nearest kin,
5 That they may keep you from
the immoral woman,
From the [d]seductress *who*
flatters with her words.
6 For at the window of my house
I looked through my lattice,
7 And saw among the simple,
I perceived among the youths,
A young man devoid of
understanding,
8 Passing along the street near
her corner;
And he took the path to her
house
9 [e]In the twilight, in the evening,
In the black and dark night.
10 And there a woman met him,
With the [f]attire of a harlot,
and a crafty heart.
11 She *was* [g]loud and rebellious,
Her feet would not stay at
home.
12 At times *she was* outside, at
times in the open square,
Lurking at every corner.
13 So she caught him and kissed
him;
With an impudent face she
said to him:
14 "*I have* peace offerings with me;
Today I have paid my vows.
15 So I came out to meet you,
Diligently to seek your face,
And I have found you.
16 I have spread my bed with
tapestry,
Colored coverings of Egyptian
linen.
17 I have perfumed my bed
With myrrh, aloes, and
cinnamon.
18 Come, let us take our fill of
love until morning;
Let us delight ourselves with
love.
19 For my husband *is* not at
home;
He has gone on a long
journey;
20 He has taken a bag of money
with him,
And will come home on the
appointed day."
21 With her enticing speech she
caused him to yield,
[h]With her flattering lips she
seduced him.
22 [i]Immediately he went after her,
as an ox goes to the
slaughter,
Or as a fool to the correction
of the stocks,*
23 Till an arrow struck his liver.
As a bird hastens to the snare,
He did not know it *would cost*
his life.
24 Now therefore, listen to me,
my children;
Pay attention to the words of
my mouth:
25 Do not let your heart turn
aside to her ways,
Do not stray into her paths;
26 For she has cast down many
wounded,
And all who were slain by her
were [j]strong *men.*
27 Her house *is* the way to [k]hell,*
Descending to the chambers of
[l]death.

In praise of wisdom

8 DOES not wisdom cry out,
And understanding lift up her
voice?
2 She takes her stand on the top
of the high hill,
Beside the way, where the
paths meet.
3 She cries out by the gates, at
the entry of the city,
At the entrance of the doors:
4 "To you, O men, I call,
And my voice *is* to the sons of
men.
5 O you simple ones, understand
prudence,

34 *a* Song 8:6
CHAPTER 7
2 *b* Lev. 18:5; Prov. 4:4; Isa. 55:3
3 *c* Dt. 6:8
5 *d* Prov. 2:16; 6:24
9 *e* Job 24:15
10 *f* Cp. Gen. 38:14–15
11 *g* Prov. 9:13
21 *h* Ps. 12:2
22 *i* Lit. *suddenly*
26 *j* Neh. 13:26; cp. Jud. 16:19–20
27 *k* See Hab. 2:5, *note;* cp. Lk. 16:23, *note*
l Prov. 9:18

*
7:22 Septuagint, Syriac, and Targum read *as a dog to bonds;* Vulgate reads *as a lamb . . . to bonds.*
7:27 Or *Sheol*

And you fools, be of an
understanding heart.
6 Listen, for I will speak of
excellent things,
And from the opening of my
lips *will come* right things;
7 For my mouth will speak truth;
Wickedness *is* an abomination
to my lips.
8 All the words of my mouth *are*
with righteousness;
Nothing crooked or perverse *is*
in them.
9 They *are* all plain to him who
understands,
And right to those who find
knowledge.
10 Receive my instruction, and
not silver,
And knowledge rather than
choice gold;
11 [a]For wisdom *is* better than
rubies,
And all the things one may
desire cannot be compared
with her.

12 "I, wisdom, dwell with
prudence,
And find out knowledge *and*
discretion.
13 The [b]fear of the LORD *is* to
hate evil;
[c]Pride and arrogance and the
evil way
And the perverse mouth I hate.
14 Counsel *is* mine, and sound
wisdom;
I *am* understanding, I have
strength.
15 [d]By me kings reign,
And rulers decree justice.
16 By me princes rule, and
nobles,
All the judges of the earth.*
17 I [e]love those who love me,
And [f]those who seek me
diligently will find me.
18 Riches and honor *are* with me,
Enduring riches and
righteousness.
19 My fruit *is* better than gold,
yes, than fine gold,
And my revenue than choice
silver.
20 I traverse the way of
righteousness,
In the midst of the paths of
justice,
21 That I may cause those who
love me to inherit wealth,
That I may fill their treasuries.

22 "The [g]LORD possessed [1]me at
the beginning of His way,
Before His works of old.
23 [h]I have been established from
everlasting,
From the beginning, before
there was ever an earth.
24 When *there were* no depths I
was brought forth,
When *there were* no fountains
abounding with water.
25 [i]Before the mountains were
settled,
Before the hills, I was brought
forth;
26 While as yet He had not made
the earth or the fields,
Or the primal dust of the
world.
27 When He prepared the
heavens, I *was* there,
When He drew a circle on the
face of the deep,
28 When He established the
clouds above,
When He strengthened the
fountains of the deep,
29 [j]When He assigned to the sea
its limit,
So that the waters would not
transgress His command,
[k]When He marked out the
foundations of the earth,
30 [l]Then I was beside Him *as* a
master craftsman;*
[m]And I was daily *His* delight,
Rejoicing always before Him,
31 Rejoicing in His inhabited
world,
And [n]my delight *was* with the
sons of men.

32 "Now therefore, listen to me,
my children,

CHAPTER 8
11
a Job 28:18; Ps. 19:10; 119:127; Prov. 3:15
13
b See Ps. 19:9, *note*
c Prov. 6:17; 16:5
15
d Dan. 2:21; Rom. 13:1
17
e 1 Sam. 2:30; Ps. 91:14; Jn. 14:21
f Jas. 1:5
22
g Prov. 3:19; Jn. 1:1
23
h Cp. Ps. 2:6; Jn. 17:5
25
i Job 15:7–8
29
j Gen. 1:9–10; Job 38:8–11; Ps. 33:7; 104:9; Jer. 5:22
k Job 38:4
30
l Jn. 1:1,2, 18
m Cp. Mt. 3:17; Jn. 8:29
31
n Ps. 16:3

*8:16 Masoretic Text, Syriac, Targum, and Vulgate read *righteousness;* Bomberg, Septuagint, and some manuscripts and editions read *earth.* 8:30 A Jewish tradition reads *one brought up.*

[1](8:22) Many have seen in portions of vv. 22–36 distinct descriptions of Christ. Thus wisdom is more than the personification of an attribute of God, or of the will of God as best for man. Of course, in no sense could it be said of Christ that he was "brought forth" (vv. 24 and 25). Yet the ascription of eternality (v. 23) and presence at and participation in creation are certainly true of Him. Such statements, when read along with Jn. 1:1–3; 1 Cor. 1:23; Col. 2:3, can refer to no one less than the eternal Son of God. See Ps. 110:1, *note;* Jn. 20:28, *note.*

For [a]blessed *are those who* keep my ways.
33 Hear instruction and be wise,
And do not disdain *it*.
34 Blessed is the man who listens to me,
Watching daily at my gates,
Waiting at the posts of my doors.
35 For whoever finds me finds [b]life,
And obtains favor from the LORD;
36 But he who sins against me wrongs his own soul;
All those who hate me love death."

Eternal wisdom praised

9 WISDOM has [c]built her house,
She has hewn out her seven pillars;
2 She has slaughtered her meat,
She has mixed her wine,
She has also furnished her table.
3 She has sent out her maidens,
She cries out from the highest places of the city,
4 "Whoever *is* simple, let him turn in here!"
As for him who lacks understanding, she says to him,
5 "Come, eat of my bread
And drink of the wine I have mixed.
6 Forsake foolishness and live,
And go in the way of understanding.
7 "He who corrects a scoffer gets shame for himself,
And he who rebukes a wicked *man only* harms himself.
8 [d]Do not correct a scoffer, lest he hate you;
[e]Rebuke a wise *man,* and he will love you.
9 Give *instruction* to a wise *man,* and he will be still wiser;
Teach a just *man,* and he will [f]increase in learning.
10 "The [g]fear of the LORD *is* the beginning of wisdom,
And the knowledge of the Holy One *is* understanding.
11 For by me your days will be multiplied,
And years of life will be added to you.
12 If you are wise, you are wise for yourself,
And *if* you scoff, you will bear *it* alone."
13 A foolish woman is [h]clamorous;
She is simple, and knows nothing.
14 For she sits at the door of her house,
On a seat *by* the highest places of the city,
15 To call to those who pass by,
Who go straight on their way:
16 "Whoever *is* simple, let him turn in here";
And *as for* him who lacks understanding, she says to him,
17 [i]"Stolen water is sweet,
And bread *eaten* in secret is pleasant."
18 But he does not know that the [j]dead *are* there,
That her guests *are* in the depths of [k]hell.*

II. Wisdom and the Fear of God as Contrasted with Folly and Sin, 10—24

10 THE proverbs of [1][l]Solomon:
A [m]wise son makes a glad father,
But a [n]foolish son *is* the grief of his mother.
2 Treasures of wickedness profit nothing,
But righteousness delivers from death.
3 The [o]LORD will not allow the righteous soul to famish,
But He casts away the desire of the wicked.
4 He who has a slack hand becomes poor,
[p]But the hand of the diligent makes rich.
5 He who gathers in [q]summer *is* a wise son;
He who sleeps in harvest *is* a son who causes shame.
6 Blessings *are* on the head of the righteous,

32 *a* Ps. 119:1–2; 128:1–2; Lk. 11:28
35 *b* Jn. 17:3
CHAPTER 9
1 *c* Mt. 16:18; Eph. 2:20–22; 1 Pet. 2:5
8 *d* Mt. 7:6 *e* Ps. 141:5
9 *f* Cp. Mt. 25:29
10 *g* See Ps. 19:9, *note*
13 *h* Prov. 7:11
17 *i* Prov. 20:17
18 *j* Prov. 2:18; 7:27 *k* See Hab. 2:5, *note;* cp. Lk. 16:23, *note*
CHAPTER 10
1 *l* Prov. 1:1; 25:1 *m* Prov. 15:20; 17:21,25; 19:13; 29:3,15 *n* See Prov. 1:7, *note*
3 *o* Ps. 10:14; 34:9–10; 37:25
4 *p* Prov. 12:24; 13:4; 21:5
5 *q* Prov. 6:8

* 9:18 Or *Sheol*

[1](10:1) Chapters 1—9; 22:17—24:34 contain connected poems; 10:1—22:16; 25—29, unrelated verses.

[a]But violence covers the mouth
of the wicked.
7 The [b]memory of the righteous
is blessed,
But the name of the wicked
will rot.
8 The wise in heart will receive
commands,
But a prating fool will fall.
9 He who walks with integrity
walks securely,
But he who perverts his ways
will become known.
10 He who winks with the eye
causes trouble,
But a prating fool will fall.
11 The mouth of the righteous *is* a
well of life,
But violence covers the mouth
of the wicked.
12 Hatred stirs up strife,
But [c]love covers all sins.
13 Wisdom is found on the lips of
him who has understanding,
But a rod *is* for the back of
him who is devoid of
understanding.
14 Wise *people* store up
knowledge,
But the mouth of the foolish *is*
near destruction.
15 The [d]rich man's wealth *is* his
strong city;
The destruction of the poor *is*
their poverty.
16 The labor of the righteous
leads to [e]life,
The wages of the wicked to
sin.
17 He who keeps instruction *is in*
the way of life,
But he who refuses correction
goes astray.
18 Whoever [f]hides hatred *has*
lying lips,
And whoever spreads [g]slander
is a fool.
19 In the multitude of words sin is
not lacking,
But he who restrains his lips *is*
wise.
20 The tongue of the righteous *is*
choice silver;
The heart of the wicked *is*
worth little.
21 The lips of the righteous feed
many,

6
a v. 11; cp. Est. 7:8
7
b Ps. 112:6; Eccl. 8:10
12
c 1 Pet. 4:8
15
d Job 31:24; Ps. 52:7; Prov. 18:11; 1 Tim. 6:17
16
e Prov. 6:23
18
f Prov. 26:24
g Ps. 101:5
22
h Ps. 37:22; cp. Gen. 24:35; 26:12; 2 Chr. 9:13–28
23
i Prov. 2:14
24
j Ps. 145:19; Mt. 5:6; 1 Jn. 5:14–15
25
k v. 30; Ps. 15:5; Prov. 12:3; Mt. 7:24–25
27
l See Ps. 19:9, *note*
30
m Ps. 37:22, 29; 125:1
31
n Ps. 37:30
CHAPTER 11
1
o Lev. 19:35–36; Dt. 25:13–16; Prov. 16:11; 20:10,23
2
p Prov. 16:18; 18:12; 29:23
3
q Prov. 13:6

But fools die for lack of
wisdom.*
22 The [h]blessing of the LORD
makes *one* rich,
And He adds no sorrow with
it.
23 To do evil *is* like [i]sport to a
fool,
But a man of understanding
has wisdom.
24 The fear of the wicked will
come upon him,
[j]And the desire of the righteous
will be granted.
25 When the whirlwind passes by,
the wicked *is* no *more,*
[k]But the righteous *has* an
everlasting foundation.
26 As vinegar to the teeth and
smoke to the eyes,
So *is* the lazy *man* to those
who send him.
27 The [l]fear of the LORD prolongs
days,
But the years of the wicked
will be shortened.
28 The hope of the righteous *will*
be gladness,
But the expectation of the
wicked will perish.
29 The way of the LORD *is*
strength for the upright,
But destruction *will come* to
the workers of iniquity.
30 The [m]righteous will never be
removed,
But the wicked will not inhabit
the earth.
31 The mouth of the righteous
brings forth [n]wisdom,
But the perverse tongue will be
cut out.
32 The lips of the righteous know
what is acceptable,
But the mouth of the wicked
what is perverse.

Contrast: righteousness and wickedness

11 [o]DISHONEST scales *are* an
abomination to the LORD,
But a just weight *is* His delight.
2 When pride comes, then comes
[p]shame;
But with the humble *is*
wisdom.
3 The integrity of the upright
will guide [q]them,

* **10:21** Literally *heart*

But the perversity of the
unfaithful will destroy them.
4 [a]Riches do not profit in the day
of wrath,
But righteousness delivers
from death.
5 The righteousness of the
[b]blameless will direct* his
way aright,
But the wicked will fall by his
own [c]wickedness.
6 The righteousness of the
upright will deliver them,
But the unfaithful will be
caught by *their* lust.

7 When a wicked man dies, *his*
expectation will [d]perish,
And the hope of the unjust
perishes.
8 The righteous is delivered from
trouble,
And it comes to the wicked
instead.
9 The hypocrite with *his* mouth
destroys his neighbor,
But through knowledge the
righteous will be delivered.
10 When it goes well with the
righteous, the city [e]rejoices;
And when the wicked perish,
there is jubilation.
11 By the blessing of the upright
the city is [f]exalted,
But it is overthrown by the
mouth of the wicked.

12 He who is devoid of wisdom
despises his neighbor,
But a man of understanding
holds his peace.
13 A talebearer reveals secrets,
But he who is of a faithful
spirit [g]conceals a matter.
14 Where *there is* no counsel, the
people fall;
But in the multitude of
counselors *there is* safety.

15 He who is [h]surety for a
stranger will suffer,
But one who hates being
surety is secure.

16 A gracious woman retains
honor,
But ruthless *men* retain riches.
17 The merciful man does good
for his own soul,
But *he who is* cruel troubles
his own flesh.
18 The wicked *man* does
deceptive work,
But he [i]who sows
righteousness *will have* a
sure reward.
19 As righteousness *leads* to [j]life,
So he who pursues evil
pursues it to his own [k]death.
20 Those who are of a perverse
heart *are* an abomination to
the LORD,
But *the* blameless in their
ways *are* His delight.
21 *Though they join* forces,* the
wicked will not go
unpunished;
But the [l]posterity of the
righteous will be delivered.

22 *As* a ring of gold in a swine's
snout,
So is a lovely woman who
lacks discretion.

23 The desire of the righteous *is*
only good,
But the expectation of the
wicked *is* [m]wrath.

24 There is *one* who scatters, yet
[n]increases more;
And there is *one* who
withholds more than is right,
But it *leads* to poverty.
25 The [o]generous soul will be
made rich,
And he who waters will also
be watered himself.
26 The people will curse [p]him
who withholds grain,
But blessing *will be* on the
head of him who sells *it*.

27 He who earnestly seeks good
finds favor,
But trouble will come to him
who seeks *evil*.

28 He who [q]trusts in his riches
will [r]fall,
But the [s]righteous will flourish
like foliage.

29 He who troubles his own
house will inherit the wind,
And the fool *will be* [t]servant
to the wise of heart.

30 The fruit of the righteous *is a*
tree of life,
And he who [u]wins souls *is*
wise.

31 If the righteous will be
recompensed on the earth,
[v]How much more the ungodly
and the sinner.

4 *a* Prov. 10:2; Ezek. 7:19; Zeph. 1:18
5 *b* See Phil. 3:12, *note* *c* Prov. 5:22
7 *d* Prov. 10:28
10 *e* Prov. 28:12
11 *f* Prov. 14:34
13 *g* Prov. 19:11
15 *h* Prov. 6:1–2
18 *i* Hos. 10:12; Gal. 6:8–9; Jas. 3:18
19 *j* Prov. 10:16; 12:28 *k* Rom. 6:23
21 *l* Ps. 112:2; Prov. 14:26
23 *m* Rom. 2:8–9
24 *n* Prov. 13:7; 19:17
25 *o* 2 Cor. 9:6–10
26 *p* Cp. Amos 8:5–6
28 *q* See Ps. 2:12, *note* *r* 1 Tim. 6:17 *s* Ps. 1:3; 52:8; 92:12; Jer. 17:8
29 *t* Prov. 14:19
30 *u* Dan. 12:3; 1 Cor. 9:19; Jas. 5:20
31 *v* Cp. 1 Pet. 4:18

* 11:5 Or *make smooth* or *straight* 11:21 Literally *hand in hand*

Contrast: righteousness and wickedness

12 WHOEVER loves instruction loves knowledge,
But he who hates correction *is* stupid.

2 A good *man* obtains favor from the LORD,
But a man of wicked intentions He will condemn.

3 A man is not established by wickedness,
But the root of the righteous cannot be [a]moved.

4 An [b]excellent* wife *is* the crown of her husband,
But she who causes shame *is* like rottenness in his bones.

5 The thoughts of the righteous *are* right,
But the counsels of the wicked *are* deceitful.

6 The words of the wicked *are*, "Lie in wait for blood,"
But the mouth of the upright will deliver them.

7 The [c]wicked are overthrown and *are* no more,
But the house of the righteous will stand.

8 A man will be commended according to his wisdom,
But he who is of a perverse heart will be [d]despised.

9 Better *is the one* who is slighted but has a servant,
Than he who honors himself but lacks bread.

10 A [e]righteous *man* regards the life of his animal,
But the tender mercies of the wicked *are* cruel.

11 He who [f]tills his land will be satisfied with [g]bread,
But he who follows frivolity *is* devoid of understanding.*

12 The wicked covet the catch of evil *men*,
But the root of the righteous yields *fruit*.

13 The wicked is ensnared by the transgression of *his* lips,
But the righteous will come through [h]trouble.

14 A man will be satisfied with good by the fruit of *his* mouth,
And the recompense of a man's hands will be [i]rendered to him.

15 The [j]way of a fool *is* right in his own eyes,
But he who heeds counsel *is* wise.

16 A fool's wrath is known at once,
But a prudent *man* [k]covers shame.

17 He *who* speaks truth declares righteousness,
But a false witness, deceit.

18 There is one who speaks like the piercings of a sword,
But the tongue of the wise *promotes* [l]health.

19 The truthful lip shall be established forever,
But a [m]lying tongue *is* but for a moment.

20 Deceit is in the heart of those who devise evil,
But counselors of peace have joy.

21 No [n]grave trouble will overtake the righteous,
But the wicked shall be filled with evil.

22 [o]Lying lips *are* an abomination to the LORD,
But those who deal truthfully *are* His delight.

23 A prudent man conceals knowledge,
But the heart of fools proclaims [p]foolishness.

24 The [q]hand of the diligent will rule,
But the lazy *man* will be put to forced labor.

25 [r]Anxiety in the heart of man causes depression,
But a good [s]word makes it glad.

26 The righteous should choose his friends carefully,
For the way of the wicked leads them astray.

27 The lazy *man* does not roast what he took in hunting,
But diligence *is* man's precious possession.

28 In the way of righteousness *is* life,
And in *its* pathway *there is* no death.

CHAPTER 12
3 *a* Prov. 10:25
4 *b* Prov. 31:23; 1 Cor. 11:7
7 *c* Ps. 37:35–37; Prov. 11:21; Mt. 7:24–27
8 *d* Prov. 18:3
10 *e* Dt. 25:4
11 *f* Gen. 3:19 *g* Prov. 28:19
13 *h* 2 Pet. 2:9
14 *i* Isa. 3:10–11
15 *j* Prov. 3:7; cp. Lk. 18:11
16 *k* Prov. 11:13
18 *l* Prov. 15:4
19 *m* Ps. 52:4–5; Prov. 19:9
21 *n* Ps. 91:10; 1 Pet. 3:13
22 *o* Prov. 6:17; 11:20; Rev. 22:15
23 *p* Prov. 13:16
24 *q* Prov. 10:4
25 *r* Prov. 15:13 *s* Isa. 50:4

* **12:4** Literally *A wife of valor* **12:11** Literally *heart*

Contrast: righteousness and wickedness

13 A WISE son *heeds* his father's
instruction,
But a [a]scoffer does not listen
to rebuke.
2 A man shall eat well by the
fruit of *his* [b]mouth,
But the soul of the unfaithful
feeds on violence.
3 He who guards his mouth
preserves his life,
But he who opens wide his lips
shall have [c]destruction.
4 The [d]soul of a lazy *man*
desires, and *has* nothing;
But the soul of the diligent
shall be made rich.
5 A righteous *man* hates lying,
But a wicked *man* is loathsome
and comes to shame.
6 [e]Righteousness guards *him*
whose way is blameless,
But wickedness overthrows the
sinner.
7 [f]There is one who makes
himself rich, yet *has*
nothing;
And one who makes himself
poor, yet *has* great riches.
8 The ransom of a man's life *is*
his riches,
But the poor does not hear
rebuke.
9 The light of the righteous
rejoices,
[g]But the lamp of the wicked
will be put out.
10 By pride comes nothing but
[h]strife,
But with the well-advised *is*
wisdom.
11 Wealth *gained by* dishonesty
will be [i]diminished,
But he who gathers [j]by labor
will increase.
12 Hope deferred makes the heart
sick,
But *when* the desire comes, *it*
is a tree of life.
13 He who despises the word will
be [k]destroyed,
But he who fears the
commandment will be
rewarded.
14 The law of the wise *is* a
fountain of life,
To turn *one* away from the
snares of [l]death.
15 Good understanding gains
[m]favor,
But the way of the unfaithful *is*
hard.
16 Every prudent *man* acts with
knowledge,
But a fool [n]lays open *his*
[o]folly.
17 A wicked messenger falls into
trouble,
But a faithful ambassador
brings [p]health.
18 Poverty and shame *will come*
to him who disdains
correction,
But he who regards a rebuke
will be honored.
19 A desire accomplished is sweet
to the soul,
But *it is* an abomination to
fools to depart from evil.
20 He who walks with wise *men*
will be wise,
But the companion of fools will
be destroyed.
21 Evil pursues sinners,
But to the righteous, good shall
be repaid.
22 A good *man* leaves an
inheritance to his children's
children,
But the [q]wealth of the sinner
is stored up for the
righteous.
23 Much food *is in* the fallow
ground of the poor,
And for lack of justice there is
waste.*
24 He who [r]spares his rod hates
his son,
But he who loves him
disciplines him promptly.
25 The righteous eats to the
satisfying of his soul,
But the stomach of the wicked
shall be in want.

Contrast: righteousness and wickedness

14 THE wise woman builds her
house,
But the foolish pulls it down
with her hands.
2 He who walks in his
uprightness fears the LORD,
But *he who is* perverse in his
ways despises Him.

CHAPTER 13
1 a Cp. 1 Sam. 2:25
2 b Prov. 12:14
3 c Ps. 39:1; Prov. 21:23
4 d Prov. 10:4
6 e Prov. 11:3–6
7 f Prov. 11:24; 12:9
9 g Job 18:5–6; 21:17; Prov. 24:20
10 h Prov. 10:12
11 i Prov. 21:6
j Lit. *with the hand*
13 k Num. 15:31; Isa. 5:24
14 l Prov. 14:27
15 m Prov. 3:4
16 n Lit. *spreads*
o Prov. 12:23; 14:33
17 p Prov. 25:13
22 q Job 27:16–17; Prov. 28:8; Eccl. 2:26
24 r Prov. 19:18; 22:15; 23:13; 29:15,17

* 13:23 Literally *what is swept away*

3 In the mouth of a fool *is* a rod
of pride,
But the lips of the wise will
preserve them.
4 Where no oxen *are*, the trough
is clean;
But much increase *comes* by
the strength of an ox.
5 A [a]faithful witness does not
lie,
But a false witness will utter
[b]lies.
6 A scoffer seeks wisdom and
does not *find it*,
But knowledge *is* [c]easy to him
who understands.
7 Go from the presence of a
foolish man,
When you do not perceive *in
him* the lips of [d]knowledge.
8 The wisdom of the prudent *is*
to understand his way,
But the folly of fools *is* deceit.
9 [e]Fools mock at [f]sin,
But among the upright *there is*
favor.
10 The heart knows its own
bitterness,
And a stranger does not share
its joy.
11 The house of the wicked will
be overthrown,
But the tent of the upright will
[g]flourish.
12 There is a way *that seems*
right to a man,
But its [h]end *is* the way of
[i]death.
13 Even in laughter the heart may
sorrow,
And the end of mirth *may be*
[j]grief.
14 The backslider in heart will be
[k]filled with his own ways,
But a good man *will be
satisfied* from [l]above.*
15 The simple believes every
word,
But the prudent considers well
his steps.
16 A wise *man* fears and departs
from evil,
But a fool rages and is
self-confident.
17 A quick-tempered *man* acts
foolishly,
And a man of wicked
intentions is hated.

CHAPTER 14
5
a Rev. 1:5; 3:14
b Prov. 12:17
6
c Prov. 8:9
7
d Prov. 23:9
9
e Prov. 10:23
f Or *a sin offering*
11
g Prov. 3:33; 12:7; 15:25
12
h Rom. 6:21
i Prov. 12:15; 16:25
13
j Eccl. 2:1–2
14
k Prov. 1:31; 12:14
l Prov. 13:2; 18:20
19
m Cp. 1 Sam. 2:36
20
n Prov. 19:7
o Lit. *many are the lovers of the rich*
p Prov. 19:4
21
q Ps. 112:9; Prov. 19:17
25
r Ezek. 3:18–21
26
s See Ps. 19:9, *note*
27
t Prov. 13:14
29
u Prov. 16:32; Jas. 1:19
31
v Prov. 17:5; Mt. 25:40–45

18 The simple inherit folly,
But the prudent are crowned
with knowledge.
19 The evil will [m]bow before the
good,
And the wicked at the gates of
the righteous.
20 The poor *man* is [n]hated even
by his own neighbor,
[o]But the rich *has* many
[p]friends.
21 He who despises his neighbor
sins;
But he who has mercy on the
[q]poor, happy *is* he.
22 Do they not go astray who
devise evil?
But mercy and truth *belong* to
those who devise good.
23 In all labor there is profit,
But idle chatter* *leads* only to
poverty.
24 The crown of the wise is their
riches,
But the foolishness of fools *is*
folly.
25 A true witness delivers [r]souls,
But a deceitful *witness* speaks
lies.
26 In the [s]fear of the LORD *there
is* strong confidence,
And His children will have a
place of refuge.
27 The [s]fear of the LORD *is* a
[t]fountain of life,
To turn *one* away from the
snares of death.
28 In a multitude of people *is* a
king's honor,
But in the lack of people *is* the
downfall of a prince.
29 [u]*He who is* slow to wrath has
great understanding,
But *he who is* impulsive*
exalts folly.
30 A sound heart *is* life to the
body,
But envy *is* rottenness to the
bones.
31 [v]He who oppresses the poor
reproaches his Maker,
But he who honors Him has
mercy on the needy.
32 The wicked is banished in his
wickedness,

*
14:14 Literally *from above himself* 14:23 Literally *talk of the lips* 14:29 Literally *short of spirit*

But the righteous has a
[a]refuge in his death.

33 Wisdom rests in the heart of
him who has understanding,
But *what is* in the heart of
fools is made known.

34 Righteousness exalts a
[b]nation,
But sin *is* a reproach to *any*
people.

35 The [c]king's favor *is* toward a
wise servant,
But his wrath *is against* him
who causes shame.

Contrast: righteousness and wickedness

15 A [d]SOFT answer turns away
wrath,
[e]But a harsh word stirs up
anger.

2 The tongue of the wise uses
knowledge rightly,
But the mouth of fools pours
forth foolishness.

3 The [f]eyes of the LORD *are* in
every place,
Keeping watch on the evil and
the good.

4 A wholesome tongue *is* a tree
of life,
But perverseness in it breaks
the spirit.

5 A fool despises his father's
instruction,
But he who receives correction
is prudent.

6 *In* the house of the righteous
there is much treasure,
But in the revenue of the
wicked is trouble.

7 The lips of the wise disperse
knowledge,
But the heart of the fool *does*
not *do* so.

8 The [g]sacrifice of the wicked *is*
an abomination to the LORD,
But the prayer of the upright *is*
His delight.

9 The way of the wicked *is* an
abomination to the LORD,
But He loves him who follows
righteousness.

10 Harsh discipline *is* for him
who forsakes the way,
And he who hates correction
will die.

11 [h]Hell* and [i]Destruction *are*
before the LORD;
So how much more the hearts
of the sons of men.

12 A scoffer does not love one
who corrects him,
Nor will he go to the wise.

13 A [j]merry heart makes a
cheerful countenance,
But by sorrow of the heart the
spirit is broken.

14 The heart of him who has
understanding seeks
knowledge,
But the mouth of fools feeds
on foolishness.

15 All the days of the afflicted *are*
evil,
But he who is of a merry heart
has a continual feast.

16 [k]Better *is* a little with the [l]fear
of the LORD,
Than great treasure with
trouble.

17 [m]Better *is* a dinner of herbs*
where love is,
Than a fatted calf with hatred.

18 A wrathful man stirs up strife,
But *he who is* slow to anger
allays contention.

19 The way of the lazy *man is*
like a hedge of thorns,
But the way of the upright *is* a
highway.

20 A wise son makes a father
glad,
But a foolish man despises his
mother.

21 Folly *is* [n]joy *to him who is*
destitute of discernment,
[o]But a man of understanding
walks uprightly.

22 Without counsel, plans go
[p]awry,
But in the multitude of
counselors they are
established.

23 A man has joy by the answer
of his mouth,
And a [q]word *spoken* in due
season, how good *it is!*

24 The [r]way of life *winds* upward
for the wise,
That he may [s]turn away from
[t]hell* below.

32
a Ps. 16:11; 73:24; 2 Tim. 4:18
34
b Prov. 11:11
35
c Mt. 24:45–47
CHAPTER 15
1
d Prov. 25:15; cp. Jud. 8:1–3
e Cp. 1 Sam. 25:10; 1 Ki. 12:13–16
3
f Job 34:21; Prov. 5:21; Jer. 16:17; 32:19; Heb. 4:13
8
g Prov. 21:27; 28:9; Isa. 1:11; 61:8; 66:3; Jer. 6:20; 7:22; Amos 5:22
11
h Job 26:6; Ps. 139:8. see Hab. 2:5, *note;* cp. Lk. 16:23, *note*
i Heb. *Abaddon*
13
j Prov. 17:22
16
k Ps. 37:16; Prov. 16:8; 1 Tim. 6:6
l See Ps. 19:9, *note*
17
m Prov. 17:1
21
n Prov. 10:23
o Eph. 5:15
22
p Prov. 11:14
23
q Prov. 25:11; cp. Isa. 50:4
24
r Phil. 3:20; Col. 3:1–2
s Prov. 14:16
t See Hab. 2:5, *note;* cp. Lk. 16:23, *note*

* 15:11 Or *Sheol* 15:17 Or *vegetables* 15:24 Or *Sheol*

25 The LORD will destroy the
house of the [a]proud,
But He will establish the
boundary of the widow.

26 The thoughts of the wicked *are*
an abomination to the LORD,
But *the words* of the pure *are*
pleasant.

27 [b]He who is greedy for gain
troubles his own house,
But he who hates bribes will
live.

28 The heart of the righteous
[c]studies how to answer,
But the mouth of the wicked
pours forth evil.

29 The LORD *is* far from the
wicked,
But He hears the prayer of the
[d]righteous.

30 The light of the eyes rejoices
the heart,
And a good report makes the
bones healthy.*

31 The ear that hears the rebukes
of life
Will abide among the wise.

32 He who disdains instruction
despises his own soul,
But he who heeds rebuke gets
understanding.

33 The [e]fear of the LORD *is* the
instruction of wisdom,
And before honor *is* [f]humility.

Contrast: righteousness and wickedness

16 THE preparations of the
heart *belong* to man,
But the answer of the tongue *is*
from the LORD.

2 All the ways of a man *are* pure
in his own [g]eyes,
But the LORD [h]weighs the
spirits.

3 [i]Commit your works to the
LORD,
And your thoughts will be
established.

4 The [j]LORD has made all for
Himself,
[k]Yes, even the wicked for the
day of doom.

5 [l]Everyone proud in heart *is* an
abomination to the LORD;
Though they join forces,* none
will go unpunished.

6 In mercy and truth
Atonement is provided for
iniquity;
And by the fear of the LORD
one departs from evil.

7 When a man's ways please the
LORD,
He makes even his enemies to
be at peace with him.

8 [m]Better *is* a little with
righteousness,
Than vast revenues without
justice.

9 A man's heart plans his way,
[n]But the LORD directs his steps.

10 Divination *is* on the lips of the
king;
His mouth must not transgress
in judgment.

11 Honest weights and scales *are*
the LORD's;
All the weights in the bag *are*
His work.

12 *It is* an abomination for kings
to commit wickedness,
For a throne is established by
righteousness.

13 Righteous lips *are* the delight
of kings,
And they love him who speaks
what is right.

14 As messengers of death *is* the
king's wrath,
But a wise man will [o]appease
it.

15 In the light of the king's face *is*
life,
And his favor *is* like a [p]cloud
of the latter rain.

16 [q]How much better to get
wisdom than gold!
And to get understanding is to
be chosen rather than silver.

17 The highway of the upright *is*
to depart from evil;
He who keeps his way
preserves his soul.

18 Pride *goes* before destruction,
And a haughty spirit before a
fall.

19 Better *to be* of a humble spirit
with the lowly,
Than to divide the spoil with
the proud.

20 He who heeds the word wisely
will find good,
And whoever [r]trusts in the
LORD, happy *is* he.

25
a Isa. 2:11
27
b Isa. 5:8; Jer. 17:11
28
c 1 Pet. 3:15
29
d Jas. 5:16
33
e See Ps. 19:9, *note*
f Prov. 18:12
CHAPTER 16
2
g Prov. 21:2
h Cp. 1 Sam. 16:7
3
i Lit. *Roll*
4
j Isa. 43:7; Rom. 11:36
k Job 21:30; Rom. 9:22
5
l Prov. 6:17; 8:13
8
m Ps. 37:16; Prov. 15:16
9
n Ps. 37:23; Prov. 20:24; Jer. 10:23
14
o Prov. 25:15
15
p Zech. 10:1
16
q Prov. 8:11,19
20
r See Ps. 2:12, *note*

*15:30 Literally *fat* 16:5 Literally *hand in hand*

21 The wise in heart will be called prudent,
And sweetness of the lips increases learning.

22 Understanding *is* a wellspring of life to him who has it.
But the correction of fools *is* folly.

23 The heart of the wise teaches his mouth,
And adds learning to his lips.

24 Pleasant words *are like* a honeycomb,
Sweetness to the soul and health to the bones.

25 There is a way *that seems* right to a man,
But its end *is* the way of [a]death.

26 The person who labors, labors for himself,
For his *hungry* mouth drives [b]him *on.*

27 An ungodly man digs up evil,
And *it is* on his lips like a burning [c]fire.

28 A perverse man sows strife,
And a [d]whisperer separates the best of friends.

29 A violent man entices his neighbor,
And leads him in a way *that is* not good.

30 He winks his eye to devise perverse things;
He purses his lips *and* brings about evil.

31 The [e]silver-haired head *is* a crown of glory,
If it is found in the way of righteousness.

32 *He who is* [f]slow to anger *is* better than the mighty,
And he who rules his spirit than he who takes a city.

33 The lot is cast into the lap,
But its every decision *is* from the LORD.

Contrast: righteousness and wickedness

17 BETTER *is* a dry morsel with quietness,
Than a house full of feasting* *with* strife.

2 A wise servant will rule over a son who causes shame,
And will share an inheritance among the brothers.

3 The [g]refining pot *is* for silver and the furnace for gold,
But the LORD [h]tests the hearts.

4 An evildoer gives heed to false lips;
A liar listens eagerly to a spiteful tongue.

5 [i]He who mocks the poor reproaches his Maker;
[j]He who is glad at calamity will not go [k]unpunished.

6 [l]Children's children *are* the crown of old men,
And the glory of children *is* their father.

7 Excellent speech is not becoming to a fool,
Much less lying lips to a prince.

8 A present *is* a precious stone in the eyes of its possessor;
Wherever he turns, he prospers.

9 He who covers a transgression seeks [m]love,
But he who repeats a matter separates friends.

10 [n]Rebuke is more effective for a wise *man*
Than a hundred blows on a fool.

11 An evil *man* seeks only rebellion;
Therefore a cruel messenger will be sent against him.

12 Let a man meet a [o]bear robbed of her cubs,
Rather than a fool in his folly.

13 [p]Whoever rewards evil for good,
Evil will not depart from his house.

14 The beginning of strife *is like* releasing water;
Therefore stop contention before a quarrel starts.

15 [q]He who justifies the wicked, and he who condemns the just,
Both of them alike *are* an abomination to the LORD.

16 Why *is there* in the hand of a fool the purchase price of wisdom,
Since *he has* no heart *for it?*

25 *a* Prov. 14:12
26 *b* Eccl. 6:7
27 *c* Jas. 3:6
28 *d* Prov. 17:9
31 *e* Prov. 20:29
32 *f* Prov. 14:29; 19:11
CHAPTER 17
3 *g* Ps. 26:2; Prov. 27:21; Jer. 17:10; Mal. 3:3 *h Test/tempt:* v. 3; Isa. 7:12. (Gen. 3:1; Jas. 1:14, *note*)
5 *i* Prov. 14:31 *j* Job 31:29; 1 Cor. 13:6; cp. Obad. 12 *k* Lit. *be held innocent*
6 *l* Ps. 127:3; 128:3
9 *m* Prov. 10:12; 1 Cor. 13:5–7
10 *n* Prov. 10:17; Mic. 7:9
12 *o* Cp. Hos. 13:8
13 *p* Ps. 109:4–5; Jer. 18:20; Rom. 12:17; 1 Th. 5:15; 1 Pet. 3:9
15 *q* Ex. 23:7; Prov. 24:24; Isa. 5:23

* 17:1 Or *sacrificial meals*

17 A friend loves at all times,
And a brother is born for adversity.

18 A man devoid of understanding shakes hands in a pledge,
And becomes surety for his friend.

19 He who loves transgression loves strife,
And he who exalts his gate seeks destruction.

20 He who has a deceitful heart finds no good,
And he who has a perverse [a]tongue falls into evil.

21 He who begets a scoffer *does so* to his sorrow,
And the father of a fool has no joy.

22 A [b]merry heart does good, *like* medicine,*
But a broken spirit dries the bones.

23 A wicked *man* accepts a bribe behind the back*
To pervert the ways of [c]justice.

24 Wisdom *is* in the sight of him who has understanding,
But the eyes of a fool *are* on the ends of the earth.

25 A [d]foolish son *is* a grief to his father,
And bitterness to her who bore him.

26 Also, to punish the righteous *is* not good,
Nor to strike princes for *their* uprightness.

27 He who has knowledge [e]spares his words,
And a man of understanding is of a calm spirit.

28 Even a fool is counted wise when he holds his peace;
When he shuts his lips, *he is considered* perceptive.

Contrast: righteousness and wickedness

18 A MAN who isolates himself seeks his own desire;
He rages against all wise judgment.

2 A fool has no delight in understanding,
But in [f]expressing his own heart.

3 When the wicked comes, contempt comes also;
And with dishonor *comes* reproach.

4 The words of a man's mouth *are* deep waters;
The wellspring of wisdom *is* a flowing brook.

5 *It is* not good to show partiality to the wicked,
Or to overthrow the righteous in [g]judgment.

6 A fool's lips enter into contention,
And his mouth calls for blows.

7 A fool's mouth *is* his destruction,
And his lips *are* the snare of his [h]soul.

8 The words of a [i]talebearer *are* like tasty trifles,*
And they go down into the inmost body.

9 He who is slothful in his work
Is a brother to him who is a great destroyer.

10 The name of the LORD *is* a strong [j]tower;
The righteous run to it and are safe.

11 The rich man's wealth *is* his [k]strong city,
And like a high wall in his own esteem.

12 Before destruction the heart of a man is haughty,
And before honor *is* [l]humility.

13 He who answers a matter before he hears *it*,
It *is* folly and shame to him.

14 The spirit of a man will sustain him in sickness,
But who can bear a broken spirit?

15 The heart of the prudent acquires knowledge,
And the ear of the wise seeks knowledge.

16 A man's [m]gift makes room for him,
And brings him before great men.

17 The first *one* to plead his cause *seems* right,

20 *a* Jas. 3:8
22 *b* Prov. 12:25; 15:13,15
23 *c* Ex. 23:8
25 *d* v. 21; Prov. 10:1; 15:20; 19:13
27 *e* Prov. 10:19; cp. Jas. 1:19
CHAPTER 18
2 *f* Eccl. 5:3
5 *g* Prov. 17:15
7 *h* Eccl. 10:12
8 *i* Lit. *whisperer.* Prov. 26:22
10 *j* 2 Sam. 22:3,51; Ps. 18:2; 61:3–4; 91:2; 144:2
11 *k* Cp. Prov. 11:28
12 *l* Prov. 15:33
16 *m* Prov. 17:8; 21:14; cp. Gen. 32:20–21; 1 Sam. 25:27

*
17:22 Or *makes medicine even better*
17:23 Literally *from the bosom* 18:8 A Jewish tradition reads *wounds.*

Until his neighbor comes and
examines him.
18 Casting [a]lots causes
contentions to cease,
And keeps the mighty apart.
19 A brother offended *is harder to*
win than a strong city,
And contentions *are* like the
bars of a castle.
20 A man's stomach shall be
satisfied from the fruit of his
mouth;
From the produce of his lips he
shall be [b]filled.
21 Death and life *are* in the
[c]power of the tongue,
And those who love it will eat
its fruit.
22 [d]*He who* finds a wife finds a
good *thing*,
And obtains favor from the
LORD.
23 The poor *man* uses entreaties,
But the rich answers [e]roughly.
24 A man *who has* friends must
himself be friendly,*
But there is a [f]friend *who*
sticks closer than a brother.

Contrast: righteousness and wickedness

19 BETTER *is* the poor who
walks in his integrity
Than *one who is* perverse in
his lips, and is a fool.
2 Also it is not good *for* a soul *to*
be without knowledge,
And he sins who hastens with
his feet.
3 The foolishness of a man
twists his way,
And his heart frets against the
LORD.
4 [g]Wealth makes many friends,
But the poor is separated from
his friend.
5 A [h]false witness will not go
unpunished,
And *he who* speaks lies will
not escape.
6 Many entreat the favor of the
nobility,
And every man *is* a friend to
one who gives gifts.
7 All the brothers of the poor
hate him;
How much more do his friends
go far from him!
He may pursue *them with*
words, *yet* they abandon
him.
8 He who gets wisdom loves his
own soul;
He who keeps understanding
will find [i]good.
9 A false witness will not go
unpunished,
And *he who* speaks lies shall
perish.
10 Luxury is not fitting for a fool,
Much less for a [j]servant to
rule over princes.
11 The discretion of a man makes
him slow to anger,
And his glory *is* to [k]overlook a
transgression.
12 The king's wrath *is* like the
roaring of a lion,
But his favor *is* [l]like dew on
the grass.
13 A foolish son *is* the ruin of his
father,
And the [m]contentions of a wife
are a continual dripping.
14 Houses and riches *are* an
inheritance from fathers,
But a [n]prudent wife *is* from
the LORD.
15 Laziness casts *one* into a deep
sleep,
And an idle person will suffer
hunger.
16 [o]He who keeps the
commandment keeps his
soul,
But he who is careless* of his
ways will die.
17 [p]He who has pity on the poor
lends to the LORD,
And He will pay back what he
has given.
18 [q]Chasten your son while there
is hope,
And do not set your heart on
his destruction.*
19 *A man of* great wrath will
suffer punishment;
For if you rescue *him*, you will
have to do it again.

18 [a] Prov. 16:33
20 [b] Prov. 14:14
21 [c] Mt. 12:37
22 [d] Prov. 19:14; 31:10–28
23 [e] Cp. Jas. 2:3
24 [f] Prov. 17:17
CHAPTER 19
4 [g] Prov. 14:20
5 [h] v. 9; Ex. 23:1; Dt. 19:16–19; Prov. 6:19; 21:28
8 [i] Prov. 16:20
10 [j] Prov. 30:21–22
11 [k] Eph. 4:32
12 [l] Hos. 14:5
13 [m] Prov. 21:9; 27:15
14 [n] Prov. 18:22
16 [o] Lk. 10:28; 11:28
17 [p] Prov. 28:27; Eccl. 11:1; Mt. 10:42; 25:40; 2 Cor. 9:6–8; Heb. 6:10; cp. Job 23:12–13
18 [q] Prov. 13:24

*18:24 Following Greek manuscripts, Targum, Syriac, and Vulgate; Masoretic Text reads *may come to ruin* 19:16 Literally *despises*, figurative of recklessness or carelessness 19:18 Literally *to put him to death*; a Jewish tradition reads *his crying*.

20 Listen to counsel and receive
instruction,
That you may be wise in your
latter days.
21 There are many plans in a
man's heart,
Nevertheless the LORD's
[a]counsel—that will stand.
22 What is desired in a man is
kindness,
And a poor man is better than
a liar.
23 The [b]fear of the LORD *leads* to
life,
And *he who has it* will abide
in satisfaction;
He will not be visited with evil.
24 A lazy *man* buries his hand in
the [c]bowl,*
And will not so much as bring
it to his mouth again.
25 Strike a scoffer, and the simple
[d]will become wary;
Rebuke one who has
understanding, *and* he will
discern knowledge.
26 He who mistreats *his* father
and chases away *his* mother
Is a son who causes shame
and brings reproach.
27 Cease listening to instruction,
my son,
And you will stray from the
words of knowledge.
28 A disreputable witness scorns
justice,
And the mouth of the wicked
devours iniquity.
29 Judgments are prepared for
scoffers,
And beatings for the backs of
fools.

Contrast: righteousness and wickedness

20 [e]WINE *is* a mocker,
Strong drink *is* a brawler,
And whoever is led astray by
it is not wise.
2 The wrath* of a king *is* like
the roaring of a lion;
Whoever provokes him to
anger sins *against* his own
life.
3 *It is* honorable for a man to
stop striving,
Since any fool can start a
quarrel.
4 The lazy *man* will not plow
because of winter;
He will beg during harvest and
have nothing.
5 Counsel in the heart of man *is*
like deep water,
But a man of understanding
will draw it out.
6 Most men will [f]proclaim each
his own goodness,
But who can find a faithful
man?
7 The righteous *man* walks in
his integrity;
His children *are* blessed after
him.
8 A king who sits on the throne
of judgment
Scatters all evil with his eyes.
9 [g]Who can say, "I have made my
heart clean,
I am pure from my sin"?
10 [h]Diverse weights *and* diverse
measures,
They *are* both alike, an
abomination to the LORD.
11 Even a child is known by his
deeds,
Whether what he does *is* pure
and right.
12 The hearing ear and the seeing
eye,
The LORD has made them both.
13 Do not love sleep, lest you
come to poverty;
Open your eyes, *and* you will
be satisfied with bread.
14 "*It is* good for nothing,"* cries
the buyer;
But when he has gone his way,
then he boasts.
15 There is gold and a multitude
of rubies,
But the lips of [i]knowledge *are*
a precious jewel.
16 Take the garment of one who
is surety *for* a stranger,
And hold it as a pledge *when*
it is for a seductress.
17 Bread gained by deceit *is*
sweet to a man,

21 [a] Ps. 33:10–11; Prov. 16:9; Isa. 46:10; Heb. 6:17
23 [b] See Ps. 19:9, *note*
24 [c] Prov. 26:15
25 [d] Lit. *will be cunning*
CHAPTER 20
1 [e] Prov. 23:29–35; Hos. 4:11; cp. Gen. 9:21; Isa. 28:7
6 [f] Cp. Prov. 25:14; Mt. 6:2; Lk. 18:11
9 [g] 1 Ki. 8:46; 2 Chr. 6:36; Job 9:30–31; 14:4; Ps. 51:5; Eccl. 7:20; 1 Jn. 1:8
10 [h] Dt. 25:13; Prov. 11:1; 16:11; Mic. 6:10–12
15 [i] Job 28:12–19; Prov. 3:13–15; 8:11

*
19:24 Septuagint and Syriac read *bosom;* Targum and Vulgate read *armpit.* **20:2** Literally *fear* or *terror* which is produced by the king's wrath **20:14** Literally *evil, evil*

But afterward his mouth will
be filled with gravel.
18 Plans are established by
counsel;
By wise counsel wage war.
19 He who goes about *as* a
talebearer reveals secrets;
Therefore do not associate
with one who flatters with
his lips.
20 [a]Whoever curses his father or
his mother,
His [b]lamp will be put out in
deep darkness.
21 An [c]inheritance gained hastily
at the beginning
Will not be blessed at the end.
22 [d]Do not say, "I will recompense
evil";
[e]Wait for the LORD, and He will
save you.
23 [f]Diverse weights *are* an
abomination to the LORD,
And dishonest scales *are* not
good.
24 A man's steps *are* of the LORD;
How then can a man
understand his own way?
25 *It is* a snare for a man to
devote rashly *something as*
holy,
And afterward to reconsider
his vows.
26 A wise king sifts out the
wicked,
And brings the threshing
wheel over them.
27 The [g]spirit of a man *is* the
lamp of the LORD,
Searching all the inner depths
of his heart.*
28 Mercy and truth preserve the
king,
And by lovingkindness he
upholds his throne.
29 The glory of young men *is*
their strength,
And the splendor of old men *is*
their [h]gray head.
30 Blows that hurt cleanse away
evil,
As *do* stripes the inner depths
of the heart.*

Contrast: righteousness and wickedness

21 THE king's heart *is* in the
hand of the LORD,
Like the rivers of water;
He [i]turns it wherever He
wishes.
2 Every way of a man *is* right in
his own eyes,
But the LORD [j]weighs the
hearts.
3 To do [k]righteousness and
justice
Is more acceptable to the LORD
than sacrifice.
4 A [l]haughty look, a proud
heart,
And the [m]plowing of the
wicked *are* sin.
5 The plans of the diligent *lead*
surely to plenty,
But *those of* everyone *who is*
hasty, surely to poverty.
6 Getting treasures by a lying
tongue
Is the fleeting fantasy of those
who seek death.*
7 The violence of the wicked will
destroy them,*
Because they refuse to do
justice.
8 The way of a guilty man *is*
perverse;*
But *as for* the pure, his work *is*
right.
9 Better to dwell in a corner of a
housetop,
Than in a house shared with a
[n]contentious woman.
10 The soul of the wicked desires
evil;
His neighbor [o]finds no favor
in his eyes.
11 When the scoffer is punished,
the simple is made [p]wise;
But when the wise is
instructed, he receives
knowledge.
12 The righteous *God* wisely
considers the house of the
wicked,
Overthrowing the wicked for
their wickedness.

20
a Ex. 21:17; Lev. 20:9; Mt. 15:4
b Job 18:5–6; Prov. 24:20
21
c Prov. 28:20; cp. Hab. 2:6
22
d Dt. 32:35; Prov. 17:13; 24:29; Rom. 12:17–19; 1 Th. 5:15; 1 Pet. 3:9
e Cp. 2 Sam. 16:12
23
f Dt. 25:13; Prov. 11:1; 16:11; Mic. 6:10–12
27
g 1 Cor. 2:11
29
h Prov. 16:31
CHAPTER 21
1
i Cp. Ezra 6:22
2
j Prov. 24:12; Lk. 16:15
3
k Cp. 1 Sam. 15:22; Prov. 15:8; Isa. 1:11; Hos. 6:6; Mic. 6:7–8
4
l Prov. 6:17
m Lit. *the light of the wicked*
9
n Prov. 19:13
10
o Cp. Jas. 2:16
11
p Prov. 19:25

*
20:27 Literally *the rooms of the belly*
20:30 Literally *the rooms of the belly*
21:6 Septuagint reads *Pursue vanity on the snares of death;* Vulgate reads *Is vain and foolish, and shall stumble on the snares of death;* Targum reads *They shall be destroyed, and they shall fall who seek death.* **21:7** Literally *drag them away* **21:8** Or *The way of a man is perverse and strange*

13 [a]Whoever shuts his ears to the cry of the poor
Will also cry himself and not be heard.

14 A gift in secret pacifies anger,
And a bribe behind the back,* strong wrath.

15 *It is* a joy for the [b]just to do justice,
But destruction *will come* to the workers of iniquity.

16 A man who wanders from the way of understanding
Will rest in the assembly of the [c]dead.

17 He who loves pleasure *will be* a poor man;
He who loves wine and oil will not be rich.

18 The wicked *shall be* a ransom for the righteous,
And the unfaithful for the upright.

19 Better to dwell in the wilderness,
Than with a contentious and angry woman.

20 *There is* desirable treasure,
And oil in the dwelling of the wise,
But a foolish man squanders it.

21 He who [d]follows righteousness and mercy
Finds life, righteousness and honor.

22 A [e]wise *man* scales the city of the mighty,
And brings down the trusted stronghold.

23 [f]Whoever guards his mouth and tongue
Keeps his soul from troubles.

24 A proud *and* haughty *man*—"Scoffer" *is* his name;
He acts with arrogant pride.

25 The [g]desire of the lazy *man* kills him,
For his hands refuse to labor.

26 He covets greedily all day long,
But the righteous [h]gives and does not spare.

27 The [i]sacrifice of the wicked *is* an abomination;
How much more *when* he brings it with wicked intent!

13 *a* Mt. 18:29–34; Jas. 2:13
15 *b Righteousness (OT):* vv. 15,21; Eccl. 7:20. (Gen. 6:9; Lk. 2:25, *note*)
16 *c* Ps. 49:14
21 *d* Prov. 15:9; Mt. 5:6; Rom. 2:7
22 *e* Prov. 24:5
23 *f* Prov. 12:13; 13:3; 18:21; Jas. 3:2
25 *g* Prov. 13:4
26 *h* Prov. 22:9; Eph. 4:28; cp. 2 Cor. 9:6–15
27 *i* Cp. 1 Sam. 15:22; Prov. 28:9
31 *j* Ps. 3:8; 37:39; Jer. 3:23
CHAPTER 22
1 *k* Eccl. 7:1
2 *l* Prov. 29:13; cp. 1 Cor. 12:21
m Job 31:15; Prov. 14:31
3 *n* Prov. 27:12
4 *o* See Ps. 19:9, *note*
6 *p* Eph. 6:4; 2 Tim. 3:15
7 *q* Jas. 2:6
8 *r* Job 4:8
9 *s* 2 Cor. 9:6
t Prov. 19:17

28 A false witness shall perish,
But the man who hears *him* will speak endlessly.

29 A wicked man hardens his face,
But *as for* the upright, he establishes* his way.

30 *There is* no wisdom or understanding
Or counsel against the LORD.

31 The horse *is* prepared for the day of battle,
But deliverance *is* of the [j]LORD.

Contrast: righteousness and wickedness

22 A [k]*GOOD* name is to be chosen rather than great riches,
Loving favor rather than silver and gold.

2 The [l]rich and the poor have this in common,
The [m]LORD *is* the maker of them all.

3 A prudent *man* foresees evil and hides himself,
But the simple pass on and are [n]punished.

4 By humility *and* the [o]fear of the LORD
Are riches and honor and life.

5 Thorns *and* snares *are* in the way of the perverse;
He who guards his soul will be far from them.

6 [p]Train up a child in the way he should go,
And when he is old he will not depart from it.

7 The [q]rich rules over the poor,
And the borrower *is* servant to the lender.

8 He who sows iniquity will reap [r]sorrow,
And the rod of his anger will fail.

9 He who has a [s]generous eye will be [t]blessed,
For he gives of his bread to the poor.

10 Cast out the scoffer, and contention will leave;

*21:14 Literally *in the bosom* 21:29 Qere and Septuagint read *understands.*

Yes, strife and reproach will
[a]cease.
11 He who loves purity of heart
And has grace on his lips,
The king *will be* his friend.

12 The eyes of the LORD preserve
knowledge,
But He overthrows the words
of the faithless.

13 The lazy *man* says, "*There is* a
lion outside!
I shall be slain in the [b]streets!"

14 The mouth of an immoral
woman *is* a deep pit;
He who is abhorred by the
LORD will fall [c]there.

15 Foolishness *is* bound up in the
heart of a child;
The [d]rod of correction will
drive it far from him.

16 He who oppresses the poor to
increase his *riches,*
And he who gives to the rich,
will surely *come* to poverty.

17 Incline your ear and hear the
words of the wise,
And apply your heart to my
knowledge;
18 For *it is* a pleasant thing if you
keep them within you;
Let them all be fixed upon
your lips,
19 So that your [e]trust may be in
the LORD;
I have instructed you today,
even you.
20 Have I not written to you
excellent things
Of counsels and knowledge,
21 That I may make you [f]know
the certainty of the words of
truth,
That you may [g]answer words
of truth
To those who send to you?

22 Do not rob the [h]poor because
he *is* poor,
Nor oppress the afflicted at the
gate;
23 For the LORD will [i]plead their
cause,
And plunder the soul of those
who plunder them.

24 Make no friendship with an
angry man,
And with a [j]furious man do
not go,
25 Lest you learn his ways

10 *a* Prov. 26:20
13 *b* Prov. 26:13
14 *c* Eccl. 7:26
15 *d* Prov. 23:13–14
19 *e* See Ps. 2:12, *note*
21 *f* Cp. Lk. 1:3–4 *g* 1 Pet. 3:15
22 *h* Ex. 23:6; Job 31:16–21; Zech. 7:10
23 *i* Ps. 140:12
24 *j* Prov. 29:22
28 *k* Dt. 19:14; 27:17
29 *l* Cp. 1 Ki. 11:28
CHAPTER 23
4 *m* Prov. 28:20; Mt. 6:19; 1 Tim. 6:9–10; Heb. 13:5
5 *n* 1 Tim. 6:17
6 *o* Dt. 15:9
9 *p* Prov. 9:8; Mt. 7:6
11 *q* *Redemption* (redeeming relative type): v. 11; Isa. 41:14. (Gen. 48:16; Isa. 59:20, *note*)

And set a snare for your soul.

26 Do not be one of those who
shakes hands in a pledge,
One of those who is surety for
debts;
27 If you have nothing *with which*
to pay,
Why should he take away your
bed from under you?

28 [k]Do not remove the ancient
landmark
Which your fathers have set.

29 Do you see a man *who* excels
in his work?
He will stand before [l]kings;
He will not stand before
unknown *men.*

Contrast: righteousness and wickedness

23 WHEN you sit down to eat
with a ruler,
Consider carefully what *is*
before you;
2 And put a knife to your throat
If you *are* a man given to
appetite.
3 Do not desire his delicacies,
For they *are* deceptive food.

4 [m]Do not overwork to be rich;
Because of your own
understanding, cease!
5 Will you set your eyes on that
which is not?
For *riches* certainly make
themselves [n]wings;
They fly away like an eagle
toward heaven.

6 Do not eat the bread of a
[o]miser,*
Nor desire his delicacies;
7 For as he thinks in his heart,
so *is* he.
"Eat and drink!" he says to you,
But his heart is not with you.
8 The morsel you have eaten,
you will vomit up,
And waste your pleasant
words.

9 [p]Do not speak in the hearing of
a fool,
For he will despise the wisdom
of your words.

10 [k]Do not remove the ancient
landmark,
Nor enter the fields of the
fatherless;
11 For their [q]Redeemer *is* mighty;

*23:6 Literally *one who has an evil eye*

He will [a]plead their cause
against you.

12 Apply your heart to
instruction,
And your ears to words of
knowledge.

13 Do not withhold [b]correction
from a child,
For *if* you beat him with a rod,
he will not die.

14 You shall beat him with a rod,
And deliver his soul from
[c]hell.*

15 My son, if your heart is wise,
My heart will rejoice—indeed,
I myself;

16 Yes, my inmost being will
rejoice
When your lips speak right
things.

17 Do not let your heart envy
sinners,
But *be zealous* for the [d]fear of
the LORD all the day;

18 For surely there is a hereafter,
And your [e]hope will not be cut
off.

19 Hear, my son, and be wise;
And guide your heart in the
way.

20 [f]Do not mix with winebibbers,
Or with gluttonous eaters of
meat;

21 For the drunkard and the
glutton will come to poverty,
And drowsiness will clothe *a*
man with rags.

22 Listen to your father who
begot you,
And do not despise your
mother when she is old.

23 Buy the truth, and do not sell
it,
Also wisdom and instruction
and understanding.

24 The father of the righteous will
greatly rejoice,
And he who begets a wise
child will delight in him.

25 Let your father and your
mother be glad,
And let her who bore you
rejoice.

26 My son, give me your heart,
And let your eyes observe my
ways.

27 For a harlot *is* a deep [g]pit,
And a [h]seductress *is* a narrow
well.

28 She also lies in wait as *for* a
victim,
And increases the unfaithful
among men.

29 Who has woe?
Who has sorrow?
Who has contentions?
Who has complaints?
Who has wounds without
cause?
Who has redness of eyes?

30 [i]Those who linger long at the
wine,
Those who go in search of
mixed wine.

31 Do not look on the wine when
it is red,
When it sparkles in the cup,
When it [j]swirls around
smoothly;

32 At the last it bites like a
serpent,
And stings like a viper.

33 Your eyes will see strange
things,
And your heart will utter
perverse things.

34 Yes, you will be like one who
lies down in the midst of the
sea,
Or like one who lies at the top
of the mast, *saying:*

35 "They have struck me, *but* I
was not hurt;
They have beaten me, but I did
not feel *it.*
When shall I awake, that I
may seek [k]another *drink?*"

Contrast: righteousness and wickedness

24 [l]DO not be envious of evil
men,
Nor desire to be with them;

2 For their heart devises
violence,
And their lips talk of
troublemaking.

3 Through wisdom a house is
built,
And by understanding it is
established;

4 By knowledge the rooms are
filled
With all precious and pleasant
riches.

5 A [m]wise man *is* strong,
Yes, a man of knowledge
increases strength;

11 *a* Ps. 140:12
13 *b* Prov. 22:6,15
14 *c* See Hab. 2:5, *note;* cp. Lk. 16:23, *note*
17 *d* See Ps. 19:9, *note*
18 *e* Ps. 58:11; Prov. 24:14
20 *f* Isa. 5:22; Mt. 24:49; Lk. 21:34; Rom. 13:13; Eph. 5:18
27 *g* Prov. 22:14 *h* Prov. 5:20
30 *i* Prov. 20:1; 21:17; Eph. 5:18
31 *j* Or *goes down smoothly*
35 *k* Isa. 56:12
CHAPTER 24
1 *l* Ps. 37:1; Prov. 23:17
5 *m* Prov. 21:22; Eccl. 9:16

* 23:14 Or *Sheol*

6 For by wise counsel you will
wage your own war,
And in a multitude of
counselors *there is* safety.

7 [a]Wisdom *is* too lofty for a fool;
He does not open his mouth in
the gate.

8 He who [b]plots to do evil
Will be called a schemer.
9 The devising of foolishness *is*
sin,
And the scoffer *is* an
abomination to men.

10 *If* you [c]faint in the day of
adversity,
Your strength *is* small.

11 [d]Deliver *those who* are drawn
toward death,
And hold back *those* stumbling
to the slaughter.
12 If you say, "Surely we did not
know this,"
Does not He who [e]weighs the
hearts consider *it?*
He who keeps your soul, does
He *not* know *it?*
And will He *not* render to *each*
man [f]according to his
deeds?
13 My son, eat honey because *it*
is good,
And the honeycomb *which is*
sweet to your taste;
14 So *shall* the knowledge of
wisdom *be* to your soul;
If you have found *it,* there is a
prospect,
And your [g]hope will not be cut
off.
15 Do not lie in wait, O wicked
man, against the dwelling of
the righteous;
Do not plunder his resting
place;
16 [h]For a righteous *man* may fall
seven times
And rise again,
But the wicked shall fall by
calamity.

17 [i]Do not rejoice when your
enemy falls,
And do not let your heart be
glad when he stumbles;
18 Lest the LORD see *it,* and it
displease Him,
And He turn away His wrath
from him.

19 Do not fret because of
evildoers,
Nor be envious of the wicked;
20 For there will be no prospect
for the evil *man;*
The [j]lamp of the wicked will
be put out.

21 My son, [k]fear the LORD and the
king;
Do not associate with those
given to change;
22 For their calamity will rise
suddenly,
And who knows the ruin those
two can bring?

23 These *things* also *belong* to the
wise:

[l]*It is* not good to show
partiality in judgment.
24 He who says to the wicked,
"You *are* righteous,"
Him the people will curse;
Nations will abhor him.
25 But those who rebuke *the*
wicked will have [m]delight,
And a good blessing will come
upon them.

26 He who gives a right answer
kisses the lips.

27 Prepare your outside work,
Make it fit for yourself in the
[n]field;
And afterward build your
house.

28 Do not be a witness against
your neighbor without cause,
For would you [o]deceive* with
your lips?
29 [p]Do not say, "I will do to him
just as he has done to me;
I will render to the man
according to his work."

30 I went by the field of the lazy
man,
And by the vineyard of the
man devoid of
understanding;
31 And there it was, all
overgrown with thorns;
Its surface was covered with
nettles;
Its stone wall was broken
down.
32 When I saw *it,* I considered *it*
well;
I looked on *it and* received
instruction:
33 A little sleep, a little slumber,

7 *a* Ps. 10:5; Prov. 14:6
8 *b* Rom. 1:30
10 *c* Heb. 12:3
11 *d* Ps. 82:4; Isa. 58:6–7; 1 Jn. 3:16
12 *e* Ps. 62:12; Jer. 32:19; Rom. 2:6 *f* Job 34:11; Rev. 2:23; 22:12
14 *g* Ps. 58:11; Prov. 23:18
16 *h* Job 5:19; Ps. 34:19; 37:24; Mic. 7:8
17 *i* Job 31:29; Ps. 35:15, 19; Obad. 12
20 *j* Ps. 37:1–2
21 *k* See Ps. 19:9, *note*
23 *l* Lev. 19:15; Dt. 1:17; 16:19; Jn. 7:24
25 *m* Prov. 28:23
27 *n* Prov. 27:23–27
28 *o* Eph. 4:25
29 *p* Prov. 20:22; Mt. 5:39–44; Rom. 12:17–19

* 24:28 Septuagint and Vulgate read *Do not deceive.*

A little folding of the hands to rest;
34 [a]So shall your poverty come *like* a prowler,
And your need like an armed man.

III. Proverbs of Solomon Selected by Men of Hezekiah, 25—29

Warnings and instructions

25 [b]THESE also *are* proverbs of Solomon which the men of [c]Hezekiah king of Judah copied:

2 [d]*It is* the glory of God to conceal a matter,
But the glory of kings *is* to [e]search out a matter.
3 *As* the heavens for height and the earth for depth,
So the heart of kings *is* unsearchable.
4 [f]Take away the dross from silver,
And it will go to the silversmith *for* jewelry.
5 Take away the wicked from before the king,
And his throne will be established in [g]righteousness.
6 Do not exalt yourself in the presence of the king,
And do not stand in the place of the great;
7 For *it is* better that he say to you,
[h]"Come up here,"
Than that you should be put lower in the presence of the prince,
Whom your eyes have seen.
8 [i]Do not go hastily to court;
For what will you do in the end,
When your neighbor has put you to shame?
9 [j]Debate your case with your neighbor,
And do not disclose [k]the secret to another;
10 Lest he who hears *it* expose your shame,
And your reputation be ruined.
11 A word fitly [l]spoken *is like* apples of gold
In settings of silver.
12 *Like* an earring of gold and an ornament of fine gold
Is a wise rebuker to an obedient ear.

34 *a* Prov. 6:9–11
CHAPTER 25
1 *b* 1 Ki. 4:32 *c* c. 700 B.C.
2 *d* Dt. 29:29; Rom. 11:33 *e* Cp. Est. 6:1
4 *f* Cp. 2 Tim. 2:20–21
5 *g* Prov. 16:12; 20:8
7 *h* Lk. 14:8–10
8 *i* Prov. 17:14; Mt. 5:25
9 *j* Mt. 18:15 *k* Or *the secret of another*
11 *l* Prov. 15:23; Isa. 50:4
14 *m* Jude 12
15 *n* Prov. 15:1; 16:14; cp. Gen. 32:4; 1 Sam. 25:24
20 *o* Cp. Dan. 6:18; Rom. 12:15
21 *p* vv. 21–22; Mt. 5:44; Rom. 12:20
22 *q* Cp. 2 Sam. 16:12
24 *r* Prov. 19:13
25 *s* Prov. 15:30

13 Like the cold of snow in time of harvest
Is a faithful messenger to those who send him,
For he refreshes the soul of his masters.
14 Whoever falsely boasts of giving
Is [m]*like* clouds and wind without rain.
15 [n]By long forbearance a ruler is persuaded,
And a gentle tongue breaks a bone.
16 Have you found honey?
Eat only as much as you need,
Lest you be filled with it and vomit.
17 Seldom set foot in your neighbor's house,
Lest he become weary of you and hate you.
18 A man who bears false witness against his neighbor
Is like a club, a sword, and a sharp arrow.
19 Confidence in an unfaithful *man* in time of trouble
Is like a bad tooth and a foot out of joint.
20 *Like* one who takes away a garment in cold weather,
And like vinegar on soda,
[o]*Is* one who sings songs to a heavy heart.
21 [p]If your enemy is hungry, give him bread to eat;
And if he is thirsty, give him water to drink;
22 For *so* you will heap coals of fire on his head,
And the [q]LORD will reward you.
23 The north wind brings forth rain,
And a backbiting tongue an angry countenance.
24 *It is* better to dwell in a corner of a housetop,
Than in a house shared with a [r]contentious woman.
25 *As* cold water to a weary soul,
So *is* [s]good news from a far country.
26 A righteous *man* who falters before the wicked

Is like a murky spring and a polluted well.

27 It is not good to eat much honey;
[a]So to seek one's own glory is not glory.

28 [b]Whoever has no rule over his own spirit
Is like a city broken down, without walls.

Warnings and instructions (contd.)

26 AS snow in summer and [c]rain in harvest,
So honor is not fitting for a fool.

2 Like a flitting sparrow, like a flying swallow,
[d]So a curse without cause shall not alight.

3 A whip for the horse,
A bridle for the donkey,
And a rod for the fool's [e]back.

4 [f]Do not answer a fool according to his folly,
Lest you also be like him.

5 [1]Answer a fool according to his folly,
Lest he be wise in his own [g]eyes.

6 He who sends a message by the hand of a fool
Cuts off his own feet and drinks violence.

7 Like the legs of the lame that hang limp
Is a proverb in the mouth of fools.

8 Like one who binds a stone in a sling
Is he who gives honor to a fool.

9 Like a thorn that goes into the hand of a drunkard
Is a proverb in the mouth of fools.

10 The great God who formed everything
Gives the fool his hire and the transgressor his wages.*

11 As a [h]dog returns to his own vomit,
So a fool repeats his folly.

12 [i]Do you see a man wise in his own eyes?
There is more hope for a fool than for him.

13 The lazy man says, "There is a lion in the road!
A fierce lion is in the streets!"

14 As a door turns on its hinges,
So does the lazy man on his bed.

15 The [j]lazy man buries his hand in the bowl;
It wearies him to bring it back to his mouth.

16 The lazy man is wiser in his own eyes
Than seven men who can answer sensibly.

17 He who passes by and meddles in a quarrel not his own
Is like one who takes a dog by the ears.

18 Like a madman who throws firebrands, arrows, and death,

19 [k]Is the man who deceives his neighbor,
And says, "I was only joking!"

20 Where there is no wood, the fire goes out;
And where there is no talebearer, strife ceases.

21 [l]As charcoal is to burning coals, and wood to fire,
So is a contentious man to kindle strife.

22 The words of a [m]talebearer are like tasty trifles,
And they go down into the inmost body.

23 Fervent lips with a wicked heart
Are like earthenware covered with silver dross.

24 He who hates, disguises it with his lips,
And lays up deceit within himself;

25 When he speaks kindly, do not believe him,
For there are seven abominations in his heart;

26 Though his hatred is covered by deceit,

27 a Prov. 27:2
28 b Prov. 16:32
CHAPTER 26
1 c Cp. 1 Sam. 12:17
2 d Cp. Num. 23:8
3 e Prov. 19:29
4 f Cp. Mt. 16:1–4; 21:24–27
5 g Rom. 12:16
11 h 2 Pet. 2:22; cp. Ex. 8:15
12 i Prov. 29:20; cp. Lk. 18:11–12; Rev. 3:17
15 j Prov. 19:24
19 k Eph. 5:4
21 l Prov. 15:18; 29:22
22 m Lit. *whisperer*. Prov. 18:8

* 26:10 The Hebrew is difficult; ancient and modern translators differ greatly.

[1](26:5) Verses 4–5 illustrate Eccl. 3:7. The apparent contradiction between these verses is best resolved by remembering two things: (1) There is nothing to be gained in answering a fool in his own manner. And (2) there may be occasions when to permit a fool to go unrefuted would confirm him in his conceit. Examples: (1) see 2 Ki. 18:36; (2) see Neh. 6:8; Job 2:9–10.

His wickedness will be
revealed before the
assembly.
27 [a]Whoever digs a pit will fall
into it,
And he who rolls a stone will
have it roll back on him.
28 A lying tongue hates *those*
who are crushed by it,
And a flattering mouth works
[b]ruin.

Warnings and instructions (contd.)

27 [c]DO not boast about
tomorrow,
For you do not know what a
day may bring forth.
2 [d]Let another man praise you,
and not your own mouth;
A stranger, and not your own
lips.
3 A stone *is* heavy and sand *is*
weighty,
But a fool's wrath *is* heavier
than both of them.
4 Wrath *is* cruel and anger a
torrent,
But [e]who *is* able to stand
before jealousy?
5 [f]Open rebuke *is* better
Than love carefully concealed.
6 Faithful *are* the wounds of a
friend,
But the kisses of an enemy *are*
[g]deceitful.
7 A satisfied soul loathes the
honeycomb,
But to a hungry soul every
bitter thing *is* sweet.
8 Like a bird that wanders from
its nest
Is a man who wanders from
his place.
9 Ointment and perfume delight
the heart,
And the sweetness of a man's
friend *gives delight* [h]by
hearty counsel.
10 Do not forsake your own
friend or your father's
friend,
Nor go to your brother's house
in the day of your calamity;
Better *is* a [i]neighbor nearby
than a brother far away.
11 [j]My son, be wise, and make my
heart glad,

27
a Ps. 7:15–16; 9:15; 10:2; 57:6; Prov. 28:10; Eccl. 10:8
28
b Prov. 29:5
CHAPTER 27
1
c Jas. 4:13–14; cp. Lk. 12:19–21
2
d Prov. 25:27
4
e 1 Jn. 3:12
5
f Prov. 28:23; cp. Gal. 2:14
6
g Mt. 26:49
9
h Lit. *from the counsel of the soul*
10
i Prov. 17:17; 18:24
11
j Prov. 10:1; 23:15–26
12
k Prov. 22:3
15
l Prov. 19:13
18
m 1 Cor. 9:7–13
20
n See Hab. 2:5, *note;* cp. Lk. 16:23, *note*
o Heb. *Abaddon*
p Lit. *not*
q Cp. Eccl. 1:8
21
r Cp. Lk. 6:26
22
s An instrument for crushing
23
t Prov. 24:27

That I may answer him who
reproaches me.
12 A prudent *man* foresees evil
and hides himself;
The simple pass on *and* are
[k]punished.
13 Take the garment of him who
is surety for a stranger,
And hold it in pledge *when* he
is surety for a seductress.
14 He who blesses his friend with
a loud voice, rising early in
the morning,
It will be counted a curse to
him.
15 A [l]continual dripping on a
very rainy day
And a contentious woman are
alike;
16 Whoever restrains her
restrains the wind,
And grasps oil with his right
hand.
17 As iron sharpens iron,
So a man sharpens the
countenance of his friend.
18 [m]Whoever keeps the fig tree will
eat its fruit;
So he who waits on his master
will be honored.
19 As in water face *reflects* face,
So a man's heart *reveals* the
man.
20 [n]Hell* and [o]Destruction are
never full;
So the eyes of man are [p]never
[q]satisfied.
21 The refining pot *is* for silver
and the furnace for gold,
And a man *is valued* by [r]what
others say of him.
22 Though you grind a fool in a
mortar with a [s]pestle along
with crushed grain,
Yet his foolishness will not
depart from him.
23 Be diligent to know the state of
your flocks,
And attend to your [t]herds;
24 For riches *are* not forever,
Nor does a crown *endure* to all
generations.
25 *When* the hay is removed, and
the tender grass shows itself,

*27:20 Or *Sheol*

And the herbs of the mountains are gathered in,
26 The lambs *will provide* your clothing,
And the goats the price of a field;
27 *You shall have* enough goats' milk for your food,
For the food of your household,
And the nourishment of your maidservants.

Warnings and instructions (contd.)

28 THE wicked [a]flee when no one pursues,
But the righteous are bold as a lion.
2 Because of the transgression of a land, many *are* its princes;
But by a man of understanding *and* knowledge
Right will be prolonged.
3 A [b]poor man who oppresses the poor
Is like a driving rain which leaves no food.
4 Those who forsake the law praise the wicked,
But [c]such as keep the law contend with them.
5 Evil men do not understand justice,
But [d]those who seek the LORD understand all.
6 Better *is* the poor who walks in his integrity
Than one perverse *in his* ways, though he *be* rich.
7 Whoever keeps the law *is* a discerning son,
But a companion of gluttons shames his father.
8 One who increases his possessions by usury and extortion
Gathers it for him who will pity the poor.
9 One who turns away his ear from hearing the law,
[e]Even his prayer *is* an abomination.
10 Whoever causes the upright to go astray in an evil way,
He himself will fall into his [f]own pit;
But the blameless will inherit good.

CHAPTER 28
1 *a* Lev. 26:17,36; Ps. 53:5
3 *b* Cp. Mt. 18:28
4 *c* 1 Ki. 18:18,21; Mt. 3:7; 14:4; cp. Eph. 5:11
5 *d* Jn. 7:17; 1 Cor 2:15; 1 Jn. 2:20, 27
9 *e* Ps. 66:18; 109:7; Prov. 15:8
10 *f* Ps. 7:15; Prov. 26:27
12 *g* Prov. 11:10; 29:2
13 *h* Ps. 32:3–5; 1 Jn. 1:8–10
15 *i* Cp. 1 Pet. 5:8
16 *j* Eccl. 10:16
17 *k* Cp. Gen. 9:6
19 *l* Prov. 20:13
20 *m* Prov. 13:11; 20:21; 23:4; 1 Tim. 6:9
21 *n* Cp. Ezek. 13:19
22 *o* Prov. 21:5
23 *p* Prov. 27:5–6

11 The rich man *is* wise in his own eyes,
But the poor who has understanding searches him out.
12 When the righteous rejoice, *there is* great [g]glory;
But when the wicked arise, men hide themselves.
13 [h]He who covers his sins will not prosper,
But whoever confesses and forsakes *them* will have mercy.
14 Happy *is* the man who is always reverent,
But he who hardens his heart will fall into calamity.
15 [i]*Like* a roaring lion and a charging bear
Is a wicked ruler over poor people.
16 A ruler who lacks understanding *is* a great [j]oppressor,
But he who hates covetousness will prolong *his* days.
17 A man burdened with [k]bloodshed will flee into a pit;
Let no one help him.
18 Whoever walks blamelessly will be saved,
But *he who is* perverse *in his* ways will suddenly fall.
19 He who tills his land will have plenty of [l]bread,
But he who follows frivolity will have poverty enough!
20 A faithful man will abound with blessings,
But [m]he who hastens to be rich will not go unpunished.
21 To show partiality *is* not good,
Because for a [n]piece of bread a man will transgress.
22 A man with an evil eye [m]hastens after riches,
And does not consider that [o]poverty will come upon him.
23 He who rebukes a man will find more [p]favor afterward
Than he who flatters with the tongue.

24 Whoever robs his father or his
mother,
And says, "*It is* no
transgression,"
The same *is* companion to a
destroyer.

25 He who is of a proud heart
stirs up strife,
But he who [a]trusts in the LORD
will be prospered.

26 He who [b]trusts in his own
heart is a fool,
But whoever walks wisely will
be delivered.

27 [c]He who gives to the poor will
not lack,
But he who hides his eyes will
have many curses.

28 When the wicked arise, men
hide themselves;
But when they perish, the
righteous increase.

Warnings and instructions (contd.)

29 HE who is [d]often rebuked,
and hardens *his* neck,
Will [e]suddenly be destroyed,
and that without remedy.

2 When the righteous are in
authority, the people
[f]rejoice;
But when a wicked *man* rules,
the people groan.

3 Whoever loves wisdom makes
his father rejoice,
But a companion of harlots
wastes *his* wealth.

4 The king establishes the land
by justice,
But he who receives bribes
overthrows it.

5 A man who [g]flatters his
neighbor
Spreads a net for his feet.

6 By transgression an evil man
is snared,
But the righteous sings and
rejoices.

7 The righteous [h]considers the
cause of the poor,
But the wicked does not
understand *such* knowledge.

8 Scoffers set a city [i]aflame,
But wise *men* turn away wrath.

9 *If* a wise man contends with a
foolish man,
Whether *the fool* rages or
laughs, *there is* no peace.

10 The [j]bloodthirsty hate the
blameless,
But the upright seek his
well-being.*

11 A fool vents all his [k]feelings,*
But a wise *man* holds them
back.

12 If a ruler pays attention to lies,
All his servants *become*
wicked.

13 The poor *man* and the
oppressor have this in
common:
The LORD gives light to the
eyes of both.

14 The king who judges the [l]poor
with truth,
His throne will be established
forever.

15 The rod and rebuke give
[m]wisdom,
But a child left *to himself*
brings shame to his mother.

16 When the wicked are
multiplied, transgression
increases;
But the righteous will see their
[n]fall.

17 Correct your son, and he will
give you rest;
Yes, he will give delight to
your soul.

18 [o]Where *there is* no [1]revelation,
the people cast off restraint;
But happy *is* he who keeps the
law.

19 A servant will not be corrected
by mere words;
For though he understands, he
will not respond.

20 Do you see a man hasty in his
words?
[p]*There is* more hope for a fool
than for him.

21 He who pampers his servant
from childhood

25 *a* See Ps. 2:12, *note*
26 *b* Prov. 3:5
27 *c* Dt. 15:7; Prov. 19:17; 22:9
CHAPTER 29
1 *d* Cp. 1 Sam. 2:25; 2 Chr. 36:16
e Prov. 6:15
2 *f* Prov. 28:12
5 *g* Prov. 26:28
7 *h* Job 29:16; Ps. 41:1
8 *i* Prov. 11:11
10 *j* Cp. Gen. 4:5–8; 1 Jn. 3:12
11 *k* Prov. 14:33
14 *l* Ps. 72:4; Isa. 11:4
15 *m* Prov. 22:15
16 *n* Ps. 37:35–36; 58:10; 91:8; 92:11
18 *o* Cp. 1 Sam. 3:1; Amos 8:11–12
20 *p* Prov. 26:12

*
29:10 Literally *soul* **29:11** Literally *spirit*

[1](29:18) The Hebrew word rendered "revelation" indicates a revelation or vision from God, such as the visions that the prophets saw. Observe, in the latter part of this verse, the parallel to God's law.

Will have him as a son in the
end.
22 An angry man stirs up strife,
And a furious man abounds in
transgression.
23 [a]A man's pride will bring him
low,
But the humble in spirit will
retain honor.
24 Whoever is a partner with a
thief hates his own life;
He swears to tell the truth,*
but reveals [b]nothing.
25 The fear of man brings a
[c]snare,
But whoever trusts in the LORD
shall be safe.
26 Many seek the ruler's favor,
But justice for man *comes*
from the LORD.
27 An unjust man *is* an
abomination to the
righteous,
And *he who is* upright in the
way *is* an abomination to the
wicked.

IV. Supplemental Proverbs by Agur and Lemuel, 30—31

The words of Agur

30 THE [d]words of Agur the son of Jakeh, *his* [e]utterance. This man declared to Ithiel—to Ithiel and Ucal:

2 Surely I *am* more stupid than
any man,
And do not have the
understanding of a man.
3 I neither learned wisdom
Nor have [f]knowledge of the
Holy One.
4 [g]Who has ascended into
heaven, or descended?
Who has gathered the wind in
His fists?
Who has bound the waters in a
garment?
Who has established all the
ends of the earth?
What *is* His [h]name, and what
is His Son's name,
If you know?
5 [i]Every word of God *is* [j]pure;
He *is* a [k]shield to those who
put their [l]trust in Him.
6 [m]Do not add to His words,
Lest He rebuke you, and you
be found a liar.

23
a Prov. 15:33; 18:12; Isa. 66:2; Mt. 23:12; Lk. 14:11; 18:14; Jas. 4:6–10; 1 Pet. 5:5–6; cp. Dan. 4:30–32; Acts 12:23
24
b Lev. 5:1
25
c Cp. Gen. 12:12; 20:2; Jn. 12:42–43
CHAPTER 30
1
d Cp. Prov. 31:1
e Or *oracle*
3
f Prov. 9:10
4
g Jn. 3:13
h Cp. Rev. 19:12
5
i Ps. 12:6; 19:8
j Lit. *purified*
k Ps. 18:30; 84:11; 115:9–11
l See Ps. 2:12, *note*
6
m Dt. 12:32
8
n Mt. 6:11; Phil. 4:19
9
o Dt. 8:12–14, 17; 31:20; 32:15; cp. Neh. 9:25–26; Hos. 13:6
11
p Ex. 21:17
12
q Prov. 16:2; cp. Lk. 18:11
13
r Prov. 21:4
16
s See Hab. 2:5, *note;* cp. Lk. 16:23, *note*
17
t Lev. 20:9; Prov. 20:20; cp. Gen. 9:22

7 Two *things* I request of You
(Deprive me not before I die):
8 Remove falsehood and lies far
from me;
Give me neither poverty nor
riches—
Feed me with the food
[n]allotted to me;
9 [o]Lest I be full and deny *You,*
And say, "Who *is* the LORD?"
Or lest I be poor and steal,
And profane the name of my
God.
10 Do not malign a servant to his
master,
Lest he curse you, and you be
found guilty.
11 *There is* a generation *that*
curses its [p]father,
And does not bless its mother.
12 *There is* a generation *that is*
pure in its own [q]eyes,
Yet is not washed from its
filthiness.
13 *There is* a generation—oh, how
[r]lofty are their eyes!
And their eyelids are lifted up.
14 *There is* a generation whose
teeth *are like* swords,
And whose fangs *are like*
knives,
To devour the poor from off
the earth,
And the needy from *among*
men.
15 The leech has two daughters—
Give *and* Give!
There are three *things that* are
never satisfied,
Four never say, "Enough!":
16 The [s]grave,*
The barren womb,
The earth *that* is not satisfied
with water—
And the fire never says,
"Enough!"
17 The eye *that* [t]mocks *his*
father,
And scorns obedience to *his*
mother,
The ravens of the valley will
pick it out,
And the young eagles will eat
it.
18 There are three *things which*
are too wonderful for me,
Yes, four *which* I do not
understand:

*29:24 Literally *hears the adjuration* 30:16 Or *Sheol*

19 The way of an eagle in the air,
The way of a serpent on a rock,
The way of a ship in the midst of the sea,
And the way of a man with a virgin.

20 This *is* the way of an adulterous woman:
She eats and wipes her mouth,
And says, "I have done no wickedness."

21 For three *things* the earth is perturbed,
Yes, for four it cannot bear up:
22 For a servant when he [a]reigns,
A fool when he is filled with food,
23 A hateful *woman* when she is married,
And a maidservant who succeeds her mistress.

24 There are four *things which* are little on the earth,
But they *are* exceedingly wise:
25 The [b]ants *are* a people not strong,
Yet they prepare their food in the summer;
26 The [c]rock badgers* are a feeble folk,
Yet they make their homes in the crags;
27 The locusts have [d]no king,
Yet they all advance in ranks;
28 The spider* skillfully grasps with its hands,
And it is in kings' palaces.

29 There are three *things which* are majestic in pace,
Yes, four *which* are stately in walk:
30 A lion, *which is* mighty among beasts
And does not turn away from any;
31 A greyhound,*
A male goat also,
And a king *whose* troops *are* with him.*

32 If you have been foolish in exalting yourself,
Or if you have devised evil,
[e]*put your* hand on *your* mouth.
33 For *as* the churning of milk produces butter,
And wringing the nose produces blood,
So the forcing of wrath produces strife.

22 *a* Prov. 19:10
25 *b* Prov. 6:6
26 *c* Ps. 104:18
27 *d* Cp. Prov. 6:7
32 *e* Job 21:5; 40:4
CHAPTER 31
1 *f* Or *oracle*
6 *g* Cp. 1 Sam. 1:10
8 *h* Job 29:15–16 *i* Cp. 1 Sam. 19:4; Est. 4:16
9 *j* Lev. 19:15; Dt. 1:16 *k* Job 29:12; Isa. 1:17; Jer. 22:16
10 *l* Prov. 12:4; 19:14
11 *m* See Ps. 2:12, *note*

The words of Lemuel: the curse of intemperance

31 THE words of King Lemuel, the [f]utterance which his mother taught him:

2 What, my son?
And what, son of my womb?
And what, son of my vows?
3 Do not give your strength to women,
Nor your ways to that which destroys kings.

4 *It is* not for kings, O Lemuel,
It is not for kings to drink wine,
Nor for princes intoxicating drink;
5 Lest they drink and forget the law,
And pervert the justice of all the afflicted.
6 Give strong drink to him who is perishing,
And wine to those who are [g]bitter of heart.
7 Let him drink and forget his poverty,
And remember his misery no more.

8 [h]Open your mouth for the speechless,
[i]In the cause of all *who are* appointed to die.*
9 Open your mouth, [j]judge righteously,
And [k]plead the cause of the poor and needy.

Portrait of the virtuous wife

10 Who* can find a [l]virtuous* wife?
For her worth *is* far above rubies.
11 The heart of her husband safely [m]trusts her;
So he will have no lack of gain.
12 She does him good and not evil
All the days of her life.
13 She seeks wool and flax,
And willingly works with her hands.

*
30:26 Or *hyraxes* 30:28 Or *lizard* 30:31 Exact identity unknown • A Jewish tradition reads *a king against whom there is no uprising.*
31:8 Literally *sons of passing away* 31:10 Verses 10 through 31 are an alphabetic acrostic in Hebrew (compare Psalm 119). • Literally *a wife of valor,* in the sense of all forms of excellence

14 She is like the merchant ships,
She brings her food from afar.
15 [a]She also rises while it is yet night,
And [b]provides food for her household,
And a portion for her maidservants.
16 She considers a field and buys it;
From her profits she plants a vineyard.
17 She girds herself with strength,
And strengthens her arms.
18 She perceives that her merchandise *is* good,
And her lamp does not go out by night.
19 She stretches out her hands to the distaff,
And her hand holds the spindle.
20 She [c]extends her hand to the poor,
Yes, she reaches out her hands to the needy.
21 She is not afraid of snow for her household,
For all her household *is* clothed with scarlet.
22 She makes tapestry for herself;
Her clothing *is* fine linen and purple.
23 [d]Her husband is known in the gates,
When he sits among the elders of the land.
24 She makes linen garments and sells *them*,
And supplies sashes for the merchants.
25 Strength and honor *are* her clothing;
She shall rejoice in time to come.
26 She opens her mouth with wisdom,
And on her tongue *is* the law of kindness.
27 She watches over the ways of her household,
And does not eat the bread of idleness.
28 Her children rise up and call her blessed;
Her husband *also*, and he praises her:
29 "Many daughters have done well,
But you excel them all."
30 Charm *is* deceitful and beauty *is* passing,
But a woman *who* [e]fears the LORD, she shall be praised.
31 Give her of the fruit of her hands,
And let her own works praise her in the gates.

15 *a* Rom. 12:11 *b* Cp. Lk. 12:42
20 *c* Eph. 4:28; Heb. 13:16
23 *d* Prov. 12:4
30 *e* See Ps. 19:9, *note*

The Book of

ECCLESIASTES

Author: Solomon *Theme:* Man's Reasoning *Date of writing:* 10th Cent. B.C.

ECCLESIASTES, the title, is taken from the Septuagint translation of the OT and is a rendition of the Hebrew word *koheleth* and implies that the author is a teacher or preacher. In good part autobiographical, Ecclesiastes reflects those experiences of Solomon, "the Preacher . . . king in Jerusalem" (1:1), which corroborate his theme, "Vanity of vanities, all is vanity." (1:2); by "vanity" Solomon means *that which is empty, without permanent value, that which leads to frustration.*

Ecclesiastes is the book of man "under the sun" reasoning about life. The philosophy it sets forth, which makes no claim to revelation but which inspiration records for our instruction, represents the world-view of one of the wisest of men, who knew that there is a holy God and that He will bring everything into judgment. Key expressions are "under the sun," "I perceived," "I said in my heart." The mood of the book is generally one of sadness: words like "labor," "toil," or "work" occur often, as do "evil" and "misfortune." The expression "grasping for the wind" occurs fully nine times; and such words as "oppression," "sorrow," and "mourning" are prominent. The concluding chapter rises to the level of the fear of the LORD and obedience to His commandments.

Ecclesiastes may be divided as follows:

I. The Preacher's Experience of the Meaninglessness of Earthly Things, 1—4.
II. Exhortations in the Light of This Experience, 5—10.
III. The Conclusion of the Matter, 11—12.

I. The Preacher's Experience of the Vanity of Earthly Things, 1—4

His theme: all is vanity (cp. 12:8)

1 THE words of the Preacher, the son of David, [a]king in Jerusalem.

2 [1]"Vanity of vanities," says the
Preacher;
"Vanity of vanities, [b]all *is*
vanity."

Theme proved: (1) the ceaseless cycle of created things

3 [c]What profit has a man from all
his labor
In which he toils under the
sun?
4 *One* generation passes away,
and *another* generation
comes;
But the [2]earth abides forever.
5 The sun also rises, and the sun
goes down,
And [d]hastens to the place
where it [e]arose.
6 The [f]wind goes toward the
south,
And turns around to the north;
The wind whirls about
continually,
And comes again on its circuit.
7 All the rivers run into the sea,
Yet the sea *is* not full;
To the place from which the
rivers come,
There they return again.
8 All things *are* full of labor;
Man cannot express *it.*
The [g]eye is not satisfied with
seeing,
Nor the ear filled with hearing.
9 [h]That which has been *is* what
will be,
That which *is* done is what will
be done,
And *there is* nothing new
under the sun.
10 Is there anything of which it
may be said,
"See, this *is* new"?
It has already been in ancient
times before us.
11 *There is* [i]no remembrance of
former *things,*
Nor will there be any
remembrance of *things* that
are to come

CHAPTER 1
1 a Prov. 1:1
2 b Ps. 39:5–6; 62:9; 144:4; Rom. 8:20
3 c Eccl. 2:22; 3:9
5 d Lit. *pants* e Ps. 19:4–6
6 f Jn. 3:8
8 g Prov. 27:20
9 h Eccl. 3:15
11 i Eccl. 2:16

---

[1](1:2) "Vanity," in Ecclesiastes, and usually in Scripture, refers not to foolish pride but to the emptiness which is the final result of all life apart from God (see Introduction). Vanity is futility. It is to be born, to toil, to suffer, to experience some transitory joy which is as nothing in view of eternity, to leave it all, and to die. See Rom. 8:20–22. "All is vanity" is the thesis developed throughout the book, stated here at the beginning and reaching its climax in 12:8.

[2](1:4) Contrast Mt. 24:35. Man "under the sun" might from his own experience mistakenly think that the earth would continue indefinitely as it now is.

By *those* who will come after.

(2) Wisdom cannot satisfy

12 I, the Preacher, was king over
Israel in Jerusalem.
13 And I set my heart to seek and
[a]search out by wisdom concerning all
that is done under heaven; [b]this burdensome task God has given to the
sons of man, by which they may be
exercised.
14 I have seen all the works that are
done under the sun; and indeed, all *is*
vanity and grasping for the wind.

15 *What is* crooked cannot be
made [c]straight,
And what is lacking cannot be
numbered.

16 I communed with my heart, saying, "Look, I have attained greatness,
and have gained more wisdom [d]than
all who were before me in Jerusalem.
My heart has understood great wisdom and knowledge."
17 And I [e]set my heart to know wisdom and to know madness and folly.
I perceived that this also is grasping
for the wind.

18 For in much wisdom *is* much
grief,
And he who increases
knowledge increases sorrow.

Proof continued: (3) pleasure and riches cannot satisfy

2 I [f]SAID in my heart, "Come now,
I will test you with [g]mirth; therefore enjoy pleasure"; but surely, this
also *was* vanity.
2 I said of laughter—"Madness!";
and of mirth, "What does it accomplish?"
3 I searched in my heart *how* [h]to
gratify my flesh with wine, while guiding my heart with wisdom, and how to
lay hold on [i]folly, till I might see what
was [j]good for the sons of men to do
under heaven all the days of their
lives.
4 I made my works great, I built
myself [k]houses, and planted myself
vineyards.
5 I made myself gardens and or-
chards, and I planted all *kinds* of fruit
trees in them.
6 I made myself water pools from
which to water the growing trees of
the grove.
7 I acquired male and female servants, and had servants born in my
house. Yes, I had greater possessions

13
a Eccl. 7:25; 8:16–17
b Gen. 3:19; Eccl. 3:10
15
c Eccl. 7:13
16
d 1 Ki. 3:12
17
e Eccl. 2:3, 12; 7:23, 25; 1 Th. 5:21
CHAPTER 2
1
f Lk. 12:19
g Prov. 14:13; Eccl. 7:4; 8:15
3
h Lit. *to draw*
i Eccl. 1:17
j v. 24; Eccl. 3:12–13; 5:18; 6:12; 8:15; 12:13
4
k 1 Ki. 7:1–12
7
l 1 Ki. 4:23
8
m 1 Ki. 9:28; 10:10,14, 21,27
9
n Eccl. 1:16
o 2 Chr. 9:22
10
p Eccl. 3:22; 5:18; 9:9
11
q Eccl. 1:2, 14
12
r Eccl. 1:17; 7:25
s Eccl. 1:9
13
t Eccl. 7:11–12, 19; 9:18; 10:10
14
u Prov. 17:24; Eccl. 8:1
v Eccl. 9:2–3; Ps. 49:10
16
w Eccl. 1:11; 4:16

of [l]herds and flocks than all who
were in Jerusalem before me.
8 I also [m]gathered for myself silver
and gold and the special treasures of
kings and of the provinces. I acquired
male and female singers, the delights
of the sons of men, *and* musical instruments* of all kinds.
9 [n]So I became great and excelled
[o]more than all who were before me in
Jerusalem. Also my wisdom remained
with me.

10 Whatever my eyes desired I
did not keep from them.
I did not withhold my heart
from any pleasure,
For my heart rejoiced in all my
labor;
And this was my [p]reward from
all my labor.
11 Then I looked on all the works
that my hands had done
And on the labor in which I
had toiled;
And indeed all *was* [q]vanity
and grasping for the wind.
There was no profit under the
sun.

(4) Wisdom is better than folly, but both have an end

12 Then I turned myself to
consider wisdom and
[r]madness and folly;
For what *can* the man *do* who
succeeds the king?—
Only what he has already
[s]done.
13 Then I saw that wisdom
[t]excels folly
As light excels darkness.
14 The [u]wise man's eyes *are* in
his head,
But the fool walks in darkness.
Yet I myself perceived
That the [v]same event happens
to them all.

15 So I said in my heart,
"As it happens to the fool,
It also happens to me,
And why was I then more
wise?"
Then I said in my heart,
"This also *is* vanity."
16 For *there is* [w]no more
remembrance of the wise
than of the fool forever,
Since all that now *is* will be
forgotten in the days to
come.

* 2:8 Exact meaning unknown

And how does a wise *man* die?
As the fool!

17 Therefore I hated life because the work that was done under the sun *was* distressing to me, for all *is* vanity and grasping for the wind.

18 Then I hated all my labor in which I had toiled under the sun, because I must [a]leave it to the man who will come after me.

19 And who knows whether he will be wise or a fool? Yet he will rule over all my labor in which I toiled and in which I have shown myself wise under the sun. This also *is* vanity.

20 Therefore I turned my heart and despaired of all the labor in which I had toiled under the sun.

21 For there is a man whose labor *is* with wisdom, knowledge, and skill; yet he must leave his heritage to a man who has not labored for it. This also *is* vanity and a great evil.

22 [b]For what has man for all his labor, and for the striving of his heart with which he has toiled under the sun?

23 For all his days *are* [c]sorrowful, and his work burdensome; even in the night his heart takes no rest. This also is vanity.

24 Nothing *is* [d]better for a man *than* that he should eat and drink, and *that* his soul should enjoy good in his labor. This also, I saw, was from the hand of God.

25 For who can eat, or who can have enjoyment, more than I?*

26 For *God* gives [e]wisdom and knowledge and joy to a man who *is* good [f]in His sight; but to the sinner He gives the work of [g]gathering and collecting, that he may give to *him who is* good before God. This also *is* vanity and grasping for the wind.

Proof continued: (5) the weary round of life

3 TO everything *there is* a
season,
A [1]time for every purpose
under heaven:

2 A time to be born,
And a time to [h]die;
A time to plant,
And a time to pluck *what is*
planted;
3 A time to kill,
And a time to heal;
A time to break down,
And a time to build up;
4 A time to [i]weep,
And a time to laugh;
A time to mourn,
And a time to dance;
5 A time to cast away stones,
And a time to gather stones;
A time to embrace,
And a time to [j]refrain from
embracing;
6 A time to gain,
And a time to lose;
A time to keep,
And a time to throw away;
7 A time to tear,
And a time to sew;
A time to keep [k]silence,
And a time to [l]speak;
8 A time to love,
And a time to [m]hate;
A time of war,
And a time of peace.

9 What profit has the worker from that in which he labors?

10 I have seen the God-given [n]task with which the sons of men are to be occupied.

11 He has made everything beautiful in its time. Also He has put eternity in their hearts, except that no one can [o]find out the work that God does from beginning to end.

12 I know that nothing *is* [p]better for them than to rejoice, and to do good in their lives,

13 and also that every man should eat and drink and enjoy the good of all his labor—it *is* the [q]gift of God.

14 I know that whatever God
does,
It shall be forever.
[r]Nothing can be added to it,
And nothing taken from it.
God does *it*, that men should
[s]fear before Him.
15 That which is has already
been,
And what is to be has already
been;
And God requires an account
of what is past.

16 [2]Moreover I saw under the sun:

18
a Ps. 49:10
22
b Eccl. 1:3; 3:9
23
c Job 5:7; 14:1
24
d Eccl. 5:18; cp. 1 Tim. 6:7
26
e Prov. 2:6; Jas. 1:5
f Lit. *before him* Gen. 7:1; Lk. 1:6
g Job 27:16–17; Prov. 28:8
CHAPTER 3
2
h See Heb. 9:27, *note*
4
i Rom. 12:15
5
j Joel 2:16; 1 Cor. 7:5
7
k Amos 5:13
l Prov. 25:11
8
m Prov. 13:5; Lk. 14:26
10
n Eccl. 2:23
11
o Eccl. 8:17
12
p Eccl. 2:3, 24
13
q 1 Cor. 7:7; Jas. 1:17; cp. Jn. 4:10; Rom. 6:23; 2 Cor. 9:15; Eph. 2:8
14
r Jas. 1:17
s See Ps. 19:9, *note*

*
2:25 Following Masoretic Text, Targum, and Vulgate; some Hebrew manuscripts, Septuagint, and Syriac read *without Him.*

[1](3:1) God's sure purpose must not be confused with fatalism, a theory proved false by God's appeals to men to repent and obey.

[2](3:16) The theory known as deism, that God is unconcerned about His world, is disproved

In the place of [a]judgment,
Wickedness *was* there;
And *in* the place of
righteousness,
Iniquity *was* there.

17 I said in my heart,
[b]"God shall judge the righteous
and the wicked,
For *there is* a time there for
every purpose and for every
work."

18 I said in my heart, "Concerning
the condition of the sons of men, God
tests them, that they may see that they
themselves are *like* animals."
19 [c]For what happens to the sons
of men also happens to animals; one
thing befalls them: as one dies, so dies
the other. Surely, they all have one
breath; man has no advantage over
animals, for all *is* vanity.
20 All go to one place: [d]all are from
the dust, and all return to dust.
21 Who knows the spirit of the sons
of men, which goes [e]upward, and the
spirit of the animal, which goes down
to the earth?*
22 So I perceived that nothing *is*
[f]better than that a man should rejoice
in his own works, for that *is* his heritage. For who can bring him to see
what will happen after him?

Life's oppressions and inequalities

4 THEN I returned and considered
all the [g]oppression that is done
under the sun:

And look! The tears of the
oppressed,
But they have no comforter—
On the [h]side of their
oppressors *there is* power,
But they have no comforter.
2 [i]Therefore I praised the dead
who were already dead,
More than the living who are
still alive.
3 Yet, better than both *is he* who
has never existed,
Who has not seen the evil
work that is done under the
sun.

4 Again, I saw that for all toil and
every skillful work a man is envied by
his neighbor. This also *is* vanity and
grasping for the wind.

5 The fool folds his hands
And consumes his own flesh.
6 [j]Better a handful *with* quietness
Than both hands full, *together
with* toil and grasping for
the wind.

7 Then I returned, and I saw vanity under the sun:

8 There is one alone, without
companion:
He has neither son nor
brother.
Yet *there is* no end to all his
labors,
Nor is his [k]eye satisfied with
riches.
[l]*But he never asks,*
"For whom do I toil and deprive
myself of [m]good?"
This also *is* vanity and a grave
misfortune.
9 Two *are* better than one,
Because they have a good
reward for their labor.
10 For if they fall, one will lift up
his companion.
But woe to him *who is* alone
when he falls,
For *he has* no one to help him
up.
11 Again, if two lie down
together, they will keep
warm;
But how can one be warm
alone?
12 Though one may be
overpowered by another,
two can withstand him.
And a threefold cord is not
quickly broken.
13 Better a poor and wise youth
Than an old and foolish king
who will be admonished no
more.
14 For he comes out of prison to
be king,
Although he was born poor in
his kingdom.
15 I saw all the living who walk
under the sun;
They were with the second
youth who stands in his
place.
16 *There was* no end of all the
people over whom he was
made king;

16 *a* Eccl. 5:8
17 *b* Eccl. 11:9; Rom. 2:6–8; 2 Cor. 5:10; 2 Th. 1:6–7
19 *c* Ps. 49:12, 20; 73:22; Eccl. 2:16
20 *d* Gen. 3:19
21 *e* Eccl. 12:7
22 *f* Eccl. 2:24
CHAPTER 4
1 *g* Eccl. 3:16; 5:8 *h* Lit. *hand*
2 *i* Job 10:18
6 *j* Prov. 15:16–17; 16:8
8 *k* Prov. 27:20; Eccl. 5:10; 1 Jn. 2:16 *l* Ps. 39:6 *m* Eccl. 2:18–21

*3:21 Septuagint, Syriac, Targum, and Vulgate read *Who knows whether the spirit . . . goes upward, and whether . . . goes downward to the earth?*

by the Scripture's emphasis on God's intervention in human affairs (Dan. 4:23–27; Jn. 3:16; 2 Pet. 3:9).

Yet those who come afterward
will not rejoice in him.
Surely this also *is* vanity and
grasping for the wind.

II. Exhortations in the Light of This Experience, 5—10

Mere religious practices cannot satisfy, vv. 1–8

5 [a]WALK prudently when you go
to the house of God; and draw
near to hear [b]rather than to give the
sacrifice of fools, for they do not know
that they do evil.

2 Do not be [c]rash with your
mouth,
And let not your heart utter
anything hastily before God.
For God *is* in heaven, and you
on earth;
Therefore let your words be
[d]few.
3 For a dream comes through
much activity,
And a fool's voice *is known* by
his many words.
4 [e]When you make a vow to God,
do not delay to [f]pay it;
For *He has* no pleasure in
fools.
Pay what you have vowed—
5 [g]Better not to vow than to vow
and not pay.

6 Do not let your [h]mouth cause
your flesh to sin, nor say before the
[i]messenger *of God* that it *was* an error. Why should God be angry at your
excuse* and destroy the work of your
hands?
7 For in the multitude of dreams
and many words *there is* also vanity.
But [j]fear God.
8 If you see the oppression of the
poor, and the violent perversion of
[k]justice and righteousness in a province, do not marvel at the matter; for
high official [l]watches over high official, and higher officials are over
them.

The futility of riches

9 Moreover the profit of the land is
for all; *even* the king is served from
the field.

10 He who loves silver will not be
satisfied with silver;
Nor he who loves abundance,
with increase.
This also *is* vanity.
11 When goods increase,
They increase who eat them;

CHAPTER 5
1
a Cp. Isa. 1:12
b 1 Sam. 15:22; Ps. 50:8; Prov. 15:8; 21:27; Hos. 6:6
2
c Prov. 20:25
d Prov. 10:19; Mt. 6:7
4
e Num. 30:2; Dt. 23:21–23; Ps. 50:14; 76:11
f Ps. 66:13–14
5
g Prov. 20:25; cp. Acts 5:1–11
6
h Prov. 6:2
i See Heb. 1:4, *note*
7
j Eccl. 12:13; see Ps. 19:9, *note*
8
k Eccl. 3:16
l Ex. 2:25; Ps. 94:3–10
15
m Job 1:21; Ps. 49:17; 1 Tim. 6:7
16
n Prov. 11:29; cp. Lk. 12:16–21
18
o Eccl. 2:24; 3:12–13; 9:7; 11:9; 1 Tim. 6:17
19
p Eccl. 6:2
q Eccl. 3:13
CHAPTER 6
2
r 1 Ki. 3:13; Ps. 17:13–14; 73:7
s Lk. 12:20; cp. Eccl. 5:13

So what profit have the
owners
Except to see *them* with their
eyes?
12 The sleep of a laboring man *is*
sweet,
Whether he eats little or much;
But the abundance of the rich
will not permit him to sleep.
13 There is a severe evil *which* I
have seen under the sun:
Riches kept for their owner to
his hurt.
14 But those riches perish
through misfortune;
When he begets a son, *there is*
nothing in his hand.
15 [m]As he came from his mother's
womb, naked shall he
return,
To go as he came;
And he shall take nothing from
his labor
Which he may carry away in
his hand.
16 And this also *is* a severe evil—
Just exactly as he came, so
shall he go.
And what profit has he [n]who
has labored for the wind?
17 All his days he also eats in
darkness,
And *he has* much sorrow and
sickness and anger.

18 Here is what I have seen: [o]*It is*
good and fitting *for one* to eat and
drink, and to enjoy the good of all his
labor in which he toils under the sun
all the days of his life which God gives
him; for it *is* his heritage.
19 [p]As for every man to whom God
has given riches and wealth, and
given him power to eat of it, to receive
his heritage and rejoice in his labor—
this *is* the [q]gift of God.
20 For he will not dwell unduly on
the days of his life, because God keeps
him busy with the joy of his heart.

The futility of life

6 THERE is an evil which I have
seen under the sun, and it *is* common among men:
2 A man to whom God has given
riches and wealth and honor, [r]so that
he lacks nothing for himself of all he
desires; [s]yet God does not give him
power to eat of it, but a foreigner con-

*5:6 Literally *voice*

sumes it. This *is* vanity, and it *is* an evil
[a]affliction.
3 If a man begets a hundred *chil-*
dren and lives many years, so that the
days of his years are many, but his
soul is not satisfied with goodness, or
[b]indeed he has no burial, I say *that* a
stillborn child *is* better than he—
4 for it comes in vanity and departs in darkness, and its name is covered with darkness.
5 Though it has not seen the sun or
known *anything*, this has more rest
than that man,
6 even if he lives a thousand years
twice—but has not seen goodness. Do
not all go to one [c]place?

7 [d]All the labor of man *is* for his
mouth,
And yet the [e]soul is not
satisfied.
8 For what more has the wise
man than the fool?
What does the poor man have,
Who knows *how* to walk
before the living?
9 Better *is* the [f]sight of the eyes
than the wandering of
desire.
This also *is* vanity and
grasping for the wind.

10 Whatever one is, he has been
named [g]already,
For it is known that he *is* man;
[h]And he cannot contend with
Him who is mightier than
he.
11 Since there are many things
that increase vanity,
How *is* man the [1]better?

12 For who knows what *is* good for
man in life, all the days of his vain life
which he passes [i]like a shadow? Who
can tell a man [j]what will happen after
him under the sun?

Human wisdom's better findings

7 A [k]GOOD name *is* better than
precious ointment,
And the day of death than the
day of one's [l]birth;
2 Better to go to the house of
mourning
Than to go to the house of
feasting,
For that *is* the end of all men;
And the living will take *it* to
[m]heart.
3 [n]Sorrow *is* better than laughter,
For by a sad countenance the
heart is made better.
4 The heart of the wise *is* in the
house of mourning,
But the heart of fools *is* in the
house of mirth.
5 [o]*It is* better to hear the rebuke
of the wise
Than for a man to hear the
song of fools.
6 For like the crackling of thorns
under a pot,
So *is* the laughter of the fool.
This also is vanity.
7 Surely oppression destroys a
wise *man's* reason,
And a [p]bribe debases the
heart.

8 The end of a thing *is* better
than its beginning;
The [q]patient in spirit *is* better
than the proud in spirit.
9 [r]Do not hasten in your spirit to
be angry,
For anger rests in the bosom of
fools.
10 Do not say,
"Why were the former days
better than these?"
For you do not inquire wisely
concerning this.
11 Wisdom *is* good with an
inheritance,
And profitable to those who
see the sun.
12 For wisdom *is* a [s]defense *as*
money *is* a defense,
But the excellence of
knowledge *is that* wisdom
gives [t]life to those who have
it.

13 Consider the work of God;
For who can make straight
what He has made crooked?
14 In the day of prosperity be
joyful,
But in the day of adversity
consider:
Surely God has appointed the
one as well as the other,
So that man can find out
nothing *that will come* after
him.

2
a Cp. Eccl. 5:19
3
b 2 Ki. 9:35; Isa. 14:19–20; Jer. 22:19
6
c Eccl. 2:14–15
7
d Prov. 16:26
e Eccl. 4:8
9
f Eccl. 11:9
10
g Eccl. 1:9; 3:15
h Job 9:32; Isa. 45:9; Jer. 49:19
12
i Ps. 102:11; 109:23; 144:4; Jas. 4:14
j Eccl. 3:22
CHAPTER 7
1
k Prov. 15:30; 22:1
l Eccl. 4:2
2
m Ps. 90:12
3
n 2 Cor. 7:10
5
o Ps. 141:5; Prov. 13:18; 15:31–32
7
p Ex. 23:8; Dt. 16:19
8
q Prov. 14:29
9
r Prov. 14:17; 16:32; Jas. 1:19
12
s Eccl. 9:18
t Prov. 3:18

[1](6:11) Compare 5:18–20. In view of the futility to which his searching into the meaning of life has led, the Preacher declares that there is little satisfaction for man beyond the pleasure of eating and drinking, and the enjoyment of the fruit of man's labor. By way of contrast, consider the spiritual tone of the Preacher's final exhortation (12:13–14).

15 I have seen everything in my
days of vanity:

There is a just *man* who
perishes in his
righteousness,
And there is a wicked *man*
who prolongs *life* in his
[a]wickedness.

16 [1]Do not be overly righteous,
Nor be overly wise:
Why should you destroy
yourself?
17 Do not be overly wicked,
Nor be foolish:
Why should you die before
your time?
18 *It is* good that you grasp this,
And also not remove your
hand from the other;
For he who [b]fears God will
escape them all.

19 Wisdom strengthens the wise
More than ten rulers of the
[c]city.

20 For *there is* not a [d]just [e]man
on earth who does good
And does not sin.
21 Also do not take to heart
everything people say,
Lest you hear your servant
cursing you.
22 For many times, also, your
own heart has known
That even you have cursed
others.

23 All this I have proved by
wisdom.
I said, "I will be wise";
But it *was* far from me.
24 As for [f]that which is far off
and [g]exceedingly deep,
Who can find it out?
25 I applied my heart to know,
To search and seek out
wisdom and the reason *of*
things,
To know the wickedness of
folly,
Even of foolishness *and*
madness.
26 And I find more [h]bitter than
death
The woman whose heart *is*
snares and nets,
Whose hands *are* fetters.
He who pleases God shall
escape from her,

15
a Eccl. 8:12–14
18
b Eccl. 3:14; 5:7; 8:12–13
19
c Eccl. 9:13–18; cp. 2 Sam. 20:15–22
20
d Righteousness (OT): v. 20; Isa. 26:7. (Gen. 6:9; Lk. 2:25, *note*)
e 1 Ki. 8:46; 2 Chr. 6:36; Prov. 20:9; Rom. 3:23; 1 Jn. 1:8
24
f Job 28:12, 20; 1 Tim. 6:16
g Rom. 11:33
26
h Prov. 5:4
28
i Cp. 1 Ki. 11:1–8
29
j Gen. 1:27
k Gen. 3:6–7
CHAPTER 8
1
l Prov. 4:8–9; 17:24
m Or *strength*
2
n 1 Chr. 29:24; Ezek. 17:18; Rom. 13:5
3
o Eccl. 10:4
p Cp. 1 Ki. 2:36–46
4
q Job 34:18
5
r Lit. *will know*
6
s Eccl. 3:17
7
t Prov. 24:22; Eccl. 6:12; 9:12; 10:14
8
u Job 14:5
v Cp. Jn. 10:18
w Dt. 20:5–8

But the sinner shall be trapped
by her.

27 "Here is what I have found,"
says the Preacher,
"*Adding* one thing to the other
to find out the reason,
28 Which my soul still seeks but I
cannot find:
One man among a thousand I
have found,
But a [i]woman among all these
I have not found.
29 Truly, this only I have found:
That God made man [j]upright,
But they have sought out many
[k]schemes."

Importance of obeying rulers

8 WHO *is* like a wise *man?*
And who knows the
interpretation of a thing?
A man's [l]wisdom makes his
face shine,
And the [m]sternness of his face
is changed.

2 I *say,* "Keep the king's commandment [n]for the sake of your oath
to God.
3 "Do not be hasty to go from his
[o]presence. Do not take your stand for
an evil thing, for he does whatever
pleases [p]him."
4 Where the word of a king *is,*
there is power;
And [q]who may say to him,
"What are you doing?"
5 He who keeps his command
[r]will experience nothing
harmful;
And a wise man's heart
discerns both time and
judgment,
6 Because for every matter there
is a time and [s]judgment,
Though the misery of man
increases greatly.
7 [t]For he does not know what
will happen;
So who can tell him when it
will occur?
8 No one has power [u]over the
spirit to retain the spirit,
And no one has power in the
day of [v]death.
There is [w]no release from that
war,
And wickedness will not

[1](7:16) Natural wisdom would suggest, as do vv. 16–17, that one might well be both moderately religious and moderately wicked.

deliver those who are given
to it.

9 All this I have seen, and applied
my heart to every work that is done
under the sun: *There is* a time in which
one man rules over another to his own
hurt.
10 Then I saw the wicked buried,
who had come and gone from the
place of holiness, and they were [a]for-
gotten* in the city where they had so
done. This also *is* vanity.
11 Because the sentence against an
evil work is not executed speedily,
therefore the heart of the sons of men
is fully set in them to do [b]evil.
12 [c]Though a sinner does evil a
hundred *times*, and his *days* are prolonged, yet I surely know that [d]it will
be well with those who [e]fear God,
who fear before Him.
13 But it will not be well with the
wicked; nor will he prolong *his* days,
which are as a shadow, because he
does not fear before God.
14 There is a vanity which occurs
on earth, that there are just *men* to
whom it happens according to the
work of the wicked; again, there are
wicked *men* to whom it happens according to the work of the [f]righteous.
I said that this also *is* vanity.
15 So I commended enjoyment, because a man has nothing better under
the sun than to eat, drink, and be
[g]merry; for this will remain with him
in his labor *all* the days of his life
which God gives him under the sun.
16 When I applied my heart to
know wisdom and to see the business
that is done on earth, even though one
sees no sleep day or night,
17 then I saw all the work of God,
that a [h]man cannot find out the work
that is done under the sun. For though
a man labors to discover *it*, yet he will
not find *it;* moreover, though a wise
man attempts to know *it*, [i]he will not
be able to find *it*.

Despite wisdom, death is certain

9 FOR I considered all this in my
heart, so that I could declare it all:
that the righteous and the wise and
their works *are* in the [j]hand of God.
People know neither love nor hatred
by anything *they see* before them.

2 All things *come* alike to all:
[k]One event *happens* to the
righteous and the wicked;
To the good,* the clean, and
the unclean;
To him who sacrifices and him
who does not sacrifice.
As is the good, so *is* the sinner;
He who takes an oath as *he*
who fears an oath.

3 This *is* an [l]evil in all that is done
under the sun: that one thing *happens*
to all. Truly the hearts of the sons of
men are full of evil; madness *is* in their
hearts while they live, and after that
they go to the dead.
4 But for him who is joined to all
the living there is hope, for a living
dog is better than a dead lion.

5 For the living know that they
will die;
But the dead know nothing,
And they have no more
reward,
For the memory of them is
[m]forgotten.
6 Also their love, their hatred,
and their envy have now
perished;
Nevermore will they have a
share
In anything done under the
sun.

7 Go, [n]eat your bread with joy,
And drink your wine with a
merry heart;
For God has already accepted
your works.
8 Let your garments always be
white,
And let your head lack no oil.

9 [o]Live joyfully with the wife
whom you love all the days of your
vain life which He has given you under the sun, all your days of vanity;
[p]for that *is* your portion in life, and in
the labor which you perform under
the sun.
10 [q]Whatever your hand finds to
do, do *it* with your [r]might; [1]for *there*
is no work or device or knowledge or

10 *a* Eccl. 2:16; 9:5
11 *b* Cp. Ex. 8:15
12 *c* Isa. 65:20; Rom. 2:5 *d* Ps. 37:11, 18–19; Prov. 1:32–33; Isa. 3:10; Mt. 25:34 *e* See Ps. 19:9, *note*
14 *f* Eccl. 7:15
15 *g* Eccl. 2:24
17 *h* Job 5:9; Eccl. 3:11; Rom. 11:33 *i* Job 9:1,10; Ps. 73:16–17
CHAPTER 9
1 *j* Dt. 33:3; Job 12:10
2 *k* Gen. 3:17–19; see Heb. 9:27, *note*
3 *l* Eccl. 7:20
5 *m* Eccl. 8:10
7 *n* Eccl. 8:15
9 *o* Lit. *See* or *Enjoy life* *p* Eccl. 2:10, 24; 3:13, 22; 5:18
10 *q* Col. 3:17 *r* Rom. 12:11; Col. 3:23

*

8:10 Some Hebrew manuscripts, Septuagint, and Vulgate read *praised.* **9:2** Septuagint, Syriac, and Vulgate read *good and bad.*

[1](9:10) This statement is no more a divine revelation concerning the state of the dead than any other conclusion of "the Preacher" (1:1). No one would quote 9:2 as a divine revelation. These reasonings of man apart from divine revelation are set down by inspiration just as the words of Satan (Gen. 3:4; Job 2:4–5; etc.) are so recorded. But that life and consciousness continue between death and resurrection is directly affirmed in Scripture (Isa. 14:9–11; Mt.

wisdom in the [a]grave where you are going.

11 I returned and saw under the sun that—

The [b]race *is* not to the swift,
Nor the battle to the strong,
Nor bread to the wise,
Nor riches to men of understanding,
Nor favor to men of skill;
But time and [c]chance happen to them all.
12 For man also does not know his time:
Like fish taken in a cruel net,
Like birds caught in a snare,
So the sons of men *are* [d]snared in an evil time,
When it falls suddenly upon them.

13 This wisdom I have also seen under the sun, and it *seemed* great to me:

14 [e]*There was* a little city with few men in it; and a great king came against it, besieged it, and built great snares* around it.

15 Now there was found in it a poor wise man, and he by his wisdom delivered the city. Yet no one remembered that same poor man.

16 Then I said:

"Wisdom *is* better than [f]strength.
Nevertheless the [g]poor man's wisdom *is* despised,
And his words are not heard.
17 Words of the wise, *spoken* quietly, *should be* heard
Rather than the shout of a ruler of fools.
18 Wisdom *is* better than weapons of war;
But [h]one sinner destroys much good."

Beware a little folly

10

DEAD flies putrefy* the perfumer's ointment,
And cause it to give off a foul odor;
So does a little folly to one respected for wisdom *and* honor.
2 A wise man's heart *is* at his right hand,
But a fool's heart at his left.
3 Even when a fool walks along the way,
He lacks wisdom,
And he shows everyone *that* [i]he *is* a fool.
4 If the spirit of the ruler rises against you,
Do not leave your [j]post;
For [k]conciliation pacifies great offenses.

5 There is an evil I have seen under the sun,
As an error proceeding from the ruler:
6 Folly is set in great [l]dignity,
While the rich sit in a lowly place.
7 [m]I have seen servants on horses,
While princes walk on the ground like servants.

8 [n]He who digs a pit will fall into it,
And whoever breaks through a wall will be bitten by a serpent.
9 He who quarries stones may be hurt by them,
And he who splits wood may be endangered by it.
10 If the ax is dull,
And one does not sharpen the edge,
Then he must use more strength;
But wisdom brings success.

11 A serpent may bite [o]when *it is* not charmed;
The babbler is no different.
12 The words of a wise man's mouth *are* [p]gracious,
But the lips of a fool shall swallow him up;
13 The words of his mouth begin with foolishness,
And the end of his talk *is* raving madness.
14 A fool also multiplies words.
No man knows what is to be;
Who can tell him what will be after him?
15 The labor of fools wearies them,
For they do not even know how to go to the city!

16 [q]Woe to you, O land, when your king *is* a child,
And your princes feast in the morning!
17 Blessed *are* you, O land, when

10 *a* See Hab. 2:5, *note;* cp. Lk. 16:23, *note*
11 *b* Jer. 9:23; Amos 2:14–15
c 1 Sam. 6:9; cp. Rom. 9:16
12 *d* Prov. 29:6; Lk. 12:20,39, 46; 17:26; 21:35; 1 Th. 5:3
14 *e* Cp. 2 Sam. 20:15–22
16 *f* Eccl. 7:12, 19
g Cp. Mk. 6:2–3
18 *h* Cp. Josh. 7

CHAPTER 10
3 *i* Prov. 13:16; 18:2
4 *j* Eccl. 8:3
k Prov. 25:15; cp. 1 Sam. 25:23–25
6 *l* Cp. Est. 3:1
7 *m* Prov. 19:10; cp. Heb. 11:36–38
8 *n* Ps. 7:15; Prov. 26:27; cp. Est. 7:9–10
11 *o* Ps. 58:4–5; Jer. 8:17
12 *p* Prov. 10:32; Lk. 4:22
16 *q* Isa. 3:4–5, 12; 5:11

*
9:14 Septuagint, Syriac, and Vulgate read *bulwarks.*
10:1 Targum and Vulgate omit *putrefy.*

22:32; Mk. 9:43–48; Lk. 16:19–31; 2 Cor. 5:6–8; Phil. 1:21–23; Rev. 6:9–11).

your king *is* the son of nobles,
And your [a]princes feast at the proper time—
For strength and not for drunkenness!
18 Because of laziness the building decays,
And [b]through idleness of hands the house leaks.
19 A feast is made for laughter,
And [c]wine makes merry;
But money answers everything.

20 [d]Do not curse the king, even in your thought;
Do not curse the rich, even in your bedroom;
For a bird of the air may carry your voice,
And a bird in flight may tell the matter.

III. The Conclusion of the Matter, 11—12

The best thing possible to the natural man

11 CAST your bread [e]upon the waters,
[f]For you will find it after many days.
2 [g]Give a serving to seven, and also to eight,
For you do not know what evil will be on the earth.

3 If the clouds are full of rain,
They empty *themselves* upon the earth;
And if a tree falls to the south or the north,
In the place where the tree falls, there it shall lie.
4 He who observes the wind will not sow,
And he who regards the clouds will not reap.

5 [h]As you do not know what *is* the way of the wind,*
[i]*Or* how the bones *grow* in the womb of her who is with child,
So you do not know the works of God who makes everything.
6 In the morning sow your seed,
And in the evening do not withhold your hand;
For you do not know which will prosper,
Either this or that,
Or whether both alike *will be* good.

7 Truly the light is [j]sweet,
And *it is* pleasant for the eyes to [k]behold the sun;
8 But if a man lives many years
And [l]rejoices in them all,
Yet let him [m]remember the days of darkness,
For they will be many.
All that is coming *is* vanity.

9 Rejoice, O young man, in your youth,
And let your heart cheer you in the days of your youth;
[n]Walk in the ways of your heart,
And in the sight of your eyes;
But know that for all these
[o]God will bring you into judgment.
10 Therefore remove sorrow from your heart,
And [p]put away evil from your flesh,
For childhood and youth *are* vanity.

Fear God; keep His commandments

12 REMEMBER now your Creator in the [q]days of your youth,
Before the difficult days come,
And the years draw near
[r]when you say,
"I have no pleasure in them":
2 While the sun and the light,
The moon and the stars,
Are not darkened,
And the clouds do not return after the rain;
3 In the day [1]when the keepers of the house tremble,

17
a Prov. 31:4
18
b Prov. 24:30–34
19
c Ps. 104:15
20
d Ex. 22:28; Acts 23:5
CHAPTER 11
1
e Isa. 32:20
f Dt. 15:10; Prov. 19:17; Mt. 10:42; 2 Cor. 9:8; Gal. 6:9–10; Heb. 6:10
2
g Ps. 112:9; Lk. 6:30; 1 Tim. 6:18–19
5
h Jn. 3:8
i Ps. 139:14–15
7
j Prov. 15:30
k Eccl. 7:11
8
l Eccl. 9:7
m Eccl. 12:1
9
n Cp. Jn. 12:35–36
o Eccl. 12:14; Rom. 2:6–11
10
p 2 Cor. 7:1; 2 Tim. 2:22
CHAPTER 12
1
q 2 Chr. 34:3; Prov. 22:6; Lam. 3:27
r Cp. 2 Sam. 19:35

* 11:5 Or *spirit*

[1](12:3) Verses 1–7, which describe the process of growing old, comprise poetry of supreme beauty and universal appeal. "The keepers of the house" may be likened to the hands; "the strong men," the legs; "the grinders," the teeth; "those that look through the windows," the eyes; "the doors," the ears; "the sound of grinding," the hum of conversation in the household. Several vivid phrases follow: rising up "at the sound of a bird" may refer either to the early rising or to the thin, high voice of the aged; being "afraid of height" may be said to picture the tottering caution of the very old. Other figures complete the description: "the almond tree," with its white blossoms, may be the white hair of old age; the "grasshopper" dragging himself along possibly portrays extreme weakness; "desire" suggests the waning of vital force; the

And the strong men bow
down;
When the grinders cease
because they are few,
And those that look through
the windows grow dim;
4 When the doors are shut in the
streets,
And the sound of grinding is
low;
When one rises up at the
sound of a bird,
And all the daughters of music
are brought low.
5 Also they are afraid of height,
And of terrors in the way;
When the almond tree
blossoms,
The grasshopper is a burden,
And desire fails.
For man goes to his [a]eternal
home,
And the [b]mourners go about
the streets.

6 *Remember your Creator* before
the silver cord is loosed,*
Or the golden bowl is broken,
Or the pitcher shattered at the
fountain,
Or the wheel broken at the
well.
7 [c]Then the dust will return to the
earth as it was,
And the [d]spirit will return to
God [e]who gave it.

8 "Vanity of vanities," says the
Preacher,
"All *is* vanity."

9 And moreover, because the
Preacher was wise, he still taught the
people knowledge; yes, he pondered
and sought out *and* [f]set in order many
proverbs.
10 The Preacher sought to find acceptable words; and *what was* written
was upright—words of truth.
11 The words of the wise are like
goads, and the words of scholars* are
like well-driven nails, given by one
Shepherd.
12 And further, my son, be admonished by these. Of making many
books *there is* no end, and much study
is wearisome to the flesh.
13 Let us hear the conclusion of the
whole matter:

[g]Fear God and keep His
[1]commandments,
For this is man's all.
14 For [h]God will bring every
work into judgment,
Including every secret thing,
Whether good or evil.

5
a Job 17:13
b Jer. 9:17
7
c Gen. 3:19; Job 34:15; Ps. 90:3
d Eccl. 3:21
e Num. 16:22; 27:16; Job 34:14; Isa. 57:16; Zech. 12:1
9
f 1 Ki. 4:32
13
g Dt. 6:2; 10:12; see Ps. 19:9, *note*
14
h Eccl. 11:9; Mt. 12:36; Acts 17:30–31; Rom. 2:16; 14:10–12; 1 Cor. 4:5; 2 Cor. 5:10

*
12:6 Following Qere and Targum; Kethib reads *removed;* Septuagint and Vulgate read *broken.*
12:11 Literally *masters of assemblies*

"eternal home," the grave. Some see in "the silver cord," "the golden bowl," "the pitcher," and "the wheel" metaphors for the spinal cord, skull, and the circulatory system; but it is better to take them simply as picturing the dissolution of soul and body.

[1](12:13) "Keep His commandments" implies a definite revelation, for the commandments are God-given, not man-made. So Solomon, after showing throughout this book the vanity of worldly things, ends by pointing his people to the commandments. This conclusion accords with both the OT and the NT in presenting (1) faith ("Fear God") and (2) works ("keep His commandments"). Cp. Eph. 2:8–10. Only the life of faith issuing in works prepares man, when judged, to stand before God.

The

SONG OF SOLOMON

Author: Solomon *Theme:* The Beloved *Date of writing:* 10th Cent. B.C.

NOWHERE in Scripture does the unspiritual mind tread upon ground so mysterious and incomprehensible as in this book, whereas saintly men and women throughout the ages have found it a source of pure and exquisite delight. That the love of the divine Bridegroom, symbolized here by Solomon's love for the Shulamite maiden, should follow the analogy of the marriage relationship seems evil only to minds that are so ascetic that marital desire itself appears to them to be unholy.

The book is the expression of pure marital love as ordained by God in creation, and the vindication of that love as against both asceticism and lust—the two profanations of the holiness of marriage. Its interpretation is threefold: (1) as a vivid unfolding of Solomon's love for a Shulamite girl; (2) as a figurative revelation of God's love for His covenant people, Israel, the wife of the LORD (Isa. 54:5–6; Jer. 2:2; Ezek. 16:8–14,20–21,32,38; Hos. 2:16,18–20); and (3) as an allegory of Christ's love for His heavenly bride, the Church (2 Cor. 11:1–2, refs., Eph. 5:25–32).

The Song of Solomon is also known as Canticles, inasmuch as it contains a number of lyrics (canticles). These songs do not tell a connected story; the narrative may be discovered by piecing together details from the various conversations and incidents in the book.

In this short writing, which contains at least fifteen geographical references, there are many exquisite expressions that describe the loveliness of womanhood and the beauty of nature.

The eight chapters of this book, which is not easy to outline, are composed of the title and thirteen canticles:

Title, 1:1.	Cant. V, 2:8–17.	Cant. X, 5:2—6:3.
Cant. I, 1:2–6.	Cant. VI, 3:1–5.	Cant. XI, 6:4—7:10.
Cant. II, 1:7–8.	Cant. VII, 3:6–11.	Cant. XII, 7:11—8:4.
Cant. III, 1:9–17.	Cant. VIII, 4:1–7.	Cant. XIII, 8:5–14.
Cant. IV, 2:1–7.	Cant. IX, 4:8—5:1.	

Title

1 THE [a]song of songs, which *is* Solomon's.

Cant. I. A Young Bride, a Shulamite Girl, 1:2–6

(The Shulamite speaks)*

2 Let him kiss me with the
kisses of his mouth—

(The daughters of Jerusalem speak)

For your* [b]love *is* better than
wine.

3 Because of the [c]fragrance of
your good ointments,
Your [d]name *is* ointment
poured forth;
Therefore the virgins love you.

(The Shulamite speaks)

4 [e]Draw me away!

(The daughters of Jerusalem speak)

We will [f]run after you.*

(The Shulamite speaks)

The king [g]has brought me into
his chambers.

(The daughters of Jerusalem speak)

We will be glad and rejoice in
you.*
We will remember your* love
more than wine.
Rightly do they love you.*

(The Shulamite speaks)

5 I *am* dark, but lovely,
O daughters of Jerusalem,
Like the tents of Kedar,
Like the curtains of Solomon.
6 Do not look upon me, because
I *am* dark,
Because the sun has tanned
me.
My mother's sons were angry
with me;
They made me the keeper of
the [h]vineyards,
But my own vineyard I have
not kept.

Cant. II. The Perplexed Bride, 1:7–8

(The Shulamite continues)

7 Tell me, O you whom I love,

CHAPTER 1

1 *a* 1 Ki. 4:32
2 *b* Song 4:10
3 *c* Cp. Jn. 12:3 *d* Cp. Eccl. 7:1
4 *e* Cp. Hos. 11:4; Jn. 6:44; 12:32 *f* Cp. Phil. 3:12–14 *g* Ps. 45:14–15; cp. Jn. 14:2; Eph. 2:6
6 *h* Song 8:11–12

*

1:2 A Palestinian young woman (compare 6:13). The speaker and audience are identified according to the number, gender, and person of the Hebrew words. Occasionally the identity is not certain.
• Masculine singular, that is, the Beloved
1:4 Masculine singular, that is, the Beloved
• Feminine singular, that is, the Shulamite
• Masculine singular, that is, the Beloved
• Masculine singular, that is, the Beloved

Where you feed *your flock,*
Where you make *it* rest at
noon.
For why should I be as one
who veils herself*
By the flocks of your
companions?

(Solomon, the shepherd-lover, replies)

8 If you do not know, O fairest
among women,
Follow in the footsteps of the
flock,
And feed your little goats
Beside the shepherds' tents.

Cant. III. Mutual Admiration,
1:9–17

(Solomon speaks)

9 I have compared you, [a]my
love,
To my filly among Pharaoh's
chariots.
10 [b]Your cheeks are lovely with
ornaments,
Your neck with chains *of gold.*

(The daughters of Jerusalem speak)

11 We will make you* ornaments
of gold
With studs of silver.

(The Shulamite speaks)

12 While the king *is* at his table,
My spikenard sends forth its
fragrance.
13 A bundle of myrrh *is* my
beloved to me,
That lies all night between my
breasts.
14 My beloved *is* to me a cluster
of [c]henna *blooms*
In the vineyards of En Gedi.

(Solomon responds)

15 Behold, you *are* [1]fair, my love!
Behold, you *are* fair!
You *have* dove's eyes.

(The Shulamite speaks)

16 Behold, you *are* [d]handsome,
my beloved!
Yes, pleasant!
Also our bed *is* green.
17 The beams of our houses *are*
cedar,
And our rafters of fir.

9
a Song 2:2, 10,13; 4:1, 7; 5:2; 6:4; cp. Jn. 15:14–15
10
b Cp. Ezek. 16:11–13
14
c Song 4:13
16
d Song 5:10–16
CHAPTER 2
3
e Song 4:16; cp. Rev. 22:1–2
5
f 2 Sam. 6:19
6
g Song 8:3
7
h Song 3:5; 5:8; 8:4

Cant. IV. The Shulamite
Is Comforted, 2:1–7

(She speaks)

2

I *AM* the rose of Sharon,
And the lily of the valleys.

(Solomon speaks)

2 Like a lily among thorns,
So is my love among the
daughters.

(The Shulamite speaks)

3 Like an apple tree among the
trees of the woods,
So *is* my beloved among the
sons.
I sat down in his shade with
great delight,
And his [e]fruit *was* sweet to my
taste.

4 He brought me to the
banqueting house,
And his banner over me *was*
love.
5 Sustain me with [f]cakes of
raisins,
Refresh me with apples,
For I *am* lovesick.

6 [g]His left hand *is* under my
head,
And his right hand embraces
me.
7 [h]I charge you, O daughters of
Jerusalem,
By the gazelles or by the does
of the field,
Do not stir up nor awaken love
Until it pleases.

Cant. V. The Shulamite
Describes a Happy Visit, 2:8–17

8 The voice of my beloved!
Behold, he comes
Leaping upon the mountains,
Skipping upon the hills.
9 My beloved is like a gazelle or
a young stag.
Behold, he stands behind [2]our
wall;
He is looking through the
windows,
Gazing through the lattice.

*
1:7 Septuagint, Syriac, and Vulgate read *wanders.*
1:11 Feminine singular, that is, the Shulamite

[1](1:15) It is comforting to know that the tender thoughts of Christ for His bride, the Church, in her unperfected state are like these expressions of Solomon to the Shulamite maiden. The varied exercises of the bride's heart are part of that inner discipline suggested in the NT (Eph. 5:25–27).

[2](2:9) "Our wall." The bride is in her own home; the bridegroom visits her there.

(The Shulamite reports Solomon's words)

10 My beloved spoke, and said to me:
"Rise up, my love, my fair one,
And come away.
11 For lo, the winter is past,
The rain is over *and* gone.
12 The flowers appear on the earth;
The time of singing has come,
And the voice of the turtledove
Is heard in our land.
13 The fig tree puts forth her green figs,
And the vines *with* the tender grapes
Give a good smell.
[a]Rise up, my love, my fair one,
And come away!

14 "O my [1b]dove, in the clefts of the [c]rock,
In the secret *places* of the cliff,
Let me see your face,
Let me hear your [d]voice;
For your voice *is* sweet,
And your face *is* lovely."

15 Catch us the [e]foxes,
The little foxes that spoil the vines,
For our vines *have* tender grapes.

(The Shulamite speaks)

16 My beloved *is* mine, and [f]I *am* his.
He feeds *his flock* among the lilies.

17 [g]Until the day [h]breaks
And the shadows flee away,
Turn, my beloved,
And be [i]like a gazelle
Or a young stag
Upon the mountains of Bether.*

Cant. VI. The Shulamite Tells of Her Troubled Dream, 3:1–5

3 BY [j]night on my bed I sought the one I love;
I sought him, but I did not find him.
2 "I will rise now," *I said,*
"And go about the city;
In the streets and in the squares
I will seek the one I love."
I sought him, but I did not find him.
3 The [k]watchmen who go about the city found me;
I said,
"Have you seen the one I love?"

4 Scarcely had I passed by them,
When I found the one I love.
I held him and would not let him go,
Until I had brought him to the house of my [l]mother,
And into the chamber of her who conceived me.

(Solomon speaks)

5 [m]I charge you, O daughters of Jerusalem,
By the gazelles or by the does of the field,
Do not stir up nor awaken love
Until it pleases.

Cant. VII. Solomon Has His Bride Brought to Jerusalem, 3:6–11

(The bride speaks)

6 [n]Who *is* this coming out of the wilderness
Like pillars of smoke,
Perfumed with myrrh and [o]frankincense,
With all the merchant's fragrant powders?

(An officer of King Solomon's guard replies)

7 Behold, it *is* Solomon's couch,
With sixty valiant men around it,
Of the valiant of Israel.
8 They all hold swords,
Being expert in war.
Every man *has* his [p]sword on his thigh
Because of fear in the night.

9 Of the wood of Lebanon
Solomon the King
Made himself a palanquin:*
10 He made its pillars *of* silver,
Its support *of* gold,
Its seat *of* purple,

13 a v. 10
14 b Song 5:2; c Cp. Jer. 48:28; d Song 8:13
15 e Cp. Ps. 80:13; Ezek. 13:4; Lk. 13:32
16 f Song 6:3; 7:10
17 g Song 4:6; h Lit. *breathes, is cool*; i v. 9; Song 8:14
CHAPTER 3
1 j Cp. Isa. 26:9
3 k Song 5:7
4 l Song 8:2
5 m Song 2:7; 8:4
6 n Song 8:5; o Cp. Mt. 2:11
8 p Cp. Ps. 45:3

*2:17 Literally *Separation*
*3:9 A portable enclosed chair

[1](2:14) There is a beautiful order here. (1) It is revealed what the bride is as seen in Christ, "My dove." In herself she is most faulty; in Him, "blameless and harmless" (Phil. 2:15), which is the very character of the dove. (2) She is sought after (Lk. 19:10); hiding among the rocks, the bride is called to by her beloved. (3) The order of approach is given: she is to come near before she speaks, "Let me see your face," then "Let me hear your voice." And (4) now that she is near and has spoken, together they will remove every hindrance to their love: "Catch us . . . the little foxes that spoil the vines."

Its [a]interior [b]paved *with* love
By the daughters of Jerusalem.

(The daughters of Jerusalem sing)

11 Go forth, O daughters of Zion,
And see King Solomon with the crown
With which his mother crowned him
On the day of his wedding,
The day of the gladness of his heart.

Cant. VIII. Solomon, the Bridegroom, Expresses His Message of Love, 4:1–7

4 BEHOLD, you *are* [c]fair, my love!
Behold, you *are* fair!
You *have* dove's eyes behind your veil.
Your hair *is* like a [d]flock of goats,
Going down from Mount Gilead.
2 Your [e]teeth *are* like a flock of shorn *sheep*
Which have come up from the washing,
Every one of which bears twins,
And none *is* barren among them.
3 Your lips *are* like a strand of scarlet,
And your mouth is lovely.
Your [f]temples behind your veil
Are like a piece of pomegranate.

10
a Probably the lining
b Or *inlaid*

CHAPTER 4
1
c Song 1:15
d Song 6:5
2
e Song 6:6
3
f Song 6:7

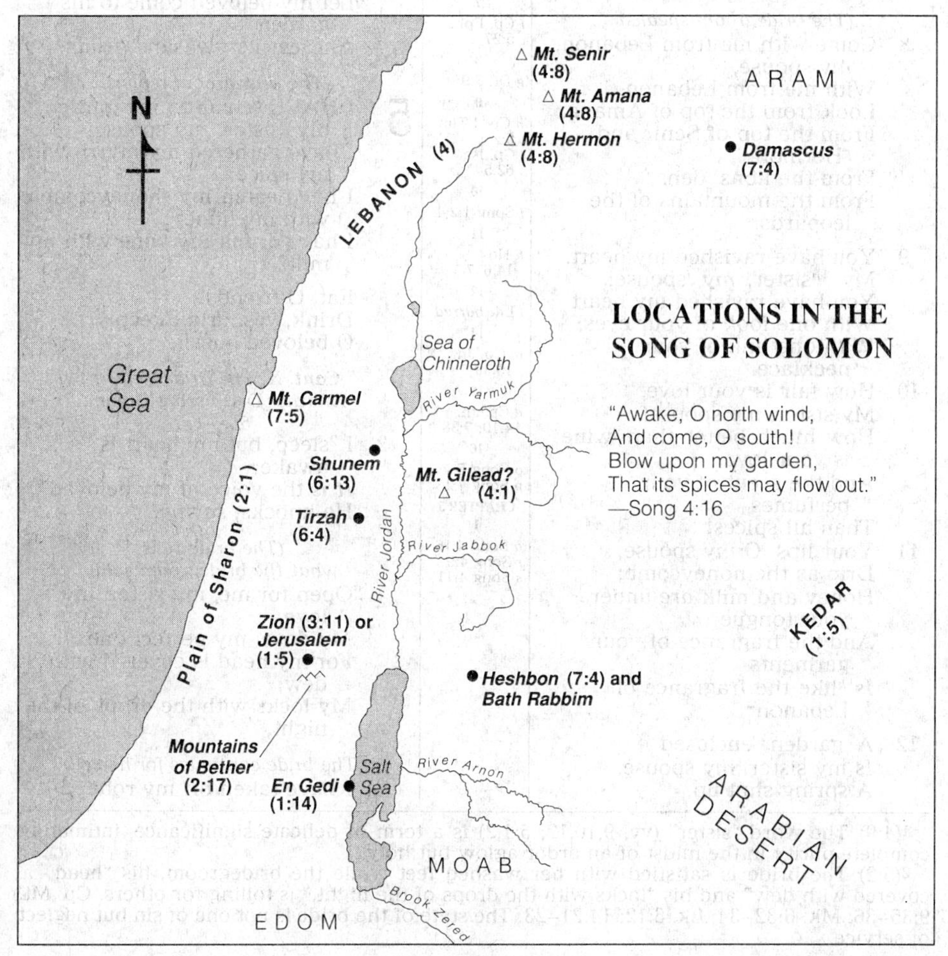

4 Your [a]neck *is* like the tower of
David,
Built for an [b]armory,
On which hang a thousand
bucklers,
All shields of mighty men.
5 Your two [c]breasts *are* like two
fawns,
Twins of a gazelle,
Which feed among the lilies.

6 [d]Until the day [e]breaks
And the shadows flee away,
I will go my way to the
mountain of myrrh
And to the hill of frankincense.

7 You *are* all fair, my love,
And *there is* no [f]spot in you.

Cant. IX. Solomon's Proposal and the Shulamite's Acceptance, 4:8—5:1

(The bridegroom speaks)

8 Come with me from Lebanon,
my spouse,
With me from Lebanon.
Look from the top of Amana,
From the top of Senir and
[g]Hermon,
From the lions' dens,
From the mountains of the
leopards.

9 You have ravished my heart,
My [1][h]sister, *my* [i]spouse;
You have ravished my heart
With one *look* of your eyes,
With one link of your
necklace.
10 How fair is your love,
My sister, *my* spouse!
How much better than [j]wine
is your love,
And the scent of your
perfumes
Than all spices!
11 Your lips, O *my* spouse,
Drip as the honeycomb;
Honey and milk *are* under
your tongue;
And the fragrance of your
garments
Is [k]like the fragrance of
Lebanon.

12 A garden [l]enclosed
Is my sister, *my* spouse,
A spring shut up,
A fountain sealed.
13 Your plants *are* an orchard of
pomegranates
With pleasant fruits,
Fragrant henna with
spikenard,
14 Spikenard and saffron,
Calamus and cinnamon,
With all trees of frankincense,
Myrrh and [m]aloes,
With all the chief spices—
15 A fountain of gardens,
A well of [n]living waters,
And streams from Lebanon.

16 Awake, O north *wind*,
And come, O south!
Blow upon my garden,
That its spices may flow out.

(The bride speaks)

[o]Let my beloved come to his
garden
And eat its pleasant [p]fruits.

(The bridegroom replies)

5 I HAVE [q]come to my garden,
my [r]sister, *my* spouse;
I have gathered my myrrh with
my spice;
I have eaten my [s]honeycomb
with my honey;
I have drunk my wine with my
milk.

Eat, O friends!
Drink, yes, drink deeply,
O beloved ones!

Cant. X. The Bride Tells of Another Distressing Dream, 5:2—6:3

2 I [2]sleep, but my heart is
awake;
It is the voice of my beloved!
He knocks, *saying,*

(The bride tells what the bridegroom said)

"Open for me, my sister, my
love,
My dove, my perfect one;
For my head is covered with
dew,
My locks with the drops of the
night."

(The bride continues for herself)

3 I have taken off my robe;

4
a Song 7:4
b Cp. Neh. 3:19
5
c Song 7:3; cp. Prov. 5:19
6
d Song 2:17
e Lit. *breathes, is cool*
7
f Cp. Eph. 5:27
8
g Dt. 3:9
9
h Cp. 1 Tim. 5:2
i Cp. Isa. 62:5
10
j Song 1:2,4
11
k Hos. 14:6–7
12
l Lit. *barred*
14
m Cp. Jn. 19:39
15
n Cp. Jn. 4:10; 7:38
16
o Song 5:1
p Song 7:13
CHAPTER 5
1
q Song 4:16
r Song 4:9
s Song 4:11

[1](4:9) The word "sister" (vv. 9,10,12; 5:1,2) is a term of delicate significance, intimating complete purity in the midst of an ardor aglow but holy.

[2](5:2) The bride is satisfied with her washed feet while the bridegroom, his "head . . . covered with dew" and his "locks with the drops of the night," is toiling for others. Cp. Mt. 9:35–36; Mk. 6:32–34; Lk. 6:12; 14:21–23. The state of the bride is not one of sin but neglect of service.

How can I put it on *again?*
I have washed my feet;
How can I defile them?
4 My beloved put his hand
By the latch *of the door,*
And my heart yearned for him.
5 I arose to open for my beloved,
And my hands dripped *with*
myrrh,
My fingers with liquid myrrh,
On the handles of the lock.

6 I opened for my beloved,
But my beloved had turned
away *and* was gone.
My heart leaped up when he
spoke.
I sought [1]him, but I could not
[a]find him;
I called him, but he gave me
no answer.
7 The [b]watchmen who went
about the city found me.
They struck me, they wounded
me;
The keepers of the walls
Took my veil away from me.
8 I charge you, O daughters of
Jerusalem,
If you find my beloved,
That you tell him I *am*
lovesick!

(The daughters of Jerusalem speak)

9 What *is* your beloved
More than *another* beloved,
[c]O fairest among women?
What *is* your beloved
More than *another* beloved,
That you so charge us?

(A full-length portrait of the bridegroom. The bride speaks)

10 My beloved *is* white and
ruddy,
[d]Chief among ten thousand.
11 His head *is like* the finest gold;
His locks *are* wavy,
And black as a raven.
12 His eyes *are* like doves
By the rivers of waters,
Washed with milk,
And fitly set.
13 His cheeks *are* like a bed of
spices,
Banks of scented herbs.
His lips *are* lilies,
Dripping liquid myrrh.
14 His hands *are* rods of gold
Set with beryl.
His body *is* carved ivory
Inlaid *with* sapphires.
15 His legs *are* pillars of marble
Set on bases of fine gold.
His countenance *is* like
Lebanon,
Excellent as the cedars.
16 His mouth *is* most sweet,
Yes, he *is* altogether lovely.
This *is* my beloved,
And this *is* my friend,
O daughters of Jerusalem!

(The daughters of Jerusalem say that they, too, would seek him)

6 WHERE has your beloved
gone,
[e]O fairest among women?
Where has your beloved
turned aside,
That [2]we may seek him with
you?

(The bride concludes)

2 My beloved has gone to his
garden,
To the beds of spices,
To feed *his flock* in the
[f]gardens,
And to gather lilies.
3 [g]I *am* my beloved's,
And my beloved *is* mine.
He feeds *his flock* among the
lilies.

Cant. XI. The Bridegroom Praises His Bride, 6:4—7:10

4 O my love, you *are as* beautiful
as Tirzah,
Lovely as [h]Jerusalem,
Awesome as *an army* with
banners!
5 Turn your eyes away from me,
For they have overcome me.
Your hair *is* like a [i]flock of
goats
Going down from Gilead.
6 Your [j]teeth *are* like a flock of
sheep
Which have come up from the
washing;
Every one bears twins,
And none *is* barren among
them.
7 Like a piece of [k]pomegranate
Are your temples behind your
veil.
8 There are sixty queens
And eighty concubines,
And [l]virgins without number.

6 *a* Song 3:1
7 *b* Song 3:3
9 *c* Song 1:8
10 *d* Lit. *distinguished, conspicuous.* Cp. Ps. 45:2

CHAPTER 6
1 *e* Song 1:8; 5:9
2 *f* Song 5:1
3 *g* Song 2:16; 7:10
4 *h* Cp. Ps. 48:2
5 *i* Song 4:1
6 *j* Song 4:2
7 *k* Song 4:3
8 *l* Song 1:3

[1](5:6) It is now the bridegroom himself who occupies her heart, not desire for personal ease.
[2](6:1) As soon as the bride witnesses to the bridegroom's own personal loveliness, a desire is awakened in the daughters of Jerusalem to find him.

9 My dove, my [a]perfect one,
Is the only one,
The only one of her mother,
The favorite of the one who bore her.
The daughters saw her
And called her blessed,
The queens and the concubines,
And they praised her.

(Solomon cites praise of his bride by the women of the court)

10 Who is she who looks forth as the morning,
Fair as the moon,
Clear as the sun,
[b]Awesome as *an army* with banners?

(The bride speaks)

11 I went down to the garden of nuts
To see the verdure of the valley,
[c]To see whether the vine had budded
And the pomegranates had bloomed.
12 Before I was even aware,
My soul had made me
As the chariots of my noble people.*

(The daughters of Jerusalem speak)

13 Return, return, O Shulamite;
Return, return, that we may look upon you!

(The bride asks)

What would you see in the Shulamite—

(The daughters of Jerusalem respond)

As it were, the dance [d]of the two camps?

(The daughters of Jerusalem express their agreement about the bride's unique beauty)

7 HOW beautiful are your feet in sandals,
[e]O prince's daughter!
The curves of your thighs *are* like jewels,
The work of the hands of a skillful workman.
2 Your navel *is* a rounded goblet;
It lacks no blended beverage.
Your waist *is* a heap of wheat
Set about with lilies.
3 Your two [f]breasts *are* like two fawns,
Twins of a gazelle.

9
a Song 5:2
10
b v. 4
11
c Song 7:12
13
d Heb. *Mahanaim.* Gen. 32:2
CHAPTER 7
1
e Cp. Ps. 45:13
3
f Song 4:5
4
g Song 4:4
10
h Song 2:16; 6:3
i Cp. Ps. 45:11
13
j Gen. 30:14

4 Your neck *is* like an ivory [g]tower,
Your eyes *like* the pools in Heshbon
By the gate of Bath Rabbim.
Your nose *is* like the tower of Lebanon
Which looks toward Damascus.
5 Your head *crowns* you like *Mount* Carmel,
And the hair of your head *is* like purple;
A king *is* held captive by *your* tresses.

(The bridegroom speaks)

6 How fair and how pleasant you are,
O love, with your delights!
7 This stature of yours is like a palm tree,
And your breasts *like* its clusters.
8 I said, "I will go up to the palm tree,
I will take hold of its branches."
Let now your breasts be like clusters of the vine,
The fragrance of your breath like apples,
9 And the roof of your mouth like the best wine.

(The bride interrupts, telling her beloved that her delights are for his enjoyment)

The wine goes *down* smoothly for my beloved,
Moving gently the lips of sleepers.*
10 I *am* my [h]beloved's,
And his [i]desire *is* toward me.

Cant. XII. The Bride Expresses Her Longing to Visit Her Home, 7:11—8:4

11 Come, my beloved,
Let us go forth to the field;
Let us lodge in the villages.
12 Let us get up early to the vineyards;
Let us see if the vine has budded,
Whether the grape blossoms are open,
And the pomegranates are in bloom.
There I will give you my love.
13 The [j]mandrakes give off a fragrance,

*6:12 Hebrew *Ammi Nadib* 7:9 Septuagint, Syriac, and Vulgate read *lips and teeth.*

And at our gates *are* pleasant
  fruits,
All [a]manner, new and old,
Which I have laid up for you,
  my beloved.

(Sensitive of the social gap between herself and the bridegroom, she implies that she is aware still that he loves her)

8 OH, that you were like my
  brother,
Who nursed at my mother's
  breasts!
If I should find you outside,
I would kiss you;
I would not be despised.
2 I would lead you *and* bring
  you
Into the [b]house of my mother,
She *who* used to instruct me.
I would cause you to drink of
  spiced wine,
Of the juice of my
  pomegranate.
3 [c]His left hand *is* under my
  head,
And his right hand embraces
  me.

(The bride quotes the bridegroom)

4 [d]I charge you, O daughters of
  Jerusalem,
Do not stir up nor awaken love
Until it pleases.

Cant. XIII. The Past Is Recalled When Baal Hamon Is Revisited, 8:5–14

(The bride's brothers speak)

5 Who *is* this coming up from
  the wilderness,
Leaning upon her beloved?

(Solomon speaks)

I awakened you under the
  apple tree.
There your mother brought
  you forth;
There she *who* bore you
  brought *you* forth.
6 [e]Set me as a seal upon your
  heart,
As a seal upon your arm;
For love *is as* strong as death,
[f]Jealousy *as* cruel as the
  [g]grave;*
Its flames *are* flames of fire,
A most vehement* flame.

13
[a] Cp. Mt. 13:52
CHAPTER 8
2
[b] Song 3:4
3
[c] Song 2:6
4
[d] Song 2:7; 3:5
6
[e] Cp. Isa. 49:16; Jer. 22:24; Hag. 2:23
[f] Prov. 6:34–35
[g] Hab. 2:5, *note;* cp. Lk. 16:23, *note*
11
[h] Cp. Mt. 21:33
[i] Cp. Isa. 7:23
12
[j] Cp. Song 1:6
14
[k] Cp. Rev. 22:17,20

(The bride speaks to Solomon)

7 Many waters cannot quench
  love,
Nor can the floods drown it.
If a man would give for love
All the wealth of his house,
It would be utterly despised.

(The bride recounts what her brothers once said)

8 We have a little sister,
And she has no breasts.
What shall we do for our sister
In the day when she is spoken
  for?
9 If she *is* a wall,
We will build upon her
A battlement of silver;
And if she *is* a door,
We will enclose her
With boards of cedar.

(The bride continues)

10 I *am* a wall,
And my breasts like towers;
Then I became in his eyes
As one who found peace.
11 Solomon had a vineyard at
  Baal Hamon;
He [h]leased the vineyard to
  keepers;
Everyone was to bring for its
  fruit
A thousand [i]silver coins.
12 [1][j]My own vineyard *is* before me.
You, O Solomon, *may have* a
  thousand,
And those who tend its fruit
  two hundred.

(The brothers speak again)

13 You who dwell in the gardens,
The companions listen for your
  voice—

(The bridegroom interrupts in pleasant repartee)

Let me hear it!

(The bride, in affectionate anticipation, responds)

14 [k]Make haste, my beloved,
And be like a gazelle
Or a young stag
On the mountains of spices.

* 8:6 Or *Sheol* • Literally *A flame of* YAH (a poetic form of *YHWH, the* LORD)

[1](8:12) The bride requests more generous pay to her brothers, showing that she has forgiven them (cp. v. 8).

The Prophetic Books

THE OT prophets were men raised up by God in times of declension and apostasy in Israel. They were primarily revivalists and patriots, speaking on behalf of God to the heart and conscience of the nation. The prophetic messages have a twofold character: (1) that which was local and for the prophet's time; and (2) that which was predictive of the divine purpose in the future. Often the prediction sprang immediately from the local circumstance (cp. Isa. 7:1–11 with vv. 12–14).

It is necessary to keep the Israelite character of the prophet in mind. Usually his predictive ministry, as well as his local and immediate ministry, has in view the covenant people, their sin and failure, and their glorious future. The Gentile is mentioned as used for the chastisement of Israel, and as judged for this, but also as sharing the grace that is yet to be shown toward Israel. The Church, corporately, is not in the vision of the OT prophet (Eph. 3:1–6). The future blessing of Israel as a nation rests upon the Palestinian Covenant of restoration and conversion (see Dt. 30:3, *note*) and the Davidic Covenant of the Kingship of the Messiah, David's Son (see 2 Sam. 7:16, *note*); and this gives to predictive prophecy its Messianic character. The final restoration of Israel is secured in the kingdom, and the source of blessing in the kingdom is the King, who is not only David's Son but also Immanuel.

But as the King is also Son of Abraham (Mt. 1:1), the promised Redeemer, and as redemption is only through the sacrifice of Christ, so Messianic prophecy of necessity presents Christ in a twofold character: (1) a suffering Messiah (e.g. Isa. 53); and (2) a reigning Messiah (e.g. Isa. 11). This duality—suffering and glory, weakness and power—involved a mystery which perplexed the prophets (Lk. 24:26–27; 1 Pet. 1:10–12).

The solution to that mystery lies, as the NT makes clear, in the two advents—the first advent to redemption through suffering; the second advent to the kingdom in glory, when the national promises to Israel will be fulfilled (cp. Mt. 1:21–23; Lk. 2:28–35; 24:46–48 with Mt. 2:2,6; 19:27–28; Lk. 1:31–33,68–75; Acts 2:30–32; 15:14–16). The prophets describe the advent in two forms which could not be contemporaneous (e.g. Zech. 9:9; contrast 14:1–9); but to them it was not revealed that, between the advent to suffering and the advent to glory, there would be accomplished certain "mysteries of the kingdom" (Mt. 13:11–17,34–35), nor that, consequent upon Messiah's rejection, the NT Church would be called out. These were, to them, mysteries "hidden in God" (Eph. 3:1–12).

Speaking broadly, then, predictive prophecy is occupied with the fulfillment of the Abrahamic, Palestinian, and Davidic Covenants. See *notes* at Gen. 12:2; Dt. 30:3, 2 Sam. 7:16.

Gentile powers are mentioned as connected with Israel. However, except in Daniel, Obadiah, Jonah, and Nahum, prophecy is not primarily concerned with Gentile world history. Daniel, as will be seen, has a distinctive character.

The predictions of the restoration of the Jews from the Babylonian captivity at the end of seventy years must be distinguished from those of the restoration of the nation from the worldwide dispersion after their rejection of Christ at His first advent. The Abrahamic, Palestinian, and Davidic Covenants (Gen. 12:1–3; Dt. 28:1—30:9; 2 Sam. 7:4–17) are the mold of predictive prophecy in its larger sense—national greatness, national disobedience, worldwide dispersion, worldwide blessing through Israel's Messiah, repentance, the second coming of Christ, the regathering of Israel and establishment of the kingdom, the conversion and blessing of Israel, and the judgment of Israel's oppressors.

The prophetic books may be divided into three groups: 1. *Pre-exilic:* Isaiah, Jeremiah, Hosea, Joel, Amos, Jonah, Micah, Nahum, Habakkuk, and Zephaniah. 2. *Exilic:* Ezekiel, Daniel, and Obadiah. 3. *Post-exilic:* Haggai, Zechariah, and Malachi. The division into major and minor prophetic writings, based upon the mere bulk of the books, is unhistoric and nonchronological.

The keys which unlock the meaning of prophecy are: the two advents of Messiah (Lk. 24:26)—the advent to suffer (Gen. 3:15; Mt. 16:21; Lk. 24:46; Acts 2:23), and the advent to reign (Dt. 30:3; Acts 1:9–11); the doctrine of the remnant (Isa. 10:20–22; Rom. 11:5, *note*); the doctrine of the day of the LORD (Isa. 2:10–22; Rev. 19:19, *note*); and the doctrine of the kingdom (OT, Gen. 1:26–28; Zech. 12:8, *note;* NT, Lk. 1:31–33; 1 Cor. 15:24, *note;* Rev. 20:4, *note*). Pivotal passages are Gen. 3:15; Dt. 28—30; Ps. 2; Isa. 7:14; 9:6–7; 53; Dan. 2 and 7.

The whole scope of prophecy must be taken into account in determining the meaning of any particular passage (2 Pet. 1:20). Hence the importance of first mastering the great themes indicated above, which in this edition of the Scriptures may be done by tracing through the body of the prophetic writings the subjects mentioned in the preceding paragraph.

CHRONOLOGICAL ORDER OF THE PROPHETS

I THE PRE-EXILIC PROPHETS

Joel	c. 850–c. 700 B.C.
Jonah	c. 800 B.C.
Amos	c. 780–755 B.C.
Hosea	c. 760–710 B.C.
Micah	c. 740 B.C.
Isaiah	c. 740–680 B.C.
Nahum	c. 666–615 B.C.
Zephaniah	c. 630–620 B.C.
Habakkuk	c. 627–586 B.C.
Jeremiah	c. 626–580 B.C.

II THE EXILIC PROPHETS

Daniel	c. 604–535 B.C.
Ezekiel	c. 593–570 B.C.
Obadiah	c. 585 B.C.

III THE POST-EXILIC PROPHETS

Haggai	520 B.C.
Zechariah	520–518 B.C.
Malachi	c. 450–400 B.C.

The Book of

ISAIAH

Author: Isaiah *Theme:* Israel's Messiah *Date of writing:* 8th Cent. B.C.

ISAIAH, whose name means *salvation of the* LORD, was the greatest of the writing prophets. He carried on his ministry in Judah during the reigns of four kings, possibly 740 to 680 B.C., a period of about sixty years during which Samaria was captured and Israel carried away, c. 722–721 B.C., and Judah was invaded by Sennacherib, 701 B.C. The themes of Isaiah's utterances reach back to the eternal counsels of God and the creation of the universe (e.g. 42:5) and look forward to the time when God will create new heavens and a new earth (65:17; 66:22). No other prophet has written with such majestic eloquence about the glory of God (see ch. 40). All the nations of the earth come within the scope of Isaiah's predictions (e.g. 2:4; 5:26; 14:6,26; 40:15,17,22; 66:18).

Whereas there are in Isaiah many important prophecies concerning Jerusalem (called by more than thirty different names), as well as prophecies about Israel, Judah, and the nations of the earth, the book sets forth the great Messianic predictions in which are foretold Christ's birth (7:14; 9:6), His Deity (9:6–7), His ministry (9:1–2; 42:1–7; 61:1–2), His death (52:1—53:12), His future millennial reign (e.g. chs. 2; 11; 65), etc.

Of all the OT prophets, Isaiah is the most comprehensive in range. No prophet is more fully occupied with the redemptive work of Christ. In no other place, in the Scriptures written under the law, is there so clear a view of grace.

The book may be divided as follows:

I. Prophecies concerning Judah, 1—12.
II. Prophecies concerning the Nations, 13—27.
III. Prophetic Warnings concerning Ephraim and Judah, 28—35.
IV. Historical Parenthesis: Sennacherib's Invasions and Hezekiah's Illness, 36—39.
V. The Greatness and Transcendence of God, 40—48.
VI. The Suffering Servant of the LORD, 49—57.
VII. Concluding Exhortations and Prophecies, 58—66.

I. Prophetic Messages concerning Judah, 1—12

God's case against Judah

1 [a]THE [b]vision of Isaiah the son of Amoz, which he saw concerning Judah and Jerusalem in the [c]days of Uzziah, Jotham, Ahaz, *and* Hezekiah, kings of Judah.

2 [1d]Hear, O heavens, and give ear, O earth!
For the LORD has spoken:
"I have nourished and brought up [e]children,
And they have rebelled against Me;
3 The ox knows its owner
And the donkey its master's crib;
But Israel [f]does not know,
My people do not consider."

4 Alas, sinful nation,
A people laden with iniquity,
A [g]brood of evildoers,
Children who are corrupters!
They have forsaken the LORD,
They have provoked to anger
The Holy One of Israel,
They have turned away backward.

5 [h]Why should you be stricken again?
You will revolt more and more.
The whole head is sick,
And the whole heart faints.
6 From the sole of the foot even to the head,
There is no soundness in it,
But wounds and bruises and putrefying sores;
They have not been closed or bound up,
Or soothed with ointment.

7 [i]Your country *is* desolate,
Your cities *are* burned with fire;
Strangers devour your land in your presence;
And *it is* desolate, as overthrown by strangers.

CHAPTER 1
1
a c. 740–c. 680 B.C.
b Num. 12:6
c 2 Chr. 26–32
2
d Cp. Dt. 32:1; Jer. 6:19; Mic. 1:2; 6:2
e Cp. Gal. 4:1–4
3
f Cp. Jer. 9:3,6
4
g Isa. 57:3–4; cp. Mt. 3:7
5
h Isa. 9:13; Jer. 2:30; 5:3
7
i Dt. 28:51–52

---

[1](1:2) The chapter, to v. 23, states the case of the LORD against Judah. Chastening, according to Dt. 28—29, has been visited upon Israel in the land (vv. 5–8), and now the time of expulsion from the land is near. But just here the LORD renews the promise of the Palestinian Covenant (see Dt. 30:3, *note*) of future restoration and exaltation (Isa. 1:26–27; 2:1–4).

8 So the daughter of Zion is left
as a booth in a vineyard,
As a hut in a garden of
cucumbers,
As a besieged city.
9 Unless the LORD of hosts
Had left to us a very small
[a]remnant,
We would have become like
[b]Sodom,
We would have been made like
Gomorrah.

Mere outward religion condemned

10 Hear the word of the LORD,
You rulers of [c]Sodom;
Give ear to the [d]law of our
God,
You people of Gomorrah:
11 "To what purpose *is* the
multitude of your sacrifices
to Me?"
Says the LORD.
"I have had enough of burnt
offerings of rams
And the fat of fed cattle.
I do not delight in the blood of
bulls,
Or of lambs or goats.
12 "When you come to [e]appear
before Me,
Who has required this from
your hand,
To trample My courts?
13 [f]Bring no more futile sacrifices;
Incense is an [g]abomination to
Me.
The New Moons, the Sabbaths,
and the calling of
assemblies—
I cannot endure iniquity and
the sacred meeting.
14 Your New Moons and your
appointed feasts
My soul hates;
They are a trouble to Me,
I am weary of bearing *them.*
15 When you spread out your
hands,
I will hide My eyes from you;
Even though you make many
prayers,
I will not [h]hear.
Your hands are full of blood.
16 "Wash yourselves, make
yourselves clean;
Put away the evil of your
doings from before My eyes.
Cease to do evil,
17 Learn to do good;
Seek justice,
Rebuke the oppressor;*
Defend the fatherless,
Plead for the widow.

Entreaty and warning

18 "Come now, and let us [i]reason
together,"
Says the LORD,
"Though your sins are like
scarlet,
They shall be as white as
[j]snow;
Though they are red like
crimson,
They shall be as wool.
19 If you are willing and obedient,
You shall eat the good of the
land;
20 But if you refuse and rebel,
You shall be devoured by the
sword";
For the mouth of the LORD has
spoken.

21 How the faithful city has
become a [k]harlot!
It was full of justice;
Righteousness lodged in it,
But now [l]murderers.
22 Your silver has become dross,
Your wine mixed with water.
23 Your princes *are* rebellious,
And companions of thieves;
Everyone loves [m]bribes,
And follows after rewards.
They do not defend the
fatherless,
Nor does the cause of the
[n]widow come before them.

24 Therefore the Lord says,
The LORD of hosts, the Mighty
One of Israel,
"Ah, I will rid Myself of My
adversaries,
And take vengeance on My
enemies.
25 I will turn My hand against
[o]you,
And [p]thoroughly [q]purge away
your [r]dross,
And take away all your alloy.
26 I will restore your [1]judges as at
the [s]first,
And your counselors as at the
beginning.
Afterward you shall be called

9 *a Remnant:* v. 9; Isa. 10:20. (Isa. 1:9; Rom. 11:5, *note*) *b* Rom. 9:29
10 *c* i.e. *Jerusalem,* Rev. 11:8 *d Law* (of Moses): vv. 10–18; Isa. 5:24. (Ex. 19:1; Gal. 3:24, *note*)
12 *e* Ex. 23:17
13 *f* vv. 11–17 *g* Cp. Isa. 66:3
15 *h* Isa. 59:1–3; Mic. 3:4
18 *i* Isa. 43:26 *j* Ps. 51:7
21 *k* Cp. Jer. 2:20 *l* Mic. 3:1–3
23 *m* Ex. 23:8; Eccl. 7:7 *n* Cp. Jas. 1:27
25 *o Israel* (prophecies): vv. 24–26; Isa. 2:2. (Gen. 12:2; Rom. 11:26, *note*) *p* Lit. *as with eye* *q Kingdom* (OT): vv. 25–26; Isa. 2:3. (Gen. 1:26; Zech. 12:8, *note*) *r* Isa. 48:10; Ezek. 22:19–22
26 *s* Jer. 33:7, 11

*1:17 Some ancient versions read *the oppressed*.

[1](1:26) Under the future kingdom the ancient method of administering the theocratic government over Israel is to be restored. See *notes* at Jud. 2:18; Mt. 19:28.

the [a]city of righteousness,
the faithful city."

27 Zion shall be redeemed with
justice,
And her penitents with
righteousness.
28 The [b]destruction of
transgressors and of sinners
shall be together,
And those who forsake the
LORD shall be consumed.
29 For they* shall be ashamed of
the [1]terebinth trees
Which you have desired;
And you shall be embarrassed
because of the gardens
Which you have chosen.
30 For you shall be as a terebinth
whose leaf fades,
And as a garden that has no
water.
31 The strong shall be as tinder,
And the work of it as a spark;
Both will burn together,
And no one shall [c]quench
them.

A vision of the coming kingdom

2 THE word that Isaiah the son of
Amoz saw concerning Judah and
Jerusalem.

2 [d]Now it shall come to [2e]pass
[f]in the latter days
That the [3]mountain of the
LORD's house
Shall be established on the top
of the mountains,
And shall be exalted above the
hills;
And all nations shall flow to it.
3 [g]Many people shall come and
say,
"Come, and let us go up to the
mountain of the LORD,
To the house of the God of
Jacob;
He will teach us His ways,
And we shall walk in His
paths."
For out of [h]Zion shall go forth
the law,
And the word of the LORD from
Jerusalem.

26
a Cp. Zech. 8:3
28
b 2 Th. 1:8–9
31
c Mk. 9:43
CHAPTER 2
2
d vv. 2–4; cp. Mic. 4:1–3
e *Israel* (prophecies): vv. 1–4; Isa. 9:7. (Gen. 12:2; Rom. 11:26, *note*)
f Cp. Gen. 49:1; see Acts 2:17, *note*
3
g Jer. 50:5; Zech. 8:21–23; 14:16–21
h *Kingdom* (OT): vv. 1–4; Isa. 4:5. (Gen. 1:26; Zech. 12:8, *note*)
5
i Cp. 1 Jn. 1:5–7
6
j Cp. Mic. 5:12
k Cp. 2 Ki. 16:7–8
7
l Cp. Dt. 17:16
m Cp. Isa. 22:18; Mic. 5:10
8
n Isa. 40:19–20
11
o Prov. 16:5

4 He shall judge between the
nations,
And rebuke many people;
They shall beat their swords
into plowshares,
And their spears into pruning
hooks;
Nation shall not lift up sword
against nation,
Neither shall they learn war
anymore.

5 O house of Jacob, come and let
us walk
In the [i]light of the LORD.

Necessity of humility in the day of the LORD

6 For You have forsaken Your
people, the house of Jacob,
Because they are filled with
eastern ways;
They *are* [j]soothsayers like the
Philistines,
And they are pleased with the
children of [k]foreigners.
7 Their land is also full of silver
and gold,
And there is no end to their
treasures;
Their land is also full of
[l]horses,
And there is no end to their
[m]chariots.
8 Their land is also full of idols;
They worship the work of their
own hands,
That which their own fingers
have [n]made.
9 People bow down,
And each man humbles
himself;
Therefore do not forgive them.
10 Enter into the rock, and hide
in the dust,
From the terror of the LORD
And the glory of His majesty.
11 The lofty looks of man shall be
[o]humbled,
The haughtiness of men shall
be bowed down,

*1:29 Following Masoretic Text, Septuagint, and Vulgate; some Hebrew manuscripts and Targum read *you.*

[1](1:29) The allusion is to the worship of idols. See *notes* at Dt. 16:21; Jud. 2:13; 3:7.
[2](2:2) Verses 2–5 are so similar to Mic. 4:1–3,5 that it has been suggested that one of these writers copied from the other. God gave both men the same vision. Micah includes an extra verse (v. 4), thus describing the vision somewhat more fully than Isaiah does. Although both prophets employ the same words, in 2:1 Isaiah stresses the fact that the vision was one that he had personally seen.
[3](2:2) A mountain, in Scripture symbolism, means a *kingdom, authority,* or *rule* (Dan. 2:35,44–45; Rev. 17:9–11; see Rev. 13:1, *note*).

And the LORD alone shall be
[a]exalted in that day.

12 For the [b]day of the LORD of
hosts
Shall come upon everything
proud and lofty,
Upon everything lifted up—
And it shall be brought low—
13 Upon all the [c]cedars of
Lebanon *that are* high and
lifted up,
And upon all the oaks of
Bashan;
14 Upon all the high mountains,
And upon all the hills *that are*
lifted up;
15 Upon every high tower,
And upon every fortified wall;
16 Upon all the [d]ships of
Tarshish,
And upon all the [e]beautiful
sloops.
17 The loftiness of man shall be
bowed down,
And the haughtiness of men
shall be brought low;
The LORD alone will be exalted
in that day,
18 But the idols He shall utterly
abolish.

19 They shall go into the [f]holes
of the rocks,
And into the [g]caves of the
earth,
From the terror of the LORD
And the glory of His majesty,
When He arises to [h]shake the
earth mightily.
20 In that day a man will [i]cast
away his idols of silver
And his idols of gold,
Which they made, *each* for
himself to worship,
To the moles and [j]bats,
21 To [k]go into the clefts of
the rocks,
And into the crags of the
rugged rocks,
From the terror of the LORD
And the glory of His majesty,
When He arises to shake the
earth mightily.

22 [l]Sever yourselves from
such a man,
Whose breath *is* in his nostrils;
For of what account is he?

National disintegration of Jerusalem and Judah through sin

3 FOR behold, the Lord, the
LORD of hosts,

11
a Isa. 5:15
12
b *Day* (of the LORD): vv. 10–21; Isa. 10:20. (Ps. 2:9; Rev. 19:19)
13
c Zech. 11:1–2; cp. Ezek. 31:3–18
16
d Cp. 1 Ki. 10:22
e Lit. *watch-towers* or *ships of pleasure*
19
f v. 10; cp. Lk. 23:30; Rev. 6:16; 9:6
g v. 21
h Cp. Hag. 2:6,21; Heb. 12:26
20
i Cp. Isa. 30:22
j Cp. Lev. 11:19
21
k vv. 10,19
22
l Ps. 146:3; Jer. 17:5
CHAPTER 3
1
m Lev. 26:26; Isa. 5:13
2
n 2 Ki. 24:14
4
o Eccl. 10:16
7
p Heb. *bind up*
8
q Mic. 3:12
9
r Gen. 19:4–9
10
s Eccl. 8:12

[m]Takes away from Jerusalem
and from Judah
The stock and the store,
The whole supply of bread and
the whole supply of water;
2 The [n]mighty man and the man
of war,
The judge and the prophet,
And the diviner and the elder;
3 The captain of fifty and the
honorable man,
The counselor and the skillful
artisan,
And the expert enchanter.

4 "I will give [o]children *to be* their
princes,
And babes shall rule over
them.
5 The people will be oppressed,
Every one by another and
every one by his neighbor;
The child will be insolent
toward the elder,
And the base toward the
honorable."

6 When a man takes hold of his
brother
In the house of his father,
saying,
"You have clothing;
You be our ruler,
And *let* these ruins *be* under
your power,"*
7 In that day he will protest,
saying,
"I cannot [p]cure *your* ills,
For in my house *is* neither food
nor clothing;
Do not make me a ruler of the
people."

8 For [q]Jerusalem stumbled,
And Judah is fallen,
Because their tongue and their
doings
Are against the LORD,
To provoke the eyes of His
glory.
9 The look on their countenance
witnesses against them,
And they declare their sin as
[r]Sodom;
They do not hide *it.*
Woe to their soul!
For they have brought evil
upon themselves.

10 "Say to the righteous [s]that *it*
shall be well *with them,*
For they shall eat the fruit of
their doings.

*3:6 Literally *hand*

11 Woe to the wicked! [a]*It shall be* ill *with him,*
For the reward of his hands shall be given him.
12 *As for* My people, children *are* their oppressors,
And women rule over them.
O My people! Those who lead you cause *you* to err,
And destroy the way of your paths."

13 The LORD stands up to plead,
And stands to judge the people.
14 The LORD will enter into judgment
With the elders of His people
And His princes:
"For you have eaten up the vineyard;
The plunder of the poor *is* in your houses.
15 What do you mean by crushing My people
And grinding the faces of the poor?"
Says the Lord GOD of hosts.

Zion's haughty women condemned

16 Moreover the LORD says:

"Because the daughters of Zion are haughty,
And walk with outstretched necks
And wanton eyes,
Walking and mincing *as* they go,
Making a jingling with their feet,
17 Therefore the Lord will strike with a scab
The crown of the head of the daughters of Zion,
And the LORD will uncover their secret parts."

18 In that day the Lord will take away the finery:
The jingling anklets, the scarves, and the crescents;
19 The pendants, the bracelets, and the veils;
20 The headdresses, the leg ornaments, and the headbands;
The perfume boxes, the charms,
21 and the rings;
The nose jewels,
22 the festal apparel, and the mantles;
The outer garments, the purses,
23 and the mirrors;
The fine linen, the turbans, and the robes.

24 And so it shall be:

Instead of a sweet smell there will be a stench;
Instead of a sash, a rope;
Instead of well-set hair, baldness;
Instead of a rich robe, a girding of sackcloth;
And branding instead of beauty.
25 Your men shall fall by the sword,
And your mighty in the war.

26 Her gates shall lament and mourn,
And she *being* desolate shall sit on the ground.

A vision of the coming kingdom (cp. Isa. 11:1–16)

4 [b]AND in that day seven women shall take hold of one man, saying,
"We will eat our own food and wear our own apparel;
Only let us be called by your name,
To take away our reproach."

2 In that [c]day the [1]Branch of the LORD shall be beautiful and glorious;
And the fruit of the earth *shall be* excellent and appealing

11 *a* Ps. 11:6; Eccl. 8:13

CHAPTER 4

1 *b* This verse concludes thought of 3:25–26

2 *c* Isa. 12:1–6

[1](4:2) A name of Christ, used in a fourfold way: (1) "the Branch of the LORD" (v. 2), i.e. the Immanuel character of Christ (Isa. 7:14) to be fully manifested to restored and converted Israel after His return in divine glory (Mt. 25:31); (2) the "Branch" of David (Isa. 11:1; Jer. 23:5; 33:15), i.e. the Messiah, "who was born of the seed of David according to the flesh" (Rom. 1:3), revealed in His earthly glory as King of kings, and Lord of lords; (3) the LORD's "Servant, the BRANCH" (Zech. 3:8), Messiah's humiliation and obedience to death according to Isa. 52:13–15; 53:1–12; Phil. 2:5–8; and (4) the "Man whose name is BRANCH" (Zech. 6:12), that is, His character as Son of Man, the "last Adam," the "second Man" (1 Cor. 15:45–47), reigning as Priest-King over the earth in the dominion given to and lost by the first Adam. Matthew is the Gospel of the Branch of David; Mark, of the LORD's Servant, the Branch; Luke, of the Man whose name is the Branch; and John, of the Branch of the LORD.

For those of Israel who have
escaped.

3 And it shall come to pass that *he
who is* left in Zion and remains in Jerusalem will be called holy—
everyone who is recorded among the
living in Jerusalem.
4 When the Lord has washed
away the filth of the daughters of
Zion, and purged the blood of Jerusalem from her midst, by the spirit of
judgment and by the spirit of burning,
5 then the LORD will create above
every dwelling place of [a]Mount Zion,
and above her assemblies, a cloud and
smoke by day and the shining of a
flaming fire by night. For over all the
glory there *will be* a covering.
6 And there will be [b]a tabernacle
for shade in the daytime from the
heat, for a place of refuge, and for a
shelter from storm and rain.

Israel, the LORD's vineyard

5 NOW let me sing to my
Well-beloved
A song of my Beloved
regarding His [c]vineyard:

My Well-beloved has a
vineyard
On a very fruitful hill.
2 He dug it up and cleared out
its stones,
And planted it with the
choicest vine.
He built a tower in its midst,
And also made a winepress in
it;
So He expected *it* to bring
forth *good* grapes,
But it brought forth wild
grapes.

3 "And now, O inhabitants of
Jerusalem and men of
Judah,
Judge, please, between Me and
My vineyard.
4 What more could have been
done to My vineyard
That I have not done in [d]it?
Why then, when I expected *it*
to bring forth *good* grapes,
Did it bring forth wild grapes?
5 And now, please let Me tell
you what I will do to My
vineyard:
I will take away its hedge, and
it shall be burned;
And break [e]down its wall, and
it shall be trampled down.
6 I will lay it [f]waste;
It shall not be pruned or dug,
But there shall come up briers
and [g]thorns.
I will also command the clouds
That they rain no rain on it."
7 For the vineyard of the LORD of
hosts *is* the house of Israel,
And the men of Judah are His
pleasant plant.
He looked for justice, but
behold, oppression;
For righteousness, but behold,
a cry *for help*.

Six woes on unfaithful Israel

8 Woe to those who join house
to house;
They add field to field,
Till *there is* no place
Where they may dwell alone in
the midst of the [h]land!
9 In my hearing the LORD of
hosts *said*,
"Truly, many houses shall be
desolate,
Great and beautiful ones,
without inhabitant.
10 For ten acres of vineyard shall
yield one [i]bath,
And a [i]homer of seed shall
yield one [i]ephah."

11 Woe to those who rise early in
the morning,
That they may follow
intoxicating drink;
Who continue until night, *till*
wine inflames them!
12 The harp and the strings,
The tambourine and flute,
And wine are in their feasts;
But they do not regard the
work of the LORD,
Nor consider the operation of
His hands.

13 Therefore [j]my people have
gone into captivity,
Because *they have* no
[k]knowledge;
Their honorable men *are*
famished,
And their multitude dried up
with thirst.
14 Therefore [l]Sheol has enlarged
itself
And opened its mouth beyond
measure;
Their glory and their multitude
and their pomp,
And he who is jubilant, shall
descend into it.
15 People shall be brought down,
Each man shall be humbled,

5 *a Kingdom* (OT): vv. 2–6; Isa. 7:14. (Gen. 1:26; Zech. 12:8, *note*)
6 *b* i.e. *a canopy*

CHAPTER 5
1 *c Parables* (OT): vv. 1–7; Jer. 13:1. (Jud. 9:8; Zech. 11:7)
4 *d* 2 Chr. 36:15
5 *e* Ps. 89:40–41
6 *f* 2 Chr. 36:19–21 *g* Isa. 7:23–25
8 *h* Mic. 2:2
10 *i* See Weights and Measures (OT), 2 Chr. 2:10, *note*
13 *j* 2 Ki. 24:14–16 *k* Hos. 4:6
14 *l* See Hab. 2:5, *note*; cp. Lk. 16:23, *note*

And the eyes of the lofty shall
be humbled.
16 But the LORD of hosts shall be
[a]exalted in judgment,
And God who is holy shall be
hallowed in righteousness.
17 Then the lambs shall feed in
their pasture,
And in the waste places of the
[b]fat ones strangers shall eat.

18 Woe to those who draw
iniquity with cords of vanity,
And sin as if with a cart rope;
19 That [c]say, "Let Him make
speed *and* hasten His work,
That we may see *it;*
And let the counsel of the Holy
One of Israel draw near and
come,
That we may know *it.*"

20 Woe to those who call evil
good, and good evil;
Who put darkness for light,
and light for darkness;
Who put bitter for sweet, and
sweet for bitter!

21 Woe to *those who are* [d]wise in
their own eyes,
And prudent in their own
sight!

22 Woe to men mighty at
drinking [e]wine,
Woe to men valiant for mixing
intoxicating drink,
23 Who [f]justify the wicked for a
bribe,
And take away justice from
the [g]righteous man!

24 Therefore, as the fire devours
the stubble,
And the flame consumes the
chaff,
So their [h]root will be as
rottenness,
And their blossom will ascend
like dust;
Because they have rejected the
[i]law of the LORD of hosts,
And despised the word of the
Holy One of Israel.
25 Therefore the anger of the
LORD is aroused against His
people;
He has stretched out His hand
against them
And stricken them,
And the hills trembled.
Their carcasses *were* as refuse
in the midst of the streets.

[j]For all this His anger is not
turned away,
But His hand *is* stretched out
still.

26 He will lift up a [k]banner to the
nations from afar,
And will [l]whistle to them from
the end of the earth;
Surely [m]they shall come with
speed, swiftly.
27 No one will be weary or
stumble among them,
No one will slumber or sleep;
Nor will the belt on their loins
be [n]loosed,
Nor the strap of their sandals
be broken;
28 Whose arrows *are* sharp,
And all their bows bent;
Their horses' hooves will seem
like flint,
And their wheels like a
whirlwind.
29 Their roaring *will be* like a
lion,
They will roar like young
lions;
Yes, they will roar
And lay hold of the prey;
They will carry *it* away safely,
And no one will deliver.
30 In that day they will roar
against them
Like the roaring of the sea.
And if *one* [o]looks to the land,
Behold, darkness *and* sorrow;
And the light is darkened by
the clouds.

Isaiah's vision

6 IN the year that [p]King Uzziah
died, I [q]saw the Lord [r]sitting on a
throne, high and lifted up, and the
train of His *robe* filled the temple.
2 Above it stood [1]seraphim; each
one had six wings: with two he covered his face, with two he [s]covered his
feet, and with two he flew.
3 And one cried to another and
said:

[t]"Holy, holy, holy *is* the LORD of
hosts;
The whole earth *is* full of His
[u]glory!"

4 And the posts of the door were
shaken by the voice of him who cried

16 [a] Isa. 2:11
17 [b] Isa. 10:16
19 [c] Cp. Jer. 17:15; 2 Pet. 3:3–4
21 [d] Prov. 3:7; Rom. 1:22; 12:16
22 [e] Cp. Isa. 56:12
23 [f] Prov. 17:15; Isa. 1:23 [g] Cp. Jas. 5:6
24 [h] Job 18:16; cp. Hos. 9:16 [i] *Law* (of Moses): vv. 24–25; Jer. 9:13. (Ex. 19:1; Gal. 3:24, *note*)
25 [j] Cp. Isa 9:12,17,21; 10:4
26 [k] Isa. 11:10, 12 [l] Zech. 10:8 [m] Cp. Dt. 28:49; Joel 2:7
27 [n] Cp. Job 12:18
30 [o] Isa. 8:22; Jer. 4:23
CHAPTER 6
1 [p] 2 Ki. 15:7 [q] Cp. 1 Ki. 22:19; Jn. 12:41; Rev. 4:2 [r] Cp. Ezek. 40:3, a theophany. See Gen. 12:7, *note*
2 [s] Ezek. 1:11
3 [t] Rev. 4:8 [u] Num. 14:21

[1](6:2) The seraphim, which are mentioned only here, appear to be angelic beings.

out, and the [a]house was filled with smoke.

5 So I said:

"Woe *is* me, for I am undone!
Because I *am* a man of
[b]unclean lips,
And I dwell in the midst of a
people of unclean lips;
For [c]my eyes have seen the
King,
The LORD of hosts."

6 Then one of the seraphim flew to
me, having in his hand a live coal
which he had taken with the tongs
from the altar.
7 And he touched my [d]mouth *with*
it, and said:

"Behold, this has touched your
lips;
Your iniquity is taken away,
And your sin purged."

8 Also I heard the voice of the
Lord, saying:

"Whom shall I send,
And who will go for Us?"

Then I said, "Here *am* I! Send [e]me."

Isaiah's new commission

9 And He said, "Go, and [f]tell this
people:

'Keep on hearing, but do not
understand;
Keep on seeing, but do not
perceive.'
10 "Make the heart of this people
dull,
And their ears heavy,
And shut their eyes;
Lest they see with their eyes,
And hear with their ears,
And understand with their
heart,
And return and be healed."

11 Then I said, "Lord, how [g]long?"
And He answered:

"Until the cities are laid waste
and without inhabitant,
The houses are without a man,
The land is utterly desolate,
12 The LORD has [h]removed men
far away,
And the forsaken places *are*
many in the midst of the
land.
13 But yet a [i]tenth *will be* in it,
And will [j]return and be for
consuming,
As a terebinth tree or as an
oak,
Whose stump *remains* when it
is cut down.
So the holy seed *shall be* its
stump."

The confederacy of Rezin and Pekah

7 NOW it came to pass in the days
of [k]Ahaz the son of Jotham, the
son of Uzziah, king of Judah, *that* Rezin king of Syria and Pekah the son of
Remaliah, king of Israel, went up to
Jerusalem to *make* war against [l]it,
but could not prevail against it.
2 And it was told to the house of
David, saying, "Syria's forces are deployed in [1]Ephraim." So his heart and
the heart of his people were moved as
the trees of the woods are moved with
the wind.
3 Then the LORD said to Isaiah, "Go
out now to meet Ahaz, you and
[m]Shear-Jashub your son, at the end of
the aqueduct from the upper pool, on
the highway to the Fuller's Field,
4 "and say to him: 'Take heed, and
be [n]quiet; do not fear or be fainthearted for these two stubs of smoking firebrands, for the fierce anger of
Rezin and Syria, and the son of Remaliah.
5 'Because Syria, Ephraim, and
the son of Remaliah have plotted evil
against you, saying,
6 "Let us go up against Judah and
trouble it, and let us make a gap in its
wall for ourselves, and set a king over
them, the son of Tabel"—
7 'thus says the Lord GOD:

"It shall not stand,
[o]Nor shall it come to pass.
8 For the head of Syria *is*
Damascus,
And the head of Damascus *is*
Rezin.
Within sixty-five years
Ephraim will be broken,
So that it will not *be* a people.
9 The head of Ephraim *is*
Samaria,
And the head of Samaria *is*
Remaliah's son.
If you will not believe,

4
a Cp. Ex. 40:34; 1 Ki. 8:10
5
b Ex. 6:12, 30
c *Inspiration:* vv. 5–9; Isa. 8:1. (Ex. 4:15; 2 Tim. 3:16, *note*)
7
d Cp. Jer. 1:9; Dan. 10:16
8
e Cp. Acts 26:19–20
9
f vv. 9–10; Mt. 13:14–15; Jn. 12:39–41; Acts 28:25–27; cp. 2 Cor. 3:14–15
11
g Cp. Ps. 79:5; 94:3; Hab. 1:2
12
h Isa. 5:9
13
i See Rom. 11:5, *note*
j See Isa. 8:18, *note*
CHAPTER 7
1
k 2 Chr. 28
l 2 Ki. 16:5,9
3
m Lit. *a remnant shall return.* Cp. Isa. 8:3
4
n Ex. 14:13; Isa. 30:15; Lam. 3:26
7
o 2 Ki. 16:5

[1](7:2) In the prophetic books Ephraim and Israel are the collective names of the ten tribes, who under Jeroboam established the northern kingdom, subsequently called Samaria (1 Ki. 21:1), and were (c. 722–721 B.C.) sent into an exile which still continues (2 Ki. 17:1–6).

Surely you shall not be
[a]established." ' "

The great sign: Immanuel, the virgin's Son

10 Moreover the LORD spoke again
to Ahaz, saying,
11 "Ask a sign for yourself from the
LORD your God; ask it either in the
depth or in the height above."
12 But Ahaz said, "I will not ask,
nor will I [b]test the LORD!"
13 Then he said, "Hear now, O
house of David! *Is it* a small thing for
you to weary men, but will you weary
my God also?
14 "Therefore the Lord Himself will
give you a [1]sign: Behold, the virgin
shall [c]conceive and bear a [d]Son, and
shall [e]call His name [f]Immanuel.
15 "Curds and [g]honey He shall eat,
[h]that He may know to refuse the evil
and choose the good.
16 "For before the Child shall know
to refuse the evil and choose the good,
the land that you dread will be forsaken by both her kings.

Prediction of an impending invasion of Judah (cp. 2 Chr. 28:1–20)

17 "The [i]LORD will bring the king of
Assyria upon you and your people
and your father's house—days that
have not come since the day that
[j]Ephraim departed from Judah."

18 And it shall come to pass in
that day
That the LORD will whistle for
the fly
That *is* in the farthest part of
the rivers of Egypt,
And for the bee that *is* in the
land of Assyria.
19 They will come, and all of
them will rest
In the desolate valleys and in
the [k]clefts of the rocks,
And on all thorns and in all
pastures.

20 In the same day the Lord will
shave with a [l]hired [2m]razor,
With those from beyond the
[n]River, with the king of
Assyria,
The head and the hair of the
legs,
And will also remove the
beard.
21 It shall be in that day
That a man will keep alive a
young cow and two sheep;
22 So it shall be, from the
abundance of milk they give,
That he will eat curds;
For curds and honey everyone
will eat who is left in the
[3]land.

23 It shall happen in that day,
That wherever there could be
a thousand vines
Worth a thousand *shekels* of
silver,
It will be for briers and thorns.
24 With arrows and bows men
will come there,
Because all the land will
become briers and thorns.

25 And to any hill which could be
dug with the hoe,
You will not go there for fear
of briers and thorns;
But it will become a range for
oxen
And a place for sheep to roam.

Overthrow of Damascus and Samaria

8 MOREOVER the LORD said to me,
"Take a large scroll, and [o]write
on it with a man's pen concerning
[p]Maher-Shalal-Hash-Baz.
2 "And I will take for Myself faithful witnesses to record, Uriah the
priest and Zechariah the son of Jeberechiah."
3 Then I went to the prophetess,
and she conceived and bore a son.
Then the LORD said to me, "Call his
name [p]Maher-Shalal-Hash-Baz;
4 "for before the child shall have
knowledge to cry 'My father' and 'My
mother,' the riches of Damascus and
the spoil of Samaria will be taken
away before the king of Assyria."
5 The LORD also spoke to me again,
saying:

6 "Inasmuch as these people
refused

9 *a* Cp. 2 Chr. 20:20
12 *b Test/tempt:* v. 12; Jer. 9:7. (Gen. 3:1; Jas. 1:14, *note*)
14 *c* Mt. 1:23
d Christ (first advent): v. 14; Isa. 9:6. (Gen. 3:15; Acts 1:11, *note*)
e Kingdom (OT): v. 14; Isa. 9:7. (Gen. 1:26; Zech. 12:8, *note*)
f Lit. *God with us*
15 *g* Cp. v. 22
h Or *when He knows*
17 *i* 2 Chr. 28:19
j 1 Ki. 12:16
19 *k* Isa. 2:19
20 *l* Isa. 10:5, 15
m 2 Chr. 28:20–21
n i.e. *the Euphrates*
CHAPTER 8
1 *o Inspiration:* v. 1; Isa. 30:8. (Ex. 4:15; 2 Tim. 3:16, *note*)
p Usually rendered, lit. *hasten the booty, hasten the spoil.* Cp. Isa. 7:3

[1](7:14) This prediction of the virgin birth of the Lord Jesus Christ is not addressed only to the faithless Ahaz, but to the whole "house of David" (v. 13). The objection that such a far-off event as the birth of Christ could be no "sign" to Ahaz is, therefore, not valid. It was a continuing prophecy addressed to the Davidic family.

[2](7:20) This is a reference to the fact that Ahaz sent gifts to Tiglath-Pileser, king of Assyria, to hire him to come and deliver him from Aram (Syria) and Israel (2 Ki. 16:5–9).

[3](7:22) Verses 20–25 describe the situation that would result from the invasion, when there would be large grazing areas but insufficient men to cultivate the fields.

The waters of [a]Shiloah that
flow softly,
And rejoice in [b]Rezin and in
Remaliah's son;
7 Now therefore, behold, the
Lord brings up over them
The waters of the [c]River,
strong and mighty—
The king of Assyria and all his
glory;
He will go up over all his
channels
And go over all his banks.
8 He will pass through Judah,
He will overflow and pass
over,
[d]He will reach up to the neck;
And the stretching out of his
wings
Will fill the breadth of Your
land, O [e]Immanuel.*

The believing remnant

9 [f]"Be shattered, O you peoples,
and be broken in pieces!
Give ear, all you from far
countries.
Gird yourselves, but be broken
in pieces;
Gird yourselves, but be broken
in pieces.
10 [g]Take counsel together, but it
will come to nothing;
Speak the word, but it will not
stand,
[h]For God *is* [1]with us."*

11 For the LORD spoke thus to me
with a strong hand, and instructed me
that I should not walk in the way of
this people, saying:

12 "Do not say, 'A [2]conspiracy,'
Concerning all that this people
call a conspiracy,
Nor be afraid of their threats,
nor be troubled.
13 The LORD of hosts, Him you
shall hallow;
Let Him *be* your fear,
And *let* Him *be* your dread.
14 He will be as a sanctuary,
But a [i]stone of stumbling and
a rock of offense
To both the houses of Israel,
As a trap and a snare to the
inhabitants of Jerusalem.
15 And many among them shall
stumble;
They shall fall and be broken,
Be snared and taken."

16 Bind up the testimony,
Seal the law among my
disciples.
17 And I will wait on the LORD,
Who hides His face from the
house of Jacob;
And I will hope in [j]Him.
18 Here am I and the children
whom the LORD has given
me!
We are for [3]signs and wonders
in Israel
From the LORD of hosts,
Who dwells in Mount Zion.

19 And when they say to you, "Seek
those who are mediums and wizards,
who whisper and mutter," should not
a people seek their God? *Should they
seek* the dead on behalf of the living?
20 To the law and to the testimony!
If they do not speak according to this
word, *it is* because *there is* no light in
them.
21 They will pass through it hard
pressed and hungry; and it shall happen, when they are hungry, that they
will be enraged and curse their king
and their God, and look upward.
22 Then they will look to the earth,
and see trouble and darkness, gloom
of anguish; and *they will be* driven
into darkness.

Christ's birth and glorious reign

9 NEVERTHELESS the gloom
will not *be* upon her who *is*
distressed,
As when [k]at first He lightly
esteemed
The land of Zebulun and the
land of Naphtali,
And [l]afterward more heavily
oppressed *her*,

6
a Or *Shelah*, Neh. 3:15; or *Siloam*, Jn. 9:7
b Cp. Isa. 7:1–9
7
c i.e. *the Euphrates*
8
d Isa. 30:28
e Isa. 7:14; Mt. 1:23
9
f Or *Make an uproar*
10
g Isa. 7:7; Acts 5:38
h Cp. Rom. 8:31
14
i *Christ* (Stone): vv. 14–15; Isa. 28:16. (Gen. 49:24; 1 Pet. 2:8)
17
j Cited in Heb. 2:13 from Septuagint Version
CHAPTER 9
1
k Or *in former times*
l Or *in the latter time He will make it glorious by the way of the sea*

* 8:8 Literally *God-With-Us* 8:10 Hebrew *Immanuel*

[1](8:10) Judah is Immanuel's land and, therefore, cannot be conquered except as Immanuel permits. Compare the end of v. 8 where the same Hebrew words are used, but rendered in our version "Immanuel." This child is the "stone of stumbling and a rock of offense" (v. 14).

[2](8:12) The reference is to the attempt to terrify Judah by the conspiracy between Syria and Samaria (Isa. 7:1–2).

[3](8:18) The primary application here is to the two sons of Isaiah, Maher-Shalal-Hash-Baz (8:1) = "Speed the Spoil, Hasten the Booty," a sign of the coming judgment of the captivity of Judah; Shear-Jashub (7:3) = "A Remnant Shall Return," a sign of the return of a remnant of Judah at the end of the seventy years of captivity (Jer. 25:11–12; Dan. 9:2). The larger and final reference is to our Lord (Heb. 2:13–14).

By the way of the sea, beyond
the Jordan,
In Galilee of the Gentiles.
2 [1]The people who walked in
darkness
Have seen a great light;
Those who dwelt in the land of
the shadow of death,
Upon them a light has shined.
3 You have multiplied the nation
And increased its joy;*
They rejoice before You
According to the joy of
harvest,
As *men* rejoice when they
divide the spoil.
4 For You have broken the yoke
of his burden
And the staff of his shoulder,
The rod of his oppressor,
As in the day of Midian.
5 For every warrior's sandal
from the noisy battle,
And garments rolled in blood,
Will be used for burning *and*
fuel of fire.
6 For unto us a [a]Child is [b]born,
Unto us a Son is given;
And the government will be
upon His shoulder.
And His name will be called
Wonderful, Counselor, Mighty
God,
Everlasting Father, Prince of
Peace.
7 Of the increase of *His*
government and peace
There will be [c]no end,
Upon the [2d]throne of David
and over His [e]kingdom,
[f]To order it and establish it
with judgment and justice
From that time forward, even
forever.
The zeal of the LORD of hosts
will perform this.

God's continuing judgment on the northern kingdom of Israel (to 10:4)

8 The LORD sent a word against
[g]Jacob,
And it has fallen on Israel.
9 All the people will know—
Ephraim and the inhabitant of
Samaria—
Who say in pride and
arrogance of heart:
10 "The bricks have fallen down,
But we will rebuild with hewn
stones;
The sycamores are cut down,
But we will replace *them* with
cedars."
11 Therefore the LORD shall set up
The adversaries of Rezin
against him,
And spur his enemies on,
12 The Syrians before and the
Philistines behind;
And they shall devour Israel
with an open mouth.

[3]For all this His anger is not
turned away,
But His hand *is* stretched out
still.

13 For the people do not turn to
Him who strikes them,
Nor do they seek the LORD of
hosts.
14 Therefore the LORD will cut off
head and tail from Israel,
Palm branch and bulrush [h]in
one day.
15 The elder and honorable, he *is*
the head;
The prophet who teaches lies,
he *is* the tail.
16 For the [i]leaders of this people
cause *them* to err,
And *those who are* led by
them are [j]destroyed.
17 Therefore the LORD will have
no joy in their young men,
Nor have mercy on their
fatherless and widows;
For everyone *is* a hypocrite
and an evildoer,
And every mouth speaks folly.

For all this His anger is not
turned away,

6
a Lk. 2:7; Jn. 3:16; 1 Jn. 4:9
b *Christ* (first advent): v. 6; Isa. 28:16. (Gen. 3:15; Acts 1:11, *note*)
7
c Dan. 2:44; Lk. 1:32–33
d *Israel* (prophecies): vv. 6–7; Isa. 11:1. (Gen. 12:2; Rom. 11:26, *note*)
e *Kingdom* (OT): vv. 6–7; Isa. 11:1. (Gen. 1:26; Zech. 12:8, *note*)
f *Christ* (second advent): vv. 6–7; Isa. 11:11. (Dt. 30:3; Acts 1:11, *note*)
8
g Gen. 32:28
14
h Cp. Rev. 18:8
16
i Mic. 3:1,5, 9
j Lit. *swallowed up*

*9:3 Following Qere and Targum; Kethib and Vulgate read *not increased joy;* Septuagint reads *Most of the people You brought down in Your joy.*

[1](9:2) Isaiah points out that the very region where Assyrian armies brought darkness and death would be the first to rejoice in the light brought by the preaching of Christ (Mt. 4:15–16).

[2](9:7) "The throne of David" is an expression as definite, historically, as "the throne of the Caesars," and does not admit of spiritualizing (Lk. 1:32–33). See Kingdom (OT), Zech. 12:8, *note;* Davidic Covenant, 2 Sam. 7:16, *note;* Acts 15:14–16.

[3](9:12) Compare the closing words of vv. 17,21 with Isa. 5:25; 10:4. The context makes it clear that, because no repentance was forthcoming from the northern kingdom of Israel, the LORD's hand of judgment will continue to be outstretched unrelentingly and will result in their captivity.

But His hand *is* stretched out still.

18 For wickedness [a]burns as the fire;
It shall devour the briers and thorns,
And kindle in the thickets of the forest;
They shall mount up *like* rising smoke.
19 Through the wrath of the LORD of hosts
The land is burned up,
And the people shall be as fuel for the fire;
[b]No man shall spare his brother.
20 And he shall snatch on the right hand
And be hungry;
He shall devour on the left hand
And not be satisfied;
Every man shall eat the flesh of his own arm.
21 Manasseh *shall devour* Ephraim, and Ephraim Manasseh;
Together they *shall be* [c]against Judah.

For all this His anger is not turned away,
But His hand *is* stretched out still.

10 "WOE to those who decree unrighteous decrees,
Who write misfortune,
Which they have prescribed
2 To rob the needy of justice,
And to take what is right from the poor of My people,
That widows may be their prey,
And *that* they may rob the fatherless.
3 What will you do in the [d]day of punishment,
And in the desolation *which* will come from [e]afar?
To whom will you flee for [f]help?
And where will you leave your glory?
4 Without Me they shall bow down among the [g]prisoners,
And they shall fall among the slain."

[h]For all this His anger is not turned away,
But His hand *is* stretched out still.

Predicted judgment on Assyria

5 "Woe to [i]Assyria, the rod of My anger
And the staff in whose hand is My indignation.
6 I will send him against an [j]ungodly nation,
And against the people of My wrath
I will [k]give him charge,
To seize the spoil, to take the prey,
And to tread them down like the mire of the streets.
7 [l]Yet he does not mean so,
Nor does his heart think so;
But *it is* in his heart to destroy,
And cut off not a few nations.
8 [m]For he says,
'*Are* not my princes altogether kings?
9 *Is* not [n]Calno like Carchemish?
Is not Hamath like Arpad?
Is not Samaria like Damascus?
10 As my hand has found the kingdoms of the idols,
Whose carved images excelled those of Jerusalem and Samaria,
11 As I have done to Samaria and her idols,
Shall I not do also to Jerusalem and her idols?' "

12 Therefore it shall come to pass,
[1]when the LORD has performed all His
work [o]on Mount Zion and on Jerusalem, *that He will say,* [p]"I will punish
the fruit of the arrogant heart of the
king of Assyria, and the glory of his
haughty looks."
13 [q]For he says:

"By the strength of my hand I have done *it,*
And by my wisdom, for I am prudent;
Also I have removed the boundaries of the people,
And have robbed their treasuries;

18 [a] Isa. 10:17; Mal. 4:1
19 [b] Mic. 7:2,6
21 [c] 2 Chr. 28:6,8
CHAPTER 10
3 [d] Hos. 9:7; cp. Lk. 19:41–44 [e] Isa. 5:26 [f] Cp. Isa. 30:1–5; 31:3
4 [g] Isa. 24:22 [h] Isa. 5:25; 9:12,17,21
5 [i] Heb. *Asshur*
6 [j] Isa. 9:17 [k] Jer. 34:22
7 [l] Cp. Gen. 50:20; Mic. 4:12; Acts 2:23–24; 1 Cor. 2:8
8 [m] vv. 9–11; cp. 2 Ki. 18:19–25; 19:10–13
9 [n] Or *Calneh,* Amos 6:2
12 [o] 2 Ki. 19:31 [p] Jer. 50:18; cp. 2 Ki. 19:35–37; Isa. 14:25
13 [q] Cp. Isa. 37:24; Ezek. 28:4; Dan. 4:30

[1](10:12) A permanent method in the divine government of the earth is illustrated here. Israel is always the center of the divine counsels earthward (Dt. 32:8). The nations are permitted to afflict Israel in chastisement for her national sins, but invariably and inevitably retribution falls upon them. Cp. Gen. 15:13–14; Dt. 30:5–7; Isa. 14:1–2; Joel 3:1–8; Mic. 5:7–9; Mt. 25:31–40.

So I have put down the
inhabitants like a valiant
man.
14 My hand has found like a nest
the riches of the people,
And as one gathers eggs *that*
are left,
I have gathered all the earth;
And there was no one who
moved *his* wing,
Nor opened *his* mouth with
even a peep."

15 Shall the ax boast itself against
him who chops with it?
Or shall the saw exalt itself
against him who saws with
it?
As if a rod could wield *itself*
against those who lift it up,
Or as if a staff could lift up, *as*
if it were not wood!
16 Therefore the Lord, the Lord*
of hosts,
Will send leanness among his
fat ones;
And under his glory
He will kindle a burning
Like the burning of a fire.
17 So the Light of Israel will be
for a fire,
And his Holy One for a flame;
It will burn and devour
His thorns and his briers in
one day.
18 And it will consume the glory
of his forest and of his
fruitful field,
Both soul and body;
And they will be as when a
sick man wastes away.
19 Then the rest of the trees of
his forest
Will be so few in number
That a child may write them.

A remnant will return

20 And it shall come to pass in
[1]that [a]day
That the [b]remnant of Israel,
And such as have escaped of
the house of Jacob,
Will never again depend on
[c]him who defeated them,
But will depend on the LORD,
the Holy One of Israel, in
truth.

20
a Day (of the LORD): vv. 20–23; Isa. 13:6. (Ps. 2:9; Rev. 19:19)
b Remnant: vv. 20–22; Isa. 11:11. (Isa. 1:9; Rom. 11:5, *note*)
c 2 Ki. 16:7
21
d Isa. 9:6
22
e vv. 22–23; Rom. 9:27–28
24
f Isa. 7:4; 8:12; 12:2
26
g Ex. 14:27
27
h Armageddon (battle of): vv. 24–34; Isa. 24:21. (Isa. 10:27; Rev. 19:17)
i Ps. 45:7; 89:20–22
28
j vv. 28–32; cp. Mic. 1:10–16

21 The remnant will return, the
remnant of Jacob,
To the [d]Mighty God.
22 For [e]though your people, O
Israel, be as the sand of the
sea,
A remnant of them will return;
The destruction decreed shall
overflow with righteousness.
23 For the Lord GOD of hosts
Will make a determined end
In the midst of all the land.

24 Therefore thus says the Lord
GOD of hosts: "O My people, who dwell
in Zion, do not be [f]afraid of the Assyrian. He shall strike you with a rod and
lift up his staff against you, in the
manner of Egypt.
25 "For yet a very little while and
the indignation will cease, as will My
anger in their destruction."
26 And the LORD of hosts will stir up
a scourge for him like the slaughter of
Midian at the rock of Oreb; *as* His rod
was on the [g]sea, so will He lift it up in
the manner of Egypt.

27 It shall come to pass in that
[h]day
That his burden will be taken
away from your shoulder,
And his yoke from your neck,
And the yoke will be destroyed
because of the [i]anointing
oil.

The Assyrians' advance and defeat
(37:7,35–36)

28 [j]He has come to Aiath,
He has passed Migron;
At Michmash he has attended
to his equipment.
29 They have gone along the
ridge,
They have taken up lodging at
Geba.
Ramah is afraid,
Gibeah of Saul has fled.
30 Lift up your voice,
O daughter of Gallim!
Cause it to be heard as far as
Laish—
O poor Anathoth!*

*
10:16 Following Bomberg; Masoretic Text and Dead Sea Scrolls read *YHWH (the LORD)*
10:30 Following Masoretic Text, Targum, and Vulgate; Septuagint and Syriac read *Listen to her, O Anathoth.*

[1](10:20) "That day" is often the equivalent of "the day of the LORD" (Isa. 2:10–22; Rev. 19:11–21). The prophecy here passes from the general to the particular, from historic and fulfilled judgments upon Assyria to the final destruction of all Gentile world power at the return of the Lord in glory. See Armageddon, Rev. 16:13–16; 19:17–21; Times of the Gentiles, Lk. 21:24 and Rev. 16:19, *notes;* The Tribulation, Ps. 2:5; Rev. 7:14, *note.*

31 Madmenah has fled,
The inhabitants of Gebim seek refuge.
32 As yet he will remain at Nob that day;
He will shake his fist at the mount of the daughter of Zion,
The hill of Jerusalem.

33 Behold, the Lord,
The LORD of hosts,
Will lop off the bough with terror;
Those of high stature *will be* hewn down,
And the haughty will be humbled.
34 He will cut down the thickets of the forest with iron,
And Lebanon will fall by the Mighty One.

Davidic kingdom to be restored by Christ: its character and extent

11 [1]THERE shall come forth a [a]Rod from the stem of [b]Jesse,
And a [c]Branch shall grow out of his roots.
2 The [d]Spirit of the LORD shall rest upon Him,
The [e]Spirit of wisdom and understanding,
The Spirit of counsel and might,
The Spirit of knowledge and of the [f]fear of the LORD.
3 His delight *is* in the [f]fear of the LORD,
And He shall not judge by the sight of His eyes,
Nor decide by the hearing of His ears;
4 But with righteousness He shall judge the poor,
And decide with equity for the meek of the earth;
He shall strike the earth with the rod of His mouth,
And with the breath of His lips He shall slay the wicked.
5 Righteousness shall be the [g]belt of His loins,
And faithfulness the belt of His waist.

6 "The wolf also shall dwell with the lamb,
The leopard shall lie down with the young goat,
The calf and the young lion and the fatling together;
And a little child shall lead them.
7 The cow and the bear shall graze;
Their young ones shall lie down together;
And the lion shall eat straw like the ox.
8 The nursing child shall play by the cobra's hole,
And the weaned child shall put his hand in the viper's den.
9 They shall not hurt nor destroy in all My holy mountain,
[h]For the earth shall be full of the knowledge of the LORD
As the waters cover the sea.

10 "And in that day there shall be a [i]Root of Jesse,
Who shall stand as [j]a banner to the people;
For the [k]Gentiles shall seek Him,
And His resting place shall be glorious."

How Christ will set up the kingdom

11 It shall come to pass in that day
That the LORD shall set His hand again the second time
To [l]recover the [m]remnant of His people who are left,
From Assyria and Egypt,
From Pathros and Cush,
From Elam and Shinar,
From Hamath and the islands of the sea.

12 He will set up a banner for the nations,
And will assemble the outcasts of Israel,
And gather together the dispersed of Judah
From the four corners of the earth.
13 Also the envy of Ephraim shall depart,
And the adversaries of Judah shall be cut off;
Ephraim shall not envy Judah,
And Judah shall not harass Ephraim.
14 But they shall fly down upon the shoulder of the Philistines toward the west;

CHAPTER 11

1

a Kingdom (OT): vv. 1–12; 12:1–6; Isa. 14:1. (Gen. 1:26; Zech. 12:8, *note*)
b Israel (prophecies): vv. 1–13; Isa. 60:1. (Gen. 12:2; Rom. 11:26, *note*)
c See Isa. 4:2, *note*

2

d Holy Spirit (OT): v. 2; Isa. 30:1. (Gen. 1:2; Zech. 12:10)
e Rev. 1:4; 4:5; 5:6; cp. 1 Cor. 12:4–11
f See Ps. 19:9, *note*

5

g Righteousness (garment): v. 5; Isa. 59:17. (Gen. 3:21; Rev. 19:8)

9

h See Hab. 2:14, *note*

10

i Rom. 15:12
j Isa. 27:12–13
k Isa. 2:2

11

l Christ (second advent): vv. 10–12; Jer. 23:6. (Dt. 30:3; Acts 1:11, *note*)
m Remnant: vv. 11–13, 16; Isa. 24:13. (Isa. 1:9; Rom. 11:5, *note*)

---

[1](11:1) This chapter is a prophetic picture of the glory of the future kingdom, which will be set up when David's Son returns in glory (Lk. 1:31–32; Acts 15:15–16).

Together they shall plunder
the people of the East;
They shall lay their hand on
Edom and Moab;
And the people of Ammon
shall obey them.
15 The LORD [a]will utterly
destroy* the tongue of the
Sea of Egypt;
With His mighty wind He will
shake His fist over the
[b]River,
And strike it in the seven
streams,
And make *men* cross over
dry-shod.
16 There will be a [c]highway for
the remnant of His people
Who will be left from Assyria,
As it was for Israel
In the day that he came up
from the land of Egypt.

Thanksgiving in the kingdom

12 AND in that day you will say:

"O LORD, I will praise You;
Though You were angry with
me,
Your anger is turned away,
and You comfort me.
2 Behold, God *is* my salvation,
I will [d]trust and not be afraid;
'For YAH, the LORD, *is* my
strength and song;
He also has become my
salvation.' "*
3 Therefore with joy you will
draw [e]water
From the wells of salvation.
4 And in that day you will say:

"Praise the LORD, call upon His
name;
Declare His deeds among the
peoples,
Make mention that His name is
exalted.
5 Sing to the LORD,
For He has done excellent
things;
This *is* known in all the earth.
6 Cry out and shout, O
inhabitant of Zion,
For great *is* the Holy One of
Israel in your [f]midst!"

II. Prophecies concerning the Nations, 13—27

The LORD summons an attacking army

13 THE [1g]burden against [2]Babylon which Isaiah the son of
Amoz saw.

2 "Lift up a banner on the high
mountain,
Raise your voice to them;
Wave your hand, that they
may enter the gates of the
nobles.
3 I have commanded My
sanctified ones;
I have also called My mighty
ones for My anger—
Those who rejoice in My
exaltation."

4 The [h]noise of a multitude in
the mountains,
Like that of many people!
A tumultuous noise of the
kingdoms of nations
gathered together!
The LORD of hosts musters
The army for battle.
5 They come from a far country,
From the end of heaven—
The [i]LORD and His weapons of
indignation,
To destroy the whole [j]land.

The day of the LORD's judgment on Babylon, picturing God's future judgment on Gentile nations

6 Wail, for the [k]day of the LORD
is at hand!
It will come as destruction
from the Almighty.
7 Therefore all hands will be
limp,
Every man's heart will [l]melt,
8 And they will be afraid.
Pangs and sorrows will take
hold of *them;*
They will be in pain as a
woman in childbirth;

15
a Isa. 50:2; 51:10–11; Zech. 10:10–11
b i.e. *the Euphrates*
16
c Isa. 19:23
CHAPTER 12
2
d See Ps. 2:12, *note*
3
e Jn. 4:10, 14; 7:37–38
6
f Zeph. 3:14–15
CHAPTER 13
1
g vv. 1–22; 14:18–23; 47:1–15; Jer. 25:12; 50:1–51:64
4
h Isa. 17:12
5
i Isa. 42:13
j Isa. 24:1; 34:2
6
k Day (of the LORD): vv. 6–16; 14:1–8; Isa. 24:1. (Ps. 2:9; Rev. 19:19)
7
l Cp. Isa. 19:1

*

11:15 Following Masoretic Text and Vulgate; Septuagint, Syriac, and Targum read *dry up*.
12:2 Exodus 15:2

[1](13:1) "Burden," which also means "oracle," is a word sometimes used in the prophetical writings to indicate a divine message of judgment.

[2](13:1) This prophecy concerning Babylon (chs. 13—14) announces the doom of the nation and city at the hands of the Medes (13:17–22), but applies the word "Babylon" to the totality of Gentile world power beginning with Nebuchadnezzar (Dan. 2:31–32,37–38) and culminating in the fourth world empire (Dan. 2:34–35,40–45) at the return of Jesus Christ to the earth as the Striking Stone. See Times of the Gentiles, Lk. 21:24 and Rev. 16:19, *notes*.

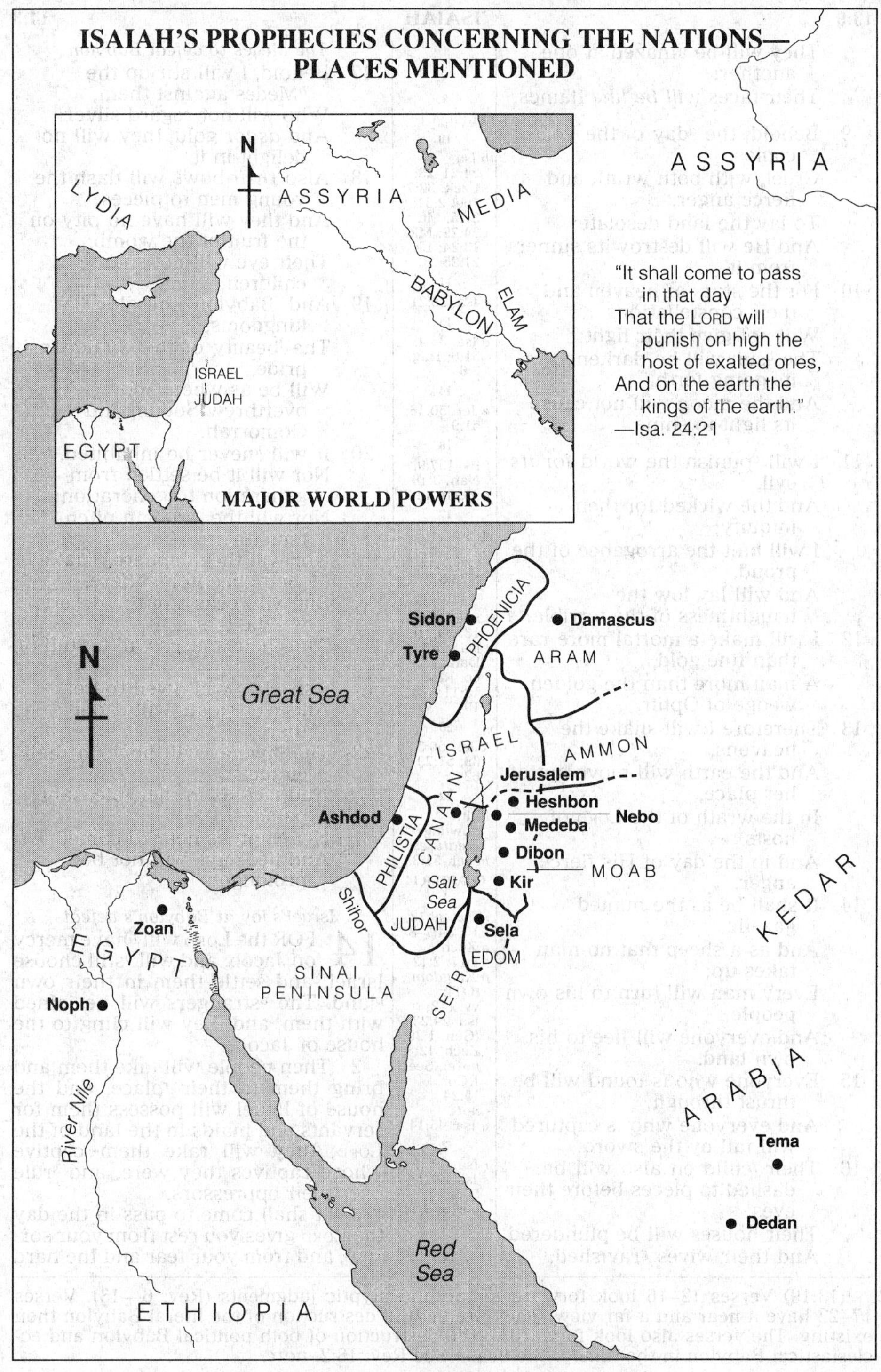

ISAIAH'S PROPHECIES CONCERNING THE NATIONS—
PLACES MENTIONED
N
LYDIA
ASSYRIA
MEDIA
BABYLON
ELAM
ISRAEL
JUDAH
EGYPT
MAJOR WORLD POWERS
ASSYRIA
"It shall come to pass
in that day
That the LORD will
punish on high the
host of exalted ones,
And on the earth the
kings of the earth."
—Isa. 24:21
PHOENICIA
Sidon
Damascus
Tyre
ARAM
N
Great Sea
ISRAEL
AMMON
Jerusalem
Heshbon
Nebo
Ashdod
Medeba
PHILISTIA
CANAAN
Dibon
Kir
MOAB
Salt Sea
KEDAR
Shihor
JUDAH
Sela
Zoan
EGYPT
EDOM
SINAI PENINSULA
SEIR
Noph
ARABIA
River Nile
Tema
Dedan
Red Sea
ETHIOPIA

They will be amazed at one
another;
Their faces *will be like* flames.

9 Behold, the [a]day of the LORD
comes,
Cruel, with both wrath and
fierce anger,
To lay the land desolate;
And He will destroy its sinners
from it.

10 For the stars of heaven and
their constellations
Will not give their light;
The [b]sun will be darkened in
its going forth,
And the moon will not cause
its light to shine.

11 "I will [c]punish the world for *its*
evil,
And the wicked for their
iniquity;
I will halt the arrogance of the
proud,
And will lay low the
haughtiness of the terrible.

12 I will make a mortal more rare
than fine gold,
A man more than the golden
wedge of Ophir.

13 [d]Therefore I will shake the
heavens,
And the earth will move out of
her place,
In the wrath of the LORD of
hosts
And in the day of His fierce
anger.

14 It shall be as the hunted
gazelle,
And as a sheep that no man
takes up;
[e]Every man will turn to his own
people,
And everyone will flee to his
own land.

15 Everyone who is found will be
thrust through,
And everyone who is captured
will fall by the sword.

16 Their [f]children also will be
dashed to pieces before their
eyes;
Their houses will be plundered
And their wives [g]ravished.

9
a Mal. 4:1
10
b Isa. 24:21–23; Ezek. 32:7; Joel 2:31; 3:15; Mt. 24:29; Mk. 13:24; Lk. 21:25
11
c Isa. 26:21
13
d Isa. 34:4; 51:6; Hag. 2:6
14
e Jer. 50:16; 51:9
16
f Ps. 137:9; Nah. 3:10
g Zech. 14:2
17
h Isa. 21:2; Jer. 51:11, 28; Dan. 5:28,31
19
i See Isa. 13:1, *note*
j Isa. 47:5; Dan. 4:30; cp. Rev. 18:11–16, 19
20
k Jer. 50:3, 39; 51:29, 62
22
l Lit. *howling creatures*
m Jer. 51:33
CHAPTER 14
1
n Isa. 49:13, 15; 54:7–8
o Zech. 1:17; 2:12
p *Kingdom (OT)*: vv. 1–2; Isa. 24:23. (Gen. 1:26; Zech. 12:8, *note*). See 1 Cor. 15:24, *note*
q Isa. 45:14
2
r Isa. 49:22
s Isa. 49:23; 54:3; 60:10; 61:5

The Medes to defeat Babylon

17 "Behold, I will stir up the
[h]Medes against them,
Who will not regard silver;
And *as for* gold, they will not
delight in it.

18 Also *their* bows will dash the
young men to pieces,
And they will have no pity on
the fruit of the womb;
Their eye will not spare
children.

19 [1]And [i]Babylon, the glory of
kingdoms,
The [j]beauty of the Chaldeans'
pride,
Will be as when God
overthrew Sodom and
Gomorrah.

20 It will [k]never be inhabited,
Nor will it be settled from
generation to generation;
Nor will the Arabian pitch
tents there,
Nor will the shepherds make
their sheepfolds there.

21 But wild beasts of the desert
will lie there,
And their houses will be full of
owls;
Ostriches will dwell there,
And wild goats will caper
there.

22 The [l]hyenas will howl in their
citadels,
And jackals in their pleasant
palaces.
Her [m]time *is* near to come,
And her days will not be
prolonged."

Israel's joy at Babylon's defeat

14 FOR the LORD will [n]have mercy
on Jacob, and will [o]still choose
Israel, and settle them in their own
[p]land. The [q]strangers will be joined
with them, and they will cling to the
house of Jacob.
2 Then people will take them and
bring them to their [r]place, and the
house of Israel will possess them for
servants and maids in the land of the
LORD; they will take them captive
whose captives they were, and [s]rule
over their oppressors.
3 It shall come to pass in the day
the LORD gives you rest from your sorrow, and from your fear and the hard

[1](13:19) Verses 12–16 look forward to the apocalyptic judgments (Rev. 6—13). Verses 17–22 have a near and a far view. They predict the destruction of the literal Babylon then existing. The verses also look forward to the destruction of both political Babylon and ecclesiastical Babylon in the time of the beast. See Rev. 18:2, *note*.

bondage in which you were made to serve,
4 that you will [a]take up this proverb against the king of Babylon, and say:

"How the oppressor has ceased,
The golden* city ceased!
5 The LORD has broken the staff
of the wicked,
The scepter of the rulers;
6 He who struck the people in
wrath with a continual
stroke,
He who ruled the nations in
anger,
Is persecuted *and* no one
hinders.
7 The whole earth is at rest *and*
quiet;
They break forth into singing.
8 Indeed the cypress trees
[b]rejoice over you,
And the cedars of Lebanon,
Saying, 'Since you were cut
down,
No woodsman has come up
against us.'

Israel taunts Babylon's fallen king

9 "Hell from beneath is excited
about you,
To meet *you* at your coming;
It stirs up the dead for you,
All the chief ones of the earth;
It has raised up from their
thrones
All the kings of the nations.
10 They all shall [c]speak and say
to you:
'Have you also become as weak
as we?
Have you become like us?
11 Your pomp is brought down to
[d]Sheol,
And the sound of your stringed
instruments;
The maggot is spread under
you,
And worms cover you.'

The overthrow of Lucifer because of pride and rebellion

12 "How you are fallen from
heaven,
O [1e]Lucifer, [f]son of the
morning!
How you are cut down to the
ground,
You who weakened the
nations!
13 For you have said in your
heart:
'I will ascend into [g]heaven,
I will exalt my throne above
the stars of God;
I will also sit on the [h]mount of
the congregation
On the farthest [i]sides of the
north;
14 I will ascend above the heights
of the clouds,
I will be like the Most High.'
15 Yet you shall be [j]brought
down to Sheol,
To the lowest depths of the
[k]Pit.
16 "Those who see you will gaze at
you,
And consider you, *saying*:
'*Is* this the man who made the
earth tremble,
Who shook kingdoms,
17 Who made the world as a
wilderness
And destroyed its cities,
Who did not open the house of
his prisoners?'

Destruction of Babylon

18 "All the kings of the nations,
All of them, sleep in glory,
Everyone in his own house;
19 But you are cast out of your
grave
Like an abominable branch,
Like the garment of those who
are slain,
Thrust through with a sword,
Who go down to the stones of
the pit,
Like a corpse trodden
underfoot.
20 You will not be joined with
them in burial,
Because you have destroyed
your land
And slain your people.
The brood of evildoers shall
[l]never be named.

4
a Isa. 13:19; cp. Hab. 2:6
8
b Isa. 55:12
10
c Ezek. 32:21
11
d See Hab. 2:5, *note;* cp. Lk. 16:23, *note*
12
e Lk. 10:18; Rev. 12:7–9
f *Satan:* vv. 12–14; Ezek. 28:12. (Gen. 3:1; Rev. 20:10)
13
g Ezek. 28:2
h Ezek. 28:14
i Ps. 48:2
15
j Cp. Mt. 11:23
k Ezek. 28:8
20
l Ps. 109:13

*14:4 Or *insolent*

[1](14:12) Verses 12–14 evidently refer to Satan who, as prince of this world system (Jn. 12:31; 14:30; 16:11; see Rev. 13:8, *note*), is the real though unseen ruler of the successive world powers, Tyre, Babylon, Medo-Persia, Greece, Rome, etc. (cp. Ezek. 28:12–14). Lucifer, "Day Star," can be none other than Satan. This significant passage points back to the beginning of sin in the universe. When Satan said, "I will," sin began. See Rev. 20:10, *note*. For other instances of addressing Satan through another, cp. Gen. 3:15; Mt. 16:22–23.

21 Prepare slaughter for his
children
Because of the iniquity of their
fathers,
Lest they rise up and possess
the land,
And fill the face of the world
with cities."

22 "For I will rise up against
them," says the LORD of
hosts,
"And [a]cut off from [b]Babylon
the name and remnant,
And offspring and posterity,"
says the LORD.
23 "I will also make it a possession
for the [c]porcupine,
And marshes of muddy water;
I will sweep it with the broom
of destruction," says the
LORD of hosts.

Judgment on Assyria

24 The LORD of hosts has sworn,
saying,
"Surely, as I have thought, so it
shall come to pass,
And as I have purposed, *so* it
shall [d]stand:
25 That I will break the [e]Assyrian
in My land,
And on My mountains tread
him underfoot.
Then his yoke shall be
removed from them,
And his burden removed from
their shoulders.
26 This *is* the [f]purpose that is
purposed against the whole
earth,
And this *is* the hand that is
stretched out over all the
nations.
27 For the LORD of hosts has
purposed,
And who will annul *it?*
His hand *is* stretched out,
And who will turn it back?"

Judgment on Philistia

28 This is the [g]burden which came
in the year that King Ahaz died.

29 "Do not rejoice, all you of
[h]Philistia,
Because the rod that struck
you is broken;
For out of the serpent's roots
will come forth a viper,
And its offspring *will be* a fiery
flying serpent.
30 The firstborn of the poor will
feed,

22
a Prov. 10:7; Isa. 26:14
b See Isa. 13:1, *note* 2
23
c Isa. 34:11; Zeph. 2:14
24
d Isa. 43:13
25
e vv. 24–27; Isa. 10:5–27; Mic. 5:5–6; Zeph. 2:13
26
f Isa. 23:9
28
g See Isa. 13:1, *note* 1
29
h vv. 29–31; Jer. 47:1–4; Ezek. 25:15–17; Zeph. 2:5; Zech. 9:6
32
i See Ps. 2:12, *note*
CHAPTER 15
1
j Dt. 2:9
k Isa. 15:1-16:14; 25:10; Jer. 25:21; 48:1–47; Amos 2:1–3; Zeph. 2:8–11
2
l See Jud. 3:7 and 1 Ki. 3:2, *notes*
3
m Jer. 48:38
4
n Jer. 48:34
5
o Isa. 16:11; Jer. 48:31

And the needy will lie down in
safety;
I will kill your roots with
famine,
And it will slay your remnant.
31 Wail, O gate! Cry, O city!
All you of [h]Philistia *are*
dissolved;
For smoke will come from the
north,
And no one *will be* alone in his
appointed times."

32 What will they answer the
messengers of the nation?
That the LORD has founded
Zion,
And the poor of His people
shall [i]take refuge in it.

Judgment on Moab

15 THE [g]burden against Moab.

Because in the night [j]Ar of
[k]Moab is laid waste
And destroyed,
Because in the night Kir of
Moab is laid waste
And destroyed,
2 He has gone up to the temple*
and Dibon,
To the [l]high places to weep.
Moab will wail over Nebo and
over Medeba;
On all their heads *will be*
baldness,
And every beard cut off.
3 In their streets they will clothe
themselves with sackcloth;
On the tops of their houses
And in their streets
Everyone will wail, [m]weeping
bitterly.
4 Heshbon and Elealeh will cry
out,
Their voice shall be heard as
far as [n]Jahaz;
Therefore the armed soldiers*
of Moab will cry out;
His life will be burdensome to
him.
5 [o]"My heart will cry out for
Moab;
His fugitives *shall flee* to Zoar,
Like a three-year-old heifer.*
For by the Ascent of Luhith
They will go up with weeping;
For in the way of Horonaim

*
15:2 Hebrew *bayith (house)* 15:4 Following Masoretic Text, Targum, and Vulgate; Septuagint and Syriac read *loins.* 15:5 Or *The Third Eglath,* an unknown city (compare Jeremiah 48:34)

They will raise up a cry of
destruction,
6 For the waters of [a]Nimrim will
be desolate,
For the green grass has
withered away;
The grass fails, there is
nothing green.
7 Therefore the abundance they
have gained,
And what they have laid up,
They will carry away to the
Brook of the Willows.
8 For the cry has gone all
around the borders of Moab,
Its wailing to Eglaim
And its wailing to Beer Elim.
9 For the waters of Dimon* will
be full of blood;
Because I will bring more upon
Dimon,*
Lions upon him who escapes
from Moab,
And on the remnant of the
land."

Moab refuses sanctuary to Israel's fugitives; her judgment soon to come

16 SEND the lamb to the ruler
of the land,
From [b]Sela to the wilderness,
To the mount of the daughter
of Zion.
2 For it shall be as a [c]wandering
bird thrown out of the nest;
So shall be the daughters of
Moab at the fords of the
[d]Arnon.
3 "Take counsel, execute
judgment;
Make your shadow like the
night in the middle of the
day;
Hide the outcasts,
Do not betray him who
escapes.
4 Let My outcasts dwell with
you, O Moab;
Be a shelter to them from the
face of the spoiler.
For the extortioner is at an
end,
Devastation ceases,
The oppressors are consumed
out of the land.
5 In mercy the [e]throne will be
established;
And One will sit on it in truth,
in the [f]tabernacle of David,
Judging and seeking justice
and hastening
[g]righteousness."

6 We have heard of the pride of
Moab—
He is very proud—
Of his haughtiness and his
pride and his wrath;
But his lies *shall* not *be* so.
7 Therefore Moab shall wail for
Moab;
Everyone shall wail.
For the foundations of Kir
Hareseth you shall mourn;
Surely *they are* stricken.
8 For the fields of Heshbon
languish,
And the vine of Sibmah;
The lords of the nations have
broken down its choice
plants,
Which have reached to Jazer
And wandered through the
wilderness.
Her branches are stretched
out,
They are gone over the [h]sea.
9 Therefore I will bewail the
vine of Sibmah,
With the weeping of Jazer;
I will drench you with my
tears,
O Heshbon and Elealeh;
For battle cries have fallen
Over your summer fruits and
your harvest.
10 [i]Gladness is taken away,
And joy from the plentiful
field;
In the vineyards there will be
no singing,
Nor will there be shouting;
No treaders will tread out wine
in the presses;
I have made their shouting
cease.
11 Therefore my [j]heart shall
resound like a harp for
Moab,
And my inner being for Kir
Heres.
12 And it shall come to pass,
When it is seen that Moab is
[k]weary on the [l]high place,
That he will come to his
sanctuary to pray;
But he will not prevail.
13 This *is* the word which the LORD

6
a Or *Nimrah,* Num. 32:3

CHAPTER 16
1
b Or *Petra.* Lit. *a rock.* 2 Ki. 14:7; Isa. 42:11
2
c Prov. 27:8
d Num. 21:13
5
e Dan. 7:14; Lk. 1:33; Rev. 11:15
f See Acts 15:13–17, *notes*
g Isa. 9:7; 11:4; 32:1
8
h Jer. 48:32
10
i Isa. 24:8; Jer. 48:33
11
j Isa. 15:5; 63:15; Jer. 48:36
12
k Cp. 1 Ki. 18:29
l Isa. 15:2. See Jud. 3:7 and 1 Ki. 3:2, *notes*

*

15:9 Following Masoretic Text and Targum; Dead Sea Scrolls and Vulgate read *Dibon;* Septuagint reads *Rimon.* • Following Masoretic Text and Targum; Dead Sea Scrolls and Vulgate read *Dibon;* Septuagint reads *Rimon.*

has spoken concerning Moab since
that time.
14 But now the LORD has spoken,
saying, "Within three years, as the
years of a hired man, the glory of
Moab will be despised with all that
great multitude, and the remnant *will*
be very small *and* feeble."

Damascus (Syria) and her ally (10 tribes) will fall

17 THE [1]burden against Damascus.

"Behold, [a]Damascus will cease
from *being* a city,
And it will be a ruinous heap.
2 The cities of [b]Aroer *are*
forsaken;*
They will be for flocks
Which lie down, and [c]no one
will make *them* afraid.
3 The fortress also will cease
from Ephraim,
The kingdom from Damascus,
And the remnant of Syria;
They will be as the [d]glory of
the children of Israel,"
Says the LORD of hosts.

4 "In that day it shall come to
pass
That the glory of Jacob will
wane,
And the fatness of his flesh
grow [e]lean.
5 It shall be [f]as when the
harvester gathers the grain,
And reaps the heads with his
arm;
It shall be as he who gathers
heads of grain
In the Valley of Rephaim.
6 Yet [g]gleaning grapes will be
left in it,
Like the shaking of an olive
tree,
Two *or* three olives at the top
of the uppermost bough,
Four *or* five in its most fruitful
branches,"
Says the LORD God of Israel.

7 In that day a man will [h]look to
his Maker,
And his eyes will have respect
for the Holy One of Israel.
8 He will not look to the altars,
The work of his hands;
He will not respect what his
[i]fingers have made,
Nor the [j]wooden images nor
the incense altars.
9 In that day his strong cities
will be as a forsaken bough*
And an uppermost branch,*
Which they left because of the
children of Israel;
And there will be desolation.

10 Because you have [k]forgotten
the God of your salvation,
And have not been mindful of
the Rock of your stronghold,
Therefore you will plant
pleasant plants
And set out foreign seedlings;
11 In the day you will make your
plant to grow,
And in the morning you will
make your seed to flourish;
But the harvest *will be* a heap
of ruins
In the day of grief and
desperate sorrow.

12 Woe to the multitude of many
people
Who make a [l]noise like the
roar of the seas,
And to the rushing of nations
That make a rushing like the
rushing of mighty waters!
13 The nations will [m]rush like the
rushing of many waters;
[n]But *God* will rebuke them and
they will flee far away,
And be [o]chased like the chaff
of the mountains before the
wind,
Like a rolling thing before the
whirlwind.
14 Then behold, at eventide,
trouble!
And before the morning, he *is*
[p]no more.
This *is* the portion of those
who plunder us,
And the lot of those who rob
us.

Woe to Ethiopia

18 WOE to the [q]land shadowed
with buzzing wings,

CHAPTER 17
1
a vv. 1–3; Jer. 49:23–27; Amos 1:3–5; Zech. 9:1
2
b Num. 32:34
c Jer. 7:33
3
d Cp. 1 Sam. 4:21; Hos. 9:11
4
e Isa. 10:16
5
f Jer. 51:33
6
g Isa. 24:13
7
h Isa. 10:20; Hos. 3:5; Mic. 7:7
8
i Isa. 2:8; 31:7
j See Dt. 16:21, *note*
10
k Isa. 51:13
12
l Isa. 13:4
13
m Cp. Isa. 33:3
n Isa. 37:29–38
o Ps. 83:13; Hos. 13:3
14
p Cp. 2 Ki. 19:35
CHAPTER 18
1
q Isa. 20:4–5; Ezek. 30:4–5,9; Zeph. 2:12; 3:10

*17:2 Following Masoretic Text and Vulgate; Septuagint reads *It shall be forsaken forever;* Targum reads *Its cities shall be forsaken and desolate.* 17:9 Septuagint reads *Hivites;* Targum reads *laid waste;* Vulgate reads *as the ploughs.* • Septuagint reads *Amorites;* Targum reads *in ruins;* Vulgate reads *corn.*

[1](17:1) There was a near fulfillment in Sennacherib's approaching invasion, but vv. 12–14 look forward also to the final invasion and battle. See Armageddon, Rev. 16:16 and 19:17, *notes.*

Which *is* beyond the rivers of [a]Ethiopia,
2 [1]Which sends ambassadors by sea,
Even in vessels of reed on the waters, *saying*,
"Go, swift messengers, to a nation tall and smooth *of skin*,
To a people terrible from their beginning onward,
A nation powerful and treading down,
Whose land the rivers divide."

3 All inhabitants of the world and dwellers on the earth:
When he [b]lifts up a banner on the mountains, you see *it;*
And when he blows a trumpet, you hear *it*.
4 For so the LORD said to me,
"I will take My rest,
And I will look from My dwelling place
Like clear heat in sunshine,
Like a cloud of dew in the heat of harvest."
5 For before the harvest, when the bud is perfect
And the sour grape is ripening in the flower,
He will both cut off the sprigs with pruning hooks
And take away *and* cut down the branches.
6 They will be left together for the mountain birds of prey
And for the beasts of the earth;
The birds of prey will summer on them,
And all the beasts of the earth will winter on them.

7 In that [c]time a present will be brought to the LORD of hosts
From* a people tall and smooth *of skin*,
And from a people terrible from their beginning onward,
A nation powerful and treading down,
Whose land the rivers divide—
To the place of the name of the LORD of hosts,
To Mount Zion.

1
a Heb. *Cush.* vv. 1–7; Ezek. 30:4–5; Zeph. 2:12
3
b Cp. Isa. 5:26; 11:10–12
7
c Isa. 14:1–3; 66:20; Mic. 4:1–8; cp. Ps. 68:31
CHAPTER 19
1
d See Isa. 13:1, *note 1*
e vv. 1–22; Jer. 9:25–26; Ezek. 29:1–30:19; Joel 3:19
f Ex. 12:12; Jer. 43:12
g Cp. Josh. 2:11; Isa. 13:7
2
h Cp. Jud. 7:22; 1 Sam. 14:16,20; 2 Chr. 20:23
3
i Isa. 8:19
4
j Isa. 20:4; Jer. 46:26; Ezek. 29:19
5
k Jer. 51:36; Ezek. 30:12
6
l i.e. *Egypt's irrigation canals*
m Or *streams* or *canals of Egypt*
7
n Or *Nile*

Egypt's decline and collapse

19 THE [d]burden against Egypt.

Behold, the LORD rides on a swift cloud,
And will come into [e]Egypt;
The [f]idols of Egypt will totter at His presence,
And the heart of Egypt will [g]melt in its midst.

2 "I will [h]set Egyptians against Egyptians;
Everyone will fight against his brother,
And everyone against his neighbor,
City against city, kingdom against kingdom.
3 The spirit of Egypt will fail in its midst;
I will destroy their counsel,
And they will consult the idols and the charmers,
The mediums and the [i]sorcerers.
4 And the Egyptians I will [j]give
Into the hand of a cruel master,
And a fierce king will rule over them,"
Says the Lord, the LORD of hosts.

5 [k]The waters will fail from the sea,
And the river will be wasted and dried up.
6 The [l]rivers will turn foul;
The [m]brooks of defense will be emptied and dried up;
The reeds and rushes will wither.
7 The papyrus reeds by the [n]River, by the mouth of the [n]River,
And everything sown by the [n]River,
Will wither, be driven away, and be no more.
8 The fishermen also will mourn;
All those will lament who cast hooks into the [n]River,
And they will languish who spread nets on the waters.
9 Moreover those who work in fine flax

*18:7 Following Dead Sea Scrolls, Septuagint, and Vulgate; Masoretic Text omits *From;* Targum reads *To.*

[1](18:2) The reference is evidently to an embassy from Egypt, resulting in the alliance denounced in chs. 30—31 and Jer. 37:7–11.

And those who weave fine
  fabric will be ashamed;
10 And its foundations will be
  broken.
All who make wages *will be*
  troubled of soul.

11 Surely the princes of Zoan *are*
  fools;
Pharaoh's wise counselors give
  foolish counsel.
[a]How do you say to Pharaoh, "I
  am the son of the wise,
The son of ancient kings?"
12 Where *are* they?
Where are your wise men?
Let them tell you now,
And let them know what the
  LORD of hosts has [b]purposed
  against Egypt.
13 The princes of Zoan have
  become fools;
The princes of [c]Noph* are
  deceived;
They have also deluded Egypt,
Those who are the mainstay of
  its tribes.
14 The LORD has mingled a
  [d]perverse spirit in her midst;
And they have caused Egypt to
  err in all her work,
As a drunken man staggers in
  his vomit.
15 Neither will there be *any* work
  for Egypt,
Which the head or tail,
Palm branch or bulrush, may
  do.*

Future restoration of Egypt and Assyria as subject to Israel in Christ's kingdom

16 In that day Egypt will [e]be like women, and will be afraid and fear because of the waving of the hand of the LORD of hosts, which He waves over it.

17 And the land of Judah will be a terror to Egypt; everyone who makes mention of it will be afraid in himself, because of the counsel of the LORD of hosts which He has [f]determined against it.

18 In that day five cities in the land of Egypt will [g]speak the language of Canaan and [h]swear by the LORD of hosts; one will be called the City of Destruction.*

19 In that day there will be an [i]altar to the LORD in the midst of the land of Egypt, and a pillar to the [j]LORD at its border.

20 And it will be for a sign and for a witness to the LORD of hosts in the land of Egypt; for they will cry to the LORD because of the oppressors, and He will send them a [k]Savior and a Mighty One, and He will deliver them.

21 Then the LORD will be known to Egypt, and the Egyptians will [l]know the LORD in that day, and will make sacrifice and [m]offering; yes, they will make a vow to the LORD and perform *it.*

22 And the LORD will strike Egypt, He will strike and [n]heal *it;* they will return to the LORD, and He will be entreated by them and heal them.

23 In that day there will be a [o]highway from Egypt to Assyria, and the Assyrian will come into Egypt and the Egyptian into Assyria, and the Egyptians will [p]serve with the Assyrians.

24 In that day Israel will be one of three with Egypt and Assyria—a blessing in the midst of the land,

25 whom the LORD of hosts shall bless, saying, "Blessed *is* Egypt My people, and Assyria the work of My hands, and [q]Israel My inheritance."

Impending conquest of Egypt and Ethiopia

20 IN the year that [r]Tartan came to Ashdod, when Sargon the king of Assyria sent him, and he fought against Ashdod and took it,

2 at the same time the LORD spoke by Isaiah the son of Amoz, saying, "Go, and remove the [s]sackcloth from your body, and take your sandals off your feet." And he did so, [t]walking naked and barefoot.

3 Then the LORD said, "Just as My servant Isaiah has walked naked and barefoot three years *for* a sign and a wonder against Egypt and [u]Ethiopia,

4 "so shall the [v]king of Assyria lead away the Egyptians as prisoners and the Ethiopians as captives, young and old, naked and barefoot, [w]with their buttocks uncovered, to the shame of Egypt.

5 [x]"Then they shall be afraid and ashamed of [u]Ethiopia their expectation and Egypt their glory.

6 "And the inhabitant of this territory will say in that day, 'Surely such *is* our expectation, wherever we flee for [y]help to be delivered from the king

---

11 *a* 1 Ki. 4:29–34; cp. Acts 7:22
12 *b* Ps. 33:11
13 *c* Jer. 2:16
14 *d* Cp. 1 Ki. 22:22
16 *e* Cp. Jer. 51:30; Nah. 3:13
17 *f* Isa. 14:24; Dan. 4:35
18 *g* Zeph. 3:9; *h* Isa. 45:23
19 *i* Isa. 56:7; 60:7; *j* Ps. 68:31
20 *k* Isa. 43:11
21 *l* Isa. 2:3–4; 11:9; *m* Zech. 14:16–18; cp. Mal. 1:11
22 *n* Dt. 32:39
23 *o* Isa. 11:16; 35:8; 40:3; 62:10; *p* Isa. 27:13
25 *q* Dt. 14:2
CHAPTER 20
1 *r* The title of the commander–in-chief of the Assyrian army. 2 Ki. 18:17
2 *s* Cp. Zech. 13:4; *t* Cp. 1 Sam. 19:24; Mic. 1:8,11
3 *u* Heb. *Cush.* Gen. 10:6
4 *v* Isa. 19:4; *w* Cp. 2 Sam. 10:4; Isa. 3:17; Jer. 13:22,26
5 *x* 2 Ki. 18:21; Isa. 30:3–7; 36:6

20:6 *y* Isa. 30:5,7; cp. 31:3

---

*

19:13 That is, ancient Memphis **19:15** Compare Isaiah 9:14–16 **19:18** Some Hebrew manuscripts, Arabic, Dead Sea Scrolls, Targum, and Vulgate read *Sun;* Septuagint reads *Asedek* (literally *Righteousness*).

of Assyria; and how shall we escape?' "

God commands Medes to take Babylon

21 THE [a]burden against the Wilderness of the Sea.

As whirlwinds in the [b]South
pass through,
So it comes from the desert,
from a terrible land.
2 A distressing vision is declared
to me;
The treacherous dealer deals
treacherously,
And the plunderer plunders.
[c]Go up, O Elam!
Besiege, O Media!
All its sighing I have made to
cease.
3 Therefore my loins are filled
with pain;
Pangs have taken hold of me,
like the pangs of a woman
in labor.
I was distressed when *I* heard
it;
I was dismayed when *I* saw *it.*
4 My heart wavered, fearfulness
frightened me;
The [d]night for which I longed
He turned into fear for me.
5 Prepare the table,
Set a watchman in the tower,
Eat and drink.
Arise, you princes,
Anoint the shield!

6 For thus has the Lord said to
me:
"Go, set a watchman,
Let him declare what he sees."
7 And he saw a chariot *with* a
pair of horsemen,
A chariot of donkeys, *and* a
chariot of camels,
And he listened earnestly with
great care.
8 Then he cried, "A lion,* my
Lord!
I stand continually on the
watchtower in the daytime;
I have sat at my post every
night.
9 And look, here comes a chariot
of men *with* a pair of
horsemen!"
Then he answered and said,
[e]"Babylon is fallen, is fallen!
And all the carved images of
her gods
He has [f]broken to the
ground."

10 Oh, my threshing and the
grain of my floor!
That which I have heard from
the LORD of hosts,
The God of Israel,
I have declared to you.

Woe to Edom

11 The [a]burden against [g]Dumah.

He calls to me out of [h]Seir,
"Watchman, what of the night?
Watchman, what of the night?"
12 The watchman said,
"The morning comes, and also
the night.
If you will inquire, inquire;
Return! Come back!"

Woe to Arabia

13 The [a]burden against [i]Arabia.

In the forest in Arabia you will
lodge,
O you [j]traveling companies of
[k]Dedanites.
14 O inhabitants of the land of
Tema,
Bring water to him who is
thirsty;
With their bread they met him
who fled.
15 For they fled from the swords,
from the drawn sword,
From the bent bow, and from
the distress of war.

16 For thus the LORD has said to me:
"Within a year, according to the year
of a hired man, all the glory of Kedar
will fail;
17 "and the remainder of the number of archers, the mighty men of the
people of Kedar, will be diminished;
for the LORD God of Israel has spoken
it."

The Valley of Vision:
woe to Jerusalem

22 THE [a]burden against the [l]Valley of Vision.

What ails you now, that you
have all gone up to the
housetops,
2 You who are full of noise,
A tumultuous city, a [m]joyous
city?
Your slain *men are* [n]not slain
with the sword,
Nor dead in battle.
3 All your rulers have fled
together;

CHAPTER 21
1
a See Isa. 13:1, *note 1*
b See Gen. 12:9, *note*
2
c Isa. 13:17; 22:6
4
d Dt. 28:67
9
e Jer. 51:8; Rev. 14:8; 18:2
f Cp. Jer. 50:2; 51:44
11
g Gen. 25:14; 1 Chr. 1:30; Josh. 15:52
h Gen. 32:3; Jer. 49:7; Ezek. 35:2; Obad. 1
13
i Jer. 25:24
j i.e. *caravans*
k Gen. 10:7; 1 Chr. 1:9, 32; Jer. 25:23; Ezek. 27:15

CHAPTER 22
1
l v. 5; cp. Jer. 7:32; 19:6
2
m Isa. 32:13
n Cp. Jer. 14:18

*
21:8 Dead Sea Scrolls read *Then the observer cried.*

They are captured by the
archers.
All who are found in you are
bound together;
They have fled from afar.
4 Therefore I said, "Look away
from me,
[a]I will weep bitterly;
Do not labor to comfort me
Because of the plundering of
the daughter of my people."

5 For *it is* a day of trouble and
treading down and
perplexity
[b]By the Lord GOD of hosts
In the Valley of Vision—
Breaking down the walls
And of crying to the mountain.
6 [c]Elam bore the quiver
With chariots of men *and*
horsemen,
And [d]Kir uncovered the shield.
7 It shall come to pass *that* your
choicest valleys
Shall be full of chariots,
And the horsemen shall set
themselves in array at the
[e]gate.

8 [f]He [g]removed the protection of
Judah.
You looked in that day to the
armor of the [h]House of the
Forest;
9 You also saw the [i]damage to
the city of David,
That it was great;
And you gathered together the
[j]waters of the lower pool.
10 You numbered the houses of
Jerusalem,
And the houses you broke
down
To fortify the wall.
11 You also [k]made a reservoir
between the two walls
For the water of the old [l]pool.
But you did [m]not look to its
Maker,
Nor did you have respect for
Him who fashioned it long
ago.

12 And in that day the Lord GOD
of hosts
[n]Called for weeping and for
mourning,
For [o]baldness and for girding
with sackcloth.
13 But instead, joy and gladness,

4
a Cp. Jer. 4:19; 9:1; Lk. 19:41
5
b Lam. 1:5; 2:2
6
c Isa. 21:2
d 2 Ki. 16:9; Isa. 15:1
7
e Cp. 2 Chr. 32:1
8
f 2 Ki. 18:15–16
g Cp. 2 Ki. 16:18
h 1 Ki. 7:2; 10:17
9
i Cp. 2 Chr. 32:5
j 2 Ki. 20:20; 2 Chr. 32:30
11
k Neh. 3:16
l 2 Chr. 32:3–4
m Cp. Isa. 5:12
12
n Joel 1:13
o Cp. Ezra 9:3
13
p Isa. 5:11, 22; cp. Lk. 17:26–29
q Isa. 56:12; 1 Cor. 15:32
14
r Cp. 1 Sam. 3:14; Ezek. 24:13
17
s Or *cover.* Cp. Est. 7:8
18
t Isa. 2:7
20
u 2 Ki. 18:18
22
v Isa. 9:6

Slaying oxen and killing sheep,
Eating meat and [p]drinking
wine:
[q]"Let us eat and drink, for
tomorrow we die!"
14 Then it was revealed in my
hearing by the LORD of hosts,
"Surely for this iniquity there
[r]will be no atonement for
you,
Even to your death," says the
Lord GOD of hosts.

Shebna replaced by Eliakim

15 Thus says the Lord GOD of hosts:

"Go, proceed to this steward,
To [1]Shebna, who *is* over the
house, *and say:*
16 'What have you here, and
whom have you here,
That you have hewn a
sepulcher here,
As he who hews himself a
sepulcher on high,
Who carves a tomb for himself
in a rock?
17 Indeed, the LORD will throw
you away violently,
O mighty man,
And will surely [s]seize you.
18 He will surely turn violently
and toss you like a ball
Into a large country;
There you shall die, and there
your glorious [t]chariots
Shall be the shame of your
master's house.
19 So I will drive you out of your
office,
And from your position he will
pull you down.*

20 'Then it shall be in that day,
That I will call My servant
[u]Eliakim the son of Hilkiah;
21 I will clothe him with your
robe
And strengthen him with your
belt;
I will commit your
responsibility into his hand.
He shall be a father to the
inhabitants of Jerusalem
And to the house of Judah.
22 The key of the house of David
I will lay on his [v]shoulder;

*22:19 Septuagint omits *he will pull you down;* Syriac, Targum, and Vulgate read *I will pull you down.*

[1](22:15) Shebna was a foreigner and a man of considerable influence who was displaced by Eliakim (vv. 20–25). Later he evidently became Hezekiah's scribe (36:3; 37:2).

So he shall open, and no one
shall shut;
And he shall shut, and no one
shall [a]open.
23 I will fasten him *as* a [b]peg in a
secure place,
And he will become a glorious
throne to his father's house.

24 'They will hang on him all the
glory of his father's house, the offspring and the posterity, all vessels of
small quantity, from the cups to all the
pitchers.
25 'In that day,' says the LORD of
hosts, 'the peg that is fastened in the
secure place will be removed and be
cut down and fall, and the burden that
was on it will be cut off; for the LORD
has spoken.' "

The fall of Tyre

23 THE [c]burden against [d]Tyre.

Wail, you ships of Tarshish!
For it is laid waste,
So that there is no house, no
harbor;
From the land of Cyprus* it is
revealed to them.
2 Be still, you inhabitants of the
coastland,
You merchants of Sidon,
Whom those who cross the sea
have filled.*
3 And on great waters the grain
of Shihor,
The harvest of the River,* *is*
her revenue;
And she is a [e]marketplace for
the nations.
4 Be ashamed, O Sidon;
For the sea has spoken,
The strength of the sea, saying,
"I do not labor, nor bring forth
children;
Neither do I rear young men,
Nor bring up virgins."
5 When the report *reaches*
Egypt,
They also will be in agony at
the report of Tyre.
6 Cross over to Tarshish;
Wail, you inhabitants of the
coastland!
7 *Is* this your [f]joyous *city*,
Whose antiquity *is* from
ancient days,
Whose feet carried her far off
to dwell?
8 Who has taken this counsel
against Tyre, the [g]crowning
city,
Whose merchants *are* princes,
Whose traders *are* the
honorable of the earth?
9 The LORD of hosts has
[h]purposed it,
To bring to dishonor the
[i]pride of all glory,
To bring into contempt all the
honorable of the earth.
10 Overflow through your land
like the River,*
O daughter of Tarshish;
There is no more strength.
11 He stretched out His hand over
the sea,
He shook the kingdoms;
The LORD has given a
commandment [j]against
Canaan
To destroy its strongholds.
12 And He said, [k]"You will
rejoice no more,
O you oppressed virgin
daughter of Sidon.
Arise, cross over to Cyprus;
There also you will have no
rest."
13 Behold, the land of the
[l]Chaldeans,
This people *which* was not;
Assyria founded it for wild
beasts of the desert.
They set up its towers,
They raised up its palaces,
And brought it to ruin.

14 [m]Wail, you ships of Tarshish!
For your strength is laid waste.

15 Now it shall come to pass in that
day that Tyre will be forgotten [n]sev-
enty years, according to the days of
one king. At the end of seventy years
it will happen to Tyre as *in* the song of
the harlot:

16 "Take a harp, go about the city,
You forgotten harlot;
Make sweet melody, sing
many songs,
That you may be
remembered."

17 And it shall be, at the end of seventy years, that the LORD will deal with
Tyre. She will return to her hire, and

22
a Here the prophecy looks forward to Christ. Rev. 3:7
23
b vv. 23–25; cp. Zech. 10:4–6; Isa. 33:20–24; 54:1–8
CHAPTER 23
1
c See Isa. 13:1, *note 1*
d vv. 1–18; Jer. 25:22; 47:4; Ezek. 26:1–21; 28:20–24; Amos 1:9–10; Zech. 9:2–4
3
e Ezek. 27:3–23
7
f Isa. 22:2
8
g Cp. Rev. 18:9–19
9
h Isa. 14:26
i Isa. 13:11; 24:4; Dan. 4:37
11
j Zech. 9:2–4
12
k Cp. Rev. 18:22
13
l Isa. 47:1
14
m Ezek. 27:25–30
15
n Cp. Jer. 25:11–12

23:1 Hebrew *Kittim*, western lands, especially Cyprus **23:2** Following Masoretic Text and Vulgate; Septuagint and Targum read *passing over the water;* Dead Sea Scrolls read *your messengers passing over the sea.* **23:3** That is, the Nile **23:10** That is, the Nile

commit fornication with all the kingdoms of the world on the face of the
earth.
18 Her gain and her pay will be [a]set
apart for the LORD; it will not be treasured nor laid up, for her gain will be
for those who dwell before the LORD,
to eat sufficiently, and for fine clothing.

Isaiah's "little apocalypse" (24—27): desolate Palestine after Babylonian invasion pictures distress in the tribulation

24 BEHOLD, the LORD [b]makes
the earth empty and makes
it waste,
[c]Distorts its surface
And scatters abroad its
inhabitants.
2 And it shall be:
As with the people, so with the
priest;
As with the servant, so with
his master;
As with the maid, so with her
mistress;
As with the buyer, so with the
seller;
As with the lender, so with the
borrower;
As with the creditor, so with
the debtor.
3 The land shall be entirely
emptied and utterly
plundered,
For the LORD has spoken this
word.

4 The earth mourns *and* fades
away,
The world languishes *and*
fades away;
The [d]haughty people of the
earth languish.
5 The earth is also [e]defiled
under its inhabitants,
Because they have
[f]transgressed the laws,
Changed the ordinance,
Broken the [g]everlasting
covenant.
6 Therefore the [h]curse has
devoured the earth,
And those who dwell in it are
desolate.
Therefore the inhabitants of
the earth are [i]burned,
And few men *are* left.
7 [j]The new wine fails, the vine
languishes,
All the merry-hearted sigh.
8 The mirth of the tambourine
ceases,
The noise of the jubilant ends,
The joy of the harp ceases.
9 They shall not drink wine with
a song;
Strong drink is bitter to those
who drink it.
10 The city of confusion is broken
down;
Every house is shut up, so that
none may go in.
11 *There is* a cry for wine in the
streets,
All joy is darkened,
The mirth of the land is gone.
12 In the city desolation is left,
And the gate is stricken with
destruction.
13 When it shall be thus in the
midst of the land [k]among
the people,
It shall be like the shaking of
an olive tree,
Like the [l]gleaning of grapes
when the vintage is done.

A spared remnant rejoices

14 They shall lift up their voice,
they shall sing;
For the majesty of the LORD
They shall cry aloud from the
sea.
15 Therefore [m]glorify the LORD in
the dawning light,
The [n]name of the LORD God of
Israel in the [o]coastlands of
the sea.
16 From the ends of the earth we
have heard songs:
"Glory to the righteous!"
But I said, "I am ruined,
ruined!
Woe to me!
The treacherous dealers have
dealt treacherously,
Indeed, the treacherous dealers
have dealt very
treacherously."

Distress of nations climaxed by God's judgments during the tribulation

17 [p]Fear and the pit and the snare
Are upon you, O inhabitant of
the earth.
18 And it shall be
That he who flees from the
noise of the fear
Shall fall into the pit,
And he who comes up from
the midst of the pit
Shall be caught in the snare;

18
a Cp. Zech. 14:20–21
CHAPTER 24
1
b Day (of the LORD): vv. 1–20; Isa. 24:21. (Ps. 2:9; Rev. 19:19)
c Or *turns it upside down.* Cp. 2 Ki. 21:13
4
d Isa. 25:11
5
e Num. 35:33
f Isa. 59:12
g 1 Chr. 16:14–19; Ps. 105:7–12; cp. Isa. 55:3
6
h Cp. Mal. 4:6
i Isa. 9:19
7
j Joel 1:10–12
13
k Remnant: v. 13; Isa. 37:32. (Isa. 1:9; Rom. 11:5, *note*)
l Isa. 17:6
15
m Isa. 25:3
n Mal. 1:11
o Isa. 42:4
17
p Jer. 48:43

For the [a]windows from on
high are open,
And the foundations of the
earth are shaken.

19 The earth is violently broken,
The earth is split open,
The earth is shaken
exceedingly.
20 The earth shall [b]reel to and fro
like a drunkard,
And shall totter like a hut;
Its transgression shall be
heavy upon it,
And it will fall, and not rise
again.

21 [c]It shall come to pass in that
day
That the LORD will [d]punish on
high the host of exalted
ones,
And on the earth the [e]kings of
the earth.
22 They will be gathered together,
As prisoners are gathered in
the pit,
And will be shut up in the
prison;
After many days they will be
punished.
23 Then the [f]moon will be
disgraced
And the sun ashamed;
For the [g]LORD of hosts will
[h]reign
On Mount Zion and in
Jerusalem
And before His elders,
gloriously.

Triumphs of the Kingdom Age

25

O LORD, You *are* my God.
I will exalt You,
I will praise Your name,
For You have done wonderful
things;
Your counsels of old *are*
faithfulness *and* truth.
2 For You have made a city a
ruin,
A fortified city a ruin,
A palace of foreigners to be a
city no more;
It will never be rebuilt.
3 Therefore the strong people
will [i]glorify You;
The city of the terrible nations
will fear You.
4 For You have been a strength
to the poor,
A strength to the needy in his
distress,
A refuge from the storm,
A shade from the heat;
For the blast of the terrible
ones *is* as a storm *against*
the wall.
5 You will reduce the noise of
aliens,
As heat in a dry place;
As heat in the shadow of a
cloud,
The song of the terrible ones
will be diminished.

6 And in this mountain
The LORD of hosts will make
for all people
A feast of choice pieces,
A feast of wines [j]on the lees,
Of fat things full of marrow,
Of well-refined wines [j]on the
lees.
7 And He will destroy on this
mountain
The surface of the [k]covering
cast over all people,
And the veil that is spread
over all nations.
8 He will [l]swallow up death
forever,
And the Lord GOD will [m]wipe
away tears from all faces;
The rebuke of His people
He will take away from all the
earth;
For the LORD has spoken.

9 And it will be said in that day:
"Behold, this *is* our God;
We have waited for Him, and
He will save us.
This *is* the LORD;
[n]We have waited for Him;
We will be glad and rejoice in
His salvation."

10 For on this mountain the hand
of the LORD will rest,
And [o]Moab shall be trampled
down under Him,
As straw is trampled down for
the refuse heap.
11 And He will spread out His
hands in their midst
As a swimmer reaches out to
swim,
And He will bring down their
[p]pride
Together with the trickery of
their hands.
12 The fortress of the high fort of
your walls
He will bring down, lay low,
And bring to the ground, down
to the dust.

18
a Cp. Gen. 7:11

20
b Tribulation (the great): v. 20; Jer. 30:7. (Ps. 2:5; Rev. 7:14)

21
c Day (of the LORD): vv. 1–23; Isa. 26:20. (Ps. 2:9; Rev. 19:19)
d Armageddon (battle of): v. 21; Isa. 26:21. (Isa. 10:27; Rev. 19:17)
e Ps. 76:12

23
f Isa. 13:10
g Isa. 60:19–20; Joel 3:16–17
h Kingdom (OT): v. 23; Isa. 32:1. (Gen. 1:26; Zech. 12:8, *note*)

CHAPTER 25

3
i Isa. 24:15

6
j i.e. *fermenting and aging.* See Jer. 48:11, *note*

7
k Cp. 2 Cor. 3:15–16

8
l Hos. 13:14; 1 Cor. 15:54; Rev. 20:14
m Rev. 7:17; 21:4

9
n Gen. 49:18; Isa. 8:17; 26:8; Ti. 2:13

10
o Isa. 15:1–16:14; Jer. 25:21; 48:1–47; Ezek. 25:8–11; Amos 2:1–3; Zeph. 2:8–11

11
p Isa. 24:4; 26:5

The worship and testimony of restored and converted Israel

26 [a]IN that day this song will be [b]sung in the land of Judah:

"We have a strong city;
God will appoint salvation *for* walls and bulwarks.
2 Open the gates,
That the righteous nation which keeps the truth may enter in.
3 You will keep *him* in perfect [c]peace,
Whose mind *is* stayed *on You,*
Because he [d]trusts in You.
4 [e]Trust in the LORD forever,
For in YAH, the LORD, *is* [f]everlasting strength.
5 For He [g]brings down those who dwell on high,
The lofty city;
He lays it low,
He lays it low to the ground,
He brings it down to the dust.
6 The foot shall tread it down—
The feet of the poor
And the steps of the needy."

7 The way of the just *is* [h]uprightness;
O Most Upright,
You weigh the path of the just.
8 Yes, in the way of Your judgments,
O LORD, we have [i]waited for You;
The desire of *our* soul *is* for Your name
And for the remembrance of You.
9 With my soul I have desired You in the night,
Yes, by my spirit within me I will seek You early;
For when Your judgments *are* in the earth,
The inhabitants of the world will learn righteousness.

10 Let grace be shown to the wicked,
Yet he will not learn righteousness;
In the land of uprightness he will deal unjustly,
And will not behold the majesty of the LORD.
11 LORD, *when* Your hand is lifted up, they will not see.
But they will see and be ashamed
For *their* envy of people;
Yes, the fire of Your enemies shall devour them.

12 LORD, You will establish peace for us,
For You have also done all our works in us.
13 O LORD our God, masters besides You
Have had dominion over us;
But by You only we make mention of Your name.
14 *They are* dead, they will not live;
They are deceased, they will not rise.
Therefore You have punished and destroyed them,
And made all their memory to [j]perish.
15 You have [k]increased the nation, O LORD,
You have increased the nation;
You are glorified;
You have expanded all the borders of the land.

In the day of God's wrath, some are sheltered (v. 20), and others are raised from the dead (v. 19)

16 LORD, [l]in trouble they have visited You,
They poured out a prayer *when* Your chastening *was* upon them.
17 As a woman with child
Is in pain and cries out in her pangs,
When she draws near the time of her delivery,
So have we been in Your sight, O LORD.
18 We have been with child, we have been in pain;
We have, as it were, brought forth wind;
We have not accomplished any deliverance in the earth,
Nor have the inhabitants of the world fallen.

19 [m]Your dead shall [1]live;

CHAPTER 26
1
a Isa. 12:1
b Cp. Rev. 5:9; 14:3
3
c Isa. 57:19; Phil. 4:6–7
d See Ps. 2:12, *note*
4
e Isa. 12:2; 50:10; 51:5
f Lit. *the rock of ages.* Dt. 32:4
5
g Isa. 25:11
7
h Righteousness (OT): v. 7; Ezek. 18:5. (Gen. 6:9; Lk. 2:25, *note*)
8
i Isa. 25:9; 33:2
14
j Eccl. 9:5; Isa. 14:22
15
k Isa. 9:3
16
l Hos. 5:15
19
m Resurrection: v. 19; Dan. 12:2. (2 Ki. 4:35; 1 Cor. 15:52, *note*). Isa. 25:8; Hos. 13:14

[1](26:19) Eliminate the supplied words "together with." In the Hebrew "body" is in the plural—"bodies." Verses 19–21, with ch. 27, constitute the LORD's answer to the plaint of Israel in vv. 11–18. "My dead bodies shall rise," i.e. the bodies of the LORD's people will rise.

Together with my dead body*
they shall arise.
Awake and sing, you who
dwell in dust;
For your dew is like the dew of
herbs,
And the earth shall cast out
the dead.

20 [a]Come, my people, [b]enter your
chambers,
And shut your doors behind
you;
Hide yourself, as it were, [c]for
a little moment,
Until the [d]indignation is past.
21 For behold, the LORD comes out
of His [e]place
To [f]punish the inhabitants of
the earth for their iniquity;
The earth will also disclose her
blood,
And will no more cover her
slain.

Restored Israel to blossom and bud

27 IN that day the LORD with His
severe sword, great and
strong,
Will punish [g]Leviathan the
fleeing serpent,
Leviathan that [h]twisted
serpent;
And He will slay the [i]reptile
that is in the sea.

2 In that day sing to her,
"A [j]vineyard of red wine!*
3 I, the LORD, [k]keep it,
I water it every moment;
Lest any hurt it,
I keep it night and day.
4 Fury is not in Me.
Who would set briers and
thorns
Against Me in battle?
I would go through them,
I would burn them together.
5 Or let him take hold of My
[l]strength,
That he may make peace with
Me;
And he shall make peace with
Me."

6 Those who come He shall
cause to take root in Jacob;
Israel shall blossom and bud,
And fill the face of the world
with fruit.

7 [m]Has He struck Israel as He
struck those who struck
him?
Or has He been slain
according to the slaughter of
those who were slain by
Him?
8 In measure, by sending it
away,
You contended with it.
He removes it by His rough
wind
In the day of the east wind.
9 Therefore by this the iniquity
of Jacob will be covered;
And this is all the fruit of
taking away his sin:
When he makes all the stones
of the altar
Like chalkstones that are
beaten to dust,
[n]Wooden images and incense
altars shall not stand.

10 Yet the fortified city will be
[o]desolate,
The habitation forsaken and
left like a wilderness;
There the calf will feed, and
there it will lie down
And consume its branches.
11 When its boughs are withered,
they will be broken off;
The women come and set them
on fire.
For it is a people of [p]no
understanding;
Therefore He who made them
will [q]not have mercy on
them,
And He who formed them will
show them no favor.

12 And it shall come to pass in
that day
That the LORD will thresh,
From the channel of the [r]River
to the Brook of Egypt;
And you will be [s]gathered one
by one,
O you children of Israel.

13 So it shall be in that day:
The great trumpet will be
blown;
They will come, who are about
to perish in the land of
Assyria,
And they who are outcasts in
the land of [t]Egypt,

20
a Cp. Mt. 11:28–30
b Cp. Ex. 12:22
c Ps. 30:5; Isa. 54:7–8
d *Day* (of the LORD): vv. 20–21; Isa. 34:8. (Ps. 2:9; Rev. 19:19)
21
e Mic. 1:3
f *Armageddon* (battle of): vv. 20–21; Isa. 34:2. (Isa. 10:27; Rev. 19:17)
CHAPTER 27
1
g Perhaps the crocodile
h Gen. 3:1; Rev. 12:9, 15
i Cp. Isa. 51:9; Ezek. 29:3
2
j Isa. 5:7
3
k Isa. 31:5
5
l Isa. 12:2; 17:10; 25:4
7
m Isa. 10:12,17; 30:30–33; 31:8–9; 37:36–38
9
n See Dt. 16:21, *note*
10
o Isa. 5:6, 17; 32:14; Jer. 26:18
11
p Dt. 32:28; Isa. 1:3
q Isa. 9:17
12
r i.e. *the Euphrates*
s Isa. 11:11; 56:8
13
t Isa. 19:22

*26:19 Following Masoretic Text and Vulgate; Syriac and Targum read *their dead bodies;* Septuagint reads *those in the tombs.* **27:2** Following Masoretic Text (Kittel's *Biblia Hebraica*), Bomberg, and Vulgate; Masoretic Text (*Biblia Hebraica Stuttgartensia*), some Hebrew manuscripts, and Septuagint read *delight;* Targum reads *choice vineyard.*

And shall [a]worship the LORD in
the holy mount at Jerusalem.

III. Prophetic Warnings concerning Ephraim and Judah, 28—35

Woe to Ephraim: their Assyrian captivity predicted

28 WOE to the crown of pride,
to the drunkards of
[b]Ephraim,
Whose glorious beauty *is* a
fading flower
Which *is* at the head of the
verdant valleys,
To those who are overcome
with wine!
2 Behold, the Lord has a mighty
and strong one,
[c]Like a tempest of hail and a
destroying storm,
Like a flood of mighty waters
overflowing,
Who will bring *them* down to
the earth with *His* hand.
3 The crown of pride, the
drunkards of Ephraim,
Will be trampled underfoot;
4 And the glorious beauty is a
fading flower
Which *is* at the head of the
verdant valley,
Like the first fruit before the
summer,
Which an observer sees;
He eats it up while it is still in
his hand.

5 In that day the LORD of hosts
will be
For a crown of glory and a
diadem of beauty
To the remnant of His people,
6 For a spirit of justice to him
who sits in judgment,
And for strength to those who
turn back the battle at the
gate.

7 But they also have [d]erred
through wine,
And through intoxicating drink
are out of the way;
The priest and the prophet
have erred through
intoxicating drink,
They are swallowed up by
wine,
They are out of the way
through intoxicating [e]drink;
They err in vision, they
stumble *in* [f]judgment.
8 For all tables are full of vomit
and filth;
No place *is clean.*

9 "Whom will he teach
knowledge?
And whom will he make to
understand the message?
Those *just* weaned from milk?
Those *just* drawn from the
breasts?
10 [g]For precept *must be* upon
precept, precept upon
precept,
Line upon line, line upon line,
Here a little, there a little."

11 For with stammering lips and
another tongue
He will speak to this people,
12 To whom He said, "This *is* the
[h]rest *with which*
You may cause the weary to
rest,"
And, "This *is* the refreshing";
Yet they would not hear.
13 But the word of the LORD was
to them,
"Precept upon precept, precept
upon precept,
Line upon line, line upon line,
Here a little, there a little,"
That they might go and fall
backward, and be broken
And snared and caught.

Ephraim's fate a warning to Judah

14 Therefore hear the word of the
LORD, you scornful men,
Who rule this people who *are*
in Jerusalem,
15 Because you have said, "We
have made a covenant with
death,
And with [i]Sheol we are in
agreement.
When the overflowing scourge
passes through,
It will not come to us,
For we have made [j]lies our
refuge,
And under falsehood we have
hidden ourselves."

16 Therefore thus says the Lord
GOD:

"Behold, I lay in Zion a [k]stone
for a foundation,
A [l]tried stone, a precious
cornerstone, a sure
foundation;
Whoever believes will not act
hastily.
17 Also I will make justice the
measuring line,
And righteousness the
plummet;

13 *a* Isa. 2:3; Zech. 14:16

CHAPTER 28

1 *b* See Isa. 7:2, *note*

2 *c* Isa. 30:30; Ezek. 13:11

7 *d* Prov. 20:1 *e* Isa. 5:11, 22; 56:12 *f* Hos. 4:11

10 *g* v. 13; cp. 2 Chr. 36:15; Jer. 25:3–4; 35:15; 44:4

12 *h* Isa. 30:15

15 *i* See Hab. 2:5, *note;* cp. Lk. 16:23, *note* *j* Isa. 9:15

16 *k Christ* (as Stone): v. 16; Isa. 32:2. (Gen. 49:24; 1 Pet. 2:8) *l Christ* (first advent): v. 16; Isa. 42:3. (Gen. 3:15; Acts 1:11, *note*)

The hail will sweep away the
refuge of lies,
And the waters will overflow
the hiding place.
18 Your covenant with death will
be annulled,
And your agreement with
[a]Sheol will not stand;
When the overflowing scourge
passes through,
Then you will be trampled
down by it.
19 As often as it goes out it will
take you;
For morning by morning it will
pass over,
And by day and by night;
It will be a terror just to
understand the report."

20 For the bed is too short to
stretch out *on*,
And the covering so narrow
that one cannot wrap
himself *in it*.
21 For the LORD will rise up as *at*
Mount [b]Perazim,
He will be angry as in the
Valley of [c]Gibeon—
That He may do His work, His
awesome work,
And bring to pass His act, His
unusual act.
22 Now therefore, do not be
mockers,
Lest your bonds be made
strong;
For I have heard from the Lord
GOD of hosts,
A [d]destruction determined
even upon the whole earth.

23 Give ear and hear my voice,
Listen and hear my speech.
24 Does the plowman keep
plowing all day to sow?
Does he keep turning his soil
and breaking the clods?
25 When he has leveled its
surface,
Does he not sow the black
cummin
And scatter the cummin,
Plant the wheat in rows,
The barley in the appointed
place,
And the [e]spelt in its place?
26 For He instructs him in right
judgment,
His God teaches him.

27 For the black cummin is not
threshed with a threshing
sledge,
Nor is a cartwheel rolled over
the cummin;
But the black cummin is
beaten out with a stick,
And the cummin with a rod.
28 Bread *flour* must be ground;
Therefore he does not thresh it
forever,
Break *it with* his cartwheel,
Or crush it *with* his horsemen.
29 This also comes from the LORD
of hosts,
Who is [f]wonderful in counsel
and excellent in [g]guidance.

Jerusalem (Ariel) and Judah warned of impending discipline

29 "WOE to [h]Ariel, to Ariel, the
city *where* David dwelt!
Add year to year;
Let feasts come around.
2 Yet I will distress Ariel;
There shall be heaviness and
sorrow,
And it shall be to Me as Ariel.
3 I will encamp against you all
around,
I will lay siege against you
with a mound,
And I will raise siegeworks
against you.
4 You shall be brought down,
You shall speak out of the
ground;
Your speech shall be low, out
of the dust;
Your voice shall be like a
medium's, out of the ground;
And your speech shall whisper
out of the dust.

5 [i]"Moreover the multitude of your
foes
Shall be like fine dust,
And the multitude of the
terrible ones
[j]Like chaff that passes away;
Yes, it shall be in an instant,
[k]suddenly.
6 You will be punished by the
LORD of hosts
With thunder and [l]earthquake
and great noise,
With storm and tempest
And the flame of devouring
fire.
7 The [m]multitude of all the
nations who fight against
Ariel,
Even all who fight against her
and her fortress,
And distress her,

18
a See Hab. 2:5, *note;* cp. Lk. 16:23, *note*
21
b 2 Sam. 5:20; 1 Chr. 14:11
c Josh. 10:10,12; 1 Chr. 14:16
22
d Isa. 10:22
25
e i.e. *a form of wheat*
29
f Ps. 92:5; Isa. 9:6
g Or *wisdom*
CHAPTER 29
1
h Lit. *Hearth of God* = Jerusalem; cp. Isa. 31:9
5
i Or *Then*
j Job 21:18; Isa. 17:13
k Isa. 47:11
6
l Zech. 14:4; Rev. 16:18–19
7
m Mic. 4:11–12; Zech. 12:9

Shall be as a dream of a night
vision.
8 It shall even be as when a
hungry man dreams,
And look—he eats;
But he awakes, and his soul is
still empty;
Or as when a thirsty man
dreams,
And look—he drinks;
But he awakes, and indeed *he*
is faint,
And his soul still craves:
So the multitude of all the
nations shall be,
Who fight against Mount
Zion."

God's reasons for the discipline

9 Pause and wonder!
Blind yourselves and be blind!
They are drunk, but not with
wine;
They stagger, but not with
intoxicating drink.
10 For the LORD has poured out on
you
The spirit of deep [a]sleep,
And has closed your eyes,
namely, the prophets;
And He has [b]covered your
heads, *namely,* the seers.

11 The whole vision has become to
you like the words of a book that is
sealed, which *men* deliver to one who
is literate, saying, "Read this, please."
And he says, "I cannot, for it *is*
sealed."
12 Then the book is delivered to
one who is illiterate, saying, "Read
this, please." And he says, "I am not
literate."
13 Therefore the LORD said:

"Inasmuch as these people draw
near with their mouths
And honor Me [c]with their lips,
But have removed their hearts
far from Me,
And their fear toward Me is
taught by the commandment
of men,
14 Therefore, behold, I will again
do a [d]marvelous work
Among this people,
A marvelous work and a
wonder;
For the [e]wisdom of their wise
men shall perish,
And the understanding of their
prudent *men* shall be
hidden."

15 Woe to those who seek deep to
hide their counsel far from
the LORD,
And their works are in the
dark;
They say, "Who [f]sees us?"
and, "Who knows us?"
16 Surely you have things turned
around!
Shall the potter be esteemed as
the clay;
For shall the thing made say of
him who made it,
"He did not make me"?
Or shall the thing formed say
of him who formed it,
"He has no [g]understanding"?

Blessing after discipline foreshadows kingdom blessing

17 *Is* it not yet a very [h]little while
Till Lebanon shall be turned
into a fruitful field,
And the fruitful field be
esteemed as a forest?
18 In that day the deaf [i]shall
hear the words of the book,
And the eyes of the blind shall
see out of obscurity and out
of darkness.
19 The [j]humble also shall
increase *their* joy in the
LORD,
And the [k]poor among men
shall rejoice
In the Holy One of Israel.
20 For the terrible one is brought
to nothing,
The scornful one is consumed,
And all who watch for iniquity
are cut off—
21 Who make a man an offender
by a word,
And lay a snare for him who
reproves in the gate,
And turn aside the just by
empty words.

22 Therefore thus says the LORD,
who [l]redeemed Abraham, concerning the house of Jacob:

"Jacob shall not now be
[m]ashamed,
Nor shall his face now grow
pale;
23 But when he sees his
[n]children,
The work of My hands, in his
midst,
They will hallow My name,
And hallow the Holy One of
Jacob,
And fear the God of Israel.

10
a Isa. 6:9–10; Rom. 11:8
b Isa. 44:18; Mic. 3:6
13
c Ps. 78:36; Ezek. 33:31; Mt. 15:8–9; Mk. 7:6–7
14
d Hab. 1:5
e Jer. 49:7; Obad. 8; 1 Cor. 1:19
15
f Ps. 10:11; 94:7; Isa. 47:10; Ezek. 8:12
16
g Isa. 45:9; cp. 64:8; Jer. 18:1–6; Rom. 9:19–21
17
h Isa. 35:1–2
18
i Isa. 35:5
19
j Isa. 11:4; Mt. 5:5
k Isa. 14:30, 32
22
l See Ex. 14:30 and Isa. 59:20, *notes*
m Isa. 45:17
23
n Isa. 49:20–26

24 These also who erred in spirit
will come to understanding,
And those who complained
will learn doctrine."

Judah warned not to make alliance with Egypt against Sennacherib

30 "WOE to the rebellious
children," says the LORD,
"Who take counsel, but not of
Me,
And who devise plans, but not
of My [a]Spirit,
[b]That they may add sin to sin;
2 Who walk to go down to
Egypt,
And have not [c]asked My
advice,
To strengthen themselves in
the strength of Pharaoh,
And to trust in the shadow of
Egypt!
3 Therefore the strength of
Pharaoh
Shall be your shame,
And [d]trust in the shadow of
Egypt
Shall be *your* [e]humiliation.
4 For his princes were at [f]Zoan,
And his ambassadors came to
[g]Hanes.
5 They were all ashamed of a
people *who* could not benefit
them,
Or be help or benefit,
But a shame and also a
reproach."

6 The [h]burden against the beasts
of the [i]South.

Through a land of trouble and
anguish,
From which *came* the lioness
and lion,
The viper and fiery flying
serpent,
They will carry their riches on
the backs of young donkeys,
And their treasures on the
humps of camels,
To a people *who* shall not
profit;
7 For the Egyptians shall help in
[j]vain and to no purpose.
Therefore I have called her
Rahab-Hem-Shebeth.*
8 Now go, [k]write it before them
on a tablet,
And note it on a scroll,
That it may be for time to
come,
Forever and ever:

9 That this *is* a [l]rebellious
people,
Lying children,
Children *who* will not hear the
law of the LORD;
10 Who say to the seers, "Do not
see,"
And to the prophets, "Do not
prophesy to us right things;
Speak to us smooth things,
prophesy [m]deceits.
11 Get out of the way,
Turn aside from the path,
Cause the Holy One of Israel
To cease from before us."

12 Therefore thus says the Holy
One of Israel:

"Because you [n]despise this
word,
And [d]trust in oppression and
perversity,
And rely on them,
13 Therefore this iniquity shall be
to you
Like a breach ready to fall,
A bulge in a high wall,
Whose breaking comes
[o]suddenly, in an instant.
14 And He shall break it like the
breaking of the potter's
vessel,
Which is broken in pieces;
He shall not spare.
So there shall not be found
among its fragments
A shard to take fire from the
hearth,
Or to take water from the
cistern."

Judah exhorted to trust the LORD

15 For thus says the Lord GOD, the
Holy One of Israel:

"In returning and [p]rest [q]you
shall be saved;
In quietness and confidence
shall be your strength."
But you would not,
16 And you said, "No, for we will
flee on horses"—
Therefore you shall flee!
And, "We will ride on swift
horses"—
Therefore those who pursue
you shall be swift!
17 [r]One thousand *shall flee* at the
threat of one,

CHAPTER 30

1
a *Holy Spirit* (OT): v. 1; Isa. 32:15. (Gen. 1:2; Zech. 12:10)
b Cp. Dt. 29:19

2
c Cp. Num. 27:21; Josh. 9:14; 1 Ki. 22:7; Jer. 21:2; 42:2–3,20

3
d See Ps. 2:12, *note*
e Cp. Isa. 20:5

4
f Isa. 19:11
g Or *Tahpanes*, Jer. 43:7

6
h See Isa. 13:1, *note*
i See Gen. 12:9, *note*

7
j Cp. Jer. 37:7

8
k *Inspiration:* v. 8; Isa. 59:21. (Ex. 4:15; 2 Tim. 3:16, *note*)

9
l Isa. 1:2; 65:2

10
m Mic. 2:11; cp. 1 Ki. 22:8; 2 Tim. 4:3–4

12
n v. 9; Lev. 26:43; Num. 15:31; Prov. 1:30; 13:13; Isa. 5:24; Ezek. 20:13,16, 24; Amos 2:4; cp. 2 Sam. 12:19; Rom. 10:17; Heb. 10:28

13
o Isa. 29:5

15
p Isa. 28:12
q Cp. Mt. 23:37

17
r Cp. Lev. 26:8; Dt. 28:25; 32:30; Josh. 23:10

*30:7 Literally *Rahab Sits Idle*

At the threat of five you shall flee,
Till you are left as a pole on top of a mountain
And as a banner on a hill.

18 Therefore the LORD will wait, that He may be [a]gracious to you;
And therefore He will be exalted, that He may have mercy on you.
For the LORD *is* a God of justice;
[b]Blessed *are* all those who [c]wait for Him.

19 For the people shall dwell in Zion at Jerusalem;
You shall [d]weep no more.
He will be very gracious to you at the sound of your cry;
When He hears it, He will [e]answer you.

20 And *though* the Lord gives you
The bread of adversity and the water of affliction,
Yet your teachers will not be moved into a corner anymore,
But your eyes shall see your teachers.

21 Your ears shall hear a word behind you, saying,
"This *is* the way, walk in it,"
Whenever you turn to the right hand
Or whenever you turn to the left.

22 You will also defile the covering of your images of silver,
And the ornament of your molded images of gold.
You will [f]throw them away as an unclean thing;
You will say to them, "Get away!"

23 [g]Then He will give the rain for your seed
With which you sow the ground,
And bread of the increase of the earth;
It will be fat and plentiful.
In that day your cattle will feed
In large pastures.

24 Likewise the oxen and the young donkeys that work the ground
Will eat cured fodder,
Which has been winnowed with the shovel and fan.

25 There will be on every high mountain
And on every high hill
Rivers *and* streams of waters,
In the day of the [h]great slaughter,
When the towers fall.

26 Moreover the light of the moon will be as the light of the sun,
And the light of the sun will be sevenfold,
As the light of seven days,
In the day that the LORD binds up the bruise of His people
And heals the stroke of their wound.

The LORD's judgment on Assyria

27 Behold, the name of the LORD comes from afar,
Burning *with* His anger,
And *His* burden *is* heavy;
His lips are full of indignation,
And His tongue like a devouring fire.

28 His [i]breath is like an overflowing stream,
Which reaches up to the neck,
To sift the nations with the sieve of futility;
And *there shall be* a bridle in the jaws of the people,
Causing *them* to err.

29 You shall have a song
As in the night *when* a holy festival is kept,
And gladness of heart as when one goes with a flute,
To come into the mountain of the LORD,
To the [j]Mighty One of Israel.

30 The LORD will cause His glorious voice to be heard,
And show the descent of His arm,
With the indignation of *His* anger
And the flame of a devouring fire,
With scattering, tempest, and hailstones.

31 For through the voice of the LORD
[k]Assyria will be beaten down,
As He strikes with the rod.

32 And *in* every place where the staff of punishment passes,
Which the LORD lays on him,

18
a Isa. 33:2
b Ps. 2:12; 34:8; Prov. 16:20; Jer. 17:7
c Isa. 26:8

19
d Isa. 25:8
e Isa. 65:24

22
f Isa. 2:20; 31:7

23
g Cp. Mt. 6:33; 1 Tim. 4:8

25
h Isa. 2:10–21; 34:2

28
i Isa. 11:4; 2 Th. 2:8

29
j Lit. *Rock.* Dt. 32:4

31
k Isa. 14:25

It will be with tambourines
and harps;
And in battles of brandishing
He will fight with it.
33 For [a]Tophet *was* established of
old,
Yes, for the king it is prepared.
He has made *it* deep and large;
Its pyre *is* fire with much
wood;
The breath of the LORD, like a
stream of brimstone,
Kindles it.

Egypt's help vain: the LORD will defend Jerusalem

31 WOE to those who go down
to [b]Egypt for help,
And rely on horses,
Who [c]trust in chariots because
they are many,
And in horsemen because they
are very strong,
But who do not look to the
Holy One of Israel,
[d]Nor seek the LORD!
2 Yet He also *is* wise and will
bring disaster,
And will not call back His
words,
But will arise against the
house of evildoers,
And against the help of those
who work iniquity.
3 Now the Egyptians *are* men,
and not God;
And their horses are flesh, and
not spirit.
When the LORD stretches out
His hand,
Both he who helps will fall,
And he who is helped will fall
down;
They all will perish [e]together.
4 For thus the LORD has spoken to
me:

[f]"As a lion roars,
And a young lion over his prey
(When a multitude of
shepherds is summoned
against him,
He will not be afraid of their
voice
Nor be disturbed by their
noise),
So the LORD of hosts will come
down
To fight for Mount Zion and
for its hill.
5 [g]Like birds flying about,
So will the LORD of hosts
defend Jerusalem.
Defending, He will also deliver
it;
Passing over, He will preserve
it."

6 Return *to Him* against whom the
children of Israel have [h]deeply revolted.
7 For in that day every man shall
[i]throw away his idols of silver and his
idols of gold—sin, which your own
hands have made for yourselves.

8 "Then Assyria shall [j]fall by a
sword not of man,
And a sword not of mankind
shall [k]devour him.
But he shall flee from the
sword,
And his young men shall
become forced labor.
9 He shall cross over to his
stronghold for fear,
And his princes shall be afraid
of the banner,"
Says the LORD,
Whose fire *is* in Zion
And whose furnace *is* in
Jerusalem.

Christ the coming righteous king

32 BEHOLD, a [1]king will [l]reign
in righteousness,
And princes will rule with
justice.
2 A man will be as a hiding
place from the wind,
And a cover from the tempest,
As rivers of water in a dry
place,
As the shadow of a great
[m]rock in a weary land.
3 [n]The eyes of those who see will
not be dim,
And the ears of those who
hear will listen.
4 Also the heart of the rash will
[o]understand knowledge,
And the tongue of the
stammerers will be ready to
speak [p]plainly.
5 The foolish person will no
longer be called generous,
Nor the miser said *to be*
bountiful;
6 For the foolish person will
speak foolishness,

33
a See Jer. 7:31, *note*

CHAPTER 31

1
b Isa. 30:1–2
c See Ps. 2:12, *note*
d Dan. 9:13; cp. Hos. 7:7

3
e Isa. 20:6; cp. Ps. 37:38; Isa. 1:28

4
f Hos. 11:10; Amos 3:8

5
g Dt. 32:11; Ps. 91:4

6
h Hos. 9:9

7
i Isa. 30:22

8
j 2 Ki. 19:35–36
k Isa. 37:36

CHAPTER 32

1
l Kingdom (OT): vv. 1–2, 14–18; Isa. 33:17. (Gen. 1:26; Zech. 12:8, *note*)

2
m Christ (as Rock): v. 2; Dan. 2:34. (Gen. 49:24; 1 Pet. 2:8)

3
n Isa. 35:5

4
o Isa. 29:24
p Cp. Isa. 35:5–6

---

[1](32:1) In chs. 32—35 the day of the LORD (Isa. 2:10–22; Rev. 19:11–21) and the kingdom age are in view.

And his heart will work
[a]iniquity:
To practice ungodliness,
To utter error against the LORD,
To keep the hungry
unsatisfied,
And he will cause the drink of
the thirsty to fail.
7 Also the schemes of the
schemer *are* evil;
He devises wicked plans
To destroy the poor with
[b]lying words,
Even when the needy speaks
justice.
8 But a generous man devises
generous things,
And by generosity he shall
stand.
9 Rise up, you women who are
at ease,
Hear my voice;
You complacent daughters,
Give ear to my speech.
10 In a year and *some* days
You will be troubled, you
complacent women;
For the vintage will fail,
The gathering will not come.
11 Tremble, you *women* who are
at ease;
Be troubled, you complacent
ones;
Strip yourselves, make
yourselves bare,
And gird *sackcloth* on *your*
waists.
12 People shall mourn upon their
breasts
For the pleasant fields, for the
fruitful vine.
13 On the land of my people will
come up thorns *and* [c]briers,
Yes, on all the happy homes *in*
the joyous city;
14 Because the palaces will be
forsaken,
The bustling city will be
deserted.
The forts and towers will
become lairs forever,
A joy of wild donkeys, a
pasture of [d]flocks—
15 Until the [e]Spirit is poured
upon us from on high,
And the wilderness becomes a
fruitful field,
And the fruitful field is
counted as a forest.
16 Then justice will dwell in the
wilderness,
And righteousness remain in
the fruitful field.
17 The work of righteousness will
be [f]peace,
And the effect of
righteousness, quietness and
[g]assurance forever.
18 My people will dwell in a
peaceful habitation,
In secure dwellings, and in
quiet [h]resting places,
19 Though hail comes down on
the forest,
And the city is brought low in
humiliation.
20 Blessed *are* you who sow
beside all waters,
Who send out freely the [i]feet
of the ox and the donkey.

Distressed Jerusalem delivered

33 WOE to you who [j]plunder,
though you *have* not *been*
plundered;
And you who deal
treacherously, though they
have not dealt treacherously
with you!
When you cease plundering,
You will be [k]plundered;
When you make an end of
dealing treacherously,
They will deal treacherously
with you.
2 O LORD, be gracious to us;
We have [l]waited for You.
Be their* arm every morning,
Our [m]salvation also in the time
of trouble.
3 At the noise of the tumult the
people shall [n]flee;
When You lift Yourself up, the
nations shall be scattered;
4 And Your plunder shall be
gathered
Like the gathering of the
caterpillar;
As the running to and fro of
locusts,
He shall run upon them.
5 The LORD is [o]exalted, for He
dwells on high;
He has filled Zion with justice
and righteousness.
6 Wisdom and knowledge will
be the stability of your
times,
And the strength of salvation;

6 *a* Prov. 24:7–9
7 *b* Jer. 5:26–28
13 *c* Isa. 7:23–25
14 *d* Isa. 27:10
15 *e Holy Spirit* (OT): v. 15; Isa. 34:16. (Gen. 1:2; Zech. 12:10)
17 *f* Ps. 119:165; Rom. 14:17; Jas. 3:18
g Assurance/security: vv. 17–18; Isa. 43:1. (Ps. 23:1; Jude 1, *note*)
18 *h* Hos. 2:18–23; Zech. 3:10
20 *i* Isa. 30:23–24
CHAPTER 33
1 *j* Isa. 21:2; Hab. 2:8
k Isa. 10:12; 14:25; 31:8
2 *l* Isa. 26:8
m Isa. 12:2
3 *n* Isa. 17:13
5 *o* Ps. 97:9

*33:2 Septuagint omits *their;* Syriac, Targum, and Vulgate read *our.*

The [a]fear of the LORD *is* His
treasure.

7 Surely their valiant ones shall
cry outside,
The [b]ambassadors of peace
shall weep bitterly.
8 The highways lie waste,
The traveling man ceases.
He has broken the covenant,
He has [c]despised the cities,*
He regards no man.
9 The earth mourns *and*
[d]languishes,
Lebanon is shamed *and*
shriveled;
Sharon is like a [e]wilderness,
And Bashan and Carmel shake
off *their fruits.*

10 "Now I will rise," says the LORD;
"Now I will be exalted,
Now I will lift Myself up.
11 You shall conceive chaff,
You shall bring forth stubble;
Your breath, *as* fire, shall
devour you.
12 And the people shall be *like*
the burnings of lime;
Like thorns cut up they shall
be burned in the fire.
13 Hear, you *who are* afar off,
what I have done;
And you *who are* near,
acknowledge My might."

The glorious result
of cleansing judgment

14 The sinners in Zion are afraid;
Fearfulness has seized the
hypocrites:
"Who among us shall dwell
with the devouring [f]fire?
Who among us shall dwell
with everlasting burnings?"
15 He who walks righteously and
speaks [g]uprightly,
He who despises the gain of
oppressions,
Who gestures with his hands,
refusing bribes,
Who stops his ears from
hearing of bloodshed,
And shuts his eyes from seeing
evil:
16 He will dwell on high;
His place of defense *will be* the
fortress of rocks;
Bread will be given him,
His water *will be* sure.

17 Your eyes will see the [1h]King
in His [i]beauty;
They will see the land that is
very far off.
18 Your heart will meditate on
[j]terror:
"Where *is* the scribe?
Where *is* he who weighs?
Where *is* he who counts the
towers?"
19 You will not see a fierce
people,
A people of obscure speech,
beyond perception,
Of a stammering tongue *that*
you cannot understand.
20 Look upon Zion, the city of
our appointed feasts;
Your eyes will see Jerusalem,
a quiet home,
A tabernacle *that* will not be
taken down;
Not one of its stakes will ever
be removed,
Nor will any of its cords be
broken.
21 But there the majestic LORD
will be for us
A place of broad rivers *and*
streams,
In which no galley with oars
will sail,
Nor majestic ships pass by
22 (For the LORD *is* our [2k]Judge,
The LORD *is* our Lawgiver,
The LORD *is* our King;
He will [l]save us);
23 Your tackle is loosed,
They could not strengthen
their mast,
They could not spread the sail.

Then the prey of great plunder
is divided;
The lame take the prey.
24 And the inhabitant will not
say, "I am sick";

6
a See Ps. 19:9, *note*
7
b 2 Ki. 18:18,37
8
c 2 Ki. 18:13–17
9
d Isa. 24:4
e See Dt. 1:1, *note*
14
f Isa. 30:27, 30; Heb. 12:29
15
g Ps. 24:3–4
17
h Kingdom (OT): vv. 17–20; Isa. 35:1. (Gen. 1:26; Zech. 12:8, *note*)
i Ps. 27:4
18
j Cp. Isa. 54:14
22
k Acts 10:42
l Isa. 25:9; 35:4

*33:8 Following Masoretic Text and Vulgate; Dead Sea Scrolls read *witnesses*; Septuagint omits *cities*; Targum reads *They have been removed from their cities.*

[1](33:17) When God's own King reigns, terror and invasion will be forever at an end (vv. 17–20; cp. 28:11).
[2](33:22) All the functions of government—judicial, legislative, and executive—will be centered in the Messianic King. The most important prayers of the New Year's liturgy of the Jews stress these fundamental ideas, to which a section of the prayers is devoted. After each group of prayers the horn *(shofar)* is blown.

The people who dwell in it *will*
be forgiven *their* [a]iniquity.

Future judgment on enemies of Israel and kingdom blessing (34—35). Armageddon in the day of the LORD (Rev. 19:17–21)

34 COME near, you nations, to
hear;
And heed, you people!
Let the earth hear, and all that
is in it,
The world and all things that
come forth from it.
2 For the [b]indignation of the
LORD *is* against all nations,
And *His* fury against all their
armies;
He has utterly [c]destroyed
them,
He has given them over to the
[d]slaughter.
3 Also their slain shall be
thrown out;
Their stench shall rise from
their corpses,
And the mountains shall be
melted with their blood.
4 All the host of heaven shall be
[e]dissolved,
And the heavens shall be
rolled up like a scroll;
All their host shall fall down
As the leaf falls from the vine,
And as *fruit* falling from a fig
tree.
5 "For My sword shall be bathed
in heaven;
Indeed it shall come down on
[f]Edom,
And on the people of My
curse, for judgment.
6 The [g]sword of the LORD is
filled with blood,
It is made overflowing with
fatness,
With the blood of lambs and
goats,
With the fat of the kidneys of
rams.
For the LORD has a sacrifice in
Bozrah,
And a great slaughter in the
land of Edom.
7 The wild oxen shall come
down with them,
And the young bulls with the
mighty bulls;
Their land shall be soaked
with blood,
And their dust saturated with
fatness."
8 For *it is* the [h]day of the LORD's
[i]vengeance,
The year of recompense for the
cause of Zion.
9 [j]Its streams shall be turned into
pitch,
And its dust into brimstone;
Its land shall become burning
pitch.
10 It shall not be quenched night
or day;
Its [k]smoke shall ascend
forever.
From generation to generation
it shall lie waste;
No one shall pass through it
forever and ever.
11 But the pelican and the
porcupine shall [l]possess it,
Also the owl and the raven
shall dwell in it.
And He shall stretch out over it
The line of [1]confusion and the
stones of emptiness.
12 They shall call its nobles to the
kingdom,
But none *shall be* there, and all
its princes shall be nothing.
13 And thorns shall come up in
its palaces,
Nettles and brambles in its
fortresses;
It shall be a habitation of
jackals,
A courtyard for ostriches.
14 The wild beasts of the desert
shall also meet with the
jackals,
And the wild goat shall bleat
to its companion;
Also the night creature shall
rest there,
And find for herself a place of
rest.
15 There the arrow snake shall
make her nest and lay
eggs
And hatch, and gather *them*
under her shadow;
There also shall the hawks be
gathered,
Every one with her mate.
16 "Search from the book of the
LORD, and read:
Not one of these shall fail;
Not one shall lack her mate.

24
a Isa. 40:2
CHAPTER 34
2
b Day (of destruction): vv. 1–8; Isa. 61:2. (Job 21:30; Rev. 20:11)
c Armageddon (battle of): vv. 1–8; Isa. 63:3. (Isa. 10:27; Rev. 19:17)
d Isa. 13:5
4
e Isa. 13:13; Mt. 24:29
5
f vv. 1–8; see Gen. 36:1, *note*
6
g Isa. 66:16
8
h Day (of the LORD) vv. 1–8; Isa. 63:1. (Ps. 2:9; Rev. 19:19)
i See Isa. 61:2, *note*
9
j Dt. 29:23
10
k Rev. 14:11; 18:18; 19:3
11
l Isa. 14:23; Zeph. 2:14; Rev. 18:2

[1](34:11) The words "confusion . . . emptiness" are translated from the Hebrew *tohu . . . wabohu* rendered "without form and void" in Gen. 1:2.

For My mouth has commanded
it, and His [a]Spirit has
gathered them.
17 He has cast the lot for them,
And His hand has divided it
among them with a
measuring line.
They shall possess it forever;
From generation to generation
they shall dwell in it."

Kingdom blessings for regathered Israel

35 THE [b]wilderness and the
wasteland shall be glad for
[c]them,
And the [d]desert shall rejoice
and blossom as the rose;
2 It shall blossom abundantly
and rejoice,
Even with joy and singing.
The glory of Lebanon shall be
given to it,
The excellence of Carmel and
Sharon.
They shall see the [e]glory of
the LORD,
The excellency of our God.

3 [f]Strengthen the weak hands,
And make firm the feeble
knees.
4 Say to those *who are*
fearful-hearted,
"Be strong, do not fear!
Behold, your God will come
with [g]vengeance,
With the recompense of God;
He will come and [h]save you."

5 [i]Then the eyes of the blind
shall be opened,
And the ears of the deaf shall
be unstopped.
6 Then the lame shall leap like a
deer,
And the tongue of the dumb
sing.
For waters shall burst forth in
the wilderness,
And streams in the desert.
7 The parched ground shall
become a pool,
And the thirsty land springs of
water;
In the habitation of jackals,
where each lay,

16
a Holy Spirit (OT): v. 16; Isa. 40:13. (Gen. 1:2; Zech. 12:10)

CHAPTER 35
1
b Isa. 32:15
c Kingdom (OT): vv. 1–10; Isa. 40:9. (Gen. 1:26; Zech. 12:8, *note*)
d Isa. 41:19; 51:3
2
e Isa. 40:5
3
f Job 4:3–4; Heb. 12:12
4
g Isa. 34:8
h Isa. 33:22
5
i Isa. 29:18
8
j Isa. 19:23
k Isa. 52:1; Joel 3:17; Rev. 21:27
l i.e. *the redeemed*
9
m Lev. 26:6; Isa. 11:9; Ezek. 34:25
n See Isa. 59:20, *note;* cp. Ex. 14:30, *note*
10
o Isa. 30:19; 65:19

CHAPTER 36
2
p 2 Ki. 18:17-20:19 is a parallel account to Isa. 36:2–39:8
3
q Isa. 22:20
r Isa. 22:15

There shall be grass with reeds
and rushes.
8 A [j]highway shall be there, and
a road,
And it shall be called the
Highway of Holiness.
The [k]unclean shall not pass
over it,
But it *shall be* for [l]others.
Whoever walks the road,
although a fool,
Shall not go astray.
9 No lion shall be there,
[m]Nor shall *any* ravenous beast
go up on it;
It shall not be found there.
But the [n]redeemed shall walk
there,
10 And the ransomed of the LORD
shall return,
And come to Zion with
singing,
With everlasting joy on their
heads.
They shall obtain joy and
gladness,
And sorrow and sighing shall
[o]flee away.

IV. Historical Parenthesis: Sennacherib's Invasions and Hezekiah's Illness, 36—39

The first invasion (2 Ki. 18:9–16)

36 NOW it came to pass in the
fourteenth year of King Hezekiah *that* [1]Sennacherib king of Assyria came up against all the fortified
cities of Judah and took them.

Sennacherib's second invasion; his attempt to terrify Jerusalem through the Rabshakeh's threats (2 Ki. 18:17–37; 2 Chr. 32:1–19)

2 [p]Then the king of Assyria sent
the [2]Rabshakeh with a great army
from Lachish to King Hezekiah at Jerusalem. And he stood by the aqueduct from the upper pool, on the highway to the Fuller's Field.
3 And [q]Eliakim the son of Hilkiah,
who was over the household,
[r]Shebna the scribe, and Joah the son
of Asaph, the recorder, came out to
him.
4 Then *the* Rabshakeh said to

[1](36:1) This verse appears simply to introduce the two Assyrian invasions, referring to the first invasion described in 2 Ki. 18:13–16 (see 2 Ki. 18:7, *note*), when Sennacherib evidently accompanied his father, Sargon, as general, and perhaps as regent also. At that time Hezekiah paid tribute. Beginning in v. 2 Isaiah describes what occurred in the second invasion (36:2—37:38; cp. 2 Ki. 18:17—19:36; 2 Chr. 32:1–4; 36:5–23), after Hezekiah turned back to God (36:5,21).

[2](36:2) Rabshakeh here and in ch. 37 is not a personal name but the title of an Assyrian official, as are Tartan, Rabsaris, and Rabmag, 2 Ki. 18:17ff.; Jer. 39:3,13.

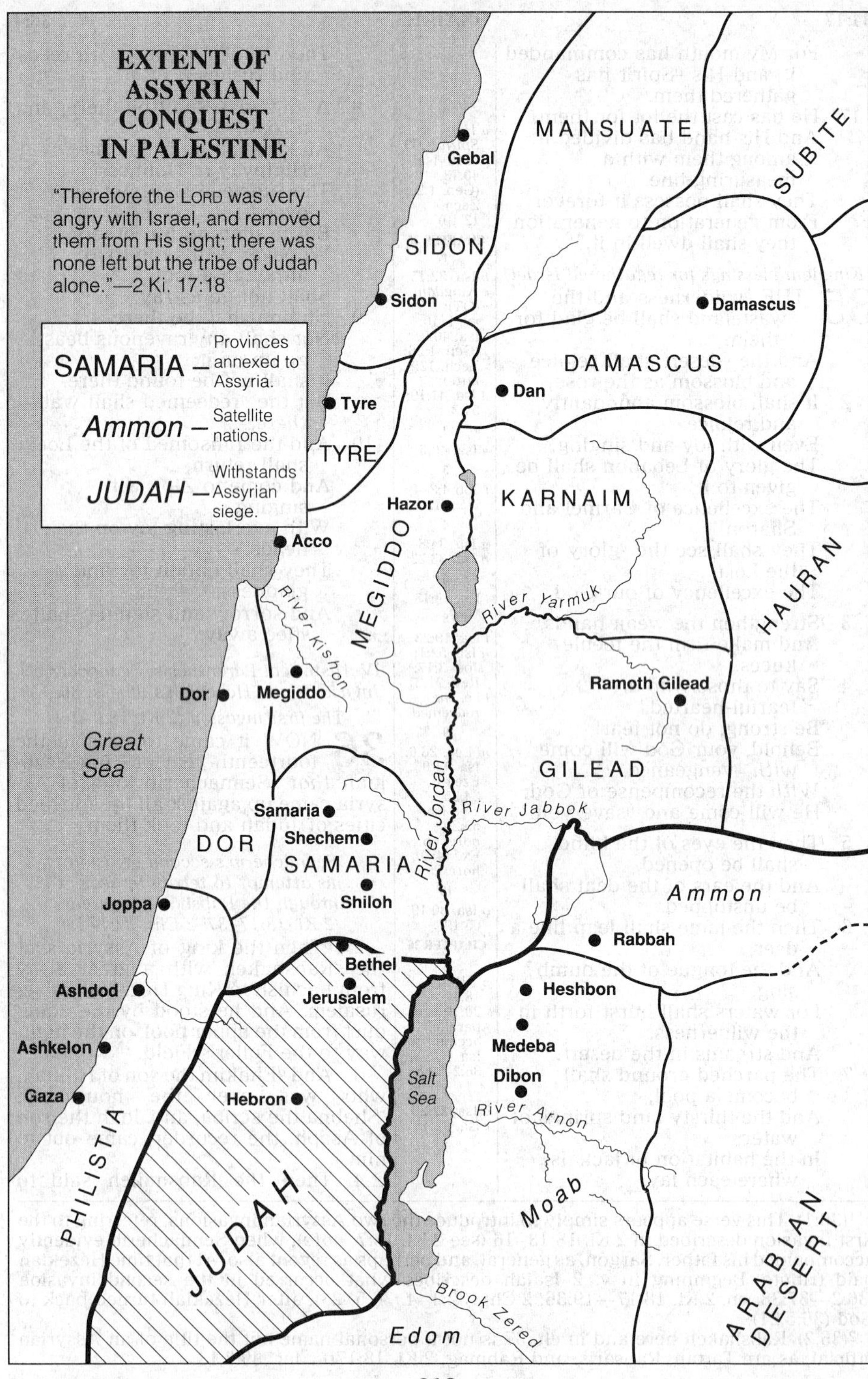
EXTENT OF ASSYRIAN CONQUEST IN PALESTINE
"Therefore the LORD was very angry with Israel, and removed them from His sight; there was none left but the tribe of Judah alone."—2 Ki. 17:18
SAMARIA – Provinces annexed to Assyria.
Ammon – Satellite nations.
JUDAH – Withstands Assyrian siege.
MANSUATE
SUBITE
Gebal
SIDON
Sidon
Damascus
DAMASCUS
Dan
Tyre
TYRE
KARNAIM
Hazor
Acco
MEGIDDO
HAURAN
River Kishon
River Yarmuk
Ramoth Gilead
Dor
Megiddo
Great Sea
GILEAD
Samaria
River Jordan
River Jabbok
DOR
Shechem
SAMARIA
Shiloh
Ammon
Joppa
Rabbah
Bethel
Jerusalem
Heshbon
Ashdod
Medeba
Ashkelon
Salt Sea
Dibon
Gaza
Hebron
River Arnon
PHILISTIA
JUDAH
Moab
ARABIAN DESERT
Brook Zered
Edom

them, "Say now to Hezekiah, 'Thus
says the great king, the king of Assyria: "What confidence is this in
which you trust?
5 "I say you speak of having plans
and power for war; but *they are* mere
words. Now in whom do you [a]trust,
that you rebel against me?
6 "Look! You are trusting in the
staff of this broken reed, Egypt, on
which if a man leans, it will go into his
hand and pierce it. So *is* Pharaoh king
of Egypt to all who [b]trust in him.
7 "But if you say to me, 'We trust
in the LORD our God,' *is it* not He
whose [c]high places and whose altars
Hezekiah has taken away, and said to
Judah and Jerusalem, 'You shall worship before this altar'?" '
8 "Now therefore, I urge you, give
a pledge to my master the king of Assyria, and I will give you two thousand
horses—if you are able on your part to
put riders on them!
9 "How then will you repel one
captain of the least of my master's servants, and put your trust in Egypt for
chariots and horsemen?
10 "Have I now come up without
the LORD against this land to destroy
it? The LORD [d]said to me, 'Go up
against this land, and destroy it.' "
11 Then Eliakim, Shebna, and Joah
said to *the* Rabshakeh, "Please speak
to your servants in Aramaic, for we
understand *it;* and do not speak to us
in Hebrew* in the hearing of the people who *are* on the wall."
12 But *the* Rabshakeh said, "Has
my master sent me to your master and
to you to speak these words, and not
to the men who sit on the wall, who
will eat and drink their own waste
with you?"
13 Then *the* Rabshakeh stood and
called out with a loud voice in Hebrew, and said, "Hear the words of the
great king, the king of Assyria!
14 "Thus says the king: 'Do not let
Hezekiah deceive you, for he will not
be able to deliver you;
15 'nor let Hezekiah make you trust
in the LORD, saying, "The LORD will
surely deliver us; this city will not be
given into the hand of the king of Assyria." '
16 "Do not listen to Hezekiah; for
thus says the king of Assyria: 'Make
peace with me *by a* present and come
out to me; and every one of you eat
from his own vine [e]and every one
from his own fig tree, and every one of
you drink the waters of his own cistern;
17 'until I come and take you away
to a land like your own land, a land of
grain and new wine, a land of bread
and vineyards.
18 '*Beware* lest Hezekiah persuade
you, saying, "The LORD will deliver
us." Has any one of the [f]gods of the
nations delivered its land from the
hand of the king of Assyria?
19 'Where *are* the gods of Hamath
and Arpad? Where *are* the gods of
Sepharvaim? Indeed, have they delivered [g]Samaria from my hand?
20 'Who among all the gods of
these lands have delivered their countries from my hand, that the LORD
should deliver Jerusalem from my
hand?' "
21 But they held their peace and answered him not a word; for the king's
commandment was, "Do not answer
him."

Hezekiah learns the Rabshakeh's words

22 Then Eliakim the son of Hilkiah,
who *was* over the household, Shebna
the scribe, and Joah the son of Asaph,
the recorder, came to Hezekiah with
their clothes [h]torn, and told him the
words of *the* Rabshakeh.

Hezekiah seeks Isaiah's help;
God's deliverance promised
(2 Ki. 19:1–7; 2 Chr. 32:20)

37 [i]AND so it was, when King
Hezekiah heard *it,* that he tore
his clothes, covered himself with
sackcloth, and went into the house of
the LORD.
2 Then he sent Eliakim, who *was*
over the household, Shebna the
scribe, and the elders of the priests,
covered with sackcloth, to Isaiah the
prophet, the son of Amoz.
3 And they said to him, "Thus says
Hezekiah: 'This day *is* a day of [j]trou-
ble and rebuke and [k]blasphemy; for
the children have come to birth, but
there is no strength to bring them
forth.
4 'It may be that the LORD your
God will hear the words of *the* Rabshakeh, whom his master the king of
Assyria has sent to [l]reproach the living God, and will rebuke the words
which the LORD your God has [m]heard.
Therefore lift up *your* prayer for the
remnant that is [n]left.' "

5
a See Ps. 2:12, *note*
6
b Ps. 146:3; Isa. 30:2
7
c 2 Ki. 18:4; see *notes* at Jud. 3:7; 1 Ki. 3:2; 15:14
10
d Cp. Isa. 10:5–6
16
e Cp. Zech. 3:10
18
f 2 Ki. 19:12; Isa. 37:12
19
g 2 Ki. 17:6
22
h i.e. *by their own hands*
CHAPTER 37
1
i 2 Ki. 19 is a parallel account with Isa. 37
3
j Isa. 22:5; 26:16; 33:2
k Or *reproach for provocation*
4
l Isa. 36:15, 18,20
m Cp. Ezek. 35:12–13
n Lit. *found*

*
36:11 Literally *Judean*

5 So the servants of King Hezekiah came to Isaiah.
6 And Isaiah said to them, "Thus
you shall say to your master, [a]'Thus
says the LORD: "Do not be afraid of the
words which you have heard, with
which the servants of the king of Assyria have blasphemed Me.
7 "Surely I will send a spirit upon
him, and he shall hear a rumor and
return to his own land; and I will cause
him to fall by the sword in his own
land." ' "

Sennacherib's blasphemous letter
(2 Ki. 19:8–13; 2 Chr. 32:17–19)

8 Then *the* Rabshakeh returned,
and found the king of Assyria warring
against Libnah, for he heard that he
had departed from Lachish.
9 And the king heard concerning
Tirhakah king of Ethiopia, "He has
come out to make war with you." So
when he heard *it*, he sent messengers
to Hezekiah, saying,
10 "Thus you shall speak to Hezekiah king of Judah, saying: 'Do not let
your God in whom you [b]trust deceive
you, saying, "Jerusalem shall not be
given into the hand of the king of Assyria."
11 'Look! You have heard what the
kings of Assyria have done to all lands
by utterly destroying them; and shall
you be delivered?
12 'Have the [c]gods of the nations
delivered those whom my fathers
have destroyed, Gozan and Haran and
Rezeph, and the people of Eden who
were in Telassar?
13 'Where *is* the king of Hamath,
the king of Arpad, and the king of the
city of Sepharvaim, Hena, and
[d]Ivah?' "

Hezekiah's prayer in the temple
(2 Ki. 19:14–19; 2 Chr. 32:20)

14 And Hezekiah received the letter from the hand of the messengers,
and read it; and Hezekiah went up to
the house of the LORD, and spread it
before the LORD.
15 Then Hezekiah [e]prayed to the
LORD, saying:
16 "O LORD of hosts, God of Israel,
the One who dwells *between* the cherubim, You *are* God, You [f]alone, of all
the kingdoms of the earth. You have
made heaven and earth.
17 [g]"Incline Your ear, O LORD, and
hear; open Your eyes, O LORD, and
see; and [h]hear all the words of Sennacherib, which he has sent to reproach the living God.
18 "Truly, LORD, the kings of Assyria have laid waste all the nations
and their [i]lands,
19 "and have cast their gods into
the fire; for they *were* [j]not gods, but
the work of men's hands—wood and
stone. Therefore they destroyed them.
20 "Now therefore, O LORD our God,
[k]save us from his hand, that all the
kingdoms of the earth may [l]know
that You *are* the LORD, You alone."

God's second answer through
Isaiah (2 Ki. 19:20–34)

21 Then Isaiah the son of Amoz
sent to Hezekiah, saying, "Thus says
the LORD God of Israel, 'Because you
have prayed to Me against Sennacherib king of Assyria,
22 'this *is* the word which the LORD
has spoken concerning him:

"The virgin, the daughter of
Zion,
Has despised you, laughed you
to scorn;
The daughter of Jerusalem
Has shaken *her* head behind
your back!
23 "Whom have you reproached
and blasphemed?
Against whom have you raised
your voice,
And lifted up your eyes on
high?
Against the Holy One of Israel.
24 By your servants you have
reproached the Lord,
And said, 'By the multitude of
my chariots
I have come up to the height of
the mountains,
To the limits of Lebanon;
I will cut down its tall cedars
And its choice cypress trees;
I will enter its farthest height,
To its fruitful forest.
25 I have dug and drunk water,
And with the soles of my feet I
have dried up
All the [m]brooks of defense.'
26 "Did you not hear [n]long ago
How I made it,
From ancient times that I
formed it?
Now I have brought it to pass,
That you should be
For crushing fortified cities
into heaps of ruins.
27 Therefore their inhabitants
[o]*had* little power;

6 *a* Cp. Isa. 7:3–8; 26:4; 30:15; 31:3
10 *b* See Ps. 2:12, *note*
12 *c* Isa. 36:18–19; cp. Isa. 10:9–11
13 *d* Or *Avva*, 2 Ki. 17:24
15 *e* *Bible prayers* (OT): vv. 14–20; Isa. 38:3. (Gen. 15:2; Hab. 3:1)
16 *f* Isa. 43:10–11
17 *g* Dan. 9:18 *h* Ps. 74:22
18 *i* 2 Ki. 15:29; 16:9; 17:24
19 *j* Isa. 40:19–20
20 *k* Isa. 33:22 *l* Ps. 83:18
25 *m* Probably the rivers of Egypt
26 *n* Isa. 25:1; 40:21; 45:21
27 *o* Lit. *were short of hand*

They were dismayed and
confounded;
They were *as* the grass of the
field
And the green herb,
As the grass on the housetops
And *grain* blighted before it is
grown.
28 "But I know your [a]dwelling
place,
Your going out and your
coming in,
And your rage against Me.
29 Because your rage against Me
and your tumult
Have come up to My ears,
[b]Therefore I will put My hook
in your nose
And My bridle in your lips,
And I will [c]turn you back
By the way which you came." '

30 "This *shall be* a sign to you:

You shall eat this year such as
grows of itself,
And the second year what
springs from the same;
Also in the third year sow and
reap,
Plant vineyards and eat the
fruit of them.
31 And the remnant who have
escaped of the house of
Judah
Shall again take root
downward,
And bear fruit upward.
32 For out of Jerusalem shall go a
[d]remnant,
And those who escape from
Mount Zion.
The [e]zeal of the LORD of hosts
will do this.

33 "Therefore thus says the LORD concerning the king of Assyria:

'He shall not come into this
city,
Nor shoot an arrow there,
Nor come before it with shield,
Nor build a siege mound
against it.
34 By the way that he came,
By the same shall he return;
And he shall not come into this
city,'
Says the LORD.
35 'For I will [f]defend this city, to
save it
For My own sake and for My
servant [g]David's sake.' "

185,000 Assyrians killed by God; Sennacherib murdered
(2 Ki. 19:35–37; 2 Chr. 32:21)

36 Then the [h]angel of the LORD
went out, and [i]killed in the camp of
the Assyrians one hundred and
eighty-five thousand; and when *peo-*
ple arose early in the morning, there
were the corpses—all dead.
37 So Sennacherib king of Assyria
departed and went away, returned
home, and remained at [j]Nineveh.
38 Now it came to pass, as he was
worshiping in the house of Nisroch his
god, that his sons Adrammelech and
Sharezer struck him down with the
sword; and they escaped into the land
of [k]Ararat. Then [l]Esarhaddon his son
reigned in his place.

Hezekiah's healing
(2 Ki. 20:1–11; 2 Chr. 32:24–30)

38 IN those [1]days [m]Hezekiah was
sick and near death. And Isa-
iah the prophet, the son of Amoz, went
to him and said to him, "Thus says the
LORD: 'Set your house in order, for you
shall die and not live.' "
2 Then Hezekiah turned his face
toward the wall, and [n]prayed to the
LORD,
3 and said, "Remember now, O
LORD, I [o]pray, how I have walked before You in truth and with a [p]loyal
heart, and have done *what is* good in
Your [q]sight." And Hezekiah wept bitterly.
4 And the word of the LORD came
to Isaiah, saying,
5 "Go and tell Hezekiah, 'Thus
says the LORD, the God of David your
father: "I have heard your prayer, I
have seen your tears; surely I will add
to your days [r]fifteen years.
6 "I will deliver you and this city
from the hand of the king of Assyria,
and I will [s]defend this city." '
7 "And this *is* the sign to you from
the LORD, that the LORD will do this
thing which He has spoken:
8 "Behold, I will bring the shadow
on the sundial, which has gone down
with the sun on the [t]sundial of Ahaz,
[2][i]ten degrees backward." So the sun

28
a Lit. *sitting*
29
b Isa. 30:28; Ezek. 38:4
c Ezek. 38:4; 39:2
32
d *Remnant:* v. 32; Isa. 46:3. (Isa. 1:9; Rom. 11:5, *note*)
e 2 Ki. 19:31; Isa. 9:7
35
f Isa. 31:5; 38:6
g 1 Ki. 11:13
36
h *Angel* (of the LORD): v. 36; Isa. 63:9. (Gen. 16:7; Jud. 2:1, *note*)
i *Miracles* (OT): v. 36; 38:8; Dan. 3:26. (Gen. 5:24; Jon. 1:17, *note*)
37
j See Jon. 3:3, *note*
38
k See Gen. 8:4
l Ezra 4:2
CHAPTER 38
1
m 2 Ki. 20:1–19 is a parallel account to Isa. 38–39
2
n Cp. Isa. 37:15
3
o *Bible prayers* (OT): v. 3; Jer. 14:7. (Gen. 15:2; Hab. 3:1)
p See Phil. 3:12, *note*
q 2 Ki. 18:3
5
r Cp. 2 Ki. 18:2,13
6
s Isa. 37:35
8
t Cp. Josh. 10:12–14

[1](38:1) Hezekiah's illness (chs. 38—39) took place prior to the events of chs. 36—37. See 2 Ki. 18:7, *note.*
[2](38:8) Scoffers have suggested that it would be impossible for the earth to reverse its

returned ten degrees on the dial by which it had gone down.

9 This is the [1]writing of Hezekiah king of Judah, when he had been sick and had recovered from his sickness:

10 I said,
"In the [a]prime of my life
I shall go to the gates of
[b]Sheol;
I am deprived of the remainder
of my years."
11 I said,
"I shall not see YAH,
The LORD* in the land of the
living;
I shall observe man no more
among the inhabitants of the
world.*
12 My life span is gone,
Taken from me like a
shepherd's [c]tent;
I have cut off my life like a
weaver.
He cuts me off from the loom;
From day until night You
make an end of me.
13 I have considered until
morning—
Like a lion,
So He breaks all my bones;
From day until night You
make an end of me.
14 Like a crane *or* a swallow, so I
chattered;
I mourned like a dove;
My eyes fail *from looking*
upward.
O LORD,* I am oppressed;
Undertake for me!
15 "What shall I say?
He has both spoken to me,*
And He Himself has done *it*.
I shall walk [d]carefully all my
years
In the bitterness of my soul.
16 O LORD, by these *things men*
live;
And in all these *things is* the
life of my spirit;
So You will restore me and
make me live.
17 Indeed *it was* for *my own*
peace
That I had great bitterness;
But You have lovingly
delivered my soul from the
pit of corruption,
For You have cast all my sins
behind Your [e]back.
18 For [b]Sheol cannot [f]thank You,
[g]Death cannot praise You;
Those who go down to the pit
cannot hope for Your truth.
19 The living, the living man, he
shall praise You,
As I *do* this day;
The father shall make known
Your truth to the children.

20 "The LORD *was ready* to save
me;
Therefore we will sing my
songs with stringed
instruments
All the days of our life, in the
house of the LORD."

21 Now [h]Isaiah had said, "Let them
take a lump of figs, and apply *it* as a
poultice on the boil, and he shall recover."
22 And [i]Hezekiah had said, "What
is the sign that I shall go up to the
house of the LORD?"

Hezekiah imprudently reveals defenses;
Babylonian captivity foretold
(2 Ki. 20:12–19; 2 Chr. 32:31)

39 AT that [j]time Merodach-
Baladan* the son of Baladan,
king of Babylon, sent letters and a present to Hezekiah, for he heard that he
had been sick and had recovered.
2 And Hezekiah was pleased with
them, and showed them the house of
his treasures—the silver and gold, the
spices and precious ointment, and all
his armory—all that was found
among his [k]treasures. There was
nothing in his house or in all his dominion that Hezekiah did not show
them.
3 Then Isaiah the prophet went to
King Hezekiah, and said to him,
"What did these men say, and from
where did they come to you?" So Hez-

10
[a] Cp. Ps. 102:24
[b] See Hab. 2:5, *note;* cp. Lk. 16:23, *note*
12
[c] Cp. 2 Cor. 5:1; 2 Pet. 1:13–14
15
[d] Cp. 1 Ki. 21:27
17
[e] *Forgiveness:* v. 17; Isa. 44:22. (Lev. 4:20; Mt. 26:28, *note*)
18
[f] Ps. 115:17
[g] See Eccl. 9:10, *note*
21
[h] 2 Ki. 20:7
22
[i] 2 Ki. 20:8
CHAPTER 39
1
[j] 2 Ki. 20:1–19 is a parallel account to Isa. 38–39
2
[k] 2 Chr. 36:18

*
38:11 Hebrew YAH, YAH • Following some Hebrew manuscripts; Masoretic Text and Vulgate read *rest;* Septuagint omits *among the inhabitants of the world;* Targum reads *land.* **38:14** Following Bomberg; Masoretic Text and Dead Sea Scrolls read *Lord.* **38:15** Following Masoretic Text and Vulgate; Dead Sea Scrolls and Targum read *And shall I say to Him;* Septuagint omits first half of this verse. **39:1** Spelled *Berodach-Baladan* in 2 Kings 20:12

rotation and that, furthermore, such reversal would destroy the world. This was a miracle, of course. The Creator is not limited by the natural laws that He instituted.

[1](38:9) Verses 10–20 contain the only extant narrative in the OT written by a king of Judah after the time of Solomon.

ekiah said, "They came to me from a
[l]far country, from Babylon."
4 And he said, "What have they
seen in your house?" So Hezekiah answered, "They have seen all that *is* in
my house; there is nothing among my
treasures that I have not shown them."
5 Then Isaiah said to Hezekiah,
"Hear the word of the LORD of hosts:
6 'Behold, the days are coming
when all that *is* in your house, and
what your fathers have accumulated
until this day, shall be [a]carried to Babylon; nothing shall be left,' says the
LORD.
7 'And they shall take away *some*
of your [b]sons who will descend from
you, whom you will beget; and they
shall be eunuchs in the palace of the
king of Babylon.' "

3 *a* Dt. 28:49; Jer. 5:15
6 *b* 2 Ki. 24:13; 25:13–15; Jer. 20:5
7 *c* Dan. 1:3–4
CHAPTER 40
2 *d* Lit. *to the heart of* *e* i.e. *hard or forced service*

8 So Hezekiah said to Isaiah, "The
word of the LORD which you have spoken *is* good!" For he said, "At least
there will be peace and truth in my
days."

V. The Greatness and Transcendence of God, 40—48

The prophet's new message

40 [1]"COMFORT, yes, comfort My
people!"
[2]Says your God.
2 "Speak [c]comfort to Jerusalem,
and cry out to her,
That her [d]warfare is ended,
That her iniquity is pardoned;
For she has received from the
LORD's hand
Double for all her sins."

---

[1](40:1) Since this part of the book never predicts exile, but speaks of it as if already present while promising deliverance, the theory has been advanced that it was not written by Isaiah but by a later unknown writer (sometimes referred to as Second Isaiah), writing shortly before the end of the exile. In support of this position it has been asserted that the literary style and theological viewpoint are different from those of the original Isaiah. Yet the similarities in style and vocabulary are far greater than the differences; in fact, Isaiah's style is distinctive. The alleged variations of theological viewpoint are never actual contradictions, but merely differences of emphasis. Such alterations of style and of theological emphasis as exist are only what would be expected, in view of the difference in the subjects discussed. There are really only two strong arguments for a difference of authorship: (1) the fact that the name of Cyrus is mentioned a century before his time; and (2) the fact that the exile is assumed rather than predicted.

The first of these is not a difficulty to one who believes in predictive prophecy. In fact, Josiah's name was predicted nearly three hundred years before his time (1 Ki. 13:2).

As to the second argument, assumption by a prophet of the standpoint of a future situation is not limited to these chapters, but is found also in other portions of the prophetic books (e.g. Isa. 9:2–4; Mic. 4:9—5:1).

Before Isaiah died, the northern kingdom had already been in exile for some time, and the continuing sin of Judah made its eventual exile absolutely certain. Isaiah and his godly followers would feel almost as if they too were already in exile. Under these circumstances it is not at all strange that the Spirit of God should lead him to assume the standpoint of the exile and to give his followers a message of deliverance that was also ideally suited to revive the spirits and encourage the faith of the godly during the exile.

The unity of Isaiah is made certain by the fact that the NT ascribes to Isaiah quotations from each of the main portions of the book. Thus in Jn. 12:37–41 citations from Isa. 53 and Isa. 6 are both ascribed to Isaiah.

Starting from the mistaken belief in different authorship of the first and last parts of Isaiah, those who have accepted this position have generally gone on to use similar arguments from vocabulary and viewpoint to divide the last part into two, which they call Second Isaiah and Third Isaiah, and then still further to subdivide each of these, as well as the first part of the book, separating the whole into a mosaic which is thought to be the work of a multiplicity of authors, writing over a period of several centuries. But there is no compelling evidence for rejecting the view of the NT writers, that the whole book is the work of Isaiah the son of Amoz (Isa. 1:1).

[2](40:1) The section of Isaiah which runs from 40:1 to 56:8 looks at Israel in exile and promises deliverance through Cyrus (e.g. 41:2,25; 44:28; 45:1–4; 46:11; 48:14–15). Mingled with the promise of deliverance is constantly increasing recognition of the fact that the exile is only the necessary result of Israel's sin (e.g. 42:19–25; 43:22–28; etc.). Therefore, unless this problem is satisfactorily dealt with, other captivities will inevitably follow. God promises that He will send His Servant to take away sin and to bring light to all the world (e.g. 42:1–7; 49:1–6; 52:13—53:12). The full view of the redemptive sufferings of Christ in Isa. 52:13—53:12 leads to the evangelical strain so prominent in this part of Isaiah (e.g. 44:22–23; 55:1–3,6–7). Isaiah also predicts Israel's return in the end time (cp. Isa. 11:12; 43:1–7; 51:11,21–23; 52:1; 54:6–10; 60:15–22; 61:7–9; 65:18–25).

The mission of John the Baptist (cp. Mt. 3:3)

3 The [a]voice of one crying in the wilderness:
"Prepare the way of the LORD;
Make straight in the desert*
A highway for our God.
4 Every valley shall be exalted
And every mountain and hill brought low;
The crooked places shall be made straight
And the rough places smooth;
5 The [b]glory of the LORD shall be revealed,
And all flesh shall see *it* together;
For the mouth of the LORD has spoken."

The greatness of God and man's insignificance

6 The voice said, "Cry out!"
And he* said, "What shall I cry?"
"All flesh *is* [c]grass,
And all its loveliness *is* like the flower of the field.
7 The grass withers, the flower fades,
Because the breath of the LORD blows upon it;
Surely the people *are* grass.
8 The grass withers, the flower fades,
But the word of our God stands forever."

9 O Zion,
[1]You who bring good tidings,
Get up into the high mountain;
O [d]Jerusalem,
You who bring good tidings,
Lift up your voice with strength,
Lift *it* up, be not afraid;
Say to the cities of Judah,
"Behold your God!"

10 Behold, the Lord GOD shall come with a strong *hand,*
And His arm shall rule for Him;
Behold, His reward *is* with Him,
And His work before Him.
11 He will feed His flock like a [e]shepherd;
He will gather the lambs with His arm,
And carry *them* in His [f]bosom,
And gently lead those who are with young.

12 Who has measured the waters* in the hollow of His hand,
Measured heaven with a span
And calculated the dust of the earth in a measure?
Weighed the mountains in scales
And the hills in a balance?
13 Who has [g]directed the [h]Spirit of the LORD,
Or *as* His counselor has taught Him?
14 With whom did He take counsel, and *who* instructed Him,
And taught Him in the path of justice?
Who [i]taught Him knowledge,
And showed Him the way of understanding?
15 Behold, the nations *are* as a drop in a bucket,
And are counted as the small dust on the scales;
Look, He lifts up the isles as a very little thing.
16 And Lebanon *is* not sufficient to burn,
Nor its beasts sufficient for a burnt offering.
17 All nations before Him *are* as [j]nothing,
And they are counted by Him less than nothing and worthless.

18 To whom then will you [k]liken God?
Or what likeness will you compare to Him?
19 The workman molds an image,
The goldsmith overspreads it with gold,

3 *a* vv. 3–5; Mk. 1:3; Lk. 3:4–6; Jn. 1:23
5 *b* Isa. 35:2
6 *c* vv. 6–8; Jas. 1:10; 1 Pet. 1:24–25
9 *d Kingdom* (OT): vv. 9–11; Isa. 62:10. (Gen. 1:26; Zech. 12:8, *note*)
11 *e* Cp. Jn. 10:11, 14–16; Heb. 13:20; 1 Pet. 2:25; 5:4
f Cp. Num. 11:12
13 *g* Rom. 11:34; 1 Cor. 2:16
h Holy Spirit (OT): v. 13; Isa. 42:1. (Gen. 1:2; Zech. 12:10)
14 *i* Job 36:22–23
17 *j* Dan. 4:35
18 *k* v. 25; Isa. 46:5; Acts 17:29

*
40:3 Following Masoretic Text, Targum, and Vulgate; Septuagint omits *in the desert.*
40:6 Following Masoretic Text and Targum; Dead Sea Scrolls, Septuagint, and Vulgate read *I.*
40:12 Following Masoretic Text, Septuagint, and Vulgate; Dead Sea Scrolls read *waters of the sea;* Targum reads *waters of the world.*

[1](40:9) In the Septuagint the clause, "who brings good tidings," is expressed by *euaggelizō* (also 41:27; 52:7; 60:6; 61:1), which in the NT is the verb often used for declaring good tidings, or preaching the Gospel (e.g. Lk. 1:19; 7:22; 8:1; Acts 8:4; 10:36; 15:35; Rom. 1:15; 1 Cor. 15:2; etc.). Our words "evangelize" and "evangelism" are derived from this Greek verb.

And the silversmith casts silver
chains.
20 Whoever *is* too impoverished
for *such* a contribution
Chooses a tree *that* will not
rot;
He seeks for himself a skillful
workman
To prepare a carved image
that will not totter.

21 [a]Have you not known?
Have you not heard?
Has it not been told you from
the beginning?
Have you not understood from
the foundations of the earth?
22 *It is* He who sits above the
[1]circle of the earth,
And its inhabitants *are* like
grasshoppers,
Who [b]stretches out the
heavens like a curtain,
And spreads them out like a
[c]tent to dwell in.
23 [d]He brings the princes to
nothing;
He makes the judges of the
earth useless.

24 Scarcely shall they be planted,
Scarcely shall they be sown,
Scarcely shall their stock take
root in the earth,
When He will also blow on
them,
And they will wither,
And the whirlwind will take
them away like stubble.

25 [e]"To whom then will you liken
Me,
Or *to whom* shall I be equal?"
says the Holy One.
26 Lift up your eyes on high,
And see who has created these
things,
Who brings out their host by
number;
He [f]calls them all by name,
By the greatness of His might
And the strength of *His* power;
Not one is missing.

27 [g]Why do you say, O Jacob,
And speak, O Israel:
"My way is hidden from the
LORD,
And [h]my just claim is passed
over by my God"?
28 Have you not known?
Have you not heard?
The everlasting God, the LORD,
The Creator of the ends of the
earth,
Neither faints nor is weary.
His [i]understanding is
unsearchable.
29 He gives power to the weak,
And to *those who have* no
might He increases strength.
30 Even the youths shall faint and
be weary,
And the young men shall
utterly fall,
31 But those who [j]wait on the
LORD
Shall [k]renew *their* strength;
They shall mount up with
wings like eagles,
They shall run and not be
weary,
They shall walk and not faint.

The living God taunts lifeless idols

41 "KEEP silence before Me, O
coastlands,
And let the people renew *their*
strength!
Let them come near, then let
them speak;
Let us [l]come near together for
judgment.

2 "Who raised up [2m]one from the
east?
Who in righteousness called
him to His [n]feet?
Who gave the nations before
him,
And made *him* rule over
kings?
Who gave *them* as the dust *to*
his sword,
As driven stubble to his bow?
3 Who pursued them, *and* passed
safely
By the way *that* he had not
gone with his feet?
4 Who has performed and done
it,

21
a Ps. 19:1; Acts 14:17; Rom. 1:19–20
22
b Job 9:8; Ps. 104:2; Isa. 42:5; 44:24; Jer. 10:12
c Ps. 19:4
23
d Ps. 107:40; cp. 1 Cor. 1:26–29
25
e v. 18; Dt. 4:15
26
f Ps. 147:4
27
g Isa. 54:7–8
h Job 34:5
28
i Eccl. 11:5; Rom. 11:33
31
j Isa. 30:15; 49:23
k Ps. 103:5
CHAPTER 41
1
l Isa. 1:18
2
m Isa. 45:1, 13
n Cp. Jud. 4:10

[1](40:22) Many hold that this verse alludes to the sphericity of the earth. Cp. Job 9:8; Ps. 104:2; Isa. 42:5; 44:24; Jer. 10:12.

[2](41:2) This verse predicts the coming of the Persian conqueror Cyrus, whose victories and rapid growth in power are ascribed to the providence of God. Cyrus came from the region to the northeast. Hence he is sometimes spoken of as coming from the east, sometimes from the north. Here he is called "one from the east," in v. 25, "one from the north." In 46:11 the emphasis is on God's work: "calling a bird of prey from the east." See also 41:25; 44:28; 45:1–4; 46:11; and 48:14–15.

Calling the generations from
the beginning?
'I, the LORD, am the first;
And with the [a]last I *am* [b]He.' "

5 The coastlands saw *it* and
feared,
The ends of the earth were
afraid;
They drew near and came.
6 Everyone helped his neighbor,
And said to his brother,
Be of good courage!"
7 So the [c]craftsman encouraged
the [d]goldsmith;
He who smooths *with* the
hammer *inspired* him who
strikes the anvil,
Saying, "It *is* ready for the
soldering";
Then he fastened it with pegs,
That it might not totter.
8 "But you, Israel, *are* My
[1]servant,
Jacob whom I have chosen,
The descendants of Abraham
My [e]friend.
9 *You* whom I have taken from
the ends of the earth,
And called from its farthest
regions,
And said to you,
'You *are* My servant,
I have chosen you and have
not cast you away:
10 [f]Fear not, for I *am* with you;
Be not dismayed, for I *am* your
God.
I will strengthen you,
Yes, I will help you,
I will uphold you with My
righteous right hand.'
11 "Behold, all those who were
incensed against you
Shall be ashamed and
disgraced;
They shall be as nothing,
And those who strive with you
shall perish.
12 You shall seek them and not
find them—
Those who contended with
you.
Those who war against you
Shall be as nothing,
As a nonexistent thing.

4
a Rev. 1:8, 17; 22:13
b Isa. 43:10; 44:6
7
c Isa. 44:13
d Isa. 40:19
8
e 2 Chr. 20:7; Jas. 2:23
10
f Isa. 43:1,5; 44:2
14
g Job 25:6
h Redemption (redeeming relative type): v. 14; Isa. 43:1. (Gen. 48:16; Isa. 59:20, *note*)
15
i Cp. Mic. 4:13
17
j Ps. 94:14; Rom. 11:2
18
k Isa. 43:20; 49:10; 55:1
19
l Perhaps the olive tree
m Isa. 35:1

13 For I, the LORD your God, will
hold your right hand,
Saying to you, 'Fear not, I will
help you.'

14 "Fear not, you [g]worm Jacob,
You men of Israel!
I will help you," says the LORD
And your [h]Redeemer, the Holy
One of Israel.
15 "Behold, I will make you into a
new threshing sledge with
sharp teeth;
You shall [i]thresh the
mountains and beat *them*
small,
And make the hills like chaff.
16 You shall winnow them, the
wind shall carry them away,
And the whirlwind shall
scatter them;
You shall rejoice in the LORD,
And glory in the Holy One of
Israel.

17 "The poor and needy seek
water, but *there is* none,
Their tongues fail for thirst.
I, the LORD, will hear them;
I, the God of Israel, will not
[j]forsake them.
18 I will open rivers in desolate
heights,
And fountains in the midst of
the valleys;
I will make the wilderness a
pool of [k]water,
And the dry land springs of
water.
19 I will plant in the wilderness
the cedar and the acacia
tree,
The myrtle and the [l]oil tree;
I will set in the [m]desert the
cypress tree *and* the pine
And the box tree together,
20 That they may see and know,
And consider and understand
together,
That the hand of the LORD has
done this,
And the Holy One of Israel has
created it.

21 "Present your case," says the
LORD.
"Bring forth your strong

[1](41:8) Three servants of the LORD are mentioned in Isaiah: (1) David (Isa. 37:35); (2) Israel the nation (Isa. 41:8–16; 43:1–10; 44:1–8,21; 45:4; 48:20); and (3) Messiah (42:1–12; ch. 49 in full, but observe especially vv. 5–7, where the Servant Christ restores the servant nation; 50:4–6; 52:13–15; 53:1–12). Israel the nation was a faithless servant but, restored and converted, will yet "thresh the mountains." Against the Servant Christ no charge of unfaithfulness or failure is brought. See Isa. 42:1, *note*.

reasons," says the [a]King of
Jacob.
22 "Let them bring forth and show
us what will happen;
Let them show the [b]former
things, what they *were*,
That we may [c]consider them,
And know the latter end of
them;
Or declare to us things to
come.
23 Show the things that are to
come hereafter,
That we may know that you
are gods;
Yes, do good or do evil,
That we may be dismayed and
see *it* together.
24 Indeed you *are* [d]nothing,
And your work *is* nothing;
He who chooses you *is* an
abomination.

25 "I have raised up one from the
[e]north,
And he shall come;
From the rising of the sun he
shall call on My name;
And he shall come against
princes as *though* mortar,
As the potter treads clay.
26 Who has declared from the
beginning, that we may
know?
And former times, that we may
say, '*He is* righteous'?
Surely *there is* no one who
shows,
Surely *there is* no one who
declares,
Surely *there is* no one who
hears your words.
27 The first time *I said* to Zion,
'Look, there they are!'
And I will give to Jerusalem
one who brings good
[f]tidings.
28 For I looked, and *there was* no
man;
I looked among them, but
there was no counselor,
Who, when I asked of them,
could answer a word.

21
a Isa. 43:15
22
b Isa. 43:9
c Lit. *set our heart upon them*
24
d Rom. 3:10–20
25
e Cp. Isa. 14:31; Jer. 1:13–14
27
f Gospel: v. 27; Isa. 52:7. (Gen. 12:3; Rev. 14:6)
CHAPTER 42
1
g Holy Spirit (OT): v. 1; Isa. 44:3. (Gen. 1:2; Zech. 12:10)
h Isa. 11:2
3
i Christ (first advent): vv. 1–7; Isa. 49:1. (Gen. 3:15; Acts 1:11, *note*)
j i.e. *a dimly burning wick.* Mt. 12:18–21
6
k Isa. 49:6; 60:3; Mt. 4:16; Lk. 2:32; Acts 13:47–48; Rom. 9:24–30; 10:19–20; 11:11–12; 15:9–12

29 Indeed they *are* all worthless;*
Their works *are* nothing;
Their molded images *are* wind
and confusion.

Christ, the Servant of the LORD

42 "BEHOLD! My [1]Servant whom
I uphold,
My Elect One *in whom* My
soul delights!
I have put My [g]Spirit upon
[h]Him;
He will bring forth justice to
the Gentiles.
2 He will not cry out, nor raise
His voice,
Nor cause His voice to be
heard in the street.
3 A [i]bruised reed He will not
break,
And [j]smoking flax He will not
quench;
He will bring forth justice for
truth.
4 He will not fail nor be
discouraged,
Till He has established justice
in the earth;
And the coastlands shall wait
for His law."

5 Thus says God the LORD,
Who created the heavens and
stretched them out,
Who spread forth the earth
and that which comes from
it,
Who gives breath to the people
on it,
And spirit to those who walk
on it:
6 "I, the LORD, have called You in
righteousness,
And will hold Your hand;
I will keep You and give You
as a covenant to the people,
[2]As a light to the [k]Gentiles,
7 To open blind eyes,
To bring out prisoners from
the prison,

*41:29 Following Masoretic Text and Vulgate; Dead Sea Scrolls, Syriac, and Targum read *nothing;* Septuagint omits the first line.

[1](42:1) There is a twofold account of the coming Servant: He is represented (1) as weak, despised, rejected, slain; and also (2) as a mighty conqueror, taking vengeance on the nations and restoring Israel (e.g. 40:10; 63:1–4). The former class of passages relate to the first advent and are fulfilled; the latter, to the second advent and are unfulfilled.

[2](42:6) The prophets connect the Gentiles with Christ in a threefold way: (1) As the Light He brings salvation to the Gentiles (Lk. 2:32; Acts 13:47–48), a distinctive feature of the Church Age (Rom. 11:17–24; Eph. 2:11–12). (2) As the Root of Jesse He is to reign over the Gentiles in His kingdom (Isa. 11:10; Rom. 15:12). See Kingdom (OT), Gen. 1:26–28; Zech. 12:8, *note*. And (3) believing Gentiles in the present age, together with believing Jews, constitute "the church which is His body" (Eph. 1:22–23). See Eph. 3:6, *note*.

Those who sit in darkness
from the prison house.

Israel, chosen, sinning, and chastened

8 I *am* the LORD, that *is* My
name;
And My glory I will not give to
another,
Nor My praise to carved
images.
9 Behold, the former things have
come to pass,
And new things I declare;
Before they spring forth I tell
you of them."

10 Sing to the LORD a new song,
And His praise from the ends
of the earth,
You who go down to the sea,
and all that is in it,
You coastlands and you
inhabitants of them!
11 Let the wilderness and its
cities lift up *their voice,*
The villages *that* Kedar
inhabits.
Let the inhabitants of [a]Sela
sing,
Let them shout from the top of
the mountains.
12 Let them give glory to the
LORD,
And declare His praise in the
coastlands.
13 The LORD shall go forth like a
mighty man;
He shall stir up *His* zeal like a
man of war.
He shall cry out, yes, shout
aloud;
He shall prevail against His
enemies.

14 "I have held My peace a long
time,
I have been still and restrained
Myself.
Now I will cry like a woman in
labor,
I will pant and gasp at once.
15 I will lay waste the mountains
and hills,
And dry up all their
vegetation;
I will make the rivers
coastlands,
And I will dry up the pools.
16 I will bring the blind by a way
they did not know;
I will lead them in paths they
have not known.
I will make darkness light
before them,
And crooked places straight.
These things I will do for
them,
And not forsake them.
17 They shall be turned back,
They shall be greatly ashamed,
Who trust in carved images,
Who say to the molded
images,
'You *are* our gods.'

18 "Hear, you deaf;
And look, you blind, that you
may see.
19 Who *is* blind but My servant,
Or deaf as My messenger
whom I send?
Who *is* blind as *he who is*
perfect,
And blind as the LORD's
servant?
20 Seeing many things, but you
do not observe;
Opening the ears, but he does
not hear."

21 The LORD is well pleased for
His righteousness' sake;
He will [b]exalt the law and
make *it* honorable.
22 But this *is* a people robbed and
plundered;
All of them are snared in
holes,
And they are hidden in prison
houses;
They are for prey, and no one
delivers;
For plunder, and no one says,
"Restore!"

23 Who among you will give ear
to this?
Who will listen and hear for
the time to come?
24 Who gave Jacob for plunder,
and Israel to the robbers?
Was it not the LORD,
He against whom we have
sinned?
[c]For they would not walk in His
ways,
Nor were they obedient to His
law.
25 Therefore He has poured on
him the fury of His anger
And the strength of battle;
It has set him on fire all
around,
Yet he [d]did not know;
And it burned him,

11
a Isa. 16:1
21
b Cp. Ps. 138:2
24
c Isa. 65:2
25
d Isa. 1:3; 5:13

Yet he did not take *it* to
[a]heart.

Israel to be redeemed and restored

43 BUT now, thus says the LORD,
who created you, O Jacob,
And He who formed you, O
Israel:
[b]"Fear not, for I have [c]redeemed
you;
I have called *you* by your
name;
You *are* [d]Mine.
2 When you pass through the
waters, I *will be* [e]with you;
And through the rivers, they
shall not overflow you.
[f]When you walk through the
fire, you shall not be burned,
Nor shall the flame scorch you.
3 For I *am* the LORD your God,
The Holy One of Israel, your
Savior;
I gave Egypt for your [g]ransom,
Ethiopia and Seba in your
place.
4 Since you were precious in My
sight,
You have been honored,
And I have [h]loved you;
Therefore I will give men for
you,
And people for your life.
5 [i]Fear not, for I *am* with you;
I will bring your descendants
from the east,
And [j]gather you from the
west;
6 I will say to the [k]north, 'Give
them up!'
And to the south, 'Do not keep
them back!'
Bring My sons from afar,
And My daughters from the
ends of the earth—
7 Everyone who is [l]called by
My name,
Whom I have [m]created for My
glory;
I have formed him, yes, I have
made him."

Israel to be God's witness

8 Bring out the blind people who
have eyes,
And the [n]deaf who have ears.
9 Let all the nations be gathered
together,
And let the people be
assembled.
Who among them can declare
this,
And show us [o]former things?
Let them bring out their
witnesses, that they may be
justified;
Or let them hear and say, "*It is*
truth."
10 [p]"You *are* My witnesses," says
the LORD,
"And My servant whom I have
chosen,
That you may know and
believe Me,
And understand that I *am* He.
[q]Before Me there was no God
formed,
Nor shall there be after Me.
11 [r]I, *even* I, *am* the LORD,
And besides Me *there is* no
savior.
12 I have declared and saved,
I have proclaimed,
And *there was* no foreign *god*
among you;
Therefore you *are* My
witnesses,"
Says the LORD, "that I *am* God.
13 Indeed before the day *was*, I
am He;
And *there is* no one who can
deliver out of My hand;
I work, and who will [s]reverse
it?"

Babylon to be destroyed; Israel, forgiven

14 Thus says the LORD, your
Redeemer,
The Holy One of Israel:
"For your sake I will send to
Babylon,
And bring them all down as
fugitives—
The Chaldeans, who rejoice in
their ships.
15 I *am* the LORD, your Holy One,
The Creator of Israel, your
[t]King."
16 Thus says the LORD, who
makes a [u]way in the sea
And a path through the mighty
waters,
17 Who brings forth the chariot
and horse,
The army and the power
(They shall lie down together,
they shall not rise;
They are extinguished, they
are quenched like a wick):
18 "Do not remember the former
things,
Nor consider the things of old.
19 Behold, I will do a new thing,
Now it shall spring forth;
Shall you not know it?

25
a Isa. 29:13

CHAPTER 43

1
b v. 5
c *Redemption* (redeeming relative type): vv. 1–14; Isa. 44:6. (Gen. 48:16; Isa. 59:20, *note*)
d *Assurance/security:* v. 1; Isa. 49:16. (Ps. 23:1; Jude 1, *note*)

2
e Jer. 30:11
f Ps. 66:12; cp. Dan. 3:25–27

3
g Prov. 11:8; 21:18; cp. Mt. 20:28; 1 Tim. 2:6

4
h Isa. 63:9

5
i Isa. 41:10, 14; 44:2; Jer. 30:10–11; 46:27–28
j Isa. 54:7

6
k Isa. 49:12

7
l Isa. 63:19; cp. Jas. 2:7
m Ps. 100:3; Isa. 29:23; cp. Jn. 3:3–5; 2 Cor. 5:17; Eph. 2:10

8
n Isa. 29:18

9
o Isa. 41:22

10
p Isa. 44:8
q Isa. 41:4; 44:6

11
r Isa. 45:21; Hos. 13:4

13
s Isa. 14:27

15
t Isa. 41:21

16
u Isa. 51:10

I will even make a road in the wilderness
And rivers in the desert.
20 The beast of the field will honor Me,
The jackals and the ostriches,
Because I give waters in the wilderness
And rivers in the desert,
To give drink to My people,
My [a]chosen.
21 This people I have formed for Myself;
They shall declare My [b]praise.

22 "But you have not called upon Me, O Jacob;
And you have been [c]weary of Me, O Israel.
23 You have not brought Me the sheep for your burnt offerings,
Nor have you honored Me with your sacrifices.
I have not caused you to serve with grain offerings,
Nor wearied you with incense.
24 You have bought Me no sweet cane with money,
Nor have you satisfied Me with the fat of your sacrifices;
But you have burdened Me with your sins,
You have [d]wearied Me with your iniquities.

25 "I, *even* I, *am* He who [e]blots out your transgressions [f]for My own sake;
[g]And I will not remember your sins.
26 Put Me in remembrance;
Let us contend together;
State your *case*, that you may be acquitted.
27 Your first father sinned,
And your [h]mediators have transgressed against Me.
28 Therefore I will profane the princes of the sanctuary;
[i]I will give Jacob to the curse,
And Israel to reproaches.

The promise of the Spirit; the folly of idolatry

44 "YET hear now, O Jacob My servant,
And Israel whom I have chosen.
2 Thus says the LORD who made you
And formed you from the womb, *who* will help you:
'Fear not, O Jacob My servant;
And you, [j]Jeshurun, whom I have chosen.
3 For I will pour water on him who is thirsty,
And floods on the dry ground;
I will pour My [k]Spirit on your descendants,
And My blessing on your offspring;
4 They will spring up among the grass
Like willows by the watercourses.'
5 One will say, 'I *am* the LORD's';
Another will call *himself* by the name of Jacob;
Another will write *with* his hand, 'The LORD's,'
And name *himself* by the name of Israel.

6 "Thus says the LORD, the King of Israel,
And his [l]Redeemer, the LORD of hosts:
[m]'I *am* the First and I *am* the Last;
Besides Me *there is* no God.
7 And who can proclaim as I do?
Then let him declare it and set it in order for Me,
Since I appointed the ancient people.
And the things that are coming and shall come,
Let them show these to them.
8 Do not fear, nor be afraid;
Have I not told you from that time, and declared *it*?
[n]You *are* My witnesses.
Is there a God besides Me?
Indeed *there is* no other Rock;
I know not *one*.' "

9 Those who make an image, all of them *are* useless,
And their precious things shall not profit;
They *are* their own witnesses;
They neither see nor know, that they may be ashamed.
10 Who would form a god or mold an image
That profits him [o]nothing?
11 Surely all his companions would be ashamed;
And the workmen, they *are* mere men.
Let them all be gathered together,
Let them stand up;
Yet they shall fear,
They shall be ashamed together.

---

20 *a Election* (corporate): vv. 20–21; Ezek. 20:5. (Dt. 7:6; 1 Pet. 5:13, *note*)

21 *b* Jer. 13:11; cp. 1 Pet. 2:9

22 *c* Mal. 1:13

24 *d* Isa. 7:13

25 *e* Isa. 44:22; Jer. 50:20; Acts 3:19
f Ezek. 36:22
g Isa. 1:18; Jer. 31:34

27 *h* Lit. *interpreters.* Mal. 2:7–8

28 *i* Ps. 79:4; Jer. 24:9; Dan. 9:11; Zech. 8:13

CHAPTER 44

2 *j* Lit. *upright.* Poetical name of Israel. Dt. 32:15; 33:5,26

3 *k Holy Spirit* (OT): v. 3; Isa. 48:16. (Gen. 1:2; Zech. 12:10)

6 *l Redemption* (redeeming relative type): v. 6; Isa. 44:22. (Gen. 48:16; Isa. 59:20, *note*)
m Isa. 41:4; 48:12; Rev. 1:8, 17; 22:13

8 *n* Isa. 43:10, 12

10 *o* Isa. 41:29; 45:20

12 The blacksmith with the tongs
works one in the coals,
Fashions it with hammers,
And works it with the strength
of his arms.
Even so, he is hungry, and his
strength fails;
He drinks no water and is
faint.

13 The [a]craftsman stretches out
his rule,
He marks one out with chalk;
He fashions it with a plane,
He marks it out with the
compass,
And makes it like the figure of
a man,
According to the beauty of a
man, that it may remain in
the house.

14 He cuts down cedars for
himself,
And takes the cypress and the
oak;
He secures *it* for himself
among the trees of the
forest.
He plants a pine, and the rain
nourishes *it*.

15 Then it shall be for a man to
burn,
For he will take some of it and
warm himself;
Yes, he kindles *it* and bakes
bread;
Indeed he makes a god and
worships *it;*
He makes it a carved image,
and falls down to it.

16 He burns half of it in the fire;
With this half he eats meat;
He roasts a roast, and is
satisfied.
He even warms *himself* and
says,
"Ah! I am warm,
I have seen the fire."

17 And the rest of it he makes
into a god,
His carved image.
He falls down before it and
worships *it*,
Prays to it and says,
"Deliver me, for you *are* my
god!"

18 They do not know nor
understand;
For He has [b]shut their eyes, so
that they cannot see,
And their hearts, so that they
cannot [c]understand.

19 And no one considers in his
heart,
Nor *is there* knowledge nor
understanding to say,
"I have burned half of it in the
fire,
Yes, I have also baked bread
on its coals;
I have roasted meat and eaten
it;
And shall I make the rest of it
an abomination?
Shall I fall down before a
block of wood?"

20 He feeds on ashes;
A [d]deceived heart has turned
him aside;
And he cannot deliver his soul,
Nor say, "*Is there* not a [e]lie in
my right hand?"

Forgiven Israel to return to their land

21 "Remember these, O Jacob,
And Israel, for you *are* My
[f]servant;
I have formed you, you *are* My
servant;
O Israel, you will not be
[g]forgotten by Me!

22 I have blotted out, like a thick
cloud, your transgressions,
And like a cloud, your sins.
[h]Return to Me, for I have
[i]redeemed you."

23 Sing, O heavens, for the LORD
has done *it!*
Shout, you lower parts of the
earth;
Break forth into singing, you
mountains,
O forest, and every tree in it!
For the LORD has [i]redeemed
Jacob,
And [j]glorified Himself in
Israel.

24 Thus says the LORD, your
[i]Redeemer,
And He who formed you from
the womb:
"I *am* the LORD, who makes all
things,
Who stretches out the heavens
all alone,
Who spreads abroad the earth
by Myself;

25 Who [k]frustrates the signs of
the babblers,
And drives diviners mad;
Who turns wise men
backward,

13
a Cp. Jer. 24:1
18
b Isa. 6:9–10; 29:10; cp. Rom. 1:18–23
c Jer. 10:14
20
d 2 Th. 2:11; 2 Tim. 3:13
e Rom. 1:25
21
f See Isa. 41:8, *note*
g Isa. 49:15
22
h Forgiveness: v. 22; Jer. 31:34. (Lev. 4:20; Mt. 26:28, *note*)
i Redemption (redeeming relative type): vv. 22–24; Isa. 47:4. (Gen. 48:16; Isa. 59:20, *note*)
23
j Isa. 49:3; 60:21
25
k Isa. 47:13

And makes their knowledge
[a]foolishness;
26 Who confirms the word of His
servant,
And performs the counsel of
His messengers;
Who says to Jerusalem, 'You
shall be inhabited,'
To the cities of Judah, 'You
shall be built,'
And I will raise up her waste
places;
27 [b]Who says to the deep, 'Be dry!
And I will dry up your rivers';

The prophecy concerning Cyrus: the restoration under Ezra and Nehemiah

28 Who says of [1c]Cyrus, '*He is*
My shepherd,
And he shall perform all My
pleasure,
Saying to Jerusalem, "You
shall be built,"
And to the [d]temple, "Your
foundation shall be laid." '

Cyrus will perform God's will

45 "THUS says the LORD to His
anointed,
To [e]Cyrus, whose right hand I
have held—
To subdue nations before him
And [f]loose the armor of kings,
To open before him the
[g]double doors,
So that the gates will not be
shut:
2 'I will go before you
And [h]make the crooked
places* straight;
[i]I will break in pieces the gates
of bronze
And cut the bars of iron.
3 I will give you the treasures of
darkness
And hidden riches of secret
places,
That you may know [j]that I,
the LORD,
Who call *you* by your name,
Am the God of Israel.
4 For Jacob My servant's sake,
And Israel My elect,
I have even called you by your
name;
I have named you, though you
have not [k]known Me.

Safety and salvation only in the LORD

5 [l]I *am* the LORD, and *there is* no
other;
There is no God besides Me.
I will gird you, though you
have not known Me,
6 [m]That they may [n]know from the
rising of the sun to its
setting
That *there is* none besides Me.
I *am* the LORD, and *there is* no
other;
7 I form the light and create
darkness,
I make peace and [o]create
[2]calamity;
I, the LORD, do all these *things*.'
8 "Rain down, you heavens, from
above,
And let the skies pour down
righteousness;
Let the earth open, let them
bring forth salvation,
And let righteousness spring
up together.
I, the LORD, have created it.
9 "Woe to him who [p]strives with
his Maker!
Let the potsherd *strive* with
the potsherds of the earth!
[q]Shall the clay say to him who
forms it, 'What are you
making?'
Or shall your handiwork *say*,
'He has no hands'?
10 Woe to him who says to *his*
father, 'What are you
begetting?'
Or to the woman, 'What have
you brought forth?' "
11 Thus says the LORD,
The Holy One of Israel, and
his Maker:
[r]"Ask Me of things to come
concerning My [s]sons;
And concerning the [t]work of
My hands, you command
Me.

25
a Isa. 29:14; 1 Cor. 1:20
27
b Jer. 50:38; 51:36
28
c Ezra 1:1; Isa. 45:1, 13
d Ezra 6:7
CHAPTER 45
1
e Isa. 44:28
f Job 12:21
g i.e. *the gates of Babylon*
2
h Isa. 40:4
i Ps. 107:16
3
j Cp. Isa. 43:1
4
k Cp. Jud. 2:10; 1 Th. 4:5
5
l Dt. 4:35, 39; 32:39; Isa. 44:8; cp. Isa. 46:9
6
m Ps. 102:15; Isa. 37:20; Mal. 1:11
n Isa. 11:9; 52:10
7
o Amos 3:6
9
p Cp. Job 40:8–9; Prov. 21:30
q Isa. 29:16; Jer. 18:6; Rom. 9:20
11
r Isa. 8:19
s Jer. 31:9
t Isa. 60:21; 64:8

*45:2 Dead Sea Scrolls and Septuagint read *mountains;* Targum reads *I will trample down the walls;* Vulgate reads *I will humble the great ones of the earth.*

[1](44:28) Compare 1 Ki. 13:2 where Josiah is mentioned by name, although 1 Kings was written two centuries before his birth.

[2](45:7) God is not the author of sin (Hab. 1:13; 2 Tim. 2:13; Ti. 1:2; Jas. 1:13; 1 Jn. 1:5). One of the meanings of the Hebrew word *ra* (often translated "evil") carries the idea of *adversity* or *calamity*, and it is evidently so employed here. God has made sorrow and wretchedness to be the sure fruits of sin.

12 I have made the earth,
And created man on it.
I—My hands—stretched out the heavens,
And all their host I have commanded.
13 I have raised him up in [a]righteousness,
And I will direct all his ways;
He shall build My [b]city
And let My exiles go free,
Not for price nor [c]reward,"
Says the LORD of hosts.

Israel's future restoration will influence other peoples

14 Thus says the LORD:

"The [d]labor of Egypt and merchandise of Cush
And of the Sabeans, men of stature,
Shall come over to you, and they shall be yours;
They shall walk behind you,
They shall come over in chains;
And they shall bow down to you.
They will make supplication to you, *saying*, 'Surely God *is* in you,
And *there is* no other;
There is no other God.' "

15 Truly You *are* God, who hide Yourself,
O God of Israel, the Savior!
16 They shall be [e]ashamed
And also disgraced, all of them;
They shall go in confusion together,
Who are makers of idols.
17 [f]*But* Israel shall be saved by the LORD
With an [g]everlasting salvation;
You shall not be ashamed or [h]disgraced
Forever and ever.

18 For thus says the LORD,
Who [1]created the heavens,
Who is God,
Who formed the earth and made it,
Who has established it,
Who did not create it in vain,
Who formed it to be [i]inhabited:
"I *am* the LORD, and *there is* no other.
19 I have not spoken in secret,
In a dark place of the earth;
I did not say to the seed of Jacob,
'Seek Me in vain';
I, the LORD, speak righteousness,
I declare things that are right.

20 "Assemble yourselves and come;
Draw near together,
You *who have* escaped from the nations.
They have no knowledge,
Who carry the wood of their carved image,
And pray to a god *that* cannot [j]save.
21 Tell and bring forth *your case;*
Yes, let them take counsel together.
Who has [k]declared this from ancient time?
Who has told it from that time?
Have not I, the LORD?
And *there is* no other God besides Me,
A just God and a Savior;
There is none besides Me.
22 [l]"Look to Me, and be saved,

13
a Cp. Isa. 41:2
b Isa. 44:28
c Cp. Isa. 52:3

14
d Ps. 68:31; 72:10–11; Isa. 14:1; 49:23; 60:9–10,14, 16; Zech. 8:22–23

16
e Isa. 44:11

17
f v. 25; Rom. 11:26
g Isa. 51:6
h Isa. 29:22

18
i Ps. 115:16; Acts 17:26

20
j Isa. 44:9

21
k Isa. 44:7

22
l Ps. 22:27; 65:5; cp. Num. 21:8–9

---

[1](45:18) This is one of the Scripture passages that suggest the Divine Judgment interpretation of Gen. 1:1–2 (see Gen. 1:2, *note*). This interpretation views the earth as having been created perfect. After an indefinite period of time, possibly in connection with Satan's sin of rebellion against the Most High (see *notes* at Isa. 14:12 and Ezek. 28:12), judgment fell upon the earth and it became "empty" or "waste" (as some translate *bohu*). Another indefinite interval elapsed after which "the Spirit of God was hovering over the face of the waters" (Gen. 1:2) in a re-creation of the earth. Some of the arguments for this viewpoint are: (1) Only the earth, not the universe, is said to have been "without form and void." (2) The face of the earth bears the marks of a catastrophe. (3) The word rendered "was" may also be translated "became," as indicated above—"*became* without form and void." (4) The Hebrew expression for "without form and void" *(tohu wabohu)* is used to describe a condition produced by divine judgment in the only other two texts where the two words appear in conjunction (Isa. 34:11, "emptiness"; Jer. 4:23, "without form and void"). (5) Such a prehistoric divine judgment would throw some light on Satan's fall and the peculiar relation he seems to sustain to the earth. And (6) this interpretation leaves room for an undetermined period of time between the original creation and divine judgment. Adam, created after the events of Gen. 1:1–2, was the first man.

All you ends of the earth!
For I *am* God, and *there is* no
other.
23 I have [a]sworn by Myself;
The word has gone out of My
mouth *in* righteousness,
And shall not return,
That to Me [b]every knee shall
bow,
Every tongue shall [c]take an
oath.
24 He shall say,
'Surely in the LORD I have
[d]righteousness and strength.
To Him *men* shall come,
And all shall be ashamed
Who are incensed against Him.
25 In the LORD all the descendants
of Israel
Shall be justified, and shall
glory.'"

The power of God and the powerlessness of idols

46 BEL bows down, Nebo
stoops;
Their idols were on the beasts
and on the cattle.
Your carriages *were* heavily
loaded,
A burden to the weary *beast*.
2 They stoop, they bow down
together;
They could not deliver the
burden,
But have themselves gone into
[e]captivity.
3 "Listen to Me, O house of
Jacob,
And all the [f]remnant of the
house of Israel,
Who have been [g]upheld *by Me*
from birth,
Who have been carried from
the womb:
4 Even to *your* old age, I *am* He,
And *even* to gray hairs I will
carry *you!*
I have made, and I will bear;
Even I will carry, and will
deliver *you*.
5 "To whom will you [h]liken Me,
and make *Me* equal
And compare Me, that we
should be alike?
6 They [i]lavish gold out of the
bag,
And weigh silver on the scales;
They hire a [j]goldsmith, and he
makes it a god;
They prostrate themselves, yes,
they worship.

23
a Gen. 22:16; Heb. 6:13
b Rom. 14:11; Phil. 2:10
c Isa. 19:18
24
d Isa. 54:17
CHAPTER 46
2
e Jer. 48:7
3
f *Remnant*: v. 3; Jer. 15:21. (Isa. 1:9; Rom. 11:5, *note*)
g Isa. 63:9
5
h Isa. 40:18
6
i Jer. 10:4
j Isa. 44:12
9
k Dt. 32:7
l Isa. 45:5
10
m Isa. 45:21; 48:3
n Ps. 33:11; Prov. 19:21; 21:30; Isa. 14:24; 25:1; Acts 5:39; Heb. 6:17
11
o See Isa. 41:2, *note*
p Isa. 44:28; 45:13
12
q Ps. 76:5
CHAPTER 47
1
r vv. 1–15; 13:1–22; 14:18–23; Jer. 25:12; 50:1–51:64

7 They bear it on the shoulder,
they carry it
And set it in its place, and it
stands;
From its place it shall not
move.
Though *one* cries out to it, yet
it cannot answer
Nor save him out of his
trouble.
8 "Remember this, and show
yourselves men;
Recall to mind, O you
transgressors.
9 [k]Remember the former things
of old,
For I *am* God, and *there is* [l]no
other;
I am God, and *there is* none
like Me,
10 [m]Declaring the end from the
beginning,
And from ancient times *things*
that are not *yet* done,
Saying, 'My [n]counsel shall
stand,
And I will do all My pleasure,'
11 Calling a bird of prey from the
[o]east,
The man who [p]executes My
counsel, from a far country.
Indeed I have spoken *it;*
I will also bring it to pass.
I have purposed *it;*
I will also do it.
12 "Listen to Me, you
[q]stubborn-hearted,
Who *are* far from
righteousness:
13 I bring My righteousness near,
it shall not be far off;
My salvation shall not linger.
And I will place salvation in
Zion,
For Israel My glory.

Judgment on Babylon

47 "COME down and sit in the
dust,
O virgin daughter of [r]Babylon;
Sit on the ground without a
throne,
O daughter of the Chaldeans!
For you shall no more be
called
Tender and delicate.
2 Take the millstones and grind
meal.
Remove your veil,
Take off the skirt,
Uncover the thigh,
Pass through the rivers.

3 Your nakedness shall be
uncovered,
Yes, your shame will be seen;
I will take vengeance,
And I will not arbitrate with a
man."

4 *As for* our [a]Redeemer, the
LORD of hosts *is* His name,
The Holy One of Israel.

5 "Sit in silence, and go into
darkness,
O daughter of the Chaldeans;
For you shall no longer be
called
The Lady of [b]Kingdoms.
6 I was [c]angry with My people;
I have profaned My
inheritance,
And given them into your
hand.
You showed them no mercy;
On the elderly you laid your
[d]yoke very heavily.
7 And you said, 'I shall be a lady
forever,'
So that you did not take these
things to [e]heart,
Nor remember the latter end of
them.

8 "Therefore hear this now, *you
who are* given to pleasures,
Who dwell securely,
Who say in your heart,
'I *am*, and *there is* no one else
besides me;
I shall not sit *as* a widow,
Nor shall I know the loss of
children';
9 But these two *things* shall
come to you
In a [f]moment, in one day:
The loss of children, and
widowhood.
They shall come upon you in
their fullness
Because of the multitude of
your sorceries,
For the great abundance of
your enchantments.

10 "For you have [g]trusted in your
wickedness;
You have said, 'No one [h]sees
me';
Your wisdom and your
knowledge have warped
you;
And you have said in your
heart,
'I *am*, and *there is* no one else
besides me.'

4
a Redemption (redeeming relative type): v. 4; Isa. 48:17. (Gen. 48:16; Isa. 59:20, *note*)
5
b Isa. 13:19; Rev. 17:18
6
c 2 Sam. 24:1; 2 Chr. 28:9; Zech. 1:15
d Dt. 28:49–50
7
e Isa. 42:25
9
f Rev. 18:8, 10
10
g See Ps. 2:12, *note*
h Isa. 29:15
11
i 1 Th. 5:3
j Isa. 29:5
13
k Cp. Isa. 44:5; Dan. 2:2
14
l Nah. 1:10; Mal. 4:1
m Jer. 51:58
n Lit. *their souls*
CHAPTER 48
1
o Jer. 5:2; cp. Jer. 4:2
2
p Mic. 3:11; Rom. 2:17

11 Therefore evil shall come upon
you;
You shall not know from
where it arises.
And trouble shall fall upon
you;
You will not be able to put it
off.
And [i]desolation shall come
upon you [j]suddenly,
Which you shall not know.

12 "Stand now with your
enchantments
And the multitude of your
sorceries,
In which you have labored
from your youth—
Perhaps you will be able to
profit,
Perhaps you will prevail.
13 You are wearied in the
multitude of your counsels;
[k]Let now the astrologers, the
stargazers,
And the monthly
prognosticators
Stand up and save you
From what shall come upon
you.
14 Behold, they shall be as
[l]stubble,
The fire shall [m]burn them;
They shall not deliver
[n]themselves
From the power of the flame;
It shall not *be* a coal to be
warmed by,
Nor a fire to sit before!
15 Thus shall they be to you
With whom you have labored,
Your merchants from your
youth;
They shall wander each one to
his quarter.
No one shall save you.

Israel reminded of God's promises

48 "HEAR this, O house of Jacob,
Who are called by the name
of Israel,
And have come forth from the
wellsprings of Judah;
Who swear by the name of the
LORD,
And make mention of the God
of Israel,
But [o]not in truth or in
righteousness;
2 For they call themselves after
the holy city,
And [p]lean on the God of
Israel;

The LORD of hosts *is* His name:

3 "I have [a]declared the former things from the beginning;
They went forth from My mouth, and I caused them to hear it.
Suddenly I did *them,* and they came to pass.
4 Because I knew that you *were* obstinate,
And your neck *was* an iron sinew,
And your brow [b]bronze,
5 Even from the beginning I have declared *it* to you;
Before it came to pass I proclaimed *it* to you,
Lest you should say, 'My idol has done [c]them,
And my carved image and my molded image
Have commanded them.'

6 "You have heard;
See all this.
And will you not declare *it?*
I have made you hear new things from this time,
Even hidden things, and you did not know them.
7 They are created now and not from the beginning;
And before this day you have not heard them,
Lest you should say, 'Of course I knew them.'
8 Surely you did not hear,
Surely you did not know;
Surely from long ago your ear was not opened.
For I knew that you would deal very treacherously,
And were called a transgressor from the [d]womb.

9 "For My name's [e]sake I will defer My anger,
And *for* My praise I will restrain it from you,
So that I do not cut you off.
10 Behold, I have [f]refined you, but not as silver;
I have tested you in the [g]furnace of affliction.
11 For My own [h]sake, for My own sake, I will do *it;*
For how should *My name* be [i]profaned?
And I will not give My glory to another.

3 *a* Isa. 44:7–8; 46:10
4 *b* Ex. 32:1–9; Dt. 32:5; Ps. 78:8; Ezek. 2:4; 3:7; Acts 7:51
5 *c* Cp. Jer. 44:15–18
8 *d* Dt. 9:24
9 *e* v. 11; Ps. 79:9; 106:8; Isa. 43:25; Ezek. 20:9, 14,22,44
10 *f* Ps. 66:10; Jer. 9:7
g Dt. 4:20; Jer. 11:4
11 *h* Cp. 48:9
i Lev. 22:2, 32
12 *j* Isa. 41:4; 44:6; Rev. 1:17; 22:13
14 *k* Isa. 47:1–15
15 *l* Cp. Isa. 41:2
16 *m* Isa. 61:1; Zech. 2:8–9,11
n *Holy Spirit* (OT): v. 16; Isa. 59:19. (Gen. 1:2; Zech. 12:10)
17 *o* *Redemption* (redeeming relative type): v. 17; Isa. 48:20. (Gen. 48:16; Isa. 59:20, *note*)
p Cp. 2 Tim. 3:16–17
q Isa. 49:10
18 *r* Ps. 81:13
s Dt. 28:1–14

12 "Listen to Me, O Jacob,
And Israel, My called:
I *am* He, I *am* the [j]First,
I *am* also the Last.
13 Indeed My hand has laid the foundation of the earth,
And My right hand has stretched out the heavens;
When I call to them,
They stand up together.

14 "All of you, assemble yourselves, and hear!
Who among them has declared these *things?*
The LORD loves him;
He shall do His pleasure on [k]Babylon,
And His arm *shall be against* the Chaldeans.
15 I, *even* I, have spoken;
Yes, I have [l]called him,
I have brought him, and his way will prosper.

16 "Come near to Me, hear this:
I have not spoken in secret from the beginning;
From the time that it was, I *was* there.
[1]And now the [m]Lord GOD and His [n]Spirit
Have* sent Me."

17 Thus says the LORD, your [o]Redeemer,
The Holy One of Israel:
"I *am* the LORD your God,
Who [p]teaches you to profit,
Who [q]leads you by the way you should go.
18 [r]Oh, that you had heeded My commandments!
[s]Then your peace would have been like a river,
And your righteousness like the waves of the sea.
19 Your descendants also would have been like the sand,
And the offspring of your [t]body like the grains of sand;
His name would not have been cut off
Nor destroyed from before Me."

20 Go forth from Babylon!

48:19 *t* Isa. 7:14; 9:6

*

48:16 The Hebrew verb is singular.

[1](48:16) This is one of the clearest of the OT intimations of the Trinity. For the speaker here is not the prophet but the LORD Himself. Cp. v. 12ff.

[a]Flee from the Chaldeans!
With a voice of singing,
Declare, proclaim this,
Utter it to the end of the earth;
Say, "The LORD has [b]redeemed
His servant Jacob!"
21 And they did not thirst
When He led them through the
deserts;
He caused the waters to flow
from the rock for them;
He also split the rock, and the
waters gushed out.
22 "*There is* no peace," says the
LORD, "for the [c]wicked."

VI. The Suffering Servant of the LORD, 49—57

The Holy One (Messiah), a light to Gentile nations (vv. 6,12) as well as to Israel (v. 7)

49 "LISTEN, O coastlands, to
[d]Me,
And take heed, you peoples
from afar!
The LORD has called Me from
the womb;
From the [e]matrix of My
mother He has made
mention of My name.
2 And He has made My mouth
like a sharp [f]sword;
In the shadow of His hand He
has hidden Me,
And made Me a polished shaft;
In His quiver He has hidden
Me."
3 "And He said to me,
'You *are* My [g]servant, O Israel,
In whom I will be [h]glorified.'
4 Then I said, 'I have labored in
vain,
I have spent my strength for
nothing and in vain;
Yet surely [i]my just reward *is*
with the LORD,
And my work with my God.' "
5 "And now the LORD says,
Who formed Me from the
womb *to be* His Servant,
To bring Jacob back to Him,
So that Israel is gathered to
Him*
(For I shall be glorious in the
eyes of the LORD,
And My God shall be My
strength),
6 Indeed He says,
'It is too small a thing that You
should be My Servant
To raise up the tribes of Jacob,
And to restore the preserved
ones of Israel;
I will also give You as a light
to the [j]Gentiles,
That You should be My
salvation to the ends of the
[k]earth.' "
7 Thus says the LORD,
The [b]Redeemer of Israel, their
Holy One,
To Him whom man [l]despises,
To Him whom the nation
abhors,
To the Servant of rulers:
[m]"Kings shall see and arise,
Princes also shall worship,
Because of the LORD who is
faithful,
The Holy One of Israel;
And He has chosen You."
8 Thus says the LORD:
"In an [n]acceptable time I have
heard You,
And in the day of salvation I
have helped You;
I will preserve You and give
You
As a [o]covenant to the people,
To restore the earth,
To cause them to inherit the
desolate heritages;
9 [p]That You may say to the
prisoners, 'Go forth,'
To those who *are* in darkness,
'Show yourselves.'

"They shall feed along the
roads,
And their pastures *shall be* on
all desolate heights.
10 They shall neither [q]hunger nor
thirst,
Neither [r]heat nor sun shall
strike them;
For He who has mercy on
them will [s]lead them,
Even by the springs of water
He will guide them.
11 I will make each of My
[t]mountains a road,
And My highways shall be
elevated.
12 Surely these shall come from
[u]afar;
Look! Those from the north
and the west,

20 *a* Jer. 50:8; Zech. 2:6–7 *b Redemption* (redeeming relative type): v. 20; 49:7; Isa. 49:26. (Gen. 48:16; Isa. 59:20, *note*)
22 *c* Isa. 57:21
CHAPTER 49
1 *d Christ* (first advent): vv. 1–6; Isa. 50:6. (Gen. 3:15; Acts 1:11, *note*) *e* Isa. 7:14; 9:6
2 *f* Cp. Hos. 6:5; Rev. 1:16; 2:16; 19:15
3 *g* Isa. 41:8 *h* Isa. 44:23; 60:21
4 *i* Isa. 50:6–9
6 *j* See Isa. 42:6, *note* *k* Acts 13:47
7 *l* Ps. 22:6; Isa. 53:3 *m* Isa. 52:15
8 *n* 2 Cor. 6:2 *o* Isa. 42:6
9 *p* Isa. 61:1
10 *q* Rev. 7:16 *r* Ps. 121:6 *s* Ps. 23:2; Isa. 48:17
11 *t* Isa. 40:4
12 *u* Isa. 43:5–6

* **49:5** Qere, Dead Sea Scrolls, and Septuagint read *is gathered to Him*; Kethib reads *not gathered*.

And these from the land of
Sinim."[1]

13 Sing, O heavens!
Be joyful, O earth!
And break out in singing, O mountains!
For the LORD has comforted His people,
And will have mercy on His afflicted.

14 But Zion said, "The LORD has forsaken me,
And my Lord has forgotten me."

15 [a]"Can a woman forget her nursing child,
And not have compassion on the son of her womb?
Surely they may forget,
Yet I will not forget you.
16 See, I have [b]inscribed you on the palms *of My hands;*
Your walls *are* continually before Me.
17 Your sons* shall make haste;
Your destroyers and those who laid you waste
Shall go away from you.
18 Lift up your eyes, look around and see;
All these gather together *and* come to you.
As I live," says the LORD,
"You shall surely clothe yourselves with them all as an ornament,
And bind them *on you* as a bride *does*.

19 "For your waste and desolate places,
And the land of your destruction,
Will even now be too small for the inhabitants;
And those who swallowed you up will be far away.
20 The children you will have,
After you have lost the others,
Will say again in your ears,
'The place *is* too small for me;
Give me a place where I may dwell.'
21 Then you will say in your heart,
'Who has begotten these for me,
Since I have lost my children and am desolate,
A captive, and wandering to and fro?
And who has brought these up?
There I was, left alone;
But these, where *were* they?' "

Gentile nations to serve Israel

22 Thus says the Lord GOD:

"Behold, I will lift My hand in an oath to the nations,
And set up My standard for the peoples;
They shall bring your sons in *their* arms,
And your daughters shall be carried on *their* shoulders;
23 Kings shall be your foster fathers,
And their queens your nursing mothers;
They shall bow down to you with *their* faces to the earth,
And lick up the dust of your feet.
Then you will know that I *am* the LORD,
For they shall not be [c]ashamed who wait for Me."

24 Shall the prey be taken from the mighty,
Or the captives of the righteous* be delivered?

25 But thus says the LORD:

"Even the captives of the mighty shall be taken away,
And the prey of the terrible be delivered;
For I will contend with him who contends with you,
And I will save your children.
26 I will feed those who oppress you with their own flesh,
And they shall be drunk with their own blood as with sweet wine.
All flesh shall [d]know
That I, the LORD, *am* your Savior,
And your [e]Redeemer, the Mighty One of Jacob."

15 a Mal. 3:17; cp. Mt. 7:11; Rom. 11:29

16 b *Assurance/security:* v. 16; Isa. 54:17. (Ps. 23:1; Jude 1, *note*). Cp. Ex. 13:9; Song 8:6

23 c Rom. 5:5; 9:33; 10:11

26 d Ps. 9:16
e *Redemption* (redeeming relative type): v. 26; Isa. 52:3. (Gen. 48:16; Isa. 59:20, *note*)

*

49:17 Dead Sea Scrolls, Septuagint, Targum, and Vulgate read *builders*. **49:24** Following Masoretic Text and Targum; Dead Sea Scrolls, Syriac, and Vulgate read *the mighty;* Septuagint reads *unjustly*.

[1](49:12) Some hold that the word *Sinim* refers to a people of the Far East, perhaps the Chinese.

The humiliation of the Holy One

50 THUS says the LORD:
"Where *is* the [a]certificate of your mother's divorce,
Whom I have put away?
Or which of My [b]creditors *is it* to whom I have sold you?
For your iniquities you have sold yourselves,
And for your transgressions your mother has been put away.
2 Why, when I came, *was there* no man?
Why, when I called, *was there* none to answer?
Is My hand shortened at all that it cannot [c]redeem?
Or have I no power to deliver?
Indeed with My [d]rebuke I dry up the sea,
I make the rivers a wilderness;
Their fish stink because *there is* no water,
And die of thirst.
3 I clothe the heavens with blackness,
And I make sackcloth their covering."

4 "The [e]Lord GOD has given Me
The tongue of the [f]learned,
That I should know how to speak
A word in season to *him who is* weary.
He awakens Me morning by morning,
He awakens My ear
To hear as the learned.
5 The Lord GOD has opened My ear;
And I was not rebellious,
[g]Nor did I turn away.
6 I gave My back to those who [h]struck *Me,*
And My cheeks to those who plucked out the beard;
I [i]did not hide My face from shame and [j]spitting.

7 "For the Lord GOD will help Me;
Therefore I will not be disgraced;
Therefore I have set My face like a [k]flint,
And I know that I will not be ashamed.
8 *He is* near who [l]justifies Me;
Who will contend with Me?
Let us stand together.
Who *is* My adversary?
Let him come near Me.
9 Surely the Lord GOD will help Me;
Who *is* he *who* will condemn Me?
Indeed they will all grow old like a [m]garment;
The moth will eat them up.

10 "Who among you [n]fears the LORD?
Who obeys the voice of His Servant?
Who walks in darkness
And has no light?
Let him [o]trust in the name of the LORD
And rely upon his God.
11 Look, all you who kindle a fire,
Who encircle *yourselves* with sparks:
Walk in the light of your fire and in the sparks you have kindled—
This you shall have from My hand:
You shall lie down in torment.

God's remnant exhorted

51 "LISTEN to Me, you who follow after righteousness,
You who seek the LORD:
Look to the rock *from which* you were hewn,
And to the hole of the pit *from which* you were dug.
2 [p]Look to Abraham your father,
And to Sarah *who* bore you;
For I called him alone,
And blessed him and increased him."

3 For the LORD will [q]comfort Zion,
He will comfort all her waste places;
He will make her wilderness like Eden,
And her desert like the [r]garden of the LORD;
Joy and gladness will be found in it,
Thanksgiving and the voice of melody.

4 "Listen to Me, My people;
And give ear to Me, O My nation:
For law will proceed from Me,
And I will make My justice rest
As a light of the peoples.
5 My righteousness *is* near,
My salvation has gone forth,

CHAPTER 50

1
a Dt. 24:1; Jer. 3:8; see Hos. 2:2, *note*
b Cp. 2 Ki. 4:1; Mt. 18:25

2
c See Ex. 14:30, and Isa. 59:20, *notes*
d Ps. 106:9; Nah. 1:4

4
e Ex. 4:11
f Cp. Jn. 8:28

5
g Mt. 26:39; Jn. 14:31; Phil. 2:8; Heb. 10:5

6
h Mt. 27:26; Jn. 18:22
i *Christ* (first advent): vv. 4–7; Isa. 52:15. (Gen. 3:15; Acts 1:11, *note*)
j Mt. 26:67; 27:30; Mk. 14:65; 15:19

7
k Ezek. 3:8–9

8
l Rom. 8:32–34

9
m Job 13:28; Ps. 102:26; Isa. 51:6,8; Heb. 1:11

10
n See Ps. 19:9, *note*
o Ps. 20:7; cp. 2 Chr. 20:20

CHAPTER 51

2
p Rom. 4:1, 16; Heb. 11:11

3
q Isa. 40:1; 52:9; Ps. 102:13
r Gen. 13:10; Joel 2:3

And My arms will judge the peoples;
The coastlands will wait upon Me,
And on My arm they will trust.
6 Lift up your eyes to the heavens,
And look on the earth beneath.
For the heavens will [a]vanish away like smoke,
The [b]earth will grow old like a garment,
And those who dwell in it will die in like manner;
But My salvation will be [c]forever,
And My righteousness will not be abolished.

7 "Listen to Me, you who know righteousness,
You people in whose heart *is* My [d]law:
Do not fear the reproach of men,
Nor be afraid of their [e]insults.
8 For the moth will eat them up like a garment,
And the worm will eat them like wool;
But My righteousness will be forever,
And My salvation from generation to generation."

9 Awake, awake, put on strength,
O arm of the LORD!
Awake as in the ancient days,
In the generations of old.
Are You not *the arm* that cut Rahab apart,
And wounded the [f]serpent?
10 *Are* [g]You not *the One* who dried up the sea,
The waters of the great deep;
That made the depths of the sea a road
For the redeemed to [h]cross over?
11 So the ransomed of the LORD shall return,
And come to Zion with singing,
With everlasting joy on their heads.
They shall obtain joy and gladness;
Sorrow and sighing shall flee away.

12 "I, *even* I, *am* He who [i]comforts you.
Who *are* you that you should be afraid
Of a man *who* will die,
And of the son of a man *who* will be made like [j]grass?
13 And you [k]forget the LORD your Maker,
Who stretched out the heavens
And laid the foundations of the earth;
You have feared continually every day
Because of the fury of the oppressor,
When *he has* prepared to destroy.
And where *is* the fury of the oppressor?
14 The captive exile hastens, that he may be loosed,
That he should not die in the pit,
And that his bread should not fail.
15 But I *am* the LORD your God,
Who divided the sea whose waves roared—
The LORD of hosts *is* His name.
16 And I have put My [l]words in your mouth;
I have covered you with the shadow of My hand,
That I may plant the heavens,
Lay the foundations of the earth,
And say to Zion, 'You *are* My people.' "

Zion's failures forgiven

17 Awake, awake!
Stand up, O Jerusalem,
You who have drunk at the hand of the LORD
The cup of His fury;
You have [m]drunk the dregs of the cup of trembling,
And drained *it* out.
18 *There is* no one to guide her
Among all the sons she has brought forth;
Nor *is there any* who takes her by the hand
Among all the sons she has brought up.
19 These two *things* have come to you;
Who will be sorry for you?—
Desolation and destruction, famine and sword—
By whom will I comfort you?
20 Your sons have fainted,
They lie at the head of all the streets,

6
a Isa. 13:13; Mt. 24:35; 2 Pet. 3:10
b Isa. 24:19–20; Heb. 1:10–12
c Isa. 45:17

7
d Jer. 31:33; Heb. 10:16
e Mt. 5:11; cp. Acts 5:41

9
f Isa. 27:1

10
g Cp. Ex. 15:1–10
h Isa. 63:11–13

12
i v. 3; 2 Cor. 1:3
j Isa. 40:6–7; Jas. 1:10

13
k Isa. 17:10; Jer. 2:32; cp. Dt. 6:12; 8:11

16
l Dt. 18:18; Isa. 59:21; Jn. 3:34

17
m Isa. 29:9; 63:6

Like an antelope in a net;
They are full of the fury of the LORD,
The rebuke of your God.

21 Therefore please hear this, you afflicted,
And drunk but not with wine.
22 Thus says your Lord,
The LORD and your God,
Who [a]pleads the cause of His people:
"See, I have taken out of your hand
The cup of trembling,
The dregs of the cup of My fury;
You shall no longer drink it.
23 [b]But I will put it into the hand of those who afflict you,
Who have said to you,*
'Lie down, that we may walk over you.'
And you have laid your body like the ground,
And as the street, for those who walk over."

Vision of Jerusalem in the Kingdom Age

52 AWAKE, awake!
Put on your strength, O Zion;
Put on your beautiful garments,
O Jerusalem, the holy city!
For the uncircumcised and the unclean
Shall no longer come to you.
2 Shake yourself from the dust, arise;
Sit down, O Jerusalem!
Loose yourself from the bonds of your neck,
O captive daughter of Zion!
3 For thus says the LORD:

"You have sold yourselves for nothing,
And you shall be [c]redeemed [d]without money."

4 For thus says the Lord GOD:

"My people went down at first
Into [e]Egypt to dwell there;
Then the Assyrian oppressed them without cause.
5 Now therefore, what have I here," says the LORD,
"That My people are taken away for nothing?
Those who rule over them
Make them [f]wail,"* says the LORD,
"And My name *is* blasphemed continually every day.
6 Therefore My people shall know My name;
Therefore *they shall know* in that day
That I *am* He who speaks:
'Behold, *it is* I.' "

7 How beautiful upon the mountains
Are the [g]feet of him who brings good [h]news,
Who proclaims peace,
Who brings glad tidings of good *things*,
Who proclaims salvation,
Who says to Zion,
"Your God reigns!"
8 Your watchmen shall lift up *their* voices,
With their voices they shall sing together;
For they shall see eye to eye
When the LORD brings back Zion.
9 Break forth into joy, sing together,
You waste places of Jerusalem!
For the LORD has comforted His people,
He has redeemed Jerusalem.
10 The LORD has made bare His holy arm
In the eyes of all the nations;
And all the ends of the earth shall see
The salvation of our God.

11 Depart! Depart! Go out from there,
Touch no unclean *thing*;
Go out from the midst of her,
Be [i]clean,
You who bear the vessels of the LORD.
12 For you shall not go out with [j]haste,
Nor go by flight;
For the [k]LORD will go before you,
And the God of Israel *will be* your [l]rear guard.

22
a Jer. 50:34
23
b Isa. 14:2; Jer. 25:17, 26–28; Zech. 12:2
CHAPTER 52
3
c *Redemption* (redeeming relative type): vv. 3,9; Isa. 54:5. (Gen. 48:16; Isa. 59:20, *note*)
d Isa. 45:13
4
e Gen. 46:6
5
f Isa. 65:14
7
g Nah. 1:15; Rom. 10:15
h *Gospel:* v. 7; Isa. 61:1. (Gen. 12:3; Rev. 14:6)
11
i 2 Cor. 6:17
12
j Cp. Ex. 12:33,39
k Mic. 2:13
l Ex. 14:19

*51:23 Literally *your soul* 52:5 Dead Sea Scrolls read *Mock;* Septuagint reads *Marvel and wail;* Targum reads *Boast themselves;* Vulgate reads *Treat them unjustly.*

Jehovah's Servant (Christ) marred and exalted

13 Behold, My [1]Servant shall deal prudently;
He shall be exalted and extolled and be very high.
14 Just as many were astonished at you,
So His visage was [2a]marred more than any man,
And His form more than the sons of men;
15 So shall [b]He [3]sprinkle* many nations.
Kings shall shut their mouths at Him;
For what had not been told them they shall [c]see,
And what they had not heard they shall consider.

The vicarious sacrifice of Christ, Jehovah's Servant
(1 Pet. 2:24–25)

53 [d]WHO has believed our report?
And to whom has the arm of the LORD been revealed?
2 For He shall grow up before Him as a tender plant,
And as a root out of dry ground.
He has no form or comeliness;
And when we see Him,
There is no beauty that we should desire Him.
3 He is [e]despised and rejected by men,
A Man of sorrows and acquainted with grief.
And we hid, as it were, *our* faces from Him;
He was despised, and we did not esteem Him.

4 Surely He has borne our griefs
And [f]carried our [4]sorrows;
Yet we esteemed Him stricken,
Smitten by God, and afflicted.
5 But He *was* wounded for our transgressions,
He was bruised for our iniquities;
The chastisement for our peace *was* upon Him,
And by His stripes we are healed.
6 All we like sheep have gone astray;
We have turned, every one, to his own way;
And the LORD has laid on Him the iniquity of us all.
7 He was oppressed and He was afflicted,
Yet He opened not His mouth;
He was led as a lamb to the slaughter,
And as a sheep before its shearers is silent,
[g]So He opened not His mouth.
8 He was [h]taken from prison and from judgment,
And who will declare His generation?

14
a Sacrifice (prophetic): 52:14–53:12; Dan. 9:26. (Gen. 3:15; Heb. 10:18, *note*)
15
b Christ (first advent): 52:13–53:12; Isa. 61:1. (Gen. 3:15; Acts 1:11, *note*)
c Rom. 15:21
CHAPTER 53
1
d Jn. 12:38; Rom. 10:16
3
e Mt. 27:30–31
4
f Mt. 8:17; 1 Pet. 2:24
7
g Mt. 26:62–63; Mk. 15:3–5; Jn. 19:9; Acts 8:32–33
8
h Mt. 27:11–26; Lk. 23:1–25

* 52:15 Or *startle*

[1](52:13) Although Christ's birth is predicted earlier (7:14; 49:1–7), the passage on Christ as the Suffering Servant of the LORD begins at this point. His humiliation in general is foretold in ch. 50. Chapter 53 contains a statement of Christ's suffering (vv. 1–3), after which that suffering is set forth as vicarious (vv. 4–6, 7–9) and victorious (vv. 10–12). Because of this sacrifice, salvation can be offered, as in ch. 55.

The marginal references in Isa. 53 indicate how frequently quotations from it were used by our Lord and the NT writers. Observe that in the Servant passages the Servant is sometimes spoken of, sometimes spoken to, and sometimes speaks Himself.

[2](52:14) The literal rendering presents a shocking picture: "His visage was marred more than any man, / And His form more than the sons of men" i.e. not human. This was the effect of the brutalities described in Mt. 26:67–68; 27:27–30.

[3](52:15) Compare the literal fulfillment of this prediction in 1 Pet. 1:1–2, where people of many nations are described as having been sprinkled with the blood of Jesus Christ. The word here translated "sprinkle" is commonly used in the Pentateuch to describe the cleansing of the vessels in the temple when the priests sprinkled blood or water upon them. Cp. Heb. 10:22.

[4](53:4) Because Matthew quotes this passage and applies it to physical disease (cp. Mt. 8:17 with context) it has been conjectured by some that disease as well as sin was included in the atoning death of Christ. But Matthew asserts that the Lord fulfilled the first part of Isa. 53:4 during the healing ministry of His service on earth. Matthew 8:17 makes no reference to Christ's atoning death for sin.

The Lord took away the diseases of men by healing them. He died for our sins, not for our diseases. For physical disease in itself is not sin; it is merely one of the results of sin. Thus Isa. 53:5–6 prophesies that Christ would bear our sins on the cross (cp. 1 Pet. 2:24–25). His death was substitutionary and atoning.

For He was cut off from the
land of the living;
For the transgressions of My
people He was stricken.
9 And they* made His grave
with the wicked—
But with the [a]rich at His
[1]death,
Because He had done no
violence,
[b]Nor *was any* deceit in His
mouth.

10 Yet it pleased the LORD to
bruise Him;
He has put *Him* to grief.
When You make His soul an
offering for sin,
He shall see *His* seed, He shall
prolong *His* days,
And the pleasure of the LORD
shall prosper in His hand.
11 He shall see the labor of His
soul,* *and* be satisfied.
By His knowledge My
righteous Servant shall
[c]justify many,
For He shall bear their
iniquities.
12 Therefore I will divide Him a
portion with the great,
And He shall divide the spoil
with the strong,
Because He [d]poured out His
soul unto death,
And He was [e]numbered with
the transgressors,
And He bore the sin of many,
And made intercession for the
[f]transgressors.

Israel, the restored "wife" of the LORD (cp. Hos. 2:1—3:5)

54 "SING, O [g]barren,
You *who* have not borne!
Break forth into singing, and
cry aloud,
You *who* have not [h]labored
with child!
For more *are* the children of
the desolate
Than the children of the
married woman," says the
LORD.
2 [i]"Enlarge the place of your tent,
And let them stretch out the
curtains of your dwellings;
Do not spare;
Lengthen your cords,
And strengthen your stakes.
3 For you shall expand to the
right and to the left,
And your descendants will
[j]inherit the nations,
And make the desolate cities
inhabited.

4 [k]"Do not fear, for you will not be
ashamed;
Neither be disgraced, for you
will not be put to shame;
For you will forget the shame
of your youth,
And will not remember the
reproach of your widowhood
anymore.
5 For your Maker *is* your
[l]husband,
The LORD of hosts *is* His name;
And your [m]Redeemer *is* the
Holy One of Israel;
He is called the God of the
whole earth.
6 For the LORD has called you
Like a woman forsaken and
grieved in spirit,
Like a youthful wife when you
were refused,"
Says your God.
7 "For a mere moment I have
forsaken you,
But with great mercies I will
[n]gather you.
8 With a little wrath I hid My
face from you for a moment;
But with everlasting kindness I
will have mercy on you,"
Says the LORD, your Redeemer.

9 "For this *is* like the waters of
Noah to Me;
For as I have sworn
That the [o]waters of Noah
would no longer cover the
earth,
So have I sworn
That I would not be angry with
[p]you, nor rebuke you.
10 For the mountains shall depart
And the hills be removed,
But My kindness shall not
depart from you,
Nor shall My covenant of
peace be removed,"
Says the LORD, who has mercy
on you.

9
a Mt. 27:57–60
b 1 Pet. 2:22
11
c Acts 13:38–39; Rom. 5:15–18
12
d Isa. 50:6; Rom. 3:25
e Mt. 27:38; Mk. 15:28; Lk. 22:37
f Lk. 23:34
CHAPTER 54
1
g Gal. 4:27
h See Mic. 4:11, *note*
2
i Isa. 49:19
3
j Isa. 14:2; 49:22–23; 60:9
4
k Isa. 41:10
5
l "*Wife*" (of the LORD): vv. 1–7; Jer. 31:32. (Isa. 54:5; Hos. 2:2). Cp. Isa. 62:4–5
m Redemption (redeeming relative type): vv. 5,8; Isa. 59:20. (Gen. 48:16; Isa. 59:20, *note*)
7
n Isa. 43:5; 56:8
9
o Gen. 8:21; 9:11; cp. Jer. 31:35–36
p Ezek. 39:29

*
53:9 Literally *he* or *He* 53:11 Following Masoretic Text, Targum, and Vulgate; Dead Sea Scrolls and Septuagint read *From the labor of His soul He shall see light.*

[1](53:9) In the Hebrew the word rendered "death" is an intensive plural. It has been suggested that it speaks of the violence of Christ's death, the very pain of which made it like a repeated death.

11 "O you afflicted one,
Tossed with tempest, *and* not comforted,
Behold, I will lay your stones with colorful gems,
And lay your foundations with sapphires.
12 I will make your pinnacles of rubies,
Your gates of crystal,
And all your walls of precious stones.
13 All your [a]children *shall be* taught by the LORD,
And great *shall be* the [b]peace of your children.
14 In righteousness you shall be established;
You shall be far from oppression, for you shall not fear;
And from terror, for it shall not come near you.
15 Indeed they shall surely assemble, *but* not because of Me.
Whoever assembles against you shall [c]fall for your sake.
16 "Behold, I have created the blacksmith
Who blows the coals in the fire,
Who brings forth an instrument for his work;
And I have created the spoiler to destroy.
17 No [d]weapon formed against you shall [e]prosper,
And every tongue *which* rises against you in judgment
You shall condemn.
This *is* the heritage of the servants of the LORD,
And their [f]righteousness *is* from Me,"
Says the LORD.

Salvation through God's grace

55 "HO! [g]Everyone who thirsts,
Come to the waters;
And you who have no money,
Come, [h]buy and eat.
Yes, come, buy wine and milk
Without money and without price.
2 Why do you spend money for *what is* not bread,
And your wages for *what* does not satisfy?
Listen carefully to Me, and eat *what is* good,
And let your soul delight itself in abundance.
3 Incline your ear, and come to Me.
Hear, and your soul shall live;
And I will make an [i]everlasting covenant with you—
The sure mercies of [j]David.
4 Indeed I have given [k]him *as* a witness to the people,
A leader and commander for the people.
5 Surely you shall call a [l]nation you do not know,
And nations *who* do not know you shall run to you,
Because of the LORD your God,
And the Holy One of Israel;
For He has glorified you."
6 [m]Seek the LORD while He may be [n]found,
Call upon Him while He is near.
7 Let the wicked forsake his way,
And the unrighteous man his [o]thoughts;
Let him return to the LORD,
And He will have mercy on him;
And to our God,
For He will abundantly pardon.
8 "For My [p]thoughts *are* not your thoughts,
Nor *are* your ways My ways," says the LORD.
9 "For *as* the heavens are higher than the earth,
So are My ways higher than your ways,
And My [q]thoughts than your thoughts.
10 "For as the rain comes down, and the snow from heaven,
And do not return there,
But water the earth,
And make it bring forth and bud,
That it may give seed to the sower
And bread to the eater,
11 So shall My word be that [r]goes forth from My mouth;
It shall not return to Me void,
But it shall accomplish what I please,
And it shall [s]prosper *in the thing* for which I sent it.
12 "For you shall go out with joy,
And be led out with peace;

13
a Jn. 6:45; cp. 1 Cor. 2:10; 1 Th. 4:9; 1 Jn. 2:20
b Cp. Isa. 48:18
15
c Isa. 41:11–16
17
d Assurance/security: v. 17; Hab. 3:19. (Ps. 23:1; Jude 1, *note*)
e Isa. 29:8
f v. 14
CHAPTER 55
1
g Mt. 5:6; Jn. 4:14; 7:37; Rev. 21:6; 22:17
h Cp. Rev. 3:18
3
i Isa. 61:8; Jer. 32:40; see 2 Sam. 7:16, *note*
j 2 Sam. 7:8–15; Ps. 89:28; Acts 13:34
4
k Cp. Jer. 30:9; Hos. 3:5
5
l Isa. 52:15; Eph. 2:11–12
6
m Heb. 3:7–15; cp. Mt. 25:11–13; Jn. 7:33–36
n Ps. 32:6; Isa. 49:8; cp. 2 Cor. 6:2
7
o Isa. 59:7; Zech. 8:17
8
p Cp. 1 Sam. 16:7
9
q Ps. 139:17–18
11
r Isa. 45:23
s Isa. 46:9–11

The mountains and the hills
Shall break forth into singing
before you,
And all the trees of the field
shall clap *their* hands.
13 Instead of the thorn shall come
up the cypress tree,
And instead of the brier shall
come up the myrtle tree;
And it shall be to the LORD for
a [a]name,
For an everlasting sign *that*
shall not be cut off."

Rewards for obedience to God

56 THUS says the LORD:
"Keep [b]justice, and do
righteousness,
For My [c]salvation *is* about to
come,
And My righteousness to be
revealed.
2 Blessed *is* the man *who* does
this,
And the son of man *who* lays
hold on it;
Who keeps from defiling the
Sabbath,
And keeps his hand from
doing any evil."
3 Do not let the son of the
foreigner
Who has [d]joined himself to the
LORD
Speak, saying,
"The LORD has utterly separated
me from His people";
Nor let the eunuch say,
"Here I am, a dry tree."
4 For thus says the LORD:
"To the eunuchs who keep My
Sabbaths,
And choose what pleases Me,
And hold fast My covenant,
5 Even to them I will give in My
house
And within My walls a place
and a name
Better than that of sons and
daughters;
I will give them* an
everlasting name
That shall not be cut off.
6 "Also the sons of the [e]foreigner
Who join themselves to the
LORD, to serve Him,
And to love the name of the
LORD, to be His [f]servants—
Everyone who keeps from
defiling the Sabbath,
And holds fast My covenant—

13
a Isa. 63:12, 14

CHAPTER 56
1
b Jer. 22:3
c Isa. 46:13; Mt. 3:2; 4:17; Rom. 13:11,12
3
d Isa. 14:1; 45:14
6
e Isa. 60:10
f Cp. Ruth 1:16
7
g Mt. 21:13; Mk. 11:17; Lk. 19:46
h Rom. 12:1; Heb. 13:15; 1 Pet. 2:5
i Isa. 60:7
8
j Ps. 147:2; Isa. 11:12; 27:12; 54:7
10
k Cp. Jer. 14:13–14
11
l Ezek. 34:2–10
12
m Isa. 28:7
n Isa. 22:13; Lk. 12:19; 1 Cor. 15:32; cp. Ps. 10:6; Prov. 23:35
o 2 Pet. 3:4

7 Even them I will bring to My
holy mountain,
And make them joyful in My
[g]house of prayer.
Their burnt offerings and their
[h]sacrifices
Will be [i]accepted on My altar;
For My house shall be called a
house of prayer for all
nations."
8 The Lord GOD, who [j]gathers
the outcasts of Israel, says,
"Yet I will gather to him
Others besides those who are
gathered to him."
9 All you beasts of the field,
come to devour,
All you beasts in the forest.
10 His watchmen *are* [k]blind,
They are all ignorant;
They *are* all dumb dogs,
They cannot bark;
Sleeping, lying down, loving to
slumber.
11 Yes, *they are* greedy dogs
Which never have enough.
And they *are* [l]shepherds
Who cannot understand;
They all look to their own
way,
Every one for his own gain,
From his *own* territory.
12 "Come," *one says,* "I will bring
wine,
And we will fill ourselves with
intoxicating [m]drink;
[n]Tomorrow will be [o]as today,
And much more abundant."

False leaders rebuked

57 THE righteous perishes,
And no man takes *it* to heart;
Merciful men *are* taken away,
While no one considers
That the righteous is taken
away from evil.
2 He shall enter into peace;
They shall rest in their beds,
Each one walking *in* his
uprightness.
3 "But come here,
You sons of the sorceress,
You offspring of the adulterer
and the harlot!
4 Whom do you ridicule?
Against whom do you make a
wide mouth
And stick out the tongue?
Are you not children of
transgression,

*56:5 Literally *him*

Offspring of falsehood,
5 Inflaming yourselves with gods
under every green tree,
[a]Slaying the children in the
valleys,
Under the clefts of the rocks?
6 Among the smooth [b]*stones* of
the stream
Is your portion;
They, they, *are* your lot!
Even to them you have poured
a drink offering,
You have offered a grain
offering.
Should I receive comfort in
[c]these?
7 "On a lofty and high mountain
You have set your bed;
Even there you went up
To offer sacrifice.
8 Also behind the doors and
their posts
You have set up your
remembrance;
For you have [d]uncovered
yourself *to those other* than
Me,
And have gone up to them;
You have enlarged your bed
And made *a covenant* with
them;
You have loved their bed,
Where you saw *their* nudity.*
9 You went to the king with
ointment,
And increased your perfumes;
You sent your [e]messengers far
off,
And *even* descended to [f]Sheol.
10 You are wearied in the length
of your way;
Yet you did not say, 'There is
[g]no hope.'
You have found the life of
your hand;
Therefore you were not
grieved.
11 "And of whom have you been
afraid, or [h]feared,
That you have lied
And not remembered Me,
Nor taken *it* to your heart?
[i]Is it not because I have held
My peace from of old
That you do not fear Me?
12 I will declare your
righteousness
And your works,
For they will not profit you.
13 When you cry out,
Let your collection *of idols*
deliver you.

CHAPTER 57

5
a Jer. 7:31; cp. 2 Ki. 23:10

6
b Jer. 3:9
c Jer. 5:9

8
d Ezek. 16:15

9
e Ezek. 23:16,40
f See Hab. 2:5, *note*; cp. Lk. 16:23, *note*

10
g Cp. Jer. 2:25

11
h Isa. 51:12–13
i Ps. 50:21; Eccl. 8:11

13
j See Ps. 2:12, *note*

14
k Isa. 62:10

15
l Job 6:10; Lk. 1:49
m Ps. 68:35; Zech. 2:13
n Ps. 34:18; 51:17; Isa. 66:2

16
o Ps. 85:5; 103:9; Mic. 7:18

17
p Jer. 6:13
q Isa. 59:2

18
r Jer. 3:22

19
s Heb. 13:15
t Acts 2:39; Eph. 2:17

20
u Job 15:20; Prov. 4:16; Jude 13

21
v Isa. 48:22

But the wind will carry them
all away,
A breath will take *them*.
But he who puts his [j]trust in
Me shall possess the land,
And shall inherit My holy
mountain."
14 And one shall say,
[k]"Heap it up! Heap it up!
Prepare the way,
Take the stumbling block out
of the way of My people."

Blessings of the contrite

15 For thus says the High and
Lofty One
Who inhabits eternity, whose
name *is* [l]Holy:
"I dwell in the high and holy
[m]*place*,
With him *who* has a [n]contrite
and humble spirit,
To revive the spirit of the
humble,
And to revive the heart of the
contrite ones.
16 For I will not contend [o]forever,
Nor will I always be angry;
For the spirit would fail before
Me,
And the souls *which* I have
made.
17 For the iniquity of his
[p]covetousness
I was angry and struck him;
I [q]hid and was angry,
And he went on backsliding in
the way of his heart.
18 I have seen his ways, and will
[r]heal him;
I will also lead him,
And restore comforts to him
And to his mourners.

19 "I create the [s]fruit of the lips:
Peace, peace to *him who is*
[t]far off and to *him who is*
near,"
Says the LORD,
"And I will heal him."
20 But the [u]wicked *are* like the
troubled sea,
When it cannot rest,
Whose waters cast up mire
and dirt.
21 [v]"*There is* no peace,"
Says my God, "for the wicked."

*57:8 Literally *hand,* a euphemism

VII. Concluding Exhortations and Prophecies, 58—66

Right and wrong fasting

58 "CRY aloud, spare not;
Lift up your voice like a trumpet;
[a]Tell My people their transgression,
And the house of Jacob their sins.
2 Yet they seek Me daily,
And delight to know My ways,
As a nation that did righteousness,
And did not forsake the ordinance of their God.
They ask of Me the ordinances of justice;
They take delight in approaching God.
3 'Why have we fasted,' [b]*they say*, 'and You have not seen?
Why have we afflicted our souls, and You take no notice?'

"In fact, in the day of your fast you find pleasure,
And exploit all your laborers.
4 [c]Indeed you fast for strife and debate,
And to strike with the fist of wickedness.
You will not fast as *you do* this day,
To make your voice heard on high.
5 Is it [d]a fast that I have chosen,
A day for a man to afflict his soul?
Is it to bow down his head like a bulrush,
And to spread out sackcloth and ashes?
Would you call this a fast,
And an acceptable day to the LORD?

6 "*Is* this not the fast that I have chosen:
To [e]loose the bonds of wickedness,
To [f]undo the heavy burdens,
To let the [g]oppressed go free,
And that you break every yoke?
7 *Is it* not to [h]share your bread with the hungry,
And that you bring to your house the poor who are cast out;
When you see the [i]naked, that you cover him,
And not hide yourself from your own [j]flesh?

Blessings on the charitable

8 Then your light shall break forth like the morning,
Your healing shall spring forth speedily,
And your righteousness shall go before you;
The [k]glory of the LORD shall be your rear guard.
9 Then you shall call, and the LORD will answer;
You shall cry, and He will say, 'Here I *am*.'

"If you take away the yoke from your midst,
The pointing of the [l]finger, and speaking wickedness,
10 *If* you extend your soul to the hungry
And satisfy the afflicted soul,
Then your light shall dawn in the darkness,
And your darkness shall *be* as the noonday.
11 The LORD will guide you continually,
And satisfy your soul in drought,
And strengthen your bones;
You shall be like a watered garden,
And like a spring of water, whose waters do not fail.
12 Those from among you
Shall build the old waste places;
You shall raise up the foundations of many generations;
And you shall be called the Repairer of the Breach,
The Restorer of Streets to Dwell In.

13 "If you turn away your foot from the [m]Sabbath,
From doing your pleasure on My holy day,
And call the Sabbath a delight,
The holy *day* of the LORD honorable,
And shall honor Him, not doing your own ways,
Nor finding your own pleasure,
Nor speaking *your own* words,
14 Then you shall delight yourself in the LORD;
And I will cause you to ride on the high hills of the earth,

CHAPTER 58

1 *a* Mic. 3:8
3 *b* Mal. 3:13–18
4 *c* Cp. 1 Ki. 21:9,12–13
5 *d* Zech. 7:5; cp. Est. 4:3; Dan. 9:3
6 *e* Lk. 4:18–19 *f* Cp. Neh. 5:1–13 *g* Jer. 34:9
7 *h* Ezek. 18:7,16; Mt. 25:35 *i* Job 31:19–22; Jas. 2:14–17; cp. Mt. 25:34–36 *j* Gen. 29:14; Neh. 5:5
8 *k* Isa. 52:12; cp. Ex. 14:19
9 *l* Cp. Prov. 6:13
13 *m* Isa. 56:2; Jer. 17:21–27

And feed you with the heritage
of Jacob your father.
The mouth of the LORD has
spoken."

The tragic nature of sin

59 BEHOLD, the LORD's hand is
not [a]shortened,
That it cannot save;
Nor His ear heavy,
That it cannot hear.
2 But your iniquities have
separated you from your
God;
And your sins have hidden *His*
face from you,
So that He will [b]not hear.
3 For your hands are defiled
with blood,
And your fingers with iniquity;
Your lips have spoken lies,
Your tongue has muttered
perversity.
4 No one calls for justice,
Nor does *any* plead for truth.
They [c]trust in [d]empty words
and speak lies;
They conceive evil and bring
forth iniquity.
5 They hatch vipers' eggs and
weave the spider's web;
He who eats of their eggs dies,
And *from* that which is
crushed a viper breaks out.
6 Their webs will not become
garments,
Nor will they cover themselves
with their works;
Their works *are* works of
iniquity,
And the act of violence *is* in
their hands.
7 Their [e]feet run to evil,
And they make haste to shed
[f]innocent blood;
Their [g]thoughts *are* thoughts
of iniquity;
Wasting and [h]destruction *are*
in their paths.
8 The way of [i]peace they have
not known,
And *there is* no justice in their
ways;
They have made themselves
crooked paths;
Whoever takes that way shall
not know peace.
9 Therefore justice is far from
us,
Nor does righteousness
overtake us;
We look for light, but there is
darkness!
For brightness, *but* we walk in
blackness!
10 We grope for the wall like the
blind,
And we grope as if *we had* no
eyes;
We stumble at noonday as at
twilight;
We are as dead *men* in
desolate places.
11 We all growl like bears,
And moan sadly like doves;
We look for justice, but *there
is* none;
For salvation, *but* it is far from
us.
12 For our [j]transgressions are
multiplied before You,
And our sins testify against us;
For our transgressions *are* with
us,
And *as for* our iniquities, we
know them:
13 In transgressing and lying
against the LORD,
And departing from our God,
Speaking oppression and
revolt,
Conceiving and uttering from
the heart words of
falsehood.
14 Justice is turned back,
And righteousness stands afar
off;
For truth is fallen in the street,
And equity cannot enter.
15 So truth fails,
And he *who* departs from evil
makes himself a [k]prey.

Then the LORD saw *it*, and it
displeased Him
That *there was* no justice.

God's search for a man; Christ the only Redeemer

16 He saw that *there was* no man,
And wondered that *there was*
[l]no intercessor;
Therefore His own arm
brought salvation for Him;
And His own righteousness, it
sustained Him.
17 [m]For He put on [n]righteousness
as a breastplate,
And a helmet of salvation on
His head;
He put on the garments of
vengeance for clothing,
And was clad with zeal as a
cloak.

CHAPTER 59

1 *a* Num. 11:23; Isa. 50:2

2 *b* Isa. 1:15

4 *c* See Ps. 2:12, *note*
d Isa. 30:12; Jer. 7:4,8

7 *e* Prov. 1:16; Rom. 3:15
f Prov. 6:17
g Isa. 55:7
h vv. 7–8; Rom. 3:16–17

8 *i* Isa. 57:20–21

12 *j* Isa. 24:5; 58:1

15 *k* Isa. 5:23; 10:2; 29:21; 32:7

16 *l* Isa. 63:5; 64:7; Ezek. 22:30

17 *m* Cp. Eph. 6:13–17
n *Righteousness* (garment): v. 17; Isa. 61:10. (Gen. 3:21; Rev. 19:8)

18 According to *their* [a]deeds,
accordingly He will repay,
Fury to His adversaries,
Recompense to His enemies;
The coastlands He will fully
repay.
19 So shall they [b]fear
The name of the LORD from the
west,
And His glory from the rising
of the sun;
When the enemy comes in like
a flood,
The [c]Spirit of the LORD will lift
up a standard against him.

20 "The [1d]Redeemer will [2]come to
[d]Zion,
And to those who turn from
transgression in Jacob,"
Says the LORD.

21 "As for Me," says the LORD, "this
is My covenant with them: My [c]Spirit
who *is* upon you, and My [e]words
which I have put in your mouth, shall
not depart from your mouth, nor from
the mouth of your descendants, nor
from the mouth of your descendants'
descendants," says the LORD, "from
this time and forevermore."

Glorious Zion in the Kingdom Age

60 ARISE, shine;
For your light has come!
And the glory of the LORD is
[f]risen upon you.
2 For behold, the darkness shall
cover the earth,
And deep darkness the people;
But the LORD will arise over
you,
And His [g]glory will be seen
upon you.
3 The Gentiles shall come to
your [h]light,
And kings to the brightness of
your rising.

4 "Lift up your eyes all around,
and see:
They all gather together, they
[i]come to you;
Your sons shall come from
afar,
And your daughters shall be
nursed at *your* side.
5 Then you shall see and become
radiant,
And your heart shall swell
with joy;
Because the [j]abundance of the
sea shall be turned to you,
The wealth of the Gentiles
shall come to you.
6 The multitude of camels shall
cover your *land,*
The dromedaries of Midian
and [k]Ephah;
All those from Sheba shall
come;
They shall bring gold and
incense,
And they shall proclaim the
praises of the LORD.
7 All the flocks of [l]Kedar shall
be gathered together to you,
The rams of Nebaioth shall
minister to you;
They shall ascend with
[m]acceptance on My altar,
And I will [n]glorify the house
of My glory.

8 "Who *are* these *who* fly like a
cloud,
And like doves to their roosts?
9 Surely the coastlands shall
wait for Me;
And the ships of Tarshish *will*
come first,
To [o]bring your sons from afar,
Their silver and their gold with
them,
To the name of the LORD your
God,
And to the Holy One of Israel,
Because He has glorified you.

18 *a* Rom. 2:6
19 *b* See Ps. 19:9, *note* *c Holy Spirit* (OT): vv. 19,21; Isa. 61:1. (Gen. 1:2; Zech. 12:10)
20 *d Redemption* (redeeming relative type): v. 20; Isa. 60:16. (Gen. 48:16; Isa. 59:20, *note*)
21 *e Inspiration:* vv. 19,21; Jer. 1:9. (Ex. 4:15; 2 Tim. 3:16, *note*)
CHAPTER 60
1 *f Israel* (prophecies): vv. 1–12; Jer. 23:3. (Gen. 12:2; Rom. 11:26, *note*)
2 *g* Isa. 4:5; cp. Rev. 21:23–24
3 *h* See Isa. 42:6, *note*
4 *i* Isa. 49:18
5 *j* Rom. 11:25–27
6 *k* Gen. 25:4
7 *l* Gen. 25:13 *m* Isa. 56:7 *n* Hag. 2:7,9
60:9 *o* Isa. 49:22

[1](59:20) Redemption, redeeming relative type, Summary: The *goel,* or redeeming relative, is a beautiful type of Christ:
(1) The redemption by a relative was of persons and an inheritance (Lev. 25:25,48; Gal. 4:5; Eph. 1:7,11,14).
(2) The redeemer must be a relative (Lev. 25:48–49; Ruth 3:12–13, see v. 9, *note;* Gal. 4:4; Heb. 2:14–15).
(3) The redeemer must be able to redeem (Ruth 4:4–6; Jer. 50:34; Jn. 10:11,18).
(4) Redemption is effected by the *goel* paying the just demand in full (Lev. 25:27; Gal. 3:13; 1 Pet. 1:18–19). See *notes* at Ex. 6:6 and Rom. 3:24.
[2](59:20) The time when the "Redeemer will come to Zion" is fixed, relatively, by Rom. 11:23–29, as following the completion of the Church. This is also the order of the great dispensational passage, Acts 15:14–17. In both, the return of the Lord to Zion follows the outcalling of the Church.

10 "The sons of [a]foreigners shall
build up your walls,
And their kings shall minister
to you;
For in My wrath I struck you,
But in My favor I have had
mercy on you.
11 Therefore your gates shall be
open continually;
They shall not be shut day or
night,
That *men* may bring to you the
wealth of the Gentiles,
And their kings in procession.
12 For the nation and kingdom
which will not serve you
shall perish,
And *those* nations shall be
utterly ruined.

13 "The glory of Lebanon shall
come to you,
The cypress, the pine, and the
box tree together,
To beautify the place of My
sanctuary;
And I will make [b]the place of
My feet glorious.
14 Also the sons of those who
afflicted you
Shall come [c]bowing to you,
And all those who despised
you shall fall prostrate at the
soles of your [b]feet;
And they shall call you The
City of the LORD,
Zion of the Holy One of Israel.

15 "Whereas you have been
forsaken and hated,
So that no one went through
you,
I will make you an eternal
excellence,
A joy of many generations.
16 You shall drink the milk of the
Gentiles,
And milk the breast of kings;
You shall know that I, the
LORD, *am* your Savior
And your [d]Redeemer, the
Mighty One of Jacob.

17 "Instead of bronze I will bring
gold,
Instead of iron I will bring
silver,
Instead of wood, bronze,
And instead of stones, iron.
I will also make your officers
peace,
And your magistrates
righteousness.
18 Violence shall no longer be
heard in your land,
Neither wasting nor
destruction within your
borders;
But you shall call your walls
Salvation,
And your gates Praise.

19 "The [e]sun shall no longer be
your light by day,
Nor for brightness shall the
moon give light to you;
But the LORD will be to you an
everlasting light,
And your God your [f]glory.
20 Your [g]sun shall no longer go
down,
Nor shall your moon withdraw
itself;
For the LORD will be your
everlasting light,
And the days of your
mourning shall be ended.
21 Also your [h]people *shall* all *be*
righteous;
They shall [i]inherit the land
forever,
The branch of My [j]planting,
The [k]work of My hands,
That I may be glorified.
22 A little one shall become a
thousand,
And a small one a strong
nation.
I, the LORD, will hasten it in its
time."

Christ's two advents in one view

61

"THE [l]Spirit of the Lord GOD
is [m]upon [n]Me,
Because the LORD has
[o]anointed Me
To preach good [p]tidings to the
poor;
He has sent Me to heal the
brokenhearted,
To proclaim liberty to the
captives,
And the opening of the prison
to *those who are* bound;
2 To proclaim the acceptable
[1]year of the LORD,

---

10 *a* Isa. 56:6; 61:5
13 *b* i.e. *the temple.* 1 Chr. 28:2; cp. Ps. 99:5; 132:7
14 *c* Isa. 45:14
16 *d Redemption* (redeeming relative type): v. 16; Isa. 63:9. (Gen. 48:16; Isa. 59:20, *note*)
19 *e* Rev. 21:23; 22:5 *f* Zech. 2:5
20 *g* Cp. Amos 8:9
21 *h* Isa. 52:1; Rev. 21:27 *i* Ps. 37:11, 22 *j* Isa. 61:3 *k* Isa. 29:23; 45:11; cp. Eph. 2:10
CHAPTER 61
1 *l Holy Spirit* (OT): v. 1; Isa. 63:10. (Gen. 1:2; Zech. 12:10) *m* Lk. 4:18–19 *n Christ* (first advent): vv. 1–2; Dan. 9:26. (Gen. 3:15; Acts 1:11, *note*) *o* Lk. 7:22; Acts 10:38 *p Gospel:* vv. 1–3; Mt. 3:1. (Gen. 12:3; Rev. 14:6)

---

[1](61:2) Observe that the Lord Jesus suspended the reading of this passage in the synagogue at Nazareth (Lk. 4:16–21) with the words "the acceptable year of the LORD." The first advent, therefore, opened the day of grace, "the acceptable year of the LORD," but does not fulfill the day of vengeance that will be accomplished when Messiah returns (2 Th. 1:7–10). Cp. Isa. 34:8; 35:4.

And the [a]day of vengeance of
our God;
To comfort all who mourn,
3 To console those who mourn
in Zion,
To give them beauty for ashes,
The oil of joy for mourning,
The garment of praise for the
spirit of heaviness;
That they may be called trees
of righteousness,
The planting of the LORD, that
He may be glorified."

Israel's primacy in the kingdom

4 And they shall rebuild the old
ruins,
They shall raise up the former
desolations,
And they shall repair the
ruined cities,
The desolations of many
generations.
5 Strangers shall stand and feed
your flocks,
And the sons of the foreigner
Shall be your plowmen and
your vinedressers.
6 But you shall be named the
priests of the LORD,
They shall call you the
servants of our God.
You shall eat the riches of the
Gentiles,
And in their glory you shall
boast.
7 Instead of your shame *you
shall have* double *honor*,
And *instead of* confusion they
shall rejoice in their portion.
Therefore in their land they
shall possess double;
Everlasting joy shall be theirs.
8 "For I, the LORD, love justice;
I hate robbery for burnt
offering;
I will direct their work in truth,
And will make with them an
everlasting [b]covenant.
9 Their descendants shall be
known among the Gentiles,
And their offspring among the
people.
All who see them shall
acknowledge them,
That they *are* the posterity
whom the LORD has blessed."
10 I will greatly rejoice in the
LORD,
My soul shall be joyful in my
God;
For He has clothed me with
the garments of salvation,
He has covered me with the
[c]robe of righteousness,
As a bridegroom decks *himself*
with ornaments,
And as a bride adorns *herself*
with her jewels.
11 For as the earth brings forth
its bud,
As the garden causes the
things that are sown in it to
spring forth,
So the Lord GOD will cause
righteousness and praise to
spring forth before all the
nations.

Divine unrest until Israel restored

62

FOR Zion's sake I will not
hold My peace,
And for Jerusalem's sake I will
not rest,
Until her righteousness goes
forth as brightness,
And her salvation as a lamp
that burns.
2 The Gentiles shall see your
righteousness,
And all [d]kings your glory.
You shall be called by a new
[e]name,
Which the mouth of the LORD
will name.
3 You shall also be a [f]crown of
glory
In the hand of the LORD,
And a royal diadem
In the hand of your God.
4 [g]You shall no longer be termed
Forsaken,
Nor shall your land any more
be termed Desolate;
But you shall be called
[h]Hephzibah,* and your land
[i]Beulah;*
For the LORD delights in you,
And your land shall be
married.
5 For *as* a young man marries a
virgin,
So shall your sons marry you;
And *as* the bridegroom rejoices
over the bride,
So shall your God rejoice over
you.

6 I have set [j]watchmen on your
walls, O Jerusalem;
They shall never hold their
peace day or night.

*62:4 Literally *My Delight Is in Her* • Literally *Married*

2
a *Day* (of destruction): v. 2; Isa. 63:4. (Job 21:30; Rev. 20:11)
8
b *Covenant* (New): v. 8; Jer. 31:31. (Isa. 61:8; Heb. 8:8, *note*)
10
c *Righteousness* (garment): v. 10; Isa. 64:6. (Gen. 3:21; Rev. 19:8)
CHAPTER 62
2
d Ps. 102:15–16; 138:4–5; 148:11,13
e vv. 4,12; Isa. 65:15; cp. Rev. 2:17
3
f Zech. 9:16
4
g Hos. 1:10; 1 Pet. 2:10
h Lit. *My delight is in her*
i Lit. *Married.* Cp. Isa. 54:5
6
j Ezek. 3:17; 33:7

You who make mention of the LORD, do not keep silent,
7 And give Him no rest till He establishes
And till He makes Jerusalem a praise in the earth.
8 The LORD has sworn by His right hand
And by the arm of His strength:
"Surely I will no longer give your grain
As food for your enemies;
And the sons of the foreigner shall not drink your new wine,
For which you have [a]labored.
9 But those who have gathered it shall eat it,
And praise the LORD;
Those who have brought it together shall drink it in My holy courts."

10 Go through,
Go through the gates!
Prepare the way for the people;
Build up,
Build up the highway!
Take out the stones,
Lift up a [b]banner for the peoples!
11 Indeed the LORD has proclaimed
To the end of the [c]world:
"Say to the daughter of Zion,
'Surely your [d]salvation is coming;
Behold, His reward *is* with Him,
And His work before Him.' "
12 And they shall call them The Holy People,
The Redeemed of the LORD;
And you shall be called Sought Out,
A City Not Forsaken.

The day of Messiah's vengeance (cp. Isa. 2:10–22; Rev. 19:11–21)

63 [e]WHO *is* this who comes from Edom,
With dyed garments from Bozrah,
This *One who is* glorious in His apparel,
Traveling in the greatness of His strength?—
"I who speak in righteousness, mighty to save."
2 Why *is* Your apparel [f]red,
And Your garments like one who treads in the winepress?
3 "I have trodden the winepress alone,
And from the peoples no one *was* with Me.
For I have [g]trodden them in My anger,
And trampled them in My fury;
Their blood is sprinkled upon My garments,
And I have stained all My robes.
4 For the [h]day of vengeance *is* in My heart,
And the year of My redeemed has come.
5 I looked, but *there was* [i]no one to help,
And I wondered
That *there was* no one to uphold;
Therefore My own arm brought salvation for Me;
And My own fury, it sustained Me.
6 I have trodden down the peoples in My anger,
Made them drunk in My fury,
And brought down their strength to the earth."

Isaiah's concern and confession for his people

7 I will mention the lovingkindnesses of the LORD
And the praises of the LORD,
According to all that the LORD has bestowed on us,
And the great goodness toward the house of Israel,
Which He has bestowed on them according to His mercies,
According to the multitude of His lovingkindnesses.
8 For He said, "Surely they *are* My people,
Children *who* will not lie."
So He became their Savior.
9 In all their affliction He was [j]afflicted,
And the [k]Angel of His Presence saved them;
In His love and in His pity He [l]redeemed them;
And He bore them and carried them
All the days of old.

8
a Cp. Lev. 26:16; Dt. 28:31; Isa. 1:7; 65:21–22
10
b *Kingdom* (OT): vv. 10–12; Isa. 65:25. (Gen. 1:26; Zech. 12:8, *note*)
11
c Ps. 22:27
d Isa. 46:13; cp. Zech. 9:9; Mt. 21:5; Jn. 12:15
CHAPTER 63
1
e *Day* (of the LORD): vv. 1–6; Isa. 66:15. (Ps. 2:9; Rev. 19:19)
2
f Cp. v. 3; the blood of his enemies
3
g *Armageddon* (battle of): vv. 1–6; Isa. 66:16. (Isa. 10:27; Rev. 19:17). See Gen. 36:1, *note*
4
h *Day* (of destruction): vv. 1–4; Mt. 25:46. (Job 21:30; Rev. 20:11)
5
i Isa. 59:16
9
j Cp. Jud. 10:16; Acts 9:5
k *Angel* (of the LORD): v. 9; Zech. 1:11. (Gen. 16:7; Jud. 2:1, *note*)
l *Redemption* (redeeming relative type): vv. 4,9,16; Jer. 31:11. (Gen. 48:16; Isa. 59:20, *note*)

10 But they [a]rebelled and grieved
His [b]Holy Spirit;
So He [c]turned Himself against
them as an enemy,
And He fought against them.

11 Then he [d]remembered the
days of old,
Moses *and* his people, *saying:*
"Where *is* He who brought
them up out of the sea
With the shepherd of His
flock?
Where *is* He who put His Holy
Spirit within them,
12 Who led *them* by the right
hand of Moses,
With His glorious arm,
[e]Dividing the water before them
To make for Himself an
everlasting name,
13 Who led them through the
deep,
As a horse in the wilderness,
That they might not stumble?"
14 As a beast goes down into the
valley,
And the Spirit of the LORD
causes him to [f]rest,
So You lead Your people,
To make Yourself a glorious
name.

15 Look down from heaven,
And see from Your habitation,
holy and glorious.
Where *are* Your zeal and Your
strength,
The yearning of Your heart
and Your mercies toward
me?
Are they restrained?
16 Doubtless You *are* our [1]Father,
Though Abraham was ignorant
of us,
And Israel does not
acknowledge us.
You, O LORD, *are* our Father;
Our Redeemer from
Everlasting *is* Your name.
17 O LORD, why have You [g]made
us stray from Your ways,
And hardened our heart from
Your [h]fear?
Return for Your servants' sake,
The tribes of Your inheritance.

10 *a* Num. 14:11; Ps. 78:40; cp. Acts 7:51; 1 Cor. 10:1–11
b Holy Spirit (OT): v. 10; Ezek. 2:2. (Gen. 1:2; Zech. 12:10)
c Ps. 106:40
11 *d* Ps. 106:44
12 *e* Ex. 14:21–22
14 *f* Cp. Ex. 33:14
17 *g* Isa. 6:9–10; Jn. 12:40
h See Ps. 19:9, *note*
CHAPTER 64
1 *i* Mic. 1:3–4
4 *j* Cp. Isa. 65:17; Jn. 14:2; 1 Cor. 2:9; Rev. 21:1
6 *k Righteousness* (garment): v. 6; Mt. 6:33. (Gen. 3:21; Rev. 19:8)

18 Your holy people have
possessed *it* but a little
while;
Our adversaries have trodden
down Your sanctuary.
19 We have become *like* those of
old, over whom You never
ruled,
Those who were never called
by Your name.

The remnant's prayer for deliverance at the return of Christ

64 OH, that You would rend the
heavens!
That You would come down!
That the mountains might
shake at Your [i]presence—
2 As fire burns brushwood,
As fire causes water to boil—
To make Your name known to
Your adversaries,
That the nations may tremble
at Your presence!
3 When You did awesome things
for which we did not look,
You came down,
The mountains shook at Your
presence.
4 For since the beginning of the
world
Men have not heard nor
perceived by the ear,
Nor has the eye seen any God
besides You,
[j]Who acts for the one who
waits for Him.
5 You meet him who rejoices
and does righteousness,
Who remembers You in Your
ways.
You are indeed angry, for we
have sinned—
In these ways we continue;
And we need to be saved.
6 But we are all like an unclean
thing,
And all [k]our righteousnesses
are like filthy rags;
We all fade as a leaf,
And our iniquities, like the
wind,
Have taken us away.

[1](63:16) Compare Isa. 1:2; 64:8. Israel collectively, the national Israel, recognizes God as the national Father (cp. Ex. 4:22–23). Doubtless the believing Israelite was born anew (cp. Jn. 3:3,5 with Lk. 13:28), but the OT Scriptures show no trace of the consciousness of personal sonship. The explanation is given in Gal. 4:1–7. The Israelite, though a child, "does not differ at all from a slave." The Spirit, as the "Spirit of His Son," could not be given to impart the consciousness of sonship until redemption had been accomplished (Gal. 4:4–6). See Adoption (Rom. 8:15; Eph. 1:5, *note*).

7 And *there is* no one who calls
on Your name,
Who stirs himself up to take
hold of You;
For You have hidden Your
face from us,
And have consumed us
because of our iniquities.

8 But now, O LORD,
You *are* our [a]Father;
We *are* the clay, and You our
[b]potter;
And all we *are* the work of
Your hand.
9 Do not be furious, O LORD,
Nor remember iniquity forever;
Indeed, please look—we all *are*
Your people!
10 Your holy cities are a
wilderness,
Zion is a wilderness,
Jerusalem a desolation.
11 Our holy and beautiful temple,
Where our fathers praised
You,
Is burned up with fire;
And all our pleasant things are
laid waste.
12 Will You restrain Yourself
because of these *things*, O
LORD?
Will You hold Your peace, and
afflict us very severely?

The LORD's answer:
no return until repentance

65 "I WAS sought by *those who*
did not ask *for Me;*
I was found by *those who* [c]did
not seek Me.
I said, 'Here I am, here I am,'
To a nation *that* was not
called by My name.
2 I have [d]stretched out My
hands all day long to a
[e]rebellious people,
Who [f]walk in a way *that is*
not good,
According to their own
thoughts;
3 A people who [g]provoke Me to
anger continually to My
face;
Who sacrifice in gardens,
And burn incense on altars of
brick;
4 Who sit among the graves,
And spend the night in the
tombs;
Who eat [h]swine's flesh,
And the broth of abominable
things is *in* their vessels;

8
a See Isa. 63:16, *note*
b Isa. 29:16; 45:9; Jer. 18:6; Rom. 9:20–21
CHAPTER 65
1
c Rom. 10:20
2
d Rom. 10:21
e Isa. 1:2,23
f Isa. 42:24
3
g Dt. 32:21
4
h Lev. 11:7; Isa. 66:17
5
i Cp. Lk. 18:9–12
7
j Ex. 20:5
k Ezek. 18:6
l Isa. 57:7; Ezek. 20:27–28
8
m Isa. 1:9; Amos 9:8–9
9
n vv. 15,22; cp. Mt. 24:22; Rom. 11:1–12
10
o Isa. 33:9; 35:2
p Josh. 7:24,26; Hos. 2:15
q Isa. 55:6
12
r 2 Chr. 36:15–16; Isa. 50:2; 66:4

5 Who say, 'Keep to yourself,
Do not come near me,
For I am [i]holier than you!'
These *are* smoke in My
nostrils,
A fire that burns all the day.
6 "Behold, *it is* written before Me:
I will not keep silence, but will
repay—
Even repay into their bosom—
7 Your iniquities and the
[j]iniquities of your fathers
together,"
Says the LORD,
"Who have burned incense on
the [k]mountains
And [l]blasphemed Me on the
hills;
Therefore I will measure their
former work into their
bosom."

8 Thus says the LORD:
"As the new wine is found in
the cluster,
And *one* says, 'Do not destroy
it,
For a blessing *is* in it,'
So will I do for My servants'
sake,
That I may not destroy them
[m]all.
9 I will bring forth descendants
from Jacob,
And from Judah an heir of My
mountains;
My [n]elect shall inherit it,
And My servants shall dwell
there.
10 [o]Sharon shall be a fold of
flocks,
And the [p]Valley of Achor a
place for herds to lie down,
For My people who have
[q]sought Me.
11 "But you *are* those who forsake
the LORD,
Who forget My holy mountain,
Who prepare a table for Gad,*
And who furnish a drink
offering for Meni.*
12 Therefore I will number you
for the sword,
And you shall all bow down to
the slaughter;
Because, when I called, you
did [r]not answer;
When I spoke, you did not
hear,

*65:11 Literally *Troop* or *Fortune*, a pagan deity
• Literally *Number* or *Destiny*, a pagan deity

But did evil before My eyes,
And chose *that* in which I do not delight."

13 Therefore thus says the Lord GOD:

"Behold, My servants shall eat,
But you shall be hungry;
Behold, My servants shall drink,
But you shall be thirsty;
Behold, My servants shall rejoice,
But you shall be ashamed;
14 Behold, My servants shall sing for joy of heart,
But you shall cry for sorrow of heart,
And wail for grief of spirit.
15 You shall leave your name as a [a]curse to My chosen;
For the Lord GOD will slay you,
And [b]call His servants by another name;
16 So that he who blesses himself in the earth
Shall bless himself in the God of truth;
And he who swears in the earth
Shall swear by the God of truth;
Because the former troubles are [c]forgotten,
And because they are hidden from My eyes.

New heavens and new earth

17 "For [1]behold, I [d]create new heavens and a new earth;
And the former shall not be remembered or come to mind.

Millennial conditions in the renewed earth with curse removed

18 But be glad and rejoice forever in what I create;
For behold, I create Jerusalem *as* a rejoicing,
And her people a joy.
19 I will [e]rejoice in Jerusalem,
And joy in My people;
The voice of [f]weeping shall no longer be heard in her,
Nor the voice of crying.
20 "No more shall an infant from there *live but a few* days,
Nor an old man who has not fulfilled his days;
For the child shall die one hundred years old,
But the sinner *being* one hundred years old shall be accursed.
21 [g]They shall build houses and inhabit *them;*
They shall plant vineyards and eat their fruit.
22 They shall not build and another inhabit;
They shall not plant and [h]another eat;
For as the days of a [i]tree, *so shall be* the days of My people,
And My elect shall long enjoy the work of their hands.
23 They shall not labor in vain,
Nor bring forth children for trouble;
For they *shall be* the descendants of the blessed of the LORD,
And their offspring with them.
24 "It shall come to pass
That before they call, I will [j]answer;
And while they are still speaking, I will [k]hear.
25 The wolf and the lamb shall feed together,
The lion shall eat straw like the ox,
And dust *shall be* the serpent's food.
They shall not [l]hurt nor destroy in all My holy [m]mountain,"
Says the LORD.

The LORD, whose throne is in heaven, rebukes hypocrisy

66 THUS says the LORD:
[n]"Heaven *is* My throne,
And earth *is* My footstool.
Where *is* the house that you will build Me?
And where *is* the place of My rest?
2 For all those *things* My hand has made,
And all those *things* exist,"
Says the LORD.
"But on this *one* will I look:

15
a Jer. 29:22; Zech. 8:13
b Isa. 62:2; cp. Acts 11:26
16
c Cp. Rev. 21:4
17
d Isa. 51:16; 66:22; 2 Pet. 3:13; Rev. 21:1
19
e Isa. 62:4–5
f Isa. 35:10; 51:11; Rev. 7:17; 21:4
21
g Ezek. 28:26; 45:4; Hos. 11:11; Amos 9:14
22
h Isa. 62:8–9
i Cp. Ps. 92:12–14
24
j Isa. 58:9
k Isa. 30:19; Dan. 9:20–23
25
l Isa. 11:6–9
m Kingdom (OT): vv. 18–25; Jer. 23:5. (Gen. 1:26; Zech. 12:8, *note*)
CHAPTER 66
1
n vv. 1–2; Acts 7:49–50; 17:24

[1](65:17) Verse 17 looks beyond the Kingdom Age to the new heavens and the new earth (see *marg.* at "create"), but vv. 18–25 describe the Kingdom Age itself. Longevity will be restored, but death, the "last enemy" (1 Cor. 15:26), will not be destroyed until after Satan's rebellion at the end of the thousand years (Rev. 20:7–14).

[a]On *him who is* poor and of a
contrite spirit,
And who trembles at My word.

3 "He who kills a bull *is as if* he
slays a man;
He who [b]sacrifices a lamb, *as
if* he breaks a dog's neck;
He who offers a grain offering,
as if he offers swine's blood;
He who burns incense, *as if* he
blesses an idol.
Just as they have chosen their
own ways,
And their soul delights in their
abominations,
4 So will I choose their
delusions,
And bring their fears on them;
Because, when I called, [c]no
one answered,
When I spoke they did not
hear;
But they did evil before My
eyes,
And chose *that* in which I do
not delight."
5 Hear the word of the LORD,
You who tremble at His word:
"Your brethren who [d]hated
you,
Who cast you out for My
name's sake, said,
'Let the LORD be [e]glorified,
That we may see your joy.'
But they shall be ashamed."
6 The sound of noise from the
city!
A voice from the temple!
The voice of the LORD,
Who fully repays His enemies!

Israel reborn in a day

7 [1]"Before she [f]was in labor, she
gave birth;
Before her pain came,
She delivered a male child.
8 Who has heard such a thing?
Who has seen such things?
Shall the earth be made to give
birth in one day?
Or shall a nation be born at
once?
For as soon as Zion was in
labor,
She gave birth to her children.
9 Shall I bring to the time of
birth, and not cause
delivery?" says the LORD.
"Shall I who cause delivery shut
up *the womb?*" says your
God.

Joy in Jerusalem in the kingdom

10 "Rejoice with Jerusalem,
And be glad with her, all you
who love her;
Rejoice for joy with her, all
you who mourn for her;
11 That you may feed and be
satisfied
With the consolation of her
bosom,
That you may drink deeply
and be delighted
With the abundance of her
glory."

12 For thus says the LORD:
"Behold, I will extend [g]peace to
her like a river,
And the glory of the [h]Gentiles
like a flowing stream.
Then you shall feed;
On *her* sides shall you be
carried,
And be dandled on *her* knees.
13 As one whom his mother
comforts,
So I will [i]comfort you;
And you shall be comforted in
Jerusalem."

14 When you see *this,* your heart
shall rejoice,
And your [j]bones shall flourish
like grass;
The hand of the LORD shall be
known to His servants,
And *His* indignation to His
enemies.
15 For behold, the LORD will come
with [k]fire
And with His chariots, like a
whirlwind,
To [l]render His anger with
fury,
And His rebuke with flames of
fire.
16 For by fire and by His [m]sword
The LORD will judge all flesh;
And the slain of the LORD shall
be [n]many.

2
a Ps. 34:18; 51:17; Isa. 57:15
3
b Isa. 1:10–17; 58:1–5; Mic. 6:7–8
4
c Isa. 65:12
5
d Isa. 60:15; cp. Lk. 6:22
e 2 Th. 1:10; Ti. 2:13
7
f vv. 7–8; see Mic. 4:11, *note*
12
g Isa. 48:18
h Isa. 61:6
13
i Isa. 51:3
14
j See Ezek. 37:1, *note*
15
k Isa. 9:5; 2 Th. 1:8
l Day (of the LORD): vv. 15–24; Jer. 25:29. (Ps. 2:9; Rev. 19:19)
16
m Armageddon (battle of): vv. 15–16; Jer. 25:29. (Isa. 10:27; Rev. 19:17)
n Isa. 34:6

[1](66:7) "Who has heard such a thing?" (v. 8). Here is something contrary to nature in that it is a supernatural plan of God. The time of Israel's labor is "the time of Jacob's trouble" (Jer. 30:7), the tribulation. Christ, a "male child," was born historically long before that time of pain (as prophesied in v. 7). But when Israel's time of labor arrives, a repentant remnant of Israel, "a nation," will be born "in one day" at the Lord's return to the earth.

17 "Those who sanctify themselves
and purify themselves,
To go to the gardens
After an *idol* in the midst,
Eating swine's flesh and the
abomination and the mouse,
Shall be [a]consumed together,"
says the LORD.

18 "For I *know* their works and
their [b]thoughts. It shall be that I will
[c]gather all nations and tongues; and
they shall come and see My glory.
19 "I will set a sign among them;
and those among them who escape I
will send to the nations: *to* Tarshish
and Pul* and Lud, who draw the bow,
and Tubal and Javan, *to* the coastlands afar off who have not heard My
fame nor seen My glory. And they
shall declare My [d]glory among the
Gentiles.
20 "Then they shall [e]bring all your
brethren for an [f]offering to the LORD
out of all nations, on horses and in
chariots and in litters, on mules and
on camels, to My holy mountain Jerusalem," says the LORD, "as the children
of Israel bring an offering in a clean
vessel into the house of the LORD.
21 "And I will also take some of
them for [g]priests *and* Levites," says
the LORD.

Forever in God's presence

22 "For as the [h]new heavens and
the new earth
Which I will make shall
remain before Me," says the
LORD,
"So shall your descendants and
your name remain.
23 And it shall come to pass
That from one New Moon to
another,
And from one Sabbath to
another,
All [i]flesh shall come to
worship before Me," says the
LORD.
24 "And they shall go forth and
look
Upon the corpses of the men
Who have transgressed against
Me.
For their [j]worm does not die,
And their fire is not quenched.
They shall be an abhorrence to
all flesh."

17 [a] Isa. 65:3–8
18 [b] Isa. 59:7 [c] Jer. 3:17
19 [d] Mal. 1:11
20 [e] Isa. 49:22 [f] Isa. 18:7
21 [g] Isa. 61:6
22 [h] Isa. 65:17; 2 Pet. 3:13; Rev. 21:1
23 [i] Zech. 14:17–21
24 [j] Mk. 9:44

*66:19 Following Masoretic Text and Targum; Septuagint reads *Put* (compare Jeremiah 46:9).

The Book of

JEREMIAH

Author: Jeremiah *Theme:* Warning and Judgment *Date of writing:* 7th Cent. B.C.

JEREMIAH (the meaning of his name is uncertain) was a young priest of Anathoth when he began to prophesy. Because of the intensely personal nature of his book, his character and life are better known to us than those of any of the other writing prophets. Sometimes called "the weeping prophet," Jeremiah was a devoted patriot, wholly committed to God and to holiness. Persecuted by his own people for his bold proclamation of the unwelcome truth about the impending captivity (19:14—20:18; chs. 37—38), he never lost his compassion for them.

Jeremiah's call came in the thirteenth year of King Josiah, 626 B.C. Zephaniah and Habakkuk were contemporaries of his earlier ministry; Daniel, of his later. His earlier prophecies, uttered during the last years of Jerusalem, were chiefly warnings to the people that unless they repented of their sins their city would be destroyed. After the fall of Jerusalem in 586 B.C., Jeremiah was given the choice by Nebuchadnezzar of either going to Babylon or staying with the poor remnant (2 Ki. 24:14) of his own people. He chose to stay and minister to the remnant. Following the murder of Gedaliah (41:7ff.), he advised his people to remain in the land, but they went to Egypt, taking Jeremiah and Baruch (43:6,7) with them. While there, Jeremiah still sought to turn the remnant back to the LORD (ch. 44). He also predicted Israel's return to the land in the end time (e.g. 23:5–8). Jeremiah probably died in Egypt.

The book may be divided as follows:

I. Prophecies of Judgment on Judah, 1—45.
II. Prophecies concerning Foreign Nations, 46—51.
III. Historical Supplement, 52.

I. Prophecies of Judgment on Judah, 1—45

Jeremiah's call and commission

1 [a]THE words of Jeremiah the son
of Hilkiah, of the [b]priests who
were in [c]Anathoth in the land of Benjamin,
2 to whom the word of the LORD
came in the days of [d]Josiah the son of
Amon, king of Judah, in the thirteenth
year of his reign.
3 It came also in the days of [e]Jehoiakim the son of Josiah, king of Judah, until the end of the eleventh year
of [f]Zedekiah the son of Josiah, king
of Judah, until the carrying away of
Jerusalem captive in the [g]fifth month.
4 Then the word of the LORD came
to me, saying:

5 "Before I formed you in the
[h]womb I knew you;
Before you were born I
[i]sanctified you;
I ordained you a prophet to the
nations."

6 Then said I:

"Ah, Lord GOD!
Behold, [j]I cannot speak, for I
am a youth."

7 But the LORD said to me:
"Do not say, 'I *am* a youth,'
For you shall go to all to
whom I send you,
And whatever I command you,
you shall speak.
8 Do not be afraid of their
[k]faces,
[l]For I *am* with you to deliver
you," says the LORD.

9 Then the LORD put forth His
[m]hand and touched my mouth, and the
LORD said to me:

"Behold, I have put My [n]words
in your mouth.
10 See, I have this day set you
over the nations and over
the kingdoms,
To root out and to pull down,
To destroy and to throw down,
To build and to plant."

Signs confirming Jeremiah's call

11 Moreover the word of the LORD
came to me, saying, "Jeremiah, what
do you see?" And I said, "I see a
[o]branch of an [1]almond tree."

CHAPTER 1
1
a c.626–c. 580 B.C.
b Cp. 1 Ki. 2:26
c Jer. 29:27
2
d 2 Ki. 21:24
3
e 2 Ki. 23:34
f See Lev. 23:2, *note*
g 2 Ki. 24:17
5
h Cp. Isa. 49:5; Gal. 1:15
i Sanctification (OT): v. 5; Dan. 4:13. (Gen. 2:3; Zech. 8:3)
6
j Cp. Ex. 4:10–12
8
k Ezek. 2:6
l Cp. Ex. 3:12; Dt. 31:6,8; Josh. 1:5
9
m Cp. Ezek. 40:3–4, a theophany. See Gen. 12:7, *note* *n Inspiration:* v. 9; Jer. 30:2. (Ex. 4:15; 2 Tim. 3:16, *note*) 1:11 *o* See Num. 17:8, *note*

---

[1](1:11) Because it flowers earlier than other trees, the almond (sounds like Hebrew for *the watcher*) signifies the near fulfillment of God's purposed judgment (v. 10).

12 Then the LORD said to me, "You
have seen well, for I am ready to perform My word."
13 And the word of the LORD came
to me the second time, saying, "What
do you see?" And I said, "I see a [1][a]boil-
ing pot, and it is facing away from the
north."
14 Then the LORD said to me:

"Out of the north calamity shall
break forth
On all the inhabitants of the
land.
15 For behold, I am [b]calling
All the families of the
kingdoms of the north," says
the LORD;
"They shall come and each one
set his throne
At the entrance of the [c]gates
of Jerusalem,
Against all its walls all around,
And against all the cities of
Judah.
16 I will utter My judgments
Against them concerning all
their wickedness,
[d]Because they have forsaken
Me,
Burned [e]incense to other gods,
And worshiped the works of
their own [f]hands.
17 "Therefore prepare yourself and
arise,
And speak to them all that I
command you.
Do not be dismayed before
their faces,
Lest I dismay you before them.
18 For behold, I have made you
this day
A [g]fortified city and an iron
pillar,
And bronze walls against the
whole land—
Against the kings of Judah,
Against its princes,
Against its priests,
And against the people of the
land.
19 They will fight against you,
But they shall not prevail
against you.
For I *am* with you," says the
LORD, "to deliver you."

13
a Ezek. 11:3,7; 24:3–14
15
b Jer. 25:9
c Jer. 39:3
16
d Dt. 28:20; Jer. 17:13
e Isa. 65:3–4; Jer. 7:9
f Isa. 37:19; Jer. 2:28
18
g Isa. 50:7; Jer. 6:27; 15:20
CHAPTER 2
2
h Ezek. 16:8; cp. Ezek. 16:22,43, 60; 23:1–21
i Dt. 2:7
3
j Ex. 19:5–6
k Gen. 12:3; Isa. 41:11; Jer. 30:15–16
5
l Isa. 5:4; Mic. 6:3
6
m Isa. 63:9, 11–13; Hos. 13:4
7
n Lit. *the land of Carmel.* Num. 13:27; 14:7–8; Dt. 8:7–9
o Isa. 24:5; Jer. 3:1
8
p Cp. Mal. 2:1–9
q Lit. *shepherds*

First message to apostate Judah: entreaty and warning (2:1—3:5)

2 MOREOVER the [2]word of the
LORD came to me, saying,
2 "Go and cry in the hearing of Jerusalem, saying, 'Thus says the LORD:

"I remember you,
The kindness of your [h]youth,
The love of your betrothal,
When you [i]went after Me in
the wilderness,
In a land not sown.
3 [j]Israel *was* holiness to the LORD,
The firstfruits of His increase.
All that devour him will
offend;
Disaster will [k]come upon
them," says the LORD.'"

4 Hear the word of the LORD, O
house of Jacob and all the families of
the house of Israel.
5 Thus says the LORD:

[l]"What injustice have your
fathers found in Me,
That they have gone far from
Me,
Have followed idols,
And have become idolaters?
6 Neither did they say, 'Where *is*
the LORD,
Who [m]brought us up out of the
land of Egypt,
Who led us through the
wilderness,
Through a land of deserts and
pits,
Through a land of drought and
the shadow of death,
Through a land that no one
crossed
And where no one dwelt?'
7 I brought you into [n]a bountiful
country,
To eat its fruit and its
goodness.
But when you entered, you
[o]defiled My land
And made My heritage an
abomination.
8 The priests did not say, 'Where
is the LORD?'
And those who handle the law
did [p]not know Me;
The [q]rulers also transgressed
against Me;

[1](1:13) The boiling pot symbolizes a raging conflict which was to descend upon the land from the north, i.e. the Babylonian invasion.
[2](2:1) The general character of the first message to Judah is threefold: the LORD (1) reminds Israel of the days of blessing and deliverance, e.g. 2:1–7; (2) reproaches them with forsaking Him, e.g. 2:13; and (3) accuses them of choosing other, and impotent, gods, e.g. 2:10–12, 26–28.

The prophets prophesied by Baal,
And walked after *things that* do not profit.

9 "Therefore I will yet [a]bring charges against you," says the LORD,
"And against your children's children I will bring charges.
10 For pass beyond the coasts of Cyprus* and see,
Send to Kedar* and consider diligently,
And see if there has been such *a* [b]*thing.*
11 Has a nation changed *its* gods,
Which *are* not gods?
But My people have changed their Glory
For *what* does not profit.
12 Be astonished, O heavens, at this,
And be horribly afraid;
Be very desolate," says the LORD.
13 "For My people have committed two evils:
They have forsaken Me, the [c]fountain of living waters,
And hewn themselves cisterns—broken cisterns that can hold no water.

14 "*Is* Israel a servant?
Is he a homeborn *slave*?
Why is he plundered?
15 The young lions roared at him, *and* growled;
They made his land waste;
His cities are burned, without inhabitant.
16 Also the people of Noph* and [d]Tahpanhes
Have broken the crown of your head.
17 Have you not brought this on yourself,
In that you have forsaken the LORD your God
When He [e]led you in the way?
18 And now why take the road to [f]Egypt,
To drink the waters of [g]Sihor?
Or why take the road to [h]Assyria,
To drink the waters of the [i]River?
19 Your own wickedness will [j]correct you,
And your backslidings will rebuke you.
Know therefore and see that *it is* an evil and bitter *thing*
That you have forsaken the LORD your God,
And the fear of Me *is* not in you,"
Says the Lord GOD of hosts.

20 "For of old I have [k]broken your yoke *and* burst your bonds;
And you [l]said, 'I will not transgress,'
When [m]on every high hill and under every green tree
You lay down, playing the harlot.
21 Yet I had planted you a noble [n]vine, a seed of highest quality.
How then have you turned before Me
Into the [o]degenerate plant of an [p]alien vine?
22 For though you wash yourself with lye, and use much soap,
Yet your iniquity is [q]marked before Me," says the Lord GOD.

23 "How can you say, 'I am [r]not polluted,
I have not gone after the Baals'?
See your way in the valley;
Know what you have done:
You are a swift dromedary breaking loose in her ways,
24 A wild donkey used to the wilderness,
That sniffs at the wind in her desire;
In her time of mating, who can turn her away?
All those who seek her will not weary themselves;
In her month they will find her.
25 Withhold your foot from being unshod, and your throat from thirst.
But you said, [s]'There is no hope.
No! For I have loved aliens, and after them I will go.'

26 "As the thief is ashamed when he is found out,
So is the house of Israel ashamed;
They and their kings and their princes, and their priests and their [t]prophets,

9
a Ezek. 20:35–36; Mic. 6:2
10
b Jer. 18:13
13
c Ps. 36:9; Jer. 17:13; cp. Jn. 4:14
16
d Jer. 43:7–9
17
e Dt. 32:10
18
f Isa. 30:1–3
g Josh. 13:3
h Hos. 5:13
i i.e. *the Euphrates*
19
j Jer. 4:18
20
k Lev. 26:13
l Ex. 19:8; Josh. 24:18; Jud. 10:16; 1 Sam. 12:10
m Isa. 57:5, 7; Jer. 3:6; cp. Dt. 12:2
21
n Isa. 5:2
o Dt. 32:32; Isa. 5:4; cp. 1:21
p i.e. *foreign* or *wild*
22
q Job 14:16–17; Jer. 17:1–2; cp. Hos. 13:12
23
r Prov. 30:12
25
s Isa. 57:10; Jer. 18:12
26
t Isa. 28:7; Jer. 5:31

*
2:10 Hebrew *Kittim,* western lands, especially Cyprus • In the northern Arabian desert, representative of the eastern cultures 2:16 That is, Memphis in ancient Egypt

27 Saying to a tree, 'You *are* my
father,'
And to a [a]stone, 'You gave
birth to me.'
For they have turned *their*
back to Me, and not *their*
face.
But in the time of their
[b]trouble
They will say, 'Arise and save
us.'
28 But [c]where *are* your gods that
you have made for
yourselves?
Let them arise,
If they can [d]save you in the
time of your trouble;
For *according to* the number of
your cities
Are your gods, O Judah.

29 "Why will you plead with Me?
You all have transgressed
against Me," says the LORD.
30 "In vain I have chastened your
children;
They [e]received no correction.
Your sword has [f]devoured
your prophets
Like a destroying lion.

31 "O generation, see the word of
the LORD!
Have I been a wilderness to
Israel,
Or a land of darkness?
Why do My people say, 'We
are lords;
We will come no more to
You'?
32 Can a virgin forget her
ornaments,
Or a bride her attire?
Yet My people have [g]forgotten
Me days without number.

33 "Why do you beautify your way
to seek love?
Therefore you have also taught
The wicked women your ways.
34 Also on your skirts is found
The blood of the lives of the
poor innocents.
I have not found it by secret
search,
But plainly on all these things.
35 Yet you [h]say, 'Because I am
innocent,
Surely His anger shall turn
from me.'
Behold, I will plead My case
against you,

27
[a] Jer. 3:9
[b] Isa. 26:16; Hos. 5:15
28
[c] Dt. 32:37; Jud. 10:14
[d] Jer. 11:12
30
[e] Jer. 5:3
[f] Neh. 9:26; Acts 7:52; 1 Th. 2:15
32
[g] Ps. 106:21; Jer. 13:25; Hos. 8:14
35
[h] Mal. 2:17; 3:8
36
[i] v. 18; Jer. 31:22; Hos. 5:13; 12:1
37
[j] Jer. 17:5; cp. 37:7–10
CHAPTER 3
1
[k] Dt. 24:1–4
2
[l] See Jud. 3:7 and 1 Ki. 3:2, *notes*
[m] v. 20
3
[n] See Jer. 14:1, *note*
4
[o] Jer. 2:2; Hos. 2:15

Because you say, 'I have not
sinned.'
36 Why do you [i]gad about so
much to change your way?
Also you shall be ashamed of
Egypt as you were ashamed
of Assyria.
37 Indeed you will go forth from
him
With your hands on your head;
For the LORD has rejected your
trusted allies,
And you will [j]not prosper by
them.

The polluted land

3 "THEY say, 'If a man divorces
his wife,
And she goes from him
And becomes another man's,
May he return to her [k]again?'
Would not that land be greatly
polluted?
But you have played the harlot
with many lovers;
Yet return to Me," says the
LORD.

2 "Lift up your eyes to the
desolate [l]heights and see:
Where have you not [m]lain *with
men?*
By the road you have sat for
them
Like an Arabian in the
wilderness;
And you have polluted the
land
With your harlotries and your
wickedness.
3 Therefore the [n]showers have
been withheld,
And there has been no latter
rain.
You have had a harlot's
forehead;
You refuse to be ashamed.
4 Will you not from this time cry
to Me,
'My Father, You *are* the guide
[o]of my youth?
5 Will He remain angry forever?
Will He keep it to the end?'
Behold, you have spoken and
done evil things,
As you were able."

Second message: future glory
conditional upon repentance (3:6—6:30)

6 The LORD [1]said also to me in the
days of Josiah the king: "Have you

[1](3:6) The general character of the second message to Judah is: (1) reproach that the

seen what backsliding [1]Israel has
done? She has gone up on every high
mountain and under every green tree,
and there played the harlot.
7 "And I said, after she had done
all these *things*, 'Return to Me.' But
she did not return. And her treacherous [a]sister Judah saw it.
8 "Then I saw that for all the
causes for which backsliding Israel
had committed adultery, I had put her
away and given her a certificate of
[b]divorce; yet her treacherous sister
Judah did not fear, but went and
played the harlot also.
9 "So it came to pass, through her
casual harlotry, that she defiled the
land and committed adultery with
[c]stones and trees.
10 "And yet for all this her treacherous sister Judah has not turned to
Me [d]with her whole heart, but in pretense," says the LORD.
11 Then the LORD said to me, "Backsliding Israel has shown herself more
righteous than treacherous Judah.
12 "Go and proclaim these words
toward the north, and say:

'Return, backsliding Israel,'
says the LORD;
'I will not cause My anger to
fall on you.
[e]For I *am* merciful,' says the
LORD;
'I will not remain angry
forever.
13 Only [f]acknowledge your
iniquity,
That you have transgressed
against the LORD your God,
And have scattered your
charms
To alien deities under every
green tree,
And you have not obeyed My
voice,' says the LORD.

14 "Return, O backsliding children," says the LORD; "for I am [g]mar-
ried to you. I will take you, one from
a city and two from a family, and I will
bring you to [h]Zion.
15 "And I will give you [i]shepherds
according to My heart, who will [j]feed
you with knowledge and understanding.
16 "Then it shall come to pass,
when you are multiplied and [k]in-
creased in the land in those days,"
says the LORD, "that they will say no
more, 'The ark of the covenant of the
LORD.' It shall not come to mind, nor
shall they remember it, nor shall they
visit *it*, nor shall it be made anymore.
17 "At that time Jerusalem shall be
called The Throne of the LORD, and all
the [l]nations shall be gathered to it, to
the name of the LORD, to Jerusalem.
No more shall they follow the dictates
of their evil hearts.
18 "In those days the [m]house of Judah shall walk with the house of Israel, and they shall come together out
of the land of the north to the land that
I have given as an inheritance to your
fathers.
19 "But I said:

'How can I put you among the
children
And give you a pleasant land,
A beautiful heritage of the
hosts of nations?'

"And I said:

'You shall call Me, [n]"My
Father,"
And not turn away from Me.'
20 Surely, *as* a wife treacherously
departs from her husband,
So have you dealt
treacherously with Me,
O house of Israel," says the
LORD.

21 A voice was heard on the
desolate [o]heights,
Weeping *and* supplications of
the children of Israel.
For they have perverted their
way;
They have forgotten the LORD
their God.

22 "Return, you backsliding
children,
And I will [p]heal your
backslidings."

"Indeed we do come to You,
For You are the LORD our God.

7 [a] Ezek. 16:46; 23:2–4
8 [b] Isa. 50:1
9 [c] Isa. 57:6; Jer. 2:27
10 [d] Hos. 7:14; cp. 2 Chr. 34:33
12 [e] Ps. 103:8–9; Jer. 31:20
13 [f] Lev. 26:40; Dt. 30:1–2; Prov. 28:13; cp. 1 Jn. 1:9
14 [g] Jer. 31:32; Hos. 2:19–20
[h] Jer. 31:6
15 [i] Jer. 23:4; Ezek. 34:23; cp. Eph. 4:11
[j] Cp. Acts 20:28
16 [k] Isa. 49:19; Jer. 23:3
17 [l] Jer. 4:2; 16:19
18 [m] Isa. 11:13; Jer. 50:4; Ezek. 37:16–22; Hos. 1:11
19 [n] Isa. 63:16
21 [o] See Jud. 3:7 and 1 Ki. 3:2, *notes*
22 [p] Hos. 6:1; 14:4

example of the LORD's chastening of the northern kingdom (2 Ki. 17:1–18) has produced no effect upon Judah, e.g. 3:6–10; (2) warning of a like chastisement impending over Judah, e.g. vv. 15–17; (3) touching appeals to return to the LORD, e.g. 3:12–14; and (4) promises of final national restoration and blessing, e.g. 3:16–18.

[1](3:6) Israel and Ephraim are the names by which the northern kingdom (the ten tribes) is usually called in the prophets. When the name Israel refers to the whole nation, the context makes it clear.

23 Truly, in vain *is salvation hoped for* from the [a]hills,
And from the multitude of mountains;
Truly, [b]in the LORD our God
Is the salvation of Israel.
24 For shame has devoured
The labor of our [c]fathers from our youth—
Their flocks and their herds,
Their sons and their daughters.
25 We lie down in our shame,
And our reproach covers us.
[d]For we have sinned against the LORD our God,
We and our fathers,
From our youth even to this day,
And have not obeyed the voice of the LORD our God."

Judgment of invasion predicted

4 "IF you will return, O Israel," says the LORD,
[e]"Return to Me;
And if you will put away your abominations out of My sight,
Then you shall not [f]be moved.
2 And you shall swear, 'The LORD lives,'
In truth, in judgment, and in righteousness;
The [g]nations shall bless themselves in Him,
And in Him they shall [h]glory."

3 For thus says the LORD to the
men of Judah and Jerusalem:

[i]"Break up your fallow ground,
And do not sow among thorns.
4 [j]Circumcise yourselves to the LORD,
And take away the foreskins of your hearts,
You men of Judah and inhabitants of Jerusalem,
Lest My fury come forth like fire,
And burn so that no one can quench *it*,
Because of the evil of your doings."

5 Declare in Judah and proclaim
in Jerusalem, and say:

[k]"Blow the trumpet in the land;
Cry, 'Gather together,'
And say, [l]'Assemble yourselves,
And let us go into the fortified cities.'
6 Set up the standard toward Zion.
Take refuge! Do not delay!
For I will bring disaster from the [m]north,
And great destruction."
7 The [1]lion has come up from his thicket,
And the [n]destroyer of nations is on his way.
He has gone forth from his place
To make your land desolate.
Your cities will be laid waste,
Without inhabitant.
8 For this, [o]clothe yourself with sackcloth,
Lament and wail.
For the fierce anger of the LORD
Has not turned back from us.
9 "And it shall come to pass in that day," says the LORD,
"*That* the heart of the king shall perish,
And the heart of the princes;
The priests shall be astonished,
And the prophets shall wonder."
10 Then I said, "Ah, Lord GOD!
Surely You have greatly [2][p]deceived this people and Jerusalem,
Saying, 'You shall have peace,'
Whereas the sword reaches to the heart."
11 At that time it will be said
To this people and to Jerusalem,
"A dry [q]wind of the desolate heights *blows* in the wilderness
Toward the daughter of My people—
Not to fan or to cleanse—
12 A wind too strong for these will come for Me;
Now I will also speak judgment against them."

23 [a] Ps. 121:1–2 [b] Ps. 3:8; Prov. 21:31; Jon. 2:9
24 [c] Jer. 14:20
25 [d] Ezra 9:7
CHAPTER 4
1 [e] Jer. 3:1, 22; Joel 2:12 [f] Jer. 7:3,7; 15:19; 35:15
2 [g] Isa. 65:16; Jer. 3:17 [h] Jer. 9:24; 1 Cor. 1:31; 2 Cor. 10:7
3 [i] Hos. 10:12
4 [j] Dt. 10:16; 30:6; Col. 2:11; cp. Jer. 9:26; Rom. 2:28–29
5 [k] Jer. 6:1 [l] Jer. 8:14
6 [m] Jer. 1:13–15; 6:1,22
7 [n] Jer. 25:9
8 [o] Isa. 22:12; Jer. 6:26
10 [p] Ezek. 14:9; cp. 2 Th. 2:11
11 [q] Jer. 51:1; Ezek. 17:10; Hos. 13:15

[1](4:7) The word "lion" is a metaphorical allusion to Nebuchadnezzar, the king of Babylon (Dan. 7:4).
[2](4:10) God never deceives His people. Jeremiah thought that God had deceived him (see Jer. 20:7, *note*), because he had failed to understand the full import of divine revelation concerning impending judgment. Actually God had plainly warned the people of Israel.

13 "Behold, he shall come up like clouds,
And his [a]chariots like a whirlwind.
His [b]horses are swifter than eagles.
Woe to us, for we are plundered!"

14 O Jerusalem, [c]wash your heart from wickedness,
That you may be saved.
How long shall your evil thoughts lodge within you?
15 For a voice declares from Dan
And proclaims affliction from Mount Ephraim:
16 "Make mention to the nations,
Yes, proclaim against Jerusalem,
That watchers come from a [d]far country
And raise their voice against the cities of Judah.
17 Like keepers of a field they are [e]against her all around,
Because she has been rebellious against Me," says the LORD.
18 "Your ways and your doings
Have procured these *things* for you.
This *is* your wickedness,
Because it is bitter,
Because it reaches to your heart."

19 O my soul, my soul!
I am pained in my very heart!
My heart makes a noise in me;
I cannot hold my peace,
Because you have heard, O my soul,
The sound of the trumpet,
The alarm of war.
20 [f]Destruction upon destruction is cried,
For the whole land is plundered.
Suddenly my [g]tents are plundered,
And my curtains in a moment.
21 How long will I see the standard,
And hear the sound of the trumpet?

22 "For My people *are* foolish,
They have [h]not known Me.
They *are* silly children,
And they have [i]no understanding.
[j]They *are* wise to do [k]evil,
But to do good they have no knowledge."

23 I beheld the earth, and indeed *it was* without form, and void;
And the heavens, they *had* no light.
24 I beheld the mountains, and indeed they trembled,
And all the [l]hills moved back and forth.
25 I beheld, and indeed *there was* no man,
And all the birds of the heavens had fled.
26 I beheld, and indeed the fruitful land *was* a [m]wilderness,
And all its cities were broken down
At the presence of the LORD,
By His fierce anger.

27 For thus says the LORD:

"The whole land shall be desolate;
Yet I will not make a [n]full end.
28 For this shall the earth mourn,
And the heavens above be black,
Because I have spoken.
I have [o]purposed and will not [p]relent,
Nor will I turn back from it.
29 The whole city shall flee from the noise of the horsemen and bowmen.
They shall go into thickets and climb up on the rocks.
Every city *shall be* forsaken,
And not a man shall dwell in it.

30 "And *when* you *are* plundered,
What will you do?
Though you clothe yourself with crimson,
Though you adorn *yourself* with ornaments of gold,
Though you [q]enlarge your eyes with paint,
In vain you will make yourself fair;
Your [r]lovers will despise you;
They will seek your life.

31 "For I have heard a voice as of a woman in labor,
The anguish as of her who brings forth her first child,
The voice of the daughter of Zion bewailing herself;
She spreads her hands, *saying,*

13 *a* Isa. 5:28 *b* Dt. 28:49; Lam. 4:19; Hos. 8:1; Hab. 1:8
14 *c* Isa. 1:16; Jas. 4:8
16 *d* Isa. 39:3; Jer. 5:15
17 *e* 2 Ki. 25:4
20 *f* Ezek. 7:25–26 *g* Jer. 10:20
22 *h* Cp. Jer. 2:8 *i* Isa. 27:11 *j* Reverse of Rom. 16:19 *k* Jer. 9:3
24 *l* Isa. 5:25; Ezek. 38:20
26 *m* Jer. 9:10
27 *n* Jer. 5:10, 18; 30:11; 46:28
28 *o* Isa. 46:10–11; Dan. 4:35 *p* See Zech. 8:14, *note*
30 *q* Ezek. 23:40 *r* Jer. 30:14; Ezek. 23:9–10,22

'Woe *is* me now, for my soul is weary
Because of murderers!'

Reasons for judgment

5 "RUN to and fro through the streets of Jerusalem;
See now and know;
And seek in her open places
If you can find a [a]man,
If there is *anyone* who executes judgment,
Who seeks the truth,
And I will pardon her.
2 [b]Though they say, 'As the LORD lives,'
Surely they swear falsely."
3 O LORD, *are* not [c]Your eyes on the truth?
You have stricken them,
But they have not grieved;
You have consumed them,
But they have refused to receive correction.
They have made their faces harder than rock;
They have [d]refused to return.
4 Therefore I said, "Surely these *are* poor.
They are foolish;
For they [e]do not know the way of the LORD,
The judgment of their God.
5 I will go to the great men and speak to them,
For [f]they have known the way of the LORD,
The judgment of their God."
But these have altogether broken the yoke
And burst the bonds.
6 Therefore a lion from the forest shall slay them,
A wolf of the deserts shall destroy them;
A leopard will watch over their cities.
Everyone who goes out from there shall be torn in pieces,
Because their transgressions are many;
Their backslidings have increased.
7 "How shall I pardon you for this?
Your children have forsaken Me
And [g]sworn by *those that* [h]*are* not gods.
When I had fed them to the full,
Then they committed adultery
And assembled themselves by troops in the harlots' houses.
8 They were *like* well-fed lusty stallions;
Every one neighed after his neighbor's wife.
9 Shall I not punish *them* for these *things?*" says the LORD.
"And shall I not [i]avenge Myself on such a nation as this?
10 "Go up on her walls and destroy,
But do not make a [j]complete end.
Take away her branches,
For they *are* not the LORD's.
11 For the house of Israel and the house of Judah
Have dealt very treacherously with Me," says the LORD.
12 They have [k]lied about the LORD,
And [l]said, "*It is* not [m]He.
Neither will evil come upon us,
Nor shall we see sword or famine.
13 And the prophets become wind,
For the word *is* not in them.
Thus shall it be done to them."
14 Therefore thus says the LORD
God of hosts:
"Because you speak this word,
Behold, I will make My words in your mouth fire,
And this people wood,
And it shall devour them.
15 Behold, [n]I will bring a nation against you from afar,
O house of Israel," says the LORD.
"It *is* a mighty nation,
It *is* an ancient nation,
A nation whose language you do not know,
Nor can you understand what they say.
16 Their quiver *is* like an open tomb;
They *are* all mighty men.
17 [o]And they shall eat up your harvest and your bread,
Which your sons and daughters should eat.
They shall eat up your flocks and your herds;
They shall eat up your vines and your fig trees;
They shall destroy your fortified cities,

CHAPTER 5
1 a Ezek. 22:30; cp. Gen. 18:23–32
2 b Isa. 48:1; Ti. 1:16
3 c 2 Chr. 16:9; Jer. 16:17
d Isa. 9:13; Jer. 7:28
4 e Jer. 8:7
5 f Mic. 3:1
7 g Josh. 23:7; Zeph. 1:5
h Dt. 32:21; Gal. 4:8; cp. 1 Cor. 8:5–6
9 i Jer. 9:9
10 j Jer. 4:27
12 k 2 Chr. 36:16
l Isa. 47:8; Jer. 23:17
m Cp. Jer. 43:1–4
15 n Dt. 28:49; Isa. 5:26; Jer. 1:15; 4:16; 6:22–23
17 o Lev. 26:16; Dt. 28:31–33

In which you [a]trust, with the
sword.

18 "Nevertheless in those days,"
says the LORD, "I will not make a
[b]complete end of you.
19 "And it will be when you say,
[c]'Why does the LORD our God do all
these *things* to us?' then you shall answer them, 'Just as you have [d]for-
saken Me and served foreign gods in
your land, so you shall serve aliens in
a land *that is* not yours.'

20 "Declare this in the house of
Jacob
And proclaim it in Judah,
saying,
21 'Hear this now, O foolish
people,
[e]Without understanding,
Who have eyes and see not,
And who have ears and hear
not:
22 Do you not fear [f]Me?' says the
LORD.
'Will you not tremble at My
presence,
Who have placed the sand as
the bound of the sea,
By a perpetual decree, that it
cannot pass beyond it?
And though its waves toss to
and fro,
Yet they cannot prevail;
Though they roar, yet they
cannot pass over it.
23 But this people has a defiant
and rebellious heart;
They have revolted and
departed.
24 They do not say in their heart,
"Let us now [g]fear the LORD our
God,
[h]Who gives rain, both the
[i]former and the latter, in its
season.
He reserves for us the
appointed weeks of the
[j]harvest."
25 Your iniquities have turned
these *things* away,
And your sins have withheld
good from you.

26 'For among My people are
found wicked *men;*
They lie in wait as one who
sets snares;
They set a trap;
They catch men.
27 As a cage is full of birds,
So their houses *are* full of
deceit.

17
a Hos. 8:14; see Ps. 2:12, *note*
18
b Jer. 30:11
19
c Dt. 29:24; 1 Ki. 9:8–9; Jer. 13:22; 16:10
d Jer. 1:16
21
e Isa. 6:9; 48:8; Jer. 6:10; Ezek. 12:2; Mt. 13:14; Jn. 12:40; Acts 28:26
22
f Jer. 2:19; 44:10
24
g See Ps. 19:9, *note*
h Ps. 147:8; Jer. 14:22; Mt. 5:45; Acts 14:17
i Dt. 11:14; Joel 2:23; Jas. 5:7
j Gen. 8:22
27
k Jer. 12:1
29
l Jer. 5:9; Mal. 3:5
30
m Jer. 23:14; Hos. 6:10; 2 Tim. 4:3
31
n Jer. 6:13; 14:14; cp. Ezek. 13:1–23
o Mic. 2:11
CHAPTER 6
1
p Neh. 3:14
q Jer. 4:6
3
r 2 Ki. 25:1–4; Jer. 4:17; 12:10
4
s Jer. 51:27; Joel 3:9

Therefore they have become
[k]great and grown rich.
28 They have grown fat, they are
sleek;
Yes, they surpass the deeds of
the wicked;
They do not plead the cause,
The cause of the fatherless;
Yet they prosper,
And the right of the needy
they do not defend.
29 Shall I not [l]punish *them* for
these *things?*' says the LORD.
'Shall I not avenge Myself on
such a nation as this?'

30 "An astonishing and [m]horrible
thing
Has been committed in the
land:
31 [n]The prophets prophesy falsely,
And the priests rule by their
own power;
And My people love *to have it*
[o]so.
But what will you do in the
end?

Jerusalem will fall amid suffering

6 "O YOU children of Benjamin,
Gather yourselves to flee from
the midst of Jerusalem!
Blow the trumpet in Tekoa,
And set up a signal-fire in
[p]Beth Haccerem;
For disaster appears out of the
[q]north,
And great destruction.
2 I have likened the daughter of
Zion
To a lovely and delicate
woman.
3 The [r]shepherds with their
flocks shall come to her.
They shall pitch *their* tents
against her all around.
Each one shall pasture in his
own place."
4 [s]"Prepare war against her;
Arise, and let us go up at
noon.
Woe to us, for the day goes
away,
For the shadows of the evening
are lengthening.
5 Arise, and let us go by night,
And let us destroy her
palaces."

6 For thus has the LORD of hosts
said:

"Cut down trees,

And build a [a]mound against
Jerusalem.
This *is* the city to be punished.
She *is* full of oppression in her
midst.
7 As a fountain wells up with
water,
So she wells up with her
wickedness.
Violence and plundering are
heard in her.
Before Me continually *are* grief
and wounds.
8 Be instructed, O Jerusalem,
[b]Lest My soul depart from you;
Lest I make you desolate,
A land not inhabited."

9 Thus says the LORD of hosts:

"They shall thoroughly glean as
a vine the remnant of Israel;
As a grape-gatherer, put your
hand back into the
branches."

10 To whom shall I speak and
give warning,
That they may hear?
Indeed their ear *is*
[c]uncircumcised,
And they cannot give heed.
Behold, the word of the LORD is
a [d]reproach to them;
They have no delight in it.
11 Therefore I am full of the fury
of the LORD.
I am [e]weary of holding *it* in.
"I will pour it out on the
children outside,
And on the assembly of young
men together;
For even the husband shall be
taken with the wife,
The aged with *him who is* full
of days.
12 And their houses shall be
[f]turned over to others,
Fields and wives together;
For I will stretch out My hand
Against the inhabitants of the
land," says the LORD.
13 "Because from the least of them
even to the greatest of them,
Everyone *is* given to
[g]covetousness;
And from the prophet even to
the [h]priest,
Everyone deals falsely.
14 They have also healed the
[i]hurt of My people slightly,
Saying, 'Peace, peace!'
When *there is* no [j]peace.

15 Were they ashamed when they
had committed abomination?
No! They were not at all
ashamed;
Nor did they know how to
blush.
Therefore they shall fall
among those who fall;
At the time I punish them,
They shall be cast down," says
the LORD.

16 Thus says the LORD:

"Stand in the [k]ways and see,
And ask for the old [l]paths,
where the good way *is*,
And walk in it;
Then you will find rest for
your souls.
But they said, 'We will not
walk *in it*.'
17 Also, I set [m]watchmen over
you, *saying*,
[n]'Listen to the sound of the
trumpet!'
But they said, 'We will not
listen.'
18 Therefore hear, you nations,
And know, O congregation,
what *is* among them.
19 [o]Hear, O earth!
Behold, I will certainly bring
[p]calamity on this people—
The [q]fruit of their thoughts,
Because they have not heeded
My words
Nor My law, but rejected it.
20 [r]For what purpose to Me
Comes frankincense from
Sheba,
And [s]sweet cane from a far
country?
Your burnt offerings *are* not
acceptable,
Nor your sacrifices sweet to
Me."
21 Therefore thus says the LORD:
"Behold, I will lay stumbling
blocks before this people,
And the fathers and the sons
together shall fall on them.
The neighbor and his friend
shall perish."

22 Thus says the LORD:

"Behold, a people comes from
the [t]north country,
And a great nation will be
raised from the farthest
parts of the earth.
23 They will lay hold on bow and
spear;

---

6 *a* Jer. 32:24
8 *b* Ezek. 23:18; Hos. 9:12
10 *c* Ex. 6:12; Jer. 5:21; 7:26; Acts 7:51 *d* Jer. 8:9
11 *e* Cp. Jer. 20:9
12 *f* Dt. 28:30; Jer. 8:10; 38:22
13 *g* Isa. 56:11; Jer. 8:10; 22:17; 23:11; Mic. 3:5,11 *h* Jer. 5:31
14 *i* Lit. *bruise* or *breach* *j* Jer. 8:11–15
16 *k* i.e. *highways* or *roads* *l* Jer. 18:15
17 *m* Isa. 62:6; Ezek. 3:17 *n* Dt. 4:1; Isa. 58:1; Jer. 25:4; cp. Lk. 16:29
19 *o* Isa. 1:2 *p* Jer. 19:3, 15 *q* Prov. 1:31
20 *r* Ps. 40:6; 50:7–9; Isa. 1:11; 66:3; Jer. 7:21–23; Amos 5:21; Mic. 6:6–8 *s* Isa. 43:24
22 *t* Jer. 1:15; 4:6; 5:15; 10:22; 50:41–43

They *are* cruel and have no
mercy;
Their voice roars like the sea;
And they ride on horses,
As men of war set in array
against you, O daughter of
Zion."

24 We have heard the report of it;
Our hands grow feeble.
Anguish has taken hold of us,
Pain as of a woman in labor.
25 Do not go out into the field,
Nor walk by the way.
Because of the sword of the
enemy,
Fear *is* on every side.
26 O daughter of my people,
Dress in sackcloth
And [a]roll about in ashes!
Make mourning *as for* an only
son, most bitter lamentation;
For the plunderer will
suddenly come upon us.

27 "I have set you *as* an assayer
and a [b]fortress among My
people,
That you may know and test
their way.
28 They *are* all stubborn rebels,
walking as slanderers.
They are bronze and iron,
They *are* all corrupters;
29 The bellows blow fiercely,
The lead is consumed by the
fire;
The smelter refines in vain,
For the wicked are not drawn
off.
30 *People* will call them [c]rejected
silver,
Because the LORD has [d]rejected
them."

Message at the temple gate (7—10)

7 THE [1]word that came to Jeremiah
from the LORD, saying,
2 "Stand in the [e]gate of the LORD's
house, and proclaim there this word,
and say, 'Hear the word of the LORD,
all *you of* Judah who enter in at these
gates to worship the LORD!' "
3 Thus says the LORD of hosts, the
God of Israel: [f]"Amend your ways
and your doings, and I will cause you
to dwell in this place.
4 [g]"Do not trust in these lying
words, saying, 'The temple of the
LORD, the temple of the LORD, the temple of the LORD *are* these.'
5 "For if you thoroughly amend
your ways and your doings, if you
thoroughly execute judgment between a man and his neighbor,
6 "*if* you do not oppress the
[h]stranger, the fatherless, and the
widow, and do not shed innocent
blood in this place, or walk after other
gods to your [i]hurt,
7 "then I will cause you to dwell in
this place, in the land that I gave to
your fathers forever and ever.
8 "Behold, you [j]trust in lying
words that cannot profit.
9 [k]"Will you steal, murder, commit adultery, swear falsely, burn incense to Baal, and walk after other
gods whom you do not know,
10 "and *then* come and stand before Me in this house which is called
by My name, and say, 'We are delivered to do all these abominations'?
11 "Has this [l]house, which is called
by My name, become a den of thieves
in your eyes? Behold, I, even I, have
seen *it*," says the LORD.
12 "But go now to My place which
was in [m]Shiloh, where I set My name
at the first, and see what I did to it
because of the wickedness of My people Israel.
13 "And now, because you have
done all these works," says the LORD,
"and I spoke to you, rising up early
and speaking, but you did not hear,
and I called you, but you did not answer,
14 "therefore I will do to the house
which is called by My name, in which
you trust, and to this place which I
gave to you and your fathers, as I have
done to [n]Shiloh.
15 "And I will cast you out of My
sight, as I have cast out all your
brethren—the whole posterity of
Ephraim.
16 "Therefore [o]do not pray for this
people, nor lift up a cry or prayer for
them, nor make intercession to Me;
for I will not hear you.
17 "Do you not see what they do in
the cities of Judah and in the streets of
Jerusalem?
18 "The children gather wood, the
fathers kindle the fire, and the women
knead dough, to make cakes for the

26 *a* Jer. 25:34; Mic. 1:10
27 *b* Jer. 1:18
30 *c* Lit. *inferior* *d* Jer. 7:29
CHAPTER 7
2 *e* Jer. 17:19
3 *f* Jer. 4:1; 26:13
4 *g* Cp. v. 8; Mic. 3:11
6 *h* Ex. 22:21–24; Jer. 22:3 *i* Dt. 6:14–15; 8:19; 11:28; 13:6–11
8 *j* See Ps. 2:12, *note*
9 *k* Ex. 20:3–17
11 *l* Mt. 21:13; Mk. 11:17; Lk. 19:46
12 *m* Josh. 18:1; Jud. 18:31
14 *n* 1 Sam. 4:10–11; Ps. 78:60; Jer. 26:6,9
16 *o* Jer. 11:14; 14:11; cp. Ex. 32:10; 1 Jn. 5:16

[1](7:1) The general character of the message in the temple gate is, like the first and second messages, one of rebuke, warning, and exhortation, but this message is addressed more to such in Judah as still maintain outwardly the worship of the LORD; it is a message to religious Judah, e.g. 7:2,9–10; 8:10–11.

[1]queen of heaven; and *they* pour out
drink offerings to other gods, that
they may provoke Me to anger.
19 "Do they [a]provoke Me to anger?" says the LORD. "*Do they* not *provoke* themselves, to the shame of their
own faces?"
20 Therefore thus says the Lord
GOD: "Behold, My anger and My fury
will be poured out on this place—on
man and on beast, on the trees of the
field and on the fruit of the ground.
And it will burn and not be quenched."
21 Thus says the LORD of hosts, the
God of Israel: "Add your [b]burnt offerings to your sacrifices and eat meat.
22 "For I did not speak to your fathers, [2]or command them in the day
that I brought them out of the land of
Egypt, [c]concerning burnt offerings or
sacrifices.
23 "But this is what I commanded
them, saying, [d]'Obey My voice, and I
will be your God, and you shall [e]be
My people. And walk in all the ways
that I have commanded you, that it
may be well with you.'
24 "Yet they [f]did not obey or incline their ear, but [g]followed the
counsels *and* the dictates of their evil
hearts, and went backward and not
forward.
25 "Since the day that your fathers
came out of the land of Egypt until this
day, I have even sent to you all My
[h]servants the prophets, daily rising up
early and sending *them*.
26 "Yet they did not obey Me or incline their ear, but stiffened their
neck. They did worse than their fathers.
27 "Therefore you shall [i]speak all
these words to them, but they will not
obey you. You shall also call to them,
but they will not answer you.
28 "So you shall say to them, 'This
is a nation that does not obey the voice
of the LORD their God nor receive correction. Truth has perished and has
been cut off from their mouth.
29 [j]'Cut off your hair and cast *it*
away, and take up a lamentation on
the desolate heights; for the LORD has
rejected and forsaken the generation
of His wrath.'
30 "For the children of Judah have
done evil in My sight," says the LORD.
"They have [k]set their abominations in
the house which is called by My name,
to pollute it.
31 "And they have built the high
places of [3]Tophet, which *is* in the Valley of the Son of Hinnom, to burn their
sons and their daughters in the fire,
which I did not command, nor did it
come into My heart.
32 "Therefore behold, the days are
coming," says the LORD, "when it will
no more be called Tophet, or the Valley of the Son of Hinnom, but the Valley of Slaughter; for they will bury in
Tophet until there is no room.
33 "The [l]corpses of this people will
be food for the birds of the heaven and
for the beasts of the earth. And no one
will [m]frighten *them away*.
34 [n]"Then I will cause to cease
from the cities of Judah and from the
streets of Jerusalem the voice of mirth
and the voice of gladness, the voice of
the bridegroom and the voice of the
bride. For the land shall be [o]desolate.

Insensitivity toward sin

8 "AT that time," says the LORD,
"they shall bring out the bones of
the kings of Judah, and the bones of
its princes, and the bones of the
priests, and the bones of the prophets,

19 *a* Dt. 32:16, 21
21 *b* Isa. 1:11; Jer. 6:20; Hos. 8:13; Amos 5:21–22
22 *c* 1 Sam. 15:22; Ps. 51:16–17; Hos. 6:6
23 *d* Ex. 15:26; Dt. 6:3; Jer. 11:4–7 *e* Ex. 19:5; Lev. 26:12
24 *f* Ps. 81:11; Jer. 11:8 *g* Dt. 29:19; Ps. 81:12
25 *h* 2 Chr. 36:15; Jer. 25:4; 29:19; Mk. 12:1–10; Lk. 11:47–49
27 *i* Jer. 1:7; cp. Ezek. 2:7
29 *j* Isa. 15:2; Jer. 48:37; Mic. 1:16; cp. Job 1:20; Jer. 16:6
30 *k* 2 Ki. 21:4, 7; 2 Chr. 33:4,7; Jer. 23:11; 32:34; Ezek. 7:20
33 *l* Jer. 9:22; Ezek. 6:5. Fulfilled in part in all the destructions of Jerusalem, this prediction looks finally toward Rev. 19:17–21 *m* Dt. 28:26; cp. Jer. 12:9
7:34 *n* Jer. 16:9; 25:10 *o* Lev. 26:33; Isa. 1:7; 3:26; Jer. 25:11

[1](7:18) The "queen of heaven" is a term used for a vile heathen goddess, mentioned only in two passages in the Bible, here and in Jer. 44:15–30. The prophets declare God's wrath on all who worship her. She is probably the same as Ashtoreth, a heathen deity referred to in Jud. 2:13; 10:6; 1 Sam. 31:10; 1 Ki. 11:5,33; and in 2 Ki. 23:13 where she is called "the abomination of the Sidonians."

[2](7:22) See Ex. 20:1, *note*, the threefold giving of the law. The command concerning burnt offerings and sacrifices was not given to the people until they had broken the Decalogue, the law of obedience.

[3](7:31) Evidently Tophet was the name of certain high places built in the Valley of the Son of Hinnom, just south of Jerusalem, on which human sacrifices were offered. Josiah defiled the place (2 Ki. 23:10) and Jeremiah predicted that the valley would become known as "the Valley of Slaughter" (v. 32). From the horror of the fires of its idolatrous rites, and its pollution by Josiah, the valley became a symbol of great burning in connection with sin. The Greek term *Gehenna* (formed from the Heb. for "Valley of Hinnom") means *place of fire* and is used twelve times in the NT as a designation for the place of eternal punishment (see Mt. 5:22, *note;* Jas. 3:6), the lake of fire prepared for the devil and his angels (Mt. 25:41).

and the bones of the inhabitants of Jerusalem, out of their graves.
2 "They shall spread them before the sun and the moon and all the host of heaven, which they have loved and which they have served and after which they have walked, which they have sought and which they have worshiped. They shall not be gathered nor buried; they shall be like refuse on the face of the earth.
3 "Then death shall be [a]chosen rather than life by all the residue of those who remain of this evil family, who remain in all the places where I have driven them," says the LORD of hosts.
4 "Moreover you shall say to them, 'Thus says the LORD:

"Will they fall and not rise?
Will one turn away and not return?
5 Why has this people slidden back,
Jerusalem, in a perpetual backsliding?
They hold fast to deceit,
They [b]refuse to return.
6 [c]I listened and heard,
But they do not speak aright.
[d]No man [e]repented of his wickedness,
Saying, 'What have I done?'
Everyone turned to his own course,
As the horse rushes into the battle.

7 [f]"Even the stork in the heavens
Knows her appointed times;
And the turtledove, the swift, and the swallow
Observe the time of their coming.
But My people [g]do not know the judgment of the LORD.

8 "How can you say, [h]'We *are* wise,
And the law of the LORD *is* with us'?
Look, the false pen of the scribe certainly works falsehood.
9 The wise men are ashamed,
They are dismayed and taken.
Behold, they have rejected the word of the LORD;
So [i]what wisdom do they have?
10 Therefore I will [j]give their wives to others,
And their fields to those who will inherit *them;*
Because from the least even to the greatest
Everyone is given to covetousness;
From the prophet even to the priest
Everyone deals falsely.
11 For they have healed the hurt of the daughter of My people slightly,
Saying, [k]'Peace, peace!'
When *there is* no peace.
12 Were they ashamed when they had committed abomination?
No! They were not at all ashamed,
Nor did they know how to blush.
Therefore they shall fall among those who fall;
In the time of their [l]punishment
They shall be cast down," says the LORD.

13 "I will surely consume them," says the LORD.
"No grapes *shall be* on the vine,
Nor figs on the fig tree,
And the leaf shall fade;
And *the things* I have given them shall [m]pass away from them." ' "

14 "Why do we sit still?
[n]Assemble yourselves,
And let us enter the fortified cities,
And let us be silent there.
For the LORD our God has put us to silence
And given us water of gall to drink,
Because we have sinned against the LORD.

15 "*We* [o]looked for peace, but no good *came;*
And for a time of health, and there was trouble!
16 The snorting of His horses was heard from Dan.
The whole land trembled at the sound of the neighing of His strong ones;
For they have come and devoured the land and all that is in it,
The city and those who dwell in it."

17 "For behold, I will send serpents among you,

CHAPTER 8

3 *a* Job 3:21–22; 7:15–16; Rev. 9:6
5 *b* Jer. 5:3; 9:3
6 *c* Ps. 14:2; cp. Isa. 30:18; 2 Pet. 3:9 *d* Mic. 7:2 *e* See Zech. 8:14, *note*
7 *f* Prov. 6:6–8; Song 2:12; Isa. 1:3; cp. Mt. 16:2–3 *g* Jer. 5:4; 9:3
8 *h* Rom. 2:17
9 *i* Isa. 44:25; Jer. 4:22
10 *j* Dt. 28:30; Jer. 6:12; Amos 5:11; Zeph. 1:13
11 *k* Ezek. 13:10
12 *l* Jer. 6:12–15
13 *m* Dt. 28:39–40; Jer. 5:17
14 *n* Jer. 4:5
15 *o* Jer. 14:19

Vipers which cannot be
charmed,
And they shall bite you," says
the LORD.

18 I would comfort myself in
sorrow;
My heart *is* [1]faint in me.
19 Listen! The voice,
The cry of the daughter of my
people
From a [a]far country:
"*Is* not the LORD in Zion?
Is not her King in her?"
"Why have they provoked Me
to anger
With their carved images—
With foreign idols?"
20 "The harvest is past,
The summer is ended,
And we are not saved!"
21 For the hurt of the daughter of
my people I am hurt.
I am mourning;
Astonishment has taken hold
of me.
22 *Is there* no [b]balm in Gilead,
Is there no physician there?
Why then is there no recovery
For the health of the daughter
of my people?

Jeremiah laments for his people

9 OH, that my head were waters,
And my eyes a fountain of
tears,
That I might [c]weep day and
night
For the slain of the daughter of
my people!
2 Oh, that I had in the
wilderness
A lodging place for travelers;
That I might leave my people,
And go from them!
For they *are* all [d]adulterers,
An assembly of treacherous
men.
3 "And *like* their bow they have
bent their tongues *for* [e]lies.
They are not valiant for the
truth on the earth.
For they proceed from [f]evil to
evil,
And they [g]do not know Me,"
says the LORD.
4 "Everyone take heed to his
neighbor,

19
a Jer. 5:15
22
b Jer. 46:11; cp. Gen. 37:25; 43:11; Jer. 51:8
CHAPTER 9
1
c Jer. 10:19
2
d Jer. 5:7–8; 23:10
3
e Hos. 4:1–2
f Jer. 4:22; 13:23
g Cp. 1 Sam. 2:12
4
h See Ps. 2:12, *note*
i Jer. 6:28
5
j Ps. 36:3–4; Isa. 59:4
7
k Isa. 1:25; 48:10; Mal. 3:3
l *Test/tempt:* v. 7; Jer. 11:20. (Gen. 3:1; Jas. 1:14, *note*)
8
m Jer. 5:26
9
n Jer. 5:9,29
11
o Isa. 25:2; Jer. 19:3,8; 26:9

And do not [h]trust any brother;
For every brother will utterly
supplant,
And every neighbor will walk
with [i]slanderers.
5 Everyone will [j]deceive his
neighbor,
And will not speak the truth;
They have taught their tongue
to speak lies;
They weary themselves to
commit iniquity.
6 Your dwelling place *is* in the
midst of deceit;
Through deceit they refuse to
know Me," says the LORD.

7 Therefore thus says the LORD of
hosts:

"Behold, [k]I will refine them and
[l]try them;
For how shall I deal with the
daughter of My people?
8 Their tongue *is* an arrow shot
out;
It speaks deceit;
One speaks peaceably to his
neighbor with his mouth,
But in his heart he [m]lies in
wait.
9 Shall I not [n]punish them for
these *things*?" says the LORD.
"Shall I not avenge Myself on
such a nation as this?"

10 I will take up a weeping and
wailing for the mountains,
And for the dwelling places of
the wilderness a
lamentation,
Because they are burned up,
So that no one can pass
through;
Nor can *men* hear the voice of
the cattle.
Both the birds of the heavens
and the beasts have fled;
They are gone.
11 [o]"I will make Jerusalem a heap
of ruins, a den of jackals.
I will make the cities of Judah
desolate, without an
inhabitant."

12 Who *is* the wise man who may
understand this? And *who is he* to
whom the mouth of the LORD has spoken, that he may declare it? Why does
the land perish *and* burn up like a wil-

[1](8:18) In chs. 8:18—9:2 and similar sections, e.g. 10:19–25; 15:15–18; 20:7–18, the prophet talks things over with himself and sometimes with God. Though these passages temporarily break the continuity, they are valuable in revealing Jeremiah's inner feelings.

derness, so that no one can pass
through?
13 And the LORD said, "Because
they have forsaken My [a]law which I
set before them, and have [b]not obeyed
My voice, nor walked according to it,
14 "but they have [c]walked according to the dictates of their own hearts
and after the Baals, [d]which their fathers taught them,"
15 therefore thus says the LORD of
hosts, the God of Israel: "Behold, I will
feed them, this people, with wormwood, and give them water of gall to
drink.
16 "I will [e]scatter them also among
the Gentiles, whom neither they nor
their fathers have known. And I will
send a sword after them until I have
consumed them."
17 Thus says the LORD of hosts:

"Consider and call for the
mourning women,
That they may come;
And send for [f]skillful wailing
women,
That they may come.
18 Let them make haste
And take up a wailing for us,
That our eyes may run with
tears,
And our eyelids gush with
water.
19 For a voice of wailing is heard
from Zion:
'How we are plundered!
We are greatly ashamed,
Because we have forsaken the
land,
Because we have been cast out
of our dwellings.' "
20 Yet hear the word of the LORD,
O women,
And let your ear receive the
word of His mouth;
Teach your daughters wailing,
And everyone her neighbor a
lamentation.
21 For death has come through
our windows,
Has entered our palaces,
To [g]kill off the children—*no
longer to be* outside!
And the young men—*no longer*
on the streets!
22 Speak, "Thus says the LORD:
'Even the carcasses of men
shall fall as refuse on the
open field,
Like cuttings after the
harvester,

13
a Law (of Moses): vv. 13–16; Ezek. 22:26. (Ex. 19:1; Gal. 3:24, *note*)
b Jer. 3:25; 7:24
14
c Jer. 7:24; 11:8; cp. 3:17
d Cp. 1 Ki. 22:52–53
16
e Lev. 26:33; Dt. 28:64; Jer. 15:2–4
17
f Amos 5:16
21
g 2 Chr. 36:17; Jer. 18:21; Ezek. 9:5–6
22
h Jer. 8:1–2
23
i Ps. 33:16–18
24
j Jer. 4:2; 1 Cor. 1:31; 2 Cor. 10:17
k Mic. 6:8; 7:18
26
l Lev. 26:41; Jer. 6:10; Ezek. 44:7; cp. Jer. 4:4; Rom. 2:28–29
CHAPTER 10
2
m Dt. 12:30; 18:9–14
3
n Isa. 44:9–20

And no one shall [h]gather
them.' "
23 Thus says the LORD:

"Let not the wise *man* glory in
his wisdom,
Let not the mighty *man* glory
in his [i]might,
Nor let the rich *man* glory in
his riches;
24 But let him who [j]glories glory
in this,
That he understands and
knows Me,
That I *am* the LORD, exercising
lovingkindness, judgment,
and righteousness in the
earth.
[k]For in these I delight," says the
LORD.

25 "Behold, the days are coming,"
says the LORD, "that I will punish all
who are circumcised with the
uncircumcised—
26 "Egypt, Judah, Edom, the people
of Ammon, Moab, and all *who are* in
the farthest corners, who dwell in the
wilderness. For all *these* nations *are*
uncircumcised, and all the house of
Israel *are* [l]uncircumcised in the
heart."

A satire on idolatry

10 HEAR the word which the
LORD speaks to you, O house of
Israel.
2 Thus says the LORD:

[m]"Do not learn the way of the
Gentiles;
Do not be dismayed at the
signs of heaven,
For the Gentiles are dismayed
at them.
3 For the customs of the peoples
are futile;
For *one* cuts a [n]tree from the
forest,
The work of the hands of the
workman, with the ax.
4 They decorate it with silver
and gold;
They fasten it with nails and
hammers
So that it will not topple.
5 They *are* upright, like a palm
tree,
And they cannot speak;
They must be carried,
Because they cannot go *by
themselves*.
Do not be afraid of them,
For they cannot do evil,

Nor can they do any [a]good."

6 Inasmuch as *there is* [b]none like You, O LORD
(You *are* great, and Your name *is* great in might),
7 Who would not [c]fear You, O King of the nations?
For this is Your rightful due.
For among all the wise *men* of the nations,
And in all their kingdoms,
There is none like You.
8 But they are altogether [d]dull-hearted and foolish;
A wooden idol *is* a worthless doctrine.
9 Silver is beaten into plates;
It is brought from Tarshish,
And [e]gold from Uphaz,
The work of the craftsman
And of the hands of the metalsmith;
Blue and purple *are* their clothing;
They *are* all the work of skillful *men.*
10 But the LORD *is* the true God;
He *is* the living God and the everlasting King.
At His wrath the earth will tremble,
And the nations will not be able to endure His indignation.

11 [1]Thus you shall say to them:
"The [f]gods that have not made the
heavens and the earth shall perish
from the earth and from under these
heavens."

12 [g]He has made the earth by His power,
He has [h]established the world by His wisdom,
And has [i]stretched out the heavens at His discretion.
13 When He utters His voice,
There is a multitude of waters in the heavens:
"And [j]He causes the vapors to ascend from the ends of the earth.
He makes lightning for the rain,
He brings the wind out of His treasuries."

5
a Isa. 41:23
6
b Isa. 46:5–9
7
c Jer. 5:22; Rev. 15:4; see Ps. 19:9, *note*
8
d Isa. 44:18
9
e Dan. 10:5
11
f 1 Cor. 8:5–6; see Ps. 16:4, *note*
12
g vv. 12–15; Gen. 1:1, 6–7; Jer. 51:15
h Ps. 93:1
i Job 9:8; Ps. 104:2; Isa. 40:22
13
j Ps. 135:7
17
k Cp. Ezek. 12:3–12
19
l vv. 19–25; see Jer. 8:18 and 20:7, *notes*
20
m Jer. 31:15
21
n Isa. 56:11
o Jer. 23:2

14 Everyone is [d]dull-hearted, without knowledge;
Every metalsmith is put to shame by an image;
For his molded image *is* falsehood,
And *there is* no breath in them.
15 They *are* futile, a work of errors;
In the time of their punishment they shall perish.
16 The Portion of Jacob *is* not like them,
For He *is* the Maker of all *things,*
And Israel *is* the tribe of His inheritance;
The LORD of hosts *is* His name.

17 [k]Gather up your wares from the land,
O inhabitant of the fortress!
18 For thus says the LORD:

"Behold, I will throw out at this time
The inhabitants of the land,
And will distress them,
That they may find *it so.*"

Prayer of the prophet

19 [l]Woe is me for my hurt!
My wound is severe.
But I say, "Truly this *is* an infirmity,
And I must bear it."
20 My tent is plundered,
And all my cords are broken;
My children have gone from me,
And they *are* [m]no more.
There is no one to pitch my tent anymore,
Or set up my curtains.
21 For the [n]shepherds have become [d]dull-hearted,
And have not sought the LORD;
Therefore they shall not prosper,
And all their flocks shall be [o]scattered.
22 Behold, the noise of the report has come,
And a great commotion out of the north country,
To make the cities of Judah desolate, a den of jackals.

[1](10:11) Instead of being in the Hebrew language like the rest of Jeremiah, this verse is in Aramaic, the language of the people among whom the Israelites were to dwell as captives. Jeremiah was telling them how to present their belief in God in the language spoken by the nations around them. Cp. Ps. 2:12.

23 O LORD, I know the [a]way of
man *is* not in himself;
It is not in man who walks to
direct his own steps.
24 O LORD, [b]correct me, but with
justice;
Not in Your anger, lest You
bring me to nothing.
25 Pour out Your fury on the
Gentiles, who do not know
You,
And on the families who do
not call on Your name;
For they have eaten up Jacob,
[c]Devoured him and consumed
him,
And made his dwelling place
desolate.

Message on the broken covenant
(11—12)

11 THE [1]word that came to Jeremiah from the LORD, saying,
2 "Hear the words of this covenant, and speak to the men of Judah
and to the inhabitants of Jerusalem;
3 "and say to them, 'Thus says the
LORD God of Israel: [d]"Cursed *is* the
man who does not obey the words of
this covenant
4 "which I commanded your fathers in the day I brought them out of
the land of Egypt, from the [e]iron furnace, saying, [f]'Obey My voice, and do
according to all that I command you;
so shall you be My people, and I will
be your God,'
5 "that I may establish the [g]oath
which I have sworn to your fathers, to
give them 'a land flowing with milk
and honey,'* as *it is* this day." ' " And
I answered and said, [h]"So be it, LORD."
6 Then the LORD said to me, "Proclaim all these words in the cities of
Judah and in the streets of Jerusalem,
saying: 'Hear the words of this covenant and [i]do them.
7 'For I earnestly exhorted your
fathers in the day I brought them up
out of the land of Egypt, until this day,
rising early and exhorting, saying,
"Obey My voice."
8 'Yet they did not obey or incline
their ear, but everyone followed the
dictates of his evil heart; therefore I
will bring upon them all the words of
this covenant, which I commanded
them to do, but *which* they have [j]not
done.' "
9 And the LORD said to me, "A conspiracy has been found among the
men of Judah and among the inhabitants of Jerusalem.
10 "They have turned back to the
iniquities of their forefathers who refused to hear My words, and they have
gone after other gods to serve them;
the house of Israel and the house of
Judah have broken My covenant
which I made with their fathers."
11 Therefore thus says the LORD:
"Behold, I will surely bring calamity
on them which they will not be able to
escape; and [k]though they cry out to
Me, I will not listen to them.
12 "Then the cities of Judah and the
inhabitants of Jerusalem will go and
cry out to the gods to whom they offer
incense, but they will not save them at
all in the time of their trouble.
13 "For *according to* the number of
your cities were your gods, O Judah;
and *according to* the number of the
streets of Jerusalem you have set up
altars to *that* shameful thing, altars to
burn incense to Baal.
14 "So do not [l]pray for this people,
or lift up a cry or prayer for them; for
I will not hear *them* in the time that
they cry out to Me because of their
trouble.

15 "What has My beloved to do in
My house,
Having done lewd deeds with
many?
And the [2]holy flesh has passed
from you.
When you do evil, then you
rejoice.
16 The LORD called your name,
Green [m]Olive Tree, Lovely *and*
of Good Fruit.
With the noise of a great
tumult
He has kindled fire on it,
And its branches are broken.

17 "For the LORD of hosts, who
planted you, has pronounced doom
against you for the evil of the house of

23
a Prov. 20:24
24
b Ps. 6:1; 38:1; Jer. 30:11; 46:28; cp. Dt. 8:5; Job 5:17; Prov. 3:11–12; 22:15; 23:13; Hab. 1:12; Jn. 15:2; Heb. 12:5–11
25
c Jer. 8:16
CHAPTER 11
3
d Dt. 27:26; Gal. 3:10
4
e Dt. 4:20; 1 Ki. 8:51; cp. Isa. 48:10
f Lev. 26:3–12; Jer. 7:23
5
g Dt. 7:12–13; Ps. 105:9–10
h Heb. *Amen*
6
i Dt. 17:19; Jas. 1:22; cp. Rom. 2:13
8
j Jer. 9:13; 13:10
11
k Ps. 18:41; Prov. 1:28; Isa. 1:15; Jer. 14:12; Ezek. 8:18; Mic. 3:4; Zech. 7:13
14
l Ex. 32:10; Jer. 7:16; 14:11; cp. 1 Jn. 5:16
16
m Ps. 52:8; cp. Rom. 11:17

*11:5 Exodus 3:8

[1](11:1) This, like the other messages, is made up of rebuke, exhortation, and warning, but in this instance these are based upon the violation of the Palestinian Covenant (see Dt. 30:3, *note*). The Assyrian and Babylonian captivities of Israel and Judah were the execution of the warning, Dt. 28:63–68.

[2](11:15) Here the LORD is asking: "To what purpose are your sacrifices? The efficacy of your sacrifices is cancelled by your sin." Cp. v. 15; Isa. 1:13–15; Hag. 2:12.

Israel and of the house of Judah, which they have done against themselves to provoke Me to anger in offering incense to Baal."

Plot against Jeremiah; prophecy against men of Anathoth

18 Now the LORD gave me knowledge *of it,* and I know *it;* for You showed me their doings.

19 But I *was* like a docile lamb brought to the [a]slaughter; and I did not know that they had devised schemes against me, *saying,* "Let us [b]destroy the tree with its fruit, and let us cut him off from the land of the living, that his name may be remembered no more."

20 But, O LORD of hosts,
You who judge righteously,
[c]Testing [d]the mind and the heart,
Let me see Your [e]vengeance on them,
For to You I have revealed my cause.

21 "Therefore thus says the LORD concerning the men of [f]Anathoth who seek your life, saying, [g]'Do not prophesy in the name of the LORD, lest you die by our hand'—

22 "therefore thus says the LORD of hosts: 'Behold, I will punish them. The young men shall die by the sword, their sons and their daughters shall [h]die by famine;

23 'and there shall be no remnant of them, for I will bring catastrophe on the men of Anathoth, *even* the year of their [i]punishment.'"

Jeremiah's prayer and God's response to him

12 [j]RIGHTEOUS *are* You, O LORD, when I plead with You;
Yet let me talk with You about *Your* judgments.
[k]Why does the way of the wicked prosper?
Why are those happy who deal so treacherously?

2 You have planted them, yes, they have taken root;
They grow, yes, they bear fruit.
[l]You *are* near in their mouth
But far from their mind.

3 But You, O LORD, know me;
You have seen me,
And You have [c]tested my heart toward You.
Pull them out like sheep for the slaughter,
And prepare them for the day of slaughter.

4 How long will the [m]land mourn,
And the herbs of every field wither?
The beasts and birds are consumed,
For the wickedness of those who dwell there,
Because they said, "He will not see our final end."

5 "If you have run with the footmen, and they have wearied you,
Then how can you contend with horses?
And *if* in the land of peace,
In which you trusted, *they wearied you,*
Then how will you do in the [n]floodplain* of the Jordan?

6 For even your brothers, the house of your father,
Even they have dealt treacherously with you;
Yes, they have called a multitude after you.
Do not believe them,
Even though they speak smooth words to you.

7 "I have forsaken My house, I have left My heritage;
I have given the dearly beloved of My soul into the hand of her enemies.

8 My heritage is to Me like a lion in the forest;
It cries out against Me;
Therefore I have [o]hated it.

9 My heritage *is* to Me *like* a speckled vulture;
The vultures all around *are* against her.
Come, assemble all the beasts of the field,
Bring them to devour!

10 "Many rulers* have destroyed My [p]vineyard,
They have trodden My portion underfoot;
They have made My pleasant portion a desolate wilderness.

11 They have made it [q]desolate;
Desolate, it mourns to Me;

---

19 [a] Cp. Isa. 53:7 [b] Jer. 18:18; 20:10; 26:8; 38:4
20 [c] *Test/tempt:* v. 20; 12:3; Jer. 17:10. (Gen. 3:1; Jas. 1:14, *note*). Ps. 7:9; Rev. 2:23 [d] Cp. 1 Sam. 16:7; 1 Chr. 28:9 [e] Jer. 15:15
21 [f] Jer. 1:1 [g] Isa. 30:10; Amos 2:12, 7:13, 16; Mic. 2:6
22 [h] Jer. 9:21
23 [i] Jer. 23:12; 46:21; 48:44; 50:27; Lk. 19:44
CHAPTER 12
1 [j] Ezra 9:15 [k] Job 12:6; 21:7; Ps. 37:35; 73:3; Mal. 3:15
2 [l] Isa. 29:13; Ezek. 33:31; Mt. 15:8; Mk. 7:6
4 [m] Jer. 23:10; Hos. 4:3
5 [n] i.e. *under such a test.* Jer. 49:19; 50:44; cp. Josh. 3:15; 1 Chr. 12:15
8 [o] Hos. 9:15
10 [p] Isa. 5:1–7
11 [q] Jer. 10:22; 22:6

---

* 12:5 Or *thicket* 12:10 Literally *shepherds* or *pastors*

The whole land is made
desolate,
Because no one takes *it* to
heart.
12 The plunderers have come
On all the desolate heights in
the wilderness,
For the sword of the LORD shall
devour
From *one* end of the land to
the *other* end of the land;
No flesh shall have peace.
13 [a]They have sown wheat but
reaped thorns;
They have put themselves to
pain *but* do not profit.
But be ashamed of your
harvest
Because of the fierce anger of
the LORD."

14 Thus says the LORD: "Against all
My evil neighbors who [b]touch the inheritance which I have caused My
people Israel to inherit—behold, I will
pluck them out of their land and pluck
out the house of Judah from among
them.
15 "Then it shall be, after I have
plucked them out, that I will return
and have [c]compassion on them and
bring them back, everyone to his heritage and everyone to his land.
16 "And it shall be, if they will learn
carefully the ways of My people, to
swear by My name, 'As the LORD lives,'
as they taught My people to swear by
Baal, then they shall be [d]established
in the midst of My people.
17 "But if they do not [e]obey, I will
utterly pluck up and destroy that nation," says the LORD.

Sign of the ruined sash

13 THUS the LORD said to me:
[f]"Go and get yourself a linen
[g]sash, and put it around your waist,
but do not put it in water."
2 So I got a sash according to the
word of the LORD, and put *it* around
my waist.
3 And the word of the LORD came
to me the second time, saying,

13
a Lev. 26:16; Dt. 28:38; Mic. 6:15; Hag. 1:6
14
b Cp. Zech. 2:8
15
c Jer. 31:20; Lam. 3:32
16
d Eph. 2:20–21; 1 Pet. 2:5
17
e Isa. 60:12
CHAPTER 13
1
f vv. 9–11
g *Parables* (OT): vv. 1–11; Jer. 18:1. (Jud. 9:8; Zech. 11:7)
9
h Lev. 26:19
i Isa. 2:10–17; 23:9; Zeph. 3:11
10
j Jer. 16:12
k Jer. 9:14; 11:8; 16:12
11
l Ex. 19:5
m Isa. 43:21
n Jer. 7:24
13
o Isa. 51:17, 21; 63:6; Jer. 25:27; 51:7
14
p Jer. 19:9–11

4 "Take the sash that you acquired, which *is* around your waist,
and arise, go to the Euphrates,* and
hide it there in a hole in the rock."
5 So I went and hid it by the [1]Eu-
phrates, as the LORD commanded me.
6 Now it came to pass after many
days that the LORD said to me, "Arise,
go to the Euphrates, and take from
there the sash which I commanded
you to hide there."
7 Then I went to the Euphrates
and dug, and I took the sash from the
place where I had hidden it; and there
was the sash, ruined. It was profitable
for nothing.
8 Then the word of the LORD came
to me, saying,
9 "Thus says the LORD: 'In this
manner I will [h]ruin the pride of Judah
and the great [i]pride of Jerusalem.
10 'This evil people, who [j]refuse to
hear My words, who [k]follow the dictates of their hearts, and walk after
other gods to serve them and worship
them, shall be just like this sash which
is profitable for nothing.
11 'For as the sash clings to the
waist of a man, so I have caused the
whole house of Israel and the whole
house of Judah to cling to Me,' says
the LORD, 'that [l]they may become My
people, for renown, for praise, and for
[m]glory; but they would [n]not hear.'
12 "Therefore you shall speak to
them this word: 'Thus says the LORD
God of Israel: "Every bottle shall be
filled with wine." ' And they will say to
you, 'Do we not certainly know that
every bottle will be filled with wine?'
13 "Then you shall say to them,
'Thus says the LORD: "Behold, I will fill
all the inhabitants of this land—even
the kings who sit on David's throne,
the priests, the prophets, and all the
inhabitants of Jerusalem—with
[o]drunkenness!
14 "And I will [p]dash them one
against another, even the fathers and
the sons together," says the LORD. "I

*13:4 Hebrew *Perath*

[1](13:5) Some have questioned the possibility of Jeremiah's having actually buried his sash at Perath (or by the Euphrates), in view of the distance and the war conditions. However, there were periods in Jeremiah's ministry when that whole area was at peace. It is not impossible that Jeremiah may have actually made a visit to Babylon, and if so, this event could easily have taken place at that time, as he might have buried the sash on his way there and might have dug it up on his way back. It is also possible to interpret the Hebrew word as meaning, not Perath but the Wadi Farah, a few miles north of Jerusalem. In this case he could have buried the sash at any time prior to the final Babylonian attack. Thus there is reason to assume that this passage describes an actual event—not a mere vision or imaginary story. Jeremiah's ruined sash served as a symbol indicating Israel's unsatisfactory life and service.

will not pity nor spare nor have
mercy, but will destroy them." ' "

15 Hear and give ear:
Do not be proud,
For the LORD has spoken.
16 [a]Give glory to the LORD your
God
Before He causes [b]darkness,
And before your feet stumble
On the dark mountains,
And while you are looking for
light,
He turns it into the shadow of
death
And makes *it* dense darkness.
17 But if you will not hear it,
My soul will [c]weep in secret
for *your* pride;
My eyes will weep bitterly
And run down with tears,
Because the LORD's flock has
been taken captive.

18 Say to the king and to the
queen mother,
"Humble yourselves;
Sit down,
For your rule shall collapse,
the crown of your glory."
19 The cities of the [d]South shall
be shut up,
And no one shall open *them;*
Judah shall be carried away
captive, all of it;
It shall be wholly carried away
captive.

20 Lift up your eyes and see
Those who come from the
[e]north.
Where *is* the flock *that* was
given to you,
Your beautiful sheep?
21 What will you say when He
punishes you?
For you have taught them
To be chieftains, to be head
over you.
Will not pangs seize you,
Like a woman in labor?
22 And if you say in your heart,
[f]"Why have these things come
upon me?"
For the greatness of your
iniquity
Your skirts have been
uncovered,
Your heels made bare.
23 Can the Ethiopian [g]change his
skin or the leopard its spots?
Then may you also do good
who are accustomed to do
evil.

24 "Therefore I will [h]scatter them
[i]like stubble
That passes away by the wind
of the wilderness.
25 This is your lot,
The portion of your measures
from Me," says the LORD,
"Because you have forgotten
Me
And [j]trusted in falsehood.
26 Therefore I will uncover your
skirts over your face,
That your shame may appear.
27 I have seen your adulteries
And your *lustful* [k]neighings,
The lewdness of your harlotry,
Your abominations on the hills
in the fields.
Woe to you, O Jerusalem!
Will you still not be made
clean?"

Message concerning the droughts
(14—15)

14 THE word of the LORD that came to Jeremiah concerning the [1]droughts.

2 "Judah mourns,
And her gates languish;
They mourn for the land,
And the cry of Jerusalem has
gone up.
3 Their nobles have sent their
lads for water;
They went to the cisterns *and*
found no water.
They returned with their
vessels empty;
They were ashamed and
confounded
And covered their heads.
4 Because the ground is parched,
For there was [l]no rain in the
land,
The plowmen were ashamed;
They covered their heads.
5 Yes, the deer also gave birth in
the field,
But left because there was no
grass.

16
a Josh. 7:19; Ps. 96:8; Mal. 2:2
b Isa. 5:30; 8:22; Amos 8:9
17
c Jer. 9:1; 14:17
19
d Jer. 52:27
20
e Jer. 10:22; 46:20
22
f Jer. 5:19; 16:10
23
g Cp. Prov. 27:22
24
h Jer. 9:16
i Ps. 1:4; Hos. 13:3
25
j See Ps. 2:12, *note*
27
k Jer. 5:8
CHAPTER 14
4
l Jer. 3:3; Ezek. 22:24

[1](14:1) The significance of a drought at this time was very great. It was one of the signs predicted in the Palestinian Covenant (Dt. 28:23–24), and had already been fulfilled in part in the reign of Ahab (1 Ki. 17:1ff.). As that sign had been followed, even though after a long interval, by the Assyrian captivity of the northern kingdom, it should have been received by Judah as a most solemn warning.

6 And the wild donkeys stood in
the desolate heights;
They sniffed at the wind like
jackals;
Their eyes failed because *there*
was no grass."

7 [a]O LORD, though our iniquities
testify against us,
Do it for Your name's sake;
For our backslidings are many,
We have sinned against You.
8 O the Hope of Israel, his
Savior in time of trouble,
Why should You be like a
stranger in the land,
And like a traveler *who* turns
aside to tarry for a night?
9 Why should You be like a man
astonished,
Like a mighty one *who*
[b]cannot save?
Yet You, O LORD, [c]*are* in our
midst,
And we are called by Your
name;
Do not leave us!

10 Thus says the LORD to this people:

[d]"Thus they have loved to
wander;
They have not restrained their
feet.
Therefore the LORD does not
accept them;
He will remember their
iniquity now,
And [e]punish their sins."

11 Then the LORD said to me, [f]"Do
not pray for this people, for *their*
good.
12 [g]"When they fast, I will not hear
their cry; and when they offer burnt
offering and grain offering, I will not
accept them. But I will consume them
by the sword, by the famine, and by
the pestilence."
13 Then I said, "Ah, Lord GOD! Behold, the prophets say to them, 'You
shall not see the sword, nor shall you
have [h]famine, but I will give you assured [i]peace in this place.' "
14 And the LORD said to me, "The
prophets prophesy [j]lies in My name.
I have [k]not sent them, commanded
them, nor spoken to them; they prophesy to you a false vision, divination, a
worthless thing, and the [l]deceit of
their heart.
15 "Therefore thus says the LORD
concerning the prophets who prophesy in My name, whom I did not send,
and who say, 'Sword and famine shall
not be in this land'—'By sword and
famine those prophets shall be [m]con-
sumed!
16 'And the people to whom they
prophesy shall be cast out in the
streets of Jerusalem because of the
famine and the sword; they will
have [n]no one to bury them—them nor
their wives, their sons nor their
daughters—for I will pour their
wickedness on them.'
17 "Therefore you shall say this
word to them:

'Let my eyes flow with [o]tears
night and day,
And let them not cease;
For the virgin daughter of my
people
Has been broken with a
mighty stroke, with a very
severe blow.
18 If I go out to the [p]field,
Then behold, those slain with
the sword!
And if I enter the city,
Then behold, those sick from
famine!
Yes, both prophet and [q]priest
go about in a land they do
not know.' "

19 Have You utterly rejected
Judah?
Has Your soul loathed Zion?
Why have You stricken us so
that *there is* no healing for
us?
We looked for peace, but *there*
was no good;
And for the time of healing,
and there was [r]trouble.
20 We acknowledge, O LORD, our
wickedness
And the iniquity of our
[s]fathers,
For we have [t]sinned against
You.'
21 Do not abhor *us*, for Your
name's sake;
Do not disgrace the throne of
Your glory.
Remember, do not break Your
covenant with us.
22 Are there any among the
[u]idols of the nations that
can cause [v]rain?
Or can the heavens give
showers?
Are You not He, O LORD our
God?
Therefore we will wait for
You,

7
a Bible prayers (OT): vv. 7–9; Jer. 32:16. (Gen. 15:2; Hab. 3:1)
9
b Cp. Isa. 59:1
c Ex. 29:45–46; Lev. 26:11–12
10
d Jer. 2:23–25
e Jer. 44:21–23
11
f Jer. 7:16; 11:14; cp. Ex. 32:10
12
g Prov. 1:28; Isa. 1:15; 58:3; Ezek. 8:18; Mic. 3:4; Zech. 7:13
13
h Cp. Jer. 15:2
i Jer. 8:11; 23:17; cp. 1 Th. 5:2–3
14
j Jer. 20:6; 23:25
k Jer. 27:15
l Jer. 23:16
15
m Ezek. 14:10
16
n Ps. 79:3; Jer. 16:4; cp. 7:32–8:3
17
o Jer. 13:17
18
p Jer. 6:25; Ezek. 7:15
q Jer. 23:11
19
r Jer. 8:15
20
s Jer. 3:25
t Ps. 106:6; Dan. 9:8
22
u Dt. 32:21
v Jer. 5:24; cp. 1 Ki. 18:41–46

Since You have made all these.

Judgment is inevitable

15 THEN the LORD said to me,
[a]"*Even* if [b]Moses and [c]Samuel
stood before Me, My mind *would* not
be favorable toward this people. Cast
them out of My sight, and let them go
forth.
2 "And it shall be, if they say to
you, 'Where should we go?' then you
shall tell them, 'Thus says the LORD:

[d]"Such as *are* for death, to
death;
And such as *are* for the sword,
to the sword;
And such as *are* for the
famine, to the famine;
And such as *are* for the
[e]captivity, to the captivity." '

3 "And I will [f]appoint over them
four forms *of destruction*," says the
LORD: "the sword to slay, the dogs to
drag, the birds of the heavens and the
beasts of the earth to devour and destroy.
4 [g]"I will hand them over to trouble, to all kingdoms of the earth, because of Manasseh the son of Hezekiah, king of Judah, for what he did in
Jerusalem.

5 "For who will have [h]pity on
you, O Jerusalem?
Or who will bemoan you?
Or who will turn aside to ask
how you are doing?
6 You have forsaken Me," says
the LORD,
"You have gone backward.
Therefore I will stretch out My
hand against you and
destroy you;
I am weary of [i]relenting!
7 And I will winnow them with a
winnowing fan in the gates
of the land;
I will [j]bereave *them* of
children;
I will destroy My people,
Since they do not [k]return from
their ways.
8 Their widows will be increased
to Me more than the sand of
the seas;
I will bring against them,
Against the mother of the
young men,
A plunderer at noonday;
I will cause anguish and terror
to fall on them [l]suddenly.

9 "She languishes who has
[m]borne seven;
She has breathed her last;
Her sun has gone down
While *it was* yet day;
She has been ashamed and
confounded.
And the remnant of them I will
deliver to the sword
Before their enemies," says the
LORD.

10 [n]Woe is me, my mother,
That you have borne me,
A man of strife and a man of
contention to the whole
earth!
I have neither lent for interest,
Nor have men lent to me for
interest.
Every one of them curses me.

11 The LORD said:

"Surely it will be well with your
[1]remnant;
Surely I will cause the enemy
to [o]intercede with you
In the time of adversity and in
the time of affliction.
12 Can anyone break iron,
The northern iron and the
bronze?
13 Your wealth and your
treasures
I will give as plunder without
price,
Because of all your sins,
Throughout your territories.
14 And I will make *you* cross over
with* your enemies
Into a [p]land *which* you do not
know;
For a fire is kindled in My
anger,
Which shall burn upon you."

CHAPTER 15

1
[a] Cp. Ezek. 14:14,20
[b] Ex. 32:11–12; Ps. 99:6
[c] 1 Sam. 7:9

2
[d] Jer. 43:11; Ezek. 5:2, 12; cp. Zech. 11:9
[e] Jer. 9:16; 16:13

3
[f] Lev. 26:16, 21,25; Ezek. 14:21

4
[g] Dt. 28:25; 2 Ki. 21:1–18; 23:26–27; 24:3–4

5
[h] Isa. 51:19

6
[i] Jer. 20:16; see Zech. 8:14, *note*

7
[j] Jer. 9:21; 18:21
[k] Isa. 9:13; Jer. 5:3; Amos 4:10–11

8
[l] Isa. 29:5

9
[m] 1 Sam. 2:5

10
[n] Jer. 20:14

11
[o] i.e. *make supplication to.* Jer. 21:2; 37:3; 42:2

14
[p] Jer. 16:13; 17:4

*15:14 Following Masoretic Text and Vulgate; Septuagint, Syriac, and Targum read *cause you to serve* (compare 17:4).

[1](15:11) The remnant, of whom Jeremiah is the representative, is carefully distinguished from the unbelieving mass of the people. They must share with the nation the coming captivity, for they too have sinned (v. 13). However, the LORD's judgment upon the nation will be but a purifying chastisement to them, and they receive a special promise (v. 11). Verses 15–18 give the answer of the remnant to vv. 11–14. Two things characterize the believing remnant always—loyalty to the Word of God, and separation from those who mock that Word (vv. 16–17. Cp. Rev. 3:8–10).

Jeremiah communes with God

15 O LORD, You know;
Remember me and visit me,
And take [a]vengeance for me
on my persecutors.
In Your enduring patience, do
not take me away.
Know that for Your sake I
have suffered rebuke.
16 Your words were found, and I
[b]ate them,
And Your word was to me the
joy and rejoicing of my
heart;
For I am called by Your name,
O LORD God of hosts.
17 I did not sit in the assembly of
the [c]mockers,
Nor did I rejoice;
I sat alone because of Your
hand,
For You have filled me with
indignation.
18 [d]Why is my pain perpetual
And my wound incurable,
Which refuses to be healed?
Will You surely be to me like
an unreliable stream,
As waters *that* fail?

19 Therefore thus says the LORD:

[e]"If you return,
Then I will bring you back;
You shall stand before Me;
If you [f]take out the precious
from the vile,
You shall be as My mouth.
Let them return to you,
But you must not return to
them.
20 And I will make you to this
people a fortified bronze
[g]wall;
And they will fight against
you,
But they shall [h]not prevail
against you;
For I *am* with you to save you
And deliver you," says the
LORD.
21 "I will deliver [i]you from the
hand of the wicked,
And I will [j]redeem you from
the grip of the terrible."

Sign of the unmarried prophet (16:1—17:18)

16 THE word of the LORD also
came to me, [1]saying,
2 "You shall [k]not take a wife, nor
shall you have sons or daughters in
this place."
3 For thus says the LORD concerning the sons and daughters who are
born in this place, and concerning
their mothers who bore them and
their fathers who begot them in this
land:
4 "They shall die gruesome
deaths; they shall not be lamented nor
shall they be [l]buried, *but* they shall
be like refuse on the face of the earth.
They shall be consumed by the sword
and by famine, and their [m]corpses
shall be meat for the birds of heaven
and for the beasts of the earth."
5 For thus says the LORD: "Do not
enter the house of mourning, nor go to
lament or bemoan them; for I have
taken away My peace from this people," says the LORD, "lovingkindness
and mercies.
6 "Both the great and the small
shall die in this land. They shall not be
buried; neither shall men lament for
them, [n]cut themselves, nor make
themselves [o]bald for them.
7 "Nor shall *men* break *bread* in
mourning for them, to comfort them
for the dead; nor shall *men* give them
the cup of consolation to drink for
their father or their mother.
8 "Also you shall not go into the
house of feasting to sit with them, to
eat and drink."
9 For thus says the LORD of hosts,
the God of Israel: "Behold, I will cause
to [p]cease from this place, before your
eyes and in your days, the voice of
mirth and the voice of gladness, the
voice of the bridegroom and the voice
of the bride.
10 "And it shall be, when you show
this people all these words, and they
say to you, [q]'Why has the LORD pronounced all this great disaster against
us? Or what *is* our iniquity? Or what *is*
our sin that we have committed
against the LORD our God?'
11 "then you shall say to them,
[r]'Because your fathers have forsaken
Me,' says the LORD; 'they have walked
after other gods and have served them
and worshiped them, and have forsaken Me and not kept My law.
12 'And you have done worse than
your fathers, for behold, each one fol-

15 [a] Jer. 11:20; 20:12
16 [b] Cp. Ezek. 3:1–3; Rev. 10:9–10
17 [c] i.e. *merrymakers*
18 [d] Jer. 10:19; see Jer. 8:18 and 20:7, *notes*
19 [e] Cp. Zech. 3:7
[f] Ezek. 22:26; 44:23; cp. 2 Cor. 6:14–18
20 [g] Jer. 1:18; 6:27; Ezek. 3:9
[h] Jer. 20:11
21 [i] *Remnant:* vv. 11–21; Jer. 23:3. (Isa. 1:9; Rom. 11:5, *note*)
[j] Cp. Ps. 71:1–5
CHAPTER 16
2 [k] Cp. 1 Cor. 7:26–27
4 [l] Jer. 14:16; 19:11
[m] Ps. 79:2; Jer. 7:33; 34:20
6 [n] Lev. 19:28; Dt. 14:1; Jer. 41:5; 47:5
[o] Cp. Isa. 15:2; 22:12; Mic. 1:16
9 [p] Isa. 24:7–8; Jer. 7:34; 25:10; Ezek. 26:13; Hos. 2:11; Rev. 18:23
10 [q] Dt. 29:24; Jer. 5:19; 13:22; 22:8
11 [r] Dt. 29:25; Jer. 22:9

[1](16:1) The sign of the unmarried prophet is interpreted by the context. The whole social life of Judah was about to be disrupted and cease from the land. But observe the promises of vv. 14–16 and Jer. 17:7–8.

lows the dictates of his own evil heart,
so that [a]no one listens to Me.
13 [b]'Therefore I will cast you out of
this land into a land that you do not
know, neither you nor your fathers;
and there you shall serve other gods
day and night, where I will not show
you favor.'
14 "Therefore behold, the [c]days
are coming," says the LORD, "that it
shall no more be said, 'The LORD lives
who brought up the children of Israel
from the land of Egypt,'
15 "but, 'The LORD lives who
brought up the children of Israel from
the land of the [d]north and from all the
lands where He had driven them.' For
I will [e]bring them back into their land
which I gave to their fathers.
16 "Behold, I will send for many
[f]fishermen," says the LORD, "and they
shall fish them; and afterward I will
send for many hunters, and they shall
hunt them from every mountain and
every hill, and out of the holes of the
rocks.
17 [g]"For My eyes *are* on all their
ways; they are not hidden from My
face, nor is their iniquity hidden from
My eyes.
18 "And first I will repay [h]double
for their iniquity and their sin, [i]because
they have defiled My land; they
have filled My inheritance with the
carcasses of their detestable and
abominable idols."

19 O LORD, my strength and my
fortress,
My refuge in the day of
affliction,
The Gentiles shall come to You
From the ends of the earth and
say,
"Surely our fathers have
inherited lies,
Worthlessness and
unprofitable *things.*"
20 Will a man make gods for
himself,
Which *are* not gods?
21 "Therefore behold, I will this
once cause them to know,
I will cause them to know
My hand and My might;
And they shall know that [j]My
name *is* the LORD.

The deceitful heart (v. 9)

17 "THE sin of Judah *is* [k]written
with a [l]pen of iron;
With the point of a diamond *it*
is [m]engraved
On the tablet of their heart,
And on the horns of your
altars,
2 While their children remember
Their altars and their [n]wooden
images
By the green trees on the high
hills.
3 O My mountain in the field,
I will give as plunder your
wealth, all your treasures,
And your [o]high places of sin
within all your borders.
4 And you, even yourself,
Shall let go of your heritage
which I gave you;
And I will cause you to serve
your enemies
In the land which you do not
know;
For you have kindled a fire in
My anger *which* shall burn
forever."

5 Thus says the LORD:

"Cursed *is* the man who trusts
in [p]man
And makes flesh his strength,
Whose heart departs from the
LORD.
6 For he shall be like a shrub in
the desert,
And shall not see when good
comes,
But shall inhabit the parched
places in the wilderness,
In a salt land *which is* not
inhabited.

7 [q]"Blessed *is* the man who trusts
in the LORD,
And whose hope is the LORD.
8 For he shall be [r]like a tree
planted by the waters,
Which spreads out its roots by
the river,
And will not fear* when heat
comes;
But its leaf will be green,
And will not be anxious in the
year of drought,
Nor will cease from yielding
fruit.

9 "The [s]heart *is* deceitful above
all *things,*
And desperately wicked;
Who can know it?
10 I, the LORD, [t]search the heart,

12 *a* Jer. 13:10
13 *b* Dt. 4:26–28; 28:36, 63–65; Jer. 15:2,14
14 *c* Isa. 11:11–12; Jer. 23:7–8; Ezek. 37:21–25
15 *d* Jer. 3:18 *e* Jer. 24:6; 30:3; 32:37
16 *f* Amos 4:2; Hab. 1:15
17 *g* Job 34:21; Prov. 5:21; 15:3; Jer. 32:19; Heb. 4:13
18 *h* Isa. 40:2; Jer. 17:18 *i* Ezek. 43:7–9
21 *j* Heb. *Jehovah (YHWH).* Ps. 83:18
CHAPTER 17
1 *k* Jer. 2:22 *l* Job 19:24 *m* Prov. 3:3, 2 Cor. 3:3
2 *n* See Dt. 16:21, *note*
3 *o* See Jud. 3:7 and 1 Ki. 3:2, *notes*
5 *p* Ps. 146:3; Isa. 31:3
7 *q* Ps. 2:12; 34:8; 125:1; 146:5; Prov. 16:20; Isa. 30:18; Jer. 39:18
8 *r* Job 8:16; Ps. 1:3
9 *s* Eccl. 9:3; Mt. 15:19
10 *t* 1 Sam. 16:7; 1 Chr. 28:9; Ps. 7:9; 139:23–24; Prov. 17:3; Jer. 11:20; 20:12; Rom. 8:27; Rev. 2:23

* 17:8 Qere and Targum read *see.*

I [a]test the mind,
Even to give every man
according to his ways,
According to the fruit of his
doings.
11 "*As* a partridge that broods but
does not hatch,
So is he who gets riches, but
not by right;
It will leave him in the midst
of his days,
And at his end he will be a
fool."
12 A glorious high throne from
the beginning
Is the place of our sanctuary.
13 O LORD, the [b]hope of Israel,
[c]All who forsake You shall be
ashamed.
"Those who depart from Me
Shall be [d]written in the earth,
Because they have forsaken
the LORD,
The fountain of living waters."
14 Heal me, O LORD, and I shall
be healed;
Save me, and I shall be saved,
For You *are* my praise.
15 Indeed they say to me,
[e]"Where *is* the word of the LORD?
Let it come now!"
16 As for me, I have not hurried
away from *being* a shepherd
who follows You,
Nor have I desired the woeful
day;
You know what came out of
my lips;
It was right there before You.
17 Do not be a terror to me;
You *are* my hope in the day of
doom.
18 Let them be ashamed who
[f]persecute me,
But do not let me be put to
shame;
Let them be dismayed,
But do not let me be dismayed.
Bring on them the day of
doom,
And destroy them with double
destruction!

Message concerning the Sabbath

19 Thus the LORD said to me: "Go
and stand in the gate of the children of
the people, by which the kings of Judah come in and by which they go out,
and in all the gates of Jerusalem;
20 "and say to them, 'Hear the word
of the LORD, you kings of Judah, and
all Judah, and all the inhabitants of
Jerusalem, who enter by these gates.
21 'Thus says the LORD: [g]"Take
heed to yourselves, and bear no burden on the Sabbath day, nor bring *it* in
by the gates of Jerusalem;
22 "nor carry a burden out of your
houses on the Sabbath day, nor do any
work, but hallow the Sabbath day, as
I commanded your fathers.
23 [h]"But they did not obey nor incline their ear, but made their neck
stiff, that they might not hear nor receive instruction.
24 "And it shall be, [i]if you heed Me
carefully," says the LORD, "to bring no
burden through the gates of this city
on the [j]Sabbath day, but hallow the
Sabbath day, to do no work in it,
25 [k]"then shall enter the gates of
this city kings and princes sitting on
the throne of David, riding in chariots
and on horses, they and their princes,
accompanied by the men of Judah and
the inhabitants of Jerusalem; and this
city shall remain forever.
26 "And they shall come from the
cities of Judah and from the places
around Jerusalem, from the land of
Benjamin and from the [l]lowland,
from the mountains and from the
[m]South, bringing burnt offerings and
sacrifices, grain offerings and incense, bringing sacrifices of praise to
the house of the LORD.
27 "But if you will not heed Me to
hallow the Sabbath day, such as not
carrying a burden when entering the
gates of Jerusalem on the Sabbath
day, then I will kindle a fire in its
gates, and it shall [n]devour the palaces
of Jerusalem, and it shall not be
[o]quenched." ' "

Sign of the potter's house (18—19)

18 THE word which came to Jeremiah from the LORD, [p]saying:
2 "Arise and go down to the [1]pot-
ter's house, and there I will cause you
to hear My words."
3 Then I went down to the potter's
house, and there he was, making
something at the wheel.

10 *a Test/tempt:* v. 10; Jer. 20:12. (Gen. 3:1; Jas. 1:14, *note*)
13 *b* Jer. 14:8 *c* Ps. 73:27; Isa. 1:28 *d* Cp. Lk. 10:20
15 *e* Isa. 5:19; Ezek. 12:22, 2 Pet. 3:4
18 *f* Jer. 15:10; 18:18
21 *g* Cp. Neh. 13:15–19; Jn. 5:10
23 *h* Jer. 7:24–26; 11:10; 16:12; 19:15
24 *i* Jer. 11:4; 26:3 *j* Ex. 16:23–30; 20:8–10; Num. 15:32–36; Dt. 5:12–14; Neh. 13:15; Isa. 58:13
25 *k* Jer. 22:4
26 *l* See Dt. 1:7, *note* *m* See Gen. 12:9, *note*
27 *n* Jer. 7:20 *o* Jer. 39:8
CHAPTER 18
1 *p Parables (OT):* vv. 1–6; Jer. 24:1. (Jud. 9:8; Zech. 11:7)

[1](18:2) In ch. 18 God explains to Jeremiah that sovereign grace is able to take the marred pot (Israel) and remake it a useful vessel (v. 4). But to the elders, in ch. 19, the prophet declares that their generation will be irreparably destroyed like a smashed fragile jar, and the fragments taken to Babylon. That generation of the nation was not restored to the land (19:10–13).

4 And the vessel that he made of
clay was [a]marred in the hand of the
potter; so he made it again into another vessel, as it seemed good to the
potter to make.
5 Then the word of the LORD came
to me, saying:
6 "O house of Israel, [b]can I not do
with you as this potter?" says the
LORD. "Look, as the [c]clay *is* in the potter's hand, so *are* you in My hand, O
house of Israel!
7 "The instant I speak concerning
a nation and concerning a kingdom, to
pluck up, to pull down, and to destroy
it,
8 "if that nation against whom I
have spoken turns from its evil, I will
[d]relent of the disaster that I thought to
bring upon [e]it.
9 "And the instant I speak concerning a nation and concerning a
kingdom, to build and to plant *it*,
10 "if it does evil in My sight so that
it does not obey My voice, then I will
relent concerning the good with
which I said I would benefit [f]it.
11 "Now therefore, speak to the
men of Judah and to the inhabitants of
Jerusalem, saying, 'Thus says the
LORD: "Behold, I am fashioning a [g]di-
saster and devising a plan against
you. Return now every one from his
evil way, and make your ways and
your doings [h]good." ' "
12 And they said, "That is [i]hope-
less! So we will walk according to our
own plans, and we will every one obey
the dictates of his evil heart."
13 Therefore thus says the LORD:

"Ask now among the Gentiles,
Who has heard such [j]things?
The virgin of Israel has done a
very horrible thing.
14 Will *a man* leave the
snow-water of Lebanon,
Which comes from the rock of
the field?
Will the cold flowing waters be
forsaken for strange waters?
15 "Because My people have
[k]forgotten Me,
They have burned incense to
worthless idols.
And they have caused
themselves to stumble in
their ways,
From the [l]ancient paths,
To walk in pathways and not
on a highway,
16 To make their land [m]desolate
and a perpetual [n]hissing;
Everyone who passes by it will
be astonished
And shake his head.
17 I will [o]scatter them as with an
east wind before the enemy;
I will show them* the back
and not the face
In the day of their calamity."

18 Then they said, "Come and let us
devise plans [p]against Jeremiah; [q]for
the law shall not perish from the
[r]priest, nor counsel from the [s]wise,
nor the word from the [t]prophet.
Come and let us attack him with the
tongue, and let us not give heed to any
of his words."

19 Give heed to me, O LORD,
And listen to the voice of those
who contend with me!
20 Shall evil be repaid for good?
For they have [u]dug a pit for
my life.
Remember that I [v]stood before
You
To speak good for them,
To turn away Your wrath from
them.
21 Therefore deliver up their
children to the famine,
And pour out their *blood*
By the force of the sword;
Let their wives *become* widows
And [w]bereaved of their
children.
Let their men be put to death,
Their young men *be* slain
By the sword in battle.
22 Let a cry be heard from their
houses,
When You bring a troop
suddenly upon them;
For they have dug a pit to take
me,
And hidden snares for my feet.
23 Yet, LORD, You know all their
counsel
Which is against me, to slay
me.
Provide [x]no atonement for
their iniquity,
Nor blot out their sin from
Your sight;
But let them be overthrown
before You.
Deal *thus* with them
In the time of Your [y]anger.

*18:17 Following Septuagint, Syriac, Targum, and Vulgate; Masoretic Text reads *look them in*.

4
a Cp. Jer. 13:7
6
b Isa. 45:9; Rom. 9:20–21
c Isa. 64:8
8
d See Zech. 8:14, *note*
e Ezek. 18:21; cp. Jon. 3:10
10
f Cp. 1 Sam. 2:30; 13:13
11
g i.e. *punishment*
h Jer. 7:3–7
12
i Jer. 2:25
13
j Jer. 2:10–11
15
k Jer. 2:13, 32; 3:21; 13:25; 17:13
l Jer. 6:16
16
m Jer. 19:8; 25:9; 49:13; 50:13
n 1 Ki. 9:8; Lam. 2:15; Mic. 6:16
17
o Jer. 13:24; 20:4–5
18
p Jer. 11:19; 17:18; 20:11
q Cp. Mal. 2:7
r Cp. Jer. 2:8
s Cp. Jer. 8:8
t Cp. Jer. 5:13
20
u Jer. 5:26
v Jer. 14:17–15:1
21
w Jer. 15:7
23
x Ps. 109:14
y Jer. 7:20

Judah, the broken flask

19 THUS says the LORD: "Go and get a potter's earthen flask, and *take* some of the elders of the people and some of the elders of the priests.

2 "And go out to the [a]Valley of the Son of Hinnom, which *is* by the entry of the Potsherd Gate; and proclaim there the words that I will tell you,

3 "and say, 'Hear the word of the LORD, O kings of Judah and inhabitants of Jerusalem. Thus says the LORD of hosts, the God of Israel: "Behold, I will bring such a catastrophe on this place, that whoever hears of it, his ears will [b]tingle.

4 [c]"Because they have forsaken Me and made this an alien place, because they have burned incense in it to other gods whom neither they, their fathers, nor the kings of Judah have known, and have filled this place with the blood of the innocents

5 "(they have also built the high places of Baal, to [d]burn their sons with fire *for* burnt offerings to Baal, which I did not command or speak, nor did it come into My mind),

6 "therefore behold, the days are coming," says the LORD, "that this place shall no more be called [e]Tophet [f]or the Valley of the Son of Hinnom, but the Valley of Slaughter.

7 "And I will make void the counsel of Judah and Jerusalem in this place, and I will cause them to [g]fall by the sword before their enemies and by the hands of those who seek their lives; their [h]corpses I will give as meat for the birds of the heaven and for the beasts of the earth.

8 "I will make this city desolate and a hissing; everyone who passes by it will be [i]astonished and hiss because of all its plagues.

9 "And I will cause them to eat the [j]flesh of their sons and the flesh of their daughters, and everyone shall eat the flesh of his friend in the siege and in the desperation with which their enemies and those who seek their lives shall drive them to despair." '

10 "Then you shall break the flask in the sight of the men who go with you,

11 "and say to them, 'Thus says the LORD of hosts: "Even so I will [k]break this people and this city, as *one* breaks a potter's vessel, which cannot be made whole again; and they shall bury *them* in Tophet till *there is* no place to bury.

12 "Thus I will do to this place," says the LORD, "and to its inhabitants, and make this city like Tophet.

13 "And the [l]houses of Jerusalem and the houses of the kings of Judah shall be defiled like the place of Tophet, because of all the houses on whose [m]roofs they have burned incense to all the host of heaven, and poured out drink offerings to other gods." ' "

14 Then Jeremiah came from Tophet, where the LORD had sent him to prophesy; and he stood in the [n]court of the Lord's house and said to all the people,

15 "Thus says the LORD of hosts, the God of Israel: 'Behold, I will bring on this city and on all her towns all the doom that I have pronounced against it, because they have stiffened their necks that they might not hear My words.' "

Jeremiah persecuted by Pashhur (19:14—20:6)

20 NOW [o]Pashhur the son of [p]Immer, the priest who *was* also chief governor in the house of the LORD, heard that Jeremiah prophesied these things.

2 Then Pashhur struck Jeremiah the prophet, and [1]put him in the stocks that *were* in the high [q]gate of Benjamin, which *was* by the house of the LORD.

3 And it happened on the next day that Pashhur brought Jeremiah out of the stocks. Then Jeremiah said to him, "The LORD has not called your name Pashhur, but [r]Magor-Missabib.

4 "For thus says the LORD: 'Behold, I will make you a terror to yourself and to all your friends; and they shall fall by the sword of their enemies, and your eyes shall see *it*. I will [s]give all Judah into the hand of the king of Babylon, and he shall carry them captive to Babylon and slay them with the sword.

5 'Moreover I will [t]deliver all the wealth of this city, all its produce, and all its precious things; all the treasures of the kings of Judah I will give into the hand of their enemies, who will

CHAPTER 19

2 *a* Josh. 15:8; 2 Ki. 23:10; Jer. 7:31; 32:35

3 *b* 1 Sam. 3:11; 2 Ki. 21:12

4 *c* Dt. 28:20; Isa. 65:11; Jer. 2:13, 17,19; 15:6; 17:13

5 *d* Lev. 18:21; 2 Ki. 17:17

6 *e* See Jer. 7:31, *note* *f* Jer. 7:32

7 *g* Lev. 26:17; Dt. 28:25 *h* Jer. 7:32–8:3; 16:4; 25:33

8 *i* Jer. 18:16; 25:9

9 *j* Lev. 26:29; Dt. 28:53; cp. 2 Ki. 6:28–29; Lam. 4:10

11 *k* Ps. 2:9; Isa. 30:14; Jer. 13:14

13 *l* Jer. 52:13 *m* 2 Ki. 23:12; Jer. 32:29; Zeph. 1:5

14 *n* Jer. 26:2–8

CHAPTER 20

1 *o* Ezra 2:37–38 *p* 1 Chr. 24:14

2 *q* Jer. 37:13

3 *r* Lit. *Terror on every side*

4 *s* Jer. 21:4–10

5 *t* 2 Ki. 20:17; 24:12–16; 25:13

[1](20:2) To be placed in the stocks was a painful experience, during which the victim's head, hands, and feet were held securely in holes cut in a single piece of timber.

plunder them, seize them, and [a]carry
them to Babylon.
6 'And you, Pashhur, and all who
dwell in your house, shall go into captivity. You shall go to Babylon, and
there you shall die, and be buried
there, you and all your friends, to
whom you have prophesied [b]lies.' "

Jeremiah complains to God

7 [c]O LORD, You [1]induced me, and
I was persuaded;
You are stronger than I, and
have prevailed.
I am in [d]derision daily;
Everyone mocks me.
8 For when I spoke, I cried out;
I shouted, "Violence and
plunder!"
Because the word of the LORD
was made to me
A reproach and a [e]derision
daily.
9 Then I said, "I will [f]not make
mention of Him,
Nor speak anymore in His
name."
But *His word* was in my heart
[g]like a burning fire
Shut up in my bones;
I was [h]weary of holding *it*
back,
And [i]I could not.
10 For I heard many mocking:
"Fear on every side!"
"Report," *they say*, "and we will
report it!"
All my acquaintances watched
for my stumbling, *saying*,
"Perhaps he can be induced;
Then we will prevail against
him,
And we will take our revenge
on him."
11 But the LORD *is* [j]with me as a
mighty, awesome One.
Therefore my [k]persecutors will
stumble, and will not prevail.
They will be greatly ashamed,
for they will not prosper.
Their everlasting confusion
will never be forgotten.
12 But, O LORD of hosts,
You who [l]test the righteous,
And see the mind and heart,
Let me see Your [m]vengeance
on them;
For I have pleaded my cause
before You.
13 Sing to the LORD! Praise the
LORD!
For He has [n]delivered the life
of the poor
From the hand of evildoers.
14 Cursed *be* the day in which I
was [o]born!
Let the day not be blessed in
which my mother bore me!
15 Let the man *be* cursed
Who brought news to my
father, saying,
"A male child has been born to
you!"
Making him very glad.
16 And let that man be like the
cities
Which the LORD overthrew,
and did not [p]relent;
Let him hear the cry in the
morning
And the shouting at noon,
17 Because he did not kill me
from the womb,
That my mother might have
been my grave,
And her womb always
enlarged *with me*.
18 Why did I come forth from the
womb to see labor and
sorrow,
That my days should be
consumed with shame?

Messages concerning Judah's last four kings: (1) Zedekiah (21:1—22:9)

21 THE word which came to Jeremiah from the LORD when
[q]King Zedekiah sent to him Pashhur
the son of Melchiah, and [r]Zephaniah
the son of Maaseiah, the priest, saying,
2 "Please [s]inquire of the LORD for
us, for Nebuchadnezzar* king of Bab-

5 a Isa. 39:6
6 b Jer. 14:14; 23:32
7 c vv. 7–18; see Jer. 8:18, *note* d Lam. 3:14
8 e Cp. 2 Chr. 36:16
9 f Cp. 1 Ki. 19:3–4; Jon. 1:1–3 g Job 32:18–19; Ps. 39:3 h Jer. 6:11; cp. Acts 4:20 i Cp. Acts 18:5
11 j Jer. 1:18–19 k Jer. 17:18
12 l *Test/tempt*: v. 12; Mal. 3:10. (Gen. 3:1; Jas. 1:14, *note*). Jer. 11:20 m Jer. 15:15
13 n Ps. 35:9–10; 109:30–31
14 o Job 3:3–6; Jer. 15:10
16 p See Zech. 8:14, *note*
CHAPTER 21
1 q 2 Ki. 24:17 r 2 Ki. 25:18; Jer. 29:25; 37:3
2 s 1 Sam. 9:9

*21:2 Hebrew *Nebuchadrezzar*, and so elsewhere

[1](20:7) Jeremiah is not accusing the LORD of misrepresentation but is giving vent to his great sorrow at the terrible situation in which he finds himself. God has called him to stand alone amid constant opposition, and has gradually led him into the position where He wants him to be—one that involves great misery for Jeremiah. In vv. 14–18 Jeremiah expresses his anguish in extreme language. Such passages in the prophetic books are not to be taken as merely the expression of sinful or erroneous human thoughts. The terrible sorrow of Jeremiah echoes the sorrow of God Himself as He sees His own people going on in sin and unbelief, ignoring His goodness toward them, and making it necessary for Him to chasten them. See Jer. 4:10, *note*.

ylon makes war against us. Perhaps
the LORD will deal with us according to
all His wonderful works, that *the king*
may go away from us."
3 Then Jeremiah said to them,
"Thus you shall say to Zedekiah,
4 'Thus says the LORD God of Israel: "Behold, I will turn back the
weapons of war that *are* in your
hands, with which you fight against
the king of Babylon and the Chaldeans* who besiege you outside the
walls; and I will assemble them in the
midst of this city.
5 "I [a]Myself will fight against you
with an [b]outstretched hand and with
a strong arm, even in anger and fury
and great wrath.
6 "I will strike the inhabitants of
this city, both man and beast; they
shall die of a great pestilence.
7 "And afterward," says the LORD,
"I will [c]deliver Zedekiah king of Judah, his servants and the people, and
such as are left in this city from the
pestilence and the sword and the famine, into the hand of Nebuchadnezzar
king of Babylon, into the hand of their
enemies, and into the hand of those
who seek their life; and he shall strike
them with the edge of the sword. He
shall not [d]spare them, or have pity or
mercy." '
8 "Now you shall say to this people, 'Thus says the LORD: "Behold, I
[e]set before you the way of life and the
way of death.
9 "He who remains in this city
shall die by the sword, by famine, and
by pestilence; but he who goes out and
defects to the Chaldeans who besiege
you, he shall [f]live, and his [g]life shall
be as a prize to him.
10 "For I have set My face against
this city for [h]adversity and not for
good," says the LORD. "It shall be
[i]given into the hand of the king of
Babylon, and he shall burn it with
[j]fire." '
11 "And concerning the house of
the king of Judah, *say*, 'Hear the word
of the LORD,
12 'O house of David! Thus says the
LORD:

"Execute judgment in the
morning;
And deliver *him who is*
plundered
Out of the hand of the
oppressor,
Lest My fury go forth like fire
And burn so that no one can
quench *it*,
Because of the evil of your
doings.

13 "Behold, [k]I *am* against you, O
inhabitant of the valley,
And rock of the plain," says
the LORD,
"Who [l]say, 'Who shall come
down against us?
Or who shall enter our
dwellings?'
14 But I will punish you
according to the [m]fruit of
your doings," says the LORD;
"I will kindle a fire in its forest,
And it shall devour all things
around it." ' "

Zedekiah warned of Jerusalem's fall

22 THUS says the LORD: "Go down
to the house of the king of Judah, and there speak this word,
2 "and say, [n]'Hear the word of the
LORD, O king of Judah, you who sit on
the throne of David, you and your servants and your people who enter these
gates!
3 'Thus says the LORD: [o]"Execute
judgment and righteousness, and deliver the plundered out of the hand of
the oppressor. Do no wrong and do no
violence to the stranger, the [p]father-
less, or the widow, nor shed innocent
blood in this place.
4 "For if you indeed do this thing,
[q]then shall enter the gates of this
house, riding on horses and in chariots, accompanied by servants and
people, kings who sit on the throne of
David.
5 "But if you will not hear these
words, I [r]swear by Myself," says the
LORD, "that this house shall become a
desolation." ' "
6 For thus says the LORD to the
house of the king of Judah:

"You *are* [s]Gilead to Me,
The head of Lebanon;
Yet I surely will make you a
wilderness,
Cities *which* are not inhabited.
7 I will prepare destroyers
against you,
Everyone with his weapons;
They shall cut down your
choice cedars
And cast *them* into the fire.
8 "And many nations will pass by

5
a Jer. 33:5; Isa. 63:10
b Cp. Ex. 6:6
7
c Jer. 32:1–5; 39:4–10
d 2 Chr. 36:17; Isa. 47:6
8
e Dt. 30:19
9
f Jer. 38:2
g Jer. 39:18
10
h Jer. 19:15
i Jer. 20:4
j 2 Chr. 36:19
13
k Ezek. 13:8
l Jer. 49:4
14
m Prov. 1:31; Isa. 3:10–11
CHAPTER 22
2
n Jer. 17:20
3
o Jer. 21:12
p Jer. 7:6; Zech. 7:10
4
q Jer. 17:25
5
r Cp. Gen. 22:16; Heb. 6:13–20
6
s Song 4:1

*21:4 Or *Babylonians*

this city; and everyone will say to his
neighbor, [a]'Why has the LORD done so
to this great city?'
9 "Then they will answer, [b]'Because they have forsaken the covenant of the LORD their God, and worshiped other gods and served them.' "

(2) Message concerning Jehoahaz (Shallum)

10 Weep not for the [c]dead, nor
bemoan him;
[d]Weep bitterly for him who
goes away,
For he shall return no more,
Nor see his native country.

11 For thus says the LORD concerning [e]Shallum the son of Josiah, king
of Judah, who reigned instead of Josiah his father, who went from this
place: "He shall not return here [f]any-
more,
12 "but he shall die in the place
where they have led him captive, and
shall see this land no more.

(3) Message concerning Jehoiakim

13 [g]"Woe to him [h]who builds his
house by unrighteousness
And his chambers by injustice,
Who uses his neighbor's
service without wages
And gives him nothing for his
work,
14 Who says, 'I will build myself
a wide house with spacious
chambers,
And cut out windows for it,
Paneling *it* with cedar
And painting *it* with
vermilion.'
15 "Shall you reign because you
enclose *yourself* in cedar?
Did not your father eat and
drink,
And do justice and
righteousness?
Then *it was* [i]well with him.
16 He judged the cause of the
poor and needy;
Then *it was* well.
Was not this knowing Me?"
says the LORD.
17 "Yet your eyes and your heart
are for nothing but your
[j]covetousness,
For shedding innocent blood,
And practicing oppression and
violence."

18 Therefore thus says the LORD
concerning Jehoiakim the son of Josiah, king of Judah:

"They shall not [k]lament for
him,
Saying, 'Alas, my brother!' or
'Alas, my sister!'
They shall not lament for him,
Saying, 'Alas, master!' or 'Alas,
his glory!'
19 He shall be [1]buried with the
[l]burial of a donkey,
Dragged and cast out beyond
the gates of Jerusalem.

(4) Message concerning Coniah (Jeconiah, Jehoiachin)

20 "Go up to Lebanon, and cry out,
And lift up your voice in
Bashan;
Cry from Abarim,
For all your lovers are
destroyed.
21 I spoke to you in your
prosperity,
But you said, 'I will not hear.'
This *has been* your manner
from your [m]youth,
That you did not obey My
voice.
22 The wind shall eat up all your
[n]rulers,
And your lovers shall go into
captivity;
Surely then you will be
ashamed and humiliated
For all your wickedness.
23 O inhabitant of Lebanon,
Making your nest in the
cedars,
How gracious will you be
when pangs come upon you,
Like the pain of a woman in
labor?

24 "*As* I live," says the LORD,
"though [o]Coniah the son of Jehoiakim, king of Judah, were the signet on
My right hand, yet I would pluck you
off;
25 "and I will give you into the hand
of those who seek your life, and into
the hand *of those* whose face you
fear—the hand of Nebuchadnezzar

8
a Dt. 29:24–25; 1 Ki. 9:8–9
9
b 2 Ki. 22:17; 2 Chr. 34:25
10
c 2 Ki. 22:20
d Jer. 14:17; Lam. 3:48
11
e 1 Chr. 3:15; or *Jehoahaz,* 2 Ki. 23:30
f 2 Ki. 23:34; 2 Chr. 36:4; Ezek. 19:4
13
g Jer. 17:11; Ezek. 22:13
h Lev. 19:13; Dt. 24:14–15; Jas. 5:4
15
i 2 Ki. 23:25; cp. Jer. 7:23; 42:6
17
j Jer. 6:13; 8:10; Lk. 12:15–20
18
k Jer. 16:4; 25:33; cp. 2 Chr. 35:24–25
19
l Jer. 8:2; 36:30
21
m Jer. 32:30; cp. 2 Ki. 24:8–9
22
n Jer. 10:21; 23:1–2
24
o Contracted from *Jeconiah,* 1 Chr. 3:16

[1](22:19) It has been claimed that the silence of the historical books about Jehoiakim's fate proves that Jeremiah prophesied wrongly. On the contrary, this prediction gives further historical information. If Jeremiah had made so precise a prediction about a contemporary and the prediction had not been fulfilled, it is unthinkable that the people would have continued to regard Jeremiah as a true prophet and to treasure his writings. Cp. Dt. 18:20–22.

king of Babylon and the hand of the
Chaldeans.
26 "So I will cast you out, and your
[a]mother who bore you, into another
country where you were not born; and
there you shall die.
27 "But to the land to which they
desire to return, there they shall not
return.

28 "Is this man Coniah a despised,
broken idol—
A vessel in which *is* no
pleasure?
Why are they cast out, he and
his descendants,
And cast into a land which
they do not know?
29 O earth, earth, earth,
Hear the word of the LORD!
30 Thus says the LORD:
'Write this man down as
[1]childless,
A man *who* shall not prosper
in his days;
For [b]none of his descendants
shall prosper,
Sitting on the throne of David,
And ruling anymore in
Judah.' "

God's true king: Messiah, the righteous Branch. Israel to be regathered

23 "WOE to the [c]shepherds who
destroy and scatter the sheep
of My pasture!" says the LORD.
2 Therefore thus says the LORD
God of Israel against the [c]shepherds
who feed My people: "You have scattered My flock, driven them away, and
not attended to them. Behold, I will
attend to you for the evil of your doings," says the LORD.
3 "But I will [2]gather the [d]remnant
of My [e]flock out of all countries where
I have driven them, and bring them
back to their folds; and they shall be
fruitful and increase.
4 "I will set up [f]shepherds over
them who will feed them; and they
shall fear no more, nor be dismayed,
nor shall they be lacking," says the
LORD.

5 "Behold, *the* days are coming,"
says the LORD,
"That I will raise to David a
[g]Branch of righteousness;
A [h]King shall reign and
prosper,
And execute judgment and
righteousness in the earth.
6 [i]In His days Judah will be
saved,
And Israel will dwell safely;
Now this *is* His name by which
He will be called:

[j]THE LORD OUR
RIGHTEOUSNESS.

7 "Therefore, behold, *the* days are
coming," says the LORD, "that they
shall no longer say, 'As the LORD lives
who brought up the children of Israel
from the land of Egypt,'
8 "but, 'As the LORD lives who
brought up and led the descendants of
the house of Israel from the north
country and [k]from all the countries
where I had driven them.' And they
shall dwell in their own [l]land."

False prophets denounced

9 My heart within me is broken
Because of the prophets;
All my bones shake.
I am like a drunken man,

26 *a* 2 Ki. 24:8, 12,15
30 *b* vv. 24–30; Jer. 36:30; see Mt. 1:11, *note;* cp. Acts 15:13, *note*
CHAPTER 23
1 *c* Jer. 22:22; Ezek. 34:1–10; Zech. 11:15–17; cp. Ezek. 34:11–31; 37:24; Zech. 11:4–14; Jn. 10:1–16
3 *d Remnant:* vv. 3–8; Jer. 31:7. (Isa. 1:9; Rom. 11:5, *note*)
e Israel (prophecies): vv. 3–8; Jer. 30:3. (Gen. 12:2; Rom. 11:26, *note*)
4 *f* Jer. 3:15; Ezek. 34:23
5 *g* See Isa. 4:2, *note*
h Kingdom (OT): vv. 5–8; Jer. 30:9. (Gen. 1:26; Zech. 12:8, *note*)
6 *i Christ* (second advent): vv. 5–6; Ezek. 37:22. (Dt. 30:3; Acts 1:11, *note*)
j Heb. *Jehovah-tsidkenu* See Ex. 34:6, *note*
23:8 *k* v. 3; Isa. 43:5–6 *l* Gen. 12:7; Jer. 16:14–15; 31:8

[1](22:30) This declaration does not mean that Coniah (or Jeconiah or Jehoiachin) would have no children, for in 1 Chr. 3:17–18 some are named (cp. Mt. 1:12). By divine judgment this king was to be written down childless, i.e. no physical descendant would occupy a place in the list of Israel's kings. Consequently, if our Lord Jesus, who is to occupy David's throne (Lk. 1:32–33), had been begotten by Mary's husband, Joseph, who was of the line of Jeconiah (Mt. 1:12,16), it would have contradicted this divine prediction. Christ's dynastic right to the throne came, through his foster father Joseph, from Jeconiah, but the physical descent of Jesus from David came through Mary, whose genealogy is traced to David through Nathan rather than through Solomon (cp. Lk. 3:31 with Mt. 1:17).

[2](23:3) This final restoration will be accomplished after a period of unexampled tribulation (Jer. 30:3–10), and in connection with the manifestation of David's righteous Branch (v. 5), *Jehovah-tsidkenu* (v. 6). This restoration is not to be confused with the return of a remnant of Judah under Ezra, Nehemiah, and Zerubbabel at the end of the seventy years' captivity (Jer. 29:10). At His first advent Christ, David's righteous Branch (Lk. 1:31–33), did not establish an *earthly* kingdom, but was crowned with thorns and crucified. Neither was Israel the nation restored, nor did the Jewish people say, "THE LORD OUR RIGHTEOUSNESS." Cp. Rom. 10:3. The prophecy is yet to be fulfilled (Acts 15:14–17).

And like a man whom wine
has overcome,
Because of the LORD,
And because of His holy
words.
10 For the land is full of
adulterers;
For because of a curse the land
mourns.
The pleasant places of the
wilderness are dried up.
Their course of life is evil,
And their might *is* not right.
11 "For both prophet and priest
are [a]profane;
Yes, in My [b]house I have
found their wickedness,"
says the LORD.
12 "Therefore their way shall be to
them
Like slippery *ways;*
In the darkness they shall be
driven on
And fall in them;
For I will bring disaster on
them,
The year of their punishment,"
says the LORD.
13 "And I have seen folly in the
prophets of Samaria:
They prophesied by Baal
And caused My people Israel
to err.
14 Also I have seen a horrible
thing in the prophets of
Jerusalem:
They commit adultery and
walk in lies;
They also strengthen the hands
of evildoers,
So that no one turns back from
his wickedness.
All of them are like [c]Sodom to
Me,
And her inhabitants like
Gomorrah.

15 "Therefore thus says the LORD of
hosts concerning the prophets:

'Behold, I will feed them with
wormwood,
And make them drink the
water of gall;
For from the prophets of
Jerusalem
Profaneness has gone out into
all the land.' "

16 Thus says the LORD of hosts:
"Do [d]not listen to the words of
the prophets who prophesy
to you.
They make you worthless;
They [e]speak a vision of their
own heart,
Not from the mouth of the
LORD.
17 They continually say to those
who despise Me,
'The LORD has said, "You shall
have peace" ';
And *to* everyone who walks
according to the dictates of
his own heart, they say,
'No evil shall come upon you.' "
18 For [f]who has stood in the
counsel of the LORD,
And has perceived and heard
His word?
Who has marked His word and
heard *it?*
19 Behold, a whirlwind of the
LORD has gone forth in
fury—
A violent whirlwind!
It will fall violently on the
head of the wicked.
20 The [g]anger of the LORD will
not turn back
Until He has executed and
performed the thoughts of
His heart.
In the [h]latter days you will
understand it perfectly.
21 [i]"I have not sent these prophets,
yet they ran.
I have not spoken to them, yet
they prophesied.
22 But if they had stood in My
counsel,
And had caused My people to
hear My words,
Then they would have turned
them from their evil way
And from the evil of their
doings.

23 "*Am* I a God near at hand,"
says the LORD,
"And not a God afar off?
24 Can anyone [j]hide himself in
secret places,
So I shall not see him?" says
the LORD;
[k]"Do I not fill heaven and
earth?" says the LORD.

25 "I have heard what the prophets
have said who prophesy lies in My
name, saying, 'I have dreamed, I have
dreamed!'
26 "How long will *this* be in the
heart of the prophets who prophesy
lies? Indeed *they are* prophets of the
deceit of their own heart,

11
a Jer. 6:13; 8:10
b Jer. 7:30; 32:34
14
c Dt. 32:32; Isa. 1:9–10
16
d Cp. Jer. 27:16; Mt. 7:15; 2 Cor. 11:13–15; 1 Jn. 4:1
e v. 21; Jer. 14:14
18
f v. 22; Ps. 25:14; cp. Ps. 1:1–2
20
g Jer. 30:24
h Gen. 49:1; Jer. 30:24; see Acts 2:17, *note*
21
i Jer. 14:14; 27:15; 29:9
24
j Ps. 139:7–12; Amos 9:2–4
k 1 Ki. 8:27; Ps. 139:8

27 “who try to make My people forget My name by their dreams which
everyone tells his neighbor, as their
fathers forgot My name for Baal.

28 “The prophet who has a dream,
let him tell a dream;
And he who has My word, let
him speak My word
faithfully.
What *is* the chaff to the
wheat?” says the LORD.
29 “*Is* not My word like a [a]fire?”
says the LORD,
“And like a [b]hammer *that*
breaks the rock in pieces?

30 “Therefore behold, [c]I *am*
against the prophets,” says the LORD,
“who steal My words every one from
his neighbor.
31 “Behold, I *am* [d]against the
prophets,” says the LORD, “who use
their tongues and say, ‘He says.’
32 “Behold, I *am* against those who
prophesy false dreams,” says the
LORD, “and tell them, and cause My
people to err by their [e]lies and by their
[f]recklessness. Yet I did not send them
or command them; therefore they
shall not [g]profit this people at all,”
says the LORD.
33 “So when these people or the
prophet or the priest ask you, saying,
‘What is the [h]oracle of the LORD?’ you
shall then say to them, ‘What oracle?’* I will even forsake you,” says
the LORD.
34 “And *as for* the prophet and the
priest and the people who say, ‘The
oracle of the LORD!’ I will even punish
that man and his house.
35 “Thus every one of you shall say
to his neighbor, and every one to his
brother, ‘What has the LORD answered?’ and, ‘What has the LORD spoken?’
36 “And the oracle of the LORD you
shall mention no more. For every
man’s word will be his oracle, for you
have [i]perverted the words of the living God, the LORD of hosts, our God.
37 “Thus you shall say to the
prophet, ‘What has the LORD answered
you?’ and, ‘What has the LORD spoken?’
38 “But since you say, ‘The oracle
of the LORD!’ therefore thus says the
LORD: ‘Because you say this word,
“The oracle of the LORD!” and I have
sent to you, saying, “Do not say, ‘The
oracle of the LORD!’ ”
39 ‘therefore behold, I, even I, will
utterly forget you and [j]forsake you,
and the city that I gave you and your
fathers, and *will cast you* out of My
presence.
40 ‘And I will bring an everlasting
reproach upon you, and a perpetual
[k]shame, which shall not be [l]forgot-
ten.’ ”

Sign of the figs: some recent deportees will be returned from Babylon, but not all

24 THE LORD showed me, and
there were [m]two baskets of figs
set before the temple of the LORD, after
Nebuchadnezzar [n]king of Babylon
had carried away captive Jeconiah the
son of Jehoiakim, king of Judah, and
the princes of Judah with the craftsmen and smiths, from Jerusalem, and
had brought them to Babylon.
2 One basket *had* very good figs,
like the figs *that are* first ripe; and the
other basket *had* very bad figs which
could not be eaten, they were so [o]bad.
3 Then the LORD said to me, “What
do you see, Jeremiah?” And I said,
“Figs, the good figs, very good; and
the bad, very bad, which cannot be
eaten, they are so bad.”
4 Again the word of the LORD came
to me, saying,
5 “Thus says the LORD, the God of
Israel: ‘Like these good figs, so will I
acknowledge those who are carried
away captive from Judah, whom I
have sent out of this place for *their
own* [p]good, into the land of the Chaldeans.
6 ‘For I will set My eyes on them
for good, and I will [q]bring them back
to this land; I will build them and not
pull *them* down, and I will plant them
and not pluck *them* up.
7 ‘Then I will give them a [r]heart to
know Me, that I *am* the LORD; and they
shall be [s]My people, and I will be their
God, for they shall return to Me with
their whole heart.
8 ‘And as the bad figs which cannot be eaten, they are so bad’—surely
thus says the LORD—‘so will I give up
Zedekiah the king of Judah, his
princes, the [t]residue of Jerusalem
who remain in this land, and those
who dwell in the land of [u]Egypt.
9 ‘I will [v]deliver them to trouble
into all the kingdoms of the earth, for
their harm, *to be* a reproach and a

29
a Jer. 5:14
b Cp. 2 Cor. 10:4–5; Heb. 4:12
30
c Dt. 18:20; Jer. 14:14–15
31
d Ezek. 13:9
32
e Jer. 20:6; 27:10; Lam. 2:14; 3:37
f Zeph. 3:4
g Jer. 7:8
33
h Cp. vv. 30–32; see Isa. 13:1, *note 1*
36
i Dt. 4:2; cp. Jer. 6:10; 8:9; 17:15; 2 Pet. 3:16
39
j v. 33; Hos. 4:6
40
k Mic. 3:5–7
l Jer. 20:11
CHAPTER 24
1
m Parables (OT): vv. 1–10; Jer. 27:1. (Jud. 9:8; Zech. 11:7)
n 2 Ki. 24:12; 2 Chr. 36:10
2
o Jer. 29:17
5
p Cp. Zech. 13:9
6
q Jer. 12:15; 23:3; 29:10
7
r Dt. 30:6; Jer. 31:31–34; Ezek. 11:19; 36:26–27
s Jer. 30:22; 31:33; 32:38
8
t Jer. 39:9
u Jer. 44:26–30
9
v Dt. 28:25, 37; 1 Ki. 9:7; 2 Chr. 7:20; Jer. 15:4; 29:18; 34:17

*
23:33 Septuagint, Targum, and Vulgate read *‘You are the burden.’*

byword, a taunt and a curse, in all places where I shall drive them.

10 'And I will send the sword, the famine, and the pestilence among them, till they are consumed from the land that I gave to them and their fathers.' "

Prophecy of the seventy years' Babylonian captivity
(v. 11; cp. Dan. 9:2)

25 THE word that came to Jeremiah concerning all the people of Judah, in the [a]fourth year of [b]Jehoiakim the son of Josiah, king of Judah (which *was* the first year of Nebuchadnezzar king of Babylon),

2 which Jeremiah the prophet spoke to all the people of Judah and to all the inhabitants of Jerusalem, saying:

3 "From the thirteenth year of Josiah the son of Amon, king of Judah, even to this day, this *is* the twenty-third year in which the word of the LORD has come to me; and I have spoken to you, rising early and speaking, but you have not listened.

4 "And the LORD has sent to you all His [c]servants the prophets, rising early and sending *them,* but you have not listened nor inclined your ear to hear.

5 "They said, [d]'Repent now everyone of his evil way and his evil doings, and dwell in the land that the LORD has given to you and your fathers forever and ever.

6 'Do not go after other gods to serve them and worship them, and do not provoke Me to anger with the works of your hands; and I will not harm you.'

7 "Yet you have not listened to Me," says the LORD, "that you might [e]provoke Me to anger with the works of your hands to your own hurt.

8 "Therefore thus says the LORD of hosts: 'Because you have not heard My words,

9 'behold, I will send and take [f]all the families of the north,' says the LORD, 'and Nebuchadnezzar the king of Babylon, [g]My servant, and will bring them against this land, against its inhabitants, and against these nations all around, and will utterly destroy them, and make them an astonishment, a [h]hissing, and perpetual desolations.

10 'Moreover I will take from them the voice of mirth and the voice of gladness, the voice of the bridegroom and the voice of the bride, the sound of the millstones and the light of the lamp.

11 'And this whole land shall be a desolation *and* an astonishment, and these nations shall serve the king of Babylon [1]seventy [i]years.

Babylon and other nations to be judged

12 'Then it will come to pass, when seventy years are completed, *that* I will punish the king of Babylon and that nation, the [j]land of the Chaldeans, for their iniquity,' says the LORD; 'and I will make it a perpetual desolation.

13 'So I will bring on that land all My words which I have pronounced against it, all that is written in this book, which Jeremiah has prophesied concerning all the nations.

14 '(For many nations and great kings shall be served by them also; and I will repay them according to their deeds and according to the works of their own hands.)' "

15 For thus says the LORD God of Israel to me: "Take this [k]wine cup of fury from My hand, and cause all the nations, to whom I send you, to drink it.

16 "And they will [l]drink and stagger and go mad because of the sword that I will send among them."

17 Then I took the cup from the LORD's hand, and made all the nations drink, to whom the LORD had sent me:

18 Jerusalem and the cities of Judah, its kings and its princes, to make them a desolation, an [m]astonishment, a hissing, and a curse, as *it is* this day;

19 Pharaoh king of [n]Egypt, his servants, his princes, and all his people;

20 all the [o]mixed multitude, all the kings of the land of Uz, all the kings of the land of the [p]Philistines (namely, Ashkelon, Gaza, Ekron, and the remnant of Ashdod);

CHAPTER 25
1 a Jer. 36:1
b 2 Ki. 24:1–2; 2 Chr. 36:4–6
4 c Jer. 7:25; 26:5
5 d 2 Ki. 17:13; Jer. 18:11; 35:15; cp. Jon. 3:10
7 e Dt. 32:21; Jer. 7:19; 32:30
9 f Jer. 34:1
g Isa. 44:28–45:1; Jer. 27:6; 43:10
h Jer. 19:8; 29:18
11 i Jer. 29:10
12 j Isa. 13:1–22; 14:18–23; 47:1–15; Jer. 50:1–51:64
15 k Job 21:20; Ps. 75:8; Isa. 51:17; Rev. 14:10
16 l Jer. 51:7; Ezek. 23:34; Nah. 3:11
18 m Jer. 29:18; 44:12
19 n Jer. 46:2–26; Ezek. 29:2-32:32; cp. Isa. 19:1–25
20 o Ezek. 30:5
p Jer. 47:1–7; Ezek. 25:16–17

[1](25:11) Compare Lev. 26:33–35; 2 Chr. 36:21; Dan. 9:2. The seventy years are considered by some to be a round number. Others find the number to be exact, counting from about 604 B.C. (the first deportation being in Jehoiakim's reign, whereas the second was in 597 B.C. in Jehoiachin's reign, and the last in Zedekiah's reign in 586 B.C.) to about 535 B.C. when the exiles returned to the land after the decree of Cyrus (Ezra 1:1–3).

21 [a]Edom, [b]Moab, and the people
of [c]Ammon;
22 all the kings of [d]Tyre, all the
kings of Sidon, and the kings of the
coastlands which *are* across the sea;
23 [e]Dedan, Tema, Buz, and all *who*
are in the farthest corners;
24 all the kings of Arabia and all
the kings of the [f]mixed multitude who
dwell in the desert;
25 all the kings of Zimri, all the
kings of [g]Elam, and all the kings of
the [h]Medes;
26 all the kings of the north, far and
near, one with another; and all the
kingdoms of the world which *are* on
the face of the earth. Also the king of
[i]Sheshach shall drink after them.
27 "Therefore you shall say to
them, 'Thus says the LORD of hosts, the
God of Israel: "Drink, be drunk, and
vomit! Fall and rise no more, because
of the sword which I will send among
you." '
28 "And it shall be, if they refuse to
take the cup from your hand to drink,
then you shall say to them, 'Thus says
the LORD of hosts: "You shall certainly
drink!
29 "For behold, I begin to bring calamity on the city which is called by
My name, and should you be utterly
unpunished? You shall not be unpunished, for [j]I will call for a [k]sword on
[1]all the inhabitants of the earth," says
the LORD of hosts.'
30 "Therefore prophesy against
them all these words, and say to them:

'The LORD will roar from on
high,
And utter His voice from His
holy habitation;
He will [l]roar mightily against
His fold.
He will give a shout, as those
who tread *the grapes*,
Against all the inhabitants of
the earth.
31 A noise will come to the ends
of the earth—
For the LORD has a
[m]controversy with the
nations;
He will [n]plead His case with
all flesh.
He will give those *who are*
wicked to the sword,' says
the LORD."

32 Thus says the LORD of hosts:
"Behold, disaster shall go forth
From nation to nation,
And a great whirlwind shall be
raised up
From the [o]farthest parts of the
earth.

33 "And at that day the slain of the
LORD shall be from *one* end of the
earth even to the *other* end of the
earth. They shall not be lamented, or
gathered, or buried; they shall become
refuse on the ground.

34 "Wail, [p]shepherds, and cry!
Roll about *in the ashes*,
You leaders of the flock!
For the days of your slaughter
and your dispersions are
fulfilled;
You shall fall like a precious
vessel.
35 And the shepherds will have
no way to flee,
Nor the leaders of the flock to
escape.
36 A voice of the cry of the
shepherds,
And a wailing of the leaders to
the flock *will be heard*.
For the LORD has plundered
their pasture,
37 And the peaceful dwellings are
cut down
Because of the fierce anger of
the LORD.
38 He has left His lair like the
lion;
For their land is desolate
Because of the fierceness of
the Oppressor,
And because of His fierce
anger."

Message in the temple court

26 IN the beginning of the reign of
Jehoiakim the son of Josiah,
king of Judah, this word came from
the LORD, saying,
2 "Thus says the LORD: 'Stand in
the court of the LORD's house, and
speak to all the cities of Judah, which
come to worship *in* the LORD's house,

---

21 *a* Jer. 49:7–22; Ezek. 25:12–14; 35:1–15; Joel 3:19; Amos 1:11–12; Obad. 1–9, 15–16 *b* Isa. 15:1-16:14; 25:10; Jer. 48:1–47; Amos 2:1–3; Zeph. 2:8–11 *c* Jer. 49:1–6; Ezek 21:28–32; 25:1–7; Amos 1:13; Zeph. 2:8–11
22 *d* Isa. 23:1–18; Jer. 47:4; Ezek. 26:1–21; 28:20–24; Amos 1:9–10; Zech. 9:2–4
23 *e* Isa. 21:13
24 *f* Ezek. 30:5
25 *g* Jer. 49:34 *h* Jer. 51:11
26 *i* Another name for *Babylon.* Jer. 51:41
29 *j Day* (of the LORD): vv. 29–38; Jer. 46:10. (Ps. 2:9; Rev. 19:19) *k Armageddon* (battle of): vv. 29–33; Ezek. 38:21. (Isa. 10:27; Rev. 19:17)
30 *l* Isa. 42:13; Joel 3:16; Amos 1:2
31 *m* Hos. 4:1; Mic. 6:2 *n* Isa. 66:16; Joel 3:2
32 *o* Jer. 31:8

25:34 *p* Jer. 23:1–2; 50:6

1(25:29) The scope of this prophecy cannot be limited to the invasion of Nebuchadnezzar. If the LORD does not spare His own city, should the nations imagine that there is no judgment for them? The prophecy leaps to the very end of the Church Age. (See *notes* on Day of the LORD, Joel 1:15; Rev. 19:19; and Armageddon, Rev. 19:17. Cp. Isa. 2:10–22).

[a]all the words that I command you to
speak to them. Do not diminish a
word.
3 'Perhaps everyone will [b]listen
and turn from his evil way, that I may
[c]relent concerning the calamity
which I purpose to bring on them because of the evil of their doings.'
4 "And you shall say to them,
'Thus says the LORD: "If you will not
listen to Me, to walk in My law which
I have set before you,
5 "to heed the words of My [d]ser-
vants the prophets whom I sent to you,
both rising up early and sending *them*
(but you have not heeded),
6 "then I will make this house like
[e]Shiloh, and will make this city a
curse to all the nations of the earth." ' "
7 So the priests and the prophets
and all the people heard Jeremiah
speaking these words in the house of
the LORD.

Priests and prophets seek Jeremiah's death

8 Now it happened, when Jeremiah had made an end of speaking all
that the LORD had commanded *him* to
speak to all the people, that the priests
and the prophets and all the people
[f]seized him, saying, "You will surely
die!
9 "Why have you prophesied in
the name of the LORD, saying, 'This
house shall be like Shiloh, and this
city shall be [g]desolate, without an inhabitant'?" And all the people were
gathered against Jeremiah in the
house of the LORD.

Princes spare Jeremiah

10 When the princes of Judah
heard these things, they [h]came up
from the king's house to the house of
the LORD and sat down in the entry of
the New Gate of the LORD's *house*.
11 And the priests and the prophets
spoke to the princes and all the people, saying, "This man deserves to
[i]die! For he has prophesied against
this city, as you have heard with your
ears."
12 Then Jeremiah spoke to all the
princes and all the people, saying:
"The LORD sent me to prophesy
against this house and against this
city with all the words that you have
heard.
13 "Now therefore, [j]amend your
ways and your doings, and obey the
voice of the LORD your God; then the
LORD will [c]relent concerning the

CHAPTER 26
2
a v. 8; Dt. 4:2; Jer. 43:1; Ezek. 3:10; Mt. 28:20; Rev. 22:19
3
b Jer. 36:3–7
c See Zech. 8:14, *note*
5
d Jer. 25:4; 29:19
6
e 1 Sam. 4:10–11; Ps. 78:60; Jer. 7:12–14
8
f Cp. Jer. 20:1–2
9
g Jer. 9:11
10
h Cp. Acts 21:31–32
11
i Jer. 38:4; cp. Mt. 26:66
13
j Jer. 7:3
16
k Cp. 1 Sam. 14:45
l Cp. Mt. 27:11–26; Acts 23:29; 25:25; 26:31
18
m Mic. 1:1
n Mic. 3:12
19
o See Ps. 19:9, *note*
p 2 Ki. 20:1–19; 2 Chr. 32:1–31; Isa. 36:1–39:8
q Jer. 18:8
21
r Cp. Neh. 6:10–11
22
s Jer. 36:12, 25
t Jer. 43:6–7

doom that He has pronounced against
you.
14 "As for me, here I am, in your
hand; do with me as seems good and
proper to you.
15 "But know for certain that if you
put me to death, you will surely bring
innocent blood on yourselves, on this
city, and on its inhabitants; for truly
the LORD has sent me to you to speak
all these words in your hearing."
16 So the princes and all the [k]peo-
ple said to the priests and the prophets, "This man does [l]not deserve to
die. For he has spoken to us in the
name of the LORD our God."
17 Then certain of the elders of the
land rose up and spoke to all the assembly of the people, saying:
18 [m]"Micah of Moresheth prophesied in the days of Hezekiah king of
Judah, and spoke to all the people of
Judah, saying, 'Thus says the LORD of
hosts:

[n]"Zion shall be plowed *like* a
field,
Jerusalem shall become heaps
of ruins,
And the mountain of the
temple*
Like the bare hills of the
forest." '

19 "Did Hezekiah king of Judah
and all Judah ever put him to death?
Did he not [o]fear the LORD and [p]seek
the LORD's favor? And the Lord [q]re-
lented concerning the doom which He
had pronounced against them. But we
are doing great evil against ourselves."
20 Now there was also a man who
prophesied in the name of the LORD,
Urijah the son of Shemaiah of Kirjath
Jearim, who prophesied against this
city and against this land according to
all the words of Jeremiah.
21 And when Jehoiakim the king,
with all his mighty men and all the
princes, heard his words, the king
sought to put him to death; but when
Urijah heard *it*, he was afraid and
[r]fled, and went to Egypt.
22 Then Jehoiakim the king sent
men to Egypt: [s]Elnathan the son of
Achbor, and *other* men *who went*
with him to [t]Egypt.
23 And they brought Urijah from
Egypt and brought him to Jehoiakim
the king, who killed him with the

*26:18 Literally *house*

sword and cast his dead body into the
graves of the common people.
24 Nevertheless the hand of [a]Ahi-
kam the son of Shaphan was with Jeremiah, so that they should not give
him into the hand of the people to put
him to death.

Sign of the yokes: surrounding nations commanded to submit to Nebuchadnezzar

27 IN the beginning of the reign of
[b]Jehoiakim* the son of Josiah,
king of Judah, this word came to Jeremiah from the LORD, [c]saying,*
2 "Thus says the LORD to me:
'Make for yourselves bonds and
[d]yokes, and put them on your neck,
3 'and send them [e]to the king of
Edom, the king of Moab, the king of
the Ammonites, the king of Tyre, and
the king of Sidon, by the hand of the
messengers who come to Jerusalem to
Zedekiah king of Judah.
4 'And command them to say to
their masters, "Thus says the LORD of
hosts, the God of Israel—thus you
shall say to your masters:
5 'I have made the earth, the man
and the beast that *are* on the ground,
by My great power and by My outstretched arm, and have [f]given it to
whom it seemed proper to Me.
6 'And now I have [d]given all these
lands into the hand of Nebuchadnezzar the king of Babylon, [g]My servant;
and the [h]beasts of the field I have also
given him to serve him.
7 'So all [i]nations shall serve him
and his son and his son's son, [j]until
the time of his land comes; and then
many nations and great kings shall
make him serve them.
8 'And it shall be, *that* the nation
and kingdom which will not serve
Nebuchadnezzar the king of Babylon,
and which will not [k]put its neck under
the yoke of the king of Babylon, that
nation I will punish,' says the LORD,
'with the sword, the famine, and the
pestilence, until I have consumed
them by his hand.
9 'Therefore do not listen to your
prophets, your diviners, your dreamers, your soothsayers, or your sorcerers, who speak to you, saying, "You
shall not serve the king of Babylon."
10 'For they prophesy a [l]lie to you,
to remove you far from your land; and
I will drive you out, and you will perish.
11 'But the nations that bring their
necks under the yoke of the king of

24
a 2 Ki. 22:12–14; Jer. 39:14; 40:5–7

CHAPTER 27
1
b Here is possibly a scribal error. Heb. reads *Jehoiakim,* but context requires *Zedekiah.* See NKJV textual note.
c *Parables* (OT): vv. 1–7; Ezek. 17:1. (Jud. 9:8; Zech. 11:7)
2
d Jer. 28:14
3
e Cp. Jer. 25:20–26
5
f Ezek. 29:18–20; Dan. 4:35
6
g Jer. 25:9; 43:10; Ezek. 29:18–20
h Dan. 2:38
7
i Jer. 25:14; cp. 50:9
j Jer. 25:12; 50:27; Dan. 5:26
8
k v. 11; cp. Jer. 38:17–23
10
l Jer. 23:16, 32; 28:15
14
m Jer. 23:16
15
n Jer. 23:21; 29:9
16
o 2 Chr. 36:7,10; Jer. 28:3; Dan. 1:2
19
p 2 Ki. 25:13; Jer. 52:17–21
20
q 2 Ki. 24:14–15; Jer. 24:1
21
r Jer. 20:5

Babylon and serve him, I will let them
remain in their own land,' says the
LORD, 'and they shall till it and dwell in
it.' " ' "
12 I also spoke to Zedekiah king of
Judah according to all these words,
saying, "Bring your necks under the
yoke of the king of Babylon, and serve
him and his people, and live!
13 "Why will you die, you and your
people, by the sword, by the famine,
and by the pestilence, as the LORD has
spoken against the nation that will not
serve the king of Babylon?
14 "Therefore do not [m]listen to the
words of the prophets who speak to
you, saying, 'You shall not serve the
king of Babylon,' for they prophesy a
lie to you;
15 "for I have [n]not sent them," says
the LORD, "yet they prophesy a lie in
My name, that I may drive you out,
and that you may perish, you and the
prophets who prophesy to you."
16 Also I spoke to the priests and to
all this people, saying, "Thus says the
LORD: 'Do not listen to the words of
your prophets who prophesy to you,
saying, [o]"Behold, the vessels of the
LORD's house will now shortly be
brought back from Babylon"; for they
prophesy a lie to you.
17 'Do not listen to them; serve the
king of Babylon, and live! Why should
this city be laid waste?
18 'But if they *are* prophets, and if
the word of the LORD is with them, let
them now make intercession to the
LORD of hosts, that the vessels which
are left in the house of the LORD, *in* the
house of the king of Judah, and at Jerusalem, do not go to Babylon.'
19 "For thus says the LORD of hosts
[p]concerning the pillars, concerning
the Sea, concerning the carts, and
concerning the remainder of the vessels that remain in this city,
20 "which Nebuchadnezzar king of
Babylon did not take, when he carried
away [q]captive Jeconiah the son of Jehoiakim, king of Judah, from Jerusalem to Babylon, and all the nobles of
Judah and Jerusalem—
21 "yes, thus says the LORD of hosts,
the God of Israel, concerning the [r]ves-
sels that remain in the house of the
LORD, and in the house of the king of
Judah and of Jerusalem:

*27:1 Following Masoretic Text, Targum, and Vulgate; some Hebrew manuscripts, Arabic, and Syriac read *Zedekiah* (compare 27:3,12; 28:1).
• Septuagint omits verse 1.

22 'They shall be [a]carried to Babylon, and there they shall be until the day that I [b]visit them,' says the LORD. 'Then I will [c]bring them up and restore them to this place.' "

Hananiah's false prophecy and death

28 AND it happened in the same year, at the beginning of the reign of Zedekiah king of Judah, in the [d]fourth year *and* in the [e]fifth month, *that* Hananiah the son of [f]Azur the prophet, who *was* from Gibeon, spoke to me in the house of the LORD in the presence of the priests and of all the people, saying,

2 "Thus speaks the LORD of hosts, the God of Israel, saying: 'I have broken the [g]yoke of the king of Babylon.

3 'Within two full years I will [h]bring back to this place all the vessels of the LORD's house, that Nebuchadnezzar king of Babylon [i]took away from this place and carried to Babylon.

4 'And I will bring back to this place [j]Jeconiah the son of Jehoiakim, king of Judah, with all the [k]captives of Judah who went to Babylon,' says the LORD, 'for I will break the yoke of the king of Babylon.' "

5 Then the prophet Jeremiah spoke to the prophet Hananiah in the presence of the priests and in the presence of all the people who stood in the house of the LORD,

6 and the prophet Jeremiah said, [l]"Amen! The LORD do so; the LORD perform your words which you have prophesied, to bring back the vessels of the LORD's house and all who were carried away captive, from Babylon to this place.

7 "Nevertheless hear now this word that I speak in your hearing and in the hearing of all the people:

8 "The prophets who have been before me and before you of old prophesied against many countries and great kingdoms—of war and disaster and pestilence.

9 "As for the [m]prophet who prophesies of [n]peace, when the word of the prophet comes to pass, the prophet will be known *as* one whom the LORD has truly [o]sent."

10 Then Hananiah the prophet took the yoke off the prophet Jeremiah's neck and broke it.

11 And Hananiah spoke in the presence of all the people, saying, "Thus says the LORD: 'Even so I will break the yoke of Nebuchadnezzar king of Babylon [p]from the neck of all nations within the space of two full years.' " And the prophet Jeremiah went his way.

12 Now the word of the LORD came to Jeremiah, after Hananiah the prophet had broken the [q]yoke from the neck of the prophet Jeremiah, saying,

13 "Go and tell Hananiah, saying, 'Thus says the LORD: "You have broken the yokes of wood, but you have made in their place yokes of iron."

14 'For thus says the LORD of hosts, the God of Israel: "I have put a [r]yoke of iron on the neck of all these nations, that they may serve Nebuchadnezzar king of Babylon; and they shall serve him. I have given him the [s]beasts of the field also." ' "

15 Then the prophet Jeremiah said to Hananiah the prophet, "Hear now, Hananiah, the LORD has not sent you, [t]but you make this people [u]trust in a [v]lie.

16 "Therefore thus says the LORD: 'Behold, I will cast you from the face of the earth. This year you shall [w]die, because you have taught [x]rebellion against the LORD.' "

17 So Hananiah the prophet died the same year in the [d]seventh month.

Message to the Jews of the first captivity

29 NOW these *are* the words of the letter that Jeremiah the prophet sent from Jerusalem to the remainder of the elders who were [1y]carried away captive—to the priests, the prophets, and all the people whom Nebuchadnezzar had carried away captive from Jerusalem to Babylon.

2 (This happened after [z]Jeconiah the king, the [aa]queen mother, the eunuchs, the princes of Judah and Jerusalem, the [bb]craftsmen, and the smiths had departed from Jerusalem.)

3 *The letter was sent* by the hand of Elasah the son of [cc]Shaphan, and Gemariah the son of Hilkiah, whom Zedekiah king of Judah sent to Babylon, to Nebuchadnezzar king of Babylon, [dd]saying,

4 Thus says the LORD of hosts,

22
a 2 Ki. 25:13; 2 Chr. 36:18
b 2 Chr. 36:21; Jer. 29:10; 32:5
c Ezra 1:7–11; 7:19

CHAPTER 28

1
d See Lev. 23:2, *note*
e Jer. 51:59
f Ezek. 11:1

2
g Jer. 27:12

3
h Jer. 27:16
i 2 Ki. 24:13; Dan. 1:2

4
j Jer. 24:1; or *Jehoiachin,* 2 Ki. 24:12; or *Coniah,* Jer. 22:24
k Cp. Jer. 20:4

6
l 1 Ki. 1:36

9
m Dt. 18:22
n Jer. 23:17; Ezek. 13:10,16
o Cp. 1 Ki. 22:28

11
p Jer. 27:7

12
q Jer. 27:2

14
r Dt. 28:48
s Jer. 27:6

15
t Jer. 29:31; Ezek. 13:22
u See Ps. 2:12, *note*
v Jer. 27:10; 29:9

16
w Jer. 20:6
x Dt. 13:5; Jer. 29:32

CHAPTER 29

1
y Jer. 27:20

2
z 2 Ki. 24:12; Jer. 22:26
aa Jer. 13:18
bb Jer. 24:1

3
cc 2 Chr. 34:8

dd vv. 4–7,28

[1](29:1) Compare 2 Ki. 24:10–16. The complete captivity of Judah came eleven years later (2 Ki. 25:1–7).

the God of Israel, to all who
were carried away captive,
whom I have caused to be
carried away from Jerusalem
to Babylon:
5 Build houses and dwell *in*
them; plant gardens and eat
their fruit.
6 Take wives and beget sons and
daughters; and take wives for
your sons and give your
daughters to husbands, so that
they may bear sons and
daughters—that you may be
increased there, and not
diminished.
7 And seek the peace of the city
where I have caused you to be
carried away captive, and
[a]pray to the LORD for it; for in
its peace you will have peace.
8 For thus says the LORD of
hosts, the God of Israel: Do not
let your prophets and your
diviners who are in your midst
[b]deceive you, nor listen to
your dreams which you cause
to be dreamed.
9 For they prophesy [c]falsely to
you in My name; I have not
sent them, says the LORD.
10 For thus says the LORD: [d]After
seventy years are completed at
Babylon, I will visit you and
perform My good word toward
you, and cause you to [e]return
to this place.
11 For I know the thoughts that I
think toward you, says the
LORD, thoughts of peace and
not of evil, to give you a future
and a hope.
12 [f]Then you will call upon Me
and go and pray to Me, and I
will [g]listen to you.
13 And you will [h]seek Me and
find *Me,* when you search for
Me with all your heart.
14 I will be [i]found by you, says
the LORD, and I will bring you
back from your captivity; I will
[j]gather you from all the
nations and from all the places
where I have driven you, says
the LORD, and I will bring you
to the place from which I
cause you to be carried away
captive.
15 Because you have said, "The
LORD has raised up prophets
for us in Babylon"—
16 [k]therefore thus says the LORD
concerning the king who sits
on the throne of David,
concerning all the people who
dwell in this city, and
concerning your brethren who
have not gone out with you
into captivity—
17 thus says the LORD of hosts:
Behold, I will send on them the
sword, the famine, and the
pestilence, and will make them
like rotten [l]figs that cannot be
eaten, they are so bad.
18 And I will pursue them with
the sword, with famine, and
with pestilence; and I will
[m]deliver them to trouble
among all the kingdoms of the
earth—to be a curse, an
[n]astonishment, a hissing, and
a reproach among all the
nations where I have driven
them,
19 because they have not heeded
My words, says the LORD,
which I sent to them by My
servants the prophets, rising
up early and sending *them;*
neither would you heed, says
the LORD.
20 Therefore hear the word of the
LORD, all you of the captivity,
whom I have sent from
Jerusalem to Babylon.
21 Thus says the LORD of hosts,
the God of Israel, concerning
Ahab the son of Kolaiah, and
Zedekiah the son of Maaseiah,
who prophesy a [o]lie to you in
My name: Behold, I will
deliver them into the hand of
Nebuchadnezzar king of
Babylon, and he shall slay
them before your eyes.
22 And because of them a [p]curse
shall be taken up by all the
captivity of Judah who *are* in
Babylon, saying, "The LORD
make you like Zedekiah and
[q]Ahab, whom the king of
Babylon roasted in the fire";
23 because they have done
disgraceful things in Israel,
have committed adultery with
their neighbors' wives, and
have spoken lying words in
My name, which I have not
commanded them. Indeed I
[r]know, and *am* a witness, says
the LORD.
24 You shall also speak to
Shemaiah the Nehelamite,
saying,

7 [a] Ezra 6:10; Neh. 1:4–11; Dan. 9:16; 1 Tim. 2:2
8 [b] Jer. 14:14, 23:21; 27:14–15; Eph. 5:6
9 [c] Jer. 28:15; 37:19
10 [d] 2 Chr. 36:21–23; Ezra 1:1–4, Jer. 25:12; 27:22; Dan. 9:2 [e] Jer. 24:6; 30:3
12 [f] Ps. 50:14–15; Dan. 9:3–19 [g] Ps. 145:19
13 [h] Lev. 26:39–42; Dt. 30:1–3
14 [i] Dt. 4:7; Ps. 32:6; 46:1; Isa. 55:6–7; Jer. 24:7 [j] Jer. 23:3,8; 30:3; 32:37
16 [k] Jer. 38:2–3, 17–23
17 [l] Jer. 24
18 [m] Dt. 28:25; 2 Chr. 29:8; Jer. 15:4; 24:9; 34:17 [n] Jer. 25:9, 18
21 [o] Jer. 14:14–15; Lam. 2:14
22 [p] Isa. 65:15 [q] Cp. Dan. 3:6
23 [r] Prov. 5:21; Jer. 16:17

25 Thus speaks the LORD of hosts,
the God of Israel, saying: You
have sent letters in your name
to all the people who *are* at
Jerusalem, to [a]Zephaniah the
son of Maaseiah the priest, and
to all the priests, saying,
26 "The LORD has made you priest
instead of Jehoiada the priest,
so that there should be officers
in the house of the LORD over
every man *who* is [b]demented
and considers himself a
prophet, that you should put
him in prison and in the
[c]stocks.
27 Now therefore, why have you
not rebuked Jeremiah of
Anathoth who makes himself a
prophet to you?
28 For he has sent to us *in*
Babylon, saying, 'This
captivity is long; build houses
and dwell *in them,* and plant
gardens and eat their fruit.' "
29 Now Zephaniah the priest read
this letter in the hearing of
Jeremiah the prophet.
30 Then the word of the LORD
came to Jeremiah, saying:
31 Send to all those in captivity,
saying,
Thus says the LORD concerning
Shemaiah the Nehelamite:
Because Shemaiah has
prophesied to you, and I have
[d]not sent him, and he has
caused you to trust in a [e]lie—
32 therefore thus says the LORD:
Behold, I will punish Shemaiah
the Nehelamite and his family:
he shall not have anyone to
dwell among this people, nor
shall he see the good that I
will do for My people, says the
LORD, because he has taught
[f]rebellion against the LORD.

The day of the LORD: "the time of Jacob's trouble" (v. 7), the tribulation

30 THE [1]word that came to Jeremiah from the LORD, saying,
2 "Thus speaks the LORD God of
Israel, saying: [g]'Write in a book for
yourself all the [h]words that I have
spoken to you.
3 'For behold, the days are coming,' says the LORD, 'that [i]I will bring
back from captivity My people Israel
and Judah,' says the LORD. 'And I will
cause them to return to the land that I
gave to their fathers, and they shall
possess it.' "
4 Now these *are* the words that the
LORD spoke concerning Israel and Judah.
5 "For thus says the LORD:
'We have heard a voice of
trembling,
Of fear, and not of peace.
6 Ask now, and see,
Whether a man is ever in labor
with child?
So why do I see every man
with his hands on his loins
Like a woman in [j]labor,
And all faces turned pale?
7 Alas! For [k]that day *is* great,
So that none *is* like it;
And it *is* the [2]time of Jacob's
trouble,
But he shall be saved out of it.

8 'For it shall come to pass in
that day,'
Says the LORD of hosts,
'*That* I will break his yoke
from your neck,
And will burst your bonds;
Foreigners shall no more
enslave them.
9 But they shall serve the LORD
their God,
And [l]David their [m]king,
Whom I will raise up for them.

10 'Therefore do not fear, O My
servant Jacob,' says the
LORD,
'Nor be dismayed, O Israel;
For behold, I will save you
from afar,
And your seed from the [n]land
of their captivity.
Jacob shall return, have rest
and be quiet,
And no one shall make *him*
afraid.

25 *a* 2 Ki. 25:18; Jer. 21:1
26 *b* 2 Ki. 9:11; Jn. 10:20; Acts 26:24; 2 Cor. 5:13 *c* Jer. 20:2
31 *d* Jer. 27:15 *e* Ezek. 13:8–16, 22–23
32 *f* Jer. 28:16
CHAPTER 30
2 *g* See Jer. 36:32, *note* *h Inspiration:* v. 2; Jer. 36:1. (Ex. 4:15; 2 Tim. 3:16, *note*)
3 *i Israel* (prophecies): vv. 1–9; Jer. 31:7. (Gen. 12:2; Rom. 11:26, *note*)
6 *j* See Mic. 4:11, *note*
7 *k Tribulation* (the great): vv. 4–7; Dan. 12:1. (Ps. 2:5; Rev. 7:14)
9 *l* Isa. 55:3–4; Ezek. 34:23; 37:24; Hos. 3:5 *m Kingdom* (OT): vv. 7–9; Jer. 33:17. (Gen. 1:26; Zech. 12:8, *note*)
10 *n* Jer. 3:18

[1](30:1) Since the book is so largely occupied with the message of judgment (1:10), these chapters are all the more significant in predicting such glorious features as: (1) the indestructibility of Israel (30:11; 31:35–37); (2) the return from exile (30:10; 31:23; 33:7); (3) the coming of the Messianic King (33:15–16); (4) the conversion of Israel (33:8,16); and (5) the realization of the New Covenant (31:31ff.; 32:39–40).

[2](30:7) The time of trouble for Jacob is identical to the tribulation. See Rev. 7:14, *note.*

11 For I *am* with [a]you,' says the
LORD, 'to save you;
[b]Though I make a full end of all
nations where I have
scattered you,
Yet I will not make a
[1]complete end of [c]you.
But I will correct you in
justice,
And will not let you go
altogether unpunished.'

12 "For thus says the LORD:

[d]'Your affliction *is* incurable,
Your wound *is* severe.
13 *There is* no one to plead your
cause,
That you may be bound up;
You have no healing
medicines.
14 All your lovers have forgotten
you;
They do not seek you;
For I have wounded you with
the wound of an enemy,
With the chastisement of a
cruel one,
For the multitude of your
iniquities,
Because your sins have
increased.
15 Why do you cry about your
affliction?
Your sorrow *is* incurable.
Because of the multitude of
your iniquities,
Because your sins have
increased,
I have done these things to
you.

16 'Therefore all those who devour
you shall be [e]devoured;
And all your adversaries, every
one of them, shall go into
[f]captivity;
Those who [g]plunder you shall
become plunder,
And all who [h]prey upon you I
will make a prey.
17 For I will [i]restore health to
you
And heal you of your wounds,'
says the LORD,
'Because they called you an
outcast *saying*:
"This *is* Zion;
No one seeks her." '

Israel to be delivered in last days

18 "Thus says the LORD:

'Behold, I will [j]bring back the
captivity of Jacob's tents,
And have mercy on his
dwelling places;
The city shall be built upon its
own mound,
And the palace shall remain
according to its own plan.
19 Then out of them shall proceed
thanksgiving
And the voice of those who
make merry;
I will [k]multiply them, and they
shall not diminish;
I will also glorify them, and
they shall not be small.
20 Their children also shall be as
before,
And their congregation shall
be established before Me;
And I will punish all who
oppress them.
21 Their nobles shall be from
among them,
And their governor shall come
from their midst;
Then I will cause him to draw
near,
And he shall [l]approach Me;
For who *is* this who pledged
his heart to approach Me?'
says the LORD.
22 'You shall be [m]My people,
And I will be your God.' "
23 [n]Behold, the whirlwind of the
LORD
Goes forth with fury,
A continuing whirlwind;
It will fall violently on the
head of the wicked.
24 The fierce anger of the LORD
will not return until He has
done it,
And until He has performed
the intents of His heart.

In the [o]latter days you will
consider it.

Joy will replace sorrow

31 "AT the same time," says the
LORD, "I will be the God of all

11 [a] Isa. 43:2–5 [b] Amos 9:8 [c] Jer. 46:27–28
12 [d] 2 Chr. 36:16; Jer. 15:18
16 [e] Ex. 23:22; Isa. 41:11; Jer. 10:25 [f] Isa. 14:2; Joel 3:8 [g] Isa. 33:1; Ezek. 39:10 [h] Jer. 2:3
17 [i] Jer. 33:6
18 [j] i.e. *cause to cease*
19 [k] Isa. 49:19–21; Jer. 23:3; 33:22
21 [l] Num. 16:5; Ps. 65:4
22 [m] Jer. 24:7; 31:1,33; 32:38; Ezek. 11:20; 36:28; 37:27
23 [n] Jer. 23:19–20
24 [o] See Acts 2:17, *note*

[1](30:11) No OT prophet is more positive of the destruction of Israel's political economy and the consequent exile of the nation than is Jeremiah, but he is also insistent that the disaster of the hour does not mean the nation's dissolution. Repeatedly the prophet assures the nation that God will not make a "complete end" of Israel (cp. 4:27; 5:10,18; 30:11; 46:28). The perpetuity of Israel as a nation is thus assured.

the families of Israel, and they shall be My [a]people."

2 Thus says the LORD:

"The people who survived the sword
Found grace in the wilderness—
Israel, when I went to give him rest."

3 The LORD has appeared of old to me, *saying:*
"Yes, I have loved you with an everlasting [b]love;
Therefore with lovingkindness I have drawn you.
4 Again I will build you, and you shall be rebuilt,
O virgin of Israel!
You shall again be adorned with your tambourines,
And shall go forth in the dances of those who rejoice.
5 You shall yet plant vines on the mountains of Samaria;
The planters shall plant and eat *them* as ordinary food.
6 For there shall be a day
When the watchmen will cry on Mount Ephraim,
'Arise, and let us go up *to* Zion,
To the LORD our God.' "

7 For thus says the LORD:

"Sing with gladness for Jacob,
And shout among the chief of the nations;
Proclaim, give praise, and say,
'O LORD, save Your people,
The [c]remnant of [d]Israel!'
8 Behold, I will bring them from the north country,
And gather them from the [e]ends of the earth,
Among them the blind and the lame,
The woman with child
And the one who labors with child, together;
A great throng shall return there.
9 They shall come with [f]weeping,
And with supplications I will lead them.
I will cause them to walk by the [g]rivers of waters,
In a straight way in which they shall not stumble;
For I am a [h]Father to Israel,
And Ephraim *is* My firstborn.

10 "Hear the word of the LORD, O nations,
And declare *it* in the isles afar off, and say,
'He who scattered Israel will gather him,
And keep him as a [i]shepherd *does* his flock.'
11 For the LORD has [j]redeemed Jacob,
And ransomed him from the hand of one stronger than he.
12 Therefore they shall come and sing in the height of Zion,
Streaming to the goodness of the LORD—
For wheat and new wine and oil,
For the young of the flock and the herd;
Their souls shall be like a well-watered garden,
And they shall sorrow no more at all.

13 "Then shall the virgin rejoice in the dance,
And the young men and the old, together;
For I will turn their mourning to joy,
Will comfort them,
And make them rejoice rather than [k]sorrow.
14 I will satiate the soul of the priests with abundance,
And My people shall be satisfied with My goodness, says the LORD."

15 Thus says the LORD:

"A voice was heard in Ramah,
Lamentation *and* bitter weeping,
Rachel [l]weeping for her children,
Refusing to be comforted for her children,
Because they *are* [m]no more."

16 Thus says the LORD:

"Refrain your voice from [n]weeping,
And your eyes from tears;
For your work shall be rewarded, says the LORD,
And they shall come back from the land of the enemy.
17 There is [o]hope in your future, says the LORD,
That *your* children shall come back to their own border.

CHAPTER 31
1 *a* Jer. 30:22
3 *b* Isa. 43:4
7 *c Remnant:* vv. 7–14; Ezek. 6:8. (Isa. 1:9; Rom. 11:5, *note*) *d Israel* (prophecies): vv. 7–14, 31–40; Ezek. 36:22. (Gen. 12:2; Rom. 11:26, *note*)
8 *e* Jer. 30:3; 32:37
9 *f* Jer. 50:4 *g* Isa 49:10 *h* Isa. 64:8
10 *i* Isa. 40:11; Ezek. 34:11–12
11 *j Redemption* (redeeming relative type): v. 11; Jer. 32:7. (Gen. 48:16; Isa. 59:20, *note*)
13 *k* Cp. Jn. 16:20
15 *l* Mt. 2:18 *m* Jer. 10:20
16 *n* Isa. 25:8; 30:19
17 *o* Jer. 29:11

18 "I have surely heard Ephraim
bemoaning himself:
'You have [a]chastised me, and I
was chastised,
Like an untrained bull;
Restore me, and I will return,
For You *are* the LORD my God.
19 Surely, after my turning, I
[b]repented;
And after I was instructed, I
struck myself on the thigh;
I was [c]ashamed, yes, even
humiliated,
Because I bore the reproach of
my youth.'
20 *Is* Ephraim My dear son?
Is he a pleasant child?
For though I spoke against
him,
I earnestly remember him still;
Therefore My heart yearns for
him;
I will surely have [d]mercy on
him, says the LORD.

21 "Set up signposts,
Make landmarks;
Set your heart toward the
highway,
The way in *which* you went.
Turn back, O virgin of Israel,
Turn back to these your cities.
22 How long will you gad about,
O you backsliding daughter?
For the LORD has created a
[1]new thing in the earth—
A woman shall encompass a
man."

23 Thus says the LORD of hosts, the
God of Israel: "They shall again use
this speech in the land of Judah and in
its cities, when I [e]bring back their
captivity: 'The LORD bless you, O home
of justice, *and* mountain of holiness!'
24 "And there shall dwell in Judah
itself, and in all its cities together,
farmers and those going out with
flocks.
25 "For I have satiated the weary
soul, and I have replenished every sorrowful soul."
26 After this I [f]awoke and looked
around, and my sleep was [g]sweet to
me.

A new covenant to be made with Israel

27 "Behold, the days are coming,
says the LORD, that I will sow the house
of Israel and the house of Judah with
the seed of man and the seed of beast.
28 [h]"And it shall come to pass, *that*
as I have watched over them to pluck
up, to break down, to throw down, to
destroy, and to afflict, so I will watch
over them to build and to plant, says
the LORD.
29 "In those days they shall say no
more:

[i]'The fathers have eaten sour
grapes,
And the children's teeth are set
on edge.'

30 "But every one shall die for his
[j]own iniquity; every man who eats
the sour grapes, his teeth shall be set
on edge.
31 [k]"Behold, the days are coming,
says the LORD, when I will make a new
[2l]covenant with the house of Israel
and with the house of Judah—
32 "not according to the covenant
that I made with their fathers in the
day *that* I took them by the hand to
lead them out of the land of Egypt, My
covenant which they broke, though I
was a [m]husband to them,* says the
LORD.

18
a Ps. 94:12; cp. Heb. 12:5–11
19
b See Zech. 8:14, *note*
c Ezek. 36:31
20
d Jer. 3:12; 12:15
23
e i.e. *cause to cease*
26
f Cp. Zech. 4:1
g Prov. 3:24
28
h The second or constructive phase of Jeremiah's ministry begins here. Cp. Jer. 1:10
29
i Ezek. 18:2–3
30
j Dt. 24:16; 2 Chr. 25:4; Ezek. 18:4,20
31
k vv. 31–34; Heb. 8:8–12; 10:16–17
l *Covenant* (New): vv. 31–34; Jer. 32:40. (Isa. 61:8; Heb. 8:8, *note*)
32
m *"Wife"* (of the LORD): v. 32; Hos. 2:2. (Isa. 54:5; Hos. 2:2)

* 31:32 Following Masoretic Text, Targum, and Vulgate; Septuagint and Syriac read *and I turned away from them.*

[1](31:22) Most contemporary Bible teachers understand the passage to mean that Israel, contrary to the practice of women, will woo the LORD, her divine husband. Older expositors almost unanimously took the verse to predict the virgin birth of the Messiah. Their arguments are: (1) The "new thing in the earth" would require an event of unprecedented character. (2) The word "created" implies an act of divine power. (3) The term "woman" demands an individual rather than the entire nation. And (4) the word "man" is properly used of God (Isa. 9:6).

[2](31:31) The New Covenant of 31:31–40 and 32:40ff. is one of the significant covenants of Scripture, and is remarkably full, stating: (1) the time of the covenant (vv. 31,33); (2) the parties to the covenant (v. 31); (3) the contrast in covenants—Mosaic and New (v. 32); (4) the terms of the covenant (v. 33); (5) the comprehensiveness of the covenant (v. 34); (6) the basic features of the covenant (v. 34): (a) knowledge of God and (b) forgiveness of sin; (7) the perpetuity of the people of the covenant (vv. 35–37); and (8) the guarantee of the covenant (the rebuilt city) (vv. 38–40). See Heb. 8:8, *note*. Although certain features of this covenant have been fulfilled for believers in the present Church Age, e.g. (6) above, the covenant remains to be realized for Israel according to the explicit statement of v. 31.

33 “But this *is* the covenant that I
will make with the house of Israel after those days, says the LORD: I will put
My [a]law in their minds, and write it on
their [b]hearts; and I will be their God,
and they shall be My people.
34 “No more shall every man teach
his neighbor, and every man his
brother, saying, ‘Know the LORD,’ for
they all shall [c]know Me, from the
least of them to the greatest of them,
says the LORD. For I will [d]forgive their
iniquity, and their sin I will remember
no more.”

35 Thus says the LORD,
Who gives the sun for a light
by day,
The ordinances of the moon
and the stars for a light by
night,
Who disturbs the sea,
And its waves roar
(The LORD of hosts *is* His
name):

36 [e]“If those ordinances depart
From before Me, says the LORD,
Then the seed of Israel shall
also cease
From being a nation before Me
forever.”

37 Thus says the LORD:

[f]“If heaven above can be
measured,
And the foundations of the
earth searched out beneath,
I will also [g]cast off all the seed
of Israel
For all that they have done,
says the LORD.

38 “Behold, the days are coming,
says the LORD, that the city shall be
built for the LORD [h]from the Tower of
Hananel to the Corner Gate.
39 “The [i]surveyor’s line shall
again extend straight forward over
the hill Gareb; then it shall turn toward Goath.
40 “And the whole valley of the
[j]dead bodies and of the ashes, and all
the fields as far as the Brook Kidron,
to the corner of the [k]Horse Gate toward the east, *shall be* [l]holy to the
LORD. It shall not be plucked up or
thrown down anymore forever.”

33
a vv. 33–34; Heb. 10:16–17
b Cp. 2 Cor. 3:3
34
c Jer. 24:7
d *Forgiveness:* v. 34; Mt. 6:12. (Lev. 4:20; Mt. 26:28, *note*)
36
e Ps. 148:3–6
37
f Jer. 33:22
g Jer. 33:24–26; Rom. 11:2–5, 26–27
38
h Neh. 3:1; 12:39; Zech. 14:10
39
i Ezek. 40:3, 5; Zech. 2:1–2
40
j Cp. Jer. 7:31–32
k 2 Chr. 23:15; Neh. 3:28
l Joel 3:17
CHAPTER 32
1
m 2 Ki. 25:1–2; Jer. 39:1, see 1 Chr. 11:11, *note*
2
n Jer. 20:2–3; 37:15; 39:13–15
3
o Jer. 26:8–9
p Jer. 21:3–7
4
q 2 Ki. 25:6; Jer. 21:7; 34:3
r Jer. 39:5–6
5
s Jer. 39:7; Ezek. 12:13
t Jer. 27:12–18
7
u *Redemption* (redeeming relative

Jeremiah imprisoned: the sign of Hanamel’s field

32 THE word that came to Jeremiah from the LORD [m]in the
tenth year of Zedekiah king of Judah,
which was the eighteenth year of Nebuchadnezzar.
2 For then the king of Babylon’s
army besieged Jerusalem, and Jeremiah the prophet was shut up in the
court of the [n]prison, which *was in* the
king of Judah’s house.
3 For Zedekiah king of Judah had
shut him up, saying, “Why do you
[o]prophesy and say, ‘Thus says the
LORD: “Behold, I will give this city into
the hand of the king of Babylon, and
he shall take [p]it;
4 “and Zedekiah king of Judah
shall not escape from the hand of the
Chaldeans, but shall surely be [q]deliv-
ered into the hand of the king of Babylon, and shall speak with him face to
face,* and see him eye to [r]eye;
5 “then he shall [s]lead Zedekiah to
Babylon, and there he shall be until I
visit him,” says the LORD; “though you
fight with the Chaldeans, you shall
[t]not succeed” ’?”
6 And Jeremiah said, “The word
of the LORD came to me, saying,
7 ‘Behold, Hanamel the son of
Shallum your uncle will come to you,
saying, “Buy my field which *is* in Anathoth, for the [u]right of redemption *is*
yours to buy *it*.” ’
8 “Then Hanamel my uncle’s son
came to me in the court of the prison
according to the word of the LORD, and
said to me, ‘Please buy my field that *is*
in Anathoth, which *is* in the country of
Benjamin; for the right of inheritance
is yours, and the redemption yours;
buy *it* for yourself.’ Then I knew that
this was the word of the LORD.
9 “So I [1]bought the field from Hanamel, the son of my uncle who *was* in
Anathoth, and weighed *out to* him the
money—seventeen [v]shekels of silver.
10 “And I signed the deed and
sealed *it*, took witnesses, and weighed
the money on the scales.
11 “So I took the purchase deed,
both that which was sealed *according*

type): vv. 7–15; Jer. 50:34. (Gen. 48:16; Isa. 59:20, *note*) **32:9** *v* See Coinage (OT), Ex. 30:13, *note*

*

32:4 Literally *mouth to mouth*

[1](32:9) Here is a sign (1) of Jeremiah’s faith in his own predictions of the restoration of Judah (v. 15), for the field was then occupied by the Babylonian army; and (2) to Judah of that coming restoration. Observe that Jeremiah was acting upon the principle of Heb. 11:1.

to the law and custom, and that which
was open;
12 "and I gave the purchase deed to
[a]Baruch the son of Neriah, son of
Mahseiah, in the presence of Hanamel
my uncle's *son,* and in the presence of
the [b]witnesses who signed the purchase deed, before all the Jews who
sat in the court of the prison.
13 "Then I charged [a]Baruch before
them, saying,
14 'Thus says the LORD of hosts, the
God of Israel: "Take these deeds, both
this purchase deed which is sealed
and this deed which is open, and put
them in an earthen vessel, that they
may last many days."
15 'For thus says the LORD of hosts,
the God of Israel: "Houses and fields
and vineyards shall be [c]possessed
again in this land." '

Jeremiah's prayer and the LORD's response

16 "Now when I had delivered the
purchase deed to Baruch the son of
Neriah, I [d]prayed to the LORD, saying:
17 'Ah, Lord GOD! Behold, [e]You
have made the heavens and the earth
by Your great power and outstretched
arm. [f]There is nothing too hard for
You.
18 '*You* show [g]lovingkindness to
thousands, and repay the iniquity of
the fathers into the bosom of their
children after them—the Great, the
Mighty God, whose name *is* the LORD
of hosts.
19 '*You are* great in counsel and
mighty in work, for [h]your eyes *are*
open to all the ways of the sons of
men, to give everyone according to his
ways and according to the fruit of his
doings.
20 'You have set signs and wonders
in the land of Egypt, to this day, and in
Israel and among *other* men; and You
have made Yourself a [i]name, as it is
this day.
21 'You [j]have brought Your people
Israel out of the land of Egypt with
signs and wonders, with a strong hand
and an outstretched arm, and with
great terror;
22 'You have given them this land,
of which You swore to their fathers to

12
a Jer. 36:4
b Isa. 8:2
15
c Jer. 31:5, 12,14
16
d Bible prayers (OT): vv. 16–25; Ezek. 9:8. (Gen. 15:2; Hab. 3:1)
17
e 2 Ki. 19:15
f Gen. 18:14; Lk. 1:37
18
g Ex. 20:6; 34:7; Dt. 5:9–10
19
h Job 34:21; Ps. 33:13; Prov. 5:21; Jer. 16:17
20
i Ex. 9:16; 1 Chr. 17:21; Isa. 63:12; Jer. 13:11; Dan. 9:15

32:21 j Ex. 6:6; 2 Sam. 7:23; Ps. 136:11–12

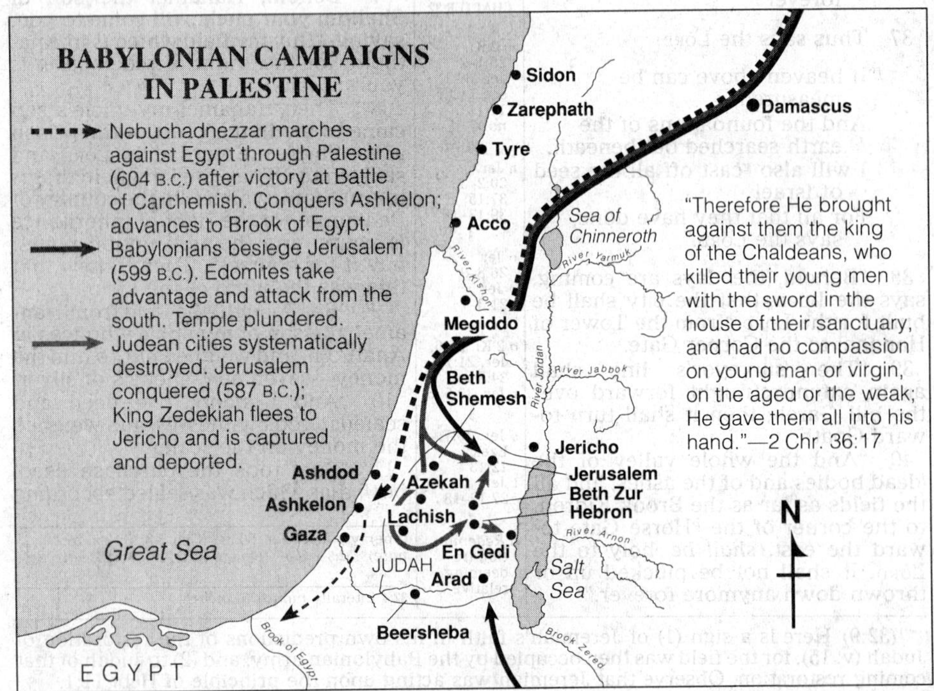
BABYLONIAN CAMPAIGNS IN PALESTINE
Nebuchadnezzar marches against Egypt through Palestine (604 B.C.) after victory at Battle of Carchemish. Conquers Ashkelon; advances to Brook of Egypt.
Babylonians besiege Jerusalem (599 B.C.). Edomites take advantage and attack from the south. Temple plundered.
Judean cities systematically destroyed. Jerusalem conquered (587 B.C.); King Zedekiah flees to Jericho and is captured and deported.
"Therefore He brought against them the king of the Chaldeans, who killed their young men with the sword in the house of their sanctuary, and had no compassion on young man or virgin, on the aged or the weak; He gave them all into his hand."—2 Chr. 36:17
Sidon
Zarephath
Damascus
Tyre
Acco
Sea of Chinneroth
River Yarmuk
River Kishon
Megiddo
River Jordan
River Jabbok
Beth Shemesh
Jericho
Jerusalem
Beth Zur
Hebron
Ashdod
Azekah
Ashkelon
Lachish
Gaza
River Arnon
En Gedi
Great Sea
JUDAH
Arad
Salt Sea
Beersheba
Brook Zered
Brook of Egypt
EGYPT
N

give them—"a [a]land flowing with milk and honey."

23 'And they came in and took possession of it, but they have not obeyed Your voice or walked in Your law. They have done nothing of all that You commanded them to do; therefore You have caused all this calamity to come upon them.

24 'Look, the [b]siege mounds! They have come to the city to take it; and the city has been given into the hand of the Chaldeans who fight against it, because of the sword and famine and pestilence. What You have spoken has happened; there You see *it!*

25 'And You have said to me, O Lord GOD, "Buy the field for money, and take witnesses"!—yet the city has been given into the hand of the Chaldeans.' "

26 Then the word of the LORD came to Jeremiah, saying,

27 "Behold, I *am* the LORD, the [c]God of all flesh. Is there anything [d]too hard for Me?

28 "Therefore thus says the LORD: 'Behold, I will give this city into the hand of the Chaldeans, into the hand of Nebuchadnezzar king of Babylon, and he shall take it.

29 'And the Chaldeans who fight against this city shall come and set fire to this city and burn it, with the houses on whose roofs they have offered incense to Baal and poured out drink offerings to other gods, to provoke Me to anger;

30 'because the children of Israel and the children of Judah have done only evil before Me from their youth. For the children of Israel have provoked Me only to anger with the work of their hands,' says the LORD.

31 'For this city has been to Me *a provocation of* My anger and My fury from the day that they built it, even to this day; [e]so I will remove it from before My face

32 'because of all the evil of the children of Israel and the children of Judah, which they have done to provoke Me to anger—[f]they, their kings, their princes, their priests, their [g]prophets, the men of Judah, and the inhabitants of Jerusalem.

33 'And they have turned to Me the [h]back, and not the face; though I taught them, rising up early and teaching *them,* yet they have not listened to receive instruction.

34 'But they set their abominations in the [i]house which is called by My name, to defile it.

35 'And they built the [j]high places of Baal which *are* in the Valley of the Son of Hinnom, to cause their sons and their daughters to pass through *the fire* to [k]Molech, which I did not command them, nor did it come into My mind that they should do this abomination, to cause Judah to sin.'

36 "Now therefore, thus says the LORD, the God of Israel, concerning this city of which you say, 'It shall be delivered into the hand of the king of Babylon by the sword, by the famine, and by the pestilence':

37 'Behold, I will [l]gather them out of all countries where I have driven them in My anger, in My fury, and in great wrath; I will bring them back to this place, and I will cause them to dwell safely.

38 'They shall be [m]My people, and I will be their God;

39 'then I will [n]give them one heart and one way, that they may fear Me forever, for the good of them and their children after them.

40 'And I will make an [o]everlasting covenant with them, that I will not turn away from doing them good; but I will put My [p]fear in their hearts so that they will not depart from Me.

41 'Yes, I will [q]rejoice over them to do them good, and I will assuredly [r]plant them in this land, with all My heart and with all My soul.'

42 "For thus says the LORD: [s]'Just as I have brought all this great calamity on this people, so I will bring on them all the good that I have promised them.

43 'And fields will be bought in this land of which you say, "*It is* desolate, without man or beast; it has been given into the hand of the Chaldeans."

44 'Men will buy fields for money, sign deeds and seal *them,* and take witnesses, in the land of [t]Benjamin, in the places around Jerusalem, in the cities of Judah, in the cities of the mountains, in the cities of the [u]lowland, and in the cities of the [v]South; for I will cause their captives to return,' says the LORD."

The prophecy of the Davidic kingdom
(see 2 Sam. 7:8–16, and note)

33 MOREOVER the word of the LORD came to Jeremiah a sec-

22 *a* Ex. 3:8,17; Jer. 11:5
24 *b* Jer. 33:4
27 *c* Num. 16:22 *d* v. 17; Mt. 19:26; cp. Num. 11:23; Isa. 59:1
31 *e* 2 Ki. 23:27
32 *f* Isa. 1:4–6; Dan. 9:8 *g* Jer. 23:14
33 *h* Cp. Ezek. 8:16
34 *i* Jer. 7:10–12, 30; 23:11
35 *j* See Jud. 3:7 and 1 Ki. 3:2, *notes* *k* Lev. 18:21; 1 Ki. 11:33
37 *l* Dt. 30:3; Jer. 23:3; 29:14; 31:10; 50:19; Ezek. 37:21
38 *m* Jer. 24:7; 30:22; 31:33
39 *n* Ezek. 11:19–20
40 *o* *Covenant* (New): vv. 37–40; Jer. 50:5. (Isa. 61:8; Heb. 8:8, *note*) *p* See Ps. 19:9, *note*
41 *q* Dt. 3:9; Zeph. 3:17 *r* Jer. 24:6; 31:28; Amos 9:15
42 *s* Jer. 31:28
44 *t* Jer. 17:26 *u* See Dt. 1:7, *note* *v* See Gen. 12:9, *note*

ond time, [a]while he was still shut up
in the court of the prison, saying,
2 "Thus says the LORD who made
[b]it, the LORD who formed it to establish it (the LORD *is* His name):
3 [c]'Call to Me, and I will answer
you, and show you great and mighty
things, which you do not know.'
4 "For thus says the LORD, the God
of Israel, concerning the houses of this
city and the houses of the kings of Judah, which have been pulled down *to*
*fortify** against the [d]siege mounds
and the sword:
5 'They come to fight with the
[e]Chaldeans, but *only* to fill their
places* with the dead bodies of men
whom I will slay in My anger and My
fury, all for whose wickedness I have
hidden My face from this city.
6 'Behold, I will bring it health and
[f]healing; I will heal them and reveal
to them the abundance of peace and
truth.
7 'And I will cause the captives of
Judah and the captives of Israel to return, and will rebuild those places as
at the first.
8 'I will [g]cleanse them from all
their iniquity by which they have
sinned against Me, and I will pardon
all their iniquities by which they have
sinned and by which they have transgressed against Me.
9 'Then it shall be to Me a [h]name
of joy, a praise, and an honor before
all nations of the earth, who shall hear
all the good that I do to them; they
shall fear and tremble for all the goodness and all the prosperity that I provide for it.'
10 "Thus says the LORD: 'Again
there shall be heard in this place—of
which you say, "It *is* desolate, without
man and without beast"—in the cities
of Judah, in the streets of Jerusalem
that are desolate, without man and
without inhabitant and without beast,
11 'the [i]voice of joy and the voice
of gladness, the voice of the bridegroom and the voice of the bride, the
voice of those who will say:

"Praise the LORD of hosts,
For the LORD *is* good,
For His mercy *endures*
forever"—

and of those *who will* bring the [j]sacri-
fice of praise into the house of the
LORD. For I will cause the captives of
the land to return as at the first,' says
the LORD.
12 "Thus says the LORD of hosts:
[k]'In this place which is desolate, without man and without beast, and in all
its cities, there shall again be a dwelling place of shepherds causing *their*
flocks to lie down.
13 'In the cities of the mountains, in
the cities of the [l]lowland, in the cities
of the [m]South, in the land of Benjamin,
in the places around Jerusalem, and in
the cities of Judah, the flocks shall
again pass under the hands of him
who counts *them*,' says the LORD.
14 'Behold, the days are coming,'
says the LORD, 'that I will perform that
[n]good thing which I have promised to
the house of Israel and to the house of
Judah:

15 [1]'In those days and at that time
I will cause to grow up to
David
A [o]Branch of righteousness;
He shall execute judgment and
righteousness in the earth.
16 In those days Judah will be
saved,
And Jerusalem will dwell
safely.
And this *is the name* by which
she will be called:
[p]THE LORD OUR
RIGHTEOUSNESS.'*

17 "For thus says the LORD: 'David
shall never [q]lack a man to sit on the
[r]throne of the house of Israel;
18 'nor shall the [s]priests, the Levites, lack a man to offer burnt offerings before Me, to kindle grain offerings, and to sacrifice continually.' "
19 And the word of the LORD came
to Jeremiah, saying,
20 "Thus says the LORD: 'If you can
break My covenant with the day and
My covenant with the night, so that
there will not be day and night in their
season,
21 'then My [t]covenant may also be
broken with David My servant, so that
he shall not have a son to reign on his
throne, and with the Levites, the
priests, My ministers.

CHAPTER 33

1 *a* See Jer. 37:11, *note*
2 *b* i.e. *the earth*
3 *c* Ps. 91:15; Isa. 55:6–7; Jer. 29:12
4 *d* Jer. 32:24
5 *e* Jer. 21:4–7; 32:5; 37:9–10
6 *f* Jer. 30:17
8 *g* Ezek. 36:25; Zech. 13:1; Heb. 9:13–14
9 *h* Isa. 55:13; 62:2–4; Jer. 13:11
11 *i* Cp. Jer. 7:34; 16:9; 25:10
j Heb. 13:15
12 *k* Isa. 65:10; Jer. 31:24; 50:19
13 *l* See Dt. 1:7, *note*
m See Gen. 12:9, *note*
14 *n* Jer. 29:10; 32:42
15 *o* See Isa. 4:2, *note*
16 *p* Heb. *Jehovah-tsidkenu.* See Ex. 34:6, *note*
17 *q* 2 Sam. 7:16; 1 Ki. 2:4; Ps. 89:29,36; Lk. 1:32,33
r Kingdom (OT): vv. 14–17; Ezek. 11:15. (Gen. 1:26; Zech. 12:8, *note*)

33:18 *s* Ezek. 44:15 **33:21** *t* 2 Sam 23:5

*
33:4 Compare Isaiah 22:10 **33:5** Compare 2 Kings 23:14 **33:16** Compare 23:5,6

[1](33:15) See *notes* on Davidic Covenant (2 Sam. 7:16); Kingdom (OT), (Gen. 1:26; Zech. 12:8); and Kingdom (NT), (1 Cor. 15:24).

22 [a]'As the host of heaven cannot
be numbered, nor the sand of the sea
measured, so will I [b]multiply the descendants of David My servant and
the [c]Levites who minister to Me.' "
23 Moreover the word of the LORD
came to Jeremiah, saying,
24 "Have you not considered what
these people have spoken, saying,
'The two families which the LORD has
chosen, He has also cast them off'?
Thus they have [d]despised My people,
as if they should no more be a nation
before them.
25 "Thus says the LORD: [e]'If My
covenant *is* not with day and night,
and if I have not appointed the ordinances of heaven and earth,
26 [f]then I will [g]cast away the descendants of Jacob and David My servant, *so* that I will not take *any* of his
descendants *to be* rulers over the descendants of Abraham, Isaac, and Jacob. For I will cause their captives to
return, and will have mercy on
them.' "

Message to Zedekiah concerning his coming captivity

34 THE word which came to Jeremiah from the LORD, [h]when
Nebuchadnezzar king of Babylon and
all his army, all the [i]kingdoms of the
earth under his dominion, and all the
people, fought against Jerusalem and
all its cities, saying,
2 "Thus says the LORD, the God of
Israel: 'Go and [j]speak to Zedekiah
king of Judah and tell him, "Thus says
the LORD: 'Behold, I will give this city
into the hand of the king of Babylon,
and he shall burn it with fire.
3 'And you shall [k]not escape from
his hand, but shall surely be taken and
delivered into his hand; your eyes
shall see the eyes of the king of Babylon, he shall speak with you [l]face to
face,* and you shall go to Babylon.' " '
4 "Yet hear the word of the LORD,
O Zedekiah king of Judah! Thus says
the LORD concerning you: 'You shall
not die by the sword.
5 'You shall die in peace; as in the
[m]ceremonies of your fathers, the former kings who were before you, so
they shall burn incense for you and
lament for you, *saying,* "Alas, lord!"
For I have pronounced the word, says
the LORD.' "
6 Then Jeremiah the prophet
spoke all these words to Zedekiah
king of Judah in Jerusalem,
7 when the king of Babylon's
army fought against Jerusalem and all
the cities of Judah that were left,
against Lachish and Azekah; for *only*
these [n]fortified cities remained of the
cities of Judah.

Princes and people rebuked: Jerusalem to be a desolation

8 *This is* the word that came to Jeremiah from the LORD, after King Zedekiah had made a covenant with all the
people who *were* at Jerusalem to proclaim liberty to them:
9 that every man should set [o]free
his male and female slave—a Hebrew
man or woman—that no one should
keep a Jewish brother in bondage.
10 Now when all the princes and all
the people, who had entered into the
covenant, heard that everyone should
set free his male and female slaves,
that no one should keep them in bondage anymore, they obeyed and let
them go.
11 But afterward they changed
their minds and made the male and
female slaves return, whom they had
set free, and brought them into subjection as male and female slaves.
12 Therefore the word of the LORD
came to Jeremiah from the LORD, saying,
13 "Thus says the LORD, the God of
Israel: 'I made a [p]covenant with your
fathers in the day that I brought them
out of the land of Egypt, out of the
house of bondage, saying,
14 "At the end of [q]seven years let
every man set free his Hebrew
brother, who has been sold to him;
and when he has served you six years,
you shall let him go free from you."
But your fathers did not obey Me nor
incline their ear.
15 'Then you recently turned and
did what was right in My sight—every
man proclaiming liberty to his neighbor; and you made a covenant before
Me in the house which is called by My
name.
16 'Then you turned around and
profaned My name, and every one of
you brought back his male and female
slaves, whom he had set at liberty, [1]at
their pleasure, and brought them back

22
a Gen. 15:5; 22:17
b Jer. 30:19; Ezek. 36:10–11
c Isa. 66:21
24
d Neh. 4:2–4; Est. 3:6–8; Ps. 44:13–14; 83:4; Ezek. 36:2
25
e v. 20; Gen. 8:22
26
f Jer. 31:37
g Rom. 11:1–2
CHAPTER 34
1
h 2 Ki. 25:1; Jer. 32:1–2; 39:1; 52:4
i Jer. 25:9; Dan. 2:37–38
2
j 2 Chr. 36:11–12
3
k 2 Ki. 25:4–5; Jer. 21:7
l Jer. 32:4; 39:5–6
5
m Or *burnings.* 2 Chr. 16:14; 21:19
7
n 2 Ki. 18:13; 19:8; 2 Chr. 11:5,9
9
o Lev. 25:39–46
13
p Ex. 24:3, 7–8
14
q Ex. 21:2; Dt. 15:12

*34:3 Literally *mouth to mouth*

[1](34:16) It was according to the law that Hebrew slaves, when they were set at liberty, could accept freedom or remain with their masters forever (Ex. 21:5–6).

into subjection, to be your male and female slaves.'

17 "Therefore thus says the LORD: 'You have not obeyed Me in proclaiming liberty, every one to his brother and every one to his neighbor. Behold, I [a]proclaim liberty to you,' says the LORD—'to the sword, to pestilence, and to famine! And I will [b]deliver you to trouble among all the kingdoms of the earth.

18 'And I will give the men who have transgressed My covenant, who have not performed the words of the covenant which they made before Me, [c]when they cut the calf in two and passed between the parts of it—

19 'the princes of Judah, the princes of Jerusalem, the eunuchs, the priests, and all the people of the land who passed between the parts of the calf—

20 'I will [d]give them into the hand of their enemies and into the hand of those who seek their life. Their dead bodies shall be for [e]meat [f]for the birds of the heaven and the beasts of the earth.

21 'And I will give Zedekiah king of Judah and his princes into the hand of their enemies, into the hand of those who seek their life, and into the hand of the king of Babylon's army which has gone back from you.

22 'Behold, I will command,' says the LORD, 'and cause them to [g]return to this city. They will fight against it and take it and burn it with fire; and I will [h]make the cities of Judah a desolation without inhabitant.' "

The Rechabites' obedience contrasted with Judah's disobedience

35 THE word which came to Jeremiah from the LORD in the days of Jehoiakim the son of Josiah, king of Judah, saying,

2 "Go to the house of the [i]Rechabites, speak to them, and bring them into the house of the LORD, into one of the [j]chambers, and give them wine to drink."

3 Then I took Jaazaniah the son of Jeremiah, the son of Habazziniah, his brothers and all his sons, and the whole house of the Rechabites,

4 and I brought them into the house of the LORD, into the chamber of the sons of Hanan the son of Igdaliah, a man of God, which *was* by the chamber of the princes, above the chamber of Maaseiah the son of Shallum, the [k]keeper of the door.

5 Then I set before the sons of the house of the Rechabites bowls full of wine, and cups; and I said to them, [l]"Drink wine."

6 But they said, "We will drink no wine, for [m]Jonadab the son of Rechab, our father, commanded us, saying, 'You shall drink [n]no wine, you nor your sons, forever.

7 'You shall not build a house, sow seed, plant a vineyard, nor have *any of these;* but all your days you shall dwell in tents, that you may [o]live many days in the land where you are sojourners.'

8 "Thus we have [p]obeyed the voice of Jonadab the son of Rechab, our father, in all that he charged us, to drink no wine all our days, we, our wives, our sons, or our daughters,

9 "nor to build ourselves houses to dwell in; nor do we have vineyard, field, or seed.

10 "But we have dwelt in tents, and have obeyed and done according to all that Jonadab our father commanded us.

11 "But it came to pass, when Nebuchadnezzar king of Babylon came up into the land, that we said, 'Come, let us [q]go to Jerusalem for fear of the army of the Chaldeans and for fear of the army of the Syrians.' So we dwell at Jerusalem."

12 Then came the word of the LORD to Jeremiah, saying,

13 "Thus says the LORD of hosts, the God of Israel: 'Go and tell the men of Judah and the inhabitants of Jerusalem, [r]"Will you not receive instruction to obey My words?" says the LORD.

14 "The words of Jonadab the son of Rechab, which he commanded his sons, not to drink wine, are performed; for to this day they drink none, and obey their father's commandment. [s]But although I have spoken to you, [t]rising early and speaking, you did not obey Me.

15 "I have also sent to you all My [u]servants the prophets, rising up early and sending *them*, saying, 'Turn now everyone from his evil way, amend your doings, and do not go after other gods to serve them; then you will [v]dwell in the land which I have given you and your fathers.' But you have not inclined your ear, nor obeyed Me.

16 "Surely the sons of Jonadab the son of Rechab have performed the

17
a Mt. 7:2; Gal. 6:7; Jas. 2:13
b Dt. 28:25, 64; Jer. 29:18
18
c Gen. 15:10,17
20
d Jer. 22:25
e Jer. 16:4
f Jer. 7:32–33; 19:7; 25:33
22
g Jer. 37:6–10
h Jer. 9:11; 44:2,6
CHAPTER 35
2
i 2 Sam. 4:2; 1 Chr. 2:55
j 1 Ki. 6:5–6, 8
4
k 2 Ki. 12:9; 25:18; 1 Chr. 9:19
5
l vv. 5–10; cp. Amos 2:12
6
m vv. 8,14, 16,19; or *Jehonadab*, 2 Ki. 10:15,23
n Lev. 10:9; Num. 6:2–4; Jud. 13:7,14; Prov. 31:4; Ezek. 44:21; Lk. 1:15
7
o Ex. 20:12; Eph. 6:2–3
8
p Eph. 6:1; Col. 3:20
11
q Jer. 4:5–7; 8:14
13
r Jer. 6:10; 17:23; 32:33
14
s 2 Chr. 36:15
t Jer. 7:13; 25:3
15
u Jer. 26:4–5; 29:19
v Jer. 7:7; 22:4; 25:5–6

commandment of their [a]father, which
he commanded them, but this people
has not obeyed Me." '
17 "Therefore thus says the LORD
God of hosts, the God of Israel: 'Behold, I will bring on Judah and on all
the inhabitants of Jerusalem all the
doom that I have pronounced against
them; [b]because I have spoken to them
but they have not heard, and I have
called to them but they have not answered.' "
18 And Jeremiah said to the house
of the Rechabites, "Thus says the LORD
of hosts, the God of Israel: 'Because
you have obeyed the commandment
of Jonadab your father, and kept all
his precepts and done according to all
that he commanded you,
19 'therefore thus says the LORD of
hosts, the God of Israel: "Jonadab the
son of Rechab shall not lack a man to
stand before Me [c]forever." ' "

Jehoiakim burns Jeremiah's scroll

36 NOW it came to pass in the
[d]fourth year of [e]Jehoiakim the
son of Josiah, king of Judah, *that* this
[f]word came to Jeremiah from the
LORD, saying:
2 "Take a [g]scroll of a book and
[h]write on it all the words that I have
spoken to you against Israel, against
Judah, and against all the nations,
from the day I spoke to you, [i]from the
days of Josiah even to this day.
3 "It [j]may be that the house of Judah will hear all the adversities which
I purpose to bring upon them, that everyone may [k]turn from his evil way,
that I may forgive their iniquity and
their sin."
4 Then Jeremiah called [l]Baruch
the son of Neriah; and Baruch wrote
on a scroll of a book, at the instruction
of Jeremiah,* all the words of the
LORD which He had spoken to him.
5 And Jeremiah commanded Bar-
uch, saying, "I *am* [m]confined, I cannot
go into the house of the LORD.
6 "You go, therefore, and read
from the scroll which you have written at my instruction,* the words of
the LORD, in the hearing of the people
in the LORD's house on the [n]day of fasting. And you shall also read them in
the hearing of all Judah who come
from their cities.
7 "It may be that they will present
their supplication before the LORD,
and everyone will turn from his evil
way. For great *is* the anger and the

16
a Heb. 12:9
17
b Prov. 1:24; Isa. 65:12; 66:4; Jer. 7:13
19
c Ex. 20:12; Eph. 6:2–3
CHAPTER 36
1
d Jer. 25:1; 45:1
e Or *Eliakim,* 2 Ki. 23:34–37
f Inspiration: vv. 1–32; Jer. 45:2. (Ex. 4:15; 2 Tim. 3:16, *note*)
2
g Isa. 8:1; Ezek. 2:9; Zech. 5:1
h See v. 32, *note*
i Jer. 25:3
3
j Jer. 26:3; Ezek. 12:3
k Jer. 18:8; cp. Jon. 3:8
4
l Jer. 32:12; 45:1
5
m Jer. 32:2; 33:1
6
n Lev. 16:29; 23:27–32; Acts 27:9
9
o See Lev. 23:2, *note*
12
p Jer. 41:1
q Jer. 26:22
16
r Cp. Amos 7:10–11

fury that the LORD has pronounced
against this people."
8 And Baruch the son of Neriah
did according to all that Jeremiah the
prophet commanded him, reading
from the book the words of the LORD in
the LORD's house.
9 Now it came to pass in the fifth
year of Jehoiakim the son of Josiah,
king of Judah, in the [o]ninth month,
that they proclaimed a fast before the
LORD to all the people in Jerusalem,
and to all the people who came from
the cities of Judah to Jerusalem.
10 Then Baruch read from the book
the words of Jeremiah in the house of
the LORD, in the chamber of Gemariah
the son of Shaphan the scribe, in the
upper court at the entry of the New
Gate of the LORD's house, in the hearing of all the people.
11 When Michaiah the son of Gemariah, the son of Shaphan, heard all
the words of the LORD from the book,
12 he then went down to the king's
house, into the scribe's chamber; and
there all the princes were sitting—
[p]Elishama the scribe, Delaiah the son
of Shemaiah, [q]Elnathan the son of
Achbor, Gemariah the son of Shaphan, Zedekiah the son of Hananiah,
and all the princes.
13 Then Michaiah declared to them
all the words that he had heard when
Baruch read the book in the hearing of
the people.
14 Therefore all the princes sent Jehudi the son of Nethaniah, the son of
Shelemiah, the son of Cushi, to Baruch, saying, "Take in your hand the
scroll from which you have read in the
hearing of the people, and come." So
Baruch the son of Neriah took the
scroll in his hand and came to them.
15 And they said to him, "Sit down
now, and read it in our hearing." So
Baruch read *it* in their hearing.
16 Now it happened, when they had
heard all the words, that they looked
in fear from one to another, and said
to Baruch, "We will surely [r]tell the
king of all these words."
17 And they asked Baruch, saying,
"Tell us now, how did you write all
these words—at his instruction?"*
18 So Baruch answered them, "He
proclaimed with his mouth all these
words to me, and I wrote *them* with
ink in the book."

*
36:4 Literally *from Jeremiah's mouth*
36:6 Literally *from my mouth* **36:17** Literally *with his mouth*

19 Then the princes said to Baruch,
"Go and [a]hide, you and Jeremiah; and
let no one know where you are."
20 And they went to the king, into
the court; but they stored the scroll in
the chamber of Elishama the scribe,
and told all the words in the hearing of
the king.
21 So the king sent Jehudi to bring
the scroll, and he took it from Elishama the scribe's chamber. And Jehudi
[b]read it in the hearing of the king and
in the hearing of all the princes who
stood beside the king.
22 Now the king was sitting in the
[c]winter house in the [d]ninth month,
with *a fire* burning on the hearth before him.
23 And it happened, when Jehudi
had read three or four columns, *that
the king* cut [e]it with the scribe's knife
and [f]cast *it* into the fire that *was* on
the hearth, until all the scroll was consumed in the fire that *was* on the
hearth.
24 Yet they were [g]not afraid, nor
did they [h]tear their garments, the king
nor any of his servants who heard all
these words.
25 Nevertheless Elnathan, Delaiah,
and Gemariah implored the king not
to burn the scroll; but he would not
listen to them.
26 And the king commanded Jerahmeel the king's* son, Seraiah the son
of Azriel, and Shelemiah the son of
Abdeel, to [i]seize Baruch the scribe
and Jeremiah the prophet, but the
LORD hid them.

Destroyed scroll replaced

27 Now after the king had burned
the scroll with the words which Baruch had written at the instruction of
Jeremiah,* the word of the LORD came
to Jeremiah, saying:
28 "Take yet another scroll, and
write on it all the former words that
were in the first scroll which Jehoiakim the king of Judah has burned.
29 "And you shall say to Jehoiakim
king of Judah, 'Thus says the LORD:
"You have burned this scroll, saying,
[j]"Why have you written in it that the
king of Babylon will certainly come
and destroy this land, and cause man
and beast to [k]cease from here?' "
30 'Therefore thus says the LORD
concerning Jehoiakim king of Judah:
"He shall have [l]no one to sit on the
throne of David, and his dead body
shall be [m]cast out to the heat of the day
and the frost of the night.
31 "I will punish him, his family,
and his servants for their iniquity; and
I will bring on them, on the inhabitants of Jerusalem, and on the men of
Judah all the doom that I have pronounced against them; but they did
not heed." ' "
32 Then Jeremiah took another
scroll and gave it to Baruch the scribe,
the son of Neriah, who wrote on it at
the instruction of Jeremiah* all the
words of the book which Jehoiakim
king of Judah had burned in the fire.
And besides, there were added to
them many similar [1]words.

Jeremiah's interview with Zedekiah

37 NOW King [n]Zedekiah the son
of Josiah reigned instead of
[o]Coniah the son of Jehoiakim, whom
Nebuchadnezzar king of Babylon
made king in the land of Judah.
2 [p]But neither he nor his servants
nor the people of the land gave heed to
the words of the LORD which He spoke
by the prophet Jeremiah.
3 And Zedekiah the king sent Jehucal the son of Shelemiah, and Zephaniah the son of Maaseiah, the priest,
to the prophet Jeremiah, saying,

19
a Cp. 1 Ki. 17:3; 18:4, 10; Jer. 26:20–24
21
b Cp. 2 Ki. 22:10
22
c Amos 3:15
d See Lev. 23:2, *note*
23
e i.e. *the scroll* (v. 21)
f Cp. Jer. 20:8; Zech. 7:12
24
g Ps. 36:1; cp. 64:5
h Cp. 1 Ki. 21:27; 2 Ki. 19:1–2; 22:11; Isa. 36:22; 37:1
26
i Cp. 1 Ki. 19:1–3,10, 14
29
j Jer. 32:3
k Jer. 25:9–11; 26:9
30
l See Jer. 22:30 and Mt. 1:11, *notes;* cp. Acts 15:16, *note*
m Jer. 22:19
CHAPTER 37
1
n 2 Ki. 24:17; 2 Chr. 36:10
o Or *Jeconiah,* 1 Chr. 3:16
2
p 2 Chr. 36:12–14

*36:26 Hebrew *Hammelech* **36:27** Literally *from Jeremiah's mouth* **36:32** Literally *from Jeremiah's mouth*

[1](36:32) This verse explains the arrangement of Jeremiah's prophecy. As the exile came nearer, God commanded Jeremiah to write down the messages that He had already given orally (30:2) and to add to them new divine promises of return from exile and of other blessings in the more distant future (30:3,10–11). Jehoiakim destroyed Jeremiah's scroll (36:23). God commanded Jeremiah to dictate a new scroll. Jeremiah did so, reproducing the contents of the previous scroll, which probably had been arranged in the order in which God had originally given them. But he added at the proper places certain other inspired discussions of the same subjects (36:32). Later on Jeremiah inserted messages received at later times but logically related to messages previously given, putting them at the appropriate places within the scroll already written, as for instance, chs. 21; 24; 27—29; 32—34. Other messages given after the new scroll was written were added in the order in which they were received, and these were followed by certain special sections (chs. 45—52). Thus the arrangement of the book is partly according to the time the messages were given, and partly according to the nature of the subject matter.

[a]"Pray now to the LORD our God for us."

4 Now Jeremiah was coming and going among the people, for they had not *yet* put him in prison.

5 Then [b]Pharaoh's army came up from Egypt; and when the Chaldeans who were besieging Jerusalem heard news of them, they departed from Jerusalem.

6 Then the word of the LORD came to the prophet Jeremiah, saying,

7 "Thus says the LORD, the God of Israel, 'Thus you shall say to the king of Judah, who sent you to Me to inquire of Me: [c]"Behold, Pharaoh's army which has come up to help you will return to Egypt, to their own land.

8 "And the Chaldeans shall come back and [d]fight against this city, and take it and burn it with fire." '

9 "Thus says the LORD: 'Do not deceive yourselves, saying, "The Chaldeans will surely depart from us," for they will not depart.

10 'For though you had defeated the whole army of the Chaldeans who fight against you, and there remained *only* wounded men among them, they would rise up, every man in his tent, and burn the city with fire.' "

Jeremiah falsely accused and imprisoned

11 And it [1]happened, when the army of the Chaldeans left *the siege* of Jerusalem for fear of Pharaoh's army,

12 that Jeremiah went out of Jerusalem to go into the land of Benjamin to claim his property there among the people.

13 And when he was in the Gate of Benjamin, a captain of the guard *was* there whose name *was* Irijah the son of Shelemiah, the son of Hananiah; and he seized Jeremiah the prophet, saying, "You are [e]defecting to the Chaldeans!"

14 Then Jeremiah said, "False! I am not defecting to the Chaldeans." But he did not listen to him. So Irijah seized Jeremiah and brought him to the princes.

15 Therefore the princes were angry with Jeremiah, and they [f]struck him and put him in prison in the [g]house of Jonathan the scribe. For they had made that the prison.

16 When Jeremiah entered the dungeon and the cells, and Jeremiah had remained there many days,

17 then Zedekiah the king sent and took him *out*. The king asked him secretly in his house, and [h]said, "Is there *any* word from the LORD?" And Jeremiah said, "There is." Then he said, "You shall be [i]delivered into the hand of the king of Babylon!"

18 Moreover Jeremiah said to King Zedekiah, "What [j]offense have I committed against you, against your servants, or against this people, that you have put me in prison?

19 "Where now *are* your prophets who prophesied to you, saying, 'The king of Babylon will not come against you or against this land'?

20 "Therefore please hear now, O my lord the king. Please, let my petition be accepted before you, and do not make me return to the house of Jonathan the scribe, lest I die there."

21 Then Zedekiah the king commanded that they should commit Jeremiah to the [k]court of the prison, and that they should give him daily a piece of bread from the bakers' street, [l]until all the bread in the city was gone. Thus Jeremiah remained in the court of the prison.

Jeremiah, released from the dungeon, gives Zedekiah final opportunity to repent

38 NOW Shephatiah the son of Mattan, Gedaliah the son of Pashhur, Jucal* the son of Shelemiah, and [m]Pashhur the son of Malchiah heard the words that Jeremiah had spoken to all the people, saying,

2 "Thus says the LORD: 'He who remains in this city shall die by the sword, by famine, and by pestilence; but he who goes over to the Chaldeans shall [n]live; his life shall be as a [o]prize to him, and he shall live.'

3 "Thus says the LORD: [p]'This city shall surely be [q]given into the hand of the king of Babylon's army, which shall take it.' "

3
a Jer. 42:2
5
b Cp. 2 Ki. 24:7; Ezek. 17:15
7
c Isa. 36:6; Ezek. 17:17
8
d Jer. 34:22; 39:2–3
13
e Cp. Jer. 18:18; 20:10; Amos 7:10; Acts 6:11; 24:5–9
15
f Jer. 20:2
g Jer. 38:26
17
h Cp. Jer. 38:14–16, 24–27
i Jer. 21:7; Ezek. 12:12–13; 17:19–21
18
j Cp. 1 Sam. 24:9, 26:18; Dan. 6:22; Jn. 10:32; Acts 25:8, 11,25
21
k Jer. 32:2; 38:13,28
l Jer. 38:9; 52:6
CHAPTER 38
1
m Jer. 21:1
2
n Jer. 21:8–9; 27:12–13
o Jer. 21:9; 45:5
3
p Jer. 21:10; 32:3
q Jer. 34:2

* 38:1 Same as *Jehucal* (compare 37:3)

[1](37:11) Five steps in Jeremiah's prison experiences are recorded: (1) He is arrested in the gate and committed to prison on the false charge of treason (37:11–15). (2) He is released from prison, but restricted to the courtyard of the prison (37:17–21). (3) He is imprisoned in the miry dungeon of Malchiah (38:6). (4) He is again released from the dungeon and kept in the prison courtyard until the capture of the city (38:17–28). And (5) he is carried in chains from the city by Nebuzaradan, captain of the guard, being finally released at Ramah (40:1–4).

4 Therefore the princes said to the king, "Please, [1]let this man be put to death, for thus he weakens the hands of the men of war who remain in this city, and the hands of all the people, by speaking such words to them. For this man does not seek the welfare of this people, but their [a]harm."

5 Then Zedekiah the king said, "Look, he *is* in your hand. [b]For the king can *do* nothing against you."

6 [c]So they took Jeremiah and cast him into the dungeon of Malchiah the king's* son, which *was* in the court of the prison, and they let Jeremiah down with ropes. And in the dungeon *there was* no water, but mire. So Jeremiah sank in the mire.

7 Now [d]Ebed-Melech the Ethiopian, one of the eunuchs, who was in the king's house, heard that they had put Jeremiah in the dungeon. When the king was sitting at the Gate of Benjamin,

8 Ebed-Melech went out of the king's house and spoke to the king, saying:

9 "My lord the king, these men have done evil in all that they have done to Jeremiah the prophet, whom they have cast into the dungeon, and he is likely to die from hunger in the place where he is. For *there is* [e]no more bread in the city."

10 Then the [2]king commanded Ebed-Melech the Ethiopian, saying, "Take from here thirty men with you, and lift Jeremiah the prophet out of the dungeon before he dies."

11 So Ebed-Melech took the men with him and went into the house of the king under the treasury, and took from there old clothes and old rags, and let them down by ropes into the dungeon to Jeremiah.

12 Then Ebed-Melech the Ethiopian said to Jeremiah, "Please put these old clothes and rags under your armpits, under the ropes." And Jeremiah did so.

4
a Cp. Jer. 29:7
5
b vv. 24–27; cp. Mt. 27:24; Jn. 12:43
6
c Lam. 3:55; see Jer. 37:11, *note*
7
d vv. 7–13; Jer. 39:15–18
9
e Jer. 37:21
14
f Jer. 21:1–2; 37:17
15
g Cp. Lk. 22:67–68
16
h Isa. 57:16
17
i Jer. 38:2; 2 Ki. 24:12, 14–16
19
j Cp. Isa. 51:12–13
k Jer. 39:9
20
l Jer. 40:9
22
m Jer. 8:10

13 So they pulled Jeremiah up with ropes and lifted him out of the dungeon. And Jeremiah remained in the court of the prison.

14 Then Zedekiah the king sent and had Jeremiah the prophet brought to him at the third entrance of the house of the LORD. And the king said to Jeremiah, "I will [f]ask you something. Hide nothing from me."

15 Jeremiah said to Zedekiah, "If I declare *it* to you, will you not surely put me to death? [g]And if I give you advice, you will not listen to me."

16 So Zedekiah the king swore secretly to Jeremiah, saying, "*As* the LORD lives, [h]who made our very souls, I will not put you to death, nor will I give you into the hand of these men who seek your life."

17 Then Jeremiah said to Zedekiah, "Thus says the LORD, the God of hosts, the God of Israel: 'If you surely [i]surrender to the king of Babylon's princes, then your soul shall live; this city shall not be burned with fire, and you and your house shall live.

18 'But if you do not surrender to the king of Babylon's princes, then this city shall be given into the hand of the Chaldeans; they shall burn it with fire, and you shall not escape from their hand.' "

19 And Zedekiah the king said to Jeremiah, "I am [j]afraid of the Jews who have [k]defected to the Chaldeans, lest they deliver me into their hand, and they abuse me."

20 But Jeremiah said, "They shall not deliver *you*. Please, obey the voice of the LORD which I speak to you. So it shall be [l]well with you, and your soul shall live.

21 "But if you refuse to surrender, this *is* the word that the LORD has shown me:

22 'Now behold, all the [m]women who are left in the king of Judah's house *shall be* surrendered to the king

*38:6 Hebrew *Hammelech*

[1](38:4) Here is the fundamental reason why the prophetic warnings of the OT and NT are unwelcome to an unreasoning optimism. Cp. 26:11.

[2](38:10) King Zedekiah did everything he could to make Jeremiah's imprisonment comfortable. He seems genuinely to have desired to help the prophet and to follow the messages that Jeremiah gave him from the LORD. However, Zedekiah was afraid of the nobles who had been brought into power by his wicked brother, Jehoiakim. Although Zedekiah wished to be a good king, his weakness and fear not only made him ineffective but also caused him to be actually a bad king. Jehoiakim, who preceded Zedekiah, had been hampered in some of his evil ways by the good nobles whom his father, Josiah, had put into power (cp. Jer. 26), but by the end of his reign Jehoiakim had succeeded in replacing most of them with the wicked men who now controlled Zedekiah.

of Babylon's princes, and those *women* shall say:

"Your close friends have set
upon you
And prevailed against you;
Your feet have sunk in the
mire,
And they have turned away
again."

23 'So they shall surrender all your wives and [a]children to the Chaldeans. [b]You shall not escape from their hand, but shall be taken by the hand of the king of Babylon. And you shall cause this city to be burned with fire.' "

24 Then Zedekiah said to Jeremiah, "Let no one know of these words, and you shall not die.

25 "But if the princes hear that I have talked with you, and they come to you and say to you, 'Declare to us now what you have said to the king, and also what the king said to you; do not hide *it* from us, and we will not put you to death,'

26 "then you shall say to them, 'I [c]presented my request before the king, that he would not make me return to [d]Jonathan's house to die there.' "

27 Then all the princes came to Jeremiah and asked him. And he told them according to all these words that the king had commanded. So they stopped speaking with him, for the conversation had not been heard.

28 Now Jeremiah [e]remained in the court of the prison until the day that Jerusalem was taken. And he was *there* when Jerusalem was taken.

Jerusalem falls: Zedekiah taken to Babylon (cp. 2 Ki. 25:1–7; 2 Chr. 36:17–21; Jer. 52:4–17)

39 IN the [f]ninth year of Zedekiah king of Judah, in the [g]tenth month, Nebuchadnezzar king of Babylon and all his army came against Jerusalem, and besieged it.

2 In the [h]eleventh year of Zedekiah, in the [g]fourth month, on the ninth *day* of the month, the city was penetrated.

3 Then all the princes of the king of Babylon came in and [i]sat in the Middle Gate: Nergal-Sharezer, Samgar-Nebo, Sarsechim, [j]Rabsaris,* Nergal-Sarezer, [j]Rabmag,* with the rest of the princes of the king of Babylon.

4 So it was, when Zedekiah the king of Judah and all the men of war saw them, that they [k]fled and went out of the city by night, by way of the king's garden, by the gate between the two walls. And he went out by way of the [l]plain.

5 But the Chaldean army pursued them and [m]overtook Zedekiah in the plains of Jericho. And when they had captured him, they brought him up to Nebuchadnezzar king of Babylon, to [n]Riblah in the land of Hamath, where he pronounced judgment on him.

6 Then the king of Babylon killed the sons of Zedekiah before his [o]eyes in Riblah; the king of Babylon also killed all the [p]nobles of Judah.

7 Moreover he put out Zedekiah's [q]eyes, and bound him with bronze fetters to carry him off to [r]Babylon.

8 And the [s]Chaldeans burned the king's house and the houses of the people with [t]fire, and [1]broke down the [u]walls of Jerusalem.

9 Then [v]Nebuzaradan the captain of the guard carried away captive to Babylon the remnant of the people who remained in the city and those who [w]defected to him, with the rest of the people who remained.

10 But Nebuzaradan the captain of the guard left in the land of Judah the [x]poor people, who had nothing, and gave them vineyards and fields at the same time.

Jeremiah released from prison

11 Now Nebuchadnezzar king of Babylon gave charge concerning Jeremiah to Nebuzaradan the captain of the guard, saying,

12 "Take him and look after him, and do him no [y]harm; but do to him just as he says to you."

13 So Nebuzaradan the captain of the guard sent Nebushasban, [j]Rabsaris, Nergal-Sharezer, [j]Rabmag, and all the king of Babylon's chief officers;

14 then they sent *someone* to [z]take Jeremiah from the court of the prison, and committed him to Gedaliah the

23 *a* Jer. 39:6; 41:10 *b* v. 18; Jer. 39:5
26 *c* Jer. 37:20 *d* Jer. 37:15
28 *e* Jer. 37:21; cp. 39:14
CHAPTER 39
1 *f* Ezek. 24:1–2 *g* See Lev. 23:2, *note*
2 *h* Jer. 1:3
3 *i* Jer. 1:15 *j* See Isa. 36:2, *note*
4 *k* Cp. Isa. 30:15–16 *l* See Dt. 1:1, *note*
5 *m* Jer. 21:7; 32:4; 38:18,23 *n* 2 Ki. 23:33
6 *o* Dt. 28:34 *p* Jer. 34:19–21
7 *q* Ezek. 12:13 *r* *Times of the Gentiles:* v. 7; Dan. 2:29. (Dt. 28:49; Rev. 16:19)
8 *s* 2 Ki. 25:9; Jer. 38:18; 52:13 *t* Jer. 21:10 *u* Neh. 1:3
9 *v* 2 Ki. 25:8 *w* Jer. 38:19
10 *x* Jer. 40:7
12 *y* Jer. 1:18–19; 15:20–21; cp. Acts 24:23
14 *z* Jer. 38:6, 13,28

*39:3 A title, probably *Chief Officer;* also verse 13
• A title, probably *Troop Commander;* also verse 13

[1](39:8) Here began "the times of the Gentiles," a mark of which is that Jerusalem is "trampled by Gentiles," i.e. under Gentile political control. This has been true from the time of King Nebuchadnezzar to this day. See *notes* on the Times of the Gentiles (Lk. 21:24; Rev. 16:19).

son of [a]Ahikam, the son of Shaphan, that he should take him home. So he dwelt among the people.

Ebed-Melech rewarded

15 Meanwhile the word of the LORD had come to Jeremiah while he was shut up in the court of the prison, saying,

16 "Go and speak to [b]Ebed-Melech the Ethiopian, saying, 'Thus says the LORD of hosts, the God of Israel: "Behold, I will bring My words upon this city for [c]adversity and not for good, and they shall be *performed* in that day before you.

17 "But I will deliver you in that day," says the LORD, "and you shall not be given into the hand of the men of whom you *are* afraid.

18 "For I will surely deliver you, and you shall not fall by the sword; but your life shall be as a [d]prize to you, [e]because you have put your [f]trust in Me," says the LORD.' "

Jeremiah remains in Judah. Gedaliah made ruler

40 THE word that came to Jeremiah from the LORD [g]after Nebuzaradan the captain of the guard had let him go from Ramah, when he had taken him bound in chains among all who were carried away captive from Jerusalem and Judah, who were carried away captive to Babylon.

2 And the captain of the guard took Jeremiah and said to him: "The LORD your God has pronounced this doom on this place.

3 "Now the LORD has brought *it*, and has done just as He said. [h]Because you *people* have sinned against the LORD, and not obeyed His voice, therefore this thing has come upon you.

4 "And now look, I free you this day from the chains that *were* on your hand. If it seems good to you to come with me to Babylon, come, and I will look after you. But if it seems wrong for you to come with me to Babylon, remain here. See, all the [i]land *is* before you; wherever it seems good and convenient for you to go, go there."

5 Now while Jeremiah had not yet gone back, *Nebuzaradan said,* "Go back to [j]Gedaliah the son of Ahikam, the son of Shaphan, [k]whom the king of Babylon has made governor over the cities of Judah, and dwell with him among the people. Or go wherever it seems convenient for you to go." So the captain of the guard gave him [l]rations and a gift and let him go.

6 Then Jeremiah went to Gedaliah the son of Ahikam, to [m]Mizpah, and dwelt with him among the people who were left in the land.

7 And when all the [n]captains of the armies who *were* in the fields, they and their men, heard that the king of Babylon had made Gedaliah the son of Ahikam governor in the land, and had committed to him men, women, children, and the [o]poorest of the land who had not been carried away captive to Babylon,

8 then they came to Gedaliah at Mizpah—[p]Ishmael the son of Nethaniah, [q]Johanan and Jonathan the sons of Kareah, Seraiah the son of Tanhumeth, the sons of Ephai the Netophathite, and [r]Jezaniah* the son of a [s]Maachathite, they and their men.

9 And Gedaliah the son of Ahikam, the son of Shaphan, took an oath before them and their men, saying, "Do not be afraid to serve the Chaldeans. Dwell in the land and serve the king of Babylon, and it shall be [t]well with you.

10 "As for me, I will indeed dwell at Mizpah and serve the Chaldeans who come to us. But you, [o]gather wine and summer fruit and oil, put *them* in your vessels, and dwell in your cities that you have taken."

11 Likewise, when all the Jews who *were* in Moab, among the Ammonites, in Edom, and who *were* in all the countries, heard that the king of Babylon had left a remnant of Judah, and that he had set over them Gedaliah the son of Ahikam, the son of Shaphan,

12 then all the Jews [u]returned out of all places where they had been driven, and came to the land of Judah, to Gedaliah at Mizpah, and gathered wine and summer fruit in abundance.

13 Moreover Johanan the son of Kareah and all the captains of the forces that *were* in the fields came to Gedaliah at Mizpah,

14 and said to him, "Do you certainly know that Baalis the king of the Ammonites has sent [p]Ishmael the son of Nethaniah to murder you?" But Gedaliah the son of Ahikam did not believe them.

15 Then Johanan the son of Kareah

14
a Jer. 26:24
16
b Jer. 38:7–13
c Dan. 9:12
18
d Jer. 21:9; 38:2; 45:5
e 1 Chr. 5:20; Ps. 37:40
f See Ps. 2:12, *note*
CHAPTER 40
1
g Jer. 39:11–14
3
h Dt. 29:24–25; Jer. 50:7; Dan. 9:11
4
i Cp. Gen. 20:15
5
j Jer. 39:14
k 2 Ki. 25:22
l Cp. Jer. 52:34
6
m Jud. 20:1
7
n 2 Ki. 25:23
o Jer. 39:10
8
p Jer. 41:1–10
q Jer. 41:11; 43:2
r Jer. 42:1
s Dt. 3:14; Josh. 12:5; cp. 2 Sam. 10:6
9
t Jer. 27:11; 38:17–20
12
u Jer. 43:5

---

* 40:8 Spelled *Jaazaniah* in 2 Kings 25:23

spoke secretly to Gedaliah in Mizpah, saying, "Let me go, please, and I will kill Ishmael the son of Nethaniah, and no one will know *it.* Why should he [a]murder you, so that all the Jews who are gathered to you would be scattered, and the [b]remnant in Judah perish?"

16 But Gedaliah the son of Ahikam said to Johanan the son of Kareah, "You shall not do this thing, for you speak [c]falsely concerning Ishmael."

Ishmael murders Gedaliah, treacherously kills others and casts their bodies into pit

41 NOW it came to pass in the [d]seventh month [e]*that* Ishmael the son of Nethaniah, the son of Elishama, of the royal family and of the officers of the king, came with ten men to Gedaliah the son of Ahikam, at [f]Mizpah. And there they ate bread together in Mizpah.

2 Then Ishmael the son of Nethaniah, and the ten men who were with him, arose and [e]struck Gedaliah the son of [g]Ahikam, the son of Shaphan, with the sword, and killed him whom the king of Babylon had made [h]governor over the land.

3 Ishmael also struck down all the Jews who were with him, *that is,* with Gedaliah at Mizpah, and the Chaldeans who were found there, the men of war.

4 And it happened, on the second day after he had killed Gedaliah, when as yet no one knew *it,*

5 that certain men came from Shechem, from Shiloh, and from Samaria, eighty men with their beards shaved and their clothes torn, having [i]cut themselves, with offerings and incense in their hand, to [j]bring *them* to the house of the LORD.

6 Now Ishmael the son of Nethaniah went out from Mizpah to meet them, weeping as he went along; and it happened as he met them that he said to them, "Come to Gedaliah the son of Ahikam!"

7 So it was, when they came into the midst of the city, that Ishmael the son of Nethaniah [k]killed them *and cast them* into the midst of a pit, he and the men who were with him.

8 But ten men were found among them who said to Ishmael, "Do not kill us, for we have treasures of wheat, barley, oil, and honey in the field." So he desisted and did not kill them among their brethren.

9 Now the pit into which Ishmael had cast all the dead bodies of the men whom he had slain, because of Gedaliah, *was* [l]the same one Asa the king had made for fear of Baasha king of Israel. Ishmael the son of Nethaniah filled it with *the* slain.

10 Then Ishmael carried away captive all the [m]rest of the people who *were* in Mizpah, the king's [n]daughters and all the people who remained in Mizpah, whom Nebuzaradan the captain of the guard had committed to Gedaliah the son of Ahikam. And Ishmael the son of Nethaniah carried them away captive and departed to go over to the [o]Ammonites.

11 But when [p]Johanan the son of Kareah and all the captains of the forces that *were* with him heard of all the evil that Ishmael the son of Nethaniah had done,

12 they took all the men and went to fight with Ishmael the son of Nethaniah; and they found him by the [q]great pool that *is* in Gibeon.

13 So it was, when all the people who *were* with Ishmael saw Johanan the son of Kareah, and all the captains of the forces who *were* with him, that they were glad.

14 Then all the people whom Ishmael had carried away captive from Mizpah turned around and came back, and went to Johanan the son of Kareah.

15 But Ishmael the son of Nethaniah escaped from Johanan with eight men and went to the Ammonites.

Johanan rescues people

16 Then Johanan the son of Kareah, and all the captains of the forces that were with him, took from Mizpah all the [r]rest of the people whom he had recovered from Ishmael the son of Nethaniah after he had murdered Gedaliah the son of Ahikam—the mighty men of war and the women and the children and the eunuchs, whom he had brought back from Gibeon.

17 And they departed and dwelt in the habitation of [s]Chimham, which is near Bethlehem, as they went on their way to [t]Egypt,

18 because of the Chaldeans; for they were [u]afraid of them, because Ishmael the son of Nethaniah had murdered Gedaliah the son of Ahikam, whom the king of Babylon had made governor in the land.

15
a Cp. 1 Sam. 26:8
b Jer. 42:2
16
c Cp. Jer. 41:2
CHAPTER 41
1
d See Lev. 23:2, *note*
e 2 Ki. 25:25
f Jer. 40:6, 10
2
g Jer. 26:24
h Jer. 40:5
5
i Cp. Dt. 14:1
j Neh. 10:34–35
7
k Ps. 55:23; Ezek. 22:27; cp. 33:24–26
9
l 1 Ki. 15:22; 2 Chr. 16:6
10
m Jer. 40:11–15
n Jer. 43:6
o Jer. 40:14
11
p Jer. 40:8, 13
12
q 2 Sam. 2:13
16
r Jer. 40:11–12; 43:4–7
17
s 2 Sam. 19:37,38
t Jer. 43:7
18
u Cp. Isa. 51:12–13; 57:11; Jer. 42:11; Lk. 12:4–5

Jeremiah warns remnant: divine judgment pronounced

42 NOW all the captains of the forces, [a]Johanan the son of Kareah, Jezaniah the son of Hoshaiah, and all the people, from the least to the greatest, came near

2 and said to Jeremiah the prophet, [b]"Please, let our petition be acceptable to you, and [c]pray for us to the LORD your God, for all this remnant (since we are [d]left *but* a few of many, as you can see),

3 "that the LORD your God may show us the [e]way in which we should walk and the thing we should do."

4 Then Jeremiah the prophet said to them, "I have heard. Indeed, I will pray to the LORD your God according to your words, and it shall be, *that* whatever the LORD answers you, I will [f]declare *it* to you. I will keep [g]nothing back from you."

5 So they said to Jeremiah, "Let the LORD be a true and faithful [h]witness between us, if we do not do according to everything which the LORD your God sends us by you.

6 "Whether *it is* pleasing or displeasing, we will [i]obey the voice of the LORD our God to whom we send you, that it may be [j]well with us when we obey the voice of the LORD our God."

7 And it happened after ten days that the word of the LORD came to Jeremiah.

8 Then he called Johanan the son of Kareah, all the captains of the forces which *were* with him, and all the people from the least even to the greatest,

9 and said to them, "Thus says the LORD, the God of Israel, to whom you sent me to present your petition before Him:

10 'If you will still remain in this land, then I will build you and not pull *you* down, and I will plant you and not pluck *you* up. For I [k]relent concerning the disaster that I have brought upon you.

11 'Do not be [l]afraid of the king of Babylon, of whom you are afraid; do not be afraid of him,' says the LORD, 'for I *am* with you, to save you and deliver you from his hand.

12 'And I will show you mercy, that he may have mercy on you and cause you to return to your own land.'

13 "But if you say, 'We will not dwell in this land,' disobeying the voice of the LORD your God,

14 "saying, 'No, but we will go to the land of [m]Egypt where we shall see no war, nor hear the sound of the trumpet, nor be hungry for bread, and there we will dwell'—

15 "Then hear now the word of the LORD, O remnant of Judah! Thus says the LORD of hosts, the God of Israel: 'If you wholly [n]set your faces to enter Egypt, and go to dwell there,

16 'then it shall be *that* the [o]sword which you feared shall overtake you there in the land of Egypt; the famine of which you were afraid shall follow close after you there *in* Egypt; and there you shall die.

17 'So shall it be with all the men who set their faces to go to Egypt to dwell there. They shall die by the sword, by famine, and by pestilence. And [p]none of them shall remain or escape from the disaster that I will bring upon them.'

18 "For thus says the LORD of hosts, the God of Israel: 'As My anger and My fury have been poured out on the inhabitants of Jerusalem, so will My fury be poured out on you when you enter Egypt. And you shall be an oath, an [q]astonishment, a curse, and a reproach; and you shall see this place no more.'

19 "The LORD has said concerning you, O remnant of Judah, [r]'Do not go to Egypt!' Know certainly that I have admonished you this day.

20 "For you were hypocrites in your hearts when you sent me to the LORD your God, saying, 'Pray for us to the LORD our God, and according to all that the LORD your God says, so declare to us and we will do *it*.'

21 "And I have this day declared *it* to you, but you have [s]not obeyed the voice of the LORD your God, or anything which He has sent you by me.

22 "Now therefore, know certainly that you shall [t]die by the sword, by famine, and by pestilence in the place where you desire to go to dwell."

Jeremiah in Egypt, warns of judgment

43 NOW it happened, when Jeremiah had stopped speaking to all the people all the [u]words of the LORD their God, for which the LORD their God had sent him to them, all these words,

2 that [v]Azariah the son of Hoshaiah, Johanan the son of Kareah, and all the proud men spoke, saying to Jer-

CHAPTER 42
1 [a] Jer. 40:8, 13
2 [b] Jer. 15:11 [c] Ex. 8:28; 1 Sam. 7:8; 12:19; 1 Ki. 13:6; Isa. 37:4; Jer. 37:3; Acts 8:24; cp. Jas. 5:16 [d] Dt. 4:27
3 [e] Ezra 8:21
4 [f] 1 Ki. 22:14 [g] 1 Sam. 3:18; Acts 20:20
5 [h] Jud. 11:10
6 [i] Ex. 24:7; Josh. 24:24; cp. Jer. 44:16 [j] Dt. 6:3; Jer. 7:23
10 [k] Jer. 18:7–8; see Zech. 8:14, *note*
11 [l] Cp. Jer. 41:18
14 [m] Jer. 41:17; 43:7
15 [n] Jer. 44:12–14; cp. Dt. 17:16; Lk. 9:51
16 [o] Ezek. 11:8
17 [p] Cp. Jer. 44:14,28
18 [q] Jer. 18:16; 24:9; 26:6; 29:18; 44:12; cp. Zech. 8:13
19 [r] Dt. 17:16
21 [s] Isa. 30:1–7
22 [t] v. 17; Ezek. 6:11
CHAPTER 43
1 [u] Jer. 42:9–18
2 [v] Or *Jezaniah*, Jer. 42:1

emiah, "You speak [a]falsely! The LORD our God has not sent you to say, 'Do not go to Egypt to dwell there.'

3 "But [b]Baruch the son of Neriah has set you against us, to deliver us into the hand of the Chaldeans, that they may put us to death or carry us away captive to [c]Babylon."

4 So Johanan the son of Kareah, all the captains of the forces, and all the people would [d]not obey the voice of the LORD, to remain in the land of Judah.

5 But Johanan the son of Kareah and all the captains of the forces took all the [e]remnant of Judah who had returned to dwell in the land of Judah, from all nations where they had been driven—

6 men, women, children, the [f]king's daughters, and [g]every person whom Nebuzaradan the captain of the guard had left with Gedaliah the son of Ahikam, the son of Shaphan, and Jeremiah the prophet and Baruch the son of Neriah.

7 [h]So they went to the land of Egypt, for they did not obey the voice of the LORD. And they went as far as [i]Tahpanhes.

8 Then the [j]word of the LORD came to Jeremiah in Tahpanhes, saying,

9 "Take large stones in your hand, and hide them in the sight of the men of Judah, in the clay in the brick courtyard which *is* at the entrance to Pharaoh's house in Tahpanhes;

10 "and say to them, 'Thus says the LORD of hosts, the God of Israel: "Behold, I will send and bring Nebuchadnezzar the king of Babylon, [k]My servant, and will set his throne above these stones that I have hidden. And he will spread his royal pavilion over them.

11 "When he comes, he shall strike the land of [l]Egypt *and deliver* to death *those appointed* for death, and to captivity [m]*those appointed* for captivity, and to the sword *those appointed* for the sword.

12 "I* will kindle a fire in the houses of the [n]gods of Egypt, and he shall burn them and carry them away captive. And he shall array himself with the land of Egypt, as a shepherd puts on his garment, and he shall go out from there in peace.

13 "He shall also break the sacred pillars of [o]Beth Shemesh* that *are* in the land of Egypt; and the houses of the gods of the Egyptians he shall burn with fire." ' "

Message to the Jews in Egypt
(cp. Jer. 43:8–13)

44

THE word that came to Jeremiah concerning all the Jews who dwell in the land of Egypt, who dwell at [p]Migdol, at Tahpanhes, at [q]Noph,* and in the country of [r]Pathros, saying,

2 "Thus says the LORD of hosts, the God of Israel: 'You have seen all the calamity that I have brought on Jerusalem and on all the cities of Judah; and behold, this day they *are* a [s]desolation, and no one dwells in them,

3 'because of their wickedness which they have committed to provoke Me to anger, in that they went to burn incense *and* to [t]serve other gods whom they did not know, they nor you nor your fathers.

4 'However I have sent to you all My servants the prophets, [u]rising early and sending *them,* saying, "Oh, do not do this abominable thing that I hate!"

5 'But they did not listen or incline their ear to turn from their wickedness, to burn no incense to other gods.

6 'So My fury and My anger were poured out and kindled in the cities of Judah and in the streets of Jerusalem; and they are wasted *and* desolate, as it is this day.'

7 "Now therefore, thus says the LORD, the God of hosts, the God of Israel: 'Why do you commit *this* great evil [v]against yourselves, to cut off from you man and woman, child and infant, out of Judah, leaving none to remain,

8 'in that you provoke Me to wrath with the works of your hands, burning incense to other gods in the land of Egypt where you have gone to dwell, that you may cut yourselves off and be a curse and a reproach among all the nations of the earth?

9 'Have you forgotten the wickedness of your fathers, the wickedness of the kings of Judah, the wickedness of their wives, your own wickedness, and the wickedness of your wives, which they committed in the land of Judah and in the streets of Jerusalem?

---

2 *a* Cp. 2 Chr. 36:12–13; cp. Jer. 42:5
3 *b* Jer. 36:4; 45:1 *c* Cp. Jer. 38:4
4 *d* 2 Ki. 25:26; cp. Jer. 42:4
5 *e* Jer. 40:11–12
6 *f* Jer. 41:10 *g* Jer. 39:10; 40:7
7 *h* Jer. 42:19 *i* An Egyptian city (called *Hanes,* Isa. 30:4) in the delta of the Nile, Jer. 2:16; 44:1; 46:14
8 *j* vv. 8–13; Jer. 41:1–30
10 *k* Jer. 25:9; 27:6; cp. Ezek. 29:18–20
11 *l* Isa. 19:1–25; Jer. 25:19 *m* Jer. 15:2; cp. Zech. 11:9
12 *n* Jer. 46:25
13 *o* Heliopolis, cp. *On,* Gen. 41:50

CHAPTER 44
1 *p* Jer. 46:13–14 *q* Jer. 2:16 *r* v. 15; Ezek. 29:14; 30:14
2 *s* Jer. 9:11; 34:22
3 *t* Dt. 13:6; 32:17; Jer. 19:4
4 *u* 2 Chr. 36:15; Jer. 7:25; 25:4; 26:5; 29:19

44:7 *v* Num. 16:38; Jer. 7:19

*

43:12 Following Masoretic Text and Targum; Septuagint, Syriac, and Vulgate read *He.*
43:13 Literally *House Of The Sun,* ancient On; later called *Heliopolis* **44:1** That is, ancient Memphis

10 'They have not been [a]humbled, to this day, nor have they [b]feared; they have not walked in My law or in My statutes that I set before you and your fathers.'

11 "Therefore thus says the LORD of hosts, the God of Israel: 'Behold, I will [c]set My face against you for catastrophe and for cutting off all Judah.

12 'And I will take the remnant of Judah who have set their faces to go into the land of Egypt to dwell there, and they shall all be consumed *and* fall in the land of Egypt. They shall be [d]consumed by the sword *and* by famine. They shall die, from the least to the greatest, by the sword and by famine; and they shall be an oath, an [e]astonishment, a curse and a reproach!

13 'For I will [f]punish those who dwell in the land of Egypt, as I have punished Jerusalem, by the sword, by famine, and by pestilence,

14 'so that none of the remnant of Judah who have gone into the land of Egypt to dwell there shall escape or survive, lest they return to the land of Judah, to which they [g]desire to return and dwell. For none shall return except those who escape.' "

15 Then [h]all the men who knew that their wives had burned incense to other gods, with all the women who stood by, a great multitude, and all the people who dwelt in the land of Egypt, in Pathros, answered Jeremiah, saying:

16 "*As for* the word that you have spoken to us in the name of the LORD, we will [i]not listen to you!

17 "But we will certainly do [j]whatever has gone out of our own mouth, to burn incense to the [k]queen of heaven and pour out drink offerings to her, as we have done, we and our fathers, our kings and our princes, in the cities of Judah and in the streets of Jerusalem. For *then* we had plenty of [l]food, were well-off, and saw no trouble.

18 "But since we stopped burning incense to the queen of heaven and pouring out drink offerings to her, we have [m]lacked everything and have been consumed by the sword and by famine."

19 *The women also said,* "And when we burned incense to the queen of heaven and poured out drink offerings to her, did we make cakes for her, to worship her, and pour out drink offerings to her without our [n]husbands' *permission?*"

10
a Jer. 6:15; 8:12; 2 Chr. 36:12; Dan. 5:22
b Jer. 5:22–24; see Ps. 19:9, *note*

11
c Lev. 17:10; 20:5–6; 26:17; Jer. 21:10; Amos 9:4

12
d Jer. 42:15–17, 22
e Jer. 42:18

13
f Jer. 43:11

14
g Jer. 22:27

15
h Cp. Prov. 11:21

16
i Cp. Jer. 42:6

17
j v. 25; cp. Num. 30:12–14; Dt. 23:23; Jud. 11:36
k See Jer. 7:18, *note*
l Cp. Ex. 16:3; Hos. 2:5–9

18
m Cp. Num. 11:5–6; Mal. 3:13–15

19
n Cp. Num. 30:6–7

22
o Jer. 25:11, 38; cp. Dt. 31:29

26
p Gen. 22:16; Heb. 6:13
q Jer. 10:6
r Neh. 9:5; Ezek. 20:39

27
s Cp. Jer. 31:28

28
t v. 14; cp. Isa. 27:13

20 Then Jeremiah spoke to all the people—the men, the women, and all the people who had given him *that* answer—saying:

21 "The incense that you burned in the cities of Judah and in the streets of Jerusalem, you and your fathers, your kings and your princes, and the people of the land, did not the LORD remember them, and did it *not* come into His mind?

22 "So the LORD could no longer bear *it,* because of the evil of your doings *and* because of the abominations which you committed. Therefore your land is a desolation, an [o]astonishment, a curse, and without an inhabitant, as *it is* this day.

23 "Because you have burned incense and because you have sinned against the LORD, and have not obeyed the voice of the LORD or walked in His law, in His statutes or in His testimonies, therefore this calamity has happened to you, as *at* this day."

24 Moreover Jeremiah said to all the people and to all the women, "Hear the word of the LORD, all Judah who *are* in the land of Egypt!

25 "Thus says the LORD of hosts, the God of Israel, saying: 'You and your wives have spoken with your mouths and fulfilled with your hands, saying, "We will surely keep our vows that we have made, to burn incense to the queen of heaven and pour out drink offerings to her." You will surely keep your vows and perform your vows!'

26 "Therefore hear the word of the LORD, all Judah who dwell in the land of Egypt: 'Behold, I have [p]sworn by My [q]great [r]name,' says the LORD, 'that My name shall no more be named in the mouth of any man of Judah in all the land of Egypt, saying, "The Lord GOD lives."

27 'Behold, I will [s]watch over them for adversity and not for good. And all the men of Judah who *are* in the land of Egypt shall be consumed by the sword and by famine, until there is an end to them.

28 'Yet a small number who [t]escape the sword shall return from the land of Egypt to the land of Judah; and all the remnant of Judah, who have gone to the land of Egypt to dwell there, shall know whose words will stand, Mine or theirs.

29 'And this *shall be* a sign to you,' says the LORD, 'that I will punish you in this place, that you may know that

My words will surely [a]stand against
you for adversity.'
30 "Thus says the LORD: 'Behold, I
will give [b]Pharaoh Hophra king of
Egypt into the hand of his enemies
and into the hand of those who seek
his life, as I gave Zedekiah king of
Judah into the hand of Nebuchadnezzar king of Babylon, his enemy who
sought his life.' "

Baruch warned of self-seeking

45 THE word that Jeremiah the
prophet spoke to [c]Baruch the
son of Neriah, when he had [d]written
these words in a book at the instruction of Jeremiah,* in the [e]fourth year
of Jehoiakim the son of Josiah, king of
Judah, saying,
2 [f]"Thus says the LORD, the God of
Israel, to you, O Baruch:
3 'You said, "Woe is me now! For
the LORD has added grief to my sorrow. I [g]fainted in my sighing, and I
find no rest." '
4 "Thus you shall say to him,
'Thus says the LORD: "Behold, what I
have built I will break down, and what
I have planted I will pluck up, that is,
this whole land.
5 "And do you seek great things
for [h]yourself? Do not seek *them;* for
behold, I will bring adversity on all
flesh," says the LORD. "But I will give
your [i]life to you as a [j]prize in all
places, wherever you go." ' "

II. Prophecies concerning
Foreign Nations, 46—51

Prophecy against Egypt

46 THE word of the LORD which
came to Jeremiah the prophet
against the [k]nations.
2 Against [l]Egypt.
Concerning the army of [m]Pha-
raoh Necho, king of Egypt, which was
by the River Euphrates in Carchemish, and which Nebuchadnezzar
king of Babylon [n]defeated in the
[o]fourth year of Jehoiakim the son of
Josiah, king of Judah:

3 "Order the buckler and shield,
And draw near to battle!
4 Harness the horses,
And mount up, you horsemen!
Stand forth with *your* helmets,
Polish the spears,
Put on the armor!
5 Why have I seen them
dismayed *and* turned back?
Their mighty ones are beaten
down;
They have speedily fled,
And did not look back,
For fear *was* all around," says
the LORD.
6 "Do not let the swift flee away,
Nor the mighty man escape;
They will [p]stumble and fall
Toward the north, by the River
Euphrates.
7 "Who *is* this coming up [q]like a
[r]flood,
Whose waters move like the
rivers?
8 Egypt rises up like a [r]flood,
And *its* waters move like the
rivers;
And he says, 'I will go up *and*
cover the earth,
I will destroy the city and its
inhabitants.'
9 Come up, O horses, and rage,
O chariots!
And let the mighty men come
forth:
The [s]Ethiopians and the
Libyans who handle the
shield,
And the [t]Lydians who handle
and bend the bow.
10 For this *is* the [u]day of the Lord
GOD of hosts,
A day of vengeance,
That He may avenge Himself
on His adversaries.
The sword shall devour;
It shall be [v]satiated and made
drunk with their blood;
For the Lord GOD of hosts has
a sacrifice
In the north country by the
River Euphrates.
11 "Go up to Gilead and take balm,
O virgin, the daughter of
Egypt;
In vain you will use many
medicines;
You shall not be cured.
12 The nations have heard of
your [w]shame,
And your cry has filled the
land;
For the mighty man has
stumbled against the mighty;
They both have fallen
together."

13 The word that the LORD spoke to
Jeremiah the prophet, how Nebuchadnezzar king of Babylon would

29 *a* Ps. 33:11
30 *b* Jer. 46:25–26; Ezek. 29:3; 30:21
CHAPTER 45
1 *c* Jer. 32:12, 16; 43:3 *d* Jer. 25:1; 36:1; 46:2 *e* Cp. Jer. 36:4–32
2 *f Inspiration:* vv. 1–2; Ezek. 2:2. (Ex. 4:15; 2 Tim. 3:16, *note*)
3 *g* Ps. 6:6; 69:3; cp. 2 Cor. 4:16; Gal. 6:9
5 *h* Cp. 1 Ki. 3:11–12; Rom. 12:16 *i* Jer. 21:9; 38:2 *j* Jer. 39:18
CHAPTER 46
1 *k* Jer. 1:10; 25:15–31
2 *l* vv. 2–26; Jer. 25:17–19; Ezek. 29:2–32:32; cp. Isa. 19:1–25 *m* 2 Ki. 23:33–35 *n* 2 Ki. 23:29; 24:7; 2 Chr. 35:20 *o* Jer. 45:1
6 *p* Dan. 11:19
7 *q* Isa. 8:7–8; Jer. 47:2; Dan. 11:22 *r* Or *the Nile*
9 *s* 1 Chr. 1:8 *t* Gen. 10:13
10 *u Day* (of the LORD): v. 10; Ezek. 30:3. (Ps. 2:9; Rev. 19:19) *v* Isa. 34:6; Zeph. 1:7

46:12 *w* Jer. 2:36

*
45:1 Literally *from Jeremiah's mouth*

come *and* [a]strike the land of Egypt.

14 "Declare in Egypt, and proclaim in [b]Migdol;
Proclaim in [c]Noph* and in [d]Tahpanhes;
Say, 'Stand fast and prepare yourselves,
For the sword devours all around you.'
15 Why are your valiant *men* swept away?
They did not stand
Because the LORD drove them away.
16 He made many fall;
Yes, one fell upon another.
And they said, 'Arise!
[e]Let us go back to our own people
And to the land of our nativity
From the oppressing sword.'
17 They cried there,
'Pharaoh, king of Egypt, *is but* a noise.
He has passed by the appointed time!'
18 "*As* I live," says the King,
Whose [f]name *is* the LORD of hosts,
"Surely as Tabor *is* among the mountains
And as Carmel by the sea, *so* he shall come.
19 O you daughter dwelling in Egypt,
Prepare yourself to go into captivity!
For [c]Noph* shall be waste and desolate, without inhabitant.
20 "Egypt *is* a very pretty heifer,
But destruction comes, it comes [g]from the north.
21 Also her mercenaries are in her midst like fat bulls,
For they also are turned back,
They have fled away together.
They did not stand,
For the day of their calamity had come upon them,
The time of their [h]punishment.
22 Her noise shall go like a serpent,
For they shall march with an army
And come against her with axes,
Like those who chop wood.
23 "They shall cut down her forest," says the LORD,
"Though it cannot be searched,
Because they *are* [i]innumerable,
And more numerous than grasshoppers.
24 The daughter of Egypt shall be ashamed;
She shall be delivered into the hand
Of the people of the north."

25 The LORD of hosts, the God of Israel, says: "Behold, I will bring punishment on [j]Amon* of No,* and Pharaoh and Egypt, with their [k]gods and
their kings—Pharaoh and those who
[l]trust in him.
26 "And I will deliver them into the
[m]hand of those who seek their lives,
into the hand of Nebuchadnezzar king
of Babylon and the hand of his servants. [n]Afterward it shall be inhabited as in the days of old," says the
LORD.

27 "But do not [o]fear, O My servant Jacob,
And do not be dismayed, O Israel!
For [1]behold, I will [p]save you from afar,
And your offspring from the land of their captivity;
Jacob shall return, have rest and be at ease;
No one shall make *him* afraid.
28 Do not fear, O Jacob My servant," says the LORD,
"For I *am* with you;
For I will make a complete end of all the nations
To which I have driven you,
But I will [q]not make a complete end of you.
[2]I will rightly [r]correct you,
For I will not leave you wholly unpunished."

13
a Isa. 19:1; Jer. 43:10–11; Ezek. 29:1–21
14
b Jer. 44:1
c Ezek. 30:13
d Ezek. 30:18
16
e Jer. 51:9
18
f Isa. 47:4; 48:2
20
g vv. 6,10; Jer. 1:14; 47:2
21
h Jer. 50:27
23
i Cp. Joel 1:4
25
j Ezek. 30:14–16; Nah. 3:8
k Jer. 43:12
l Isa. 30:1–5; 31:1–3; see Ps. 2:12, *note*
26
m Jer. 44:30; Ezek. 32:11
n Ezek. 29:11–14
27
o Isa. 41:13–14; 43:5; 44:2; Jer. 30:10–11
p Isa. 11:11; Jer. 23:3–4
28
q Jer. 4:27; Amos 9:8–9
r Jer. 30:11

*
46:14 That is, ancient Memphis **46:19** That is, ancient Memphis **46:25** A sun god • That is, ancient Thebes

[1](46:27) Here is one of the many prophecies having a double view—a near and far fulfill-ment.
[2](46:28) Here is one of the many answers to the question: "Did God reject His people?" (Rom. 11:1).

Prophecy against Philistia and Phoenicia

47 THE word of the LORD that came to Jeremiah the prophet against the [a]Philistines, before Pharaoh attacked Gaza.
2 Thus says the LORD:

"Behold, [b]waters rise out of the
north,
And shall be an overflowing
flood;
They shall overflow the land
and all that is in it,
The city and those who dwell
within;
Then the men shall cry,
And all the inhabitants of the
land shall wail.
3 At the noise of the stamping
hooves of his strong horses,
At the rushing of his chariots,
At the rumbling of his wheels,
The fathers will not look back
for *their* children,
Lacking courage,
4 Because of the day that comes
to plunder all the
[c]Philistines,
To cut off from [d]Tyre and
Sidon every helper who
remains;
For the LORD shall plunder the
Philistines,
The [e]remnant of the country
of [f]Caphtor.
5 [g]Baldness has come upon Gaza,
Ashkelon is cut off
With the remnant of their
valley.
How long will you cut
yourself?

6 "O you [h]sword of the LORD,
How long until you are quiet?
Put yourself up into your
scabbard,
Rest and be still!
7 How can it be quiet,
Seeing the LORD has given it a
[i]charge
Against Ashkelon and against
the seashore?
There He has appointed it."

Prophecy against Moab

48 AGAINST [j]Moab.
Thus says the LORD of hosts, the God of Israel:

"Woe to [k]Nebo!
For it is plundered,
[l]Kirjathaim is shamed *and*
taken;
The high stronghold* is
shamed and dismayed—
2 No more praise of Moab.
In [m]Heshbon they have devised
evil against her:
'Come, and let us cut her off as
a nation.'
You also shall be cut down, O
[n]Madmen!*
The sword shall pursue you;
3 A voice of crying *shall be* from
[o]Horonaim:
'Plundering and great
destruction!'

4 "Moab is destroyed;
Her little ones have caused a
cry to be heard;*
5 For in the Ascent of Luhith
they ascend with continual
weeping;
For in the descent of Horonaim
the enemies have heard a
cry of destruction.

6 "Flee, save your lives!
And be like the juniper* in the
wilderness.
7 For because you have trusted
in your works and your
[p]treasures,
You also shall be taken.
And [q]Chemosh shall go forth
into captivity,
His priests and his princes
together.
8 And the [r]plunderer shall come
against every city;
No one shall escape.
The valley also shall perish,
And the plain shall be
destroyed,
As the LORD has spoken.

9 "Give wings to Moab,
That she may flee and get
away;
For her cities shall be desolate,
Without any to dwell in them.
10 Cursed *is* he who does the
work of the LORD deceitfully,
And cursed *is* he who keeps
back his sword from blood.

11 "Moab has been at ease from
his* youth;

CHAPTER 47
1
a vv. 1–4; Isa. 14:29–31; Ezek. 25:15–17; Zeph. 2:5; Zech. 9:6
2
b Isa. 8:7; Jer. 46:7–8
4
c Isa. 14:29–31
d Isa. 23:1–18; Jer. 25:22; Ezek. 26:1–21; 28:20–24; Amos 1:9–10; Zech. 9:2–4
e Ezek. 25:16; Amos 1:8
f Dt. 2:23
5
g Zeph. 2:4
6
h Dt. 32:41; Ezek. 21:3–5
7
i Ezek. 14:17

CHAPTER 48
1
j vv.1–47; 25:21; Isa. 15:1–16:14; 25:10; Ezek. 28:8–11; Amos 2:1–3; Zeph. 2:8–11
k Isa. 15:2
l Num. 32:37
2
m Jer. 49:3
n Isa. 10:31
3
o Isa. 15:5
7
p Jer. 9:23; 1 Tim. 6:17
q Isa. 46:1–2; cp. 1 Ki. 11:7
8
r v. 18

*
48:1 Hebrew *Misgab* 48:2 A city of Moab
48:4 Following Masoretic Text, Targum, and Vulgate; Septuagint reads *Proclaim it in Zoar.*
48:6 Or *Aroer,* a city of Moab 48:11 The Hebrew uses masculine and feminine pronouns interchangeably in this chapter.

He has [a]settled on his [1b]dregs,
And has not been emptied from vessel to vessel,
Nor has he gone into captivity.
Therefore his taste remained in him,
And his scent has not changed.

12 "Therefore behold, the days are coming," says the LORD,
"That I shall send him wine-workers
Who will tip him over
And empty his vessels
And break the bottles.
13 Moab shall be ashamed of [c]Chemosh,
[d]As the house of Israel was ashamed of [e]Bethel, their confidence.
14 "How can you say, 'We *are* mighty
And strong men for the war'?
15 Moab is plundered and gone up *from* her cities;
Her chosen young men have gone down to the slaughter," says the King,
Whose name *is* the LORD of hosts.

16 "The calamity of Moab *is* near at hand,
And his affliction comes quickly.
17 Bemoan him, all you who are around him;
And all you who know his name,
Say, 'How the strong staff is broken,
The beautiful rod!'

18 "O daughter inhabiting Dibon,
Come down from *your* glory,
And sit in thirst;
For the plunderer of Moab has come against you,
He has destroyed your strongholds.
19 O inhabitant of [f]Aroer,
Stand by the way and watch;
Ask him who flees
And her who escapes;
Say, 'What has happened?'
20 Moab is shamed, for he is broken down.
Wail and cry!
Tell it in Arnon, that Moab is plundered.

11
a Zeph. 1:12
b i.e. *he is contented*
13
c Isa. 46:1–2; cp. 1 Ki. 11:7
d Cp. 1 Ki. 12:25–29
e 1 Ki. 13:32–34
19
f Dt. 2:36; Isa. 17:2
24
g Amos 2:2
25
h See Dt. 33:17, *note*
27
i Zeph. 2:8
j Lam. 2:15; cp. Mic. 7:8–10
28
k Song 2:14
29
l Isa. 16:6; Zeph. 2:10
m Jer. 49:16
31
n Cp. Ps. 102:1–14
o Isa. 16:7, 11
32
p Num. 21:32; Isa. 16:8–9

21 "And judgment has come on the plain country:
On Holon and Jahzah and Mephaath,
22 On Dibon and Nebo and Beth Diblathaim,
23 On Kirjathaim and Beth Gamul and Beth Meon,
24 On [g]Kerioth and Bozrah,
On all the cities of the land of Moab,
Far or near.
25 The [h]horn of Moab is cut off,
And his arm is broken," says the LORD.

26 "Make him drunk,
Because he exalted *himself* against the LORD.
Moab shall wallow in his vomit,
And he shall also be in derision.
27 For was not Israel a [i]derision to you?
Was he found among thieves?
For whenever you speak of him,
You [j]shake *your head in scorn.*
28 You who dwell in Moab,
Leave the cities and dwell in the rock,
And be like the [k]dove *which* makes her nest
In the sides of the cave's mouth.

29 "We have heard the [l]pride of Moab
(He *is* exceedingly proud),
Of his loftiness and arrogance and [m]pride,
And of the haughtiness of his heart."

30 "I know his wrath," says the LORD,
"But it *is* not right;
His lies have made nothing right.
31 Therefore I will wail for Moab,
And I will cry out for all Moab;
I* will [n]mourn for the men of [o]Kir Heres.
32 O vine of Sibmah! I will weep for you with the weeping of [p]Jazer.

*48:31 Following Dead Sea Scrolls, Septuagint, and Vulgate; Masoretic Text reads *He.*

[1](48:11) The dregs (or "lees," Isa. 25:6) are the sediment at the bottom of a container of wine.

Your plants have gone over
the sea,
They reach to the sea of Jazer.
The plunderer has fallen on
your summer fruit and your
vintage.
33 Joy and [a]gladness are taken
From the plentiful field
And from the land of Moab;
I have caused wine to fail from
the winepresses;
No one will tread with joyous
shouting—
Not joyous shouting!
34 [b]"From the cry of Heshbon to
[c]Elealeh and to Jahaz
They have uttered their voice,
From Zoar to Horonaim,
Like a three-year-old heifer;*
For the waters of Nimrim also
shall be desolate.
35 "Moreover," says the LORD,
"I will cause to cease in Moab
The one who offers *sacrifices*
in the high places
And burns incense to his gods.
36 Therefore My heart shall wail
like flutes for Moab,
And like flutes My heart shall
wail
For the men of Kir Heres.
Therefore the riches they have
acquired have perished.
37 "For every head *shall be* bald,
and every beard clipped;
On all the hands *shall be* cuts,
and on the loins sackcloth—
38 A general lamentation
On all the [d]housetops of Moab,
And in its streets;
For I have [e]broken Moab like
a vessel in which *is* no
pleasure," says the LORD.
39 "They shall wail:
'How she is broken down!
How Moab has turned her
back with shame!'
So Moab shall be a derision
And a dismay to all those
about her."
40 For thus says the LORD:

"Behold, one shall [f]fly like an
eagle,
And spread his wings over
Moab.
41 [g]Kerioth is taken,
And the strongholds are
surprised;
The mighty men's hearts in
Moab on that day shall be
Like the heart of a woman in
birth pangs.
42 And Moab shall be destroyed
as a people,
Because he exalted *himself*
against the LORD.
43 Fear and the pit and the snare
shall be upon you,
O inhabitant of Moab," says
the LORD.
44 "He who flees from the fear
shall fall into the pit,
And he who gets out of the pit
shall be caught in the
[h]snare.
For upon Moab, upon it I will
bring
The year of their
[i]punishment," says the
LORD.

45 "Those who fled stood under
the shadow of Heshbon
Because of exhaustion.
But a fire shall come out of
Heshbon,
A flame from the midst of
[j]Sihon,
And shall [k]devour the brow of
Moab,
The crown of the head of the
sons of tumult.
46 Woe to you, O Moab!
The people of Chemosh perish;
For your sons have been taken
captive,
And your daughters captive.
47 "Yet I will [l]bring back the
captives of Moab
In the [m]latter days," says the
LORD.

Thus far *is* the judgment of
Moab.

Prophecy against Ammon

49 AGAINST the [n]Ammonites.
Thus says the LORD:

"Has Israel no sons?
Has he no heir?
Why *then* does Milcom*
inherit Gad,
And his people dwell in its
cities?
2 [o]Therefore behold, the days are
coming," says the LORD,
"That I will cause to be heard
an alarm of war
In [p]Rabbah of the Ammonites;

33 *a* Isa. 16:10
34 *b* Isa. 15:4–6 *c* Num. 32:3,37
38 *d* Isa. 15:3 *e* Jer. 22:28
40 *f* Dt. 28:49; Jer. 49:22; Hab. 1:8; cp. Dan. 7:4; Hos. 8:1
41 *g* Amos 2:2
44 *h* Isa. 24:17–18; Amos 5:19 *i* Jer. 46:21
45 *j* Ps. 135:11 *k* Num. 24:17
47 *l* Jer. 49:6 *m* Jer. 49:39
CHAPTER 49
1 *n* vv. 1–6; Jer. 25:21; Ezek. 21:28–32; 25:1–7; Amos 1:13; Zeph. 2:8–11
2 *o* Amos 1:13–15 *p* Ezek. 21:20; 25:5

*
48:34 Or *The Third Eglath*, an unknown city (compare Isaiah 15:5) **49:1** Hebrew *Malcam*, literally *their king*, a god of the Ammonites; also called *Molech* (compare verse 3)

It shall be a desolate mound,
And her villages shall be
burned with fire.
Then Israel shall take
possession of his
inheritance," says the LORD.

3 "Wail, O [a]Heshbon, for Ai is
plundered!
Cry, you daughters of Rabbah,
Gird yourselves with
sackcloth!
Lament and run to and fro by
the walls;
For Milcom shall go into
captivity
With his priests and his
princes together.
4 Why do you [b]boast in the
valleys,
Your flowing valley, O
backsliding daughter?
Who trusted in her [c]treasures,
saying,
'Who will come against me?'
5 Behold, I will bring fear upon
you,"
Says the Lord GOD of hosts,
"From all those who are around
you;
You shall be driven out,
everyone headlong,
And no one will gather those
who wander off.
6 But [d]afterward I will bring
back
The captives of the people of
Ammon," says the LORD.

Prophecy against Edom

7 [1][e]Against Edom.
Thus says the LORD of hosts:

"*Is* wisdom no more in
[f]Teman?
Has counsel perished from the
prudent?
Has their wisdom [g]vanished?
8 Flee, turn back, dwell in the
depths, O inhabitants of
Dedan!
For I will bring the calamity of
Esau upon him,
The time *that* I will [h]punish
him.
9 If grape-gatherers came to you,
Would they not leave *some*
gleaning [i]grapes?
If thieves by night,
Would they not destroy until
they have enough?
10 But I have made Esau [j]bare;
I have uncovered his secret
places,
And he shall not be able to
hide himself.
His descendants are plundered,
His brethren and his
neighbors,
And he *is* no more.
11 Leave your fatherless children,
I will preserve *them* alive;
And let your widows [k]trust in
Me."

12 For thus says the LORD: "Behold,
those whose judgment *was* not to
drink of the cup have assuredly
drunk. And *are* you the one who will
altogether go unpunished? You shall
not go unpunished, but you shall
surely drink *of it.*
13 "For I have sworn by Myself,"
says the LORD, "that [l]Bozrah shall become a desolation, a reproach, a
waste, and a curse. And all its cities
shall be perpetual wastes."

14 [m]I have heard a message from
the LORD,
And an ambassador has been
sent to the nations:
"Gather together, come against
her,
And rise up to battle!
15 "For indeed, I will make you
small among nations,
Despised among men.
16 Your fierceness has deceived
you,
The [n]pride of your heart,
O you who dwell in the clefts
of the rock,
Who hold the height of the
hill!
Though you make your nest as
high as the eagle,
I will bring you down from
there," says the LORD.

17 "Edom also shall be an
astonishment;
Everyone who goes by it will
be [o]astonished
And will hiss at all its plagues.
18 [p]As in the overthrow of Sodom
and Gomorrah
And their neighbors," says the
LORD,
"No one shall remain there,
Nor shall a son of man dwell
in it.

19 "Behold, he shall come up like a

3
a Jer. 48:2
4
b Jer. 9:23
c Jer. 48:7
6
d v. 39; Jer. 48:47
7
e vv. 7–22; Jer. 25:21; Ezek. 25:12–14; 35:1–15; Joel 3:19; Amos 1:11–12; Obad. 1–9, 15–16
f Gen. 36:11; Job 2:11
g Jer. 8:9
8
h Jer. 9:9
9
i Obad. 5–6
10
j Mal. 1:3
11
k See Ps. 2:12, *note*
13
l Isa. 34:6; 63:1; Amos 1:12
14
m vv. 14–16
16
n Jer. 48:29
17
o vv. 17–22; see Gen. 36:1, *note*
18
p Gen. 19:24–25; Dt. 29:23; Jer. 50:40; Amos 4:11

[1](49:7) Observe that this passage (vv. 7–17) is strikingly similar to Obadiah, e.g. Obad. 8–9.

lion from the floodplain* of the Jordan
Against the dwelling place of the strong;
But I will suddenly make him run away from her.
And who *is* a chosen *man that* I may appoint over her?
For who *is* like Me?
Who will arraign Me?
And who *is* that shepherd
Who will withstand Me?"

20 Therefore hear the counsel of the LORD that He has taken against Edom,
And His purposes that He has proposed against the inhabitants of Teman:
[a]Surely the least of the flock shall draw them out;
Surely He shall make their dwelling places desolate with them.
21 The earth shakes at the noise of their fall;
At the cry its noise is heard at the [b]Red Sea.
22 Behold, He shall come up and fly like the eagle,
And spread His wings over Bozrah;
The heart of the mighty men of Edom in that day shall be
Like the heart of a woman in birth pangs.

Prophecy against Damascus (Syria)

23 [c]Against Damascus.

[d]"Hamath and [e]Arpad are shamed,
For they have heard bad news.
They are fainthearted;
There is trouble on the sea;
It cannot be quiet.
24 Damascus has grown feeble;
She turns to flee,
And fear has seized *her*.
Anguish and sorrows have taken her like a woman in labor.
25 Why is the city of praise not deserted, the city of My joy?
26 Therefore her [f]young men shall fall in her streets,
And all the men of war shall be cut off in that day," says the LORD of hosts.
27 "I will kindle a fire in the wall of Damascus,
And it shall consume the palaces of [g]Ben-Hadad."

20 *a* Jer. 50:45
21 *b* Lit. *sea of reeds*
23 *c* vv. 23–27; Isa. 17:1–3; Amos 1:3, 5; Zech. 9:1 *d* Jer. 39:5; Zech. 9:2 *e* Isa. 37:13
26 *f* Jer. 50:30; 51:4
27 *g* Amos 1:4
28 *h* Isa. 21:16–17; Ezek. 27:21
31 *i* Ezek. 38:11 *j* Num. 23:9; cp. Dt. 33:28; Mic. 7:14
32 *k* v. 36; Ezek. 5:10
33 *l* Jer. 9:11; 10:22; Mal. 1:3
34 *m* Gen. 10:22; Jer. 25:25; Ezek. 32:24 *n* 2 Ki. 24:17–18

Prophecy against Kedar (Arabians) and Hazor

28 Against [h]Kedar and against the kingdoms of Hazor, which Nebuchadnezzar king of Babylon shall strike. Thus says the LORD:

"Arise, go up to Kedar,
And devastate the men of the East!
29 Their tents and their flocks they shall take away.
They shall take for themselves their curtains,
All their vessels and their camels;
And they shall cry out to them,
'Fear *is* on every side!'
30 "Flee, get far away! Dwell in the depths,
O inhabitants of Hazor!" says the LORD.
"For Nebuchadnezzar king of Babylon has taken counsel against you,
And has conceived a plan against you.
31 "Arise, go up to the wealthy nation that [i]dwells securely," says the LORD,
"Which has neither gates nor bars,
Dwelling [j]alone.
32 Their camels shall be for booty,
And the multitude of their cattle for plunder.
I will [k]scatter to all winds those in the farthest corners,
And I will bring their calamity from all its sides," says the LORD.
33 "Hazor shall be a dwelling for [l]jackals, a desolation forever;
No one shall reside there,
Nor son of man dwell in it."

Prophecy against Elam

34 The word of the LORD that came
to Jeremiah the prophet against
[m]Elam, in the [n]beginning of the reign
of Zedekiah king of Judah, saying,
35 "Thus says the LORD of hosts:

'Behold, I will break the bow of Elam,
The foremost of their might.
36 Against Elam I will bring the four winds

*49:19 Or *thicket*

From the four quarters of
heaven,
And scatter them toward all
those winds;
There shall be no nations
where the outcasts of Elam
will not go.
37 For I will cause Elam to be
dismayed before their
enemies
And before those who seek
their life.
I will bring disaster upon
them,
My fierce anger,' says the
LORD;
'And I will send the sword after
them
Until I have consumed them.
38 I will set My throne in Elam,
And will destroy from there
the king and the princes,'
says the LORD.
39 'But it shall come to pass in the
latter days:
I will [a]bring back the captives
of Elam,' says the LORD."

Prophecy against Babylon

50 THE word that the LORD spoke
against [b]Babylon *and* against
the land of the Chaldeans by Jeremiah
the prophet.

2 "Declare among the nations,
Proclaim, and set up a
standard;
Proclaim—do not conceal *it*—
Say, 'Babylon is [c]taken, [d]Bel
is shamed.
Merodach* is broken in
pieces;
Her idols are humiliated,
Her images are broken in
pieces.'
3 For out of the north a nation
comes up against her,
Which shall make her land
desolate,
And [e]no one shall dwell
therein.
They shall move, they shall
depart,
Both man and beast.
4 "In those days and in that
time," says the LORD,
"The children of Israel shall
come,
They and the children of Judah
together;
With continual weeping they
shall come,
And seek the LORD their God.
5 They shall ask the way to
Zion,
With their faces toward it,
saying,
'Come and let us join ourselves
to the LORD
In a perpetual [f]covenant
That will not be forgotten.'
6 "My people have been lost
[g]sheep.
Their shepherds have led them
[h]astray;
They have turned them away
on the mountains.
They have gone from
mountain to hill;
They have forgotten their
resting place.
7 All who found them have
devoured them;
And their adversaries said,
'We have [i]not offended,
Because they have sinned
against the LORD, the
habitation of justice,
The LORD, the hope of their
fathers.'
8 "Move from the midst of
Babylon,
[j]Go out of the land of the
Chaldeans;
And be like the rams before
the flocks.
9 For behold, [k]I will raise and
cause to come up against
Babylon
An assembly of great nations
from the north country,
And they shall [l]array
themselves against her;
From there she shall be
captured.
Their arrows *shall be* like
those of an expert warrior;*
[m]None shall return in vain.
10 And Chaldea shall become
plunder;
All who plunder her shall be
satisfied," says the LORD.
11 "Because you were glad,
because you [n]rejoiced,
You destroyers of My heritage,
Because you have grown fat
like a heifer threshing grain,
And you bellow like bulls,
12 Your mother shall be deeply
ashamed;

39
a v. 49:6; see Acts 2:17, *note*

CHAPTER 50
1
b chs. 50:1-51:64; Jer. 25:12; Isa. 13:1–22; 14:18–22; 47:1–15
2
c Isa. 21:9; cp. Rev. 14:8; 18:2
d Isa. 46:1
3
e vv. 39–40; Isa. 13:17–20
5
f Covenant (New): vv. 4–5; Mt. 26:28. (Isa. 61:8; Heb. 8:8, *note*)
6
g v. 17; Isa. 53:6; cp. Ezek. 34:11–31; 1 Pet. 2:25
h Jer. 23:1; Ezek. 34:2
7
i Jer. 40:2–3; Zech. 11:5
8
j Isa. 48:20; Jer. 51:6, 45
9
k vv. 3,41; Jer. 51:27
l vv. 14,29
m Cp. 2 Sam. 1:22
11
n Cp. Ps. 35:19

*
50:2 A Babylonian god; sometimes spelled *Marduk*
50:9 Following some Hebrew manuscripts, Septuagint, and Syriac; Masoretic Text, Targum, and Vulgate read *a warrior who makes childless.*

She who bore you shall be
ashamed.
Behold, the least of the nations
shall be a [a]wilderness,
A dry land and a desert.
13 Because of the wrath of the
LORD
She shall not be inhabited,
But she shall be wholly
desolate.
Everyone who goes by
Babylon shall be [b]horrified
And hiss at all her plagues.
14 "Put yourselves in array against
Babylon all around,
All you who bend the bow;
Shoot at her, spare no arrows,
For she has sinned against the
LORD.
15 Shout against her all around;
She has given her hand,
Her foundations have fallen,
Her walls are [c]thrown down;
For it *is* the [d]vengeance of the
LORD.
Take vengeance on her.
As she has done, so do to her.
16 Cut off the sower from
Babylon,
And him who handles the
sickle at harvest time.
For fear of the oppressing
sword
Everyone shall turn to his own
people,
And everyone shall flee to his
[e]own land.

17 "Israel *is* like [f]scattered sheep;
The lions have driven *him*
away.
First the king of [g]Assyria
devoured him;
Now at last this
Nebuchadnezzar king of
Babylon has broken his
bones."
18 Therefore thus says the LORD of
hosts, the God of Israel:
"Behold, I will punish the king
of Babylon and his land,
As I have punished the king of
[h]Assyria.
19 But I will [i]bring back Israel to
his home,
And he shall feed on Carmel
and Bashan;
His soul shall be satisfied on
Mount Ephraim and Gilead.
20 In those days and in that
time," says the LORD,
"The [j]iniquity of Israel shall be
sought, but *there shall be*
none;
And the sins of Judah, but they
shall not be found;
For I will pardon those [k]whom
I preserve.

21 "Go up against the land of
Merathaim, against it,
And against the inhabitants of
[l]Pekod.
Waste and utterly destroy
them," says the LORD,
"And do according to all that I
have commanded you.
22 A sound of battle *is* in the
land,
And of great destruction.
23 How the [m]hammer of the
whole earth has been cut
apart and broken!
How Babylon has become a
desolation among the
nations!
I have laid a snare for you;
24 You have indeed been
[n]trapped, O Babylon,
And you were not aware;
You have been found and also
caught,
Because you have [o]contended
against the Lord.
25 The LORD has opened His
armory,
And has brought out the
weapons of His indignation;
For this *is* the work of the
Lord GOD of hosts
In the land of the Chaldeans.
26 Come against her from the
farthest border;
Open her storehouses;
Cast her up as heaps of ruins,
And destroy her utterly;
Let nothing of her be left.
27 Slay all her bulls,
Let them go down to the
slaughter.
Woe to them!
For their day has come, the
time of their punishment.
28 The voice of those who flee
and escape from the land of
Babylon
Declares in Zion the
vengeance of the LORD our
God,
The vengeance of His temple.

29 "Call together the archers
against Babylon.
All you who bend the bow,
encamp against it all
around;

12
a Jer. 51:43
13
b Jer. 49:17
15
c Jer. 51:58
d Jer. 51:6, 11
16
e Isa. 13:14; Jer. 51:9
17
f v. 6; 2 Ki. 24:10,14; Jer. 2:15
g 2 Ki. 15:29; 17:6; 18:9–13
18
h Ezek. 31:3,11–12
19
i Jer. 32:37; 33:12; Ezek. 11:17
20
j Num. 23:21; Jer. 31:34
k Isa. 1:9
21
l Ezek. 23:23
23
m Jer. 51:20–24
24
n Dan. 5:30–31
o Isa. 45:9

Let none of them escape.*
Repay her according to her work;
According to all she has done, do to her;
For she has been [a]proud against the LORD,
Against the Holy One of Israel.
30 Therefore her young men shall fall in the streets,
And all her men of war shall be cut off in that day," says the LORD.
31 "Behold, I *am* against you,
O most haughty one!" says the Lord GOD of hosts;
"For your day has come,
The time *that* I will [b]punish you.*
32 The most [c]proud shall stumble and fall,
And no one will raise him up;
I will kindle a fire in his cities,
And it will devour all around him."

33 Thus says the LORD of hosts:
"The children of Israel *were* oppressed,
Along with the children of Judah;
All who took them captive have held them fast;
They have refused to let them go.
34 Their [d]Redeemer *is* strong;
The LORD of hosts *is* His name.
He will thoroughly plead their [e]case,
That He may give rest to the land,
And disquiet the inhabitants of Babylon.

35 "A sword *is* against the Chaldeans," says the LORD,
"Against the inhabitants of Babylon,
And against her princes and her [f]wise men.
36 A sword *is* against the soothsayers, and they will be fools.
A sword *is* against her mighty men, and they will be dismayed.
37 A sword *is* against their horses,
Against their chariots,
And against all the [g]mixed peoples who *are* in her midst;
And they will become like [h]women.
A sword *is* against her [i]treasures, and they will be robbed.
38 A drought* *is* against her waters, and they will be dried up.
For it *is* the land of carved images,
And they are insane with *their* idols.

39 "Therefore the wild desert beasts shall dwell *there* with the [j]jackals,
And the ostriches shall dwell in it.
It shall be inhabited no more forever,
Nor shall it be dwelt in from generation to generation.
40 [k]As God overthrew Sodom and Gomorrah
And their neighbors," says the LORD,
"*So* no one shall reside there,
Nor son of man [l]dwell in it.

41 "Behold, a people shall come from the north,
And a great nation and many kings
Shall be raised up from the ends of the earth.
42 They shall hold the bow and the lance;
They *are* [m]cruel and shall not show mercy.
Their voice shall roar like the sea;
They shall ride on horses,
Set in array, like a man for the battle,
Against you, O daughter of Babylon.

43 "The king of Babylon has [n]heard the report about them,
And his hands grow feeble;
Anguish has taken hold of him,
Pangs as of a woman in [o]childbirth.

44 "Behold, he shall come up like a lion from the floodplain* of the Jordan

29
a Isa. 47:10; cp. Dan. 4:37
31
b Jer. 6:15
32
c Isa. 26:5; Mal. 4:1
34
d *Redemption* (redeeming relative type): v. 34; Lam. 3:58. (Gen. 48:16; Isa. 59:20, *note*)
e Isa. 51:22
35
f Jer. 51:57
37
g Jer. 25:20, 24
h Jer. 51:30
i Prov. 11:4; Jer. 49:4
39
j Lit. *howling creatures.* Jer. 51:37
40
k Gen. 19:24–25; Isa. 13:19; Jer. 49:18
l Isa. 13:20
42
m Isa. 13:17–18
43
n Jer. 51:31
o Jer. 6:24

*
50:29 Qere, some Hebrew manuscripts, Septuagint, and Targum add *to her.* **50:31** Following Masoretic Text and Targum; Septuagint and Vulgate read *The time of your punishment.* **50:38** Following Masoretic Text, Targum, and Vulgate; Syriac reads *sword;* Septuagint omits *A drought is.* **50:44** Or *thicket*

Against the dwelling place of
the strong;
But I will make them suddenly
run away from her.
And who *is* a chosen *man that*
I may appoint over her?
For who *is* like Me?
Who will arraign Me?
And who *is* that shepherd
Who will [a]withstand Me?"

45 Therefore hear the counsel of
the LORD that He has taken
against Babylon,
And His [b]purposes that He has
proposed against the land of
the Chaldeans:
[c]Surely the least of the flock
shall draw them out;
Surely He will make their
dwelling place desolate with
them.
46 At the noise of the taking of
Babylon
The earth trembles,
And the cry is heard among
the nations.

Babylon judged by the LORD for sins against Israel

51 THUS says the LORD:
"Behold, I will raise up against
[d]Babylon,
Against those who dwell in
Leb Kamai,*
A destroying wind.
2 And I will send winnowers to
Babylon,
Who shall winnow her and
empty her land.
For in the day of doom
They shall be [e]against her all
around.
3 Against *her* let the archer bend
his bow,
And lift himself up against *her*
in his armor.
Do not spare her young men;
Utterly destroy all her army.
4 Thus the slain shall fall in the
land of the Chaldeans,
And *those* thrust through in
her streets.
5 For Israel is [f]not forsaken, nor
Judah,
By his God, the LORD of hosts,
Though their land was filled
with sin against the Holy
One of Israel."

6 [g]Flee from the midst of
Babylon,
And every one save his life!
Do not be cut off in her
iniquity,
For this *is* the time of the
LORD's vengeance;
He shall recompense her.
7 [h]Babylon *was* a golden cup in
the LORD's hand,
That made all the earth drunk.
The [i]nations drank her wine;
Therefore the nations are
[j]deranged.
8 [k]Babylon has suddenly fallen
and been destroyed.
[l]Wail for her!
Take balm for her pain;
Perhaps she may be healed.
9 We would have healed
Babylon,
But she is not healed.
Forsake her, and let us go
everyone to his own country;
For her judgment reaches to
heaven and is lifted up to
the skies.
10 The LORD has [m]revealed our
righteousness.
Come and let us declare in
Zion the work of the LORD
our God.

11 Make the arrows bright!
Gather the shields!
The [n]LORD has raised up the
spirit of the kings of the
Medes.
For His [o]plan *is* against
Babylon to destroy it,
Because it *is* the [p]vengeance of
the LORD,
The vengeance for His temple.
12 [q]Set up the standard on the
walls of Babylon;
Make the guard strong,
Set up the watchmen,
Prepare the ambushes.
For the LORD has both [r]devised
and done
What He spoke against the
inhabitants of Babylon.
13 O you who dwell by many
waters,
Abundant in treasures,
Your end has come,
The measure of your
covetousness.
14 The LORD of hosts has sworn
by Himself:
"Surely I will fill you with men,
as with locusts,

44
a Job 41:10; Jer. 49:19
45
b Jer. 51:29
c Jer. 49:19–20
CHAPTER 51
1
d Isa. 47:1; Jer. 50:1
2
e Jer. 50:14
5
f Jer. 33:24–26; 46:28
6
g Jer. 50:8; cp. Rev. 18:4
7
h Cp. Rev. 17:4
i Cp. Rev. 18:3
j Jer. 25:15–16
8
k Isa. 21:9; Jer. 50:2; cp. Rev. 14:8; 18:2
l Cp. Rev. 18:9
10
m Ps. 37:6
11
n Isa. 13:17
o Jer. 50:45
p Jer. 50:28
12
q v. 27; Nah. 2:1; 3:14
r vv. 1–4

*51:1 A code word for *Chaldea* (Babylonia); may be translated *The Midst of Those Who Rise Up Against Me*

And they shall lift up a shout
against you."

15 [a]He has made the earth by His
power;
He has established the world
by His wisdom,
And [b]stretched out the heaven
by His understanding.
16 When He utters *His* voice—
There is a multitude of waters
in the heavens:
"He causes the vapors to ascend
from the ends of the earth;
He makes lightnings for the
rain;
He brings the wind out of His
treasuries."*

17 Everyone is dull-hearted,
without knowledge;
Every [c]metalsmith is put to
shame by the carved image;
For his molded image *is*
falsehood,
And *there is* no breath in
them.
18 They *are* futile, a work of
errors;
In the time of their
[d]punishment they shall
perish.
19 The Portion of Jacob *is* not
like them,
For He *is* the Maker of all
things;
And *Israel is* the tribe of His
inheritance.
The LORD of hosts *is* His name.

20 "You *are* My [e]battle-ax *and*
weapons of war:
For with you I will break the
nation in pieces;
With you I will destroy
kingdoms;
21 With you I will break in pieces
the horse and its rider;
With you I will break in pieces
the chariot and its rider;
22 With you also I will break in
pieces man and woman;
With you I will break in pieces
old and young;
With you I will break in pieces
the young man and the
maiden;
23 With you also I will break in
pieces the shepherd and his
flock;
With you I will break in pieces
the [f]farmer and his yoke of
oxen;
And with you I will break in
pieces governors and rulers.

24 "And I will repay Babylon
And all the inhabitants of
Chaldea
For all the evil they have done
In Zion in your sight," says the
LORD.

25 "Behold, I *am* against you, [g]O
destroying mountain,
Who destroys all the earth,"
says the LORD.
"And I will stretch out My hand
against you,
Roll you down from the rocks,
And make you a burnt
mountain.
26 They shall not take from you a
stone for a corner
Nor a stone for a foundation,
But you shall be [h]desolate
forever," says the LORD.

27 Set up a banner in the land,
Blow the trumpet among the
nations!
Prepare the [i]nations against
her,
Call the kingdoms together
against her:
Ararat, Minni, and Ashkenaz.
Appoint a general against her;
Cause the horses to come up
like the bristling locusts.
28 Prepare against her the
nations,
With the kings of the Medes,
Its governors and all its rulers,
All the land of his dominion.
29 And the land will tremble and
sorrow;
For every [j]purpose of the LORD
shall be performed against
Babylon,
To make the land of Babylon a
desolation without
[k]inhabitant.
30 The mighty men of Babylon
have ceased fighting,
They have remained in their
strongholds;
Their might has failed,
They became *like* women;
They have burned her dwelling
places,
The bars of her *gate* are
broken.
31 One runner will run to meet
another,

15 a vv. 15–19; Jer. 10:12–16 b Job 9:8; Ps. 104:2; Isa. 40:22
17 c Jer. 10:14
18 d Jer. 48:44
20 e Cp. Isa. 10:5,15; Jer. 50:23
23 f Amos 5:16
25 g Zech. 4:7; see Isa. 13:1, *note 2*
26 h Jer. 50:26, 40
27 i Jer. 50:9
29 j Jer. 50:45 k Isa. 13:20

* 51:16 Psalm 135:7

And one messenger to meet
another,
To show the king of Babylon
that his city is taken on *all*
sides;
32 The passages are blocked,
The reeds they have burned
with fire,
And the men of war are
terrified.

33 For thus says the LORD of hosts,
the God of Israel:
"The daughter of Babylon *is*
like a [a]threshing floor
When it is time to thresh her;
Yet a little while
And the time of her harvest
will come."

34 "Nebuchadnezzar the king of
Babylon
Has devoured me, he has
crushed me;
He has made me an [b]empty
vessel,
He has swallowed me up like a
monster;
He has filled his stomach with
my delicacies,
He has spit me out.
35 Let the violence *done* to me
and my flesh *be* upon
Babylon,"
The inhabitant of Zion will
say;
"And my blood be upon the
inhabitants of Chaldea!"
Jerusalem will say.

36 Therefore thus says the LORD:
"Behold, I will [c]plead your case
and take vengeance for you.
I will dry up her sea and make
her springs dry.
37 Babylon shall become a heap,
A [d]dwelling place for [e]jackals,
An [f]astonishment and a
hissing,
Without an inhabitant.
38 They shall roar together like
lions,
They shall growl like lions'
whelps.
39 In their excitement I will
prepare their feasts;
I will make them drunk,
That they may rejoice,
And sleep a perpetual sleep
And not awake," says the
LORD.
40 "I will bring them down
Like lambs to the slaughter,
Like rams with male goats.

41 "Oh, how [g]Sheshach* is taken!
Oh, how the [h]praise of the
whole earth is seized!
How Babylon has become
desolate among the nations!
42 The [i]sea has come up over
Babylon;
She is covered with the
multitude of its waves.
43 Her [j]cities are a desolation,
A dry land and a wilderness,
A land where [k]no one dwells,
Through which no son of man
passes.
44 I will punish [l]Bel in Babylon,
And I will bring out of his
mouth what he has
swallowed;
And the nations shall not
stream to him anymore.
Yes, the wall of Babylon shall
fall.

45 "My people, [m]go out of the
midst of her!
And let everyone [n]deliver
himself from the fierce anger
of the LORD.
46 And lest your heart faint,
And you fear for the [o]rumor
that *will be* heard in the land
(A rumor will come *one* year,
And after that, in *another* year
A rumor *will come*,
And violence in the land,
Ruler against ruler),
47 Therefore behold, the days are
coming
That I will bring judgment on
the [p]carved images of
Babylon;
Her whole land shall be
ashamed,
And all her slain shall fall in
her midst.
48 [q]Then the heavens and the
earth and all that *is* in them
Shall sing joyously over
Babylon;
For the plunderers shall come
to her from the north," says
the LORD.

49 As Babylon *has caused* the
slain of Israel to fall,
So at Babylon the slain of all
the earth shall fall.
50 You who have escaped the
sword,
Get away! Do not stand still!

33 *a* Isa. 21:10; Dan. 2:35
34 *b* Isa. 24:1
36 *c* Ps. 140:12; Jer. 50:34
37 *d* Isa. 13:22; Jer. 50:39; cp. Rev. 18:2 *e* Jer. 49:33 *f* Jer. 44:22
41 *g* Jer. 25:26 *h* Isa. 13:19; Jer. 49:25; Dan. 4:30
42 *i* Cp. Isa. 8:7–8
43 *j* Jer. 50:39–40 *k* Isa. 13:20
44 *l* Jer. 50:2
45 *m* Jer. 51:6; 50:8; cp. Rev. 18:4 *n* Cp. Gen. 19:12–16; Acts 2:40
46 *o* Cp. Mt. 24:6–7
47 *p* Isa. 21:9; Jer. 50:2
48 *q* Isa. 44:23; 48:20; 49:13; cp. Rev. 18:20

* 51:41 A code word for *Babylon* (compare Jeremiah 25:26)

[a]Remember the LORD afar off,
And let Jerusalem come to
your mind.
51 We are ashamed because we
have heard reproach.
Shame has covered our faces,
For strangers [b]have come into
the sanctuaries of the LORD's
house.
52 "Therefore behold, the days are
coming," says the LORD,
"That I will bring judgment on
her [c]carved images,
And throughout all her land
the wounded shall groan.
53 [d]Though Babylon were to
mount up to heaven,
And though she were to fortify
the height of her strength,
Yet from Me plunderers would
come to her," says the LORD.
54 The sound of a cry *comes* from
Babylon,
And great destruction from the
land of the Chaldeans,
55 Because the LORD is plundering
Babylon
And silencing her loud voice,
Though her waves roar like
great waters,
And the noise of their voice is
uttered,
56 Because the plunderer comes
against her, against Babylon,
And her mighty men are
taken.
Every one of their bows is
broken;
For the LORD *is* the God of
recompense,
He will surely [e]repay.
57 "And I will make drunk
Her princes and [f]wise men,
Her governors, her deputies,
and her mighty men.
And they shall sleep a
perpetual sleep
And not awake," says the
[g]King,
Whose name *is* the LORD of
hosts.

58 Thus says the LORD of hosts:

"The broad walls of Babylon
shall be utterly [h]broken,
And her high gates shall be
burned with fire;
The people will labor in vain,
And the nations, because of
the fire;
And they shall be [i]weary."

59 The word which Jeremiah the
prophet commanded Seraiah the son
of [j]Neriah, the son of Mahseiah,
when he went with Zedekiah the king
of Judah to Babylon in the fourth year
of his reign. And Seraiah *was* the
quartermaster.
60 So Jeremiah [k]wrote in a book all
the evil that would come upon Babylon, all these words that are written
against Babylon.
61 And Jeremiah said to Seraiah,
"When you arrive in Babylon and see
it, and read all these words,
62 "then you shall say, 'O LORD, You
have spoken against this place to cut
it off, so that none shall remain in it,
neither man nor beast, but it shall be
desolate [l]forever.'
63 "Now it shall be, when you have
finished reading this book, [m]*that* you
shall tie a stone to it and throw it out
into the Euphrates.
64 "Then you shall say, 'Thus Babylon shall sink and not rise from the
catastrophe that I will bring upon her.
And they shall be weary.' " [n]Thus far
are the words of Jeremiah.

III. Historical Supplement, 52

An appendix: second account of overthrow of Judah (cp. 2 Ki. 25:1–26; Jer. 39:1–10)

52 ZEDEKIAH [o]*was* twenty-one
years old when he became
king, and he reigned eleven years in
Jerusalem. His mother's name *was*
Hamutal the daughter of Jeremiah of
[p]Libnah.
2 He also did evil in the sight of the
LORD, according to all that Jehoiakim
had done.
3 For because of the anger of the
LORD *this* happened in Jerusalem and
Judah, till He finally cast them out
from His presence. Then Zedekiah
[q]rebelled against the king of Babylon.
4 Now it came to pass in the
[r]ninth year of his reign, in the [s]tenth
month, on the tenth *day* of the month,
that Nebuchadnezzar king of Babylon and all his army came against
Jerusalem and encamped against it;
and *they* built a siege wall against it
all around.
5 So the city was besieged until
the eleventh year of King Zedekiah.
6 By the [s]fourth month, on the
ninth day of the month, the famine
had become so severe in the city that
there was no food for the people of the
land.
7 Then the city wall was broken

50 a Dt. 4:29–31; Ezek. 6:9
51 b Ps. 74:3–8; Jer. 52:13; Lam. 1:10
52 c Isa. 21:9; Jer. 50:2
53 d Jer. 49:16; Amos 9:2; Obad. 4
56 e Jer. 51:24; Ps. 94:1; Jer. 50:29
57 f Jer. 50:35 g Jer. 46:18; 48:15
58 h Jer. 50:15 i Hab. 2:13
59 j Jer. 32:12
60 k Jer. 36:2
62 l Isa. 13:20; 14:22–23; Jer. 50:3
63 m Cp. Rev. 18:21
64 n Cp. Job 31:40; Ps. 72:20
CHAPTER 52
1 o 2 Ki. 24:18; 2 Chr. 36:11 p Josh. 10:29
3 q 2 Chr. 36:13
4 r Cp. Ezek. 24:1–2 s See Lev. 23:2, *note*

through, and all the men of war fled
and went out of the city at night by
way of the gate between the two walls,
which *was* by the king's garden, even
though the Chaldeans *were* near the
city all around. And they went by way
of the [a]plain.
8 But the army of the Chaldeans
pursued the king, and they [b]overtook
Zedekiah in the plains of Jericho. All
his army was scattered from him.
9 So they took the king and
brought him up to the king of Babylon
at Riblah in the land of Hamath, and
he pronounced judgment on him.
10 Then the king of Babylon killed
the sons of Zedekiah before his eyes.
And he killed all the princes of Judah
in Riblah.
11 He also [c]put out the eyes of Zedekiah; and the king of Babylon bound
him in bronze fetters, took him to Babylon, and put him in prison till the day
of his death.
12 [d]Now in the [e]fifth month, on the
tenth *day* of the month (which *was* the
nineteenth year of King Nebuchadnezzar king of Babylon), Nebuzaradan, the captain of the guard, *who*
served the king of Babylon, came to
Jerusalem.
13 He [f]burned the house of the
LORD and the king's house; all the
houses of Jerusalem, that is, all the
houses of the great, he burned with
fire.
14 And all the army of the Chaldeans who *were* with the captain of the
guard broke down all the walls of Jerusalem all around.
15 Then Nebuzaradan the captain
of the guard carried away captive
some of the poor people, the rest of the
people who remained in the city, the
defectors who had deserted to the
king of Babylon, and the rest of the
craftsmen.
16 But Nebuzaradan the captain of
the guard left *some* of the poor of the
land as vinedressers and [g]farmers.
17 [h]The bronze pillars that *were* in
the house of the LORD, and the carts
and the bronze Sea that *were* in the
house of the LORD, the Chaldeans
broke in pieces, and carried all their
bronze to Babylon.
18 They also took away the pots,
the shovels, the trimmers, the bowls,
the spoons, and all the bronze utensils
with which the priests ministered.
19 The basins, the firepans, the
bowls, the pots, the lampstands, the
spoons, and the cups, whatever *was*
solid gold and whatever *was* solid silver, the captain of the guard took
away.
20 The two pillars, one Sea, the
twelve bronze bulls which *were* under
it, and the carts, which King Solomon
had made for the house of the LORD—
the bronze of all these articles was beyond [i]measure.
21 Now *concerning* the [j]pillars: the
height of one pillar *was* eighteen cubits, a measuring line of twelve [k]cu-
bits could measure its circumference,
and its thickness *was* four fingers; *it*
was hollow.
22 A capital of bronze *was* on it;
and the height of one capital *was* five
cubits, with a network and pomegranates all around the capital, all of
bronze. The second pillar, with pomegranates was the same.
23 There were ninety-six pomegranates on the sides; all the [l]pome-
granates, all around on the network,
were one hundred.
24 The captain of the guard took
[m]Seraiah the chief priest, [n]Zephaniah
the second priest, and the three doorkeepers.
25 He also took out of the city an
officer who had charge of the men of
war, seven men of the king's close associates who were found in the city,
the principal scribe of the army who
mustered the people of the land, and
sixty men of the people of the land
who were found in the midst of the
city.
26 And Nebuzaradan the captain of
the guard took these and brought
them to the king of Babylon at Riblah.
27 Then the king of Babylon struck
them and put them to death at Riblah
in the land of Hamath. Thus Judah
was carried away captive from its own
land.
28 [o]These *are* the people whom
Nebuchadnezzar carried away captive: in the seventh year, three thousand and twenty-three Jews;
29 in the eighteenth year of Nebuchadnezzar he carried away captive
from Jerusalem eight hundred and
thirty-two persons;
30 in the twenty-third year of Nebuchadnezzar, Nebuzaradan the captain
of the guard carried away captive of
the Jews seven hundred and forty-five
persons. All the persons *were* four
thousand six hundred.
31 [p]Now it came to pass in the
thirty-seventh year of the captivity of

7
a See Dt. 1:1, *note*
8
b Jer. 21:7, 32:4; 37:17; cp. 38:17
11
c Ezek. 12:13
12
d vv. 12–21; 2 Ki. 25:8–21
e See Lev. 23:2, *note*
13
f 2 Chr. 36:19; Isa. 64:11
16
g Jer. 31:24
17
h vv. 17–20; Jer. 27:19–22; cp. 1 Ki. 7:15–20
20
i 1 Ki. 7:47
21
j 1 Ki. 7:15; 2 Ki. 25:17; 2 Chr. 3:15
k See Weights and Measures (OT), 2 Chr. 2:10, *note*
23
l 1 Ki. 7:20
24
m 2 Ki. 25:18
n Jer. 21:1; 29:25
28
o 2 Ki. 24:12, 14–16; cp. Ezra 2:1–65; Neh. 7:6–67 ; Dan. 1:1–7
31
p vv. 31–34; 2 Ki. 25:27–30

Jehoiachin king of Judah, in the
[a]twelfth month, on the twenty-fifth
day of the month, *that* Evil-
Merodach* king of Babylon, in the
first *year* of his reign, [b]lifted up the
head of Jehoiachin king of Judah and
brought him out of prison.

32 And he spoke kindly to him and
gave him a more prominent seat than
those of the kings who *were* with him
in Babylon.

33 So Jehoiachin changed from his
prison garments, and he [c]ate bread
regularly before the king all the days
of his life.

34 And as for his provisions, there
was a regular ration given him by the
king of Babylon, a portion for each
day until the day of his death, all the
days of his life.

31
a See Lev. 23:2, *note*
b Cp. Gen. 40:13–20

33
c i.e. *he dined at the king's table,* cp. 2 Sam. 9:13

---

*52:31 Or *Awil-Marduk*

The Book of

LAMENTATIONS

Author: Jeremiah *Theme:* Mourning for Jerusalem *Date of writing:* 6th Cent. B.C.

LAMENTATIONS, composed of five elegies lamenting the destruction of Jerusalem, is undoubtedly the work of Jeremiah. In literary form it is in good part alphabetic, somewhat on the order of Ps. 119. Thus in chs. 1 and 2 a new letter of the Hebrew alphabet begins each of the twenty-two verses. In ch. 3 there are sixty-six verses, arranged in twenty-two groups of three verses, each of which in succession begins with a new letter. The fifth chapter, although not alphabetical, contains twenty-two verses in a plaintive meter which—the second half of each verse being shorter than the first—conveys a somber effect of diminuendo.

The deeper significance of Lamentations lies in the fact that Jeremiah's intense burden of sympathy for Jerusalem discloses the love and sorrow of the LORD for the very people whom He is chastening, a burden similar to that which the Lord Jesus Christ expressed in His lament over Jerusalem (Mt. 23:37–39).

The book may be divided as follows:

I. The Desolation of Jerusalem, 1.
II. The Day of the LORD's Anger, 2.
III. The Nation's Affliction and God's Faithfulness, 3.
IV. Horrors of the Siege of Jerusalem, 4.
V. A Plaintive Prayer to the LORD, 5.

I. The Desolation of Jerusalem

1 HOW [a]lonely sits the city
That was full of people!
[b]*How* like a widow is she,
Who *was* great among the nations!
The [c]princess among the provinces
Has become a slave!

2 She weeps bitterly in the night,
Her tears *are* on her cheeks;
Among all her lovers
She has none to comfort *her*.
All her friends have dealt treacherously with her;
They have become her enemies.

3 [d]Judah has gone into captivity,
Under affliction and hard servitude;
She dwells among the nations,
She finds no [e]rest;
All her persecutors overtake her in dire straits.

4 The roads to Zion mourn
Because no one comes to the set feasts.
All her gates are [f]desolate;
Her priests sigh,
Her virgins are afflicted,
And she *is* in bitterness.

5 Her adversaries have become the [g]master,
Her enemies prosper;
For the LORD has afflicted her
[h]Because of the multitude of her transgressions.
Her children have gone into captivity before the enemy.

6 And from the daughter of Zion
All her splendor has departed.
Her princes have become like deer
That find no [i]pasture,
That flee without strength
Before the pursuer.

7 In the days of her affliction and roaming,
Jerusalem [j]remembers all her pleasant things
That she had in the days of old.
When her people fell into the hand of the enemy,
With no one to help her,
The adversaries saw her
And mocked at her downfall.*

8 [k]Jerusalem has sinned gravely,
Therefore she has become vile.*
All who honored her despise her
Because they have seen her nakedness;
Yes, she sighs and turns away.

9 Her uncleanness *is* in her skirts;

CHAPTER 1

1
a Isa. 3:26
b Isa. 47:7–9
c Ezra 4:20

3
d Jer. 52:27
e Dt. 28:65; cp. Mt. 11:28–30

4
f Isa. 27:10

5
g Dt. 28:44
h Jer. 30:14–15; 52:28; Dan. 9:7, 16

6
i Cp. Jn. 10:9

7
j Ps. 137:1

8
k 1 Ki. 8:46

*1:7 Vulgate reads *her Sabbaths.* 1:8 Septuagint and Vulgate read *moved* or *removed*.

She did not consider her [a]destiny;
Therefore her collapse was awesome;
She had no comforter.
"O LORD, behold my affliction,
For *the* enemy is exalted!"

10 The adversary has spread his hand
Over all her pleasant things;
For she has seen the nations [b]enter her sanctuary,
Those whom You commanded
[c]Not to enter Your assembly.

11 All her people sigh,
They seek bread;
They have given their valuables for food to restore life.
"See, O LORD, and consider,
For I am scorned."

12 "*Is it* nothing to you, all you who pass by?
Behold and see
[d]If there is any sorrow like my sorrow,
Which has been brought on me,
Which the LORD has inflicted
In the day of His fierce anger.

13 "From above He has sent fire into my bones,
And it overpowered them;
He has [e]spread a net for my feet
And turned me back;
He has made me desolate
And faint all the day.

14 "The [f]yoke of my transgressions was bound;*
They were woven together by His hands,
And thrust upon my neck.
He made my strength fail;
The Lord delivered me into the hands of *those whom* I am not able to withstand.

15 "The Lord has trampled underfoot all my mighty *men* in my midst;
He has called an assembly against me
To crush my young men;
The Lord trampled *as* in a [1]winepress
The virgin daughter of Judah.

9 *a* Dt. 32:29; Isa. 47:7; Jer. 5:31
10 *b* Jer. 51:51 *c* Dt. 23:3
12 *d* Dan. 9:12
13 *e* Ezek. 12:13; 17:20
14 *f* Dt. 28:48
16 *g* Eccl. 4:1
17 *h* Jer. 4:31 *i* 2 Ki. 24:2–4
18 *j* Ps. 119:75; Dan. 9:14
20 *k* Dt. 32:25; Ezek. 7:15
21 *l* Ps. 35:15; Jer. 48:27; 50:11; Obad. 12 *m* Isa. 13; Jer. 46
22 *n* Ps. 137:7–8; Jer. 30:16

16 "For these *things* I weep;
My eye, my eye overflows with water;
Because the [g]comforter, who should restore my life,
Is far from me.
My children are desolate
Because the enemy prevailed."

17 Zion spreads out her hands,
But no one comforts [h]her;
The LORD has commanded concerning Jacob
That those [i]around him *become* his adversaries;
Jerusalem has become an unclean thing among them.

18 "The LORD is [j]righteous,
For I rebelled against His commandment.
Hear now, all peoples,
And behold my sorrow;
My virgins and my young men
Have gone into captivity.

19 "I called for my lovers,
But they deceived me;
My priests and my elders
Breathed their last in the city,
While they sought food
To restore their life.

20 "See, O LORD, that I *am* in distress;
My soul is troubled;
My heart is overturned within me,
For I have been very rebellious.
Outside the [k]sword bereaves,
At home *it is* like death.

21 "They have heard that I sigh,
But no one comforts me.
All my enemies have heard of my trouble;
They are [l]glad that You have done *it*.
Bring on the [m]day You have announced,
That they may become like me.

22 "Let all their wickedness come before You,
And [n]do to them as You have done to me
For all my transgressions;
For my sighs *are* many,
And my heart *is* faint."

*1:14 Following Masoretic Text and Targum; Septuagint, Syriac, and Vulgate read *watched over*.

[1](1:15) A winepress is at times used to picture divine judgment (Isa. 63:3; Rev. 14:19–20; 19:15).

II. The Day of the LORD*'s Anger*

2 HOW the Lord has covered the
daughter of Zion
With a [a]cloud in His anger!
He [b]cast down from heaven to
the earth
The beauty of Israel,
And did not remember His
[c]footstool
In the day of His anger.

2 The Lord has swallowed up
and has [d]not pitied
All the dwelling places of
Jacob.
He has thrown down in His
wrath
The strongholds of the
daughter of Judah;
He has brought *them* down to
the ground;
He has profaned the kingdom
and its princes.

3 He has cut off in fierce anger
Every [e]horn of Israel;
He has drawn back His [f]right
hand
From before the enemy.
He has blazed against Jacob
like a flaming fire
Devouring all around.

4 [g]Standing like an enemy, He
has bent His bow;
With His right hand, like an
adversary,
He has slain all *who were*
pleasing to His eye;
On the tent of the daughter of
Zion,
He has poured out His fury
like fire.

5 The Lord was like an enemy.
He has swallowed up Israel,
[h]He has swallowed up all her
palaces;
He has destroyed her
strongholds,
And has increased mourning
and lamentation
In the daughter of Judah.

6 He has [i]done violence to His
[j]tabernacle,
As if it were a garden;
He has destroyed His place of
[k]assembly;
The LORD has caused
The appointed feasts and
Sabbaths to be forgotten in
Zion.
In His burning indignation He
has [l]spurned the king and
the priest.

7 The Lord has spurned His
altar,
He has [m]abandoned His
sanctuary;
He has given up the walls of
her palaces
Into the hand of the enemy.
They have made a [n]noise in
the house of the LORD
As on the day of a set feast.

8 The LORD has purposed to
destroy
The [o]wall of the daughter of
Zion.
He has [p]stretched out a line;
He has not withdrawn His
hand from destroying;
Therefore He has caused the
rampart and wall to lament;
They languished together.

9 Her gates have sunk into the
ground;
He has destroyed and broken
her bars.
Her [q]king and her princes *are*
among the nations;
The Law *is* no *more*,
And her prophets find [r]no
vision from the LORD.

10 The elders of the daughter of
Zion
Sit on the ground *and* keep
silence;
They throw dust on their heads
And gird themselves with
sackcloth.
The virgins of Jerusalem
Bow their heads to the ground.

11 [s]My eyes fail with tears,
My heart is troubled;
My bile is poured on the
ground
Because of the destruction of
the daughter of my people,
Because the children and the
infants
Faint in the streets of the city.

12 They say to their mothers,
"Where *is* grain and wine?"
As they swoon like the
wounded
In the streets of the city,
As their life is poured out
In their mothers' bosom.

13 [t]How shall I console you?
To what shall I liken you,
O daughter of Jerusalem?

CHAPTER 2

1
a Lam. 3:44
b Cp. Mt. 11:23
c Ezek. 43:7

2
d vv. 17,21; Lam. 3:43

3
e See Dt. 33:17, *note*
f Ps. 74:11

4
g Isa. 63:10

5
h 2 Ki. 25:9; Jer. 52:13

6
i Ps. 80:12; 89:40; Isa. 5:5; Jer. 7:14
j Or *booth*, or *hedge*
k Jer. 52:13
l Isa. 43:28

7
m Ezek. 24:21
n Ps. 74:3–8

8
o Jer. 52:14
p 2 Ki. 21:13; Isa. 34:11

9
q Dt. 28:36; 2 Ki. 24:15; 25:7; Lam. 1:3; 4:20
r Mic. 3:6

11
s Ps. 6:7; Lam. 3:48

13
t Lam. 1:12; Dan. 9:12

What shall I compare with
you, that I may comfort you,
O virgin daughter of Zion?
For your ruin *is* spread wide as
the sea;
Who can heal you?

14 Your prophets have seen for
you
False and [a]deceptive visions;
They have not [b]uncovered
your iniquity,
To bring back your captives,
But have envisioned for you
false [c]prophecies and
delusions.

15 [d]All who pass by clap *their*
hands at you;
They hiss and shake their
heads
At the daughter of Jerusalem:
"*Is* this the city that is called
'The [e]perfection of beauty,
The joy of the whole earth'?"

16 All your enemies have opened
their mouth against you;
They hiss and gnash *their*
teeth.
They say, "We have swallowed
her up!
Surely this *is* the [f]day we have
waited for;
We have found *it*, we have
seen *it!*"

17 The LORD has done what He
[g]purposed;
He has fulfilled His [1]word
Which He commanded in days
of old.
He has thrown down and has
not pitied,
And He has caused an enemy
to rejoice over you;
He has exalted the [h]horn of
your adversaries.

18 Their heart cried out to the
Lord,
"O wall of the daughter of Zion,
[i]Let tears run down like a river
day and night;
Give yourself no relief;
Give your eyes no rest.

19 "Arise, cry out in the night,
At the beginning of the
watches;
[j]Pour out your heart like water
before the face of the Lord.
Lift your hands toward Him

14
a Jer. 23:25–29; 29:8–9; 37:19
b Cp. Isa. 58:1
c Jer. 23:33–36
15
d 1 Ki. 9:8; Jer. 18:16; Nah. 3:19
e Ps. 48:2; 50:2; Ezek. 16:14
16
f Lam. 1:21; Obad. 12–15
17
g Ps. 89:42; Ezek. 5:11; cp. Dt. 32:4; Ps. 33:11
h See Dt. 33:17, *note*
18
i Jer. 14:17; Lam. 1:16
19
j Ps. 62:8
20
k Lev. 26:29; Dt. 28:53; Jer. 19:9; Lam. 4:10; Ezek. 5:10
21
l Jer. 18:21
22
m Jer. 16:2–4; 44:7
CHAPTER 3
1
n Cp. Jer. 15:15–18
4
o Job 16:8
6
p Ps. 88:5–6; 143:3
7
q Job 3:23; 19:8; Hos. 2:6

For the life of your young
children,
Who faint from hunger at the
head of every street."

20 "See, O LORD, and consider!
To whom have You done this?
[k]Should the women eat their
offspring,
The children they have
cuddled?*
Should the priest and prophet
be slain
In the sanctuary of the Lord?

21 "Young and old lie
On the ground in the streets;
My virgins and my young men
Have fallen by the [l]sword;
You have slain *them* in the
day of Your anger,
You have slaughtered *and* not
pitied.

22 "You have invited as to a feast
day
The terrors that surround me.
In the day of the LORD's anger
There was no refugee or
survivor.
Those whom I have borne and
brought up
My enemies have [m]destroyed."

III. The Nation's Affliction and God's Faithfulness

Jeremiah shares his nation's affliction

3 I *AM* the man *who* has seen
[n]affliction by the rod of His
wrath.
2 He has led me and made *me*
walk
In darkness and not *in* light.
3 Surely He has turned His hand
against me
Time and time again
throughout the day.

4 [o]He has aged my flesh and my
skin,
And broken my bones.
5 He has besieged me
And surrounded *me* with
bitterness and woe.
6 [p]He has set me in dark places
Like the dead of long ago.

7 [q]He has hedged me in so that I
cannot get out;
He has made my chain heavy.

* **2:20** Vulgate reads *a span long.*

[1](2:17) Sometimes God must act in sovereign judgment in order to fulfill His Word. Cp. Lev. 26:16; Dt. 28:15.

8 [a]Even when I cry and shout,
He shuts out my prayer.
9 He has blocked my ways with hewn stone;
He has made my paths crooked.
10 He *has been* to me a bear lying in wait,
Like a lion in ambush.
11 He has turned aside my ways and torn me in pieces;
He has made me desolate.
12 [b]He has bent His bow
And set me up as a target for the arrow.
13 He has caused the arrows of His quiver
To pierce my loins.*
14 I have become the [c]ridicule of all my people—
Their taunting [d]song all the day.
15 [e]He has filled me with bitterness,
He has made me drink wormwood.
16 He has also broken my teeth with gravel,
And covered me with ashes.
17 You have moved my soul far from peace;
I have forgotten prosperity.
18 And I said, "My strength and my hope
Have perished from the LORD."
19 Remember my affliction and roaming,
The wormwood and the gall.
20 My soul still remembers
And sinks within me.
21 This I recall to my mind,
Therefore I have [f]hope.

Jeremiah speaks of God's faithfulness

22[1][g]*Through* the LORD's mercies we are not consumed,
Because His compassions fail [h]not.
23 [i]*They are* new every morning;
Great *is* Your faithfulness.
24 "The LORD *is* [j]my portion," says my soul,
"Therefore I [k]hope in Him!"
25 The LORD *is* good to those who [l]wait for Him,
To the soul *who* seeks Him.
26 *It is* good that *one* should [m]hope and [n]wait quietly
For the salvation of the LORD.
27 *It is* good for a man to bear
The yoke in his youth.
28 Let him sit alone and keep silent,
Because *God* has laid *it* on him;
29 Let him put his mouth in the dust—
There may yet be hope.
30 Let him give *his* cheek to the one who [o]strikes him,
And be full of reproach.
31 [p]For the Lord will not cast off forever.
32 Though He causes grief,
Yet He will show compassion
According to the multitude of His mercies.
33 [q]For He does not afflict willingly,
Nor grieve the children of men.
34 To crush under one's feet
All the prisoners of the earth,
35 To turn aside the justice *due* a man
Before the face of the Most High,
36 Or subvert a man in his cause—
[r]The Lord does not approve.
37 Who *is* he *who* speaks and it comes to pass,
When the Lord has not commanded *it?*
38 *Is it* [s]not from the mouth of the Most High
That woe and well-being proceed?
39 Why should a living man complain,
A man for the punishment of his sins?

A call to self-judgment and confession

40 Let us search out and examine our ways,
And turn back to the LORD;
41 Let us lift our hearts and hands
To God in heaven.

8 *a* Job 30:20; Ps. 22:2
12 *b* Job 7:20; 16:12; Ps. 38:2
14 *c* Jer. 20:7 *d* Ps. 69:12
15 *e* Jer. 9:15
21 *f* Ps. 130:7
22 *g* Mal. 3:6 *h* Ps. 78:38; Jer. 3:12; 30:11
23 *i* Isa. 33:2
24 *j* Ps. 16:5; 73:26; 119:57; Jer. 10:16 *k* Jer. 17:17; Mic. 7:7
25 *l* Ps. 130:6; Isa. 30:18
26 *m* Rom. 4:16–18; cp. 1 Pet. 1:13 *n* Ex. 14:13; Isa. 7:4
30 *o* Cp. Mt. 27:30; Mk. 15:19; Lk. 22:63; Jn. 18:22
31 *p* Ps. 77:7; 94:14; Isa. 54:7–10
33 *q* Isa. 28:21; Ezek. 33:11; Heb. 12:10
36 *r* Hab. 1:13
38 *s* Contra. Jas. 3:10–11

* 3:13 Literally *kidneys*

[1](3:22) This beautiful passage (vv. 22–27) sounds a note of hope and trust amid the gloom of the book. Even his grief cannot blind the prophet to the abiding faithfulness of the LORD (cp. also vv. 31–33,40–41,55–58).

42 We have transgressed and rebelled;
You have not pardoned.

43 You have covered *Yourself* with anger
And pursued us;
You have slain *and* not pitied.
44 You have covered Yourself with a cloud,
That prayer should not pass through.
45 [a]You have made us an offscouring and refuse
In the midst of the peoples.
46 All our enemies
Have [b]opened their mouths against us.
47 Fear and a snare have come upon us,
Desolation and destruction.
48 My eyes overflow with rivers of [c]water
For the destruction of the daughter of my people.

49 My eyes flow and do not cease,
Without interruption,
50 [d]Till the LORD from heaven
Looks down and sees.
51 My eyes bring suffering to my soul
Because of all the daughters of my city.

Jeremiah's prison experience

52 My enemies without cause
Hunted me down like a bird.
53 They silenced* my life in the pit
And threw stones at me.
54 The waters flowed over my head;
I said, "I am cut off!"

55 [e]I called on Your name, O LORD,
From the lowest [f]pit.
56 You have heard my voice:
"Do not hide Your ear
From my sighing, from my cry for help."
57 [g]You drew near on the day I called on You,
And said, [h]"Do not fear!"

58 O Lord, You have pleaded the case for my soul;
You have [i]redeemed my life.
59 O LORD, You have seen *how* I am wronged;
Judge my case.
60 You have seen all their vengeance,
All their schemes against me.

45
a 1 Cor. 4:13
46
b Lam. 2:16
48
c Jer. 14:17; Lam. 2:11
50
d Isa. 63:15
55
e Ps. 130:1; Jon. 2:2
f Jer. 38:6–13
57
g Jas. 4:8
h Isa. 41:10, 14; Dan. 10:12
58
i *Redemption* (redeeming relative type): v. 58; Hos. 13:14. (Gen. 48:16; Isa. 59:20, *note*)
62
j v. 14
64
k Ps. 28:4; Jer. 11:20; 2 Tim. 4:14
CHAPTER 4
1
l Cp. Ezek. 7:19–22
2
m Isa. 30:14; Jer. 19:11; 2 Cor. 4:7
6
n Ezek. 16:48
o Gen. 19:24–25

61 You have heard their reproach, O LORD,
All their schemes against me,
62 The lips of my enemies
And their [j]whispering against me all the day.
63 Look at their sitting down and their rising up;
I *am* their taunting song.

64 [k]Repay them, O LORD,
According to the work of their hands.
65 Give them a veiled* heart;
Your curse *be* upon them!
66 In Your anger,
Pursue and destroy them
From under the heavens of the LORD.

IV. Horrors of the Siege of Jerusalem

4 HOW the gold has become [l]dim!
How changed the fine gold!
The stones of the sanctuary are scattered
At the head of every street.

2 The precious sons of Zion,
Valuable as fine gold,
How they are regarded as [m]clay pots,
The work of the hands of the potter!

3 Even the jackals present their breasts
To nurse their young;
But the daughter of my people *is* cruel,
Like ostriches in the wilderness.

4 The tongue of the infant clings
To the roof of its mouth for thirst;
The young children ask for bread,
But no one breaks *it* for them.

5 Those who ate delicacies
Are desolate in the streets;
Those who were brought up in scarlet
Embrace ash heaps.

6 The punishment of the iniquity of the daughter of my people
Is greater than the punishment of the [n]sin of Sodom,
[o]Which was overthrown in a moment,
With no hand to help her!

*

3:53 Septuagint reads *put to death.* **3:65** A Jewish tradition reads *sorrow of.*

7 Her Nazirites* were brighter than snow
And whiter than milk;
They were more ruddy in body than rubies,
Like sapphire in their appearance.

8 *Now* their appearance is blacker than soot;
They go unrecognized in the streets;
Their skin clings to their bones,
It has become as dry as wood.

9 *Those* slain by the sword are better off
Than *those* who die of hunger;
For these [a]pine away,
Stricken *for lack* of the fruits of the [b]field.

10 The hands of the compassionate [c]women
Have cooked their own [d]children;
They became food for them
In the destruction of the daughter of my people.

11 The LORD has fulfilled His fury,
[e]He has poured out His fierce anger.
He [f]kindled a fire in Zion,
And it has devoured its foundations.

12 The kings of the earth,
And all inhabitants of the world,
Would not have believed
That the adversary and the enemy
Could [g]enter the gates of Jerusalem—

13 [h]Because of the sins of her prophets
And the [1]iniquities of her priests,
Who shed in her midst
The blood of the just.

14 They wandered blind in the streets;
They have defiled themselves with blood,
So that no one would touch their garments.

15 They cried out to them,
"Go away, [i]unclean!
Go away, go away,
Do not touch us!"
When they fled and wandered,
Those among the nations said,
"They shall no longer dwell *here.*"

16 The face* of the LORD scattered them;
He no longer regards them.
The people do not respect the priests
Nor show favor to the elders.

17 Still our eyes failed us,
Watching vainly for our help;
In our watching we watched
For a nation *that* could not save *us.*

18 They tracked our steps
So that we could not walk in our streets.
[j]Our end was near;
Our days were over,
For our end had come.

19 Our pursuers were swifter
Than the eagles of the heavens.
They pursued us on the mountains
And lay in wait for us in the wilderness.

20 The breath of our nostrils, the anointed of the LORD,
Was caught in their pits,
Of whom we said, "Under his shadow
We shall live among the nations."

21 [k]Rejoice and be glad, O daughter of [l]Edom,
You who dwell in the land of [m]Uz!
The cup shall also pass over to you
And you shall become drunk and make yourself naked.

22 *The punishment of* your iniquity is [n]accomplished,
O daughter of Zion;
He will no longer send you into captivity.
He will [o]punish your iniquity,
O daughter of Edom;
He will uncover your sins!

9
a Lev. 26:39
b Jer. 16:4
10
c Dt. 28:56–57
d Dt. 28:53–55; 2 Ki. 6:29; Jer. 19:9; Lam. 2:20
11
e Jer. 7:20
f Dt. 32:22; Jer. 21:14
12
g Jer. 21:13
13
h Jer. 5:31; 6:13; 14:14; 23:11,21; 32:32; Ezek. 22:26,28; Zeph. 3:4
15
i Cp. Lev. 13:45–46
18
j Ezek. 7:2–3,6; Amos 8:2
21
k Cp. Eccl. 11:9
l Ps. 83:3–6; Jer. 25:21, 27; 49:7–22
m See Job 1:1, *note*
22
n Isa. 40:2
o Ps. 137:7

*4:7 Or *nobles* 4:16 Targum reads *anger.*

[1](4:13) Verses 13–14 are a drastic example of the far-reaching consequences of corrupt spiritual leadership.

V. A Plaintive Prayer to the LORD

5 REMEMBER, O LORD, what has come upon us;
Look, and behold our reproach!
2 [a]Our inheritance has been turned over to aliens,
And our houses to foreigners.
3 We have become orphans and waifs,
Our mothers *are* like [b]widows.
4 We pay for the water we drink,
And our wood comes at a price.
5 *They* pursue at our [c]heels;*
We labor *and* have no rest.
6 We have given our hand *to* the Egyptians
And the [d]Assyrians, to be satisfied with bread.
7 Our fathers sinned *and are* no more,
But we bear their iniquities.
8 Servants rule over us;
There is none to deliver *us* from their hand.
9 We get our bread *at the risk* of our lives,
Because of the sword in the wilderness.
10 Our skin is hot as an oven,
Because of the fever of famine.
11 They [e]ravished the women in Zion,
The maidens in the cities of Judah.
12 Princes were hung up by their hands,
And elders were not respected.
13 Young men [f]ground at the millstones;
Boys staggered under *loads of* wood.
14 The elders have ceased *gathering at* the gate,
And the young men from their [g]music.
15 The joy of our heart has ceased;
Our dance has turned into [h]mourning.
16 The crown has fallen *from* our head.
Woe to us, for we have sinned!
17 Because of this our heart is faint;
Because of these *things* our eyes grow dim;
18 Because of Mount Zion which is [i]desolate,
With foxes walking about on it.
19 [j]You, O LORD, remain forever;
Your throne from generation to generation.
20 Why do You forget us forever,
And forsake us for so long a time?
21 [k]Turn us back to You, O LORD, and we will be restored;
Renew our days as of old,
22 Unless You have utterly rejected us,
And are very angry with us!

CHAPTER 5
2 *a* Ps. 79:1
3 *b* Jer. 15:8; 18:21
5 *c* Dt. 28:48; Jer. 28:14
6 *d* Jer. 2:18; Hos. 5:13
11 *e* Isa. 13:16; Zech. 14:2
13 *f* Jud. 16:21
14 *g* Jer. 7:34
15 *h* Amos 8:10
18 *i* Isa. 27:10
19 *j* Ps. 9:7; 10:16; 29:10; 90:2; 102:12; 145:13; Hab. 1:12
21 *k* Ps. 80:3,7, 19; Jer. 31:18

* 5:5 Literally *necks*

The Book of

EZEKIEL

Author: Ezekiel *Theme:* Judgment and Glory *Date of writing:* 6th Cent. B.C.

EZEKIEL, a priest whose name means *God will strengthen*, was among the Jewish exiles carried away to Babylon between the first and final deportations of Judah (2 Ki. 24:11–16). His book shows him as a man of stern integrity and strong purpose, completely devoted to the practices of his priestly religion. Like Daniel and the Apostle John, he prophesied outside the land of Judah; and his prophecy, like theirs, follows the method of symbol and vision. Unlike the pre-exilic prophets, whose ministry was primarily either to Judah or to the ten-tribe kingdom, or to both, Ezekiel was the voice of the LORD to "the whole house of Israel." In marked contrast with Jeremiah, all of the material in Ezekiel's prophecy is arranged in chronological order as God revealed it to him.

Speaking broadly, the purpose of Ezekiel's ministry was to keep before the generation born in exile the national sins which had brought Israel so low (e.g. Ezek. 14:23); to sustain the faith of the exiles by predictions of national restoration, of the execution of justice upon their oppressors, and of national glory under the Davidic monarchy.

Observe that the glory of the LORD departed from the city just before the destruction of Jerusalem (11:23); this glory will return to Jerusalem in the millennial period (43:2). No temple in Jerusalem has known the presence of the glory of God in this manner since 586 B.C.

The book may be divided as follows:

I. The Call of Ezekiel, 1—3.
II. Warnings of Judgment on Jerusalem, 4—24.
III. Judgments on the Gentile Nations, 25—32.
IV. Ezekiel's Responsibility as Watchman, 33.
V. Predictions of Events to Take Place at the End of the Age, When Israel is Again in Her Own Land, 34—39.
VI. The Millennial Temple and Its Worship, 40:1—47:12.
VII. The Division of the Land during the Millennial Age, 47:13—48:35.

I. The Call of Ezekiel, 1—3

Occasion of Ezekiel's first vision: the glory of the LORD

1 NOW it came to pass in the thirti-
eth year, in the [a]fourth *month*, on
the fifth *day* of the month, as I *was*
among the captives [b]by the River
[c]Chebar, *that* the heavens were
[d]opened and I saw visions* of God.
2 On the fifth *day* of the month,
which *was* in the [e]fifth year of King
Jehoiachin's captivity,
3 the word of the LORD came expressly to Ezekiel the [1]priest, the son
of Buzi, in the land of the Chaldeans*
by the River Chebar; and the [f]hand of
the LORD was upon him there.
4 Then I looked, and behold, a
whirlwind was coming out of the
north, a great cloud with raging fire
engulfing itself; and [2]brightness *was*
all around it and radiating out of its

CHAPTER 1

1
a See Lev. 23:2, *note*
b v. 3; Ezek. 3:15, 23; 10:15
c A large canal between the Euphrates and Tigris Rivers
d Mt. 3:16; Acts 7:56; Rev. 4:1

2
e c. 593 B.C.

1:3 *f* 1 Ki. 18:46; 2 Ki. 3:15; Ezek. 3:14,22; 8:1; 33:22; 37:1; 40:1

*

1:1 Following Masoretic Text, Septuagint, and Vulgate; Syriac and Targum read *a vision*. 1:3 Or *Babylonians*, and so elsewhere in this book

[1](1:3) Since Ezekiel was a priest, it is possible to trace priestly indications throughout his prophecy. His visions of the divine glory (chs. 1 and 10) are reminiscent of the Shekinah in the Mosaic system. The stages of the departure of the glory (chs. 8—11) are described by one familiar with the priestly order. Chapters 40—48 are admittedly couched in terms understandable only in the framework of the Levitical appointments. Even details of the priesthood, such as the prohibition against defilement of the priest (4:13ff.), and the profanation of the Sabbath (20:12ff.; 22:8) are found.

[2](1:4) In exile, far from the sight of the glory of God's earthly temple, surrounded by the pomp of idolatry, Ezekiel received a vision of the majesty and wonder of God's glory, showing that his God was more magnificent than anything to be found in heathenism, and impressing on his mind the greatness of the unseen God of Israel. The vision indicated that the affairs of the world are not directed by impersonal laws of nature, but by a living Spirit (vv. 20–21). Above the babel of man's plans, the authoritative voice of God speaks (v. 24). The four faces in the vision (v. 10) prefigure the four aspects in which God would reveal Himself when He incarnated Himself in human flesh as Messiah. On the right is the lion, symbol of kingship (Mt.). On the left is the ox, symbol of the Servant (Mk.). The face of a man represents His

midst like the color of amber, out of
the midst of the fire.
5 Also from within it *came* the
likeness of four [1]living creatures. And
this *was* their appearance: they had
the likeness of a man.
6 Each one had four faces, and
each one had four wings.
7 Their legs *were* straight, and the
soles of their feet *were* like the soles of
calves' feet. They sparkled like the
color of burnished bronze.
8 The hands of a man *were* under
their wings on their four sides; and
each of the four had faces and wings.
9 Their wings touched one another. *The creatures* did not turn
when they went, but each one went
straight [a]forward.
10 As for the [b]likeness of their
[c]faces, [d]*each* had the face of a man;
each of the four had the face of a lion
on the right side, each of the four had
the face of an ox on the left side, and
each of the four had the face of an
eagle.
11 Thus *were* their faces. [e]Their
wings stretched upward; two *wings* of
each one touched one another, and
two covered their bodies.
12 And each one [f]went straight
forward; they went [g]wherever the
spirit wanted to go, and they did not
turn when they went.
13 As for the likeness of the living
creatures, their appearance *was* like
burning coals of fire, like the appearance of torches going back and forth
among the living creatures. The fire
was bright, and out of the fire went
lightning.
14 And the living creatures ran
back and forth, in [h]appearance like a
flash of lightning.
15 Now as I looked at the living
creatures, behold, a wheel *was* on the
earth beside each living creature with
its four faces.
16 The appearance of the wheels
and their workings *was* [i]like the color
of beryl, and all four had the same
likeness. The appearance of their
workings *was*, as it were, a wheel in
the middle of a wheel.
17 When they moved, they went toward any one of four directions; they
did not turn aside when they went.
18 As for their rims, they were so
high they were awesome; and their
rims *were* [j]full of eyes, all around the
four of them.
19 When the living creatures went,
the wheels went beside them; and
when the living creatures were lifted
up from the earth, the wheels were
lifted up.
20 Wherever the spirit wanted to
go, they went, *because* there the spirit
went; and the wheels were lifted together with them, for the spirit of the
living creatures* *was* in the wheels.
21 When those went, *these* went;
when those [k]stood, *these* stood; and
when those were lifted up from the
earth, the wheels were lifted up together with them, for the spirit of the
living creatures* *was* in the wheels.
22 The likeness of the firmament
above the heads of the living creatures* *was* like the color of an awesome [l]crystal, stretched out [m]over
their heads.
23 And under the firmament their
wings *spread out* straight, one toward
another. Each one had two which covered one side, and each one had two
which covered the other side of the
body.
24 When they went, I heard the
noise of their [n]wings, like the [o]noise
of many waters, [p]like the voice of the
Almighty, a tumult like the noise of an
army; and when they stood still, they
let down their wings.
25 A voice came from above the firmament that *was* over their heads;

9 *a* Ezek. 10:20–22
10 *b* Cp. Rev. 4:7 *c* Ezek. 10:14 *d* Cp. Num. 2:3,10,18, 25
11 *e* Cp. Isa. 6:2
12 *f* Ezek. 10:11 *g* v. 20
14 *h* Zech. 4:10
16 *i* Dan. 10:6
18 *j* Ezek. 10:12; Rev. 4:6,8
21 *k* Cp. Num. 9:15–23
22 *l* Rev. 4:6 *m* Ezek. 10:1
24 *n* Ezek. 3:13 *o* Ezek. 43:2; Rev. 1:15 *p* Job 37:4–5; Ps. 29:3–4; 68:33

*
1:20 Literally *living creature;* Septuagint and Vulgate read *spirit of life;* Targum reads *creatures.*
1:21 Literally *living creature;* Septuagint and Vulgate read *spirit of life;* Targum reads *creatures.*
1:22 Following Septuagint, Targum, and Vulgate; Masoretic Text reads *living creature.*

perfect humanity (Lk.). The eagle, soaring overhead, symbolizes His Deity (Jn.). Cp. also Rev. 4:7.

[1](1:5) These are identified as the cherubim in 10:20. The cherubim are symbolic of God's holy presence and unapproachability. They are celestial beings who guard and vindicate the righteousness of God (cp. Gen. 3:24; Ex. 26:1,31; 36:8,35), the mercy of God (cp. Ex. 25:22; 37:9), and the government of God (cp. 1 Sam. 4:4; Ps. 80:1; 99:1; Ezek. 1:22,26). In the holy of holies God's glory dwelt between the cherubim (Ps. 80:1; cp. Ex. 25:10–22). Some think that the living creatures of Rev. 4 are cherubim (besides points of similarity, observe dissimilarity to the cherubim in number of wings: Ezek. 1:6; 10:21; Rev. 4:8; cp. Isa. 6:2). This dissimilarity may indicate that these beings have power to appear in different forms for purposes of symbolic revelation.

whenever they stood, they let down
their wings.
26 And above the firmament over
their heads *was* the likeness of a
throne, in appearance [a]like a sapphire stone; on the likeness of the
throne *was* a likeness with the appearance of a [b]man high above [c]it.
27 Also from the appearance of His
waist and upward I saw, as it were, the
color of amber with the appearance of
fire all around within it; and from the
appearance of His waist and downward I saw, as it were, the appearance
of fire with brightness all around.
28 [d]Like the appearance of a rainbow in a cloud on a rainy day, so *was*
the appearance of the brightness all
around it. This *was* the appearance of
the likeness of the [e]glory of the LORD.
So when I saw *it,* [f]I fell on my
face, and I heard a voice of One speaking.

Ezekiel commissioned

2 AND He said to me, [1]"Son of man,
[g]stand on your feet, and I will
speak to you."
2 Then the [h]Spirit [i]entered me
when He [j]spoke to me, and set me on
my feet; and I heard Him who spoke to
me.
3 And He said to me: "Son of man,
I am sending you to the children of
Israel, to a rebellious nation that has
[k]rebelled against Me; they and their
fathers have transgressed against Me
to this very day.
4 "For *they are* impudent and
[l]stubborn children. I am sending you
to them, and you shall say to them,
'Thus says the Lord GOD.'
5 "As for them, whether they hear
or whether they [m]refuse—for they *are*
a [n]rebellious house—yet they will
know that a prophet has been among
them.
6 "And you, son of man, do [o]not
be afraid of them nor be afraid of their
words, though briers and thorns *are*
with you and you dwell among scorpions; do not be afraid of their words or
dismayed by their looks, though they
are a rebellious house.

26
a Ex. 24:10
b Evidently a Christophany. Cp. Isa. 6:1; Jn. 12:41
c Ezek. 8:2
28
d Rev. 4:3; 10:1
e Ezek. 3:12,23
f Ezek. 3:23; Dan. 8:17; Acts 9:4; Rev. 1:17
CHAPTER 2
1
g Dan. 10:11
2
h *Holy Spirit* (OT): v. 2; Ezek. 3:24. (Gen. 1:2; Zech. 12:10)
i Ezek. 3:24
j *Inspiration:* v. 2; Amos 3:7. (Ex. 4:15; 2 Tim. 3:16, *note*)
3
k Ezek. 5:6; 20:8,13,18
4
l Isa. 48:4; Jer. 5:3; 6:15
5
m Isa. 6:9–10; Ezek. 3:11; cp. Mt. 10:12–15
n Ezek. 3:26
6
o Isa. 51:12; Jer. 1:8; Ezek. 3:9
8
p Cp. Num. 20:10–13
q Ezek. 3:1–3
CHAPTER 3
6
r Jon. 3:5–10
7
s Jn. 15:20, 23
9
t Isa. 50:7; Jer. 1:18; 15:20; Mic. 3:8

7 "You shall speak My words to
them, whether they hear or whether
they refuse, for they *are* rebellious.
8 "But [p]you, son of man, hear
what I say to you. Do not be rebellious
like that rebellious house; open your
mouth and [q]eat what I give you."
9 Now when I looked, there was a
hand stretched out to me; and behold,
a scroll of a book *was* in it.
10 Then He spread it before me;
and *there was* writing on the inside
and on the outside, and written on it
were lamentations and mourning and
woe.

Ezekiel, God's watchman

3 MOREOVER He said to me, "Son
of man, eat what you find; eat this
scroll, and go, speak to the house of
Israel."
2 So I opened my mouth, and He
caused me to eat that scroll.
3 And He said to me, "Son of man,
feed your belly, and fill your stomach
with this scroll that I give you." So I
[2]ate, and it was in my mouth like
honey in sweetness.
4 Then He said to me: "Son of
man, go to the house of Israel and
speak with My words to them.
5 "For you *are* not sent to a people
of unfamiliar speech and of hard language, *but* to the house of Israel,
6 "not to many people of unfamiliar speech and of hard language,
whose words you cannot understand.
Surely, had I sent you to them, they
would have [r]listened to you.
7 "But the house of Israel will not
listen to you, because they will [s]not
listen to Me; for all the house of Israel
are impudent and hard-hearted.
8 "Behold, I have made your face
strong against their faces, and your
forehead strong against their foreheads.
9 [t]"Like adamant stone, harder
than flint, I have made your forehead;
do not be afraid of them, nor be dismayed at their looks, though they *are*
a rebellious house."

[1](2:1) The expression "son of man" is a common Semitic way of indicating an individual man (Ps. 4:2; 57:4; 58:1; 144:3; Jer. 49:18,33; 50:40; 51:43). God addresses Ezekiel about ninety times by this title. In Dan. 7:13 the term is used to show that an actual man will come in the clouds of heaven to receive a worldwide kingdom. From this use in Daniel it came to refer to the glorious Messiah, and in such a sense Jesus utilized it, calling Himself "the Son of Man" nearly eighty times in the Gospels.

[2](3:3) Compare Ezek. 2:10; Rev. 10:9. Whatever its message, the Word of God is sweet to faith because it is the Word of God.

10 Moreover He said to me: "Son of
man, receive into your heart all My
words that I speak to you, and hear
with your ears.
11 "And go, get to the captives, to
the children of your people, and speak
to them and tell them, 'Thus says the
Lord GOD,' whether they hear, or
whether they [a]refuse."
12 Then the Spirit lifted me up, and
I heard behind me a great thunderous
voice: "Blessed *is* the [b]glory of the
LORD from His place!"
13 *I* also *heard* the [c]noise of the
wings of the living creatures that
touched one another, and the noise of
the wheels beside them, and a great
thunderous noise.
14 So the Spirit lifted me up and
took me away, and I went in [d]bitter-
ness, in the heat of my spirit; but the
[e]hand of the LORD was strong upon
me.
15 Then I came to the captives at
Tel Abib, who dwelt by the River Chebar; and I sat where they sat, and remained there astonished among them
[f]seven days.
16 Now it [g]came to pass at the end
of seven days that the word of the
LORD came to me, saying,
17 "Son of man, I have made you a
[h]watchman for the house of Israel;
therefore hear a word from My mouth,
and give them [i]warning from Me:
18 "When I say to the wicked, 'You
shall surely die,' and you give him no
warning, nor speak to warn the
wicked from his wicked way, to save
his life, that same wicked *man* [j]shall
die in his iniquity; but his blood I will
require at your hand.
19 "Yet, if you warn the wicked,
and he does not turn from his wickedness, nor from his wicked way, he
shall die in his iniquity; [k]but you have
delivered your soul.
20 "Again, when a righteous *man*
turns from his righteousness and commits [l]iniquity, and I lay a stumbling
block before him, he shall die; because you did not give him warning,

11
a Ezek. 2:5
12
b Ezek. 1:28; 8:4
13
c Ezek. 1:24; 10:5
14
d Cp. Jer. 20:9
e 2 Ki. 3:15; Ezek. 1:3; 8:1; 37:1
15
f Job 2:13
16
g Jer. 42:7
17
h Isa. 52:8; 62:6; Jer. 6:17; Ezek. 33:7–9; cp. Isa. 56:10
i Lev. 19:17; Prov. 14:25; Isa. 58:1
18
j Ezek. 33:6; Jn. 8:21,24
19
k v. 21; Isa. 49:4–5; Acts 18:6; 20:26
20
l Ezek. 18:24
21
m Cp. Jas. 5:19–20
22
n Or *valley.* Ezek. 8:4
24
o Holy Spirit (OT): vv. 12,14, 24; Ezek. 8:3. (Gen. 1:2; Zech. 12:10)
25
p Ezek. 4:8
26
q Cp. Ezek. 24:27; 29:21
r Hos. 4:17; Amos 8:11

he shall die in his sin, and his righteousness which he has done shall not
be remembered; but his blood I will
require at your hand.
21 "Nevertheless if you warn the
righteous *man* that the righteous
should not sin, and he does not sin, he
shall surely live because he took
warning; also you will have delivered
your [m]soul."
22 Then the hand of the LORD was
upon me there, and He said to me,
[1]"Arise, go out into the [n]plain, and
there I shall talk with you."
23 So I arose and went out into the
[n]plain, and behold, the glory of the
LORD stood there, like the glory which
I saw by the River Chebar; and I fell on
my face.
24 Then the [o]Spirit entered me and
set me on my feet, and spoke with me
and said to me: "Go, shut yourself inside your house.
25 "And you, O son of man, surely
they will put [p]ropes on you and bind
you with them, so that you cannot go
out among them.
26 "I will make your tongue cling to
the roof of your mouth, so that you
shall be [q]mute and [r]not be one to rebuke them, for they *are* a [a]rebellious
house.
27 [s]"But when I speak with you, I
will open your mouth, and you shall
say to them, 'Thus says the Lord GOD.'
He who hears, let him hear; and he
who refuses, let him refuse; for they
are a rebellious house.

II. Warnings of Judgment on Jerusalem, 4—24

Signs of coming judgment of Jerusalem: (1) the clay tablet

4 "YOU also, son of man, [2]take a
clay tablet and lay it before you,
and portray on it a city, Jerusalem.
2 [t]"Lay siege against it, build a
[u]siege wall against it, and heap up a
mound against it; set camps against it

3:27 *s* Ex. 4:11–12; Ezek. 33:22 **4:2** *t* Jer. 6:6 *u* 2 Ki. 25:1

[1](3:22) Evidently this command to arise and go to the plain where the LORD appeared to him, as at the River Chebar, was given to Ezekiel after he had carried out the commission of vv. 17–21 and the people had turned against him. Then the LORD struck Ezekiel mute (v. 26), so that he was obliged to communicate by symbolic actions. Only when God had a special message to give through him could he speak (v. 27). This condition continued until the prophecy of judgment upon Jerusalem was fulfilled (24:25–27; 33:21–22).

[2](4:1) The symbolic actions during the prophet's inability to speak were testimonies to the past wickedness and chastisement of the house of Israel (the whole nation), and prophetic of a coming seige. They are therefore intermediate between the siege of 2 Ki. 24:10–16, at which time Ezekiel was carried to Babylon, and the siege of 2 Ki. 25:1–11, eleven years later.

also, and place battering rams against
it all around.
3 "Moreover take for yourself an
iron plate, and set it *as* an iron wall
between you and the city. Set your
face against it, and it shall be [a]be-
sieged, and you shall lay siege against
it. This *will be* a [b]sign to the house of
Israel.
4 "Lie also on your left side, and
lay the iniquity of the house of Israel
upon it. *According* to the number of
the days that you lie on it, you shall
bear their iniquity.
5 "For I have laid on you the years
of their iniquity, according to the
number of the [1]days, three hundred
and ninety days; so you shall bear the
iniquity of the house of Israel.
6 "And when you have completed
them, lie again on your right side; then
you shall bear the iniquity of the
house of Judah forty days. I have laid
on you a day for each year.
7 "Therefore you shall set your
face toward the siege of Jerusalem;
your arm *shall be* uncovered, and you
shall prophesy against it.
8 "And surely I will [c]restrain you
so that you cannot turn from one side
to another till you have ended the days
of your siege.

(2) Defiled bread

9 "Also take for yourself wheat,
barley, beans, lentils, millet, and spelt;
put them into one vessel, and make
bread of them for yourself. *During* the
number of days that you lie on your
side, three hundred and ninety days,
you shall eat it.
10 "And your food which you eat
shall be by weight, twenty shekels a
day; from time to time you shall eat it.
11 "You shall also drink water by
measure, one-sixth of a [d]hin; from
time to time you shall drink.
12 "And you shall eat it *as* barley
cakes; and bake it using fuel of human
waste in their sight."
13 Then the LORD said, "So [e]shall
the children of Israel eat their defiled
bread among the Gentiles, where I
will drive them."
14 So I said, [f]"Ah, Lord GOD! Indeed I have never defiled myself from
my youth till now; I have never eaten
what died of [g]itself or was torn by
beasts, nor has [h]abominable flesh
ever come into my mouth."
15 Then He said to me, "See, I am
giving you cow dung instead of human waste, and you shall prepare
your bread over it."
16 Moreover He said to me, "Son of
man, surely I will cut off the [i]supply
of bread in Jerusalem; they shall eat
bread by weight and with anxiety, and
shall drink water by measure and with
[j]dread,
17 "that they may lack bread and
water, and be dismayed with one another, and [k]waste away because of
their iniquity.

(3) The razor and the hair

5 "AND you, son of man, take a
sharp sword, take it as a barber's
razor, and [l]pass *it* over your head and
your beard; then take scales to weigh
and divide the hair.
2 "You shall burn with fire one-
third in the midst of the [m]city, when
the days of the siege are finished; then
you shall take one-third and strike
around *it* with the sword, and one-
third you shall scatter in the wind: I
will draw out a sword after [n]them.
3 [o]"You shall also take a small
number of them and bind them in the
edge of your *garment*.
4 "Then take some of them again
and throw them into the midst of the
fire, and burn them in the fire. From
there a fire will go out into all the
house of Israel.
5 "Thus says the Lord GOD: 'This *is*
Jerusalem; I have set her in the midst
of the nations and the countries all
around her.
6 'She has rebelled against My
judgments by doing wickedness more
than the nations, and against My statutes more than the countries that *are*
all around her; for they have refused
My judgments, and they have not
walked in My statutes.'
7 "Therefore thus says the Lord
GOD: 'Because you have multiplied
disobedience more than the nations
that *are* all around you, have not
walked in My statutes nor kept My
judgments, nor even done* according
to the judgments of the nations that
are all around you'—
8 "therefore thus says the Lord
GOD: 'Indeed I, even I, *am* against you
and will execute judgments in your
midst in the sight of the nations.

CHAPTER 4
3 a Jer. 39:1–2 b Ezek. 12:6,11; 24:24,27; cp. Isa. 20:2–4; Jer. 13:1–11
8 c Ezek. 3:25
11 d See Weights and Measures (OT), 2 Chr. 2:10, *note*
13 e Hos. 9:3; cp. Dan. 1:8
14 f Acts 10:14 g Lev. 17:15; 22:8; Ezek. 44:31 h Dt. 14:3; Isa. 65:4; 66:17
16 i Lev. 26:26; Ps. 105:16; Isa. 3:1; Ezek. 5:16; 14:13 j Lam. 5:4
17 k Lam. 4:9; Ezek. 24:23
CHAPTER 5
1 l Cp. Lev. 21:5; Ezek. 44:20
2 m Cp. Ezek. 4:1–2 n Lev. 26:25; Lam. 1:20
3 o Jer. 40:6; 52:16

*5:7 Following Masoretic Text, Septuagint, Targum, and Vulgate; many Hebrew manuscripts and Syriac read *but have done* (compare 11:12).

[1](4:5) Each day Ezekiel carried out this symbolism for a few hours.

9 [a]'And I will do among you what I have never done, and the like of which I will never do again, because of all your abominations.

10 'Therefore fathers shall eat *their* sons in your midst, and sons shall eat their fathers; and I will execute judgments among you, and all of you who remain I will [b]scatter to all the winds.

11 'Therefore, *as* I live,' says the Lord GOD, 'surely, because you have [c]defiled My sanctuary with all your detestable things and with all your abominations, therefore I will also diminish *you;* [d]My eye will not spare, nor will I have any pity.

12 'One-third of you shall die of the pestilence, and be consumed with famine in your midst; and one-third shall fall by the sword all around you; and I will [e]scatter another third to all the winds, and I will draw out a sword after [f]them.

13 'Thus shall My anger be spent, and I will cause My fury to rest upon them, and I will be [g]avenged; and they shall know that I, the LORD, have [h]spoken *it* in My zeal, when I have spent My fury upon them.

14 'Moreover I will make you a [i]waste and a reproach among the nations that *are* all around you, in the sight of all who pass by.

15 'So it* shall be a [j]reproach, a taunt, a [k]lesson, and an [l]astonishment to the nations that *are* all around you, when I execute judgments among you in anger and in fury and in furious rebukes. I, the LORD, have spoken.

16 'When I send against them the terrible arrows of famine which shall be for destruction, which I will send to destroy you, I will increase the famine upon you and cut off your supply of bread.

17 'So I will send against you famine and wild [m]beasts, and they will bereave you. Pestilence and blood shall pass through you, and I will bring the sword against you. I, the LORD, have spoken.' "

Idolaters to be punished;
a remnant to be spared (v. 8)

6 NOW the word of the LORD came to me, saying:

2 "Son of man, set your face toward the [n]mountains of Israel, and prophesy against them,

3 "and say, 'O mountains of Israel, hear the word of the Lord GOD! Thus says the Lord GOD to the mountains, to the hills, to the ravines, and to the valleys: "Indeed I, *even* I, will bring a sword against you, and I will [o]destroy your high places.

4 "Then your altars shall be desolate, your incense altars shall be broken, and I will [o]cast down your slain *men* before your idols.

5 "And I will lay the corpses of the children of Israel before their idols, and I will scatter your [p]bones all around your altars.

6 "In all your dwelling places the cities shall be laid waste, and the high places shall be desolate, so that your altars may be laid waste and made desolate, your idols may be broken and made to cease, your incense altars may be cut down, and your works may be abolished.

7 "The slain shall fall in your midst, and you shall know that I *am* the LORD.

8 "Yet I will leave a [q]remnant, so that you may have *some* who escape the sword among the nations, when you are [r]scattered through the countries.

9 "Then those of you who escape will [s]remember Me among the nations where they are carried captive, because I was crushed by their adulterous heart which has departed from Me, and by their eyes which play the harlot after their idols; they will [t]loathe themselves for the evils which they committed in all their abominations.

10 "And they shall know that I *am* the LORD; I have not said in vain that I would bring this calamity upon them."

Idolaters to be slain

11 'Thus says the Lord GOD: [u]"Pound your fists and stamp your feet, and say, 'Alas, for all the evil abominations of the house of Israel! For they shall [r]fall by the sword, by famine, and by pestilence.

12 'He who is far off shall die by the pestilence, he who is near shall fall by the sword, and he who remains and is besieged shall die by the famine. [v]Thus will I spend My fury upon them.

13 'Then you shall know that I *am* the LORD, when their slain are among their idols all around their altars, [w]on

9 *a* Lam. 4:6; Dan. 9:12; cp. Mt. 24:21
10 *b* v. 12; Lev. 26:33; Dt. 28:64; Ezek. 12:14; Zech. 2:6
11 *c* Jer. 7:9–11; Ezek. 8:5–6,16 *d* Ezek. 7:4, 9; 8:18; 9:10
12 *e* vv. 2,10; Jer. 9:16; Ezek. 6:8 *f* Jer. 43:10–11; 44:27
13 *g* Isa. 1:24 *h* Ezek. 36:6; 38:19
14 *i* Lev. 26:31–32; Neh. 2:17
15 *j* Dt. 28:37; 1 Ki. 9:7; Ps. 79:4; Jer. 24:9; Lam. 2:15 *k* Isa. 26:9; cp. 1 Cor. 10:11 *l* Jer. 25:11
17 *m* Dt. 32:24; Ezek. 14:15
CHAPTER 6
2 *n* Ezek. 36:1
3 *o* Lev. 26:30; see Jud. 3:7 and 1 Ki. 3:2, *notes*
5 *p* Cp. 2 Ki. 23:14,16, 20; Jer. 8:1–2
8 *q Remnant:* vv. 8, 11–14; Ezek. 9:4. (Isa. 1:9; Rom. 11:5, *note*) *r* Ezek. 5:12
9 *s* Dt. 4:29; Jer. 51:50 *t* Ezek. 20:43

6:11 *u* Ezek. 21:14 **6:12** *v* Ezek. 5:13 **6:13** *w* vv. 4–5; Jer. 3:6

*

5:15 Septuagint, Syriac, Targum, and Vulgate read *you.*

every high hill, on all the [a]mountain-
tops, [b]under every green tree, and under every thick oak, wherever they offered sweet incense to all their idols.
14 'So I will stretch out My hand
against them and make the land desolate, yes, more desolate than the wilderness toward Diblah, in all their
dwelling places. Then they shall know
that I *am* the LORD.' " ' "

Babylonian invasion near

7 MOREOVER the word of the LORD
came to me, saying,
2 "And you, son of man, thus says
the Lord GOD to the land of Israel:

[c]'An end! The end has come
upon the four corners of the
land.
3 Now the end *has come* upon
you,
And I will send My anger
against you;
I will judge you [d]according to
your ways,
And I will repay you for all
your abominations.
4 [e]My eye will not spare you,
Nor will I have pity;
But I will repay your ways,
And your abominations will be
in your midst;
Then you shall [f]know that I
am the LORD!'
5 "Thus says the Lord GOD:

'A disaster, a singular
[g]disaster;
Behold, it has come!
6 An end has come,
The end has come;
It has dawned for you;
Behold, it has come!
7 Doom has come to you, you
who dwell in the land;
The [h]time has come,
A day of trouble *is* near,
And not of rejoicing in the
mountains.
8 Now upon you I will soon pour
out My fury,
And spend My anger upon
you;
I will judge you according to
your ways,
And I will repay you for all
your abominations.
9 'My eye will not spare,
Nor will I have pity;

13
a Hos. 4:13
b Isa. 57:5
CHAPTER 7
2
c vv. 3,6; Amos 8:2; cp. Mt. 24:6,13–14
3
d Rom. 2:6
4
e v. 9; Ezek. 5:11; 8:18; 9:10
f v. 27; Ezek. 6:7; 12:20
5
g 2 Ki. 21:12–13
7
h v. 12; Zeph. 1:14–15

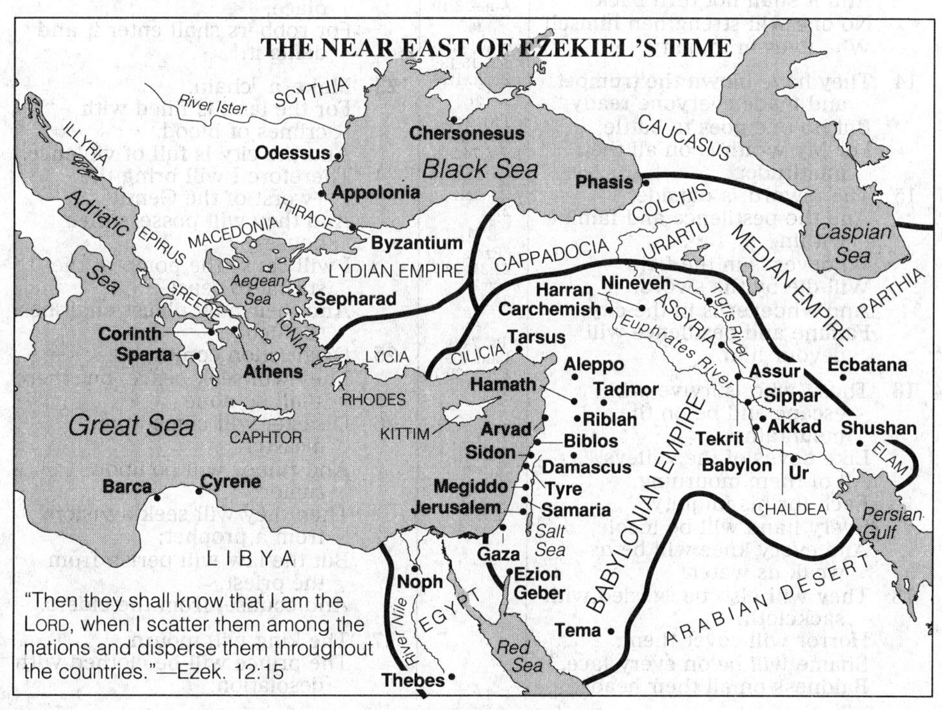

"Then they shall know that I am the LORD, when I scatter them among the nations and disperse them throughout the countries."—Ezek. 12:15

I will repay you according to
your ways,
And your abominations will be
in your midst.
Then you shall know that I *am*
the LORD who strikes.

10 'Behold, the day!
Behold, it has come!
Doom has gone out;
The rod has blossomed,
Pride has budded.
11 Violence has risen up into a
rod of wickedness;
None of them *shall remain,*
None of their multitude,
None of them;
Nor *shall there be* wailing for
them.
12 The [a]time has come,
The day draws [b]near.

'Let not the buyer [c]rejoice,
Nor the seller [d]mourn,
For wrath *is* on their whole
multitude.
13 For the seller shall not return
to what has been sold,
Though he may still be alive;
For the vision concerns the
whole multitude,
And it shall not turn back;
No one will strengthen himself
Who lives in iniquity.

14 'They have blown the trumpet
and made everyone ready,
But no one goes to battle;
For My wrath *is* on all their
multitude.
15 The [e]sword *is* outside,
And the pestilence and famine
within.
Whoever *is* in the field
Will die by the sword;
And whoever *is* in the city,
Famine and pestilence will
devour him.

16 'Those who [f]survive will
escape and be on the
mountains
Like doves of the valleys,
All of them mourning,
Each for his iniquity.
17 [g]Every hand will be feeble,
And every knee will be *as*
weak *as* water.
18 They will also be [h]girded with
sackcloth;
Horror will cover them;
Shame *will be* on every face,
Baldness on all their heads.

12
a v. 7
b Cp. 1 Cor. 7:29–31; Jas. 5:8–9
c Prov. 20:14
d Isa. 24:2
15
e Jer. 14:18; Lam. 1:20; Ezek. 5:12
16
f Ezek. 6:8; 14:22
17
g Isa. 13:7; Jer. 6:24; Ezek. 21:7
18
h Isa. 3:24; 15:2–3; Jer. 48:37; Amos 8:10
19
i Prov. 11:4; Jer. 15:13; Zeph. 1:18
21
j 2 Ki. 24:13; Jer. 20:5
k Ps. 74:2–8
23
l Cp. Jer. 27:2
24
m Ezek. 21:31; 28:7
n Ezek. 24:21
26
o Ps. 74:9; Lam. 2:9; Ezek. 20:1, 3

19 'They will throw their silver
into the streets,
And their gold will be like
refuse;
[i]Their silver and their gold will
not be able to deliver them
In the day of the wrath of the
LORD;
They will not satisfy their
souls,
Nor fill their stomachs,
Because it became their
stumbling block of iniquity.

The temple to be profaned by Babylonians

20 'As for the beauty of his
ornaments,
He set it in majesty;
But they made from it
The images of their
abominations—
Their detestable things;
Therefore I have made it
Like refuse to them.
21 I will give it as [j]plunder
Into the hands of strangers,
And to the wicked of the earth
as spoil;
And they shall [k]defile it.
22 I will turn My face from them,
And they will defile My secret
place;
For robbers shall enter it and
defile it.

23 'Make a [l]chain,
For the land is filled with
crimes of blood,
And the city is full of violence.
24 Therefore I will bring the
[m]worst of the Gentiles,
And they will possess their
houses;
I will cause the pomp of the
strong to cease,
And their holy places shall be
[n]defiled.
25 Destruction comes;
They will seek peace, but *there
shall be* none.
26 Disaster will come upon
disaster,
And rumor will be upon
rumor.
[o]Then they will seek a vision
from a prophet;
But the law will perish from
the priest,
And counsel from the elders.
27 'The king will mourn,
The prince will be clothed with
desolation,

And the hands of the common
people will tremble.
I will do to them according to
their way,
And according to what they
deserve I will judge them;
Then they shall [1]know that I
am the LORD!' "

Another vision of glory

8 [a]AND it came to pass in the sixth
[b]year, in the [c]sixth *month,* on the
fifth *day* of the month, as I sat in my
house with the [d]elders of Judah sitting before me, that the hand of the
Lord GOD fell upon me there.
2 Then I looked, and there was a
likeness, like the appearance of fire—
from the appearance of His waist and
downward, fire; and from His waist
and upward, like the appearance of
brightness, like the color of [e]amber.
3 He stretched out the form of a
hand, and took me by a [2]lock of my
hair; and the [f]Spirit [g]lifted me up between earth and heaven, and brought
me in [3]visions of God to Jerusalem, to
the door of the north gate of the inner
court, [h]where the seat of the image of
jealousy *was,* [i]which provokes to
jealousy.
4 And behold, the [j]glory of the
God of Israel *was* there, like the vision
that I saw in the [k]plain.

The temple defiled

5 Then He said to me, "Son of
man, lift your eyes now toward the
north." So I lifted my eyes toward the
north, and there, north of the altar
gate, was this image of jealousy in the
entrance.
6 Furthermore He said to me, "Son
of man, do you see what they are doing, the great [l]abominations that the
house of Israel commits here, to make
Me go far away from My sanctuary?
Now turn again, you will see greater
abominations."
7 So He brought me to the door of
the court; and when I looked, there
was a hole in the wall.
8 Then He said to me, "Son of
man, dig into the wall"; and when I
dug into the wall, there was a door.
9 And He said to me, "Go in, and
see the wicked abominations which
they are doing there."
10 So I went in and saw, and
there—every [m]sort of [n]creeping thing,
abominable beasts, and all the idols of
the house of Israel, portrayed all
around on the walls.
11 And there stood before them
[o]seventy men of the elders of the
house of Israel, and in their midst
stood Jaazaniah the son of Shaphan.
Each man had a censer in his hand,
and a thick cloud of incense went up.
12 Then He said to me, "Son of
man, have you seen what the elders of
the house of Israel do in the dark, every man in the room of his idols? For
they say, 'The LORD does [p]not see us,
the LORD has forsaken the land.' "
13 And He said to me, "Turn again,
and you will see greater abominations
that they are doing."
14 So He brought me to the door of
the north gate of the LORD's house; and
to my dismay, women were sitting
there weeping for [q]Tammuz.
15 Then He said to me, "Have you
seen *this,* O son of man? Turn again,
you will see greater abominations
than these."
16 So He brought me into the inner
court of the LORD's house; and there, at
the door of the temple of the LORD,
[r]between the porch and the altar,
were about [s]twenty-five men with
their backs toward the temple of the

CHAPTER 8

1
a Cp. Ezek. 1:1–2
b c. 592 B.C.
c See Lev. 23:2, *note*
d Ezek. 14:1; 20:1; 33:31

2
e Ezek. 1:27

3
f Holy Spirit (OT): v. 3; Ezek. 11:1. (Gen. 1:2; Zech. 12:10)
g Acts 8:39; cp. 2 Cor. 12:2–4
h Jer. 7:30; 32:34; Ezek. 5:11
i Dt. 32:16, 21

4
j Ezek. 3:12; 9:3
k Or *valley.* Ezek. 1:28; 3:22–23

6
l 2 Ki. 23:4–5

10
m Ex. 20:4; Dt. 4:16–18
n Rom. 1:23

11
o Num. 11:16,25

12
p Isa. 29:15; Ezek. 9:9

14
q i.e. *the Greek Adonis*

16
r Joel 2:17
s Ezek. 11:1

[1](7:27) Divine justice is one of the evidences of the living God. Just as the LORD announces through Ezekiel that retribution upon the wicked leaders of Israel will convince them that He is the LORD ("they shall know that I am the LORD"), so in the final judgment of the wicked the ultimate justice of God will leave no doubt of His reality.

[2](8:3) It had been a year or more since Ezekiel was required to shave off the hair of his head and his beard, so that his hair had had ample time to grow in. Cp. Ezek. 1:1; 5:1.

[3](8:3) The four visions of ch. 8 emphasize the profanation of God in the very temple set aside to His worship. Idolatry was present and unchecked (vv. 5,10–11); women were participating in the immoral cult of Tammuz; and sun worshipers brazenly turned their backs to the temple (v. 16). Although Ezekiel was actually by the River Chebar (1:1,3; 3:23; 10:15,20,22; 43:3), in a vision he was transported back to Jerusalem. These profanations going on in the temple area were shown to the prophet so that he might justify to the new generation, born and growing up in Assyria and Babylon, the righteousness of God in the present chastening. Because of sins like these, past and present, the captivities were necessitated. This strain continues through the book to 33:21. Interspersed with the various visions are promises of restoration and blessing to be brought about by Israel's repentance. See Israel (Gen. 12:2–3; Rom. 11:26, *note*); also Kingdom (OT) (Gen. 1:26–28; Zech. 12:6–8 and *note* at v. 8).

LORD and their faces toward the east,
and they were worshiping the [a]sun
toward the east.
17 And He said to me, "Have you
seen *this,* O son of man? Is it a trivial
thing to the house of Judah to commit
the abominations which they commit
here? For they have filled the land
with violence; then they have returned to provoke Me to anger. Indeed
they [b]put the branch to their nose.
18 "Therefore I also will act in fury.
My eye will not [c]spare nor will I have
pity; and though they [d]cry in My ears
with a loud voice, I will not hear
them."

Vision of the slaying in Jerusalem

9 THEN He called out in my hearing with a loud voice, saying, "Let
those who have charge over the city
draw near, each *with* a deadly
weapon in his hand."
2 And suddenly six men came
from the direction of the upper gate,
which faces north, each with his
battle-ax in his hand. One man among
them *was* clothed with [e]linen and had
a writer's inkhorn at his side. They
went in and stood beside the bronze
altar.
3 Now the [f]glory of the God of Israel had [1]gone up from the cherub,
where it had been, to the threshold of
the temple.* And He called to the man
clothed with linen, who *had* the
writer's inkhorn at his side;
4 and the LORD said to him, "Go
through the midst of the city, through
the midst of Jerusalem, and put a
mark on the [g]foreheads of the [h]men
who sigh and cry over all the abominations that are done within it."
5 To the others He said in my
hearing, "Go after him through the
city and [i]kill; do not let your eye
spare, nor have any pity.
6 [j]"Utterly slay old *and* young
men, maidens and little children and
women; but do not come near anyone
on whom *is* the mark; and [k]begin at
My sanctuary." So they began with
the [l]elders who *were* before the temple.
7 Then He said to them, "Defile
the temple, and fill the courts with the
slain. Go out!" And they went out and
killed in the city.
8 So it was, that while they were
killing them, I was left *alone;* and I fell
on my face and cried out, and [m]said,
"Ah, Lord GOD! Will You destroy all
the remnant of Israel in pouring out
Your fury on Jerusalem?"
9 Then He said to me, "The iniquity of the house of Israel and Judah *is*
exceedingly great, and the [n]land is
full of bloodshed, and the city full of
perversity; for they say, 'The LORD has
forsaken the land, and the LORD does
[o]not see!'
10 "And as for Me also, My eye will
[p]neither spare, nor will I have pity,
but I will recompense their deeds on
their own head."
11 Just then, the man clothed with
linen, who *had* the inkhorn at his side,
reported back and said, "I have done
as You commanded me."

Vision of God's glory departing from the temple at Jerusalem (v. 18)

10 AND I looked, and there in the
[q]firmament that was above the
head of the cherubim, there appeared
something like a sapphire stone, having the appearance of the likeness of
a throne.
2 Then He spoke to the man
[r]clothed with linen, and said, "Go in
among the wheels, under the cherub,
fill [s]your hands with [t]coals of fire
from among the cherubim, and [u]scat-
ter *them* over the city." And he went in
as I watched.
3 Now the cherubim were standing on the south side of the temple*
when the man went in, and the [v]cloud
filled the inner court.
4 Then the glory of the LORD went
up from the cherub, *and paused* over
the threshold of the temple; and the
[w]house was filled with the cloud, and
the court was full of the brightness of
the LORD's [x]glory.
5 And the [y]sound of the wings of
the cherubim was heard *even* in the
outer court, like the [z]voice of Almighty God when He speaks.

16 *a* Dt. 4:19; 2 Ki. 23:5, 11; Jer. 8:6
17 *b* i.e. *an insulting gesture*
18 *c* Ezek. 5:11 *d* Prov. 1:28; Isa. 1:15; Jer. 11:11; 14:12; Mic. 3:4; Zech. 7:13
CHAPTER 9
2 *e* Ezek. 10:2
3 *f* Ezek. 3:23; 8:4; 10:4, 18; 11:22, 23
4 *g* Rev. 7:3; 9:4; 20:4; cp. Ex. 12:7,23; Rev. 13:16–17 *h Remnant:* v. 4; Ezek. 11:16. (Isa. 1:9; Rom. 11:5, *note*)
5 *i* Ezek. 7:9
6 *j* 2 Chr. 36:17 *k* 1 Pet. 4:17 *l* Ezek. 8:11–12
8 *m Bible prayers (OT):* v. 8; Dan. 9:3. (Gen. 15:2; Hab. 3:1)
9 *n* Ezek. 8:17; cp. 2 Ki. 21:16 *o* Ezek. 8:12
10 *p* Ezek. 5:11; 8:18; 11:21
CHAPTER 10
1 *q* Ezek. 1:22,23,25, 26
2 *r* Ezek. 9:2, 3; Dan. 10:5 *s* Lit. *the hollow of your hands* *t* Cp. Isa. 6:6 *u* Cp. Rev. 8:5
10:3 *v* 1 Ki. 8:10–11 **10:4** *w* Ezek. 43:5 *x* Ezek. 11:22–23 **10:5** *y* Ezek. 1:24; 3:13 *z* Ps. 29:3–5,7–9

*
9:3 Literally *house* **10:3** Literally *house*, also in verses 4 and 18

[1](9:3) It is noteworthy that to Ezekiel the priest was given the vision of the glory of the LORD departing (1) from the cherubim to the threshold of the temple (v. 3; 10:4); (2) from the threshold (10:18); (3) from temple and city to the mountain on the east of Jerusalem, Olivet (11:23); and (4) returning to the millennial temple to abide (43:2–5).

6 Then it happened, when He
commanded the man clothed in linen,
saying, "Take fire from among the
wheels, from among the cherubim,"
that he went in and stood beside the
wheels.
7 And the cherub stretched out his
hand from among the cherubim to the
fire that *was* among the cherubim,
and took *some of it* and put *it* into the
hands of the *man* clothed with linen,
who took *it* and went out.
8 The cherubim appeared to have
the form of a man's hand under their
[a]wings.
9 And when I looked, there were
[b]four wheels by the cherubim, one
wheel by one cherub and another
wheel by each other cherub; the
wheels appeared *to have* the color of
a beryl stone.
10 *As for* their appearance, all four
looked alike—as it were, a wheel in
the middle of a wheel.
11 [c]When they went, they went toward *any of* their four directions; they
did not turn aside when they went, but
followed in the direction the head was
facing. They did not turn aside when
they went.
12 And their whole [d]body, with
their back, their hands, their wings,
and the wheels that the four had, *were*
[e]full of eyes all around.
13 As for the wheels, they were
called in my hearing, "Wheel."
14 Each one had [f]four [g]faces: the
first face *was* the face of a cherub, the
second face the face of a man, the
third the face of a lion, and the fourth
the face of an eagle.
15 And the cherubim were lifted up.
[h]This *was* the living creature I saw by
the River Chebar.
16 When the cherubim went, the
wheels went beside them; and when
the cherubim lifted their wings to
mount up from the earth, the same
wheels also did not turn from beside
them.
17 When *the cherubim** stood still,
the wheels stood still, and when *one**
was lifted up, *the other** lifted itself
up, for the [i]spirit of the living creature
was in [i]them.
18 Then the glory of the LORD [j]de-
parted from the threshold of the temple and stood over the cherubim.
19 And the cherubim lifted their
wings and mounted up from the earth
in my sight. When they went out, the
wheels *were* beside them; and they
stood at the door of the [k]east gate of
the LORD's house, and the glory of the
God of Israel *was* above them.
20 [l]This *is* the living creature I saw
under the God of Israel by the River
Chebar, and I knew they *were* cherubim.
21 Each one had four faces and
each one four wings, and the likeness
of the hands of a man *was* under their
wings.
22 And the likeness of their faces
was the same *as* the faces which I had
seen by the River Chebar, their appearance and their persons. They
each went straight [m]forward.

Wicked leaders to be judged

11 THEN the [n]Spirit lifted me up
and brought me to the [o]East
Gate of the LORD's house, which faces
eastward; and there at the door of the
gate were [p]twenty-five men, among
whom I saw Jaazaniah the son of [q]Az-
zur, and Pelatiah the son of Benaiah,
princes of the people.
2 And He said to me: "Son of man,
these *are* the men who [r]devise iniquity and give wicked counsel in this
city,
3 "who say, '*The time is* not near
to build houses; this *city is* the caldron, and we *are* the meat.'
4 "Therefore prophesy against
them, prophesy, O son of man!"
5 Then the [n]Spirit of the LORD fell
upon me, and said to me, "Speak!
'Thus says the LORD: "Thus you have
said, O house of Israel; for I [s]know the
things that come into your mind.
6 "You have [t]multiplied your
slain in this city, and you have filled its
streets with the slain."
7 'Therefore thus says the Lord
GOD: "Your slain whom you have laid
in its midst, they *are* the meat, and this
city is the [u]caldron; but I shall [v]bring
you out of the midst of it.
8 "You have [w]feared the sword;
and I will bring a sword upon you,"
says the Lord GOD.
9 "And I will bring you out of its
midst, and deliver you into the hands
of [x]strangers, and execute judgments
on you.
10 [y]"You shall fall by the sword. I
will judge you at the border of Israel.
Then you shall know that I *am* the
LORD.
11 "This *city* shall not be your caldron, nor shall you be the meat in its

*
10:17 Literally *they* • Literally *they* • Literally *they*

8
a Ezek. 1:8
9
b Ezek. 1:15
11
c Ezek. 1:17
12
d Lit. *flesh*
e Rev. 4:6,8
14
f Ezek. 1:6, 10–11; Rev. 4:7
g vv. 21–22
15
h See Ezek. 1:5, *note*
17
i Ezek. 1:21
18
j v. 4
19
k Ezek. 11:1
20
l Ezek. 10:15; 1:22
22
m Ezek. 1:9, 12
CHAPTER 11
1
n *Holy Spirit* (OT): vv. 1,5; Ezek. 11:24. (Gen. 1:2; Zech. 12:10)
o Ezek. 10:19
p Ezek. 8:16
q Cp. Jer. 28:1
2
r Mic. 2:1
5
s Jer. 16:17; 17:10; cp. 1 Chr. 28:9
6
t Ezek. 22:2–3
7
u v. 3; cp. Ezek. 24:3–11; Mic. 3:3
v Cp. 2 Ki. 25:18–21
8
w Jer. 42:16
9
x Dt. 28:36
10
y Jer. 39:6; 52:10

midst. I will judge you at the border of Israel.

12 "And you shall know that I *am* the LORD; for you have not walked in My statutes nor executed [a]My judgments, but have done according to the customs of the Gentiles which *are* all around you." ' "

13 Now it happened, while I was prophesying, that Pelatiah the son of Benaiah died. Then I fell on my face and cried with a loud voice, and said, "Ah, Lord GOD! Will You make a complete end of the remnant of Israel?"

Promise of restoration of remnant of Israel to the land

14 Again the word of the LORD came to me, saying,

15 "Son of man, your brethren, your relatives, your countrymen, and [b]all the house of Israel in its entirety, *are* those about whom the inhabitants of Jerusalem have said, 'Get far away from the LORD; this land has been given to us as a possession.'

16 "Therefore say, 'Thus says the Lord GOD: "Although I have cast them far off among the Gentiles, and although I have [c]scattered them among the countries, yet I shall be a little [1d]sanctuary for them in the countries where they have gone." '

17 "Therefore say, 'Thus says the Lord GOD: "I will [e]gather you from the peoples, assemble you from the countries where you have been scattered, and I will give you the land of Israel." '

18 "And they will go there, and they will take away all its [f]detestable things and all its abominations from there.

19 "Then I will [g]give them one heart, and I will [h]put a new spirit within them,* and take the stony heart out of their flesh, and give them a heart of flesh,

20 "that they may walk in My statutes and keep My judgments and do them; and [i]they shall be My people, and I will be their God.

21 "But *as for those* whose hearts follow the desire for their detestable things and their abominations, I will recompense their deeds on their own heads," says the Lord GOD.

Vision of glory departing from Mount of Olives (cp. Ezek. 43:1–4)

22 So the cherubim lifted up their wings, with the wheels beside them, and the glory of the God of Israel *was* high above them.

23 And the [j]glory of the LORD [k]went up from the midst of the [2]city and stood on the mountain, which *is* on the east side of the city.

24 Then the [l]Spirit took me up and brought me in a vision by the Spirit of God into Chaldea,* to those in captivity. And the vision that I had seen went up from me.

25 So I spoke to those in captivity of all the things the LORD had shown me.

Sign of Ezekiel's preparation for moving; the prince to be taken captive

12 NOW the word of the LORD came to me, saying:

2 "Son of man, you dwell in the midst of a rebellious house, which has eyes to see but does [m]not see, and ears to hear but does [m]not hear; for they *are* a rebellious house.

3 "Therefore, son of man, prepare your belongings for [n]captivity, and go into captivity by day in their sight. You shall go from your place into captivity to another place in their sight. [o]It may be that they will consider, though they *are* a rebellious house.

4 "By day you shall bring out your belongings in their sight, as though going into [n]captivity; and at evening you shall go in their sight, like those who go into captivity.

5 "Dig through the wall in their sight, and carry your belongings out through it.

6 "In their sight you shall bear *them* on *your* shoulders *and* carry *them* out at twilight; you shall cover your face, so that you cannot see the

12 *a* Ezek. 20:24
15 *b Kingdom* (OT): vv. 14–20; Ezek. 16:13. (Gen. 1:26; Zech. 12:8, *note*)
16 *c Remnant:* vv. 16–21; Joel 2:32. (Isa. 1:9; Rom. 11:5, *note*) *d* Isa. 8:14
17 *e* Isa. 11:11–16; Jer. 24:6; Ezek. 28:25; 34:13; 36:24
18 *f* Ezek. 37:23
19 *g* Jer. 32:39; Ezek. 36:26 *h* Jer. 31:33; cp. Ps. 51:10; Ezek. 18:31
20 *i* Jer. 24:7; Ezek. 14:11; 36:28; 37:27
23 *j* Ezek. 8:4; 9:3; 10:4, 18; 43:4 *k* Cp. 1 Ki. 8:5–11; Ezra 3:12; Ezek. 43:2–5
24 *l Holy Spirit* (OT): v. 24; Ezek. 36:27. (Gen. 1:2; Zech. 12:10)
CHAPTER 12
2 *m* Jer. 5:21; Mt. 13:13–14; cp. Jn. 9:39–41 12:3 *n* Jer. 10:17–18 *o* Cp. Jer. 36:3; Lk. 20:13; 2 Tim. 2:25

* **11:19** Literally *you* **11:24** Or *Babylon*, and so elsewhere in this book

[1](11:16) Even in drastic judgment, as in the case of the dispersion of Israel, God provides for His people a place of refuge. This refuge, called here "a little sanctuary," is the LORD Himself (cp. Ps. 90:1; 91:9; Isa. 4:6). So with all of God's own, Gentile as well as Jew, in the midst of deserved judgment there is still a sanctuary of refuge and peace in Him.

[2](11:23) The departure of the divine glory (the visible symbol of God's presence) from the temple, marks the end of the theocratic kingdom in OT history. On the mount of transfiguration the glory of God was manifested to our Lord's disciples (Mt. 17:1–5; cp. also Jn. 1:14; 2 Cor. 4:6; Jas. 2:1; 2 Pet. 1:16–18). The visible glory will return when the kingdom is restored to Israel (Ezek. 43:1–7; Rev. 21:22–24).

ground, for I have made you a [a]sign to
the house of Israel."
7 So I did as I was commanded. I
brought out my belongings by day, as
though going into captivity, and at
evening I dug through the wall with
my hand. I brought *them* out at twilight, *and* I bore *them* on *my* shoulder
in their sight.
8 And in the morning the word of
the LORD came to me, saying,
9 "Son of man, has not the house
of Israel, the rebellious house, said to
you, [b]'What are you doing?'
10 "Say to them, 'Thus says the
Lord GOD: "This [c]burden *concerns* the
prince in Jerusalem and all the house
of Israel who are among them." '
11 "Say, 'I *am* a sign to you. As I
have done, so shall it be done to them;
they shall be carried away into captivity.'
12 "And the [d]prince who *is* among
them shall bear *his belongings* on *his*
shoulder at twilight and go out. They
shall dig through the wall to carry
them out through it. He shall cover his
face, so that he cannot see the ground
with *his* eyes.
13 "I will also spread My net over
him, and [e]he shall be caught in My
snare. I will bring him to Babylon, *to*
the land of the Chaldeans; yet he shall
[f]not see it, though he shall die there.
14 "I will [g]scatter to every wind all
who *are* around him to help him, and
all his troops; and I will draw out the
sword after them.
15 "Then they shall [h]know that I
am the LORD, when I scatter them
among the nations and disperse them
throughout the countries.
16 "But I will spare a few of their
men from the sword, from famine, and
from pestilence, that they may declare
all their abominations among the
Gentiles wherever they go. Then they
shall know that I *am* the LORD."

Full captivity near at hand
(cp. 2 Ki. 25:1–10)

17 Moreover the word of the LORD
came to me, saying,
18 "Son of man, eat your bread with
quaking, and drink your water with
trembling and [i]anxiety.
19 "And say to the people of the
land, 'Thus says the Lord GOD to the
inhabitants of Jerusalem *and* to the
land of Israel: "They shall eat their
bread with [i]anxiety, and drink their
water with dread, so that her land may
be emptied of all who are in it, because
of the violence of all those who dwell
in it.
20 "Then the cities that are inhabited shall be laid waste, and the land
shall become desolate; and you shall
know that I *am* the LORD." ' "
21 And the word of the LORD came
to me, saying,
22 "Son of man, what *is* this proverb *that* you *people* have about the
land of Israel, which says, 'The [j]days
are prolonged, and every vision fails'?
23 "Tell them therefore, 'Thus says
the Lord GOD: "I will lay this proverb
to rest, and they shall no more use it as
a proverb in Israel." But say to them,
"The [k]days are at hand, and the fulfillment of every vision.
24 "For no more shall there be any
[l]false vision or flattering divination
within the house of Israel.
25 "For I *am* the LORD. I speak, and
the word which I speak will come to
pass; it will no more be postponed;
[1]for in your days, O rebellious house,
I will say the [m]word and [n]perform it,"
says the Lord GOD.' "
26 Again the word of the LORD came
to me, saying,
27 "Son of man, look, the house of
Israel is saying, 'The vision that he
sees *is* [o]for many days *from now*, and
he prophesies of times far off.'
28 "Therefore say to them, 'Thus
says the Lord GOD: "None of My words
will be postponed any more, but the
word which I speak [p]will be done,"
says the Lord GOD.' "

Lying prophets condemned

13 AND the word of the LORD
came to me, saying,
2 "Son of man, prophesy [q]against
the prophets of Israel who prophesy,
and say to those who prophesy out of
their own [r]heart, 'Hear the word of
the LORD!' "
3 Thus says the Lord GOD: "Woe to
the foolish prophets, who follow their
own spirit and have seen nothing!
4 "O Israel, your prophets are like
foxes in the deserts.

6 [a] v. 11; Ezek. 4:3; 24:24; see Isa. 8:18, *note*
9 [b] Ezek. 24:19; cp. 17:12; 20:49
10 [c] See Isa. 13:1, *note* 1
12 [d] Jer. 39:4; 52:7
13 [e] Jer. 32:4–5; 39:5; 52:8–9 [f] Jer. 52:11
14 [g] 2 Ki. 25:4–5; Ezek. 5:10
15 [h] vv. 16,20; Ps. 9:16; Ezek. 6:7, 14; 11:10
18 [i] Ezek. 4:16
22 [j] v. 27; Jer. 5:12; 17:15; Ezek. 11:3; cp. 2 Pet. 3:4
23 [k] Joel 2:1; Zeph. 1:14
24 [l] Jer. 14:13–16; Ezek. 13:6; cp. Zech. 13:2–4
25 [m] v. 28; Isa. 55:11; Dan. 9:12; Lk. 21:33 [n] Num. 23:19; Isa. 14:24
27 [o] v. 22; Dan. 10:14
28 [p] v. 25; Jer. 4:7; cp. Mt. 24:48–50
CHAPTER 13
2 [q] Isa. 28:7; Jer. 23:1–40; Lam. 2:14; Ezek. 22:25–28 [r] Jer. 14:14

[1](12:25) It must be borne in mind that, although the prophet was in Babylon, he prophesied as though he were in the land. This was during the eleven years' interval between the first and the final deportation. See Ezek. 8:3, *note*.

5 [a]"You have not gone up into the gaps to build a wall for the house of Israel to stand in battle on the day of the LORD.

6 "They have envisioned [b]futility and false divination, saying, 'Thus says the LORD!' But the LORD has [c]not sent them; yet they hope that the word may be confirmed.

7 "Have you not seen a futile vision, and have you not spoken false divination? You say, 'The LORD says,' but I have not spoken."

8 Therefore thus says the Lord GOD: "Because you have spoken nonsense and envisioned lies, therefore I *am* indeed against you," says the Lord GOD.

9 "My hand will be [d]against the prophets who envision futility and who [e]divine lies; they shall not be in the assembly of My people, [f]nor be written in the record of the house of Israel, nor shall they enter into the land of Israel. Then you shall know that I *am* the Lord GOD.

10 "Because, indeed, because they have seduced My people, saying, [g]'Peace!' when *there is* no [h]peace—and one builds a wall, and they [i]plaster it with [j]untempered *mortar*—

11 "say to those who plaster *it* with [j]untempered *mortar*, that it will fall. There will be [k]flooding rain, and you, O great hailstones, shall fall; and a stormy wind shall tear *it* down.

12 "Surely, when the wall has fallen, will it not be said to you, 'Where *is* the mortar with which you plastered *it*?'"

13 Therefore thus says the Lord GOD: "I will cause a stormy wind to break forth in My fury; and there shall be a flooding rain in My anger, and great hailstones in fury to consume *it*.

14 "So I will break down the wall you have plastered with [j]untempered *mortar*, and bring it down to the ground, so that its foundation will be uncovered; it will fall, and you shall be consumed in the midst of it. Then you shall [l]know that I *am* the LORD.

15 "Thus will I accomplish My wrath on the wall and on those who have plastered it with [j]untempered *mortar;* and I will say to you, 'The wall *is* no *more*, nor those who plastered it,

16 '*that is*, the prophets of Israel who prophesy concerning Jerusalem, and who [m]see visions of peace for her when *there is* no peace,'" says the Lord GOD.

17 "Likewise, son of man, set your face against the daughters of your people, who prophesy out of their own heart; prophesy against them,

18 "and say, 'Thus says the Lord GOD: "Woe to the *women* who sew *magic* charms on their sleeves* and make veils for the heads of people of every height to hunt souls! [n]Will you hunt the souls of My people, and keep yourselves alive?

19 "And will you profane Me among My people for handfuls of barley and [o]for pieces of bread, killing people who should not die, and keeping people alive who should not live, by your lying to My people who listen to lies?"

20 'Therefore thus says the Lord GOD: "Behold, I *am* against your *magic* charms by which you hunt souls there like birds. I will tear them from your arms, and let the souls go, the souls you hunt like birds.

21 "I will also tear off your veils and deliver My people out of your hand, and they shall no longer be as prey in your hand. Then you shall know that I *am* the LORD.

22 "Because with [p]lies you have made the heart of the righteous sad, whom I have not made sad; and you have [q]strengthened the hands of the wicked, so that he does not turn from his wicked way to save his life.

23 "Therefore you shall no longer envision [r]futility nor practice divination; for I will deliver My people out of your hand, and you shall know that I *am* the LORD."'"

Idolatrous elders of Israel condemned

14 NOW some of the elders of Israel [s]came to me and sat before me.

2 And the word of the LORD came to me, saying,

3 "Son of man, these men have set up their idols in their hearts, and put before them [t]that which causes them to stumble into iniquity. Should I let Myself be [u]inquired of at all by them?

4 "Therefore speak to them, and say to them, 'Thus says the Lord GOD: "Everyone of the house of Israel who sets up his idols in his heart, and puts before him what causes him to stumble into iniquity, and then comes to the prophet, I the LORD will answer him who comes, according to the multitude of his idols,

5
a Ezek. 22:30; cp. Ps. 106:23, 30
6
b Jer. 29:8–9
c Jer. 27:8–15
9
d Jer. 23:30
e Jer. 20:3–6
f Ezra 2:59, 62; cp. Neh. 7:5
10
g Jer. 14:13; cp. Jer. 28:9
h Cp. Jer. 37:19
i Ezek. 22:28
j i.e. *whitewash*
11
k Ezek. 38:22
14
l vv. 9,21, 23; Ezek. 14:8
16
m Jer. 6:14
18
n Cp. 2 Pet. 2:14
19
o 1 Sam. 2:15–17; Prov. 28:21; Mic. 3:5; Rom. 16:18; 1 Pet. 5:2
22
p Jer. 28:15
q Jer. 23:14
23
r v. 6; Ezek. 12:24; Mic. 3:5–6
CHAPTER 14
1
s Ezek. 8:1; 20:1; cp. 33:31
3
t Ezek. 7:19
u Ezek. 20:31; cp. 2 Ki. 3:13

*13:18 Literally *over all the joints of My hands;* Vulgate reads *under every elbow;* Septuagint and Targum read *on all elbows of the hands.*

5 "that I may seize the house of
Israel by their heart, because they are
all estranged from Me by their idols." '
6 "Therefore say to the house of
Israel, 'Thus says the Lord GOD: "Repent, turn away from your idols, and
[a]turn your faces away from all your
abominations.
7 "For anyone of the house of Israel, or of the strangers who dwell in
Israel, who separates himself from Me
and sets up his idols in his heart and
puts before him what causes him to
stumble into iniquity, then comes to a
prophet to [b]inquire of him concerning
Me, I the LORD will answer him by Myself.
8 "I will [c]set My face against that
man and [d]make him a sign and a
proverb, and I will cut him off from the
midst of My people. Then you shall
[e]know that I *am* the LORD.
9 "And if the prophet is induced to
speak anything, I the LORD have [f]in-
duced that prophet, and I will stretch
out My hand against him and destroy
him from among My people Israel.
10 "And they shall bear their iniquity; the punishment of the prophet
shall be the same as the punishment of
the one who inquired,
11 [g]"that the house of Israel may no
longer stray from Me, nor be profaned
anymore with all their transgressions,
but that they may be My people and I
[h]may be their God," says the Lord
GOD.' "

Jerusalem on no account to be spared

12 The word of the LORD came
again to me, saying:
13 "Son of man, when a land sins
against Me by persistent unfaithfulness, I will stretch out My hand
against it; I will cut off its supply of
bread, send famine on it, and cut off
man and beast from it.
14 "Even *if* these three men, Noah,
[1]Daniel, and Job, were in it, they
would [i]deliver *only* themselves by
their righteousness," says the Lord
GOD.
15 "If I cause wild [j]beasts to pass
through the land, and they empty it,
and make it so desolate that no man

6
a Isa. 55:6–7; Ezek. 18:30–32
7
b Cp. Jer. 37:17–21
8
c Lev. 17:10; 20:3,5,6; Jer. 44:11; Ezek. 15:7
d Num. 26:10; Dt. 28:37; Ezek. 5:15
e Ezek. 13:14
9
f 1 Ki. 22:23; Job 12:16; Isa. 66:4; Jer. 4:10; 2 Th. 2:11; cp. Ps. 81:11–12; Isa. 63:17
11
g Ps. 119:67,71; Jer. 31:18–19; Heb. 12:11
h Ezek. 11:20; 34:30
14
i vv. 16,18, 20; cp. Gen. 19:15–25
15
j Ezek. 5:17
16
k Ezek. 15:8; 33:28–29
17
l Ezek. 25:13; Zeph. 1:3
19
m 2 Sam. 24:15; Ezek. 38:22
21
n Jer. 15:2–3
22
o Ezek. 12:16
p Ezek. 6:8
23
q Cp. Ezek.

may pass through because of the
beasts,
16 "*even though* these three men
were in it, *as* I live," says the Lord GOD,
"they would deliver neither sons nor
daughters; only they would be delivered, and the land would be [k]desolate.
17 "Or *if* I bring a sword on that
land, and say, 'Sword, go through the
land,' and I [l]cut off man and beast
from it,
18 "even *though* these three men
were in it, *as* I live," says the Lord GOD,
"they would deliver neither sons nor
daughters, but only they themselves
would be delivered.
19 "Or *if* I send a [m]pestilence into
that land and pour out My fury on it in
blood, and cut off from it man and
beast,
20 "even *though* Noah, Daniel, and
Job *were* in it, *as* I live," says the Lord
GOD, "they would deliver neither son
nor daughter; they would deliver *only*
themselves by their righteousness."
21 For thus says the Lord GOD:
"How much more it shall be when I
send My [n]four severe judgments on
Jerusalem—the sword and famine
and wild beasts and pestilence—to cut
off man and beast from it?
22 "Yet behold, there shall be left in
it a [o]remnant who will be [p]brought
out, *both* sons and daughters; surely
they will come out to you, and you will
see their ways and their doings. Then
you will be comforted concerning the
disaster that I have brought upon Jerusalem, all that I have brought upon
it.
23 "And they will [q]comfort you,
when you see their ways and their doings; and you shall know that I have
done nothing [r]without cause that I
have done in it," says the Lord GOD.

Parable of the useless vine
(cp. Isa. 5:1–24)

15 THEN the word of the LORD
came to me, saying:
2 "Son of man, how is the wood of
the [2s]vine *better* than any other

16:54 r Jer. 22:8–9 **15:2** s Cp. Ps. 80:8–16; Isa. 5:1–7; Jer. 2:21; Ezek. 19:10–14; Hos. 10:1; Jn. 15:6

[1](14:14) Many see here important contemporaneous testimony to the historicity and character of Daniel, who was still living when Ezekiel wrote. Cp. vv. 16,18,20; also Jer. 15:1. It is a tribute to Daniel's character that he, though still a young man, is linked with Noah and Job.

[2](15:2) The vine, as described by Ezekiel, symbolizes unregenerate man in general and sinful Israel in particular. Just as the vine wood is tough, twisted, unworkable, and fit only for fuel, so Israel, recalcitrant in sin, is fit only for judgment.

Whereas in ch. 15 (and in Isa. 5 also) the vine pictures only judgment, in Jn. 15 Christ uses

wood, the vine branch which is among
the trees of the forest?
3 "Is wood taken from it to make
any object? Or can *men* make a peg
from it to hang any vessel on?
4 "Instead, it is thrown into the
[a]fire for fuel; the fire devours both
ends of it, and its middle is burned. Is
it useful for *any* work?
5 "Indeed, when it was whole, no
object could be made from it. How
much less will it be useful for *any*
work when the fire has devoured it,
and it is burned?
6 "Therefore thus says the Lord
GOD: 'Like the wood of the [b]vine
among the trees of the forest, which I
have given to the fire for fuel, so I will
give up the inhabitants of Jerusalem;
7 'and I will [c]set My face against
them. They will go out from *one* fire,
but *another* fire shall devour them.
Then you shall know that I *am* the
LORD, when I set My face against them.
8 'Thus I will make the land desolate, because they have persisted in
unfaithfulness,' says the Lord GOD."

The LORD's grace to unfaithful Jerusalem

16 AGAIN the word of the LORD
came to me, saying,
2 "Son of man, cause Jerusalem to
know her [d]abominations,
3 "and say, 'Thus says the Lord
GOD to Jerusalem: "Your birth and
your nativity *are* from the land of Canaan; your father *was* an [e]Amorite
and your mother a [f]Hittite.
4 "*As for* your nativity, [g]on the
day you were born your navel cord
was not cut, nor were you washed in
water to cleanse *you;* you were not
rubbed with salt nor wrapped in
swaddling cloths.
5 "No eye pitied you, to do any of
these things for you, to have compassion on you; but you were thrown out
into the open field, when you yourself
were loathed on the day you were
born.
6 "And when I passed by you and
saw you struggling in your own blood,
I said to you in your blood, 'Live!' Yes,
I said to you in your blood, 'Live!'

CHAPTER 15
4
a Cp. Isa. 27:11
6
b Cp. Ezek. 17:3–10
7
c Lev. 17:10; Ezek. 14:8
CHAPTER 16
2
d vv. 15–34; Ezek. 8:9–17
3
e Gen. 15:16; Dt. 7:1; Josh. 24:15
f See 2 Ki. 7:6, *note*
4
g Cp. Hos. 2:3
8
h Cp. Jer. 2:2
i Gen. 22:16–18
j Ex. 24:6–8
k Ex. 19:5
11
l i.e. *a necklace*
12
m Cp. Gen. 24:47; Isa. 3:21
13
n Kingdom (OT): vv. 13–14; Ezek. 20:33. (Gen. 1:26; Zech. 12:8, *note*)
14
o Ps. 50:2; cp. Lam. 2:15
15
p See Ps. 2:12, *note*
q Cp. Dt. 32:15; Jer. 7:4; Mic. 3:11
r Isa. 1:21; 57:8; Jer. 2:20; 3:2,6, 20; Ezek. 23:11–20; Hos. 1:2
16
s vv. 16,24, 25,31,39; see Jud. 3:7 and 1 Ki. 3:2, *notes*

7 "I made you thrive like a plant in
the field; and you grew, matured, and
became very beautiful. *Your* breasts
were formed, your hair grew, but you
were naked and bare.
8 "When I passed by you again
and looked upon you, indeed your
time *was* the time of [h]love; so I spread
My wing over you and covered your
nakedness. Yes, I [i]swore an oath to
you and entered into a [j]covenant with
you, and [k]you became Mine," says the
Lord GOD.
9 "Then I washed you in water;
yes, I thoroughly washed off your
blood, and I anointed you with oil.
10 "I clothed you in embroidered
cloth and gave you sandals of badger
skin; I clothed you with fine linen and
covered you with silk.
11 "I adorned you with ornaments,
put bracelets on your wrists, and a
[l]chain on your neck.
12 "And I put a jewel [m]in your nose,
earrings in your ears, and a beautiful
crown on your head.
13 "Thus you were adorned with
gold and silver, and your clothing *was*
of fine linen, silk, and embroidered
cloth. You ate *pastry of* fine flour,
honey, and oil. You were exceedingly
beautiful, and succeeded to [n]royalty.
14 "Your fame went out among the
nations because of your [o]beauty, for it
was perfect through My splendor
which I had bestowed on you," says
the Lord GOD.

She becomes a harlot

15 "But you [p]trusted [q]in your own
beauty, [1][r]played the harlot because of
your fame, and poured out your harlotry on everyone passing by who
would have it.
16 "You took some of your garments and adorned multicolored
[s]high places for yourself, and played
the harlot on them. *Such* things
should not happen, nor be.
17 "You have also taken your beautiful jewelry from My gold and My silver, which I had given you, and made

it to portray the living union between Himself and the believer. Here the intrinsic worthlessness of the wood is wholly subordinated to the single, positive function of the vine—that of bearing fruit. Thus our Lord takes the figure of the vine wood, representative in Ezekiel of humanity ruined in sin, and transforms it into the parable of Himself as the Vine and Christians as His branches, bearing fruit for Him.

1(16:15) An expression that, in the spiritual realm, denotes worship of the gods of the nations.

for yourself male images and played
the harlot with them.
18 "You took your embroidered
garments and covered them, and you
set My oil and My incense before
them.
19 "Also My food which I gave
you—the pastry of fine flour, oil, and
honey *which* I fed you—you set it before them as sweet incense; and *so* it
was," says the Lord GOD.
20 "Moreover you took your sons
and your daughters, whom you bore
to Me, and these you [a]sacrificed to
them to be devoured. *Were* your *acts*
of harlotry a small matter,
21 "that you have slain My children
and offered them up to them by causing them to pass through *the* [b]*fire*?
22 "And in all your abominations
and acts of harlotry you did not remember the days of your [c]youth,
when you were naked and bare, struggling in your blood.
23 "Then it was so, after all your
wickedness—'Woe, woe to you!' says
the Lord GOD—
24 "*that* you also built for yourself
a shrine, and [d]made a high place for
yourself in every street.
25 "You built your high places at
the head of every road, and made your
beauty to be abhorred. You offered
yourself to everyone who passed by,
and multiplied your acts of harlotry.
26 "You also committed harlotry
with the [e]Egyptians, your very fleshly
neighbors, and increased your acts of
harlotry to [f]provoke Me to anger.
27 "Behold, therefore, I stretched
out My hand against you, diminished
your allotment, and gave you up to the
will of those who hate you, the daughters of the [g]Philistines, who were
[h]ashamed of your lewd behavior.
28 "You also played the harlot with
the [i]Assyrians, because you were in-
satiable; indeed you played the harlot
with them and still were not satisfied.
29 "Moreover you multiplied your
acts of harlotry as far as the land of
the trader, [j]Chaldea; and even then
you were not satisfied.
30 "How degenerate is your heart!"
says the Lord GOD, "seeing you do all
these *things*, the deeds of a [k]brazen
harlot.
31 "You erected your shrine at the
head of every road, and built your
high place in every street. Yet you
were not like a harlot, because you
scorned [l]payment.
32 "*You are* an adulterous wife,

20 *a* Ps. 106:37–38; Isa. 57:5; Jer. 7:31
21 *b* 2 Ki. 17:17; Jer. 19:5; Ezek. 20:31; 23:37
22 *c* vv. 43,60; Jer. 2:2; Hos. 11:1
24 *d* Ps. 78:58; Isa. 57:7; Jer. 2:20; 3:2
26 *e* Ezek. 20:7–8 *f* Dt. 31:20
27 *g* Isa. 9:12; Ezek. 25:15 *h* Cp. Rom. 2:24
28 *i* 2 Ki. 16:7–10; 2 Chr. 28:20–21; Jer. 2:18, 36; Ezek. 23:12
29 *j* Ezek. 23:14–17
30 *k* Cp. Jer. 3:3
31 *l* Isa. 52:3
33 *m* Isa. 57:8–9; cp. Hos. 8:9–10
37 *n* Lam. 1:2, 19; Ezek. 23:22; Hos. 2:10
38 *o* Lev. 20:10; Dt. 22:22
40 *p* Ezek. 23:45–47
41 *q* Dt. 13:16; 2 Ki. 25:9; Jer. 39:8; 52:13
42 *r* Ezek. 5:13; 21:17

who takes strangers instead of her
husband.
33 "Men make payment to all harlots, but you made your [m]payments to
all your lovers, and hired them to
come to you from all around for your
harlotry.
34 "You are the opposite of *other*
women in your harlotry, because no
one solicited you to be a harlot. In that
you gave payment but no payment
was given you, therefore you are the
opposite."

Her judgment prophesied

35 'Now then, O harlot, hear the
word of the LORD!
36 'Thus says the Lord GOD: "Because your filthiness was poured out
and your nakedness uncovered in
your harlotry with your lovers, and
with all your abominable idols, and
because of the blood of your children
which you gave to them,
37 "surely, therefore, I will gather
all your [n]lovers with whom you took
pleasure, all those you loved, *and* all
those you hated; I will gather them
from all around against you and will
uncover your nakedness to them, that
they may see all your nakedness.
38 "And I will judge you [o]as women
who break wedlock or shed blood are
judged; I will bring blood upon you in
fury and jealousy.
39 "I will also give you into their
hand, and they shall throw down your
shrines and break down your high
places. They shall also strip you of
your clothes, take your beautiful jewelry, and leave you naked and bare.
40 "They shall also bring up an [p]as-
sembly against you, and they shall
stone you with stones and thrust you
through with their swords.
41 "They shall [q]burn your houses
with fire, and execute judgments on
you in the sight of many women; and
I will make you cease playing the harlot, and you shall no longer hire lovers.
42 "So I will lay to [r]rest My fury
toward you, and My jealousy shall depart from you. I will be quiet, and be
angry no more.
43 "Because you did not remember
the days of your youth, but agitated
Me* with all these *things*, surely I will

* **16:43** Following Septuagint, Syriac, Targum, and Vulgate; Masoretic Text reads *were agitated with Me.*

also [a]recompense your deeds on *your own* head," says the Lord GOD. "And you shall not commit lewdness in addition to all your abominations.

44 "Indeed everyone who quotes proverbs will use *this* proverb against you: 'Like mother, like daughter!'

45 "You *are* your mother's daughter, loathing husband and children; and you *are* the [b]sister of your sisters, who [c]loathed their husbands and children; your mother *was* a [d]Hittite and your father an Amorite.

46 "Your elder sister *is* [e]Samaria, who dwells with her daughters to the north of you; and your younger sister, who dwells to the south of you, *is* Sodom and her daughters.

47 "You did not walk in their ways nor act according to their abominations; but, as *if that were* too little, you became [f]more corrupt than they in all your ways.

48 "As I live," says the Lord GOD, "neither your sister [g]Sodom nor her daughters have done as you and your daughters have done.

49 "Look, this was the iniquity of your sister Sodom: She and her daughter had [h]pride, [i]fullness of food, and abundance of [j]idleness; neither did she strengthen the hand of the poor and [k]needy.

50 "And they were haughty and [l]committed abomination before Me; therefore I took them away as I saw *fit*.*

51 "Samaria did not commit [m]half of your sins; but you have multiplied your abominations more than they, and have [n]justified your sisters by all the abominations which you have done.

52 "You who [o]judged your sisters, bear your own shame also, because the sins which you committed were more abominable than theirs; they are more righteous than you. Yes, be disgraced also, and bear your own shame, because you [n]justified your sisters.

53 [p]"When I bring back their captives, the captives of Sodom and her daughters, and the captives of Samaria and her daughters, then *I will also bring back* the captives of your captivity among them,

54 "that you may bear your own shame and be disgraced by all that you did when you comforted them.

55 "When your sisters, Sodom and her daughters, return to their former state, and Samaria and her daughters return to their former state, then you and your daughters will return to your former state.

56 "For your sister Sodom was not a byword in your mouth in the days of your pride,

57 "before your wickedness was uncovered. It was like the time of the [q]reproach of the daughters of Syria* and all *those* around her, and of the daughters of the Philistines, who despise you everywhere.

58 "You have paid for your lewdness and your abominations," says the LORD.

59 'For thus says the Lord GOD: "I will deal with you as you have done, who despised the oath by breaking the covenant.

Yet God will fulfill His covenants

60 "Nevertheless I will [1][r]remember My [2]covenant with you in the days of your youth, and I will establish an [s]everlasting covenant with you.

61 "Then you will remember your ways and be [t]ashamed, when you receive your older and your younger sisters; for I will give them to you for daughters, but not because of My covenant with you.

62 "And I will [u]establish My covenant with you. Then you shall know that I *am* the LORD,

63 "that you may [v]remember and be ashamed, and [w]never open your mouth anymore because of your shame, when I provide you an atonement for all you have done," says the Lord GOD.' "

43 *a* Ezek. 9:10; 11:21; 22:31
45 *b* Ezek. 23:2–4 *c* Cp. Zech. 11:8 *d* See 2 Ki. 7:6, *note*
46 *e* Cp. Jer. 3:8–11
47 *f* 2 Ki. 21:9; Ezek. 5:6; cp. Mt. 12:41–42
48 *g* Isa. 3:9; Lam. 4:6; Mt. 10:15; 11:24; Rev. 11:8
49 *h* Cp. Ps. 138:6 *i* Cp. Isa. 22:13 *j* Cp. Amos 6:4–6 *k* Jer. 5:28; cp. Ezek. 18:7–8
50 *l* Cp. Gen. 13:13; 18:20; 19:5
51 *m* Ezek. 23:11 *n* i.e. *made them appear righteous*
52 *o* Cp. Rom. 2:1
53 *p* vv. 60–61; cp. Isa. 1:9
57 *q* 2 Ki. 16:5; 2 Chr. 28:18
60 *r* Lev. 26:42–45; Ps. 106:45 *s* Isa. 55:3; Jer. 32:40; 50:5; Ezek. 37:26
61 *t* Jer. 50:4–5; Ezek. 6:9; 20:43

16:62 *u* Hos. 2:19–20 **16:63** *v* Ezek. 36:31–32 *w* Ps. 39:9; Rom. 3:19

*

16:50 Vulgate reads *you saw;* Septuagint reads *he saw;* Targum reads *as was revealed to Me.*
16:57 Following Masoretic Text, Septuagint, Targum, and Vulgate; many Hebrew manuscripts and Syriac read *Edom.*

[1](16:60) It must ever be a source of encouragement to God's people to have the assurance from His Word that He remains faithful even when they themselves are unfaithful (2 Tim. 2:13). There could be no hope of salvation were this not true.

[2](16:60) In its first use in this verse, the word "covenant" alludes to the Palestinian Covenant (see Dt. 30:3, *note*); in its second usage, to the New Covenant (see Heb. 8:8, *note*).

Parable of the two eagles (vv. 3,7)

17 AND the word of the LORD came to me, [a]saying,
2 "Son of man, pose a riddle, and
speak a [b]parable to the house of Israel,
3 "and say, 'Thus says the Lord
GOD:

"A great eagle with large wings
and long pinions,
Full of feathers of various
colors,
Came to Lebanon
And took from the cedar the
highest branch.
4 He cropped off its topmost
young twig
And carried it to a land of
trade;
He set it in a city of
merchants.
5 Then he took some of the seed
of the land
And planted it in a fertile field;
He placed *it* by abundant
waters
And set it like a willow tree.
6 And it grew and became a
spreading vine of low
stature;
Its branches turned toward
him,
But its roots were under it.
So it became a vine,
Brought forth branches,
And put forth shoots.
7 "But there was another* great
eagle with large wings and
many feathers;
And behold, this vine bent its
roots toward him,
And stretched its branches
toward him,
From the garden terrace where
it had been planted,
That he might water it.
8 It was planted in good soil by
many waters,
To bring forth branches, bear
fruit,
And become a majestic vine." '
9 "Say, 'Thus says the Lord GOD:
"Will it thrive?
[c]Will he not pull up its roots,
Cut off its fruit,
And leave it to wither?
All of its spring leaves will
wither,
And no great power or many
people
Will be needed to pluck it up
by its roots.
10 Behold, *it is* planted,
Will it thrive?
Will it not utterly wither when
the [d]east wind touches it?
It will wither in the garden
terrace where it grew." ' "

Zedekiah's rebellion against Nebuchadnezzar and its result (2 Ki. 24:17–20; 25:1–10)

11 Moreover the word of the LORD
came to me, saying,
12 "Say now to the [e]rebellious
house: 'Do you not know what these
things mean?' Tell *them,* 'Indeed the
[f]king of Babylon went to Jerusalem
and took its king and princes, and led
them with him to Babylon.
13 'And he took the king's [g]offspring,
made a covenant with him,
and put him under oath. He also took
away the mighty of the land,
14 'that the kingdom might be
brought low and not lift itself up, *but*
that by keeping his covenant it might
stand.
15 'But he [h]rebelled against him by
sending his ambassadors to Egypt,
that they might give him horses and
many people. Will he prosper? Will he
who does such *things* escape? Can he
break a covenant and still be delivered?
16 '*As* I live,' says the Lord GOD,
'surely [1]in the place *where* the king
dwells who made him king, whose
oath he despised and whose covenant
he broke—with him in the midst of
Babylon he shall [i]die.
17 [j]'Nor will Pharaoh with *his*
mighty army and great company do
anything in the war, [k]when they heap
up a siege mound and build a wall to
cut off many persons.
18 'Since he despised the oath by
breaking the covenant, and in fact
[l]gave his hand and still did all these
things, he shall not escape.' "
19 Therefore thus says the Lord
GOD: "*As* I live, surely My oath which
he despised, and My covenant which
he broke, I will recompense on his
own head.
20 "I will spread My net over him,

CHAPTER 17
1 *a Parables* (OT): vv. 1–14; Ezek. 19:1. (Jud. 9:8; Zech. 11:7)
2 *b* Ezek. 20:49; 24:3
9 *c* Cp. 2 Ki. 25:7
10 *d* Ezek. 19:12; Hos. 13:15
12 *e* Ezek. 2:3–5 *f* v. 3; 2 Ki. 24:11–16
13 *g* Jer. 37:1
15 *h* 2 Ki. 24:20; 2 Chr. 36:13; Jer. 52:3
16 *i* Jer. 52:11; Ezek. 12:13
17 *j* Jer. 37:7; Ezek. 29:6 *k* Jer. 52:4; Ezek. 4:2
18 *l* Cp. 1 Chr. 29:24; Lam. 5:6

*17:7 Following Septuagint, Syriac, and Vulgate; Masoretic Text and Targum read *one.*

[1](17:16) Nebuchadnezzar, who made Zedekiah king, reigned in Babylon.

and he shall be taken in My snare. I
will bring him to Babylon and try him
there for the treason which he committed against Me.
21 "All his fugitives* with all his
troops shall fall by the sword, and
those who remain shall be [a]scattered
to every wind; and you shall know
that I, the LORD, have spoken."
22 Thus says the Lord GOD: "I will
take also *one* of the highest [b]branches
of the high cedar and set *it* out. I
will crop off from the topmost of its
young twigs a [c]tender one, and will
[d]plant *it* on a high and prominent
mountain.
23 "On the [e]mountain height of Israel I will [f]plant it; and it will bring
forth boughs, and bear fruit, and be a
majestic cedar. [g]Under it will dwell
birds of every sort; in the shadow of its
branches they will dwell.
24 "And all the trees of the field
shall know that I, the LORD, have
brought down the high tree and exalted the low tree, dried up the green
tree and made the dry tree [h]flourish;
I, the LORD, have spoken and have
done *it*."

God's justice defended; personal judgment for personal sin

18 THE word of the LORD came to
me again, saying,
2 "What do you mean when you
use this proverb concerning the land
of Israel, saying:

'The fathers have eaten sour
grapes,
And the children's teeth are set
on [i]edge'?

3 "As I live," says the Lord GOD,
"you shall no longer use this proverb
in Israel.

4 "Behold, all souls are [j]Mine;
The soul of the father
As well as the soul of the son
is Mine;
The [k]soul who sins shall die.
5 But if a man is [l]just
And does what is lawful and
right;
6 If he has not eaten on the
[m]mountains,
Nor lifted up his eyes to the
idols of the house of Israel,
Nor defiled his neighbor's
wife,
Nor approached a woman
[n]during her impurity;
7 If he has not oppressed
anyone,
But has restored to the debtor
his [o]pledge;
Has robbed no one by
violence,
But has given his bread to the
[p]hungry
And covered the naked with
[q]clothing;
8 If he has not exacted [r]usury
Nor taken any increase,
But has withdrawn his hand
from iniquity
And executed true judgment
between man and man;
9 *If* he has walked in My statutes
And kept My judgments
faithfully—
He *is* just;
He shall surely [s]live!"
Says the Lord GOD.

10 "If he begets a son *who is* a
robber
Or a [t]shedder of blood,
Who does any of these *things*
11 And does none of those *duties,*
But has eaten on the
mountains
Or defiled his neighbor's wife;
12 If he has oppressed the poor
and needy,
Robbed by violence,
Not restored the pledge,
Lifted his eyes to the idols,
Or committed abomination;
13 If he has exacted usury
Or taken increase—
Shall he then live?
He shall not live!
If he has done any of these
abominations,
He shall surely die;
His [u]blood shall be upon him.

14 "*If,* however, he begets a son
Who sees all the sins which his
father has done,
And considers but does not do
[v]likewise;
15 *Who* has not eaten on the
mountains,
Nor lifted his eyes to the idols
of the house of Israel,
Nor defiled his neighbor's
wife;

21
a Ezek. 12:15; 22:15
22
b Isa. 4:2; 11:1; Jer. 23:5–6; 33:15; Zech. 3:8; 6:12
c Isa. 53:2
d Ps. 2:6
23
e Isa. 2:2–3; Ezek. 20:40; Mic. 4:1
f Cp. Isa. 62:1–7
g Cp. Ezek. 31:6; Dan. 4:12
24
h Ezek. 37:3; Amos 9:11; Rom. 11:23–24
CHAPTER 18
2
i Jer. 31:29; Lam. 5:7
4
j Num. 16:22
k v. 20; Rom. 6:23
5
l *Righteousness* (OT): vv. 5–9; Hab. 2:4. (Gen. 6:9; Lk. 2:25, *note*)
6
m vv. 11,15; Ezek. 22:9
n Lev. 18:19; 20:18
7
o Ex. 22:26; Dt. 24:12–13
p Dt. 15:11
q Isa. 58:7
8
r Ex. 22:25; Lev. 25:36–37; Dt. 23:19
9
s Ezek. 20:11; Amos 5:4
10
t Gen. 9:6; Ex. 21:12; Num. 35:31
13
u Lev. 20:9, 11–13,16, 27

18:14 *v* Prov. 23:24

*17:21 Following Masoretic Text and Vulgate; many Hebrew manuscripts and Syriac read *choice men;* Targum reads *mighty men;* Septuagint omits *All his fugitives.*

16 Has not oppressed anyone,
Nor withheld a pledge,
Nor robbed by violence,
But has given his bread to the hungry
And covered the naked with clothing;
17 *Who* has withdrawn his hand from the poor*
And not received usury or increase,
But has executed My judgments
And walked in My statutes—
He shall not die for the iniquity of his father;
He shall surely live!

18 "*As for* his father,
Because he cruelly oppressed,
Robbed his brother by violence,
And did what *is* not good among his people,
Behold, he shall die for his iniquity.

19 "Yet you say, 'Why should the
son not bear the [a]guilt of the father?'
Because the son has done what is lawful and right, and has kept all My statutes and observed them, he shall
surely live.
20 "The [b]soul who sins shall die.
The [c]son shall not bear the guilt of the
father, nor the father bear the guilt of
the son. The [d]righteousness of the
righteous shall be upon himself, and
the [e]wickedness of the wicked shall
be upon himself.
21 "But if a wicked man [f]turns
from all his sins which he has committed, keeps all My statutes, and does
what is lawful and right, he shall
surely live; he shall not die.
22 "None of the transgressions
which he has committed shall be remembered against him; because of the
righteousness which he has done, he
shall [g]live.
23 [h]"Do I have any pleasure at all
that the wicked should die?" says the
Lord God, "*and* not that he should turn
from his ways and [i]live?
24 "But when a righteous man
turns away from his righteousness
and commits [j]iniquity, and does according to all the abominations that
the wicked *man* does, shall he live?
[1]All the righteousness which he has
done shall [k]not be remembered; because of the unfaithfulness of which
he is guilty and the sin which he has
committed, because of them he shall
[l]die.
25 "Yet you say, 'The [m]way of the
Lord is not fair.' Hear now, O house of
Israel, is it not My way which is fair,
and your ways which are not fair?
26 "When a righteous *man* turns
away from his righteousness, commits iniquity, and dies in it, it is because of the iniquity which he has
done that he dies.
27 "Again, when a wicked *man*
turns away from the wickedness
which he committed, and does what is
lawful and right, he preserves himself
alive.
28 "Because he considers and turns
away from all the transgressions
which he committed, he shall surely
live; he shall not die.
29 "Yet the house of Israel says,
'The way of the Lord is not fair.' O
house of Israel, is it not My ways
which are fair, and your ways which
are not fair?
30 "Therefore I will judge you, O
house of Israel, every one according to
his ways," says the Lord God. [n]"Repent, and turn from all your transgressions, so that iniquity will not be your
ruin.
31 [o]"Cast away from you all the
transgressions which you have committed, and get yourselves a [p]new
heart and a new spirit. For why should
you die, O house of Israel?
32 [q]"For I have no pleasure in the
death of one who dies," says the Lord
God. "Therefore turn and [r]live!"

19 *a* Ex. 20:5; Dt. 5:9; 2 Ki. 23:26; 24:3–4
20 *b* Ezek. 18:4 *c* Dt. 24:16; 2 Ki. 14:6; 2 Chr. 25:4; Jer. 31:29–30 *d* Isa. 3:10–11 *e* Rom. 2:9
21 *f* v. 27; Ezek. 33:12,19
22 *g* Ps. 18:20–24
23 *h* Lam. 3:33; Ezek. 18:32; 33:11; 1 Tim. 2:4; 2 Pet. 3:9 *i* Cp. 2 Cor. 2:5–11
24 *j* Ezek. 33:18 *k* Cp. Gal. 3:3–4 *l* Cp. Prov. 21:16; Jer. 18:1–10
25 *m* v. 29; Ezek. 33:17,20
30 *n* Mt. 3:2; Rev. 2:5; see Zech. 8:14 and Acts 17:30, *notes*
31 *o* Isa. 1:16; 55:7; Eph. 4:22–23 *p* Ps. 51:10; Jer. 32:39; Ezek. 11:19; 36:26
32 *q* v. 23; Lam. 3:33; Ezek. 33:11; 2 Pet. 3:9 *r* Prov. 4:2

*18:17 Following Masoretic Text, Targum, and Vulgate; Septuagint reads *iniquity* (compare verse 8).

[1](18:24) This and similar passages in Ezekiel (e.g. 3:17–21; 33:10–20) have been understood by some to teach that a Christian may lose his righteous standing before God. But in support of the security of the believer it should be observed that these passages in Ezekiel do not necessarily teach the eternal loss of a saved person, because the word "righteous" may refer to ceremonial religion (cp. Mt. 5:20) and not to "the righteousness which is from God by faith" (cp. Phil. 3:7–9). Moreover, the punishment threatened may refer only to physical death rather than to eternal death. In any case, these texts in Ezekiel must be considered in the light of such NT affirmations as Jn. 10:28; Rom. 5:8–9; 8:38–39; Phil. 1:6; etc. that so clearly teach the security of the believer.

Lament for the princes of Israel

19 "MOREOVER take up a [a]lamentation for the princes of Israel,
2 "and say:

'What *is* your mother? A [b]lioness:
She lay down among the lions;
Among the young lions she nourished her cubs.
3 She brought up one of her cubs,
And he became a [c]young lion;
He learned to catch prey,
And he devoured men.
4 The nations also heard of him;
He was trapped in their pit,
And they brought him with chains to the land of [d]Egypt.

5 'When she saw that she waited, *that* her hope was lost,
She took [e]another of her cubs *and* made him a young lion.
6 He roved among the lions,
And became a young lion;
He learned to catch prey;
He devoured men.
7 He knew their desolate places,*
And laid waste their cities;
The land with its fullness was desolated
By the noise of his roaring.
8 [f]Then the nations set against him from the provinces on every side,
And spread their net over him;
He was trapped in their pit.
9 They put him in a cage [g]with chains,
And brought him to the king of Babylon;
They brought him in nets,
That his voice should no longer be heard on the mountains of Israel.

10 'Your mother *was* like a [h]vine in your bloodline,*
Planted by the waters,
Fruitful and full of branches
Because of many waters.
11 She had strong branches for scepters of rulers.
She towered in stature above the thick branches,
And was seen in her height amid the dense foliage.
12 But she was [i]plucked up in fury,
She was cast down to the ground,
And the east wind dried her fruit.
Her strong branches were broken and withered;
The fire consumed them.
13 And now she *is* planted in the wilderness,
In a dry and thirsty land.
14 [j]Fire has come out from a rod of her branches
And devoured her fruit,
So that she has no strong [k]branch—a scepter for ruling.' "

This *is* a lamentation, and has become a lamentation.

God's dealing with Israel vindicated

20 IT came to pass in the [l]seventh
[m]year, in the [n]fifth *month,* on
the tenth *day* of the month, *that* certain of the elders of Israel came to inquire of the LORD, and [o]sat before me.
2 Then the word of the LORD came
to me, saying,
3 "Son of man, speak to the elders
of Israel, and say to them, 'Thus says
the Lord GOD: "Have you come to inquire of Me? *As* I live," says the Lord
GOD, "I will [p]not be inquired of by
you." '
4 "Will you judge them, son of
man, will you judge *them?* Then make
known to them the abominations of
their fathers.
5 "Say to them, 'Thus says the
Lord GOD: "On the day when I [q]chose
Israel and raised My hand in an oath
to the descendants of the house of Jacob, and made Myself known to them
in the land of Egypt, I raised My hand
in an oath to them, saying, 'I *am* the
LORD your God.'
6 "On that day I raised My hand in
an oath to them, to [r]bring them out of
the land of Egypt into a land that I had
searched out for them, [s]'flowing with
milk and honey,' the glory of all lands.
7 "Then I said to them, 'Each of
you, throw away the abominations
which are before his eyes, and do not
[t]defile yourselves with the idols of
Egypt. I *am* the LORD your God.'
8 "But they rebelled against Me

CHAPTER 19

1 *a* Parables (OT): vv. 1–14; Ezek. 23:1. (Jud. 9:8; Zech. 11:7)

2 *b* Symbol of Judah, Gen. 49:9; 1 Ki. 10:18–20

3 *c* *Jehoahaz (Shallum),* vv. 3–4; 2 Ki. 23:31–32; 2 Chr. 36:1–2; Jer. 22:10–12

4 *d* 2 Ki. 23:33–34

5 *e* *Jehoiachin (Jeconiah, Coniah),* vv. 5–9; 2 Ki. 24:8–16; Jer. 22:24–30

8 *f* 2 Ki. 24:2

9 *g* Lit. *with hooks*

10 *h* Symbol of Judah, Isa. 5:1–7; Jer. 2:21; Ezek. 15:1–15

12 *i* Jer. 31:27–28

14 *j* *Zedekiah,* vv. 10–14; 2 Ki. 24:17–20
k Cp. Ps. 110:2

CHAPTER 20

1 *l* Cp. Ezek. 1:1; 8:1; 24:1
m c. 591 B.C.
n See Lev. 23:2, *note*
o Ezek. 8:1; 14:1

3 *p* Ezek. 7:26; 14:3

5 *q* Election (corporate): v. 5; Hos. 11:1. (Dt. 7:6; 1 Pet. 5:13, *note*)

20:6 *r* Ex. 3:8,17; Dt. 8:7–9; Jer. 32:22 *s* v. 15; Ex. 3:8,17; 13:5; 33:3; Jer. 11:5; 32:22
20:7 *t* Lev. 17:7; 18:3; Dt. 29:16–18; Josh. 24:14

*

19:7 Septuagint reads *He stood in insolence;* Targum reads *He destroyed its palaces;* Vulgate reads *He learned to make widows.* **19:10** Literally *blood.* Following Masoretic Text, Syriac, and Vulgate; Septuagint reads *like a flower on a pomegranate tree;* Targum reads *in your likeness.*

and would not obey Me. They did not
all cast away the abominations which
were before their eyes, [a]nor did they
forsake the idols of Egypt. Then I said,
'I will pour out My fury on them and
fulfill My anger against them in the
midst of the land of Egypt.'
9 "But I [b]acted for My name's
sake, that it should not be profaned
before the Gentiles among whom they
were, in whose sight I had made Myself [c]known to them, to bring them
out of the land of Egypt.
10 "Therefore I made them go out
of the land of Egypt and brought them
into the wilderness.
11 "And [d]I gave them My statutes
and showed them My judgments,
'which, *if* a man does, he shall [e]live by
them.'
12 "Moreover I also gave them My
[f]Sabbaths, to be a sign between them
and Me, that they might know that I
am the LORD who sanctifies them.
13 "Yet the house of Israel rebelled
against Me in the wilderness; they did
not walk in My statutes; they despised
My judgments, 'which, *if* a man does,
he shall live by them'; and they greatly
defiled My Sabbaths. Then I said I
would pour out My fury on them in the
wilderness, to consume them.
14 "But I acted for My name's
[1]sake, that it should not be profaned
before the Gentiles, in whose sight I
had brought them out.
15 [g]"So I also raised My hand in an
oath to them in the wilderness, that I
would not bring them into the land
which I had given *them,* 'flowing with
milk and honey,' the glory of all lands,
16 "because they despised My judgments and did not walk in My statutes,
but profaned My Sabbaths; [h]for their
heart went after their idols.
17 "Nevertheless My eye spared
them from destruction. I did not make
an end of them in the wilderness.
18 "But I said to their children in the
wilderness, 'Do not walk in the statutes of your fathers, nor observe their
judgments, nor defile yourselves with
their idols.
19 'I *am* the LORD your God: Walk in
My statutes, keep My judgments, and
do them;
20 [i]'hallow My Sabbaths, and they
will be a sign between Me and you,
that you may know that I *am* the LORD
your God.'
21 "Notwithstanding, the [j]children
rebelled against Me; they did not walk
in My statutes, and were not careful to
observe My judgments, 'which, *if* a
man does, he shall live by them'; but
they profaned My Sabbaths. Then I
said I would pour out My fury on them
and fulfill My anger against them in
the wilderness.
22 "Nevertheless I withdrew My
hand and acted for My name's sake,
that it should not be profaned in the
sight of the Gentiles, in whose sight I
had brought them out.
23 "Also I raised My hand in an
oath to those in the wilderness, that I
would [k]scatter them among the Gentiles and disperse them throughout
the countries,
24 "because they had not executed
My judgments, but had despised My
statutes, profaned My Sabbaths, and
their eyes were fixed on their fathers'
idols.
25 "Therefore I also [l]gave them up
to statutes *that were* not good, and
judgments by which they could not
live;
26 "and I pronounced them unclean
because of their ritual gifts, in that
they caused all [m]their firstborn to pass
through *the fire,* that I might make
them desolate and that they might
know that I am the LORD." '
27 "Therefore, son of man, speak to
the house of Israel, and say to them,
'Thus says the Lord GOD: "In this too
your fathers have [n]blasphemed Me,
by being unfaithful to Me.
28 "When I brought them into the
land *concerning* which I had raised
My hand in an oath to give them, and
they saw all the high hills and all the
thick trees, there they offered their
sacrifices and provoked Me with their
offerings. There they also sent up
their sweet aroma and poured out
their drink offerings.
29 "Then I said to them, 'What *is*
this high place to which you go?' So its
name is called [o]Bamah to this day." '
30 "Therefore say to the house of

8
a Cp. Ex. 32:1–9
9
b vv. 14,22; cp. Ex. 32:9–14; Num. 12:11–24; Dt. 9:1–29; Ezek. 36:16–38
c Josh. 2:10; 9:9–10
11
d Ex. 20:1; Dt. 4:8; Neh. 9:13–14; Ps. 147:19–20
e Lev. 18:5
12
f Ex. 20:8; 31:13; 35:2; Dt. 5:12
15
g Num. 14:28–30; Ps. 95:11; 106:26
16
h Num. 15:39; Ps. 78:37; Amos 5:25–26; Acts 7:42–43
20
i v. 12; Isa. 58:13–14; Jer. 17:22
21
j Num. 25:1–2; Dt. 9:23–24; 31:27
23
k Lev. 26:33; Dt. 28:64; Ps. 106:27; Jer. 15:4
25
l v. 39; Ps. 81:12; Rom. 1:24; 2 Th. 2:11
26
m Cp. Ex. 13:1–16
27
n Isa. 65:7; Rom. 2:24
29
o i.e. *High place.* vv. 28–29; see Jud. 3:7 and 1 Ki. 3:2, *notes*

[1](20:14) "For My name's sake" expresses one of God's motives in dealing with humanity. Although it means so little to most men, the name of the LORD is infinitely precious to Him. See 36:20, where the LORD says of unfaithful Israel, "they profaned My holy name," and the following verse, where He says of Himself, "I had concern for My holy name." Consistent with His holiness, God is concerned to vindicate the honor of His name.

Israel, 'Thus says the Lord GOD: "Are
you defiling yourselves in the manner
of your [a]fathers, and committing harlotry according to their [b]abomina-
tions?
31 "For when you offer your gifts
and make your sons pass through the
fire, you defile yourselves with all
your idols, even to this day. So shall I
be inquired of by you, O house of Israel? *As* I live," says the Lord GOD, "I
will [c]not be inquired of by you.
32 "What you have in your mind
shall never be, when you say, 'We will
be like the Gentiles, like the families in
other countries, serving wood and
stone.'

God will establish Israel in her land

33 "*As* I live," says the Lord GOD,
"surely with a mighty hand, with an
outstretched arm, and with fury
poured out, I [d]will [e]rule over you.
34 "I will bring you out from the
peoples and gather you out of the
countries where you are scattered,
with a mighty hand, with an outstretched arm, and with fury poured
out.
35 "And I will bring you into the
wilderness of the peoples, and there I
will plead My case with you face to
face.
36 [f]"Just as I pleaded My case with
your fathers in the wilderness of the
land of Egypt, so I will plead My case
with you," says the Lord GOD.
37 "I will make you [g]pass under the
[1]rod, and I will bring you into the bond
of the [h]covenant;
38 "I will [i]purge the rebels from
among you, and those who transgress
against Me; I will bring them out of the
country where they dwell, but they
shall not enter the land of Israel. Then
you will know that I *am* the LORD.
39 "As for you, O house of Israel,"
thus says the Lord GOD: [j]"Go, serve
every one of you his idols—and
hereafter—if you will not obey Me;
but profane My holy name no more
with your gifts and your idols.
40 "For on My holy mountain, on
the mountain height of Israel," says
the Lord GOD, "there [k]all the house of
Israel, all of them in the land, shall
serve Me; there I will [l]accept them,
and there I will require your offerings
and the firstfruits of your sacrifices,
together with all your holy things.
41 "I will accept you as a sweet
aroma when I bring you out from the
peoples and gather you out of the
countries where you have been scattered; and I will be hallowed in you
before the Gentiles.
42 "Then you shall know that I *am*
the LORD, [m]when I bring you into the
land of Israel, into the country *for*
which I raised My hand in an oath to
give to your fathers.
43 "And there you shall remember
your ways and all your doings with
which you were defiled; and you shall
[n]loathe yourselves in your own sight
because of all the evils that you have
committed.
44 "Then you shall know that I *am*
the LORD, when I have dealt with you
for My name's sake, not according to
your wicked ways nor according to
your corrupt doings, O house of Israel," says the Lord GOD.' "
45 Furthermore the word of the
LORD came to me, saying,
46 "Son of man, set your face toward the south; preach against the
south and prophesy against the forest
land, the South,*
47 "and say to the forest of the
South, 'Hear the word of the LORD!
Thus says the Lord GOD: "Behold, I
will kindle a fire in you, and it shall
devour every green tree and every dry
tree in you; the blazing flame shall not
be quenched, and all faces [o]from the
south to the north shall be scorched by
it.
48 "All flesh shall see that I, the
LORD, have kindled it; it shall not be
quenched." ' "
49 Then I said, "Ah, Lord GOD! They
say of me, 'Does he not speak [p]para-
bles?' "

Signs of the sighing prophet:
parable of the sword of the LORD

21 AND the word of the LORD
came to me, saying,
2 "Son of man, set your face to-

30 *a* Jud. 2:19 *b* Jer. 7:26; 16:12
31 *c* Ezek. 20:3
33 *d Judgments* (the seven): vv. 33–44; Dan. 7:22. (1 Sam. 7:14; Rev. 20:12, *note*) *e Kingdom* (OT): vv. 33–44; Ezek. 34:13. (Gen. 1:26; Zech. 12:8, *note*)
36 *f* Num. 14:21–23, 28–29
37 *g* Lev. 27:32; Jer. 33:13 *h* Ps. 89:30–34; Ezek. 16:60,62
38 *i* Amos 9:9–10; Zech. 13:8–9; Mal. 3:3; 4:1–3
39 *j* Jud. 10:14; Ps. 81:12; Amos 4:4
40 *k* Ezek. 37:22,24 *l* Isa. 60:7; Ezek. 43:27; Zech. 8:20–22; Mal. 3:4; cp. Rom. 12:1
42 *m* Ezek. 11:17; 34:13; 36:24
43 *n* Lev. 26:39; Ezek. 6:9; 36:31; cp. Hos. 5:15
47 *o* Ezek. 21:4

20:49 *p* Ezek. 12:9; 17:2; cp. Mt. 13:10–13

* **20:46** Hebrew *Negev*

[1](20:37) The passage is a prophecy of future judgment upon Israel, regathered from all nations (Gen. 12:3; see *notes* at Isa. 1:26 and Rom. 11:26). The issue of this judgment determines who of Israel in that day will enter kingdom blessing (Ps. 50:1–7; Ezek. 20:33–44; Mal. 3:2–5; 4:1–2). Regarding other judgments, see *notes* at Mt. 25:32; Jn. 12:31; 1 Cor. 11:31; 2 Cor. 5:10; Jude 6; Rev. 20:12.

ward Jerusalem, [a]preach against the
holy places, and prophesy against the
land of Israel;
3 "and say to the land of Israel,
'Thus says the LORD: "Behold, I *am*
[b]against you, and I will draw My
sword out of its sheath and cut off
both [c]righteous and wicked from you.
4 "Because I will cut off both righteous and wicked from you, therefore
My sword shall go out of its sheath
against [d]all flesh from south *to* north,
5 "that all flesh may know that I,
the LORD, have drawn My sword out of
its sheath; it shall not return anymore." '
6 [e]"Sigh therefore, son of man,
with a breaking heart, and sigh with
bitterness before their eyes.
7 "And it shall be when they say to
you, 'Why are you sighing?' that you
shall answer, 'Because of the news;
when it comes, every heart will melt,
all hands will be [f]feeble, every spirit
will faint, and all knees will be weak
as water. Behold, it is coming and
shall be brought to pass,' says the
Lord GOD."
8 Again the word of the LORD came
to me, saying,
9 "Son of man, prophesy and say,
'Thus says the LORD!' Say:

'A [g]sword, a sword is
sharpened
And also polished!
10 Sharpened to make a dreadful
slaughter,
Polished to flash like lightning!
Should we then make mirth?
It despises the scepter of My
son,
As it does all wood.
11 And He has given it to be
polished,
That it may be handled;
This sword is sharpened, and it
is polished
To be given into the hand of
the slayer.'

12 "Cry and wail, son of man;
For it will be against My
people,
Against all the [h]princes of
Israel.
Terrors including the sword
will be against My people;
Therefore strike *your* thigh.

13 "Because *it is* a testing,
And what if *the sword*
despises even the scepter?
The scepter shall be no *more*,"
says the Lord GOD.

14 "You therefore, son of man,
prophesy,
And [i]strike *your* hands
together.
The third time let the sword do
double *damage*.
It *is* the sword *that* slays,
The sword that slays the great
men,
That enters their private
chambers.
15 I have set the point of the
sword against all their gates,
That the heart may melt and
many may stumble.
Ah! *It is* made bright;
It is grasped for slaughter:
16 "Swords at the ready!
Thrust right!
Set your blade!
Thrust left—
Wherever your edge is
ordered!
17 "I also will beat [j]My fists
together,
And I will cause My [k]fury to
rest;
I, the LORD, have spoken."

Jerusalem's doom inevitable

18 The word of the LORD came to me
again, saying:
19 "And son of man, appoint for
yourself two ways for the sword of the
king of Babylon to go; both of them
shall go from the same land. Make a
sign; put *it* at the head of the road to
the city.
20 "Appoint a road for the sword to
go to [l]Rabbah of the Ammonites, and
to Judah, into [m]fortified Jerusalem.
21 "For the king of Babylon stands
at the parting of the road, at the fork
of the two roads, to use divination: he
shakes the arrows, he consults the images, he looks at the [n]liver.
22 "In his right hand is the divination for Jerusalem: to set up battering
rams, to call for a slaughter, to lift the
voice with shouting, to set battering
rams against the gates, to heap up a
siege mound, and to build a wall.
23 "And it will be to them like a
false divination in the eyes of those
who have sworn [o]oaths with them;
but he will bring their iniquity to remembrance, that they may be taken.
24 "Therefore thus says the Lord
GOD: 'Because you have made your iniquity to be remembered, in that your
transgressions are uncovered, so that

CHAPTER 21
2 [a] Cp. Amos 7:16
3 [b] Ezek. 5:8 [c] Job 9:22; cp. Ezek. 14:14
4 [d] Ezek. 20:47
6 [e] Isa. 22:4; Jer. 4:19; Lk. 19:41
7 [f] Ezek. 7:17
9 [g] vv. 15,28; Dt. 32:41; Ezek. 5:1
12 [h] Cp. Ezek. 22:6
14 [i] Ezek. 6:11
17 [j] v. 15; Ezek. 22:13 [k] Ezek. 16:42; 24:13
20 [l] Jer. 49:2; Ezek. 25:5; Amos 1:14 [m] Ps. 48:12–13
21 [n] Cp. Prov. 16:33; 21:1
23 [o] Ezek. 17:16,18

in all your doings your sins appear—
because you have come to remembrance, you shall be taken in hand.

No Davidic king till Messiah comes to reign (vv. 26–27; Rev. 19:11—20:6)

25 'Now to you, O [a]profane, wicked
prince of Israel, whose day has come,
whose iniquity *shall* end,
26 'thus says the Lord GOD:

"Remove the turban, and take
off the crown;
Nothing *shall remain* the same.
Exalt the humble, and humble
the exalted.
27 [b]Overthrown, overthrown,
I will make it overthrown!
[c]It shall be no *longer*,
Until He comes whose [1]right it
is,
And I will give it *to* [d]*Him*." '

28 "And you, son of man, prophesy
and say, 'Thus says the Lord GOD
[e]concerning the Ammonites and concerning their reproach,' and say:

'A sword, a sword *is* drawn,
Polished for slaughter,
For consuming, for flashing—
29 While they see [f]false visions
for you,
While they divine a lie to you,
To bring you on the necks of
the wicked, the slain
[g]Whose day has come,
Whose iniquity *shall* end.
30 'Return *it* to its sheath.
I will [h]judge you
In the place where you were
created,
In the [i]land of your nativity.
31 I will pour out My indignation
on you;
I will blow against you with
the fire of My wrath,
And deliver you into the hands
of brutal men *who are*
skillful to [j]destroy.
32 You shall be fuel for the fire;
Your blood shall be in the
midst of the land.
You shall not be remembered,
For I the LORD have spoken.' "

Sins of Israel enumerated

22

MOREOVER the word of the
LORD came to me, saying,
2 "Now, son of man, will you
judge, will you judge the bloody city?
Yes, show her all her abominations!
3 "Then say, 'Thus says the Lord
GOD: "The city sheds [k]blood in her
own midst, that her time may come;
and she makes idols within herself to
defile herself.
4 "You have become guilty by the
blood which you have [l]shed, and
have defiled yourself with the idols
which you have made. You have
caused your days to draw near, and
have come to *the end of* your years;
[m]therefore I have made you a reproach to the nations, and a mockery
to all countries.
5 "*Those* near and *those* far from
you will mock you as infamous *and*
full of tumult.
6 "Look, the [n]princes of Israel:
each one has used his power to shed
blood in you.
7 "In you they have [o]made light of
father and mother; in your midst they
have oppressed the stranger; in you
they have mistreated the [p]fatherless
and the widow.
8 "You have despised My holy
things and profaned My Sabbaths.
9 "In you are men who [q]slander to
cause bloodshed; in you are those who
eat on the mountains; in your midst
they commit lewdness.
10 "In you men uncover their fathers' nakedness; in you they violate
women who are [r]set apart during
their impurity.
11 "One commits abomination with
his [s]neighbor's wife; another lewdly
defiles his [t]daughter-in-law; and another in you violates his sister, his father's [u]daughter.
12 "In you they take [v]bribes to shed
blood; you take usury and increase;
you have made profit from your
neighbors by extortion, and have
[w]forgotten Me," says the Lord GOD.
13 "Behold, therefore, I beat My
fists at the dishonest profit which you
have made, and at the bloodshed
which has been in your midst.
14 "Can your heart endure, or can
your hands remain strong, in the days
when I shall deal with you? I, the LORD,
have spoken, and will do *it*.

25 *a* 2 Chr. 36:13; Jer. 52:2; Ezek. 12:10; 17:19
27 *b* Cp. Hag. 2:7,22 *c* v. 13; Gen. 49:10; Lk. 1:32–33; Jn. 1:49 *d* Ps. 2:6; 72:6–7; Jer. 23:5–6
28 *e* vv. 28,32; Jer. 25:21; 49:1–6; Ezek. 25:1–7; Amos 1:13; Zeph. 2:8–11
29 *f* Ezek. 13:6–9; 22:28 *g* v. 25; Job 18:20; Ps. 37:13; Isa. 10:3; Ezek. 7:2,3,7
30 *h* Gen. 15:14 *i* Ezek. 16:3
31 *j* Jer. 6:22–23; 51:20–21; Hab. 1:6–10
CHAPTER 22
3 *k* Ezek. 24:6–7
4 *l* Cp. 2 Ki. 21:16 *m* Dt. 28:37; 1 Ki. 9:7; Ezek.5:14; Dan. 9:16
6 *n* Isa. 1:23; Mic. 3:1–3; Zeph. 3:3
7 *o* Lev. 20:9; Dt. 27:16 *p* Ex. 22:22; Jer. 5:28
9 *q* Jer. 9:4
10 *r* Lev. 18:19; 20:18; Ezek. 18:6

22:11 *s* Jer. 5:8; Ezek. 18:11 *t* Lev. 18:15 *u* Lev. 18:9 **22:12** *v* Ex. 23:8; Dt. 16:19; 27:25 *w* Dt. 32:18; Jer. 3:21; Ezek. 23:35

[1](21:27) The Lord Jesus is the only one "whose right it is." When He finishes overturning men's affairs and thrones, He will take His own throne and rule over the world from Jerusalem (Gen. 49:10; Isa. 2:1–4).

15 "I will scatter you among the nations, disperse you throughout the
countries, and remove your filthiness
completely from you.
16 "You shall defile yourself in the
sight of the nations; then you shall
know that I *am* the LORD." ' "

Parable of the dross in the furnace

17 The word of the LORD came to
me, saying,
18 "Son of man, the house of Israel
has become [a]dross to Me; they *are* all
bronze, tin, iron, and lead, in the midst
of a [b]furnace; they have become dross
from silver.
19 "Therefore thus says the Lord
GOD: 'Because you have all become
dross, therefore behold, I will gather
you into the midst of Jerusalem.
20 '*As men* gather silver, bronze,
iron, lead, and tin into the midst of a
furnace, to blow fire on it, to [c]melt *it;*
so I will gather *you* in My anger and in
My fury, and I will leave *you there* and
melt you.
21 'Yes, I will gather you and [d]blow
on you with the fire of My wrath, and
you shall be melted in its midst.
22 'As silver is melted in the midst
of a furnace, so shall you be melted in
its midst; then you shall know that I,
the LORD, have [e]poured out My fury
on you.' "

Sins of the leaders and people

23 And the word of the LORD came
to me, saying,
24 "Son of man, say to her: 'You *are*
a land that is [f]not cleansed* or rained
on in the day of indignation.'
25 "The [g]conspiracy of her prophets* in her midst is like a roaring lion
tearing the prey; they have devoured
people; they have taken [h]treasure and
precious things; they have made
many widows in her midst.
26 "Her [i]priests have violated My
[j]law and [k]profaned My holy things;
they have [l]not distinguished between
the holy and unholy, nor have they
made known *the difference* between
the unclean and the clean; and they
have hidden their eyes from My Sabbaths, so that I am profaned among
them.

18
a Ps. 119:119; Isa. 1:22; Jer. 6:28
b Prov. 17:3; Isa. 48:10
20
c Isa. 1:25; Jer. 9:7
21
d vv. 20–22
22
e v. 31; Ezek. 20:8, 33
24
f Jer. 2:30; Ezek. 24:13
25
g Jer. 11:9; Hos. 6:9
h Mic. 3:11; Zeph. 3:3–4
26
i Jer. 32:32; Lam. 4:13
j *Law* (of Moses): v. 26; Dan. 9:11. (Ex. 19:1; Gal. 3:24, *note*)
k Lev. 22:2; 1 Sam. 2:29
l Lev. 10:10
27
m v. 6; Isa. 1:23; Mic. 3:1–3, 9–11; Zeph. 3:3
28
n i.e. *whitewash*
o Jer. 23:25–32; Ezek. 21:29
29
p Ex. 23:9
30
q Ps. 106:23
r Isa. 59:16; Jer. 5:1
CHAPTER 23
1
s *Parables* (OT): vv. 1–17; Ezek. 24:3. (Jud. 9:8; Zech. 11:7)

27 "Her [m]princes in her midst *are*
like wolves tearing the prey, to shed
blood, to destroy people, and to get
dishonest gain.
28 "Her prophets plastered them
with [n]untempered *mortar,* seeing
false visions, and divining [o]lies for
them, saying, 'Thus says the Lord
GOD,' when the LORD had not spoken.
29 "The people of the land have
used oppressions, committed robbery,
and mistreated the poor and needy;
and they wrongfully [p]oppress the
stranger.
30 [1]"So I sought for a man among
them who would make a wall, and
[q]stand in the gap before Me on behalf
of the land, that I should not destroy it;
but I found [r]no one.
31 "Therefore I have poured out My
indignation on them; I have consumed
them with the fire of My wrath; and I
have recompensed their deeds on
their own heads," says the Lord GOD.

Parable of Oholah (Israel) and Oholibah (Judah)

23 THE word of the LORD came
again to me, [s]saying:

2 "Son of man, there were two
women,
The [t]daughters of one mother.
3 They committed [2]harlotry in
Egypt,
They committed harlotry in
their youth;
Their breasts were there
embraced,
Their virgin bosom was there
pressed.
4 Their names: Oholah the elder
and Oholibah her [u]sister;
[v]They were Mine,
And they bore sons and
daughters.
As for their names,

23:2 *t* Ezek. 16:44–46 **23:4** *u* Jer. 3:6–7 *v* Ezek. 16:8,20; see Hos. 2:2, *note*

*
22:24 Following Masoretic Text, Syriac, and Vulgate; Septuagint reads *showered upon.* **22:25** Following Masoretic Text and Vulgate; Septuagint reads *princes;* Targum reads *scribes.*

[1](22:30) Jeremiah was in Jerusalem at that time, but of what value were his prayers for a people who would not repent (Jer. 11:14; cp. Ps. 66:18)?

[2](23:3) This dark parable of Oholah and Oholibah unmasks the loathsome nature of unfaithfulness to God and provides a corrective for any light view of apostasy. The picture, revolting though it is, shows the awfulness of spiritual adultery whereby the LORD's people, who are one with Him as bride with bridegroom, repudiate their union with Him and give themselves to the service of the world, the flesh, and the devil. Cp. Jas. 4:4.

Samaria *is* [a]Oholah, and
Jerusalem *is* [b]Oholibah.

5 "Oholah played the harlot even
though she was Mine;
And she lusted for her lovers,
the neighboring Assyrians,
6 *Who were* clothed in purple,
Captains and rulers,
All of them desirable young
men,
Horsemen riding on horses.
7 Thus she committed her
harlotry with them,
All of them choice men of
Assyria;
And with all for whom she
lusted,
With all their idols, she defiled
herself.
8 She has never given up her
harlotry *brought* from Egypt,
For in her youth they had lain
with her,
Pressed her virgin bosom,
And poured out their
immorality upon her.
9 "Therefore I have delivered her
Into the hand of her lovers,
Into the hand of the Assyrians,
For whom she lusted.
10 They [c]uncovered her
nakedness,
Took away her sons and
daughters,
And slew her with the sword;
She became a byword among
women,
For they had executed
judgment on her.

11 "Now although her sister Oholibah saw *this*, she became [d]more corrupt in her lust than she, and in her
harlotry more corrupt than her sister's
harlotry.

12 "She lusted for the neighboring
[e]Assyrians,
Captains and rulers,
Clothed most gorgeously,
Horsemen riding on horses,
All of them desirable young
men.
13 Then I saw that she was
defiled;
Both *took* the same way.
14 But she increased her harlotry;
She looked at men portrayed
on the wall,
Images of [f]Chaldeans
portrayed in vermilion,
15 Girded with belts around their
waists,
Flowing turbans on their
heads,
All of them looking like
captains,
In the manner of the
Babylonians of Chaldea,
The land of their nativity.
16 As [g]soon as her eyes saw
them,
She lusted for them
And sent [h]messengers to them
in Chaldea.
17 "Then the Babylonians came to
her, into the bed of love,
And they defiled her with their
immorality;
So she was defiled by them,
and alienated herself from
them.
18 She revealed her harlotry and
uncovered her nakedness.
Then [i]I [j]alienated Myself
from her,
As I had alienated Myself from
her sister.

19 "Yet she multiplied her harlotry
In calling to remembrance the
days of her youth,
When she had played the
harlot in the land of [k]Egypt.
20 For she lusted for her
paramours,
Whose flesh *is like* the flesh of
donkeys,
And whose issue *is like* the
issue of horses.
21 Thus you called to
remembrance the lewdness
of your youth,
When the [l]Egyptians pressed
your bosom
Because of your youthful
breasts.

The Babylonian invasion

22 "Therefore, Oholibah, thus says
the Lord GOD:

[m]'Behold, I will stir up your
lovers against you,
From whom you have
alienated yourself,
And I will bring them against
you from every side:
23 The Babylonians,
All the Chaldeans,
[n]Pekod, Shoa, Koa,
All the Assyrians with them,
All of them desirable young
men,
Governors and rulers,
Captains and men of renown,
All of them riding on horses.

4
a Meaning *(She has) her own tent.* See 2 Chr. 10:16 and Hos. 1:10, *notes*
b Meaning *My tent (is) in her.* See 2 Ki. 17:23, *note*
10
c Ezek. 16:37
11
d Ezek. 16:51–52
12
e Ezek. 16:28; cp. 2 Ki. 16:8, 17–18; 2 Chr. 28:19–25
14
f Jer. 50:2; Ezek. 8:10; 16:29
16
g Cp. v. 23; Isa. 57:8
h Isa. 57:9
18
i Jer. 6:8
j Ps. 78:59; 106:40; Jer. 12:8
19
k v. 3; Lev. 18:3
21
l Ezek. 16:26
22
m v. 28; Ezek. 16:37–41
23
n Jer. 50:21

24 And they shall come against
you
With chariots, wagons, and
war-horses,
With a horde of people.
They shall array against you
Buckler, shield, and helmet all
around.

'I will delegate judgment to
them,
And they shall judge you
according to their
judgments.
25 I will set My [a]jealousy against
you,
And they shall deal furiously
with you;
They shall remove your nose
and your ears,
And your remnant shall fall by
the sword;
They shall take your sons and
your daughters,
And your remnant shall be
devoured by fire.
26 They shall also [b]strip you of
your clothes
And take away your beautiful
jewelry.

27 'Thus I will make you cease
your lewdness and your
harlotry
Brought from the land of
Egypt,
So that you will not lift your
eyes to them,
Nor remember Egypt
anymore.'

28 "For thus says the Lord GOD:
'Surely I will deliver you [c]into the
hand of those you hate, into the hand
of those from whom [d]you alienated
yourself.
29 [e]'They will deal hatefully with
you, take away all you have worked
for, and leave you naked and bare.
The nakedness of your harlotry shall
be uncovered, both your lewdness and
your harlotry.
30 'I will do these *things* to you because you have gone as a harlot after
the Gentiles, because you have become defiled by their idols.
31 'You have walked in the way of
your sister; therefore I will put her
[f]cup in your hand.'
32 "Thus says the Lord GOD:

'You shall drink of your sister's
cup,
The deep and wide one;
[g]You shall be laughed to scorn
And held in derision;
It contains much.
33 You will be filled with
drunkenness and sorrow,
The cup of horror and
desolation,
The cup of your sister
Samaria.
34 You shall [h]drink and drain it,
You shall break its shards,
And tear at your own breasts;
For I have spoken,'
Says the Lord GOD.

35 "Therefore thus says the Lord
GOD:

[1]'Because you have [i]forgotten
Me and cast Me behind your
back,
Therefore you shall bear the
penalty
Of your lewdness and your
harlotry.' "

Judgment of Oholah and Oholibah

36 The LORD also said to me: "Son of
man, will you judge Oholah and Oholibah? Then [j]declare to them their
abominations.
37 "For they have committed adultery, and [k]blood *is* on their hands.
They have committed adultery with
their idols, and even sacrificed their
[l]sons whom they bore to Me, passing
them through *the fire,* to devour *them.*
38 "Moreover they have done this
to Me: They have [m]defiled My sanctuary on the same day and profaned My
Sabbaths.
39 "For after they had [n]slain their
children for their idols, on the same
day they came into My sanctuary to
profane it; and indeed [o]thus they have
done in the midst of My house.
40 "Furthermore you sent for men
to come from afar, to whom a [p]mes-
senger *was* sent; and there they came.
And you washed yourself for them,
[q]painted your eyes, and adorned
yourself with ornaments.
41 "You sat on a stately couch, with
a table prepared before it, on which
you had [r]set My incense and My oil.
42 "The sound of a carefree multitude *was* with her, and [s]Sabeans *were*
brought from the wilderness with men

25 *a* Ex. 34:14; Ezek. 36:5–6; Zeph. 1:18; cp. Jas. 4:4–5
26 *b* Isa. 3:18–23; Ezek. 16:39
28 *c* Jer. 21:7–10; Ezek. 16:37–41 *d* v. 17
29 *e* Dt. 28:48
31 *f* vv. 31–34; Jer. 7:14–15; 25:15–18
32 *g* Ezek. 22:4–5
34 *h* Ps. 75:8; Isa. 51:17
35 *i* Jer. 2:32; 3:21; 13:25; Ezek. 22:12
36 *j* Cp. Lam. 2:14
37 *k* Ezek. 22:3 *l* Ezek. 16:20–21, 36,45; 20:26,31
38 *m* Ezek. 5:11
39 *n* i.e. *sacrificed* *o* 2 Ki. 21:2–7
40 *p* Isa. 57:9 *q* 2 Ki. 9:30; Jer. 4:30
41 *r* Prov. 7:17; Ezek. 16:18–19; Hos. 2:8
42 *s* Or *drunkards.* Heb. uncertain

[1](23:35) Whereas God is faithful in remembering His covenant with His people (see Ezek. 16:60, *note*), when they forget Him they must expect chastening from Him (Heb. 12:6).

of the common sort, who put bracelets on their wrists and beautiful crowns on their heads.

43 "Then I said concerning *her who had grown* old in adulteries, 'Will they commit harlotry with her now, and she *with them?*'

44 "Yet they went in to her, as men go in to a woman who plays the harlot; thus they went in to Oholah and Oholibah, the lewd women.

45 "But righteous men will [a]judge them after the manner of adulteresses, and after the manner of women who shed blood, because they *are* adulteresses, and blood *is* on their hands.

46 "For thus says the Lord GOD: 'Bring up an assembly against them, give them up to trouble and plunder.

47 'The assembly shall stone them with [b]stones and execute them with their swords; they shall [c]slay their sons and their daughters, and burn their houses with fire.

48 'Thus I will cause lewdness to cease from the land, that all women may be [d]taught not to practice your lewdness.

49 'They shall repay you for your lewdness, and you shall pay for your idolatrous sins. Then you shall know that I *am* the Lord GOD.' "

Parable of the boiling pot

24 AGAIN, in the [e]ninth [f]year, in the [g]tenth month, on the tenth *day* of the month, the word of the LORD came to me, saying,

2 "Son of man, write down the name of the [h]day, this very day—the king of Babylon started his siege against Jerusalem this very day.

3 "And utter a [i]parable to the rebellious house, and say to them, 'Thus says the Lord GOD:

"Put on a pot, set *it* on,
And also pour water into it.
4 Gather pieces *of meat* in it,
Every good piece,
The thigh and the shoulder.
Fill *it* with choice cuts;
5 Take the choice of the flock.
Also pile *fuel* bones under it,
Make it boil well,
And let the cuts simmer in it."

6 'Therefore thus says the Lord GOD:

[j]"Woe to the bloody city,
To the pot whose scum *is* in it,
And whose scum is not gone
from it!
Bring it out piece by piece,
On which no [k]lot has fallen.
7 For her blood is in her midst;
She set it on top of a rock;
She did not [l]pour it on the
ground,
To cover it with dust.
8 That it may raise up fury and
take vengeance,
I have set her blood on top of
a rock,
That it may not be covered."

9 'Therefore thus says the Lord GOD:

[m]"Woe to the bloody city!
I too will make the pyre great.
10 Heap on the wood,
Kindle the fire;
Cook the meat well,
Mix in the spices,
And let the cuts be burned up.

11 "Then set the pot empty on the
coals,
That it may become hot and its
bronze may burn,
That its filthiness may be
[n]melted in it,
That its scum may be
consumed.
12 She has grown weary with lies,
And her great scum has not
gone from her.
Let her scum *be* in the fire!
13 In your [o]filthiness *is* lewdness.
Because I have cleansed you,
and you were not cleansed,
You will [p]not be cleansed of
your filthiness anymore,
[q]Till I have caused My fury to
rest upon you.
14 [r]I, the LORD, have spoken *it;*
[s]It shall come to pass, and I will
do *it;*
I will not hold back,
Nor will I spare,
Nor will I [t]relent;
According to your ways
And according to your deeds
They* will judge you,"
Says the Lord GOD.' "

Death of Ezekiel's wife: a sign

15 Also the word of the LORD came to me, saying,

16 "Son of man, behold, I take away from you the desire of your eyes with one stroke; yet you shall [u]neither mourn nor weep, nor shall your tears run down.

17 "Sigh in silence, make no

45
a Ezek. 16:38
47
b Lev. 20:10; cp. Jn. 8:1–11
c 2 Chr. 36:17,19; Ezek. 24:21
48
d Dt. 13:11; Ezek. 22:15; cp. 2 Pet. 2:6
CHAPTER 24
1
e Cp. Ezek. 1:1; 20:1; 26:1
f c. 589 B.C.
g See Lev. 23:2, *note*
2
h 2 Ki. 25:1
3
i *Parables* (OT): vv. 3–6; Ezek. 31:3. (Jud. 9:8; Zech. 11:7)
6
j v. 9; Ezek. 22:2–4
k Joel 3:3; Obad. 11; Nah. 3:10
7
l Lev. 17:13; Dt. 12:16, 24
9
m Nah. 3:1; Hab. 2:12
11
n Ezek. 22:15–22
13
o Ezek. 23:36–48
p Jer. 6:28–30; Ezek. 22:24
q Ezek. 5:13; 8:18; 16:42
14
r 1 Sam. 15:29
s Num. 23:19; Isa. 55:11
t See Zech. 8:14, *note*
16
u Jer. 16:5

*24:14 Septuagint, Syriac, Targum, and Vulgate read *I.*

mourning for the dead; bind your turban on your head, and [a]put your sandals on your feet; do not cover *your* lips, and do not eat man's bread *of sorrow*."

18 So I spoke to the people in the morning, and at evening my wife died; and the next morning I did as I was commanded.

19 And the people said to me, [b]"Will you not tell us what these *things signify* to us, that you [c]behave so?"

20 Then I answered them, "The word of the LORD came to me, saying,

21 'Speak to the house of Israel, "Thus says the Lord GOD: 'Behold, I will [d]profane My sanctuary, your arrogant boast, the desire of your eyes, the delight of your soul; and your [e]sons and daughters whom you left behind shall fall by the sword.

22 'And you shall do as I have done; you shall not cover *your* lips nor eat man's bread *of sorrow*.

23 'Your turbans shall be on your heads and your sandals on your feet; you shall neither mourn nor weep, but you shall [f]pine away in your iniquities and mourn with one another.

24 'Thus [g]Ezekiel is a sign to you; according to all that he has done you shall do; and when this comes, you shall know that I *am* the Lord GOD.' "

25 'And you, son of man—*will it* not *be* in the day when I take from them their stronghold, their joy and their glory, the desire of their eyes, and that on which they set their minds, their sons and their daughters:

26 'on that day one who [h]escapes will come to you to let *you* hear *it* with *your* ears;

27 'on that day your mouth will be [i]opened to him who has escaped; you shall speak and no longer be [j]mute. Thus you will be a [k]sign to them, and they shall know that I *am* the LORD.' "

III. Judgments on the Gentile Nations, 25—32

Prophecy against Ammon

25 THE word of the LORD came to me, saying,

2 "Son of man, set your face against the [1]Ammonites, and prophesy against them.

3 "Say to the Ammonites, 'Hear the word of the Lord GOD! Thus says the Lord GOD: [m]"Because you said, 'Aha!' against My sanctuary when it was profaned, and against the land of Israel when it was desolate, and against the house of Judah when they went into captivity,

4 "indeed, therefore, I will deliver you as a possession to the [n]men of the East, and they shall set their encampments among you and make their dwellings among you; they shall eat your fruit, and they shall drink your milk.

5 "And I will make Rabbah a stable for camels and Ammon a resting place for flocks. Then you shall know that I *am* the LORD."

6 'For thus says the Lord GOD: [o]"Because you clapped *your* hands, stamped your feet, and rejoiced in heart with all your disdain for the land of Israel,

7 "indeed, therefore, I will stretch out My hand against you, and give you as plunder to the [p]nations; I will cut you off from the peoples, and I will cause you to perish from the countries; I will destroy you, and you shall know that I *am* the LORD."

Prophecy against Moab

8 [2]'Thus says the Lord GOD: "Because [q]Moab and Seir say, 'Look! The house of Judah *is* like all the nations,'

9 "therefore, behold, I will clear the territory of Moab of cities, of the cities on its frontier, the glory of the country, Beth Jeshimoth, Baal Meon, and [r]Kirjathaim.

10 "To the men of the East I will give it as a possession, together with the Ammonites, that the Ammonites may not be remembered among the nations.

11 "And I will execute judgments upon Moab, and they shall know that I *am* the LORD."

17 [a] Cp. 2 Sam. 15:30
19 [b] Ezek. 12:9; 37:18 [c] vv. 16–17
21 [d] Lam. 2:7; Ezek. 7:24 [e] Jer. 16:3–4
23 [f] Lev. 26:39; Ezek. 33:10
24 [g] v. 27; Ezek. 4:3; 12:6,11; cp. Isa. 20:3
26 [h] Ezek. 33:21
27 [i] Ezek. 33:22 [j] Cp. Ezek. 3:26 [k] v. 24
CHAPTER 25
2 [l] Jer. 25:21; 49:1–6; Ezek. 21:28–32; Amos 1:13; Zeph. 2:8–11
3 [m] Prov. 17:5; cp. Jer. 33:24; Ezek. 26:2; 36:2
4 [n] Cp. Jer. 49:2; Ezek. 21:20
6 [o] Lam. 2:15
7 [p] Cp. Isa. 36:18–20
8 [q] Isa. 15:1–16:14; 25:10; Jer. 25:21; 48:1–47; Amos 2:1–3; Zeph. 2:8–11

25:9 [r] Jer. 48:23

[1](25:2) During the course of the seige of Jerusalem, Ezekiel turned his attention entirely to prophecies concerning foreign nations (25:1—32:32).

[2](25:8) The prophecies upon Gentile powers (see v. 2, *note*) have doubtless had partial fulfillments of which history and the present condition of those cities and countries bear witness, but the mention of the day of the LORD (30:3) makes it evident that a fulfillment in the final sense is still future. See Day of the LORD (Isa. 2:10–22; Joel 1:15 and Rev. 19:19, *notes*); also Armageddon (Rev. 16:13–16; 19:17, *note*). Those countries are once more to be the battleground of the nations.

Prophecy against Edom

12 'Thus says the Lord GOD: [a]"Because of what [b]Edom did against the house of Judah by taking vengeance, and has greatly offended by avenging itself on them,"

13 'therefore thus says the Lord GOD: "I will also stretch out My hand against Edom, cut off man and beast from it, and make it desolate from Teman; Dedan shall fall by the sword.

14 "I will lay My vengeance on Edom by the hand of My people Israel, that they may do in Edom according to My anger and according to My fury; and they shall know My vengeance," says the Lord GOD.

Prophecy against Philistia

15 'Thus says the Lord GOD: [1]"Because the [c]Philistines dealt vengefully and took vengeance with a spiteful heart, to destroy because of the old hatred,"

16 'therefore thus says the Lord GOD: "I will stretch out My hand against the Philistines, and I will cut off the Cherethites and destroy the remnant of the seacoast.

17 "I will execute great vengeance on them with furious rebukes; and they shall [d]know that I *am* the LORD, when I lay My vengeance upon them." ' "

Judgment on Tyre

26 AND it came to pass in the [e]eleventh [f]year, on the first *day* of the month, *that* the word of the LORD came to me, saying,

2 "Son of man, [g]because Tyre has said against Jerusalem, [h]'Aha! She is broken who *was* the gateway of the peoples; now she is turned over to me; I shall be filled; she is laid waste.'

3 "Therefore thus says the Lord GOD: 'Behold, I *am* against you, O Tyre, and will cause many nations to come up against you, as the sea causes its waves to come up.

4 'And they shall destroy the walls of Tyre and break down her towers; I will also scrape her dust from her, and make her like the top of a rock.

5 'It shall be *a place for* spreading nets in the midst of the sea, for I have spoken,' says the Lord GOD; 'it shall become plunder for the nations.

6 'Also her daughter *villages* which *are* in the fields shall be slain by the sword. Then they shall know that I am the LORD.'

7 "For thus says the Lord GOD: 'Behold, I will bring against Tyre from the north [i]Nebuchadnezzar* king of Babylon, [j]king of kings, with horses, with chariots, and with horsemen, and an army with many people.

8 'He will slay with the sword your daughter *villages* in the fields; he will heap up a siege mound against you, build a wall against you, and raise a defense against you.

9 'He will direct his battering rams against your walls, and with his axes he will break down your towers.

10 'Because of the abundance of his horses, their dust will cover you; your walls will shake at the noise of the horsemen, the wagons, and the chariots, when he enters your gates, as men enter a city that has been breached.

11 'With the hooves of his [k]horses he will trample all your streets; he will slay your people by the sword, and your strong pillars will fall to the ground.

12 'They will plunder your riches and pillage your merchandise; they will break down your walls and destroy your pleasant houses; they will lay your stones, your timber, and your soil in the [l]midst of the water.

13 'I will put an end to the [m]sound of your songs, and the sound of your harps shall be heard no more.

14 'I will [2]make you like the top of a rock; you shall be *a place for* spreading nets, and you shall never be re-

12
a 2 Chr. 28:17; Ps. 137:7; Obad. 10–14
b Jer. 25:21; 49:7–22; Ezek. 35:1–15; Joel 3:19; Amos 1:11–12; Obad. 1–9, 15–16

15
c Isa. 14:29–31; Jer. 47:1–4; Zeph. 2:5; Zech. 9:6

17
d Cp. vv. 5, 7,11,14

CHAPTER 26

1
e Cp. Ezek. 24:1; 29:1, 17
f c. 587 B.C.

2
g Isa. 23; Jer. 25:22; 47:4; Amos 1:9; Zech. 9:2
h Cp. Ezek. 25:3; 36:2

7
i Jer. 27:3–6; Ezek. 29:18
j Ezra 7:12; Dan. 2:37

11
k Hab. 1:8

12
l Ezek. 27:27,32

13
m Isa. 14:11; 24:8; Jer. 7:34; 16:9; 25:10

* **26:7** Hebrew *Nebuchadrezzar,* and so elsewhere in this book

[1](25:15) The Philistines' sustained animosity toward Israel, remembered chiefly from Goliath's challenge to David, required God's judgment upon them.

[2](26:14) The fate predicted for Tyre is unique and has been remarkably fulfilled. At the time of Ezekiel, Tyre was on the coast of Phoenicia at the shore of the Mediterranean Sea. As Ezekiel predicted, Nebuchadnezzar conquered and destroyed the city. He had no reason, however, to fulfill v. 12 by casting its ruins into the sea. Some of the people from Tyre escaped to an island and built a new city there. Three hundred years later Alexander the Great, desiring to conquer this island city, built a causeway to it and threw all the remains of ancient Tyre (called *Palaeotyrus* by the Greeks) into the sea, fulfilling Ezek. 26:12. The old city of Tyre has never been rebuilt, but has remained like the top of a rock. Remains of ancient Sidon (28:20–24) have been excavated, and a flourishing town now stands on its old site, but the remains of ancient Tyre are in the sea under Alexander's causeway.

built, for I the LORD have spoken,' says
the Lord GOD.
15 "Thus says the Lord GOD to Tyre:
'Will the [a]coastlands not shake at the
sound of your fall, when the wounded
cry, when slaughter is made in the
midst of you?
16 'Then all the [b]princes of the sea
will come down from their thrones,
lay aside their robes, and take off their
embroidered garments; they will
clothe themselves with trembling;
they will sit on the ground, [c]tremble
every moment, and be [d]astonished at
you.
17 'And they will take up a [e]lamen-
tation for you, and say to you:

"How you have perished,
O one inhabited by seafaring
men,
O renowned city,
Who was [f]strong at sea,
She and her inhabitants,
Who caused their terror *to be*
on all her inhabitants!
18 Now the [a]coastlands tremble
on the day of your fall;
Yes, the coastlands by the sea
are troubled at your
[g]departure." '

19 "For thus says the Lord GOD:
'When I make you a desolate city, like
cities that are not inhabited, when I
bring the deep upon you, and great
waters cover you,
20 'then I will bring you down
[h]with those who descend into the Pit,
to the people of old, and I will make
you dwell in the lowest part of the
earth, in places desolate from antiquity, with those who go down to the
Pit, so that you may never be inhabited; and I shall establish glory in the
land of the living.
21 'I will make you a [i]terror, and
you *shall be* no *more;* [j]though you are
sought for, you will never be found
[k]again,' says the Lord GOD."

Lament over Tyre
(cp. Rev. 18:1–24)

27 THE word of the LORD came
again to me, saying,
2 "Now, son of man, take up a
[l]lamentation for Tyre,
3 "and say to Tyre, [m]'You who are
situated at the entrance of the sea,
merchant of the peoples on many
coastlands, thus says the Lord GOD:

"O Tyre, you have said,
'I *am* perfect in [n]beauty.'

15
a Isa. 41:5
16
b Isa. 23:8
c Ezek. 32:10
d Ezek. 27:35
17
e Ezek. 27:2–36
f Josh. 19:29
18
g Cp. Isa. 23:5
20
h Ezek. 32:18,24; cp. Isa. 14:9–10
21
i Ezek. 27:36
j Ps. 37:10, 36; Ezek. 28:19
k Cp. Jer. 51:64
CHAPTER 27
2
l vv. 2–36; cp. Ezek. 28:11–19
3
m Ezek. 26:17
n Cp. Isa. 13:19; Ezek. 28:12
6
o Isa. 2:12–13
p Or *deck*
7
q i.e. *as an awning*
8
r 1 Ki. 9:27
9
s Ps. 83:7
12
t Gen. 10:4; 2 Chr. 20:36; Ezek. 38:13
13
u Joel 3:4–6; cp. Rev. 18:13
14
v Gen. 10:3; Ezek. 38:6

4 Your borders *are* in the midst
of the seas.
Your builders have perfected
your beauty.
5 They made all *your* planks of
fir trees from Senir;
They took a cedar from
Lebanon to make you a
mast.
6 *Of* [o]oaks from Bashan they
made your oars;
The company of Ashurites
have inlaid your [p]planks
With ivory from the coasts of
Cyprus.*
7 Fine embroidered linen from
Egypt was what you spread
for your sail;
Blue and purple from the
coasts of Elishah was what
[q]covered you.
8 "Inhabitants of Sidon and
Arvad were your oarsmen;
Your [r]wise men, O Tyre, were
in you;
They became your pilots.
9 Elders of [s]Gebal and its wise
men
Were in you to caulk your
seams;
All the ships of the sea
And their oarsmen were in you
To market your merchandise.
10 "Those from Persia, Lydia,*
and Libya*
Were in your army as men of
war;
They hung shield and helmet
in you;
They gave splendor to you.
11 Men of Arvad with your army
were on your walls *all*
around,
And the men of Gammad were
in your towers;
They hung their shields on
your walls *all* around;
They made your beauty
perfect.

12 [t]"Tarshish *was* your merchant
because of your many luxury goods.
They gave you silver, iron, tin, and
lead for your goods.
13 "Javan, Tubal, and Meshech
were your traders. They bartered human [u]lives and vessels of bronze for
your merchandise.
14 "Those from the house of [v]To-

*
27:6 Hebrew *Kittim,* western lands, especially Cyprus **27:10** Hebrew *Lud* • Hebrew *Put*

garmah traded for your wares with
horses, steeds, and mules.
15 "The men of [a]Dedan *were* your
traders; many isles *were* the market of
your hand. They brought you ivory
tusks and ebony as payment.
16 "Syria *was* your merchant because of the abundance of goods you
made. They gave you for your wares
emeralds, purple, embroidery, fine
linen, corals, and rubies.
17 "Judah and the land of Israel
were your traders. They traded for
your merchandise [b]wheat of Minnith,
millet, honey, oil, and balm.
18 "Damascus *was* your merchant
because of the abundance of goods
you made, because of your many luxury items, with the wine of Helbon
and with white wool.
19 "Dan and Javan paid for your
wares, traversing back and forth.
Wrought iron, cassia, and cane were
among your merchandise.
20 "Dedan *was* your merchant in
saddlecloths for riding.
21 "Arabia and all the princes of
[c]Kedar *were* your regular merchants.
They traded with you in lambs, rams,
and goats.
22 "The merchants of Sheba and
Raamah *were* your merchants. They
traded for your wares the choicest
spices, all kinds of precious stones,
and gold.
23 [d]"Haran, Canneh, Eden, the
merchants of [e]Sheba, Assyria, *and*
Chilmad *were* your merchants.
24 "These *were* your merchants in
choice items—in purple clothes, in
embroidered garments, in chests of
multicolored apparel, in sturdy woven
cords, which were in your marketplace.

25 "The ships of Tarshish were
carriers of your
merchandise.
You were filled and very
glorious in the midst of the
seas.
26 Your oarsmen brought you
into many waters,
But the [f]east wind broke you
in the midst of the seas.

27 "Your riches, wares, and
merchandise,
Your mariners and pilots,
Your caulkers and
merchandisers,
All your men of war who *are*
in you,
And the entire company which
is in your midst,
Will fall into the midst of the
seas on the day of your ruin.
28 The common-land will shake
at the sound of the cry of
your pilots.

29 "All who handle the oar,
The [g]mariners,
All the pilots of the sea
Will come down from their
ships *and* stand on the
shore.
30 They will make their voice
heard because of you;
They will cry bitterly and cast
dust on their [h]heads;
They will roll about in ashes;
31 They will shave themselves
completely [i]bald because of
you,
Gird themselves with
sackcloth,
And weep for you
With bitterness of heart *and*
bitter wailing.
32 In their wailing for you
They will take up a
[j]lamentation,
And lament for you:
[k]'What *city is* like Tyre,
[l]Destroyed in the midst of the
sea?
33 'When your wares went out by
sea,
You satisfied many people;
You enriched the kings of the
earth
With your many luxury goods
and your merchandise.
34 But you are broken by the seas
in the depths of the waters;
Your merchandise and the
entire company will fall in
your midst.
35 All the inhabitants of the isles
will be [m]astonished at you;
Their kings will be greatly
afraid,
And *their* countenance will be
troubled.
36 The merchants among the
peoples will hiss at you;
You will become a [n]horror,
and *be* [o]no more
forever.' " ' "

Tyre's proud ruler rebuked

28 THE word of the LORD came to
me again, saying,
2 "Son of man, say to the prince of
Tyre, 'Thus says the Lord GOD:

15 [a] Gen. 10:7; Isa. 21:13
17 [b] 1 Ki. 5:9, 11; Ezra 3:7; Acts 12:20
21 [c] Jer. 49:28
23 [d] Gen. 11:31; 2 Ki. 19:12 [e] Gen. 25:3
26 [f] Ps. 48:7; Jer. 18:17; Acts 27:14
29 [g] Cp. Rev. 18:17–19
30 [h] Cp. Rev. 18:19
31 [i] Ezek. 29:18
32 [j] Ezek. 26:17 [k] Cp. Rev. 18:18 [l] Ezek. 26:4–5
35 [m] Ezek. 26:16
36 [n] Ezek. 26:21 [o] Ps. 37:10, 36; Ezek. 28:19

[a]"Because your heart *is* [b]lifted
up,
And you say, 'I *am* a [c]god,
I sit *in* the seat of gods,
In the midst of the [d]seas,'
Yet you *are* a man, and not a
god,
Though you set your heart as
the heart of a god
3 (Behold, you *are* wiser than
[e]Daniel!
There is no secret that can be
hidden from you!
4 With your wisdom and your
understanding
You have gained [f]riches for
yourself,
And gathered gold and silver
into your treasuries;
5 By your great wisdom in
[g]trade you have increased
your riches,
And your heart is lifted up
because of your [h]riches),"

6 'Therefore thus says the Lord
GOD:

"Because you have set your
heart as the heart of a god,
7 Behold, therefore, I will bring
[i]strangers against you,
The most [j]terrible of the
nations;
And they shall draw their
swords against the beauty of
your wisdom,
And defile your splendor.
8 They shall throw you down
into the [k]Pit,
And you shall die the death of
the slain
In the midst of the seas.

9 "Will you still say before him
who slays you,
'I *am* a [c]god'?
But you *shall be* a man, and
not a god,
In the hand of him who slays
you.
10 You shall die the death of the
uncircumcised
By the hand of aliens;
For I have spoken," says the
Lord GOD.' "

Satan, the real king of Tyre, who instigated the earthly ruler (cp. Isa. 14:12–17)

11 Moreover the word of the LORD
came to me, saying,
12 "Son of man, take up a [l]lamen-
tation for the king of Tyre, and say to
him, 'Thus says the Lord GOD:

[1]"You *were* the [m]seal of
perfection,
Full of wisdom and [n]perfect in
beauty.
13 You were in Eden, the garden
of God;
Every precious stone *was* your
covering:
The sardius, topaz, and
diamond,
Beryl, onyx, and jasper,
Sapphire, turquoise, and
emerald with gold.
The workmanship of your
timbrels and pipes
Was prepared for you on the
day you were created.

14 "You *were* the anointed
[o]cherub who covers;
I established you;
You were on the holy
[p]mountain of God;
You walked back and forth in
the midst of fiery stones.
15 You *were* perfect in your ways
from the day you were
created,
Till [q]iniquity was found in
you.

16 "By the abundance of your
trading
You became filled with
violence within,
And you sinned;
Therefore I cast you as a
profane thing
Out of the mountain of God;
And I destroyed you, O
covering cherub,
From the midst of the fiery
stones.

17 "Your heart was lifted up
because of your beauty;
You corrupted your wisdom

CHAPTER 28
2
a Cp. Mt. 24:15; see v. 12, *note*
b Jer. 49:16; Ezek. 31:10
c Isa. 14:13–14
d Ezek. 27:27
3
e Ezek. 14:14; Dan. 1:20
4
f Zech. 9:1–3
5
g Ezek. 27:12–25
h Cp. Ps. 52:7; Hos. 13:6
7
i Ezek. 26:7
j Ezek. 7:24; 21:31; 30:11
8
k Isa. 14:15
12
l Ezek. 27:2
m Ezek. 27:3
n *Satan:* vv. 12–15; Zech. 3:1. (Gen. 3:1; Rev. 20:10)
14
o v. 16; Ex. 25:20
p Isa. 14:13
15
q Isa. 14:12

[1](28:12) Here in vv. 11–17, as in Isa. 14:12–17, the language goes beyond the king of Tyre to Satan, inspirer and unseen ruler of all such pomp and pride as that of Tyre. Gen. 3:14–15 and Mt. 16:23 are other instances of thus indirectly addressing Satan. The unfallen state of Satan is here described; his fall is written in Isa. 14. See Rev. 20:10, *note*. Moreover, the vision is not of Satan in his own person, but of Satan fulfilling himself through an earthly king who arrogates to himself divine honors, so that the prince of Tyre foreshadows the beast (Dan. 7:8; Rev. 19:20).

for the sake of your
splendor;
I cast you to the ground,
I laid you before kings,
That they might gaze at you.
18 "You defiled your sanctuaries
By the multitude of your
iniquities,
By the iniquity of your trading;
Therefore I brought fire from
your midst;
It devoured you,
And I turned you to ashes
upon the earth
In the sight of all who saw
you.
19 All who knew you among the
peoples are astonished at
you;
[a]You have become a horror,
And *shall be* no [1b]more
forever." ' "

Prophecy against Sidon

20 Then the word of the LORD came
to me, saying,
21 "Son of man, set your face toward Sidon, and prophesy against
her,
22 "and say, 'Thus says the Lord
GOD:

"Behold, I *am* against you, O
[c]Sidon;
I will be [d]glorified in your
midst;
And they shall know that I *am*
the LORD,
When I execute judgments in
her and am hallowed in her.
23 [e]For I will send pestilence upon
her,
And blood in her streets;
The wounded shall be judged
in her midst
By the sword against her on
every side;
Then they shall know that I
am the LORD.

24 "And there shall no longer be a
[f]pricking brier or a painful thorn for
the house of Israel from among all
who are around them, who [g]despise
them. Then they shall know that I *am*
the Lord GOD."

Future regathering of Israel

25 'Thus says the Lord GOD: "When
I have [h]gathered the house of Israel
from the peoples among whom they
are scattered, and am hallowed in
them in the sight of the Gentiles, then
they will dwell in their own land
which I gave to My servant Jacob.
26 "And they will [i]dwell safely
there, build houses, and plant [j]vine-
yards; yes, they will dwell securely,
when I execute judgments on all those
around them who despise them. Then
they shall know that I *am* the LORD
their God." ' "

Prophecy against Egypt

29 IN the [k]tenth [l]year, in the
[m]tenth *month,* on the twelfth
day of the month, the word of the LORD
came to me, saying,
2 "Son of man, set your face
against Pharaoh king of Egypt, and
prophesy against him, and against all
[n]Egypt.
3 "Speak, and say, 'Thus says the
Lord GOD:

[o]"Behold, I *am* against you,
O Pharaoh king of Egypt,
O great [p]monster who lies in
the midst of his rivers,
Who has said, 'My River* *is*
my own;
I have made *it* for myself.'
4 But I will put [q]hooks in your
jaws,
And cause the fish of your
rivers to stick to your scales;
I will bring you up out of the
midst of your rivers,
And all the fish in your rivers
will stick to your scales.
5 I will leave you in the
wilderness,
You and all the fish of your
rivers;
You shall fall on the open
[r]field;
You shall not be picked up [s]or
gathered.*
I have given you as food
To the beasts of the field

19 *a* Ezek. 26:21 *b* Ezek. 27:36
22 *c* vv. 20–24; Isa. 23:1–18; Jer. 25:22; 47:4; Ezek. 26:1–21; Amos 1:9–10; Zech. 9:2–4 *d* Ex. 14:4, 17; Ezek. 39:13
23 *e* Jer. 47:4
24 *f* Num. 33:55; Josh. 23:13 *g* v. 26; Ezek. 16:57; 25:6–7
25 *h* Isa. 11:12; Ezek. 11:17; 20:41; 34:13; 37:21
26 *i* Jer. 23:6; Ezek. 36:28 *j* Jer. 31:5; Amos 9:14
CHAPTER 29
1 *k* Cp. Ezek. 26:1; 29:17 *l* c. 588 B.C. *m* See Lev. 23:2, *note*
2 *n* 29:1–30:19; Isa. 19:1–22; Joel 3:19
3 *o* v. 10; Jer. 44:30; Ezek. 28:22 *p* Isa. 51:9; Ezek. 32:2
4 *q* Isa. 37:29; Ezek. 38:4
5 *r* Ezek. 32:4–6 *s* Jer. 8:2; 16:4; 25:33

* **29:3** That is, the Nile **29:5** Following Masoretic Text, Septuagint, and Vulgate; some Hebrew manuscripts and Targum read *buried.*

[1](28:19) Verses 1–19 contain references to the ruler and the king of Tyre (vv. 1,12); to Satan (v. 12, see *note 1*); and evidently to the city of Tyre (vv. 7–8,18–19). Other Scriptures make clear that neither the destiny of unsaved men nor of Satan involves cessation of being (Mt. 18:8; 25:41,46; Mk. 3:29; 2 Th. 1:9; Heb. 6:2; Jude 6,13; Rev. 14:11; 20:10). Existence on earth is what is involved here.

And to the birds of the
heavens.

6 "Then all the inhabitants of
Egypt
Shall know that I *am* the LORD,
Because they have been a
[a]staff of reed to the house of
Israel.
7 When they took hold of you
with the hand,
You [b]broke and tore all their
shoulders;*
When they leaned on you,
You broke and made all their
backs quiver."

8 'Therefore thus says the Lord
GOD: "Surely I will bring a sword upon
you and cut off from you man and
beast.
9 "And the land of Egypt shall become [c]desolate and waste; then they
will know that I *am* the LORD, because
he said, 'The River *is* mine, and I have
made *it*.'
10 "Indeed, therefore, I *am* against
you and against your rivers, and I will
make the land of Egypt utterly waste
and desolate, [d]from Migdol* *to* Syene, as far as the border of Ethiopia.
11 "Neither foot of man shall pass
through it nor foot of beast pass
through it, and it shall be uninhabited
forty years.
12 "I will make the land of Egypt
desolate in the midst of the countries
that are desolate; and among the cities *that are* laid waste, her cities shall
be desolate forty years; and I will
[e]scatter the Egyptians among the nations and disperse them throughout
the countries."
13 'Yet, thus says the Lord GOD: "At
the end of forty years I will [f]gather
the Egyptians from the peoples
among whom they were scattered.
14 "I will bring back the captives of
Egypt and cause them to return to the
land of Pathros, to the land of their
origin, and there they shall be a lowly
kingdom.
15 "It shall be the lowliest of kingdoms; it shall never again exalt itself
above the nations, for I will diminish
them so that they will not rule over the
nations anymore.
16 "No longer shall it be the [g]confi-
dence of the house of Israel, but will
remind them of *their* iniquity when

6
a 2 Ki. 18:21; Isa. 36:6; Ezek. 17:15
7
b Jer. 37:5–8
9
c Ezek. 30:7–8
10
d Ex. 14:2; Jer. 44:1
12
e Ezek. 30:23
13
f Jer. 46:26
16
g Isa. 20:5; 30:1–3; 36:4–6; Lam. 4:17
17
h Cp. v. 1; Ezek. 30:20
i c. 571 B.C.
j See Lev. 23:2, *note*
18
k Jer. 27:6; Ezek. 26:7–8
l Ezek. 27:31
19
m Jer. 43:10–13; Ezek. 30:10
21
n Ps. 132:17; see Dt. 33:17, *note*
CHAPTER 30
3
o Ezek. 7:7, 12; Joel 2:1; Zeph. 1:7
p *Day* (of the LORD): v. 3; Ezek. 38:14. (Ps. 2:9; Rev. 19:19)
4
q Heb. *Cush.* Isa. 18:1–7; Zeph. 2:12
5
r Jer. 25:20, 24

they turned to follow them. Then they
shall know that I *am* the Lord GOD." ' "
17 And it came to pass in the
[h]twenty-seventh [1][i]year, in the [j]first
month, on the first *day* of the month,
that the word of the LORD came to me,
saying,
18 "Son of man, [k]Nebuchadnezzar
king of Babylon caused his army to
labor strenuously against Tyre; every
head *was* made [l]bald, and every
shoulder rubbed raw; yet neither he
nor his army received wages from
Tyre, for the labor which they ex-
pended on it.
19 "Therefore thus says the Lord
GOD: 'Surely I will give the land of
Egypt to [m]Nebuchadnezzar king of
Babylon; he shall take away her
wealth, carry off her spoil, and remove her pillage; and that will be the
wages for his army.
20 'I have given him the land of
Egypt *for* his labor, because they
worked for Me,' says the Lord GOD.
21 'In that day I will cause the
[n]horn of the house of Israel to spring
forth, and I will open your mouth to
speak in their midst. Then they shall
know that I *am* the LORD.' "

Lament over Egypt's fall

30 THE word of the LORD came to
me again, saying,
2 "Son of man, prophesy and say,
'Thus says the Lord GOD:

"Wail, 'Woe to the day!'
3 For the [o]day *is* near,
Even the [p]day of the LORD *is*
near;
It will be a day of clouds, the
time of the Gentiles.
4 The sword shall come upon
Egypt,
And great anguish shall be in
[q]Ethiopia,
When the slain fall in Egypt,
And they take away her
wealth,
And her foundations are
broken down.

5 [q]"Ethiopia, Libya,* Lydia,* all
the [r]mingled people, Chub, and the
men of the lands who are allied, shall
fall with them by the sword."

*
29:7 Following Masoretic Text and Vulgate; Septuagint and Syriac read *hand.* **29:10** Or *tower* **30:5** Hebrew *Put* • Hebrew *Lud*

[1](29:17) Although Ezekiel did not receive this particular message during the siege of Jerusalem, but seventeen years later, he inserted it here in connection with his previous messages
concerning Egypt.

6 'Thus says the LORD:

"Those who uphold Egypt shall
fall,
And the pride of her power
shall come down.
From Migdol *to* Syene
Those within her shall fall by
the sword,"
Says the Lord GOD.
7 "They shall be [a]desolate in the
midst of the desolate
countries,
And her cities shall be in the
midst of the cities *that are*
laid waste.
8 Then they will know that I *am*
the LORD,
When I have set a fire in Egypt
And all her helpers are
destroyed.
9 On that day [b]messengers shall
go forth from Me in ships
To make the [c]careless
Ethiopians afraid,
And great anguish shall come
upon them,
As on the day of Egypt;
For indeed it is coming!"

10 'Thus says the Lord GOD:

"I will also make a multitude of
Egypt to cease
By the hand of
[d]Nebuchadnezzar king of
Babylon.
11 He and his people with him,
the most [e]terrible of the
nations,
Shall be brought to destroy the
land;
They shall draw their swords
against Egypt,
And fill the land with the slain.
12 I will make the [f]rivers dry,
And sell the land into the hand
of the wicked;
I will make the land waste,
and all that is in it,
By the hand of aliens.
I, the LORD, have spoken."

13 'Thus says the Lord GOD:

"I will also [g]destroy the idols,
And cause the images to cease
from Noph;*
There shall [h]no longer be
princes from the land of
Egypt;
I will put fear in the land of
Egypt.
14 I will make [i]Pathros desolate,
Set fire to Zoan,
And execute judgments in
[j]No.
15 I will pour My fury on Sin,*
the strength of Egypt;
I will cut off the multitude of
[j]No,
16 And set a fire in Egypt;
Sin shall have great pain,
No shall be split open,
And Noph *shall be in* distress
daily.
17 The young men of Aven* and
Pi Beseth shall fall by the
sword,
And these *cities* shall go into
captivity.
18 At Tehaphnehes* the day shall
also be darkened,*
When I break the yokes of
Egypt there.
And her arrogant strength
shall cease in her;
As for her, a cloud shall cover
her,
And her daughters shall go
into captivity.
19 Thus I will [k]execute judgments
on Egypt,
Then they shall know that I
am the LORD." ' "

God promises Babylon victory over Egypt

20 And it came to pass in the eleventh [l]year, in the [m]first *month,* on the
seventh *day* of the month, *that* the
word of the LORD came to me, [n]saying,
21 "Son of man, I have broken the
arm of Pharaoh king of Egypt; and
see, it has not been bandaged for
[o]healing, nor a splint put on to bind it,
to make it strong enough to hold a
sword.
22 "Therefore thus says the Lord
GOD: 'Surely I *am* [p]against Pharaoh
king of Egypt, and will break his
[q]arms, both the strong one and the
one that was broken; and I will make
the sword fall out of his hand.
23 'I will [r]scatter the Egyptians
among the nations, and disperse them
throughout the countries.
24 'I will strengthen the arms of the
king of Babylon and put My sword in
his hand; but I will break Pharaoh's
arms, and he will groan before him
with the groanings of a mortally
wounded *man.*

7
a Ezek. 29:12
9
b Cp. Isa. 18:1–2
c i.e. *unsuspecting.* Cp. Isa. 47:8–11; Ezek. 38:10–12
10
d Jer. 27:6; Ezek. 26:7–8
11
e Ezek. 28:7; 31:12
12
f Isa. 19:5–6; cp. Ezek. 29:3, 9
13
g Isa. 19:1; Jer. 43:12; 46:25; Zech. 13:2
h Zech. 10:11
14
i Jer. 44:1; Ezek. 29:14
j i.e. *Thebes*
19
k Ps. 9:16; Ezek. 5:8; 25:11
20
l c. 587 B.C.
m See Lev. 23:2, *note*
n vv. 21–26; cp. Ezek. 32:1–16
21
o Jer. 46:11
22
p Jer. 46:25
q Cp. Ps. 37:17
23
r v. 26; Ezek. 29:12

*
30:13 That is, ancient Memphis **30:15** That is, ancient Pelusium **30:17** That is, ancient On (Heliopolis) **30:18** Spelled *Tahpanhes* in Jeremiah 43:7 and elsewhere • Following many Hebrew manuscripts, Bomberg, Septuagint, Syriac, Targum, and Vulgate; Masoretic Text reads *refrained.*

25 'Thus I will strengthen the arms of the king of Babylon, but the arms of Pharaoh shall fall down; they shall [a]know that I *am* the LORD, when I put My sword into the hand of the king of Babylon and he stretches it out against the land of Egypt.

26 'I will scatter the Egyptians among the nations and disperse them throughout the countries. Then they shall know that I *am* the LORD.' "

Parable of the cedar of Lebanon: Pharaoh's pride rebuked

31 NOW it came to pass in the [b]eleventh year, in the [c]third [d]*month*, on the first *day* of the month, *that* the word of the LORD came to me, saying,

2 "Son of man, say to Pharaoh king of Egypt and to his multitude:

'Whom are you like in your
greatness?
3 [e]Indeed [f]Assyria *was* a [g]cedar
in Lebanon,
With fine branches that shaded
the forest,
And of high stature;
And its top was among the
[h]thick boughs.
4 The [i]waters made it grow;
Underground waters gave it
height,
With their rivers running
around the place where it
was planted,
And sent out rivulets to all the
trees of the field.

5 'Therefore its height was
exalted above all the trees of
the field;
Its boughs were multiplied,
And its branches became long
because of the abundance of
water,
As it sent them out.
6 All the [j]birds of the heavens
made their nests in its
boughs;
Under its branches all the
beasts of the field brought
forth their young;
And in its shadow all great
nations made their home.
7 'Thus it was beautiful in
greatness and in the length
of its branches,
Because its roots reached to
abundant waters.
8 The cedars in the [k]garden of
God could not hide it;
The fir trees were not like its
boughs,
And the chestnut* trees were
not like its branches;
No tree in the garden of God
was like it in beauty.
9 I made it beautiful with a
multitude of branches,
So that all the trees of Eden
envied it,
That *were* in the garden of
God.'

10 "Therefore thus says the Lord GOD: 'Because you have increased in height, and it set its top among the [h]thick boughs, and its heart was [l]lifted up in its height,

11 'therefore I will deliver it into the hand of the [m]mighty one of the nations, and he shall surely deal with it; I have driven it out for its wickedness.

12 'And aliens, the most [n]terrible of the nations, have cut it down and left it; its branches have fallen on the [o]mountains and in all the valleys; its boughs lie [p]broken by all the rivers of the land; and all the peoples of the earth have gone from under its shadow and left it.

13 [q]'On its ruin will remain all the
birds of the heavens,
And all the beasts of the field
will come to its branches—

14 'So that no trees by the waters may ever again exalt themselves for their height, nor set their tops among the [h]thick boughs, that no tree which drinks water may ever be high enough to reach up to them.

'For they have all been
delivered to death,
To the [r]depths of the earth,
Among the children of men
who go down to the Pit.'

15 "Thus says the Lord GOD: 'In the day when it [s]went down to [t]hell, I caused mourning. I covered the deep because of it. I restrained its rivers, and the great waters were held back. I caused Lebanon to mourn for it, and all the trees of the field wilted because of it.

16 'I made the nations shake at the sound of its fall, when I [u]cast it down to [v]hell together with those who descend into the Pit; and all the trees of Eden, the choice and best of Lebanon,

25
[a] Ps. 9:16
CHAPTER 31
1
[b] Ezek. 30:20; 32:1
[c] See Lev. 23:2, *note*
[d] Cp. Jer. 52:5–6
3
[e] *Parables (OT)*: vv. 3–14; Ezek. 37:1. (Jud. 9:8; Zech. 11:7)
[f] vv. 3–18; cp. Book of Nahum
[g] Cp. Dan. 4:10; Amos 2:9
[h] Or *clouds*
4
[i] Ezek. 29:3–9
6
[j] Ezek. 17:23; Dan. 4:12
8
[k] Gen. 2:8; 13:10; Ezek. 28:13
10
[l] Cp. 2 Chr. 32:25; Isa. 10:12; Ezek. 28:17; Dan. 5:20
11
[m] Ezek. 30:10
12
[n] Ezek. 30:11; 32:12
[o] Ezek. 32:5
[p] Ezek. 30:24–25
13
[q] Isa. 18:6; Ezek. 32:4
14
[r] Ezek. 32:18
15
[s] Ezek. 32:22–23
[t] See Hab. 2:5, *note*
16
[u] Isa. 14:15
[v] See Lk. 16:23, *note*

* 31:8 Hebrew *armon*

all that drink water, were [a]comforted
in the [b]depths of the earth.
17 'They also went down to [c]hell
with it, with those *slain* by the sword;
and *those who were* its *strong* arm
dwelt in its shadows among the nations.
18 'To which of the trees in Eden
will you then be likened in glory and
greatness? Yet you shall be brought
down with the trees of Eden to the
[b]depths of the earth; you shall [d]lie in
the midst of the uncircumcised, with
those slain by the sword. This *is* Pharaoh and all his multitude,' says the
Lord GOD."

Further lament over Pharaoh and Egypt

32 AND it came to pass in the
[e]twelfth [f]year, in the [g]twelfth
month, on the first *day* of the month,
that the word of the LORD came to me,
saying,
2 "Son of man, take up a lamentation for Pharaoh king of Egypt, and
say to him:

'You are like a young lion
among the nations,
And you *are* like a [h]monster in
the seas,
[i]Bursting forth in your rivers,
Troubling the waters with your
feet,
And fouling their rivers.'

3 "Thus says the Lord GOD:

'I will therefore spread My net
over you with a company of
many people,
And they will draw you up in
My net.
4 Then I will [j]leave you on the
land;
I will cast you out on the open
fields,
And cause to settle on you all
the [k]birds of the heavens.
And with you I will fill the
beasts of the whole earth.
5 I will lay your flesh on the
[l]mountains,
And fill the valleys with your
carcass.
6 'I will also water the land with
the flow of your blood,
Even to the mountains;
And the riverbeds will be full
of you.
7 When *I* put out your light,
I will [m]cover the heavens, and
make its stars dark;

16
a Ezek. 32:31; cp. Isa. 14:9–11; contrast Lk. 16:19–31
b Ezek. 32:18
17
c See Lk. 16:23, *note*
18
d Ezek. 28:10; 32:19,21,24
CHAPTER 32
1
e Ezek. 31:1; 33:21
f c. 586 B.C.
g See Lev. 23:2, *note*
2
h Ezek. 29:3
i Jer. 46:7–8
4
j Ezek. 29:5
k Isa. 18:6; Ezek. 31:13
5
l Ezek. 31:12
7
m Isa. 13:10; Joel 2:31; 3:15 Amos 8:9; Mt. 24:29; Rev. 6:12–13
10
n Cp. Ezek. 28:19
11
o Jer. 46:26; Ezek. 30:4
12
p Ezek. 30:11; 31:12
16
q v. 2; Ezek. 2:10; 19:1,14; 26:17; 27:2,32; 28:12

I will cover the sun with a
cloud,
And the moon shall not give
her light.
8 All the bright lights of the
heavens I will make dark
over you,
And bring darkness upon your
land,'
Says the Lord GOD.

9 'I will also trouble the hearts of
many peoples, when I bring your destruction among the nations, into the
countries which you have not known.
10 'Yes, I will make many peoples
[n]astonished at you, and their kings
shall be horribly afraid of you when I
brandish My sword before them; and
they shall tremble *every* moment, every man for his own life, in the day of
your fall.'
11 "For [o]thus says the Lord GOD:
'The sword of the king of Babylon
shall come upon you.
12 'By the swords of the mighty
warriors, all of them the most [p]terri-
ble of the nations, I will cause your
multitude to fall.

'They shall plunder the pomp
of Egypt,
And all its multitude shall be
destroyed.
13 Also I will destroy all its
animals
From beside its great waters;
The foot of man shall muddy
them no more,
Nor shall the hooves of
animals muddy them.
14 Then I will make their waters
clear,
And make their rivers run like
oil,'
Says the Lord GOD.

15 'When I make the land of
Egypt desolate,
And the country is destitute of
all that once filled it,
When I strike all who dwell in
it,
Then they shall know that I
am the LORD.

16 'This *is* the [q]lamentation
With which they shall lament
her;
The daughters of the nations
shall lament her;
They shall lament for her, for
Egypt,
And for all her multitude,'
Says the Lord GOD."

17 It came to pass also in the
twelfth [a]year, on the fifteenth *day* of
the month, [b]that the word of the LORD
came to me, saying:

18 "Son of man, [c]wail over the
multitude of Egypt,
And cast them down to the
[d]depths of the earth,
Her and the daughters of the
famous nations,
With those who go down to
the Pit:
19 [e]'Whom do you surpass in
beauty?
Go down, be placed with the
uncircumcised.'

20 "They shall fall in the midst of
those slain by the sword;
She is delivered to the sword,
[f]Drawing her and all her
multitudes.
21 The [g]strong among the mighty
Shall speak to him out of the
midst of [h]hell
With those who help him:
'They have gone down,
They lie with the
uncircumcised, slain by the
sword.'

22 [i]"Assyria *is* there, and all her
company,
With their graves all around
her,
All of them slain, fallen by the
sword.
23 Her [j]graves are set in the
recesses of the Pit,
And her company is all around
her grave,
All of them slain, fallen by the
sword,
Who caused terror in the land
of the living.

24 "There *is* [k]Elam and all her
multitude,
All around her grave,
All of them slain, fallen by the
sword,
Who have gone down
uncircumcised to the [d]lower
parts of the earth,
Who caused their terror in the
land of the living;
Now they bear their shame
with those who go down to
the Pit.
25 They have set her [l]bed in the
midst of the slain,
With all her multitude,
With her graves all around it,

17
a c. 586 B.C.
b 32:1; 33:21
18
c Cp. Mic. 1:8
d Ezek. 31:14
19
e Ezek. 31:2,18
20
f Ps. 28:3
21
g v. 27; Isa. 1:31; 14:9–10
h See Hab. 2:5, *note;* cp. Lk. 16:23, *note*
22
i Ezek. 31:3, 16
23
j Isa. 14:15
24
k Jer. 49:34
25
l Ps. 139:8
26
m Gen. 10:2; Ezek. 27:13; 38:2
27
n Isa. 14:18–19
29
o Isa. 9:25–26; 34:5–6; Ezek. 25:12–14
30
p Jer. 25:26; Ezek. 38:6, 15; 39:2
31
q Ezek. 31:16; cp. Isa. 14:9–11; contrast Lk. 16:19–31

All of them uncircumcised,
slain by the sword;
Though their terror was
caused
In the land of the living,
Yet they bear their shame
With those who go down to
the Pit;
It was put in the midst of the
slain.

26 "There *are* [m]Meshech and Tubal
and all their multitudes,
With all their graves around it,
All of them uncircumcised,
slain by the sword,
Though they caused their
terror in the land of the
living.
27 They do [n]not lie with the
mighty
Who are fallen of the
uncircumcised,
Who have gone down to [h]hell
with their weapons of war;
They have laid their swords
under their heads,
But their iniquities will be on
their bones,
Because of the terror of the
mighty in the land of the
living.
28 Yes, you shall be broken in the
midst of the uncircumcised,
And lie with *those* slain by the
sword.

29 "There *is* [o]Edom,
Her kings and all her princes,
Who despite their might
Are laid beside *those* slain by
the sword;
They shall lie with the
uncircumcised,
And with those who go down
to the Pit.
30 There *are* the princes of the
[p]north,
All of them, and all the
Sidonians,
Who have gone down with the
slain
In shame at the terror which
they caused by their might;
They lie uncircumcised with
those slain by the sword,
And bear their shame with
those who go down to the
Pit.

31 "Pharaoh will see them
And be [q]comforted over all his
multitude,
Pharaoh and all his army,

Slain by the sword,"
Says the Lord GOD.

32 "For I have caused My terror in
the land of the living;
And he shall be placed in the
midst of the uncircumcised
With *those* slain by the sword,
Pharaoh and all his multitude,"
Says the Lord GOD.

IV. Ezekiel's Responsibility as Watchman, 33

His solemn duty to sound warning

33 AGAIN the word of the LORD
came to me, saying,
2 "Son of man, speak to the children of your people, and say to them:
'When I bring the sword upon a land,
and the people of the land take a man
from their territory and make him
their [a]watchman,
3 'when he sees the sword coming
upon the land, if he blows the trumpet
and warns the people,
4 'then whoever hears the sound
of the trumpet and does [b]not take
warning, if the sword comes and takes
him away, his blood shall be on his
own [c]head.
5 'He heard the sound of the trumpet, but did not take warning; his
blood shall be upon himself. But he
who takes warning will save his life.
6 'But if the watchman sees the
sword coming and does not blow the
trumpet, and the people are not
warned, and the sword comes and
takes *any* person from among them,
he is taken away in his iniquity; but
his blood I will require at the watchman's hand.'
7 "So you, son of man: I have
made you a [d]watchman for the house
of Israel; therefore you shall hear a
word from My mouth and warn them
for Me.
8 "When I say to the wicked, 'O
wicked *man*, you shall surely die!' and
you do not speak to warn the wicked
from his way, that wicked *man* shall
die in his iniquity; but his blood I will
require at your hand.
9 "Nevertheless if you warn the
wicked to turn from his way, and he
does not turn from his way, he shall
die in his iniquity; but you have delivered your soul.
10 "Therefore you, O son of man,
say to the house of Israel: 'Thus you
say, "If our transgressions and our
sins *lie* upon us, and we [e]pine away in
them, how can we then [f]live?" '
11 "Say to them: '*As* I live,' says the
Lord GOD, [g]'I have no pleasure in the
death of the wicked, but that the
wicked [h]turn from his way and live.
Turn, turn from your evil ways! For
[i]why should you die, O house of Israel?'
12 "Therefore you, O son of man,
say to the children of your people:
'The [j]righteousness of the righteous
man shall not deliver him in the day of
his transgression; as for the wickedness of the wicked, he shall not fall
because of it in the day that he turns
from his wickedness; nor shall the
righteous be able to live because of *his*
righteousness in the day that he sins.'
13 "When I say to the righteous
that he shall surely live, [k]but he trusts
in his own righteousness and commits
iniquity, none of his righteous works
shall be remembered; but because of
the iniquity that he has [l]committed,
he shall die.
14 "Again, when I say to the
wicked, 'You shall surely die,' if he
turns from his sin and does what is
lawful and right,
15 "*if* the wicked [m]restores the
pledge, [n]gives back what he has stolen, and walks in the statutes of life
without committing iniquity, he shall
surely live; he shall not die.
16 [o]"None of his sins which he has
committed shall be remembered
against him; he has done what is lawful and right; he shall surely live.
17 "Yet the children of your people
say, 'The way of the LORD is not fair.'
But it is their way which is not fair!
18 "When the righteous turns from
his righteousness and commits iniquity, he shall [p]die because of it.
19 "But when the wicked turns
from his wickedness and does what is
lawful and right, he shall [q]live because of it.
20 "Yet you say, 'The [r]way of the
LORD is not fair.' O house of Israel, I
will judge every one of you according
to his own ways."

Word comes of Jerusalem's capture; Ezekiel's speech returns

21 And it came to pass in the
twelfth [s]year of our captivity, in the
[t]tenth *month*, on the fifth *day* of the
month, *that* one who had [u]escaped
from Jerusalem came to me and said,
"The city has been captured!"
22 Now the hand of the LORD had
been upon me the evening before the
man came who had escaped. And He

CHAPTER 33

2
a v. 7; cp. 2 Sam. 18:24–25; 2 Ki. 9:17; Hos. 9:8

4
b Jer. 6:17; Zech. 1:4
c Acts 18:6

7
d Isa. 62:6; Ezek. 3:17–21

10
e Ezek. 24:23
f Cp. Ezek. 37:11

11
g 2 Sam. 14:14; Lam. 3:33; Ezek. 18:23,32; Hos. 11:8; 2 Pet. 3:9
h Ezek. 18:21,30; Hos. 14:1, 4; Acts 3:19
i Ezek. 18:31

12
j Ezek. 3:20; 18:24–26, 27

13
k Cp. Rom. 10:1–13
l Ezek. 3:20; 18:1–4,24

15
m Ezek. 18:7
n Ex. 22:1–4; Lev. 6:2, 4–5; Num. 5:6–7; Lk. 19:8

16
o Isa. 1:18

18
p Cp. Gal. 3:3–4

19
q Cp. Jer. 18:1–10

20
r v. 17; Ezek. 18:25,29

21
s c. 586 B.C.
t Cp. Jer. 39:1–2; see Lev. 23:2, *note*
u Ezek. 24:26

had [a]opened my mouth; so when he came to me in the morning, my mouth was opened, and I was no longer mute.

Hearers but not doers of the Word

23 Then the word of the LORD came to me, saying:

24 "Son of man, they who inhabit those ruins in the land of Israel are saying, [b]'Abraham was only one, and he inherited the land. But we *are* many; the land has been given to us as a [c]possession.'

25 "Therefore say to them, 'Thus says the Lord GOD: "You eat *meat* with [d]blood, you lift up your eyes toward your idols, and shed blood. Should you then possess the [e]land?

26 "You rely on your sword, you commit abominations, and you defile one another's [f]wives. Should you then possess the land?" '

27 "Say thus to them, 'Thus says the Lord GOD: "*As* I live, surely those who *are* in the ruins shall fall by the sword, and the one who *is* in the open field I will give to the beasts to be devoured, and those who *are* in the strongholds and caves shall die of the pestilence.

28 "For I will make the land most [g]desolate, her arrogant strength shall cease, and the mountains of Israel shall be so desolate that no one will pass through.

29 "Then they shall know that I *am* the LORD, when I have made the land most desolate because of all their abominations which they have committed." '

30 "As for you, son of man, the children of your people are talking about you beside the walls and in the doors of the houses; and they speak to one another, everyone saying to his brother, 'Please come and hear what the word is that comes from the LORD.'

31 "So they come to you as people do, they [h]sit before you *as* My people, and they [i]hear your words, but they do not do them; for with their [j]mouth they show much love, *but* their hearts pursue their *own* gain.

32 "Indeed you *are* to them as a very lovely song of one who has a pleasant voice and can play well on an instrument; for they hear your words, but they do [k]not do them.

33 "And when this comes to pass—surely it will come—then they will [l]know that a prophet has been among them."

22
a Ezek. 3:26–27; 24:27
24
b Isa. 51:2; Mt. 3:9; Jn. 8:39; Acts 7:5
c Ezek. 11:15
25
d Lev. 17:10–14
e Dt. 29:28
26
f Ezek. 22:11
28
g Jer. 44:2, 6,22; Ezek. 36:34–35
31
h Ezek. 8:1; 14:1; 20:1
i Isa. 58:2; Ezek. 14:1; 20:1
j Ps. 78:36–37; Isa. 29:13; Jer. 12:2; 1 Jn. 3:18
32
k Mt. 7:21–28; Jas. 1:22–25
33
l 1 Sam. 3:20; Ezek. 2:5
CHAPTER 34
2
m vv. 2–10; Jer. 23:1; Ezek. 22:25; Zech. 11:17
3
n Isa. 56:11
o Ezek. 33:25–26; Mic. 3:1–3; Zech. 11:5
4
p v. 8; cp. v. 16; Zech. 11:15–17
q Lk. 15:4
r Cp. 1 Pet. 5:2–4
5
s Jer. 10:21
t v. 8; Isa. 56:9; Jer. 12:9
6
u Jer. 50:6; 1 Pet. 2:25
10
v Ezek. 13:8
w Ezek. 3:18; Heb. 13:17
x Ezek. 13:23

V. Prediction of Events to Take Place at the End of the Age, When Israel Is Again in Her Own Land, 34—39

Message to the faithless shepherds of Israel

34 AND the word of the LORD came to me, saying,

2 "Son of man, prophesy against the shepherds of Israel, prophesy and say to them, 'Thus says the Lord GOD to the shepherds: [m]"Woe to the shepherds of Israel who feed themselves! Should not the shepherds feed the flocks?

3 "You [n]eat the fat and clothe yourselves with the wool; you [o]slaughter the fatlings, *but* you do not feed the flock.

4 "The [p]weak you have not strengthened, nor have you healed those who were sick, nor bound up the broken, nor brought back what was driven away, nor [q]sought what was lost; but with [r]force and cruelty you have ruled them.

5 "So they were [s]scattered because *there was* no shepherd; and they [t]became food for all the beasts of the field when they were scattered.

6 "My sheep [u]wandered through all the mountains, and on every high hill; yes, My flock was scattered over the whole face of the earth, and no one was seeking or searching *for them."*

7 'Therefore, you shepherds, hear the word of the LORD:

8 "*as* I live," says the Lord GOD, "surely because My flock became a prey, and My flock became food for every beast of the field, because *there was* no shepherd, nor did My shepherds search for My flock, but the shepherds fed themselves and did not feed My flock"—

9 'therefore, O shepherds, hear the word of the LORD!

10 'Thus says the Lord GOD: "Behold, I *am* [v]against the shepherds, and I will [w]require My flock at their hand; I will cause them to cease feeding the sheep, and the shepherds shall feed themselves no more; for I will [x]deliver My flock from their mouths, that they may no longer be food for them."

Israel to be restored: the Davidic kingdom to be set up

11 'For thus says the Lord GOD: "Indeed I Myself will search for My sheep and seek them out.

12 “As a [1a]shepherd seeks out his
flock on the day he is among his scattered sheep, so will I seek out My
sheep and deliver them from all the
places where they were scattered on a
cloudy and dark day.
13 “And I will [b]bring them out from
the peoples and gather them from the
countries, and will bring them to their
own [c]land; I will feed them on the
mountains of Israel, in the valleys and
in all the inhabited places of the country.
14 “I will [d]feed them in good pasture, and their fold shall be on the high
mountains of Israel. There they shall
lie down in a good fold and feed in rich
pasture on the mountains of Israel.
15 “I will feed My flock, and I will
make them lie down,” says the Lord
GOD.
16 “I will [e]seek what was lost and
bring back what was driven away,
bind up the broken and strengthen
what was sick; but I will destroy the
fat and the strong, and feed them in
judgment.”
17 ‘And *as for* you, O My flock, thus
says the Lord GOD: “Behold, I shall
judge between sheep and sheep, between rams and goats.
18 “*Is it* too little for you to have
eaten up the good pasture, that you
must tread down with your feet the
residue of your pasture—and to have
drunk of the clear waters, that you
must foul the residue with your feet?
19 “And *as for* My flock, they eat
what you have [f]trampled with your
feet, and they drink what you have
fouled with your feet.”
20 ‘Therefore thus says the Lord
GOD to them: “Behold, I Myself will
judge between the fat and the lean
sheep.
21 “Because you have pushed with
side and shoulder, butted all the
[g]weak ones with your horns, and scattered them abroad,
22 “therefore I will save My flock,
and they shall no longer be a prey; and
I will judge between sheep and sheep.
23 “I will establish [h]one shepherd
over them, and he shall feed them—

12
a Jer. 31:10
13
b Isa. 65:9–10; Jer. 23:3; Ezek. 11:17; 20:41; 28:25; 36:24; 37:21–22
c Kingdom (OT): vv. 11–15, 22–25; Ezek. 37:21. (Gen. 1:26; Zech. 12:8, *note*)
14
d Jer. 3:15
16
e v. 4; Isa. 40:11; Mic. 4:6; Mt. 18:11; Mk. 2:17; Lk. 5:32
19
f Jer. 12:10
21
g Cp. Lk. 13:14–16
23
h Isa. 11:1–5,10; 40:11; Jer. 23:4–5; Hos. 1:11; Jn. 10:11; Heb. 13:20; 1 Pet. 2:25; 5:4
24
i v. 30; Ex. 29:45; Ezek. 37:27
j Ezek. 37:24–26
25
k Ezek. 37:26; see Heb. 8:8, *notes*
l Lev. 26:6; Isa. 11:6–9; 35:9; Hos. 2:18
26
m Gen. 12:2; Isa. 19:24; Zech. 8:13

My servant David. He shall feed them
and be their shepherd.
24 “And [i]I, the LORD, will be their
God, and My servant [j]David a prince
among them; I, the LORD, have spoken.
25 “I will make a [k]covenant of
peace with them, and cause [l]wild
beasts to cease from the land; and
they will dwell safely in the wilderness and sleep in the woods.
26 “I will make them and the places
all around My hill a [m]blessing; and I
will cause showers to come down in
their season; there shall be showers of
blessing.
27 “Then the trees of the field shall
yield their fruit, and the earth shall
yield her increase. They shall be safe
in their land; and they shall know that
I *am* the LORD, when I have [n]broken
the bands of their yoke and delivered
them from the hand of those who en-
slaved them.
28 “And they shall no longer be a
prey for the nations, nor shall beasts
of the land devour them; but they shall
[o]dwell safely, and no one shall make
them afraid.
29 “I will raise up for them a garden
of renown, and they shall [p]no longer
be consumed with hunger in the land,
nor [q]bear the shame of the Gentiles
anymore.
30 “Thus they shall know that I, the
LORD their God, *am* with them, and
they, the house of Israel, *are* [r]My people,” says the Lord GOD.’ ”
31 “You are My flock, the flock of
My pasture; you *are* men, *and* I *am*
your God,” says the Lord GOD.

Prophecy against Mount Seir (Edom)

35 MOREOVER the word of the
LORD came to me, saying,
2 “Son of man, set your face
against [s]Mount Seir and prophesy
against it,
3 “and say to it, ‘Thus says the
Lord GOD:

34:27 *n* Lev. 26:13; Jer. 2:20 **34:28** *o* v. 25; Jer. 30:10; 46:27 **34:29** *p* Ezek. 36:29 *q* Ezek. 36:6,15 **34:30** *r* Ezek. 14:11; 36:28 **35:2** *s* vv. 1–15; Jer. 25:21; 49:7–22; Ezek. 25:12–14; Joel 3:19; Amos 1:11–12; Obad. 1–9,15–16

[1](34:12) In its Messianic and evangelical import, this passage (vv. 11–31) is like a window letting the light of dawn into a hall of judgment. Verses 12,14–16,22 look forward to the LORD of Ps. 23 and the Good Shepherd of Jn. 10; but the primary reference is to Israel—“there shall be showers of blessing” (v. 26), the people “shall be safe on their land” (v. 27), “they shall no longer be a prey for the nations” (v. 28). Verses 23–30 speak of a restoration yet future, for the remnant which returned to Palestine after the captivity was continually under the Gentile yoke until they were driven from the land in A.D. 70.

"Behold, O Mount Seir, I *am*
against you;
I will stretch out My hand
against you,
And make you most desolate;
4 I shall lay your cities waste,
And you shall be desolate.
Then you shall know that I *am*
the LORD.

5 [a]"Because you have had an ancient hatred, and have shed *the blood*
of the children of Israel by the power
of the sword at the time of their calamity, *when* their iniquity *came to an*
end,
6 "therefore, *as* I live," says the
Lord GOD, "I will prepare you for
[b]blood, and blood shall pursue you;
since you have not hated blood, therefore blood shall pursue you.
7 "Thus I will make Mount Seir
most desolate, and cut off from it the
one who leaves and the one who returns.
8 "And I will fill its mountains
with the slain; on your hills and in
your valleys and in all your ravines
those who are slain by the sword shall
fall.
9 "I will make you perpetually
[c]desolate, and your cities shall be uninhabited; then you shall know that I
am the LORD.
10 "Because you have said, 'These
[d]two nations and these two countries
shall be mine, and we will [e]possess
them,' although the LORD was [f]there,
11 "therefore, *as* I live," says the
Lord GOD, "I will do according to your
anger and according to the envy
which you showed in your hatred
against them; and I will make Myself
known among them when I judge you.
12 "Then you shall know that I *am*
the LORD. I have [g]heard all your [h]blas-
phemies which you have spoken
against the mountains of Israel, saying, 'They are desolate; they are given
to us to consume.'
13 "Thus with your mouth you have
boasted against Me and multiplied
your [i]words against Me; I have heard
them."
14 'Thus says the Lord GOD: [j]"The
whole earth will rejoice when I make
you desolate.
15 "As you [k]rejoiced because the
inheritance of the house of Israel was
desolate, [l]so I will do to you; you shall
be desolate, O Mount Seir, as well as
all of Edom—all of it! Then they shall
know that I *am* the LORD." '

Restoration of Israel to the land

36 [1]"AND you, son of man, prophesy to the mountains of Israel,
and say, 'O mountains of Israel, hear
the word of the LORD!
2 'Thus says the Lord GOD: "Because the enemy has said of you,
[m]'Aha! The ancient [n]heights have become our possession,' " '
3 "therefore prophesy, and say,
'Thus says the Lord GOD: "Because
they made *you* desolate and swallowed you up on every side, so that
you became the possession of the rest
of the nations, and [o]you are taken up
by the lips of [p]talkers and slandered
by the people"—
4 'therefore, O mountains of Israel, hear the word of the Lord GOD!
Thus says the Lord GOD to the mountains, the hills, the rivers, the valleys,
the desolate wastes, and the cities that
have been forsaken, which became
plunder and [q]mockery to the rest of
the nations all around—
5 'therefore thus says the Lord
GOD: "Surely I have spoken in My
burning jealousy against the rest of
the nations and against all [r]Edom,
who gave My land to themselves as a
[s]possession, with wholehearted joy
and spiteful minds, in order to plunder
its open country." '
6 "Therefore prophesy concerning the land of Israel, and say to the
mountains, the hills, the rivers, and
the valleys, 'Thus says the Lord GOD:
"Behold, I have spoken in My jealousy
and My fury, because you have
[t]borne the shame of the nations."
7 'Therefore thus says the Lord
GOD: "I have raised My hand in an
oath that surely the nations that *are*
around you shall [u]bear their own
shame.
8 "But you, O mountains of Israel,
you shall shoot forth your branches
and yield your fruit to My people Israel, for they are about to come.
9 "For indeed I *am* for you, and I
will turn to you, and you shall be tilled
and sown.

CHAPTER 35
5 *a* Ps. 137:7
6 *b* Isa. 63:1–6
9 *c* v. 4
10 *d* Cp. Ezek. 37:22 *e* Ps. 83:4–12 *f* Ezek. 48:35
12 *g* Zeph. 2:8 *h* Isa. 52:5
13 *i* Ezek. 36:3
14 *j* Isa. 65:13–14
15 *k* 35:12; 36:4–7; Obad. 12, 15 *l* Lam. 4:21

CHAPTER 36
2 *m* Jer. 33:24; Ezek. 25:3; 26:2 *n* See Jud. 3:7 and 1 Ki. 3:2, *notes*
3 *o* Dt. 28:37; 1 Ki. 9:7; Lam. 2:15; Dan. 9:16 *p* 35:13
4 *q* Ps. 79:4; Jer. 48:27
5 *r* Ezek. 25:12–14; 35:1–2 *s* 35:10
6 *t* v. 15; Ps. 74:10; 123:3–4; Ezek. 34:29
7 *u* Jer. 25:9, 15,29

[1](36:1) The order in this and succeeding prophecies is (1) restoration of the land (36:1–15); (2) restoration of the people (36:16—37:28); (3) judgment on Israel's enemies (38:1—39:24); and (4) that which concerns the worship of the LORD that He may dwell among His people (40:1—47:12).

10 "I will [a]multiply men upon you,
all the house of Israel, all of it; and the
cities shall be inhabited and the ruins
rebuilt.
11 "I will multiply upon you man
and beast; and they shall increase and
bear young; I will make you inhabited
as in former times, and do [b]better *for
you* than at your beginnings. Then you
shall know that I *am* the LORD.
12 "Yes, I will cause men to walk on
you, My people Israel; they shall take
[c]possession of you, and you shall be
their inheritance; no more shall you
[d]bereave them *of children.*"
13 'Thus says the Lord GOD: "Because they say to you, 'You devour
men and bereave your nation *of children,*'
14 "therefore you shall devour men
no more, nor bereave your nation anymore," says the Lord GOD.
15 "Nor will I let you hear the
taunts of the nations anymore, nor
[e]bear the reproach of the peoples anymore, nor shall you cause your nation
to stumble anymore," says the Lord
GOD.'"
16 Moreover the word of the LORD
came to me, saying:
17 "Son of man, when the house of
Israel dwelt in their own land, they
[f]defiled it by their own ways and
deeds; to Me their way was like the
uncleanness of a woman in her customary impurity.
18 "Therefore I poured out My fury
on them for the blood they had shed
on the land, and for their idols *with
which* they had defiled it.
19 "So I [g]scattered them among the
nations, and they were dispersed
throughout the countries; I judged
them according to their ways and
their deeds.
20 "When they came to the nations,
wherever they went, they [h]profaned
My holy name—when they said of
them, [1]'These *are* the people of the
LORD, *and* yet they have gone out of
His land.'
21 "But I had concern for My holy
name, which the house of Israel had
profaned among the nations wherever
they went.
22 "Therefore say to the house of
Israel, 'Thus says the Lord GOD: "I do
not do *this* for your sake, [i]O house of
Israel, but for [j]My holy name's sake,
which you have profaned among the
nations wherever you went.
23 "And I will sanctify My great
name, which has been profaned
among the nations, which you have
profaned in their midst; and the nations shall know that I *am* the LORD,"
says the Lord GOD, "when I am [k]hal-
lowed in you before their eyes.
24 "For I will [l]take you from
among the nations, gather you out of
all countries, and bring you into your
own land.
25 "Then I will [m]sprinkle clean water on you, and you shall be clean; I
will cleanse you from all your filthiness and from all your idols.

Ezekiel's statement of the new covenant

26 "I will give you a [n]new heart and
put a new spirit within you; I will take
the heart of stone out of your flesh and
give you a heart of flesh.
27 "I will put My [o]Spirit within you
and cause you to walk in My statutes,
and you will keep My judgments and
do *them.*
28 "Then you shall [p]dwell in the
land that I gave to your fathers; you
shall be [q]My people, and I will be your
God.
29 "I will deliver you from all your
[r]uncleannesses. I will call for the
grain and multiply it, and bring no
famine upon you.
30 "And I will multiply the fruit of
your trees and the increase of your
fields, so that you need never again
bear the reproach of famine among
the nations.
31 "Then you will [s]remember your
evil ways and your deeds that *were*
not good; and you will [t]loathe yourselves in your own sight, for your iniquities and your abominations.
32 [u]"Not for your sake do I do *this,*"
says the Lord GOD, "let it be known
to you. Be ashamed and confounded
for your own ways, O house of Israel!
33 'Thus says the Lord GOD: "On the
day that I cleanse you from all your
iniquities, I will also enable *you* to

10 *a* Isa. 49:19–21; Jer. 33:12, 22
11 *b* Isa. 51:3; cp. Job 42:12; Rev. 21:1–4, 23–27; 22:1–5
12 *c* Obad. 17 *d* Cp. Lam. 1:20
15 *e* Ezek. 34:29
17 *f* Lev. 18:25, 27–28; Jer. 2:7
19 *g* Dt. 28:64
20 *h* Isa. 52:5; Rom. 2:24
22 *i Israel* (prophecies): vv. 22–38; Ezek. 37:21. (Gen. 12:2; Rom. 11:26, *note*) *j* Ezek. 20:44
23 *k* Ezek. 20:41; 28:22; 38:23; 39:7,25
24 *l* Ezek. 34:13
25 *m* Isa. 52:15; Heb. 10:22
26 *n* Jer. 32:39; Ezek. 11:19
27 *o Holy Spirit* (OT): vv. 26–27; Ezek. 37:1. (Gen. 1:2; Zech. 12:10)
28 *p* Ezek. 28:25; 37:25 *q* Jer. 30:22; Ezek. 11:20; 37:27 **36:29** *r* Zech. 13:1 **36:31** *s* Ezek. 16:63 *t* Ezek. 6:9; 20:43 **36:32** *u* v. 22; Dt. 9:5

[1](36:20) This is an expression of scorn. The world has only contempt for those who profess to be God's people but whose lives are inconsistent with their profession.

dwell in the cities, and the ruins shall
be rebuilt.
34 "The desolate land shall be tilled
instead of lying desolate in the sight of
all who pass by.
35 "So they will say, 'This land that
was desolate has become like the
[a]garden of Eden; and the wasted, desolate, and ruined cities *are now* fortified *and* inhabited.'
36 "Then the nations which are left
all around you shall know that I, the
LORD, have rebuilt the ruined places
and planted what was desolate. I, the
LORD, have spoken *it*, and I will do *it*."
37 'Thus says the Lord GOD: "I will
also let the house of Israel [b]inquire of
Me to do this for them: I will increase
their men like a flock.
38 "Like a flock *offered as* holy *sacrifices*, like the flock at Jerusalem on
its feast days, so shall the ruined cities
be filled with flocks of men. Then they
shall know that I *am* the LORD."' "

Vision of valley of dry bones:
Israel's restoration

37 THE hand of the LORD came
upon me and brought me out in
the [c]Spirit of the LORD, and [d]set me
down in the midst of the valley; and it
was full of [1]bones.
2 Then He caused me to pass by
them all around, and behold, *there
were* very many in the open valley;
and indeed *they were* very dry.
3 And He said to me, "Son of man,
can these bones live?" So I answered,
"O Lord GOD, You know."
4 Again He said to me, "Prophesy
to these bones, and say to them, 'O dry
bones, hear the word of the LORD!
5 'Thus says the Lord GOD to these
bones: "Surely I will cause breath to
enter into you, and you shall live.
6 "I will put sinews on you and
bring flesh upon you, cover you with
skin and put breath in you; and you
shall live. Then you shall know that I
am the LORD." ' "
7 So I prophesied as I was commanded; and as I prophesied, there
was a noise, and suddenly a rattling;
and the bones came together, bone to
bone.
8 Indeed, as I looked, the sinews
and the flesh came upon them, and the
skin covered them over; but *there was*
no breath in them.
9 Also He said to me, "Prophesy to
the breath, prophesy, son of man, and
say to the breath, 'Thus says the Lord
GOD: "Come from the four winds, O
breath, and breathe on these slain,
that they may [e]live." ' "
10 So I prophesied as He commanded me, and breath came into
them, and they lived, and stood upon
their feet, an [f]exceedingly great
army.

Vision explained

11 Then He said to me, "Son of
man, these bones are the [g]whole
house of Israel. They indeed say, 'Our
bones are dry, our hope is [h]lost, and
we ourselves are cut off!'
12 "Therefore prophesy and say to
them, 'Thus says the Lord GOD: "Behold, O My people, I will [i]open your
graves and cause you to come up from
your [j]graves, and bring you into the
land of Israel.
13 "Then you shall know that I *am*
the LORD, when I have opened your
graves, O My people, and brought you
up from your graves.
14 "I will put My [c]Spirit in you, and
you shall live, and I will place you in
your own land. Then you shall know
that I, the LORD, have spoken *it* and
performed *it*," says the LORD.' "

Sign of the two sticks

15 Again the word of the LORD came
to me, [d]saying,
16 "As for you, son of man, take a
stick for yourself and write on it: 'For
Judah and for the children of Israel,
his companions.' Then take another
stick and write on it, 'For Joseph, the
stick of Ephraim, and *for* all the house
of Israel, his companions.'
17 "Then join them one to another
for yourself into one stick, and they
will become [k]one in your hand.
18 "And when the children of your
people speak to you, saying, 'Will you
not show us what you *mean* by
these?'—
19 "say to them, 'Thus says the
Lord GOD: "Surely I will take the stick
of Joseph, which *is* in the hand of

35 *a* Isa. 51:3; Ezek. 28:13; Joel 2:3
37 *b* Ezek. 14:3; 20:3, 31
CHAPTER 37
1 *c Holy Spirit* (OT): vv. 1,14; Ezek. 39:29. (Gen. 1:2; Zech. 12:10) *d Parables* (OT): vv. 1–14, 15–28; Zech. 6:9. (Jud. 9:8; Zech. 11:7)
9 *e* v. 5; Ps. 104:30
10 *f* Jer. 33:22
11 *g* Ezek. 36:10 *h* Cp. Ezek. 33:10
12 *i* Cp. Dt. 32:39 *j* Isa. 26:19; 66:14; Dan. 12:2; Hos. 13:14
17 *k* Jer. 50:4; Hos. 1:11

[1](37:1) Having announced the restoration of the nation (36:24–38), the LORD now gives in vision and symbol the method of its accomplishment. Verse 11 gives the clue. The bones represent the whole house of Israel living at the time of restoration. The graves (v. 12) are the nations where they dwell. The order is: (1) bringing the people out (v. 12); (2) bringing them in (v. 12); (3) their conversion (v. 13); and (4) their being filled with the Spirit (v. 14). The symbol follows. The two sticks are Judah and the ten tribes; united, they are one nation (vv. 19–28).

Ephraim, and the tribes of Israel, his
companions; and I will join them with
it, with the stick of Judah, and make
them one stick, and they will be one in
My hand."'
20 "And the sticks on which you
write will be in your hand before their
eyes.
21 "Then say to them, 'Thus says
the Lord GOD: "Surely I will take the
[a]children of Israel from among the
nations, wherever they have gone,
and will [b]gather them from every
side and [c]bring them into their own
land;
22 "and I will make them one nation in the land, on the mountains of
Israel; and one [d]king shall be king
over them all; they shall no longer be
two nations, nor shall they ever be divided into two kingdoms again.
23 "They shall not defile themselves anymore with their idols, nor
with their detestable things, nor with
any of their transgressions; but I will
deliver them from all their dwelling
places in which they have sinned, and
will [e]cleanse them. Then they shall
be My people, and I will be their
God.
24 [f]"David My servant *shall be*
king over them, and they shall all have
one shepherd; they shall also walk in
My judgments and observe My statutes, and do them.
25 "Then they shall dwell in the
land that I have given to Jacob My
servant, where your fathers dwelt;
and they shall dwell there, they, their
children, and their children's children, [g]forever; and [h]My servant David *shall be* their prince forever.
26 "Moreover I will make a [i]cov-
enant of peace with them, and it shall
be an everlasting covenant with them;
I will establish them and multiply
them, and I will set My sanctuary in
their midst forevermore.
27 "My tabernacle also shall be
with them; indeed I will be their God,
and they shall be My people.
28 "The nations also will know that
I, the LORD, sanctify Israel, when My
sanctuary is in their midst forevermore."'"

21
a Israel (prophecies): vv. 21–28; Ezek. 39:25. (Gen. 12:2; Rom. 11:26, *note*)
b Jer. 32:37; Ezek. 36:24
c Kingdom (OT): vv. 21–28; Dan. 2:35. (Gen. 1:26; Zech. 12:8, *note*)
22
d Christ (second advent): vv. 21–22; Dan. 7:14. (Dt. 30:3; Acts 1:11, *note*)
23
e Ezek. 36:25–29
24
f Isa. 40:11; Jer. 23:5; 30:9; Ezek. 34:23–24; Hos. 3:5; Lk. 1:32
25
g Isa. 60:21; Joel 3:20; Amos 9:15
h Ps. 89:3–4
26
i Isa. 55:3; Jer. 32:40; Ezek. 34:24–25; see Heb. 8:8, *notes*
CHAPTER 38
2
j 38:1–39:24; Rev. 20:8
k Gen. 10:2
l Ezek. 32:26
3
m See v. 2, *note*
4
n 2 Ki. 19:28
o Isa. 43:17
6
p Gen. 10:2–3
q Ezek.

Prophecy against Gog: future invasion of Palestine by northern confederacy

38 NOW the word of the LORD
came to me, saying,
2 "Son of man, set your face
against [1][j]Gog, of the land of [k]Magog,
the prince of Rosh,* [l]Meshech, and
Tubal, and prophesy against him,
3 "and say, 'Thus says the Lord
GOD: "Behold, I *am* against you, O
[m]Gog, the prince of Rosh, Meshech,
and Tubal.
4 "I will [n]turn you around, put
hooks into your jaws, and [o]lead you
out, with all your army, horses, and
horsemen, all splendidly clothed, a
great company *with* bucklers and
shields, all of them handling swords.
5 "Persia, Ethiopia,* and Libya*
are with them, all of them *with* shield
and helmet;
6 [p]"Gomer and all its troops; the
house of [q]Togarmah *from* the far
north and all its troops—many people
are with you.
7 "Prepare yourself and be ready,
you and all your companies that are
gathered about you; and be a guard
for them.
8 [r]"After many days you will be
visited. In the latter years you will
come into the land of those brought
back from the sword *and* gathered
from many people on the mountains
of Israel, which had long been desolate; they were brought out of the nations, and now all of them dwell
[s]safely.
9 "You will ascend, coming like a
storm, covering the land like a cloud,
you and all your troops and many peoples with you."
10 'Thus says the Lord GOD: "On
that day it shall come to pass *that*
thoughts will arise in your mind, and
you will make an evil plan:
11 "You will say, 'I will go up
against a land of [t]unwalled villages; I

27:14 **38:8** *r* Isa. 24:22 *s* Ezek. 34:25; 39:26
38:11 *t* Jer. 49:31; Zech. 2:4

38:2 Targum, Vulgate, and Aquila read *chief prince of* (also verse 3). **38:5** Hebrew *Cush* • Hebrew *Put*

[1](38:2) The reference is to the powers in the north of Europe, headed by Russia. The whole passage should be read in connection with Zech. 12:1–4; 14:1–9; Mt. 24:14–30; Rev. 14:14–20; 19:17–21. Gog is probably the prince; Magog, his land. Russia and the northern powers have long been the persecutors of dispersed Israel, and it is congruous both with divine justice and with the covenants of God that destruction should fall in connection with the attempt to exterminate the remnant of Israel in Jerusalem. The entire prophecy belongs to the yet future day of the LORD (see *notes* at Joel 1:15; Rev. 19:19).

will go to a peaceful people, who dwell safely, all of them dwelling without walls, and having neither bars nor gates'—

12 "to take plunder and to take booty, to stretch out your hand against the waste places *that are again* inhabited, and against a people gathered from the nations, who have acquired livestock and goods, who dwell in the midst of the land.

13 [a]"Sheba, [b]Dedan, the merchants of [c]Tarshish, and all their young lions will say to you, 'Have you come to take plunder? Have you gathered your army to take booty, to carry away silver and gold, to take away livestock and goods, to take great plunder?' " '

14 "Therefore, son of man, prophesy and say to [d]Gog, 'Thus says the Lord GOD: "On that [e]day when My people Israel dwell safely, will you not know *it?*

15 "Then you will come from your place out of the far north, you and many peoples with you, all of them riding on horses, a great company and a mighty army.

16 "You will come up against My people Israel like a cloud, to cover the land. It will be in the [f]latter days that I will bring you against My land, so that the nations may [g]know Me, when I am [h]hallowed in you, O [d]Gog, before their eyes."

17 'Thus says the Lord GOD: [i]"Are *you* he of whom I have spoken in former days by My servants the prophets of Israel, who prophesied for years in those days that I would bring you against them?

18 "And it will come to pass at the same time, when [d]Gog comes against the land of Israel," says the Lord GOD, "*that* My fury will show in My face.

19 "For in My jealousy *and* in the fire of My wrath I have spoken: [j]'Surely in that day there shall be a great earthquake in the land of Israel,

20 'so that the fish of the sea, the birds of the heavens, the beasts of the field, all creeping things that creep on the earth, and all men who *are* on the face of the earth shall shake at My presence. The [k]mountains shall be thrown down, the steep places shall fall, and every wall shall fall to the ground.'

21 "I will call for a [l]sword against Gog throughout all My mountains," says the Lord GOD. [m]"Every man's sword will be against his brother.

13
a Ezek. 27:22
b Ezek. 27:20
c Ezek. 27:12

14
d See v. 2, *note*
e *Day* (of the LORD): 38:14–39:29; Joel 2:1. (Ps. 2:9; Rev. 19:19)

16
f v. 8; cp. Dan. 2:28; 10:14; see Acts 2:17, *note*
g Ezek. 35:11
h Ezek. 28:22

17
i Cp. 1 Pet. 1:10–11

19
j Joel 3:16; Hag. 2:6–7; Rev. 16:18

20
k Jer. 4:24; Nah. 1:5–6

21
l *Armageddon* (battle of): 38:1–39:24; Joel 3:9. (Isa. 10:27; Rev. 19:17)
m 1 Sam. 14:20

22
n Ezek. 13:11

23
o v. 16; Ps. 9:16; Ezek. 37:28; 39:7

CHAPTER 39

1
p See 38:2, *note*

2
q Ezek. 38:8

4
r Ezek. 38:4
s Ezek. 33:27

6
t Ezek. 38:22

7
u Ezek. 36:23
v Ezek. 38:16

8
w Rev. 16:17; 21:6

22 "And I will bring him to judgment with pestilence and bloodshed; I will rain down on him, on his troops, and on the many peoples who *are* with him, [n]flooding rain, great hailstones, fire, and brimstone.

23 "Thus I will magnify Myself and sanctify Myself, and I will be [o]known in the eyes of many nations. Then they shall know that I *am* the LORD." '

Prophecy against Gog (continued): destruction of invaders

39 "AND you, son of man, prophesy against [p]Gog, and say, 'Thus says the Lord GOD: "Behold, I *am* against you, O Gog, the prince of [p]Rosh,* Meshech, and Tubal;

2 "and I will [q]turn you around and lead you on, bringing you up from the far north, and bring you against the mountains of Israel.

3 "Then I will knock the bow out of your left hand, and cause the arrows to fall out of your right hand.

4 "You shall fall upon the [r]mountains of Israel, you and all your troops and the peoples who *are* with you; I will give you to birds of prey of every sort and *to* the beasts of the field to be [s]devoured.

5 "You shall fall on the open field; for I have spoken," says the Lord GOD.

6 "And I will send [t]fire on Magog and on those who live in security in the coastlands. Then they shall know that I *am* the LORD.

7 "So I will make My holy name known in the midst of My people Israel, and I will not *let them* [u]profane My holy name anymore. Then the nations shall [v]know that *I am* the LORD, the Holy One in Israel.

8 "Surely it is coming, and [w]it shall be done," says the Lord GOD. "This *is* the day of which I have spoken.

9 "Then those who dwell in the cities of Israel will go out and set on fire and burn the weapons, both the shields and bucklers, the bows and arrows, the javelins and spears; and they will make fires with them for seven years.

10 "They will not take wood from the field nor cut down *any* from the forests, because they will make fires with the weapons; and they will [x]plunder those who plundered them,

39:10 *x* Isa. 14:2

*

39:1 Targum, Vulgate, and Aquila read *chief prince of.*

and pillage those who pillaged them,"
says the Lord GOD.

11 "It will come to pass in that day *that* I will give [a]Gog a burial place there in Israel, the valley of those who pass by east of the sea; and it will obstruct travelers, because there they will bury Gog and all his multitude. Therefore they will call *it* the Valley of [b]Hamon Gog.

12 "For seven months the house of Israel will be burying them, in order to [c]cleanse the land.

13 "Indeed all the people of the land will be burying, and they will gain [d]renown for it on the day that I am glorified," says the Lord GOD.

14 "They will set apart men regularly employed, with the help of a search party,* to pass through the land and bury those bodies remaining on the ground, in order to cleanse it. At the end of seven months they will make a search.

15 "The search party will pass through the land; and *when anyone* sees a man's bone, he shall set up a marker by it, till the buriers have buried it in the Valley of [b]Hamon Gog.

16 "*The* name of *the* city *will* also *be* Hamonah. Thus they shall cleanse the land." '

17 "And as for you, son of man, thus says the Lord GOD, 'Speak to every sort of bird and to every beast of the field:

"Assemble yourselves and
come;
Gather together from all sides
to My [e]sacrificial meal
Which I am sacrificing for you,
A great sacrificial meal on the
mountains of Israel,
That you may eat flesh and
drink blood.
18 You shall eat the flesh of the
mighty,
Drink the blood of the princes
of the earth,
Of rams and lambs,
Of goats and bulls,
All of them [f]fatlings of
Bashan.
19 You shall eat fat till you are
full,
And drink blood till you are
drunk,
At My sacrificial meal
Which I am sacrificing for you.
20 You shall be filled at My table
With horses and riders,
With mighty men
And with all the men of war,"
says the Lord GOD.

21 "I will [g]set My glory among the nations; all the nations shall see My judgment which I have executed, and My hand which I have laid on them.

22 "So the house of Israel shall know that I *am* the LORD their God from that day forward.

23 "The Gentiles shall [h]know that the house of Israel went into captivity for their iniquity; because they were unfaithful to Me, therefore I [i]hid My face from them. I gave them into the hand of their enemies, and they all fell by the sword.

24 "According to their uncleanness and according to their transgressions I have dealt with them, and hidden My face from them." '

Israel restored and converted

25 "Therefore thus says the Lord GOD: [j]'Now I will bring back the captives of Jacob, and have mercy on the [k]whole house of Israel; and I will be jealous for My holy name—

26 'after they have borne their shame, and all their unfaithfulness in which they were unfaithful to Me, when they dwelt safely in their *own* land and no one made *them* afraid.

27 [l]'When I have brought them back from the peoples and gathered them out of their enemies' lands, and I am hallowed in them in the sight of many nations,

28 [m]'then they shall know that I *am* the LORD their God, who sent them into captivity among the nations, but also brought them back to their land, and left none of them captive any longer.

29 [n]'And I will not hide My face from them anymore; for I shall have poured out My [o]Spirit on the house of Israel,' says the Lord GOD."

VI. The Millennial Temple and Its Worship, 40:1—47:12

Vision of the man with the measuring rod

40 IN the twenty-fifth [p]year of our captivity, at the beginning of the year, on the tenth *day* of the month, in the fourteenth year after the city was [q]captured, on the very same day the hand of the LORD was upon me; and He took me there.

2 In the visions of God He [r]took me into the land of Israel and set me on a very high mountain; on it toward

11
a See 38:2, *note*
b i.e. *multitude of Gog*
12
c Cp. Dt. 21:23
13
d Jer. 33:9; Zeph. 3:19–20
17
e Zeph. 1:7
18
f Dt. 32:14
21
g Ezek. 38:23
23
h Ezek. 36:18–20, 23
i Isa. 59:2
25
j *Israel* (prophecies): vv. 25–29; Hos. 3:5. (Gen. 12:2; Rom. 11:26, *note*)
k Ezek. 20:40; Hos. 1:11
27
l Ezek. 28:25–26
28
m v. 22; Ezek. 34:30
29
n Isa. 54:8–9
o *Holy Spirit* (OT): v. 29; Ezek. 43:5. (Gen. 1:2; Zech. 12:10)
CHAPTER 40
1
p c. 573 B.C.
q 2 Ki. 25:1–4; Jer. 39:2–3; 52:4–7
2
r Ezek. 3:14; 37:1

* 39:14 Literally *those who pass through*

the south *was* something like the structure of a city.

3 He took me there, and behold, *there was* a [a]man whose appearance *was* like the appearance of bronze. He had a line of flax and a measuring [b]rod in his hand, and he stood in the gateway.

4 And the man said to me, "Son of man, [c]look with your eyes and hear with your ears, and fix your mind on everything I show you; for you *were* brought here so that I might show *them* to you. [d]Declare to the house of Israel everything you see."

Vision of the millennial temple

5 Now [1]there was a wall all around the outside of the temple.* In the man's hand was a measuring rod six [b]cubits *long, each being a* cubit and a handbreadth; and he measured the width of the wall structure, one [b]rod; and the height, one rod.

6 Then he went to the gateway which faced [e]east; and he went up its stairs and measured the threshold of the gateway, *which was* one rod wide, and the other threshold *was* one rod wide.

7 Each [f]gate chamber *was* one rod long and one rod wide; between the gate chambers *was a space of* five cubits; and the threshold of the gateway by the vestibule of the inside gate *was* one rod.

8 He also measured the vestibule of the inside gate, one rod.

9 Then he measured the vestibule of the gateway, eight cubits; and the gateposts, two cubits. The vestibule of the gate *was* on the inside.

10 In the eastern gateway *were* three gate chambers on one side and three on the other; the three *were* all the same size; also the gateposts were of the same size on this side and that side.

3
a Theophanies: vv. 3–4; Dan. 8:15. (Gen. 12:7, *note;* Dan. 10:5). Ezek. 43:6
b See Weights and Measures (OT), 2 Chr. 2:10, *note*

4
c Ezek. 44:5
d Ezek. 43:10

6
e Ezek. 43:1

7
f Perhaps a guard room

16
g 1 Ki. 6:4
h 1 Ki. 6:29, 32,35

17
i Ezek. 42:1; cp. Rev. 11:2
j 1 Ki. 6:5; 2 Chr. 31:11
k Cp. Ezek. 45:5

11 He measured the width of the entrance to the gateway, ten cubits; *and* the length of the gate, thirteen cubits.

12 *There was* a space in front of the gate chambers, one cubit *on this side* and one cubit on that side; the gate chambers *were* six cubits on this side and six cubits on that side.

13 Then he measured the gateway from the roof of *one* gate chamber to the roof of the other; the width *was* twenty-five cubits, as door faces door.

14 He measured the gateposts, sixty cubits high, and the court all around the gateway *extended* to the gatepost.

15 *From* the front of the entrance gate to the front of the vestibule of the inner gate *was* fifty cubits.

16 *There were* [g]beveled window *frames* in the gate chambers and in their intervening archways on the inside of the gateway all around, and likewise in the vestibules. *There were* windows all around on the inside. And on each gatepost *were* [h]palm trees.

17 Then he brought me into the [i]outer court; and *there were* [j]chambers and a pavement made all around the court; [k]thirty chambers faced the pavement.

18 The pavement was by the side of the gateways, corresponding to the length of the gateways; *this was* the lower pavement.

19 Then he measured the width from the front of the lower gateway to the front of the inner court exterior, one hundred cubits toward the east and the north.

20 On the [i]outer court was also a gateway facing north, and he measured its length and its width.

21 Its gate chambers, three on this side and three on that side, its gate-

* 40:5 Literally *house,* and so elsewhere in this book

[1](40:5) The last nine chapters of Ezekiel have posed numerous problems for expositors. Five explanations have been offered: (1) Some feel these chapters describe the Solomonic temple before its destruction in 586 B.C. This is not possible because of disagreement in detail with the accounts in the books of Kings and Chronicles. (2) Some hold it is a description of the restoration temple completed in the sixth century B.C. This view is also untenable, because the descriptions do not tally. (3) Others maintain that the chapters portray an ideal temple never realized. This position does not explain why the portrayal is presented, nor why there is so much detail. (4) Still another view is the claim that the picture is one of the Church and its blessings in this age. This view does not explain the symbolism, nor why large areas of Christian doctrine are omitted. And (5) the preferable interpretation is that Ezekiel gives a picture of the millennial temple. Judging from the broad context of the prophecy (the time subsequent to Israel's regathering and conversion) and the testimony of other Scripture (Isa. 66; Ezek. 6; 14), this interpretation is in keeping with God's prophetic program for the millennium. The Church is not in view here, but rather it is a prophecy for the consummation of Israel's history on earth.

posts and its archways, had the same measurements as the first gate; its length *was* fifty cubits and its width twenty-five cubits.

22 Its windows and those of its archways, and also its palm trees, *had* the same measurements as the gateway facing east; it was ascended by seven steps, and its archway *was* in front of it.

23 A gate of the inner court was opposite the northern gateway, just as the eastern *gateway;* and he measured from gateway to gateway, one hundred cubits.

24 After that he brought me toward the south, and there a gateway was facing south; and he measured its gateposts and archways according to these same measurements.

25 *There were* windows in it and in its archways all around like those windows; its length *was* fifty cubits and its width twenty-five cubits.

26 Seven steps led up to it, and its archway *was* in front of them; and it had palm trees on its gateposts, one on this side and one on that side.

27 *There was* also a gateway on the inner court, facing south; and he measured from gateway to gateway toward the south, one hundred cubits.

28 Then he brought me to the inner court through the southern gateway; he measured the southern gateway according to these same measurements.

29 Also its gate chambers, its gateposts, and its archways *were* according to these same measurements; *there were* windows in it and in its archways all around; *it was* fifty cubits long and [a]twenty-five [b]cubits wide.

30 *There were* archways all around, twenty-five cubits long and five cubits wide.

31 Its archways faced the outer court, palm trees *were* on its gateposts, and going up to it *were* eight steps.

32 And he brought me into the inner court facing east; he measured the gateway according to these same measurements.

33 Also its gate chambers, its gateposts, and its archways *were* according to these same measurements; and *there were* windows in it and in its archways all around; *it was* fifty cubits long and twenty-five cubits wide.

34 Its archways faced the outer court, and palm trees *were* on its gateposts on this side and on that side; and going up to it *were* eight steps.

35 Then he brought me to the north gateway and measured *it* according to these same measurements—

36 also its gate chambers, its gateposts, and its archways. It had windows all around; its length *was* fifty cubits and its width twenty-five cubits.

37 Its gateposts faced the outer court, palm trees *were* on its gateposts on this side and on that side, and going up to it *were* eight steps.

38 *There was* a chamber and its entrance by the gateposts of the gateway, where they [c]washed the burnt offering.

39 In the vestibule of the gateway *were* two tables on this side and two tables on that side, on which to slay the burnt offering, the [d]sin offering, and the [e]trespass offering.

40 At the outer side of the vestibule, [f]as one goes up to the entrance of the northern gateway, *were* two tables; and on the other side of the vestibule of the gateway *were* two tables.

41 Four tables *were* on this side and four tables on that side, by the side of the gateway, eight tables on which they slaughtered *the sacrifices.*

42 *There were* also four tables of [g]hewn stone for the burnt offering, one cubit and a half long, one cubit and a half wide, and one cubit high; on these they laid the instruments with which they slaughtered the burnt offering and the sacrifice.

43 Inside *were* hooks, a [h]handbreadth wide, fastened all around; and the flesh of the sacrifices *was* on the tables.

Chambers of the singers and priests

44 Outside the inner gate *were* the chambers for the [i]singers in the inner court, one facing south at the side of the northern gateway, and the other facing north at the side of the southern gateway.

45 Then he said to me, "This chamber which faces south *is* for the priests who [j]have charge of the temple.

46 "The chamber which faces north *is* for the priests who [k]have charge of the altar; these *are* the sons of [l]Zadok, from the sons of Levi, who come near the LORD to minister to Him."

47 And he measured the court, one hundred cubits long and one hundred cubits wide, foursquare. The altar *was* in front of the temple.

29
a vv. 21,25, 33,36
b See Weights and Measures (OT), 2 Chr. 2:10, *note*
38
c 2 Chr. 4:6
39
d Lev. 4:2–3
e Lev. 5:6; 6:6; 7:1
40
f i.e. *at the step*
42
g Cp. Ex. 20:25
43
h See Weights and Measures (OT), 2 Chr. 2:10, *note*
44
i 1 Chr. 6:31–32; 16:41–43; 25:1–7
45
j Lev. 8:35; Num. 3:27–28,32, 38; 18:5; 1 Chr. 9:23; 2 Chr. 13:11; Ps. 134:1
46
k Lev. 6:12–13
l 1 Ki. 2:35; Ezek. 43:19; 44:15–16

48 Then he brought me to the [a]vestibule of the temple and measured the doorposts of the vestibule, five cubits on this side and five cubits on that side; and the width of the gateway was three cubits on this side and three cubits on that side.

49 The length of the vestibule *was* twenty cubits, and the width eleven cubits; and by the steps which led up to it *there were* [b]pillars by the doorposts, one on this side and another on that side.

The holy and most holy place, side chambers, the rear buildings and interior

41

THEN he [c]brought me into the sanctuary* and measured the doorposts, six cubits wide on one side and six cubits wide on the other side—the width of the tabernacle.

2 The width of the entryway *was* ten cubits, and the side walls of the entrance *were* five cubits on this side and five cubits on the other side; and he measured its length, forty cubits, and its width, twenty cubits.

3 Also he went [d]inside and measured the doorposts, two cubits; and the entrance, six cubits *high;* and the width of the entrance, seven cubits.

4 He measured the length, twenty cubits; and the width, twenty cubits, beyond the sanctuary; and he said to me, [e]"This *is* the [f]Most Holy *Place.*"

5 Next, he measured the wall of the temple, six [g]cubits. The width of each side chamber all around the temple *was* four cubits on every side.

6 The side [h]chambers *were* in three stories, one above the other, thirty chambers in each story; they rested on ledges which *were* for the side chambers all around, that they might be supported, but [i]not fastened to the wall of the temple.

7 [j]As one went up from story to story, the side chambers became wider all around, because their supporting ledges in the wall of the temple ascended like steps; therefore the width of the structure increased as one went up *from* the lowest *story* to the highest by way of the middle one.

8 I also saw an elevation all around the temple; it was the foundation of the side chambers, a full [g]rod, *that is,* six cubits *high.*

9 The thickness of the outer wall of the side chambers *was* five cubits, and so also the remaining terrace by the place of the side chambers of the temple.

10 And between *it and* the *wall* chambers was a width of twenty cubits all around the temple on every side.

11 The doors of the side chambers opened on the terrace, one door toward the north and another toward the south; and the width of the terrace *was* five cubits all around.

12 The building that faced the separating courtyard at its western end *was* seventy cubits wide; the wall of the building *was* five cubits thick all around, and its length ninety cubits.

13 So he measured the temple, one [k]hundred cubits long; and the separating courtyard with the building and its walls *was* one hundred cubits long;

14 also the width of the eastern face of the temple, including the separating courtyard, *was* one hundred cubits.

15 He measured the length of the building behind it, facing the separating courtyard, with its [l]galleries on the one side and on the other side, one hundred cubits, as well as the inner temple and the porches of the court,

16 their doorposts and the [m]beveled window frames. And the galleries all around their three stories opposite the threshold were paneled with [n]wood from the ground to the windows—the windows were covered—

17 from the space above the door, even to the inner room,* as well as outside, and on every wall all around, inside and outside, [1]by measure.

18 And *it was* made with [o]cherubim and [p]palm trees, a palm tree between cherub and cherub. *Each* cherub had two faces,

19 so that the face of a [q]man *was* toward a palm tree on one side, and the face of a young lion toward a palm tree on the other side; thus *it was* made throughout the temple all around.

20 From the floor to the space above the door, and on the wall of the sanctuary, cherubim and palm trees *were* carved.

21 The [r]doorposts of the temple *were* square, *as was* the front of the

48
a 1 Ki. 6:3; 2 Chr. 3:4
49
b 1 Ki. 7:15–21; 2 Chr. 3:17; cp. Rev. 3:12
CHAPTER 41
1
c Ezek. 40:2–3
3
d i.e. *to the inner room*
4
e 1 Ki. 6:20; 2 Chr. 3:8
f Ex. 26:33–34; Heb. 9:3–8
5
g See Weights and Measures (OT), 2 Chr. 2:10, *note*
6
h 1 Ki. 6:5
i 1 Ki. 6:6,10
7
j Cp. 1 Ki. 6:8
13
k Ezek. 40:47
15
l Ezek. 42:3, 5
16
m 1 Ki. 6:4; Ezek. 40:16,25
n 1 Ki. 6:15
18
o 1 Ki. 6:29; 2 Chr. 3:7
p 2 Chr. 3:5; Ezek. 40:16
19
q Ezek. 1:10; 10:14
21
r 1 Ki. 6:33

*41:1 Hebrew *heykal,* here the main room of the temple, sometimes called the *holy place* (compare Exodus 26:33) 41:17 Literally *house,* here *the Most Holy Place*

1(41:17) Every detail, however small it may seem, is important in the work of the LORD.

sanctuary; their appearance was similar.
22 The [a]altar *was* of wood, three
cubits high, and its length two cubits.
Its corners, its length, and its sides
were of wood; and he said to me, "This
is the [b]table that *is* before the LORD."
23 [c]The temple and the sanctuary
had two doors.
24 The doors had two [d]panels
apiece, two folding panels: two *panels*
for one door and two panels for the
other *door.*
25 Cherubim and palm trees *were*
carved on the doors of the temple just
as they *were* carved on the walls. A
wooden canopy *was* on the front of
the vestibule outside.
26 *There were* beveled window
frames and palm trees on one side and
on the other, on the sides of the
vestibule—also on the side chambers
of the temple and on the canopies.

The priests' chambers and final measurements of the temple

42 THEN he [e]brought me out into
the [f]outer court, by the way toward the [g]north; and he brought me
into the [h]chamber which *was* opposite the [i]separating courtyard, and
which *was* opposite the building toward the north.
2 Facing the length, *which was*
one hundred [j]cubits (the width was
fifty cubits), was the north door.
3 Opposite the inner court of
twenty *cubits,* and opposite the
[f]pavement of the outer court, *was*
[k]gallery against gallery in three *stories.*
4 In front of the chambers, toward
the inside, *was* a walk ten cubits wide,
at a distance of one cubit; and their
doors faced north.
5 Now the upper chambers *were*
shorter, because the galleries took
away *space* from them more than
from the lower and middle stories of
the building.
6 For they *were* in three *stories*
and did not have pillars like the pillars
of the courts; therefore *the upper level*
was shortened more than the lower
and middle levels from the ground up.
7 And a wall which *was* outside
ran parallel to the chambers, at the
front of the chambers, toward the
outer court; its length *was* fifty cubits.
8 The length of the chambers toward the outer court *was* fifty cubits,
whereas that facing the temple *was*
one [l]hundred cubits.
9 At the lower chambers *was* the
entrance on the east side, as one goes
into them from the outer court.
10 Also *there were* chambers in the
thickness of the wall of the court
toward the east, opposite the separating courtyard and opposite the
building.
11 *There was* a walk in front of
them also, and their appearance *was*
like the chambers which *were* toward
the north; they *were* as long and
as wide as the others, and all their
exits and entrances *were* according to
plan.
12 And corresponding to the doors
of the chambers that *were* facing
south, as one enters them, *there was* a
door in front of the walk, the way directly in front of the wall toward the
east.
13 Then he said to me, "The north
chambers *and* the south chambers,
which *are* opposite the separating
courtyard, *are* the holy chambers
where the priests who [m]approach the
LORD [n]shall eat the most holy offerings. There they shall lay the most
holy offerings—the [o]grain offering,
the sin offering, and the trespass
offering—for the place *is* holy.
14 "When the priests enter them,
they shall not go out of the holy *chamber* into the outer court; but there they
shall [p]leave their [q]garments in which
they minister, for they *are* holy. They
shall put on other garments; then they
may approach *that* which *is* for the
people."
15 Now when he had finished measuring the inner temple, he brought
me out through the gateway that faces
toward the [r]east, and measured it all
around.
16 He measured the east side with
the measuring rod,* five hundred
[j]rods by the measuring rod all
around.
17 He measured the north side, five
hundred rods by the measuring rod all
around.
18 He measured the south side, five
hundred rods by the measuring rod.
19 He came around to the west side
and measured five hundred rods by
the measuring rod.
20 He measured it on the four sides;
it had a [s]wall all around, [t]five hundred *cubits* long and five hundred
wide, to separate the holy areas from
the [u]common.

22
a Ex. 30:1; 1 Ki. 6:20
b Ex. 25:23–30; Lev. 24:6
23
c 1 Ki. 6:31–35
24
d 1 Ki. 6:34
CHAPTER 42
1
e Ezek. 41:4
f Ezek. 40:17
g Ezek. 40:20
h Ezek. 41:12,15
i vv. 10,13
2
j See Weights and Measures (OT), 2 Chr. 2:10, *note*
3
k Ezek. 41:15
8
l Ezek. 41:13–14
13
m Ezek. 43:19
n Lev. 6:16, 26
o Lev. 2:3, 10; 6:14, 17,25,29; 7:1; 10:13–14; Num. 18:9–10
14
p Ezek. 44:19
q Cp. Ex. 29:5–9; Lev. 8:7,13
15
r Ezek. 40:6
20
s Ezek. 40:5
t Ezek. 45:2
u Ezek. 44:23

*
42:16 Compare 40:5

Vision of glory of the Lord *filling the temple (cp. Ezek. 11:22–24)*

43 AFTERWARD he brought me to the gate, the gate that faces toward the [a]east.

2 And behold, the [b]glory of the God of Israel came from the way of the east. His [c]voice *was* like the sound of many waters; and the earth shone with His [d]glory.

3 *It was* like the appearance of the vision which I saw—like the vision which I saw [1]when I came to destroy the city. The visions *were* like the vision which I saw by the River Chebar; and I fell on my face.

4 And the [e]glory of the Lord came into the temple by way of the gate which faces toward the east.

5 The [f]Spirit lifted me up and brought me into the inner court; and behold, the glory of the Lord [g]filled the temple.

The place of the throne in the coming kingdom

6 Then I heard *Him* speaking to me from the temple, while a [h]man stood beside me.

7 And He said to me, "Son of man, *this is* the [i]place of My throne and the place of the soles of My feet, where I will [j]dwell in the midst of the children of Israel forever. No more shall the house of Israel defile My holy name, they nor their kings, by their harlotry or with the carcasses of their kings on their [k]high places.

8 "When they set their threshold by My threshold, and their doorpost by My doorpost, with a wall between them and Me, they [l]defiled My holy name by the abominations which they committed; therefore I have consumed them in My anger.

9 "Now let them put their harlotry and the carcasses of their kings far away from Me, and I will dwell in their midst forever.

10 "Son of man, describe the temple to the house of Israel, that they may be ashamed of their iniquities; and let them measure the pattern.

CHAPTER 43

1 a Ezek. 42:15

2 b Ezek. 9:3; 10:18,19
c Ezek. 1:24; Rev. 1:15; 14:2; 19:6
d Ezek. 10:4; Rev. 18:1

4 e Ezek. 11:23

5 f Holy *Spirit* (OT): v. 5; Joel 2:28. (Gen. 1:2; Zech. 12:10)
g Ex. 40:34; 1 Ki. 8:10–11; Ezek. 44:4

6 h Ezek. 1:26

7 i Ps. 99:1; Isa. 60:13
j Ezek. 37:26–28
k Ezek. 6:5, 13

8 l Ezek. 44:7

11 m Ezek. 44:5
n Ezek. 11:20

12 o Ezek. 40:2

13 p Ex. 27:1–8
q See Weights and Measures (OT), 2 Chr. 2:10, *note*

14 r Ezek. 45:19

15 s Ex. 27:2

16 t Ex. 27:1

11 "And if they are ashamed of all that they have done, make known to them the design of the temple and its arrangement, its exits and its entrances, its entire design and all its [m]ordinances, all its forms and all its laws. Write *it* down in their sight, so that they may keep its whole design and all its ordinances, and [n]perform them.

12 "This *is* the law of the temple: The whole area surrounding the [o]mountaintop *is* most holy. Behold, this *is* the law of the temple.

Measure of the altar of sacrifice

13 "These are the measurements of the [p]altar in cubits (the [q]*cubit is* one cubit and a [q]handbreadth): the base one cubit high and one cubit wide, with a rim all around its edge of one [q]span. This *is* the height of the altar:

14 "from the base on the ground to the lower [r]ledge, two cubits; the width of the ledge, one cubit; from the smaller ledge to the larger ledge, four cubits; and the width of the ledge, *one* cubit.

15 "The altar hearth *is* four cubits high, with four [s]horns extending upward from the hearth.

16 "The altar hearth *is* twelve cubits long, twelve wide, [t]square at its four corners;

17 "the ledge, fourteen *cubits* long and fourteen wide on its four sides, with a rim of half a cubit around it; its base, one cubit all around; and its [u]steps face toward the east."

18 And He said to me, "Son of man, thus says the Lord God: 'These *are* the ordinances for the altar on the day when it is made, for sacrificing [v]burnt offerings on it, and for [w]sprinkling blood on it.

The offerings

19 [2]'You shall give a young [x]bull for a sin offering to the [y]priests, the

43:17 *u* Cp. Ex. 20:26 **43:18** *v* Ex. 40:29 *w* Lev. 1:5
43:19 *x* Ex. 29:10–12; Lev. 8:14–15; Ezek. 45:18–19
y Ezek. 44:15

[1](43:3) Obviously it was not Ezekiel who came to destroy the city of Jerusalem for her sins, but the Lord Himself. On the basis of the requirements of the context, the reading in some six manuscripts, the version of Theodotion and that of the Vulgate, the best reading is "when He came to destroy the city." A possible rendering, and perhaps preferable, would be to read the final letter of the disputed word as a well-known abbreviation for "Lord," thus giving us the reading "when the Lord came to destroy the city."

[2](43:19) A problem is posed by this paragraph (vv. 19–27). Since the NT clearly teaches that animal sacrifices do not in themselves cleanse away sin (Heb. 10:4) and that the one sacrifice of the Lord Jesus Christ that was made at Calvary completely provides for such expiation (cp. Heb. 9:12,26,28; 10:10,14), how can there be a fulfillment of such a prophecy? Two answers

Levites, who are of the seed of [a]Za-
dok, who [b]approach Me to minister to
Me,' says the Lord GOD.
20 'You shall take some of its blood
and put *it* on the four horns of the
altar, on the four corners of the ledge,
and on the rim around it; thus you
shall cleanse it and make atonement
for it.
21 'Then you shall also take the bull
of the sin offering, and [c]burn it in the
appointed place of the temple, [d]out-
side the sanctuary.
22 'On the second day you shall offer a kid of the goats without blemish
for a sin offering; and they shall
cleanse the altar, as they cleansed *it*
with the bull.
23 'When you have finished cleansing *it*, you shall offer a young bull
without blemish, and a ram from the
flock without blemish.
24 'When you offer them before the
LORD, the priests shall throw [e]salt on
them, and they will offer them up *as* a
burnt offering to the LORD.
25 'Every day for [f]seven days you
shall prepare a goat *for* a sin offering;
they shall also prepare a young bull
and a ram from the flock, both without
blemish.
26 'Seven days they shall make
atonement for the altar and purify it,
and so consecrate *it*.
27 'When these days are over it
shall be, on the [g]eighth day and thereafter, that the priests shall offer your
burnt offerings and your peace offerings on the altar; and I will accept
you,' says the Lord GOD."

Gate for the prince
to eat bread before the LORD

44 THEN He brought me back to
the outer gate of the sanctuary
which faces toward the east, but it *was*
shut.
2 And the LORD said to me, "This
gate shall be shut; it shall not be
opened, and no man shall enter by it,
because the LORD God of Israel has
[h]entered by it; therefore it shall be
shut.
3 "*As for* the [1][i]prince, *because* he
is the prince, he may sit in it to [j]eat
bread before the LORD; [k]he shall enter
by way of the vestibule of the gateway, and go out the same way."

The glory fills the house

4 Also He brought me by way of
the north gate to the front of the temple; so I looked, and behold, the
[l]glory of the LORD filled the house of
the LORD; and I fell on my face.
5 And the LORD said to me, "Son of
man, [m]mark well, see with your eyes
and hear with your ears, all that I say
to you concerning all the [n]ordinances
of the house of the LORD and all its
laws. Mark well who may enter the
house and all who go out from the
sanctuary.
6 "Now say to the rebellious, to the
house of Israel, 'Thus says the Lord
GOD: "O house of Israel, let Us [o]have
no more of all your abominations.
7 "When you brought in [p]foreign-
ers, [q]uncircumcised in heart and uncircumcised in flesh, to be in My sanctuary to defile it—My house—and
when you offered My food, the fat and
the blood, then they broke My covenant because of all your abominations.
8 "And you have not kept charge
of My holy things, but you have set
others to keep charge of My sanctuary
for you."

The priests of the future temple

9 'Thus says the Lord GOD: "No
[p]foreigner, uncircumcised in heart or
uncircumcised in flesh, shall enter My
sanctuary, including any foreigner
who *is* among the children of Israel.
10 "And the [r]Levites who went far
from Me, when Israel went astray,
who strayed away from Me after their
idols, they shall bear their iniquity.
11 "Yet they shall be ministers in
My sanctuary, *as* gatekeepers of the
house and ministers of the house; they
shall slay the burnt offering and the
sacrifice for the people, and they shall
stand before them to minister to them.
12 "Because they ministered to
them before their idols and caused the
house of Israel to fall into iniquity,

19
a Ezek. 40:46
b Cp. Num. 16:5–40
21
c Ex. 29:14
d Heb. 13:11; cp. Lev. 4:12, *note*
24
e Lev. 2:13
25
f Ex. 29:35–37; Lev. 8:33
27
g Lev. 9:1–4
CHAPTER 44
2
h Ezek. 43:2–4
3
i Ezek. 37:25; 45:7
j Cp. Gen. 31:54; 1 Cor. 10:18
k Ezek. 46:2,8
4
l Ezek. 3:23; 43:5
5
m Ezek. 40:4
n Ezek. 43:11
6
o Ezek. 45:9; 1 Pet. 4:3
7
p Num. 18:4; Zech. 14:21; cp. Acts 21:28
q Jer. 9:26
10
r 2 Ki. 23:8; cp. 2 Chr. 29:4–5

have been suggested: (1) Such sacrifices, if actually offered, will be memorial in character. They will, according to this view, look back to our Lord's work on the cross, as the offerings of the old covenant anticipated His sacrifice. They would, of course, have no expiatory value. And (2) the reference to sacrifices is not to be taken literally, in view of the putting away of such offerings, but is rather to be regarded as a presentation of the worship of redeemed Israel, in her own land and in the millennial temple, using the terms with which the Jews were familiar in Ezekiel's day.

[1](44:3) This prince is not the Messiah, as shown by his actions in chs. 44—46.

therefore I have [a]raised My hand in an oath against them," says the Lord GOD, "that they shall bear their iniquity.
13 "And they shall [b]not come near Me to minister to Me as priest, nor come near any of My holy things, nor into the Most Holy *Place;* but they shall bear their shame and their abominations which they have committed.
14 "Nevertheless I will make them [c]keep charge of the temple, for all its work, and for all that has to be done in it.
15 "But the priests, the Levites, the [d]sons of Zadok, who kept charge of My sanctuary when the children of Israel went astray from Me, they shall come near Me to minister to Me; and they [e]shall stand before Me to offer to Me the fat and the blood," says the Lord GOD.
16 "They shall [f]enter My sanctuary, and they shall come near My table to minister to Me, and they shall keep My charge.
17 "And it shall be, whenever they enter the gates of the inner court, that [g]they shall put on linen garments; no wool shall come upon them while they minister within the gates of the inner court or within the house.
18 "They shall have linen turbans on their heads and linen trousers on their bodies; they shall not clothe themselves with *anything that causes* sweat.
19 "When they go out to the outer court, to the *outer* court to the people, they shall take off their garments in which they have ministered, [h]leave them in the holy chambers, and put on other garments; and in their holy garments they shall [i]not sanctify the people.
20 "They shall neither [j]shave their heads nor let their hair grow [k]long, but they shall keep their hair well trimmed.
21 "No priest shall [l]drink wine when he enters the inner court.
22 "They shall not take as wife a [m]widow or a divorced woman, but take virgins of the descendants of the house of Israel, or widows of priests.
23 "And they shall [n]teach My people *the difference* between the holy and the unholy, and cause them to [o]discern between the unclean and the clean.
24 "In [p]controversy they shall stand as judges, *and* judge it according to My judgments. They shall keep My laws and My statutes in all My appointed meetings, and they shall hallow My Sabbaths.
25 "They shall not defile *themselves* by coming near a dead person. Only for father or mother, for son or daughter, for brother or unmarried sister may they defile themselves.
26 "After he is cleansed, they shall count [q]seven days for him.
27 "And on the day that he goes to the sanctuary to minister in the sanctuary, he must offer his [r]sin offering in the inner court," says the Lord GOD.
28 "It shall be, in regard to their inheritance, *that* [s]I *am* their inheritance. You shall give them no [t]possession in Israel, for I *am* their possession.
29 "They shall eat the grain offering, the sin offering, and the trespass offering; every [u]dedicated thing in Israel shall be theirs.
30 "The [v]best of all firstfruits of any kind, and every sacrifice of any kind from all your sacrifices, shall be the priest's; also you shall give to the priest the first of your ground meal, to cause a blessing to rest on your house.
31 "The priests [w]shall not eat anything, bird or beast, that died naturally or was torn *by wild beasts.*

The LORD's district of land

45 "MOREOVER, when you [x]divide the land by lot into inheritance, you shall set apart a [y]district for the LORD, a holy section of the land; its length *shall be* twenty-five thousand *cubits,* and the width ten thousand. It *shall be* holy throughout its territory all around.
2 "Of this there shall be a square plot for the sanctuary, [z]five hundred by five hundred *rods,* with fifty [aa]cubits around it for an open space.
3 "So this is the district you shall measure: twenty-five thousand *cubits* long and ten thousand wide; in it shall be the [bb]sanctuary, the Most Holy *Place.*
4 "It shall be a holy *section* of the land, belonging to the priests, the ministers of the sanctuary, who come near to minister to the LORD; it shall be a place for their houses and a holy place for the sanctuary.
5 "*An area* twenty-five thousand

12 *a* Isa. 9:16
13 *b* 2 Ki. 23:9
14 *c* Num. 18:4; 1 Chr. 23:28,32
15 *d* 1 Sam. 2:35; 2 Sam. 15:27; Ezek. 43:19; 48:11 *e* Dt. 10:8
16 *f* Num. 18:7–8
17 *g* Ex. 28:39–43; 39:27–29
19 *h* Ezek. 42:14 *i* Lev. 6:27; cp. Ezek. 46:20; Mt. 23:17–19
20 *j* Lev. 21:5 *k* Num. 6:5
21 *l* Lev. 10:9
22 *m* Lev. 21:7, 13–14
23 *n* Lev. 10:10–11; Ezek. 22:26; Mal. 2:7 *o* Lev. 20:25
24 *p* Dt. 17:8; 2 Chr. 19:8–10
26 *q* Num. 19:13–19
27 *r* Lev. 5:3,6
28 *s* Num. 18:20; Dt. 10:9; 18:1–2; Josh. 13:14,33 *t* Ezek. 45:4
29 *u* Lev. 27:28
30 *v* Cp. Ex. 13:2; Num. 3:13
31 *w* Lev. 22:8; Dt. 14:21

45:1 *x* Num. 26:52–56 *y* Ezek. 48:8–9 **45:2** *z* Ezek. 42:20 *aa* See Weights and Measures (OT), 2 Chr. 2:10, *note* **45:3** *bb* Ezek. 48:10

cubits long and ten thousand wide shall belong to the Levites, the ministers of the temple; they shall have twenty chambers as a possession.*

6 "You shall appoint as the property of the city *an area* [a]five thousand *cubits* wide and twenty-five thousand long, adjacent to the district of the holy *section;* it shall belong to the whole house of Israel.

Section for the prince

7 "The [b]prince shall have *a section* on one side and the other of the holy district and the city's property; and bordering on the holy district and the city's property, extending westward on the west side and eastward on the east side, the length *shall be* side by side with one of the *tribal* portions, from the west border to the east border.

8 "The land shall be his possession in Israel; and My princes shall no more oppress My people, but they shall [c]give *the rest of* the land to the house of Israel, according to their tribes."

9 'Thus says the Lord GOD: [d]"Enough, O princes of Israel! Remove violence and plundering, execute justice and righteousness, and stop dispossessing My people," says the Lord GOD.

10 "You shall have [e]honest scales, an honest [f]ephah, and an honest [f]bath.

11 "The ephah and the bath shall be of the same measure, so that the bath contains one-tenth of a [f]homer, and the ephah one-tenth of a homer; their measure shall be according to the homer.

12 "The [g]shekel *shall be* twenty [g]gerahs; twenty shekels, twenty-five shekels, *and* fifteen shekels shall be your [g]mina.

13 "This *is* the offering which you shall offer: you shall give one-sixth of an ephah from a homer of wheat, and one-sixth of an ephah from a homer of barley.

14 "The ordinance concerning oil, the bath of oil, *is* one-tenth of a bath from a [f]kor. A kor *is* a homer or ten baths, for ten baths *are* a homer.

15 "And one lamb shall be given from a flock of two hundred, from the rich pastures of Israel. These shall be for grain offerings, burnt offerings, and peace offerings, to make atonement for them," says the Lord GOD.

16 "All the people of the land shall [h]give this offering for the prince in Israel.

17 "Then it shall be the [i]prince's part *to give* burnt offerings, grain offerings, and drink offerings, at the feasts, the New Moons, the Sabbaths, and at all the appointed seasons of the house of Israel. He shall prepare the sin offering, the grain offering, the burnt offering, and the peace offerings to make atonement for the house of Israel."

18 'Thus says the Lord GOD: "In the [j]first *month,* on the first *day* of the month, you shall take a young bull without blemish and cleanse the sanctuary.

19 "The priest shall take some of the blood of the sin offering and put *it* on the doorposts of the temple, on the four corners of the ledge of the altar, and on the gateposts of the gate of the inner court.

20 "And so you shall do on the seventh *day* of the month for everyone who has [k]sinned unintentionally or in ignorance. Thus you shall make atonement for the temple.

21 [l]"In the first *month,* on the fourteenth day of the month, you shall observe the Passover, a feast of seven days; unleavened bread shall be eaten.

22 "And on that day the prince shall prepare for himself and for all the people of the land a [m]bull *for* a sin offering.

23 "On the seven days of the feast he shall prepare a burnt offering to the LORD, seven bulls and seven rams without blemish, daily for seven days, and a kid of the goats daily *for* a sin offering.

24 "And he shall prepare a grain offering of one [f]ephah for each bull and one ephah for each ram, together with a [f]hin of oil for each ephah.

25 "In the [j]seventh *month,* on the [n]fifteenth day of the month, at the feast, he shall do likewise for seven days, according to the sin offering, the burnt offering, the grain offering, and the oil."

The prince to worship first; then he is to lead the people in worship

46 'THUS says the Lord GOD: "The gateway of the inner court that faces toward the east shall be shut the six [o]working days; but on the Sabbath

6 *a* Ezek. 48:15
7 *b* Ezek. 44:3; 48:21
8 *c* Ezek. 48:1–7, 23–29; cp. Josh. 11:23
9 *d* Ezek. 44:6
10 *e* Lev. 19:36; Prov. 16:11 *f* See Weights and Measures (OT), 2 Chr. 2:10, *note*
12 *g* See Coinage (OT), Ex. 30:13, *note;* cp. 2 Chr. 2:10, *note*
16 *h* Cp. Ex. 30:14–15
17 *i* Ezek. 46:4–12
18 *j* See Lev. 23:2, *note*
20 *k* Lev. 4:27
21 *l* Ex. 12:1–24; Lev. 23:5–8; Num. 9:2–3; 28:16–17; Dt. 16:1
22 *m* Lev. 4:14
25 *n* Lev. 23:33–43; Num. 29:12–38
CHAPTER 46
1 *o* Ex. 20:9

*45:5 Following Masoretic Text, Targum, and Vulgate; Septuagint reads *a possession, cities of dwelling.*

it shall be opened, and on the day of
the New Moon it shall be opened.
2 "The prince shall [a]enter by way
of the vestibule of the gateway from
the outside, and stand by the gatepost.
The priests shall prepare his burnt offering and his peace offerings. He
shall worship at the threshold of the
gate. Then he shall go out, but the gate
shall not be shut until evening.
3 "Likewise the [b]people of the
land shall worship at the entrance to
this gateway before the LORD on the
Sabbaths and the New Moons.
4 "The burnt offering that the
prince [c]offers to the LORD on the [d]Sab-
bath day *shall be* six lambs without
blemish, and a ram without blemish;
5 "and the grain offering *shall be*
one [e]ephah for a ram, and the grain
offering for the lambs, as much as he
wants to give, as well as a [e]hin of oil
with every ephah.
6 "On the day of the New Moon *it*
shall be a young bull without blemish,
six lambs, and a ram; they shall be
without blemish.
7 "He shall prepare a grain offering of an [e]ephah for a bull, an ephah
for a ram, as much as he wants to give
for the lambs, and a [e]hin of oil with
every ephah.
8 "When the prince enters, he
shall go in by way of the vestibule of
the gateway, and go out the same way.
9 "But when the people of the land
come [f]before the LORD on the appointed feast days, whoever enters by
way of the north [g]gate to worship
shall go out by way of the south gate;
and whoever enters by way of the
south gate shall go out by way of the
north gate. He shall not return by way
of the gate through which he came,
but shall go out through the opposite
gate.
10 "The prince shall then be [h]in
their midst. When they go in, he shall
go in; and when they go out, he shall
go out.
11 "At the festivals and the appointed feast days the grain offering
shall be an [e]ephah for a bull, an ephah
for a ram, as much as he wants to give
for the lambs, and a [e]hin of oil with
every ephah.
12 "Now when the prince makes a
voluntary burnt offering or voluntary
peace offering to the LORD, the gate
that faces toward the east shall then
be opened for him; and he shall prepare his burnt offering and his peace
offerings as he did on the Sabbath
day. Then he shall go out, and after he
goes out the gate shall be shut.
13 "You shall daily make a burnt
offering to the LORD *of* a lamb of the
first year without blemish; you shall
prepare it every [i]morning.
14 "And you shall prepare a grain
offering with it every morning, a sixth
of an [e]ephah, and a third of a [e]hin of
oil to moisten the fine flour. This grain
offering is a perpetual ordinance, to
be made regularly to the LORD.
15 "Thus they shall prepare the
lamb, the grain offering, and the oil, *as*
a [j]regular burnt offering every morning."
16 'Thus says the Lord GOD: "If the
prince gives a [k]gift *of some* of his inheritance to any of his sons, it shall
belong to his sons; it is their possession by inheritance.
17 "But if he gives a gift of some of
his inheritance to one of his servants,
it shall be his until the [l]year of liberty,
after which it shall return to the
prince. But his inheritance shall belong to his sons; it shall become theirs.
18 "Moreover the [m]prince shall not
take any of the people's inheritance
by [n]evicting them from their property; he shall provide an inheritance
for his sons from his own property, so
that none of My people may be [o]scat-
tered from his property." ' "

Place for boiling and baking

19 Now he brought me through the
[p]entrance, which *was* at the side of
the gate, into the holy [q]chambers of
the priests which face toward the
north; and there a place *was* situated
at their extreme western end.
20 And he said to me, "This *is* the
place where the priests shall [r]boil the
trespass offering and the sin offering,
and where they shall [s]bake the grain
offering, so that they do not bring
them out into the outer court to [t]sanc-
tify the people."
21 Then he brought me out into the
outer court and caused me to pass by
the four corners of the court; and in
fact, in every corner of the court *there*
was another court.
22 In the four corners of the court
were enclosed courts, forty [e]*cubits*
long and thirty wide; all four corners
were the same size.
23 *There was* a row *of building*
stones all around in them, all around
the four of them; and cooking hearths
were made under the rows of stones
all around.

2 *a* Ezek. 44:3
3 *b* Cp. Lk. 1:10
4 *c* Ezek. 45:17 *d* Num. 28:9–10
5 *e* See Weights and Measures (OT), 2 Chr. 2:10, *note*
9 *f* Ex. 34:23; Dt. 16:16–17; Ps. 84:7 *g* Ezek. 48:31,33
10 *h* Cp. 2 Sam. 6:14–15; 1 Chr. 29:20
13 *i* Cp. Num. 28:3–5
15 *j* Ex. 29:42; Num. 28:6
16 *k* Cp. 2 Chr. 21:3
17 *l* Lev. 25:10
18 *m* Ezek. 45:8; cp. Isa. 11:3–4 *n* Cp. 1 Ki. 21:19; Mic. 2:1–2 *o* Cp. Ezek. 34:3–6
19 *p* Ezek. 42:9 *q* Ezek. 42:13
20 *r* 2 Chr. 35:13 *s* Lev. 2:4–5,7 *t* Ezek. 44:19

24 And he said to me, "These *are*
the kitchens where the ministers of
the temple shall boil the sacrifices of
the people."

The river of the sanctuary
(cp. Zech. 14:8–9; Rev. 22:1–2)

47 THEN he brought me back to
the door of the temple; and
there was [a]water, flowing from under
the threshold of the temple toward the
east, for the front of the temple faced
east; the water was flowing from under the right side of the temple, south
of the altar.
2 He brought me out by way of the
north gate, and led me around on the
outside to the outer gateway that faces
[b]east; and there was water, running
out on the right side.
3 And when the [c]man went out to
the east with the line in his hand, he
measured one thousand [d]cubits, and
he brought me through the waters; the
water *came up to my* ankles.
4 Again he measured one thousand and brought me through the waters; the water *came up to my* knees.
Again he measured one thousand and
brought me through; the water *came
up to my* waist.
5 Again he measured one thou-
sand, *and it was* a river that I could not
cross; for the water was too deep, water in which one must swim, a river
that could not be crossed.
6 He said to me, "Son of man, have
you seen *this*?" Then he brought me
and returned me to the bank of the
river.
7 When I returned, there, along
the bank of the river, *were* very many
[e]trees on one side and the other.
8 Then he said to me: "This water
flows toward the eastern region, goes
down into the [f]valley, and enters the
sea. *When it* reaches the sea, *its* waters are healed.
9 "And it shall be *that* every living
thing that moves, wherever the [g]riv-
ers go, will live. There will be a very
great multitude of fish, because these
waters go there; for they will be
healed, and everything will live wherever the river goes.
10 "It shall be *that* fishermen will
stand by it from En Gedi to En Eglaim;
they will be *places* for spreading their
nets. Their fish will be of the same
kinds as the fish of the [h]Great Sea,
exceedingly many.
11 "But its swamps and marshes
will not be healed; they will be given
over to salt.
12 "Along the bank of the river, on
this side and that, will grow all *kinds
of* trees used for food; their [i]leaves
will not wither, and their fruit will not
fail. They will bear fruit every month,
because their water flows from the
sanctuary. Their fruit will be for food,
and their [i]leaves for [j]medicine."

VII. The Division of the Land
during the Millennial Age, 47:13—48:35

Borders of the land (cp. Gen. 15:18–21)

13 Thus says the Lord GOD: "These
are the [k]borders by which you shall
divide the land as an inheritance
among the twelve tribes of Israel. [l]Jo-
seph *shall have two* portions.
14 "You shall inherit it equally with
one another; for I [m]raised My hand in
an oath to give it to your fathers, and
this land shall fall to you as your inheritance.
15 "This *shall be* the border of the
land on the north: from the [h]Great
Sea, *by* the [n]road to Hethlon, as one
goes to [o]Zedad,
16 [o]"Hamath, [p]Berothah, Sibraim
(which *is* between the border of Damascus and the border of Hamath), to
Hazar Hatticon (which *is* on the border of Hauran).
17 "Thus the boundary shall be
from the Sea to [q]Hazar Enan, the border of Damascus; and as for the north,
northward, it is the border of Hamath.
This is the north side.
18 "On the east side you shall mark
out the border from between Hauran
and Damascus, and between Gilead
and the land of Israel, along the Jordan, and along the eastern side of the
sea. *This is* the east side.
19 "The south side, toward the
South,* *shall be* from Tamar to the
[r]waters of [s]Meribah by Kadesh,
along the brook to the [h]Great Sea.
This is the south side, toward the
South.
20 "The west side *shall be* the
[h]Great Sea, from the *southern* boundary until one comes to a point opposite
Hamath. This *is* the west side.
21 "Thus you shall [t]divide this land
among yourselves according to the
tribes of Israel.
22 "It shall be that you will divide it
by [u]lot as an inheritance for your-

CHAPTER 47

1
a vv. 1–12; Ps. 46:4; Joel 3:18; Zech. 13:1; 14:8; Rev. 22:1

2
b Ezek. 44:1–2

3
c Ezek. 40:3
d See Weights and Measures (OT), 2 Chr. 2:10, *note*

7
e v. 12; Isa. 60:13; Rev. 22:2

8
f See Dt. 1:1, *note*

9
g Lit. *two rivers*

10
h Num. 34:6; Josh. 23:4; Ezek. 48:28

12
i Ps. 1:3; Jer. 17:8; cp. Job 8:16
j Rev. 22:2

13
k Num. 34:1–29
l Cp. Gen. 48:5; 1 Chr. 5:1

14
m Gen. 12:7; 13:15; 15:7; 17:8; 26:3; 28:13; Ezek. 20:5–6,28, 42

15
n Ezek. 48:1
o Num. 34:8

16
p 2 Sam. 8:8

17
q Num. 34:9

19
r Num. 20:13; Dt. 32:51; Ps. 81:7
s Ezek. 48:28

21
t Ezek. 45:1

22
u Num. 26:55–56

*47:19 Hebrew *Negev*

selves, and for the [a]strangers who dwell among you and who bear children among you. [b]They shall be to you as native-born among the children of Israel; they shall have an inheritance with you among the tribes of Israel.

23 "And it shall be *that* in whatever tribe the stranger dwells, there you shall give *him* his inheritance," says the Lord GOD.

Division of the land among seven of the tribes (cp. Josh. 13:1—19:51)

48 "NOW these *are* the names of the tribes: From the [1c]northern border along the road to Hethlon at the entrance of Hamath, to Hazar Enan, the border of Damascus northward, in the direction of Hamath, *there shall be* one *section for* [d]Dan from its east to its west side;

2 "by the border of Dan, from the east side to the west, one *section for* [e]Asher;

3 "by the border of Asher, from the east side to the west, one *section for* [f]Naphtali;

4 "by the border of Naphtali, from the east side to the west, one *section for* [g]Manasseh;

5 "by the border of Manasseh, from the east side to the west, one *section for* [h]Ephraim;

6 "by the border of Ephraim, from the east side to the west, one *section for* [i]Reuben;

7 "by the border of Reuben, from the east side to the west, one *section for* [j]Judah;

District of land for the sanctuary

8 "by the border of Judah, from the east side to the west, shall be the [2k]district which you shall set apart, twenty-five thousand *cubits* in width, and *in* length the same as one of the *other* portions, from the east side to the west, with the [l]sanctuary in the center.

9 "The district that you shall set apart for the LORD *shall be* twenty-five thousand *cubits* in length and ten thousand in width.

District of the land for the priests and Levites

10 "To these—to the priests—the holy district shall belong: on the north twenty-five thousand *cubits in length,* on the west ten thousand in width, on the east ten thousand in width, and on the south twenty-five thousand in length. The sanctuary of the LORD shall be in the center.

11 [m]"*It shall be* for the priests of the sons of Zadok, who are sanctified, who have kept My charge, who did not go astray when the children of Israel went astray, [n]as the Levites went astray.

12 "And *this* district of land that is set apart shall be to them a thing most [o]holy by the border of the Levites.

13 "Opposite the border of the priests, the [p]Levites *shall have an area* twenty-five thousand *cubits* in length and ten thousand in width; its entire length *shall be* twenty-five thousand and its width ten thousand.

14 [q]"And they shall not sell or exchange any of it; they may not alienate this [r]best *part* of the land, for *it is* holy to the LORD.

15 "The five thousand *cubits* in width that remain, along the edge of the twenty-five thousand, shall be for [s]general use by the city, for dwellings and [t]common-land; and the city shall be in the center.

16 "These *shall be* its measurements: the north side four thousand five hundred *cubits,* the south side four thousand five hundred, the east side four thousand five hundred, and the west side four thousand five hundred.

17 "The common-land of the city shall be: to the north two hundred and fifty *cubits,* to the south two hundred and fifty, to the east two hundred and fifty, and to the west two hundred and fifty.

18 "The rest of the length, alongside the district of the holy *section, shall be* ten thousand *cubits* to the east and ten thousand to the west. It shall be adjacent to the district of the holy *section,* and its produce shall be food for the workers of the city.

19 "The workers of the city, from all the tribes of Israel, shall cultivate it.

20 "The entire district *shall be* twenty-five thousand *cubits* by twenty-five thousand *cubits,* four-

22
a Isa. 14:1; 56:6–7; cp. Eph. 3:6; Rev. 7:9–10
b Cp. Rom. 10:12; Gal. 3:28; Col. 3:11
CHAPTER 48
1
c Ezek. 47:15
d Josh. 19:40–48
2
e Josh. 19:24–31
3
f Josh. 19:32–39
4
g Josh. 13:29–31; 17:1–11, 17–18
5
h Josh. 16:5–10; 17:8–10, 14–18
6
i Josh. 13:15–23
7
j Josh. 15:1–63
8
k Ezek. 45:1–6
l vv. 10,21; Ezek. 45:3–4; cp. Isa. 12:6
11
m Ezek. 40:46; 44:15
n Ezek. 44:10
12
o Ezek. 45:4
13
p Ezek. 45:5
14
q Cp. Lev. 25:32–34; 27:10,28,33
r Ezek. 44:30
15
s Ezek. 42:20
t Ezek. 45:2

1(48:1) The portion of land provided for each of the twelve tribes runs in parallel strips, east from the Mediterranean Sea, starting with Dan in the north and ending with Gad at the south.

2(48:8) The word (Heb. *t^erûmâh*) translated here, in v. 9, and in 45:1 as "district" denotes something *lifted up* and describes a presentation to the LORD alone. Here the offering consists of land. In other passages (Ex. 29:27; Num. 15:19, etc.) it is an animal or grain offering.

square. You shall set apart the holy
district with the property of the city.

District for the prince

21 "The [a]rest *shall belong* to the
prince, on one side and on the other of
the holy district and of the city's property, next to the twenty-five thousand
cubits of the *holy* district as far as the
eastern border, and westward next to
the twenty-five thousand as far as the
western border, adjacent to the *tribal*
portions; *it shall belong* to the prince.
It shall be the holy district, and the
[b]sanctuary of the temple *shall be* in
the center.
22 "Moreover, apart from the possession of the Levites and the possession of the city *which are* in the midst
of what *belongs* to the prince, *the area*
between the border of Judah and the
border of [c]Benjamin shall belong to
the prince.

Portion of land for the other tribes

23 "As for the rest of the tribes,
from the east side to the west, Benjamin *shall have* one *section;*
24 "by the border of Benjamin,
from the east side to the west, [d]Sim-
eon *shall have* one *section;*
25 "by the border of Simeon, from
the east side to the west, [e]Issachar
shall have one *section;*
26 "by the border of Issachar, from
the east side to the west, [f]Zebulun
shall have one *section;*
27 "by the border of Zebulun, from
the east side to the west, [g]Gad *shall
have* one *section;*
28 "by the border of Gad, on the
south side, toward the South,* the
border shall be from Tamar *to* the
[h]waters of Meribah *by* Kadesh, along
the brook to the [i]Great Sea.
29 "This *is* the land which you shall
[j]divide by lot as an inheritance
among the tribes of Israel, and these
are their portions," says the Lord GOD.

The city and its gates

30 "These *are* the exits of the city.
On the north side, measuring four
thousand five hundred *cubits*
31 "(the [k]gates of the city *shall be*
named after the tribes of Israel), the
three gates northward: one gate for
Reuben, one gate for Judah, and one
gate for Levi;
32 "on the east side, four thousand
five hundred *cubits,* three gates: one
gate for Joseph, one gate for Benjamin, and one gate for Dan;
33 "on the south side, measuring
four thousand five hundred *cubits,*
three gates: one gate for Simeon, one
gate for Issachar, and one gate for
Zebulun;
34 "on the west side, four thousand
five hundred *cubits* with their three
gates: one gate for Gad, one gate for
Asher, and one gate for Naphtali.
35 "All the way around *shall be*
eighteen thousand *cubits;* and the
name of the city from *that* day *shall
be:* THE [l]LORD *IS* [1m]THERE."

21
a Ezek. 45:7
b vv. 8,10
22
c Josh. 18:21–28
24
d Josh. 19:1–9
25
e Josh. 19:17–23
26
f Josh. 19:10–16
27
g Josh. 13:24–28
28
h Ezek. 47:19
i Ezek. 47:10
29
j Ezek. 47:14, 21–22
31
k vv. 31–34; Rev. 21:10–14
35
l Heb. *Jehovah-shammah.* See Ex. 34:6, *note*
m Joel 3:21; Zech. 2:10; Rev. 21:3; 22:3

* 48:28 Hebrew *Negev*

[1](48:35) Ezekiel begins and ends with God. Between the great vision of God in ch. 1 and these closing words, "THE LORD IS THERE," is the unsparing record of man's failure and sin, judged by God. But His judgment works to His glory, and the book ends with the one thing that makes heaven what it is, the Presence of the LORD.

The Book of

DANIEL

Author: Daniel *Theme:* Rise and Fall of Kingdoms *Date of writing:* 6th Cent. B.C.

THE Book of Daniel, like Revelation in the NT, is called an apocalypse, as are also Isaiah 24—27 (the Isaiah Apocalypse), and the visions in Zechariah. "Apocalypse" means *unveiling*. When wickedness seemed supreme in the world, and evil powers were dominant, an apocalypse was given to show the real situation behind that which was apparent, and to indicate the eventual victory of righteousness upon the earth. Apocalyptic writing uses many figures and symbols. God used this literary form to convey His truth to His people.

The author of this book, Daniel, whose name means *God is my judge*, was taken in his youth to Babylon in the first deportation under Nebuchadnezzar. He soon excelled in wisdom in this land famous for its wise men, and ultimately rose to become first among the three highest officers of the Medo-Persian Empire (5:29; 6:1–3). His life in Babylon extended to at least 530 B.C.

Daniel is a book of kings and kingdoms, of thrones and dominions. While including a number of historical records, it embodies prophecies of the sequence of kingdoms in "the times of the Gentiles" (Lk. 21:24; see Rev. 16:19, *note*) and portrays the end of this period. It voices the only prophecy in the OT (9:24–27) that sets the time of Christ's first advent.

The historical events in Daniel, occurring at the beginning of the times of the Gentiles, illustrate events prophetically set forth in the book as taking place at the end of this period and culminating catastrophically in the termination of Gentile world rule at the return of Christ, the Messiah. Thus, the persecution of the children of God in chs. 3 and 6 foreshadows the more severe and universal persecution of God's people to take place at the end of this age (7:25; 8:24; 12:1); likewise, the blasphemous repudiation of the God of Israel, as in 5:1–4; 6:5–12, will appear in a more universal form and even greater intensity at the end of the age (7:25; 9:26; 11:37,38).

This book is referred to or quoted many times in the NT (cp. especially our Lord's reference to Daniel in Mt. 24:15; Mk. 13:14) and is the key to Revelation. It exercised a great influence upon the early church; its scheme of four successive empires dominated European historiography until the middle of the eighteenth century.

The book may be divided as follows:

I. Daniel's Early Life in the Babylonian Court, 1.
II. Nebuchadnezzar's Vision of the Statue, 2.
III. The Deliverance of the Three Hebrew Youths from the Fiery Furnace, 3.
IV. The Vision and Humbling of Nebuchadnezzar, 4.
V. Daniel's Experiences under Belshazzar and Darius, 5—6.
VI. Daniel's Vision of the Four Beasts, 7.
VII. The Prophecy of the Defeat of the Persians by the Greeks, and the Desecration of the Temple, 8.
VIII. Daniel's Prayer and the Prophecy of the Seventy Weeks, 9.
IX. Daniel's Final Vision, 10—12.

I. Daniel's Early Life in the Babylonian Court, 1

Daniel in the palace of Nebuchadnezzar

1 IN the [1]third [a]year of the reign of
[b]Jehoiakim king of Judah, Nebuchadnezzar king of Babylon came to
Jerusalem and besieged it.
2 And the Lord gave Jehoiakim
king of Judah into his hand, with
[c]some of the articles of the house of
God, which he carried into the land of
Shinar to the house of his god; and he
brought the articles into the treasure
house of his god.

CHAPTER 1

1

a c. 605 B.C.
b 2 Ki. 24:1–2; 2 Chr. 36:5–7; Jer. 25:1; 52:12–30. Daniel was deported about 8 years before Ezekiel

2

c Jer. 27:19–20; Dan. 5:1–3

3 Then the king instructed Ashpe-
naz, the master of his eunuchs, to
bring some of the children of Israel
and some of the [d]king's descendants
and some of the nobles,
4 young men in whom *there was*
no blemish, but good-looking, gifted
in all wisdom, possessing knowledge
and quick to understand, who *had*
ability to serve in the king's palace,
and whom they might teach the language and literature of the Chaldeans.
5 And the king appointed for them

1:3 *d* 2 Ki. 20:18; Isa. 39:7

---

[1](1:1) This is Jehoiakim's third year, Babylonian reckoning (fourth year, Hebrew reckoning, Jer. 25:1). Babylonians called the first year "the year of accession." Daniel was in the first of three deportations (see Jer. 25:11, *note*). The year was about 605 B.C.

a daily provision of the king's delicacies and of the wine which he drank,
and three years of training for them,
so that at the end of *that time* they
might serve before the king.
6 Now from among those of the
sons of Judah were Daniel, Hananiah,
Mishael, and Azariah.
7 To them the chief of the eunuchs
gave names: he gave Daniel *the name*
[a]Belteshazzar; to Hananiah, Shadrach; to Mishael, Meshach; and to
Azariah, Abed-Nego.

Daniel's purpose of heart

8 But Daniel purposed in his heart
that he would not [b]defile himself with
the portion of the king's delicacies,
nor with the [c]wine which he drank;
therefore he requested of the chief of
the eunuchs that he might not defile
himself.
9 Now [d]God had brought Daniel
into the favor and goodwill of the chief
of the eunuchs.
10 And the chief of the eunuchs
said to Daniel, "I fear my lord the king,
who has appointed your food and
drink. For why should he see your
faces looking worse than the young
men who *are* your age? Then you
would endanger my head before the
king."
11 So Daniel said to the steward*
whom the chief of the eunuchs had set
over Daniel, Hananiah, Mishael, and
Azariah,
12 "Please test your servants for ten
days, and let them give us vegetables
to eat and water to drink.
13 "Then let our appearance be examined before you, and the appearance of the young men who eat the
portion of the king's delicacies; and as
you see fit, *so* deal with your servants."
14 So he consented with them in
this matter, and tested them ten days.
15 And at the end of ten days their
features appeared [e]better and fatter
in flesh than all the young men who
ate the portion of the king's delicacies.
16 Thus the steward took away
their portion of delicacies and the
wine that they were to drink, and gave
them vegetables.
17 As for these four young men,
God [f]gave them [g]knowledge and skill
in all literature and wisdom; and Daniel had [h]understanding in all visions
and dreams.
18 Now at the end of the days, when
the king had said that they should be
brought in, the chief of the eunuchs
brought them in before Nebuchadnezzar.
19 Then the king interviewed*
them, and among them all none was
found like Daniel, Hananiah, Mishael,
and Azariah; therefore they [i]served
before the king.
20 And in all matters of [j]wisdom
and understanding about which the
king examined them, he found them
ten times better than all the magicians
and astrologers who *were* in all his
realm.
21 Thus Daniel [k]continued until
the first year of King Cyrus.

II. Nebuchadnezzar's Vision of the Image, 2

The forgotten dream

2 NOW in the second [l]year of Nebuchadnezzar's reign, Nebuchadnezzar had dreams; and his spirit was
so troubled that his sleep left him.
2 Then the king gave the command to [m]call the magicians, the astrologers, the sorcerers, and the
[n]Chaldeans to tell the king his
dreams. So they came and stood before the king.
3 And the king said to them, "I
have had a dream, and my spirit is
anxious to know the dream."
4 Then the Chaldeans spoke to the
king in [1]Aramaic, "O king, live forever! Tell your servants the dream,
and we will give the interpretation."
5 The king answered and said to
the Chaldeans, "My decision is firm: if
you do not make known the dream to
me, and its interpretation, you shall be
cut in pieces, and your houses shall be
made an ash heap.
6 "However, if you tell the dream
and its interpretation, you shall receive from me gifts, rewards, and
great honor. Therefore tell me the
dream and its interpretation."
7 They answered again and said,
"Let the king tell his servants the

7
a Dan. 2:26; 4:8,9,18, 19; 5:12. Identical in meaning with *Belshazzar*

8
b Cp. Lev. 11:1–47
c Cp. 1 Cor. 10:21; see Num. 6:2, *note*

9
d Gen. 39:21; Ps. 106:46; Prov. 16:7; Acts 7:10; 27:3

15
e Cp. Ex. 23:25

17
f v. 20; 1 Ki. 3:12,28; 2 Chr. 1:10–12; Lk. 21:15; Jas. 1:5–7
g Cp. Acts 7:22
h 2 Chr. 26:5; cp. Ezek. 28:3–4

19
i Gen. 41:46; Prov. 22:29

20
j Lit. *wisdom of understanding*

21
k Daniel was to see the return of the remnant of Judah at the end of the 70 years, Jer. 25:11–12; 29:10. He actually lived beyond the first year of Cyrus, Dan. 10:1

CHAPTER 2

1
l c. 602 B.C. See Dan. 1:1, *note*

2
m Gen. 41:8; Isa. 47:12–13
n Reput-
edly the wisest men of ancient times; cp. v. 13, *wise*

*
1:11 Hebrew *Melzar,* also in verse 16
1:19 Literally *talked with them*

[1](2:4) Aramaic, the language spoken at the court of Nebuchadnezzar, was later used as the official language of the whole western section of the Persian Empire.

dream, and we will give its interpretation."
8 The king answered and said, "I
know for certain that you would gain
time, because you see that my decision is firm:
9 "if you do not make known the
dream to me, *there is only* one decree
for you! For you have agreed to speak
lying and corrupt words before me till
the time has changed. Therefore tell
me the dream, and I shall know that
you can give me its interpretation."
10 The Chaldeans answered the
king, and said, "There is not a man on
earth who can tell the king's matter;
therefore no king, lord, or ruler has
ever asked such things of any magi-
cian, astrologer, or Chaldean.
11 "*It is* a difficult thing that the
king requests, and there is no other
who can tell it to the king except the
[a]gods, whose dwelling is not with
flesh."
12 For this reason the king was angry and very furious, and gave the
command to destroy all the wise *men*
of Babylon.
13 So the decree went out, and they
began killing the wise *men;* and they
sought [b]Daniel and his companions,
to kill *them.*

Daniel requests time;
prays for wisdom

14 Then with counsel and wisdom
Daniel answered Arioch, the [c]captain
of the king's guard, who had gone out
to kill the wise *men* of Babylon;
15 he answered and said to Arioch
the king's captain, "Why is the decree
from the king so urgent?" Then Arioch
made the decision known to Daniel.
16 So Daniel went in and asked the
king to give him time, that he might
tell the king the interpretation.
17 Then Daniel went to his house,
and made the decision known to Hananiah, Mishael, and Azariah, his companions,
18 that they might [d]seek [e]mercies
from the God of heaven concerning
this secret, so that Daniel and his companions might not perish with the rest
of the wise *men* of Babylon.

The secret revealed to Daniel

19 Then the [f]secret was revealed to
Daniel in a night vision. So Daniel
blessed the God of heaven.
20 Daniel answered and said:
"Blessed be the name of God
forever and ever,

11
a Dan. 5:11; cp. 1 Cor. 8:5–6
13
b Dan. 1:19–20
14
c Lit. *executioner,* v. 24
18
d Cp. Est. 4:15–17; Isa. 37:4; Jer. 33:3; Mt. 18:19; Acts 12:5
e Dan. 9:9
19
f Prov. 3:32; Amos 3:7
20
g v. 23; 1 Chr. 29:11–12; Job 12:13; Ps. 147:5; Jer. 32:19; Mt. 6:13; Rom. 11:33; cp. Dan. 1:17
21
h Cp. Dan. 7:25
i Ps. 31:15
j Job 12:18; Ps. 75:6–7; Dan. 4:35
22
k vv. 28,47; Job 15:8; Ps. 25:14; Prov. 3:32; cp. Dan. 4:9; Mt. 6:6
l Ps. 139:12; Isa. 45:7; Jer. 23:24
m 1 Tim. 6:16
23
n Ps. 21:2
24
o v. 14
p Cp. Acts 27:24
28
q Gen. 40:8; 41:16
r See Gen. 49:1 and Acts 2:17, *notes*
29
s *Times of the Gentiles:* vv. 27–45; Dan. 4:17. (Dt. 28:49; Rev. 16:19)

[g]For wisdom and might are His.
21 And He [h]changes the [i]times
and the seasons;
[j]He removes kings and raises
up kings;
He gives wisdom to the wise
And knowledge to those who
have understanding.
22 He [k]reveals deep and secret
things;
He knows what *is* in the
[l]darkness,
And [m]light dwells with Him.

23 "I thank You and praise You,
O God of my fathers;
You have given me wisdom
and might,
And have now made known to
me what we [n]asked of You,
For You have made known to
us the king's demand."

24 Therefore Daniel went to [o]Ari-
och, whom the king had appointed to
destroy the wise *men* of Babylon. He
went and said thus to him: "Do not
destroy the wise *men* of Babylon;
[p]take me before the king, and I will
tell the king the interpretation."
25 Then Arioch quickly brought
Daniel before the king, and said thus
to him, "I have found a man of the
captives* of Judah, who will make
known to the king the interpretation."
26 The king answered and said to
Daniel, whose name *was* Belteshazzar, "Are you able to make known to
me the dream which I have seen, and
its interpretation?"
27 Daniel answered in the presence
of the king, and said, "The secret
which the king has demanded, the
wise *men,* the astrologers, the magicians, and the soothsayers cannot declare to the king.
28 "But there is a [q]God in heaven
who reveals secrets, and He has made
known to King Nebuchadnezzar what
will be in the [r]latter days. Your
dream, and the visions of your head
upon your bed, were these:
29 "As for you, O king, thoughts
came *to* your *mind while* on your bed,
about what would come to pass after
this; and He who reveals secrets has
made known to you [s]what will be.
30 "But as for me, this secret has
not been revealed to me because I
have more wisdom than anyone living, but for *our* sakes who make
known the interpretation to the king,

*
2:25 Literally *of the sons of the captivity*

and that you may know the thoughts
of your heart.

The dream; the great image

31 "You, O king, were watching;
and behold, a great [1]image! This great
image, whose splendor *was* excellent,
stood before you; and its form *was*
awesome.
32 "This image's head *was* of fine
gold, its chest and arms of silver, its
belly and [a]thighs of bronze,
33 "its legs of iron, its feet partly of
iron and partly of clay.*
34 "You watched while a [b]stone
was cut out without hands, which
struck the image on its feet of iron and
clay, and broke them in pieces.
35 [c]"Then the iron, the clay, the
bronze, the silver, and the gold were
crushed together, and became like
[d]chaff from the summer threshing
floors; the wind carried them away so
that no trace of them was found. And
the stone that struck the image [e]be-
came a great [2]mountain and filled the
whole earth.

The interpretation:
first world empire. Babylon
under Nebuchadnezzar (cp. 7:4)

36 "This *is* the dream. Now we will
tell the interpretation of it before the
king.
37 "You, O king, *are* a king of kings.
For the God of heaven has given you
a kingdom, power, strength, and
glory;
38 "and [3]wherever the children of
men dwell, or the beasts of the field
and the birds of the heaven, He has
given *them* into your hand, and has
made you ruler over them all—you
are this head of gold.

Second and third world empires:
Medo-Persia (cp. 7:5; 8:20) and
Greece (cp. 7:6; 8:21)

39 "But after you shall arise another kingdom inferior to yours; then
another, a third kingdom of bronze,
which shall rule over all the earth.

Fourth world empire: Rome
(cp. 7:7; 9:26)

40 "And the [f]fourth kingdom shall
be as strong as iron, inasmuch as iron
breaks in pieces and shatters everything; and like iron that crushes, *that*
kingdom will break in pieces and
crush all the others.
41 "Whereas you saw the feet and
toes, partly of potter's clay and partly

32
a Lit. *sides*
34
b Christ (Stone): vv. 34–35; Dan. 2:45. (Gen. 49:24; 1 Pet. 2:8)
35
c Dan. 7:23–27; Rev. 16:14; see Rev. 19:17, *note*
d Ps. 1:4; Mt. 3:12
e Kingdom (OT): vv. 34–45; Dan. 7:14. (Gen. 1:26; Zech. 12:8, *note*)
40
f Dan. 7:7, 23

*
2:33 Or *baked clay*, and so in verses 34,35, and 42

[1](2:31) The vision prophetically portrays the course of world empire and its destruction by Christ, who called this period "the times of the Gentiles" (Lk. 21:24; see Rev. 16:19, *note*). The four metals composing the statue are explained as symbolizing four empires (vv. 38–40), not necessarily possessing the inhabited earth but divinely authorized to do so (v. 38), and fulfilled in Babylon, Medo-Persia, Greece (under Alexander), and Rome. The latter power is seen divided, first into two (the legs), fulfilled in the eastern and western Roman Empires, and then into ten (the toes) (see Dan. 7:26, *note*). As a whole, the statue gives the imposing outward greatness and splendor of the Gentile world power.

The Striking Stone (2:34–35) destroys the Gentile world system (in its final form) by a sudden and irremediable blow, not by the gradual processes of conversion and assimilation; and then and not before, does the Stone become a mountain which fills "the whole earth" (cp. Dan. 7:26–27). Such a destruction of the Gentile monarchy system did not occur at the first advent of Christ. On the contrary, He was put to death by the sentence of an officer of the fourth empire, which was then at the zenith of its power. After Christ's death the western part of the Roman Empire fell in A.D. 476 and the eastern part in 1453, but no other world empire has superseded Rome because only four empires will precede Christ's return and rule. The interposition of the Church Age between the first and second advents of Christ, as revealed in the NT, is not a part of this vision. The deadly wound suffered by the fourth empire will not be healed by the restoration of the empire until the Church Age has been completed by the rapture of the Church (Rev. 13:3). Thus Gentile world power still continues, and the crushing blow is still suspended. The detail of the end-time is given in Dan. 7 and Rev. 13—19. It is important to observe that (1) Gentile world power is to end in a sudden catastrophic judgment (see Armageddon, Rev. 16:13–16; 19:17, *note*); and (2) it is immediately to be followed by the kingdom of heaven. The God of the heavens will not set up His kingdom until after the destruction of the Gentile world system. It is noteworthy that Gentile world dominion begins and ends with a great statue, or image (Dan. 2:31; Rev. 13:14–15).

This Stone must not be identified with the Church, as some hold, for the task of the Church is never said to be the destruction of the nations of the earth.

[2](2:35) A mountain is one of the biblical symbols of a kingdom. See Isa. 2:2, *note*.

[3](2:38) Universal dominion is indicated. It was never fully realized, but divine authority was given for it. See v. 31, *note*.

of iron, the kingdom shall be divided; [1]yet the strength of the iron shall be in it, just as you saw the iron mixed with ceramic clay.

42 "And *as* the toes of the feet *were* partly of iron and partly of clay, [a]so the kingdom shall be partly strong and partly fragile.

43 "As you saw iron mixed with ceramic clay, they will mingle with the seed of men; but they will not adhere to one another, just as iron does not mix with clay.

Christ's kingdom to be established on earth (see Mt. 3:2, note)

44 [2]"And in the days of these kings the God of heaven will set up a [b]kingdom which shall never be destroyed; and the kingdom shall not be left to other people; it shall [c]break in pieces and consume all these kingdoms, and it shall stand forever.

45 "Inasmuch as you saw that the [d]stone was cut out of the mountain without hands, and that it broke in pieces the iron, the bronze, the clay, the silver, and the gold—the great God has made known to the king what will come to pass after this. The dream is certain, and its interpretation is sure."

Daniel promoted

46 [e]Then King Nebuchadnezzar fell on his face, prostrate before Daniel, and commanded that they should present an offering and incense to him.

47 The king answered Daniel, and said, "Truly [f]your God *is* the God of [g]gods, the Lord of kings, and a [h]revealer of secrets, since you could reveal this secret."

48 [i]Then the king [j]promoted Daniel and gave him many great gifts; and he made him ruler over the whole province of Babylon, and chief administrator over all the wise *men* of Babylon.

49 Also [3]Daniel petitioned the king, and he set [k]Shadrach, Meshach, and Abed-Nego over the affairs of the province of Babylon; but Daniel *sat* in the gate* of the king.

42
a Dan. 7:24
44
b Isa. 9:6–7; Dan. 7:14, 27; Lk. 1:32–33
c Ps. 2:9; Isa. 60:12
45
d Christ (Stone): vv. 44–46; Zech. 4:7. (Gen. 49:24; 1 Pet. 2:8)
46
e Cp. vv. 27–30; Acts 10:25
47
f Dan. 3:28–29; 4:34–37
g Dt. 10:17; cp. 1 Cor. 8:5–6
h vv. 22,28
48
i Prov. 14:35; 21:1
j Dan. 5:11; cp. Gen. 41:39–43
49
k Dan. 1:7
CHAPTER 3
1
l Cp. Rev. 13:14–15
m See Weights and Measures (OT), 2 Chr. 2:10, *note*

III. The Deliverance of the Three Hebrew Youths from the Fiery Furnace, 3

Nebuchadnezzar's pride: the image of gold

3 NEBUCHADNEZZAR the king made an [l]image of gold, whose height *was* sixty cubits *and* its width six [m]cubits. He set it up in the plain of Dura, in the province of Babylon.

2 And King Nebuchadnezzar sent *word* to gather together the satraps, the administrators, the governors, the counselors, the treasurers, the judges, the magistrates, and all the officials of the provinces, to come to the dedication of the image which King Nebuchadnezzar had set up.

3 So the satraps, the administrators, the governors, the counselors, the treasurers, the judges, the magistrates, and all the officials of the provinces gathered together for the dedication of the image that King Nebuchadnezzar had set up; and they stood before the image that Nebuchadnezzar had set up.

4 Then a herald cried aloud: "To you it is commanded, O peoples, nations, and languages,

5 "*that* at the time you hear the sound of the horn, flute, harp, lyre, *and* psaltery, in symphony with all kinds of music, you shall fall down

*2:49 That is, the king's court

[1](2:41) From the head of gold (v. 38) to the iron of the fourth kingdom (Rome) there is deterioration in fineness, but increase in strength (v. 40). Then comes the deterioration of the fourth kingdom in that very quality—strength. (1) Deterioration by division: the kingdom is divided into two, the legs (eastern and western empires), and these are again divided into kingdoms, the number of which, when the Stone strikes the image, will be ten (toes, v. 42; cp. 7:23–24). And (2) deterioration by admixture: the iron mixed with the clay.

[2](2:44) This passage fixes, in relation to other predicted events, the time when the millennial kingdom will be established. It will be "in the days of these kings," i.e. the days of the ten kings (cp. 7:24–27) symbolized by the toes of the image. The ten kings did not exist at the advent of Messiah, nor was the federation even possible until the dissolution of the Roman Empire and the rise of the present nationalistic world system. See Kingdom (OT) (Gen. 1:26; Zech. 12:8, *note*); Kingdom (NT) (Lk. 1:31–33; Rev. 20:4); also *notes* at Mt. 3:2; 6:33; and 1 Cor. 5:24. In vv. 44–45 the method by which the millennial kindgom will be established is repeated from vv. 34–35, i.e. the Striking Stone will crush the statue that represents the world powers that are inimical to God. (See v. 31, *note;* cp. Ps. 2:5 with 2:6; Zech. 14:1–8 with 14:9.)

[3](2:49) Contrast Gen. 19:1, Lot, the compromiser with Daniel, the resolute. To sit in the gate of the king was to be in the place of authority.

and [a]worship the gold image that
King Nebuchadnezzar has set up;
6 "and whoever does not fall down
and [1]worship shall be cast immediately into the midst of a burning fiery
furnace."
7 So at that time, when all the people heard the sound of the horn, flute,
harp, *and* lyre, in symphony with all
kinds of music, all the people, nations,
and languages fell down *and* worshiped the gold image which King
Nebuchadnezzar had set up.

Daniel's three companions refuse to worship the image

8 Therefore at that time certain
[b]Chaldeans came forward and [c]ac-
cused the Jews.
9 They spoke and said to King
Nebuchadnezzar, "O king, live forever!
10 "You, O king, have made a decree that everyone who hears the
sound of the horn, flute, harp, lyre,
and psaltery, in symphony with all
kinds of music, shall fall down and
worship the gold image;
11 "and whoever does not fall down
and worship shall be cast into the
midst of a burning fiery furnace.
12 "There are certain Jews [d]whom
you have set over the affairs of the
province of Babylon: Shadrach, Meshach, and Abed-Nego; these men, O
king, have [e]not paid due regard to
you. They do not serve your gods or
worship the gold image which you
have set up."
13 Then Nebuchadnezzar, in [f]rage
and fury, gave the command to bring
Shadrach, Meshach, and Abed-Nego.
So they brought these men before the
king.
14 Nebuchadnezzar spoke, saying
to them, "*Is it* true, Shadrach, Meshach, and Abed-Nego, *that* you do
not serve my [g]gods or worship the
gold image which I have set up?
15 "Now if you are ready at the time
you hear the sound of the horn, flute,
harp, lyre, *and* psaltery, in symphony
with all kinds of music, and you fall
down and worship the image which I
have made, *good!* But if you do not
worship, you shall be cast immediately into the midst of a burning fiery
furnace. And [h]who *is* the god who will
deliver you from my hands?"
16 Shadrach, Meshach, and Abed-
Nego answered and said to the king,
"O Nebuchadnezzar, we have no need
to answer you in this matter.
17 "If that *is the case,* our [i]God
whom we serve is able to [j]deliver us
from the burning fiery furnace, [2]and
He will deliver *us* from your hand, O
king.
18 [k]"But if not, let it be known to
you, O king, that we do not serve your
gods, nor will we [l]worship the gold
image which you have set up."

Daniel's companions protected in tribulation

19 Then Nebuchadnezzar was full
of fury, and the expression on his face
changed toward Shadrach, Meshach,
and Abed-Nego. He spoke and commanded that they heat the furnace
seven times more than it was usually
heated.
20 And he commanded certain
mighty men of valor who *were* in his
army to bind Shadrach, Meshach, and
Abed-Nego, *and* cast *them* into the
burning fiery furnace.
21 Then these men were bound in
their coats, their trousers, their turbans, and their *other* garments, and
were cast into the midst of the burning
fiery furnace.
22 Therefore, because the king's
command was urgent, and the furnace
exceedingly hot, the flame of the fire
killed those men who took up Shadrach, Meshach, and Abed-Nego.
23 And these three men, Shadrach,
Meshach, and Abed-Nego, fell down
bound into the midst of the burning
fiery furnace.
24 Then King Nebuchadnezzar was
[m]astonished; and he rose in haste *and*
spoke, saying to his counselors, "Did
we not cast three men bound into the

5
a vv. 7,10, 15; cp. Dan. 9:27; Mt. 24:15; 2 Th. 2:4
8
b vv. 8–12; cp. v. 29
c Ezra 4:6, 12; Est. 3:8–9
12
d Dan. 2:49
e Dan. 1:8; 6:12–13
13
f Dan. 2:12
14
g Cp. Jer. 50:2
15
h Ex. 5:2; cp. Isa. 36:18–20
17
i Jer. 1:8; 15:20–21; 42:11; Dan. 6:19–22; cp. Ps. 27:1; Isa. 26:3; 51:12–13; Jer. 30:7–9
j 1 Sam. 17:37; Jer. 1:8; 15:20–21; 42:11; Dan. 6:16, 19–22
18
k Job 13:15; cp. Acts 4:19
l Ex. 20:3–5; Lev. 19:4
24
m Dan. 4:19

[1](3:6) Here is a case of enforced state religion, involving the worship of a man-made image. This phenomenon, appearing at the beginning of the times of the Gentiles and continuing from time to time through history (e.g. Roman emperor worship, Japanese Shinto shrines, and Soviet veneration of Lenin), will reappear at the end of the age when, not only the dragon, but the beast and the image of the beast also will be worshiped under compulsion (Rev. 13:4–15; 14:9–11; 19:20; 20:4; cp. 2 Th. 2:4). There will be increasing stress upon worship at the end of the age, but it will be satanically directed.

[2](3:17) These three Jews were faithful to God, although they were far from their homeland. They are a fitting illustration of the Jewish remnant in the last days (Isa. 1:9; Rom. 11:5), who will be faithful in the furnace of the great tribulation (Ps. 2:5; Rev. 7:14).

midst of the fire?" They answered and
said to the king, "True, O king."
25 "Look!" he answered, "I see four
men loose, [a]walking in the midst of
the fire; and they are [b]not hurt, and
the [c]form of the fourth is like [d]the Son
of God."*

Nebuchadnezzar recognizes the deliverance to be of God

26 Then Nebuchadnezzar [e]went
near the mouth of the burning fiery
furnace *and* spoke, saying, "Shadrach, Meshach, and Abed-Nego, servants of the [f]Most High God, come
out, and come *here.*" Then Shadrach,
Meshach, and Abed-Nego [g]came
from the midst of the fire.
27 And the satraps, administrators,
governors, and the king's counselors
gathered together, and they saw these
men on whose bodies the [h]fire had no
power; the hair of their head was not
singed nor were their garments affected, and the smell of fire was not on
them.
28 Nebuchadnezzar spoke, saying,
"Blessed be the God of Shadrach, Meshach, and Abed-Nego, who sent His
[i]Angel* and delivered His servants
who trusted in Him, and they have
frustrated the king's word, and
yielded their bodies, that they should
not serve nor worship any god except
their own God!

Nebuchadnezzar's decree and the promotion of the three Hebrew young men

29 "Therefore I make a [j]decree
that any people, nation, or language
which speaks anything amiss against
the [k]God of Shadrach, Meshach, and
Abed-Nego shall be cut in pieces, and
their houses shall be made an ash
heap; because there is no other God
who can deliver like this."
30 Then the king promoted Shadrach, Meshach, and Abed-Nego in
the province of Babylon.

IV. The Vision and Humbling of Nebuchadnezzar, 4

The king's proclamation to all nations

4 NEBUCHADNEZZAR the king,

[l]To all peoples, nations, and
languages that dwell in all the
earth:

Peace be multiplied to you.

2 I thought it good to declare the
signs and wonders that the
Most High God has worked for
me.

3 How great *are* His signs,
And how mighty His wonders!
His kingdom *is* an [m]everlasting
kingdom,
And His dominion *is* from
generation to generation.

Nebuchadnezzar's vision of a great tree

4 I, Nebuchadnezzar, was at rest
in my house, and flourishing in
my palace.
5 I saw a dream which made me
afraid, and the thoughts on my
bed and the visions of my head
troubled me.
6 Therefore I issued a decree to
bring in all the wise *men* of
Babylon before me, that they
might make known to me the
interpretation of the dream.
7 Then the magicians, the
astrologers, the Chaldeans, and
the soothsayers came in, and I
told them the dream; but they
did not make known to me its
interpretation.
8 But at last Daniel came before
me (his name *is* Belteshazzar,
according to the name of my
god; in him *is* the Spirit of the
Holy [n]God), and I told the
dream before him, *saying:*
9 "Belteshazzar, chief of the
magicians, because I know that
the Spirit of the Holy [n]God *is*
in you, and no secret troubles
you, explain to me the visions
of my dream that I have seen,
and its interpretation.
10 "These *were* the visions of my
head *while* on my bed:

I was looking, and behold,
A [o]tree in the midst of the
earth,
And its height was great.
11 The tree grew and became
strong;
Its height reached to the
heavens,
And it could be seen to the
ends of all the earth.
12 Its leaves *were* lovely,
Its fruit abundant,
And in it *was* food for all.
The [p]beasts of the field found
shade under it,

25
a Cp. Ps. 91:3–9
b Isa. 43:2
c Cp. Phil. 2:6–8
d Cp. 1 Cor. 8:5–6

26
e *Miracles* (OT): vv. 19–27; Dan. 6:22. (Gen. 5:24; Jon. 1:17, *note*)
f Dan. 4:2–3,17, 34–35
g Cp. Dt. 4:20; 1 Ki. 8:51; Jer. 11:4

27
h Heb. 11:34

28
i Ps. 34:7–8; Isa. 37:36; Dan. 6:22; Acts 5:19; 12:7; see Heb. 1:4, *note*

29
j Dan. 6:26
k Dan. 2:46–47; 4:34–37; cp. Dt. 4:35,39; Isa. 44:8; 45:5; 46:9; 1 Cor. 8:5–6

CHAPTER 4

1
l Dan. 2:37–38; 3:29

3
m 2 Sam. 7:16; Ps. 89:35–37; Dan. 7:13–14; Lk. 1:31–33

8
n Dan. 5:11, 14; cp. 1 Cor. 8:5–6

10
o v. 22. Symbol of a great king; cp. Ezek. 31:1–14

12
p Jer. 27:6

*3:25 Or *a son of the gods* 3:28 Or *angel*

The birds of the heavens dwelt
in its branches,
And all flesh was fed from it.

13 "I saw in the visions of my
head *while* on my bed, and
there was a [a]watcher, a [b]holy
one, coming down from
heaven.
14 He cried aloud and said thus:

[c]'Chop down the tree and cut off
its branches,
Strip off its leaves and scatter
its fruit.
Let the beasts get out from
under it,
And the birds from its
branches.
15 Nevertheless leave the stump
and roots in the earth,
Bound with a band of iron and
bronze,
In the tender grass of the field.
Let it be wet with the dew of
heaven,
And *let* him graze with the
beasts
On the grass of the earth.
16 Let his heart be changed from
that of a man,
Let him be given the heart of a
beast,
And let [d]seven times* pass
over him.

17 'This decision *is* by the decree
of the watchers,
And the sentence by the word
of the holy ones,
In order [e]that the living may
know
[f]That the Most High [1]rules in
the [g]kingdom of men,
[h]Gives it to whomever He will,
And sets over it the [i]lowest of
men.'

18 "This dream I, King
Nebuchadnezzar, have seen.
Now you, Belteshazzar, declare
its interpretation, since all the
wise *men* of my kingdom are
not able to make known to me
the interpretation; but you *are*
able, for the Spirit of the Holy
[j]God *is* in you."

13
a vv. 17,23
b Sanctification (OT): v. 13; Joel 1:14. (Gen. 2:3; Zech. 8:3)
14
c Cp. Mt. 3:10; 7:19; Lk. 13:6–9
16
d The number of completeness
17
e Ps. 9:16; 83:18
f vv. 25,32; Dan. 2:21; 5:21
g Times of the Gentiles: vv. 17,25, 32; Dan. 7:2. (Dt. 28:49; Rev. 16:19)
h Jer. 27:5–7; Ezek. 29:18–20; Dan. 2:37; 5:18
i 1 Sam. 2:8; Dan. 11:21
18
j vv. 8,9; Dan. 5:11, 14; cp. 1 Cor. 8:5–6
19
k Dan. 7:15, 28; 8:27
l Cp. 2 Sam. 18:32
22
m Dan. 2:37–38

Daniel interprets the vision

19 Then Daniel, whose name was
Belteshazzar, was astonished
for a time, and his thoughts
[k]troubled him. *So* the king
spoke, and said, "Belteshazzar,
do not let the dream or its
interpretation trouble you."
Belteshazzar answered and
said, "My lord, *may* the
[l]dream concern those who
hate you, and its interpretation
concern your enemies!
20 The tree that you saw, which
grew and became strong,
whose height reached to the
heavens and which *could be
seen* by all the earth,
21 whose leaves *were* lovely and
its fruit abundant, in which
was food for all, under which
the beasts of the field dwelt,
and in whose branches the
birds of the heaven had their
home—
22 it *is* [m]you, O king, who have
grown and become strong; for
your greatness has grown and
reaches to the heavens, and
your dominion to the end of
the earth.
23 And inasmuch as the king saw
a watcher, a holy one, coming
down from heaven and saying,
'Chop down the tree and
destroy it, but leave its stump
and roots in the earth, *bound*
with a band of iron and bronze
in the tender grass of the field;
let it be wet with the dew of
heaven, and let him graze with
the beasts of the field, till
seven times pass over him';
24 this is the interpretation, O
king, and this is the decree of
the Most High, which has
come upon my lord the king:
25 They shall drive you from
men, your dwelling shall be
with the beasts of the field,
and they shall make you eat
grass like oxen. They shall wet
you with the dew of heaven,
and seven times shall pass

* **4:16** Possibly *seven years,* and so in verses 23,25, and 32

[1](4:17) This divine rule refers to the universal kingdom of God, which (1) includes all things; (2) always exists without interruption; (3) never fails in its purposes; and (4) is generally administered providentially (see vv. 25,32,34–35; cp. Ps. 103:19; 148:8). This kingdom should be distinguished from the mediatorial kingdom of Christ, though the latter issues from it (cp. Dan. 7:9–14) and will finally be merged with it (1 Cor. 15:24).

over you, [1]till you know that
the Most High rules in the
kingdom of men, and gives it
to whomever He [a]chooses.
26 And inasmuch as they gave the
command to leave the stump
and roots of the tree, your
kingdom shall be assured to
you, after you come to know
that Heaven rules.
27 Therefore, O king, let my
advice be acceptable to you;
[b]break off your sins by *being*
righteous, and your iniquities
by showing mercy to *the* poor.
Perhaps there may be a
[c]lengthening of your
prosperity."

The vision fulfilled;
the king's restoration

28 All *this* came upon King
Nebuchadnezzar.
29 At the end of the [d]twelve
months he was walking about
the royal palace of Babylon.
30 The king spoke, saying, "Is not
this [e]great Babylon, that [f]I
have built for a royal dwelling
by my mighty power and for
the honor of my majesty?"
31 [g]While the word *was still* in
the king's mouth, a voice fell
from heaven: [h]"King
Nebuchadnezzar, to you it is
spoken: the kingdom has
departed from you!
32 And they shall drive you from
men, and your dwelling *shall*
be with the beasts of the field.
They shall make you eat grass
like oxen; and seven times
shall pass over you, until you
know that the Most High rules
in the kingdom of men, and
gives it to whomever He
chooses."
33 That very hour the word was
fulfilled concerning
Nebuchadnezzar; he was
driven from men and ate grass
like oxen; his body was wet
with the dew of heaven till his
hair had grown like eagles'
feathers and his nails like
birds' *claws.*
34 And at the end of the time* I,
Nebuchadnezzar, lifted my
eyes to heaven, and my
understanding returned to me;
and [2]I blessed the Most High
and praised and honored Him
who lives forever:

For His dominion *is* an
[i]everlasting dominion,
And His kingdom *is* from
generation to generation.
35 All the inhabitants of the earth
are reputed as [j]nothing;
He does [k]according to His will
in the army of heaven
And *among* the inhabitants of
the earth.
No one can [l]restrain His hand
Or [m]say to Him, "What have
You done?"

36 At the same time my reason
returned to me, and for the
glory of my kingdom, my
honor and splendor returned to
me. My counselors and nobles
resorted to me, I was [n]restored
to my kingdom, and excellent
majesty was added to me.
37 Now I, Nebuchadnezzar,
[o]praise and extol and honor
the King of heaven, all of
whose works *are* [p]truth, and
His ways justice. And those
who walk in pride He is able
to [q]put down.

V. Daniel's Experiences
under Belshazzar and Darius, 5—6

Belshazzar defiles the temple vessels

5 BELSHAZZAR the king made a
great feast for a thousand of his
lords, and drank wine in the presence
of the thousand.
2 While he tasted the wine, Belshazzar gave the command to bring
the gold and silver vessels which his
[3]father Nebuchadnezzar had taken
from the temple which *had been* in Je-

25 a Cp. Prov. 21:1
27 b Prov. 28:13; Isa. 55:7; Ezek. 18:21–22; Rom. 2:9–11 c 1 Ki. 21:29; cp. Jon. 3:4–10
29 d Cp. 2 Pet. 3:9
30 e Isa. 13:19 f Cp. v. 37; Ezek. 29:3
31 g Cp. Dan. 5:5; Acts 12:20–23; 1 Th. 5:3 h vv. 31–37; cp. Lk. 12:16–20
34 i Ps. 10:16; Dan. 2:44; 7:14; Mic. 4:7; Lk. 1:33
35 j Isa. 40:17 k Ps. 135:6 l Isa. 43:13 m Isa. 45:9; Jer. 18:6; Rom. 9:20; 1 Cor. 2:16
36 n 2 Chr. 20:20; Prov. 22:4
37 o Dan. 2:46–47; 3:28–29 p Ps. 33:4 q Ex. 18:11; Dan. 5:20

* 4:34 Literally *days*

[1](4:25) This discipline was effective. Cp. v. 30 with v. 37.
[2](4:34) Progress may be traced in Nebuchadnezzar's apprehension of the true God: (1) "God is the God of gods [one among the national or tribal gods, but greater than they], the Lord [*Adonai,* meaning *Master*] of kings, and a revealer of secrets" (2:47). (2) He is still a Hebrew Deity, but Master of angels and a God who responds to faith (3:28). And (3) here (vv. 34–35) the king rises into a true apprehension of God. Cp. Darius, 6:25–27.
[3](5:2) The word "father" is used here, as it is frequently employed in the Scriptures, to indicate an ancestor; e.g. David is spoken of as the father of Jesus (Lk. 1:31–32). Probably Belshazzar was the grandson of Nebuchadnezzar through his mother.

rusalem, that the king and his lords, his wives, and his concubines might drink from them.

3 Then they brought the gold [a]vessels that had been taken from the temple of the house of God which *had been* in Jerusalem; and the king and his lords, his wives, and his concubines drank from them.

4 They drank wine, and praised the gods of gold and silver, bronze and iron, wood and stone.

The handwriting on the wall

5 [b]In the same hour the fingers of a man's hand appeared and wrote opposite the lampstand on the plaster of the wall of the king's palace; and the king saw the part of the hand that wrote.

6 Then the king's countenance changed, and his thoughts [c]troubled him, so that the [d]joints of his hips were loosened and his knees knocked against each other.

7 The king cried aloud to bring in the [e]astrologers, the Chaldeans, and the soothsayers. The king spoke, saying to the wise *men* of Babylon, "Whoever reads this writing, and tells me its interpretation, shall be clothed with purple and *have* a chain of gold around his neck; and he shall be the third ruler in the kingdom."

8 Now all the king's wise *men* came, but they could not read the writing, or make known to the king its interpretation.

9 Then King Belshazzar was greatly troubled, his [f]countenance was changed, and his lords were astonished.

Daniel interprets the writing

10 The queen, because of the words of the king and his lords, came to the banquet hall. The queen spoke, saying, "O king, live forever! Do not let your thoughts trouble you, nor let your countenance change.

11 "There is a man in your kingdom in whom *is* the Spirit of the Holy [g]God. And in the days of your father, light and understanding and wisdom, like the wisdom of the gods, were found in him; and King Nebuchadnezzar your [h]father—your father the king—made him chief of the magicians, astrologers, Chaldeans, *and* soothsayers.

12 "Inasmuch as an excellent spirit, knowledge, understanding, interpreting dreams, solving riddles, and explaining enigmas* were found in this Daniel, whom the king named Belteshazzar, now let Daniel be called, and he will give the interpretation."

13 Then Daniel was brought in before the king. The king spoke, and said to Daniel, "*Are* you that Daniel who is one of the captives* from Judah, whom my [h]father the king brought from Judah?

14 "I have heard of you, that the Spirit of [i]God *is* in you, and *that* light and understanding and excellent wisdom are found in you.

15 "Now the wise *men*, the astrologers, have been brought in before me, that they should read this writing and make known to me its interpretation, but they could not give the interpretation of the thing.

16 "And I have heard of you, that you can give interpretations and explain enigmas. Now if you can read the writing and make known to me its interpretation, you shall be clothed with purple and *have* a chain of gold around your neck, and shall be the [1]third ruler in the kingdom."

17 Then Daniel answered, and said before the king, "Let your [j]gifts be for yourself, and give your rewards to another; yet I will read the writing to the king, and make known to him the interpretation.

18 "O king, the Most High God [k]gave [2]Nebuchadnezzar your father a

CHAPTER 5
3
a 2 Chr. 36:10
5
b Cp. Dan. 4:31; Lk. 12:19–20; 1 Th. 5:2–3
6
c Cp. Isa. 21:1–4
d i.e. *the strength of his legs gave way*
7
e Isa. 47:13
9
f Lit. (Aram.) *brightnesses,* v. 6
11
g v. 14; Dan. 4:8,9, 18; cp. 1 Cor. 8:5–6
h See v. 2, *note*
14
i v. 11; Dan. 4:8,9,18; cp. 1 Cor. 8:5–6
17
j Cp. Gen. 14:22–23; 2 Ki. 5:16
18
k Jer. 27:5–7; Dan. 2:37–38; 4:17

*
5:12 Literally *untying knots,* and so in verse 16
5:13 Literally *of the sons of the captivity*

[1](5:16) Belshazzar was co-ruler with his father (see v. 18, *note*); so Daniel was next to the kings in power.

[2](5:18) The biblical order of the monarchs of Daniel's time is as follows:

(1) Nebuchadnezzar (c. 604–562 B.C.) with whom the captivity of Judah and "the times of the Gentiles" (see Lk. 21:24 and Rev. 16:19, *notes*) began, and who established the first of the four world monarchies (2:37–38; 7:4).

(2) Belshazzar (c. 553–539 B.C.), the Bel-sharusur of the inscriptions, eldest son of Nabonidus and co-regent with his father.

(3) Darius, the Mede (c. 539 B.C.–?), 5:31; 6:1–27; 9:1. Concerning this Darius, secular history awaits further discoveries. It is conjectured that he was Gobryas (Gubaru), a Median official whom Cyrus made ruler of Babylon after the conquest.

(4) Cyrus (c. 539–530 B.C.), with whose rise to power the Medo-Persian world empire came

kingdom and majesty, glory and
honor.
19 "And because of the majesty that
He gave him, all peoples, nations, and
languages trembled and feared before
him. Whomever he wished, he [a]exe-
cuted; whomever he wished, he kept
alive; whomever he wished, he set up;
and whomever he wished, he put
down.
20 "But when his heart was lifted
up, and his spirit was [b]hardened in
pride, he was deposed from his kingly
throne, and they took his glory from
him.
21 "Then he was [c]driven from the
sons of men, his heart was made like
the beasts, and his dwelling *was* with
the wild donkeys. They fed him with
grass like oxen, and his body was wet
with the dew of heaven, till he knew
that the Most High God [d]rules in the
kingdom of men, and appoints over it
whomever He chooses.
22 "But you his son, Belshazzar,
have not humbled your heart, although you knew all this.
23 "And you have [e]lifted yourself
up against the Lord of heaven. They
have brought the [f]vessels of His
house before you, and you and your
lords, your wives and your concubines, have drunk wine from them.
And you have praised the gods of silver and gold, bronze and iron, wood
and stone, which do not see or hear or
know; and the [g]God who *holds* your
breath in His hand and owns all your
[h]ways, you have not glorified.
24 "Then the fingers* of the hand
were sent from Him, and this writing
was written.
25 "And this is the inscription that
was written:

[1]MENE, MENE, TEKEL,
UPHARSIN.

26 "This *is* the interpretation of

19
a Dan. 2:12–13; 3:6
20
b Dan. 4:30; cp. 4:37
21
c Dan. 4:30–33
d Ex. 9:14–16; Ezek. 17:24; Dan. 2:21; 4:25,32, 34–35
23
e Cp. Num. 14:41; Job 9:4; Isa. 37:23; Jer. 50:29
f vv. 2–4; Ex. 40:9; Num. 18:3; Isa. 52:11; Heb. 9:21
g Acts 17:24–26; Rom. 1:21; 3:23
h Prov. 20:24; Jer. 10:23
28
i v. 31; Dan. 9:1; cp. Isa. 13:17; 21:2; Jer. 51:11–28
30
j Cp. Jer. 51:1–5
31
k Dan. 2:39
CHAPTER 6
1
l Cp. Est. 1:1
3
m Dan. 1:17; 2:48; 5:11
n Cp. Gen. 42:6; Est. 10:3
4
o Cp. Dan. 3:8; Mt. 27:18

each word. MENE: God has numbered
your kingdom, and finished it;
27 "TEKEL: You have been weighed
in the balances, and found wanting;
28 "PERES: Your kingdom has been
divided, and [i]given to the Medes and
Persians."*
29 Then Belshazzar gave the command, and they clothed Daniel with
purple and *put* a chain of gold around
his neck, and made a proclamation
concerning him that he should be the
[2]third ruler in the kingdom.
30 That very night Belshazzar, king
of the Chaldeans, was [j]slain.
31 And Darius the Mede [3]received
the [k]kingdom, *being* about sixty-two
years old.

Daniel under Darius

6 IT pleased Darius to set [l]over the
kingdom one hundred and twenty
satraps, to be over the whole kingdom;
2 and over these, three governors,
of whom Daniel *was* one, that the satraps might give account to them, so
that the king would suffer no loss.
3 Then this Daniel [m]distinguished
himself above the governors and satraps, because an excellent spirit *was*
in him; and the king gave thought to
[n]setting him over the whole realm.

The governors and satraps plot against Daniel

4 So the governors and satraps
sought to find *some* [o]charge against
Daniel concerning the kingdom; but
they could find no charge or fault, because he *was* faithful; nor was there
any error or fault found in him.
5 Then these men said, "We shall
not find any charge against this Dan-

*

5:24 Literally *palm* **5:28** Aramaic *Paras*, consonant with *Peres*

fully into existence (2:39; 7:5). In verses 1–4 of ch. 8 the Median power is seen as the lesser of the two horns of the ram; the Persian power of Cyrus, as the higher horn which appeared last. Under Cyrus, who was named more than a century before his birth (Isa. 44:28—45:4), the return of the Jewish remnant to Palestine began (Ezra 1:1–4). See Dan. 11:2, *notes.*

[1](5:25) Each of the three Aramaic words has a double sense. "MENE" (from *mena, to number*) is repeated for emphasis. God has numbered the days of the Babylonian kingdom. "TEKEL" (from *tekal, to weigh*) indicates that the kingdom has been morally evaluated by God, and found lacking. "PERES" (from *peres, to divide;* "Persians" comes from *paras*) is a prediction that the kingdom is to be divided and given to the Persians. "UPHARSIN" (*u* is Aramaic for *and,* as in Hebrew) is the plural of PERES.

[2](5:29) Daniel was made third ruler (see vv. 7 and 16) because Nabonidus, the last king of Babylon, had elevated his son Belshazzar to be co-regent over the kingdom in Babylon while he himself resided in Tema in Arabia.

[3](5:31) Darius was probably made king under Cyrus, the Persian "king of kings" (cp. 9:1).

iel unless we find *it* against him [a]concerning the law of his God."

6 So these governors and satraps thronged before the king, and said thus to him: "King Darius, live forever!

7 "All the governors of the kingdom, the administrators and satraps, the counselors and advisors, have [b]consulted together to establish a royal statute and to make a firm decree, that whoever petitions any [c]god or man for thirty days, [d]except you, O king, shall be cast into the den of lions.

8 "Now, O king, establish the decree and sign the writing, so that it cannot be changed, [e]according to the law of the Medes and Persians, which does not alter."

9 Therefore King Darius signed the written decree.

Daniel's steadfastness in prayer

10 Now when Daniel [f]knew that the writing was signed, he went home. And in his upper room, with his windows open [g]toward Jerusalem, he knelt down on his knees [h]three times that day, and [i]prayed and gave thanks before his God, as was his custom since early days.

11 Then these men assembled and found Daniel praying and making supplication before his God.

12 And they went before the king, and spoke concerning the king's decree: "Have you not signed a decree that every man who petitions any [c]god or man within thirty days, [d]except you, O king, shall be cast into the den of lions?" The king answered and said, "The thing *is* true, according to the law of the Medes and Persians, which does not alter."

13 So they answered and said before the king, "That Daniel, who is one of the [j]captives* from Judah, does not show due [k]regard for you, O king, or for the decree that you have signed, but makes his petition three times a day."

14 And the king, when he heard *these* words, was greatly [l]displeased with himself, and set *his* heart on Daniel to deliver him; and he [m]labored till the going down of the sun to deliver him.

15 Then these men approached the king, and said to the king, "Know, O king, that *it is* the law of the Medes and Persians that no decree or statute which the king establishes may be changed."

Daniel in the lions' den

16 So the king gave the command, and they brought Daniel and cast *him* into the den of lions. *But* the king spoke, saying to Daniel, "Your God, whom you serve continually, He will [n]deliver you."

17 Then a stone was brought and laid on the mouth of the den, and the king sealed it with his own signet ring and with the signets of his lords, that the purpose concerning Daniel might not be changed.

18 Now the king went to his palace and spent the night fasting; and no musicians* were brought before him. Also his sleep went from him.

19 Then the [o]king arose very early in the morning and went in haste to the den of lions.

20 And when he came to the den, he cried out with a lamenting voice to Daniel. The king spoke, saying to Daniel, "Daniel, servant of the living God, has your God, whom you serve continually, been [p]able to deliver you from the lions?"

21 Then Daniel said to the king, "O king, live forever!

22 "My God [q]sent His [r]angel and [s]shut the lions' mouths, so that they have not hurt me, because I was found innocent before Him; and also, O king, I have done no wrong before you."

23 Now the king was exceedingly glad for him, and commanded that they should take Daniel up out of the den. So Daniel was taken up out of the den, and no injury whatever was found on him, because he believed in his God.

24 And the king gave the command, and they [t]brought those men who had accused Daniel, and they cast *them* into the den of lions—them, their children, and their wives; and the lions overpowered them, and broke all their bones in pieces before they ever came to the bottom of the den.

The decree of Darius

25 Then King Darius wrote:

> [u]To all peoples, nations, and languages that dwell in all the earth:
>
> Peace be multiplied to you.

26 I make a decree that in every

5
a Cp. Acts 24:13–21; 1 Pet. 4:12–16
7
b Ps. 59:3; 62:4; 64:2–6
c Cp. 1 Cor. 8:5–6
d Cp. Rev. 13:15
8
e vv. 12,15; Est. 1:19
10
f Cp. Acts 20:22–24
g 1 Ki. 8:29–30, 46–48; Ps. 5:7; Jon. 2:4
h Cp. Ps. 55:17
i Phil. 4:6; 1 Th. 5:17–18
13
j Dan. 5:13
k Dan. 3:12; cp. Est. 3:8; Acts 5:29
14
l Cp. Mk. 6:26
m Cp. Ps. 49:7
16
n Ps. 34:7, 19; 37:39–40; 50:15; Mt. 27:43; Col. 1:13; 1 Th. 1:10; 2 Pet. 2:9
19
o Dan. 3:24
20
p Gen. 18:14; Jer. 32:17; Lk. 1:37; cp. Jn. 11:38–44
22
q *Miracles* (OT): vv. 16–23; Jon. 1:17. (Gen. 5:24; Jon. 1:17, *note*). Acts 12:11
r Dan. 3:28; see Heb. 1:4, *note*
s Cp. Heb. 11:33
24
t Cp. Est. 7:1–10; 9:5–16; Dan. 3:22
25
u Dan. 4:1

*
6:13 Literally *of the sons of the captivity*
6:18 Exact meaning unknown

dominion of my kingdom *men*
must tremble and fear before
the God of Daniel.

[a]For He *is* the living God,
And steadfast forever;
His kingdom *is the one* which
shall not be destroyed,
And His dominion *shall endure*
to the end.
27 He delivers and rescues,
And He works signs and
wonders
In heaven and on earth,
Who has delivered Daniel from
the power of the lions.

28 So this Daniel prospered in the
reign of Darius and in the reign of Cyrus the Persian.

VI. Daniel's Vision
of the Four Beasts, 7

The dream (cp. 2:31–43)

7 IN the [b]first year of Belshazzar
king of Babylon, Daniel had a
dream and visions of his head *while*
on his bed. Then he [c]wrote down the
dream, telling the main facts.*
2 Daniel spoke, saying, "I saw in
my vision by night, and behold, the
four winds of heaven were stirring up
the Great [1d]Sea.
3 "And [e]four great [2]beasts came
up from the sea, each different from
the other.

First world empire: Babylon
(cp. 2:37–38)

4 "The first *was* like a [f]lion, and
had [g]eagle's wings. I watched till its

26
a Cp. Dan. 2:47; 3:28–29; 4:3,34–35

CHAPTER 7
1
b c. 553 B.C.
c Cp. Rev. 1:19
2
d Times of the Gentiles: vv. 2–27; Joel 3:12. (Dt. 28:49; Rev. 16:19)
3
e Cp. v. 17
4
f Cp. Jer. 4:7 with Jer. 25:9
g Cp. Ezek. 17:3 with Ezek. 17:12
h Dan. 4:16, 34
6
i Cp. Dan. 8:22
7
j See Dt. 33:17, *note*
8
k The Beast: vv. 8,11; Dan. 7:24. (Dan. 7:8; Rev. 19:20)

wings were plucked off; and it was
lifted up from the earth and made to
stand on two feet like a man, and a
[h]man's heart was given to it.

Second world empire: Medo-Persia
(cp. 2:39; 8:20)

5 "And suddenly another beast, a
second, like a bear. It was raised up on
one side, and *had* [3]three ribs in its
mouth between its teeth. And they
said thus to it: 'Arise, [4]devour much
flesh!'

Third world empire: Greece
(cp. 2:39; 8:21–22; 10:20; 11:2–4)

6 "After this I looked, and there
was another, like a [5]leopard, which
had on its back [i]four wings of a bird.
The beast also had four heads, and
dominion was given to it.

Fourth world empire: Rome
(cp. vv. 23–24; 2:40–43; 9:26)

7 "After this I saw in the night visions, and behold, a fourth beast,
dreadful and terrible, exceedingly
strong. It had huge iron teeth; it was
devouring, breaking in pieces, and
trampling the residue with its feet. It
was different from all the beasts that
were before it, and it had ten [j]horns.

Rome: final form of fourth world
empire; the ten kings and
the little horn (vv. 24–27;
see v. 14, note)

8 "I was considering the [j]horns,
and there was another horn, a [6k]little

*
7:1 Literally *the head* (or *chief*) *of the words*

[1](7:2) "Sea" in Scripture imagery stands for the populace, the unorganized mass of mankind (Isa. 60:5; Mt. 13:47; Lk. 21:25; Rev. 13:1).

[2](7:3) The monarchy vision of Nebuchadnezzar (ch. 2) covers the same order of fulfillment as Daniel's beast vision, but with this difference: Nebuchadnezzar saw the imposing outward power and splendor of "the times of the Gentiles" (Lk. 21:24; cp. Rev. 16:19, *note*), whereas Daniel saw the true character of Gentile world government as rapacious and warlike, established and maintained by force. It is remarkable that the heraldic insignia of the Gentile nations are all beasts or birds of prey.

[3](7:5) This is a possible reference to the threefold dominion of the second empire, Media, Persia, Babylonia.

[4](7:5) That is, Lydia, Babylonia, Egypt, etc.

[5](7:6) An allusion to the swiftness of Alexander's conquests.

[6](7:8) The vision is of the end of Gentile world dominion. The former Roman Empire (the iron kingdom of 2:33–35,40–44; 7:7) will have ten horns (i.e. kings, Rev. 17:12), corresponding to the ten toes of the image. As Daniel considers this vision of the ten kings, there rises up among them a "little horn" (king), who subdues three of the ten kings so completely that the separate identity of their kingdoms is destroyed. Seven kings of the ten are left, and the "little horn," who is "the prince who is to come" of 9:26, the "abomination" of 12:11 and Mt. 24:15, and the "beast rising up out of the sea" of Rev. 13:1–10. He will be the head of the restored fourth world empire (Beast, see Rev. 19:20, *note*). Some expositors also equate with him the "willful king" of 11:36–45, and the "man of sin" of 2 Th. 2:3–8.

one, coming up among them, before whom three of the first horns were plucked out by the roots. And there, in this horn, *were* eyes like the eyes of a man, and a mouth speaking pompous words.

The coming of the Son of Man (vv. 9–14; cp. Mt. 24:27–30; 25:31–34; Rev. 19:11–21)

9 "I watched till thrones were put
in place,
And the [1]Ancient of Days was
seated;
His garment *was* [a]white as
snow,
And the hair of His head *was*
like pure [b]wool.
His throne *was* a fiery flame,
Its wheels a burning [c]fire;
10 A fiery stream issued
And came forth from before
Him.
A thousand thousands
ministered to Him;
[d]Ten thousand times ten
thousand stood before Him.
The court* was seated,
And the books were opened.

11 "I watched then because of the
sound of the pompous words which
the [e]horn was speaking; I watched till
the beast was slain, and its body destroyed and given to the [f]burning
flame.
12 "As for the rest of the beasts,
they had their dominion taken away,
yet their lives were prolonged for a
season and a time.

Scene in heaven before coming of Son of Man (cp. Rev. 5:1–14)

13 "I was [g]watching in the night
visions,
And behold, *One* like [h]the Son
of Man,
Coming with the [i]clouds of
heaven!
He came to the Ancient of
Days,
[2]And they brought Him near
before Him.
14 Then to [3]Him was given
dominion and glory and a
[j]kingdom,
That all peoples, nations, and
languages should serve Him.
His dominion *is* an everlasting
[k]dominion,
Which shall not pass away,
And His kingdom *the one*
Which shall not be destroyed.

The interpretation of beast vision

15 "I, Daniel, was grieved in my
spirit within *my* body, and the visions
of my head troubled me.
16 "I came near to one of those who
stood by, and asked him the truth of
all this. So he told me and made
known to me the interpretation of
these things:
17 'Those great beasts, which are
four, *are* four kings* *which* arise out
of the earth.
18 'But the [4]saints of the Most High
shall receive the kingdom, and pos-

9 *a* Cp. Mk. 9:3 *b* Cp. Rev. 1:14 *c* Cp. Ezek. 10:2,6
10 *d* Rev. 5:11
11 *e* See Dt. 33:17, *note* *f* Rev. 19:20; 20:10
13 *g* Cp. Rev. 5:6–10 *h* Lit. *a son* *i* Mt. 26:64
14 *j Kingdom* (OT): vv. 9, 13–14; Hos. 3:4. (Gen. 1:26; Zech. 12:8, *note*). Isa. 16:5 *k Christ* (second advent): vv. 13–14; Hos. 3:5. (Dt. 30:3; Acts 1:11, *note*)

*7:10 Or *judgment* 7:17 Representing their kingdoms (compare verse 23)

[1](7:9) This title, while referring here and in v. 13 to God the Father, has equal application to Christ, e.g. v. 22; Rev. 1:8,13–18. Cp. Ps. 45:6; 93:2; Mic. 5:2; Hab. 1:12.

[2](7:13) This scene is identical with that of Rev. 5:6–10. There the ascription of praise concerning those who are "kings and priests" (see Dan. 7:18, *note*) ends with the words, "and we shall reign on the earth." Revelation 6 opens the "distress" of Ps. 2:5, introductory to setting the king on Zion (Ps. 2:6; Rev. 20:4). The vision (7:9–14) reverses the order of events as they will be fulfilled. Verse 13 describes the scene in heaven (cp. Rev. 5:6–10) which, in fulfillment, precedes the events which Daniel sees in vision in vv. 9–12. The order of fulfillment will be: (1) the investiture of the Son of Man with the kingdom (Dan. 7:13,14; Rev. 5:6–10); (2) the "distress" of Ps. 2:5, fully described in Mt. 24:21–22; Rev. 6–18; (3) the return of the Son of Man in glory to deliver the blow of 2:45 (Dan. 7:9–11; Rev. 19:11–21); and (4) God's judgment of individuals among the nations and the setting up of the kingdom (Dan. 7:10,26–27; Mt. 25:31–46; Rev. 20:1–6).

[3](7:14) Verses 13–14 are identical with Rev. 5:1–7, and precede the fulfillment of Dan. 2:34–35. Verses 13–14 and Rev. 5:1–7 describe the investiture of the Son of Man and Son of David with the kingdom authority, while Dan. 2:34–35 describes the crushing blow (see Armageddon, Rev. 16:13–16; 19:17, *note*) which destroys Gentile world power, thus clearing the way for the actual setting up of the kingdom of heaven. Verses 34–35 and Rev. 19:19–21 describe the same event.

[4](7:18) See "saints" in vv. 22,25, and 27 also. That the Church saints, i.e. believers of the Church Age, will also share this rule seems evident in that the Church, having part in the first resurrection, will "reign with Him [Christ] a thousand years" (Rev. 20:6). Cp. Rom. 8:17; 2 Tim. 2:10–12; 1 Pet. 2:9; Rev. 1:6; 3:21; 5:10.

sess the kingdom forever, even forever
and ever.'
19 "Then I wished to [a]know the
truth about the fourth beast, which
was different from all the others, exceedingly dreadful, *with* its teeth of
iron and its nails of bronze, *which* devoured, broke in pieces, and trampled
the residue with its feet;
20 "and the ten horns that *were* on
its head, and the other *horn* which
came up, before which three fell,
namely, that [b]horn which had eyes
and a mouth which spoke pompous
words, whose appearance *was* greater
than his fellows.
21 "I was watching; and the same
[b]horn was making war against the
[c]saints, and prevailing against them,
22 "until the Ancient of Days came,
and a [d]judgment was made *in favor* of
the [e]saints of the Most High, and the
time came for the saints to possess
the kingdom.
23 "Thus he said:

'The fourth beast shall be
A fourth kingdom on earth,
Which shall be different from
all *other* kingdoms,
And shall devour the whole
earth,
Trample it and break it in
pieces.

Satan's blasphemous leader

24 The [f]ten horns *are* ten kings
Who shall arise from this
kingdom.
And [g]another shall rise after
them;
He shall be different from the
first *ones*,
And shall subdue three kings.
25 He shall [h]speak *pompous*
words against the Most
High,
Shall persecute* the saints of
the Most High,
And shall intend to change
times and law.
Then *the saints* shall be given
into his hand
For a [1]time and times and half
a time.

26 'But the [i]court shall be seated,
[2]And they shall [j]take away his
dominion,
To consume and destroy *it*
forever.
27 Then the kingdom and
dominion,
And the greatness of the
kingdoms under the whole
heaven,
Shall be given to the people,
the saints of the Most High.
His kingdom *is* an [k]everlasting
kingdom,
And all dominions shall serve
and obey Him.'

28 "This *is* the end of the account.*
As for me, Daniel, my thoughts
greatly troubled me, and my countenance changed; but I kept the matter
in my heart."

19 [a] See v. 18, *note*
20 [b] See Dt. 33:17, *note*
21 [c] Rev. 13:7
22 [d] *Judgments* (the seven): vv. 21–27; Joel 3:1. (2 Sam. 7:14; Rev. 20:12, *note*) [e] Cp. 1 Cor. 6:2–3
24 [f] Rev. 13:1 [g] *The Beast*: vv. 20–26; Dan. 8:25. (Dan. 7:8; Rev. 19:20).
25 [h] Rev. 13:1–6
26 [i] v. 10; Dan. 2:35; cp. Rev. 16:14; 19:17–19, 21 [j] Rev. 19:20
27 [k] vv. 13–14; 2 Sam. 7:16; Ps. 89:35–37; Dan. 4:3; Lk. 1:31–33

* 7:25 Literally *wear out* 7:28 Literally *the word*

[1](7:25) The terms found in the OT and NT referring to specific lengths of time in future events require careful consideration, so as to avoid fantastic speculations. The first occurrence of a reference to a period of three and one-half years in the prophetic future is the expression "time and times and half a time" found here. It is also in Dan. 12:7 and Rev. 12:14. This is the same length of time as one-half of the final seven-year period (9:27), and is likewise the period of time expressed in the term "forty-two months" (Rev. 11:2; 13:5), or "one thousand two hundred and sixty days" (Rev. 12:6).

The three-and-one-half-year period seems to be a reference to the last half of Daniel's seventieth week, also known as the great tribulation.

[2](7:26) The end of Gentile world power. (1) In the beast vision of ch. 7, the fourth beast (v. 7) is declared to be "the fourth kingdom," i.e. the Roman Empire, the "iron" kingdom of ch. 2. The "ten horns" upon the fourth beast (Roman Empire), v. 7, are declared to be "ten kings who shall arise from this kingdom" (v. 24), answering to the ten toes of the image vision of ch. 2. The ten kingdoms, including the regions formerly ruled by Rome, will constitute, therefore, the form in which the fourth or Roman Empire will exist when the whole fabric of Gentile world domination is struck by the stone "cut out of the mountain without hands," i.e. Christ (2:44–45; 7:9). But (2) Daniel sees a "little horn" rise and subdue three of the ten kings (vv. 24–26). His distinguishing mark is hatred of God and believers. He is not to be confused with the little horn of ch. 8, a prophecy fulfilled in Antiochus Epiphanes (see 8:9, *note*). In Rev. 13 additional particulars of the little horn of Dan. 7 are given (see Rev. 13:1, *note*).

VII. The Prophecy of the Defeat of the Persians by the Greeks, and the Desecration of the Temple, 8

The vision of the ram and male goat

8 [1]IN the [a]third year of the reign of King Belshazzar a [2]vision appeared *to* me—to me, Daniel—after the one that appeared to me the first time.

2 I saw in the vision, and it so happened while I was looking, that I *was* in Shushan, the citadel, which *is* in the province of Elam; and I saw in the vision that I was by the River Ulai.

3 Then I lifted my eyes and saw, and there, standing beside the river, was a [b]ram which had two horns, and the two horns *were* high; but one *was* [c]higher than the other, and the higher *one* came up last.

4 I saw the ram pushing westward, northward, and southward, so that no animal could withstand him; nor *was there any* that could deliver from his hand, but he did according to his will and became great.

5 And as I was considering, suddenly a [d]male goat came from the west, across the surface of the whole earth, without touching the ground; and the goat *had* a notable [e]horn between his eyes.

6 Then he came to the ram that had two horns, which I had seen standing beside the river, and ran at him with furious power.

7 And I saw him confronting the ram; he was moved with rage against him, attacked the ram, and broke his two horns. There was no power in the ram to withstand him, but he cast him down to the ground and trampled him; and there was no one that could deliver the ram from his hand.

8 Therefore the male goat grew very great; but when he became strong, the large [e]horn was broken, and in place of it [f]four notable ones came up toward the four winds of heaven.

The little horn

9 And out of one of them came a [3]little [e]horn which grew exceedingly great toward the south, toward the east, and toward the Glorious *Land.*

10 And it grew up to the host of heaven; and it cast down *some* of the host and *some* of the stars to the ground, and trampled them.

11 He even [g]exalted *himself* as high as the Prince of the host; and by him the daily *sacrifices* were taken away, and the place of His sanctuary was cast down.

12 Because of transgression, an army was given over *to the horn* to oppose the daily *sacrifices;* and he cast truth down to the ground. He did *all this* and [h]prospered.

13 Then I heard a [i]holy one speaking; and *another* holy one said to that certain *one* who was speaking, "How long *will* the vision *be, concerning* the daily *sacrifices* and the transgression of [4]desolation, the giving of both the

CHAPTER 8
1
[a] c. 551 B.C.
3
[b] v. 20
[c] Dan. 7:5
5
[d] v. 21
[e] Dan. 11:3; see Dt. 33:17, *note*
8
[f] v. 22; Dan. 7:6; 11:4
11
[g] Cp. Isa. 14:13
12
[h] Dan. 11:36
13
[i] Dan. 4:13, 17

[1](8:1) The remarkably precise predictions in chs. 8 and 11 about the reign, character, and antecedents of Antiochus Epiphanes, the Hellenistic king who cruelly persecuted the Jews 400 years after the time of Nebuchadnezzar, were advanced by Porphyry, an anti-Christian philosopher of the third century A.D., as proof that the Book of Daniel could not have been written before that time. This view has been followed by many modern critics but should not keep any believer in predictive prophecy from accepting the traditional date.

[2](8:1) This chapter gives details concerning the second and third world kingdoms: the silver and bronze kingdoms of ch. 2; and the bear and leopard kingdoms of ch. 7, i.e. the Medo-Persian and Grecian (Macedonian) kingdoms of history. At the time of this vision (8:1), the first world empire was nearing its end. Belshazzar was the last ruler of that monarchy in the city of Babylon. See *notes* at 5:2,18,29.

[3](8:9) The little horn of this verse (cp. v. 23) was fulfilled (171–164 B.C.) in the historical Antiochus Epiphanes, who came out of Syria (one of the four prominent kingdoms of vv. 8,22), and persecuted the Jews and profaned the temple at Jerusalem. He is not to be confused with the little horn of 7:8, who is yet to come in the tribulation period (see vv. 9–13,23). The little horn of 7:8 will rise from the ten horns into which the fourth empire (Roman) will be divided, whereas the little horn of ch. 8 comes out of one of the four horns (vv. 9,22) into which the third empire (Grecian) is divided after Alexander's death (vv. 21–22) in the latter time of the four kingdoms of Alexander's generals (v. 23). Both little horns are violent in their hatred of the Jews and of God, and in their profaning of the temple at Jerusalem (cp. 7:25 and 8:10–12).

[4](8:13) Seven times in Daniel desolation is spoken of: (1) of the sanctuary (8:13), fulfilled by Antiochus Epiphanes, 171–164 B.C.; (2) of the sanctuary (9:17), alluding to its condition in Daniel's time, when the Jews were in exile; (3) generally, of the land (9:18), also referring to Daniel's time; (4) of the sanctuary (9:26), fulfilled in A.D. 70 in the destruction of city and temple after the cutting off of Messiah (Lk. 21:20); and (5), (6), and (7) of the sanctuary, by the beast,

sanctuary and the host to be trampled
underfoot?"
14 And he said to me, [1]"For two
thousand three hundred days;* then
the sanctuary shall be cleansed."

The interpretation of the vision

15 Then it happened, when I, Daniel, had seen the vision and was seeking the meaning, that suddenly there
stood before me one having the appearance of a [a]man.
16 And I heard a man's voice between *the banks of* the Ulai, who
called, and said, [b]"Gabriel, make this
man understand the vision."
17 So he came near where I stood,
and when he came I was afraid and
fell on my face; but he said to me, "Understand, son of man, that the vision
refers to the [2]time of the end."
18 Now, as he was speaking with
me, I was in a [c]deep sleep with my
face to the ground; but he touched me,
and stood me upright.
19 And he [d]said, "Look, I am making known to you what shall happen
in the latter time of the indignation;
for at the appointed time the end *shall
be.*

The identity of the ram

20 "The [3]ram which you saw, having the two [e]horns—*they are* the
kings of Media and Persia.

The male goat and his successors

21 "And the male goat *is* the kingdom* of Greece. The large [e]horn that
is between its eyes *is* the [f]first king.
22 "As for the broken *horn* and the
[4]four that stood up in its place, four
kingdoms shall arise out of that nation, but not with its power.

The king with fierce features

23 "And in the latter time of their
kingdom,
When the transgressors have
reached their fullness,
A [5]king shall arise,
Having fierce features,
Who understands sinister
schemes.
24 His power shall be mighty, but
not by his [g]own power;
He shall destroy fearfully,
And shall prosper and thrive;
He shall destroy the mighty,
and *also* the holy people.

25 "Through [h]his cunning
He shall cause deceit to
prosper under his rule;*
And he shall exalt *himself* in
his heart.
He shall destroy many in *their*
prosperity.
He shall [i]even rise against the
Prince of princes;
But he shall be broken without
human means.*

26 "And the vision of the evenings
and mornings
Which was told is true;
Therefore [j]seal up the vision,
For *it refers* to many days *in
the future.*"

27 And I, Daniel, fainted and was
sick for days; afterward I arose and
went about the king's business. I was
astonished by the vision, but no one
understood it.

*VIII. Daniel's Prayer, and
the Prophecy of the Seventy Weeks, 9*

*The vision of the seventy
weeks (vv. 1–27)*

9 IN the [k]first year of Darius the
son of Ahasuerus, of the lineage
of the Medes, who was made king
over the realm of the Chaldeans—

15 *a Theophanies:* v. 15; Dan. 10:5. (Gen. 12:7, *note;* Dan. 10:5)
16 *b* Dan. 9:21; Lk. 1:19,26
18 *c* Dan. 10:9
19 *d* v. 20
20 *e* See Dt. 33:17, *note*
21 *f* i.e. *Alexander the Great*
24 *g* Cp. 2 Th. 2:9
25 *h The Beast:* vv. 24–25; Dan. 9:26. (Dan. 7:8; Rev. 19:20)
i Rev. 19:19–20
26 *j* Dan. 12:4, 9
CHAPTER 9
1 *k* c. 539 B.C.

*
8:14 Literally *evening-mornings* 8:21 Literally *king,* representing his kingdom (compare 7:17,23) 8:25 Literally *hand* • Literally *hand*

9:27; 11:31; 12:11. Cp. Mt. 24:15; Mk. 13:14; 2 Th. 2:3,8–12; Rev. 13:14–15.

[1](8:14) This prediction was fulfilled during the bitter persecution under Antiochus Epiphanes and in the cleansing of the sanctuary in Jerusalem.

[2](8:17) Two "ends" seems to be in view here: (1) historically, the end of the third empire (Grecian) of Alexander, out of one of the divisions of which (Syria) the little horn of v. 9 (Antiochus Epiphanes) arose; and (2) prophetically, the end of "the times of the Gentiles" (see Lk. 21:24 and Rev. 16:19, *notes*)—Daniel's final time of the end (see Dan. 12:4, *note*).

[3](8:20) Compare vv. 3–4. The higher horn, which came up last, was Persia. The other was Media, which was dominant at first. Cp. 6:12.

[4](8:22) The four kingdoms into which Alexander's empire was divided (4th Cent. B.C.): Macedonia, Syria, Egypt, and Asia Minor. See Dan. 11:4, *note.*

[5](8:23) Concerning this sinister figure there are three views: (1) Some think he is the "king of the North" referred to in 11:40. (2) Others regard him as a type of the Roman beast of the end time (7:23–27). And (3) some see in this king a direct prophecy of the final Roman beast, thus identifying his geographical origin.

2 in the first year of his reign I, Daniel, understood by the books the number of the years *specified* by the word of the LORD through Jeremiah the prophet, that He would accomplish [1]seventy years in the desolations of Jerusalem.

Daniel's confession and prayer

3 Then I [a]set my face toward the Lord God to make request by [2b]prayer and supplications, with fasting, sackcloth, and ashes.

4 And I [b]prayed to the LORD my God, and made confession, and said, "O Lord, great and awesome God, who keeps His covenant and mercy with those who love Him, and with those who keep His commandments,

5 "we have sinned and committed iniquity, we have done wickedly and rebelled, even by departing from Your precepts and Your judgments.

6 "Neither have we heeded Your servants the prophets, who spoke in Your name to our kings and our princes, to our fathers and all the people of the land.

7 "O Lord, righteousness *belongs* to You, but to us shame of face, as *it is* this day—to the men of Judah, to the inhabitants of Jerusalem and all Israel, those near and those far off in all the countries to which You have driven them, because of the unfaithfulness which they have committed against You.

8 "O Lord, to us *belongs* shame of face, to our kings, our princes, and our fathers, because we have sinned against You.

9 "To the Lord our God *belong* mercy and forgiveness, though we have rebelled against Him.

10 "We have not obeyed the voice of the LORD our God, to walk in His laws, which He set before us by His servants the prophets.

11 "Yes, all Israel has transgressed Your [c]law, and has departed so as not to obey Your voice; therefore the curse and the oath written in the Law of Moses the servant of God have been poured out on us, because [d]we have sinned against Him.

12 "And He has [e]confirmed His words, which He spoke against us and against our judges who judged us, by bringing upon us a great disaster; for under the whole heaven such has [f]never been done as what has been done to Jerusalem.

13 "As *it is* written in the [g]Law of Moses, all this disaster has come upon us; yet we have not made our prayer before the LORD our God, that we might turn from our iniquities and understand Your truth.

14 "Therefore the LORD has [h]kept the disaster in mind, and brought it upon us; for the LORD our God *is* righteous in all the works which He does, though we have not obeyed His voice.

15 "And now, O Lord our God, who brought Your people out of the land of Egypt with a mighty hand, and made Yourself a [i]name, as *it is* this day—we have sinned, we have done wickedly!

16 "O Lord, according to all Your righteousness, I pray, let Your anger and Your fury be turned away from Your city [j]Jerusalem, Your holy mountain; because for our sins, and for the iniquities of our fathers, Jerusalem and Your people *are* a reproach to all *those* around us.

17 "Now therefore, our God, hear the prayer of Your servant, and his supplications, and for the Lord's sake cause Your face to shine on Your sanctuary, which is desolate.

18 "O my God, incline Your ear and hear; open Your eyes and see our desolations, and the city which is called by Your name; for we do not present our supplications before You because of our righteous deeds, but because of Your great mercies.

19 "O Lord, hear! O Lord, forgive! O Lord, listen and act! Do not delay for Your own sake, my God, for Your city and Your people are called by Your name."

The seventy weeks of years

20 Now while I *was* speaking, [k]praying, and confessing my sin and the sin of my people Israel, and presenting my supplication before the LORD my God for the holy mountain of my God,

21 yes, while I *was* speaking in prayer, the man [l]Gabriel, whom I had

3
a Dan. 10:15
b *Bible prayers* (OT): vv. 3–21; Jon. 2:1. (Gen. 15:2; Hab. 3:1)
11
c *Law* (of Moses): vv. 8–13; Mal. 4:4. (Ex. 19:1; Gal. 3:24, *note*)
d Neh. 1:6; Ps. 106:6; cp. Isa. 6:5
12
e Jer. 44:2–6; Lam. 2:17
f Lam. 1:12; 2:13
13
g Lev. 26:14–45; Dt. 28:15–68
14
h Jer. 31:28; 44:27
15
i Jer. 32:20
16
j v. 20; Ps. 122:6; Jer. 29:7; cp. Zech. 8:1–8
20
k Cp. Ps. 145:18–19; Isa. 65:24
21
l Dan. 8:16; Lk. 1:19,26

[1](9:2) The "books" were Jeremiah's writings (Jer. 25:11, where see *note;* 29:10).

[2](9:3) In vv. 4–19 is recorded Daniel's prayer, which arose from the study of the prophetic Scriptures (v. 2; cp. Jer. 25) and was a fulfillment of the prophetic portion of Solomon's prayer (1 Ki. 8:33–36). Here there are adoration (v. 4), confession (vv. 5–15), and petition (vv. 16–19). Prophetic study is intended to lead to a deeper spiritual life.

seen in the vision at the beginning,
being caused to fly swiftly, reached
me about the time of the evening offering.
22 And he informed *me,* and talked
with me, and said, "O Daniel, I have
now come forth to give you skill to
understand.
23 "At the beginning of your supplications the command went out, and I
have come to tell *you,* for you *are*
greatly [a]beloved; therefore consider
the matter, and understand the vision:

23
a Dan. 10:11,19
24
b i.e. *Daniel's people*
c Heb. *kaphar, atone for.* See Ex. 29:33, *note*

24 "Seventy [1]weeks are determined
For [b]your people and for your
holy city,
To finish the transgression,
To [c]make an end of* sins,
To make reconciliation for
iniquity,
To bring in everlasting
righteousness,
To seal up vision and
prophecy,

*9:24 Following Qere, Septuagint, Syriac, and Vulgate; Kethib and Theodotion read *To seal up.*

[1](9:24) Daniel's prophecy of the seventy "weeks" ('sevens') (vv. 24–27) provides the chronological frame for Messianic prediction from Daniel to the establishment of the kingdom on earth and also a key to its interpretation. Its main features are as follows:

(1) The entire prophecy is concerned primarily with Daniel's "people" and their "holy city"—i.e. Israel and Jerusalem.

(2) Two princes are mentioned; the first is named the "Messiah the Prince" (v. 25); the second is described as "the prince who is to come" (v. 26), a reference to the little horn of ch. 7:8, whose "people" would destroy the rebuilt Jerusalem after the cutting off of the Messianic Prince (v. 26).

(3) The "seventy weeks" of the prophecy are weeks of years, an important sabbatical time-measure in the Jewish calendar. Violation of the command to observe the sabbatical year brought the judgment of the Babylonian captivity and determined its length of seventy years. Cp. Lev. 25:1–22; 26:33–35; 2 Chr. 36:19–21; Dan. 9:2. Compare also Gen. 29:26–28 for use of "week" to indicate seven years.

(4) These 490 prophetic years are each 360 days long. This is proved by the biblical references to the seventieth week of seven years, which is divided into two halves (v. 27), the latter half being variously designated as "a time and times, and half a time" (Dan. 7:25; cp. Rev. 12:14); forty-two months (Rev. 11:2; 13:5); or 1260 days (Rev. 11:3; 12:6). In this connection it should be remembered that, in the grand sweep of prophecy, prophetic time is invariably so near as to give full warning, so indeterminate as to give no satisfaction to mere curiosity (cp. Mt. 24:36; Acts 1:7).

(5) The beginning of the seventy weeks is fixed as "the going forth of the command to restore and build Jerusalem" and its wall (v. 25). The only decree in Scripture authorizing the rebuilding of the city and its wall is recorded in Neh. 2; dated in "the month of Nisan, in the twentieth year of King Artaxerxes" (i.e. 445 B.C.), it is well attested in ancient history. From this date as a beginning, the first sixty-nine weeks reach to "the Messiah, the Prince."

(6) At a later time, after the "sixty-two weeks" which follow the first "seven weeks" (i.e. after sixty-nine weeks), two important events will take place: (1) Messiah will be "cut off" and will have none of His regal rights ("but not for Himself"). And (2) the rebuilt city and sanctuary will again be destroyed, this time by "the people" of another "prince" who is yet to come. It is generally agreed that these two events were fulfilled in the death of Christ (A.D. 29) and the destruction of Jerusalem by Rome in A.D. 70. Both events are placed before the seventieth week of v. 27. Hence a period of at least forty-one years between the death of Christ and the destruction of Jerusalem must intervene between the sixty-ninth and seventieth weeks.

(7) The main events of the final "one week" (v. 27) are as follows: (1) There is a seven-year "covenant" made by the future Roman prince (the "little horn" of 7:8) with the Jews. (2) In the middle of the week there is a forcible interruption of the Jewish ritual of worship by the Roman prince who introduces "abomination" that renders the sanctuary desolate. (3) At the same time he launches persecution against the Jews. And (4) the end of the seventieth week brings judgment upon the desolator and also brings "everlasting righteousness" (v. 24—i.e. the blessings of the Messianic kingdom).

The proof that this final week has not yet been fulfilled is seen in the fact that Christ definitely relates its main events to His second coming (Mt. 24:6,15). Hence, during the interim between the sixty-ninth and seventieth weeks there must lie the whole period of the Church set forth in the NT but not revealed in the OT. The interpretation which assigns the last of the seventy weeks to the end of the age is found in the Church Fathers. When this seventieth week was referred to during the first two and one-half centuries of the Christian Church, it was almost always assigned to the end of the age. Irenaeus places the appearance of Antichrist at the end of the age in the last week; in fact, he asserts that the time of Antichrist's tyranny will last just one-half of the week, three years and six months. So likewise Hippolytus states that Daniel "indicates the showing forth of the seven years which shall be in the last times."

And to anoint the [a]Most Holy.

25 "Know therefore and
understand,
That from the going forth of
the command
To restore and build Jerusalem
Until Messiah the Prince,
There shall be seven weeks
and sixty-two weeks;
The street* shall be built
again, and the wall,*
Even in troublesome times.

26 "And after the sixty-two weeks
[b]Messiah shall be [c]cut off, [d]but
not for Himself;
And the people of the [e]prince
who is to come
Shall destroy the city and the
sanctuary.
The end of it *shall be* with a
flood,
And till the [f]end of the war
desolations are determined.
27 Then he shall [g]confirm a
covenant with many for one
week;
But in the middle of the week
He shall bring an end to
sacrifice and offering.
And on the wing of
abominations shall be one
who makes desolate,
Even until the consummation,
which is determined,
Is poured out on the
[h]desolate."

IX. Daniel's Final Vision, 10—12

The vision of the glory of God

10 IN the [i]third year of Cyrus
king of Persia a message was
revealed to Daniel, whose [j]name was
called Belteshazzar. The message *was*
true, but the appointed time *was*
long;* and he understood the message, and had understanding of the vision.
2 In those days I, Daniel, was
mourning three full [1]weeks.
3 I ate no pleasant food, no meat
or wine came into my mouth, nor did
I anoint myself at all, till three whole
weeks were fulfilled.
4 Now on the twenty-fourth day of
the [k]first month, as I was by the side
of the great river, that *is*, the Tigris,*
5 I lifted my eyes and looked, and
behold, a certain [l]man clothed in
[m]linen, whose [n]waist *was* girded with
gold of Uphaz!
6 His body *was* like beryl, his face
like the appearance of [o]lightning, his
eyes like [p]torches of fire, his arms and
feet like burnished [q]bronze in color,
and the sound of his words like the
voice of a multitude.
7 And I, Daniel, alone saw the vision, for the men who were with me
did [r]not see the vision; but a great
terror fell upon them, so that they fled
to hide themselves.
8 Therefore I was left alone when
I saw this great vision, and no strength
[s]remained in me; for my vigor was
turned to frailty in me, and I retained
no strength.
9 Yet I heard the sound of his
words; and while I heard the sound of
his words I was in a deep sleep on my
face, with my face to the ground.

Conflict: holy and unholy angels

10 [2]Suddenly, a hand touched me,
which made me tremble on my knees
and *on* the palms of my hands.
11 And he said to me, "O Daniel,
man greatly beloved, understand the
words that I speak to you, and stand
upright, for I have now been sent to
you." While he was speaking this
word to me, I stood trembling.
12 Then he said to me, "Do not fear,
Daniel, for from the first day that you
set your heart to understand, and to
humble yourself before your God,
your words were heard; and I have
come because of your words.
13 "But the [3]prince of the kingdom
of Persia withstood me twenty-one
days; and behold, [t]Michael, one of the
chief princes, came to help me, for I
had been left alone there with the
kings of Persia.
14 "Now I have come to make you

24 *a* Lit. *a most holy place*

26 *b* Christ (first advent): vv. 24–26; Hos. 11:1. (Gen. 3:15; Acts 1:11, *note*)

c Sacrifice (prophetic): v. 26; Zech. 12:10. (Gen. 3:15; Heb. 10:18, *note*)

d Or *and shall have nothing.* That is, nothing of the *regal* glory which was rightly His.

e The Beast: vv. 26–27; Dan. 11:36. (Dan. 7:8; Rev. 19:20)

f Lit. *till the end shall be war; desolations are determined.* Cp. Mt. 24:6–14

27 *g* Or *make a firm covenant*

h Lit. *desolator*

CHAPTER 10

1 *i* c. 536 B.C.

j Dan. 1:7

4 *k* See Lev. 23:2, *note*

5 *l* Theophanies: vv. 4–9, 16–17. (Gen. 12:7, *note;* Dan. 10:5). See v. 10, *note*

m Ezek. 9:2; 10:2

n Cp. Rev.

1:13 **10:6** *o* Cp. Rev. 1:16 *p* Cp. Rev. 1:14 *q* Cp. Rev. 1:15 **10:7** *r* Cp. Acts 22:9 **10:8** *s* Cp. Ex. 3:2–10; Isa. 6:1–10; Rev. 1:12–19 **10:13** *t* v. 21; Dan. 12:1; Jude 9; Rev. 12:7

*

9:25 Or *open square* • Or *moat* **10:1** Or *and of great conflict* **10:4** Hebrew *Hiddekel*

[1](10:2) Here and in v. 3 the Hebrew text reads "weeks of days" so as to distinguish these weeks from the weeks of years in ch. 9:24–27.

[2](10:10) Verses 10–15 probably introduce an angel. Verses 4–9, 16–17 are theophanies.

[3](10:13) Compare v. 20. The intimation is clear that, as the holy angels are sent forth on behalf of the heirs of salvation, so demons are concerned on behalf of the world system of Satan (Jn. 7:7; Rev. 13:8).

understand what will happen to your people in the [a]latter days, for the vision *refers* to *many* days yet *to come.*"

15 When he had spoken such words to me, I turned my face toward the ground and became speechless.

16 And suddenly, *one* having the likeness of the sons* of men touched my lips; then I opened my mouth and spoke, saying to him who stood before me, "My lord, because of the vision my sorrows have overwhelmed me, and I have retained no strength.

17 "For how can this servant of my lord talk with you, my lord? As for me, no strength remains in me now, nor is any breath left in me."

18 Then again, *the one* having the likeness of a man touched me and strengthened me.

19 And he said, "O man greatly beloved, fear not! Peace *be* to you; be strong, yes, be strong!" So when he spoke to me I was strengthened, and said, "Let my lord speak, for you have strengthened me."

20 Then he said, "Do you know why I have come to you? And now I must return to fight with the prince of Persia; and when I have gone forth, indeed the prince of Greece will come.

21 "But I will tell you what is noted in the Scripture of Truth. (No one upholds me against these, except Michael your prince.

14
a See Acts 2:17, *note*

CHAPTER 11

1
b c. 539 B.C.
c Dan. 5:31; 9:1

3
d Cp. Dan. 8:21–26
e vv. 16,36

4
f Zech. 2:6; cp. Rev. 7:1

5
g vv. 8–9

6
h Cp. v. 13

From Darius to the man of sin
(11:1—12:13)

11 "ALSO in the [b]first year of [c]Darius the Mede, I, *even* I, stood up to confirm and strengthen him.)

2 "And now I will tell you the truth: [1]Behold, [2]three more kings will arise in Persia, and the fourth shall be far richer than *them* all; by his strength, through his riches, he shall stir up all against the realm of Greece.

3 "Then a mighty [3][d]king shall arise, who shall rule with great dominion, and do [e]according to his will.

4 "And when he has arisen, his kingdom shall be broken up and [4]divided toward the [f]four winds of heaven, but not among his posterity nor according to his dominion with which he ruled; for his kingdom shall be uprooted, even for others besides these.

5 "Also the [5]king of the South shall become strong, as well as *one* of his princes; and he shall gain power over him and have dominion. His dominion *shall be* a [g]great dominion.

6 "And [h]at the end of *some* years they shall join forces, for the daughter of the [6]king of the South shall go to the king of the North to make an agreement; but she shall not retain the power of her authority, and neither he nor his authority* shall stand; but she

*
10:16 Theodotion and Vulgate read *the son;* Septuagint reads *a hand.* **11:6** Literally *arm*

[1](11:2) The spirit of prophecy here returns to that which more immediately concerned Daniel and his royal masters—the near future of the empire in which he was so great a personage. Four kings were yet to follow in Medo-Persia. Then will come Alexander the "mighty king" of Greece (v. 3). The division of Alexander's empire into four parts (v. 4), as already predicted (8:22), is foretold. The turbulent course of affairs in two parts of the disintegrated Alexandrian empire, Syria and Egypt, is then traced down to v. 20. Here Antiochus Epiphanes, the little horn of ch. 8, occupies the vision down to v. 36. His pollution of the sanctuary is again mentioned. See 8:9, *note.* From v. 36 the interpretation is of the willful king and his activities in the end-time. See Dan. 11:36, *note.*

[2](11:2) The three kings of Persia are probably Cyrus II (550–530 B.C.) referred to in Ezra 1:1 and 2 Chr. 36:22–23; Cambyses, 529–522 B.C., not referred to in the OT; and Darius I Hystaspes, 521–486 B.C. (Ezra 5; 6). The fourth king is either Ahasuerus, 486–465 B.C. (Ezra 4:6) or Artaxerxes I, 465–424 B.C. (Ezra 7:11–26).

[3](11:3) The "mighty king" is Alexander the Great who died c. 323 B.C. He is referred to also in 7:6; 8:5–8,21–22.

[4](11:4) Following Alexander's death the empire was divided among four of his generals: Cassander, ruling Macedonia; Lysimachus, ruling Thrace and Asia Minor; Ptolemy I, ruling Egypt, whose successors, the Ptolemies, ruled from 323–30 B.C.; and Seleucus, ruling Syria and the remainder of the Near East, whose successors, known as the Seleucids, ruled until c. 65 B.C.

[5](11:5) The "king of the South" here is Ptolemy I Soter, 323–285 B.C., and the strong one is Seleucus I Nicator, 312–281, the most powerful of all those ruling in the once-united empire of Alexander. Daniel's prophecy here passes over the second Seleucid king, Antiochus I Soter, 281–261 B.C., though it does speak of a union of these two royal lines through marriage.

[6](11:6) This "king of the South" is Ptolemy II Philadelphus, 285–246 B.C. The daughter was Berenice.

shall be given up, with those who brought her, and with him who begot her, and with him who strengthened her in *those* times.

7 "But from a [1]branch of her roots *one* shall arise in his place, who shall come with an army, enter the fortress of the king of the North, and deal with them and prevail.

8 "And he shall also carry their gods captive to Egypt, with their princes* *and* their precious articles of silver and gold; and he shall continue *more* years than the king of the North.

9 "Also *the king of the North* shall come to the kingdom of the king of the South, but shall return to his own land.

10 [2]"However his sons shall stir up strife, and assemble a multitude of great forces; and *one* shall certainly come and overwhelm and pass through; then he shall return to his fortress and stir up strife.

11 "And the king of the South shall be [a]moved with [b]rage, and go out and fight with him, with the king of the North, who shall muster a great multitude; but the [c]multitude shall be given into the hand of his *enemy*.

12 "When he has taken away the multitude, his heart will be lifted up; and he will cast down tens of thousands, but he will not prevail.

13 "For the king of the North will return and muster a multitude greater than the former, and shall certainly come at the end of some years with a great army and much equipment.

14 "Now in those times many shall rise up against the [3]king of the South. Also, violent men* of your people shall exalt themselves in fulfillment of the vision, but they shall [d]fall.

15 "So the [4]king of the North shall come and [e]build a siege mound, and take a fortified city; and the forces* of the South shall not withstand *him*. Even his choice troops *shall have* no strength to resist.

16 "But he who comes against him shall do according to his own will, and no one shall stand against him. He shall stand in the Glorious Land with destruction in his power.*

17 "He shall also [f]set his face to enter with the strength of his whole kingdom, and upright ones* with him; thus shall he do. And he shall give him the daughter of women to destroy it; but she shall not stand *with him*, or be for him.

18 "After this he shall turn his face to the [g]coastlands, and shall take many. But a ruler shall bring the reproach against them to an end; and with the [h]reproach removed, he shall turn back on him.

19 "Then he shall turn his face toward the fortress of his own land; but he shall [i]stumble and fall, and [j]not be found.

20 "There shall arise in his place one who imposes taxes *on* the glorious kingdom; but within a few days he shall be destroyed, but not in anger or in battle.

Antiochus Epiphanes, the Syrian king who will hurt Israel

21 "And in his place shall [k]arise a vile [5]person, to whom they will not give the honor of royalty; but he shall come in peaceably, and seize the kingdom by intrigue.

22 "With the force* of a [l]flood they shall be swept away from before him and be broken, and also the prince of the covenant.

23 "And after the league *is made* with him he shall act [m]deceitfully, for he shall come up and become strong with a small *number of* people.

24 "He shall enter [n]peaceably, even into the [o]richest places of the province; and he shall do *what* his fathers have not done, nor his forefathers: he shall disperse among them the plunder, spoil, and riches; and he shall devise his plans against the strongholds, but *only* for a time.

11
a Prov. 16:14
b Dan. 8:7
c Ps. 33:16; cp. Eccl. 9:11
14
d Job 9:13
15
e Ezek. 4:2; 17:17
17
f 2 Ki. 12:17; Ezek. 4:3,7
18
g Isa. 66:19; Jer. 2:10; 31:10; Zeph. 2:11
h Cp. Hos. 12:14
19
i Ps. 27:2; Jer. 46:6
j Ps. 37:36; Ezek. 26:21
21
k vv. 24,32
22
l Dan. 9:26
23
m Cp. Gen. 3:1
24
n v. 21
o Cp. Neh. 9:25; Ezek. 34:14

*
11:8 Or *molded images* 11:14 Or *robbers*, literally *sons of breakage* 11:15 Literally *arms* 11:16 Literally *hand* 11:17 Or *bring equitable terms* 11:22 Literally *arms*

[1](11:7) The reference in vv. 7–9 is to Ptolemy III Euergetes, 246–222 B.C. In v. 11, the "king of the South" is Ptolemy IV Philopator, 222–203 B.C.

[2](11:10) The two rulers of Syria are Seleucus III Ceraunus (sometimes called Soter) 226–223 B.C. and Antiochus III the Great, 223–187 B.C., whose activities continue through v. 19.

[3](11:14) This "king of the South" is Ptolemy V Epiphanes, 203–181 B.C., whose activities continue down through v. 24.

[4](11:15) The "king of the North" is Seleucus IV Philopator, 187–175 B.C.

[5](11:21) This northern king (vv. 21–35) is none other than Antiochus IV Epiphanes, 175–164 B.C., the great persecutor of the Jews and type of Antichrist.

25 [1]"He shall stir up his power and his courage against the king of the South with a great army. And the king of the South shall be stirred up to battle with a very great and mighty army; but he shall not stand, for they shall devise plans against him.

26 "Yes, those who eat of the portion of his delicacies shall destroy him; his army shall be swept away, and many shall fall down slain.

27 "Both these kings' hearts *shall be* bent on evil, and they shall [a]speak lies at the same table; but it shall not prosper, for the end *will* still *be* at the appointed [b]time.

28 "While returning to his land with great riches, his heart shall be *moved* against the holy covenant; so he shall do *damage* and return to his own land.

29 "At the appointed time he shall return and go toward the south; but it shall not be like the former or the latter.

30 "For ships from Cyprus* shall come against him; therefore he shall be grieved, and return in rage against the holy covenant, and do *damage.* So he shall return and show regard for those who forsake the holy covenant.

31 "And forces* shall be mustered by him, and they shall [2c]defile the sanctuary fortress; then they shall take away the daily *sacrifices,* and place *there* the abomination of desolation.

32 "Those who do wickedly against the covenant he shall corrupt with flattery; but the people who know their God shall be [d]strong, and carry out *great exploits.*

27
a Cp. Jer. 9:3–5
b Dan. 8:19; Hab. 2:3
31
c Dan. 8:11–13
32
d e.g. *the Maccabees.* c. 168 and following
36
e The Beast: vv. 36–45; Dan. 12:11. (Dan. 7:8; Rev. 19:20)
f Cp. Rev. 13:5–6
g Cp. 1 Cor. 8:5–6
37
h Isa. 14:13; 2 Th. 2:4
40
i Dan. 12:4, 9

33 "And those of the people who understand shall instruct many; yet *for many* days they shall fall by sword and flame, by captivity and plundering.

34 "Now when they fall, they shall be aided with a little help; but many shall join with them by intrigue.

35 "And *some* of those of understanding shall fall, to refine them, purify *them,* and make *them* white, *until* the time of the end; because *it is* still for the appointed time.

Prophecy concerning the willful king

36 "Then the [3]king shall do according to his own will: [e]he shall exalt and magnify himself above every god, shall [f]speak blasphemies against the God of [g]gods, and shall prosper till the wrath has been accomplished; for what has been determined shall be done.

37 "He shall regard neither the [g]God* of his fathers nor the desire of women, nor regard any [g]god; for he shall [h]exalt himself above *them* all.

38 "But in their place he shall honor a god of fortresses; and a [g]god which his fathers did not know he shall honor with gold and silver, with precious stones and pleasant things.

39 "Thus he shall act against the strongest fortresses with a foreign [g]god, which he shall acknowledge, *and* advance *its* glory; and he shall cause them to rule over many, and divide the land for gain.

40 "At the [i]time of the end the king

*
11:30 Hebrew *Kittim,* western lands, especially Cyprus **11:31** Literally *arms* **11:37** Or *gods*

[1](11:25) Verses 25–28 record the first campaign of Antiochus Epiphanes against Egypt.

[2](11:31) Verses 31–35 record the desolation of the Jerusalem temple by Antiochus Epiphanes.

[3](11:36) Here the prophetic foreview, having traced (vv. 3–20) the two parts of Alexander's empire (Syria and Egypt) which had to do with Palestine and the Jews up till the time of Antiochus Epiphanes, and having described his career (vv. 21–35), overleaps the Church Age and centuries to "the time of the end" (v. 35). Prophecy at this point does not concern itself with history as such but only with history as it affects Israel and the Holy Land. Antiochus Epiphanes was insignificant as compared with many historical personages whom the Bible does not mention, but he scourged the people of God and defiled His holy altar by offering a sow upon it. His attitude and actions toward Israel brought him into prophetic light.

The identity of the willful king is variously interpreted. Some expositors consider him to be the little horn of ch. 7 and the head of the revived Roman Empire. He will disregard all pagan gods ("gods of his fathers," NKJV note) and the Messianic hope, and will honor the god of war (the "god of fortresses"). He is identified as a supreme ruler, who will "magnify himself above every god."

Another view considers him an unregenerate Jew in the Holy Land in league with the Roman beast (7:8ff.), who is an unbelieving Gentile in Rome (Rev. 17:9ff.). The willful king disregards the God of Israel ("the God of his fathers"); cares nothing for the hope of Messiah ("the desire of [Jewish] women"); and honors the Roman beast (the "god of fortresses"), Rev. 13:11–18.

The doom of the willful king is at the second coming of Christ (v. 45).

of the South shall attack him; and the
king of the North shall come against
him like a whirlwind, with chariots,
horsemen, and with many ships; and
he shall enter the countries, overwhelm *them,* and pass through.
41 “He shall also enter the Glorious
Land, and many *countries* shall be
overthrown; but these shall escape
from his hand: Edom, Moab, and the
prominent people of Ammon.
42 “He shall stretch out his hand
against the countries, and the land of
[a]Egypt shall not escape.
43 “He shall have power over the
treasures of gold and silver, and over
all the precious things of Egypt; also
the Libyans and Ethiopians *shall follow* at his heels.
44 “But news from the east and the
north shall trouble him; therefore he
shall go out with great fury to destroy
and annihilate many.
45 “And he shall plant the tents of
his [b]palace between the seas and the
glorious holy mountain; yet he shall
come to his end, and no one will help
him.

The great tribulation

12 “AT that time Michael shall
stand up,
The great prince who stands
watch over the sons of your
people;
And there shall be a time of
trouble,
[c]Such as never was since there
was a nation,
Even to that time.
And at that time your people
shall be delivered,
Every one who is found
written in the book.

The resurrections

2 And [1]many of those who sleep
in the dust of the earth shall
[d]awake,
Some to everlasting life,
Some to shame *and* everlasting
contempt.
3 Those who are [e]wise shall
shine
[f]Like the brightness of the
firmament,
And those who [g]turn many to
righteousness
Like the stars forever and
ever.

God's last message to Daniel

4 “But you, Daniel, shut up the
words, and seal the book until the
[2]time of the end; many shall [h]run to
and fro, and knowledge shall increase.”
5 Then I, Daniel, looked; and there
stood [i]two others, one on this river-
bank and the other on that river-
bank.
6 And *one* said to the man clothed
in [j]linen, who *was* above the waters
of the river, “How long shall the fulfillment of these wonders *be?*”
7 Then I heard the man clothed in
linen, who *was* above the waters of
the river, when he [k]held up his right
hand and his left hand to heaven, and
swore by Him who lives forever,
that *it shall be* for a time, times, and
half *a time;* and when the power of
the holy people has been completely
shattered, all these *things* shall be
finished.
8 Although I heard, I did not understand. Then I said, “My lord, what
shall be the end of these *things?*”

42
a Joel 3:19
45
b See Dan. 11:2, *note*
CHAPTER 12
1
c Tribulation (the great): v. 1; Mt. 24:21. (Ps. 2:5; Rev. 7:14)
2
d Resurrection: vv. 2, 13; Hos. 13:14. (2 Ki. 4:35; 1 Cor. 15:52, *note*)
3
e Prov. 3:35; Dan. 11:33
f Rewards: vv. 2–3; Mt. 5:12. (Dan. 12:3; 1 Cor. 3:14, *note*)
g Prov. 11:30; Jas. 5:19–20
4
h Amos 8:12
5
i Dan. 10:5–6,16
6
j Ezek. 9:2
7
k Cp. Rev. 10:5–6

[1](12:2) This resurrection concerns Daniel's people (v. 1), i.e. the Jews (cp. 9:15–16,20,24; 10:14), and is selective; not all, but “many” (v. 2), restricted to those written in the “book” (v. 1). The latter part of v. 2 may be rendered as follows: “*These* [i.e. the ones who awake] to everlasting life; but *those* [i.e. those left in the grave who are yet to awake] to shame and everlasting contempt.” This resurrection will occur after the tribulation and concerns OT believers and tribulation believers—not the Church, which will be translated before the tribulation.

[2](12:4) In Daniel the expression “the time of the end” or its equivalent occurs in 8:17–19; 9:26; 11:35,40,45; 12:4,6,9. Summary: (1) The time of the end in Daniel begins with the violation by “the prince who is to come” (i.e. little horn, “man of sin,” “beast”) of his covenant with the Jews for the restoration of the temple and sacrifice (9:27), and his presentation of himself as God (9:27; 11:36–38; Mt. 24:15; 2 Th. 2:4; Rev. 13:4–6), and ends with his destruction by the appearing of the Lord in glory (2 Th. 2:8; Rev. 19:19–20). (2) The duration of the “time of the end” is three and one-half years, coinciding with the last half of the seventieth week of Daniel (7:25; 12:7; Rev. 13:5). And (3) this “time of the end” is the “time of Jacob's trouble” (Jer. 30:7); “a time of trouble, such as never was since there was a nation” (Dan. 12:1); “great tribulation, such as has not been since the beginning of the world until this time, no, nor ever shall be” (Mt. 24:21). The NT, especially Revelation, adds many details.

9 And he said, "Go *your way,* Daniel, for the words *are* closed up and
sealed till the time of the end.
10 "Many shall be purified, made
white, and refined, but the wicked
shall do wickedly; and none of the
wicked shall understand, but the wise
shall understand.
11 "And from the time *that* the
daily *sacrifice* is taken away, and the
[a]abomination [b]of desolation is set up,
there shall be one thousand two hundred and ninety days.
12 "Blessed *is* he who waits, and
comes to the [1]one thousand three hundred and thirty-five days.
13 "But you, go *your way* till the
end; for you shall rest, and will arise
to your inheritance at the end of the
days."

11
a See Dan. 9:24, *note*
b *The Beast:* v. 11; Mt. 24:15. (Dan. 7:8; Rev. 19:20)

[1](12:12) Three periods of "days" date from the "abomination" (i.e. the blasphemous assumption of Deity by the beast, v. 11; Mt. 24:15; 2 Th. 2:4): (1) Twelve hundred and sixty days to the destruction of the beast (7:25; 12:7; Rev. 13:5; 19:19–20). This is also the duration of the great tribulation (cp. 12:4, *note*). (2) Dating from the same event is a period of 1290 days, an addition of thirty days (12:11). And (3) again forty-five days are added, and with them the promise of v. 12. No account is directly given of that which occupies the interval of seventy-five days between the end of the tribulation and the full blessing of v. 12. It is suggested that the explanation may be found in the prophetic descriptions of the events following the war of Armageddon (Rev. 16:13–16; see 19:17, *note*). The beast is destroyed and Gentile world dominion ended by the Striking Stone at the end of the 1260 days, but the scene is, so to speak, filled with the debris of the image which the "wind" must carry away before full blessing comes (2:35).

The Book of

HOSEA

Author: Hosea *Theme:* Redeeming Love *Date of writing:* 8th Cent. B.C.

HOSEA, whose name means *the* LORD *saves*, carried on his ministry during the days of four different kings of Judah—Uzziah, Jotham, Ahaz, and Hezekiah; and of Jeroboam II, the king of Israel. Hosea was a contemporary of Amos in Israel, and of Isaiah and Micah in Judah, and his ministry continued after the first, or Assyrian, captivity of the northern kingdom.

The theme of the opening chapters of Hosea's prophecy is the unfaithfulness of Israel, set forth in terms of the marriage relationship, a familiar figure of speech depicting God's relation to His chosen people (Ex. 34:15–16; Lev. 17:7; 20:5–6; Dt. 32:16,21; Isa. 54:5). Israel's forsaking of the LORD was brought home to Hosea in the adulterous acts of his own wife, so that his personal experiences became an allegory of God's experience with Israel. She was not only unfaithful, but her sin also took its character from the exalted relationship into which she had been brought.

The major truths of the book are: (1) God suffers when His people are unfaithful to Him; (2) God cannot condone sin; and (3) God will never cease to love His own and, consequently, He seeks to win back those who have forsaken Him.

The book may be divided as follows:

I. The Prophet's Tragic Experience, 1—3.
II. An Indictment of Israel, 4—8.
III. Retribution on Israel, 9—10.
IV. God's Unceasing Love for Israel, 11:1—13:8.
V. The Ultimate Restoration of Israel, 13:9—14:9.

I. The Prophet's Tragic Experience, 1—3

Introduction

1 THE word of the LORD that came to Hosea the son of Beeri, in the days of [a]Uzziah, [b]Jotham, [c]Ahaz, *and* [d]Hezekiah, kings of Judah, and in the days of [e]Jeroboam the son of Joash, king of Israel.

The marriage: birth of Jezreel

2 When the LORD began to speak by Hosea, the LORD said to Hosea:

"Go, [1]take yourself a wife of
harlotry
And children of harlotry,
For the [f]land has committed
great harlotry
By departing from the LORD."

3 So he went and took Gomer the daughter of Diblaim, and she conceived and bore him a son.

4 Then the LORD said to him:

"Call his name Jezreel,
For in a little *while*
I will avenge the bloodshed of
[g]Jezreel on the house of
Jehu,
And [h]bring an end to the
kingdom of the house of
Israel.
5 It shall come to pass in that
day
That I will break the bow of
Israel in the Valley of
Jezreel."

Birth of Lo-Ruhamah

6 And she conceived again and bore a daughter. Then *God* said to him:

"Call her name [i]Lo-Ruhamah,
For I will no longer have
mercy on the house of Israel,
But I will utterly take them
away.*
7 Yet [j]I will have mercy on the
house of Judah,
Will save them by the LORD
their God,

CHAPTER 1

1
a 2 Chr. 26; Isa. 1:1; Amos 1:1
b 2 Chr. 27; Mic. 1:1
c 2 Chr. 28
d 2 Chr. 29:1–32:33
e 2 Ki. 14:23–29

2
f Dt. 31:16; Jud. 2:17; Ps. 73:27; Jer. 2:13; Ezek. 16:1–59; 23:1–49

4
g Meaning *scattered.* 2 Ki. 10:1–14
h 2 Ki. 17:6, 23; 18:11

6
i Meaning *no mercy.* Isa. 27:11

7
j 2 Ki. 19:34–35

* 1:6 Or *That I may forgive them at all*

---

[1](1:2) God did not command Hosea to take an immoral wife but permitted him to carry out his desire to marry Gomer, warning him that she would be unfaithful, and using the prophet's tragic experience as a basis for portraying God's relation to Israel during a period of unfaithfulness.

Hosea's marriage is no less historical because his children were given symbolic names as a message to Israel (vv. 4,6,9). Cp. Isa. 8:18.

And will not save them by
bow,
Nor by sword or battle,
By horses or horsemen."

Birth of Lo-Ammi

8 Now when she had weaned Lo-
Ruhamah, she conceived and bore a
son.
9 Then *God* said:

"Call his name [a]Lo-Ammi,
For you *are* not My people,
And I will not be your *God*.

Future restoration of Israel (to 2:1)

10 "Yet the number of the children
of [1]Israel
Shall be as the [b]sand of the
sea,
Which cannot be measured or
numbered.
And it shall come to pass
In the place where it was said
to them,
'You *are* not My [c]people,'*
There it shall be said to them,
'*You are* sons of the living
God.'
11 [d]Then the children of Judah
and the children of Israel
Shall be gathered together,
And appoint for themselves
one head;
And they shall come up out of
the land,
For great *will be* the day of
Jezreel!

2 SAY to your brethren, [e]'My
people,'*
And to your sisters, [f]'Mercy*
is shown.'

Chastisement of Israel (2 Ki. 17:1–18)

2 "Bring charges against your
mother, bring charges;
For [2]she *is* [g]not My [h]wife, nor
am I her Husband!
Let her put away her harlotries
from her sight,
And her adulteries from
between her breasts;
3 Lest I [i]strip her naked
And expose her, as in the day
she was [j]born,
And make her like a
wilderness,
And set her like a dry land,
And slay her with thirst.
4 "I will not have mercy on her
children,
For they *are* the children of
harlotry.
5 For their mother has played
the harlot;
She who conceived them has
behaved shamefully.
For she said, 'I will [k]go after
my lovers,
Who give *me* my bread and
my water,
My wool and my linen,
My oil and my drink.'
6 "Therefore, behold,
I will [l]hedge up your way with
thorns,
And wall her in,
So that she cannot find her
paths.
7 She will chase her lovers,
But not overtake them;
Yes, she will seek them, but
not find *them*.
Then she will say,
'I will go and return to my
[m]first husband,
For then *it was* [n]better for me
than now.'
8 For she did not know
That I [o]gave her grain, new
wine, and oil,

9 *a* Meaning *not my people*
10 *b* Gen. 22:17 *c* Rom. 9:26
11 *d* Isa. 11:11–13; Jer. 3:18; 50:4; Ezek. 34:23; 37:15–28
CHAPTER 2
1 *e* Cp. Hos. 1:9 *f* Cp. Hos. 1:6
2 *g* Isa. 50:1 *h* "*Wife*" (of the LORD): vv. 1–23. (Isa. 54:5; Hos. 2:2)
3 *i* Jer. 13:22, 26; Ezek. 16:37–39 *j* Ezek. 16:4–7,22
5 *k* Ezek. 23:5
6 *l* Lam. 3:7,9
7 *m* Isa. 54:5–8 *n* Cp. Ezek. 16:8–14
8 *o* Ezek. 16:19

*
1:10 Hebrew *lo-ammi* (compare verse 9)
2:1 Hebrew *Ammi* (compare 1:9,10) • Hebrew *Ruhamah* (compare 1:6)

[1](1:10) "Israel" in Hosea usually refers to the ten tribes forming the northern kingdom as distinguished from "Judah," the tribes of Judah and Benjamin, forming the southern kingdom which adhered to the Davidic family. Cp. 1 Ki. 12:1–20. The promise of 1:10—2:1 yet awaits fulfillment. See Israel (Gen. 12:2–3; Rom. 11:26, *note*).

[2](2:2) "Wife" of the LORD, Summary: Marriage is one of many figures used in Scripture to emphasize the relationship of God to men. This illustration is used in both OT and NT to picture love, intimacy, privilege, and responsibility. In the OT, as here in vv. 16–23, Israel is described as the wife of the LORD, though now disowned because of disobedience. Nevertheless eventually, upon repentance, Israel will be restored. This relationship is not to be confused with that of the Church to Christ (Jn. 3:29). In the mystery of the divine Trinity both are true. The NT speaks of the Church as a virgin espoused to one husband (2 Cor. 11:1–2), which could never be said of an adulterous wife restored in grace. Israel is, then, to be the restored and forgiven wife of the LORD; the Church is the virgin wife of the Lamb (Jn. 3:29; Rev. 19:6–8). Israel will be the LORD's earthly wife (ch. 2:23); the Church, the Lamb's heavenly bride (Rev. 19:7).

And multiplied her silver and
gold—
Which they prepared for Baal.

9 "Therefore I will return and
take away
My grain in its time
And My new wine in its
season,
And will take back My wool
and My linen,
Given to cover her nakedness.
10 Now I will [a]uncover her
lewdness in the sight of her
lovers,
And no one shall deliver her
from My hand.
11 I will also cause all her mirth
to [b]cease,
Her feast days,
Her New Moons,
Her Sabbaths—
All her appointed feasts.

12 "And I will destroy her vines
and her fig trees,
Of which she has said,
'These *are* my wages that my
lovers have given me.'
So I will make them a forest,
And the beasts of the field
shall eat them.
13 I will punish her
For the days of the [c]Baals to
which she burned incense.
She decked herself with her
earrings and jewelry,
And went after her lovers;
But Me she forgot," says the
LORD.

Restoration of Israel, the adulterous wife

14 "Therefore, behold, I will allure
her,
Will bring her into the
wilderness,
And speak comfort to her.
15 I will give her her vineyards
from there,
And the Valley of [d]Achor as a
door of hope;
She shall sing there,
As in the days of her youth,
As in the day when she came
up from the land of Egypt.

16 "And it shall be, in that day,"
Says the LORD,
"*That* you will call Me [e]'My
Husband,'*
And no longer call Me 'My
Master,'*
17 For I will take from her mouth
the names of the Baals,
And they shall be remembered
by their name no more.
18 In that day I will make a
covenant for them
With the [f]beasts of the field,
With the birds of the air,
And *with* the creeping things
of the ground.
Bow and sword of battle I will
shatter from the earth,
To make them lie down
[g]safely.

19 "I will betroth you to Me
forever;
Yes, I will [1]betroth you to Me
In righteousness and justice,
In lovingkindness and mercy;
20 I will betroth you to Me in
faithfulness,
And you shall know the LORD.

21 "It shall come to pass in that
day
That I will answer," says the
LORD;
"I will answer the heavens,
And they shall answer the
earth.
22 The earth shall answer
With grain,
With new wine,
And with oil;
They shall answer Jezreel.*
23 Then I will [2h]sow her for
Myself in the earth,
And I will have mercy on *her
who had* not obtained
mercy;*
Then I will say to *those who
were* not My [i]people,*
'You *are* My people!'
And they shall say, '*You are*
my God!' "

The future Davidic kingdom, when Israel will fear the LORD

3 THEN the LORD said to me, "Go
again, love a woman *who is* loved

10 *a* Ezek. 16:37
11 *b* Jer. 7:34; 16:9
13 *c* i.e. *heathen gods and idols*
15 *d* i.e. *trouble.* Josh. 7:26; Isa. 65:10
16 *e* v. 7
18 *f* Isa. 11:6–9 *g* Isa. 32:18
23 *h* Amos 9:15 *i* Zech. 13:9; cp. Rom. 9:25–26; Eph. 2:11–22; 1 Pet. 2:10

* 2:16 Hebrew *Ishi* • Hebrew *Baali* 2:22 Literally *God Will Sow* 2:23 Hebrew *lo-ruhamah* • Hebrew *lo-ammi*

[1](2:19) The grace of God is beautifully set forth in the verb "betroth" which signifies, in the original, *to woo a virgin.* Cp. Num. 23:21.

[2](2:23) This verse plays upon the literal meaning of the children's names. See Hos. 1:2, *notes;* cp. Hos. 2:1.

by a lover* and is committing adultery, just like the love of the LORD for
the children of Israel, who look to
other gods and love *the* [a]raisin cakes
of the pagans."
2 So I bought her for myself for
fifteen *shekels* of silver, and one and
one-half [b]homers of barley.
3 And I said to her, "You shall stay
with me many days; you shall not play
the harlot, nor shall you have a man—
so, too, *will I be* toward you."
4 For the children of Israel shall
abide many days [c]without [d]king or
prince, without sacrifice or [1]sacred
pillar, without ephod or teraphim.
5 [2]Afterward the children of Israel
shall [e]return and seek the LORD their
God and David their [f]king. They shall
fear the LORD and His goodness in the
latter days.

II. An Indictment of Israel, 4—8

The LORD's charge against the sinful nation

4 HEAR the word of the LORD,
You children of Israel,
For the LORD *brings* a [g]charge
against the inhabitants of
the land:

"There is no truth or mercy
Or knowledge of God in the
land.
2 *By* swearing and lying,
Killing and stealing and
committing adultery,
They break all restraint,
With bloodshed upon
bloodshed.
3 [h]Therefore the land will mourn;
And everyone who dwells
there will waste away
With the beasts of the field
And the birds of the air;
Even the fish of the sea will be
taken away.
4 "Now let no man contend, or
rebuke another;
For your people *are* like those
who [i]contend with the
priest.
5 Therefore you shall stumble in
the day;
The prophet also shall stumble
with you in the night;
And I will destroy your
mother.

Israel's willful ignorance

6 [j]My people are destroyed for
[3]lack of knowledge.
Because you have rejected
knowledge,
I also will reject you from
being priest for Me;
[k]Because you have forgotten
the law of your God,
I also will forget your children.
7 "The more they increased,
The more they sinned against
Me;
[l]I will change* their glory*
into shame.
8 They eat up the sin of My
people;
They set their heart on their
iniquity.
9 And it shall be: [m]like people,
like priest.
So I will punish them for their
ways,
And reward them for their
deeds.
10 For they shall [n]eat, but not
have enough;
They shall commit harlotry,
but not increase;
Because they have ceased
obeying the LORD.

CHAPTER 3

1

a Heb. *ashishah.* Cakes of raisins were used in some of the sacrificial feasts of the Canaanites

2

b See Weights and Measures (OT), 2 Chr. 2:10, *note*

4

c *Kingdom* (OT): vv. 4–5; Joel 3:12. (Gen. 1:26; Zech. 12:8, *note*)

d Hos. 10:3; cp. Jn. 19:15

5

e *Israel* (prophecies): vv. 4–5; Joel 3:1. (Gen. 12:2; Rom. 11:26, *note*)

f *Christ* (second advent): vv. 4–5; Mic. 4:7. (Dt. 30:3; Acts 1:11, *note*)

CHAPTER 4

1

g Hos. 12:2; Mic. 6:2; cp. Jer. 25:31

3

h Jer. 4:28; 12:4; Amos 5:16; 8:8; Zeph. 1:3

4

i Dt. 17:12

4:6 *j* Isa. 5:13 *k* Ezek. 22:26 **4:7** *l* 1 Sam. 2:30; Mal. 2:9 **4:9** *m* Jer. 5:30–31; 2 Tim. 4:3–4 **4:10** *n* Lev. 26:26; Hag. 1:6

*

3:1 Literally *friend* or *husband* **4:7** Following Masoretic Text, Septuagint, and Vulgate; scribal tradition, Syriac, and Targum read *They will change.* • Following Masoretic Text, Septuagint, Syriac, Targum, and Vulgate; scribal tradition reads *My glory.*

[1](3:4) This prediction has been remarkably fulfilled in the condition of Israel since the time of Christ. Scattered, without political unity under a king or a prince, and performing no sacrifices since the destruction of the temple by the Romans in A.D. 70, they have yet retained their identity and avoided idolatrous worship of sacred stones or idols.

[2](3:5) Chapter 3 is one of the classic OT passages describing Israel's past, present, and future. Her idolatrous past is illustrated by Gomer's unfaithfulness to Hosea (vv. 1–2), despite which Hosea is commanded to love her and buy her back "as the LORD loves the Israelites," a love which led Him to pay the purchase price of the blood of the cross to redeem Israel, the basis of her restoration. The present condition of Israel is illustrated and plainly prophesied in vv. 3–4. Her future is declared in v. 5, showing her repentance toward God who, in His faithfulness, will restore her.

[3](4:6) This is one of the best known and most frequently quoted passages in Hosea.

11 "Harlotry, wine, and new wine
enslave the heart.

Israel's persistent idolatry

12 My people ask counsel from
their wooden *idols,*
And their staff [a]informs them.
For the spirit of harlotry has
caused *them* to stray,
And they have played the
harlot against their God.
13 They offer [b]sacrifices on the
mountaintops,
And burn incense on the hills,
Under oaks, poplars, and
terebinths,
Because their shade *is* good.
[c]Therefore your daughters
commit harlotry,
And your brides commit
adultery.

14 "I will not punish your
daughters when they commit
harlotry,
Nor your brides when they
commit adultery;
For *the men* themselves go
apart with harlots,
And offer sacrifices with a
ritual harlot.*
Therefore people *who* do not
understand will be trampled.

15 "Though you, Israel, play the
harlot,
Let not Judah offend.
Do not come up to Gilgal,
Nor go up to [d]Beth Aven,
Nor swear an oath, *saying,* 'As
the LORD lives'—

16 "For Israel is [e]stubborn
Like a stubborn calf;
Now the LORD will let them
forage
Like a lamb in open country.

17 [f]"Ephraim *is* joined to [g]idols,
[h]Let him alone.
18 Their drink is rebellion,
They commit harlotry
continually.
Her rulers dearly love
dishonor.*
19 The wind has wrapped her up
in its wings,
And they shall be ashamed
because of their sacrifices.

The LORD's face is withdrawn

5

"HEAR this, O priests!
Take heed, O house of Israel!
Give ear, O house of the king!
For yours *is* the judgment,
Because you have been a snare
to Mizpah
And a net spread on Tabor.
2 The revolters are deeply
involved in slaughter,
Though I rebuke them all.
3 I know Ephraim,
And Israel is not hidden from
Me;
For now, O Ephraim, you
commit harlotry;
Israel is defiled.

4 "They do not direct their deeds
Toward turning to their God,
For the spirit of harlotry is in
their midst,
And they do not know the
LORD.
5 The [i]pride of Israel testifies to
his face;
Therefore Israel and Ephraim
stumble in their iniquity;
Judah also stumbles with
them.

6 "With their flocks and herds
They shall go to [j]seek the
LORD,
But they will not find *Him;*
He has withdrawn Himself
from them.
7 They have dealt treacherously
with the LORD,
For they have begotten pagan
children.
Now a New Moon shall devour
them and their heritage.

8 [k]"Blow the ram's horn in Gibeah,
The trumpet in Ramah!
Cry aloud *at* [d]Beth Aven,
'*Look* behind you, O Benjamin!'
9 Ephraim shall be desolate in
the day of rebuke;
Among the tribes of Israel I
make known what is sure.

10 "The princes of Judah are like
those who [l]remove a
landmark;
I will pour out my wrath on
them like water.
11 Ephraim is [m]oppressed *and*
broken in judgment,
Because he willingly walked
by *human* precept.
12 Therefore I *will be* to Ephraim
like a moth,
And to the house of Judah like
[n]rottenness.

12
a i.e. *speaks like an oracle*
13
b Isa. 1:29; 57:5,7; Ezek. 6:13; 20:28
c Amos 7:17; Rom. 1:28–32
15
d Josh. 7:2; Hos. 10:8
16
e Jer. 3:6; 7:24; 8:5; Zech. 7:11
17
f Hosea uses this name for Israel, the northern kingdom, 37 times. See 6:4, *marg.*
g Cp. Hos. 14:8
h Mt. 15:14
CHAPTER 5
5
i Hos. 7:10
6
j Prov. 1:28; Isa. 1:15; Jer. 11:11; Ezek. 8:18; Mic. 3:4; Jn. 7:34
8
k Hos. 8:1; Joel 2:1
10
l Dt. 19:14; 27:17
11
m Dt. 28:33
12
n Prov. 12:4

*
4:14 Compare Deuteronomy 23:18 4:18 Hebrew is difficult; a Jewish tradition reads *Her rulers shamefully love, 'Give!'.*

13 "When Ephraim saw his
sickness,
And Judah *saw* his wound,
Then Ephraim [a]went to
Assyria
And sent to King Jareb;
Yet he cannot cure you,
Nor heal you of your wound.
14 For I *will be* like a [b]lion to
Ephraim,
And like a young lion to the
house of Judah.
I, *even* I, will tear *them* and go
away;
I will take *them* away, and no
one shall rescue.

A remnant in the last days

15 I will return again to My place
[1]Till they acknowledge their
offense.
Then they will seek My face;
In their affliction they will
earnestly seek Me."

6

[c]COME, and let us [d]return to
the LORD;
For He has torn, but He will
[e]heal us;
He has stricken, but He will
bind us up.
2 After two days He will revive
us;
On the third day He will raise
us up,
That we may live in His sight.
3 Let us know,
Let us pursue the knowledge
of the LORD.
His going forth is established
as the morning;
He will come to us like the
rain,
Like the latter *and* former rain
to the earth.

The LORD laments Ephraim's (Israel's) sin

4 "O [f]Ephraim, what shall I do to
you?
O Judah, what shall I do to
you?
For your faithfulness is like a
morning cloud,
And like the early dew it goes
away.
5 Therefore I have hewn *them*
by the prophets,
I have slain them by the words
of My mouth;
And your judgments *are like*
light *that* goes forth.
6 For I desire [g]mercy and [h]not
sacrifice,
And the knowledge of God
more than burnt offerings.

7 "But like men* they
transgressed the covenant;
There they dealt treacherously
with Me.
8 [i]Gilead *is* a city of evildoers
And defiled with blood.
9 As bands of robbers lie in wait
for a man,
So the company of [j]priests
[k]murder on the way to
Shechem;
Surely they commit [l]lewdness.
10 I have seen a horrible thing in
the house of Israel:
There *is* the harlotry of
Ephraim;
Israel is defiled.
11 Also, O Judah, a [m]harvest is
appointed for you,
When I return the captives of
My people.

Ephraim's iniquity

7

"WHEN I would have healed
Israel,
Then the iniquity of Ephraim
was uncovered,
And the wickedness of
[n]Samaria.
For they have committed
fraud;
A thief comes in;
A band of robbers takes spoil
outside.
2 They do not consider in their
hearts
That I [o]remember all their
wickedness;
Now their own deeds have
surrounded them;
They are before My face.
3 They make a [p]king glad with
their wickedness,
And [q]princes with their lies.

4 "They *are* all adulterers.
Like an oven heated by a
baker—
He ceases stirring *the fire* after
kneading the dough,
Until it is leavened.
5 In the day of our king

13
a Hos. 7:11; 10:6
14
b Hos. 13:7–8
CHAPTER 6
1
c Isa. 1:18
d See Rom. 11:5, *note*
e Hos. 14:4
4
f Meaning *fruitful.* Hos. 11:8
6
g Mt. 9:13; 12:7
h Isa. 1:12–13; Mic. 6:6–8
8
i Hos. 12:11
9
j Hos. 5:1
k Jer. 7:9–10
l Ezek. 22:9
11
m Cp. Jer. 51:33; Joel 3:13
CHAPTER 7
1
n Ezek. 23:4–8
2
o Hos. 5:3
3
p Hos. 1:1
q Mic. 7:3

*6:7 Or *like Adam*

[1](5:15) Taken with Mt. 23:37–39, this passage gives in broad outline the course of Israel's future restoration to God.

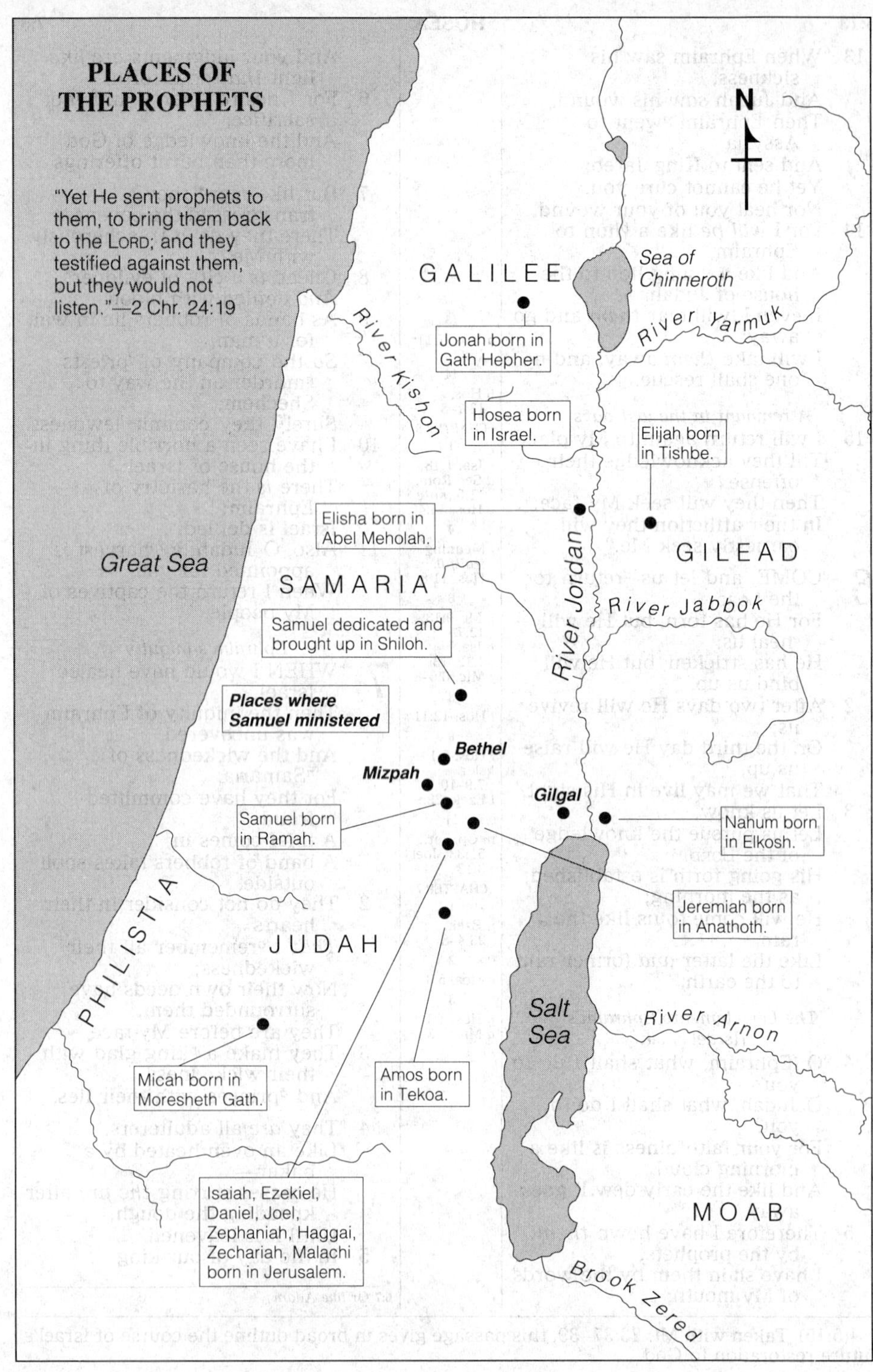
PLACES OF THE PROPHETS
"Yet He sent prophets to them, to bring them back to the LORD; and they testified against them, but they would not listen."—2 Chr. 24:19
N
GALILEE
Sea of Chinneroth
River Yarmuk
River Kishon
Jonah born in Gath Hepher.
Hosea born in Israel.
Elijah born in Tishbe.
Elisha born in Abel Meholah.
GILEAD
River Jordan
Great Sea
SAMARIA
River Jabbok
Samuel dedicated and brought up in Shiloh.
Places where Samuel ministered
Bethel
Mizpah
Gilgal
Samuel born in Ramah.
Nahum born in Elkosh.
Jeremiah born in Anathoth.
PHILISTIA
JUDAH
Salt Sea
River Arnon
Micah born in Moresheth Gath.
Amos born in Tekoa.
Isaiah, Ezekiel, Daniel, Joel, Zephaniah, Haggai, Zechariah, Malachi born in Jerusalem.
MOAB
Brook Zered

Princes have made *him* sick,
inflamed with [a]wine;
He stretched out his hand with
[b]scoffers.
6 They prepare their heart like
an oven,
While they lie in wait;
Their baker* sleeps all night;
In the morning it burns like a
flaming fire.
7 They are all hot, like an oven,
And have devoured their
judges;
All their kings have fallen.
[c]None among them calls upon
[d]Me.
8 "Ephraim has [e]mixed himself
among the peoples;
Ephraim is a cake unturned.
9 Aliens have devoured his
strength,
But he does [f]not know *it;*
Yes, gray hairs are here and
there on him,
Yet he does not know *it.*
10 And the [g]pride of Israel
testifies to his face,
But they do not return to the
LORD their God,
Nor seek Him for all this.

11 [h]"Ephraim also is like a silly
dove, without sense—
They call to [i]Egypt,
They go to [j]Assyria.
12 Wherever they go, I will
[k]spread My net on them;
I will bring them down like
birds of the air;
I will chastise them
According to what their
congregation has heard.
13 "Woe to them, for they have
fled from Me!
Destruction to them,
Because they have
transgressed against Me!
Though I [l]redeemed them,
Yet they have spoken lies
against Me.
14 They did [m]not cry out to Me
with their heart
When they wailed upon their
beds.

"They assemble together for*
grain and new [n]wine,
They rebel against Me;*
15 Though I disciplined *and*
strengthened their arms,
Yet they devise evil against
Me;

5
a Isa. 28:1
b Isa. 28:14
7
c Isa. 64:7
d Cp. Jer. 10:25
8
e Ps. 106:35
9
f Isa. 42:25
10
g Hos. 5:5
11
h Hos. 11:11
i Isa. 30:3
j Hos. 5:13; 8:9
12
k Ezek. 12:13
13
l Ex. 18:18
14
m Job 35:9–10; Ps. 78:36; Jer. 3:10; Zech. 7:5
n Amos 2:8
16
o Dt. 28:68; Hos. 8:13; 9:3
CHAPTER 8
2
p Hos. 5:15
4
q 1 Ki. 12:20; 2 Ki. 15:23,25
6
r Isa. 40:19
7
s Cp. Hos. 10:13
t Hos. 7:9

16 They return, *but* not to the
Most High;*
They are like a treacherous
bow.
Their princes shall fall by the
sword
For the cursings of their
tongue.
This *shall be* their derision in
the land of [o]Egypt.

Reaping the whirlwind

8 "*SET* the trumpet* to your
mouth!
He shall come like an eagle
against the house of the
LORD,
Because they have
transgressed My covenant
And rebelled against My law.
2 [p]Israel will cry to Me,
'My God, we know You!'
3 Israel has rejected the good;
The enemy will pursue him.

4 [q]"They set up kings, but not by
Me;
They made princes, but I did
not acknowledge *them.*
From their silver and gold
They made idols for
themselves—
That they might be cut off.
5 Your calf is rejected, O
Samaria!
My anger is aroused against
them—
How long until they attain to
innocence?
6 For from Israel *is* even this:
A [r]workman made it, and it *is*
not God;
But the calf of Samaria shall
be broken to pieces.

7 "They [s]sow the wind,
And reap the whirlwind.
The stalk has no bud;
It shall never produce meal.
If it should produce,
[t]Aliens would swallow it up.
8 Israel is swallowed up;
Now they are among the
Gentiles
Like a vessel in which *is* no
pleasure.

*
7:6 Following Masoretic Text and Vulgate; Syriac and Targum read *Their anger;* Septuagint reads *Ephraim.* 7:14 Following Masoretic Text and Targum; Vulgate reads *thought upon;* Septuagint reads *slashed themselves for* (compare 1 Kings 18:28). • Following Masoretic Text, Syriac, and Targum; Septuagint omits *They rebel against Me;* Vulgate reads *They departed from Me.* 7:16 Or *upward* 8:1 Hebrew *shophar,* ram's horn

9 For they have gone up to
[a]Assyria,
Like a wild donkey alone by
itself;
Ephraim has hired lovers.
10 Yes, though they have hired
among the nations,
Now I will gather them;
And they shall sorrow a little,*
Because of the burden* of the
king of princes.

11 "Because Ephraim has made
many altars for sin,
They have become for him
altars for sinning.
12 I have written for him the
[b]great things of My law,
But they were considered a
strange thing.
13 *For* the sacrifices of My
offerings they sacrifice flesh
and eat *it*,
But the LORD does [c]not accept
them.
[d]Now He will remember their
iniquity and punish their
sins.
They shall return to Egypt.

14 "For Israel has [e]forgotten his
Maker,
And has built temples;*
Judah also has multiplied
fortified [f]cities;
But I will send fire upon his
cities,
And it shall devour his
palaces."

III. Retribution on Israel, 9—10

Ephraim punished and cast away

9 DO [g]not rejoice, O Israel, with
joy like *other* peoples,
For you have played the harlot
against your God.
You have made love *for* hire
on every threshing floor.
2 The threshing floor and the
winepress
Shall not feed them,
And the new wine shall fail in
her.

3 They shall not dwell in the
[h]LORD's land,
But [i]Ephraim shall return to
Egypt,
And shall [j]eat unclean *things*
in Assyria.
4 They shall not offer wine
offerings to the LORD,
Nor shall their [k]sacrifices be
pleasing to Him.
It shall be like bread of
mourners to them;
All who eat it shall be defiled.
For their bread *shall be* for
their *own* life;
It shall not come into the
house of the LORD.

5 What will you do in the
appointed day,
And in the day of the feast of
the LORD?
6 For indeed they are gone
because of destruction.
Egypt shall gather them up;
Memphis shall bury them.
[l]Nettles shall possess their
valuables of silver;
Thorns *shall be* in their tents.

7 The days of punishment have
come;
The days of recompense have
come.
Israel [m]knows!
The prophet *is* a [n]fool,
The spiritual man *is* insane,
Because of the greatness of
your iniquity and great
enmity.
8 The [o]watchman of Ephraim *is*
with my God;
But the prophet *is* a fowler's*
snare in all his ways—
Enmity in the house of his
God.
9 They are deeply corrupted,
As in the days of [p]Gibeah.
He will remember their
iniquity;
He will punish their sins.

10 "I found Israel
Like grapes in the [q]wilderness;
I saw your fathers
As the [r]firstfruits on the fig
tree in its first season.
But they went to [s]Baal Peor,
And separated themselves *to*
that shame;
They became an abomination
like the thing they loved.
11 *As for* Ephraim, their glory
shall fly away like a bird—
No birth, no pregnancy, and
no conception!
12 Though they bring up their
children,
Yet I will bereave them to the
last man.

9
a Hos. 7:11; 12:1
12
b Dt. 4:6–8; Ps. 119:18; 147:19–20
13
c Jer. 6:20; Hos. 6:6; 9:4
d Hos. 9:9; Amos 8:7
14
e Dt. 32:18
f Num. 32:17; 2 Ki. 18:13
CHAPTER 9
1
g Isa. 22:12–13
3
h Lev. 25:23; Jer. 2:7; 16:18
i Hos. 11:5
j Ezek. 4:13; cp. Dan. 1:8
4
k Hos. 8:13; Amos 5:22
6
l Isa. 5:6; 32:13; 34:13; Hos. 10:8
7
m Isa. 10:3; cp. Lk. 19:44
n Lam. 2:14; Ezek. 13:3–10
8
o Jer. 6:17; 31:6; Ezek. 3:17; 33:7
9
p Jud. 19:1–30
10
q Jer. 2:2
r Isa. 28:4; Mic. 7:1
s Num. 25:3; Ps. 106:28

*8:10 Or *begin to diminish* • Or *oracle* 8:14 Or *palaces* 9:8 That is, one who catches birds in a trap or snare

Yes, woe to them when I
depart from them!
13 Just as I saw Ephraim like
[a]Tyre, planted in a pleasant
place,
So Ephraim will bring out his
children to the murderer."

14 Give them, O LORD—
What will You give?
Give them a miscarrying
womb
And dry breasts!

15 "All their wickedness *is* in
[b]Gilgal,
For there I hated them.
Because of the evil of their
deeds
I will drive them from My
house;
I will love them no more.
All their princes *are*
[c]rebellious.
16 Ephraim is [d]stricken,
Their root is dried up;
They shall bear no fruit.
Yes, were they to bear
children,
I would kill the darlings of
their womb."

17 My God will [e]cast them away,
Because they did not obey
Him;
And they shall be [f]wanderers
among the nations.

"Break up your fallow ground" (10:12)

10 ISRAEL empties *his* vine;
He brings forth fruit for
himself.
According to the multitude of
his [g]fruit
He has increased the altars;
According to the bounty of his
land
They have embellished *his*
sacred pillars.
2 Their heart is divided;
Now they are held guilty.
He will break down their
altars;
He will ruin their sacred
pillars.

3 For now they say,
"We have [h]no king,
Because we did not fear the
LORD.
And as for a king, what would
he do for us?"
4 They have spoken words,
Swearing falsely in making a
covenant.

13
a Ezek. 27:3–4
15
b Hos. 4:15; 12:11
c Hos. 5:2
16
d Hos. 5:11
17
e 2 Ki. 17:20; Zech. 10:6
f Lev. 26:33
CHAPTER 10
1
g Cp. Hos. 14:8
3
h Hos. 13:11
4
i Heb. *rosh, a poisonous plant.* Cp. Dt. 29:18
5
j 1 Ki. 12:28–29; Hos. 8:5–6; 13:2
k Hos. 9:11
6
l Hos. 5:13
8
m Hos. 4:15; see Jud. 3:7 and 1 Ki. 3:2, *notes*
n 1 Ki. 13:34
o Lk. 23:30; Rev. 6:16
9
p Hos. 9:9
q Jud. 20
11
r Jer. 50:11
12
s Jer. 4:3
t Hos. 6:3
u Or *teaches you righteousness*

Thus judgment springs up like
[i]hemlock in the furrows of
the field.

5 The inhabitants of Samaria
fear
Because of the [j]calf* of Beth
Aven.
For its people mourn for it,
And its priests shriek for it—
Because its [k]glory has
departed from it.
6 *The idol* also shall be carried
to Assyria
As a present for King [l]Jareb.
Ephraim shall receive shame,
And Israel shall be ashamed of
his own counsel.

7 *As for* Samaria, her king is cut
off
Like a twig on the water.
8 Also the [m]high places of Aven,
the [n]sin of Israel,
Shall be destroyed.
The thorn and thistle shall
grow on their altars;
They shall say to the
mountains, [o]"Cover us!"
And to the hills, "Fall on us!"

9 "O Israel, you have sinned from
the days of [p]Gibeah;
There they stood.
The [q]battle in Gibeah against
the children of iniquity*
Did not overtake them.
10 When *it is* My desire, I will
chasten them.
Peoples shall be gathered
against them
When I bind them for their two
transgressions.*
11 Ephraim *is* a trained [r]heifer
That loves to thresh *grain;*
But I harnessed her fair neck,
I will make Ephraim pull *a
plow.*
Judah shall plow;
Jacob shall break his clods."

12 Sow for yourselves
righteousness;
Reap in mercy;
[s]Break up your fallow ground,
For *it is* time to seek the LORD,
Till He [t]comes and [u]rains
righteousness on you.

13 You have plowed wickedness;
You have reaped iniquity.

*
10:5 Literally *calves* **10:9** So read many Hebrew manuscripts, Septuagint, and Vulgate; Masoretic Text reads *unruliness.* **10:10** Or *in their two habitations*

You have eaten the fruit of
lies,
Because you [a]trusted in your
own way,
In the multitude of your
mighty men.
14 Therefore tumult shall arise
among your people,
And all your fortresses shall be
plundered
As [b]Shalman plundered Beth
Arbel in the day of battle—
A mother dashed in pieces
upon *her* children.
15 Thus it shall be done to you, O
Bethel,
Because of your great
wickedness.
At dawn the king of Israel
Shall be cut off utterly.

IV. God's Unceasing Love for Israel, 11:1—13:8

The LORD's past relationship with His people

11 "WHEN Israel *was* a child, I
loved him,
And out of Egypt I [c]called
[d]My [1e]son.
2 *As* they called them,*
So they [f]went from them;*
They sacrificed to the Baals,
And burned incense to carved
images.
3 "I taught Ephraim to walk,
Taking them by their [g]arms;*
But they did not know that I
healed them.
4 I drew them with gentle
cords,*
With bands of love,
And [h]I was to them as those
who take the yoke from
their neck.*
I stooped *and* fed them.

5 "He shall not return to the land
of Egypt;
But the Assyrian shall be his
king,
Because they refused to repent.
6 And the sword shall slash in
his cities,
Devour his districts,
And consume *them,*
Because of their own counsels.
7 My people are bent on
backsliding from Me.

13
a See Ps. 2:12, *note*
14
b Or *Shalmaneser,* 2 Ki. 17:3; 18:9
CHAPTER 11
1
c Election (corporate): v. 1; Mt. 24:22. (Dt. 7:6; 1 Pet. 5:13, *note*)
d Ex. 4:22; Mt. 2:15
e Christ (first advent): v. 1; Mic. 5:2. (Gen. 3:15; Acts 1:11, *note*)
2
f 2 Ki. 17:13–15
3
g Dt. 32:10–11
4
h Lev. 26:13
8
i Gen. 14:8; 19:24–25; Dt. 29:23
j See Zech. 8:14, *note*
11
k Isa. 11:11
l Ezek. 34:27–28
CHAPTER 12
1
m Job 15:2–3; Hos. 8:7
n Hos. 8:9

Though they call to the Most
High,*
None at all exalt *Him.*
8 "How can I give you up,
Ephraim?
How can I hand you over,
Israel?
How can I make you like
[i]Admah?
How can I set you like
Zeboiim?
My heart churns within Me;
My [j]sympathy is stirred.
9 I will not execute the
fierceness of My anger;
I will not again destroy
Ephraim.
For I *am* God, and not man,
The Holy One in your midst;
And I will not come with
terror.*
10 "They shall walk after the LORD.
He will roar like a lion.
When He roars,
Then *His* sons shall come
trembling from the west;
11 They shall come trembling like
a bird from Egypt,
Like a dove from the land of
[k]Assyria.
And I will [l]let them dwell in
their houses,"
Says the LORD.
12 "Ephraim has encircled Me with
lies,
And the house of Israel with
deceit;
But Judah still walks with God,
Even with the Holy One* *who
is* faithful.

Further rebuke of Ephraim's sin

12 "EPHRAIM [m]feeds on the
wind,
And pursues the east wind;
He daily increases lies and
desolation.
Also they make a covenant
with the [n]Assyrians,

*
11:2 Following Masoretic Text and Vulgate; Septuagint reads *Just as I called them;* Targum interprets as *I sent prophets to a thousand of them.* • Following Masoretic Text, Targum, and Vulgate; Septuagint reads *from My face.* 11:3 Some Hebrew manuscripts, Septuagint, Syriac, and Vulgate read *My arms.* 11:4 Literally *cords of a man* • Literally *jaws* 11:7 Or *upward* 11:9 Or *I will not enter a city* 11:12 Or *holy ones*

[1](11:1) This is a reference not only to the exodus of Israel from Egypt but also to the fact that all of God's dealings with Israel were based upon the love that He would show in calling His Son, the Lord Jesus Christ, back from the comparative safety of Egypt in order that He might suffer and die to accomplish His great redemptive work. Cp. Mt. 2:15.

And oil is carried to Egypt.

2 "The LORD also *brings* a [q]charge
against Judah,
And will punish Jacob
according to his ways;
According to his deeds He will
recompense him.
3 He took his brother by the
[b]heel in the womb,
And in his strength he
[c]struggled with God.
4 Yes, he struggled with the
[d]Angel and prevailed;
He wept, and sought favor
from Him.
He found Him *in* [e]Bethel,
And there He spoke to us—
5 That is, the LORD God of hosts.
The LORD *is* His [f]memorable
name.
6 So you, by *the help of* your
God, [g]return;
Observe mercy and justice,
And wait on your God
continually.

7 "A cunning Canaanite!
Deceitful scales *are* in his
hand;
He loves to oppress.
8 And Ephraim said,
'Surely I have become rich,
I have found wealth for myself;
In all my labors
They shall find in me no
iniquity that *is* sin.'
9 "But I *am* the LORD your God,
Ever since the land of Egypt;
I will again make you dwell in
[h]tents,
As in the days of the appointed
feast.
10 I have also spoken by the
[i]prophets,
And have multiplied visions;
I have given symbols through
the witness of the prophets."
11 Though [j]Gilead *has* idols—
Surely they are vanity—
Though they sacrifice bulls in
[k]Gilgal,
Indeed their altars *shall be*
heaps in the furrows of the
field.
12 Jacob [l]fled to the country of
Syria;
[m]Israel served for a spouse,
And for a wife he tended
sheep.
13 [n]By a prophet the LORD brought
Israel out of Egypt,
And by a prophet he was
preserved.
14 Ephraim [o]provoked *Him* to
anger most bitterly;
Therefore his Lord will leave
the guilt of his bloodshed
upon him,
And return his reproach upon
him.

Ephraim's continuing wickedness

13 [p]WHEN Ephraim spoke,
trembling,
He exalted *himself* in Israel;
But when he offended through
Baal *worship,* he died.
2 Now they sin more and more,
And have made for themselves
molded images,
Idols of their silver, according
to their skill;
All of it *is* the work of
craftsmen.
They say of them,
"Let the men who sacrifice*
[q]kiss the [r]calves!"
3 Therefore they shall be like the
morning cloud
And like the early dew that
passes away,
Like chaff blown off from a
threshing floor
And like smoke from a
chimney.

4 "Yet I *am* the LORD your God
Ever since the land of Egypt,
And you shall know no God
but Me;
For *there is* no [s]savior besides
Me.
5 I knew you in the wilderness,
In the land of great drought.
6 When they had pasture, they
were filled;
They were filled and their
heart was exalted;
Therefore they forgot Me.
7 "So I will be to them like a lion;
Like a leopard by the road I
will lurk;
8 I will meet them [t]like a bear
deprived *of her cubs;*
I will tear open their rib cage,
And there I will devour them
like a lion.
The wild beast shall tear them.

V. The Ultimate Restoration of Israel, 13:9—14:9

9 "O Israel, you are destroyed,*

2
a Hos. 4:1; Mic. 6:2
3
b Gen. 25:26
c Gen. 32:24–28
4
d See Heb. 1:4, *note*
e Gen. 28:12–19; 35:9–15
5
f Ex. 3:15
6
g Hos. 14:1; Mic. 6:8
9
h Cp. Zech. 14:16–19; Rev. 7:15–17
10
i 2 Ki. 17:13
11
j Hos. 6:8
k Hos. 9:15
12
l Gen. 28:5; Dt. 26:5
m Gen. 29:20,28
13
n Ex. 12:50–51; 13:3; Ps. 77:20; Isa. 63:11–12; Mic. 6:4
14
o Ezek. 18:10–13; cp. 1 Ki. 12:25-13:5; 15:30; 2 Ki. 17:11–23
CHAPTER 13
1
p Cp. Josh. 4:14; Job 29:21–25
2
q An act of homage. Cp. 1 Ki. 19:18; Ps. 2:12
r Hos. 10:5
4
s Isa. 45:21–22; 1 Tim. 2:5
8
t 2 Sam. 17:8; Prov. 17:12

*13:2 Or *those who offer human sacrifice*
13:9 Literally *it* or *he destroyed you*

But your help* *is* from Me.
10 I will be your King;*
Where *is any other,*
That he may save you in all
your cities?
And your judges to whom you
said,
'Give me a king and princes'?
11 I [1]gave you a king in My
anger,
And [2]took *him* away in My
wrath.

12 "The iniquity of Ephraim *is*
bound up;
His sin *is* stored up.
13 The sorrows of a woman in
childbirth shall come upon
him.
He *is* an unwise son,
For he should not stay long
where children are born.

14 "I will ransom them from the
power of the [a]grave;*
I will [b]redeem them from
death.
O [c]Death, I will be your
plagues!*
O [d]Grave,* I will be your
destruction!*
[3]Pity is hidden from My eyes.

15 Though he is fruitful among
his brethren,
An east wind shall come;
The wind of the LORD shall
come up from the
wilderness.
Then his spring shall become
dry,
And his fountain shall be dried
up.
He shall plunder the treasury
of every desirable prize.
16 Samaria is held guilty,*
For she has [e]rebelled against
her God.
They shall fall by the sword,
Their infants shall be dashed
in pieces,
And their women with child
[f]ripped open.

Israel's future blessing, when God's anger is turned away

14 O ISRAEL, [g]return to the
LORD your God,
For you have stumbled
because of your iniquity;
2 Take words with you,
And return to the LORD.
Say to Him,
"Take away all iniquity;
Receive *us* graciously,
For we will offer the
[h]sacrifices* of our lips.
3 Assyria shall [i]not save us,
We will not ride on horses,
Nor will we say anymore to
the work of our hands,
'*You are* our gods.'
For in You the fatherless finds
mercy."

4 "I will heal their [j]backsliding,
I will [k]love them freely,
For My anger has turned away
from [4]him.
5 I will be like the [l]dew to
Israel;
He shall grow like the lily,
And lengthen his roots like
Lebanon.
6 His branches shall spread;
His [m]beauty shall be like an
olive tree,
And his fragrance like
Lebanon.
7 Those who dwell under his
shadow shall return;
They shall be revived *like*
grain,
And grow like a vine.
Their scent* *shall be* like the
wine of Lebanon.

8 "Ephraim *shall say,*
'What have I to do anymore
with idols?'
I have heard and observed
him.
I *am* like a green cypress tree;

14
a Resurrection: v. 14; Mt. 9:25. (2 Ki. 4:35; 1 Cor. 15:52, *note*)
b Redemption (redeeming relative type): v. 14. (Gen. 48:16; Isa. 59:20, *note*)
c 1 Cor. 15:55
d See Hab. 2:5, *note*
16
e 2 Ki. 18:12
f 2 Ki. 15:16
CHAPTER 14
1
g Hos. 12:6; Joel 2:13
2
h i.e. *praise.* Ps. 69:30–31; Heb. 13:15
3
i Hos. 7:11; 10:13; 12:1
4
j Jer. 14:7
k Eph. 1:6
5
l Job 29:19; Prov. 19:12
6
m Ps. 52:8; 128:3

*
• Literally *in your help* **13:10** Septuagint, Syriac, Targum, and Vulgate read *Where is your king?* **13:14** Or *Sheol* • Septuagint reads *where is your punishment?* • Or *Sheol* • Septuagint reads *Where is your sting?* **13:16** Septuagint reads *shall be disfigured* **14:2** Literally *bull calves;* Septuagint reads *fruit.* **14:7** Literally *remembrance*

[1](13:11) This doubtless refers either to Saul (1 Sam. 15:22–23) or to Jeroboam I (1 Ki. 14:14–16; 15:30).
[2](13:11) The allusion appears to be to the northern kingdom's last king, Hoshea.
[3](13:14) God will not change His announced purpose.
[4](14:4) Hosea closes his book with the heartening word of forgiveness. When Israel responds to the LORD's loving plea to return to Him (vv. 1–3), then will follow the gracious healing of their backsliding, the free bestowal of His love, the turning away of His anger, the future blessing of their restoration, and their final repudiation of idolatry (vv. 4–8).

[a]Your fruit is found in Me."

9 Who *is* wise?
Let him understand these things.
Who is prudent?
Let him know them.
For the ways of the LORD *are* right;
The righteous walk in them,
But transgressors stumble in them.

8 *a* Jn. 15:4; cp. Hos. 10:1; Jas. 1:17

The Book of

JOEL

Author: Joel *Theme:* Day of the LORD *Date of writing:* 9th or 8th Cent. B.C.

THE Book of Joel, whose name means *the LORD (Jehovah) is God,* is difficult to date because no Israelite king or foreign nation is mentioned in it. Many think that it was written in the time of Jehoash. It describes the invasion of Judah by a plague of locusts that destroyed everything in its path and impoverished the people (1:1—2:11). In this situation the prophet urged the people to turn to the LORD (2:12–17). God's merciful answer follows. The passage at 2:18–19 shows the LORD accepting the repentance of the people and promising that He will not only remove from them the plague of locusts (2:20), but that He will also restore to them all that the locusts have eaten (2:23–25). In 2:28ff. the prophet looks far into the future at coming judgment and coming joys. The locust invasion, now only a matter of history, may be taken as a harbinger of invasions of human armies which are yet to come. Great blessings which God promises to pour out upon His people in the latter days are described.

Joel may be divided into three parts:

I. The Present Chastisement and Its Removal, 1:1—2:27.
II. The Promise of the Spirit, 2:28–29.
III. The Future Deliverance in the Coming Day of the LORD, 2:30—3:21.

I. The Present Chastisement and Its Removal, 1:1—2:27

Introduction

1 THE word of the LORD that came to [a]Joel the son of Pethuel.

2 Hear this, you elders,
And give ear, all you inhabitants of the land!
Has *anything like* this happened in your days,
Or even in the days of your fathers?
3 [b]Tell your children about it,
Let your children *tell* their children,
And their children another generation.

Desolation by locusts

4 What the [1c]chewing locust* left, the swarming [d]locust has eaten;
What the swarming locust left, the crawling locust has eaten;
And what the crawling locust left, the consuming locust has eaten.

5 Awake, you [e]drunkards, and weep;
And wail, all you drinkers of wine,
Because of the new wine,
For it has been cut off from your mouth.
6 For a [f]nation has come up against My land,
Strong, and without number;

CHAPTER 1
1
a Acts 2:16
3
b Ex. 10:2; Ps. 78:4; Isa. 38:19
4
c Amos 4:9
d Isa. 33:4
5
e Isa. 5:11; 28:1; Hos. 7:5
6
f Joel 2:2,11

* 1:4 Exact identity of these locusts is unknown.

---

[1](1:4) Some expositors understand these words to be different stages of the locusts' development. The essential fact is that, according to the usual method of the Spirit in prophecy, some local circumstance is shown to be of spiritual significance, and is made the occasion of a far-reaching prophecy (e.g. Isa. 7:1–14, where the Syrian invasion and the unbelief of Ahaz give occasion to the great prophecy of v. 14). Here in Joel a plague of locusts is shown to have symbolic significance (1:13–14), portraying a coming invasion (2:1–11) if repentance is not forthcoming (2:12–17). This impending "day of the LORD" in judgment becomes a foreshadowing of that great climactic day of the LORD, not yet fulfilled (Isa. 2:12, *refs.*).

The picture foreshadows the end-time of Israel's age, of "the times of the Gentiles" (Lk. 21:24; Rev. 16:19); of the battle of Armageddon (Rev. 16:14; 19:11–21); of the regathering of Israel (see Rom. 11:26, *note*); and of kingdom blessing.

The order of events during Israel's last days may be: (1) the invasion of Palestine from the north by Gentile world powers (Joel 2:1–10; Armageddon, Rev. 16:14, *refs.*); (2) the Lord's army and destruction of the invaders (Rev. 19:11–21); (3) the repentance of Judah in the land (2:12–17; Dt. 30:3, *note*); (4) the answer of the LORD (2:18–27); (5) the outpouring of the Spirit in Israel's "last days" (2:28–29); (6) the return of the Lord in glory and the setting up of the kingdom (2:30–32; Acts 15:15–17) by the regathering of the nation and the judgment of the nations (3:1–16); and (7) permanent kingdom blessing (3:17–21; Zech. 14:1–21; see Mt. 25:32, *note*).

His teeth *are* the teeth of a lion,
And he has the fangs of a fierce lion.
7 He has laid waste My vine,
And ruined My fig tree;
He has stripped it bare and thrown *it* away;
Its branches are made white.

8 Lament like a virgin girded with sackcloth
For the husband of her youth.
9 The grain offering and the drink offering
Have been cut off from the house of the LORD;
The priests [a]mourn, who minister to the LORD.
10 The field is wasted,
The land [b]mourns;
For the grain is ruined,
The new wine is dried up,
The oil [c]fails.

11 Be ashamed, you [d]farmers,
Wail, you vinedressers,
For the wheat and the barley;
Because the harvest of the field has perished.
12 The vine has dried up,
And the fig tree has withered;
The pomegranate tree,
The palm tree also,
And the apple tree—
All the trees of the field are withered;
Surely [e]joy has withered away from the sons of men.

13 Gird yourselves and lament, you priests;
Wail, you who minister before the altar;
Come, lie all night in sackcloth,
You who minister to my God;
For the grain offering and the drink offering
Are withheld from the house of your God.

Desolation by starvation and drought

14 [f]Consecrate a [g]fast,
Call a sacred assembly;
Gather the elders
And all the inhabitants of the land
Into the house of the LORD your God,
And cry out to the LORD.

15 Alas for the day!
For the [1]day of the LORD *is* [h]at hand;
It shall come [i]as destruction from the Almighty.
16 Is not the food [j]cut off before our eyes,
Joy and gladness from the house of our God?
17 The seed shrivels under the clods,
Storehouses are in shambles;
Barns are broken down,
For the grain has withered.
18 How the [k]animals groan!
The herds of cattle are restless,
Because they have no pasture;
Even the flocks of sheep suffer punishment.*

19 O LORD, to You I cry out;
For fire has devoured the open pastures,
And a flame has burned all the trees of the field.
20 The beasts of the field also cry out to You,
For the water brooks are dried up,
And fire has devoured the open pastures.

The victorious invading army from the north (v. 20), Assyria

2 BLOW the trumpet in Zion,
And sound an alarm in My holy mountain!
Let all the inhabitants of the land tremble;
For the [l]day of the LORD is coming,
For it is at hand:

9
a Joel 2:17
10
b Hos. 4:3
c Isa. 24:7
11
d Amos 5:16
12
e Isa. 16:10; 24:11
14
f Sanctification (OT): vv. 13–14; Zech. 8:3. (Gen. 2:3; Zech. 8:3)
g Joel 2:15–16
15
h See Mt. 4:17, *note*
i Isa. 13:6; Ezek. 7:2–12
16
j Isa. 3:1–7; Amos 4:6–9
18
k Jer. 12:4; 14:5–6
CHAPTER 2
1
l Day (of the LORD): 1:15; 2:1–11; Joel 2:31. (Ps. 2:9; Rev. 19:19)

*1:18 Septuagint and Vulgate read *are made desolate.*

[1](1:15) The term "day of the LORD [Jehovah]" is that period of time when the LORD openly intervenes in the affairs of men, when man's day has closed (Cp. 1 Cor. 4:3). It will be inaugurated with the rapture of the Church (1 Cor. 15:50–58; 1 Th. 4:13–18). Since the prophets saw historical events from God's viewpoint, they saw the unity of God's world program. Thus they discerned that visitations of God in their time were near foreshadowings of an ultimate fulfillment. In this sense the term is frequently used by Joel.

The day of the LORD in prophetic times will cover the time of the coming tribulation (Rev. 6—19) and the reign of Christ on David's throne (Rev. 20). It will be brought to an end by the judgment of the great white throne (Rev. 20:11–15) and the ushering in of the new heavens and earth, called "the day of God" (2 Pet. 3:10–13). See Rev. 19:19, *note*.

2 A day of darkness and
gloominess,
A day of clouds and thick
darkness,
Like the morning *clouds*
spread over the mountains.
A people *come*, [a]great and
strong,
The [b]like of whom has never
been;
Nor will there ever be any
such after them,
Even for many successive
generations.

3 A fire devours before them,
And behind them a flame
burns;
The land *is* [c]like the Garden of
Eden before them,
And behind them a desolate
wilderness;
Surely nothing shall escape
them.
4 Their appearance is like the
appearance of [d]horses;
And like swift steeds, so they
run.
5 With a noise like chariots
Over mountaintops they leap,
Like the noise of a flaming fire
that devours the stubble,
Like a strong people set in
battle array.

6 Before them the people writhe
in pain;
All faces are drained of color.*
7 They run like mighty men,
They climb the wall like men
of war;
Every one marches in
formation,
And they do not break [e]ranks.
8 They do not push one another;
Every one marches in his own
column.*
Though they lunge between
the weapons,
They are not cut down.*
9 They run to and fro in the city,
They run on the wall;
They climb into the houses,
They enter at the windows like
a thief.
10 The earth quakes before them,
The heavens tremble;
The sun and moon grow
[f]dark,
And the stars diminish their
brightness.
11 The LORD gives [g]voice before
His [1]army,
For His camp is very great;
For strong *is the One* who
executes His word.
For the [h]day of the LORD *is*
great and very terrible;
Who can endure it?

Only repentance can avert invasion

12 "Now, therefore," says the LORD,
[i]"Turn to Me with all your heart,
With fasting, with weeping,
and with mourning."
13 So rend your heart, and not
your garments;
Return to the LORD your God,
For He *is* gracious and
merciful,
Slow to anger, and of great
[j]kindness;
And He [k]relents from doing
harm.
14 Who knows [l]*if* He will turn
and [k]relent,
And leave a blessing behind
Him—
A grain offering and a drink
offering
For the LORD your God?

15 Blow the trumpet in Zion,
Consecrate a fast,
Call a sacred assembly;
16 Gather the people,
Sanctify the congregation,
Assemble the elders,
Gather the children and
nursing babes;
Let the bridegroom go out
from his chamber,
And the bride from her
dressing room.
17 Let the priests, who minister to
the LORD,
Weep between the porch and
the altar;
Let them say, "Spare Your
people, O LORD,
And do not give Your heritage
to reproach,

2 *a* Joel 1:6 *b* Dan. 12:1
3 *c* Gen. 2:8; 13:10; Isa. 51:3
4 *d* Cp. Rev. 9:7–9
7 *e* Prov. 30:27
10 *f* Isa. 13:10; Joel 3:15
11 *g* Jer. 25:30; Joel 3:16; Amos 1:2 *h* Jer. 30:7; Amos 5:18; Zeph. 1:15
12 *i* Dt. 4:29; Jer. 4:1; Ezek. 33:11; Hos. 12:6; 14:1
13 *j* Ex. 34:6 *k* See Zech. 8:14, *note*
14 *l* 2 Sam. 12:22; Jer. 26:3; Jon. 3:9

*2:6 Septuagint, Targum, and Vulgate read *gather blackness.* 2:8 Literally *his own highway* • That is, they are not halted by losses

[1](2:11) In vv. 1–10 the advancing locust plague becomes illustrative of an invading army. (A locust's head resembles a horse's head in miniature.) Verse 11 states that the LORD will bring this army against His people to discipline them for their sin unless they open their hearts in abject and full repentance (vv. 12–17). Only thus can the invasion of the northern (Assyrian) army be averted (v. 20).

That the nations should rule
over them.
Why should they say among
the peoples,
'Where *is* their God?' "

Deliverance promised if Israel repents

18 Then the LORD will be zealous
for His land,
And pity His people.
19 The LORD will answer and say
to His people,
"Behold, I will send you grain
and new wine and oil,
And you will be satisfied by
them;
I will no longer make you a
reproach among the nations.

20 "But I will remove far from you
the northern *army*,
And will drive him away into a
barren and desolate land,
With his face toward the
eastern sea
And his back toward the
western sea;
His stench will come up,
And his foul odor will rise,
Because he has done
monstrous things."

21 Fear not, O land;
Be glad and rejoice,
For the LORD has done
marvelous things!
22 Do not be afraid, you beasts of
the field;
For the open pastures are
springing up,
And the tree bears its fruit;
The fig tree and the vine yield
their strength.
23 Be glad then, you children of
Zion,
And rejoice in the LORD your
God;
For He has given you the
former [a]rain faithfully,*
And He will cause the rain to
come down for you—
The former rain,
And the latter rain in the first
month.
24 The threshing floors shall be
full of wheat,
And the vats shall overflow
with new wine and oil.
25 "So I will restore to you the
years that the swarming
locust has eaten,
The crawling locust,
The consuming locust,
And the chewing locust,*
My great army which I sent
among you.
26 You shall eat in plenty and be
satisfied,
And praise the name of the
LORD your God,
Who has dealt wondrously
with you;
And My people shall never be
put to [b]shame.
27 Then you shall know that I *am*
in the midst of Israel:
I *am* the LORD your God
And there is [c]no other.
My people shall never be put
to shame.

II. The Promise of the Spirit, 2:28–29

28 [d]"And it shall come to pass
afterward
That I will pour out [1e]My
Spirit on [2]all flesh;
Your sons and your daughters
shall prophesy,
Your old men shall dream
dreams,
Your young men shall see
visions.
29 And also on *My* menservants
and on *My* maidservants
I will pour out My Spirit in
those days.

III. The Future Deliverance in the Coming Day of the LORD, 2:30—3:21

The signs preceding the day of the LORD (cp. Isa. 13:9–10; 24:21–23; Ezek. 32:7–10; Mt. 24:29–30)

30 "And I will show wonders in
the heavens and in the
earth:
Blood and fire and pillars of
smoke.

23
a Dt. 11:14; Jer. 5:24; Hos. 6:3; Jas. 5:7
26
b Isa. 45:17
27
c Isa. 45:6
28
d vv. 28–32; Acts 2:17–21
e Holy Spirit (OT): vv. 28–29; Mic. 2:7. (Gen. 1:2; Zech. 12:10)

*
2:23 Or *the teacher of righteousness*
2:25 Compare 1:4

[1](2:28) Compare Acts 2:17. Peter did not state that Joel's prophecy was fulfilled on the day of Pentecost. The details of Joel 2:30–32 (cp. Acts 2:19–20) were not realized at that time. Peter quoted Joel's prediction as an illustration of what was taking place in his day, and as a guarantee that God would yet completely fulfill all that Joel had prophesied. The time of that fulfillment is stated here ("afterward," cp. Hos. 3:5), i.e. in the latter days when Israel turns to the LORD. See also Gen. 49:1, *note*.

[2](2:28) The fulfillment of Moses' desire (Num. 11:29). Cp. Isa. 32:15; 44:3–4; Ezek. 36:27–28; 37:14; 39:29; Zech. 12:10.

31 The sun shall be turned into darkness,
And the moon into blood,
Before the coming of the great and awesome [a]day of the LORD.
32 And it shall come to pass
That whoever calls on the name of the LORD
Shall be saved.
For in Mount Zion and in Jerusalem there shall be deliverance,
As the LORD has said,
Among the [b]remnant whom the LORD calls.

The restoration of Israel (cp. Isa. 11:10–12; Jer. 23:5–8; Ezek. 37:21–28; Acts 15:15–17)

3 "FOR behold, in those days
[c]and at that time,
[d]When I bring back the captives of Judah and Jerusalem,

Judgment of Gentile nations (Zech. 12:2–3; 14:9; see Mt. 25:32, note)

2 I will also gather all nations,
And bring them down to the [e]Valley of [f]Jehoshaphat;
And I will enter into judgment with them there
On account of My people, My heritage Israel,
Whom they have scattered among the nations;
They have also divided up My land.
3 They have cast lots for My people,
Have given a boy *as payment* for a harlot,
And sold a girl for wine, that they may drink.
4 "Indeed, what have you to do with Me,
O Tyre and Sidon, and all the coasts of Philistia?
Will you retaliate against Me?
But if you retaliate against Me,
Swiftly and speedily I will return your retaliation upon your own head;
5 Because you have taken My silver and My gold,
And have carried into your temples My prized possessions.
6 Also the people of Judah and the people of Jerusalem
You have sold to the Greeks,

31
a Day (of the LORD): vv. 28–32; 3:9–21; Amos 2:16. (Ps. 2:9; Rev. 19:19)
32
b Remnant: v. 32; Amos 5:15. (Isa. 1:9; Rom. 11:5, *note*)
CHAPTER 3
1
c Judgments (the seven): vv. 1–14; Mt. 7:23. (1 Sam. 7:14; Rev. 20:12, *note*)
d Israel (prophecies): vv. 1–8, 15–20; Zech. 10:6. (Gen. 12:2; Rom. 11:26, *note*)
2
e v. 12
f Meaning *the LORD judges*
9
g Lit. *Sanctify,* i.e. by sacrifices and proper rites. Jer. 6:4, cp. 1 Sam. 7:8–9
h Armageddon (battle of): vv. 9–14; Obad. 15. (Isa. 10:27; Rev. 19:17)
12
i Kingdom (OT): vv. 12, 16–21; Amos 9:11. (Gen. 1:26; Zech. 12:8, *note*)
j Times of the Gentiles: vv. 2, 11–14; Lk. 21:24. (Dt. 28:49; Rev. 16:19)

That you may remove them far from their borders.
7 "Behold, I will raise them
Out of the place to which you have sold them,
And will return your retaliation upon your own head.
8 I will sell your sons and your daughters
Into the hand of the people of Judah,
And they will sell them to the Sabeans,*
To a people far off;
For the LORD has spoken."
9 Proclaim this among the nations:
[1][g]"Prepare for [h]war!
Wake up the mighty men,
Let all the men of war draw near,
Let them come up.
10 Beat your plowshares into swords
And your pruning hooks into spears;
Let the weak say, 'I *am* strong.'"
11 Assemble and come, all you nations,
And gather together all around.
Cause Your mighty ones to go down there, O LORD.
12 "Let the nations be wakened, and come up to the Valley of Jehoshaphat;
For there I will [i]sit to [j]judge all the surrounding nations.
13 Put in the sickle, for the harvest is [k]ripe.
Come, go down;
For the winepress is full,
The vats overflow—
For their wickedness *is* great."
14 Multitudes, multitudes in the valley of decision!
For the day of the LORD *is* near in the valley of decision.
15 The sun and moon will grow dark,
And the stars will diminish their brightness.

3:13 *k* Rev. 14:17–20

*3:8 Literally *Shebaites* (compare Isaiah 60:6 and Ezekiel 27:22)

[1](3:9) Verses 9–15 refer to Armageddon; vv. 15–21 are parallel with 2:30–32.

16 The LORD also will roar from
Zion,
And utter His voice from
Jerusalem;
The heavens and earth will
shake;
But the LORD will be a shelter
for His people,
And the strength of the
children of Israel.
17 "So you shall know that I *am*
the LORD your God,
Dwelling in Zion My [a]holy
mountain.
Then Jerusalem shall be holy,
And no aliens shall ever pass
through her again."

Final restoration. Full kingdom blessing (see Zech. 12:8, note)

18 And it will come to pass in
that day
That the mountains shall drip
with new wine,
The hills shall flow with milk,
And all the brooks of Judah
shall be flooded with water;
A [b]fountain shall flow from
the house of the LORD
And water the Valley of
Acacias.
19 "Egypt shall be a desolation,
And Edom a desolate
wilderness,
Because of violence *against*
the people of Judah,
For they have shed innocent
blood in their land.
20 But Judah shall abide forever,
And Jerusalem from
generation to generation.
21 For I will acquit them of the
guilt of bloodshed, whom I
had not acquitted;
For the LORD dwells in Zion."

17
a Obad. 16; Zech. 8:3

18
b Ps. 46:4; Ezek. 47:1; Zech. 14:8; Rev. 22:1

The Book of

AMOS

Author: Amos *Theme:* Judgment on Sin *Date of writing:* 8th Cent. B.C.

AMOS, whose name is related to a verb meaning *to bear a load*, was burdened over the sin of the northern kingdom in the eighth century B.C. Whereas Hosea was crushed with a sense of the unfaithfulness of Israel to the love of God, Amos was outraged at the violence they had done to the justice and righteousness of God. The note he strikes in his prophecy is the counterpart and corollary to the message uttered by Hosea. The words most descriptive of Amos's message are: "But let justice run down like water, and righteousness like a mighty stream." (5:24). Social justice is inseparable from true piety.

The book may be divided as follows:

I. The Pronouncement of Judgment, 1—2.
II. Inevitable Divine Judgment Because of Sin, 3—4.
III. God Pleads with Israel to Return to Him, 5:1–15.
IV. Some Phenomena in Relation to Coming Judgment, 5:16—9:10.
V. The Final Restoration of Israel, 9:11–15.

I. The Pronouncement of Judgment, 1—2

Introduction

1 THE words of Amos, who was among the [a]sheepbreeders* of Tekoa, which he saw concerning Israel in the days of [b]Uzziah king of Judah, and in the days of [c]Jeroboam the son of Joash, king of Israel, two years before the [d]earthquake.

2 And he said:

"The LORD roars from Zion,
And utters His voice from Jerusalem;
The pastures of the shepherds mourn,
And the top of Carmel withers."

Judgments on surrounding cities and nations

3 [1]Thus says the LORD:

"For three transgressions of [e]Damascus, and for [2]four,
I will not turn away its *punishment*,
Because they have [f]threshed Gilead with implements of iron.
4 But I will send a [g]fire into the house of Hazael,
Which shall devour the palaces of [h]Ben-Hadad.
5 I will also [i]break the *gate* [3]bar of Damascus,
And cut off the inhabitant from the Valley of Aven,
And the one who holds the scepter from Beth Eden.
The people of Syria shall go captive to Kir,"
Says the LORD.

6 Thus says the LORD:

"For three transgressions of [j]Gaza, and for four,
I will not turn away its *punishment*,
Because they took captive the whole captivity
To deliver *them* up to Edom.
7 But I will send a fire upon the wall of Gaza,
Which shall devour its palaces.
8 I will cut off the inhabitant from Ashdod,
And the one who holds the scepter from Ashkelon;
I will turn My hand against Ekron,
And the remnant of the Philistines shall perish,"
Says the Lord GOD.

9 Thus says the LORD:

CHAPTER 1

1
a Amos 7:14
b 2 Ki. 15:1–7; 2 Chr. 26:1–23; Isa. 1:1; Hos. 1:1; called *Azariah* in 2 Ki. 14:21
c 2 Ki. 14:23–29
d Isa. 42:13; Jer. 25:30; Joel 3:16; Zech. 14:5

3
e vv. 3–5; Isa. 17:1–3; Jer. 49:23–27; Zech. 9:1
f 2 Ki. 10:32–33

4
g Jer. 49:27
h 1 Ki. 20:1; 2 Ki. 6:24

5
i 2 Ki. 14:28; Isa. 8:4; Jer. 51:30

6
j Jer. 47:1,5; Zeph. 2:4

*1:1 Compare 2 Kings 3:4

---

[1](1:3) Observe Amos's method of prophesying. Beginning with denunciation of Israel's enemies (cp. vv. 3,6,9,11,13; and 2:1), he wins a hearing from a hostile crowd. Moving nearer, he speaks of the sin of Judah (2:4). Finally, having gained the sympathy of his hearers, he points out the sin of Israel itself (3:1). Isaiah used a similar method (Isa. 28).

[2](1:3) "For three transgressions . . . and for four" is an expression indicating a measure of full iniquity and inevitable judgment.

[3](1:5) The gates of ancient cities were secured by heavy bars. It was gates such as these that Samson carried away from Gaza's entrance (Jud. 16:3).

"For three transgressions of
[a]Tyre, and for four,
I will not turn away its
punishment,
Because they delivered up the
whole captivity to Edom,
And did not remember the
covenant of brotherhood.
10 But I will send a fire upon the
wall of Tyre,
Which shall devour its
palaces."

11 Thus says the LORD:

"For three transgressions of
[b]Edom, and for four,
I will not turn away its
punishment,
Because he pursued his
[c]brother with the sword,
And cast off all pity;
His anger tore perpetually,
And he kept his wrath forever.
12 But I will send a fire upon
Teman,
Which shall devour the palaces
of Bozrah."

13 Thus says the LORD:

"For three transgressions of the
people of [d]Ammon, and for
four,
I will not turn away its
punishment,
Because they ripped open the
women with child in Gilead,
That they might enlarge their
territory.
14 But I will kindle a fire in the
wall of Rabbah,
And it shall devour its palaces,
Amid shouting in the day of
battle,
And a tempest in the day of
the whirlwind.
15 Their king shall go into
[e]captivity,
He and his princes together,"
Says the LORD.

Judgments on surrounding cities and nations (continued)

2 THUS says the LORD:

[f]"For three transgressions of
Moab, and for four,
I will not turn away its
punishment,
Because he burned the bones
of the king of Edom to lime.
2 But I will send a fire upon
Moab,
And it shall devour the palaces
of Kerioth;
Moab shall die with tumult,
With shouting *and* trumpet
sound.
3 And I will cut off the judge
from its midst,
And slay all its princes with
him,"
Says the LORD.

Judgment on God's people: Judah and Israel

4 Thus says the LORD:

"For three transgressions of
[g]Judah, and for four,
I will not turn away its
punishment,
Because they have despised
the law of the LORD,
And have [h]not kept His
commandments.
Their lies lead them [i]astray,
Lies which their fathers
followed.
5 But I will send a fire upon
Judah,
And it shall devour the
[j]palaces of Jerusalem."

6 Thus says the LORD:

"For three transgressions of
[k]Israel, and for four,
I will not turn away its
punishment,
Because they sell the righteous
for silver,
And the [l]poor for a pair of
sandals.
7 They pant after* the dust of
the earth *which is* on the
head of the poor,
And pervert the way of the
humble.
A man and his father go in to
the [m]*same* girl,
To [n]defile My holy name.
8 They lie down by every altar
on clothes taken in pledge,
And drink the wine of the
condemned *in* the house of
their god.

9 "Yet *it was* I *who* destroyed the
[o]Amorite before them,
Whose height *was* like the
[p]height of the cedars,
And he *was as* strong as the
oaks;
Yet I destroyed his fruit above

9 *a* vv. 9–10; Isa. 23:1–18; Jer. 25:22; 47:4; Ezek. 26:1–21; 28:20–24; Zech. 9:2–4
11 *b* vv. 11–12; Jer. 25:21; 49:7–22; Ezek. 25:12–14; 35:1–15; Joel 3:19; Obad. 1–9, 15–16 *c* Obad. 10
13 *d* Jer. 25:21; 49:1–6; Ezek. 21:28–32; 25:1–7; Zeph. 2:8–11
15 *e* Jer. 49:3
CHAPTER 2
1 *f* Isa. 15:1–16:14; 25:10; Jer. 25:21; 48:1–47; Ezek. 25:8–11; Zeph. 2:8–11
4 *g* 2 Ki. 17:19; Hos. 12:2; Amos 3:2 *h* Lev. 26:14–15, 43 *i* Isa. 9:15–16; Hab. 2:18
5 *j* By Nebuchadnezzar's army in c. 586 B.C.
6 *k* Jud. 2:17–20; 2 Ki. 17:7–18; 18:12; Ezek. 22:1–13, 23–29 *l* Amos 4:1; 5:11; 8:6; Mic. 2:2; 3:3
7 *m* Lev. 18:6–8; cp. Gen. 35:22; 2 Sam. 16:22; 1 Cor. 5:1 *n* Lev. 20:3; Ezek. 36:20–22
2:9 *o* Gen. 15:16; Josh. 10:12 *p* Ezek. 31:3

★ **2:7** Or *trample on*

And his roots beneath.
10 Also *it was* I *who* brought you
up from the land of Egypt,
And led you forty years
through the wilderness,
To possess the land of the
Amorite.
11 I raised up some of your sons
as [a]prophets,
And some of your young men
as [b]Nazirites.
Is it not so, O you children of
Israel?"
Says the LORD.
12 "But you gave the Nazirites
wine to drink,
And commanded the prophets
saying,
'Do not [c]prophesy!'

13 "Behold, [d]I am weighed down
by you,
As a cart full of sheaves is
weighed down.
14 Therefore flight shall perish
from the swift,
The strong shall not strengthen
his power,
Nor shall the mighty deliver
himself;
15 He shall not stand who
handles the bow,
The swift of foot shall not
escape,
Nor shall he who rides a horse
deliver himself.
16 The most courageous men of
might
Shall flee naked in that [e]day,"
Says the LORD.

II. Inevitable Divine Judgment Because of Sin, 3—4

All twelve tribes guilty

3 HEAR this word that the LORD has
spoken against you, O children of
Israel, against the [1]whole family
which I brought up from the land of
Egypt, saying:

2 "You only have I [f]known of all
the families of the earth;
[2]Therefore I will punish you for
all your iniquities."

3 [3]Can two [g]walk together,
unless they are agreed?
4 Will a lion roar in the forest,
when he has no prey?
Will a young lion cry out of his
den, if he has caught
nothing?
5 Will a bird fall into a snare on
the earth, where there is no
trap for it?
Will a snare spring up from
the earth, if it has caught
nothing at all?
6 If a trumpet is blown in a city,
will not the people [h]be
afraid?
If there is [i]calamity in a city,
will not the LORD have done
it?
7 Surely the Lord GOD does
nothing,
Unless He [j]reveals His secret
to His servants the
[k]prophets.
8 A lion has roared!
Who will not fear?
The Lord GOD has spoken!
[l]Who can but prophesy?
9 "Proclaim in the palaces at
Ashdod,
And in the palaces in the land
of Egypt, and say:
'Assemble on the mountains of
Samaria;
See great tumults in her midst,
And the oppressed within her.
10 For they do [m]not know to do
right,'
Says the LORD,
'Who store up violence and
robbery in their palaces.' "
11 Therefore thus says the Lord
GOD:

"An adversary *shall be* all
around the land;
He shall sap your strength
from you,
And your palaces shall be
plundered."
12 Thus says the LORD:

11
a Num. 12:6; cp. Dt. 18:15–19
b Num. 6:1–8
12
c Isa. 30:10
13
d Or *I weigh you down*
16
e Day (of the LORD): vv. 14–16; Amos 5:18. (Ps. 2:9; Rev. 19:19)
CHAPTER 3
2
f By covenant relationship. Dt. 4:32–37
3
g Lev. 26:23–24
6
h Or *run together*
i Cp. Isa. 45:7; Jer. 4:6; Jas. 1:13,17
7
j Cp. Gen. 18:17
k Inspiration: vv. 7–8; Mic. 3:8. (Ex. 4:15; 2 Tim. 3:16, *note*)
8
l Jer. 20:9; Mic. 3:8; Acts 4:20; 5:20,29; 1 Cor. 9:16
10
m Jer. 4:22

---

[1](3:1) The language here, and the expression "house of Jacob" (v. 13), evidently give the prophecy a wider application than to Israel, the ten-tribe northern kingdom, though the judgment was executed first upon this kingdom (2 Ki. 17:18–23).

[2](3:2) The LORD's controversy with the Gentile cities which hated Israel is brief: "I will send a fire" (2:2). But Israel had been brought into the place of privilege and so of responsibility, and the LORD's indictment is detailed and unsparing. Cp. Mt. 11:23; Lk. 12:47–48; 1 Pet. 4:17; 2 Pet. 2:4; Jude 6.

[3](3:3) Observe the seven result-cause questions in vv. 3–6, concluding with the challenge: "If there is calamity in a city, will not the LORD have done it?"

"As a shepherd takes from the
mouth of a lion
Two legs or a piece of an ear,
So shall the children of Israel
be taken out
Who dwell in Samaria—
In the corner of a bed and on
the edge* of a couch!
13 Hear and testify against the
house of Jacob,"
Says the Lord GOD, the God of
hosts,
14 "That in the day I punish Israel
for their transgressions,
I will also visit *destruction* on
the altars of [a]Bethel;
And the horns of the altar
shall be cut off
And fall to the ground.
15 I will destroy the winter house
along with the summer
house;
The houses of ivory shall
perish,
And the great houses shall
have an end,"
Says the LORD.

The LORD scorns Bethel's sacrifices

4 HEAR this word, you [b]cows of
Bashan, who *are* on the
mountain of Samaria,
Who oppress the [c]poor,
Who crush the needy,
Who say to your husbands,*
"Bring *wine*, let us [d]drink!"
2 The Lord GOD has sworn by
His [e]holiness:
"Behold, the days shall come
upon you
When He will take you away
with fishhooks,
And your posterity with
fishhooks.
3 You will go out *through*
broken *walls*,
Each one straight ahead of her,
And you will be cast into
Harmon,"
Says the LORD.
4 "Come to [1][f]Bethel and
transgress,
At Gilgal multiply
transgression;
Bring your [g]sacrifices every
morning,
Your tithes every three days.*
5 Offer a sacrifice of
[h]thanksgiving with [i]leaven,
Proclaim *and* announce the
freewill offerings;
For [j]this you love,
You children of Israel!"
Says the Lord GOD.

Unheeded chastening

6 "Also I gave you cleanness of
teeth in all your cities.
And [k]lack of bread in all your
places;
[l]Yet you have not returned to
Me,"
Says the LORD.
7 "I also withheld rain from you,
When *there were* still three
months to the harvest.
I made it rain on one city,
I withheld rain from another
city.
One part was rained upon,
And where it did not rain the
part withered.
8 So two *or* three cities
wandered to another city to
drink water,
But they were not satisfied;
Yet you have not returned to
Me,"
Says the LORD.
9 "I blasted you with blight and
mildew.
When your gardens increased,
Your vineyards,
Your fig trees,
And your olive trees,
The [m]locust devoured *them;*
Yet you have not returned to
Me,"
Says the LORD.
10 "I sent among you a plague
after the manner of [n]Egypt;
Your young men I killed with
a sword,
Along with your captive
[o]horses;
I made the stench of your
camps come up into your
nostrils;
Yet you have not returned to
Me,"
Says the LORD.
11 "I overthrew *some* of you,

14
a Amos 4:4
CHAPTER 4
1
b Ps. 22:12; Ezek. 39:18
c Amos 2:6
d Prov. 23:20
2
e Ps. 89:35
4
f Amos 3:14
g Amos 5:21–22
5
h See Lev. 7:13, *note*
i *Leaven:* v. 5; Mt. 13:33. (Gen. 19:3; Mt. 13:33, *note*)
j Cp. Col. 2:18
6
k Dt. 11:17; Hag. 1:6
l vv. 8–9; 2 Chr. 28:22; Jer. 5:3; Hag. 2:17; cp. Heb. 12:9
9
m Joel 1:4
10
n Dt. 28:60
o Cp. 2 Ki. 13:7

*

3:12 The Hebrew is uncertain. 4:1 Literally *their lords* or *their masters* 4:4 Or *years* (compare Deuteronomy 14:28)

[1](4:4) Compare 1 Ki. 12:25–33. Any altar at Bethel, after the establishment of the LORD's worship at Jerusalem, was of necessity schismatic and idolatrous (Dt. 12:4–14). Cp. Jn. 4:21–24; also Mt. 18:20; Heb. 13:10–14.

As God [a]overthrew Sodom
and Gomorrah,
And you were like a firebrand
plucked from the burning;
Yet you have not returned to
Me,"
Says the LORD.

12 "Therefore thus will I do to you,
O Israel;
Because I will do this to you,
[b]Prepare to meet your God, O
Israel!"

13 For behold,
He who forms mountains,
And creates the wind,
Who [c]declares to man what
his* thought *is*,
And makes the morning
darkness,
Who treads the high places of
the earth—
The LORD God of hosts *is* His
name.

III. God Pleads with Israel to Return to Him, 5:1–15

5 HEAR this word which I take up
against you, a lamentation, O
house of Israel:

2 The virgin of Israel has fallen;
She will rise no more.
She lies forsaken on her land;
There is [d]no one to raise her
up.

3 For thus says the Lord GOD:

"The city that goes out by a
thousand
Shall have a hundred left,
And that which goes out by a
hundred
Shall have ten left to the house
of Israel."

4 For thus says the LORD to the
house of Israel:

[e]"Seek Me and live;
5 But do not seek [f]Bethel,
Nor enter Gilgal,
Nor pass over to Beersheba;
For Gilgal shall surely go into
captivity,
And Bethel shall come to
nothing.
6 [g]Seek the LORD and live,
Lest He break out like fire *in*
the house of Joseph,
And devour *it*,
With no one to quench *it* in
Bethel—
7 You who turn justice to
wormwood,
And lay righteousness to rest
in the earth!"

8 He made the Pleiades and
[h]Orion;
He turns the shadow of death
into morning
And makes the day dark as
night;
He calls for the waters of the
sea
And pours them out on the
face of the earth;
The LORD *is* His name.
9 He rains ruin upon the strong,
So that fury comes upon the
fortress.

10 They [i]hate the one who
rebukes in the gate,
And they abhor the one who
speaks uprightly.
11 [j]Therefore, because you tread
down the poor
And take grain taxes from
him,
Though you have [k]built houses
of hewn stone,
Yet you shall not dwell in
them;
You have planted pleasant
vineyards,
But you shall not drink wine
from them.
12 For I [l]know your manifold
transgressions
And your mighty sins:
Afflicting the just *and* taking
bribes;
Diverting the poor *from justice*
at the gate.
13 Therefore the prudent keep
silent at that time,
For it *is* an evil time.

14 Seek good and not evil,
That you may live;
So the LORD God of hosts will
be with you,
As you have spoken.
15 Hate evil, love good;
Establish justice in the gate.
It may be that the LORD God of
hosts
Will be gracious to the
[m]remnant of Joseph.

IV. Some Phenomena in Relation to the Coming of the LORD, 5:16—9:10

The day of the LORD

16 Therefore the LORD God of hosts,
the Lord, says this:

11 a Gen. 19:24–25; Isa. 13:19; Jer. 49:18; Lam. 4:6
12 b 4:2; cp. Jer. 5:22; Mt. 24:44
13 c Ps. 139:2; Dan. 2:28, 30
CHAPTER 5
2 d Cp. Amos 9:11
4 e v. 6; Dt. 4:29; 2 Chr. 15:2; Jer. 29:13
5 f Amos 3:14; 4:4
6 g Isa. 55:3, 6–7
8 h Job 9:9; 38:31
10 i Isa. 66:5; cp. Jer. 17:16–18
11 j Amos 2:6 k Dt. 28:30, 38–39; Mic. 6:15; Zeph. 1:13; Hag. 1:6
12 l Hos. 5:3
15 m *Remnant:* v. 15; Mic. 2:12. (Isa. 1:9; Rom. 11:5, *note*)

* 4:13 Or *His*

"*There shall be* wailing in all
streets,
And they shall say in all the
highways,
'Alas! Alas!'
They shall call the farmer to
mourning,
And skillful lamenters to
wailing.
17 In all vineyards *there shall be*
wailing,
For I will pass through you,"
Says the LORD.
18 Woe to you who desire the
[a]day of the LORD!
For what good *is* the day of the
LORD to you?
It *will be* darkness, and not
light.
19 It *will be* as though a man fled
from a lion,
And a bear met him!
Or *as though* he went into the
house,
Leaned his hand on the wall,
And a serpent bit him!
20 *Is* not the day of the LORD
darkness, and not light?
Is it not very dark, with no
brightness in it?

Worship without righteousness an abomination to the LORD

21 "I hate, I despise your feast
days,
And I do not [b]savor your
sacred assemblies.
22 Though you offer Me burnt
offerings and your grain
offerings,
I will not accept *them*,
Nor will I regard your fattened
peace offerings.
23 Take away from Me the noise
of your songs,
For I will not hear the melody
of your stringed instruments.
24 But let justice run down like
water,
And righteousness like a
mighty stream.
25 "Did you offer Me [c]sacrifices
and offerings
In the wilderness forty years,
O house of Israel?
26 You also carried Sikkuth*
your king*
And Chiun,* your idols,
The star of your gods,
Which you made for
yourselves.
27 Therefore I will send you into
[d]captivity beyond
Damascus,"
Says the LORD, whose [e]name *is*
the God of hosts.

Woe to those at ease in a time of unrighteousness

6 [f]WOE to you *who are* at [g]ease
in Zion,
And [h]trust in Mount Samaria,
Notable persons in the chief
nation,
To whom the house of Israel
comes!
2 Go over to [i]Calneh and see;
And from there go to [j]Hamath
the great;
Then go down to Gath of the
Philistines.
Are you better than these
kingdoms?
Or is their territory greater
than your territory?
3 *Woe to* you who put [k]far off
the day of doom,
Who cause the seat of violence
to come near;
4 Who lie on beds of [1]ivory,
Stretch out on your couches,
Eat lambs from the flock
And calves from the midst of
the stall;
5 Who sing idly to the sound of
stringed instruments,
And invent for yourselves
[l]musical instruments [m]like
David;
6 Who [n]drink wine from bowls,
And anoint yourselves with the
best ointments,
But are not grieved for the
affliction of Joseph.
7 Therefore they shall now go
[o]captive as the first of the
captives,
And those who recline at
banquets shall be removed.
8 The Lord GOD has [p]sworn by
Himself,
The LORD God of hosts says:
"I abhor the [q]pride of Jacob,
And hate his palaces;

18 *a Day* (of the LORD): vv. 18–20; Obad. 15. (Ps. 2:9; Rev. 19:19)
21 *b* Isa. 1:11–15; 66:3; Jer. 6:20; Hos. 9:4; Mic. 6:6–8
25 *c* vv. 25–27; Dt. 32:17–19; Neh. 9:18–21; Acts 7:42–43
27 *d* Amos 7:11,17; Mic. 4:10
e Amos 4:13
CHAPTER 6
1 *f* Lk. 6:24
g Ps. 123:4; Isa. 32:9–11; Zeph. 1:12
h Isa. 31:1; Jer. 49:4
2 *i* Or *Calno*, Isa. 10:9; cp. Gen. 10:10
j 2 Ki. 18:34
3 *k* Isa. 56:12; Amos 9:10; Mt. 24:37–39; cp. 2 Pet. 3:3–7
5 *l* Amos 5:23; 8:10; cp. 1 Chr. 15–16
m 1 Chr. 23:5
6 *n* Amos 4:1
7 *o* Amos 5:27
8 *p* Jer. 51:14; Heb. 6:13–17
q Ps. 47:4; Ezek. 24:21; Amos 8:7

*5:26 A pagan deity • Septuagint and Vulgate read *tabernacle of Moloch*. • A pagan deity

[1](6:4) The luxury and extravagance in which the northern kingdom lived have been fully attested by the archaeological findings of ivory figures and ivory panels in the homes of ancient Samaria.

Therefore I will deliver up *the* city
And all that is in it."

9 Then it shall come to pass, that if
[a]ten men remain in one house, they
shall die.
10 And when a relative *of the dead,*
with one who will burn *the bodies,*
picks up the bodies* to take them out
of the house, he will say to one inside
the house, "*Are there* any more with
you?" Then someone will say, "None."
And he will say, "Hold your tongue!
For we dare not mention the name of
the LORD."

11 For behold, the LORD gives a command:
He will break the [b]great house into bits,
And the little house into pieces.

12 Do horses run on rocks?
Does *one* plow *there* with oxen?
Yet you have turned [c]justice into gall,
And the fruit of righteousness into [d]wormwood,

13 You who rejoice over Lo Debar,*
Who say, "Have we not taken [e]Karnaim* for ourselves
By our own strength?"

14 "But, behold, I will raise up a nation against you,
O house of Israel,"
Says the LORD God of hosts;
"And they will afflict you from the entrance of Hamath
To the Valley of the [f]Arabah."

Warning through visions
(cp. 8:1—9:10)

7 THUS the Lord GOD showed me:
Behold, He formed locust swarms
at the beginning of the late crop; indeed *it was* the late crop after the
king's mowings.
2 And so it was, when they had
finished eating the grass of the land,
that I said:

"O Lord GOD, forgive, I pray!
Oh, that Jacob may stand,
For he *is* small!"

3 *So* the LORD [g]relented concerning this.
"It shall not be," said the LORD.

9 *a* Cp. Amos 5:3
11 *b* Cp. 2 Ki. 25:9
12 *c* Isa. 59:13–14 *d* Amos 5:7
13 *e* See Dt. 33:17, *note*
14 *f* See Dt. 1:1, *note*
CHAPTER 7
3 *g* See Zech. 8:14, *note*
9 *h* See Jud. 3:7 and 1 Ki. 3:2, *notes* *i* v. 11; 2 Ki. 15:8–10
10 *j* 1 Ki. 12:31–32; 13:33 *k* 1 Ki. 13:32; Amos 4:4 *l* Cp. Jer. 26:8–11; 38:4
11 *m* Amos 5:27; 6:7
12 *n* Cp. Mt. 8:34
13 *o* Cp. Jer. 11:21; Amos 2:12; 5:10; Acts 4:18

4 Thus the Lord GOD showed me:
Behold, the Lord GOD called for conflict by fire, and it consumed the great
deep and devoured the territory.
5 Then I said:

"O Lord GOD, cease, I pray!
Oh, that Jacob may stand,
For he *is* small!"

6 *So* the LORD [g]relented concerning this.
"This also shall not be," said the Lord GOD.

7 Thus He showed me: Behold, the
Lord stood on a wall *made* with a
plumb line, with a plumb line in His
hand.
8 And the LORD said to me, "Amos,
what do you see?" And I said, "A
plumb line." Then the Lord said:

"Behold, I am setting a [1]plumb line
In the midst of My people Israel;
I will not pass by them anymore.

9 The [h]high places of Isaac shall be desolate,
And the sanctuaries of Israel shall be laid waste.
I will rise with the sword [i]against the house of Jeroboam."

Amaziah sends accusation against
Amos to Jeroboam

10 Then Amaziah the [j]priest of
[k]Bethel sent to Jeroboam king of Israel, saying, "Amos has [l]conspired
against you in the midst of the house
of Israel. The land is not able to bear
all his words.

11 "For thus Amos has said:

'Jeroboam shall die by the sword,
And Israel shall surely be led away [m]captive
From their own land.'"

12 Then Amaziah said to Amos:

[n]"Go, you seer!
Flee to the land of Judah.
There eat bread,
And there prophesy.

13 But [o]never again prophesy at Bethel,
For it *is* the king's sanctuary,

*
6:10 Literally *bones* 6:13 Literally *Nothing*
• Literally *Horns,* symbol of strength

[1](7:8) The plumb line is a symbol of judgment according to righteousness. Cp. Isa. 28:17; 34:11; Lam. 2:8.

And it *is* the royal residence."

The answer of Amos

14 Then Amos answered, and said
to Amaziah:

"I *was* no prophet,
Nor *was* I a son of a prophet,
But I *was* a [a]sheepbreeder*
And a tender of sycamore
fruit.
15 Then the LORD took me as I
followed the flock,
And the LORD said to me,
'Go, [b]prophesy to My people
Israel.'
16 Now therefore, hear the word
of the LORD:
You say, 'Do not prophesy
against Israel,
And do not spout against the
house of Isaac.'
17 "Therefore thus says the LORD:

'Your wife shall be a harlot in
the city;
Your sons and daughters shall
fall by the sword;
Your land shall be divided by
survey line;
You shall die in a [c]defiled
land;
And Israel shall surely be led
away captive
From his own land.'"

Basket of summer fruit: Israel's impending captivity

8 THUS the Lord GOD showed me:
Behold, a [d]basket of [e]summer
fruit.
2 And He said, "Amos, what do
you see?" So I said, "A basket of summer fruit." Then the LORD said to me:

"The end has come upon My
people Israel;
I will [f]not pass by them
anymore.
3 And the songs of the temple
Shall be wailing in that day,"
Says the Lord GOD—
"Many dead bodies everywhere,
They shall be thrown out in
silence."

4 Hear this, you who swallow
up* the needy,
And make the poor of the land
fail,
5 Saying:

"When will the New Moon be
past,
That we may sell grain?
And the Sabbath,
That we may trade wheat?
Making the [g]ephah small and
the shekel large,
Falsifying the scales by
[h]deceit,
6 That we may buy the [i]poor for
silver,
And the needy for a pair of
sandals—
Even sell the bad wheat?"

7 The LORD has sworn by the
pride of Jacob:
"Surely I will never forget any
of their works.
8 Shall the land not tremble for
this,
And everyone mourn who
dwells in it?
All of it shall swell like the
River,*
Heave and subside
Like the River of Egypt.
9 "And it shall come to pass in
that day," says the Lord GOD,
"That I will make the sun go
down at noon,
And I will darken the earth in
broad daylight;
10 I will turn your feasts into
[j]mourning,
And all your songs into
lamentation;
I will bring sackcloth on every
waist,
And baldness on every head;
I will make it like mourning
for an only *son*,
And its end like a bitter day.

11 "Behold, the days are coming,"
says the Lord GOD,
"That I will send a famine on
the land,
Not a famine of bread,
Nor a thirst for water,
[k]But of hearing the words of the
LORD.
12 They shall wander from sea to
sea,
And from north to east;
They shall run to and fro,
seeking the word of the
LORD,
But shall [l]not find *it*.

13 "In that day the fair virgins
And strong young men

14 *a* Amos 1:1
15 *b* Amos 3:8
17 *c* 2 Ki. 17:6; Ezek. 4:13; Hos. 9:3
CHAPTER 8
1 *d* Cp. Jer. 24:1–3 *e* i.e. *soon to perish*
2 *f* Amos 7:8
5 *g* See Weights and Measures (OT), 2 Chr. 2:10, *note* *h* Lev. 19:35–36; Dt. 25:13–15
6 *i* Amos 2:6
10 *j* Lam. 5:15; Ezek. 7:18
11 *k* Mic. 3:6–7; cp. 1 Sam. 3:1; 28:6; 2 Chr. 15:3
12 *l* Ezek. 7:26; 20:3

*7:14 Compare 2 Kings 3:4 8:4 Or *trample on* (compare 2:7) 8:8 That is, the Nile; some Hebrew manuscripts, Septuagint, Syriac, Targum, and Vulgate read *River* (compare 9:5); Masoretic Text reads *the light*.

Shall faint from thirst.
14 Those who swear by the [a]sin*
of Samaria,
Who say,
'As your god lives, O Dan!'
And, 'As the [b]way of
Beersheba lives!'
They shall fall and never rise
again."

The final prophecy of dispersion
(cp. v. 9 and Dt. 28:63–68)

9 I SAW the Lord [1]standing by the
altar, and He said:
"Strike the doorposts, that the
thresholds may shake,
And break them on the heads
of them all.
I will slay the last of them with
the sword.
He who flees from them shall
not get away,
And he who escapes from
them shall not be delivered.
2 [c]"Though they dig into [d]hell,*
From there My hand shall take
them;
[e]Though they climb up to
heaven,
From there I will bring them
down;
3 And though they [f]hide
themselves on top of Carmel,
From there I will search and
take them;
Though they hide from My
sight at the bottom of the
sea,
From there I will command the
serpent, and it shall bite
them;
4 Though they go into captivity
before their enemies,
From there I will command the
sword,
And it shall slay them.
I will set My eyes on them for
[g]harm and not for good."
5 The Lord GOD of hosts,
He who touches the earth and
it melts,
And all who dwell there
mourn;
All of it shall swell like the
[h]River,

14
a Hos. 8:5
b Acts 9:2; 18:25; 19:9,23; 24:14

CHAPTER 9
2
c Ps. 139:8; Jer. 23:24
d See Hab. 2:5, *note*
e Job 20:6; Jer. 51:53; Obad. 4; Mt. 11:23
3
f Jer. 23:24
4
g Jer. 21:10; 39:16; 44:11
5
h i.e. *the Nile*
6
i Amos 4:13; 5:27
7
j Cp. Isa. 20:4
8
k Jer. 30:11
9
l See Ps. 72:1, *note*
m Isa. 65:8–16
10
n Isa. 28:15; Jer. 5:12
11
o vv. 11–12; Acts 15:16–17
p Kingdom (OT): vv. 11–15; Mic. 4:1. (Gen. 1:26; Zech. 12:8, *note*)

And subside like the [h]River of
Egypt.
6 He who builds His layers in
the sky,
And has founded His strata in
the earth;
Who calls for the waters of the
sea,
And pours them out on the
face of the earth—
The LORD *is* His [i]name.

7 "*Are* you not like the people of
[j]Ethiopia to Me,
O children of Israel?" says the
LORD.
"Did I not bring up Israel from
the land of Egypt,
The Philistines from Caphtor,
And the Syrians from Kir?

8 "Behold, the eyes of the Lord
GOD *are* on the sinful
kingdom,
And I will destroy it from the
face of the earth;
Yet I will [k]not utterly destroy
the house of Jacob,"
Says the LORD.

9 "For surely I will command,
And will [l]sift the house of
Israel among all nations,
As *grain* is sifted in a sieve;
[m]Yet not the smallest grain shall
fall to the ground.
10 All the sinners of My people
shall die by the sword,
Who say, 'The calamity shall
[n]not overtake nor confront
us.'

V. The Final Restoration
of Israel, 9:11–15

The LORD's second advent and the
re-establishment of the Davidic kingdom

11 "On that [o]day I will raise up
The tabernacle* of [p]David,
which has [2]fallen down,
And repair its damages;
I will raise up its ruins,
And rebuild it as in the days of
old;

*
8:14 Or *Ashima*, a Syrian goddess 9:2 Or *Sheol*
9:11 Literally *booth*, figure of a deposed dynasty

[1](9:1) The position of the Lord (*Adonai*) is significant. The altar usually speaks of mercy through judgment upon a substitutionary sacrifice (cp. Jn. 12:31–33), but when altar and sacrifice are despised, the altar becomes a place of judgment only.

[2](9:11) The Davidic monarchy, pictured by a tabernacle (lit. "booth"), was in a degraded condition. Cp. Isa. 11:1. On the basis of this verse the Talmudic rabbis called Messiah *Bar Naphli* ("the son of the fallen"). But He will arise (Mal. 4:2).

12 That they may possess the
remnant of [a]Edom,
And all the Gentiles who are
called by My name,"
Says the LORD who does [1]this
thing.

Israel's restoration in the kingdom

13 "Behold, the days are coming,"
says the LORD,
"When the plowman shall
[b]overtake the reaper,
And the treader of grapes him
who sows seed;
The mountains shall drip with
sweet wine,
And all the hills shall flow
with it.
14 I will [c]bring back the captives
of My people Israel;
They shall build the waste
cities and inhabit *them;*
They shall plant vineyards and
drink wine from them;
They shall also make gardens
and eat fruit from them.
15 [d]I will plant them in their land,
[2]And no longer shall they be
pulled up
From the land I have given
them,"
Says the LORD your God.

12
a Isa. 11:14
13
b i.e. *there will be continuous productivity*
14
c Isa. 60:4
15
d Isa. 60:21; Jer. 32:41; Ezek. 34:28; 37:25; Joel 3:20

[1](9:12) The ancient Greek translation rendered this verse as follows: "That the rest of mankind may seek [the LORD], and all the nations upon whom My name is called," says the LORD, who does all these things. Strange as it may seem to those who are unfamiliar with the Hebrew language, the Hebrew text may be rendered this way, with little more than the change of one letter. The corruption of this letter must have occurred after the time of the apostles, for James thus quoted the verse at the Jerusalem Council, and based his decision upon it (Acts 15:14–17). There were learned men present, some of them hostile to his view, who would certainly have shouted him down if he had based his decision upon a reading different from that which existed in the then current Hebrew manuscripts.

[2](9:15) Amos's single prophecy of future blessing (9:11–15) details (1) the restoration of the Davidic dynasty (v. 11); (2) the conversion of the nations (v. 12); (3) the fruitfulness of the land (v. 13); (4) Israel's return from captivity (v. 14); (5) the rebuilding of the waste cities (v. 14); and (6) Israel's permanent settlement in the holy land (v. 15).

The Book of
OBADIAH

Author: Obadiah *Theme:* Doom of Edom *Date of writing:* 6th Cent. B.C.

OBADIAH is completely unknown, apart from the meaning of his name (*servant* or *worshiper of the* LORD). The date of his prophecy is not certain, but internal evidence seems best to point to about 585 B.C., the year after the destruction of Jerusalem by Nebuchadnezzar, the king of Babylon. Some scholars suggest a much earlier date, however, i.e. around the 9th century.

The book, which in literary form is a "doom song," has a single theme—judgment upon Edom, the nation descended from Esau. In Obadiah's time Sela (later called Petra) was the capital of Edom. Its unique ruins, cut out of solid cliffs of rose-colored rock and long hidden in the arid regions south of the Dead Sea, were discovered in A.D. 1812 and stand as a silent witness to the fulfillment of the prophecy.

The book may be divided as follows:

I. The Pronouncement of Doom upon Edom, vv. 1–9.
II. The Cause of This Doom, vv. 10–14.
III. Edom in the Day of the LORD, vv. 15–21.

I. The Pronouncement of Doom upon Edom, vv. 1–9

Introduction.

The deceitfulness of pride

THE VISION of Obadiah.
Thus says the Lord GOD
[a]concerning [1]Edom
(We have heard a report from
the LORD,
And a messenger has been
sent among the nations,
saying,
"Arise, and let us rise up
against her for battle"):
2 "Behold, I will make you small
among the nations;
You shall be greatly despised.
3 The [b]pride of your heart has
deceived you,
You who dwell in the [2]clefts of
the rock,
Whose habitation is high;
You who say in your heart,
'Who will bring me down to the
ground?'
4 Though you ascend *as* high as
the eagle,
And though you set your nest
among the stars,
From there I will [c]bring you
down," says the LORD.
5 "If thieves had come to you,
If robbers by night—
Oh, how you will be cut off!—
Would they not have stolen till
they had enough?
If [d]grape-gatherers had come
to you,
Would they not have left *some*
gleanings?
6 "Oh, how Esau shall be
searched out!
How his hidden treasures shall
be sought after!
7 All the men in your
confederacy
Shall force you to the border;
The men at peace with you
Shall deceive you *and* prevail
against you.
Those who eat your bread
shall lay a trap* for you.
No one is aware of it.
8 [e]"Will I not in that day," says the
LORD,
"Even destroy the wise *men*
from [f]Edom,
And understanding from the
mountains of Esau?
9 Then your mighty men, O
[g]Teman, shall be dismayed,
To the end that everyone from
the mountains of Esau
May be cut off by [3]slaughter.

1 *a* vv. 1–9, 15–16; Jer. 25:21; 49:7–22; Ezek. 25:12–14; 35:1–15; Joel 3:19; Amos 1:11–12
3 *b* Jer. 49:16; cp. Ezek. 28:2
4 *c* Mal. 1:4; cp. Isa. 14:12–15
5 *d* Jer. 49:9
8 *e* See Jer. 49:7, *note*
f See Gen. 36:1, *note*
9 *g* Gen. 36:11; 1 Chr. 1:45; Job 2:11; Jer. 49:20. Teman was noted for its wisdom, Jer. 49:7

* v.7 Or *wound*, or *plot*

[1](v. 1) The enmity between Jacob and Esau (Gen. 36), the founder of Edom, persisted through the centuries (Ex. 15:15; Num. 20:14ff.; Ps. 83:6; Isa. 63:1–6; Joel 3:19; etc.). The sin of Edom was pride (v. 3), which led to violation of the bond between brothers (vv. 10–14).

[2](v. 3) The allusion is to Petra, the great cliff-city which, in Obadiah's time, was called Sela. See Introduction.

[3](v. 9) The destruction described here (cp. Jer. 49:7–22; Ezek. 25:12–14) was probably at

II. The Cause of This Doom, vv. 10–14

10 "For [a]violence against your
brother Jacob,
Shame shall cover you,
And you shall be [b]cut off
forever.
11 In the day that you [c]stood on
the other side—
In the day that strangers
carried [d]captive his
forces,
When foreigners entered his
gates
And cast lots for Jerusalem—
Even you *were* as one of
them.

12 "But you should not have gazed
on the day of your brother
In the day of his captivity;*
Nor should you have [e]rejoiced
over the children of Judah
In the day of their destruction;
Nor should you have spoken
proudly
In the day of distress.
13 You should not have entered
the gate of My people
In the day of their calamity.
Indeed, you should not have
gazed on their affliction
In the day of their calamity,
Nor laid *hands* on their
substance
In the day of their calamity.
14 You should not have stood at
the crossroads
To cut off those among them
who escaped;
Nor should you have delivered
up those among them who
remained
In the day of distress.

III. Edom in the Day of the LORD, vv. 15–21

15 "For the [f]day of the LORD
[g]upon all the nations *is*
near;
As you have done, it shall be
done to you;
Your reprisal shall return upon
your own head.
16 For as you drank on my holy
mountain,
So shall all the nations drink
continually;
Yes, they shall drink, and
swallow,
And they shall be as though
they had never been.

Future deliverance for Jacob; judgment on Esau

17 "But on Mount Zion there shall
be [h]deliverance,
And there shall be [1]holiness;
The house of Jacob shall
possess their possessions.
18 The house of Jacob shall be a
fire,
And the house of Joseph a
flame;
But the house of [2]Esau *shall be*
stubble;
They shall kindle them and
devour them,
And no survivor shall *remain*
of the [i]house of Esau,"
For the LORD has spoken.

19 The [j]South [k]shall possess the
mountains of Esau,
[l]And the [m]Lowland shall
possess Philistia.
They shall possess the fields of
Ephraim
And the fields of Samaria.
Benjamin *shall possess* Gilead.
20 And the captives of this host of
the children of Israel
Shall possess the land of the
Canaanites
As far as Zarephath.
The captives of Jerusalem who
are in Sepharad
Shall possess the cities of the
[j]South.

10
a Ezek. 25:12–13
b Joel 3:19
11
c Ps. 83:5–8
d Probably the deportation by Nebuchadnezzar, c. 586 B.C.
12
e Ezek. 35:15; 36:5
15
f *Day* (of the LORD): vv. 15–21; Zeph. 1:7. (Ps. 2:9; Rev. 19:19)
g *Armageddon* (battle of): vv. 15–18; Zeph. 3:8. (Isa. 10:27; Rev. 19:17)
17
h Joel 2:32
18
i vv. 9,10, 16; cp. Isa. 63:1–6
19
j See Gen. 12:9, *note*
k Isa. 11:14; Amos 9:12
l Zeph. 2:7
m See Dt. 1:7, *note*

* v.12 Literally *on the day he became a foreigner*

the hands of the Arabs. As a result Edom was almost devoid of popultion during the Persian period. The presence of Arabs in the neighborhood is shown by the aggression of Geshem, the Arab, the enemy of Nehemiah (Neh. 6:1–2). Later a mixture of Arabs with the remainder of the Edomites became quite a factor in the region of Petra, the former capital of Edom, establishing there a kingdom called the Nabataean kingdom, as well as in southern Palestine, which was largely in the hands of the Edomites. The Greeks and Romans called the Edomites Idumeans, another form of the same name. King Herod was an Edomite.

[1](v. 17) "There shall be holiness." Here Obadiah points to the essential element of the Messianic kingdom. Because the LORD's kingdom must be a holy kingdom, man who is by himself unholy can never establish it. Only the Holy One of Israel can set up a holy kingdom.

[2](v. 18) Edom will be revived (cp. Isa. 11:14) in the latter days.

21 Then [1]saviors shall come to
Mount Zion
To judge the mountains of
Esau,
And the [a]kingdom shall be the
[2b]LORD's.

21 *a* See Zech. 12:8 and 1 Cor. 15:24, *notes* *b* Ps. 22:28; Dan. 2:44; 7:14; Zech. 14:9; Rev. 11:15

[1](v. 21) Saviors or deliverers on the earth, as in Jud. 3:9,15, will serve under the Lord Jesus Christ, the King of kings (Rev. 19:16; cp. also Rev. 20:4).

[2](v. 21) This final verse is clearly Messianic. Short though his book is, Obadiah concludes, as do so many of the other prophets, with the promise of future deliverance for Israel in the kingdom.

The Book of

JONAH

Author: Jonah *Theme:* God's Mercy *Date of writing:* 8th Cent. B.C.

JONAH was a prophet of Israel who lived about the time of Jeroboam II (2 Ki. 14:25). His name means *dove,* and he occupies a unique place as the first foreign missionary. The historical character of Jonah's preservation in the great fish and his preaching to the inhabitants of Nineveh is attested by Christ, who likens the prophet's experience to His own burial and resurrection (Mt. 12:38–42).

A masterpiece of condensed narration, this book has suffered from overemphasis upon the miracle of the great fish (see 1:17, *note*). However, neither deletion nor rationalization solves the difficulty of the miracle which remains an object of faith, not explanation. The Book of Jonah is full of the supernatural; aside from the great fish, there are the vine, the worm, the east wind, and, greatest of all, the repentance of the entire city of Nineveh.

Jonah's character and God's dealing with him foreshadow the subsequent history of the nation of Israel: outside the land, a trouble to the Gentiles, yet witnessing to them; cast out, but miraculously preserved; in future deepest distress calling upon the LORD as Savior, finding deliverance and then becoming missionaries to the Gentiles (Zech. 8:7–23). But chiefly Jonah typifies Christ as the Sent-One, raised from the dead, and carrying salvation to the Gentiles.

The book may be divided as follows:

I. The Disobedience and Flight of Jonah, 1:1–11.
II. Jonah and the Great Fish, 1:12—2:10.
III. The Greatest Revival in History, 3.
IV. The Wideness of God's Mercy, 4.

I. The Disobedience and Flight of Jonah, 1:1–11

Introduction

1 NOW the word of the LORD came
to [1a]Jonah the son of Amittai,
saying,

Jonah flees from the LORD

2 "Arise, go to [b]Nineveh, that
[c]great city, and cry out against it; for
their wickedness has come up before
Me."
3 But Jonah arose to flee to Tarshish from the presence of the LORD.
He went down to [d]Joppa, and found a
ship going to [e]Tarshish; so he paid the
fare, and went down into it, to go with
them to Tarshish [f]from the presence
of the LORD.
4 But the LORD [g]sent out a great
[h]wind on the sea, and there was a
mighty tempest on the sea, so that the
ship was about to be broken up.
5 Then the [i]mariners were afraid;
and every man cried out to his god,
and threw the cargo that *was* in the
ship into the sea, to lighten the load.*
But Jonah had gone down into the
lowest parts of the ship, had lain
down, and was fast asleep.
6 So the captain came to him, and
said to him, "What do you mean,
sleeper? Arise, call on your God; perhaps your God will consider us, so
that we may not perish."
7 And they said to one another,
"Come, let us cast [j]lots, that we may
know for whose cause this trouble *has*
come upon us." So they cast lots, and
the lot fell on Jonah.
8 Then they said to him, "Please
tell us! For whose cause *is* this trouble
upon us? What is your occupation?
And where do you come from? What
is your country? And of what people
are you?"
9 So he said to them, "I *am* a Hebrew; and I [k]fear the LORD, the God of
heaven, [l]who made the sea and the
dry *land.*"
10 Then the men were exceedingly
afraid, and said to him, "Why have
you done this?" For the men knew that
he fled from the presence of the LORD,
because he had told them.
11 Then they said to him, "What
shall we do to you that the sea may be
calm for us?"—for the sea was growing more tempestuous.

CHAPTER 1
1
a 2 Ki. 14:25; Mt. 12:39–41; 16:4; Lk. 11:29–30, 32
2
b Isa. 37:37; see Nah. 1:1, *note*
c Gen. 10:11–12; Jon. 4:11; see Jon. 3:3, *note*
3
d The place of Peter's vision, Acts 10:5
e Isa. 23:1
f Gen. 4:16; Job 1:12; 2:7; cp. Ps. 139:7–10
4
g Lit. *hurled.* Cp. Ps. 148:8
h Ps. 107:25–28
5
i Probably the famous Phoenicians

1:7 *j* Prov. 16:33 1:9 *k* See Ps. 19:9, *note* *l* Neh. 9:6; Ps. 146:6; Acts 17:24

*1:5 Literally *from upon them*

---

[1](1:1) The prophet's home was Gath Hepher of Zebulun (2 Ki. 14:25), north of Nazareth in Galilee. Compare the misstatement quoted in Jn. 7:52.

II. Jonah and the Great Fish, 1:12—2:10

Jonah swallowed by the fish

12 And he said to them, "Pick [a]me
up and throw me into the sea; then the
sea will become calm for you. For I
know that this great tempest *is* because of me."
13 Nevertheless the men rowed
hard to return to land, but they could
[b]not, for the sea continued to grow
more tempestuous against them.
14 Therefore they cried out to the
LORD and said, "We pray, O LORD,
please do not let us perish for this
man's life, and do not charge us with
innocent [c]blood; for You, O LORD,
have done as it [d]pleased You."
15 So they picked up Jonah and
threw him into the sea, and the sea
[e]ceased from its raging.
16 Then the men feared the LORD
exceedingly, and offered a sacrifice to
the LORD and took vows.
17 Now the LORD had [1f]prepared a
[g]great fish to swallow Jonah. And Jonah was in the belly of the fish [h]three
days and three nights.

Jonah's prayer; the LORD's answer

2 THEN Jonah [2i]prayed to the LORD
his God from the fish's belly.
2 And he said:

"I [j]cried out to the LORD
because of my affliction,
And He answered me.
"Out of the belly of [k]Sheol I
cried,
And You heard my voice.
3 For You cast me into the deep,
Into the heart of the seas,
And the floods surrounded me;
All Your [l]billows and Your
waves passed over me.
4 Then I [m]said, 'I have been cast
out of Your sight;
Yet I will look again toward
Your holy temple.'
5 The [n]waters surrounded me,
even to my soul;
The deep closed around me;
Weeds were wrapped around
my head.
6 I went down to the moorings
of the mountains;
The earth with its bars *closed*
behind me forever;
Yet You have brought up my
life from the pit,
O LORD, my God.

7 "When my soul fainted within
me,
I remembered the LORD;
And my prayer went *up* to
You,
Into Your holy temple.

8 "Those who regard worthless
idols
Forsake their own Mercy.
9 But I will sacrifice to You
With the voice of thanksgiving;
I will pay what I have [o]vowed.
[p]Salvation *is* of the [q]LORD."

10 So the LORD [g]spoke to the fish,
and it vomited Jonah onto dry *land.*

III. The Greatest Revival in History, 3

Nineveh repents and is spared

3 NOW the word of the LORD came
to Jonah the second time, saying,
2 "Arise, go to [r]Nineveh, that
great city, and preach to it the message that I tell you."
3 So Jonah arose and went to Nineveh, according to the word of the
LORD. Now Nineveh was an exceedingly great city, a three-day [3]journey
in extent.

12 *a* Cp. 2 Sam. 24:17
13 *b* Prov. 21:30
14 *c* Cp. Gen. 9:5–6 *d* Dan. 4:35
15 *e* Ps. 107:29
17 *f* Lit. *appointed, ordered.* Jon. 4:6,7, 8 *g Miracles* (OT): 1:17–2:10. (Gen. 5:24; Jon. 1:17, *note*) *h* Mt. 12:40
CHAPTER 2
1 *i Bible prayers* (OT): vv. 1–9; Hab. 3:1. (Gen. 15:2; Hab. 3:1)
2 *j* Ps. 18:4–6; 120:1; 130:1; 142:1; Lam. 3:55–56 *k* Ps. 86:13; 88:1–7; see Hab. 2:5, *note*
3 *l* Ps. 42:7
4 *m* Ps. 31:22
5 *n* Ps. 69:1; Lam. 3:54
9 *o* Eccl. 5:4–5 *p* The theme of the Bible
q Jer. 3:23 3:2 *r* See Nah. 1:1, *note*

[1](1:17) No other miracle of Scripture has called forth so much unbelief. It has been claimed that a whale could not swallow a man, yet types of whales have been found that could easily do so. However, the word used here, like the one in Mt. 12:40, does not mean *whale* but *sea monster,* possibly the whale shark or rhinodon, the largest of all fish, sometimes attaining a length of seventy feet. The real miracle is not the swallowing but the fact that Jonah was alive when he was cast out of the great fish on to the dry land. After all, a miracle is what might be expected of divine love, interposing for good in a physically and morally disordered universe (Rom. 8:19–23).

[2](2:1) That Jonah prayed implies that he was alive and conscious. The prayer is full of passages from the Psalms, indicating that Jonah had stored the Word of God in his heart. Cp. Rom. 15:4.

[3](3:3) Nineveh was one of the greatest cities of ancient times. So large was its metropolitan area that it would take three days to go through it. This statement in Jonah was much questioned before the rise of modern archaeology. Excavations in Mesopotamia have fully confirmed the statements in Jonah, Nahum, and other parts of the OT about the greatness of

4 And Jonah began to enter the
city on the first day's walk. Then he
cried out and said, "Yet [1]forty days,
and Nineveh shall be overthrown!"
5 So the [a]people of Nineveh [b]be-
lieved God, proclaimed a fast, and put
on sackcloth, from the greatest to the
least of them.
6 Then word came to the king of
Nineveh; and he arose from his throne
and laid aside his robe, covered *himself* with sackcloth and sat in ashes.
7 And he caused *it* to be proclaimed and published throughout
Nineveh by the [c]decree of the king
and his nobles, saying,

Let neither man nor beast,
herd nor flock, taste anything;
do not let them eat, or drink
water.
8 But let man and beast be
covered with sackcloth, and
cry mightily to God; yes, let
every one turn from his evil
way and from the violence that
is in his hands.
9 Who can tell [d]*if* God will turn
and [e]relent, and turn away
from His fierce anger, so that
we may not perish?

10 Then God saw their works, that
they turned from their evil way; and
God [e]relented from the disaster that
He had said He would bring upon
them, and He did [2f]not do it.

IV. The Wideness of God's Mercy, 4

Jonah's displeasure

4 BUT it [3]displeased Jonah exceedingly, and he became [g]angry.
2 So he prayed to the LORD, and
said, "Ah, LORD, was not this what I

CHAPTER 3
5
a Mt. 12:41
b *Faith:* v. 5; Hab. 2:4. (Gen. 3:20; Heb. 11:39, *note*)
7
c Dan. 3:29
9
d Dan. 4:27; Joel 2:14; Amos 5:15
e See Zech. 8:14, *note*
10
f Jer. 18:8
CHAPTER 4
1
g Cp. Lk. 15:28
2
h Ex. 34:6; Ps. 86:5; Joel 2:13
4
i Cp. Mt. 20:15
5
j Cp. 1 Ki. 19:9–13
6
k Four prepared things. Cp. Jon. 1:17; 4:7,8

said when I was still in my country?
Therefore I fled previously to Tarshish; for I know that You *are* a [h]gra-
cious and merciful God, slow to anger
and abundant in lovingkindness, One
who [e]relents from doing harm.
3 "Therefore now, O LORD, please
take my life from me, for *it is* better for
me to die than to live!"

Jonah rebuked by the LORD

4 Then the LORD said, "*Is it* right
for you to be [i]angry?"
5 So Jonah went out of the city
and [j]sat on the east side of the city.
There he made himself a shelter
and sat under it in the shade, till he
might see what would become of the
city.
6 And the LORD God [k]prepared a
plant* and made it come up over Jonah, that it might be shade for his
head to deliver him from his misery.
So Jonah was very grateful for the
plant.
7 But as morning dawned the next
day God prepared a worm, and it *so*
damaged the plant that it withered.
8 And it happened, when the sun
arose, that God prepared a vehement
east wind; and the sun beat on Jonah's
head, so that he grew faint. Then he
wished death for himself, and said,
"*It is* better for me to die than to
live."
9 Then God said to Jonah, "*Is it*
right for you to be angry about the
plant?" And he said, "*It is* right for me
to be angry, even to death!"
10 But the LORD said, "You have had
pity on the [4]plant for which you have
not labored, nor made it grow, which

*4:6 Hebrew *kikayon,* exact identity unknown

Nineveh. Yet in 612 B.C. Nineveh was so completely destroyed by its enemies that even its location was forgotten. See 3:4, *note*.

[1](3:4) The message of Jonah, as is so often the case in prophetic books, was ethically conditioned. If Nineveh repented, it would be spared; if it refused, it was to be destroyed.

Since God knew that Nineveh would ultimately reject His Word and would turn to even greater wickedness than before, the prediction of destruction is given in absolute form. Never was a city more terribly destroyed than was Nineveh. The whole Book of Nahum is devoted to predicting this terrible utter destruction. The forty-day element was ethically conditioned, and the time was lengthened at the occurrence of the great temporary revival described here in ch. 3. Compare the similar postponement of a predicted catastrophe in 1 Ki. 21:29.

[2](3:10) This is the greatest revival in recorded history; no physical miracle in this book compares with the marvel and extent of this spiritual miracle.

[3](4:1) The old nature resists the display of God's grace to any of His creatures. An example is Jonah's own admission in 4:2.

[4](4:10) In these last verses the great missionary lesson of the book is sharply drawn: Are the souls of men not worth as much as a vine? Like Jonah, God's people today are often more concerned about the material benefits so freely bestowed upon us by God than about the destiny of a lost world.

came up in a night and perished in a
night.
11 "And should I not pity [a]Nineveh,
that [b]great city, in which are more
than one hundred and twenty thousand persons who cannot discern between their right hand and their left—and much livestock?"

11 [a]See Nah. 1:1, *note* [b] See Jon. 3:3, *note*

The Book of

MICAH

Author: Micah *Theme:* Judgment and Kingdom *Date of writing:* 8th Cent. B.C.

MICAH, whose name means *Who is like the LORD?*, prophesied in the eighth century B.C. as a contemporary of Isaiah (cp. 1:1 with Isa. 1:1). He came from the small town of Moresheth, about twenty miles southwest of Jerusalem. There are many similarities between passages in Isaiah and Micah (cp. Mic. 4:1–5 with Isa. 2:2–4). Jeremiah mentions Micah by name (Jer. 26:18) and relates him to the reign of Hezekiah, and our Lord quotes Mic. 7:6 in Mt. 10:35–36. Samaria, Jerusalem, all Judah, Israel, and the nations are the subject of the prophecy. Assyria is the prominent foreign power. The messages are particularly to the capital cities, Samaria and Jerusalem, as the centers of influence in the nation. God pleads with Israel and Judah to turn to Him from their sin, setting forth the Assyrian as the rod of His wrath, and He concludes with promises of future glory under the Messiah and His righteous reign.

The book may be divided as follows:

I. Condemnation and Captivity, 1—2.
II. Rebuke, and Restoration in the Kingdom, 3—5.
III. Pleading, and Assurance of Mercy, 6—7.

I. Condemnation and Captivity, 1—2

Introduction

1 THE word of the LORD that came to [a]Micah of Moresheth in the days of [b]Jotham, Ahaz, *and* Hezekiah, kings of Judah, which he saw concerning Samaria and Jerusalem.

Judgment on Israel

2 Hear, all you peoples!
Listen, O earth, and all that is in it!
Let the Lord GOD be a witness against you,
The Lord from His holy temple.
3 For behold, the LORD is [1]coming out of His place;
He will come down
And tread on the [c]high places of the earth.
4 The mountains will melt under Him,
And the valleys will split
Like wax before the fire,
Like waters poured down a steep place.
5 All this is for the transgression of Jacob
And for the sins of the house of Israel.
What *is* the transgression of Jacob?
Is it not Samaria?
And what *are* the [d]high places of Judah?
Are they not Jerusalem?

Assyria will destroy Samaria and reach the gate of Jerusalem

6 [2]"Therefore I will make Samaria a heap of ruins in the field,
Places for planting a vineyard;
I will pour down her stones into the valley,
And I will uncover her foundations.
7 All her carved images shall be beaten to pieces,
And all her [3e]pay as a harlot shall be burned with the fire;
All her idols I will lay desolate,
For she gathered *it* from the [f]pay of a harlot,
And they shall return to the pay of a harlot."
8 Therefore I will wail and howl,
I will go stripped and naked;
I will make a wailing like the [g]jackals
And a mourning like the ostriches,
9 For her wounds *are* incurable.

CHAPTER 1

1
a Jer. 26:18
b 2 Ki. 15:5, 7,32–38; 2 Chr. 27:1–9; Isa. 1:1; Hos. 1:1

3
c Dt. 32:13; 33:29; Amos 4:13

5
d 1 Ki. 15:14; see Jud. 3:7 and 2 Ki. 3:2, *notes;* cp. Amos 4:4, *note*

7
e Hos. 2:5, 12
f Dt. 23:18

8
g Job 30:29

---

[1](1:3) These words predict Shalmaneser's destruction of the northern kingdom, Sennacherib's invasion, and Nebuchadnezzar's invasion.

[2](1:6) In vv. 6–16 the Assyrian invasion is described. Cp. 2 Ki. 17:1–18. This is the local circumstance which gives rise to the prophecy of the greater invasion in the last days (4:11–13), when the Lord will deliver His people at the Battle of Armageddon (Rev. 16:13–16; see Rev. 19:17, *note*).

[3](1:7) This "pay as a harlot" probably was costly vessels that had been given to heathen temples.

For it has come to Judah;
It has come to the gate of My
people—
To Jerusalem.

10 Tell *it* not in [a]Gath,
Weep not at all;
In Beth Aphrah*
Roll yourself in the dust.
11 Pass by in naked shame, you
inhabitant of Shaphir;
The inhabitant of Zaanan*
does not go out.
Beth Ezel mourns;
Its place to stand is taken
away from you.
12 For the inhabitant of Maroth
pined* for [b]good,
But [c]disaster came down from
the LORD
To the gate of Jerusalem.
13 O inhabitant of [d]Lachish,
Harness the chariot to the
swift steeds
(She *was* the beginning of sin
to the daughter of Zion),
For the transgressions of Israel
were [e]found in you.
14 Therefore you shall give
presents to Moresheth
Gath;*
The houses of [f]Achzib* *shall
be* a lie to the kings of
Israel.
15 I will yet bring an heir to you,
O inhabitant of Mareshah;*
The glory of Israel shall come
to [g]Adullam.
16 Make yourself bald and cut off
your hair,
Because of your precious
children;
Enlarge your baldness like an
eagle,
For they shall go from you into
[h]captivity.

Reasons for judgment

2 WOE to those who devise
iniquity,
And work out evil on their
beds!
At [i]morning light they
practice it,
[1]Because it is in the [j]power of
their hand.
2 They [k]covet fields and take
them by [l]violence,
Also houses, and seize *them*.
So they oppress a man and his
house,
A man and his inheritance.

3 Therefore thus says the LORD:
"Behold, against this [m]family I
am devising [n]disaster,
From which you cannot
remove your necks;
Nor shall you walk haughtily,
For this *is* an evil time.
4 In that day *one* shall take up a
proverb against you,
And lament with a bitter
lamentation, saying:
'We are utterly destroyed!
He has changed the heritage of
my people;
How He has removed *it* from
me!
To a turncoat He has divided
our fields.' "

5 Therefore you will have no one
to determine boundaries* by
lot
In the assembly of the LORD.
6 [2]"Do not prattle," *you say to
those* who prophesy.
So they shall not prophesy to
you;*
They shall not return insult for
insult.*
7 *You who are* named the house
of Jacob:
"Is the [o]Spirit of the LORD
restricted?
Are these His [p]doings?
Do not My words do good
To him who walks uprightly?
8 "Lately My people have risen
up as an enemy—
You pull off the robe with the
garment
From those who trust *you*, as
they pass by,
Like men returned from war.
9 The women of My people you
cast out
From their pleasant houses;
From their children
You have taken away My
glory forever.

10
a 2 Sam. 1:20
12
b Isa. 59:9–11
c Amos 3:6
13
d Isa. 36:2
e Ezek. 23:11
14
f Josh. 15:44
15
g 2 Chr. 11:7
16
h Amos 7:11,17; Mic. 4:10
CHAPTER 2
1
i Hos. 7:6–7
j Cp. Prov. 3:27
2
k Isa. 5:8
l Cp. Ahab and Naboth, 1 Ki. 21:1–16
3
m Ex. 20:5; Jer. 8:3
n Amos 5:13
7
o Holy Spirit (OT): v. 7; Mic. 3:8. (Gen. 1:2; Zech. 12:10)
p Cp. Isa. 28:21; Ezek. 33:11; Mic. 7:18

*
1:10 Literally *House of Dust* 1:11 Literally *Going Out* 1:12 Literally *was sick* 1:14 Literally *Possession of Gath* • Literally *Lie* 1:15 Literally *Inheritance* 2:5 Literally *one casting a surveyor's line* 2:6 Literally *to these* • Vulgate reads *He shall not take shame.*

[1](2:1) Their principle was "might makes right." Observe the LORD's viewpoint (vv. 3–5).
[2](2:6) The chief reason for the rise of the false prophets was the unpopular character of the message of the true prophets, who called the nation back to God.

10 "Arise and depart,
For this *is* not *your* rest;
Because it is defiled, it shall destroy,
Yes, with utter destruction.
11 If a man should walk in a false spirit
And speak a lie, *saying,*
'I will prophesy to you of wine and drink,'
Even he would be the [a]prattler of this people.

Deliverance promised

12 "I will surely assemble all of you, O Jacob,
I will surely gather the [b]remnant of Israel;
I will put them together like sheep of the [c]fold,*
Like a flock in the midst of their pasture;
They shall make a loud noise because of [d]*so many* people.
13 The one who breaks open will come up before them;
They will break out,
Pass through the gate,
And go out by it;
Their king will pass before them,
With the LORD at their head."

II. Rebuke, and Restoration in the Kingdom, 3—5

Faithless leaders rebuked

3 AND I said:
"Hear now, O heads of Jacob,
And you [e]rulers of the house of Israel:
Is it not for you to know [f]justice?
2 You who hate good and love evil;
Who strip the skin from My people,*
And the flesh from their bones;
3 Who also eat the flesh of My people,
Flay their skin from them,
Break their bones,
And chop *them* in pieces
Like *meat* for the pot,
Like flesh in the [g]caldron."
4 Then they will cry to the LORD,
But He will [h]not hear them;
He will even hide His face from them at that time,
Because they have been evil in their deeds.

5 Thus says the LORD concerning the [i]prophets
Who make my people stray;
Who chant "Peace"
While they chew with their teeth,
But who prepare war against him
Who puts nothing into their mouths:
6 "Therefore you shall have night without vision,
And you shall have darkness without divination;
The sun shall go down on the prophets,
And the day shall be dark for [j]them.
7 So the seers shall be ashamed,
And the diviners abashed;
Indeed they shall all cover their lips;
For *there is* no answer from God."
8 But truly I am full of [k]power by the [l]Spirit of the LORD,
And of justice and might,
To declare to Jacob his [m]transgression
And to Israel his sin.

Jerusalem to be destroyed

9 Now hear this,
You heads of the house of Jacob
And rulers of the house of Israel,
Who abhor justice
And pervert all equity,
10 Who build up Zion with [n]bloodshed
And Jerusalem with iniquity:
11 Her heads judge for a [o]bribe,
Her priests teach for pay,
And her prophets [1]divine for money.
Yet they lean on the LORD, and say,
"Is not the LORD among us?
No harm can come upon us."
12 [p]Therefore because of you
[q]Zion shall be plowed *like* a field,
Jerusalem shall become heaps of ruins,

11
a Isa. 30:10; Jer. 5:30–31; 2 Tim. 4:3–4
12
b *Remnant:* vv. 12–13; Mic. 4:1. (Isa. 1:9; Rom. 11:5, *note*)
c Cp. 2 Ki. 3:4
d Jer. 33:22
CHAPTER 3
1
e Ezek. 22:27
f Jer. 5:5
3
g Ezek. 11:7; cp. Ezek. 24:3–14
4
h Jer. 11:11
5
i Jer. 6:13; Ezek. 13:19
6
j Isa. 29:10; Jer. 23:33–40; Ezek. 13:23
8
k *Inspiration:* v. 8; Hab. 2:2. (Ex. 4:15; 2 Tim. 3:16, *note*)
l *Holy Spirit* (OT): v. 8; Hag. 2:5. (Gen. 1:2; Zech. 12:10)
m Isa. 58:1
10
n Hab. 2:12
11
o Mic. 7:3; cp. Isa. 1:23; Jer. 6:13
12
p Fulfilled A.D. 70. Cp. Lk. 21:20–24
q Jer. 26:18

*2:12 Hebrew *Bozrah* 3:2 Literally *them*

[1](3:11) Fortune-telling, or "divining," is never referred to in the OT in a good sense. Cp. Balaam, Num. 23—24.

And the mountain of the
temple*
Like the bare hills of the
forest.

Vision of earth's golden age

4 [a]NOW it shall come to pass in
the [1]latter days
That the [2]mountain of the
LORD's house
Shall be established on the
[b]top of the mountains,
And shall be exalted above the
hills;
And peoples shall flow to [c]it.
2 Many nations shall come and
say,
"Come, and let us go up to the
mountain of the LORD,
To the house of the God of
Jacob;
He will teach us His ways,
And we shall walk in His
paths."
For out of Zion the law shall
go forth,
And the word of the LORD from
Jerusalem.
3 He shall judge between many
peoples,
And rebuke strong nations afar
off;
They shall beat their swords
into plowshares,
And their spears into pruning
hooks;
Nation shall not lift up sword
against nation,
Neither shall they learn war
anymore.
4 But everyone shall sit under
his vine and under his fig
tree,
And no one shall make *them*
afraid;
For the mouth of the LORD of
hosts has spoken.
5 For all people walk each in the
name of his god,
But we will walk in the name
of the LORD our God
Forever and ever.

Israel to be regathered

6 "In that day," says the LORD,
"I will assemble the lame,
I will gather the [d]outcast
And those whom I have
afflicted;
7 I will make the lame a
remnant,
And the outcast a strong
nation;
So the [e]LORD will [f]reign over
them in Mount Zion
From now on, even forever.
8 And you, O tower of the flock,
The stronghold of the daughter
of Zion,
To you shall it come,
Even the former dominion
shall come,
The kingdom of the daughter
of Jerusalem."

Intervening Babylonian captivity

9 Now why do you cry aloud?
Is there no king in your midst?
Has your counselor perished?
For pangs have seized you like
a woman in labor.
10 Be in pain, and labor to bring
forth,
O daughter of Zion,
Like a woman in birth pangs.
For now you shall go forth
from the city,
You shall dwell in the field,
And to [g]Babylon you shall go.
There you shall be [h]delivered;
There the [i]LORD will [j]redeem
you
From the hand of your
enemies.

Armageddon predicted

11 Now also [3]many nations have
gathered against you,

CHAPTER 4

1
a vv. 1–4; Isa. 2:2–4; see Acts 2:17, *note*
b Kingdom (OT): vv. 1–5; Mic. 5:2. (Gen. 1:26; Zech. 12:8, *note*)
c Remnant: vv. 1–7; Mic. 5:3. (Isa. 1:9; Rom. 11:5, *note*)

6
d Ezek. 34:16

7
e Christ (second advent): vv. 6–7; Hag. 2:6. (Dt. 30:3; Acts 1:11, *note*)
f Isa. 24:23

10
g Amos 5:27
h Through Cyrus. Cp. Isa. 44:28; 45:1–4
i Isa. 45:13
j Ps. 18:7

*3:12 Literally *house*

[1](4:1) Micah 4:1–3 and Isa. 2:2–4 are practically identical. The Spirit of God gave both prophets the same revelation because of its surpassing importance. It is impossible to prove that either prophet was quoting the other.

[2](4:1) In vv. 1–4 there are some general predictions concerning the kingdom. In Scripture a mountain is sometimes the symbol of a great earthly power (Dan. 2:35); hills, of smaller powers. The prediction asserts (1) the ultimate establishment of the kingdom, with Jerusalem for the capital (v. 2); (2) the universality of the future kingdom (v. 2); (3) its character—peace (v. 3); and (4) its effect—prosperity (v. 4). Cp. Isa. 2:1–5; 11:1–12.

[3](4:11) Having described the future kingdom (vv. 1–8) and glanced at the Babylonian captivity (vv. 9–10), Micah looks forward into the last days to refer to the great battle (see Armageddon, Rev. 16:13–16; 19:17, *note*) which immediately precedes the setting up of the Messianic kingdom. See Kingdom (OT) (Gen. 1:26–28; Zech. 12:8, *note*); also, Kingdom (NT) (Lk. 1:31–33; 1 Cor. 15:24, *note*).

Who say, "Let her be defiled,
And let our eye look upon
Zion."
12 But they do [a]not know the
thoughts of the LORD,
Nor do they understand His
counsel;
For He will gather them like
sheaves to the threshing
floor.

13 [b]"Arise and [c]thresh, O daughter
of Zion;
For I will make your [d]horn
iron,
And I will make your hooves
bronze;
You shall beat in pieces many
peoples;
I will consecrate their gain to
the LORD,
And their substance to the
Lord of the whole earth."

Birth and rejection of the King
(cp. Mt. 2:1–6; 27:24–37)

5 NOW gather yourself in
troops,
O daughter of troops;
He has laid siege against us;
They will strike the [e]judge of
Israel with a rod on the
cheek.

2 "But you, Bethlehem
[f]Ephrathah,
Though you are little among
the thousands of Judah,
Yet [g]out of [h]you shall come
forth to Me
The One to be [i]Ruler in Israel,
Whose goings forth *are* from
of old,
From [1]everlasting."

Interval between the rejection
and the return of the King

3 Therefore He shall give them
up,

12
a Cp. Isa. 10:7
13
b Zech. 12:1–8; 14:14
c Isa. 41:15
d See Dt. 33:17, *note*
CHAPTER 5
1
e King Zedekiah in the Babylonian invasion
2
f Gen. 35:19
g Mt. 2:5–12; Lk. 2:4,11; Jn. 7:42
h Christ (first advent): v. 2; Zech. 9:9. (Gen. 3:15; Acts 1:11, *note*)
i Kingdom (OT): vv. 2,4; Zeph. 3:15. (Gen. 1:26; Zech. 12:8, *note*)
3
j Remnant: vv. 3–9; Mic. 7:18. (Isa. 1:9; Rom. 11:5, *note*)
4
k Ps. 72:8; Isa. 52:13; Zech. 9:10; Lk. 1:32
5
l vv. 5–6; Isa. 10:5–27; 14:24–27; Zeph. 2:13
6
m Gen. 10:8–12
n Isa. 14:25

Until the time *that* she who is
in labor has given birth;
Then the [j]remnant of His
brethren
Shall return to the children of
Israel.
4 And He shall stand and feed
His flock
In the strength of the LORD,
In the majesty of the name of
the LORD His God;
And they shall abide,
For now He [k]shall be great
To the ends of the earth;
5 And this *One* shall be peace.

When the [l]Assyrian comes
into our land,
And when he treads in our
palaces,
Then we will raise against him
Seven shepherds and eight
princely men.
6 They shall waste with the
sword the land of Assyria,
And the [m]land of Nimrod at its
entrances;
Thus He shall [n]deliver *us* from
the Assyrian,
When he comes into our land
And when he treads within our
borders.

7 Then the remnant of Jacob
Shall be in the midst of many
peoples,
Like [o]dew from the LORD,
Like showers on the grass,
That tarry for no man
Nor wait for the sons of men.
8 And the remnant of Jacob
Shall be among the Gentiles,
In the midst of many peoples,
Like a [p]lion among the beasts
of the forest,
Like a young lion among
flocks of sheep,

5:7 *o* Gen. 27:28 5:8 *p* Num. 24:9

In ch. 5:2 the scene shifts from the great battle (yet future) to the birth and rejection of the King, Messiah (Mt. 27:24–25,37). This is followed by the statement that Israel will be abandoned "until the time that she who is in labor has given birth" (v. 3). There is a twofold "labor" of Israel: (1) that which brings forth the "male Child" (Christ) (Rev. 12:1–2,5); and (2) that which, in the last days, brings forth a believing remnant out of the still unbelieving nation (v. 3; 4:10; Jer. 30:6–11). Both aspects are combined in Isa. 66. In Isa. 66:7 there is the male Child (Christ) of Rev. 12:1–2,5; in Isa. 66:8–24, the remnant, established in kingdom blessing. The meaning of Mic. 5:3 is that, from the rejection of Christ at His first coming, the LORD will abandon Israel until the believing remnant appear; then He stands and shepherds in His proper strength as the LORD (v. 4); He is the defense of His people as in 4:3,11–13; and afterward the remnant go as missionaries to Israel and to all the world (5:7–8; Zech. 8:23).

[1](5:2) The Ruler comes from Bethlehem in time, but His activities have been from eternity. His goings forth were in creation, preservation, providences, theophanies, and redemptive activity. The eternal preexistence of the Messiah is thus strongly presented.

Who, if he passes through,
Both treads down and tears in pieces,
And none can deliver.
9 Your hand shall be lifted against your adversaries,
And all your enemies shall be cut off.

10 "And it shall be in that day," says the LORD,
"That I will [a]cut off your [b]horses from your midst
And destroy your [c]chariots.
11 I will cut off the cities of your land
And throw down all your strongholds.
12 I will cut off sorceries from your hand,
And you shall have no soothsayers.
13 Your carved images I will also cut off,
And your sacred pillars from your midst;
You shall no more worship the work of your hands;
14 I will pluck your [d]wooden images from your midst;
Thus I will destroy your cities.
15 And I will execute vengeance in anger and fury
On the nations that have not heard."*

III. Pleading, and Assurance of Mercy, 6—7

The LORD's past and present controversy with Israel (vv. 1–5; 10–16)

6 HEAR now what the LORD says:
"Arise, plead your case before the mountains,
And let the hills hear your voice.
2 Hear, O you mountains, the LORD's complaint,
And you strong foundations of the earth;
For the LORD has a [e]complaint against His people,
And He will contend with Israel.

3 "O My people, what have I [f]done to you?
And how have I [g]wearied you?
Testify against Me.
4 For I brought you up from the land of Egypt,
I [h]redeemed you from the house of bondage;
And I sent before you Moses, Aaron, and Miriam.
5 O My people, remember now
What [i]Balak king of Moab counseled,
And what Balaam the son of Beor answered him,
From Acacia Grove* to Gilgal,
That you may know the righteousness of the LORD."

What the LORD requires of man

6 With what shall I come before the LORD,
And bow myself before the High God?
Shall I come before Him with burnt offerings,
With calves a year old?
7 Will the LORD be [j]pleased with thousands of rams,
Ten thousand rivers of oil?
Shall I give my [1]firstborn *for* my transgression,
The fruit of my body *for* the sin of my soul?

8 He has [k]shown you, O man, what *is* good;
And what does the LORD [2]require of you
But [l]to do justly,
To love mercy,
And to walk humbly with your God?

9 The LORD's voice cries to the city—
Wisdom shall see Your name:

"Hear the rod!
Who has appointed it?
10 Are there yet the treasures of wickedness
In the house of the wicked,
And the short measure *that is* an abomination?
11 Shall I count pure *those* with the wicked scales,

10
a Zech. 9:10
b Dt. 17:16
c Isa. 2:7; 22:18

14
d See Dt. 16:21, *note*

CHAPTER 6
2
e Isa. 1:18; Hos. 12:2

3
f Isa. 5:4; Jer. 2:5
g Isa. 43:22–23; Mal. 1:13

4
h See Ex. 14:30 and Isa. 52:20, *notes*

5
i Num. 23:7–10, 18–24; 24:3–9, 15–24

7
j Ps. 40:6–8; 51:16–17; Isa. 1:12–13; 66:3; Jer. 6:20; Hos. 9:4; Amos 5:21–22

8
k Dt. 10:12; 1 Sam. 15:22; Hos. 6:6; 12:6
l Gen. 18:19; Isa. 1:17

*
5:15 Or *obeyed* 6:5 Hebrew *Shittim* (compare Numbers 25:1; Joshua 2:1, 3:1)

[1](6:7) The law claimed the firstborn of man and beast for the LORD (Ex. 13:2,12). The firstborn of beasts were sacrificed. However, the sacrifice of children was forbidden on pain of death (Lev. 18:21; 20:2–5; Dt. 12:31; 18:10). They were redeemed (Ex. 13:13). This passage does not teach that human sacrifice was common in Israel; it merely reveals the futility of such a practice.

[2](6:8) Old Testament piety was essentially concerned with the ethical, not with externals.

And with the bag of deceitful
[a]weights?
12 For her rich men are full of
[b]violence,
Her inhabitants have spoken
lies,
And their tongue is deceitful in
their mouth.
13 "Therefore I will also make *you*
sick by striking you,
By making *you* desolate
because of your sins.
14 You shall eat, but not be
satisfied;
Hunger* *shall be* in your
midst.
You may carry *some* away,*
but shall not save *them;*
And what you do rescue I will
give over to the sword.
15 [c]"You shall sow, but not reap;
You shall tread the olives, but
not anoint yourselves with
oil;
And *make* sweet wine, but not
drink wine.
16 For the statutes of [d]Omri are
kept;
All the works of [e]Ahab's
house *are done;*
And you walk in their
counsels,
That I may make you a
desolation,
And your inhabitants a hissing.
Therefore you shall bear the
reproach of My people."*

The prophet confesses the truth of the LORD's indictment

7 WOE is me!
For I am like those who gather
summer fruits,
Like those who glean vintage
grapes;
There is no cluster to eat
Of the first-ripe fruit *which* my
soul desires.
2 The faithful *man* has [f]perished
from the earth,
And *there is* no one upright
among men.
They all lie in wait for blood;
Every man hunts his brother
with a net.

3 That they may successfully do
evil with both hands—
The prince asks *for gifts,*
The judge *seeks* a [g]bribe,
And the great *man* utters his
evil desire;
So they scheme together.
4 The best of them *is* like a
brier;
The most upright *is sharper*
than a thorn hedge;
The day of your watchman and
your punishment comes;
Now shall be their perplexity.

5 Do [h]not [i]trust in a friend;
Do not put your confidence in
a companion;
Guard the doors of your mouth
From her who lies in your
[j]bosom.
6 For son dishonors father,
Daughter rises against her
mother,
Daughter-in-law against her
mother-in-law;
A man's enemies *are* the men
of his own [k]household.

Submission to the LORD; ascription of praise

7 [1]Therefore I will look to the
LORD;
I will [l]wait for the God of my
salvation;
My God will hear me.

8 Do not rejoice over me, my
enemy;
When I fall, I will [m]arise;
When I sit in darkness,
The LORD *will be* a light to me.
9 I will bear the indignation of
the LORD,
Because I have [n]sinned against
Him,
Until He pleads my [o]case
And executes justice for me.
He will bring me forth to the
light;
I will see [p]His righteousness.
10 Then *she who is* my enemy
will see,
And shame will cover her who
said to me,
"Where is the LORD your God?"
My eyes will see her;

11 *a* Lev. 19:36; Hos. 12:7
12 *b* Mic. 2:2
15 *c* Dt. 28:38–40; Amos 5:11; Zeph. 1:13; Hag. 1:6
16 *d* 1 Ki. 16:25–26 *e* 1 Ki. 16:30; 21:25–26; 2 Ki. 21:3
CHAPTER 7
2 *f* Isa. 57:1
3 *g* Mic. 3:11
5 *h* Jer. 9:4 *i* See Ps. 2:12, *note* *j* Dt. 28:56
6 *k* Mt. 10:36
7 *l* Ps. 130:5; Isa. 25:9; Lam. 3:24–25
8 *m* Prov. 24:16; 2 Cor. 4:9
9 *n* Lam. 3:39–40 *o* Jer. 50:34 *p* Rom. 10:1–4; 11:23–27

*
6:14 Or *Emptiness* or *Humiliation* • Targum and Vulgate read *You shall take hold.* 6:16 Following Masoretic Text, Targum, and Vulgate; Septuagint reads *of nations.*

[1](7:7) Verses 7–20 are, primarily, the confession and intercession of the prophet, who identifies himself with Israel. Cp. Dan. 9:3–19. Intercession was a part of the prophetic office (Gen. 20:7; Jer. 27:18). But Micah's prayer voices also the heart exercise of the remnant in the last days. Such is prophecy, an intermingling of the near and the far. Cp. Ps. 22:1; Mt. 27:46.

Now she will be trampled
down
Like mud in the streets.

11 *In* the day when your [a]walls
are to be built,
In that day the decree shall go
far and wide.*
12 *In* that day they* shall [b]come
to you
From Assyria and the fortified
cities,*
From the fortress* to the
[c]River,
From sea to sea,
And mountain *to* mountain.
13 Yet the land shall be desolate
Because of those who dwell in
it,
And for the fruit of their
deeds.

14 Shepherd Your people with
Your staff,
The flock of Your heritage,
Who dwell solitarily *in* a
woodland,
In the midst of Carmel;
Let them feed *in* Bashan and
Gilead,
As in days of old.

15 [d]"As in the days when you came
out of the land of Egypt,
I will show them* [e]wonders."

16 The nations shall see and be
ashamed of all their might;
They shall put *their* hand over
their mouth;
Their ears shall be deaf.
17 They shall [f]lick the dust like a
serpent;
They shall crawl from their
holes like snakes of the
earth.
[g]They shall be afraid of the
LORD our God,
And shall fear because of You.
18 Who *is* a God like [1]You,
[2h]Pardoning iniquity
And passing over the
transgression of the
[i]remnant of His heritage?

He does not retain His anger
[j]forever,
Because He delights *in* [k]mercy.
19 He will again have compassion
on us,
And will subdue our iniquities.

You will [l]cast all our* sins
Into the depths of the sea.
20 You will [m]give truth to Jacob
And mercy to Abraham,
Which You have sworn to our
fathers
From days of old.

11
a Amos 9:11
12
b Isa. 19:23–25
c i.e. *the Euphrates*
15
d Ps. 78:12
e Ex. 34:10
17
f Ps. 72:9; Isa. 49:23
g Jer. 33:9
18
h Ex. 34:7,9; Isa. 43:25
i *Remnant:* v. 18; Zeph. 2:7. (Isa. 1:9; Rom. 11:5, *note*)
j Ps. 103:8–9
k Ezek. 33:11
19
l Cp. Isa. 38:17; 43:25; 44:22; Jer. 31:34; Heb. 8:12; 10:17
20
m Lk. 1:72–73

*

7:11 Or *the boundary shall be extended*
7:12 Literally *he*, collective of the captives
• Hebrew *arey mazor*, possibly *cities of Egypt*
• Hebrew *mazor*, possibly *Egypt* **7:15** Literally *him*, collective for the captives **7:19** Literally *their*

[1](7:18) Here is a play on the prophet's name, which means *Who is like the* LORD?
[2](7:18) Verses 18–20 are read in the synagogue on the Day of Atonement. Annually the orthodox Jew, at a river or running stream, symbolically empties his pockets of his sins, casting them into the water (see v. 19).

The Book of

NAHUM

Author: Nahum *Theme:* Nineveh's Doom *Date of writing:* 7th Cent. B.C.

NAHUM means *comfort (of God)* and is related to the name Nehemiah. Nahum prophesied during the seventh century B.C. His book forms the sequel to the Book of Jonah. The repentance under Jonah delayed the judgment of God for about a century. Nahum's prophecy may be dated between the destruction of Thebes or No Amon (3:8) by Ashurbanipal in 666 B.C. and the capture of Nineveh by the Babylonians and their allies in 612 B.C. The style of Nahum is lyric poetry of a high order, which some have considered the most impassioned in all the prophets. All concede that his messages are vivid and forceful.

The book may be divided as follows:

I. The Character of God, 1:1–8.
II. God's Punishment of His Enemies, 1:9–15.
III. The Destruction of Nineveh Detailed, 2.
IV. The Cause of the Destruction, 3.

I. The Character of God, 1:1–8

Introduction

1 THE [a]burden* against [1b]Nineveh. The book of the vision of Nahum the Elkoshite.

The holiness of the LORD; judgment on Nineveh

2 [2]God *is* jealous, and the LORD avenges;
The LORD avenges and *is* furious.
The LORD will take vengeance on His adversaries,
And He reserves *wrath* for His enemies;
3 [c]The LORD *is* slow to anger and great in power,
And will not at all acquit *the* wicked.

[d]The LORD has His way
In the whirlwind and in the storm,
And the clouds *are* the dust of His feet.
4 He rebukes the sea and makes it dry,
And dries up all the rivers.
[3]Bashan and Carmel wither,
And the flower of Lebanon wilts.
5 The mountains quake before Him,
The hills melt,
And the earth heaves* at His presence,
Yes, the world and all who dwell in it.

6 [e]Who can stand before His indignation?
And who can endure the fierceness of His anger?
His fury is poured out like fire,
And the rocks are thrown down by Him.

7 The LORD *is* [f]good,
A stronghold in the day of trouble;
And [g]He knows those who trust in Him.
8 But with an overflowing flood
He will make an utter end of its place,

CHAPTER 1

1
a See Isa. 13:1, *note*
b Gen. 10:11; 2 Ki. 19:36; Jon. 1:2; 4:11; Nah. 2:8; 3:7; Zeph. 2:13; Mt. 12:41; Lk. 11:32; see Jon. 3:3 and 4, *notes*

3
c Ex. 34:6–7; Neh. 9:17; Ps. 103:8; Jon. 4:2; 2 Pet. 3:9
d Cp. Ps. 18:7–15; 97:2; 104:3; Hab. 3:5, 11–12

6
e Mal. 3:2

7
f Ps. 25:8; 37:39–40; 100:5; Jer. 33:11; Lam. 3:25
g Ps. 1:6; 2 Tim. 2:19; see Ps. 2:12, *note*

*1:1 Or *oracle* 1:5 Targum reads *burns.*

---

[1](1:1) Nineveh, the capital of the ancient Assyrian Empire, was noted for its cruelty and violence (Jon. 3:8). This is confirmed by the ancient records found there. Under the preaching of Jonah in the eighth century B.C., the city and king had turned to God (Jon. 3:3–10). But in the time of Nahum, a century or more later, the city had wholly departed from God. The message of Nahum, therefore, though given perhaps a generation before the destruction of the city, is not a call to repentance but an unrelieved warning of judgment (1:9; 3:10). Such is the way of God; light rejected brings destruction.

[2](1:2) The great ethical lesson of Nahum is that the character of God makes Him not only "slow to anger" (v. 3) and a refuge to those who trust Him (v. 7), but also one who "will not at all acquit the wicked" (v. 3). He can be "just and the justifier of the one who has faith in Jesus" (Rom. 3:26), but only because His holy law has been vindicated in the cross.

[3](1:4) Bashan, Carmel, and Lebanon are known to have been among the most fertile regions of Palestine.

And darkness will pursue His
enemies.

II. God's Punishment of His Enemies, 1:9–15

9 What do you conspire against
the LORD?
He will make an utter end *of
it.*
Affliction will not rise up a
second time.
10 For while tangled *like* thorns,
And while drunken *like*
drunkards,
They shall be devoured like
stubble fully dried.
11 From you comes forth *one*
Who plots evil against the
LORD,
A wicked [1]counselor.

12 Thus says the LORD:

"Though *they are* [2]safe, and
likewise many,
Yet in this manner they will be
[a]cut down
When he passes through.
Though I have afflicted you,
I will afflict you [b]no more;
13 For now I will break off his
yoke from you,
And burst your bonds apart."

14 The LORD has given a
command concerning you:
"Your name shall be
perpetuated no longer.
Out of the house of your gods
I will cut off the carved image
and the molded image.
I will dig your [3c]grave,
For you are [d]vile."

12
a Isa. 10:16–19
b Cp. Isa. 54:7–8
14
c Ezek. 32:22–23
d Nah. 3:6
15
e Isa. 40:9; 52:7; Rom. 10:15
f Isa. 29:7–8

The joyful news

15 Behold, on the mountains
The [e]feet of him who brings
[4]good tidings,
Who proclaims peace!
O Judah, keep your appointed
feasts,
Perform your vows.
For the wicked one shall no
more pass through you;
He is [f]utterly cut off.

III. The Destruction of Nineveh Detailed, 2

2 [5]HE who scatters* has come up
before your face.
Man the fort!
Watch the road!
Strengthen *your* flanks!
Fortify *your* power mightily.

2 For the LORD will restore the
excellence of Jacob
Like the excellence of Israel,
For the emptiers have emptied
them out
And ruined their vine
branches.

3 The shields of his mighty men
are made [6]red,
The valiant men *are* in scarlet.
The chariots *come* with
flaming torches
In the day of his preparation,
And the spears are
brandished.*
4 The chariots rage in the
streets,

*2:1 Vulgate reads *he who destroys.* 2:3 Literally *the cypresses are shaken;* Septuagint and Syriac read *the horses rush about;* Vulgate reads *the drivers are stupefied.*

[1](1:11) It is generally agreed that the invader is Sennacherib, king of Assyria, who threatened Judah in the fourteenth year of Hezekiah's reign. Cp. 2 Ki. 18:13—19:37; Isa. 36—37.

[2](1:12) In the context the expression "safe, and likewise many," although a literal translation of the Hebrew, does not seem to make much sense. Actually the Hebrew here represents a transliteration of a long-forgotten Assyrian legal formula. Excavation in the ruins of ancient Nineveh, buried since 612 B.C., has brought to light thousands of ancient Assyrian tablets, dozens of which contain this Assyrian legal formula. It proves, on investigation, to indicate joint and separate responsibility for carrying out an obligation. Nahum quotes the LORD as using this Assyrian formula in speaking to the Assyrians, saying in effect, "Even though your entire nation joins as one person to resist Me, nevertheless I shall overcome you." As the words would have been equally incomprehensible to the later Hebrew copyists, their retention is striking evidence of the care of the scribes in copying exactly what they found in the manuscripts, and testifies to God's providential preservation of the Biblical text.

[3](1:14) This denotes the complete destruction of Nineveh by the Medes and Babylonians, which occurred in 612 B.C.

[4](1:15) The words in Isa. 52:7 speak of deliverance from Babylon; here, from Assyria in 612 B.C. Paul applies the words in Rom. 10:15 to the Gospel of Christ, which announces eternal deliverance from sin.

[5](2:1) That is, the Medo-Babylonian forces under Cyaxares and Nabopolassar.

[6](2:3) The invaders were especially fond of red.

They [a]jostle one another in the
broad roads;
They seem like torches,
They run like [1]lightning.

5 He remembers his nobles;
They stumble in their walk;
They make haste to her walls,
And the defense is prepared.
6 The gates of the rivers are
opened,
And the palace is dissolved.
7 It is decreed:*
She shall be led away captive,
She shall be brought up;
And her maidservants shall
lead *her* as with the voice of
doves,
Beating their breasts.

8 Though Nineveh of old *was*
like a pool of water,
Now they flee away.
"Halt! Halt!" *they cry;*
But no one [b]turns back.
9 Take spoil of silver!
Take spoil of [c]gold!
There is no end of treasure,
Or wealth of every desirable
prize.
10 She is empty, desolate, and
waste!
The heart melts, and the knees
shake;
Much pain *is* in every side,
And all their faces are drained
of color.*

11 Where *is* the dwelling of the
[d]lions,
And the feeding place of the
young lions,
Where the lion walked, the
lioness *and* lion's cub,
And no one made *them* afraid?
12 The lion tore in pieces enough
for his cubs,
Killed for his lionesses,
[e]Filled his caves with prey,
And his dens with flesh.

13 [f]"Behold, I *am* against you,"
says the LORD of hosts, "I will burn
your* chariots in smoke, and the
sword shall devour your young lions;
I will cut off your prey from the earth,
and the voice of your [g]messengers
shall be heard no more."

IV. The Cause of the Destruction, 3

As Nineveh sowed, so must she reap

3 WOE to the [h]bloody city!
It *is* all full of lies *and* robbery.
Its victim never departs.
2 The noise of a whip
And the noise of rattling
wheels,
Of galloping horses,
Of clattering chariots!
3 Horsemen charge with bright
sword and glittering spear.
There is a multitude of slain,
A great number of bodies,
[2]Countless corpses—
They stumble over the
corpses—
4 Because of the multitude of
harlotries of the seductive
harlot,
The [i]mistress of sorceries,
Who sells nations through her
harlotries,
And families through her
sorceries.

5 "Behold, I *am* [j]against you,"
says the LORD of hosts;
"I will lift your skirts over your
face,
I will show the nations your
nakedness,
And the kingdoms your shame.
6 I will cast abominable filth
upon you,
Make you [k]vile,
And make you a spectacle.
7 It shall come to pass *that* all
who look upon you
Will flee from you, and say,
[l]'Nineveh is laid waste!
Who will bemoan her?'
Where shall I seek comforters
for you?"

8 Are you better than [3][m]No
Amon*

CHAPTER 2
4 [a] Nah. 3:2
8 [b] Cp. Jer. 46:5; 47:3
9 [c] Ezek. 7:19; Zeph. 1:18
11 [d] Job 4:10–11; Ezek. 19:2–7
12 [e] Isa. 10:6; Jer. 51:34
13 [f] Ezek. 29:3; 38:3; 39:1; Nah. 3:5
[g] 2 Ki. 18:17–25; 19:9–13,23

CHAPTER 3
1 [h] Ezek. 22:2–3; 24:6–9; Hab. 2:12
4 [i] Isa. 47:9–12; Rev. 18:2–3
5 [j] Nah. 2:13
6 [k] Nah. 1:14
7 [l] Jon. 3:3; 4:11; see Nah. 1:1, *note*
8 [m] Jer. 46:25; Ezek. 30:15–16

*
2:7 Hebrew *Huzzab* 2:10 Compare Joel 2:6
2:13 Literally *her* 3:8 That is, ancient Thebes; Targum and Vulgate read *populous Alexandria*.

[1](2:4) The Assyrian war chariots moved with unprecedented speed.
[2](3:3) The striking cruelty of the Assyrians in battle is amply attested by the cuneiform inscriptions found by excavators at Nineveh.
[3](3:8) The fall of well-fortified Thebes (Hebrew *No Amon*) in Egypt to Ashurbanipal in 661 B.C. (vv. 8–10) is here used as a solemn warning to proud Nineveh that she will also fall, despite her excellent defenses (vv. 14–19). Nahum's prophecy against Nineveh was fulfilled c. 612 B.C. when she fell to Nebuchadnezzar, who led the assault on behalf of his father, Nabopolassar of Babylon.

That was situated by the
River,*
That had the waters around
her,
Whose rampart *was* the sea,
Whose wall *was* the sea?
9 [a]Ethiopia and Egypt *were* her
strength,
And *it was* boundless;
[b]Put and [c]Lubim were your*
helpers.
10 Yet she *was* carried away,
She went into [d]captivity;
Her young children also were
dashed to pieces
At the head of every street;
They cast [e]lots for her
honorable men,
And all her great men were
bound in chains.
11 You also will be drunk;
You will be hidden;
You also will seek refuge from
the enemy.
12 All your strongholds *are* [f]fig
trees with ripened figs:
If they are shaken,
They fall into the mouth of the
eater.
13 Surely, your people in your
midst *are* [g]women!
The gates of your land are
wide open for your enemies;
Fire shall devour the bars of
your *gates.*

14 Draw your water for the siege!
Fortify your strongholds!
Go into the clay and tread the
mortar!
Make strong the brick kiln!
15 There the fire will devour you,
The sword will cut you off;
It will eat you up like a locust.

Make yourself many—like the
[h]locust!
Make yourself many—like the
swarming locusts!
16 You have multiplied your
[i]merchants more than the
stars of heaven.
The locust plunders and flies
away.
17 Your commanders *are* like
swarming locusts,
And your generals like great
grasshoppers,
Which camp in the hedges on
a cold day;
When the sun rises they flee
away,
And the place where they *are*
is not known.

18 Your shepherds slumber, O
king of Assyria;
Your nobles rest *in the dust.*
Your people are scattered on
the mountains,
And no one gathers them.
19 Your injury *has* no healing,
Your wound is severe.
[j]All who hear news of you
Will clap *their* hands over you,
For upon whom has not your
wickedness passed
[1]continually?

9
a Heb. *Cush*
b Gen. 10:6; Ezek. 27:10
c i.e. *the Libyans.* 2 Chr. 12:3; 16:8; Jer. 46:9; Ezek. 30:5; 38:5; Dan. 11:43
10
d Cp. Isa. 19:4; 20:4
e Joel 3:3; Obad. 11
12
f Rev. 6:12–13
13
g Isa. 19:16; Jer. 51:30
15
h Joel 1:4
16
i Rev. 18:3, 11–19
19
j Job 27:23; Lam. 2:15; Zeph. 2:15; cp. Isa. 14:8

*
• Literally *rivers,* that is, the Nile and the surrounding canals **3:9** Septuagint reads *her.*

[1](3:19) For all who accept evil as a matter of course, Nahum provides a corrective. Those who criticize him as harsh and unfeeling might better ask themselves whether they have ever been morally indignant against the crying injustices and outrageous wickedness of their time.

The Book of

HABAKKUK

Author: Habakkuk *Theme:* From Doubt to Faith *Date of writing:* 7th Cent. B.C.

HABAKKUK, whose name means *embrace*, prophesied to Judah concerning the impending invasion by the Chaldeans (1:6). The conditions of 1:2–4 are corroborated by the record in 2 Ki. 21—22; moral and spiritual decline marked the life of the nation.

Habakkuk was a man of a deeply tender nature and spiritual character. He manifested a great love for his people, fulfilling the position of watchman over them. His questions and doubts arose from his jealousy for the holiness and justice of God. The prophet was perplexed over God's permission of evil in Judah, and even more so over God's use of Babylon as the rod of correction for His people. The answer to his questions is found in 2:4, which is the key verse of the book and is quoted in Rom. 1:17; Gal. 3:11; Heb. 10:38. It sets forth the cause of life and death. Sin must issue in destruction; faith invariably leads to spiritual life. The theophany in ch. 3, reminiscent of that at Mount Sinai, is one of the grandest in the Bible. (Cp. Ezek. 40:3–4; see Gen. 12:7, *note*.) The reference in 3:19 to "stringed instruments" may suggest that the prophet was a Levite and a musician.

The book may be divided as follows:

I. The Perplexity of the Prophet, 1:1—2:1.
II. The Answer of God, 2:2–20.
III. The Triumphant Faith of Habakkuk, 3.

I. The Perplexity of the Prophet, 1:1—2:1

Introduction

1 THE [1]burden which the prophet Habakkuk saw.

The problem: Why is sin unjudged?

2 O LORD, how long shall I cry,
And You will not hear?
Even cry out to You,
[a]"Violence!"
And You will [b]not save.
3 Why do You show me
[2]iniquity,
And cause *me* to see trouble?
For plundering and violence
are before me;
There is strife, and contention
arises.
4 Therefore the law is powerless,
And justice never goes forth.
For the wicked surround the
righteous;
Therefore perverse judgment
proceeds.

The LORD's answer

5 "Look among the nations and
watch—
Be utterly astounded!
For *I will* work a work in your
days
Which you would not believe,
though it were told *you*.
6 For indeed I am [c]raising up
the [3]Chaldeans,
A bitter and hasty [d]nation
Which marches through the
breadth of the earth,
To possess dwelling places
that are not theirs.
7 They are terrible and dreadful;
Their [4]judgment and their
dignity proceed from
[e]themselves.
8 Their horses also are [f]swifter
than leopards,
And more fierce than evening
wolves.
Their chargers charge ahead;
Their cavalry comes from afar;
They fly as the [g]eagle *that*
hastens to eat.
9 "They all come for violence;
Their faces are set *like* the east
wind.
They gather captives like sand.
10 They scoff at kings,

CHAPTER 1

2
a Mic. 2:1–2; 3:1–3
b Job 21:5–16; cp. Ps. 73:1–16

6
c Dt. 28:49–50; 2 Ki. 24:2; 2 Chr. 36:17; Mic. 4:10
d Ezek. 7:24; 21:31

7
e Cp. Jer. 39:5–9

8
f Jer. 4:13
g Job 9:26; 39:29–30; Lam. 4:19; Hos. 8:1; Mt. 24:28; Lk. 17:37

---

[1](1:1) The "burden" (or oracle; see Isa. 13:1, *note*) is not Habakkuk's question in vv. 2–4, nor the one in 1:12—2:1, but the LORD's answer to both of these questions.

[2](1:3) Like Asaph (Ps. 73) and Job, Habakkuk is perplexed by the affliction of the godly and the prosperity of the ungodly. The key to the solution is 2:4.

[3](1:6) The Chaldeans were Semites, descendants from Chesed, son of Nahor, brother of Abraham (Gen. 22:22). Habakkuk sees the Chaldeans as the rod of God's anger on the kingdom of Judah, as Isaiah (5:26–30) saw the Assyrians as the agent of God's punishment on the kingdom of Israel (Isa. 10:5).

[4](1:7) The Chaldeans, recognizing no superiors, were a law unto themselves.

And princes are scorned by
them.
They deride every stronghold,
For they heap up earthen
mounds and seize it.
11 Then *his* mind* changes, and
he transgresses;
He commits offense,
Ascribing this power to his
god."

Habakkuk's perplexity:
How can God use wicked Babylon?

12 Are You not [a]from everlasting,
O LORD my God, my Holy One?
We shall not die.
O LORD, You have appointed
them for judgment;
[b]O Rock, You have marked
them for [c]correction.
13 *You are* of purer eyes than to
[d]behold evil,
And cannot look on
wickedness.
Why do You look on those
who deal treacherously,
And hold Your tongue when
the wicked devours
A *person* more righteous than
he?
14 *Why* do You make men like
fish of the sea,
Like creeping things *that have*
no ruler over them?
15 They take up all of them with
a hook,
They catch them in their net,
And gather them in their
dragnet.
Therefore they rejoice and are
glad.
16 Therefore they sacrifice to
their net,
And burn incense to their
dragnet;
Because by them their share *is*
sumptuous
And their food plentiful.
17 Shall they therefore empty
their net,
And continue to slay nations
without pity?

2 I WILL stand my watch
And set myself on the rampart,
And watch to see what He will
say to me,
And what I will answer when I
am corrected.

II. The Answer of God, 2:2–20
The just shall live by faith

2 Then the LORD answered me and
said:

[e]"Write the vision
And make *it* plain on tablets,
That he may [1]run who reads it.
3 For the vision *is* yet for an
[2]appointed time;
But at the end it will speak,
and it will [f]not lie.
Though it tarries, [g]wait for it;
Because it will surely come,
It will not tarry.

4 "Behold the proud,
His soul is not [h]upright in him;
But the [3]just shall live by his
[i]faith.

12
a Ps. 90:2; 93:2
b Dt. 32:4
c Isa. 10:5–7; Jer. 25:9
13
d i.e. *look with favor upon*
CHAPTER 2
2
e Inspiration: vv. 2–4; Zech. 7:7. (Ex. 4:15; 2 Tim. 3:16, *note*)
3
f Ezek. 12:24–25
g Ps. 27:13–14; Jas. 5:7–8; 2 Pet. 3:9
4
h Righteousness (OT): v. 4; Mal. 3:18. (Gen. 6:9; Lk. 2:25, *note*)
i Faith: v. 4; Mt. 8:10. (Gen. 3:20; Heb. 11:39, *note*)

*1:11 Literally *spirit* or *wind*

[1](2:2) Not, as usually quoted, "that he who runs may read," but "that he may run who reads"; i.e. as a messenger of the vision. Cp. Zech. 2:4–5.

[2](2:3) To the watching prophet comes the response of the vision (vv. 2–20). Three elements are to be distinguished: (1) The moral judgment of the LORD upon the evils practiced by Israel (vv. 5–13, 15–19). (2) The future purpose of God that "the earth will be filled with the knowledge of the glory of the LORD, as the waters cover the sea" (v. 14). That this revelation awaits the return of the Lord in glory is shown (a) by the parallel passage in Isa. 11:9–12; and (b) by the quotation of v. 3 in Heb. 10:37–38, where the "it" of the vision becomes "He" and refers to the return of the Lord. It is then, after the vision is fulfilled, that "the knowledge of the glory," etc. shall fill the earth. But (3) meantime, "the just shall live by his faith." This great evangelical word is applied to Jews and Gentiles in Rom. 1:17; to the Gentiles in Gal. 3:11–14; and to Hebrews especially in Heb. 10:38. This opening of life to faith alone, makes possible not only the salvation of the Gentiles, but also the existence of a believing remnant in Israel while the nation, as such, is in blindness and unbelief (see Rom. 11:1 and 5, *notes*), with neither priesthood nor temple, and consequently unable to keep the ordinances of the law. Such is the LORD! In disciplinary government His ancient Israel is cast out of the land and judicially blinded (2 Cor. 3:12–15), but in covenanted mercy the individual Jew may resort to the simple faith of Abraham (Gen. 15:6; Rom. 4:1–5) and be saved. This, however, does not set aside the Palestinian and Davidic Covenants (see Dt. 30:3 and 2 Sam. 7:16, *notes*), for "the earth will be filled," etc. (v. 14), and the LORD will again be in His temple (v. 20). Cp. Rom. 11:25–27.

[3](2:4) Here is the central theme of the Bible. The cause of life and death is presented. Trust in God brings life (Gen. 15:6; Jn. 3:16; Rom. 6:23); pride leads to death, because it will not

5 "Indeed, because he
transgresses by wine,
He is a proud man,
And he does not stay at home.
Because he [a]enlarges his
desire as [1]hell,*
And he *is* like death, and
cannot be satisfied,
He gathers to himself all
nations
And heaps up for himself all
peoples.

6 "Will not all these [b]take up a
proverb against him,
And a taunting riddle against
him, and say,
'Woe to him who increases
What is not his—how long?
And to him who loads himself
with many pledges'?*
7 Will not your creditors* rise
up suddenly?
Will they not awaken who
oppress you?
And you will become their
booty.
8 [c]Because you have plundered
many nations,
All the remnant of the people
shall plunder you,
Because of men's blood
And the violence of the land
and the city,
And of all who dwell in it.

9 "Woe to him who covets evil
gain for his house,
That he may [d]set his nest on
high,
That he may be delivered from
the power of disaster!
10 You give shameful counsel to
your house,
Cutting off many peoples,
And sin *against* your soul.
11 For the stone will cry out from
the wall,
And the beam from the
timbers will answer it.

12 "Woe to him who builds a town
with bloodshed,
Who establishes a city by
iniquity!
13 Behold, [e]*is it* not of the LORD
of hosts
That the peoples labor to feed
the fire,*
And nations weary themselves
in vain?
14 [2]For the earth will be filled
With the knowledge of the
glory of the LORD,
As the waters cover the sea.

15 "Woe to him who gives drink to
his neighbor,
Pressing* *him to* your bottle,
Even to make *him* drunk,
That you may look on his
nakedness!
16 You are filled with shame
instead of glory.
You also—drink!
And be exposed as
uncircumcised!*
The cup of the LORD's right
hand *will be* turned against
you,
And utter shame will be on
your glory.
17 For the violence *done to*
Lebanon will cover you,
And the plunder of beasts
which made them afraid,
Because of men's blood
And the violence of the land
and the city,
And of all who dwell in it.

5
a Isa. 5:14
6
b Mic. 2:4
8
c Isa. 33:1; Jer. 27:7; Ezek. 39:10
9
d Jer. 49:16; Obad. 4
13
e Or *it is not of the* LORD, etc., i.e. *though permitted in His providence, not His plan.* Cp. Mic. 4:2–4

*
2:5 Or *Sheol* 2:6 Syriac and Vulgate read *thick clay.* 2:7 Literally *those who bite you* 2:13 Literally *for what satisfies fire,* that is, for what is of no lasting value 2:15 Literally *Attaching* or *Joining* 2:16 Dead Sea Scrolls and Septuagint read *And reel!;* Syriac and Vulgate read *And fall fast asleep!*

accept by faith the grace of God (Rom. 1:17; Gal. 3:11; Heb. 10:38).

[1](2:5) The Hebrew *Sheol* is, in the OT, the place to which the dead go. (1) Often, therefore, it is spoken of as the equivalent of the grave, where all human activities cease; the terminus toward which all human life moves (e.g. Gen. 42:38; Job 14:13; Ps. 88:3). (2) To the man "under the sun," the natural man, who of necessity judges from appearances, *Sheol* seems no more than the grave—the end and total cessation, not only of the activities of life, but also of life itself (Eccl. 9:5,10). But (3) Scripture reveals *Sheol* as a place of sorrow (2 Sam. 22:6; Ps. 18:5; 116:3), into which the wicked are turned (Ps. 9:17), and where they are fully conscious (Isa. 14:9–17; Ezek. 32:21). Compare Jon. 2:2; what the belly of the great fish was to Jonah, *Sheol* is to those who are therein. The *Sheol* of the OT and *Hades* of the NT are identical. See Lk. 16:23, *note.*

[2](2:14) Compare Isa. 11:9, which fixes the time when "the earth will be filled with the knowledge of the glory of the LORD," etc. It is when David's righteous Branch has set up the kingdom. See Davidic Covenant, 2 Sam. 7:16, *note;* Kingdom (OT), Gen. 1:26–28; Zech. 12:8, *note;* Kingdom (NT), Lk. 1:31–33; 1 Cor. 15:24, *note.*

18 "What profit is the image, that
its maker should carve it,
The molded image, a teacher
of lies,
That the maker of its mold
should trust in it,
To make mute idols?
19 Woe to him who says to wood,
'Awake!'
To silent stone, 'Arise! It shall
teach!'
Behold, it is overlaid with gold
and silver,
Yet in it there is no breath at
all.
20 [a]"But the LORD is in His holy
temple.
Let all the earth keep silence
before Him."

III. The Triumphant Faith of Habakkuk, 3

3 A [1b]PRAYER of Habakkuk the
prophet, on [c]Shigionoth.

2 O LORD, I have heard your
speech *and* was afraid;
O LORD, revive Your work in
the midst of the years!
In the midst of the years make
it known;
In wrath remember mercy.
3 [2d]God came from Teman,
The Holy One from Mount
Paran. [e]Selah

His glory covered the heavens,
And the earth was full of His
praise.
4 *His* brightness was like the
light;
He had rays *flashing* from His
hand,
And there His power *was*
hidden.
5 Before Him went pestilence,
And fever followed at His feet.

6 He stood and measured the
earth;
He looked and startled the
nations.
And the everlasting mountains
were scattered,
The perpetual hills bowed.
His ways *are* everlasting.
7 I saw the tents of [f]Cushan in
affliction;
The curtains of the land of
Midian trembled.

8 O LORD, were *You* displeased
with the rivers,
Was Your anger against the
rivers,
Was Your wrath against the
sea,
That You rode on Your horses,
Your chariots of salvation?
9 Your bow was made quite
ready;
Oaths were sworn over *Your*
arrows.* Selah

You divided the earth with
rivers.
10 The mountains saw You *and*
trembled;
The overflowing of the water
passed by.
The deep uttered its voice,
And lifted its hands on high.
11 The [g]sun and moon stood still
in their habitation;
At the light of Your arrows
they went,
At the shining of Your
glittering spear.

12 You marched through the land
in indignation;
You trampled the nations in
anger.
13 You went forth for the
salvation of Your people,
For salvation with Your
Anointed.
You struck the head from the
house of the wicked,
By laying bare from
foundation to neck. Selah

20
a Zeph. 1:7; Zech. 2:13
CHAPTER 3
1
b *Bible prayers* (OT): vv. 1–19. (Gen. 15:2; Hab. 3:1)
c Probably musical instruments
3
d Cp. Ezek. 40:3–4, a theophany. See Gen. 12:7, *note*
e See Ps. 3:2, *note*
7
f Or *Ethiopia*
11
g Josh. 10:12–13

*3:9 Literally *rods* or *tribes* (compare verse 14)

[1](3:1) Bible prayers (OT), Summary: Prayer is an integral part of worship, in the OT and in the NT. In the OT the petitions and supplications of God's people are based upon His character and the divine covenants. OT saints, often acting in the priestly office of representing the people before the LORD, frequently appeal to the honor of the name of God and the steadfastness of His word as they plead with the Almighty to fulfill on their behalf the promises that He has graciously made to them as His covenant people (Gen. 15:2–3; 18:23–32; Ex. 32:11–14; 2 Sam. 7:18–29; 1 Ki. 8:22–53; 18:36–37; Dan. 9:3–19). For Bible prayers (NT), see Lk. 11:2, *note*.

[2](3:3) This theophany recalls the events of the Exodus and Sinai, which form the background for God's future deliverance of His people (v. 13) and His judgment of their enemies (v. 12).

14 You thrust through with his
own arrows
The head of his villages.
They came out like a
whirlwind to scatter me;
Their rejoicing was like
feasting on the poor in
secret.
15 [a]You walked through the sea
with Your horses,
Through the heap of great
waters.
16 When I heard, my body
trembled;
My lips quivered at *the* voice;
Rottenness entered my bones;
And I trembled in myself,
That I might rest in the day of
trouble.
When he comes up to the
people,
He will invade them with his
troops.

15
a v. 8; Ps. 77:19
18
b Isa. 41:16; 61:10
19
c Assurance/security: vv. 17–19; Jn. 3:16. (Ps. 23:1; Jude 1, *note*)
d 2 Sam. 22:34; Ps. 18:33
e Dt. 32:13; 33:29

17 Though the fig tree may not
blossom,
Nor fruit be on the vines;
Though the labor of the olive
may fail,
And the fields yield no food;
Though the flock may be cut
off from the fold,
And there be no herd in the
stalls—
18 Yet I will [1b]rejoice in the LORD,
I will joy in the God of my
salvation.
19 The LORD God* is my
[c]strength;
He will make my feet like
[d]deer's *feet*,
And He will make me walk on
my [e]high hills.

To the [2]Chief Musician. With my stringed instruments.

*
3:19 Hebrew *YHWH Adonai*

[1](3:18) Verses 17–18 declare that Habakkuk's love for God, like that of any devoted believer, is not based on what he expects God to give him. Even if God should send him suffering and loss, he declares, he will still rejoice in the God of his salvation. Here is one of the strongest manifestations of faith in the Scriptures.

[2](3:19) This is a musical notation for the choirmaster for the temple liturgy.

The Book of

ZEPHANIAH

Author: Zephaniah *Theme:* Day of the LORD *Date of writing:* 7th Cent. B.C.

ZEPHANIAH, which means *the* LORD *hides* or *protects*, was a great-great-grandson of King Hezekiah (1:1). The internal evidence of the book shows that he prophesied during the reign of King Josiah, probably before the great revival of 621 B.C. Stirred by the moral declension of his time, he foresaw the fall of Jerusalem which, in his inspired vision, became a figure of the day of the LORD. Not only so, but he also looked forward to the judgment of the Gentiles and the restoration of Israel in the Messianic kingdom.

A leading theme of Zephaniah is the day of the LORD, a future event that he describes with vivid power. Zephaniah uses the term, "day of the LORD," more than any other prophet except Joel, yet he pleads with Judah to "seek the LORD" that they might be "hidden in the day of the LORD's anger" (2:3).

The book may be divided as follows:

I. The Coming Invasion of Nebuchadnezzar, a Figure of the Day of the LORD, 1:1—2:3.
II. Predictions of Judgments of Surrounding Nations, 2:4–15.
III. The Moral State of Israel: Captivity Will Come, 3:1–7.
IV. Future Judgment of the Gentiles, Followed by Kingdom Blessing under Messiah, 3:8–20.

I. The Coming Invasion of Nebuchadnezzar, a Figure of the Day of the LORD, 1:1—2:3

Introduction

1 THE word of the LORD which came to Zephaniah the son of Cushi, the son of Gedaliah, the son of Amariah, the son of Hezekiah, in the days of [a]Josiah the son of Amon, king of Judah.

The coming judgment of Judah

2 "I will utterly consume everything
From the face of the land,"
Says the LORD;
3 "I will consume man and beast;
I will consume the birds of the heavens,
The fish of the sea,
And the [b]stumbling blocks*
along with the wicked.
I will cut off man from the face of the land,"
Says the LORD.

4 "I will stretch out My hand against Judah,
And against all the inhabitants of Jerusalem.
I will cut off every trace of Baal from this place,
The names of the [c]idolatrous priests* with the *pagan* priests—
5 Those who worship the host of heaven [d]on the housetops;
Those who worship and swear *oaths* by the LORD,
But who *also* swear by [1]Milcom;
6 Those who have turned back from *following* the LORD,
And have not sought the LORD, nor inquired of Him."

7 Be silent in the presence of the Lord GOD;
[2]For the [e]day of the LORD *is* at hand,
For the LORD has prepared a [f]sacrifice;
He has invited* His guests.

CHAPTER 1
1 a 2 Ki. 22:1–23:30; 2 Chr. 34:1–35:27; Jer. 1:2; 22:11
3 b Cp. Ezek. 7:19
4 c 2 Ki. 23:5
5 d 2 Ki. 23:12; Jer. 19:13
7 e *Day* (of the LORD): vv. 7–18; Zech. 12:2. (Ps. 2:9; Rev. 19:19)
f Dt. 28:26; Jer. 46:10; Ezek. 39:17–19

*1:3 Figurative of idols 1:4 Hebrew *chemarim*
1:7 Literally *set apart, consecrated*

---

[1](1:5) Milcom, Molech (Lev. 18:21; 1 Ki. 11:5), was an idol of the Ammonites.

[2](1:7) In predictive prophecy, such as Zephaniah's portrayal of the day of the LORD, the near and far view are often merged. From a distance a great mountain range appears as a single barrier against the sky, although it actually comprises many foothills and intermediate summits separated by extensive valleys from the ultimate heights. So Zephaniah, seeing in the impending fall of Jerusalem the nearest aspect of the day of the LORD, can say that it is "at hand" (v. 7) and "hastens quickly" (v. 14); whereas, towering in the distant future of unfulfilled prophecy, the final Day of the LORD awaits the return of Christ in glory. It is then that all earth-judgment will culminate, to be followed by the restoration and blessing of Israel and the nations in the kingdom. See Day of the LORD (Isa. 2:10–22; see Joel 1:15 and Rev. 19:19, *notes*); Israel (Gen. 12:2–3; Rom. 11:26).

8 "And it shall be,
In the day of the LORD's
sacrifice,
That I will punish the princes
and the king's children,
And all such as are clothed
with foreign apparel.
9 In the same day I will punish
All those who [1]leap over the
threshold,*
Who fill their masters' houses
with violence and deceit.

10 "And there shall be on that
day," says the LORD,
"The sound of a mournful cry
from the Fish [a]Gate,
A wailing from the Second
Quarter,
And a loud crashing from the
hills.
11 Wail, you inhabitants of
[2]Maktesh!*
For all the merchant people
are cut down;
All those who handle money
are cut off.

12 "And it shall come to pass at
that time
That I will search Jerusalem
with lamps,
And punish the men
Who are [b]settled in
complacency,*
Who say in their heart,
'The LORD will not do good,
Nor will He do evil.'
13 Therefore their goods shall
become booty,
And their houses a desolation;
They shall build houses, but
not inhabit *them;*
They shall plant vineyards, but
[c]not drink their wine."

14 [3]The great day of the LORD *is*
near;
It is near and hastens quickly.
The noise of the day of the
LORD is bitter;
There the mighty men shall
cry out.
15 [d]That day *is* a day of wrath,
A day of trouble and distress,
A day of devastation and
desolation,
A day of darkness and
gloominess,
A day of clouds and thick
darkness,
16 A day of trumpet and alarm
Against the fortified cities
And against the high towers.

17 "I will bring distress upon men,
And they shall walk like
[e]blind men,
[f]Because they have sinned
against the LORD;
Their blood shall be poured
out like dust,
And their flesh like refuse."

18 [g]Neither their silver nor their
gold
Shall be able to deliver them
In the day of the LORD's wrath;
But the whole land shall be
devoured
By the fire of His jealousy,
For He will make speedy
riddance
Of all those who dwell in the
land.

Zephaniah's call to repentance

2 [h]GATHER yourselves together,
yes, gather together,
O [i]undesirable nation,
2 Before the decree is issued,
Or the day passes like chaff,
Before the LORD's fierce anger
comes upon you,
Before the day of the LORD's
anger comes upon you!
3 Seek the LORD, all you meek of
the earth,
Who have upheld His justice.
Seek righteousness, seek
humility.
It [j]may be that you will be
hidden
In the day of the LORD's anger.

*II. Predictions of Judgments
of Surrounding Nations, 2:4–15*

4 For [k]Gaza shall be forsaken,
And Ashkelon desolate;
They shall drive out Ashdod at
noonday,
And Ekron shall be uprooted.
5 Woe to the inhabitants of the
seacoast,
The nation of the Cherethites!

10 *a* Now called the Damascus Gate
12 *b* Amos 6:1
13 *c* Dt. 28:39
15 *d* Isa. 22:5
17 *e* Dt. 28:29 *f* Cp. Jer. 3:25; 44:23
18 *g* Ezek. 7:19
CHAPTER 2
1 *h* Joel 1:14 *i* Lit. *shameless.* Cp. Jer. 3:3
3 *j* Joel 2:14
4 *k* Jer. 47:1, 5; Zech. 9:5

*
1:9 Compare 1 Samuel 5:5 1:11 Literally *Mortar,* a market district of Jerusalem 1:12 Literally *on their lees,* that is, settled like the dregs of wine

[1](1:9) "Leap over the threshold" may suggest the zeal of their plundering expeditions.
[2](1:11) Maktesh was a depression in Jerusalem where the market places were situated.
[3](1:14) Verses 14–16 are the basis of the ancient Latin hymn, *Dies Irae* ("Day of Wrath").

The word of the LORD *is* against you,
O Canaan, land of the [a]Philistines:
"I will destroy you;
So there shall be no inhabitant."

6 The seacoast shall be pastures,
With shelters* for shepherds and folds for flocks.

7 The coast shall be for the [b]remnant of the house of Judah;
They shall feed *their* flocks there;
In the houses of Ashkelon they shall lie down at evening.
For the LORD their God will intervene for them,
And [c]return their captives.

8 "I have heard the reproach of [d]Moab,
And the insults of the people of [e]Ammon,
With which they have reproached My people,
And made arrogant threats against their borders.

9 Therefore, as I live,"
Says the LORD of hosts, the God of Israel,
"Surely Moab shall be like Sodom,
And the people of Ammon like [f]Gomorrah—
Overrun with weeds and saltpits,
And a perpetual desolation.
The residue of My people shall plunder them,
And the remnant of My people shall possess them."

10 This they shall have for their pride,
Because they have reproached and made arrogant threats
Against the people of the LORD of hosts.

11 The LORD *will be* awesome to them,
For He will reduce to nothing all the gods of the earth;
People shall worship Him,
Each one from his place,
Indeed all the shores of the nations.

12 "You [g]Ethiopians also,
You shall be slain by My sword."

13 And He will stretch out His hand against the north,
Destroy [h]Assyria,
And make [i]Nineveh a desolation,
As dry as the wilderness.

14 The herds shall lie down in her midst,
Every beast of the nation.
Both the pelican and the bittern
Shall lodge on the capitals *of* her *pillars;*
Their voice shall sing in the windows;
Desolation *shall be* at the threshold;
For He will lay bare the cedar work.

15 This is the rejoicing city
That dwelt [j]securely,
That said in her heart,
"I *am it,* and *there is* none besides me."
How has she become a desolation,
A place for beasts to lie down!
Everyone who passes by her
Shall hiss and shake his fist.

III. The Moral State of Israel; Captivity Will Come, 3:1–7

3 WOE to her who is rebellious and polluted,
To the oppressing city!

2 She has not obeyed *His* voice,
She has not received correction;
She has not [k]trusted in the LORD,
She has not drawn near to her God.

3 Her [l]princes in her midst *are* roaring lions;
Her judges *are* evening wolves
That leave not a bone till morning.

4 Her [m]prophets are insolent, treacherous people;
Her [n]priests have polluted the sanctuary,
They have done violence to the law.

5 The LORD *is* righteous in her midst,
He will do no unrighteousness.
Every morning He brings His justice to light;
He never fails,

5
a Ezek. 25:15–17
7
b Remnant: vv. 1–3, 7–9; Zeph. 3:13. (Isa. 1:9; Rom. 11:5, *note*)
c Zeph. 3:19–20
8
d vv. 8–11; Amos 2:1–3
e vv. 8–11; Amos 1:13
9
f Dt. 29:23
12
g Isa. 18:1–7; Ezek. 30:4–5
13
h Isa. 10:5–27; 14:24–27; Mic. 5:5–6
i See Nah. 1:1, *note*
15
j Isa. 47:8
CHAPTER 3
2
k See Ps. 2:12, *note*
3
l Ezek. 22:27
4
m Ezek. 22:25; Mic. 3:5,11
n Ezek. 22:26; Mal. 2:7–8

---

*2:6 Literally *excavations,* either underground huts or cisterns

But the unjust knows no
shame.

6 "I have cut off nations,
Their fortresses are devastated;
I have made their streets
desolate,
With none passing by.
Their cities are destroyed;
There is no one, no inhabitant.

7 I said, 'Surely you will [a]fear
Me,
You will receive instruction'—
So that her dwelling would not
be cut off,
Despite everything for which I
punished her.
But they rose early and
corrupted all their deeds.

IV. Future Judgment of the Gentiles, Followed by Kingdom Blessing under Messiah, 3:8–20

8 "Therefore [b]wait for Me," says
the LORD,
"Until the day I rise up for
plunder;*
My determination *is* to [c]gather
the [d]nations
To My assembly of kingdoms,
[e]To pour on them My
indignation,
All my fierce anger;
All the earth shall be devoured
With the fire of My jealousy.

Israel's cleansing

9 "For [1]then I will restore to the
peoples a [2]pure [f]language,
That they all may call on the
name of the LORD,
To serve Him with one accord.

10 From beyond the rivers of
Ethiopia
My worshipers,
The daughter of My dispersed
ones,
Shall bring My offering.

11 In that day you shall not be
shamed for any of your
deeds
In which you transgress
against Me;
For then I will take away from
your midst
Those who [g]rejoice in your
pride,
And you shall no longer be
haughty
In My holy mountain.

12 I will leave in your midst
A meek and humble people,
And they shall [h]trust in the
name of the LORD.

13 The [i]remnant of Israel shall
do no unrighteousness
And speak no lies,
Nor shall a deceitful tongue be
found in their mouth;
For they shall [j]feed *their*
flocks and lie down,
And no one shall make *them*
afraid."

Israel's restoration and blessing; the King in the kingdom

14 Sing, O daughter of Zion!
Shout, O Israel!
Be glad and rejoice with all
your heart,
O daughter of Jerusalem!

15 The LORD has taken away your
judgments,
He has cast out your enemy.
The [k]King of Israel, the LORD,
is in your [3]midst;
You shall see* disaster no
more.

16 In that day [l]it shall be said to
Jerusalem:
"Do not fear;
Zion, let not your hands be
weak.

17 The LORD your God in your
midst,
The Mighty One, will save;
He will [m]rejoice over you with
gladness,

7
a See Ps. 19:9, *note*
8
b Mic. 7:7; Hab. 2:3
c Isa. 66:18; Joel 3:2; Mic. 4:12; Mt. 25:32
d Cp. Zech. 12:9; 14:3
e Armageddon (battle of): vv. 8,15; Zech. 10:3. (Isa. 10:27; Rev. 19:17)
9
f Isa. 19:18
11
g Isa. 2:12; 5:15
12
h See Ps. 2:12, *note*
13
i Remnant: vv. 13–20; Hag. 1:14. (Isa. 1:9; Rom. 11:5, *note*)
j Ezek. 34:13–15
15
k Kingdom (OT): vv. 13–20; Zech. 6:13. (Gen. 1:26; Zech. 12:8, *note*)
16
l Isa. 35:3–4
17
m Dt. 30:9; Isa. 62:5; 65:19; Jer. 32:41

*

3:8 Septuagint and Syriac read *for witness;* Targum reads *for the day of My revelation for judgment;* Vulgate reads *for the day of My resurrection that is to come.* **3:15** Some Hebrew manuscripts, Septuagint, and Bomberg read *see;* Masoretic Text and Vulgate read *fear.*

[1](3:9) In Zephaniah the conversion of "the peoples" is stated out of the usual prophetic order, in which the blessing of Israel and the setting up of the kingdom precede the conversion of the Gentiles. See Zech. 12:1,8, with *notes.* But the passage gives clear testimony as to when the conversion of the nations will occur. It is after the smiting of the nations. Compare Isa. 11:9 with context; Ps. 2:5–8; Dan. 2:34–35; Acts 15:15–17; Rev. 19:19—20:6.

[2](3:9) The prophet is not foretelling a universal language, as though to reverse the consequences of Babel, but the conversion of the nations, a spiritual transformation readily discernible in their purified speech.

[3](3:15) That this, and all like passages in the prophets (see Kingdom (OT), Gen. 1:26–28; Zech. 12:8, *note*), cannot refer to anything which occurred at the first coming of Christ is clear from the context. Precisely the reverse is true. See, e.g., Isa. 11:1, *note.*

He will [a]quiet *you* with His
[1]love,
He will rejoice over you with
singing."

18 "I will gather those who sorrow
over the appointed
assembly,
Who are among you,
To whom its reproach *is* a
burden.
19 Behold, at that time
I will deal with all who afflict
you;
I will save the lame,
And gather those who were
driven out;
I will appoint them for praise
and fame
In every land where they were
put to shame.
20 At that time I will [b]bring you
back,
Even at the time I gather you;
For I will give you [2]fame and
praise
Among all the peoples of the
earth,
When I return your captives
before your eyes,"
Says the LORD.

17
a Or *be quiet in,* a love too great for words

20
b Isa. 11:12; 27:12; 56:8; Ezek. 28:25; 34:13; 37:21; Amos 9:14

[1](3:17) For the LORD's own, His final word is not of anger, as with the unbelieving nations, but of love, as expressed in this beautiful verse. When it comes to His people, chastised and forgiven, the LORD rests His case in love and rejoicing.
[2](3:20) This is the fulfillment of Israel's destiny, as stated in Dt. 26:19.

The Book of

HAGGAI

Author: Haggai *Theme:* Rebuilding the Temple *Date of writing:* 6th Çent. B.C.

HAGGAI, whose name means *festive*, was one of the early post-captivity prophets. His ministry was to rebuke the returned exiles for their delay in rebuilding the temple and to encourage them to set to work. Haggai was a contemporary of Zechariah (Ezra 5:1–2).

The five messages that make up the Book of Haggai are among the most precisely dated of all prophecies, the year, month, and day being specified in each case (1:1,15; 2:1,10,20). Such expressions as "then the word of the LORD came" and "Thus says the LORD of hosts" occur about nineteen times in the two chapters of the prophecy.

The book may be divided according to the five messages of Haggai, as follows:

I. The First Message of Rebuke, 1:1–11.
II. The First Message of Encouragement, 1:12–15.
III. The Second Message of Encouragement: the Future Glory of the Temple, 2:1–9.
IV. The Second Message of Rebuke, 2:10–19.
V. The Third Message of Encouragement: the Final Overthrow of Gentile World Power, 2:20–23.

I. The First Message of Rebuke, 1:1–11

Introduction

1 IN the [a]second year of King [1]Darius, in the [b]sixth month, on the first [c]day of the month, the word of the LORD came by [2d]Haggai the prophet to [3e]Zerubbabel the son of Shealtiel, governor of Judah, and to [f]Joshua the son of Jehozadak, the high priest, saying,

2 "Thus speaks the LORD of hosts, saying: 'This people says, "The [4]time has not come, the time that the LORD's house should be built." ' "

The condition of the exiles: God's discipline because of disobedience

3 Then the word of the LORD came by Haggai the prophet, saying,

4 "*Is it* time for you yourselves to dwell in your paneled houses, and this temple* *to lie* [g]in ruins?"

5 Now therefore, thus says the LORD of hosts: [h]"Consider your ways!

6 "You have [i]sown much, and
bring in little;
You eat, but do not have
enough;
You drink, but you are not
filled with drink;
You clothe yourselves, but no
one is warm;
And he who earns wages,
Earns wages *to put* into a bag
with holes."

7 Thus says the LORD of hosts: [h]"Consider your ways!

8 "Go up to the [j]mountains and bring wood and build the temple, that I may take pleasure in it and be glorified," says the LORD.

9 "*You* looked for much, but indeed *it came to* little; and when you brought it home, I [k]blew it away. Why?" says the LORD of hosts. "Because of My house that *is in* ruins, while every one of you runs to his own house.

10 "Therefore the [l]heavens above you withhold the dew, and the earth withholds its fruit.

11 "For I called for a [m]drought on the land and the mountains, on the grain and the new wine and the oil, on whatever the ground brings forth, on

CHAPTER 1
1
[a] Ezra 4:24; Hag. 2:10; Zech. 1:1,7
[b] See Lev. 23:2, *note*
[c] Cp. Hag. 1:15; 2:1
[d] Ezra 5:1; 6:14
[e] 1 Chr. 3:19; Ezra 2:2; Neh. 7:7; Zech. 4:6; Mt. 1:12–13
[f] Or *Jeshua*. Ezra 3:2; Neh. 12:1; Zech. 3:1–5
4
[g] Cp. 2 Sam. 7:2
5
[h] i.e. *Lay to heart*
6
[i] Dt. 28:38–40
8
[j] Ezra 3:7
9
[k] Indicative of God's displeasure

1:10 [l] Dt. 28:23–24 1:11 [m] Cp. Mal. 3:9–11

*1:4 Literally *house*, and so in verse 8

---

[1](1:1) The dating of a Hebrew prophecy by the reign of a Gentile monarch, in this instance Darius I Hystaspis, reveals that the times of the Gentiles were in progress (Lk. 21:24). For similar instances, cp. Dan. 2:1; 7:1; etc.

[2](1:1) Haggai's prophecy should be compared with the prophecy of Zechariah, his contemporary, and also with the historical record in the Book of Ezra, as follows: Hag. 1:1–11 with Ezra 4:24—5:1; Hag. 1:12–15 with Ezra 5:2 and Zech. 1:1–6; Hag. 2:10–23 with Zech. 1:7—6:15. Also cp. Ezra 5:3–17; 6:1–13 with Zech. 7—8.

[3](1:1) Zerubbabel and Joshua were not only religious leaders, but prominent men in civic life also.

[4](1:2) Contrast with this David's concern in 2 Sam. 7:2.

men and livestock, and on [1]all the labor of *your* hands."

II. The First Message
of Encouragement, 1:12–15

The work recommenced

12 Then Zerubbabel the son of Shealtiel, and [a]Joshua the son of Jehozadak, the high priest, with all the remnant of the people, obeyed the voice of
the LORD their God, and the words of
Haggai the prophet, as the LORD their
God had sent him; and the people
[b]feared the presence of the LORD.
13 Then Haggai, the LORD's messenger, spoke the LORD's message to
the people, saying, "I *am* with you,
says the LORD."
14 So the LORD [c]stirred up the spirit
of Zerubbabel the son of Shealtiel,
governor of Judah, and the spirit of
Joshua the son of Jehozadak, the high
priest, and the spirit of all the [d]rem-
nant of the people; and they came and
[e]worked on the house of the LORD of
hosts, their God,
15 on the twenty-fourth [f]day of the
sixth month, in the second year of
King Darius.

III. The Second Message
of Encouragement: the Future Glory
of the Temple, 2:1–9

The temples

2 IN the [g]seventh *month,* on the
[2]twenty-first of the month, the
word of the LORD came by Haggai the
prophet, saying:
2 "Speak now to Zerubbabel the
son of Shealtiel, governor of Judah,
and to Joshua the son of Jehozadak,
the high priest, and to the remnant of
the people, saying:
3 [h]'Who is left among you who
saw this [3]temple* in its former glory?
And how do you see it now? In comparison with it, *is this* not in your eyes
as nothing?
4 'Yet now be strong, Zerubbabel,'
says the LORD; 'and be strong,
[i]Joshua, son of Jehozadak, the high
priest; and be strong, all you people of
the land,' says the LORD, 'and work; for
I *am* with you,' says the LORD of hosts.
5 '*According to* the word that I
[j]covenanted with you when you came
out of Egypt, so My [k]Spirit remains
among you; do not fear!'
6 "For thus says the LORD of hosts:
[l]'Once more (it *is* a little while) I will
[m]shake heaven and earth, the sea and
dry land;
7 'and I will shake all nations, and
they shall come to the Desire of All
Nations,* and I will fill this temple
with [n]glory,' says the LORD of hosts.
8 'The silver *is* Mine, and the gold
is Mine,' says the LORD of hosts.
9 'The [o]glory of this latter [4]temple
shall be greater than the former,' says
the LORD of hosts. 'And in this place I
will give [5]peace,' says the LORD of
hosts."

IV. The Second Message
of Rebuke, 2:10–19

God's message of cleansing
and blessing

10 On the [p]twenty-fourth *day* of the
ninth *month,* in the second year of Darius, the word of the LORD came by
Haggai the prophet, saying,
11 "Thus says the LORD of hosts:

12 *a* Or *Jeshua.* Ezra 3:2; Neh. 12:1; Zech. 3:1–5 *b* See Ps. 19:9, *note*
14 *c* 2 Chr. 36:22; Ezra 1:1 *d Remnant:* v. 14; Zech. 8:6. (Isa. 1:9; Rom. 11:5, *note*) *e* Ezra 5:2
15 *f* Cp. v. 1; 2:1
CHAPTER 2
1 *g* Cp. v. 10; see Lev. 23:2, *note*
3 *h* Ezra 3:12–13
4 *i* Or *Jeshua.* Not the same man as in Josh. 1:1ff.; Ezra 2:2
5 *j* Ex. 29:45; 33:12–14 *k Holy Spirit* (OT): v. 5; Zech. 4:6. (Gen. 1:2; Zech. 12:10)
6 *l* Heb. 12:26 *m Christ* (second advent): vv. 6–7; Zech. 2:10. (Dt. 30:3; Acts 1:11, *note*). Cp. Ezek. 21:27; Dan. 2:44; Joel 3:16 **2:7** *n* 1 Ki. 8:11; Isa. 60:7; Zech. 2:5 **2:9** *o* Or *the future glory of this house shall be greater than the former* **2:10** *p* v. 20

* **2:3** Literally *house,* and so in verses 7 and 9
2:7 Or *the desire of all nations*

[1](1:11) The principle of Mt. 6:33 is valid in every generation.

[2](2:1) This was the seventh day of the Feast of Tabernacles (Lev. 23:39–44; cp. Jn. 7:37ff.).

[3](2:3) The prophet calls the old men who remembered Solomon's temple, to witness to the new generation how greatly that structure exceeded the present in magnificence; and he then utters a prophecy (vv. 7–9) which can only refer to the future kingdom temple described by Ezekiel. It is certain that the restoration temple and all subsequent structures, including Herod's, were far inferior in costliness and splendor to Solomon's. The present period is described in Hos. 3:4–5. Verse 6 is quoted in Heb. 12:26–27. Verse 7, "I will shake all nations," refers to the great tribulation and is followed by the coming of Christ in glory, as in Mt. 24:29–30. "The Desire of All Nations" (LXX, "the riches of all nations" i.e. the treasures or desirable things) is an expression that refers ultimately to Christ, in whom all true riches culminate. See Mal. 3:1, *note.*

[4](2:9) In a broad sense all the temples (i.e. Solomon's, Ezra's, Herod's, that which will be used by the unbelieving Jews under covenant with the beast [Dan. 9:27; Mt. 24:15; 2 Th. 2:3–4], and Ezekiel's future kingdom temple [Ezek. 40—47]) are looked upon as though they are the "house of the LORD," since they all *profess* to be that. For that reason Christ purified the temple of His day, erected though it was by an Idumean usurper to please the Jews (Mt. 21:12–13).

[5](2:9) Peace will be bestowed through the Prince of Peace (Isa. 9:6–7; cp. Mic. 5:5).

'Now, ask the priests *concerning the*
law, saying,
12 "If one carries holy meat in the
fold of his garment, and with the edge
he touches bread or stew, wine or oil,
or any food, will it become holy?"'"
Then the priests answered and said,
"No."
13 And Haggai said, "If *one who is*
[1a]unclean *because* of a dead body
touches any of these, will it be unclean?" So the priests answered and
said, "It shall be unclean."
14 Then Haggai answered and said,
"'So is this people, and so is this nation before Me,' says the LORD, 'and so
is every work of their hands; and what
they offer there is unclean.
15 'And now, carefully [b]consider
from this day forward: from before
stone was laid upon stone in the temple of the LORD—
16 'since those *days,* when *one*
came to a heap of [c]twenty ephahs,
there were *but* ten; when *one* came to
the wine vat to draw out fifty baths
from the press, there were *but* twenty.
17 'I struck you with [d]blight and
mildew and hail in all the labors of
your hands; [e]yet you did not *turn* to
Me,' says the LORD.
18 [b]'Consider now [f]from this day
forward, from the twenty-fourth day
of the ninth month, from the day that
the foundation of the LORD's temple
was [g]laid—[b]consider it:
19 'Is the seed still in the barn? As
yet the vine, the fig tree, the pomegranate, and the olive tree have not
yielded *fruit. But* from this day I will
[h]bless *you.*'"

V. The Third Message of Encouragement: the Final Overthrow of Gentile World Power, 2:20–23

20 And again the word of the LORD
came to Haggai on the twenty-fourth
day of the month, saying,
21 "Speak to [i]Zerubbabel, governor of Judah, saying:

'I will shake heaven and earth.
22 I will [j]overthrow the throne of
kingdoms;
I will destroy the strength of
the Gentile kingdoms.
I will overthrow the chariots
And those who ride in them;
The horses and their riders
shall come down,
Every one by the sword of his
brother.

23 'In that day,' says the LORD of
hosts, 'I will take you, [2]Zerubbabel My
servant, the son of Shealtiel,' says the
LORD, 'and will make you like a [3k]sig-
net *ring;* for I have [l]chosen you,' says
the LORD of hosts."

13 *a* Lev. 22:4–6; Num. 19:22
15 *b* i.e. *lay to heart*
16 *c* Cp. Lev. 26:26; Hag. 1:6–11
17 *d* Dt. 28:22; Amos 4:9 *e* Amos 4:6–11
18 *f* vv. 15–19; cp. Zech. 8:9–12 *g* Ezra 5:16
19 *h* Mal. 3:10
21 *i* Hag. 1:1–14; cp. Ezra 5:2; Zech. 4:6–10
22 *j* Dan. 2:34–35, 44–45; Rev. 19:11–21
23 *k* Song 8:6; Jer. 22:24 *l* Isa. 42:1; 43:10

[1](2:13) The principle is illuminated by Lev. 6:18; 22:4–6; and Num. 19:11. The Mosaic law held that moral cleanness could not be transmitted, but moral uncleanness could. The long disobedience of the nation rendered their work unprofitable before God.

[2](2:23) The Messianic line came through Zerubbabel as a descendant of David (Mt. 1:12; Lk. 3:27).

[3](2:23) The signet ring is a symbol of royal authority.

The Book of
ZECHARIAH

Author: Zechariah *Theme:* Messiah's Advents *Date of writing:* 6th Cent. B.C.

ZECHARIAH, whose name means *the LORD remembers*, was a prophet of the restoration from Babylon. As a contemporary of Haggai (cp. 1:1 with Hag. 1:1), he began his ministry in the second year of Darius I Hystaspis, 520 B.C. His messages cover events beginning with the rebuilding of the temple and concluding with the millennium.

Expositors, both Jewish and Christian, have complained of the difficulty of the book. This is due largely to the visions of chs. 1—6. But no OT prophet has more prophecy concerning Christ, Israel, and the nations in so short a space than has Zechariah. He predicts the second coming of Christ, His reign, His priesthood, His kingship, His humanity, His Deity, His building of the temple of the LORD, His coming in lowliness, His bringing of permanent peace, His rejection and betrayal for thirty pieces of silver, His return to Israel as the crucified One, and His being struck by the sword of the LORD.

Zechariah's predictions of other prophetic events of the end-time are equally clear and significant. In the last chapter alone the prophet discloses the last siege of Jerusalem, the initial victory of the enemies of Israel, the cleaving of the Mount of Olives, the LORD's defense of Jerusalem by His visible appearing on Olivet, judgment on the confederated nations, the topographical changes in the land of Israel, the Feast of Tabernacles in the millennium, and the ultimate holiness of Jerusalem and her people.

The book may be divided as follows:

I. Call to Repentance, 1:1–6.
II. A Series of Eight Visions to Comfort Jerusalem, 1:7—6:15.
III. The Delegation from Bethel concerning Fasting, 7—8.
IV. Prophecies concerning the End of Israel's Age and the Return and Reign of Christ, 9—14.

I. Call to Repentance, 1:1–6
Introduction

1 IN the [a]eighth month of the second year of [b]Darius, the word of
the LORD came to [c]Zechariah the son
of Berechiah, the son of [d]Iddo the
prophet, saying,

A solemn warning
and call to repentance

2 "The LORD has been very angry
with your fathers.
3 "Therefore say to them, 'Thus
says the LORD of hosts: [e]"Return to
Me," says the LORD of hosts, "and I
will return to you," says the LORD of
hosts.
4 "Do not be like your fathers,
to whom the [f]former prophets
preached, saying, 'Thus says the LORD
of hosts: "Turn now from your evil
ways and your evil deeds." ' But they
[g]did not hear nor heed Me," says the
LORD.

5 "Your fathers, where *are* they?
And the prophets, do they live
forever?
6 Yet surely My words and My
statutes,
Which I commanded My
servants the prophets,
Did they not overtake your
fathers?

"So they returned and said:

'Just as the LORD of hosts
determined to do to us,
According to our ways and
according to our deeds,
So He has dealt with us.' " ' "

II. A Series of Eight Visions
to Comfort Jerusalem, 1:7—6:15

(1) The rider on the red horse

7 On the twenty-fourth day of the
[a]eleventh month, which is the month
Shebat, in the second year of Darius,
the word of the LORD came to Zechariah the son of Berechiah, the son of
Iddo the prophet:
8 I [1]saw by night, and behold, a

CHAPTER 1

1
a See Lev. 23:2, *note*
b v. 7; Ezra 4:24; 6:15; Hag. 1:1; Zech. 7:1
c Ezra 5:1; 6:14
d Neh. 12:4, 16

3
e Mal. 3:7

4
f Pre–exilic prophets. 2 Chr. 24:19; Zech. 7:7
g 2 Chr. 36:15–16

---

[1](1:8) Zechariah's first vision (vv. 8–17) reveals Judah in dispersion, Jerusalem under adverse possession, and the Gentile nations at rest about it. This condition still continues, and the LORD's answer to the intercession of the angel sweeps on to the end-time of Gentile domination, when "the LORD will again comfort Zion," etc. (vv. 16–17; Isa. 40:1–5). See Kingdom (OT) (Gen. 1:26–28; Zech. 12:8, *note*).

man riding on a [1]red horse, and it
stood among the myrtle trees in the
[a]hollow; and behind him *were* horses:
red, sorrel, and white.
9 Then I said, [b]"My lord, what *are*
these?" So the [c]angel who talked with
me said to me, "I will show you what
they *are*."
10 And the man who stood among
the myrtle trees answered and said,
"These *are the ones* whom the LORD
has sent to walk to and fro throughout
the earth."
11 So they answered the [d]Angel of
the LORD, who stood among the myrtle
trees, and said, "We have walked to
and fro throughout the earth, and behold, all the earth is resting quietly."

The LORD *displeased with the nations*

12 Then the [d]Angel of the LORD answered and said, "O LORD of hosts,
[e]how long will You not have mercy on
Jerusalem and on the cities of Judah,
against which You were angry these
[f]seventy years?"
13 And the LORD answered the [d]an-
gel who talked to me, *with* good *and*
comforting words.
14 So the [d]angel who spoke with
me said to me, "Proclaim, saying,
'Thus says the LORD of hosts:

"I am [g]zealous for Jerusalem
And for Zion with great zeal.
15 I am exceedingly angry with
the nations at ease;
For I was a little angry,
And they helped—*but* with
evil *intent*."

16 'Therefore thus says the LORD:

"I am [h]returning to Jerusalem
with mercy;
My [i]house [j]shall be built in
it," says the LORD of hosts,
"And a *surveyor's* [k]line shall be
stretched out over
Jerusalem." '

17 "Again proclaim, saying, 'Thus
says the LORD of hosts:

"My cities shall again spread
out through prosperity;
The LORD will again [l]comfort
Zion,
And will again [m]choose
Jerusalem." ' "

(2) The four horns and four craftsmen

18 [2]Then I raised my eyes and
looked, and there *were* four [n]horns.
19 And I said to the [d]angel who
talked with me, "What *are* these?" So
he answered me, "These *are* the horns
that have scattered Judah, Israel, and
Jerusalem."
20 Then the LORD showed me four
[3]craftsmen.
21 And I said, "What are these coming to do?" So he said, "These *are* the
[o]horns that scattered Judah, so that
no one could lift up his head; but the
craftsmen* are coming to terrify
them, to cast out the [p]horns of the nations that lifted up *their* horn against
the land of Judah to scatter it."

(3) The man with the measuring line in his hand

2 [4]THEN I raised my eyes and
looked, and behold, a man with a
[q]measuring line in his hand.
2 So I said, "Where are you going?" And he said to me, "To measure
Jerusalem, to see what *is* its width and
what *is* its length."
3 And there *was* the [d]angel who
talked with me, going out; and another angel was coming out to meet
him,

8 *a* i.e. *a shady place* or *glen*
9 *b* Zech. 4:4–5,13; 6:4 *c* See Heb. 1:4, *note*
11 *d Angel* (of the LORD): vv. 9, 11–14,19; 2:3; Zech. 3:1. (Gen. 16:7; Jud. 2:1, *note*). See Heb. 1:4, *note*
12 *e* Ps. 74:10; Jer. 12:4; cp. Rev. 6:10 *f* 2 Chr. 36:21; Jer. 25:11–12; 29:10; Dan. 9:2
14 *g* Joel 2:18; Zech. 8:2; cp. 2 Cor. 11:2
16 *h* Zech. 2:10–11 *i* Ezra 6:14–15; Hag. 1:4; Zech. 4:9 *j* 2 Chr. 36:23; Ezra 1:2–3; Isa. 44:28 *k* Zech. 2:1–12
17 *l* Isa. 40:1–2; 51:3 *m* Isa. 14:1; Zech. 2:12
18 *n* Lam. 2:17

1:21 *o* See v. 18, *note;* Dt. 33:17, *note* *p* v. 19; Ps. 75:10 2:1 *q* Jer. 31:39

* 1:21 Literally *these*

[1](1:8) Compare Rev. 6:4. The whole period of Gentile world power is characterized by the red horse, i.e. by the sword. Cp. also Dan. 9:26; Mt. 24:6–7.

[2](1:18) A horn is sometimes used as a symbol of a Gentile king (Dan. 7:24; Rev. 17:12), and the vision is of the four world empires (Dan. 2:36–44; 7:3–7), which have "scattered Judah, Israel, and Jerusalem" (v. 19). See Dt. 33:17, *note*.

[3](1:20) The four craftsmen may denote the four judgments of Ezek. 14:21 ("the sword and famine and wild beasts and pestilence"), and in turn the four horsemen and horses of Rev. 6:1–8. See v. 18, *note*.

[4](2:1) The measuring line (or rod) is used by Ezekiel (40:3,5) as a symbol of preparation for rebuilding the city and temple in the Kingdom Age. Here it has that meaning, as the context shows (vv. 4–13). The subject of the vision is the restoration of nation and city. In no sense has this prophecy been fulfilled. The order is: (1) the LORD in glory in Jerusalem (v. 5) (cp. Mt. 24:29–30); (2) the restoration of Israel (v. 6); (3) the judgment of the LORD upon the nations (vv. 8–9) (cp. Mt. 25:31–32); and (4) the full blessing of the earth (vv. 10–13). See Kingdom (OT) (Gen. 1:26–28; Zech. 12:8, *note;* Israel, Gen. 12:2–3; Rom. 11:26, *note*).

Jerusalem in the Kingdom Age

4 who said to him, "Run, speak to
this young man, saying: 'Jerusalem
shall be inhabited *as* towns without
walls, because of the multitude of men
and livestock in it.
5 'For I,' says the LORD, 'will be a
wall of fire all around her, and I will be
the glory in her midst.' "
6 "Up, up! Flee from the land of the
north," says the LORD; "for I have
spread you abroad like the four winds
of heaven," says the LORD.
7 "Up, Zion! Escape, you who
dwell with the daughter of [a]Babylon."
8 For thus says the LORD of hosts:
"He sent Me after glory, to the nations
which plunder you; for he who
touches you touches the [b]apple of His
eye.
9 "For surely I will shake My hand
against them, and they shall become
spoil for their servants. Then you will
know that the LORD of hosts has sent
Me.
10 "Sing and rejoice, O daughter of
Zion! For behold, [c]I am coming and I
will [d]dwell in your midst," says the
LORD.
11 "Many nations shall be joined to
the LORD in that day, and they shall
become My people. And I will dwell in
your midst. Then you will know that
the LORD of hosts has sent Me to you.
12 "And the LORD will [e]take possession of Judah as His inheritance in the
[1]Holy Land, and will again choose Jerusalem.
13 [f]"Be silent, all flesh, before the
LORD, for He is aroused from His holy
habitation!"

(4) Joshua the high priest;
the LORD's servant, the BRANCH

3 THEN he showed me [2]Joshua the
high priest standing before the
[g]Angel of the LORD, and [h]Satan standing at his right hand to oppose him.
2 And the LORD said to Satan, "The
LORD rebuke you, Satan! The LORD
who has chosen Jerusalem rebuke
you! *Is* this not a [3]brand plucked from
the fire?"
3 Now Joshua was [i]clothed with
filthy garments, and was standing before the [g]Angel.
4 Then He answered and spoke to
those who stood before Him, saying,
"Take away the filthy garments from
him." And to him He said, "See, I have
removed your iniquity from you, and
I will [j]clothe you with rich robes."
5 And I said, "Let them put a clean
turban on his head." So they put a
clean turban on his head, and they put
the clothes on him. And the [g]Angel of
the LORD stood by.
6 Then the [g]Angel of the LORD admonished Joshua, saying,
7 "Thus says the LORD of hosts:

'If you will walk in My ways,
And if you will [k]keep My
command,
Then you shall also judge My
house,
And likewise have charge of
My courts;
I will give you places to walk
Among these who stand here.

8 'Hear, O Joshua, the high
priest,
You and your companions who
sit before you,
For they are a wondrous sign;
For behold, I am bringing forth
My Servant the [l]BRANCH.
9 For behold, the [m]stone
That I have laid before Joshua:
Upon the stone *are* [n]seven
eyes.
Behold, I will engrave its
inscription,'
Says the LORD of hosts,
'And I will remove the iniquity
of that land in one day.
10 In [4]that day,' says the LORD of
hosts,
'Everyone will invite his
neighbor

CHAPTER 2

7
a Isa. 48:20; Jer. 51:6

8
b Dt. 32:10; Ps. 17:8

10
c *Christ* (second advent): vv. 10–12; Zech. 6:13. (Dt. 30:3; Acts 1:11, *note*)
d Same Heb. word as *Shekinah*

12
e Dt. 32:9; Ps. 33:12; Jer. 10:16

13
f Hab. 2:20; Zeph. 1:7

CHAPTER 3

1
g *Angel* (of the LORD): vv. 1,3,5–6; Zech. 4:1. (Gen. 16:7; Jud. 2:1, *note*)
h *Satan:* vv. 1–2; Mt. 4:1. (Gen. 3:1; Rev. 20:10)

3
i Isa. 64:6; cp. Phil. 3:1–9

4
j Gen. 3:21

7
k Lev. 8:35; Ezek. 44:16

8
l See Isa. 4:2, *note*

9
m See 1 Pet. 2:8, *note*
n Zech. 4:10; cp. Rev. 5:6

---

[1](2:12) This is the only place in the Bible where the term "Holy Land" is used.

[2](3:1) The purpose of this vision was to set forth the reinstatement of Israel into their priestly office. Cp. Ex. 19:5–6. It discloses: (1) the change from self-righteousness to the righteousness of God (see Rom. 3:21, *note*), of which Paul's experience in Phil. 3:1–9 is the illustration, as it is also the foreshadowing of the conversion of Israel; and (2) in type, the preparation of Israel for receiving the LORD's Branch (see Isa. 4:2, *note*). The refusal of the Jews to abandon self-righteousness for the righteousness of God blinded them to the presence of the Branch in their midst at His first advent (Rom. 10:1–4; 11:7–8). Compare Zech. 6:12–15, which speaks of the manifestation of the Branch in glory (v. 13) as the Priest-King, when Israel will receive Him. See Heb. 5:6, *note*.

[3](3:2) "A brand plucked from the fire," i.e. retrieved for God's future purpose.

[4](3:10) Verse 10 marks the time of fulfillment as in the future kingdom. It speaks of a

Under his vine and under his
fig tree.' "

(5) The golden lampstand
and the two olive trees

4 NOW the [a]angel [b]who talked
with me came back and wakened
me, as a man who is wakened out of
his sleep.
2 And he said to me, "What do you
see?" [1]So I said, "I am looking, and
there *is* a lampstand of solid gold with
a bowl on top of it, and on the *stand*
[c]seven lamps with seven pipes to the
seven lamps.
3 [d]"Two olive trees *are* by it, one
at the right of the bowl and the other
at its left."
4 So I answered and spoke to the
angel who talked with me, saying,
"What *are* these, my lord?"
5 Then the angel who talked with
me answered and said to me, "Do you
not know what these are?" And I said,
"No, my lord."
6 So he answered and said to me:

"This *is* the word of the LORD to
[e]Zerubbabel:
'Not by might nor by [f]power,
but by My [g]Spirit,'
Says the LORD of hosts.
7 'Who *are* you, O great
[h]mountain?
Before Zerubbabel *you shall*
become a plain!
And he shall bring forth the
[i]capstone
With shouts of "Grace, grace
to it!" ' "

Zerubbabel to finish
rebuilding the temple

8 Moreover the word of the LORD
came to me, saying:

CHAPTER 4
1
a Angel (of the LORD): v. 1; Zech. 5:5. (Gen. 16:7; Jud. 2:1, *note*)
b Zech. 1:9; 3:1
2
c Ex. 25:37; Rev. 4:5
3
d Rev. 11:3–4
6
e Hag. 1:1
f Isa. 30:1; Hos. 1:7; Hag. 2:4–5
g Holy Spirit (OT): v. 6; Zech. 12:10. (Gen. 1:2; Zech. 12:10)
7
h Jer. 51:25
i Christ (Stone): v. 7; Mt. 7:24. (Gen. 49:24; 1 Pet. 2:8)
9
j Ezra 3:8–11; 5:16
k Ezra 6:14–15; cp. Zech. 6:12–13
10
l Cp. Neh. 4:2–4; Hag. 2:3
m Zech. 3:9
n 2 Chr. 16:9
14
o Cp. Rev. 11:3–12

9 "The hands of Zerubbabel
Have [j]laid the foundation of
this temple;*
His hands shall also [k]finish *it.*
Then you will know
That the LORD of hosts has sent
Me to you.
10 For who has despised the day
of [l]small things?
For these seven rejoice to see
The plumb line in the hand of
Zerubbabel.
They are the [m]eyes of the
LORD,
Which [n]scan to and fro
throughout the whole
earth."

11 Then I answered and said to
him, "What *are* these two olive trees—
at the right of the lampstand and at its
left?"
12 And I further answered and said
to him, "What *are these* two olive
branches that *drip* into the recepta-
cles* of the two gold pipes from which
the golden *oil* drains?"
13 Then he answered me and said,
"Do you not know what these *are?*"
And I said, "No, my lord."
14 So he said, "These *are* the [o]two
anointed ones, who stand beside the
Lord of the whole earth."

(6) The flying scroll

5 THEN I turned and raised my
eyes, and saw there a [2]flying
scroll.
2 And he said to me, "What do you
see?" So I answered, "I see a flying

*
4:9 Literally *house* 4:12 Literally *into the hands of*

security which Israel has never known since the captivity, nor will know until the kingdom comes. Cp. Isa. 11:1–9.

[1](4:2) In this vision the lampstand represents God's witness before the world. In the time of Zechariah this witness was maintained by Israel. In the Church Age it is maintained by the Church (cp. Rev. 1:12,13,20; 2:1,5; etc.). Although the Church will be removed at the rapture (1 Th. 4:13–17; etc.), God will still maintain a witness in the world. The two olive trees represent two phases of God's government, one the priestly and the other the kingly. From these two olive trees the oil was carried to the lampstand. Oil is the uniform symbol of the Holy Spirit. See Acts 2:4, *note.*

The two olive trees represent Joshua and Zerubbabel, whose witness in that day is the prototype of the two witnesses of Rev. 11:3–12. Actually no human being can be the real source of the power that actuates God's witness. It is only as Joshua, Zerubbabel, or any other human being represents Christ, the true Priest-King, that he fulfills this vision. In their fullest significance the two olive trees speak of Christ, the LORD's Priest-King (cp. Ps. 110:4).

[2](5:1) A scroll, in Scripture symbolism, denotes the written word, whether of God or man (Ezra 6:2; Jer. 36:2,4,6, etc.; Ezek. 3:1–3, etc.). Zechariah's sixth vision is of the rebuke of sin by the Word of God. The two sins mentioned really transgress both tablets of the law. To steal is to set aside our neighbor's right; to swear is to set aside God's claim to reverence. As always, the law can only curse (v. 3; Gal. 3:10–14).

scroll. Its length *is* twenty [a]cubits and
its width ten cubits."
3 Then he said to me, "This *is* the
curse that goes out over the face of the
whole [b]earth: 'Every thief shall be expelled,' according *to* this side of *the*
scroll; and, 'Every perjurer shall be
expelled,' according *to* that side of it."
4 "I will send out *the curse,*" says
the LORD of hosts;
"It shall enter the house of the
[c]thief
And the house of the one who
[d]swears falsely by My name.
It shall remain in the midst of
his house
And [e]consume it, with its
timber and stones."

(7) The basket and the women

5 Then the [f]angel who talked with
me came out and said to me, "Lift your
eyes now, and see what this *is* that
goes forth."
6 So I asked, [1]"What *is* it?" And he
said, "It *is* a [a]basket* that is going
forth." He also said, "This *is* their resemblance throughout the [b]earth:
7 "Here *is* a lead disc lifted up, and
this *is* a woman sitting inside the basket";
8 then he said, "This *is* Wickedness!" And he thrust her down into the
basket, and threw the lead cover*
over its mouth.
9 Then I raised my eyes and
looked, and there *were* two women,
coming with the wind in their wings;
for they had wings like the wings of a
[g]stork, and they lifted up the basket
between earth and heaven.
10 So I said to the [f]angel who
talked with me, "Where are they carrying the basket?"
11 And he said to me, "To build a
house for it in the land of [h]Shinar;

CHAPTER 5

2
a See Weights and Measures (OT), 2 Chr. 2:10, *note*

3
b Or *land,* i.e. *Palestine*

4
c Ex. 20:15; Lev. 19:11
d Ex. 20:7; Lev. 19:12; Isa. 48:1; Jer. 5:2
e Cp. Prov. 3:33

5
f *Angel* (of the LORD): vv. 5,10; 6:4–5; Zech. 12:8. (Gen. 16:7; Jud. 2:1, *note*)

9
g Lev. 11:13,19

11
h i.e. *Babylon,* Dan. 1:2

CHAPTER 6

6
i v. 8; cp. Jer. 1:14; Ezek. 1:4

9
j *Parables* (OT): vv. 9–15; Zech. 11:7. (Jud. 9:8; Zech. 11:7)

when it is ready, *the basket* will be set
there on its base."

(8) The four chariots

6 THEN I turned and raised my
eyes and looked, and behold,
[2]four chariots *were* coming from between two mountains, and the mountains *were* mountains of bronze.
2 With the first chariot *were* red
horses, with the second chariot black
horses,
3 with the third chariot white
horses, and with the fourth chariot
dappled horses—strong *steeds.*
4 Then I answered and said to the
[f]angel who talked with me, "What *are*
these, my lord?"
5 And the [f]angel answered and
said to me, "These *are* four spirits of
heaven, who go out from *their* station
before the Lord of all the earth.
6 "The one with the black horses is
going to the [i]north country, the white
are going after them, and the dappled
are going toward the south country."
7 Then the strong *steeds* went out,
eager to go, that they might walk to
and fro throughout the earth. And He
said, "Go, walk to and fro throughout
the earth." So they walked to and fro
throughout the earth.
8 And He called to me, and spoke
to me, saying, "See, those who go toward the north country have given
rest to My Spirit in the north country."

The symbolic crowning of Joshua

9 Then the word of the LORD came
to me, [j]saying:
10 "Receive *the gift* from the
captives—from Heldai, Tobijah, and
Jedaiah, who have come from
Babylon—and go the same day and

*

5:6 Hebrew *ephah,* a measuring container, and so elsewhere 5:8 Literally *stone*

[1](5:6) In the vision of the measuring basket there is a blending of elements from Zechariah's time with those of the far distant future. The basket is employed to indicate how the measure of Israel's sins had accumulated in that day. Compare, for the figure of a measure, 2 Sam. 8:2; Jer. 51:13; Hab. 3:6–7; Mt. 7:2; 23:32. For such iniquity there must be, first of all, the restraint of God in order that the righteous may be permitted to live in the land; this is symbolized by the basket's lead cover. Second, evil must be completely eradicated from the land and carried back to the seat of idolatry and defiance of God, namely, Babylon; this is indicated by the flight of the basket to Babylon, its base. Cp. Rev. 18.

[2](6:1) The interpretation of the eighth vision must be governed by the authoritative declaration of v. 5. The four chariots with their horses do not symbolize the four world empires of Daniel, but "four spirits of heaven, who go out from their station before the LORD of all the earth." These spirits are angels (Lk. 1:19; Heb. 1:14). They have also a ministry earthward, and of like nature with the spirits of Zech. 6:1–8, i.e. judgment. The symbol (chariots and horses) is in perfect harmony with this. Always in Scripture symbolism, they stand for the power of God earthward in judgment (Jer. 46:9–10; Joel 2:3–11; Nah. 3:1–7). The vision, then, speaks of the LORD's judgments upon the Gentile nations north and south in the day of the LORD (Isa. 2:10–22; Rev. 19:11–21).

enter the house of Josiah the son of
Zephaniah.
11 "Take the silver and [a]gold,
make an elaborate [1]crown, and set *it*
on the head of [b]Joshua the son of Jehozadak, the high priest.
12 "Then speak to him, saying,
'Thus says the LORD of hosts, saying:

"Behold, the Man whose name
is the [c]BRANCH!
From His place He shall
branch out,
And He shall build the temple
of the LORD;
13 Yes, He shall build the temple
of the LORD.
He shall bear the [d]glory,
And shall sit and rule on His
[e]throne;
So He shall be a [f]priest on His
[g]throne,
And the counsel of peace shall
be between them both." '

14 "Now the elaborate crown shall
be for a memorial in the temple of the
LORD for Helem,* Tobijah, Jedaiah,
and Hen the son of Zephaniah.
15 "Even those from afar shall
come and build the temple of the LORD.
Then you shall know that the LORD of
hosts has sent Me to you. And *this*
shall come to pass if you diligently
obey the voice of the LORD your God."

11
a Cp. Ezra 7:14–16; 8:26–30
b Hag. 1:1; Zech. 3:1–5
12
c See Isa. 4:2, *note*
13
d Isa. 11:10; 22:24
e *Kingdom* (OT): vv. 11–13; Zech. 12:8. (Gen. 1:26; Zech. 12:8, *note*)
f Ps. 110:4
g *Christ* (second advent): vv. 11–13; Zech. 12:10. (Dt. 30:3; Acts 1:11, *note*)
CHAPTER 7
1
h Cp. Ezra 6:15; Zech. 1:1
i See Lev. 23:2, *note*
5
j Zech. 8:19
k Isa. 1:11–12; 58:1–9
6
l Dt. 12:7; 14:26; 1 Chr. 29:29; cp.

III. The Delegation from Bethel concerning Fasting, 7—8

The question

7 NOW in the [h]fourth year of King
Darius it came to pass *that* the
word of the LORD came to Zechariah,
on the fourth day of the ninth month,
[i]Chislev,
2 when [2]*the people** sent Sherez-
zer,* with Regem-Melech and his
men, *to* the house of God,* to pray
before the LORD,
3 *and* to ask the priests who *were*
in the house of the LORD of hosts, and
the prophets, saying, "Should I weep
in the fifth month and fast as I have
done for so many years?"

The answer of the LORD: their fasts were mere form

4 Then the word of the LORD of
hosts came to me, saying,
5 "Say to all the people of the land,
and to the priests: 'When you [j]fasted
and mourned in the fifth and seventh
months during those seventy years,
did you really fast for Me—for [k]Me?
6 [l]'When you eat and when you
drink, do you not eat and drink *for*
yourselves?

1 Cor. 10:31; 11:20–22

*
6:14 Following Masoretic Text, Targum, and Vulgate; Syriac reads *for Heldai* (compare verse 10); Septuagint reads *for the patient ones.*
7:2 Literally *they* (compare verse 5) • Or *Sar-Ezer* • Hebrew *Bethel*

[1](6:11) Following the earth-judgments symbolized in the war chariots (6:1–8) comes the manifestation of Christ in His kingdom glory (vv. 9–15). This is the invariable prophetic order: first, the judgments of the day of the LORD (Isa. 2:10–22; Rev. 19:11–21); then, the kingdom (cp. Ps. 2:5 with 2:6; Isa. 3:24–26 with 4:2–6; 10:33–34 with 11:1–10; Rev. 19:19–21 with 20:4–6). This is set forth symbolically by the crowning of Joshua, which was not a vision but was actually done (cp. Ezek. 37:16–22). The fulfillment in the Branch will infinitely transcend the symbol. He "shall bear the glory" (v. 13; Mt. 16:27; 24:30; 25:31) as the Priest-King on His own throne (vv. 12–13; Heb. 7:1–3). Christ is now a Priest but is still in the holiest within the veil (Heb. 9:11–14,24; cp. Lev. 16:15) and seated on the Father's throne (Rev. 3:21). He has not yet come out to take His own throne (Heb. 9:28). It was to keep alive this larger hope of Israel that this crown was made for the symbolical crowning of Joshua; it was to be laid up in the temple as a memorial.

[2](7:2) The mission of these Jews concerned a fast day instituted by the Jews during the captivity in commemoration of the destruction of Jerusalem, wholly of their own will and without warrant from the Word of God. In the beginning there was doubtless sincere contrition in the observance of the day; now it had become a mere ceremonial. The Jews sent from Bethel would be rid of it, but seek authority from the priests. The whole matter, like much in modern pseudo-Christianity, was extra-biblical, formal, and futile. The LORD takes the occasion to send a divine message to the inquirers. That message is in five parts: (1) Their fast was a mere religious form; they should rather have given heed to the "former prophets" (vv. 4–7; cp. Isa. 1:12; Mt. 15:1–10). (2) They are told why their prayer of seventy years has not been answered (vv. 8–14; cp. Ps. 66:18; Isa. 1:14–17). (3) The unchanged purpose of the LORD and the blessing of Israel in the kingdom are alluded to (8:1–8; compare a like order in Isa. 1:24–31 with 2:1–4). (4) The messengers of the captivity are exhorted to hear "the prophets who spoke in the day the foundation was laid," i.e. Haggai and Zechariah, and to do justly; then all their fasts and feasts will become gladness and joy (8:9–19). And (5) they are assured that Jerusalem is yet to be the religious center of the earth (8:20–23; cp. Isa. 2:1–3; Zech. 14:16–21).

7 '*Should you* not *have obeyed* the
[a]words which the LORD proclaimed
through the [b]former prophets when
Jerusalem and the cities around it
were inhabited and prosperous, and
the [c]South and the [d]Lowland were inhabited?' "

Why their prayers were unanswered

8 Then the word of the LORD came
to Zechariah, saying,
9 "Thus says the LORD of hosts:

'Execute true justice,
Show mercy and compassion
Everyone to his brother.
10 Do not oppress the widow or
the fatherless,
The alien or the poor.
Let none of you [e]plan evil in
his heart
Against his brother.'

11 "But they refused to heed,
shrugged their shoulders, and stopped
their ears so that they could [f]not hear.
12 "Yes, they made their hearts like
flint, refusing to hear the law and the
words which the LORD of hosts had
sent by His Spirit through the [g]former
prophets. Thus great [h]wrath came
from the LORD of hosts.
13 "Therefore it happened, *that*
just as He proclaimed and they would
[i]not hear, so they called out and I
would not listen," says the LORD of
hosts.
14 "But I [j]scattered them with a
whirlwind among all the nations
which they had not known. Thus the
land became desolate after them, so
that no one passed through or returned; for they made the pleasant
land desolate."

The LORD will restore Israel in the kingdom

8 AGAIN the word of the LORD of
hosts came, saying,
2 "Thus says the LORD of hosts:

'I am [k]zealous for Zion with
great zeal;
With great fervor I am zealous
for her.'

3 "Thus says the LORD:

'I will [l]return to Zion,
And [m]dwell in the midst of
Jerusalem.
Jerusalem shall be called the
City of Truth,
The Mountain of the LORD of
hosts,
The [1n]Holy Mountain.'

4 "Thus says the LORD of hosts:

[o]'Old men and old women shall
again sit
In the streets of Jerusalem,
Each one with his staff in his
hand
Because of great age.
5 The streets of the city
Shall be [p]full of boys and girls
Playing in its streets.'

6 "Thus says the LORD of hosts:

'If it is marvelous in the eyes of
the [q]remnant of this people
in [2]these days,
Will it also be marvelous in
My eyes?'
Says the LORD of hosts.

7 "Thus says the LORD of hosts:

'Behold, I will save My people
from the land of the east
And from the land of the west;
8 I will [r]bring them *back*,
And they shall dwell in the
midst of Jerusalem.
They shall be [s]My people
And I will be their God,
In truth and righteousness.'

Exhortation to hear the prophets

9 "Thus says the LORD of hosts:

'Let your hands be strong,
You who have been hearing in
these days

7
a Inspiration: v. 7; Mt. 2:5. (Ex. 4:15; 2 Tim. 3:16, *note*)
b Zech. 1:4
c See Gen. 12:9, *note*
d See Dt. 1:1, *note*
10
e Ezek. 18:5; 45:9; Mic. 6:6–8; Zech. 8:16
11
f Jer. 17:23
12
g Neh. 9:30
h Dan. 9:11–12
13
i Prov. 1:24–28; Isa. 1:15; Jer. 11:11
14
j Lev. 26:33; Dt. 4:27; 28:64; Neh. 1:8
CHAPTER 8
2
k Joel 2:18; Zech. 1:14; cp. 2 Cor. 11:2
3
l Zech. 1:16
m Zech. 2:10–11
n Sanctification (OT): v. 3. (Gen. 2:3; Zech. 8:3). Isa. 11:9; Jer. 31:23
4
o Cp. Isa. 65:20
5
p Jer. 30:19–20
6
q Remnant: vv. 6–8, 11–12; Zech. 11:7. (Isa. 1:9; Rom. 11:5, *note*)
8
r Zeph. 3:20
s Jer. 30:22; 31:1,33; Zech. 13:9

[1](8:3) Sanctification, Holiness (OT), Summary: In the OT various forms of the words *consecrate, dedicate, sanctify,* and *holiness* are renderings of one Hebrew word. The terms are used of persons and of things, and have an identical meaning, i.e. *set apart.* Only when used of God Himself (e.g. Lev. 11:45), or of the holy angels (e.g. Dan. 4:13), is any inward moral quality necessarily implied. Doubtless a priest or other person set apart to the service of God, whose whole will and desire went with his setting apart, experienced progressively an inner detachment from evil. See Mt. 4:5 and Rev. 22:11, *notes.*

[2](8:6) The remnant in vv. 6,11,12 refers to the remnant of Judah which returned from Babylon, among whom Zechariah was prophesying. See Rom. 11:5, *note.*

These words by the mouth of
the [1][a]prophets,
Who *spoke* in the day the
foundation was laid
For the house of the LORD of
hosts,
That the temple might be built.
10 For before these days
There were no wages for man
nor any hire for beast;
There was no peace from the
enemy for whoever went out
or came in;
For I set all men, everyone,
against his neighbor.

11 [b]'But now I *will* not *treat* the
remnant of this people as in the former days,' says the LORD of hosts.

12 [c]'For the seed *shall be*
prosperous,
The vine shall give its fruit,
The ground shall give her
increase,
And the heavens shall give
their dew—
I will cause the remnant of this
people
To possess all these.
13 And it shall come to pass
That just as you were a curse
among the nations,
O house of Judah and house of
Israel,
So I will save you, and [d]you
shall be a blessing.
Do not fear,
Let your hands be strong.'

14 "For thus says the LORD of hosts:
'Just as I determined to punish
you
When your fathers provoked
Me to wrath,'
Says the LORD of hosts,
'And I would not [2]relent,
15 So again in these days
I am determined to do good
To Jerusalem and to the house
of Judah.
Do not fear.
16 These *are* the things you shall
[e]do:
[f]Speak each man the truth to
his neighbor;
Give judgment in your gates
for truth, justice, and peace;
17 Let none of you think evil in
your* heart against your
neighbor;
And do not love a false oath.
For all these *are things* that I
hate,'
Says the LORD."

18 Then the word of the LORD of
hosts came to me, saying,
19 "Thus says the LORD of hosts:

'The fast of the [g]fourth *month,*
The fast of the [g]fifth,
The fast of the [g]seventh,
And the fast of the [g]tenth,
Shall be joy and gladness and
[h]cheerful feasts
For the house of Judah.
Therefore love truth and
peace.'

Jerusalem to be the religious center of the earth

20 "Thus says the LORD of hosts:

'Peoples shall yet come,
Inhabitants of many cities;
21 The inhabitants of one *city*
shall go to another, saying,
"Let us continue to go and pray
before the LORD,
And [i]seek the LORD of hosts.
I myself will go also."
22 Yes, [j]many peoples and strong
nations
Shall come to seek the LORD of
hosts in Jerusalem,
And to pray before the LORD.'

23 "Thus says the LORD of hosts: 'In
[3]those days ten men from every language of the nations shall [k]grasp the
sleeve of a Jewish man, saying, "Let
us go with you, for we have heard *that*
God *is* with you." ' "

*8:17 Literally *his*

9 [a] Ezra 5:1–2; 6:14; Hag. 2:4; Zech. 4:9
11 [b] Hag. 2:15–19
12 [c] Lit. *For the seed of peace, the vine*
13 [d] Gen. 12:2; Isa. 19:24–25; Ezek. 34:26; Zeph. 3:20; cp. Ruth 4:11–12
16 [e] Zech. 7:9–10 [f] Eph. 4:25
19 [g] See Lev. 23:2, *note* [h] Cp. Zech. 7:3,5
21 [i] Isa. 2:2–3
22 [j] Isa. 66:23; Zech. 14:16–21
23 [k] Isa. 45:14

[1](8:9) Haggai and Zechariah, who were in Jerusalem when the Temple was begun (Ezra 5:1–2).
[2](8:14) Repentance (OT), Summary: In the OT, "repentance" is one of the English words used to translate the Hebrew *nacham, to be eased* or *comforted.* It is used of both God and man. *Relent* is usually used for God in the NKJV. Notwithstanding the literal meaning of *nacham,* it is evident, from a study of all the passages, that the sacred writers use it in the sense of *metanoia* in the NT, meaning *a change of mind.* See Mt. 3:2; Acts 17:30, *note.* As in the NT, such change of mind is often accompanied by contrition and self-judgment. When applied to God, the word is used phenomenally, according to OT custom. God seems to change His mind. The phenomena are such as, in the case of a man, would indicate a change of mind.
[3](8:23) That is, in the days when Jerusalem has been made the center of earth's worship,

IV. Prophecies concerning the End of Israel's Age and the Return and Reign of Christ, 9—14

Destruction of cities surrounding Israel

9 THE [a]burden of the word of
the LORD
Against the land of Hadrach,
And [b]Damascus its resting
place
(For the eyes of men
And all the tribes of Israel
Are on the LORD);
2 Also *against* Hamath, *which*
borders on it,
And *against* [c]Tyre and Sidon,
though they are very wise.
3 For Tyre built herself a tower,
Heaped up silver like the dust,
And gold like the mire of the
streets.
4 Behold, the LORD will cast her
out;
He will destroy her power in
the sea,
And she will be devoured by
fire.
5 Ashkelon shall see *it* and fear;
Gaza also shall be very
sorrowful;
And [d]Ekron, for He dried up
her expectation.
The king shall perish from
Gaza,
And Ashkelon shall not be
inhabited.
6 "A mixed race shall settle in
[e]Ashdod,
And I will cut off the pride of
the [f]Philistines.
7 I will take away the blood
from his mouth,
And the abominations from
between his teeth.
But he who remains, even he
shall be for our God,
And shall be like a leader in
Judah,
And Ekron like a Jebusite.
8 I will [g]camp around My house
Because of the army,
[1]Because of him who passes by
and him who returns.
No more shall an oppressor
pass through them,
For now I have seen with My
eyes.

Prophecy of Messiah's triumphal entry at first advent

9 "Rejoice greatly, O daughter of
Zion!
Shout, O daughter of
Jerusalem!
[2]Behold, your [h]King is coming
to you;
[i]He *is* just and having
salvation,
Lowly and riding on a donkey,
A colt, the foal of a donkey.

Future deliverance of Judah and Ephraim (Israel)

10 [3]I will cut off the chariot from
Ephraim
And the horse from Jerusalem;
The [j]battle bow shall be cut
off.
He shall speak peace to the
nations;
His [k]dominion *shall be* 'from
sea to sea,
And from the River to the ends
of the earth.'
11 "As for you also,
Because of the blood of your
covenant,
I will set your [l]prisoners free
from the waterless pit.
12 Return to the [m]stronghold,
You prisoners of [n]hope.
Even today I declare

CHAPTER 9
1 *a* See Isa. 13:1, *note* *b* Isa. 17:1
2 *c* vv. 2–4; Isa. 23:1–18; Jer. 25:22; 47:4; Ezek. 26:1–21; 28:20–24; Amos 1:9–10
5 *d* Zeph. 2:4–5
6 *e* Amos 1:8 *f* Ezek. 25:15–17
8 *g* Zech. 2:5
9 *h* Mt. 21:1–10; Mk. 11:1–10; Lk. 19:29–40; Jn. 12:12–15 *i Christ* (first advent): v. 9; Zech. 11:13. (Gen. 3:15; Acts 1:11, *note*)
10 *j* Ps. 46:9; Isa. 2:4; Hos. 2:18; Mic. 4:3 *k* Ps. 72:8
11 *l* Cp. Isa. 24:17–23, where vv. 21,23 fix the time as the day of the LORD. See Rev. 19:19, *note*
12 *m* Jer. 16:19. See context *n* Jer. 17:13; cp. Heb. 6:18–19

from v. 14

in the millennial age. Verse 23 explains: the Jew (cp. Remnant, Isa. 1:9; see Rom. 11:5, *note*) will then be the missionary.

[1](9:8) This refers to the advance and return of Alexander (v. 13) after the battle of Issus. He subdued the cities mentioned in vv. 1–6, and afterward returned to Greece without harming Jerusalem. But the greater meaning converges on the yet future last days (see Acts 2:17, *note*), as the latter part of v. 8 shows, for many oppressors have passed through Jerusalem since the days of Alexander.

[2](9:9) The events following this manifestation of Christ as King are recorded in the Gospels. The real faith of the multitude who cried "Hosanna" is given in Mt. 21:11. So little was Jesus deceived by His apparent reception as King that He wept over Jerusalem and announced its impending destruction, fulfilled in A.D. 70. Cp. Lk. 19:38–44. The same multitude soon cried, "Crucify him."

[3](9:10) After the King is introduced in v. 9, the following verses look forward to the end time and the kingdom.

That I will restore [a]double to
you.
13 For I have bent Judah, My
bow,
Fitted the bow with Ephraim,
[b]And raised up your sons, O
Zion,
Against your sons, O Greece,
And made you like the sword
of a mighty man."
14 Then the LORD will be seen
over them,
And His [c]arrow will go forth
like lightning.
The Lord GOD will blow the
trumpet,
And go with whirlwinds from
the south.
15 The LORD of hosts will [d]defend
them;
They shall devour and subdue
with slingstones.
They shall drink *and* roar as if
with wine;
They shall be filled *with blood*
like basins,
Like the corners of the altar.
16 The LORD their God will [e]save
them in that day,
As the flock of His people.
For they *shall be like* the
[f]jewels of a crown,
Lifted like a banner over His
land—
17 For how great is its* goodness
And how great its* [g]beauty!
Grain shall make the young
men thrive,
And new wine the young
women.

Future strengthening of Judah and Ephraim

10 ASK the LORD for [h]rain
In the time of the [1]latter
rain.*
The LORD will make flashing
clouds;
He will give them showers of
rain,
Grass in the field for everyone.
2 For the idols* speak delusion;
The diviners envision [i]lies,
And tell false dreams;
They comfort in vain.
Therefore *the people* wend
their way like [j]sheep;
They are in trouble [k]because
there is no shepherd.
3 "My anger is kindled against
the [l]shepherds,
And I will punish the
goatherds.
For the LORD of hosts will visit
His flock,
The house of Judah,
And will make them as His
royal horse in the [m]battle.
4 From him [2]comes the
cornerstone,
From him the tent peg,
From him the battle bow,
From him every ruler*
together.
5 They shall be like mighty men,
Who tread down *their enemies*
In the mire of the streets in the
battle.
They shall fight because the
LORD is with them,
And the riders on horses shall
be put to shame.
6 "I will strengthen the house of
Judah,
And I will save the house of
Joseph.
I will bring them back,
Because I have [n]mercy on
them.
[o]They shall be as though I had
not cast them aside;
For I *am* the LORD their God,
And I will [p]hear them.
7 *Those of* Ephraim shall be like
a mighty man,
And their heart shall rejoice as
if with wine.
Yes, their children shall see *it*
and be glad;

12
a Isa. 61:7
13
b Lit. *I will raise up*
14
c Hab. 3:11
15
d Zech. 12:8
16
e Jer. 31:10–11
f Isa. 62:3; Mal. 3:17
17
g Ps. 45:1–16
CHAPTER 10
1
h Joel 2:23
2
i Jer. 27:9; Ezek. 13
j Jer. 50:6, 17
k Ezek. 34:5–8
3
l Jer. 25:34–36; Ezek. 34:2; Zech. 11:17
m *Armageddon* (battle of): v. 3; Zech. 12:2. (Isa. 10:27; Rev. 19:17)
6
n Zech. 1:16
o *Israel* (prophecies): vv. 6–12; Mt. 24:31. (Gen. 12:2; Rom. 11:26, *note*)
p Zech. 13:9

*
9:17 Or *His* • Or *His* 10:1 That is, spring rain
10:2 Hebrew *teraphim* 10:4 Or *despot*

[1](10:1) Compare Hos. 6:3; Joel 2:23–32; Zech. 12:10. There are both a physical and spiritual meaning: rain as of old will be restored to Palestine, but also there will be a mighty effusion of the Spirit upon restored Israel.

[2](10:4) The tense is futuristic: "From him [Judah] will come the cornerstone [Ex. 17:6; see 1 Pet. 2:8, *note*], from him the tent peg [Isa. 22:23–24], from him the battle bow," etc. The whole scene is of the events which cluster around the deliverance of Israel at the time of the invasion of Palestine from the north (Ezek. 38—39) and the final liberation which will be completely effected by the return of the Lord (Rev. 19:11–21); but previously He strengthens the hard-pressed Israelites (Mic. 4:13; Zech. 9:13–15; 10:5–7; 12:2–6; 14:14). That there may have been a fulfillment in the Maccabean victories can neither be affirmed nor denied from Scripture, but the ultimate fulfillment, when Christ comes again, is certain.

Their heart shall rejoice in the
LORD.
8 I will [a]whistle for them and
gather them,
For I will [b]redeem them;
And they shall [c]increase as
they once increased.

The dispersion and regathering of Israel

9 "I will [d]sow them among the
peoples,
And they shall [e]remember Me
in far countries;
They shall live, together with
their children,
And they shall return.
10 I will also bring them back
from the land of Egypt,
And gather them from Assyria.
I will bring them into the land
of Gilead and Lebanon,
Until no *more room* is found
for them.
11 He shall pass through the sea
with affliction,
And strike the waves of the
sea:
All the depths of the [f]River
shall dry up.
Then the pride of [g]Assyria
shall be brought down,
And the scepter of Egypt shall
depart.
12 "So I will strengthen them in
the LORD,
And they shall walk up and
down in His name,"
Says the LORD.

Messiah the true Shepherd rejected at His first advent

11 OPEN your doors, O
Lebanon,
That fire may devour your
cedars.
2 Wail, O cypress, for the [h]cedar
has fallen,
Because the mighty *trees* are
ruined.
Wail, O oaks of Bashan,
For the thick forest has come
down.
3 *There is* the sound of wailing
[i]shepherds!
For their glory is in ruins.
There is the sound of roaring
lions!
For the pride* of the Jordan is
in ruins.

4 Thus says the LORD my God,
"Feed the flock for slaughter,
5 "whose owners slaughter them
and feel [j]no guilt; those who sell them
say, 'Blessed be the LORD, for I am
[k]rich'; and their shepherds do [l]not
pity them.
6 "For I will no longer pity the inhabitants of the land," says the LORD.
"But indeed I will give everyone into
his neighbor's hand and into the hand
of his king. They shall attack the land,
and I will not deliver *them* from their
hand."
7 So I fed the flock for slaughter,
in particular the [m]poor of the flock.* I
took for myself [1]two [n]staffs: [2]the one
I called Beauty,* and the other I called
Bonds;* and I fed the flock.
8 I dismissed the three shepherds
in one month. My soul loathed them,
and their soul also abhorred me.
9 Then I said, "I will not feed you.
Let what is dying die, and what is
[o]perishing perish. Let those that are
left eat each other's flesh."
10 And I took my staff, Beauty, and
cut it in two, that I might break the
covenant which I had made with all
the [p]peoples.
11 So it was broken on that day.

8 *a* Isa. 5:26 *b* See Ex. 6:6 and Isa. 59:20, *notes* *c* Zech. 2:4
9 *d* Hos. 2:23 *e* Dt. 30:1
11 *f* i.e. *the Nile* *g* Zeph. 2:13
CHAPTER 11
2 *h* Ezek. 31:3
3 *i* Jer. 25:34
5 *j* Jer. 50:7 *k* Hos. 12:8 *l* Ezek. 34:2–3
7 *m Remnant:* vv. 7,11; Mal. 3:16. (Isa. 1:9; Rom. 11:5, *note*) *n Parables (OT):* vv. 7–14. (Jud. 9:8; Zech. 11:7)
9 *o* Jer. 15:2
10 *p* i.e. *all nations*

*11:3 Or *floodplain, thicket* 11:7 Following Masoretic Text, Targum, and Vulgate; Septuagint reads *for the Canaanites.* • Or *Grace,* and so in verse 10 • Or *Unity,* and so in verse 14

[1](11:7) The scene belongs to the first advent. "Beauty" and "Bonds"—literally, "Graciousness" and "Binders" (unifiers)—signify first, God's protection over Israel by His restraint upon the nations; then, the brotherly ties within the nation itself. With the breaking of the first staff, Judah was abandoned to the destruction foretold in vv. 1–6, which was fulfilled in A.D. 70. The breaking of the second staff meant the destruction of the inner bond of the nation, resulting in the internal strife and divisions that contributed largely to the downfall of the Jewish state in A.D. 70. The order of this chapter is: (1) the wrath against the land (vv. 1–6), fulfilled in the destruction of Jerusalem after the rejection of Christ (Lk. 19:41–44); (2) the cause of that wrath in the betrayal and rejection of Christ (vv. 7–14); and (3) the rise of the "worthless shepherd," the beast (Dan. 7:8; Rev. 19:20), and his destruction (vv. 15–17).

[2](11:7) Parables (OT), Summary: A parable is a similitude used to teach or enforce a truth. The OT parables fall into three classes: (1) the story-parable, of which Jud. 9:7–15 is an instance; (2) parabolic discourses, e.g. Isa. 5:1–7; and (3) parabolic actions, e.g. Ezek. 37:16–22.

Thus the [1]poor* of the flock, who
were watching me, knew that it *was*
the word of the LORD.
12 Then I said to them, "If it is
agreeable to you, give *me* my wages;
and if not, refrain." [a]So they weighed
out for my wages thirty *pieces* of silver.
13 And the LORD said to me, "Throw
it to the potter"—that princely price
they set on me. So I took the [b]thirty
pieces of silver and threw them into
the house of the LORD for the potter.
14 Then I cut in two my other staff,
Bonds, that I might break the brotherhood between Judah and Israel.

The foolish shepherd to be overthrown

15 [2]And the LORD said to me, "Next,
take for yourself the implements of a
[c]foolish shepherd.
16 "For indeed I will raise up a
shepherd in the land *who* will not care
for those who are [d]cut off, nor seek
the young, nor heal those that are broken, nor feed those that still stand. But
he will eat the flesh of the fat and tear
their hooves in [e]pieces.

17 [f]"Woe to the worthless
shepherd,
Who leaves the flock!
A sword *shall be* against his
arm
And against his right eye;
His arm shall completely
wither,
And his right eye shall be
totally blinded."

Jerusalem to be attacked
but Judah to be delivered

12 THE [3]burden* of the word of
the LORD against Israel. Thus
says the LORD, who stretches out the
heavens, lays the foundation of the
earth, and forms the spirit of man
within him:

12
a Mt. 26:15; 27:9–10
13
b Christ (first advent): vv. 11–13; Zech. 13:7. (Gen. 3:15; Acts 1:11, *note*). Cp. Ex. 21:32
15
c Isa. 56:11
16
d i.e. *perishing*
e Ezek. 34:1–10; Mic. 3:1–3
17
f Jer. 23:1; Ezek. 34:2; Jn. 10:12–13
CHAPTER 12
2
g Day (of the LORD): 12:1–13:9; Zech. 14:1. (Ps. 2:9; Rev. 19:19)
h Armageddon (battle of): vv. 1–9; Zech. 14:3. (Isa. 10:27; Rev. 19:17)
8
i Kingdom (OT): vv. 6–8; Zech. 14:16. (Gen. 1:26; Zech. 12:8, *note*). See Gen. 1:26, *note*
j Angel (of the LORD): v. 8. (Gen. 16:7; Jud. 2:1, *note*). See Heb.

2 [g]"Behold, I will make Jerusalem
a cup of drunkenness to all the surrounding peoples, when they lay
[h]siege against Judah and Jerusalem.
3 "And it shall happen in that day
that I will make Jerusalem a very
heavy stone for all peoples; all who
would heave it away will surely be cut
in pieces, though all nations of the
earth are gathered against it.
4 "In that day," says the LORD, "I
will strike every horse with confusion,
and its rider with madness; I will open
My eyes on the house of Judah, and
will strike every horse of the peoples
with blindness.
5 "And the governors of Judah
shall say in their heart, 'The inhabitants of Jerusalem *are* my strength in
the LORD of hosts, their God.'
6 "In that day I will make the governors of Judah like a firepan in the
woodpile, and like a fiery torch in the
sheaves; they shall devour all the surrounding peoples on the right hand
and on the left, but Jerusalem shall be
inhabited again in her own place—
Jerusalem.
7 "The LORD will save the tents
of Judah first, so that the glory of
the house of David and the glory
of the inhabitants of Jerusalem shall
not become greater than that of
Judah.
8 "In that day the LORD will defend
the inhabitants of Jerusalem; the one
who is feeble among them in that day
shall be like David, and the [i]house of
[4]David *shall be* like God, like the [j]An-
gel of the LORD before them.
9 "It shall be in that day *that* I will

1:4, *note*

*
11:11 Following Masoretic Text, Targum, and Vulgate; Septuagint reads *the Canaanites.*
12:1 Or *oracle*

[1](11:11) The "poor of the flock," i.e. the "remnant according to the election of grace" (Rom. 11:5), are those Jews who did not wait for the manifestation of Christ in glory but believed in Him at His first coming and subsequently. Of them it is said that they "were watching me," and "knew."

[2](11:15) The reference is to the coming beast; no other personage of prophecy in any sense meets the description. He who came in His Father's name was rejected. The alternative is one who comes in his own name (Jn. 5:43; Rev. 13:4–8).

[3](12:1) Chapters 12—14 form one prophecy, the general theme of which is the return of the Lord and the establishment of the kingdom. The order is: (1) the siege of Jerusalem preceding the battle of Armageddon (vv. 1–3); (2) the battle itself (vv. 4–9); (3) the pouring out of the Spirit and the personal revelation of Christ to the family of David and the remnant in Jerusalem, not merely as the glorious Deliverer but also as the One whom Israel pierced and has long rejected (v. 10); (4) the godly sorrow which follows that revelation (vv. 11–14); and (5) the cleansing fountain (Zech. 13:1) then to be opened effectually to Israel.

[4](12:8) Kingdom (OT), Summary (see also Kingdom [NT] Lk. 1:33; 1 Cor. 15:24, *note*):
I. Dominion over the Earth before the Call of Abraham.

seek to destroy all the nations that come against Jerusalem.

The Spirit poured out: the pierced One revealed to the repentant and delivered remnant

10 "And I will [a]pour on the house of David and on the inhabitants of Jerusalem the [1b]Spirit of grace and supplication; then they will look on [c]Me

10 a Joel 2:28–29 b Holy Spirit (OT): v. 10. (Gen. 1:2; Zech. 12:10) c Christ (second advent): vv. 9–10; Zech. 14:4. (Dt. 30:3; Acts 1:11, *note*)

(1) Dominion over creation was given to the first man and woman (Gen. 1:26–28). Through the fall this dominion was lost, Satan becoming "ruler of this world" (Mt. 4:8–10; Jn. 14:30).

(2) After the flood, the principle of human government was established under the covenant with Noah (Gen. 9:6; see Gen. 9:16, *note*). Biblically, this is still the charter of all government.

II. The Theocratic Kingdom in Israel. (See also 1 Sam. 8:7, *note*.) The call of Abraham involved, with much else, the creation of a distinctive people through whom great purposes of God toward the human race might be worked out (see Israel, Gen. 12:1–3; Rom. 11:26, *note*). Among these purposes is the establishment of a worldwide kingdom. The history of the divine mediatorial rule in Israel is as follows:

(1) Its establishment under Moses (Ex. 19:3–7; cp. Ex. 3:1–10; 24:12).

(2) Its administration under leader-judges (Josh. 1:1–5; Jud. 2:16–18).

(3) Its administration under kings (1 Sam. 10:1,24; 16:1–13; 1 Ki. 9:1–5).

(4) Its end at the captivity (Ezek. 21:25–27; cp. Jer. 27:6–8; Dan. 2:36–38).

III. The Future Restoration of the Theocratic Kingdom.

(1) The Davidic Covenant (2 Sam. 7:8–16 [see v. 16, *note*]; Ps. 89:3–4,20–21,28–37).

(2) The exposition of the Davidic Covenant by the prophets (Isa. 1:25–26 [see v. 26, *note*] to Zech. 12:6–8). They describe the kingdom as follows:

(a) It will be Davidic, to be established under David's heir, who is to be born of a virgin, therefore truly man, but also "Immanuel," "Mighty God, Everlasting Father, Prince of Peace" (Isa. 7:13–14; 9:6–7; 11:1; Jer. 23:5; Ezek. 34:23; 37:24; Hos. 3:4–5).

(b) It will be a kingdom heavenly in origin, principle, and authority (Dan. 2:34–35,44–45), but set up on the earth, with Jerusalem as the capital (Isa. 2:2–4; 4:3,5; 24:23; 33:20; 62:1–7; Jer. 23:5; 31:38–40; Joel 3:1,16–17).

(c) The kingdom is to be established first over regathered, restored, and converted Israel, and is then to become universal (Ps. 2:6–8; 22:1–31; 24:1–10; Isa. 1:2–3; 11:1,10–13; 60:12; Jer. 23:5–8; 30:7–11; Ezek. 20:33–40; 37:21–25; Zech. 9:10; 14:16–19).

(d) The moral characteristics of the kingdom are to be righteousness and peace. The meek, not the proud, will inherit the earth; longevity will be greatly increased; the knowledge of the LORD will be universal; beast-ferocity will be removed; absolute equity will be enforced; and open sin will be visited with instant judgment; whereas the enormous majority of earth's inhabitants will be saved (Ps. 2:9; Isa. 11:4,6–9; 26:9; 65:20; Zech. 14:16–21). The NT (Rev. 20:1–5) adds a detail of immense significance—the removal of Satan from the scene. It is impossible to conceive to what heights of spiritual, intellectual, and physical perfection humanity will attain in this, its coming age of righteousness and peace (Ps. 72:1–10; Isa. 11:4–9).

(e) The kingdom is to be established by power, not persuasion, and is to follow divine judgment upon the Gentile world powers (Ps. 2:4–9; Isa. 9:7; Dan. 2:35,44–45; 7:26–27; Zech. 14:1–19). See Zech. 6:11, *note*.

(f) The restoration of Israel and the establishment of the kingdom are connected with the advent of the LORD, yet future (Dt. 30:3–5; Ps. 2:1–9; Zech. 14:4).

(g) The chastisement reserved for disobedience in the house of David (2 Sam. 7:14; Ps. 89:30–33) fell in the captivities and worldwide dispersion. Since that time, though a remnant returned under prince Zerubbabel, Jerusalem has generally been under the political authority of Gentiles. Even today, under Israeli rule, Gentiles control many important sites within the Holy City. The Davidic Covenant has not been abrogated (Ps. 89:33–37), however, but is yet to be fulfilled (Acts 15:14–17).

[1](12:10) Holy Spirit (OT), Summary: (1) The personality and Deity of the Holy Spirit appear from the attributes ascribed to Him and from His works. (2) He is revealed as sharing the work of creation and, therefore, as omnipotent (Gen. 1:2; Job 26:13; 33:4; Ps. 104:30); omnipresent (Ps. 139:7); striving with men (Gen. 6:3); enlightening (Job 32:8); enduing with constructive skill (Ex. 28:3; 31:3); giving physical strength (Jud. 14:6,19), executive ability, and wisdom (Jud. 3:10; 6:34; 11:29; 13:25); enabling men to receive and utter divine revelations (Num. 11:25; 2 Sam. 23:2); and, generally, empowering the servants of God (Ps. 51:12; Joel 2:28; Mic. 3:8; Zech. 4:6). (3) He is called holy (Ps. 51:11); good (Ps. 143:10); the Spirit of judgment and burning (Isa. 4:4); the Spirit of the LORD, of wisdom, understanding, counsel, might, knowledge, the fear of the LORD (Isa. 11:2), and of grace and supplication (Zech. 12:10). (4) In the OT the Holy Spirit acts in free sovereignty, coming upon men and even upon a dumb animal as He wills; nor are conditions set forth (as in the NT) by compliance with which any one may receive the Spirit. The indwelling of every believer by the abiding Spirit is a NT blessing consequent upon the death and resurrection of Christ (Jn. 7:39; 16:7; Acts 2:33; Gal. 3:1–6).

whom [a]they [b]pierced. Yes, they will
mourn for Him as one mourns for *his*
only *son,* and grieve for Him as one
grieves for a firstborn.
11 "In that day there shall be a great
[c]mourning in Jerusalem, like the
mourning at Hadad Rimmon in the
plain of Megiddo.*
12 [d]"And the land shall mourn, every family by itself: the family of the
house of David by itself, and their
wives by themselves; the family of the
house of Nathan by itself, and their
wives by themselves;
13 "the family of the house of Levi
by itself, and their wives by themselves; the family of Shimei by itself,
and their wives by themselves;
14 "all the families that remain, every family by itself, and their wives by
themselves.

Cleansing of the remnant

13 "IN that [e]day a [f]fountain shall
be opened for the house of David and for the inhabitants of Jerusalem, for sin and for [g]uncleanness.

False prophets to be ashamed

2 "It shall be in that day," says the
LORD of hosts, "*that* I will [h]cut off the
names of the idols from the land, and
they shall no longer be remembered. I
will also cause the [i]prophets and the
unclean spirit to depart from the land.
3 "It shall come to pass *that* if anyone still prophesies, then his father
and mother who begot him will say to
him, 'You shall [j]not live, because you
have spoken lies in the name of the
LORD.' And his father and [k]mother
who begot him shall thrust him
through when he prophesies.
4 "And it shall be in that day *that*
every prophet will be ashamed of his
vision when he prophesies; they will
not wear a robe of coarse hair to deceive.
5 "But he will say, 'I *am* no
prophet, I *am* a farmer; for a man
taught me to keep cattle from my
youth.'
6 "And *one* will say to [1]him, 'What
are these wounds between your
arms?'* Then he will answer, '*Those*
with which I was wounded in the
house of my friends.'

Prophecy of the true prophet, Messiah
(cp. Mt. 26:31; Mk. 14:27)

7 "Awake, O sword, against My
Shepherd,
Against the Man who is My
Companion,"
Says the LORD of hosts.
[l]"Strike the [m]Shepherd,
And the [n]sheep will be
scattered;
Then I will turn My hand
against the little ones.

Israel to be refined and delivered

8 [2]And it shall come to pass in all
the land,"
Says the LORD,
"*That* [o]two-thirds in it shall be
cut off *and* die,
But *one*-third shall be left in it:
9 I will bring the *one*-third
through the fire,
Will [p]refine them as silver is
refined,
And [q]test them as gold is
tested.
They will [r]call on My name,
And I will answer them.
I will say, 'This *is* My people';

10 *a* Jn. 19:37; Rev. 1:7 *b Sacrifice* (prophetic): v. 10; Mt. 26:28. (Gen. 3:15; Heb. 10:18, *note*). Ps. 22:16
11 *c* Mt. 24:30; Rev. 1:7
12 *d* Mt. 24:30
CHAPTER 13
1 *e* Zech. 12:2 *f* Ps. 36:9; 1 Jn. 1:9; cp. Ps. 51:2,7; 65:3; Isa. 1:16–18; Mal. 3:2–3 *g* Ezek. 36:25
2 *h* Hos. 2:17 *i* Jer. 23:14–15
3 *j* Dt. 18:20 *k* Dt. 13:6–11
7 *l Christ* (first advent): v. 7; Mal. 3:1. (Gen. 3:15; Acts 1:11, *note*) *m* Mt. 26:31, 67; Mk. 14:27,65; 15:19 *n* Cp. Jn. 10:1–14
8 *o* Ezek. 5:2–4,12
9 *p* Isa. 48:10; Ezek. 20:38; Mal. 3:3 *q* See Jas. 1:14, *note* *r* Zeph. 3:9

★ 12:11 Hebrew *Megiddon* 13:6 Or *hands*

And (5) the OT contains predictions of a future pouring out of the Spirit upon Israel (Ezek. 37:14; 39:29), and upon "all flesh" (Joel 2:28–29). The expectation of Israel, therefore, was twofold—of the coming of Messiah-Immanuel, and of such a pouring out of the Spirit as the prophets described. See Holy Spirit, Acts 2:4, *note.*

[1](13:6) This verse is best understood as an evasive reply of a false prophet in the last days. It carries on and concludes the subject begun in v. 2. By no valid interpretation may it be referred to the Lord Jesus Christ. There is no clear change of subject between vv. 5 and 6 such as exists between vv. 6 and 7. Christ would not claim that He was not a prophet (cp. Dt. 18:15–18); He was not a farmer; He was not bought or sold from His youth. Verse 7 does speak of Christ, as Mt. 26:31 and Mk. 14:27 attest.

[2](13:8) This chapter now returns to the subject of 12:10. Verses 8–9 refer to the sufferings of the remnant (Isa. 1:5; Rom. 11:9) preceding the great battle. Then ch. 14 is a recapitulation of the whole matter. The order is: (1) the gathering of the nations, 14:2 (see Armageddon, Rev. 16:13–16; 19:17, *note*); (2) the deliverance, 14:3; (3) the return of Christ to the Mount of Olives, and the physical change of the scene, 14:4–8; and (4) the setting up of the kingdom, and full earthly blessing, 14:9–21.

And each one will [a]say, 'The
LORD *is* my God.' "

The LORD's triumphant return to earth to bring deliverance

14 BEHOLD, the [b]day of the
LORD is coming,
And your spoil will be divided
in your midst.
2 For I will [c]gather all the
nations to battle against
Jerusalem;
The city shall be taken,
The houses rifled,
And the women ravished.
Half of the city shall go into
captivity,
But the remnant of the people
shall not be cut off from the
city.
3 Then the LORD will go forth
And [d]fight against those
nations,
As He fights in the day of
battle.

The visible return in glory: physical changes in Palestine (vv. 4,10)

4 And in that day His feet will
[e]stand on the Mount of
[f]Olives,
Which faces Jerusalem on the
east.
[1]And the Mount of Olives shall
be split in two,
From east to west,
Making a very large valley;
Half of the mountain shall
move toward the north
And half of it toward the
south.
5 Then you shall flee *through*
My mountain valley,
For the mountain valley shall
reach to Azal.
Yes, you shall flee
As you fled from the
[g]earthquake
In the days of Uzziah king of
Judah.

Thus the [h]LORD my God will
come,
And all the saints with You.*

6 It shall come to pass in that
day
That there will be no light;
The lights will diminish.
7 It shall be one day
Which is known to the LORD—
Neither day nor night.
But at evening time it shall
happen
That it will be light.

The river of the sanctuary (cp. Ezek. 47:1–12; Rev. 22:1–2)

8 And in that day it shall be
That living waters shall flow
from Jerusalem,
Half of them toward the
eastern sea
And half of them toward the
western sea;
In both summer and winter it
shall occur.

The kingdom set up on the earth

9 And the LORD shall be [i]King
over all the [2]earth.
In that day it shall be—
"The LORD *is* one,"*
And His name one.

10 All the land shall be turned into
a [j]plain from Geba to Rimmon south
of Jerusalem. *Jerusalem** shall be
raised up and inhabited in her place
from Benjamin's Gate to the place of
the First Gate and the Corner Gate,
and *from* the [k]Tower of Hananel to
the king's winepresses.

11 *The people* shall dwell in it;
And no longer shall there be
utter destruction,
But Jerusalem shall be [l]safely
inhabited.

12 And this shall be the plague with
which the LORD will strike all the people who fought against Jerusalem:

Their flesh shall dissolve while
they stand on their feet,
Their eyes shall dissolve in
their sockets,
And their tongues shall
dissolve in their mouths.

*

14:5 Or *you;* Septuagint, Targum, and Vulgate read *Him.* 14:9 Compare Deuteronomy 6:4
14:10 Literally *She*

9
a Hos. 2:23

CHAPTER 14
1
b *Day* (of the LORD): vv. 1–21; Mal. 4:1. (Ps. 2:9; Rev. 19:19)
2
c Zech. 12:2–3
3
d *Armageddon* (battle of): vv. 1–5; Mt. 24:28. (Isa. 10:27; Rev. 19:17)
4
e *Christ* (second advent): vv. 3–4; Mt. 10:23. (Dt. 30:3; Acts 1:11, *note*)
f Acts 1:9–12
5
g Amos 1:1
h Mt. 24:30–31; 25:31; Jude 14; cp. Dt. 33:2
9
i Jer. 23:5–6; Rev. 11:15
10
j See Dt. 1:1, *note*
k Jer. 31:38
11
l Ezek. 34:25–28; Hos. 2:18

[1](14:4) Verse 5 implies that the cleavage of the Mount of Olives is due to an earthquake, and this is confirmed by Isa. 29:6; Rev. 16:18–19. In both passages the context, as here in vv. 1–3, associates the earthquake with the Gentile invasion under the beast (Dan. 7:8; Rev. 19:20). Not one of the related events of this chapter occurred at the first coming of Christ, closely associated though He then was with the Mount of Olives.
[2](14:9) This will be the answer to the prayer of Mt. 6:10. Cp. Dan. 2:44–45; 7:27. See Kingdom (NT), Lk. 1:31–33; 1 Cor. 15:24, *note.*

13 It shall come to pass in that day
That a great panic from the LORD will be among them.
Everyone will seize the hand of his neighbor,
And raise his hand against his neighbor's hand;
14 Judah also will fight at Jerusalem.
And the wealth of all the surrounding nations
Shall be gathered together:
Gold, silver, and apparel in great abundance.

15 Such also shall be the plague
On the horse *and* the mule,
On the camel and the donkey,
And on all the cattle that will be in those camps.
So *shall* this plague *be*.

The worship and spirituality of the kingdom

16 And it shall come to pass *that*
everyone who is left of all the nations
which came against Jerusalem shall
[a]go up from year to year to [b]worship
the [c]King, the LORD of hosts, and to
keep the [d]Feast of Tabernacles.

17 And it shall be *that* whichever of
the families of the earth do not come
up to Jerusalem to worship the King,
the LORD of hosts, on them there will
be [e]no rain.
18 If the family of [f]Egypt will not
come up and enter in, they *shall have*
no *rain;* they shall receive the plague
with which the LORD strikes the nations who do not come up to keep the
Feast of Tabernacles.
19 This shall be the punishment of
Egypt and the punishment of all the
nations that do not come up to keep
the Feast of Tabernacles.
20 In that day [g]"HOLINESS TO
THE LORD" shall be *engraved* on the
[h]bells of the horses. The [i]pots in the
LORD's house shall be like the bowls
before the altar.
21 Yes, every pot in Jerusalem and
Judah shall be holiness to the LORD of
hosts.* Everyone who sacrifices shall
come and take them and [j]cook in
them. In that day there shall no longer
be a [k]Canaanite in the house of the
LORD of hosts.

16 *a* Isa. 2:2–3; 60:6–9; 66:18–21; Mic. 4:1–2 *b* Isa. 27:13 *c Kingdom* (OT): vv. 16–21. (Gen. 1:26; Zech. 12:8, *note*) *d* Lev. 23:34–43
17 *e* Isa. 60:12
18 *f* Isa. 19:21
20 *g* Ex. 28:36; 39:30; Isa. 23:18; Jer. 2:3 *h* Or *bridles* *i* Ezek. 46:20
21 *j* The flesh of the sacrifices will be boiled in these pots *k* Isa. 35:8; Ezek. 44:9; Joel 3:17; Rev. 21:27; 22:15

* 14:21 Or *on every pot . . . shall be (engraved) "HOLINESS TO THE LORD OF HOSTS"*

The Book of

MALACHI

Author: Malachi *Theme:* Formalism Rebuked *Date of writing:* 5th Cent. B.C.

MALACHI means *my messenger*, which is probably an abbreviated form of *the messenger of the LORD*. Apart from the meaning of his name, nothing is known of Malachi. This final message of the OT contains the prophecy of John the Baptist's ministry, the fulfillment of which begins the NT. Malachi develops his main theme, which is the corruption of the priests and the sins of the people against the family and their miserliness toward God, followed by questions from those addressed and statements proving the original assertions, a dialectic form of discussion which later became quite popular in Judaism.

The book may be divided as follows:

I. Israel Pretends to be Unaware of God's Love, 1:1–5.
II. The Priests Deny Despising the Name of the LORD, 1:6—2:9.
III. Israel's Sins against One Another and against the Family, 2:10–17.
IV. The Coming of the Forerunner, John the Baptist, 3:1–5.
V. Two Groups of Israel Contrasted: Those Withholding Tithes versus the Faithful Remnant, 3:6–18.
VI. The Coming Day of the LORD, and the Return of Christ, 4:1–6.

I. Israel Pretends to be Unaware of God's Love, 1:1–5

Introduction

1 THE burden* of the word of the LORD to Israel by Malachi.

The LORD's love for His chosen people, Israel

2 "I have [a]loved you," says the LORD.
"Yet you say, [b]'In what way have You loved us?'
Was not Esau Jacob's brother?"
Says the LORD.
"Yet [c]Jacob I have loved;
3 But Esau I have [1]hated,
And [d]laid waste his mountains and his heritage
For the jackals of the wilderness."

4 Even though [e]Edom has said,
"We have been impoverished,
But we will return and build the desolate places,"

Thus says the LORD of hosts:

"They may build, but I will [f]throw down;
They shall be called the Territory of Wickedness,
And the people against whom the LORD will have indignation forever.
5 Your eyes shall see,
And you shall say,
'The LORD is [g]magnified beyond the border of Israel.'

II. The Priests Deny Despising the Name of the LORD, 1:1—2:9

Sins of the restoration priests

6 "A son [h]honors *his* father,
And a servant *his* master.
[2]If then I am the [i]Father,
Where *is* My honor?
And if I *am* a Master,
Where *is* My reverence?
Says the LORD of hosts
To you priests who despise My name.
Yet you say, [b]'In what way

CHAPTER 1
2
a Dt. 4:37; 7:7–8
b Mal. 2:17; 3:7
c Rom. 9:13
3
d Ezek. 35:9,15
4
e i.e. *Esau's descendants*. Gen. 25:30
f Jer. 49:16–18
5
g Mic. 5:4
6
h Ex. 20:12; Mt. 15:4–8; Eph. 6:2–3
i Isa. 63:16; 64:8; Jer. 31:9

* 1:1 Or *oracle*

---

[1](1:3) The statement that God loved Jacob but hated Esau, must be taken as relative rather than absolute. Special blessings were promised to Esau and his descendants (Gen. 27:38–40). However, the spiritual insight of Jacob was far greater, and Jacob was the one through whom the promised seed was to come. The comparison of the good things done for Jacob with those done for Esau is like the difference between loving and hating. Compare Lk. 14:26, the statement that if a man does not hate his father and mother he cannot be a disciple of Christ. Love for father and mother is commanded in the Scripture. No Christian can hate his father and mother. What is meant is that his love for Christ should be so great that, in comparison, the love for father and mother would seem almost like hate.

[2](1:6) See Isa. 63:16, *note*. The relationship here is national, not personal (Jer. 3:18–19); here, apparently, the Jews were calling the LORD "Father" but were yielding Him no filial obedience. Cp. Jn. 8:37–39; Rom. 9:1–8.

have we despised Your
name?'
7 "You offer [1]defiled food on My
altar,
But say,
[a]'In what way have we defiled
You?'
By saying,
'The table of the LORD is
[2]contemptible.'
8 And [b]when you offer the blind
as a sacrifice,
Is it not evil?
And when you offer the lame
and sick,
Is it not evil?
Offer it then to your governor!
Would he be pleased with you?
Would he accept you
favorably?"
Says the LORD of hosts.
9 "But now entreat God's favor,
That He may be gracious to us.
While this is being *done* by
your hands,
Will He accept you favorably?"
Says the LORD of hosts.
10 [c]"Who *is there* even among you
who would shut the doors,
So that you would not kindle
fire *on* My altar in vain?
I have no pleasure in you,"
Says the LORD of hosts,
"Nor will I accept an offering
from your hands.
11 [3]For from the rising of the sun,
even to its going down,
My name *shall be* great among
the Gentiles;
In every place incense *shall be*
offered to My [4]name,
And a pure offering;
For My name shall be great
among the nations,"
Says the LORD of hosts.
12 "But you profane it,
In that you say,
'The table of the LORD* is
defiled;
And its fruit, its food, *is*
contemptible.'
13 You also say,
'Oh, what a [d]weariness!'
And you sneer at it,"
Says the LORD of hosts.
"And you bring the stolen, the
lame, and the sick;
Thus you bring an offering!
Should I accept this from your
hand?"
Says the LORD.
14 "But cursed *be* the deceiver
Who has in his flock a male,
And takes a vow,
But sacrifices to the Lord what
is [e]blemished—
For I *am* a great King,"
Says the LORD of hosts,
"And My name *is to be* [f]feared
among the nations.

Priests to be disciplined by God

2 "AND now, O [g]priests, this
commandment is for you.
2 If you will not hear,
And if you will not take *it* to
heart,
To give glory to My name,"
Says the LORD of hosts,
"I will send a curse upon you,
And I will [h]curse your
blessings.
Yes, I have cursed them
[i]already,
Because you do not take *it* to
heart.
3 "Behold, I will rebuke your
descendants
And spread [j]refuse on your
faces,
The refuse of your solemn
feasts;
And *one* will take you away
with it.
4 Then you shall know that I
have sent this
commandment to you,
That My covenant with Levi
may continue,"
Says the LORD of hosts.
5 "My [k]covenant was with him,
one of life and peace,
And I gave them to him *that
he might* fear *Me;*
So he feared Me

7
a Mal. 2:17; 3:7
8
b Dt. 15:19–23
10
c Or *I would that one among you would shut the doors* [of the temple]. Cp. Isa. 1:11–15
13
d Isa. 43:22
14
e Lev. 22:18–20
f Zeph. 2:11
CHAPTER 2
1
g Mal. 1:6
2
h Israel's distinctive blessings would turn to curses. Cp. Dt. 28:3–14 with 15–35
i Mal. 3:9
3
j Ex. 29:14
5
k Reference to godly Levites. Num. 25:10–13; Dt. 33:8–9

*1:12 Following Bomberg; Masoretic Text reads *Lord.*

[1](1:7) The very sins that provoked Nehemiah (Neh. 5:1–13; 7:63–65; 9:4ff.; 13:23–27) are condemned by Malachi: (1) defilement of the priesthood; (2) foreign marriages after divorce from Jewish wives; and (3) neglect of the tithe and offerings.

[2](1:7) Contempt was shown by the offering of forbidden sacrifices (vv. 7–8; cp. Dt. 15:21).

[3](1:11) So it would have been had Israel been true to the LORD (cp. Isa. 45:5–6). So it will be one day despite Israel's past failures.

[4](1:11) This is a prediction concerning the millennial age (cp. Ezek. 40—48).

And was reverent before My
name.
6 The [a]law of truth* was in his
mouth,
And injustice was not found on
his lips.
He walked with Me in peace
and equity,
And turned many away from
iniquity.

7 "For the lips of a priest should
[b]keep knowledge,
And *people* should [c]seek the
law from his mouth;
For he is the messenger of the
LORD of hosts.
8 But [d]you have departed from
the way;
You have caused many to
stumble at the law.
You have corrupted the
covenant of Levi,"
Says the LORD of hosts.
9 "Therefore I also have made
you contemptible and base
Before all the people,
Because you have not kept My
ways
But have shown [e]partiality in
the law."

III. Israel's Sins against One Another and against the Family, 2:10–17

Sins against brotherhood

10 Have we not all one Father?
Has not one God created us?
Why do we deal treacherously
with one [f]another
By profaning the covenant of
the fathers?

Sins against God in the family

11 Judah has dealt treacherously,
And an abomination has been
committed in Israel and in
Jerusalem,
For Judah has [g]profaned
The LORD's holy *institution*
which He loves:
He has married the daughter
of a foreign god.
12 May the LORD cut off from the
tents of Jacob
The man who does this, being
awake and aware,*
Yet who brings an offering to
the LORD of hosts!

6
a Dt. 33:10
7
b i.e. *guard*
c Num. 27:21; Dt. 17:8–11
8
d Ungodly Levites
9
e Dt. 1:17; Mic. 3:11; 1 Tim. 5:21
10
f Cp. Jer. 9:4–5
11
g Ezra 9:1–2
14
h Mal. 3:5
15
i Gen. 2:24
j Cp. Ezra 9:2
16
k *Deity* (names of): v. 16; Mal. 3:18. (Gen. 1:1; Mal. 3:18)
l Mt. 19:6–8
17
m Mal. 1:2,6
n Isa. 5:20
o Jer. 17:15

13 And this is the second thing
you do:
You cover the altar of the LORD
with tears,
With weeping and crying;
So He does not regard the
offering anymore,
Nor receive *it* with goodwill
from your hands.
14 Yet you say, "For what
reason?"
Because the LORD has been
witness
Between you and the wife of
your youth,
With whom you have dealt
[h]treacherously;
Yet she is your companion
And your wife by covenant.
15 But did He not make *them*
[i]one,
Having a remnant of the
Spirit?
And why one?
He seeks [j]godly offspring.
Therefore take heed to your
spirit,
And let none deal
treacherously with the wife
of his youth.

16 "For the LORD [k]God of Israel
says
That He [1]hates [l]divorce,
For it covers one's garment
with violence,"
Says the LORD of hosts.
"Therefore take heed to your
spirit,
That you do not deal
treacherously."

Sin of insincere religious profession

17 You have wearied the LORD
with your words;
Yet you say,
[m]"In what way have we wearied
Him?"
In that you say,
[n]"Everyone who does evil
Is good in the sight of the
LORD,
And He delights in them,"
Or, "Where *is* the God of
[o]justice?"

*
2:6 Or *true instruction* 2:12 Talmud and Vulgate read *teacher and student.*

[1](2:16) This verse does not contradict Dt. 24:1, where divorce is permitted by the law of Moses, not prescribed. Cp. Mt. 19:3–9.

IV. The Coming of the Forerunner, John the Baptist, 3:1–6

A parenthetic passage

3 "BEHOLD, I send [a]My
messenger,
And he will prepare the way
before Me.
And the [1]Lord, whom you
seek,
Will [b]suddenly come to His
temple,
Even the [c]Messenger of the
covenant,
In whom you delight.
Behold, He is [d]coming,"
Says the LORD of hosts.

2 "But who can [e]endure the day
of His coming?
And [f]who can stand when He
appears?
For He *is* like a refiner's [g]fire
And like launderers' soap.
3 He will sit as a [2h]refiner and a
purifier of silver;
He will purify the sons of Levi,
And purge them as gold and
silver,
That they may [i]offer to the
LORD
An offering in righteousness.
4 "Then the offering of Judah and
Jerusalem
Will be pleasant to the LORD,
As in the days of old,
As in former years.
5 And I will come near you for
judgment;
I will be a swift witness
Against sorcerers,
Against adulterers,
Against [j]perjurers,
Against those who [k]exploit
wage earners and [l]widows
and orphans,
And against those who turn
away an [m]alien—
Because they do not fear Me,"
Says the LORD of hosts.
6 "For I *am* the LORD, I do not
[n]change;
Therefore you are not
consumed, O sons of Jacob.

V. Two Groups of Israel Contrasted, 3:7–18

The people have robbed God

7 Yet from the days of your
fathers
You have gone away from My
ordinances
And have not kept *them*.
[o]Return to Me, and I will return
to you,"
Says the LORD of hosts.
"But you said,
[p]'In what way shall we return?'
8 "Will a man rob God?
Yet you have robbed Me!
But you say,
'In what way have we robbed
You?'
[q]In tithes and offerings.
9 You are cursed with a curse,
For you have robbed Me,
Even this whole nation.
10 [r]Bring all the tithes into the
storehouse,
That there may be food in My
house,
And [s]try Me now in this,"
Says the LORD of hosts,
"If I will not open for you the
windows of heaven
And pour out for you *such*
blessing
That *there will* not *be room*
enough *to receive it*.
11 "And I will rebuke the devourer
for your sakes,
So that he will not destroy the
fruit of your ground,
Nor shall the vine fail to bear
fruit for you in the field,"
Says the LORD of hosts;
12 "And all nations will call you
blessed,
For you will be a delightful
land,"
Says the LORD of hosts.

CHAPTER 3

1
a Mt. 11:10; Mk. 1:2; Lk. 7:27
b God's answer to the last question in 2:17
c See Jud. 2:1, *note*
d Christ (first advent): v. 1; Mt. 1:18. (Gen. 3:15; Acts 1:11, *note*)

2
e Jer. 10:10; Joel 2:11; Nah. 1:6; Mal. 4:1
f Rev. 6:17
g Isa. 4:4; Mt. 3:10–12

3
h Isa. 1:25; Zech. 13:9
i 1 Pet. 2:5

5
j Lev. 19:12; Zech. 5:4; Jas. 5:12
k Lev. 19:13; Jas. 5:4
l Ex. 22:22
m Dt. 24:17

6
n Num. 23:19; Rom. 11:29; Jas. 1:17

7
o Zech. 1:3
p Mal. 1:2,6

8
q Neh. 13:10–12

10
r Prov. 3:9–10
s *Test/tempt:* v. 10; Mal. 3:15. (Gen. 3:1; Jas. 1:14, *note*)

[1](3:1) The first part of v. 1 is quoted of John the Baptist (Mt. 11:10; Mk. 1:2; Lk. 7:27), but the next words, "the Lord whom you seek," etc., are nowhere quoted in the NT. The reason is obviously that, in everything except Christ's first advent, the picture in vv. 2–5 of the LORD who suddenly comes to His temple (Hab. 2:20) is one of judgment, not of grace. Malachi, in common with other OT prophets, saw both advents of Messiah blended in one horizon, but did not see the separating interval described in Mt. 13 which was consequent upon the rejection of the King (Mt. 13:16–17). Still less was the Church Age in his vision (Eph. 3:3–6; Col. 1:25–27). "My messenger" (v. 1) is John the Baptist; the "Messenger of the covenant" is Christ in both of His advents, but with special reference to the events which are to follow His second coming.

[2](3:3) Malachi reveals God in several relationships to Israel: Father, Lord, God, and Judge.

13 "Your words have been harsh
against Me,"
Says the LORD,
"Yet you say,
'What have we spoken against
You?'
14 You have said,
'It is useless to serve God;
What profit *is it* that we have
kept His ordinance,
And that we have walked as
mourners
Before the LORD of hosts?
15 So now we call the proud
blessed,
For those who do wickedness
are raised up;
They even [a]tempt God and go
free.'"

The faithful remnant; the LORD's book of remembrance

16 Then [b]those who feared the
LORD spoke to one another,
And the LORD listened and
heard *them;*
So a book of remembrance
was written before Him
For those who fear the LORD
And who meditate on His
name.
17 "They shall be Mine," says the
LORD of hosts,
"On the day that I make them
My jewels.*
And I will spare them
As a man spares his own son
who serves him."
18 Then you shall again discern
Between the [c]righteous and
the wicked,
Between one who serves
[1d]God
And one who does not serve
Him.

15
a *Test/tempt:* v. 15; Mt. 4:1. (Gen. 3:1; Jas. 1:14, *note*)
16
b *Remnant:* vv. 16–18; Rom. 9:27. (Isa. 1:9; Rom. 11:5, *note*)
18
c *Righteousness* (OT): v. 18; Mt. 1:19. (Gen. 6:9; Lk. 2:25, *note*)
d *Deity* (names of): v. 18. (Gen. 1:1; Mal. 3:18)

* 3:17 Literally *special treasure*

[1](3:18) Deity (OT)—its revelation, Summary: God is revealed in the OT (1) through His names as follows:

CLASS	ENGLISH FORM	HEBREW EQUIVALENT
Primary	God	*El, Elah,* or *Elohim,* Gen.1:1, *note*
	LORD	*YHWH (Jehovah),* Gen.2:4; Ex. 34:6, *note*
	Lord	*Adon,* or *Adonai,* Gen.15:2, *note*
Compound with *El*=God	Almighty God	*El Shaddai,* Gen.17:1, *note*
	Most High, or God Most High	*El Elyon,* Gen.14:18, *note*
	Everlasting God	*El Olam,* Gen.21:33, *note*
	Mighty God	*El Gibbor,* Isa.9:6–7
Compound with *YHWH (Jehovah)* =LORD	LORD God	*YHWH (Jehovah) Elohim,* Gen.2:4; Ex. 34:6, *note*
	Lord GOD	*Adonai YHWH (Jehovah),* Gen.15:2, *note*
	LORD of hosts	*YHWH (Jehovah) Sabaoth,* 1 Sam.1:3, *note*

This revelation of God by His names is invariably made in connection with some particular need of His people, and there can be no need of man to which these names do not answer as showing that man's true resource is in God. Even human failure and sin but to evoke new and fuller revelations of the divine fullness.

(2) The OT Scriptures reveal the existence of a Supreme Being, the Creator of the universe and of man, the Source of all life and of all intelligence, who is to be worshiped and served by men and angels. This Supreme Being is One, but, in some manner not fully revealed in the OT, is a unity in plurality. This is shown by the use of the plural pronoun in the interrelation of Deity as evidenced in Gen. 1:26; 3:22; Ps. 110:1; and Isa. 6:8. That the interrelation of Deity includes that of Father and Son is directly asserted in Ps. 2:7 (with Heb. 1:5); likewise the Spirit is distinctly recognized in His personality, and to Him are ascribed all the divine attributes (e.g. Gen. 1:2; Num. 11:25; 24:2; Jud. 3:10; 6:34; 11:29; 13:25; 14:6,19; 15:14; 2 Sam. 23:2; Job 26:13; 33:4; Ps. 106:33; 139:7; Isa. 40:7; 59:19; 63:10. See Zech. 12:10, *note*).

(3) The incarnation is intimated in the theophanies, or appearances of God in human form (e.g. Gen. 18:1,13,17–22; 32:24–30), and distinctly predicted in the promises connected with redemption (e.g. Gen. 3:15) and with the Davidic Covenant (e.g. Isa. 7:13–14; 9:6–7; Jer. 23:5–6). The revelation of Deity in the NT so illuminates that of the OT that the latter is seen to be, from Genesis to Malachi, the foreshadowing of the coming incarnation of God in Jesus the Christ. In promise, covenant, type, and prophecy the OT points forward to Him.

(4) The revelation of God to man is one of authority and of redemption. He requires righteousness from man, but saves the unrighteous through sacrifice; and in His redemptive dealings with man all the divine persons and attributes are brought into manifestation. The

VI. The Coming Day of the LORD *and the Return of Christ, 4:1–6*

4 "FOR behold, the day is
[a]coming,
Burning like an oven,
And all the proud, yes, all who
do wickedly will be stubble.
And the day which is coming
shall [b]burn them up,"
Says the LORD of hosts,
"That will leave them neither
[1]root nor branch.
2 But to you who [c]fear My name
The Sun of Righteousness shall
arise
With healing in His wings;
And you shall go out
And grow fat like stall-fed
calves.
3 You shall trample the wicked,
For they shall be ashes under
the soles of your feet
On the day that I do *this*,"
Says the LORD of hosts.
4 "Remember the [d]Law of Moses,
My servant,
Which I commanded him in
Horeb for all Israel,
With the statutes and
judgments.

Elijah to come again before the day of the LORD *(cp. Rev. 11:3–6)*

5 Behold, I will send you [e]Elijah
the prophet
Before the coming of the great
and dreadful day of the
LORD.
6 And he will [f]turn
The hearts of the fathers to the
children,
And the hearts of the children
to their fathers,
Lest I come and strike the
earth with a [2]curse."

CHAPTER 4

1

a Day (of the LORD): 3:17–4:6; Mt. 24:29. (Ps. 2:9; Rev. 19:19)
b Isa. 9:18–19; cp. 2 Pet. 3:10

2

c See Ps. 19:9, *note*

4

d Law (of Moses): v. 4; Mt. 4:4. (Ex. 19:1; Gal. 3:24, *note*)

5

e Mt. 11:10–14; 17:11–13

6

f Lk. 1:17

OT reveals the justice of God as fully as His mercy, but never in opposition to His mercy. The flood, e.g., was an unspeakable mercy to unborn generations. From Genesis to Malachi He is revealed as the seeking God who has no pleasure in the death of the wicked, and who heaps up before the sinner every possible motive to persuade him to faith and obedience.

(5) In the experience of the OT men of faith, their God inspires reverence but never slavish fear; they exhaust the resources of language to express their love and adoration in view of His lovingkindness and tender mercy. This adoring love of His saints is the triumphant answer to those who pretend to find the OT revelation of God cruel and repellent. It is in harmony, not contrast, with the NT revelation of God in Christ.

(6) Those passages which attribute to God bodily parts and human emotions (e.g. Ex. 33:11,20–23; Dt. 29:20; 2 Chr. 16:9; Jer. 15:6) are metaphorical and mean that in the infinite being of God there exists that which answers spiritually to these things—eyes, a hand, feet, etc.; and the jealousy and anger attributed to Him are the emotions of perfect love in view of the havoc of sin.

(7) In the OT revelation there is a true sense in which, wholly apart from sin or infirmity, God is like His creature, man (Gen. 1:27); and the supreme and perfect revelation of God, toward which the OT points, is a revelation in and through a perfect Man, the Lord Jesus Christ, God's unique Son.

[1](4:1) This verse gives no basis for the error of annihilationism. It describes physical death, not the state of the soul after death. The unsaved are in conscious eternal woe (Rev. 14:10–11; 20:11–15), as the saved are in conscious eternal bliss (Rev. 21:1–7).

[2](4:6) Genesis reveals the entrance of the curse into the human family (Gen. 3); the last word of the OT shows the curse still persisting (Mal. 4:6); Matthew begins (1:1) with Him who came to remove the curse (Gal. 3:13; Rev. 21:3–5; 22:3).

From Malachi to Matthew

THE close of the OT canon left Israel in two divisions. Most of the nation was dispersed throughout the Persian Empire, more as colonists than as captives. A remnant, chiefly of the tribe of Judah, with Zerubbabel, a prince of the Davidic family, and the survivors of the priests and Levites had returned to the land under the permissive decrees of Cyrus and his successors (Dan. 5:18, and 9:24, *notes*), and had re-established the temple worship. It is on this remnant that the interest of the student of Scripture centers; and this interest concerns both their political and religious history.

I. Politically, the fortunes of the Palestinian Jews are linked to the history of the Gentile world powers foretold by Daniel (Dan. 2 and 7).

1. The Persian rule continued about one hundred years after the close of the OT canon, and seems to have been mild and tolerant, allowing to the high priest, along with his religious functions, a measure of civil power, but under the governors of Syria. In this period the rival worship of Samaria, which began during the Israelite monarchy, was developed and its own temple established.

2. In 334 B.C. Syria fell under the power of the third of the world empires, the Greco-Macedonian Empire of Alexander. That conqueror was induced to treat the Jews with much favor; but upon the breaking up of his empire, Judea fell between the anvil and the hammer of Syria and Egypt, coming first under the power of Syria, but later under Egypt as ruled by the Ptolemaic kings. During this period (323–198 B.C.) great numbers of Jews were established in Egypt, and the Septuagint (LXX) translation of the OT was begun (c. 285 B.C.).

In 198 B.C. Judea was conquered by Antiochus III the Great, and annexed to Syria. At this time the land was divided into the five provinces familiar to readers of the Gospels—Galilee, Samaria, Judea (these three being often collectively called Judea), Trachonitis, and Perea. The Jews were at first permitted to regulate their own lives by their own laws under a high priest and a council. In 171 B.C. Antiochus IV Epiphanes (the "little" horn of Dan. 8:9), after repeated interferences with the temple and priesthood, plundered Jerusalem, profaned the temple, and killed many of the inhabitants. In 168 B.C. Antiochus offered a sow upon the great altar and erected an altar to Jupiter. This is the "desolation" of Dan. 8:13. The temple worship was forbidden; the people were condemned to eat swine's flesh.

The excesses of Antiochus provoked the revolt of the Maccabees, one of the most heroic pages of history. Mattathias, the first of the Maccabees, a priest of great sanctity and energy of character, began the revolt with a band of godly and determined Jews pledged to free their nation and restore its ancient worship. He was succeeded by his son Judas, known in history as Maccabeus, probably from the Hebrew word for "hammer." He was assisted by four brothers, of whom Simon is best known.

In 165 B.C. Judas regained possession of Jerusalem and purified and rededicated the temple, an event celebrated in the Jewish Feast of the Dedication. Judas, who was slain in battle, was succeeded by his brother, Jonathan. In him the civil and priestly authority were united (143 B.C.). Under Jonathan, his brother Simon, and his nephew John Hyrcanus I, the Hasmonean line of priest-rulers was established by treaty with Rome. An account of the history of Antiochus Epiphanes and the Maccabees is found in the apocryphal book, I Maccabees.

3. After some years, there was a civil war in Judea, which was ended in 63 B.C. by the Roman conquest of Judea and Jerusalem by Pompey. Pompey left Hyrcanus II, the last of the Hasmoneans, a nominal sovereignty, but with Antipater, an Idumean, wielding the actual power. In 47 B.C. Antipater was made procurator of Judea by Julius Caesar. Antipater appointed his son, Herod, governor of Galilee. Following Caesar's assassination, disorder broke out in Judea, and Herod fled to Rome. There, in 40 B.C., he was appointed king of the Jews; on his return he conciliated the people by his marriage with Mariamne (38 B.C.), the granddaughter of Hyrcanus II, and appointed her brother, the Maccabean Aristobulus III, high priest. When Jesus Christ was born, Herod was king.

II. The religious history of the Jews during the long period from Malachi (c. 400 B.C.) to Christ follows the course of the troubled political history as to outer ceremonies, the high priestly office, and the temple worship. But of greater importance than these are the efforts and means by which the faith of Israel was nurtured and kept alive.

1. The experience of the captivity seems to have destroyed the Jews' tendency to idolatry. Their problem during the captivity, when they were deprived of temple and priest, was to maintain the exalted spiritual and moral ideals given them by the older prophets. Afterward, during the intertestamental period, the problem continued. Despite the revival of temple and priesthood, the struggle became one of preserving the prophetic faith of the Jews in the midst of outward persecution and sordid divisions within.

2. The external means to this end was the synagogue, an institution which formed no part of the biblical order of national life and which did not develop as a separate entity until after the time of Malachi. Its origin is obscure, but its roots may go back to the captivity when the Jews, who were without the temple and its rites, met on the Sabbath

for prayer. Such meetings, which would give opportunity for the reading of Scripture, would require some order of procedure as well as some authority for the restraint of disorder. Whatever its precise beginnings were, the synagogue doubtless grew out of the necessities of the situation in which the Jews were placed during the closing centuries of the pre-Christian era. It served the vital purpose of maintaining familiarity with the inspired writings. Upon these the spiritual life of the true Israel (Rom. 9:6, *note*) was nourished.

3. Also during this period there was created that mass of tradition, comment, and interpretation, known as *Mishna, Gemara* (forming the *Talmud*), *Midrashim*, and *Kabbala*, that was so superimposed upon the law that obedience was transferred from the law itself to the traditional interpretations.

4. During this same period there arose the two great sects known in the Gospel narratives as Pharisees and Sadducees. (See Mt. 3:7, with *notes*.) The Herodians were a political party rather than a sect.

Among these people, the Jews—governed under Rome by an Idumean usurper, torn by bitter religious controversies, and maintaining an elaborate religious ritual—appeared Jesus, the Son of God, the Christ, and the Savior of the world.

THE NEW TESTAMENT

Words of Christ
in Red

The Four Gospels

THE FOUR GOSPELS record the eternal being, human ancestry, birth, life and ministry, death, resurrection, and ascension of Jesus the Christ, Son of God and Son of Man. Taken together, they set forth, not a biography but a Person.

The fact that the four Gospels present a Person rather than a complete biography indicates the spirit in which they should be approached. What is most important is to see and know through these narratives Him whom they reveal. It is of less importance to endeavor to piece together a full account of His life from these inspired records (Jn. 21:25). For some adequate reason it did not please God to cause to be written a full biography of His Son. The years up to the beginning of His ministry are passed over in a silence that is broken but once, and that in a few verses in Luke's Gospel (Lk. 2:40–52). It is wise to respect the divine reticence.

But the four Gospels, though designedly incomplete as a story, are complete as a revelation. We may not know everything that Jesus did, but we may know Him. In four great narratives, each of which in some respects supplements the other three, we have Jesus Christ Himself.

This is the essential respect in which these narratives differ from biography or portraiture. "The words that I speak to you are spirit, and they are life" (Jn. 6:63). The believing student finds here the living Christ.

The distinctive part that each evangelist has in this presentation of the living Christ is briefly noted in the separate introductions to the Gospels, but it may be profitable to make some general suggestions for study and interpretation.

I. The OT is the inspired introduction to the NT, and whoever comes to the study of the four Gospels with a mind saturated with the OT foreview of Christ—His Person, work, and kingdom—will be greatly helped in understanding them. Into the Gospels are woven OT quotation, allusion, and type. The very first verse of the NT drives the reader back to the OT; and the risen Christ took His disciples back to the Hebrew Scriptures for an explanation of His sufferings and glory (Lk. 24:27,44). One of His last acts was the opening of their understanding that they might comprehend the OT in relation to Himself (Lk. 24:45).

Therefore, in approaching the study of the Gospels, the mind should be freed, so far as possible, from such presuppositions as that the Church is to be equated with the true Israel, and that the OT promises to Israel and the foreview of the kingdom relate only to the Church. Interpretations are not true because they are familiar. It should not, therefore, be assumed that "the throne of . . . David" (Lk. 1:32) is synonymous with the Father's throne (Rev. 3:21), or that "the house of Jacob" (Lk. 1:33) is the Church composed of both Jew and Gentile.

II. The mission of Jesus was initially to the Jews (Mt. 10:5–6; 15:23–25; John 1:11). He was "born under the law" (Gal. 4:4), and was "a servant to the circumcision for the truth of God, to confirm the promises made to the fathers" (Rom. 15:8) and to fulfill the law that grace might abound. Therefore, a strong legal and Jewish coloring is to be expected up to the cross (Mt. 5:17–19; cp. Mt. 10:5–6; 15:22–28; 23:2; Mk. 1:44; etc.). The Sermon on the Mount is closely related to law in the highest spiritual sense, for it demands as the condition of blessing (Mt. 5:3–9) that perfect character which only grace through divine power creates (Gal. 5:22–23).

III. The doctrines of grace are developed in the Epistles, not in the Gospels; but they are implicit in the Gospels, because they rest upon the death and resurrection of Christ and upon the great germinal truths He taught, truths of which the Epistles are the unfolding. The Christ of the Gospels is the perfect manifestation of grace.

IV. The Gospels do not develop the doctrine of the Church. The word "church" occurs in Matthew only. After His rejection as King and Savior by the Jews, our Lord, announcing a mystery until that moment "hidden in God" (Eph. 3:3–10), said, "I will build My church" (Mt. 16:18). It was, therefore, yet future; but His personal ministry had gathered out the believers who were, on the Day of Pentecost, made by the baptism with the Spirit the first members of "the church which is His body" (Eph. 1:23; cp. 1 Cor. 12:12–13).

The Gospels present a group of Jewish disciples, associated on earth with a Messiah in humiliation. The Epistles present a Church which is the body of Christ, made up of the regenerate who are associated with Him "in the heavenlies," co-heirs with Him of the Father, co-rulers with Him of the coming kingdom; and, as to the earth, although strangers and pilgrims, yet His witnesses and the instruments for doing His will among men (Acts 1:8; 1 Cor. 12:12–13; 2 Cor. 5:14–21; Eph. 1:3–14,20–23; 2:4–6; 1 Pet. 2:11).

V. The Gospels present Christ in His three offices of Prophet, Priest, and King.

As Prophet His ministry resembles that of the OT prophets. But it is the nature and dignity of His Person that makes Him the unique Prophet. Of old, God spoke through the prophets; now He speaks in the Son (Heb. 1:1–2). The OT prophet was a voice from God; the Son is God Himself (Dt. 18:18–19).

The prophet in any dispensation is God's messenger to His people, first, to establish truth; and, second, when His people are in declension and apostasy, to call them back to truth. The prophet's message, therefore, is usually one of rebuke and appeal. At times, however, as when his message of rebuke and appeal is not heeded, he becomes a foreteller of things to come. In this, too, Christ is like the other prophets; most of His predictive ministry occurs after His rejection as King.

The sphere and character of Christ's kingly office are defined in the Davidic Covenant (2 Sam. 7:16, *note*), as interpreted by the prophets and confirmed by the NT. Whereas the NT in no way abrogates or changes the Davidic Covenant or its interpretation, it adds details which were not in the original covenant. The Sermon on the Mount is an elaboration of the idea of righteousness as the predominant characteristic of the kingdom (Isa. 11:2–5; Jer. 23:5–6; 33:14–16). The OT prophet saw in one horizon, so to speak, the suffering and glory of Messiah (1 Pet. 1:10–11). The NT shows that His suffering and glory are separated by the present Church Age, and points forward to the Lord's return as the time when the Davidic Covenant of blessing through power will be fulfilled (Lk. 1:30–33; Acts 2:29–36; 15:14–17), just as the Abrahamic Covenant of blessing through suffering was fulfilled at His first coming (Acts 3:24–25; Gal. 3:6–14).

Christ is never called King of the Church. "The King" is indeed one of His divine titles, and the Church joins Israel in exalting "the King eternal, immortal, invisible" (Ps. 10:16; 1 Tim. 1:17). The Church is to reign under Him. The Holy Spirit is now calling out, not the subjects but the co-heirs and co-rulers of the kingdom (Rom. 8:15–18; 1 Cor. 6:2–3; 2 Tim. 2:11–12; Rev. 1:6; 3:21; 5:10).

Christ's priestly office is the complement of His prophetic office. The prophet represents God to the people; the priest represents the people to God. Because the people are sinful he, the priest, must be a sacrificer; because they are needy, he must be a compassionate intercessor (Heb. 5:1–2; 8:1–3). So Christ on the cross entered upon His high priestly work, offering Himself without spot to God (Heb. 9:14), as now He exercises an ever-living intercession for His people (Heb. 7:25). John 17 provides the pattern of that continuing intercession.

VI. In the Gospels, primary interpretation should be distinguished from moral application. Much in the Gospels that belongs in strict interpretation to the Jews or the kingdom is yet such a revelation of the mind of God and is so based on eternal principles as to have a moral application to the people of God, whatever their dispensational position. It is always true that "the pure in heart" are blessed because they "see God" and that "woe" is the portion of religious formalists whether under law or grace.

VII. Special emphasis rests upon that to which all four Gospels bear united testimony.

1. In all alike there is revealed the one unique Person. The pen is a different pen, the incidents in which He is seen are sometimes different incidents, but He is always the same Christ.

2. All the evangelists record the ministry of John the Baptist.

3. All record the feeding of the five thousand.

4. All record Christ's offer of Himself as King, according to Zech. 9:9.

5. All record the betrayal by Judas; the denial by Peter.

6. All record the trial and crucifixion of Christ.

7. All record the bodily resurrection of Christ.

8. All record events occurring during the forty days of the post-resurrection ministry of Christ—a ministry keyed to a new note of universality and of power.

9. All point forward to His second coming.

And this record is so presented as to testify that the supreme business that brought Him into the world was His death and resurrection; that all that precedes these was preparation, and that from them flow all the blessings God ever has bestowed or ever will bestow upon man.

VIII. Since the first three Gospels contain so much material in common that they may be arranged as a synopsis, they are called the Synoptic Gospels. Careful readers of the NT will observe the similarities among and also the differences peculiar to these Gospels. That they contain dissimilarities is not surprising in view of the fact that each of these three Gospels is written for a particular purpose—Matthew to present Jesus as King, Mark to present Him as Servant, and Luke to present Him as Son of Man.

Matthew may have been the first Gospel written. It is thought that Mark's account reflects, in its subject matter, Peter's view of our Lord. That there were in existence many early accounts of the life and work of Christ is plain from Luke's prologue to his Gospel (Lk.1:1–4).

As for John, this Gospel is in a class by itself. Probably written later than the Synoptics, it does not outline the life of our Lord but, in keeping with the writer's declared aim to present Jesus as the Son of God (Jn. 20:30–31), selects its material including much that is not in the first three Gospels.

An effort has been made by certain scholars to trace the forms or patterns into which the earliest traditions about Christ were put for oral repetition. These forms are supposed to have provided material for the Gospels and are also thought to have been so thoroughly shaped by the needs of the early Church as to preclude a full historical basis for all the events recorded in the Gospels. In its effort to explain the differences in the Gospels, this critical view raises a question concerning the historical accuracy of the whole record. However, it fails to recognize evidence which supports the historicity of the Gospels. It may also be observed that selectivity of material does not necessarily mean distortion of fact, nor is the use of reliable tradition incompatible with the inspiration of the Gospel records.

The important thing to keep in mind is the established fact that these Gospels are inspired historical documents of genuine authenticity and full integrity. Moreover, the believer in Christ knows in his own life the reality of the living Lord, who is so faithfully and yet so variously presented in the Synoptics and in John's Gospel.

The Gospel According to

MATTHEW

Author: Matthew *Theme:* Christ, the King *Date of writing:* c. A.D. 50

MATTHEW, called also Levi, was the writer of the First Gospel. His name appears seventh or eighth in the NT lists of the apostles (Mt. 10:3; Mk. 3:18; Lk. 6:15). Matthew was a Jew who collected taxes for the Roman government. He was thus despised by loyal Jews.

Written originally for the Jews, the Gospel of Matthew presents Christ as the Son of David and the Son of Abraham. Because He is portrayed as King, His genealogy is traced to King David; and the place of His birth, Bethlehem, the home of David, is emphasized. Seven times in this Gospel Christ is spoken of as "the Son of David" (1:1; 9:27; 12:23; 15:22; 20:30; 21:9; 22:42). Only in Matthew does Christ speak of "the throne of His glory" (19:28; cp. 25:31). Moreover, only here in the Gospels is Jerusalem referred to as "the holy city" (4:5) and "the city of the great King" (5:35). Since it is the Gospel of the King, Matthew is also the Gospel of the kingdom; in it the word "kingdom" appears more than fifty times and the expression "the kingdom of heaven," which is found nowhere else in the NT, appears about thirty times.

Matthew, more than any of the Gospel writers, identifies events and utterances in the life of our Lord with OT predictions, e.g. 1:22; 2:15,17,23; 4:14; 12:17; 13:14; 21:4; 26:54,56; 27:9,35.

Matthew may be divided as follows:

I. The King Introduced: His Genealogy, Birth, and Early Life, 1—4.
II. The Principles of the Rule of the King: the Sermon on the Mount, 5—7.
III. The Authority of the King Manifested and Rejected, 8—12.
IV. The Mysteries of the Kingdom: the Period Between the King's Two Advents, 13.
V. The Ministry of the Rejected King, 14—23.
VI. The Predicted Return of the King: the Olivet Discourse, 24—25.
VII. The Death and Resurrection of the King, 26—28.

CHAPTER 1
1
a vv. 1–17
b 1 Sam. 16:1–14; 2 Sam. 7:12–29; Ps. 132:11
c Gen. 12:1–4; 13:15–18; 15:1–6; 17:1–8; 22:15–18
2
d Gen. 21:1–8; 26:1–5
e Gen. 25:19–28; 28:1–4, 10–15
f Gen. 29:35
3
g Gen. 38:24–30;

I. The King Introduced: His Genealogy, Birth, and Early Life, 1—4

Genealogy of Jesus through Solomon (v. 7) and foster father, Joseph (v. 16; cp. Lk. 3:23–38)

1 THE book of the [1a]geneal-
ogy of Jesus Christ, the Son
of [b]David, the Son of [c]Abra-
ham:
2 Abraham begot [d]Isaac,
Isaac begot [e]Jacob, and Jacob
begot [f]Judah and his brothers.
3 Judah begot [g]Perez and
Zerah by Tamar, Perez begot
Hezron, and Hezron begot
Ram.
4 Ram begot Amminadab,
Amminadab begot Nahshon,
and Nahshon begot Salmon.
5 Salmon begot [h]Boaz by
Rahab, Boaz begot Obed by
Ruth, Obed begot Jesse,
6 and Jesse begot David the
king.
David the king begot Sol-
omon by her *who had been the*
*wife** of [i]Uriah.
7 Solomon begot [j]Reho-
boam, Rehoboam begot [k]Abi-
jah, and Abijah begot Asa.*
8 Asa begot [l]Jehoshaphat,
Jehoshaphat begot Joram, and
Joram begot [2m]Uzziah.

*
1:6 Words in italic type have been added for clarity. They are not found in the original Greek. 1:7 NU-Text reads *Asaph.*

Ruth 4:18–22
5
h Ruth 2:1; 4:1–13
6
i 2 Sam. 11:3
7
j 1 Ki. 11:43
k 2 Chr. 11:20
8
l 1 Chr. 3:10
m 2 Ki. 15:13

---

[1](1:1) There are two genealogies of our Lord—here and at Lk. 3:23–38 (where see *note* at v. 23). The genealogy in Matthew begins with Abraham, founder of the Hebrew nation, and concludes with Joseph, the husband of Mary. Luke's genealogy begins with Joseph and carries the Messianic line back as far as Adam. Matthew inserts historical data, Luke does not. The list in Matthew is divided into three sections.

The last individual in these genealogies in the OT records is Zerubbabel (Mt. 1:13; Lk. 3:27). There are some omissions, as between Joram and Uzziah (Mt. 1:8), for which see 2 Ki. 8:24 and 1 Chr. 3:11. Women are mentioned in the Matthew genealogy, contrary to usual custom (cp. 1 Chr. 1—8).

[2](1:8) Uzziah (called Azariah, 2 Ki. 14:21) was not the son, but the great-great-grandson of Joram. Cp. 2 Ki. 8:25; 13:1—15:38; 2 Chr. 22—25. The wording of each succession may some-

9 Uzziah begot Jotham, Jotham begot [a]Ahaz, and Ahaz begot Hezekiah.

10 Hezekiah begot Manasseh, Manasseh begot Amon,* and Amon begot [b]Josiah.

11 Josiah begot [1]Jeconiah and his brothers about the time they were carried away to Babylon.

12 And after they were brought to [c]Babylon, Jeconiah begot [d]Shealtiel, and Shealtiel begot [e]Zerubbabel.

13 Zerubbabel begot Abiud, Abiud begot Eliakim, and Eliakim begot Azor.

14 Azor begot Zadok, Zadok begot Achim, and Achim begot Eliud.

15 Eliud begot Eleazar, Eleazar begot Matthan, and Matthan begot Jacob.

16 And Jacob begot Joseph the husband of [f]Mary, [2]of whom was born Jesus who is called [3]Christ.

17 So all the generations from Abraham to David *are* [4]fourteen generations, from David until the captivity in Babylon *are* fourteen generations, and from the captivity in Babylon until the Christ *are* fourteen generations.

Conception and birth of Jesus (Lk. 1:26–38; 2:1–7; Jn. 1:1–2,14)

18 [g]Now the birth of Jesus Christ was as follows: After His mother Mary was betrothed to Joseph, before they came together, she was found with child of the Holy [h]Spirit.

19 Then Joseph her husband, being a [i]just *man,* and not wanting to make her a public example, was minded to put her away [j]secretly.

20 But while he thought about these things, behold, [k]an angel of the Lord appeared to him in a dream, saying, "Joseph, son of David, do not be afraid to take to you Mary your wife, for that which is conceived in her is of the Holy [h]Spirit.

21 "And she will bring forth a [l]Son, and you shall call His name [m]JESUS, for He will [n]save His people from their [o]sins."

22 So all this was done that it might be fulfilled which was spoken [p]by the Lord through the prophet, saying:

23 *"Behold, the virgin shall be with child, and bear a Son, and they shall call His name* [5]*Immanuel,"** which is translated, "God with us."

24 Then Joseph, being aroused from sleep, did as the angel of the Lord commanded him and took to him his wife,

25 and did not know her till

*1:10 NU-Text reads *Amos.* 1:23 Words in oblique type in the New Testament are quoted from the Old Testament.

9
a 2 Ki. 15:38
10
b 1 Ki. 13:2
12
c 2 Ki. 24:11–16; 2 Chr. 36:20–21; Jer. 29:1–4
d 1 Chr. 3:17
e Ezra 2:2; 3:8; see 1 Chr. 3:19, *note*
16
f Mt. 13:55; Mk. 6:3; Lk. 8:19; see Lk. 1:27, *note*
18
g Christ (first advent): vv. 18–25; Mt. 2:4. (Gen. 3:15; Acts 1:11, *note*)
h Holy Spirit (NT): vv. 18,20; Mt. 3:11. (Mt. 1:18; Acts 2:4, *note*)
19
i Righteousness (OT): v. 19; Mt. 5:20. (Gen. 6:9; Lk. 2:25, *note*)
j Cp. Dt. 24:1
20
k See Jud. 2:1 and Heb. 1:4, *notes*
21
l Isa. 7:14; 9:6–7
m Gk. form of Heb. *Jehoshua,* meaning *Jehovah is salvation*
n Jn. 1:29; see Rom. 1:16, *note*
o See Rom. 3:23, *note*
22
p Isa. 7:14

times indicate that a man is a more remote ancestor than an immediate father.

[1](1:11) In Jer. 22:24–30 a curse is pronounced upon this former king of Judah. There it is predicted that none of his descendants should prosper sitting on David's throne. Had our Lord been the natural son of Joseph, who was descended from Jeconiah, He could never reign in power and righteousness because of the curse. But Christ came through Mary's line, not Joseph's. As the adopted son of Joseph, the curse upon Jeconiah's seed did not affect Him.

[2](1:16) The changed expression here is important. It is no longer "begot," but "the husband of Mary, by whom [fem. sing.] was born Jesus." Jesus was not begotten of natural generation.

[3](1:16) "Christ" (*Christos* means *anointed*), the Greek form of the Hebrew *Messiah* (Dan. 9:25–26), is the official name of our Lord, as "Jesus" is His human name (Lk. 1:31; 2:21). The name, or title, "Christ," connects Him with the entire OT foreview (see Zech. 12:8, *note*) of a coming Prophet (Dt. 18:15–19), Priest (Ps. 110:4), and King (2 Sam. 7:12–13). As these were typically anointed with oil (1 Ki. 19:16; cp. Ex. 29:7; 1 Sam. 16:13 respectively), so Jesus was anointed with the Holy Spirit (Mt. 3:16; Mk. 1:10–11; Lk. 3:21–22; Jn. 1:32–33), thus becoming officially identified as the Christ.

[4](1:17) As in the genealogies of the OT (Gen. 5; 1 Chr. 1—9), certain generations are omitted here in order to make the arrangement uniform. Cp. 1 Chr. 3:11–12; Ezra 7:1–5. The list may have been put in this form for purposes of memorization. Memorization is aided by the fact that each of the triads of names concludes with an important era in Israel's history, i.e. David's reign, the Babylonian captivity, and the advent of the promised Messiah.

[5](1:23) Why was Jesus not actually called "Immanuel"? According to Hebrew usage the name does not represent a title but a characterization, as in Isa. 1:26 and 9:6. The name "Immanuel" shows that He really was "God with us." Thus the Deity of Christ is stressed at the very beginning of Matthew.

25
a Gk. form of Heb. *Jehoshua,* meaning *Jehovah is salvation*

CHAPTER 2
1
b c. 5 B.C.
c Cp. Mic. 5:2
2
d Kingdom (NT): vv. 2, 5–6; Mt. 3:2. (Mt. 2:2; 1 Cor. 15:24, *note*)
4
e Christ (first advent): vv. 1–6; Mt. 4:16. (Gen. 3:15; Acts 1:11, *note*)
5
f Inspiration: vv. 5–6; Mt. 2:15. (Ex. 4:15; 2 Tim. 3:16, *note*)

she had brought forth her firstborn Son.* And he called His
name [a]JESUS.

Visit of the wise men

2 NOW [b]after Jesus was
[1c]born in Bethlehem of Judea in the days of [2]Herod the
king, behold, [3]wise men from
the East came to Jerusalem,
2 saying, "Where is He who
has been born [d]King of the
Jews? For we have seen His star
in the East and have come to
worship Him."
3 When Herod the king
heard *this,* he was troubled, and
all Jerusalem with him.
4 And when he had gath-
ered all the chief priests and
[4]scribes of the people together,
he inquired of them where [e]the
Christ was to be born.
5 So they said to him, "In
Bethlehem of Judea, for thus it
is [f]written by the prophet:

6 *'But you, [g]Bethlehem, in*
the land of Judah,
Are not the least among
the rulers of Judah;
For out of you shall
come a Ruler
Who will shepherd My
people Israel.' "

7 Then Herod, when he had
secretly called the wise men, determined from them what time
the [h]star appeared.
8 And he sent them to Bethlehem and said, "Go and search
carefully for the young Child,
and when you have found *Him,*
bring back word to me, that I
may come and worship Him
also."
9 When they heard the king,
they departed; and behold, the
star which they had seen in the
East went before them, till it

6
g Mic. 5:2; Jn. 7:42
7
h Num. 24:17

* 1:25 NU-Text reads *a Son.*

[1](2:1) In the 708th year from the foundation of Rome (46 B.C. by Christian reckoning) Julius Caesar established the Julian calendar, beginning the year with January 1st. But it was not until the sixth century A.D. that Dionysius Exiguus, a Scythian monk living in Rome, who was confirming the Easter cycle, originated the system of reckoning time from the birth of Christ. Gradually this usage spread, being adopted in England by the Synod of Whitby in 664, until it gained universal acceptance. In 1582 Pope Gregory XIII reformed the Julian calendar. However, more accurate knowledge shows that the earlier reckonings of the time of Christ's birth were in error by several years. Thus it is now agreed that the birth of Christ should be placed c. 6–4 B.C.

[2](2:1) The Herod mentioned here (vv. 1,3,7,12,13,16,19,22) and in Lk. 1:5 is known to history as Herod the Great. His family was nominally Jewish but actually Idumaean (Edomite, see Gen. 36:1, *note*). The Romans had appointed his grandfather, Antipas (died 78 B.C.) governor of Idumaea, and Julius Caesar had made his father, Antipater, procurator of Judea (47–43 B.C.). The Roman triumvir, Mark Antony, appointed Herod the Great tetrarch of Galilee in 37 B.C. He greatly increased the splendor of Jerusalem, erecting the temple, which was the center of Jewish worship in the time of our Lord.

Herod's slaughter of the infants at Bethlehem (v. 16) was in keeping with his cruel character. Herod died in March, 4 B.C., and was succeeded by a son, Archelaus (Mt. 2:22). For other members of the Herodian family, see Mk. 6:14, *note.*

[3](2:1) "Wise men" (or "magi") is from the Greek *magoi,* a Persian word for men expert in the study of the stars. There is no evidence that these magi were only three in number or that they were kings. Their interest aroused by the star that signalized Christ's birth, they journeyed to Judea to seek the newborn King of the Jews. They arrived some months after His birth. When Herod sent them to Bethlehem, the star reappeared and led them to the Christ Child.

[4](2:4) "Scribes" were so called because it was their office to make copies of the Scriptures, to classify and teach the precepts of the oral law (see Pharisees, Mt. 3:7, *note*), and to keep careful count of every letter in the OT writings. Such an office was necessary in a religion of law and precept, and was an OT function (2 Sam. 8:17; 20:25; 1 Ki. 4:3; Jer. 8:8; 36:10,12,26). To this legitimate work the teachers added a record of rabbinical decisions on questions of ritual *(Halachoth);* the new code resulting from those decisions *(Mishna);* the Hebrew sacred legends *(Gemara,* forming with the *Mishna,* the *Talmud*); commentaries on the OT *(Midrashim);* reasonings upon these *(Hagada);* and, finally, mystical interpretations which found in Scripture meanings other than the grammatical, lexical, and obvious ones (the *Kabbala*), not unlike the allegorical method of Origen. In our Lord's time, the Pharisees considered it orthodox to receive this mass of writing which had been superimposed upon and had obscured the Scripture.

came and stood over where the
young Child was.
10 When they saw the star,
they rejoiced with exceedingly
great joy.
11 And when they had come
into the house, they saw the
young Child with Mary His
mother, and fell down and worshiped Him. And when they had
opened their treasures, they
presented [a]gifts to Him: gold,
frankincense, and myrrh.
12 Then, being divinely
warned in a dream that they
should not return to Herod, they
departed for their own country
another way.

Flight into Egypt

13 Now when they had departed, behold, [b]an angel of the
Lord appeared to Joseph in a
dream, saying, "Arise, take the
young Child and His mother,
flee to Egypt, and stay there until I bring you word; for [c]Herod
will seek the young Child to destroy Him."
14 When he arose, he took
the young Child and His mother
by night and departed for
Egypt,
15 and was there until the
death of Herod, that it might be
fulfilled which was [d]spoken by
the Lord through the prophet,
saying, [1]*"Out of Egypt I called
My Son."*

Herod puts innocent children to death

16 Then Herod, when he saw
that he was deceived by the
wise men, was exceedingly angry; and he sent forth and put to
death all the male children who
were in Bethlehem and in all its
districts, from two years old and
under, according to the time
which he had determined from
the [e]wise men.
17 Then was fulfilled what
was [d]spoken by Jeremiah the
prophet, saying:
18 *"A voice was heard in
Ramah,
Lamentation, weeping,
and great mourning,
Rachel weeping for her
children,
Refusing to be
comforted,
Because they are no
more."*

Return from Egypt to Nazareth (cp. Lk. 2:39–40; also read Lk. 2:41–52)

19 Now [f]when Herod was
dead, behold, an [g]angel of the
Lord appeared in a dream to Joseph in Egypt,
20 [h]saying, "Arise, take the
young Child and His mother,
and go to the land of Israel, [i]for
those who [j]sought the young
Child's life are dead."
21 Then he arose, took the
young Child and His mother,
and came into the land of Israel.
22 But when he heard that
[k]Archelaus was reigning over
Judea instead of his father
Herod, he was afraid to go
there. And being warned by
God in a [l]dream, he turned
aside into the region of Galilee.
23 And he came and dwelt in
a city called Nazareth, that it
might be fulfilled which was
[d]spoken by the prophets, [2]"He
shall be called a Nazarene."

Ministry of John the Baptist (Mk. 1:1–8; Lk. 3:1–20; Jn. 1:6–8,15–37)

3 IN those days John the Baptist came [m]preaching in the
wilderness of Judea,
2 and [n]saying, [o]"Repent,
for [p]the [3]kingdom of heaven is
[q]at hand!"

11
a Cp. Ps. 72:10–11; Isa. 60:6
13
b See Jud. 2:1 and Heb. 1:4, *notes*
c See Mk. 6:14, *note*
15
d *Inspiration:* vv. 15, 17–18,23; Mt. 3:3. (Ex. 4:15; 2 Tim. 3:16, *note*). Cp. Isa. 11:1; Jer. 31:15; Hos. 11:1
16
e See Mt. 2:1, *note 3*

19
f c. 4 B.C. See Mk. 6:14, *note*
g See Heb. 1:4, *note*
20
h Lk. 2:14
i Cp. Ex. 4:19
j v. 16
22
k Son of Herod the Great. See Mt. 2:1, *note*
l Mt. 2:13,19
CHAPTER 3
1
m *Gospel:* vv. 1–2; Mt. 4:17. (Gen. 12:3; Rev. 14:6)
2
n See Acts 17:30, *note*
o *Repentance:* vv. 2, 8,11; Mt. 4:17. (Mt. 3:2; Acts 17:30, *note*)
p *Kingdom* (NT): v. 2; Mt. 4:17. (Mt. 2:2; 1 Cor. 15:24, *note*)
q See Mt. 4:17, *note*

---

[1](2:15) The words quoted are from Hos. 11:1, and the passage illustrates the principle that prophetic utterances often have a latent and deeper meaning than at first appears. Israel, nationally, was a son (Ex. 4:22), but Christ was the greater Son. Compare Isa. 41:8 with Isa. 42:1–4 and 52:13–14, where the servant-nation and the Servant-Son are both in view; also Rom. 9:4–5.

[2](2:23) "He shall be called a Nazarene" probably refers to Isa. 11:1, where the Messiah is spoken of as "a Rod [*netzer*] from the stem of Jesse."

[3](3:2) The expression "kingdom of heaven" (lit. "of the heavens"), one that is peculiar to Matthew, refers to the rule of the heavens, i.e. the rule of the God of heaven over the earth (cp. Dan. 2:44; 4:25,32). The kingdom of heaven is similar in many respects to the kingdom of God and is often used synonymously with it, though emphasizing certain features of divine

3 For this is he who was [a]spoken of by the prophet Isaiah, saying:

"The voice of one crying
in the wilderness:
'Prepare the way of the
LORD;
Make His paths
[b]straight.' "

4 Now John himself was clothed in camel's hair, with a [c]leather belt around his waist; and his food was locusts and wild honey.

5 Then Jerusalem, all Judea, and all the region around the Jordan went out to him
6 and were baptized by him in the Jordan, confessing their [d]sins.
7 But when he saw many of the [1]Pharisees and [2]Saddducees coming to his baptism, he said

3
a Inspiration: v. 3; Mt. 4:4. (Ex. 4:15; 2 Tim. 3:16, *note*). Cp. Isa. 40:3
b Ezek. 1:7

4
c Cp. 2 Ki. 1:8

6
d See Rom. 3:23, *note*

government. When contrasted with the universal kingdom of God, the kingdom of heaven includes only men on earth, excluding angels and other creatures. The kingdom of heaven is the earthly sphere of profession as shown by the inclusion of those designated as wheat and tares, the latter of which are cast out of the kingdom (Mt. 13:41), and is compared to a net containing both the good and bad fish which are later separated (Mt. 13:47).

The kingdom of heaven is revealed in three aspects in Matthew: (1) As "at hand" (see 4:17, *note 4*), the kingdom is offered in the Person of the King, of whom John the Baptist is the forerunner (Mt. 3:1). (2) As fulfilled in the present age, the kingdom of heaven is presented in seven "mysteries" (Mt. 13), revealing the character of the rule of heaven over the earth between the first and second comings of the Lord. And (3) as fulfilled after the second coming of Christ, the kingdom of heaven will be realized in the future millennial kingdom as predicted by Daniel (Dan. 2:34–36,44–45) and covenanted to David (2 Sam. 7:12–16; see Zech. 12:8, *note*). This millennial form of the kingdom of heaven is wholly future and will be set up after the return of the King in glory (Mt. 24:29—25:46; Acts 15:14–17; see Mt. 6:33, *note*).

[1](3:7) Called "Pharisees" from a Hebrew word meaning *separate.* After the ministry of the post-exilic prophets ceased, godly men called *Chasidim* (saints) arose who sought to keep alive reverence for the law among the descendants of the Jews who returned from the Babylonian captivity. This movement degenerated into the Pharisaism of our Lord's day—a letter-strictness which overlaid the law with traditional interpretations held to have been communicated by the LORD to Moses as oral explanations of equal authority with the law itself (cp. Mt. 15:2–3; Mk. 7:8–13; Gal. 1:14).

The Pharisees were strictly a sect. A member was a *chaber* (i.e. "united," Jud. 20:11) and was obligated to remain true to the principles of Pharisaism. They were moral, zealous, and self-denying, but self-righteous (Lk. 18:9) and destitute of the sense of sin and need (Lk. 7:39). They were the foremost persecutors of Jesus Christ and the objects of His unsparing denunciation, e.g. Mt. 23:1–36; Lk. 11:42–44.

[2](3:7) The Sadducees were a Jewish sect that denied the existence of angels or other spirits, and all miracles, especially the resurrection of the body. They were the religious rationalists of the time (Mk. 12:18–23; Acts 23:8), and were strongly entrenched in the Sanhedrin and

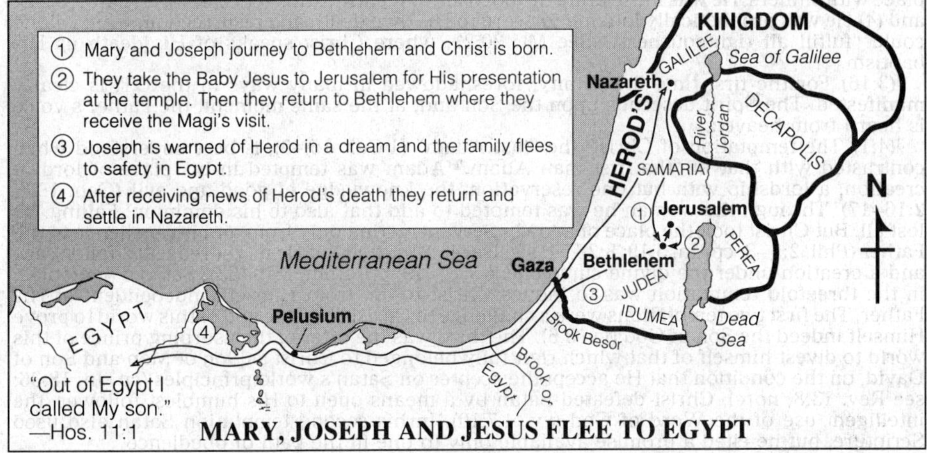
① Mary and Joseph journey to Bethlehem and Christ is born.
② They take the Baby Jesus to Jerusalem for His presentation at the temple. Then they return to Bethlehem where they receive the Magi's visit.
③ Joseph is warned of Herod in a dream and the family flees to safety in Egypt.
④ After receiving news of Herod's death they return and settle in Nazareth.
HEROD'S KINGDOM
GALILEE
Sea of Galilee
Nazareth
River Jordan
DECAPOLIS
SAMARIA
Jerusalem
PEREA
N
Mediterranean Sea
Gaza
Bethlehem
JUDEA
IDUMEA
Dead Sea
Brook Besor
Brook of Egypt
Pelusium
EGYPT
"Out of Egypt I called My son." —Hos. 11:1
MARY, JOSEPH AND JESUS FLEE TO EGYPT

to them, [a]"Brood of vipers!
Who warned you to flee from
the wrath to come?
8 "Therefore bear fruits worthy of repentance,
9 "and do not think to say to
yourselves, 'We have Abraham
as *our* father.' For I say to you
that God is able to raise up children to Abraham from these
stones.
10 "And even now the ax is
laid to the root of the trees.
Therefore every tree which
does not bear good fruit is [b]cut
down and thrown into the fire.
11 "I indeed baptize you with
water unto repentance, but He
who is coming after me is
mightier than I, whose sandals I
am not worthy to carry. He will
baptize you with the Holy
[c]Spirit and [d]fire.*
12 "His winnowing fan *is* in
His hand, and He will thoroughly clean out His threshing
floor, and gather His wheat into
the barn; but He will burn up the
chaff with unquenchable fire."

Baptism of Jesus (Mk. 1:9–11; Lk. 3:21–22; cp. Jn. 1:31–34)

13 [e]Then Jesus came from
Galilee to John at the Jordan to
be baptized by him.
14 And John *tried to* prevent
Him, saying, "I need to be baptized by You, and are You coming to me?"
15 But Jesus answered and
said to him, [1]"Permit *it to be so*
now, for thus it is fitting for us
to fulfill all [f]righteousness."
Then he allowed Him.
16 When He had been bap-
tized, [2]Jesus came up immediately from the water; and behold, the [g]heavens were opened
to Him, and He* saw the Spirit
of God descending like a dove
and alighting upon Him.
17 And suddenly a voice
came from heaven, saying,
[h]"This is My beloved Son, in
whom I am well pleased."

Temptation of Jesus (Mk. 1:12–13; Lk. 4:1–13; cp. Gen. 3:6; 1 Jn. 2:16)

4 [3]THEN Jesus was led up by
the [c]Spirit into the wilderness to be [i]tempted by the
[j]devil.
2 And when He had fasted

*
3:11 M-Text omits *and fire.* 3:16 Or *he*

7
a Lit. *Offspring*
10
b Mt. 7:19
11
c *Holy Spirit* (NT): vv. 11,16; 4:1; Mt. 10:20. (Mt. 1:18; Acts 2:4, *note*)
d Acts 2:3
13
e c. A.D. 26
15
f See 1 Jn. 3:7, *note*
16
g Cp. Ezek. 1:1; Acts 7:56; Rev. 4:1
17
h Lit. *This is My Son, the Beloved.* Mt. 17:5; Mk. 9:7; Lk. 9:35; cp. Isa. 42:1; Eph. 1:3–6
CHAPTER 4
1
i *Test/tempt:* vv. 1,3,7; Mt. 6:13. (Gen. 3:1; Jas. 1:14, *note*)
j *Satan:* vv. 1, 5,8,10–11; Mt. 12:26. (Gen. 3:1; Rev. 20:10)

priesthood (Acts 4:1–2; 5:17). The Sadducees are identified with no affirmative doctrine, but were mere deniers of the supernatural.

1(3:15) Why the Lord, who needed no repentance, should insist upon receiving a rite which signified confession (v. 6) and repentance (v. 11) is nowhere directly explained. It may be suggested that: (1) Jesus was now to enter into His mediatorial office as Prophet, Priest, and King and, as the Aaronic high priest publicly entered his office in a special ceremony (Ex. 29:4–7), so our Lord's baptism signifies His entering His ministry; (2) our Lord's baptism was the means for His introduction as Messiah to His people (Jn. 1:31–34); (3) by thus taking His place with sinners, He was illustrating the doctrine of identification (cp. Isa. 53:12; 2 Cor. 5:21); and (4) He was prophetically looking forward to His own death and resurrection, which alone could "fulfill all righteousness." See Mt. 20:22, where Christ speaks of His death as His baptism.

2(3:16) For the first time the Trinity, foreshadowed in many ways in the OT, is clearly manifested. The Spirit descends upon the Son and, at the same moment, the Father's voice is heard from heaven.

3(4:1) The temptation of Christ, the "last Adam" (1 Cor. 15:45), is best understood when contrasted with that of "the first man Adam." Adam was tempted in his place of lord of creation, a lordship with but one reservation, the knowledge of good and evil (Gen. 1:26; 2:16–17). Through the woman he was tempted to add that also to his dominion. Falling, he lost all. But Christ took the place of a lowly Servant, acting only from and in obedience to the Father (Phil. 2:5–8; cp. Jn. 5:19; 8:28,54; see Isa. 41:8, *note*), that He might redeem a fallen race and a creation under the divine curse (Gen. 3:17–19; cp. Rom. 8:19–23). Satan's one object in the threefold temptation was to induce Christ to act from Himself, independent of His Father. The first two temptations were a challenge to Christ from the god of this world to prove Himself indeed the Son of God (vv. 3,6). The third was the offer of the usurping prince of this world to divest himself of that which rightfully belonged to Christ as Son of Man and Son of David, on the condition that He accept the scepter on Satan's world principles (cp. Jn. 18:36; see Rev. 13:8, *note*). Christ defeated Satan by a means open to His humblest follower, the intelligent use of the Word of God (vv. 4,7,10). In his second temptation Satan also used Scripture, but he cited a promise available only to one in the path of obedience.

[a]forty days and forty nights, afterward He was hungry.
3 Now when the tempter
came to Him, he said, "If You
are the Son of God, command
that these stones become
bread."
4 But He answered and
said, [b]"It is [c]written, [d]'*Man
shall not live by bread alone,
but by every word that proceeds
from the mouth of God.'*"
5 Then the devil took Him
up into the [1][e]holy city, set Him
on the pinnacle of the temple,
6 and said to Him, "If You
are the Son of God, throw Yourself down. For it is [c]written:

> [f]'*He shall give His [g]angels*
> *charge over you,'*

and,

> *'In their hands they shall*
> *bear you up,*
> *Lest you dash your foot*
> *against a stone.'*"

7 Jesus said to him, "It is
[c]written again, [d]'*You shall not
tempt the [h]*LORD *your God.'*"
8 Again, the devil took Him
up on an exceedingly high
mountain, and [i]showed Him all
the kingdoms of the [2]world and
their glory.
9 And he said to Him, "All
these things I will give You if
You will fall down and worship
me."
10 Then Jesus said to him,
"Away with you,* Satan! For it
is [c]written, [d]'*You shall worship
the* LORD *your God, and Him
only you shall [j]serve.'*"
11 Then the devil [k]left Him,
and behold, [g]angels came and
ministered to Him.

*Jesus begins His public
ministry in Capernaum
(Mk. 1:14; Lk. 4:14–15)*

12 Now when Jesus heard
that John had been put in
prison, He departed to Galilee.
13 And leaving Nazareth, He
came and dwelt in Capernaum,
which is by the sea, in the regions of Zebulun and Naphtali,
14 that it might be fulfilled
which was [c]spoken by Isaiah
the prophet, saying:

> 15 *"The land of Zebulun and*
> *the land of Naphtali,*
> *By the way of the sea,*
> *beyond the Jordan,*
> *Galilee of the Gentiles:*
> 16 *The people who sat in*
> *darkness have seen a*
> *great [l]light,*
> *And upon those who sat*
> *in the region and*
> *shadow of death*
> [m]*Light has dawned."**

17 From that [3]time Jesus began to [n]preach and to say,
[o]"Repent, for the [p]kingdom of
heaven [q]is [4]at hand."

*Jesus' first disciples (Mk. 1:16–20;
cp. Lk. 5:1–11; Jn. 1:35–42)*

18 And Jesus, walking by the

*4:10 M-Text reads *Get behind Me.*
4:16 Isaiah 9:1–2

2
a Cp. Ex. 34:28; 1 Ki. 19:8
4
b Dt. 8:3
c *Inspiration:* vv. 4, 6–7,10, 14–16; Mt. 5:18. (Ex. 4:15; 2 Tim. 3:16, *note*). Isa. 9:1–2
d *Law* (of Moses): vv. 4,7,10; Mt. 5:17. (Ex. 19:1; Gal. 3:24, *note*)
5
e *Sanctification* (NT): v. 5; Mt. 7:6. (Mt. 4:5; Rev. 22:11)
6
f Ps. 91:11–12
g See Heb. 1:4, *note*
7
h Dt. 6:16
8
i 1 Jn. 2:15–17; cp. Rev. 21:10

10
j Dt. 6:13; 10:20
11
k Jas. 4:7
16
l *Christ* (first advent): vv. 13–16; Mt. 12:18. (Gen. 3:15; Acts 1:11, *note*)
m Isa. 42:6–7
17
n *Gospel:* v. 17; Mt. 4:23. (Gen. 12:3; Rev. 14:6)
o *Repentance:* v. 17; Mt. 9:13. (Mt. 3:2; Acts 17:30, *note*)
p *Kingdom* (NT): v. 17; Mt. 4:23. (Mt. 2:2; 1 Cor. 15:24, *note*)
q See Mt. 3:2, *note*

---

[1](4:5) In the NT one Greek word, *hagios,* in its various forms, is rendered, "holy," "holiness," "consecrated," "sanctify," and "sanctified." Like the Heb. *qodesh,* it signifies *set apart.*

[2](4:8) The Greek word *kosmos* means *order, arrangement,* and so, with the Greeks, *beauty;* for order and arrangement, in the sense of system, are at the bottom of the Greek conception of beauty. Sometimes *kosmos* means *world.* When the word is employed in the NT for humanity, the world of men, it denotes organized humanity—humanity in families, tribes, nations. The word for chaotic, unorganized humanity—the mere mass of men—is *thalassa,* the "sea" of men (e.g. Rev. 13:1). For "world" *(kosmos)* in the bad ethical sense, see Rev. 13:8, *note.*

[3](4:17) The phrase "from that time" is used by Matthew to indicate two sharply contrasted phases of our Lord's teaching ministry. The first begins here with His proclamation of the kingdom as "at hand." The second comes at 16:21 when, following Israel's rejection of the King and His kingdom, Christ begins to declare openly the necessity of His death and resurrection.

[4](4:17) The biblical term "at hand" or "near" is never a positive affirmation that the person or thing said to be at hand will immediately appear, but only that that person or thing has the quality of imminency. When Christ appeared to the Jewish people, the next thing, in the order of revelation as they understood it, should have been the setting up of the Davidic kingdom. Yet God had predicted the rejection and crucifixion of the King (Ps. 22; Isa. 53). The long period of the secret form of the kingdom (Mt. 13:11), the worldwide preaching of the cross, and the out-calling of the Church was as yet locked up in the secret counsels of God (Mt. 13:11,17; Eph. 3:3–12).

20
a Mt. 19:27
23
b Gospel: v. 23; Mt. 9:35. (Gen. 12:3; Rev. 14:6)
c Kingdom (NT): v. 23; 5:2–12; Mt. 5:19. (Mt. 2:2; 1 Cor. 15:24, *note*)
24
d Mk. 1:32–33; Lk. 4:40; see Mk. 3:15, *note*

Sea of Galilee, saw [1]two brothers, Simon called Peter, and Andrew his brother, casting a net
into the sea; for they were fishermen.
19 Then He said to them,
"Follow Me, and I will make you
fishers of men."
20 They immediately [a]left
their nets and followed Him.
21 Going on from there, He
saw two other brothers, [2]James
the son of Zebedee, and John
his brother, in the boat with
Zebedee their father, mending
their nets. He called them,
22 and immediately they left
the boat and their father, and
followed Him.

Early ministry in Galilee

23 And Jesus went about all
Galilee, teaching in their synagogues, preaching the [b]gospel
of the [c]kingdom, and healing
all kinds of sickness and all
kinds of disease among the people.
24 Then His fame went
throughout all Syria; and they
[d]brought to Him all sick people
who were afflicted with various
diseases and torments, and
those who were [e]demon-
possessed, [f]epileptics, and par-
alytics; and He healed them.
25 Great [g]multitudes followed Him—from Galilee, and
from Decapolis, Jerusalem, Judea, and beyond the Jordan.

II. The Principles and the Rule of the Kingdom: the Sermon on the Mount, 5—7

The Sermon on the Mount (Lk. 6:20–49): the Beatitudes

5 AND seeing the multitudes,
He [h]went up on a moun-
tain, and when He was seated
His disciples came to Him.
2 Then He opened His
mouth and [i]taught them, [3]say-
ing:

3 [j]"Blessed *are* the poor in spirit,
For theirs is the [4c]kingdom of heaven.
4 Blessed *are* those who mourn,
For they shall be comforted.
5 Blessed *are* the [k]meek,
For they shall inherit the earth.

e See Mt. 7:22, *note*
f Cp. Lk. 8:26–39
25
g Mt. 5:1; 8:1, 18; Mk. 3:7–8
CHAPTER 5
1
h Mt. 14:23; 15:29; 17:1
2
i Mt. 7:29; Mk. 10:1; 12:35; Jn. 8:2
3
j Prov. 16:19; Isa. 66:2
5
k Ps. 22:26; 25:9; 37:11; 147:6; 149:4; Isa. 29:19

---

[1](4:18) Peter and Andrew were already disciples (Jn. 1:35–42). This is a call to service.

[2](4:21) Four persons are called by this name in the NT: (1) James, the son of Zebedee, an apostle (Mt. 10:2) and the brother of the Apostle John, apart from whom he is never mentioned and with whom, together with Peter, he was admitted to the special intimacy of our Lord (Mt. 17:1; Mk. 5:37; 9:2; 14:33). He was martyred by Herod (Acts 12:2). (2) James, the son of Alphaeus, who was one of the twelve apostles (Mt. 10:3). He is called James "the Less" (Mk. 15:40). (3) James, the Lord's half brother (Mt. 13:55; Mk. 6:3; Gal. 1:19). The younger children of Mary did not believe in Jesus during His earthly life (Jn. 7:5) but joined His followers after His resurrection (Acts 1:14). James became the leader of the Jerusalem church (Acts 12:17; 15:13; 21:18; Gal. 1:19; 2:9,12) and wrote the Epistle of James. And (4) James, the father of the Apostle Judas (Lk. 6:16; Acts 1:13).

[3](5:2) The beatific character and attitude described by our Lord in vv. 3–12 are unattainable by self-effort, but are wrought in the Christian by the work of the indwelling Holy Spirit. Cp. 1 Cor. 3:16; Gal. 5:22–23.

[4](5:3) Having announced the kingdom of heaven as "at hand," the King now, in the Sermon on the Mount (Mt. 5—7), declares to His disciples (5:1) the principles of that kingdom.

1. In this sermon our Lord reaffirms the Mosaic law of the OT theocratic kingdom as the governing code in His coming kingdom on earth (5:17), and declares that the attitude of men toward this law will determine their place in the kingdom (5:19).

2. Christ here also declares that He has come to fulfill the Law (5:17), which He now proceeds to do in part in the Sermon on the Mount: (a) by showing that the divine law deals with thoughts and motives as well as overt acts (5:27–28; 6:1–6); and, (b) by abrogating certain concessions made formerly because of the hardness of men's hearts (5:31–32; cp. 19:8).

3. In the Sermon on the Mount, Christ sets forth the perfect standard of righteousness demanded by the law (5:48), thus demonstrating that all men are sinners, habitually falling short of the divine standard, and that, therefore, salvation by works of law is an impossibility.

4. Although the law, as expressed in the Sermon on the Mount, cannot save sinners (Rom. 3:20), and the redeemed of the present age are not under law (Rom. 6:14), nevertheless both the Mosaic law and the Sermon on the Mount are a part of Holy Scripture which is inspired by God and therefore "profitable for doctrine, for reproof, for correction, for instruction in righteousness" (2 Tim. 3:16) for the redeemed of all ages.

6 Blessed *are* those who
[a]hunger and thirst
for [b]righteousness,
For they shall be filled.
7 Blessed *are* the merciful,
For they shall obtain
mercy.
8 Blessed *are* the [c]pure in
heart,
For they shall see God.
9 Blessed *are* the
peacemakers,
For they shall be called
sons of God.
10 Blessed are those who
are persecuted for
[d]righteousness' sake,
For theirs is the
[e]kingdom of heaven.

11 "Blessed are [1]you when they revile and persecute you, and say all kinds of evil against you falsely for My sake.

12 "Rejoice and be exceedingly [f]glad, for great *is* your [g]reward in heaven, for so they [h]persecuted the [i]prophets who were before you.

The Similitudes
(Mk. 4:21–23; Lk. 8:16–18)

13 "You are the [j]salt of the earth; but if the salt loses its flavor, how shall it be seasoned? It is then good for nothing but to be thrown out and [k]trampled underfoot by men.

14 "You are the [l]light of the [m]world. A city that is set on a hill cannot be hidden.

15 "Nor do they light a lamp and put it under a basket, but on a [n]lampstand, and it gives light to all *who are* in the house.

16 "Let your light so shine before men, that they may see your good works and glorify your Father in heaven.

Relation of Christ to the Law

17 "Do not think that I came to destroy the [2][o]Law or the Prophets. I did not come to destroy but to fulfill.

18 "For assuredly, I say to you, till heaven and earth pass away, [p]one [q]jot or one [r]tittle will by no means pass from the law till all is fulfilled.

19 "Whoever therefore breaks one of the least of these [o]commandments, and teaches men so, shall be called least in the [s]kingdom of heaven; but whoever does and teaches *them*, he shall be called great in the kingdom of heaven.

20 "For I say to you, that unless your [d]righteousness [t]exceeds *the* [u]*righteousness* of the [v]scribes and [w]Pharisees, you will by no means enter the [s]kingdom of heaven.

First reconciliation, then sacrifice

21 "You have [o]heard that it was [p]said to those of old, *'You shall not* [x]*murder*, and whoever murders will be in danger of the judgment.'

22 "But I say to you that whoever is angry with his brother without a cause* shall be in danger of the judgment. And whoever says to his brother, [y]'Raca!' shall be in danger of the council. But whoever says, 'You fool!' shall be in danger of [3]hell fire.

* 5:22 NU-Text omits *without a cause*.

6
a Lk. 1:53; cp. Isa. 55:1; Lk. 15:17
b See Rom. 10:10, *note*
8
c Ps. 24:4
10
d See 1 Jn. 3:7, *note*
e See Mt. 3:2, *note*
12
f 1 Pet. 4:14
g *Rewards:* v. 12; Mt. 6:1. (Dan. 12:3; 1 Cor. 3:14, *note*)
h Acts 7:52
i Cp. Heb. 11:32–40
13
j *Parables* (NT): vv. 13–16; Mt. 7:24. (Mt. 5:13; Lk. 21:29)
k Cp. Ps. 119:118
14
l Jn. 8:12
m Gk. *kosmos.* See Mt. 4:8, *note*
15
n Cp. Phil. 2:15

17
o *Law* (of Moses): vv. 17–19, 21; Mt. 5:27. (Ex. 19:1; Gal. 3:24, *note*)
18
p *Inspiration:* vv. 18, 21; Mt. 5:27. (Ex. 4:15; 2 Tim. 3:16, *note*)
q Smallest Hebrew letter
r Minute ornament over Hebrew letter
19
s *Kingdom* (NT): vv. 19–20; Mt. 5:35. (Mt. 2:2; 1 Cor. 15:24, *note*)
20
t Cp. Lk. 18:11–12; Rom. 3:20; 9:31; 10:3; Phil. 3:5–7
u *Righteousness* (OT): v. 20; Mt. 13:17. (Gen. 6:9; Lk. 2:25, *note*)
v See Mt. 2:4, *note*
w See Mt. 3:7, *note*
21
x See Ex. 20:13, *note*
22
y Lit. *Empty,* an abusive epithet

[1](5:11) The change from the third person "those" (vv. 3–10) to the second person "you," etc. (vv. 11–16) is significant. Most of the Sermon on the Mount is addressed directly to the disciples as subjects of the kingdom of heaven.

[2](5:17) Christ's relation to the Law of Moses may be thus summarized: (1) Christ was made under the law (Gal. 4:4). (2) He lived in perfect obedience to the law (Mt. 17:5; Jn. 8:46; 1 Pet. 2:21–23). (3) He was a minister of the law to the Jews, clearing it from rabbinical sophistries, enforcing it upon those who professed to obey it (e.g. Lk. 10:25–37), but confirming the promises made to the fathers under the Mosaic Covenant (Rom. 15:8; see Ex. 19:5, *note*). (4) He fulfilled the types of the law by His holy life and sacrificial death (Heb. 9:11–28). (5) He bore, vicariously, the curse of the law, so that the Abrahamic Covenant (see Gen. 12:2, *note*) might avail all who believe (Gal. 3:13–14). (6) He brought out, by His redemptive work, all who believe—from the place of servants under the law to the place of sons (Gal. 4:1–7). And (7) He mediated by His blood the New Covenant (see Heb. 8:8, *note*) of assurance and grace in which all believers stand (Rom. 5:2), so establishing the "law of Christ" (Gal. 6:2, refs.) with its precepts of righteous living made possible by the indwelling Spirit.

[3](5:22) Greek *geenna* equals Gehenna, the place in the Valley of Hinnom where, anciently, human sacrifices were offered (2 Chr. 33:6; Jer. 7:31), and where the continuous burning of rubbish illustrated for the Jewish people unending judgment upon the wicked. The word

23 "Therefore if you bring
your gift to the altar, and there
remember that your brother has
[a]something against you,
24 "leave your gift there before the altar, and go your way.
First be reconciled to your
brother, and then come and offer your gift.
25 "Agree with your [b]adver-
sary quickly, while you are on
the way with him, lest your adversary deliver you to the judge,
the judge hand you over to the
officer, and you be thrown into
prison.
26 "Assuredly, I say to you,
you will by no means get out of
there till you have paid the last
[1c]penny.

Lust, adultery, and divorce
(cp. Mt. 19:3–11; Mk. 10:2–12;
1 Cor. 7:1–16)

27 "You have [d]heard that it
was [e]said to those of old,*
[f]'*You shall not commit adul-*
tery.'
28 "But I say to you that whoever [g]looks at a woman to lust
for her has already committed
adultery with her in his heart.
29 "If your right eye causes
you to [h]sin, pluck it out and cast
it from you; for it is more profitable for you that one of your
members perish, than for your
whole body to be cast into [i]hell.
30 "And if your right hand
causes you to [h]sin, cut it off and
cast *it* from you; for it is more
profitable for you that one of
your members perish, than for
your whole body to be cast into
[i]hell.
31 "Furthermore it has been
[e]said, [f]'Whoever divorces his
wife, let him give her a [j]certifi-
cate of divorce.'
32 "But I say to you that whoever divorces his wife for any
reason except sexual immorality* [k]causes her to commit
adultery; and whoever marries
a woman who is divorced commits adultery.

Perjury and retaliation forbidden

33 "Again you have heard
that it was [e]said to those of old,
[f]'You [l]shall not swear falsely,
but shall [m]perform your oaths to
the [n]Lord.'

23 [a] Rom. 14:19
25 [b] Lk. 12:58–59; cp. Prov. 25:8–9; Jas. 3:13–18
26 [c] See Coinage (NT), v. 26, *note*
27 [d] Ex. 20:14
[e] *Inspiration:* vv. 27, 31,33; Mt. 5:38. (Ex. 4:15; 2 Tim. 3:16, *note*)
[f] *Law* (of Moses): vv. 27,31,33; Mt. 5:38. (Ex. 19:1; Gal. 3:24, *note*)
28 [g] 2 Sam. 11:2–5; Mt. 15:19; Jas. 1:14–15; cp. Job 31:1; Prov. 6:25
29 [h] Lit. *stumble*
[i] Gk. *geenna.* See Mt. 5:22, *note*
31 [j] Dt. 24:1; cp. Gen. 2:23–24; Jer. 3:1
32 [k] Lk. 16:18; cp. 1 Cor. 7:12
33 [l] Lev. 19:12
[m] Num. 30:2
[n] Dt. 23:23

*5:27 NU-Text and M-Text omit *to those of old.* 5:32 Or *fornication*

occurs in Mt. 5:22,29,30; 10:28; 18:9; 23:15,33; Mk. 9:43,45,47; Lk. 12:5; Jas. 3:6. In every instance except the last, the word was spoken by Jesus Christ in most solemn warning of the consequences of sin. He described it as the place where "their worm does not die and the fire is not quenched" (Mk. 9:48). It is called "lake of fire" etc. in Rev. 19:20; 20:10,14,15. See Death, the second (Jn. 8:24; Rev. 21:8); also Lk. 16:23, *note.*

[1](5:26) Coinage (NT). In NT times, not only Roman but Greek, Syrian, and Egyptian coins were in common circulation, some of them with local imitations of varying value. Estimates differ widely as to the proper value of these coins in terms of late twentieth-century American dollars, the variation depending on whether the value of gold, silver, or purchasing power is made the basis. Moreover, the U.S. dollar value of precious metals varies from day to day.

The most common coin was (1) the Roman denarius, a silver coin about two-thirds the size of an American quarter, worth about 16 cents and representing an ordinary day's wages for a laborer (Mt. 18:28; 20:2,9,10,13; 22:19; Mk. 6:37; 12:15; 14:5; Lk. 7:41; 10:35; 20:24; Jn. 6:7; 12:5; Rev. 6:6). (2) The Greek equivalent was the drachma, mentioned only in Lk. 15:8. Some locally coined drachmas were worth less. (3) The "didrachma," i.e. a double drachma, cited in Mt. 17:24, was probably coined locally and used for payment of the temple tax. (4) The "pieces of silver" (Mt. 26:15; 27:3,5,6,9) were probably tetradrachmas, i.e. a coin worth four drachmas, corresponding to the OT shekel (cp. Zech. 11:12,13). (5) But the coins in Acts 19:19, described as "pieces of silver," were probably Greek drachmas. (6) The stater, a silver coin equivalent to four Greek drachmas or one shekel, and worth about 64 cents, is referred to in Mt. 17:27. It was the exact amount of the tax for two people, i.e. Christ and Peter. Gold staters, not mentioned in the Bible, were half the weight of the silver stater. The Roman aureus, a gold coin, is not mentioned in the NT except indirectly as "gold" in Mt. 10:9. Many coins were issued of copper or bronze. (7) A coin referred to as "copper" (Gk. *chalkos*) in Mt. 10:9 and Mk. 6:8, and as "money" in Mk. 12:41 was probably a small Greek or Roman coin worth about one-half cent. (8) The "penny" (Gk. *kodrantes*) of Mt. 5:26, transliterated as *quadrans* in Mk. 12:42, was worth about one-fourth cent. (9) Four pennies made one "copper coin" (Gk. *assarion,* Mt. 10:29; Lk 12:6), worth about one cent. And (10) the "mite" (Gk. *lepton*), the smallest coin (Mk. 12:42; Lk. 12:59; 21:2), was one-half a penny and worth about one-eighth cent.

Sums of money were indicated by "mina" (Gk. *mna*), worth 100 denarii, and by "talents" worth 6,000 denarii. For coinage (OT), see Ex. 30:13, note.

34 "But I say to you, [a]do not swear at all: neither by heaven, for it is God's throne;

35 "nor by the earth, for it is His footstool; nor by Jerusalem, for it is the city [b]of the great [c]King.

36 "Nor shall you swear by your head, because you cannot make one hair white or black.

37 "But let your 'Yes' be 'Yes,' and your 'No,' 'No.' For whatever is more than these is from the evil one.

38 "You have heard that it was [d]said, [e]*'An eye for an [f]eye and a tooth for a tooth.'*

39 "But I tell you not to resist an evil person. But whoever slaps you on your right cheek, turn the other to him also.

40 "If anyone wants to sue you and take away your tunic, let him have *your* cloak also.

41 "And whoever compels you to go one mile, go with him two.

42 [g]"Give to him who asks you, and from him who wants to borrow from you do not turn away.

Love of enemies enjoined
(Lk. 6:27–36)

43 "You have [h]heard that it was [d]said, [f]*'You shall love your neighbor* and hate your enemy.'

44 "But I say to you, love your enemies, [i]bless those who curse you, [j]do good to those who hate you, and [k]pray for those who spitefully use you and persecute you,*

45 "that you may be sons of your Father in heaven; for He [l]makes His sun rise on the evil and on the good, and sends rain on the just and on the unjust.

46 "For if you love those who love you, what reward have you? Do not even the [m]tax collectors do the same?

47 "And if you greet your brethren* only, what do you do more *than others*? Do not even the tax collectors* do so?

48 "Therefore you shall be [1]perfect, just as your Father in heaven is perfect.

Religious ostentation rebuked

6 "TAKE heed that you do not do your [2]charitable deeds before men, to be seen by them. Otherwise you have no [n]reward from your Father in heaven.

2 "Therefore, when you do a charitable deed, do not sound a trumpet before you as the hypocrites do in the synagogues and in the streets, that they may have glory from men. Assuredly, I say to you, they have their reward.

3 "But when you [o]do a charitable deed, do not let your left hand know what your right hand is doing,

4 "that your charitable deed may be in secret; and your Father who sees in secret will Himself [p]reward you openly.*

5 "And when you pray, you shall not be like the hypocrites. For they love to pray standing in the synagogues and on the corners of the streets, that they may be seen by men. Assuredly, I say to you, they have their reward.

6 "But you, when you pray, go into your room, and when you have shut your door, pray to your Father who *is* in the secret *place;* and your Father who sees in secret will reward you openly.*

7 "And when you pray, do not use [q]vain repetitions as the heathen *do.* For they think that they will be heard for their many words.

8 "Therefore do not be like them. For your Father [r]knows the things you have need of before you ask Him.

34
a Jas. 5:12; cp. Mt. 26:63; 2 Cor. 2:17; 1 Th. 2:5
35
b Mt. 5:3,19; 6:10
c Kingdom (NT): v. 35; Mt. 6:10. (Mt. 2:2; 1 Cor. 15:24, *note*)
38
d Inspiration: vv. 38, 43; Mt. 8:17. (Ex. 4:15; 2 Tim. 3:16, *note*)
e Ex. 21:24; Lev. 24:20; Dt. 19:21
f Law (of Moses): vv. 38,43; Mt. 7:12. (Ex. 19:1; Gal. 3:24, *note*)
42
g Dt. 15:7–11; Lk. 6:30–34; 1 Tim. 6:18
43
h Lev. 19:18; Dt. 23:3–6
44
i i.e. *pray for*
j Rom. 12:20
k Cp. Lk. 23:34; Acts 7:60
45
l Ps. 65:9–13; Lk. 12:16–17; Acts 14:17
46
m They were Jews employed by the Roman government

CHAPTER 6
1
n Rewards: vv. 1,4,6; Mt. 6:18. (Dan. 12:3; 1 Cor. 3:14, *note*)
3
o Cp. Mt. 8:4; Rom. 12:8
4
p Lk. 14:12–14; Phil. 4:19; 2 Tim. 1:16–18
7
q Cp. 1 Ki. 18:26,29; Mt. 26:39–44; Lk. 18:1–8
8
r Rom. 8:26–27

*
5:44 NU-Text omits three clauses from this verse, leaving, *"But I say to you, love your enemies and pray for those who persecute you."* 5:47 M-Text reads *friends.* • NU-Text reads *Gentiles.* 6:4 NU-Text omits *openly.* 6:6 NU-Text omits *openly.*

[1](5:48) The word implies full development, growth into maturity of godliness. See Phil. 3:12, *note;* cp. also 1 Jn. 1:8,10.

[2](6:1) The expression refers to religious externalities. Although others may observe these acts, this fact must not be the motive behind the deeds.

9
[a] Lk. 11:1–4; Jn. 16:24; Eph. 6:18; Jude 20
[b] *Bible prayers* (NT): vv. 9–13; Mt. 8:2. (Mt. 6:9; Lk. 11:2, *note*)
[c] Mt. 5:9,16
[d] Mal. 1:11

10
[e] *Kingdom* (NT): v. 10; Mt. 7:21. (Mt. 2:2; 1 Cor. 15:24, *note*)
[f] See Mt. 3:2, *note*

11
[g] Cp. Prov. 30:8–9

12
[h] *Forgiveness:* vv. 12, 14–15; Mt. 9:2. (Lev. 4:20; Mt. 26:28, *note*)
[i] i.e. *sin.* See Rom. 3:23, *note*

13
[j] *Test/tempt:* v. 13; Mt. 16:1. (Gen. 3:1; Jas. 1:14, *note*)
[k] Jn. 17:15; 2 Tim. 4:18; 2 Pet. 2:9

16
[l] Lk. 18:12; cp. Isa. 58:3–7

Instruction in praying
(cp. Lk. 11:1–4, where see note)

9 "In this [a]manner, therefore, [1b]pray:

[c]Our Father in heaven,
Hallowed be Your
[d]name.
10 Your [e]kingdom [f]come.
Your will be done
On earth as *it is* in
heaven.
11 Give us this day our
[g]daily bread.
12 And [h]forgive us our
[i]debts,
[2]As we forgive our
debtors.
13 And do not lead us into
[j]temptation,
But [k]deliver us from the
evil one.
[3]For Yours is the
kingdom and the
power and the glory
forever. Amen.*

14 "For if you forgive men their trespasses, your heavenly Father will also [h]forgive you.
15 "But if you do not forgive men their trespasses, neither will your Father forgive your trespasses.
16 "Moreover, when you [l]fast, do not be like the hypocrites, with a sad countenance. For they disfigure their faces that they may appear to men to be fasting. Assuredly, I say to you, they have their reward.
17 "But you, when you fast, anoint your head and wash your face,
18 "so that you do not appear to men to be fasting, but to your Father who *is* in the secret *place;* and your Father who sees in secret will [m]reward you openly.*

Treasure in heaven

19 "Do not lay up for yourselves [n]treasures on earth, where moth and rust destroy and where thieves break in and steal;
20 "but lay up for yourselves treasures in [o]heaven, where neither moth nor rust destroys and where thieves do not break in and steal.
21 "For where your treasure is, there your heart will be also.
22 "The lamp of the body is the eye. If therefore your eye is good, your whole body will be full of light.
23 "But if your eye is [p]bad, your whole body will be full of darkness. If therefore the light that is in you is darkness, how great *is* that darkness!
24 "No one can serve [q]two masters; for either he will hate the one and love the other, or else he will be loyal to the one and despise the other. You cannot serve God and mammon.

*6:13 NU-Text omits *For Yours* through *Amen.* 6:18 NU-Text and M-Text omit *openly.*

18
[m] *Rewards:* v. 18; Mt. 10:41. (Dan. 12:3; 1 Cor. 3:14, *note*)

19
[n] Prov. 23:4; 1 Tim. 6:6–11; Jas. 5:2

20
[o] Mt. 19:21; cp. Col. 3:1; 1 Tim. 6:19

23
[p] i.e. *defective*

24
[q] Lk. 16:13; cp. 1 Ki. 18:21; 2 Ki. 17:41; Gal. 1:10; Jas. 4:4; 1 Jn. 2:15; Rev. 3:15–16

[1](6:9) Verses 9–13 contain what is familiarly known as The Lord's Prayer. It is His prayer in that He is its author. It was intended to be a model prayer for the disciples: "In this manner, therefore, pray." See Lk. 11:2, *note.*

[2](6:12) The problem raised by the conditional nature of this petition for forgiveness may be explained as follows: In the fully developed doctrine of Christian salvation there are two areas of divine forgiveness. The first area is that of the forgiveness that comes to the sinner at the time of justification, and deals with the guilt of his sins in a total sense (Eph. 1:7). To this forgiveness there is attached but one condition, i.e. to receive it once for all by faith in Christ (Rom. 4:5–8). The second area of forgiveness covers the relation of the divine Father to those who have become His children and deals specifically with the matter of fellowship whenever it is broken by sin. To obtain such forgiveness we must confess and forsake the sin (1 Jn. 1:9; cp. Ps. 66:18 and Prov. 28:13). The forgiveness mentioned here in v. 12 belongs in this second area, because it occurs in a prayer given to disciples of Christ (5:2) who could call upon God as their Father (6:9,26). The ultimate motive for forgiving our debtors is based upon the grace of God, and appears later in the progress of revelation (Eph. 4:32; Col. 3:13).

[3](6:13) This doxology does not appear in the oldest Greek manuscripts, and, in those which do include it, there are variations. The account by Luke omits it altogether (Lk. 11:2–4). Many eminent textual authorities believe that it was added by later hands, perhaps to make the prayer more suitable for public worship. The doxology, however, is biblical, for its main ideas seem clearly to parallel a prayer of David recorded in 1 Chr. 29:11—"Yours, O LORD, is . . . the power and the glory . . . [and] the kingdom." Moreover, the majority of Gk. manuscripts do contain the doxology.

The cure for care

25 "Therefore I say to you, [a]do not worry about your life, what you will eat or what you will drink; nor about your body, what you will put on. Is not life more than food and the body more than clothing?

26 "Look at the birds of the air, for they neither sow nor reap nor gather into barns; yet your heavenly Father feeds them. Are you not of more value than they?

27 "Which of you by worrying can add one [b]cubit to his stature?

28 "So why do you worry about clothing? Consider the lilies of the field, how they grow: they neither toil nor spin;

29 "and yet I say to you that even [c]Solomon in all his glory was not arrayed like one of these.

30 "Now if God so clothes the grass of the field, which today is, and tomorrow is thrown into the oven, *will He* not much more *clothe* you, O you of little faith?

31 "Therefore do not worry, saying, 'What shall we eat?' or 'What shall we drink?' or 'What shall we wear?'

32 "For after all these things the Gentiles seek. For your heavenly Father [d]knows that you need all these things.

33 "But seek first the kingdom of [1]God and His [e]righteousness, and all these things shall be added to you.

34 [f]"Therefore do not worry about tomorrow, for tomorrow will worry about its own things. Sufficient for the day *is* its own trouble.

25
a v. 31; Lk. 12:22–31; Phil. 3:18–19; 4:6–7; Heb. 13:5–6
27
b See Weights and Measures (NT), Acts 27:28, *note*
29
c Cp. 1 Ki. 10
32
d v. 8; Phil. 4:19; cp. Ex. 3:7–8; Dt. 2:7; Ps. 103:14
33
e Righteousness (garment): v. 33; Rom. 2:7. (Gen. 3:21; Rev. 19:8)
34
f Jas. 4:13,14

Unjust criticism forbidden
(Lk. 6:37–42)

7 [g]"JUDGE not, that you be not judged.

2 "For with what judgment you judge, you will be judged; and with the [h]measure you use, it will be measured back to you.

3 "And why do you look at the [i]speck in your brother's eye, but do not consider the plank in your own eye?

4 "Or how can you say to your brother, 'Let me remove the speck from your eye'; and look, a plank *is* in your own eye?

5 "Hypocrite! First remove the plank from your own eye, and then you will see clearly to remove the speck from your brother's eye.

6 "Do not give what is [j]holy to the [k]dogs; nor cast your pearls before swine, lest they trample them under their [l]feet, and turn and tear you in pieces.

Encouragement to pray
(see Lk. 11:2, note)

7 "Ask, and it will be [m]given to you; seek, and you will find; knock, and it will be opened to you.

8 "For everyone who asks receives, and he who seeks finds, and to him who knocks it will be opened.

9 "Or what man is there among you who, if his son asks for bread, will give him a stone?

10 "Or if he asks for a fish, will he give him a serpent?

11 "If you then, being evil, know how to give [n]good gifts to your children, how much more will your Father who is in heaven give good things to those who ask Him!

CHAPTER 7
1
g Rom. 14:4, 10,13; 1 Cor. 4:3–5; 5:12
2
h Mk. 4:24–25; 2 Cor. 9:6
3
i Rom. 2:1; cp. 1 Cor. 10:12; Gal. 6:1
6
j Sanctification (NT): v. 6; Mt. 23:17. (Mt. 4:5; Rev. 22:11)
k Cp. Mt. 15:26
l Cp. Heb. 10:29
7
m Mt. 21:22; Mk. 11:24; Lk. 11:9–13; 18:1–8; Jn. 15:7; Jas. 1:5; 1 Jn. 3:22
11
n Ps. 84:11; Isa. 63:7; Rom. 8:32; Jas. 1:17; 1 Jn. 3:1

[1](6:33) The expression, "the kingdom of God" (Mt. 12:28), although used in many cases as synonymous with the kingdom of heaven, is to be distinguished from it in some instances (see Mt. 3:2, *note*): (1) The kingdom of God is at times viewed as everlasting and universal, i.e. the rule of the sovereign God over all creatures and things (Ps. 103:19; Dan. 4:3). In this sense the kingdom of God includes the kingdom of heaven. (2) The kingdom of God is also used to designate the sphere of salvation entered only by the new birth (Jn. 3:5–7) in contrast with the kingdom of heaven as the sphere of profession which may be real or false (see Mt. 13:3, *note;* 25:1,11–12). And (3) since the kingdom of heaven is in the earthly sphere of the universal kingdom of God, the two have many things in common and in some contexts the terms are interchangeable.

Like the kingdom of heaven, the kingdom of God is realized in the rule of God in the present age and will also be fulfilled in the future millennial kingdom. It continues forever in the eternal state (cp. Dan. 4:3).

The golden rule
(Lk. 6:31; cp. Eph. 4:32)

12 "Therefore, whatever you want men to do to you, do also to them, for this is the [a]Law and the [b]Prophets.

Two ways contrasted (cp. Ps. 1)

13 "Enter by the [c]narrow gate; for wide *is* the gate and broad *is* the way that leads to destruction, and there are many who go in by it.

14 "Because* narrow *is* the gate and difficult *is* the way which leads to [d]life, and there are few who find it.

False and true teachers
(Lk. 6:43–45)

15 "Beware of [e]false prophets, who come to you in sheep's clothing, but inwardly they are ravenous wolves.

16 "You will know them by their fruits. Do men gather grapes from thornbushes or [f]figs from thistles?

17 "Even so, every good tree bears good fruit, but a bad tree bears bad fruit.

18 "A good tree cannot bear bad fruit, nor *can* a bad tree bear good fruit.

19 "Every tree that does not bear good fruit is [g]cut down and thrown into the fire.

20 "Therefore by their fruits you will know them.

False profession (Lk. 6:46)

21 "Not everyone who [h]says to Me, 'Lord, Lord,' shall enter the [i]kingdom of heaven, but he who [j]does the will of My Father in heaven.

22 "Many will say to Me in that day, 'Lord, Lord, have we not prophesied in Your name, cast out [1]demons in Your name, and done many wonders in Your name?'

23 "And then I will declare to them, 'I never knew you; [k]depart from Me, you who [l]practice lawlessness!'

Parable of two builders
and two foundations (Lk. 6:47–49)

24 "Therefore whoever hears these sayings of Mine, and does them, I will [m]liken him to a wise man who built his house on the [n]rock:

25 "and the rain descended, the floods came, and the winds blew and beat on that house; and it did not fall, for it was founded on the rock.

26 "But everyone who hears these sayings of Mine, and does not do them, will be like a foolish man who built his house on the sand:

27 "and the rain descended, the floods came, and the winds blew and beat on that house;

*7:14 NU-Text and M-Text read *How . . . !*

12
a Law (of Moses): v. 12; Mt. 8:4. (Ex. 19:1; Gal. 3:24, *note*)
b See Lk. 2:25, *note*

13
c Mk. 10:23–27; Lk. 13:24; Jn. 10:7,9

14
d Life (eternal): v. 14; Mt. 18:8. (Mt. 7:14; Rev. 22:19)

15
e Jer. 23:16; Ezek. 22:28; Mk. 13:22; Lk. 6:26; 2 Pet. 2:1; 1 Jn. 4:1; cp. Dt. 13:1–5; Rev. 13:11–17; 19:20

16
f Jas. 3:12

19
g Mt. 3:10; Lk. 13:6–9; Jn. 15:2,6; cp. Mt. 25:41–46

21
h Lk. 13:25; cp. Isa. 29:13; 2 Tim. 3:5; Ti. 1:16
i Kingdom (NT): vv. 21–23; Mt. 8:11. (Mt. 2:2; 1 Cor. 15:24, *note*). See Mt. 3:2, *note*
j Rom. 2:13; Jas. 1:22–25

23
k Judgments (the seven): v. 23; Mt. 13:40. (1 Sam. 7:14; Rev. 20:12, *note*)
l See Rom. 3:23, *note*

24
m Parables (NT): vv. 24–27; Mt. 9:16. (Mt. 5:13; Lk. 21:29)
n Christ (Rock): vv. 24–25; Mt. 16:18. (Gen. 49:24; 1 Pet. 2:8)

[1](7:22) The Greek *daimonia* means "demons," never "devils." There is only one devil (Gk. *diabolos*), i.e. Satan.

To the reality and personality of demons the NT Scriptures bear abundant testimony. As to their origin, nothing is clearly revealed, but they are not to be confused with the angels mentioned in 2 Pet. 2:4; Jude 6. Summary: (1) Demons are spirits (Mt. 12:43,45), Satan's emissaries (Mt. 12:26–27), and so numerous as to make Satan's power practically ubiquitous (Mk. 5:9). (2) They are capable of entering and controlling both men and animals (Mk. 5:2–5,11–13), and earnestly seek embodiment, without which, apparently, they are powerless for evil (Mt. 12:43–44; Mk. 5:10–12). (3) Demon influence and demon possession are discriminated in the NT. Instances of the latter are Mt. 4:24; 8:16,28,33; 9:32; 12:22; Mk. 1:32; 5:15–16,18; Lk. 8:36; Acts 8:7; 16:16. (4) Demons are unclean, sullen, violent and malicious (Mt. 8:28; 9:33; 10:1; 12:43; Mk. 1:23; 5:3–5; 9:17,20; Lk. 6:18; 9:39). (5) They know Jesus Christ as Most High God and recognize His supreme authority (Mt. 8:31–32; Mk. 1:23–24; Acts 19:15; Jas. 2:19). (6) They know their eternal fate to be one of torment (Mt. 8:29; Lk. 8:31). (7) They inflict physical maladies (Mt. 12:22; 17:15–18; Lk. 13:16). However, mental disease is to be distinguished from the disorder of mind due to demonic control. (8) Demon influence may manifest itself in religious asceticism (1 Tim. 4:1–3), degenerating into uncleanness. (9) The sign of demon influence in religion is departure from the faith, i.e. the body of revealed truth in the Scriptures (1 Tim. 4:1). (10) The demons maintain a conflict with Christians who would be spiritual (Eph. 6:12; 1 Tim. 4:1–3). The Christian's resources are prayer and bodily control (Mt. 17:21), "the whole armor of God" (Eph. 6:13–18). (11) All unbelievers are open to demon possession (Eph. 2:2). (12) Exorcism in the name of Jesus Christ (Acts 16:18) was practiced for demon possession. And (13) one of the awful features of the apocalyptic judgments in which this age will end is an emergence of demons out of the bottomless pit (Rev. 9:1–11,20).

and it fell. And great was its fall."

Effect of sermon on hearers

28 And so it was, when Jesus had ended these sayings, that the people were astonished at His [a]teaching,

29 for He taught them as one having authority, and not as the scribes.

III. The Authority of the King Manifested and Rejected, 8—12

Jesus cleanses a leper
(Mk. 1:40–45; Lk. 5:12–14)

8 WHEN He had come down from the mountain, great multitudes followed Him.

2 And [1]behold, a [b]leper came and [c]worshiped Him, [d]saying, [2]"Lord, if You are willing, You can make me clean."

3 Then Jesus put out *His* hand and touched him, saying, "I am willing; be cleansed." Immediately his leprosy [e]was [f]cleansed.

4 And Jesus said to him, "See that you tell no one; but go your way, show yourself to the priest, and offer the [g]gift that [h]Moses [i]commanded, as a testimony to them."

Jesus heals a centurion's servant
(Lk. 7:1–10)

5 Now when Jesus had entered Capernaum, a [3j]centurion came to Him, pleading with Him,

6 saying, "Lord, my servant is lying at home paralyzed, dreadfully tormented."

7 And Jesus said to him, "I will come and heal him."

8 The centurion answered and said, "Lord, I am not worthy that You should come under my roof. But only speak a word, and my servant will be healed.

9 "For I also am a man under [k]authority, having soldiers under me. And I say to this *one*, 'Go,' and he goes; and to another, 'Come,' and he comes; and to my servant, 'Do this,' and he does *it*."

10 When Jesus heard *it*, He [l]marveled, and said to those who followed, "Assuredly, I say to you, I have not found such great [m]faith, not even in Israel!

11 "And I say to you that many will come from east and west, and sit down with Abraham, Isaac, and Jacob in the [n]kingdom of heaven.

12 "But the sons of the kingdom will be cast out into outer darkness. There will be weeping and gnashing of [o]teeth."

13 Then Jesus said to the centurion, "Go your way; and [p]as you have [m]believed, *so* let it be done for you." And his servant was [q]healed that same hour.

Peter's mother-in-law healed
(Mk. 1:29–34; Lk. 4:38–41)

14 Now when Jesus had come into Peter's house, He saw his wife's mother lying sick with a fever.

15 So He [r]touched her hand, and the [s]fever [q]left her. And she arose and [t]served them.*

16 When evening had come, they brought to Him many who were [u]demon-possessed. And He [v]cast out the spirits with a word, and healed all who were sick,

17 that it might be fulfilled

* 8:15 NU-Text and M-Text read *Him*.

28
a Mt. 13:54; Mk. 1:22; Lk. 4:32

CHAPTER 8

2
b Lev. 13:1–46; cp. Num. 12:10–15; 2 Ki. 5:1–14, 20–27; 15:5; 2 Chr. 26:16–19; see Ex. 4:6 and Lev. 13:2, *notes*
c Mt. 2:11; 9:18; 15:25; Jn. 9:38
d Bible prayers (NT): v. 2; Mt. 8:25. (Mt. 6:9; Lk. 11:2, *note*)

3
e Mt. 11:5; Lk. 4:27
f Miracles (NT): vv. 2–3, 5–17; Mt. 8:26. (Mt. 8:3; Acts 28:8, *note*)

4
g Lev. 14:4–32; Dt. 24:8; Mk. 1:44; Lk. 5:14; cp. Mt. 5:17 with Rom. 3:21
h Law (of Moses): v. 4; Mt. 11:13. (Ex. 19:1; Gal. 3:24, *note*)
i Lev. 14:4–32; Dt. 24:8. Contrast Rom. 3:21 with Mt. 5:17

5
j Mt. 27:54; Acts 10:1; see Acts 27:1, *note*

9
k Cp. Mk. 1:27; Lk. 9:1

10
l Cp. Mt. 15:21–28
m Faith: vv. 10,13; Mt. 9:2. (Gen. 3:20; Heb. 11:39, *note*)

11
n Kingdom (NT): vv. 11–12; Mt. 9:35. (Mt. 2:2; 1 Cor. 15:24, *note*)

12
o Lk. 13:28

13
p Cp. Mt. 9:22,29; Lk. 7:50; 8:48, 50
q Miracles (NT): vv. 2–3, 5–17; Mt. 8:26. (Mt. 8:3; Acts 28:8, *note*)

15
r Cp. v. 3
s Cp. Jn. 4:52
t Cp. Lk. 8:2–3

16
u See Mt. 7:22, *note*
v See Mk. 3:15, *note*

---

[1](8:2) In chs. 5—7 the King declares the principles of the kingdom; in chs. 8—9 He gives proof of His power to banish from the earth the consequences of sin and to control the elements of nature.

[2](8:2) Greek *Kurios.* This is the first occurrence of the word, as applied to Jesus, with His evident sanction. In itself the word means *master,* and is so used of human relationships in, e.g. Mt. 6:24; 15:27; Mk. 13:35; Eph. 6:9. But the general use of the word in the NT is as a divine title (over 650 times), translated either "Lord" or "Master." Both uses, divine and human, are brought together in Eph. 6:9 and Col. 4:1. It is the Greek equivalent of the Heb. *Adonai* (see Gen. 15:2, *note*), but it is also used in the NT to translate the Heb. *Jehovah* (LORD; see Ex. 34:6, *note*), e.g. Mt. 1:20,22; 2:15; 3:3; 4:7,10; 11:25; 21:9; Mk. 12:29–30; Lk. 1:68; 2:9. Both of these OT titles of Deity are rendered by *Kurios* in one sentence (Mt. 22:44). Our Lord used it of His Father (Mt. 4:7,10; etc.). But the most frequent use of *Kurios* is as a divine title of Jesus. That the intent is to identify Jesus Christ with the OT Deity is evident from Mt. 3:3; 12:8; 21:9 (Ps. 118:26); 22:43–45 (Ps. 110); Lk. 1:43; Jn. 14:8–10; 20:28; Acts 9:5 (Ps. 2). See Jn. 20:28, *note.*

[3](8:5) In the Roman army a centurion was a captain over one hundred men.

which was [a]spoken by Isaiah the prophet, saying:

"He Himself [b]took our infirmities
And bore our sicknesses."

Discipleship tested (Lk. 9:57–62)

18 And when Jesus saw great multitudes about Him, He gave a command to depart to the other side.

19 Then a certain scribe came and said to Him, "Teacher, I will follow You wherever You [c]go."

20 And Jesus [d]said to him, "Foxes have holes and birds of the air *have* nests, but the [1]Son of Man has nowhere to lay *His* head."

21 Then another of His disciples said to Him, "Lord, let me first go and bury my [e]father."

22 But Jesus said to him, "Follow Me, and let the [f]dead bury their own dead."

Jesus stills winds and waves (Mk. 4:36–41; Lk. 8:22–25)

23 Now when He got into a boat, His disciples followed Him.

24 And suddenly a great tempest arose on the sea, so that the boat was covered with the waves. But He was asleep.

25 Then His disciples came to *Him* and awoke Him, [g]saying, "Lord, save us! We are perishing!"

26 But He said to them, [h]"Why are you fearful, O you of [i]little faith?" Then He arose and rebuked the winds and the sea, and there was a great [j]calm.

27 So the men marveled, saying, "Who can this be, that even the winds and the sea obey Him?"

Jesus casts out demons at Gergesa (Mk. 5:1–21; Lk. 8:26–40)

28 When He had come to the other side, to the country of the Gergesenes,* there met Him two [k]demon-possessed *men*, coming out of the tombs, exceedingly fierce, so that no one could pass that way.

29 And suddenly they cried out, saying, [l]"What have we to do with You, Jesus, You Son of God? Have You come here to [m]torment us before the [n]time?"

30 Now a good way off from them there was a herd of many swine feeding.

31 So the [k]demons begged Him, saying, "If You cast us out, permit us to go away* into the [o]herd of swine."

32 And He said to them, "Go." So when they had [p]come out, they went into the herd of swine. And suddenly the whole herd of swine ran violently down the steep place into the sea, and perished in the water.

33 Then those who kept *them* fled; and they went away into the city and told everything, including what *had happened* to the [k]demon-possessed *men*.

34 And behold, the whole city came out to meet Jesus. And when they saw Him, they begged *Him* to [q]depart from their region.

*8:28 NU-Text reads *Gadarenes*.
8:31 NU-Text reads *send us*.

17
a *Inspiration*: v. 17; Mt. 10:14. (Ex. 4:15; 2 Tim. 3:16, *note*). Isa. 53:4; cp. Mt. 1:22–23
b Cp. 2 Cor. 5:21; 1 Pet. 2:24
19
c Cp. Mt. 26:24
20
d Cp. Lk. 2:7; 1 Cor. 4:11
21
e Cp. 1 Ki. 19:20
22
f *Death* (spiritual): v. 22; Lk. 9:60. (Gen. 2:17; Eph. 2:5, *note*)
25
g *Bible prayers* (NT): v. 25; Mt. 9:18. (Mt. 6:9; Lk. 11:2, *note*)
26
h Cp. Isa. 44:8
i Cp. Mt. 17:20; Mk. 16:17–18
j *Miracles* (NT): vv. 24–32; Mt. 9:7. (Mt. 8:3; Acts 28:8, *note*). Cp. Ps. 107:23–35
28
k See Mt. 7:22, *note*
29
l Mk. 1:24; cp. 1 Ki. 17:18; Acts 24:25; 2 Cor. 6:14
m Cp. Mt. 25:41 with Rev. 19:20
n Cp. 2 Pet. 2:4
31
o Cp. Mt. 7:6; Lk. 15:15–16
32
p *Miracles* (NT): vv. 24–32; Mt. 9:7. (Mt. 8:3; Acts 28:8, *note*)
34
q v. 29; cp. Amos 7:12; Lk. 4:29; Acts 16:39

1(8:20) The name "Son of Man" is based on the great Messianic passage in Dan. 7:13. Cp. Mt. 16:28; 19:28; 25:31; 26:64; Mk. 14:62; Lk. 22:69. Our Lord uses this term about eighty times to refer to Himself. It is His name as the representative Man, in the sense of 1 Cor. 15:45–47, as Son of David is distinctively His Jewish name, and Son of God His divine name. Our Lord constantly uses this term as implying that His mission (e.g. Mt. 11:19; Lk. 19:10), His death and resurrection (e.g. Mt. 12:40; 20:18; 26:2), and His second coming (e.g. Mt. 24:37–44; Lk. 12:40) transcend in scope and result all merely Jewish limitations. When Nathanael confesses Him as "King of Israel," our Lord's answer is, "You will see greater things . . . the angels of God ascending and descending upon the Son of Man" (Jn. 1:50–51). When His messengers are cast out by the Jews, His thought leaps forward to the time when the Son of Man comes again to the human race (cp. Mt. 10:5–6 with v. 23). It is in this name also that universal judgment is committed to Him (Jn. 5:22,27). It is also a name indicating that in Him is fulfilled the OT foreview of blessing through a coming Man (see Gen. 1:26, *note 2*; 3:15; 12:3; Ps. 8:4; 80:17; Isa. 7:14; 9:6–7; 32:2).

Paralytic man healed
(Mk. 2:3–12; Lk. 5:18–26)

9 SO He got into a boat, crossed over, and came to His [a]own city.

2 Then behold, they brought to Him a paralytic lying on a bed. When Jesus saw their [b]faith, He said to the paralytic, "Son, be of good cheer; your sins are [c]forgiven you."

3 And at once some of the [d]scribes said within themselves, "This Man [e]blasphemes!"

4 But Jesus, knowing their thoughts, said, "Why do you think evil in your hearts?

5 "For which is easier, to [f]say, '*Your* [g]sins are [c]forgiven you,' or to say, 'Arise and walk'?

6 "But that you may [h]know that the [i]Son of Man has [j]power on earth to [c]forgive [g]sins"—then He said to the paralytic, "Arise, take up your bed, and go to your house."

7 And he [k]arose and departed to his house.

8 Now when the multitudes saw *it*, they [l]marveled* and glorified God, who had given such power to men.

Call of Matthew (Levi)
(Mk. 2:14; Lk. 5:27–29)

9 As Jesus passed on from there, He saw a man named Matthew sitting at the tax office. And He said to him, [m]"Follow Me." So he arose and followed Him.

Jesus answers the Pharisees
(Mk. 2:15–20; Lk. 5:29–35)

10 Now it happened, as Jesus sat at the table in the house, *that* behold, many tax collectors and sinners came and sat down with Him and His disciples.

11 And when the [n]Pharisees saw *it*, they [o]said to His disciples, "Why does your Teacher eat with tax collectors and [g]sinners?"

12 When Jesus heard *that*, He said to them, "Those who are [p]well have no need of a physician, but those who are sick.

13 "But go and learn what *this* means: [q]'*I desire mercy and not sacrifice.*' For I did not come to call the [r]righteous, but [g]sinners, to [s]repentance."*

14 Then the disciples of John came to Him, saying, "Why do we and the [t]Pharisees fast [u]often,* but Your disciples do not fast?"

15 And Jesus said to them, "Can the friends of the bridegroom mourn as long as the bridegroom is with them? But the days will come when the bridegroom will be taken away from them, and then they will fast.

Parable of the cloth and wineskins
(Mk. 2:21–22; Lk. 5:36–39)

16 "No one puts a piece of unshrunk [v]cloth on an old garment; for the patch pulls away from the garment, and the tear is made worse.

17 "Nor do they put new wine into old wineskins, or else the wineskins break, the wine is spilled, and the wineskins are ruined. But they put new wine into new wineskins, and both are [w]preserved."

Two miracles of healing
(Mk. 5:21–43; Lk. 8:40–56)

18 While He spoke these things to them, behold, a ruler came and worshiped Him, [x]saying, "My daughter has just died, but come and lay Your hand on her and she will live."

19 So Jesus arose and followed him, and so *did* His [y]disciples.

20 And suddenly, a woman who had a [z]flow of blood for twelve years came from behind and [aa]touched the hem of His [bb]garment.

21 For she [x]said to herself, "If only I may touch His garment, I shall be made [cc]well."

22 But Jesus turned around, and when He saw her He said, "Be of good cheer, daughter; your [b]faith has [k]made you [cc]well." And the woman was made well from that hour.

23 When Jesus came into the ruler's house, and saw the flute

*
9:8 NU-Text reads *were afraid.*
9:13 NU-Text omits *to repentance.*
9:14 NU-Text brackets *often* as disputed.

CHAPTER 9

1
a Mt. 4:13; 11:23

2
b Faith: vv. 2, 22; Mt. 9:29. (Gen. 3:20; Heb. 11:39, *note*)
c Forgiveness: vv. 2, 5–6; Mt. 12:31. (Lev. 4:20; Mt. 26:28, *note*)

3
d See Mt. 2:4, *note*
e Cp. Mk. 3:28–30

5
f Cp. Mk. 1:27; Lk. 7:41–50
g See Rom. 3:23, *note*

6
h Cp. 1 Jn. 5:20
i See Mt. 8:20, *note*
j Or *authority.* Jn. 3:35; 5:27; cp. Acts 4:7–12

7
k Miracles (NT): vv. 2–7, 18–25; Mt. 9:30. (Mt. 8:3; Acts 28:8, *note*)

8
l Mt. 8:27; Jn. 7:15; cp. Acts 5:11

9
m Cp. Mt. 4:18–22

11
n Cp. Lk. 7:36–39; see Mt. 3:7, *note*
o Mt. 11:19; Lk. 5:30; 15:2; 19:7

12
p Lk. 18:9–14; Jn. 9:39–41

13
q Hos. 6:6; Mt. 12:7
r See Rom. 10:10, *note*
s Repentance: v. 13; Mt. 11:20. (Mt. 3:2; Acts 17:30, *note*)

14
t See Mt. 3:7, *note*
u Mt. 11:18

16
v Parables (NT): vv. 16–17; Mt. 13:3. (Mt. 5:13; Lk. 21:29)

17
w Cp. Jn. 1:17

18
x Bible prayers (NT): vv. 18, 21; Mt. 9:27. (Mt. 6:9; Lk. 11:2, *note*)

19
y Mt. 10:2–4

20
z Lev. 15:19–33; cp. Lev. 18:19; 20:18
aa Mt. 5:27; Lk. 8:43–44; cp. Mt. 8:3
bb Mt. 14:36; Mk. 6:56

21
cc See Lk. 7:44, *note*

players and the noisy crowd
wailing,
24 He said to them, "Make
room, for the girl is not dead,
but sleeping." And they ridiculed Him.
25 But when the crowd was
put outside, He went in and
[a]took her by the hand, and the
girl [b]arose.
26 And the [c]report of this
went out into all that land.

Two blind men
and a demoniac healed

27 When Jesus departed
from there, [d]two blind men followed Him, crying out and
[e]saying, [f]"Son of David, have
mercy on us!"
28 And when He had come
into the house, the blind men
came to Him. And Jesus said to
them, "Do you believe that I am
able to do this?" They said to
Him, "Yes, Lord."
29 Then He touched their
eyes, saying, "According to
your [g]faith let it be to you."
30 And their eyes were
[h]opened. And Jesus sternly
warned them, saying, "See *that*
no one knows *it*."
31 But when they had de-
parted, they spread the [c]news
about Him in all that country.
32 As they went out, behold,
they brought to Him a man,
mute and [i]demon-possessed.
33 And when the demon
[h]was cast out, the mute spoke.
And the multitudes marveled,
saying, "It was never seen like
this in Israel!"
34 But the [j]Pharisees said,
"He casts out [i]demons by the
ruler of the demons."
35 Then Jesus went about all
the cities and villages, teaching
in their synagogues, preaching
the [k]gospel of the [l]kingdom,
and healing every sickness and
every disease among the [m]peo-
ple.*

Jesus' compassion
for the multitudes (Mk. 6:5–6)

36 But when He saw the multitudes, He was moved with
compassion for them, because
they were weary* and scattered, like sheep having no
shepherd.
37 Then He said to His disciples, "The harvest truly *is* plentiful, but the laborers *are* few.
38 "Therefore pray the Lord
of the harvest to [n]send out laborers into His harvest."

The twelve apostles sent forth
(Mk. 6:7–13; Lk. 9:1–6)

10 AND when He had
called His twelve disci-
ples to *Him*, He gave them
[o]power *over* unclean spirits, to
cast them out, and to heal all
kinds of sickness and all kinds
of disease.
2 Now the names of the
twelve [1]apostles are these: first,
Simon, who is called Peter, and

25
a Mt. 8:3,15; Mk. 1:31; cp. Eph. 2:4–7
b Resurrection: vv. 23–25; Mt. 10:8. (2 Ki. 4:35; 1 Cor. 15:52, *note*)
26
c Mt. 4:24
27
d Mt. 20:29–34
e Bible prayers (NT): v. 27; Mt. 11:25. (Mt. 6:9; Lk. 11:2, *note*)
f Mt. 15:22; Lk. 18:38,39
29
g Faith: v. 29; Mt. 15:28. (Gen. 3:20; Heb. 11:39, *note*)
30
h Miracles (NT): vv. 27–30, 32–35; Mt. 11:5. (Mt. 8:3; Acts 28:8, *note*)
32
i See Mt. 7:22, *note*
34
j See Mt. 3:7, *note*
35
k Gospel: v. 35; Mt. 10:7. (Gen. 12:3; Rev. 14:6)
l Kingdom (NT): v. 35; Mt. 10:7. (Mt. 2:2; 1 Cor. 15:24, *note*)
m Mt. 4:23; see Mk. 3:15, *note*
38
n Mt. 28:19–20; Eph. 4:11–12; cp. Acts 13:2–21:8
CHAPTER 10
1
o Lk. 10:17

*
9:35 NU-Text omits *among the people.*
9:36 NU-Text and M-Text read *harassed.*

[1](10:2) The word "apostle" (Gk. *apostolos)* means *a messenger, one sent forth with orders.* It is used concerning our Lord Himself (Heb. 3:1). Elsewhere it is used of the twelve, who were called to that office by our Lord during His earthly ministry; of Paul, called to the apostleship by the risen and ascended Lord; of Barnabas (Acts 14:14), specially designated by the Holy Spirit (Acts 13:2); and of Matthias, chosen by lot to take the place of Judas Iscariot (Acts 1:15–26). Although Matthias is never actually referred to as an apostle, it is said of him: "And he was numbered with the eleven apostles."

The "signs of an apostle" were: (1) They were chosen directly by the Lord Himself or, as in the case of Barnabas, by the Holy Spirit (Mt. 10:1–2; Mk. 3:13–14; Lk. 6:13; Acts 9:6,15; 13:2; 22:10,14–15; Rom. 1:1). (2) They were endued with sign-gifts, miraculous powers which were the divine credentials of their office (Mt. 10:1; Acts 5:15–16; 16:16–18; 28:8–9). (3) Their relation to the kingdom was that of heralds, announcing, to Israel only (Mt. 10:5–6), the kingdom as at hand (see Mt. 4:17, *note 4*), and manifesting kingdom powers (Mt. 10:7–8). (4) Our Lord delegated, first to Peter (Mt. 16:19) and then to the remainder of the apostolate (Mt. 18:18; Jn. 20:21–23) on behalf of all Christians, the authority to deal with men's sins through the Gospel, under the figure of "the keys of the kingdom." (5) The apostles' future relation to the kingdom will be that of judges over the twelve tribes (Mt. 19:28). (6) Consequent upon the rejection of the kingdom and the revelation of the mystery hidden in God (Mt. 16:18; Eph. 3:1–12), the Church, the apostolic office was invested with a new endowment, the baptism with the Holy Spirit (Acts 2:1–4); a new power, that of imparting the Spirit to Jewish believers in Christ; a new relation, that of foundation stones of the new temple (Eph. 2:20–22); and a

Andrew his brother; [a]James the
son of Zebedee, and John his
brother;
3 Philip and Bartholomew;
Thomas and Matthew the tax
collector; James the *son* of Alphaeus, and Lebbaeus, whose
surname was* Thaddaeus;
4 Simon the Cananite,* and
Judas Iscariot, who also betrayed Him.
5 These twelve Jesus sent
out and commanded them, saying: "Do not go into the way of
the [1]Gentiles, and do not enter a
city of the Samaritans.
6 "But go rather to the [b]lost
sheep of the house of Israel.
7 "And as you go, [c]preach,
saying, 'The [d]kingdom of
heaven is [e]at hand.'
8 "Heal the sick, cleanse the
lepers, [f]raise the dead,* cast
out [g]demons. Freely you have
received, freely give.
9 "Provide neither [h]gold
nor [h]silver nor copper in your
money belts,
10 "nor bag for *your* journey,
nor two tunics, nor sandals, nor
staffs; for a [i]worker is worthy
of his food.
11 "Now whatever city or
town you enter, inquire who in
it is worthy, and stay there till
you go out.
12 "And when you go into a
household, greet it.
13 "If the household is worthy, let your peace come upon it.
But if it is not worthy, let your
peace return to you.
14 "And whoever will not receive you nor hear your [j]words,
when you depart from that
house or city, [k]shake off the
dust from your feet.
15 "Assuredly, I say to you, it
will be more [l]tolerable for the
land of Sodom and Gomorrah
in the [m]day of judgment than for
that city!

The Gospel of the kingdom
to be proclaimed
before Christ's return (vv. 7,23)

16 "Behold, I [2]send you out as
[n]sheep in the midst of wolves.
Therefore be wise as [o]serpents
and harmless as [p]doves.
17 "But beware of men, for
they will deliver you up to councils and scourge you in their
synagogues.
18 "You will be brought before governors and kings for
My sake, as a testimony to them
and to the Gentiles.
19 "But when they deliver
you up, [q]do not worry about
how or what you should speak.
For it will [r]be given to you in
that hour what you should
speak;
20 "for it is not you who
speak, but the [s]Spirit of your
Father who speaks in you.
21 "Now brother will deliver
up brother to death, and a father
his child; and children will rise
up against parents and cause
them to be put to death.
22 "And you will be hated by

*
10:3 NU-Text omits *Lebbaeus, whose surname was.* **10:4** NU-Text reads *Cananaean.* **10:8** NU-Text reads *raise the dead, cleanse the lepers;* M-Text omits *raise the dead.*

2
a See Mt. 4:21, *note*
6
b Gk. *apollumi.* Jer. 50:6; see Jn. 3:16, *note 3*
7
c Gospel: v. 7; Mt. 11:5. (Gen. 12:3; Rev. 14:6)
d Kingdom (NT): v. 7; Mt. 11:11. (Mt. 2:2; 1 Cor. 15:24, *note*)
e See Mt. 4:17, *note*
8
f Resurrection: v. 8; Mt. 17:3. (2 Ki. 4:35; 1 Cor. 15:52, *note*)
g See Mt. 7:22, *note*
9
h See Coinage (NT), Mt. 5:26, *note*
10
i Lk. 10:7; 1 Cor. 9:4–14
14
j Inspiration: v. 14; Mt. 11:10. (Ex. 4:15; 2 Tim. 3:16, *note*)
k Lk. 10:10–11
15
l Mt. 11:22
m Day (of judgment): v. 15; Mt. 11:22. (Mt. 10:15; Rev. 20:11)
16
n Lk. 10:3; cp. Mt. 7:15
o Cp. 2 Cor. 12:16; Eph. 5:15; Col. 4:5
p Cp. Phil. 2:14–16
19
q Cp. Mt. 6:25,31,34
r Mk. 13:11; Lk. 12:11–12; 21:14–15
20
s Holy Spirit (NT): v. 20; Mt. 12:18. (Mt. 1:18; Acts 2:4, *note*). Cp. 2 Sam. 23:2; Acts 4:5–12; 6:10

new function, that of preaching the glad tidings of salvation, through the crucified and risen Lord, to Jew and Gentile alike. And (7) it is implied that an apostle was one who was an eyewitness of the resurrection of Christ (Acts 1:22; 1 Cor. 9:1), i.e. he must have seen the risen Lord. There is no NT record that Barnabas, called an apostle in Acts 14:14, saw Christ after His resurrection, but if such a qualification was implicit in apostleship, he must have been such an eyewitness.

[1](10:5) The instructions for this mission differ from the Great Commission given just before our Lord's ascension. (1) Here the mission is to Israel only, avoiding Gentiles and Samaritans, whereas the Great Commission sends the disciples "into all the world" (Mt. 28:16–20; Mk. 16:15–18; Lk. 24:46–48; Acts 1:8). And (2) here the twelve, being heralds of Israel's King, are to depend upon the hospitality of each village that they enter (vv. 9–14), whereas at the end of His ministry Christ commands those who are to preach the Gospel in His absence to do the opposite (Lk. 22:35–36). See also the practice implied in 3 Jn. 7.

[2](10:16) The scope of vv. 16–23 reaches beyond the personal ministry of the twelve. They cover not only the sphere of service in a general sense during this age, but the words of v. 23 make it apparent that they have in view particularly the preaching of the remnant (Isa. 1:9; see Rom. 11:5, *note*) in the tribulation (Ps. 2:5; see Rev. 7:14, *note*), and immediately preceding the return of Christ in glory (see Dt. 30:3, *note;* Acts 1:11, *note*). The remnant then will not have gone over the cities of Israel until the Lord comes.

22
a Mt. 24:13; Mk. 13:13; cp. Gal. 6:9; Rev. 2:10
23
b Mt. 24:14; Mk. 13:10
c See Mt. 8:20, *note*
d Christ (second advent): v. 23; Mt. 16:27. (Dt. 30:3; Acts 1:11, *note*)
25
e Jn. 8:48,52
f Title of a heathen deity. Mt. 9:34; 12:24; Mk. 3:22; Lk. 11:15
26
g Mk. 4:22; Lk. 8:17; 12:2–3; 1 Cor. 4:5
27
h Acts 5:20; cp. Col. 1:6, 23
28
i Isa. 8:13; Lk. 12:5; cp. 2 Cor. 5:11
j Gk. *geenna.* See Mt. 5:22, *note*
29
k Lk. 12:6–7
l See Coinage (NT), Mt. 5:26, *note*
30
m Lk. 21:18; Acts 27:34
32
n Ps. 119:46; Lk. 12:8; cp. Rev. 3:8

all for My name's sake. But he
who [a]endures to the end will be
[1]saved.
23 "When they persecute you
in this city, flee to another. For
assuredly, I say to you, you will
not have [b]gone through the cities of Israel before the [c]Son of
Man [d]comes.

The cost and compensations of discipleship

24 "A disciple is not above
his teacher, nor a servant above
his master.
25 "It is enough for a disciple
that he be like his teacher, and
a servant like his master. If they
have [e]called the master of the
house [f]Beelzebub,* how much
more *will they call* those of his
household!
26 "Therefore do not fear
them. For there is [g]nothing covered that will not be revealed,
and hidden that will not be
known.
27 "Whatever I tell you in the
dark, [h]speak in the light; and
what you hear in the ear, preach
on the housetops.
28 "And do not fear those
who kill the body but cannot kill
the soul. But rather [i]fear [2]Him
who is able to destroy both soul
and body in [j]hell.
29 "Are not two [k]sparrows
sold for a [l]copper coin? And
not one of them falls to the
ground apart from your Father's will.
30 "But the very [m]hairs of
your head are all numbered.
31 "Do not fear therefore;
you are of more value than
many sparrows.
32 "Therefore whoever [n]con-
fesses Me before men, him I will
also confess before My Father
who is in heaven.
33 "But whoever denies Me
before men, him I will also
[o]deny before My Father who is
in heaven.
34 "Do not think that I came
to bring [3]peace on earth. I did
not come to bring peace but a
sword.
35 "For I have come to *'set a
man [p]against his father, a
daughter against her mother,
and a daughter-in-law against
her mother-in-law'*;
36 "and *'a man's enemies will
be those of his own household.'*
37 "He who loves father or
mother more than Me is not
worthy of Me. And he who loves
son or daughter more than Me
is not [q]worthy of Me.
38 "And he who does not
take his cross and follow after
Me is not worthy of Me.
39 "He who finds his life will
lose it, and he who loses his life
for My sake will find it.
40 [r]"He who receives you receives Me, and he who receives
Me receives Him who sent Me.
41 "He who receives a
prophet in the name of a
prophet shall receive a prophet's [s]reward. And he who receives a [t]righteous man in the
name of a righteous man shall
receive a righteous man's [s]re-
ward.
42 "And whoever [u]gives one
of these little ones only a cup of
cold *water* in the name of a disciple, assuredly, I say to you, he
shall by no means lose his [s]re-
ward."

Jesus eulogizes John the Baptist (Lk. 7:18–35)

11 NOW it came to pass,
when Jesus finished com-

33
o Mk. 8:38; Lk. 9:26; 12:9; 2 Tim. 2:12
35
p Mic. 7:6; Lk. 12:53; cp. Jn. 9:18–23
37
q Lk. 14:26; cp. Dt. 33:9; 2 Cor. 5:16
40
r Lk. 9:48; Jn. 12:44; cp. Mt. 25:40,45; Gal. 4:14
41
s *Rewards:* vv. 41–42; Mt. 16:27. (Dan. 12:3; 1 Cor. 3:14, *note*)
t See Rom. 10:10; and 1 Jn. 3:7, *notes*
42
u Mk. 9:41; cp. 1 Ki. 18:4; Mt. 18:5–6; Lk. 21:1–4

*10:25 NU-Text and M-Text read *Beelzebul*

[1](10:22) The word "saved" is used here, not in the sense of the salvation of the soul but of deliverance out of persecution.

[2](10:28) The reference is not to Satan, as many suppose, but to God who alone has power to "destroy both soul and body in hell."

[3](10:34) Compare Jn. 14:27. Four references to peace may be mentioned: (1) "Peace with God" (Rom. 5:1); this peace is the work of Christ into which the individual enters by faith (Eph. 2:14–17; Rom. 5:1). (2) "Peace from God" (Rom. 1:7; 1 Cor. 1:3, etc.), which is to be found in the salutation of all the epistles bearing Paul's name, and which emphasizes the source of all true peace. (3) "Peace of God" (Phil. 4:7), inward peace, the state of the soul of the Christian who, having entered into peace with God, has committed all his anxieties to God through prayer and supplication with thanksgiving (Lk. 7:50; Phil. 4:6–7); this phrase emphasizes the quality or the nature of the peace granted. And (4) peace on earth (Ps. 72:7; 85:10; Isa. 9:6–7; 11:1–12), universal peace on the earth during the millennium.

manding His twelve disciples, that He departed from there to [a]teach and to preach in their cities.

2 And when [1b]John had heard in prison about the works of Christ, he sent two of* his disciples

3 and said to Him, "Are You the [c]Coming One, or do we look for another?"

4 Jesus answered and said to them, "Go and tell John the things which you hear and see:

5 "*The* [d]blind [e]see and *the* lame walk; *the* lepers are cleansed and *the* deaf hear; *the* dead are raised up and *the* poor have the [f]gospel [g]preached to them.

6 "And blessed is he who is not [h]offended because of Me."

7 As they departed, Jesus began to say to the multitudes concerning John: "What did you go out into the wilderness to see? A reed shaken by the wind?

8 "But what did you go out to see? A man clothed in soft garments? Indeed, those who wear soft *clothing* are in kings' houses.

9 "But what did you go out to see? A prophet? Yes, I say to you, and more than a prophet.

10 "For this is *he* of whom it is [i]written:

'Behold, I send My
messenger before Your
face,
Who will prepare Your
way before You.'

11 "Assuredly, I say to you, among those born of women there has not risen one greater than John the Baptist; but he who is [j]least in the [k]kingdom of heaven is [2]greater than he.

12 "And from the days of John the Baptist until now the [k]kingdom of heaven [l]suffers [3]violence, and the violent take it by force.

13 "For all the prophets and the [m]law [i]prophesied until John.

14 "And if you are willing to receive *it,* [n]he is [o]Elijah who is to come.

15 "He who has ears to hear, let him hear!

16 "But to what shall I liken this generation? It is like children sitting in the marketplaces and calling to their companions,

17 "and saying:

'We played the flute for
you,
And you did not
dance;
We mourned to you,
And you did not
lament.'

18 "For John came neither eating nor drinking, and they say, 'He has a [p]demon.'

19 "The [q]Son of Man came [r]eating and drinking, and they say, 'Look, a glutton and a winebibber, a friend of tax collectors and [s]sinners!' But wisdom is justified by her children."*

Jesus denounces the indifferent

20 [4]Then He began to rebuke the [t]cities in which most of His

*
11:2 NU-Text reads *by* for *two of.*
11:19 NU-Text reads *works.*

CHAPTER 11

1
a Lk. 23:5

2
b Mt. 4:12; 14:3; Mk. 6:17

3
c Gen. 49:10; Dt. 18:15,18

5
d Miracles (NT): v. 5; Mt. 12:13. (Mt. 8:3; Acts 28:8, *note*). Lk. 4:18–19
e Mt. 9:27–30; Jn. 9:1–7; cp. Isa. 29:18–19; 35:4–6
f Gospel: v. 5; Mt. 24:14. (Gen. 12:3; Rev. 14:6)
g Isa. 61:1

6
h Cp. Mt. 13:57; 24:10; 26:31; cp. Rom. 9:33; 1 Cor. 1:23

10
i Inspiration: vv. 10, 13–14; Mt. 12:3. (Ex. 4:15; 2 Tim. 3:16, *note*). Isa. 40:3; Mal. 3:1

11
j Cp. Eph. 3:4–10; Heb. 11:40; 1 Pet. 1:10–12
k Kingdom (NT): vv. 11–12; Mt. 13:11. (Mt. 2:2; 1 Cor. 15:24, *note*)

12
l Lk. 16:16; cp. Lk. 5:19–20

13
m Law (of Moses): v. 13; Mt. 12:5. (Ex. 19:1; Gal. 3:24, *note*)

14
n See Mt. 17:10, *note*
o Mt. 17:12; Lk. 1:17; cp. Mal. 4:5

18
p See Mt. 7:22, *note*

19
q See Mt. 8:20, *note*
r Mt. 9:10; Lk. 5:29–32; 7:36; Jn. 2:1–11
s See Rom. 3:23, *note*

20
t Lk. 10:13–15; see Mk. 8:23, *note*

[1](11:2) John is in prison, the King is rejected, and John's faith wavers. So the Lord encourages and exhorts His servant (vv. 4–6). Cp. Jn. 15:20.

[2](11:11) Positionally greater, not morally. John the Baptist was as great, in strength of character, as any man "born of women" but, as to the kingdom, his ministry was to announce that it was at hand. The kingdom did not then come but was rejected, and John was martyred and the King subsequently crucified. The least in the kingdom, when it is set up in glory (see Kingdom [NT], Lk. 1:31–33; 1 Cor. 15:24, *note*) will be greater than John in the fullness of the Lord's power and glory. It is not heaven which is in question, but Messiah's earthly kingdom. See Mt. 3:2, *note;* 6:33, *note.*

[3](11:12) It has been much disputed whether the violence (force) here is external, as against the kingdom in the persons of John the Baptist and Jesus; or that, considering the opposition of the scribes and Pharisees, only the violently resolute would press into it. Both things are true. The King and His herald suffered violence, and this is the primary and greater meaning; but also, some were resolutely becoming disciples. Cp. Lk. 16:16.

[4](11:20) The kingdom of heaven, announced as at hand by John the Baptist, by the King Himself, and by the twelve, and attested by mighty works, has been morally rejected. The

20
a Repentance: vv. 20–21; Mt. 12:41. (Mt. 3:2; Acts 17:30, *note*)
22
b Day (of judgment): vv. 20–24; Mt. 12:36. (Mt. 10:15; Rev. 20:11)
23
c See Lk. 16:23, *note*
d Gen. 13:13; 18:20; 19:24; Lk. 17:28
25
e Bible prayers (NT): vv. 25–26; Mt. 14:30. (Mt. 6:9; Lk. 11:2, *note*)
f Lk. 10:21; cp. Ps. 8:2; 1 Cor. 1:19–31

mighty works had been done,
because they did not [a]repent:
21 "Woe to you, Chorazin!
Woe to you, Bethsaida! For if
the mighty works which were
done in you had been done in
Tyre and Sidon, they would
have repented long ago in sackcloth and ashes.
22 "But I say to you, it will be
more tolerable for Tyre and Sidon in the [b]day of judgment
than for you.
23 "And you, Capernaum,
who are exalted to heaven, will
be* brought down to [c]Hades;
for if the mighty works which
were done in you had been done
in [d]Sodom, it would have remained until this day.
24 "But I say to you that it
shall be more tolerable for the
land of Sodom in the day of
judgment than for you."

The new message: personal discipleship

25 At that time Jesus answered and [e]said, "I thank You,
Father, Lord of heaven and
earth, that You have [f]hidden
these things from *the* wise and
prudent and have revealed
them to babes.
26 "Even so, Father, for so it
seemed good in Your sight.
27 "All things have been delivered to Me by My Father, and
no one knows the Son except
the Father. Nor does anyone
know the Father [g]except the
Son, and *the one* to whom the
Son wills to reveal *Him.*
28 [1]"Come to [h]Me, all *you*
who labor and are heavy laden,
and I will give you rest.
29 "Take My yoke upon you
and learn from Me, for [i]I am
gentle and lowly in heart, and
you will find rest for your souls.
30 "For My yoke *is* easy and
My burden is light."

Christ is Lord of the Sabbath
(Mk. 2:23–28; Lk. 6:1–5)

12 AT that time Jesus went
through the grainfields
on the [2j]Sabbath. And His disciples were hungry, and began

*11:23 NU-Text reads *will you be exalted to heaven? No, you will be.*

27
g Cp. Jn. 1:18; 14:9–10
28
h Jn. 6:35–37; cp. Jn. 1:38–39
29
i Zech. 9:9; Phil. 2:5–8; cp. Jn. 13:3–15; 1 Jn. 2:6
CHAPTER 12
1
j Sabbath: vv. 1–13; Mt. 24:20. (Gen. 2:3; Mt. 12:1, *note*)

places chosen for the testing of the nation, Chorazin, Bethsaida, etc., having rejected both John and Jesus, the rejected King now speaks of judgment. The official rejection was later (Mt. 27:21–25).

[1](11:28) The new message of Jesus. The rejected King now turns from the rejecting nation and offers, not the kingdom but rest and service to all who are in conscious need of His help. It is a pivotal point in the ministry of Jesus.

[2](12:1) "Sabbath," from Heb. *shabbath* (Gk. *sabbaton*), means *cessation from labor, rest.* (1) The Sabbath appears in Scripture as the day of God's rest in the finished work of creation (Gen. 2:2–3). During the long period from Eden to Sinai, no mention is made of it. Then the Sabbath was revealed to Israel (Ex. 16:23; Neh. 9:13–14), made a part of the law (Ex. 20:8–11), and invested with the character of a "sign" between the LORD and Israel, and a perpetual reminder to Israel of their separation to God (Ex. 31:13–17). It was observed by complete rest (Ex. 35:2–3); and by the LORD's express order a man was put to death for gathering sticks on the Sabbath day (Num. 15:32–36). Apart from maintaining the continued burnt offering (Num. 28:9), and its connection with the annual feasts (Ex. 12:16; Lev. 23:3,8; Num. 28:25), the seventh-day Sabbath was never made a day of sacrifice, worship, or any manner of religious service. It was simply and only a day of complete rest for man and beast, a humane provision for man's needs. In Christ's words, "The Sabbath was made for man, and not man for the Sabbath" (Mk. 2:27). (2) Our Lord found the observance of the day encrusted with rabbinical evasions and restrictions (Mt. 12:2), wholly unknown to the law, so that He was Himself held to be a Sabbath-breaker by the religious authorities of the time. The Sabbath will be again observed during the tribulation period (Mt. 24:20–21) and the Kingdom Age (Isa. 66:23). (3) The Christian first-day-rest perpetuates in the dispensation of the Church the principle that one-seventh of the time is especially sacred, but in all other respects is in contrast with the Sabbath. One is the seventh day; the other the first. The Sabbath commemorates God's creation-rest; the first day, Christ's resurrection. On the seventh day God rested; on the first day Christ was ceaselessly active. The Sabbath commemorates a finished creation; the first day, a finished redemption. The Sabbath was a day of legal obligation; the first day, one of voluntary worship and service. The Sabbath is mentioned in Acts only in connection with the Jews, and in the balance of the NT but twice (Col. 2:16; Heb. 4:4). In these passages the seventh-day Sabbath is explained to be, not a day to be observed by the Christians, but a type of the present rest into which the believer will enter when he "has himself also ceased from his works" and trusts Christ.

to [a]pluck heads of grain and to
eat.
2 And when the Pharisees
saw *it*, they said to Him, "Look,
Your disciples are doing what is
[1]not lawful to do on the Sabbath!"
3 But He said to them,
"Have you [b]not [c]read [2]what
David did when he was hungry,
he and those who were with
him:
4 "how he entered the house
of God and ate the [d]showbread
which was not lawful for him to
eat, nor for those who were with
him, but only for the priests?
5 "Or have you not read in
the [e]law that on the Sabbath the
priests in the temple profane the
Sabbath, and are blameless?
6 "Yet I say to you that in
this place there is *One* [f]greater
than the temple.
7 "But if you had known
what *this* means, *'I desire*
[g]mercy and not sacrifice,' you
would not have condemned the
guiltless.
8 "For the [h]Son of Man is
Lord even* of the Sabbath."

Jesus heals on the Sabbath
(Mk. 3:1–5; Lk. 6:6–11)

9 Now when He had de-
parted from there, He went into
their synagogue.
10 And behold, there was a
man who had a withered hand.
And they asked Him, saying, "Is
it lawful to heal on the
Sabbath?"—that they might accuse Him.
11 Then He said to them,
"What man is there among you
who has one sheep, and if it falls
into a pit on the Sabbath, will
not lay hold of it and lift *it* out?
12 "Of how much more value
then is a man than a sheep?
Therefore it is lawful to do
[i]good on the Sabbath."
13 Then He said to the man,
"Stretch out your hand." And he
stretched *it* out, and it was [j]re-
stored as whole as the other.

Many others healed (Mk. 3:6–12)

14 Then the Pharisees went
out and plotted against Him,
how they might [k]destroy Him.
15 But when Jesus knew *it*,
He withdrew from there. And
great multitudes* followed
Him, and He healed them all.
16 Yet He [l]warned them not
to make Him known,
17 that it might be fulfilled
which was [c]spoken by Isaiah
the prophet, saying:

18 *"Behold! My [m]Servant*
whom I have chosen,
My [n]Beloved in whom
My soul is well
pleased!
I will put My [o]Spirit
upon Him,
And He will declare
justice to the [3]Gentiles.
19 *He will not quarrel nor*
cry out,
Nor will anyone hear His
voice in the streets.
20 *A bruised reed He will*
not break,
And smoking flax He
will not quench,
Till He sends forth
justice to victory;
21 *And in His name*
Gentiles will [p]trust."

22 Then one was brought
to Him who was [q]demon-
possessed, blind and mute; and
He [j]healed him, so that the
blind and* mute man both
spoke and saw.
23 And all the multitudes
were amazed and said, "Could
this be the [r]Son of David?"

The Pharisees blaspheme
the Holy Spirit
(Mk. 3:22–30; Lk. 11:14–23)

24 Now when the [s]Pharisees
heard *it* they said, "This *fellow*

*
12:8 NU-Text and M-Text omit *even*.
12:15 NU-Text brackets *multitudes* as disputed.
12:22 NU-Text omits *blind and*.

1 *a* Dt. 23:25
3 *b* Ex. 31:15; 35:2; cp. Num. 15:32–36; Lk. 13:14
c *Inspiration:* vv. 3–5, 17–21; Mt. 12:39. (Ex. 4:15; 2 Tim. 3:16, *note*)
4 *d* Cp. Ex. 29:32–33; Lev. 8:31; see Ex. 25:30, *note*
5 *e* *Law* (of Moses): v. 5; Mt. 15:3. (Ex. 19:1; Gal. 3:24, *note*)
6 *f* 2 Chr. 6:18; Isa. 66:1–2
7 *g* 1 Sam. 15:22; Hos. 6:6; Mic. 6:6–8; Mt. 9:13
8 *h* vv. 32,40; see Mt. 8:20, *note*
12 *i* Cp. Lk. 14:1–6
13 *j* *Miracles* (NT): vv. 10–13, 22; Mt. 14:20. (Mt. 8:3; Acts 28:8, *note*)
14 *k* Ps. 2:2; Mt. 27:1; Mk. 3:6; Lk. 6:11; Jn. 5:18
16 *l* Mt. 8:4; 9:30; 17:9
18 *m* vv. 18–21; Isa. 42:1–4
n *Christ* (first advent): vv. 18–24; Mt. 18:11. (Gen. 3:15; Acts 1:11, *note*)
o *Holy Spirit* (NT): v. 18; Mt. 12:31. (Mt. 1:18; Acts 2:4, *note*)
21 *p* i.e. *hope*
22 *q* See Mt. 7:22, *note;* 2 Th. 2:9
23 *r* Mt. 9:27; 21:9
24 *s* See Mt. 3:7, *note*

[1](12:2) It was lawful to glean grain (Dt. 23:24–25), but not on the Sabbath.
[2](12:3) Jesus' action (vv. 1–8) is highly significant. "What David did" refers to the time of his rejection and persecution by Saul (1 Sam. 21:6). Jesus here is not so much the rejected Savior as the rejected King.
[3](12:18) The rejected King of Israel will turn to the Gentiles (contrast Mt. 10:5–6). In fulfillment this awaited the official rejection, and the crucifixion and resurrection of Christ (Lk. 24:46–48; Acts 9:15; 13:46; 28:25–28; Rom. 11:11).

does not cast out demons [a]ex-
cept by Beelzebub,* the ruler of
the [b]demons."
25 But Jesus knew their
thoughts, and said to them: "Every kingdom divided against itself is brought to desolation,
and every city or house divided
against itself will not stand.
26 "If [c]Satan casts out Satan,
he is divided against himself.
How then will his kingdom
stand?
27 "And if I cast out [d]demons
by Beelzebub, by whom do your
[e]sons cast *them* out? Therefore
they shall be your judges.
28 "But if I [f]cast out [d]de-
mons by the Spirit of God,
surely the kingdom of God has
come upon you.
29 "Or how can one enter a
strong man's house and plunder
his goods, unless he first binds
the strong man? And then he
will plunder his house.
30 "He who is not with Me is
against Me, and he who does
not gather with Me scatters
abroad.

The unpardonable sin: ascribing to Satan the works of the Holy Spirit (Mk. 3:28–30)

31 "Therefore I say to you,
every [g]sin and blasphemy will
be [h]forgiven men, but the [1]blas-
phemy *against* the [i]Spirit will
not be forgiven men.
32 "Anyone who speaks a
word against the [j]Son of Man,
it will be forgiven him; but whoever speaks against the Holy
[i]Spirit, it will not be forgiven
him, either in this [k]age or in the
age to come.

Destiny in words

33 "Either make the [l]tree
good and its fruit good, or else
make the tree bad and its fruit
bad; for a tree is known by *its*
fruit.
34 [m]"Brood of vipers! How
[n]can you, being evil, speak
good things? For out of the
abundance of the heart the
mouth speaks.
35 "A good man out of the
good treasure of his heart*
brings forth good things, and an
evil man out of the evil treasure
brings forth evil things.
36 "But I say to you that for
every idle word men may
speak, they will give account of
it in the [o]day of judgment.
37 "For by your words you
will be justified, and by your
words you will be condemned."

The sign of the prophet Jonah (Lk. 11:29–32; cp. Jon. 1:17)

38 Then [p]some of the scribes
and Pharisees answered, saying, "Teacher, we want to see a
[q]sign from You."
39 But He answered and said
to them, "An evil and adulterous
generation seeks after a sign,
and no sign will be given to it
except the [r]sign of the prophet
Jonah.
40 "For as Jonah was three
days and three nights in the
belly of the [s]great fish, so will
the [j]Son of Man be three days
and three nights in the heart of
the [t]earth.
41 "The men of [u]Nineveh
will rise up in the judgment with
this generation and condemn it,
because they [v]repented at the
preaching of [2]Jonah; and indeed a greater than Jonah *is*
here.

*

12:24 NU-Text and M-Text read *Beelzebul*
12:35 NU-Text and M-Text omit *of his heart.*

24
a vv. 24–28; Mt. 9:34
b See Mt. 7:22, *note;* 2 Th. 2:9
26
c Satan: vv. 26–27; Mt. 13:19. (Gen. 3:1; Rev. 20:10)
27
d See Mt. 7:22, *note*
e Cp. Lk. 9:49–50; 10:17; Acts 19:13–16
28
f 1 Jn. 3:8
31
g See Rom. 3:23, *note*
h Forgiveness: vv. 31–32; Mt. 18:21. (Lev. 4:20; Mt. 26:28, *note*)
i Holy Spirit (NT): vv. 28, 31–32; Mt. 22:43. (Mt. 1:18; Acts 2:4, *note*)
32
j See Mt. 8:20, *note*
k Gk. *aiōn.* See Mk. 10:30, *note*
33
l Mt. 7:17–18; Lk. 6:43–44

34
m Mt. 3:7; 23:33
n Cp. Lk. 6:45; Rom. 8:7–8; Jas. 3:10
36
o Day (of judgment): vv. 36, 41–42; Mk. 6:11. (Mt. 10:15; Rev. 20:11)
38
p See Mt. 2:4 and 3:7, *notes*
q vv. 38–40; Mt. 16:1–4; Mk. 8:11–12; cp. Mt. 16:4; Lk. 11:29–32; 1 Cor. 1:22
39
r Inspiration: vv. 39–41; Mt. 12:42. (Ex. 4:15; 2 Tim. 3:16, *note*)
40
s Gk. *kētos, a sea monster.* See Jon. 1:17, *note;* cp. Job 7:12; Ezek. 32:2
t Mt. 27:63
41
u Jon. 3:5–9; see Nah. 1:1, *note*
v Repentance: v. 41; Mt. 21:29. (Mt. 3:2; Acts 17:30, *note*)

[1](12:31) The "blasphemy against the Spirit" consisted in ascribing to Satan the work of the Holy Spirit (cp. v. 24). Such a sin was unpardonable because of the unusual circumstances of their rejection of Christ. This most serious sin of the Pharisees was the climax of their continual denial of the obvious truth that the miracles of Jesus represented the power of God (e.g. 9:33–34), so that Jesus' message was heaven-authenticated. Their folly in deliberately apostatizing by ascribing to the devil the mighty works of Christ by the Holy Spirit is summarized by our Lord in Mt. 23:13–36 and Lk. 11:52. Anyone who is concerned about his rejection of Christ has obviously not committed this "unpardonable sin," and can still come to Christ.

[2](12:41) The fact that, in this key passage where our Lord uses the experience of Jonah to predict His burial, the other four references—i.e. to the men of Nineveh, the queen of Sheba, Solomon, and Christ Himself ("a greater than Solomon")—are plainly historical, confirms the historicity of Jonah. For the Lord would hardly include a mythical figure, as some call Jonah, in the identical context with these four historical references.

The sign of the queen of Sheba
(cp. 2 Chr. 9:1–12)

42 [a]"The [b]queen of the South will rise up in the judgment with this generation and condemn it, for she came from the ends of the earth to hear the wisdom of Solomon; and indeed a greater than Solomon *is* here.

Worthlessness of self-reformation
(Lk. 11:24–26)

43 "When an unclean [c]spirit goes out of a man, [d]he goes through dry places, seeking rest, and finds none.

44 "Then [d]he says, 'I will return to my house from which I came.' And when he comes, he finds *it* empty, swept, and put in order.

45 "Then he goes and takes with him seven other [c]spirits more wicked than himself, and they enter and dwell there; and the last *state* of that man is [e]worse than the first. [1]So shall it also be with this wicked [f]generation."

The new relationships
(Mk. 3:31–35; Lk. 8:19–21)

46 [2]While He was still talking to the multitudes, behold, His mother and brothers stood outside, seeking to speak with Him.

47 Then one said to Him, "Look, [g]Your mother and Your brothers are standing outside, seeking to speak with You."

48 But He answered and said to the one who told Him, "Who is My mother and who are My [h]brothers?"

49 And He stretched out His hand toward His disciples and said, "Here are My mother and My [i]brothers!

50 "For [j]whoever does the will of My Father in heaven is My brother and sister and mother."

IV. The Mysteries of the Kingdom: the Period between the King's Two Advents, 13

(1) The sower and the soils
(Mk. 4:1–25; Lk. 8:4–15)

13 ON the same day Jesus went out of the house and sat by the sea.

2 And great multitudes were gathered together to Him, so that He got into a [k]boat and sat; and the whole multitude stood on the shore.

3 Then He [3]spoke many things to them in [l]parables, saying: "Behold, a [4m]sower went out to sow.

4 "And as he sowed, some *seed* fell by the wayside; and the birds came and devoured them.

5 "Some fell on stony places, where they did not have much earth; and they immediately sprang up because they had no depth of earth.

6 "But when the sun was up they were scorched, and because they had no root they withered away.

7 "And some fell among thorns, and the thorns sprang up and choked them.

8 "But others fell on good ground and yielded a crop: some a hundredfold, some sixty, some thirty.

42
a Inspiration: vv. 39–42; Mt. 13:14. (Ex. 4:15; 2 Tim. 3:16, *note*)
b 1 Ki. 10:1–13
43
c Cp. Mk. 7:25–26; see Mt. 7:22, *note*
d i.e. *the unclean spirit*
45
e 2 Pet. 2:20; cp. Heb. 6:4–6
f See Mt. 24:34, *note*
47
g Mt. 13:55–56; Jn. 2:12; Acts 1:14
48
h Cp. Dt. 33:9; Lk. 2:49
49
i Jn. 20:17; Rom. 8:29
50
j Cp. Jn. 15:14
CHAPTER 13
2
k Lk. 5:3
3
l *Parables (NT):* vv. 3–52; Mt. 18:12. (Mt. 5:13; Lk. 21:29). Mk. 4:2; Lk. 8:4
m vv. 3–9

[1](12:45) Again the rejected King announces judgment (cp. 11:20–24). Israel, in the center of the Pharisaic revival of outward religious strictness, was like a man out of whom a demon had come, i.e. of his own volition. He would come back and find an empty house, etc. The application is to those who are depending upon self-reformation.

[2](12:46) Rejected by Israel, those of His own race (cp. Rom. 9:3), our Lord intimates the formation of the new family of faith which will overstep the racial claims that Israel has known to this time and will receive all those ("whoever," v. 50) who will be His disciples. Cp. Jn. 6:28–29.

[3](13:3) The seven parables of ch. 13, called by our Lord "mysteries of the kingdom of heaven" (v. 11), taken together describe the result of the presence of the Gospel in the world during the present age, that is, the time of seed-sowing which began with our Lord's personal ministry and will end with the "harvest" (vv. 40–43). The result is the mingled tares and wheat, good fish and bad, in the sphere of Christian profession. It is Christendom.

[4](13:3) The figure marks a new beginning. To labor in God's vineyard (Israel, Isa. 5:1–7) is one thing; to go forth sowing the seed of the Word in a field which is the world, quite another (cp. Mt. 10:5). One-fourth of the seed takes permanent root, and the result is "wheat" (v. 25; 1 Pet. 1:23), or "sons of the kingdom" (v. 38). This parable (vv. 3–9) is treated throughout as foundational to the mysteries of the kingdom of heaven. It is interpreted by our Lord Himself (vv. 18–23).

9 “He who has [a]ears to
hear, let him hear!”

(Private explanation
to disciples vv. 10–17)

10 And the disciples came
and said to Him, “Why do You
speak to them in parables?”
11 He answered and said to
them, “Because it has been
given to you to know the [1b]mys-
teries of the [c]kingdom of
heaven, but to them it has not
been given.
12 “For whoever has, to him
more will be given, and he will
have abundance; but whoever
does not have, even what he has
will be taken away from [d]him.
13 “Therefore I speak to
them in parables, [e]because seeing they do not see, and hearing
they do not hear, nor do they
understand.
14 “And in them the [f]proph-
ecy of Isaiah is fulfilled, which
says:

‘Hearing you will hear
and shall not
understand,
And seeing you will see
and not [g]perceive;
15 *For the hearts of this*
people have [h]grown
dull.
Their ears are hard of
hearing,
And their eyes they have
[i]closed,
Lest they should see with
their eyes and hear
with their ears,
Lest they should
understand with their
hearts and turn,
So that I should [j]heal*
them.’•

16 “But blessed *are* your eyes
for they see, and your ears for
they [k]hear;
17 “for assuredly, I say to you
that many [2]prophets and [l]righ-
teous *men* [m]desired to see what
you see, and did not see *it*, and
to hear what you hear, and did
not hear *it*.
18 [n]“Therefore hear the parable of the sower:
19 “When anyone hears the
word of the [c]kingdom, and
does not understand *it*, then
the wicked [o]*one* comes and
snatches away what was sown
in his heart. This is he who received seed by the wayside.
20 “But he who received the
seed on stony places, this is he
who hears the word and immediately receives it with joy;
21 “yet he has no root in himself, but endures only for a
while. For when [p]tribulation or
persecution arises because of
the word, immediately he stumbles.
22 “Now he who received
seed among the thorns is he
who hears the word, and the
cares of this [q]world and the deceitfulness of riches choke the
word, and he becomes [r]unfruit-
ful.
23 “But he who received seed

* 13:15 NU-Text and M-Text read *would.*
• Isaiah 6:9–10

9
a Mt. 11:15; cp. Rev. 2:7
11
b Mk. 4:10–11; cp. Mic. 4:12; 1 Cor. 2:10
c Kingdom (NT): vv. 3–52; Mt. 16:19. (Mt. 2:2; 1 Cor. 15:24, *note*)
12
d Mt. 25:29
13
e Jn. 8:43; cp. Jn. 7:16–17; 9:39–41
14
f Inspiration: vv. 14–15; Mt. 13:35. (Ex. 4:15; 2 Tim. 3:16, *note*)
g Jn. 6:36; cp. Dt. 29:3–4
15
h Cp. Heb. 5:11
i Lk. 19:42
j Acts 28:26–27
16
k Prov. 20:12; Lk. 10:23–24; cp. Mt. 16:17
17
l Righteousness (OT): v. 17; Mt. 21:32. (Gen. 6:9; Lk. 2:25, *note*)
m Cp. Jn. 8:56
18
n vv. 18–23
19
o Satan: v. 19; Mt. 13:38. (Gen. 3:1; Rev. 20:10)
21
p Acts 14:22; cp. Heb. 6:4–6 with 10:34
22
q Gk. *aiōn.* See Mk. 10:30, *note*
r Cp. Prov. 11:28; 1 Tim. 6:9, 17

[1](13:11) A “mystery” in Scripture is a previously hidden truth now divinely revealed. This chapter shows clearly for the first time that there will be an interval between Christ’s first and second advents (vv. 17,35; cp. 1 Pet. 1:10–12). The greater mysteries are: (1) the mysteries of the kingdom of heaven (Mt. 13:3–50); (2) the mystery of Israel’s blindness during this age (Rom. 11:25, with context); (3) the mystery of the translation of living saints at the end of this age (1 Cor. 15:51–52; 1 Th. 4:13–17); (4) the mystery of the NT Church as one body composed of Jews and Gentiles (Eph. 3:1–12; Rom. 16:25; Eph. 6:19; Col. 4:3); (5) the mystery of the Church as the bride of Christ (Eph. 5:23–32); (6) the mystery of the in-living Christ (Gal. 2:20; Col. 1:26–27); (7) the “mystery of God, . . . and of Christ,” i.e. Christ as the incarnate fullness of the Godhead embodied, in whom all the divine wisdom for man subsists (1 Cor. 2:7; Col. 2:2,9); (8) the mystery of the processes by which godlikeness is restored to man (1 Tim. 3:16); (9) the mystery of lawlessness (2 Th. 2:7; cp. Mt. 13:33); (10) the mystery of the seven stars (Rev. 1:20); and (11) the mystery of Babylon (Rev. 17:5,7).

[2](13:17) The OT prophets saw in one blended vision the rejection and crucifixion of the King (see Heb. 10:18, *note*), and also His glory as David’s Son (see Zech. 12:8, *note*), but “what, or what manner of time the Spirit of Christ who was in them was indicating when He testified beforehand the sufferings of Christ and the glories that would follow,” was not revealed to them—only that the vision was not for themselves (1 Pet. 1:10–12). That revelation Christ makes in these parables. A period of time is to intervene between His sufferings and His glory. That interval is occupied with the “mysteries of the kingdom of heaven” described here.

on the good ground is he who
hears the word and under-
stands *it,* who indeed bears
[a]fruit and produces: some a
hundredfold, some sixty, some
thirty."

(2) The tares among the wheat
(cp. vv. 36–43)

24 [1]Another parable He put
forth to them, saying: "The
[b]kingdom of heaven is like a
man who sowed [c]good seed in
his field;
25 "but while men slept, his
enemy came and sowed [d]tares
among the wheat and went his
way.
26 "But when the grain had
sprouted and produced a crop,
then the tares also appeared.
27 "So the servants of the
owner came and said to him,
'Sir, did you not sow good seed
in your field? How then does it
have tares?'
28 "He said to them, 'An enemy has done this.' The servants said to him, 'Do you want
us then to go and gather them
up?'
29 "But he said, 'No, lest
while you gather up the tares
you also uproot the [e]wheat with
them.
30 'Let [f]both grow together
until the harvest, and at the time
of harvest I will say to the reapers, [2]"First gather together the
tares and bind them in bundles
to burn them, but gather the
wheat into my barn." ' "

(3) The mustard seed
(Mk. 4:30–32)

31 [3]Another parable He put
forth to them, saying: "The
[b]kingdom of heaven is like a
[g]mustard seed, which a man
took and sowed in his field,
32 "which indeed is the least
of all the seeds; but when it is
grown it is greater than the
herbs and becomes a [h]tree, so
that the birds of the air come
and nest in its branches."

(4) The leaven (Lk. 13:20–21)

33 [4]Another parable He

23
a Jn. 15:5; Phil. 1:11; Col. 1:6
24
b See Mt. 3:2, *note*
c Cp. 2 Tim. 3:15–17; 1 Pet. 1:23; 1 Jn. 3:9
25
d Cp. Acts 20:29–30; Jude 8–13, 16–19
29
e Cp. Mt. 3:12
30
f Cp. Phil. 3:18–19; 2 Th. 3:6; 2 Tim. 2:19
31
g Lk. 13:18–19
32
h Ezek. 17:22–24; 31:3–9; cp. Dan. 4:20–22

[1](13:24) This parable (vv. 24–30) is also interpreted by our Lord (vv. 36–43). Here the "good seed" is not the "word," as in the first parable (vv. 19,23), but rather that which the Word has produced (1 Pet. 1:23), i.e. the children of the kingdom. These are providentially "sown" (v. 37), i.e. scattered here and there in the "field" of the "world" (v. 38). The "world" here is both geographic and ethnic—the earth-world, and also the world of men. The wheat of God at once becomes the scene of Satan's activity. Where children of the kingdom are gathered, there, "among the wheat" (vv. 25,38,39), Satan sows "sons of the wicked one," who profess to be children of the kingdom and, in outward ways, are so like the true children that only the angels may, in the end, be trusted to separate them (vv. 40–43). So great is Satan's power of deception that the tares often really suppose themselves to be children of the kingdom (7:21–23). Many other parables and exhortations have this mingled condition in view (e.g. 22:11–14; 25:1–13,14–30; Lk. 18:10–14; Heb. 6:4–9). Indeed, it characterizes Matthew from ch. 13 to the end. The parable of the wheat and the tares is not a description of the world, but of that which professes to be the kingdom. Not all unbelievers are called children of the devil; only those who have willfully rejected the light are so designated (cp. v. 38; Jn. 8:38–44).

[2](13:30) This will have its fulfillment at the end of the age (v. 40), when Christ returns to reign. The wicked will be destroyed. The Church, translated before the tribulation, will be gathered into the millennial kingdom, together with those living believers who have survived the tribulation period (v. 43; 24:13; 25:31,34) and the resurrected righteous men and women of all the previous ages.

[3](13:31) The parable of the mustard seed suggests the rapid but unsubstantial growth of the mystery aspect of the kingdom (see 13:3, *note 3*) from a small beginning (Acts 1:15; 2:41; 1 Cor. 1:26) to a great place on the earth.

[4](13:33) It was common practice to retain a lump of leavened or fermented dough from a former baking and use it to leaven new dough. Under the Mosaic law, however, leaven was forbidden in bread used in the Feast of Unleavened Bread and the Passover (Ex. 12:8,15–20; Lev. 23:6–8), and similar exclusion of leaven applied to offerings placed on the altar (Ex. 23:18; 34:25; Lev. 2:11; 6:17). The only exceptions were the use of leaven in the two wave loaves offered as firstfruits (Lev. 23:17) and some of the cakes of bread offered with the thank offerings (Lev. 7:13, *note*).

Leaven, which brings about fermentation, is uniformly regarded in Scripture as typifying the presence of impurity or evil (Ex. 12:15,19; 13:7; Lev. 2:11; Dt. 16:4; Mt. 16:6,12; Mk. 8:15; Lk. 12:1; 1 Cor. 5:6–9; Gal. 5:9). The two wave loaves, representing Israel and the Gentiles as forming the Church, contained leaven in recognition of imperfections in the believers (see Lev.

spoke to them: "The [a]kingdom
of heaven is like [b]leaven, which
a woman took and hid in three
[c]measures* of meal till it was
[d]all leavened."
34 All these things Jesus
spoke to the multitude in parables; and without a parable He
did not speak to them,
35 that it might be [e]fulfilled
which was spoken by the
prophet, saying:

"I will open My mouth in
parables;
I will utter things kept
secret from the
foundation of the
[f]world."

(Second mystery [vv. 24–30] explained)

36 Then Jesus sent the multitude away and went into the
house. And His disciples came
to Him, saying, [g]"Explain to us
the parable of the tares of the
field."
37 He answered and said to
them: "He who sows the good
seed is the [h]Son of Man.
38 "The field is the [f]world,
the good seeds are the sons of
the [a]kingdom, but the tares are
the sons of the [i]wicked *one.*
39 "The enemy who sowed
them is the [i]devil, the harvest is
the [j]end of the [k]age, and the
reapers are the [l]angels.
40 [m]"Therefore as the tares
are gathered and burned in the
fire, so it will be at the [j]end of
this [k]age.
41 "The [h]Son of Man will
send out His [l]angels, and they
will gather out of His [a]kingdom
all things that offend, and those
who practice lawlessness,
42 "and will cast them into
the furnace of fire. There will be
wailing and gnashing of teeth.
43 [1]"Then the [n]righteous will
[o]shine forth as the sun in the
kingdom of their Father. He
who has ears to hear, let him
hear!

(5) The hidden treasure

44 "Again, the [a]kingdom of
heaven is like [p]treasure [2]hidden
in a field, which a man found

* 13:33 Greek *sata,* approximately two pecks in all

33 *a* See Mt. 3:2, *note*; *b Leaven:* v. 33; Mt. 16:6. (Gen. 19:3; Mt. 13:33, *note*); *c* See Weights and Measures (NT), Acts 27:28, *note*; *d* 1 Cor. 5:6; Gal. 5:9
35 *e Inspiration:* v. 35; Mt. 15:7. (Ex. 4:15; 2 Tim. 3:16, *note*). Ps. 78:2; *f* Gk. *kosmos.* See Mt. 4:8, *note*
36 *g* Mk. 4:33–34
37 *h* See Mt. 8:20, *note*
38 *i Satan:* vv. 38–39; Mt. 16:23. (Gen. 3:1; Rev. 20:10)
39 *j* See Mt. 24:3, *note*; *k* Gk. *aiōn.* See Mk. 10:30, *note*; *l* See Heb. 1:4, *note*
40 *m Judgments* (the seven): vv. 40–43; Mt. 13:49. (1 Sam. 7:14; Rev. 20:12, *note*)
43 *n* See Rom. 10:10, *note*; *o* Cp. Dan. 12:3
44 *p* Cp. Ex. 19:5

23:17, *note*). The use of leaven in the flour seems intended likewise to represent evil within the kingdom of heaven. The teaching that leaven in this parable represents the beneficent influence of the Gospel pervading the world has no Scriptural justification. Nowhere in Scripture does leaven represent good; the idea of a converted world at the end of the age is contradicted by the presence of tares among the wheat and bad fish among the good in the kingdom itself. Although biblical truth has a beneficial moral influence on the world, the mingling of leaven is not the method of divine salvation or enlargement of the kingdom. Tares never become wheat. The parable is, therefore, a warning that true doctrine, represented by the flour, would be corrupted by false doctrine (cp. 1 Tim. 4:1–3; 2 Tim. 2:17–18; 4:3–4; 2 Pet. 2:1–3).

Summary: (1) Leaven, as a symbolic or typical substance, is always mentioned in the OT in an evil sense (Gen. 19:3, marg.). (2) The use of the word in the NT explains its symbolic meaning. It is "malice and wickedness" as contrasted with "sincerity and truth" (1 Cor. 5:6–8). It is evil doctrine (Mt. 16:12) in its threefold form of Pharisaism, Sadduceeism, and Herodianism (Mt. 16:6; Mk. 8:15). The leaven of the Pharisees was externalism in religion (Mt. 23:14–16,23–28); of the Sadducees, skepticism as to the supernatural and as to the Scriptures (Mt. 22:23,29); of the Herodians, worldliness—a Herod party among the Jews (Mt. 22:16–21; Mk. 3:6). And (3) the use of the word in Mt. 13:33 is congruous with its meaning elsewhere in the Scriptures, as denoted in the paragraphs above.

[1](13:43) The kingdom does not become the kingdom of the Father until Christ, having "put all enemies under His feet," including the last enemy, death, "delivers the kingdom to God and Father" (1 Cor. 15:24–28). There is triumph over death at the first resurrection (1 Cor. 15:54–55), but death, "the last enemy," is not destroyed until the end of the millennium (Rev. 20:14).

[2](13:44) The interpretation of the parable of the treasure which makes the buyer of the field to be a sinner who is seeking Christ, has no warrant in the parable itself. The field is declared to be the world (v. 38). The seeking sinner does not buy, but forsakes the world to gain Christ. Furthermore, the sinner has nothing to sell; neither is Christ for sale or hidden in a field; nor, having found Christ, does the sinner hide Him again (cp. Mk. 7:24; Acts 4:20). At every point the interpretation breaks down.

The field is the world (v. 38), which was purchased by our Lord at the priceless cost of His own blood in order that He might have the treasure (1 Pet. 1:18). As Israel was God's treasure

and hid; and for joy over it he
goes and [a]sells all that he has
and buys that field.

(6) The pearl of great price

45 "Again, the [b]kingdom of
heaven is like a merchant seeking beautiful [1]pearls,
46 "who, when he had found
one pearl of great price, went
and sold all that he had and
bought it.

(7) The dragnet

47 "Again, the [b]kingdom of
heaven is like a [2]dragnet that
was cast into the sea and gathered some of every [c]kind,
48 "which, when it was full,
they drew to shore; and they sat
down and [d]gathered the good
into vessels, but threw the bad
away.
49 "So it will be at the [e]end of
the [f]age. The [g]angels will come
forth, [h]separate the wicked
from among the [i]just,
50 "and cast them into the
furnace of fire. There will be
wailing and gnashing of teeth."
51 Jesus said to them,*
"Have you understood all these
things?" They said to Him, "Yes,
Lord."*•

(8) The householder

52 Then He said to them,
"Therefore every [j]scribe instructed concerning* the [b]king-
dom of heaven is like a householder who brings out of his
treasure *things* new and old."

Last visit to Nazareth
(Mk. 6:1–6; contrast Lk. 4:16–32)

53 Now it came to pass, when
Jesus had finished these parables, that He departed from
there.
54 When He had come to His
own country, He taught them in
their synagogue, so that they
were [k]astonished and said,
"Where did this *Man* get this
wisdom and *these* mighty
works?
55 "Is this not the [l]carpen-
ter's son? Is not His mother
called Mary? And His brothers
[m]James, Joses,* Simon, and Judas?
56 "And His sisters, are they
not all with us? Where then did
this *Man* get all these things?"
57 So they were [n]offended at

44
a Cp. Isa. 53:4–10
45
b See Mt. 3:2, *note*
47
c Mt. 22:9
48
d Cp. Mt. 24:31; Mt. 25:31–46
49
e See Mt. 24:3, *note*
f Gk. *aiōn.* See Mk. 10:30, *note*
g See Heb. 1:4, *note*
h Judgments (the seven): v. 49; Mt. 16:27. (1 Sam. 7:14; Rev. 20:12, *note*)
i See Rom. 10:10, *note*

52
j See Mk. 12:34, *note*
54
k Jn. 7:15
55
l Jn. 6:42; cp. Jn. 7:41,48, 52
m See Mt. 4:21, *note*
57
n Mt. 11:6

*
13:51 NU-Text omits *Jesus said to them.*
• NU-Text omits *Lord.* 13:52 Or *for.*
13:55 NU-Text reads *Joseph.*

in OT times (Ex. 19:5; Ps. 135:4), so there is at the present time "a remnant [of Israel] according to the election of grace" (Rom. 11:5). Those who compose the remnant are no longer reckoned as Jews (Gal. 3:28) but as members of the "one body" together with saved Gentiles (Eph. 2:14–18; 4:4) and thus Christ's inheritance (Eph. 1:18) and His joy (Heb. 12:2).

[1](13:45) The true Church is the pearl of great price. Its formation covers a large part of the period of the mysteries of the kingdom, and is itself called a mystery (Rom. 16:25–26; Eph. 3:3–12; 5:32; Col. 1:24–27). A pearl is an illustration of the Church: (1) A pearl is formed by accretion, and that not mechanically but vitally, as Christ adds to the Church (Acts 2:41,47; 5:14; 11:24; Eph. 2:21; Col. 2:19). And (2) Christ, having given Himself for the pearl, is now preparing it for presentation to Himself (Eph. 5:25–27). The kingdom is not the Church, but the true children of the kingdom during the fulfillment of these mysteries, baptized by one Spirit into one body (1 Cor. 12:12–13), compose the Church, the pearl.

[2](13:47) The parable of the dragnet presents, as does that of the wheat and the tares, the mystery of the kingdom as the sphere of profession, but with this difference: there Satan was the active agent; here the admixture is more the result of the tendency of a movement to gather to itself that which is not really of it. The kingdom of heaven is like a net which, cast into the sea of humanity, gathers of every kind, good and bad. These remain together in the net (v. 49) and not merely in the sea until the end of the age. It is not even a converted net, much less a converted sea. Much violence has been done to sound exegesis by the notion that the world is to be converted in this age. Against that notion stands our Lord's own interpretation of the parables of the sower, the wheat and the tares, and the net.

Such, then, is the mystery form of the kingdom (see Mt. 3:2, *note;* 6:33, *note*). It is the sphere of Christian profession during this age. It is a mingled body of true and false, wheat and tares, good and bad. It is defiled by formalism, doubt, and worldliness. But within it Christ sees the true children of the true kingdom who, at the end, are to "shine forth like the sun." In the great field, the world, He sees His treasure that He redeems for His own through His cross. Thus, in this aspect of the kingdom, He sees the Church, His body and bride composed of believing Israelites and Gentiles and for joy sells all that He has (2 Cor. 8:9) and buys the field, the treasure, and the pearl.

Him. But Jesus said to them, "A [a]prophet is not without [b]honor except in his own [c]country and in his own house."

58 Now He did not do many mighty works there [d]because of their unbelief.

V. The Ministry of the Rejected King, 14—23

Murder of John the Baptist (Mk. 6:14–29; Lk. 9:7–9)

14 AT that time [e]Herod the tetrarch heard the report about Jesus

2 and said to his servants, "This is John the Baptist; he is risen from the dead, and therefore these powers are at work in him."

3 For Herod had laid hold of John and bound him, and put *him* in [f]prison for the sake of [g]Herodias, his brother [h]Philip's wife.

4 Because John had said to him, "It is not lawful for you to have her."

5 And although he wanted to put him to death, he feared the multitude, because they counted him as a prophet.

6 But when Herod's birthday was celebrated, the [i]daughter of Herodias danced before them and pleased Herod.

7 Therefore he promised with an oath to give her whatever she might ask.

8 So she, having been prompted by her mother, said, "Give me [j]John the Baptist's head here on a platter."

9 And the king was [k]sorry; nevertheless, because of the oaths and because of those who sat with him, he commanded *it* to be given to *her*.

10 So he sent and had John beheaded in prison.

11 And his head was brought on a platter and given to the girl, and she brought *it* to her mother.

12 Then his disciples came and took away the body and buried it, and went and told Jesus.

13 When Jesus heard *it*, He [l]departed from there by boat to a deserted place by Himself. But when the multitudes heard it,

57
a Cp. Jn. 4:44
b See Lk. 24:19, *note*
c Cp. Jn. 1:11; 5:43
58
d Jn. 5:44, 46–47
CHAPTER 14
1
e Herod Antipas, son of Herod, the Great. See Mk. 6:14, *note*
3
f Mt. 4:12
g See Mk. 6:14, *note*
h Herod Philip. See Mk. 6:14, *note*
6
i Salome. See Mk. 6:14, *note*
8
j Acts 7:52
9
k Cp. Jud. 11:30–40; Dan. 6:13–17
13
l Mt. 12:15

they followed Him on foot from the cities.

14 And when Jesus went out He saw a great multitude; and He was moved with [m]compassion for them, and healed their sick.

Five thousand fed (Mk. 6:30–44; Lk. 9:10–17; Jn. 6:1–14)

15 When it was evening, His disciples came to Him, saying, "This is a deserted place, and the hour is already late. Send the multitudes away, that they may go into the villages and buy themselves food."

16 But Jesus said to them, "They do not need to go away. You [n]give them something to eat."

17 And they said to Him, "We have here only five loaves and two fish."

18 He said, "Bring them here to Me."

19 Then He [o]commanded the multitudes to sit down on the grass. And He took the five loaves and the two fish, and looking up to heaven, He [p]blessed and broke and gave the loaves to the disciples; and the disciples gave to the multitudes.

20 [q]So they all ate and were filled, and they took up twelve baskets full of the fragments that [r]remained.

21 Now those who had eaten were about five thousand men, besides women and children.

Jesus walks on the water (Mk. 6:45–52; Jn. 6:15–21)

22 Immediately Jesus made His disciples get into the boat and go before Him to the other side, while He [s]sent the multitudes away.

23 And when He had sent the multitudes away, He went up on the [t]mountain by Himself to pray. Now when evening came, He was alone there.

24 But the boat was now in the middle of the sea,* tossed by the waves, for the wind was contrary.

25 Now in the [u]fourth watch

*14:24 NU-Text reads *many furlongs away from the land.*

14
m Mt. 9:36; Mk. 6:34
16
n vv. 16–21; cp. Mt. 15:32–39
19
o Cp. Jn. 2:5
p Jn. 6:23; cp. Jn. 11:41–42; 1 Cor. 11:24
20
q Miracles (NT): vv. 19–21, 24; Mt. 14:25. (Mt. 8:3; Acts 28:8, *note*)
r Cp. 2 Ki. 4:1–7,42–44; Mt. 15:27
22
s Cp. Mk. 5:31
23
t Lk. 9:28; Jn. 6:15
25
u 3–6 a.m. See Jn. 19:14, *note*

of the night Jesus went to them,
[a]walking on the sea.
26 And when the disciples
saw Him walking on the sea,
they were troubled, saying, [b]"It
is a ghost!" And they cried out
for fear.
27 But immediately Jesus
spoke to them, saying, "Be of
good [c]cheer! It is I; do not be
afraid."
28 And Peter answered Him
and said, "Lord, if it is You,
command me to come to You on
the water."
29 So He said, "Come." And
when Peter had come down out
of the boat, he [a]walked on the
water to go to Jesus.
30 But when he saw that the
[d]wind *was* boisterous,* he was
afraid; and beginning to sink he
cried out, saying, [e]"Lord, save
me!"
31 And immediately Jesus
stretched out *His* hand and
caught him, and said to him, "O
you of [f]little faith, why did you
[g]doubt?"
32 And when they got into
the boat, the wind [a]ceased.
33 Then those who were in
the boat came and* worshiped
Him, saying, "Truly You are the
[h]Son of God."

Healing in Gennesaret
(Mk. 6:53–56)

34 When they had crossed
over, they came to the land of *
Gennesaret.
35 And when the men of that
place recognized Him, they sent
out into all that surrounding region, brought to Him all who
were sick,
36 and begged Him that they
might only [i]touch the hem of
His garment. And as many as
touched *it* were [a]made perfectly [j]well.

God's commandments versus
man's tradition (Mk. 7:1–13)

15 THEN the scribes and
Pharisees who were
from Jerusalem came to Jesus,
saying,
2 "Why do Your disciples
transgress the [k]tradition of the
elders? For they do not wash
their hands when they eat
bread."
3 He answered and said to
them, "Why do you also transgress the [l]commandment of
God because of your tradition?
4 "For God [m]commanded,
saying, *'Honor your father and*
your mother'; and, *'He who*
curses father or mother, let him
[n]*be put to death.'*
5 "But you say, 'Whoever
says to his father or mother,
"Whatever profit you might
have received from me *is* a [o]gift
to God"—
6 'then he need not honor
his father or mother.'* Thus
you have made the [l]command-
ment* of God of [p]no effect by
your tradition.
7 "Hypocrites! Well did Isaiah prophesy about you, [q]say-
ing:

8 *'These people draw near*
to Me with their
mouth,
And honor Me with*
their [r]lips,
But their heart is far
from Me.
9 *And in vain they*
worship Me,
Teaching as doctrines
the commandments of
[s]*men.'"*

Diagnosis of the heart of man
(Mk. 7:14–23)

10 When He had called the
multitude to *Himself*, He said to
them, "Hear and understand:
11 [t]"Not what goes into the
mouth defiles a man; but what
comes out of the mouth, this defiles a man."
12 Then His disciples came
and said to Him, "Do You know
that the [u]Pharisees were offended when they heard this
saying?"
13 But He answered and
said, "Every plant which My
heavenly Father has not planted
will be uprooted.
14 "Let them alone. They are
[v]blind leaders of the blind. And

*
14:30 NU-Text brackets *that* and *boisterous* as disputed. **14:33** NU-Text omits *came and.* **14:34** NU-Text reads *came to land at.* **15:6** NU-Text omits *or mother.* • NU-Text reads *word.* **15:8** NU-Text omits *draw near to Me with their mouth, And.*

25
a *Miracles* (NT): vv. 24–33, 35–36; Mt. 15:28. (Mt. 8:3; Acts 28:8, *note*)
26
b Cp. Acts 12:15
27
c Acts 23:11; 27:22,25,36; cp. Ps. 46:1–5; Isa. 41:10; 43:1–2
30
d Cp. Lk. 8:22–25
e *Bible prayers* (NT): v. 30; Mt. 15:22. (Mt. 6:9; Lk. 11:2, *note*)
31
f Mt. 6:30; 8:26; cp. Jas. 1:6–7
g Cp. Mt. 21:21
33
h Ps. 2:7; Mt. 16:16; 27:54; Lk. 4:41; Jn. 1:49; 6:69; Acts 8:37; Rom. 1:4
36
i Mk. 5:24–34
j Mt. 9:21–22; 12:13; 15:28,31
CHAPTER 15
2
k Cp. Mt. 23:16–18; Lk. 11:38

3
l *Law* (of Moses): vv. 3–4,6; Mt. 19:7. (Ex. 19:1; Gal. 3:24, *note*). Ex. 20:12; 21:17
4
m Ex. 20:1
n Lev. 20:9; Dt. 27:16; Prov. 30:17; cp. 1 Tim. 5:4–8
5
o Mt. 5:23–24
6
p Cp. Prov. 28:24
7
q *Inspiration:* vv. 7–9; Mt. 16:4. (Ex. 4:15; 2 Tim. 3:16, *note*). Isa. 29:13
8
r Ps. 78:36; Ezek. 33:31
9
s Col. 2:22; Ti. 1:14
11
t Cp. Rom. 14:14–23; Col. 2:20–23; 1 Tim. 4:4–5; Ti. 1:15
12
u See Mt. 3:7, *note*
14
v Mt. 23:16, 24; Lk. 6:39; Rom. 2:19

if the blind leads the blind, both will fall into a ditch."

15 Then Peter answered and said to Him, "Explain this parable to us."

16 So Jesus said, "Are you also still without understanding?

17 "Do you not yet understand that whatever enters the mouth goes into the stomach and is eliminated?

18 "But those things which proceed out of the mouth come from the [a]heart, and they defile a man.

19 "For out of the heart proceed [b]evil thoughts, murders, adulteries, fornications, thefts, false witness, blasphemies.

20 "These are [c]*the things* which defile a man, but to eat with unwashed hands does not defile a man."

Jesus and the Syro-Phoenician woman (Mk. 7:24–30)

21 Then Jesus went out from there and departed to the region of Tyre and Sidon.

22 And behold, a woman of Canaan came from that region and [d]cried out to Him, saying, "Have mercy on me, O Lord, [e]Son of David! My daughter is severely [f]demon-possessed."

23 But He answered her not a word. And His disciples came and urged Him, saying, "Send her away, for she cries out after us."

24 But He answered and said, "I was not sent except to the [g]lost sheep of the [h]house of Israel."

25 Then she came and worshiped Him, [d]saying, "Lord, [i]help me!"

26 But He answered and said, "It is not good to take the children's bread and throw *it* to the little [j]dogs."

27 And she [d]said, "Yes, Lord, yet even the little dogs eat the crumbs which fall from their masters' table."

28 Then Jesus answered and said to her, "O woman, [k]great *is* your [l]faith! Let it be to you [m]as you desire." And her daughter was [n]healed from that very hour.

Further healing (cp. Mk. 7:31–37)

29 Jesus departed from there, skirted the Sea of Galilee, and went up on the mountain and sat down there.

30 Then great multitudes came to Him, having with them *the* lame, blind, mute, maimed, and many others; and they laid them down at Jesus' [o]feet, and He healed them.

31 So the multitude marveled when they saw *the* mute speaking, *the* maimed made whole, *the* lame walking, and *the* blind seeing; and they [p]glorified the God of Israel.

Four thousand fed (Mk. 8:1–9)

32 Now Jesus called His disciples to *Himself* and said, "I have [q]compassion on the multitude, because they have now continued with Me three days and have nothing to eat. And I do not want to send them away hungry, lest they faint on the way."

33 Then His disciples said to Him, "Where could we get enough bread in the wilderness to fill such a great [r]multitude?"

34 Jesus said to them, "How many loaves do you have?" And they said, "Seven, and a few little fish."

35 So He commanded the multitude to sit down on the ground.

36 And He took the seven loaves and the fish and gave thanks, broke *them* and gave *them* to His disciples; and the disciples *gave* to the multitude.

37 [n]So they all ate and were filled, and they took up seven large baskets full of the fragments that were left.

38 Now those who ate were four thousand men, besides women and children.

39 And He sent away the multitude, got into the boat, and came to the region of Magdala.*

The blind Pharisees rebuked (Mk. 8:10–14)

16 THEN the [s]Pharisees and [s]Sadducees came, and [t]testing Him asked that He

* 15:39 NU-Text reads *Magadan*.

18
a Mt. 12:34; see Mk. 7:21, *note*
19
b Prov. 6:14; Rom. 1:29–32; Gal. 5:19–21
20
c Cp. Col. 3:5,8
22
d Bible prayers (NT): vv. 22, 25,27; Mt. 26:39. (Mt. 6:9; Lk. 11:2, *note*)
e Mt. 1:1; 22:41–42; cp. Ps. 132:11
f See Mt. 7:22, *note*
24
g Gk. *apollumi.* See Jn. 3:16, *note 3*
h Mt. 10:6; Rom. 15:8
25
i Cp. Ps. 145:18
26
j Mt. 7:6
28
k Lk. 7:9; contrast Mk. 6:6
l Faith: v. 28; Mt. 17:20. (Gen. 3:20; Heb. 11:39, *note*)
m Cp. Mt. 9:27–29; 21:21–22; Lk. 4:25–27
n Miracles (NT): vv. 21–28, 32–39; Mt. 16:10. (Mt. 8:3; Acts 28:8, *note*)

30
o Mk. 7:25; Lk. 7:38; 8:41; 10:39
31
p Lk. 5:25,26; 19:37–38; cp. Mt. 11:20–24
32
q Mt. 9:36; 14:14; 20:34; cp. Ps. 86:15; 111:4; 145:8
33
r Cp. Mt. 14:15–21
CHAPTER 16
1
s See Mt. 3:7, *notes*
t Test/tempt: v. 1; Mt. 19:3. (Gen. 3:1; Jas. 1:14, *note*)

would show them a sign from heaven.

2 He answered and said to them, "When it is evening you say, '*It will be* fair weather, for the sky is red';

3 "and in the morning, '*It will be* foul weather today, for the sky is red and threatening.' Hypocrites!* You know how to discern the face of the sky, but you cannot *discern* the signs of the [a]times.

4 "A wicked and adulterous [b]generation seeks after a sign, and no sign shall be given to it except the [c]sign of the prophet* Jonah." And He left them and departed.

5 Now when His disciples had come to the other side, they had forgotten to take bread.

Symbol of leaven explained
(Mk. 8:15–21)

6 Then Jesus said to them, "Take heed and beware of the [d]leaven of the Pharisees and the Sadducees."

7 And they reasoned among themselves, saying, "*It is* because we have taken no bread."

8 But Jesus, being aware of *it,* said to them, "O you of little faith, why do you reason among yourselves because you have brought no bread?*

9 "Do you not yet understand, or [e]remember the five loaves of the five thousand and how many baskets you took up?

10 [f]"Nor the seven loaves of the four thousand and [g]how many large baskets you took up?

11 "How is it you do not understand that I did not speak to you concerning bread?—*but* to beware of the [d]leaven of the Pharisees and Sadducees."

12 Then they understood that He did not tell *them* to beware of the [d]leaven of bread, but of the [h]doctrine of the [i]Pharisees and [i]Sadducees.

Peter's confession of Christ
(Mk. 8:27–30; Lk. 9:18–21; cp. Jn. 6:68–69)

13 When Jesus came into the region of Caesarea Philippi, He asked His disciples, saying, [j]"Who do [k]men say that I, the [l]Son of Man, am?"

14 So they said, "Some *say* [m]John the Baptist, some Elijah, and others Jeremiah or [n]one of the prophets."

15 He said to them, "But who do [o]you say that I am?"

16 Simon Peter answered and said, "You are the [p]Christ, the Son of the living God."

First mention of the Church

17 Jesus answered and said to him, "Blessed are you, Simon [q]Bar-Jonah, for [r]flesh and blood has not revealed *this* to you, but My [s]Father who is in heaven.

18 "And I also say to you that you are [1]Peter, and on this [t]rock I will build My [2u]church, and the gates of [v]Hades shall not prevail against it.

19 "And I will give you the [3w]keys of the [x]kingdom of heaven, and whatever you bind on earth will be bound in heaven, and whatever you loose

*
16:3 NU-Text omits *Hypocrites.*
16:4 NU-Text omits *the prophet.*
16:8 NU-Text reads *you have no bread.*

3
a Cp. Jer. 8:7
4
b Prov. 30:12; cp. Mt. 21:23–27
c *Inspiration:* v. 4; Mt. 19:4. (Ex. 4:15; 2 Tim. 3:16, *note*)
6
d *Leaven:* vv. 6,11–12; Mk. 8:15. (Gen. 19:3; Mt. 13:33, *note*). Lk. 12:1; cp. 1 Cor. 5:6–8; Gal. 5:9
9
e Mt. 14:15–21; Mk. 6:30–44; Lk. 9:10–17; Jn. 6:1–14
10
f Mt. 15:32–38; Mk. 8:1–9
g *Miracles* (NT): vv. 9–10; Mt. 17:18. (Mt. 8:3; Acts 28:8, *note*)
12
h Cp. Gal. 1:6–9; Col. 2:4,8,18
i See Mt. 3:7, *notes*
13
j Cp. Mt. 21:10
k Cp. Jn. 5:41
l vv. 27,28; see Mt. 8:20, *note*
14
m Mt. 14:2
n Mt. 21:11
15
o Jn. 6:67
16
p Mt. 14:33; Jn. 6:69; Acts 8:37; 9:20; cp. Mt. 26:69–75
17
q Meaning *son of Jonah*
r Cp. Jn. 6:63–65
s Mt. 11:27; 1 Cor. 2:10; Gal. 1:16; cp. Jn. 1:12–13; 1 Jn. 4:15; 5:1,5
18
t *Christ* (Rock): v. 18; Mt. 21:42. (Gen. 49:24; 1 Pet. 2:8)
u *Church* (the true): v. 18; Acts 2:47. (Mt. 16:18; Heb. 12:23)
v See Lk. 16:23, *note*
19
w Mk. 13:34
x *Kingdom* (NT): v. 19; Mt. 16:27. (Mt. 2:2; 1 Cor. 15:24, *note*)

[1](16:18) In the Greek there is a play upon words in this statement: "You are Peter [*petros, a stone*], and upon this rock [*petra, a massive rock*] I will build My church." It is upon Christ Himself that the Church is built. See what the Apostle Peter writes (1 Pet. 2:4–8); compare also Paul's statement (1 Cor. 3:11).

[2](16:18) The word "church" (Gk. *ekklēsia,* from a verb meaning *to call out*) is used of any assembly and in itself implies no more than a gathering of people who have been called forth, e.g. the town meeting at Ephesus (Acts 19:41), and Israel, called out of Egypt and assembled in the wilderness (Acts 7:38). Israel was a "church," but not in any sense the NT church—the primary point of similarity being that both were "called out" and by the same God. See Acts 7:38 and Heb. 12:23, *notes.*

[3](16:19) These are not the keys of the Church but of the kingdom of heaven in the sense of ch. 13, i.e. the sphere of Christian profession. A key is a badge of power or authority (cp. Isa. 22:22; Rev. 3:7). The apostolic history explains and limits this trust, for it was Peter who opened the door of Christian opportunity to Israel on the Day of Pentecost (Acts 2:38–42) and to Gentiles in the house of Cornelius (Acts 10:34–48). There was no assumption by Peter of any other authority (Acts 15:7–11). In the council James, not Peter, seems to have presided

on earth will be loosed* in
heaven."
20 Then He [1]commanded His
disciples that they should tell no
one that He was [a]Jesus the
Christ.

Christ foretells His death
and resurrection
(Mk. 8:31–33; Lk. 9:22)

21 From that time Jesus began to show to His disciples that
He must go to Jerusalem, and
[b]suffer many things from the elders and chief priests and
[c]scribes, and be killed, and be
raised the third day.
22 Then Peter took Him aside
and began to rebuke Him, saying, "Far be it from You, Lord;
this shall not happen to You!"
23 But He turned and said to
Peter, "Get behind Me, [d]Satan!
You are an offense to Me, for
you are not mindful of the
things of God, but the things of
men."

Cost of discipleship
(Mk. 8:34–38; Lk. 9:23–26)

24 Then Jesus said to His disciples, "If anyone desires to
come after Me, let him deny
himself, and [e]take up his cross,
and [f]follow Me.
25 "For whoever desires to
save his life will lose it, but whoever loses his life for My sake
will find it.
26 "For what [g]profit is it to a
man if he gains the whole
[h]world, and loses his own soul?
Or what will a man give in exchange for his soul?
27 "For the Son of Man will
[i]come in the [j]glory of His Father with His angels, and then
He will [k]reward each [l]accord-
ing to his works.
28 "Assuredly, I say to you,
there are some standing here
who shall not taste death till
they see the Son of Man coming
in His [j]kingdom."

The transfiguration:
a foreview of the future kingdom
(Mk. 9:2–13; Lk. 9:28–36)

17 NOW after six days Jesus took Peter, [m]James,
and John his brother, led them
up on a high mountain by themselves;
2 and He [2]was [j]transfig-
ured before them. His face
shone like the sun, and His
clothes became as white as the
light.
3 And behold, Moses and
Elijah [n]appeared to them, talking with Him.
4 Then Peter answered and
said to Jesus, "Lord, it is good
for us to be here; if You wish, let
us* make here three tabernacles: one for You, one for Moses, and one for Elijah."
5 While he was still speaking, behold, a bright cloud overshadowed them; and suddenly a
[o]voice came out of the cloud,

*16:19 Or *will have been bound . . . will have been loosed* 17:4 NU-Text reads *I will.*

20
a Many mss. omit the word *Jesus*
21
b Mt. 17:12; 20:17–19
c See Mt. 2:4, *note*
23
d Satan: v. 23; Mt. 25:41. (Gen. 3:1; Rev. 20:10)
24
e Acts 14:22; 2 Cor. 4:10–11; 2 Tim. 3:12
f 1 Pet. 2:21
26
g Lk. 12:20–21; cp. Jas. 5:1–6
h Gk. *kosmos.* See Mt. 4:8, *note*

27
i Christ (second advent): vv. 27–28; Mt. 19:28. (Dt. 30:3; Acts 1:11, *note*)
j Kingdom (NT): vv. 27–28; 17:1–5; Mt. 18:1. (Mt. 2:2; 1 Cor. 15:24, *note*). Cp. Rev. 1:13–16
k Rewards: v. 27; Mt. 24:47. (Dan. 12:3; 1 Cor. 3:14, *note*)
l Judgments (the seven): v. 27; Mt. 22:13. (1 Sam. 7:14; Rev. 20:12, *note*)
CHAPTER 17
1
m See Mt. 4:21, *note*
3
n Resurrection: v. 3; Mt. 17:9. (2 Ki. 4:35; 1 Cor. 15:52, *note*)
5
o Jn. 12:28–30

(Acts 15:19; cp. Gal. 2:11–14). Peter claimed no more for himself than to be an apostle by gift (1 Pet. 1:1) and an elder by office (1 Pet. 5:1).

The power of binding and loosing was shared (Mt. 18:18) by the apostles and other believers (Jn. 20:22–23, where see *note;* cp. Lk. 24:33). An illustration of Peter's use of this authority as related to forgiveness (Jn. 20:23) is given in Acts 10:43. See also Paul's use of it in Acts 13:38–39. The keys of death and the place of departed spirits are held by the Lord Jesus Christ alone (Rev. 1:18).

[1](16:20) The disciples had been proclaiming Jesus as the Christ, i.e. the covenanted King of a kingdom promised to the Jews and at hand. The Church, on the contrary, must be built upon testimony to Him as crucified, risen from the dead, ascended, and made "head over all things to the church" (Eph. 1:20–23). The former testimony was ended; the new testimony was not yet ready because the blood of the new covenant had not yet been shed, but our Lord began to speak of His death and resurrection (v. 21). It is a turning point of immense significance.

[2](17:2) The transfiguration scene contains, in miniature, all the elements of the future kingdom in manifestation (2 Pet. 1:15–21): (1) the Lord Jesus, not in humiliation but in glory (v. 2); (2) Moses, in glory, representative of the redeemed who have passed through death into the kingdom (Mt. 13:43; cp. Lk. 9:30–31); (3) Elijah, in glory, representative of the redeemed who have entered the kingdom by translation (1 Cor. 15:50–53; 1 Th. 4:13–17); (4) Peter, James, and John, not glorified, representatives, for the moment, of Israel in the flesh in the future kingdom (Ezek. 37:21–27); and (5) the crowd at the foot of the mountain (v. 14), representative of those who are to be brought into the kingdom after it is established over Israel (Isa. 11:10–12; etc.).

saying, "This is My beloved [a]Son, in whom I am well pleased. Hear Him!"

6 And when the disciples heard *it,* they fell on their faces and were greatly afraid.

7 But Jesus came and touched them and said, "Arise, and do not be afraid."

8 When they had lifted up their eyes, they saw no one but Jesus only.

9 Now as they came down from the mountain, Jesus commanded them, saying, "Tell the vision to no one until the Son of Man is risen [b]from the dead."

10 And His disciples asked Him, saying, [1]"Why then do the scribes say that Elijah must come first?"

11 Jesus answered and said to them, "Indeed, [c]Elijah is coming first* and will restore all things.

12 "But I say to you that Elijah has come already, and they did not know him but did to him whatever they wished. Likewise the Son of Man is also about to suffer at their hands."

13 Then the disciples understood that He spoke to them of John the Baptist.

The powerless disciples: the mighty Christ (Mk. 9:14–29; Lk. 9:37–43)

14 And when they had come to the multitude, a man came to Him, [d]kneeling down to Him and saying,

15 "Lord, have mercy on my son, for he is an epileptic* and [e]suffers severely; for he often falls into the fire and often into the water.

16 "So I brought him to Your disciples, but they could not cure him."

17 Then Jesus answered and said, "O [f]faithless and [g]perverse generation, how long shall I be with you? How long shall I bear with you? Bring him here to Me."

18 And Jesus [h]rebuked the [i]demon, and it came out of him; and the child was [j]cured from that very hour.

19 Then the disciples came to Jesus privately and said, [k]"Why could we not cast it out?"

20 So Jesus said to them, "Because of your [l]unbelief;* for assuredly, I say to you, if you have [m]faith as a mustard seed, you will say to this mountain, 'Move from here to there,' and it will move; and nothing will be impossible for you.

21 "However, this kind does not go out except by prayer and [n]fasting."*

Jesus again foretells His death and resurrection (Mk. 9:30–32; Lk. 9:43–45)

22 Now while they were staying* in Galilee, Jesus said to them, "The [o]Son of Man is about to be [p]betrayed into the hands of men,

23 "and they will kill Him, and the third day He will be raised up." And they were exceedingly [q]sorrowful.

The miracle of the temple tax from the mouth of a fish (cp. Mk. 12:13–17)

24 When they had come to Capernaum,* those who received the [r]*temple* tax came to Peter and said, "Does your Teacher not pay the *temple* tax?"

25 He said, "Yes." And when he had come into the house, Jesus anticipated him, saying, "What do you think, Simon? From whom do the kings of the earth take customs or taxes,

5 *a* Mt. 3:17; 2 Pet. 1:17
9 *b Resurrection:* v. 9; Mt. 22:23. (2 Ki. 4:35; 1 Cor. 15:52, *note*)
11 *c* Mal. 4:5; Mt. 11:14; Lk. 1:17
14 *d* Mk. 1:40
15 *e* Cp. Mt. 15:22
17 *f* Cp. Jn. 20:27 *g* Dt. 32:5; Phil. 2:15
18 *h* Lk. 4:41 *i* See Mt. 7:22, *note* *j Miracles* (NT): vv. 14–18, 24–25; Mt. 17:27. (Mt. 8:3; Acts 28:8, *note*)
19 *k* v. 16
20 *l* Mt. 16:8; 21:21; Lk. 17:6 *m Faith:* vv. 19–21; Mt. 21:32. (Gen. 3:20; Heb. 11:39, *note*)
21 *n* Cp. Acts 13:2–3; 1 Cor. 7:5
22 *o* See Mt. 8:20, *note* *p* Mt. 20:17–19; Mk. 9:31; 10:33; Lk. 18:31–33; Acts 2:23
23 *q* Mt. 26:22; Jn. 16:6
24 *r* See Coinage (NT), Mt. 5:26, *note;* cp. Ex. 30:13

*
17:11 NU-Text omits *first.* **17:15** Literally *moonstruck* **17:20** NU-Text reads *little faith.* **17:21** NU-Text omits this verse. **17:22** NU-Text reads *gathering together.* **17:24** NU-Text reads *Capharnaum* (here and elsewhere).

[1](17:10) Compare Mal. 3:1; 4:5–6; Mt. 11:14; Mk. 9:11–13; Lk. 1:17. All the passages must be taken together. (1) Christ confirms the specific and still unfulfilled prophecy of Mal. 4:5–6: "Elijah is coming first and will restore all things." Here, as in Malachi, the prediction fulfilled in John the Baptist, and that yet to be fulfilled in Elijah, are kept distinct. (2) But John the Baptist had come already, and with a ministry so completely in the spirit and power of Elijah's future ministry (Lk. 1:17) that in a typical sense, it could be said: "Elijah has come already." Compare Mt. 10:40; Phile. 12,17, where the same thought of identification, although still preserving personal distinction, occurs (cp. Jn. 1:21).

from their sons or from [a]strangers?"

26 Peter said to Him, "From strangers." Jesus said to him, "Then the sons are free.

27 "Nevertheless, lest we [b]offend them, go to the sea, cast in a hook, and take the fish that comes up first. And when you have opened its mouth, you will [c]find a [d]piece of money;* take that and give it to them for Me and you."

Childlike faith necessary for entrance into the kingdom of heaven
(Mk. 9:33–50; Lk. 9:46–50)

18 AT that time the disciples came to Jesus, saying, "Who then is [e]greatest in the [f]kingdom of heaven?"

2 Then Jesus called a little [g]child to Him, set him in the midst of them,

3 and said, "Assuredly, I say to you, unless you [h]are converted and become as little children, you will by no means enter the [f]kingdom of heaven.

4 "Therefore whoever humbles himself as this little child is the greatest in the [f]kingdom of heaven.

5 "Whoever receives one little child like this in My name receives Me.

6 "But whoever causes one of these little ones who believe in Me to [i]sin, it would be better for him if a millstone were hung around his neck, and he were drowned in the depth of the sea.

The Father's concern for His own: parable of the lost sheep
(Lk. 15:3–7)

7 "Woe to the [j]world because of offenses! For offenses must come, but woe to that man by whom the offense comes!

8 [k]"If your hand or foot causes you to [i]sin, cut it off and cast *it* from you. It is better for you to enter into [l]life lame or maimed, rather than having two hands or two feet, to be cast into the everlasting fire.

9 "And if your eye causes you to [i]sin, pluck it out and cast *it* from you. It is better for you to enter into life with one eye, rather than having two eyes, to be cast into [m]hell fire.

10 "Take heed that you do not despise one of these little ones, for I say to you that in heaven their [n]angels always see the face of My Father who is in heaven.

11 "For the [o]Son of Man has [p]come to [q]save that which was [r]lost.*

12 "What do you think? [s]If a man has a hundred sheep, and one of them goes astray, does he not leave the ninety-nine and go to the mountains to seek the one that is straying?

13 "And if he should find it, assuredly, I say to you, he rejoices more over that *sheep* than over the ninety-nine that did not go astray.

14 "Even so it is not the [t]will of your Father who is in heaven that one of these little ones should perish.

Discipline and forgiveness in the church; agreement in prayer
(Lk. 17:3–4)

15 "Moreover if your [u]brother [v]sins against you, go and tell him his fault between you and him alone. If he hears you, you have gained your brother.

16 "But if he will not hear, take with you one or two more, that *'by the mouth of [w]two or three witnesses every word may be established.'*

17 "And if he refuses to hear them, tell *it* to the [x]church. But if he refuses even to hear the church, let him be to you like a [y]heathen and a tax collector.

18 "Assuredly, I say to you, whatever you [z]bind on earth will be bound in heaven, and whatever you loose on earth will be loosed in heaven.

19 "Again I say* to you that if two of you agree on earth concerning anything that they [aa]ask, it will be done for them by My Father in heaven.

20 "For where two or three are gathered [bb]together in My

*

17:27 Greek *stater*, the exact amount to pay the temple tax (didrachma) for two.
18:11 NU-Text omits this verse.
18:19 NU-Text and M-Text read *Again, assuredly, I say.*

25
a Isa. 60:10–17; cp. Isa. 49:22–23
27
b Lit. *cause them to stumble*
c Miracles (NT): vv. 24–27; Mt. 19:2. (Mt. 8:3; Acts 28:8, *note*)
d See Coinage (NT), Mt. 5:26, *note;* cp. Ex. 30:13
CHAPTER 18
1
e Lk. 22:24–27; cp. Mt. 20:20–28
f Kingdom (NT): vv. 1–4; Mt. 18:23. (Mt. 2:2; 1 Cor. 15:24, *note*)
2
g Mt. 19:14; Mk. 10:15; Lk. 18:14–17; cp. Ps. 131:2; 1 Cor. 14:20
3
h Lit. *turn about*
6
i Lit. *stumble*
7
j Gk. *kosmos.* See Mt. 4:8, *note*
8
k Mt. 5:29,30
l Life (eternal): vv. 8–9; Mt. 19:16. (Mt. 7:14; Rev. 22:19)
9
m Gk. *geenna.* See Mt. 5:22, *note.* Lit. *the gehenna of fire*
10
n See Heb. 1:4, *note*
11
o See Mt. 8:20, *note*
p Christ (first advent): v. 11; Mt. 21:5. (Gen. 3:15; Acts 1:11, *note*)
q See Rom. 1:16, *note*
r Gk. *apollumi.* See Jn. 3:16, *note 3*
12
s Parables (NT): vv. 12–14; Mt. 18:23. (Mt. 5:13; Lk. 21:29)
14
t 1 Tim. 2:4
15
u Lev. 19:17; Gal. 6:1–2; Eph. 4:30–32; Jas. 5:19–20
v See Rom. 3:23, *note*
16
w Dt. 19:15; Jn. 8:17; 2 Cor. 13:1; 1 Tim. 5:19; cp. Mt. 18:19
17
x Or *assembly.* Cp. 1 Cor. 5:3–5; 6:1–5
y Cp. 1 Cor. 5:9–13
18
z Jn. 20:22–23; see Mt. 16:19, *note*
19
aa 1 Jn. 3:22; 5:14; cp. 1 Pet. 3:7
20
bb Acts 20:7; 1 Cor. 14:26

name, I am there in the midst of them."

21 Then Peter came to Him and said, "Lord, how [a]often shall my brother [b]sin against me, and I [c]forgive him? Up to seven times?"

22 Jesus said to him, "I do not say to you, up to seven times, but up to [d]seventy times seven.

23 "Therefore the [e]kingdom of heaven is [f]like a certain king who wanted to settle accounts with his servants.

24 "And when he had begun to settle accounts, one was brought to him who owed him ten thousand [g]talents.

25 "But as he was [h]not able to pay, his master commanded that he be sold, with his wife and children and all that he had, and that payment be made.

26 "The servant therefore fell down before him, saying, 'Master, have patience with me, and I will pay you all.'

27 "Then the master of that servant was moved with compassion, released him, and [c]forgave him the debt.

28 "But that servant went out and found one of his fellow servants who owed him a hundred [g]denarii; and he laid hands on him and took *him* by the throat, saying, 'Pay me what you owe!'

29 "So his fellow servant fell down at his feet* and begged him, saying, 'Have patience with me, and I will pay you all.'*

30 "And he [i]would not, but went and threw him into prison till he should pay the debt.

31 "So when his fellow servants saw what had been done, they were very grieved, and came and told their master all that had been done.

32 "Then his master, after he had called him, said to him, 'You wicked servant! I [c]forgave you [j]all that debt because you begged me.

33 'Should you not also have had compassion on your fellow servant, just as I had pity on you?'

34 "And his master was angry, and delivered him to the [1]torturers until he should pay all that was due to him.

35 "So My heavenly Father also will do to you if each of you, from his heart, does not forgive his brother his trespasses."*

Jesus teaches concerning divorce (cp 5:31–32; Mk. 10:1—12; Luke 16:18; Rom. 7:1–3; 1 Cor. 7:10–16)

19 NOW it came to pass, when Jesus had finished these sayings, *that* He [k]departed from Galilee and came to the region of Judea beyond the Jordan.

2 And great multitudes followed Him, and He [l]healed them there.

3 The Pharisees also came to Him, [m]testing Him, and saying to Him, "Is it lawful for a man to divorce his wife for *just* any reason?"

4 And He answered and said to them, [2]"Have you not [n]read [o]that He who made* *them* at the beginning *'made them male and female,'**

5 "and said, *'For this reason a man shall leave his father and mother and be joined to his wife, and* [p]*the two shall become one flesh'*?

6 "So then, they are no longer two but one flesh. Therefore what God has joined together, let not man separate."

7 They said to Him, "Why then did Moses [q]command to give a certificate of divorce, and to put her away?"

8 He said to them, [3]"Moses, because of the [r]hardness of your hearts, permitted you to di-

*

18:29 NU-Text omits *at his feet.* • NU-Text and M-Text omit *all.*
18:35 NU-Text omits *his trespasses.*
19:4 NU-Text reads *created.* • Genesis 1:27; 5:2

21
a Cp. v. 15
b See Rom. 3:23, *note*
c Forgiveness: vv. 21–22, 27,32,35; Mt. 26:28. (Lev. 4:20; Mt. 26:28, *note*)

22
d Mt. 6:14; Mk. 11:25; Col. 3:13; cp. Ps. 78:40

23
e Kingdom (NT): vv. 23–34; Mt. 19:12. (Mt. 2:2; 1 Cor. 15:24, *note*)
f Parables (NT): vv. 23–35; Mt. 20:1. (Mt. 5:13; Lk. 21:29)

24
g See Coinage (NT), Mt. 5:26, *note*

25
h Cp. Rom. 3:19–20; 5:8

30
i Cp. Eph. 4:31–32; Col. 3:12–13

32
j Lk. 7:41–43

CHAPTER 19

1
k Jn. 10:40

2
l Miracles (NT): v. 2; Mt. 20:34. (Mt. 8:3; Acts 28:8, *note*)

3
m Test/tempt: v. 3; Mt. 22:18. (Gen. 3:1; Jas. 1:14, *note*)

4
n Inspiration: vv. 4–6; Mt. 21:4. (Ex. 4:15; 2 Tim. 3:16, *note*)
o Cp. Jn. 1:3; Eph. 3:9

5
p Gen. 2:24; 1 Cor. 6:16; cp. Eph. 5:21–33

7
q Law (of Moses): vv. 7–8; Mt. 19:18. (Ex. 19:1; Gal. 3:24, *note*)

8
r Heb. 3:15; cp. Rom. 8:3; Heb. 7:18–19

[1](18:34) Here is justice on the ground of law. Compare the grace of God offered to sinners (Rom. 3:21–26; 6:23; see also Jn. 1:17, *note*).

[2](19:4) Compare Gen. 1:27; 2:23–24. Observe in vv. 4–6 Jesus' confirmation of the Genesis narrative of the creation.

[3](19:8) Compare Dt. 24:1–4. Our Lord here confirms the Mosaic authorship of Deuteronomy.

8
a Mal. 2:16
11
b vv. 11–12; cp. Jn. 16:12; 1 Cor. 7:2–6,9
12
c 1 Cor. 7:7–8,17; cp. 1 Tim. 4:1–3
d *Kingdom* (NT): vv. 12, 14,23–24; Mt. 19:28. (Mt. 2:2; 1 Cor. 15:24, *note*)
e Cp. 1 Cor. 7:32–35
13
f Mt. 20:31
14
g Mt. 18:3–4; cp. 1 Pet. 2:2
16
h Cp. Rom. 7:18
i *Life* (eternal): vv. 16–17; Mt. 19:29. (Mt. 7:14; Rev. 22:19)

vorce your [a]wives, but from the beginning it was not so.

9 "And I say to you, whoever divorces his wife, except for sexual immorality,* and marries another, commits adultery; and whoever marries her who is divorced commits adultery."

10 His disciples said to Him, "If such is the case of the man with *his* wife, it is better not to marry."

11 But He said to them, [b]"All cannot accept this saying, but only *those* to whom it has been given:

12 "For there are eunuchs who were born thus from *their* mother's womb, and there are eunuchs who were made eunuchs by men, and there are eunuchs who have [c]made themselves eunuchs for the [d]kingdom of heaven's [e]sake. He who is able to accept *it,* let him accept *it.*"

Jesus blesses little children
(Mk. 10:13–16; Lk. 18:15–17)

13 Then little children were brought to Him that He might put *His* hands on them and pray, but the disciples [f]rebuked them.

14 But Jesus said, "Let the little children come to Me, and do not forbid them; for of [g]such is the [d]kingdom of heaven."

15 And He laid *His* hands on them and departed from there.

The rich young ruler
(Mk. 10:17–27;
Lk. 18:18–27; cp. Lk. 10:25–30)

16 Now behold, one came and [1]said to Him, "Good* Teacher, what [h]good thing shall I do that I may have [i]eternal life?"

17 So He said to him, "Why do you call Me good?* No one *is* [j]good but One, *that is,* God.* But if you want to enter into life, [k]keep the commandments."

18 He said to Him, [l]"Which ones?" Jesus said, "*'You shall not murder,' 'You shall not commit adultery,' 'You shall not steal,' 'You shall not bear false witness,'*

19 *'Honor your father and your mother,'** and, *'You shall love your* [m]*neighbor as yourself.'* "

20 The young man said to Him, "All these things I have [n]kept from my youth.* What do I still lack?"

21 Jesus said to him, "If you want to be [o]perfect, go, sell what you have and give to the poor, and you will have treasure in heaven; and come, follow Me."

22 But when the young man heard that saying, he went away sorrowful, for he had great possessions.

23 Then Jesus said to His disciples, "Assuredly, I say to you that it is hard for a [p]rich man to [q]enter the [d]kingdom of heaven.

24 "And again I say to you, it is easier for a camel to go through the eye of a [r]needle [s]than for a rich man to enter the kingdom of God."

25 When His disciples heard *it,* they were greatly astonished, saying, "Who then can be [t]saved?"

26 But Jesus looked at *them*

17
j Ps. 25:8; 34:8; Nah. 1:7; Rom. 2:4
k Lev. 18:5; Dt. 4:40; 6:17; 7:11; 11:22; 28:9; Gal. 3:10; cp. Rom. 3:19; 10:1–5
18
l *Law* (of Moses): vv. 18–20; Mt. 22:24. (Ex. 19:1; Gal. 3:24, *note*)
19
m Lev. 19:18; Mt. 5:43; 22:39; Lk. 10:29–37; Rom. 13:9; Gal. 5:14; Jas. 2:8
20
n Phil. 3:6–7; contrast vv. 7–9
21
o See Mt. 5:48, *note*
23
p Mt. 13:22; 1 Tim. 6:9–10; Jas. 5:1–3; cp. Jas. 2:5
q Cp. Jn. 3:5
24
r Gk. *raphis, a sewing needle*
s Cp. Mt. 7:13–14
25
t Cp. Mt. 13:3–9; see Rom. 1:16, *note*

*

19:9 Or *fornication* **19:16** NU-Text omits *Good.* **19:17** NU-Text reads *Why do you ask Me about what is good?* • NU-Text reads *There is One who is good.* **19:19** Exodus 20:12–16 Deuteronomy 5:16–20 **19:20** NU-Text omits *from my youth.*

[1](19:16) The rich young man made four mistakes, each of which was met by the Lord with unerring wisdom: (1) His mistake about the Person of Christ, thinking Him only a good teacher, was answered by the inescapable dilemma—either He is God or He is not a good man (v. 17). (2) His mistake about the way of eternal life, supposing it could be earned by works, was met by confronting him with the high demands of divine law (v. 17). (3) His mistake about himself, thinking he had kept the law (v. 20), was answered by testing him as to works of righteousness (v. 21) and opening his eyes to his failure (v. 22). And (4) his most tragic mistake was in not heeding the final words of Christ, "Come, follow Me" (v. 21); for therein was offered gracious hope for a sinner. In the Lord's explanation to the disciples, after the incident, He made it clear that salvation is never won by human attainment, but that "with God all things are possible" (vv. 24–26)—even the salvation of those who love riches. Salvation has always been by God's grace to the sinner, through his faith in Christ's atoning sacrifice. See Jn. 1:17, *note.*

and said to them, "With men
this is impossible, but with God
all things are [a]possible."

The apostles' reward now
and in the future kingdom
(Mk. 10:28–31; Lk. 18:28–30)

27 Then Peter answered and
said to Him, "See, we have left
all and followed You. Therefore
what shall we have?"
28 So Jesus said to them,
"Assuredly I say to you, that in
the [1]regeneration, [b]when the
Son of Man sits on the [c]throne
of His glory, you who have followed
Me will also sit on twelve
thrones, [2]judging the twelve
tribes of Israel.
29 "And everyone who has
left houses or brothers or sisters
or father or mother or wife* or
children or lands, for My
name's sake, shall receive a
hundredfold, and inherit eternal
[d]life.
30 "But [e]many *who are* first
will be last, and the last first.

Parable of the laborers

20 "FOR the [c]kingdom of
heaven is [3][f]like a landowner
who went out early in the
morning to hire laborers for his
vineyard.
2 "Now when he had agreed
with the laborers for a [g]denarius
a day, he sent them into his
vineyard.
3 "And he went out about
the [h]third hour and saw others
standing idle in the marketplace,
4 "and said to them, 'You
also go into the vineyard, and
whatever is right I will give
you.' So they went.
5 "Again he went out about
the [i]sixth and the [j]ninth hour,
and did likewise.
6 "And about the [k]eleventh
hour he went out and found others
standing idle,* and said to
them, 'Why have you been
standing here idle all day?'
7 "They said to him, 'Because
no one hired us.' He said
to them, 'You also go into the
vineyard, and whatever is right
you will receive.'*
8 "So when [l]evening had
come, the owner of the vineyard
said to his steward, 'Call the laborers
and give them *their*
wages, beginning with the last
to the first.'
9 "And when those came
who *were hired* about the [k]eleventh
hour, they each [m]received
a denarius.
10 "But when the first came,
they supposed that they would
receive more; and they likewise
[n]received each a denarius.
11 "And when they had received
it, they [o]complained
against the landowner,
12 "saying, 'These last *men*
have worked *only* one hour, and
you made them [p]equal to us
who have borne the burden and
the heat of the day.'
13 "But he answered one of
them and said, 'Friend, I am doing
you no wrong. Did you not
agree with me for a denarius?
14 'Take *what is* yours and
go your way. I wish to give to
this last man *the same* as to
you.
15 'Is it not lawful for me to
do [q]what I wish with my own
things? Or is your eye evil because
I am good?'
16 "So the [r]last will be first,
and the first last. For many are
called, but few chosen."*

*
19:29 NU-Text omits *or wife.*
20:6 NU-Text omits *idle.* **20:7** NU-Text omits the last clause of this verse.
20:16 NU-Text omits the last sentence of this verse.

26
a Gen. 18:14; Num. 11:23; Isa. 59:1; Jer. 32:17
28
b Christ (second advent): v. 28; Mt. 23:39. (Dt. 30:3; Acts 1:11, *note*)
c Kingdom (NT): vv. 27–28; 20:1–16; Mt. 20:21. (Mt. 2:2; 1 Cor. 15:24, *note*). Mt. 25:31; Lk. 1:31–33; Rev. 3:21
29
d Life (eternal): v. 29; Mt. 25:46. (Mt. 7:14; Rev. 22:19)
30
e Mt. 20:16; Lk. 13:30; cp. Mt. 21:31
CHAPTER 20
1
f Parables (NT): vv. 1–16; Mt. 21:28. (Mt. 5:13; Lk. 21:29). Mt. 21:33; cp. Isa. 5:7; Mt. 28:19; Jn. 15:1–5
2
g See Coinage (NT), Mt. 5:26, *note*
3
h 9 a.m. See Jn. 19:14, *note*
5
i Noon
j 3 p.m.
6
k 5 p.m.
8
l 2 Cor. 5:10
9
m Cp. 1 Cor. 9:24–25; 2 Tim. 4:7–8; see 1 Cor. 3:14, *note*
10
n Cp. Lk. 10:42
11
o Cp. Rom. 14:10–13
12
p Cp. Lk. 17:7–10; 1 Cor. 9:16–17
15
q Rom. 9:20–21; cp. Eph. 1:3–11; 2:4–8
16
r Mt. 19:30; cp. Mt. 22:14

[1](19:28) The word "regeneration," (Gk. *palingenesia* meaning *new birth, renewal, re-creation)* occurs only one other time in the NT, in Ti. 3:5. There it refers to the Christian's new birth; here, to the re-creation of the social order and renewal of the earth (Isa. 11:6–9; Rom. 8:19–23) when the kingdom comes. See Restoration (Acts 3:21, *note*); Kingdom, OT (Zech. 12:8, *note*); Kingdom, NT (1 Cor. 15:24, *note*).

[2](19:28) Our Lord's prediction discloses how the promise of Isa. 1:26 will be fulfilled when the kingdom is set up. The kingdom will be administered over Israel through the apostles, according to the ancient theocratic judgeship (Jud. 2:18).

[3](20:1) The complaint of these laborers (vv. 11–12) reveals their character. They had been dealt with fairly; they protested because others had been dealt with generously.

Jesus again predicts His death and resurrection
(Mk. 10:32–34; Lk. 18:31–34; cp. also Mt. 12:28–42; 16:21–28; 17:22–23)

17 Now Jesus, going up to Jerusalem, took the twelve disciples aside on the road and said to them,

18 "Behold, we are going up to Jerusalem, and the [a]Son of Man will be betrayed to the chief priests and to the scribes; and they will condemn Him to death,

19 "and deliver Him to the [b]Gentiles to [c]mock and to [d]scourge and to [e]crucify. And the third day He will [f]rise again."

Christ's response to request of the mother of James and John
(Mk. 10:35–45)

20 Then the mother of Zebedee's sons came to Him with her sons, kneeling down and asking something from Him.

21 And He said to her, "What do you wish?" She said to Him, "Grant that these two sons of mine may [g]sit, one on Your right hand and the other on the left, in Your [h]kingdom."

22 But Jesus answered and said, "You do not know what you ask. Are you able to drink the [i]cup that I am about to drink, and be baptized with the baptism that I am baptized with?"* They said to Him, "We are able."

23 So He said to them, "You will indeed drink My cup, and be baptized with the baptism that I am baptized [j]with;* but to [h]sit on My right hand and on My left is not Mine to give, but *it is for those* for whom it is prepared by My Father."

24 And when the ten heard *it,* they were greatly [k]displeased with the two brothers.

25 But Jesus called them to *Himself* and said, "You know that the rulers of the Gentiles lord it over them, and those who are great exercise authority over them.

26 "Yet it shall [l]not be so among you; but whoever desires to become great among you, let him be your [m]servant.

27 "And whoever desires to be first among you, let him be your slave—

28 "just as the [n]Son of Man did not come to be served, but to serve, and to give His life a [o]ransom for many."

Sight restored to two blind men
(Mk. 10:46–52; cp. Lk. 18:35–43, and see note 0 below)

29 Now as they went out of Jericho, a great multitude followed Him.

30 And behold, [1]two blind men sitting by the road, when they heard that Jesus was passing by, cried out, saying, "Have mercy on us, O Lord, [p]Son of David!"

31 Then the multitude [q]warned them that they should be quiet; but they cried out all the more, saying, "Have mercy on us, O Lord, Son of David!"

32 So Jesus stood still and called them, and said, "What do you want Me to do for you?"

33 They said to Him, "Lord, that our eyes may be opened."

34 So Jesus had [r]compassion and touched their eyes. And [s]immediately their eyes received sight, and they followed Him.

---

*

20:22 NU-Text omits *and be baptized with the baptism that I am baptized with.*
20:23 NU-Text omits *and be baptized with the baptism that I am baptized with.*

18
a Mt. 26:47–57
19
b Mt. 27:2
c Mt. 26:67–68
d Mt. 27:26
e Mt. 27:35; Acts 3:13–15
f Mt. 28:5–6; Mk. 16:6,9; Lk. 24:5–8
21
g v. 23; cp. Mt. 19:28; Rev. 3:21–22
h Kingdom (NT): vv. 21, 23; Mt. 21:5. (Mt. 2:2; 1 Cor. 15:24, *note*). Mt. 25:31; Lk. 1:31–33; Rev. 3:21
22
i Mt. 26:39, 42; Lk. 22:41–42; Jn. 18:11; cp. Isa. 53:2–5; Mt. 27:46; 2 Cor. 5:21; Gal. 3:13; 1 Pet. 2:24; 3:18
23
j Acts 12:2; Rev. 1:9
24
k Cp. Mt. 18:1; Lk. 22:23–27
26
l Mt. 23:11; 1 Pet. 5:3
m Mt. 23:11; Mk. 9:35; 10:43; Jn. 13:1–16; 1 Cor. 9:19–22
28
n Phil. 2:7; see Mt. 8:20, *note*
o Isa. 53:6, 10–11; 2 Cor. 5:21; 1 Tim. 2:5–6; Ti. 2:14; 1 Pet. 1:18–19; see *notes* at Ex. 14:30; Isa. 59:20; and Rom. 3:24
30
p 2 Sam. 7:14–17; Ps. 89:3–5, 19–37; Isa. 11:10–12; Ezek. 37:21–25; Mt. 1:1; Lk. 1:31,32; Acts 15:14–17
31
q Mt. 19:13
34
r Mt. 9:36; 14:14; 15:32; 18:27
s Miracles (NT): vv. 30–34; Mt. 21:19. (Mt. 8:3; Acts 28:8, *note*)

---

[1](20:30) A twofold discrepancy is alledged to exist between the account of this miracle in Mt. 20:29–34 and those in Mk. 10:46–52 and Lk. 18:35–43: the subjects, and time of the healing. Two blind men were involved; Bartimaeus, the more active, is mentioned by name in Mark. Nothing is known of the other. Luke states that the time of the healing was before Christ entered Jericho; Matthew and Mark place it at His departure from the city. An explanation is possible on one of two grounds: (1) the healing could have taken place after our Lord left the old Jericho, and was drawing near the new Jericho, which Herod the Great had built some distance away; and (2) the blind men could have entreated the Lord for healing when He approached the city, but were healed as He departed from it.

The King's public offer of Himself as King
(Mk. 11:1–10; Lk. 19:29–38; Jn. 12:12–19; cp. Zech. 9:9)

CHAPTER 21
1
21 [a]NOW when they drew near Jerusalem, and came to Bethphage,* at the Mount of Olives, then Jesus sent two disciples,
2 saying to them, "Go into the village opposite you, and immediately you will find a donkey tied, and a colt with her. Loose *them* and bring *them* to Me.
3 "And if anyone says anything to you, you shall say, 'The Lord has [b]need of them,' and immediately he will send them."
4 All* this was done that it might be [1]fulfilled which was [c]spoken by the prophet, saying:
5 *"Tell the daughter of Zion,*
'Behold, your [d]King is [e]coming to you,
Lowly, and sitting on a donkey,
*A colt, the foal of a donkey.'"**
6 So the disciples went and did as Jesus commanded them.
7 They brought the donkey and the colt, laid their clothes on them, and set *Him** on them.
8 And a very great multitude spread their [f]clothes on the road; others cut down branches from the trees and spread *them* on the road.
9 Then the multitudes who went before and those who followed cried out, saying:

"Hosanna to the Son of David!
[c]'*Blessed is He who comes in the name of the* LORD!'
Hosanna in the highest!"

10 And when He had come into Jerusalem, all the city was moved, saying, "Who is this?"
11 So the multitudes said, "This is Jesus, the [g]prophet from Nazareth of Galilee."

Jesus drives traders from Temple
(Mk. 11:15–18; Lk. 19:45–47; cp. Jn. 2:13–16)

12 Then Jesus went into the temple of God* and drove out all those who bought and sold in the temple, and overturned the tables of the money changers

1
a vv. 1–9; cp. Zech. 14:4–9. The two advents are in striking contrast
3
b Cp. Ps. 50:10
4
c Inspiration: vv. 4–5,9; Mt. 21:13. (Ex. 4:15; 2 Tim. 3:16, *note*). Ps. 118:26
5
d Kingdom (NT): vv. 1–9; Mt. 22:2. (Mt. 2:2; 1 Cor. 15:24, *note*)
e Christ (first advent): vv. 4–5; Mt. 21:37. (Gen. 3:15; Acts 1:11, *note*)
8
f Cp. 2 Ki. 9:13
11
g Dt. 18:15, 18; Mt. 2:23; 16:14; Lk. 4:16–29; Jn. 6:14; 7:40; 9:17; Acts 3:22–23; see Lk. 24:19, *note*

*
21:1 M-Text reads *Bethsphage.*
21:4 NU-Text omits *All.* 21:5 Zechariah 9:9 21:7 NU-Text reads *and He sat.*
21:12 NU-Text omits *of God.*

[1](21:4) Here was the King's final and official offer of Himself, in accord with the prophecy of Zech. 9:9. Acclaimed by an unthinking multitude whose real belief is expressed in v. 11, but with no welcome from the official representatives of the nation, He was soon to hear the multitude shout: "Crucify Him!" (27:22,23; cp. Mk. 15:13,14; Lk. 23:21).

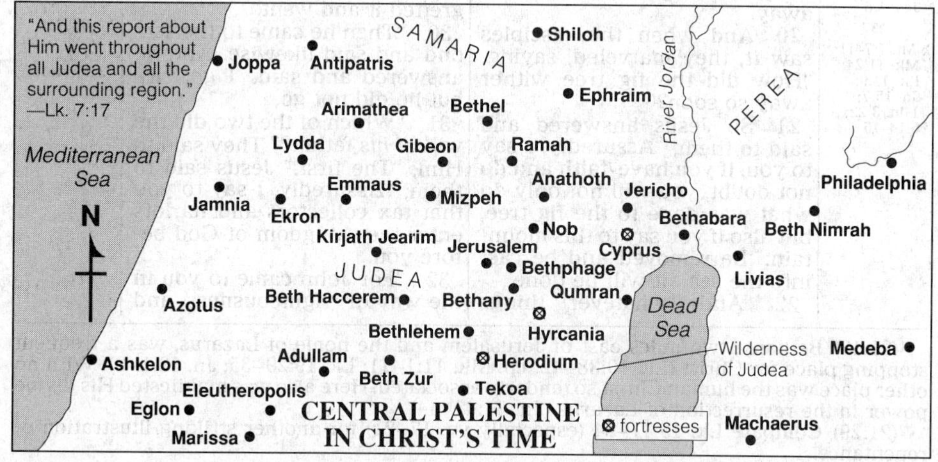

and the seats of those who sold
doves.
13 And He said to them, "It is
[a]written, [b]*'My house shall be*
called a house of prayer,' but
you have made it a *'den of*
thieves.' "
14 Then *the* [c]blind and *the*
lame came to Him in the temple,
and He healed them.
15 But when the chief priests
and scribes saw the wonderful
things that He did, and the children crying out in the temple
and saying, "Hosanna to the
[d]Son of David!" they were indignant
16 and said to Him, "Do You
hear what these are saying?"
And Jesus said to them, "Yes.
Have you never [a]read,

> [e]*'Out of the mouth of*
> *babes and nursing*
> *infants*
> *You have perfected*
> *praise'?"*

17 Then He left them and
[f]went out of the city to [1]Beth-
any, and He lodged there.

The barren fig tree
(Mk. 11:12–14,20–26)

18 Now in the morning, as He
returned to the city, He was
[g]hungry.
19 And seeing a [h]fig tree by
the road, He came to it and
found nothing on it but leaves,
and said to it, "Let no fruit grow
on you ever again." Immediately the fig tree [i]withered
away.
20 And when the disciples
saw *it,* they marveled, saying,
"How did the fig tree wither
away so soon?"
21 So Jesus answered and
said to them, "Assuredly, I say
to you, if you have [j]faith and do
not doubt, you will not only do
what was done to the fig tree,
but also if you say to this mountain, 'Be removed and be cast
into the sea,' it will be done.
22 "And [k]whatever things
you ask in prayer, believing,
you will receive."

Jesus' authority challenged
(Mk. 11:27–33; Lk. 20:1–8)

23 Now when He came into
the temple, the chief priests and
the elders of the people confronted Him as He was teaching, and said, "By what authority are You doing these things?
And who gave You this authority?"
24 But Jesus answered and
said to them, "I also will ask you
one thing, which if you tell Me,
I likewise will tell you by what
authority I do these things:
25 "The [l]baptism of [m]John—
where was it from? From
heaven or from men?" And they
[n]reasoned among themselves,
saying, "If we say, 'From
heaven,' He will say to us, 'Why
then did you not believe him?'
26 "But if we say, 'From
men,' we [o]fear the multitude,
for all count John as a
[p]prophet."
27 So they answered Jesus
and said, "We do not know."
And He said to them, [q]"Neither
will I tell you by what authority
I do these things.

Parable of the two sons

28 "But what do you think?
[r]A man had two sons, and he
came to the first and said, 'Son,
go, work today in my [s]vine-
yard.'
29 "He answered and said, 'I
will not,' but afterward he [2][t]re-
gretted it and went.
30 "Then he came to the second and said likewise. And he
answered and said, 'I go, sir,'
but he did not go.
31 "Which of the two did the
will of *his* father?" They said to
Him, "The first." Jesus said to
them, "Assuredly, I say to you
that tax collectors and harlots
enter the [u]kingdom of God before you.
32 "For John came to you in
the way of [v]righteousness, and

13
a Inspiration: vv. 13, 16; Mt. 21:42. (Ex. 4:15; 2 Tim. 3:16, *note*)
b Isa. 56:7; Jer. 7:11
14
c Cp. Lk. 14:21; Acts 3:1–10
15
d Mt. 1:1; Jn. 7:42; cp. Jer. 23:5–6
16
e Ps. 8:2; cp. 1 Cor. 1:26–29
17
f Mk. 11:11
18
g Mk. 11:12–14; cp. Jn. 4:6
19
h Lit. *a solitary fig tree.* Lk. 13:6–9
i Miracles (NT): vv. 18–22; Mk. 1:26. (Mt. 8:3; Acts 28:8, *note*)
21
j Mt. 17:20; Lk. 17:6; 1 Cor. 13:2; Jas. 1:6
22
k Mt. 7:7–11; Mk. 11:24; Lk. 11:9; Jn. 15:7; 1 Jn. 3:22; 5:14–15

25
l Jn. 1:29–34; see Acts 8:12, *note*
m Jn. 1:15–28
n Cp. Lk. 5:21
26
o v. 46; Mt. 14:5; Lk. 20:6; cp. Prov. 29:25; Mk. 6:25
p Mt. 14:5
27
q Cp. v. 32; Mt. 3:3
28
r Parables (NT): vv. 28–32; Mt. 21:33. (Mt. 5:13; Lk. 21:29)
s v. 33; Mt. 20:1; cp. Isa. 5:7; Mt. 28:19; Jn. 15:1–5
29
t Repentance: v. 29; Mk. 1:4. (Mt. 3:2; Acts 17:30, *note*)
31
u See Mt. 6:33, *note*
32
v Righteousness (OT): v. 32; Mt. 27:19. (Gen. 6:9; Lk. 2:25, *note*)

[1](21:17) Bethany, two miles east of Jerusalem and the home of Lazarus, was a frequent stopping place for Christ (Lk. 10:38–42; cp. Mk. 11:1–11; Lk. 19:29–35; Jn. 12:1–8). With no other place was the human Christ so tenderly associated. Here also was manifested His divine power in the resurrection of Lazarus (Jn. 11:41–44).

[2](21:29) Compare Lk. 15:11–24 (especially vv. 17–21) for another striking illustration of repentance.

you did not believe him; but tax
collectors and harlots [a]believed
him; and when you saw *it,* you
did not afterward relent and believe him.

Parable of the landowner
(Mk. 12:1–9; Lk. 20:9–19;
cp. Isa. 5:1–7)

33 "Hear another [b]parable:
There was a certain landowner
who planted a vineyard and set
a hedge around it, dug a winepress in it and built a tower. And
he leased it to vinedressers and
went into a far country.
34 "Now when vintage-time
drew near, he sent his servants
to the [c]vinedressers, that they
might receive its fruit.
35 "And the vinedressers
took his servants, beat one,
killed one, and stoned another.
36 "Again he sent other servants, more than the first, and
they did likewise to them.
37 "Then last of all he [d]sent
his [e]son to them, saying, 'They
will respect my son.'
38 "But when the vinedressers saw the son, they said
among themselves, 'This is the
[f]heir. Come, let us [g]kill him
and seize his inheritance.'
39 "So they took him and cast
him out of the vineyard and
killed *him.*
40 "Therefore, when the
owner of the vineyard comes,
what will he do to those vinedressers?"
41 They said to Him, "He will
destroy those wicked men mis-
erably, and lease *his* vineyard to
other vinedressers who will
render to him the fruits in their
seasons."
42 Jesus said to them, "Have
you never [h]read in the Scriptures:

'The [i]stone which the
builders rejected
Has become the [j]chief
cornerstone.
This was the LORD's
doing,
And it is marvelous in
our eyes'?

43 "Therefore I say to [k]you,
the [1][l]kingdom of God will be
taken from you and given to a
nation bearing the fruits of it.
44 "And whoever falls on this
[2][i]stone will be broken; but on
whomever it falls, it will grind
him to powder."
45 Now when the chief
priests and [m]Pharisees heard
His parables, they perceived
that He was speaking of them.
46 But when they sought to
lay hands on Him, they [n]feared
the multitudes, because they
took Him for a prophet.

Parable of the marriage feast
(Lk. 14:16–24)

22 AND Jesus answered
and spoke to them again
by [b]parables and said:
2 "The [o]kingdom of heaven
is like a certain king who arranged a marriage for his son,
3 "and sent out his servants
to call those who were invited to
the [p]wedding; and they were
not willing to come.
4 "Again, he sent out other
servants, saying, 'Tell those
who are invited, "See, I have
prepared my dinner; my oxen
and fatted cattle *are* killed, and

32
a Faith: v. 32; Mk. 2:5. (Gen. 3:20; Heb. 11:39, *note*)
33
b Parables (NT): vv. 33–43; 22:1–14; Mt. 24:32. (Mt. 5:13; Lk. 21:29)
34
c Jn. 15:1; Jas. 5:7–8
37
d Christ (first advent): v. 37; Mt. 26:31. (Gen. 3:15; Acts 1:11, *note*)
e Jn. 3:16
38
f Heb. 1:2; cp. Rom. 8:16–17
g Ps. 2:2; Jn. 11:53; Acts 4:26–28

42
h Inspiration: v. 42; Mt. 22:31. (Ex. 4:15; 2 Tim. 3:16, *note*). Ps. 118:22–23
i Christ (Stone): vv. 42,44; Mk. 12:10. (Gen. 49:24; 1 Pet. 2:8)
j v. 5; Isa. 29:16; Mk. 12:10; Acts 4:11; Eph. 2:20; 1 Pet. 2:6–7
43
k i.e. *national Israel, the barren vine* (vv. 33–41). Cp. Isa. 5:1–7
l See Mt. 6:33, *note*
45
m See Mt. 3:7, *note*
46
n v. 26; Mt. 14:5; Mk. 11:18,32
CHAPTER 22
2
o Kingdom (NT): vv. 2–14; Mt. 23:13. (Mt. 2:2; 1 Cor. 15:24, *note*)
3
p Or *marriage feast*

[1](21:43) Our Lord here uses the expression "kingdom of God," referring to a sphere of genuine faith in God, in contrast with His usual expression "kingdom of heaven." The kingdom of God is declared to be "taken from you," i.e. taken from the scribes and Pharisees represented in the parable as the wicked vinedressers, and given to a people who will bring forth the fruits of salvation. This passage teaches that unbelieving scribes and Pharisees would not be saved, because of their rejection of the Son. Others who will manifest the fruits of salvation take their place. Neither in the present age nor in the future millennium is the kingdom of God the exclusive possession of either Israel or the Gentiles.

[2](21:44) Christ as the Stone is revealed in a threefold way: (1) To Israel, Christ, coming not in Messianic glory but in the form of a Servant, is a Stumbling Stone and Rock of offense (Isa. 8:14–15; Rom. 9:32–33; 1 Cor. 1:23; 1 Pet. 2:8). (2) To the Church, Christ is the Foundation Stone and the Chief Cornerstone (1 Cor. 3:11; Eph. 2:20–22; 1 Pet 2:4–5). And (3) to the Gentile world powers (see Times of the Gentiles, Lk. 21:24, *note;* Rev. 16:19, *note*), Christ is to be the Striking Stone of destruction (Dan. 2:34). Israel stumbled over Christ; the Church is built upon Christ; Gentile world dominion will be crushed by Christ. See Armageddon, Rev. 16:13–16; 19:17, *note.*

all things *are* ready. Come to
the [a]wedding." '
5 "But they made light of it
and went their ways, one to his
own farm, another to his business.
6 "And the rest seized his
servants, treated *them* spitefully, and killed *them.*
7 "But when the king heard
about it, he was furious. And he
sent out his armies, destroyed
those murderers, and burned up
their city.
8 "Then he said to his servants, 'The [a]wedding is ready,
but those who were invited
were not worthy.
9 [b]'Therefore go into the
highways, and as many as you
find, invite to the [a]wedding.'
10 "So those servants went
out into the [c]highways and
gathered together all whom
they found, both bad and good.
And the [a]wedding *hall* was
filled with guests.
11 "But when the king came
in to see the guests, he saw a
man there who did not have on
a wedding garment.
12 "So he said to him,
[d]'Friend, how did you come in
here without a [e]wedding garment?' And he was [f]speechless.
13 "Then the king said to the
servants, 'Bind him hand and
foot, take him away, and* cast
him into [g]outer darkness; there
will be weeping and gnashing of
teeth.'
14 "For [h]many are called, but
few *are* chosen."

Jesus answers the Herodians
(Mk. 12:13–17; Lk. 20:20–26)

15 [1]Then the Pharisees went
and plotted how they might entangle Him in *His* talk.
16 And they sent to Him their
disciples with the [2i]Herodians,
saying, "Teacher, we know that
You are true, and teach the way
of God in truth; nor do You care
about anyone, for You do not
regard the person of men.
17 "Tell us, therefore, what
do You think? Is it lawful to pay
[j]taxes to Caesar, or not?"
18 But Jesus perceived their
wickedness, and said, "Why do
you [k]test Me, *you* hypocrites?
19 "Show Me the tax money."
So they brought Him a [l]denar-
ius.
20 And He said to them,
"Whose image and inscription
is this?"
21 They said to Him, "Caesar's." And He said to them,
"Render therefore to Caesar the
things that are [m]Caesar's, and to
God the things that are [n]God's."
22 When they had heard
these words, they marveled,
and left Him and went their
way.

Jesus answers the Sadducees
(Mk. 12:18–27; Lk. 20:27–38)

23 The same day the Sadducees, who say there is no [o]res-
urrection, came to Him and
asked Him,
24 saying: "Teacher, Moses
[p]said that if a man dies, having
no children, his brother shall
marry his wife and raise up offspring for his brother.
25 "Now there were with us
seven brothers. The first died
after he had married, and having no offspring, left his wife to
his brother.
26 "Likewise the second also,
and the third, even to the seventh.
27 "Last of all the woman
died also.
28 "Therefore, in the resurrection, [q]whose wife of the
seven will she be? For they all
had her."
29 Jesus answered and said
to them, [3]"You are mistaken,

*22:13 NU-Text omits *take him away and.*

4
a Or *mar-riage feast*
9
b The world-wide call. Mt. 28:16–20; Rev. 22:17
10
c Mt. 13:47–48; Acts 28:28; cp. Rom. 10:18; 15:19; Col. 1:5–6,23
12
d Cp. Mt. 26:50
e Contrast Rom. 10:1–13 with Phil. 3:7–9
f Rom. 3:19
13
g Judgments (the seven): v. 13; Mt. 23:33. (1 Sam. 7:14; Rev. 20:12, *note*)
14
h Mt. 20:16; cp. Isa. 65:2
16
i Mk. 3:6; see v. 15, *note*

17
j Cp. Mt. 17:24–27
18
k Test/ tempt: v. 18; Mt. 22:35. (Gen. 3:1; Jas. 1:14, *note*)
19
l See Coinage (NT), Mt. 5:26, *note*
21
m Rom. 13:1–7; 1 Pet. 2:13–17
n 1 Cor. 3:23; 6:19–20; 12:27
23
o Resurrection: vv. 23–31; Mt. 26:32. (2 Ki. 4:35; 1 Cor. 15:52, *note*)
24
p Law (of Moses): v. 24; Mt. 22:36. (Ex. 19:1; Gal. 3:24, *note*). Dt. 25:5
28
q Cp. 1 Tim. 1:4; 4:7; 6:4; 2 Tim. 2:23–26

[1](22:15) Verses 15–46 record our Lord's meetings with the representatives of Israel—the Herodians, the Sadducees, and the Pharisees (see 3:7, *note*). Although He answered their questions and put them to silence (v. 46), they did not repent and turn to Him in faith. The only message left for them was the woes of ch. 23.

[2](22:16) Not a sect but a political party that supported the Herod dynasty.

[3](22:29) "You are mistaken" (from the Greek verb *planaō*) carries the idea of being deceived. Thus Jesus' answer to the Sadducees' question gives the three incapacities of the rationalist: (1) self-deception (Rom. 1:21–22); (2) ignorance of the spiritual content of Scripture (Acts 13:27); and (3) disbelief in the intervention of divine power (2 Pet. 3:4–9).

not knowing the Scriptures nor the power of God.
30 "For in the resurrection they neither marry nor are given in marriage, but are [a]like angels of God* in heaven.
31 "But concerning the resurrection of the dead, have you not [b]read what was spoken to you by God, saying,
32 [c]'*I am the God of Abraham, the God of Isaac, and the God of Jacob*'? God is not the God of the dead, but of the living."
33 And when the multitudes heard *this,* they were astonished at His teaching.

Jesus answers the Pharisees
(Mk. 12:28–34; cp. Lk. 10:25–28)

34 But when the [d]Pharisees heard that He had silenced the [d]Sadducees, they gathered together.
35 Then one of them, a [1]lawyer, asked *Him a question,* [e]testing Him, and saying,
36 "Teacher, which *is* the [f]great commandment in the [g]law?"
37 Jesus said to him, "'*You shall [h]love the* LORD *your God with all your heart, with all your soul, and with all your mind.*'
38 "This is *the* first and great commandment.
39 "And *the* second *is* like it: '*You shall love your [i]neighbor as yourself.*'
40 "On these two commandments hang [j]all the Law and the Prophets."

Jesus questions the Pharisees concerning the Messiah
(Mk. 12:35–37; Lk. 20:41–44)

41 While the [d]Pharisees were gathered together, Jesus [2]asked them,
42 saying, "What do you think about the Christ? Whose Son is He?" They said to Him, "*The* [k]*Son* of David."
43 He said to them, "How then does David in the [l]Spirit call Him '*Lord,*' saying:

44 [m]'*The* LORD *said to my Lord,*
"Sit at My right hand,
Till I make Your enemies
Your footstool"'?

45 "If David then calls Him '*Lord,*' how is He his Son?"
46 And no one was able to answer Him a word, nor from that day on did anyone dare question Him anymore.

The marks of a Pharisee
(Mk. 12:38–40; Lk. 20:45–47)

23 THEN Jesus spoke to the multitudes and to His disciples,
2 [3]saying: "The scribes and the Pharisees sit in Moses' [4]seat.
3 "Therefore whatever they tell you to observe,* *that* observe and do, but do not do according to their works; for they say, and do not do.
4 "For they [n]bind heavy burdens, hard to bear, and lay *them* on men's shoulders; but they *themselves* will not move them with one of their fingers.
5 "But all their works they do to [o]be seen by men. They make their [5]phylacteries broad and enlarge the borders of their garments.
6 "They love the best places at feasts, the best seats in the synagogues,
7 "greetings in the market-

*
22:30 NU-Text omits *of God.*
23:3 NU-Text omits *to observe.*

30
a 1 Jn. 3:2; see Heb. 1:4, *note*
31
b *Inspiration:* vv. 31–32; Mt. 24:15. (Ex. 4:15; 2 Tim. 3:16, *note*)
32
c Gen. 17:7; 26:24; 28:21; Ex. 3:6; Acts 7:26
34
d See Mt. 3:7, *notes*
35
e *Test/tempt:* v. 35; Mt. 26:41. (Gen. 3:1; Jas. 1:14, *note*)
36
f Cp. Mt. 5:17–48
g *Law* (of Moses): vv. 36–40; Mt. 23:23. (Ex. 19:1; Gal. 3:24, *note*)
37
h Dt. 6:5; 10:12; cp. Rom. 3:19; Gal. 3:10
39
i Lev. 19:18; Mt. 19:19; Rom. 13:9; Gal. 5:14; cp. Lk. 10:29–37
40
j Mt. 7:12; Rom. 13:10; 1 Tim. 1:5
42
k Mt. 1:1; 21:9
43
l *Holy Spirit* (NT): v. 43; Mt. 28:19. (Mt. 1:18; Acts 2:4, *note*)
44
m Ps. 110:1
CHAPTER 23
4
n Cp. Mt. 11:29–30; Lk. 11:46; Acts 15:10; Rom. 2:17–24; Gal. 5:1; 6:13; Col. 2:16
5
o Mt. 6:1,2,5, 16

[1](22:35) The Greek word *nomikos* is translated "lawyer" here and in Lk. 7:30; 10:25; 11:45,46,52; 14:3; Ti. 3:13. In the Matthean and Lucan references it describes men expert in the *Jewish* law, normally called "scribes" (cp. Ezra 7:6,10). In Titus it probably refers to one who was expert in *Roman* law.

[2](22:41) Jesus' question was not personal but doctrinal; "Whose Son is the Messiah?" Cp. Jn. 19:7; Acts 2:25–36; Rom. 1:3–4.

[3](23:2) Verses 1–12 introduce the woes that Christ pronounced upon the scribes and Pharisees, and particularly emphasize the pride and self-exaltation of these interpreters of the law. The woes are expressed in the most severe language Christ ever used.

[4](23:2) Moses' seat has reference to the position of a teacher of the law of Moses. Cp. Ezra 7:6,25–26. The law is to be honored, but not the hypocritical teachers of it.

[5](23:5) Compare Dt. 6:8, which describes the proper and spiritual use of God's commandments.

places, and to be called by men, 'Rabbi, Rabbi.'

8 "But you, do not be called 'Rabbi'; for One is your Teacher, the Christ,* and you are all brethren.

9 "Do not call anyone on earth your father; for One is your Father, He [a]who is in heaven.

10 "And do not be called teachers; for One is your Teacher, the Christ.

11 "But he who is greatest among you shall be your servant.

12 "And whoever exalts himself will be humbled, and he who humbles himself will be exalted.

Jesus announces seven woes on the Pharisees
(Mk. 12:38–40; Lk. 20:47)

13 "But woe to you, scribes and Pharisees, hypocrites! For you shut up the [b]kingdom of heaven against men; for you neither go in *yourselves,* nor do you allow those who are entering to go in.

14 "Woe to you, scribes and Pharisees, hypocrites! For you devour widows' houses, and for a pretense make long prayers. Therefore you will receive greater condemnation.*

15 "Woe to you, scribes and Pharisees, hypocrites! For you travel land and sea to win one proselyte, and when he is won, you make him twice as much a son of [c]hell as yourselves.

16 "Woe to you, [d]blind guides, who say, 'Whoever swears by the temple, it is nothing; but whoever swears by the gold of the temple, he is obliged *to perform it.*'

17 [e]"Fools and blind! For which is greater, the gold or the temple that [f]sanctifies* the gold?

18 "And, 'Whoever swears by the altar, it is nothing; but whoever swears by the gift that is on it, he is obliged *to perform it.*'

19 "Fools and blind! For which is greater, the gift or the altar that [f]sanctifies the gift?

20 "Therefore he who swears by the altar, swears by it and by all things on it.

21 "He who swears by the temple, swears by it and by Him who dwells* in it.

22 "And he who swears by heaven, swears by the throne of God and by Him who sits on it.

23 "Woe to you, scribes and Pharisees, hypocrites! For you pay [g]tithe of mint and [1]anise and cummin, and have [h]neglected the weightier *matters* of the [i]law: justice and mercy and faith. These you ought to have done, without leaving the others undone.

24 "Blind guides, who strain out a gnat and swallow a camel!

25 "Woe to you, scribes and Pharisees, hypocrites! For you cleanse the outside of the cup and dish, but inside they are full of extortion and self-indulgence.*

26 "Blind Pharisee, first cleanse the inside of the cup and dish, that the outside of them may be clean also.

27 "Woe to you, scribes and Pharisees, hypocrites! For you are like [j]whitewashed tombs which indeed appear beautiful outwardly, but inside are full of dead *men's* bones and all uncleanness.

28 "Even so you also outwardly appear righteous to men, but inside you are full of hypocrisy and [k]lawlessness.

29 "Woe to you, scribes and Pharisees, hypocrites! Because you [l]build the tombs of the prophets and adorn the monuments of the righteous,

30 "and say, 'If we had lived

9
a Mt. 5:16,48; 6:1,9,14,26, 32; 7:11
13
b *Kingdom* (NT): v. 13; Mt. 23:39. (Mt. 2:2; 1 Cor. 15:24, *note*)
15
c Gk. *geenna.* See Mt. 5:22, *note*
16
d Mt. 15:14; cp. Isa. 56:10–11; Mal. 2:8
17
e Cp. Eph. 5:15
f *Sanctification* (NT): vv. 17,19; Mt. 24:15. (Mt. 4:5; Rev. 22:11)

23
g Lk. 11:42; 18:12
h 1 Sam. 15:22; Isa. 1:11–17; Hos. 6:6; Mic. 6:8
i *Law* (of Moses): v. 23; Mk. 1:44. (Ex. 19:1; Gal. 3:24, *note*)
27
j Lk. 11:44; Acts 23:3; cp. Phil. 3:4–6
28
k See Rom. 3:23, *note*
29
l Lk. 11:47–48

*
23:8 NU-Text omits *the Christ.*
23:14 NU-Text omits this verse.
23:17 NU-Text reads *sanctified.*
23:21 M-Text reads *dwelt.* 23:25 M-Text reads *unrighteousness.*

[1](23:23) Under the prescription in Dt. 14:22–23, the rabbis of Jesus' day included these spices as part of the tithe of grain. Mint is, perhaps, the "horse mint" *(Mentha longifolia),* the more common of several varieties growing wild in the Holy Land today. Anise *(Anethum graveolens)* resembles parsley and its aromatic, oval-shaped seeds are not unlike caraway. Cumin *(Cuminum cyminum)* is an herb of the carrot family, not common in Bible lands today.

31
a Acts 7:51–52
32
b 1 Th. 2:15–16
33
c Judgments (the seven): vv. 33,35; Mt. 24:51. (1 Sam. 7:14; Rev. 20:12, *note*)
d Gk. *geenna.* See Mt. 5:22, *note*
34
e The Jews' treatment of the apostles is proved, vv. 31–33
f Lk. 11:49; Jn. 16:2; Acts 7:54–60
g Acts 5:40; 2 Cor. 11:24–25
35
h Rev. 18:24
37
i Lk. 19:41–42; cp. Isa. 22:4
j vv. 31,34; Neh. 9:26; 2 Chr. 24:20–21; 36:15–16; Mt. 21:35–36

in the days of our fathers, we
would not have been partakers
with them in the blood of the
prophets.'
31 "Therefore you are witnesses against yourselves that
you are [a]sons of those who
murdered the prophets.
32 "Fill up, then, the measure
of your [b]fathers' *guilt.*
33 "Serpents, brood of vipers! How can you escape [c]the
condemnation of [d]hell?
34 "Therefore, indeed, I
[e]send you prophets, wise men,
and scribes: *some* of them you
will [f]kill and crucify, and *some*
of them you will [g]scourge in
your synagogues and persecute
from city to city,
35 "that on you may come
[h]all the righteous blood shed on
the earth, from the blood of
righteous [1]Abel to the blood of
Zechariah, son of [2]Berechiah,
whom you murdered between
the temple and the altar.
36 "Assuredly, I say to you,
all these things will [3]come upon
this generation.

Jesus laments over Jerusalem
(Lk. 13:34–35; cp. Ps. 118:26; Jer. 22:5)

37 [i]"O Jerusalem, Jerusalem, the one who kills the
prophets and [j]stones those who
are sent to her! How often I
wanted to [k]gather your children together, as a hen gathers
her chicks under *her* [l]wings,
but you were not willing!
38 "See! Your house is left to
you desolate;
39 "for I say to you, you shall
see Me no more [4m]till you say,
[n]*'Blessed is He who comes in*
the name of the LORD!' "*

VI. The Predicted Return of the King: the Olivet Discourse, 24—25

The Olivet Discourse: the temple to be destroyed
(Mk. 13:1–2; Lk. 21:5–6)

24 THEN Jesus went out
and [5]departed from the
temple, and His disciples came
up to show Him the buildings of
the temple.
2 And Jesus said to them,
"Do you not see all these things?
Assuredly, I say to you, [o]not
one stone shall be left here upon
another, that shall not be
thrown down."

The disciples' two questions: "When" and "What?"
(Mk. 13:3–4; Lk. 21:7)

3 Now as He sat on the
Mount of Olives, the disciples
came to Him privately, saying,
[6]"Tell us, [p]when will these

* 23:39 Psalm 118:26

k Mt. 11:28–30
l Cp. Ps. 17:8; 91:4
39
m Kingdom (NT): v. 39; Mt. 24:14. (Mt. 2:2; 1 Cor. 15:24, *note*)
n Christ (second advent): v. 39; Mt. 24:3. (Dt. 30:3; Acts 1:11, *note*)
CHAPTER 24
2
o Cp. 1 Ki. 9:7–9; Ps. 79:1; Isa. 64:11; Jer. 26:18; Mic. 3:12; Lk. 19:44
3
p vv. 27,37, 39; Lk. 17:20–37; 1 Th. 5:2–3

[1](23:35) Our Lord here confirms the record of Gen. 4:8–10. Cp. Heb. 12:24.

[2](23:35) This was probably the actual father of this martyr, Zechariah, who is designated in 2 Chronicles as son of his famous grandfather, Jehoiada, who had died at the advanced age of 130 before Zechariah began his ministry. Cp. 2 Chr. 24:15,20–22; 36:16; Lk. 11:51.

[3](23:36) Compare Rev. 18:21–24. Thus history runs. Judgment falls upon one generation for the sins of centuries. The prediction of v. 36 was fulfilled in the destruction of Jerusalem in A.D. 70.

[4](23:39) Observe the "tills" or "untils" of Israel's blessing: (1) Israel must say, "Blessed is He" (v. 39; cp. Rom. 10:3–4). (2) Gentile world power must run its course (Lk. 21:24; cp. Dan. 2:34–35). And (3) the elect number of the Gentiles and Jews must be brought into the Church (Acts 15:13–18). Then "the Deliverer will come out of Zion," etc. (Rom. 11:25–27).

[5](24:1) The Lord Jesus leaves that which He abandons to judgment. See Mk. 8:21–23 (with *note* at v. 23) in the light of Mt. 11:21–22. Cp. Rev. 18:4.

[6](24:3) Chapter 24, with Lk. 21:20–24, answers the twofold question. The order is as follows: "When will these things be?"—i.e. destruction of the temple and city. The answer is in Lk. 21:20,24. The remainder of Mt. 24:3 really constitutes a single question: "And what will be the sign of Your coming, and of the end of the age?" The answer is in vv. 4–33. Verses 4–14 have a double interpretation: They give (1) the character of the age—wars, international unrest, famines, pestilences, persecutions, and false Christs (cp. Dan. 9:26). This is not the description of a converted world. But (2) the same answer applies in a specific way to the end of the age, i.e. Daniel's seventieth week (see Dan. 9:24, *note*). All that has characterized the age gathers into awful intensity at the end. Verse 14 has specific reference to the proclamation of the good news that the kingdom is again "at hand" (Rev. 14:6–7; see Rom. 11:5, *note*). Verse 15 gives the sign of the abomination (see Dan. 9:24, *note*)—the man of sin, or beast (2 Th. 2:3–8; cp. Dan. 9:27; 12:11; Rev. 13:4–7).

This introduces the great tribulation (Ps. 2:5; see Rev. 7:14, *note*), which runs its awful things be? And what *will be* the sign of Your [a]coming, and of the end of the [b]age?"

Daniel's seventieth week of years (Dan. 9:27): the end time (Mk. 13:5–13; cp. Lk. 21:8–11)

4 And Jesus answered and said to them: "Take heed that no one deceives you.

5 "For [c]many will come in My name, saying, 'I am the [d]Christ,' and will deceive many.

6 "And you will hear of [e]wars and rumors of wars. See that you are not troubled; for all* *these things* must come to pass, but the end is not yet.

7 "For [f]nation will rise against nation, and kingdom against kingdom. And there will be [g]famines, pestilences,* and [h]earthquakes in various places.

8 "All these *are* the beginning of sorrows.

9 "Then they will [i]deliver you up to tribulation and kill you, and you will be hated by all nations for My name's sake.

10 "And then [j]many will be offended, will betray one another, and will hate one another.

11 "Then many [k]false prophets will rise up and deceive many.

12 "And because [l]lawlessness will abound, the love of many will grow [m]cold.

13 "But he who endures to the end shall be [1]saved.

14 "And this [n]gospel of the [o]kingdom will be preached in all the [p]world as a witness to all the nations, and then the end will come.

The middle of Daniel's seventieth week: the abomination of desolation (Mk. 13:14–18; cp. Lk. 21:20–23)

15 "Therefore when you see the [q]'*abomination of desolation*,'* [r]spoken of by Daniel the prophet, standing in the [s]holy place" **(whoever reads, let him understand),**

16 [2]"then let those who are in Judea flee to the mountains.

17 "Let him who is on the housetop not go down to take anything out of his house.

18 "And let him who is in the field not go back to get his clothes.

19 "But woe to those who are pregnant and to those who are nursing babies in those days!

20 "And pray that your flight may not be in winter or on the [t]Sabbath.

The great tribulation (latter half of week). (Mk. 13:19–23; cp. Ps. 2:5; Lk. 21:23–24; see Rev. 7:14, note)

21 "For then there will be [u]great tribulation, such as has not been since the beginning of the [v]world until this time, no, nor ever shall be.

22 "And unless those days were shortened, no flesh would be saved; but for the [w]elect's sake those days will be shortened.

3
a Christ (second advent): v. 3; Mt. 24:27. (Dt. 30:3; Acts 1:11, *note*)
b Gk. *aiōn*. See Mk. 10:30, *note*
5
c v. 24; Jn. 5:43; 1 Jn. 2:18
d Antichrist: vv. 4–5,11; Mt. 24:24. (Mt. 24:5; Rev. 13:11, *note*)
6
e Rev. 6:2–4
7
f Hag. 2:22
g Rev. 6:5–6
h Cp. Rev. 6:12
9
i Mt. 10:17–18; Lk. 21:12; Jn. 15:20–21; Rev. 2:10
10
j Cp. Dan. 12:10
11
k Acts 20:29; 2 Pet. 2:1; Rev. 13:11; 19:20
12
l See Rom. 3:23, *note*
m 2 Th. 2:3; 2 Tim. 3:1–3; cp. Rev. 3:15–16
14
n Gospel: v. 14; Mt. 26:13. (Gen. 12:3; Rev. 14:6)
o Kingdom (NT): v. 14; Mt. 24:30. (Mt. 2:2; 1 Cor. 15:24, *note*)
p Gk. *oikoumenē*. See Lk. 2:1, *note*
15
q The Beast: v. 15; Mk. 13:14. (Dan. 7:8; Rev. 19:20)
r Inspiration: v. 15; Mt. 24:37. (Ex. 4:15; 2 Tim. 3:16, *note*)
s Sanctification (NT): v. 15; Mt. 25:31. (Mt. 4:5; Rev. 22:11)
20
t Sabbath: v. 20; Mt. 28:1. (Gen. 2:3; Mt. 12:1, *note*)
21
u Tribulation (the great): vv. 21–22, 29; Mk. 13:19. (Ps. 2:5; Rev. 7:14)
v Gk. *kosmos*. See Mt. 4:8, *note*
22
w Election (corporate): v. 22; Mt. 24:24. (Dt. 7:6; 1 Pet. 5:13, *note*)

*
24:6 NU-Text omits *all*. **24:7** NU-Text omits *pestilences*. **24:15** Daniel 11:31; 12:11

course of three and a half years, culminating in the battle of Rev. 19:19–21 (see Rev. 19:19, *note*), at which time Christ becomes the Striking Stone of Dan. 2:34. The detail of this period (vv. 15–28) is: (1) the abomination in the holy place (v. 15), causing sacrifice to cease; (2) the warning (vv. 16–20) to believing Jews who will then be in Judea; (3) the great tribulation, with renewed warning about false Christs (vv. 21–26); (4) the sudden striking of the Gentile world power (vv. 27–28); (5) the glorious appearing of the Lord, visible to all nations, and the regathering of Israel (vv. 29–31); (6) the sign of the fig tree (vv. 32–33); and (7) warnings, applicable to this present age over which these events are ever impending (vv. 34–51; cp. Phil. 4:5). Careful study of Dan. 2; 7; 9; and Rev. 13 will make the interpretation clear. See, also, Remnant (Isa. 1:9; Rom. 11:5, *note*).

[1](24:13) The reference is not to the salvation of the soul of the believer who endures persecution, but to his deliverance by the Lord's return.

[2](24:16) Compare Lk. 21:20–24. The passage in Luke refers in express terms to a destruction of Jerusalem which was fulfilled by Titus in A.D. 70; the passage in Matthew alludes to a future crisis in Jerusalem after the manifestation of the "abomination." See Beast (Dan. 7:8; Rev. 19:20, *note*); and Armageddon (Rev. 16:13–16; 19:17, *note*). As the circumstances in both cases will be similar, so are the warnings. In the former case Jerusalem was destroyed; in the latter it will be delivered by divine interposition.

23 "Then if anyone says to
you, 'Look, here *is* the Christ!'
or 'There!' do not believe *it*.
24 "For [a]false christs and
false prophets will rise and
show great signs and wonders
to deceive, if possible, even the
[b]elect.
25 "See, I have told you beforehand.
26 "Therefore if they say to
you, 'Look, He is in the desert!'
do not go out; *or* 'Look, *He is* in
the inner rooms!' do not believe
it.
27 "For as the [c]lightning
comes from the east and flashes
to the west, so also will the
[d]coming of the [e]Son of Man be.
28 [1]"For wherever the [f]car-
cass is, there the eagles will be
gathered together.

The King's return to earth
at the close of the tribulation
(Mk. 13:24–27; Lk. 21:29–33)

29 "Immediately after the
tribulation of [g]those days the
sun will be darkened, and the
moon will not give its light;
the stars will fall from heaven,
and the powers of the heavens
will be shaken.
30 "Then the sign of the [e]Son
of Man will appear in heaven,
and then all the tribes of the
earth will [h]mourn, and they will
see the Son of Man [d]coming on
the [i]clouds of heaven with
power and great [j]glory.
31 "And He will send His
[k]angels with a great sound of a
trumpet, and they [l]will gather
together His [b]elect from the
four winds, from one end of
heaven to the other.

Parable of the fig tree
(Mk. 13:28–31; Lk. 21:29–33)

32 "Now learn this [m]parable
from the fig tree: When its
branch has already become tender and puts forth leaves, you
know that summer *is* near.
33 "So you also, when you
see all these things, know that
[n]it is near—at the doors!
34 "Assuredly, I say to you,
[o]this [2]generation will by no
means pass away till all these
things take place.
35 [p]"Heaven and earth will
pass away, but My words will
by no means pass away.

Watchfulness enjoined
(Mk. 13:32–37; Lk. 21:34–36)

36 "But of [d]that [g]day and
hour no one [q]knows, not even
the [k]angels of heaven,* but My
Father only.
37 "But as the [r]days of Noah
were, so also will the [d]coming
of the [e]Son of Man be.
38 "For as in the days before
the flood, they were eating and
drinking, marrying and giving
in marriage, until the day that
Noah entered the ark,
39 "and did not know until
the flood came and took them
all away, so also will the [d]com-
ing of the [e]Son of Man be.
40 "Then two *men* will be in
the field: one will be taken and
the other left.
41 "Two *women will be*
grinding at the mill: one will be
taken and the other left.
42 [s]"Watch therefore, for you
do [t]not know what hour* your
Lord is [d]coming.
43 "But know this, that if the
master of the house had known
what hour the thief would come,
he would have watched and not
allowed his house to be broken
into.
44 "Therefore you also be
[u]ready, for the [e]Son of Man is

*
24:36 NU-Text adds *nor the Son.*
24:42 NU-Text reads *day.*

24
a *Antichrist:* vv. 23–24; Jn. 5:43. (Mt. 24:5; Rev. 13:11, *note*)
b *Election* (corporate): vv. 24,31; Mk. 13:20. (Dt. 7:6; 1 Pet. 5:13, *note*)
27
c Lk. 17:24
d *Christ* (second advent): vv. 27,30, 36–45; Mt. 24:46. (Dt. 30:3; Acts 1:11, *note*)
e See Mt. 8:20, *note*
28
f *Armageddon* (battle of): vv. 27–28; Lk. 17:37. (Isa. 10:27; Rev. 19:17)
29
g *Day* (of the LORD): vv. 29–31, 36; Mt. 25:31. (Ps. 2:9; Rev. 19:19)
30
h Cp. Zech. 12:10–14
i Dan. 7:13
j *Kingdom* (NT): vv. 30–31; Mt. 25:1. (Mt. 2:2; 1 Cor. 15:24, *note*)
31
k See Heb. 1:4, *note*
l *Israel* (prophecies): v. 31; Mk. 13:27. (Gen. 12:2; Rom. 11:26, *note*)
32
m *Parables* (NT): vv. 32–33; Mt. 25:1. (Mt. 5:13; Lk. 21:29)
33
n Or *He.* Cp. 1 Th. 5:1–5
34
o Mt. 23:36
35
p 1 Pet. 1:23–25; 2 Pet. 3:10
36
q vv. 42,44; Acts 1:7; cp. Zech. 14:7
37
r *Inspiration:* vv. 37–38; Mt. 26:24. (Ex. 4:15; 2 Tim. 3:16, *note*). Gen. 6:5–8; 1 Pet. 3:20
42
s Mt. 25:13; 1 Th. 5:6
t v. 50
44
u Lk. 12:35–40

[1](24:28) The meaning of this somewhat puzzling verse is illuminated in the final dialogue between God and Job (Job 39:27–30). The spiritual application here is that, where moral corruption exists, divine judgment falls.

[2](24:34) The word "generation" (Gk. *genea*), though commonly used in Scripture of those living at one time, could not here mean those alive at the time of Christ, as none of "these things"—i.e. the worldwide preaching of the kingdom, the tribulation, the return of the Lord in visible glory, and the regathering of the elect—occurred then. The expression "this generation" here (1) may mean that the future generation which will endure the tribulation and see the signs, will also see the consummation, the return of the Lord; or (2) it may be used in the sense of *race* or *family*, meaning that the nation or family of Israel will be preserved "till all these things take place," a promise wonderfully fulfilled to this day.

[a]coming at an hour you do not expect.

45 "Who then is a [1]faithful and wise servant, whom his master made ruler over his household, to give them [b]food in due season?

46 "Blessed *is* that servant whom his master, when he [a]comes, will find so doing.

47 "Assuredly, I say to you that he will [c]make him ruler over all his goods.

48 "But if that evil servant says in his heart, 'My master is [d]delaying his [a]coming,'*

49 "and begins to beat *his* fellow servants, and to eat and drink with the drunkards,

50 "the master of that servant will [a]come on a day when he is not looking for *him* and at an hour that he is [e]not aware of,

51 "and will cut him in two and [f]appoint *him* his portion with the hypocrites. There shall be weeping and gnashing of teeth.

The parable of the ten virgins

25 [2]"THEN the [g]kingdom of heaven shall be [h]likened to ten virgins who took their lamps and went out to meet the [i]bridegroom.

2 "Now five of them were wise, and five *were* foolish.

3 "Those who *were* foolish took their lamps and took no oil with them,

4 "but the wise took oil in their vessels with their lamps.

5 "But while the bridegroom was delayed, they all slumbered and slept.

6 "And at midnight a cry was *heard:* 'Behold, the bridegroom is coming;* go out to meet him!'

7 "Then all those virgins arose and [j]trimmed their lamps.

8 "And the foolish said to the wise, 'Give us *some* of your oil, for our lamps are going out.'

9 "But the wise answered, saying, '*No,* lest there should not be enough for us and you; but go rather to those who sell, and buy for yourselves.'

10 "And while they went to buy, the bridegroom [a]came, and those who were ready went in with him to the [k]wedding; and the door was shut.

11 "Afterward the other virgins came also, saying, 'Lord, Lord, [l]open to us!'

12 "But he answered and said, 'Assuredly, I say to you, I do [m]not know you.'

13 [n]"Watch therefore, for you [o]know neither the day nor the hour* in which the [p]Son of Man is [a]coming.

The parable of the talents

14 "For *the* [q]*kingdom of heaven is* like a man traveling to a far country, *who* called his own servants and delivered his goods to them.

15 "And to one he gave five [r]talents, to another two, and to another one, to each according to his own ability; and immediately he went on a journey.

16 "Then he who had received the five talents went and [s]traded with them, and made another five talents.

17 "And likewise he who *had received* two gained two more also.

18 "But he who had received one went and dug in the ground, and [t]hid his lord's money.

19 "After a long time the lord of those servants came and [u]settled accounts with them.

20 "So he who had received five [r]talents came and brought five other talents, saying, 'Lord, you delivered to me five talents; look, I have gained five more talents besides them.'

21 "His lord said to him,

44
a Christ (second advent): vv. 36–50; 25:10–13; Mt. 25:31. (Dt. 30:3; Acts 1:11, *note*)
45
b Cp. 1 Pet. 5:2–4
47
c *Rewards:* v. 47; Mt. 25:21. (Dan 12:3; 1 Cor. 3:14, *note*)
48
d 2 Pet. 3:4–9; cp. Heb. 10:37; Rev. 22:7, 12,20
50
e Mk. 13:32
51
f *Judgments* (the seven): v. 51; Mt. 25:28. (1 Sam. 7:14; Rev. 20:12, *note*). Mt. 7:21–23; 25:3–12; 2 Pet. 2:20–22
CHAPTER 25
1
g *Kingdom* (NT): vv. 1–46; Mt. 26:29. (Mt. 2:2; 1 Cor. 15:24, *note*)
h *Parables* (NT): vv. 1–30; Mk. 2:21. (Mt. 5:13; Lk. 21:29)
i Syr. and Vul. add *and the bride*
7
j Cp. Lk. 12:35

10
k Or *marriage feast*
11
l Lk. 13:25–30
12
m Mt. 7:21–23
13
n Mk. 13:35; 1 Th. 5:6
o Mt. 24:36, 42
p See Mt. 8:20, *note*
14
q See Mt. 3:2, *note*
15
r See Coinage (NT), Mt. 5:26, *note*
16
s Cp. Eph. 5:16; 1 Tim. 4:12; 2 Pet. 1:5–8
18
t Cp. Prov. 26:15; 1 Pet. 4:10; 2 Pet. 1:9–12
19
u Cp. Rom. 14:10–12; 1 Cor. 3:9–17; 2 Cor. 5:10

*
24:48 NU-Text omits *his coming.*
25:6 NU-Text omits *is coming.*
25:13 NU-Text omits the rest of this verse.

[1](24:45) Compare Lk. 12:42–48; 1 Cor. 4:2. The Lord commends faithfulness rather than ability.

[2](25:1) This part of the Olivet Discourse goes beyond the "sign" questions of the disciples (24:3) and presents our Lord's return in three aspects: (1) as testing profession, vv. 1–13; (2) as testing service, vv. 14–30; and (3) as testing individual Gentiles, vv. 31–46.

21
a Lk. 16:10; 1 Cor. 4:2; 2 Tim. 4:7–8
b Rewards: vv. 21–23, 28–29, 34–40; Mk. 9:41. (Dan. 12:3; 1 Cor. 3:14, *note*)
c Ps. 16:11; Jn. 15:10–11; cp. Zeph. 3:17; Heb. 12:1–2
22
d See Coinage (NT), Mt. 5:26, *note*
24
e Jude 15; cp. Mt. 20:11–12
26
f Mt. 18:32; Lk. 19:22; cp. Mt. 24:48–50
28
g Judgments (the seven): vv. 28–30; Mt. 25:41. (1 Sam. 7:14; Rev. 20:12, *note*)
29
h Mt. 13:12; Mk. 4:25; Lk. 8:18; 19:26; Jn. 15:2
30
i Mt. 7:23; 8:12; 24:51
j Ps. 112:10
31
k See Mt. 8:20, *note*

[1]'Well *done,* good and faithful
servant; you were [a]faithful over
a few things, I will [b]make you
ruler over many things. Enter
into the [c]joy of your lord.'
22 "He also who had received
two [d]talents came and said,
'Lord, you delivered to me two
talents; look, I have gained two
more talents besides them.'
23 "His lord said to him,
'Well *done,* good and faithful
servant; you have been faithful
over a few things, I will [b]make
you ruler over many things. Enter into the [c]joy of your lord.'
24 "Then he who had re-
ceived the one [d]talent came and
said, 'Lord, I knew you to be a
[e]hard man, reaping where you
have not sown, and gathering
where you have not scattered
seed.
25 'And I was afraid, and
went and hid your talent in the
ground. Look, *there* you have
what is yours.'
26 "But his lord answered
and said to him, 'You [f]wicked
and lazy servant, you knew that
I reap where I have not sown,
and gather where I have not
scattered seed.
27 'So you ought to have de-
posited my money with the
bankers, and at my coming I
would have received back my
own with interest.
28 [g]'Therefore take the talent from him, and [b]give *it* to
him who has ten talents.
29 'For to everyone who
[h]has, more will be [b]given, and
he will have abundance; but
from him who does not have,
even what he has will be [g]taken
away.
30 'And [g]cast the unprofitable servant into the outer darkness. [i]There will be weeping
and [j]gnashing of teeth.'

Judgment of individual Gentiles at Christ's return to earth

31 "When the [k]Son of Man
[l]comes in His glory, and all the
[m]holy* [n]angels with Him, [o]then
He will sit on the throne of His
[p]glory.
32 [2]"All the nations will be
gathered before Him, and He
will separate them one from another, as a shepherd divides *his*
sheep from the goats.
33 "And He will set the
[q]sheep on His right hand, but
the goats on the left.
34 "Then the King will say to
those on His right hand, 'Come,
you blessed of My Father, [b]in-
herit the [p]kingdom prepared
for you from the foundation of
the [r]world:
35 'for I was [s]hungry and
you gave Me food; I was thirsty
and you gave Me drink; I was a
stranger and you took Me in;
36 'I *was* naked and you
clothed Me; I was sick and you
visited Me; I was in prison and
you came to Me.'
37 "Then the [t]righteous will

*
25:31 NU-Text omits *holy.*

l Christ (second advent): v. 31; Mt. 26:64. (Dt. 30:3; Acts 1:11, *note*)
m Sanctification (NT): v. 31; Mt. 27:53. (Mt. 4:5; Rev. 22:11)
n See Heb. 1:4, *note*
o Day (of the LORD): vv. 31–46; Mt. 26:29. (Ps. 2:9; Rev. 19:19)
p See Mt. 3:2, *note*
33
q Ps. 79:13; 100:3; Jn. 10:11,27–28; cp. Zech. 10:3
34
r Gk. *kosmos.* See Mt. 4:8, *note*
35
s Mt. 4:2; 21:18
37
t See Rom. 10:10, *note*

[1](25:21) The same commendation is gained by the servant with two talents (v. 23) as by the one with five talents, because both were equally faithful.

[2](25:32) This judgment of individual Gentiles is to be distinguished from other judgments in Scripture, such as the judgment of the Church (2 Cor. 5:10–11), the judgment of Israel (Ezek. 20:33–38), and the judgment of the wicked after the millennium (Rev. 20:11–15). The time of this judgment is "when the Son of Man comes in His glory," i.e. at the second coming of Christ after the tribulation. The subjects of this judgment are "all the nations," i.e. all Gentiles (Gk. *ethnē*) then living on earth. Three classes of individuals are mentioned: (1) sheep, saved Gentiles; (2) goats, unsaved Gentiles; and (3) brethren, the people of Israel. The scene is on earth; no books are opened; it deals with the living rather than with those translated or raised from the dead. The test of this judgment is the treatment by individual Gentiles of those whom Christ calls "My brethren" living in the preceding tribulation period when Israel is fearfully persecuted (cp. Gen. 12:3). The good works mentioned are the proof but not the ground of faith and salvation. The fact that the righteous and the unrighteous are still mingled and require separation after the establishment of Christ's throne on earth makes evident that no rapture, i.e. translation of the saints, could have taken place at the time of Christ's coming to the earth after the tribulation. In such a case the separation here described would have already occurred before the establishment of the throne. The sheep are Gentiles saved on earth during the period between the rapture and Christ's second coming to the earth. For the other six important judgments see Jn. 12:31, *note;* 1 Cor. 11:31, *note;* 2 Cor. 5:10, *note;* Ezek. 20:37, *note;* Jude 6, *note;* and Rev. 20:12, *note.*

answer Him, saying, 'Lord, when did we see You hungry and feed *You,* or thirsty and give *You* drink?

38 'When did we see You a stranger and take *You* in, or naked and clothe *You?*

39 'Or when did we see You sick, or in prison, and come to You?'

40 "And the King will answer and say to them, 'Assuredly, I say to you, inasmuch as you did *it* to one of the least of these My brethren, you [a]did *it* to Me.'

41 "Then He will also say to those on the left hand, [b]'Depart from Me, you cursed, into the everlasting fire prepared for the [c]devil and his [d]angels:

42 'for [e]I was hungry and you gave Me no food; I was thirsty and you gave Me no drink;

43 'I was a stranger and you did not take Me in, naked and you did not clothe Me, sick and in prison and you did not visit Me.'

44 "Then they also will answer Him,* saying, 'Lord, when did we see You hungry or thirsty or a stranger or naked or sick or in prison, and did not [f]minister to You?'

45 "Then He will answer them, saying, 'Assuredly, I say to you, [g]inasmuch as you did not do *it* to one of the least of these, you did not do *it* to Me.'

46 "And these will go away [b]into everlasting [h]punishment, but the [i]righteous into [j]eternal life."

VII. The Death and Resurrection of the King, 26—28

Jewish authorities plot death of Jesus (Mk. 14:1–2; Lk. 22:1–2)

26 NOW it came to pass, when Jesus had finished all these sayings, *that* He said to His disciples,

2 "You know that after two days is the [k]Passover, and the [l]Son of Man will be delivered up to be crucified."

3 Then the chief priests, the

40
a Mt. 10:40–42; Mk. 9:41; cp. Heb. 6:10

41
b Judgments (the seven): vv. 41–46; Lk. 14:14. (1 Sam. 7:14; Rev. 20:12, *note*)
c Satan: v. 41; Mk. 1:13. (Gen. 3:1; Rev. 20:10)
d See Heb. 1:4, *note*

42
e vv. 35,44

44
f Cp. Lk. 8:3

45
g Prov. 14:31; cp. Zech. 2:8; Acts 9:2,4–5

46
h Day (of destruction): v. 46; Lk. 21:22. (Job 21:30; Rev. 20:11)
i See Rom. 10:10, *note*
j Life (eternal): v. 46; Mk. 10:17. (Mt. 7:14; Rev. 22:19)

CHAPTER 26

2
k See Ex. 12:11, *note*
l See Mt. 8:20, *note*

[m]scribes,* and the elders of the people assembled at the palace of the high priest, who was called Caiaphas,

4 and [n]plotted to take Jesus by trickery and kill *Him.*

5 But they said, "Not during the feast, lest there be an uproar among the [o]people."

Jesus anointed for His burial by Mary of Bethany (Mk. 14:3–9; Jn. 12:1–8)

6 And when Jesus was in Bethany at the house of Simon the [p]leper,

7 a [q]woman came to Him having an alabaster flask of very costly fragrant oil, and she poured *it* on His [1]head as He sat *at the table.*

8 But when His disciples saw *it,* they were indignant, saying, "Why this waste?

9 "For this fragrant oil might have been sold for much and given to *the* poor."

10 But when Jesus was aware of *it,* He said to them, "Why do you trouble the woman? For she has done a good work for Me.

11 "For you have the poor with [r]you always, but [s]Me you do not have always.

12 "For in pouring this fragrant oil on My body, she did *it* [t]for My [u]burial.

13 "Assuredly, I say to you, wherever this [v]gospel is preached in the whole [w]world, what this woman has done will also be told as a memorial to her."

Judas agrees to betray Jesus (Mk. 14:10–11; Lk. 22:3–6)

14 Then one of the twelve, called Judas Iscariot, went to the chief priests

15 and said, "What are you willing to give me if I [x]deliver Him to you?" And they counted out to him thirty [y]pieces of silver.

16 So from that time he

*25:44 NU-Text and M-Text omit *Him.*
26:3 NU-Text omits *the scribes.*

3
m See Mt. 2:4, *note*

4
n Jn. 11:47; Acts 4:25–28

5
o Mt. 21:26

6
p Mt. 8:2; cp. Lk. 15:2

7
q i.e. *Mary of Bethany.* Mk. 16:9

11
r Dt. 15:11
s Lk. 5:34–35; Jn. 14:19; 16:28

12
t Lit. *to prepare Me for*
u Jn. 19:38–42; cp. Mk. 16:1

13
v Gospel: v. 13; Mt. 26:55. (Gen. 12:3; Rev. 14:6)
w Gk. *kosmos.* See Mt. 4:8, *note*

15
x vv. 47–50; cp. Jn. 11:57
y Mt. 27:3; cp. Zech. 11:12–13; see Coinage (NT), Mt. 5:26, *note*

[1](26:7) Compare Jn. 12:3. The ordinary anointing of hospitality and honor was of the feet (Lk. 7:38) and head (Lk. 7:46). But Mary of Bethany, who alone of our Lord's followers had comprehended His thrice-repeated announcement of His coming death and resurrection, invested the anointing with the deeper meaning of the preparation of His body for burying.

sought opportunity to betray Him.

Preparation for the Passover (Mk. 14:12–16; Lk. 22:7–13)

17 Now on the first *day* of the *Feast of* the Unleavened Bread the disciples came to Jesus, saying to Him, "Where do You want us to prepare for You to eat the Passover?"

18 And He said, "Go into the city to a certain man, and say to him, 'The Teacher says, [a]"My time is at hand; I will keep the Passover at your house with My disciples." ' "

19 So the disciples did as Jesus had directed them; and they prepared the Passover.

The last Passover (Mk. 14:17–21; Lk. 22:14–20,24–30; cp. Jn. 13:1–12)

20 When evening had come, He [1]sat down with the twelve.

21 Now as they were eating, He said, "Assuredly, I say to you, one of you will [b]betray Me."

22 And they were exceedingly sorrowful, and each of them began to say to Him, "Lord, is it I?"

23 He answered and said, "He who [c]dipped *his* hand with Me in the dish will [b]betray Me.

24 "The Son of Man indeed goes just as it is [d]written of Him, but [e]woe to that man by whom the Son of Man is [b]betrayed! [f]It would have been good for that man if he had not been born."

25 Then Judas, who was betraying Him, answered and said, "Rabbi, is it I?" He said to him, "You have said it."

The Lord's Supper instituted (Mk. 14:22–25; Lk. 22:17–20; cp. 1 Cor. 11:23–34; Jn. 13:12–30)

26 And as they were eating, Jesus took [g]bread, blessed* and broke *it*, and gave *it* to the disciples and said, "Take, eat; this is My [h]body."

27 Then He took the cup, and gave thanks, and gave *it* to them, saying, "Drink from it, all of you.

28 "For this is My [i]blood of the [j]new* [k]covenant, which is shed for many for the [2][l]remission of [m]sins.

29 "But I say to you, I will not drink of this fruit of the vine from now on until that [n]day when I drink it new with you in My Father's [o]kingdom."

(Here read John 14)

Jesus foretells Peter's denial (Mk. 14:26–31; Lk. 22:31–34; Jn. 13:31–38)

30 And when they had sung a hymn, they went out to the Mount of Olives.

31 Then Jesus said to them, "All of you will be made to

*

26:26 M-Text reads *gave thanks for.*
26:28 NU-Text omits *new.*

18
a v. 2; Lk. 9:51; Jn. 12:23; 13:1; 17:1; cp. Jn. 7:30; 8:20
21
b Jn. 6:70–71; 13:21
23
c Ps. 41:9; 55:12–14; Jn. 13:18,26
24
d Inspiration: v. 24; Mt. 26:31. (Ex. 4:15; 2 Tim. 3:16, *note*). Cp. Isa. 53
e Mt. 27:3–5; Lk. 17:1; Acts 1:16–20
f Jn. 17:12; Acts 1:25

26
g 1 Cor. 10:16
h 1 Pet. 2:24
28
i Sacrifice (prophetic): v. 28; Mt. 27:35. (Gen. 3:15; Heb. 10:18, *note*)
j Covenant (New): v. 28; Mk. 14:24. (Isa. 61:8; Heb. 8:8, *note*)
k Ex. 24:8
l Forgiveness: v. 28; Mk. 2:5. (Lev. 4:20; Mt. 26:28, *note*)
m See Rom. 3:23, *note*
29
n Day (of the LORD): v. 29; Mk. 13:24. (Ps. 2:9; Rev. 19:19)
o Kingdom (NT): v. 29; Mt. 26:64. (Mt. 2:2; 1 Cor. 15:24, *note*)

---

[1](26:20) The order of events on this solemn evening appears to have been: (1) Jesus partakes of the Passover with the apostles, and rebukes their contention (Mt. 26:20; Mk. 14:17; Lk. 22:14–16,24–30); (2) washes their feet (Jn. 13:1–20); (3) identifies Judas as the traitor (Mt. 26:21–25; Mk. 14:18–21; Lk. 22:21–23; Jn. 13:21–29); (4) Judas withdraws, the others profess loyalty (Jn. 13:30–38; cp. Mt. 26:31–35; Mk. 14:27–31; Lk. 22:31–38); (5) Jesus institutes the Lord's Supper (Mt. 26:26–29; Mk. 14:22–25; Lk. 22:17–20); (6) addresses the eleven in the upper room (Jn. 14); (7) again on the way to Gethsemane (Jn. 15—16); (8) intercedes with the Father for His own (Jn. 17); and (9) agonizes in the garden, is betrayed and arrested (Mt. 26:30,36–50; Mk. 14:26,32–52; Lk. 22:39–53; Jn. 18:1–12).

[2](26:28) Forgiveness, Summary: The Greek word here (also in Acts 10:43; Heb. 9:22) means *to send off* or *away*. And this, throughout Scripture, is the one fundamental meaning of forgiveness—to separate the sin from the sinner. Distinction must be made between divine and human forgiveness: (1) Human forgiveness means the remission of a penalty deserved, whereas the divine forgiveness, in type and fulfillment in both OT and NT, always follows the execution of the penalty. "The priest shall make atonement for his sin that he has committed, and it shall be forgiven him" (Lev. 4:35). "This is My blood of the new covenant, which is shed for many for the remission [sending away] of sins" (Mt. 26:28). "Without shedding of blood there is no remission" (Heb. 9:22). See Sacrifice (Gen. 4:4 and Heb. 10:18, *notes*). The sin of the justified believer interrupts his fellowship; it is forgiven upon confession, but always on the ground of Christ's propitiating sacrifice (1 Jn. 1:6–9; 2:2). And (2) human forgiveness rests upon and results from the divine forgiveness. In many passages this is assumed rather than stated, but the principle is declared in Mt. 18:32–33; Eph. 4:32.

stumble because of Me this night, for it is [a]written:

'I will strike the
[b]Shepherd,
And the sheep of the
flock will be scattered.'

32 "But after I have been [c]raised, I will go before you to Galilee."

33 Peter answered and said to Him, "Even if all are made to stumble because of You, I will never be made to stumble."

34 Jesus said to him, "Assuredly, I say to you that this night, before the [d]rooster crows, you will deny Me three times."

(Here read John 15—17)

35 Peter said to Him, "Even if I have to die with You, I will not deny You!" And so said all the disciples.

Jesus' agony in the garden
(Mk. 14:32–42; Lk. 22:39–46; Jn. 18:1)

36 Then Jesus came with them to a place called Gethsemane, and said to the disciples, "Sit here while I go and pray over there."

37 And He took with Him Peter and the two sons of Zebedee, and He began to be sorrowful and deeply [e]distressed.

38 Then He said to them, "My soul is exceedingly sorrowful, even to death. Stay here and watch with Me."

The first prayer
(Mk. 14:35; Lk. 22:41–42)

39 He went a little farther and fell on His face, and [f]prayed, saying, "O My Father, if it is possible, let this [1g]cup pass from Me; nevertheless, not as I will, [h]but as You *will*."

The sleeping disciples
(Mk. 14:37–40; Lk. 22:45–46)

40 Then He came to the disciples and found them sleeping, and said to Peter, "What? Could you not watch with Me one hour?

41 "Watch and pray, lest you enter into [i]temptation. [j]The spirit indeed *is* willing, but the flesh *is* weak."

The second prayer
(Mk. 14:39; Lk. 22:44)

42 Again, a second time, He went away and [f]prayed, saying, "O My Father, if this cup cannot pass away from Me unless* I drink it, Your will be done."

43 And He came and found them asleep again, for their eyes were heavy.

The third prayer (Mk. 14:41)

44 So He left them, went away again, and [f]prayed the third time, saying the same words.

45 Then He came to His disciples and said to them, "Are *you* still sleeping and resting? Behold, the hour is at hand, and the Son of Man is being [k]betrayed into the hands of [l]sinners.

46 "Rise, let us be going. See, My betrayer is at hand."

Jesus' betrayal and arrest
(Mk. 14:43–50; Lk. 22:47–53; Jn. 18:3–11)

47 And while He was still speaking, behold, Judas, one of the twelve, with a great multitude with swords and clubs, [m]came from the chief priests and elders of the people.

48 Now His betrayer had given them a sign, saying, "Whomever I [n]kiss, He is the One; seize Him."

49 Immediately he went up to Jesus and said, "Greetings, Rabbi!" and [o]kissed Him.

50 But Jesus said to him, [2p]"Friend, why have you

*26:42 NU-Text reads *if this may not pass away unless.*

31
a Inspiration: v. 31; Mt. 26:54. (Ex. 4:15; 2 Tim. 3:16, *note*). Zech. 13:7; cp. Jn. 16:32
b Christ (first advent): v. 31; Mt. 27:9. (Gen. 3:15; Acts 1:11, *note*)

32
c Resurrection: v. 32; Mt. 27:52. (2 Ki. 4:35; 1 Cor. 15:52, *note*)

34
d v. 74; Jn. 18:27; cp. Mk. 13:35

37
e Isa. 53:3; Lam. 1:12; Jn. 12:27

39
f Bible prayers (NT): vv. 39, 42,44; Mt. 27:46. (Mt. 6:9; Lk. 11:2, *note*). Cp. 2 Cor. 12:8
g vv. 42,44; Heb. 5:7–9; cp. Gen. 22:6–8
h Ps. 40:8; Jn. 5:30; 6:38; Phil. 2:8; cp. 2 Sam. 15:26

41
i Test/tempt: v. 41; Mk. 1:13. (Gen. 3:1; Jas. 1:14, *note*)
j Ps. 103:14–16; Rom. 7:15; 8:23; Gal. 5:17; cp. Rom. 7:18–25; 8:13

45
k Mt. 17:22–23; 20:18–19
l See Rom. 3:23, *note*

47
m Acts 1:16

48
n Cp. v. 50; Ps. 55:13

49
o Prov. 27:6; cp. 2 Sam. 15:5; 20:9–10; Rom. 16:16

50
p Ps. 41:9; cp. Ps. 55:12–14

[1](26:39) The "cup" must be interpreted by our Lord's own use of that symbol in speaking of His approaching sacrificial death (20:22; Jn. 18:11). In view of Jn. 10:17–18, He could have been in no fear of an unwilling death. The value of the account of the agony in the garden is in the evidence that it affords that He knew fully what the agony of the cross would mean when His soul would be made an offering for sin (Isa. 53:10)—the hiding of the Father's face. Knowing completely what the cost would be, He voluntarily paid it.

[2](26:50) Here is one of the most touching things in the Bible. The Lord still reaches out to Judas in friendship while he is about to betray Him.

come?" Then they came and laid hands on Jesus and took Him.

51 And suddenly, one of those *who were* with Jesus stretched out *his* hand and drew his sword, struck the servant of the high priest, and cut off his ear.

52 But Jesus said to him, "Put your sword in its place, for all who take the [a]sword will perish* by the sword.

53 "Or do you think that I cannot now pray to My Father, and He will provide Me with more than [b]twelve [1]legions of [c]angels?

54 "How then could the [d]Scriptures be [e]fulfilled, that it must happen thus?"

55 In that hour Jesus said to the multitudes, "Have you come out, as against a robber, with swords and clubs to take Me? I sat daily with you, [f]teaching in the temple, and you did not seize Me.

56 "But all this was done that the [d]Scriptures of the prophets might be [e]fulfilled." Then all the disciples [g]forsook Him and fled.

Jesus brought before Caiaphas and Sanhedrin (Mk. 14:53–65; cp. Jn. 18:12,19–24)

57 And those who had laid hold of Jesus [2]led *Him* away to [h]Caiaphas the high priest, where the scribes and the elders were assembled.

58 But [i]Peter followed Him at a distance to the high priest's courtyard. And he went in and [j]sat with the servants to see the end.

59 Now the chief priests, the elders,* and all the council sought [k]false testimony against Jesus to put Him to death,

60 but found none. Even though many false witnesses came forward, they found none.* But at last two false witnesses* came forward

61 and said, "This *fellow* said, 'I am able to [l]destroy the temple of God and to build it in three days.' "

62 And the high priest arose and said to Him, "Do You answer nothing? What *is it* these men testify against You?"

63 But Jesus [m]kept silent. And the high priest answered and said to Him, "I [n]put You under oath by the living God: Tell us if You are the Christ, the Son of God!"

64 Jesus said to him, "*It is as* you said. Nevertheless, I say to you, hereafter you will see the [o]Son of Man [p]sitting at the right hand of the Power, and [q]coming on the clouds of heaven."

65 Then the high priest [r]tore his clothes, saying, "He has spoken blasphemy! What further need do we have of witnesses? Look, now you have heard His [s]blasphemy!

66 "What do you think?" They answered and said, "He is deserving of death."

67 Then they [t]spat in His face and beat Him; and others

*26:52 M-Text reads *die.* **26:59** NU-Text omits *the elders.* **26:60** NU-Text puts a comma after *but found none,* does not capitalize *Even,* and omits *they found none.* • NU-Text omits *false witnesses.*

52
a Gen. 9:6; Rev. 13:10
53
b Cp. 2 Ki. 6:17; Dan. 7:10; Lk. 2:13–14
c See Heb. 1:4, *note*
54
d Inspiration: vv. 54, 56; Mt. 27:9. (Ex. 4:15; 2 Tim. 3:16, *note*)
e v. 24; Isa. 50:6; 53:2–11; Lk. 24:25–27, 44–46; Jn. 19:28; Acts 17:3; 13:29; 26:23; cp. Dan. 9:24–26
55
f Gospel: v. 55; Mt. 28:19. (Gen. 12:3; Rev. 14:6)
56
g Cp. 2 Tim. 4:10,16
57
h Lk. 22:54
58
i Jn. 18:15–16
j Cp. Ps. 1:1

59
k Ex. 20:16; Ps. 35:11
61
l Mt. 27:40; Jn. 2:19–22
63
m Isa. 53:7; Mt. 27:12, 14; Acts 8:32
n Lk. 22:67–71
64
o See Mt. 8:20, *note*
p Kingdom (NT): v. 64; Mt. 27:37. (Mt. 2:2; 1 Cor. 15:24, *note*)
q Christ (second advent): v. 64; Mk. 8:38. (Dt. 30:3; Acts 1:11, *note*)
65
r Num. 14:6; cp. Lev. 10:6; 21:10
s Jn. 10:30–36
67
t Isa. 50:6; 52:14; Mt. 27:30; Lk. 22:63–65

[1](26:53) At that time a Roman legion comprised between 3,000 and 6,000 men.

[2](26:57) The order of events following the arrest of the Lord Jesus appears to have been: (1) The Jewish trial of Jesus, composed of three stages: (a) the preliminary hearing before Annas (Jn. 18:12–14,19–24); (b) the informal trial before Caiaphas and the Sanhedrin, presumably before dawn (Mt. 26:57–68; Mk. 14:53–65; Lk. 22:54,63–65; Jn. 18:24); and (c) the formal trial by the Sanhedrin (Mt. 27:1; Mk. 15:1; Lk. 22:66–71). (2) Associated with (1) but before (3) were Peter's denials (Mt. 26:58,69–75; Mk. 14:54,66–72; Lk. 22:54–62; Jn. 18:15–18,25–27) and Judas' suicide (Mt. 27:3–10; Acts 1:18–19). (3) The Gentile trial of Jesus, composed of three stages: (a) Jesus was questioned by Pilate the first time (Mt. 27:2,11–14; Mk. 15:1–5; Lk. 23:1–5; Jn. 18:28–38); (b) Pilate sent Jesus to Herod (Lk. 23:6–12); and (c) Herod sent Jesus back to Pilate, who released Barabbas (Mt. 27:15–26; Mk. 15:6–15; Lk. 23:13–25; Jn. 18:39–40). Then (4) Jesus was crowned with thorns and brutally beaten by the Roman soldiers (Mt. 27:27–30; Mk. 15:16–19; Jn. 19:1–3). (5) As Christ was led forth to be crucified, the cross was laid on Simon (Mt. 27:31–32; Mk. 15:20–21; Lk. 23:26). And (6) on the way to Golgotha, Jesus warned the weeping women of judgment yet to fall on Jerusalem (Lk. 23:27–31). For the order of events at the crucifixion, see Mt. 27:33, *note.*

[a]struck *Him* with the palms of their hands,

68 saying, "Prophesy to us, Christ! Who is the one who struck You?"

Peter's three denials
(Mk. 14:66–72; Lk. 22:55–62; Jn. 18:15–18,25–27)

69 Now Peter sat outside in the courtyard. And a servant girl came to him, saying, "You also were with Jesus of Galilee."

70 But he denied it before *them* all, saying, "I do not know what you are saying."

71 And when he had gone out to the gateway, another [1]*girl* saw him and said to those *who were* there, "This *fellow* also was with Jesus of Nazareth."

72 But again he denied with an oath, "I do not know the Man!"

73 And a little later those who stood by came up and said to Peter, "Surely you also are *one* of them, for your [b]speech betrays you."

74 Then he began to [c]curse and swear, *saying,* "I do not know the Man!" Immediately a rooster [d]crowed.

75 And Peter remembered the word of Jesus who had said to him, "Before the rooster crows, you will deny Me three times." So he went out and wept bitterly.

Jesus delivered to Pilate
(Mk. 15:1; Lk. 23:1; Jn. 18:28)

27 WHEN morning came, all the chief priests and elders of the people plotted against Jesus to put Him to death.

2 And when they had bound Him, they led Him away and delivered Him to Pontius* Pilate the governor.

Judas' unavailing remorse
(cp. Acts 1:16–19)

3 Then Judas, His betrayer, seeing that He had been condemned, was remorseful and brought back the thirty [e]pieces of silver to the chief priests and elders,

4 saying, "I have [f]sinned by betraying [g]innocent blood." And they said, "What *is that* to us? You see *to it!*"

5 Then he threw down the [e]pieces of silver in the temple and departed, and went and [h]hanged himself.

6 But the chief priests took the silver [e]pieces and said, "It is not lawful to put them into the treasury, because they are the price of blood."

7 And they consulted together and bought with them the potter's field, to bury strangers in.

8 Therefore that field has been [i]called the Field of Blood to this day.

9 Then was fulfilled what was [j]spoken by [2]Jeremiah the prophet, saying, *"And they took the thirty [e]pieces of silver, the value of [k]Him who was priced,* whom they of the children of Israel priced,

10 *"and gave them for the potter's field, as the* LORD *[l]directed me."**

Jesus examined by Pilate
(Mk. 15:2–5; Lk. 23:2–3; Jn. 18:29–38)

11 Now Jesus stood before the governor. And the governor asked Him, saying, "Are You the King of the Jews?" Jesus said to him, [m]"*It is as* you say."

12 And while He was being accused by the chief priests and elders, He answered [n]nothing.

*

27:2 NU-Text omits *Pontius.*
27:10 Jeremiah 32:6–9

67
a Mic. 5:1; Jn. 19:3; cp. 1 Pet. 2:20–23
73
b Cp. Acts 2:7–11
74
c Contrast Mt. 16:16–17
d v. 34

CHAPTER 27
3
e Mt. 26:15; cp. Zech. 11:12–13; see Coinage (NT), Mt. 5:26, *note*
4
f Cp. Ex. 10:16; Num. 22:34; Josh. 7:20; 1 Sam. 15:24; see Rom. 3:23, *note*
g Cp. 1 Sam. 19:5
5
h Acts 1:18; cp. 1 Sam. 31:4; 2 Sam. 17:23
8
i Acts 1:19
9
j *Inspiration:* vv. 9–10; Mt. 27:35. (Ex. 4:15; 2 Tim. 3:16, *note*)
k *Christ* (first advent): vv. 9–10, 34–35,50; Mt. 28:6. (Gen. 3:15; Acts 1:11, *note*)
10
l Zech. 11:12–13
11
m v. 37; 1 Tim. 6:13
12
n v. 14; Acts 8:32; cp. Isa. 53:7

[1](26:71) Compare v. 69; Mk. 14:69; Lk. 22:58; Jn. 18:25. Regarding the alleged discrepancies in these accounts, it should be said that an excited crowd had gathered, and Peter was interrogated in two places: with the guards (v. 58), where the first charge was made (v. 69); and in the gateway (v. 71), where a great number of people would be gathered. Here the second and third interrogations were made by another girl and by the crowd (vv. 71,73; Jn. 18:25).

[2](27:9) There may be an allusion to Jer. 18:1–4 and 19:1–3, but the reference is distinctly to Zech. 11:12–13. A Talmudic tradition states that the prophetic writings were placed in the canon in this order: Jeremiah, Ezekiel, Isaiah, etc. Many Hebrew manuscripts follow this order. Thus Matthew cited the passage as from the roll of the prophets and by the name of the first book.

13 Then Pilate said to Him,
"Do You not hear how many
things they testify against
You?"
14 But He answered him not
one word, so that the governor
marveled greatly.

Jesus or Barabbas? (Mk. 15:6–15;
Lk. 23:13–25; cp. Jn. 18:38–40)

15 Now at the feast the governor was accustomed to releasing to the multitude one
prisoner whom they wished.
16 And at that time they had
a notorious prisoner called Barabbas.*
17 Therefore, when they had
[1]gathered together, Pilate said
to them, "Whom do you want
me to release to you? Barabbas,
or Jesus who is called Christ?"
18 For he knew that they had
handed Him over because of
[a]envy.
19 While he was [b]sitting on
the judgment seat, his wife sent
to him, saying, "Have nothing to
do with that [c]just Man, for I
have suffered many things today in a dream because of Him."
20 But the chief priests and
elders persuaded the multitudes
that they should ask for Barabbas and destroy Jesus.
21 The governor answered
and said to them, [d]"Which of
the two do you want me to release to you?" They said, [e]"Barabbas!"
22 Pilate said to them, "What
then shall I do with Jesus who is
called Christ?" *They* all said to
him, "Let Him be crucified!"
23 Then the governor said,
[f]"Why, what evil has He
[g]done?" But they cried out all
the more, saying, "Let Him be
crucified!"
24 When Pilate saw that he
could [h]not prevail at all, but
rather *that* a tumult was rising,
he took water and [i]washed *his*
hands before the multitude,
saying, "I am innocent of the
blood of this [c]just Person.* You
see *to it*."
25 And all the people an-
swered and said, "His [j]blood *be*
on us and on our children."
26 Then he released Barabbas to them; and when he had
[k]scourged Jesus, he delivered
Him to be crucified.

The King crowned with thorns;
He is then led to the place
of crucifixion
(Mk. 15:16–23; Lk. 23:26–32;
Jn. 19:16–17)

27 Then the soldiers of the
governor took Jesus into the
Praetorium and gathered the
whole garrison around Him.
28 And they [l]stripped Him
and put a [m]scarlet robe on Him.
29 When they had twisted a
crown of [n]thorns, they put *it* on
His head, and a reed in His right
hand. And they bowed the knee
before Him and mocked Him,
saying, "Hail, King of the Jews!"
30 Then they [o]spat on Him,
and took the reed and struck
Him on the head.
31 And when they had
mocked Him, they took the robe
off Him, put His *own* clothes on
Him, and led Him away to be
crucified.
32 Now as they came out,
they found a man of Cyrene, Si-

*27:16 NU-Text reads *Jesus Barabbas*.
27:24 NU-Text omits *just*.

18
a Mt. 21:38; Jn. 15:22–25; cp. Gen. 37:11; Dan. 3:8–12; 6:1–4
19
b Cp. Rev. 20:11–15
c *Righteousness* (OT): vv. 19,24; Mk. 6:20. (Gen. 6:9; Lk. 2:25, *note*)
21
d Cp. Dt. 30:15–20; Josh. 24:15; 1 Ki. 18:21
e Acts 3:14; cp. Jn. 5:43; 2 Th. 2:3–8
23
f Acts 3:13
g Cp. Jer. 26:16; Acts 23:29; 25:25
24
h Cp. 1 Sam. 15:24; Jer. 38:5; Dan. 6:15
i Cp. Dt. 21:6–7; Job 9:30–31; Prov. 30:20
25
j Dt. 19:10; cp. Gen. 4:10; Josh. 2:19; 2 Sam. 1:16; Mt. 23:35; Acts 5:28
26
k Isa. 53:5; Jn. 19:1
28
l Jn. 19:2
m Lk. 23:11; cp. Ps. 69:19
29
n Cp. Gen. 3:18; Gal. 3:13
30
o Isa. 50:6; Mt. 26:67

[1](27:17) There were two legal systems that condemned Christ: the Jewish and the Roman, the very two which underlie modern jurisprudence. The arrest and proceedings under Annas, Caiaphas, and the Sanhedrin were under Jewish law; those under Pilate and Herod were under Roman law. The Jewish trial was illegal in several particulars: (1) The judge was not impartial and did not protect the accused. There is no evidence that the quorum of twenty-three judges was present; the judges took part in the arrest; and they were hostile (Mt. 26:62–63). (2) The arrest was unlawful because it was carried out under no formal accusation. (3) In criminal trials all sessions had to be started and carried on only during the day. Night sessions were illegal. (4) A verdict of guilty could not be rendered on the same day as the conclusion of the trial. It had to be given on the next day. (5) The search for hostile testimony was illegal (Mt. 26:59; Mk. 14:56; Jn. 11:53). (6) No accused could be convicted on his own evidence, yet they sought replies and admissions from Christ to condemn Him (Mt. 26:63–66; Jn. 18:19). And (7) no valid legal evidence was presented against Him.

After Pilate declared Christ innocent (Mt. 27:24), his subsequent acts were all contrary to the letter and spirit of Roman law.

mon by name. Him they compelled to [a]bear His cross.

Jesus crucified (Mk. 15:22–32; Lk. 23:33–43; Jn. 19:17–24)

33 [1]And when they had come to a place called [b]Golgotha, that is to say, Place of a Skull,
34 they gave Him [c]sour* wine mingled with gall to drink. But when He had tasted *it,* He would not drink.
35 [d]Then they [e]crucified Him, and divided His garments, casting lots,* that it might be fulfilled which was [f]spoken by the prophet:

> *"They divided My [g]garments among them,*
> *And for My clothing they cast lots."*

36 Sitting down, they kept watch over Him there.
37 And they put up over His head the accusation written against Him:

[2]THIS IS JESUS THE [h]KING OF THE JEWS.

38 Then two robbers were [e]crucified with Him, one on the right and another on the left.
39 And those who passed by blasphemed Him, wagging their heads
40 and saying, "You who destroy the temple and build *it* in three days, save Yourself! If You are the Son of God, come down from the cross."
41 Likewise the chief priests also, mocking with the scribes and elders,* said,
42 "He [i]saved others; Himself He cannot save. If He is the [h]King of Israel,* let Him now come down from the cross, and we will believe Him.*
43 "He [j]trusted in God; let Him deliver Him now if He will have Him; for He said, 'I am the Son of God.' "
44 Even the robbers who were crucified with Him reviled Him with the same thing.

Jesus' death fulfills the law (Mk. 15:33–41; Lk. 23:44–49; Jn. 19:30–37; Heb. 9:3–8; 10:19–20)
The dispensation of law ends: see Acts 2:1, note

45 Now from the [k]sixth hour until the [l]ninth hour there was darkness over all the land.
46 And about the [l]ninth hour Jesus cried out with a loud voice, [m]saying, [n]"Eli, Eli, lama sabachthani?" that is, [3f]*"My God, My God, why have You forsaken Me?"**
47 Some of those who stood there, when they heard *that,* said, "This Man is calling for Elijah!"
48 Immediately one of them ran and took a sponge, filled *it* with [c]sour wine and put *it* on a

32
a Cp. 2 Cor. 4:10
33
b See Mk. 15:22, *note*
34
c v. 48; Ps. 69:21
35
d c. A.D. 29
e Sacrifice (of Christ): vv. 33–35, 38; Mk. 14:24. (Gen. 3:15; Heb. 10:18, *note*)
f Inspiration: vv. 35, 46; Mt. 28:20. (Ex. 4:15; 2 Tim. 3:16, *note*)
g Ps. 22:18
37
h Kingdom (NT): vv. 37, 42; Mk. 1:14. (Mt. 2:2; 1 Cor. 15:24, *note*)
42
i Mt. 18:11; Jn. 3:14–15; cp. Ps. 22:7–8; see Rom. 1:16, *note*
43
j See Ps. 2:12, *note*
45
k Noon. See Jn. 19:14, *note*
l 3 p.m. See Jn. 19:14, *note*
46
m Bible prayers (NT): v. 46; Mk. 5:23. (Mt. 6:9; Lk. 11:2, *note*)
n See Mk. 15:35, *note*

*
27:34 NU-Text omits *sour.* **27:35** NU-Text and M-Text omit the rest of this verse. **27:41** M-Text reads *with the scribes, the Pharisees, and the elders.* **27:42** NU-Text reads *He is the King of Israel!* • NU-Text and M-Text read *we will believe in Him.* **27:46** Psalm 22:1

[1](27:33) The order of events at the crucifixion: (1) The arrival at Golgotha (v. 33; Mk. 15:22; Lk. 23:33; Jn. 19:17). (2) The offer of the stupefying drink is refused (v. 34; Mk. 15:23). (3) Jesus is crucified between two robbers (vv. 35–38; Mk. 15:24–28; Lk. 23:33–38; Jn. 19:18). (4) He utters the first cry from the cross, "Father, forgive," etc. (Lk. 23:34). (5) The soldiers divide His garments (v. 35; Mk. 15:24; Lk. 23:34; Jn. 19:23). (6) The Jews mock Jesus (vv. 39–43; Mk. 15:29–32; Lk. 23:35). (7) The robbers revile Him, but one repents and believes (v. 44; Mk. 15:32; Lk. 23:39–43). (8) The second cry from the cross, "Today you will be with Me," etc. (Lk. 23:43). (9) The third cry, "Woman, behold your son," etc. (Jn. 19:26–27). (10) The darkness (v. 45; Mk. 15:33; Lk. 23:44). (11) The fourth cry, "My God," etc. (vv. 46–47; Mk. 15:34–36). (12) The fifth cry, "I thirst!" (Jn. 19:28). (13) The sixth cry, "It is finished!" (Jn. 19:30). (14) The seventh cry, "Father, into Your hands," etc. (Lk. 23:46). And (15) our Lord dismisses His spirit (v. 50; Mk. 15:37; Lk. 23:46; Jn. 19:30).

[2](27:37) Compare Mk. 15:26; Lk. 23:38; Jn. 19:19. These accounts supplement but do not contradict each other. No one of the evangelists quotes the entire inscription. All have "the King of the Jews." Matthew and Luke add to this the further words, "This is"; Matthew quotes the name "Jesus"; while John gives the additional words, "of Nazareth." The narratives combined give the entire inscription: "This is [Mt., Lk.] Jesus [Mt., Jn.] of Nazareth [Jn.] the King of the Jews" [all].

[3](27:46) Psalm 22 is predictive of this terrible cry; Ps. 22:3 gives the answer to the question.

50
a Jn. 10:18; 1 Cor. 15:3
b Acts 5:5,10
51
c Cp. Ex. 26:31–33; 35:12; 40:3
52
d Resurrection: vv. 52–53; Mt. 28:6. (2 Ki. 4:35; 1 Cor. 15:52, *note*)
53
e Sanctification (NT): v. 53; Mk. 6:20. (Mt. 4:5; Rev. 22:11)
54
f Mt. 14:33; cp. Mt. 16:16; Jn. 1:49; 6:69; Acts 8:37
56
g Son of Alphaeus. See Mt. 4:21, *note*

reed, and offered it to Him to
drink.
49 The rest said, "Let Him
alone; let us see if Elijah will
come to save Him."
50 And Jesus cried out again
with a loud voice, and [a]yielded
up [1]His [b]spirit.
51 Then, [c]behold, the [2]veil of
the temple was torn in two from
top to bottom; and the earth
quaked, and the rocks were
split,
52 and the [3]graves were
opened; and many bodies of the
saints who had fallen asleep
[d]were raised;
53 and coming out of the
graves after His resurrection,
they went into the [e]holy city
and appeared to many.
54 So when the centurion
and those with him, who were
guarding Jesus, saw the earthquake and the things that had
happened, they feared greatly,
saying, [f]"Truly this was the
Son of God!"
55 And many women who
followed Jesus from Galilee,
ministering to Him, were there
looking on from afar,
56 among whom were Mary
Magdalene, Mary the mother of
[g]James and Joses,* and the
mother of Zebedee's sons.

Jesus buried (Mk. 15:42–47; Lk. 23:50–56; Jn. 19:38–42)

57 Now when evening had
come, there came a rich man
from Arimathea, named Jo-
seph, who himself had also become a disciple of Jesus.
58 This man went to Pilate
and asked for the body of Jesus.
Then Pilate commanded the
body to be given to him.
59 When Joseph had taken
the body, he wrapped it in a
clean linen cloth,
60 and laid it in [h]his new
tomb which he had hewn out of
the rock; and he rolled a large
stone against the door of the
tomb, and departed.
61 And Mary Magdalene was
there, and the other Mary, sitting opposite the tomb.

The tomb sealed and guarded

62 On the next day, which
followed the Day of Preparation, the chief priests and Pharisees gathered together to Pilate,
63 saying, "Sir, we remember, while He was still alive,
how that [i]deceiver said, [j]'After
three days I will rise.'
64 "Therefore command that
the tomb be made secure until
the third day, lest His disciples
come by night* and steal Him
away, and say to the people, 'He
has risen from the dead.' So the
last deception will be worse
than the first."
65 Pilate said to them, "You
have a guard; go your way,
make *it* as secure as you know
how."
66 So they went and made

60
h Isa. 53:9
63
i Cp. 2 Cor. 6:8
j Mt. 12:40; 16:21; 17:23; 20:19; 26:61; Mk. 8:31; 10:34; Lk. 9:22; 18:33; 24:6–7; Jn. 2:19

*
27:56 NU-Text reads *Joseph.*
27:64 NU-Text omits *by night.*

[1](27:50) The Greek phrases used here and in Jn. 19:30 are unique in the NT. In fifteen other Bible verses, "breathed one's last," or "yielded up the spirit," is used to translate a single Hebrew or Greek word meaning *breathe out* or *expire.* This is true of the description of the death of Jesus in Mk. 15:37,39 and Lk. 23:46. But in Mt. 27:50 and Jn. 19:30 alone these expressions translate Greek phrases of three words, meaning *give over the spirit* or *deliver up the spirit.* The death of Jesus was different from that of any other man. No one could take His life from Him except as He was willing to permit it (Jn. 10:18). Christ chose to die so that we might live.

[2](27:51) The veil that was torn divided the Holy Place from the Most Holy Place, into which only the high priest might enter on the Day of Atonement (see Ex. 26:31, *note;* Lev. 16:1–30). The tearing of that veil, which was a type of the human body of Christ (Heb. 10:20), signified that a "new and living way" was opened for all believers into the very presence of God, with no other sacrifice or priesthood except Christ's (cp. Heb. 9:1–8; 10:19–22).

[3](27:52) Although the graves were opened at the time of Christ's death (vv. 50–51), the bodies did not arise until "after His resurrection" (v. 53). Christ is the firstborn from among the dead (Col. 1:18; Rev. 1:5) and "the firstfruits of those who have fallen asleep" (1 Cor. 15:20). It is not said that these bodies returned to their graves. The wave sheaf (Lev. 23:10–12) typifies the resurrection of Christ, but it would appear from the symbol used that plurality is implied. It was a single "grain of wheat" that fell into the ground in the crucifixion and entombment of Christ (Jn. 12:24); it was a sheaf which came forth in resurrection. The inference is that these saints went with the risen Christ into heaven.

the tomb secure, sealing the
stone and setting the guard.

Christ's resurrection, and events of that day (cp. Mk. 16:1–14; Lk. 24:1–49; Jn. 20:1–23)

28 NOW [1]after the [a]Sab-
bath, as the first *day* of
the week began to [2]dawn, Mary
Magdalene and the other Mary
came to see the tomb.
2 And behold, there was a
great earthquake; for an [b]angel
of the Lord descended from
heaven, and came and rolled
back the stone from the door,*
and sat on it.
3 [c]His countenance was like
lightning, and his clothing as
white as snow.
4 And the guards shook for
fear of him, and became like
[d]dead *men.*
5 But the [e]angel answered
and said to the women, [f]"Do
not be afraid, for I know that
you seek Jesus who was crucified.
6 "He is not here; for [g]He is
[h]risen, as He said. Come, see
the place where the Lord lay.
7 "And go quickly and tell
His disciples that He is [h]risen
from the dead, and indeed He is
going before you into [i]Galilee;
there you will see Him. Behold,
I have told you."
8 So they went out quickly
from the tomb with fear and
great joy, and ran to bring His
disciples word.
9 And as they went to tell
His disciples,* behold, [3]Jesus
met them, saying, "Rejoice!" So
they came and held Him by the
feet and worshiped Him.
10 Then Jesus said to them,
"Do not be afraid. Go *and* tell
My [j]brethren to go to Galilee,
and there they will see Me."

The soldiers bribed

11 Now while they were going, behold, some of the [k]guard
came into the city and reported
to the chief priests all the things
that had happened.
12 When they had assembled
with the elders and consulted
together, they [l]gave a large
sum of money to the soldiers,
13 saying, "Tell them, 'His
disciples came at night and
stole Him *away* while we slept.'
14 "And if this comes to the
governor's ears, we will [m]ap-
pease him and make you secure."
15 So they took the money
and did as they were instructed;
and this saying is commonly reported among the Jews until
this day.

Jesus in Galilee: His great commission (cp. Mk. 16:15–18; Lk. 24:46–48; Jn. 17:18; 20:21; Acts 1:8; 1 Cor. 15:6)

16 Then the eleven disciples
went away into Galilee, to the
mountain which Jesus had appointed for them.
17 When they saw Him, they
worshiped Him; but some
[n]doubted.
18 And Jesus came and
spoke to them, saying, [o]"All authority has been given to Me in
heaven and on earth.

*28:2 NU-Text omits *from the door.*
28:9 NU-Text omits the first clause of this verse.

CHAPTER 28
1
a Sabbath: v. 1; Mk. 2:23. (Gen. 2:3; Mt. 12:1, *note*)
2
b See Jud. 2:1 and Heb. 1:4, *notes*
3
c Cp. Dan. 10:6; Rev. 10:1
4
d Rev. 1:17
5
e v. 2
f Cp. Rom. 8:15; 2 Tim. 1:7
6
g Christ (first advent): vv. 5–6; Mk. 11:9. (Gen. 3:15; Acts 1:11, *note*)
h Resurrection: vv. 1–7; Mk. 5:42. (2 Ki. 4:35; 1 Cor. 15:52, *note*)
7
i Mt. 26:32
10
j Ps. 22:22; Jn. 20:17; Heb. 2:11–12
11
k Mt. 27:65
12
l Cp. Mt. 26:14–16
14
m Cp. Acts 12:19
17
n Jn. 20:24–29
18
o Dan. 7:13–14; Jn. 3:35; 5:22; 17:2; 1 Cor. 15:27; Eph. 1:22; Heb. 1:2

[1](28:1) The Sabbaths end; the first day begins as a Christian memorial. See Mt. 12:1, *note.* Cp. Jn. 20:19; Acts 20:7; 1 Cor. 16:2; Rev. 1:10.

[2](28:1) Combining the four narratives, the order of events on the resurrection morning would seem to be as follows: In the early morning, the women went to the tomb of Jesus to anoint His body, even though they did not know how they could get into the tomb (Mk. 16:2–3). There were the three, Mary Magdalene, Mary (the mother of James, Mk. 16:1; Lk. 24:10), and Salome, followed by other women who had accompanied Jesus from Galilee (Lk. 23:55—24:1). The three women found the stone had been removed by an angel (Mt. 28:2). Mary Magdalene hurried to tell Peter and John, who ran toward the tomb (Jn. 20:2–4). Meanwhile, Mary the mother of James, Salome, and then the other women arrived at the tomb, entered it and saw angels who assured them Jesus had risen. They ran from the tomb in fear and joy to inform His disciples (Mt. 28:8). Peter and John arrived at the tomb, entered, observed, and left (Jn. 20:4–10). Mary Magdalene returned to the tomb, stood weeping, and Jesus revealed Himself to her (Jn. 20:11–18). As the other women were on their way to tell His disciples, Jesus appeared to them (Mt. 28:9–10). For other post-resurrection appearances of our Lord, see Jn. 20:16, *note.*

[3](28:9) For the order of our Lord's post-resurrection appearances, see Jn. 20:16, *note.*

19
a Gospel: vv. 19–20; Mk. 1:1. (Gen. 12:3; Rev. 14:6)
b See Acts 8:12, *note*
c Or *into*
d Holy Spirit (NT): v. 19; Mk. 1:8. (Mt. 1:18; Acts 2:4, *note*)
20
e Inspiration: vv. 19–20; Mk. 1:2. (Ex. 4:15; 2 Tim. 3:16, *note*)
f Mt. 18:20; Acts 4:31; 18:10; 23:11
g Gk. *aiōn.* See Mk. 10:30, *note*

19 "Go therefore* and [a]make disciples of all the nations, [b]baptizing them [c]in the [1]name of the Father and of the Son and of the Holy [d]Spirit,
20 "teaching them to observe all things [e]that I have commanded you; and lo, I am [f]with you always, *even* to the end of the [g]age." Amen.*

*28:19 M-Text omits *therefore.*
28:20 NU-Text omits *Amen.*

[1](28:19) In the progress of revelation the one true God appears clearly in the NT as existing in three divine Persons: named here "the Father," and "the Son," and "the Holy Spirit." Compare also Mt. 3:16–17; 1 Cor. 12:4–6; 2 Cor. 13:14; Eph. 2:18; 4:4–6; 5:18–20; 1 Pet. 1:2; Jude 20–21.

1. Each of these divine Persons possesses His own personal characteristics and is clearly distinguished from the other Persons (cp. Jn. 14:16–17,26; 15:26; 16:7–15). Yet the three Persons are equal in being, power, and glory: each being called "God" (Jn. 6:27; Heb. 1:8; Acts 5:3–4); each possessing all the divine attributes (Jas. 1:17; Heb. 13:8; 9:14); each performing divine works (Jn. 5:21; Rom. 8:11); and each receiving divine honors (Jn. 5:23; 2 Cor. 13:14).

2. With reference to the order of their activities, the Father is first, the Son is second, and the Holy Spirit is third; the general formula being as follows: *from* the Father (1 Cor. 8:6), *through* the Son (Jn. 3:17), *by* the Holy Spirit (Eph. 3:5), and *to* the Father (Eph. 2:18). Even so, however, no one of the Persons acts independently of the other Persons; there is always mutual concurrence, as our Lord said, "My Father has been working until now, and I have been working" (Jn. 5:17); and, "The Son can do nothing of Himself" (Jn. 5:19); and again, "I and My Father are one" (Jn. 10:28–30).

3. In the NT revelation of God as a tri-personal Being, there is no retreat from the stern monotheism of the OT (cp. Dt. 6:4–5 with Mk. 12:29–30 and Rom. 3:30). The three divine Persons are *one* God, not three gods. It was necessary in the OT to emphasize first the divine unity in order to guard against polytheistic tendencies. But even in the OT, read in the light of the NT, a plurality of Persons appears within the one true God (cp. Gen. 1:26; Isa. 6:8; 48:12 with 48:16).

4. The Trinity of God is confessedly a great mystery, something wholly beyond the possibility of complete explanation. But we can guard against error by holding fast to the facts of divine revelation: that (1) with respect to His *Being* or essence, God is *one;* (2) with respect to His *Personality,* God is *three;* and (3) we must neither divide the essence, nor confuse the Persons. Yet, in spite of its mystery, the doctrine of the divine Trinity has always proved to be rich in spiritual and practical values.

5. The importance attached to the divine Trinity, in NT revelation, appears in the fact that the doctrine is firmly embedded in two formulas which are constantly repeated in the hearing of the church: (1) the formula of baptism (Mt. 28:19); and (2) the formula of benediction (2 Cor. 13:14).

For names of Deity, see *notes* at Gen. 1:1; 14:18; 15:2; 17:1; 21:33; Ex. 34:6; 1 Sam. 1:3; Mal. 3:18. Also see *notes* at Lord, Mt. 8:2; Word *(Logos),* Jn. 1:1; Lord (Deity of Christ), Jn. 20:28; Holy Spirit, Acts 2:4.

The Gospel According to

MARK

Author: Mark *Theme:* Christ, the Servant *Date of writing:* c. A.D. 68

MARK, the author of the Second Gospel, was a native of Jerusalem. His mother's name was Mary (Acts 12:12); his father is not known to us. John Mark is not named in the Gospels but appears in The Acts when, with his uncle, Barnabas, he accompanied Paul on the first missionary journey as far as Perga, where he turned back for reasons that are not given (Acts 13:13). Rejected by Paul, he went with Barnabas to Cyprus (Acts 15:38–40). During Paul's later years, however, Mark was at his side (Col. 4:10; Phil. 24) and was sent for by Paul shortly before the apostle's execution (2 Tim. 4:11). Peter referred to Mark as "my son" (1 Pet. 5:13). From the early days of the church, Mark's Gospel has been thought to reflect Peter's view of Christ.

Although it is the briefest of the Gospels, Mark's narrative is often more vivid and detailed than the parallel accounts in Matthew and Luke—e.g. the story of the demoniac of Gadara (5:1–20). Written principally for the Roman world, this Gospel presents Christ as the Servant of the Lord, sent to accomplish a specific work for God. Therefore, it is a book of deeds more than words, and contains no long discourses and few parables. The word "immediately" occurs more than thirty times. As the Servant of the Lord, Christ fulfills such Messianic prophecies as Isa. 42:1–21; 49:1–7; 50:4–11; 52:13—53:12; Zech. 3:8. Because He is presented as a servant, a genealogy is not needed. An unusual number of passages give insight into the feelings of our Lord (cp. 3:5; 7:34; 10:21). Although Christ is set forth in Mark in His servant character, the strong emphasis upon His miracles points to His power as the Son of God.

The Gospel may be divided as follows:

I. The Introduction of the Servant to His Public Ministry, 1:1–13.
II. The Work Accomplished by the Servant, 1:14—13:37.
III. The Servant's Obedience unto Death, 14—15.
IV. The Resurrection and Ascension of the Victorious Servant, 16.

CHAPTER 1

1
a Mt. 1:1; 3:13; Lk. 3:21
b Gospel: vv. 1,14–15; Mk. 2:2. (Gen. 12:3; Rev. 14:6)
2
c Inspiration: v. 2; Mk. 1:44. (Ex. 4:15; 2 Tim. 3:16, *note*)
d Some mss. read, *Isaiah, the prophet.* Cp. v. 3; Isa. 40:3
e Mal. 3:1
4
f See Acts 8:12, *note*
g Repentance: v. 4; Mk. 2:17. (Mt. 3:2; Acts 17:30, *note*)
h See Rom. 3:23, *note*

I. The Introduction of the Servant to His Public Ministry, 1:1–13

Ministry of John the Baptist (Mt. 3:1–12; Lk. 3:1–20; Jn. 1:6–8, 15–37)

1 THE [a]beginning of the [b]gospel of Jesus Christ, the Son of God.

2 As it is [c]written in the [d]Prophets:

[e]*"Behold, I send My messenger before Your face,*
Who will prepare Your way before You."
3 *"The voice of one crying in the wilderness:*
'Prepare the way of the LORD;
Make His paths straight.' "

4 John came baptizing in the wilderness and preaching a [f]baptism of [g]repentance for the remission of [h]sins.

5 Then all the land of Judea, and those from Jerusalem, went out to him and were all baptized by him in the Jordan River, confessing their [h]sins.

6 Now John was clothed with camel's hair and with a leather belt around his waist, and he ate locusts and wild honey.

7 And he preached, saying, "There [i]comes One after me who is mightier than I, whose sandal strap I am not worthy to stoop down and loose.

8 "I indeed baptized you with water, but He will baptize you with the Holy [j]Spirit."

Baptism of Jesus (Mt. 3:13–17; Lk. 3:21–22)

9 It came to pass in those days *that* Jesus [k]came from Nazareth of Galilee, and was baptized by John in the Jordan.

10 And immediately, coming up from* the water, He saw the [l]heavens parting and the Spirit [m]descending upon Him like a dove.

11 Then a voice came from heaven, "You are My [n]beloved

7
i Acts 13:25
8
j Holy Spirit (NT): vv. 8,10,12; Mk. 3:29. (Mt. 1:18; Acts 2:4, *note*)
9
k c. A.D. 26
10
l Ezek. 1:1
m Acts 10:38
11
n Mt. 17:5

* 1:10 NU-Text reads *out of.*

Son, in whom I am well
pleased."

Temptation of Jesus
(Mt. 4:1–11; Lk. 4:1–13)

12 Immediately the Spirit
drove Him into the wilderness.
13 And He was there in the
wilderness forty days, [a]tempted
by [b]Satan, and was with the
wild beasts; and the angels ministered to Him.

II. The Work Accomplished
by the Servant, 1:14—13:37

First tour of Galilee
(Mt. 4:12–17; Lk. 4:14)

14 Now after John was put in
prison, Jesus came to Galilee,
preaching the gospel of the
[c]kingdom* of God,
15 and saying, "The time is
fulfilled, and the kingdom of
God is [d]at hand. Repent, and
believe in the gospel."

Jesus' first disciples
(Mt. 4:18–22; Lk. 5:1–11;
cp. Jn. 1:35–49)

16 And as He walked by the
Sea of Galilee, He saw Simon
and Andrew his brother casting
a net into the sea; for they were
fishermen.
17 Then Jesus said to them,
"Follow Me, and I will make you
become [e]fishers of men."
18 They immediately [f]left
their nets and followed Him.
19 When He had gone a little
farther from there, He saw
James the *son* of Zebedee, and
John his brother, who also *were*
in the boat mending their nets.
20 And immediately He
called them, and they [g]left their
father Zebedee in the boat with
the hired servants, and went after Him.

Jesus casts out demons
at Capernaum (Lk. 4:31–37)

21 Then they went into Capernaum, and immediately on
the Sabbath He entered the
[h]synagogue and taught.
22 And they were [i]aston-
ished at His teaching, for He
taught them as one having authority, and not as the [j]scribes.
23 Now there was a man in
their synagogue with an [k]un-
clean spirit. And he cried out,
24 saying, "Let *us* alone!

13
a Test/tempt: vv. 12–13; Mk. 8:11. (Gen. 3:1; Jas. 1:14, *note*)
b Satan: v. 13; Mk. 3:23. (Gen. 3:1; Rev. 20:10)
14
c Kingdom (NT): vv. 14–15; Mk. 4:11. (Mt. 2:2; 1 Cor. 15:24, *note*)
15
d See Mt. 4:17, *note 4*
17
e Mt. 13:47–48; cp. Jer. 16:16
18
f Cp. Mk. 10:28–30
20
g Cp. Mt. 10:37
21
h Mt. 4:23; Lk. 4:16; 13:10
22
i v. 27; Mt. 7:28–29; 13:54
j See Mt. 2:4, *note*
23
k Mt. 12:43; Mk. 5:2; 7:25; Lk. 4:33

[l]What have we to do with You,
Jesus of Nazareth? Did You
come to destroy us? I [m]know
who You are—the [n]Holy One of
God!"
25 But Jesus rebuked him,
saying, "Be quiet, and come out
of him!"
26 And when the unclean
spirit had convulsed him and
cried out with a loud voice, he
[o]came out of him.
27 Then they were all
amazed, so that they questioned
among themselves, saying,
"What is this? What new doctrine *is* this? For with authority* He commands even the unclean spirits, and they obey
Him."
28 And immediately His
[p]fame spread throughout all the
region around Galilee.

Peter's mother-in-law healed
(Mt. 8:14–15; Lk. 4:38–39)

29 Now as soon as they had
come out of the synagogue, they
entered the house of Simon and
Andrew, with James and John.
30 But Simon's wife's mother
lay sick with a fever, and they
told Him about her at once.
31 So He came and took her
by the hand and lifted her up,
and immediately the fever left
her. And she served them.

Further healing and preaching
(Mt. 8:16–17; Lk. 4:40–44)

32 At evening, when the sun
had set, they brought to Him
[q]all who were sick and those
who were [r]demon-possessed.
33 And the whole city was
gathered together at the door.
34 [s]Then He healed many
who were sick with various diseases, and [t]cast out many [r]de-
mons; and He [u]did not allow the
demons to speak, because they
knew Him.
35 Now in the morning, having risen a long while before
daylight, He went out and departed to a solitary place; and
there He [v]prayed.
36 And Simon and those *who*
were with Him searched for
Him.

24
l Mt. 8:28–29; Mk. 5:7–8; Lk. 8:28
m v. 34; Mk. 3:11; Lk. 4:41; Jas. 2:19
n Ps. 16:10
26
o Miracles (NT): vv. 23–26, 30–31, 32–34,39; Mk. 1:42. (Mt. 8:3; Acts 28:8, *note*)
28
p Mt. 4:24; 9:31
32
q Mt. 11:4–5; Lk. 9:11
r See Mt. 7:22, *note*
34
s See Mk. 3:15, *note*
t Mt. 9:33; Lk. 13:32
u Mk. 3:12
35
v Mt. 26:39, 44; Mk. 6:46; Lk. 5:16; 6:12; 9:28–29; Heb. 5:7

*
1:14 NU-Text omits *of the kingdom.*
1:27 NU-Text reads *What is this? A new doctrine with authority.*

37 When they found Him, they said to Him, [a]"Everyone is [b]looking for You."

38 But He said to them, "Let us go into the next towns, that I may preach there also, because [c]for this purpose I have come forth."

39 And He was [d]preaching in their synagogues throughout all Galilee, and [e]casting out [f]demons.

A leper healed
(Mt. 8:2–4; Lk. 5:12–14)

40 Now a [g]leper came to Him, imploring Him, kneeling down to Him and saying to Him, "If You are willing, You [h]can make me clean."

41 Then Jesus, moved with [i]compassion, stretched out *His* hand and touched him, and said to him, "I am willing; be cleansed."

42 As soon as He had spoken, [j]immediately the leprosy [k]left him, and he was cleansed.

43 And He strictly warned him and sent him away at once,

44 and said to him, "See that you say nothing to anyone; but go your way, show yourself to the priest, and offer for your cleansing [l]those things which [m]Moses [n]commanded, as a testimony to them."

45 However, he went out and began to proclaim *it* freely, and to spread the matter, so that Jesus could no longer openly enter the city, but was outside in deserted places; and they came to Him from every direction.

A paralytic man healed
(Mt. 9:1–8; Lk. 5:17–26)

2 AND again He entered Capernaum after *some* days, and it was heard that He was in the house.

2 Immediately* many gathered together, so that there was no longer room to receive *them,* not even near the door. And He [o]preached the word to them.

3 Then they came to Him, bringing a [p]paralytic who was carried by four *men.*

4 And when they could not come near Him because of the crowd, they uncovered the roof where He was. So when they had broken through, they let down the bed on which the paralytic was lying.

5 When Jesus saw their [q]faith, He said to the paralytic, "Son, your [r]sins are [s]forgiven you."

6 And some of the [t]scribes were sitting there and reasoning in their hearts,

7 "Why does this *Man* speak blasphemies like this? Who can [u]forgive sins but God alone?"

8 But immediately, when Jesus perceived in His spirit that they reasoned thus within themselves, He said to them, "Why do you reason about these things in your hearts?

9 "Which is easier, to say to the paralytic, '*Your* sins are forgiven you,' or to say, 'Arise, take up your bed and walk'?

10 "But that you may know that the [v]Son of Man has power on earth to forgive sins"—He said to the paralytic,

11 "I say to you, arise, take up your bed, and go to your house."

12 Immediately he [k]arose, took up the bed, and went out in the presence of them all, so that all were amazed and [w]glorified God, saying, "We never saw *anything* like this!"

Call of Levi (Matthew)
(Mt. 9:9–15; Lk. 5:27–35)

13 Then He went out again by the sea; and all the multitude came to Him, and He taught them.

14 As He passed by, He saw Levi the *son* of Alphaeus sitting at the tax office. And He said to him, [x]"Follow Me." So he arose and [y]followed Him.

15 Now it happened, as He was dining in *Levi's* house, that many [z]tax collectors and [r]sinners also sat together with Jesus and His disciples; for there were many, and they followed Him.

16 And when the [t]scribes and* Pharisees saw Him eating with the tax collectors and sinners, they said to His disciples, "How *is it* that He eats and

*
2:2 NU-Text omits *Immediately.*
2:16 NU-Text reads *of the.*

37
a Mt. 4:25; Jn. 3:26; 12:19
b Heb. 11:6; cp. Jn. 7:34, 36

38
c Isa. 61:1–2; Mk. 10:45; Jn. 17:8

39
d Mt. 4:23; cp. 2 Tim. 4:2
e v. 26; Mk. 5:8,13; 7:29–30
f See Mt. 7:22, *note*

40
g Lev. 13:24–25, 44–46; cp. 2 Ki. 5:1–14; 15:5; see Ex. 4:6 and Lev. 13:2, *notes*
h Cp. Jer. 32:17

41
i Lk. 7:13; cp. Heb. 4:15

42
j v. 31; Mt. 15:28; Mk. 5:29
k *Miracles* (NT): vv. 40–42; 2:3–12; Mk. 3:5. (Mt. 8:3; Acts 28:8, *note*)

44
l Lev. 14:1–32; see Lev. 14:3, *note*
m *Law* (of Moses): v. 44; Mk. 7:8. (Ex. 19:1; Gal. 3:24, *note*)
n *Inspiration:* v. 44; Mk. 7:6. (Ex. 4:15; 2 Tim. 3:16, *note*)

CHAPTER 2

2
o *Gospel:* v. 2; Mk. 8:35. (Gen. 12:3; Rev. 14:6)

3
p Mt. 4:24; 8:6; Acts 8:7; 9:33

5
q *Faith:* vv. 3–5; Mk. 5:34. (Gen. 3:20; Heb. 11:39, *note*)
r See Rom. 3:23, *note*
s *Forgiveness:* vv. 5–10; Mk. 3:28. (Lev. 4:20; Mt. 26:28, *note*)

6
t See Mt. 2:4, *note*

7
u Dan. 9:9; cp. Jn. 1:1, 14 with Jn. 8:11

10
v See Mt. 8:20, *note*

12
w Mt. 15:31; Phil. 2:11

14
x Mt. 4:19; 8:22; 19:21; Jn. 1:43; 12:26; 21:22
y Lk. 18:28; cp. Lk. 22:54

15
z They were Jews employed by the Roman government

drinks with tax collectors and sinners?"

17 When Jesus heard *it,* He said to them, "Those who are well have no need of a physician, but those who are sick. I did not come to call *the* [a]righteous, but sinners, to [b]repentance."*

18 The disciples of John and of the [c]Pharisees were fasting. Then they came and said to Him, "Why do the disciples of John and of the Pharisees fast, but Your disciples do not fast?"

19 And Jesus said to them, "Can the friends of the bridegroom fast while the [d]bridegroom is with them? As long as they have the [d]bridegroom with them they cannot fast.

20 "But the days will come when the bridegroom will be [e]taken away from them, and then they will fast in those days.

Parable of the cloth and wineskins
(cp. Mt. 9:16–17; Lk. 5:36–39)

21 "No one [f]sews a piece of unshrunk cloth on an old garment; or else the new piece pulls away from the old, and the tear is made worse.

22 "And no one puts new wine into old wineskins; or else the new wine bursts the wineskins, the wine is spilled, and the wineskins are [g]ruined. But new wine must be put into new wineskins."

Jesus is Lord of the Sabbath
(Mt. 12:1–8; Lk. 6:1–5)

23 Now it happened that He went through the grainfields on the [h]Sabbath; and as they went His disciples began to [i]pluck the heads of grain.

24 And the [c]Pharisees said to Him, "Look, why do they do what is [j]not lawful on the Sabbath?"

25 But He said to them, "Have you never read [k]what David did when he was in need and hungry, he and those with him:

26 "how he went into the house of God *in the days* of Abiathar the high priest, and [l]ate the [m]showbread, which is not lawful to eat except for the priests, and also gave some to those who were with him?"

27 And He said to them, "The Sabbath was made for man, and not man for the [n]Sabbath.

28 "Therefore the [o]Son of Man is also Lord of the Sabbath."

Jesus heals on the Sabbath
(Mt. 12:9–14; Lk. 6:6–11)

3 AND He entered the synagogue again, and a man was there who had a withered hand.

2 So they [p]watched Him closely, whether He would [q]heal him on the Sabbath, so that they might accuse Him.

3 And He said to the man who had the withered hand, "Step forward."

4 Then He said to them, "Is it lawful on the Sabbath to do good or to do evil, to save life or to kill?" But they kept silent.

5 And when He had looked around at them with anger, being grieved by the [r]hardness of their hearts, He said to the man, "Stretch out your hand." And he stretched *it* out, and his hand was [s]restored as whole as the other.*

Many others healed
(Mt. 12:15–16; Lk. 6:17–19)

6 Then the [t]Pharisees went out and immediately plotted with the [u]Herodians against Him, how they might destroy Him.

7 But Jesus withdrew with His disciples to the sea. And a great multitude from Galilee followed Him, and from Judea

8 and Jerusalem and Idumea and beyond the Jordan; and those from Tyre and Sidon, a great multitude, when they heard how [v]many things He was doing, came to Him.

9 So He told His disciples that a small boat should be kept ready for Him because of the multitude, lest they should crush Him.

10 For He healed [w]many, so that as many as had afflictions pressed about Him to [x]touch Him.

*
2:17 NU-Text omits *to repentance.*
3:5 NU-Text omits *as whole as the other.*

17
a See Rom. 10:10, *note*
b Repentance: v. 17; Mk. 6:12. (Mt. 3:2; Acts 17:30, *note*)
18
c See Mt. 3:7, *note 1*
19
d Jn. 3:29; cp. Mt. 22:2–14; Eph. 5:25–32; Rev. 19:7
20
e Acts 1:9
21
f Parables (NT): vv. 21–22; Mk. 3:23. (Mt. 5:13; Lk. 21:29)
22
g Gk. *apollumi.* See Jn. 3:16, *note 3*
23
h Sabbath: vv. 23–28; 3:2–4; Mk. 6:2. (Gen. 2:3; Mt. 12:1, *note*)
i Dt. 23:25
24
j Ex. 20:10; 31:15; cp. Num. 15:32–36
25
k 1 Sam. 21:1–6
26
l Cp. Ex. 29:32–33
m Lev. 24:5–9; see Ex. 25:30, *note*

27
n Gen. 2:3; Ex. 23:12; Dt. 5:14; Neh. 9:14; Ezek. 20:12; cp. Isa. 58:13–14
28
o See Mt. 8:20, *note*
CHAPTER 3
2
p Ps. 37:32; Lk. 14:1; 20:20
q Lk. 13:14
5
r Zech. 7:12
s Miracles (NT): vv. 1–5,10; Mk. 4:39. (Mt. 8:3; Acts 28:8, *note*)
6
t Mk. 12:13; see Mt. 3:7, *note 1*
u See Mt. 22:16, *note*
8
v Or *great.* Mk. 5:19
10
w Lk. 7:21
x Mt. 9:21; Mk. 6:56

11 And the unclean spirits, whenever they saw Him, fell down before Him and cried out, [a]saying, "You are the [b]Son of God."

12 But He sternly [c]warned them that they should not make Him known.

The twelve chosen
(Mt. 10:1–4; Lk. 6:12–16)

13 And He went up on the mountain and [d]called to *Him* those He Himself wanted. And they came to Him.

14 Then He appointed twelve,* that they might be with Him and that He might send them out to preach,

15 [1]and to have [e]power to heal sicknesses and* to cast out [f]demons:

16 Simon,* to whom He gave the name [g]Peter;

17 [h]James the *son* of Zebedee and John the brother of James, to whom He gave the name Boanerges, that is, "Sons of Thunder";

18 Andrew, Philip, Bartholomew, [i]Matthew, Thomas, [h]James the *son* of Alphaeus, [j]Thaddaeus, Simon the Cananite;

19 and Judas Iscariot, who also betrayed Him. And they went into a house.

20 Then the multitude came together again, so that they could not so much as eat bread.

21 But when His [k]own people heard *about this,* they went out to lay hold of Him, for they said, "He is [l]out of His mind."

The unpardonable sin
(Mt. 12:31–32; Lk. 11:14–21)

22 And the [m]scribes who came down from Jerusalem said, "He has Beelzebub," and, "By the [n]ruler of the [f]demons He casts out demons."

23 So He called them to *Himself* and said to them in [o]parables: "How can [p]Satan cast out Satan?

24 "If a kingdom is divided against itself, that kingdom cannot stand.

25 "And if a house is divided against itself, that house [q]cannot stand.

26 "And if [p]Satan has risen up against himself, and is divided, he cannot stand, but has an end.

27 "No one can [r]enter a strong man's house and plunder his goods, unless he first binds the strong man. And then he will plunder his house.

28 "Assuredly, I say to you, all [s]sins will be [t]forgiven the sons of men, and whatever blasphemies they may utter;

29 "but he who blasphemes against the Holy [u]Spirit never has forgiveness, but [v]is subject to eternal condemnation"—

30 because they [w]said, "He has an unclean spirit."

The new relationships
(Mt. 12:46–50; Lk. 8:19–21)

31 Then His brothers and His mother came, and standing outside they sent to Him, calling Him.

32 And a multitude was sitting around Him; and they said to Him, "Look, Your mother and Your brothers* are outside seeking You."

33 But He answered them, saying, "Who is My mother, or My brothers?"

34 And He looked around in a circle at those who sat about Him, and said, "Here are My mother and My [k]brothers!

35 "For [2]whoever does the [x]will of God is My brother and My sister and mother."

The parable of the sower and the soils (Mt. 13:1–17; Lk. 8:4–10)

4 AND again He began to teach by the sea. And a great multitude was gathered to Him, so that He got into a boat and sat *in it* on the sea; and the whole multitude was on the land facing the sea.

2 Then He taught them

*
3:14 NU-Text adds *whom He also named apostles.* **3:15** NU-Text omits *to heal sicknesses and.* **3:16** NU-Text reads *and He appointed the twelve: Simon . . . .* **3:32** NU-Text and M-Text add *and Your sisters.*

11
a Mk. 1:24; Lk. 4:41
b Mt. 8:29; 14:33; Mk. 1:1; 5:7; Lk. 8:28; cp. Jas. 2:19
12
c Mk. 1:34
13
d Mk. 6:7
15
e Lk. 9:1
f See Mt. 7:22, *note*
16
g Mt. 16:18; cp. Jn. 1:42
17
h See Mt. 4:21, *note*
18
i Or *Levi,* Mk. 2:14
j Or *Judas,* Jn. 14:22
21
k v. 34; Mt. 13:55; Mk. 6:3; Jn. 2:12; see Jn. 15:15, *note*
l Acts 26:24; 2 Cor. 5:13
22
m See Mt. 2:4, *note*
n Jn. 12:31; 14:30; 16:11; Eph. 2:2
23
o Parables (NT): vv. 23–27; Mk. 4:2. (Mt. 5:13; Lk. 21:29)
p Satan: vv. 22–23, 26; Mk. 4:15. (Gen. 3:1; Rev. 20:10)
25
q Cp. Jud. 7:22
27
r Mt. 12:29
28
s See Rom. 3:23, *note*
t Forgiveness: v. 28; 4:12; Mk. 11:25. (Lev. 4:20; Mt. 26:28, *note*)
29
u Holy Spirit (NT): v. 29; Mk. 12:36. (Mt. 1:18; Acts 2:4, *note*)
v Or *is guilty of an eternal sin.* Lk. 12:10; Acts 7:51; cp. Heb. 6:4–6; 10:26–29
30
w v. 22; Mt. 9:34; Jn. 7:20; 8:48, 52; 10:20; cp. Isa. 5:20; 1 Cor. 12:3
35
x Eph. 6:6; Heb. 10:36; 1 Pet. 4:2; 1 Jn. 2:17

[1](3:15) Observe that there is a distinction between common sicknesses and demon possession.
[2](3:35) To do God's will is to enter into an everlasting relationship with Christ (1 Jn. 2:17).

many things by [a]parables, and said to them in His teaching:

3 "Listen! Behold, a sower went out to sow.

4 "And it happened, as he sowed, *that* some *seed* fell by the [b]wayside; and the birds of the air* came and devoured it.

5 "Some fell on [c]stony ground, where it did not have much earth; and immediately it sprang up because it had no depth of earth.

6 "But when the sun was up it was scorched, and because it had [d]no root it withered away.

7 "And some *seed* fell among thorns; and the [e]thorns grew up and choked it, and it yielded no crop.

8 "But other *seed* fell on [f]good ground and yielded a crop that sprang up, increased and produced: some thirtyfold, some sixty, and some a hundred."

9 And He said to them,* "He who has ears to hear, let him hear!"

10 But when He was alone, those around Him with the twelve asked Him about the parable.

11 And He said to them, "To you it has been given to [g]know the mystery of the [h]kingdom of God; but to those who are outside, all things come in parables,

12 "so that

'Seeing they may see and
not perceive,
And hearing they may
hear and not
understand;
Lest they should [i]turn,
And their sins be
*forgiven them.'"**

The parable explained
(Mt. 13:18–23; Lk. 8:11–15)

13 And He said to them, "Do you not understand this parable? How then will you understand all the parables?

14 "The sower [j]sows the word.

15 "And these are the ones by the [k]wayside where the word is sown. When they hear, [l]Satan comes immediately and takes away the word that was sown in their hearts.

16 "These likewise are the ones sown on [m]stony ground who, when they hear the word, immediately receive it with gladness;

17 "and they have no [n]root in themselves, and so endure only for a time. Afterward, when tribulation or persecution arises for the word's sake, immediately they stumble.

18 "Now these are the ones sown among [o]thorns; *they are* the ones who hear the word,

19 "and the [p]cares of this [q]world, the [r]deceitfulness of riches, and the desires for other things entering in choke the word, and it becomes unfruitful.

20 "But these are the ones sown on [s]good ground, those who hear the word, accept *it*, and bear [t]fruit: some thirtyfold, some sixty, and some a hundred."

Parable of the lamp (cp. Mt. 5:15–16; Lk. 8:16–18; 11:33–36)

21 Also He said to them, [a]"Is a lamp brought to be put under a basket or under a bed? Is it not to be set on a lampstand?

22 "For there is nothing hidden which will not be [u]revealed, nor has anything been kept secret but that it should come to light.

23 "If anyone has ears to hear, let him hear."

24 Then He said to them, "Take heed what you hear. With the same measure you use, it will be [v]measured to you; and to you who hear, more will be given.

25 "For whoever [w]has, to him more will be given; but whoever does not have, even what he has will be taken away from him."

Parable of spiritual growth

26 And He said, [a]"The [x]kingdom of God is as if a man should scatter [y]seed on the ground,

27 "and should sleep by night and rise by day, and the seed should sprout and [z]grow, he himself does not know how.

*

4:4 NU-Text and M-Text omit *of the air.*
4:9 NU-Text and M-Text omit *to them.*
4:12 Isaiah 6:9–10

CHAPTER 4

2
a Parables (NT): vv. 2–23, 26–29; Mk. 4:30. (Mt. 5:13; Lk. 21:29)
4
b v. 15
5
c v. 16
6
d v. 17
7
e vv. 18–19
8
f v. 20
11
g Mt. 11:25; 1 Cor. 2:10–16; 2 Cor. 4:6; cp. Mt. 16:7; 1 Cor. 1:18–31; see Mt. 13:11, *note*
h Kingdom (NT): vv. 2–34; Mk. 9:1. (Mt. 2:2; 1 Cor. 15:24, *note*)
12
i Acts 3:19
14
j v. 3; Lk. 8:1; cp. Eph. 3:8
15
k v. 4
l Satan: v. 15; Mk. 8:33. (Gen. 3:1; Rev. 20:10)
16
m v. 5
17
n v. 6
18
o v. 7
19
p Lk. 21:34; cp. Lk. 14:16–24
q Gk. *aiōn.* See Mk. 10:30, *note*
r Prov. 23:5; Eccl. 5:13; Lk. 18:24; 1 Tim. 6:9–10,17; cp. Acts 5:1–10
20
s v. 8; cp. 2 Th. 2:13
t Jn. 15:5; Rom. 7:4
22
u Eccl. 12:14; Mt. 10:26–27; Lk. 12:3; 1 Cor. 4:5; cp. Rev. 20:12
24
v Mt. 7:2; Lk. 6:38; 2 Cor. 9:6
25
w Mt. 13:12; 25:29
26
x v. 11; see Mt. 6:33, *note*
y v. 14; Mt. 13:24–30, 36–43; Lk. 8:1; cp. 1 Pet. 1:23, 25; 1 Jn. 3:9; 5:18
27
z 2 Cor. 3:18; 2 Pet. 3:18; cp. Job 17:9; Ps. 1:3; 92:13–14

28 "For the earth [a]yields crops by itself: first the blade, then the head, after that the full grain in the head.

29 "But when the grain ripens, immediately he puts in the sickle, because the [b]harvest has come."

Parable of the mustard seed (see Mt. 13:31–32, note; Lk. 13:18–19)

30 [c]Then He said, "To what shall we liken the kingdom of God? Or with what parable shall we picture it?

31 "*It is* like a mustard seed which, when it is sown on the ground, is smaller than all the seeds on earth;

32 "but when it is sown, it grows up and [d]becomes greater than all herbs, and shoots out large branches, so that the [e]birds of the air may nest under its shade."

33 And with many such [f]parables He spoke the word to them as they were [g]able to hear *it*.

34 But without a parable He did not speak to them. And when they were alone, He [h]explained all things to His disciples.

Jesus stills the wind and the sea (Mt. 8:23–27; Lk. 8:22–25)

35 On the same day, when evening had come, He said to them, "Let us cross over to the other side."

36 Now when they had left the multitude, they took Him along in the boat as He was. And other little boats were also with Him.

37 And a [i]great windstorm arose, and the waves beat into the boat, so that it was already filling.

38 But He was in the stern, asleep on a pillow. And they awoke Him and said to Him, [j]"Teacher, [k]do You not care that we are perishing?"

39 Then He arose and [l]rebuked the wind, and said to the sea, [m]"Peace, be still!" And the wind [n]ceased and there was a great calm.

40 But He said to them, "Why are you so fearful? [o]How *is it* that you have no faith?"*

41 And they feared exceedingly, and said to one another, [p]"Who can this be, that even the wind and the sea obey Him!"

Jesus casts out demons at Gadara (Mt. 8:28–34; Lk. 8:26–39)

5 THEN they came to the other side of the sea, to the country of the Gadarenes.*

2 And when He had come out of the boat, immediately there met Him out of the tombs a man with an [q]unclean spirit,

3 who had *his* dwelling among the tombs; and no one could bind him,* not even with chains,

4 because he had often been bound with shackles and chains. And the chains had been pulled apart by him, and the shackles broken in pieces; neither could anyone tame him.

5 And always, night and day, he was in the mountains and in the tombs, crying out and cutting himself with stones.

6 When he saw Jesus from afar, he ran and worshiped Him.

7 And he cried out with a loud voice and said, "What have I to do with You, Jesus, Son of the Most High God? I [r]implore You by God that You do not torment me."

8 For He said to him, [s]"Come out of the man, unclean spirit!"

9 Then He asked him, "What *is* your name?" And he answered, saying, "My name *is* [t]Legion; for we are many."

10 Also he begged Him earnestly that He would not send them out of the country.

11 Now a large herd of [u]swine was feeding there near the mountains.

12 So all the [v]demons begged Him, saying, "Send us to the swine, that we may enter them."

13 And at once Jesus* [w]gave them permission. Then the unclean spirits [n]went out and entered the swine (there were about two thousand); and the

*

4:40 NU-Text reads *Have you still no faith?*
5:1 NU-Text reads *Gerasenes.*
5:3 NU-Text adds *anymore.* 5:13 NU-Text reads *And He gave.*

28
a Jn. 12:24; cp. 1 Cor. 3:6–7
29
b Mt. 13:30, 39; cp. Isa. 51:11; 57:1–2; Rev. 14:14–16
30
c *Parables* (NT): vv. 30–32; Mk. 12:1. (Mt. 5:13; Lk. 21:29)
32
d Cp. Ezek. 17:22–24; 31:3–9; Dan. 4:20–22
e vv. 4,15
33
f Mt. 13:34–35
g Cp. Jn. 16:12; 1 Cor. 3:1–2
34
h v. 11; Lk. 24:27,45
37
i Cp. Job 38:1; Jon. 1:4
38
j Mt. 23:8–10
k Ps. 44:23; cp. Ps. 69:1–2; 1 Pet. 5:7
39
l Mk. 9:25; Lk. 4:39
m Ps. 65:7; 89:9; 93:4; 104:6–7; cp. Ps. 107:27–30
n *Miracles* (NT): vv. 37–41; 5:2–13; Mk. 5:29. (Mt. 8:3; Acts 28:8, *note*)
40
o Mt. 14:31–32; cp. Mk. 16:14; Lk. 24:25
41
p Cp. Mt. 14:33; Mk. 1:27; 7:37
CHAPTER 5
2
q Mk. 1:23; 7:25; Rev. 16:13–14
7
r Mt. 26:63; Mk. 1:24; Acts 19:13; cp. Lk. 4:41
8
s Mk. 1:25; 9:25; Acts 16:18; cp. 1 Jn. 3:8
9
t v. 13; cp. Mk. 16:9
11
u Lev. 11:7–8; Dt. 14:8; Lk. 15:15–16
12
v See Mt. 7:22, *note*
13
w Lk. 4:36; cp. Job 12:16; Col. 2:10; Heb. 2:8; 1 Pet. 3:22

herd ran violently down the steep place into the sea, and drowned in the sea.

14 So those who fed the swine [a]fled, and they told *it* in the city and in the country. And they went out to see what it was that had happened.

15 Then they came to Jesus, and saw the one *who had been* [b]demon-possessed and had the legion, [c]sitting and [d]clothed and in his right mind. And they were afraid.

16 And those who saw it told them how it happened to him *who had been* demon-possessed, and about the swine.

17 Then they began to plead with Him to [e]depart from their region.

18 And when He got into the boat, he who had been demon-possessed begged Him that he might be with Him.

19 However, Jesus did not permit him, but said to him, "Go home to your friends, and tell them what great things the Lord has done for you, and how He has had compassion on you."

20 And he departed and began to [f]proclaim in Decapolis all that Jesus had done for him; and all [g]marveled.

Two miracles of healing
(Mt. 9:18–26; Lk. 8:40–56)

21 Now when Jesus had crossed over again by boat to the other side, a great multitude gathered to Him; and He was by the sea.

22 And behold, one of the [h]rulers of the synagogue came, Jairus by name. And when he saw Him, he fell at His feet

23 and [i]begged Him earnestly, saying, "My little daughter lies at the point of death. Come and [j]lay Your hands on her, that she may be healed, and she will live."

24 So *Jesus* went with him, and a great multitude followed Him and thronged Him.

25 Now a certain woman had a [k]flow of blood for [l]twelve years,

26 and had suffered many things from many physicians. She had spent all that she had and was no better, but rather grew worse.

27 When she heard about Jesus, she came behind *Him* in the crowd and [m]touched His garment.

28 For she said, "If only I may touch His clothes, I shall be made well."

29 Immediately the fountain of her blood was dried up, and she felt in *her* body that she was [n]healed of the affliction.

30 And Jesus, immediately knowing in Himself that [o]power had gone out of Him, turned around in the crowd and said, "Who touched My clothes?"

31 But His disciples said to Him, "You see the multitude thronging You, and You say, 'Who touched Me?' "

32 And He looked around to see her who had done this thing.

33 But the woman, [p]fearing and trembling, knowing what had happened to her, came and fell down before Him and told Him the whole truth.

34 And He said to her, "Daughter, your [q]faith has made you well. [r]Go in peace, and be healed of your affliction."

35 While He was still speaking, *some* came from the ruler of the synagogue's *house* who said, "Your daughter is dead. Why trouble the Teacher any further?"

36 As soon as Jesus heard the word that was spoken, He said to the ruler of the synagogue, "Do not be afraid; only [s]believe."

37 And He permitted no one to follow Him except Peter, James, and John the brother of James.

38 Then He came to the house of the ruler of the synagogue, and saw a tumult and those who [t]wept and [u]wailed loudly.

39 When He came in, He said to them, "Why make this commotion and weep? The child is [v]not dead, but [w]sleeping."

40 And they ridiculed Him. But when He had put them all outside, He took the father and the mother of the child, and

14
a Cp. Jn. 10:12–13
15
b Mt. 4:24; 8:16; Mk. 1:32; see Mt. 7:22, *note*
c Lk. 10:39; cp. Mt. 11:28–30
d Isa. 61:10; cp. Rev. 3:5; 4:4
17
e Acts 16:39; cp. Lk. 4:29
20
f Ex. 15:2; Ps. 66:16
g Mt. 9:8,33; Jn. 5:20; 7:21; Acts 3:12; 4:13
22
h Acts 13:15
23
i Bible prayers (NT): vv. 23, 28; Mk. 7:26. (Mt. 6:9; Lk. 11:2, *note*)
j Mt. 8:15; Mk. 6:5; 7:32; 8:23, 25; 16:18; Lk. 4:40; Acts 9:17; 28:8
25
k Lev. 15:19, 25
l Cp. v. 42

27
m Mt. 14:35–36; Mk. 3:10; 6:56
29
n Miracles (NT): vv. 22–43; Mk. 6:5. (Mt. 8:3; Acts 28:8, *note*)
30
o Lk. 6:19
33
p Ps. 89:7
34
q Faith: vv. 28,34; Mk. 7:29. (Gen. 3:20; Heb. 11:39, *note*)
r 1 Sam. 1:17; 20:42; 2 Ki. 5:19; Lk. 7:50
36
s v. 34; Mk. 9:23; Jn. 11:40; cp. Rom. 4:17–20
38
t Mk. 16:10; Acts 9:39
u Cp. Mt. 13:42,50; Rev. 18:15, 19
39
v Jn. 11:4
w Death (physical): v. 39; Lk. 16:22. (Gen. 2:17; Heb. 9:27, *note*)

those *who were* with Him, and
entered where the child was lying.
41 Then He took the child by
the hand, and said to her, "Tali-
tha, cumi," which is translated,
"Little girl, I say to you, arise."
42 Immediately the girl
[a]arose and walked, for she was
twelve years *of age.* And they
were [b]overcome with great
amazement.
43 But He commanded them
strictly that [c]no one should
know it, and said that *something* should be given her to eat.

Jesus visits Nazareth
(Mt. 13:54–58; see Lk. 4:16, note)

6 THEN He went out from
there and came to His own
country, and His disciples followed Him.
2 And when the [d]Sabbath
had come, He began to teach in
the synagogue. And many hearing *Him* were [e]astonished, saying, "Where *did* this Man *get*
these things? And what wisdom
is this which is given to Him,
that such mighty works are performed by His hands!
3 "Is this not the carpenter,
the Son of Mary, and brother of
James, Joses, Judas, and Simon? And are not His sisters
here with us?" So they were [f]of-
fended at Him.
4 But Jesus said to them, "A
[g]prophet is not without honor
except in his own country,
among his own relatives, and in
his own house."
5 Now He could do no
mighty work there, except that
He laid His hands on a few sick
people and [h]healed *them.*
6 And He marveled because
of their [i]unbelief. Then He
went about the villages in a circuit, [j]teaching.

The twelve sent forth to preach
and heal (Mt. 10:1–42; Lk. 9:1–6)

7 And He called the twelve
to *Himself,* and began to [k]send
them out [l]two *by* two, and gave
them power over unclean spirits.
8 He commanded them to
take nothing for the journey except a staff—no [m]bag, no bread,
no [n]copper in *their* money
belts—
9 but to [o]wear sandals, and
not to put on two tunics.
10 Also He said to them, "In
whatever place you enter a
house, stay there till you depart
from that place.
11 "And whoever* will not
receive you nor hear you, when
you depart from there, shake off
the dust under your feet as a testimony against them.• As-
suredly, I say to you, it will be
more tolerable for Sodom and
Gomorrah in the [p]day of judgment than for that city!"
12 So they went out and
preached that *people* should
[q]repent.
13 And they [r]cast out many
[s]demons, and [t]anointed with
oil many who were sick, and
[h]healed *them.*

Murder of John the Baptist
(Mt. 14:1–14; Lk. 9:7–9)

14 Now King [1]Herod heard *of
Him,* for His name had become
well known. And he said, "John
the Baptist is risen from the

* 6:11 NU-Text reads *whatever place.*
• NU-Text omits the rest of this verse.

42
a Resurrection: v. 42; Mk. 9:4. (2 Ki. 4:35; 1 Cor. 15:52, *note*). Jn. 5:21
b Mk. 1:27; 7:37
43
c Mt. 12:16–19
CHAPTER 6
2
d Sabbath: v. 2; Mk. 16:1. (Gen. 2:3; Mt. 12:1, *note*)
e Mt. 7:28; Lk. 4:32; Acts 4:13
3
f Cp. Rom. 9:32; 1 Pet. 2:7–8
4
g Lk. 4:24; Jn. 4:44
5
h Miracles (NT): vv. 5, 13; Mk. 6:42. (Mt. 8:3; Acts 28:8, *note*)
6
i Mt. 17:17, 20; Heb. 3:18–19; 4:2
j Mt. 4:23; 9:35; Lk. 4:31,44; 13:22; Acts 10:38; Eph. 2:17; cp. Isa. 61:1–3
7
k Mt. 28:19–20; Mk. 3:14
l Eccl. 4:9–10; cp. Ex. 4:14–16; Dt. 17:6; Mt. 18:16; Rev. 11:3
8
m Lk. 10:4; 22:35; cp. 1 Cor. 9:14
n Cp. 2 Ki. 12:9–10
9
o Cp. Eph. 6:15
11
p Day (of judgment): v. 11; Lk. 10:12. (Mt. 10:15; Rev. 20:11)
12
q Repentance: v. 12; Lk. 3:3. (Mt. 3:2; Acts 17:30, *note*)
13
r See Mk. 3:15, *note*
s See Mt. 7:22, *note*
t Jas. 5:14

[1](6:14) The Herodian family is important in NT history. In addition to the father, Herod the Great, and his son and successor, Archelaus (see Mt. 2:1, *note*), three other sons are named in the NT: (1) Herod Antipas (mentioned here, v. 14ff.; Mt. 14:1; Lk. 3:1), tetrarch of Galilee and Perea (4 B.C. until banished, A.D. 39). (2) Herod Philip (Boëthos), mentioned here as Philip (v. 17; Mt. 14:3; Lk. 3:19). (3) Another Herod Philip (Lk. 3:1), tetrarch of territory east of Jordan (4 B.C.–A.D. 33).

Two children of another son of Herod the Great, Aristobulus (a son not included in the NT), are also named: Herodias (mentioned here, v. 17ff.; Mt. 14:3) and Herod Agrippa I (Acts 12:1,6,18–24).

It was Herodias, who had been married to her uncle, Herod Philip (Boëthos) but left him to live with another uncle, Herod Antipas, whom John the Baptist rebuked (vv. 14–29; Mt. 14:1–14). Herodias' daughter is not named in the NT. She is mentioned only as "Herodias' daughter" (v. 22ff.; Mt. 14:6–11), but from other sources it is known that her name was Salome, whose first husband was her great uncle (the Philip of Lk. 3:1).

Others of the Herodian family named in the NT are three children of Herod Agrippa I: (1)

dead, and therefore [a]these powers are at work in him."
15 Others [b]said, "It is Elijah."
And others said, "It is the
[c]Prophet, or* like one of the
prophets."
16 But when Herod heard, he
said, "This is John, whom I beheaded; he has been raised
from the dead!"
17 For Herod himself had
sent and laid hold of John, and
bound him in prison for the
sake of [d]Herodias, his brother
[d]Philip's wife; for he had married her.
18 Because John had [e]said to
Herod, "It is not [f]lawful for you
to have your brother's wife."
19 Therefore Herodias held it
against him and wanted to kill
him, but she could not;
20 for Herod feared John,
knowing that he *was* a [g]just and
[h]holy man, and he protected
him. And when he heard him,
he did many things, and heard
him gladly.
21 Then an opportune day
came when Herod on his birthday gave a feast for his nobles,
the high officers, and the chief
men of Galilee.
22 And when Herodias'
[i]daughter herself came in and
danced, and pleased Herod and
those who sat with him, the king
said to the girl, "Ask me whatever you want, and I will give *it*
to you."
23 He also swore to her,
"Whatever you ask me, I will
give you, up to half my kingdom."
24 So she went out and said
to her mother, "What shall I
ask?" And she said, "The head
of John the Baptist!"
25 Immediately she came in
with haste to the king and
asked, saying, "I want you to
give me at once the head of
John the Baptist on a platter."
26 And the king was exceedingly sorry; *yet,* because of the
oaths and because of those who
sat with him, he did not want to
refuse her.
27 Immediately the king sent
an executioner and com-
manded his head to be brought.
And he went and beheaded him
in prison,
28 brought his head on a
platter, and gave it to the girl;
and the girl gave it to her
mother.
29 When his disciples heard
of it, they came and [j]took away
his corpse and laid it in a tomb.

The apostles return to Jesus after first preaching tour
(Lk. 9:10)

30 Then the apostles gathered to Jesus and [k]told Him all
things, both what they had done
and what they had taught.
31 And He said to them,
"Come aside by yourselves to a
deserted place and rest a while."
For there were many coming
and going, and they did not
even have time to eat.

Five thousand fed
(Mt. 14:13–21; Lk. 9:10–17; Jn. 6:5–13)

32 So they departed to a deserted place in the boat by
themselves.
33 But the multitudes* saw
them departing, and many
[l]knew Him and ran there on
foot from all the cities. They arrived before them and came together to Him.
34 And Jesus, when He came
out, saw a great multitude and
was moved with [m]compassion
for them, because they were
like [n]sheep not having a shepherd. So He began to [o]teach
them many things.
35 When the day was now far
spent, His disciples came to
Him and said, "This is a deserted place, and already the
hour *is* late.
36 "Send them away, that
they may go into the surrounding country and villages and

*
6:15 NU-Text and M-Text omit *or.*
6:33 NU-Text and M-Text read *they.*

14
a Or *mighty works.* Lk. 19:37
15
b Mt. 16:14; Mk. 8:28; Lk. 9:19; cp. Jn. 1:21
c Mt. 21:11; see Lk. 24:19, *note*
17
d See v. 14, *note*
18
e Cp. 2 Tim. 4:2
f Lev. 18:16, 20,21; cp. 1 Cor. 6:9–10; Heb. 13:4
20
g Righteousness (OT): v. 20; Lk. 1:6. (Gen. 6:9; Lk. 2:25, *note*)
h Sanctification (NT): v. 20; Mk. 8:38. (Mt. 4:5; Rev. 22:11)
22
i Salome. See v. 14, *note*

29
j 1 Ki. 13:29–30; Mt. 27:58–61; Acts 8:2
30
k Lk. 10:17
33
l v. 54; Col. 1:6
34
m Mt. 9:36; Heb. 5:2; cp. Heb. 2:17; 4:15
n Num. 27:17; 1 Ki. 22:17; Zech. 10:2; cp. Ezek. 34
o Isa. 48:17; 61:1–3

Herod Agrippa II (Acts 25:13ff.; 26:1,2,27–32); (2) Drusilla (Acts 24:24); and (3) Bernice (Acts 25:13; 26:30).

Thus it will be observed that two or more names of each of three successive generations after Herod the Great are mentioned in the NT.

buy themselves bread;* for they have nothing to eat."

37 But He answered and said to them, "You give them something to eat." And they said to Him, [a]"Shall we go and buy two hundred [b]denarii worth of bread and give them *something* to eat?"

38 But He said to them, [c]"How many loaves do you have? Go and see." And when they found out they said, [d]"Five, and two fish."

39 Then He [e]commanded them to make them all sit down in groups on the green grass.

40 So they sat down in [f]ranks, in hundreds and in fifties.

41 And when He had taken the five loaves and the two fish, He [g]looked up to heaven, [h]blessed and broke the loaves, and gave *them* to His disciples to set before them; and the two fish He divided among *them* all.

42 So they all ate and were [i]filled.

43 And they took up [j]twelve baskets full of fragments and of the fish.

44 Now those who had eaten the loaves were about* [k]five thousand men.

Jesus walks on the water
(Mt. 14:22–32; Jn. 6:15–21)

45 Immediately He made His disciples get into the boat and go before Him to the other side, to Bethsaida, while He sent the multitude away.

46 And when He had sent them away, He [l]departed to the mountain to pray.

47 Now when evening came, the boat was in the middle of the sea; and He *was* alone on the land.

48 Then He saw them straining at rowing, for the wind was [m]against them. Now about the [n]fourth watch of the night He [o]came to them, [p]walking on the sea, and would have passed them by.

49 And when they saw Him walking [q]on the sea, they supposed it was a [r]ghost, and cried out;

50 for they all saw Him and were troubled. But immediately He talked with them and said to them, [s]"Be of good cheer! It is I; do not be [t]afraid."

51 Then He went up into the boat to them, and the wind [u]ceased. And they were greatly [v]amazed in themselves beyond measure, and marveled.

52 For they had [w]not understood about the loaves, because their heart was [x]hardened.

Jesus heals at Gennesaret
(Mt. 14:34–36)

53 When they had crossed over, they [y]came to the land of Gennesaret and anchored there.

54 And when they came out of the boat, immediately the people [z]recognized Him,

55 ran through that whole surrounding region, and began to [aa]carry about on beds those who were sick to wherever they heard He was.

56 Wherever He entered into villages, cities, or in the country, they laid the sick in the marketplaces, and begged Him that they might just [bb]touch the [cc]hem of His garment. And as many as touched Him [l]were made well.

God's commandments
versus man's traditions
(Mt. 15:1–9)

7 THEN the [dd]Pharisees and some of the scribes came together to Him, having come from Jerusalem.

2 Now when* they saw some of His disciples eat bread with defiled, that is, with [ee]unwashed hands, they [ff]found fault.

3 For the Pharisees and all the Jews do not eat unless they wash *their* hands in a special way, holding the [gg]tradition of the elders.

4 *When they come* from the marketplace, they do not eat unless they wash. And there are many other things which they have received and hold, *like* the washing of cups, pitchers, copper vessels, and couches.

5 Then the Pharisees and

*
6:36 NU-Text reads *something to eat* and omits the rest of verse. **6:44** NU-Text and M-Text omit *about.* **7:2** NU-Text omits *when* and *they found fault.*

37
a Cp. Num. 11:13,22; Mt. 15:33; Mk. 8:4
b See Coinage (NT), Mt. 5:26, *note*
38
c Cp. 2 Ki. 4:2–6
d Cp. Mt. 15:34; Mk. 8:5
39
e Mt. 15:35; Mk. 8:6
40
f Cp. 1 Cor. 14:33,40
41
g Jn. 11:41–42
h Mt. 15:36; 26:26; Mk. 8:7; Lk. 24:30; cp. Dt. 8:3,10; 1 Sam. 9:13; 1 Tim. 4:4–5
42
i Miracles (NT): vv. 37–44, 47–51, 55–56; Mk. 7:30. (Mt. 8:3; Acts 28:8, *note*)
43
j Cp. 2 Chr. 31:10; Mal. 3:10; Mk. 8:8
44
k Cp. Mt. 15:38; Mk. 8:9
46
l Mk. 1:35; Lk. 5:16
48
m Cp. Isa. 54:11
n 3–6 a.m. See Jn. 19:14, *note*
o Cp. Ps. 46:1
p Cp. Job 9:8
49
q Cp. Jn. 1:3; Col. 1:16; Heb. 1:2
r Mt. 14:26; Lk. 24:37; cp. Job 4:15–16

50
s Mt. 9:2; Jn. 16:33
t Isa. 41:10; cp. Ps. 46:1–5; Isa. 43:1–2
51
u Ps. 107:29; cp. Mk. 4:35–41
v Mk. 1:27; 2:12; 5:42; 7:37
52
w Mt. 16:9–11; cp. Mk. 8:17–18; Jn. 6:26
x Isa. 63:17; Mk. 3:5; 16:14; cp. Jer. 17:9; Heb. 3:8,13
53
y Cp. Ps. 107:30
54
z v. 33
55
aa Cp. Mk. 2:3–5
56
bb Mt. 9:20; Mk. 5:27
cc Num. 15:38–39
CHAPTER 7
1
dd See Mt. 3:7, *note 1*
2
ee Mt. 15:20
ff Cp. Mt. 9:11,14
3
gg Gal. 1:14; 1 Pet. 1:18

scribes asked Him, "Why do
Your disciples not walk according to the [1]tradition of the elders, but eat bread with unwashed hands?"
6 He answered and said to
them, "Well did Isaiah prophesy
of you [a]hypocrites, as it is
[b]written:

'This people honors Me
with their lips,
But their [2]heart is far
from Me.
7 *And in vain they*
worship Me,
Teaching [c]as doctrines
the commandments of
men.'

8 "For laying aside the
[d]commandment of God, you
hold the tradition of men*—the
washing of pitchers and cups,
and many other such things you
do."
9 He said to them, "*All too*
well you [e]reject the commandment of God, that you may keep
your tradition.
10 "For Moses [b]said, *'Honor*
your father and your mother';
and, *'He who curses father or*
mother, let him [f]be put to
death.'
11 "But you say, 'If a man
says to his father or mother,
"Whatever profit you might
have received from me *is*
Corban"—' (that is, a [3]gift *to*
God),
12 "then you no longer let
him do anything [g]for his father
or his mother,
13 "making the word of God
of no effect through your tradition which you have handed
down. And many such things
you do."

Diagnosis of the heart of man
(Mt. 15:10–20)

14 When He had called all
the multitude to *Himself*, He
said to them, "Hear Me, everyone, and [h]understand:
15 "There is nothing that
[i]enters a man from outside
which can defile him; but the
things which [j]come out of him,
those are the things that [k]defile
a man.
16 "If anyone has ears to
[l]hear, let him hear!"*
17 When He had entered a
house away from the crowd, His
disciples asked Him concerning
the parable.
18 So He said to them, [m]"Are
you thus without understanding
also? Do you not perceive that
whatever enters a man from
outside cannot defile him,
19 "because it does not enter
his heart but his [n]stomach, and
is eliminated, *thus* purifying all
foods?"*
20 And He said, [o]"What
comes out of a man, that defiles
a man.
21 "For from within, out of
the [4p]heart of men, [q]proceed
evil thoughts, [r]adulteries, [s]for-
nications, [t]murders,
22 "thefts, [u]covetousness,
wickedness, [v]deceit, [w]lewd-
ness, an evil eye, [x]blasphemy,
[y]pride, foolishness.
23 "All these evil things come
from within and defile a man."

Jesus and the
Syro-Phoenician woman
(Mt. 15:21–28)

24 From there He arose and
went to the region of Tyre and
Sidon.* And He entered a
house and wanted no one to
know *it*, but He could not be
[z]hidden.

*
7:8 NU-Text omits the rest of this verse.
7:16 NU-Text omits this verse.
7:19 NU-Text ends quotation with *eliminated,* setting off the final clause as Mark's comment that Jesus has declared all foods clean. 7:24 NU-Text omits *and Sidon.*

6
a Mt. 23:13, 14,15,23,25, 27,29; cp. 2 Tim. 3:5
b Inspiration: vv. 6, 10; Mk. 9:12. (Ex. 4:15; 2 Tim. 3:16, *note*). Isa. 29:13
7
c v. 5; Col. 2:8; cp. Col. 2:16,18–23; see Mt. 3:7, *notes*
8
d Law (of Moses): vv. 8–10; Mk. 10:3. (Ex. 19:1; Gal. 3:24, *note*)
9
e Prov. 1:25; Jer. 7:23–24; Isa. 24:5
10
f Ex. 20:12; 21:17; Lev. 20:9; Dt. 21:18–21; Prov. 20:20
12
g Cp. 1 Tim. 5:8

14
h Mt. 16:9,11, 12
15
i Cp. 1 Cor. 8:8
j Cp. Rom. 14:17; see Mk. 7:21, *note*
k Isa. 59:3; Heb. 12:15
16
l v. 14; Mt. 11:15; cp. Prov. 20:12; Mt. 13:16
18
m Isa. 28:9–11; 1 Cor. 3:2; Heb. 5:11
19
n 1 Cor. 6:13
20
o Ps. 39:1; Mt. 12:34–37; Jas. 3:6
21
p Gen. 6:5; 8:21; Prov. 6:18; Jer. 17:9; cp. Mt. 12:34
q Gal. 5:19–21
r 1 Th. 4:3; cp. 1 Cor. 10:8
s Cp. 1 Pet. 4:15
t 2 Pet. 2:14
22
u Lk. 12:15
v Rom. 1:28–29
w 1 Pet. 4:3
x Rev. 2:9
y 1 Jn. 2:16
24
z Mk. 2:1–2

[1](7:5) The tradition of the elders is what was called the "oral law," which was alleged to have been handed down from Moses. It is actually a traditional interpretation of the written law. Cp. v. 7, marg.

[2](7:6) "Man looks at the outward appearance, but the LORD looks at the heart" (1 Sam. 16:7).

[3](7:11) The sense of the latter part of v. 11 and of v. 12 is: "that is to say, 'I have dedicated to God that which would relieve your need.' No longer do you Pharisees and scribes let him use it for his father or mother."

[4](7:21) Here in vv. 21–23 the Lord Jesus presents, in their logical order, the three forms in which sin appears: (1) in human nature—"out of the heart of men"; (2) in the human mind—"evil thoughts"; and (3) in human action—"adulteries, fornications, murders, thefts," etc.

25 For a woman whose young daughter had an unclean spirit heard about Him, and she came and [a]fell at His feet.

26 The woman was a Greek, a Syro-Phoenician by birth, and she kept [b]asking Him to cast the [c]demon out of her daughter.

27 But Jesus said to her, "Let the children be filled first, for it is not good to take the children's bread and throw *it* to the little dogs."

28 And she answered and said to Him, "Yes, Lord, yet even the little dogs under the table eat from the children's crumbs."

29 Then He said to her, [d]"For this saying go your way; the [c]demon has gone out of your daughter."

30 And when she had come to her house, she found the demon [e]gone out, and her daughter lying on the bed.

Further healing (Mt. 15:29–31)

31 Again, departing from the region of Tyre and Sidon, He came through the midst of the region of Decapolis to the Sea of Galilee.

32 Then they brought to Him one who was deaf and had an impediment in his speech, and they begged Him to put His hand on him.

33 And He took him [f]aside from the multitude, and put His fingers in his ears, and He [g]spat and touched his tongue.

34 Then, [h]looking up to heaven, He [i]sighed, and said to him, "Ephphatha," that is, [j]"Be opened."

35 [e]Immediately his ears were opened, and the impediment of his tongue was loosed, and he spoke plainly.

36 Then He commanded them that they should tell no one; but the more He commanded them, the more widely they proclaimed *it*.

37 And they were [k]astonished beyond measure, saying, "He has done all things well. He [l]makes both the deaf to hear and the mute to speak."

25
a Mk. 5:22; Jn. 11:32; Rev. 1:17
26
b Bible prayers (NT): v. 26; Mk. 9:24. (Mt. 6:9; Lk. 11:2, *note*)
c See Mt. 7:22, *note*
29
d Faith: v. 29; Mk. 9:24. (Gen. 3:20; Heb. 11:39, *note*)
30
e Miracles (NT): vv. 25–30, 32–37; 8:1–9; Mk. 8:25. (Mt. 8:3; Acts 28:8, *note*)
33
f Mk. 5:40; cp. 1 Ki. 17:19; 2 Ki. 4:33; Acts 9:40
g Mk. 8:23; Jn. 9:6
34
h Mt. 14:19; Mk. 6:41; Jn. 11:41
i Mk. 8:12; Jn. 11:33,38
j Cp. Ps. 33:9
37
k Mk. 6:51; 10:26
l Mt. 12:22

Four thousand fed (Mt. 15:32–39)

8 IN those days, the multitude being very great and having [m]nothing to eat, Jesus called His disciples *to Him* and said to them,

2 "I have [n]compassion on the multitude, because they have now continued with Me three days and have nothing to eat.

3 "And if I send them away hungry to their own houses, they will faint on the way; for some of them have come from afar."

4 Then His disciples answered Him, [o]"How can one satisfy these people with bread here in the wilderness?"

5 He asked them, "How many [p]loaves do you have?" And they said, "Seven."

6 So He commanded the multitude to [q]sit down on the ground. And He took the seven loaves and gave thanks, broke *them* and gave *them* to His disciples to set before *them;* and they set *them* before the multitude.

7 They also had a [r]few small fish; and having blessed them, He said to set them also before *them.*

8 So they ate and [e]were [s]filled, and they took up seven large baskets of [t]leftover fragments.

9 Now those who had eaten were about four thousand. And He sent them away,

Symbol of leaven explained (Mt. 16:1–12)

10 immediately got into the boat with His disciples, and came to the region of Dalmanutha.

11 Then the [u]Pharisees came out and began to [v]dispute with Him, seeking from Him a [w]sign from heaven, [x]testing Him.

12 But He [y]sighed deeply in His spirit, and said, "Why does this generation seek a sign? Assuredly, I say to you, [z]no sign shall be given to this generation."

13 And He left them, and getting into the boat again, departed to the other side.

CHAPTER 8
1
m Mt. 14:15; Mk. 6:36; Lk. 9:12
2
n Mt. 9:36; 14:14; Mk. 1:41; 6:34
4
o Cp. Num. 11:21–22; Ps. 78:19–20; Mt. 14:17; Mk. 6:37; Lk. 9:13; Jn. 6:5,7
5
p Mk. 6:38; Jn. 6:9
6
q Cp. 1 Cor. 14:33,40
7
r Cp. 1 Ki. 17:8–16; 2 Ki. 4:1–7; 2 Chr. 14:11; Ps. 37:16
8
s Cp. Dt. 8:10
t Cp. 2 Ki. 4:42–44
11
u See Mt. 3:7, *note 1*
v Mt. 22:23–24
w Mt. 12:38; Lk. 11:16; Jn. 2:18; 6:30; 1 Cor. 1:22
x Test/tempt: v. 11; Mk. 10:2. (Gen. 3:1; Jas. 1:14, *note*)
12
y Mk. 7:34
z Mt. 12:39

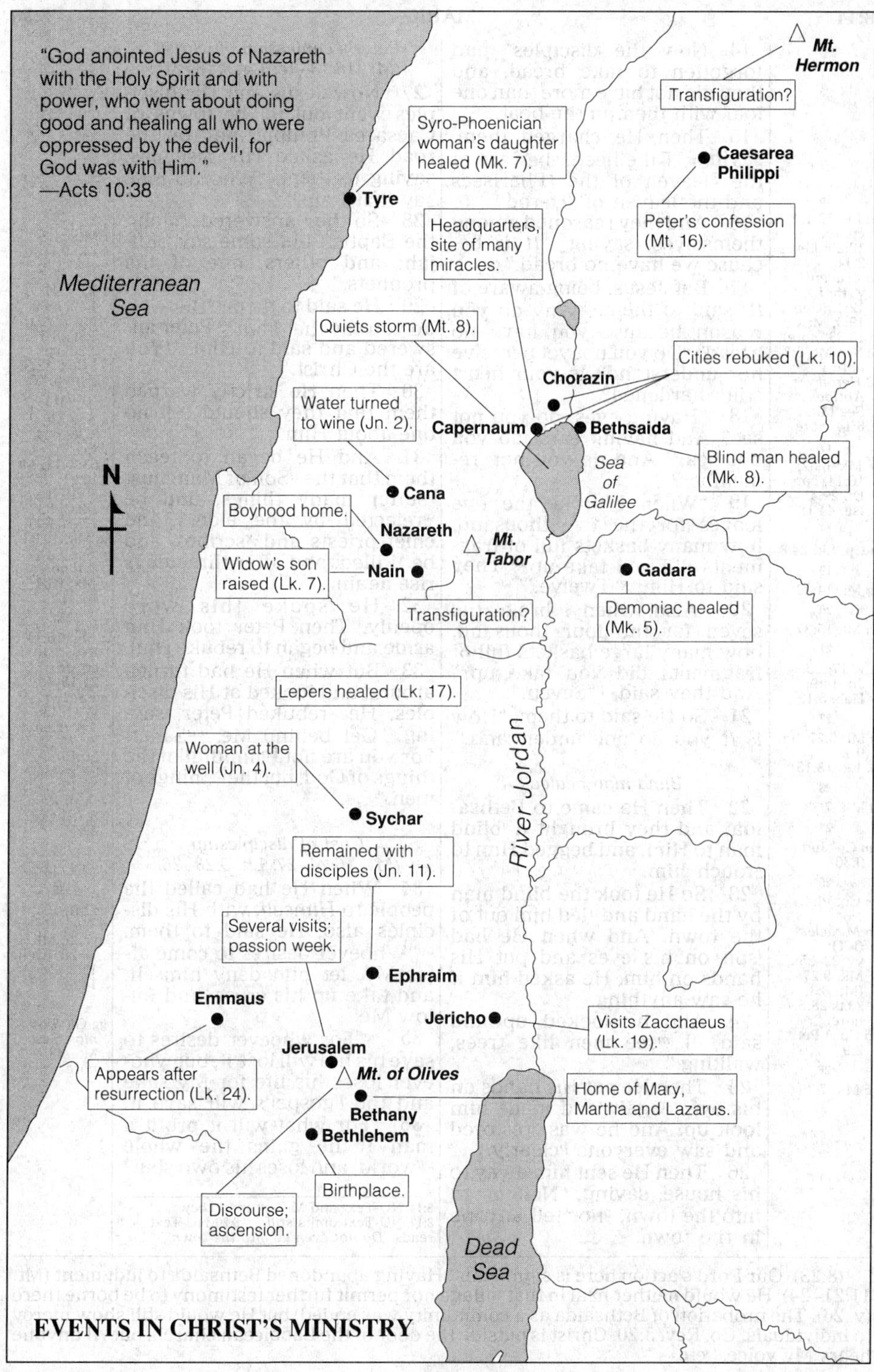
"God anointed Jesus of Nazareth with the Holy Spirit and with power, who went about doing good and healing all who were oppressed by the devil, for God was with Him."
—Acts 10:38
Mt. Hermon
Transfiguration?
Syro-Phoenician woman's daughter healed (Mk. 7).
Caesarea Philippi
Tyre
Peter's confession (Mt. 16).
Headquarters, site of many miracles.
Mediterranean Sea
Quiets storm (Mt. 8).
Cities rebuked (Lk. 10).
Chorazin
Water turned to wine (Jn. 2).
Capernaum
Bethsaida
Blind man healed (Mk. 8).
Sea of Galilee
N
Cana
Boyhood home.
Nazareth
Mt. Tabor
Widow's son raised (Lk. 7).
Nain
Gadara
Demoniac healed (Mk. 5).
Transfiguration?
Lepers healed (Lk. 17).
River Jordan
Woman at the well (Jn. 4).
Sychar
Remained with disciples (Jn. 11).
Several visits; passion week.
Ephraim
Emmaus
Jericho
Visits Zacchaeus (Lk. 19).
Jerusalem
Appears after resurrection (Lk. 24).
Mt. of Olives
Home of Mary, Martha and Lazarus.
Bethany
Bethlehem
Birthplace.
Discourse; ascension.
Dead Sea

EVENTS IN CHRIST'S MINISTRY

14 Now the disciples* had forgotten to take bread, and they did not have more than one loaf with them in the boat.

15 Then He charged them, saying, "Take heed, [a]beware of the [b]leaven of the [c]Pharisees and the leaven of [d]Herod."

16 And they reasoned among themselves, saying, "*It is* because we have no bread."

17 But Jesus, being aware of *it*, said to them, "Why do you reason because you have no bread? [e]Do you not yet perceive nor understand? Is your heart still* hardened?

18 "Having eyes, do you not see? And having ears, do you not hear? And do you not [f]remember?

19 "When I broke the five loaves for the five thousand, how many baskets full of fragments did you take up?" They said to Him, [g]"Twelve."

20 "Also, when I broke the seven for the four thousand, how many large baskets full of fragments did you take up?" And they said, [h]"Seven."

21 So He said to them, "How *is it* you do not [i]understand?"

Blind man healed

22 Then He came to Bethsaida; and they brought a [j]blind man to Him, and begged Him to [k]touch him.

23 So He took the blind man by the hand and [1]led him out of the town. And when He had [l]spit on his eyes and put His hands on him, He asked him if he saw anything.

24 And he looked up and said, "I [m]see men like trees, walking."

25 Then He put *His* hands on his eyes [n]again and made him look up. And he was [o]restored and saw everyone [p]clearly.

26 Then He sent him away to his house, saying, "Neither go into the town, [q]nor tell anyone in the town."*

Peter's confession of Christ
(Mt. 16:13–16; Lk. 9:18–21)

27 Now Jesus and His disciples went out to the towns of Caesarea Philippi; and on the road He asked His disciples, saying to them, "Who do men say that I am?"

28 So they answered, [r]"John the Baptist; but some *say,* [s]Elijah; and others, one of the prophets."

29 He said to them, "But who do you say that I am?" Peter answered and said to Him, [t]"You are the Christ."

30 Then He strictly warned them that they should tell no one about Him.

31 And He began to teach them that the [u]Son of Man must [v]suffer many things, and be [w]rejected by the elders and chief priests and [x]scribes, and be [y]killed, and after three days rise again.

32 He spoke this word openly. Then Peter took Him aside and began to rebuke Him.

33 But when He had turned around and looked at His disciples, He [z]rebuked Peter, saying, "Get behind Me, [aa]Satan! For you are not [bb]mindful of the things of God, but the [cc]things of men."

Cost of discipleship
(Mt. 16:24–27; Lk. 9:23–26)

34 When He had called the people to *Himself,* with His disciples also, He said to them, [dd]"Whoever desires to come after Me, let him deny himself, and take up his cross, and follow Me.

35 [ee]"For whoever desires to save his life will lose it, but whoever loses his life for My sake and the [ff]gospel's will save it.

36 "For what will it profit a man if he gains the whole [gg]world, and loses his own soul?

*

8:14 NU-Text and M-Text read *they.* **8:17** NU-Text omits *still.* **8:26** NU-Text reads *"Do not even go into the town."*

15
a Lk. 12:1; cp. Ex. 12:20; Lev. 2:11
b *Leaven:* v. 15; Lk. 12:1. (Gen. 19:3; Mt. 13:33, *note*)
c See Mt. 3:7, *note 1*
d *Herod Antipas.* See Mk. 6:14, *note*
17
e Mk. 6:52; 16:14; cp. Dt. 29:4; Isa. 44:18
18
f Cp. Lk. 24:8
19
g Mt. 14:20
20
h Mt. 15:37
21
i v. 17; cp. Jn. 14:9; Heb. 5:12
22
j Mt. 9:27; Jn. 9:1
k Lk. 18:15
23
l Mk. 7:33
24
m Cp. Jud. 9:36
25
n Cp. Phil. 1:6
o *Miracles* (NT): vv. 22–25; Mk. 9:27. (Mt. 8:3; Acts 28:8, *note*)
p Cp. 1 Pet. 2:9
26
q Mk. 7:36

28
r Mt. 14:2
s Lk. 9:8
29
t Jn. 1:41; 4:42; 6:69; 11:27; Acts 2:36; 8:37; 9:20; cp. 1 Cor. 12:3; 1 Jn. 5:1,5
31
u See Mt. 8:20, *note*
v Isa. 53:3–11; Mt. 16:21; 20:19; Lk. 18:31–33; 1 Pet. 1:11
w Mk. 10:33
x See Mt. 2:4, *note*
y Mk. 9:31; 10:34
33
z Mk. 16:14; Rev. 3:19; cp. Jn. 21:15–19
aa *Satan:* v. 33; Lk. 4:8. (Gen. 3:1; Rev. 20:10)
bb Cp. Mt. 16:17
cc Cp. Rom. 8:7; 1 Cor. 2:14
34
dd Lk. 14:27
35
ee Mt. 10:39
ff *Gospel:* v. 35; Mk. 10:29. (Gen. 12:3; Rev. 14:6)
36
gg Gk. *kosmos.* See Mt. 4:8, *note*

[1](8:23) Our Lord's action here is significant. Having abandoned Bethsaida to judgment (Mt. 11:21–24), He would neither heal in that village nor permit further testimony to be borne there (v. 26). The probation of Bethsaida as a community was ended, but He would still show mercy to individuals. Cp. Rev. 3:20. Christ is outside the door of the Laodicean church, but "If anyone hears My voice," etc.

37 "Or what will a man give in exchange for his soul?

38 "For whoever is [a]ashamed of Me and My words in this adulterous and sinful generation, of him the Son of Man also will be [b]ashamed when He [c]comes in the glory of His Father with the [d]holy [e]angels."

The transfiguration
(Mt. 17:1–8; Lk. 9:28–36)

9 AND He said to them, "Assuredly, I say to you that there are some standing here who will not taste death till they [f]see the [g]kingdom of God present with power."

2 Now after six days Jesus took Peter, James, and John, and led them up on a high mountain apart by themselves; and He was [h]transfigured before them.

3 His clothes became shining, exceedingly [i]white, like snow, such as no launderer on earth can whiten them.

4 And Elijah [j]appeared to them with Moses, and [k]they were talking with Jesus.

5 Then Peter answered and said to Jesus, "Rabbi, it is good for us to be here; and let us make three tabernacles: one for You, one for Moses, and one for Elijah"—

6 because he did not know what to say, for they were greatly afraid.

7 And a [l]cloud came and overshadowed them; and a voice came out of the cloud, saying, "This is [m]My beloved Son. [n]Hear Him!"

8 Suddenly, when they had looked around, they saw no one anymore, but [o]only Jesus with themselves.

9 Now as they came down from the mountain, He commanded them that they should tell no one the things they had seen, till the [p]Son of Man had risen from the dead.

10 So they kept this word to themselves, questioning [q]what the rising from the dead meant.

11 And they asked Him, saying, "Why do the [r]scribes say that [s]Elijah must come first?"

12 Then He answered and told them, "Indeed, Elijah is coming first and restores all things. And how is it [t]written concerning the Son of Man, that He must suffer many things and be [u]treated with contempt?

13 "But I say to you that Elijah has also come, and they did to him whatever they wished, as it is written of him."

The powerless disciples:
the mighty Christ
(Mt. 17:14–21; Lk. 9:37–42)

14 And when He came to the disciples, He saw a great multitude around them, and scribes disputing with them.

15 Immediately, when they saw Him, all the people were greatly amazed, and running to *Him,* greeted Him.

16 And He asked the scribes, "What are you discussing with them?"

17 Then one of the crowd answered and said, "Teacher, I brought You my son, who has a mute spirit.

18 "And wherever it seizes him, it throws him down; he foams at the mouth, gnashes his teeth, and becomes rigid. So I spoke to Your disciples, that they should cast it out, but they could [v]not."

19 He answered him and said, "O [w]faithless generation, how long shall I be with you? How long shall I bear with you? Bring him to Me."

20 Then they brought him to Him. And when he saw Him, immediately the [x]spirit convulsed him, and he fell on the ground and wallowed, foaming at the mouth.

21 So He asked his father, "How long has this been happening to him?" And he said, "From childhood.

22 "And often he has thrown him both into the fire and into the water to destroy him. But if You can do anything, have compassion on us and help us."

23 Jesus said to him, [y]"If you can believe,* all things *are* possible to him who believes."

24 Immediately the father of

38
a 2 Tim. 1:8–9
b Cp. Mt. 10:32–33
c Christ (second advent): v. 38; Mk. 13:26. (Dt. 30:3; Acts 1:11, *note*)
d Sanctification (NT): v. 38; Lk. 1:35. (Mt. 4:5; Rev. 22:11)
e See Heb. 1:4, *note*

CHAPTER 9
1
f See Mt. 17:2, *note*
g Kingdom (NT): vv. 1–4; Mk. 10:37. (Mt. 2:2; 1 Cor. 15:24, *note*)
2
h Cp. Heb. 2:9
3
i Dan. 7:9; Mt. 28:3
4
j Resurrection: vv. 4–5; Mk. 16:6. (2 Ki. 4:35; 1 Cor. 15:52, *note*)
k Cp. Rom. 3:21
7
l Ex. 40:34; 1 Ki. 8:10; Acts 1:9; Rev. 1:7
m Ps. 2:7; Isa. 42:1; Mk. 1:11; 2 Pet. 1:17
n Acts 3:22; cp. Heb. 2:3
8
o Cp. Jn. 3:30; 6:68
9
p See Mt. 8:20, *note*
10
q Jn. 2:19–22; cp. Lk. 24:25–27
11
r See Mk. 12:34, *note*
s See Mt. 17:10, *note*

12
t Inspiration: v. 12; Mk. 10:5. (Ex. 4:15; 2 Tim. 3:16, *note*). Isa. 53:2–11
u Lk. 23:11; Acts 4:11
18
v Cp. vv. 28–29
19
w Jn. 4:48
20
x Mk. 1:26
23
y Jn. 11:40

*9:23 NU-Text reads *"If You can! All things. . . ."*

the child cried out and said with tears, [a]"Lord, [b]I believe; [c]help my unbelief!"

25 When Jesus saw that the people came running together, He [d]rebuked the unclean spirit, saying to it: "Deaf and dumb spirit, I command you, come out of him and enter him no more!"

26 Then *the spirit* cried out, convulsed him greatly, and came out of him. And he became as one dead, so that many said, "He is dead."

27 But Jesus took him by the hand and lifted him up, and he [e]arose.

28 And when He had come into the house, His disciples asked Him privately, "Why could we not cast it out?"

29 So He said to them, "This kind can come out by nothing but [f]prayer and fasting."*

Jesus foretells His death and resurrection
(Mt. 17:22–23; Lk. 9:43–45)

30 Then they departed from there and passed through Galilee, and He did not want anyone to know *it*.

31 For He taught His disciples and said to them, "The [g]Son of Man is being [h]betrayed into the hands of men, and they will [i]kill Him. And after He is killed, He will [j]rise the third day."

32 But they did [k]not understand this saying, and were afraid to ask Him.

Humility, the secret of greatness
(Mt. 18:1–6; Lk. 9:46–48)

33 Then He came to Capernaum. And when He was in the house He asked them, "What was it you disputed among yourselves on the road?"

34 But they kept silent, for on the road they had [l]disputed among themselves who *would be the* [m]greatest.

35 And He sat down, called the twelve, and said to them, "If anyone desires to be [n]first, he shall be last of all and [o]servant of all."

36 Then He took a little [p]child and set him in the midst of them. And when He had taken him in His arms, He said to them,

37 "Whoever receives one of these little children in My name [q]receives Me; and whoever receives Me, receives not Me but Him who sent Me."

Sectarianism rebuked
(Lk. 9:49–50)

38 Now John answered Him, saying, "Teacher, we saw someone who does not follow us casting out [r]demons in Your name, and we forbade him because he does not follow us."

39 But Jesus said, "Do not forbid him, for no one who works a miracle in My name can [s]soon afterward speak evil of Me.

40 "For he who is not against us is [t]on our* side.

41 "For whoever gives you a [u]cup of water to drink in My name, because you belong to Christ, assuredly, I say to you, he will by no means lose his [v]reward.

Jesus' solemn warning of hell

42 "But whoever causes one of these little ones who believe in Me to stumble, it would be better for him if a millstone were hung around his neck, and he were thrown into the sea.

43 "If your [w]hand causes you to sin, cut it off. It is better for you to enter into life maimed, rather than having two hands, to go to [x]hell, into the fire that shall never be quenched—

44 "where

'Their worm does not die,
And the fire is not
*quenched.'**

45 "And if your foot causes you to sin, cut it off. It is better for you to enter life lame, rather than having two feet, to be cast into [x]hell, into the fire that shall never be quenched—

46 "where

'Their worm does not die,
And the fire is not
*quenched.'**

*
9:29 NU-Text omits *and fasting.*
9:40 M-Text reads *against you is on your side.* **9:44** NU-Text omits this verse.
9:46 NU-Text omits the last clause of verse 45 and all of verse 46.

24
a Bible prayers (NT): v. 24; Mk. 10:47. (Mt. 6:9; Lk. 11:2, *note*)
b Faith: vv. 23–24; Mk. 10:52. (Gen. 3:20; Heb. 11:39, *note*)
c Lk. 17:5
25
d Mk. 1:25
27
e Miracles (NT): vv. 17–27; Mk. 10:52. (Mt. 8:3; Acts 28:8, *note*)
29
f Jas. 5:16
31
g See Mt. 8:20, *note*
h Lk. 24:20
i Mt. 16:21; Lk. 18:33; Acts 2:23
j Mt. 20:19; 1 Cor. 15:4
32
k Lk. 2:50; 18:34
34
l Prov. 13:10
m Lk. 22:24
35
n Cp. 1 Cor. 15:9 with Mt. 23:2–8
o Mt. 20:26–27; 23:11; Mk. 10:43–44; Lk. 22:26–27
36
p Mk. 10:13–16

37
q Mt. 10:40; cp. Mt. 25:40
38
r See Mt. 7:22, *note*
39
s Cp. Acts 19:13–16
40
t Cp. Mt. 12:30
41
u Mt. 10:42; cp. Mt. 25:35,40; Heb. 6:10
v Rewards: v. 41; Lk. 6:23. (Dan. 12:3; 1 Cor. 3:14, *note*)
43
w Mt. 5:29–30; 18:8–9; cp. Gal. 2:20; Col. 3:5–10
x Gk. *geenna.* See Mt. 5:22, *note*

47 "And if your eye causes you to sin, [a]pluck it out. It is better for you to enter the kingdom of God with one eye, rather than having two eyes, to be cast into [b]hell fire—

48 "where

'Their [c]worm does not die,
And the [d]fire is not quenched.'

49 "For everyone will be seasoned with [e]fire,* and every sacrifice will be [f]seasoned with salt.

50 "Salt *is* good, but if the salt [g]loses its flavor, how will you season it? Have [h]salt in yourselves, and have [i]peace with one another."

Jesus teaches concerning divorce
(Mt. 5:31–32; 19:1–9; Lk. 16:18; cp. Rom. 7:1–3; 1 Cor. 7:10–16)

10 THEN He arose from there and came to the region of Judea by the other side of the Jordan. And multitudes gathered to Him again, and as He was accustomed, He taught them again.

2 The [j]Pharisees came and asked Him, "Is it lawful for a man to divorce *his* wife?" [k]testing Him.

3 And He answered and said to them, "What did Moses [l]command you?"

4 They said, "Moses permitted *a man* to [m]write a certificate of divorce, and to dismiss *her*."

5 And Jesus answered and said to them, "Because of the hardness of your heart he [n]wrote you this precept.

6 "But from the beginning of the creation, [o]God *'made them male and female.'*

7 *'For this reason a man shall [p]leave his father and mother and be joined to his wife,*

8 *'and the two shall become one flesh'*; so then they are no longer two, but one flesh.

9 "Therefore what God has joined together, let not man separate."

10 In the house His disciples also asked Him again about the same *matter*.

11 So He said to them, "Whoever divorces his wife and marries another commits [q]adultery against her.

12 "And if a woman divorces her husband and marries another, she commits adultery."

Jesus blesses little children
(Mt. 19:13–15; Lk. 18:15–17)

13 Then they brought little children to Him, that He might touch them; but the disciples rebuked those who brought *them*.

14 But when Jesus saw *it*, He was [1]greatly displeased and said to them, "Let the little children come to Me, and do not forbid them; for of such is the [r]kingdom of God.

15 "Assuredly, I say to you, [s]whoever does not receive the kingdom of God as a little child will [t]by no means enter it."

16 And He took them up in His arms, laid *His* hands on them, and [2]blessed them.

The rich young ruler
(Mt. 19:16–30; Lk. 18:18–30; cp. Lk. 10:25)

17 Now as He was going out on the road, one came running, knelt before Him, and asked Him, "Good Teacher, what shall I [u]do that I may inherit [v]eternal life?"

18 So Jesus said to him, [3]"Why do you call Me good? No one *is* good but One, *that is,* [w]God.

19 "You know the [l]commandments: [x]*'Do not commit adultery,' 'Do not [y]murder,' 'Do not steal,' 'Do not bear false witness,'* [z]'Do not defraud,' *'Honor your father and your mother.'* "*

20 And he answered and said

47
a Cp. Rom. 8:13
b Gk. *geenna.* See Mt. 5:22, *note*
48
c Isa. 66:24; cp. Lk. 16:24–26
d Jer. 7:20; Rev. 21:8
49
e Mt. 3:11
f Lev. 2:13
50
g Mt. 5:13
h Col. 4:6
i Rom. 14:19
CHAPTER 10
2
j See Mt. 3:7, *note*
k Test/tempt: v. 2; Mk. 12:15. (Gen. 3:1; Jas. 1:14, *note*)
3
l Law (of Moses): vv. 3–8, 19–20; Mk. 12:19. (Ex. 19:1; Gal. 3:24, *note*)
4
m Dt. 24:1–4
5
n Inspiration: vv. 4–9; Mk. 11:17. (Ex. 4:15; 2 Tim. 3:16, *note*)
6
o Gen. 1:27; 2:21–25; 5:1–2
7
p Eph. 5:31
11
q Ex. 20:14
14
r See Mt. 6:33, *note*
15
s Mt. 18:3–4
t Lk. 13:28
17
u vv. 19,21; Jn. 6:28; Acts 2:37; cp. Rom. 9:31–32; 10:2–3; Gal. 2:16; 3:10–12
v Life (eternal): v. 17; Mk. 10:30. (Mt. 7:14; Rev. 22:19)
18
w 1 Sam. 2:2
19
x Ex. 20:12–17; Jas. 2:11
y See Ex. 20:13, *note*
z Cp. Rom. 13:7–10

---

* **9:49** NU-Text omits the rest of this verse.
10:19 Exodus 20:12–16; Deuteronomy 5:16–20

---

[1](10:14) Literally, "moved with indignation," an unusual expression relating to the Lord Jesus.
[2](10:16) In Hebrew custom this was the act of a father. Cp. Gen. 27:38.
[3](10:18) In paraphrase this question might read: "Believing Me to be only a human teacher, why do you call Me good?"

to Him, "Teacher, all these things I have [a]kept from my youth."

21 Then Jesus, looking at him, loved him, and said to him, "One thing you lack: Go your way, [b]sell whatever you have and give to the poor, and you will have [c]treasure in heaven; and come, [d]take up the cross, and follow Me."

22 But he was sad at this word, and [e]went away sorrowful, for he had great possessions.

"With God all things are possible"

23 Then Jesus looked around and said to His disciples, [f]"How hard it is for those who have [g]riches to enter the [h]kingdom of God!"

24 And the disciples were [1]astonished at His words. But Jesus answered again and said to them, "Children, how hard it is for those who [i]trust in riches* to enter the kingdom of God!

25 "It is easier for a camel to go through the eye of a [jk]needle than for a rich man to enter the kingdom of God."

26 And they were [l]greatly astonished, saying among themselves, "Who then can be [m]saved?"

27 But Jesus looked at them and said, "With men *it is* impossible, but not with God; for with God all things are [n]possible."

Faithfulness to the Lord will be rewarded

28 Then Peter began to say to Him, "See, we have [o]left all and followed You."

29 So Jesus answered and said, "Assuredly, I say to you, there is no one who has left house or brothers or sisters or father or mother or wife* or children or lands, for My sake and the [p]gospel's,

30 "who shall not [q]receive a hundredfold now in this time—houses and brothers and sisters and mothers and children and lands, with [r]persecutions—and in the [2]age to come, [s]eternal life.

31 "But many *who are* [t]first will be last, and the last first."

Jesus again foretells His death and resurrection (Mt. 20:17–19; Lk. 18:31–33)

32 Now they were on the road, going up to Jerusalem, and Jesus was going before them; and they were amazed. And as they followed they were afraid. Then He took the twelve aside again and began to [u]tell them the things that would happen to Him:

33 "Behold, we are going up to Jerusalem, and the [v]Son of Man will be betrayed to the chief priests and to the [w]scribes; and they will condemn Him to death and deliver Him to the Gentiles;

34 "and they will mock Him, and scourge Him, and spit on Him, and kill Him. And the third day He will rise again."

Christ's response to request of James and John (Mt. 20:20–28)

35 Then James and John, the sons of Zebedee, came to Him, saying, "Teacher, we want You to do for us whatever we [x]ask."

36 And He said to them, "What do you want Me to do for you?"

37 They said to Him, "Grant us that we may sit, one on Your right hand and the other on Your left, in Your [y]glory."

38 But Jesus said to them, "You do not know what you ask. Are you able to drink the [z]cup that I drink, and be baptized with the [aa]baptism that I am baptized with?"

39 They said to Him, "We are able." So Jesus said to them,

*10:24 NU-Text omits *for those who trust in riches.* 10:29 NU-Text omits *or wife.*

20 *a* Phil. 3:6
21 *b* Lk. 12:33; cp. Acts 2:45; 4:34 *c* Mt. 6:20; cp. Lk. 16:11 *d* Mk. 8:34
22 *e* Cp. 2 Tim. 4:10
23 *f* Cp. Job 31:24–25,28; 1 Cor. 1:26; 1 Tim. 6:9–10 *g* Mk. 4:19 *h* See Mt. 6:33, *note*
24 *i* Ps. 52:7; Prov. 11:28; 1 Tim. 6:17
25 *j* Gk. *raphis, a sewing needle* *k* Mt. 13:22; 19:24
26 *l* Mk. 6:51; 7:37 *m* Cp. Heb. 7:25; see Rom. 1:16, *note*
27 *n* Job 42:2; Jer. 32:17; Lk. 1:37; cp. Gen. 18:14; Num. 11:23
28 *o* Lk. 5:11; cp. Phil. 3:7–9
29 *p Gospel:* v. 29; Mk. 13:10. (Gen. 12:3; Rev. 14:6)
30 *q* Lk. 18:29–30; cp. 2 Chr. 25:9 *r* 1 Th. 3:3; 2 Tim. 3:12; 1 Pet. 4:12–13 *s Life* (eternal): v. 30; Lk. 10:25. (Mt. 7:14; Rev. 22:19)
31 *t* Mt. 20:16; Lk. 13:30
32 *u* Mk. 8:31; 9:12,31
33 *v* See Mt. 8:20, *note* *w* See Mt. 2:4, *note*
35 *x* Jas. 4:3; cp. Jer. 45:5
37 *y Kingdom* (NT): v. 37; Mk. 11:10. (Mt. 2:2; 1 Cor. 15:24, *note*)
38 *z* Mt. 26:39, 42; Mk. 14:36; Lk. 22:41–42; Jn. 18:11; cp. 1 Pet. 3:18 *aa* Lk. 12:50

[1](10:24) The disciples were amazed. To the Jewish people temporal prosperity was a token of divine favor. See, e.g. Dt. 28:1–12.

[2](10:30) The Greek noun *aiōn,* here translated "age" (v. 30), has various connotations: *a period of time* (e.g. the Mosaic age; the Church age) and, in certain contexts *eternity* or *forever.* It is also translated "world" (Lk. 16:8; Rom. 12:2). However, "world" is normally the translation of the Gk. *kosmos* (see Mt. 4:8 and Rev. 13:8, *notes*) or of the Gk. *oikoumenē* (see Lk. 2:1, *note*).

[1a]"You will indeed drink the cup that I drink, and with the baptism I am baptized with you will be baptized;

40 "but to sit on My right hand and on My left is not Mine to give, but *it is for those* [b]for whom it is prepared."

41 And when the ten heard *it*, they began to be greatly displeased with James and John.

42 But Jesus called them to *Himself* and said to them, "You know that those who are considered rulers over the Gentiles lord it over them, and their great ones exercise authority over them.

43 "Yet it shall not be so among you; but whoever desires to become great among you shall be your [c]servant.

44 "And whoever of you desires to be first shall be slave of all.

45 "For even the [d]Son of Man did not come to be served, but to [e]serve, and to give His [f]life a [g]ransom for many."

Bartimaeus receives his sight
(Mt. 20:29–34; cp. Lk. 18:35–43)

46 Now they came to Jericho. As He went out of Jericho with His disciples and a great multitude, [h]blind Bartimaeus, the son of Timaeus, sat by the road begging.

47 And when he heard that it was Jesus of Nazareth, he began to cry out and [i]say, "Jesus, [j]Son of David, [k]have mercy on me!"

48 Then many warned him to be quiet; but he cried out all the more, "Son of David, have mercy on me!"

49 So Jesus stood still and [l]commanded him to be called. Then they called the blind man, saying to him, "Be of good cheer. Rise, He is calling you."

50 And throwing aside his garment, he rose and came to Jesus.

51 So Jesus answered and said to him, "What do you want Me to do for you?" The blind man said to Him, "Rabboni, that I may [m]receive my sight."

52 Then Jesus said to him, "Go your way; your [n]faith has made you well." And immediately he [o]received his sight and followed Jesus on the road.

The triumphal entry of Jesus
(Mt. 21:1–9; Lk. 19:28–38;
Jn. 12:12–18; cp. Zech. 9:9)

11 NOW when they drew near Jerusalem, to [p]Bethphage* and [q]Bethany, at the [r]Mount of Olives, He sent two of His disciples;

2 and He said to them, "Go into the village opposite you; and as soon as you have entered it you will find a colt tied, on which no one has sat. Loose it and bring *it*.

3 "And if anyone says to you, 'Why are you doing this?' say, 'The [s]Lord has need of it,' and immediately he will send it here."

4 So they went their way, and found the* colt tied by the door outside on the street, and they loosed it.

5 But some of those who stood there said to them, "What are you doing, loosing the colt?"

6 And they spoke to them just as Jesus had commanded. So they let them go.

7 Then they brought the colt to Jesus and threw their clothes on it, and He [t]sat on it.

8 And many spread their clothes on the road, and others cut down leafy [u]branches from the trees and spread *them* on the road.

9 Then those who went before and those who followed cried out, saying:

"Hosanna!
'Blessed is He who
[v]comes in the name of
*the LORD!'**
10 Blessed *is* the [w]kingdom
of our father David
That comes in the name
of the Lord!*
Hosanna in the highest!"

*
11:1 M-Text reads *Bethsphage.*
11:4 NU-Text and M-Text read *a.*
11:9 Psalm 118:26 **11:10** NU-Text omits *in the name of the Lord.*

39
a Mt. 10:17–18, 21–22; 24:9; Jn. 16:33; Acts 12:2
40
b Mt. 25:34; Jn. 17:2,6, 24; Rom. 8:30; Heb. 11:16
43
c Mt. 23:11; cp. 1 Cor. 9:19–23
45
d See Mt. 8:20, *note*
e Lk. 22:27; cp. Phil. 2:7–8
f Or *soul.* Gk. *psuchē.* Isa. 53:10–12
g 2 Cor. 5:21; 1 Tim. 2:5–6; Ti. 2:14; see Rom. 3:24, *note*
46
h See Mt. 20:30, *note*
47
i Bible prayers (NT): vv. 47–48, 51; Mk. 14:35. (Mt. 6:9; Lk. 11:2, *note*)
j Jer. 23:5; Mt. 22:42; Rom. 1:3–4; Rev. 22:16
k Mt. 15:22; Lk. 17:13
49
l Cp. Ps. 86:15; Heb. 4:15
51
m Cp. Mt. 7:7–8 with Isa. 35:5

52
n Faith: v. 52; Lk. 5:20. (Gen. 3:20; Heb. 11:39, *note*)
o Miracles (NT): vv. 46–52; 11:12–14, 20–21; Lk. 4:39. (Mt. 8:3; Acts 28:8, *note*)
CHAPTER 11
1
p Meaning *house of unripe figs*
q See Mt. 21:17, *note*
r Mk. 13:3; Lk. 22:39; Acts 1:12; cp. Zech. 14:4
3
s Cp. Ps. 50:10
7
t Cp. 1 Ki. 1:33
8
u Cp. Lev. 23:40
9
v Christ (first advent): vv. 9–10; Mk. 12:6. (Gen. 3:15; Acts 1:11, *note*)
10
w Kingdom (NT): v. 10; Lk. 1:33. (Mt. 2:2; 1 Cor. 15:24, *note*)

[1](10:39) James and John would suffer martyrdom and exile respectively (Acts 12:2; Rev. 1:9).

11 And Jesus went into Jerusalem and into the [a]temple. So when He had looked around at all things, as the hour was already late, He went out to [b]Bethany with the twelve.

The barren fig tree
(Mt. 21:18–21)

12 Now the next day, when they had come out from Bethany, He was [c]hungry.

13 And seeing from afar a [d]fig tree having [1]leaves, He went to see if perhaps He would find something on it. When He came to it, He found nothing but leaves, for it was not the season for figs.

14 In response Jesus said to it, "Let no one eat fruit from you ever again." And His disciples heard *it.*

Jesus drives traders from temple
(Mt. 21:12–16; Lk. 19:45–47; cp. Jn. 2:13–16)

15 So they came to Jerusalem. Then Jesus went into the temple and began to drive out those who bought and sold in the temple, and overturned the tables of the money changers and the seats of those who sold [e]doves.

16 And He would not allow anyone to carry wares through the temple.

17 Then He taught, saying to them, "Is it not [f]written, [g]*'My house shall be called a house of prayer for all nations'*? But you have made it a [h]*'den of thieves.'* "

18 And the [i]scribes and chief priests heard it and [j]sought how they might destroy Him; for they [k]feared Him, because all the people were [l]astonished at His teaching.

19 When evening had come, He went out of the city.

The prayer of faith
(cp. 1 Jn. 5:14–15)

20 Now in the morning, as they passed by, they saw the [m]fig tree dried up from the roots.

21 And Peter, remembering, said to Him, "Rabbi, look! The fig tree which You cursed has withered away."

22 So Jesus answered and said to them, [n]"Have faith in God.

23 "For assuredly, I say to you, whoever says to this mountain, 'Be removed and be cast into the sea,' and does not doubt in his heart, but [o]believes that those things he says will be done, he will have whatever he says.

24 "Therefore I say to you, whatever things you ask when you pray, [p]believe that you receive *them,* and you will [q]have *them.*

A forgiving spirit required

25 "And whenever you stand praying, if you have anything against anyone, [r]forgive him, that your Father in heaven may also [s]forgive you your trespasses.

26 [t]"But if you do not forgive, neither will your Father in heaven forgive your trespasses."*

Jesus' authority challenged
(Mt. 21:23–27; Lk. 20:1–8)

27 Then they came again to Jerusalem. And as He was walking in the temple, the chief priests, the [i]scribes, and the elders came to Him.

28 And they said to Him, "By what [u]authority are You doing these things? And who gave You this authority to do these things?"

29 But Jesus answered and said to them, "I also will ask you one question; then answer Me, and I will [v]tell you by what authority I do these things:

30 "The [w]baptism of John—was it from heaven or from men? Answer Me."

31 And they reasoned among themselves, saying, "If we say, 'From heaven,' He will say, 'Why then did you not believe him?'

32 "But if we say, 'From men' "—they feared the people,

* 11:26 NU-Text omits this verse.

11
a vv. 15–17; cp. Mal. 3:1
b See Mt. 21:17, *note*
12
c Mt. 4:2
13
d Cp. Lk. 13:6–9
15
e Lev. 14:22; cp. Lk. 2:24
17
f *Inspiration:* v. 17; Mk. 12:10. (Ex. 4:15; 2 Tim. 3:16, *note*)
g Isa. 56:7
h Jer. 7:11
18
i See Mt. 2:4, *note*
j Ps. 2:2
k Cp. v. 32; Mt. 21:46
l Mt. 7:28; Mk. 1:22; 6:2
20
m vv. 13–14

22
n Lit. *faith of God.* Cp. 1 Cor. 12:9; Eph. 2:8
23
o Mt. 17:20; cp. 1 Cor. 13:2
24
p Jas. 1:5–6
q Mt. 7:7–11; Jn. 14:13–14; 15:7; 16:24; 1 Jn. 5:14–15
25
r Mt. 6:14; 18:23–35; Eph. 4:32; Col. 3:13; see Mt. 6:12, *note*
s *Forgiveness:* vv. 25–26; Lk. 5:20. (Lev. 4:20; Mt. 26:28, *note*)
26
t Mt. 18:35; cp. Mt. 6:12
28
u Jn. 5:27
29
v Cp. v. 33
30
w Mk. 1:4–5, 8; Lk. 7:29–30; cp. Jn. 1:25–34

[1](11:13) Fig trees which have retained their leaves through the winter usually have figs also. It was still too early for new leaves or fruit.

for all [a]counted John to have been a prophet indeed.

33 So they answered and said to Jesus, [b]"We do not know." And Jesus answered and said to them, "Neither will I tell you by what authority I do these things."

Parable of the vineyard owner (Mt. 21:33–46; Lk. 20:9–19; cp. Isa. 5:1–7)

12 THEN He began to speak to them in [c]parables: [1d]"A man planted a vineyard and set a hedge around *it*, dug *a place for* the wine vat and built a tower. And he leased it to vinedressers and went into a far country.

2 "Now at vintage-time he sent a servant to the vinedressers, that he might receive some of the fruit of the vineyard from the vinedressers.

3 "And they took *him* and beat him and sent *him* away empty-handed.

4 "Again he sent them another servant, and at him they threw stones,* wounded *him* in the head, and sent *him* away shamefully treated.

5 "And again he sent another, and him they killed; and [e]many others, [f]beating some and [g]killing some.

6 "Therefore still having one son, his beloved, he also [h]sent him to them last, saying, 'They will respect my son.'

7 "But those vinedressers said among themselves, 'This is the heir. Come, let us kill him, and the inheritance will be ours.'

8 "So they took him and [i]killed *him* and cast *him* out of the vineyard.

9 "Therefore what will the owner of the vineyard do? He will come and destroy the vinedressers, and give the vineyard to others.

10 "Have you not even read this [j]Scripture:

'The [k]stone which the builders rejected
Has become the chief cornerstone.
11 *This was the* LORD'S *doing,*
And it is marvelous in our eyes'?"

12 And they sought to lay hands on Him, but [l]feared the multitude, for they knew He had spoken the parable against them. So they left Him and went away.

Jesus answers the Herodians (Mt. 22:15–22; Lk. 20:19–26)

13 Then they sent to Him some of the [m]Pharisees and the [n]Herodians, to [o]catch Him in *His* words.

14 When they had come, they said to Him, "Teacher, we know that You are true, and care about no one; for You do not [p]regard the person of men, but teach the [q]way of God in truth. Is it lawful to pay taxes to Caesar, [r]or not?

15 "Shall we pay, or shall we not pay?" But He, knowing their [s]hypocrisy, said to them, "Why do you [t]test Me? Bring Me a [u]denarius that I may see *it*."

16 So they brought *it*. And He said to them, "Whose image and inscription *is* this?" They said to Him, "Caesar's."

17 And Jesus answered and said to them, [v]"Render to Caesar the things that are Caesar's, and to [w]God the things that are God's." And they marveled at Him.

Jesus answers the Sadducees (Mt. 22:23–33; Lk. 20:27–38)

18 Then *some* [x]Sadducees,

*12:4 NU-Text omits *and at him they threw stones.*

32
a Mt. 14:5
33
b Cp. Jer. 8:7; Rom. 1:18; 2 Cor. 4:3–4
CHAPTER 12
1
c Mt. 13:10–15
d Parables (NT): vv. 1–11; Mk. 13:28. (Mt. 5:13; Lk. 21:29)
5
e Cp. Jer. 7:25
f 2 Chr. 36:16; cp. Mt. 23:34
g Cp. Acts 7:52
6
h Christ (first advent): vv. 6–8; Mk. 14:27. (Gen. 3:15; Acts 1:11, *note*)
8
i Acts 2:23
10
j Inspiration: vv. 10–11; Mk. 12:26. (Ex. 4:15; 2 Tim. 3:16, *note*)
k Christ (Stone): v. 10; Lk. 20:17. (Gen. 49:24; 1 Pet. 2:8). Ps. 118:22–23
12
l Mk. 11:32
13
m See Mt. 3:7, *note*
n See Mt. 22:16, *note*
o Lk. 11:54
14
p Cp. Acts 10:34–35
q Acts 18:26; cp. Jn. 10:1; 2 Pet. 2:15, 21
r Cp. Lk. 23:2
15
s Mt. 23:28; Lk. 12:1
t Test/tempt: vv. 13–15; Lk. 4:2. (Gen. 3:1; Jas. 1:14, *note*)
u See Coinage (NT), Mt. 5:26, *note*
17
v Cp. Mt. 17:25–27; Rom. 13:7
w Eccl. 5:4–5
18
x Acts 23:8; see Mt. 3:7, *note*

[1](12:1) This parable (vv. 1–9), addressed to the religious leaders of Israel—"the chief priests, the scribes, and the elders" (11:27)—illustrates God's dealings with the nation and their rejection of His proffered love and of their responsibilities to Him. The "man" (v. 1) is God Himself; the vineyard is Israel (v. 1; cp. Isa. 5:1–7); the servants (vv. 2–5) are the OT prophets and John the Baptist; the "son, his beloved" whom they killed (vv. 6–8), is Jesus Himself (cp. Heb. 1:1–3); and the destruction of the vinedressers (v. 9) is a prediction regarding Jerusalem's fall in A.D. 70 (cp. Lk. 21:20–24). That the chief priests, the scribes, and elders recognized that it was they of whom Christ spoke is recorded in v. 12. The words of the Lord discovered and laid bare the thoughts and intents of their hearts (cp. Heb. 4:12).

who say there is no resurrection, came to Him; and they asked Him, saying:

19 "Teacher, [a]Moses wrote to us that [b]if a man's brother dies, and leaves *his* wife behind, and leaves no children, his brother should take his wife and raise up offspring for his brother.

20 "Now there were seven brothers. The first took a wife; and dying, he left no offspring.

21 "And the second took her, and he died; nor did he leave any offspring. And the third likewise.

22 "So the seven had her and left no offspring. Last of all the woman died also.

23 "Therefore, in the resurrection, when they rise, whose wife will she be? For all seven had her as wife."

24 Jesus answered and said to them, "Are you not therefore mistaken, because you do not know the Scriptures nor the power of God?

25 "For when they rise [c]from the dead, they neither marry nor are given in marriage, but are like [d]angels in heaven.

26 "But concerning the dead, that they [e]rise, have you not [1][f]read in the [a]book of Moses, in the *burning* bush *passage,* how God [g]spoke to him, saying, *'I am the God of Abraham, the God of Isaac, and the God of Jacob'*?

27 [h]"He is not the God of the dead, but the God of the living. You are therefore greatly mistaken."

Jesus answers the Pharisees (Mt. 22:34–40; cp. Lk. 10:25–37)

28 Then [i]one of the scribes came, and having heard them reasoning together, perceiving* that He had answered them well, asked Him, "Which is the [2]first commandment of all?"

29 Jesus answered him, "The first of all the commandments is: [j]*'Hear, O Israel, the* LORD *our God, the* LORD *is* [k]*one.*

30 *'And you shall* [l]*love the* LORD *your God with all your heart, with all your soul, with all your mind, and with all your strength.'* This *is* the first commandment.*

31 "And the second, like *it, is* this: [m]*'You shall love your neighbor as yourself.'* There is no other commandment greater than [n]these."

32 So the [o]scribe said to Him, "Well *said,* Teacher. You have spoken the [p]truth, for there is one God, and there is no other but He.

33 "And to love Him with all the heart, with all the understanding, with all the soul,* and with all the strength, and to love one's neighbor as oneself, [q]is more than all the whole burnt offerings and sacrifices."

34 Now when Jesus saw that he answered [r]wisely, He said to him, "You are [3]not far from the [s]kingdom of God." But after that no one dared question Him.

Jesus questions the Pharisees concerning Messiah (Mt. 22:41–46; Lk. 20:41–44)

35 Then Jesus answered and said, while He taught in the temple, "How *is it* that the [o]scribes say that the Christ is the [t]Son of David?

36 "For [4]David himself [f]said by the Holy [u]Spirit:

'The LORD *said to my Lord,*
"Sit at My right hand,
*Till I make Your enemies Your footstool."'**

37 "Therefore David himself calls Him *'Lord'*; how is He *then*

*
12:28 NU-Text reads *seeing.*
12:30 NU-Text omits this sentence.
12:33 NU-Text omits *with all the soul.*
12:36 Psalm 110:1

19
a *Law* (of Moses): vv. 19,26, 28–31; Lk. 1:6. (Ex. 19:1; Gal. 3:24, *note*)
b Dt. 25:5; cp. Ruth 1:11–13
25
c Or *from among*
d See Heb. 1:4, *note*
26
e Jn. 5:25, 28–29; Acts 26:8; Rom. 4:17; Rev. 20:12–13
f *Inspiration:* vv. 26, 36; Mk. 13:14. (Ex. 4:15; 2 Tim. 3:16, *note*)
g Ex. 3:1–10, 12
27
h Cp. Rom. 14:9
28
i See Mk. 12:34, *note*

29
j See Dt. 6:4, *note*
k v. 32; Isa. 44:8; 45:22; 46:9; 1 Cor. 8:6
30
l Dt. 10:12; 30:6; see Dt. 6:5, *note*
31
m Lev. 19:18; Mt. 19:19; Gal. 5:14; cp. Rom. 13:10
n Rom. 13:9
32
o See Mt. 2:4, *note*
p Jn. 1:14,17; 14:6
33
q Cp. Ps. 51:16–17; Mic. 6:7–8
34
r Cp. 1 Tim. 1:5
s See Mt. 6:33, *note*
35
t Cp. Rom. 1:3–4
36
u *Holy Spirit* (NT): v. 36; Mk. 13:11. (Mt. 1:18; Acts 2:4, *note*)

[1](12:26) Our Lord here affirms the historicity and inspiration of Ex. 3.
[2](12:28) The scribes divided the whole law into 613 precepts.
[3](12:34) The scribe was not far, in knowledge, from the kingdom of God. He knew the very law which utterly condemns even the best man—the true office of the law. Cp. Rom. 3:19; 10:3–5; Gal. 3:10,22–24.
[4](12:36) The Lord Jesus Christ here affirms both the Davidic authorship and the inspiration of Ps. 110.

his [a]Son?" And the common people heard Him gladly.

38 Then He said to them in His teaching, "Beware of the [b]scribes, who desire to go around in long robes, *love* greetings in the marketplaces,

39 "the [c]best seats in the synagogues, and the best places at feasts,

40 "who devour widows' houses, and for a [d]pretense make long prayers. These will receive greater condemnation."

The widow's mites (Lk. 21:1–4)

41 Now Jesus sat opposite the treasury and saw how the people put money into the [e]treasury. And many *who were* rich put in much.

42 Then one poor widow came and threw in two [f]mites,* which make a [g]quadrans.

43 So He called His disciples to *Himself* and said to them, "Assuredly, I say to you that this poor widow has put in more than all those who have given to the treasury;

44 "for they all put in out of their abundance, but she out of her [h]poverty put in all that she had, her whole livelihood."

The Olivet Discourse (Mt. 24—25): the disciples' two questions (Mt. 24:3; Lk. 21:7)

13 THEN as He went out of the temple, one of His disciples said to Him, "Teacher, see what manner of stones and what buildings *are here!*"

2 And Jesus answered and said to him, "Do you see these great [i]buildings? Not *one* stone shall be [j]left upon another, that shall not be thrown down."

3 Now as He sat on the Mount of Olives opposite the temple, [k]Peter, [l]James, [m]John, and [n]Andrew asked Him privately,

4 "Tell us, when will these things be? And what *will be* the sign when all these things will be fulfilled?"

Daniel's seventieth week of years (Dan. 9:27); the end time (Mt. 24:4–14; cp. Lk. 21:8–11)

5 And Jesus, answering them, began to say: "Take heed that no one [o]deceives you.

6 "For many will [p]come in My name, saying, 'I am *He,*' and will deceive many.

7 "But when you hear of wars and rumors of wars, do not be troubled; for *such things* must happen, but the [q]end *is* not yet.

8 "For nation will rise against nation, and [r]kingdom against kingdom. And there will be [s]earthquakes in various places, and there will be [t]famines and troubles.* These *are* the beginnings of [u]sorrows.

9 "But watch out for yourselves, for they will [v]deliver you up to councils, and you will be beaten in the synagogues. You will be brought* before rulers and kings for My sake, for a testimony to them.

10 "And the [w]gospel must first be preached to all the nations.

11 "But when they arrest *you* and deliver you up, do not worry beforehand, or premeditate* what you will speak. But whatever is given you in that hour, speak that; for it is not you who speak, but the Holy [x]Spirit.

12 "Now brother will betray brother to death, and a father *his* child; and children will rise up against parents and cause them to be put to death.

13 "And you will be [y]hated by all for My name's sake. But he who endures to the [z]end shall be [aa]saved.

The middle of the week: the abomination of desolation (Mt. 24:15–20)

14 "So when you see the [bb]'*abomination of desolation,*' [cc]spoken of by Daniel the prophet,* standing where [dd]it ought not" (let the reader understand), [ee]"then let those who are in Judea flee to the mountains.

15 "Let him who is on the housetop not go down into the house, nor enter to take anything out of his house.

16 "And let him who is in the

*
12:42 Greek *lepta,* very small copper coins worth a fraction of a penny **13:8** NU-Text omits *and troubles.* **13:9** NU-Text and M-Text read *will stand.* **13:11** NU-Text omits *or premeditate.* **13:14** NU-Text omits *spoken of by Daniel the prophet.*

37
a Acts 2:29–31
38
b See Mt. 2:4, *note*
39
c Lk. 14:7
40
d Cp. 1 Th. 2:5
41
e Cp. 2 Ki. 12:9–10
42
f Smallest coin. See Coinage (NT), Mt. 5:26, *note*
g See Coinage (NT), Mt. 5:26, *note*
44
h 2 Cor. 8:2; cp. 2 Cor. 8:5,12
CHAPTER 13
2
i Cp. Jn. 2:20
j Lk. 19:44; cp. 1 Ki. 9:7; Mic. 3:12
3
k Mt. 16:18; Mk. 1:16
l Mk. 1:19; see Mt. 4:21, *note*
m Mk. 1:19
n Jn. 1:40
5
o Jer. 29:8; Eph. 5:6; Col. 2:8; 2 Th. 2:3; cp. 1 Jn. 4:1; Rev. 20:8

6
p v. 22; cp. Jn. 5:43
7
q Cp. Jer. 4:27; 5:10, 18
8
r Hag. 2:22
s Cp. Rev. 6:12
t Cp. Rev. 6:5–6
u Lit. *birth pangs*
9
v Mt. 10:17; Acts 12:4
10
w Gospel: v. 10; Mk. 14:9. (Gen. 12:3; Rev. 14:6)
11
x Holy Spirit (NT): v. 11; Lk. 1:15. (Mt. 1:18; Acts 2:4, *note*)
13
y Mt. 10:22
z The end of the tribulation. See Mt. 24:13, *note*
aa Cp. Rev. 20:4
14
bb The Beast: v. 14; Jn. 5:43. (Dan. 7:8; Rev. 19:20)
cc Inspiration: v. 14; Mk. 14:21. (Ex. 4:15; 2 Tim. 3:16, *note*)
dd Or *he.* Dan. 11:36; 12:11; 2 Th. 2:4
ee Cp. Lk. 21:20–24 where see *notes*

field not go back to get his clothes.

17 "But woe to those who are pregnant and to those who are nursing babies in those days!

18 "And pray that your flight may not be in winter.

The great tribulation
(latter half of week)
(Mt. 24:21–28;
cp. Ps. 2:5; see Rev. 7:14, note)

19 "For *in* those days there will be [a]tribulation, such as has not been since the beginning of the creation which God created until this time, nor ever shall be.

20 "And unless the Lord had shortened those days, no flesh would be saved; but for the [b]elect's sake, whom He chose, He shortened the days.

21 "Then if anyone says to you, 'Look, here *is* the Christ!' or, 'Look, *He is* there!' do not believe it.

22 "For false christs and false prophets will rise and show signs and [c]wonders to deceive, if possible, even the [b]elect.

23 "But take heed; see, I have [d]told you all things beforehand.

Christ's return to the earth
at the close of the tribulation
(Mt. 24:29–31; Lk. 21:25–28)

24 "But in those [e]days, after that tribulation, the sun will be darkened, and the moon will not give its light;

25 "the stars of heaven will fall, and the powers in the heavens will be [f]shaken.

26 "Then they will see the [g]Son of Man coming in the [h]clouds with great power and glory.

27 "And then He will send His [i]angels, and [j]gather together His [b]elect from the four winds, from the farthest part of earth to the farthest part of heaven.

Parable of the fig tree
(Mt. 24:32–33; Lk. 21:29–31)

28 "Now learn this [k]parable from the fig tree: When its branch has already become tender, and puts forth leaves, you know that summer is near.

29 "So you also, when you see these things happening, know that it* is near—at the doors!

30 "Assuredly, I say to you, this [l]generation will by no means pass away till all these things take place.

31 [m]"Heaven and earth will pass away, but My words will by no means pass away.

Watchfulness enjoined
(Mt. 24:36–51)

32 "But of that day and hour [n]no one knows, not even the [i]angels in heaven, nor the Son, but only the [o]Father.

33 "Take heed, [p]watch and pray; for you do not know when the time is.

34 "*It is* like a man going to a far country, who left his house and gave [q]authority to his servants, and to each his work, and commanded the doorkeeper to watch.

35 [r]"Watch therefore, [s]for you do not know when the master of the house is coming—in the evening, at midnight, at the crowing of the rooster, or in the morning—

36 "lest, coming suddenly, he find you [t]sleeping.

37 "And what I say to you, I say to [u]all: Watch!"

III. The Servant's Obedience
unto Death, 14—15

Jewish authorities plot death
of Jesus (Mt. 26:2–5; Lk. 22:1–2)

14 AFTER two days it was the [v]Passover and *the Feast* of [w]Unleavened Bread. And the chief priests and the [x]scribes [y]sought how they might take Him by trickery and put *Him* to death.

2 But they said, "Not during the feast, lest there be an uproar of the [z]people."

Jesus anointed by
Mary of Bethany
(Mt. 26:6–13; Jn. 12:1–8)

3 And being in Bethany at the house of Simon the leper, as He [aa]sat at the table, a woman came having an alabaster flask of very costly oil of spikenard. Then she broke the flask and poured *it* on His [bb]head.

4 But there were some who

*13:29 Or *He*

19
a Tribulation (the great): vv. 14–23; Lk. 21:20. (Ps. 2:5; Rev. 7:14)
20
b Election (corporate): vv. 20,22,27; Lk. 18:7. (Dt. 7:6; 1 Pet. 5:13, *note*)
22
c Dt. 13:1–3; Rev. 13:13–14
23
d Jn. 16:1–4
24
e Day (of the LORD): vv. 24–37; Lk. 17:30. (Ps. 2:9; Rev. 19:19)
25
f Isa. 13:10; 34:4; Heb. 12:26
26
g Christ (second advent): vv. 26, 32–33, 35–36; Mk. 14:62. (Dt. 30:3; Acts 1:11, *note*). See Mt. 8:20, *note*
h Dan. 7:13
27
i See Heb. 1:4, *note*
j Israel (prophecies): v. 27; Lk. 1:33. (Gen. 12:2; Rom. 11:26, *note*)
28
k Parables (NT): vv. 28–29; Lk. 5:36. (Mt. 5:13; Lk. 21:29)

30
l See Mt. 24:34, *note*
31
m 2 Pet. 3:7, 10,12
32
n Mt. 25:13
o Acts 1:7
33
p 1 Th. 5:6; 1 Pet. 4:7
34
q Mt. 16:19
35
r Mk. 14:38; 1 Cor. 16:13; 2 Tim. 4:5
s Cp. Lk. 12:39–40; 21:34; Rom. 13:11; 2 Pet. 3:10
36
t Cp. Mt. 25:1–13
37
u Cp. Acts 2:39; Rom. 10:12; 1 Cor. 9:19–23
CHAPTER 14
1
v vv. 12–21; Ex. 12
w v. 12; Lk. 22:1
x See Mt. 2:4, *note*
y Cp. Acts 4:25–28
2
z Cp. Mt. 21:26
3
aa Lk. 7:37
bb See Mt. 26:7, *note*

were indignant among themselves, and said, "Why was this fragrant oil wasted?

5 "For it might have been sold for more than three hundred [a]denarii and given to the poor." And they [b]criticized her sharply.

6 But Jesus said, "Let her alone. Why do you trouble her? She has done a good work for Me.

7 [c]"For you have the poor with you always, and whenever you wish you may do them good; [d]but Me you do not have always.

8 "She has done what she could. She has come beforehand to [e]anoint My body for burial.

9 "Assuredly, I say to you, wherever this [f]gospel is [g]preached in the whole [h]world, what this woman has done will also be told as a memorial to her."

Judas agrees to betray Jesus (Mt. 26:14–16; Lk. 22:3–6)

10 Then [i]Judas Iscariot, one of the twelve, went to the chief priests to betray Him to them.

11 And when they heard *it,* they were glad, and promised to [j]give him money. So he sought how he might conveniently betray Him.

Preparation for the Passover (Mt. 26:17–19; Lk. 22:7–13)

12 Now on the [k]first day of Unleavened Bread, when they [l]killed the [m]Passover *lamb,* His disciples said to Him, "Where do You want us to go and prepare, that You may eat the Passover?"

13 And He sent out two of His disciples and said to them, "Go into the city, and a man will meet you carrying a pitcher of water; follow him.

14 "Wherever he goes in, say to the master of the house, 'The Teacher says, "Where is the guest room in which I may eat the Passover with My disciples?"'

15 "Then he will show you a large upper room, furnished *and* prepared; there make ready for us."

16 So His disciples went out, and came into the city, and found it just as He had said to them; and they prepared the Passover.

The last Passover (Mt. 26:20–24; Lk. 22:14,21–23; Jn. 13:18–19)

17 [1]In the evening He came with the twelve.

18 Now as they sat and ate, Jesus said, "Assuredly, I say to you, [n]one of you who eats with Me will betray Me."

19 And they began to be [o]sorrowful, and to say to Him one by one, "*Is* it I?" And another *said,* "*Is* it I?"*

20 He answered and said to them, "*It is* one of the twelve, who dips with Me in the dish.

21 "The Son of Man indeed goes just [p]as it is [q]written of Him, but [r]woe to that man by whom the [s]Son of Man is betrayed! [t]It would have been good for that man if he had never been born."

The Lord's Supper instituted (Mt. 26:26–29; Lk. 22:17–20; cp. 1 Cor. 11:23–26; Jn. 13:12–30)

22 And as they were eating, Jesus took [u]bread, blessed and broke *it,* and gave *it* to them and said, "Take, eat;* this is My [v]body."

23 Then He took the cup, and when He had given thanks He gave *it* to them, and they all [w]drank from it.

24 And He said to them, "This is My [x]blood of the [y]new* [z]covenant, which is shed for many.

25 "Assuredly, I say to you, I will no longer drink of the fruit of the vine until that day when I drink it new in the [aa]kingdom of God."

Jesus foretells Peter's denial (Mt. 26:30–35; Lk. 22:31–34; Jn. 13:36–38)

26 And when they had [bb]sung a hymn, they went out to the Mount of Olives.

*
14:19 NU-Text omits this sentence.
14:22 NU-Text omits *eat.* **14:24** NU-Text omits *new.*

5
a See Coinage (NT), Mt. 5:26, *note*
b Mt. 20:11; Jn. 6:61
7
c Dt. 15:11
d Jn. 7:33; 8:21; 14:2, 12; 16:10,17, 28
8
e Cp. Jn. 19:40
9
f *Gospel:* v. 9; Mk. 16:15. (Gen. 12:3; Rev. 14:6)
g Mt. 28:19–20; Mk. 16:15; Lk. 24:47
h Gk. *kosmos.* See Mt. 4:8, *note*
10
i Ps. 41:9; 55:12–14; Mt. 10:2–4
11
j Cp. Ex. 21:32; 1 Tim. 6:10
12
k Ex. 12:8
l i.e. *sacrificed*
m See Ex. 12:11, *note*

18
n Jn. 6:70–71
19
o Cp. Mt. 9:15
21
p Cp. Acts 2:23
q *Inspiration:* v. 21; Mk. 14:27. (Ex. 4:15; 2 Tim. 3:16, *note*)
r Acts 1:16–20; cp. Mt. 18:7
s See Mt. 8:20, *note*
t Cp. Mt. 18:6
22
u 1 Cor. 10:16
v 1 Pet. 2:24
23
w Cp. 1 Cor. 10:4,21
24
x *Sacrifice* (prophetic): v. 24; Mk. 15:25. (Gen. 3:15; Heb. 10:18, *note*). Cp. Lev. 17:11; Heb. 9:14–22
y *Covenant* (New): v. 24; Lk. 22:20. (Isa. 61:8; Heb. 8:8, *note*)
z Ex. 24:8
25
aa See Mt. 6:33, *note*
26
bb Cp. Ps. 47:6–7; Eph. 5:19

[1](14:17) For the order of events on the night of the Passover Supper, see Mt. 26:20, *note.*

27 Then Jesus said to them,
[a]"All of you will be [b]made to
stumble because of Me this
night,* for it is [c]written:

'I will [d]strike the
[e]Shepherd,
And the sheep will be
scattered.'

28 "But after I have been
raised, I will [f]go before you to
Galilee."
29 Peter said to Him, "Even if
all are made to stumble, yet I
will not *be*."
30 Jesus said to him, "Assuredly, I say to you that today,
even this night, before the
rooster crows twice, you will
deny Me three times."
31 But he spoke more vehemently, "If I have to die with
You, I will not deny You!" [g]And
they all said likewise.

Jesus' agony in the garden
(Mt. 26:36–46; Lk. 22:39–46;
Jn. 18:1)

32 Then they came to a place
which was named Gethsemane;
and He said to His disciples, "Sit
here while I pray."
33 And He [h]took Peter,
James, and John with Him, and
He began to be troubled and
deeply distressed.
34 Then He said to them, "My
soul is exceedingly [i]sorrowful,
even to death. Stay here and
watch."

The first prayer
(Mt. 26:39; Lk. 22:41–42)

35 He went a little farther,
and fell on the ground, and
[j]prayed that if it were possible,
the hour might pass from Him.
36 And He said, [k]"Abba, Father, all things *are* possible for
You. Take this [l]cup away from
Me; [m]nevertheless, not what I
will, but [n]what You *will*."
37 Then He came and found
them sleeping, and said to Peter, "Simon, are you sleeping?
Could you not watch one hour?
38 [o]"Watch and pray, lest
you enter into temptation. The
spirit indeed *is* willing, but the
[p]flesh *is* weak."

The second prayer
(Mt. 26:42; Lk. 22:44)

39 Again He went away and
prayed, and spoke the same
words.
40 And when He returned,
He found them asleep again, for
their eyes were heavy; and they
did not know what to answer
Him.

The third prayer (Mt. 26:44)

41 Then He came the third
time and said to them, "Are you
still sleeping and resting? It is
enough! The [q]hour has come;
behold, the [r]Son of Man is being betrayed into the hands of
[s]sinners.
42 "Rise, let us be going. See,
My betrayer is at hand."

Jesus' betrayal and arrest
(Mt. 26:47–56; Lk. 22:47–53;
Jn. 18:3–11)

43 And immediately, while
He was still speaking, [t]Judas,
one of the twelve, with a great
[u]multitude with swords and
clubs, came from the chief
priests and the [v]scribes and the
elders.
44 Now His betrayer had
given them a signal, saying,
"Whomever I [w]kiss, He is the
One; seize Him and lead *Him*
away safely."
45 As soon as He had come,
immediately he went up to Him
and said to Him, "Rabbi,
Rabbi!" and kissed Him.
46 Then they laid their hands
on Him and took Him.
47 And one of those who
stood by drew his sword and
struck the servant of the high
priest, and cut off his ear.
48 Then Jesus answered and
said to them, "Have you come
out, as against a robber, with
swords and clubs to take Me?
49 "I was daily with you in
the temple [x]teaching, and you
did not seize Me. But the Scriptures must be [y]fulfilled."
50 Then they all [z]forsook
Him and fled.
51 Now a certain young man
followed Him, having a linen
cloth thrown around *his* naked
body. And the young men laid
hold of him,
52 and he left the linen cloth
and fled from them naked.

27
a Jn. 16:32
b Cp. Mt. 11:6
c *Inspiration:* v. 27; Mk. 15:28. (Ex. 4:15; 2 Tim. 3:16, *note*)
d Isa. 53:5,10; Zech. 13:7
e *Christ* (first advent): v. 27; Mk. 16:6. (Gen. 3:15; Acts 1:11, *note*)
28
f Mk. 16:7
31
g Cp. v. 50
33
h Mk. 5:37; 9:2; 13:3
34
i Isa. 53:3–4; Jn. 12:27
35
j *Bible prayers* (NT): vv. 35–36, 39,41; Mk. 15:34. (Mt. 6:9; Lk. 11:2, *note*)
36
k Aram. *Father.* Cp. Rom. 8:15; Gal. 4:6
l See Mt. 26:39, *note*
m Jn. 4:34
n Cp. Ps. 40:7–8
38
o Lk. 21:36
p Rom. 7:18, 21–24; see Jude 23, *note*

41
q Jn. 17:1
r See Mt. 8:20, *note*
s See Rom. 3:23, *note*
43
t Mk. 14:10
u Ps. 3:1
v See Mt. 2:4, *note*
44
w Prov. 27:6; cp. 2 Sam. 20:9–10
49
x Mt. 21:23; cp. Mt. 4:23; 9:35; Lk. 13:10; 23:5
y Cp. Isa. 53:7–8; Dan. 9:26
50
z Cp. v. 31; 2 Tim. 4:10, 16

*14:27 NU-Text omits *because of Me this night.*

Jesus is brought before the high priest and Sanhedrin (Mt. 26:57–68; Jn. 18:12–14,19–24)

53 [1]And they led Jesus away to the [a]high priest; and with him were [b]assembled all the [c]chief priests, the elders, and the [d]scribes.

54 But [e]Peter followed Him at a distance, right into the courtyard of the high priest. And he sat with the servants and warmed himself at the fire.

55 Now the chief priests and all the council [f]sought testimony against Jesus to put Him to death, but [g]found none.

56 For many bore [h]false witness against Him, but their testimonies did not agree.

57 Then some rose up and bore false witness against Him, saying,

58 "We heard Him say, 'I will [i]destroy this temple made with hands, and within three days I will build another made [j]without hands.'"

59 But not even then did their testimony agree.

60 And the high priest stood up in the midst and asked Jesus, saying, [k]"Do You answer nothing? What *is it* these men testify against You?"

61 But He [l]kept silent and answered nothing. Again the high priest asked Him, saying to Him, [m]"Are You the Christ, the Son of the Blessed?"

62 Jesus said, "I am. And you will see the [n]Son of Man [o]sitting at the right hand of the Power, and [p]coming with the clouds of heaven."

63 Then the high priest [q]tore his clothes and said, "What further need do we have of witnesses?

64 "You have heard the [r]blasphemy! What do you think?" And they all condemned Him to be deserving of [s]death.

65 Then some began to [t]spit on Him, and to blindfold Him, and to beat Him, and to say to Him, "Prophesy!" And the officers [u]struck Him with the palms of their hands.*

Peter's three denials (Mt. 26:69–75; Lk. 22:56–62; Jn. 18:16–18,25–27)

66 Now [v]as Peter was below in the courtyard, one of the servant girls of the high priest came.

67 And when she saw Peter warming himself, she looked at him and said, "You also were with [w]Jesus of Nazareth."

68 But he denied it, saying, "I neither know nor understand what you are saying." And he went out on the porch, and a rooster [x]crowed.

69 And the servant girl saw him again, and began to say to those who stood by, "This is one of them."

70 But he denied it again. And a little later those who stood by said to Peter again, "Surely you are *one* of them; for you are a Galilean, and your speech shows *it*."*

71 Then he began to [y]curse and swear, "I do not know this Man of whom you speak!"

72 A second time *the* rooster [x]crowed. Then Peter called to mind the word that Jesus had said to him, "Before the rooster crows twice, you will deny Me three times." And when he thought about it, he wept.

The Sanhedrin delivers Jesus to Pilate (Mt. 27:1–2,11–15; Lk. 23:1–7,13–18; Jn. 18:28–40; 19:1–16)

15 IMMEDIATELY, in the morning, the chief priests held a [z]consultation with the elders and [d]scribes and the whole council; and they bound Jesus, led *Him* away, and [aa]delivered *Him* to Pilate.

2 Then Pilate asked Him, "Are You the [bb]King of the Jews?" He answered and said to him, "*It is as* you say."

3 And the chief priests accused Him of many things, but He [cc]answered nothing.

4 Then Pilate asked Him again, saying, "Do You answer

53
a Jn. 11:49,51
b v. 55; Mk. 15:1
c Mt. 16:21; 27:12; Lk. 9:22; 23:23; Jn. 7:32; 18:3; 19:6
d See Mt. 2:4, *note*
54
e Jn. 18:15
55
f Cp. Ps. 27:12; 35:11
g Cp. Dan. 6:4; 1 Pet. 3:16
56
h Ex. 20:16; Ps. 35:11; Prov. 6:16–19; 19:5
58
i Cp. Mk. 15:29
j 2 Cor. 5:1
60
k Mk. 15:3–5
61
l Isa. 53:7; Jn. 19:9; Acts 8:32; 1 Pet. 2:23; cp. Ps. 38:13–14; 39:9
m Lk. 22:67
62
n See Mt. 8:20, *note*
o Ps. 110:1; Mt. 25:31; Lk. 1:32; cp. Rev. 4:2
p Christ (second advent): v. 62; Lk. 9:26. (Dt. 30:3; Acts 1:11, *note*). Cp. Dan. 7:13
63
q Cp. Num. 14:6; Acts 14:13–14
64
r Jn. 10:33, 36; cp. Rev. 13:6
s Jn. 19:7
65
t Isa. 50:6
u See Isa. 52:14, *note*

66
v Cp. Jn. 13:36–38
67
w Mk. 10:47; Jn. 1:45; Acts 10:38
68
x Cp. v. 30; Jn. 13:38
71
y Cp. Mk. 14:29,31; 1 Cor. 10:12
CHAPTER 15
1
z Ps. 2:2; Acts 2:23; 4:27–28
aa Lk. 18:32; Acts 3:13
2
bb Mt. 2:2; Jn. 19:19
3
cc Isa. 53:7; Jn. 19:9; Acts 8:32

---

*14:65 NU-Text reads *received Him with slaps.* 14:70 NU-Text omits *and your speech shows it.*

[1](14:53) For the order of events following the arrest of the Lord Jesus, see Mt. 26:57, *note.*

[a]nothing? See how many things they testify against You!"*

5 But Jesus still answered nothing, so that Pilate marveled.

Jesus or Barabbas? (Mt. 27:16–26; Lk. 23:16–25; Jn. 18:40)

6 Now at the feast he was accustomed to releasing one prisoner to them, whomever they requested.

7 And there was one named Barabbas, *who was* chained with his fellow rebels; they had committed murder in the rebellion.

8 Then the multitude, crying aloud,* began to ask *him to do* just as he had always done for them.

9 But Pilate answered them, saying, [b]"Do you want me to release to you the King of the Jews?"

10 For he knew that the chief priests had handed Him over because of [c]envy.

11 But the chief priests stirred up the crowd, so that he should [d]rather release Barabbas to them.

12 Pilate answered and said to them again, "What then do you want me to do *with Him* whom you call the [e]King of the Jews?"

13 So they cried out again, "Crucify Him!"

14 Then Pilate said to them, "Why, [f]what evil has He done?" But they cried out all the more, "Crucify Him!"

15 So Pilate, wanting to gratify the [g]crowd, released Barabbas to them; and he delivered Jesus, after he had scourged *Him,* to be [h]crucified.

Jesus is crowned with thorns (Mt. 27:27–31)

16 Then the soldiers led Him away into the hall called Praetorium, and they called together the whole garrison.

17 And they clothed Him with purple; and they twisted a crown of [i]thorns, put it on His *head,*

18 and began to salute Him, "Hail, King of the Jews!"

19 Then they [j]struck Him on the head with a reed and spat on Him; and bowing the knee, they worshiped Him.

20 And when they had [k]mocked Him, they took the purple off Him, put His own clothes on Him, and led Him out to crucify Him.

21 Then they compelled a certain man, Simon a Cyrenian, the father of Alexander and [l]Rufus, as he was coming out of the country and passing by, to bear His cross.

22 And they [m]brought Him to the place [1]Golgotha, which is translated, Place of a Skull.

23 Then they gave Him wine mingled with myrrh to [2][n]drink, but He did not take *it.*

Jesus is crucified (Mt. 27:33–56; Lk. 23:33–49; Jn. 19:17–37)

24 [3]And [o]when they crucified Him, they [p]divided His garments, casting lots for them to determine what every man should take.

25 Now it was the [q]third hour, and they [r]crucified Him.

26 And the [s]inscription of His accusation was written above:

THE KING OF THE JEWS.

27 [t]With Him they also crucified two robbers, one on His right and the other on His left.

28 So the Scripture was fulfilled* which [u]says, *"And He was numbered with the transgressors."**

29 And those who passed by [v]blasphemed Him, [w]wagging their heads and saying, "Aha! *You* who [x]destroy the temple and build *it* in three days,

*
15:4 NU-Text reads *of which they accuse You.* 15:8 NU-Text reads *going up.* 15:28 Isaiah 53:12 • NU-Text omits this verse.

4
a Mt. 26:62–63; Mk. 14:60–61
9
b See Mt. 27:17, *note*
10
c Prov. 27:4; cp. Jn. 12:19
11
d Acts 3:14; cp. Jn. 1:11
12
e Ps. 2:6; Isa. 9:7; Jer. 23:5; 33:15; Mic. 5:2
14
f Isa. 53:9; Jn. 8:46; 1 Pet. 2:21–23; cp. Acts 3:13
15
g Cp. Mk. 6:26
h Isa. 53:8

17
i Cp. Gen. 3:18
19
j Isa. 50:6; 53:5; Mk. 14:65; cp. Ps. 69:7,19; Isa. 52:14
20
k Ps. 35:16; Mk. 10:34; Lk. 22:63; 23:11
21
l Cp. Rom. 16:13
22
m Heb. 13:12; cp. Gal. 2:20; Heb. 13:13
23
n v. 36
24
o c. A.D. 29
p Ps. 22:18
25
q 9 a.m. See Jn. 19:14, *note*
r *Sacrifice* (of Christ): vv. 22–26; Lk. 22:20. (Gen. 3:15; Heb. 10:18, *note*)
26
s See Mt. 27:37, *note*
27
t Isa. 53:9,12; Lk. 22:37
28
u *Inspiration:* v. 28; Lk. 1:3. (Ex. 4:15; 2 Tim. 3:16, *note*)
29
v Ps. 22:6–7; 69:7
w Ps. 109:25; cp. Lam. 2:15
x Mk. 14:58; Jn. 2:19–21

---

[1](15:22) "Golgotha" is the Aramaic word for "skull," and is used also in Mt. 27:33; Jn. 19:17.

[2](15:23) Wine and myrrh mixed together composed a stupefying drink which was sometimes given to those who were in great pain in suffering such as must be endured in crucifixion.

[3](15:24) For the order of events at the crucifixion, see Mt. 27:33, *note.*

30 "save Yourself, and come
down from the cross!"
31 Likewise the chief priests
also, [a]mocking among themselves with the [b]scribes, said,
"He saved [c]others; [d]Himself He
cannot save.
32 "Let the Christ, the King
of Israel, descend now from the
cross, that we may [e]see and believe."* Even those who were
crucified with Him reviled Him.
33 Now when the [f]sixth hour
had come, there was darkness
over the whole land until the
[g]ninth hour.
34 And at the ninth hour Jesus cried out with a loud voice,
[h]saying, [i]"Eloi, Eloi, lama sabachthani?" which is translated, *"My God, My God, why
have You forsaken Me?"*
35 Some of those who stood
by, when they heard *that,* said,
"Look, He is calling for [1]Elijah!"
36 Then someone ran and
filled a sponge full of sour wine,
put *it* on a reed, and [j]offered *it*
to Him to drink, saying, "Let
Him alone; let us see if Elijah
will come to take Him down."
37 And Jesus cried out with a
loud voice, and [k]breathed His
last.
38 Then the [l]veil of the temple was torn in two from [2]top to
bottom.
39 So when the centurion,
who stood opposite Him, saw
that He cried out like this and
[k]breathed His last,* he said,
"Truly this Man was the [m]Son of
God!"
40 There were also women
looking on from afar, among
whom were [n]Mary Magdalene,
Mary the mother of [o]James the
Less and of Joses, and Salome,
41 who also followed Him
and ministered to Him when He
was in Galilee, and many other
women who came up with Him
to Jerusalem.

Jesus is buried (Mt. 27:57–61; Lk. 23:50–56; Jn. 19:28–42)

42 Now when evening had
come, [p]because it was the Preparation Day, that is, the day before the Sabbath,
43 Joseph of Arimathea, a
prominent council member,
who was himself [q]waiting for
the [r]kingdom of God, coming
and taking courage, went in to
Pilate and asked for the body of
Jesus.
44 Pilate marveled that He
was already dead; and sum-
moning the centurion, he asked
him if He had been dead for
some time.
45 So when he found out
from the centurion, he granted
the body to Joseph.
46 Then he bought fine linen,
took Him down, and wrapped
Him in the linen. And he [s]laid
Him in a tomb which had been
hewn out of the rock, and rolled
a stone against the door of the
tomb.
47 And [n]Mary Magdalene
and Mary *the mother* of Joses
observed where He was laid.

IV. The Resurrection and Ascension of the Victorious Servant, 16

Christ's resurrection and events of that day (cp. Mt. 28:1–15; Lk. 24:1–49; Jn. 20:1–23)

16 [3]NOW when the [t]Sab-
bath was past, [n]Mary
Magdalene, Mary *the mother* of
James, and Salome bought
spices, that they might come
and [u]anoint Him.
2 [v]Very early in the morning, on the first *day* of the week,
they came to the tomb when the
sun had risen.
3 And they said among
themselves, [w]"Who will roll

*

15:32 M-Text reads *believe Him.*
15:39 NU-Text reads *that He thus breathed His last.*

31
a Lk. 18:32
b See Mt. 2:4, *note*
c Lk. 7:14–15; Jn. 11:43–44
d Cp. Jn. 3:14–15 with Heb. 9:22
32
e Cp. Mt. 16:4; Lk. 16:31; Jn. 20:29
33
f 12 noon. See Jn. 19:14, *note*
g 3 p.m.
34
h Bible prayers (NT): v. 34; Lk. 2:28. (Mt. 6:9; Lk. 11:2, *note*)
i Ps. 22:1; see Mt. 27:46, *note*
36
j Ps. 69:21
37
k See Mt. 27:50, *note*
38
l See Mt. 27:51, *note*
39
m Mt. 14:33; Mk. 3:11; Lk. 1:35; Jn. 1:34; 3:18; 10:36; 20:31; Acts 8:37; 9:20
40
n Cp. Lk. 8:2–3; see Lk. 1:27, *note*
o Son of Alphaeus. See Mt. 4:21, *note*

42
p Cp. Ex. 34:25; Dt. 21:22–23
43
q Cp. Lk. 2:38
r See Mt. 6:33, *note*
46
s Isa. 53:9
CHAPTER 16
1
t Sabbath: v. 1; Lk. 4:16. (Gen. 2:3; Mt. 12:1, *note*)
u Mk. 14:8
2
v See Mt. 28:1, *note*
3
w Cp. Ex. 14:13–16

[1](15:35) Our Lord was speaking in Aramaic (v. 34). The pronunciation of the first word of His cry from the cross, *"Eloi"* is very similar to the Hebrew pronunciation of "Elijah," or its Greek counterpart, "Elias."

[2](15:38) God tore the veil "from top to bottom." The way into the Holiest was now opened for the believer into the very presence of God, Christ having made atonement for sin and having glorified God thereby. Cp. Heb. 9:8,24; 10:19–22.

[3](16:1) For the order of events on the day of Christ's resurrection, and His other post-resurrection appearances, see Mt. 28:1, *note;* Jn. 20:16, *note.*

away the stone from the door of
the tomb for us?"
4 But when they looked up,
they saw that the stone had
been rolled away—for it was
very large.
5 And entering the tomb,
they saw a young man clothed
in a long white robe sitting on
the right side; and they were
alarmed.
6 But he said to them, "Do
not be alarmed. You seek Jesus
of Nazareth, who was crucified.
[a]He is [b]risen! He is not here.
See the place where they laid
Him.
7 "But go, tell His disciples—and Peter—that He is
going before you into Galilee;
there you will see Him, [c]as He
said to you."
8 So they went out quickly*
and fled from the tomb, for they
trembled and were amazed.
And they said nothing to anyone, for they were afraid.
9 [1]Now when *He* rose early
on the first *day* of the week, He
[d]appeared first to Mary Magdalene, out of whom He had cast
seven [e]demons.
10 She went and told those
who had been with Him, as they
mourned and wept.
11 And when they heard that
He was alive and had been seen
by her, they did [f]not believe.
12 After that, He appeared in
another form to two of them as
they walked and went into the
country.
13 And they went and told *it*
to the rest, *but* they did not believe them either.
14 Later He appeared to the
[2]eleven as they sat at the table;
and He rebuked their unbelief
and hardness of heart, because
they did not believe those who
had seen Him after He had
risen.

Christ's commission to the eleven
(Lk. 24:46–48; cp. Mt. 28:16–20;
Jn. 17:18; 20:21; Acts 1:8)

15 And He said to them, "Go
into [g]all the [h]world and preach
the [i]gospel to every creature.
16 "He who [j]believes and is
[k]baptized will be [l]saved; but he
who does not believe will be
condemned.
17 "And these [m]signs will follow those who believe: In My
name they will [n]cast out [e]de-
mons; they will [o]speak with
new tongues;
18 "they* will take up [p]ser-
pents; and if they drink anything deadly, it will by no
means hurt them; they will lay
hands on the sick, and they will
recover."

The ascension
(Lk. 24:49–53; Acts 1:6–11)

19 So then, after the Lord
had spoken to them, He was
[q]received up into heaven, and
[r]sat down at the right hand of
God.
20 And they went out and
preached everywhere, the Lord
working with *them* and confirming the [i]word through the
accompanying [s]signs. Amen.*

*
16:8 NU-Text and M-Text omit *quickly*.
16:18 NU-Text reads *and in their hands they will*.
16:20 Verses 9–20 are bracketed in NU-Text as not original. They are lacking in Codex Sinaiticus and Codex Vaticanus, although nearly all other manuscripts of Mark contain them.

6
a *Christ* (first advent): vv. 6–7; Lk. 1:31. (Gen. 3:15; Acts 1:11, *note*)
b *Resurrection:* vv. 6,9, 11–12,14; Lk. 7:15. (2 Ki. 4:35; 1 Cor. 15:52, *note*)
7
c Mk. 14:28
9
d See Jn. 20:16, *note*
e See Mt. 7:22, *note*
11
f vv. 13,14

15
g Col. 1:6
h Gk. *kosmos*. See Mt. 4:8, *note*
i *Gospel:* vv. 15,20; Lk. 2:10. (Gen. 12:3; Rev. 14:6)
16
j Jn. 3:16; Acts 16:30–31; Rom. 10:8–10
k See Acts 8:12, *note*
l See Rom. 1:16, *note*
17
m Acts 5:12
n Acts 8:7
o Acts 2:4
18
p Acts 28:3–6
19
q Acts 1:9; Rev. 4:2
r 1 Pet. 3:22
20
s Heb. 2:4

[1](16:9) Verses 9–20 are not found in the two most ancient manuscripts, the Sinaiticus and Vaticanus; others have them with partial omissions and variations. But the passage is quoted by Irenaeus and Hippolytus in the second or third century.

[2](16:14) "The eleven" is here used as a collective term, not necessarily implying that eleven persons were present. See Lk. 24:33; cp. 1 Cor. 15:5; see also Mt. 28:16, where "eleven disciples" implies a definite number of persons.

The Gospel According to

LUKE

Author: Luke *Theme:* Christ, the Man *Date of writing:* c. A.D. 60

LUKE, who wrote the Third Gospel and Acts, was known as "the beloved physician" (Col. 4:14). He was a companion and fellow worker with Paul (Phil. 24). Compare the Introduction to Acts.

This book, the longest of the Gospels, was written principally for the Greeks. Its emphasis is upon the perfect humanity of Christ, whom it presents as the Son of Man, the human-divine Person, and whose genealogy it traces to Adam. Luke's narrative of the birth and infancy of the Lord is from the point of view of the virgin mother. He alone tells of Christ's boyhood and reveals more of His prayer life than the other Synoptics. The parables found in this Gospel show Christ's concern for lost humanity. In the accounts of certain miracles, the trained observation of a physician is evident.

Luke is in many ways the Gospel of compassion, stressing, as it does, the Lord's sympathy for the brokenhearted, the sick, the mistreated, and the bereaved. It also shows the ministry of women to Christ. Along with its presentation of the Son of Man, the book emphasizes the worldwide scope of salvation. Luke alone records the parables of the lost sheep, the lost coin, and the lost son (15:3–32) and the mission of the seventy (10:1–24).

The Gospel of Luke may be divided as follows:

I. Introduction, 1:1–4.
II. The Birth, Baptism, Genealogy, and Temptation of Christ, 1:5—4:13.
III. The Public Ministry of the Son of Man, to the Triumphal Entry, 4:14—19:27.
IV. The Rejection of Christ, and His Death, 19:28—23:56.
V. Christ's Resurrection, Commission to the Disciples, and Ascension, 24:1–53.

CHAPTER 1
1
a Jn. 20:31
2
b Mk. 1:1; Jn. 15:27; Acts 1:21–22
c Acts 1:3; 10:39; Heb. 2:3; 1 Pet. 5:1; 2 Pet. 1:16; 1 Jn. 1:1
d Cp. Eph. 3:7–8
e Acts 1:2
3
f Inspiration: vv. 1–4; Lk. 1:70. (Ex. 4:15; 2 Tim. 3:16, *note*)
g Acts 1:1
4
h v. 1
5
i Herod the Great. See Mt. 2:1, *note*
j v. 39

I. The Introduction, 1:1–4

1 INASMUCH as many have
taken in hand to set in order
a narrative of those [a]things
which have been fulfilled*
among us,
2 just as those who from the
[b]beginning were [c]eyewitnesses
and [d]ministers of the word [e]de-
livered them to us,
3 it seemed good to me also,
having had perfect understanding of all things [1]from the very
first, to [f]write to you an orderly
account, most excellent [g]The-
ophilus,
4 that you may know the
certainty of those [h]things in
which you were instructed.

II. The Birth, Baptism, Genealogy, and Temptation of Christ, 1:5—4:13

John the Baptist's birth foretold

5 There was in the days of
[i]Herod, the king of [j]Judea, a
certain priest named Zacharias,
of the [k]division of [l]Abijah. His
[m]wife *was* of the daughters of
Aaron, and her name *was* Elizabeth.
6 And they were both [n]righ-
teous before God, walking in all
the [o]commandments and ordinances of the Lord blameless.
7 But they had no child,
[p]because Elizabeth was barren,
and they were both well advanced in years.
8 So it was, that while he
was serving as priest before
God in the order of his division,
9 according to the custom of
the priesthood, his lot fell to
[q]burn incense when he went
into the temple of the Lord.
10 And the whole multitude
of the people was praying outside at the hour of incense.
11 Then an [r]angel of the

*1:1 Or *are most surely believed*

k 1 Chr. 24:1, 10
l Neh. 12:4
m Lev. 21:13–14; cp. 2 Cor. 6:14–18
6
n Righteousness (OT): vv. 5–6; Lk. 2:25. (Gen. 6:9; Lk. 2:25, *note*)
o Law (of Moses): v. 6; Lk. 2:23. (Ex. 19:1; Gal. 3:24, *note*)
7
p Cp. Gen. 18:11–14
9
q Ex. 30:7–8
11
r See Heb. 1:4, *note*

---

[1](1:3) "From the very first" is from the Gk. *anōthen* (adv., from *anō*, which can mean "up," "upward," or "above"), which is translated elsewhere by "from above" (Jn. 3:31; 19:11; Jas. 1:17; 3:15,17; but cp. Acts 26:5, where it is translated "from the first"). Luke's use of *anōthen* is an affirmation that his knowledge of these things, derived from those who had been eyewitnesses from the beginning (v. 2), was confirmed by revelation. In like manner Paul had doubtless heard from the eleven the story of the institution of the Lord's Supper; but he also had it by revelation from the Lord (1 Cor. 11:23) and his writing, like Luke's knowledge, thus became firsthand and not simply traditional. Observe, too, Luke's expression "in order," an emphatic term to indicate his purpose of presenting the Gospel record in an orderly fashion.

Lord appeared to him, standing
on the right side of the altar of
incense.
12 And when Zacharias saw
him, he was [a]troubled, and fear
fell upon him.
13 But the [b]angel said to him,
"Do not be afraid, Zacharias,
for your [c]prayer is heard; and
your wife [d]Elizabeth will [e]bear
you a son, and you shall call his
name [f]John.
14 "And you will have joy
and gladness, and many will
[g]rejoice at his birth.
15 "For he will be [h]great in
the sight of the Lord, and shall
[i]drink neither wine nor strong
drink. He will also be filled with
the Holy [j]Spirit, even from his
mother's womb.
16 "And he will [k]turn many
of the children of Israel to the
Lord their God.
17 [l]"He will also go before
Him in the spirit and power of
Elijah, *'to turn the hearts of the
fathers to the children,'** and
the disobedient to the wisdom
of the just, to make ready a people prepared for the Lord."
18 And Zacharias said to the
angel, "How shall I know this?
[m]For I am an old man, and my
wife is well advanced in years."
19 And the angel answered
and said to him, "I am [n]Gabriel,
who stands in the presence of
God, and was sent to speak to
you and bring you these glad
[o]tidings.
20 "But behold, you will be
[p]mute and not able to speak until the day these things take
place, because you did not believe my words which will be
fulfilled in their own time."
21 And the people waited for
Zacharias, and marveled that
he lingered so long in the temple.
22 But when he came out, he
could not speak to them; and
they perceived that he had seen
a vision in the temple, for he
[q]beckoned to them and remained speechless.
23 So it was, as soon as the
days of his service were completed, that he departed to his
[r]own house.
24 Now after those days his
wife [s]Elizabeth [t]conceived;
and she hid herself five months,
saying,
25 "Thus the Lord has dealt
with me, in the days when He
looked on *me,* to [u]take away my
reproach among people."

The annunciation of Jesus' birth

26 Now in the [v]sixth month
the [b]angel [w]Gabriel was sent by
God to a city of Galilee named
Nazareth,
27 to a [x]virgin betrothed to a
man whose name was Joseph,
of the house of David. The virgin's name *was* [1]Mary.
28 And having come in, the
angel said to her, "Rejoice,
[y]highly favored *one,* the Lord *is*
with you; blessed *are* you
among women!"*
29 But when she saw *him,**
she was [z]troubled at his saying,
and considered what manner of
greeting this was.
30 Then the angel said to her,
"Do not be afraid, Mary, for you
have found [aa]favor with God.

*
1:17 Malachi 4:5–6 **1:28** NU-Text omits *blessed are you among women.*
1:29 NU-Text omits *when she saw him.*

12 [a] v. 29; Lk. 2:9
13 [b] See Heb. 1:4, *note* [c] Cp. Gen. 25:21 [d] v. 24 [e] v. 57 [f] vv. 60,63
14 [g] v. 58
15 [h] Lk. 7:24–28 [i] Cp. Lev. 10:9; Num. 6:2–4 [j] *Holy Spirit* (NT): vv. 15,17; Lk. 1:35. (Mt. 1:18; Acts 2:4, *note*)
16 [k] vv. 76–79; cp. Dan. 12:3
17 [l] See Mt. 17:10, *note*
18 [m] Cp. Gen. 17:17
19 [n] Meaning *man of God.* Dan 8:16; 9:21 [o] Lk. 2:10
20 [p] v. 22; cp. Ezek. 3:24–27
22 [q] Cp. vv. 20, 62
23 [r] Cp. 1 Chr. 9:22–25
24 [s] vv. 5,13 [t] v. 36; cp. Gen. 21:2
25 [u] Gen. 30:23; cp. Isa. 4:1
26 [v] See Lev. 23:2, *note 2* [w] Meaning *man of God.* Dan. 8:16; 9:21
27 [x] Mt. 1:18
28 [y] Or *endued with grace.* v. 30; cp. Dan. 9:23; 10:19
29 [z] v. 12
30 [aa] v. 28; Lk. 2:52

[1](1:27) Six Marys are to be distinguished in the NT: (1) Mary, the mother of Jesus, always clearly identified by the context. (2) Mary, the mother of the Apostle James (called "the Less," Mk. 15:40) and wife of Clopas (Jn. 19:25), who may be identified with Alphaeus (Mt. 10:3; Mk. 3:18; Lk. 6:15). She was evidently the cousin of Mary, the mother of Jesus. This Mary watched the crucifixion (Mt. 27:56; Mk. 15:40; Jn. 19:25), visited the garden tomb (Mk. 15:47; 16:1; Lk. 24:10), and was presumably among the women who saw the risen Lord on the resurrection day (Mt. 28:7–9; Lk. 24:9,22–24). She is normally mentioned only in connection with one or both of her sons. Some have conjectured that this Mary was the sister of Mary, the mother of Jesus, but it is highly improbable that two sisters would have the same name. (3) Mary of Bethany, sister of Martha and Lazarus, mentioned by name only in Lk. 10:39,42; Jn. 11:1,2,19,20,28,31,32,45; 12:3, but referred to in Mt. 26:7; Mk. 14:3–9. (4) Mary Magdalene, a woman of Magdala, "out of whom [Jesus] had cast seven demons" (Mk. 16:9). She is never mentioned apart from the identifying word "Magdalene" and is not to be confused with the sinful woman who anointed the Savior's feet in a city of Galilee (Lk. 7:36–50). (5) Mary, the mother of John Mark, and sister of Barnabas (Acts 12:12). And (6) Mary, a Christian woman of Rome, to whom Paul sent his salutation (Rom. 16:6).

31 "And behold, you will [a]conceive in your womb and bring forth a [b]Son, and shall call His [c]name JESUS.
32 "He will be great, and will be called the Son of the [d]Highest; and the Lord God will [e]give Him the [f]throne of His [g]father David.
33 "And He [h]will reign over the house of Jacob [i]forever, and of His [j]kingdom there will be no end."

Jesus' miraculous conception

34 Then Mary said to the angel, "How can this be, [k]since I do not know a man?"
35 And the angel answered and said to her, "*The* Holy [l]Spirit will come upon you, and the power of the Highest will overshadow you; therefore, also, that [m]Holy One who is to be born will be called the [n]Son of God.
36 "Now indeed, Elizabeth your relative has also conceived a son in her old age; and this is now the sixth month for her who was called barren.
37 [o]"For with God nothing will be impossible."
38 Then Mary said, "Behold the maidservant of the Lord! [p]Let it be to me according to your word." And the angel departed from her.

Mary visits Elizabeth

39 Now Mary arose in those days and went into the hill country with haste, to a city of Judah,
40 and entered the house of Zacharias and greeted Elizabeth.
41 And it happened, when Elizabeth heard the greeting of Mary, that the babe leaped in her womb; and Elizabeth was [q]filled with the Holy [l]Spirit.
42 Then she spoke out with a loud voice and said, [r]"Blessed *are* you among women, and blessed *is* the fruit of your womb!
43 "But why *is* this *granted* to me, that the mother of my Lord should [s]come to me?
44 "For indeed, as soon as the voice of your greeting sounded in my ears, the babe leaped in my womb for joy.
45 [t]"Blessed *is* she who [u]believed, for there will be a fulfillment of those things which were told her from the Lord."

Mary's "Magnificat"
(cp. 1 Sam. 2:1–10)

46 And Mary said:

"My soul magnifies the Lord,
47 And my spirit has [v]rejoiced in [w]God my [x]Savior.
48 For He has [y]regarded the lowly state of His maidservant;
For behold, henceforth all generations will call me blessed.
49 For He who is mighty has done [z]great things for me,
And [aa]holy *is* His name.
50 And His [bb]mercy *is* on those who [cc]fear Him
From generation to generation.
51 He has shown strength with His [dd]arm;
He has scattered *the* [ee]proud in the imagination of their hearts.
52 [ff]He has put down the mighty from *their* thrones,
And exalted *the* lowly.
53 He has [gg]filled *the* hungry with good things,
And *the* rich He has sent away empty.
54 He has helped His [hh]servant Israel,
In remembrance of *His* mercy,
55 [ii]As He [jj]spoke to our [kk]fathers,
To Abraham and to his [ll]seed forever."

56 And Mary remained with her about three months, and returned to her house.

John is born and named

57 Now Elizabeth's full time came for her to be delivered, and she brought forth a son.
58 When her neighbors and relatives heard how the Lord

---

31 *a* Isa. 7:14; Mt. 1:21; Gal. 4:4
b Christ (first advent): vv. 31–35; Lk. 2:7. (Gen. 3:15; Acts 1:11, *note*)
c Lk. 2:21; Phil. 2:9–11

32 *d* vv. 35,76
e 2 Sam. 7:12; Isa. 9:6–7; Jer. 23:5
f 2 Sam. 7:14–17
g Mt. 1:1

33 *h Israel* (prophecies): vv. 32–33; Lk. 1:68. (Gen. 12:2; Rom. 11:26, *note*)
i Dan. 2:44; 7:14,27; Mic. 4:7; Heb. 1:8; 2 Pet. 1:11
j Kingdom (NT): vv. 32–33; Lk. 8:10. (Mt. 2:2; 1 Cor. 15:24, *note*)

34 *k* Cp. Mt. 1:18–20

35 *l Holy Spirit* (NT): vv. 35,41; Lk. 1:67. (Mt. 1:18; Acts 2:4, *note*)
m Sanctification (NT): v. 35; Lk. 1:70. (Mt. 4:5; Rev. 22:11)
n Ps. 2:7; Mt. 14:33; Jn. 1:34; 20:31; Acts 8:37; Rom. 1:1–4; Heb. 1:2,8

37 *o* Mt. 19:26; cp. Gen. 18:14

38 *p* Cp. Rom. 6:13

41 *q* Acts 6:3

42 *r* v. 28

43 *s* Cp. Mt. 3:14

45 *t* Jn. 20:29
u Cp. Heb. 11:11

47 *v* Hab. 3:18
w 1 Tim. 1:1; Ti. 3:4
x See Rom. 1:16, *note*

48 *y* Cp. 1 Sam. 1:11; Ps. 138:6

49 *z* Ps. 71:19; 126:2–3
aa Ps. 111:9; Rev. 4:8

50 *bb* Ex. 34:6–7; Ps. 103:17
cc See Ps. 19:9, *note*

51 *dd* Ps. 98:1
ee 1 Pet. 5:5

52 *ff* 1 Sam. 2:7–8

53 *gg* Mt. 5:6

54 *hh* Isa. 41:8

55 *ii* Gal. 3:16
jj See Heb. 8:8, *note*
kk Rom. 11:28
ll Gen. 17:19

had shown great mercy to her, they [a]rejoiced with her.

59 So it was, on the [b]eighth day, that they came to circumcise the child; and they would have called him by the name of his father, Zacharias.

60 His mother answered and said, "No; he shall be called [c]John."

61 But they said to her, "There is no one among your relatives who is called by this name."

62 So they made signs to his father—what he would have him called.

63 And he asked for a writing tablet, and wrote, saying, "His name is John." So they all marveled.

64 Immediately his mouth was [d]opened and his tongue *loosed,* and he spoke, praising God.

65 Then fear came on all who dwelt around them; and all these sayings were discussed throughout all the hill country of Judea.

66 And all those who heard *them* kept *them* in their [e]hearts, saying, "What kind of child will this be?" And the hand of the Lord was with him.

Zacharias' "Benedictus"

67 Now his father Zacharias was [f]filled with the Holy [g]Spirit, and prophesied, saying:

68 [h]"Blessed *is* the Lord God of Israel,
For He has [i]visited and [j]redeemed His [k]people,

69 And has raised up a [l]horn of [m]salvation for us
In the house of His servant David,

70 [n]As He [o]spoke by the mouth of His [p]holy prophets,
Who *have been* [q]since the [r]world began,

71 That we should be saved from our enemies
And from the hand of all who hate us,

72 To perform the mercy *promised* to our fathers
And to remember His [p]holy [s]covenant,

73 The [t]oath which He swore to our father Abraham:

74 To grant us that we,
Being delivered from the hand of our enemies,
Might serve Him without fear,

75 In [p]holiness and [u]righteousness before Him all the days of our life.

76 "And you, child, will be called the [v]prophet of the Highest;
For you [w]will go before the face of the Lord to prepare His ways,

77 To give [x]knowledge of [m]salvation to His people
By the remission of their [y]sins,

78 Through the tender mercy of our God,
With which the [z]Dayspring from on high has visited* us;

79 To give [aa]light to those who sit in darkness and the shadow of death,
To [bb]guide our feet into the way of peace."

80 So the [cc]child grew and became strong in spirit, and was in the deserts till the day of his manifestation to Israel.

Jesus is born in Bethlehem
(Mt. 1:18–25; 2:1; cp. Jn. 1:14)

2 AND it came to pass in those days *that* a decree went out from Caesar Augustus that all the [1]world should be [dd]registered.

2 This census first took place while Quirinius was governing Syria.

3 So all went to be registered, everyone to his own city.

4 Joseph also went up from Galilee, out of the city of Naza-

* 1:78 NU-Text reads *shall visit.*

58
a v. 14; Rom. 12:15
59
b Gen. 17:12; Lev. 12:3; Phil. 3:5
60
c vv. 13,63
64
d v. 20
66
e Lk. 2:18
67
f v. 41
g Holy Spirit (NT): v. 67; Lk. 2:25. (Mt. 1:18; Acts 2:4, *note*)
68
h 1 Ki. 1:48; Ps. 106:48
i Cp. Lk. 2:27–32
j See Ex. 6:6 and Rom. 3:24, *notes*
k Israel (history): vv. 68–79; Lk. 13:35. (Gen. 12:2; Rom. 11:26, *note*)
69
l 2 Sam. 22:3; see Dt. 33:17, *note*
m See Rom. 1:16, *note*
70
n Rom. 1:2
o Inspiration: vv. 70–79; Lk. 3:4. (Ex. 4:15; 2 Tim. 3:16, *note*)
p Sanctification (NT): vv. 70,72,75; Lk. 2:23. (Mt. 4:5; Rev. 22:11)
q Acts 3:21
r Gk. *aiōn.* See Mk. 10:30, *note*

72
s See Gen. 12:2, *note*
73
t Gen. 22:16–18
75
u Eph. 4:24; see Rom. 10:10, *note*
76
v Mt. 11:9
w v. 17; Lk. 7:27
77
x Mk. 1:4
y See Rom. 3:23, *note*
78
z Or *Sunrising.* Cp. Mal. 4:2; 2 Pet. 1:19
79
aa Isa. 9:2; Acts 26:18
bb Jn. 10:4
80
cc Cp. Lk. 2:40
CHAPTER 2
1
dd Acts 5:37

[1](2:1) The "world" (Gk. *oikoumenē,* signifying *the inhabited earth*) when it has political reference in the NT, speaks of the Roman Empire or the Roman world.

reth, into Judea, to the city of David, which is called [a]Bethlehem, because he was of the [b]house and lineage of David,

5 to be registered with Mary, his betrothed wife,* who was with child.

6 So it was, that while they were there, the days were completed for her to be delivered.

7 [c]And she [d]brought forth her firstborn Son, and wrapped Him in swaddling cloths, and laid Him in a manger, because there was no room for them in the inn.

Angelic announcement of Jesus' birth

8 Now there were in the same country shepherds living out in the fields, keeping watch over their flock by night.

9 And behold,* an [e]angel of the Lord stood before them, and the glory of the Lord shone around them, and they were greatly afraid.

10 Then the angel said to them, [f]"Do not be afraid, for behold, I bring you good [g]tidings of great joy which will be to [h]all people.

11 "For there is born to you this day in the city of David a [i]Savior, who is Christ the Lord.

12 "And this *will be* the sign to you: You will find a Babe wrapped in swaddling cloths, lying in a manger."

13 And suddenly there was with the angel a multitude of the heavenly host praising God and saying:

14 "Glory to God in the highest,
And on earth [j]peace, goodwill toward men!"*

Shepherds visit the Baby Jesus

15 So it was, when the [k]angels had gone away from them into heaven, that the shepherds said to one another, "Let us now go to Bethlehem and see this thing that has come to pass, which the Lord has made known to us."

16 And they came with haste and found Mary and Joseph, and the Babe lying in a manger.

17 Now when they had seen *Him,* they made widely* known the saying which was told them concerning this Child.

18 And all those who heard *it* marveled at those things which were told them by the shepherds.

19 But Mary kept all these things and pondered *them* in her heart.

20 Then the shepherds returned, glorifying and [l]praising God for all the things that they had heard and seen, as it was told them.

Jesus presented at the temple in Jerusalem (cp. Ex. 13:12,15)

21 And when [m]eight days were completed for the circumcision of the Child,* His name was called [n]JESUS, the name given by the [k]angel [o]before He was conceived in the womb.

22 Now when the [p]days of her purification according to the law of Moses were completed, they brought Him to Jerusalem to present *Him* to the Lord

23 [q](as it is written in the [r]law of the Lord, [s]*"Every male who opens the womb shall be called [t]holy to the LORD"*),

24 and to offer a sacrifice [u]according to what is said in the law of the Lord, *"A pair of turtledoves or two young pigeons."*

Simeon's adoration and prophecy

25 And behold, there was a man in Jerusalem whose name was Simeon, and this man was [1v]just and devout, waiting for the Consolation of Israel, and

*2:5 NU-Text omits *wife.* 2:9 NU-Text omits *behold.* 2:14 NU-Text reads *toward men of goodwill.* 2:17 NU-Text omits *widely.* 2:21 NU-Text reads *for His circumcision.*

4
a Mic. 5:2
b See Mt. 1:1, *note*
7
c c. 5 B.C.
d *Christ* (first advent): vv. 1–7; Lk. 2:26. (Gen. 3:15; Acts 1:11, *note*)
9
e See Heb. 1:4, *note;* cp. Jud. 2:1, *note*
10
f Lk. 1:13,30
g *Gospel:* vv. 10–11; Lk. 4:18. (Gen. 12:3; Rev. 14:6)
h Gen. 12:3; Isa. 49:6
11
i See Rom. 1:16, *note*
14
j See Mt. 10:34, *note*
15
k See Heb. 1:4, *note*

20
l Lk. 19:37
21
m Gen. 17:12; Lev. 12:3; cp. Lk. 1:59
n Mt. 1:21
o Lk. 1:31; cp. Lk. 1:13
22
p Lev. 12:2–6
23
q Ex. 14:19; 22:29; Lev. 27:26; Dt. 18:4; Neh. 10:36; cp. Jas. 1:18
r *Law* (of Moses): vv. 23–24, 39; Lk. 4:4. (Ex. 19:1; Gal. 3:24, *note*)
s Ex. 13:2,12; Num. 3:13; 8:17
t *Sanctification* (NT): v. 23; Lk. 9:26. (Mt. 4:5; Rev. 22:11)
24
u Lev. 12:8
25
v *Righteousness* (OT): vv. 25,37; Lk. 23:47. (Gen. 6:9; Lk. 2:25, *note*)

[1](2:25) Righteousness (OT), Summary: The words "righteous" and "just" are used to translate the Heb. *yashar,* "upright"; *tsaddiq,* "just." In these words but one idea inheres: the righteous or just man is so called because he is right with God; and he is right with God because he has observed "all the commandments and ordinances of the Lord" (Lk. 1:6; cp. Rom. 10:5; Phil. 3:6). The OT righteous man was not sinless (Eccl. 7:20) but one who, for his sins, trusted the coming Messiah and offered in faith the required sacrifice (e.g. Lev.

the Holy [a]Spirit was upon him.
26 And it had been revealed
to him by the Holy [a]Spirit that
he would not see death before
he had seen the Lord's [b]Christ.
27 So he came by the Spirit
into the temple. And when the
parents brought in the Child Jesus, to do for Him according to
the custom of the law,
28 he took Him up in his
arms and blessed God and
[c]said:

29 "Lord, now You are
letting Your servant
[d]depart in peace,
[e]According to Your word;
30 For my eyes have seen
Your [f]salvation
31 Which You have
prepared before the
face of all peoples,
32 A [g]light to *bring*
revelation to the
Gentiles,
And the glory of Your
people Israel."

33 And Joseph and His
mother* marveled at those
things which were spoken of
Him.
34 Then Simeon blessed
them, and said to Mary His
mother, "Behold, this *Child* is
destined for the fall and [h]rising
of many in Israel, and for a sign
which will be [i]spoken against
35 "(yes, a sword will [j]pierce
through your own soul also),
that the thoughts of many
hearts may be revealed."

Anna's testimony to Christ

36 Now there was one, Anna,
a [k]prophetess, the daughter of
Phanuel, of the tribe of [l]Asher.
She was of a great age, and had
lived with a husband seven
years from her virginity;
37 and this woman *was* a
[m]widow of about eighty-four
years,* who did not depart
from the temple, but served *God*
with fastings and [n]prayers
night and day.
38 And coming in that in-
stant she gave thanks to the
Lord,* and spoke of Him to all
those who [o]looked for [p]re-
demption in Jerusalem.

Return to Nazareth: the silent years (after events of Mt. 2)

39 So when they had performed all things according to
the law of the Lord, they returned to Galilee, to their *own*
city, Nazareth.
40 [q]And the Child grew and
became strong in spirit,* filled
with [r]wisdom; and the [s]grace
of God was upon Him.

Jesus' visit to His "Father's house" in Jerusalem

41 His parents went to [t]Jeru-
salem every year at the Feast of
the [u]Passover.
42 And when He was twelve
years old, they went up to Jerusalem according to the [v]custom
of the feast.
43 When they had finished
the [w]days, as they returned, the
Boy Jesus lingered behind in Jerusalem. And Joseph and His
mother* did not know *it;*
44 but supposing Him to
have been in the company, they
went a day's journey, and
sought Him among *their* relatives and acquaintances.
45 So when they [x]did not
find Him, they returned to Jerusalem, seeking Him.
46 Now so it was *that* after
three days they found Him in
the temple, sitting in the midst
of the [y]teachers, both listening
to them and asking them questions.
47 And all who heard Him
were [z]astonished at His understanding and answers.
48 So when they saw Him,
they were [aa]amazed; and His
mother said to Him, "Son, why
have You done this to us? Look,
Your father and I have sought
You anxiously."
49 And He said to them,
"Why did you seek Me? Did you
not know that I must be [bb]about
[cc]My Father's business?"
50 But they did [dd]not understand the statement which He
spoke to them.

---

25 *a Holy Spirit* (NT): vv. 25–27; Lk. 3:16. (Mt. 1:18; Acts 2:4, *note*)
26 *b Christ* (first advent): vv. 26–32; Lk. 9:56. (Gen. 3:15; Acts 1:11, *note*)
28 *c Bible prayers* (NT): vv. 28–32; Lk. 5:12. (Mt. 6:9; Lk. 11:2, *note*)
29 *d* v. 26; cp. Gen. 46:30
e v. 26
30 *f* Gen. 49:18; see Rom. 1:16, *note*
32 *g* Isa. 49:6; 60:1–3; Mt. 4:13–16; Acts 13:47; cp. Acts 28:28; Rom. 9:22–24
34 *h* Mt. 21:44; 1 Cor. 1:23–24; 1 Pet. 2:7
i Acts 28:22; 1 Pet. 2:12; 4:14
35 *j* Jn. 19:25
36 *k* Cp. Ex. 15:20; Acts 21:9
l Josh. 19:24
37 *m* Cp. 1 Tim. 5:9–13
n 1 Tim. 5:5
38 *o* v. 25; Lam. 3:25–26; cp. Lk. 24:21
p Cp. Isa. 52:9; see Rom. 3:24, *note*
40 *q* Cp. Lk. 1:80
r 1 Cor. 1:24, 30
s See Jn. 1:17, *note*
41 *t* Jn. 4:20
u Lk. 22:15; see Ex. 12:11, *note*
42 *v* Ex. 23:14–15
43 *w* Ex. 12:15
45 *x* Cp. Jn. 7:33–36
46 *y* Lk. 5:17
47 *z* Mt. 7:28; Mk. 1:22; Lk. 4:22
48 *aa* Jn. 7:15,46
49 *bb* Jn. 9:4
cc Jn. 4:34; 5:17,36; cp. Ps. 40:8
50 *dd* Lk. 9:45; 18:34; cp. Mk. 8:18

2:33 NU-Text reads *And His father and mother.* **2:37** NU-Text reads *a widow until she was eighty-four.* **2:38** NU-Text reads *to God.* **2:40** NU-Text omits *in spirit.* **2:43** NU-Text reads *And His parents.*

4:27–35). Compare Righteousness (NT), Rom. 10:10, *note*, and Paul's contrast, Phil. 3:4–9.

Jesus grows in wisdom, stature, and favor

51 Then He went down with them and came to Nazareth, and was subject to them, but His mother [a]kept all these things in her heart.

52 And Jesus [b]increased in [c]wisdom and stature, [d]and in favor with God and men.

Ministry of John the Baptist (Mt. 3:1–11; Mk. 1:1–8; Jn. 1:6–8,15–37)

3 NOW in the fifteenth year of the reign of Tiberius Caesar, [e]Pontius Pilate being governor of Judea, [f]Herod being [1]tetrarch of Galilee, his brother [g]Philip tetrarch of Iturea and the region of Trachonitis, and Lysanias tetrarch of Abilene,

2 while Annas and [h]Caiaphas were high priests,* the word of God came to [i]John the son of Zacharias in the wilderness.

3 And he went into all the region around the Jordan, preaching a baptism of [j]repentance for the remission of [k]sins,

4 as it is [l]written in the book of the words of Isaiah the prophet, [m]saying:

"The voice of one crying in the wilderness:
'Prepare the way of the L*ORD;*
Make His paths straight.
5 *Every valley shall be filled*
And every mountain and hill brought low;
The crooked places shall be made straight
And the rough ways smooth;
6 *And all flesh shall see the [n]salvation of God.' "*

7 Then he said to the multitudes that came out to be baptized by him, [o]"Brood of vipers! Who warned you to flee from the wrath to come?

8 "Therefore bear fruits [p]worthy of repentance, and do not begin to say to yourselves, [q]'We have Abraham as *our* father.' For I say to you that God is able to raise up children to Abraham from these stones.

9 "And even now the ax is laid to the root of the trees. [r]Therefore every tree which does not bear good fruit is cut down and thrown into the fire."

10 So the people asked him, saying, [s]"What shall we do then?"

11 He answered and said to them, "He who has two tunics, let him [t]give to him who has none; and he who has food, let him do [u]likewise."

12 Then tax collectors also came to be baptized, and said to him, "Teacher, [v]what shall we do?"

13 And he said to them, "Collect no more than what is appointed for you."

14 Likewise the soldiers asked him, saying, "And [w]what shall we do?" So he said to them, "Do not intimidate anyone or accuse [x]falsely, and be content with your [y]wages."

15 Now as the people were in expectation, and all reasoned in their hearts about John, whether he was the Christ *or* not,

16 John answered, saying to all, "I indeed [z]baptize you with water; but One mightier than I is coming, whose sandal strap I am not worthy to loose. He will [aa]baptize you with the Holy [bb]Spirit and fire.

17 "His winnowing fan *is* in His hand, and He will thoroughly clean out His threshing floor, [cc]and gather the wheat into His barn; but the chaff He will burn with unquenchable fire."

18 And with many other exhortations he preached to the people.

19 But [dd]Herod the tetrarch, being rebuked by him concerning [ee]Herodias, his brother [ff]Philip's wife,* and for all the evils which Herod had done,

20 also added this, above all, that he shut John up in prison.

*
3:2 NU-Text and M-Text read *in the high priesthood of Annas and Caiaphas.*
3:19 NU-Text reads *his brother's wife.*

51
a v. 19; cp. Dan. 7:28
52
b v. 40; cp. 1 Sam. 2:21
c Isa. 11:2–3; Col. 2:2–3
d 1 Sam. 2:26; Prov. 3:1–4; cp. Acts 2:47; Rom. 14:18
CHAPTER 3
1
e Mt. 27:2
f Herod Antipas. Mt. 14:1; see Mk. 6:14, *note*
g Herod Philip, son of Herod the Great. Mt. 14:3; see Mk. 6:14, *note*
2
h Jn. 11:49; 18:13; Acts 4:6
i Lk. 1:13
3
j Repentance: vv. 3, 8; Lk. 5:32. (Mt. 3:2; Acts 17:30, *note*)
k See Rom. 3:23, *note*
4
l Inspiration: vv. 4–6; Lk. 4:4. (Ex. 4:15; 2 Tim. 3:16, *note*)
m Isa. 40:3–5; Mk. 1:3
6
n Isa. 52:10; Rom. 10:8–18; see Rom. 1:16, *note*
7
o Mt. 12:34
8
p 2 Cor. 7:9–11; cp. Mt. 7:20
q Cp. Rom. 9:6,8; Gal. 3:29; 6:15

9
r Lk. 13:5–9
10
s Acts 2:37–38; 16:30–31
11
t Cp. Jas. 2:14–20
u Isa. 58:7; cp. 1 Tim. 6:17–18
12
v Cp. vv. 10, 14
14
w Cp. vv. 10, 12
x Ex. 20:16; 23:1
y Cp. Mt. 20:1–14
16
z See Acts 8:12, *note*
aa Jn. 7:39; Acts 2:1–4
bb Holy Spirit (NT): v. 16; Lk. 3:22. (Mt. 1:18; Acts 2:4, *note*)
17
cc Mt. 13:24–30
19
dd Herod Antipas. v. 1; Mt. 14:1; see Mk. 6:14, *note*
ee See Mk. 6:14, *note*
ff Herod Philip, son of Herod the Great. See Mk. 6:14, *note*

[1](3:1) A tetrarch, who governed a fourth part of a province, was sometimes called a king.

Baptism of Jesus (Mt. 3:13–17;
Mk. 1:9–11; cp. Jn. 1:31–34)

21 When all the people were
[a]baptized, it came to pass that
Jesus also was [b]baptized; and
while He [c]prayed, the heaven
was [d]opened.
22 And the Holy [e]Spirit descended in bodily form like a
dove upon Him, and a voice
came from heaven which said,
"You are My beloved Son; in
You I am well [f]pleased."

Genealogy of Mary,
mother of Jesus,
in David's line through Nathan
(v. 31; cp. Mt. 1:1–16)

23 Now Jesus Himself began
His ministry at about [g]thirty
years of age, being (as was supposed) *the* [h]son of Joseph, *the*
[1]*son* of Heli,
24 *the son* of Matthat,* *the*
son of Levi, *the son* of Melchi,
the son of Janna, *the son* of Joseph,
25 *the son* of Mattathiah, *the*
son of Amos, *the son* of Nahum,
the son of Esli, *the son* of Nag-
gai,
26 *the son* of Maath, *the son*
of Mattathiah, *the son* of Semei,
the son of Joseph, *the son* of Judah,
27 *the son* of Joannas, *the*
son of Rhesa, *the son* of [i]Zerub-
babel, *the son* of Shealtiel, *the*
son of Neri,
28 *the son* of Melchi, *the son*
of Addi, *the son* of Cosam, *the*
son of Elmodam, *the son* of Er,
29 *the son* of Jose, *the son* of
Eliezer, *the son* of Jorim, *the*
son of Matthat, *the son* of Levi,
30 *the son* of Simeon, *the son*
of Judah, *the son* of Joseph, *the*
son of Jonan, *the son* of Eliakim,
31 *the son* of Melea, *the son*
of Menan, *the son* of Mattathah,
the son of Nathan, *the son* of
David,
32 *the son* of Jesse, *the son* of
Obed, *the son* of Boaz, *the son*
of Salmon, *the son* of Nahshon,
33 *the son* of Amminadab,
the son of Ram, *the son* of Hezron, *the son* of Perez, *the son* of
Judah,
34 *the son* of Jacob, *the son*
of Isaac, *the son* of Abraham,
the son of Terah, *the son* of Nahor,
35 *the son* of Serug, *the son*
of Reu, *the son* of Peleg, *the son*
of Eber, *the son* of Shelah,
36 *the son* of Cainan, *the son*
of [j]Arphaxad, *the son* of Shem,
the son of Noah, *the son* of Lamech,
37 *the son* of Methuselah, *the*
son of Enoch, *the son* of Jared,
the son of Mahalalel, *the son* of
Cainan,
38 *the son* of Enosh, *the son*
of Seth, *the son* of Adam, *the*
son of God.

21
a See Acts 8:12, *note*
b C. A.D. 26
c Cp. Lk. 9:29
d Ezek. 1:1; cp. Acts 7:56; Rev. 4:1; 11:19; 15:5; 19:11

22
e Holy Spirit (NT): v. 22; Lk. 4:1. (Mt. 1:18; Acts 2:4, *note*)
f Mt. 17:5; 2 Pet. 1:17

23
g Cp. Num. 4:3,35,39,47
h Lk. 4:22; Jn. 6:42

27
i Ezra 2:2; 3:8; see 1 Chr. 3:19, *note*

36
j Gen. 10:22, 24; 11:10–13; 1 Chr. 1:17–18

* 3:24 This and several other names in the genealogy are spelled somewhat differently in the NU-Text. Since the New King James Version uses the Old Testament spelling for persons mentioned in the New Testament, these variations, which come from the Greek, have not been footnoted.

[1](3:23) The genealogies of our Lord recorded in Mt. 1:1–17 and Lk. 3:23–38 have their similarities and their differences. Though the Lucan genealogy goes back to Adam and that of Matthew goes only to Abraham, they are both in absolute agreement in the generations between Abraham and David. It is with the son of David that the great difference begins, for Luke traces our Lord's ancestry from David through Nathan, whereas Matthew uses the royal line through Solomon. It is true that the names Shealtiel, Zerubbabel, and possibly Matthat (Matthan in Mt.) appear subsequently in both, but otherwise the lists are entirely different. Indeed in one, Jacob is spoken of as Joseph's father; whereas in the other, Heli is presumably so presented.

Two views have been maintained by equally godly and learned scholars. Some believe both genealogies are of Joseph, but that the one in Matthew gives the legal descendants of David to establish our Lord's claim to the Davidic throne, while Luke gives the particular line to which Joseph actually belonged. The second list, then, is spoken of as the collateral line and is eligible for royal duty when the legal line is incapacitated or becomes extinct.

A far simpler solution, and in all probability the true one, is that since every man has two genealogies—one through his father and another through his mother—so Matthew presents Joseph's genealogy (the Lord's foster or legal father, not his actual father), whereas Luke presents Mary's genealogy. This view is supported by linguistic and historical evidence and is held by many students of the Bible. In addition, appeal may be made to Num. 27:1–11 and 36:1–12 to give Scriptural precedent for the substitution of Joseph's name in Lk. 3:23. At the same time it avoids the judgment spoken of in Jer. 22:28–30 (see Mt. 1:11, *note*).

CHAPTER 4
1
a Isa. 11:2; 61:1
b Holy Spirit (NT): vv. 1,14; Lk. 11:13. (Mt. 1:18; Acts 2:4, *note*)
c Ezek. 3:12; Lk. 2:27; cp. 1 Ki. 18:12; Acts 8:39
2
d Cp. Gen. 3:15
e Test/ tempt: vv. 1–13; Lk. 8:13. (Gen. 3:1; Jas. 1:14, *note*)
f Cp. Ex. 34:28; 1 Ki. 19:8; Acts 1:3
g Mk. 11:12
3
h Mk. 3:11; Jn. 20:31
4
i Inspiration: vv. 4,8; Lk. 4:10. (Ex. 4:15; 2 Tim. 3:16, *note*). Cp. Eph. 6:17
j Law (of Moses): vv. 4,8; Lk. 4:12. (Ex. 19:1; Gal. 3:24, *note*)
k Dt. 8:3; cp. Jn. 6:22–58
5
l Gk. *oikoumene*. See Lk. 2:1, *note*
6
m Cp. Rev. 13:2
n Cp. Jn. 12:31; 14:30; 2 Cor. 4:4
o Rev. 13:7
7
p Cp. Gen. 3:1–7
8
q Satan: vv. 2–13; Lk. 8:12. (Gen. 3:1; Rev. 20:10)
r Dt. 6:13; 10:20
4:9 s Cp. Jn. 12:3

Temptation of Jesus (Mt. 4:1–11; Mk. 1:12–13; cp. Gen. 3:6; 1 Jn. 2:16)

4 THEN Jesus, being [a]filled
with the Holy [b]Spirit, returned from the Jordan and was
[c]led by the Spirit into* the wilderness,
2 [d]being [e]tempted for [f]forty
days by the devil. And in those
days He ate nothing, and afterward, when they had ended, He
was [g]hungry.
3 And the devil said to Him,
"If You are the [h]Son of God,
command this stone to become
bread."
4 But Jesus answered him,
saying, "It is [i]written, [j]'*Man
shall not live by* [k]*bread alone,
but by every word of God.*'"*
5 Then the devil, taking
Him up on a high mountain,
showed Him* all the kingdoms
of the [l]world in a moment of
time.
6 And the devil said to Him,
"All this [m]authority I will give
You, and their glory; for *this*
has been [n]delivered to me, and
I [o]give it to whomever I wish.
7 "Therefore, if You will
worship before me, [p]all will be
Yours."
8 And Jesus answered and
said to him, "Get behind Me,
[q]Satan!* For* it is [i]written,
[j]'*You shall* [r]*worship the* LORD
*your God, and Him only you
shall serve.*'"
9 Then he brought Him to
Jerusalem, [s]set Him on the pinnacle of the temple, and said to
Him, "If You are the [h]Son of

*

4:1 NU-Text reads *in.* 4:4 NU-Text omits *but by every word of God.* 4:5 NU-Text reads *And taking Him up, he showed Him.* 4:8 NU-Text omits *Get behind Me, Satan.* • NU-Text and M-Text omit *For.*

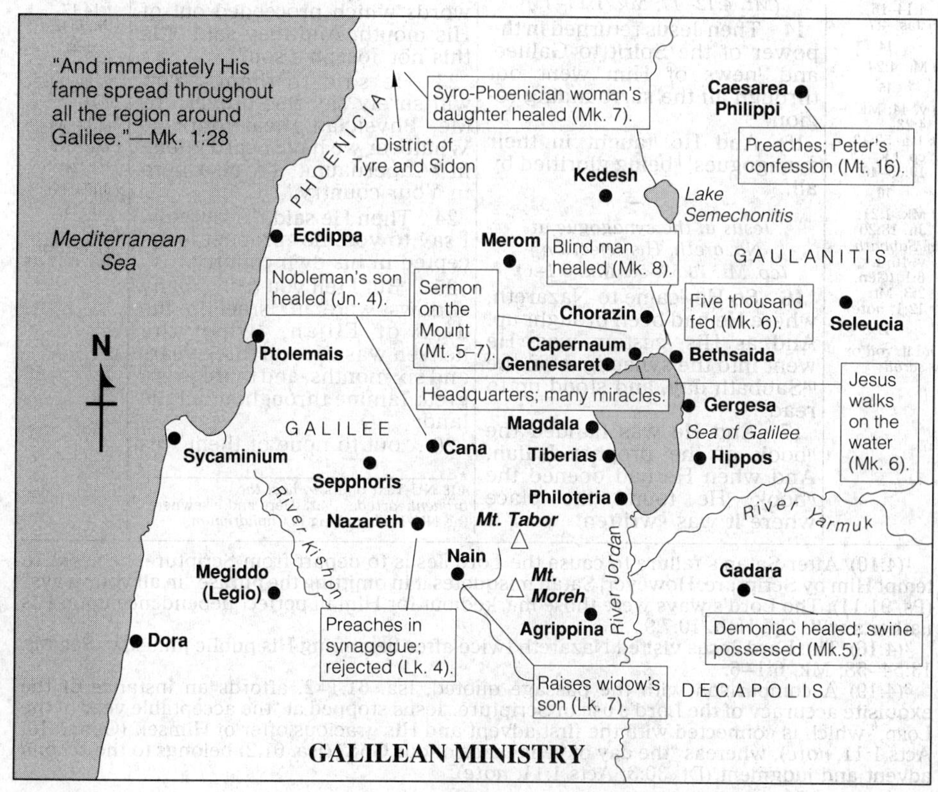

GALILEAN MINISTRY

9
a Cp. 1 Pet. 5:8
10
b *Inspiration:* vv. 10, 12,17–19; Lk. 6:3. (Ex. 4:15; 2 Tim. 3:16, *note*). Cp. Eph. 6:17
c Ps. 91:11–12
d See Heb. 1:4, *note*
12
e *Law* (of Moses): v. 12; Lk. 5:14. (Ex. 19:1; Gal. 3:24, *note*)
f Dt. 6:16; cp. 1 Cor. 10:9
13
g Heb. 4:14–16
h Jas. 4:7
14
i Mt. 4:24
15
j v. 44; Mt. 4:23
k Isa. 52:13; cp. Lk. 19:35–40
16
l Mk. 1:21; Jn. 18:20
m *Sabbath:* v. 16; Lk. 6:1. (Gen. 2:3; Mt. 12:1, *note*)
17
n Lit. *roll* or *scroll*

God, [a]throw Yourself down
from here.
10 "For it is [1b]written:

[c]'He shall give His [d]angels
charge over you,
To keep you,'

11 "and,

'In their hands they shall
bear you up,
Lest you dash your foot
against a stone.'"

12 And Jesus answered and
said to him, "It has been [b]said,
[e]'You shall not [f]tempt the LORD
your God.'"
13 Now when the devil had
ended every [g]temptation, he
[h]departed from Him until an
opportune time.

III. The Public Ministry
of the Son of Man, to the
Triumphal Entry,
4:14—19:27

First tour of Galilee
(Mt. 4:12–17; Mk. 1:14–15)

14 Then Jesus returned in the
power of the Spirit to Galilee,
and [i]news of Him went out
through all the surrounding region.
15 And He [j]taught in their
synagogues, [k]being glorified by
all.

Jesus in the synagogue at
Nazareth; His rejection
(cp. Mt. 13:53–58; Mk. 6:1–6)

16 So He [2]came to Nazareth,
where He had been brought up.
And as His [l]custom was, He
went into the synagogue on the
[m]Sabbath day, and stood up to
read.
17 And He was handed the
[n]book of the prophet Isaiah.
And when He had opened the
[n]book, He found the place
where it was [b]written:

18 [o]*"The Spirit of the* LORD *is*
upon Me,
Because He has anointed
Me
To preach the [p]gospel to
the poor;
He has sent Me to heal
*the brokenhearted,**
To proclaim liberty to
the captives
And recovery of sight to
the blind,
To [q]set at liberty those
who are oppressed;
19 *To proclaim the*
[3]acceptable year of the
LORD."

20 Then He closed the [n]book,
and gave *it* back to the atten-
dant and [r]sat down. And the
eyes of all who were in the synagogue were fixed on Him.
21 And He began to say to
them, "Today this Scripture is
[s]fulfilled in your hearing."
22 So all bore witness to Him,
and marveled at the [t]gracious
words which proceeded out of
His mouth. And they said, [u]"Is
this not Joseph's son?"
23 He said to them, "You
will surely say this proverb to
Me, 'Physician, [v]heal yourself!
Whatever we have heard [w]done
in [x]Capernaum,* do also here
in Your country.'"
24 Then He said, "Assuredly,
I say to you, no [y]prophet is accepted in his own country.
25 "But I tell you truly, many
widows were in Israel in the
days of Elijah, [z]when the
heaven was shut up three years
and six months, and there was a
great famine throughout all the
land;
26 "but to none of them was

*4:18 NU-Text omits *to heal the brokenhearted.* 4:23 Here and elsewhere the NU-Text spelling is *Capharnaum.*

18
o Isa. 61:1–2
p *Gospel:* v. 18; Lk. 7:22. (Gen. 12:3; Rev. 14:6)
q Dan. 9:24; Jn. 8:32; cp. Rev. 22:1–5
20
r i.e. *to teach.* Mt. 5:1; Lk. 5:3; Jn. 8:2
21
s Mt. 1:22–23; Acts 13:29
22
t Ps. 45:2; Jn. 1:14,17
u Jn. 6:42
23
v Cp. Mt. 27:40; Lk. 5:31
w Mt. 11:23–24
x Mt. 4:13
24
y Jn. 4:44
25
z 1 Ki. 17:1–7; cp. Jas. 5:17–18

[1](4:10) After Satan's failure to cause the Lord Jesus to depart from Scripture, he seeks to tempt Him by Scripture. However, Satan misquotes it in omitting the phrase "in all your ways" (Ps. 91:11). The Lord's ways were those marked out for Him in perfect dependence upon His Father's will. Cp. Heb. 10:7,9.

[2](4:16) The Lord Jesus visited Nazareth twice after beginning His public ministry. See Mt. 13:54–58; Mk. 6:1–6.

[3](4:19) A comparison with the passage quoted, Isa. 61:1–2, affords an instance of the exquisite accuracy of the Lord's use of Scripture. Jesus stopped at "the acceptable year of the LORD," which is connected with the first advent and His gracious offer of Himself (Gen. 3:15; Acts 1:11, *note*), whereas "the day of vengeance of our God" (Isa. 61:2) belongs to the *second* advent and judgment (Dt. 30:3; Acts 1:11, *note*).

Elijah sent [a]except to Zarephath,* *in the region* of [b]Sidon,
to a woman *who was* a widow.
27 "And many lepers were in
Israel in the time of Elisha the
prophet, and none of them was
cleansed [c]except Naaman the
Syrian."
28 So all those in the synagogue, when they heard these
things, were [d]filled with wrath,
29 [e]and rose up and thrust
Him out of the city; and they led
Him to the brow of the hill on
which their city was built, that
they might throw Him down
over the cliff.
30 Then [f]passing through
the midst of them, He went His
way.

Jesus casts out demons at Capernaum (Mk. 1:21–28)

31 Then He went down to Capernaum, a city of Galilee, and
was [g]teaching them on the Sabbaths.
32 And they were [h]aston-
ished at His teaching, [i]for His
word was with authority.
33 Now in the synagogue
there was a man who had a
spirit of an unclean [j]demon.
And he cried out with a loud
voice,
34 saying, "Let *us* alone!
What have we to do with You,
Jesus of Nazareth? Did You
come to destroy us? I know who
You are—the [k]Holy One of
God!"
35 But Jesus rebuked him,
saying, "Be quiet, and come out
of him!" And when the [j]demon
had thrown him in *their* midst,
it came out of him and did not
hurt him.
36 Then they were all
amazed and spoke among
themselves, saying, "What a
word this *is!* [l]For with authority and power He commands
the unclean spirits, and they
come out."
37 And the [m]report about
Him went out into every place
in the surrounding region.

Peter's mother-in-law and others healed (Mt. 8:14–17; Mk. 1:29–34)

38 Now He arose from the
synagogue and entered Simon's
house. But Simon's wife's

26
a 1 Ki. 17:8–16
b Cp. Mt. 15:21–28
27
c 2 Ki. 5:1–15
28
d Lk. 6:11
29
e Lk. 17:25; Jn. 8:37; 10:31; cp. Acts 5:33
30
f Jn. 8:59; 10:39
31
g v. 15
32
h Mt. 7:28–29
i v. 36; Jn. 6:63; 8:26, 28,38,47; 12:49–50; cp. Ti. 2:15
33
j See Mt. 7:22, *note*
34
k Ps. 16:10; Isa. 49:7; Lk. 1:35
36
l v. 32
37
m vv. 14–15; cp. Mic. 5:4; Mk. 1:45

mother was sick with a high fever, and they [n]made request of
Him concerning her.
39 So He stood over her and
[o]rebuked the fever, and it [p]left
her. And immediately she arose
and [q]served them.
40 When the sun was setting,
[r]all those who had any that
were sick with various diseases
brought them to Him; and He
laid His hands on every one of
them and healed them.
41 And [j]demons also came
out of many, [s]crying out and
saying, [t]"You are the Christ,*
the Son of God!" And He, [u]re-
buking *them,* did not allow
them to speak, for they [v]knew
that He was the Christ.
42 Now when it was day, He
departed and went into a [w]de-
serted place. And the crowd
sought Him and came to Him,
and tried to keep Him from
leaving them;
43 but He said to them, "I
must [x]preach the [y]kingdom of
God to the other cities also, because for this purpose I have
been sent."
44 And He was [z]preaching in
the synagogues of Galilee.*

Jesus calls first disciples (Mt. 4:18–22; Mk. 1:16–20; cp. Jn. 1:35–51; 21:1–8)

5 SO it was, as the multitude
pressed about Him to [aa]hear
the word of God, that He stood
by the Lake of Gennesaret,
2 and saw two boats standing by the lake; but the fishermen had gone from them and
were washing *their* nets.
3 Then He got into one of
the boats, which was Simon's,
and asked him to put out a little
from the land. And He [bb]sat
down and taught the multitudes
from the boat.
4 When He had stopped
speaking, He said to Simon,
"Launch out into the deep and
[cc]let down your nets for a
[dd]catch."
5 But Simon answered and
said to Him, "Master, we have
[ee]toiled all night and caught
[ff]nothing; nevertheless [gg]at

38
n v. 12; Mk. 5:23
39
o Lk. 8:24
p Miracles (NT): vv. 38–41; 5:4–5; Lk. 5:6. (Mt. 8:3; Acts 28:8, *note*)
q Cp. Lk. 8:2–3
40
r Cp. v. 40 with v. 41; see Mk. 3:15, *note*
41
s Acts 8:7
t Mk. 8:29; cp. Mk. 14:61
u vv. 34–35
v Mk. 3:11; cp. Acts 19:15
42
w Lk. 9:10
43
x Mk. 1:14; Jn. 9:4
y See Mt. 6:33, *note*
44
z Mt. 4:23; 9:35
CHAPTER 5
1
aa Acts 13:44; cp. Rom. 10:17
3
bb Jn. 8:2
4
cc vv. 5,19; cp. Mk. 2:4
dd v. 9
5
ee Cp. Mk. 6:48
ff Jn. 21:3
gg Ps. 33:9; cp. Mt. 8:8

*4:26 Greek *Sarepta* 4:41 NU-Text omits *the Christ.* 4:44 NU-Text reads *Judea.*

Your word I will let down the net."

6 And when they had done this, they [a]caught a great number of fish, and their net was breaking.

7 So they signaled to *their* partners in the [b]other boat to come and help them. And they came and filled both the boats, so that they began to sink.

8 When Simon Peter saw *it,* he [c]fell down at Jesus' knees, saying, [d]"Depart from me, for I am a sinful man, O Lord!"

9 For he and all who were with him were [e]astonished at the catch of fish which they had taken;

10 and so also *were* James and John, the sons of Zebedee, who were partners with Simon. And Jesus said to Simon, [f]"Do not be afraid. From now on you will [g]catch men."

11 So when they had brought their boats to land, they [h]forsook all and followed Him.

A leper cleansed
(Mt. 8:2–4; Mk. 1:40–45)

12 And it happened when He was in a certain city, that behold, a man who was full of [i]leprosy saw Jesus; and he fell on *his* face and implored Him, [j]saying, "Lord, if You are [1]willing, You [k]can make me clean."

13 Then He put out *His* hand and touched him, saying, "I am willing; be cleansed." [l]Immediately the leprosy [a]left him.

14 And He charged him to tell no one, "But go and [m]show yourself to the priest, and make an offering for your cleansing, as a testimony to them, [n]just as Moses [o]commanded."

15 However, the [p]report went around concerning Him all the more; and great multitudes came together to hear, and to be healed by Him of their infirmities.

6
a Miracles (NT): vv. 4–9, 12–14, 18–25; Lk. 6:8. (Mt. 8:3; Acts 28:8, *note*)
7
b vv. 2–3
8
c Cp. Rev. 5:8,14
d Cp. Mt. 8:34
9
e Mk. 5:42; 10:24,26
10
f Cp. Mt. 8:26
g Cp. Ezek. 47:9–10
11
h Mt. 19:27; Mk. 8:34–35; 10:28–31; Lk. 9:59–62; Jn. 12:26; cp. Phil. 3:7–8
12
i Lev. 13–14
j Bible prayers (NT): v. 12; Lk. 8:24. (Mt. 6:9; Lk. 11:2, *note*)
k Cp. Gen. 18:14; Jer. 32:17,27; Mt. 8:8
13
l Mt. 20:34; Lk. 8:44; Jn. 5:9
14
m Lk. 17:14
n Lev. 13:1–3; 14:2–32
o Law (of Moses): vv. 14,17; Lk. 10:26. (Ex. 19:1; Gal. 3:24, *note*)
15
p Mk. 1:45

A paralytic healed
(Mt. 9:2–8; Mk. 2:1–12)

16 So He Himself *often* [q]withdrew into the wilderness and [r]prayed.

17 Now it happened on a certain day, as He was teaching, that there were [s]Pharisees and teachers of the law sitting by, who had come out of every town of Galilee, Judea, and Jerusalem. And the power of the Lord was *present* to heal them.*

18 Then behold, men brought on a bed a man who was paralyzed, whom they sought to bring in and lay before Him.

19 And when they could not find how they might bring him in, because of the crowd, they went up on the housetop and let him down with *his* bed through the tiling into the midst [t]before Jesus.

20 When He saw their [u]faith, He said to him, "Man, your [v]sins are [w]forgiven you."

21 And the [x]scribes and the Pharisees began to reason, saying, "Who is this who speaks [y]blasphemies? Who can forgive sins but [z]God alone?"

22 But when Jesus [aa]perceived their thoughts, He answered and said to them, "Why are you reasoning in your hearts?

23 "Which is easier, to say, 'Your sins are forgiven you,' or to say, 'Rise up and walk'?

24 "But that you may know that the [bb]Son of Man has [cc]power on earth to forgive sins"—He said to the man who was paralyzed, [dd]"I say to you, arise, take up your bed, and go to your house."

25 Immediately he [a]rose up before them, took up what he had been lying on, and departed

* 5:17 NU-Text reads *present with Him to heal.*

16
q Lk. 9:10
r Mt. 14:23; Mk. 1:35; Lk. 6:12; 9:18; 11:1
17
s See Mt. 3:7, *note 1*
19
t Mt. 15:30
20
u Faith: vv. 18–20; Lk. 7:9. (Gen. 3:20; Heb. 11:39, *note*)
v See Rom. 3:23, *note*
w Forgiveness: vv. 20, 24; Lk. 6:37. (Lev. 4:20; Mt. 26:28, *note*)
21
x See Mt. 2:4, *note*
y Mt. 26:65; Jn. 10:33
z Ps. 130:4; Isa. 43:25
22
aa Lk. 9:47; Jn. 2:25
24
bb See Mt. 8:20, *note*
cc Mt. 28:18
dd Mk. 2:11; 5:41; Lk. 7:14

[1](5:12) The leper honored Christ by recognizing His power to heal, and begged Him, "if You are willing," to heal his leprosy. Similarly the Christian should recognize Christ's power to heal, but should always pray, "if You are willing" (1 Jn. 5:14). Even the Lord Jesus prayed, "Not My will, but Yours, be done" (Lk. 22:42). Paul prayed three times that his "thorn in the flesh" might be removed, but when God willed not to do so, Paul realized that God had a wise and good purpose in asking him to continue to bear it (2 Cor. 12:7–9; Rom. 8:28).

to his own house, [a]glorifying
God.
26 And they were all amazed,
and they [b]glorified God and
were filled with fear, saying,
"We have seen strange things
today!"

Call of Levi (Matthew): Jesus questioned by scribes and Pharisees (Mt. 9:9–15; Mk. 2:13–20)

27 After these things He
went out and saw a tax collector
named [c]Levi, sitting at the tax
office. And He said to him,
[d]"Follow Me."
28 So he left all, rose up, and
[e]followed Him.
29 Then Levi gave Him a
great feast in his own house.
And there were a great number
of tax collectors and others who
sat down with them.
30 And their [f]scribes and
the [g]Pharisees* complained
against His disciples, saying,
[h]"Why do You eat and drink
with tax collectors and [i]sin-
ners?"
31 Jesus answered and said
to them, "Those who are well
have no need of a physician, but
those who are [j]sick.
32 "I have not come to call
the [k]righteous, but sinners, to
[l]repentance."
33 Then they said to Him,
"Why do* the disciples of John
[m]fast often and make prayers,
and likewise those of the Pharisees, but Yours eat and drink?"
34 And He said to them, "Can
you make the friends of the
bridegroom fast while the
[n]bridegroom is with them?
35 "But the days will come
when the bridegroom will be
taken away from them; then
they will fast in those days."

Parable of cloth and wineskins (Mt. 9:16–17; Mk. 2:21–22)

36 Then He spoke a [o]parable
to them: "No one puts a piece
from a new garment on an old
one;* otherwise the new makes
a tear, and also the piece that
was *taken* out of the new does
not match the old.
37 "And no one puts new
wine into old wineskins; or else
the new wine will burst the

25
a Lk. 17:15, 18; Acts 3:8
26
b Lk. 7:16
27
c Or *Matthew*, Mt. 9:9
d Mk. 8:34; Lk. 9:59; Jn. 12:26; 21:19,22
28
e Mt. 4:22; 19:27; Mk. 10:28
30
f See Mt. 2:4, *note*
g See Mt. 3:7, *note 1*
h Mt. 11:19; Lk. 15:2
i See Rom. 3:23, *note*
31
j Cp. Lk. 15:1–32; 19:1–10
32
k See Rom. 10:10, *note*
l *Repentance:* v. 32; Lk. 10:13. (Mt. 3:2; Acts 17:30, *note*)
33
m Lk. 7:33
34
n Jn. 3:29; cp. Eph. 5:25–32; Rev. 19:7–9
36
o *Parables* (NT): vv. 36–39; Lk. 6:39. (Mt. 5:13; Lk. 21:29)

wineskins and be spilled, and
the wineskins will be ruined.
38 "But new wine must be put
into new wineskins, and both
are preserved.*
39 "And no one, having drunk
old *wine,* immediately* desires
new; for he says, 'The old is
better.' "*

Jesus is Lord of the Sabbath (Mt. 12:1–8; Mk. 2:23–28)

6 NOW it happened on the
second [p]Sabbath after the
first* that He went through the
grainfields. And His disciples
plucked the heads of [q]grain and
ate *them,* rubbing *them* in *their*
hands.
2 And some of the [g]Phari-
sees said to them, "Why are you
doing what is not lawful to do
on the [r]Sabbath?"
3 But Jesus answering them
said, "Have you not even [s]read
this, [t]what David did when he
was hungry, he and those who
were with him:
4 "how he went into the
house of God, took and ate the
[u]showbread, and also gave
some to those with him, which
is not lawful for any but the
priests to eat?"
5 And He said to them, "The
[v]Son of Man is also Lord of the
Sabbath."

Jesus heals on the Sabbath (Mt. 12:9–14; Mk. 3:1–6)

6 Now it happened on another [p]Sabbath, also, that He
entered the synagogue and
taught. And a man was there
whose right hand was withered.
7 So the scribes and [g]Phari-
sees watched Him closely,
whether He would [w]heal on the
Sabbath, that they might find
an [x]accusation against Him.
8 But He [y]knew their
thoughts, and said to the man
who had the withered hand,
"Arise and stand here." And he
[z]arose and stood.
9 Then Jesus said to them, "I

CHAPTER 6
1
p *Sabbath:* vv. 1–7,9; Lk. 13:10. (Gen. 2:3; Mt. 12:1, *note*)
q Dt. 23:25
2
r Ex. 20:10
3
s *Inspiration:* vv. 3–4; Lk. 7:27. (Ex. 4:15; 2 Tim. 3:16, *note*)
t 1 Sam. 21:6
4
u See Ex. 25:30, *note*
5
v See Mt. 8:20, *note*
7
w Lk. 13:14; 14:1–6
x Lk. 20:20
8
y Mt. 9:4; Jn. 2:24–25; cp. 1 Sam. 16:7
z *Miracles* (NT): vv. 6–10; Lk. 7:10. (Mt. 8:3; Acts 28:8, *note*)

*
5:30 NU-Text reads *But the Pharisees and their scribes.* **5:33** NU-Text omits *Why do,* making the verse a statement. **5:36** NU-Text reads *No one tears a piece from a new garment and puts it on an old one.* **5:38** NU-Text omits *and both are preserved.* **5:39** NU-Text omits *immediately.* • NU-Text reads *good.* **6:1** NU-Text reads *on a Sabbath.*

will ask you one thing: [a]Is it
lawful on the Sabbath to do
good or to do [b]evil, to save life
or to destroy?"*
10 And when He had looked
around at them all, He said to
the man,* "Stretch out your
hand." And he did so, and his
hand was restored as whole as
the other.*
11 But they were filled with
[c]rage, and discussed with one
another what they might do to
Jesus.
12 Now it came to pass in
those days that He went out to
the mountain to pray, and continued all night in [d]prayer to
God.

The twelve chosen
(cp. Mt. 10:2–4; Mk. 3:13–19)

13 And when it was day, He
called His disciples to *Himself;*
and from them He [e]chose
[f]twelve whom He also named
apostles:
14 Simon, whom He also
named Peter, and Andrew his
brother; James and John; Philip
and Bartholomew;
15 Matthew and Thomas;
James the *son* of Alphaeus, and
Simon called the Zealot;
16 Judas *the son* of [g]James,
and [h]Judas Iscariot who also
became a traitor.

The Sermon on the Level Place
(cp. Mt. 5—7, Sermon
on the Mount)

17 And He came down with
them and stood on a level place
with a crowd of His disciples
and a great multitude of people
from all Judea and Jerusalem,
and from the seacoast of Tyre
and Sidon, who came to hear
Him and be healed of their diseases,
18 as well as those who were
tormented with unclean spirits.
And they were healed.
19 And the whole multitude
[i]sought to [j]touch Him, for
power went out from Him and
healed *them* all.

The Beatitudes (Mt. 5:3–12)

20 Then He lifted up His eyes
toward His disciples, and said:
"Blessed *are you* poor,
For yours is the
[k]kingdom of God.
21 [l]Blessed *are you* who
hunger now,
For you shall be
[m]filled.
[n]Blessed *are you* who
weep now,
For you shall [o]laugh.
22 Blessed are you when
men hate you,
And [p]when they
exclude you,
And revile *you,* and
cast out your name
as evil,
For the [q]Son of Man's
sake.
23 [r]Rejoice in that day and
leap for joy!
For indeed your
[s]reward *is* great in
heaven,
For in like manner
their [t]fathers did to
the prophets.
24 "But [u]woe to you who are
rich,
For [v]you have received
your consolation.
25 [w]Woe to you who are full,
For you shall hunger.
[x]Woe to you who laugh
now,
For you shall mourn
and [y]weep.
26 [z]Woe to you* when all*
men speak well of
you,
For so did their fathers
to the false prophets.
27 [aa]"But I say to you who
hear: [bb]Love your enemies, do
good to those who hate you,
28 [cc]"bless those who curse
you, and [dd]pray for those who
spitefully use you.
29 "To him who strikes you
on the *one* cheek, offer the other
also. [ee]And from him who takes
away your cloak, do not withhold *your* tunic either.
30 [ff]"Give to everyone who
asks of you. And from him who
takes away your goods do not
ask *them* back.
31 "And just as you want

*
6:9 M-Text reads *to kill.* **6:10** NU-Text and M-Text read *to him.* • NU-Text omits *as whole as the other.*
6:26 NU-Text and M-Text omit *to you.* • M-Text omits *all.*

9
a Jn. 7:23
b Cp. Jas. 4:17
11
c Lk. 4:28
12
d Mt. 14:23; Mk. 1:35; Lk. 5:16; 9:18; 11:1
13
e Jn. 6:70
f vv. 14–16; Mt. 10:1; cp. Acts 1:13
16
g See Mt. 4:21, *note*
h Lk. 22:3–6
19
i Mt. 14:36
j Mk. 5:27–28; Lk. 8:44–47

20
k See Mt. 6:33, *note*
21
l Isa. 55:1
m Rev. 7:16
n Isa. 61:3; Rev. 7:17
o Ps. 126:5
22
p Jn. 16:2
q See Mt. 8:20, *note*
23
r Acts 5:41; Jas. 1:2
s *Rewards:* v. 23; Lk. 6:35. (Dan. 12:3; 1 Cor. 3:14, *note*)
t Acts 7:51
24
u Lk. 12:21; Jas. 5:1–6
v Mt. 6:2; Lk. 16:25
25
w Isa. 65:13
x Prov. 14:13
y Jas. 4:9
26
z Cp. 1 Jn. 4:5
27
aa vv. 27–36; cp. Mt. 5:39–48
bb Rom. 12:20
28
cc Rom. 12:14
dd Cp. Lk. 23:34; Acts 7:60
29
ee Cp. 1 Cor. 6:7; 1 Pet. 2:19–20
30
ff Dt. 15:7–8; Prov. 3:27; Mt. 5:42; cp. 1 Jn. 3:17

men to do to you, you also do to them likewise.

32 "But if you love those who love you, what credit is that to you? For even [a]sinners love those who love them.

33 "And if you do good to those who do good to you, what credit is that to you? For even sinners do the same.

34 "And if you lend *to those* from whom you hope to receive back, what credit is that to you? For even sinners lend to sinners to receive as much back.

35 "But [b]love your enemies, [c]do good, and [d]lend, hoping for nothing in return; and your [e]reward will be great, and you will be sons of the Most High. For He is kind to the unthankful and evil.

36 [f]"Therefore be merciful, just as your Father also is merciful.

37 [g]"Judge not, and you shall not be judged. Condemn not, and you shall not be condemned. [h]Forgive, and you will be [i]forgiven.

38 [j]"Give, and it will be given to you: good measure, pressed down, shaken together, and running over will be put into your bosom. For with the same measure that you use, it will be measured back to you."

39 And He spoke a [k]parable to them: "Can the [l]blind lead the blind? Will they not both fall into the ditch?

40 "A [m]disciple is not above his teacher, but everyone who is perfectly trained will be like his teacher.

41 "And why do you look at the speck in your brother's eye, but do not perceive the plank in your own eye?

42 "Or how can you say to your brother, 'Brother, let me remove the speck that *is* in your eye,' when you yourself do not see the plank that *is* in your own eye? Hypocrite! [n]First remove the plank from your own eye, and then you will see clearly to remove the speck that is in your brother's eye.

43 [o]"For a good tree does not bear bad fruit, nor does a bad tree bear good fruit.

44 "For every tree is known by its own fruit. For *men* do not gather figs from thorns, nor do they gather grapes from a bramble bush.

45 [p]"A good man out of the good treasure of his heart brings forth good; and an evil man out of the evil treasure of his heart* brings forth evil. For out of the abundance of the heart his [q]mouth speaks.

Parable of two builders and two foundations (Mt. 7:24–27)

46 "But why do you call Me [r]'Lord, Lord,' and not do the things which I say?

47 "Whoever comes to Me, and hears My sayings and [s]does them, I will show you whom he is like:

48 [k]"He is like a man building a house, who [t]dug deep and laid the foundation on the [u]rock. And when the [v]flood arose, the stream beat vehemently against that house, and [w]could not shake it, for it was founded on the rock.*

49 "But he who heard and did nothing is like a man who built a house on the earth without a foundation, against which the stream beat vehemently; and immediately it fell.* And the [x]ruin of that house was great."

Jesus heals a centurion's servant (Mt. 8:5–13)

7 NOW when He concluded all His sayings in the hearing of the people, He entered Capernaum.

2 And a certain centurion's servant, who was dear to him, was sick and ready to die.

3 So when he heard about Jesus, he sent elders of the Jews to Him, pleading with Him to come and heal his servant.

4 And when they came to Jesus, they begged Him earnestly, saying that the one for whom He should do this was [y]deserving,

5 "for he loves our nation, and has built us a synagogue."

6 Then Jesus went with them. And when He was already not far from the house,

*

6:45 NU-Text omits *treasure of his heart.*
6:48 NU-Text reads *for it was well built.*
6:49 NU-Text reads *collapsed.*

32
a See Rom. 3:23, *note*
35
b Rom. 13:10
c Heb. 13:16
d Lev. 25:35–37
e Rewards: v. 35; Lk. 19:17. (Dan. 12:3; 1 Cor. 3:14, *note*)
36
f Eph. 4:32; cp. 1 Pet. 3:9
37
g vv. 37–46; Rom. 14:4; 1 Cor. 4:5
h Mt. 18:21–35
i Forgiveness: v. 37; Lk. 7:48. (Lev. 4:20; Mt. 26:28, *note*)
38
j Prov. 28:27; see 2 Cor. 8:1, *note*
39
k Parables (NT): vv. 39, 47–49; Lk. 7:41. (Mt. 5:13; Lk. 21:29)
l Mt. 15:14; 23:16; Rom. 2:19
40
m Mt. 10:24; Jn. 15:20
42
n Cp. Gal. 6:4
43
o Mt. 12:33; Jas. 3:12

45
p Mt. 12:34–35
q Prov. 15:2, 28; 16:23; 18:21; cp. Mt. 12:36–37; Jas. 3:10
46
r Mt. 25:11–12; Lk. 13:25; cp. 1 Cor. 12:3
47
s Jn. 14:21; Jas. 1:22–25
48
t Cp. Mt. 13:5
u Cp. 1 Cor. 3:11
v Cp. Ps. 32:6
w Cp. 1 Jn. 2:17
49
x Cp. Prov. 1:29–31
CHAPTER 7
4
y Cp. vv. 6,7

7
[a] Ps. 33:9;
107:20; cp.
Lk. 4:36;
Jn. 11:43
8
[b] Mk. 13:34
9
[c] Cp. Mt.
15:28
[d] *Faith:* v. 9;
Lk. 7:50.
(Gen. 3:20;
Heb. 11:39,
note)
[e] Cp. Rom.
3:1–2
10
[f] *Miracles*
(NT):
vv. 2–10,
12–15,22;
Lk. 8:2. (Mt.
8:3; Acts
28:8, *note*)
13
[g] Lam. 3:32;
Jn. 11:35;
Heb. 4:15
[h] Lk. 8:52
14
[i] Mk. 5:41;
cp. Eph.
5:14
15
[j] Mt. 11:5;
Lk. 8:55;
Jn. 11:44
[k] *Resurrection:* vv. 15,
22; Lk. 8:55.
(2 Ki. 4:35;
1 Cor.
15:52, *note*)
[l] 1 Ki. 17:23;
2 Ki. 4:36
16
[m] Lk. 1:65
[n] Lk. 5:26
[o] v. 39; see
Lk. 24:19,
note
[p] Lk. 1:68;
cp. Ex. 4:31

the centurion sent friends to
Him, saying to Him, "Lord, do
not trouble Yourself, for I am
not worthy that You should enter under my roof.
7 "Therefore I did not even
think myself worthy to come to
You. But [a]say the word, and my
servant will be healed.
8 "For I also am a man
placed under [b]authority, having soldiers under me. And I say
to one, 'Go,' and he goes; and to
another, 'Come,' and he comes;
and to my servant, 'Do this,' and
he does *it.*"
9 When Jesus heard these
things, He [c]marveled at him,
and turned around and said to
the crowd that followed Him, "I
say to you, I have not found
such great [d]faith, not even in
[e]Israel!"
10 And those who were sent,
returning to the house, found
the servant [f]well who had been
sick.*

A widow's son raised from the dead

11 Now it happened, the day
after, *that* He went into a city
called Nain; and many of His
disciples went with Him, and a
large crowd.
12 And when He came near
the gate of the city, behold, a
dead man was being carried
out, the only son of his mother;
and she was a widow. And a
large crowd from the city was
with her.
13 When the Lord saw her,
He had [g]compassion on her and
said to her, [h]"Do not weep."
14 Then He came and
touched the open coffin, and
those who carried *him* stood
still. And He said, "Young man,
I say to you, [i]arise."
15 So he who was dead [j]sat
[k]up and began to speak. And
He [l]presented him to his
mother.
16 Then [m]fear came upon all,
and they [n]glorified God, saying,
"A great [o]prophet has risen up
among us"; and, "God has [p]vis-
ited His people."
17 And this report about Him
went throughout all Judea and
all the surrounding region.
18 Then the disciples of John
[q]reported to him concerning all
these things.

Jesus eulogizes John the Baptist (Mt. 11:2–19)

19 And John, calling two of
his disciples to *him,* sent *them*
to Jesus,* saying, "Are You the
[r]Coming One, or do we look for
another?"
20 When the men had come
to Him, they said, "John the
Baptist has sent us to You, saying, 'Are You the Coming One,
or do we look for another?' "
21 And that very hour He
cured many of infirmities, afflictions, and evil spirits; and to
many blind He gave sight.
22 Jesus answered and said
to them, "Go and [s]tell John the
[t]things you have seen and
heard: [u]that *the* blind [v]see, *the*
lame [w]walk, *the* lepers are
[x]cleansed, *the* deaf [y]hear, *the*
dead are [z]raised, *the* poor have
the [aa]gospel [bb]preached to them.
23 "And blessed is *he* who is
not [cc]offended because of Me."
24 When the messengers of
John [1]had departed, He began
to speak to the multitudes concerning John: "What did you go
out into the wilderness to see? A
reed shaken by the wind?
25 "But what did you go out
to see? A man clothed in [dd]soft
garments? Indeed those who
are gorgeously appareled and
[ee]live in luxury are in kings'
courts.
26 "But what did you go out
to see? A prophet? Yes, I say to
you, and more than a prophet.
27 "This is *he* of whom it is
[ff]written:

[gg]*'Behold, I send My*
messenger before Your
face,
Who will prepare Your
way before You.'

28 "For I say to you, among
those born of women there is
not a [hh]greater prophet than

18
[q] Mt. 11:2–5
19
[r] Mic. 5:2;
Zech. 9:9;
Mal. 3:1–3
22
[s] Cp. Mt.
28:7; Mk.
5:19
[t] Cp. Acts
26:16
[u] Isa. 35:5
[v] Jn. 9:7
[w] Mt. 15:31
[x] Lk.
17:12–14
[y] Mk. 7:37
[z] vv. 14–15
[aa] *Gospel:*
v. 22; Lk.
8:1. (Gen.
12:3; Rev.
14:6)
[bb] Isa. 61:1–3
23
[cc] Cp. 1 Pet.
2:8
25
[dd] Cp. Mt.
3:4
[ee] Cp. 1 Ki.
3:13;
4:21–27
27
[ff] *Inspiration:* v. 27;
Lk. 18:31.
(Ex. 4:15;
2 Tim. 3:16,
note)
[gg] Isa. 40:3;
Mal. 3:1; cp.
Lk. 1:16–17,
76; Jn. 1:23
28
[hh] Lk. 1:15

*
7:10 NU-Text omits *who had been sick.*
7:19 NU-Text reads *the Lord.*

[1](7:24) Having gently reproved John the Baptist's doubt, the Lord bears witness concerning him before others. The Lord Jesus knows when to reprove, and also where and when to praise.

John the Baptist;* but he who is least in the kingdom of God is greater than he."

29 And when all the people heard *Him,* even the tax collectors justified God, having been [a]baptized with the baptism of John.

30 But the [b]Pharisees and [c]lawyers rejected the [d]will of God for themselves, not having been baptized by him.

31 And the Lord said,* "To what then shall I liken the men of this generation, and what are they like?

32 "They are like children sitting in the marketplace and calling to one another, saying:

'We played the flute for
you,
And you did not
dance;
We mourned to you,
And you did not weep.'

33 "For [e]John the Baptist came [f]neither eating bread nor drinking wine, and you say, 'He has a [g]demon.'

34 "The [h]Son of Man has come [i]eating and drinking, and you say, 'Look, a glutton and a winebibber, a friend of tax collectors and [j]sinners!'

35 "But [k]wisdom is justified by all her children."

Jesus anointed in Pharisee's house

36 Then one of the [b]Pharisees asked Him to eat with him. And He went to the Pharisee's house, and sat down to eat.

37 And behold, a woman in the city who was a [j]sinner, when she knew that *Jesus* sat at the table in the Pharisee's house, brought an [l]alabaster flask of fragrant oil,

38 and stood at His feet behind *Him* [m]weeping; and she began to wash His [n]feet with her tears, and wiped *them* with the [o]hair of her head; and she kissed His feet and anointed *them* with the fragrant oil.

39 Now when the Pharisee who had invited Him saw *this,* he spoke to himself, saying, "This man, if He were a [p]prophet, would know who and what manner of woman *this is* who is touching Him, for she is a [j]sinner."

Parable of two debtors

40 And Jesus answered and said to him, "Simon, I have something to say to you." So he said, "Teacher, say it."

41 [q]"There was a certain creditor who had two debtors. One owed five hundred [r]denarii, and the other fifty.

42 "And when they had nothing with which to repay, he freely [s]forgave them both. Tell Me, therefore, which of them will love him more?"

43 Simon answered and said, "I suppose the *one* whom he forgave more." And He said to him, "You have rightly judged."

44 Then He turned to the woman and said to [1]Simon, "Do you see this woman? I entered your house; you gave Me no [t]water for My feet, but she has washed My feet with her tears and wiped *them* with the hair of her head.

45 "You gave Me no [u]kiss, but this woman has not ceased to kiss My feet since the time I came in.

46 "You did not anoint My [v]head with oil, but this woman has anointed My [w]feet with fragrant oil.

47 "Therefore I say to you, her sins, *which are* many, are forgiven, for she loved much. But to whom little is forgiven, *the same* loves little."

48 Then He said to her, [x]"Your [j]sins are [y]forgiven."

49 And those who sat at the table with Him began to say to

*

7:28 NU-Text reads *there is none greater than John.* 7:31 NU-Text and M-Text omit *And the Lord said.*

29
a See Acts 8:12, *note*
30
b See Mt. 3:7, *note 1*
c See Mt. 22:35, *note*
d Or *counsel.* Cp. Acts 20:27
33
e Mt. 3:1
f Mt. 3:4; Lk. 1:15
g See Mt. 7:22, *note*
34
h See Mt. 8:20, *note*
i v. 36; Lk. 15:2
j See Rom. 3:23, *note*
35
k Mt. 11:19; cp. 1 Cor. 1:21–24
37
l Cp. Mt. 26:7
38
m Cp. Zech. 12:10
n Cp. Isa. 52:7
o Cp. 1 Cor. 11:15
39
p v. 16; see Lk. 24:19, *note*
41
q Parables (NT): vv. 41–43; Lk. 8:4. (Mt. 5:13; Lk. 21:29)
r See Coinage (N.T.), Mt. 5:26, *note*
42
s Cp. Ps. 32:1–5; 51:1–3; 103:3; Isa. 1:18; 43:25; 44:22
44
t Gen. 18:4; cp. 1 Tim. 5:10
45
u Rom. 16:16; cp. Mt. 26:48–49
46
v Eccl. 9:8; cp. Ps. 23:5
w Cp. Jn. 13:3–15
48
x Mt. 9:2
y Forgiveness: vv. 47–48; Lk. 11:4. (Lev. 4:20; Mt. 26:28, *note*)

[1](7:44) See Jas. 2:14–26. When Jesus would justify the woman in the eyes of Simon, He points to her works, for only through her works could Simon see the proof of her faith; but when He would send the woman away in peace, He points to her faith (v. 50), not her works. See Ti. 2:14; 3:4–8. The believer should never base his assurance on his own works (cp. Mt. 7:22–23); assurance rests completely on the finished work of Christ. See Assurance (Isa. 32:17; Jude 1, *note*).

themselves, [a]"Who is this who even forgives sins?"

50 Then He said to the woman, "Your [b]faith has saved you. Go in peace."

Women who ministered to Jesus on preaching tours

8 NOW it came to pass, afterward, that He went through every city and village, preaching and bringing the [c]glad tidings of the [d]kingdom of God. And the twelve *were* with Him,

2 [e]and certain [f]women who had been [g]healed of evil spirits and infirmities—Mary called [h]Magdalene, out of whom had come seven [i]demons,

3 and Joanna the wife of Chuza, [j]Herod's steward, and Susanna, and many others who provided for Him* from their substance.

Parable of the sower and the soils (Mt. 13:1–23; Mk. 4:1–20)

4 And when a great multitude had gathered, and they had come to Him from every city, He spoke by a [k]parable:

5 "A sower went out to sow his seed. And as he sowed, some fell by the wayside; and it was trampled down, and the birds of the air devoured it.

6 "Some fell on rock; and as soon as it sprang up, it withered away because it lacked moisture.

7 "And some fell among thorns, and the thorns sprang up with it and choked it.

8 "But others fell on good ground, sprang up, and yielded a crop a hundredfold." When He had said these things He cried, [l]"He who has ears to hear, let him hear!"

9 Then His disciples asked Him, saying, "What does this parable mean?"

10 And He said, "To you it has been given to know the [m]mysteries of the [n]kingdom of God, but to the rest *it is given* in parables, [o]that

'Seeing they may not see,
And hearing they may
not understand.'

11 "Now the parable is this: The [p]seed is the [q]word of God.

12 "Those by the wayside are the ones who hear; then the [r]devil comes and [s]takes away the word out of their [t]hearts, lest they should believe and be [u]saved.

13 "But the ones on the rock *are those* who, when they hear, receive the word with joy; and these [v]have no root, who believe for a while and in time of [w]temptation fall away.

14 "Now the ones *that* fell among [x]thorns are those who, when they have heard, go out and are choked with cares, [y]riches, and pleasures of life, and bring no fruit to maturity.

15 "But the ones *that* fell on the [z]good ground are those who, having heard the word with a noble and good heart, [aa]keep *it* and bear fruit with [bb]patience.

Parable of the lighted lamp (Mt. 5:15–16; Mk. 4:21–23; Lk. 11:33–36)

16 "No one, when he has lit a lamp, covers it with a [cc]vessel or puts *it* under a bed, but sets *it* on a [dd]lampstand, that those who enter may see the [ee]light.

17 "For [ff]nothing is secret that will not be [gg]revealed, nor *anything* hidden that will not be known and come to light.

18 "Therefore take heed how you hear. [hh]For whoever has, to him *more* will be given; and whoever does not have, even what he seems to [ii]have will be taken from him."

New relationships (Mt. 12:46–50; Mk. 3:31–35)

19 Then [jj]His mother and brothers came to Him, and could not approach Him because of the crowd.

20 And it was told Him *by some,* who said, "Your mother and Your brothers are standing outside, desiring to see You."

21 But He answered and said to them, "My mother and My brothers are these who hear the word of God and [kk]do it."

*8:3 NU-Text and M-Text read *them.*

49
a Lk. 5:21
50
b Faith: v. 50; Lk. 8:48. (Gen. 3:20; Heb. 11:39, *note*)
CHAPTER 8
1
c Gospel: v. 1; Lk. 9:6. (Gen. 12:3; Rev. 14:6)
d See Mt. 6:33, *note*
2
e See Mk. 3:15, *note*
f Mk. 15:41
g Miracles (NT): v. 2; Lk. 8:24. (Mt. 8:3; Acts 28:8, *note*)
h Mk. 16:9
i See Mt. 7:22, *note*
3
j Herod Antipas. See Mk. 6:14, *note*
4
k Parables (NT): vv. 4–18; Lk. 10:30. (Mt. 5:13; Lk. 21:29)
8
l Mt. 11:15; Mk. 7:16; Lk. 14:35
10
m See Mt. 13:11, *note*
n Kingdom (NT): v. 10; Lk. 9:26. (Mt. 2:2; 1 Cor. 15:24, *note*)
o Cp. Dt. 29:3–4; Isa. 6:9–10; Acts 28:26–27

11
p 1 Pet. 1:23
q Lk. 5:1; 11:28
12
r Satan: v. 12; Lk. 10:18. (Gen. 3:1; Rev. 20:10)
s Cp. 1 Cor. 2:11
t Cp. v. 15
u See Rom. 1:16, *note*
13
v v. 6
w Test/tempt: v. 13; Lk. 10:25. (Gen. 3:1; Jas. 1:14, *note*). 2 Tim. 4:10
14
x v. 7
y Mt. 19:23; 1 Tim. 6:9–10
15
z v. 8
aa Cp. Jas. 1:22
bb Rom. 2:7; Heb. 10:36; Jas. 5:7–8
16
cc A measuring container
dd Rev. 1:20
ee Mt. 5:14
17
ff Mt. 10:26; Lk. 12:2; 1 Cor. 4:5
gg Eccl. 12:14; 2 Cor. 5:10
18
hh Mt. 25:29
ii Mt. 13:12
19
jj Mt. 13:55–56; Acts 1:14
21
kk v. 15

Jesus stills the wind and the sea
(Mt. 8:23–27; Mk. 4:35–41)

22 Now it happened, on a certain day, that He got into a boat with His disciples. And He said to them, "Let us cross over to the other side of the lake." And they launched out.

23 But as they sailed He fell asleep. And a windstorm came down on the lake, and they were filling *with water,* and were in jeopardy.

24 And they came to Him and awoke Him, [a]saying, "Master, Master, we are perishing!" Then He arose and rebuked the wind and the raging of the water. And they [b]ceased, and there was a calm.

25 But He said to them, [c]"Where is your faith?" And they were afraid, and marveled, saying to one another, [d]"Who can this be? For He commands even the winds and water, and they obey Him!"

Jesus casts out demons at Gadara
(Mt. 8:28–34; Mk. 5:1–20)

26 Then they sailed to the country of the Gadarenes,* which is opposite Galilee.

27 And when He stepped out on the land, there met Him a certain man from the city who had [e]demons for a long time. And he wore no clothes,* nor did he live in a house but in the [f]tombs.

28 When he saw Jesus, he [g]cried out, fell down before Him, and with a loud voice said, [h]"What have I to do with You, Jesus, [i]Son of the [j]Most High God? I beg You, do not torment me!"

29 For He had commanded the unclean spirit to come out of the man. For it had often seized him, and he was kept under guard, bound with chains and shackles; and he [k]broke the bonds and was driven by the [e]demon into the wilderness.

30 Jesus asked him, saying, "What is your name?" And he said, "Legion," because many [e]demons had entered him.

31 And they begged Him that He would not command them to go out into the [l]abyss.

32 Now a herd of many [m]swine was feeding there on the mountain. So they begged Him that He would permit them to enter them. And He [n]permitted them.

33 Then the [e]demons [b]went out of the man and entered the swine, and the herd ran violently down the steep place into the lake and drowned.

34 When those who fed *them* saw what had happened, they fled and told *it* in the city and in the country.

35 Then they went out to see what had happened, and came to Jesus, and found the man from whom the [e]demons had departed, [o]sitting at the [p]feet of Jesus, [q]clothed and in his [r]right mind. And they were afraid.

36 They also who had seen *it* told them by what means he who had been [e]demon-possessed was healed.

37 Then the whole multitude of the surrounding region of the Gadarenes* [1][s]asked Him to [t]depart from them, for they were seized with great [u]fear. And He got into the boat and returned.

38 Now the man from whom the [e]demons had departed [v]begged Him that he might be with Him. But Jesus sent him away, saying,

39 "Return to your own house, and [w]tell what great things God has done for you." And he went his way and [x]proclaimed throughout the whole city what great things Jesus had done for him.

40 So it was, when Jesus returned, that the multitude welcomed Him, for they were all [y]waiting for Him.

*

8:26 NU-Text reads *Gerasenes.*
8:27 NU-Text reads *who had demons and for a long time wore no clothes.*
8:37 NU-Text reads *Gerasenes.*

24 *a Bible prayers* (NT): v. 24; Lk. 9:38. (Mt. 6:9; Lk. 11:2, *note*)
b Miracles (NT): vv. 24, 27–35; Lk. 8:55. (Mt. 8:3; Acts 28:8, *note*)
25 *c* Lk. 9:41; cp. Mt. 8:10
d Lk. 4:36; 5:26; cp. Ps. 107:23–32
27 *e* See Mt. 7:22, *note*
f Cp. Prov. 21:16
28 *g* Mk. 1:26; 9:26; cp. Acts 16:16–17
h Mk. 1:23–24; cp. Jas. 2:19
i Lk. 4:41; cp. Phil. 2:10–11
j Cp. Gen. 14:19
29 *k* Cp. Rom. 8:7

31 *l* Cp. Rev. 20:1–3
32 *m* Lev. 11:7; Dt. 14:8; cp. 2 Pet. 2:22
n Cp. Job 12:16
35 *o* Mt. 11:28
p Mt. 28:9; Mk. 7:25; Lk. 10:39; 17:16; Jn. 11:32
q Cp. Phil. 3:9
r 2 Tim. 1:7
37 *s* Mk. 1:24; Lk. 4:34
t Job 21:14; Acts 16:39; cp. Lk. 4:29–30
u Lk. 5:26
38 *v* Lk. 18:43
39 *w* Cp. Lk. 5:14–15
x Cp. Mt. 11:20; Jn. 4:48
40 *y* Cp. Lk. 12:35–40

[1](8:37) Unconscious of their own need, the Gadarenes asked the Lord to depart; for His power terrified and condemned them. At the same time the man who had been healed begged the Lord that he might follow Him.

Two miracles of healing
(Mt. 9:18–26; Mk. 5:21–43)

41 And behold, there came a man named Jairus, and he was a [a]ruler of the synagogue. And he fell down at Jesus' [b]feet and begged Him to come to his house,

42 for he had an [c]only daughter about twelve years of age, and she was [d]dying. But as He went, the multitudes thronged Him.

43 Now a woman, having a [e]flow of blood for twelve years, who had spent all her livelihood on physicians and could not be healed by any,

44 came from behind and [f]touched the border of His garment. And immediately her flow of blood stopped.

45 And Jesus said, "Who touched Me?" When all denied it, Peter and those with him* said, "Master, the multitudes throng and press You, and You say, 'Who touched Me?' "*

46 But Jesus said, "Somebody touched Me, for I perceived [g]power going out from Me."

47 Now when the woman saw that she was not hidden, she came trembling; and falling down before Him, she [h]declared to Him in the presence of all the people the reason she had touched Him and how she was healed immediately.

48 And He said to her, "Daughter, be of good cheer;* [i]your [j]faith has made you well. [k]Go in peace."

49 While He was still speaking, someone came from the ruler of the synagogue's *house,* saying to him, "Your daughter is dead. Do not trouble the Teacher."*

50 But when Jesus heard *it,* He answered him, saying, "Do not be afraid; only [l]believe, and she will be made well."

51 When He came into the house, He permitted no one to go in* [m]except Peter, James, and John,* and the father and mother of the girl.

52 Now all wept and mourned for her; but He said, [n]"Do not weep; she is not dead, but [o]sleeping."

53 And they ridiculed Him, knowing that she was dead.

54 But He put them all outside,* took her by the hand and called, saying, "Little girl, [p]arise."

55 Then her spirit [q]returned, and she [r]arose immediately. And He commanded that she be given *something* to eat.

56 And her parents were astonished, but He [s]charged them to tell no one what had happened.

The twelve sent forth
(Mt. 10:1–15; cp. Mk. 6:7–13)

9 [t]THEN He called His [u]twelve disciples together and [v]gave them power and authority over all [w]demons, and to cure diseases.

2 He sent them to preach the [x]kingdom of God and to heal the sick.

3 And He said to them, "Take [y]nothing for the journey, neither staffs nor bag nor bread nor money; and do not have two tunics apiece.

4 [z]"Whatever house you enter, stay there, and from there depart.

5 "And whoever will not receive you, when you go out of that city, [aa]shake off the very dust from your feet as a testimony against them."

6 So they departed and went through the towns, preaching the [bb]gospel and healing everywhere.

7 Now [cc]Herod the tetrarch heard of all that was done by Him; and he was perplexed, because it was said by some that [dd]John had risen from the dead,

8 and by some that [ee]Elijah had appeared, and by others that one of the old prophets had risen again.

9 Herod said, "John I have beheaded, but who is this of whom I hear such things?" So he sought to [ff]see Him.

10 And the apostles, when

*

8:45 NU-Text omits *and those with him.* • NU-Text omits *and You say, 'Who touched Me?'* 8:48 NU-Text omits *be of good cheer.* 8:49 NU-Text adds *anymore.* 8:51 NU-Text adds *with Him.* • NU-Text and M-Text read *Peter, John, and James.* 8:54 NU-Text omits *put them all outside.*

41
a Cp. Jn. 7:48
b Mt. 28:9; Mk. 7:25; Lk. 10:39; 17:16; Jn. 11:32

42
c Cp. Lk. 9:38
d Lk. 7:2

43
e Lev. 15:19–22

44
f Mk. 6:56; Lk. 5:13; cp. Acts 5:15; 19:12; Rom. 4:4–5

46
g Cp. Lk. 5:17

47
h Cp. Rom. 10:10

48
i Lk. 7:50
j *Faith:* v. 48; Lk. 17:5. (Gen. 3:20; Heb. 11:39, *note*)
k Jn. 8:11

50
l Mk. 11:22–24

51
m Mt. 17:1; 26:37; Mk. 13:3

52
n Lk. 7:13
o Jn. 11:11

54
p Lk. 7:14; cp. Jn. 5:25, 28

55
q *Miracles* (NT): vv. 41–55; 9:1; Lk. 9:17. (Mt. 8:3; Acts 28:8, *note*)
r *Resurrection:* v. 55; Lk. 9:31. (2 Ki. 4:35; 1 Cor. 15:52, *note*)

56
s Mt. 9:30

CHAPTER 9

1
t See Mk. 3:15, *note*
u vv. 10,12; Mt. 10:2
v Mk. 16:17–18; Jn. 14:12
w See Mt. 7:22, *note*

2
x See Mt. 6:33, *note*

3
y Lk. 10:4; 22:35

4
z Cp. Phil. 4:11

5
aa Lk. 10:10–11

6
bb *Gospel:* v. 6; Lk. 20:1. (Gen. 12:3; Rev. 14:6)

7
cc *Herod Antipas.* See Mk. 6:14, *note*
dd Cp. Mk. 6:14–29

8
ee Cp. 2 Ki. 2:1–11

9
ff Cp. Lk. 23:6–12

they had [a]returned, told Him all that they had done. Then He took them and went aside privately into a [b]deserted place belonging to the city called Bethsaida.

11 But when the multitudes knew *it,* they followed Him; and He received them and spoke to them about the [c]kingdom of God, and healed those who had [1]need of healing.

Five thousand fed (Mt. 14:15–21; Mk. 6:32–44; Jn. 6:5–13)

12 When the day began to wear away, the twelve came and said to Him, "Send the multitude away, that they may go into the surrounding towns and country, and lodge and get provisions; for we are in a deserted place here."

13 But He said to them, "You give them something to eat." And they said, "We have no more than five loaves and two fish, unless we go and buy food for all these people."

14 For there were about five thousand men. Then He said to His disciples, "Make them sit down in groups of fifty."

15 And they did so, and made them all sit down.

16 Then He took the five loaves and the two fish, and looking up to heaven, He [d]blessed and broke *them,* and gave *them* to the disciples to set before the multitude.

17 So they all ate and were [e]filled, and twelve baskets of the [f]leftover fragments were taken up by them.

Peter's confession of Christ (Mt. 16:13–20; Mk. 8:27–30)

18 And it happened, as He was alone praying, *that* His disciples joined Him, and He asked them, saying, "Who do the crowds say that I am?"

19 So they answered and said, [g]"John the Baptist, but some *say* [h]Elijah; and others *say* that one of the old prophets has risen again."

20 He said to them, "But who do you say that I am?" [i]Peter answered and said, "The Christ of God."

21 And He strictly warned and commanded them to tell this to no one,

Jesus foretells His death and resurrection (Mt. 16:21–27; Mk. 8:31–33)

22 saying, "The [j]Son of Man [k]must suffer many things, and be rejected by the elders and chief priests and [l]scribes, and be killed, and be raised the third day."

Cost of discipleship (Mt. 16:24–27; Mk. 8:34–38)

23 Then He said to *them* all, [m]"If anyone desires to come after Me, let him deny himself, and take up his cross daily,* and follow Me.

24 [n]"For whoever desires to save his life will lose it, but whoever loses his life for My sake will save it.

25 "For what profit is it to a man [o]if he gains the whole [p]world, and is himself destroyed or lost?

26 "For whoever is [q]ashamed of Me and My words, of him the [j]Son of Man will be [r]ashamed when He [s]comes in His *own* [t]glory, and *in His* Father's, and of the [u]holy [v]angels.

The transfiguration (Mt. 17:1–8; Mk. 9:2–8)

27 "But I tell you truly, there are some standing here who shall not taste death till they [w]see the kingdom of God."

28 [x]Now it came to pass, about eight days after these sayings, that He took Peter, John, and James and went up on the mountain to pray.

29 As He prayed, the appearance of His face was altered, and His robe *became* white *and* [y]glistening.

30 And behold, [z]two men talked with Him, who were [aa]Moses and [bb]Elijah,

*
9:23 M-Text omits *daily.*

10 *a* Mk. 6:30 *b* Mt. 14:13
11 *c* See Mt. 6:33, *note*
16 *d* Lk. 22:19; 24:30
17 *e Miracles* (NT): vv. 12–17; Lk. 9:42. (Mt. 8:3; Acts 28:8, *note*) *f* Cp. 2 Ki. 4:42–44
19 *g* v. 7 *h* v. 8
20 *i* Jn. 6:68–69
22 *j* See Mt. 8:20, *note* *k* Lk. 18:31–33 *l* See Mt. 2:4, *note*
23 *m* Mt. 10:38; Mk. 8:34–38; Lk. 14:27; cp. Phil. 3:7–11
24 *n* Jn. 12:25
25 *o* Lk. 16:19–31; Acts 1:18,25 *p* Gk. *kosmos.* See Mt. 4:8, *note*
26 *q* Rom. 1:16 *r* Mt. 10:32–33; cp. 2 Tim. 1:8 *s Christ* (second advent): v. 26; Lk. 13:35. (Dt. 30:3; Acts 1:11, *note*). Mt. 25:31 *t Kingdom* (NT): vv. 26–36; Lk. 10:22. (Mt. 2:2; 1 Cor. 15:24, *note*) *u Sanctification* (NT): v. 26; Jn. 10:36. (Mt. 4:5; Rev. 22:11) *v* See Heb. 1:4, *note*
27 *w* Mt. 16:28; cp. 2 Pet. 1:16–18
28 *x* See Mt. 17:2, *note*
29 *y* Cp. Ex. 34:29–35; 2 Cor. 4:6
30 *z* Cp. Rom. 3:21 *aa* Heb. 11:23–29 *bb* 2 Ki. 2:1–11

[1](9:11) Compare Lk. 4:40; Rom. 5:20. Wherever need is acknowledged, the Lord is ready to meet it. Since the need of bodily healing is keenly felt, sometimes men are inclined to put it first. However, spiritual need is greater and, in fact, is often the greatest where there is the least consciousness of it, e.g. Rev. 3:17.

31 who [a]appeared [b]in glory and spoke of His [c]decease which He was about to accomplish at Jerusalem.

32 But Peter and those with him were heavy with [d]sleep; and when they were fully awake, they saw His glory and the two men who stood with Him.

33 Then it happened, as they were parting from Him, *that* Peter said to Jesus, "Master, it is good for us to be here; and let us make [e]three tabernacles: one for You, one for Moses, and one for Elijah"—not knowing what he said.

34 While he was saying this, a cloud came and overshadowed them; and they were fearful as they entered the [f]cloud.

35 And a voice came out of the cloud, saying, [g]"This is My beloved Son.* Hear Him!"

36 When the voice had ceased, Jesus was found alone. But they kept quiet, and told no one in those days any of the things they had seen.

Powerless disciples: the mighty Christ (Mt. 17:14–21; Mk. 9:14–29)

37 Now it happened on the next day, when they had come down from the mountain, that a great multitude met Him.

38 Suddenly a man from the multitude cried out, [h]saying, "Teacher, I implore You, look on my son, for he is my only child.

39 "And behold, a spirit seizes him, and he suddenly cries out; it convulses him so that he foams *at the mouth;* and it departs from him with great difficulty, bruising him.

40 "So I implored Your disciples to cast it out, but they could not."

41 Then Jesus answered and said, "O [i]faithless and perverse generation, how long shall I be with you and bear with you? Bring your son here."

42 And as he was still coming, the [j]demon threw him down and convulsed *him.* Then Jesus rebuked the unclean spirit, [k]healed the child, and gave him back to his father.

43 And they were all amazed at [l]the majesty of God. But while everyone marveled at all the things which Jesus did, He said to His disciples,

Jesus again foretells His death (Mt. 17:22–23; Mk. 9:30–32)

44 "Let these words [m]sink down into your ears, for the [n]Son of Man is about to be [o]betrayed into the hands of men."

45 [p]But they did not understand this saying, and it was hidden from them so that they did not perceive it; and they were afraid to ask Him about this saying.

Humility, the secret of greatness (Mt. 18:1–6; Mk. 9:33–37)

46 Then a [q]dispute arose among them as to which of them would be greatest.

47 And Jesus, [r]perceiving the thought of their heart, took a little [s]child and set him by Him,

48 and said to them, [t]"Whoever receives this little child in My name receives Me; and [u]whoever receives Me [v]receives Him who sent Me. For he who is [w]least among you all will be great."

Sectarianism rebuked (Mt. 9:38–40)

49 Now John answered and said, "Master, we saw someone casting out [j]demons in Your name, and we forbade him because he does not follow with [x]us."

50 But Jesus said to him, [y]"Do not forbid *him,* for he who is not against us* is [z]on our* side."

Jesus again passes through Samaria

51 Now it came to pass, when the time had come for Him to be received up, that He [aa]steadfastly set His face to go to Jerusalem,

52 and sent messengers before His face. And as they went, they entered a village of the Samaritans, to prepare for Him.

53 But they did not receive

31
a *Resurrection:* vv. 30–31; Lk. 14:14. (2 Ki. 4:35; 1 Cor. 15:52, *note*)
b Cp. Phil. 3:21; Col. 3:4; 1 Jn. 3:2
c Or *departure, exodus.* Cp. 1 Pet. 1:10–12
32
d Mt. 26:40, 43
33
e Cp. vv. 19–20; Jn. 14:8–11
34
f Ex. 13:21; Acts 1:9
35
g Mt. 3:17
38
h *Bible prayers* (NT): vv. 38–40; Lk. 10:21. (Mt. 6:9; Lk. 11:2, *note*)
41
i Cp. Jn. 14:12
42
j See Mt. 7:22, *note*
k *Miracles* (NT): vv. 38–42; Lk. 11:14. (Mt. 8:3; Acts 28:8, *note*)
43
l 2 Pet. 1:16
44
m Cp. vv. 31, 45; Mt. 17:22
n See Mt. 8:20, *note*
o v. 22; Mk. 10:33
45
p Lk. 2:50
46
q Lk. 22:24–27
47
r Mt. 9:4; Jn. 2:24–25
s Lk. 18:17
48
t Mt. 18:5
u Mt. 10:40; Jn. 12:44
v Jn. 13:20
w 1 Cor. 15:9; Eph. 3:8
49
x Cp. 1 Cor. 3:5–8
50
y Cp. Num. 11:26–30
z Cp. Lk. 11:23; Phil. 1:15–18
51
aa Isa. 50:7; cp. Mt. 26:53–54; Heb. 12:2

---

*9:35 NU-Text reads *This is My Son, the Chosen One.* 9:50 NU-Text reads *you.*
• NU-Text reads *your.*

Him, because His face was *set*
for the journey to Jerusalem.
54 And when His disciples
[a]James and John saw *this,* they
said, "Lord, do You want us to
command fire to come down
from heaven and consume
them, just as [b]Elijah did?"*
55 But He turned and re-
buked them,* and said, "You do
not know what manner of
[c]spirit you are of.
56 "For the [d]Son of Man did
not [e]come to destroy men's
lives but to [f]save *them.*"* And
they went to another village.

Discipleship tested
(Mt. 8:19–22)

57 Now it happened as they
journeyed on the road, *that*
someone said to Him, "Lord, I
will follow You wherever You
go."
58 And Jesus said to him,
"Foxes have holes and birds of
the air *have* nests, but the [d]Son
of Man [g]has nowhere to lay *His*
head."
59 Then He said to another,
"Follow Me." But he said, "Lord,
let me first go and [h]bury my father."
60 Jesus said to him, "Let the
[i]dead bury their own [j]dead,
but you go and preach the
[k]kingdom of God."
61 And another also said,
"Lord, I will follow You, but let
me first go *and* bid them farewell who are at my house."
62 But Jesus said to him, "No
one, having put his hand to the
plow, and looking [l]back, is [m]fit
for the [k]kingdom of God."

The seventy sent forth
(contra. Mt. 10)

10 AFTER these things the
Lord appointed seventy
others also,* and sent them two
by two before His face into every city and place where He
Himself was about to go.
2 Then He said to them,
"The [n]harvest truly *is* great, but
the laborers *are* few; therefore
pray the Lord of the harvest to
send out [o]laborers into His harvest.
3 "Go your way; behold, I
send you out as lambs among
wolves.

54
a Mk. 3:17
b v. 30; 2 Ki. 1:10,12
55
c Rom. 8:15; 2 Tim. 1:7
56
d See Mt. 8:20, *note*
e Christ (first advent): v. 56; Lk. 19:38. (Gen. 3:15; Acts 1:11, *note*)
f Lk. 19:10; Jn. 3:17; 12:47; see Rom. 1:16, *note*
58
g Lk. 2:7; 8:23; cp. 1 Cor. 4:11
59
h Cp. Lk. 18:28–30
60
i Death (spiritual): v. 60; Lk. 15:24. (Gen. 2:17; Eph. 2:5, *note*)
j See Heb. 9:27, *note*
k See Mt. 6:33, *note*
62
l Cp. Gen. 19:17,26; Phil. 3:13–14
m 2 Tim. 4:10
CHAPTER 10
2
n Mt. 9:37; Jn. 4:35
o 1 Cor. 3:9

4 [p]"Carry neither money
bag, [q]knapsack, nor sandals;
and [r]greet no one along the
road.
5 "But whatever house you
enter, first say, [s]'Peace to this
house.'
6 "And if a son of peace is
there, your peace will rest on it;
if not, it will return to you.
7 "And remain in the same
house, eating and drinking such
things as they give, [t]for the laborer is worthy of his wages. Do
not go from house to house.
8 "Whatever city you enter,
and they receive you, eat such
things as are set before you.
9 "And heal the sick there,
and say to them, 'The [k]kingdom
of God has come near to you.'
10 "But whatever city you enter, and they do not receive you,
go out into its streets and say,
11 'The very dust of your city
which clings to us* we [u]wipe
off against you. Nevertheless
know this, that the [k]kingdom of
God has come near you.'
12 "But* I say to you that it
will be more [v]tolerable in that
[w]Day for Sodom than for that
city.

Jesus denounces the indifferent
(Mt. 11:20–24)

13 [x]"Woe to you, Chorazin!
Woe to you, Bethsaida! For if
the mighty works which were
done in you had been done in
Tyre and Sidon, they would
have [y]repented long ago, sitting
in sackcloth and ashes.
14 "But it will be more tolerable for Tyre and Sidon at the
judgment than for you.
15 "And you, Capernaum,
who are [z]exalted to heaven,
will be brought down to [aa]Ha-
des.*
16 "He who [bb]hears you hears
Me, he who [cc]rejects you rejects
Me, and he who rejects Me rejects Him who sent Me."
17 Then the seventy* re-

4
p Lk. 9:3
q Cp. Lk. 22:35
r Cp. Gen. 24:33,56; 2 Ki. 4:29
5
s 1 Sam. 25:6; cp. Isa. 57:21
7
t 1 Tim. 5:18
11
u Lk. 9:5; Acts 13:51
12
v Lam. 4:6; cp. Lk. 12:47; Heb. 2:3; 10:26
w Day (of judgment): vv. 12–15; Lk. 11:31. (Mt. 10:15; Rev. 20:11)
13
x See Mt. 11:20 and Mk. 8:23, *notes*
y Repentance: v. 13; Lk. 11:32. (Mt. 3:2; Acts 17:30, *note*)
15
z Cp. Isa. 14:13,15
aa See Lk. 16:23, *note*
16
bb Cp. Mt. 16:19; 18:18
cc 1 Th. 4:8; cp. Jn. 5:23; 13:20

*
9:54 NU-Text omits *just as Elijah did.*
9:55 NU-Text omits the rest of this verse.
9:56 NU-Text omits the first sentence of this verse. **10:1** NU-Text reads *seventy-two others.* **10:11** NU-Text reads *our feet.*
10:12 NU-Text and M-Text omit *But.*
10:15 NU-Text reads *will you be exalted to heaven? You will be thrust down to Hades!*
10:17 NU-Text reads *seventy-two.*

turned with joy, saying, "Lord, even the [a]demons are subject to us in Your name."

18 And He said to them, "I saw [b]Satan [c]fall like lightning from heaven.

19 "Behold, I give you the authority to [d]trample on serpents and scorpions, and over all the power of the enemy, and nothing shall by any means hurt you.

20 "Nevertheless do not rejoice in this, that the spirits are subject to you, but rather* rejoice because your names are [e]written in heaven."

21 In that hour Jesus rejoiced in [f]the Spirit and [g]said, "I thank You, Father, Lord of heaven and earth, that You have hidden these things from *the* wise and prudent and revealed them to babes. Even so, Father, for so it seemed good in Your sight.

22 "All* things have been [h]delivered to Me by My Father, and no one knows who the Son is except the Father, [i]and who the Father is except the Son, and *the one* to whom the Son wills to reveal *Him.*"

23 Then He turned to *His* disciples and said privately, [j]"Blessed *are* the eyes which see the things you see;

24 "for I tell you that many [k]prophets and kings have desired to see what you see, and have not seen *it,* and to hear what you hear, and have not heard *it.*"

A lawyer questions Jesus
(cp. Mt. 22:34–40; Mk. 12:28–34)

25 And behold, a certain lawyer stood up and [l]tested Him, saying, "Teacher, what shall I do to inherit [m]eternal life?"

26 He said to him, "What is written in the [n]law? What is your reading *of it?*"

27 So he answered and said, [o]"'*You shall love the* LORD *your God with all your heart, with all your soul, with all your strength, and with all your mind,*' and '*your neighbor as yourself.*'"

28 And He said to him, "You have answered rightly; do this and you will live."

29 But he, wanting to [p]justify himself, said to Jesus, "And who is my neighbor?"

Parable of the good Samaritan

30 Then Jesus answered and [q]said: "A certain *man* went down from Jerusalem to Jericho, and fell among thieves, who stripped him of his clothing, wounded *him,* and departed, leaving *him* half dead.

31 "Now by chance a certain priest came down that road. And when he saw him, he passed by on the other side.

32 "Likewise a Levite, when he arrived at the place, came and looked, and passed by on the other side.

33 "But a certain [r]Samaritan, as he journeyed, came where he was. And when he saw him, he had [s]compassion.

34 "So he went to *him* and bandaged his wounds, pouring on oil and wine; and he set him on his own animal, brought him to an inn, and took care of him.

35 "On the next day, when he departed,* he took out two [t]denarii, gave *them* to the innkeeper, and said to him, 'Take care of him; and whatever more you spend, when I come again, I will repay you.'

36 "So which of these three do you think was neighbor to him who fell among the thieves?"

37 And he said, "He who showed mercy on him." Then Jesus said to him, [u]"Go and do likewise."

Martha and Mary in contrast

38 Now it happened as they went that He entered a certain village; and a certain woman named [v]Martha welcomed Him into her house.

39 And she had a sister called [w]Mary, who also sat at Jesus'* feet and heard His [x]word.

40 But Martha was distracted with much serving, and she approached Him and said, "Lord, do You not [y]care that my sister has left me to serve alone?

*
10:20 NU-Text and M-Text omit *rather.* **10:22** M-Text reads *And turning to the disciples He said, "All ....* **10:35** NU-Text omits *when he departed.* **10:39** NU-Text reads *the Lord's.*

17
a See Mt. 7:22, *note*
18
b Satan: v. 18; Lk. 11:18. (Gen. 3:1; Rev. 20:10)
c Jn. 12:31; cp. Isa. 14:12–19; Jn. 16:11; Rev. 12:8–9
19
d Mk. 16:18; cp. Acts 28:5
20
e Isa. 4:3; Dan. 12:1; cp. Ex. 32:32; Ps. 69:28; Rev. 13:8
21
f Some mss. read *the Holy Spirit*
g Bible prayers (NT): v. 21; Lk. 11:2. (Mt. 6:9; Lk. 11:2, *note*)
22
h Kingdom (NT): v. 22; Lk. 11:2. (Mt. 2:2; 1 Cor. 15:24, *note*). Jn. 3:35; Heb. 2:8
i Jn. 1:18
23
j Mt. 13:16
24
k 1 Pet. 1:10–11; cp. Jn. 8:56
25
l Test/tempt: v. 25; Lk. 11:4. (Gen. 3:1; Jas. 1:14, *note*)
m Life (eternal): vv. 25–28; Lk. 12:15. (Mt. 7:14; Rev. 22:19)
26
n Law (of Moses): vv. 26–27; Lk. 16:16. (Ex. 19:1; Gal. 3:24, *note*)
27
o Lev. 19:18; Dt. 6:5; Mt. 19:19

29
p Lk. 16:15; cp. Gal. 3:11
30
q Parables (NT): vv. 30–37; Lk. 11:5. (Mt. 5:13; Lk. 21:29)
33
r Jn. 4:9
s Lk. 15:20
35
t See Coinage (NT), Mt. 5:26, *note*
37
u Prov. 14:21; Mt. 9:13; 12:7; cp. Mic. 6:8
38
v Jn. 11:1; 12:2
39
w Jn. 11:1; 19–20,28–32
x Lk. 4:32; Jn. 4:41; cp. Jn. 5:38
40
y Cp. 1 Pet. 5:7

41
a Mk. 4:19; Lk. 21:34; cp. Mt. 6:25–34
42
b Ps. 27:4; cp. Lk. 18:22

CHAPTER 11
2
c *Bible prayers* (NT): vv. 2–4; Lk. 15:18. (Mt. 6:9; Lk. 11:2, *note*)
d *Kingdom* (NT): v. 2; Lk. 12:32. (Mt. 2:2; 1 Cor. 15:24, *note*)
4
e *Forgiveness:* v. 4; Lk. 17:3. (Lev. 4:20; Mt. 26:28, *note*)
f See Rom. 3:23, *note*
g Eph. 4:32; see Mt. 6:12, *note*
h Cp. Lk. 22:46; 1 Cor. 10:13; Jas. 1:13–15
i *Test/tempt:* v. 4; Lk. 11:16. (Gen. 3:1; Jas. 1:14, *note*)

Therefore tell her to help me."
41 And Jesus* answered and
said to her, "Martha, Martha,
you are [a]worried and troubled
about many things.
42 "But [b]one thing is needed,
and Mary has chosen that good
part, which will not be taken
away from her."

Christ's instruction about prayer
(cp. Mt. 6:9–15)

11 NOW it came to pass, as
He was praying in a cer-
tain place, when He ceased,
that one of His disciples said to
Him, "Lord, teach us to pray, as
John also taught his disciples."
2 So He said to them,
"When you pray, [1c]say:

Our Father in heaven,*
Hallowed be Your name.
Your [d]kingdom come.*
Your will be done
On earth as *it is* in
heaven.
3 Give us day by day our
daily bread.
4 And [e]forgive us our
[f]sins,
For we also [g]forgive
everyone who is
indebted to us.
And do not [h]lead us into
[i]temptation,
But deliver us from the
evil one."*

Parable of the persistent friend
5 And He said to them,
[j]"Which of you shall have a
friend, and go to him at midnight and say to him, 'Friend,
lend me three loaves;
6 'for a friend of mine has
come to me on his journey, and
I have nothing to set before
him';
7 "and he will answer from
within and say, 'Do not trouble
me; the door is now shut, and
my children are with me in bed;
I cannot rise and give to you'?
8 "I say to you, though he
will not rise and give to him because he is his friend, yet because of his [k]persistence he will
rise and give him as many as he
needs.
9 "So I say to you, [l]ask, and
it will be given to you; [m]seek,
and you will find; knock, and it
will be opened to you.
10 "For everyone who asks
receives, and he who seeks
finds, and to him who knocks it
will be opened.

Parable of fatherhood
11 [j]"If a son asks for bread*
from any father among you, will

5
j *Parables* (NT): vv. 5–8, 11–13; Lk. 11:33. (Mt. 5:13; Lk. 21:29). Mt. 7:9–10
8
k Cp. Lk. 18:1–8
9
l Ps. 50:14–15; Jer. 33:3; Mk. 11:24; Jn. 15:7; Jas. 1:5–6; 1 Jn. 3:22; 5:14–15
m Isa. 55:6

*
10:41 NU-Text reads *the Lord.*
11:2 NU-Text omits *Our* and *in heaven.*
• NU-Text omits the rest of this verse.
11:4 NU-Text omits *But deliver us from the evil one.* **11:11** NU-Text omits the words from *bread* through *for* in the next sentence.

[1](11:2) Bible prayers (NT), Summary: This well-loved prayer which our Lord taught His disciples, known as The Lord's Prayer, was evidently given upon two separate occasions and under different circumstances, and with some variations: first, in the Sermon on the Mount, while Christ was warning His disciples against ostentatious formality in prayer (cp. Mt. 5:1 with 6:5–13, where see *notes*); and second, at an unnamed "certain place" in response to the request of one of the disciples, "Lord, teach us to pray" (Lk. 11:1–4). Although the Lord's Prayer was obviously not given to be used only as a form, the two accounts teach us many precious lessons about the nature of prayer.

(1) Such prayer is based upon the relationship of God as the Father of all who truly believe in His Son (Jn. 1:13), for only these can truly say, "Our Father" (Mt. 6:9). (2) It must begin with the attitude of worship: "Hallowed be Your name"—an acknowledgement of the absolute holiness of all that God is and does. (3) In the sense of petition, prayer must put first the kingdom and its coming down from heaven. (4) True prayer accepts in advance the will of God, whether known or unknown, whether to grant or to withhold. (5) Prayer should always envision the divine will and kingdom as objectives which will certainly be realized on earth. (6) In the meantime the children of God may be properly concerned in prayer with present physical needs. (7) Prayer may be hindered when the fellowship of the children with their Father is broken because of sin (Mt. 6:12,15). And (8) the children of God must be divinely taught "to pray," not merely *how* to pray (Lk. 11:1). This prayer, as originally given, does not specify in detail the complete doctrine of prayer for the Church, although it contains it in germ. The element of thanksgiving is not specifically mentioned (cp. Phil. 4:6–7), yet surely thanksgiving is implicit in "Hallowed be Your name"; for who can hallow God, i.e. hold Him sacred and offer worship to Him, without thanksgiving? Later, in the progress of divine revelation, our Lord gave the definite command to believers to pray in His name (Jn. 16:23–24).

he give him a stone? Or if *he*
asks for a fish, will he give him
a serpent instead of a fish?
12 "Or if he asks for an egg,
will he offer him a scorpion?
13 "If you then, being evil,
know how to give [a]good gifts to
your children, how much more
will *your* heavenly Father [1]give
the [b]Holy Spirit to those who
ask Him!"

A demoniac boy healed

14 And He was casting out a
[c]demon, and it was mute. So it
was, when the demon had
[d]gone out, that the mute spoke;
and the multitudes marveled.

Pharisees blaspheme
the Holy Spirit
(Mt. 12:24–30; Mk. 3:22–30)

15 But some of them said,
"He casts out [c]demons by [e]Be-
elzebub,* the ruler of the demons."
16 Others, [f]testing *Him*,
sought from Him a sign from
heaven.
17 But He, [g]knowing their
thoughts, said to them: "Every
kingdom divided against itself
is brought to desolation, and a
house *divided* against a house
falls.
18 "If [h]Satan also is divided
against himself, how will his
kingdom stand? Because you
say I cast out [c]demons by Beelzebub.
19 "And if I [i]cast out [c]de-
mons [e]by Beelzebub, by whom
do your sons cast *them* out?
Therefore they will be your
judges.
20 "But if I cast out [c]demons
with the [j]finger of God, surely
the kingdom of God has come
upon you.
21 "When a strong man, fully
armed, guards his own palace,
his goods are in peace.
22 "But when a [k]stronger
than he comes upon him and
overcomes him, he [l]takes from
him all his armor in which he
trusted, and divides his spoils.
23 "He who is not with Me is
[m]against Me, and he who does
not gather with Me scatters.

Worthlessness of self-reformation
(Mt. 12:43–45)

24 "When an [n]unclean spirit
goes out of a man, he goes
through dry places, seeking
rest; and finding none, he says,
'I will return to my house from
which I came.'
25 "And when he comes, he
finds *it* [o]swept and put in order.
26 "Then he goes and takes
with *him* seven other spirits
more wicked than himself, and
they enter and dwell there; and
the last *state* of that man is
[p]worse than the first."
27 And it happened, as He
spoke these things, that a certain woman from the crowd
raised her voice and said to
Him, [q]"Blessed *is* the womb
that bore You, and *the* breasts
which nursed You!"
28 But He said, "More than
that, [r]blessed *are* those who
hear the word of God and keep
it!"

The sign of Jonah
(Mt. 12:38–41)

29 And while the crowds
were thickly gathered together,
He began to say, "This is an
evil generation. It seeks a [s]sign,
and no sign will be given to it
except the [t]sign of Jonah the
prophet.*
30 "For [u]as Jonah became a
sign to the Ninevites, so also the
[v]Son of Man will be to this generation.
31 "The [w]queen of the South
will rise up in the [x]judgment
with the men of this generation
and condemn them, for she
came from the ends of the earth
to hear the wisdom of Solomon;
and indeed a [y]greater than Solomon *is* here.
32 "The men of Nineveh will

*
11:15 NU-Text and M-Text read *Beelzebul*
11:29 NU-Text omits *the prophet.*

13
a Jas. 1:17
b Holy Spirit (NT): v. 13; Lk. 12:10. (Mt. 1:18; Acts 2:4, *note*)
14
c See Mt. 7:22, *note*
d Miracles (NT): v. 14; Lk. 13:13. (Mt. 8:3; Acts 28:8, *note*)
15
e Mt. 9:34
16
f Test/tempt: v. 16; Lk. 20:23. (Gen. 3:1; Jas. 1:14, *note*)
17
g Mt. 9:4
18
h Satan: v. 18; Lk. 13:16. (Gen. 3:1; Rev. 20:10)
19
i Cp. Mk. 9:38
20
j Ex. 8:19; cp. Jn. 3:2; Acts 2:22
22
k Cp. Heb. 2:14–15; Rev. 20:2–3
l Cp. 1 Jn. 4:4

23
m Cp. Lk. 9:50
24
n Mk. 1:27; 3:11; 5:13; Acts 5:16; 8:7
25
o Cp. 1 Cor. 3:16; Eph. 3:16–17; 5:18
26
p Cp. Jn. 5:14; Heb. 6:4–8; 10:26–29
27
q Lk. 1:28,48
28
r Ps. 1:1–2; 112:1; 119:1–2; Isa. 48:17–18; Jas. 1:25; cp. Mt. 7:21; Lk. 8:21
29
s 1 Cor. 1:22
t Mt. 12:39
30
u v. 32; Jon. 1:17; 3:3–10
v See Mt. 8:20, *note*
31
w 1 Ki. 10:1–9; 2 Chr. 9:1–8
x Day (of judgment): vv. 31–32; Jn. 5:22. (Mt. 10:15; Rev. 20:11)
y Isa. 9:6; Rom. 9:5; cp. Phil. 2:9–11

[1](11:13) To the Jew this promise was undoubtedly new and staggering, for it indicates that in advance of the fulfillment of Joel 2:28–29, all might receive the Holy Spirit. It should be kept in mind, however, that in accordance with the promise, as recorded in Lk. 24:49; Jn. 7:38–39; 14:16–17; Acts 1:4–5, and with the historic fact stated in Rom. 8:9,15; 1 Cor. 6:19; 2 Cor. 1:22; Gal. 4:6; 1 Jn. 2:20,27, for the Christian to go back to Lk. 11:13 is to forget Pentecost and to ignore the truth that now every believer has the indwelling Spirit. See Acts 2:4, *note*.

rise up in the judgment with this
generation and condemn it, for
they [a]repented at the preaching
of Jonah; and indeed a [b]greater
than Jonah *is* here.

Parable of lighted lamp
(Mt. 5:14–16; Mk. 4:21–22;
cp. Lk. 8:16)

33 [c]"No one, when he has lit
a lamp, puts *it* in a secret place
or under a basket, but on a
lampstand, that those who
come in may see the light.
34 "The [d]lamp of the body is
the eye. Therefore, when your
eye is good, your whole body
also is full of light. But when
your eye is bad, your body also
is full of darkness.
35 "Therefore take heed that
the light which is in you is not
darkness.
36 "If then your whole body
is [e]full of light, having no part
dark, *the* whole *body* will be
full of light, as when the bright
shining of a lamp gives you
light."
37 And as He spoke, a certain
[f]Pharisee asked Him to dine
with him. So He went in and sat
down to eat.
38 When the Pharisee saw *it*,
he marveled that He had not
first [g]washed before dinner.

Woes to the Pharisees
(cp. Mt. 23:13–35)

39 Then the Lord said to him,
"Now you Pharisees make the
outside of the cup and dish
clean, but your [h]inward part is
full of greed and wickedness.
40 "Foolish ones! Did not
[i]He who made the outside
make the inside also?
41 "But rather [j]give alms of
such things as you have; then
indeed all things are clean to
you.
42 "But woe to you Phari-
sees! For you tithe mint and rue
and all manner of herbs, and
[k]pass by justice and the [l]love of
God. These you ought to have
done, without leaving the others undone.
43 "Woe to you Pharisees!
For you [m]love the best seats in
the synagogues and greetings
in the marketplaces.
44 "Woe to you, scribes and
Pharisees, hypocrites!* [n]For
you are like [o]graves which are
not seen, and the men who walk
over *them* are not aware of
them."
45 Then one of the [p]lawyers
answered and said to Him,
"Teacher, by saying these
things You reproach us also."
46 And He said, "Woe to you
also, [p]lawyers! For you [q]load
men with burdens hard to bear,
and [r]you yourselves do not
touch the burdens with one of
your fingers.
47 "Woe to you! For you
build the tombs of the prophets,
and your fathers [s]killed them.
48 "In fact, you bear witness
that you approve the deeds of
your fathers; for they indeed
killed them, and you build their
tombs.
49 "Therefore the [t]wisdom
of God also said, 'I will send
them prophets and apostles,
and *some* of them they will kill
and persecute,'
50 "that the blood of all the
prophets which was shed from
the foundation of the [u]world
may be [v]required of this generation,
51 [w]"from the blood of Abel
to the blood of Zechariah who
perished between the altar and
the temple. Yes, I say to you, it
shall be required of this generation.
52 "Woe to you [p]lawyers!
For you have taken away the
[x]key of knowledge. You did not
enter in yourselves, and those
who were entering in you [y]hin-
dered."
53 And as He said these
things to them,* the [z]scribes
and the Pharisees began to as-
sail *Him* vehemently, and to
cross-examine Him about many
things,
54 lying in wait for Him, and
[aa]seeking to catch Him in something He might say, that they
might accuse Him.*

*
11:44 NU-Text omits *scribes and Pharisees, hypocrites.* **11:53** NU-Text reads *And when He left there.* **11:54** NU-Text omits *and seeking* and *that they might accuse Him.*

32
a Repentance: v. 32; Lk. 13:3. (Mt. 3:2; Acts 17:30, *note*)
b Isa. 9:6; Rom. 9:5; cp. Phil. 2:9–11
33
c Parables (NT): vv. 33–36; Lk. 12:16. (Mt. 5:13; Lk. 21:29)
34
d Mt. 6:22–23; Acts 26:16–18
36
e Cp. Ps. 119:18
37
f See Mt. 3:7, *note 1*
38
g Mk. 7:2–3
39
h Gen. 6:5; cp. Jas. 4:8
40
i Gen. 1:26–27
41
j Lk. 12:33
42
k Mic. 6:7–8; cp. 1 Sam. 15:22
l Jn. 5:42
43
m Mt. 23:6; Mk. 12:38
44
n Cp. Acts 23:3
o Ps. 5:9; cp. Num. 19:16
45
p See Mt. 22:35, *note*
46
q Mt. 23:4
r Cp. Rom. 2:17–24
47
s Acts 7:52
49
t Prov. 1:20
50
u Gk. *kosmos.* See Mt. 4:8, *note*
v Cp. Jer. 51:56; Rev. 18:24
51
w 2 Chr. 36:16; see Mt. 23:35, *notes*
52
x Cp. Mt. 16:19
y Cp. Mal. 2:7; Mk. 7:13
53
z See Mt. 2:4, *note*
54
aa Mk. 12:13

Jesus warns of false doctrine (leaven) of Pharisees (cp. Mt. 16:6–12; Mk. 8:14–21)

12 IN the meantime, when an innumerable multitude of people had gathered together, so that they trampled one another, He began to say to His disciples first *of all,* "Beware of the [a]leaven of the [b]Pharisees, which is [c]hypocrisy.

2 [d]"For there is nothing covered that will not be [e]revealed, nor hidden that will not be known.

3 "Therefore whatever you have spoken in the dark will be heard in the light, and what you have spoken in the ear in [f]inner rooms will be proclaimed on the housetops.

4 "And I say to you, My [g]friends, do not be afraid of those who kill the body, and after that have no more that they can do.

5 "But I will show you whom you should fear: Fear Him who, after He has killed, has power to cast into [h]hell; yes, I say to you, [i]fear Him!

6 "Are not five sparrows sold for two [j]copper coins?* And [k]not one of them is forgotten before God.

7 "But the very hairs of your head are all numbered. Do not fear therefore; you are of more value than many sparrows.

8 "Also I say to you, [l]whoever confesses Me [m]before men, him the [n]Son of Man also will confess before the [o]angels of God.

9 "But he who [p]denies Me before men will be denied before the [o]angels of God.

10 "And anyone who speaks a word against the [n]Son of Man, it will be [q]forgiven him; but to him who blasphemes against the Holy [r]Spirit, it will not be forgiven.

11 "Now when they bring you to the synagogues and magistrates and authorities, [s]do not worry about how or what you should answer, or what you should say.

12 "For the Holy [r]Spirit will [t]teach you in that very hour what you ought to say."

13 Then one from the crowd said to Him, "Teacher, tell my brother to divide the inheritance with me."

14 But He said to him, "Man, who made Me a [u]judge or an arbitrator over you?"

15 And He said to them, "Take heed and beware of covetousness,* for one's [v]life does not consist in the abundance of the things he possesses."

Parable of the rich fool

16 Then He spoke a [w]parable to them, saying: "The ground of a certain rich man yielded plentifully.

17 "And he thought within himself, saying, 'What shall I do, since I have no room to store my crops?'

18 "So he said, [x]'I will do this: I will pull down my barns and build greater, and there I will store all my crops and my goods.

19 'And I will say to my soul, [y]"Soul, you have many goods laid up for many years; take your ease; [z]eat, drink, *and* be merry." '

20 "But God said to him, [aa]'Fool! [bb]This night your soul will be required of you; then [cc]whose will those things be which you have provided?'

21 "So *is* he who lays up treasure for himself, and is not [dd]rich toward God."

22 Then He [ee]said to His disciples, "Therefore I say to you, [ff]do not worry about your life, what you will eat; nor about the body, what you will put on.

23 "Life is more than food, and the [gg]body *is more* than clothing.

24 "Consider the ravens, for they neither sow nor reap, which have neither storehouse nor barn; and God [hh]feeds them. Of how much more value are you than the birds?

25 "And which of you by worrying can add one [ii]cubit to his stature?

26 "If you then are not able to do *the* least, why are you anxious for the rest?

---

*

12:6 Greek *assarion,* a coin of very small value **12:15** NU-Text reads *all covetousness.*

CHAPTER 12

1
a *Leaven:* v. 1; Lk. 13:21. (Gen. 19:3; Mt. 13:33, *note*)
b See Mt. 3:7, *note 1*
c Mt. 16:12; Lk. 11:39

2
d vv. 2–9; cp. Mt. 10:26–33
e 1 Cor. 4:5

3
f Cp. Mt. 6:6

4
g Jn. 15:15

5
h Gk. *geenna.* See Mt. 5:22, *note*
i Ps. 119:120

6
j See Coinage (NT), Mt. 5:26, *note*
k Mt. 6:26

8
l 1 Sam. 2:30; Mt. 10:32; Rom. 10:9
m Ps. 119:46
n See Mt. 8:20, *note*
o See Heb. 1:4, *note*

9
p Mt. 10:33; Mk. 8:38; 2 Tim. 2:12

10
q Mt. 12:31–32
r *Holy Spirit* (NT): vv. 10,12; Lk. 24:49. (Mt. 1:18; Acts 2:4, *note*)

11
s Mt. 10:19; cp. Lk. 21:12–15

12
t Jn. 14:26; cp. Ex. 4:12

14
u Cp. Jn. 18:36

15
v *Life* (eternal): v. 15; Lk. 18:18. (Mt. 7:14; Rev. 22:19)

16
w *Parables* (NT): vv. 16–21; Lk. 12:35. (Mt. 5:13; Lk. 21:29)

18
x Cp. Hab. 2:9; Jas. 4:13–15

19
y Cp. Prov. 27:1
z Eccl. 2:24; 3:13; 5:18; 8:15; cp. 1 Cor. 15:32

20
aa Or *senseless one*
bb Ps. 52:5; cp. Dan. 5:30; Acts 12:23
cc Ps. 39:6

21
dd Jas. 5:1–5; cp. Ps. 52:7

22
ee vv. 22–31; cp. Mt. 6:25–34
ff Phil. 4:6

23
gg Cp. Ps. 139:14

24
hh Job 38:41; Ps. 147:9

25
ii See Weights and Measures (NT), Acts 27:28, *note*

27 "Consider the lilies, how they grow: they neither toil nor spin; and yet I say to you, even [a]Solomon in all his glory was not arrayed like one of these.

28 "If then God so clothes the grass, which today is in the field and tomorrow is thrown into the oven, how much more *will He clothe* you, O *you* of [b]little faith?

29 "And do not seek what you should eat or what you should drink, nor have an anxious mind.

30 "For all these things the nations of the [c]world seek after, and your Father [d]knows that you need these things.

31 "But seek the [e]kingdom of God, and all these things* shall be added to you.

32 "Do not fear, little flock, for it is your Father's good pleasure to [f]give you the [g]kingdom.

33 [h]"Sell what you have and give [i]alms; provide yourselves money bags which do not grow old, a [j]treasure in the heavens that does not fail, where no thief approaches nor moth destroys.

34 [k]"For where your treasure is, there your heart will be also.

Parable and warnings pertinent to Christ's second coming (Mt. 24:37—25:30)

35 [l]"Let your waist be [m]girded and *your* [n]lamps burning;

36 "and you yourselves be like men who wait for their master, when he will return from the wedding, that when he comes and knocks they may open to him immediately.

37 [o]"Blessed *are* those servants whom the master, when he [p]comes, will find [q]watching. Assuredly, I say to you that he will gird himself and have them sit down *to eat,* and will come and serve them.

38 "And if he should come in the [r]second watch, or come in the [s]third watch, and find *them* so, blessed are those servants.

39 "But know this, that if the master of the house had known what hour the [t]thief would come, he would have watched and* not allowed his house to be broken into.

40 "Therefore you also be ready, for the [u]Son of Man is coming at an hour you do not expect."

Parable of testing of servants

41 Then Peter said to Him, "Lord, do You speak this parable *only* to us, or to all *people?*"

42 And the Lord said, [l]"Who then is that [v]faithful and wise steward, whom *his* master will make ruler over his household, to give *them their* portion of food in due season?

43 "Blessed *is* that servant whom his master will find so doing when he comes.

44 "Truly, I say to you that he will make him [w]ruler over all that he has.

45 "But if that servant says in his heart, 'My master is [x]delaying his coming,' and begins to beat the male and female servants, and to eat and drink and be drunk,

46 "the master of that servant will come on a [y]day when he is not looking for *him,* and at an hour when he is not aware, and will cut him in two and appoint *him* his portion with the unbelievers.

47 "And [z]that servant who [aa]knew his master's will, and did not prepare *himself* or do according to his will, shall be beaten with many *stripes.*

48 [bb]"But he who did not know, yet committed things deserving of stripes, shall be beaten with few. For everyone to whom much is given, from him much will be required; and to whom much has been committed, of him they will ask the more.

Christ a divider of men in spiritual matters

49 "I came to send [cc]fire on the earth, and how I wish it were already kindled!

50 "But I have a [dd]baptism to be baptized with, and how distressed I am till it is [ee]accomplished!

51 [ff]"Do *you* suppose that I came to give peace on earth? I

*12:31 NU-Text reads *His kingdom, and these things.* 12:39 NU-Text reads *he would not have allowed.*

27
a 1 Ki. 10:4–7
28
b Mt. 6:30; 8:26; 14:31; 16:8
30
c Gk. *kosmos.* See Mt. 4:8, *note*
d Mt. 6:31–32; cp. 2 Chr. 16:9
31
e See Mt. 6:33, *note*
32
f Dan. 7:18, 27; Lk. 22:29
g *Kingdom* (NT): v. 32; Lk. 13:18. (Mt. 2:2; 1 Cor. 15:24, *note*). See Mt. 3:2, *note*
33
h Mt. 19:21; cp. Acts 2:44–45; 4:34–35
i Lk. 11:41
j Mt. 6:20
34
k Cp. Col. 3:1–3
35
l *Parables* (NT): vv. 35–39, 42–48; Lk. 13:6. (Mt. 5:13; Lk. 21:29)
m Eph. 6:14; 1 Pet. 1:13
n Mt. 5:16
37
o Mt. 24:46; cp. 2 Tim. 4:7–8; 1 Pet. 5:1–4; 2 Pet. 1:10–11
p Cp. Rev. 22:20
q Cp. Mt. 25:1–13
38
r 9 p.m. to midnight. See Jn. 19:14, *note*
s Midnight to 3 a.m.
39
t 1 Th. 5:2; Rev. 16:15
40
u See Mt. 8:20, *note*
42
v Mt. 24:45–46; cp. Lk. 19:15–19
44
w Mt. 25:21; Rev. 3:21
45
x 2 Pet. 3:3–4
46
y 1 Th. 5:3
47
z Cp. Num. 15:30; Dt. 25:2; Lk. 10:12
aa Jas. 4:17; cp. Jn. 9:41
48
bb Lev. 5:17; cp. 1 Tim. 1:12–13
49
cc v. 51
50
dd Mt. 20:18, 22–23
ee Jn. 12:27; 19:30
51
ff Mt. 10:34

tell you, not at all, but rather [a]division.

52 "For from now on five in one house will be divided: three against two, and two against three.

53 [b]"Father will be divided against son and son against father, mother against daughter and daughter against mother, mother-in-law against her daughter-in-law and daughter-in-law against her mother-in-law."

54 Then He also said to the multitudes, [c]"Whenever you see a cloud rising out of the west, immediately you say, 'A shower is coming'; and so it is.

55 "And when you see the [d]south wind blow, you say, 'There will be hot weather'; and there is.

56 "Hypocrites! You can discern the face of the sky and of the earth, but how *is it* you do not discern [e]this time?

57 "Yes, and why, even of yourselves, do you not judge what is right?

58 [f]"When you go with your adversary to the magistrate, make every effort along the way to settle with him, lest he drag you to the judge, the judge deliver you to the officer, and the officer throw you into prison.

59 "I tell you, you shall not depart from there till you have paid the very last [g]mite."

Men must not judge but repent

13 THERE were present at that season some who told Him about the [h]Galileans whose blood Pilate had mingled with their sacrifices.

2 And Jesus answered and said to them, "Do you suppose that these Galileans were worse [i]sinners than all *other* Galileans, because they suffered such things?

3 "I tell you, no; but unless you [j]repent you will all likewise perish.

4 "Or those eighteen on whom the tower in Siloam fell and killed them, do you think that they were worse [i]sinners than all *other* men who dwelt in Jerusalem?

5 "I tell you, no; but [k]unless you [j]repent you will all likewise perish."

Parable of fig tree: judgment delayed (contra. Mt. 21:18–21; Mk. 11:12–14,20–26)

6 He also spoke this [l]parable: "A certain *man* had a fig tree planted in his vineyard, and he came seeking fruit on it and found none.

7 "Then he said to the keeper of his vineyard, 'Look, for [m]three years I have come seeking fruit on this fig tree and find none. [n]Cut it down; why does it use up the ground?'

8 "But he answered and said to him, 'Sir, let it alone this year also, until I dig around it and fertilize *it*.

9 'And if it bears fruit, *well.* But if not, after that* you can [o]cut it down.'"

A cripple cured on the Sabbath

10 Now He was teaching in one of the [p]synagogues on the [q]Sabbath.

11 And behold, there was a woman who had a spirit of infirmity eighteen years, and was bent over and could in no way raise *herself* up.

12 But when Jesus saw her, He called *her* to *Him* and said to her, "Woman, you are loosed from your [r]infirmity."

13 And He laid *His* hands on her, and immediately she was [s]made straight, and glorified God.

14 But the ruler of the synagogue answered with indignation, because Jesus had [t]healed on the [q]Sabbath; and he said to the crowd, [u]"There are six days on which men ought to work; therefore come and be healed on them, and not on the Sabbath day."

15 The Lord then answered him and said, [v]"Hypocrite!* [w]Does not each one of you on the Sabbath loose his ox or donkey from the stall, and lead *it* away to water it?

16 "So ought not this woman,

*

13:9 NU-Text reads *And if it bears fruit after that, well. But if not, you can cut it down.* 13:15 NU-Text and M-Text read *Hypocrites.*

51
a Jn. 9:16; Acts 14:4
53
b Mt. 10:36; cp. Mic. 7:6
54
c Mt. 16:2–3
55
d Job 37:17
56
e Lk. 19:41–44; cp. 1 Cor. 1:19–27
58
f Prov. 25:8; Mt. 5:25; cp. Isa. 55:6; Heb. 3:7–15
59
g Smallest coin. See Coinage (NT), Mt. 5:26, *note;* cp. Mt. 18:34; 2 Th. 1:9
CHAPTER 13
1
h Cp. Acts 5:37
2
i See Rom. 3:23, *note*
3
j *Repentance:* vv. 3, 5; Lk. 15:7. (Mt. 3:2; Acts 17:30, *note*)

5
k Cp. Ezek. 18:30
6
l *Parables* (NT): vv. 6–9; Lk. 13:18. (Mt. 5:13; Lk. 21:29)
7
m Cp. Lev. 19:23
n Cp. Ex. 32:10; Rom. 2:2–16
9
o Jn. 15:2
10
p Cp. Acts 18:4
q *Sabbath:* vv. 10, 14–16; Lk. 14:1. (Gen. 2:3; Mt. 12:1, *note*)
12
r Lk. 7:21; 8:2; cp. Rom. 8:26; Heb. 4:15
13
s *Miracles* (NT): vv. 11–13; Lk. 14:4. (Mt. 8:3; Acts 28:8, *note*)
14
t Lk. 6:6–11; 14:1–6; Jn. 5:16
u Ex. 20:9; 23:12
15
v Mt. 7:5; 23:13
w Cp. Lk. 14:3–5

being a [a]daughter of Abraham, whom [b]Satan has bound—think of it—for eighteen years, be loosed from this bond on the Sabbath?"

17 And when He said these things, all His adversaries were [c]put to shame; and all the multitude rejoiced for all the glorious things that were [d]done by Him.

Parables of mustard seed and leaven repeated (see Mt. 13:31–33, notes; Mk. 4:30–32)

18 Then He said, "What is the [e]kingdom of God like? And [f]to what shall I compare it?

19 "It is like a [g]mustard seed, which a man took and put in his garden; and it grew and became a large* tree, and the birds of the air nested in its branches."

20 And again He said, [f]"To what shall I liken the [e]kingdom of God?

21 "It is like [h]leaven, which a woman took and hid in three [i]measures* of meal till it was all leavened."

Teachings on the way to Jerusalem

22 And He went through the cities and villages, teaching, and journeying toward Jerusalem.

23 Then one said to Him, "Lord, are there [j]few who are [k]saved?" And He said to them,

24 "Strive to enter through the [l]narrow gate, for many, I say to you, will seek to enter and will not be able.

25 "When once the Master of the house has risen up and [m]shut the [n]door, and you begin to stand outside and knock at the door, saying, [o]'Lord, Lord, open for us,' and He will answer and say to you, 'I do not know you, where you are from,'

26 "then you will begin to [1]say, 'We ate and drank in Your presence, and You taught in our streets.'

27 "But He will say, 'I tell you I do [p]not know you, where you are from. Depart from Me, all you [q]workers of iniquity.'

28 [r]"There will be weeping and gnashing of teeth, when you see Abraham and Isaac and Jacob and all the prophets in the [s]kingdom of God, and yourselves thrust out.

29 [t]"They will come from the east and the west, from the north and the south, and sit down in the [s]kingdom of God.

30 [u]"And indeed there are last who will be first, and there are first who will be last."

31 On that very day* some [v]Pharisees came, saying to Him, "Get out and depart from here, for [w]Herod wants to kill You."

32 And He said to them, "Go, tell that fox, 'Behold, I cast out [x]demons and perform cures today and tomorrow, and the third *day* I shall [y]be perfected.'

33 "Nevertheless I must journey today, tomorrow, and the *day* following; for it cannot be that a prophet should perish outside of Jerusalem.

Jesus laments over Jerusalem (Mt. 23:37–39; Lk. 19:41–44; cp. Ps. 118:26; Jer. 22:5)

34 "O Jerusalem, Jerusalem, the one who [z]kills the prophets and stones those who are sent to her! [aa]How often I wanted to [bb]gather your children together, as a hen *gathers* her brood under *her* wings, but you were [cc]not willing!

35 "See! Your house is left to you [dd]desolate; and assuredly,* I say to you, you shall not see Me [ee]until *the time* comes when you say, [ff]'*Blessed is He who* [gg]*comes in the name of the* LORD!' "•

Mercy is proper every day (cp. Mt. 12:9–13)

14 NOW it happened, as He went into the house of one of the rulers of the [v]Pharisees to eat bread on the [hh]Sabbath, that they watched Him closely.

2 And behold, there was a

*13:19 NU-Text omits *large*. 13:21 Greek *sata*, approximately two pecks in all
13:31 NU-Text reads *In that very hour.*
13:35 NU-Text and M-Text omit *assuredly*.
• Psalm 118:26

16
a Cp. Lk. 19:9; Rom. 4:9–12
b *Satan:* v. 16; Lk. 22:3. (Gen. 3:1; Rev. 20:10)
17
c Cp. Isa. 45:24; 1 Pet. 3:16
d Mk. 5:19,20
18
e *Kingdom* (NT): vv. 18–21; Lk. 19:38. (Mt. 2:2; 1 Cor. 15:24, *note*). See Mt. 6:33, *note*
f *Parables* (NT): vv. 18–21; Lk. 14:7. (Mt. 5:13; Lk. 21:29)
19
g Cp. Mt. 17:20
21
h *Leaven:* v. 21; 1 Cor. 5:6. (Gen. 19:3; Mt. 13:33, *note*)
i See Weights and Measures (NT), Acts 27:28, *note*
23
j Mt. 7:14; 20:16
k See Rom. 1:16, *note*
24
l Mt. 7:13; cp. Lk. 9:23; 14:33
25
m Mt. 25:10; Rev. 22:11
n Cp. Rev. 3:20
o Mt. 7:23; cp. Lk. 6:46
27
p Mt. 25:12; cp. Mt. 25:41–46
q Ti. 1:16
28
r Mt. 8:12
s See Mt. 3:2 and 6:33, *notes*
29
t Cp. Isa. 49:6–12; Rev. 5:9
30
u Mt. 19:30
31
v See Mt. 3:7, *note 1*
w *Herod Antipas*, son of Herod the Great. See Mk. 6:14, *note*
32
x See Mt. 7:22, *note*
y Jn. 17:4–5; 19:30; Heb. 10:12–13
34
z 2 Chr. 24:20–21; 36:15–16
aa Cp. Neh. 9:26–27
bb Cp. Dt. 32:11–12; Ps. 91:4
cc Cp. Prov. 1:24–25
35
dd *Israel* (history): vv. 34–35; Lk. 19:43. (Gen. 12:2; Rom. 11:26, *note*). Cp. Dan. 9:27; Lk. 21:24
ee See Mt. 23:39, *note*
ff Mt. 21:9
gg *Christ* (second advent): v. 35; Lk. 17:30. (Dt. 30:3; Acts 1:11, *note*). Isa. 62:11; Mk. 11:10
CHAPTER 14
1
hh *Sabbath:* vv. 1,3,5; Lk. 23:54. (Gen. 2:3; Mt. 12:1, *note*)

[1](13:26) Christian activity must not be equated with salvation, e.g. Judas Iscariot.

certain man before Him who had dropsy.

3 And Jesus, answering, spoke to the [a]lawyers and Pharisees, saying, "Is it lawful to [b]heal on the Sabbath?"*

4 But they kept silent. And He took *him* and [c]healed him, and let him go.

5 Then He answered them, saying, "Which of you, having a donkey* or an ox that has fallen into a pit, will not immediately pull him out on the Sabbath day?"

6 And they could not answer Him regarding these things.

Parable of the ambitious guest

7 So He told a [d]parable to those who were invited, when He noted how they chose the best places, saying to them:

8 "When you are invited by anyone to a wedding feast, do not sit down in the best place, lest one more honorable than you be invited by him;

9 "and he who invited you and him come and say to you, 'Give place to this man,' and then you begin with shame to take the lowest place.

10 "But when you are invited, go and sit down in the [e]lowest place, so that when he who invited you comes he may say to you, 'Friend, go up [f]higher.' Then you will have glory in the presence of those who sit at the table with you.

11 "For [g]whoever exalts himself will be humbled, [h]and he who humbles himself will be exalted."

12 Then He also said to him who invited Him, "When you give a dinner or a supper, do not ask your friends, your brothers, your relatives, nor rich neighbors, lest they also invite you back, and you be repaid.

13 "But when you give a feast, invite *the* [i]poor, *the* maimed, *the* lame, *the* blind.

14 "And you will be [j]blessed, because they cannot repay you; for you shall be [k]repaid at the [l]resurrection of the just."

Parable of the great supper
(cp. Mt. 22:1–14)

15 Now when one of those who sat at the table with Him heard these things, he said to Him, [m]"Blessed *is* he who shall eat bread* in the [n]kingdom of God!"

16 Then He said to him, [d]"A certain man gave a great supper and invited many,

17 "and sent his servant at supper time to say to those who were invited, 'Come, for all things are now ready.'

18 "But they all with one *accord* began to make [o]excuses. The first said to him, [p]'I have bought a piece of ground, and I must go and see it. I ask you to have me excused.'

19 "And another said, 'I have bought five yoke of oxen, and I am going to test them. I ask you to have me excused.'

20 "Still another said, 'I have married a wife, and therefore I cannot come.'

21 "So that servant came and reported these things to his master. Then the master of the house, being angry, said to his servant, [q]'Go out quickly into the [r]streets and lanes of the city, and bring in here *the* [s]poor and *the* maimed and *the* lame and *the* blind.'

22 "And the servant said, 'Master, it is done as you commanded, and still there is [t]room.'

23 "Then the master said to the servant, 'Go out into the highways and hedges, and [u]compel *them* to come in, that my house may be filled.

24 'For I say to you that [v]none of those men who were invited shall [w]taste my supper.' "

Discipleship tested
(cp. Mt. 10:37–39)

25 Now great multitudes went with Him. And He turned and said to them,

26 [x]"If anyone comes to Me and does not [1]hate his father

3
a See Mt. 22:35, *note*
b Lk. 4:18
4
c Miracles (NT): vv. 2–4; Lk. 17:14. (Mt. 8:3; Acts 28:8, *note*)
7
d Parables (NT): vv. 7–11, 16–24; Lk. 14:28. (Mt. 5:13; Lk. 21:29)
10
e Cp. Prov. 15:33; 18:12
f Cp. Prov. 25:6–7
11
g Mt. 23:12; Lk. 18:14; cp. Ps. 18:27; Prov. 29:23
h Cp. Job 22:29; Isa. 57:15; Jas. 4:6,10; 1 Pet. 5:5
13
i Cp. Neh. 8:10,12
14
j Mt. 25:34–40
k Judgments (the seven): v. 14; Jn. 5:22. (1 Sam. 7:14; Rev. 20:12, *note*)
l Resurrection: v. 14; Lk. 20:35. (2 Ki. 4:35; 1 Cor. 15:52, *note*). Jn. 5:29; Acts 24:15

15
m Rev. 19:9
n See Mt. 6:33, *note*
18
o Cp. Isa. 30:15; Mt. 23:37; Jn. 5:40
p Cp. Mt. 6:24
21
q Cp. Mt. 28:18–19; Acts 13:46
r Cp. Prov. 1:20–23
s Cp. 1 Sam. 2:8; Jas. 2:5
22
t Cp. 2 Pet. 3:9
23
u Cp. 2 Cor. 5:20
24
v Cp. Prov. 1:24–31; Mt. 21:43; Heb. 12:25
w Cp. Heb. 3:15–19
26
x Cp. Dt. 13:6–11

---

* 14:3 NU-Text adds *or not.* 14:5 NU-Text and M-Text read *son.* 14:15 M-Text reads *dinner.*

---

[1](14:26) Terms which define the emotions or affections are frequently comparative. Natural

and mother, wife and children, brothers and sisters, yes, and his [a]own life also, he cannot be My disciple.

27 "And [b]whoever does not bear his cross and come after Me cannot be My disciple.

Three parables about counting the cost of discipleship (vv. 28–35). (1) The tower

28 [c]"For which of you, intending to build a tower, does not sit down first and count the cost, whether he has *enough* to finish *it*—

29 "lest, after he has laid the foundation, and is not able to finish, all who see *it* begin to mock him,

30 "saying, 'This man began to build and was not able to [d]finish.'

(2) The king contemplating war

31 [c]"Or what king, going to make war against another king, does not sit down first and [e]consider whether he is able with ten thousand to meet him who comes against him with twenty thousand?

32 "Or else, while the other is still a great way off, he sends a [f]delegation and asks [g]conditions of peace.

33 "So likewise, whoever of you does not [h]forsake [i]all that he has cannot be My disciple.

(3) The flavorless salt (cp. Mt. 5:13; Mk. 9:50)

34 [j]"Salt *is* good; but if the salt has lost its flavor, how shall it be seasoned?

35 "It is neither fit for the land nor for the dunghill, *but* men throw it out. He who has ears to hear, let him hear!"

Three parables concerning joy over repentance (vv. 1–32)

15 THEN all the tax collectors and the [k]sinners drew near to Him to hear Him.

2 And the [l]Pharisees and [m]scribes complained, saying, "This Man receives sinners and [n]eats with them."

(1) The lost sheep (cp. Mt. 18:12–14)

3 So He spoke this [j]parable to them, saying:

4 "What man of you, having a hundred sheep, if he [o]loses one of them, does not leave the ninety-nine in the wilderness, and go after the one which is [p]lost until he [q]finds it?

5 "And when he has found *it*, he lays *it* on his shoulders, rejoicing.

6 "And when he comes home, he calls together *his* friends and neighbors, saying to them, [r]'Rejoice with me, for I have found my sheep which was [s]lost!'

7 "I say to you that likewise there will be more joy in heaven over one [k]sinner who repents than over ninety-nine [t]just persons who [u]need no [v]repentance.

(2) The lost coin

8 "Or what woman, having ten [w]silver coins,* if she loses one coin, does not light a lamp, sweep the house, and search carefully until she finds *it?*

9 "And when she has found *it*, she calls *her* friends and neighbors together, saying, 'Rejoice with me, for I have found the piece which I [s]lost!'

10 "Likewise, I say to you, there is [x]joy in the presence of the [y]angels of God over one [k]sinner who [v]repents."

(3) The lost son (vv. 11–32)

11 Then He said: "A certain man had two sons.

12 "And the younger of them said to *his* father, 'Father, give me the portion of goods that falls *to me*.' So he divided to them *his* [z]livelihood.

13 "And not many days after, the younger son gathered all together, journeyed to a far coun-

* 15:8 Greek *drachma*, a valuable coin often worn in a ten-piece garland by married women

26
a Rev. 12:11
27
b Lk. 9:23; cp. 2 Tim. 3:12
28
c *Parables* (NT): vv. 28–35; 15:3–32; Lk. 16:1. (Mt. 5:13; Lk. 21:29)
30
d Cp. Heb. 6:11
31
e Cp. Prov. 20:18
32
f Cp. Lk. 12:58
g Cp. Job 22:21
33
h Mt. 19:27; cp. 2 Tim. 4:10
i Cp. Phil. 3:7–8
34
j *Parables* (NT): vv. 28–35; 15:3–32; Lk. 16:1. (Mt. 5:13; Lk. 21:29). Mk. 9:49; Col. 4:6
CHAPTER 15
1
k See Rom. 3:23, *note*
2
l See Mt. 3:7, *note*
m See Mt. 2:4, *note 4*

n Mt. 9:10–15; cp. Gal. 2:11–14
4
o 1 Pet. 2:25
p Gk. *apollumi.* v. 24; see Jn. 3:16, *note 3*
q Cp. Ezek. 34:11–16; Jn. 10:11–14
6
r Rom. 12:15
s Lk. 19:10
7
t See 1 Jn. 3:7, *note*
u Mk. 2:17
v *Repentance:* vv. 7, 10,18,21; Lk. 16:30. (Mt. 3:2; Acts 17:30, *note*)
8
w Gk. *drachmē.* See Coinage (NT), Mt. 5:26, *note*
10
x Cp. Acts 11:18
y See Heb. 1:4, *note*
12
z Mk. 12:44

affection is to be, as compared with the Christian's devotedness to Christ, as if it were hate. See Mt. 12:47–50, where Christ illustrates this principle in His own Person. But in the Lord the natural affections are sanctified and lifted to the level of the divine love (cp. Jn. 19:26–27; Eph. 5:25–28).

try, and there wasted his possessions with [a]prodigal living.

14 “But when he had spent all, there arose a severe famine in that land, and he began to be in want.

15 “Then he went and joined himself to a citizen of that country, and he sent him into his fields to feed [b]swine.

16 “And he would gladly have filled his stomach with the pods that the swine ate, and no one gave him *anything*.

17 “But when he came to himself, he said, ‘How many of my father’s hired servants have bread enough and to spare, and I perish with hunger!

18 ‘I will arise and go to my father, and will [c]say to him, “Father, [d]I have [e]sinned against heaven and before you,

19 “and I am no longer worthy to be called your son. Make me like one of your hired servants.” ’

20 “And he arose and came to his father. But when he was still a [f]great way off, his father saw him and had [g]compassion, and ran and fell on his neck and kissed him.

21 “And the son [c]said to him, ‘Father, I have [e]sinned against heaven and in your sight, and am no longer worthy to be called your son.’

22 “But the father said to his servants, [h]‘Bring* out the [i]best robe and put *it* on him, and put a ring on his hand and sandals on *his* feet.

23 ‘And bring the fatted calf here and kill *it*, and let us eat and be merry;

24 ‘for this my son was [j]dead and is [k]alive again; he was [l]lost and is found.’ And they began to be [m]merry.

25 “Now his older son was in the field. And as he came and drew near to the house, he heard music and dancing.

26 “So he called one of the servants and asked what these things meant.

27 “And he said to him, ‘Your brother has come, and because he has received him safe and sound, your father has killed the fatted calf.’

28 “But he was angry and would not go in. Therefore his father came out and pleaded with him.

29 “So he answered and said to *his* father, ‘Lo, these many years I have been serving you; I never transgressed your commandment at any time; and [n]yet you never gave me a young goat, that I might make merry with my friends.

30 ‘But as soon as this son of yours came, who has devoured your livelihood with harlots, you killed the fatted calf for him.’

31 “And he said to him, ‘Son, you are always with me, and all that I have is yours.

32 ‘It was right that we should make merry and be glad, for your brother was [j]dead and is alive again, and was lost and is [o]found.’ ”

Parable of the unjust steward: the proper use of money

16 HE also said to His disciples: [p]“There was a certain rich man who had a [q]steward, and an accusation was brought to him that this man was wasting his goods.

2 “So he called him and said to him, ‘What is this I hear about you? Give an [r]account of your stewardship, for you can no longer be steward.’

3 “Then the steward said within himself, ‘What shall I do? For my master is taking the stewardship away from me. I cannot dig; I am ashamed to beg.

4 ‘I have resolved what to do, that when I am put out of the stewardship, they may receive me into their houses.’

5 “So he called every one of his master’s debtors to *him*, and said to the first, ‘How much do you owe my master?’

6 “And he said, ‘A hundred [s]measures* of oil.’ So he said to him, ‘Take your bill, and sit down quickly and write fifty.’

7 “Then he said to another, ‘And how much do you owe?’ So he said, ‘A hundred [s]mea-

13
a Cp. Prov. 23:21; 29:3
15
b Cp. Lev. 11:7–8
18
c *Bible prayers* (NT): vv. 18–19, 21; Lk. 16:24. (Mt. 6:9; Lk. 11:2, *note*)
d Ex 9:27; 10:16; Num. 22:34; Josh. 7:20; 1 Sam. 15:24,30; 26:21; 2 Sam. 12:13; 24:10,17; Ps. 51:4; Mt. 27:4; cp. Lev. 26:40–42; 1 Ki. 8:46–53; Lk. 18:13; 1 Jn. 1:9; 2:1–2
e See Rom. 3:23, *note*
20
f Cp. Acts 2:39; Eph. 2:13,17
g Jer. 3:12; Mt. 9:36
22
h Cp. Zech. 3:3–5
i Cp. Isa. 61:10; Gal. 3:27; Phil. 3:8–9; Rev. 19:8; see Rom. 10:10, *note*
24
j *Death* (spiritual): vv. 24,32; Jn. 5:24. (Gen. 2:17; Eph. 2:5, *note*)
k Cp. Rom. 6:13; Eph. 2:1–6
l Gk. *apollumi*. v. 24; see Jn. 3:16, *note 3*
m v. 32; cp. Isa. 35:10

29
n Cp. Mt. 20:11–15
32
o Cp. Lk. 15:3–7
CHAPTER 16
1
p *Parables* (NT): vv. 1–9; Lk. 17:7. (Mt. 5:13; Lk. 21:29)
q Cp. Lk. 12:42–47
2
r Rom. 14:12; 2 Cor. 5:10; 1 Pet. 4:5; cp. Eccl. 11:9–10
6
s See Weights and Measures (NT), Acts 27:28, *note*

*
15:22 NU-Text reads *Quickly bring.*
16:6 Greek *batos*, eight or nine gallons each (Old Testament *bath*)

sures* of wheat.' And he said to him, 'Take your bill, and write eighty.'

8 "So the master commended the unjust steward because he had dealt shrewdly. For the sons of this [a]world are more shrewd in their generation than the sons of [b]light.

9 "And I say to you, [c]make friends for yourselves by [d]unrighteous mammon, that when you fail,* they may receive you into an everlasting home.

10 "He who *is* faithful in *what is* least is faithful also in much; and he who is unjust in *what is* least is unjust also in much.

11 "Therefore if you have not been faithful in the unrighteous mammon, who will commit to your trust the [e]true *riches?*

12 "And if you have not been faithful in what is [f]another man's, who will give you what is your [g]own?

13 [h]"No servant can serve two masters; for either he will hate the one and love the other, or else he will be loyal to the one and despise the other. [i]You cannot serve God and mammon."

Jesus rebukes greed

14 Now the [j]Pharisees, who were [k]lovers of money, also heard all these things, and they derided Him.

15 And He said to them, "You are those who [l]justify yourselves [m]before men, but God [n]knows your hearts. For what is highly esteemed among men is an [o]abomination in the sight of God.

16 "The [p]law and the prophets *were* until [q]John. Since that time the [r]kingdom of God has been preached, and everyone is pressing into it.

17 "And it is easier for heaven and earth to [s]pass away than for one [t]tittle of the [p]law to [u]fail.

Jesus teaches concerning divorce (Mt. 5:31–32; 19:1–9; Mk. 10:1–12; cp. Rom. 7:1–3; 1 Cor. 7:10–16)

18 "Whoever divorces his wife and marries another commits [v]adultery; and whoever marries her who is divorced from *her* husband commits adultery.

The rich man and Lazarus

19 [1]"There was a certain rich man who was clothed in purple and fine linen and fared sumptuously every day.

20 "But there was a certain beggar named Lazarus, full of sores, who was laid at his gate,

21 "desiring to be fed with the crumbs which fell* from the rich man's table. Moreover the dogs came and licked his sores.

22 "So it was that the beggar [w]died, and was carried by the [x]angels to [y]Abraham's bosom. The rich man also died and was buried.

23 "And being in [z]torments in [2][aa]Hades, he lifted up his eyes

*16:7 Greek *koros,* ten or twelve bushels each (Old Testament *kor*) 16:9 NU-Text reads *it fails.* 16:21 NU-Text reads *with what fell.*

8
a Gk. *aiōn.* See Mk. 10:30, *note*
b Jn. 12:36; Eph. 5:8; 1 Th. 5:5
9
c Cp. 1 Tim. 6:17–19
d Cp. Mk. 10:24; Jas. 5:1–3
11
e Cp. 2 Cor. 6:10; Eph. 1:18; 1 Tim. 6:17; Rev. 3:18
12
f Cp. Lk. 19:13
g 1 Pet. 1:3–4
13
h Cp. Josh. 24:15
i Mt. 6:24; Gal. 1:10; cp. 1 Jn. 2:15; Jas. 4:4
14
j See Mt. 3:7, *note 1*
k Mt. 23:14; cp. Ti. 1:11
15
l Lk. 10:29; cp. Rom. 4:2; Gal. 3:11
m Mt. 6:2,5, 16; cp. Mt. 23:28
n 1 Sam. 16:7; 1 Chr. 28:9; 2 Chr. 6:30; Ps. 7:9; Prov. 15:11; Jer. 17:10
o Ps. 10:3; Prov. 6:16–19; 16:5; cp. Ti. 1:16
16
p *Law* (of Moses): vv. 16–17; Lk. 16:29. (Ex. 19:1; Gal. 3:24, *note*)
q Mt. 3:1–12
r See Mt. 6:33, *note*
17
s Mt. 5:18
t Minute ornament over Heb. letter
u Isa. 40:8; 1 Pet. 1:24–25
18
v Cp. Mt. 5:27–28
22
w *Death* (physical): v. 22; Lk. 20:36. (Gen. 2:17; Heb. 9:27, *note*)
x See Heb. 1:4, *note*
y Mt. 8:11; cp. Jas. 2:5
23
z See Lk. 16:23, *note;* cp. Hab. 2:5, *note*
aa Cp. Rev. 14:11

[1](16:19) Verses 19–31 are not said to be a parable. Rich men and beggars were common. There is no reason why Jesus may not have had in mind a particular case. In no parable is an individual named, as here (v. 20).

[2](16:23) The Greek word *Hadēs,* like its Hebrew equivalent, *Sheol,* is used in two ways:

(1) To indicate the condition of the unsaved between death and the great white throne judgment (Rev. 20:11–15). Luke 16:23–24 shows that the lost in *Hadēs* are conscious, possess full use of their faculties, memory, etc., and are in torment. This continues until the final judgment of the lost (2 Pet. 2:9), when all the unsaved, and *Hadēs* itself, will be cast into the lake of fire (Rev. 20:13–15).

(2) To indicate, in general, the condition of all departed human spirits between death and the resurrection. This usage is found occasionally in the OT but rarely, if ever, in the NT (cp. Gen. 37:35; 42:38; 44:29,31). It should not lead anyone to think that there is a possibility of change from one state to the other after death, for v. 23 shows that when the unsaved man who was in *Hadēs* saw Abraham and Lazarus, they were "afar off," and v. 26 states that between the two places there is a great gulf fixed, so that no one can cross from one to the other.

Some interpreters think that Eph. 4:8–10 indicates that a change in the place of the departed believers occurred at the resurrection of Christ. It is certain that now all who are saved go at and saw Abraham afar off, and Lazarus in his bosom.

24 "Then he cried and [a]said, 'Father Abraham, have mercy on me, and send Lazarus that he may dip the tip of his finger in water and cool my tongue; for I am [b]tormented in this flame.'

25 "But Abraham said, 'Son, remember that in your lifetime you [c]received your good things, and likewise Lazarus evil things; but now he is comforted and you are tormented.

26 'And besides all this, between us and you there is a great gulf fixed, so that those who want to pass from here to you cannot, nor can those from there pass to us.'

27 "Then he [a]said, 'I beg you therefore, father, that you would send him to my father's house,

28 'for I have five brothers, that he may testify to them, lest they also come to this place of torment.'

29 "Abraham said to him, 'They have [d]Moses and the prophets; let them [e]hear [f]them.'

30 "And he [a]said, 'No, father Abraham; but if one goes to them from the dead, they will [g]repent.'

31 "But he said to him, [h]'If they do not [e]hear [d]Moses and the prophets, neither will they be [i]persuaded though one rise from the dead.' "

Instructions regarding offending, forgiving, and faith
(cp. Mt. 18:1–7,18–35)

17 THEN He said to the disciples, "It is impossible that no offenses should [j]come, but [k]woe *to him* through whom they do come!

2 "It would be better for him if a millstone were hung around his neck, and he were thrown into the sea, than that he should offend one of these little ones.

3 "Take heed to yourselves. If your brother [l]sins against you,* [m]rebuke him; and if he [g]repents, [n]forgive him.

4 "And if he [o]sins against you seven times in a day, and seven times in a day returns to you,* saying, 'I repent,' [p]you shall forgive him."

5 And the apostles [a]said to the Lord, "Increase our [q]faith."

6 So the Lord said, [r]"If you have faith as a mustard seed, you can say to this mulberry tree, 'Be pulled up by the roots and be planted in the sea,' and it would obey you.

Earnest service is our duty

7 "And [s]which of you, having a servant plowing or tending sheep, will say to him when he has come in from the field, 'Come at once and sit down to eat'?

8 "But will he not rather say to him, 'Prepare something for my supper, and gird yourself and serve me till I have eaten and drunk, and afterward you will eat and drink'?

9 "Does he thank that servant because he did the things that were commanded him? I think not.*

10 "So likewise you, when you have done all those things which you are commanded, say, [t]'We are unprofitable servants. We have done what was our duty to do.' "

Ten lepers cleansed

11 Now it happened as He went to [u]Jerusalem that He passed through the midst of Samaria and Galilee.

12 Then as He entered a certain village, there met Him ten men who were [v]lepers, who stood afar off.

13 And they lifted up *their*

*
17:3 NU-Text omits *against you.*
17:4 M-Text omits *to you.* 17:9 NU-Text ends verse with *commanded;* M-Text omits *him.*

24
a Bible prayers (NT): vv. 24, 27,30; 17:5; Lk. 17:13. (Mt. 6:9; Lk. 11:2, *note*)
b Mk. 9:42–48; cp. Heb. 10:31

25
c Job 21:13; Lk. 6:24; Jas. 5:5

29
d Law (of Moses): vv. 29,31; Lk. 18:20. (Ex. 19:1; Gal. 3:24, *note*)
e Cp. Acts 3:22–23
f Isa. 8:20; Jn. 5:39; Acts 15:21; 2 Tim. 3:15

30
g Repentance: vv. 30–31; 17:3–4; Lk. 24:47. (Mt. 3:2; Acts 17:30, *note*)

31
h Jn. 5:46
i Cp. Rom. 10:1–21; 11:7–10

CHAPTER 17

1
j 1 Cor. 11:19
k Mt. 18:6–7; 26:24; Mk. 9:42; Jude 11; cp. 2 Th. 1:6

3
l Mt. 18:15; see Rom. 3:23, *note*
m Gal. 6:1; cp. Prov. 17:10
n Forgiveness: vv. 3–4; Lk. 23:34. (Lev. 4:20; Mt. 26:28, *note*)

4
o See Rom. 3:23, *note*
p Cp. Col. 3:12–14

5
q Faith: vv. 5–6; Lk. 17:19. (Gen. 3:20; Heb. 11:39, *note*)

6
r Mt. 17:20; Mk. 9:23

7
s Parables (NT): vv. 7–10; Lk. 18:1. (Mt. 5:13; Lk. 21:29)

10
t Cp. Isa. 64:6; Mt. 25:37–40; 1 Cor. 9:16–17; Phile. 11

11
u Lk. 9:51

12
v Num. 5:2; cp. 2 Ki. 7:3–10

once into the presence of Christ (2 Cor. 5:8; Phil. 1:23). Jesus told the penitent thief: "today you will be with Me in Paradise" (Lk. 23:43). Paul was "caught up to the third heaven . . . into Paradise (2 Cor. 12:1–4). Paradise is a place of great joy and bliss, but this bliss is not complete until the spirit is reunited with a glorified body at the resurrection of the just (1 Cor. 15:51–54; 1 Th. 4:16–17). Though both *Sheol* and *Hadēs* are sometimes translated "grave" (cp. Gen. 37:35), they never indicate a burial place but, rather, the state of the spirit after death. See also Hab. 2:5, *note.*

voices and [a]said, "Jesus, Master, have mercy on us!"

14 So when He saw *them,* He said to them, "Go, show yourselves to the [b]priests." And so it was that as they went, they were [c]cleansed.

15 And one of them, when he saw that he was healed, returned, and with a loud [a]voice [d]glorified God,

16 and fell down on *his* face at His feet, giving Him thanks. And he was a [e]Samaritan.

17 So Jesus answered and said, "Were there not ten cleansed? But where *are* the nine?

18 "Were there not any found who returned to give glory to God except this foreigner?"

19 And He said to him, "Arise, go your way. [f]Your [g]faith has [c]made you well."

The kingdom in its present aspect (see Lk. 17:21, note; cp. Lk. 19:11–27)

20 Now when He was asked by the Pharisees when the [h]kingdom of God would come, He answered them and said, "The kingdom of God does not come with [i]observation;

21 "nor will they say, 'See here!' or 'See there!'* For indeed, the [h]kingdom of God is [1][j]within you."

Jesus foretells His second coming (see Dt. 30:3, note, and Acts 1:9–11, note)

22 Then He said to the disciples, "The [k]days will come when you will desire to see one of the days of the [l]Son of Man, and you will not see *it.*

23 "And they will say to you, [m]'Look here!' or 'Look there!'* [n]Do not go after *them* or follow *them.*

24 "For as the lightning that flashes out of one *part* under heaven shines to the other *part* under heaven, so also the [l]Son of Man will be in His day.

25 "But first He must suffer many things and be [o]rejected by this generation.

26 [p]"And as it [q]was in the [r]days of [s]Noah, so it will be also in the days of the [l]Son of Man:

27 "They ate, they drank, they married wives, they were given in marriage, until the [t]day that Noah entered the ark, and the flood came and [u]destroyed them all.

28 "Likewise as it was also in the days of Lot: They ate, they drank, they bought, they sold, they planted, they built;

29 "but on the [v]day that Lot went out of Sodom it rained fire and brimstone from heaven and destroyed *them* all.

30 "Even so will it be in the [w]day when the [l]Son of Man is [x]revealed.

31 "In that day, he who is on the housetop, and his goods *are* in the house, let him not come down to take them away. And likewise the one who is in the field, let him not turn back.

32 "Remember Lot's [y]wife.

33 [z]"Whoever seeks to save his life will lose it, and whoever loses his life will preserve it.

34 "I tell you, in that night there will be two *men* in one bed: the one will be taken and the other will be left.

35 [aa]"Two *women* will be grinding together: the one will be taken and the other left.

36 "Two *men* will be in the field: the one will be taken and the other left."*

37 And they answered and said to Him, "Where, Lord?" So

13
a Bible prayers (NT): vv. 13, 15–16; Lk. 18:11. (Mt. 6:9; Lk. 11:2, *note*)
14
b Lev. 13:1–59; Mt. 8:4; Lk. 5:14
c Miracles (NT): vv. 14, 19; Lk. 18:43. (Mt. 8:3; Acts 28:8, *note*)
15
d Lk. 5:25; 18:43
16
e 2 Ki. 17:24; Lk. 9:52–53; Jn. 4:9
19
f Mt. 9:22
g Faith: v. 19; Lk. 18:42. (Gen. 3:20; Heb. 11:39, *note*)
20
h See Mt. 6:33, *note*
i Or *outward show.* Jn. 18:36; see v. 21, *note*
21
j Mt. 12:28; Rom. 14:17
22
k Mt. 9:15
l See Mt. 8:20, *note*
23
m Mt. 24:23; cp. Lk. 21:8
n Cp 1 Jn. 4:1

25
o Lk. 9:22
26
p Mt. 24:37–39
q Gen. 6:5–7
r Gen. 6:8–13
s 1 Pet. 3:20
27
t Gen. 7:1–16
u Gen. 7:19–23; cp. 1 Th. 5:3
29
v Gen. 19:29; 2 Pet. 2:6–7
30
w Day (of the LORD): vv. 30–37; Lk. 21:27. (Ps. 2:9; Rev. 19:19)
x Christ (second advent): vv. 30–31; Lk. 18:8. (Dt. 30:3; Acts 1:11, *note*)
32
y Gen. 19:26
33
z Mt. 16:25
35
aa Mt. 24:40–41

*17:21 NU-Text reverses *here* and *there.*
17:23 NU-Text reverses *here* and *there.*
17:36 NU-Text and M-Text omit verse 36.

[1](17:21) The Greek word *entos* carries the force of *in the midst.* It could not be said of a self-righteous, Christ-rejecting Pharisee that the kingdom of God, as to its spiritual content, was "within" his *heart.* Our Lord's whole answer, designedly enigmatic to the Pharisees (cp. Mt. 13:10–13), has a dispensational meaning. The kingdom in its outward form, as covenanted to David (2 Sam. 7:16, *note*) and described by the prophets (Zech. 12:8, *note*) had been rejected by the Jews, so that, during this present age, it would "not come with observation" (lit. "outward show") but in the hearts of men (see Lk. 19:11–12; Acts 1:6–8, *note;* Rom. 14:17). Meantime, the kingdom was actually "in the midst" of the Pharisees in the persons of the King and His disciples. Ultimately the kingdom of heaven will come visibly to earth at our Lord's second coming. See v. 24.

He said to them, [a]"Wherever the body is, there the eagles will be gathered together."

Two parables on prayer
(vv. 1–14)

(1) Persistence rewarded

18 THEN He spoke a [b]parable to them, that men [c]always ought to pray and not lose heart,

2 saying: "There was in a certain city a judge who did not fear God nor regard man.

3 "Now there was a widow in that city; and she came to him, saying, 'Get justice for me from my adversary.'

4 "And he would not for a while; but afterward he said within himself, 'Though I do not fear God nor regard man,

5 'yet because this widow troubles me I will avenge her, lest by her continual coming she weary me.' "

6 Then the Lord said, "Hear what the unjust judge said.

7 "And shall God not avenge His own [d]elect who cry out day and night to Him, though He bears [e]long with them?

8 "I tell you that He will avenge them speedily. Nevertheless, when the [f]Son of Man [g]comes, will He really find [1h]faith on the earth?"

(2) The Pharisee and tax collector: proper and improper attitudes

9 Also He spoke this [b]parable to some who [i]trusted in themselves that they were [j]righteous, and despised others:

10 "Two men went up to the temple to pray, one a Pharisee and the other a tax collector.

11 "The [k]Pharisee stood and [l]prayed thus with himself, 'God, I thank You that I am not like other men—extortioners, unjust, adulterers, or even as this tax collector.

12 'I fast twice a week; I give tithes of all that I possess.'

13 "And the tax collector, standing afar off, would not so much as raise *his* eyes to heaven, but beat his breast, saying, 'God, be [2m]merciful to me a [n]sinner!'

14 "I tell you, this man went down to his house [o]justified *rather* than the other; for everyone who exalts himself will be humbled, and [p]he who humbles himself will be exalted."

Jesus blesses little children
(Mt. 19:13–15; Mk. 10:13–16)

15 Then they also brought infants to Him that He might touch them; but when the disciples saw *it*, they [q]rebuked them.

16 But Jesus called them to *Him* and said, "Let the little children come to Me, and do not forbid them; for of [r]such is the [s]kingdom of God.

17 "Assuredly, I say to you, whoever does not receive the kingdom of God as a little child will by no means enter it."

The rich young ruler
(Mt. 19:16–30; Mk. 10:17–31; cp. Lk. 10:25–37)

18 Now a certain ruler asked Him, saying, "Good Teacher, what shall I do to inherit [t]eternal life?"

19 So Jesus said to him, "Why do you call Me good? No one *is* good but [u]One, *that is*, God.

20 "You [v]know the [w]commandments: *'Do not commit adultery,' 'Do not [x]murder,' 'Do not steal,' 'Do not bear false witness,' 'Honor your father and your mother.'* "

21 And he said, "All [y]these things I have kept from my youth."

37
a Armageddon (battle of): v. 37; Rev. 16:14. (Isa. 10:27; Rev. 19:17)

CHAPTER 18

1
b Parables (NT): vv. 1–14; Lk. 19:11. (Mt. 5:13; Lk. 21:29)
c Rom. 12:12; 1 Th. 5:17

7
d Election (corporate): v. 7; Jn. 6:37. (Dt. 7:6; 1 Pet. 5:13, *note*)
e Cp. 2 Pet. 3:9

8
f See Mt. 8:20, *note*
g Christ (second advent): v. 8; Lk. 21:27. (Dt. 30:3; Acts 1:11, *note*)
h Lit. *the faith. Apostasy:* v. 8; 2 Th. 2:3. (Lk. 18:8; 2 Tim. 3:1, *note*)

9
i Prov. 30:12
j See Rom. 10:3, *note*

11
k See Mt. 3:7, *note 1*
l Bible prayers (NT): vv. 11–13; Lk. 18:38. (Mt. 6:9; Lk. 11:2, *note*). Cp. Isa. 1:15; Rev. 3:17

13
m i.e. *propitiated*
n See Rom. 3:23, *note*

14
o Justification: v. 14; Acts 13:39. (Lk. 18:14; Rom. 3:28, *note*)
p Mt. 23:12; cp. Jas. 4:6; 1 Pet. 5:5–6

15
q v. 39

16
r Mt. 18:3
s See Mt. 6:33, *note*

18
t Life (eternal): vv. 18, 30; Jn. 1:4. (Mt. 7:14; Rev. 22:19)

19
u Ps. 86:5; 119:68

20
v Mk. 10:19
w Law (of Moses): v. 20; Lk. 20:28. (Ex. 19:1; Gal. 3:24, *note*). Ex. 20:3–17; Dt. 5:7–21
x See Ex. 20:13, *note*

21
y Phil. 3:6

---

[1](18:8) The reference is not to personal faith but to belief in the whole body of revealed truth. (Cp. Rom. 1:5; 1 Cor. 16:13; 2 Cor. 13:5; Col. 1:23; 2:7; Ti. 1:13; Jude 3. See v. 8 *marg.*, Apostasy; 2 Tim. 3:1, *note*).

[2](18:13) Greek *hilaskomai,* used in the Septuagint and NT in connection with the mercy seat (Ex. 25:17,18,21; Heb. 9:5). An instructed Jew, the tax collector was thinking, not of mercy alone, but of the blood-sprinkled mercy seat (Lev. 16:5, *note;* see also Propitiation, Rom. 3:25, *note*). His prayer might be paraphrased, "Be toward me as You are when You look on the atoning blood." The Bible knows nothing of divine forgiveness apart from sacrifice (see Mt. 26:28, *note*).

22 So when Jesus heard
these things, He said to him,
"You still [a]lack one thing. Sell
all that you have and distribute
to the poor, and you will have
[b]treasure in heaven; and come,
follow Me."
23 But when he [c]heard this,
he became very [d]sorrowful, for
he was very rich.
24 And when Jesus saw that
he became very sorrowful, He
said, [e]"How hard it is for those
who have riches to enter the
kingdom of God!
25 "For it is easier for a camel
to go through the eye of a [f]nee-
dle than for a rich man to enter
the [g]kingdom of God."
26 And those who heard it
said, "Who then can be
[h]saved?"
27 But He said, "The things
which are impossible with men
are [i]possible with God."

Reward for sacrifice

28 Then Peter said, "See, we
have [j]left all* and followed
You."
29 So He said to them, "Assuredly, I say to you, there is no
one who has left house or parents or brothers or wife or children, for the sake of the [g]king-
dom of God,
30 "who shall not receive
[k]many times more in this present time, and in the [l]age to
come eternal life."

Jesus again foretells His death and resurrection (Mt. 20:17–19; Mk. 10:32–34)

31 Then He took the twelve
aside and said to them, "Behold,
we are [m]going up to Jerusalem,
and all things that are [n]written
by the prophets concerning the
[o]Son of Man will be accomplished.
32 "For He will be [p]delivered
to the Gentiles and will be
mocked and insulted and spit
upon.
33 "They will scourge *Him*
and kill Him. And the third day
He will rise again."
34 But they understood none
of these things; this saying was
[q]hidden from them, and they
did not know the things which
were spoken.

Bartimaeus receives his sight (Mk. 10:46–52; cp. Mt. 20:29–34)

35 Then it happened, as He
was coming near Jericho, that a
certain [r]blind man sat by the
road begging.
36 And hearing a multitude
passing by, he asked what it
meant.
37 So they told him that Jesus of Nazareth was passing by.
38 And he cried out, [s]saying,
"Jesus, [t]Son of David, have
mercy on me!"
39 Then those who went before [u]warned him that he
should be quiet; but he cried out
all the more, [t]"Son of David,
have mercy on me!"
40 So Jesus stood still and
commanded him to be brought
to Him. And when he had come
near, He asked him,
41 saying, "What do you
want Me to do for you?" He
[s]said, "Lord, that I may receive
my sight."
42 Then Jesus said to him,
"Receive your sight; your [v]faith
has [w]made you well."
43 And immediately he [x]re-
ceived his sight, and followed
Him, [y]glorifying God. And all
the people, when they saw *it*,
gave praise to God.

Conversion of Zacchaeus

19 THEN *Jesus* entered and
passed through [z]Jeri-
cho.
2 Now behold, *there was* a
man named Zacchaeus who
was a chief tax collector, and he
was rich.
3 And he sought to [aa]see
who Jesus was, but could not
because of the crowd, for he
was of short stature.
4 So he ran ahead and
climbed up into a sycamore tree
to see Him, for He was going to
pass that *way*.
5 And when Jesus came to
the place, He looked up and saw
him,* and said to him, "Zacchaeus, make haste and come
down, for today I must [bb]stay at
your house."
6 So he made haste and

*
18:28 NU-Text reads *our own*.
19:5 NU-Text omits *and saw him*.

22
a Cp. Jas. 2:10
b Mt. 6:19–20; 1 Tim. 6:19
23
c Cp. Ezek. 33:31
d Cp. Mt. 6:24
24
e Mt. 19:24; Mk. 10:24; 1 Tim. 6:9–10; cp. Prov. 11:28
25
f Gk. *raphis*, a sewing needle
g See Mt. 6:33, *note*
26
h See Rom. 1:16, *note*
27
i Job 42:2; Jer. 32:17
28
j Mt. 19:27; cp. Phil. 3:7–9
30
k Cp. Job 42:10–17
l Gk. *aiōn*. See Mk. 10:30, *note*
31
m Lk. 9:51
n *Inspiration*: vv. 31–33; Lk. 19:46. (Ex. 4:15; 2 Tim. 3:16, *note*). Ps. 22; Isa. 53
o See Mt. 8:20, *note*
32
p Mt. 17:22; Lk. 23:1; Acts 3:13
34
q Mk. 9:32; Lk. 9:45

35
r See Mt. 20:30, *note*
38
s *Bible prayers* (NT): vv. 38, 41; Lk. 22:32. (Mt. 6:9; Lk. 11:2, *note*)
t Mt. 9:27
39
u v. 15
42
v *Faith*: v. 42; Lk. 23:42. (Gen. 3:20; Heb. 11:39, *note*)
w Or *saved you*. See Rom. 1:16, *note*
43
x *Miracles* (NT): v. 43; Lk. 22:51. (Mt. 8:3; Acts 28:8, *note*)
y Lk. 5:26; Acts 4:21
CHAPTER 19
1
z Josh. 6:26; 1 Ki. 16:34
3
aa Jn. 12:21
5
bb Cp. Jn. 14:23

came down, and received Him
joyfully.
7 But when they saw *it*, they
all complained, saying, "He has
gone to be a guest with a man
who is a [a]sinner."
8 Then Zacchaeus stood
and said to the Lord, "Look,
Lord, I give half of my goods to
the [b]poor; and if I have taken
anything from anyone by false
accusation, I [c]restore [1]four-
fold."
9 And Jesus said to him,
"Today [d]salvation has come to
this house, because he also is a
son of [e]Abraham;
10 "for the [f]Son of Man has
come to [g]seek and to [d]save that
which was lost."

The ten minas: parable of long journey (see Lk. 17:21, note, and Acts 1:6–8, note)

11 Now as they heard these
things, He spoke another [h]para-
ble, because He was near Jerusalem and because they thought
the [i]kingdom of God would appear [j]immediately.
12 Therefore He said: "A certain nobleman went into a [k]far
country to receive for himself a
kingdom and to return.
13 "So he called ten of his
[l]servants, delivered to them ten
[m]minas,* and said to them,
[n]'Do business till I come.'
14 "But his citizens hated
him, and sent a delegation after
him, saying, 'We will [o]not have
this *man* to [p]reign over us.'
15 "And so it was that when
he returned, having received
the [i]kingdom, he then commanded these servants, to
whom he had given the
[m]money, to be called to him,
that he might know how much
every man had gained by trading.
16 "Then came the first, saying, 'Master, your [m]mina has
earned ten minas.'
17 "And he said to him,
[q]'Well *done,* good servant; because you were [r]faithful in a
very little, [s]have authority over
ten cities.'
18 "And the second came,
saying, 'Master, your mina has
earned five [m]minas.'
19 "Likewise he said to him,
'You also be over five cities.'
20 "Then another came, saying, 'Master, here is your mina,
which I have kept put away in a
handkerchief.
21 'For I [t]feared you, because you are an austere man.
You collect what you did not deposit, and reap what you did not
sow.'
22 "And he said to him, 'Out
of your own [u]mouth I will judge
you, *you* wicked servant. You
knew that I was an austere man,
collecting what I did not deposit
and [v]reaping what I did not
sow.
23 'Why then did you not put
my [m]money in the bank, that at
my coming I might have collected it with interest?'
24 "And he said to those who
stood by, 'Take the [m]mina from
him, and [s]give *it* to him who
has ten minas.'
25 ("But they said to him,
'Master, he has ten minas.')
26 'For I say to you, that [w]to
everyone who has will be given;
and from him who does not
have, even what he has will be
taken away from him.
27 'But bring here those [x]en-
emies of mine, who did not want
me to reign over them, and
[y]slay *them* before me.' "

IV. The Rejection of Christ, and His Death, 19:28—23:56

Triumphal entry of Jesus (Mt. 21:1–9; Mk. 11:1–10; Jn. 12:12–19; cp. Zech. 9:9)

28 When He had said this, He
went on [z]ahead, going up to Jerusalem.
29 And it came to pass, when
He drew near to Bethphage*
and [aa]Bethany, [bb]at the mountain called [cc]Olivet, *that* He sent
two of His disciples,
30 saying, "Go into the village opposite *you,* where as you
enter you will find a colt tied, on
which [dd]no one has ever sat.
Loose it and bring *it here.*

*
19:13 The *mina* (Greek *mna,* Hebrew *minah*) was worth about three months' salary.
19:29 M-Text reads *Bethsphage.*

7
a Lk. 5:30; 15:2; see Rom. 3:23, *note*
8
b Ps. 41:1
c Cp. Lev. 6:1–5; Num. 5:6–7; Prov. 6:30–31
9
d See Rom. 1:16, *note*
e Gal. 3:7
10
f See Mt. 8:20, *note*
g Mt. 9:13; Mk. 2:17; 10:45; Lk. 5:32; Rom. 5:8
11
h Parables (NT): vv. 11–27; Lk. 20:9. (Mt. 5:13; Lk. 21:29)
i See Mt. 6:33, *note*
j Cp. Lk. 17:20–21
12
k Mt. 25:14; Mk. 13:34
13
l Cp. Lk. 12:37–38; 17:10
m See Coinage (NT), Mt. 5:26, *note*
n Cp. 1 Pet. 4:10–11; 5:2–4
14
o Cp. Ps. 2:2–3; Mt. 21:38; Jn. 1:11
p Cp. 1 Cor. 15:25; Rev. 11:15
17
q Mt. 25:21, 23
r Lk. 16:10; cp. 1 Cor. 4:2
s Rewards: vv. 17–19, 24–26; 1 Cor. 3:8. (Dan. 12:3; 1 Cor. 3:14, *note*). Cp. Rev. 2:26–28

21
t Cp. Rom. 8:15; 2 Tim. 1:6–7; Jas. 2:19
22
u 2 Sam. 1:16; Job 15:6; Mt. 12:37; cp. Rom. 3:19; Ti. 3:11
v Mt. 25:26
26
w Mt. 13:12; Mk. 4:25; Lk. 8:18
27
x Cp. 1 Cor. 15:25; Heb. 10:13
y Cp. Ps. 2:9; Isa. 63:1–6; Rev. 19:11–21
28
z Mk. 10:32; Lk. 9:51
29
aa Mt. 26:6; Jn. 12:1
bb v. 37; cp. Zech. 14:4
cc Jn. 8:1; Acts 1:12
30
dd Cp. Lk. 23:53

[1](19:8) This was in strict accord with Jewish standards of rectitude (Ex. 22:1).

31 "And if anyone asks you,
'Why are you loosing *it?*' thus
you shall say to him, [a]'Because
the Lord has need of it.' "
32 So those who were sent
went their way and found *it* just
[b]as He had said to them.
33 But as they were loosing
the colt, the owners of it said to
them, "Why are you loosing the
colt?"
34 And they said, "The Lord
has need of him."
35 Then they brought him to
Jesus. And they threw their own
clothes on the colt, and they set
Jesus on him.
36 And as He went, *many*
spread their clothes on the road.
37 Then, as He was now
drawing near the descent of the
[c]Mount of Olives, the whole
multitude of the disciples began
to [d]rejoice and praise God with
a loud voice for all the mighty
works they had seen,
38 saying:

[e]" '*Blessed is the [f]King
who [g]comes in the
[h]name of the LORD!*'
[i]Peace in heaven and
glory in the highest!"

39 And some of the [j]Phari-
sees called to Him from the
crowd, "Teacher, [k]rebuke Your
disciples."
40 But He answered and said
to them, "I tell you that if these
should keep silent, the [l]stones
would immediately cry out."

Jesus again laments over Jerusalem
(cp. Mt. 23:37–39; Lk. 13:34–35)

41 Now as He drew near, He
saw the city and [m]wept over it,
42 [1]saying, [n]"If you had
known, even you, especially in
this [o]your day, the things *that*
[p]*make* for your [q]peace! But
now they are hidden from your
eyes.
43 [r]"For days will come upon
you when your enemies will
build an embankment around
you, surround you and close
you in on every side,
44 [s]"and level you, and your
children within you, to the
ground; and they will not leave
in you one stone upon another,
because you did not know the
time of your [t]visitation."

Jesus drives traders from temple
(Mt. 21:12–13; Mk. 11:15–18; cp. Jn. 2:13–16)

45 Then He went into the
temple and began to drive out
those who bought and sold in
it,*
46 saying to them, "It is
[u]written, *'My house is** a
[v]*house of prayer,'* but you have
made it a *'den of thieves.'* "
47 And He was [w]teaching
daily in the temple. But the chief
priests, the [x]scribes, and the
leaders of the people sought to
[y]destroy Him,
48 and were unable to do
anything; for all the people
were very attentive to [z]hear
Him.

Jesus' authority challenged
(Mt. 21:23–27; Mk. 11:27–33)

20

NOW it happened on
one of those days, as He
[w]taught the people in the temple
and preached the [aa]gospel, *that*
the chief priests and the
[x]scribes, together with the elders, confronted *Him*
2 and spoke to Him, saying,
"Tell us, [bb]by what authority are
You doing these things? Or who
is he who gave You this authority?"
3 But He answered and said
to them, "I also will ask you one
thing, and answer Me:
4 "The [cc]baptism of John—
was it from heaven or from
men?"
5 And they reasoned among
themselves, saying, [dd]"If we say,
'From heaven,' He will say,
'Why then* did you not believe
him?'
6 "But if we say, 'From
men,' all the people will stone
us, for they are persuaded that
John was a [ee]prophet."
7 So they answered [ff]that
they did not know where *it was*
from.
8 And Jesus said to them,

*
19:45 NU-Text reads *those who were selling.* **19:46** NU-Text reads *shall be.* **20:5** NU-Text and M-Text omit *then.*

31
a Cp. Ps. 50:10
32
b Lk. 22:13
37
c Jn. 8:1; Acts 1:12
d Lk. 13:17; 18:43
38
e Ps. 118:26; Lk. 13:35; cp. 1 Tim. 1:17
f Kingdom (NT): v. 38; Lk. 22:29. (Mt. 2:2; 1 Cor. 15:24, *note*)
g Christ (first advent): v. 38; Lk. 20:13. (Gen. 3:15; Acts 1:11, *note*)
h Cp. Jn. 5:43
i Cp. Lk. 2:14; Rom. 5:1; Eph. 2:14
39
j See Mt. 3:7, *note 1*
k Cp. Phil. 2:15
40
l Cp. Hab. 2:11
41
m Isa. 53:3; Jn. 11:35; cp. Rom. 12:15
42
n Cp. Dt. 5:29; 32:29; Isa. 48:18
o Ps. 95:7–8; Heb. 3:13
p Lk. 1:77–79; Acts 10:36; cp. Dan. 9:24
q Rom. 5:1
43
r Israel (prophecies): vv. 41–44; Lk. 21:20. (Gen. 12:2; Rom. 11:26, *note*)
44
s 1 Ki. 9:7; Mt. 24:2; Mk. 13:2; Lk. 21:6

t Lk. 1:68; Jn. 12:35
46
u Inspiration: v. 46; Lk. 20:17. (Ex. 4:15; 2 Tim. 3:16, *note*)
v Isa. 56:7; Jer. 7:11
47
w Lk. 21:37; 22:53
x See Mt. 2:4, *note*
y Lk. 20:19; Jn. 7:19
48
z Lk. 21:38
CHAPTER 20
1
aa Gospel: v. 1; Lk. 24:47. (Gen. 12:3; Rev. 14:6)
2
bb Cp. Acts 4:7,10
4
cc Jn. 1:26,31
5
dd Cp. Jn. 5:33–36
6
ee Mt. 14:5; Mk. 6:20; Lk. 7:24–29
7
ff Job 24:13; cp. Rom. 1:18,21; 2 Cor. 4:3; 2 Th. 2:10

[1](19:42) As perfect Man, He wept; as Son of God, He warned (cp. Isa. 10:1–4).

"Neither will I tell you by what authority I do these things."

Parable of the vineyard owner
(Mt. 21:33–46; Mk. 12:1–9; cp. Isa. 5:1–7)

9 Then He began to tell the people this [a]parable: "A certain man planted a [b]vineyard, leased it to vinedressers, and went into a far country for a long time.

10 "Now at vintage-time he [c]sent a servant to the vinedressers, that they might give him some of the fruit of the vineyard. But the vinedressers beat him and sent *him* away empty-handed.

11 "Again he sent another servant; and they beat him also, treated *him* shamefully, and sent *him* away empty-handed.

12 "And again he sent a third; and they wounded him also and cast *him* out.

13 "Then the owner of the vineyard said, 'What shall I do? I will [d]send my beloved son. Probably they will respect *him* when they see him.'

14 "But when the vinedressers saw him, they reasoned among themselves, saying, 'This is the [e]heir. Come, [f]let us kill him, that the inheritance may be [g]ours.'

15 "So they cast him out of the vineyard and [h]killed *him*. Therefore what will the owner of the vineyard do to them?

16 "He will come and [i]destroy those vinedressers and give the vineyard to [j]others." And when they heard *it* they said, "Certainly not!"

17 Then He looked at them and said, "What then is this that is [k]written:

[l]*'The [m]stone which the*
builders rejected
Has become the chief
cornerstone'?

18 "Whoever falls on that stone will be [n]broken; [o]but on whomever it falls, it will grind him to powder."

Jesus answers the Herodians
(Mt. 22:15–22; Mk. 12:13–17)

19 And the chief priests and the [p]scribes that very hour sought to lay hands on Him, but they feared the people*—for they knew He had spoken this parable against them.

20 So they watched *Him*, and sent spies who pretended to be righteous, that they might seize on His words, in order to deliver Him to the power and the authority of the governor.

21 Then they asked Him, saying, "Teacher, we know that You say and teach rightly, and You do not show personal favoritism, but teach the way of God in truth:

22 "Is it lawful for us to pay taxes to Caesar or not?"

23 But He perceived their craftiness, and said to them, "Why do you [q]test Me?*

24 "Show Me a [r]denarius. Whose image and inscription does it have?" They answered and said, "Caesar's."

25 And He said to them, [s]"Render therefore to Caesar the things that are Caesar's, and to God the things that are God's."

26 But they could not catch Him in His words in the presence of the people. And they [t]marveled at His answer and kept silent.

Jesus answers the Sadducees
(Mt. 22:23–33; Mk. 12:18–27)

27 Then some of the [u]Sadducees, who deny that there is a resurrection, came to *Him* and asked Him,

28 saying: "Teacher, [v]Moses wrote to us *that* if a man's brother dies, having a wife, and he dies without children, his [w]brother should take his wife and raise up offspring for his brother.

29 "Now there were seven brothers. And the first took a wife, and died without children.

30 "And the second* took her as wife, and he died childless.

31 "Then the third took her, and in like manner the seven

9
a Parables (NT): vv. 9–18; Lk. 21:29. (Mt. 5:13; Lk. 21:29)
b Ps. 80:8; cp. Isa. 5:1–7
10
c 2 Ki. 17:13–14; 2 Chr. 36:15–16; Acts 7:52; 1 Th. 2:15; cp. Heb. 11:32–39
13
d Christ (first advent): vv. 13–15; Jn. 1:14. (Gen. 3:15; Acts 1:11, *note*). Jn. 3:16; Rom. 8:3; Gal. 4:4; Heb. 1:1–2
14
e Heb. 1:1–3
f Mt. 27:21–23
g Jn. 11:47–48
15
h Lk. 23:33; Acts 2:22–23; 3:15
16
i Cp. Prov. 1:24–31
j Jn. 1:11–13; Rom. 11:11
17
k Inspiration: v. 17; Lk. 20:37. (Ex. 4:15; 2 Tim. 3:16, *note*). See Mt. 21:44, *note*
l Ps. 118:22; 1 Pet. 2:7–8
m Christ (Stone): vv. 17–18; Jn. 7:38. (Gen. 49:24; 1 Pet. 2:8)
18
n Isa. 8:14–15
o Dan. 2:34–35, 44–45
19
p See Mt. 2:4, *note*

23
q Test/tempt: vv. 21–23; Lk. 22:28. (Gen. 3:1; Jas. 1:14, *note*)
24
r See Coinage (NT), Mt. 5:26, *note*
25
s Mt. 17:24–27; Rom. 13:7; 1 Pet. 2:13–17
26
t Cp. Col. 4:6
27
u Mt. 16:1,6, 12; Acts 4:1–2; 23:6–8; see Mt. 3:7, *note*
28
v Law (of Moses): v. 28; Lk. 24:27. (Ex. 19:1; Gal. 3:24, *note*). Dt. 25:5–6
w Cp. Gen. 38:8–10

*
20:19 M-Text reads *but they were afraid.*
20:23 NU-Text omits *Why do you test Me?*
20:30 NU-Text ends verse 30 here.

also; and they left no children,* and died.

32 "Last of all the woman died also.

33 "Therefore, in the resurrection, whose wife does she become? For all seven had her as wife."

34 Jesus answered and said to them, "The sons of this [a]age marry and are given in marriage.

35 "But those who are [b]counted worthy to attain that [a]age, and the [c]resurrection from the dead, neither marry nor are given in marriage;

36 "nor can they [d]die anymore, for they are equal to the [e]angels and are sons of God, [f]being sons of the resurrection.

37 "But even [g]Moses [h]showed in the *burning* bush *passage* that the dead are raised, when he called the Lord *'the God of Abraham, the God of Isaac, and the God of Jacob.'*

38 "For He is not the God of the dead but of the [i]living, for all live to Him."

Jesus questions and denounces the scribes (cp. Mt. 22:41—23:36; Mk. 12:35–40)

39 Then some of the [j]scribes answered and said, "Teacher, You have spoken well."

40 But after that they dared not question Him anymore.

41 And He said to them, "How can they say that the Christ is the [k]Son of David?

42 "Now David himself [h]said in the Book of Psalms:

[l]*'The* LORD *said to my*
Lord,
"Sit at My right hand,
43 *Till I make Your enemies*
Your footstool."'

44 "Therefore David calls Him *'Lord'*; [m]how is He then his Son?"

45 Then, in the hearing of all the people, He said to His disciples,

46 [n]"Beware of the [j]scribes, who desire to go around in long robes, love [o]greetings in the marketplaces, the [p]best seats in the synagogues, and the best places at feasts,

47 "who [q]devour widows' houses, and for a [r]pretense make long prayers. These will receive [s]greater condemnation."

The widow's mites (Mk. 12:41–44)

21

AND He looked up and saw the rich putting their gifts into the treasury,

2 and He saw also a certain [t]poor widow putting in two [u]mites.

3 So He said, "Truly I say to you that this poor widow has put in more than all;

4 "for all these out of their abundance have put in offerings for God,* but she out of her poverty put in [v]all the livelihood that she had."

The Olivet Discourse (vv. 5–38) (Mt. 24—25; Mk. 13)

5 Then, as some spoke of the [w]temple, how it was adorned with beautiful stones and donations, He said,

6 "These things which you see—the days will come in which [x]not *one* stone shall be left upon another that shall not be thrown down."

The disciples' two questions: When and What? (Mt. 24:3; Mk. 13:4)

7 So they asked Him, saying, "Teacher, but when will these things be? And what sign *will there be* when these things are about to take place?"

Daniel's seventieth week of years (Dan. 9:27): the end time (Mt. 24:4–14; Mk. 13:5–13)

8 [y]And He said: "Take heed that you not be [z]deceived. For many will come in My name, saying, 'I am *He*,' and, 'The time has drawn near.' Therefore* do not go after them.

9 "But when you hear of [aa]wars and commotions, do not be terrified; for these things must come to pass first, but the end *will not come* immediately."

10 Then He said to them, "Nation will rise against nation, and kingdom against kingdom.

11 "And there will be great

34
a Gk. *aiōn.* See Mk. 10:30, *note*
35
b Phil. 3:11; cp. Lk. 21:36; 2 Th. 1:5; Rev. 3:4
c Resurrection: vv. 27–38; Lk. 24:6. (2 Ki. 4:35; 1 Cor. 15:52, *note*)
36
d Death (physical): v. 36; Rom. 5:14. (Gen. 2:17; Heb. 9:27, *note*). Cp. 1 Cor. 15:42,49,52
e See Heb. 1:4, *note*
f Rom. 8:23; 1 Jn. 3:2
37
g Ex. 3:1–6; Acts 7:30–32
h Inspiration: vv. 37, 42–43; Lk. 21:22. (Ex. 4:15; 2 Tim. 3:16, *note*)
38
i Rom. 14:8–9; Heb. 11:16
39
j See Mt. 2:4, *note*
41
k Mt. 1:1; Lk. 18:38; cp. Isa. 9:6–7
42
l vv. 41–44; Ps. 110:1; Acts 2:34–35
44
m Acts 13:22–23; Rom. 1:3; 9:4–5
46
n Lk. 12:1
o Lk. 11:43
p Lk. 14:7
47
q Mt. 23:14
r Mt. 6:5–6
s Cp. Lk. 10:12–14

CHAPTER 21
2
t 2 Cor. 6:10
u Smallest coin. See Coinage (NT), Mt. 5:26, *note*
4
v 2 Cor. 8:12
5
w Cp. Jn. 2:19–21
6
x Isa. 64:10–11; Lam. 2:6–9; Mic. 3:12; Lk. 19:41–44
8
y See Mt. 24:3, *note*
z Eph. 5:6; 2 Th. 2:3; 1 Jn. 4:1; cp. 2 Cor. 11:13–15; 2 Tim. 3:13; Rev. 12:9
9
aa Rev. 6:4

*
20:31 NU-Text and M-Text read *the seven also left no children.* **21:4** NU-Text omits *for God.* **21:8** NU-Text omits *Therefore.*

[a]earthquakes in various places,
and famines and pestilences;
and there will be fearful sights
and great signs from heaven.

Suffering of apostles and believers prior to seventieth week

12 "But before all these
things, [b]they will lay their
hands on you and persecute
you, delivering *you* up to the
synagogues and prisons. You
will be brought before kings
and rulers for My name's sake.
13 "But it will turn out for you
as an occasion for [c]testimony.
14 "Therefore settle *it* in your
hearts not to meditate beforehand on what you will answer;
15 "for I will give you a
mouth and wisdom which all
your adversaries will not be
able to contradict or resist.
16 "You will be betrayed
even by parents and brothers,
relatives and friends; and they
will put *some* of you to death.
17 "And you will be hated by
all for My name's sake.
18 "But not a hair of your
head shall be lost.
19 "By your patience possess
your souls.

Destruction of Jerusalem foretold

20 "But [1]when you see Jerusalem [d]surrounded by armies,
then know that its [e]desolation
is near.
21 "Then let those who are in
Judea flee to the mountains, let
those who are in the midst of
her depart, and let not those
who are in the country enter
her.

11
a Rev. 6:12
12
b Jn. 16:2; Rev. 2:10
13
c Phil. 1:12–14
20
d Israel (prophecies): v. 20; Jn. 1:31. (Gen. 12:2; Rom. 11:26, *note*)
e Tribulation (the great): vv. 20–26; Rev. 3:10. (Ps. 2:5; Rev. 7:14)

22 "For these are the [f]days of
vengeance, that [g]all things
which are [h]written may be fulfilled.
23 "But woe to those who are
pregnant and to those who are
nursing babies in those days!
For there will be great distress
in the land and wrath upon this
people.
24 "And they will fall by the
edge of the sword, and be led
away captive into all nations.
And Jerusalem will be [2]tram-
pled by Gentiles until the [i]times
of the Gentiles are fulfilled.

Return of Christ to earth at the close of the tribulation
(Mt. 24:27–31; Mk. 13:24–27)

25 "And there will be [j]signs
in the sun, in the moon, and in
the stars; and on the earth distress of nations, with [k]perplex-
ity, the sea and the waves roaring;
26 "men's hearts failing them
from fear and the expectation of
those things which are coming
on the earth, for the powers of
the heavens will be shaken.
27 "Then they will see the
[l]Son of Man [3m]coming [n]in a
cloud with power and great
glory.
28 "Now when these things
begin to happen, look up and lift
up your heads, because your
[o]redemption draws near."

Parable of the fig tree
(Mt. 24:32–35; Mk. 13:28–31)

29 Then He spoke to them a
[4p]parable: "Look at the fig tree,
and all the trees.

22
f Day (of destruction): v. 22; Lk. 21:35. (Job 21:30; Rev. 20:11)
g Isa. 65:12–15
h Inspiration: v. 22; Lk. 22:22. (Ex. 4:15; 2 Tim. 3:16, *note*)
24
i Times of the Gentiles: v. 24; Rev. 11:2. (Dt. 28:49; Rev. 16:19)
25
j Isa. 13:9–10, 13; 2 Pet. 3:10–12
k Cp. 2 Chr. 15:5–6
27
l See Mt. 8:20, *note*
m Christ (second advent): v. 27; Jn. 14:3. (Dt. 30:3; Acts 1:11, *note*). 2 Th. 1:7–10
n Day (of the LORD): v. 27; Lk. 21:34. (Ps. 2:9; Rev. 19:19)
28
o See Rom. 3:24, *note*
29
p Parables (NT): vv. 29–33. (Mt. 5:13; Lk. 21:29)

---

[1](21:20) Two sieges of Jerusalem are in view in the Olivet Discourse, the one fulfilled in A.D. 70, and the other yet to be fulfilled at the end of the age. Here the reference is to the siege by Titus, A.D. 70, when the city was taken and vv. 20–24 literally fulfilled. These horrors illustrate the conditions in Palestine at the time of the end, but neither v. 20 nor v. 24 is included in the accounts of the Olivet Discourse given by Matthew and Mark. The references in Mt. 24:15–28 and Mk. 13:14–26 are to the final siege, when the city will be taken by enemies but delivered by the return of the Lord to the earth (Rev. 19:11–21; Zech. 14:2–4). In Lk. the sign is Jerusalem being surrounded by armies (21:20); in Mt. 24:15 and Mk. 13:14 the sign is the abomination of desolation in the Holy Place (2 Th. 2:4; Rev. 13:12–15).

[2](21:24) The "times of the Gentiles" began with the captivity of Judah under Nebuchadnezzar (2 Chr. 36:1–21). Since that time Jerusalem has been, as Christ said, "trampled by Gentiles." See *marg.* also.

[3](21:27) This is clearly the return of Christ in which He comes to the earth, not His return to translate the Church. Signs in the sun, moon, and stars, and the shaking of the heavens do not accompany the rapture but are phenomena that will take place after the Church is gone (cp. 2 Pet. 3:10–13; Rev. 6:12–17).

[4](21:29) Parables (NT), Summary: In the NT, as in the OT, a parable is a similitude used to teach or enforce a truth (see Zech. 11:7, *note*). No one in Scripture record is as generous in the use of the parabolic method of teaching as Christ, who employs it liberally to illustrate

30 "When they are already
budding, you see and know for
yourselves that summer is now
near.
31 "So you also, when you
see these things happening,
know that the [a]kingdom of God
is [b]near.
32 "Assuredly, I say to you,
this [c]generation will by no
means pass away till all things
take place.
33 [d]"Heaven and earth will
pass away, but My [e]words will
by no means pass away.

Watchfulness enjoined
(Mt. 24:36–51; Mk. 13:32–37)

34 "But take heed to yourselves, lest your hearts be
weighed down with carousing,
[f]drunkenness, and [g]cares of
this life, and that [h]Day come on
you unexpectedly.
35 [i]"For [j]it will come as a
snare on all those who dwell on
the face of the whole earth.
36 [k]"Watch therefore, and
[l]pray always that you may be
counted [m]worthy* to escape all
these things that will come to
pass, and to stand before the
Son of Man."
37 And in the daytime He
was teaching in the temple, but
at night He went out and stayed
on the mountain called Olivet.
38 Then early in the morning
all the people came to Him in
the temple to hear Him.

Judas agrees to betray Jesus
(Mt. 26:14–16; Mk. 14:1–2,10–11)

22 NOW the Feast of Un-
leavened Bread drew
near, which is called [n]Passover.
2 And the chief priests and
the [o]scribes sought how they
might kill Him, for they feared
the people.
3 Then [p]Satan entered Judas, surnamed Iscariot, who
was numbered among the
[q]twelve.
4 So he went his way and
conferred with the chief priests
and captains, how he might betray Him to them.
5 And they were glad, and
[r]agreed to give him money.
6 So he promised and
sought opportunity to [s]betray
Him to them in the absence of
the multitude.

Preparation for the Passover
(Mt. 26:17–19; Mk. 14:12–16)

7 Then came the Day of Unleavened Bread, when the Passover must be killed.
8 And He sent Peter and
John, saying, "Go and prepare
the Passover for us, that we may
eat."
9 So they said to Him,
"Where do You want us to prepare?"
10 And He said to them, "Behold, when you have entered
the city, a man will meet you
carrying a pitcher of water; follow him into the house which he
enters.
11 "Then you shall say to the
master of the house, 'The
Teacher says to you, [t]"Where is
the guest room where I may eat
the [n]Passover with My disciples?" '
12 "Then he will show you a
large, furnished upper room;
there make ready."
13 So they went and [u]found
it just as He had said to them,
and they prepared the Passover.

The last Passover (Mt. 26:20;
Mk. 14:17; Jn. 13:1–17)

14 [1]When the hour had come,
He sat down, and the [q]twelve*
apostles with Him.
15 Then He said to them,
"With *fervent* desire I have de-

31
a See Mt. 6:33, *note*
b See Mt. 4:17, *note*
32
c See Mt. 24:34, *note*
33
d Isa. 51:6; Heb. 1:10–11; 2 Pet. 3:7, 10,12
e Isa. 40:8; Lk. 16:17; 1 Pet. 1:24–25
34
f Rom. 13:13
g Lk. 8:14
h Day (of the LORD): vv. 34–35; Acts 2:20. (Ps. 2:9; Rev. 19:19)
35
i 1 Th. 5:2–3; 2 Pet. 3:10; Rev. 16:15
j Day (of destruction): v. 35; 2 Th. 1:8. (Job 21:30; Rev. 20:11)
36
k Mt. 25:13
l Lk. 18:1; Eph. 6:18; Col. 4:2; 1 Th. 5:17
m Lk. 20:35
CHAPTER 22
1
n See Ex. 12:11, *note*
2
o See Mt. 2:4, *note*
3
p Satan: vv. 3–6; Lk. 22:31. (Gen. 3:1; Rev. 20:10)
q Mt. 10:2–4

5
r Zech. 11:12; cp. 1 Tim. 6:10
6
s vv. 3–6, 21–23, 47–48; Ps. 41:9
11
t Cp. Lk. 2:7
13
u Lk. 19:32

*21:36 NU-Text reads *may have strength.*
22:14 NU-Text omits *twelve.*

important spiritual truths, with stories of things familiar in the natural realm. Asked by His disciples why He spoke in parables, our Lord admitted two purposes: that (a) His followers might know the mysteries of the kingdom; and (b) those whose hearts were hardened might neither hear nor understand the same doctrine (Mt. 13:10–17). Parables in the NT fall into three classifications: (1) general, e.g. Mk. 9:50; Lk. 10:30–37; 18:9–14; Rom. 7:1–6; (2) pertaining to the Church Age, e.g. Mt. 13:3–9,18–23; and (3) relating to the Messianic kingdom, e.g. Mt. 24:45–51; Lk. 14:16–24.

[1](22:14) For the order of events on the night of the Passover Supper, see Mt. 26:20, *note.*

15
a Cp. Heb. 9:11–12,26 with Heb. 10:1–9
b Cp. 1 Cor. 5:7
16
c v. 30; cp. Rev. 19:9
17
d v. 20
18
e See Mt. 6:33, *note*

sired to [a]eat [b]this Passover
with you before I suffer;
16 "for I say to you, I will no
longer eat of it [c]until it is fulfilled in the kingdom of God."
17 The He took the [d]cup,
and gave thanks, and said,
"Take this and divide *it* among
yourselves;
18 "for I say to you,* I will
not drink of the fruit of the vine
until the [e]kingdom of God
comes."

The Lord's Supper instituted (Mt. 26:26–29; Mk. 14:22–25; cp. Jn. 13:12–30; 1 Cor. 11:23–26)

19 And He took bread, gave
thanks and broke *it*, and gave *it*
to them, saying, "This is My
[f]body which is given for you;
[g]do this in remembrance of
Me."
20 Likewise He also *took* the
cup after supper, saying, "This
cup *is* the [h]new covenant in My

19
f 1 Pet. 2:24
g 1 Cor. 11:23–26
20
h Covenant (New): v. 20; Rom. 11:27. (Isa. 61:8; Heb. 8:8, *note*)

*22:18 NU-Text adds *from now on.*

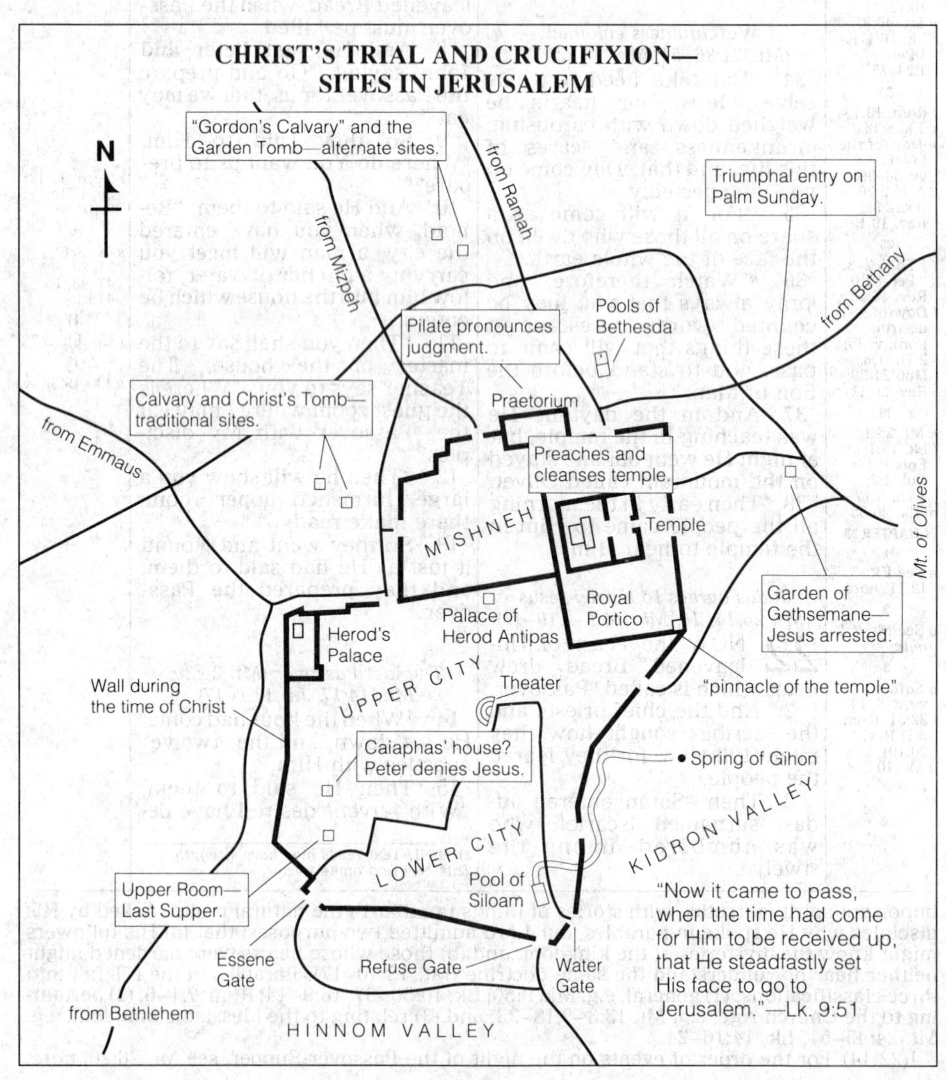

[a]blood, which is [b]shed for you.

Jesus predicts His betrayal
(Mt. 26:21–25; Mk. 14:18–21;
Jn. 13:18–30)

21 "But behold, the hand of
My [c]betrayer *is* with Me on the
table.
22 "And truly the [d]Son of
Man goes [e]as it [f]has been determined, but woe to that man
by whom He is betrayed!"
23 Then they began to question among themselves, which
of them it was who would do
this thing.

Renewed strife over who should be
the greatest (Mt. 20:20–28;
Mk. 9:33–37; 10:35–45;
Jn. 13:1–17)

24 Now there was also a dispute among them, as to which of
them should be considered the
[g]greatest.
25 And He said to them, "The
kings of the Gentiles exercise
lordship over them, and those
who exercise authority over
them are called 'benefactors.'
26 [h]"But not so *among* you;
on the contrary, he who is greatest among you, let him be as the
younger, and he who governs as
he who serves.
27 "For who *is* greater, he
who sits at the table, or he who
serves? *Is* it not he who sits at
the table? Yet I am among you
as the One who [i]serves.

The apostles' reward
in future kingdom (Mt. 19:27–30;
Mk. 10:28–31; cp. Rev. 3:31)

28 "But you are those who
have continued with Me in My
[j]trials.
29 "And I bestow upon you a
[k]kingdom, just as My Father bestowed *one* upon Me,
30 "that you may eat and
drink at My table in My kingdom, and [l]sit on thrones [m]judg-
ing the twelve [n]tribes of Israel."

20
a 1 Cor. 10:16
b *Sacrifice* (of Christ): vv. 19–20; Lk. 23:33. (Gen. 3:15; Heb. 10:18, *note*)
21
c Jn. 13:21, 26–27
22
d See Mt. 8:20, *note*
e Jn. 17:12; Acts 2:23
f *Inspiration:* vv. 22, 37; Lk. 23:30. (Ex. 4:15; 2 Tim. 3:16, *note*). Ps. 41:9; 55:12–14
24
g v. 26; Lk. 9:46–48
26
h 1 Pet. 5:3
27
i Lk. 12:37; Phil. 2:7; cp. 1 Cor. 9:19
28
j *Test/tempt:* vv. 28, 31–32; Lk. 22:40. (Gen. 3:1; Jas. 1:14, *note*). Cp. Heb. 4:15
29
k *Kingdom* (NT): vv. 29–30; Lk. 23:42. (Mt. 2:2; 1 Cor. 15:24, *note*). See Mt. 3:2, *note*
30
l Mt. 19:28; Rev. 3:21
m Cp. 1 Cor. 6:2
n Cp. Rev. 7:4–8; 21:12

Jesus foretells Peter's denial
(Mt. 26:30–35; Mk. 14:26–31;
Jn. 13:36–38)

31 And the Lord said,* "Simon, Simon! Indeed, [o]Satan
has [p]asked for you, that he may
[j]sift *you* as [1]wheat.
32 "But I have [q]prayed for
you, that your faith should not
fail; and when you have returned to *Me*, [r]strengthen your
brethren."
33 But he said to Him, "Lord,
I am ready to go with You, both
to prison and to death."
34 Then He said, "I tell you,
Peter, the rooster shall not crow
this day before you will [s]deny
three times that you know Me."

Disciples warned of
coming conflict
(cp. Jn. 14—16;
contra. Mt. 10:9–13)

35 And He said to them,
[t]"When I sent you without
money bag, knapsack, and sandals, did you lack anything?" So
they said, "Nothing."
36 Then He said to them,
"But now, he who has a money
bag, let him take *it*, and likewise
a knapsack; and he who has no
sword, let him sell his garment
and buy one.
37 "For I say to you that this
which is [f]written must still be
accomplished in [2]Me: *'And He*
was [u]*numbered with the*
[v]*transgressors.'* For the things
concerning Me have an end."
38 So they said, "Lord, look,
here *are* two swords." And He
said to them, "It is enough."

Jesus' agony in the garden
(Mt. 26:36–46; Mk. 14:32–42;
cp. Heb. 5:7–8)

39 Coming out, He went to
the [w]Mount of Olives, as He was
accustomed, and His disciples
also followed Him.
40 When He came to the
place, He said to them, "Pray

*
22:31 NU-Text omits *And the Lord said.*

31
o *Satan:* v. 31; Jn. 8:44. (Gen. 3:1; Rev. 20:10)
p 1 Pet. 5:8
32
q *Bible prayers* (NT): v. 32; Lk. 22:42. (Mt. 6:9; Lk. 11:2, *note*)
r Jn. 21:15–17; 2 Pet. 1:10–15
34
s Cp. Rev. 3:8
35
t Lk. 9:3; 10:4; cp. 1 Ki. 17:2–6
37
u Isa. 53:12; Mk. 15:28. For divine imputation see Jas. 2:23, *note*
v See Rom. 3:23, *note*
39
w Lk. 21:37

[1](22:31) Peter was, as it were, the wheat; his self-confidence, the chaff. Cp. Jn. 5:24; 10:28; Rom. 6:1–2; 1 Jn. 1:8; 2:1.

[2](22:37) At this point Christ emphatically applies to Himself a portion of Isa. 53. Therefore, to deny that the fifty-third chapter of Isaiah predicts Christ's suffering is to contradict the Savior's own interpretation of the prophecy. For another authentication of the central meaning of Isa. 53, see Acts 8:32–35.

that you may not enter [a]into [b]temptation."

41 And He was withdrawn from them about a stone's throw, and He knelt down and prayed,

42 [c]saying, "Father, if it is Your will, take this [d]cup away from Me; nevertheless [e]not My will, but Yours, be done."

43 Then [f]an [g]angel appeared to Him from heaven, strengthening Him.

44 And being in agony, He prayed more earnestly. Then His sweat became like great drops of blood falling down to the ground.*

45 When He rose up from prayer, and had come to His disciples, He found them [1]sleeping from sorrow.

46 Then He said to them, "Why do you [h]sleep? Rise and [i]pray, lest you enter into [b]temptation."

Jesus betrayed by Judas (Mt. 26:47–54; Mk. 14:43–47; Jn. 18:2–11)

47 And while He was still speaking, behold, a [j]multitude; and he who was called [k]Judas, one of the twelve, went before them and drew near to Jesus to kiss Him.

48 But Jesus said to him, "Judas, are you betraying the [l]Son of Man with a [m]kiss?"

49 When those around Him saw what was going to happen, they said to Him, "Lord, shall we strike with the sword?"

50 And one of them struck the servant of the high priest and cut off his right ear.

51 But Jesus answered and said, "Permit even this." And He touched his ear and [n]healed him.

52 Then Jesus said to the chief priests, captains of the temple, and the elders who had come to Him, "Have you come out, as against a [o]robber, with swords and clubs?

53 "When I was with you daily in the [p]temple, you did not try to seize Me. But this is your [q]hour, and the power of darkness."

Jesus' arrest; Peter's three denials (Mt. 26:55–58,69–75; Mk. 14:48–54,66–72; Jn. 18:15–18,25–27)

54 [2]Having arrested Him, they [r]led *Him* and brought Him into the high priest's house. But Peter followed [s]at a distance.

55 Now when they had kindled a fire in the midst of the courtyard and sat down together, Peter sat [t]among them.

56 And a certain servant girl, seeing him as he sat by the fire, looked intently at him and said, "This man was also with Him."

57 But he [u]denied Him,* saying, "Woman, I do not know Him."

58 And after a little while another saw him and said, "You also are of them." But Peter said, "Man, I am not!"

59 Then after about an hour had passed, another confidently affirmed, saying, "Surely this *fellow* also was with Him, for he is a [v]Galilean."

60 But Peter said, "Man, I do not know what you are saying!" Immediately, while he was still speaking, the rooster* crowed.

61 And the Lord turned and [w]looked at Peter. Then Peter [x]remembered the word of the Lord, how He had said to him, [y]"Before the rooster crows,* you will deny Me three times."

62 So Peter went out and [z]wept bitterly.

Jesus mocked and beaten (Mt. 26:67–68; Mk. 14:65; Jn. 18:22–23)

63 [aa]Now the men who held Jesus mocked Him and [bb]beat Him.

64 And having blindfolded

40
a Lk. 11:4
b *Test/tempt:* vv. 40,46; Jn. 6:6. (Gen. 3:1; Jas. 1:14, *note*)

42
c *Bible prayers* (NT): v. 42; Lk. 23:34. (Mt. 6:9; Lk. 11:2, *note*)
d See Mt. 26:39, *note*
e Jn. 4:34; 5:30; 6:38; 8:29

43
f Mt. 4:11
g See Heb. 1:4, *note*

46
h Lk. 9:32
i 1 Chr. 16:11; Lk. 18:1; Eph. 6:18; 1 Th. 5:17

47
j Cp. Ps. 3:6; 27:3
k Acts 1:16–17

48
l See Mt. 8:20, *note*
m Prov. 27:6; cp. Ps. 2:12

51
n *Miracles* (NT): vv. 50–51; Jn. 2:9. (Mt. 8:3; Acts 28:8, *note*)

52
o Lk. 23:32

53
p Lk. 19:47–48
q Jn. 12:27; cp. Acts 2:23

54
r Isa. 53:7–8; Acts 8:32; cp. Lk. 4:1
s Cp. Mk. 14:50; Jn. 21:19

55
t Cp. Gen. 12:11–16; 19:1–16; Ps. 1:1; 2 Cor. 6:17–18; Jas. 4:4

57
u vv. 58,60

59
v Acts 1:11; 2:7

61
w Cp. Ps. 32:8; Isa. 66:2
x v. 34; cp. Ezek. 16:63; Rev. 2:5
y Jn. 13:38

62
z Cp. 2 Cor. 7:10–11

63
aa Ps. 69:1,4, 7–9
bb Isa. 50:6

*
22:44 NU-Text brackets verses 43 and 44 as not in the original text. **22:57** NU-Text reads *denied it.* **22:60** NU-Text and M-Text read *a rooster.* **22:61** NU-Text adds *today.*

[1](22:45) Peter was sleeping while his Master was praying (v. 45), and resisting while his Master was submitting (vv. 49–51; cp. Jn. 18:10). He followed at a distance (v. 54), sat down among his Lord's enemies (v. 55), and denied the Lord, the faith, and the brotherhood (vv. 57,58,60).

[2](22:54) For the order of events following Christ's arrest, see Mt. 26:57, *note.*

Him, they [a]struck Him on the
face and asked Him,* saying,
"Prophesy! Who is the one who
struck You?"
65 And many other things
they blasphemously spoke
against Him.

Jesus before the Sanhedrin
(Mt. 26:59–68; 27:1; Mk. 14:55–65;
15:1; Jn. 18:19–24)

66 As soon as it was day, the
elders of the people, both chief
priests and [b]scribes, [c]came together and led Him into their
council, saying,
67 [d]"If You are the Christ,
tell us." But He said to them, "If
I tell you, you will [e]by no means
believe.
68 "And if I also ask *you,* you
will by no means answer Me or
let *Me* go.*
69 [f]"Hereafter the [g]Son of
Man will [h]sit on the right hand
of the power of God."
70 Then they all said, "Are
You then the Son of God?" So
He said to them, "You *rightly*
say that [i]I am."
71 And they said, "What further [j]testimony do we need?
For we have [k]heard it ourselves
from His own mouth."

Jesus before Pilate
(Mt. 27:2,11–14;
Mk. 15:1–5; Jn. 18:28–38)

23 THEN the whole [l]multi-
tude of them arose and
led Him to [m]Pilate.
2 And they began to [n]ac-
cuse Him, saying, "We found
this *fellow* [o]perverting the* nation, and [p]forbidding to pay
taxes to Caesar, saying that He
Himself is Christ, a [q]King."
3 Then Pilate asked Him,
saying, "Are You the King of the
Jews?" He answered him and
said, [r]"*It is as* you say."
4 So Pilate said to the chief
priests and the crowd, [s]"I find
no fault in this Man."
5 But they were the more
fierce, saying, "He [t]stirs up the
people, teaching throughout all
Judea, beginning from Galilee
to this place."

Pilate sends Jesus to Herod

6 When Pilate heard of
[u]Galilee,* he asked if the Man
were a Galilean.
7 And as soon as he knew
that He belonged to [v]Herod's
jurisdiction, he sent Him to
[w]Herod, who was also in Jerusalem at that time.
8 Now when [v]Herod saw
Jesus, he was exceedingly glad;
for he had [x]desired for a long
time to see Him, because he had
[y]heard many things about Him,
and he hoped to see some miracle done by Him.
9 Then he questioned Him
with many words, but He answered him [z]nothing.
10 And the chief priests and
[b]scribes stood and vehemently
accused Him.
11 Then [v]Herod, with his
men of war, treated Him with
contempt and [aa]mocked *Him,*
arrayed Him in a gorgeous
robe, and sent Him back to Pilate.
12 That very day Pilate and
Herod became friends [bb]with
each other, for previously they
had been at enmity with each
other.

Herod sends Jesus back to Pilate,
who seeks to release Him
(Mt. 27:15–26; Mk. 15:6–15;
Jn. 18:39—19:16)

13 Then Pilate, when he had
[cc]called together the chief
priests, the rulers, and the people,
14 said to them, "You have
brought this Man to me, as one
who [dd]misleads the people. And
indeed, having examined *Him*
in your presence, I have found
[ee]no fault in this Man concerning those things of which you
[dd]accuse Him;
15 "no, neither did [v]Herod,
for I sent you back to him;* and
indeed [ff]nothing deserving of
death has been done by Him.
16 "I will therefore chastise
Him and [gg]release *Him*"
17 (for it was necessary for
him to release one to them at the
feast).*
18 And they all cried out at
once, saying, [hh]"Away with this

64
a Zech. 13:7
66
b See Mt. 2:4, *note*
c Ps. 2:2; Acts 4:26
67
d v. 70; Jn. 10:24
e Lk. 20:5–7
69
f Cp. Acts 7:55–56 with Rev. 1:7
g See Mt. 8:20, *note*
h Ps. 110:1; Heb. 1:3; cp. Dan. 7:13–14
70
i Jn. 10:30
71
j Cp. Mk. 14:55–59
k Jn. 19:7
CHAPTER 23
1
l Lk. 22:47
m Lk. 3:1; 13:1; cp. Jn. 19:1–16
2
n v. 14; Lk. 5:29; 6:7
o v. 14
p Cp. Mt. 17:27; Lk. 20:19–26
q Jn. 19:12; cp. Acts 17:7
3
r 1 Tim. 6:13
4
s v. 14; Mt. 27:19; cp. 2 Cor. 5:21; 1 Pet. 2:22
5
t Cp. Lk. 14:25–27; Jn. 6:15
6
u Jn. 7:41

7
v Herod Antipas. See Mk. 6:14, *note*
w Lk. 3:1
8
x Lk. 9:9
y Mt. 14:1; Mk. 6:14
9
z Isa. 53:7; Jn. 19:9
11
aa v. 36; Isa. 53:3
12
bb Acts 4:26–27; cp. Ps. 2:1–6
13
cc See Acts 23:1, *note*
14
dd v. 2
ee v. 4; cp. Dan. 6:4
15
ff Cp. Jer. 26:16; Acts 23:29; 28:18
16
gg Cp. Acts 5:40–41
18
hh Cp. Mt. 8:34; Mk. 6:3; Lk. 4:28–29; Jn. 1:11; 5:43; 12:48

*
22:64 NU-Text reads *And having blindfolded Him, they asked Him.* **22:68** NU-Text omits *also* and *Me or let Me go.* **23:2** NU-Text reads *our.* **23:6** NU-Text omits *of Galilee.* **23:15** NU-Text reads *for he sent Him back to us.* **23:17** NU-Text omits verse 17.

Man, and [a]release to us Barabbas"—

19 who had been thrown into prison for a certain rebellion made in the city, and for murder.

20 Pilate, therefore, wishing to release Jesus, again called out to them.

21 But they shouted, saying, [b]"Crucify *Him,* crucify Him!"

22 Then he said to them the third time, "Why, what evil has He done? I have found [c]no reason for death in Him. I will therefore [d]chastise Him and let *Him* go."

23 But they were insistent, demanding with loud voices that He be crucified. And the voices of these men and of the chief priests prevailed.*

24 So Pilate [e]gave sentence that it should be as they requested.

25 [f]And he released to them* the one they requested, who for rebellion and murder had been thrown into prison; but he delivered Jesus to their will.

On the way to the place of crucifixion (Mt. 27:31–32; Mk. 15:20–21; Jn. 19:16–17)

26 Now as they led Him away, they laid hold of a certain man, Simon a Cyrenian, who was coming from the country, and on him they laid the cross that he might bear *it* after Jesus.

27 And a great multitude of the people followed Him, and [g]women who also mourned and [h]lamented Him.

28 But Jesus, turning to them, said, "Daughters of Jerusalem, do not weep for Me, but [i]weep for yourselves and for your children.

29 "For indeed the days are coming in which they will say, 'Blessed *are* the barren, wombs that never bore, and breasts which never nursed!'

30 "Then they will begin [j]'*to say to the mountains,* [k]*"Fall on us!" and to the hills, "Cover us!"'*

31 "For if they do these things in the [1]green wood, what will be done in the dry?"

32 There were also two others, [l]criminals, led with Him to be put to death.

Jesus is crucified (Mt. 27:33–43; Mk. 15:22–32; Jn. 19:17–22)

33 [2]And [m]when they had come to the place called [n]Calvary, there they [o]crucified Him, and the criminals, one on the right hand and the other on the left.

34 Then Jesus [p]said, "Father, [q]forgive them, for they do not know what they do."* And they divided His garments and cast lots.

35 And the [3]people stood looking on. But even the rulers with them sneered, saying, "He saved others; let Him save Himself if He is the Christ, the chosen of God."

36 The soldiers also mocked Him, coming and offering Him [r]sour wine,

37 and saying, "If You are the King of the Jews, [s]save Yourself."

38 And an inscription also was written over Him in letters of Greek, Latin, and Hebrew:*

THIS IS THE KING OF THE JEWS.

*
23:23 NU-Text omits *and of the chief priests.* 23:25 NU-Text and M-Text omit *to them.* 23:34 NU-Text brackets the first sentence as a later addition. 23:38 NU-Text omits *written* and *in letters of Greek, Latin, and Hebrew.*

18 *a* Acts 3:13–15
21 *b* Cp. Ps. 69:20; Jn. 7:7; 15:18, 25
22 *c* vv. 4,14 *d* v. 16
24 *e* Cp. Dt. 1:17
25 *f* Isa. 53:8; cp. Prov. 17:15
27 *g* Cp. Lk. 8:2–3 *h* Cp. Acts 8:2
28 *i* Cp. Lk. 19:41
30 *j Inspiration:* v. 30; Lk. 24:25. (Ex. 4:15; 2 Tim. 3:16, *note*) *k* Hos. 10:8; Rev. 6:16–17; 9:6
32 *l* vv. 33,39; Isa. 53:12
33 *m* c. A.D. 29 *n* Or *the skull.* See Mk. 15:22, *note* *o Sacrifice* (of Christ): v. 33; Lk. 23:46. (Gen. 3:15; Heb. 10:18, *note*)
34 *p Bible prayers* (NT): v. 34; Lk. 23:42. (Mt. 6:9; Lk. 11:2, *note*) *q Forgiveness:* v. 34; Acts 2:38. (Lev. 4:20; Mt. 26:28, *note*). Isa. 53:12; Mt. 5:44
36 *r* Ps. 69:21
37 *s* v. 35

[1](23:31) The saying is probably a proverb in the form of an *a fortiori* argument. If the Romans condemned to death the one they admitted to be innocent, how would they deal in the future with those whom they found guilty?

[2](23:33) For the order of events at the crucifixion of Christ, see Mt. 27:33, *note.*

[3](23:35) Jesus crucified is the touchstone revealing what the world is: "The people stood looking on" in stolid indifference; the rulers, who wanted religion but without a divine Christ crucified for their sins, mocked (Mt. 27:41); the brutal "blasphemed Him" (v. 39); the conscious sinner prayed (v. 42); and the covetous sat down before the cross and played their sordid game (Mt. 27:35–36). The cross is the judgment of this world (Jn. 12:31).

39
a v. 35
41
b 2 Cor. 5:21; Heb. 7:26; 1 Pet. 2:21–24
42
c *Bible prayers* (NT): vv. 42, 46; Jn. 4:15. (Mt. 6:9; Lk. 11:2, *note*)
d *Faith:* vv. 42–43; Jn. 1:12. (Gen. 3:20; Heb. 11:39, *note*)
e *Kingdom* (NT): vv. 37–38, 42; Jn. 1:49. (Mt. 2:2; 1 Cor. 15:24, *note*). See Mt. 3:2, *note*
43
f Rev. 2:7; cp. 2 Cor. 12:2, 4; see Lk. 16:23, *note*
44
g i.e. noon till 3 p.m. See Jn. 19:14, *note*
45
h Heb. 9:3; 10:19–20
46
i Ps. 31:5; 1 Pet. 2:23
j *Sacrifice* (of Christ): v. 46; Jn. 1:29. (Gen. 3:15; Heb. 10:18, *note*)
k See Mt. 27:50, *note*
47
l *Righteousness* (OT): vv. 47,50; Acts 10:22. (Gen. 6:9; Lk. 2:25, *note*). See Rom. 10:10, *note*
48
m Cp. Zech. 12:10; Rev. 1:7

The repentant robber
(cp. Mt. 27:44;
Mk. 15:32)

39 Then [1]one of the criminals who were hanged blasphemed Him, saying, "If You are the Christ,* [a]save Yourself and us."

40 But the other, answering, rebuked him, saying, "Do you not even fear God, seeing you are under the same condemnation?

41 "And we indeed justly, for we receive the due reward of our deeds; but this Man has done [b]nothing wrong."

42 Then he [c]said to Jesus, "Lord,* [d]remember me when You come into Your [e]kingdom."

43 And Jesus said to him, [2]"Assuredly, I say to you, today you will be with Me in [f]Paradise."

Darkness from sixth
to ninth hour;
Jesus dismisses His spirit
(Mt. 27:45–56; Mk. 15:33–41;
Jn. 19:28–30)

44 Now it was* about the sixth hour, and there was darkness over all the earth [g]until the ninth hour.

45 Then the sun was darkened,* and the [h]veil of the temple was torn in two.

46 And when Jesus had cried out with a loud voice, He [c]said, "Father, [i]'*into Your hands I commit My spirit.*'" Having said this, [j]He [k]breathed His last.

47 So when the centurion saw what had happened, he glorified God, saying, "Certainly this was a [l]righteous Man!"

48 And the whole crowd who came together to that sight, seeing what had been done, [m]beat their breasts and returned.

49 But all His acquaintances, and the [n]women who followed Him from Galilee, [o]stood at a distance, watching these things.

Jesus is buried (Mt. 27:57–61;
Mk. 15:42–47; Jn. 19:38–42)

50 Now behold, *there was* a man named Joseph, a council member, a good and [l]just man.

51 He had [p]not consented to their decision and deed. *He was* from Arimathea, a city of the Jews, who himself was also [q]waiting* for the [r]kingdom of God.

52 This man went to Pilate and asked for the body of Jesus.

53 Then he took it down, wrapped it in linen, and [s]laid it in a tomb *that was* hewn out of the rock, where [t]no one had ever lain before.

54 That day was the [u]Preparation, and the [v]Sabbath drew near.

55 And the [n]women who had come with Him from Galilee followed after, and they observed the tomb and how His body was laid.

56 Then they returned and [w]prepared spices and fragrant oils. And they rested on the Sabbath [x]according to the commandment.

V. Christ's Resurrection,
Commission to the Disciples,
and Ascension, 24
The resurrection and events of
that day (cp. Mt. 28:1–15;
Mk. 16:1–11; Jn. 20:1–18)

24 NOW [3]on the [y]first *day* of the week, very early in the morning, they, and certain *other women* with them,* came

49
n Cp. Lk. 8:1–3; 24:22
o Ps. 38:11
51
p Cp. Gen. 37:21–22; 42:21–22; Prov. 1:10; 1 Tim. 5:22
q Cp. Lk. 2:25,38
r See Mt. 6:33, *note*
53
s Isa. 53:9
t Cp. Lk. 19:30
54
u Mt. 27:62
v *Sabbath:* vv. 54,56; Jn. 5:9. (Gen. 2:3; Mt. 12:1, *note*)
56
w Mk. 16:1
x Ex. 20:10; see Mt. 12:1, *note*
CHAPTER 24
1
y See Acts 20:7, *note*

*

23:39 NU-Text reads *Are You not the Christ?* 23:42 NU-Text reads *And he said, "Jesus, remember me.* 23:44 NU-Text adds *already.* 23:45 NU-Text reads *obscured.* 23:51 NU-Text reads *who was waiting.* 24:1 NU-Text omits *and certain other women with them.*

[1](23:39) When the two criminals were hanged beside the Lord, the one was no better than the other. Mark says, "Even those who were crucified with Him reviled Him" (Mark 15:32). It is only the grace of God in the cross of Christ that can instantly transform a sinner's belligerence into an attitude of saving faith and confession. The repentant thief began to see (1) the justice of his own punishment (v. 41); (2) the sinless character of Christ (v. 41); (3) the Deity of Christ (v. 42); (4) a living Christ beyond the grave (v. 42); and (5) a kingdom beyond the cross, with Jesus as its coming King (v. 42).

[2](23:43) One criminal was saved, so that none needs to despair; but only one, so that none may presume.

[3](24:1) For the order of events on the resurrection morning, see Mt. 28:1, *note.*

to the tomb [a]bringing the spices
which they had prepared.
2 But they found the [b]stone
rolled away from the tomb.
3 Then they went in and
[c]did not find the body of the
Lord Jesus.
4 And it happened, as they
were greatly* perplexed about
this, that behold, [d]two men
stood by them in shining garments.
5 Then, as they were afraid
and bowed *their* faces to the
earth, they said to them, "Why
do you seek the [e]living among
the [f]dead?
6 "He is not here, but is
[g]risen! [h]Remember how He
spoke to you when He was still
in Galilee,
7 "saying, 'The [i]Son of Man
must be [j]delivered into the
hands of [k]sinful men, and be
crucified, and the third day rise
again.' "
8 And they [l]remembered
His words.
9 Then they returned from
the tomb and told all these
things to the eleven and to all
the rest.
10 It was Mary Magdalene,
[m]Joanna, [n]Mary *the mother* of
[o]James, and the other *women*
with them, who told these
things to the apostles.
11 And their words [p]seemed
to them like idle tales, and they
did not believe them.
12 But [q]Peter arose and ran
to the tomb; and stooping down,
he saw the linen cloths lying*
by themselves; and he departed,
marveling to himself at what
had happened.

Jesus reveals Himself to two Emmaus disciples (Mk. 16:12–13)

13 [1]Now behold, two of them
were traveling that same day to
a village called Emmaus, which
was seven [r]miles* from Jerusalem.
14 And they [s]talked together
of all these things which had
happened.
15 So it was, while they conversed and reasoned, that [t]Je-
sus Himself drew near and went
with them.
16 But their eyes were restrained, so that they did not
[u]know Him.
17 And He said to them,
[v]"What kind of conversation *is*
this that you have with one another as you walk and are
sad?"*
18 Then the one whose name
was Cleopas answered and said
to Him, "Are You the only
stranger in Jerusalem, and have
You not known the things
which happened there in these
days?"
19 And He said to them,
"What things?" So they said to
Him, "The things concerning
Jesus of Nazareth, who was a
[2w]Prophet mighty in deed and
word before God and all the
people,
20 "and how the chief priests
and our rulers [x]delivered Him
to be condemned to death, and
crucified Him.
21 "But we were hoping that
it was He who was going to [y]re-
deem Israel. Indeed, besides all
this, today is the third day since
these things happened.
22 "Yes, and certain [z]women
of our company, who arrived at
the tomb early, astonished us.
23 "When they did not find
His body, they came saying that
they had also seen a vision of
[aa]angels who said He was alive.
24 "And [bb]certain of those
who were with us went to the
tomb and found *it* just as the
women had said; but Him they
did not see."
25 Then He said to them, "O
foolish ones, and slow of heart

*

24:4 NU-Text omits *greatly.*
24:12 NU-Text omits *lying.* **24:13** Literally *sixty stadia* **24:17** NU-Text reads *as you walk? And they stood still, looking sad.*

1 *a* Lk. 23:56; cp. Mt. 26:12; Mk. 14:8; Jn. 12:7
2 *b* Cp. Jn. 11:38–41
3 *c* v. 23
4 *d* Cp. Acts 1:10
5 *e* Lit. *Him who lives*
f See Heb. 9:27, *note*
6 *g Resurrection:* vv. 1–7; Lk. 24:46. (2 Ki. 4:35; 1 Cor. 15:52, *note*)
h Cp. v. 8
7 *i* See Mt. 8:20, *note*
j Lk. 9:44; 18:31–33; cp. Acts 2:22–24
k See Rom. 3:23, *note*
8 *l* Lk. 9:22,44; Jn. 2:19–22
10 *m* Lk. 8:3
n See Lk. 1:27, *note*
o See Mt. 4:21, *note*
11 *p* Cp. v. 25
12 *q* v. 34
13 *r* See Weights and Measures (NT), Acts 27:28, *note*
14 *s* Cp. Dt. 6:7; Mal. 3:16
15 *t* See Jn. 20:16, *note*
16 *u* Jn. 20:14; 21:4
17 *v* Cp. v. 14
19 *w* Mt. 21:11; Lk. 9:19; Jn. 3:2; 6:14
20 *x* Lk. 23:1; Acts 13:27–28
21 *y* Cp. Acts 1:6; see Rom. 3:24, *note*
22 *z* v. 10; Lk. 23:55
23 *aa* See Heb. 1:4, *note*
24 *bb* v. 12

[1](24:13) For post-resurrection appearances of our Lord, see Jn. 20:16, *note.*
[2](24:19) Christ possessed in perfection the credentials of a true prophet (see Dt. 13:4 and 1 Cor. 12:10, *notes*). Not only was He able, by His own power, to perform miracles, but also His message was completely harmonious with the Word of God, He Himself being the living Word. He told forth divine truth and foretold the divine prophetic program. Christ was Prophet, Priest (Zech. 6:9–13), and King (Mt. 2:2; Rev. 19:11–16).

to believe in all that the prophets have [a]spoken!
26 [b]"Ought not the Christ to
have suffered these things and
to enter into His [c]glory?"
27 And [d]beginning at [e]Mo-
ses and all the [f]Prophets, He
expounded to them in [g]all the
[a]Scriptures the things concerning [1h]Himself.
28 Then they drew near to
the village where they were going, and He indicated that He
would have gone farther.
29 But they [i]constrained
Him, saying, [j]"Abide with us,
for it is toward evening, and the
day is far spent." And He went
in to stay with them.
30 Now it came to pass, as He
sat at the table with them, that
He [k]took bread, blessed and
broke *it,* and gave it to them.
31 Then their [l]eyes were
opened and they knew Him;
and He vanished from their
sight.
32 And they said to one another, "Did not our heart burn
within us while He talked with
us on the road, and while He
opened the Scriptures to us?"

Further appearances of the risen Lord on resurrection day (Mk. 16:14; Jn. 20:19–25. See also Jn. 20:26—21:25)

33 So they rose up that very
hour and returned to Jerusalem,
and found the [m]eleven and
those *who were* with them gathered together,
34 saying, "The Lord is risen
indeed, and has [n]appeared to
Simon!"
35 And they told about the
things *that had happened* on
the road, and how He was
known to them in the breaking
of bread.
36 Now as they said these
things, Jesus Himself stood in
the midst of them, and said to
them, "Peace to you."
37 But they were terrified
and frightened, and supposed
they had seen a [o]spirit.
38 And He said to them,
"Why are you troubled? And
why do doubts arise in your
hearts?
39 "Behold My hands and My
feet, that it is I Myself. [p]Handle
Me and see, for a [q]spirit does
not have flesh and bones as you
see I have."
40 When He had said this, He
showed them His hands and His
feet.*
41 But while they still did not
believe for joy, and marveled,
He said to them, "Have you any
food here?"
42 So they gave Him a piece
of a broiled fish and some honeycomb.*
43 And He took *it* and [r]ate in
their presence.

The Gospel to be given to all (Mt. 28:18–20; Mk. 16:15–18; Jn. 17:18; 20:21; Acts 1:8)

44 Then He said to them,
"These *are* the words which I
spoke to you while I was still
with you, that all things must be
fulfilled which were [a]written in
the [e]Law of Moses and *the*
Prophets and *the* [s]Psalms concerning Me."
45 And He opened their understanding, that they might
comprehend the Scriptures.
46 Then He said to them,
"Thus it is [a]written, and thus it
was necessary for the Christ to
suffer and to [t]rise* from the
dead the third day,
47 "and that [u]repentance and
remission of sins should be
[v]preached in His name to all nations, beginning at Jerusalem.
48 "And you are witnesses of
these things.

The ascension (Mk. 16:19–20; Acts 1:9–11)

49 "Behold, I send the
[w]Promise of My Father upon
you; but tarry in the city of Jeru-

25
a Inspiration: vv. 25, 27,44–47; Jn. 1:45. (Ex. 4:15; 2 Tim. 3:16, *note*)
26
b Acts 17:2–3; Heb. 2:9–10
c 1 Pet. 1:10–12
27
d Gen. 3:15; 22:18; 26:4; 49:10; Num. 21:9; Dt. 18:15
e Law (of Moses): vv. 27,44; Jn. 1:17. (Ex. 19:1; Gal. 3:24, *note*)
f Isa. 7:14; 40:10; 53:2–12; Jer. 23:5; 33:14; Ezek. 34:23; 37:25; Dan. 9:24–26; Mal. 3:1; 4:2; Jn. 1:45
g Cp. Acts 8:31–35; 17:2–3
h Ps. 132:11; Jn. 5:39; Rom. 1:1–6
29
i Gen. 19:2–3
j Jn. 14:23
30
k Mk. 8:6; Lk. 9:16; cp. 1 Cor. 11:23–32
31
l Cp. Ps. 119:18; Jn. 9:1–41; 1 Jn. 3:2
33
m See Mk. 16:14, *note*
34
n 1 Cor. 15:5
37
o Mk. 6:49
39
p Jn. 20:27; 1 Jn. 1:1
q 1 Cor. 15:50
43
r Acts 10:39–41
44
s See Ps. 118:29, *note*
46
t Resurrection: v. 46; Jn. 2:22. (2 Ki. 4:35; 1 Cor. 15:52, *note*)
47
u Repentance: v. 47; Acts 2:38. (Mt. 3:2; Acts 17:30, *note*)
v Gospel: v. 47; Jn. 3:16. (Gen. 12:3; Rev. 14:6)
49
w Holy Spirit (NT): v. 49; Jn. 1:32. (Mt. 1:18; Acts 2:4, *note*)

---

* **24:40** Some printed New Testaments omit this verse. It is found in nearly all Greek manuscripts. **24:42** NU-Text omits *and some honeycomb.* **24:46** NU-Text reads *written, that the Christ should suffer and rise.*

---

[1](24:27) Cleopas and his companion on the Emmaus Road had the inestimable privilege of hearing the incarnate Word, Christ the risen Lord, explain the written Word, the Holy Scriptures. In doing so, the Lord Jesus gave them the great key to the understanding of Scripture—that He Himself is its subject and that in Him the entire Book finds its unity.

salem* until you are endued
with power from on high."
50 And He led them out [a]as
far as Bethany, and He lifted up
His hands and blessed them.
51 Now it came to pass, while
He [1]blessed them, that He was
parted from them and carried
[b]up into heaven.
52 And they worshiped Him,
and returned to Jerusalem with
great joy,
53 and were continually in
the temple praising and* blessing God. Amen.*

50 a i.e. *toward*
51 b Acts 1:9–11; see 2 Cor. 12:2, *note*

*
24:49 NU-Text omits *of Jerusalem.*
24:53 NU-Text omits *praising and.*
• NU-Text omits *Amen.*

[1](24:51) The attitude of our Lord here characterizes His relationship to His people in the Church Age. It is an attitude of fullness of grace; an ascended Lord is blessing a believing people with spiritual blessings.

The Gospel According to

JOHN

Author: John *Theme:* Christ in His Deity *Date of writing:* C. A.D. 85–90

JOHN, the writer of this Gospel, was the son of Zebedee and one of the twelve. Along with his brother, James, and with Peter, he belonged to the inner circle of disciples, a group that was near Christ on such occasions as the transfiguration and the agony in Gethsemane. It was to John that our Lord on the cross commended His mother. John appears with Peter in the first part of Acts and is referred to by Paul as one of the three "pillars" of the Church (Gal. 2:9). His other writings are the Epistles bearing his name, and Revelation.

John's purpose in the Fourth Gospel was, as he plainly declares, "that you may believe that Jesus is the Christ, the Son of God, and that believing you may have life in His name" (20:31). Therefore, he presents Christ as the Son of God (1:34,49; etc.), who was sent from God (3:2; 6:46; etc.) and always spoke the message God gave Him (3:34; 7:16–17; etc.). In accordance with the purpose of this Gospel, the words "believe" and "life," and the titles, "Son" and "Son of God," are used many more times than in the Synoptic Gospels. Other characteristic words of John are "true," "truth," "love," "witness," and "world" (Gk. *kosmos*). John alone records the great "I am" declarations of Christ (6:35; 8:12; 10:7,11; 11:25; 14:6) and gives the sayings of Christ introduced by the solemn "Most assuredly," literally, "Amen, amen" (1:51; 5:19,24,25, etc.). Moreover, he alone reports the great controversy between Christ and His enemies (chs. 7—12).

The Gospel of John may be divided as follows:

I. The Prologue: The Eternal Word Incarnate in the Son of God, 1:1–14.
II. The Witness of John the Baptist to the Son of God, 1:15–34.
III. The Son of God Manifesting His Power in Public Ministry, 1:35—12:50.
IV. The Private Ministry of the Son of God, 13—17.
V. The Sacrifice of the Son of God, 18—19.
VI. The Manifestation of the Son of God in Resurrection, 20.
VII. The Epilogue: The Risen Son of God, the Master of Life and Service, 21.

I. The Prologue:
The Eternal Word Incarnate
in the Son of God, 1:1–14

The Deity of Jesus Christ
(cp. Jn. 10:30; Heb. 1:5–13)

1 IN the [a]beginning was the
[1]Word, and the [b]Word was
[c]with God, and the Word was
[d]God.
2 He was in the beginning
with God.

The preincarnate work
of the Son of God
(cp. Col. 1:16–17; Heb. 1:2)

3 [e]All things were made
through Him, and without Him
nothing was made that was
made.
4 In Him was [f]life, and the
life was the [g]light of men.
5 And the light shines in the
[h]darkness, and the darkness
did not comprehend* it.

Witness of John the Baptist
(see also vv. 15–34)

6 [i]There was a [j]man sent
from God, whose name *was*
John.
7 This man came for a [k]wit-
ness, to bear witness of the
Light, that all through him
might [l]believe.
8 He was not that Light, but
was sent to bear witness of that
[m]Light.

Jesus Christ, the true Light:
rejected and received
(Jn. 3:17–21; 8:12; 9:5; 12:46)

9 That was the true Light

* 1:5 Or *overcome*

CHAPTER 1

1
a 1 Jn. 1:1
b Rev. 19:13
c Jn. 17:5
d 1 Jn. 5:20

3
e Eph. 3:9; Col. 1:16–17; cp. Gen. 1:1–2:23

4
f *Life* (eternal): v. 4; Jn. 3:15. (Mt. 7:14; Rev. 22:19). Jn. 4:14; 17:3; 1 Jn. 5:12
g Cp. Ps. 36:9

5
h Cp. Jn. 3:19

6
i C. A.D. 26
j Mal. 3:1; Mt. 3:1–17; Mk. 1:1–11; Lk. 3:1–22

7
k Jn. 3:25–36; 5:33–35
l Jn. 3:16

8
m Isa. 9:2; 49:6

---

[1](1:1) Greek *Logos* (Aram. *Memra,* used as a designation of God in the Targums, i.e. Aramaic translations of the OT). The Greek word means, (1) *a thought* or *concept;* and (2) *the expression* or *utterance of that thought.* As a designation of Christ, therefore, *Logos* is peculiarly suitable because (1) in Him are embodied all the treasures of the divine wisdom, the collective thought of God (1 Cor. 1:24; Eph. 3:10–11; Col. 2:2–3); and (2) He is, from eternity, but especially in His incarnation, the utterance or expression of the Person and thought of Deity (Jn. 1:3–5,9,14–18; 14:9–11; Col. 2:9). In the Being, Person, and work of Christ, Deity is expressed.

which gives light to every man
coming into the [a]world.*
10 He was in the [a]world, and
the [a]world was made through
Him, and the [a]world did [b]not
know Him.
11 [1]He came to His own, and
His own did not receive Him.
12 But as many as received
Him, to them He gave the [c]right
to become [d]children of God, to
those who [e]believe in His
name:
13 who were born, not of
blood, nor of the will of the
flesh, nor of the will of man, but
of God.

The Word made flesh (Jn. 14:9; cp. Mt. 1:18–23; Lk. 1:30–35; 2:11; 1 Tim. 3:16)

14 And the [f]Word [g]became
[h]flesh and dwelt among us, and
we [i]beheld His glory, the glory
as of the only begotten of the
Father, full of [j]grace and
[k]truth.

II. The Witness of John the Baptist to the Son of God, 1:15–34

John bears witness (Mt. 3:1–17; Mk. 1:1–11; Lk. 3:1–22)

15 John bore [l]witness of
Him and cried out, saying, "This
was He of whom I said, 'He who
comes after me is preferred before me, for He was before
me.' "
16 And* of His fullness we
have all received, and [j]grace
for grace.
17 For the [m]law was given
through Moses, *but* [2j]grace and
[k]truth came through Jesus
Christ.
18 No one has [3]seen God at
any time. The only begotten
Son,* who is in the bosom of
the Father, He has [n]declared
Him.
19 Now this is the testimony
of John, when the Jews sent
priests and Levites from Jerusalem to ask him, "Who are you?"
20 He confessed, and did not
deny, but confessed, "I am not
the Christ."
21 And they asked him,
"What then? [o]Are you Elijah?"
He said, "I am not." "Are you
[p]the Prophet?" And he answered, "No."
22 Then they said to him,
"Who are you, that we may give
an answer to those who sent us?
What do you say about yourself?"

*

1:9 Or *That was the true Light which, coming into the world, gives light to every man.* 1:16 NU-Text reads *For.*
1:18 NU-Text reads *only begotten God.*

9
a Gk. *kosmos.* See Mt. 4:8, *note*
10
b Acts 13:27; cp. 1 Cor. 2:8
12
c Lit. *authority*
d Cp. 1 Jn. 5:1–2
e *Faith:* v. 12; Jn. 1:49. (Gen. 3:20; Heb. 11:39, *note*)
14
f v. 1; Rev. 19:13
g 1 Tim. 3:16
h *Christ* (first advent): v. 14; Jn. 3:13. (Gen. 3:15; Acts 1:11, *note*)
i 2 Pet. 1:16–18
j *Grace:* vv. 14, 16–17; Acts 4:33. (Jn. 1:14; Jn. 1:17, *note*)
k Jn. 14:6; 18:37; cp. Eph. 4:21
15
l Mal. 3:1

17
m *Law* (of Moses): v. 17; Jn. 1:45. (Ex. 19:1; Gal. 3:24, *note*)
18
n Lit. *led forth, expounded* Cp. Jn. 14:9
21
o See Mt. 17:10, *note*
p Dt. 18:15; Jn. 6:14; 7:40

---

[1](1:11) Another rendering would be: "He came to His own things, and His own people did not receive Him."

[2](1:17) Grace, Summary: (1) Grace is "the kindness and the love of God our Savior . . . not by works of righteousness which we have done . . . having been justified by His grace" (Ti. 3:4,5,7). As a principie, therefore, grace is set in contrast with law (Rom. 11:6), under which God demands righteousness from men, as, under grace, He gives righteousness to men (Rom. 3:21–24; 8:3–4; Gal. 2:16; Phil. 3:9). Law is connected with Moses and works; grace, with Christ and faith (Jn. 1:17; Rom. 10:4–10). Under law, blessings accompany obedience (Dt. 28:1–6); grace bestows blessings as a free gift (Rom. 4:3–5; Eph. 2:8).

(2) In its fullness, grace began with the ministry of Christ involving His death and resurrection, for He came to die for sinners (Jn. 1:17; Mt. 11:28–30; 16:21; 20:28; Rom. 3:24–26; 4:24–25). Under the former dispensation, law was shown to be powerless to secure righteousness and life for a sinful race (Gal. 3:21–22). Prior to the cross man's salvation was through faith (Gen. 15:6; Rom. 4:3), being grounded on Christ's atoning sacrifice, anticipated by God (Rom. 3:25; see Gen. 1:28, heading, *note*, par. 3); now it is clearly revealed that salvation and righteousness are received by faith in the crucified and resurrected Savior (Jn. 1:12–13; 5:24; 1 Jn. 5:11–13), with holiness of life and good works following as the fruit of salvation (Jn. 15:16; Rom. 8:2–4; Eph. 2:8–10; Ti. 2:11–14).

(3) There was grace before Christ came, as witnessed by the provision of sacrifice for sinners (Ex. 20:24–26; Lev. 5:17–18; 17:11). The difference between the former age and the present age, therefore, is not a matter of *no* grace and *some* grace, but rather that today grace reigns (Rom. 5:21), in the sense that the only Being who has a right to judge sinners (Jn. 5:22) is now seated on a throne of grace (Heb. 4:14–16), not imputing to the world their trespasses (2 Cor. 5:19).

[3](1:18) Compare Gen. 32:30; Ex. 24:10; 33:18; Jud. 6:22; 13:22; Rev. 22:4. No man has ever seen God in His spiritual Being or Essence. But in His OT appearances (see Gen. 12:7, *note* 2), and especially in Jesus Christ incarnate, God has been seen by men (Jn. 14:8–9; 1 Jn. 1:1–2).

23 He said: "I *am*

'The voice of one crying
in the wilderness:
[a]*"Make straight the way of*
the LORD,*" '*

as the prophet Isaiah said."

24 Now those who were sent were from the Pharisees.

25 And they asked him, saying, "Why then do you [b]baptize if you are not the Christ, [c]nor Elijah, nor [d]the Prophet?"

26 John answered them, saying, "I [b]baptize with water, but there stands One among you whom you do [e]not know.

27 "It is He who, coming after me, is [f]preferred before me, whose sandal strap I am not worthy to [g]loose."

28 These things were done in Bethabara* beyond the Jordan, where John was baptizing.

29 The next day John saw Jesus coming toward him, and said, "Behold! The [h]Lamb of God who [i]takes away the [j]sin of the [k]world!

30 "This is He of whom I said, 'After me comes a Man who is [f]preferred before me, for He was before me.'

31 "I did not know Him; but that He [l]should be revealed to Israel, therefore I came [b]baptizing with water."

32 And John bore witness, saying, "I saw the [m]Spirit descending from heaven like a dove, and He [n]remained upon Him.

33 "I did not know Him, but He who sent me to [b]baptize with water said to me, 'Upon whom you see the [m]Spirit descending, and remaining on Him, this is He who baptizes with the Holy Spirit.'

34 "And I have seen and testified that this is the [o]Son of God."

III. The Son of God Manifesting His Power in Public Ministry, 1:35—12:50

Jesus' first converts

35 Again, the next [p]day, John stood with two of his disciples.

36 And looking at Jesus as He walked, he said, "Behold the [h]Lamb of God!"

37 The two disciples heard him speak, and they [q]followed Jesus.

38 Then Jesus turned, and seeing them following, said to them, "What do you [r]seek?" They said to Him, "Rabbi" (which is to say, when translated, Teacher), "where are You staying?"

39 He said to them, [1]"Come and see." They came and saw where He was [s]staying, and [t]remained with Him that day (now it was about the [u]tenth hour).

40 One of the two who heard John *speak,* and followed Him, was [v]Andrew, Simon Peter's brother.

41 He first found his own brother Simon, and said to him, "We have found the [w]Messiah" (which is translated, the Christ).

42 And he brought him to Jesus. Now when Jesus looked at him, He said, "You are Simon the son of Jonah.* You shall be called [x]Cephas" (which is translated, A Stone).

43 The following day Jesus wanted to go to Galilee, and He [y]found [z]Philip and said to him, "Follow Me."

44 Now Philip was from Bethsaida, the city of Andrew and Peter.

45 Philip found Nathanael and said to him, "We have found Him of whom Moses in the [aa]law, and also the prophets, [bb]wrote—Jesus of Nazareth, the [cc]son of Joseph."

46 And Nathanael said to him, "Can anything good come out of [dd]Nazareth?" Philip said to him, "Come and see."

47 Jesus saw Nathanael coming toward Him, and said of him, "Behold, an Israelite indeed, in whom is no [ee]deceit!"

48 Nathanael said to Him, "How do You know me?" Jesus answered and said to him, "Be-

*1:28 NU-Text and M-Text read *Bethany.*
1:42 NU-Text reads *John.*

23
a Isa. 40:3
25
b See Acts 8:12, *note*
c See Mt. 17:10, *note*
d Dt. 18:15; Jn. 6:14; 7:40
26
e Jn. 4:10; 8:19; 9:30; Acts 13:27
27
f Jn. 3:31; Col. 1:17–18; cp. Heb. 1:4; 3:3
g Acts 13:25
29
h Sacrifice (of Christ): vv. 29,36; Jn. 3:14. (Gen. 3:15; Heb. 10:18, *note*). Isa. 53:7; Mt. 1:21; 1 Cor. 5:7; 1 Pet. 1:18–19
i Or *bears.* Gal. 1:4; Eph. 5:2; Ti. 2:14; Heb. 9:26; 1 Pet. 2:24; 1 Jn. 3:5; Rev. 1:5
j See Rom. 3:23, *note* Jn. 3:31; Col. 1:17–18; cp. Heb. 1:4; 3:3
k Gk. *kosmos.* See Mt. 4:8, *note*
31
l Israel (prophecies): v. 31; Acts 2:30. (Gen. 12:2; Rom. 11:26, *note*). Cp. Lk. 2:26,38
32
m Holy Spirit (NT): vv. 32–33; Jn. 3:5. (Mt. 1:18; Acts 2:4, *note*)
n Isa. 11:2; 42:1; 61:1; Acts 10:38
34
o Jn. 11:27
35
p C. A.D. 26

37
q Mt. 4:20,22; cp. Jn. 10:27; 12:26
38
r Cp. Mk. 1:37; Lk. 4:42; 19:3; Jn. 6:24; 12:21
39
s Cp. Lk. 9:58
t Cp. Rev. 3:20
u 10 a.m. See Jn. 19:14, *note*
40
v Mt. 4:18; Mk. 1:29; 13:3; Jn. 6:8; 12:22
41
w i.e. *the Anointed.* Dan. 9:25; Jn. 4:25
42
x Aramaic. See Mt. 16:18, *note 1*
43
y Cp. Mt. 18:12; Lk. 19:10; Jn. 5:14; 9:35
z Mt. 10:3; Jn. 6:5; 12:21,22; 14:8,9
45
aa Law (of Moses): v. 45; Jn. 7:19. (Ex. 19:1; Gal. 3:24, *note*). Lk. 24:27
bb Inspiration: v. 45; Jn. 2:17. (Ex. 4:15; 2 Tim. 3:16, *note*). Dt. 18:15
cc Lk. 3:23
46
dd Cp. Lk. 4:16–30; Jn. 7:41,52
47
ee Ps. 32:2; cp. Rom. 2:28–29

[1](1:39) This was the call to discipleship in contrast with the call to special service that is recorded in Mt. 4:18–22.

fore Philip called you, when you were under the fig tree, I saw you."

49 Nathanael answered and said to Him, "Rabbi, [a]You are the [b]Son of God! You are the [c]King of Israel!"

50 Jesus answered and said to him, "Because I said to you, 'I saw you under the fig tree,' do you [a]believe? You will see greater things than these."

51 And He said to him, [d]"Most assuredly, I say to you, hereafter* you shall see heaven open, and the [e]angels of God ascending and descending upon the [f]Son of Man."

The first miracle: at Cana

2 ON the third day there was a [g]wedding in Cana of Galilee, and the [h]mother of Jesus was there.

2 Now both Jesus and His disciples were invited to the wedding.

3 And when they ran out of wine, the mother of Jesus said to Him, "They have no wine."

4 Jesus said to her, [i]"Woman, what does your concern have to do with Me? My hour has not yet come."

5 His mother said to the servants, "Whatever He says to you, do *it*."

6 Now there were set there six waterpots of stone, according to the manner of [j]purification of the Jews, containing twenty or thirty [k]gallons apiece.

7 Jesus said to them, "Fill the waterpots with water." And they filled them up to the brim.

8 And He said to them, "Draw *some* out now, and take *it* to the master of the feast." And they took *it*.

9 When the master of the feast had tasted the water that was [l]made wine, and did not know where it came from (but the servants who had drawn the water knew), the master of the feast called the bridegroom.

10 And he said to him, "Every man at the beginning sets out the good wine, and when the *guests* have well drunk, then the inferior. You have kept the good wine until now!"

11 This [m]beginning of signs Jesus did in Cana of Galilee, and manifested His [n]glory; and His disciples [a]believed in Him.

12 After this He went down to [o]Capernaum, He, His [p]mother, His [q]brothers, and His disciples; and they did not stay there many days.

The first Passover (cp. Jn. 6:4; 11:55). First purification of temple (cp. later purification, Mt. 21:12–13; Mk. 11:15–17; Lk. 19:45–56)

13 Now the [r]Passover of the Jews was at hand, and Jesus went up to Jerusalem.

14 And He [s]found in the [t]temple those who sold [u]oxen and sheep and doves, and the money changers doing business.

15 When He had made a whip of cords, He [v]drove them all [w]out of the temple, with the sheep and the oxen, and poured out the changers' money and overturned the tables.

16 And He said to those who sold doves, "Take these things away! Do not make My Father's house a house of merchandise!"

17 Then His disciples remembered that it was [x]written, [y]*"Zeal for Your house has eaten* Me up."*

18 So the Jews answered and said to Him, "What [z]sign do You show to us, since You do these things?"

19 Jesus answered and said to them, [aa]"Destroy this temple, and in three days I will raise it up."

20 Then the Jews said, "It has taken forty-six years to build this temple, and will You raise it up in three days?"

21 But He was speaking of the [bb]temple of His body.

22 Therefore, when He had [cc]risen from the dead, His disciples [dd]remembered that He had said this to them;* and they believed the Scripture and the word which Jesus had said.

23 Now when He was in Jerusalem at the [r]Passover, during the feast, many [a]believed in

*

1:51 NU-Text omits *hereafter.*
2:17 NU-Text and M-Text read *will eat.*
2:22 NU-Text and M-Text omit *to them.*

49
a Faith: vv. 49–50; 2:11,23; Jn. 4:39. (Gen. 3:20; Heb. 11:39, *note*)
b Jn. 11:27
c Kingdom (NT): vv. 49–51; Jn. 12:13. (Mt. 2:2; 1 Cor. 15:24, *note*)

51
d Jn. 5:19,24, 25; 6:26,32, 47,53; 8:34, 51,58; 10:1, 7; 12:24; 13:16,20,21; 14:12; 16:20,23
e See Heb. 1:4, *note*
f See Mt. 8:20, *note*

CHAPTER 2

1
g Heb. 13:4
h Jn. 19:25

4
i Common form of addressing females. Cp. Jn. 19:26; 20:13

6
j Mt. 15:2; Mk. 7:3; Lk. 11:39
k See Weights and Measures (NT), Acts 27:28, *note*

9
l Miracles (NT): vv. 1–11; Jn. 2:23. (Mt. 8:3; Acts 28:8, *note*). Jn. 4:46

11
m Jn. 4:54
n Jn. 1:14

12
o Mt. 4:13; Jn. 4:46
p See Lk. 1:27, *note*
q Mt. 12:46; 13:55

13
r c. A.D. 26. Cp. Jn. 6:4; 11:55; 18:28; see Ex. 12:11, *note*

14
s Cp. 2 Chr. 36:14; Jer. 7:30; Ezek. 44:7–8; Zeph. 3:4
t Mal. 3:1
u Cp. Lev. 17:3–4

15
v Cp. Jer. 10:10; Nah. 1:6
w Cp. Lev. 19:30; Eccl. 5:1

17
x Inspiration: v. 17; Jn. 3:14. (Ex. 4:15; 2 Tim. 3:16, *note*)
y Ps. 69:9

18
z Jn. 6:30; cp. Mt. 12:38

19
aa Mt. 26:61; 27:40

21
bb Cp. 1 Cor. 6:19

22
cc Resurrection: v. 22; Jn. 5:21. (2 Ki. 4:35; 1 Cor. 15:52, *note*)
dd Jn. 12:16; cp. Jn. 14:26

23
a Miracles (NT): v. 23; 3:2; Jn. 4:46. (Mt. 8:3; Acts 28:8, *note*)
b Jn. 5:36; Acts 2:22
24
c Mt. 9:4; Jn. 16:30; Rev. 2:23
CHAPTER 3
1
d See Mt. 3:7, *note 1*
e Jn. 7:50–51; 19:39
2
f Jn. 2:23
g Acts 10:38
3
h Jn. 1:13; Gal. 6:15; Eph. 2:10; Ti. 3:5; Jas. 1:18; 1 Pet. 1:23; See Eph. 4:24, *note*
i Lit. *from above.* vv. 5,7
j See Mt. 6:33, *note*
5
k See v. 3, *note*
l Cp. Ezek. 36:25–27; Jn. 4:14; Eph. 5:26; Ti. 3:5–6
m Holy Spirit (NT): vv. 5–6,8; Jn. 3:34. (Mt. 1:18; Acts 2:4, *note*)
6
n 1 Cor. 15:50; see Jude 23,

His name when they saw the
[a]signs which He [b]did.
24 But Jesus did not commit
Himself to them, because He
[c]knew all *men,*
25 and had no need that anyone should testify of man, for
He knew what was in man.

Jesus and Nicodemus: the new birth

3 THERE was a man of the
[d]Pharisees named [e]Nico-
demus, a ruler of the Jews.
2 This man came to Jesus by
night and said to Him, "Rabbi,
we know that You are a teacher
come from God; for no one can
[f]do these [a]signs that You do
unless [g]God is with him."
3 Jesus answered and said
to him, "Most assuredly, I say to
you, [h]unless one is [1]born
[i]again, he cannot see the
[j]kingdom of God."
4 Nicodemus said to Him,
"How can a man be born when
he is old? Can he enter a second
time into his mother's womb
and be born?"
5 Jesus answered, "Most assuredly, I say to you, unless one
is [k]born of [l]water and the
[m]Spirit, he cannot enter the
[j]kingdom of God.
6 "That which is born of the
flesh is [n]flesh, and that which is
[k]born of the [m]Spirit is spirit.
7 "Do not marvel that I said
to you, 'You must be [k]born
again.'
8 "The wind blows where it
wishes, and you hear the sound
of it, but cannot tell where it
comes from and where it goes.
So is everyone who is [k]born of
the [m]Spirit."
9 Nicodemus answered and
said to Him, "How can these
things be?"
10 Jesus answered and said
to him, "Are you the teacher of
Israel, and do not know these
things?
11 "Most assuredly, I say to
you, [o]We speak what We know
and testify what We have seen,
and you do not receive Our witness.
12 "If I have told you [p]earthly
things and you do not believe,
how will you believe if I tell you
[q]heavenly things?
13 "No one has [r]ascended to
heaven but He who [s]came
down from heaven, *that is,* the
[t]Son of Man who is in heaven.*
14 "And [u]as Moses [v]lifted up
the serpent in the wilderness,
even so must the [t]Son of Man
be lifted up,
15 "that whoever [w]believes
in Him should not perish but*
have eternal [x]life.
16 [y]"For God so [z]loved the
[aa]world that He [v]gave His only
begotten [bb]Son, that whoever
[2][w]believes in Him should not
[3]perish but [cc]have everlasting
[x]life.

cc Assurance/security: v. 16; Jn. 5:24. (Ps. 23:1; Jude 1, *note*)

*
3:13 NU-Text omits *who is in heaven.*
3:15 NU-Text omits *not perish but.*

note
11
o v. 32; Jn. 8:14
12
p Cp. Phil. 3:19
q Cp. 1 Cor. 2:14
13
r Cp. Prov. 30:4
s Christ (first advent): v. 13; Jn. 3:31. (Gen. 3:15; Acts 1:11, *note*)
t See Mt. 8:20, *note*
14
u Inspiration: v. 14; Jn. 4:37. (Ex. 4:15; 2 Tim. 3:16, *note*). Num. 21:9
v Sacrifice (of Christ): vv. 14,16; Jn. 6:33. (Gen. 3:15; Heb. 10:18, *note*)
15
w Jn. 6:47
x Life (eternal): vv. 15–16; Jn. 3:36. (Mt. 7:14; Rev. 22:19)
16
y Gospel: vv. 16–17; Acts 5:42. (Gen. 12:3; Rev. 14:6)
z Rom. 5:8; 1 Jn. 4:9
aa Gk. *kosmos.* See Mt. 4:8, *note*
bb Isa. 9:6

[1](3:3) Regeneration: (1) The necessity of the new birth grows out of the incapacity of the natural man to "see" or "enter" the kingdom of God. However gifted, moral, or refined he may be, the natural man is absolutely blind to spiritual truth and impotent to enter the kingdom; for he can neither obey, understand, nor please God (vv. 3,5–6; cp. Ps. 51:5; Jer. 17:9; Mk. 7:21–23; 1 Cor. 2:14; Rom. 8:7–8; Eph. 2:3. See Mt. 6:33, *note*). (2) The new birth is not a reformation of the old nature (Rom. 6:6, *note*), but a creative act of the Holy Spirit (Jn. 3:5; cp. 1:12–13; 2 Cor. 5:17; Eph. 2:10; 4:24). (3) The condition of the new birth is faith in Christ crucified (Jn. 3:14,15; cp. 1:12–13; Gal. 3:24). (4) Through the new birth the believer becomes a member of the family of God (Gal. 3:26; 1 Pet. 1:23) and a partaker of the divine nature, the life of Christ Himself (Gal. 2:20; Eph. 2:10; 4:24; Col. 1:27; 2 Pet. 1:4; 1 Jn. 5:10–12). And (5) in view of Ezek. 36:24–26, Nicodemus should have known about the new birth. Observe the correspondence between the "clean water," the "new spirit," and the "new heart" of the Ezekiel passage and the "water," "Spirit," and new birth ("born again") of Jn. 3:3,7.

[2](3:16) In the NT belief denotes more than intellectual assent to a fact. The word (Gk. *pistis,* noun; *pisteuō,* verb) means *adherence to, committal to, faith in, reliance upon, trust in* a person or an object, and this involves not only the consent of the mind, but an act of the heart and will of the subject. "Whoever believes in Him" is equivalent to "whoever trusts in or commits himself to Him [Christ]." Belief, then, is synonymous with faith, which in the NT consists of believing and receiving what God has revealed. See Faith, Heb. 11:39, *note.*

[3](3:16) Greek *apollumi,* translated "ruined," Mk. 2:22; "lost," Mt. 10:6; 15:24; Lk. 15:4,6,32.

17 "For God did not send His Son into the [a]world to [b]condemn the [a]world, but that the [a]world through Him might be [c]saved.

18 [d]"He who [e]believes in Him is not [f]condemned; but he who does not believe is [f]condemned already, because he has not believed in the name of the only begotten Son of God.

19 "And this is the [g]condemnation, that the light has come into the [a]world, and men loved darkness rather than light, because their deeds were evil.

20 "For everyone practicing evil hates the light and does not come to the light, lest his deeds should be [h]exposed.

21 "But he who does the truth comes to the [i]light, that his deeds may be clearly seen, that they have been [j]done in God."

Last testimony of John the Baptist

22 After these things Jesus and His disciples came into the land of Judea, and there He remained with them and [k]baptized.

23 Now John also was baptizing in Aenon near Salim, because there was much water there. And they [l]came and were [k]baptized.

24 For John had not yet been thrown into [m]prison.

25 Then there arose a dispute between *some* of John's disciples and the Jews about purification.

26 And they came to John and said to him, "Rabbi, He who was with you beyond the Jordan, to whom you have [n]testified—behold, He is [o]baptizing, and all are [p]coming to Him!"

27 John answered and said, "A man can [q]receive nothing unless it has been given to him from heaven.

28 "You yourselves bear me witness, that I [r]said, 'I am not the Christ,' but, 'I have been [s]sent before Him.'

29 "He who has the [t]bride is the bridegroom; but the friend of the bridegroom, who stands and hears him, rejoices greatly because of the bridegroom's voice. Therefore this joy of mine is fulfilled.

30 [u]"He must increase, but I *must* decrease.

31 "He who [v]comes from [w]above is [x]above all; he who is of the earth is earthly and speaks of the earth. He who comes from heaven is above all.

32 "And what He has seen and heard, that He [y]testifies; and no one receives His testimony.

33 "He who has received His testimony has certified that God is true.

34 "For [z]He whom God has [v]sent speaks the words of God, for God does not give the [aa]Spirit by measure.

35 "The Father [bb]loves the Son, and has given all things into His hand.

36 "He who [e]believes in the Son [1]has everlasting [cc]life; and he who does not believe the Son shall not see life, but the [dd]wrath of God abides on him."

Jesus leaves for Galilee

4 THEREFORE, when the Lord knew that the [ee]Pharisees had heard that Jesus made and baptized more disciples than John

2 (though Jesus Himself did [ff]not [o]baptize, but His disciples),

3 He left Judea and departed again to Galilee.

4 But He needed to go through Samaria.

Jesus and the Samaritan woman

5 So He came to a city of Samaria which is called Sychar, near the plot of ground that [gg]Jacob [hh]gave to his son Joseph.

6 Now [gg]Jacob's [ii]well was

17
a Gk. *kosmos.* See Mt. 4:8, *note*
b Or *judge*
c Lk. 9:56; see Rom. 1:16, *note*
18
d Jn. 6:40,47; Rom. 8:1
e Jn. 6:47
f Or *judged*
19
g Or *judgment*
20
h Eph. 5:13
21
i See 1 Jn. 1:7, *note*
j Jn. 15:4–5; 1 Cor. 15:10
22
k Cp. Jn. 4:2; see Acts 8:12, *note*
23
l Mt. 3:5–6
24
m Mt. 4:12; cp. Mt. 14:3
26
n Jn. 1:7
o See Acts 8:12, *note*
p Mk. 2:2; 3:10; 5:24; Lk. 8:19
27
q Rom. 12:5–8; 1 Cor. 3:5–6; 4:7; Heb. 5:4; 1 Pet. 4:10–11
28
r Jn. 1:19–27
s Mal. 3:1
29
t *Bride* (of Christ): v. 29; Rom. 7:4. (Jn. 3:29; Rev. 19:7, *note*)
30
u Isa. 9:7
31
v *Christ* (first advent): vv. 31,34; Jn. 4:26. (Gen. 3:15; Acts 1:11, *note*)
w Jn. 8:23
x Jn. 13:13; Col. 1:17–18
32
y Jn. 15:15
34
z Jn. 7:16
aa *Holy Spirit* (NT): v. 34; Jn. 4:14. (Mt. 1:18; Acts 2:4, *note*)
35
bb Jn. 5:20
36
cc *Life* (eternal): v. 36; Jn. 4:14. (Mt. 7:14; Rev. 22:19)
dd Rom. 1:18; Eph. 5:6; 1 Th. 1:10
CHAPTER 4
1
ee See Mt. 3:7, *note 1*
2
ff Cp. 1 Cor. 1:17
5
gg Gen. 33:19
hh Gen. 48:22; Josh. 24:32
6
ii Cp. Gen. 29:2

In no NT instance does it signify cessation of conscious existence or of consciousness. Instead, it indicates here that state of conscious suffering which continues eternally and is the inevitable result of sin. See 1 Cor. 5:5, *note.*

[1](3:36) Eternal life is not only a future hope but the present possession of everyone who believes in Christ.

there. Jesus therefore, [1]being
[a]wearied from *His* journey, sat
thus by the well. It was about
the [b]sixth hour.
7 A woman of Samaria
came to draw water. Jesus said
to her, "Give Me a drink."
8 For His disciples had gone
away into the city to buy food.
9 Then the woman of Sa-
maria said to Him, "How is it
that You, being a Jew, ask a
drink from me, a Samaritan
woman?" For Jews have no
[c]dealings with [d]Samaritans.
10 Jesus answered and said
to her, "If you knew the [e]gift of
God, and who it is who says to
you, 'Give Me a drink,' you
would have asked Him, and He
would have given you [f]living
water."
11 The woman said to Him,
"Sir, You have nothing to draw
with, and the well is deep.
Where then do You get that
[f]living water?
12 "Are You [g]greater than
our father Jacob, who gave us
the well, and drank from it himself, as well as his sons and his
livestock?"
13 Jesus answered and said
to her, "Whoever drinks of this
water will thirst again,
14 "but whoever drinks of the
water that I shall give him will
never thirst. But the [h]water that
I shall give him will become in
him a [i]fountain of [j]water
[k]springing up into everlasting
[l]life."
15 The woman [m]said to Him,
"Sir, give me this water, that I
may not thirst, nor come here to
draw."
16 Jesus said to her, "Go, call
your husband, and come here."
17 The woman answered and
said, "I have no husband." Jesus
said to her, "You have well said,
'I have no husband,'
18 "for you have had five
husbands, and the one whom
you now have is not your husband; in that you spoke truly."
19 The woman said to Him,
"Sir, I perceive that You are a
[n]prophet.
20 "Our fathers worshiped
on this [o]mountain, and you
Jews say that in [p]Jerusalem is
the place where one ought to
worship."
21 Jesus said to her,
"Woman, believe Me, the hour
is coming when you will neither
on this mountain, nor in Jerusalem, worship the Father.
22 "You worship what you do
not know; we know what we
worship, for [q]salvation is of the
Jews.
23 "But the hour is coming,
and now is, when the true worshipers will [r]worship the Father in spirit and truth; for the
Father is seeking such to worship Him.
24 [s]"God *is* [t]Spirit, and
those who worship Him must
[r]worship in spirit and truth."
25 The woman said to Him, "I
know that Messiah is [u]coming"
(who is called Christ). "When
He comes, He will tell us all
things."
26 Jesus said to her, [v]"I who
speak to you am [w]*He*."
27 And at this *point* His disciples came, and they [x]marveled
that He talked with a woman;
yet no one said, "What do You
seek?" or, "Why are You talking
with her?"
28 The woman then left her
waterpot, went her way into the
city, and said to the men,
29 [y]"Come, see a Man who
told me all things that I ever did.
Could this be the Christ?"
30 Then they went out of the
city and came to Him.
31 In the meantime His disciples urged Him, saying, "Rabbi,
eat."
32 But He said to them, "I
have food to eat of which you do
not know."
33 Therefore the disciples
said to one another, "Has anyone brought Him *anything* to
eat?"
34 Jesus said to them, "My
food is to do the [z]will of Him
who sent Me, and to [aa]finish His
work.
35 "Do you not say, 'There
are still four months and *then*
comes the [bb]harvest'? Behold, I

6
a Cp. Heb. 4:15
b 6 p.m. See Jn. 19:14, *note;* cp. Gen. 24:11
9
c Acts 10:28
d vv. 39,40; 2 Ki. 17:24; cp. Mt. 10:5–6; Lk. 9:52; 10:33; 17:16; Jn. 8:48
10
e Rom. 5:15
f Jn. 7:38
12
g Cp. Jn. 8:53; Heb. 1:1–2:8
14
h *Holy Spirit* (NT): v. 14; Jn. 7:39. (Mt. 1:18; Acts 2:4, *note*)
i i.e. *the indwelling Spirit.* Cp. Jn. 7:37–39
j Cp. Ex. 17:6
k Jn. 7:37–38
l *Life* (eternal): v. 14; Jn. 4:36. (Mt. 7:14; Rev. 22:19)
15
m *Bible prayers* (NT): v. 15; Jn. 4:49. (Mt. 6:9; Lk. 11:2, *note*)
19
n See Lk. 24:19, *note*

20
o Gen. 12:6–8; 33:18; Jud. 9:7
p Dt. 12:5; 1 Ki. 9:3; Ps. 122:1–9; see Amos 4:4, *note*
22
q See Rom. 1:16, *note*
23
r Mt. 18:20; Heb. 13:10–14
24
s See Jn. 1:18, *note*
t Or *spirit.* Reference to Holy Spirit is debatable. Cp. 2 Cor. 3:17–18
25
u Dt. 18:15
26
v Jn. 6:35,41, 48,51; 8:12; 9:5; 10:7,9, 11,14; 11:25; 14:6; 15:1,5; Rev. 1:8,17; cp. Ex. 3:14; Isa. 43:11–15
w *Christ* (first advent): v. 26; Jn. 5:43. (Gen. 3:15; Acts 1:11, *note*). Jn. 9:37
27
x Cp. v. 9; Acts 10:28; 11:3; Gal. 2:12
29
y Cp. Ps. 66:16
34
z Ps. 40:7–8; Heb. 10:9
aa Jn. 17:4; 19:30; cp. Acts 20:24; 2 Tim. 4:7
35
bb Gen. 8:22

[1](4:6) Observe that, in His humanity, Jesus experienced the same physical limitations that all men know. Cp. Heb. 4:15–16.

say to you, lift up your eyes and look at the fields, for they are already white for [a]harvest!

36 "And he who reaps receives [b]wages, and gathers [c]fruit for eternal [d]life, that [e]both he who sows and he who reaps may rejoice together.

37 "For in this the [f]saying is true: [g]'One sows and another reaps.'

38 "I sent you to reap that for which you have not labored; [h]others have labored, and you have entered into their labors."

Jesus and the Samaritans

39 And many of the [i]Samaritans of that city [j]believed in Him because of the word of the woman who testified, "He told me all that I *ever* did."

40 So when the [i]Samaritans had come to Him, they urged Him to stay with them; and He stayed there two days.

41 And many more [j]believed because of His own [k]word.

42 Then they said to the woman, "Now we [j]believe, not because of what you said, for we ourselves have heard *Him* and we know that this is indeed the Christ,* the [l]Savior of the [m]world."

43 Now after the two days He departed from there and went to Galilee.

44 For Jesus Himself testified [n]that a [o]prophet has no honor in his own country.

45 So when He came to Galilee, the Galileans received Him, having [p]seen all the things He did in Jerusalem at the feast; for they also had gone to the feast.

Jesus heals a nobleman's son

46 So Jesus came again to Cana of Galilee where He had [q]made the water wine. [r]And there was a certain [s]nobleman whose son was sick at Capernaum.

47 When he heard that Jesus had come out of Judea into Galilee, he went to Him and implored Him to come down and heal his son, for he was at the point of death.

48 Then Jesus said to him, "Unless you *people* see [t]signs and wonders, you will by no means believe."

49 The nobleman [u]said to Him, "Sir, come down before my child dies!"

50 Jesus said to him, [v]"Go your way; your son lives." So the man [j]believed the [k]word that Jesus spoke to him, and he went his way.

51 And as he was now going down, his servants met him and told *him,* saying, [w]"Your son lives!"

52 Then he inquired of them the hour when he got better. And they said to him, "Yesterday at the [x]seventh hour the fever [q]left him."

53 So the father knew that *it was* at the same hour in which Jesus said to him, [y]"Your son lives." And he himself [j]believed, and his whole household.

54 This again *is* the [z]second sign Jesus did when He had come out of Judea into Galilee.

Another feast of the Jews: healing of the crippled man at pool of Bethesda

5 AFTER this there was a [aa]feast of the Jews, and Jesus [bb]went up to Jerusalem.

2 Now there is in Jerusalem by the Sheep [cc]*Gate* a pool, which is called in Hebrew, Bethesda,* having five porches.

3 In these lay a great multitude of sick people, blind, lame, paralyzed, waiting for the moving of the water.

4 For an [dd]angel went down at a certain time into the pool and stirred up the water; then whoever stepped in first, after the stirring of the water, was made well of whatever disease he had.*

5 Now a certain man was there who had an [ee]infirmity thirty-eight years.

6 When Jesus saw him lying there, and knew that he already had been *in that condition* a long time, He said to him, [ff]"Do you want to be made well?"

*4:42 NU-Text omits *the Christ.*
5:2 NU-Text reads *Bethzatha.*
5:4 NU-Text omits *waiting for the moving of the water* at the end of verse 3, and all of verse 4.

35
a Mt. 9:37
36
b Cp. Ps. 126:6
c Rom. 6:22
d *Life* (eternal): v. 36; Jn. 5:24. (Mt. 7:14; Rev. 22:19)
e 1 Th. 2:19
37
f *Inspiration:* v. 37; Jn. 5:46. (Ex. 4:15; 2 Tim. 3:16, *note*). Mic. 6:15
g 1 Cor. 3:5–9
38
h Jer. 44:4; 1 Pet. 1:12
39
i Cp. Lk. 9:52–53
j *Faith:* vv. 39, 41–42,50,53; Jn. 5:46. (Gen. 3:20; Heb. 11:39, *note*)
41
k Lk. 4:32; Jn. 6:63; cp. Mk. 13:31; Jn. 7:46; 12:48
42
l See Rom. 1:16, *note*
m Gk. *kosmos.* See Mt. 4:8, *note*
44
n Mt. 13:57; Mk. 6:4; Lk. 4:24
o See Lk. 24:19, *note*
45
p Jn. 2:13,23; cp. Lk. 19:37
46
q *Miracles* (NT): vv. 46–54; 5:2–6; Jn. 5:9. (Mt. 8:3; Acts 28:8, *note*)
r Cp. Mt. 8:5–13; Lk. 7:1–10
s Or *ruler*
48
t Jn. 6:30

49
u *Bible prayers* (NT): v. 49; Jn. 11:41. (Mt. 6:9; Lk. 11:2, *note*)
50
v Cp. Mk. 7:29–30
51
w v. 53; cp. Ps. 111:7; Ezek. 12:25
52
x 7 o'clock. See Jn. 19:14, *note*
53
y v. 51
54
z Cp. Jn. 2:11
CHAPTER 5
1
aa Lev. 23:2; Dt. 16:16
bb Jn. 2:13
2
cc Neh. 3:1; 12:39
4
dd See Heb. 1:4, *note*
5
ee Cp. Mt. 8:17; Lk. 5:15; 13:11; 2 Cor. 12:10; Gal. 4:13; 1 Tim. 5:23; Heb. 4:15
6
ff Cp. v. 40

7 The [a]sick man answered
Him, "Sir, [b]I have no man to put
me into the pool when the water
is stirred up; but while I am
coming, another steps down before me."
8 Jesus said to him, [c]"Rise,
take up your bed and walk."
9 And immediately the man
was [d]made well, took up his
bed, and walked. And that day
was the [e]Sabbath.
10 The Jews therefore said to
him who was cured, "It is the
[e]Sabbath; it is not [f]lawful for
you to carry your bed."
11 He answered them, "He
who made me well said to me,
[g]'Take up your bed and walk.' "
12 Then they asked him,
"Who is the Man who said to
you, 'Take up your bed and
walk'?"
13 But the one who was
[h]healed did not know who it
was, for Jesus had [i]withdrawn,
a multitude being in *that* place.
14 Afterward Jesus found
him in the temple, and said to
him, "See, you have been made
well. [j]Sin no more, lest a worse
thing come upon you."
15 The man departed and
told the Jews that it was Jesus
who had made him well.
16 For this reason the Jews
[k]persecuted Jesus, and sought
to kill Him,* because He had
done these things on the [e]Sab-
bath.

Jesus claims equality with the Father

17 But Jesus answered them,
"My Father has been working
until now, and I have been
[l]working."
18 Therefore the Jews sought
all the more to [m]kill Him, because He not only broke the
[e]Sabbath, but also said that
[n]God was [1]His Father, [o]making
Himself equal with God.
19 Then Jesus answered and
said to them, [p]"Most assuredly,
I say to you, the Son can do
[2]nothing of Himself, but what
He sees the Father [q]do; for
whatever He does, the Son also
does in like manner.
20 "For the Father [r]loves the
Son, and [s]shows Him all things
that He Himself does; and He
will show Him greater works
than these, that you may marvel.
21 "For as the Father [t]raises
the dead and gives life to *them,*
even so the Son [u]gives life to
whom He will.
22 "For the Father judges no
one, but has committed [v]all
[w]judgment to the Son,
23 "that all should honor the
Son just as they honor the Father. He who does not honor the
Son does not honor the Father
who sent Him.
24 [p]"Most assuredly, I say to
you, he who hears My word and
[x]believes in Him who sent Me
has everlasting [y]life, and shall
[z]not come into [v]judgment, but
has passed from [aa]death into
life.

The two resurrections

25 "Most assuredly, I say to
you, the [3]hour is coming, and
now is, when the dead will hear
the voice of the Son of God; and
those who hear [t]will [y]live.
26 "For [bb]as the Father has
life in Himself, so He has
granted the Son to have [cc]life in
Himself,
27 "and has given Him au-
thority to execute [w]judgment
also, because He is the Son of
Man.
28 "Do not marvel at this; for
the [dd]hour is coming in which all
who are in the graves will [ee]hear
His voice
29 [ff]"and [t]come forth—those
who have done good, [z]to the

* 5:16 NU-Text omits *and sought to kill Him.*

7
a Cp. Lk. 13:11; Acts 3:2
b Cp. Ps. 142:4
8
c Cp. Mt. 9:6
9
d *Miracles* (NT): vv. 2–9; Jn. 6:14. (Mt. 8:3; Acts 28:8, *note*)
e *Sabbath:* vv. 9–10,16, 18; Jn. 7:22. (Gen. 2:3; Mt. 12:1, *note*)
10
f Jer. 17:21–22; see Mt. 12:1, *note*
11
g v. 8
13
h Lk. 13:14; 22:51
i Lk. 4:30
14
j See Rom. 3:23, *note*
16
k Lk. 4:29; Jn. 8:37; 10:39
17
l Jn. 9:4; 17:4
18
m Jn. 7:1,19; cp. Lk. 6:11; Jn. 7:7; 15:18,25
n v. 17; cp. Jn. 10:36; 19:7
o Jn. 10:30, 33; Phil. 2:6
19
p Jn. 1:51; 5:19,24,25; 6:26,32,47, 53; 8:34,51, 58; 10:1,7; 12:24; 13:16,20,21; 14:12; 16:20,23
q Lit. *doing*
20
r Mt. 3:17
s Mt. 11:27

21
t *Resurrection:* vv. 21, 25,29; Jn. 6:40. (2 Ki. 4:35; 1 Cor. 15:52, *note*)
u Jn. 11:25; cp. Eph. 2:1,5; Col. 2:13
22
v *Judgments* (the seven): vv. 22,24; Jn. 5:29. (1 Sam. 7:14; Rev. 20:12, *note*)
w *Day* (of judgment): vv. 22,27; Jn. 5:29. (Mt. 10:15; Rev. 20:11). Dan. 7:9–10; Acts 17:31
24
x Jn. 6:47
y *Life* (eternal): vv. 24–25; Jn. 5:29. (Mt. 7:14; Rev. 22:19)
z *Assurance/security:* vv. 24,29; Jn. 6:39. (Ps. 23:1; Jude 1, *note*)
aa *Death* (spiritual): vv. 24–25; Jn. 8:51. (Gen. 2:17; Eph. 2:5, *note*)
26
bb Ps. 36:9
cc Jn. 1:4; 14:6; 1 Cor. 15:45; Dan. 7:9–10; Acts 17:31
28
dd See v. 25, *note*
ee 1 Th. 4:15–17
29
ff Dan. 12:2

[1](5:18) Literally, "His own Father" (Gk. *patera idion*). It is clear that the Jews understood that Jesus was claiming to be God. Cp. 10:33.

[2](5:19) Some have mistakenly said that Jesus was here disclaiming equality with the Father. On the contrary, the whole context argues the opposite (vv. 18 where see *note,* 23,26). Our Lord is simply saying that He and the Father work together (cp. v. 17).

[3](5:25) Since this "hour" of spiritual regeneration has already lasted for over nineteen centuries, it is also possible for the future "hour" of physical resurrection (vv. 28–29) to extend over a thousand years—the righteous to be raised at the beginning; the wicked, at the end. See Rev. 20.

resurrection of [a]life, and those
who have done evil, to the [b]res-
urrection [c]of [d]condemnation.

Confirmatory witnesses to Jesus

30 "I can of Myself do nothing. As I hear, I judge; and My
[b]judgment is righteous, because I do not seek My own will
but the will of the Father who
sent Me.
31 "If I bear [1]witness of Myself, My witness is not true.
32 "There is [e]another who
bears witness of Me, and I know
that the witness which He witnesses of Me is true.

(1) Witness of John the Baptist

33 "You have sent to John,
and he has borne witness to the
truth.
34 "Yet I do not receive testimony from man, but I say these
things that you may be [f]saved.
35 "He was the burning and
shining lamp, and you were
willing for a time to rejoice in
his light.

(2) Witness of Jesus' works

36 "But I have a greater witness than John's; for the works
which the Father has given Me
to [g]finish—the very [h]works
that I do—bear witness of Me,
that the Father has sent Me.

(3) Witness of the Father
(cp. Mt. 3:17)

37 "And the Father Himself,
who sent Me, has testified of
Me. You have neither heard His
voice at any time, nor [i]seen His
form.
38 "But you do not have His
word abiding in you, because
whom He sent, Him you do not
believe.

(4) Witness of Scripture
(cp. Lk. 24:27,44)

39 "You [j]search the Scriptures, for in them you think you
have eternal [a]life; and these are
they which testify of Me.
40 "But you are not willing to
come to Me that you may have
[a]life.
41 "I do not receive honor
from men.
42 "But I know you, that you
do not have the love of God in
you.
43 "I have [k]come in My Father's name, and you do not receive Me; if [l]another comes in
his own [m]name, him you will receive.
44 "How can you believe,
who receive honor from one another, and do not seek the honor
that *comes* from the only God?
45 "Do not think that I shall
accuse you to the Father; there
is *one* who accuses you—
Moses, in whom you [n]trust.
46 "For if you believed Moses, you would [o]believe Me; for
he [p]wrote about Me.
47 "But if you do [q]not believe
his [p]writings, how will you believe My words?"

Another Passover:
five thousand fed
(Mt. 14:15–21; Mk. 6:32–44;
Lk. 9:12–17)

6 [2]AFTER these things Jesus
went over the Sea of [r]Gali-
lee, which is *the Sea* of [s]Tibe-
rias.
2 Then a great multitude
followed Him, because they saw
His signs which He performed
on those who were [t]diseased.
3 And Jesus went up on the
mountain, and there He sat with
His disciples.
4 Now the [u]Passover, a
feast of the Jews, was near.
5 Then Jesus lifted up *His*
eyes, and seeing a great multitude coming toward Him, He
said to [v]Philip, "Where shall we
buy bread, that these may eat?"
6 But this He said to [w]test
him, for He Himself knew what
He would do.
7 Philip answered Him,
[x]"Two hundred [y]denarii worth

29
a Life (eternal): vv. 29, 39–40; Jn. 6:27. (Mt. 7:14; Rev. 22:19)
b Day (of judgment): vv. 29–30; Jn. 12:48. (Mt. 10:15; Rev. 20:11). Dan. 7:9–10; Acts 17:31
c Judgments (the seven): v. 29; Jn. 19:16. (1 Sam. 7:14; Rev. 20:12, *note*)
d Rev. 20:11–15
32
e v. 37
34
f See Rom. 1:16, *note*
36
g Jn. 17:4
h Jn. 9:16; 10:38
37
i See Jn. 1:18, *note*
39
j Cp. Dt. 17:19; Acts 17:11
43
k Christ (first advent): v. 43; Jn. 6:33. (Gen. 3:15; Acts 1:11, *note*)
l The Beast: v. 43; 2 Th. 2:3. (Dan. 7:8; Rev. 19:20)
m Antichrist: v. 43; 2 Cor. 11:4. (Mt. 24:5; Rev. 13:11, *note*)
45
n Cp. Ps. 118:9; see Ps. 2:12, *note*
46
o Faith: v. 46; Jn. 6:69. (Gen. 3:20; Heb. 11:39, *note*)
p Inspiration: vv. 46–47; Jn. 6:31. (Ex. 4:15; 2 Tim. 3:16, *note*)
47
q Lk. 16:31
CHAPTER 6
1
r Or *Chinnereth,* Num. 34:11; or *Chinneroth,* Josh. 12:3
s Jn. 21:1
2
t Mt. 4:23; 8:16; 9:35; 14:36; 15:30; 19:2
4
u c. A.D. 27. Cp. Jn. 2:13; 11:55; 18:28; see Ex. 12:11, *note*
5
v Jn. 1:43
6
w Test/tempt: v. 6; Jn. 8:6. (Gen. 3:1; Jas. 1:14, *note*)
7
x Cp. Num. 11:21–22
y See Coinage (NT), Mt. 5:26, *note*

[1](5:31) Compare Jn. 8:14. The statement here (5:31) might be paraphrased as follows: "If I testify about Myself, you will say My testimony is not valid." Against this charge our Lord, in defending His Messianic claims, urges the biblical rule of evidence which requires two or three witnesses (Num. 35:30; Dt. 17:6; Jn. 8:17–18). The additional witnesses are cited in vv. 32–47.

[2](6:1) There are many events in our Lord's ministry which took place between ch. 5:47 and 6:1, i.e. the period between Mt. 4:12 and 14:12.

of bread is not sufficient for
them, that every one of them
may have a little."
8 One of His disciples, [a]An-
drew, Simon Peter's brother,
said to Him,
9 "There is a lad here who
has five barley loaves and two
small fish, but what are they
among so [b]many?"
10 Then Jesus said, "Make
the people sit down." Now there
was much grass in the place. So
the men sat down, in number
about five thousand.
11 And Jesus took the loaves,
and when He had [c]given thanks
He distributed *them* to the disciples, and the disciples* to those
sitting down; and likewise of
the fish, as much as they
wanted.
12 So when they were filled,
He said to His disciples, "Gather
up the fragments that remain,
so [d]that nothing is lost."
13 Therefore they gathered
them up, and filled twelve baskets with the fragments of the
five barley loaves which were
left over by those who had
eaten.
14 Then those men, when
they had seen the [e]sign that Jesus did, said, "This is truly [f]the
Prophet who is to come into the
[g]world."

Jesus walks on the water
(Mt. 14:22–32; Mk. 6:45–52)

15 Therefore when Jesus
perceived that they were about
to come and take Him by force
to make Him [h]king, He departed again to the mountain by
Himself alone.
16 [i]Now when evening came,
His disciples went down to the
sea,
17 got into the boat, and went
over the sea toward Capernaum. And it was already dark,
and Jesus had not come to
them.
18 Then the sea arose be-
cause a [j]great wind was blowing.
19 So when they had rowed
about three or four [k]miles,*
they saw Jesus [e]walking on the
[l]sea and drawing near the boat;
and they were [m]afraid.
20 But He said to them, [n]"It is
I; do not be afraid."
21 Then they willingly received Him into the boat, and
immediately the boat was at the
land where they were going.

Jesus, the bread of life

22 On the following day,
when the people who were
standing on the other side of the
sea saw that there was no other
boat there, except that one
which His disciples had entered,* and that Jesus had not
entered the boat with His disciples, but His disciples had gone
away alone—
23 however, other boats
came from Tiberias, near the
[o]place where they ate bread after the Lord had given thanks—
24 when the people therefore
saw that Jesus was not there,
nor His disciples, they also got
into boats and came to Capernaum, [p]seeking Jesus.
25 And when they found Him
on the other side of the sea, they
said to Him, "Rabbi, when did
You come here?"
26 Jesus answered them and
said, [q]"Most assuredly, I say to
you, you seek Me, not because
you saw the signs, but because
you [r]ate of the loaves and were
filled.
27 [s]"Do not labor for the
food which perishes, but for the
food which [t]endures to everlasting [u]life, which the [v]Son of
Man will [w]give you, because
God the Father has [x]set His seal
on Him."
28 Then they said to Him,
"What shall we do, that we may
work the works of God?"
29 Jesus answered and said
to them, "This is the work of
God, that you [y]believe in Him
whom He sent."

Jesus, sent from heaven

30 Therefore they said to
Him, "What [z]sign will You perform then, that we may see it
and believe You? What work
will You do?
31 "Our fathers ate the

*
6:11 NU-Text omits *to the disciples, and the disciples.* **6:19** Literally *twenty-five or thirty stadia* **6:22** NU-Text omits *that* and *which His disciples had entered.*

8
a Jn. 1:40
9
b Cp. 2 Ki. 4:42–44
11
c v. 23; cp. 1 Sam. 9:13; Mt. 26:26; 1 Tim. 4:4–5
12
d Cp. Gen. 41:35–36; Prov. 21:20
14
e *Miracles* (NT): vv. 5–14, 16–21; Jn. 9:7. (Mt. 8:3; Acts 28:8, *note*)
f Gen. 49:10; Dt. 18:15, 18; Jn. 1:21; 7:40; Acts 3:22; 7:37; cp. Mt. 21:11
g Gk. *kosmos.* See Mt. 4:8, *note*
15
h Jn. 18:36
16
i Mt. 14:23; Mk. 6:47
18
j Cp. 1 Ki. 19:11; Job 1:19; Jon. 1:4; Mk. 4:37; Acts 27:14
19
k See Weights and Measures (NT), Acts 27:28, *note*
l Cp. Job 9:8; Isa. 43:16
m Mt. 17:6
20
n Isa. 43:1–2
23
o v. 11
24
p Mk. 1:37; Lk. 4:42; cp. Lk. 19:3; Jn. 12:21
26
q Jn. 1:51; 5:19,24,25; 6:26,32,47, 53; 8:34,51, 58; 10:1,7; 12:24; 13:16,20,21; 14:12; 16:20,23
r vv. 11–12
27
s Mt. 6:19; cp. Eccl. 2:11; 4:8; Isa. 55:2
t vv. 54–58; cp. Col. 3:1–2
u *Life* (eternal): v. 27; Jn. 6:33. (Mt. 7:14; Rev. 22:19)
v See Mt. 8:20, *note*
w Eph. 2:8–9
x Ps. 2:7; Isa. 42:1; Acts 2:22; 2 Pet. 1:17; cp. Jn. 3:33
29
y 1 Jn. 3:23
30
z Mt. 12:38

[a]manna in the desert; as it is [b]written, *'He gave them bread from heaven to eat.'* "*

32 Then Jesus said to them, [c]"Most assuredly, I say to you, Moses did not give you the bread from heaven, but [d]My Father gives you the true bread from heaven.

33 "For the bread of God [e]is He who [f]comes down from heaven and [g]gives [h]life to the [i]world."

34 Then they said to Him, "Lord, give us this bread always."

35 And Jesus said to them, [j]"I am the bread of [h]life. He who comes to Me shall never [k]hunger, and he who [l]believes in Me shall never [m]thirst.

36 "But I said to you that you have [n]seen Me and yet do [o]not believe.

37 "All that the Father [p]gives Me will come to Me, and [q]the one who comes to Me I will by no means cast out.

38 "For I have [f]come down from heaven, not to do My own will, [r]but the [g]will of Him who sent Me.

39 "This is the will of the Father who sent Me, that of all He has given Me I should lose [s]nothing, but should raise it up at the last [t]day.

40 "And this is the will of Him who sent Me, that everyone who sees the Son and believes in Him may have everlasting [h]life; and I will [u]raise him up at the last [t]day."

41 The Jews then complained about Him, because He said, [j]"I am the bread which [f]came down from heaven."

42 And they said, [v]"Is not this Jesus, the son of Joseph, whose father and mother we know? How is it then that He says, 'I have [f]come down from heaven'?"

43 Jesus therefore answered and said to them, "Do not murmur among yourselves.

44 "No one can [w]come to Me unless the Father who sent Me [x]draws him; and I will raise him up at the last [t]day.

45 "It is [b]written in the prophets, *'And they shall all be taught by God.'* Therefore everyone who has heard and learned* from the Father comes to Me.

46 "Not that anyone has seen the Father, except He who is from God; He has seen the Father.

47 [c]"Most assuredly, I say to you, he who believes in Me* has everlasting [h]life.

48 [j]"I [y]am the bread of life.

49 "Your fathers ate the [a]manna in the wilderness, and are [z]dead.

50 "This is the bread which [f]comes down from heaven, that one may eat of it and not die.

51 [j]"I [y]am the living bread which [f]came down from heaven. If anyone eats of this bread, he will [h]live [s]forever; and the bread that I shall give is My flesh, which I shall [g]give for the life of the [aa]world."

52 The Jews therefore quarreled among themselves, saying, "How can this Man give us *His* flesh to eat?"

53 Then Jesus said to them, [c]"Most assuredly, I say to you, unless you eat the flesh of the Son of Man and drink His blood, you have no life in you.

54 [bb]"Whoever eats My flesh and drinks My blood has eternal [h]life, and I will raise him up at the last [t]day.

55 "For My flesh is food indeed,* and My blood is drink indeed.

56 [cc]"He who eats My flesh and drinks My blood abides in Me, and I in him.

57 "As the living Father sent Me, and I live because of the Father, so he who feeds on Me will [h]live because of Me.

58 "This is the [dd]bread which [f]came down from heaven—not [ee]as your fathers ate the [a]manna, and are dead. He who eats this bread will [h]live forever."

59 These things He said in the synagogue as He taught in Capernaum.

*

6:31 Exodus 16:4; Nehemiah 9:15; Psalm 78:24 **6:45** M-Text reads *hears and has learned.* **6:47** NU-Text omits *in Me.* **6:55** NU-Text reads *true food* and *true drink.*

31
a Ex. 16:4–35; Num. 11:6–9; 21:5; Dt. 8:3
b *Inspiration:* vv. 31, 45; Jn. 7:42. (Ex. 4:15; 2 Tim. 3:16, *note*). Isa. 54:13

32
c Jn. 1:51; 5:19,24,25; 6:26,32,47, 53; 8:34,51, 58; 10:1,7; 12:24; 13:16,20,21; 14:12; 16:20,23
d Jn. 3:13,16

33
e vv. 48,58
f *Christ* (first advent): vv. 33,38, 41–42, 50–51,58; Jn. 7:29. (Gen. 3:15; Acts 1:11, *note*)
g *Sacrifice* (of Christ): vv. 33,38,51; Jn. 10:11. (Gen. 3:15; Heb. 10:18, *note*)
h *Life* (eternal): vv. 33, 35,40,47,51, 54,57–58; Jn. 6:63. (Mt. 7:14; Rev. 22:19)
i Gk. *kosmos.* See Mt. 4:8, *note*

35
j Jn. 6:35,41, 48,51; 8:12, 58; 9:5; 10:7,9,11,14; 11:25; 14:6; 15:1,5; Rev. 1:8,17; cp. Ex. 3:14; Isa. 43:11–15
k Rev. 7:16
l v. 29
m Isa. 55:1–2; Jn. 4:14; cp. Mt. 5:6

36
n Jn. 15:24
o Jn. 10:26

37
p *Election* (personal): v. 37; Jn. 6:65. (Dt. 7:6; 1 Pet. 5:13, *note*)
q Isa. 1:18; 55:7; Mt. 11:28; Lk. 23:42–43; 1 Tim. 1:15; Heb.

4:15–16; 7:25; Rev. 22:17

38
r Ps. 40:7–8; Mt. 26:39; Jn. 4:34; 5:30

39
s *Assurance/security:* vv. 39,51; Jn. 10:28. (Ps. 23:1; Jude 1, *note*)
t See Acts 2:17, *note*

40
u *Resurrection:* v. 40; Jn. 11:23. (2 Ki. 4:35; 1 Cor. 15:52, *note*)

42
v Mt. 13:55

44
w v. 37
x Eph. 2:8–9; Phil. 1:29; 2:12–13

48
y vv. 33,35; Gal. 2:20; Col. 3:3–4

49
z Cp. 1 Cor. 10:1–5

51
aa Gk. *kosmos.* See Mt. 4:8, *note*

54
bb v. 40

56
cc Cp. vv. 47–48 with vv. 53–54

58
dd vv. 32–35, 48–51
ee v. 31; Ex. 16:14–35

Discipleship tested by doctrine
(cp. Mt. 8:19–22; 10:36)

60 Therefore many of His disciples, when they heard *this*, said, "This is a hard saying; [a]who can understand it?"

61 When Jesus knew in Himself that His disciples complained about this, He said to them, "Does this [b]offend you?

62 "*What* then if you should see the [c]Son of Man [d]ascend where He was before?

63 "It is the [e]Spirit who [f]gives life; the [g]flesh profits nothing. The [h]words that I speak to you are spirit, and *they* are [i]life.

64 "But there are some of you who do [j]not believe." For Jesus knew from the beginning who they were who did not believe, and who would [k]betray Him.

65 And He said, "Therefore I have said to you that no one can come to Me unless it has been [l]granted to him by My Father."

Peter confesses his faith
(cp. Mt. 16:13–20; Mk. 8:27–30; Lk. 9:18–21)

66 From that *time* many of His disciples went [m]back and walked with Him no more.

67 Then Jesus said to the twelve, "Do you also want to go away?"

68 But Simon Peter answered Him, "Lord, to whom shall we go? You have the words of eternal [i]life.

69 "Also we have come to [n]believe and know that You are the Christ, the Son of the living God."*

70 Jesus answered them, "Did I not choose you, the twelve, and one of you is a [o]devil?"

71 He spoke of [p]Judas Iscariot, *the son* of Simon, for it was he who would [q]betray Him, being one of the twelve.

Christ's unbelieving brothers press Him to go to Jerusalem

7 AFTER these things Jesus walked in Galilee; for He did not want to walk in Judea, because the Jews* sought to [r]kill Him.

2 Now the Jews' [s]Feast of Tabernacles was at hand.

3 His brothers therefore said to Him, "Depart from here and go into Judea, that Your disciples also may see the works that You are doing.

4 "For no one does anything in secret while he himself seeks to be known openly. If You do these things, show Yourself to the [t]world."

5 For [u]even His [v]brothers did not believe in Him.

6 Then Jesus said to them, "My [w]time has not yet come, but your time is always ready.

7 "The [x]world cannot [y]hate you, but it hates Me because I testify of it that its works are evil.

8 "You go up to this [s]feast. I am not yet* going up to this feast, for My [w]time has not yet fully come."

9 When He had said these things to them, He remained in Galilee.

Jesus at the Feast of Tabernacles

10 But when His [v]brothers had gone up, then He also went up to the [s]feast, not openly, but as it were in [z]secret.

11 Then the Jews sought Him at the feast, and said, "Where is He?"

12 [aa]And there was much complaining among the people concerning Him. Some said, "He is good"; others said, "No, on the contrary, He deceives the people."

13 However, no one spoke openly of Him for [bb]fear of the Jews.

14 Now about the middle of the [s]feast Jesus went up into the temple and [cc]taught.

15 And the Jews [dd]marveled, saying, "How does this Man know letters, having never [ee]studied?"

16 Jesus* answered them and said, "My doctrine is not Mine, but [ff]His who sent Me.

17 "If anyone wills to do His will, he shall know concerning the [gg]doctrine, [hh]whether it is from God or *whether* I speak on My own *authority*.

*6:69 NU-Text reads *You are the Holy One of God.* 7:1 That is, the ruling authorities 7:8 NU-Text omits *yet.* 7:16 NU-Text and M-Text read *So Jesus.*

60
a Cp. Mk. 9:32
61
b Lit. *cause you to stumble*
62
c See Mt. 8:20, *note*
d Acts 1:9; cp. Jn. 20:17
63
e Gen. 2:7
f 1 Cor. 15:45
g Jn. 3:6
h v. 68; Jn. 14:24
i *Life* (eternal): vv. 63, 68; Jn. 8:12. (Mt. 7:14; Rev. 22:19)
64
j Jn. 10:25–26
k v. 70
65
l *Election* (personal): v. 65; Jn. 13:18. (Dt. 7:6; 1 Pet. 5:13, *note*)
66
m Lk. 9:62; cp. 1 Jn. 2:19
69
n *Faith:* v. 69; Jn. 7:31. (Gen. 3:20; Heb. 11:39, *note*)
70
o Gk. *diabolos, adversary,* usually referring to Satan. See Rev. 20:10, *note*
71
p Jn. 12:4; 13:2,26
q Mt. 26:14–16
CHAPTER 7
1
r Mt. 21:38; 26:4; Jn. 5:18; 7:19, 25; 8:37,40
2
s Lev. 23:34; Dt. 16:13–15; Neh. 8:14,18

4
t Gk. *kosmos.* See Mt. 4:8, *note*
5
u Ps. 69:8
v Mt. 12:46; 13:55; cp. Acts 1:14
6
w Cp. Mt. 26:18,45; Jn. 12:23; 13:1; 17:1
7
x Gk. *kosmos.* See Rev. 13:8, *note*
y Cp. Jn. 15:18–19
10
z Cp. Jn. 11:56
12
aa Cp. Jn. 9:16
13
bb Jn. 9:22
14
cc Mt. 4:23; 5:2; 7:29; Mk. 6:34; Lk. 4:15; 5:3; Jn. 8:2
15
dd Mt. 13:54; 15:31; 22:22,33
ee An allusion to the fact that Jesus had not attended a rabbinical school
16
ff Dt. 18:15, 18–19
17
gg Or *teaching*
hh Cp. Jn. 8:28,47; 12:49; 14:10,24; 17:8

18 "He who speaks from himself seeks his own glory; but He who [a]seeks the glory of the One who sent Him is true, and [b]no unrighteousness is in Him.

19 "Did not Moses give you the [c]law, yet none of you keeps the law? Why do you seek to kill Me?"

20 The people answered and said, "You have a [d]demon. Who is seeking to kill You?"

21 Jesus answered and said to them, "I did one work, and you all marvel.

22 "Moses therefore gave you [e]circumcision (not that it is from Moses, but [c]from the fathers), and you circumcise a man on the [f]Sabbath.

23 "If a man receives circumcision on the Sabbath, so that the [c]law of Moses should not be broken, are you angry with Me because I made a man [g]completely well on the [f]Sabbath?

24 "Do not judge according to appearance, but judge with [h]righteous judgment."

25 Now some of them from Jerusalem said, "Is this not He whom they seek to [i]kill?

26 "But look! He speaks boldly, and they say nothing to Him. [j]Do the rulers know indeed that this is truly* the Christ?

27 [k]"However, we know where this Man is from; but when the Christ comes, no one knows where He is from."

28 Then Jesus cried out, as He taught in the temple, saying, "You both know Me, and you know where I am from; and I have not come of Myself, but He who sent Me is true, whom you do not know.

29 "But* I know Him, for I am [l]from Him, and He sent Me."

30 Therefore they sought to take Him; but no one laid a hand on Him, because His [m]hour had not yet come.

31 And many of the people [n]believed in Him, and said, "When the Christ [l]comes, will He do more signs than these which this *Man* has done?"

32 The [o]Pharisees heard the crowd murmuring these things concerning Him, and the Pharisees and the chief priests sent officers to take Him.

33 Then Jesus said to them,* [p]"I shall be with you a little while longer, and *then* I [q]go to Him who sent Me.

34 "You will seek Me and not find *Me*, and where I am you [r]cannot come."

35 Then the Jews said among themselves, "Where does He intend to go that we shall not find Him? Does He intend to go to the [s]Dispersion among the [t]Greeks and teach the Greeks?

36 "What is this thing that He said, 'You will seek Me and not find Me, and where I am you cannot come'?"

The great prophecy concerning the Holy Spirit for power (Acts 2:2–4; cp. Jn. 4:14)

37 On the [u]last day, that great *day* of the feast, Jesus stood and cried out, saying, "If anyone thirsts, let him come to Me and drink.

38 "He who believes in Me, as the Scripture has said, out of his heart will [v]flow rivers of living [w]water."

39 But this He spoke concerning the Spirit, whom those believing* in Him would receive; for the Holy* [x]Spirit was not yet *given*, because Jesus was not yet [y]glorified.

Divided opinion about Jesus

40 Therefore many* from the crowd, when they heard this saying, [n]said, "Truly this [z]is the Prophet."

41 Others [n]said, "This is [aa]the Christ." But some said, "Will the Christ come out of Galilee?

42 "Has not the Scripture [bb]said that the Christ [l]comes from the seed of David and from the town of Bethlehem, where David was?"

43 So there was a division among the people because of Him.

44 Now some of them wanted to take Him, but no one laid hands on Him.

45 Then the officers came to

---

18 *a* Jn. 8:50; cp. Phil. 2:3–8
b Jn. 8:46; 2 Cor. 5:21; Heb. 4:15; 7:26; 1 Pet. 1:19; 2:22

19 *c Law* (of Moses): vv. 19, 22–23; Jn. 7:49. (Ex. 19:1; Gal. 3:24, *note*)

20 *d* See Mt. 7:22, *note*

22 *e* Gen. 17:9–14
f Sabbath: vv. 22–23; Jn. 9:14. (Gen. 2:3; Mt. 12:1, *note*)

23 *g* Cp. Jn. 5:1–16

24 *h* See 1 Jn. 3:7, *note*

25 *i* Mt. 21:38; 26:4; Lk. 22:2; Jn. 5:18; 8:37, 40

26 *j* v. 48; cp. Jn. 12:42

27 *k* Mt. 13:55

29 *l Christ* (first advent): vv. 29,31,42; Jn. 8:42. (Gen. 3:15; Acts 1:11, *note*)

30 *m* Jn. 8:20

31 *n Faith:* vv. 31, 40–41; Jn. 8:30. (Gen. 3:20; Heb. 11:39, *note*)

32 *o* See Mt. 3:7, *note 1*

33 *p* Jn. 13:33
q Mk. 16:19; Lk. 24:51; Acts 1:9; Heb. 9:24; 1 Pet. 3:22

34 *r* Mt. 5:20; 1 Cor. 6:9; 15:50; Rev. 21:27

35 *s* Jas. 1:1
t See Eph. 3:6, *note*

37 *u* Lev. 23:36

38 *v Christ* (Rock): vv. 37–39; Acts 4:11. (Gen. 49:24; 1 Pet. 2:8)
w Isa. 12:3; 43:20; 44:3; 55:1; Jn. 6:35; Rev. 21:6; 22:17

39 *x Holy Spirit* (NT): vv. 38–39; Jn. 14:16. (Mt. 1:18; Acts 2:4, *note*). Jn. 16:7
y Jn. 13:31; 17:5; cp. Acts 3:13

40 *z* Dt. 18:15, 18; Jn. 6:14; see Lk. 24:19, *note*

41 *aa* Jn. 4:42; 6:69

42 *bb Inspiration:* v. 42; Jn. 8:17. (Ex. 4:15; 2 Tim. 3:16, *note*). 2 Sam. 7:12; Ps. 132:11; Jer. 23:5; Mic. 5:2; Lk. 2:4

---

*

7:26 NU-Text omits *truly*. **7:29** NU-Text and M-Text omit *But*. **7:33** NU-Text and M-Text omit *to them*. **7:39** NU-Text reads *who believed*. • NU-Text omits *Holy*. **7:40** NU-Text reads *some*.

the chief priests and [a]Phari-
sees, who said to them, "Why
have you not brought Him?"
46 The officers answered,
[b]"No man ever spoke like this
Man!"
47 Then the [a]Pharisees answered them, "Are you also deceived?
48 [c]"Have any of the rulers
or the [a]Pharisees believed in
Him?
49 "But this crowd that does
not know the [d]law is accursed."
50 Nicodemus [e](he who came
to Jesus by night,* being one of
them) said to them,
51 "Does our [d]law judge a
man before it [f]hears him and
knows what he is doing?"
52 They answered and said
to him, "Are you also from Galilee? Search and look, [g]for no
prophet has arisen* out of Galilee."
53 [1]And everyone went to his
own house.*

The scribes and Pharisees accuse a woman caught in adultery

8 BUT Jesus went to the
Mount of Olives.
2 Now early* in the morn-
ing He came again into the temple, and all the people came to
Him; and He sat down and
[h]taught them.
3 Then the [i]scribes and
[a]Pharisees brought to Him a
woman caught in adultery. And
when they had set her in the
midst,
4 they said to Him,
"Teacher, this woman was
caught* in [j]adultery, in the
very act.
5 "Now Moses, in the [d]law,
commanded* us that such
should be [k]stoned.* But what
do You say?"*
6 This they said, [l]testing
Him, that they [m]might have
something of which to accuse
Him. But Jesus stooped down
and wrote on the ground with
His finger, as though He did not
hear.*
7 So when they continued
asking Him, He raised Himself
up* and said to them, "He who
is without [n]sin among you, [o]let
him throw a stone at her first."
8 And again He stooped
down and wrote on the ground.
9 Then those who heard *it,*
being convicted by *their* conscience,* went out one by one,
beginning with the oldest *even*
to the last. And Jesus was left
[p]alone, and the woman standing in the midst.
10 When Jesus had raised
Himself up and saw no one but
the woman, He said to her,*
"Woman, where are those [q]ac-
cusers of yours?* Has no one
condemned you?"
11 She said, "No one, Lord."
And Jesus said to her, "Neither
do I [r]condemn you; go and*
[n]sin no more."

The central conflict between Jesus and the Pharisees: the origin of Christ. He is the light of the world (cp. Jn. 1:9)

12 Then Jesus spoke to them
again, saying, [s]"I am the [t]light
of the [u]world. He who [v]follows
Me shall not walk in darkness,
but have the light of [w]life."
13 The [a]Pharisees therefore
said to Him, "You bear witness
of Yourself; Your witness is not
true."
14 Jesus answered and said
to them, "Even if I bear witness
of Myself, My witness is true,
for I know where I came from
and where I am going; but you

*

7:50 NU-Text reads *before.* 7:52 NU-Text reads *is to rise.* 7:53 The words *And everyone* through *sin no more* (8:11) are bracketed by NU-Text as not original. They are present in over 900 manuscripts.
8:2 M-Text reads *very early.* 8:4 M-Text reads *we found this woman.* 8:5 M-Text reads *in our law Moses commanded.*
• NU-Text and M-Text read *to stone such.* • M-Text adds *about her.*
8:6 NU-Text and M-Text omit *as though He did not hear.* 8:7 M-Text reads *He looked up.* 8:9 NU-Text and M-Text omit *being convicted by* their *conscience.*
8:10 NU-Text omits *and saw no one but the woman;* M-Text reads *He saw her and said.*
• NU-Text and M-Text omit *of yours.*
8:11 NU-Text and M-Text add *from now on.*

45
a See Mt. 3:7, *note 1*
46
b Mt. 13:54, 56; Lk. 4:22
48
c v. 26; cp. Lk. 8:41; Jn. 12:42; 1 Cor. 1:26–29
49
d Law (of Moses): vv. 49,51; 8:5; Jn. 8:17. (Ex. 19:1; Gal. 3:24, *note*)
50
e Jn. 3:1–2
51
f Dt. 1:16; 19:15
52
g v. 41; cp. Jn. 1:46
CHAPTER 8
2
h v. 28; Jn. 18:20
3
i See Mt. 2:4, *note*
4
j Ex. 20:14; Mt. 5:27; 19:9; Rom. 7:3; cp. Mt. 5:28–32; 1 Cor. 6:9; 2 Pet. 2:14
5
k Lev. 20:10; Dt. 22:22–24; cp. Num. 5:11–31
6
l Test/tempt: v. 6; Acts 5:9. (Gen. 3:1; Jas. 1:14, *note*)
m Mt. 22:15; cp. Jn. 18:31

7
n See Rom. 3:23, *note*
o Dt. 17:7; cp. Mt. 7:1–5; Rom. 2:1,22
9
p Cp. Mt. 22:22
10
q Cp. Lk. 12:14
11
r Cp. Mt. 11:19; Lk. 7:39; 19:7; Rom. 5:8; 1 Tim. 1:15; see Rom. 1:16, *note*
12
s Jn. 6:35,41, 48,51; 8:12, 58; 9:5; 10:7,9,11,14; 11:25; 14:6; 15:1,5; Rev. 1:8,17; cp. Ex. 3:14; Isa. 43:11–15
t Isa. 9:2; Mal. 4:2; Jn. 9:5; 2 Tim. 1:10
u Gk. *kosmos.* See Mt. 4:8, *note*
v 1 Th. 5:5
w Life (eternal): v. 12; Jn. 10:10. (Mt. 7:14; Rev. 22:19)

[1](7:53) Although Jn. 7:53—8:11 is not found in some ancient manuscripts, the immediate context, beginning with Christ's declaration, "I am the light of the world" (8:12) seems clearly to have its occasion in the conviction wrought in the hearts of the Pharisees as recorded in 8:9, and also helps to explain the Pharisees' words in 8:41. It is therefore to be considered a genuine part of the Gospel.

do not know where I come from and where I am going.

15 "You judge according to the [a]flesh; I judge no one.

16 "And yet if I do judge, My judgment is true; for I am not alone, but I *am* with the Father who sent Me.

17 "It is also [b]written in your [c]law that the testimony of two men is true.

18 "I am One who bears witness of Myself, and the [d]Father who sent Me bears witness of Me."

19 Then they said to Him, "Where is Your Father?" Jesus answered, "You know neither Me nor My Father. [e]If you had known Me, you would have known My Father also."

20 These words Jesus spoke in the treasury, as He taught in the temple; and no one laid hands on Him, for His [f]hour had not yet come.

21 Then Jesus said to them again, "I am going away, and you will seek Me, and will [g]die in your [h]sin. Where I go you [i]cannot come."

22 So the Jews said, "Will He [j]kill Himself, because He says, 'Where I go you cannot come'?"

23 And He said to them, "You are from beneath; [k]I am from above. You are of this [l]world; I am not of this [l]world.

24 "Therefore I said to you that you will [g]die in your [h]sins; for if you do not believe that I am *He,* you will [g]die in your [h]sins."

25 Then they said to Him, "Who are You?" And Jesus said to them, "Just what I have been [m]saying to you from the beginning.

26 "I have many things to say and to judge concerning you, but He who sent Me is true; and I speak to the [l]world those things which I heard from Him."

27 They did not understand that He spoke to them of the Father.

28 Then Jesus said to them, "When you [n]lift up the [o]Son of Man, then you will know that I am *He,* and *that* I do nothing of Myself; but as My Father taught Me, I [p]speak these things.

29 "And He who sent Me is with Me. The Father has not left Me alone, for I always do those things that please Him."

30 As He spoke these words, many [q]believed in Him.

31 Then Jesus said to those Jews who [q]believed Him, "If you [r]abide in My [s]word, you are My disciples indeed.

32 "And you shall know the [t]truth, and the truth shall make you free."

33 They answered Him, [u]"We are Abraham's descendants, and have never been in bondage to anyone. How *can* you say, 'You will be made free'?"

34 Jesus answered them, [v]"Most assuredly, I say to you, whoever commits [h]sin is a [w]slave of [h]sin.

35 "And a slave does [x]not abide in the house forever, *but* a son [y]abides forever.

36 "Therefore if the Son makes you free, you shall be [z]free indeed.

37 "I know that you are [1]Abraham's descendants, but you seek to [aa]kill Me, because My word has no place in you.

38 "I [bb]speak what I have seen with My Father, and you do what you have seen with* your father."

39 They answered and said to Him, "Abraham is our father." Jesus said to them, "If you were Abraham's children, you would do the works of Abraham.

40 "But now you seek to kill Me, a Man who has told you the [t]truth [b]which I heard from God. Abraham did not do this.

41 "You do the deeds of your father." Then they said to Him, "We were not [cc]born of fornication; [dd]we have one Father—God."

42 Jesus said to them, "If God were your Father, you would love Me, for I proceeded forth and [ee]came from God; nor have

*8:38 NU-Text reads *heard from.*

15
a Flesh: v. 15; Rom. 7:5. (Jn. 8:15; Jude 23)
17
b Inspiration: vv. 17, 40; Jn. 10:34. (Ex. 4:15; 2 Tim. 3:16, *note*). Dt. 17:6; 19:15
c Law (of Moses): v. 17; Jn. 9:16. (Ex. 19:1; Gal. 3:24, *note*)
18
d Jn. 5:37
19
e Cp. Jn. 14:7
20
f Jn. 2:4; 7:30
21
g Death (the second): vv. 21,24; Jn. 11:26. (Jn. 8:21; Rev. 20:14, *note*)
h See Rom. 3:23, *note*
i Jn. 7:34
22
j Cp. vv. 37, 40
23
k Jn. 6:35,41, 48,51; 8:12, 58; 9:5; 10:7,9,11,14; 11:25; 14:6; 15:1,5; Rev. 1:8,17; cp. Ex. 3:14; Isa. 43:11–15
l Gk. *kosmos.* See Mt. 4:8 and Rev. 13:8, *notes*
25
m Jn. 4:26
28
n Jn. 3:14; 12:32,34
o See Mt. 8:20, *note*

p Dt. 18:15, 18–19; Jn. 12:49
30
q Faith: vv. 30–31; Jn. 9:7. (Gen. 3:20; Heb. 11:39, *note*)
31
r v. 51; Jn. 14:15,23; cp. Jn. 17:6; 1 Jn. 2:3; Rev. 3:8
s Cp. v. 37
32
t Jn. 1:14,17; 14:6
33
u v. 37; Lk. 3:8; cp. Jn. 8:39–40
34
v Jn. 1:51; 5:19,24,25; 6:26,32,47, 53; 8:34,51, 58; 10:1,7; 12:24; 13:16,20,21; 14:12; 16:20,23
w Prov. 5:22; 2 Pet. 2:19; cp. Mt. 12:34; Rom. 6:14–23
35
x Cp. Gen. 21:10; Gal. 4:30
y Cp. Rom. 8:15–17
36
z Rom. 8:2; 2 Cor. 3:17; Gal. 5:1
37
aa v. 40; cp. v. 22
38
bb Jn. 14:10, 24
41
cc Cp. Mt. 1:18–25
dd Cp. Ti. 1:16
42
ee Christ (first advent): v. 42; Jn. 9:39. (Gen. 3:15; Acts 1:11, *note*)

[1](8:37) All Jews are natural descendants of Abraham, but are not necessarily his spiritual posterity. Cp. Rom. 9:6–8; Gal. 3:6–14.

I come of Myself, but [a]He sent Me.

43 "Why do you not understand My speech? Because you are not able to listen to My word.

44 "You are of *your* [1]father the [b]devil, and the [c]desires of your father you want to [d]do. He was a murderer from the beginning, and *does not* stand in the truth, because there is no truth in him. When he speaks [e]a lie, he speaks from his own *resources,* for he is a liar and the father of it.

45 "But because I tell the truth, you do not believe Me.

46 "Which of you [f]convicts Me of sin? And if I tell the truth, why do you not believe Me?

47 "He who is of God [g]hears God's words; therefore you do not hear, because you are not of God."

48 Then the Jews answered and said to Him, "Do we not say rightly that You are a [h]Samaritan and [i]have a [j]demon?"

49 Jesus answered, "I do not have a demon; but I honor My Father, and [k]you dishonor Me.

50 "And I do not [l]seek My *own* glory; there is One who seeks and judges.

51 [m]"Most assuredly, I say to you, [n]if anyone keeps My word he shall never see [o]death."

52 Then the Jews said to Him, "Now we know that You [p]have a [j]demon! Abraham is [q]dead, and the prophets; and You say, 'If anyone keeps My word he shall never taste death.'

53 "Are You [r]greater than our father Abraham, who is dead? And the prophets are dead. [s]Who do You make Yourself out to be?"

54 Jesus answered, [t]"If I honor Myself, My honor is nothing. [u]It is My Father who honors Me, of whom you say that He is your* God.

55 "Yet [v]you have not known Him, but I know Him. And if I say, 'I do not know Him,' I shall be a liar like you; but I do know Him and [w]keep His word.

56 "Your father Abraham rejoiced to see My day, and he [x]saw *it* and was glad."

57 Then the Jews said to Him, "You are not yet fifty years old, and have You seen Abraham?"

58 Jesus said to them, [m]"Most assuredly, I say to you, [y]before Abraham was, [z]I AM."

59 Then they [aa]took up stones to throw at Him; but Jesus hid Himself and went out of the temple,* [bb]going through the midst of them, and so passed by.

Jesus heals man born blind

9 NOW as *Jesus* passed by, He saw a man who was blind from birth.

2 And His disciples asked Him, saying, "Rabbi, who [cc]sinned, this man or his parents, that he was born blind?"

3 Jesus answered, "Neither this man nor his parents [cc]sinned, but [dd]that the works of God should be revealed in him.

4 "I* must [ee]work the works of Him who sent Me while it is [ff]day; *the* night is coming when no one can work.

5 "As long as I am in the [gg]world, [z]I am the [hh]light of the [gg]world."

6 When He had said these things, He spat on the ground and made [ii]clay with the saliva; and He anointed the eyes of the blind man with the clay.

7 And He said to him, "Go, wash in the pool of Siloam" (which is translated, Sent). So he [jj]went and [kk]washed, and came back [ll]seeing.

8 Therefore the neighbors and those who previously had seen that he was blind* said, "Is not this he who sat and begged?"

9 Some said, "This is he." Others *said,* "He is like him."* He said, "I am *he.*"

10 Therefore they said to

42
a Gal. 4:4
44
b Satan: v. 44; Jn. 12:31. (Gen. 3:1; Rev. 20:10). Ezek. 28:12–17
c 1 Jn. 2:16–17
d 1 Jn. 3:8–10
e Lit. *the lie.* Gen. 3:4–5
46
f 1 Jn. 3:5
47
g Lk. 8:15
48
h 2 Ki. 17:24; cp. Mt. 10:5–6; Lk. 9:52; 10:33; 17:16; Jn. 4:9,39,40
i v. 52; Jn. 7:20; 10:20
j See Mt. 7:22, *note*
49
k Jn. 5:41; cp. Jn. 12:28
50
l Jn. 7:18; Phil. 2:6–8
51
m Jn. 1:51; 5:19,24,25; 6:26,32,47, 53; 8:34,51, 58; 10:1,7; 12:24; 13:16,20,21; 14:12; 16:20,23
n Jn. 5:24; 11:26
o Death (spiritual): v. 51; Rom. 6:16. (Gen. 2:17; Eph. 2:5, *note*)
52
p v. 48; Jn. 7:20; 10:20
q Cp. Zech. 1:5; Heb. 11:13
53
r Cp. Jn. 4:12; Heb. 3:3
s Jn. 10:33; 19:7
54
t v. 50; Jn. 5:31–32
u Acts 3:13; cp. Jn. 16:14; 17:1
55
v v. 19; Jn. 7:28–29
w v. 29; Jn.

15:10
56
x Heb. 11:13
58
y Mic. 5:2; Jn. 17:5; Heb. 7:3; Rev. 22:13
z Jn. 6:35,41, 48,51; 8:12, 58; 9:5; 10:7,9,11,14; 11:25; 14:6; 15:1,5; Rev. 1:8,17; cp. Ex. 3:14; Isa. 43:11–15
59
aa Jn. 10:31; 11:8
bb Lk. 4:30; Jn. 10:39
CHAPTER 9
2
cc See Rom. 3:23, *note*
3
dd Jn. 11:4
4
ee Jn. 4:34; 5:19,36; 17:4
ff Jn. 11:9–10; 12:35
5
gg Gk. *kosmos.* See Mt. 4:8, *note*
hh Jn. 1:5,9; 3:19; 8:12; 12:35,46
6
ii vv. 11,14, 15; cp. Mk. 7:33; 8:23
7
jj Faith: v. 7; Jn. 9:38. (Gen. 3:20; Heb. 11:39, *note*)
kk Cp. 2 Ki. 5:1–14
ll Miracles (NT): vv. 1–11; Jn. 11:44. (Mt. 8:3; Acts 28:8, *note*)

---

*
8:54 NU-Text and M-Text read *our.*
8:59 NU-Text omits the rest of this verse.
9:4 NU-Text reads *We.* **9:8** NU-Text reads *a beggar.* **9:9** NU-Text reads *"No, but he is like him."*

---

[1](8:44) That this satanic fatherhood cannot be limited to the Pharisees is made clear in 1 Jn. 3:8–10.

him, [1]"How were your eyes opened?"

11 He answered and said, "A Man called Jesus made clay and anointed my eyes and said to me, 'Go to the pool of* Siloam and wash.' So I went and washed, and I received sight."

12 Then they said to him, "Where is He?" He said, "I do not know."

13 They brought him who formerly was blind to the [a]Pharisees.

14 Now it was a [b]Sabbath when Jesus made the clay and opened his eyes.

15 Then the [a]Pharisees also asked him again how he had received his sight. He said to them, "He put clay on my eyes, and I washed, and I see."

16 Therefore some of the [a]Pharisees said, "This Man is [c]not from God, because He does not [d]keep the [b]Sabbath." Others said, "How can a man who is a sinner do such signs?" And there was a [e]division among them.

17 They said to the blind man again, "What do you say about Him because He opened your eyes?" He said, "He is a [f]prophet."

18 But the Jews did not believe concerning him, that he had been blind and received his sight, until they called the parents of him who had received his sight.

19 And they asked them, saying, "Is this your son, who you say was born blind? How then does he now see?"

20 His [g]parents answered them and said, "We know that this is our son, and that he was born blind;

21 "but by what means he now sees we do not know, or who opened his eyes we do not know. He is of age; ask him. He will speak for himself."

22 His parents said these *things* because they [h]feared the Jews, for the Jews had agreed already that if anyone confessed *that* He *was* Christ, he would be [i]put [2]out of the synagogue.

23 Therefore his parents said, "He is of age; ask him."

24 So they again called the man who was blind, and said to him, "Give God the glory! We [j]know that this Man is a sinner."

25 He answered and said, "Whether He is a sinner *or not* I do not know. One thing I know: that though I was blind, now I see."

26 Then they said to him again, "What did He do to you? How did He open your eyes?"

27 He answered them, "I told you already, and you did not listen. Why do you want to hear *it* again? Do you also want to become His disciples?"

28 Then they reviled him and said, "You are His disciple, but we are Moses' disciples.

29 "We know that God [k]spoke to [l]Moses; *as for* this *fellow*, we do not know [m]where He is from."

30 The man answered and said to them, "Why, this is a marvelous thing, that you do not know where He is from; yet He has opened my eyes!

31 "Now we know that God does [n]not hear [o]sinners; but if anyone is a worshiper of God and does His will, He hears him.

32 "Since the [p]world began it has been unheard of that anyone opened the eyes of one who was born blind.

33 "If this Man were not from God, He could do [q]nothing."

34 They answered and said to him, "You were completely [r]born in sins, and are you teaching us?" And they [s]cast him out.

Jesus affirms His Deity

35 Jesus heard that they had cast him out; and when He had [t]found him, He said to him, "Do

*9:11 NU-Text omits *the pool of.*

13
a See Mt. 3:7, *note 1*

14
b *Sabbath:* vv. 14,16; Jn. 19:31. (Gen. 2:3; Mt. 12:1, *note*)

16
c Cp. v. 33; Jn. 3:2
d *Law* (of Moses): v. 16; Jn. 18:31. (Ex. 19:1; Gal. 3:24, *note*)
e Jn. 7:12,43; 10:19

17
f Jn. 4:19; 6:14; see Lk. 24:19, *note*

20
g Cp. Mt. 10:35

22
h Jn. 7:13; 12:42; 19:38
i v. 34; Jn. 16:2

24
j v. 16

29
k Ex. 19:19–20; 33:11; 34:29; Num. 12:6–8
l Jn. 5:45–47; cp. Acts 13:27
m Jn. 7:27–28; 8:14

31
n Job 27:8–9; Ps. 18:41; 66:18; Prov. 15:29; 28:9; Mic. 3:4; Zech. 7:13; cp. Ps. 34:15; Jas. 5:16
o See Rom. 3:23, *note*

32
p Gk. *aiōn.* See Mk. 10:30, *note*

33
q Jn. 5:19; 14:10–11

34
r Ps. 51:5
s v. 22

35
t Jn. 5:14; cp. Mt. 18:12; Lk. 19:10

[1](9:10) Observe the progress in the healed man's apprehension of the Person of Christ: (1) "A Man called Jesus" (v. 11); (2) "He is a prophet" (v. 17); (3) "if anyone is a worshiper of God and does His will" (v. 31); and (4) "and he worshiped Him" (v. 38).

[2](9:22) For a Jew to be put out of the synagogue meant that he was ostracized by everyone.

you [a]believe in the [b]Son of
God?"*
36 He answered and said,
[c]"Who is He, Lord, that I may
believe in Him?"
37 And Jesus said to him,
"You have both seen Him and it
is [d]He who is talking with you."
38 Then he said, "Lord, I [e]be-
lieve!" And he [f]worshiped Him.
39 And Jesus said, "For
[g]judgment I have [h]come into
this [i]world, that those who do
not see may see, and that those
who see may be made [j]blind."
40 Then *some* of the Pharisees who were with Him heard
these words, and said to Him,
[k]"Are we blind also?"
41 Jesus said to them, [l]"If
you were blind, you would have
no [m]sin; but now you say, 'We
see.' Therefore your [m]sin [n]re-
mains.

Jesus as the good Shepherd
(cp. Ps. 23; Heb. 13:20; 1 Pet. 5:4)

10 [o]"MOST assuredly, I say
to you, he who does not
enter the sheepfold by the door,
but climbs up some other [p]way,
the same is a thief and a robber.
2 "But he who enters by the
door is the shepherd of the
sheep.
3 "To him the doorkeeper
opens, and the sheep [q]hear his
voice; and he calls his own
sheep by [r]name and [s]leads
them out.
4 "And when he brings out
his own sheep, he goes before
them; and the sheep follow him,
for they know his voice.
5 "Yet they will by no
means follow a [t]stranger, but
will flee from him, for they do
not know the voice of strangers."
6 Jesus used this [u]illustra-
tion, but they did not understand the things which He
spoke to them.
7 Then Jesus said to them
again, [o]"Most assuredly, I say
to you, [1][v]I am the door of the
sheep.
8 "All who *ever* came before
Me* are thieves and robbers,
but the sheep did not hear them.
9 [v]"I am the door. If anyone
enters by Me, he will be [w]saved,
and will go in and out and find
pasture.
10 "The thief does not come
except to steal, and to kill, and
to destroy. I have [h]come that
they may have [x]life, and that
they may have *it* more [y]abun-
dantly.
11 [v]"I am the good [z]shep-
herd. The good shepherd [aa]gives
His life for the sheep.
12 "But a hireling, *he who is*
not the shepherd, one who does
not own the sheep, sees the wolf
coming and [bb]leaves the sheep
and flees; and the wolf catches
the sheep and scatters them.
13 "The hireling flees because he is a hireling and does
not care about the sheep.
14 [v]"I am the good [z]shep-
herd; and I [cc]know My *sheep,*
and [dd]am known by My own.
15 "As the Father knows Me,
even so I know the Father; and
I [aa]lay down My life [ee]for the
sheep.
16 "And [2]other sheep I have
which are not of this fold; them
also I must bring, and they will
hear My voice; and there will be
one [ff]flock *and* one [z]shepherd.
17 "Therefore My Father
[gg]loves Me, because I [aa]lay down
My life that I may take it again.
18 "No one takes it from Me,
but I [aa]lay it down of Myself. I
have power to lay it down, and
I have power to take it [hh]again.
This [ii]command I have received
from My Father."

10:17 *gg* Jn. 5:20 **10:18** *hh* Jn. 2:19 *ii* Jn. 14:31; 17:4; cp. Heb. 10:5–9

*
9:35 NU-Text reads *Son of Man.*
10:8 M-Text omits *before Me.*

35
a Jn. 1:7; 16:31
b Mt. 2:15; 3:17; 14:33; 16:16; 17:5; Lk. 1:35; Jn. 1:34; 3:18; 10:36; 11:27; Acts 9:20; 1 Jn. 4:15; 5:13
36
c Cp. Rom. 10:14
37
d Jn. 4:26
38
e Faith: vv. 36–38; Jn. 10:42. (Gen. 3:20; Heb. 11:39, *note*)
f Mt. 8:2; cp. Jn. 20:16–17, 26–28
39
g Cp. Jn. 3:16–17
h Christ (first advent): v. 39; 10:10; Jn. 11:27. (Gen. 3:15; Acts 1:11, *note*)
i Gk. *kosmos.* See Mt. 4:8, *note*
j Cp. Ezek. 12:2
40
k Cp. Mt. 13:13; Rom. 2:19
41
l Cp. Jn. 15:22–24
m See Rom. 3:23, *note*
n Cp. Mt. 23:27–33
CHAPTER 10
1
o Jn. 1:51; 5:19,24,25; 6:26,32,47, 53; 8:34,51, 58; 10:1,7; 12:24; 13:16,20,21; 14:12; 16:20,23
p Cp. Jn. 14:6
3
q v. 27
r Jn. 20:16; cp. Rev. 2:17
s Cp. Jn. 9:34–38
5
t vv. 12–13; 2 Cor. 11:13–15; cp. Isa. 56:10–12; Jer. 50:6
6
u Lit. *proverb,* i.e. figure of speech. Jn. 16:25,29; 2 Pet. 2:22
7
v Jn. 6:35,41, 48,51; 8:12, 58; 9:5; 10:7,9,11,14; 11:25; 14:6; 15:1,5; Rev. 1:8,17; cp. Ex. 3:14; Isa. 43:11–15
9
w See Rom. 1:16, *note*
10
x Life (eternal): v. 10; Jn. 10:28. (Mt. 7:14; Rev. 22:19)
y Cp. Jn. 7:37–39
11
z v. 2; Gen. 49:24; Isa. 40:11; Ezek. 34:23; Heb. 13:20; 1 Pet. 2:25; 5:4
aa Sacrifice (of Christ): vv. 11,15, 17–18; Jn. 12:24. (Gen. 3:15; Heb. 10:18, *note*)
12
bb Cp. Zech. 11:15–17
14
cc Nah. 1:7; Jn. 6:64; 2 Tim. 2:19
dd v. 4; 2 Tim. 1:12
15
ee 1 Jn. 3:16
16
ff Jn. 11:52; 17:21; Eph. 2:13–16; 3:1–6; Col. 3:10–11

[1](10:7) The shepherd work of our Lord has three aspects: (1) As the "good shepherd" He lays down His life for the sheep (v. 11) and is, therefore, "the door" by which "if anyone enters by Me, he will be saved" (v. 9). This answers to Ps. 22. (2) He is the "great Shepherd," who was "brought up . . . from the dead" (Heb. 13:20) to care for and make perfect the sheep. This answers to Ps. 23. And (3) He is the "Chief Shepherd" who is coming in glory to give crowns of reward to the faithful shepherds (1 Pet. 5:4). This answers to Ps. 24.

[2](10:16) The "other sheep" are not of the Jewish fold, but are Gentiles. Cp. Isa. 56:8; Jn. 17:20; Acts 15:7–9; Eph. 2:11–19.

19 Therefore there was a [a]division again among the Jews because of these sayings.

20 And many of them said, "He has a [b]demon and is [1]mad. Why do you listen to Him?"

21 Others said, "These are not the words of one who has a [b]demon. Can a demon open the eyes of the blind?"

Jesus asserts His Deity
(Jn. 5:26–27; 14:9; 20:28–29)

22 Now it was the Feast of Dedication in Jerusalem, and it was winter.

23 And Jesus walked in the temple, in Solomon's porch.

24 Then the Jews surrounded Him and said to Him, "How long do You [c]keep us in doubt? If You are the Christ, tell us plainly."

25 Jesus answered them, "I told you, and you do not believe. The works that I do in My Father's name, they [d]bear witness of Me.

26 "But you do not believe, [e]because you are not of My sheep, as I said to you.*

27 "My sheep hear My voice, and I [f]know them, and they follow Me.

28 "And I [g]give them eternal [h]life, and they shall [i]never perish; neither shall anyone snatch them out of My hand.

29 "My Father, who has given *them* to Me, is greater than all; and no one is able to snatch *them* out of My Father's hand.

30 "I and *My* Father [j]are one."

31 Then the Jews [k]took up stones again to stone Him.

32 Jesus answered them, "Many good works I have shown you from My Father. For which of those works do you stone Me?"

33 The Jews answered Him, saying, "For a good work we do not stone You, but for [l]blasphemy, and because You, being a Man, make Yourself God."

34 Jesus answered them, "Is it not [m]written in your law, *'I said, [n]"You are gods"'*?

35 "If He called them gods, to whom the word of God [m]came (and the Scripture [o]cannot be broken),

36 "do you say of Him whom the Father [p]sanctified and [q]sent into the [r]world, 'You are blaspheming,' because I said, 'I am the Son of God'?

37 "If I do not do the works of My Father, do not believe Me;

38 "but if I do, though you do not believe Me, believe the [s]works, that you may know and believe* [t]that the Father [j]*is* in Me, and I in Him."

39 Therefore they sought again to seize Him, but He escaped out of their hand.

Jesus withdraws from Jerusalem

40 And He went away again beyond the Jordan to the place where John was [u]baptizing at first, and there He stayed.

41 Then many came to Him and said, "John performed no sign, but all the things that John [v]spoke about this Man were true."

42 And many [w]believed in Him there.

Jesus raises Lazarus
of Bethany from the dead

11 NOW a certain *man* was sick, Lazarus of Bethany, the town of [x]Mary and her sister [y]Martha.

2 It was *that* Mary who anointed the Lord with fragrant oil and wiped His feet with her hair, whose brother Lazarus was sick.

3 Therefore the sisters sent to Him, saying, "Lord, behold, he whom You love is sick."

4 When Jesus heard *that*, He said, "This sickness is [z]not unto death, but [aa]for the glory of God, that the Son of God may be glorified through it."

5 Now Jesus loved Martha and her sister and Lazarus.

6 So, when He heard that he

*
10:26 NU-Text omits *as I said to you.*
10:38 NU-Text reads *understand.*

19
a Jn. 9:16
20
b See Mt. 7:22, *note*
24
c Lit. *keep us in suspense*
25
d v. 38; Mt. 11:4; Jn. 2:11; 20:30; cp. Jn. 3:2
26
e Jn. 8:47
27
f Nah. 1:7; Jn. 6:64; 2 Tim. 2:19
28
g Rom. 6:23; cp. Mt. 11:28; 16:19; Lk. 10:19; Jn. 4:14; 6:51; 14:27
h Life (eternal): v. 28; Jn. 11:25. (Mt. 7:14; Rev. 22:19)
i Assurance/security: vv. 28–29; Jn. 11:26. (Ps. 23:1; Jude 1, *note*). Rom. 8:35–39; 1 Pet. 1:5
30
j Jn. 17:21–24; cp. Jn. 15:23
31
k Jn. 8:59
33
l Mt. 9:3
34
m Inspiration: vv. 34–35; Jn. 12:14. (Ex. 4:15; 2 Tim. 3:16, *note*)
n Ps. 82:6
35
o Mt. 5:17–18
36
p Sanctification (NT): v. 36; Jn. 17:17. (Mt. 4:5; Rev. 22:11). Lk. 1:35
q Jn. 5:23,24, 36,37; 6:44, 57; 7:16,18; 8:16,18
r Gk. *kosmos.* See Mt. 4:8, *note*
38
s Jn. 5:36
t Jn. 14:10
40
u Mt. 3:6; see Acts 8:12, *note*
41
v Jn. 1:29,36; 3:28–36; 5:33
42
w Faith: v. 42; Jn. 11:22. (Gen. 3:20; Heb. 11:39, *note*)
CHAPTER 11
1
x See Lk. 1:27, *note*
y Lk. 10:40; Jn. 12:2
4
z v. 11; cp. Mt. 9:24
aa Cp. Jn. 14:13; 17:1

[1](10:20) This accusation was doubtless occasioned by Christ's claim to be "the good shepherd" (vv. 11,14), who would be identified by informed Jews as the covenant-God of Ps. 23. Cp. Jn. 10:33.

was sick, He stayed two more days in the place where He was.

7 Then after this He said to *the* disciples, "Let us go to Judea again."

8 *The* disciples said to Him, "Rabbi, lately the Jews sought to [a]stone You, and are You going there again?"

9 Jesus answered, "Are there not twelve hours in the day? If anyone walks in the day, he does not stumble, because he sees the [b]light of this [c]world.

10 "But if one walks in the [d]night, he stumbles, because the [b]light is not in him."

11 These things He said, and after that He said to them, "Our friend Lazarus [e]sleeps, but I go that I may [f]wake him up."

12 Then His disciples said, "Lord, if he sleeps he will [g]get well."

13 However, Jesus spoke of his death, but they thought that He was speaking about taking rest in sleep.

14 Then Jesus said to them [h]plainly, "Lazarus is dead.

15 "And I am glad for your sakes that I was not there, that you may believe. Nevertheless let us go to him."

16 Then [i]Thomas, who is called the Twin, said to his fellow disciples, "Let us also go, that we may die with Him."

17 So when Jesus came, He found that he had already been in the tomb four days.

18 Now Bethany was near Jerusalem, about two [j]miles* away.

19 And many of the [k]Jews had joined the women around Martha and Mary, to comfort them concerning their brother.

20 Then Martha, as soon as she heard that Jesus was coming, went and met Him, but Mary was [l]sitting in the house.

21 Now Martha said to Jesus, "Lord, if You had been here, my brother would not have died.

22 "But even now I [m]know that whatever You [n]ask of God, God will give You."

23 Jesus said to her, "Your brother will [o]rise again."

24 Martha said to Him, "I know that he will rise again in the [o]resurrection at the last [p]day."

25 Jesus said to her, [q]"I [r]am the [o]resurrection and the [s]life. He who [t]believes in Me, though he may [u]die, he shall live.

26 "And whoever lives and [t]believes in Me shall [v]never [w]die. Do you believe this?"

27 She said to Him, "Yes, Lord, I [m]believe that [x]You are the Christ, the Son of God, who is to [y]come into the [z]world."

28 And when she had said these things, she went her way and secretly called Mary her sister, saying, "The Teacher has come and is calling for you."

29 As soon as she heard *that*, she arose quickly and came to Him.

30 Now Jesus had not yet come into the town, but was* in the place where Martha met Him.

31 Then the Jews who were with her in the house, and comforting her, when they saw that Mary rose up quickly and went out, followed her, saying, "She is going to the tomb to weep there."*

32 Then, when Mary came where Jesus was, and saw Him, she [aa]fell down at His feet, saying to Him, "Lord, if You had been here, my brother would not have died."

33 Therefore, when Jesus saw her weeping, and the Jews who came with her weeping, He groaned in the spirit and was troubled.

34 And He said, "Where have you laid him?" They said to Him, "Lord, come and see."

35 Jesus [bb]wept.

36 Then the Jews said, "See how He [cc]loved him!"

37 And some of them said, "Could not this Man, who opened the eyes of the [dd]blind, also have kept this man from dying?"

38 Then Jesus, [ee]again groaning in Himself, came to the tomb. It was a [ff]cave, and a [gg]stone lay against it.

39 Jesus said, "Take away

*

11:18 Literally *fifteen stadia*
11:30 NU-Text adds *still.* **11:31** NU-Text reads *supposing that she was going to the tomb to weep there.*

8
a Jn. 8:59; 10:31
9
b Isa. 9:2; Jn. 1:4,7,8,9; 3:19–21; 5:35; 8:12; 9:5; 12:35–36,46
c Gk. *kosmos.* See Mt. 4:8, *note*
10
d Cp. Jn. 3:19
11
e Mt. 9:24; cp. Acts 7:60; 1 Cor. 15:51
f Cp. 1 Th. 4:13–17
12
g Lit. *be saved* or *restored*
14
h Cp. Jn. 10:24
16
i Jn. 14:5; 20:24–29
18
j See Weights and Measures (NT), Acts 27:28, *note*
19
k vv. 31,33,45
20
l Cp. Isa. 26:3
22
m Faith: vv. 22,27; Jn. 11:45. (Gen. 3:20; Heb. 11:39, *note*)
n Cp. v. 41; Jn. 17:9
23
o Resurrection: vv. 23–25; Jn. 11:44. (2 Ki. 4:35; 1 Cor. 15:52, *note*)

24
p See Acts 2:17, *note*
25
q Jn. 6:35,41, 48,51; 8:12, 58; 9:5; 10:7,9,11,14; 11:25; 14:6; 15:1,5; Rev. 1:8,17; cp. Ex. 3:14; Isa. 43:11–15
r Jn. 5:21; 6:39–40; Rev. 1:18
s Life (eternal): vv. 25–26; Jn. 12:25. (Mt. 7:14; Rev. 22:19)
t Jn. 3:16
u 1 Cor. 15:22; Heb. 9:27
26
v Assurance/security: v. 26; Jn. 14:19. (Ps. 23:1; Jude 1, *note*)
w Death (the second): v. 26; Rom. 8:13. (Jn. 8:21; Rev. 20:14, *note*)
27
x Mt. 16:16; Jn. 6:69
y Christ (first advent): v. 27; Jn. 12:13. (Gen. 3:15; Acts 1:11, *note*)
z Gk. *kosmos.* See Mt. 4:8, *note*
32
aa Mk. 5:22; 7:25; Rev. 1:17
35
bb Lk. 19:41; cp. Heb. 4:15
36
cc v. 3
37
dd Jn. 9:1–11
38
ee v. 33
ff Cp. Gen. 23:19
gg Mt. 27:60, 66

the [a]stone." Martha, the sister
of him who was dead, said to
Him, "Lord, by this time there is
a [b]stench, for he has been *dead*
four days."
40 Jesus said to her, "Did I
not say to you that if you would
believe you would see the
[c]glory of God?"
41 Then they took away the
stone *from the place* where the
dead man was lying.* And Jesus lifted up *His* eyes and [d]said,
"Father, I thank You that You
have heard Me.
42 "And I know that You always [e]hear Me, but because of
the people who are [f]standing
by I said *this,* that they may believe that You sent Me."
43 Now when He had said
these things, He [g]cried with a
[h]loud voice, "Lazarus, come
forth!"
44 And he who had died
[i]came [j]out bound hand and
foot with [k]graveclothes, and his
face was wrapped with a cloth.
Jesus said to them, [l]"Loose
him, and let him go."

Many are converted
(cp. Jn. 12:10–11): Pharisees
conspire to kill Jesus

45 Then many of the Jews
who had come to Mary, and had
seen the things Jesus did, [m]be-
lieved in Him.
46 But some of them went
away to the Pharisees and [n]told
them the things Jesus did.
47 Then the chief priests and
the [o]Pharisees gathered a
[p]council and said, [q]"What shall
we do? For this Man works
many signs.
48 "If we let Him alone like
this, [r]everyone will believe in
Him, and the Romans will come
and take away both our place
and nation."
49 And one of them, [s]Caia-
phas, being high priest that
year, said to them, "You know
nothing at all,
50 "nor do you consider that
it is expedient for us* that [t]one
man should die for the people,
and not that the whole nation
should perish."
51 Now this he did not say on
his own *authority;* but being
high priest that year he prophesied that Jesus would die for the
nation,
52 and [u]not for that nation
only, but also that He would
[v]gather together in one the children of God who were scattered
abroad.
53 Then, from that day on,
they plotted [w]to put Him to
death.
54 Therefore Jesus no longer
[x]walked openly among the
Jews, but went from there into
the country near the wilderness, to a city called Ephraim,
and there remained with His
disciples.
55 And the [y]Passover of the
Jews was near, and many went
from the country up to Jerusalem before the Passover, to [z]pu-
rify themselves.
56 Then they [aa]sought Jesus,
and spoke among themselves as
they stood in the temple, "What
do you think—that He will not
come to the feast?"
57 Now both the chief priests
and the Pharisees had given a
command, that if anyone knew
where He was, he should report
it, that they might [bb]seize Him.

Jesus anointed by Mary
of Bethany
(Mt. 26:6–13; Mk. 14:3–9)

12 THEN, six days before
the [y]Passover, Jesus
came to [cc]Bethany, where Lazarus was who had been dead,*
whom He had [j]raised from the
dead.
2 There they made Him a
supper; and [dd]Martha served,
but Lazarus was one of those
who sat at the table with Him.
3 [ee]Then [1]Mary took a
[ff]pound of very costly oil of
[gg]spikenard, anointed the feet of

*
11:41 NU-Text omits *from the place where the dead man was lying.* **11:50** NU-Text reads *you.* **12:1** NU-Text omits *who had been dead.*

39
a Mt. 27:60, 66
b Cp. Acts 13:36–37
40
c v. 4; Jn. 17:4
41
d Bible prayers (NT): vv. 41–42; Jn. 12:27. (Mt. 6:9; Lk. 11:2, *note*)
42
e v. 22; cp. 1 Ki. 18:36–37
f Cp. Jn. 12:29–30
43
g Cp. Mt. 8:8; Jn. 5:25
h Cp. 1 Th. 4:16
44
i Miracles (NT): vv. 38–44; Jn. 20:19. (Mt. 8:3; Acts 28:8, *note*)
j Resurrection: v. 44; 12:1; Jn. 12:9. (2 Ki. 4:35; 1 Cor. 15:52, *note*). Mt. 11:5; Lk. 7:14–15; 8:54–55
k Jn. 19:40; 20:5–7
l Cp. Rom. 8:2; Gal. 5:1
45
m Faith: v. 45; Jn. 12:11. (Gen. 3:20; Heb. 11:39, *note*)
46
n Jn. 5:15
47
o See Mt. 3:7, *note 1*
p vv. 47–53; Ps. 2:2; Mt. 26:3
q Cp. Acts 4:16
48
r Cp. Jn. 6:15
49
s Mt. 26:3
50
t Jn. 18:14; cp. Jn. 18:39

52
u Cp. Isa. 49:6; 2 Cor. 5:14; 1 Jn. 2:2
v Ps. 22:27; Jn. 10:16; Eph. 2:14–17; cp. Rom. 16:26
53
w Mt. 12:14; 26:4; 27:1; Lk. 6:11; 19:47; 22:2; Jn. 5:16
54
x Jn. 7:1
55
y c. A.D. 28. Cp. Jn. 2:13; 6:4; 18:28; see Ex. 12:11, *note*
z Num. 9:10, 13; 31:19–20; Lk. 2:22; cp. Jn. 18:28; Acts 21:26
56
aa Jn. 7:11
57
bb Mt. 26:14–16; cp. Jn. 18:2–9
CHAPTER 12
1
cc Jn. 11:1
2
dd Lk. 10:40–41; cp. Mt. 11:29–30
3
ee Jn. 11:2; cp. Lk. 7:37–38
ff See Weights and Measures (NT), Acts 27:28, *note*
gg Song 1:12

[1](12:3) As Martha served the Lord, and Lazarus had communion with Him (v. 2), so Mary offered the worship of a grateful heart. Others before Mary had come to the Lord's feet to have their need met; she came to give Him His due. Although two other evangelists, Matthew and Mark, record Mary's act, John alone gives her name.

4
a Jn. 13:26
5
b See Coinage (NT), Mt. 5:26, *note*
6
c Cp. Jn. 6:70–71
8
d Cp. Dt. 15:11
e v. 35; Mk. 14:7; Jn. 17:11
9
f Resurrection: vv. 9, 17; Jn. 20:9. (2 Ki. 4:35; 1 Cor. 15:52, *note*)
11
g Jn. 7:31; 11:45
h Faith: v. 11; Jn. 12:42. (Gen. 3:20; Heb. 11:39, *note*)
12
i See Mt. 21:4, *note*
13
j Cp. Lev. 23:40
k Lit. *Oh, save.* Ps. 118:25–26
l Christ (first advent): v. 13; Jn. 12:47. (Gen. 3:15; Acts 1:11, *note*)
m Kingdom (NT): v. 13; Jn. 18:33. (Mt. 2:2; 1 Cor. 15:24, *note*)
14
n Inspiration: vv. 14–15; Jn. 12:38. (Ex. 4:15; 2 Tim. 3:16, *note*). Zech. 9:9

Jesus, and wiped His feet with her hair. And the house was filled with the fragrance of the oil.
4 But one of His disciples, [a]Judas Iscariot, Simon's *son,* who would betray Him, said,
5 "Why was this fragrant oil not sold for three hundred [b]denarii* and given to the poor?"
6 This he said, not that he cared for the poor, but because he was a [c]thief, and had the money box; and he used to take what was put in it.
7 But Jesus said, "Let her alone; she has kept* this for the day of My burial.
8 "For the [d]poor you have with you always, but [e]Me you do not have always."
9 Now a great many of the Jews knew that He was there; and they came, not for Jesus' sake only, but that they might also see Lazarus, whom He had [f]raised from the dead.
10 But the chief priests plotted to put Lazarus to death also,
11 because on account of him [g]many of the Jews went away and [h]believed in Jesus.

Jesus enters the city of Jerusalem
(Mt. 21:1–9; Mk. 11:1–10; Lk. 19:29–38; cp. Zech. 9:9; Rev. 19:11–16)

12 The next day a great multitude that had come to the feast, [i]when they heard that Jesus was coming to Jerusalem,
13 took [j]branches of palm trees and went out to meet Him, and cried out:

[k]"Hosanna!
'Blessed is He who
[l]comes in the name of the LORD!'
The [m]King of Israel!"

14 Then Jesus, when He had found a young donkey, sat on it; as it is [n]written:

15 [o]*"Fear not, daughter of Zion;*
Behold, your King is coming,
Sitting on a donkey's colt."

16 His disciples did [p]not understand these things at first; but when Jesus was glorified, then they remembered that these things were written about Him and *that* they had done these things to Him.
17 Therefore the people, who were with Him when He called Lazarus out of his tomb and [f]raised him from the dead, [q]bore witness.
18 For this reason the people also met Him, because they heard that He had done this sign.
19 The [r]Pharisees therefore said among themselves, "You see that you are accomplishing nothing. Look, the [s]world has [t]gone after Him!"

Certain Greeks seek an interview with Jesus

20 Now there were certain [u]Greeks among those who came up to worship at the feast.
21 Then they came to [v]Philip, who was from Bethsaida of Galilee, and asked him, saying, "Sir, we wish to see Jesus."
22 Philip came and told Andrew, and in turn Andrew and Philip told Jesus.

Jesus foretells His crucifixion

23 But Jesus answered them, saying, "The [1][w]hour has come that the [x]Son of Man should be glorified.
24 [y]"Most assuredly, I say to you, [2]unless a grain of wheat falls into the ground and dies, it

15
o Isa. 40:9
16
p Cp. Jn. 2:22
17
q v. 11
19
r See Mt. 3:7, *note*
s Gk. *kosmos.* See Mt. 4:8, *note*
t Cp. Jn. 11:47–48
20
u Mk. 7:26; Acts 17:4; 18:4; 19:10; 20:21; 21:28; Rom. 1:14,16; 1 Cor. 1:22
21
v Jn. 1:43–44; 14:8–11
23
w Mt. 26:18, 45; Jn. 13:1; 17:1
x See Mt. 8:20, *note*
24
y Jn. 1:51; 5:19,24,25; 6:26,32,47, 53; 8:34,51, 58; 10:1,7; 12:24; 13:16,20,21; 14:12; 16:20,23

*
12:5 About one year's wages for a worker.
12:7 NU-Text reads *that she may keep.*

[1](12:23) The hour of human decision was now past, as far as the establishment of the kingdom was concerned (Lk. 19:41–44). The King had been rejected by His own nation and, therefore, the predicted temporal blessings of that kingdom for both Jews and Gentiles (Isa. 60:1–4; 62:1–4) had to be deferred until the King's return in glory (Acts 15:16–17). But now a greater hour has arrived—the hour of the King's glorification through death and resurrection (Jn. 12:23–24,28); this hour, set by the determined purpose and foreknowledge of God, will bring eternal life to all who believe, whether Jews or Gentiles (8:24,32).

[2](12:24) Chapters 12—17 are a progression according to the order of approach to God in the tabernacle types. Chapter 12, in which Christ speaks of His death, answers to the bronze

24
a Sacrifice (of Christ): vv. 24, 32–33; Jn. 19:18. (Gen. 3:15; Heb. 10:18, *note*)
25
b Mk. 8:35
c Gk. *kosmos.* See Rev. 13:8, *note*
d Life (eternal): v. 25; Jn. 12:50. (Mt. 7:14; Rev. 22:19)
26
e Mt. 16:24
f Jn. 14:3; 17:24
g Cp. Jn. 14:21,23; 2 Tim. 4:7–8
27
h Cp. Heb. 5:7–8
i Bible prayers (NT): vv. 27–28; Jn. 17:1. (Mt. 6:9; Lk. 11:2, *note*)
j Jn. 18:37
28
k Mt. 3:17; 17:5
29
l See Heb. 1:4, *note*
31
m Satan: v. 31; Jn. 13:2. (Gen. 3:1; Rev. 20:10). Jn. 14:30
32
n Jn. 3:14; 8:28
34
o Ps. 102:26–27; Isa. 9:6–7
35
p Jn. 7:33
q Jn. 11:10; 1 Jn. 2:9–11

remains alone; but if it [a]dies, it
produces much grain.
25 [b]"He who loves his life
will lose it, and he who hates his
life in this [c]world will keep it for
eternal [d]life.
26 "If anyone serves Me, let
him [e]follow Me; and [f]where I
am, there My servant will be
also. If anyone serves Me, him
My Father will [g]honor.
27 "Now My soul is troubled,
and what shall I [h]say? [i]'Father,
save Me from this hour'? [j]But
for this purpose I came to this
hour.
28 "Father, glorify Your
name." Then a [k]voice came
from heaven, *saying,* "I have
both glorified *it* and will glorify
it again."
29 Therefore the people who
stood by and heard *it* said that
it had thundered. Others said,
"An [l]angel has spoken to Him."
30 Jesus answered and said,
"This voice did not come because of Me, but for your sake.
31 "Now is the [1]judgment of
this [c]world; now the [m]ruler of
this world will be cast out.
32 "And I, if I am [n]lifted up
from the earth, will draw all
peoples to Myself."
33 This He said, signifying by
what [a]death He would die.
34 The people answered
Him, "We have heard from the
law that the [o]Christ remains
forever; and how *can* You say,
'The Son of Man must be lifted
up'? Who is this Son of Man?"
35 Then Jesus said to them,
[p]"A little while longer the light
is with you. Walk while you
have the light, lest darkness
overtake you; [q]he who walks in
darkness does not know where
he is going.

36 "While you have the light,
believe in the light, that you
may become [r]sons of light."
These things Jesus spoke, and
departed, and was hidden from
them.
37 But although He had done
so many [s]signs before them,
they did not believe in Him,
38 that the word of Isaiah the
prophet might be fulfilled,
which he [t]spoke:

"Lord, who has believed
our report?
And to whom has the
arm of the L*ORD been*
revealed?"

39 Therefore they could not
believe, because Isaiah [t]said
again:

40 *"He has* [u]*blinded their*
eyes and hardened
their hearts,
[v]*Lest they should see with*
their eyes,
Lest they should
understand with their
hearts and turn,
So that I should heal
them."

41 These things Isaiah said
[w]when* he saw His glory and
spoke of Him.
42 Nevertheless even among
the rulers many [x]believed in
Him, but because of the Pharisees they did not confess *Him,*
lest they should be put out of the
synagogue;
43 [y]for they loved the praise
of men more than the praise of
God.
44 Then Jesus cried out and
said, "He who believes in Me,
[z]believes not in Me but in [aa]Him
who sent Me.

*
12:41 NU-Text reads *because.*

36
r Lk. 16:8
37
s Jn. 11:47
38
t Inspiration: vv. 38–41; Jn. 12:48. (Ex. 4:15; 2 Tim. 3:16, *note*). Isa. 6:10; 53:1
40
u Cp. Rom. 11:25
v Mt. 13:14
41
w Isa. 6:1
42
x Faith: v. 42; Jn. 14:1. (Gen. 3:20; Heb. 11:39, *note*)
43
y Cp. Jn. 5:44; Acts 12:1–3; 24:27; 25:9
44
z Jn. 3:16,18, 36; 11:25,26
aa Jn. 5:24

---

alter of burnt offering, a figure of the cross. The next step between the altar and the Most Holy Place is the laver (Ex. 30:17–21), answering to ch. 13, where Christ washes the disciples' feet. In chs. 14—16, with His now purified believer-priests (1 Pet. 2:5), the High Priest enters into and shares the blessed fellowship of the Holy Place. In ch. 17, the High Priest enters alone into the Most Holy Place to intercede for His own blood-purchased people (Heb. 7:24–28). That intercession is not for the salvation but the keeping and blessing of those for whom He prays. His death (assumed as accomplished, 17:4) has saved them.

[1](12:31) This judgment refers to Jesus Christ as bearing the believer's sins, which have been judged in the Person of Jesus Christ "lifted up" on the cross. The result was death for Christ and justification for the believer, who can never again be put in jeopardy (5:24; Rom. 5:9; 8:1; 2 Cor. 5:21; Gal. 3:13; Heb. 9:26–28; 10:10,14–17; 1 Pet. 2:24; 3:18). For other judgments, see 1 Cor. 11:31, *note;* 2 Cor. 5:10, *note;* Mt. 25:32, *note;* Ezek. 20:37, *note;* Jude 6, *note;* Rev. 20:12, *note.*

45
a Jn. 14:9
46
b vv. 35–36; Jn. 1:4–5; 8:12
c Gk. *kosmos.* See Mt. 4:8, *note*
d Jn. 3:16,18, 36; 11:25,26
47
e Christ (first advent): vv. 46–47; Jn. 16:27. (Gen. 3:15; Acts 1:11, *note*)
f See Rom. 3:24, *note*
g Gk. *kosmos.* See Mt. 4:8, *note*
48
h Inspiration: v. 48; Jn. 13:18. (Ex. 4:15; 2 Tim. 3:16, *note*)
i Day (of judgment): v. 48; Acts 17:31. (Mt. 10:15; Rev. 20:11). See Acts 2:17, *note*
50
j Life (eternal): v. 50; Jn. 14:6. (Mt. 7:14; Rev. 22:19)
k Jn. 8:28
CHAPTER 13
1
l Jn. 12:23; 17:1
m v. 34; Jn. 15:9; cp. Rom. 8:35–39
2
n Satan: v. 2; Jn. 13:27. (Gen. 3:1; Rev. 20:10)

45 "And he who sees Me
[a]sees Him who sent Me.
46 "I have come *as* a [b]light
into the [c]world, that whoever
[d]believes in Me should not
abide in darkness.
47 "And if anyone hears My
words and does not believe,* I
do not judge him; for I did not
[e]come to judge the [c]world but
to [f]save the [g]world.
48 "He who rejects Me, and
does not receive My words, has
that which judges him—the
word that I have [h]spoken will
judge him in the last [i]day.
49 "For I have not spoken on
My own *authority;* but the Father who sent Me gave Me a
command, what I should say
and what I should speak.
50 "And I know that His
command is everlasting [j]life.
Therefore, whatever I speak,
just as the Father has told Me,
so I [k]speak."

IV. The Private Ministry of the Son of God, 13—17

Jn. 13—14 were spoken in the upper room (cp. Mk. 14:14–16)

13 NOW [1]before the feast of
the Passover, when Jesus knew that His [l]hour had
come that He should depart
from this [c]world to the Father,
having loved His own who were
in the [c]world, He [m]loved them
to the end.

The last Passover: Jesus washes disciples' feet (Mt. 26:20–24; Mk. 14:17; Lk. 22:14,21–23)

2 And supper being ended,*
the [n]devil having already put it
into the heart of Judas Iscariot,
Simon's *son,* to betray Him,
3 Jesus, knowing that the
Father had [o]given all things
into His hands, and that He had
[p]come from God and was [q]going to God,
4 rose from supper and
[r]laid aside His garments, took a
towel and girded Himself.
5 After that, He poured
[s]water into a basin and [t]began
to [u]wash the disciples' feet, and
to wipe *them* with the towel
with which He was girded.
6 Then He came to Simon
Peter. And *Peter* said to Him,
"Lord, [v]are You washing my
feet?"
7 Jesus answered and said
to him, "What I am doing you do
not [w]understand now, but you
will know after this."
8 Peter said to Him, "You
shall never wash my feet!" Jesus answered him, "If I do not
wash you, you have [x]no part
with Me."
9 Simon Peter said to Him,
"Lord, not my feet only, but also
my hands and *my* head!"
10 Jesus said to him, "He who
is [2]bathed needs only to wash
his feet, but is [y]completely
clean; and you are clean, but not
all of you."
11 For He [z]knew who would
betray Him; therefore He said,
"You are not all clean."
12 So when He had [aa]washed
their feet, taken His garments,
and sat down again, He said to
them, "Do you know what I
have done to you?
13 "You call Me [bb]Teacher

*12:47 NU-Text reads *keep them.*
13:2 NU-Text reads *And during supper.*

3
o Jn. 5:20–23; 17:2
p Jn. 8:42; 16:28
q Jn. 17:11; 20:17
4
r Cp. Lk. 22:27; Phil. 2:7–8
5
s Cp. Eph. 5:26
t Cp. Mt. 20:25–28; Mk. 9:35
u v. 12; cp. Gen. 18:4; 19:2; 24:32; 43:24; 1 Sam. 25:41; 2 Sam. 11:8; Lk. 7:44
6
v Cp. Mt. 3:14
7
w Jn. 12:16; 16:12
8
x Cp. Gen. 35:2–3; Eph. 4:30
10
y 1 Cor. 1:30; 6:11; cp. 1 Jn. 3:9
11
z Jn. 6:64; 18:4
12
aa vv. 5,14
13
bb Mt. 23:8, 10; Eph. 6:9

[1](13:1) For the order of all of the events on the night of the Passover Supper, see Mt. 26:20, *note.*

[2](13:10) The words "bathed" and "wash" in this verse are translated from two different Greek words. The first is from the Gk. *louō* and denotes complete ablution. "Wash" is from the Gk. *niptō,* which is the usual NT word for washing the hands or feet (e.g. Mt. 15:2; Jn. 9:15; 1 Tim. 5:10).

The underlying imagery is of an oriental returning from the public baths to his house. His feet would acquire defilement and require cleansing, but not his body. So the believer is cleansed as before the law from all sin "once for all" (Heb. 10:1–12), but needs throughout his earthly life to bring his daily sins to the Father in confession, so that he may abide in unbroken fellowship with the Father and with the Son (1 Jn. 1:1–10). The blood of Christ answers forever to all the law could say as to the believer's guilt, but he needs constant cleansing from the defilement of sin. See Eph. 5:25–27; 1 Jn. 5:6. Typically, the order of approach to the presence of God was, first, the bronze altar of sacrifice; then, the laver of cleansing (Ex. 40:6–7). See, also, the order in Ex. 30:17–21. Christ will not have communion with a defiled saint, but He can and will cleanse him.

and Lord, and you say well, for so I am.

14 "If I then, *your* Lord and Teacher, have washed your feet, [a]you also ought to wash one another's feet.

15 "For I have given you an [b]example, that you should [c]do as I have done to you.

16 "Most assuredly, I say to you, a [d]servant is not greater than his master; nor is he who is sent greater than he who sent him.

17 [e]"If you know these things, blessed are you if you do them.

18 "I do not speak concerning all of you. I know whom I have [f]chosen; but that the [g]Scripture may be [h]fulfilled, '*He who eats bread with Me* has lifted up his heel against Me.*'

19 "Now I tell you [i]before it comes, that when it does come to pass, you may believe that I am *He.*

20 [j]"Most assuredly, I say to you, he who [k]receives whomever I send receives Me; and he who receives Me receives Him who sent Me."

Jesus predicts His betrayal (Mt. 26:21–25; Mk. 14:18–21; Lk. 22:21–23)

21 When Jesus had said these things, He was troubled in spirit, and testified and said, [l]"Most assuredly, I say to you, one of you will [m]betray Me."

22 Then the disciples looked at one another, perplexed about whom He spoke.

23 Now there was leaning on Jesus' bosom one of His disciples, [n]whom Jesus loved.

24 Simon Peter therefore motioned to him to ask who it was of whom He spoke.

25 Then, leaning back* on Jesus' breast, he said to Him, "Lord, who is it?"

26 Jesus answered, "It is he to whom I shall give a piece of bread when I have dipped *it.*" And having dipped the bread, He gave *it* to Judas Iscariot, *the son* of Simon.

27 Now after the piece of bread, [o]Satan [p]entered him. Then Jesus said to him, "What you do, do quickly."

28 But no one at the table knew for what reason He said this to him.

29 For some thought, because Judas had the [q]money box, that Jesus had said to him, "Buy *those things* we need for the feast," or that he should give something to the poor.

30 Having received the piece of bread, he then went out immediately. And it was [r]night.

31 So, when he had gone out, Jesus said, "Now the [s]Son of Man is glorified, and God is [t]glorified in Him.

32 "If God is [t]glorified in Him, God will also glorify Him in Himself, and glorify Him immediately.

33 "Little children, I shall be with you a [u]little while longer. You will seek Me; and [v]as I said to the Jews, 'Where I am going, you cannot come,' so now I say to you.

34 "A new commandment I give to you, that you [w]love [x]one another; as I have loved you, that you also love one another.

35 "By this all will know that you are My disciples, if you have [w]love for [x]one another."

Jesus foretells Peter's denial (Mt. 26:30–35; Mk. 14:26–31; Lk. 22:31–34)

36 Simon Peter said to Him, "Lord, where are You going?" Jesus answered him, "Where I am [y]going you cannot follow Me now, [z]but you shall follow Me afterward."

37 Peter said to Him, "Lord, why can I not follow You now? I will [aa]lay down my life for Your sake."

38 Jesus answered him, "Will you lay down your life for My sake? [j]Most assuredly, I say to you, the rooster shall not [bb]crow till you have denied Me three times.

*13:18 NU-Text reads *My bread.*
13:25 NU-Text and M-Text add *thus.*

14
a Cp. Rom. 12:10; Gal. 6:1–2; 1 Pet. 5:5
15
b 1 Pet. 2:21–24; cp. Phil. 2:5; 1 Jn. 2:6
c Cp. Mt. 7:12
16
d Jn. 15:20
17
e Jas. 1:25
18
f *Election* (personal): v. 18; Jn. 15:16. (Dt. 7:6; 1 Pet. 5:13, *note*)
g Jn. 17:12
h *Inspiration:* v. 18; Jn. 14:10. (Ex. 4:15; 2 Tim. 3:16, *note*). Ps. 41:9
19
i Jn. 14:29
20
j Jn. 1:51; 5:19,24,25; 6:26,32,47, 53; 8:34,51, 58; 10:1,7; 12:24; 13:16,20,21; 14:12; 16:20,23
k Mt. 10:40; cp. 2 Cor. 5:20
21
l Ps. 41:9; Jn. 6:64
23
m Jn. 19:26; 20:2; 21:7, 20,24
26
n Mt. 10:4; Jn. 6:70–71; 12:4; Acts 1:16
27
o *Satan:* v. 27; Jn. 14:30. (Gen. 3:1; Rev. 20:10)
p Lk. 22:3
29
q Jn. 12:6
30
r Cp. Jn. 18:3
31
s See Mt. 8:20, *note*
t Jn. 14:13; 17:4; 1 Pet. 4:11
33
u Jn. 12:35; 14:19; 16:16–19; cp. Heb. 10:37
v Jn. 7:34; 8:21
34
w *Law* (of Christ): vv. 34–35; Jn. 14:15. (Jn. 13:34; 2 Jn. 5). Jn. 15:12–13; 1 Jn. 3:16
x 1 Jn. 3:14; cp. 1 Cor. 13:1; 1 Jn. 4:20
36
y Jn. 14:2; 16:5
z Jn. 21:18; 2 Pet. 1:14
37
aa Mk. 14:29; Lk. 22:33
38
bb Jn. 18:25–27

CHAPTER 14

1

a v. 27; cp. Isa. 43:1–2
b Faith: v. 1; Jn. 17:20. (Gen. 3:20; Heb. 11:39, *note*)

2

c Mt. 25:34; Heb. 11:16

3

d Christ (second advent): v. 3; Jn. 14:28. (Dt. 30:3; Acts 1:11, *note*)

5

e Mt. 10:3; Jn. 11:16; 20:24–29; 21:2

6

f Jn. 6:35,41, 48,51; 8:12, 58; 9:5; 10:7,9,11,14; 11:25; 14:6; 15:1,5; Rev. 1:8,17; cp. Ex. 3:14; Isa. 43:11–15
g Heb. 10:19–20; cp. Mt. 7:14; Lk. 1:79
h Jn. 1:14,17; 18:37
i Life (eternal): v. 6; Jn. 17:2. (Mt. 7:14; Rev. 22:19)
j 1 Tim. 2:5; cp. Heb. 8:6; 9:15,24; 12:24; 1 Jn. 2:1
k Jn. 10:7–9; Acts 4:12

7

l Cp. v. 10; Jn. 10:30; 17:11,22

9

m Jn. 12:45

10

n v. 20; Jn.

Jesus comforts His apostles: He announces His coming for them

14 [a]"LET not your heart be
troubled; you [b]believe in
God, believe also in Me.
2 "In My Father's house are
many mansions;* if *it were* not
so, I would have told you. I go to
[c]prepare a place for you.*
3 "And if I go and prepare a
place for you, I will [d]come
again and [1]receive you to Myself; that where I am, *there* you
may be also.
4 "And where I go you
know, and the way you know."
5 [e]Thomas said to Him,
"Lord, we do not know where
You are going, and how can we
know the way?"
6 Jesus said to him, [f]"I am
the [g]way, the [h]truth, and the
[i]life. [j]No one comes to the Father [k]except through Me.

Jesus and the Father are one

7 [l]"If you had known Me,
you would have known My Father also; and from now on you
know Him and have seen Him."
8 Philip said to Him, "Lord,
show us the Father, and it is sufficient for us."
9 Jesus said to him, "Have I
been with you so long, and yet
you have not known Me, Philip?
[m]He who has seen Me has seen
the Father; so how can you say,
'Show us the Father'?
10 "Do you not believe that [n]I
am in the Father, and the Father
in Me? The [o]words that I speak
to you I do not speak on My own
authority; but the Father who
dwells in Me [p]does the works.
11 "Believe Me that I *am* in
the Father and the Father in Me,
or else believe Me for the sake
of the [q]works themselves.
12 [r]"Most assuredly, I say to
you, he who believes in Me, the
works that I do he will do also;
and greater *works* than these he
will do, because I go to My Father.

New privilege in prayer

13 "And whatever you [s]ask
in My name, that I will do, that
the Father may be [t]glorified in
the Son.
14 "If you ask* anything in
My name, I will do *it.*

Promise of Spirit's indwelling

15 "If you [u]love Me, keep*
My commandments.
16 "And I will pray the Father, and He will [v]give you another [2w]Helper, that [x]He may
abide with you forever—
17 "the [x]Spirit of [y]truth,
whom the [z]world [aa]cannot receive, because it neither sees
Him nor knows Him; but you
know Him, for He dwells with
you and will be [bb]in you.
18 "I will not leave you orphans; I will come to you.
19 "A little while longer and
the [z]world will see Me no more,
but you will see Me. [cc]Because I
live, [dd]you will live also.
20 "At that day you will know
that [n]I *am* in My Father, and
you in [3]Me, and I in you.

1 Jn. 3:24 **14:19** *cc* Rom. 5:10; 2 Cor. 4:10
dd Assurance/ security: vv. 19–20; Jn. 17:11. (Ps. 23:1; Jude 1, *note*)

*

14:2 Literally *dwellings* • NU-Text adds a word which would cause the text to read either *if it were not so, would I have told you that I go to prepare a place for you?* or *if it were not so I would have told you; for I go to prepare a place for you* **14:14** NU-Text adds *Me.* **14:15** NU-Text reads *you will keep.*

1:18; 10:38; 17:21,23; cp. 2 Cor. 4:4; Col. 1:15
o Inspiration: v. 10; Jn. 14:24. (Ex. 4:15; 2 Tim. 3:16, *note*). Dt. 18:18; Jn. 12:49; 17:8
p Cp. Jn. 7:16; 8:28; 12:49

11

q Jn. 5:36

12

r Jn. 1:51; 5:19,24,25; 6:26,32,47, 53; 8:34,51, 58; 10:1,7; 12:24; 13:16,20,21; 14:12; 16:20,23

13

s v. 14; Jn. 15:16; 16:23–24
t Jn. 13:31

15

u Law (of Christ): v. 15; Jn. 14:21. (Jn. 13:34; 2 Jn. 5)

16

v See Lk. 11:13, *note*
w See 1 Jn. 2:1, *note*
x Holy Spirit (NT): vv. 16–18; Jn. 14:26. (Mt. 1:18; Acts 2:4, *note*)

17

y Jn. 16:13; 1 Jn. 4:6
z Gk. *kosmos.* See Rev. 13:8, *note*
aa 1 Cor. 2:14
bb Jn. 7:38–39; 1 Cor. 6:19; 2 Cor. 6:16;

[1](14:3) As a part of this discourse, which has been of comfort to the Church throughout the centuries, the Lord gives a promise of His personal return for His own people, a doctrine that is expanded by the Apostle Paul in 1 Th. 4:13–18. This aspect of Christ's return is to be distinguished from His coming to the earth to establish His kingdom (Rev. 19:11–16).

[2](14:16) Greek *paraklētos* meaning *one called alongside to help;* thus, *a helper, a comforter;* in 1 Jn. 2:1, "an Advocate with the Father." Christ is the Christian's Paraclete with the Father when the Christian sins; the Holy Spirit is the Christian's indwelling Paraclete to help his ignorance and infirmity, and to make intercession (Rom. 8:26–27). See Holy Spirit, Acts 2:4, *note.* Furthermore, Christ also intercedes as well as advocates (Rom. 8:34; Heb. 7:25).

[3](14:20) The new relationship described in the words "you in Me, and I in you" introduces the NT mystery of the body of Christ. The position of the Church in Christ, as composed of members of His body (cp. Eph. 3:1–7), and the truth of Christ as indwelling the believer (cp. Col. 1:24–27) are central features in the Pauline doctrine of the Church, and are here revealed to the disciples for the first time by Christ. The living union of the members of the body is

21 "He who has My commandments and [1]keeps them, it is he who loves Me. And he who [a]loves Me will be loved by My Father, and I will love him and manifest Myself to him."

22 Judas (not Iscariot) said to Him, "Lord, how is it that You will manifest Yourself to us, and not to the [b]world?"

23 Jesus answered and said to him, "If anyone [a]loves Me, he will keep My word; and My Father will love him, and We will come to him and make Our home with him.

24 "He who does not love Me does not keep My words; and the [c]word which you hear is not Mine but the Father's who sent Me.

25 "These things I have spoken to you while being present with you.

26 "But the [d]Helper, the [e]Holy [f]Spirit, whom the Father will [g]send in My name, He will [h]teach you all things, and bring to your [i]remembrance all things that I said to you.

Christ's bequest of peace

27 [j]"Peace I leave with you, [k]My peace I give to you; not as the [b]world gives do I give to you. Let not your heart be [l]troubled, neither let it be afraid.

28 "You have heard Me say to you, 'I am going away and [m]coming *back* to you.' If you loved Me, you would rejoice because I said,* 'I am [n]going to the Father,' for My Father is greater than I.

29 "And now I have told you before it comes, that when it does come to pass, you may [o]believe.

30 "I will no longer talk much with you, for the [p]ruler of this [b]world is coming, and he has [q]nothing in Me.

31 "But that the [r]world may know that I love the Father, and as the Father gave Me [s]commandment, so I do. Arise, let us go from here.

The Vine and the branches

15 [t]"I AM the [2]true [u]vine, and My Father is the vinedresser.

2 "Every branch in Me that does [v]not bear fruit He takes away;* and every *branch* that bears fruit He [3]prunes, that it may bear [w]more fruit.

3 "You are already [x]clean because of the word which I have spoken to you.

4 [y]"Abide in Me, and I in you. As the branch cannot bear fruit of itself, unless it [4]abides in the vine, neither can you, unless you abide in Me.

5 [t]"I am the vine, you *are* the branches. He who abides in Me, and I in him, bears much [z]fruit; for without Me you can do [aa]nothing.

6 "If anyone does not abide in Me, he is cast out as a branch and is withered; and they gather them and throw *them* into the fire, and they are burned.

7 "If you abide in Me, and My words [bb]abide in you, you will* ask what you desire, and it shall be [cc]done for you.

8 "By this My Father is [dd]glo-

*
14:28 NU-Text omits *I said.* **15:2** Or *lifts up* **15:7** NU-Text omits *you will.*

21
a Law (of Christ): vv. 21,23; Jn. 15:17. (Jn. 13:34; 2 Jn. 5)
22
b Gk. *kosmos.* See Rev. 13:8, *note*
24
c Inspiration: v. 24; Jn. 15:25. (Ex. 4:15; 2 Tim. 3:16, *note*). Dt. 18:18; Jn. 12:49; 17:8
26
d See 1 Jn. 2:1, *note*
e Holy Spirit (NT): v. 26; Jn. 15:26. (Mt. 1:18; Acts 2:4, *note*)
f See Lk. 11:13, *note*
g Jn. 15:26
h 1 Cor. 2:13; cp. 1 Jn. 2:27
i Jn. 2:22; 12:16
27
j See Mt. 10:34, *note*
k Jn. 16:33
l v. 1
28
m Christ (second advent): v. 28; Jn. 16:16. (Dt. 30:3; Acts 1:11, *note*)
n Jn. 7:33; 16:5; 17:11
29
o Jn. 13:19
30
p Satan: v. 30; Jn. 17:15. (Gen. 3:1; Rev. 20:10). Jn. 12:31; 16:11; 2 Cor. 4:4; Eph. 2:2
q Jn. 8:46; 2 Cor. 5:21; Heb. 4:15; 1 Pet. 1:19; 2:22
31
r Gk. *kosmos.* See Mt. 4:8, *note*
s Jn. 10:18; Phil. 2:8
CHAPTER 15
1
t Jn. 6:35,41, 48,51; 8:12, 58; 9:5; 10:7,9,11,14; 11:25; 14:6; 15:1,5; Rev. 1:8,17; cp. Ex. 3:14; Isa. 43:11–15
u Cp. Jn. 1:4; 11:25; 1 Jn. 5:12
2
v Cp. Mt. 25:30
w Mt. 13:12; cp. Rom. 5:3–4; Heb. 12:5–11
3
x Jn. 13:10
4
y vv. 5–7; Jn. 17:23; Eph. 3:17; see 2 Pet. 3:18, *note*
5
z Gal. 5:22–23; cp. Col. 3:12–17
aa 2 Cor. 3:5; cp. Lk. 5:4–11; Jn. 6:44; 21:3–6; Phil. 4:13
7
bb 1 Jn. 2:14
cc Jn. 14:13
8
dd Ps. 22:23; Jn. 13:31; 17:4; 1 Pet. 4:11

---

explained by Christ in the figure of the vine and the branches (Jn. 15:1–11).

[1](14:21) Observe that the Lord correlates love for Him with obedience to Him. To love Christ means to care enough about Him to keep His commandments (vv. 23–24). But we cannot keep His commandments unless we search the Scriptures to find out what they are.

[2](15:1) Christ is the "true vine"—"true" in contrast with Israel. See Isa. 5:1–7.

[3](15:2) Three conditions of a fruitful life are shown here: (1) cleansing, vv. 2–3; cp. Jn. 13:10, *note;* (2) abiding, v. 4, *note;* and (3) obedience, vv. 10,12. (See Law of Christ, Gal. 6:2; 2 Jn. 5, *note*).

[4](15:4) To abide in Christ is, on the one hand, to have no known sin unjudged and unconfessed, no interest into which He is not brought, no life which He cannot share. On the other hand, the "abiding" one takes all burdens to Him, and draws all wisdom, life, and strength from Him. It is not unceasing consciousness of these things, and of Him, but that nothing is allowed in the life which separates from Him. See Fellowship, 1 Jn. 1:3–7; Communion, 1 Cor. 10:16.

rified, that you bear [1]much fruit;
so you will be My disciples.
9 "As the Father [a]loved Me,
I also have loved you; abide in
My love.
10 "If you keep My com-
mandments, you will abide in
My love, just as I have kept My
Father's commandments and
abide in His love.
11 "These things I have spoken to you, that My joy may remain in you, and *that* your joy
may be full.
12 [b]"This is My [c]command-
ment, that you love one another
as I have loved you.
13 "Greater love has no one
than this, than to [d]lay down
one's life for his friends.
14 "You are My friends if you
do whatever I [e]command you.

New intimacy

15 [2]"No longer do I call you
servants, for a servant does not
know what his master is doing;
but I have called you friends, for
all things that I heard from My
Father I have made [f]known to
you.
16 "You did not choose Me,
but I [g]chose you and appointed
you that you should go and bear
fruit, and *that* your fruit should
remain, that whatever you ask
the Father [h]in My name He may
give you.
17 "These things I command
you, that you [i]love one another.

The world's attitude toward believers in Christ

18 "If the [j]world hates you,
you know that it [k]hated Me before *it hated* you.
19 "If you were of the [j]world,
the [j]world would love its own.
Yet because you are not of the
[j]world, but I [g]chose you [l]out of
the [m]world, therefore the
[j]world [n]hates you.
20 "Remember the word that
I [o]said to you, 'A servant is not
greater than his master.' If they

9 *a* Jn. 5:20; 17:26
12 *b* Jn. 13:34 *c* Rom. 12:9
13 *d* 1 Jn. 3:16; cp. Jn. 10:11,15,17, 18; 13:37, 38; 1 Jn. 3:16
14 *e* v. 10; Mt. 28:20; Jn. 14:15,21; Acts 10:42; 1 Jn. 3:23–24
15 *f* Cp. Gen. 18:17 with 2 Chr. 20:7
16 *g Election* (personal): vv. 16,19; Acts 1:2. (Dt. 7:6; 1 Pet. 5:13, *note*) *h* Jn. 16:23,24
17 *i Law* (of Christ): v. 17; Jn. 17:26. (Jn. 13:34; 2 Jn. 5)
18 *j* Gk. *kosmos.* See Rev. 13:8, *note* *k* v. 25
19 *l Separation:* v. 19; Jn. 17:6. (Gen. 12:1; 2 Cor. 6:17, *note*) *m* Gk. *kosmos.* See Mt. 4:8, *note* *n* Jn. 17:14; cp. Jn. 7:7
20 *o* Jn. 13:16

persecuted Me, they will also
persecute you. If they kept My
word, they will keep yours also.
21 "But all these things they
will do to you for My name's
sake, because they do not know
Him who sent Me.
22 "If I had not come and spoken to them, they would have
no [p]sin, but now they have no
[q]excuse for their sin.
23 [r]"He who hates Me hates
My Father also.
24 "If I had not done among
them the works which no one
else did, they would have no
[p]sin; but now they have [s]seen
and also hated both Me and My
Father.
25 "But *this happened* that
the word might be fulfilled
which is [t]written in their law,
[u]*'They hated Me without a*
cause.'
26 "But when the [v]Helper
comes, whom I shall send to you
from the Father, the [w]Spirit of
truth who proceeds from the Father, He will testify of Me.
27 "And you also will bear
[t]witness, because you have
been with Me from the [x]begin-
ning.

Jesus warns of persecution (cp. Mt. 24:9–10; Lk. 21:16–19)

16 "THESE things I have
spoken to you, that you
should not be made to stumble.
2 "They will [y]put you out of
the synagogues; yes, the time is
coming that whoever kills you
will [z]think that he offers God
service.
3 "And these things they
will do to you* because they
have [aa]not known the Father nor
Me.
4 "But these things I have
told you, that when the* time
comes, you may remember that
I told you of them. And these

*
16:3 NU-Text and M-Text omit *to you.*
16:4 NU-Text reads *their.*

22 *p* See Rom. 3:23, *note* *q* Cp. 1 Th. 2:5; 1 Pet. 2:16
23 *r* v. 24; cp. v. 18
24 *s* Jn. 14:9
25 *t Inspiration:* vv. 25, 27; Jn. 16:13. (Ex. 4:15; 2 Tim. 3:16, *note*) *u* Ps. 35:19; 69:4
26 *v* See Jn. 14:16 and 1 Jn. 2:1, *notes* *w Holy Spirit* (NT): vv. 26–27; Jn. 16:7. (Mt. 1:18; Acts 2:4, *note*)
27 *x* Mk. 3:14; Lk. 1:2
CHAPTER 16
2 *y* Jn. 9:22; cp. Jn. 9:34 *z* Cp. Acts 7:57–60; 8:1; Phil. 3:4–6
3 *aa* Jn. 8:19; Acts 13:27; cp. Jn. 14:9

[1](15:8) There are four degrees in fruit-bearing: (1) no fruit ("does not bear fruit," v. 2); (2) "fruit" (v. 2); (3) "more fruit" (v. 2); and (4) "much fruit" (vv. 5,8). As we bear "much fruit," the Father is glorified in us. The fruit may be converts (Rom. 1:13); Christian character—the fruit of the Spirit (Gal. 5:22–23); and conduct—the fruits of righteousness (Rom. 6:21–22; Phil. 1:11). The moralities and graces of Christianity, which are the fruit of the Spirit, are often imitated but never duplicated.

[2](15:15) Observe the progressive intimacy between the Lord and His disciples, as recorded in John's Gospel: (1) servants (13:13,16); (2) friends (15:15); and (3) brethren (20:17).

things I did not say to you at the [a]beginning, because I was with you.

5 "But now I [b]go away to Him who sent Me, and none of you asks Me, 'Where are You going?'

6 "But because I have said these things to you, [c]sorrow has filled your heart.

Threefold work of the Spirit toward the world

7 "Nevertheless I tell you the truth. It is to your advantage that I go away; for if I do not go away, [d]the [e]Helper will not come to you; but if I [f]depart, I will [g]send Him to you.

8 "And when He has [g]come, He will convict the [h]world of [i]sin, [j]and of [k]righteousness, and of judgment:

9 "of sin, [l]because they do not believe in Me;

10 "of righteousness, [m]because I [b]go to My Father and you see Me no more;

11 "of judgment, [n]because the ruler of this [o]world is judged.

After His ascension Christ to continue to reveal truth through the Spirit

12 [1]"I still have many things to say to you, but you cannot bear *them* now.

13 "However, when He, the [d]Spirit of truth, has come, He will [p]guide you into all truth; for He will not speak on His own *authority,* but whatever He [q]hears He will speak; and He will [r]tell you things to come.

14 [s]"He will glorify Me, for He will take of what is Mine and declare *it* to you.

15 [t]"All things that the Father has are Mine. Therefore I said that He will take of Mine and declare *it* to you.*

Jesus speaks of His death, resurrection, and second advent

16 "A [u]little while, and you will not see Me; and again a little while, and you will [v]see Me, because I [b]go to the Father."

17 Then *some* of His disciples said among themselves, "What is this that He says to us, 'A little while, and you will not see Me; and again a little while, and you will see Me'; and, 'because I [b]go to the Father'?"

18 They said therefore, "What is this that He says, 'A little while'? We do not know what He is saying."

19 Now Jesus [w]knew that they desired to ask Him, and He said to them, "Are you inquiring among yourselves about what I said, 'A little while, and you will not see Me; and again a little while, and you will see Me'?

20 [x]"Most assuredly, I say to you that you will weep and [y]lament, but the [h]world will [z]rejoice; and you will be sorrowful, but your sorrow will be turned into [aa]joy.

21 "A woman, when she is in [bb]labor, has sorrow because her hour has come; but as soon as she has given birth to the child, she no longer remembers the anguish, for joy that a human

*

16:15 NU-Text and M-Text read *He takes of Mine and will declare it to you.*

4
a Mk. 3:14; Lk. 1:2
5
b vv. 5,16–17; Jn. 7:33; 13:33; 14:28; 17:11
6
c Mt. 17:23; Jn. 16:20,22
7
d *Holy Spirit* (NT): vv. 7–11, 13–14; Jn. 20:22. (Mt. 1:18; Acts 2:4, *note*)
e See Jn. 14:16 and 1 Jn. 2:1, *notes*
f Mk. 16:19; Lk. 24:51; Acts 1:9–11
g Acts 1:8; 2:1–4; see Lk. 11:13, *note*
8
h Gk. *kosmos.* See Mt. 4:8, *note*
i See Rom. 3:23, *note*
j Cp. Acts 24:25
k See Rom. 3:21, *note*
9
l Cp. 1 Jn. 5:10
10
m Cp. Jn. 14:12
11
n Cp. Jn. 12:31; Rom. 16:20
o Gk. *kosmos.* See Rev. 13:8, *note*
13
p Jn. 14:26
q *Inspiration:* v. 13; Jn. 17:8. (Ex. 4:15; 2 Tim. 3:16, *note*)
r Cp. 1 Cor. 2:9–12; Eph. 3:5
14
s Jn. 15:26
15
t Cp. Jn. 10:30; 14:10; 17:22
16
u vv. 16–19; Jn. 7:33; 12:35; 13:33; 14:19
v *Christ* (second advent): vv. 16–19; Jn. 21:22. (Dt. 30:3; Acts 1:11, *note*)
19
w Cp. Mt. 12:25; 22:18; Mk. 2:8; Lk. 6:8; 11:17; Jn. 2:25
20
x Jn. 1:51; 5:19,24,25; 6:26,32,47, 53; 8:34,51, 58; 10:1,7; 12:24; 13:16,20,21; 14:12; 16:20,23
y Mk. 16:10; Lk. 24:17
z Cp. Rev. 11:10
aa Lk. 24:32, 41; cp. Jer. 31:13
21
bb Gen. 3:16; Isa. 13:8; 42:14; 1 Th. 5:3

[1](16:12) Observe Christ's preauthentication of the NT Scriptures: (1) He expressly declared that He was leaving "many things" unrevealed (v. 12). (2) He promised that this revelation would be completed after the Spirit came (v. 13, "guide you into all truth"). (3) He outlined in advance exactly the elements of NT revelation: (a) historical—"bring to your remembrance all things that I said to you" (14:26); (b) doctrinal—interpretation of the historical facts, "teach you all things" (14:26; 16:14); and (c) prophetic—"tell you things to come" (16:13). (4) He chose certain persons to receive and witness to the revelations (Mt. 28:19; Jn. 15:27; 16:13; Acts 1:8; 9:15–17). (5) He gave to their words, when speaking for Him in the Spirit, precisely the same authority as His own words (Mt. 10:14–15; Lk. 10:16; Jn. 13:20; 15:20; 17:20; see e.g. 1 Cor. 14:37 for Paul's consciousness of this authority). (6) That Christ expected this new revelation would be recorded is evident from such passages as Jn. 17:20 and Acts 1:8, for only thus could the accurate witness of the chosen writers reach all nations after they had passed away. And (7) that some of the new revelation was recorded by men outside the original apostolic group (e.g. Mark and Luke) is explained by the fact that there were "prophets" in the early Church who, like Paul, were chosen by the ascended Christ (Eph. 4:11), and who not only received new revelation (Eph. 3:4–5) but also recorded it in "Scriptures" (Rom. 16:25–26). See 2 Tim. 3:16, *note.*

21
a Gk. *kosmos.* See Mt. 4:8, *note*
22
b 1 Pet. 1:8
23
c Jn. 1:51; 5:19,24,25; 6:26,32,47, 53; 8:34,51, 58; 10:1,7; 12:24; 13:16,20,21; 14:12; 16:20,23
d Mt. 7:7–8; Jn. 14:13; 15:7,16; cp. Eph. 6:18; Jas. 1:5–6; 4:2–3; 1 Jn. 3:22; 5:14
e v. 26; cp. Lk. 24:47; Jn. 20:31; Acts 3:6; 16:18; Eph. 5:20
24
f Jn. 17:13; cp. Rom. 14:17
g Jn. 15:11
25
h v. 29; Jn. 10:6
i Jn. 7:13
27
j Jn. 14:21,23
k *Christ* (first advent): vv. 27–28, 30; Jn. 17:8. (Gen. 3:15; Acts 1:11, *note*)
29
l Cp. v. 25
30
m Jn. 21:17; cp. 1 Chr. 28:9; 2 Chr. 6:30; Jn. 2:24–25; 6:64; Acts

being has been born into the
[a]world.
22 “Therefore you now have
sorrow; but I will see you again
and your heart will rejoice, and
your [b]joy no one will take from
you.
23 “And in that day you will
ask Me nothing. [c]Most assuredly,
I say to you, whatever
you [d]ask the Father [e]in My
name He will give you.
24 “Until now you have
asked nothing in My name.
[d]Ask, and you will receive, that
your [f]joy may be [g]full.
25 “These things I have spoken
to you in figurative language;
but the time is coming
when I will no longer speak to
you in [h]figurative language, but
I will tell you [i]plainly about the
Father.
26 “In that day you will ask in
My name, and I do not say to
you that I shall pray the Father
for you;
27 “for the Father Himself
[j]loves you, because you have
loved Me, and have believed
that I [k]came forth from God.
28 “I [k]came forth from the
Father and have come into the
[a]world. Again, I leave the
[a]world and go to the Father.”
29 His disciples said to Him,
“See, now You are speaking
[i]plainly, and using no [l]figure
of speech!
30 “Now we are sure that
You [m]know all things, and have
no need that anyone should
question You. By this we believe
that You [k]came forth from
God.”
31 Jesus answered them, “Do
you now believe?
32 “Indeed the hour is coming,
yes, has now come, that you
will be [n]scattered, each to his
own, and will leave Me alone.
And yet I am not alone, because
the Father is with Me.
33 “These things I have spoken
to you, that in Me you may
have [o]peace. In the [p]world you
will* have tribulation; but be of
good cheer, I have [q]overcome
the [p]world.”

Christ's high priestly, intercessory prayer

17 JESUS spoke these
words, lifted up His eyes
to heaven, and [1][r]said: “Father,
the hour has come. [2]Glorify
Your Son, that Your Son also
may glorify You,
2 “as You have given Him
authority over all flesh, that He
should* [3]give eternal [s]life to as
many as You have [4]given Him.
3 “And this is eternal [s]life,
that they may [t]know You, the
only true God, and Jesus Christ
whom You have sent.
4 “I have glorified You on
the earth. I have [u]finished the
work which You have given Me
to do.
5 “And now, O Father, glorify
Me together with Yourself,
with the glory which [v]I had
with You before the [a]world
was.

*16:33 NU-Text and M-Text omit *will.*
17:2 M-Text reads *shall.*

1:24; Rom. 8:27
32
n Zech. 13:7; Mt. 26:31; Acts 8:1
33
o See Mt. 10:34, *note*
p Gk. *kosmos.* See Rev. 13:8, *note*
q Cp. 1 Cor. 15:24
CHAPTER 17
1
r *Bible prayers* (NT): vv. 1–26; Acts 1:24. (Mt. 6:9; Lk. 11:2, *note*)
2
s *Life* (eternal): vv. 2–3; Jn. 20:31. (Mt. 7:14; Rev. 22:19)
3
t Jer. 9:23–24
4
u Dan. 9:24; Jn. 4:34; 19:30
5
v Prov. 8:22–30; Jn. 1:1–2

[1](17:1) This chapter constitutes the Lord's own prayer to His Father. Compare the prayer that He taught to His disciples, known as The Lord's Prayer (Mt. 6:9–13; Lk. 11:2–4. See also *notes*). Here in ch. 17 the reader may look deeply into the heart of the Son of God. The petitions are personal and intercessory, Christ's high priestly prayer. See also next *note* and Jn. 17:2, *notes.*

[2](17:1) Observe the seven petitions in this prayer: (1) that Jesus may be glorified as the Son who has glorified the Father (v. 1; cp. Phil. 2:9–11); (2) for restoration to the eternal glory (v. 5); (3) for the safety of believers from (a) the world (v. 11) and (b) the evil one (v. 15); (4) for the sanctification of believers (v. 17); (5) for the spiritual unity of believers (vv. 21–23); (6) that the world may believe (v. 21); and (7) that believers may be with Him in heaven to behold and share His glory (v. 24). In vv. 1–5 the Lord prays for Himself; in vv. 6–19 He prays for His disciples; and in vv. 20–26 He prays for all Christians throughout the whole age.

[3](17:2) Christ's gifts to those whom the Father gave Him are: eternal life (v. 2); the Father's name (vv. 6,26; cp. 20:17); the Father's words (vv. 8,14); His own joy (v. 13); and His own glory (v. 22).

[4](17:2) Seven times Jesus speaks of Christians as given to Him by the Father (vv. 2,6 [twice], 9,11,12,24). Jesus Christ is God's love gift to the world (3:16), and believers are the Father's love gift to Jesus Christ. It is Christ who commits the Christian to the Father for safekeeping, so that the believer's security rests upon the Father's faithfulness to His Son Jesus Christ.

6 "I have manifested Your name to the men whom You have given Me [a]out of the [b]world. [c]They were Yours, You gave them to Me, and they have kept Your word.

7 "Now they have known that all things which You have given Me are from You.

8 "For I have given to them the [d]words which You have given Me; and they have received *them,* and have known surely that I [e]came forth from You; and they have believed that [f]You sent Me.

9 "I pray for them. I do not pray for the [g]world but for those whom You have given Me, for they are Yours.

10 "And all Mine are Yours, and Yours are Mine, and I am glorified in them.

11 "Now I am no longer in the [b]world, but these are in the world, and I [h]come to You. Holy Father, [i]keep through Your name those whom You have given Me,* that they may be one as We *are.*

12 "While I was with them in the [b]world,* I kept them in Your name. Those whom You gave Me I have kept;* and [j]none of them is [k]lost except the son of perdition, that the [d]Scripture might be [l]fulfilled.

13 "But now I [h]come to You, and these things I speak in the [b]world, that they may have My joy fulfilled in themselves.

14 "I have given them Your [d]word; and the [g]world has [m]hated them because they are [a]not of the [g]world, just as I am not of the [g]world.

15 "I do not pray that You should take them out of the [b]world, [n]but that You should [i]keep them from [o]the evil one.

16 "They are not of the [g]world, just as I am [a]not of the [g]world.

17 [p]"Sanctify them by Your truth. [q]Your [d]word is truth.

18 "As You [e]sent Me into the [b]world, I also have [r]sent them into the [b]world.

19 "And for their sakes I [p]sanctify Myself, that they also may be [s]sanctified by the truth.

20 "I do not pray for these alone, but also for those who will* [t]believe in Me through their word;

21 "that they all may be one, [u]as You, Father, *are* in Me, and I in You; that they also may be one in Us, that the [b]world may believe that [f]You [e]sent Me.

22 "And the [v]glory which You gave Me I have given them, that they may be one just as We are one:

23 "I in them, and You in Me; that they may be made [w]perfect in one, and that the [b]world may know that You have [e]sent Me, and have loved them as You have loved Me.

24 "Father, I [i]desire that they also whom You gave Me may be [x]with Me where I am, that they may behold My glory which You have given Me; for You loved Me before the foundation of the [b]world.

25 "O righteous Father! The [b]world has not known You, but I have known You; and these have known that You sent Me.

26 "And I have declared to them Your [y]name, and will declare *it,* that the [z]love with which You loved Me may be [aa]in them, and I in them."

V. The Sacrifice of the Son of God, 18—19

Jesus in Gethsemane
(Mt. 26:36–46; Mk. 14:32–42; Lk. 22:39–46)

18 WHEN Jesus had spoken these words, He went out with His disciples over the Brook [bb]Kidron, where there was a garden, which He and His disciples entered.

Jesus' betrayal and arrest
(Mt. 26:47–56; Mk. 14:43–50; Lk. 22:47–54)

2 And Judas, who betrayed Him, also knew the place; for Jesus often [cc]met there with His disciples.

3 Then Judas, having received a detachment *of troops,* and officers from the chief priests and [dd]Pharisees, came

*
17:11 NU-Text and M-Text read *keep them through Your name which You have given Me.* **17:12** NU-Text omits *in the world.* • NU-Text reads *in Your name which You gave Me. And I guarded them* (or *it*). **17:20** NU-Text and M-Text omit *will.*

6
a Separation: vv. 6, 14,16; Rom. 12:2. (Gen. 12:1; 2 Cor. 6:17, *note*)
b Gk. *kosmos.* See Mt. 4:8, *note*
c Ezek. 18:4; Rom. 14:8
8
d Inspiration: vv. 8, 12,14,17; Jn. 19:24. (Ex. 4:15; 2 Tim. 3:16, *note*)
e Christ (first advent): vv. 8,18,21, 23; Acts 1:9. (Gen. 3:15; Acts 1:11, *note*)
f Dt. 18:15,18
9
g Gk. *kosmos.* See Rev. 13:8, *note*
11
h Mk. 16:19; Lk. 24:51; Acts 1:9; Heb. 4:14; 9:24; 1 Pet. 3:22
i Assurance/security: vv. 11,15,24; Acts 2:21. (Ps. 23:1; Jude 1, *note*)
12
j Jn. 6:39
k See Jn. 3:16, *note*
l Ps. 41:9
14
m Mt. 24:9; Lk. 6:22; 21:17; Jn. 15:19
15
n 2 Th. 3:3; 2 Tim. 4:18; 2 Pet. 2:9; 1 Jn. 5:18
o Satan: v. 15; Acts 5:3. (Gen. 3:1; Rev. 20:10)
17
p Sanctification (NT): vv. 17,19; Acts 3:21. (Mt. 4:5; Rev. 22:11)
q Ps. 119:9; Jn. 15:3; Eph. 5:26
18
r Jn. 20:21
19
s v. 17; cp. Heb. 2:11
20
t Faith: v. 20; Jn. 20:8. (Gen. 3:20; Heb. 11:39, *note*). Acts 1:8
21
u Rom. 12:5; Eph. 4:4,6; Gal. 3:28; cp. Acts 4:32
22
v 2 Cor. 3:18
23
w See Mt. 5:48 and Phil. 3:12, *notes*
24
x Jn. 14:3; 1 Th. 4:17
26
y Ex. 34:5–7
z Law (of Christ): v. 26; Rom. 5:5. (Jn. 13:34; 2 Jn. 5)
aa Eph. 3:17–19; cp. 1 Jn. 4:16
CHAPTER 18
1
bb Cp. 2 Sam. 15:23
2
cc Cp. Lk. 21:37
3
dd See Mt. 3:7, *note 1*

there with lanterns, torches,
and weapons.
4 Jesus therefore, [a]know-
ing all things that would come
upon Him, [b]went forward and
said to them, "Whom are you
seeking?"
5 They answered Him, [c]"Jesus of Nazareth." Jesus said to
them, "I am *He.*" And Judas,
who [d]betrayed Him, also
[e]stood with them.
6 Now when He said to
them, "I am *He,*" they drew back
and [f]fell to the ground.
7 Then He asked them
again, "Whom are you seeking?" And they said, "Jesus of
Nazareth."
8 Jesus answered, "I have
told you that I am *He.* Therefore, if you seek Me, let these go
their way,"
9 that the saying might be
fulfilled which He [g]spoke, "Of
those whom You gave Me I
have lost none."

Peter strikes Malchus

10 Then Simon Peter, having
a [h]sword, drew it and struck the
high priest's servant, and [i]cut
off his right ear. The servant's
name was Malchus.
11 So Jesus said to Peter,
"Put your sword into the sheath.
[j]Shall I not drink the [k]cup
which My Father has given
Me?"

Jesus brought before high priest (through v. 27; Mt. 26:57–68; Mk. 14:53–65; Lk. 22:63–71)

12 Then the detachment *of*
troops and the captain and the
officers of the Jews arrested Jesus and bound Him.
13 And they [1]led Him away
to [l]Annas first, for he was the
father-in-law of [m]Caiaphas who
was high priest that year.
14 Now it was Caiaphas who
advised the Jews [n]that it was
expedient that one man should
die for the people.

(Interlude: Peter's three denials; see also vv. 25–27; Mt. 26:69–75; Mk. 14:66–72; Lk. 22:54–62)

15 And Simon Peter [o]fol-
lowed Jesus, and so *did* [p]an-
other* disciple. Now that disciple was known to the high
priest, and went with Jesus into
the courtyard of the high priest.
16 But Peter stood at the door
outside. Then the other disciple,
who was known to the high
priest, went out and spoke to
her who kept the door, and
brought Peter in.
17 Then the servant girl who
kept the door said to Peter,
"You are not also *one* of this
Man's disciples, are you?" He
said, "I am [q]not."
18 Now the servants and officers who had made a [r]fire of
coals stood there, for it was
cold, and they warmed themselves. And Peter stood with
them and warmed himself.
19 The high priest then asked
Jesus about His disciples and
His [s]doctrine.
20 Jesus answered him, "I
spoke [t]openly to the [u]world. I
always taught [v]in synagogues
and [w]in the temple, where the
Jews always meet,* and in secret I have said nothing.
21 "Why do you ask Me? Ask
[x]those who have heard Me
what I said to them. Indeed they
know what I said."
22 And when He had said
these things, one of the officers
who stood by [y]struck Jesus
with the palm of his hand, saying, "Do You answer the high
priest like that?"
23 Jesus answered him, "If I
have spoken evil, bear witness
of the evil; but if [z]well, why do
you strike Me?"
24 Then [aa]Annas sent Him
bound to [bb]Caiaphas the high
priest.
25 Now Simon Peter stood
and warmed himself. Therefore
they said to him, "You are not
also *one* of His disciples, are
you?" He denied *it* and said, "I
am [q]not!"
26 One of the servants of the
high priest, a relative *of him*
whose ear Peter cut off, said,
"Did I not see you in the garden
with Him?"

4
a Jn. 13:1,3; 19:28
b Cp. Lk. 9:51; Heb. 12:2
5
c Mt. 21:11; Mk. 1:24; 14:67; 16:6; Lk. 18:37; 24:19; Jn. 1:45; 19:19; Acts 2:22; 3:6; 4:10; 6:14; 10:38; 22:8; 26:9
d Ps. 41:9
e Cp. Ex. 23:2; Ps. 1:1; Prov. 24:1; 2 Cor. 6:14
6
f Cp. Ps. 27:2
9
g Jn. 6:39; 17:12; cp. 1 Cor. 10:13
10
h Cp. Lk. 22:38,49–50
i v. 26
11
j Cp. 1 Sam. 3:18; Acts 21:14
k Cp. Mt. 20:22; 26:39; Mk. 14:36; Lk. 22:42
13
l Lk. 3:2; Acts 4:6
m Mt. 26:3; Jn. 11:49
14
n Jn. 11:49–50
15
o Mk. 14:54
p Jn. 20:2–5
17
q vv. 17, 25–27; Mt. 26:34; cp. Mt. 10:33; Acts 3:14; 2 Tim. 2:12
18
r Cp. Jn. 21:9
19
s Or *teaching.* Mk. 4:2; Jn. 7:16–17; 2 Jn. 9
20
t Jn. 8:26; cp. Jn. 10:24; 16:25,29
u Gk. *kosmos.* See Mt. 4:8, *note*
v Jn. 6:59
w Mk. 14:49; Jn. 7:14,28
21
x Mk. 12:37
22
y Isa. 50:6; cp. 1 Ki. 22:24; Job 16:10; Jer. 20:2; Mic. 5:1; Acts 23:2
23
z Cp. 1 Pet. 2:19,23
24
aa v. 13; Lk. 3:2; Acts 4:6
bb vv. 13,14; Jn. 11:49

*

18:15 M-Text reads *the other.*
18:20 NU-Text reads *where all the Jews meet.*

[1](18:13) For the order of events following Christ's arrest, see Mt. 26:57, *note.*

27
[a] vv. 17, 25–27; Mt. 26:34; cp. Mt. 10:33; Acts 3:14; 2 Tim. 2:12
[b] Mt. 26:34; Jn. 13:38
28
[c] Cp. Mt. 23:23; Mk. 7:4; Acts 10:28; Gal. 4:9–10; 5:1; Col. 2:20–23; Heb. 9:10
[d] c. A.D. 29. Cp. Jn. 2:13; 6:4; 11:55; see Ex. 12:11, *note*
29
[e] Mt. 27:11–14; Mk. 15:2–5
31
[f] *Law* (of Moses): v. 31; Jn. 19:7. (Ex. 19:1; Gal. 3:24, *note*). Lev. 24:16; cp. Acts 18:15
32
[g] Mt. 20:17–19
[h] Jn. 3:14; 12:32–33
33
[i] *Kingdom* (NT): vv. 33–34, 36–37,39; 19:3; Jn. 19:14. (Mt. 2:2; 1 Cor. 15:24, *note*). Lk. 23:2–3
36
[j] 1 Tim. 6:13
[k] Gk. *ek, out of;* or *according to*
[l] Gk. *kosmos.* See Rev. 13:8, *note*
[m] Cp. Ps. 45:6; Isa. 9:6–7; Dan. 2:44; Zech. 9:9; Rom.

27 Peter then [a]denied again;
and immediately a [1b]rooster
crowed.

Jesus before Pilate
(Mt. 27:2,11–14;
Mk. 15:1–5; Lk. 23:1–7,13–15)

28 Then they led Jesus from
Caiaphas to the Praetorium,
and it was early morning. But
they themselves did not go into
[c]the Praetorium, lest they
should be defiled, but that they
might eat the [d]Passover.
29 [e]Pilate then went out to
them and said, "What accusation do you bring against this
Man?"
30 They answered and said
to him, "If He were not an evildoer, we would not have delivered Him up to you."
31 Then Pilate said to them,
"You take Him and judge Him
according to your [f]law." Therefore the Jews said to him, "It is
not lawful for us to put anyone
to death,"
32 that the saying of Jesus
might be fulfilled which He
[g]spoke, [h]signifying by what
death He would die.
33 Then Pilate entered the
Praetorium again, called Jesus,
and said to Him, "Are You the
[i]King of the Jews?"
34 Jesus answered him, "Are
you speaking for yourself about
this, or did others tell you this
concerning Me?"
35 Pilate answered, "Am I a
Jew? Your own nation and the
chief priests have delivered You
to me. What have You done?"
36 Jesus [j]answered, "My
[i]kingdom is [2]not [k]of this
[l]world. If My [m]kingdom were
of this [l]world, My servants
would [n]fight, so that I should
not be delivered to the Jews; but
now My kingdom is not from
[o]here."
37 Pilate therefore said to
Him, "Are You a king then?" Jesus answered, [3]"You say *rightly*
that I am a king. For this cause
I was born, and for this cause I
have come into the [p]world,
[q]that I should bear [r]witness to
the [s]truth. Everyone who is of
the truth [t]hears My voice."
38 Pilate said to Him, "What
is truth?" And when he had said
this, he went out again to the
Jews, and said to them, "I find
[u]no fault in Him at all."

Jesus condemned:
Barabbas preferred
(Mt. 27:15–21; Mk. 15:6–11;
Lk. 23:18–19)

39 "But you have a custom
that I should release someone to
you at the [d]Passover. Do you
therefore want me to release to
you the [i]King of the Jews?"
40 Then they all cried again,
saying, [v]"Not this Man, but Barabbas!" Now Barabbas was a
robber.

Jesus crowned with thorns
(Mt. 27:27–30; Mk. 15:16–18)

19 SO then Pilate took Jesus and [w]scourged *Him.*
2 And the soldiers twisted a
crown of thorns and put *it* on
His head, and they put on Him a
purple robe.
3 Then they said,* "Hail,
[i]King of the Jews!" And they
[x]struck Him with their hands.

Pilate makes final effort
to release Jesus (Mt. 27:22–26;
Mk. 15:12–15; Lk. 23:20–25)

4 Pilate then went out
again, and said to them, "Behold, I am bringing Him out to
you, that you may know that I
find [y]no fault in Him."
5 Then Jesus came out,

*19:3 NU-Text reads *And they came up to Him and said.*

14:17; Col. 1:13
[n] Cp. Mt. 26:53
[o] Cp. Jn. 6:15
37
[p] Gk. *kosmos.* See Mt. 4:8, *note*
[q] Mt. 5:17; 20:28; Lk. 4:43; 12:49; 19:10; Jn. 3:17; 9:39; 10:10; 12:47
[r] Isa. 55:4; Rev. 1:5
[s] Jn. 14:6
[t] Jn. 8:47; 10:27
38
[u] Isa. 53:9; Jn. 19:4,6; 1 Pet. 2:22–24
40
[v] Acts 3:14
CHAPTER 19
1
[w] Mt. 27:26; Mk. 15:15
3
[x] Isa. 50:6; cp.1 Ki. 22:24; Acts 23:2
4
[y] Isa. 53:9; Jn. 18:38; 1 Pet. 2:22–24

[1](18:27) This was not a particular rooster; it was the time in the morning designated as "cockcrow." Cp. Mk. 13:35; 14:30,72.

[2](18:36) This verse has erroneously been taken to mean that Christ was disavowing that His kingdom would be established on earth. Apart from the incompatibility of such a view with the entire testimony of Scripture (cp. Lk. 1:33; Rev. 11:15), it conflicts with the remainder of the verse. Earthly kingdoms are inaugurated, carried on, and brought to an end by human force, but His kingdom would be ushered in and maintained by His personal appearance and omnipotence.

[3](18:37) This is a clear, affirmative answer, according to the Greek idiom, though English requires the addition of "rightly" or a similar word. Observe what follows in the text: "for this cause I was born," etc.

wearing the crown of thorns and the purple robe. And *Pilate* said to them, [a]"Behold the Man!"

6 Therefore, when the chief priests and officers saw Him, they cried out, saying, "Crucify *Him,* crucify *Him!*" Pilate said to them, "You take Him and crucify *Him,* for I find [b]no fault in Him."

7 The Jews answered him, "We have a law, and according to our* [c]law He ought to die, because He made Himself the Son of God."

8 Therefore, when Pilate heard that saying, [d]he was the more afraid,

9 and went again into the Praetorium, and said to Jesus, "Where are You from?" But Jesus gave him [e]no answer.

10 Then Pilate said to Him, "Are You not speaking to me? Do You not know that I have [f]power to crucify You, and [f]power to release You?"

11 Jesus answered, [g]"You could have no [f]power at all against Me unless it had been [h]given you from above. Therefore [i]the one who delivered Me to you has the greater [j]sin."

12 From then on Pilate sought to release Him, but the Jews cried out, saying, "If you let this Man go, you are not Caesar's friend. Whoever makes himself a king speaks against [k]Caesar."

13 [l]When Pilate therefore heard that saying, he brought Jesus out and sat down in the judgment seat in a place that is called *The* Pavement, but in Hebrew, Gabbatha.

14 Now it was the Preparation Day of the Passover, and about the [1m]sixth hour. And he said to the Jews, "Behold your [n]King!"

15 But they cried out, "Away with *Him,* away with *Him!* Crucify Him!" Pilate said to them, "Shall I crucify your [n]King?" The chief priests answered, "We have no [o]king but Caesar!"

Jesus is crucified (Mt. 27:31–50; Mk. 15:19–37; Lk. 23:26–46)

16 [2]Then he delivered Him to them to be [p]crucified. So they took Jesus and led *Him* away.*

17 And He, bearing His cross, [q]went out to a place called *the Place* of a Skull, which is called in Hebrew, [r]Golgotha,

18 where they [s]crucified Him, and [t]two others with Him, one on either side, and Jesus in the center.

19 Now Pilate wrote a title and put *it* on the cross. And the writing was:

JESUS OF NAZARETH,
THE [n]KING OF THE JEWS.

20 Then many of the Jews read this title, for the place where Jesus was crucified was near the city; and it was written in [u]Hebrew, [v]Greek, *and* Latin.

21 Therefore the chief priests of the Jews said to Pilate, "Do not write, 'The King of the Jews,' but, 'He said, "I am the King of the Jews." ' "

22 Pilate answered, "What I have written, I have written."

23 Then the soldiers, when they had crucified Jesus, took His garments and made four parts, to each soldier a part, and also the tunic. Now the tunic was without seam, woven from the top in one piece.

24 They said therefore among themselves, "Let us not tear it, but cast lots for it, whose it shall be," that the [w]Scripture might be fulfilled which [x]says:

"They divided My
garments among them,

*19:7 NU-Text reads *the law.*
19:16 NU-Text omits *and led Him away.*

5
a Cp. Jn. 1:29
6
b Isa. 53:9; Jn. 18:38; 1 Pet. 2:22–24
7
c Law (of Moses): v. 7; Acts 3:22. (Ex. 19:1; Gal. 3:24, *note*). Lev. 24:16
8
d Cp. Mt. 27:19
9
e Isa. 53:7; Lk. 23:9
10
f Or *authority.* Jn. 10:18
11
g Cp. Lk. 22:53; Jn. 7:30; Acts 4:27–28
h Jn. 3:27; Rom. 13:1
i Mk. 14:44; Jn. 18:3
j See Rom. 3:23, *note*
12
k Cp. Lk. 23:2; Acts 17:7
13
l Dt. 1:17; 1 Sam. 15:24; Prov. 29:25; Isa. 51:12; Acts 4:19
14
m 6 a.m. See *note*
n Kingdom (NT): vv. 14–15, 19–22; Acts 1:6. (Mt. 2:2; 1 Cor. 15:24, *note*)
15
o Cp. Hos. 3:4
16
p Judgments (the seven): vv. 16–18; Acts 10:42. (1 Sam. 7:14; Rev. 20:12, *note*)
17
q Num. 15:36; Heb. 13:12; see Num. 19:2, *note*
r See Mk. 15:22, *note*
18
s Sacrifice (of Christ): v. 18; Jn. 19:34. (Gen. 3:15; Heb. 10:18, *note*)
t Isa. 53:12
20
u Cp. 2 Ki. 18:26; Acts 21:40; 22:2; 26:14
v Cp. Acts 21:37
24
w Inspiration: v. 24; Jn. 19:28. (Ex. 4:15; 2 Tim. 3:16, *note*)
x Ps. 22:18

[1](19:14) John uses Roman time with the hours starting at 12 midnight and 12 noon, as is done today. However, the Synoptics use Hebrew reckoning, beginning with sunrise (i.e. 6 a.m.; 7 a.m. being the first hour, etc.). This is apparent from the care with which the Gospels specify particular hours in relation to the crucifixion. Our Lord was put on the cross at 9 a.m. ("third hour" Mk. 15:25); darkness was over the land from noon until 3 p.m. ("sixth" till "ninth hour," Mt. 27:45–46; Mk. 15:33–34; Lk. 23:44). Thus here the "sixth hour" could not be Hebrew time (noon), but rather 6 a.m., "when morning came" (Mt. 27:1–2). Acts uses Hebrew time.

[2](19:16) For the order of events at the crucifixion, see Mt. 27:33, *note.*

And for My clothing they
cast lots."

Therefore the soldiers did these
things.
25 Now there [a]stood by the
cross of Jesus His [b]mother, and
His mother's sister, [c]Mary the
wife of Clopas, and [c]Mary Magdalene.
26 When Jesus therefore
saw His mother, and the [d]disci-
ple [e]whom He loved standing
by, He said to His mother,
[f]"Woman, behold your son!"
27 Then He said to the disciple, "Behold your mother!" And
from that hour that disciple
took her to his own *home.*
28 After this, Jesus, knowing* that all things were now
[g]accomplished, [h]that the
[i]Scripture might be fulfilled,
said, "I thirst!"
29 Now a vessel full of [j]sour
wine was sitting there; and they
filled a sponge with sour wine,
put *it* on hyssop, and put *it* to
His mouth.
30 So when Jesus had re-
ceived the sour wine, He said,
[1]"It is finished!" And bowing
His head, He [k]gave up His
spirit.

Events following His death
(Mt. 27:51–56; Mk. 15:38–41;
Lk. 23:45,47–49)

31 Therefore, because it was
the [l]Preparation *Day,* that the
bodies should [m]not remain on
the cross on the [n]Sabbath (for
that Sabbath was a [o]high day),
the Jews asked Pilate that their
legs might be broken, and *that*
they might be taken away.
32 Then the soldiers came
and broke the legs of the first
and of the other who was crucified [p]with Him.
33 But when they came to Jesus and saw that He was already [q]dead, they did not break
His legs.
34 But one of the soldiers
[r]pierced His side with a spear,
and immediately [s]blood and
water came out.
35 And he who has seen has
testified, and his testimony is
[t]true; and he knows that he is
telling the truth, so that you
may [u]believe.
36 For these things were
done that the [i]Scripture should
be fulfilled, [v]*"Not one of His*
bones shall be broken."
37 And again another
[i]Scripture says, [w]*"They shall*
look on Him whom they
pierced."

Jesus is buried
(Mt. 27:57–66; Mk. 15:42–47;
Lk. 23:50–56)

38 After this, Joseph of Arimathea, being a disciple of Jesus, but secretly, for [x]fear of the
Jews, asked Pilate that he might
take away the body of Jesus;
and Pilate gave *him* permission.
So he came and took the body of
Jesus.
39 And [y]Nicodemus, who at
first came to Jesus by night, also
came, bringing a mixture of
[z]myrrh and aloes, about a hundred [aa]pounds.
40 Then they took the body
of Jesus, and bound it in [bb]strips
of linen with the spices, as the
custom of the Jews is to bury.
41 Now in the place where
He was [cc]crucified there was a
garden, and in the garden a new
tomb in which [dd]no one had yet
been laid.
42 So there they [ee]laid Jesus,
because of the Jews' [l]Prepara-
tion *Day,* for the tomb was
nearby.

VI. The Manifestation of the Son
of God in Resurrection, 20
The resurrection and events
of that day (cp. Mt. 28:1–15;
Mk. 16:1–14; Lk. 24:1–32)

20 [2]NOW on the [ff]first *day*
of the week [c]Mary Mag-
dalene [gg]went to the tomb early,
while it was still dark, and saw
that the [hh]stone had been taken
away from the tomb.
2 Then she ran and came to
Simon Peter, and to the [ii]other
disciple, [jj]whom Jesus loved,
and said to them, "They have

*19:28 M-Text reads *seeing.*

25
a Mt. 27:55–56; Mk. 15:40–41; Lk. 23:49
b Cp. Lk. 2:35
c See Lk. 1:27, *note*
26
d Cp. Jn. 18:15
e Jn. 13:23; 20:2; 21:7, 20,24
f Jn. 2:4
28
g Cp. v. 30
h vv. 24,36,37
i Inspiration: vv. 28–29, 36–37; Jn. 20:9. (Ex. 4:15; 2 Tim. 3:16, *note*)
29
j Ps. 69:21
30
k See Mt. 27:50, *note*
31
l Mt. 27:62; Mk. 15:42; Lk. 23:54
m Dt. 21:23; cp. Josh. 8:29; 10:26
n Sabbath: v. 31; Acts 13:14. (Gen. 2:3; Mt. 12:1, *note*)
o Ex. 12:16; Lev. 23:6–7
32
p Cp. Gal. 2:20; 6:14; Col. 2:20
33
q Cp. Jn. 10:18
34
r Cp. Jn. 20:20,25,27
s Sacrifice (of Christ): v. 34; Acts 13:23. (Gen. 3:15; Heb. 10:18, *note*). Mt. 26:28; Rom. 5:9; 1 Pet. 1:18–19; 1 Jn. 1:7; 5:6,8; Rev. 1:5; 7:14

35
t Jn. 21:24; cp. 3 Jn. 12
u Jn. 20:31
36
v Ps. 34:20; cp. Ex. 12:46; Num. 9:12
37
w Zech. 12:10; Rev. 1:7
38
x Jn. 7:13; cp. Jn. 12:42
39
y Jn. 3:1–2; 7:50
z Mt. 2:11; cp. Ps. 45:8
aa See Weights and Measures (NT), Acts 27:28, *note*
40
bb Jn. 20:7; cp. Jn. 11:44
41
cc vv. 17–18
dd Cp. Mk. 11:2
42
ee Isa. 53:9
CHAPTER 20
1
ff Acts 20:7; 1 Cor. 16:2; see Mt. 28:1, *note 1*
gg See Mt. 28:1, *note 2*
hh Mt. 27:60, 66
2
ii Jn. 21:23–24
jj Jn. 13:23; 19:26; 21:7, 20,24

[1](19:30) "It is finished!" was the shout of victory. See Jn. 4:34; 17:4; Rom. 10:4; Gal. 3:13; Heb. 10:5–10.
[2](20:1) For the order of events on the resurrection day, see Mt. 28:1, *note 2.*

2
a vv. 13,15
3
b Jn. 21:23–24
5
c Jn. 20:7; cp. Jn. 11:44
6
d Cp. Jn. 21:7
e Jn. 19:40
7
f Or *face cloth.* Jn. 11:44
8
g vv. 2,3,4; Jn. 21:23,24
h Faith: v. 8; Jn. 20:29. (Gen. 3:20; Heb. 11:39, *note*)
9
i Inspiration: v. 9; Jn. 20:31. (Ex. 4:15; 2 Tim. 3:16, *note*). Ps. 16:10
j Resurrection: vv. 9, 14; Jn. 21:14. (2 Ki. 4:35; 1 Cor. 15:52, *note*)

[a]taken away the Lord out of the tomb, and we do not know where they have laid Him."

3 Peter therefore went out, and the [b]other disciple, and were going to the tomb.

4 So they both ran together, and the [b]other disciple outran Peter and came to the tomb first.

5 And he, stooping down and looking in, saw the [c]linen cloths lying *there;* yet he did not go in.

6 Then Simon Peter came, following him, and [d]went into the tomb; and he saw the [e]linen cloths lying *there,*

7 and the [f]handkerchief that had been around His head, not lying with the linen cloths, but folded together in a place by itself.

8 Then the [g]other disciple, who came to the tomb first, went in also; and he saw and [h]believed.

9 For as yet they did not know the [i]Scripture, that He must [j]rise again from the dead.

10 Then the disciples [k]went away again to their own homes.

Jesus appears to Mary Magdalene

11 But Mary stood outside by the tomb weeping, and as she wept she stooped down *and looked* into the tomb.

12 And she saw two [l]angels in white sitting, one at the head and the other at the feet, where the body of Jesus had lain.

13 Then they said to her, "Woman, why are you weeping?" She said to them, "Because they have taken away my Lord, and I do not know where they have laid Him."

14 Now when she had said this, she turned around and saw [j]Jesus standing *there,* and did not [m]know that it was Jesus.

15 Jesus said to her, "Woman, why are you weeping? [n]Whom are you seeking?" She, supposing Him to be the gardener, said to Him, "Sir, if You have carried Him away, tell me where You have laid Him, and I will take Him away."

16 Jesus said to her,

10
k Cp. Jn. 21:3
12
l See Heb. 1:4, *note*
14
m Cp. Lk. 24:16; Jn. 21:4
15
n Cp. Jn. 18:4

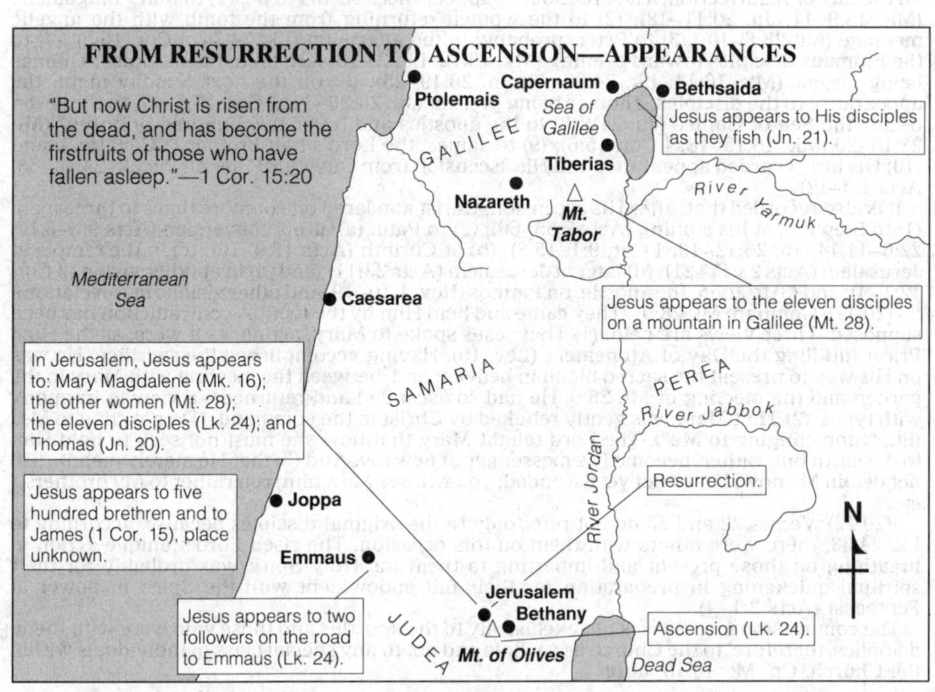

FROM RESURRECTION TO ASCENSION—APPEARANCES
"But now Christ is risen from the dead, and has become the firstfruits of those who have fallen asleep."—1 Cor. 15:20
Ptolemais
Capernaum
Bethsaida
Sea of Galilee
Jesus appears to His disciples as they fish (Jn. 21).
GALILEE
Tiberias
Nazareth
Mt. Tabor
River Yarmuk
Mediterranean Sea
Caesarea
Jesus appears to the eleven disciples on a mountain in Galilee (Mt. 28).
In Jerusalem, Jesus appears to: Mary Magdalene (Mk. 16); the other women (Mt. 28); the eleven disciples (Lk. 24); and Thomas (Jn. 20).
SAMARIA
PEREA
River Jabbok
River Jordan
Resurrection.
Jesus appears to five hundred brethren and to James (1 Cor. 15), place unknown.
Joppa
Emmaus
N
Jerusalem
Bethany
Jesus appears to two followers on the road to Emmaus (Lk. 24).
JUDEA
Mt. of Olives
Ascension (Lk. 24).
Dead Sea

[1][a]"Mary!" She turned and said to Him,* "Rabboni!" (which is to say, Teacher).

17 Jesus said to her, [2]"Do not cling to Me, for I have not yet [b]ascended to My Father; but go to My [c]brethren and say to them, 'I am ascending to [d]My Father and your Father, and *to* My God and your God.' "

18 [e]Mary Magdalene came and told the disciples that she had seen the Lord,* and *that* He had spoken these things to her.

Jesus appears to the disciples, Thomas being absent (Mk. 16:14; Lk. 24:33–49)

19 Then, the same day at evening, being the first *day* of the week, when the doors were shut where the disciples were assembled,* for [f]fear of the Jews, Jesus [g]came and stood in the midst, and said to them, [h]"Peace *be* with you."

20 When He had said this, He [i]showed them *His* hands and His side. [j]Then the disciples were glad when they saw the Lord.

21 So Jesus said to them again, [k]"Peace to you! As the Father has sent Me, I also [l]send you."

22 And when He had said this, He [m]breathed on [3]*them,* and said to them, "Receive the Holy [n]Spirit.

23 [o]"If you forgive the [p]sins of any, they are forgiven them; if you retain the *sins* of any, they are retained."

Jesus appears to the disciples, Thomas being present

24 Now Thomas, called the [q]Twin, one of the twelve, was not with them when Jesus came.

25 The other disciples therefore said to him, "We have seen the Lord." So he said to them,

*

20:16 NU-Text adds *in Hebrew.* **20:18** NU-Text reads *disciples, "I have seen the Lord,"* . . . **20:19** NU-Text omits *assembled.*

16
a Jn. 10:3
17
b Lk. 24:5; Acts 1:9; Heb. 4:14
c Heb. 2:11
d Jn. 17:11
18
e See Lk. 1:27, *note*
19
f Jn. 9:22; 19:38; cp. Acts 12:12–17
g Miracles (NT): v. 19; Jn. 20:26. (Mt. 8:3; Acts 28:8, *note*)
h v. 21; Jn. 14:27; Eph. 2:17; see Mt. 10:34, *note*
20
i Acts 1:3; cp. 1 Jn. 1:1
j Cp. Jn. 16:20–22
21
k v. 19; see Mt. 10:34, *note*
l Mt. 28:18–20; Jn. 17:18
22
m Cp. Gen. 2:7; Ezek. 37:9
n Holy Spirit (NT): v. 22; Acts 1:2. (Mt. 1:18; Acts 2:4, *note*). Cp. Jn. 14:25–26; see Lk. 11:13, *note*
23
o Cp. Mt. 16:19; 18:18
p See Rom. 3:23, *note*
24
q Jn. 11:16

[1](20:16) During the forty days between His resurrection and ascension, the Lord Jesus is recorded to have appeared to His own followers on ten occasions, the first five of these being on the day of resurrection. The order of the appearances seems to be: (1) to Mary Magdalene (Mk. 16:9–11; Jn. 20:11–18); (2) to the women returning from the tomb with the angelic message (Mt. 28:8–10); (3) to Peter, probably in the afternoon (Lk. 24:34; 1 Cor. 15:5); (4) to the Emmaus disciples toward evening (Mk. 16:12; Lk. 24:13–32); (5) to the disciples, Thomas being absent (Mk. 16:14; Lk. 24:36–43; Jn. 20:19–25); (6) on the next Sunday night, the appearance to the disciples, Thomas being present (Jn. 20:26–31; 1 Cor. 15:5); (7) to the seven beside the Sea of Galilee (Jn. 21); (8) to the apostles and "over five hundred brethren" (Mt. 28:16–20; Mk. 16:15–18; 1 Cor. 15:6); (9) to James, the Lord's half brother (1 Cor. 15:7); and (10) His last recorded appearance and His ascension from Olivet (Mk. 16:19–20; Lk. 24:44–53; Acts 1:3–12).

It is also recorded that, after His ascension, Christ appeared one or more times to three men: (1) to Stephen, at his stoning (Acts 7:55–60); (2) to Paul: (a) at his conversion (Acts 9:3–8,17; 22:6–11,14–15; 26:12–19; 1 Cor. 9:1; 15:8); (b) at Corinth (Acts 18:9–10); (c) in the temple at Jerusalem (Acts 22:17–21); (d) later at Jerusalem (Acts 23:11); and (e) in another vision (2 Cor. 12:1–4); and (3) to John, the apostle, on Patmos (Rev. 1:10–19, and other visions in Revelation).

[2](20:17) Compare Mt. 28:9: "They came and held Him by the feet." A contradiction has been supposed. Three views are held: (1) That Jesus spoke to Mary, acting, as it were, as the High Priest fulfilling the Day of Atonement (Lev. 16). Having accomplished the sacrifice, He was on His way to present the sacred blood in heaven; and, between the meeting with Mary in the garden and the meeting of Mt. 28:9, He had so ascended and returned—a view in harmony with types. (2) That Mary was gently rebuked by Christ in the command, "Do not cling to Me" (lit., "Stop clinging to Me"). The Lord taught Mary that now she must not seek to hold Him to the earth but, rather, become His messenger of new joy. And (3) that He merely meant: "Do not detain Me now; I have not yet ascended; you will see Me again; run rather to My brothers," etc.

[3](20:22) Verses 22 and 23 do not refer only to the original disciples because, according to Lk. 24:33, there were others with them on this occasion. The risen Lord's unique action in breathing on those present and imparting to them the Holy Spirit was probably for their spiritual quickening in preparation for their full endowment with the Spirit in power at Pentecost (Acts 2:1–4).

The commission of v. 23 was not exclusively to the apostles and those who were with them; it applies, therefore, to the Church as a whole and not to any special class of individuals within the Church. Cp. Mt. 16:19, *note.*

25
a Cp. Zech. 12:10; Jn. 4:48
26
b Jn. 11:16
c *Miracles* (NT): v. 26; 21:3–4; Jn. 21:6. (Mt. 8:3; Acts 28:8, *note*)
d v. 19; see Mt. 10:34, *note*
27
e Mk. 16:14
28
f Cp. Jn. 1:49; 9:35–38; Phil. 2:10–11
29
g *Faith:* v. 29; Acts 2:44. (Gen. 3:20; Heb. 11:39, *note*). Rom. 10:6–9
h Cp. Rom. 4:18–20; 2 Cor. 5:7; 1 Pet. 1:8–9
30
i Jn. 21:25
31
j *Inspiration:* v. 31; Jn. 21:24. (Ex. 4:15; 2 Tim. 3:16, *note*)

"Unless I [a]see in His hands the
print of the nails, and put my
finger into the print of the nails,
and put my hand into His side,
I will not believe."
26 And after eight days His
disciples were again inside, and
[b]Thomas with them. Jesus
came, the doors being shut, and
[c]stood in the midst, and said,
[d]"Peace to you!"
27 Then He said to Thomas,
"Reach your finger here, and
look at My hands; and reach
your hand *here,* and put *it* into
My side. Do not be [e]unbeliev-
ing, but believing."
28 And Thomas answered
and said to Him, [f]"My [1]Lord
and my God!"
29 Jesus said to him,
"Thomas,* because you have
seen Me, you have [g]believed.
[h]Blessed *are* those who have
not seen and *yet* have [g]be-
lieved."

Purpose of John's Gospel

30 And truly Jesus did
[i]many other signs in the presence of His disciples, which are
not written in this book;
31 but these are [j]written that
[k]you may believe that Jesus [l]is
the Christ, the Son of God, and
that believing you may have
[m]life in His name.

VII. The Epilogue: the Risen Son of God, the Master of Life and Service, 21

Jesus appears to seven apostles at Sea of Galilee

21 AFTER these things Jesus showed Himself
again to the disciples at the
[n]Sea of Tiberias, and in this
way He showed *Himself:*
2 Simon Peter, [o]Thomas
called the Twin, [p]Nathanael of
[q]Cana in Galilee, the [r]*sons* of
Zebedee, and two others of His
disciples were together.

Christ and our service: (1) in self-will, under human leadership

3 Simon Peter said to them,
"I am going fishing." They said
to him, "We are going with you
also." They went out and immediately* got into the boat, and
that night they caught nothing.
4 But when the morning
had now come, Jesus stood on

*
20:29 NU-Text and M-Text omit *Thomas.*
21:3 NU-Text omits *immediately.*

k Jn. 19:35; 1 Jn. 5:13
l Lk. 2:11; 1 Jn. 5:1; cp. Mt. 16:16; Lk. 4:41; Jn. 1:41; 7:41; 11:27; Acts 17:3
m *Life* (eternal): v. 31; Acts 2:28. (Mt. 7:14; Rev. 22:19)
CHAPTER 21
1
n Jn. 6:1
2
o Jn. 20:24
p Jn. 1:45–51
q Jn. 2:1
r Mt. 4:21

[1](20:28) The Deity of Jesus Christ is declared in Scripture:

(1) The OT both intimates and explicitly predicts His Deity. (a) The theophanies intimate the appearance of God in human form, and His ministry thus to man (Gen. 16:7–14; 18:2–23, especially v. 17; cp. 32:28 with Hos. 12:3–5; Ex. 3:2–14). (b) The Messiah is expressly declared to be the Son of God (Ps. 2:2–9), and God (cp. Ps. 45:6–7 with Heb. 1:8–9; Ps. 110:1 with Mt. 22:44; Acts 2:34 and Heb. 1:13; Ps. 110:4 with Heb. 5:6; 6:20; 7:17–21; Zech. 6:13). (c) His virgin birth was foretold as the means through which God could be Immanuel, God with us (cp. Isa. 7:13–14 with Mt. 1:22–23). (d) The Messiah is expressly invested with the divine names (Isa. 9:6–7). (e) In a prophecy of His death He is called "the Man who is . . . Companion" to the LORD (cp. Zech. 13:7 with Mt. 26:31). And (f) His eternal Being is declared (cp. Mic. 5:2 with Mt. 2:6; Jn. 7:42).

(2) Christ Himself affirmed His Deity. (a) He applied to Himself the Jehovistic I AM. (Jn. 4:26; 6:20; 8:24,28,58; 18:5,6). The pronoun "He" appears in translation (4:26 and 18:5,6), but not in the Greek. In 8:56–59 the Jews correctly understood this as the Lord's claim to full Deity (cp. Jn. 10:33). (b) He claimed to be the *Adonai* of the OT (Mt. 22:42–45. See Gen. 15:2, *note*). (c) He asserted His identity with the Father (Mt. 28:19; Mk. 14:62; Jn. 10:30. That the Jews so understood is shown by Jn. 10:31–33; 14:8–9; 17:5). (d) He exercised the chief prerogative of God—the forgiveness of sins (Mk. 2:5–7); Lk. 7:48–50). (e) He asserted omnipresence (Mt. 18:20; Jn. 3:13); omniscience (Jn. 11:11–14, when Jesus was fifty miles away; Mk. 11:6–8); omnipotence (Mt. 28:18; Lk. 7:14; Jn. 5:21–23; 6:19); mastery over nature, and creative power (Lk. 9:16–17; Jn. 2:9; 10:28). And (f) He received and approved human worship of Himself (Mt. 14:33; 28:9; Jn. 20:28–29).

(3) The NT writers ascribe divine titles to Christ (Jn. 1:1; 20:28; Acts 20:28; Rom. 1:4; 9:5; 2 Th. 1:12; 1 Tim. 3:16; Ti. 2:13; Heb. 1:8; 1 Jn. 5:20).

(4) The NT writers ascribe divine perfections and attributes to Christ (Mt. 11:28; 18:20; 28:20; Jn. 1:2; 2:23–25; 3:13; 5:17; 21:17; Heb. 1:3,11–12 with Heb. 13:8; Rev. 1:8,17–18; 11:17; 22:13).

(5) The NT writers ascribe divine works to Christ (Jn. 1:3,10; Col. 1:16–17; Heb. 1:3).

(6) The NT writers teach that supreme worship should be paid to Christ (Acts 7:59–60; 1 Cor. 1:2; 2 Cor. 13:14; Phil. 2:9–11; Heb. 1:6; Rev. 1:5–6; 5:12–13).

(7) The holiness and resurrection of Christ confirm His Deity (Jn. 8:46; Rom. 1:4).

the shore; yet the disciples did
not [a]know that it was Jesus.

(2) Barren result of service in self-will

5 Then Jesus said to them,
"Children, have you any food?"
They answered Him, "No."

(3) Fruitfulness of Christ-directed service

6 And He said to them,
[b]"Cast the net on the right side
of the boat, and you will find
some." So they cast, and [c]now
they were not able to draw it in
because of the multitude of fish.
7 Therefore that disciple
[d]whom Jesus loved said to Peter,
"It is the [e]Lord!" Now when
Simon Peter heard that it was
the Lord, he [f]put on *his* outer
garment (for he had removed
it), and plunged into the sea.
8 But the other disciples
came in the little boat (for they
were not far from land, but
about two hundred [g]cubits),
dragging the net with fish.
9 Then, as soon as they had
come to land, they saw a [h]fire of
coals there, [i]and [j]fish laid on
it, and bread.
10 Jesus said to them, "Bring
some of the fish which you have
just caught."
11 Simon Peter went up and
dragged the net to land, full of
large fish, one hundred and
fifty-three; and although there
were so many, the net [k]was not
broken.

4 *a* Jn. 20:14
6 *b* Cp. Lk. 5:3–7
c *Miracles* (NT): vv. 3–6; Acts 3:7. (Mt. 8:3; Acts 28:8, *note*)
7 *d* vv. 20,24; Jn. 13:23; 20:2
e Cp. Lk. 24:30–31
f Cp. Jn. 21:18
8 *g* See Weights and Measures (NT), Acts 27:28, *note*
9 *h* Cp. Jn. 18:18
i Cp. Mt. 14:15–21; 15:32–39
j Cp. Mt. 17:24–27
11 *k* Cp. Lk. 5:6

(4) Christ's provision for His servants (cp. Lk. 22:35; Phil. 4:19)

12 Jesus said to them,
[l]"Come *and* eat breakfast." Yet
none of the disciples dared
ask Him, "Who are You?"—
knowing that it was the Lord.
13 Jesus then came and
[m]took the bread and gave it to
them, and likewise the fish.
14 This *is* now the [n]third time
Jesus showed Himself to His
disciples after He was [o]raised
from the dead.

(5) Love, the only proper motive in service (1 Cor. 13; 2 Cor. 5:14; Rev. 2:4–5)

15 So when they had eaten
breakfast, Jesus said to Simon
Peter, "Simon, *son* of Jonah,*
do you [1]love Me [p]more than
these?" He said to Him, "Yes,
Lord; You know that I love
You." He said to him, [q]"Feed
[2]My lambs."
16 He said to him again a second
time, "Simon, *son* of Jonah,*
do you love Me?" He said
to Him, "Yes, Lord; You know
that I love You." He said to him,
[r]"Tend My [s]sheep."
17 He said to him the [t]third
time, "Simon, *son* of Jonah,* do
you [3]love Me?" Peter was
grieved because He said to him
the third time, "Do you love
Me?" And he said to Him, "Lord,
You know all things; You know

*21:15 NU-Text reads *John.* 21:16 NU-Text reads *John.* 21:17 NU-Text reads *John.*

12 *l* Cp. Gen. 7:1; Isa. 1:18; 55:1; Mt. 11:28; Rev. 22:17
13 *m* Cp. Lk. 24:29–32
14 *n* Cp. Jn. 20:19,26
o *Resurrection:* v. 14; Acts 1:3. (2 Ki. 4:35; 1 Cor. 15:52, *note*)
15 *p* i.e. *than the other disciples do*
q vv. 16,17; Acts 20:28; 1 Tim. 4:16; 1 Pet. 5:2
16 *r* Or *Nurture.* 1 Pet. 5:2
s Ps. 79:13; Mt. 10:16; 15:24; 25:33; 26:31; cp. Jn. 10:1–16
17 *t* Cp. Jn. 13:38; 18:15–27

[1](21:15) In vv. 15–17 two different Greek verbs are used for "love": *agapaō, to love deeply,* used of divine love in 14:21, and of the love which the law demands (Lk. 10:27); and *phileō, to be fond of,* a love of lesser degree than *agapaō,* as between friends. In the first two instances, where the Lord asks Peter, "Do you love Me?" He uses *agapaō;* but Peter, remembering his three denials of the Lord and aware now of his own weakness, does not dare to reply with as strong a word as *agapaō.* Instead, he employs *phileō* in his reply, "Yes, Lord; You know that I love You." When the Lord inquires the third time, "Do you love Me," He uses the lesser word, *phileō.* And again the humbled disciple replies: "Lord, You know all things; You know that I love [*phileō*] You."

[2](21:15) Christ's threefold repetition of the pronoun "My"—"My lambs . . . My sheep . . . My sheep" (vv. 15,16,17)—reminds all Christians who hold responsibility over others that the persons under them belong, first of all, to Christ. Pastors, missionaries, teachers, and parents are but undershepherds to whose care Christ's sheep are committed. Cp. Heb. 13:20; 1 Pet. 5:3.

[3](21:17) With his confidence in himself greatly shaken through having so recently denied his Lord, Peter feels unworthy to express his love to Christ by the strong word *agapaō,* and therefore uses the weaker word *phileō.* See 21:15, *note 1.* Jesus now condescends to Peter's self-evaluation, saying, in effect: "Even if you do not trust your own emotions far enough to apply the word *agapaō* to them, you still should feed my sheep." Our duty to Christ should depend, not upon the strength of our subjective feelings, but upon our realization of what He has done for us.

that I love You." Jesus said to
him, "Feed My [a]sheep.

(6) The Master reveals to Peter that He determines the time and manner of His servants' death

18 [b]"Most assuredly, I say to
you, when you were younger,
you girded yourself and walked
where you [c]wished; but when
you are old, you will stretch out
your hands, and another will
gird you and carry *you* where
you do [d]not wish."
19 This He spoke, [e]signify-
ing [f]by what death he would
glorify God. And when He had
spoken this, He said to him,
[g]"Follow Me."

(7) All His servants will not die (cp. 1 Cor. 15:51–52; 1 Th. 4:14–18)

20 Then Peter, turning
around, saw the disciple [h]whom
Jesus loved following, [i]who also
had leaned on His breast at the
supper, and said, "Lord, who is
the one who betrays You?"
21 Peter, seeing him, said to
Jesus, "But Lord, what *about*
this man?"
22 Jesus said to him, "If I will
that he remain [j]till I [k]come,
what *is that* to you? [g]You follow Me."
23 Then this saying went out
among the brethren that this
disciple would not die. Yet Jesus did not say to him that he
would not die, but, "If I will that
he remain [j]till I [k]come, what *is
that* to you?"
24 This is the [h]disciple who
[l]testifies of these things, and
[m]wrote these things; and we
know that his testimony is true.
25 And there are also [n]many
other things that Jesus did,
which if they were written one
by one, I suppose that even the
[o]world itself could not contain
the books that would be written.
Amen.

17
a Ps. 79:13; Mt. 10:16; 15:24; 25:33; 26:31; cp. Jn. 10:1–16
18
b Jn. 1:51; 5:19,24,25; 6:26,32,47, 53; 8:34,51, 58; 10:1,7; 12:24; 13:16,20,21; 14:12; 16:20,23
c v. 3
d Acts 12:3–4
19
e Cp. Jn. 12:33; 18:32
f 2 Pet. 1:13–14
g Mt. 4:19; 16:24; cp. Lk. 14:28–33
20
h vv. 7,24; Jn. 13:23; 20:2
i Jn. 13:25
22
j Jn. 14:3; 1 Th. 1:10; 5:23
k Christ (second advent): vv. 22–23; Acts 1:11. (Dt. 30:3; Acts 1:11, *note*)
24
l Jn. 19:35
m Inspiration: v. 24; Acts 1:1. (Ex. 4:15; 2 Tim. 3:16, *note*)
25
n Jn. 20:30
o Gk. *kosmos.* See Mt. 4:8, *note*

THE ACTS

of the Apostles

Author: Luke *Theme:* First Century Missions *Date of writing:* c. A.D. 60

THE BOOK OF ACTS, written by Luke, the author of the Third Gospel, is a continuation of that narrative. Luke wrote more of the NT than any other individual. The physician and companion of Paul (see Acts 16:10, *note*), he was the first historian of the early years of the Church.

The book has often been called "The Acts of the Holy Spirit." The Holy Spirit is referred to more than fifty times in this one book, particularly in relation to baptism with the Holy Spirit, being filled with the Holy Spirit, and being led by the Holy Spirit. Acts begins with Luke's second account of the ascension of the Lord and terminates with Paul's residence in Rome as a prisoner, covering a period of more than thirty years.

This book is of highest importance because it is the only inspired account of the beginning and early work of the Church. It clarifies some of the historical references in the Pauline Epistles. Its place in the NT canon identifies it as the bridge from the Gospels to the Epistles. It is the primary textbook for the study of missionary principles, the defense of the faith, the Person and work of the Holy Spirit, and the methods and themes of Christian preaching.

Acts may be divided as follows:

I. The Waiting Church, 1.
II. From Pentecost to the Conversion of Saul, 2—8.
III. From the Conversion of Saul to the First Missionary Journey, 9—12.
IV. The First Missionary Journey, 13—14.
V. The Council at Jerusalem, 15:1–35.
VI. The Second Missionary Journey, 15:36—18:22.
VII. The Third Missionary Journey, 18:23—21:14.
VIII. From Jerusalem to Rome, 21:15—28:31.

CHAPTER 1

I. The Waiting Church, 1

Introduction: Christ's 40-day ministry

1 THE [a]former account I
made, O [b]Theophilus, of all
that Jesus began both to do and
teach,
2 until the day in which He
was taken up, after He through
the Holy [c]Spirit had given commandments
to the apostles
whom He had [d]chosen,
3 to whom He also [e]presented
Himself [f]alive after His
suffering by many infallible
proofs, being seen by them during
[1]forty days and speaking of
the things pertaining to the
[g]kingdom of God.
4 And being assembled together
with *them,* He commanded
them not to depart
from Jerusalem, but to wait for
the Promise of the Father,
"which," *He said,* "you have
[h]heard from Me;
5 "for John truly [i]baptized
with water, but you shall be
[j]baptized with the Holy [c]Spirit
not many days from now."
6 Therefore, when they had
come together, they asked Him,
saying, "Lord, will You at this
time restore the [2k]kingdom to
Israel?"
7 And He said to them, "It is
not for you to [l]know times or
seasons which the Father has
put in His own authority.

The commission to evangelize the world (cp. Mt. 28:18–20; Mk. 16:15–18; Lk. 24:47–48; Jn. 20:21–22)

8 "But you shall receive

1
a i.e. *The Gospel according to Luke. Inspiration:* v. 1; Acts 1:16. (Ex. 4:15; 2 Tim. 3:16)
b Lk. 1:3
2
c Holy Spirit (NT): vv. 2,5; Acts 1:8. (Mt. 1:18; Acts 2:4, *note*)
d Election (personal): v. 2; Acts 6:5. (Dt. 7:6; 1 Pet. 5:13, *note*)
3
e c. A.D. 29
f Resurrection: vv. 2–3; Acts 1:22. (2 Ki. 4:35; 1 Cor. 15:52, *note*)
g See Mt. 6:33, *note*
4
h Jn. 14:16–17,26
5
i See Acts 8:12, *note*
j Mt. 3:11; see Acts 2:4, *note*, par. (5)
6
k Kingdom (NT): vv. 6–7; Acts 2:30. (Mt. 2:2; 1 Cor. 15:24, *note*). See Mt. 3:2, *note*
7
l Mt. 24:36

---

[1](1:3) This is the only reference in the Bible to the length of Christ's postresurrection ministry on the earth.

[2](1:6) For forty days the risen Lord had been instructing the apostles about the kingdom of God, teaching them out of the Scriptures (Lk. 24:27,32,44–45). One point was left untouched, i.e. the time when He would restore the kingdom to Israel; hence the apostles' question. Observe that the Lord did not rebuke them for their inquiry about the restoration of the kingdom. Their question was a valid one. But His answer was in accord with His repeated teaching: the time is God's secret (Mt. 24:36,42,44; 25:13; cp. 1 Th. 5:1).

8
a See Acts 19:2, *note*
b *Holy Spirit* (NT): vv. 8,16; Acts 2:4. (Mt. 1:18; Acts 2:4, *note*)
c Acts 8:5
d Col. 1:23; Rev. 14:6
9
e *Christ* (first advent): vv. 9–11; Acts 2:22. (Gen. 3:15; Acts 1:11, *note*)
f Mk. 16:19; Heb. 4:14; 9:24; 1 Pet. 3:22
g See Lk. 24:51 and 2 Cor. 12:2, *notes*
h Cp. Mt. 24:30; 1 Th. 4:17; Rev. 1:7; 11:12
10
i Cp. 2 Cor. 12:2
11
j *Christ* (second advent): v. 11; Acts 3:20. (Dt. 30:3;

power [a]when the Holy [b]Spirit
has come upon you; and you
shall be [1]witnesses to Me* in Jerusalem, and in all Judea and
[c]Samaria, and to the [d]end of
the earth."
9 Now when He had spoken these things, while they
watched, [e]He was [f]taken [g]up,
and a [h]cloud received Him out
of their sight.

The promise of Christ's return to the earth

10 And while they looked
steadfastly toward [i]heaven as
[e]He [f]went [g]up, behold, two
men stood by them in white apparel,
11 who also said, "Men of
Galilee, why do you stand gazing up into heaven? [e]This *same*
Jesus, who was [f]taken [g]up
from you into heaven, will so
[2j]come in like manner as you
saw Him go into heaven."

Waiting for the Spirit (cp. v. 5)

12 Then they returned to Jerusalem from the mount called
Olivet, which is near Jerusalem,
a Sabbath [k]day's journey.
13 And when they had en-
tered, they went up into [l]the upper room where they were staying: [m]Peter, James, John, and
Andrew; Philip and Thomas;
Bartholomew and Matthew;
James *the son* of Alphaeus and
Simon the Zealot; and Judas
the son of [n]James.
14 These all [o]continued with
one accord in prayer and supplication,* with the women and
Mary the mother of Jesus, and
with His [p]brothers.

Matthias chosen to take Judas' place

15 And in those days [q]Peter
stood up in the midst of the disciples* (altogether the number
of names was about a hundred
and twenty), and said,
16 "Men *and* brethren, this
Scripture had to be fulfilled,
which the Holy [b]Spirit [r]spoke
before by the mouth of David
concerning [s]Judas, who became a guide to those who arrested Jesus;

*

1:8 NU-Text reads *My witnesses.*
1:14 NU-Text omits *and supplication.*
1:15 NU-Text reads *brethren.*

Acts 1:11, *note*)
12
k See Weights and Measures (NT), Acts 27:28, *note*
13
l Cp. Mk. 14:15; Jn. 20:19
m Mt. 10:2
n See Mt. 4:21, *note*
14
o Cp. Eph. 6:18
p Cp. Jn. 7:5
15
q Cp. Acts 2:14–40
16
r *Inspiration:* v. 16; Acts 1:20. (Ex. 4:15; 2 Tim. 3:16, *note*)
s Ps. 41:9

[1](1:8) This command, specifying the geographical areas to be evangelized, was carried out in exactly the order prescribed here. The work of evangelizing in Jerusalem began at 2:1; in Judea and Samaria, at 8:5; and throughout the remainder of the earth, at 8:26.

[2](1:11) The Two Advents, Summary: (1) The OT foreview of the coming Messiah is presented in two aspects—that of rejection and suffering (e.g. in Isa. 53); and that of earthly glory and power (e.g. in Isa. 11; Jer. 23; Ezek. 37). Often these two aspects blend in one passage (e.g. Ps. 22). The prophets themselves were perplexed by this seeming contradiction (1 Pet. 1:10–11). It was solved by partial fulfillment. In due time the Messiah, born of a virgin according to Isaiah's prophecy (7:14), appeared among men and began His ministry by announcing the predicted kingdom as "at hand" (Mt. 4:17, *note* 4). The rejection of King and kingdom followed. (2) Thereupon the rejected King announced His approaching crucifixion, resurrection, departure, and return (Mt. 12:38–40; 16:1–4,21,27; 24; 25; Lk. 12:35–46; 17:20–36; 18:31–34; 19:12–27). (3) He uttered predictions concerning the course of events between His departure and return (Mt. 13:1–50; 16:18; 24:4–26). And (4) this promised return of Christ is a prominent theme in Acts, the Epistles, and Revelation.

Taken together the NT teachings concerning the return of Jesus Christ may be summarized as follows:

(1) The return of Christ will be personal and corporeal, in two stages: *to the air* before the Tribulation—usually called the Rapture (1 Th. 4:14–17; Phil. 3:20–21; Rev. 3:10); then He will return *to the earth* after the Tribulation (Acts 1:11; Mt. 23:39; 24:30; 25:31; Rev. 19:11–16).

(2) His coming has a threefold relation: to the Church, to Israel, and to the nations:

(a) To the Church, the descent of the Lord into the air, to raise believers who have died and to change the living Christians, is a constant expectation and hope (1 Cor. 15:51–52; Phil. 3:20; 1 Th. 1:10; 4:13–17; 1 Tim. 6:14; Ti. 2:13; Rev. 22:20).

(b) To Israel, the return of the Lord to the earth is to accomplish the yet unfulfilled prophecies of Israel's national regathering, conversion, and establishment in peace and power under the Davidic Covenant (2 Sam. 7:16, *note;* cp. Acts 15:14–17 with Zech. 14:1–9). See Kingdom (OT), 2 Sam. 7:8–17; Zech. 12:8, *note;* (NT), Lk. 1:31–33; 1 Cor. 15:24, *note*.

(c) To the Gentile nations, the return of Christ is to bring the destruction of the present political world system (Dan. 2:34–35; Rev. 19:11, *note*), and the judgment of Mt. 25:31–46, followed by world-wide Gentile conversion and participation in the blessings of the kingdom (Isa. 2:2–4; 11:10; 60:3; Zech. 8:3,20–23; 14:16–21).

18
[a] Mt. 27:3–10; cp. Zech. 11:12–13; 2 Pet. 2:15
20
[b] *Inspiration:* v. 20; Acts 2:16. (Ex. 4:15; 2 Tim. 3:16, *note*)
[c] Ps. 69:25
[d] Ps. 109:8
[e] Gk. *episkopē, overseership.* See Ti. 1:5, *note*
22
[f] See Acts 8:12, *note*

17 "for he was numbered
with us and obtained a part in
this ministry."
18 (Now this man [a]pur-
chased a field with the wages of
iniquity; and falling headlong,
he burst open in the middle and
all his entrails gushed out.
19 And it became known to
all those dwelling in Jerusalem;
so that field is called in their
own language, Akel Dama, that
is, Field of Blood.)
20 "For it is [b]written in the
book of Psalms:

[c]*'Let his dwelling place be*
desolate,
And let no one live in it';

and,

[d]*'Let another take his*
[e]*office.'*

21 "Therefore, of these men
who have accompanied us all
the time that the Lord Jesus
went in and out among us,
22 "beginning from the [f]bap-
tism of John to that day when
He was [g]taken up from us, one
of these must become a witness
with us of His [h]resurrection."
23 And they proposed two:
Joseph called Barsabas, who
was surnamed Justus, and Matthias.
24 And they [i]prayed and
said, "You, O Lord, who know
the [j]hearts of all, show which of
these two You have chosen
25 "to take part in this ministry and apostleship from which
Judas by [k]transgression fell,
that he might go to his own
place."
26 And they cast their lots,
and the lot fell on Matthias. And
he was [l]numbered with the
eleven apostles.

II. From Pentecost to the Conversion of Saul, 2—8

Sixth dispensation: the Church. Pentecost: the Spirit sent from heaven
(Jn. 7:37–39; cp. 1 Cor. 12:12–13)

2 [m]WHEN the [1n]Day of Pentecost had fully come, they

[g] vv. 9–11
[h] *Resurrection:* v. 22; Acts 2:24. (2 Ki. 4:35; 1 Cor. 15:52, *note*)
24
[i] *Bible prayers (NT):* vv. 24–25; Acts 4:24. (Mt. 6:9; Lk. 11:2, *note*)
[j] 1 Sam. 16:7
25
[k] See Rom. 3:23, *note*
26
[l] v. 17
CHAPTER 2
1
[m] c. A.D. 29
[n] Acts 20:16; see Lev. 23:16, *note*

[1](2:1) *The Sixth Dispensation: the Church.* A new age was announced by our Lord Jesus Christ in Mt. 12:47—13:52. The Church was clearly prophesied by Him in Mt. 16:18 (cp. Mt. 18:15–19), purchased by the shedding of His blood on Calvary (Rom. 3:24–25; 1 Cor. 6:20; 1 Pet. 1:18–19), and constituted as the Church after His resurrection and ascension at Pentecost when, in accordance with His promise (Acts 1:5), individual believers were for the first time baptized with the Holy Spirit into a unified spiritual organism, likened to a body of which Christ is the Head (1 Cor. 12:12–13; Col. 2:19). Because of the emphasis upon the Holy Spirit, this age has also been called "the dispensation of the Spirit."

The point of testing in this dispensation is the Gospel of our Lord Jesus Christ, the message of good news about His death and resurrection (Jn. 19:30; Acts 4:12; 1 Cor. 15:3–5; 2 Cor. 5:21; etc.). The continuing, cumulative revelation of the previous dispensations combines with this fuller revelation to emphasize the utter sinfulness and lostness of man and the adequacy of the historically completed work of Christ to save by grace through faith all who come to God by Him (Jn. 14:6; Acts 10:43; 13:38–39; Rom. 3:21–26; Eph. 2:8–9; 1 Tim. 4:10; Heb. 10:12–14; 11:6). As those saved individuals who compose Christ's true Church fulfill the Lord's command to preach the Gospel to the ends of the earth (Mk. 16:15; Lk. 24:46–48; Acts 1:8), God, during this age, is taking out from Jews and Gentiles "a people for His name" (Acts 15:14), called "the Church" and henceforth carefully distinguished from both Jews and Gentiles as such (1 Cor. 10:32; Gal. 3:27–28; Eph. 2:11–18; 3:5–6).

The Lord Jesus warned that during the whole period, while the Church is being formed by the Holy Spirit, many will reject His Gospel, and many others will pretend to believe in Him and will become a source of spiritual corruption and hindrance to His purpose in this age, in the professing church. These will bring apostasy, particularly in the last days (Mt. 13:24–30,36–40,47–49; 2 Th. 2:5–8; 1 Tim. 4:1–2; 2 Tim. 3:1; 4:3–4; 2 Pet. 2:1–2; 1 Jn. 2:18–20).

The Church Age will be brought to a close by a series of prophesied events, the chief of which are: (1) The translation of the true Church from the earth to meet her Lord in the air at a point of time known to God but unrevealed to men, and ever held before believers as an imminent and happy hope, encouraging them in loving service and holiness of life. This event is usually called "the rapture" (see 1 Th. 4:17, *note*). (2) The judgments of the seventieth week of Daniel, called "the tribulation" (see Rev. 7:14, *note*), which will fall upon mankind in general but will include the unsaved portion of the professing church, which will have gone into apostasy and thus be left behind on earth when the true Church is translated to heaven. This final form of the apostate church is described in Rev. 17 as "the harlot" which will first "ride" the political power ("beast"), only to be overthrown and absorbed by that power (cp. Rev. 18:2, *note*). And (3) the return from heaven to earth of our Lord Jesus Christ in power and glory,

were all with one accord* in
one place.
2 And suddenly there came
a sound from heaven, as of a
rushing mighty [a]wind, and it
filled the whole house where
they were sitting.

3 Then there appeared to
them divided tongues, as of fire,
and *one* sat upon each of them.
4 And they were all filled
with the [1]Holy [b]Spirit and be-

2 *a* Cp. Jn. 3:8

4 *b* *Holy Spirit* (NT): vv. 2–4; Acts 2:17. (Mt. 1:18; Acts 2:4, *note*)

*2:1 NU-Text reads *together.*

bringing with Him His Church, to set up His millennial kingdom of righteousness and peace (see Rev. 19:11 and 17, *notes*). For *notes* on other dispensations, see Innocence (Gen. 1:28); Conscience (Moral Responsibility) (Gen. 3:7); Human Government (Gen. 8:15); Promise (Gen. 12:1); Law (Ex. 19:1); Kingdom (Rev. 20:4).

[1](2:4) The Holy Spirit, NT, Summary: (1) The Holy Spirit is revealed as a divine Person. This is expressly declared (e.g. Jn. 14:16–17,26; 15:26; 16:7–15; cp. Mt. 28:19), and everywhere implied.

(2) The revelation concerning Him is progressive: (a) In the OT (see Zech. 12:10, *note*) He comes upon whom He will, apparently without reference to conditions in them. (b) During His earth-life Christ taught His disciples (Lk. 11:13) that they might receive the Spirit through prayer to the Father. (c) At the close of His ministry He promised that He would Himself pray to the Father, and that in answer to His prayer the Helper would come to abide (Jn. 14:16–17). (d) On the evening of His resurrection He came to the disciples in the upper room and breathed on them saying, "Receive the Holy Spirit" (Jn. 20:22), but He instructed them to wait before beginning their ministry until the Spirit should come upon them (Lk. 24:49; Acts 1:8). (e) On the day of Pentecost the Spirit came upon the whole body of believers (Acts 2:1–4). (f) After Pentecost the Spirit was imparted to such as believed, in some cases by the laying on of hands (Acts 8:17; 9:17). And (g) with Peter's experience in the conversion of Cornelius (Acts 10) it became clear that the norm for this age was that Jew and Gentile were to be saved on precisely the same conditions, and the Holy Spirit was to be given without delay to those who met the one essential condition of trust in Christ (Acts 10:44; 11:15–18). This is the permanent fact for the entire Church Age. Every believer is born of the Spirit (Jn. 3:3–6; 1 Jn. 5:1); indwelt by the Spirit, whose presence makes the believer's body a temple (1 Cor. 6:19; cp. Rom. 8:9–15; Gal. 4:6; 1 Jn. 2:27); and baptized with the Spirit (1 Cor. 12:12–13; 1 Jn. 2:20,27), thus sealing him for God (Eph. 1:13; 4:30).

(3) The NT distinguishes between having the Spirit, which is true of all believers, and being filled with the Spirit, which is the Christian's privilege and duty (cp. Acts 2:4 with 4:29–31;

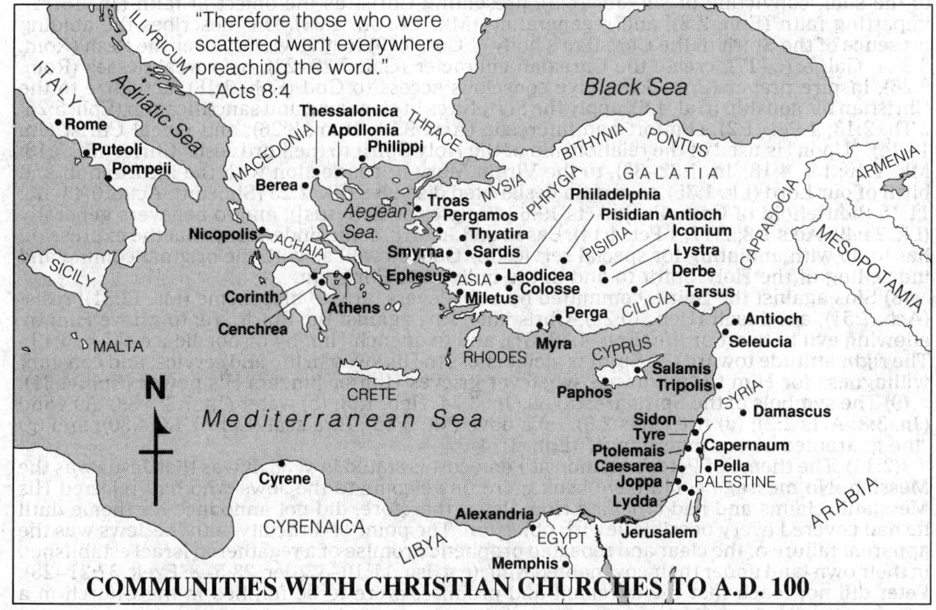

COMMUNITIES WITH CHRISTIAN CHURCHES TO A.D. 100

gan to speak with [a]other
tongues, as the Spirit gave them
utterance.
5 And there were [b]dwelling
in Jerusalem Jews, [c]devout
men, from [d]every nation under
heaven.
6 And when this sound oc-
curred, the [e]multitude came together, and were confused, because everyone heard them
speak in his own language.
7 Then they were all
[f]amazed and marveled, saying
to one another, "Look, are not
all these who speak [g]Galileans?
8 "And how *is it that* we
hear, each in our own language
in which we were born?
9 "Parthians and Medes and
Elamites, those dwelling in
Mesopotamia, Judea and [h]Cap-
padocia, [h]Pontus and [h]Asia,

10 "Phrygia and [i]Pamphylia,
Egypt and the parts of Libya
adjoining [j]Cyrene, visitors from
Rome, both Jews and [k]prose-
lytes,
11 "Cretans and Arabs—we
hear them speaking in our own
tongues the wonderful works of
God."
12 So they were all amazed
and perplexed, saying to one
another, "Whatever could this
mean?"
13 Others mocking said,
"They are full of new wine."

Peter's sermon. Theme: Jesus is Lord and Christ (v. 36)

14 But Peter, standing up
with the eleven, raised his voice
and [1]said to them, "Men of Judea and all who [l]dwell in Jeru-

4 *a* Cp. Ps. 68:18
5 *b* v. 14; *c* Acts 8:2; cp. Lk. 2:25; *d* vv. 9–11
6 *e* Acts 4:32
7 *f* v. 12; *g* Lk. 13:1; Jn. 4:45; cp. Mk. 14:70; Lk. 23:6
9 *h* 1 Pet. 1:1
10 *i* Cp. Acts 13:13; *j* Cp. Acts 11:20; *k* Cp. Ex. 12:48
14 *l* v. 5

Eph. 1:13–14 with 5:18). There is one baptism with the Spirit, but many fillings with the Spirit.

(4) The Holy Spirit is related to Christ in His conception (Mt. 1:18–20; Lk. 1:35), baptism (Mt. 3:16; Mk. 1:10; Lk. 3:22; Jn. 1:32–33), walk and service (Lk. 4:1,14), resurrection (Rom. 8:11), and as His witness throughout this age (Jn. 15:26; 16:8–11,13–14).

(5) The Spirit forms the Church (Mt. 16:18; Heb. 12:23, *note*) by baptizing all believers into the body of Christ (1 Cor. 12:12–13; cp. the universal address, 1 Cor. 1:1–2); imparts gifts for service to every member of that body (1 Cor. 12:7–11,27–30); guides the members in their service (Acts 16:6–7); and is Himself the power of that service (Acts 1:8; 2:4; 1 Cor. 2:4).

(6) The Spirit abides in a company of believers, making of them, corporately, a temple (1 Cor. 3:16–17).

(7) The NT indicates a threefold personal relationship of the Spirit to the believer: "with," "in," and "upon" (Jn. 14:16–17; 1 Cor. 6:19; Acts 1:8). "With" indicates the approach of God to the soul, convicting of sin (Jn. 16:9), presenting Christ as the object of faith (Jn. 16:14), imparting faith (Eph. 2:8), and regenerating (Mk. 1:8; Jn. 1:33). "In" describes the abiding presence of the Spirit in the Christian's body (1 Cor. 6:19) to give victory over the flesh (Rom. 8:2–4; Gal. 5:16–17), create the Christian character (Gal. 5:22–23), help weaknesses (Rom. 8:26), inspire prayer (Eph. 6:18), give conscious access to God (Eph. 2:18), actualize to the Christian his sonship (Gal. 4:6), apply the Scriptures in cleansing and sanctification (Eph. 5:26; 2 Th. 2:13; 1 Pet. 1:2), comfort and intercede (Acts 9:31; Rom. 8:26), and reveal Christ (Jn. 16:14). "Upon" is used of the relationship of the Holy Spirit to the Lord Jesus Christ (Mt. 3:16; Mk. 1:10; Lk. 4:18; Jn. 1:32–33), to the Virgin Mary in connection with the incarnation and birth of our Lord (Lk. 1:35), to certain designated disciples (Lk. 2:25 [Simeon]; Acts 10:44–45; 11:15 [household of Cornelius]; Acts 19:6 [disciples at Ephesus]), and to believers generally (Lk. 24:49; Acts 1:8; 2:17; 1 Pet. 4:14). Based on Lk. 4:18, some understand that the expression has to do with anointing for special service for God, as well as with the original coming and indwelling of the Holy Spirit to and in the individual Christian.

(8) Sins against the Spirit, committed by unbelievers, are: to blaspheme (Mt. 12:31), resist (Acts 7:51), and insult (Heb. 10:29). Christians' sins against the Spirit are: to grieve Him by allowing evil in heart or life (Eph. 4:30–31), and to quench Him by disobedience (1 Th. 5:19). The right attitude toward the Spirit is yieldedness to His sway in life and service, and constant willingness for Him to "put away" whatever grieves Him or hinders His power (Eph. 4:31).

(9) The symbols of the Spirit are: (a) oil (Jn. 3:34; Heb. 1:9); (b) water (Jn. 7:38–39); (c) wind (Jn. 3:8; Acts 2:2); (d) fire (Acts 2:3); (e) a dove (Mt. 3:16); (f) a seal (Eph. 1:13; 4:30); and (g) "the guarantee of our inheritance" (Eph. 1:14).

[1](2:14) The theme of Peter's sermon at Pentecost is stated in v. 36. It was that Jesus was the Messiah. No message could have been more unwelcome to the Jews who had rejected His Messianic claims and had crucified Him. Peter, therefore, did not announce his theme until he had covered every possible Jewish objection. The point of difficulty with the Jews was the apparent failure of the clear and repeated prophetic promise of a regathered Israel established in their own land under their covenanted King (e.g. Isa. 11:10–12; Jer. 23:5–8; Ezek. 37:21–28). Peter did not teach that the covenant and promises were to be fulfilled in the Church in a

salem, let this be known to you, and heed my words.

Explanation: This is the Spirit (cp. Joel 2:28–32)

15 "For these are not drunk, as you suppose, since it is *only* the [a]third hour of the day.
16 "But this is what was [b]spoken [c]by the prophet Joel:

17 *'And it shall come to*
pass in the [1]last days, says God,
That I will pour out of
My [d]Spirit on all flesh;
Your sons and your
daughters shall
prophesy,
Your young men shall
see visions,
Your old men shall
dream dreams.
18 *And on My menservants*
and on My
maidservants
I will pour out My
[d]Spirit in those days;
And they shall prophesy.
19 *I will show wonders in*
heaven above
And signs in the earth
beneath:
Blood and fire and vapor
of smoke.
20 *[e]The sun shall be turned*
into darkness,
And the moon into
blood,
Before the coming of the
great and awesome
[f]day of the LORD.
21 *And it shall come to pass*
That [g]whoever calls on
the name of the LORD
[h]Shall be [i]saved.'

Exposition: Jesus is risen and exalted as Lord and Christ. (David foretold this, vv. 25–31; cp. Ps. 16:8–11)

22 "Men of Israel, hear these words: [j]Jesus of Nazareth, a Man attested by God to you [k]by miracles, wonders, and signs which God did through Him in your midst, as you yourselves also know—
23 "Him, being delivered by the [l]determined purpose and [m]foreknowledge of God, you have taken* by lawless hands, have crucified, and put to death;
24 "whom God [n]raised up, having loosed the pains of death, because it was not possible that He should be held by it.
25 "For David [b]says concerning Him:

'I foresaw the LORD
always before my face,
For He is at my right
hand, that I may not
be shaken.
26 *Therefore my heart*
rejoiced, and my
tongue was glad;
Moreover my flesh also
will rest in hope.
27 *For You will not leave*
my soul in [o]Hades,
Nor will You allow Your
Holy One to see
[p]corruption.
28 *You have made known*
to me the ways of
[q]life;

*2:23 NU-Text omits *have taken.*

15
a 9 a.m. See Jn. 19:14, *note*
16
b *Inspiration:* vv. 16–21, 25–28; Acts 2:30. (Ex. 4:15; 2 Tim. 3:16, *note*)
c vv. 17–21; Joel 2:28–32
17
d *Holy Spirit* (NT): vv. 17–18; Acts 2:33. (Mt. 1:18; Acts 2:4, *note*)
20
e Isa. 13:10; Ezek. 32:7; Mt. 24:29; Mk. 13:24–25; Lk. 21:25; Rev. 6:12
f *Day* (of the LORD): vv. 19–20; 1 Cor. 5:5. (Ps. 2:9; Rev. 19:19)
21
g Rom. 10:13
h *Assurance/security:* v. 21; Rom. 8:38. (Ps. 23:1; Jude 1, *note*)
i See Rom. 1:16, *note*
22
j *Christ* (first advent): vv. 22–32; Acts 3:13. (Gen. 3:15; Acts 1:11, *note*)
k Jn. 5:36
23
l Acts 4:28
m *Foreknowledge:* v. 23; Rom. 8:29. (Acts 2:23; 1 Pet. 1:20)
24
n *Resurrection:* vv. 24, 27,30–32; Acts 3:15. (2 Ki. 4:35; 1 Cor. 15:52, *note*)
27
o See Lk. 16:23, *note*
p Acts 13:30–37
28
q *Life* (eternal): v. 28; Acts 3:15. (Mt. 7:14; Rev. 22:19)

so-called "spiritual" sense, but showed from Ps. 16 that David himself understood that the dead and risen Christ would fulfill the covenant and sit on his (David's) throne (vv. 25–32). In precisely the same way James (Acts 15:13–17) met the difficulty. See Kingdom (OT), Gen. 1:26–28; Zech. 12:8, *note;* (NT), Lk. 1:31–33; 1 Cor. 15:24, *note.*

[1](2:17) A distinction should be observed between "the last days" when the prediction relates to Israel (Isa. 2:2; Mic. 4:1, "latter" in some versions; see also Num. 24:14; Dt. 31:29; Jer. 23:20; 30:24; 49:39; Ezek. 38:16; Dan. 2:28; 10:14; Hos. 3:5), and the "last days" when the prediction relates to the Church (2 Tim. 3:1–8; Heb. 1:1–2; Jas. 5:3; 2 Pet. 3:1–9; see also such passages as 1 Tim. 4:1; 1 Pet. 1:5,20; 1 Jn. 2:18; Jude 18). While Acts 2:17 is part of this context and therefore relates to the Church, it should be remembered that it has reference to Israel as well and, therefore, points to a future day (see Joel 2:28, *note*). When "last days" is used of the Church, the plural form ("days") should be distinguished from the singular ("day"). The "last day" (Jn. 6:39,40,44,54; 11:24) in this usage refers to the resurrection. (In Jn. 12:48 it is used of the time when unbelievers will be judged.) The "last days," as related to the Church, began with the advent of Christ (Heb. 1:2), but the expression has special reference to the time of declension and apostasy at the end of the age (2 Tim. 3:1). The "last days," as related to Israel, are the days which, though begun in sorrow, issue in Israel's exaltation and blessing (cp. Jer. 30:4–10), i.e. the Kingdom Age (Isa. 2:2–4; Mic. 4:1–7). They are "last days," not with reference to this dispensation but in respect to the whole of Israel's history. Cp. Gen. 49:1, *note.*

You will make me full of
joy in Your
*presence.'**

29 "Men *and* brethren, let *me* speak freely to you of the patriarch David, that he is both [a]dead and buried, and his tomb is with us to this day.

30 "Therefore, being a prophet, and knowing that God had [b]sworn with an [c]oath to him that of the fruit of his body, according to the flesh, [d]He would raise up the Christ to sit on his [e]throne,*

31 "he, foreseeing this, spoke concerning the resurrection of the Christ, that His soul was not left in [f]Hades, nor did His flesh see [g]corruption.

32 "This Jesus God has raised up, of which we are all [h]witnesses.

33 "Therefore being [i]exalted to the right hand of God, and having received from the Father the [j]promise of the Holy [k]Spirit, He poured out this [l]which you now see and hear.

34 "For David did not ascend into the heavens, but he [b]says himself:

[m]*'The* LORD *said to my*
Lord,
[i]*"Sit at My right hand,*
35 *Till I make Your enemies*
Your footstool."'

36 "Therefore let all the house of Israel know assuredly that God has [i]made this Jesus, whom you [n]crucified, both Lord and Christ."

Exhortation: Repent
and be baptized

37 Now when they heard *this,* they were cut to the heart, and said to Peter and the rest of the apostles, "Men *and* brethren, what shall we do?"

38 Then Peter said to them, [o]"Repent, and let every one of you be [p]baptized in the name of Jesus Christ for the [q]remission of [r]sins; and you shall receive the gift of the Holy [k]Spirit.

39 "For the [d]promise is to you and to your children, and to all who are afar off, as many as the Lord our God will call."

40 And with many other words he testified and exhorted them, saying, "Be saved from this perverse [s]generation."

Extension: three thousand saved
and baptized; the first church

41 Then those who gladly* received his word were baptized; and that day about three thousand souls were added *to them.*

42 And they continued steadfastly in the apostles' [t]doctrine and [1]fellowship, in the breaking of bread, and in prayers.

43 Then [u]fear came upon every soul, and [v]many wonders and signs were done through the apostles.

44 Now all who [w]believed were together, and had all things in [x]common,

45 and sold their possessions and goods, and divided them among all, as anyone had need.

46 So continuing daily with one accord in the temple, and breaking bread from house to house, they ate their food with gladness and simplicity of heart,

47 praising God and having favor with all the people. And the Lord added to the [y]church* daily those who were being [z]saved.

The first apostolic miracle:
the lame man healed

3 NOW Peter and John went up together to the temple at the hour of prayer, the [aa]ninth *hour.*

2 And a certain man lame from his mother's womb was carried, whom they laid daily at the gate of the temple which is called Beautiful, to ask alms from those who entered the temple;

3 who, seeing Peter and

29
a Cp. 1 Ki. 2:10
30
b Inspiration: vv. 30–31, 34–35; Acts 3:18. (Ex. 4:15; 2 Tim. 3:16, *note*)
c 2 Sam. 7:12; Ps. 132:11
d Israel (prophecies): vv. 29–32, 39; Acts 13:17. (Gen. 12:2; Rom. 11:26, *note*)
e Kingdom (NT): v. 30; Acts 15:16. (Mt. 2:2; 1 Cor. 15:24, *note*)
31
f See Lk. 16:23, *note*
g Acts 13:30–37
32
h Acts 3:15
33
i Acts 5:31
j Lk. 24:49
k Holy Spirit (NT): vv. 33, 38–39; Acts 4:8. (Mt. 1:18; Acts 2:4, *note*)
l Acts 2:1–11
34
m Ps. 110:1; Mt. 22:44
36
n v. 23
38
o Repentance: v. 38; Acts 3:19. (Mt. 3:2; Acts 17:30, *note*)
p See Acts 8:12, *note*
q Forgiveness: v. 38; Acts 5:31. (Lev. 4:20; Mt. 26:28, *note*)
r See Rom. 3:23, *note*

40
s See Mt. 24:34, *note*
42
t Or *teaching*
43
u See Ps. 19:9, *note*
v Acts 2:22; 4:30; 5:12; 6:8; 14:3; 15:12
44
w Faith: v. 44; Acts 3:16. (Gen. 3:20; Heb. 11:39, *note*)
x See Acts 4:32, *note*
47
y Church (the true): vv. 41–47; Acts 4:32. (Mt. 16:18; Heb. 12:23)
z See Rom. 1:16, *note*
CHAPTER 3
1
aa 3 p.m. See Jn. 19:14, *note*

*
2:28 Psalm 16:8–11 **2:30** NU-Text omits *according to the flesh, He would raise up the Christ* and completes the verse with *He would seat one on his throne.*
2:41 NU-Text omits *gladly.* **2:47** NU-Text omits *to the church.*

[1](2:42) Among the factors which were present in the earliest days of the Church were the following: fellowship, prayer, preaching, doctrine, divine illumination, baptism, the Lord's Supper, miracles, and joy. See also 4:32, *note.*

John about to go into the temple, asked for alms.
4 And fixing his eyes on
him, with John, Peter said,
"Look at us."
5 So he gave them his attention, expecting to receive something from them.
6 Then Peter said, "Silver
and gold I do not have, but what
I do have I give you: [a]In the
name of Jesus Christ of Nazareth, rise up and walk."
7 And he took him by the
right hand and lifted *him* up,
and immediately his feet and
ankle bones [b]received strength.
8 So he, leaping up, stood
and walked and entered the
temple with them—walking,
leaping, and praising God.
9 And [c]all the people saw
him walking and praising God.
10 Then they knew that it
was he who sat begging alms at
the Beautiful Gate of the temple; and they were filled with
wonder and amazement at what
had happened to him.
11 Now as the lame man who
was healed held on to Peter and
John, all the people ran together to them in the [d]porch
which is called Solomon's,
greatly amazed.

Peter's second sermon. Theme: The covenants will be fulfilled

12 So when Peter saw *it,* he
responded to the people: "Men
of Israel, why do you marvel at
this? Or why look so intently at
us, as though by our own power
or godliness we had made this
man walk?
13 "The God of Abraham,
Isaac, and Jacob, the God of our
fathers, glorified His Servant
[e]Jesus, whom you delivered up
and denied in the presence of
Pilate, when he was determined
to let *Him* go.
14 "But you denied the Holy
One and the Just, and [f]asked
for a murderer to be granted to
you,
15 "and killed the [g]Prince of
[h]life, whom God [i]raised from
the dead, of which we are [j]wit-
nesses.
16 "And His name, through
[k]faith in His name, has made
this man strong, whom you see
and know. Yes, the faith which
comes through Him has given
him this perfect soundness in
the presence of you all.
17 "Yet now, brethren, I
know that you did *it* in [l]igno-
rance, as *did* also your rulers.
18 "But those things which
God [m]foretold by the mouth of
all His prophets, that [n]the
Christ would suffer, He has thus
fulfilled.
19 [o]"Repent therefore and be
[p]converted, that your [q]sins
may be blotted out, so that times
of refreshing may come from
the presence of the Lord,
20 [1]"and that He may [r]send
Jesus Christ, who was preached
to you before,*
21 "whom heaven must re-
ceive until the times of [2]res-
toration of all things, which
God has [m]spoken by the mouth
of all His [s]holy prophets since
the [t]world began.
22 "For [u]Moses truly [m]said to
the fathers, *'The* L*ORD your God
will raise up for you a* [v]*Prophet
like me from your brethren.
Him you shall hear in all things,
whatever He says to you.*

* 3:20 NU-Text and M-Text read *Christ Jesus, who was ordained for you before.*

6
a Acts 4:10
7
b Miracles (NT): vv. 1–8; Acts 5:12. (Mt. 8:3; Acts 28:8, *note*)
9
c Acts 4:16, 21
11
d Jn. 10:23; Acts 5:12
13
e Christ (first advent): vv. 12–15; Acts 3:26. (Gen. 3:15; Acts 1:11, *note*)
14
f Jn. 18:40
15
g Lit. *Author*
h Life (eternal): v. 15; Acts 5:20. (Mt. 7:14; Rev. 22:19)
i Resurrection: v. 15; Acts 4:2. (2 Ki. 4:35; 1 Cor. 15:52, *note*)
j Acts 5:32
16
k Faith: v. 16; Acts 4:4. (Gen. 3:20; Heb. 11:39, *note*)
17
l Acts 17:30; cp. Lev. 4:2; 1 Tim. 1:13
18
m Inspiration: vv. 18, 21–22; Acts 3:25. (Ex. 4:15; 2 Tim. 3:16, *note*)
n Lit. *His Christ*
19
o Repentance: v. 19; Acts 5:31. (Mt. 3:2; Acts 17:30, *note*)
p Lit. *turned again*
q See Rom. 3:23, *note*
20
r Christ (second advent): vv. 20–21; Rom. 11:26. (Dt. 30:3; Acts 1:11, *note*)
21
s Sanctification (NT): v. 21; Acts 4:27. (Mt. 4:5; Rev. 22:11)
t Gk. *aiōn.* See Mk. 10:30, *note*
22
u Law (of Moses): v. 22; Acts 5:34. (Ex. 19:1; Gal. 3:24, *note*). Dt. 18:15, 18,19; Acts 7:37
v See Lk. 24:19, *note*

[1](3:20) The appeal to repent and the promise of "times of refreshing" refer to the OT prophecy that prior to the second advent of the Messiah the godly remnant of the nation Israel will repent and turn to God in preparation for the millennial blessing to follow the second advent (cp. Dt. 30:1–3; Zech. 12:10–14). The nation as a whole rejected Peter's entreaty and, though individuals believed in Christ and were saved, there was no fulfillment of the requirements of national repentance.

[2](3:21) The word "restoration" is rendered from the Greek noun *apokatastasis* meaning *restoration to a former state* (cp. Acts 1:6). The meaning is limited by the words: "which God has spoken by the mouth of all His holy prophets since the world began." The prophets speak of the restoration of Israel to the land (see Israel, Gen. 12:2–3; Rom. 11:26; also Palestinian Covenant, Dt. 30:3, *note*); and of the restoration of the theocracy under David's Son (see Davidic Covenant, 2 Sam. 7:16, *note;* Kingdom [OT], Gen. 1:26–28; Zech. 12:8, *note*). No prediction of the conversion and restoration of the wicked dead is found in the prophets or elsewhere. Cp. Rev. 20:11–15.

23 *'And it shall be that every soul who will not hear that Prophet shall be utterly destroyed from among the people.'*

24 "Yes, and [a]all the prophets, from Samuel and those who follow, as many as have spoken, have also foretold* these days.

25 "You are sons of the prophets, and of the [b]covenant which God made with [c]our fathers, [d]saying to Abraham, *'And in your seed all the families of the earth shall be blessed.'**

26 "To you [e]first, God, having raised up His Servant Jesus, [f]sent Him to bless you, in turning away every one *of you* from your [g]iniquities."

First persecution

4 NOW as they spoke to the people, the priests, the captain of the temple, and the [h]Sadducees came upon them,

2 being greatly disturbed that they taught the people and preached in Jesus the [i]resurrection from the dead.

3 And they laid hands on them, and put *them* in custody until the next day, for it was already evening.

4 However, many of those who heard the word [j]believed; and the number of the men came to be about five thousand.

Peter addresses the Sanhedrin

5 And it came to pass, on the next day, that their rulers, elders, and [k]scribes,

6 as well as [l]Annas the high priest, [l]Caiaphas, John, and Alexander, and as many as were of the family of the high priest, were gathered together at Jerusalem.

7 And when they had set them in the midst, they asked, "By [m]what power or by what name have you done this?"

8 Then [n]Peter, filled with the Holy [o]Spirit, said to them, "Rulers of the people and elders of Israel:

9 "If we this day are judged for a good deed *done* to a helpless man, by what means he has been made well,

10 [1]"let it be known to you all, and to all the people of Israel, that by the [p]name of [f]Jesus Christ of Nazareth, whom you crucified, [q]whom God [i]raised from the dead, by Him this man stands here before you whole.

11 [r]"This is the [s]*'stone which was rejected by you builders, which has become the chief cornerstone.'*

12 "Nor is there [t]salvation in any other, for there is [u]no other name under heaven given among men by which we must be saved."

Sanhedrin forbids further preaching in the name of Jesus

13 Now when they saw the boldness of Peter and John, and perceived that they were [v]uneducated and untrained men, they marveled. And they realized that they had been [w]with Jesus.

14 And seeing the man who had been healed standing with them, they could say nothing against it.

15 But when they had commanded them to go aside out of the council, they conferred among themselves,

16 saying, [x]"What shall we do to these men? For, indeed, that a notable miracle has been done through them *is* evident to all who dwell in Jerusalem, and we cannot [2]deny *it*.

17 "But so that it spreads no further among the people, let us severely threaten them, that from now on they speak to no man in this [p]name."

18 So they called them and commanded them [y]not to speak at all nor teach in the [p]name of Jesus.

19 But Peter and John [z]answered and said to them, "Whether it is right in the sight of God to listen to you more than to God, you judge.

24
a Lk. 24:25
25
b See Gen. 12:2, *note*
c Lit. *your*
d Inspiration: v. 25; Acts 4:25. (Ex. 4:15; 2 Tim. 3:16, *note*)
26
e Rom. 1:16; cp. Rom. 2:9–10
f Christ (first advent): v. 26; 4:10–11; Acts 4:26. (Gen. 3:15; Acts 1:11, *note*)
g See Rom. 3:23, *note*
CHAPTER 4
1
h Mt. 22:23; see Mt. 3:7, *note* 2
2
i Resurrection: vv. 2, 10; Acts 4:33. (2 Ki. 4:35; 1 Cor. 15:52, *note*)
4
j Faith: v. 4; Acts 4:32. (Gen. 3:20; Heb. 11:39, *note*)
5
k See Mt. 2:4, *note*
6
l Lk. 3:2; Jn. 11:49; 18:13
7
m Mt. 21:23
8
n Cp. Lk. 12:11–12
o Holy Spirit (NT): v. 8; Acts 4:31. (Mt. 1:18; Acts 2:4, *note*)

10
p Acts 3:6,16
q Acts 2:24
11
r Ps. 118:22; Mt. 21:42
s Christ (Stone): v. 11; Rom. 9:32. (Gen. 49:24; 1 Pet. 2:8)
12
t See Rom. 1:16, *note*
u Jn. 14:6; 1 Tim. 2:5
13
v Cp. Mt. 11:25; 1 Cor. 1:27
w Cp. Jn. 7:15–17
16
x Cp. Jn. 11:47
18
y Acts 5:28; cp. Amos 2:12; 7:13
19
z Acts 5:29; cp. 1 Cor. 9:16

*
3:24 NU-Text and M-Text read *proclaimed.*
3:25 Genesis 22:18; 26:4; 28:14

[1](4:10) There is no record that here or at any later time the Sanhedrin ever attempted to deny the fact of Christ's resurrection.

[2](4:16) The Sanhedrin could not deny that a miracle had been done, but they would not admit it either.

20 [a]"For we cannot but
speak the things which we
[b]have seen and heard."
21 So when they had further
threatened them, they let them
go, finding no way of punishing
them, [c]because of the people,
since they all [d]glorified God for
what had been [e]done.
22 For the man was over
forty years old on whom this
miracle of healing had been
performed.

Christians again filled with the Spirit (cp. Acts 2:1–4)

23 And being let go, they
went to their own [f]*companions*
and reported all that the chief
priests and elders had said to
them.
24 So when they heard that,
they [g]raised their voice to God
with one accord and said:
"Lord, You *are* God, [h]who made
heaven and earth and the sea,
and all that is in them,
25 "who by the mouth of
Your servant David* have
[i]said:

'Why did the nations
rage,
And the people plot vain
things?
26 *The kings of the earth*
took their stand,
And the rulers were
[1]*gathered together*
Against the [j]*LORD and*
against His [k]*Christ.'*

27 "For truly against Your
[l]holy [m]Servant Jesus, whom
You anointed, both [n]Herod and
Pontius Pilate, with the Gentiles
and the people of Israel, were
gathered together
28 "to do whatever Your
hand and Your purpose [o]deter-
mined before to be done.
29 "Now, Lord, look on their
threats, and grant to Your servants that with all boldness they
may [p]speak Your word,
30 "by stretching out Your
hand to heal, and that signs and
wonders may be done through
the name of Your [l]holy [q]Ser-
vant Jesus."
31 And when they had
prayed, the place where they
were assembled together was
shaken; and they were all filled
with the Holy [r]Spirit, and they
spoke the word of God with
boldness.

Voluntary sharing among believers at Jerusalem (cp. Acts 2:42–47)

32 Now the multitude of
[s]those who [t]believed were of
[u]one heart and one soul; neither
did anyone say that any of the
things he possessed was his
own, but they had all things in
[2]common.
33 And with great power the
apostles gave [v]witness to the
[w]resurrection of the Lord Jesus.
And great [x]grace was upon
them all.
34 Nor was there anyone
among [s]them who lacked; for
all who were possessors of
lands or houses sold them, and
brought the proceeds of the
things that were sold,
35 and laid *them* at the apostles' feet; and they distributed to
each as anyone had need.
36 And Joses,* who was also
named Barnabas by the apostles (which is translated Son of
[y]Encouragement), a Levite of
the country of Cyprus,
37 having land, sold *it*, and
brought the money and laid *it* at
the apostles' feet.

*4:25 NU-Text reads *who through the Holy Spirit, by the mouth of our father, Your servant David.* 4:36 NU-Text reads *Joseph.*

20
a Cp. Job 32:19; Jer. 20:9; Amos 3:8
b 1 Jn. 1:1,3
21
c Cp. Acts 5:26
d Mt. 15:31; cp. 1 Chr. 29:11
e Acts 3:7–8
23
f Acts 2:44–46
24
g *Bible prayers* (NT): vv. 24–30; Acts 7:59. (Mt. 6:9; Lk. 11:2, *note*)
h Ex. 20:11
25
i *Inspiration:* v. 25; Acts 7:2. (Ex. 4:15; 2 Tim. 3:16, *note*). See Ps. 2:6, *note*
26
j *Christ* (first advent): vv. 26–27; Acts 7:52. (Gen. 3:15; Acts 1:11, *note*)
k i.e. *Anointed.* Ps. 2:2
27
l *Sanctification* (NT): vv. 27,30; Acts 6:13. (Mt. 4:5; Rev. 22:11)
m v. 30; cp. Acts 3:13
n Lk. 23:11–12. This is *Herod Antipas,* son of Herod, the Great. See Mk. 6:14, *note*
28
o Acts 2:23
29
p Cp. Acts 19:8; Eph. 6:19
30
q v. 27
31
r *Holy Spirit* (NT): v. 31; Acts 5:3. (Mt. 1:18; Acts 2:4, *note*)
32
s *Church* (the true): vv. 32,34; Acts 5:11. (Mt. 16:18; Heb. 12:23)
t *Faith:* v. 32; Acts 5:14. (Gen. 3:20; Heb. 11:39, *note*)
u Cp. Jn. 17:21
33
v Acts 1:22
w *Resurrection:* v. 33; Acts 5:30. (2 Ki. 4:35; 1 Cor. 15:52, *note*)
x *Grace:* v. 33; Acts 11:23. (Jn. 1:14; Jn. 1:17, *note*)
36
y Or *Exhortation*

[1](4:26) The Greek word for "gathered together" is used for the gathering of harvest (Mt. 25:24,26) and often for the gathering of powerful groups determined to put Jesus to death—i.e. the Pharisees (Jn. 11:47), the chief priests (Mt. 26:3,57), and the band of soldiers (Mt. 27:27). It is also employed for the gathering together of the kings of the earth by demons at the end of the age (Rev. 16:14,16; cp. Ps. 2:2).

[2](4:32) The experience of the Christians of the Jerusalem church in sharing their possessions is not to be taken as normative for all Christian churches or communities. This voluntary sharing of possessions in the time of persecution is a beautiful evidence of the oneness of the believers. However, it should be observed that this communal sharing was (1) voluntary (v. 32; cp. 5:4); (2) in a time of persecution (v. 29); and (3) evidently restricted to the Jerusalem church.

Ananias and Sapphira lie to the Holy Spirit

5 BUT a certain man named Ananias, with Sapphira his wife, sold a possession.

2 And he [a]kept back *part* of the proceeds, his wife also being aware *of it,* and brought a certain [b]part and laid *it* at the apostles' feet.

3 But Peter said, "Ananias, [c]why has [d]Satan filled your heart to [1]lie to the Holy [e]Spirit and keep back *part* of the price of the land for yourself?

4 "While it remained, was it not your own? And after it was sold, was it not in your own control? Why have you conceived this thing in your heart? You have not lied to men [f]but to God."

5 Then Ananias, hearing these words, fell down and breathed his last. So great fear came upon all those who heard these things.

6 And the [g]young men arose and wrapped him up, [h]carried *him* out, and buried *him.*

7 Now it was about three hours later when his wife came in, not knowing what had happened.

8 And Peter answered her, "Tell me whether you sold the land for so much?" She said, "Yes, for so much."

9 Then Peter said to her, "How is it that you have agreed together to [i]test the [e]Spirit of the Lord? Look, the feet of those who have buried your husband *are* at the door, and they will carry you out."

10 Then immediately she fell down at his feet and breathed her last. And the [h]young men came in and found her dead, and carrying *her* out, buried *her* by her husband.

11 So great fear came upon all the [j]church and upon all who heard these things.

Mighty miracles at Jerusalem

12 And through the hands of the apostles many [k]signs and wonders were [l]done among the people. And they were all with one accord in Solomon's [m]Porch.

13 Yet none of the rest dared join them, but the people esteemed them highly.

14 And [n]believers were increasingly [j]added to the Lord, multitudes of both men and women,

15 so that they brought the sick out into the streets and laid *them* on beds and couches, that at least the [o]shadow of Peter passing by might fall on some of them.

16 Also a multitude gathered from the surrounding cities to Jerusalem, [p]bringing sick people and those who were tormented by unclean spirits, and they were all [l]healed.

Second persecution

17 Then the high priest rose up, and all those who *were* with him (which is the sect of the [q]Sadducees), and they were filled with [r]indignation,

18 and [s]laid their [t]hands on the apostles and put them in the common [u]prison.

19 [v]But at night an [w]angel of the Lord [l]opened the prison doors and [x]brought them out, and said,

20 "Go, stand in the temple and [y]speak to the people all the words of this [z]life."

21 And when they heard *that,* they entered the temple early in the morning and taught. But the high priest and those with him came and called the [aa]council together, with all the elders of the children of Israel, and sent to the prison to have them brought.

22 But when the officers came and did not find them in the prison, they returned and reported,

23 saying, "Indeed we found the prison shut securely, and the guards standing outside* before the doors; but when we opened them, we [bb]found no one inside!"

*5:23 NU-Text and M-Text omit *outside.*

CHAPTER 5

2

a Cp. Josh. 7:11–12; Mal. 3:8–9; 1 Tim. 6:10
b Cp. Acts 4:34–37

3

c Cp. 1 Chr. 21:1; Mt. 13:19; Jn. 13:2,27; Eph. 6:11, 16; 1 Pet. 5:8
d Satan: v. 3; Acts 10:38. (Gen. 3:1; Rev. 20:10)
e Holy Spirit (NT): vv. 3,9; Acts 5:32. (Mt. 1:18; Acts 2:4, *note*)

4

f Cp. Num. 16:11; 1 Sam. 8:7; Lk. 10:16; 1 Th. 4:8

6

g Lit. *younger*
h Cp. Lev. 10:4

9

i Test/tempt: v. 9; Acts 15:10. (Gen. 3:1; Jas. 1:14, *note*)

11

j Church (the true): vv. 11,14; Acts 6:1. (Mt. 16:18; Heb. 12:23)

12

k Acts 2:43; 4:30; 6:8; 14:3; 15:12
l Miracles (NT): vv. 12, 15–16, 18–25; Acts 8:6. (Mt. 8:3; Acts 28:8, *note*)

m Acts 3:11

14

n Faith: v. 14; Acts 6:5. (Gen. 3:20; Heb. 11:39, *note*)

15

o Cp. Acts 19:12

16

p See Mk. 3:15, *note*

17

q See Mt. 3:7, *note 2*
r Lit. *jealousy.* Cp. Mt. 27:18; Acts 13:45

18

s Cp. Lk. 21:12
t Contrast Acts 6:6
u Acts 4:3; 16:37

19

v Cp. Lk. 21:13
w See Jud. 2:1, *note*
x Cp. Acts 12:7–11

20

y Cp. Ti. 2:15
z Life (eternal): v. 20; Acts 11:18. (Mt. 7:14; Rev. 22:19)

21

aa See Acts 23:1, *note*

23

bb Cp. 2 Sam. 22:2; Jer. 1:8; Dan. 6:27; 2 Cor. 1:10

[1](5:3) The sin of Ananias and Sapphira consisted in lying, not in keeping back their property. Observe especially v. 4.

24 Now when the high priest,* the captain of the temple, and the chief priests heard these things, they wondered what the outcome would be.

25 So one came and told them, saying,* "Look, the men whom you put in prison are standing in the temple and teaching the people!"

26 Then the captain went with the officers and brought them without violence, for they [a]feared the people, lest they should be stoned.

27 And when they had brought them, they set *them* before the [b]council. And the high priest asked them,

28 saying, "Did we not strictly* [c]command you not to teach in this name? And look, you have filled Jerusalem with your [d]doctrine, and intend to bring this Man's [e]blood on us!"

The answer of the apostles

29 But Peter and the *other* apostles answered and said: "We [f]ought to obey God rather than men.

30 "The God of our fathers [g]raised up Jesus whom you murdered by hanging on a tree.

31 "Him God has [h]exalted to His right hand *to be* [i]Prince and [j]Savior, to give [k]repentance to Israel and [l]forgiveness of [m]sins.

32 "And we are His [n]witnesses to these things, and *so* also *is* the Holy [o]Spirit whom God has given to those who obey Him."

Gamaliel's counsel: "Take heed"

33 When they heard *this,* they were [1p]furious and plotted to kill them.

34 Then one in the council stood up, a [q]Pharisee named [r]Gamaliel, a teacher of the [s]law held in respect by all the people, and commanded them to put the apostles outside for a little while.

35 And he said to them: "Men of Israel, take heed to yourselves what you intend to do regarding these men.

36 "For some time ago Theudas rose up, claiming to be somebody. A number of men, about four hundred, joined him. He was slain, and all who [t]obeyed him were scattered and came to [u]nothing.

37 "After this man, Judas of Galilee rose up in the days of the [v]census, and drew away many people after him. He also perished, and all who [t]obeyed him were dispersed.

38 "And now I say to you, keep away from these men and let them alone; for if this plan or this work is of men, it will come to [u]nothing;

39 "but if it is of God, you cannot overthrow it—lest you even be found to fight against God."

The apostles beaten and commanded to silence

40 And they agreed with him, and when they had called for the apostles and [w]beaten *them,* they commanded that they should not speak in the [x]name of Jesus, and let them go.

41 So they departed from the presence of the council, [y]rejoicing that they were counted worthy to suffer shame for His* name.

42 And daily in the temple, and in every house, they did not cease teaching and [z]preaching Jesus *as* the Christ.

Internal dissension overcome by love

6 NOW in those days, when *the* [aa]*number of* the disciples was multiplying, there arose a complaint against the Hebrews by the Hellenists,* because their widows were neglected in the daily distribution.

2 Then the twelve summoned the multitude of the disciples and said, "It is not desirable that we should leave the word of God and serve tables.

3 "Therefore, brethren, seek

5:24 NU-Text omits *the high priest.*
5:25 NU-Text and M-Text omit *saying.*
5:41 NU-Text reads *the name;* M-Text reads *the name of Jesus.* 6:1 That is, Greek-speaking Jews

26
a Cp. Mt. 21:26; Mk. 11:32; 12:12; Lk. 20:19; 22:2; Acts 4:21
27
b See Acts 23:1, *note*
28
c Acts 4:17–18
d Or *teaching.* Acts 2:42; 13:12
e Cp. Mt. 27:25
29
f Cp. Acts 4:19–20
30
g Resurrection: v. 30; Acts 9:41. (2 Ki. 4:35; 1 Cor. 15:52, *note*)
31
h Mk. 16:19; Acts 2:33; Phil. 2:9–11
i Acts 3:15; Rev. 1:5
j See Rom. 1:16, *note*
k Repentance: v. 31; Acts 8:22. (Mt. 3:2; Acts 17:30, *note*)
l Forgiveness: v. 31; Acts 8:22. (Lev. 4:20; Mt. 26:28, *note*)
m See Rom. 3:23, *note*
32
n Lk. 24:48; Acts 1:22; 10:39; 13:31; 1 Pet. 5:1
o Holy Spirit (NT): v. 32; Acts 6:3. (Mt. 1:18; Acts 2:4, *note*)
33
p Acts 7:54
34
q See Mt. 3:7, *note 1*
r Acts 22:3
s Law (of Moses): v. 34; Acts 6:13. (Ex. 19:1; Gal. 3:24, *note*)

36
t Or *believed*
u Cp. Isa. 8:10
37
v Cp. Lk. 2:1
40
w Mt. 10:17; Acts 16:22–23; 21:32; 2 Cor. 11:25
x Cp. Jas. 2:7
41
y Mt. 5:10–12; 1 Pet. 4:13
42
z Gospel: v. 42; 6:2, 4; Acts 8:4. (Gen. 12:3; Rev. 14:6)
CHAPTER 6
1
aa Church (the true): vv. 1–7; Acts 8:1. (Mt. 16:18; Heb. 12:23)

[1](5:33) Compare Acts 2:37. The Gospel, when preached in the power of the Holy Spirit, often convicts or enrages.

out from among you seven men of *good* [a]reputation, full of the Holy [b]Spirit and wisdom, whom we may appoint over this [c]business;

4 "but we will give ourselves continually to prayer and to the ministry of the word."

5 And the saying pleased the whole multitude. And they [1d]chose Stephen, a man full of [e]faith and the Holy [b]Spirit, and [f]Philip, Prochorus, Nicanor, Timon, Parmenas, and Nicolas, a proselyte from Antioch,

6 whom they set before the apostles; and when they had prayed, they laid [2]hands on them.

7 Then the word of God spread, and the number of the disciples multiplied greatly in Jerusalem, and a great many of the priests were obedient to the faith.

8 And Stephen, full of [e]faith* and power, did great [g]wonders and signs among the people.

Third persecution: Stephen brought before the council

9 Then there arose some from what is called the Synagogue of the Freedmen (Cyrenians, Alexandrians, and those from Cilicia and Asia), disputing with Stephen.

10 And they were [h]not able to resist the wisdom and the [b]Spirit by which he spoke.

11 [i]Then they secretly induced men to say, "We have heard him speak blasphemous words against Moses and God."

12 And they stirred up the people, the elders, and the [j]scribes; and they came upon *him*, seized him, and brought *him* to the council.

13 They also set up [k]false witnesses who said, "This man does not cease to speak blasphemous* words against this [l]holy place and the [m]law;

14 "for we have heard him say that this [n]Jesus of Nazareth will destroy this place and [o]change the customs which Moses delivered to us."

15 And all who sat in the council, looking steadfastly at him, [p]saw his face as the face of an [q]angel.

Stephen addresses Sanhedrin on the unbelief of Israel

7 THEN the high priest said, "Are these things so?"

2 And he said, [r]"Brethren and fathers, [s]listen: The [t]God of glory appeared to our father Abraham when he was in Mesopotamia, before he dwelt in [u]Haran,

3 "and said to him, [v]*'Get out of your country and from your relatives, and come to a land that I will show you.'**

4 [w]"Then he came out of the land of the Chaldeans and dwelt in [u]Haran. And from there, when his father was [x]dead, He moved him to this land in which you now dwell.

5 "And *God* gave him no inheritance in it, not even *enough* to set his foot on. But even [y]when *Abraham* had no child, He [z]promised to give it to him for a possession, and to his descendants after him.

6 "But God spoke in this way: that his descendants would [aa]dwell in a foreign land, and that they would bring them into [bb]bondage and oppress *them* four hundred years.

7 *'And the nation to whom they will be in bondage I will* [cc]*judge,'** said God, *'and after that they shall* [dd]*come out and serve Me in this place.'**

8 "Then He gave him the [ee]covenant of circumcision; and so *Abraham* [ff]begot Isaac and circumcised him on the eighth day; and Isaac [gg]*begot* Jacob,

*

6:8 NU-Text reads *grace.* 6:13 NU-Text omits *blasphemous.* 7:3 Genesis 12:1 7:7 Genesis 15:14 • Exodus 3:12

3
a 1 Tim. 3:7
b *Holy Spirit* (NT): vv. 3,5,10; Acts 7:51. (Mt. 1:18; Acts 2:4, *note*)
c Phil. 1:1; 1 Tim. 3:8–13
5
d *Election* (personal): vv. 3–6; Acts 9:15. (Dt. 7:6; 1 Pet. 5:13, *note*)
e *Faith:* vv. 5, 8; Acts 8:12. (Gen. 3:20; Heb. 11:39, *note*)
f Acts 8:5; 21:8
8
g Acts 2:43; 5:12; 8:15; 14:3
10
h Cp. Lk. 21:15
11
i Cp. Mt. 26:59–60; Lk. 23:2; Acts 24:5–9
12
j See Mt. 2:4, *note*
13
k Cp. Ex. 20:16
l *Sanctification* (NT): v. 13; Acts 7:33. (Mt. 4:5; Rev. 22:11)
m *Law* (of Moses): vv. 13–14; Acts 7:37. (Ex. 19:1; Gal. 3:24, *note*)
14
n Acts 10:38
o Cp. Acts 25:8
15
p Cp. Ex. 34:29–30; 2 Cor. 3:7, 18
q See Heb. 1:4, *note*
CHAPTER 7
2
r Cp. Acts 22:1
s *Inspiration:* vv. 2–53; Acts 8:28. (Ex. 4:15; 2 Tim. 3:16, *note*)
t Ps. 29:3
u Gen. 11:31, 32
3
v See Gen. 12:2, *note*
4
w Heb. 11:8–10
x Gen. 11:32
5
y Cp. Gen. 18:10–14
z Gen. 12:7; 15:7; 17:8
6
aa Gen. 15:13–14; 47:11–12
bb Ex. 1:8–14; 12:40–41
7
cc Ex. 14:13–31
dd Josh. 3:1–17
8
ee Gen. 17:9–14
ff Gen. 21:1–5
gg Gen. 25:21–26

[1](6:5) It is interesting to observe that these men were all Hellenists (see 6:1, *marg.*), as their Grecian names indicate.

[2](6:6) The laying on of hands sometimes accompanied prayer (Mt. 19:13,15) and was also used as a sign of healing (Mk. 5:23; 6:5, etc.), a symbol for the impartation of the Holy Spirit (Acts 8:17,19; 9:17; 19:6), and a token of ordination for special service (Acts 6:6; 13:3; 1 Tim. 4:14, etc.).

and Jacob [a]*begot* the twelve patriarchs.
9 "And the patriarchs, becoming [b]envious, [c]sold Joseph
into Egypt. But [d]God was with
him
10 "and delivered him out of
all his troubles, and gave him
[e]favor and wisdom in the presence of Pharaoh, king of Egypt;
and he [f]made him governor
over Egypt and all his house.
11 "Now a [g]famine and great
trouble came over all the land of
Egypt and Canaan, and our fathers found no sustenance.
12 "But [h]when Jacob heard
that there was grain in Egypt,
he sent out our fathers first.
13 "And the [i]second *time* Joseph was made known to his
brothers, and Joseph's family
became known to the Pharaoh.
14 "Then Joseph sent and
called his father Jacob and all
his [1]relatives to *him*, seventy-
five* people.
15 "So Jacob [j]went down to
Egypt; and he [k]died, he and our
fathers.
16 "And they were [l]carried
back to Shechem and laid in the
tomb that Abraham bought for
a sum of money from the sons of
[2]Hamor, [m]*the father* of Shechem.
17 "But when the [n]time of the
promise drew near which God
had [o]sworn to Abraham, the
people [p]grew and multiplied in
Egypt
18 "till another king [q]arose
who did not know Joseph.
19 "This man dealt treacherously with our people, and [r]op-
pressed our forefathers, making them expose their babies, so
that they might not live.
20 "At this time Moses was
[s]born, and was [t]well pleasing
to God; and he was brought up
in his father's house for three
months.
21 "But when he was [u]set
out, [v]Pharaoh's daughter took
him away and brought him up
as her own son.
22 "And Moses was learned
in all the wisdom of the Egyptians, and was [w]mighty in
words and deeds.
23 [x]"Now when he was forty
years old, it came into his heart
to visit his brethren, the children of Israel.
24 "And seeing one of *them*
suffer wrong, he defended and
avenged him who was op-
pressed, and struck down the
Egyptian.
25 "For he supposed that his
brethren would have understood that God would deliver
them by his hand, but they did
not understand.
26 "And the next day he appeared to two of them as they
were fighting, and *tried to* reconcile them, saying, 'Men, you
are brethren; why do you wrong
one another?'
27 "But he who did his neighbor wrong pushed him away,
saying, [3][y]*'Who made you a*
ruler and a judge over us?
28 *'Do you want to kill me as*
you did the Egyptian yester-
day?'
29 "Then, at this saying, Moses [z]fled and became a dweller
in the land of Midian, where he
[aa]had two sons.
30 [bb]"And when forty years
had passed, an [cc]Angel of the

*7:14 Or *seventy* (compare Exodus 1:5)

8
a Gen. 29:28–30:24; 35:16–18
9
b Gen. 37:11; cp. Mt. 27:18; Acts 5:17
c Gen. 37:28
d Gen. 39:2
10
e Cp. Dan. 1:9
f Gen. 41:38–44
11
g Gen. 41:54–56
12
h Gen. 42:1
13
i Gen. 45:4–16
15
j Gen. 46:5–7
k Gen. 49:33
16
l Gen. 50:13
m Or *in Shechem*
17
n vv. 6–7; Ex. 2:23–25
o See Gen. 12:2, *note*
p Ex. 1:7–9; Ps. 105:24
18
q Ex. 1:8
19
r Ex. 1:7–22
20
s Ex. 2:1–2
t Heb. 11:23
21
u Ex. 2:3–4
v Ex. 2:5–10
22
w Cp. Lk. 24:19
23
x vv. 23–29; Ex. 2:11–15
27
y Ex. 2:14; cp. Lk. 12:14
29
z Heb. 11:27
aa Ex. 2:21–22; 4:20
30
bb vv. 30–35; Ex. 3:1–10
cc See Jud. 2:1, *note*

---

[1](7:14) Compare Gen. 46:26, *note*. There is no real contradiction. The "house of Jacob" numbered seventy, but the "relatives" would include the wives of Jacob's sons.

[2](7:16) A contradiction between vv. 15–16 and Gen. 23:17; 33:19 is frequently asserted. A solution of the problem has been suggested in several ways: (1) a scribal error in naming Abraham in Acts 7:16 (but only one manuscript omits the name); (2) a telescoping of the accounts in Gen. 23 and 33 (understandable in view of Stephen's situation and the need for brevity); and (3) Abraham actually did buy two burial places (Gen. 23:17; Acts 7:15–16). The first, near Hebron, he bought from Ephron, the Hittite, in the presence of the children of Heth. The second, near Shechem, he bought from the sons of Hamor. Later Jacob must have repurchased the second in "the parcel of land . . . from the children of Hamor, Shechem's father" (Gen. 33:18–19). Since Abraham, Isaac, and Jacob were buried at Hebron (Gen. 49:31; 50:13), Stephen's reference to "our fathers" buried in Shechem (v. 16) must be restricted to Joseph and other members of the family (Josh. 24:32; Acts 7:15–16).

[3](7:27) But he became their ruler and judge. Cp. Lk. 19:14.

Lord* appeared to him in a flame of fire in a bush, in the wilderness of Mount Sinai.

31 "When Moses saw *it*, he marveled at the sight; and as he drew near to observe, the voice of the Lord came to him,

32 *"saying, 'I am the God of your fathers—the God of Abraham, the God of Isaac, and the God of Jacob.'** And Moses trembled and dared not look.

33 *'Then the* LORD *said to him,* [a]*"Take your sandals off your feet, for the place where you stand is* [b]*holy ground.*

34 [c]*"I have surely seen the oppression of My people who are in Egypt; I have heard their groaning and have come down to deliver them. And now come, I will* [d]*send you to Egypt."'**

35 "This Moses whom they rejected, saying, [e]*'Who made you a ruler and a judge?'* is the one God sent *to be* a ruler and a deliverer by the hand of the [f]Angel who appeared to him in the bush.

36 "He [g]brought them out, [h]after he had shown wonders and signs in the land of Egypt, and in the Red Sea, and in the wilderness [i]forty years.

37 "This is that Moses who [j]said to the children of Israel, *'The* LORD *your God will raise up for you a* [k]*Prophet like me from your brethren. Him you shall hear.'**

38 "This is he who was in the [1]congregation in the wilderness with the [f]Angel who spoke to him on Mount Sinai, and *with* our fathers, the one who received the living [l]oracles to give to us,

39 "whom our fathers [m]would not obey, but rejected. And in their hearts they turned back to Egypt,

40 [n]"saying to Aaron, *'Make us gods to go before us; as for this Moses who brought us out of the land of Egypt, we do not know what has become of him.'*

41 "And they [o]made a calf in those days, offered sacrifices to the idol, and [p]rejoiced in the works of their own hands.

42 "Then God turned and gave them up to worship the host of heaven, as it is written in the book of the Prophets:

[q]*'Did you offer Me*
slaughtered animals
and sacrifices during
forty years in the
wilderness,
O house of Israel?

43 *You also took up the*
tabernacle of Moloch,
And the star of your god
Remphan,
Images which you made
to worship;
And [r]*I will carry you*
away beyond
Babylon.'

44 "Our fathers had the [s]tabernacle of witness in the wilderness, as He appointed, instructing Moses to make it [t]according to the pattern that he had seen,

45 "which our fathers, having received it in turn, also [u]brought with Joshua into the land possessed by the Gentiles, whom God drove out before the face of our fathers until the [v]days of David,

46 "who found favor before God and [w]asked to find a dwelling for the God of Jacob.

47 "But Solomon [x]built Him a house.

48 "However, the Most High does [y]not dwell in temples made with hands, as the prophet says:

49 [z]*'Heaven is My throne,*
And earth is My
footstool.
What house will you
build for Me? says the
LORD,
Or what is the place of
My rest?

*
7:30 NU-Text omits *of the Lord.*
7:32 Exodus 3:6,15 7:34 Exodus 3:5,7–8,10
7:37 NU-Text and M-Text omit *Him you shall hear.*

33
a Cp. Josh. 5:15
b Sanctification (NT): v. 33; Acts 20:32. (Mt. 4:5; Rev. 22:11)
34
c Ex. 2:24–25
d Ps. 105:26
35
e Ex. 2:14
f See Jud. 2:1, *note*
36
g Ex. 12:41; Dt. 6:21,23
h Dt. 6:22; Ps. 78:12–13; cp. Acts 2:43; 5:12; 6:8; 8:13; 14:3
i Num. 14:33
37
j Law (of Moses): v. 37; Acts 7:53. (Ex. 19:1; Gal. 3:24, *note*)
k Dt. 18:15, 18–19
38
l Rom. 3:2; Heb. 5:12; 1 Pet. 4:11
39
m Ps. 95:8–11
40
n Ex. 32:1
41
o Ex. 32:2–4
p Ex. 32:6, 18–19
42
q Amos 5:25–27
43
r 2 Chr. 36:11–21; Jer. 25:9–12
44
s Or *tent of testimony*
t Ex. 25:1–27:19; Heb. 8:5
45
u Josh. 3:1–4:11
v 2 Sam. 6:2–15
46
w 2 Sam. 7:1–13; 1 Ki. 8:17; 1 Chr. 22:7; Ps. 132:4–5
47
x 1 Ki. 5:1–6:38; 8:20–21
48
y 2 Chr. 2:6; Acts 17:24
49
z Isa. 66:1–2; cp. 1 Ki. 8:27

[1](7:38) The original meaning of *ekklēsia* was *a gathering out of citizens in a public place for deliberation.* The Septuagint used it to signify the assembly of Israel. Here it is employed in its most general sense of a called-out meeting. In most instances in the NT the term indicates the body of believers, the church local or universal.

50 *Has My hand not* [a]*made*
all these things?'

51 "*You* [b]stiff-necked and
[c]uncircumcised in heart and
ears! You always resist the Holy
[d]Spirit; as your fathers *did,* so
do you.
52 "Which of the prophets
did your fathers not [e]perse-
cute? And they killed those who
foretold the [f]coming of the Just
One, of whom you now have become the betrayers and murderers,
53 "who have received the
[g]law by the direction of [h]angels
and have not kept *it.*"

Stephen, the first martyr.
First mention of Saul of Tarsus
(v. 58), later called Paul (13:9)

54 [1]When they heard these
things they were [i]cut to the
heart, and they gnashed at him
with *their* teeth.
55 But he, being full of the
Holy [d]Spirit, gazed into heaven
and saw the [j]glory of God, and
Jesus standing at the right hand
of God,
56 and said, "Look! I see the
heavens opened and the [k]Son
of Man standing at the right
hand of God!"
57 Then they cried out with a
loud voice, stopped their ears,
and ran at him with one accord;
58 and they cast *him* out of
the city and stoned *him.* And the
witnesses laid down their
clothes at the feet of a young
man named [l]Saul.
59 And they stoned Stephen
as he was calling on *God* and
[m]saying, "Lord Jesus, [n]receive
my spirit."
60 Then he knelt down and
[m]cried out with a loud voice,
"Lord, [o]do not charge them
with this [p]sin." And when he
had said this, he fell [q]asleep.

Fourth persecution: Saul takes
leading part (cp. Gal. 1:13–14)

8 NOW Saul was consenting
to his death. At that time a
great persecution arose against
the [r]church which was at Jerusalem; and they were all [s]scat-
tered throughout the regions of
Judea and Samaria, except the
apostles.
2 And devout men carried
Stephen *to his burial,* and made
great lamentation over him.
3 As for Saul, he made
havoc of the [t]church, entering
every house, and dragging off
men and women, committing
them to prison.

The first missionaries
(cp. Acts 11:19–21)

4 Therefore those who were
scattered [u]went everywhere
[2v]preaching the word.

Philip's ministry at Samaria
(The case of Simon, the sorcerer)

5 Then [w]Philip [x]went down
to the* city of Samaria and
[v]preached Christ to them.
6 And the multitudes with
one accord heeded the things
spoken by Philip, hearing and
seeing the [y]miracles which he
did.
7 For [z]unclean spirits, crying with a loud voice, came out
of many who were possessed;
and many who were paralyzed
and lame were healed.
8 And there was great joy in
that city.
9 But there was a certain
man called Simon, who previously practiced [aa]sorcery in the
city and astonished the people
of Samaria, claiming that he
was someone great,
10 to whom they all gave
heed, from the least to the greatest, saying, "This man is the
great power of God."
11 And they heeded him because he had astonished them
with his [aa]sorceries for a long
time.
12 But when they [bb]believed
[w]Philip as he [v]preached the
things concerning the [cc]king-

*8:5 Or *a*

50
a Ps. 102:25
51
b Ex. 32:9
c Cp. Dt. 10:16; 30:6; Jer. 4:4; Rom. 2:29; Col. 2:11
d Holy Spirit (NT): vv. 51,55; Acts 8:15. (Mt. 1:18; Acts 2:4, *note*)
52
e 2 Chr. 36:16; Jer. 2:30; Mt. 23:35
f Christ (first advent): v. 52; Acts 10:36. (Gen. 3:15; Acts 1:11, *note*)
53
g Law (of Moses): v. 53; Acts 10:14. (Ex. 19:1; Gal. 3:24, *note*)
h See Heb. 1:4, *note*
54
i Acts 5:33
55
j Ex. 24:17
56
k See Mt. 8:20, *note*
58
l Acts 22:20
59
m Bible prayers (NT): vv. 59–60; Acts 9:6. (Mt. 6:9; Lk. 11:2, *note*)
n Cp. Lk. 23:46; 1 Pet. 4:19
60
o Cp. Lk. 23:34
p See Rom. 3:23, *note*
q Cp. 1 Cor. 15:51; 1 Th. 4:13–17

CHAPTER 8
1
r Church (the true): v. 1; Acts 12:1. (Mt. 16:18; Heb. 12:23)
s Acts 11:19; see Acts 1:8, *note*
3
t Churches (local): v. 3; Acts 9:31. (Acts 8:3; Phil. 1:1, *note*)
4
u Mt. 10:23
v Gospel: vv. 4–5,12; Acts 8:14. (Gen. 12:3; Rev. 14:6)
5
w Acts 6:5
x See Acts 1:8, *note*
6
y Miracles (NT): vv. 6–7; Acts 8:13. (Mt. 8:3; Acts 28:8, *note*)
7
z See Mt. 7:22, *note*
9
aa Dt. 18:10–11; cp. 2 Ki. 17:17; Acts 13:6; Rev. 18:23; 21:8
12
bb Faith: v. 12; Acts 8:13. (Gen. 3:20; Heb. 11:39, *note*)
cc See Mt. 6:33, *note*

[1](7:54) False witnesses had been brought to testify before the council against Stephen (6:9–14). Stephen bore true witness against them, quoting the testimony of writings which they acknowledged to be inspired. He spoke of the persistent rejection of God and His servants by the nation, until at length the truth was brought home to them and aroused the maddened enmity in their hearts.

[2](8:4) Here began witness concerning Christ to all nations (v. 1; cp. Lk. 24:47; Acts 1:8, *note*).

13
a Faith: vv. 13–14; Acts 8:37. (Gen. 3:20; Heb. 11:39, *note*)
b Miracles (NT): v. 13; Acts 8:39. (Mt. 8:3; Acts 28:8, *note*)
14
c Acts 5:12, 29,40
d Gospel: v. 14; Acts 8:25. (Gen. 12:3; Rev. 14:6)
e Cp. Acts

dom of God and the name of Jesus Christ, both men and
women were [1]baptized.
13 Then Simon himself also
[a]believed; and when he was
baptized he continued with
Philip, and was amazed, seeing
the [b]miracles and signs which
were done.
14 Now when the [c]apostles
who were at Jerusalem heard
that Samaria had [a]received the
[d]word of God, they sent [e]Peter
and John to them,
15 who, when they had come
down, prayed for them that they
might receive the Holy [f]Spirit.
16 For as yet He had [g]fallen
upon none of them. They had
only been [h]baptized in the
[i]name of the Lord Jesus.
17 Then they [j]laid hands on
them, and they received the
Holy [f]Spirit.
18 And when Simon saw that
through the [j]laying on of the
apostles' hands the Holy [f]Spirit
was given, he offered them
[k]money,
19 saying, "Give me this

age (NT), Mt. 5:26, *note*

3:1–11
15
f Holy Spirit (NT): vv. 15–18; Acts 8:19. (Mt. 1:18; Acts 2:4, *note*)
16
g Cp. Acts 2:38
h See v. 12, *note*
i Mt. 28:19
17
j Acts 19:6; cp. Dt. 34:9
18
k See Coin-

[1](8:12) The practice of baptizing with water is introduced into the NT during the ministry of John the Baptist, whose baptism is referred to as "for the remission of sins," or, "baptism of repentance" (Mk. 1:4; Lk. 3:3; etc.). Christ Himself was baptized by John (Mt. 3:13–17; etc.). In His case it was certainly not for the reasons mentioned but as a symbol of His identification with mankind.

Before His ascension, the Lord Jesus commanded His disciples to preach the Gospel to all the world, baptizing all who believed this saving message in the name of the Father, the Son, and the Holy Spirit (Mt. 28:19; Mk. 16:15–16). This command was faithfully obeyed by the early Church beginning with the day of Pentecost (Acts 2:38,41; 8:12–13,36–38; 9:18; 10:48; 16:14–15,32–33; 18:8; 19:5; 22:13–16).

Baptism has, since the apostolic age, been practiced by every major group in the Christian church and, in Protestant communions, is recognized as one of two sacraments—the other being the Lord's Supper. Since early in the Church's history three different modes of baptism have been used: aspersion (sprinkling); affusion (pouring); and immersion (dipping).

John the Baptist, and our Lord also, prophesied a baptism with the Holy Spirit (Mt. 3:11; Jn. 1:33; Acts 1:5; 11:16). See 1 Cor. 12:12–13; Acts 2:4, *note* on Holy Spirit, paragraph (5).

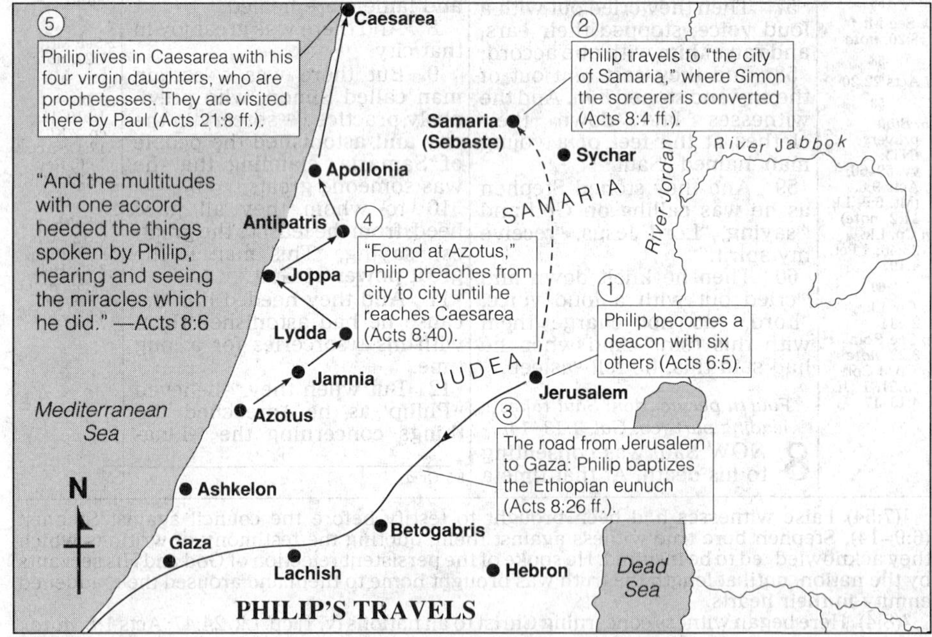
5
Philip lives in Caesarea with his four virgin daughters, who are prophetesses. They are visited there by Paul (Acts 21:8 ff.).
Caesarea
2
Philip travels to "the city of Samaria," where Simon the sorcerer is converted (Acts 8:4 ff.).
Samaria (Sebaste)
Sychar
River Jabbok
River Jordan
Apollonia
"And the multitudes with one accord heeded the things spoken by Philip, hearing and seeing the miracles which he did." —Acts 8:6
SAMARIA
Antipatris
4
"Found at Azotus," Philip preaches from city to city until he reaches Caesarea (Acts 8:40).
Joppa
1
Philip becomes a deacon with six others (Acts 6:5).
Lydda
Jamnia
JUDEA
Jerusalem
Mediterranean Sea
Azotus
3
The road from Jerusalem to Gaza: Philip baptizes the Ethiopian eunuch (Acts 8:26 ff.).
N
Ashkelon
Betogabris
Gaza
Lachish
Hebron
Dead Sea
PHILIP'S TRAVELS

power also, that anyone on
whom I lay hands may receive
the Holy [a]Spirit."
20 But Peter said to him,
"Your [b]money [c]perish with
you, because you thought that
the [d]gift of God could be purchased with money!
21 "You have neither part
nor portion in this matter, for
your [e]heart is not right in the
sight of God.
22 [f]"Repent therefore of this
your wickedness, and pray God
if perhaps the thought of your
[e]heart may be [g]forgiven you.
23 "For I see that you are poisoned by [h]bitterness and bound
by [i]iniquity."
24 Then Simon answered
and said, [j]"Pray to the Lord for
me, that none of the things
which you have spoken may
come upon me."
25 So when they had [k]testi-
fied and preached the word of
the Lord, they returned to Jerusalem, preaching the [l]gospel
[m]in many villages of the Samaritans.

Philip and the Ethiopian treasurer

26 Now [n]an [o]angel of the
Lord spoke to [p]Philip, saying,
"Arise and [q]go [r]toward the
south along the road which
goes down from Jerusalem to
Gaza." This is desert.
27 So he arose and went. And
behold, a man of [s]Ethiopia, a
eunuch of great authority under
Candace the queen of the Ethiopians, who had charge of all her
treasury, and had [t]come to Jerusalem to worship,
28 was returning. And sitting
in his chariot, he was reading
Isaiah the [u]prophet.
29 Then the [a]Spirit said to
Philip, "Go near and overtake
this chariot."
30 So Philip ran to him, and
heard him reading the [u]prophet
Isaiah, and said, [v]"Do you understand what you are reading?"
31 And he said, [w]"How can I,
unless someone [x]guides me?"
And he asked Philip to come up
and sit with him.
32 The place in the [u]Scrip-
ture which he read was this:

[y]*"He was led as a sheep to*
the slaughter;
And as a lamb before its
shearer is silent,
[z]*So He opened not His*
mouth.
33 *In His humiliation His*
[aa]*justice was taken*
away,
And who will declare His
generation?
For His life is [bb]*taken*
from the earth."

34 So the eunuch answered
Philip and said, "I ask you, of
whom does the prophet say this,
of himself or [cc]of some other
man?"
35 Then Philip opened his
mouth, and [dd]beginning at this
Scripture, [l]preached Jesus to
him.
36 Now as they went down
the road, they came to some water. And the eunuch said, "See,
here is water. What hinders me
from being [ee]baptized?"
37 Then Philip said, [ff]"If you
believe with all your heart, you
may." And he answered and
said, "I [gg]believe that Jesus
Christ is the Son of God."*
38 So he commanded the
chariot to stand still. And both
Philip and the eunuch went
down into the water, and he
[ee]baptized him.
39 Now when they came up
out of the water, the [a]Spirit of
the Lord [hh]caught Philip away,
so that the eunuch saw him no
more; and he went on his way
[ii]rejoicing.
40 But Philip was found at
Azotus. And passing through,
he preached in all the cities till
he came to [jj]Caesarea.

III. From the Conversion of Saul to the First Missionary Journey, 9—12

Saul's conversion
(Acts 22:1–16; 26:9–18)

9 [kk]THEN [ll]Saul, still breathing threats and murder
against the disciples of the
Lord, went to the high priest
2 and asked [mm]letters from
him to the synagogues of Da-

* 8:37 NU-Text and M-Text omit this verse. It is found in Western texts, including the Latin tradition.

19
a Holy Spirit (NT): vv. 15–19, 29,39; Acts 9:17. (Mt. 1:18; Acts 2:4, *note*)
20
b See Coinage (NT), Mt. 5:26, *note*
c Cp. 2 Ki. 5:16
d Acts 2:38
21
e Jer. 17:9; cp. Mt. 15:8, 19
22
f Repentance: v. 22; Acts 11:18. (Mt. 3:2; Acts 17:30, *note*)
g Forgiveness: v. 22; Acts 13:38. (Lev. 4:20; Mt. 26:28, *note*)
23
h Cp. Jer. 4:18; Eph. 4:31
i See Rom. 3:23, *note*
24
j Cp. Ex. 8:8; Num. 21:7; Jer. 42:2
25
k Cp. Ps. 66:16; 107:2; Isa. 63:7
l Gospel: vv. 25,35; Acts 9:20. (Gen. 12:3; Rev. 14:6)
m See Acts 1:8, *note*
26
n See Jud. 2:1, *note*
o See Heb. 1:4, *note*
p Acts 6:5
q Mt. 28:19
r Or *at noon*
27
s Ps. 68:31
t 1 Ki. 8:41–42; cp. Jn. 12:20
28
u Inspiration: vv. 28, 30,32–33; Acts 10:43. (Ex. 4:15; 2 Tim. 3:16, *note*)
30
v Cp. Lk. 24:45
31
w Cp. Rom. 10:14–15
x Cp. Jn. 16:13
32
y Isa. 53:7–8
z Mt. 26:62–63; 27:12,14; Jn. 19:9
33
aa Lk. 23:1–25
bb Lk. 23:33–46
34
cc Cp. Acts 2:30–31; 1 Pet. 1:10–11; Rev. 19:10
35
dd Cp. Lk. 24:27–45; Acts 10:43; 17:2–3
36
ee Acts 16:33; see Acts 8:12, *note*
37
ff Rom. 10:9–10
gg Faith: v. 37; Acts 9:42. (Gen. 3:20; Heb. 11:39, *note*)
39
hh Miracles (NT): vv. 39–40; Acts 9:18. (Mt. 8:3; Acts 28:8, *note*). Cp. 1 Ki. 18:12; 2 Cor. 12:2
ii Cp. Acts 16:34
40
jj Acts 21:8
CHAPTER 9
1
kk A.D. 31–33
ll Acts 7:57; 8:1,3; 26:10–11
2
mm Acts 22:5

mascus, so that if he found any who were [a]of the Way, whether men or women, he might bring them bound to Jerusalem.

3 As he journeyed he came near Damascus, and suddenly a [b]light shone around him from heaven.

4 Then he fell to the ground, and heard a voice saying to him, "Saul, Saul, why are you persecuting [1]Me?"

5 And he said, "Who are You, Lord?" Then the Lord said, "I am [c]Jesus, whom you are persecuting.* It *is* hard for you to kick against the [d]goads."

6 So he, trembling and astonished, [e]said, "Lord, what do You want me to do?" Then the Lord *said* to him, "Arise and go into the city, and you will be told what you must do."

7 And the men who journeyed with him stood speechless, hearing a [2]voice [f]but seeing no one.

8 Then Saul arose from the ground, and when his eyes were opened he saw [g]no one. But they led him by the hand and brought *him* into Damascus.

9 And he was three days without sight, and neither ate nor drank.

10 Now there was a certain disciple at Damascus named Ananias; and to him the Lord said in a vision, "Ananias." And he said, "Here I am, Lord."

11 So the Lord *said* to him, "Arise and go to the street called Straight, and inquire at the house of Judas for *one* called Saul of Tarsus, for behold, he is praying.

12 "And in a vision he has seen a man named Ananias coming in and putting *his* hand on him, so that he might receive his sight."

13 Then Ananias answered, "Lord, I have [h]heard from many about this man, how much harm he has done to Your saints in Jerusalem.

14 "And here he has authority from the chief priests to bind all who call on Your name."

15 But the Lord said to him, "Go, for he is a [i]chosen vessel of Mine to bear My name before [j]Gentiles, [k]kings, and the [l]children of Israel.

16 "For I will show him how many things he must [m]suffer for My [n]name's sake."

Saul filled with the Spirit

17 And Ananias went his way and entered the house; and [o]laying his hands on him he said, [p]"Brother Saul, the Lord Jesus,* who appeared to you on the road as you came, has sent me that you may [q]receive your sight and be [r]filled with the Holy [s]Spirit."

Saul baptized

18 Immediately there fell from his eyes *something* like scales, and he [t]received his sight at once; and he arose and was baptized.

19 So when he had received food, he was strengthened. Then Saul spent some days with the disciples at Damascus.

Saul preaches at Damascus

20 Immediately he [u]preached the Christ* in the synagogues, [3]that He is the Son of God.

21 Then all who heard were amazed, and said, "Is this not he who destroyed those who called on this name in Jerusalem, and

2
- *a* Jn. 14:6

3
- *b* Acts 22:6; 26:13

5
- *c* Cp. Acts 2:36
- *d* Acts 26:14

6
- *e* *Bible prayers* (NT): v. 6; Acts 22:10. (Mt. 6:9; Lk. 11:2, *note*)

7
- *f* Cp. Dt. 4:12; Dan. 10:7

8
- *g* Lit. *nothing*

13
- *h* Cp. vv. 1–2; Gal. 1:23

15
- *i* *Election* (personal): vv. 15–16; Acts 10:41. (Dt. 7:6; 1 Pet. 5:13, *note*)
- *j* Rom. 1:5; 11:13; Gal. 2:7; Eph. 3:7–8; 2 Tim. 4:17; see Eph. 3:6, *note*
- *k* Cp. Acts 26:1–2; 27:24
- *l* Acts 21:40; Rom. 1:16; 9:1–5; see Rom. 11:26, *note*

16
- *m* Acts 20:23; 2 Cor. 11:23–28; 12:7–10; Gal. 6:17; Phil. 1:29–30
- *n* 2 Cor. 4:11; cp. Rev. 2:3

17
- *o* Cp. v. 12
- *p* Cp. 2 Cor. 2:13; Phile. 1; Rev. 1:9
- *q* Cp. Jn. 9:1–15
- *r* Cp. Eph. 5:19
- *s* *Holy Spirit* (NT): v. 17; Acts 9:31. (Mt. 1:18; Acts 2:4, *note*)

18
- *t* *Miracles* (NT): vv. 17–18; Acts 9:34. (Mt. 8:3; Acts 28:8, *note*)

20
- *u* *Gospel:* v. 20; Acts 9:27. (Gen. 12:3; Rev. 14:6)

*

9:5 NU-Text and M-Text omit the last sentence of verse 5 and begin verse 6 with *But arise and go.* **9:17** M-Text omits *Jesus.* **9:20** NU-Text reads *Jesus.*

[1](9:4) The Lord identifies himself with His people.

[2](9:7) Compare 22:9; 26:14. A contradiction has been imagined. The three statements should be taken together. The men heard the "voice" as a sound (Gk. *phōnē*) but did not hear the actual words "Saul, Saul," etc.

[3](9:20) Compare 2:36. Peter, while maintaining the Deity of Jesus ("God has made this Jesus, whom you crucified "both Lord and Christ"), gives special prominence to His Messiahship. Paul, fresh from the vision of the glory, puts the emphasis on His Deity. Peter's charge was that the Jews had crucified the Son of David (Acts 2:25–30); Paul's, that they had crucified the Lord of glory (1 Cor. 2:8). The point was, not that the Christ was God, a truth plainly taught by Isaiah (Isa. 7:14; 9:6–7), but that Jesus, the crucified Nazarene, was the Christ and therefore God the Son.

has come here for that purpose, so that he might bring them [a]bound to the chief priests?"

22 [1]But Saul increased all the more in strength, and confounded the Jews who dwelt in Damascus, proving that this *Jesus* is the Christ.

Saul escapes to Jerusalem

23 Now after many days were past, the Jews [b]plotted to kill him.

24 But their plot became [c]known to Saul. And they watched the gates day and night, to kill him.

25 Then the disciples took him by night and [d]let *him* down through the wall in a large basket.

26 And when Saul had [2]come to Jerusalem, he tried to join the disciples; but they were all [e]afraid of him, and did not believe that he was a disciple.

27 But [f]Barnabas took him and brought *him* to the apostles. And he declared to them how he had seen the Lord on the road, and that He had spoken to him, and how he had [g]preached [h]boldly at Damascus in the name of Jesus.

28 So he was with them at Jerusalem, coming in and going out.

29 And he spoke [h]boldly in the name of the Lord Jesus and disputed against the Hellenists, but they attempted to kill him.

Saul returns to Tarsus

30 When the brethren found out, they brought him down to Caesarea and sent him out to Tarsus.

31 Then the [i]churches* throughout all Judea, Galilee, and Samaria had peace and were [j]edified. And walking in the [k]fear of the Lord and in the [l]comfort of the Holy [m]Spirit, they were [n]multiplied.

Peter's ministry resumed: Aeneas healed

32 Now it came to pass, as Peter went through [o]all *parts of the country*, that he also came down to the saints who dwelt in Lydda.

33 There he found a certain man named Aeneas, who had been bedridden eight years and was [p]paralyzed.

34 And Peter said to him, "Aeneas, [q]Jesus the Christ heals you. Arise and make your bed." Then he [r]arose immediately.

35 So all who dwelt at Lydda and Sharon saw him and [s]turned to the Lord.

Peter raises Dorcas from the dead

36 At Joppa there was a certain disciple named Tabitha, which is translated [t]Dorcas. This woman was [u]full of good works and charitable deeds which she did.

37 But it happened in those days that she became sick and died. When they had washed her, they laid *her* in an upper room.

38 And since Lydda was near Joppa, and the disciples had heard that Peter was there, they sent two men to him, imploring *him* not to delay in coming to them.

39 Then Peter arose and went with them. When he had come, they brought *him* to the upper room. And all the [v]widows stood by him weeping, showing the tunics and garments which Dorcas had made while she was with them.

40 But Peter [w]put them all out, and knelt down and prayed. And turning to the body he said, "Tabitha, arise." And she opened her eyes, and when she saw Peter she sat up.

41 Then he gave her *his* hand and lifted her up; and when he

*
9:31 NU-Text reads *church . . . was edified.*

21 *a* v. 2
23 *b* Cp. Acts 23:12–15
24 *c* Cp. Acts 23:16
25 *d* Cp. Josh. 2:15; 1 Sam. 19:12; 2 Cor. 11:32–33
26 *e* Cp. Acts 9:1–2,13–14
27 *f* Acts 4:36; 11:22–26 *g Gospel:* v. 27; Acts 10:36. (Gen. 12:3; Rev. 14:6) *h* vv. 20,22
31 *i Churches* (local): v. 31; Acts 11:22. (Acts 8:3; Phil. 1:1, *note*) *j* Eph. 4:16,29 *k* Ps. 34:9; cp. Heb. 12:28; see Ps. 19:9, *note* *l* Jn. 14:16; cp. Phil. 2:1–2 *m Holy Spirit* (NT): v. 31; Acts 10:19. (Mt. 1:18; Acts 2:4, *note*) *n* v. 42; Acts 16:5
32 *o* Cp. Acts 8:4
33 *p* Cp. Mt. 9:2–8
34 *q* Acts 3:6,16; 4:10 *r Miracles* (NT): vv. 33–40; Acts 9:41. (Mt. 8:3; Acts 28:8, *note*)
35 *s* Acts 11:21; 15:19; cp. 26:18,20
36 *t* Meaning *gazelle* *u* Cp. 1 Tim. 2:10; 5:10
39 *v* Cp. Acts 6:1
40 *w* Cp. 2 Ki. 4:33; Mt. 9:25; Mk. 5:40

[1](9:22) It seems probable that vv. 22–25 refer to Paul's labors in Damascus after his return from Arabia (Gal. 1:17). The "many days" (v. 23) may represent the "three years" of Gal. 1:18, which intervened between Paul's return to Damascus and his visit to Peter.

[2](9:26) Acts records four visits of Paul to Jerusalem after his conversion: (1) 9:23–30. This seems identical with the visit of Gal. 1:18–19. The apostles of Acts 9:27 were Peter and James, the Lord's half brother. (2) 11:30. Paul may have been in Jerusalem during the events of 12:1–24. See v. 25. (3) 15:1–30; Gal. 2:2–10. And (4) 21:17—23:35.

had called the saints and [a]wid-
ows, he [b]presented her [c]alive.
42 And it became known
throughout all Joppa, and many
[d]believed on the Lord.
43 So it was that he stayed
many days in Joppa with Simon, a tanner.

The Gospel goes to the Gentiles:
Cornelius sends for Peter

10 THERE was a certain
man in [e]Caesarea called
Cornelius, a [f]centurion of what
was called the Italian Regiment,
2 a [g]devout *man* and one
who [h]feared God with all his
household, who gave alms generously to the people, and
prayed to God always.
3 About the [i]ninth hour of
the day he saw clearly in a [j]vi-
sion an [k]angel of God coming in
and saying to him, "Cornelius!"
4 And when he observed
him, he was [l]afraid, and said,
"What is it, lord?" So he said to
him, [m]"Your prayers and your
alms have come up for a [n]me-
morial before God.
5 "Now [o]send men to Joppa,
and send for Simon whose surname is Peter.
6 "He is lodging with Si-
mon, a tanner, whose house is
by the sea.* He will tell you
what you must do."
7 And when the [k]angel who
spoke to him had departed, Cornelius called two of his household servants and a devout soldier from among those who
waited on him [p]continually.
8 So [q]when he had ex-
plained all *these* things to them,
he sent them to Joppa.

Peter's vision of a great sheet

9 [r]The next day, as they
went on their journey and drew
near the city, Peter went up on
the housetop to [s]pray, about the
[t]sixth hour.
10 Then he became very hungry and wanted to eat; but while
they made ready, he fell into a
[u]trance
11 and [v]saw heaven [w]opened
and an object like a great [1]sheet
bound at the four corners, descending to him and let down to
the earth.
12 In it were all kinds of four-
footed animals of the earth,
wild beasts, creeping things,
and birds of the [x]air.
13 And a voice came to him,
"Rise, Peter; kill and eat."
14 But Peter said, "Not so,
Lord! For I have never eaten
anything common or [y]un-
clean."
15 And a voice *spoke* to him
again the second time, [z]"What
God has cleansed you must not
call common."
16 This was done [aa]three
times. And the object was taken
up into heaven again.
17 Now while Peter wondered within himself what this
[v]vision which he had seen
meant, behold, the men who
had been sent from Cornelius
had made inquiry for Simon's
house, and stood before the
gate.
18 And they called and asked
whether [bb]Simon, whose surname was Peter, was lodging
there.
19 While Peter thought about
the [v]vision, the [cc]Spirit said to
him, "Behold, three men are
seeking you.
20 "Arise therefore, go down

*10:6 NU-Text and M-Text omit the last sentence of this verse.

41
a Cp. Acts 6:1
b Miracles (NT): vv. 36–42; Acts 12:7. (Mt. 8:3; Acts 28:8, *note*)
c Resurrection: vv. 40–41; Acts 10:40. (2 Ki. 4:35; 1 Cor. 15:52, *note*). Acts 20:12
42
d Faith: v. 42; Acts 10:45. (Gen. 3:20; Heb. 11:39, *note*). Jn. 11:45; 12:11
CHAPTER 10
1
e Acts 8:40; 23:23
f Cp. Lk. 7:2–10; see Acts 27:1, *note*
2
g Acts 2:5
h Ps. 34:9; cp. Heb. 12:28; see Ps. 19:9, *note*
3
i 3 p.m. See Jn. 19:14, *note;* cp. Mt. 27:46; Acts 3:1; 10:30
j vv. 10–17; cp. Acts 9:10–12
k See Jud. 2:1 and Heb. 1:4, *notes*
4
l Cp. Lk. 24:37
m v. 2
n Cp. Mt. 26:13; Heb. 6:9–10
5
o Acts 11:13–14
7
p Cp. Acts 2:42,46; 6:4; 8:13
8
q Cp. Acts 15:12,14; 21:19
9
r vv. 9–48; cp. Acts 11:5–18
s Cp. Dan. 6:10–11
t Noon. See Jn. 19:14, *note*
10
u Cp. Acts 22:17
11
v vv. 11–16
w Ezek. 1:1; Mt. 3:16; Acts 7:56; Rev. 4:1
12
x Lit. *heaven*
14
y Law (of Moses): v. 14; Acts 13:15. (Ex. 19:1; Gal. 3:24, *note*). Lev. 11:1–47; cp. Isa. 66:17; Ezek. 4:14; Dan. 1:8
15
z Cp. v. 28; Mt. 15:11; Rom. 14:14, 17,20; 1 Tim. 4:4; Ti. 1:15
16
aa Cp. Mt. 26:34,75
18
bb v. 5
19
cc Holy Spirit (NT): v. 19; Acts 10:38. (Mt. 1:18; Acts 2:4, *note*)

[1](10:11) Although this vision is admittedly symbolic, Peter's experience recorded here was a definite revelation to him that God had made a major change in His dealings with mankind (v. 28). Peter demurred at God's command (v. 14), but the Spirit of God was insistent that he should adjust his thinking and action to this change (vv. 13,15–16,19–20,28,34–35,45,47; 11:12,17–18). The animals and birds represented both Gentiles ("unclean" according to the law) and Jews (ceremonially "clean"). They were present together in this sheet let down from heaven (cp. Jn. 17:18), declared cleansed by God (vv. 15,34–35), and then caught up to heaven (v. 16). The revelation of the Church was not given alone to Paul. Paul himself says that it was revealed "by the Spirit to His holy apostles and [NT] prophets [both words plural]" (Eph. 3:5). This revelation to Peter, reported to Gentiles at Caesarea (Acts 10:24–29) and Jews at Jerusalem (Acts 11:1–11), plainly teaches that God is calling out both Gentiles and Jews to Himself in this age (Eph. 2:11–22). This was Peter's own evaluation of what God did through him at Caesarea (Acts 15:7–11,14; see Jn. 14:20, *note*).

and [a]go with them, [b]doubting
nothing; for I have sent them."
21 Then Peter went down to
the men who had been sent to
him from Cornelius,* and said,
"Yes, I am he whom you seek.
[c]For what reason have you
come?"
22 And they said, [d]"Cornelius *the* centurion, a [e]just man,
one who fears God and has a
[f]good reputation among all the
nation of the Jews, was divinely
instructed by a holy [g]angel to
summon you to his house, and
to hear words from you."

Peter goes to Caesarea

23 Then he invited them in
and lodged *them.* On the next
day Peter went away with them,
and [h]some brethren from Joppa
accompanied him.
24 And the following day
they entered Caesarea. Now
Cornelius was waiting for them,
and had called together his relatives and close friends.
25 As Peter was coming in,
Cornelius met him and [i]fell
down at his feet and worshiped
him.
26 But Peter lifted him up,
saying, "Stand up; I myself am
also a [j]man."
27 And as he talked with him,
he went in and found [k]many
who had come together.
28 Then he said to them,
"You know how [l]unlawful it is
for a Jewish man to keep company with or go to one of another nation. But [m]God has
shown me that I should not call
any man common or unclean.
29 "Therefore I came without
objection as soon as I was sent
for. I ask, then, for [n]what reason have you sent for me?"
30 So Cornelius said, "Four
days ago I was [o]fasting until
this hour; and at the [p]ninth
hour* I prayed in my house,
and behold, a man stood before
me in bright clothing,
31 "and said, 'Cornelius,
your prayer has been heard,
and your alms are remembered
in the sight of God.
32 'Send therefore to Joppa
and call Simon here, whose surname is Peter. He is lodging in
the house of Simon, a tanner, by
the sea.* When he comes, he
will speak to you.'
33 "So I sent to you immediately, and you have done well to
come. Now therefore, we are all
present before God, to hear all
the things commanded you by
God."

Peter's sermon to Gentiles in the house of Cornelius. Theme: Salvation through faith (cp. Acts 2:14–41)

34 Then Peter opened *his*
mouth and said: "In truth I perceive that God [q]shows no partiality.
35 "But in every nation whoever fears Him and works
[r]righteousness is [s]accepted by
Him.
36 "The word which *God*
sent to the children of Israel,
[t]preaching [u]peace through Jesus Christ—He is Lord of all—
37 "that word you know,
which was proclaimed throughout all Judea, and began from
Galilee after the baptism which
John preached:
38 "how [v]God anointed Jesus of Nazareth with the Holy
[w]Spirit and with power, who
[x]went about doing good and
healing all who were oppressed
by the [y]devil, for [z]God was
with Him.
39 "And we are [aa]witnesses of
all things which He did both in
the land of the Jews and in Jerusalem, whom they* [bb]killed by
hanging on a tree.
40 "Him God [cc]raised up on
the third day, and showed Him
openly,
41 [dd]"not to all the people, but
to [aa]witnesses [ee]chosen before
by God, *even* to us who [ff]ate and
drank with Him after He arose
from the dead.
42 "And He commanded us
to [t]preach to the people, and to
testify that it is He who was ordained by God *to be* [gg]Judge of
the living and the dead.
43 "To Him all the prophets

20
a Cp. Acts 16:9–10
b i.e. *making no distinction.* Cp. Rom. 4:20
21
c v. 29; cp. Lk. 18:41
22
d vv. 1–2; see Acts 27:1, *note*
e *Righteousness* (OT): v. 22; Rom. 1:17. (Gen. 6:9; Lk. 2:25, *note*)
f Cp. Acts 22:12; 1 Tim. 3:7
g See Jud. 2:1, *note*
23
h v. 45; Acts 11:12
25
i Cp. Acts 16:29
26
j Cp. Acts 14:11–18; Rev. 19:10; 22:8–9
27
k v. 24
28
l Cp. Jn. 4:9; 18:28; Acts 11:3; Gal. 2:12–14
m v. 15; cp. Acts 15:8–9
29
n v. 21
30
o Cp. Ex. 34:28; 1 Sam. 7:6; 1 Ki. 19:8; Ezra 10:6; Dan. 10:3; Lk. 4:1–2; Acts 9:9; 13:2–3; 14:23; 27:33
p 3 p.m. See Jn. 19:14, *note*

34
q Dt. 10:17; Rom. 2:11; cp. Rom. 3:29–30; 10:12–13
35
r See Rom. 10:10, *note*
s Ps. 15:1–2
36
t *Gospel:* vv. 36–37, 42–43; Acts 11:1. (Gen. 12:3; Rev. 14:6)
u *Christ* (first advent): vv. 34–43; Acts 13:23. (Gen. 3:15; Acts 1:11, *note*)
38
v Isa. 61:1–3
w *Holy Spirit* (NT): v. 38; Acts 10:44. (Mt. 1:18; Acts 2:4, *note*)
x Mt. 4:23
y *Satan:* v. 38; Acts 13:10. (Gen. 3:1; Rev. 20:10)
z Jn. 3:2; 8:29
39
aa Acts 1:8
bb Acts 2:23
40
cc *Resurrection:* vv. 40–41; Acts 13:30. (2 Ki. 4:35; 1 Cor. 15:52, *note*)
41
dd Cp. Jn. 14:22
ee *Election* (corporate): v. 41; Acts 13:17. (Dt. 7:6; 1 Pet. 5:13, *note*)
ff Lk. 24:30, 41–43
42
gg *Judgments* (the seven): v. 42; Acts 17:31. (2 Sam. 7:14; Rev. 20:12, *note*)

*

10:21 NU-Text and M-Text omit *who had been sent to him from Cornelius.*
10:30 NU-Text reads *Four days ago to this hour, at the ninth hour.* **10:32** NU-Text omits the last sentence of this verse.
10:39 NU-Text and M-Text add *also.*

43
a Inspiration: v. 43; Acts 13:15. (Ex. 4:15; 2 Tim. 3:16, note)
b Jn. 3:16,18
43
c Acts 13:38–39
d See Rom. 3:23, note
44
e Holy Spirit (NT): vv. 44–45, 47; Acts 11:12. (Mt. 1:18; Acts 2:4, note)
f Cp. Acts 11:15
45
g Cp. Acts 15:5
h Faith: v. 45; Acts 11:17. (Gen. 3:20; Heb. 11:39, note)
i Cp. Acts 2:1–4
j See Eph. 3:6, note
48
k See Acts 8:12, note

[a]witness that, through His name, whoever [b]believes in Him will receive [c]remission of [d]sins."

The Spirit also given to Gentile believers

44 [1]While Peter was still
speaking these words, the Holy
[e]Spirit [f]fell upon all those who
heard the word.
45 And those of the [g]circum-
cision who [h]believed were astonished, as many as came with
Peter, because the gift of the
Holy [e]Spirit had been [i]poured
out on the [j]Gentiles also.
46 For they heard them
speak with tongues and magnify God. Then Peter answered,
47 "Can anyone forbid water,
that these should not be baptized who have received the
Holy [e]Spirit just as we *have?*"
48 And he commanded them
to be [k]baptized in the name of
the Lord. Then they asked him
to stay a few days.

Peter vindicates his ministry to Gentiles

11 NOW the apostles and
brethren who were in Ju-
dea heard that the [j]Gentiles
had also received the [l]word of
God.
2 And when Peter came up
to Jerusalem, those of the [g]cir-
cumcision contended with him,
3 saying, "You went in to
uncircumcised men and ate
with them!"
4 But Peter explained *it* to
them in order from the beginning, saying:
5 [m]"I was in the city of
Joppa praying; and in a trance I
saw a vision, [n]an object descending like a great sheet, let
down from heaven by four corners; and it came to me.
6 "When I observed it in-
tently and considered, I saw
four-footed animals of the
earth, wild beasts, creeping
things, and birds of the [o]air.
7 "And I heard a voice say-

CHAPTER 11
1
l Gospel: v. 1; Acts 11:19. (Gen. 12:3; Rev. 14:6)
5
m vv. 5–18; cp. Acts 10:9–48
n vv. 5–10; cp. Acts 10:11–16
6
o Lit. *heaven*

[1](10:44) Up to this point the Gospel had been offered principally to the Jews, though some Gentile proselytes may have been included in the conversions on the Day of Pentecost, and Philip had previously preached in Samaria (Acts 8). Through Peter's experience with Cornelius it is made plain that the norm for this age, for both Jews and Gentiles, is for the Holy Spirit to be given without delay, human mediation, or conditions other than simple faith in Jesus Christ for both Jew and Gentile.

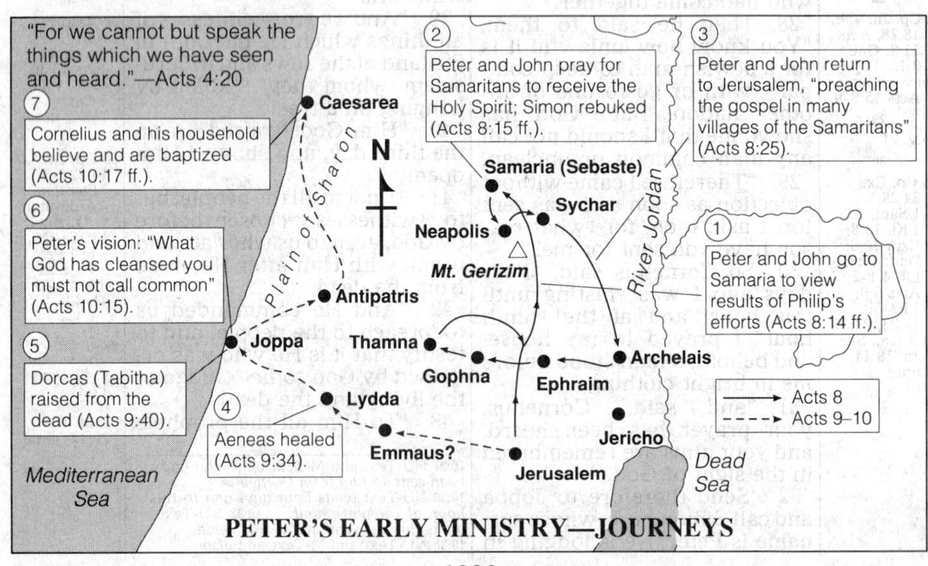
"For we cannot but speak the things which we have seen and heard."—Acts 4:20
7
Cornelius and his household believe and are baptized (Acts 10:17 ff.).
6
Peter's vision: "What God has cleansed you must not call common" (Acts 10:15).
5
Dorcas (Tabitha) raised from the dead (Acts 9:40).
4
Aeneas healed (Acts 9:34).
2
Peter and John pray for Samaritans to receive the Holy Spirit; Simon rebuked (Acts 8:15 ff.).
3
Peter and John return to Jerusalem, "preaching the gospel in many villages of the Samaritans" (Acts 8:25).
1
Peter and John go to Samaria to view results of Philip's efforts (Acts 8:14 ff.).
Caesarea
Plain of Sharon
N
Samaria (Sebaste)
Sychar
Neapolis
Mt. Gerizim
River Jordan
Antipatris
Joppa
Thamna
Gophna
Ephraim
Archelais
Lydda
Emmaus?
Jericho
Jerusalem
Dead Sea
Mediterranean Sea
Acts 8
Acts 9–10
PETER'S EARLY MINISTRY—JOURNEYS

ing to me, 'Rise, Peter; kill and eat.'

8 "But I said, 'Not so, Lord! For nothing common or unclean has at any time entered my mouth.'

9 "But the voice answered me again from heaven, 'What God has cleansed you must not call common.'

10 "Now this was done three times, and all were drawn up again into heaven.

11 [a]"At that very moment, three men stood before the house where I was, having been sent to me from Caesarea.

12 "Then the [b]Spirit told me to go with them, [c]doubting nothing. Moreover these [d]six brethren accompanied me, and we entered the man's house.

13 "And he told us how he had seen an [e]angel standing in his house, who said to him, 'Send men to Joppa, and call for Simon whose surname is Peter,

14 'who will tell you words by which you and all your household will be [f]saved.'

15 "And as I began to speak, the [b]Holy Spirit fell upon them, [g]as upon us at the beginning.

16 "Then I remembered the word of the Lord, how He [h]said, 'John indeed [i]baptized with water, but you shall be [j]baptized with the [b]Holy Spirit.'

17 "If therefore God gave them the same gift [g]as *He gave* us when we [k]believed on the Lord Jesus Christ, [l]who was I that I could withstand God?"

18 When they heard these things they became silent; and they glorified God, saying, "Then God has also granted to the [m]Gentiles [n]repentance to [o]life."

The church at Antioch and the new name: Christians

19 Now those who were scattered after the [p]persecution that arose over Stephen traveled as far as Phoenicia, Cyprus, and Antioch, [q]preaching the word to no one but the Jews only.

20 But some of them were men from Cyprus and Cyrene, who, when they had come to Antioch, spoke to the [r]Hellenists, [q]preaching the Lord Jesus.

21 And the hand of the Lord was with them, and a great number [k]believed and [s]turned to the Lord.

22 Then news of these things came to the ears of the [t]church in Jerusalem, and they sent out [u]Barnabas to go as far as Antioch.

23 When he came and had seen the [v]grace of God, he was glad, and encouraged them all that with purpose of heart they should continue with the Lord.

24 For he was a [w]good man, full of the [b]Holy Spirit and of [k]faith. And a great many people were [s]added to the Lord.

25 Then Barnabas departed for [x]Tarsus to seek Saul.

26 And when he had found him, he brought him to Antioch. So it was that for a whole year they assembled with the [t]church and taught a great many people. And the disciples were first called [y]Christians in Antioch.

The church at Antioch sends gift to Jerusalem believers

27 And in these days [z]prophets came from Jerusalem to Antioch.

28 Then one of them, named [aa]Agabus, stood up and showed by the [b]Spirit that there was going to be a great famine throughout all the [bb]world, which also happened in the days of [cc]Claudius Caesar.

29 Then the disciples, each according to his ability, determined to send relief to the brethren dwelling in Judea.

30 This they also did, and sent it to the [dd]elders [ee]by the hands of Barnabas and Saul.

Fifth persecution: Peter arrested

12 NOW about that time [ff]Herod the king stretched out *his* hand to harass some from the [gg]church.

2 Then he [hh]killed [ii]James the brother of [1]John with the sword.

3 And because he saw that it pleased the Jews, he proceeded

11
a vv. 11–18; cp. Acts 10:17–48
12
b Holy Spirit (NT): vv. 12, 15–17,24,28; Acts 13:2. (Mt. 1:18; Acts 2:4, *note*)
c i.e. *making no distinction*
d Cp. Mt. 18:16
13
e See Jud. 2:1, *note*
14
f See Rom. 1:16, *note*
15
g Acts 2:1–4; 15:7–9
16
h Mk. 1:8
i See Acts 8:12, *note*
j See Acts 2:4, *note*, par. (5)
17
k Faith: vv. 17–18, 21,24; Acts 13:12. (Gen. 3:20; Heb. 11:39, *note*)
l Cp. Job 9:12–14; Dan. 4:35; Rom. 11:33–36
18
m See Eph. 3:6, *note*
n Repentance: v. 18; Acts 13:24. (Mt. 3:2; Acts 17:30, *note*). 2 Cor. 7:10
o Life (eternal): v. 18; Acts 13:46. (Mt. 7:14; Rev. 22:19)
19
p Cp. Acts 8:1
q Gospel: vv. 19–20; Acts 12:24. (Gen. 12:3; Rev. 14:6)

20
r Cp. Acts 6:1
21
s Acts 9:35; 14:1
22
t Churches (local): vv. 22,26; Acts 13:1. (Acts 8:3; Phil. 1:1, *note*)
u Acts 4:36
23
v Grace: v. 23; Acts 13:43. (Jn. 1:14; Jn. 1:17, *note*)
24
w See 1 Jn. 3:7, *note*
25
x Acts 9:11
26
y Cp. Acts 26:28; 1 Pet. 4:16
27
z Acts 13:1; cp. Acts 15:32
28
aa Acts 21:10
bb Gk. *oikoumene*. See Lk. 2:1, *note*
cc Acts 18:2
30
dd Elders: v. 30; Acts 14:23. (Acts 11:30; Ti. 1:5, *note*)
ee Acts 12:25
CHAPTER 12
1
ff Herod Agrippa I. See Mk. 6:14, *note*
gg Church (the true): v. 1; Acts 12:5. (Mt. 16:18; Heb. 12:23)
2
hh Cp. 2 Chr. 24:20–22; Mk. 6:21–29; Lk. 11:49–51; Acts 7:54–60; Heb. 11:37; Rev. 6:9
ii See Mt. 4:21, *note*

---

[1](12:2) This is the last reference to the Apostle John in Acts.

further to seize Peter also. Now it was *during* the Days of Unleavened Bread.

4 So when he had [a]arrested him, he put *him* in prison, and delivered *him* to four [b]squads of soldiers to keep him, intending to bring him before the people after Passover.

Peter miraculously released from prison

5 Peter was therefore kept in prison, but [c]constant* [d]prayer was offered to God for him by the [e]church.

6 And when [f]Herod was about to bring him out, that night Peter was sleeping, bound with two chains between two soldiers; and the guards before the door were keeping the prison.

7 Now behold, an [g]angel of the Lord stood by *him*, and a light shone in the prison; and he struck Peter on the side and [h]raised him up, saying, "Arise quickly!" And his chains [i]fell off *his* hands.

8 Then the [g]angel said to him, "Gird yourself and tie on your sandals"; and so he did. And he said to him, "Put on your garment and follow me."

9 So he went out and followed him, and did not know that what was done by the [g]angel was real, but thought he was seeing a vision.

10 When they were past the first and the second guard posts, they came to the iron gate that leads to the city, which [i]opened to them [j]of its own accord; and they went out and went down one street, and immediately the [g]angel departed from him.

11 And when Peter had come to himself, he said, "Now I know for certain that the Lord has [k]sent His [g]angel, and has [l]delivered me from the hand of [f]Herod and *from* all the expectation of the Jewish people."

12 So, when he had considered *this*, he [m]came to the house of [n]Mary, the mother of [o]John whose surname was Mark, [p]where many were gathered together praying.

13 And as Peter knocked at the door of the gate, a girl named Rhoda came to answer.

14 When she recognized Peter's voice, because of *her* gladness she did not open the gate, but ran in and announced that Peter stood before the gate.

15 But they said to her, "You are beside yourself!" Yet she kept insisting that it was so. So they said, "It is his angel."

16 Now Peter continued knocking; and when they opened *the door* and saw him, they were astonished.

17 But motioning to them with his hand to keep silent, he [q]declared to them how the Lord had brought him out of the prison. And he said, "Go, tell these things to [r]James and to the brethren." And he departed and went to another place.

18 Then, as soon as it was day, there was no small stir among the soldiers about what had become of Peter.

19 But when [f]Herod had searched for him and not found him, he examined the guards and commanded that *they* should be [s]put to death. And he went down from Judea to Caesarea, and stayed *there*.

Herod blasphemes and dies

20 Now [f]Herod had been very angry with the people of [t]Tyre and Sidon; but they came to him with one accord, and having made Blastus the king's personal aide their friend, they asked for peace, because their country was supplied with food by the king's *country*.

21 So on a set day [f]Herod, arrayed in royal apparel, sat on his throne and gave an oration to them.

22 And the people kept shouting, "The voice of a [u]god and not of a man!"

23 Then immediately an [g]angel of the Lord [v]struck him, because he did not [w]give glory to God. And he was eaten by worms and [x]died.

24 But the [y]word of God grew and [e]multiplied.

25 And [z]Barnabas and Saul

*12:5 NU-Text reads *constantly* (or *earnestly*).

4
a Jn. 21:18
b i.e. *squads of four men each*
5
c Cp. Rom. 1:9; 1 Th. 1:2–3; 2:13; 5:17; 2 Tim. 1:3
d Cp. Eph. 6:18; Jas. 5:16
e *Church* (the true): vv. 5, 24; Acts 20:28. (Mt. 16:18; Heb. 12:23)
6
f Herod Agrippa I. See Mk. 6:14, *note*
7
g Cp. Acts 5:19–20; see Jud. 2:1, *note*
h Or *aroused him*
i *Miracles* (NT): vv. 7–11; Acts 13:11. (Mt. 8:3; Acts 28:8, *note*). Cp. Acts 5:19
10
j Cp. Acts 16:26
11
k Ps. 34:7; cp. Dan. 3:28; 6:22
l Cp. Job 5:19; 2 Pet. 2:9
12
m Cp. Acts 4:23
n See Lk. 1:27, *note*
o Acts 13:5, 13; 15:37; 2 Tim. 4:11; Phile. 24; 1 Pet. 5:13
p v. 5; cp. Isa. 65:24

17
q Cp. Ps. 66:16
r See Mt. 4:21, *note*
19
s Cp. Acts 16:27
20
t Mt. 11:21
22
u Cp. Acts 14:11; 28:6
23
v Cp. 1 Sam. 25:38; 2 Sam. 6:7; 2 Ki. 6:18; 15:5; 19:35; 1 Chr. 21:7; 2 Chr. 26:20
w Cp. Ex. 5:2; 2 Chr. 26:16; 32:25; Isa. 10:13; 14:13; 47:10; Ezek. 28:2; 31:10; Dan. 4:30; 5:23; Obad. 3
x Cp. Acts 5:5,10
24
y *Gospel:* v. 24; Acts 13:5. (Gen. 12:3; Rev. 14:6). Isa. 55:11
25
z Acts 11:30

25
a Acts 11:30
b Acts 12:12; 15:37

CHAPTER 13

1
c Churches (local): vv. 1–3; Acts 14:23. (Acts 8:3; Phil. 1:1, *note*)
d Lit. *the foster brother of*
e Herod Agrippa I. See Mk. 6:14, *note*

2
f Holy Spirit (NT): vv. 2,4,9; Acts 13:52. (Mt. 1:18; Acts 2:4, *note*)

3
g See Acts 6:6, *note*

5
h Gospel: vv. 5,7; Acts 13:12. (Gen. 12:3; Rev. 14:6)

returned from* Jerusalem when
they had [a]fulfilled *their* ministry, and they also took with
them [b]John whose surname was
Mark.

IV. The First Missionary Journey, 13—14

Set apart by Holy Spirit

13 NOW in the [c]church that
was at Antioch there
were certain prophets and
teachers: Barnabas, Simeon
who was called Niger, Lucius of
Cyrene, Manaen [d]who had
been brought up with [e]Herod
the tetrarch, and Saul.
2 As they ministered to the
Lord and fasted, the Holy
[f]Spirit said, "Now separate to
Me Barnabas and Saul for the
work to which I have called
them."
3 Then, having fasted and
prayed, and [g]laid hands on
them, they sent *them* away.
4 So, being sent out by the
Holy [f]Spirit, they went down to
Seleucia, and from there they
sailed to Cyprus.
5 And when they arrived in
Salamis, they [h]preached the
word of God in the synagogues
of the Jews. They also had John
as *their* assistant.

Opposition from Satan

6 Now when they had gone
through the island* to Paphos,
they found a certain [1]sorcerer, a
false prophet, a Jew whose
name *was* Bar-Jesus,
7 who was with the proconsul, Sergius Paulus, an intelligent man. This man called for
Barnabas and Saul and sought
to hear the [h]word of God.
8 But Elymas the sorcerer
(for so his name is translated)
withstood them, seeking to turn
the proconsul away from the
faith.
9 Then Saul, who also *is*
called Paul, filled with the Holy
[f]Spirit, looked intently at him
10 and said, "O full of all deceit and all fraud, *you* son of the
[i]devil, *you* enemy of all [j]righ-
teousness, will you not cease
perverting the straight ways of
the Lord?
11 "And now, indeed, the
hand of the Lord *is* upon you,
and you shall be blind, not see-

10
i Satan: v. 10; Acts 26:18. (Gen. 3:1; Rev. 20:10)
j See Rom. 10:10, *note*

*
12:25 NU-Text and M-Text read *to.*
13:6 NU-Text reads *the whole island.*

[1](13:6) "Sorcerer," from the Greek noun *magos,* is the same word that is rendered "wise men" ("Magi," Gk. *magoi*) in Mt. 2:1, where see *note 3.*

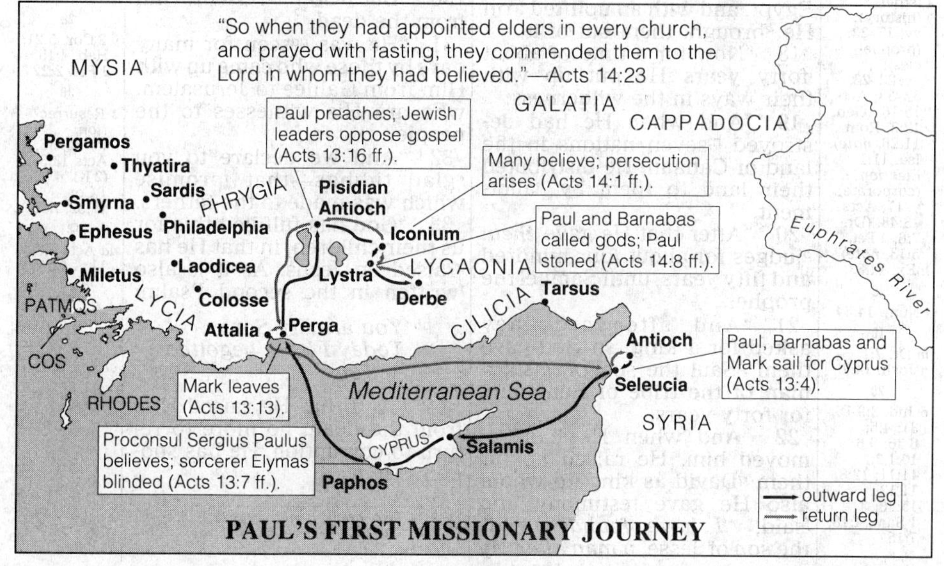
"So when they had appointed elders in every church, and prayed with fasting, they commended them to the Lord in whom they had believed."—Acts 14:23
MYSIA
GALATIA
CAPPADOCIA
Paul preaches; Jewish leaders oppose gospel (Acts 13:16 ff.).
Many believe; persecution arises (Acts 14:1 ff.).
Paul and Barnabas called gods; Paul stoned (Acts 14:8 ff.).
Pergamos
Thyatira
Smyrna
Sardis
PHRYGIA
Pisidian Antioch
Ephesus
Philadelphia
Iconium
Miletus
Laodicea
Lystra
LYCAONIA
Euphrates River
PATMOS
LYCIA
Colosse
Derbe
Tarsus
CILICIA
Attalia
Perga
COS
Antioch
Paul, Barnabas and Mark sail for Cyprus (Acts 13:4).
Seleucia
Mark leaves (Acts 13:13).
Mediterranean Sea
RHODES
SYRIA
Proconsul Sergius Paulus believes; sorcerer Elymas blinded (Acts 13:7 ff.).
CYPRUS
Salamis
Paphos
outward leg
return leg
PAUL'S FIRST MISSIONARY JOURNEY

ing the sun for a time." And immediately a dark mist [a]fell on him, and he went around seeking someone to lead him by the hand.

12 Then the proconsul [b]believed, when he saw what had been done, being astonished at the [c]teaching of the Lord.

13 Now when Paul and his party set sail from Paphos, they came to Perga in Pamphylia; and John, [d]departing from them, returned to Jerusalem.

Justification by faith preached by Paul at Antioch in Pisidia (vv. 38–39)

14 But when they departed from Perga, they came to Antioch in Pisidia, and went into the synagogue on the [e]Sabbath day and sat down.

15 And after [f]the reading of the [g]Law and the Prophets, the rulers of the synagogue sent to them, saying, "Men *and* brethren, if you have any word of exhortation for the people, say on."

16 Then Paul stood up, and motioning with *his* hand said, "Men of Israel, and you who [h]fear God, listen:

17 [i]"The God of this people Israel* [j]chose our fathers, and exalted the people when they dwelt as strangers in the land of Egypt, and with an uplifted arm He [k]brought them out of it.

18 "Now for a time of about [l]forty years He put up with their ways in the wilderness.

19 "And when He had destroyed [m]seven nations in the land of Canaan, He distributed their land to them by [n]allotment.

20 "After that He gave *them* [o]judges for about four hundred and fifty years, until Samuel the prophet.

21 "And afterward they asked for a king; so God gave them [p]Saul the son of Kish, a man of the tribe of Benjamin, for forty years.

22 "And when He had removed him, He raised up for them [q]David as king, to whom also He gave testimony and [f]said, [r]'*I have found David** the *son* of Jesse, *a man after My own heart,* who will do all My will.'

23 "From this man's seed, according to *the* [i]promise, God [s]raised up for Israel a [t]Savior—Jesus—*

24 "after John had first preached, before His coming, the baptism of [u]repentance to all the people of Israel.

25 "And as John was finishing his course, he said, 'Who do you think I am? I am not *He.* But behold, [v]there comes One after me, the sandals of whose feet I am not worthy to loose.'

26 "Men *and* brethren, sons of the family of Abraham, and [w]those among you who fear God, to you the word of this [x]salvation has been sent.

27 "For those who dwell in Jerusalem, and their rulers, because they did not know Him, nor even the voices of the Prophets which are read every [e]Sabbath, have fulfilled *them* in condemning *Him.*

28 "And though they found [y]no cause for death *in Him,* they asked Pilate that He should be [t]put to death.

29 "Now when they had fulfilled all that was [f]written concerning Him, they took *Him* down from the tree and laid *Him* in a tomb.

30 "But God [z]raised Him from the dead.

31 "He was [aa]seen for many days by those who came up with Him from Galilee to Jerusalem, who are His witnesses to the people.

32 "And we declare to you [c]glad tidings—that [i]promise which was made to the fathers.

33 "God has fulfilled this for us their children, in that He has [z]raised up Jesus. As it is also [f]written in the second Psalm:

[bb]*'You are My Son,*
Today I have begotten
You.'

34 "And that He raised Him from the dead, no more to return to corruption, He has spoken [cc]thus:

*

13:17 M-Text omits *Israel.* **13:22** Psalm 89:20 **13:23** M-Text reads *for Israel salvation.*

11
a Miracles (NT): vv. 8–12; Acts 14:10. (Mt. 8:3; Acts 28:8, *note*). Cp. Gen. 19:11; 2 Ki. 6:18

12
b Faith: v. 12; Acts 13:48. (Gen. 3:20; Heb. 11:39, *note*)
c Gospel: vv. 12, 32–39; Acts 13:44. (Gen. 12:3; Rev. 14:6)

13
d Acts 15:38

14
e Sabbath: vv. 14,27; Acts 13:42. (Gen. 2:3; Mt. 12:1, *note*)

15
f Inspiration: vv. 15, 22–42; Acts 13:47. (Ex. 4:15; 2 Tim. 3:16, *note*)
g Law (of Moses): v. 15; Acts 13:39. (Ex. 19:1; Gal. 3:24, *note*)

16
h See Ps. 19:9, *note*

17
i Israel (history): vv. 17–23; (prophecies): vv. 22–23, 32–33; Acts 15:16. (Gen. 12:2; Rom. 11:26, *note*). Isa. 11:1
j Election (corporate): v. 17; Acts 13:48. (Dt. 7:6; 1 Pet. 5:13, *note*)
k Ex. 14:8

18
l Num. 14:34

19
m Dt. 7:1
n Josh. 14:2

20
o Jud. 3:9,15, 31; 4:5; 6:36; 9:6; 10:1,3; 11:11; 12:8, 11,13; 15:20; 1 Sam. 4:18; 7:15

21
p 1 Sam. 10:20–24

22
q 1 Sam. 16:12–13; see Zech. 12:8, *note*
r 1 Sam. 13:14

23
s Christ (first advent): vv. 23–25; Acts 17:31. (Gen. 3:15; Acts 1:11, *note*)
t Sacrifice (of Christ): vv. 23, 28–29; Acts 17:3. (Gen. 3:15; Heb. 10:18, *note*)

24
u Repentance: v. 24; Acts 17:30. (Mt. 3:2; Acts 17:30, *note*). Mt. 3:11

25
v Jn. 1:27

26
w Isa. 55:1
x See Rom. 1:16, *note*

28
y 2 Cor. 5:21; Heb. 4:15; 1 Pet. 2:22

30
z Resurrection: vv. 30–36; Acts 13:37. (2 Ki. 4:35; 1 Cor. 15:52, *note*)

31
aa Acts 1:3, 11; 1 Cor. 15:5–8

33
bb Ps. 2:7

34
cc Isa. 55:3

'I will give you the sure
mercies of David.'

35 "Therefore He also says in another *Psalm:*

'You will not allow Your
[a]Holy One to see
corruption.'

36 "For David, after he had served his own generation by the will of God, fell asleep, was buried with his fathers, and saw corruption;
37 "but He whom God [b]raised up saw no corruption.
38 "Therefore let it be known to you, brethren, that through this Man is preached to you the [c]forgiveness of [d]sins;
39 "and by Him [e]everyone who believes is [f]justified from all things from which you could not be justified by the [g]law of Moses.
40 "Beware therefore, lest what has been spoken in the prophets come upon you:

41 *'Behold, you despisers,*
Marvel and perish!
For I [h]work a work in
your days,
A work which you will
by no means believe,
Though one were to
declare it to you.'"

42 So when the Jews went out of the synagogue,* the Gentiles begged that these words might be preached to them the next [i]Sabbath.
43 Now when the congregation had broken up, many of the Jews and devout proselytes followed Paul and Barnabas, who, speaking to them, persuaded them to continue in the [j]grace of God.

The Jews oppose Paul
(cp. vv. 6,50),
who turns to the Gentiles
(cp. Acts 18:6; 28:25)

44 On the next [i]Sabbath almost the whole city came together to hear the [k]word of God.
45 But when the Jews saw the multitudes, they were filled with envy; and contradicting and blaspheming, they opposed the things spoken by Paul.
46 Then Paul and Barnabas grew bold and said, "It was necessary that the [k]word of God should be spoken to you [l]first; but since you [m]reject it, and judge yourselves unworthy of everlasting [n]life, behold, we turn to the Gentiles.
47 "For so the Lord has [o]commanded us:

[p]*'I have set you as a light*
to the Gentiles,
That you should be for
[q]salvation to the ends
of the earth.'"

48 Now when the Gentiles heard this, they were glad and glorified the word of the Lord. And as many as had been [r]appointed to eternal [n]life [s]believed.
49 And the word of the Lord was being [k]spread throughout all the region.
50 But the Jews stirred up the devout and prominent women and the chief men of the city, raised up [t]persecution against Paul and Barnabas, and expelled them from their region.
51 But they [1u]shook off the dust from their feet against them, and came to Iconium.
52 And the disciples were filled with [v]joy and [w]with the Holy [x]Spirit.

The work in Iconium;
many believe

14 NOW it happened in Iconium that they went together to the synagogue of the Jews, and so spoke that a great [y]multitude both of the Jews and of the [z]Greeks [s]believed.
2 But the [aa]unbelieving Jews stirred up the [bb]Gentiles and poisoned their minds against the brethren.
3 Therefore they stayed there a long time, speaking boldly in the Lord, who was bearing witness to the [k]word of His [j]grace, granting signs and

* 13:42 Or *And when they went out of the synagogue of the Jews;* NU-Text reads *And when they went out of the synagogue, they begged.*

35
a Ps. 16:10
37
b Resurrection: vv. 30–37; Acts 17:3. (2 Ki. 4:35; 1 Cor. 15:52, *note*)
38
c Forgiveness: v. 38; Acts 26:18. (Lev. 4:20; Mt. 26:28, *note*)
d See Rom. 3:23, *note*
39
e Jn. 3:16
f Justification: v. 39; Rom. 2:13. (Lk. 18:14; Rom. 3:28, *note*)
g Law (of Moses): v. 39; Acts 15:1. (Ex. 19:1; Gal. 3:24, *note*)
41
h Hab. 1:5
42
i Sabbath: vv. 42,44; Acts 15:21. (Gen. 2:3; Mt. 12:1, *note*)
43
j Grace: v. 43; 14:3; Acts 14:26. (Jn. 1:14; Jn. 1:17, *note*)
44
k Gospel: vv. 44, 46–49; 14:3; Acts 14:7. (Gen. 12:3; Rev. 14:6)

46
l Mt. 10:6; Acts 3:26; Rom. 1:16
m Lit. *thrust it from you*
n Life (eternal): vv. 46, 48; Rom. 2:7. (Mt. 7:14; Rev. 22:19)
47
o Inspiration: v. 47; Acts 15:15. (Ex. 4:15; 2 Tim. 3:16, *note*)
p Isa. 49:6
q See Rom. 1:16, *note*
48
r Election (personal): v. 48; Acts 14:23. (Dt. 7:6; 1 Pet. 5:13, *note*). See 1 Pet. 1:20 and Eph. 1:5, *notes*
s Faith: v. 48; 14:1; Acts 14:9. (Gen. 3:20; Heb. 11:39, *note*)
50
t Acts 7:52; 2 Tim. 3:11
51
u Mt. 10:14
52
v Cp. Mt. 5:12; Acts 5:41; 1 Pet. 1:6–9
w Acts 2:4; 4:8,31; 13:9
x Holy Spirit (NT): v. 52; Acts 15:8. (Mt. 1:18; Acts 2:4, *note*)
CHAPTER 14
1
y Cp. Acts 13:44–45
z Acts 17:4; 18:4; 19:10; 20:21; 21:28; Rom. 1:14,16; 1 Cor. 1:22
2
aa Cp. Acts 13:45; 2 Th. 3:2
bb See Eph. 3:6, *note*

1(13:51) This was in accord with the Lord's instructions (Lk. 9:5; 10:11).

[a]wonders to be done by their hands.

4 But the multitude of the city was [b]divided: part sided with the Jews, and part with the apostles.

The work in Derbe and Lystra;
a cripple healed

5 And when a violent attempt was made by both the Gentiles and Jews, with their rulers, to [c]abuse and stone them,

6 they became aware of it and [d]fled to Lystra and Derbe, cities of Lycaonia, and to the surrounding region.

7 And they were preaching the [e]gospel there.

8 And in Lystra a [f]certain man without strength in his feet was sitting, a cripple from his mother's womb, who had never walked.

9 *This* man heard Paul speaking. Paul, observing him intently and seeing that he had [g]faith to be healed,

10 said with a loud voice, "Stand up straight on your feet!" And he [h]leaped and walked.

11 Now when the people saw what Paul had done, they raised their voices, saying in the Lycaonian *language*, "The [i]gods have come down to us in the likeness of men!"

12 And Barnabas they called Zeus, and Paul, Hermes, because he was the chief speaker.

13 Then the priest of Zeus, whose temple was in front of their city, brought oxen and garlands to the gates, intending to [j]sacrifice with the multitudes.

14 But when the apostles Barnabas and Paul heard this, they tore their clothes and ran in among the multitude, crying out

15 and saying, "Men, why are you doing these things? [k]We also are men with the same nature as you, and preach to you that you should turn from these [l]useless things to the living God, who made the heaven, the earth, the sea, and all things that are in them,

16 "who in bygone generations [m]allowed all nations to walk in their own ways.

17 "Nevertheless He did not leave Himself without [n]witness, in that He did good, gave us [o]rain from heaven and fruitful seasons, filling our hearts with [p]food and gladness."

18 And with these sayings they could scarcely restrain the multitudes from [i]sacrificing to them.

Paul stoned at Lystra

19 Then Jews from Antioch and Iconium came there; and having persuaded the multitudes, they stoned Paul *and* dragged *him* out of the city, supposing him to be [q]dead.

20 However, when the disciples gathered around him, he rose up and went into the city. And the next day he departed with Barnabas to Derbe.

Elders appointed in every church

21 And when they had preached the [e]gospel to that city and made many disciples, they returned to Lystra, Iconium, and Antioch,

22 strengthening the souls of the disciples, [r]exhorting *them* to continue in the faith, and *saying*, "We must through many [s]tribulations enter the [t]kingdom of God."

23 So when they [u]had [v]appointed [w]elders in every [x]church, and prayed with fasting, they [y]commended them to the Lord in whom they had [g]believed.

24 And after they had passed through Pisidia, they came to Pamphylia.

25 Now when they had [e]preached the word in Perga, they went down to Attalia.

Return to Antioch;
report to church

26 From there they sailed to Antioch, where they had been [z]commended to the [aa]grace of God for the work which they had completed.

27 Now when they had come and gathered the [x]church together, they reported all that God had done with them, and that He had opened the door of [g]faith to the [bb]Gentiles.

3
a Acts 5:12; Heb. 2:4; cp. Mk. 16:20; Rom. 15:19; 1 Cor. 2:4

4
b Lk. 12:51; cp. Jn. 9:16; Acts 17:4–5; 19:9; 28:24

5
c 2 Tim. 3:11

6
d Mt. 10:23

7
e *Gospel:* vv. 7,21,25; Acts 15:7. (Gen. 12:3; Rev. 14:6)

8
f Cp. Acts 3:2

9
g *Faith:* vv. 9, 23,27; Acts 15:5. (Gen. 3:20; Heb. 11:39, *note*)

10
h *Miracles* (NT): vv. 8–10; Acts 16:18. (Mt. 8:3; Acts 28:8, *note*)

11
i Cp. Acts 12:22; 28:6

13
j Cp. Dan. 2:46

15
k Cp. Acts 10:26; Jas. 5:17; Rev. 22:9
l Cp. Isa. 44:9–10; 1 Cor. 8:4

16
m Cp. Acts 17:30

17
n Acts 17:24–26; Rom. 1:19–20
o Ps. 147:8; Jer. 5:24
p Ps. 145:16

19
q 2 Cor. 12:1–4

22
r Cp. Acts 11:23
s 2 Tim. 3:12
t See Mt. 6:33, *note*

23
u *Election* (personal): v. 23; Acts 15:7. (Dt. 7:6; 1 Pet. 5:13, *note*)
v Lit. *chose,* i.e. *by raising of hands*
w *Elders:* v. 23; Acts 15:2. (Acts 11:30; Ti. 1:5, *note*)
x *Churches* (local): vv. 23,27; Acts 15:3. (Acts 8:3; Phil. 1:1, *note*)
y Cp. Acts 20:32

26
z Cp. Acts 13:1–3
aa *Grace:* v. 26; Acts 15:11. (Jn. 1:14; Jn. 1:17, *note*)

27
bb See Eph. 3:6, *note*

28 So they stayed there a long time with the disciples.

V. The Council at Jerusalem, 15:1–35

Circumcision question settled; the legalizers from Judea

CHAPTER 15

15 AND [a]certain *men* came down from Judea and [b]taught the brethren, [c]"Unless you are circumcised according to the [d]custom of Moses, you cannot be [e]saved."

Paul and Barnabas go to Jerusalem

2 Therefore, when Paul and Barnabas had no small dissension and dispute with them, they determined that Paul and Barnabas and certain others of them should [f]go up to Jerusalem, to the apostles and [g]elders, about this question.

3 So, being sent on their way by the [h]church, they passed through Phoenicia and Samaria, describing the [i]conversion of the [i]Gentiles; and they caused great joy to all the brethren.

4 [j]And when they had come to Jerusalem, they were received by the [h]church and the apostles and the [g]elders; and they reported all things that God had done with them.

5 But some of the sect of the [k]Pharisees who [l]believed rose up, saying, "It is necessary to circumcise them, and to command *them* to keep the [d]law of Moses."

Peter's rebuttal: Why place Gentile believers under yoke of law?

6 Now the apostles and [g]elders came together to consider this matter.

7 And when there had been much [m]dispute, Peter rose up and said to them: "Men and brethren, you know that a good while ago God [n]chose among us, that [o]by my mouth the [i]Gentiles should hear the word of the [p]gospel and believe.

8 "So God, who [q]knows the heart, acknowledged them by giving them the Holy [r]Spirit, just as *He did* to us,

9 "and made no distinction between us and them, [s]purifying their hearts by [l]faith.

10 "Now therefore, why do you [t]test God by putting a [u]yoke on the neck of the disciples which neither our fathers nor we were able to bear?

11 "But we believe that through the [v]grace of the Lord Jesus Christ* we shall be [e]saved in the same manner as [w]they."

Paul and Barnabas testify

12 Then all the multitude kept silent and listened to Barnabas and Paul declaring how many miracles and wonders God had worked through them among the [i]Gentiles.

James announces decision of council: (1) the outcalling of Gentiles agrees with promises to Israel

13 And after they had become silent, [x]James answered, saying, [1]"Men *and* brethren, listen to me:

14 "Simon has declared how

*15:11 NU-Text and M-Text omit *Christ.*

1
a Cp. Gal. 2:12
b Cp. Gal. 3:1–5; 5:2–4
c Cp. Col. 2:11–14
d *Law* (of Moses): vv. 1,5; Acts 15:21. (Ex. 19:1; Gal. 3:24, *note*). Gen. 17:10–11; Lev. 12:3
e See Rom. 1:16, *note*
2
f Cp. Gal. 2:1
g *Elders:* vv. 2,4,6; Acts 15:22. (Acts 11:30; Ti. 1:5, *note*)
3
h *Churches* (local): vv. 3–4; Acts 15:22. (Acts 8:3; Phil. 1:1, *note*)
i See Eph. 3:6, *note*
4
j c. A.D. 49
5
k See Mt. 3:7, *note 1*
l *Faith:* vv. 5, 9; Acts 16:1. (Gen. 3:20; Heb. 11:39, *note*)

7
m Or *questioning*
n *Election* (personal): v. 7; Acts 22:14. (Dt. 7:6; 1 Pet. 5:13, *note*)
o See Mt. 16:19, *note*
p *Gospel:* v. 7; Acts 15:35. (Gen. 12:3; Rev. 14:6)
8
q Acts 1:24; cp. 1 Chr. 28:9; Heb. 4:12
r *Holy Spirit* (NT): v. 8; Acts 15:28. (Mt. 1:18; Acts 2:4, *note*). Acts 10:44–45
9
s Cp. Jn. 15:3; 1 Cor. 6:11
10
t *Test/tempt:* v. 10; Acts 20:19. (Gen. 3:1; Jas. 1:14, *note*)
u Cp. Mt. 11:28–30
11
v *Grace:* v. 11; Acts 15:40. (Jn. 1:14; Jn. 1:17, *note*)
w Cp. Gal. 2:14–16
13
x Acts 12:17; see Mt. 4:21, *note*

[1](15:13) This important passage shows God's program for this age. It is necessary to observe the purpose of James in his decision. He is not simply arguing that Gentiles can be saved. This is clearly taught in many passages in the OT and was recognized by the apostles at their conference described in Acts 11 (note especially v. 18). The problem is circumcision. Must Gentiles become Jews before they become Christians? James declares that Amos 9:12 shows that, at the return of Christ, there will not only be believing Jews (here called "the rest of mankind") but also (translating NKJV "even" by "and") believing Gentiles "who are called by My name" (v. 17). Thus the passage, as explained by James, shows the following elements in the divine plan: (1) The taking out from among the Gentiles of a people for His name, the distinctive work of the present or Church Age. The Church is the *ekklēsia*—the "called-out assembly." The Gospel has never anywhere converted all but everywhere has called out some. No mention is made in this passage of gathering out the remnant from Israel in this age (cp. Rom. 11:5), because this was not the issue in dispute at the Jerusalem Council. (2) "After this [i.e. the out-calling] I will return." James quotes from Amos 9:11–12. The verses which follow in Amos describe the final regathering of Israel, which the other prophets invariably connect with the fulfillment of the Davidic Covenant (e.g. Isa. 11:1,10–12; Jer. 23:5–8). (3) "And will

God at the first visited the Gentiles to take out of them a people
for His name.
15 "And with this the words
of the prophets agree, just as it
is [a]written:

16 [b]*'After this I will* [1]*return*
And will rebuild the
tabernacle of [c]*David,*
which has fallen
down;
I will rebuild its ruins,
And I will set it up;
17 *So that the rest of*
mankind may seek the
LORD,
Even all the Gentiles
who are called by My
name,
Says the LORD who does
*all these things.'**
18 "Known to God from
[d]eternity are all His works.*

(2) Gentiles are not under the law

19 [2]"Therefore I judge that
we should not trouble those
from among the [e]Gentiles who
are turning to God,
20 "but that we [f]write to
them to abstain from things polluted by idols, *from* sexual immorality,* *from* things strangled, and *from* blood.
21 "For Moses has had
throughout many generations
those who [g]preach him in every
city, being read in the synagogues every [h]Sabbath."
22 Then it pleased the apostles and [i]elders, with the whole
[j]church, to send chosen men of
their own company to Antioch
with Paul and Barnabas,
namely, Judas who was also
named Barsabas,* and Silas,
leading men among the brethren.
23 They wrote this *letter* by
them:

The apostles, the [i]elders,
and the brethren,
To the brethren who are
of the [e]Gentiles in
Antioch, Syria, and
Cilicia:
Greetings.
24 Since we have heard that
some who went out from
us have troubled you
with words, [k]unsettling
your souls, saying, "*You*
must be circumcised and
keep the law"*—to
whom we gave no *such*
commandment—
25 it seemed good to us,
being assembled with
one accord, to send
chosen men to you with
our beloved Barnabas
and Paul,
26 [l]men who have risked
their lives for the name
of our Lord Jesus Christ.
27 We have therefore sent
Judas and Silas, who will
also report the same
things by word of mouth.

15 *a Inspiration:* vv. 15–17; Acts 17:2. (Ex. 4:15; 2 Tim. 3:16, *note*). Cp. Isa. 54:1–5; Hos. 3:5

16 *b Israel* (prophecies): vv. 16–17; Acts 26:7. (Gen. 12:2; Rom. 11:26, *note*)
c Kingdom (NT): vv. 14–17; Acts 17:7. (Mt. 2:2; 1 Cor. 15:24, *note*)

18 *d* Gk. *aiōn.* See Mk. 10:30, *note*

19 *e* See Eph. 3:6, *note*

20 *f* Acts 21:25; cp. Lev. 17:14–15

21 *g Law* (of Moses): vv. 20–21; Acts 18:13. (Ex. 19:1; Gal. 3:24, *note*)
h Sabbath: v. 21; Acts 16:13. (Gen. 2:3; Mt. 12:1, *note*)

22 *i Elders:* vv. 22–23; Acts 16:4. (Acts 11:30; Ti. 1:5, *note*)
j Churches (local): v. 22; Acts 15:41. (Acts 8:3; Phil. 1:1, *note*)

24 *k* Gal. 1:7

26 *l* Acts 13:50; 14:19; 1 Cor. 15:30; 2 Cor. 11:23–26

*15:17 Amos 9:11–12 **15:18** NU-Text reads *Says the Lord, who makes these things known from eternity (of old).* **15:20** Or *fornication* **15:22** NU-Text and M-Text read *Barsabbas.* **15:24** NU-Text omits *saying, "You must be circumcised and keep the law".*

rebuild the tabernacle of David, which has fallen down." Christ took the title to David's throne back to heaven with Him, assuring that David will never lack a man to sit on his throne, and looking forward to the re-establishment of Davidic rule over Israel (2 Sam. 7:8–17; Lk. 1:31–33). (4) "That the rest of mankind [Israelites] may seek the LORD" (cp. Zech. 12:7–8; 13:1–2). And (5) "And (Gk. *kai*) all the Gentiles," etc. (cp. Mic. 4:2; Zech. 8:21–22). This is also the order of Rom. 11:24–27.

[1](15:16) With the exception of the first five words, vv. 16–18 are quoted from Amos 9:11–12. James quoted from the LXX, which here preserved the original text (see Amos 9:12, *note*). Amos 9:11 begins with the words "on that day." James introduced his quotation in such a way as to show what day Amos was talking about, namely, the time after the present world-wide witness (Acts 1:8), when Christ will return. James showed that there will be Gentile believers at that time as well as Jewish believers; hence he concluded that Gentiles are not required to become Jewish proselytes by circumcision.

[2](15:19) The scope of the decision goes far beyond the mere question of circumcision. The whole question of the relation of the law to Gentile believers had been put in issue (v. 5), and their exemption is declared in the decision (vv. 19,24). The decision might be otherwise stated in the terms of Rom. 6:14: "You are not under law but under grace." Gentile believers were to show grace by abstaining from the practices offensive to godly Jews (vv. 20–21,28–29; cp. Rom. 14:12–17; 1 Cor. 8:1–13).

28
a Holy Spirit (NT): v. 28; 16:6–7; Acts 19:2. (Mt. 1:18; Acts 2:4, *note*)
29
b Acts 21:25; cp. Lev. 17:14–15
c Cp. 1 Cor. 8:1–13
d 1 Cor. 5:1; 6:18; 7:2; Col. 3:5; 1 Th. 4:3
e Cp. Dt. 4:9; 23:9; Prov. 4:23; 1 Tim. 5:22; Jas. 1:27; 1 Jn. 5:21; Jude 21
30
f v. 23
31
g Or *exhortation*
32
h Acts 11:27; 1 Cor. 12:28,29; Eph. 4:11; Rev. 18:20
35
i Cp. Acts 11:26
j Gospel: vv. 35–36; Acts 16:10. (Gen. 12:3; Rev. 14:6)
36
k Cp. Acts 13:2
37
l Acts 12:12, 25; cp. Acts 13:5; Col. 4:10; 2 Tim. 4:11; Phile. 24
38
m Acts 13:13

(3) Gentile believers must not cause Jews to stumble

28 For it seemed good to
the [a]Holy Spirit, and to
us, to lay upon you no
greater burden than
these necessary things:
29 [b]that you abstain from
[c]things offered to idols,
from blood, from things
strangled, and from
[d]sexual immorality.* If
you [e]keep yourselves
from these, you will do
well.
Farewell.

Judas and Silas go to Antioch

30 So when they were sent
off, they came to Antioch; and
when they had gathered the
multitude together, they delivered the [f]letter.
31 When they had read it,
they rejoiced over its [g]encour-
agement.
32 Now Judas and Silas,
themselves being [1h]prophets
also, exhorted and strengthened the brethren with many
words.
33 And after they had stayed
there for a time, they were sent
back with greetings from the
brethren to the apostles.*
34 However, it seemed good
to Silas to remain there.*
35 Paul and Barnabas also
remained in [i]Antioch, teaching
and [j]preaching the word of the
Lord, with many others also.

VI. The Second Missionary Journey, 15:36—18:22

Paul and Silas depart; Barnabas and Mark go to Cyprus

36 Then after some days
[k]Paul said to Barnabas, "Let us
now go back and visit our brethren in every city where we have
[j]preached the word of the Lord,
and see how they are doing."
37 Now Barnabas was determined to take with them [l]John
called Mark.
38 But Paul insisted that they
should not take with them the
one who had [m]departed from
them in Pamphylia, and had not
gone with them to the work.
39 Then the contention became so sharp that they parted
from one another. And so [2]Bar-
nabas took Mark and sailed to
[n]Cyprus;
40 but Paul chose [o]Silas and
departed, [p]being commended
by the brethren to the [q]grace of
God.
41 And he went through
Syria and Cilicia, strengthening
the [r]churches.

Timothy circumcised and added to missionary party

16 THEN he came to
[s]Derbe and Lystra. And
behold, a certain disciple was
there, named Timothy, *the* son
of a certain Jewish [t]woman
who [u]believed, but his father
was Greek.
2 He was [v]well spoken of by
the brethren who were at Lystra
and Iconium.
3 Paul wanted to have him
go on with him. And he took
him and [w]circumcised him because of the Jews who were in
that region, for they all knew
that his father was Greek.
4 And as they went through
the cities, they delivered to
them the [x]decrees to keep,
which were determined by the
apostles and [y]elders at Jerusalem.
5 So the [r]churches were
strengthened in the faith, and
increased in number [z]daily.

The Spirit guides to Troas; the Macedonian vision; Luke joins party (v. 10)

6 Now when they had gone
through Phrygia and the region
of [aa]Galatia, they were forbidden by the [a]Holy Spirit to
preach the word in Asia.
7 After they had come to
Mysia, they tried to go into Bithynia, but the [a]Spirit* did not
permit them.
8 So passing by Mysia, they
came down to Troas.

39
n Acts 4:36; 13:4
40
o v. 22
p Cp. Acts 14:26
q Grace: v. 40; Acts 18:27. (Jn. 1:14; Jn. 1:17, *note*)
41
r Churches (local): v. 41; 16:5; Acts 18:22. (Acts 8:3; Phil. 1:1, *note*)
CHAPTER 16
1
s Acts 14:6
t i.e. *Eunice*, 2 Tim. 1:5; cp. 1 Cor. 7:14; Eph. 6:4; 2 Tim. 3:15
u Faith: v. 1; Acts 16:14. (Gen. 3:20; Heb. 11:39, *note*)
2
v Cp. 1 Sam. 18:30; Prov. 22:1; Eccl. 7:1; Acts 6:3; 10:22; 22:12; 2 Cor. 8:18; 1 Tim. 3:7; 3 Jn. 12
3
w Cp. 1 Cor. 9:19–20; Gal. 2:3; 5:6; 6:15
4
x Acts 15:19–21
y Elders: v. 4; Acts 20:17. (Acts 11:30; Ti. 1:5, *note*)
5
z Acts 2:47
6
aa Acts 18:23; Gal. 1:1–2

*
15:29 Or *fornication* **15:33** NU-Text reads *to those who had sent them.*
15:34 NU-Text and M-Text omit this verse.
16:7 NU-Text adds *of Jesus.*

[1](15:32) The NT gift of prophecy is defined in 1 Cor. 14:3.
[2](15:39) This is the last time Barnabas is mentioned in Acts.

9 And a [a]vision appeared to Paul in the night. A man of Macedonia stood and [b]pleaded with him, saying, "Come over to Macedonia and help us."

10 Now after he had seen the [c]vision, immediately [1]we sought to go [d]to Macedonia, concluding that the Lord had called us to preach the [e]gospel to them.

Paul enters Europe; goes to Philippi

11 Therefore, sailing from Troas, we ran a straight course to Samothrace, and the next *day* came to Neapolis,

12 and from there to [f]Philippi, which is the foremost city of that part of Macedonia, a [g]colony. And we were staying in that city for some days.

13 And on the [h]Sabbath day we went out of the city to the riverside, [i]where prayer was customarily made; and we sat down and [e]spoke to the women who met *there.*

First convert in Europe: Lydia

14 Now a certain woman named Lydia heard *us.* She was a seller of purple from the city of [j]Thyatira, who worshiped God. The Lord [k]opened her [l]heart to [m]heed the [e]things spoken by Paul.

15 And when she and her [n]household were [o]baptized, she begged *us,* saying, "If you have judged me to be [p]faithful to the Lord, come to my house and [q]stay." So she [r]persuaded us.

A demon cast out: Paul and Silas beaten

16 Now it happened, as we went to prayer, that a certain slave girl possessed with a [s]spirit of divination met us, who brought her masters [t]much profit by fortune-telling.

17 This girl followed Paul and us, and [u]cried out, saying, "These men are the servants of the Most High God, who pro-

9
a Cp. Acts 9:10
b Here the Gospel turns to Europe

10
c v. 9
d 2 Cor. 2:13
e *Gospel:* vv. 10, 13–14; Acts 16:31. (Gen. 12:3; Rev. 14:6)

12
f Phil. 1:1
g i.e. *a Roman colony*

13
h *Sabbath:* v. 13; Acts 17:2. (Gen. 2:3; Mt. 12:1, *note*)
i Lit. *where we supposed there was a place of prayer*

14
j Rev. 1:11; 2:18,24
k *Faith:* v. 14; Acts 16:34. (Gen. 3:20; Heb. 11:39, *note*). Cp. Jn. 6:44
l Cp. 2 Cor. 4:6
m Cp. Acts 8:6

15
n Cp. Jn. 4:53; Acts 11:14
o See Acts 8:12, *note*
p Cp. Phil. 4:3; 2 Jn. 4–11
q Cp. Mt. 10:11; 1 Pet. 4:9
r Cp. Lk. 24:29; Heb. 13:2

16
s Lit. *a spirit, a Python,* i.e. *a demon.* See Mt. 7:22, *note*
t Cp. Acts 19:24

17
u Cp. Mk. 1:34

[1](16:10) The change here from "they" (vv. 6–8) to "we" indicates that at Troas Luke, the narrator, joined Paul's company.

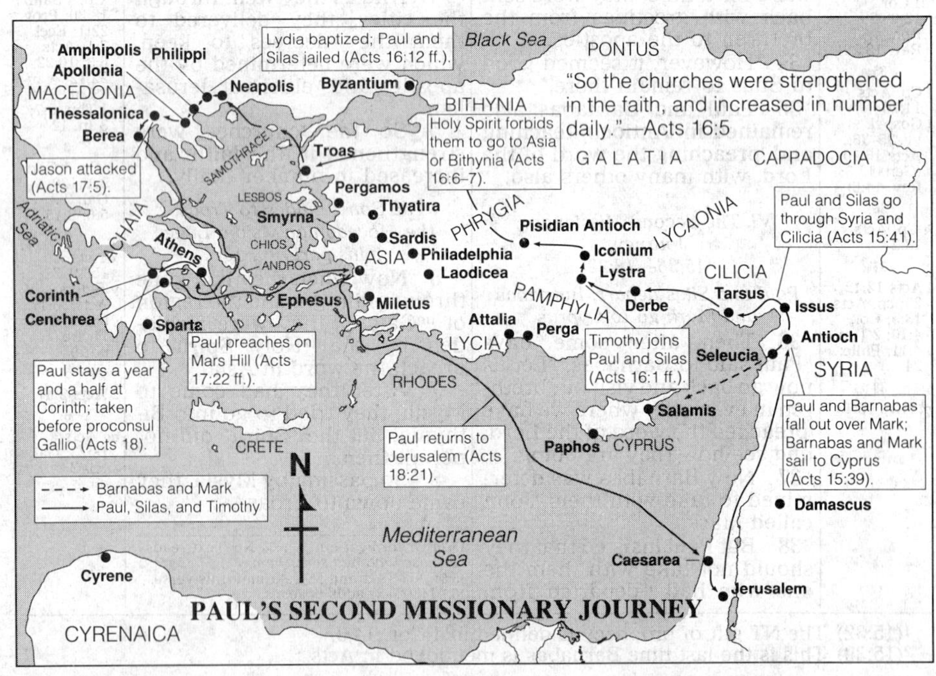

PAUL'S SECOND MISSIONARY JOURNEY

claim to us the way of [a]salvation.”

18 And this she did for many days. But Paul, greatly annoyed, turned and said to the [b]spirit, “I command you in the name of Jesus Christ to [c]come out of her.” And he [d]came out that very hour.

19 But when her masters [e]saw that their hope of profit was gone, they seized Paul and Silas and dragged *them* into the marketplace to the authorities.

20 And they brought them to the magistrates, and said, “These men, being Jews, exceedingly [f]trouble our city;

21 “and they teach customs [g]which are not lawful for us, being [h]Romans, to receive or observe.”

22 Then the multitude rose up together against them; and the magistrates tore off their clothes and commanded *them* to be beaten with rods.

23 And when they had [i]laid many [j]stripes on them, they threw *them* into [k]prison, commanding the jailer to keep them securely.

24 Having received such a charge, he put them into the inner prison and fastened their feet in the [l]stocks.

Philippian jailer converted

25 But at midnight Paul and Silas were [m]praying and [n]singing hymns to God, and the prisoners were listening to them.

26 Suddenly there was a great [o]earthquake, so that the foundations of the prison were shaken; and immediately all the [p]doors were opened and everyone’s chains were loosed.

27 And the keeper of the prison, awaking from sleep and seeing the prison doors open, supposing the prisoners had fled, drew his sword and was about to [q]kill himself.

28 But Paul called with a loud voice, saying, “Do yourself no harm, for we are all here.”

29 Then he called for a light, ran in, and fell down trembling before Paul and Silas.

Faith: the only condition of salvation

30 And he brought them out and said, “Sirs, [r]what must I do to be [a]saved?”

31 So they [s]said, [t]“Believe on the Lord Jesus Christ, and you will be [a]saved, you and your [u]household.”

32 Then they spoke the [s]word of the Lord to him and to all who were in his [u]house.

33 And he took them the same hour of the night and washed *their* [j]stripes. And immediately he and all his family were [v]baptized.

34 Now when he had brought them into his house, he set food before them; and he [w]rejoiced, having [x]believed in God with all his [u]household.

Paul released by Roman praetors

35 And when it was day, the magistrates sent the officers, saying, “Let those men go.”

36 So the keeper of the prison reported these words to Paul, saying, “The magistrates have sent to let you go. Now therefore depart, and go in peace.”

37 But Paul said to them, “They have [j]beaten us openly, uncondemned [y]Romans, *and* have thrown *us* into prison. And now do they put us out secretly? No indeed! Let them come themselves and get us out.”

38 And the officers told these words to the magistrates, and they were afraid when they heard that they were [y]Romans.

39 Then they came and pleaded with them and brought *them* out, and [z]asked *them* to depart from the city.

40 So they went out of the prison and entered *the house of* Lydia; and when they had seen the brethren, they [aa]encouraged them and departed.

Paul visits Thessalonica; church founded there

17 NOW when they had passed through Amphipolis and Apollonia, they came to [bb]Thessalonica, where there was a synagogue of the Jews.

2 Then Paul, [cc]as his custom was, went in to them, and for

17
a See Rom. 1:16, *note*
18
b Lit. *a spirit, a Python,* i.e. *a demon.* See Mt. 7:22, *note*
c Cp. Mk. 5:8
d *Miracles* (NT): vv. 16–18; Acts 19:11. (Mt. 8:3; Acts 28:8, *note*)
19
e Cp. Mk. 5:16–17; Acts 19:25–26
20
f Acts 17:6; cp. 1 Ki. 18:17
21
g Cp. Est. 3:8
h Cp. vv. 37, 38
23
i 1 Th. 2:2
j 2 Cor. 6:5; cp. Acts 11:24; 1 Pet. 2:24
k Cp. Acts 8:3
24
l Cp. Jer. 20:2–3
25
m Cp. 1 Th. 3:10; Jas. 5:16
n Cp. Col. 3:16
26
o Cp. 1 Ki. 19:11; Mt. 27:51; 28:2; Rev. 6:12; 11:19
p Cp. Acts 5:19; 12:10
27
q Cp. Acts 12:19

30
r Cp. Jn. 6:28–29; Acts 2:37
31
s *Gospel:* vv. 31–32; Acts 17:11. (Gen. 12:3; Rev. 14:6)
t Jn. 3:16; Acts 13:38–39; Rom. 10:9–11
u Cp. Jn. 4:53; Acts 11:14
33
v See Acts 8:12, *note*
34
w Cp. Acts 2:46; Rom. 15:13
x *Faith:* v. 34; Acts 17:4. (Gen. 3:20; Heb. 11:39, *note*)
37
y Cp. Acts 22:25–29; 25:11–12
39
z Cp. Lk. 8:37
40
aa Or *exhorted.* Cp. vv. 9,15,39; Acts 14:22
CHAPTER 17
1
bb 1 Th. 1:1; 2 Th. 1:1
2
cc v. 10; Acts 9:20; 13:5, 14; 14:1; 18:4; 19:8; cp. Lk. 4:16

2
a Sabbath: v. 2; Acts 18:4. (Gen. 2:3; Mt. 12:1, *note*)
b 1 Th. 2:1–16
c Inspiration: vv. 2, 11; Acts 23:5. (Ex. 4:15; 2 Tim. 3:16, *note*)
3
d Sacrifice (of Christ): v. 3; Acts 20:28. (Gen. 3:15; Heb. 10:18, *note*). Cp. Lk. 24:26,46
e Resurrection: v. 3; Acts 17:18. (2 Ki. 4:35; 1 Cor. 15:52, *note*)
f Acts 18:5, 28; cp. Jn. 6:69; 11:27; see Acts 9:20, *note*
4
g Cp. Acts 13:44–45; 14:1,4
h Faith: vv. 4, 12; Acts 17:34. (Gen. 3:20; Heb. 11:39, *note*)
i Cp. Acts 13:50; Phil. 4:3
5
j Acts 13:45; cp. Mt. 27:18
k Rom. 16:21
6
l Acts 14:19; 16:19
7
m Kingdom (NT): v. 7; Rom. 15:12. (Mt. 2:2; 1 Cor. 15:24, *note*). Cp. Lk. 23:2; Jn. 19:12

three [a]Sabbaths [b]reasoned
with them from the [c]Scriptures,
3 explaining and demon-
strating [1]that the Christ had to
[d]suffer and [e]rise again from the
dead, and *saying,* "This [f]Jesus
whom I preach to you is the
Christ."
4 [g]And some of them were
[h]persuaded; and a great multitude of the devout Greeks, and
not a few of the [i]leading
women, joined Paul and Silas.

Jews riot at Thessalonica

5 But the Jews who were
not persuaded, becoming [j]envi-
ous,* took some of the evil men
from the marketplace, and
gathering a mob, set all the city
in an uproar and attacked the
house of [k]Jason, and sought to
bring them out to the people.
6 But when they did not find
them, they [l]dragged Jason and
some brethren to the [2]rulers of
the city, crying out, "These who
have turned the world upside
down have come here too.
7 "Jason has harbored
them, and these are all acting
contrary to the decrees of Caesar, saying there is another
[m]king—Jesus."
8 And they troubled the
crowd and the rulers of the city
when they heard these things.
9 So when they had taken
security from Jason and the
rest, they let them go.

Paul and Silas at Berea

10 Then the brethren immediately sent Paul and Silas away
by night to Berea. When they
arrived, they went into the synagogue of the Jews.
11 These were more fair-
minded than those in Thessalonica, in that they received the
[n]word with all [o]readiness, and
[p]searched the [c]Scriptures daily
to find out whether these things
were so.
12 [3]Therefore many of them
[h]believed, and also not a few of
the [q]Greeks, prominent women
as well as men.
13 But when the [r]Jews from
Thessalonica learned that the
word of God was [n]preached by
Paul at Berea, [s]they came there
also and [t]stirred up the crowds.
14 Then immediately the
brethren [u]sent Paul away, to go
to the sea; but both Silas and
Timothy remained there.
15 So those who conducted
Paul brought him to Athens;
and [v]receiving a command for
Silas and [w]Timothy to come to
him with all speed, they departed.

Paul alone at Athens

16 Now while Paul waited for
them at Athens, his spirit was
[x]provoked within him when he
saw that the city was given over
to idols.
17 Therefore he reasoned in
the synagogue with the Jews
and with the *Gentile* worshipers, and in the marketplace
daily with those who happened
to be there.
18 Then* certain [4]Epicurean
and Stoic philosophers encountered him. And some said,
"What does this babbler want to
say?" Others said, "He seems to
be a proclaimer of foreign

*17:5 NU-Text omits *who were not persuaded;* M-Text omits *becoming envious.* 17:18 NU-Text and M-Text add *also.*

11
n Gospel: vv. 11,13; Acts 17:18. (Gen. 12:3; Rev. 14:6)
o Cp. Acts 16:14
p Jn. 5:39; cp. Lk. 16:29; Acts 26:22–23
12
q v. 4
13
r v. 5
s v. 5; cp. Lk. 11:52; 1 Th. 2:15
t Cp. v. 8
14
u Cp. Mt. 10:23
15
v Acts 18:5
w Cp. 1 Th. 3:1–2
16
x Cp. Ex. 32:19–20; Ps. 119:158

[1](17:3) Paul's argument was twofold: that (1) according to the Scriptures, the Christ (Messiah) had to suffer and rise again; and (2) Jesus of Nazareth was that Messiah.

[2](17:6) The Greek word is *politarchēs.* At this point the historicity of Acts has been attacked on the ground that the magistrates of Thessalonica were not called "politarchs." However, an inscription on the Arch of Galerius over the Egnatian Way corroborates the usage of this title in Thessalonica.

[3](17:12) Here is an illustration of Jn. 5:46. Believing the OT, many of the Bereans believed the Gospel of Christ.

[4](17:18) The Epicureans were disciples of Epicurus, 341–270 B.C., who abandoned as hopeless the search by reason for pure truth (cp. Jn. 18:38), seeking instead true pleasure through experience. The Stoics were disciples of Zeno, 336–264 B.C. This philosophy was founded on human self-sufficiency, inculcated stern self-repression and solidarity of the race. Paul's sermon (vv. 22–32) contains a most remarkable refutation of the specific views of both of these schools, which were extremely widespread in the apostolic world. As a result of the sermon "some men joined him and believed" (v. 34).

18
[a] *Gospel:* vv. 18–20; Acts 18:11. (Gen. 12:3; Rev. 14:6)
[b] 1 Cor. 15:12
[c] *Resurrection:* vv. 18, 31–32; Acts 20:12. (2 Ki. 4:35; 1 Cor. 15:52, *note*). Cp. Acts 17:32

19
[d] The highest court of Athens, which met on Mars' Hill, west of the Acropolis. v. 22
[e] Or *teaching*

22
[f] v. 19

23
[g] Cp. Rom. 1:19–21; 1 Cor. 1:21

24
[h] Gk. *kosmos.* See Mt. 4:8, *note*
[i] Acts 7:48–50

25
[j] Cp. Ps. 50:8–15
[k] Gen. 2:7; Isa. 42:5; Dan. 5:23

26
[l] Dt. 32:8; Job 12:23; Dan. 4:35

27
[m] Ps. 139:7–10; Jer. 23:23–24

28
[n] Cp. Rom. 14:8

[1]gods," because he [a]preached
to them [b]Jesus and the [c]resur-
rection.
19 And they took him and
brought him to the [d]Areopagus,
saying, "May we know what
this new [e]doctrine *is* of which
you speak?
20 "For you are bringing
some strange things to our ears.
Therefore we want to know
what these things mean."
21 For all the Athenians and
the foreigners who were there
spent their time in nothing else
but either to tell or to hear some
new thing.

Paul's sermon on the Areopagus.
Theme: God will judge the world
by the resurrected Lord Jesus

22 Then Paul stood in the
midst of the [f]Areopagus and
said, "Men of Athens, I perceive
that in all things you are very
religious;
23 "for as I was passing
through and considering the objects of your worship, I even
found an altar with this inscription:

[g]TO THE UNKNOWN GOD.

Therefore, the One whom you
worship without knowing, Him
I proclaim to you:
24 "God, who made the
[h]world and everything in it,
since He is Lord of heaven and
earth, does not [i]dwell in temples made with hands.
25 "Nor is He [j]worshiped
with men's hands, as though He
needed anything, since He
[k]gives to all life, breath, and all
things.
26 "And He has made from
one blood* every nation of men
to dwell on all the face of the
earth, and has determined their
preappointed times and the
[l]boundaries of their dwellings,
27 "so that they should seek
the Lord, in the hope that they
might grope for Him and find
Him, though He is [m]not far from
each one of us;
28 [n]"for in Him we live and
move and have our being, as
also some of your own poets
have said, [2]'For we are also His
offspring.'
29 "Therefore, since we are
the [3]offspring of God, we ought
not to think that the Divine Nature is like [o]gold or silver or
stone, something shaped by art
and man's devising.
30 "Truly, these times of ignorance God [p]overlooked, but
now commands all men everywhere to [4q]repent,
31 "because He has ap-
pointed a [r]day on which He will
[s]judge the [t]world in righteousness by the [u]Man whom He has
ordained. He has given assurance of this to all by [v]raising
Him from the dead."
32 And when they heard of
the [v]resurrection of the dead,
some [w]mocked, while others
said, "We will hear you [x]again
on this *matter.*"
33 So Paul departed from
among them.
34 However, some men
joined him and [y]believed,

Heb. 11:39, *note*)

*17:26 NU-Text omits *blood.*

29
[o] Ps. 115:4–7; Isa. 40:18–19; cp. Dan. 3:1

30
[p] Cp. Acts 14:16; Rom. 3:25
[q] *Repentance:* v. 30; Acts 19:4. (Mt. 3:2; Acts 17:30, *note*)

31
[r] *Day* (of judgment): v. 31; Rom. 2:5. (Mt. 10:15; Rev. 20:11)
[s] *Judgments* (the seven): v. 31; Acts 24:25. (2 Sam. 7:14; Rev. 20:12, *note*). Ps. 9:8; 96:13; 98:9
[t] Gk. *oikoumenē.* See Lk. 2:1, *note*
[u] *Christ* (first advent): v. 31; Acts 18:5. (Gen. 3:15; Acts 1:11, *note*). Jn. 5:22; Acts 10:42
[v] *Resurrection:* vv. 18, 31–32; Acts 20:12. (2 Ki. 4:35; 1 Cor. 15:52, *note*). Rom. 1:4; Rev. 1:18

32
[w] Cp. 1 Cor. 1:18; 15:12
[x] Cp. Acts 24:25

34
[y] *Faith:* v. 34; Acts 18:8. (Gen. 3:20;

[1](17:18) The term here rendered "gods" is commonly used in Greek writings for pagan gods. It is used nowhere else in the NT in this sense, but occurs fifty times for evil spirits and is, therefore, usually translated "demons."

[2](17:28) This verse comprises quotations from two poets—Epimenides and Aratus.

[3](17:29) "Offspring" is from the Gk. *genos* meaning *race.* The reference is to the creation-work of God, in which He made man (i.e. mankind, the race in Adam) in His own likeness, Gen. 1:26–27, thus rebuking the thought that "the Divine Nature is like gold," etc. The word "Father" is not used, nor does the passage affirm anything concerning fatherhood or sonship, which are relationships based upon faith and the new birth. Cp. Jn. 1:12–13; Gal. 3:26; 4:1–7; 1 Jn. 5:1.

[4](17:30) "Repent" is the translation of a Greek verb *metanoeō,* meaning *to have another mind, to change the mind,* and is used in the NT to indicate a change of mind in respect to sin, God, and self. This change of mind may, especially in the case of Christians who have fallen into sin, be preceded by sorrow (2 Cor. 7:8–11); but sorrow for sin, though it may cause repentance, is not repentance. The son in Mt. 21:28–29 illustrates true repentance. Repentance is not an act separate from faith, but saving faith includes and implies that change of mind which is called repentance (see Heb. 11:39, *note.* Cp. Zech. 8:14, *note*).

among them Dionysius the Areopagite, a woman named Damaris, and others with them.

Founding of the church at Corinth

18 AFTER these things Paul departed from Athens and went to [1]Corinth.

2 And he found a certain Jew named [a]Aquila, born in Pontus, who had recently come from Italy with his wife Priscilla (because Claudius had commanded all the Jews to depart from Rome); and he came to them.

3 So, because he was of the same trade, he stayed with them and worked; for by occupation they were [b]tentmakers.

4 And he reasoned in the synagogue every [c]Sabbath, and [d]persuaded both Jews and [e]Greeks.

5 When Silas and Timothy had come from Macedonia, Paul was [f]compelled by the Spirit, and testified to the Jews *that* [g]Jesus *is* the Christ.

6 But [h]when they opposed him and blasphemed, he shook *his* garments and said to them, "Your blood *be* upon your *own* heads; I *am* clean. From now on I will go to the [i]Gentiles."

7 And he departed from there and entered the house of a certain *man* named Justus,* *one* who worshiped God, whose house was next door to the synagogue.

8 Then [j]Crispus, the ruler of the synagogue, [k]believed on the Lord with all his household. And many of the Corinthians, hearing, [k]believed and were baptized.

9 Now the Lord spoke to Paul in the night by a vision, "Do not be afraid, but speak, and do not keep silent;

10 "for I am with you, and no one will attack you to hurt you; for I have many people in this city."

11 And he continued *there* a year and six months, [l]teaching the word of God among them.

Gallio's indifference

12 When Gallio was proconsul of Achaia, the Jews with one accord rose up against Paul and brought him to the judgment seat,

13 saying, "This *fellow* persuades men to worship God contrary to the [m]law."

14 And when Paul was about to open *his* mouth, Gallio said to the Jews, "If it were a matter of wrongdoing or wicked crimes, O Jews, there would be reason why I should bear with you.

15 "But if it is a [n]question of words and names and your own [m]law, look *to it* yourselves; for I do not want to be a judge of such *matters*."

16 And he drove them from the judgment seat.

17 Then all the Greeks* took [o]Sosthenes, the ruler of the synagogue, and beat *him* before the judgment seat. But Gallio took no notice of these things.

Paul takes a Jewish vow
(cp. Rom. 6:14; 2 Cor. 3:7–14; Gal. 3:23–28)

18 So Paul still remained a good while. Then he took leave of the brethren and sailed for Syria, and [a]Priscilla and Aquila *were* with him. He had *his* hair [p]cut off at Cenchrea, for he had taken a vow.

19 And he came to Ephesus, and left them there; but he himself entered the synagogue and [q]reasoned with the Jews.

20 When they asked *him* to stay a longer time with them, he did not consent,

21 but took leave of them, saying, "I must by all means keep this coming feast in Jerusalem;* but I will return again to you, [r]God willing." And he sailed from Ephesus.

22 And when he had landed at [s]Caesarea, and gone up and greeted the [t]church, he went down to Antioch.

VII. The Third Missionary Journey, 18:23—21:14

23 After he had spent some time *there*, he departed and

*18:7 NU-Text reads *Titius Justus*.
18:17 NU-Text reads *they all*.
18:21 NU-Text omits *I must* through *Jerusalem*.

CHAPTER 18

2
a Rom. 16:3; 1 Cor. 16:19; 2 Tim. 4:19

3
b Cp. Acts 20:34; 1 Cor. 4:12; 1 Th. 2:9; 2 Th. 3:8

4
c *Sabbath:* v. 4; Col. 2:16. (Gen. 2:3; Mt. 12:1, *note*)
d Lit. *sought to persuade*
e Acts 14:1; 17:4; 19:10; 20:21; 21:28; Rom. 1:14,16; 1 Cor. 1:22

5
f Cp. 2 Cor. 5:14
g *Christ* (first advent): v. 5; Acts 19:4. (Gen. 3:15; Acts 1:11, *note*)

6
h Cp. Acts 13:46; 28:25–29
i Acts 13:46–48; 28:28; see Eph. 3:6, *note*

8
j 1 Cor. 1:14
k *Faith:* v. 8; Acts 18:27. (Gen. 3:20; Heb. 11:39, *note*)

11
l *Gospel:* v. 11; Acts 19:10. (Gen. 12:3; Rev. 14:6)

13
m *Law* (of Moses): vv. 13,15; Acts 21:20. (Ex. 19:1; Gal. 3:24, *note*)

15
n Acts 23:29

17
o 1 Cor. 1:1

18
p Acts 21:24; cp. Num. 6:18

19
q Cp. Acts 17:2–3,17; 18:4; 19:8

21
r Cp. 1 Cor. 4:19; Heb. 6:3; Jas. 4:15

22
s Acts 8:40
t *Churches* (local): v. 22; Acts 20:17. (Acts 8:3; Phil. 1:1, *note*)

[1](18:1) A city in Greece that was known for idolatry and the evil conduct of its citizens.

23
[a] Cp. Acts 16:6
[b] Cp. 1 Th. 3:2,13
24
[c] Acts 19:1; 1 Cor. 1:12; 3:4; 16:12; Ti. 3:13
25
[d] Lit. *taught orally,* i.e. *not by revelation.* Cp. Gal. 1:11–12
[e] Cp. Rom. 12:11
[f] Mt. 3:1–11; Mk. 1:7–8; Lk. 3:16–17; Jn. 1:26
26
[g] Lit. *precisely*

went over the region of [a]Galatia and Phrygia in order, [b]strengthening all the disciples.

(Apollos at Ephesus and Corinth)

24 Now a certain Jew named
[c]Apollos, born at Alexandria,
an eloquent man *and* mighty in
the [1]Scriptures, came to Ephesus.
25 This man had been [d]instructed in the way of the Lord;
and being [e]fervent in spirit, he
spoke and taught accurately the
things of the Lord, though he
knew only the [f]baptism of
John.
26 So he began to speak
boldly in the synagogue. When
Aquila and Priscilla heard him,
they took him aside and explained to him the way of God
more [g]accurately.
27 And when he desired to
cross to Achaia, the brethren
wrote, exhorting the disciples to
receive him; and when he arrived, he greatly helped those
who had [h]believed through
[i]grace;
28 for he vigorously refuted
the Jews publicly, showing
from the Scriptures [2]that Jesus
is the Christ.

Paul at Ephesus: disciples of John the Baptist become Christians

19 AND it happened, while
Apollos was at Corinth,
that Paul, having passed
through the [j]upper regions,
came to Ephesus. And finding
some disciples
2 he said to them, "Did you
receive the Holy [k]Spirit [3]when

27
[h] *Faith:* v. 27; Acts 19:18. (Gen. 3:20; Heb. 11:39, *note*)
[i] *Grace:* v. 27; Acts 20:24. (Jn. 1:14; Jn. 1:17, *note*)
CHAPTER 19
1
[j] Acts 18:23
2
[k] *Holy Spirit* (NT): v. 2; Acts 19:6. (Mt. 1:18; Acts 2:4, *note*)

[1](18:24) The NT Scriptures were not then written; thus the OT is referred to here.

[2](18:28) This seems to be as far as Apollos' ministry went—that Jesus was the long expected Messiah (Acts 19:3). Apollos appears to have known nothing yet of the doctrines of justification through the blood of Christ and sanctification through the Holy Spirit.

[3](19:2) In both this passage and 1:8 the Greek participles have been translated sometimes in such a way that some have concluded that the gift of the Holy Spirit was granted to believers some time after the exercise of faith on their part. The original language allows no such interpretation. The literal translation of 1:8 is: "But you shall receive power, the Holy Spirit

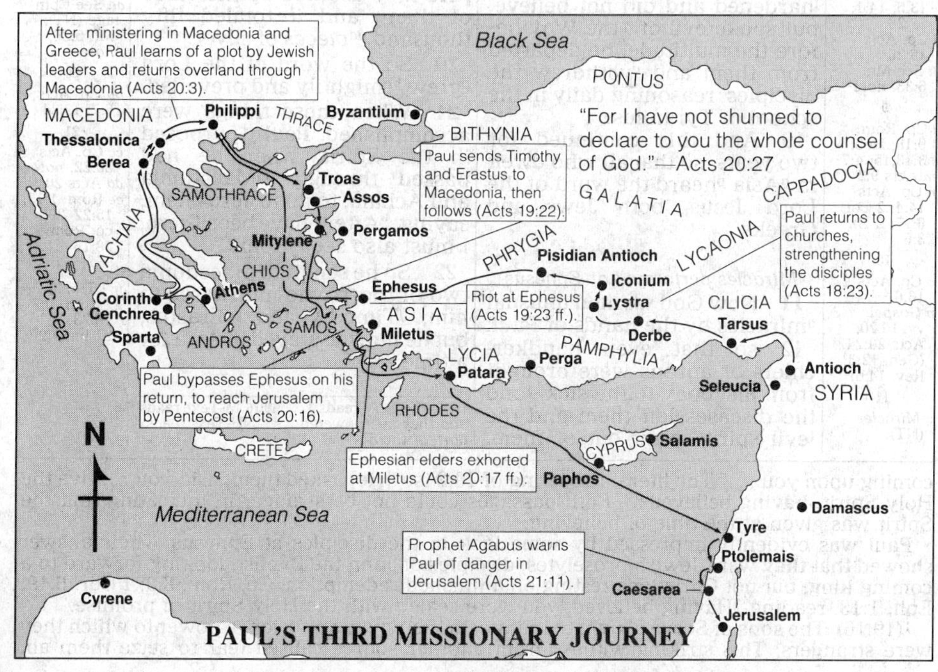

you believed?" So they said to him, "We have not so much as heard whether there is a Holy [a]Spirit."

3 And he said to them, [b]"Into what then were you baptized?" So they said, "Into John's baptism."

4 Then Paul said, "John indeed baptized with a [c]baptism of [d]repentance, saying to the people that they should believe on Him who would [e]come after him, that is, on Christ Jesus."

5 When they heard *this,* they were [f]baptized in the [g]name of the Lord Jesus.

6 And when Paul had laid hands on them, the Holy [a]Spirit came upon them, and they spoke with [h]tongues and prophesied.

7 Now the men were about twelve in all.

Paul teaches in Ephesus for nearly three years (vv. 9–10; 20:31)

8 And he [i]went into the synagogue and spoke [j]boldly for three months, reasoning and persuading concerning the things of the [k]kingdom of God.

9 But when some were [l]hardened and did not believe, but spoke evil of [m]the Way before the multitude, he departed from them and [n]withdrew the disciples, reasoning daily in the school of Tyrannus.

10 And this continued for two years, so that all who dwelt in [o]Asia [p]heard the word of the Lord Jesus, both Jews and Greeks.

Miracles performed at Ephesus

11 Now God worked unusual [q]miracles by the hands of Paul,

12 so that even handkerchiefs or aprons were brought from his [r]body to the sick, [s]and the diseases left them and the [t]evil spirits went out of them.

13 Then some of the itinerant Jewish exorcists took it upon themselves to call the name of the Lord Jesus over those who had evil spirits, saying, "We* exorcise you by the Jesus whom Paul [u]preaches."

14 Also there were seven sons of Sceva, a Jewish chief priest, who did so.

15 And the [t]evil spirit answered and said, [v]"Jesus I know, and Paul I know; but who are you?"

16 Then the man in whom the evil spirit was leaped on them, [1]overpowered* them, and prevailed against them,* so that they fled out of that house naked and wounded.

17 This became known both to all Jews and Greeks dwelling in Ephesus; and [w]fear fell on them all, and the name of the Lord Jesus was magnified.

18 And many who had [x]believed came [y]confessing and telling their deeds.

19 Also, many of those who had practiced [z]magic brought their books together and burned *them* in the sight of all. And they counted up the value of them, and *it* totaled fifty thousand [aa]*pieces* of silver.

20 So the word of the Lord [p]grew [bb]mightily and prevailed.

21 When these things were accomplished, Paul [cc]purposed in the Spirit, when he had passed through [dd]Macedonia and Achaia, to go to Jerusalem, saying, "After I have been there, I must also see [ee]Rome."

22 So he sent into Macedonia two of those who ministered to him, [ff]Timothy and [gg]Erastus, but he himself stayed in Asia for a time.

*

19:13 NU-Text reads *I.* **19:16** M-Text reads *and they overpowered.* • NU-Text reads *both of them.*

2
a Holy Spirit (NT): vv. 2,6; Acts 20:23. (Mt. 1:18; Acts 2:4, *note*)
3
b Cp. Rom. 6:3; 1 Cor. 12:13; Gal. 3:27
4
c Mt. 3:1–11; Mk. 1:7–8; Lk. 3:16–17; Jn. 1:26
d Repentance: v. 4; Acts 20:21. (Mt. 3:2; Acts 17:30, *note*)
e Christ (first advent): v. 4; Acts 26:23. (Gen. 3:15; Acts 1:11, *note*)
5
f See Acts 8:12, *note*
g Mt. 28:19; Acts 8:16
6
h Cp. Mk. 16:17; Acts 2:4; 10:46; 1 Cor. 12:10; 14:1–40
8
i Cp. Acts 13:5; 14:1; 18:26
j Cp. Acts 18:26
k See Mt. 6:33, *note*
9
l Cp. Rom. 9:18; Heb. 3:13,15; 4:7
m Acts 9:2
n Cp. Acts 14:4; 2 Cor. 6:17; 2 Th. 3:6
10
o Cp. Acts 16:6
p Gospel: vv. 10,20; Acts 20:24. (Gen. 12:3; Rev. 14:6)
11
q Miracles (NT): vv. 11–12; Acts 20:12. (Mt. 8:3; Acts 28:8, *note*)
12
r Cp. Mk. 6:56
s See Mk. 3:15, *note*
t See Mt. 7:22, *note*
13
u 1 Cor. 1:23; 2:2
15
v Cp. Mk. 1:23–24; Acts 16:16–18; Jas. 2:19
17
w Cp. Lk. 1:65; 7:16; Acts 5:5,11
18
x Faith: v. 18; Acts 21:20. (Gen. 3:20; Heb. 11:39, *note*)
y Cp. Mt. 3:6; 1 Cor. 14:24–25
19
z Cp. Dt. 18:10–14
aa See Coinage (NT), Mt. 5:26, *note*
20
bb Cp. Acts 6:7; 12:24
21
cc Cp. Acts 20:22, *note*
dd Acts 20:1
ee Rom. 1:13; 15:22–29; cp. Rom. 28:16
22
ff 1 Tim. 1:2
gg Rom. 16:23; 2 Tim. 4:20

coming upon you . . ." The literal rendering of 19:2 is: "[He] asked them, 'Did you receive the Holy Spirit, having believed?' " Both passages could not be stronger in indicating that the Spirit was given at the time of believing.

Paul was evidently impressed by some lack in the disciples at Ephesus. Their answer showed that they were Jewish proselytes, disciples of John the Baptist, looking forward to a coming king, but not Christians resting on a finished redemption. Cp. Rom. 8:9; 1 Cor. 6:19; Eph. 1:13, reading "Having believed, you were sealed with the Holy Spirit of promise."

[1](19:16) The sons of Sceva sought to imitate, to their own confusion, a power to which they were strangers. This striking witness from another source caused fear to seize them all.

Uproar at Ephesus

23 And about that time there arose a great commotion [a]about the Way.

24 For a certain man named Demetrius, a silversmith, who made silver shrines of Diana, brought no small profit to the craftsmen.

25 He called them together with the workers of similar occupation, and said: "Men, you know that we have our prosperity by this [b]trade.

26 "Moreover you see and hear that not only at Ephesus, but throughout almost all Asia, this Paul has persuaded and turned away many people, saying that they are [c]not gods which are made with hands.

27 "So not only is this [b]trade of ours in danger of falling into disrepute, but also the temple of the great goddess Diana may be despised and her magnificence destroyed,* whom all Asia and the [d]world worship."

28 Now when they heard *this,* they were full of wrath and cried out, saying, "Great *is* [1]Diana of the Ephesians!"

29 So the whole city was filled with confusion, and rushed into the theater with one accord, having seized [e]Gaius and [f]Aristarchus, Macedonians, Paul's travel companions.

30 And when Paul wanted to go in to the people, the disciples would not allow him.

31 Then some of the officials of Asia, who were his friends, sent to him pleading that he would not venture into the theater.

32 [g]Some therefore cried one thing and some another, for the assembly was [h]confused, and most of them did not know why they had come together.

33 And they drew [i]Alexander out of the multitude, the Jews putting him forward. And Alexander [j]motioned with his hand, and wanted to make his defense to the people.

34 But when they found out that he was a Jew, all with one voice cried out for about two hours, "Great *is* Diana of the Ephesians!"

35 And when the city clerk had quieted the crowd, he said: "Men of Ephesus, what man is there who does not know that the city of the Ephesians is temple guardian of the great goddess Diana, and of the *image* which fell down from Zeus?

36 "Therefore, since these things cannot be denied, you ought to be quiet and do nothing rashly.

37 "For you have brought these men here who are neither robbers of temples nor blasphemers of your* goddess.

38 "Therefore, if [k]Demetrius and his fellow craftsmen have a case against anyone, the courts are open and there are proconsuls. Let them bring charges against one another.

39 "But if you have any other inquiry to make, it shall be determined in the lawful assembly.

40 "For we are in danger of being called in question for today's [l]uproar, there being no reason which we may give to account for this [m]disorderly gathering."

41 And when he had said these things, he dismissed the assembly.

Paul preaches in Macedonia and Greece

20 AFTER the [l]uproar had ceased, Paul called the disciples to *himself,* [n]embraced *them,* and departed to go to [o]Macedonia.

2 Now when he had gone over that region and encouraged them with many words, he came to [p]Greece

3 and stayed three months. And when the Jews [q]plotted against him as he was about to

23
a i.e. *concerning Christ.* Jn. 14:6
25
b Cp. Acts 16:16–19
26
c Cp. 1 Chr. 16:26; Isa. 2:8; Jer. 2:11; 11:12; 16:20; Dan. 5:4; Acts 17:29; 1 Cor. 8:5; 12:2; Gal. 4:8; Rev. 13:14–15
27
d Gk. *oikoumenē.* See Lk. 2:1, *note*
29
e Acts 20:4; Rom. 16:23; 1 Cor. 1:14; 3 Jn. 1
f Acts 20:4; 27:2; Col. 4:10; Phile. 24
32
g v. 29
h Cp. Acts 21:34
33
i 1 Tim. 1:20; 2 Tim. 4:14
j Cp. Acts 12:17
38
k vv. 24–27
40
l 19:29–41; cp. Acts 21:31–32
m Or *seditious meeting*
CHAPTER 20
1
n Cp. v. 37
o 1 Cor. 16:5; 1 Tim. 1:3
2
p Acts 17:15; 18:1
3
q Cp. Acts 9:23–24; 23:12; 25:3; 2 Cor. 11:26

*19:27 NU-Text reads *she be deposed from her magnificence.* 19:37 NU-Text reads *our.*

[1](19:28) Gk. *Artemis,* an ancient and mythological goddess of the moon, the outdoors, and all forms of life and fertility. "Diana" is her Roman name. Artemis of the Ephesians was a particular image of the goddess, which was reputed to have fallen from heaven (v. 35). Cp. Dt. 16:21, *note;* Jud. 2:13, *note.*

sail to Syria, he decided to return through Macedonia.
4 And Sopater of Berea accompanied him to Asia—also
[a]Aristarchus and Secundus of
the Thessalonians, and [b]Gaius
of Derbe, and [c]Timothy, and
[d]Tychicus and [e]Trophimus of
Asia.
5 These men, going ahead,
waited for us at [f]Troas.

Paul at Troas seven days; church gathers on first day of week

6 But [g]we sailed away from
Philippi after the [h]Days of Unleavened Bread, and in five
days joined them at Troas,
where we stayed seven days.
7 Now on the [1]first *day* of
the week, when the disciples
came together to [i]break bread,
Paul, ready to depart the next
day, spoke to them and continued his message until midnight.
8 There were many lamps in
the [j]upper room where they*
were gathered together.
9 And in a window sat a certain young man named Eutychus, who was sinking into a
deep sleep. He was overcome
by sleep; and as Paul continued
speaking, he fell down from the
third story and was taken up
dead.
10 But Paul went down, [k]fell
on him, and embracing *him*
said, "Do not trouble yourselves, for his life is in him."
11 Now when he had come
up, had broken bread and

4
a Acts 19:29; 27:2; Col 4:10; Phile. 24
b Acts 19:29; Rom. 16:23; 1 Cor. 1:14; 3 Jn. 1
c 1 Tim. 1:2
d Eph. 6:21; Col. 4:7–8; 2 Tim. 4:12; Ti. 3:12
e Acts 21:29; 2 Tim. 4:20
5
f 2 Cor. 2:12; 2 Tim. 4:13
6
g The first person plural pronoun indicates that here Luke joins the apostles
h See Ex. 12:11, *note*
7
i Cp. Mt. 26:26–28; Acts 2:42; 1 Cor. 11:23–33
8
j Cp. Acts 1:13
10
k Cp. 1 Ki. 17:21–22; 2 Ki. 4:34–35

eaten, and talked a long while,
even till daybreak, he departed.
12 And they [l]brought the
young man in [m]alive, and they
were not a little comforted.

From Troas to Miletus

13 Then we went ahead to
the ship and sailed to Assos,
there intending to take Paul on
board; for so he had given orders, intending himself to go on
foot.
14 And when he met us at Assos, we took him on board and
came to Mitylene.
15 We sailed from there, and
the next *day* came opposite
Chios. The following *day* we arrived at Samos and stayed at
Trogyllium. The next *day* we
came to Miletus.
16 For Paul had decided to
sail past Ephesus, so that he
would not have to spend time in
Asia; for he was hurrying to be
at Jerusalem, if possible, on the
Day of [n]Pentecost.

Paul's farewell to the Ephesian elders

17 From Miletus he sent to
Ephesus and called for the [o]el-
ders of the [p]church.
18 And when they had come
to him, he said to them: "You
know, from the first day that I
came to Asia, in what manner I
always lived among you,
19 "serving the Lord with all
humility, with many tears and

*20:8 NU-Text and M-Text read *we*.

12
l *Miracles* (NT): vv. 9–12; Acts 22:13. (Mt. 8:3; Acts 28:8, *note*)
m *Resurrection:* v. 12; Acts 24:15. (2 Ki. 4:35; 1 Cor. 15:52, *note*)
16
n Acts 2:1; 1 Cor. 16:8
17
o *Elders:* v. 17; Acts 21:18. (Acts 11:30; Ti. 1:5, *note*)
p *Churches* (local): v. 17; Rom. 16:1. (Acts 8:3; Phil. 1:1, *note*)

[1](20:7) Although Paul was in Troas seven days (v. 6), apparently neither he nor the local church met for the breaking of bread until the first day of the week (v. 7).

The fact that Paul and others sometimes attended Sabbath services in Jewish synagogues (17:1–3) does not prove that the apostolic Church kept the seventh day as a special day of worship. It only shows that the early missionaries took the Gospel message wherever and whenever they found people gathered together (5:19–20; 13:5; 16:13,25–33; 17:17,19,22; 18:7; 19:9; 25:6,23). This witness was carried on daily (2:47; 17:17; 19:9) in every possible way (1 Cor. 9:19–22).

The early churches were specifically warned against submitting themselves to the bondage of any legalistic observance of Sabbath days (Col. 2:16, cp. Gal. 4:9–11). On the other hand, in the exercise of their Christian liberty (Rom. 14:5–6), these same churches voluntarily chose the first day of the week as an appropriate time for fellowship and worship (Acts 20:7; 1 Cor. 16:2), the day on which the Lord arose and repeatedly appeared to His disciples (Jn. 20:19–24,25–29). It was a new day for a new people belonging to a new creation (2 Cor. 5:17), a day of commemoration and joy, service (Mt. 28:10), and spiritual rest (Heb. 4:9–10). Contrast Sabbath, Mt. 12:1, *note*.

This observance of the first day of the week is corroborated by the early fathers: in the writings of Barnabas (c. A.D. 100), Ignatius (A.D. 107), Justin Martyr (A.D. 145–150), and Irenaeus (A.D. 155–202). The edict of Laodicea (4th Century A.D.) did not change the day of worship from the seventh to the first day of the week, as sometimes alleged, but rather put the stamp of official approval upon an observance already long established in the early churches.

[a]trials which happened to me
by the plotting of the Jews;
20 “how I kept back nothing
that was helpful, but proclaimed it to you, and taught
you publicly and from house to
house,
21 [b]“testifying to Jews, and
also to Greeks, [c]repentance toward God and faith toward our
Lord Jesus Christ.
22 “And see, now I go bound
in the [1]spirit to Jerusalem, not
knowing the things that will
happen to me there,
23 “except that the Holy
[d]Spirit testifies in every city,
saying that chains and tribulations [e]await me.
24 “But none of these things
move me; nor do I count my life
dear to myself,* so that I may
finish my race with joy, and the
ministry which I received from
the Lord Jesus, to testify to the
[f]gospel of the [g]grace of God.
25 “And indeed, now I know
that you all, among whom I
have gone preaching the [h]king-
dom of God, will see my face no
more.
26 “Therefore I testify to you
this day that I *am* [i]innocent of
the blood of all *men.*
27 [j]“For I have not shunned
to declare to you the whole
counsel of God.
28 [k]“Therefore take heed to
yourselves and to all the [l]flock,
among which the Holy [d]Spirit
has made you overseers, to
shepherd the [m]church of God*
which He [n]purchased with His
own blood.
29 “For I know this, that after
my departure savage [2][o]wolves
will [p]come in among you, not
sparing the flock.
30 “Also [q]from among yourselves men will rise up, speaking perverse things, to draw
away the disciples after themselves.
31 “Therefore watch, and remember that for [r]three years I
did not cease to warn everyone
night and day with [s]tears.
32 “So now, brethren, I
[t]commend you to God and to
the [f]word of His grace, which is
able to [u]build you up and give
you an [v]inheritance among all
those who are [w]sanctified.
33 “I have coveted no one’s
silver or gold or apparel.
34 “Yes,* you yourselves
know that these [x]hands have
provided for my necessities,
and for those who were with
me.
35 [y]“I have shown you in every way, by laboring like this,
that you must support the weak.
And remember the words of the
Lord Jesus, that He said, [z]‘It is
more blessed to give than to receive.’ ”
36 And when he had said
these things, he [aa]knelt down
and prayed with them all.
37 Then they all [bb]wept
freely, and fell on Paul’s neck
and kissed him,
38 sorrowing most of all for
the words which he spoke, that
they would see his face no
more. And they accompanied
him to the ship.

Paul and his party sail from Miletus to Tyre

21 NOW it came to pass,
that when we had de-
parted from them and set sail,
running a straight course we
came to Cos, the following *day*
to Rhodes, and from there to
Patara.
2 And finding a ship sailing
over to Phoenicia, we went
aboard and set sail.
3 When we had sighted Cy-
prus, we passed it on the left,
sailed to Syria, and landed at
Tyre; for there the ship was to
unload her cargo.

19
a Test/tempt: v. 19; 1 Cor. 7:5. (Gen. 3:1; Jas. 1:14, *note*)
21
b Acts 19:10; cp. Acts 14:1; 17:4; 18:4
c Repentance: v. 21; Acts 26:20. (Mt. 3:2; Acts 17:30, *note*)
23
d Holy Spirit (NT): vv. 23,28; Acts 21:4. (Mt. 1:18; Acts 2:4, *note*)
e Acts 21:4, 11,33
24
f Gospel: vv. 24,32; Acts 26:23. (Gen. 12:3; Rev. 14:6)
g Grace: v. 24; Rom. 1:5. (Jn. 1:14; Jn. 1:17, *note*)
25
h See Mt. 6:33, *note*
26
i Cp. Ezek. 3:18
27
j Cp. 2 Cor. 4:2
28
k Cp. Col. 4:17; 1 Tim. 4:16
l Cp. Isa. 40:11; Lk. 12:32
m Church (the true): v. 28; Rom. 7:4. (Mt. 16:18; Heb. 12:23)
n Sacrifice (of Christ): v. 28; Acts 26:23. (Gen. 3:15; Heb. 10:18, *note*)
29
o Cp. Mt. 7:15; 10:16; Jn. 10:12
p Cp. Mt. 13:25
30
q 1 Tim. 1:20; 2 Tim. 1:15; cp. 1 Jn. 2:19
31
r Cp. Acts 19:10
s v. 19
32
t Cp. Acts 14:23
u Cp. 1 Cor. 3:9–15; Eph. 2:19–22
v 1 Pet. 1:3–5
w Sanctification (NT): v. 32; Acts 21:28. (Mt. 4:5; Rev. 22:11)
34
x Cp. Acts 18:3; 1 Cor. 4:12; 1 Th. 2:9; 2 Th. 3:8
35
y i.e. *In every way I have given you an example*
z Cp. Lk. 14:12
36
aa Cp. 1 Ki. 8:54; 2 Chr. 6:13; Ezra 9:5; Ps. 95:6; Isa. 45:23; Dan. 6:10; Lk. 22:41; Acts 7:60; 9:40; 21:5; Eph. 3:14
37
bb Acts 21:13

*
20:24 NU-Text reads *But I do not count my life of any value or dear to myself.*
20:28 M-Text reads *of the Lord and God.*
20:34 NU-Text and M-Text omit *Yes.*

[1](20:22) Paul’s motive in going to Jerusalem seems to have been his great affection for the Jews (Rom. 9:1–5) and his hope that the gifts of the Gentile churches, sent by him to poor saints at Jerusalem (Rom. 15:25–28), would open the hearts of the law-bound Jewish believers to the “gospel of the grace of God” (Acts 20:24).

[2](20:29) Two sources of apostasy are: (1) false teachers from outside of the Church (2 Cor. 11:13–15; 2 Pet. 2:1–3); and (2) ambitious leaders within the Church (1 Jn. 2:18–19; 3 Jn. 9–10).

At Tyre seven days; the Holy Spirit forbids Paul to go to Jerusalem

4 And finding disciples,* we stayed there seven days. They told Paul through the [a]Spirit [b]not to go up to Jerusalem.

5 When we had come to the end of those days, we departed and went on our way; and they all accompanied us, with wives and children, till *we were* out of the city. And we [c]knelt down on the shore and prayed.

6 When we had taken our leave of one another, we boarded the ship, and they returned home.

On to Ptolemais and Caesarea, where Holy Spirit again warns Paul

7 And when we had finished *our* voyage from Tyre, we came to Ptolemais, greeted the brethren, and stayed with them one day.

8 On the next *day* we who were Paul's companions* departed and came to [d]Caesarea, and entered the house of [e]Philip the evangelist, who was *one* of the [f]seven, and stayed with him.

9 Now this man had four virgin daughters who prophesied.

10 And as we stayed many days, a certain prophet named [g]Agabus came down from Judea.

11 When he had come to us, he took Paul's belt, bound his *own* hands and feet, and said, "Thus says the Holy [a]Spirit, 'So shall the Jews at Jerusalem [h]bind the man who owns this belt, and deliver *him* into the hands of the Gentiles.' "

12 Now when we heard these things, both we and those from that place pleaded with him not to go up to Jerusalem.

13 Then Paul answered, "What do you mean by [i]weeping and breaking my heart? For I am [j]ready not only to be [h]bound, but also to [k]die at Jerusalem for the [l]name of the Lord Jesus."

14 So when he would not be persuaded, we ceased, saying, "The [m]will of the Lord be done."

VIII. From Jerusalem to Rome, 21:15—28:31

Paul goes to Jerusalem

15 And after those days we packed and went up to Jerusalem.

16 Also some of the disciples from [n]Caesarea went with us and brought with them a certain Mnason of Cyprus, an early disciple, with whom we were to lodge.

At Jerusalem, Paul takes a Jewish vow involving blood sacrifice, and enters the temple (cp. Heb. 10:2,4,9–12)

17 And when we had come to Jerusalem, the brethren received us gladly.

18 On the following *day* Paul went in with us to [o]James, and all the [p]elders were present.

19 When he had greeted them, he [q]told in detail those things which God had done among the [r]Gentiles through his [s]ministry.

20 And when they heard *it*, they glorified the Lord. And they said to him, "You see, brother, how many [t]myriads of Jews there are who have [u]believed, and [v]they are all zealous for the [w]law;

21 "but they have been informed about you that you teach all the Jews who are among the [r]Gentiles to forsake [w]Moses, saying that they ought not to [x]circumcise *their* children nor to walk according to the customs.

22 "What then? The assembly must certainly meet, for they will* hear that you have come.

23 "Therefore do what we tell you: We have four men who have taken a [y]vow.

24 "Take them and be [z]purified with them, and pay their expenses so that they may shave *their* heads, and that all may know that those things of which they were informed concerning you are nothing, but

*

21:4 NU-Text reads *the disciples*.
21:8 NU-Text omits *who were Paul's companions*. **21:22** NU-Text reads *What then is to be done? They will certainly*.

CHAPTER 21

4
a Holy Spirit (NT): vv. 4,11; Acts 28:25. (Mt. 1:18; Acts 2:4, *note*)
b Acts 21:12; cp. Acts 20:22–23; 22:17–21

5
c Cp. 1 Ki. 8:54; 2 Chr. 6:13; Ezra 9:5; Ps. 95:6; Isa. 45:23; Dan. 6:10; Lk. 22:41; Acts 7:60; 9:40; 21:5; Eph. 3:14

8
d Acts 8:40
e Acts 8:5
f Acts 6:5

10
g Acts 11:28

11
h Acts 21:33; 22:25; cp. 20:23

13
i Acts 20:37
j Cp. Rom. 1:15; 2 Tim. 4:6
k Cp. Acts 20:24; 2 Cor. 12:15; Phil. 3:8; 2 Tim. 2:10
l Cp. Acts 3:6,16; 4:10, 12,17,18,30; 5:28,40,41; 8:12,16; 9:14,15,21, 27,29; 10:43, 48; 15:14,17, 26; 16:18; 19:5,13,17; 22:16; 26:9

14
m Cp. Mt. 6:10; 26:42

16
n v. 8

18
o See Mt. 4:21, *note*
p Elders: v. 18; Phil. 1:1. (Acts 11:30; Ti. 1:5, *note*)

19
q Cp. Acts 15:4
r See Eph. 3:6, *note*
s Acts 20:24; 1 Tim. 2:7; cp. Rom. 1:1

20
t Cp. Acts 2:41; 4:4
u Faith: v. 20; Acts 21:25. (Gen. 3:20; Heb. 11:39, *note*)
v Cp. Rom. 10:2–4; Gal. 1:14
w Law (of Moses): vv. 20–21; Acts 21:24. (Ex. 19:1; Gal. 3:24, *note*)

21
x Cp. Gen. 17:9–14

23
y Probably according to Num. 6:1–7; cp. Acts 18:18; Col. 2:14–17

24
z v. 26

that you yourself also walk orderly and keep the [a]law.
25 "But concerning the
[b]Gentiles who [c]believe, we
have [d]written *and* decided that
they should observe no such
thing,* except that they should
keep themselves from *things* offered to idols, from [e]blood,
from things strangled, and from
[f]sexual immorality."
26 Then [g]Paul took the men,
and the next day, having been
purified with them, entered the
[h]temple to announce the expi-
ration of the days of [i]purifica-
tion, at which time an [g]offering
should be made for each one of
them.

Paul seized in the temple

27 Now when the seven days
were almost ended, the Jews
from Asia, seeing him in the
temple, [j]stirred up the whole
crowd and laid hands on him,
28 crying out, "Men of Israel,
help! This is the man who
teaches all *men* everywhere
against the people, the [a]law,
and this place; and furthermore
he also brought Greeks into the
temple and has defiled this
[k]holy place."
29 (For they had previously*
seen [l]Trophimus the Ephesian
with him in the city, whom they
supposed that Paul had brought
into the temple.)
30 And all the city was [m]dis-
turbed; and the people ran
together, seized Paul, and
[n]dragged him out of the temple;
and immediately the doors were
shut.

Paul rescued and bound
by Roman soldiers

31 Now as they were [o]seek-
ing to kill him, news came to the
commander of the garrison that
all Jerusalem was in an [p]up-
roar.
32 He immediately took soldiers and [q]centurions, and ran
down to them. And when they
saw the commander and the
soldiers, they stopped beating
Paul.
33 [r]Then the [s]commander
came near and took him, and
commanded *him* to be [t]bound
with two chains; and he asked
who he was and what he had
done.
34 And some among the multitude cried one thing and some
another. So when he could not
ascertain the truth because of
the tumult, he commanded him
to be taken into the [u]barracks.
35 When he reached the
stairs, he had to be carried by
the soldiers because of the violence of the mob.
36 For the multitude of the
people followed after, crying
out, [v]"Away with him!"
37 Then as Paul was about to
be led into the barracks, he said
to the [1]commander, "May I
speak to you?" He replied, "Can
you speak Greek?
38 "Are you not [w]the Egyptian who some time ago stirred
up a rebellion and led the four
thousand assassins out into the
wilderness?"
39 But Paul said, [x]"I am a
Jew from Tarsus, in Cilicia, a
citizen of no mean city; and I
implore you, permit me to speak
to the people."
40 So when he had given him
permission, Paul stood on the
stairs and motioned with his
hand to the people. And when
there was a great silence, he
spoke to *them* in the [y]Hebrew
language, saying,

Paul's defense before the mob;
he recounts his conversion
(cp. Acts 9:1–18; 26:9–18)

22 "BRETHREN and fa-
thers, hear my [z]defense
[aa]before you now."
2 And when they heard that
he spoke to them in the [bb]He-
brew language, they kept all the
more silent. Then he said:
3 [cc]"I [x]am indeed a Jew,
born in Tarsus of Cilicia, but
brought up in this city at the feet
of [dd]Gamaliel, taught according
to the strictness of our fathers'
[a]law, and was [ee]zealous toward
God [ff]as you all are today.

*21:25 NU-Text omits *that they should observe no such thing, except.*
21:29 M-Text omits *previously.*

24
a Law (of Moses): vv. 24,26,28; 22:3; Acts 22:12. (Ex. 19:1; Gal. 3:24, *note*)
25
b See Eph. 3:6, *note*
c Faith: v. 25; Acts 22:19. (Gen. 3:20; Heb. 11:39, *note*)
d See Acts 15:19, *note*
e Gen. 9:4; cp. Lev. 17:14–15
f Cp. 1 Th. 4:3–5
26
g Contrast Acts 21:4; (cp. Gal. 2:2–6) with Rom. 10:1–12; cp. Rom. 3:9–10, 19–20,28; 4:3–5; 5:1–2; 6:14; 7:1–4,6; 8:3–4; Gal. 2:15–16, 18–19; 3:10, 24–25; 4:9–11, 21–31; Phil. 3:7–9; Heb. 9:14–15,28; 10:17–18; 13:11–14
h Acts 24:18
i Cp. Jas. 4:8; 1 Pet. 1:22
27
j Cp. Acts 6:12; 13:50; 14:2; 17:13
28
k Sanctification (NT): v. 28; Acts 26:18. (Mt. 4:5; Rev. 22:11)
29
l Acts 20:4; 2 Tim. 4:20
30
m Cp. Mt. 21:10
n Cp. Acts 14:19; 16:19
31
o 2 Cor. 11:23
p Cp. v. 38; Acts 17:5; 19:40
32
q See Acts 27:1, *note*
33
r c. A.D. 56
s Acts 24:7
t Acts 21:11; 22:25; cp. 20:23
34
u v. 37; Acts 22:24; 23:10,16,32
36
v Acts 22:22; cp. Lk. 23:18
38
w Acts 5:36
39
x 2 Cor. 11:22; Phil. 3:4–6; cp. Acts 16:38; 22:25,28
40
y Acts 22:2
CHAPTER 22
1
z vv. 1–23. For Paul's defense speeches, see Acts 28:17, *note*
aa Cp. Lk. 12:11; 1 Pet. 3:15
2
bb Acts 21:40
3
cc vv. 3–16
dd Acts 5:34
ee Gal. 1:14
ff Cp. Rom. 10:2

[1](21:37) A commander (Gk. *chiliarch*) was a Roman tribune. There were six of them in a legion of 6000 men.

4 "I [a]persecuted this Way to the death, binding and delivering into prisons both men and women,

5 "as also the high priest bears me witness, and all the council of the [b]elders, from whom I also received letters to the brethren, and went to Damascus [c]to bring in chains even those who were there to Jerusalem to be punished.

6 "Now it happened, as I journeyed and came near Damascus at about noon, suddenly a great light from heaven shone around me.

7 "And I fell to the ground and [d]heard a voice saying to me, 'Saul, Saul, why are [e]you persecuting Me?'

8 "So I answered, 'Who are You, Lord?' And He said to me, 'I am Jesus of Nazareth, whom you are persecuting.'

9 "And those who were with me indeed saw the light and were afraid,* but they did [f]not hear the [g]voice of Him who spoke to me.

10 "So I [h]said, 'What shall I do, Lord?' And the Lord said to me, 'Arise and go into Damascus, and there you will be told all things which are appointed for you to [i]do.'

11 "And since I could not see for the glory of that light, being led by the hand of those who were with me, I came into Damascus.

12 "Then a certain Ananias, a devout man according to the [j]law, having a [k]good testimony with all the Jews who dwelt *there,*

13 "came to me; and he stood and said to me, 'Brother Saul, receive your sight.' And at that same hour I [l]looked up at him.

14 "Then he said, 'The God of our fathers has [m]chosen [n]you that you should [o]know His will, and see the [p]Just One, and [d]hear the voice of His mouth.

15 'For you will be His [q]witness to all men of what you have seen and heard.

16 'And now why are you waiting? Arise and be [r]baptized, and [s]wash away your [t]sins, calling on the name of the Lord.'

The Lord had warned Paul to leave Jerusalem and go to the Gentiles

17 "Now it happened, [1]when I returned to Jerusalem and was praying in the temple, that I was in a [u]trance

18 "and saw Him saying to me, 'Make haste and get [v]out of Jerusalem quickly, for they will not receive your testimony concerning Me.'

19 "So I [h]said, 'Lord, they know that in every synagogue I imprisoned and beat those who [w]believe on You.

20 'And when the blood of Your [x]martyr Stephen was shed, [y]I also was standing by consenting to his death,* and guarding the clothes of those who were killing him.'

21 "Then He said to me, 'Depart, [z]for I will send you far from here to the [aa]Gentiles.'"

Paul's defense interrupted; he asserts rights as Roman citizen

22 And they listened to him until this word, and *then* they raised their voices and said, [bb]"Away with such a *fellow* from the earth, for he is not fit to live!"

23 Then, as they cried out and tore off *their* clothes and threw dust into the air,

24 the [cc]commander ordered him to be brought into the barracks, and said that he should be [dd]examined under scourging, so that he might know why they shouted so against him.

25 And as they [ee]bound him with thongs, Paul [ff]said to the centurion who stood by, "Is it lawful for you to scourge a man who is a [gg]Roman, and uncondemned?"

26 When the [hh]centurion heard *that,* he went and told the commander, saying, "Take care what you do, for this man is a Roman."

*

22:9 NU-Text omits *and were afraid.*
22:20 NU-Text omits *to his death.*

4
a Acts 8:3; 1 Tim. 1:13
5
b Acts 23:14; 24:1; 25:15
c Acts 9:2
7
d Cp. Jn. 3:29; 10:4, 27; 18:37; Rev. 3:20
e Cp. Isa. 63:9; Zech. 2:8; Mt. 25:45; 1 Cor. 12:26
9
f Cp. Dan. 10:7
g See Acts 9:7, *note*
10
h Bible prayers (NT): vv. 10, 19–20; Eph. 1:16. (Mt. 6:9; Lk. 11:2, *note*). Cp. Acts 8:3
i Cp. Acts 2:37–38
12
j Law (of Moses): v. 12; Acts 23:3. (Ex. 19:1; Gal. 3:24, *note*)
k Cp. 1 Tim. 3:7–10
13
l Miracles (NT): vv. 6–13; Acts 28:5. (Mt. 8:3; Acts 28:8, *note*)
14
m Election (personal): v. 14; Rom. 8:33. (Dt. 7:6; 1 Pet. 5:13, *note*)
n Gal. 1:15
o Eph. 1:9; cp. Col. 1:9; Heb. 13:20–21
p Acts 3:14; 7:52
15
q Cp. Acts 23:11
16
r See Acts 8:12, *note*
s Acts 2:38; cp. 1 Cor. 5:7; 2 Cor. 7:1; 2 Tim. 2:21; Jas. 4:8; 1 Jn. 3:2–3
t See Rom. 3:23, *note*
17
u vv. 17–21; cp. Acts 10:10
18
v v. 21; cp. Acts 21:4
19
w Faith: v. 19; Acts 24:14. (Gen. 3:20; Heb. 11:39, *note*)
20
x Cp. Rev. 2:13; 17:6
y Acts 7:54–8:1
21
z Acts 9:15; 13:2,47; Rom. 11:13; Gal. 2:7–8; Eph. 3:7–8
aa See Eph. 3:6, *note*
22
bb Acts 21:36; cp. 1 Th. 2:16
24
cc See Acts 21:37, *note*
dd v. 29
25
ee Cp. Acts 21:11
ff vv. 25–30; see Acts 28:17, *note*
gg Acts 16:37; 23:27; 25:16
26
hh See Acts 27:1, *note*

[1](22:17) This was probably on the occasion of Paul's first visit to Jerusalem after his conversion (Acts 9:26ff.).

29
a v. 24
b Cp. Acts 21:11
30
c Cp. Acts 4:15; 5:27, 34,41; 6:12, 15; 23:15; 24:20
CHAPTER 23
1
d vv. 1–10. For Paul's defense speeches, see Acts 28:17, *note*
e Acts 24:16; 2 Cor. 1:12; 2 Tim. 1:3; Heb. 13:18; cp. 1 Pet. 3:15–16; 1 Jn. 3:21
2
f Cp Acts 24:1; 25:2
g Cp. 1 Ki. 22:24; Isa. 50:6; Mt. 27:30; Jn. 18:22
3
h Cp. Jn. 18:23
i Cp. Mt. 23:27
j *Law* (of Moses): vv. 3,5; Acts 23:29. (Ex. 19:1; Gal. 3:24, *note*)
5
k *Inspiration:* v. 5; Acts 24:14. (Ex. 4:15; 2 Tim. 3:16, *note*). Ex. 22:28; cp. Lev. 19:15
6
l See Mt. 3:7, *notes*

27 Then the commander came and said to him, "Tell me, are you a Roman?" He said, "Yes."

28 The commander answered, "With a large sum I obtained this citizenship." And Paul said, "But I was [1]born *a citizen.*"

29 Then immediately those who were about to [a]examine him withdrew from him; and the commander was also afraid after he found out that he was a Roman, and because he had [b]bound him.

Paul brought before the Sanhedrin

30 The next day, because he wanted to know for certain why he was accused by the Jews, he released him from *his* bonds, and commanded the chief priests and all their [c]council to appear, and brought Paul down and set him before them.

23 THEN Paul, looking earnestly at the [2]council, [d]said, "Men *and* brethren, [e]I have lived in all good conscience before God until this day."

2 And the high priest [f]Ananias commanded those who stood by him to [g]strike him on the mouth.

3 Then Paul [h]said to him, "God will strike you, *you* [i]whitewashed wall! For you sit to judge me according to the [j]law, and do you command me to be struck contrary to the law?"

4 And those who stood by said, "Do you revile God's high priest?"

5 Then Paul said, "I did not know, brethren, that he was the high priest; for it is [k]written, *'You shall not speak evil of a ruler of your people.'*"

Paul appeals to the Pharisees

6 But when Paul perceived that one part were [l]Sadducees and the other [l]Pharisees, he cried out in the council, "Men *and* brethren, I am a Pharisee, the son of a Pharisee; concerning the hope and [m]resurrection of the dead I am being judged!"

7 And when he had said this, a dissension arose between the Pharisees and the Sadducees; and the assembly was divided.

8 For Sadducees say that there is no [m]resurrection—and no [n]angel or spirit; but the Pharisees confess both.

9 Then there arose a loud outcry. And the [o]scribes of the Pharisees' party arose and protested, saying, "We find no evil in this man; but if a spirit or an [n]angel has spoken to him, let us not fight against God."*

10 Now when there arose a great dissension, the commander, fearing lest Paul might be pulled to pieces by them, commanded the soldiers to go down and take him by force from among them, and bring *him* into the barracks.

The Lord's grace to Paul

11 But the following night the [p]Lord [q]stood by him and said, [r]"Be of good cheer, Paul; for as you have testified for Me in [s]Jerusalem, so you must also [t]bear witness at [u]Rome."

A conspiracy under oath to kill Paul

12 And when it was day, [v]some of the Jews banded together and bound themselves under an oath, saying that they would neither eat nor drink till they had [w]killed Paul.

13 Now there were more than forty who had formed this conspiracy.

14 They came to the chief priests and [x]elders, and said, "We have bound ourselves under a great oath that we will eat nothing until we have killed Paul.

15 "Now you, therefore, to-

*

23:9 NU-Text omits last clause and reads *what if a spirit or an angel has spoken to him?*

m Acts 24:15, 21; 26:6–8; 28:20
8
n See Jud. 2:1 and Heb. 1:4, *notes*
9
o See Mt. 2:4, *note*
11
p Cp. Ps. 46:1–7; Mt. 28:20
q Cp. Acts 18:9–11; 27:23–24
r Cp. Mt. 9:2; 14:27; Jn. 16:33; Acts 27:22,25,36
s Acts 21:18–19; 22:1–21
t Cp. Jn. 1:7–8; 15:27
u Acts 28:23
12
v Cp. Jn. 16:2–3
w Acts 9:23–24; 25:3 26:21; 27:42
14
x Acts 4:5,23; 6:12; 22:5; 24:1; 25:15

---

[1](22:28) Paul was born as a Roman through a father who held Roman citizenship.

[2](23:1) For the fifth time the Sanhedrin was compelled to ajudicate the claims of Christ and His followers concerning His Person. Other occasions were the trials of (1) Jesus (Lk. 22:66–71); (2) Peter and John (Acts 4:5–22); (3) the twelve (Acts 5:21–40); and (4) Stephen (Acts 6:12—7:60).

gether with the [a]council, suggest to the [b]commander that he be brought down to you tomorrow,* as though you were going to make further inquiries concerning him; but we are [c]ready to kill him before he comes near."

16 So when Paul's sister's son heard of their ambush, he went and entered the barracks and told Paul.

17 Then Paul called one of the [d]centurions to *him* and said, "Take this young man to the commander, for he has something to tell him."

18 So he took him and brought *him* to the commander and said, "Paul the [e]prisoner called me to *him* and asked *me* to bring this young man to you. He has something to say to you."

19 Then the commander took him by the hand, went aside, and asked privately, "What is it that you have to tell me?"

20 And he said, "The Jews have agreed to ask that you bring Paul down to the [a]council tomorrow, as though they were going to inquire more fully about him.

21 "But do not yield to them, for more than forty of them [f]lie in wait for him, men who have bound themselves by an [g]oath that they will neither eat nor drink till they have [h]killed him; and now they are ready, waiting for the promise from you."

22 So the commander let the young man depart, and commanded *him*, "Tell no one that you have revealed these things to me."

Paul removed by night to Caesarea

23 And he called for two [d]centurions, saying, "Prepare two hundred soldiers, seventy horsemen, and two hundred spearmen to go to [i]Caesarea at the [j]third hour of the [k]night;

24 "and provide mounts to set Paul on, and bring *him* safely to Felix the governor."

25 He wrote a [l]letter in the following manner:

26 Claudius Lysias,
To the most excellent
governor Felix:
Greetings.

27 This man was [m]seized by the Jews and was about to be killed by them. Coming with the troops I rescued him, having learned that he was a [n]Roman.

28 And when I wanted to know the reason they accused him, I brought him before their [a]council.

29 I found out that he was accused concerning [o]questions of their [p]law, but had [q]nothing charged against him deserving of death or chains.

30 And when it was told me that the Jews lay in wait for the man,* I sent him immediately to you, and also commanded his accusers to state before you the charges against him.
Farewell.

31 Then the soldiers, as they were commanded, took Paul and brought *him* by night to [r]Antipatris.

32 The next day they left the horsemen to go on with him, and returned to the barracks.

33 When they came to [i]Caesarea and had delivered the [s]letter to the governor, they also presented Paul to him.

34 And when the governor had read *it*, he asked what province he was from. And when he understood that *he was* from [t]Cilicia,

35 he said, "I will hear you when your [u]accusers also have come." And he commanded him to be kept in Herod's Praetorium.

Paul before Felix, the governor

24 NOW after five days [v]Ananias the high priest came down with the elders and a certain orator *named* Tertul-

*
23:15 NU-Text omits *tomorrow*.
23:30 NU-Text reads *there would be a plot against the man.*

15
a Cp. Acts 4:15; 5:27, 34,41; 6:12, 15; 22:30; 24:20
b See Acts 21:37, *note*
c Cp. Ps. 37:32–33
17
d See Acts 27:1, *note*
18
e Cp. Eph. 3:1
21
f v. 30; cp. Lk. 11:53–54
g vv. 12–14
h Acts 9:23–24; 25:3; 26:21; 27:42
23
i Acts 8:40
j 9 p.m. See Jn. 19:14, *note*
k Cp. Acts 9:25; 17:10
25
l vv. 26–30
27
m Acts 21:30, 33
n Acts 16:37; 22:25; 25:16
29
o Cp. Acts 18:14–15; 25:19
p *Law* (of Moses): v. 29; Acts 24:6. (Ex. 19:1; Gal. 3:24, *note*)
q Acts 25:25; 26:31; cp. 25:11; 28:18
31
r Located about 40 mi. from Jerusalem. It was named by Herod the Great for his father, Antipater
33
s Acts 23:26–30
34
t Acts 21:39
35
u Acts 24:1; cp. 24:19; 25:16
CHAPTER 24
1
v Acts 23:2; 25:2

lus. These gave evidence to the
governor against Paul.

The accusation

2 And when he was called
upon, Tertullus began his [a]ac-
cusation, saying: "Seeing that
through you we enjoy great
peace, and prosperity is being
brought to this nation by your
foresight,
3 "we accept *it* always and
in all places, most noble Felix,
with all thankfulness.
4 "Nevertheless, not to be
tedious to you any further, I beg
you to hear, by your courtesy, a
few words from us.
5 "For we have found this
man a plague, a creator of dissension among all the Jews
throughout the [b]world, and a
ringleader of the sect of the
[c]Nazarenes.
6 "He even tried to [d]profane
the temple, and we seized him,*
and wanted to [e]judge him according to our [f]law.
7 "But the [g]commander
Lysias came by and with great
violence [h]took *him* out of our
hands,
8 [i]"commanding his [j]ac-
cusers to come to you. By exam-
ining him yourself you may ascertain all these things of which
we [a]accuse him."
9 And the Jews also as-
sented,* maintaining that these
things were so.

Paul's defense before Felix

10 Then Paul, after the governor had nodded to him to
speak, [k]answered: "Inasmuch
as I know that you have been for
many years a judge of this nation, I do the more cheerfully
[l]answer for myself,
11 "because you may ascertain that it is no more than
twelve days since I went up [m]to
Jerusalem to worship.
12 "And they neither found
me in the temple disputing with
anyone nor inciting the crowd,
either in the synagogues or in
the city.
13 "Nor can they prove the
things of which they now [a]ac-
cuse me.
14 "But this I confess to you,
that according to the Way
which they call a sect, so I worship the God of my [n]fathers,
[o]believing all things which are

2
a Cp. Mt. 27:12
5
b Gk. *oikoumenē*. See Lk. 2:1, *note*
c See Mt. 2:23, *note*
6
d Acts 21:28
e Cp. Jn. 18:31
f *Law* (of Moses): v. 6; Acts 24:14. (Ex. 19:1; Gal. 3:24, *note*)
7
g See Acts 21:37, *note*
h Acts 23:10
8
i Acts 23:30
j Acts 24:1; cp. 24:19; 25:16
10
k vv. 10–23. For Paul's defense speeches, see Acts 28:17, *note*
l Cp. 1 Pet. 3:15
11
m Acts 21:15
14
n Cp. 2 Tim. 1:3
o *Faith:* v. 14; Acts 27:25. (Gen. 3:20; Heb. 11:39, *note*)

*
24:6 NU-Text ends the sentence here and omits the rest of verse 6, all of verse 7, and the first clause of verse 8. **24:9** NU-Text and M-Text read *joined the attack.*

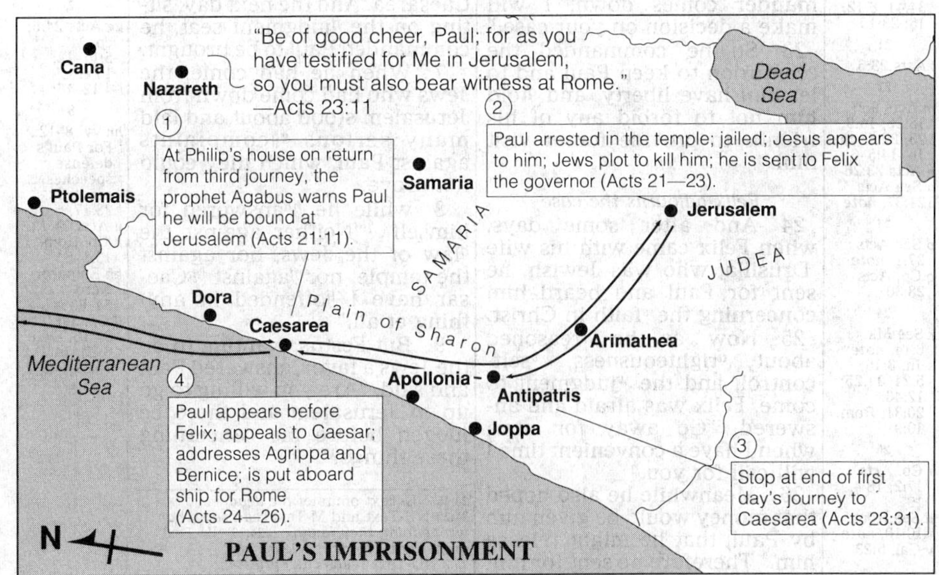
"Be of good cheer, Paul; for as you have testified for Me in Jerusalem, so you must also bear witness at Rome."
—Acts 23:11
Cana
Nazareth
Dead Sea
1
At Philip's house on return from third journey, the prophet Agabus warns Paul he will be bound at Jerusalem (Acts 21:11).
2
Paul arrested in the temple; jailed; Jesus appears to him; Jews plot to kill him; he is sent to Felix the governor (Acts 21—23).
Ptolemais
Samaria
SAMARIA
Jerusalem
JUDEA
Dora
Plain of Sharon
Caesarea
Arimathea
Mediterranean Sea
4
Apollonia
Antipatris
Joppa
Paul appears before Felix; appeals to Caesar; addresses Agrippa and Bernice; is put aboard ship for Rome (Acts 24—26).
3
Stop at end of first day's journey to Caesarea (Acts 23:31).
N
PAUL'S IMPRISONMENT

[a]written in the [b]Law and in the [c]Prophets.

15 "I have [d]hope in God, which they themselves also accept, that there [e]will be a [f]resurrection of *the* dead,* both of *the* just and *the* unjust.

16 "This *being* so, I myself always strive to have a [g]conscience without offense toward God and men.

17 "Now after many years I came to bring [h]alms and offerings to my nation,

18 [i]"in the midst of which some Jews from Asia found me [j]purified in the temple, neither with a mob nor with tumult.

19 "They ought to have been here before you to object if they had anything against me.

20 "Or else let those who are *here* themselves say if they found any wrongdoing* in me while I stood before the [k]council,

21 "unless *it is* for this one statement which I cried out, standing among them, [l]'Concerning the [f]resurrection of the dead I am being judged by you this day.' "

22 But when Felix heard these things, having more accurate knowledge of *the* [m]Way, he adjourned the proceedings and said, "When [n]Lysias the [o]commander comes down, I will make a decision on your case."

23 So he commanded the [p]centurion to keep Paul and to let *him* have liberty, and [q]told him not to forbid any of his friends to provide for or visit him.

Felix adjourns the case

24 And after some days, when Felix came with his wife [r]Drusilla, who was Jewish, he sent for Paul and heard him concerning the [s]faith in Christ.

25 Now as he [t]reasoned about [u]righteousness, [v]self-control, and the [w]judgment to come, Felix was afraid and answered, "Go away for now; when I have a convenient time I will call for you."

26 Meanwhile he also hoped that money would be given him by Paul, that he might release him.* Therefore he sent for him more often and conversed with him.

Two years at Caesarea

27 But after two years Porcius Festus succeeded Felix; and Felix, wanting to [x]do the Jews a favor, left Paul [y]bound.

Paul before Festus, the new governor

25 NOW when Festus had come to the province, after three days he went up from [z]Caesarea to Jerusalem.

2 Then the [aa]high priest* and the chief men of the Jews informed him against Paul; and they petitioned him,

3 asking a favor against him, that he would summon him to Jerusalem—while *they* [bb]lay in ambush along the road to [cc]kill him.

4 But Festus answered that Paul should be kept at Caesarea, and that he himself was going *there* shortly.

5 "Therefore," he said, "let those who have authority among you go down with *me* and accuse this man, [dd]to see if there is any fault in him."

6 And when he had remained among them [ee]more than ten days, he went down to Caesarea. And the next day, sitting on the [ff]judgment seat, he commanded Paul to be brought.

7 When he had come, the Jews who had come down from Jerusalem stood about and laid many serious [gg]complaints against Paul, which they could not prove,

8 while he [hh]answered for himself, [ii]"Neither against the [b]law of the Jews, nor against the temple, nor [jj]against [kk]Caesar have I [ll]offended in anything at all."

9 But Festus, wanting to do the Jews a favor, answered Paul and said, "Are you willing to go up to Jerusalem and there be judged before me concerning these things?"

*

24:15 NU-Text omits *of the dead.* **24:20** NU-Text and M-Text read *say what wrongdoing they found.* **24:26** NU-Text omits *that he might release him.* **25:2** NU-Text reads *chief priests.*

14
a Inspiration: v. 14; Acts 26:22. (Ex. 4:15; 2 Tim. 3:16, *note*)
b Law (of Moses): v. 14; 25:8; Acts 28:23. (Ex. 19:1; Gal. 3:24, *note*)
c Acts 3:18, 21; 13:40; 26:22–23

15
d Acts 23:6; 26:6–7; 28:20
e Dan. 12:2; Jn. 5:28–29
f Resurrection: vv. 15, 21; Acts 25:19. (2 Ki. 4:35; 1 Cor. 15:52, *note*)

16
g Acts 23:1; 2 Cor. 1:12; 2 Tim. 1:3; Heb. 13:18; cp. 1 Pet. 3:15–16; 1 Jn. 3:21

17
h Acts 11:29–30; cp. 2 Cor. 8:1–9:15

18
i Acts 21:27
j Acts 21:26

20
k Cp Acts 4:15; 5:27, 34,41; 6:12, 15; 23:15

21
l Acts 23:6

22
m Acts 9:2; 18:26; 19:9, 23; 22:4; cp. Jn. 14:5–6
n Acts 23:26
o See Acts 21:37, *note*

23
p See Acts 27:1, *note*
q Cp. Acts 28:30

24
r See Mk. 6:14, *note*
s Jn. 3:15; 5:24; 11:25; 12:46; 20:31; Rom. 10:9

25
t Cp. Acts 17:2; 18:4, 19
u See Rom. 10:10, *note*
v Gal. 5:23
w Judgments (the seven): v. 25; Rom. 1:32. (2 Sam. 7:14; Rev. 20:12, *note*)

27
x Cp. Mk. 15:15; Acts 12:3; 25:9
y Acts 25:14

CHAPTER 25

1
z Acts 8:40

2
aa Acts 24:1

3
bb Cp. Acts 23:14–16,21
cc Acts 9:23–24; 23:12; 26:21; 27:42

5
dd Cp. 1 Sam. 24:11; Ps. 7:3–6

6
ee Some mss. read *no more than eight or ten days*
ff Cp. Jn. 19:13

7
gg Acts 24:5; cp. Mt. 5:11–12; 1 Pet. 4:12–16

8
hh vv. 8–12. For Paul's defense speeches, see Acts 28:17, *note*
ii Acts 24:12
jj Cp. Rom. 13:1–5
kk Emperor Nero, A.D. 54–68
ll Cp. Jer. 37:18; Dan. 6:22; Jn. 10:32

Paul appeals his case to Caesar

10 So Paul said, "I stand at Caesar's [a]judgment seat, where I [b]ought to be judged. To the Jews I [c]have done no wrong, as you very well know.

11 "For if I am an offender, or have committed anything deserving of death, I do not object to dying; but if there is nothing in these things of which these men accuse me, no one can deliver me to them. [d]I appeal to Caesar."

12 Then Festus, when he had conferred with the [e]council, answered, "You have [d]appealed to Caesar? To [f]Caesar you shall go!"

Festus recounts case to King Agrippa

13 And after some days King [g]Agrippa and [h]Bernice came to Caesarea to greet Festus.

14 When they had been there many days, Festus laid Paul's case before the king, saying: "There is a certain man left [i]a prisoner by Felix,

15 "about whom the chief priests and the [j]elders of the Jews informed *me*, when I was in Jerusalem, asking for a judgment against him.

16 "To them I answered, 'It is not the custom of the [b]Romans to deliver any man to destruction* before the accused meets the [k]accusers face to face, and has opportunity to answer for himself concerning the charge against him.'

17 "Therefore when they had come together, without any delay, the next day I sat on the [a]judgment seat and commanded the man to be brought in.

18 "When the [k]accusers stood up, they brought no accusation against him of such things as I supposed,

19 "but had some [l]questions against him about their own religion and about a certain Jesus, who had died, whom Paul affirmed to be [m]alive.

20 "And because I was uncertain of such [l]questions, I asked whether he was willing to go to Jerusalem and there be judged concerning these matters.

10
a Cp. Jn. 19:13
b Acts 16:37; 22:25; 23:27
c Cp. Jer. 37:18; Dan. 6:22; Jn. 10:32
11
d Acts 26:32; 28:19; cp. 23:11; 27:24
12
e Cp. Mt. 12:14
f Emperor Nero, A.D. 54–68
13
g Herod Agrippa II. See Mk. 6:14, *note*
h See Mk. 6:14, *note*
14
i Acts 24:27
15
j Acts 4:5,23; 6:12; 22:5; 23:14; 24:1
16
k Acts 23:35; 24:1; cp. 24:19
19
l Acts 23:29; cp. 18:14–15
m *Resurrection:* v. 19; Acts 26:6. (2 Ki. 4:35; 1 Cor. 15:52, *note*)

21 "But when Paul [n]appealed to be reserved for the decision of [f]Augustus, I commanded him to be kept till I could send him to [f]Caesar."

22 Then Agrippa said to Festus, "I also would like to [o]hear the man myself." "Tomorrow," he said, "you shall hear him."

Agrippa prepares to hear Paul

23 So the next day, when Agrippa and Bernice had come with great pomp, and had entered the auditorium with the [p]commanders and the prominent men of the city, at Festus' command [q]Paul was brought in.

24 And Festus said: "King Agrippa and all the men who are here present with us, you see this man about whom the whole assembly of the Jews petitioned me, both at Jerusalem and here, [r]crying out that he was not fit to live any longer.

25 "But when I found that he had committed [s]nothing deserving of death, and that he himself had appealed to Augustus, I decided to send him.

26 "I have nothing certain to write to my lord concerning him. Therefore I have brought him out before you, and especially before [t]you, King Agrippa, so that after the examination has taken place I may have something to write.

27 "For it seems to me unreasonable to send a prisoner and not to specify the charges against him."

Paul's defense before Agrippa
(cp. Acts 9:1–18; 22:1–16)

26 THEN [u]Agrippa said to Paul, "You are permitted to speak for yourself." So Paul stretched out his hand and [v]answered for himself:

2 "I think myself [w]happy, King Agrippa, because today I shall answer [x]for myself before you concerning all the things of which I am [y]accused by the Jews,

3 "especially because you are expert in all [z]customs and questions which have to do with

*

25:16 NU-Text omits *to destruction,* although it is implied.

21
n Acts 25:11–12
22
o Cp. Lk. 23:8
23
p See Acts 21:37, *note*
q Acts 9:15
24
r Acts 21:36
25
s Acts 23:29; 26:31
26
t Cp. Acts 26:2–3
CHAPTER 26
1
u Herod Agrippa II. See Mk. 6:14. *note*
v vv. 1–32. For Paul's defense speeches, see Acts 28:17, *note*
2
w 1 Pet. 3:14; 4:14; cp. Phil. 4:11
x 1 Pet. 3:15–16
y Acts 21:28; 24:5–6
3
z Cp. Acts 6:14

the Jews. Therefore I beg you to hear me patiently.

4 "My manner of life from my youth, which was spent from the beginning among my own nation at Jerusalem, all the Jews know.

5 "They knew me from the first, if they were willing to testify, that according to the strictest sect of our religion I lived a [a]Pharisee.

6 "And now I stand and am [b]judged for the [c]hope of the [d]promise made by God to our fathers.

7 "To this [d]*promise* our [e]twelve [f]tribes, earnestly serving *God* night and day, hope to attain. For this [c]hope's sake, King Agrippa, I am [g]accused by the Jews.

8 "Why should it be thought incredible by you that God [c]raises the [h]dead?

9 "Indeed, I myself thought I must do many things [i]contrary to the name of [j]Jesus of Nazareth.

10 "This I also did [k]in Jerusalem, and many of the [l]saints I shut up in prison, having received [m]authority from the chief priests; and when they were [n]put to death, I [o]cast my vote against *them*.

11 "And I punished them often in every synagogue and compelled *them* to blaspheme; and being exceedingly enraged against them, I persecuted *them* even to foreign cities.

12 "While thus occupied, as I journeyed to Damascus with authority and commission from the chief priests,

13 "at midday, O king, along the road I saw a light from heaven, brighter than the sun, shining around me and those who journeyed with me.

14 "And when we all had fallen to the ground, I [p]heard a voice speaking to me and saying in the [q]Hebrew language, 'Saul, Saul, why are you persecuting Me? *It is* hard for you to kick against the [r]goads.'

15 "So I said, 'Who are You, Lord?' And He said, 'I am Jesus, whom you are persecuting.

16 'But [s]rise and stand on your feet; for I have appeared to you for this [t]purpose, to [u]make you a [v]minister and a witness both of the things which you have seen and of the things which I will yet reveal to you.

17 'I will deliver you from the *Jewish* people, as well as *from* the [w]Gentiles, to whom I now* send you,

18 'to open their eyes, *in order* to turn *them* from darkness to light, and *from* the power of [x]Satan to God, that they may receive [y]forgiveness of [z]sins and an [aa]inheritance among those who are [bb]sanctified by faith in Me.'

19 "Therefore, King Agrippa, I was not disobedient to the heavenly vision,

20 "but [cc]declared first to those in Damascus and in Jerusalem, and throughout all the region of Judea, and *then* to the [w]Gentiles, that they should [dd]repent, turn to God, and do works befitting [dd]repentance.

21 "For these reasons the Jews seized me in the temple and tried to [ee]kill *me*.

22 "Therefore, having obtained help from God, to this day I stand, witnessing both to small and great, saying no other things than those which the prophets and Moses [ff]said would come—

23 [1]"that the [gg]Christ would [hh]suffer, that He would be the first to [c]rise from the dead, and would proclaim [ii]light to the *Jewish* people and to the [w]Gentiles."

Personal appeal to Agrippa

24 Now as he thus made his defense, Festus said with a loud voice, "Paul, you are [jj]beside yourself! Much learning is driving you mad!"

25 But he said, "I am not mad,

*26:17 NU-Text and M-Text omit *now*.

5
a See Mt. 3:7, *note 1*
6
b Acts 23:6
c Resurrection: vv. 6–8,23; Acts 28:20. (2 Ki. 4:35; 1 Cor. 15:52, *note*)
d Acts 13:32–33; cp. Gen. 3:15; 22:18; 49:10
7
e Cp. Ex. 1:1–5; 28:21; Jas. 1:1
f Israel (prophecies): vv. 6–7; Rom. 9:4. (Gen. 12:2; Rom. 11:26, *note*)
g Acts 21:28; 24:5–6
8
h Cp. v. 23
9
i 1 Cor. 15:9; 1 Tim. 1:12–13
j Acts 2:22; 10:38
10
k Acts 8:1–3; Gal. 1:13
l See Rom. 1:7, *note*
m Acts 9:14
n Cp. Rev. 6:9; 20:4
o Cp. Acts 7:58
14
p See Acts 9:7, *note*
q Cp. Jn. 5:2; 19:20; Acts 21:40; 22:2
r Acts 9:5
16
s Cp. Ezek. 2:1; Dan. 10:11
t Cp. Isa. 14:27
u Cp. Acts 22:14–15
v Eph. 3:6–8
17
w See Eph. 3:6, *note*
18
x Satan: v. 18; Rom. 16:20. (Gen. 3:1; Rev. 20:10)
y Forgiveness: v. 18; Rom. 4:7. (Lev. 4:20; Mt. 26:28, *note*)
z See Rom. 3:23, *note*
aa Acts 20:32; Eph. 1:11; Col. 1:12; 1 Pet. 1:3–5
bb Sanctification (NT): v. 18; Rom. 1:2. (Mt. 4:5; Rev. 22:11)
20
cc See Acts 1:8, *note*
dd Repentance: v. 20; Rom. 2:4. (Mt. 3:2; Acts 17:30, *note*)
21
ee Acts 9:23–24; 23:12; 25:3; 27:42
22
ff Inspiration: vv. 22–23; Acts 28:23. (Ex. 4:15; 2 Tim. 3:16, *note*)
23
gg Christ (first advent): v. 23; Rom. 1:3. (Gen. 3:15; Acts 1:11, *note*)
hh Sacrifice (of Christ): v. 23; Rom. 3:25. (Gen. 3:15; Heb. 10:18, *note*)
ii Gospel: v. 23; Acts 28:31. (Gen. 12:3; Rev. 14:6)
24
jj Cp. Jn. 10:20

[1](26:23) Here in substance is the Gospel that Paul preached and that believers ought always to proclaim, "that Christ died for our sins according to the Scriptures, and that He was buried, and that He rose again the third day according to the Scriptures" (1 Cor. 15:3–4). Of course, the apostle expounded these truths but the kernel of the Gospel is here.

most noble Festus, but speak the words of truth and reason.

26 "For the king, before whom I also speak freely, [a]knows these things; for I am convinced that none of these things escapes his attention, since this thing was not done in a corner.

27 "King Agrippa, do you believe the prophets? I know that you do [b]believe."

28 Then Agrippa said to Paul, [1]"You almost persuade me to become a Christian."

29 And Paul said, "I would to God that not only you, but also all who hear me today, might become [c]both almost and altogether such as I am, except for these chains."

30 When he had said these things, the king stood up, as well as the governor and Bernice and those who sat with them;

31 and when they had gone aside, they talked among themselves, saying, "This man is doing [d]nothing deserving of death or chains."

32 Then Agrippa said to Festus, "This man might have been set [e]free if he had not [f]appealed to Caesar."

Paul sent to Rome

27 AND when it was decided that [g]we should sail to Italy, they delivered Paul and some other prisoners to *one* named Julius, a [2]centurion of the Augustan Regiment.

2 So, entering a ship of Adramyttium, we put to sea, meaning to sail along the coasts of Asia. [h]Aristarchus, a Macedonian of Thessalonica, was with us.

3 And the next *day* we landed at Sidon. And Julius [i]treated Paul kindly and gave *him* liberty to go to his friends and receive care.

4 When we had put to sea from there, we sailed under *the shelter of* Cyprus, because the winds were contrary.

5 And when we had sailed over the sea which is off Cilicia and Pamphylia, we came to Myra, *a city* of Lycia.

6 There the [j]centurion found an [k]Alexandrian ship sailing to [l]Italy, and he put us on board.

7 When we had sailed slowly many days, and arrived with difficulty off Cnidus, the wind not permitting us to proceed, we sailed under *the shelter of* [m]Crete off Salmone.

8 Passing it with difficulty, we came to a place called Fair Havens, near the city *of* Lasea.

9 Now when much time had been spent, and sailing was now [n]dangerous because the [3]Fast was already over, Paul advised them,

10 saying, "Men, I [o]perceive that this voyage will end with disaster and much loss, not only of the cargo and ship, but also our lives."

11 Nevertheless the centurion was more persuaded by the helmsman and the owner of the ship than by the things spoken by Paul.

12 And because the harbor was not suitable to winter in, the majority advised to set sail from there also, if by any means they could reach Phoenix, a harbor of Crete opening toward the southwest and northwest, *and* winter *there*.

13 When the south wind blew softly, supposing that they had obtained *their* desire, putting out to sea, they sailed close by Crete.

The storm

14 But not long after, a [p]tempestuous head wind arose, called Euroclydon.*

15 So when the ship was

26
a Acts 26:3
27
b Cp. Jas. 2:19
29
c Lit. *both in a little and in much*
31
d Acts 25:25
32
e Acts 28:18
f Acts 25:11; cp. 23:11
CHAPTER 27
1
g Cp. Acts 20:6; 21:1; 28:16; see Acts 16:10, *note*
2
h Acts 19:29; 20:4; Col. 4:10; Phile. 24
3
i Cp. Prov. 16:7
6
j See v. 1, *note*
k Acts 28:11
l v. 1
7
m Ti. 1:5
9
n Cp. 2 Cor. 11:25
10
o Cp. Amos 3:7
14
p Cp. Ps. 107:25

*27:14 NU-Text reads *Euraquilon.*

[1](26:28) Agrippa's answer to Paul's question in v. 27 probably did not mean that he was on the brink of becoming a Christian, but that he realized that Paul was trying to use Agrippa's belief in the prophets (vv. 22–23,27) to lead him to agreement with what Paul had said about Christ.

[2](27:1) A Roman centurion commanded 100 soldiers.

[3](27:9) This fast, or feast, was the Jewish Day of Atonement, commemorated on the tenth day of the seventh month (Lev. 23:27; also Lev. 23:2, *note* 2).

caught, and could not head into the wind, we let *her* drive.

16 And running under *the shelter of* an island called Clauda,* we secured the skiff with difficulty.

17 When they had taken it on board, they used cables to undergird the ship; and fearing lest they should run aground on the Syrtis* *Sands,* they struck sail and so were driven.

18 And because we were exceedingly tempest-tossed, the next *day* they lightened the ship.

19 On the third *day* we [a]threw the ship's tackle overboard with our own hands.

20 Now when neither sun nor stars appeared for many days, and no small tempest beat on *us,* all hope that we would be saved was finally given up.

The leadership of Paul

21 But after long abstinence from food, then Paul stood in the midst of them and said, "Men, you should have [b]listened to me, and not have sailed from Crete and incurred this disaster and loss.

22 "And now [c]I urge you to [d]take heart, for there will be no loss of life among you, but only of the ship.

23 "For there [e]stood by me this night an [f]angel of the God to whom I belong and whom I serve,

24 "saying, [g]'Do not be afraid, Paul; you must be brought before Caesar; and indeed God has granted you [h]all those who sail with you.'

25 "Therefore [d]take heart, men, for I [i]believe God that it will be just as it was told me.

26 "However, we must run aground on a certain [j]island."

27 Now when the fourteenth night had come, as we were driven up and down in the Adriatic *Sea,* about midnight the sailors sensed that they were drawing near some land.

28 And they took soundings and found *it* to be twenty [1]fathoms; and when they had gone a little farther, they took soundings again and found *it* to be fifteen [k]fathoms.

29 Then, fearing lest we should run aground on the rocks, they dropped four anchors from the stern, and prayed for day to come.

30 And as the sailors were seeking to escape from the ship, when they had let down the skiff into the sea, under pretense of putting out anchors from the prow,

31 Paul said to the centurion

*

27:16 NU-Text reads *Cauda.* 27:17 M-Text reads *Syrtes.*

19
a Cp. Jon. 1:5
21
b vv. 9–10
22
c Cp. 1 Sam. 30:6; Ps. 112:7; 2 Cor. 1:4; 4:8–9
d Cp. Acts 18:9–11; 23:11
23
e Cp. Acts 23:11; 2 Tim. 4:17
f See Jud. 2:1, *note*
24
g Cp. Isa. 41:10,13,14; 43:1
h vv. 43–44; cp. Gen. 18:23–33
25
i Faith: v. 25; Acts 28:24. (Gen. 3:20; Heb. 11:39, *note*). Num. 23:19; Lk. 1:45; Ti. 1:2
26
j Acts 28:1
28
k See v. 28, *note*

[1](27:28) Weights and Measures (NT). Weights and measures in the NT are based upon Hebrew, Greek, and Roman usage; e.g. "rod" (Gk. *kalamos*) is a unit of measurement employed by the Israelites in OT times (Ezek. 40:5, Heb. *kaneh*); "furlong" (Gk. *stadion*) is distinctly a Greek unit; whereas the NT "pound" (Gk. *litra,* from the Latin *libra*) is a Roman measure that was considerably lighter than the U.S. pound weight. New Testament standards of measurement can be ascertained with reasonable accuracy. See the following tables.

(1) Linear Measures. The unit of linear measurement in NT times was the cubit, approximately 18 inches in length. The table: 4 cubits = 1 fathom, or about 6 feet; 6 long cubits (Ezek. 40:5) = 1 rod (measuring), or about 10 feet; 400 cubits = 1 furlong (stadion), or about 600 feet; 5 furlongs (stadia) = a Sabbath day's journey, or about three-fifths of a mile.

The Sabbath day's journey is mentioned only once in the Bible (Acts 1:12). It was evidently the distance between Jerusalem and the Mount of Olives. But from what point in Jerusalem to what area of Olivet? According to limits set by the ancient rabbis, a Sabbath day's journey was 2000 cubits, or three-fifths of a mile. This measure may have been determined by the distance that the children of Israel were required to allow between themselves and the ark of the covenant at the passage of the Jordan (Josh. 3:4); for the rabbis may have assumed that the same limit prevailed between the tents of the people and the tabernacle—a distance that the Israelites would need to walk in order to worship.

(2) Dry Measures. Gk. *choinix* (Rev. 6:6) = 1 quart; 1 measure, Gk. *koros* (Lk. 16:7) = about 10 bushels.

(3) Liquid Measures. Gk. *metretes* (Jn. 2:6) = 10 gallons; Gk. *batos* (Lk. 16:6) = about 8 gallons.

(4) Weights. 1 pound, Gk. *litra* (Jn. 12:3) = 1 pint, or (Jn. 19:39) about ¾ lb.

For Weights and Measures (OT), see 2 Chr. 2:10, *note.*

and the soldiers, [a]"Unless these
men stay in the ship, you cannot
be saved."
32 Then the soldiers cut
away the ropes of the [b]skiff and
let it fall off.
33 And as day was about to
dawn, Paul implored *them* all to
take food, saying, "Today is the
fourteenth day you have waited
and continued without food,
and eaten nothing.
34 "Therefore I urge you to
take nourishment, [c]for this is
for your survival, [d]since not a
hair will fall from the head of
any of you."
35 And when he had said
these things, he took bread and
gave [e]thanks to God in the presence of them all; and when he
had [f]broken *it* he began to eat.
36 Then they were all en-
couraged, and also took food
themselves.
37 And in all we were two
hundred and [g]seventy-six persons on the ship.
38 So when they had eaten
enough, they [h]lightened the
ship and threw out the wheat
into the sea.

The ship founders, but all escape

39 When it was day, they did
[i]not recognize the land; but
they observed a bay with a
beach, onto which they planned
to run the ship if possible.
40 And they let go the anchors and left *them* in the sea,
meanwhile loosing the rudder
ropes; and they hoisted the
mainsail to the wind and made
for shore.
41 But striking a place where
two seas met, they ran the ship
aground; and the prow stuck
fast and remained immovable,
but the stern was being broken
up by the violence of the waves.
42 And the soldiers' [j]plan
was to kill the prisoners, lest
any of them should swim away
and escape.
43 But the centurion, wanting to [k]save Paul, kept them
from *their* purpose, and commanded that those who could
swim should jump *overboard*
first and get to land,
44 and the rest, some on
boards and some on *parts* of the
ship. And [l]so it was that they
[m]all [n]escaped safely to land.

The landing on Malta;
miracle of viper's bite
(cp. Mk. 16:18)

28 NOW when they had
[n]escaped, they then
[o]found out that the island was
called Malta.
2 And the [p]natives showed
us unusual kindness; for they
kindled a fire and [q]made us all
welcome, because of the rain
that was falling and because of
the cold.
3 But when Paul had gath-
ered a bundle of sticks and laid
them on the fire, a viper came
out because of the heat, and fastened on his hand.
4 So when the natives saw
the creature hanging from his
hand, they said to one another,
"No doubt this man is a murderer, whom, though he has escaped the sea, yet [r]justice does
not allow to live."
5 But he shook off the creature into the fire and suffered
[s]no harm.
6 However, they were ex-
pecting that he would swell up
or suddenly fall down dead. But
after they had looked for a long
time and saw no harm come to
him, they [t]changed their minds
and said that he was a [u]god.

Father of Publius is healed

7 In that region there was
an estate of the leading citizen
of the island, whose name was
Publius, who received us and
entertained us [v]courteously for
three days.
8 And it happened that the
father of Publius lay sick of a
fever and dysentery. Paul went
in to him and [w]prayed, and he
[x]laid his hands on him and
[1][s]healed him.
9 So when this was done,
the rest of those on the island
who had diseases also came and
were [s]healed.
10 They also honored us in
many ways; and when we de-

31
a vv. 22–25; cp. Ezek. 36:36; Lk. 4:9–12
32
b vv. 16,30
34
c Cp. Mt. 15:32
d Cp. Mt. 10:30; Lk. 21:18
35
e 1 Tim. 4:4
f Cp. Mt. 14:19; Lk. 24:30; Acts 2:42; 20:11
37
g Some MSS. read *about*
38
h Cp. vv. 18–19
39
i Cp. Acts 28:1
42
j Cp. v. 12
43
k Cp. Prov. 16:7

44
l v. 22; cp. 2 Cor. 1:8, 10
m v. 24
n Cp. Gen. 19:15–16; 1 Sam. 17:37; Dan. 3:27; 6:22; Jon. 2:10; Acts 5:18–19; 12:7; 16:26
CHAPTER 28
1
o v. 39
2
p v. 4; cp. Rom. 1:14; 1 Cor. 14:11; Col. 3:11
q Cp. Heb. 13:2
4
r Cp. v. 6
5
s *Miracles* (NT): vv. 3–6,8–9; Rev. 11:11. (Mt. 8:3; Acts 28:8, *note*). Mk. 16:18; Lk. 10:19
6
t v. 4
u Acts 12:22; 14:11; cp. Acts 10:25; Rev. 22:8–9
7
v Cp. Acts 27:3; 1 Pet. 3:8
8
w Cp. Jas. 5:14–15
x Acts 19:11; cp. Mk. 16:18; 1 Cor. 12:9, 28

[1](28:8) Miracles in NT times authenticated the witness of God's messengers.

parted, they provided such
things as were [a]necessary.

10
a Phil 4:19

Paul arrives at Rome

11 After three months we
sailed in an [b]Alexandrian ship
whose figurehead was the
[c]Twin Brothers, which had
wintered at the island.
12 And landing at Syracuse,
we stayed three days.
13 From there we circled
round and reached Rhegium.
And after one day the south
wind blew; and the next day we
came to Puteoli,
14 where we found [d]breth-
ren, and were invited to stay
with them seven days. And so
we went toward Rome.
15 And from there, when the
brethren heard about us, they
came to meet us as far as Appii
Forum and Three Inns. When
Paul saw them, he thanked God
and took [e]courage.
16 [f]Now when we came to
[g]Rome, the [h]centurion delivered the prisoners to the captain
of the guard; but Paul was permitted to dwell by himself with
[i]the soldier who guarded him.

11
b Acts 27:6
c Gk. *Dioskouri,* Zeus's sons Castor and Pollux
14
d Rom. 1:8; cp. Mt. 23:8; Lk. 8:21; Jn. 21:23; Rom. 8:29; Heb. 2:11; Rev. 12:10; 19:10
15
e Cp. Josh. 1:6–7,9; Ps. 27:14
16
f c. A.D. 60; see v. 30, *note*
g Cp. Acts 19:21; 23:11
h See Acts 27:1, *note*
i Acts 24:23; 27:3

Paul witnesses to the Jews in Rome

17 And it came to pass after
three days that Paul called the
leaders of the [1]Jews together.
So when they had come to-
gether, he [j]said to them: "Men
and brethren, though I have
done [k]nothing against our people or the customs of our fathers, yet I was [l]delivered as a
prisoner from Jerusalem into
the hands of the Romans,
18 "who, when they had examined me, [m]wanted to let *me*
go, because there was [k]no
cause for putting me to death.
19 "But when the Jews*
spoke against *it,* I was compelled to [n]appeal to Caesar, not

17
j vv. 17–28. For Paul's defense speeches, see v. 17, *note*
k Acts 23:29; 26:31
l Acts 21:33
18
m Acts 26:32
19
n Acts 25:11

*28:19 That is, the ruling authorities

[1](28:17) Paul's defense before the Jews at Rome concludes a series of important documentations of his innocence, which may have been presented as part of his defense when he later appeared before Caesar. They are before (1) the Jerusalem mob (22:1–23); (2) the commander (22:24–30); (3) the Sanhedrin (23:1–10); (4) Felix (24:10–23); (5) Festus (25:8–12); (6) King Agrippa II (26:1–32); and (7) Jews at Rome (28:17–28).

PAUL'S FOURTH MISSIONARY JOURNEY

that I had anything of which to
accuse my nation.
20 “For this reason therefore
I have called for you, to see *you*
and speak with *you,* because for
the [a]hope of Israel I am bound
with this [b]chain.”
21 Then they said to him,
“We neither received letters
from Judea concerning you, nor
have any of the brethren who
came reported or spoken any
evil of you.
22 “But we desire to hear
from you what you think; for
concerning this [c]sect, we know
that it is [d]spoken against everywhere.”
23 So when they had ap-
pointed him a day, many came
to him at *his* lodging, to whom
he [e]explained and solemnly
testified of the [f]kingdom of
God, persuading them concerning Jesus from both the [g]Law of
Moses and [h]the Prophets, from
morning till evening.
24 And some were [i]per-
suaded by the things which
were spoken, and some disbelieved.

Paul turns to the Gentiles
(cp. Acts 13:44; 18:6)

25 So when they did not
agree among themselves, they
departed after Paul had said
one word: “The Holy [j]Spirit
spoke rightly [h]through [k]Isaiah
the prophet to our* fathers,
26 “saying,

'Go to this people and
say:
“Hearing you will hear,
and shall not
understand;
And seeing you will see,
and not perceive;
27 *For the hearts of this*
people have grown
dull.
Their ears are hard of
hearing,
And their eyes they have
closed,
Lest they should see with
their eyes and hear
with their ears,
Lest they should
understand with their
hearts and turn,
So that I should heal
them.” '

28 “Therefore let it be known
to you that the [l]salvation of
God has been sent to the [m]Gen-
tiles, and they will hear it!”
29 And when he had said
these words, the Jews departed
and had a great dispute among
themselves.*

Two years in rented house at
Rome

30 Then Paul dwelt two
whole years in [1]his own rented
house, and received all who
came to him,
31 [n]preaching the [f]kingdom
of God and teaching the things
which concern the Lord Jesus
Christ with all confidence, no
one forbidding him.

* 28:25 NU-Text reads *your.* 28:29 NU-Text omits this verse.

20
a Resurrection: v. 20; Rom. 1:4. (2 Ki. 4:35; 1 Cor. 15:52, *note*). Acts 23:6; 24:15; 26:6–8
b Eph. 3:1; 6:20; 2 Tim. 1:8
22
c Cp. Acts 24:5,14–16
d Cp. Lk. 2:34; 1 Pet. 2:12; 4:14
23
e Cp. Gen. 49:10; Num. 24:17; Mal. 3:1; 4:2
f See Mt. 6:33, *note*
g Law (of Moses): v. 23; Rom. 2:12. (Ex. 19:1; Gal. 3:24, *note*)
h Inspiration: vv. 23, 25–27; Rom. 1:2. (Ex. 4:15; 2 Tim. 3:16, *note*)
24
i Faith: v. 24; Rom. 1:5. (Gen. 3:20; Heb. 11:39, *note*)
25
j Holy Spirit (NT): v. 25; Rom. 5:5. (Mt. 1:18; Acts 2:4, *note*)
k Isa. 6:9–10; Mt. 13:14–15; Jn. 12:40–41
28
l See Rom. 1:16, *note*
m See Eph. 3:6, *note*
31
n Gospel: v. 31; Rom. 1:1. (Gen. 12:3; Rev. 14:6)

[1](28:30) It has been much disputed whether Paul endured two Roman imprisonments from A.D. 60 to 68, or one. The tradition from Clement to Eusebius favors two imprisonments with a year of liberty between them. It has been pointed out that the leaving of Trophimus sick at Miletus (2 Tim. 4:20) could not have been an occurrence of Paul's last journey to Jerusalem, for then Trophimus was not left (Acts 20:4; 21:29); nor could it have been on his journey to Rome to appear before Caesar, for then he did not touch at Miletus. To make this incident possible, there must have been a release from the first imprisonment and an interval of ministry and travel.

The Epistles of Paul

THE EPISTLES OF PAUL have a distinctive character. The OT contains prophecies of the cross, the resurrection, and the return of Christ. In it Israel has a leading place through history and also through prophecy of the future Messianic kingdom. But "hidden in God" (Eph. 3:9) was a period not specifically revealed in the OT—the interval after the crucifixion and resurrection of Christ, and before His return in glory. Also not specifically revealed in the OT was God's purpose in calling out of the world the Church, which is Christ's body. In Mt. 16:17–19 the Lord announced that purpose but without explaining how, when, or of whom the Church would be built. Elsewhere in the Gospels He instituted the two sacraments or ordinances of the Church—baptism (Mt. 28:18–20) and the Lord's Supper (Mt. 26:26–29; Mk. 14:22–25; Lk. 22:19–20); in the discourse on the night before His crucifixion (Jn. 14—17), He set forth the relationship of His body, the Church, to Himself. But it is in the Epistles that the order, position, privileges, and duties of the Church are most fully given.

It is these things that constitute the scope of the Epistles of Paul. They develop the doctrine of the Church. In his letters to seven of the churches (in Rome, Corinth, Galatia, Ephesus, Philippi, Colosse, and Thessalonica), the Church as the body of Christ, the "mystery, which from the beginning of the ages has been hidden in God" (Eph. 3:9), is revealed. Moreover, in these Epistles the Church is instructed about her unique place in the counsels and purposes of God.

Although Christ taught that the Church is an organism, through Paul was given the detailed revelation of the body of Christ in its heavenly calling, promise, and destiny. Through him there were also unfolded the organization and administration of local churches (1 Timothy and Titus). The fact that Christ is coming for His Church, introduced in Jn. 14:3, was revealed more fully through Paul in 1 Cor. 15:51–58 and 1 Th. 4:13–18, where he teaches that "we shall not all sleep," that "the dead in Christ will rise first," and that believers living at His return will be "changed" and "caught up . . . to meet the Lord in the air."

The doctrine of grace found in the teaching of Christ is also given further revelation through Paul. More fully than any other NT writer, Paul expounds the nature and purpose of the law; the ground and means of the believer's justification, sanctification, and glorification; the interpretation of the death and resurrection of Christ; and the position, conduct, expectation, and service of the believer. Paul, converted by the personal ministry of the risen Lord, is distinctively the witness to the glorified Christ, the Head of the Church which is His body.

The chronological order of the Pauline Epistles is generally considered to be as follows: 1 and 2 Thessalonians, Galatians, 1 Corinthians, Romans, 2 Corinthians, Ephesians, Colossians, Philemon, Philippians, 1 Timothy, Titus, and 2 Timothy. The Pauline authorship of Hebrews has not been proved.

Two significant periods in the life of Paul are passed over in comparative silence—his stay in Arabia (Gal. 1:17), from which he returned with the Gospel as set forth in Galatians and Romans, and the two years in prison (Acts 24:27) between his arrest in the temple at Jerusalem and his journey under guard to Rome.

It was inevitable for a man of Paul's intellect and training, a devoted Jew who had been such a bitter enemy of Christianity, to seek the underlying principles of the Gospel. Immediately after his conversion he preached Jesus as the Messiah; but the relation of the Gospel to the law and, in lesser degree, to the great Jewish promises needed clear explanation. In Arabia this explanation was given Paul "through the revelation of Jesus Christ" (Gal. 1:11–12). The result was that he taught salvation by grace through faith wholly apart from the works of the law.

Furthermore, the Gospel proclaimed by Paul brings the believer into great relationships—to the Father, to the Son, to the Holy Spirit, and to the future purposes of God. It brings not only salvation from sin and its consequences, but also salvation into a blessed place in the divine counsels. And the Church in its deepest aspect and function requires inspired explanation. Such are the chief themes of the Epistles written by Paul from Rome and commonly called the Prison Epistles (Ephesians, Colossians, Philemon, and Philippians). It is possible that these crowning revelations were received through the apostle's disciplined meditation and prayerful seeking during the silent years at Caesarea.

The Epistle of Paul the Apostle to the

ROMANS

Author: Paul *Theme:* Gospel of God *Date of writing:* c. A.D. 57–58

THE EPISTLE TO THE ROMANS was written from Corinth during the Apostle Paul's third visit to that city (2 Cor. 13:1; cp. Acts 20:2). It is rightly placed first among the Epistles because it is the most complete exposition in the NT of the central truths of Christianity. The Epistle had its occasion in the intention of Paul to visit the Roman Christians and his desire to communicate to them the great doctrines of grace that had been revealed to him.

The theme of the Epistle is "the gospel of God" (1:1). This is the widest possible designation of the whole body of redemption truth. It relates to the whole world because there is "no partiality" (2:11) with Him who is "the God of the Jews" and "of the Gentiles also" (3:29). Accordingly all humanity is found guilty (3:19,23) and a justification is revealed which is sufficient for man's need and received through faith alone (3:28). Romans states the divine provision of God's grace whereby He is able to declare sinners as righteous through the atoning work of His righteous Son. It goes on to set forth the nature of the new life which all justified persons may enjoy through the power of the indwelling Holy Spirit. Following this the Epistle reveals God's sovereign wisdom and grace in working out His purpose through the unfaithfulness of Israel. It closes by laying on all Christians the obligation of recipients of "the mercies of God" (12:1) to live lives of consecrated service. The key expression of the book is "the righteousness of God" (1:17; 3:21,22).

The Epistle may be divided as follows:

Introduction and Theme, 1:1–17.
I. The Whole World Guilty before God, 1:18—3:20.
II. Justification by Faith in Christ, 3:21—5:21.
III. Sanctification through Union with Christ in His Death and Resurrection, 6—8.
IV. The Problem of Jewish Unbelief, 9—11.
V. Christian Life and Service for the Glory of God, 12:1—15:13.
Conclusion: The Outflow of Christian Love, 15:14—16:27.

CHAPTER 1
1
a 1 Cor. 1:1; 15:9
b *Gospel:* vv. 1–4,9; Rom. 1:15. (Gen. 12:3; Rev. 14:6)
2
c *Inspiration:* v. 2; Rom. 1:17. (Ex. 4:15; 2 Tim. 3:16, *note*)
d *Sanctification* (NT): vv. 2,4; Rom. 6:19. (Mt. 4:5; Rev. 22:11)
3
e *Christ* (first advent): vv. 3–5; Rom. 8:3. (Gen. 3:15; Acts 1:11, *note*). See

Introduction and Theme: The Righteousness of God, 1:1–17

1 PAUL, a bondservant of Jesus Christ, called *to be* an
[a]apostle, separated to the [b]gospel of God
2 which He [c]promised before through His prophets in the
[d]Holy Scriptures,
3 concerning His Son Jesus
Christ our Lord, who was [e]born
of the seed of David according
to the flesh,
4 *and* declared *to be* the
[f]Son of God with power according to the Spirit of [d]holiness, by the [g]resurrection from
the dead.
5 Through Him we have received [h]grace and [a]apostleship
for obedience to the [i]faith
among all nations for His name,
6 among whom you also are
the called of Jesus Christ;
7 To all who are in Rome,
beloved of God, called *to be*
[1]saints:
[h]Grace to you and peace
from God our Father and the
Lord Jesus Christ.
8 First, I thank my God
through Jesus Christ for you all,
that your [i]faith is spoken of
throughout the whole [j]world.
9 For God is my witness,
whom I serve with my spirit in
the [b]gospel of His Son, that
without ceasing I make mention
of you always in my prayers,
10 making request if, by
some means, now at last I may

Mt. 4:8, *note*

Lk. 3:23, *note*
4
f Acts 9:20; Heb. 1:2
g *Resurrection:* v. 4; Rom. 4:24. (2 Ki. 4:35; 1 Cor. 15:52, *note*)
5
h *Grace:* vv. 5,7; Rom. 3:24. (Jn. 1:14; Jn. 1:17, *note*). Rom. 15:15–16
i *Faith:* vv. 5, 8; Rom. 1:12. (Gen. 3:20; Heb. 11:39, *note*). Cp. Rom. 10:1–11; 16:26
8
j Gk. *kosmos.* See

---

[1](1:7) In the NT the word "saint" always refers to a sanctified person, one set apart to God inviolably for His possession and service. (Compare the related Greek words *hagios* and *hagiazō* rendered "saint" and "sanctify" respectively.) This aspect of Christian sanctification is positional, being based on the atoning blood of Christ (Heb. 13:12; cp. 10:10–14). In this sense, all believers are saints regardless of their progress in experience and growth. Thus according to Rom. 1:7, believers are not called to become saints (as the verb *"to be,"* supplied in the English translation, might seem to suggest). They *are* saints, and that by divine call, just as Paul was an apostle by divine call (1:1).

find a way in the will of God to
come to you.
11 For I long to see you, that
I may impart to you some spiritual gift, so that you may be
established—
12 that is, that I may be encouraged together with you by
the mutual [a]faith both of you
and me.
13 Now I do not want you to
be unaware, brethren, that I often planned to come to you (but
was hindered until now), that I
might have some fruit among
you also, just as among the
other [b]Gentiles.
14 I am a debtor both to
[c]Greeks and to barbarians,
both to [d]wise and to unwise.
15 So, as much as is in me, *I*
am ready to preach the [e]gospel
to you who are in Rome also.
16 For I am not ashamed of
the [e]gospel of Christ,* for it is
the [f]power of God to [1]salvation
for everyone who [a]believes, for
the Jew [g]first and also for the
[c]Greek.
17 For in it [h]the righteousness of God is revealed from
faith to faith; as it is [i]written,
"The [j]just shall live by [a]faith."

I. The Whole World Guilty before God, 1:18—3:20

(1) The wrath of God revealed

18 For the [2]wrath of God is
revealed from heaven against
all ungodliness and [k]unrigh-
teousness of men, who suppress
the [l]truth in unrighteousness,

(2) The universe a revelation of the power and Deity of God

19 because what may be
known of God is manifest in
them, for God has [m]shown *it* to
them.
20 For since the [n]creation of
the [o]world His invisible *attri-*
butes are clearly seen, being
understood by the things that
are [n]made, *even* His eternal
[p]power and [q]Godhead, so that
they are [r]without excuse,

(3) Stages of Gentile world unbelief

21 because, although they
knew God, they did not glorify
Him as God, nor were thankful,
but became futile in their
thoughts, and their [s]foolish
hearts were darkened.
22 Professing to be [d]wise,
they became fools,
23 and [t]changed the glory of
the [u]incorruptible God into an
image made like corruptible
man—and birds and four-
footed animals and [v]creeping
things.

(4) Result of Gentile world unbelief

24 Therefore [w]God also gave
them up to uncleanness, in the

* 1:16 NU-Text omits *of Christ.*

12 *a Faith:* vv. 12, 16–17; Rom. 3:22. (Gen. 3:20; Heb. 11:39, *note*). Cp. Rom. 10:1–11; 16:26

13 *b* See Eph. 3:6, *note*

14 *c* Acts 14:1; 17:4; 18:4; 19:10; 20:21; 21:28; 1 Cor. 1:22

d Cp. Isa. 19:11–12; Acts 7:22

15 *e Gospel:* vv. 15–16; Rom. 2:16. (Gen. 12:3; Rev. 14:6)

16 *f* 1 Cor. 1:18, 24

g Acts 3:26

17 *h* i.e. *a righteousness of which God is the source.* Cp. v. 18

i Inspiration: v. 17; Rom. 2:24. (Ex. 4:15; 2 Tim. 3:16, *note*). Hab. 2:4; Gal. 3:11; Heb. 10:38

j Righteousness (OT): v. 17; Rom. 2:26. (Gen. 6:9; Lk. 2:25, *note*)

18 *k* Rom. 6:13; 2 Th. 2:10; 2 Pet. 2:13; 1 Jn. 5:17

l v. 25

19 *m* Cp. Ps. 19:1–6; Acts 14:15–17; 17:22–29; see Rom. 3:2, *note*

20 *n* See Gen. 1:1, *note* 4

o Gk. *kosmos.* See Mt. 4:8, *note*

p Cp. Isa. 40:26,28

q Or *Deity.* Col. 2:9

r Cp. Rom. 2:14–15

21 *s* Cp. Eph. 4:17–19

23 *t* Cp. Jer. 2:11

u 1 Tim. 1:17; 6:15–16

v Cp. Ezek. 8:10

24 *w* vv. 26,28; Ps. 81:12; cp. Acts 7:42; 2 Th. 2:11–12

[1](1:16) The Hebrew and Greek words for "salvation" imply the ideas of deliverance, safety, preservation, healing, and soundness: "Salvation" is the great inclusive word of the Gospel, gathering into itself all the redemptive acts and processes: as justification, redemption, grace, propitiation, imputation, forgiveness, sanctification, and glorification. Salvation is in three tenses: (1) The Christian *has been* saved from the guilt and penalty of sin (Lk. 7:50; 1 Cor. 1:18; 2 Cor. 2:15; Eph. 2:5,8; 2 Tim. 1:9) and is safe. (2) The Christian *is being* saved from the habit and dominion of sin (Rom. 6:14; 8:2; 2 Cor. 3:18; Gal. 2:19–20; Phil. 1:19; 2:12–13; 2 Th. 2:13). And (3) the Christian *will be* saved at the Lord's return, from all the bodily infirmities that are the result of sin and God's curse upon the sinful world (Rom. 8:18–23; 1 Cor. 15:42–44), and brought into entire conformity to Christ (Rom. 13:11; Heb. 10:36; 1 Pet. 1:5; 1 Jn. 3:2). Salvation is by grace through faith, is a free gift and wholly without works (Rom. 3:27–28; 4:1–8; 6:23; Eph. 2:8). The divine order is: first salvation, then works (Eph. 2:9–10; Ti. 3:5–8).

[2](1:18) In the progress of its argument, the Epistle emphasizes certain aspects of the divine nature and activity: (1) the wrath of God against all forms of human sin and the certainty of its judgment (1:18—3:20); (2) the righteousness of God, both as a divine attribute and also a divine provision in saving sinners (3:21—8:39); (3) the sovereignty and wisdom of God in dealing with the problem of unbelief in Israel (9:1—11:36); and (4) the will of God for Christians in their various relationships (12:1—14:23). In addition to these emphases, the Epistle speaks generally of the goodness of God, as represented by His forbearance and longsuffering (2:4); His love (5:5,8; 8:39); and His mercy (11:30–32). Above all, from its opening salutation (1:7) to the final benediction (16:24), Romans reveals God as the God of all grace, who offers salvation to a world which deserves nothing but judgment, and saves all who believe in his Son, Jesus Christ. The infinite reach of this grace is set forth in 5:20: "But where sin abounded, grace abounded much more."

lusts of their hearts, to dishonor
their bodies among themselves,
25 who exchanged the truth
of God for the lie, and worshiped and served the creature
rather than the Creator, who is
blessed forever. Amen.
26 For this reason God gave
them up to vile passions. For
even their women exchanged
the natural use for what is
against nature.
27 Likewise also the men,
leaving the natural use of the
woman, burned in their lust for
one another, men with men
committing what is shameful,
and receiving in themselves the
penalty of their error which was
due.
28 And even as they did not
like to retain God in *their*
knowledge, God gave them
over to a debased mind, to do
those things which are not [a]fit-
ting;
29 being filled with all unrighteousness, sexual immorality,* wickedness, covetousness,
maliciousness; full of envy,
murder, strife, deceit, evil-
mindedness; *they are* whisperers,
30 backbiters, haters of God,
violent, proud, boasters, inven-
tors of evil things, disobedient
to parents,
31 undiscerning, untrustworthy, unloving, unforgiving,* unmerciful;
32 who, knowing the righ-
teous [b]judgment of God, that
those who practice such things
are deserving of death, not only
do the same but also approve of
those who practice them.

(5) Gentile pagan moralizers
no better than other pagans

2 THEREFORE you are [c]in-
excusable, O man, whoever
you are who judge, [d]for in
whatever you [1]judge another
you condemn yourself; for you
who judge practice the same
things.
2 But we know that the
[2b]judgment of God is according
to truth against those who practice such things.
3 And do you think this, O
man, [d]you who judge those
practicing such things, and doing the same, that you will escape the [b]judgment of God?
4 Or do you despise the
[e]riches of His goodness, [f]for-
bearance, and [g]longsuffering,
not knowing that the goodness
of God [h]leads you to [i]repen-
tance?
5 But in accordance with
your hardness and your impenitent heart you are treasuring up
for yourself wrath in the [j]day of
wrath and revelation of the
righteous [b]judgment of God,
6 who *"will [k]render to each*
one according to his deeds":*
7 eternal [l]life to those who
by patient continuance in [3m]do-
ing good seek for glory, honor,
and [n]immortality;
8 but to those who are [o]self-
seeking and do not obey the
truth, but obey unrighteousness—indignation and wrath,
9 tribulation and anguish,
on every soul of man who does
evil, of the Jew first and also of
the Greek;
10 but glory, honor, and
peace to everyone who [m]works
what is good, to the Jew first
and also to the Greek.
11 For [p]there is no partiality
with God.
12 For as many as have
[q]sinned without law will also

28
a Eph. 5:4
32
b Judgments (the seven): v. 32; 2:2–3, 5–11; Rom. 2:12. (2 Sam. 7:14; Rev. 20:12, *note*)
CHAPTER 2
1
c Rom. 1:20
d Mt. 7:1–5

4
e Rom. 9:23; Eph. 1:7; 2:4,7
f Rom. 3:25
g Ex. 34:6
h 2 Pet. 3:9, 15
i Repentance: v. 4; Rom. 11:29. (Mt. 3:2; Acts 17:30, *note*)
5
j Day (of judgment): v. 5; Rom. 2:16. (Mt. 10:15; Rev. 20:11)
6
k Prov. 24:12
7
l Life (eternal): v. 7; Rom. 5:21. (Mt. 7:14; Rev. 22:19)
m Righteousness (garment): vv. 7, 10; Rom. 13:14. (Gen. 3:21; Rev. 19:8)
n Or *incorruption.* 1 Cor. 15:53–54
8
o Cp. 2 Cor. 12:20; Gal. 5:19–20; Phil. 2:3; Jas. 3:14,16
11
p Dt. 10:17; Acts 10:34
12
q See Rom. 3:23, *note*

*1:29 NU-Text omits *sexual immorality.*
1:31 NU-Text omits *unforgiving.*
2:6 Psalm 62:12

[1](2:1) The judging here is moral in nature, i.e. ability to discern between right and wrong. The moralists of v. 1 were not condemned by Paul for their moral judgment but for their sin; they did the very things which they rightly judged to be wrong in other men.

[2](2:2) The basic principles of divine judgment are set forth in vv. 1–16 as follows: it will be according to (1) truth (v. 2), i.e. an objective standard of conduct; (2) deeds (v. 6); (3) the light enjoyed (vv. 11–15); and (4) the Gospel by which the secret thoughts and motives of men are judged (v. 16).

[3](2:7) In vv. 7 and 13 the cases are hypothetical. Paul is not teaching the possibility of salvation by works but is, rather, showing why all men without exception are lost. As he later states, no man has continued in doing good, nor is he a doer of the law (cp. 3:19–20). The means of justification for sinners, entirely by faith in Christ, is set forth in 3:21—8:39.

perish without law, and as
many as have [a]sinned in the
[b]law will be [c]judged by the law
13 (for not the hearers of the
law *are* just in the sight of God,
but the doers of the law will be
[d]justified;
14 for when [e]Gentiles, who
do not have the law, by nature
do the things in the law, these,
although not having the law,
are a law to themselves,
15 who show the [f]work of
the law written in their hearts,
their [g]conscience also bearing
witness, and between themselves *their* thoughts accusing
or else excusing *them*)
16 in the [h]day when God will
[c]judge the [i]secrets of men [j]by
Jesus Christ, according to my
[k]gospel.

(6) The Jew, knowing the law, is condemned by the law

17 Indeed* you are called a
Jew, and [l]rest on the [b]law, and
make your boast in God,
18 and know *His* will, and approve the things that are excellent, being instructed out of the
[b]law,
19 and are confident that you
yourself are a guide to the
[m]blind, a light to those who are
in darkness,
20 an instructor of the foolish, a teacher of babes, having
the form of knowledge and
truth in the law.
21 You, therefore, who teach
another, do you not teach yourself? You who preach that a
man should not steal, do you
steal?
22 You who say, "Do not
commit adultery," do you commit adultery? You who abhor
idols, do you [n]rob temples?
23 You who make your boast
in the [b]law, do you dishonor
God through [a]breaking the
law?
24 For *"the name of God is*
[o]*blasphemed among the* [e]*Gen-*
*tiles because of you,"** [p]as it is
[q]written.
25 For circumcision is indeed
profitable if you keep the [b]law;
but if you are a [a]breaker of the
law, your [r]circumcision has become uncircumcision.
26 [s]Therefore, if an uncircumcised man keeps the [t]righ-
teous requirements of the law,
will not his uncircumcision be
counted as circumcision?
27 And will not the physically uncircumcised, if he fulfills the [b]law, judge you who,
even with *your* written *code* and
circumcision, *are* a [a]transgres-
sor of the law?
28 [u]For he is not a Jew who *is*
one outwardly, nor *is* circumcision that which *is* outward in
the flesh;
29 [v]but *he is* a Jew who *is one*
inwardly; and circumcision *is*
that of the [w]heart, [x]in the
[1]Spirit, not in the letter; whose
praise *is* not from men but from
God.

(7) Advantage of the Jew makes his condemnation greater

3 WHAT [y]advantage then
has the Jew, or what *is* the
profit of circumcision?
2 Much in every way!
Chiefly [z]because to them were
committed the [2b]oracles of God.
3 For what if some did not
believe? [aa]Will their [bb]unbelief
make the [cc]faithfulness of God
without effect?
4 Certainly not! Indeed, let
God be true but every man a
liar. As it is [q]written:

[dd]*"That You may be*
[d]justified in Your
words,
And may overcome
when You are judged."

*
2:17 NU-Text reads *But if.* 2:24 Ezekiel 36:22

12
a See Rom. 3:23, *note*
b *Law* (of Moses): vv. 12–15, 17–18, 22–23, 25–27; 3:2; Rom. 3:19. (Ex. 19:1; Gal. 3:24, *note*)
c *Judgments* (the seven): vv. 5–12,16; Rom. 5:16. (2 Sam. 7:14; Rev. 20:12, *note*)
13
d *Justification:* v. 13; 3:4; Rom. 3:20. (Lk. 18:14; Rom. 3:28, *note*)
14
e See Eph. 3:6, *note*
15
f 1 Cor. 5:1
g Acts 24:25
16
h *Day* (of judgment): v. 16; Heb. 9:27. (Mt. 10:15; Rev. 20:11)
i Cp. Lk. 8:17
j Acts 10:42
k *Gospel:* v. 16; Rom. 10:8. (Gen. 12:3; Rev. 14:6)
17
l v. 23; cp. Jn. 5:45; 9:28–29
19
m Cp. Mt. 15:14
22
n Cp. Acts 19:37

24
o Ezek. 16:27; cp. Acts 13:45
p Isa. 52:5
q *Inspiration:* v. 24; 3:4; Rom. 3:10. (Ex. 4:15; 2 Tim. 3:16, *note*)
25
r Gen. 17:10–14; cp. Josh. 5:3; Acts 16:3; 1 Cor. 7:18; Gal. 2:3; 5:2; 6:12
26
s Cp. Eph. 2:11
t *Righteousness* (OT): v. 26; Rom. 4:3. (Gen. 6:9; Lk. 2:25, *note*)
28
u Gal. 6:15; see Rom. 9:6, *note*
29
v Cp. Phil. 3:3; Col. 2:11
w Dt. 30:6; cp. Jer. 4:4; 9:24–26; 1 Cor. 7:19
x See 2 Cor. 3:6, *note*
CHAPTER 3
1
y Cp. Rom. 9:3–5
2
z Dt. 4:5–8; Ps. 147:19
3
aa Cp. 2 Tim. 2:13; Heb. 4:2
bb Cp. Heb. 3:12; 4:11
cc Cp. Rom. 11:29
4
dd Ps. 51:4

[1](2:29) True Judaism was not merely a matter of external observances or precise keeping of ordinances but of a heart attitude toward God. As Paul says in v. 29, it is not in the letter but in the spirit. The Judaism that bases everything on minute and external observances (cp. Rom. 2:28–29) is not true Judaism but a perversion, and was condemned by the Lord Jesus Christ (Mt. 15:6).

[2](3:2) In proving the guilt of the world Paul brings the witness of three forms of divine revelation, i.e. God's will as it is revealed in the law and the prophets: (1) against the pagan, the witness of creation (1:19–20); (2) against the moralist, the witness of conscience (2:15); and (3) against the Jew, the witness of the Scriptures.

5
a See Rom. 3:21, *note*
b Cp. Rom. 6:19; Gal. 3:15

6
c Gk. *kosmos.* See Mt. 4:8, *note*

7
d See v. 23, *note*

9
e Cp. Rom. 1:18–2:24
f Cp. Gen. 6:5; Isa. 1:6; 64:6; Jer. 16:12; 2 Pet. 2:12

10
g vv. 10–12; Ps. 14:1–3; Eccl. 7:20
h Inspiration: vv. 10–18; Rom. 4:3. (Ex. 4:15; 2 Tim. 3:16, *note*)
i See Rom. 10:10, *note*

13
j vv. 13–18; Ps. 5:9; 10:7; 36:1; 140:3; Isa. 59:7–8

5 But if our unrighteousness
demonstrates the [a]righteous-
ness of God, what shall we say?
Is God unjust who inflicts
wrath? (I [b]speak as a man.)
6 Certainly not! For then
how will God judge the [c]world?
7 For if the truth of God has
increased through my lie to His
glory, why am I also still judged
as a [d]sinner?
8 And *why* not *say,* "Let us
do evil that good may come"?—
as we are slanderously reported
and as some affirm that we say.
Their condemnation is just.

(8) The final verdict:
the whole world guilty before God

9 What then? Are we better
than they? Not at all. For we
have [e]previously charged both
Jews and Greeks that they are
[f]all under [d]sin.
10 [g]As it is [h]written:

"There is none [i]righteous,
no, not one;
11 *There is none who*
understands;
There is none who seeks
after God.
12 *They have all turned*
aside;
They have together
become unprofitable;
There is none who does
*good, no, not one."**
13 [j]*"Their throat is an open*
tomb;
With their tongues they
have practiced deceit";
"The poison of asps is
under their lips";
14 *"Whose mouth is full of*
cursing and
bitterness."
15 *"Their feet are swift to*
shed blood;
16 *Destruction and misery*
are in their ways;
17 *And the way of peace*
they have not known."
18 *"There is no fear of God*
before their eyes."

19 Now we know that what-
ever the [k]law says, it says to
those who are under the law,
that every mouth may be
[l]stopped, and all the world may
[m]become guilty before God.
20 Therefore by the deeds of
the law [n]no flesh will be [o]justi-
fied in His sight, for by the [k]law
is the knowledge of [d]sin.

II. Justification by Faith
in Christ, 3:31—5:21

(1) Justification defined

21 But now the [1]righteous-
ness of God apart from the law
is revealed, being witnessed by
the [k]Law and the Prophets,
22 even the [a]righteousness
of God, through faith in Jesus
Christ, to all and on all* who
[p]believe. For there is no difference;
23 for all have [2]sinned and
fall short of the glory of God,
24 being [o]justified [q]freely by
His [r]grace through the [3]re-

*
3:12 Psalm 53:1–3; Ecclesiastes 7:20
3:22 NU-Text omits *and on all.*

19
k Law (of Moses): vv. 19–21, 27–28,31; Rom. 4:13. (Ex. 19:1; Gal. 3:24, *note*)
l Cp. Ezek. 16:63
m i.e *to be under the judicial sentence of God.*

20
n Ps. 143:2; Gal. 2:16
o Justification: vv. 20, 24; Rom. 3:26. (Lk. 18:14; Rom. 3:28, *note*)

22
p Faith: v. 22; Rom. 3:25. (Gen. 3:20; Heb. 11:39, *note*)

24
q i.e. *as a gift*
r Grace: v. 24; Rom. 4:4. (Jn. 1:14; Jn. 1:17, *note*)

[1](3:21) The righteousness of God is all that God demands and approves, and is ultimately found in Christ Himself, who fully met in our stead every requirement of the law. Through imputation Christ "became for us. . . righteousness" (1 Cor. 1:30; cp. Lev. 25:47–52; Rom. 3:26; 4:6; 10:4; 2 Cor. 5:21; Phil. 3:9; Jas. 2:23).

[2](3:23) Sin, Summary: The literal meanings of the Hebrew and Greek words variously rendered "sin," "sinner," etc. disclose the true nature of sin in its manifold manifestations. Sin is (1) transgression, an overstepping of the law, the divine boundary between good and evil (Ps. 51:1; Rom. 2:23); (2) iniquity, an act inherently wrong, whether expressly forbidden or not (Rom. 1:21–23); (3) error, a departure from right (Rom. 1:18; 1 Jn. 3:4); (4) missing the mark, a failure to meet the divine standard (Rom. 3:23); (5) trespass, the intrusion of self-will into the sphere of divine authority (Eph. 2:1); (6) lawlessness, or spiritual anarchy (1 Tim. 1:9); and (7) unbelief, or an insult to the divine veracity (Jn. 16:9). Sin (1) originated with Satan (Isa. 14:12–14); (2) entered the world through Adam (Rom. 5:12); (3) was, and is, universal, Christ alone excepted (Rom. 3:23; 1 Pet. 2:22); (4) incurs the penalties of spiritual and physical death (Gen. 2:17; 3:19; Ezek. 18:4,20; Rom. 6:23); and (5) has no remedy but in the sacrificial death of Christ (Acts 4:12; Heb. 9:26) made available by faith (Acts 13:38–39). Sin may be summarized as threefold: (1) *an act,* the violation of, or want of obedience to, the revealed will of God; (2) *a state,* absence of righteousness; and (3) *a nature,* enmity toward God.

[3](3:24) "Redemption" means *to deliver by paying a price.* The work of Christ fulfilling the OT types and prophecies of redemption is set forth in three principal Greek words: (1)

demption that is in Christ Jesus,
25 whom God [a]set forth *as* a [1]propitiation by His blood, through [b]faith, to demonstrate His [c]righteousness, because in His [d]forbearance God had passed over the [e]sins that were [f]previously committed,
26 to demonstrate at the present time His [c]righteousness, that He might be just and the [g]justifier of the one who has [b]faith in Jesus.
27 Where *is* boasting then? It is excluded. By what law? Of works? No, but by the law of [b]faith.
28 Therefore we conclude that a man is [2g]justified by [b]faith apart from the deeds of the law.

(2) Justification a universal remedy

29 Or *is He* the God of the Jews only? *Is He* not also the God of the [h]Gentiles? Yes, of the [h]Gentiles also,
30 since *there is* one God who will [g]justify the [i]circumcised by faith and the [j]uncircumcised through [b]faith.

(3) Justification by faith honors the law

31 Do we then make void the law through [b]faith? Certainly not! On the contrary, we establish the [3]law.

(4) Justification by faith illustrated in OT in Abraham and David (cp. vv. 18–25)

4 WHAT then shall we say that [k]Abraham our [l]father

25
a Sacrifice (of Christ): v. 25; Rom. 4:25. (Gen. 3:15; Heb. 10:18, *note*)
b Faith: vv. 25–31; Rom. 4:3. (Gen. 3:20; Heb. 11:39, *note*)
c See Rom. 3:21, *note*
d Rom. 2:4
e See v. 23, *note*
f i.e. *since Adam.* Cp. Heb. 9:15
26
g Justification: vv. 26, 28,30; Rom. 4:2. (Lk. 18:14; Rom. 3:28, *note*)
29
h See Eph. 3:6, *note*
30
i Cp. Rom. 2:25–29
j Cp. Gen. 15:6 with Gen. 17:9–14
CHAPTER 4
1
k Gen. 11:27–25:9
l vv. 11,12; Lk. 3:8; Jn. 8:53; Jas. 2:21

Agorazō, to buy in the market (from *agora, market*). Man is viewed as a slave "sold under sin" (Rom. 7:14) and under sentence of death (Ezek. 18:4; Jn. 3:18–19; Rom. 6:23) but subject to redemption by the purchase price of the blood of the Redeemer (1 Cor. 6:20; 7:23; 2 Pet. 2:1; Rev. 5:9; 14:3–4). (2) *Exagorazō, to buy out of the market,* i.e. to purchase and remove from further sale (Gal. 3:13; 4:5; Eph. 5:16; Col. 4:5), speaking of the finality of the work of redemption. And (3) *lutroō, to loose* or *set free* (Lk. 24:21; Ti. 2:14; 1 Pet.1:18), noun form, *lutrōsis* (Lk. 2:38; Heb. 9:12). Compare also "redeemed" (lit. *to make redemption,* Gk. *epoiēsen lutrōsin,* Lk. 1:68), and "deliverance" (intensive form, *apolutrōsis*) used commonly to indicate release of a slave (Lk. 21:28; Rom. 3:24; 8:23; 1 Cor. 1:30; Eph. 1:7,14; 4:30; Col. 1:14; Heb. 9:15; 11:35). Redemption is by sacrifice and by power (Ex. 14:30, *note*); Christ paid the price, the Holy Spirit makes deliverance actual in experience (Rom. 8:2). See Ex. 14:30, *note;* Isa. 59:20, *note* 1; Rom. 1:16, *note.*

[1](3:25) "Propitiation" is translated from the Gk. *hilastērion,* meaning *that which expiates* or *propitiates,* or *the gift which procures propitiation.* The word is also used in the NT for the place of propitiation, the "mercy seat" (Heb. 9:5), i.e. the lid of the ark (compare frequent similar use in the OT Septuagint, Ex. 25:18ff.). The cover of the ark (mercy seat) was sprinkled with atoning blood on the Day of Atonement (Lev. 16:14), representing that the righteous sentence of the law had been executed, changing a place of judgment into a place of mercy (Heb. 9:11–15; cp. "throne of grace," Heb. 4:14–16; place of communion, Ex. 25:21–22). Another Greek word, *hilasmos,* is used for Christ as our "propitiation" (1 Jn. 2:2; 4:10) and for "atonement" in the OT (cp. Lev. 25:9, Septuagint). The thought in the OT sacrifices and in the NT fulfillment is that Christ completely satisfied the just demands of a holy God for judgment on sin by His death on the cross. God, foreseeing the cross, is declared righteous in forgiving sins in the OT period as well as in justifying sinners under the new covenant (Rom. 3:25–26; cp. Ex. 29:33, *note*). Propitiation is not placating a vengeful God but, rather, it is satisfying the righteousness of a holy God, thereby making it possible for Him to show mercy righteously.

[2](3:28) Justification, Summary: The words "justified" and "righteousness" are translations of similar Greek words (verb, *dikaioō, to declare righteous, to justify;* noun, *dikaiosunē, righteousness;* adjective, *dikaios, righteous*). The believing sinner is justified, i.e. treated as righteous because Christ, "who knew no sin," bore his sins on the cross, being made "sin for us, that we might become the righteousness of God in Him" (2 Cor. 5:21). Justification is an act of divine reckoning and does not mean to *make* a person righteous. Justification (1) originates in grace (Rom. 3:24; Ti. 3:4–5); (2) is through the redemptive and propitiatory work of Christ who fulfilled the law (Rom. 3:24–25; 5:9); (3) is by faith, not works (Rom. 3:28–30; 4:5; 5:1; Gal. 2:16; 3:8,24); and (4) may be defined as *the judicial act of God whereby He justly declares and treats as righteous the one who believes in Jesus Christ.* The justified believer has been declared by the Judge Himself (Rom. 3:31) to have nothing laid to his charge (Rom. 8:1,31–34).

[3](3:31) The sinner establishes the law in its right use and honor by confessing his guilt and just condemnation. Christ, on the sinner's behalf, establishes the law by obediently keeping its precepts (Mt. 5:17–18; Gal. 4:4–5), and by enduring its penalty, death.

has found according to the
flesh?*
2 For if Abraham was [a]jus-
tified by [b]works, he has *something* to boast about, but not before God.
3 For what does the Scripture [c]say? [d]"*Abraham* [e]*believed God, and it was* [1][f]*accounted to him* [g]*for* [h]*righteousness.*"*
4 Now to him who [i]works,
the wages are not [f]counted as
[j]grace but as debt.
5 But to him who does [k]not
work but [e]believes on Him who
[a]justifies the ungodly, his faith
is accounted for righteousness,
6 just as David also [c]de-
scribes the blessedness of the
man to whom God imputes
[l]righteousness apart from
[i]works:

7 [m]"*Blessed are those whose*
[n]lawless deeds are
[o]forgiven,
And whose [n]sins are
[p]covered;
8 *Blessed is the man to*
whom the LORD *shall*
not impute [n]sin."

(5) Justification is apart from ordinances

9 *Does* this blessedness
then *come* upon the [q]circum-
cised *only*, or upon the [r]uncir-
cumcised also? For we say that
[e]faith was [f]accounted to Abraham for [h]righteousness.
10 How then was it ac-
counted? While he was [q]cir-
cumcised, or [r]uncircumcised?
Not while circumcised, but
while uncircumcised.
11 And he received the sign
of circumcision, a seal of the
[l]righteousness of the [e]faith
which *he had while still* uncircumcised, that he might be the
father of all those who [e]believe,
though they are uncircumcised,
that righteousness might be
[f]imputed to them also,
12 and the father of circumcision to those who not only *are* of
the circumcision, but who also
walk in the steps of the [e]faith

2
a *Justification:* vv. 2,5; Rom. 4:25. (Lk. 18:14; Rom. 3:28, *note*)
b See Rom. 2:7 and Jas 2:26, *notes*
3
c *Inspiration:* vv. 3, 6–7,17–23; Rom. 8:36. (Ex. 4:15; 2 Tim. 3:16, *note*)
d Gal. 3:6
e *Faith:* vv. 3, 5,9–13, 16–23; Rom. 4:24. (Gen. 3:20; Heb. 11:39, *note*)
f *Imputation:* vv. 3–6, 8–11,22; Rom. 4:23. (Gen. 15:6; Jas. 2:23). See Rom. 4:3, *note*
g i.e. *with a view to*
h *Righteousness* (OT): vv. 3,9,22; Rom. 5:7. (Gen. 6:9; Lk. 2:25, *note*)
4
i See Rom. 2:7, *note*
j *Grace:* vv. 4,16; Rom. 5:2. (Jn. 1:14; Jn. 1:17, *note*)
5
k Gal. 2:16; Eph. 2:8–9
6
l See Rom. 10:10, *note*
7
m Ps. 32:1–2
n See Rom. 3:23, *note*
o *Forgiveness:* v. 7; 2 Cor. 2:10. (Lev. 4:20; Mt. 26:28, *note*)
p See Ex. 29:33 and Lev. 16:6, *notes*
9
q Cp. Rom. 2:25–29
r Cp. Gen. 15:6 with Gen. 17:9–14

which our father [s]Abraham
had while still uncircumcised.

(6) Justification is apart from the law

13 For the [t]promise that he
would be the heir of the [u]world
was not to Abraham or to his
seed through the [v]law, but
through the [l]righteousness of
[e]faith.
14 For if those who are of the
law *are* heirs, faith is made void
and the promise made of no effect,
15 because the law brings
about wrath; for where there is
no law *there is* no [n]transgres-
sion.
16 Therefore *it is* of [e]faith
that *it might be* according to
[j]grace, so that the promise
might be sure to all the seed, not
only to those who are of the
[v]law, but also to those who are
of the faith of Abraham, who is
the father of us all
17 (as it is [c]written, *"I have
made you a* [t]*father of many nations"**) in the presence of Him
whom he believed—God, who
[w]gives life to the dead and calls
those things which do not exist
as though they did;
18 who, contrary to hope, in
[x]hope [e]believed, so that he became the [t]father of many nations, according to what was
[c]spoken, [y]*"So shall your descendants be."*
19 And not being weak in
faith, he did not consider his
own body, already dead (since
he was about a hundred years
old), [z]and the deadness of
Sarah's womb.
20 He did not waver at the
[t]promise of God through unbelief, but was strengthened in
faith, giving glory to God,
21 and being fully convinced
that what He had [t]promised He
was also able to perform.
22 And therefore *"it was* [f]*accounted to him for* [h]*righteousness."**

12
s Rom. 4:18–22
13
t See Gen. 12:2, *note*
u Gk. *kosmos.* See Mt. 4:8, *note*
v *Law* (of Moses): vv. 13–16; Rom. 5:13. (Ex. 19:1; Gal. 3:24, *note*)
17
w Jn. 5:21; 6:63; 1 Cor. 15:22,36,45; 2 Cor. 3:6; 1 Tim. 6:13; 1 Pet. 3:18
18
x Cp. Rom. 8:24–25
y Gen. 15:5
19
z Heb. 11:11

*4:1 Or *Abraham our (fore)father according to the flesh has found?* 4:3 Genesis 15:6 4:17 Genesis 17:5 4:22 Genesis 15:6

[1](4:3) The Greek word *logizomai* occurs eleven times in this chapter (vv. 3,4,5,6,8,9,10,11,22,23,24), translated by the English verbs "account," "count," and "impute." It means *to put to one's account.*

23 Now it was not written for
his sake alone that it was [a]im-
puted to him,
24 but also for us. It shall be
[a]imputed to us who [b]believe in
Him who [c]raised up Jesus our
Lord from the dead,
25 who was [d]delivered up
because of our offenses, and
was raised [1]because of our [e]jus-
tification.

(7) Results of justification

5 THEREFORE, having been
[e]justified by [b]faith, we
have* [f]peace with God
through our Lord Jesus Christ,
2 through whom also we
[g]have access by faith into this
[h]grace in which we stand, and
rejoice in hope of the glory of
God.
3 And not only *that,* but we
also glory in [i]tribulations,
knowing that tribulation produces perseverance;
4 and perseverance, char-
acter; and character, hope.
5 Now hope does not disappoint, because the [j]love of God
has been poured out in our
hearts by the Holy [k]Spirit who
was given to us.
6 For when we were still
without strength, in due time
Christ [d]died for the ungodly.
7 For scarcely for a [l]righ-
teous man will one die; yet perhaps for a good man someone
would even dare to die.
8 But God demonstrates
[m]His own love toward us, in that
while we were still [n]sinners,
Christ [d]died for us.
9 Much more then, having
now been [e]justified by His
[d]blood, we shall be [o]saved from
wrath through Him.
10 For if when we were enemies we were [p]reconciled to
God through the [d]death of His
Son, much more, having been
reconciled, we shall be [o]saved
[q]by His life.
11 And not only *that,* but we
also rejoice in God through our
Lord Jesus Christ, through
whom we have now received
[p]the reconciliation.

(8) Justification compared and contrasted with condemnation

12 [2]Therefore, just as
through one man [n]sin entered
the [r]world, and death through
sin, and thus death spread to all
men, because all [3]sinned—
13 (For until the [s]law [n]sin
was in the [r]world, but sin is not
imputed when there is no law.
14 Nevertheless [t]death
reigned from [4]Adam to Moses,
even over those who had not
[n]sinned according to the likeness of the transgression of
Adam, who is a type of Him who
was to come.

2:17; Heb. 9:27, *note*)

*5:1 Another ancient reading is, *let us have peace.*

23 *a Imputation:* v. 22–24; Gal. 3:6. (Gen. 15:6; Jas. 2:23). See Rom. 4:3, *note*
24 *b Faith:* v. 24; 5:1–2; Rom. 6:8. (Gen. 3:20; Heb. 11:39, *note*) *c Resurrection:* vv. 24–25; Rom. 6:4. (2 Ki. 4:35; 1 Cor. 15:52, *note*)
25 *d Sacrifice* (of Christ): v. 25; 5:6–11; Rom. 8:3. (Gen. 3:15; Heb. 10:18, *note*) *e Justification:* v. 25; 5:1,9; Rom. 5:16. (Lk. 18:14; Rom. 3:28, *note*)
CHAPTER 5
1 *f* Isa. 53:5; Acts 10:36
2 *g* Lit. *have obtained* *h Grace:* v. 2; Rom. 5:15. (Jn. 1:14; Jn. 1:17, *note*)
3 *i* Jn. 16:33
5 *j Law* (of Christ): vv. 5,8; Rom. 12:9. (Jn. 13:34; 2 Jn. 5) *k Holy Spirit* (NT): v. 5; Rom. 8:2. (Mt. 1:18; Acts 2:4, *note*)
7 *l Righteousness* (OT): v. 7; Rom. 8:4. (Gen. 6:9; Lk. 2:25, *note*)
8 *m* Jn. 3:16–17 *n* See Rom. 3:23, *note*
9 *o* See Rom. 1:16, *note*
10 *p Reconciliation:* vv. 10–11; Rom. 11:15. (Rom. 5:10; Col. 1:20) *q* Lit. *in.* Jn. 14:19; Col. 3:3–4
12 *r* Gk. *kosmos.* See Mt. 4:8, *note*
13 *s Law* (of Moses): v. 13; Rom. 5:20. (Ex. 19:1; Gal. 3:24, *note*)
14 *t Death* (physical): vv. 12, 14–16; Rom. 5:17. (Gen.

[1](4:25) It was "because of our offenses" that Christ died (2 Cor. 5:21; 1 Pet. 2:24). He was raised again and exalted at God's right hand "because of" the fact that we were "justified by his blood" (Rom. 5:9). His resurrection is the proof that our sins are gone.

[2](5:12) The "therefore" relates back to 3:19–23 and may be regarded as a continuation of the discussion of the universality of sin, interrupted by the passage on justification and its results (3:24—5:11).

[3](5:12) The first sin wrought the moral ruin of the race. The demonstration is simple. (1) Death is universal (vv. 12,14); all die—little children, moral people, and religious people equally with the depraved. For a universal effect there must be a universal cause; that cause is a state of universal sin (v. 12). (2) But this universal state must have had a cause. It did. The consequence of Adam's sin was that the "many were made sinners" (v. 19): "through one man's offense judgment came to all men" (v. 18). (3) Personal sins are not meant here. From Adam to Moses death reigned (v. 14) although, there being no law, personal guilt was not imputed (v. 13). Accordingly, from Gen. 4:7 to Ex. 29:14 the sin offering is not once mentioned. Then, since physical death from Adam to Moses was not due to the sinful acts of those who die (v. 13), it follows that it was due to a universal sinful state, or nature, and that state is declared to be our inheritance from Adam. And (4) the moral state of fallen man is described in Scripture (Gen. 6:5; 1 Ki. 8:46; Ps. 14:1–3; 39:5; Jer. 17:9; Mt. 18:11; Mk. 7:20–23; Jn. 3:6; Rom. 1:21; 2:1–29; 3:9–19; 7:24; 8:7; 1 Cor. 2:14; 2 Cor. 3:14; 4:4; Gal. 5:19–21; Eph. 2:1–3,11–12; 4:18–22; Col. 1:21; Heb. 3:13; Jas. 4:4). See 1 Cor. 15:22, *note*.

[4](5:14) In 5:12–21 the contrast is between Adam, sin, death (vv. 12–14) and Christ, righteousness, life (v. 21). There is no contrasting term in vv. 12–14 for the word "grace" in v. 21.

15 But the free gift *is* not like
the offense. For if by the one
man's offense many died, much
more the [a]grace of God and
the gift by the grace of the one
Man, Jesus Christ, abounded to
many.
16 And the gift *is* not like
that which came through the
one who [b]sinned. For the [c]judg-
ment *which came* from one *offense resulted* in condemnation,
but the free gift *which came*
from many offenses *resulted* in
[d]justification.
17 For if by the one
man's [b]offense [e]death reigned
through the one, much more
those who receive abundance
of [a]grace and of the gift of
[f]righteousness will reign in
life through the [g]One, Jesus
Christ.)
18 Therefore, as through one
man's [b]offense *judgment* came
to all men, resulting in condemnation, even so through [g]one
Man's [f]righteous act *the free
gift came* to all men, resulting
in [d]justification of life.
19 For as by one man's disobedience many were made
[b]sinners, so also by [g]one Man's
[h]obedience many will be made
righteous.
20 Moreover the [i]law [j]en-
tered that the offense might
abound. But where [b]sin
abounded, [a]grace [k]abounded
much more,
21 so that as [1]sin reigned in
[e]death, even so [a]grace might
reign through [f]righteousness
to eternal [l]life through Jesus
Christ our Lord.

15
a Grace: vv. 15,17, 20–21; 6:1; Rom. 6:14. (Jn. 1:14; Jn. 1:17, *note*)
16
b See Rom. 3:23, *note*
c Judgments (the seven): vv. 16,18; Rom. 8:1. (2 Sam. 7:14; Rev. 20:12, *note*)
d Justification: vv. 16, 18; Rom. 8:30. (Lk. 18:14; Rom. 3:28, *note*)
17
e Death (physical): vv. 14–17, 21; 6:9; Rom. 8:38. (Gen. 2:17; Heb. 9:27, *note*)
f See Rom. 3:21 and 10:10, *notes*
g 1 Cor. 15:21,45
19
h Phil. 2:8
20
i Law (of Moses): v. 20; Rom. 6:14. (Ex. 19:1; Gal. 3:24, *note*)
j Cp. Gal. 3:19–25
k 1 Tim. 1:14; cp. Lk. 7:47
21
l Life (eternal): v. 21; Rom. 6:22. (Mt. 7:14; Rev. 22:19)

III. Sanctification through Union with Christ in His Death and Resurrection, 6—8

Deliverance from the power of indwelling sin

(1) By union with Christ in death and resurrection

6 WHAT shall we say then?
Shall we continue in [m]sin
that [n]grace may abound?
2 Certainly not! How shall
we who [o]died to [m]sin live any
longer in it?
3 [2]Or do you not know that
as many of us as were [p]baptized
into Christ Jesus were baptized
into His death?
4 Therefore we were buried
with Him through [p]baptism
into death, that just as Christ
was [q]raised from the dead by
the glory of the Father, even so
we also should walk in newness
of life.
5 For if we have been united
together in the likeness of His
death, certainly we also shall be
in the likeness of *His* [q]resurrec-
tion,
6 knowing this, that our [3]old
man was crucified with *Him*,
that the body of [m]sin might be
[r]done away with, that we
should no longer be slaves of
sin.
7 For he who has died has
been freed from [m]sin.
8 Now if we died with
Christ, we [s]believe that we
shall also [t]live with Him,
9 knowing that Christ, having been [q]raised from the dead,
dies no more. [e]Death no longer
has dominion over Him.
10 For *the death* that He
died, He died to [m]sin [u]once for

CHAPTER 6
1
m See Rom. 3:23 and 5:21, *notes*
n Grace: vv. 15,17, 20–21; 6:1; Rom. 6:14. (Jn. 1:14; Jn. 1:17, *note*). See 2 Pet. 3:18, *note*
2
o vv. 7, 11; Gal. 5:24; Col. 3:3; 1 Pet. 2:24
3
p Col. 2:12
4
q Resurrection: vv. 4–5,9; Rom. 7:4. (2 Ki. 4:35; 1 Cor. 15:52, *note*)
6
r i.e. *rendered inoperative*
8
s Faith: v. 8; Rom. 9:30. (Gen. 3:20; Heb. 11:39, *note*)
t 2 Tim. 2:11
10
u Heb. 10:10–12,14

It is grace that makes the difference between condemnation in Adam and justification in Christ.

[1](5:21) "Sin" in chs. 6 and 7 is man's nature in distinction from "sins," which are manifestations of that nature. Compare 1 Jn. 1:8 with 1 Jn. 1:10, where this distinction also appears.

[2](6:3) In ch. 6 there are four key words which indicate the believer's personal responsibility in relation to God's sanctifying work: (1) to "know" the facts of our union and identification with Christ in His death and resurrection (vv. 3,6,9); (2) to "reckon" these facts to be true concerning ourselves (v. 11); (3) to "present" ourselves once for all as alive from the dead for God's possession and use (vv. 13,16,19); and (4) to "obey" in the realization that sanctification can proceed only as we are obedient to the will of God as revealed in His Word (vv. 16–17).

[3](6:6) The expression "old man" occurs elsewhere (Eph. 4:22; Col. 3:9) and means all that man was in Adam, both morally and judicially, i.e. the man of old, the corrupt human nature, the inborn tendency to evil in all men. In Rom. 6:6 it is the natural man himself; in Eph. 4:22 and Col. 3:9 his ways. Positionally, in the reckoning of God, the "old man" has been crucified, and the believer is exhorted to make this good in experience, reckoning it to be so by definitely "putting off" the old man and "putting on" the new. (Col. 3:8–14). See Eph. 4:24, *note*.

all; but *the life* that He lives, He
lives to God.

(2) By counting oneself dead
to the old life, and by yielding
the new life to God

11 [a]Likewise you also,
[1]reckon yourselves to be dead
indeed to [b]sin, but alive to God
in Christ Jesus our Lord.
12 Therefore do not let [b]sin
reign in your mortal body, that
you should obey it in its [c]lusts.
13 And do not present your
members *as* instruments of
[d]unrighteousness to [b]sin, but
[e]present yourselves to God as
being alive from the dead, and
your members *as* instruments
of [f]righteousness to God.

(3) By deliverance from the
principle of works through death,
and by the Spirit (i.e., as in 8:2)

14 For [b]sin shall not have dominion over you, for you are not
under [g]law but under [h]grace.
15 [2]What then? Shall we [b]sin
because we are not under [g]law
but under [h]grace? Certainly
not!
16 Do you not know that to
whom you present yourselves
slaves to [i]obey, you are that
one's slaves whom you obey,
whether of [b]sin *leading* to
[j]death, or of obedience *leading*
to [f]righteousness?
17 But God be thanked that
though you were slaves of [b]sin,
yet you obeyed from the heart
that form of doctrine to which
you were delivered.
18 And having been set free
from [b]sin, you became slaves of
[f]righteousness.
19 I speak in human *terms*
because of the weakness of
your flesh. For just as you presented your members *as* slaves
of uncleanness, and of [b]law-
lessness *leading* to *more* [b]law-
lessness, so now [e]present your
members *as* slaves *of* [f]righ-
teousness for [k]holiness.
20 For when you were slaves
of [b]sin, you were free in regard
to [f]righteousness.
21 What fruit did you have
then in the things of which you
are now ashamed? For the end
of those things *is* [j]death.
22 But now having been set
free from [b]sin, and having become slaves of God, you have
your fruit to holiness, and the
end, everlasting [l]life.
23 For the wages of [b]sin *is*
[j]death, but the gift of God *is*
eternal [l]life in Christ Jesus our
Lord.

(4) The believer united to Christ,
the new "husband"

7 OR do you not know, brethren (for I speak to those
who know the law), that the
[g]law has dominion over a man
as long as he lives?
2 For the woman who has a
husband is [m]bound by the [g]law
to *her* husband as long as he
[n]lives. But if the husband dies,
she is released from the law of
her husband.
3 So then if, while *her* husband lives, she marries another
man, she will be called an
[o]adulteress; but if her husband
dies, she is free from that law,
so that she is no adulteress,
though she has married another
man.
4 Therefore, my brethren,
you also [p]have become dead to
the [g]law through the [q]body of
Christ, that you may be [r]mar-
ried to another—to Him who
was [s]raised from the dead, that
we should bear fruit to God.
5 For when we were in the
[t]flesh, the sinful passions which
were aroused by the law were

11
a Lit. *Even so*
b See Rom. 3:23 and 5:21, *notes*
12
c Ex. 20:17; Rom. 7:7
13
d Rom. 1:18; 2 Th. 2:10; 2 Pet. 2:13; 1 Jn. 5:17
e i.e. *yield once for all.* Cp. Rom. 12:1
f See Rom. 3:21 and 10:10, *notes*
14
g Law (of Moses): vv. 14–15; 7:1–6; Rom. 7:7. (Ex. 19:1; Gal. 3:24, *note*)
h Grace: vv. 14–15; Rom. 9:23. (Jn. 1:14; Jn. 1:17, *note*). See 2 Pet. 3:18, *note*
16
i Prov. 5:22
j Death (spiritual): vv. 16,21,23; Rom. 7:10. (Gen. 2:17; Eph. 2:5, *note*)
19
k Sanctification (NT): vv. 19,22; Rom. 7:12. (Mt. 4:5; Rev. 22:11)
22
l Life (eternal): vv. 22–23; Rom. 8:6. (Mt. 7:14; Rev. 22:19)
CHAPTER 7
2
m Cp. Gen. 2:24; Mt. 5:32; Mk. 10:9
n 1 Cor. 7:39
3
o Cp. Lev. 20:10; Mt. 19:9; 1 Cor. 6:9; 2 Pet. 2:14
4
p Lit. *were made dead*
q Church (the true): v. 4; Rom. 11:25. (Mt. 16:18; Heb. 12:23)
r Bride (of Christ): v. 4; 2 Cor. 11:2. (Jn. 3:29; Rev. 19:7, *note*)
s Resurrection: v. 4; Rom. 8:11. (2 Ki. 4:35; 1 Cor. 15:52, *note*)
5
t Flesh: v. 5; Rom. 7:14. (Jn. 8:15; Jude 23)

[1](6:11) "Reckon" here does not mean *suppose* but *count on, rely upon.*

[2](6:15) The old relation to the law and sin, and the new relation to Christ and life are illustrated by the effect of death upon slavery (vv. 16–23), and marriage (7:1–6). (1) The old slavery was nominally to the law but, since the law had no delivering power, the real master continued to be sin in the nature. The end was death. The law could not give life, and sin (here personified as the old man) results in death. But death in another form, i.e. crucifixion with Christ, has intervened (6:6) to free the servant from his double bondage to sin (6:6–7) and to the law (7:4,6). And (2) this effect of death is further illustrated by widowhood. Death dissolves the marriage relation (7:1–3). As natural death frees a wife from the law of marriage, so crucifixion with Christ sets the believer free from the law (the old husband) and makes him eligible to "be married to another," i.e. the risen Christ (7:4). Cp. Gal. 3:24, *note.*

at work in our members to bear
[a]fruit to death.
6 But now we have been delivered from the law, having
died to what we were held by, so
that we should serve in the newness of the Spirit and not *in* the
oldness of the [b]letter.

(5) The believer is not made holy by the law

7 What shall we say then? *Is*
the law sin? Certainly not! On
the contrary, I would not have
known [c]sin except through the
[d]law. For I would not have
known [e]covetousness unless
the law had said, [f]*"You shall*
*not covet."**
8 But [c]sin, taking opportunity by the commandment, produced in me all *manner of evil*
desire. For apart from the law
sin *was* dead.
9 I was alive once without
the law, but [1]when the commandment came, [c]sin revived
and I [g]died.
10 And the commandment,
which *was* to *bring* [h]life, I found
to *bring* [i]death.
11 For [c]sin, taking occasion
by the commandment, deceived
me, and by it killed *me.*
12 Therefore the [d]law *is*
holy, and the commandment
[j]holy and just and good.
13 Has then what is good become death to me? Certainly
not! But [c]sin, that it might appear sin, was producing death
in me through what is good, so
that sin through the commandment might become exceed-
ingly [c]sinful.
14 For we know that the [d]law
is spiritual, but I [k]am [2]carnal,
sold under [c]sin.

(6) The strife of the two natures

15 For what [3]I am doing, I do
not understand. For what I will
to do, that I do not practice; but
what I hate, that I do.
16 If, then, I do what I will not
to do, I agree with the [d]law that
it is good.
17 But now, *it is* no longer I
who do it, but [c]sin that dwells in
me.

*7:7 Deuteronomy 5:21

5
a Cp. Gal. 5:19–21
6
b See 2 Cor. 3:6, *note*
7
c See Rom. 3:23 and 5:21, *notes*
d *Law* (of Moses): vv. 7–9, 12–14,16; Rom. 7:22. (Ex. 19:1; Gal. 3:24, *note*)
e Cp. Mt. 5:27–30
f Ex. 20:17
9
g Cp. Jas. 1:14–15
10
h Lev. 18:5
i *Death* (spiritual): v. 10; Rom. 8:2. (Gen. 2:17; Eph. 2:5, *note*)

12
j *Sanctification* (NT): v. 12; Rom. 11:16. (Mt. 4:5; Rev. 22:11)
14
k *Flesh:* v. 14; Rom. 7:18. (Jn. 8:15; Jude 23)

[1](7:9) Verses 7–25 are autobiographical. Paul's religious experience was in three strongly marked phases: (1) He was a godly Jew under the law. That the passage does not refer to that period is clear from his own explicit statements elsewhere. At that time he held himself to be "blameless" as concerning the law (Phil. 3:6). He had lived "in all good conscience" (Acts 23:1). (2) With his conversion came new light upon the law itself. He now perceived it to be "spiritual" (v. 14). He now saw that, so far from having kept it, he was condemned by it. He had supposed himself to be "alive," but now the commandment really "came" (v. 9) and he "died." Just when the apostle passed through the experience of Rom. 7:7–25 we are not told. Perhaps it was during the days of physical blindness at Damascus (Acts 9:9); perhaps in Arabia (Gal. 1:17). It is the experience of a redeemed man, continuing to act as though he were under the law, and not yet fully aware of the delivering power of the Holy Spirit (cp. Rom. 8:2). And (3) with the great revelations afterward embodied in Galatians and Romans, the apostle's experience entered its third phase. He now knew himself to be "dead to the law through the body of Christ," and, in the power of the indwelling Spirit, "free from the law of sin and death" (8:2); while "the righteous requirement of the law" was met in him (not by him) as he walked according to the Spirit (8:4).

[2](7:14) This is Paul's description of the Adamic nature and of the believer who lives under the power of it. In other places (1 Cor. 3:1,3; 2 Cor. 10:4) he calls such behavior "carnal." "Natural" is the apostle's characteristic word for the unrenewed man (1 Cor. 15:44,46), as "spiritual" designates the renewed man who lives in the Spirit (1 Cor. 3:1; Gal. 6:1).

[3](7:15) In this passage (vv. 15–25) of profound spiritual and psychological insight, the apostle personifies the struggle of the two natures within the believer—the old or Adamic nature, and the divine nature received through the new birth (1 Pet. 1:23; 2 Pet. 1:4; cp. Gal. 2:20; Col. 1:27). The frequent use of the first personal pronoun here and in the preceding section (vv. 7–14), dealing with the believer and the law, shows that self-effort can neither achieve holiness through keeping the law nor win the struggle against indwelling sin. But ch. 6, presenting the way of victory over sin through identification with Christ in His death and resurrection, and ch. 8, showing the work of the Holy Spirit on the believer's behalf, use the first personal pronoun only incidentally (6:19; 8:18,38). In vv. 15–25 the "I" that is Saul of Tarsus and the "I" that is Paul the apostle are at war, and Paul is in a state of defeat; whereas in ch. 8 Paul is victorious through the Spirit who delivers him, a victory anticipated by the despairing cry, "Who will deliver me from this body of death?" (7:24), with its admission of man's total inability to deliver himself from the bondage of sin.

18 For I know that in me (that
is, in my [a]flesh) nothing good
dwells; for to will is present
with me, but *how* to perform
what is good I do not find.
19 For the good that I will *to*
do, I do not do; but the evil I will
not *to do,* that I practice.
20 Now if I do what I will not
to do, it is no longer I who do it,
but [b]sin that dwells in me.
21 I find then a [1]law, that evil
is present with me, the one who
wills to do good.
22 For I delight in the [c]law of
God according to the inward
man.
23 But I see another law in
my members, [d]warring against
the law of my mind, and bringing me into captivity to the law
of [b]sin which is in my members.
24 O [e]wretched man that I
am! [f]Who will deliver me
[g]from this body of death?
25 I thank God—through Jesus Christ our Lord! So then,
with the mind I myself serve the
[c]law of God, but with the [a]flesh
the law of [b]sin.

(7) The Spirit delivers from the old nature, producing righteousness

8 *THERE is* therefore now
no [h]condemnation to those
who are [i]in Christ Jesus,*
[2]who do not walk according to
the flesh, but according to the
Spirit.
2 For the law of the [3][j]Spirit
of life [i]in Christ Jesus has made
me free from the law of [b]sin and
[k]death.
3 For what the [c]law could
[l]not do in that it was weak
through the [a]flesh, God *did* by
[m]sending His own Son in the
likeness of sinful flesh, [n]on account of sin: He [h]condemned
[b]sin in the flesh,
4 that the [o]righteous requirement of the [c]law might be
fulfilled in us who do not [p]walk
according to the flesh but according to the [j]Spirit.

(8) Conflict of the Spirit with the old nature (cp. Gal. 5:16–18)

5 For those who live according to the [a]flesh set their minds
on the things of the flesh, but
those *who live* according to the
[j]Spirit, the things of the [j]Spirit.
6 For to be [q]carnally
minded *is* [k]death, but to be spiritually minded *is* [r]life and
peace.
7 Because the [s]carnal mind
is enmity against God; for it is
not subject to the [c]law of God,
nor indeed can be.
8 So then, those who are in
the flesh cannot please God.
9 But you are not in the
[a]flesh but in the [j]Spirit, if indeed the [j]Spirit of God dwells
in you. Now if anyone does not
have the [j]Spirit of Christ, he is
not His.
10 And if Christ *is* in you, the
body *is* dead because of [b]sin,
but the [j]Spirit *is* life because of
righteousness.
11 But if the [j]Spirit of Him
who [t]raised Jesus from the
dead dwells in you, He who
raised Christ from the dead will
also give life to your mortal
bodies [u]through His [j]Spirit
who dwells in you.
12 Therefore, brethren, we
are debtors—not to the [a]flesh,
to live according to the flesh.

*8:1 NU-Text omits the rest of this verse.

18
a *Flesh:* vv. 18,25; 8:3,5,7,9,12; Rom. 8:13. (Jn. 8:15; Jude 23)
20
b See Rom. 3:23 and 5:21, *notes*
22
c *Law* (of Moses): vv. 22,25; 8:3–4,7; Rom. 9:4. (Ex. 19:1; Gal. 3:24, *note*)
23
d Gal. 5:17
24
e Cp. Dt. 28:67; Prov. 13:15
f Cp. Rom. 8:2
g Rom. 8:11; 1 Cor. 15:51–52; 1 Th. 4:14–17
CHAPTER 8
1
h *Judgments* (the seven): vv. 1,3; Rom. 14:10. (2 Sam. 7:14; Rev. 20:12, *note*)
i Cp. 1 Cor. 1:30
2
j *Holy Spirit* (NT): vv. 2,4–5, 9–11; Rom. 8:13. (Mt. 1:18; Acts 2:4, *note*)
k *Death* (spiritual): vv. 2,6; Rom. 8:13. (Gen. 2:17; Eph. 2:5, *note*)
3
l Cp. Acts 15:10; Gal. 3:21; Heb. 7:18
m *Christ* (first advent): v. 3; Rom. 9:5. (Gen. 3:15; Acts 1:11, *note*)
n *Sacrifice* (of Christ): v. 3; Rom. 8:32. (Gen. 3:15; Heb. 10:18, *note*)
4
o *Righteousness* (OT): v. 4; Rom. 9:30. (Gen. 6:9; Lk. 2:25, *note*)
p Rom. 6:4; 2 Cor. 5:7; Gal. 5:16; Eph. 4:1; 5:2,15; 1 Jn. 1:7; 2:6
6
q i.e. *fleshly*
r *Life* (eternal): vv. 6, 10; 2 Cor. 2:16. (Mt. 7:14; Rev. 22:19). 1 Jn. 5:12
7
s i.e. the mind of the flesh
11
t *Resurrection:* v. 11; Rom. 8:34. (2 Ki. 4:35; 1 Cor. 15:52, *note*)
u Some MSS. read *because of*

[1](7:21) Six "laws" are to be differentiated in Romans: (1) the law of Moses, which condemns (3:19); (2) law as a principle (3:21); (3) the law of faith, which excludes self-righteousness (3:27); (4) the law of sin in the members, which is victorious over the law of the mind (7:21,23,25); (5) the law of the mind, which consents to the law of Moses but cannot do it because of the law of sin in the members (7:16,23); and (6) the law of the Spirit, having power to deliver the believer from the law of sin which is in his members, and his conscience from condemnation by the Mosaic law. Moreover the Spirit works in the yielded Christian the very righteousness which Moses' law requires (8:2,4).

[2](8:1) The last thirteen words of v. 1 may be copied from v. 4, where they express the result of "no condemnation." However, these words do occur in the majority of mss. and may simply express a further description of "those who are in Christ Jesus."

[3](8:2) Up to now in Romans the Holy Spirit has been mentioned four times (1:4; 2:29; 5:5; 7:6); in this chapter alone He is mentioned nineteen times. Redemption is by blood and by power (see Ex. 14:30, *note*). Rom. 3:21—5:11 speaks of the redemptive price; ch. 8, of redemptive power.

13
a Flesh: v. 13; Rom. 13:14. (Jn. 8:15; Jude 23)
b Death (spiritual): v. 13; 2 Cor. 3:7. (Gen. 2:17; Eph. 2:5, *note*). *Death* (the second): v. 13; Rev. 2:11. (Jn. 8:21; Rev. 20:14, *note*)
c Holy Spirit (NT): vv. 13–16, 23,26–27; Rom. 9:1. (Mt. 1:18; Acts 2:4, *note*)
d Col. 3:5–10
15
e Adoption: vv. 15,23; Gal. 4:5. (Rom. 8:15; Eph. 1:5)
f Gal. 4:6
17
g Cp. Gal. 3:29; Ti. 3:7; Heb. 1:14; 6:17
h Cp. Acts 5:41; 9:16; Heb. 11:25; Jas. 5:10; 1 Pet. 2:20; 5:10
i Cp. Mt. 13:43; Phil. 3:21; Col. 3:4; Rev. 22:5
18
j 2 Cor. 4:17
19
k vv. 20–23; cp. Gen. 3:17–19
l Cp. Mt. 13:40–43; 1 Jn. 3:2
21
m Cp. Rom. 7:23; 2 Tim. 2:26; 2 Pet. 2:19
n 2 Cor. 3:17; Gal. 5:1,13

13 For if you live according
to the [a]flesh you will [b]die; but if
by the [c]Spirit you [d]put to death
the deeds of the body, you will
live.

(9) The believer is made a son and heir (cp. Gal. 4:4)

14 For as many as are led by
the [c]Spirit of God, these are
sons of God.
15 For you did not receive the
spirit of bondage again to fear,
but you received the [c]Spirit of
[e]adoption by whom we [f]cry
out, "Abba, Father."
16 The [c]Spirit Himself bears
witness with our spirit that we
are [1]children of God,
17 and if children, then
[g]heirs—heirs of God and joint
heirs with Christ, if indeed we
[h]suffer with *Him,* that we may
also be [i]glorified together.

(10) The glorious deliverance ahead (cp. Gen. 3:18–19)

18 For I consider that the
[h]sufferings of this present time
are [j]not worthy *to be compared*
with the [i]glory which shall be
revealed in us.
19 For the earnest expectation of the [k]creation eagerly
waits for the [l]revealing of the
sons of God.
20 For the [k]creation was subjected to futility, not willingly,
but because of Him who subjected *it* in hope;
21 because the [k]creation itself also will be delivered from
the [m]bondage of corruption into
the glorious [n]liberty of the children of God.
22 For we know that the
whole [2]creation groans and labors with birth pangs together
until now.
23 Not only *that,* but we also
who have the firstfruits of the
[c]Spirit, even we ourselves
groan within ourselves, eagerly
waiting for [o]the [e]adoption, the
[p]redemption of our body.
24 For we were [q]saved in this
hope, but hope that is seen is not
hope; for why does one still
hope for what he sees?
25 But if we hope for what we
do not see, we eagerly wait for
it with perseverance.

(11) The Spirit an indwelling Intercessor (cp. Heb. 7:25)

26 Likewise the [c]Spirit also
helps in our weaknesses. For we
do not know [r]what we should
pray for as we ought, but the
Spirit Himself makes intercession for us* with groanings
which cannot be [3]uttered.
27 Now He who searches the
hearts knows what the mind of
the [c]Spirit *is,* because He
makes intercession for the
saints according to *the will of*
God.

(12) God's eternal, unfailing purpose through the Gospel

28 And we know [4]that all
things work together for good
to those who love God, to those
who are the called according to
His purpose.
29 For whom He [s]foreknew,
He also [t]predestined *to be* conformed to the [u]image of His
Son, that He might be the firstborn among many brethren.
30 Moreover whom He [t]pre-
destined, these He also [v]called;
whom He called, these He also
[w]justified; and whom He justified, these He also glorified.
31 What then shall we say to

*8:26 NU-Text omits *for us.*

23
o Lit. *the placing as sons*
p Eph. 1:14; 4:30; Phil. 3:20–21; see Rom. 3:24, *note*
24
q See Rom. 1:16, *note*
26
r i.e. *how to pray*
29
s Foreknowledge: v. 29; Rom. 11:2. (Acts 2:23; 1 Pet. 1:20)
t Predestination: vv. 29–30; 1 Cor. 2:7. (Rom. 8:29; Eph. 1:11). See 1 Pet. 1:20, *note*
u Cp. 1 Cor. 15:48–49
30
v Eph. 4:4
w Justification: v. 30; Rom. 8:33. (Lk. 18:14; Rom. 3:28, *note*)

[1](8:16) "Children" is from the Gk. *teknon,* meaning *one born, a child,* and so in vv. 17,21; not, as in v. 14, "sons" (Gk. *huios*). Compare Gal. 4:1,7, where babyhood and sonhood are contrasted; also Adoption (Rom. 8:15,23; Eph. 1:5, *note*).

[2](8:22) Adam drew down into his ruin the old creation, of which he was lord and head. Christ will bring into moral unity with God, and into eternal life, all of the new creation of which He is Lord and Head (Eph. 1:22–23). Even the animal and material creation, cursed for man's sake (Gen. 3:17), will be delivered by Christ (vv. 19–22; cp. Isa. 11:6–9).

[3](8:26) When Christians are so troubled as to find great difficulty in praying, the Holy Spirit is interceding for them with divine intensity ("groanings") that expresses their needs perfectly to God.

[4](8:28) Observe, in the last clause of this verse, that God's purpose, not His foreknowledge, is first in the order of the chain of verbs occurring in vv. 28–30.

32
a Sacrifice (of Christ): vv. 32,34; Rom. 14:9. (Gen. 3:15; Heb. 10:18, *note*)
33
b Election (corporate): v. 33; Rom. 9:11. (Dt. 7:6; 1 Pet. 5:13, *note*)
c Justification: v. 33; 1 Cor. 4:4. (Lk. 18:14; Rom. 3:28, *note*)
34
d Resurrection: v. 34; Rom. 10:9. (2 Ki. 4:35; 1 Cor. 15:52, *note*)
e Heb. 7:25; 9:24
36
f Inspiration: v. 36; 9:4; Rom. 9:6. (Ex. 4:15; 2 Tim. 3:16, *note*)
g Ps. 44:22
37
h 2 Cor. 2:14; 1 Jn. 5:4
38
i Assurance/security: vv. 38–39; Rom. 10:9. (Ps. 23:1;

these [1]things? If God *is* for us,
who *can be* against us?
32 He who did not spare His
own Son, but [a]delivered Him up
for us all, how shall He not with
Him also freely give us all
things?
33 Who shall bring a charge
against God's [b]elect? *It is* God
who [c]justifies.
34 Who *is* he who condemns?
It is Christ who [d]died, and furthermore is also [d]risen, who is
even at the right hand of God,
who also makes [e]intercession
for us.

(13) The believer is made secure

35 Who shall separate us
from the love of Christ? *Shall*
tribulation, or distress, or persecution, or famine, or nakedness,
or peril, or sword?
36 As it is [f]written:

[g]*"For Your sake we are*
killed all day long;
We are accounted as
sheep for the
slaughter."

37 Yet in all these things we
are more than [h]conquerors
through Him who loved us.
38 For I am [i]persuaded that
neither [j]death nor life, nor [k]an-
gels nor principalities nor powers, nor things present nor
things to come,
39 nor height nor depth, nor
any other created thing, shall be
able to separate us from the love
of God which is in Christ Jesus
our Lord.

IV. The Problem of Jewish Unbelief, 9—11

God's sovereign wisdom and grace in working out His purpose despite the unfaithfulness of Israel (9:11)

(1) Paul's solicitude for Israel

9 I TELL the truth in Christ, I
am not lying, my con-
science also bearing me witness
in the Holy [l]Spirit,
2 that I have great sorrow
and continual grief in my heart.
3 For I could wish that I myself were [m]accursed from Christ
for my brethren, my countrymen* according to the flesh,

(2) Israel's privileges

4 who are [n]Israelites, to
whom *pertain* the adoption, the
glory, the [o]covenants, the giving of the [p]law, the service *of*
God, and the [f]promises;
5 of whom *are* the fathers
and from whom, according to
the flesh, Christ [q]*came,* who is
over all, *the* eternally blessed
God. Amen.

* 9:3 Or *relatives*

Jude 1, *note*)
j Death (physical): v. 38; Rom. 14:8. (Gen. 2:17; Heb. 9:27, *note*)
k See Heb. 1:4, *note*
CHAPTER 9
1
l Holy Spirit (NT): v. 1; Rom. 14:17. (Mt. 1:18; Acts 2:4, *note*)
3
m Cp. Ex. 32:32
4
n Israel (prophecies): vv. 1–8; Rom. 10:1. (Gen. 12:2; Rom. 11:26, *note*)
o See Heb. 8:8, *note*
p Law (of Moses): v. 4; Rom. 9:32. (Ex. 19:1; Gal. 3:24, *note*)
5
q Christ (first advent): v. 5; Gal. 4:4. (Gen. 3:15; Acts 1:11, *note*)

[1](8:31) If the Epistle to the Romans may be likened to a great cathedral of Christian truth, then ch. 8 is the highest of the towering spires of that divine revelation. The grandeur of the theme is shown in the largeness of its references to God; the sweep of its revelation which includes past, present, and future—from creation to eternity; the good news of its message about God's answer to sin's tyranny; its lovely and soul-sustaining homily on suffering; and its closing triumphant note on the security of the believer.

God the Father is seen as Judge (vv. 30,33), as Benefactor (v. 32), as Ruler of history (vv. 28–30), as the Lord who searches hearts (v. 27), calls men (v. 28), justifies and glorifies believers (v. 30); above all, He is shown as the God of love (v. 39) who "did not spare His own Son, but delivered Him up for us all" (v. 32).

God the Son is revealed as the Firstborn among many brethren (v. 29), the Deliverer (vv. 1–4), the Indweller of His people (v. 10), the Lord with whom we are to be glorified (v. 17), the Savior of our souls (v. 34).

God the Spirit is gloriously presented as the Source of power (v. 4), life, and peace (v. 6), as the Lifegiver (v. 11), and Indweller (vv. 9,11). He leads (v. 14), witnesses to our spirits (v. 16), and intercedes (v. 26). He is the Spirit of our sonship (v. 15) and the Firstfruits of our redemption (v. 23).

The chapter speaks of men as well. The man devoid of the Spirit cannot please God (vv. 6–8). The Christian knows weaknesses (v. 26) but may live by the Spirit (v. 13) as God's heir (v. 17); moreover, his body, as well as his spirit, is involved in God's plan of redemption (v. 23); and, best of all, he is to be conformed to the image of God's Son (v. 29).

The opening verses of the chapter summarize chs. 5—8. The closing verses are a rock upon which assurance may stand forever. Yet this assurance is accomplished by moral means; for God's great objective which must be realized is for His children "to be conformed to the image of His Son."

(3) Natural posterity not identical with spiritual posterity

6 But it is not that the [a]word of God has taken no effect. [1]For they *are* not all Israel who *are* of Israel,

7 nor *are they* all [b]children because they are the seed of Abraham; but, [c]*"In Isaac your seed shall be called."*

(The distinction illustrated)

8 That is, those who *are* the [b]children of the flesh, these *are* not the [b]children of God; but the [b]children of the [d]promise are counted as the seed.

9 For this *is* the [a]word of promise: [e]*"At this time I will come and Sarah shall have a son."*

10 And not only *this,* but when [f]Rebecca also had conceived by one man, *even* by our father Isaac

11 (for *the children* not yet being born, nor having done any good or evil, that the purpose of God according to [g]election might stand, not of works but of Him who calls),

12 it was [a]said to her, [h]*"The older shall serve the younger."*

13 As it is [a]written, [i]*"Jacob I have loved, but Esau I have hated."*

(4) God's mercy is under His sovereign will

14 What shall we say then? *Is there* [j]unrighteousness with God? Certainly not!

15 For He [a]says to Moses, [k]*"I will have mercy on whomever I will have* [l]*mercy, and I will have compassion on whomever I will have* [m]*compassion."*

16 So then *it is* not of him who wills, nor of him who runs, [n]but of [o]God who shows mercy.

17 For the Scripture [a]says to the Pharaoh, [p]*"For this very purpose I have raised you up, that I may show My power in you, and that My name may be declared in all the earth."*

18 Therefore He has mercy on whom He wills, and whom He wills He [q]hardens.

19 You will say to me then, "Why does He still find fault? For who has resisted His will?"

20 But indeed, O man, who are you to reply against God? [r]Will the thing formed say to him who formed *it,* "Why have you made me like this?"

21 Does not the potter have power over the clay, from the same lump to [s]make one vessel for honor and another for dishonor?

22 *What* if God, wanting to show *His* wrath and to make His power known, endured with much longsuffering the vessels of wrath prepared for destruction,

23 and that He might make known the [t]riches of His glory on the vessels of mercy, which He had [u]prepared beforehand for glory,

24 *even* us whom He [v]called, [w]not [x]of the Jews only, but also [x]of the Gentiles?

(5) The prophets foretold the blinding of Israel and mercy to Gentiles

25 As He [a]says also in Hosea:

[y]*"I will call them My*
people, who were not
My people,
And her beloved, who
was not beloved."

26 *"And it shall come to*
pass in the place
where it was [a]*said to*
them,
[z]*'You are not My people,'*
There they shall be
called [aa]*sons of the*
living God."

27 Isaiah also [a]cries out concerning Israel:

[bb]*"Though the number of*
the children of Israel

6
a Inspiration: vv. 6,9, 12–13,15,17, 25–28; Rom. 9:29. (Ex. 4:15; 2 Tim. 3:16, *note*)
7
b See Rom. 8:16, *note*
c Gen. 21:12
8
d Cp. Gal. 4:22–31
9
e Gen. 18:10; Heb. 11:11
10
f Gen. 25:21
11
g Election (personal): v. 11; Rom. 11:5. (Dt. 7:6; 1 Pet. 5:13, *note*)
12
h Gen. 25:23
13
i Mal. 1:2–3; cp. Heb. 11:20
14
j Rom. 1:18, 6:13; 2 Th. 2:10; 2 Pet. 2:13; 1 Jn. 5:17
15
k Ex. 33:19
l Cp. Ps. 103:11
m Cp. Ps. 78:38; Lam. 3:32
16
n Cp. Dan. 9:18; Eph. 2:4–6; Ti. 3:5
o Cp. Jn. 1:13; 1 Cor. 3:7
17
p Ex. 9:16
18
q Ex. 4:21
20
r Isa. 29:16; 45:9; Jer. 18:6; Dan. 4:35
21
s Cp. 2 Tim. 2:20–21
23
t Grace: v. 23; Rom. 11:5. (Jn. 1:14; Jn. 1:17, *note*)
u Cp. Eph. 1:3–12
24
v Rom. 8:28
w vv. 24–30; Isa. 42:6–7
x Lit. *from among.* Cp. Acts. 15:14
25
y Hos. 2:23
26
z Hos. 1:10
aa Gk. *huios.* Mt. 5:9; Lk. 20:36
27
bb Isa. 10:22–23

[1](9:6) The distinction is between Israel according to the flesh, the mere natural posterity of Abraham, and Israelites who through faith are also Abraham's spiritual children. Gentiles who believe are also of Abraham's spiritual seed; but here the apostle is not considering them but only the two kinds of Israelites—the natural and the spiritual Israel (Rom. 4:1–3; Gal. 3:6–7. Cp. Jn. 8:37–39). See Rom. 11:1, *note.*

The NT indicates no distinction between the terms Jew, Israelite, and Hebrew. All are used by Paul concerning himself (Acts 21:39; Rom. 11:1; Phil. 3:5).

27
a Remnant: vv. 27,29; Rom. 11:5. (Isa. 1:9; Rom. 11:5, *note*)
b See Rom. 1:16, *note*
28
c See Rom. 10:10, *note*
d Isa. 10:23
29
e Inspiration: vv. 29, 33; 10:5–8, 11; Rom. 10:15. (Ex. 4:15; 2 Tim. 3:16, *note*)
f Lit. LORD *of hosts.* Isa. 1:9; see 1 Sam. 1:3, *note*
30
g See Eph. 3:6, *note*
h Righteousness (OT): v. 30; 10:5; Gal. 3:21. (Gen. 6:9; Lk. 2:25, *note*)
i Faith: vv. 30–33; 10:6,9–11; Rom. 10:14. (Gen. 3:20; Heb. 11:39, *note*)
31
j See Rom. 3:21, *note*
32
k Law (of Moses): v. 32; 10:4–5; Rom. 13:8. (Ex. 19:1; Gal. 3:24, *note*)
l Christ (Stone): vv. 32–33; 1 Cor. 1:23. (Gen. 49:24; 1 Pet. 2:8)
33
m Ps. 118:22; Isa. 8:14; 28:16; Mt. 21:42; 1 Pet. 2:6
n Rom. 5:5
CHAPTER 10
1
o Israel (prophecies): vv. 1–4;

be as the sand of the
sea,
The [a]remnant will be
[b]saved.
28 *For He will finish the*
work and cut it short
in [c]righteousness,
*Because the [d]*LORD *will*
make a short work
*upon the earth."**

29 And as Isaiah [e]said before:

*"Unless the [f]*LORD *of*
Sabaoth had left us a
[a]seed,
We would have become
like Sodom,
And we would have been
made like Gomorrah."

30 What shall we say then?
That [g]Gentiles, who did not
pursue [h]righteousness, have attained to [c]righteousness, even
the [c]righteousness of [i]faith;
31 but Israel, pursuing the
law of [j]righteousness, has not
attained to the law of righteousness.*
32 Why? Because *they did*
not *seek it* by faith, but as it
were, by the works of the
[k]law.* For they stumbled at
that stumbling [l]stone.
33 As it is [e]written:

[m]"Behold, I lay in Zion a
stumbling [l]stone and
rock of offense,
And whoever [i]believes
on Him will [n]not be
put to shame."

(6) Apparent failure of the promises to Israel explained by their unbelief

10 BRETHREN, my heart's
desire and prayer to God
for [o]Israel* is that they may be
[b]saved.
2 For I bear them witness
that they have a [p]zeal for God,
but not according to knowledge.
3 For they being ignorant
of God's [c]righteousness, and
seeking to establish their own
[1j]righteousness, have not submitted to the [c]righteousness of
God.
4 For Christ *is* the end of the
[k]law for [c]righteousness to everyone who believes.
5 For Moses [e]writes about
the [h]righteousness which is of
the [k]law, [q]*"The man who does*
those things shall live by them."
6 But the [c]righteousness of
[i]faith speaks in this way, [r]*"Do*
not say in your heart, 'Who will
ascend into heaven?' " (that is,
to bring Christ down *from*
above)
7 or, *" 'Who will descend*
into the abyss?' " (that is, to
bring Christ up from the dead).
8 But what does it [e]say?
"The word is near you, in your
mouth and in your heart" (that
is, the [s]word of faith which we
preach):
9 [t]that if you confess with
your mouth the [u]Lord Jesus
and [i]believe in your heart that
God has [v]raised Him from the
dead, you [w]will be [b]saved.
10 For with the heart one
[i]believes unto [2]righteousness,
and with the mouth confession
is made unto [b]salvation.
11 For the Scripture [e]says,
[x]*"Whoever [i]believes on Him*
*will not be put to shame."**
12 For there is no [y]distinc-
tion between Jew and Greek,
for the same Lord over all is rich
to all who call upon Him.
13 For *"whoever calls on the*
*name of the [z]*LORD *[w]shall be*
[b]saved."

(7) World-wide outreach of the Gospel;
God would have all to be saved

14 How then shall they call
on Him in whom they have not
believed? And how shall they

*
9:28 NU-Text reads *For the Lord will finish the work and cut it short upon the earth.*
9:31 NU-Text omits *of righteousness.*
9:32 NU-Text reads *by works.*
10:1 NU-Text reads *them.* 10:11 Isaiah 28:16

Rom. 11:1. (Gen. 12:2; Rom. 11:26, *note*)
2
p Cp. Acts 22:3
5
q Lev. 18:5; Gal. 3:12
6
r vv. 6–8; Dt. 30:12–14
8
s Gospel: v. 8; Rom. 10:15. (Gen. 12:3; Rev. 14:6)
9
t Mt. 10:32; Lk. 12:8; cp. Acts 8:37
u i.e. *Jesus as Lord.* Cp. 1 Cor. 12:3
v Resurrection: v. 9; Rom. 14:9. (2 Ki. 4:35; 1 Cor. 15:52, *note*). Rom. 4:24
w Assurance/security: vv. 9,13; 1 Cor. 3:22. (Ps. 23:1; Jude 1, *note*)
11
x Cp. Isa. 49:23
12
y Rom. 3:22; Gal. 3:28
13
z Joel 2:32; Acts 2:21

[1](10:3) The word "righteousness" here (and in the passages carrying a marginal reference to this verse) alludes to legal righteousness or self-righteousness, the futile effort of man to work out under law a character which God can approve. See Rev. 19:8, *note.*

[2](10:10) "Righteousness" here (and in the passages carrying a marginal reference to this verse) alludes to that righteousness of God which is judicially reckoned to all who believe on the Lord Jesus Christ, i.e. Christians are the righteous. See 3:21, *note.*

[a]believe in Him of whom they
have not heard? And how shall
they hear without a preacher?
15 And how shall they
preach unless they are sent? As
it is [b]written:

[c]"How beautiful are the
feet of those who
preach the [d]gospel of
*peace,**
Who bring glad tidings
of good things!"

16 But they have not all
obeyed the [d]gospel. For Isaiah
[b]says, *[e]"Lord, who has [a]be-*
lieved our report?"
17 So then [a]faith *comes* by
hearing, and hearing by the
[d]word of God.
18 But I say, have they not
heard? Yes indeed:

[f]"Their sound has [b]gone
out to all the earth,
And their words to the
ends of the [g]world."

19 But I say, did Israel not
know? First Moses [b]says:

[h]"I will provoke you to
jealousy by those who
are not a nation,
I will move you to anger
by a foolish nation."

20 But Isaiah is very bold and
[b]says:

[i]"I was found by those
who did not seek Me;
I was made manifest to
[j]those who did not
ask for Me."

21 But to Israel he [b]says:

[k]"All day long I have
stretched out My
hands
To a disobedient and
[l]contrary people."

(8) The spiritual in Israel
are, like Paul, finding
salvation in Christ

11 I SAY then, [m]has God
[1]cast away His [n]people?
[o]Certainly not! For I also am an
Israelite, of the seed of Abraham, *of* the tribe of Benjamin.
2 God has not cast away His
people whom He [p]foreknew. Or
do you not know what the
Scripture [b]says of Elijah, how
he pleads with God against Israel, saying,
3 *[q]"*LORD*, they have killed*
Your prophets and torn down
Your altars, and I alone am left,
and they seek my life"?
4 But what does the divine
response [b]say to him? *[r]"I have*
reserved for Myself seven thou-
sand men who have not bowed
the knee to Baal."
5 Even so then, at this present time there is a [2s]remnant

*10:15 NU-Text omits *preach the gospel of peace, Who.*

14
a Faith: vv. 14, 16–17; Rom. 11:20. (Gen. 3:20; Heb. 11:39, *note*)
15
b Inspiration: vv. 15–16, 18–21; 11:2–4; Rom. 11:8. (Ex. 4:15; 2 Tim. 3:16, *note*)
c Isa. 52:7; Nah. 1:15
d Gospel: vv. 15–18; Rom. 11:28. (Gen. 12:3; Rev. 14:6)
16
e Isa. 53:1
18
f Ps. 19:4
g Gk. *oikoumenē.* See Lk. 2:1, *note*
19
h Dt. 32:21; cp. Rom. 11:11
20
i Isa. 65:1
j Cp. Isa. 42:6–7
21
k Isa. 65:2
l Cp. Acts 13:45

CHAPTER 11
1
m Ps. 94:14; Jer. 46:28
n Israel (prophecies): vv. 1, 8–10; Rom. 11:23. (Gen. 12:2; Rom. 11:26, *note*)
o 1 Sam. 12:22; Jer. 31:37
2
p Foreknowledge: v. 2; 1 Pet. 1:20. (Acts 2:23; 1 Pet. 1:20)
3
q 1 Ki. 19:10, 14
4
r 1 Ki. 19:18
5
s Remnant: vv. 1–7; Rom. 11:23. (Isa. 1:9; Rom. 11:5, *note*). Isa. 1:9

[1](11:1) That Israel has not been forever set aside is the theme of this chapter. (1) The salvation of Paul proves that there is still a remnant of Israel (v. 1). (2) The doctrine of the remnant proves it (vv. 2–6). (3) The present national unbelief was foreseen (vv. 7–10). (4) Israel's unbelief is the Gentile opportunity (vv. 11–25). (5) Israel is judicially broken off from the good olive tree, Christ (vv. 17–22). (6) They are to be grafted in again (vv. 23–24). And (7) the promised Deliverer will come out of Zion and the nation will be saved (vv. 25–29). That the Christian now inherits the distinctive Jewish promises is not taught in Scripture. The Christian is of the heavenly seed of Abraham (Gen. 15:5–6; Gal. 3:29) and partakes of the spiritual blessings of the Abrahamic Covenant (Gen. 12:2, *note*); but Israel as a nation always has its own place and is yet to have its greatest exaltation as the earthly people of God. See Israel (Gen. 12:2–3; Rom. 11:26, *note*); Kingdom (OT) (Gen. 1:26–28; Zech. 12:8, *note*).

[2](11:5) Remnant, Summary: In the history of Israel a remnant may be discerned, a spiritual Israel within the national Israel. In Elijah's time 7000 had not bowed the knee to Baal (1 Ki. 19:18). In Isaiah's time, Israel had been reduced to only a "very small remnant" (Isa. 1:9), for whose sake God still held back from destroying the nation. During the captivities the remnant appears in Jews like Esther, Mordecai, Ezekiel, Daniel, Shadrach, Meshach, and Abednego. At the end of the seventy years of Babylonian captivity it was the remnant that returned under Ezra and Nehemiah. At the advent of our Lord, John the Baptist, Simeon, Anna, and those "who looked for redemption in Jerusalem" (Lk. 2:38) were the remnant. During the Church Age the remnant is composed of believing Jews (Rom. 11:4–5). But an important aspect of the remnant is prophetic. During the great tribulation a remnant out of all Israel will turn to Jesus as Messiah, the "sealed" Israelites of Rev. 7:3–8. It is inferred by many students of Scripture that the great multitude of Gentiles of Rev. 7:9 will be saved by the witness of the 144,000 of vv. 3–8. Some of these will undergo martyrdom (Rev. 6:9–11), some will be spared to enter

according to the [a]election of [b]grace.

6 And if by [b]grace, then *it is* no longer of works; otherwise grace is no longer grace.* But if *it is* of works, it is no longer grace; otherwise work is no longer work.

(9) National Israel is temporarily set aside but not cast away permanently

7 What then? [c]Israel has not obtained what it seeks; but the [a]elect have obtained it, and the rest were [d]blinded.

8 Just as it is [e]written:

[f]*"God has given them a*
spirit of stupor,
Eyes that they should
not see
And ears that they
should not hear,
To this very day."

9 And David [e]says:

[g]*"Let their table become a*
snare and a trap,
A stumbling block and a
recompense to them.

10 *Let their eyes be*
darkened, so that they
do not see,
And bow down their
back always."

11 I say then, have they stumbled that they should fall? Certainly not! But through their fall, to provoke them to [h]jealousy, [i]salvation *has come* to the [j]Gentiles.

12 Now if their fall *is* riches for the [k]world, and their failure riches for the [j]Gentiles, [l]how much more their fullness!

(10) Gentiles warned: Israel's blindness is only "in part" (v. 25)

13 For I speak to you [j]Gentiles; inasmuch as I am an [m]apostle to the Gentiles, I magnify my ministry,

14 if by any means I may provoke to jealousy *those who are* my flesh and [l]save some of them.

15 For if their being cast away *is* the [n]reconciling of the [k]world, what *will* their acceptance *be* [o]but life from the dead?

16 For if the firstfruit *is* [p]holy, the lump *is* also *holy;* and if the root *is* [p]holy, so *are* the branches.

17 And if some of the branches were broken off, and you, being a wild olive tree, were grafted in among them, and with them became a partaker of the root and fatness of the [1]olive tree,

18 do not boast against the branches. But if you do boast, *remember that* you do not support the root, but the root supports you.

19 You will say then, "Branches were broken off that I might be grafted in."

20 Well *said.* Because of [q]unbelief they were broken off, and you stand by [r]faith. Do not be haughty, but fear.

21 [s]For if God did not spare the natural branches, He may not spare you either.

22 Therefore consider the goodness and severity of God: on those who fell, severity; but toward you, goodness,* if you continue in *His* goodness. Otherwise you also will be cut off.

23 And [t]they also, if they do not [u]continue in [q]unbelief, will be grafted in, for God is able to graft [v]them in again.

24 For if you were cut out of the olive tree which is wild by nature, and were grafted contrary to nature into a cultivated olive tree, how much more will these, who *are* natural *branches,* be grafted into their own olive tree?

25 For I do not desire, brethren, that you should be ignorant of this [w]mystery, lest you should be wise in your own opinion, that blindness in part has happened to Israel until the

5
a Election (corporate): vv. 5,7; Rom. 11:28. (Dt. 7:6; 1 Pet. 5:13, *note*)
b Grace: vv. 5–6; Rom. 12:3. (Jn. 1:14; Jn. 1:17, *note*). See 2 Pet. 3:18, *note*
7
c Rom. 9:31; cp. 10:13
d 2 Cor. 3:14
8
e Inspiration: vv. 8–10; Rom. 11:26. (Ex. 4:15; 2 Tim. 3:16, *note*)
f Dt. 29:3–4; Isa. 29:10; Mt. 13:14; Jn. 12:40; Acts 28:26–27
9
g Ps. 69:22
11
h Dt. 32:21; Rom. 10:19
i See Rom. 1:16, *note*
j Isa. 42:6–7; Acts 28:28; see Eph. 3:6, *note*
12
k Gk. *kosmos.* See Mt. 4:8, *note*
l Cp. Ps. 72:8–11; Isa. 49:6; 60:3
13
m Acts 9:15; 22:21; Gal. 1:16; 2:7–9; Eph. 3:8

15
n Reconciliation: v. 15; 2 Cor. 5:18. (Rom. 5:10; Col. 1:20)
o Isa. 26:16–19; cp. Ezek. 37:1–14; Hos. 6:1–3
16
p Sanctification (NT): v. 16; Rom. 12:1. (Mt. 4:5; Rev. 22:11)
20
q Heb. 3:19; cp. Rom. 9:32
r Faith: v. 20; Rom. 12:3. (Gen. 3:20; Heb. 11:39, *note*)
21
s Cp. Heb. 4:1–13
23
t Remnant: vv. 23–27; Rev. 6:11. (Isa. 1:9; Rom. 11:5, *note*)
u 2 Cor. 3:16
v Israel (prophecies): vv. 23–26; Rom. 11:27. (Gen. 12:2; Rom. 11:26, *note*)
25
w Church (the true): v. 25; Rom. 12:5. (Mt. 16:18; Heb. 12:23). See Mt. 13:11, *note*

*
11:6 NU-Text omits the rest of this verse.
11:22 NU-Text adds *of God.*

the millennial kingdom (Zech. 12:6—13:9). Many of the Psalms express prophetically, the joys and sorrows of the tribulation remnant.

[1](11:17) The olive root represents the blessings promised to Abraham's seed. Though Gentiles do not, by faith in Christ, inherit Israel's particular promises, they do receive the blessing promised to "all the families of the earth" (Gen. 12:3; cp. Gal. 3:6–9).

26
a See Rom. 1:16, *note*
b *Inspiration:* v. 26; Rom. 12:19. (Ex. 4:15; 2 Tim. 3:16, *note*)
c i.e. *Redeemer.* Isa. 59:20–21
d *Christ* (second advent): v. 26; 1 Cor. 1:7. (Dt. 30:3; Acts 1:11, *note*)
27
e *Covenant* (New): v. 27; 1 Cor. 11:25. (Isa. 61:8; Heb. 8:8, *note*)
f *Israel* (prophecies): vv. 23–27; 1 Cor. 10:1. (Gen. 12:2; Rom. 11:26, *note*)
g See Rom. 3:23, *note*
28
h *Gospel:* v. 28; Rom. 15:16. (Gen. 12:3; Rev. 14:6)
i *Election* (corporate): v. 28; Rom. 16:13. (Dt. 7:6; 1 Pet. 5:13, *note*)
29
j *Repentance:* v. 29; 2 Cor. 7:9. (Mt. 3:2; Acts 17:30, *note*)
32
k Gal. 3:22
34
l 1 Cor. 2:16; cp. Isa. 40:13
36
m Col. 1:16; Heb. 2:10

[1]fullness of the Gentiles has
come in.

(11) Repentant Israel
will yet be saved through the
Deliverer (cp. Isa. 66:8)

26 And so all Israel will be
[a]saved,* as it is [b]written:

"The [c]Deliverer will
[d]come out of Zion,
And He will turn away
ungodliness from
[2]Jacob;
27 *For this is My [e]covenant*
with them,
When I take away [f]their
[g]sins."

28 Concerning the [h]gospel
they are enemies for your sake,
but concerning the [i]election
they are beloved for the sake of
the fathers.
29 For the gifts and the calling of God *are* [j]irrevocable.
30 For as you were once disobedient to God, yet have now
obtained mercy through their
disobedience,
31 even so these also have
now been disobedient, that
through the mercy shown you
they also may obtain mercy.
32 For God has committed
them [k]all to disobedience, that
He might have mercy on all.

(12) God's matchless wisdom

33 Oh, the depth of the riches
both of the wisdom and knowledge of God! How unsearchable
are His judgments and His ways
past finding out!
34 *"For who has known the*
[l]mind of the LORD?
Or who has become His
*counselor?"**
35 *"Or who has first given to*
Him
And it shall be repaid to
*him?"**

36 For of Him and through
Him and to Him *are* [m]all things,
to whom *be* glory forever.
Amen.

V. Christian Life and Service
for the Glory of God, 12:1—15:13

(1) Dedication

12 I BESEECH you there-
fore, brethren, by the
[n]mercies of God, that you [o]pre-
sent your bodies a living [p]sacri-
fice, [q]holy, acceptable to God,
which is your reasonable [r]ser-
vice.
2 And [s]do not be con-
formed to this [t]world, but be
[u]transformed by the renewing
of your mind, that you may
prove [v]what *is* that good and
acceptable and perfect will of
God.

(2) Service through gifts
of the Spirit

3 For I say, through the
[w]grace given to me, to everyone
who is among you, not to think
of himself more highly than he
ought to think, but to think soberly, as God has [x]dealt to each
one a measure of [y]faith.
4 For as we have many
members in one body, but all
the members do not have the
same function,
5 so we, *being* many, are
one [z]body in Christ, and individually members of [aa]one another.
6 Having then gifts differing
according to the [w]grace that is
[bb]given to us, *let us use them:* if

*
11:26 Or *delivered* 11:34 Jeremiah 23:18
11:35 Job 41:11

CHAPTER 12
1
n Rom. 3:21–8:39
o i.e. *present once for all.* Cp. Rom. 6:12–13
p vv. 1–2; Phil. 4:18; see Heb. 10:18, *note*
q *Sanctification* (NT): vv. 1–2; Rom. 15:16. (Mt. 4:5; Rev. 22:11)
r Rendered *divine service,* Heb. 9:1
2
s *Separation:* v. 2; 1 Cor. 10:20. (Gen. 12:1; 2 Cor. 6:17, *note*)
t Lit. *age*
u Rendered *transfigured,* Mt. 17:2; Mk. 9:2
v Cp. Eph. 5:1–21
3
w *Grace:* vv. 3,6; Rom. 15:15. (Jn. 1:14; Jn. 1:17, *note*). See 2 Pet. 3:18, *note*
x vv. 3–8; cp. 1 Cor. 12:4–11; Eph. 4:7–16
y *Faith:* v. 3; Rom. 12:6. (Gen. 3:20; Heb. 11:39, *note*)
5
z *Church* (the true): v. 5; Rom. 16:23. (Mt. 16:18; Heb. 12:23)
aa 1 Cor. 10:17; Gal. 3:28
6
bb Jn. 3:27

[1](11:25) The "fullness of the Gentiles" is the completion of the purpose of God in this age, i.e. the outcalling from among the Gentiles of a people for Christ's name, "the church, which is His body" (Eph. 1:22–23). Cp. Acts 15:14; 1 Cor. 12:12–13; Eph. 4:11–13. It must be distinguished from "the times of the Gentiles" (Lk. 21:24).

[2](11:26) Israel, Summary: Israel, so named from the grandson of Abraham, was chosen for a fourfold mission: (1) to witness to the unity of God in the midst of universal idolatry (cp. Dt. 6:4 with Isa. 43:10–12); (2) to illustrate to the nations the blessedness of serving the true God (Dt. 33:26–29; 1 Chr. 17:20–21; Ps. 144:15); (3) to receive, preserve, and transmit the Scriptures (Dt. 4:5–8; Rom. 3:1–2); and (4) to be the human channel for the Messiah (Gen. 3:15; 12:3; 22:18; 28:10–14; 49:10; 2 Sam. 7:12–16; Isa. 7:14; 9:6; Mt. 1:1; Rom. 1:3). According to the prophets Israel, regathered from all nations, restored to her own land and converted, is yet to have her greatest earthly exaltation and glory. See Kingdom (OT) (Gen. 1:26–28; Zech. 12:8, *note*); (NT) (Mt. 2:2; 1 Cor. 15:24, *note*); Davidic Covenant (2 Sam. 7:16, *note*).

prophecy, *let us prophesy* in proportion to our [a]faith;

7 or ministry, *let us use it* in *our* ministering; he who teaches, in teaching;

8 he who exhorts, in exhortation; he who gives, with liberality; he who leads, with diligence; he who shows mercy, with cheerfulness.

(3) The Christian and those within God's family

9 *Let* [b]love *be* without hypocrisy. Abhor what is evil. Cling to what is good.

10 *Be* kindly affectionate to one another with brotherly [b]love, in honor giving preference to one another;

11 not lagging in diligence, fervent in spirit, serving the Lord;

12 rejoicing in hope, patient in tribulation, continuing [c]steadfastly in prayer;

13 [d]distributing to the needs of the saints, given to hospitality.

14 [e]Bless those who persecute you; bless and do not curse.

15 Rejoice with those who rejoice, and weep with those who weep.

16 Be of the same mind toward one another. Do not set your mind on high things, but associate with the humble. Do not be wise in your own opinion.

(4) The Christian and those outside of God's family

17 Repay no one [f]evil for evil. Have regard for good things in the sight of all men.

18 If it is possible, as much as depends on you, live peaceably with all men.

19 Beloved, do not avenge yourselves, but *rather* give place to wrath; for it is [g]written, [h]*"Vengeance is Mine, I will repay,"* says the Lord.

20 Therefore

[i]*"If your enemy is hungry,*
feed him;
If he is thirsty, give him
a drink;
For in so doing you will
heap coals of fire on
his head."

21 Do not be overcome by evil, but [j]overcome evil with good.

(5) The Christian and government

13 LET every soul be [k]subject to the governing authorities. For there is no authority except from God, and the authorities that exist are [l]appointed by God.

2 Therefore whoever resists the authority [m]resists the ordinance of God, and those who resist will bring judgment on themselves.

3 For rulers are not a terror to good works, but to evil. Do you want to be unafraid of the authority? [n]Do what is good, and you will have praise from the same.

4 For he is God's [o]minister to you for good. But if you do evil, be afraid; for he does not bear the sword in vain; for he is God's [1][o]minister, an avenger to *execute* wrath on him who practices evil.

5 Therefore *you* must be subject, not only because of wrath but also for [p]conscience' sake.

6 For because of this you also pay [q]taxes, for they are God's [r]ministers attending continually to this very thing.

7 Render therefore to [s]all their due: [q]taxes to whom taxes *are due,* customs to whom customs, fear to whom fear, honor to whom honor.

(6) The law of love toward neighbors (cp. Lk. 10:29–37)

8 [t]Owe no one anything except to [b]love one another, for he

6
a Faith: v. 6; Rom. 13:11. (Gen. 3:20; Heb. 11:39, *note*)

9
b Law (of Christ): vv. 9–10; 13:8–15:2; Rom 13:10. (Jn. 13:24; 2 Jn. 5)

12
c 1 Th. 5:17

13
d Heb. 13:16; 1 Pet. 4:9

14
e v. 20; Lk. 6:28; cp. Mt. 5:44

17
f 1 Pet. 3:9

19
g Inspiration: v. 19; Rom. 14:11. (Ex. 4:15; 2 Tim. 3:16, *note*)
h Dt. 32:35

20
i Prov. 25:21–22; cp. Mt. 5:44

21
j 12:1–2

CHAPTER 13

1
k 13:5; Ti. 3:1; 1 Pet. 2:13
l Cp. Dan 4:17; cp. Jn. 19:11

2
m Cp. Acts 23:2–5; 2 Pet. 2:10–11

3
n Cp. 1 Pet. 2:14; 3:13; 4:15

4
o Or *servant*

5
p Acts 24:16; cp. Rom. 9:1; 2 Cor. 1:12; 1 Tim. 1:5,19; 1 Pet. 3:16

6
q Cp. Mt. 17:24–27
r Or *servants*

7
s Cp. Mk. 12:17; 1 Pet. 2:17–18

8
t Cp. Lev. 19:13

[1](13:4) In vv. 1–4 the apostle points out that orderly government is part of God's provision, even in a wicked world. No ruler exercises control except as God permits (Dan. 4:17). Under normal circumstances the Christian is to be obedient to the law of the land. This does not mean that he is to obey regulations that are immoral or anti-Christian. In such cases it is his duty to obey God rather than men (Acts 5:29; cp. Dan. 3:16–18; 6:10ff. See also Gen. 8:15 and 9:16, with their *notes*).

who loves another has [a]fulfilled the [b]law.

9 For the commandments, [c]*"You shall not commit adultery," "You shall not* [d]*murder," "You shall not steal," "You shall not bear false witness,"** *"You shall not covet,"** and if *there is* any other commandment, are *all* summed up in this saying, namely, *"You shall love your neighbor as yourself."**

10 [e]Love [f]does no harm to a neighbor; therefore love *is* the fulfillment of the [b]law.

11 And *do* this, knowing the time, that now *it is* high time to awake out of sleep; for now [g]our [h]salvation *is* [i]nearer than when we *first* [j]believed.

12 The night is far spent, the day is at hand. [k]Therefore let us cast off the works of darkness, and let us put on the [l]armor of light.

13 Let us walk properly, as in the day, not in revelry and drunkenness, not in lewdness and lust, not in strife and [m]envy.

14 But [n]put on the Lord Jesus Christ, and make no provision for the [o]flesh, to *fulfill its* lusts.

(7) The Christian and debatable things (cp. 1 Cor. 8:1—10:33)

(a) The principle of individual responsibility

14 RECEIVE one who is weak in the faith, *but* not to disputes over doubtful things.

2 For one believes he may eat all things, but he who is weak eats *only* vegetables.

3 Let not him who eats despise him who does not eat, and let not him who does not eat [1]judge him who eats; for God has received him.

4 Who are you to [p]judge another's servant? To his own master he stands or falls. Indeed, he will be made to stand, for God is able to make him stand.

5 One person esteems *one* day above another; another esteems every day *alike.* Let each be fully convinced in his own mind.

6 He who observes the day, observes *it* to the Lord;* and he who does not observe the day, to the Lord he does not observe *it.* He who eats, eats to the Lord, for he gives God thanks; and he who does not eat, to the Lord he does not eat, and gives God thanks.

7 For none of us [q]lives to himself, and no one dies to himself.

8 For if we [r]live, we live to the Lord; and if we [s]die, we die to the Lord. Therefore, whether we live or die, we are the Lord's.

9 For to this end Christ [t]died and [u]rose* and lived again, that He might be [v]Lord of both the dead and the living.

10 But why do you [w]judge your brother? Or why do you show contempt for your brother? For we shall all [x]stand before the [y]judgment seat of Christ.*

11 For it is [z]written:

[aa]*"As I live, says the* LORD,
Every knee shall bow to
Me,
And every tongue shall
confess to God."

12 So then each of us shall

*

13:9 NU-Text omits *"You shall not bear false witness."* • Deuteronomy 5:17–19,21 • Leviticus 19:18
14:6 NU-Text omits the rest of this sentence. **14:9** NU-Text omits *and rose.*
14:10 NU-Text reads *of God.*

8
a Gal. 5:13–14
b Law (of Moses): vv. 8–10; 1 Cor. 7:19. (Ex. 19:1; Gal. 3:24, *note*)
9
c Ex. 20:13–17
d See Ex. 20:13, *note*
10
e Law (of Christ): 13:8–15:2; 1 Cor. 4:21. (Jn. 13:34; 2 Jn. 5)
f Cp. 1 Cor. 13:1–13
11
g The full result of salvation in glory. 1 Jn. 3:2
h See Rom. 1:16, *note*
i Cp. 1 Cor. 7:29; Jas. 5:8
j Faith: v. 11; Rom. 14:22. (Gen. 3:20; Heb. 11:39, *note*)
12
k Eph. 5:11
l Eph. 6:11
13
m Or jealousy
14
n Righteousness (garment): v. 14; Col. 3:12. (Gen. 3:21; Rev. 19:8)
o Flesh: v. 14; 1 Cor. 3:1. (Jn. 8:15; Jude 23)
CHAPTER 14
4
p Jas. 4:11–12
7
q Cp. 1 Cor. 6:19–20
8
r 2 Cor. 5:14–15
s Death (physical): v. 8; 1 Cor. 3:22. (Gen. 2:17; Heb. 9:27, *note*)
9
t Sacrifice (of Christ): v. 9; Rom. 14:15. (Gen. 3:15; Heb. 10:18, *note*)
u Resurrection: v. 9; 1 Cor. 6:14. (2 Ki. 4:35; 1 Cor. 15:52, *note*)
v Acts 10:36
10
w Cp. Mt. 7:1–2
x 2 Cor. 5:10
y Judgments (the seven): v. 10; 1 Cor. 3:13. (2 Sam. 7:14; Rev. 20:12, *note*)
11
z Inspiration: v. 11; Rom. 15:3. (Ex. 4:15; 2 Tim. 3:16, *note*)
aa Isa. 45:23; Phil. 2:10–11

[1](14:3) In this passage (14:1—15:3) Paul presents principles of guidance respecting practices about which Christians differ. Although he uses as examples meat sacrificed to idols and the keeping of ceremonial days, the principles involved apply to believers in every age. Convictions about what constitutes Christian conduct sometimes reflect ecclesiastical and social backgrounds, but the principles written in this passage are timeless. They may be stated as follows: Christians (1) are not to judge the practice of other Christians in respect to doubtful things (v. 3); (2) are personally accountable to God for their actions (v. 12); (3) are not to do anything that will put a stumbling block before their brethren (v. 13); (4) have Christian liberty regarding what they do (vv. 14,20); (5) are to do what will edify their brethren (v. 19); (6) should, for the sake of their weaker brethren, voluntarily abstain from certain practices (v. 21); (7) are to do only what can be done without self-condemnation (v. 22); and (8) are to follow the example of Christ, who did not live to please Himself (15:1–3).

give account of himself to God.

(b) The principle of a neighbor's good

13 Therefore let us not [a]judge one another anymore, but rather resolve this, not to put a stumbling block or a cause to fall in *our* brother's way.

14 I know and am convinced by the Lord Jesus that *there is* [b]nothing unclean of itself; but [c]to him who considers anything to be unclean, to him *it is* unclean.

15 Yet if your brother is [d]grieved because of *your* food, you are no longer walking in love. Do not destroy with your food the one for whom Christ [e]died.

16 Therefore do not let your good be spoken of as evil;

17 for the [f]kingdom of God is not eating and drinking, but [g]righteousness and [h]peace and joy in the Holy [i]Spirit.

18 For he who serves Christ in these things* *is* [j]acceptable to God and approved by men.

19 Therefore let us pursue the things *which make* for [h]peace and the things by which one may [k]edify another.

20 Do not destroy the work of God for the sake of food. All things indeed *are* pure, but *it is* evil for the man who eats with [d]offense.

21 *It is* good neither to eat meat nor drink wine nor *do anything* by which your brother stumbles or is offended or is made weak.*

(c) The principle of God's glory

22 Do you have [l]faith?* Have *it* to yourself before God. Happy *is* he who does not [m]condemn himself in what he approves.

23 But he who [c]doubts is condemned if he eats, because *he does* not *eat* from faith; for whatever *is* not from [l]faith is [n]sin.*

15

WE then who are strong ought to bear with the scruples of the weak, and not to please ourselves.

2 Let each of us please *his* neighbor for *his* good, leading to [k]edification.

3 For even Christ did not [o]please Himself; but as it is [p]written, [q]*"The reproaches of those who reproached You fell on Me."*

(8) Jewish and Gentile believers are one in salvation

4 For whatever things were written before were [p]written [r]for our learning, that we through the patience and comfort of the Scriptures might have hope.

5 Now may the God of patience and comfort grant you to

13
a Cp. Mt. 7:1–2
14
b Cp. Acts 10:15
c Cp. 1 Cor. 10:24–33
15
d Cp. 1 Cor. 8:9–13
e *Sacrifice* (of Christ): v. 15; 1 Cor. 1:23. (Gen. 3:15; Heb. 10:18, *note*)
17
f See Mt. 6:33, *note*
g See Rom. 10:10, *note*
h Rom. 8:6
i *Holy Spirit* (NT): v. 17; Rom. 15:13. (Mt. 1:18; Acts 2:4, *note*)
18
j 2 Cor. 5:9
19
k 1 Th. 5:11

22
l *Faith:* vv. 22–23; 15:13; Rom. 16:26. (Gen. 3:20; Heb. 11:39, *note*)
m 1 Jn. 3:21
23
n See Rom. 3:23, *note*
CHAPTER 15
3
o Phil. 2:5–8
p *Inspiration:* vv. 3–4; Rom. 15:9. (Ex. 4:15; 2 Tim. 3:16, *note*)
q Ps. 69:9
4
r Rom. 4:23–24; 1 Cor. 10:11; 2 Tim. 3:16–17

*

14:18 NU-Text reads *this.* 14:21 NU-Text omits *or is offended or is made weak.* 14:22 NU-Text reads *The faith which you have—have.* 14:23 M-Text puts Romans 16:25–27 here.

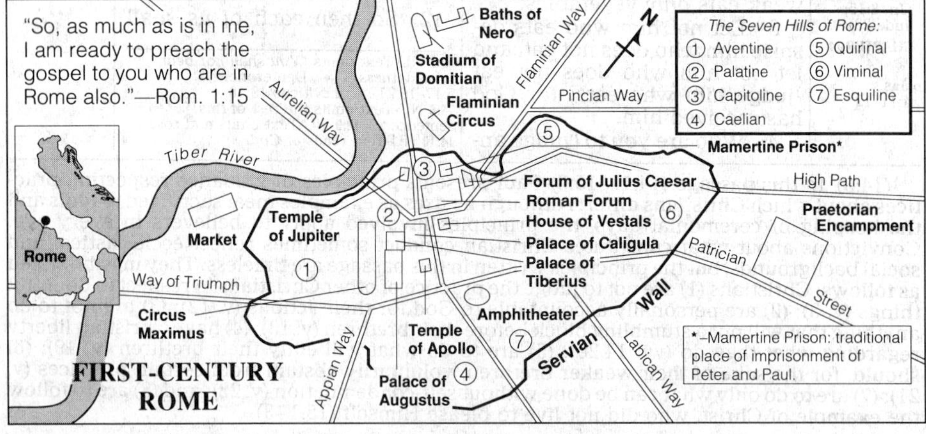

be [a]like-minded toward one another, according to Christ Jesus,

6 that you may with one mind *and* one mouth [b]glorify the God and Father of our Lord Jesus Christ.

7 Therefore [c]receive one another, just as Christ also received us,* to the glory of God.

8 Now I say that Jesus Christ has become a servant to the circumcision for the truth of God, to confirm the [d]promises *made* to the fathers,

9 and that the Gentiles might [b]glorify God for *His* mercy, as it is [e]written:

> [f]*"For this reason I will*
> *confess to You among*
> *the [g]Gentiles,*
> *And sing to Your*
> *name."**

10 And again he [e]says:

> [h]*"Rejoice, O [g]Gentiles,*
> *with His people!"*

11 And [e]again:

> [i]*"Praise the* LORD, *all you*
> *[g]Gentiles!*
> *Laud Him, all you*
> *peoples!"*

12 And [e]again, Isaiah says:

> [j]*"There shall be a root of*
> *Jesse;*
> *And He who shall rise to*
> *[k]reign over the*
> *[g]Gentiles,*
> *In Him the [g]Gentiles*
> *shall hope."*

13 Now may the God of hope fill you with all [l]joy and [m]peace in believing, that you may abound in hope by the power of the Holy [n]Spirit.

Conclusion: The Outflow of Christian Love, 15:14—16:27

Paul speaks of his coming journey to Jerusalem, Rome, and Spain

14 Now I myself am confident concerning you, my [o]brethren, that you also are full of goodness, filled with all knowledge, able also to admonish one another.*

15 Nevertheless, brethren, I have [e]written more boldly to you on *some* points, as reminding you, because of the [p]grace given to me by God,

16 that I might be a [q]minister of Jesus Christ to the [g]Gentiles, ministering the [r]gospel of God, that the [s]offering of the [g]Gentiles might be acceptable, [t]sanctified by the Holy [n]Spirit.

17 Therefore I have reason to glory in Christ Jesus in the things *which pertain* to God.

18 For I will not dare to speak of any of those things which Christ has not accomplished through me, in word and deed, to make the [g]Gentiles [u]obedient—

19 [v]in mighty signs and wonders, by the power of the [n]Spirit of God, [w]so that from Jerusalem and round about to Illyricum I have [x]fully preached the [r]gospel of Christ.

20 And [y]so I have made it my aim to preach the [r]gospel, not where Christ was named, lest I should build on another man's foundation,

21 but as it is [e]written:

> [z]*"To whom He was not*
> *announced, they shall*
> *see;*
> *And those who have not*
> *heard shall*
> *understand."*

22 For this reason I also have been much [aa]hindered from coming to you.

23 But now no longer having a place in these parts, and having a [bb]great desire these many years to come to you,

24 whenever I journey to Spain, I shall come to you.* For I hope to see you on my journey, and to be helped on my way there by you, if first I may [cc]enjoy your *company* for a while.

25 But now I am [dd]going to Jerusalem to minister to the [ee]saints.

26 For it pleased those from Macedonia and Achaia to make a certain [ff]contribution for the poor among the [ee]saints who are in Jerusalem.

27 It pleased them indeed,

*

15:7 NU-Text and M-Text read *you.* 15:9 2 Samuel 22:50 15:14 M-Text reads *others.* 15:24 NU-Text omits *I shall come to you* (and joins *Spain* with the next sentence).

5
a 1 Cor. 1:10; Phil. 1:27
6
b Cp. 1 Cor. 10:31; 1 Pet. 4:11
7
c Rom. 14:1
8
d Rom. 9:4
9
e Inspiration: vv. 9–12,15, 21; Rom. 16:26. (Ex. 4:15; 2 Tim. 3:16, *note*)
f Ps. 18:49
g See Eph. 3:6, *note*
10
h Dt. 32:43
11
i Ps. 117:1
12
j Isa. 11:1,10
k Kingdom (NT): v. 12; 1 Cor. 15:24. (Mt. 2:2; 1 Cor. 15:24, *note*)
13
l Rom. 12:12; 14:17
m Rom. 8:6
n Holy Spirit (NT): vv. 13,16,19; Rom. 15:30. (Mt. 1:18; Acts 2:4, *note*)
14
o Mt. 23:8; Lk. 8:21; Jn. 21:23; Rom. 8:29; Heb. 2:11, 17; Rev. 12:10; 19:10
15
p Grace: v. 15; Rom. 16:20. (Jn. 1:14; Jn. 1:17, *note*). See 2 Pet. 3:18, *note*; Rom. 1:5
16
q Acts 9:15; 22:21; Rom. 11:13; Gal. 1:16; 2:7–9; Eph. 3:8
r Gospel: vv. 16, 19–20; Rom. 16:25. (Gen. 12:3; Rev. 14:6)
s Isa. 26:20
t Sanctification (NT): v. 16; 1 Cor. 1:2. (Mt. 4:5; Rev. 22:11)
18
u Rom. 1:5
19
v Cp. Heb. 2:2–4
w See Acts 8:4, *note*
x Cp. Acts 20:27
20
y Lit. *being ambitious to preach*
21
z Isa. 52:15
22
aa Rom. 1:13
23
bb Acts 19:21; 23:11; Rom. 1:10–11
24
cc Rom. 1:12
25
dd Acts 24:17
ee Cp. Rom. 1:7; 8:27; 12:13; 16:2
26
ff 2 Cor. 8:1–9:15

and they are their debtors. For if
the Gentiles have been partakers of their spiritual things,
their duty is also to minister to
them in material things.
28 Therefore, when I have
performed this and have sealed
to them this fruit, I shall go by
way of you to Spain.
29 But I know that when I
come to you, I shall come in the
[a]fullness of the blessing of the
gospel* of Christ.
30 Now I beg you, brethren,
through the Lord Jesus Christ,
and through the love of the
[b]Spirit, that you [c]strive together with me in prayers to
God for me,
31 that I may be delivered
from those in Judea who do not
believe, and that my service for
Jerusalem may be acceptable to
the [d]saints,
32 that I may come to you
with [e]joy by the will of God, and
may be refreshed together with
you.
33 Now the [f]God of peace *be*
with you all. Amen.

Personal expressions
of greetings and love

16 I [g]COMMEND to you
Phoebe our sister, who is
a [h]servant of the [i]church in
Cenchrea,
2 that you may receive her
in the Lord [j]in a manner worthy of the saints, and assist her
in whatever business she has
need of you; for indeed she has
been a helper of many and of
myself also.
3 Greet [k]Priscilla and Aquila, my fellow workers in
Christ Jesus,
4 who risked their own
necks for my life, to whom not
only I give thanks, but also all
the churches of the [l]Gentiles.
5 Likewise *greet* the
[i]church that is in their house.
Greet my beloved Epaenetus,
who is the firstfruits of Achaia*
to Christ.
6 Greet Mary, who [m]labored
much for us.
7 Greet Andronicus and Junia, my [n]countrymen and my
fellow prisoners, who are of
note among the [o]apostles, who
also were [p]in Christ before me.
8 Greet Amplias, my be-
loved in the Lord.
9 Greet Urbanus, our fellow
worker in Christ, and Stachys,
my beloved.
10 Greet Apelles, approved
in Christ. Greet those who are
of the *household* of Aristobulus.
11 Greet Herodion, my coun-
tryman.* Greet those who are
of the *household* of Narcissus
who are in the Lord.
12 Greet Tryphena and Try-
phosa, who have labored in the
Lord. Greet the beloved Persis,
who labored much in the Lord.
13 Greet Rufus, [q]chosen in
the Lord, and his mother and
mine.
14 Greet Asyncritus, Phle-
gon, Hermas, Patrobas, Hermes, and the brethren who are
with them.
15 Greet Philologus and
Julia, Nereus and his sister, and
Olympas, and all the [a]saints
who are with them.
16 Greet one another with a
holy kiss. The* [i]churches of
Christ greet you.
17 Now I urge you, brethren,
note those who cause divisions
and offenses, contrary to the
[r]doctrine which you learned,
and avoid them.
18 For those who are such do
not serve our Lord Jesus*
Christ, but their own [s]belly,
and by smooth words and flattering speech deceive the hearts
of the simple.
19 For your obedience has
become known to all. Therefore
I am glad on your behalf; but I
want you to be wise in what is
good, and simple concerning
evil.
20 And the God of peace will
crush [t]Satan under your feet
shortly. The [u]grace of our Lord
Jesus Christ *be* with you. Amen.
21 Timothy, my fellow
worker, and Lucius, Jason, and
Sosipater, my countrymen,
greet you.
22 I, Tertius, who wrote *this*
epistle, greet you in the Lord.
23 Gaius, my host and *the*

*

15:29 NU-Text omits *of the gospel.* **16:5** NU-Text reads *Asia.* **16:11** Or *relative* **16:16** NU-Text reads *All the churches.* **16:18** NU-Text and M-Text omit *Jesus.*

29
a Cp. Rom. 1:11; Eph. 3:8,19
30
b Holy Spirit (NT): v. 30; 1 Cor. 2:4. (Mt. 1:18; Acts 2:4, *note*)
c 2 Cor. 1:11
31
d Cp. Rom. 1:7; 8:27; 12:13; 16:2
32
e Cp. Phile. 20; 3 Jn. 4
33
f Rom. 16:20; 1 Cor. 14:33; 2 Cor. 13:11; Phil. 4:9; 1 Th. 5:23; 2 Th. 3:16; Heb. 13:20
CHAPTER 16
1
g Cp. 2 Cor. 3:1–3; Phil. 2:29–30
h Lit. deaconess
i Churches (local): vv. 1,5,16; 1 Cor. 1:2. (Acts 8:3; Phil. 1:1, *note*)
2
j Phil. 1:27
3
k Acts 18:2, 18,26; 1 Cor. 16:19; 2 Tim. 4:19
4
l See Eph. 3:6, *note*
6
m Cp. v. 12; Phil. 4:3
7
n vv. 11–21
o Acts 1:13, 26
p Cp. Gal. 1:22

13
q Election (personal): v. 13; Gal. 1:15. (Dt. 7:6; 1 Pet. 5:13, *note*)
17
r Or *teaching.* Rom. 6:17
18
s Cp. Ezek. 13:17–19
20
t Satan: v. 20; 1 Cor. 5:5. (Gen. 3:1; Rev. 20:10)
u Grace: v. 20; Rom. 16:24. (Jn. 1:14; Jn. 1:17, *note*)

host of the whole [a]church,
greets you. Erastus, the treasurer of the city, greets you, and
Quartus, a brother.

Benediction

24 The [b]grace of our Lord Jesus Christ *be* with you all.
Amen.*
25 Now to Him who is able
to establish you according to
my [c]gospel and the preaching
of Jesus Christ, according to
the revelation of the [d]mystery
[e]kept secret since the world began
26 but now has been made
manifest, and by the prophetic
[f]Scriptures has been made
known to all nations, according
to the commandment of the
everlasting God, [g]for obedience
to the [h]faith—
27 to God, alone wise, *be*
glory through Jesus Christ forever. Amen.*

23
a Church (the true): vv. 23,25; 1 Cor. 3:9. (Mt. 16:18; Heb. 12:23). Eph. 3:1–12; see Mt. 13:11, *note*

24
b Grace: v. 24; 1 Cor. 1:3. (Jn. 1:14; Jn. 1:17, *note*)

25
c Gospel: v. 25; 1 Cor. 1:17. (Gen. 12:3; Rev. 14:6)
d i.e. *the Church*
e Lit. *kept in silence through times eternal*

26
f Inspiration: vv. 25–26; 1 Cor. 1:19. (Ex. 4:15; 2 Tim. 3:16, *note*)
g Rom. 1:5

h Faith: v. 26; 1 Cor. 1:21. (Gen. 3:20; Heb. 11:39, *note*)

*
16:24 NU-Text omits this verse.
16:27 M-Text puts Romans 16:25–27 after Romans 14:23.

The First Epistle of Paul the Apostle to the

CORINTHIANS

Author: Paul *Theme:* Christian Conduct *Date of writing:* C. A.D. 56

THE FIRST EPISTLE TO THE CORINTHIANS was written by the Apostle Paul at the close of his three years' residence in Ephesus (Acts 20:31; 1 Cor. 16:5–8). Paul's relation to the church at Corinth is set forth in Acts 18:1–18.

The occasion of this Epistle was a letter of inquiry concerning such things as marriage and the use of foods offered to idols (7:1; 8:1–13), but the apostle was also greatly troubled by reports from Corinth of deepening divisions, increasing contentions, and other problems (1:10–12), and by a case of incest which had not been judged by the church (5:1–2).

The main thrust of the Epistle is correction of error brought about more by the carnality of the believers at Corinth than by heresy. While Paul defends his apostleship because it involves the authority of the doctrine revealed through him, the letter is not a treatise but an expression of his grief, solicitude, and holy indignation on account of the unspiritual and immoral condition of the Corinthian church.

The subjects treated are various but may all be related to the general theme, Christian conduct. Even the tremendous revelation of the truth concerning the resurrection is made to bear upon that theme (15:58). And in spite of the dark overcast created by the difficulties in the church, it is in this Epistle that Paul presents his exquisite hymn of Christian love (ch. 13), as well as the most comprehensive treatment of the resurrection of the body to be found in the Word of God (ch. 15).

The Epistle may be divided as follows:

Introduction, 1:1–9.
I. Divisions in the Corinthian Church, 1:10—4:21.
II. Immorality Rebuked; Discipline Commanded, 5:1—6:8.
III. The Sanctity of the Body; Christian Marriage, 6:9—7:40.
IV. Things Offered to Idols; Limitations of Christian Liberty, 8:1—11:1.
V. Christian Order and the Lord's Supper, 11:2–34.
VI. Spiritual Gifts and Their Use in Love, 12:1—14:40.
VII. The Resurrection of the Dead, 15.
Conclusion: Instructions and Personal Greetings, 16.

CHAPTER 1

Introduction, 1:1–9

The believer's standing in grace through Christ (cp. Rom. 5:1–2; Eph. 1:3–14)

1 PAUL, [a]called *to be* an apostle of Jesus Christ through the will of God, and [b]Sosthenes *our* brother,

2 To the [c]church of God which is at Corinth, to [1]those who are [d]sanctified in Christ Jesus, [e]called *to be* [f]saints, with all who in every place call on the name of Jesus Christ our Lord, both theirs and ours:

3 [g]Grace to you and peace from God our Father and the Lord Jesus Christ.

4 I thank my God always concerning you for the [g]grace of God which was given to you by Christ Jesus,

5 that you were enriched in everything by Him [h]in all utterance and all knowledge,

6 even as the testimony of Christ was confirmed in you,

7 so that you come short in no gift, eagerly waiting for the

1
a Lit. *a called apostle.* Acts 9:15; 22:21; Rom. 11:13; Gal. 1:16; 2:7–9; Eph. 3:8
b Acts 18:17
2
c Churches (local): v. 2; 1 Cor. 4:17. (Acts 8:3; Phil. 1:1, *note*)
d Sanctification (NT): v. 2; 1 Cor. 1:30. (Mt. 4:5; Rev. 22:11)
e Eph. 4:1; 1 Th. 2:12
f Cp. Rom. 1:7; 8:27; 12:13; 15:25; 16:2
3
g Grace: vv. 3–7; 1 Cor. 3:10. (Jn. 1:14; Jn. 1:17, *note*). vv. 4–7; see 2 Pet. 3:18, *note*
5
h Cp. 1 Cor. 12:8; 2 Cor. 8:7

[1](1:2) Verses 2–9, in contrast with vv. 10–13, illustrate a distinction constantly made in the Epistles between the believer's standing in Christ Jesus, in the family of God, and his walk, or actual state. Christian standing in grace is the result of the work of Christ, and is fully entered the moment that Christ is received by faith (Jn. 1:12–13; Rom. 8:1,15–17; 1 Cor. 1:2,30; 12:12–13; Gal. 3:26; Eph. 1:3–14; 2:4–9; 1 Pet. 2:9; Rev. 1:6; 5:9–10). The weakest, most ignorant, and fallible believer has precisely the same relationships in grace as the most illustrious saint. All the work of God on his behalf, the application of the Word to walk and conscience (Jn. 17:17; Eph. 5:26), the divine chastenings (1 Cor. 11:32; Heb. 12:10), the ministry of the Spirit (Eph. 4:11–12), the difficulties and trials of daily life (1 Pet. 4:12–13), and the final transformation at the appearing of Christ (1 Jn. 3:2) have for their object to make the Christian's character conform to his exalted standing in Christ. He grows *in* grace, not *into* grace.

[1a]revelation of our Lord Jesus
Christ,
8 who will also confirm you
to the end, *that you may be*
[b]blameless in the [2c]day of our
Lord Jesus Christ.
9 God *is* [d]faithful, by whom
you were [e]called into the [f]fel-
lowship of His Son, Jesus Christ
our Lord.

I. Divisions in the Corinthian Church, 1:10—4:21

(1) Human wisdom divides the body (vv. 10–17)

10 Now I plead with you,
[g]brethren, by the name of our
Lord Jesus Christ, that you all
speak the same thing, and *that*
there be no [h]divisions among
you, but *that* you be perfectly
joined together in the same
mind and in the same judgment.
11 For it has been declared to
me concerning you, my [g]breth-
ren, by those of Chloe's *household,* that there are contentions
among you.
12 Now I say this, that each
of you says, "I am of Paul," or "I
am of [i]Apollos," or "I am of
[j]Cephas," or "I am of Christ."
13 Is Christ divided? Was
Paul crucified for you? Or were
you [k]baptized in the name of
Paul?
14 I thank God that I [k]bap-
tized [l]none of you except
[m]Crispus and [n]Gaius,
15 lest anyone should say
that I had [k]baptized in my own
name.
16 Yes, I also [k]baptized the
household of [o]Stephanas. Besides, I do not know whether I
baptized any other.
17 For Christ did not send me
to [k]baptize, but to preach the
[p]gospel, not with wisdom of
words, lest the cross of Christ
should be made of no effect.

(2) Human wisdom contrasted with the wisdom of God (i.e., the cross)

18 For the [p]message of the
cross is [q]foolishness to those
who are [r]perishing, but to us
who are being [s]saved it is the
power of God.
19 For it is [t]written:

> [u]*"I will destroy the wisdom of the wise,*
> *And bring to nothing the understanding of the prudent."*

20 [v]Where *is* the wise?
Where *is* the scribe? Where *is*
the disputer of this [w]age? Has
not God made foolish the [x]wis-
dom of this [y]world?
21 For since, in the [z]wisdom
of God, the world through [x]wis-
dom did [aa]not know God, it
pleased God through the foolishness of the [p]message
preached to [s]save those who
[bb]believe.
22 For Jews request a [cc]sign,
and Greeks seek after wisdom;
23 but we [p]preach Christ
[dd]crucified, to the Jews a stumbling [ee]block and to the Greeks*
[q]foolishness,
24 but to those who are

* 1:23 NU-Text reads *Gentiles.*

7
a Christ (second advent): v. 7; 1 Cor. 4:5. (Dt. 30:3; Acts 1:11, *note*)
8
b Col. 1:22; 1 Th. 3:13; 5:23
c Day (of Christ): v. 8; 1 Cor. 3:13. (1 Cor. 1:8, *note;* 2 Tim. 4:8)
9
d 1 Cor. 10:13
e Eph. 4:1; 1 Th. 2:12
f 1 Jn. 1:3
10
g Mt. 23:8; Lk. 8:21; Jn. 21:23; Rom. 8:29; 15:14; Heb. 2:11,17; Rev. 12:10; 19:10
h Or *schism*
12
i Acts 18:24; 19:1; 1 Cor. 3:4; 16:12; Ti. 3:13
j i.e. *Simon Peter.* Jn. 1:42
13
k See Acts 8:12, *note*
14
l Jn. 4:2
m Acts 18:8
n Acts 19:29; 20:4; Rom. 16:23; 3 Jn. 1
16
o 1 Cor. 16:15,17
17
p Gospel: vv. 17–18, 21,23; 1 Cor. 2:1. (Gen. 12:3; Rev. 14:6)
18
q 1 Cor. 2:14
r See Jn. 3:16, *note 3*
s See Rom. 1:16, *note*
19
t Inspiration: v. 19; 1 Cor. 1:31. (Ex. 4:15; 2 Tim. 3:16, *note*)
u Isa. 29:14
20
v Isa. 19:12; 33:18
w Gk. *aiōn.* See Mk. 10:30, *note*
x 1 Cor. 3:19
y Gk. *kosmos.* See Rev. 13:8, *note*
21
z Dan. 2:20; Rom. 11:33
aa Cp. Rom. 1:21
bb Faith: v. 21; 1 Cor. 2:5. (Gen. 3:20; Heb. 11:39, *note*)
22
cc Jn. 2:18
23
dd Sacrifice (of Christ): v. 23; 1 Cor. 5:7. (Gen. 3:15; Heb. 10:18, *note*)
ee Christ (Stone): v. 23; 1 Cor. 10:4. (Gen. 49:24; 1 Pet. 2:8)

[1](1:7) Three words are prominently employed in connection with the return of the Lord: (1) *Parousia,* also used by Paul of the coming of Stephanas (1 Cor. 16:17), of Titus (2 Cor. 7:6,7), and of his own coming to Philippi (Phil. 1:26). The word means *personal presence,* and is used of the return of the Lord as that event relates to the blessing of Christians (1 Cor. 15:23; 1 Th. 4:14–17) and to the destruction of the man of sin (2 Th. 2:8). (2) *Apokalupsis,* employed here, and meaning *unveiling, revelation.* This word emphasizes the visibility of the Lord's return. It is used of the Lord (2 Th. 1:7; 1 Pet. 1:7,13; 4:13), of the sons of God in connection with the Lord's return (Rom. 8:19), and of the man of sin (2 Th. 2:3,6,8), and always implies perceptibility. And (3) *epiphaneia,* translated "brightness" (2 Th. 2:8) or "manifestation" in some other versions. It means *an appearing,* and is used of both advents (first advent, 2 Tim. 1:10; second advent, 2 Th. 2:8; 1 Tim. 6:14; 2 Tim. 4:1,8; Ti. 2:13).

[2](1:8) The expression "the day of our Lord Jesus Christ," identified with His coming (v. 7), is the period of blessing for the Church beginning with the rapture. This coming day is referred to as "the day of the Lord Jesus" (1 Cor. 5:5; 2 Cor. 1:14), "the day of Jesus Christ" (Phil. 1:6), and "the day of Christ" (Phil. 1:10; 2:16). "The day of Christ" in all six references in the NT is described as relating to the reward and blessing of the Church at the rapture in contrast with the expression "the day of the LORD" (cp. Isa. 2:12; *marg.;* Joel 1:15, *note;* Rev. 19:19, *note*), which is related to judgment on unbelieving Jews and Gentiles, and blessing on millennial saints (Zeph. 3:8–20).

[a]called, both [b]Jews and Greeks, Christ the power of God and the [c]wisdom of God.

25 Because the foolishness of God is wiser than men, and the weakness of God is stronger than men.

(3) The Corinthian believers were not of the wise

26 For you see your [a]calling, [d]brethren, that not many wise according to the flesh, not many mighty, not many noble, *are called.*

27 But God has [e]chosen the foolish things of the [f]world to put to shame the wise, and God has chosen the weak things of the [f]world to put to shame the things which are mighty;

28 and the base things of the [f]world and the things which are despised God has chosen, and the things which are not, to bring to nothing the things that are,

29 that no flesh should glory in His presence.

30 But of Him you are in Christ Jesus, who became for us wisdom from God—and [g]righteousness and [h]sanctification and [i]redemption—

31 that, as it is [j]written, [k]*"He who glories, let him glory in the* Lord."

(4) The Christian revelation owes nothing to human wisdom

(a) Paul did not rely on it

2 AND I, [d]brethren, when I came to you, did not come with excellence of speech or of wisdom declaring to you the [l]testimony* of God.

2 For I determined not to know anything among you except Jesus Christ and Him crucified.

3 I was with you in weakness, in fear, and in much trembling.

4 And my speech and my [l]preaching *were* not with persuasive words of human* wisdom, but in demonstration of the [m]Spirit and of power,

5 that your [n]faith should not be in the wisdom of men but in the [o]power of God.

6 However, we speak wisdom among those who are [p]mature, yet not the wisdom of this [q]age, nor of the rulers of this [q]age, who are coming to nothing.

7 But we [j]speak the wisdom of God in a [r]mystery, the hidden *wisdom* which God [s]ordained before the [q]ages for our glory,

8 which none of the rulers of this [q]age knew; for had they known, they would not have [t]crucified the Lord of glory.

(b) Spiritual truths are not of human wisdom but revealed by God

9 But as it is [j]written:

[u]*"Eye has not seen, nor*
ear heard,
Nor have entered into
the heart of man
The things which God
has prepared for those
who love Him."

10 But God has [v]revealed *them* to us through His [m]Spirit. For the Spirit searches all things, yes, the deep things of God.

11 For what man knows the things of a man except the [w]spirit of the man which is in him? Even so no one knows the things of God except the [m]Spirit of God.

12 Now we have received, not the spirit of the [x]world, but the [m]Spirit who is from God, that we might know the things that have been freely given to us by God.

(c) The revealed things are taught in words given by the Spirit

13 These things we also [l]speak, not in [1]words which

*
2:1 NU-Text reads *mystery.* 2:4 NU-Text omits *human.*

24
a Eph. 4:1; 1 Th. 2:12
b Cp. Rom. 1:16; 2:10
c Dan. 2:20; Rom. 11:33
26
d Mt. 23:8; Lk. 8:21; Jn. 21:23; Rom. 8:29; 15:14; Heb. 2:11,17; Rev. 12:10; 19:10
27
e Ps. 8:2; Mt. 11:25
f Gk. *kosmos.* See Mt. 4:8, *note*
30
g 2 Cor. 5:21; see Rom. 3:21, *note*
h *Sanctification* (NT): v. 30; 1 Cor. 3:17. (Mt. 4:5; Rev. 22:11)
i See Rom. 3:24, *note*
31
j *Inspiration:* v. 31; 2:7–10; 1 Cor. 2:13. (Ex. 4:15; 2 Tim. 3:16, *note*)
k Jer. 9:24; 2 Cor. 10:17
CHAPTER 2
1
l *Gospel:* vv. 1–13; 1 Cor. 4:15. (Gen. 12:3; Rev. 14:6)

4
m *Holy Spirit* (NT): vv. 4,10–12; 1 Cor. 2:13. (Mt. 1:18; Acts 2:4, *note*)
5
n *Faith:* v. 5; 1 Cor. 3:5. (Gen. 3:20; Heb. 11:39, *note*)
o Rom. 1:16; 1 Th. 1:5
6
p See Phil. 3:12, *note*
q Gk. *aiōn.* See Mk. 10:30, *note*
7
r See Mt. 13:11, *note*
s *Predestination:* v. 7; Eph. 1:5. (Rom. 8:29; Eph. 1:11). See 1 Pet. 1:20, *note*
8
t Mt. 27:33–50
9
u Isa. 64:4
10
v Jn. 14:26; 16:13; Eph. 3:5; cp. Jn. 15:15; Eph. 1:9–10; Col. 1:26
11
w Job. 32:8; Eccl. 12:7; 1 Cor. 6:20; Jas. 2:26
12
x Gk. *kosmos.* 1 Cor. 7:31,33; see Rev. 13:8, *note*

1(2:13) "Words . . . which the Holy Spirit teaches."

(1) The writers of Scripture affirm, where the subject is mentioned by them at all, that the words of their writings are divinely taught. This, of necessity, refers to the original documents, not to translations and versions; but the labors of competent scholars have brought some of our English versions to a remarkable degree of reliability, so that no essential truth of Scrip-

man's wisdom [a]teaches but which the [b]Holy* Spirit teaches, comparing spiritual things with spiritual.

(d) The revealed things are spiritually discerned

14 But the [1]natural man does not receive the things of the [b]Spirit of God, for they are foolishness to him; nor can he know *them,* because they are spiritually discerned.

15 But he who is spiritual [c]judges all things, yet he himself is *rightly* [d]judged by no one.

16 For *"who has known the [e]mind of the LORD that he may instruct Him?"* But we have the mind of Christ.

(5) A carnal state prevents spiritual growth

3 AND I, brethren, could not speak to you as to spiritual *people* but as to [f]carnal, as to babes in Christ.

2 I fed you with [g]milk and not with solid food; for until now you were not able *to receive it,* and even now you are still not able;

3 for you are still [f]carnal. For where *there are* envy, strife, and divisions among you, are you not [f]carnal and behaving like *mere* men?

4 For when one says, "I am of Paul," and another, "I *am* of [h]Apollos," are you not [f]carnal?

(6) God alone counts in Christian service (cp. v. 7)

5 Who then is Paul, and who *is* Apollos, but [i]ministers through whom you [j]believed, as the Lord gave to each one?

6 I planted, Apollos watered, but God gave the increase.

7 So then [k]neither he who plants is anything, nor he who waters, but God who gives the increase.

8 Now he who plants and he who waters are [2]one, and each one will receive his own [l]reward according to his own labor.

(7) Christian service and its reward

9 For we are God's [m]fellow workers; you are God's [n]field, *you are* God's [o]building.

10 According to the [p]grace of God which was given to me, as a wise master builder I have [q]laid the foundation, and another builds on it. But let each one take heed how he builds on it.

(a) The only foundation: Jesus Christ

11 For no other [r]foundation can anyone lay than that which is laid, which is Jesus Christ.

(b) Two kinds of ministry and their result

12 Now if anyone [s]builds on this foundation *with* gold, silver, precious stones, wood, hay, straw,

13 each one's work will become clear; for the [t]Day will

*2:13 NU-Text omits *Holy.*

13
a *Inspiration:* v. 13; 1 Cor. 3:19. (Ex. 4:15; 2 Tim. 3:16, *note*)
b *Holy Spirit* (NT): vv. 13–14; 1 Cor. 3:16. (Mt. 1:18; Acts 2:4, *note*)
15
c Or *examines*
d Or *examined*
16
e Rom. 11:34; cp. Isa. 40:13
CHAPTER 3
1
f i.e. *fleshly. Flesh:* vv. 1–4; 2 Cor. 1:17. (Jn. 8:15; Jude 23). See Rom. 7:14, *note*
2
g Cp. 1 Pet. 2:2
4
h Acts 18:24; 19:1; 1 Cor. 1:12; 16:12; Ti. 3:13
5
i 2 Cor. 3:6
j *Faith:* v. 5; 1 Cor. 12:9. (Gen. 3:20; Heb. 11:39, *note*)
7
k Cp. Jn. 15:5
8
l *Rewards:* vv. 8,14; 1 Cor. 9:25. (Dan. 12:3; 1 Cor. 3:14, *note*)
9
m 2 Cor. 6:1; cp. Mk. 16:20
n Cp. vv. 6–8
o *Church* (the true): vv. 9, 16–17; 1 Cor. 6:15. (Mt. 16:18; Heb. 12:23). Zech. 6:12–13
10
p *Grace:* v. 10; 1 Cor. 15:10. (Jn. 1:14; Jn. 1:17, *note*). See 2 Pet. 3:18, *note.*
q Cp. Rom. 15:20
11
r Eph. 2:20
12
s See Rev. 19:8, *note*
13
t *Day* (of Christ): v. 13; 2 Cor. 1:14. (1 Cor. 1:8, *note;* 2 Tim. 4:8)

ture is ever under any question. And (2) 1 Cor. 2:9–14 gives the process by which a truth passes from the mind of God to the minds of His people. (a) The unseen things of God are undiscoverable by the natural man (v. 9). (b) These unseen things God has revealed to chosen men (vv. 10–12). (c) The revealed things are communicated in Spirit-taught words (v. 13). This implies neither mechanical dictation nor the effacement of the writer's personality, but only that the Spirit infallibly guides in the choice of words from the writer's own vocabulary (v. 13). And (d) these Spirit-taught words, in which the revelation has been expressed, are discerned, as to their full spiritual content, only by the spiritual among believers (1 Cor. 2:15–16). See also 2 Tim. 3:16, *note.*

[1](2:14) Paul divides men into three classes: (1) *psuchikos,* meaning *of the senses, sensual,* (Jas. 3:15; Jude 19), *natural,* i.e. the Adamic man, unrenewed through the new birth (Jn. 3:3,5); (2) *pneumatikos,* meaning *spiritual,* i.e. the renewed man as Spirit-filled and walking in the Spirit in full communion with God (Eph. 5:18–20); and (3) *sarkikos,* meaning *carnal, fleshly,* i.e. the renewed man who, walking "according to the flesh" (Rom. 8:4), remains a babe in Christ (1 Cor. 3:1–4). The natural man may be learned, gentle, eloquent and fascinating, but the spiritual content of Scripture is absolutely hidden from him; and the worldly Christian is able to comprehend only its simplest truths, "milk" (1 Cor. 3:2).

[2](3:8) Paul refutes the notion that he and Cephas (Peter) and Apollos are at variance, mere theologians and rival founders of sects; they "are one." See v. 22; 1 Cor. 16:12.

declare it, because it will be revealed by fire; and the fire will
[a]test each one's work, of what
sort it is.
14 If anyone's work which he
has built on *it* endures, he will
receive a [1]reward.
15 If anyone's work is
burned, he will suffer loss; but
he himself will be [b]saved, yet so
as through fire.
16 Do you not know that you
are the [2]temple of God and *that*
the [c]Spirit of God dwells in
you?
17 If anyone defiles the temple of God, God will destroy
him. For the temple of God is
[d]holy, which *temple* you are.
18 Let no one deceive himself. If anyone among you
seems to be wise in this [e]age, let
him become a fool that he may
become wise.
19 [f]For the wisdom of this
world is foolishness with God.
For it is [g]written, [h]*"He catches
the wise in their own craftiness"*;
20 and [g]again, [i]*"The* LORD
knows the [j]*thoughts of the
wise, that they are futile."*
21 Therefore let no one boast
in men. For all things are yours:
22 whether Paul or [k]Apollos
or [l]Cephas, or the [m]world or
life or [n]death, or things present
or things to come—all are
[o]yours.
23 And [p]you *are* Christ's,
and Christ *is* God's.

(c) Judgment of Christ's servants
is not committed to men

4 LET a man so consider us,
as [q]servants of Christ and
stewards of the [r]mysteries of
God.
2 Moreover it is required in
stewards that one be found
[s]faithful.
3 But with me it is a very
small thing that I should be
judged by you or by a human
court.* In fact, I do not even
judge myself.
4 For I know of nothing
against myself, yet I am not
[t]justified by this; but He who
judges me is the Lord.
5 Therefore judge nothing
before the time, until the Lord
[u]comes, who will both bring to
[v]light the hidden things of darkness [a]and [w]reveal the counsels
of the hearts. Then each one's
praise will come from God.
6 Now these things, [x]breth-
ren, I have figuratively transferred to myself and [y]Apollos
for your sakes, that you may
learn in us not to think beyond
what is written, that none of you
may be puffed up on behalf of
one against the other.
7 For who makes you differ
from another? And [z]what do
you have that you did not receive? Now if you did indeed receive *it,* why do you boast as if
you had not received *it?*
8 [aa]You are already full! You
are already rich! You have
reigned as kings without us—
and indeed I could wish you did
reign, [bb]that we also might reign
with you!

(8) The apostolic example
of humility and patience

9 For I think that God has
displayed us, the apostles, last,
as men condemned to death; for
we have been made a [cc]specta-
cle to the [m]world, both to [dd]an-
gels and to men.
10 We *are* [ee]fools for Christ's
sake, but you *are* wise in Christ!
We *are* weak, but you *are*
strong! You *are* distinguished,
but we *are* dishonored!
11 To the present hour we
both hunger and thirst, and we
are poorly clothed, and beaten,
and [ff]homeless.

* 4:3 Literally *day*

13
a *Judgments* (the seven): vv. 13–15; 4:5; 1 Cor. 5:13. (2 Sam. 7:14; Rev. 20:12, *note*). 2 Cor. 5:10
15
b See Rom. 1:16, *note*
16
c *Holy Spirit* (NT): v. 16; 1 Cor. 6:11. (Mt. 1:18; Acts 2:4, *note*)
17
d *Sanctification* (NT): v. 17; 1 Cor. 6:11. (Mt. 4:5; Rev. 22:11)
18
e Gk. *aiōn.* See Mk. 10:30, *note*
19
f Cp. 1 Cor. 1:20–25
g *Inspiration:* vv. 19–20; 1 Cor. 4:14. (Ex. 4:15; 2 Tim. 3:16, *note*)
h Job 5:13
20
i Ps. 94:11
j Or *reasonings*
22
k Acts 18:24; 19:1; 1 Cor. 1:12; 16:12; Ti. 3:13
l i.e. *Simon Peter.* Jn. 1:42
m Gk. *kosmos.* See Rev. 13:8, *note*
n *Death* (physical): v. 22; 1 Cor. 15:21. (Gen. 2:17; Heb. 9:27, *note*)
o *Assurance/security:* vv. 22–23; Eph. 1:14. (Ps. 23:1; Jude 1, *note*)
23
p Rom. 14:8
CHAPTER 4
1
q Rom. 13:6; 2 Cor. 3:6
r See Mt. 13:11, *note*
2
s Or *trustworthy*
4
t *Justification:* v. 4; 1 Cor. 6:11. (Lk. 18:14; Rom. 3:28, *note*)
5
u *Christ* (second advent): v. 5; 1 Cor. 15:23. (Dt. 30:3; Acts 1:11, *note*)
v Mt. 10:26
w 1 Cor. 3:13
6
x Mt. 23:8; Lk. 8:21; Jn. 21:23; Rom. 8:29; 15:14; Heb. 2:11,17; Rev. 12:10; 19:10
y Acts 18:24; 19:1; 1 Cor. 1:12; 3:4; 16:12; Ti. 3:13
7
z Jn. 3:27; cp. 1 Cor. 12:4–11; Jas. 1:17
8
aa Cp. vv. 9–12
bb Cp. Rev. 3:21; 5:10
9
cc Heb. 10:33
dd See Heb. 1:4, *note*
10
ee Cp. Acts 26:24–25
11
ff Cp. Mt. 8:20

[1](3:14) God, in the NT Scriptures, offers to the lost, salvation; and for the faithful service of the saved, He offers rewards. The passages are easily distinguished by remembering that salvation is invariably spoken of as a free gift (e.g. Jn. 4:10; Rom. 6:23; Eph. 2:8–9), whereas rewards are earned by works (Mt. 10:42; Lk. 19:17; 1 Cor. 9:24–25; 2 Tim. 4:7–8; Rev. 2:10; 22:12). A further distinction is that salvation is a present possession (Lk. 7:50; Jn. 3:36; 5:24; 6:47), whereas rewards are a future attainment, to be given at the rapture (2 Tim. 4:8; Rev. 22:12).

[2](3:16) The temple here is the Church, the body of Christ, as distinguished from the temple in 6:19, which is the physical body of the individual Christian.

12
[a] Acts 18:3; 20:34
[b] Cp. Mt. 5:44
[c] Cp. Acts 7:60
13
[d] Gk. *kosmos.* See Rev. 13:8, *note*
[e] Cp. Acts 22:22
14
[f] *Inspiration:* v. 14; 5:9,11; 1 Cor. 7:10. (Ex. 4:15; 2 Tim. 3:16, *note*)
[g] Gk. *teknon, child.* Gal. 4:19
15
[h] *Gospel:* vv. 15,17; 1 Cor. 9:12. (Gen. 12:3; Rev. 14:6)
16
[i] 1 Cor. 11:1; Phil. 3:17
17
[j] 1 Tim. 1:2
[k] *Churches* (local): v. 17; 1 Cor. 6:4. (Acts 8:3; Phil. 1:1, *note*)
20
[l] See Mt. 6:33, *note*
[m] 1 Cor. 2:4
21
[n] *Law* (of Christ): v. 21; 1 Cor. 8:9. (Jn. 13:34; 2 Jn. 5)
CHAPTER 5
1
[o] 1 Cor. 6:13; Gal. 5:19; Eph. 5:3; Col. 3:5; 1 Th. 4:3; cp. 2 Cor. 12:21; Jude 7
[p] Lev. 18:6–8
2
[q] 4:18
[r] Cp. 2 Cor. 7:7–10

12 And we [a]labor, working
with our own hands. Being [b]re-
viled, we [c]bless; being persecuted, we endure;
13 being defamed, we en-
treat. We have been made as the
filth of the [d]world, the [e]off-
scouring of all things until now.
14 I do not [f]write these
things to shame you, but as my
beloved [g]children I warn *you.*
15 For though you might
have ten thousand instructors
in Christ, yet *you do* not *have*
many fathers; for in Christ Jesus I have begotten you through
the [h]gospel.
16 Therefore I urge you, [i]im-
itate me.
17 For this reason I have sent
[j]Timothy to you, who is my beloved and faithful [g]son in the
Lord, who will remind you of
my ways in Christ, as I [h]teach
everywhere in every [k]church.

(9) Apostolic authority

18 Now some are puffed up,
as though I were not coming to
you.
19 But I will come to you
shortly, if the Lord wills, and I
will know, not the word of those
who are puffed up, but the
power.
20 For the [l]kingdom of God
is not in word but in [m]power.
21 What do you want? Shall I
come to you with a rod, or in
[n]love and a spirit of gentleness?

II. Immorality Rebuked;
Discipline Commanded, 5:1—6:8

5 IT is actually reported *that*
there is [o]sexual immorality
among you, and such sexual immorality as is not even named*
among the Gentiles—that a
man has his father's [p]wife!

Indifference to evil in the church
the result of divisions

2 And you are [q]puffed up,
and have not rather [r]mourned,
that he who has done this deed
might be taken away from
among you.
3 For I indeed, as absent in
body but present in spirit, have
already judged (as though I
were present) him who has so
done this deed.
4 In the [s]name of our Lord
Jesus Christ, when you are
gathered together, along with
my spirit, with the [t]power of
our Lord Jesus Christ,
5 deliver such a one to [u]Sa-
tan for the [1]destruction of the
flesh, [v]that his spirit may be
[w]saved in the [x]day of the Lord
Jesus.*
6 Your glorying *is* not good.
Do you not know that a little
leaven [y]leavens the whole
lump?
7 Therefore purge out the
old leaven, that you may be a
new lump, since you truly are
unleavened. For indeed Christ,
our [z]Passover, was [aa]sacrificed
for us.*
8 Therefore let us keep the
[bb]feast, not with old leaven, nor
with the leaven of malice and
wickedness, but with the unleavened *bread* of sincerity and
truth.

In the world, not of it

9 I [f]wrote to you in my epistle [cc]not to keep company with
sexually immoral people.
10 Yet *I* certainly *did* not
mean with the sexually immoral people of this [dd]world, or
with the covetous, or extortioners, or idolaters, since then you
would need to go out of the
[dd]world.
11 But now I have [f]written to
you [cc]not to keep company with
anyone named a brother, who is
sexually immoral, or covetous,
or an idolater, or a reviler, or a
drunkard, or an extortioner—
not even to eat with such a person.
12 For what *have* I *to do* with
judging those also who are

*
5:1 NU-Text omits *named.* 5:5 NU-Text omits *Jesus.* 5:7 NU-Text omits *for us.*

4
[s] Mt. 18:20
[t] 2 Cor. 12:9
5
[u] *Satan:* v. 5; 1 Cor. 7:5. (Gen. 3:1; Rev. 20:10)
[v] Cp. Prov. 23:14
[w] See Rom. 1:16, *note*
[x] *Day* (of the LORD): v. 5; 1 Th. 5:2. (Ps. 2:9; Rev. 19:19). Cp. 1 Cor. 1:8, *note*
6
[y] *Leaven:* vv. 6–8; Gal. 5:9. (Gen. 19:3; Mt. 13:33, *note*)
7
[z] See Ex. 12:11, *note*
[aa] *Sacrifice* (of Christ): v. 7; 1 Cor. 6:20. (Gen. 3:15; Heb. 10:18, *note*)
8
[bb] Cp. Ex. 12:14–20
9
[cc] Cp. Mt. 18:17; 2 Th. 3:6,14
10
[dd] Gk. *kosmos.* See Mt. 4:8, *note*

[1](5:5) "Destruction" is from the Gk. *olethros,* which is used also in 1 Th. 5:3; 2 Th. 1:9; 1 Tim. 6:9; Heb. 11:28; 1 Cor. 10:10. These and approximately twenty other words are rendered by "destroy," "destruction," "perish," "defile," and similar words. The most extensively used word is *apollumi* (in various combinations). There is no thought in these various words of annihilation but of something that is ruined and thus unsuitable or unable to fulfill its original purpose, e.g. Mt. 9:17. See Jn. 3:16, *note 3.*

[a]outside? Do you not judge
those who are inside?
13 But those who are [a]out-
side God [b]judges. Therefore
[c]*"put away from yourselves the*
evil person."

Christians forbidden to go
to law against each other
before unbelievers

6 DARE any of you, having a
matter against another, go
to law before the unrighteous,
and not before the [d]saints?
2 Do you not know that the
[d]saints will [b]judge the [e]world?
And if the [e]world will be judged
by you, are you unworthy to
judge the smallest matters?
3 Do you not know that
we shall [b]judge [f]angels? How
much more, things that pertain
to this life?
4 If then you have judg-
ments concerning things pertaining to this life, do you appoint those who are least
esteemed by the [g]church to
judge?
5 I say this to your shame. Is
it so, that there is not a wise man
among you, not even one, who
will be able to judge between
his [h]brethren?
6 But brother goes to law
against brother, and that before
unbelievers!
7 Now therefore, it is already an utter failure for you
that you go to law against one
another. Why do you not rather
accept wrong? Why do you not
rather *let yourselves* be
cheated?
8 No, you yourselves do
wrong and cheat, and *you do*
these things *to your* [h]brethren!

III. The Sanctity of the Body;
Christian Marriage, 6:9—7:40

The body is holy: (1) because
it is washed and justified

9 Do you not know that the
[i]unrighteous will not inherit
the [j]kingdom of God? Do not be
deceived. Neither fornicators,
nor idolaters, nor adulterers,
nor homosexuals,* nor [k]sod-
omites,
10 nor thieves, nor covetous,
nor drunkards, nor revilers, nor
extortioners will inherit the
[j]kingdom of God.
11 And such were some of
you. But you were [l]washed, but
you were [m]sanctified, but you
were [n]justified in the [o]name of
the Lord Jesus and by the
[p]Spirit of our God.
12 All things are lawful for
me, but all things are not [q]help-
ful. All things are lawful for me,
but I will not be brought under
the power of any.

(2) Because it is the Lord's

13 Foods for the stomach and
the stomach for foods, [1]but God
will destroy both it and them.
Now the body *is* not for [r]sexual
immorality but for the Lord,
and the Lord for the body.
14 And God both [s]raised up
the Lord and will also raise us
up by His power.
15 Do you not know that
your bodies are [t]members of
Christ? [2]Shall I then take the
members of Christ and make
them members of a harlot? Certainly not!
16 Or do you not know that
he who is joined to a harlot is
one body *with her*? For [u]*"the*
two," He says, *"shall become*
one flesh."
17 But he who is [t]joined [v]to
the Lord is one spirit *with Him*.
18 Flee [r]sexual immorality.
Every [w]sin that a man does is
outside the body, but he who
commits sexual immorality
[w]sins against his own body.

(3) Because it is God's temple

19 Or do you not know that
your body is [x]the temple of the
Holy [p]Spirit *who is* in you,
whom you have from God, and
you are not your [y]own?
20 For you were [z]bought at a
price; therefore glorify God in

* 6:9 That is, catamites

12
a Mk. 4:11
13
b *Judgments* (the seven): v. 13; 6:2–3; 1 Cor. 11:31. (2 Sam. 7:14; Rev. 20:12, *note*)
c Cp. Dt. 17:7; 19:19; 22:21,24; 24:7
CHAPTER 6
1
d Dan. 7:22; Mt. 19:28; cp. Rom. 1:7; 8:27; 12:13; 15:25; 16:2
2
e Gk. *kosmos*. See Mt. 14:8, *note*
3
f See Heb. 1:4, *note*
4
g *Churches* (local): v. 4; 1 Cor. 7:17. (Acts 8:3; Phil. 1:1, *note*)
5
h Mt. 23:8; Lk. 8:21; Jn. 21:23; Rom. 8:29; 15:14; Heb. 2:11,17; Rev. 12:10; 19:10
9
i Rom. 1:18; 6:13; 2 Th. 2:10; 2 Pet. 2:13; 1 Jn. 5:17
j See Mt. 6:33, *note*
k Cp. Rom. 1:26–27
11
l Cp. Eph. 5:26; Ti. 3:5; see Jn. 3:3, *note*
m *Sanctification* (NT): v. 11; 1 Cor. 7:14. (Mt. 4:5; Rev. 22:11)
n *Justification:* v. 11; Gal. 2:16. (Lk. 18:14; Rom. 3:28, *note*)
o Cp. Acts 3:6,16; 4:10, 12,17,18,30; 5:28,40,41; 8:12,16; 9:14,15,21, 27,29; 10:43, 48; 15:14,17, 26; 16:18; 19:5,13,17; 21:13; 22:16; 26:9
p *Holy Spirit* (NT): vv. 11,19; 1 Cor. 7:40. (Mt. 1:18; Acts 2:4, *note*)
12
q Or *profitable*
13
r 1 Cor. 5:1; Gal. 5:19; Eph. 5:3; Col. 3:5; 1 Th. 4:3; cp. 2 Cor. 12:21; Jude 7
14
s *Resurrection:* v. 14; 1 Cor. 15:4. (2 Ki. 4:35; 1 Cor. 15:52, *note*)
15
t *Church* (the true): vv. 15,17; 1 Cor. 10:17. (Mt. 16:18; Heb. 12:23)
16
u Gen. 2:24; Mt. 19:5
17
v Cp. Rom. 7:4; 2 Cor. 11:2; Eph. 5:30
18
w See Rom. 3:23, *note*
19
x Lit. *a temple*. Cp. Jn. 2:21
y Cp. Rom. 14:7–9
20
z *Sacrifice* (of Christ): v. 20; 1 Cor. 7:23. (Gen. 3:15; Heb. 10:18, *note*)

[1](6:13) Observe that gluttony, as well as impurity, is a sin against God.
[2](6:15) Both the authority of the Seventh Commandment and the apostle's appeal to the Christian's sacredness as a member of the body of Christ forbid unequivocally immorality of every kind.

your body* and in your spirit, which are God's.

(4) Because God has established marriage

7 NOW concerning the things of which you wrote to me: *It is* good for a man not to touch a woman.

2 Nevertheless, because of [a]sexual immorality, let each man have his own wife, and let each woman have her own husband.

3 Let the husband render to his wife the [b]affection due her, and likewise also the wife to her husband.

4 The wife does not have authority over her own body, but the husband *does*. And likewise the husband does not have authority over his own body, but the wife *does*.

5 Do not deprive one another except with consent for a time, that you may give yourselves to fasting and prayer; and come together again so that [c]Satan does not [d]tempt you because of your lack of self-control.

6 But I say this as a concession, not as a commandment.

7 For I wish that all men were even as I myself. But each one has his own [e]gift from God, one in this manner and another in that.

8 But I say to the unmarried and to the widows: It is good for them if they remain even as I am;

9 but if they cannot exercise self-control, [f]let them marry. For it is better to marry than to burn *with passion*.

Regulation of marriage between believers

10 Now to the married I command, *yet* not I [g]but the [h]Lord: A wife is not to depart from *her* husband.

11 But even if she does depart, let her remain unmarried or be reconciled to *her* husband. And a husband is not to [i]divorce *his* wife.

12 But to the rest I, not the Lord, [1][g]say: If any brother has a wife who does not believe, and she is willing to live with him, let him not [j]divorce her.

13 And a woman who has a husband who does not believe, if he is willing to live with her, let her not divorce him.

14 For the unbelieving husband is [k]sanctified by the wife, and the unbelieving wife is [k]sanctified by the husband; otherwise your children would be [l]unclean, but now they are [k]holy.

15 But if the unbeliever departs, let him depart; a brother or a sister is not under bondage in such *cases*. But God has called us to [m]peace.

16 For how do you know, O wife, whether you will [n]save *your* husband? Or how do you know, O husband, whether you will [n]save *your* wife?

Remain in the place of calling

17 But as God has distributed to each one, as the Lord has called each one, so let him walk. And so I [o]ordain in [p]all the [q]churches.

18 Was anyone called while circumcised? Let him not become uncircumcised. Was anyone called while uncircumcised? Let him [r]not be circumcised.

19 [s]Circumcision is nothing and uncircumcision is nothing, but [t]keeping the [u]commandments of God *is what matters*.

20 Let each one remain in the same calling in which he was called.

21 Were you called *while* a slave? Do not be concerned about it; but if you can be made free, rather use *it*.

22 For he who is called in the Lord *while* a slave is the Lord's

*6:20 NU-Text ends the verse at *body*.

CHAPTER 7

2
a 1 Cor. 5:1; Gal. 5:19; Eph. 5:3; Col. 3:5; 1 Th. 4:3; cp. 2 Cor. 12:21; Jude 7

3
b Cp. Eccl. 9:9; 1 Pet. 3:7

5
c Satan: v. 5; 2 Cor. 2:11. (Gen. 3:1; Rev. 20:10)
d Test/tempt: v. 5; 1 Cor. 10:9. (Gen. 3:1; Jas. 1:14, *note*)

7
e Cp. Mt. 19:11

9
f Cp. Jn. 2:1–2; 1 Tim. 5:14; Heb. 13:4

10
g Inspiration: vv. 10, 12; 1 Cor. 7:29. (Ex. 4:15; 2 Tim. 3:16, *note*)
h Mk. 10:6–10

11
i Or *leave*

12
j Or *leave her*

14
k Sanctification (NT): v. 14; 1 Cor. 7:34. (Mt. 4:5; Rev. 22:11)
l Cp. Mal. 2:14–15

15
m Cp. Rom. 12:18; 2 Cor. 13:11

16
n See Rom. 1:16, *note*

17
o Cp. Acts 16:4; Heb. 13:17
p 2 Cor. 11:28
q Churches (local): v. 17; 1 Cor. 10:32. (Acts 8:3; Phil. 1:1, *note*)

18
r Cp. Acts 15:1–2, 24–29; Gal. 5:1–6

19
s Gen. 17:10–14; cp. Josh. 5:3; Acts 16:3; Rom. 2:25; Gal. 2:3; 5:2; 6:12
t Cp. 1 Sam. 15:22; Jer. 7:22–23; Mt. 5:19; Jn. 15:14; 1 Jn. 2:3
u Law (of Moses): v. 19; 1 Cor. 9:8. (Ex. 19:1; Gal. 3:24, *note*)

[1](7:12) In vv. 1–12 the contrast is not between inspired teaching and uninspired teaching, as some have supposed. In vv. 10–11 Paul is repeating in substance something already taught by the Lord (Mt. 19:3–9); but in v. 12 he is dealing with a situation not covered by our Lord's teaching. Instead of disclaiming inspiration for what he writes in v. 12, the apostle is actually claiming for his own words here the same authority as for the words of Christ Himself. So also in vv. 25,40. Cp. 1 Cor. 14:37.

freedman. Likewise he who is
called *while* [a]free is Christ's
slave.
23 You were [b]bought [c]at a
[d]price; do not become slaves of
men.
24 [e]Brethren, let each one remain with [f]God in that *state* in
which he was called.

Apostolic advice to the unmarried

25 Now concerning virgins: I
have no commandment from
the Lord; yet I give judgment as
one whom the Lord in His
[g]mercy *has made* [h]trustworthy.
26 I suppose therefore that
this is good because of the present [i]distress—that *it is* good
for a man to remain as he is:
27 Are you bound to a wife?
Do not seek to be loosed. Are
you loosed from a wife? Do not
seek a wife.
28 But even if you do marry,
you have not [j]sinned; and if a
virgin marries, she has not
sinned. Nevertheless such will
have trouble in the flesh, but I
would spare you.
29 But this I [k]say, [e]brethren,
the [l]time *is* short, so that from
now on even those who have
wives should be as though they
had none,
30 those who weep as though
they did not weep, those who
rejoice as though they did not
rejoice, those who buy as
though they did not possess,
31 and those who use this
[m]world as not misusing *it*. [n]For
the form of this [m]world is passing away.
32 But I want you to be without care. He who is unmarried
[o]cares for the things of the
Lord—how he may please the
Lord.
33 But he who is married
cares about the things of the
[m]world—how he may please *his*
wife.
34 There is* a difference between a wife and a virgin. The
unmarried woman [o]cares about
the things of the Lord, that she
may be [p]holy both in body and
in spirit. But she who is married
cares about the things of the
[q]world—how she may please
her husband.
35 And this I [k]say for your
own profit, not that I may put a
leash on you, but for what is
proper, and that you may serve
the Lord without [r]distraction.
36 But if any man thinks he is
behaving improperly toward
his virgin, if she is past the
flower of youth, and thus it must
be, let him do what he wishes.
He does not [j]sin; let them
marry.
37 Nevertheless he who
stands steadfast in his heart,
having no necessity, but has
power over his own will, and
has so determined in his heart
that he will keep his virgin,*
does well.
38 So then he who gives *her**
in marriage does well, but he
who does not give *her* in marriage does better.
39 A wife is bound by law as
long as her husband lives; but if
her husband dies, she is at liberty to be married to whom she
wishes, [s]only in the Lord.
40 But she is happier if she
remains as she is, according to
my [k]judgment—and I think I
also have the [t]Spirit of God.

IV. Things Offered to Idols;
Limitations of Christian Liberty
8:1—11:1

8 NOW [u]concerning things
offered to [v]idols: We know
that we all have knowledge.
Knowledge puffs up, but love
edifies.
2 And if anyone thinks that
he knows anything, he knows
nothing yet as he ought to
know.
3 But if anyone loves God,
this one is known by Him.
4 Therefore concerning the
eating of things offered to idols,
we know that an idol *is* nothing
in the [q]world, and that *there is*
no other God but one.
5 For even if there are so-
called [w]gods, whether in
heaven or on earth (as there are
many gods and many lords),
6 [x]yet for us *there is* one
God, the Father, of whom *are* all
things, and we for Him; and one
Lord Jesus Christ, through

*7:34 M-Text adds *also*. 7:37 Or *virgin daughter* 7:38 NU-Text reads *his own virgin*.

22
a Jn. 8:36; Rom. 6:18, 22
23
b See Rom. 3:24, *note*
c 1 Cor. 6:20; 1 Pet. 1:18–19; Rev. 5:9
d Sacrifice (of Christ): v. 23; 1 Cor. 8:11. (Gen. 3:15; Heb. 10:18, *note*)
24
e Mt. 23:8; Lk. 8:21; Jn. 21:23; Rom. 8:29; 15:14; Heb. 2:11,17; Rev. 12:10; 19:10
f Eph. 6:5–8; Col. 3:22–24
25
g 2 Cor. 4:1
h 1 Tim. 1:12
26
i Or *necessity*
28
j See Rom. 3:23, *note*
29
k Inspiration: vv. 29, 35,40; 1 Cor. 9:9. (Ex. 4:15; 2 Tim. 3:16, *note*)
l 1 Pet. 4:7; cp. 2 Pet. 3:8
31
m Gk. *kosmos*. See Rev. 13:8, *note*
n Cp. Ps. 39:6; Jas. 4:14
32
o Cp. 1 Tim. 5:5
34
p Sanctification (NT): v. 34; 1 Cor. 9:13. (Mt. 4:5; Rev. 22:11)
q Gk. *kosmos*. See Mt. 4:8, *note*

35
r Cp. Lk. 10:39–42
39
s Cp. 2 Cor. 6:14
40
t Holy Spirit (NT): v. 40; 1 Cor. 12:3. (Mt. 1:18; Acts 2:4, *note*)
CHAPTER 8
1
u Cp. Rom. 14:1–15:3
v Cp. Acts 15:20
5
w See Ps. 16:4, *note*
6
x Mal. 2:10; Eph. 4:6

[a]whom *are* all things, and through whom [b]we *live.*

7 However, *there is* not in everyone that knowledge; for some, [c]with consciousness of the idol, until now eat *it* as a thing offered to an idol; and their conscience, being weak, is defiled.

8 But food does not commend us to God; for neither if we eat are we the better, nor if we do not eat are we the worse.

9 But beware lest somehow this [d]liberty of yours become a [e]stumbling block to those who are weak.

10 For if anyone sees you who have knowledge eating in an idol's temple, will not the conscience of him [f]who is weak be emboldened to eat those things offered to idols?

11 And because of your knowledge shall the weak brother perish, for whom Christ [g]died?

12 But when you thus [h]sin against the [h]brethren, and wound their weak conscience, you [i]sin against Christ.

13 Therefore, if food makes my brother stumble, I will never again eat meat, [j]lest I make my brother stumble.

Paul vindicates his apostleship (cp. Gal. 1:11—2:21)

9 AM I not an [k]apostle? Am I not free? Have I not [1][l]seen Jesus Christ our Lord? Are you not my work in the Lord?

2 If I am not an [m]apostle to others, yet doubtless I am to you. For you are the seal of my [m]apostleship in the Lord.

3 My defense to those who examine me is this:

4 Do we have no right to eat and drink?

5 Do we have no right to take along a believing wife, as *do* also the other apostles, the brothers of the Lord, and [n]Cephas?

6 Or *is it* only [o]Barnabas and I *who* have no right to [p]refrain from working?

6 *a* Jn. 1:3; Col. 1:17; Heb. 1:2 *b* Rom. 5:11; Rev. 4:11; 5:9–10
7 *c* Or *accustomed to idols*
9 *d* *Law* (of Christ): vv. 9–13; 1 Cor. 9:21. (Jn. 13:34; 2 Jn. 5) *e* Rom. 14:13; cp. 1 Jn. 2:10
10 *f* Or *if he is weak*
11 *g* *Sacrifice* (of Christ): v. 11; 1 Cor. 10:16. (Gen. 3:15; Heb. 10:18, *note*)
12 *h* See Rom. 3:23, *note* *i* Mt. 23:8; Lk. 8:21; Jn. 21:23; Rom. 8:29; 15:14; Heb. 2:11,17; Rev. 12:10; 19:10
13 *j* Cp. Mt. 18:6; Rom. 14:21; 1 Cor. 9:22
CHAPTER 9
1 *k* Acts 9:15; 22:21; Rom. 11:13; Gal. 1:16; 2:7–9; Eph. 3:8 *l* 1 Cor. 15:8
2 *m* Acts 9:15; 22:21; Rom. 11:13 Gal. 1:16; 2:7–9; Eph. 3:8
5 *n* i.e. *Simon Peter.* Jn. 1:42
6 *o* Acts 4:36 *p* Cp. Gal. 6:6; 2 Th. 3:8–9

Those who preach the Gospel are to live by means of the Gospel

7 Who ever goes to war at his own expense? [q]Who plants a vineyard and does not eat of its fruit? Or who tends a flock and does not drink of the milk of the flock?

8 Do I say these things as a *mere* man? Or does not the [r]law say the same also?

9 For it is [s]written in the [r]law of Moses, [t]*"You shall not muzzle an ox while it treads out the grain."* Is it oxen God is concerned about?

10 Or does He say *it* altogether for our sakes? [u]For our sakes, no doubt, *this* is [s]written, that he who plows should plow in hope, and he who threshes in hope should be partaker of his hope.

11 If we have sown spiritual things for you, *is it* a great thing if we reap your [v]material things?

12 If others are partakers of *this* right over you, *are* we not even more? [w]Nevertheless we have not used this right, but endure all things lest we hinder the [x]gospel of Christ.

13 Do you not know that those who minister the [y]holy things eat *of the things* of the [z]temple, and those who serve at the altar partake of *the offerings of* the altar?

14 Even so the [aa]Lord has commanded that those who preach the [x]gospel should live from the gospel.

15 But I have used [bb]none of these things, nor have I [s]written these things that it should be done so to me; for it *would be* better for me to die than that anyone should make my boasting void.

16 For if I preach the [x]gospel, I have nothing to boast of, for [cc]necessity is laid upon me; yes, woe is me if I do not preach the gospel!

17 For if I do this willingly, I have a reward; but if against my will, I have been entrusted with a stewardship.

18 What is my reward then?

7 *q* Cp. Dt. 20:6; Prov. 27:18
8 *r* *Law* (of Moses): vv. 8–9; 1 Cor. 9:20. (Ex. 19:1; Gal. 3:24, *note*)
9 *s* *Inspiration:* vv. 9–10,15; 1 Cor. 10:7. (Ex. 4:15; 2 Tim. 3:16, *note*) *t* Dt. 25:4; 1 Tim. 5:18
10 *u* Cp. Rom. 4:23–24; 2 Tim. 3:16
11 *v* Rom. 15:27
12 *w* Cp. 2 Cor. 11:7,9 *x* *Gospel:* vv. 12,14, 16–18; 1 Cor. 9:23. (Gen. 12:3; Rev. 14:6)
13 *y* *Sanctification* (NT): v. 13; 2 Cor. 7:1. (Mt. 4:5; Rev. 22:11) *z* Num. 18:8–31
14 *aa* Lk. 10:7–8
15 *bb* Cp. Acts 20:34; 1 Cor. 4:12
16 *cc* Cp. Jer. 20:9; Rom. 1:14–15

[1](9:1) Paul saw Him at his conversion on the Damascus Road (Acts 9:3–6; 22:6–10; 26:12–18).

That when I preach the gospel, I may present the gospel of Christ* without charge, that I may not abuse my authority in the gospel.

The method and reward of true ministry

19 For though I am free from all *men,* I have made myself a servant to all, that I might win the more;

20 and to the Jews I became as a Jew, that I might win Jews; to those *who are* under the [a]law, as under the law,* that I might win those *who are* under the law;

21 to those *who are* without law, as without law (not being [1]without [a]law toward God,* but under [b]law toward Christ*), that I might win those *who are* without law;

22 to the weak I became as* weak, that I might [c]win the weak. I have become all things to all *men,* that I might by all means [d]save some.

23 Now this I do for the [e]gospel's sake, that I may be partaker of it with *you.*

24 Do you not know that those who run in a race all run, but one receives the prize? [f]Run in such a way that you may obtain *it.*

25 And everyone who competes *for the prize* is temperate in all things. Now they *do it* to obtain a perishable crown, but we *for* [g]an [h]imperishable *crown.*

26 Therefore I run thus: not with uncertainty. Thus I fight: not as *one who* beats the air.

27 But I discipline my body and bring *it* into subjection, lest, when I have preached to others, I myself should become [2]disqualified.

Israel in the wilderness

10

MOREOVER, brethren, I do not want you to be unaware that all our [i]fathers were under the [j]cloud, all passed through the [k]sea,

2 all were [l]baptized into Moses in the cloud and in the sea,

3 all ate the same spiritual [m]food,

4 and all drank the same spiritual drink. For they [n]drank of that spiritual [o]Rock that followed them, and that Rock was Christ.

5 But with most of them God was not well pleased, for *their bodies* were [p]scattered in the wilderness.

6 Now these things [q]became our examples, to the intent that we should not lust after evil things as they also lusted.

7 And do not become idolaters as *were* some of them. As it is [r]written, [s]*"The people sat down to eat and drink, and rose up to play."*

8 Nor let us commit [t]sexual immorality, as [u]some of them did, and in one day twenty-three thousand [3]fell;

9 nor let us [v]tempt [w]Christ, as some of them also [x]tempted, and were destroyed by [y]serpents;

10 nor complain, as some of them also [z]complained, and were destroyed by the destroyer.

Wilderness experiences an example

11 Now all* these things [aa]happened to them as exam-

20
a Law (of Moses): vv. 20–21; 1 Cor. 14:21. (Ex. 19:1; Gal. 3:24, *note*)
21
b Law (of Christ): v. 21; 1 Cor. 13:1. (Jn. 13:34; 2 Jn. 5)
22
c Cp. Rom. 15:1; 1 Th. 5:14
d See Rom. 1:16, *note*
23
e Gospel: v. 23; 1 Cor. 15:1. (Gen. 12:3; Rev. 14:6)
24
f Cp. Phil. 3:14; 1 Tim. 6:12; Heb. 12:1–2
25
g Cp. 2 Tim. 4:8; Jas. 1:12; 1 Pet. 5:4; Rev. 2:10; 3:11
h Rewards: vv. 24–25; 2 Cor. 5:10. (Dan. 12:3; 1 Cor. 3:14, *note*)
CHAPTER 10
1
i Israel (history): vv. 1–10; 2 Cor. 3:7. (Gen. 12:2; Rom. 11:26, *note*)
j Ex. 13:21–22
k Ex. 14:21–22
2
l Cp. Rom. 6:3
3
m Ex. 16:4–36
4
n Ex. 17:5–7
o Christ (Rock): v. 4; Eph. 2:20. (Gen. 49:24; 1 Pet. 2:8). Cp. Jn. 4:13–14; 7:37–39
5
p Cp. Num. 14:26–45
6
q i.e. *happened as figures or types for us*
7
r Inspiration: v. 7; 1 Cor. 10:11. (Ex. 4:15; 2 Tim. 3:16; *note*)
s Ex. 32:6
8
t 1 Cor. 5:1; 6:13; Gal. 5:19; Eph. 5:3; Col. 3:5; 1 Th. 4:3; cp. 2 Cor. 12:21; Jude 7
u Num. 25:1–9
9
v Test/tempt: v. 9; 1 Cor. 10:13. (Gen. 3:1; Jas. 1:14, *note*)
w i.e. *the Lord.* Ex. 17:2,7
x Num. 21:5
y Num. 21:6–9
10
z Num. 14:2–29; cp. 26:63–65
11
aa v. 6; cp. Heb. 8:5

*9:18 NU-Text omits *of Christ.* 9:20 NU-Text adds *though not being myself under the law.* 9:21 NU-Text reads *God's law.* • NU-Text reads *Christ's law.* 9:22 NU-Text omits *as.* 10:11 NU-Text omits *all.*

[1](9:21) The expression might be rendered, "not lawless toward God, but inlawed to Christ." See Law (of Christ), Gal. 6:2; 2 Jn. 5. It is another way of saying that they are not under the law, but under [the rule of] grace (Rom. 6:14). In view of v. 20, where Paul has explicitly asserted the contrary, it is evident that Paul regarded himself as not being "under law."

[2](9:27) "Disqualified" is translated from the Gk. *adokimos,* meaning *disapproved. Dokimos,* without the negating *a,* is rendered "approved" in Rom. 14:18; 16:10; 1 Cor. 11:19; 2 Cor. 10:18; 2 Tim. 2:15; and Jas. 1:12. The prefix simply changes the word to a negative, i.e. *not approved,* or *disapproved.* The apostle is writing of service, not of salvation. He is not expressing fear that he may fail of salvation but of his crown. See Rewards (Dan. 12:3; 1 Cor. 3:14, *note*).

[3](10:8) There is an apparent discrepancy between this figure and that written in Num. 25:9. The latter has to do with the number of deaths "in the plague." But see 1 Chr. 11:11, *note.*

ples, and they were [a]written for our admonition, upon whom the ends of the [b]ages have come.

12 Therefore let him who thinks he stands take heed lest he fall.

13 No [c]temptation has overtaken you except such as is common to man; but God *is* faithful, who will not allow you to be tempted beyond what you are able, but with the temptation will also make the way of escape, that you may be able to bear *it*.

14 Therefore, my beloved, flee from idolatry.

15 I speak as to wise men; judge for yourselves what I [a]say.

Separation essential at the Lord's Table

16 The cup of blessing which we bless, [d]is it not the communion of the [e]blood of Christ? The bread which we break, is it not the communion of the body of Christ?

17 For we, *though* many, are one bread *and* one [f]body; for we all partake of that one [g]bread.

18 Observe Israel after the flesh: Are not those who eat of the sacrifices [h]partakers of the altar?

19 What am I saying then? That an [i]idol is anything, or what is offered to idols is anything?

20 Rather, that the things which the Gentiles sacrifice [j]they sacrifice to [k]demons and not to God, and I do [l]not want you to have [m]fellowship with [k]demons.

21 You cannot drink the cup of the Lord and the cup of [k]demons; you cannot partake of the [n]Lord's table and of the table of [k]demons.

22 Or do we provoke the Lord to [o]jealousy? Are we stronger than He?

The law of love in relation to eating and drinking (cp. Rom. 14:1–23)

23 All things are lawful for me,* but not all things are [p]helpful; all things are lawful for me,* but not all things [q]edify.

24 Let no one seek his own, but each one the [r]other's *well-being*.

25 Eat whatever is sold in the meat market, asking no questions for conscience' sake;

26 for *"the earth is the* [s]*LORD's, and all its fullness."*

27 If any of those who do not believe invites you *to dinner*, and you desire to go, eat whatever is set before you, asking no question for conscience' sake.

28 But if anyone says to you, "This was offered to idols," [t]do not eat it for the sake of the one who told you, and for conscience' sake;* for *"the earth is the LORD's, and all its fullness."**

29 "Conscience," I say, not your own, but that of the other. For why is my liberty judged by another *man's* conscience?

30 But if I partake with thanks, why am I evil spoken of for *the food* over which I give thanks?

31 Therefore, whether you eat or drink, or whatever you do, do all to the glory of God.

32 Give no offense, either to the Jews or to the Greeks or to [u]the [v]church of God,

33 just as I also please all *men* in all *things*, not seeking my own profit, but the *profit* of [w]many, that they may be [x]saved.

11 [y]IMITATE me, just as I also *imitate* Christ.

V. Christian Order and the Lord's Supper, 11:2–34

2 Now I praise you, [z]brethren, that you remember me in all things and [aa]keep the traditions just as I delivered *them* to you.

3 But I want you to know that the [bb]head of every man is Christ, the [cc]head of [1]woman *is*

*
10:23 NU-Text omits *for me.* • NU-Text omits *for me.* **10:28** NU-Text omits the rest of this verse. • Psalm 24:1

11
a Inspiration: vv. 11, 15; 1 Cor. 14:21. (Ex. 4:15; 2 Tim. 3:16, *note*)
b Gk. *aiōn.* See Mk. 10:30, *note*
13
c Test/tempt: v. 13; 2 Cor. 11:3. (Gen. 3:1; Jas. 1:14, *note*)
16
d Mt. 26:26–28
e Sacrifice (of Christ): v. 16; 1 Cor. 11:24. (Gen. 3:15; Heb. 10:18, *note*)
17
f Church (the true): v. 17; 1 Cor. 12:13. (Mt. 16:18; Heb. 12:23)
g Or *loaf.* Cp. 1 Cor. 11:23–26; 12:12–13
18
h Lev. 7:6
19
i 1 Cor. 8:4
20
j Dt. 32:17
k See Mt. 7:22, *note*
l Separation: vv. 20–21; 2 Cor. 6:17. (Gen. 12:1; 2 Cor. 6:17, *note*)
m Transl. *communion* in v. 16. Cp. 2 Cor. 6:14–7:1
21
n 1 Cor. 11:23–29
22
o Cp. Dt. 32:21

23
p 1 Cor. 6:12
q Cp. Rom. 14:19
24
r Phil. 2:4
26
s Ps. 24:1
28
t Cp. 1 Cor. 8:10
32
u Churches (local): v. 32; 1 Cor. 11:16. (Acts 8:3; Phil. 1:1, *note*)
v Church (visible): v. 32; 1 Cor. 12:28. (1 Cor. 10:32; 1 Tim. 3:15)
33
w Cp. Rom. 15:2; 1 Cor. 9:22
x See Rom. 1:16, *note*
CHAPTER 11
1
y 1 Cor. 4:16
2
z Mt. 23:8; Lk. 8:21; Jn. 21:23; Rom. 8:29; 15:14; Heb. 2:11,17; Rev. 12:10; 19:10
aa Cp. 2 Th. 2:15
3
bb Eph. 4:15
cc Gen. 3:16; Eph. 5:23

[1](11:3) Compare Gen. 3:16. The woman's veil or covering for her head is symbolic of her subordination (v. 10). According to v. 5 the covering seems to have been definitely connected with women praying or prophesying in the meetings of the church (vv. 7–8).

man, and the head of Christ *is* God.

4 Every man praying or prophesying, having *his* head covered, dishonors his head.

5 But every woman who prays or [a]prophesies with *her* head uncovered dishonors her head, for that is one and the same as if her head were shaved.

6 For if a woman is not covered, let her also be shorn. But if it is shameful for a woman to be shorn or shaved, let her be covered.

7 For a man indeed ought not to cover *his* head, since he is the [b]image and glory of God; but woman is the glory of man.

8 For man is not from woman, but woman [c]from man.

9 Nor was man created for the woman, but woman [d]for the man.

10 For this reason the woman ought to have *a symbol of* [e]authority on *her* head, because of the [f]angels.

11 Nevertheless, neither *is* man independent of woman, nor woman independent of man, in the Lord.

12 For as woman *came* from man, even so man also *comes* through woman; [g]but all things are from God.

13 Judge among yourselves. Is it proper for a woman to pray to God with her head uncovered?

14 Does not even nature itself teach you that if a man has long hair, it is a dishonor to him?

15 But if a woman has long hair, it is a glory to her; for *her* hair is given to her* for a [h]covering.

16 But if anyone seems to be contentious, we have no such custom, nor *do* the [i]churches of God.

Disorders at the Lord's Table rebuked

17 Now in giving these instructions I do [j]not praise *you*, since you come together not for the better but for the worse.

18 For first of all, when you come together as a [i]church, I [k]hear that there are [l]divisions among you, and in part I believe it.

19 For there must also be [m]factions among you, that those who are approved may be [n]recognized among you.

20 Therefore when you come together in one place, [o]it is not to eat the Lord's Supper.

21 For in eating, each one takes his own supper ahead of *others;* and one is [p]hungry and another is drunk.

22 What! Do you not have houses to eat and drink in? Or do you despise the [i]church of God and shame those who have nothing? What shall I say to you? Shall I praise you in this? I do [q]not praise *you.*

Order and meaning of the Lord's Table

23 For I received from the Lord that which I also delivered to you: [1]that the Lord Jesus on the *same* night in which He was betrayed took bread;

24 and when He had given thanks, He broke *it* and [r]said, "Take, eat;* this is My body which is [s]broken* for you; do this in [t]remembrance of Me."

25 In the same manner *He* also *took* the cup after supper, saying, "This cup is the new [u]covenant in My [s]blood. This do, as often as you drink *it,* in remembrance of Me."

26 For as often as you eat this bread and drink this cup, you proclaim the Lord's [s]death till He comes.

27 Therefore whoever eats this bread or drinks *this* cup of the Lord in an [v]unworthy manner will be guilty of the body and blood* of the Lord.

28 But let a man examine himself, and so let him eat of the bread and drink of the cup.

29 For he who eats and drinks in an [w]unworthy man-

*11:15 M-Text omits *to her.* **11:24** NU-Text omits *Take, eat.* • NU-Text omits *broken.* **11:27** NU-Text and M-Text read *the blood.*

5
a Cp. Acts 21:9
7
b Gen. 1:27; 5:1
8
c Gen. 2:21–22; cp. 1 Tim. 2:13
9
d Gen. 2:18
10
e See v. 3, *note*
f i.e. *the presence of the angels*
12
g Cp. Prov. 16:4; Rom. 11:36; 1 Cor. 8:6
15
h Or *veil*
16
i *Churches* (local): vv. 16–34; 1 Cor. 14:4. (Acts 8:3; Phil. 1:1, *note*)
17
j v. 22

18
k 1 Cor. 1:11–12
l Or *schisms*
19
m Or *sects*
n Cp. 1 Jn. 2:19
20
o Or *you cannot eat*
21
p Cp. Jude 12
22
q v. 17
24
r Mt. 26:26–28
s *Sacrifice* (of Christ): vv. 24–26; 1 Cor. 15:3. (Gen. 3:15; Heb. 10:18, *note*)
t Cp. Ex. 12:14
25
u *Covenant* (New): v. 25; 2 Cor. 3:6. (Isa. 61:8; Heb. 8:8, *note*)
27
v Cp. vv. 17–22,28–29
29
w Cp. vv. 17–22,28–29

[1](11:23) The Lord's Supper is one of the two ordinances or sacraments of the Church for this age, the other being water baptism (see Acts 8:12, *note*).

ner* eats and drinks [a]judgment
to himself, not discerning the
Lord's* body.
30 For this reason many *are*
weak and sick among you, and
many [b]sleep.
31 For if we would [1c]judge
ourselves, we would not be
[d]judged.
32 But when we are judged,
we are [e]chastened by the Lord,
that we may not be condemned
with the [f]world.
33 Therefore, my brethren,
when you [g]come together to
eat, wait for one another.
34 But if anyone is hungry,
[h]let him eat at home, lest you
come together for judgment.
And the rest I will set in order
when I come.

VI. Spiritual Gifts and Their Use in Love, 12:1—14:40

12 NOW concerning [2]spiri-
tual *gifts,* [i]brethren, I do
not want you to be ignorant:
2 You know that* you were
Gentiles, carried away to these
[j]dumb [k]idols, however you
were led.
3 Therefore I make known
to you that no one speaking [l]by
the [m]Spirit of God calls Jesus
[n]accursed, and no one can say
that Jesus is Lord except by the
Holy Spirit.

True ministry is the exercise of spiritual gifts (cp. Eph. 4:7–16)

4 There are diversities of
[3o]gifts, but the same [m]Spirit.
5 There are differences of
ministries, but the same Lord.
6 And there are diversities
of [p]activities, but it is the same
God who works all in all.
7 But the manifestation of
the [m]Spirit is given to each one
for the profit *of all:*
8 for to one is given the
word of wisdom through the
[m]Spirit, to another the word of
knowledge through the same
Spirit,
9 to another [q]faith by the
same [m]Spirit, to another gifts of
[r]healings by the same* Spirit,
10 to another the working of
[s]miracles, to another [4]proph-
ecy, to another [t]discerning of
spirits, to another *different*
kinds of [u]tongues, to another
the interpretation of tongues.
11 But one and the same
[m]Spirit works all these things,
distributing to each one individually as He wills.

Every believer is a member of Christ's body, with a definite ministry

12 For as the body is one and
has many members, but all the
members of that one body, being many, are one body, so also
is Christ.
13 For by one [m]Spirit we
were all baptized into one
[v]body—[w]whether [x]Jews or
[y]Greeks, whether slaves or

29 *a* Cp. v. 32
30 *b* Cp. 1 Jn. 5:16–17
31 *c* Cp. 2 Cor. 13:5 *d Judgments* (the seven): v. 31; 2 Cor. 5:10. (2 Sam. 7:14; Rev. 20:12, *note*)
32 *e* Heb. 12:5–10 *f* Gk. *kosmos.* See Mt. 4:8, *note*
33 *g* vv. 18,20; 1 Cor. 14:26
34 *h* Cp. vv. 21–22
CHAPTER 12
1 *i* Mt. 23:8; Lk. 8:21; Jn. 21:23; Rom. 8:29; 15:14; Heb. 2:11,17; Rev. 12:10; 19:10
2 *j* Cp. Ps. 115:4–8; Isa. 44:9–20 *k* Cp. Acts 15:20
3 *l* Cp. 1 Jn. 4:2 *m Holy Spirit* (NT): vv. 3–11,13; 2 Cor. 1:22. (Mt. 1:18; Acts 2:4, *note*) *n* Gk. *anathema.* Cp. 1 Cor. 16:22
4 *o* vv. 4–11; Rom. 12:3–8; cp. 1 Cor. 12:28–31
6 *p* Or *workings*
9 *q Faith:* v. 9; 1 Cor. 13:2. (Gen. 3:20; Heb. 11:39, *note*) *r* Mt. 10:1; Mk. 3:15; 16:18; cp. Mk. 6:13; Jas. 5:14–15
10 *s* Cp. Jn. 14:12; Acts 3:1–11; 14:8–10; 20:6–12 *t* 1 Jn. 4:1 *u* Acts 2:4–11
13 *v Church* (the true): v. 13; 1 Cor. 12:27. (Mt. 16:18; Heb. 12:23) *w* Cp. Gal. 3:28 *x* Rom. 3:29; cp. Rom. 1:16; 2:9,10; 12:2; Col. 3:11 *y* See Eph. 3:6, *note*

*
11:29 NU-Text omits *in an unworthy manner.* • NU-Text omits *Lord's.*
12:2 NU-Text and M-Text add *when.*
12:9 NU-Text reads *one.*

[1](11:31) Self-judgment is not so much the Christian's moral condemnation of his own ways or habits, as of himself for allowing such ways. Self-judgment avoids chastisement. If self-judgment is neglected, the Lord judges, and the result is chastisement, but never condemnation (v. 32; 2 Sam. 7:14–15; 12:13–14; 1 Cor. 5:5; 1 Tim. 1:20; Heb. 12:7). For other judgments, see *notes* at Ezek. 20:37; Mt. 25:32; Jn. 12:31; 2 Cor. 5:10; Jude 6; Rev. 20:12.

[2](12:1) The Greek word is plural *(pneumatika)* and refers to things pertaining to the Holy Spirit. It gives the key to chs. 12—14. Chapter 12 concerns the Spirit in relation to the body of Christ. This relation is twofold: (1) The baptism with the Spirit forms the body by uniting believers to Christ, the risen and glorified Head, and to each other (vv. 12–13). The symbol of the body thus formed is the natural, human body (v. 12), and all the analogies are freely used (vv. 14–26). And (2) to each Christian is given a spiritual enablement and capacity for specific service. None is destitute of such a gift (vv. 7,11,27), but in their distribution the Spirit acts in free sovereignty (v. 11). There is no room for self-choosing; Christian service is simply the ministry of such a gift or gifts as the individual may have received (cp. Rom. 12:4–8). The gifts are diverse (vv. 6,8–10,28–30), but all are equally honorable because they are bestowed by the same Spirit, administered under the same Lord, and energized by the same God.

[3](12:4) Compare Eph. 4:8,11–12. The Holy Spirit bestows gifts for service to men. Christ gives the gifted men to the churches.

[4](12:10) The NT prophet is not primarily a foreteller but, rather, a forthteller, one whose gift enables him to speak to others "edification and exhortation and comfort" (14:3).

free—and have all been made
to drink into* one Spirit.
14 [a]For in fact the body is not
one member but many.
15 If the foot should say, "Because I am not a hand, I am not
of the body," is it therefore not
of the body?
16 And if the ear should say,
"Because I am not an eye, I am
not of the body," is it therefore
not of the body?
17 If the whole body *were* an
eye, where *would be* the hearing? If the whole *were* hearing,
where *would be* the smelling?
18 But now God has [b]set the
members, each one of them, in
the body just as He pleased.
19 And if they *were* all one
member, where *would* the body
be?
20 But now indeed *there are*
many members, yet one body.
21 And the eye cannot say to
the hand, "I have no need of
you"; nor again the head to the
feet, "I have no need of you."
22 No, much rather, those
members of the body which
seem to be weaker are necessary.
23 And those *members* of the
body which we think to be less
honorable, on these we bestow
greater honor; and our unpresentable *parts* have greater
modesty,
24 but our presentable *parts*
have no need. But God composed the body, having given
greater honor to that *part* which
lacks it,
25 that there should be no
[c]schism in the body, but *that*
the members should have the
same care for one another.
26 And if one member suf-
fers, [d]all the members suffer
with *it;* or if one member is honored, all the members rejoice
with *it.*
27 Now you are the [e]body of
Christ, and [f]members individually.
28 [g]And God has appointed
these in the [h]church: first
[i]apostles, second [j]prophets,
third [k]teachers, after that [l]mir-
acles, then gifts of [m]healings,
[n]helps, administrations, varieties of [o]tongues.
29 *Are* all apostles? *Are* all
prophets? *Are* all teachers? *Are*
all workers of miracles?
30 Do all have gifts of healings? Do all speak with
tongues? Do all interpret?
31 But earnestly desire the
best* gifts. And yet I show you
a [1]more excellent way.

Ministry gifts must be exercised in love

13 THOUGH I speak with
the tongues of men and
of [p]angels, but have not [q]love, I
have become sounding brass or
a clanging cymbal.
2 [g]And though I have *the
gift of* prophecy, and understand all mysteries and all
knowledge, and though I have
all [r]faith, so that I could remove
[s]mountains, but have not love, I
am nothing.
3 And though I [t]bestow all
my goods to feed *the poor,* and
though I give my body to be
burned,* but have not love, it
profits me nothing.
4 Love suffers long *and* is
[u]kind; love does not [v]envy; love
does not [w]parade itself, is not
[x]puffed up;
5 does not behave [y]rudely,
does not [z]seek its own, is not
[aa]provoked, thinks no [bb]evil;
6 does not rejoice in [cc]iniq-
uity, but rejoices [dd]in the truth;
7 bears all things, believes
all things, [ee]hopes all things, endures all things.
8 Love [ff]never fails. But
whether *there are* prophecies,
they will fail; whether *there are*
tongues, they will cease;
whether *there is* knowledge, it
will vanish away.
9 For we know in part and
we prophesy [gg]in part.
10 [hh]But when that which is
perfect has come, then that

14
a vv. 14–26
18
b Cp. v. 28; Rom. 12:3–8; Eph. 4:11
25
c Or *division.* Cp. 1 Cor. 1:11–12
26
d Cp. Josh. 7:1–26
27
e Church (the true): vv. 27–28; 2 Cor. 11:2. (Mt. 16:18; Heb. 12:23). Col. 1:18,24; 2:19
f Eph. 5:30
28
g Cp. 12:8–11
h Church (visible): vv. 28–30; 1 Cor. 15:9. (1 Cor. 10:32; 1 Tim. 3:15)
i Eph. 2:20
j Eph. 4:11
k Acts 13:1
l Gal. 3:5
m Mk. 16:18
n Cp. Acts 16:9
o Cp. Acts 2:1–11

CHAPTER 13
1
p See Heb. 1:4, *note*
q Law (of Christ): 13:1–14:1. 1 Cor. 14:1. (Jn. 13:34; 2 Jn. 5)
2
r Faith: v. 2; 1 Cor. 13:13. (Gen. 3:20; Heb. 11:39, *note*)
s Cp. Mt. 17:20–21
3
t Cp. Mt. 6:1–2
4
u Eph. 4:32
v Gal. 5:26
w Cp. Rom. 1:30; 2 Tim. 3:2
x Cp. 1 Cor. 4:6,18,19
5
y Cp. Phil. 4:8
z Cp. Phil. 2:4
aa Cp. Eph. 4:2
bb Cp. Rom. 12:9
6
cc See Rom. 3:23, *note*
dd Or *with*
7
ee Cp. Heb. 6:19
8
ff Cp. Eph. 3:17–19
9
gg Cp. 1 Cor. 8:2
10
hh Cp. 1 Jn. 3:2

*12:13 NU-Text omits *into.* 12:31 NU-Text reads *greater.* 13:3 NU-Text reads *so I may boast.*

[1](12:31) Chapter 13 continues the *pneumatika* begun in ch. 12 (see 12:1, *note*). Gifts are good, but only if ministered in love (13:1–2). Benevolence is good, but not apart from love (v. 3). Love is described (vv. 4–7). Love is better than our present incomplete knowledge (vv. 8–12), even greater than faith and hope (v. 13).

12
[a] Cp. Nah. 1:7; Jn. 10:14; 1 Cor. 8:3; 2 Tim. 2:19
13
[b] *Faith:* v. 13; 1 Cor. 14:22. (Gen. 3:20; Heb. 11:39, *note*)
[c] Cp. Heb. 6:19
CHAPTER 14
1
[d] *Law* (of Christ): 13:1–14:1; 1 Cor. 16:14. (Jn. 13:34; 2 Jn. 5)
[e] Cp. 1 Th. 5:20
2
[f] vv. 13,19
[g] Lit. *listens to* or *hears*
3
[h] See v. 1, *note*
[i] v. 26; Rom. 14:19; 15:2; 2 Cor. 10:8; 12:19; Eph. 4:12,29
[j] 1 Tim. 4:13; 2 Tim. 4:2; Ti. 1:9; 2:15; Heb. 3:13; 10:25
[k] v. 31; cp. Phil. 2:1
4
[l] *Churches* (local): vv. 4–5,12; 1 Cor. 14:23. (Acts 8:3; Phil. 1:1, *note*)
5
[m] Cp. Num. 11:25–29
6
[n] Mt. 23:8; Lk. 8:21; Jn. 21:23; Rom. 8:29; 15:14; Heb. 2:11,17; Rev. 12:10; 19:10
[o] Cp. 2 Cor. 12:1; Eph. 1:17; 3:3
[p] Cp. 2 Tim. 3:16

which is in part will be done
away.
11 When I was a child, I
spoke as a child, I understood as
a child, I thought as a child; but
when I became a man, I put
away childish things.
12 For now we see in a mirror, dimly, but then face to face.
Now I know in part, but then I
shall know just as I also am
[a]known.
13 And now abide [b]faith,
[c]hope, love, these three; but the
greatest of these *is* love.

Prophecy is the superior gift

14 PURSUE [d]love, and desire spiritual *gifts,* but
[1]especially that you may
[e]prophesy.
2 For he who speaks in a
[f]tongue does not speak to men
but to God, for no one [g]under-
stands *him;* however, in the
spirit he speaks mysteries.
3 But he who [h]prophesies
speaks [i]edification and [j]ex-
hortation and [k]comfort to men.
4 He who speaks in a tongue
edifies himself, but he who
[h]prophesies [i]edifies the
[l]church.
5 I wish you all spoke with
tongues, but [m]even more that
you prophesied; for* he who
[h]prophesies *is* greater than he
who speaks with tongues, unless indeed he interprets, that
the [l]church may receive [i]edifi-
cation.
6 But now, [n]brethren, if I
come to you speaking with
tongues, what shall I profit you
unless I speak to you either by
[o]revelation, by knowledge, by
prophesying, or by [p]teaching?
7 Even things without life,
whether flute or harp, when
they make a sound, unless they
make a distinction in the
sounds, how will it be known
what is piped or played?
8 For if the trumpet makes
an uncertain sound, who will
prepare for battle?
9 So likewise you, unless
you utter by the tongue words
easy to understand, how will it
be known what is spoken? For
you will be speaking into the
air.
10 There are, it may be, so
many kinds of languages in the
[q]world, and none of them *is*
without significance.
11 Therefore, if I do not know
the meaning of the language, I
shall be a [r]foreigner to him who
speaks, and he who speaks *will
be* a foreigner to me.
12 Even so you, since you are
zealous for spiritual *gifts, let it
be* for the edification of the
[l]church *that* you seek to excel.
13 Therefore let him who
speaks in a tongue pray that he
may [s]interpret.
14 For if I pray in a tongue,
my spirit prays, but my understanding is unfruitful.
15 What is *the conclusion*
then? I will pray with the spirit,
and I will also pray with the understanding. I will [t]sing with
the spirit, and I will also sing
with the understanding.
16 Otherwise, if you bless
with the spirit, how will he who
occupies the place of the uninformed say [u]"Amen" at your
giving of thanks, since he does
not understand what you say?
17 For you indeed give
thanks well, but the other is not
[i]edified.
18 I thank my God I speak
with tongues more than you all;
19 yet in the church I would
rather speak five words with
my understanding, that I may
teach others also, than ten thousand words in a tongue.

*14:5 NU-Text reads *and.*

10
[q] Gk. *kosmos.* See Mt. 4:8, *note*
11
[r] Acts 28:4; Rom. 1:14; Col. 3:11; cp. Acts 28:2
13
[s] 1 Cor. 12:10
15
[t] Cp. Eph. 5:19; Col. 3:16
16
[u] 1 Chr. 16:36; Neh. 8:6; Rev. 5:14; 7:12; cp. Dt. 27:15–26

[1](14:1) The subject is still the *pneumatika* (see 12:1, *note*). Chapter 12 describes the gifts and the body, the Church; ch. 13 depicts the love which alone gives ministry of gifts any value; ch. 14 regulates the ministry of gifts in the primitive, apostolic assembly of believers in Christ. (1) The important gift is that of prophecy (v. 1). The NT prophet was not merely a preacher, but an inspired preacher through whom, until the NT was written, new revelations suited to the new dispensation were given (14:29–30). (2) Tongues and the sign gifts are to cease; meanwhile they must be used with restraint, and only if an interpreter is present (vv. 1–19,27–28). (3) In the primitive Church there was liberty for the ministry of all the gifts which might be present, but for prophecy more especially (vv. 23–26,31,39). And (4) these injunctions are declared to be "the commandments of the Lord" (vv. 36–37).

20 [a]Brethren, do not be
[b]children in understanding;
however, in malice be [c]babes,
but in understanding be mature.
21 In the [d]law it is [e]written:

[f]*"With men of other*
tongues and other lips
I will speak to this
people;
And yet, for all that, they
will not hear Me,"

says the Lord.
22 Therefore tongues are for
a [g]sign, not to those who [h]be-
lieve but to unbelievers; but
prophesying is not for unbelievers but for those who [h]believe.

Regulations for the ministry of spiritual gifts in the local church

23 Therefore if the whole
[i]church comes together in one
place, and all speak with
tongues, and there come in
those who are uninformed or
unbelievers, will they not [j]say
that you are out of your mind?
24 But if all prophesy, and an
unbeliever or an uninformed
person comes in, he is convinced by all, he is convicted by
all.
25 And thus* the secrets of
his heart are revealed; and so,
falling down on *his* face, he will
worship God and report that
[k]God is truly among you.
26 How is it then, [a]brethren?
Whenever you come [i]together,
each of you has a [l]psalm, has a
[m]teaching, has a tongue, has a
[n]revelation, has an [o]interpreta-
tion. Let all things be done for
edification.
27 If anyone [1]speaks in a
tongue, *let there be* [p]two or at
the most three, *each* in turn, and
let one interpret.
28 But if there is no interpreter, let him keep silent in
[i]church, and let him speak to
himself and to God.
29 Let two or three prophets
speak, and let the others judge.
30 But if *anything* is revealed
to another who sits by, let the
first keep silent.
31 For you can all prophesy
one by one, that all may learn
and all may be encouraged.
32 And the spirits of the
prophets are subject to the
prophets.
33 For God is not *the author*
of [q]confusion but of peace, as in
all the [i]churches of the [r]saints.
34 Let your* women keep silent in the [i]churches, for they
are not permitted to speak; but
they are to be [s]submissive, as
the law also [e]says.
35 And if they want to learn
something, let them ask their
own husbands at home; for it is
shameful for women to speak in
[i]church.
36 Or did the word of God
come *originally* from you? Or
[t]*was it* you only that it
reached?
37 If anyone thinks himself
to be a prophet or spiritual, let
him acknowledge that the
things which I [e]write to you are
the commandments of the Lord.
38 But if anyone is ignorant,
let him be ignorant.*
39 Therefore, [a]brethren, desire earnestly to [u]prophesy, and
do not forbid to speak with
tongues.
40 Let all things be done decently and in order.

VII. The Resurrection of the Dead, 15

(1) Fact of the resurrection of Christ

15 MOREOVER, [v]breth-
ren, I declare to you the

*14:25 NU-Text omits *And thus.* 14:34 NU-Text omits *your.* 14:38 NU-Text reads *If anyone does not recognize this, he is not recognized.*

20 a Mt. 23:8; Lk. 8:21; Jn. 21:23; Rom. 8:29; 15:14; Heb. 2:11,17; Rev. 12:10; 19:10
b Cp. Jer. 4:22; Eph. 4:14; Heb. 5:12
c Cp. 1 Cor. 3:1

21 d *Law* (of Moses): v. 21; 1 Cor. 15:56. (Ex. 19:1; Gal. 3:24, *note*)
e *Inspiration:* vv. 21, 34,37; 1 Cor. 15:3. (Ex. 4:15; 2 Tim. 3:16, *note*)
f Isa. 28:11–12; cp. Dt. 28:49

22 g Mk. 16:17
h *Faith:* v. 22; 1 Cor. 15:2. (Gen. 3:20; Heb. 11:39, *note*)

23 i *Churches* (local): vv. 23,26,28, 33–35; 1 Cor. 16:1. (Acts 8:3; Phil. 1:1, *note*)
j Cp. Acts 2:12–13

25 k Cp. Isa. 45:14

26 l Cp. Eph. 5:19; Col. 3:16
m Cp. 2 Tim. 3:16
n Cp. 2 Cor. 12:1; Eph. 1:17; 3:3
o Cp. v. 13

27 p Cp. v. 40

33 q Cp. Jas. 3:16
r Cp. Rom. 1:7; 8:27; 12:13; 15:25; 16:2

34 s Cp. Gen. 3:16; 1 Cor. 11:3; Eph. 5:22; 1 Tim. 2:11–13; 1 Pet. 3:1–5

36 t Cp. Isa. 2:3; Lk. 24:47; Rom. 15:19

39 u 14:1

CHAPTER 15

1 v Mt. 23:8; Lk. 8:21; Jn. 21:23; Rom. 8:29; 15:14; Heb. 2:11,17; Rev. 12:10; 19:10

[1](14:27) The exercise of the gift of tongues was not to be forbidden in the early Church (v. 39), but this exercise was strictly circumscribed by certain rules outlined in vv. 27–40: (1) Not more than two or three at a meeting may thus speak (v. 27). (2) These must speak in turn (v. 27). (3) If no one is able to interpret what is said, the speaker is to be silent (vv. 27–28). (4) Those who speak must be in control of their faculties, because God is not the author of confusion (vv. 32–33). (5) Women are not permitted to speak at the meetings of the church (vv. 34–36). And (6) these rules must be regarded as "the commandments of the Lord," and their observance is a mark of true spirituality (v. 37). Undue preoccupation with tongues indicates spiritual childishness (vv. 19–20).

[1][a]gospel which I preached to
you, which also you received
and in which you stand,
2 by which also you are
[b]saved, if you hold fast that
word which I preached to you—
unless you [c]believed in vain.
3 For I delivered to you first
of all that which I also received:
that Christ [d]died for our [e]sins
[f]according to the [g]Scriptures,
4 and that He was buried,
and that He [h]rose again the
third day [f]according to the
[i]Scriptures,
5 and that He was seen by
[j]Cephas, [k]then by the twelve.
6 After that He was seen by
over five hundred [l]brethren at
once, of whom the greater part
remain to the present, but some
have fallen asleep.
7 After that He was seen by
James, then by all the apostles.
8 Then last of all He was
[m]seen by me also, as by one
[2]born out of due time.
9 For I am the least of the
apostles, who am not worthy to
be called an [n]apostle, because I
persecuted the [o]church of God.
10 But by the [p]grace of God I
am what I am, and His [p]grace
toward me was not in vain; but
I labored more abundantly than
they all, yet not I, but the [p]grace
of God *which was* with me.
11 Therefore, whether *it was*
I or they, so we preach and so
you [c]believed.

(2) Importance of Christ's resurrection

12 Now if Christ is preached
that He has been [h]raised from
the dead, [q]how do some among
you say that there is no resurrection of the dead?
13 But if there is no resurrection of the dead, then Christ is
not risen.
14 And if Christ is not risen,
then our preaching *is* empty
and your [c]faith *is* also empty.
15 Yes, and we are found
false witnesses of God, because
we have testified of God that He
raised up Christ, whom He did
not raise up—if in fact the dead
do not rise.
16 For if *the* dead do not rise,
then Christ is not risen.
17 And if Christ is not risen,
your [c]faith *is* futile; you are still
in your [r]sins!
18 Then also those who have
fallen [s]asleep in Christ have
perished.
19 If in this life only we have
hope in Christ, we are of all men
the most pitiable.

(3) Order of the resurrections

20 But now Christ is [h]risen
from the dead, *and* has become
the [t]firstfruits of those who
have fallen [s]asleep.
21 For since by man [u]*came*
[v]death, by Man also *came* the
resurrection of the dead.
22 For as in [3]Adam all die,
[w]even so in Christ all shall [x]be
made alive.
23 But each one in his own
order: Christ the firstfruits, af-

1
a Gospel: vv. 1–4; 2 Cor. 1:19. (Gen. 12:3; Rev. 14:6)
2
b See Rom. 1:16, *note*
c Faith: vv. 2, 11,14,17; 2 Cor. 1:24. (Gen. 3:20; Heb. 11:39, *note*)
3
d Sacrifice (of Christ): v. 3; 2 Cor. 5:14. (Gen. 3:15; Heb. 10:18, *note*)
e See Rom. 3:23, *note*
f Inspiration: vv. 3–4; 1 Cor. 15:45. (Ex. 4:15; 2 Tim. 3:16, *note*)
g Ps. 22; Isa. 53
4
h Resurrection: vv. 4, 12–17, 20–23; 1 Cor. 15:35. (2 Ki. 4:35; 1 Cor. 15:52, *note*)
i Gen. 1:9–13; 2 Ki. 20:8; Ps. 16:9–11; Jon. 1:17; 2:10; Hos. 6:2; cp. Mt. 12:39–40; Lk. 24:46–47; Acts 13:32–37,44
5
j i.e. *Simon Peter.* Lk. 24:34
k See Mk. 16:14, *note*
6
l Mt. 23:8; Lk. 8:21; Jn. 21:23; Rom. 8:29; 15:14; Heb. 2:11,17; Rev. 12:10; 19:10
8
m Acts 9:4
9
n Acts 9:15; 22:21; Rom. 11:13; Gal. 1:16; 2:7–9; Eph. 3:8
o Church (visible): v. 9; Gal. 1:13. (1 Cor. 10:32; 1 Tim. 3:15)
10
p Grace: v. 10; 1 Cor. 16:23. (Jn. 1:14; Jn. 1:17, *note*). See 2 Pet. 3:18, *note*
12
q Cp. Acts 26:8
17
r Cp. Jn. 8:21,24; see Rom. 3:23, *note*
18
s Job 14:12; Ps. 13:3; cp. Jn. 11:12
20
t Cp. Jas. 1:18
21
u Gen. 3:19; Ezek. 18:4; Rom. 5:12; 6:23; Heb. 9:27
v Death (physical): vv. 21–22; 1 Cor. 15:26. (Gen. 2:17; Heb. 9:27, *note*)
15:22 *w* Cp. Rom. 5:17 *x* Jn. 5:28–29

[1](15:1) In vv. 1–8 the apostle outlines the Gospel of God's grace. (1) It concerns a Person—the Christ of the Scriptures and history. (2) It concerns His death—"for our sins according to the Scriptures." And (3) it concerns His resurrection—likewise "according to the Scriptures." His burial is asserted as the evidence of His death; and that He was seen alive is declared as the proof of His resurrection. This is the Gospel that Paul preached; that the early Church accepted; and by which men are saved (vv. 1–2).

[2](15:8) "One born out of due time" (Gk. *tō ektrōmati*), i.e. prematurely. Paul thinks of himself here as an Israelite whose time to be born again had not come nationally (cp. Mt. 23:39), so that his conversion by the appearing of the Lord in glory (Acts 9:3–6) was an illustration, or instance, before the time of the future national conversion of Israel. See Ezek. 20:35–38; Hos. 2:14–17; Zech. 12:10—13:6; Rom. 11:25–27; 1 Tim. 1:16.

[3](15:22) Adam is a contrasting type of Christ (vv. 45–47; cp. Rom. 5:14–19). (1) "The first man Adam became a living being" (Gen. 2:7), i.e. he derived life from another, God. "The last Adam became a life-giving spirit." Far above deriving life, He was Himself the fountain of life, and He gave that life to others (Jn. 1:4; 5:21; 10:10; 12:24; 1 Jn. 5:12). (2) In origin "the first man was of the earth, made of dust; the second Man is the Lord from heaven" (1 Cor. 15:47). And (3) each is the head of a creation and these also are in contrast: "in Adam all die . . . in Christ all shall be made alive"; the Adamic creation is "flesh," whereas the new creation is "spirit" (Jn. 3:6).

23
a Christ (second advent): v. 23; Phil. 3:20. (Dt. 30:3; Acts 1:11, *note*)
24
b v. 28
c Kingdom (NT): v. 24; Eph. 5:5. (Mt. 2:2; 1 Cor. 15:24, *note*)
25
d Ps. 110:1; Mt. 22:44
26
e Cp. 2 Tim. 1:10; Rev. 21:4
f Death (physical): v. 26; 1 Cor. 15:54. (Gen. 2:17; Heb. 9:27, *note*)
27
g Ps. 8:6
28
h v. 24
i Cp. Ps. 21:13; 47:9; 57:11; 99:5; 108:5; 118:28; Isa. 12:4; 25:1
j Cp. 1 Cor. 11:3

terward those *who are* Christ's
at His [a]coming.
24 [b]Then *comes* the end,
when He delivers the [1c]king-
dom to God the Father, when He
puts an end to all rule and all
authority and power.
25 For He must reign [d]till He
has put all enemies under His
feet.
26 The last enemy *that* will
be [e]destroyed *is* [f]death.
27 For *"He has put* [g]*all things
under His feet."* But when He
says "all things are put under
Him," it is evident that He who
put all things under Him is excepted.
28 Now when all things are
made subject to Him, [h]then the
Son Himself will also be subject
to Him who put all things under
Him, that [i]God may be [j]all in
all.

(4) Moral value of the resurrection

29 Otherwise, what will they
do who are baptized for the
[2]dead, if the dead do not rise at
all? Why then are they baptized
for the dead?
30 And why do we stand in
[k]jeopardy every hour?
31 I affirm, by the [l]boasting
in you which I have in Christ
Jesus our Lord, I [m]die daily.
32 If, in the manner of men, I
have fought with beasts at
[n]Ephesus, what advantage *is it*
to me? If *the* dead do not rise,
[o]*"Let us eat and drink, for tomorrow we die!"*
33 [p]Do not be deceived: "Evil
[q]company corrupts good habits."
34 [r]Awake to [s]righteous-
ness, and do not [t]sin; for some
do not have the [u]knowledge of
God. I speak *this* to your shame.

(5) Body of resurrection

35 But someone will say,
[v]"How are the dead [w]raised up?
And with what body do they
come?"
36 Foolish one, what you sow
is not made alive unless it [x]dies.
37 And what you sow, you do
not sow that body that shall be,
but mere grain—perhaps wheat
or some other *grain.*
38 But God gives it a body as
He pleases, and to each seed its
own body.

15:36 *x* Jn. 12:24

30
k Cp. 2 Cor. 11:26
31
l Or *rejoicing.* Cp. Phil. 3:3
m Cp. Rom. 8:36; 2 Cor. 4:10–12
32
n Cp. 2 Cor. 1:8
o Isa. 22:13
33
p Cp. Gal. 6:7
q Cp. Ps. 1:1; Prov. 4:14; 13:20; 1 Cor. 5:11; Eph. 4:29
34
r Cp. Rom. 13:11; Eph. 5:14
s Cp. Eph. 6:14
t See Rom. 3:23, *note*
u Mt. 22:29
35
v Cp. Ezek. 37:3
w Resurrection: vv. 35–41; 1 Cor. 15:42. (2 Ki. 4:35; 1 Cor. 15:52, *note*)

[1](15:24) Kingdom (NT), Summary: See Kingdom (OT) (Gen. 1:26–28; Zech. 12:8, *note*). Kingdom truth is developed in the NT in the following order: (1) The promise of the kingdom to David and his descendants, and described in the prophets (2 Sam. 7:8–17, and *notes;* Zech. 12:8), enters the NT absolutely unchanged (Lk. 1:31–33). The King was born in Bethlehem (Mt. 2:1; cp. Mic. 5:2) of a virgin (Mt. 1:18–25; cp. Isa. 7:14). (2) The kingdom announced as "at hand" (Mt. 4:17, *note 4*) by John the Baptist, by the King, and by the twelve, was rejected by the Jews, first morally (Mt. 11:20, *note*), and afterward officially (Mt. 21:42–43), and the King, crowned with thorns, was crucified. (3) In anticipation of His official rejection and crucifixion, the King revealed the "mysteries" of the kingdom of heaven (Mt. 13:11, *note*) to be fulfilled in the interval between His rejection and His return in glory (Mt. 13:1–50). (4) Afterward He announced His purpose to "build" His Church (Mt. 16:18, *marg.* and notes; cp. Eph. 3:9–11), another "mystery" which is being fulfilled in this present age contemporaneously with "the mysteries of the kingdom of heaven." The "mysteries of the kingdom of heaven" and the "mystery" of the Church (Eph. 3:9–11) occupy for the most part the same period, i.e. this present age. (5) The mysteries of the kingdom will be brought to an end by the "harvest" (Mt. 13:39–43,49–50) at the return of the King in glory, the Church having previously been caught up to meet Him in the air (1 Th. 4:13–17). (6) Upon His return the King will restore the Davidic monarchy in His own Person, regather dispersed Israel, establish His power over all the earth, and reign 1000 years (Mt. 24:27–30; Acts 15:14–17; Rev. 20:1–10). And (7) the kingdom of heaven (Mt. 3:2, *note*), thus established under David's divine Son, has for its object the restoration of the divine authority in the earth, which may be regarded as a revolted province of the great kingdom of God (Mt. 6:33, *note*). The Kingdom Age of 1000 years constitutes the seventh dispensation (Rev. 20:4, *note*). When Christ defeats the last enemy, death (vv. 24–26), then He will deliver up the kingdom to "God the Father," that "God [i.e. the triune God—Father, Son, and Holy Spirit] may be all in all" (v. 28). The eternal throne is that "of God and of the Lamb" (Rev. 22:1).

[2](15:29) Paul is not here speaking of baptizing living believers in place of either believers or unbelievers who have died. There is no assignment of saving efficacy to baptism. The argument is: Of what value is it for one to trust Christ and be baptized in the ranks left vacant by the believing dead, if there is no resurrection for believers? Why place life in jeopardy and forfeit the benefits of this life, if there is no life after death?

39 All flesh *is* not the same
flesh, but *there is* one *kind of*
flesh* of men, another flesh of
animals, another of fish, *and* another of birds.
40 *There are* also celestial
bodies and terrestrial bodies;
but the glory of the celestial *is*
one, and the *glory* of the terrestrial *is* another.
41 *There is* one glory of the
sun, another glory of the moon,
and another glory of the stars;
for *one* star differs from *an-*
other star in glory.
42 So also *is* the [a]resurrec-
tion of the dead. *The body* is
sown in corruption, it is raised
in incorruption.
43 It is sown in dishonor, it is
raised in glory. It is sown in
weakness, it is [b]raised in
power.
44 It is sown a natural body,
it is raised a [c]spiritual body.
There is a natural body, and
there is a [c]spiritual body.
45 And so it is [d]written,
[e]*"The first man Adam became a*
living being." The last Adam *be-*
came a [f]life-giving spirit.
46 However, the [c]spiritual is
not first, but the natural, and afterward the [c]spiritual.
47 The first man *was* of the
earth, *made* of dust; the second
Man *is* the Lord* from heaven.
48 As *was* the *man* of dust, so
also *are* those *who are made* of
dust; and as *is* the [c]heavenly
Man, so also *are* those *who are*
[c]heavenly.
49 And as we have borne the
[g]image of the *man* of dust, we
shall also bear* the [h]image of
the [c]heavenly *Man*.
50 Now this I say, brethren,
that flesh and blood cannot inherit the [i]kingdom of God; nor
does corruption inherit incorruption.

(6) Mystery of the resurrection
(cp. 1 Th. 4:14–17)

51 Behold, I tell you a [j]mys-
tery: We shall not all [k]sleep, but
we shall all be changed—
52 in a moment, in the twinkling of an eye, at the last trumpet. For the trumpet will sound,
and the dead will be [1][l]raised incorruptible, and we shall be
[l]changed.
53 For this corruptible must
put on [m]incorruption, and this
mortal *must* put on [n]immortal-
ity.

42
a Resurrection: vv. 35–54; 2 Cor. 1:9. (2 Ki. 4:35; 1 Cor. 15:52, *note*)
43
b Cp. Phil. 3:21
44
c Cp. Jn. 3:6; Phil. 3:21
45
d Inspiration: v. 45; 1 Cor. 15:54. (Ex. 4:15; 2 Tim. 3:16, *note*)
e Gen. 2:7
f Cp. Jn. 5:21; Rom. 8:11
49
g Gen. 5:3
h Rom. 8:29
50
i See Mt. 6:33, *note*
51
j See Mt. 13:11, *note*
k Job 14:12; Ps. 13:3; cp. Jn. 11:12
52
l Cp. 1 Jn. 3:2
53
m Cp. 2 Tim. 1:10
n Cp. 2 Cor. 5:4

*
15:39 NU-Text and M-Text omit *of flesh.*
15:47 NU-Text omits *the Lord.*
15:49 M-Text reads *let us also bear.*

[1](15:52) Resurrection, Summary: (1) The resurrection of the dead was believed by the patriarchs (cp. Gen. 22:5 with Heb. 11:19; Job 19:25–27) and revealed through the prophets (Isa. 26:19; Dan. 12:2,13; Hos. 13:14), and miracles of the dead restored to life are recorded in the OT (2 Ki. 4:32–35; 13:21). (2) Jesus Christ restored life to the dead (Mt. 9:25; Lk. 7:12–15; Jn. 11:43–44), and predicted His own resurrection (Jn. 10:18; Lk. 24:1–8). (3) A resurrection of bodies followed the resurrection of Christ (Mt. 27:52–53), and the apostles raised the dead (Acts 9:36–41; 20:9–10). (4) Two resurrections are yet future, which are inclusive of "all who are in the graves" (Jn. 5:28). These are distinguished as the "first resurrection," which is one of life (Jn. 5:28–29; 1 Cor. 15:22–23; 1 Th. 4:14–17; Rev. 20:4–6), and a second resurrection, which is one of condemnation, i.e. judgment (Jn. 5:28–29; Rev. 20:5–6,11–13). They are separated by a period of 1000 years (Rev. 20:5). The "first resurrection," that pertaining to life, will occur at the second coming of Christ (1 Cor. 15:23), the believers of the Church Age meeting Him in the air (1 Th. 4:16–17), and the martyrs of the tribulation period being raised at the close of the tribulation, when Christ returns to earth to inaugurate the millennium. Old Testament believers will likewise share in the first resurrection. Some hold that these will be raised with the Church (1 Th 4:16–17; 1 Cor. 15:51–53), prior to the tribulation; others hold that it is more harmonious with the OT Scriptures to include the OT believers with those who rise after the tribulation (Rev. 20:4–6), because both Isaiah and Daniel mention the resurrection of OT saints as taking place following a time of great trouble (Isa. 26:16–21; Dan. 12:1–3). (5) The mortal body will be related to the resurrection body as grain sown is related to the harvest (1 Cor. 15:37–38); the resurrection body will be incorruptible, glorious, powerful, and spiritual (1 Cor. 15:42–44,49). (6) The bodies of living believers will, at the same time, be instantaneously changed (1 Cor. 15:50–53; Phil. 3:20–21). This change of the living, and resurrection of the dead in Christ, is called the "redemption of our body" (Rom. 8:23; cp. Eph. 1:13–14). And (7) after the 1000 years the resurrection leading to judgment (Jn. 5:29) will occur. The resurrection body of the wicked dead is not described. They will be judged according to their works, and will be cast into the lake of fire (Rev. 20:7–15).

(The believers' ultimate victory
over death is a motive for
faithful service)

54 So when this corruptible
has put on [a]incorruption, and
this mortal has put on [b]immor-
tality, then shall be brought to
pass the [c]saying that is [d]writ-
ten: [e]*"Death is swallowed up in*
victory."
55 *"O* [e]*Death, where is your*
sting?
[f]*O Hades, where is your*
*victory?"**
56 The sting of [e]death *is*
[g]sin, and the [h]strength of sin *is*
the [i]law.
57 But thanks *be* to God, who
gives us the [j]victory through
our Lord Jesus Christ.

(7) Practical value
of the resurrection

58 [k]Therefore, my beloved
brethren, be steadfast, immovable, always abounding in the
work of the Lord, knowing that
your labor is not in vain in the
Lord.

Conclusion: Instructions and
Personal Greetings, 16

16 NOW concerning the
[l]collection for the saints,
as I have given orders to the
[m]churches of Galatia, so you
must do also:
2 On the [1n]first *day* of the
week let each one of you lay
something aside, storing up as
he may prosper, that there be no
[o]collections when I come.
3 And when I come, whom-
ever you approve by *your* letters
I will send to bear your gift to
Jerusalem.
4 But if it is fitting that I go
also, they will go with me.
5 Now I will [p]come to you
when I pass through [q]Macedo-
nia (for I am passing through
Macedonia).
6 And it may be that I will
remain, or even spend the winter with you, that you may send
me on my journey, wherever I
go.
7 For I do not wish to see
you now on the way; but I hope
to stay a while with you, [r]if the
Lord permits.
8 But I will tarry in Ephesus
until [s]Pentecost.
9 For a great and effective
door has opened to me, and
there are many [t]adversaries.
10 And if [u]Timothy comes,
see that he may be with you
without fear; for he [v]does the
work of the Lord, as I also *do.*
11 Therefore let no one [w]de-
spise him. But send him on his
journey in peace, that he may
come to me; for I am waiting for
him with the brethren.
12 Now concerning *our*
brother [x]Apollos, I strongly
urged him to come to you with
the brethren, but he was quite
unwilling to come at this time;
however, he will come when he
has a convenient time.
13 [y]Watch, [z]stand fast in the
faith, be brave, be strong.
14 Let all *that* you *do* be done
with [aa]love.
15 I urge you, brethren—you
know the household of [bb]Steph-
anas, that it is the firstfruits of
Achaia, and *that* they have devoted themselves to the ministry of the saints—
16 that you also [cc]submit to
such, and to everyone who
works and labors with *us.*
17 I am glad about the [dd]com-
ing of Stephanas, Fortunatus,
and Achaicus, for what was
lacking on your part they [ee]sup-
plied.
18 For they refreshed my
spirit and yours. Therefore acknowledge such men.
19 The [m]churches of Asia
greet you. Aquila and [ff]Priscilla
greet you heartily in the Lord,
with the [m]church that is in their
[gg]house.
20 All the brethren greet you.
Greet one another with a holy
[hh]kiss.
21 The salutation with my
own hand—Paul's.

54 *a* Cp. 2 Tim. 1:10 *b* Cp. 2 Cor. 5:4 *c* Isa. 25:8 *d* *Inspiration:* v. 54; 2 Cor. 2:3. (Ex. 4:15; 2 Tim. 3:16, *note*) *e* *Death* (physical): vv. 54–56; 2 Cor. 5:1. (Gen. 2:17; Heb. 9:27, *note*)
55 *f* Cp. Hos. 13:14
56 *g* See Rom. 3:23, *note* *h* Cp. Rom. 5:20; 7:13 *i* *Law* (of Moses): v. 56; 2 Cor. 3:7. (Ex. 19:1; Gal. 3:24, *note*)
57 *j* 2 Cor. 2:14; cp. 1 Jn. 5:4
58 *k* Cp. 2 Pet. 3:14

CHAPTER 16
1 *l* Cp. 2 Cor. 8:1–9:5 *m* *Churches* (local): vv. 1,19; 2 Cor. 1:1. (Acts 8:3; Phil. 1:1, *note*)
2 *n* Cp. Acts 20:7 *o* See 2 Cor. 8:1, *note*
5 *p* 2 Cor. 1:15 *q* Acts 19:21–22
7 *r* Jas. 4:15
8 *s* Lev. 23:15–22
9 *t* Cp. Phil. 3:18
10 *u* 2 Tim. 1:2 *v* Cp. Phil. 2:19–22
11 *w* 1 Tim. 4:12; cp. Lk. 10:16; 1 Th. 4:8
12 *x* See Acts 18:24, *note*
13 *y* Cp. 1 Pet. 5:8 *z* Cp. 2 Th. 2:15
14 *aa* *Law* (of Christ): v. 14; 2 Cor. 2:4. (Jn. 13:34; 2 Jn. 5)
15 *bb* 1 Cor. 1:16
16 *cc* Eph. 5:21
17 *dd* Gk. *parousia,* meaning *personal presence* *ee* Cp. Phil. 2:30
19 *ff* Acts 18:2, 18,26; Rom. 16:3; 1 Cor. 16:19; 2 Tim. 4:19 *gg* Cp. Col. 4:15
20 *hh* Cp. Rom. 16:16; 2 Cor. 13:12; 1 Th. 5:26; 1 Pet. 5:14

*
15:55 NU-Text reads *O Death, where is your victory? O Death, where is your sting?*

[1](16:2) The essential features of Christian giving are stated here: (1) the time of the giving; (2) the regularity of the giving; (3) the participants in giving; (4) the basis of the giving; and (5) the manner of the giving. For further details see 2 Cor. 8—9, with 2 Cor. 8:1, *note.*

23
a Grace: v. 23; 2 Cor. 1:2. (Jn. 1:14; Jn. 1:17, *note*)

22 If anyone does not love
the Lord Jesus Christ, let him be
accursed.* O Lord, come!*
23 The [a]grace of our Lord Jesus Christ *be* with you.
24 My love *be* with you all in
Christ Jesus. Amen.

*16:22 Greek *anathema* • Aramaic *Maranatha*

The Second Epistle of Paul the Apostle to the

CORINTHIANS

Author: Paul *Theme:* Paul's Authority *Date of writing:* C. A.D. 57

THE SECOND EPISTLE TO THE CORINTHIANS was written within a year of the first letter to the same church. Paul's spiritual burden was great; for, in addition to the problems with which the apostle had to deal in his first letter, a wave of distrust in relation to Paul himself had now swept through the church. Some said he was not sincere; others even questioned whether he had apostolic authority. Consequently, Paul here defends his authority by placing before the church the overwhelming evidence of his sincerity in serving God. Thus this Epistle is very personal and autobiographical.

Here, then, is an unusual accumulation of words expressing suffering of mind, heart, and body: "affliction," "anguish," "beaten," "conflicts," "distresses," "fastings," "labors," "perils," "sorrow," "stripes," "suffered," "sufferings," "tears," "tumults," "weak," and "weakness." At the same time the words "comfort" and "comforted" are found here more frequently than in other Pauline writings; also such words as "joy," "rejoicing," and "triumph" are prominent. No other Christian could match the sufferings and achievements recorded in chs. 10—12.

The Epistle may be divided as follows:

Introduction, 1:1–11.
I. Paul's Principles of Action in His Ministry, 1:12—7:16.
II. Concerning the Collection for the Poor at Jerusalem, 8:1—9:15.
III. Paul's Defense of His Apostolic Authority, 10:1—13:10.
Conclusion, 13:11–14.

Introduction, 1:1–11

1 PAUL, an [a]apostle of Jesus
Christ by the will of God,
and [b]Timothy *our* brother,

To the [c]church of God
which is at Corinth, with all the
[d]saints who are in all Achaia:

2 [e]Grace to you and peace
from God our Father and the
Lord Jesus Christ.

3 Blessed *be* the God and
Father of our Lord Jesus Christ,
the Father of mercies and God
of all comfort,
4 who [f]comforts us in all
our tribulation, that we may be
able to comfort those who are in
any trouble, with the comfort
with which we ourselves are
comforted by God.
5 For as the [g]sufferings of
Christ abound in us, so our consolation
also abounds through
Christ.
6 Now if we are afflicted, [1]*it
is* for your consolation and [h]salvation,
which is effective for enduring
the same sufferings
which we also suffer. Or if we
are comforted, *it is* for your consolation
and [h]salvation.
7 And our hope for you *is*
steadfast, because we know
that [i]as you are partakers of the
sufferings, so also *you will partake*
of the consolation.
8 For we do not want you to
be ignorant, [j]brethren, of our
[k]trouble which came to us in
Asia: that we were burdened
beyond measure, above
strength, so that we despaired
even of life.
9 Yes, we had the [l]sentence
of death in ourselves, that we
should not [m]trust in ourselves
but in God who [n]raises the
dead,
10 who delivered us from so
great a [o]death, and does* deliver
us; in whom we [p]trust that
He will still deliver *us*,
11 you also helping together
in prayer for us, that thanks
may be given by many persons
on our* behalf for the gift
granted to us through many.

I. Paul's Principles of Action in His Ministry, 1:12—7:16

12 For our boasting is this:
the [q]testimony of our conscience
that we conducted our-

*1:10 NU-Text reads *shall.* 1:11 M-Text reads *your behalf.*

CHAPTER 1
1
a Acts 9:15; 22:21; Rom. 11:13; Gal. 1:16; 2:7–9; Eph. 3:8
b 1 Cor. 16:10
c Churches (local): v. 1; 2 Cor. 8:1. (Acts 8:3; Phil. 1:1, *note*)
d Cp. Rom. 1:7; 8:27; 12:13; 15:25; 16:2
2
e Grace: v. 2; 2 Cor. 1:12. (Jn. 1:14; Jn. 1:17, *note*). See 2 Pet. 3:18, *note*
4
f Isa. 51:12; 66:13
5
g 2 Cor. 4:10; Phil. 3:10; Col. 1:24
6
h See Rom. 1:16, *note*
7
i Rom. 8:17
8
j Mt. 23:8; Lk. 8:21; Jn. 21:23; Rom. 8:29; 15:14; Heb. 2:11,17; Rev. 12:10; 19:10
k Acts 19:23–41
9
l Cp. Mt. 27:24–26
m Cp. Jer. 17:5
n Resurrection: v. 9; 2 Cor. 4:14. (2 Ki. 4:35; 1 Cor. 15:52, *note*)
10
o Cp. 1 Sam. 7:12; Job 5:19–22; Ps. 34:19,22; 2 Pet. 2:9
p Or *hope.* Jer. 17:7; 1 Tim. 4:10
12
q Cp. Acts 24:16

---

[1](1:6) What Paul and Timothy suffered for the sake of the Lord Jesus, and the encouragement that they received, were intended to encourage others also to suffer for Christ's sake.

selves in the [a]world in simplicity and godly [b]sincerity, not with fleshly [c]wisdom but by the [d]grace of God, and more abundantly toward you.

13 For we are not writing any other things to you than what you read or understand. Now I [e]trust you will understand, even to the end

14 (as also you have understood us in part), that we are your boast as you also *are* ours, in the [f]day of the Lord Jesus.

Paul explains his delay

15 And in this confidence I intended to come to you before, that you might have a second benefit—

16 to [g]pass by way of you to Macedonia, to come again from Macedonia to you, and be helped by you on my way to Judea.

17 Therefore, when I was planning this, did I do it lightly? Or the things I plan, do I plan according to the [h]flesh, that with me there should be Yes, Yes, and No, No?

18 But *as* God *is* [i]faithful, our word to you was not Yes and No.

19 For the [j]Son of God, Jesus Christ, who was [k]preached among you by us—by me, [l]Silvanus, and [m]Timothy—was not Yes and No, but in Him was Yes.

20 For all the [n]promises of God in Him *are* Yes, and in Him [o]Amen, to the glory of God through us.

21 Now He who establishes us with you in Christ and has [p]anointed us *is* God,

22 who also has [q]sealed us and given us the [r]Spirit in our hearts as a guarantee.

23 Moreover I call God as witness against my soul, that to spare you I came [s]no more to Corinth.

24 Not that we have dominion over your [t]faith, but are fellow workers for your joy; for by [t]faith you stand.

Repentance not to be regretted

2 BUT I determined this within myself, that I would not come again to you in [u]sorrow.

2 For if I make you [v]sorrowful, then who is he who makes me glad but the one who is made sorrowful by me?

3 And I [w]wrote this very thing to you, lest, when I came, I should have sorrow over those from whom I ought to have joy, having confidence in you all that my joy is *the joy* of you all.

4 For out of much affliction and anguish of heart I [w]wrote to you, with many tears, not that you should be grieved, but that you might know the [x]love which I have so abundantly for you.

5 But if anyone has caused grief, he has not grieved me, but all of you to some extent—not to be too severe.

6 This punishment which *was* [y]*inflicted* by the majority *is* sufficient for such a man,

7 so that, on the contrary, you *ought* rather to forgive and comfort *him,* lest perhaps such a one be swallowed up with too much sorrow.

8 Therefore I urge you to reaffirm *your* [x]love to him.

9 For to this end I also [w]wrote, that I might put you to the test, whether you are obedient in all things.

10 Now whom you [z]forgive anything, I also *forgive.* For if indeed I have [z]forgiven anything, I have forgiven* that one for your sakes in the presence of Christ,

11 lest [aa]Satan should take advantage of us; for we are not ignorant of his [bb]devices.

12 Furthermore, when I came to Troas to *preach* Christ's [k]gospel, and a [cc]door was opened to me [dd]by the Lord,

13 I had no rest in my spirit, because I did not find [ee]Titus my brother; but taking my leave of them, I departed for Macedonia.

New covenant ministry:
(1) it is triumphant

14 Now thanks *be* to God who always leads us in triumph in Christ, and through us dif-

---

*2:10 NU-Text reads *indeed, what I have forgiven, if I have forgiven anything, I did it for your sakes.*

12
a Gk. *kosmos.* See Mt. 4:8, *note*
b 2 Cor. 2:17
c Cp. 1 Cor. 1:17
d Grace: v. 12; 2 Cor. 4:15. (Jn. 1:14; Jn. 1:17, *note*). See 2 Pet. 3:18, *note*
13
e Or *hope.* Jer. 17:7; 1 Tim. 4:10
14
f Day (of Christ): v. 14; Phil. 1:6. (1 Cor. 1:8, *note;* 2 Tim. 4:8)
16
g 1 Cor. 16:3–6
17
h Flesh: v. 17; 2 Cor. 5:16. (Jn. 8:15; Jude 23)
18
i 1 Jn. 5:20
19
j Mk. 1:1; Lk. 1:35; Jn. 1:34; 20:31; 1 Jn. 5:5,20
k Gospel: v. 19; 2:12; 2 Cor. 4:2. (Gen. 12:3; Rev. 14:6)
l 1 Th. 1:1; 2 Th. 1:1; 1 Pet. 5:12
m 2 Cor. 1:1
20
n Rom. 15:8–9
o 1 Chr. 16:36; Neh. 8:6; 1 Cor. 14:16; Rev. 5:14; 7:12; cp. Dt. 27:15–26
21
p 1 Jn. 2:20
22
q Eph. 1:13–14
r Holy Spirit (NT): v. 22; 2 Cor. 3:3. (Mt. 1:18; Acts 2:4, *note*)
23
s Cp. 1 Cor. 4:21
24
t Faith: v. 24; 2 Cor. 4:13. (Gen. 3:20; Heb. 11:39, *note*)

CHAPTER 2
1
u Cp. 2 Cor. 12:20–21; 13:10
2
v 2 Cor. 7:8
3
w Inspiration: vv. 3–4,9; 2 Cor. 4:13. (Ex. 4:15; 2 Tim. 3:16, *note*)
4
x Law (of Christ): vv. 4,8; 2 Cor. 5:14. (Jn. 13:34; 2 Jn. 5)
6
y 1 Cor. 5:4–5
10
z Forgiveness: v. 10; Eph. 1:7. (Lev. 4:20; Mt. 26:28, *note*)
11
aa Satan: v. 11; 2 Cor. 4:4. (Gen. 3:1; Rev. 20:10)
bb Cp. 2 Cor. 11:3; Eph. 6:11; 2 Th. 2:9
12
cc Cp. 1 Cor. 16:9
dd Lit. *in*
13
ee 2 Cor. 7:6, 13; 8:6; Ti. 1:4

15
a See Rom. 1:16, *note*
b See Jn. 3:16, *note 3*
16
c *Life* (eternal): v. 16; 3:6; 2 Cor. 4:10. (Mt. 7:14; Rev. 22:19)
d Cp. 2 Cor. 3:5
17
e 2 Cor. 1:12
CHAPTER 3
2
f 1 Cor. 9:2
3
g *Holy Spirit* (NT): vv. 3,6,8; 2 Cor. 3:17. (Mt. 1:18; Acts 2:4, *note*)
h Ex. 24:12
i i.e. *The Ten Commandments*
j Cp. Jer. 31:33; Ezek. 11:19
4
k Or *confidence*
5
l Cp. 1 Cor. 15:10
6
m *Covenant* (New): v. 6; Heb. 8:8.

fuses the fragrance of His
knowledge in every place.
15 For we are to God the fragrance of Christ among those
who are being [a]saved and
among those who are [b]perish-
ing.
16 To the one *we are* the
aroma of death *leading* to death,
and to the other the aroma of
life *leading* to [c]life. And who *is*
[d]sufficient for these things?
17 For we are not, as so
many,* peddling the word of
God; but as of [e]sincerity, but as
from God, we speak in the sight
of God in Christ.

The ministry: (2) accredited

3 DO we begin again to commend ourselves? Or do we
need, as some *others,* epistles of
commendation to you or *letters*
of commendation from you?
2 [f]You are our epistle written in our hearts, known and
read by all men;
3 clearly *you are* an epistle
of Christ, ministered by us,
written not with ink but by the
[g]Spirit of the living God, not
[h]on [i]tablets of stone but on tablets of [j]flesh, *that is,* of the
heart.

4 And we have such [k]trust
through Christ toward God.
5 Not that we are sufficient
of ourselves to think of anything as *being* from ourselves,
but our sufficiency *is* from
[l]God,

The ministry: (3) spiritual and glorious, not legal

6 who also made us suffi-
cient as ministers of the new
[m]covenant, not of the letter but
of the Spirit;* for the [1]letter
kills, but the [g]Spirit [n]gives
[c]life.
7 But if the ministry of
[o]death, written *and* engraved
[p]on [i]stones, [q]was glorious, so
that the [r]children of Israel
could not look steadily at the
face of Moses because of the
glory of his countenance, which
glory was passing away,
8 how will the [s]ministry of
the [g]Spirit not be more glorious?
9 For if the ministry of condemnation *had* glory, the ministry of [t]righteousness exceeds
much more in glory.
10 For even what was made
glorious had no glory in this re-

*
2:17 M-Text reads *the rest.* 3:6 Or *spirit*

(Isa. 61:8; Heb. 8:8, *note*)
n Jn. 6:63
7
o *Death* (spiritual): v. 7; Eph. 2:5. (Gen. 2:17; Eph. 2:5, *note*)
p *Law* (of Moses): v. 7; 2 Cor. 3:15. (Ex. 19:1; Gal. 3:24, *note*)
q Lit. *came with glory*
r *Israel* (history): v. 7; 2 Cor. 3:13. (Gen. 12:2; Rom. 11:26, *note*)
8
s Cp. Gal. 3:3–5
9
t See Rom. 3:21, *note*

[1](3:6) Compare Rom. 2:29; 7:6. "The letter" is a Paulinism for the law, as "spirit" in other passages is his word for the relationships and powers of new life in Christ Jesus. Here in ch. 3 is presented a series of contrasts between law and spirit, between the old covenant and the new. The contrast is not between two methods of interpretation, literal and spiritual, but between two methods of divine dealing: one, through the law; the other, through the Holy Spirit.

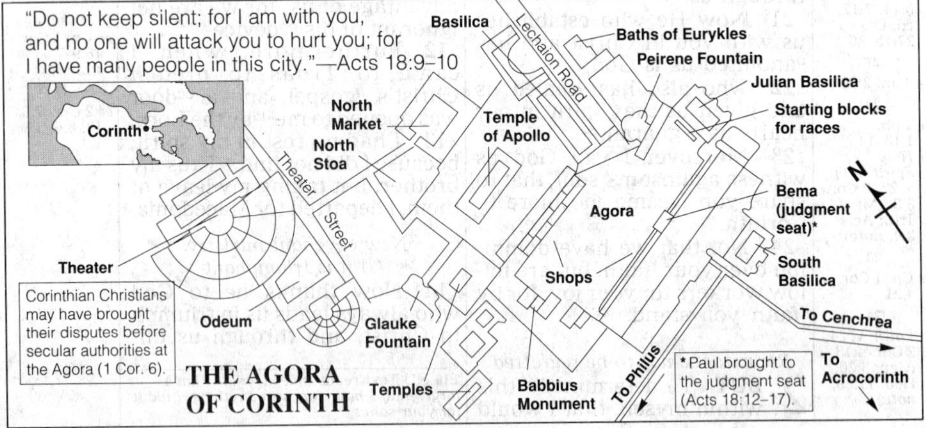

spect, because of the glory that
[a]excels.
11 For if what is [1]passing
away *was* glorious, what remains *is* much more glorious.
12 Therefore, since we have
such hope, we use great boldness of speech—
13 unlike [b]Moses, *who* put a
veil over his face so that the
[c]children of Israel could not
look steadily at the end of what
was passing away.
14 But their minds were
[d]blinded. For until this day the
same veil remains unlifted in
the reading of the Old [e]Testa-
ment, because the *veil* is taken
away in Christ.
15 But even to this day, when
[f]Moses is read, a [g]veil lies on
their heart.
16 Nevertheless [c]when one
turns to the Lord, the veil is
taken away.
17 Now the Lord is the
[h]Spirit; and where the Spirit of
the Lord *is,* there *is* [i]liberty.
18 But we all, with unveiled
face, beholding as in a mirror
the glory of the Lord, are being
[2j]transformed into the same
image from glory to glory, just
as by the [h]Spirit of the Lord.

The ministry: (4) honest,
not deceitful

4 THEREFORE, since we
have this ministry, as we
have received mercy, we do
[k]not lose heart.

(Because the truth taught is
commended by the life)

2 But we have renounced
the hidden things of shame, not
walking in craftiness nor handling the [l]word of God deceitfully, but by manifestation of
the truth commending our-
selves to every man's conscience in the sight of God.

(Because not self but Christ
Jesus as Lord is preached)

3 But even if our [l]gospel is
[m]veiled, it is veiled to those who
are [n]perishing,
4 whose minds [o]the [p]god of
this [q]age has blinded, who do
not believe, lest the light of the
[l]gospel of the glory of Christ,
who is the image of God, should
shine on them.
5 For we do not preach ourselves, but Christ Jesus the
Lord, and ourselves your bondservants for Jesus' sake.
6 For it is the God who
[r]commanded light to shine out
of darkness, who has [s]shone in
our hearts to *give* the light of the
knowledge of the glory of God
in the face of Jesus Christ.

(Because the power is of God
alone; cp. 1 Cor. 2:1–5)

7 But we have this treasure
in earthen vessels, that the excellence of the power may be of
God and not of [t]us.

The ministry: (5) suffering

8 *We are* hard pressed on
every side, yet not crushed; *we*
are perplexed, but not in despair;
9 persecuted, but not [u]for-
saken; struck down, but not
[v]destroyed—
10 always carrying about in
the body the [w]dying of the Lord
Jesus, that the [x]life of Jesus also
may be manifested in our body.
11 For we who live are always delivered to death for Jesus' sake, that the life of Jesus
also may be manifested in our
mortal flesh.
12 So then death is working
in us, but life in you.
13 And since we have the
same spirit of faith, according
to what is [y]written, [z]*"I* [aa]*be-*
lieved and therefore I spoke,"

10
a Or *sur-passes*
13
b Ex. 34:33
c Israel (history): vv. 13–15; (prophecies): v. 16; Rev. 7:4. (Gen. 12:2; Rom. 11:26, *note*)
14
d Rom. 11:7–8
e Or *Covenant*
15
f Law (of Moses): vv. 14–15; Gal. 2:16. (Ex. 19:1; Gal. 3:24, *note*)
g Cp. Isa. 6:9–10
17
h Holy Spirit (NT): vv. 17–18; 2 Cor. 5:5. (Mt. 1:18; Acts 2:4, *note*)
i Gal. 5:1,13; cp. Isa. 61:1
18
j Rom. 8:29–30
CHAPTER 4
1
k 4:16
2
l Gospel: vv. 2–5; 2 Cor. 8:18. (Gen. 12:3; Rev. 14:6)

3
m Cp. 2 Cor. 3:14
n See Jn. 3:16, *note 3*
4
o Satan: v. 4; 2 Cor. 11:3. (Gen. 3:1; Rev. 20:10)
p Jn. 12:31
q Gk. *aiōn.* See Mk. 10:30, *note*
6
r Gen. 1:3
s Cp. 2 Pet. 1:19
7
t Cp. 2 Cor. 3:5
9
u Heb. 13:5; cp. Mt. 28:20
v Cp. Mic. 7:8
10
w Lit. *putting to death.* Cp. 1 Cor. 15:31
x Life (eternal): vv. 10–12; 2 Cor. 5:4. (Mt. 7:14; Rev. 22:19)
13
y Inspiration: v. 13; 2 Cor. 6:2. (Ex. 4:15; 2 Tim. 3:16, *note*)
z Ps. 116:10
aa Faith: v. 13; 2 Cor. 5:7. (Gen. 3:20; Heb. 11:39, *note*)

[1](3:11) God's moral law proceeds from the righteousness of God and can never be abolished. The Mosaic law, as an expression of this moral law is "passing away" in that it has been superseded by another law, i.e. the standards of grace revealed in the NT. The believer is now under law to Christ (1 Cor. 9:21, and *note;* cp. Rom. 8:2–4). Although the Christian is not under the Mosaic law as a rule of life, some of the law of Moses is restated in the NT, i.e. nine of the Ten Commandments are included. The Mosaic law still constitutes a revelation of the righteousness of God and remains as a part of Scripture which "is profitable for doctrine, for reproof, for correction, for instruction in righteousness, that the man of God may be complete, thoroughly equipped for every good work" (2 Tim. 3:16–17; cp. Rom. 15:4).

[2](3:18) "Transformed." In the Greek the same word (*metamorphoō*) is rendered "transfigured" in Mt. 17:2; Mk. 9:2.

we also believe and therefore
speak,
14 knowing that He who
[a]raised up the Lord Jesus will
also [a]raise us up with Jesus,
and will present *us* with you.
15 For all things *are* for your
sakes, that [b]grace, having
spread through the many, may
cause thanksgiving to abound
to the glory of God.
16 Therefore we do [c]not lose
heart. Even though our outward
man is perishing, yet the [d]in-
ward *man* is being [e]renewed
day by day.
17 For our [f]light affliction,
which is but for a moment, is
working for us a far more exceeding *and* eternal weight of
glory,
18 while we do not look at the
things which are seen, but at the
things which are [g]not seen. For
the things which are seen *are*
temporary, but the things which
are not seen *are* eternal.

The ministry: (6) its ambition (v. 9)

5 FOR we know that if our
earthly house, *this* tent, is
[h]destroyed, we have a building
from God, a house [i]not made
with hands, eternal in the heavens.
2 For in this we groan, earnestly desiring to be clothed
with our habitation which is
from heaven,
3 if indeed, having been
clothed, we shall not be found
naked.
4 For we who are in *this* tent
groan, being burdened, not because we want to be unclothed,
but further clothed, that mortality may be swallowed up by
[j]life.
5 Now He who has prepared
us for this very thing *is* God,
who also has given us the
[k]Spirit as a guarantee.
6 So *we are* always confident, knowing that while we are
at home in the body we are absent from the Lord.
7 For we walk by [l]faith, not
by sight.
8 We are confident, yes,
well pleased rather to be [h]ab-
sent from the body and to be
present with the Lord.
9 Therefore we make it our
aim, whether present or absent,
to be well pleasing to Him.
10 [1]For we must all appear
before the [m]judgment seat of
Christ, that each one may receive the things *done* in the
body, according to what he has
done, whether [n]good or bad.

The ministry: (7) its moving motives

11 Knowing, therefore, the
[o]terror of the Lord, we persuade men; but we are well
known to God, and I also [p]trust
are well known in your con-
sciences.
12 For we do not commend
ourselves again to you, but give
you opportunity to boast on our
behalf, that you may have *an*
answer for those who boast in
appearance and not in heart.
13 For if we are beside ourselves, *it is* for God; or if we are
of sound mind, *it is* for you.
14 For the [q]love of Christ
compels us, because we judge
thus: that if One [r]died for all,
[2]then all died;
15 and He [r]died for all, that
those who live should live no
longer for themselves, but for
Him who died for them and
[a]rose again.
16 Therefore, from now on,
we regard no one according to
the [s]flesh. Even though we
have known Christ [t]according
to the flesh, yet now we know
Him thus no longer.
17 Therefore, if anyone *is* in
Christ, *he is* a new creation; old
things have passed away; be-

14
a *Resurrection:* v. 14; 5:15; 2 Cor. 13:4. (2 Ki. 4:35; 1 Cor. 15:52, *note*)
15
b *Grace:* v. 15; 2 Cor. 6:1. (Jn. 1:14; Jn. 1:17, *note*). See 2 Pet. 3:18, *note*
16
c 4:1; Gal. 6:9; cp. Rev. 2:3
d Cp. Job 32:8
e Col. 3:10; cp. Isa. 40:31
17
f Cp. Rom. 8:18
18
g Heb. 11:1; cp. 2 Cor. 5:7
CHAPTER 5
1
h *Death* (physical): vv. 1,8; 2 Cor. 7:10. (Gen. 2:17; Heb. 9:27, *note*)
i Mk. 14:58
4
j *Life* (eternal): v. 4; Gal. 2:20. (Mt. 7:14; Rev. 22:19)
5
k *Holy Spirit* (NT): v. 5; 2 Cor. 6:6. (Mt. 1:18; Acts 2:4, *note*)

7
l *Faith:* v. 7; 2 Cor. 6:15. (Gen. 3:20; Heb. 11:39, *note*)
10
m *Judgments* (the seven): v. 10; 2 Cor. 13:5. (1 Sam. 7:14; Rev. 20:12, *note*)
n *Rewards:* v. 10; Eph. 6:8. (Dan. 12:3; 1 Cor. 3:14, *note*)
11
o Or *fear.* Cp. Mt. 10:28
p Or *hope*
14
q *Law* (of Christ): v. 14; 2 Cor. 6:6. (Jn. 13:34; 2 Jn. 5)
r *Sacrifice* (of Christ): vv. 14–15; 2 Cor. 5:18. (Gen. 3:15; Heb. 10:18, *note*)
16
s *Flesh:* v. 16; 2 Cor. 7:1. (Jn. 8:15; Jude 23)
t i.e. *from the human viewpoint*

---

[1](5:10) The judgment of the believer's works, not sins, is under discussion here. His sins have been atoned for and are remembered no more forever (Heb. 10:17); but every work must come into judgment (Mt. 12:36; Rom. 14:10; Gal. 6:7; Eph. 6:8; Col. 3:24–25). The result is reward or loss of the reward, but "he himself [the Christian] shall be saved" (1 Cor. 3:11–15). This judgment occurs at the return of Christ for His Church (1 Cor. 4:5; 2 Tim. 4:8; Rev. 22:12). For other judgments, see *notes* at Ezek. 20:37; Mt. 25:32; Jn. 12:31; 1 Cor. 11:31; Jude 6; Rev. 20:12.

[2](5:14) All believers are regarded by God as having died with Christ (Rom. 6:6). We must, therefore, count upon this as being so, and live accordingly (see Rom. 6:11, *note*).

hold, all things have become
[a]new.
18 Now all things *are* of God,
who has [b]reconciled us to Himself [c]through Jesus Christ, and
has given us the ministry of
[b]reconciliation,
19 that is, that God was in
Christ [b]reconciling the [d]world
to Himself, not [e]imputing their
[f]trespasses to them, and has
committed to us the word of
[b]reconciliation.
20 Now then, we are [g]ambas-
sadors for Christ, as though
God were pleading through us:
we implore *you* on Christ's behalf, be [b]reconciled to God.
21 For He [c]made Him who
knew no sin *to be* [f]sin for us,
that we might become the
[h]righteousness of God in Him.

The ministry: (8) supernatural

6 WE then, *as* workers together *with Him* also plead
with *you* not to receive the
[i]grace of God in vain.
2 For He [j]says:

[k]"*In an acceptable time I*
have heard you,
And in the day of
[l]*salvation I have*
helped you."

Behold, now *is* the accepted
time; behold, now *is* the day of
salvation.
3 We give no offense in anything, that our ministry may not
be blamed.
4 But in all *things* we commend ourselves as [m]ministers of
God: in much patience, in tribulations, in needs, in distresses,
5 in stripes, in imprisonments, in tumults, in labors, in
sleeplessness, in fastings;
6 by purity, by knowledge,
by longsuffering, by kindness,
by the Holy [n]Spirit, by sincere
[o]love,
7 by the word of truth, by
the power of God, by the armor
of [p]righteousness on the right
hand and on the left,
8 by honor and dishonor, by
evil report and good report; as
deceivers, and *yet* true;
9 as unknown, and *yet* well
known; as [q]dying, and behold
we live; as chastened, and *yet*
not killed;
10 as sorrowful, yet always
rejoicing; as poor, yet making
many [r]rich; as having nothing,
and *yet* possessing all things.

Appeal to separation
and cleansing

11 O Corinthians! We have
spoken openly to you, our heart
is wide open.
12 You are not restricted by
us, but you are restricted by
your *own* affections.
13 Now in return for the
same (I speak as to children),
you also be open.
14 Do not be [s]unequally
yoked together with unbelievers. For what fellowship has
[t]righteousness with [u]lawless-
ness? And what communion
has light with darkness?
15 And what accord has
Christ with Belial? Or what part
has a [v]believer with an unbeliever?
16 And what agreement has
the [w]temple of God with idols?
For you* are the [x]temple of the
living God. As God has [j]said:

[y]"*I will dwell in them*
And walk among them.
[z]*I will be their God,*
And they shall be My
people."*

17 Therefore

[aa]"*Come out from among*
them
And be [1bb]*separate,* [j]*says*
the Lord.

*6:16 NU-Text reads *we.* • Jeremiah 32:38

17
a Rom. 6:3–10; Col. 3:3
18
b Reconciliation: vv. 18–20; Eph. 2:16. (Rom. 5:10; Col. 1:20)
c Sacrifice (of Christ): vv. 18–19, 21; 2 Cor. 13:4. (Gen. 3:15; Heb. 10:18, *note*)
19
d Gk. *kosmos.* See Mt. 4:8, *note*
e See Phile. 18, *note*
f See Rom. 3:23, *note*
20
g Eph. 6:20
21
h 1 Cor. 1:30; see Rom. 3:21, *note*
CHAPTER 6
1
i Grace: v. 1; 2 Cor. 8:1. (Jn. 1:14; Jn. 1:17, *note*). See 2 Pet. 3:18, *note*
2
j Inspiration: vv. 2, 16–17; 2 Cor. 6:18. (Ex. 4:15; 2 Tim. 3:16, *note*)
k Isa. 49:8
l See Rom. 1:16, *note*
4
m 1 Cor. 4:1
6
n Holy Spirit (NT): v. 6; 2 Cor. 13:14. (Mt. 1:18; Acts 2:4, *note*)
o Law (of Christ): v. 6; 2 Cor. 8:8. (Jn. 13:34; 2 Jn. 5)

7
p See 1 Jn. 3:7, *note*
9
q 2 Cor. 4:11
10
r 2 Cor. 8:9
14
s Eph. 5:6–7; cp. Dt. 7:2–3; 1 Jn. 1:6
t See Rom. 10:10, *note*
u Rom. 1:18; 6:13; 2 Th. 2:10; 2 Pet. 2:13; 1 Jn. 5:17
15
v Faith: v. 15; 2 Cor. 8:7. (Gen. 3:20; Heb. 11:39, *note*)
16
w Gk. *naos,* the sanctuary itself
x 1 Cor. 3:16–17; 6:19
y Ezek. 37:26–27
z Lev. 26:12; Jer. 31:33; Zech. 8:8
17
aa Num. 33:51–56; Isa. 52:11
bb Separation: vv. 14–17; 1 Tim. 6:11. (Gen. 12:1; 2 Cor. 6:17, *note*)

[1](6:17) Separation, Summary: (1) Separation in Scripture is twofold: (a) *from* whatever is contrary to the mind of God; and (b) *to* God Himself. The underlying principle is that in a moral universe it is impossible for God fully to bless and use His children who are in compromise or complicity with evil. (2) Separation from evil implies (a) separation in desire, motive, and act, from the world, in the ethically bad sense of this present world system (see Rev. 13:8, *note*); and (b) separation from false teachers, who are described as being "vessels . . . for dishonor" (2 Tim. 2:20–21; 2 Jn. 9–11). (3) Separation is not from contact with evil in the world or the church, but from complicity with and conformity to it (vv. 14–18; cp. Jn. 17:15; Gal. 6:1). And (4) the reward of separation is the full manifestation of the divine fatherhood (vv. 17–18);

Do not touch what is
unclean,
*And I will receive you."**
18 *"I will [a]be a Father to*
you,
And you shall be My
[b]sons and daughters,
[c]Says the LORD
*Almighty."**

7 THEREFORE, having these [c]promises, beloved, let us cleanse ourselves from all filthiness of the [d]flesh and spirit, [e]perfecting [f]holiness in the fear of God.

The heart of Paul

2 Open *your hearts* to us. We have wronged no one, we have corrupted no one, we have cheated no one.

3 I do not say *this* to condemn; for I have said before that you are in our hearts, to die together and to live together.

4 Great *is* my boldness of speech toward you, great *is* my boasting on your behalf. I am filled with comfort. I am exceedingly joyful in all our tribulation.

5 For indeed, when we came to Macedonia, our bodies had no rest, but we were troubled on every side. Outside *were* conflicts, inside *were* fears.

6 Nevertheless God, who [g]comforts the downcast, comforted us by the coming of [h]Titus,

7 and not only by his coming, but also by the consolation with which he was comforted in you, when he told us of your earnest desire, your mourning, your zeal for me, so that I rejoiced even more.

8 For even if I made you [i]sorry with my letter, I do not regret it; though I did regret it. For I perceive that the same epistle made you sorry, though only for a while.

9 Now I rejoice, not that you were made sorry, but that your sorrow led to [j]repentance. For you were made sorry in a godly manner, that you might suffer loss from us in nothing.

10 For godly [k]sorrow produces [j]repentance *leading* to [l]salvation, not to be regretted; but the sorrow of the [m]world produces [n]death.

11 For observe this very thing, that you sorrowed in a godly manner: What diligence it produced in you, *what* [o]clearing *of yourselves, what* indignation, *what* fear, *what* vehement desire, *what* zeal, *what* vindication! In all *things* you proved yourselves to be [p]clear in this matter.

12 Therefore, although I [c]wrote to you, *I did* not *do it* for the sake of him who had done the wrong, nor for the sake of him who suffered wrong, but that our care for you in the sight of God might appear to you.

13 Therefore we have been comforted in your comfort. And we rejoiced exceedingly more for the joy of Titus, because his spirit has been refreshed by you all.

14 For if in anything I have boasted to him about you, I am not ashamed. But as we spoke all things to you in truth, even so our boasting to Titus was found true.

15 And his [q]affections are greater for you as he remembers the [r]obedience of you all, how with fear and trembling you received him.

16 Therefore I rejoice that I have [s]confidence in you in everything.

II. Concerning the Collection for the Poor at Jerusalem, 8:1—9:15

(1) Example of Macedonia

8 [1]MOREOVER, [t]brethren, we make known to you the

18
a Jer. 31:9
b Jn. 1:12; Rom. 8:14; Gal. 4:5–7; Phil. 2:15; 1 Jn. 3:1
c Inspiration: vv. 16–18; 7:1,12; 2 Cor. 8:15. (Ex. 4:15; 2 Tim. 3:16, *note*)

CHAPTER 7

1
d Flesh: v. 1; 2 Cor. 10:2. (Jn. 8:15; Jude 23)
e See Mt. 5:48, *note*
f Sanctification (NT): v. 1; Eph. 1:4. (Mt. 4:5; Rev. 22:11)

6
g Isa. 49:13; 2 Cor. 1:3
h 2 Cor. 2:13

8
i 2 Cor. 2:2

9
j Repentance: vv. 9–11; 2 Cor. 12:21. (Mt. 3:2; Acts 17:30, *note*)

10
k Ps. 32:10
l See Rom. 1:16, *note*
m Gk. *kosmos.* See Rev. 13:8, *note*
n Death (physical): v. 10; Phil. 1:21. (Gen. 2:17; Heb. 9:27, *note*)

11
o Eph. 5:11
p 2 Cor. 2:5–11

15
q Cp. Jn. 13:35; 15:12; 1 Th. 3:12; 1 Pet. 1:22
r 2 Cor. 2:9

16
s 2 Cor. 2:3; 8:22; cp. 2 Th. 3:4

CHAPTER 8

1
t Mt. 23:8; Lk. 8:21; Jn. 21:23; Rom. 8:29; 15:14; Heb. 2:11,17; Rev. 12:10; 19:10

*
6:17 Ezekiel 20:34,41 6:18 2 Samuel 7:14

unhindered communion and worship (see Heb. 13:13–15), and fruitful service (2 Tim. 2:21), as world conformity involves the loss of these, though not of salvation. Here, as in all else, Christ is the model. He was "holy, harmless, undefiled, separate from sinners" (Heb. 7:26), and yet He was in such contact with them for their salvation that the Pharisees, who illustrate the mechanical and ascetic conception of separation (Mt. 3:7, *note 1*), judged Him as having lost His Nazirite character (Lk. 7:39). Cp. 1 Cor. 9:19–23; 10:27.

1(8:1) In 2 Cor. 8—9, the apostle epitomizes the Christian doctrine of giving. It may be thus

[a]grace of God bestowed on the
[b]churches of Macedonia:
2 that in a great trial of affliction the [c]abundance of their
joy and their deep poverty
abounded in the riches of their
liberality.
3 For I bear witness that according to *their* ability, yes, and
beyond *their* ability, *they were*
freely willing,
4 imploring us with much
urgency that we would receive*
the gift and the fellowship of the
ministering to the [d]saints.
5 And not *only* as we had
hoped, but they first [e]gave
themselves to the Lord, and
then to us by the [f]will of God.
6 So we urged [g]Titus, that
as he had begun, so he would
also complete this [a]grace in you
as well.

(2) Example of Christ

7 But as you abound in
everything—in [h]faith, in
[i]speech, in knowledge, in all
diligence, and in your love for
us—*see* that you [j]abound in
this [a]grace also.
8 I [k]speak not by commandment, but I am testing the sincerity of your [l]love by the diligence of others.
9 For you know the [a]grace
of our Lord Jesus Christ, that
though He was rich, yet for your
sakes He became [m]poor, that
you through His poverty might
become [n]rich.
10 And in this I give advice: It
is to your advantage not only to
be doing what you began and
were [o]desiring to do a year ago;
11 but now you also must
complete the doing *of it;* that as
there was a readiness to [p]desire
it, so *there* also *may be* a completion out of what *you* have.
12 For if there is first a [p]will-
ing mind, *it is* accepted according to what one has, *and* not according to what he does [q]not
have.
13 For *I do* not *mean* that others should be eased and you
burdened;
14 but by an equality, *that*
now at this time your abundance *may supply* their lack,
that their abundance also may
supply your lack—that there
may be [r]equality.
15 As it is [s]written, [t]*"He*
who gathered much had noth-
ing left over, and he who gath-
ered little had no lack."

(3) Trusted representatives

16 But thanks *be* to God who
puts* the same earnest care for
you into the heart of [g]Titus.
17 For he not only accepted
the exhortation, but being more
diligent, he went to you of his
own accord.
18 And we have sent with
him the [u]brother whose praise
is in the [v]gospel throughout all
the [b]churches,
19 and not only *that,* but
who was also chosen by the
[b]churches to travel with us with
this gift, which is administered
by us to the glory of the Lord
Himself and *to show* your ready
mind,
20 avoiding this: that anyone
should blame us in this lavish
gift which is administered by
us—
21 [w]providing honorable
things, not only in the sight of
the Lord, but also in the sight of
men.
22 And we have sent with
them our brother whom we
have often proved diligent in
many things, but now much
more diligent, because of the
great confidence which *we have*
in you.

1
a Grace: vv. 1,6–7,9; 2 Cor. 9:8. (Jn. 1:14; Jn. 1:17, *note*). See 2 Pet. 3:18, *note*
b Churches (local): vv. 1,18–19; 2 Cor. 8:23. (Acts 8:3; Phil. 1:1, *note*)
2
c Cp. Ex. 35:4–5, 20–29; 36:3–7
4
d Cp. Rom. 1:7; 8:27; 12:13; 15:25; 16:2
5
e Rom. 12:1–2
f Eph. 6:6
6
g 2 Cor. 12:18
7
h Faith: v. 7; 2 Cor. 10:15. (Gen. 3:20; Heb. 11:39, *note*)
i 1 Cor. 1:5
j 2 Cor. 9:8
8
k Cp. 1 Cor. 7:6
l Law (of Christ): v. 8; 2 Cor. 8:24. (Jn. 13:34; 2 Jn. 5)
9
m Cp. Lk. 9:58; Phil. 2:6–7
n Rom. 9:23; Eph. 1:7; Rev. 3:18
10
o 2 Cor. 9:2
11
p See v. 1, *note*
12
q Cp. Prov. 3:27; Mk. 12:41–44
14
r Cp. Acts 4:32–37
15
s Inspiration: v. 15; 2 Cor. 9:9. (Ex. 4:15; 2 Tim. 3:16, *note*)
t Ex. 16:18
18
u 2 Cor. 12:18; cp. Mt. 12:50; Acts 9:17; 21:20
v Gospel: v. 18; 2 Cor. 9:13. (Gen. 12:3; Rev. 14:6)
21
w Cp. Prov. 3:4; 1 Pet. 2:12

*
8:4 NU-Text and M-Text omit *that we would receive,* thus changing text to *urgency for the favor and fellowship . . . .*
8:16 NU-Text reads *has put.*

summarized: (1) It is a "grace," i.e. a disposition created by the Spirit (8:7). (2) In contrast with the law, which imposed giving as a divine requirement, Christian giving is voluntary, and a test of sincerity and love (8:8–12; 9:1–2,5,7). (3) The privilege is universal, belonging, according to ability, to rich and poor (8:1–3,12–15. Cp. 1 Cor. 16:1–2). (4) Giving is to be proportioned to income (8:12–14; cp. 1 Cor. 16:2). The OT proportion was the tithe, a proportion which antedates the law (Gen. 14:20), as well as numerous stated offerings. And (5) the rewards of Christian giving are (a) joy (8:2); (b) increased ability to give in proportion to that which has been already given (9:7–11); (c) increased thankfulness to God (9:12); and (d) God and the Gospel glorified (9:13–14). See 1 Cor. 16:2, *note.*

23 If *anyone inquires* about [a]Titus, *he is* my partner and fellow worker concerning you. Or if our brethren *are inquired about, they are* [b]messengers of the [c]churches, the glory of Christ.

24 Therefore show to them, and* before the [c]churches the proof of your [d]love and of our [e]boasting on your behalf.

(4) Encouragement: no man can outgive God

9 NOW concerning the [f]ministering to the [g]saints, it is [h]superfluous for me to write to you;

2 for I know your willingness, about which I boast of you to the Macedonians, that Achaia was ready a [i]year ago; and your zeal has stirred up the majority.

3 Yet I have sent the brethren, lest our boasting of you should be in vain in this respect, that, as I said, you may be ready;

4 lest if *some* Macedonians come with me and find you unprepared, we (not to mention you!) should be ashamed of this confident boasting.*

5 Therefore I thought it necessary to exhort the brethren to go to you ahead of time, and prepare your generous gift beforehand, which *you had* previously promised, that it may be ready as *a matter of* generosity and not as a grudging obligation.

6 But this *I say:* He who sows sparingly will also reap sparingly, and he who sows [j]bountifully will also reap bountifully.

7 *So let* each one *give* as he purposes in his heart, [k]not grudgingly or of [l]necessity; for God loves a [m]cheerful giver.

8 And God *is* able to make all [n]grace abound toward you, that you, always having all sufficiency in all *things,* may have an abundance for every good work.

9 As it is [o]written:

[p]*"He has dispersed abroad,*
He has given to the poor;
His [q]righteousness
endures forever."

10 Now may* He who supplies seed to the sower, and bread for food, supply and multiply the seed you have *sown* and [r]increase the fruits of your [q]righteousness,

11 while *you are* [s]enriched in everything for all liberality, which causes thanksgiving through us to God.

12 For the administration of this service not only supplies the needs of the [g]saints, but also is abounding through many thanksgivings to God,

13 while, through the proof of this ministry, they glorify God for the obedience of your confession to the [t]gospel of Christ, and for *your* liberal sharing with them and all *men,*

14 and by their prayer for you, who long for you because of the exceeding [n]grace of God in you.

15 [u]Thanks *be* to God for His indescribable [v]gift!

III. Paul's Defense of His Apostolic Authority (cp. Gal. 1:11—2:21), 10:1—13:10

(1) Divine authentication

10 NOW I, Paul, myself am [w]pleading with you by the meekness and gentleness of Christ—who in [x]presence *am* lowly among you, but being absent am bold toward you.

2 But I [w]beg *you* that when I am present I may not be bold [y]with that confidence by which I intend to be bold against some, who think of us as if we walked according to the [z]flesh.

3 For though we walk in the flesh, we do not war according to the [z]flesh.

4 For the [aa]weapons of our [bb]warfare *are* not [cc]carnal but mighty in God for pulling down strongholds,

5 casting down arguments and every high thing that exalts itself against the knowledge of God, bringing every thought

*
8:24 NU-Text and M-Text omit *and.*
9:4 NU-Text reads *this confidence.*
9:10 NU-Text reads *Now He who supplies . . . will supply . . . .*

23
a v. 16; 2 Cor. 7:13–14
b Cp. Phil. 2:25
c Churches (local): vv. 23–24; 2 Cor. 11:8. (Acts 8:3; Phil. 1:1, *note*)
24
d Law (of Christ): v. 24; 2 Cor. 10:5. (Jn. 13:34; 2 Jn. 5)
e 2 Cor. 7:4, 14
CHAPTER 9
1
f 2 Cor. 8:4
g Cp. Rom. 1:7; 8:27; 12:13; 15:25; 16:2
h Cp. 1 Th. 4:9
2
i 2 Cor. 8:10
6
j Lit. *with blessings.* Prov. 11:24–26; 19:17; 22:9; cp. Gal. 6:7–8
7
k Cp. Dt. 15:7–10; Rom. 12:8
l Cp. 2 Cor. 8:8
m Gk. *hilaros,* whence Eng. *hilarious.* Cp. Ex. 25:2
8
n Grace: vv. 8,14; 2 Cor. 12:9. (Jn. 1:14; Jn. 1:17, *note*). See 2 Pet. 3:18, *note*
9
o Inspiration: v. 9; 2 Cor. 13:2. (Ex. 4:15; 2 Tim. 3:16, *note*)
p Ps. 112:9

q See 1 Jn. 3:7, *note*
10
r Cp. Hos. 10:12; Phil. 1:11
11
s Cp. Prov. 10:22; 13:7; 2 Cor. 8:9; Eph. 1:18; Rev. 2:9
13
t Gospel: v. 13; 2 Cor. 10:14. (Gen. 12:3; Rev. 14:6)
15
u Cp. Ps. 68:19; Dan. 2:23; 1 Cor. 15:57; 1 Th. 5:18
v Jn. 3:16; 4:10; Rom. 6:23; 8:32; Eph. 2:8
CHAPTER 10
1
w Cp. Rom. 12:1
x v. 10
2
y Cp. 1 Cor. 4:21
z Flesh: vv. 2–3; 2 Cor. 11:18. (Jn. 8:15; Jude 23)
4
aa Cp. 1 Sam. 17:45; Rom. 13:12; 2 Cor. 6:7; Eph. 6:11–17; 1 Th. 5:8
bb Cp. Rom. 7:23; 1 Tim. 6:12
cc i.e. *fleshly*

into captivity [a]to the [b]obedi-
ence of Christ,
6 and being ready to punish
all disobedience when your
[c]obedience is fulfilled.
7 Do you look at things according to the [d]outward appearance? If anyone is convinced in himself that he is
Christ's, let him again consider
this in himself, that just as he *is*
Christ's, even so [e]we *are*
Christ's.*
8 For even if I should boast
somewhat more about our [f]au-
thority, which the Lord gave
us* for [g]edification and not for
your destruction, I shall not be
ashamed—
9 lest I seem to terrify you
by letters.
10 "For *his* letters," they say,
"*are* weighty and powerful, but
his bodily presence *is* [h]weak,
and *his* speech [i]contemptible."
11 Let such a person con-
sider this, that what we are in
word by letters when we are absent, such *we will* also *be* in
deed when we are present.
12 For [j]we dare not class
ourselves or compare ourselves
with those who commend themselves. But they, measuring
themselves by themselves, and
comparing themselves among
themselves, are not wise.
13 We, however, will not
boast beyond measure, but
[k]within the limits of the sphere
which God appointed us—a
sphere which especially includes you.
14 For we are not over-
extending ourselves (as though
our authority did not extend to
you), for it was to you that we
came with the [l]gospel of Christ;
15 not boasting of things beyond measure, *that is,* [m]in other
men's labors, but having hope,
that as your [n]faith is increased,
we shall be greatly enlarged by
you in our sphere,
16 to preach the [l]gospel in
the *regions* [o]beyond you, *and*
not to boast in [m]another man's
sphere of accomplishment.
17 But *"he who glories, let*
him [p]*glory in the* LORD."
18 For not he who [q]com-
mends himself is approved, but
whom the Lord commends.

(2) Godly jealousy

11 OH, that you would bear
with me in a little folly—
and indeed you do bear with
me.
2 For I am jealous for you
with godly jealousy. For I have
[1][r]betrothed you to one husband, that I may present [s]*you*
as a chaste virgin to Christ.

(3) Warning against false teachers

3 But I fear, lest somehow,
as the [t]serpent [u]deceived Eve
by his [v]craftiness, so your
minds may be corrupted from
the simplicity* that is in Christ.
4 For if he who comes
preaches [w]another Jesus whom
we have not preached, or *if* you
receive a different spirit which
you have not received, or a different gospel which you have
not accepted—[x]you may well
put up with it!
5 For I consider that I am
not at all [y]inferior to the most
eminent apostles.
6 Even though *I am* [z]un-
trained in speech, yet *I am* not
in [aa]knowledge. But [bb]we have
been thoroughly manifested*
among you in all things.
7 Did I commit [cc]sin in humbling myself that you might be
exalted, because I preached the
[l]gospel of God to you [dd]free of
charge?
8 I robbed other [ee]churches,
taking wages *from them* to minister to you.
9 And when I was present
with you, and in need, I was a
burden to no one, for what I
lacked the brethren who came
from Macedonia supplied. And
in everything I kept myself from
being burdensome to you, and
so I will keep *myself.*
10 As the truth of Christ is in
me, no one shall stop me from

*
10:7 NU-Text reads *even as we are.*
10:8 NU-Text omits *us.* **11:3** NU-Text adds *and purity.* **11:6** NU-Text omits *been.*

5
a Law (of Christ): v. 5; 2 Cor. 12:15. (Jn. 13:34; 2 Jn. 5)
b Cp. Mt. 7:24–25
6
c Cp. 2 Cor. 2:9
7
d Cp. 1 Sam. 16:7; Mt. 23:27; Jn. 7:24; 2 Cor. 5:12
e Rom. 14:8
8
f 2 Cor. 13:10; cp. 1 Tim. 1:20; Ti. 3:10
g Rom. 14:19; 15:2; 1 Cor. 14:3,26; 2 Cor. 12:19; Eph. 4:12,29
10
h Cp. 2 Cor. 12:7; Gal. 4:13–14
i 2 Cor. 11:6; cp. 1 Cor. 1:17; 2:1,4
12
j Cp. 2 Cor. 3:1
13
k Cp. Rom. 12:3
14
l Gospel: vv. 14,16; 11:7; Gal. 1:7. (Gen. 12:3; Rev. 14:6)
15
m Cp. Rom. 15:20
n Faith: v. 15; Gal. 2:16. (Gen. 3:20; Heb. 11:39, *note*)
16
o Cp. Mt. 28:19; Mk. 16:15; Lk. 24:47
17
p Jer. 9:24; 1 Cor. 1:31
18
q Cp. 1 Cor. 4:5

CHAPTER 11
2
r Bride (of Christ): v. 2; Eph. 5:25. (Jn. 3:29; Rev. 19:7, *note*)
s Church (the true): v. 2; Eph. 1:22. (Mt. 16:18; Heb. 12:23)
3
t Satan: v. 3; 2 Cor. 11:14. (Gen. 3:1; Rev. 20:10)
u Test/tempt: v. 3; Gal. 4:14. (Gen. 3:1; Jas. 1:14, *note*)
v Cp. 2 Cor. 2:11; Eph. 6:11; 2 Th. 2:9; Rev. 12:9; 20:7–8
4
w Antichrist: vv. 3–4; 1 Jn. 2:18. (Mt. 24:5; Rev. 13:11, *note*)
x Paul speaks ironically
5
y 2 Cor. 12:11
6
z 2 Cor. 10:10
aa Eph. 3:4
bb i.e. *we have made this clear to you*
7
cc See Rom. 3:23, *note*
dd 1 Cor. 9:18; 2 Cor. 12:13; cp. Acts 18:3; 1 Cor. 4:12
8
ee Churches (local): v. 8; 2 Cor. 11:28. (Acts 8:3; Phil. 1:1, *note*)

[1](11:2) Union with Christ is likened to the marriage relationship (see Eph. 5:32, *note*).

this boasting in the regions of
Achaia.
11 Why? Because I do not
[a]love you? God knows!
12 But what I do, I will also
continue to do, that I may cut
off the opportunity from those
who desire an opportunity to be
regarded just as we are in the
things of which they boast.
13 For such *are* [b]false apostles, deceitful workers, transforming themselves into apostles of Christ.
14 And no wonder! For [c]Sa-
tan himself transforms himself
into an [d]angel of light.
15 Therefore *it is* no great
thing if his ministers also transform themselves into ministers
of [e]righteousness, whose end
will be according to their works.

(4) Paul's unwilling boasting
(11:16—12:18)

16 I say again, let no one
think me a fool. If otherwise, at
least receive me as a fool, that
I also may boast a little.
17 What I speak, I [f]speak not
according to the Lord, but as it
were, foolishly, in this confidence of boasting.
18 Seeing that many boast
according to the [g]flesh, I also
will boast.
19 For you put up with fools
gladly, since you *yourselves* are
wise!
20 For you put up with it [h]if
one brings you into bondage, [i]if
one devours *you*, [j]if one takes
from you, [k]if one exalts himself, if one strikes you on the
face.
21 To *our* [l]shame I say that
we were too weak for that! But
in whatever anyone is bold—
I speak foolishly—I am bold
also.
22 Are they [m]Hebrews? So
am I. Are they Israelites? So *am*
I. Are they the seed of Abraham? So *am* I.
23 Are they [n]ministers of
Christ?—I speak as a fool—I
am more: in labors more abundant, in stripes above measure,
in prisons more frequently, in
deaths often.
24 From the Jews five times
I received [o]forty [p]*stripes* minus
one.
25 Three times I was [q]beaten
with rods; once I was [r]stoned;
three times I was [s]shipwrecked;
a night and a day I have been in
the deep;
26 *in* [t]journeys often, *in* perils of waters, *in* perils of robbers, *in* perils of *my own* [u]coun-
trymen, *in* perils of the Gentiles,
in perils in the city, *in* perils in
the wilderness, *in* perils in the
sea, *in* perils among false brethren;
27 in weariness and toil, in
sleeplessness often, in hunger
and thirst, in [v]fastings often, in
cold and nakedness—
28 besides the other things,
what comes upon me daily:
my deep [w]concern for all the
[x]churches.
29 [y]Who is weak, and I am
not weak? Who is made to
stumble, and I do not burn *with
indignation*?
30 If I must boast, I will
[z]boast in the things which concern my infirmity.
31 The God and Father of our
Lord Jesus Christ, who is
[aa]blessed forever, knows that I
am not lying.
32 In [bb]Damascus the governor, under Aretas the king, was
guarding the city of the Damascenes with a garrison, desiring
to arrest me;
33 but I was let down in a
basket through a window in the
wall, and escaped from his
hands.

Paul's thorn in the flesh

12 IT is doubtless* not profitable for me to boast.
I will come to [cc]visions and
[dd]revelations of the Lord:
2 I know a man in Christ
who fourteen years ago—
whether in the body I do not
know, or whether out of the
body I do not know, God
knows—such a one was

*
12:1 NU-Text reads *necessary, though not profitable, to boast.*

11
a 2 Cor. 12:15
13
b Cp. Mt. 7:15; 24:11, 24; 2 Pet. 2:1; 1 Jn. 4:1
14
c *Satan:* v. 14; 2 Cor. 12:7. (Gen. 3:1; Rev. 20:10)
d Cp. 2 Cor. 2:11; Eph. 6:11
15
e See 1 Jn. 3:7, *note*
17
f Cp. 1 Cor. 7:6
18
g *Flesh:* v. 18; Gal. 3:3. (Jn. 8:15; Jude 23)
20
h Cp. Gal. 2:4; 4:9; 2 Pet. 2:19
i Cp. Mt. 23:14; Lk. 20:47; Gal. 5:15
j Cp. Acts 20:29–30
k Cp. Mt. 23:12
21
l Cp. 2 Cor. 10:10
22
m Phil. 3:4–6
23
n Cp. 2 Cor. 3:6; Eph. 3:7–8; Col. 1:23
24
o Dt. 25:3
p 2 Cor. 6:5; cp. 1 Pet. 2:24
25
q Acts 16:22–23; 21:32
r Acts 14:5,19
s Acts 27:1–44
26
t See Acts 9:26, *note*
u Acts 9:23–24; 17:5
27
v Acts 9:9; 13:2–3; 14:23
28
w Acts 15:36; 20:17–21,31; 2 Cor. 7:12; 12:20; Gal. 4:11; 1 Th. 3:10
x *Churches* (local): v. 28; 2 Cor. 12:13. (Acts 8:3; Phil. 1:1, *note*)
29
y Cp. 2 Cor. 2:4
30
z 2 Cor. 12:5, 9,10
31
aa Rom. 9:5
32
bb Acts 9:19–25
CHAPTER 12
1
cc vv. 2–4; Acts 16:9; 18:9; 22:17–18; 23:11; 26:13–15; 27:23
dd Acts 9:3–6; Gal. 2:2

[1]caught up to the [2]third heaven.

3 And I know such a man—whether in the body or out of the body I do not know, God knows—

4 how he was caught up into [a]Paradise and heard inexpressible words, which it is not lawful for a man to utter.

5 Of such a one I will boast; yet of myself I will not [b]boast, except in my infirmities.

6 For though I might desire to boast, I will not be a fool; for I will speak the truth. But I refrain, lest anyone should think of me above what he sees me *to be* or hears from me.

7 And lest I should be exalted above measure by the abundance of the revelations, a [3c]thorn in the flesh was given to me, a messenger of [d]Satan to buffet me, lest I be exalted above measure.

8 Concerning this thing I pleaded with the Lord [e]three times that it might depart from me.

9 And He said to me, "My [f]grace is sufficient for you, for My strength is made perfect in weakness." Therefore most gladly I will rather boast in my [g]infirmities, that the power of Christ may rest upon me.

10 Therefore I take pleasure in [g]infirmities, in reproaches, in needs, in persecutions, in distresses, for Christ's sake. For when I am weak, then I am strong.

(5) Warning

11 I have become a fool in boasting;* you have compelled me. For I ought to have been commended by you; for in nothing was I [h]behind the most eminent apostles, [i]though I am nothing.

12 Truly the [j]signs of an apostle were accomplished among you with all perseverance, in signs and [k]wonders and mighty [l]deeds.

13 For what is it in which you were inferior to other [m]churches, except that I myself was not burdensome to you? Forgive me this wrong!

14 Now *for* the [n]third time I am ready to come to you. And I will not be burdensome to you; [o]for I do not seek yours, but you. For the children ought not to lay up for the parents, but the parents for the children.

15 And I will very gladly spend and be spent for your souls; though the more abundantly I [p]love you, the less I am loved.

16 But be that *as it may,* I did not burden you. Nevertheless, being crafty, I caught you by cunning!

17 Did I take advantage of you by any of those whom I sent to you?

18 I urged Titus, and sent our [q]brother with *him.* Did Titus take advantage of you? Did we not walk in the same spirit? Did *we* not *walk* in the same steps?

19 Again, do you think* that we excuse ourselves to you? We speak before God in Christ. But *we do* all things, beloved, for your [r]edification.

20 For I fear lest, [s]when I come, I shall not find you such as I wish, and *that* I shall be found by you such as you do not wish; lest *there* [t]*be* conten-

* 12:11 NU-Text omits *in boasting.*
12:19 NU-Text reads *You have been thinking for a long time. . . .*

4
a Lk. 23:43; Rev. 2:7; see Lk. 16:23, *note*
5
b vv. 9–10; 2 Cor. 11:30
7
c Gal. 4:14
d Satan: v. 7; Eph. 2:2. (Gen. 3:1; Rev. 20:10)
8
e Cp. Mt. 26:44
9
f Grace: v. 9; 2 Cor. 13:14. (Jn. 1:14; Jn. 1:17, *note*). See 2 Pet. 3:18, *note*
g Or *weaknesses*
11
h 2 Cor. 11:5; cp. 1 Cor. 15:10
i Cp. Lk. 17:10
12
j Acts 14:3; cp. Heb. 2:4
k Acts 15:12
l Acts 14:8–10; 16:16–18; 19:11–12; 20:6–12; 28:1–10
13
m Churches (local): v. 13; Gal. 1:2. (Acts 8:3; Phil. 1:1, *note*)
14
n 13:1
o Cp. 1 Cor. 10:24,33; 1 Th. 2:8
15
p Law (of Christ): v. 15; Gal. 5:6. (Jn. 13:34; 2 Jn. 5)
18
q 2 Cor. 8:18
19
r Rom. 14:19; 15:2; 1 Cor. 14:3,26; 2 Cor. 10:8; Eph. 4:12,29
20
s 13:2; cp. 1 Cor. 4:21; 2 Cor. 13:10
t Cp. Gal. 5:19–21

[1](12:2) Whereas first century cosmology was different from that of today, when the Bible speaks about a subject such as heaven, which is outside the earthly realm, it can only use the phenomenal language common to men today as well as in the first century. The NT is no more to be criticized for speaking of heaven as being "up" than a scientist is to be charged with ignorance when he speaks of the sun rising and setting.

[2](12:2) The "third heaven" is the abode of God, the first heaven being that of the clouds, and the second heaven that of the stars.

[3](12:7) Paul's "thorn in the flesh" was probably some kind of bodily weakness or disease; possibly it may have been an eye affliction (see Gal. 6:11, *note*). Undoubtedly the reason that its particular nature is not disclosed is so that Paul's consolations may avail for all to whom any type of "thorn" is given. For God's people, weakness, infirmity, and even disease may be divinely permitted: (1) to cause them to be humble (v. 7); (2) to caution them against presumption in prayer (v. 8); and (3) to exhibit the all-sufficiency of God's grace (v. 9).

tions, jealousies, outbursts of wrath, selfish ambitions, backbitings, whisperings, conceits, tumults;

21 lest, [a]when I come again, my God will humble me among you, and I shall mourn for many who have [b]sinned before and have not [c]repented of the uncleanness, fornication, and lewdness which they have practiced.

(6) Exhortation: "Examine yourselves"

13 THIS *will be* the [d]third *time* I am coming to you. *"By the mouth of two or three [e]witnesses every word shall be established."*

2 I have told you before, and foretell as if I were present the second time, and now being absent I [f]write* to those who have [b]sinned before, and to all the rest, that if I come again I will not spare—

3 since you seek a proof of Christ speaking in me, who is not weak toward you, but mighty in you.

4 For though He was [g]crucified in weakness, yet He [h]lives by the power of God. For we also are weak in Him, but we shall live with Him by the power of God toward you.

5 [i]Examine yourselves *as to* whether you are in the [j]faith. [k]Test yourselves. Do you not know yourselves, that Jesus Christ is in you?—unless indeed you are disqualified.

6 But I [l]trust that you will know that we are not disqualified.

7 Now I* pray to God that you do no evil, not that we should appear approved, but that you should do what is honorable, though we may seem disqualified.

8 [m]For we can do nothing against the truth, but for the truth.

9 For we are glad when we are weak and you are strong. And this also we pray, that you may be [n]made complete.

10 Therefore I [f]write these things being absent, lest being present I should use [o]sharpness, according to the [p]authority which the Lord has given me for edification and not for destruction.

Conclusion, 13:11–14

11 Finally, brethren, [q]farewell. Become [n]complete. Be of good comfort, be of one mind, live in peace; and the God of love and peace will be with you.

12 Greet one another with a holy kiss.

13 All the saints greet you.

14 The [r]grace of the Lord Jesus Christ, and the love of God, and the communion of the Holy [s]Spirit *be* with you all. Amen.

*13:2 NU-Text omits *I write.* 13:7 NU-Text reads *we.*

21
a 13:2; cp. 1 Cor. 4:21; 2 Cor. 13:10
b See Rom. 3:23, *note*
c Repentance: v. 21; 2 Tim. 2:25. (Mt. 3:2; Acts 17:30, *note*)

CHAPTER 13

1
d 12:14
e Dt. 19:15

2
f Inspiration: vv. 2, 10; Gal. 1:11. (Ex. 4:15; 2 Tim. 3:16, *note*)

4
g Sacrifice (of Christ): v. 4; Gal. 1:4. (Gen. 3:15; Heb. 10:18, *note*)
h Resurrection: v. 4; Gal. 1:1. (2 Ki. 4:35; 1 Cor. 15:52, *note*)

5
i Judgments (the seven): v. 5; Gal. 3:13. (1 Sam. 7:14; Rev. 20:12, *note*)
j Cp. 1 Cor. 16:13
k Cp. 2 Pet. 1:10

6
l Or *hope*

8
m Cp. Prov. 21:30

9
n Or *perfected.* See Phil. 3:12, *note*

10
o 1 Cor. 4:21
p 2 Cor. 10:8

11
q Or *rejoice*

14
r Grace: v. 14; Gal. 1:3. (Jn. 1:14; Jn. 1:17, *note*)
s Holy Spirit (NT): v. 14; Gal. 3:2. (Mt. 1:18; Acts 2:4, *note*)

The Epistle of Paul the Apostle to the

GALATIANS

Author: Paul *Theme:* Salvation by Grace *Date of writing:* c. A.D. 49 or 52

THE EPISTLE TO THE GALATIANS is addressed to a group of churches in Galatia, which was located in the center of what is now known as Asia Minor. The original inhabitants were Phrygians, with a religion of nature worship. Many Jews lived in these cities. The Galatians were noted for their impetuosity, fickleness, and love for new and curious things. Paul visited Galatia on both his first missionary journey (Acts 13:51; 14:8,20, Iconium, Lystra, and Derbe being situated in southern Galatia), and on his third (Acts 18:23), although of his labor in founding these churches there is no record. On his second missionary journey the apostle was forbidden by the Holy Spirit to preach there (Acts 16:6).

At the time Paul was writing, the Galatian churches were facing a double threat, involving purity of doctrine and purity of conduct. Certain individuals had come into the area who would "pervert the gospel of Christ" (1:7; 5:10). They insisted that, while salvation was of Christ, works were also necessary for salvation. To this Judaizing, i.e. legalistic error, the Galatians were already beginning to yield (1:6; 3:1), thus returning to a bondage of observing days, months, seasons, years, etc. (4:10). Paul overwhelmingly destroys all arguments in favor of mixing the law with faith by pointing out that Abraham was justified by faith alone 430 years before the giving of the Mosaic law. The apostle answers the complementary error—that a believer is made spiritually mature by keeping the law—by setting forth the truth of the sanctifying power of the Holy Spirit, and the richness of life available when He rules the Christian whom He indwells.

The Epistle may be divided as follows:

Introduction, 1:1–5.
I. Occasion of the Epistle: the Galatians' Departure from the True Gospel, 1:6–9.
II. Paul's Defense of His Apostolic Ministry, 1:10—2:21.
III. Justification Is Wholly by Faith, Apart from the Law, 3:1–24.
IV. The Rule of the Believer's Life Is Gracious, Not Legal, 3:25—5:1.
V. Characteristics Displayed in the Life of a Christian Justified by Faith Alone, 5:2–26.
VI. The Outworking of the New Life in Christ Jesus, 6:1–16.
Conclusion, 6:17–18.

CHAPTER 1

1
a Resurrection: v. 1; Eph. 1:20. (2 Ki. 4:35; 1 Cor. 15:52, *note*)
2
b Churches (local): v. 2; Gal. 1:22. (Acts 8:3; Phil. 1:1, *note*)
3
c Grace: vv. 3,6; Gal. 1:15. (Jn. 1:14; Jn. 1:17, *note*). See 2 Pet. 3:18, *note*
4
d Sacrifice (of Christ): v. 4; Gal. 2:20. (Gen.

Introduction:
Salutation, 1:1–5

1 PAUL, an apostle (not from
men nor through man, but
through Jesus Christ and God
the Father who [a]raised Him
from the dead),
2 and all the brethren who
are with me,

To the [b]churches of Galatia:

3 [c]Grace to you and peace
from God the Father and our
Lord Jesus Christ,
4 who [d]gave Himself for
our [e]sins, that He might [f]deliver
us from this present evil
[g]age, [h]according to the will of
our God and Father,
5 to whom *be* glory forever
and ever. Amen.

I. The Occasion of the Epistle:
the Galatians' Departure from the
True Gospel, 1:6–9

6 I marvel that you are turning
away so soon from Him who
[i]called you in the [1c]grace of
Christ, to a different gospel,
7 which is not [j]another; but
there are some who [k]trouble
you and want to [l]pervert the
[m]gospel of Christ.
8 But even if we, or an [n]angel
from heaven, preach any
other [m]gospel to you than what
we have preached to you, let
him be [o]accursed.
9 As we have said before, so
now I say again, if anyone
preaches any other [m]gospel to

note o Gk. *anathema.* 1 Cor. 16:22

3:15; Heb. 10:18, *note*)
e See Rom. 3:23, *note*
f Gal. 6:14; Col. 2:20
g Gk. *aiōn*
h Cp. 1 Jn. 2:15–17
6
i 1 Cor. 1:2; Eph. 4:1; 1 Th. 2:12
7
j Cp. Acts 4:12
k Gal. 5:10,12
l 2 Cor. 2:17; cp. 2 Cor. 11:13–14
m Gospel: vv. 7–9; Gal. 1:11. (Gen. 12:3; Rev. 14:6)
8
n Cp. 1 Ki. 13:18; see Heb. 1:4,

---

[1](1:6) The test of the Gospel is grace. If the message excludes grace, or mingles law with grace as the means either of justification or sanctification (2:21; 3:1–3), or denies the fact or guilt of sin which alone gives grace its occasion and opportunity, it is "a different" gospel, and the preacher of it is under the anathema of God (vv. 8–9).

you than what you have received, let him be [a]accursed.

II. Paul's Defense of His Apostolic Ministry, 1:10—2:21

10 [1]For do I now persuade
men, or God? Or do I seek to
[b]please men? For if I still
pleased men, I would not be a
bondservant of Christ.
11 But I make known to you,
brethren, that the [c]gospel
which was preached by me is
[d]not according to man.
12 For I neither received it
from man, nor was I taught *it*,
but *it came* [d]through the [e]reve-
lation of Jesus Christ.
13 For you have heard of my
former conduct in Judaism,
how I persecuted the [f]church of
God beyond measure and *tried*
to destroy it.
14 And I advanced in [2]Juda-
ism beyond many of my contemporaries in my own nation,
being more exceedingly [g]zeal-
ous for the traditions of my fathers.
15 But when it pleased God,
who [h]separated me from my
mother's womb and [i]called *me*
through His [j]grace,
16 to [e]reveal His Son [k]in me,
that I might [c]preach Him
among the [l]Gentiles, I did not
immediately [m]confer with
[n]flesh and blood,
17 nor did I go up to Jerusalem to those *who were* apostles
before me; but I went to Arabia,
and returned again to Damascus.
18 Then after three years I
[o]went up to Jerusalem to see
Peter,* and remained with him
fifteen days.
19 But I saw none of the other
apostles except [p]James, the
Lord's brother.
20 (Now *concerning* the
things which I [d]write to you, indeed, before God, I do not lie.)
21 Afterward I went into the
regions of Syria and Cilicia.
22 And I was unknown by
face to the [q]churches of Judea
which *were* in Christ.
23 But they were [r]hearing
only, "He who formerly [s]perse-
cuted us now [c]preaches the
faith which he once *tried to* destroy."
24 And they [t]glorified God
in me.

Behind the scenes at the first church council at Jerusalem (cp. Acts 15)

2 THEN after [u]fourteen years
I went up again to Jerusalem with Barnabas, and also
took Titus with *me*.
2 And I went up by revelation, and [d]communicated to
them that [c]gospel which I
preach among the Gentiles,
but [v]privately to those who
were of reputation, lest by any
means I might run, or had run,
[w]in vain.
3 Yet not even Titus who
was with me, being a Greek,
[x]was compelled to be [y]circum-
cised.
4 And *this occurred* be-
cause of [z]false brethren secretly brought in (who came in
by stealth to spy out our [aa]liberty
which we have in Christ Jesus,
that they might bring us into
bondage),
5 to whom we did not yield
submission [bb]even for an hour,
that the truth of the [c]gospel
might continue with you.

*1:18 NU-Text reads *Cephas*.

9
a Gk. *anathema*. 1 Cor. 16:22
10
b 1 Th. 2:4
11
c Gospel: vv. 11–12, 16,23; 2:2,5; Gal. 2:7 (Gen. 12:3; Rev. 14:6)
d Inspiration: vv. 11–12, 20; 2:2; Gal. 3:8. (Ex. 4:15; 2 Tim. 3:16, *note*)
12
e Eph. 3:3–5; cp. Acts 9:1–20; 22:1–16; 26:9–18
13
f Church (visible): v. 13; Phil. 3:6. (1 Cor. 10:32; 1 Tim. 3:15)
14
g Phil. 3:6
15
h Cp. Isa. 49:1–5; Jer. 1:5
i Election (personal): v. 15; Eph. 1:4. (Dt. 7:6; 1 Pet. 5:13, *note*). Rom. 8:30
j Grace: v. 15; Gal. 2:9. (Jn. 1:14; Jn. 1:17, *note*). See 2 Pet. 3:18, *note*
16
k 2 Cor. 4:5–7
l See Eph. 3:6, *note*
m Cp. 1:1
n Cp. Mt. 16:17
18
o Acts 9:26

19
p See Mt. 4:21, *note*
22
q Churches (local): v. 22; Phil. 1:1. (Acts 8:3; Phil. 1:1, *note*)
23
r Acts 9:20–21
s Acts 8:3
24
t Acts 11:18
CHAPTER 2
1
u Acts 15:2
2
v Acts 15:1–4
w Cp. Phil. 2:16
3
x Cp. Eph. 2:15; Col. 2:14; Heb. 7:18; 8:13
y Cp. Acts 15:5–21; Gal. 5:2
4
z Cp. 2 Cor. 11:26; Jude 4
aa Gal. 5:1,13
5
bb Cp. Acts 15:7–11

[1](1:10) The demonstration is as follows: (1) The Galatians know Paul, that he is no seeker after popularity (v. 10). (2) He puts his known character back of the assertion that his Gospel of grace was a revelation from God (vv. 11–12). (3) As for the legalizers, Paul himself had been a foremost Jew, and had forsaken Judaism for something better (vv. 13–14). (4) He had preached grace years before he saw any of the other apostles (vv. 15–24). (5) When he did meet the other apostles, they had nothing to add to his revelation (2:1–6). (6) The other apostles fully recognized Paul's apostleship (2:7–10). And (7) if the legalizers pleaded Peter's authority, the answer was that Peter himself had claimed none when he was rebuked by Paul (2:11–21).

[2](1:14) The expression, "Judaism" (vv. 13,14, Gk. *Ioudaismos*), refers to the Jewish way of belief and life. A word for "religion" (Gk. *threskeia*, meaning *religious service*) is used in the NT: (1) for external observances (Acts 26:5; Jas. 1:26; Col. 2:18, "worship"); and (2) in the sense of a believer's good works (Jas. 1:27). It is never used as synonymous with salvation or spirituality.

6 But from those who seemed to be something—whatever they were, it makes no difference to me; God [a]shows personal favoritism to no man—for those who seemed *to be something* added nothing to me.

7 But on the contrary, when they saw that the [b]gospel for the [c]uncircumcised had been committed to me, as *the gospel* for the [d]circumcised *was* to Peter

8 (for He who worked effectively in Peter for the apostleship to the [d]circumcised also [e]worked effectively in me toward the [c]Gentiles),

9 and when [f]James, Cephas, and John, who seemed to be pillars, perceived the [g]grace that had been given to me, they gave me and Barnabas the right hand of fellowship, [h]that we *should go* to the [i]Gentiles and they to the circumcised.

10 *They desired* only that we should remember the poor, the very thing which I also was eager to do.

Paul reviews how he withstood Peter at Antioch

11 Now when Peter* had come to [j]Antioch, I withstood him to his face, because he was to be blamed;

12 for before certain men came from James, he would [k]eat with the Gentiles; but when they came, he withdrew and separated himself, fearing those who were of the circumcision.

13 And the rest of the Jews also played the hypocrite with him, so that even [l]Barnabas was carried away with their hypocrisy.

14 But when I saw that they were not straightforward about the truth of the [b]gospel, I said to Peter before *them* all, "If you, being a Jew, live in the manner of Gentiles and not as the Jews, why do you* compel Gentiles to live as Jews?*

The Christian is dead to the law; its sentence has been executed

15 [1]"We *who are* Jews by nature, and not [m]sinners of the Gentiles,

16 "knowing that a man is not [n]justified [o]by the works of the [p]law but by faith in [q]Jesus Christ, even we have [r]believed in Christ Jesus, that we might be [n]justified by faith in Christ and not [o]by the works of the [p]law; for by the works of the law no flesh shall be [n]justified.

17 "But if, while [2]we seek to be justified [s]by Christ, we ourselves also are found sinners, *is* Christ therefore a minister of [m]sin? Certainly not!

18 "For if I [t]build again those things which I destroyed, I make myself a [m]transgressor.

19 "For I through the [p]law [u]died to the law that I might live to God.

The Christian life is the outliving of the inliving Christ (cp. Gal. 5:15–23)

20 "I have been [v]crucified with Christ; it is [w]no longer I who live, but Christ lives in me; and the [x]*life* which [y]I now live in the flesh I live by faith in the Son of God, who loved me and [z]gave Himself for me.

To mingle law with grace in justification nullifies grace

21 "I do not set aside the [g]grace of God; for if [aa]righteousness *comes* through the [p]law, then Christ died [bb]in vain."

*

2:11 NU-Text reads *Cephas*. 2:14 NU-Text reads *how can you*. • Some interpreters stop the quotation here.

6
a Acts 10:34; Rom. 2:11
7
b Gospel: vv. 7,14; Gal. 3:8. (Gen. 12:3; Rev. 14:6)
c Acts 9:15; 22:21; Rom. 11:13
d 1 Pet. 1:1
8
e Cp. 1 Cor. 9:2; 2 Cor. 3:2; 12:12
9
f See Mt. 4:21, *note*
g Grace: vv. 9,21; Gal. 5:4. (Jn. 1:14; Jn. 1:17, *note*). See 2 Pet. 3:18, *note*
h Acts 13:3
i See Eph. 3:6, *note*
11
j Cp. Acts 11:19–26; 15:1
12
k Acts 11:2–3
13
l Cp. Acts 15:37–39

15
m See Rom. 3:23, *note*
16
n Justification: v. 16; Gal. 3:8. (Lk. 18:14; Rom. 3:28, *note*)
o Rom. 3:20
p Law (of Moses): vv. 16,19,21; Gal. 3:2. (Ex. 19:1; Gal. 3:24, *note*)
q Lit. *Christ Jesus*
r Faith: v. 16; Gal. 3:2. (Gen. 3:20; Heb. 11:39, *note*)
17
s Cp. Rom. 8:1; Gal. 5:6
18
t Cp. Gal. 5:2–4
19
u Rom. 7:4
20
v Gal. 6:14
w See Eph. 4:24, *note*
x Life (eternal): v. 20; Gal. 6:8. (Mt. 7:14; Rev. 22:19)
y Rom. 6:8–11; Eph. 2:4–6; Col. 3:1–4
z Sacrifice (of Christ): v. 20; Gal. 3:1. (Gen. 3:15; Heb. 10:18, *note*)
21
aa See Rom. 10:10, *note*
bb Cp. 1 Cor. 15:17

---

[1](2:15) Paul here quotes from his words to Peter when he withstood Peter at Antioch (v. 11), in order to show the Galatians that, whatever the legalists may have pretended, Peter and he were in perfect accord doctrinally. Paul appealed to his common belief of Peter and himself as a rebuke of Peter's inconsistent practice.

[2](2:17) That is, "we" Jews. See Rom. 3:19–23. The passage might be thus paraphrased: If we Jews, in seeking to be justified by faith in Christ, take our places as mere sinners, like the Gentiles, is it therefore Christ who makes us sinners? By no means. It is by putting ourselves again under law after seeking justification through Christ, that we act as if we were still unjustified sinners, seeking to become righteous through law-works. Cp. Gal. 5:1–4.

CHAPTER 3

1
a Sacrifice (of Christ): vv. 1,13; Gal. 4:5. (Gen. 3:15; Heb. 10:18, *note*)

2
b Holy Spirit (NT): vv. 2–3,5,14; Gal. 4:6. (Mt. 1:18; Acts 2:4, *note*)
c Law (of Moses): vv. 2,5, 10–18; Gal. 3:19. (Ex. 19:1; Gal. 3:24, *note*)
d Rom. 10:17
e Faith: vv. 2, 5–9,11–12; Gal. 3:22. (Gen. 3:20; Heb. 11:39, *note*)

3
f See Phil. 3:12, *note*
g Flesh: v. 3; Gal. 4:23. (Jn. 8:15; Jude 23)

5
h Cp. Acts 9:17; 10:44

6
i Gen. 15:6
j Imputation: v. 6; Jas. 2:23. (Gen. 15:6; Jas. 2:23)

8
k Justification: vv. 8, 11; Gal. 3:24. (Lk. 18:14; Rom. 3:28, *note*)
l See Eph. 3:6, *note*
m Gospel: v. 8; Gal. 4:13. (Gen. 12:3; Rev. 14:6)
n Inspiration: vv. 8, 10–11,13, 15–18; Gal. 3:22. (Ex. 4:15; 2 Tim. 3:16, *note*)
o Gen. 12:3

10
p Dt. 27:26

III. Justification Is Wholly by Faith Apart from the Law, 3:1–24

(1) The gift of the Spirit is by faith

3 O FOOLISH Galatians! Who has bewitched you that you should not obey the truth,* before whose eyes Jesus Christ was clearly portrayed among you* as [a]crucified?

2 This only I want to learn from you: Did you receive the [b]Spirit by the works of the [c]law, or by the [d]hearing of [e]faith?

3 Are you so foolish? Having begun in the [b]Spirit, are you now being made [f]perfect by the [g]flesh?

4 Have you suffered so many things in vain—if indeed *it was* in vain?

5 Therefore He who [h]supplies the [b]Spirit to you and works miracles among you, *does He do it* by the works of the [c]law, or by the [d]hearing of [e]faith?—

(2) The Abrahamic Covenant is a covenant of faith (cp. Rom. 4)

6 [i]just as Abraham [e]*“believed God, and it was [j]accounted to him for righteousness.”*

7 Therefore know that *only* those who are of [e]faith are sons of Abraham.

8 And the Scripture, foreseeing that God would [k]justify the [l]Gentiles by [e]faith, preached the [m]gospel to Abraham beforehand, [n]*saying,* [o]*“In you all the nations shall be blessed.”**

9 So then those who *are* of [e]faith are blessed with believing Abraham.

(3) The person under law-works is under the curse of the law

10 For as many as are of the works of the [c]law are under the curse; for it is [n]written, [p]*“Cursed is everyone who does not continue in all things which are [n]written in the book of the [c]law, to do them.”*

11 But that no one is [k]justified by the [c]law in the sight of God *is* [n]evident, for [q]*“the just shall live by [e]faith.”*

12 Yet the [c]law is not of [e]faith, but [r]*“the man who does them shall live by them.”*

(4) Christ has borne the curse of the law

13 Christ has [s]redeemed us from the curse of the [c]law, having [a]become a [t]curse for us (for it is [n]written, [u]*“Cursed is everyone who hangs on a tree”*),

14 that the [v]blessing of Abraham might come upon the [w]Gentiles in Christ Jesus, that we might receive the promise of the [b]Spirit through faith.

15 Brethren, I [n]speak in the manner of men: Though *it is* only a man's covenant, yet *if it is* confirmed, no one annuls or adds to it.

16 Now [x]to Abraham and his Seed were the [n]promises made. He does not say, “And to seeds,” as of many, but as of [y]one, *“And to your Seed,”** who is Christ.

(5) The law did not add a new condition to the Abrahamic Covenant of faith

17 And this I [n]say, *that* the [c]law, which was four hundred and thirty years later, cannot annul the covenant that was confirmed before by God in Christ,* that it should make the promise of no effect.

18 For if the inheritance *is* of the [c]law, *it is* no longer of promise; but God gave *it* to Abraham by promise.

(6) The intent of the law is condemnation, and a preparatory discipline

19 [1][z]What purpose then *does*

11
q Hab. 2:4; Rom. 1:17

12
r Lev. 18:5

13
s See Rom. 3:24, *note*
t Judgments (the seven): v. 13; Gal. 6:4. (1 Sam. 7:14; Rev. 20:12, *note*)
u Dt. 21:23

14
v v. 8; Rom. 4:1–5
w Rom. 3:29–30

16
x Gen. 13:15
y Gen. 22:18

19
z Lit. *Why, then, the law?*

*
3:1 NU-Text omits *that you should not obey the truth.* • NU-Text omits *among you.* 3:8 Genesis 18:18; 22:18; 26:4; 28:14 3:16 Genesis 12:7; 24:7 3:17 NU-Text omits *in Christ.*

1(3:19) The answer to this question is sixfold: (1) The law was added because of transgressions, i.e. to give to sin the character of transgression. (a) Men had been sinning before Moses but, in the absence of law, their sins were not put to their account (Rom. 5:13); the law gave to sin the character of transgression, i.e. of personal guilt. (b) Furthermore, since men not only continued to sin after the law was given, but were provoked to transgress by the very law which forbade it (Rom. 7:8), the law conclusively proved the inveterate sinfulness of man's

19
a Law (of Moses): vv. 10–24; Gal. 4:21. (Ex. 19:1; Gal. 3:24, *note*)
b i.e. *in order that sin might be shown to be transgression.* Rom. 4:15
c Gal. 4:4
21
d Righteousness (OT): v. 21; Phil. 3:6. (Gen. 6:9; Lk. 2:25, *note*)
22
e Inspiration: v. 22; Gal. 4:1. (Ex. 4:15; 2 Tim. 3:16,

the [a]law *serve?* It was added
[b]because of transgressions, till
the [c]Seed should come to whom
the promise was made; *and it*
was appointed through angels
by the hand of a mediator.
20 Now a mediator does not
mediate for one *only*, but God is
one.
21 *Is* the [a]law then against
the promises of God? Certainly
not! For if there had been a law
given which could have given
life, truly [d]righteousness would
have been by the [a]law.
22 But the [e]Scripture has
confined [f]all under [g]sin, that
the promise by [h]faith in Jesus
Christ might be given to those
who believe.
23 But before faith came, we
were kept under guard by the
[a]law, kept for the faith which
would afterward be revealed.
24 Therefore the [1a]law was
our tutor [i]*to bring us* to Christ,
that we might be [j]justified by
[h]faith.

IV. The Rule of the Believer's Life Is Gracious, Not Legal, 3:25—5:1

25 But after [h]faith has come,
we are no longer under a [2]tutor.

(1) The justified believer is a son in the family of God

26 For you are all [k]sons of
God through [h]faith in Christ Jesus.
27 For as many of you as
were [l]baptized into Christ have
put on Christ.
28 [m]There is neither Jew nor
Greek, [n]there is neither slave

note)
f Cp. Rom. 3:9–20
g See Rom. 3:23, *note*
h Faith: vv. 22, 24–26; Gal. 5:5. (Gen. 3:20; Heb. 11:39, *note*)
24
i Or *until*
j Justification: v. 24; Gal. 5:4. (Lk. 18:14; Rom. 3:28, *note*)
26
k See Eph. 1:5, *note*
27
l Rom. 6:3
28
m Rom. 10:12; Col. 3:11
n 1 Cor. 12:13

---

nature (Rom. 7:11–13). (2) The law, therefore, "has confined all under sin" (cp. Rom. 3:19–20,23). (3) The law was an *ad interim* dealing, "till the Seed should come" (v. 19). (4) The law shut sinful man up to faith as the only avenue of escape (v. 23). (5) The law was to the Jews what the child-discipliner (Gk. *paidagōgos*) was in a Greek household, a custodian of children in their minority, and it had this character to or until Christ (vv. 23–25, *note;* 4:1–2). And (6) Christ having come, the believer is no longer under the child-discipliner (i.e. the law, v. 25), but has become a disciple (i.e. learner) of Christ Himself (Mt. 11:29; Lk. 10:39; Jn. 17:6–8; Ti. 2:11–13).

[1](3:24) I. The law of Moses, Summary: (1) The Mosaic Covenant was given to Israel in three parts: (a) the commandments, expressing the righteous will of God (Ex. 20:1–26); (b) the judgments, governing the social life of Israel (Ex. 21:1—24:11); and (c) the ordinances, governing the religious life of Israel (Ex. 24:12; 31:18). (2) The commandments and ordinances were one complete and inseparable whole. When an Israelite sinned, he was held "blameless" if he brought the required offering (Lk. 1:6; Phil. 3:6). (3) Law, as a method of the divine dealing with man, characterized the dispensation extending from the giving of the law to the death of Jesus Christ (Gal. 3:13–14,23–24). And (4) the attempt of legalistic teachers (e.g. Acts 15:1–31; Gal. 2:1–5) to mingle law with grace as the divine method for this present dispensation of the Church, brought out the true relation of the law to the Christian.

II. The Christian doctrine of the law: (1) Law is in contrast with grace. Under the latter God bestows the righteousness which, under law, He demanded (Ex. 19:5; Jn. 1:17; Rom. 3:21, *note;* 10:3–10; 1 Cor. 1:30). (2) The law is, in itself, holy, just, good, and spiritual (Rom. 7:12–14). (3) Before the law the whole world is guilty, and the law is therefore of necessity a ministry of condemnation, death, and the divine curse (Rom. 3:19; 2 Cor. 3:7–9; Gal. 3:10). (4) Christ bore the curse of the law, and redeemed the believer both from the curse and from the dominion of the law (Gal. 3:13; 4:5–7). (5) Law neither justifies a sinner nor sanctifies a believer (Gal. 2:16; 3:2–3,11–12). (6) The believer is both dead to the law and redeemed from it, so that he is "not under law, but under grace" (Rom. 6:14; 7:4; Gal. 2:19; 4:4–7; 1 Tim. 1:8–9). And (7) under the new covenant of grace the principle of obedience to the divine will is produced inwardly (Heb. 10:16). So far is the life of the believer from the anarchy of self-will that he is "under law toward Christ" (1 Cor. 9:21), and the new "law of Christ" (Gal. 6:2; 2 Jn. 5) is his delight; whereas, through the indwelling Spirit, the righteousness of the law is fulfilled in him (Rom. 8:2–4; Gal. 5:16–18). The commandments are used in the distinctively Christian Scriptures as an instruction in righteousness (2 Tim. 3:16–17; cp. Rom. 13:8–10; 1 Cor. 9:8–9; Eph. 6:1–3).

[2](3:25) "Tutor" is translated from the Gk. *paidagōgos*, meaning *child-discipliner* or *child-leader.* In the Greek and Roman world the pedagogue was the custodian or guardian in the education and life of minor children. The argument does not turn upon the extent or nature of the pedagogue's authority, but upon the fact that it wholly ceased when the "child" (4:1) became a son (4:1–6), when the minor became an adult. The adult "son" does voluntarily that which formerly he did in fear of the pedagogue. But even if he does not, it is no longer an issue between the son and the pedagogue (the law), but between the son and God, his Father. Cp. Heb. 12:5–10; 1 Jn. 2:1–2.

nor free, there is neither male
nor female; for you are all [a]one
in Christ Jesus.
29 And if you *are* Christ's,
then you are Abraham's [b]seed,
and [c]heirs according to the
promise.

4 NOW I [d]say *that* the heir,
as long as he is a child, does
not differ at all from a slave,
though he is master of all,
2 but is under guardians
and stewards until the time appointed by the father.
3 Even so we, when we were
children, were in bondage under the [e]elements of the world.

(2) The believer is redeemed from under the law

4 But when the fullness of
the time had come, God [f]sent
forth His Son, born* of a
[g]woman, born under the law,
5 to [h]redeem those who
were [i]under the law, that we
might receive the [j]adoption as
sons.

(3) The Spirit confirms the believer's sonship (see Eph. 1:5, note)

6 And because you are sons,
God has sent forth the [k]Spirit of
His Son into your hearts, crying
out, [l]"Abba, Father!"
7 Therefore you are no longer a slave but a son, and if a
son, then an [c]heir of* God
through Christ.

(4) Legalism is an elementary religion

8 But then, indeed, when
you did not know God, you
[m]served those which by nature
are not gods.
9 But now after you have
known God, or rather are
known by God, how *is it that*
you turn [n]again to the weak and
beggarly [e]elements, to which
you desire again to be in bondage?
10 You [o]observe days and
months and seasons and years.
11 I am [p]afraid for you, lest I
have labored for you in vain.
12 Brethren, I urge you to become like me, for I *became* like
you. You have not [q]injured me
at all.
13 You know that because of
physical [r]infirmity I preached
the [s]gospel to you at the first.
14 And my [t]trial which was
in my flesh you did not despise
or reject, but you received me as
an angel of God, *even* as Christ
Jesus.

(5) In legalism the Galatians have lost their blessing

15 What* then was the blessing you *enjoyed*? For I bear you
witness that, if possible, you
would have plucked out your
own eyes and given them to
me.
16 Have I therefore become
your enemy because I tell you
the truth?
17 They zealously court you,
but for no good; yes, they want
to exclude you, that you may be
zealous for them.
18 But it is good to be zealous
in a good thing always, and not
only when I am present with
you.

(6) The two systems, law and grace, cannot co-exist

19 My [1]little children, for
whom I [u]labor in birth again
until Christ is formed in you,
20 [v]I would like to be present
with you now and to change my
tone; for I have doubts about
you.
21 Tell me, you who desire to
be under the [w]law, do you not
[x]hear the law?
22 For it is [d]written [y]that
Abraham had two sons: the one
by a bondwoman, the other by a
freewoman.
23 But he *who was* of the
bondwoman was born according to the [z]flesh, and he of the
freewoman through [aa]promise,
24 which things are sym-

*
4:4 Or *made* 4:7 NU-Text reads *through God* and omits *through Christ*. 4:15 NU-Text reads *Where*.

28
a 1 Cor. 12:13; Eph. 2:15–16
29
b Rom. 4:11; Gal. 3:7
c Rom. 8:17
CHAPTER 4
1
d Inspiration: vv. 1, 22; Gal. 4:27. (Ex. 4:15; 2 Tim. 3:16, *note*)
3
e Cp. Col. 2:8,20
4
f Christ (first advent): v. 4; Eph. 2:17. (Gen. 3:15; Acts 1:11, *note*). Jn. 16:28
g Gen. 3:15; Isa. 7:14; Mt. 1:25
5
h Sacrifice (of Christ): v. 5; Eph. 1:7. (Gen. 3:15; Heb. 10:18, *note*)
i Gal. 3:13
j Adoption: v. 5; Eph. 1:5. (Rom. 8:15; Eph. 1:5)
6
k Holy Spirit (NT): v. 6; Gal. 4:29. (Mt. 1:18; Acts 2:4, *note*)
l Rom. 8:15
8
m Cp. 1 Th. 1:9
9
n Gal. 3:1–3
10
o Cp. Col. 2:16
11
p Cp. v. 20
12
q Cp. 2 Cor. 2:5
13
r See Gal. 6:11, *note*
s Gospel: v. 13; Eph. 1:13. (Gen. 12:3; Rev. 14:6)
14
t Test/tempt: v. 14; Gal. 6:1. (Gen. 3:1; Jas. 1:14, *note*)
19
u Cp. 1 Cor. 4:15
20
v Cp. 2 Cor. 13:1–2
21
w Law (of Moses): v. 21; Gal. 5:3. (Ex. 19:1; Gal. 3:24, *note*)
x Cp. Rom. 3:19–20
22
y Gen. 16:15; 21:2
23
z Flesh: v. 23; Gal. 5:13. (Jn. 8:15; Jude 23)
aa Gen. 17:15–19

[1](4:19) The allegory (vv. 22–31) is addressed to justified but immature believers (cp. 1 Cor. 3:1–2) who, under the influence of legalistic teachers, "desire to be under the law." It has, therefore, no application to a sinner seeking justification. It raises and answers (for the fifth time in this Epistle) the question: Is the believer under the law? (2:19–21; 3:1–3,25–26; 4:4–6,9–31).

bolic. For these are the* two [a]covenants: the one from Mount [b]Sinai which gives birth to [c]bondage, which is Hagar—
25 for this Hagar is Mount Sinai in Arabia, and corresponds to Jerusalem which now is, and is in bondage with her children—
26 but the Jerusalem [d]above is free, which is the mother of us all.
27 For it is [e]written:

[f]"Rejoice, O barren,
You who do not bear!
Break forth and shout,
You who are not in labor!
For the desolate has many more children
Than she who has a husband."

28 Now [g]we, brethren, as Isaac *was,* are children of [h]promise.
29 But, as he who was born according to the flesh then [i]persecuted him *who was born* according to the [j]Spirit, even so *it is* now.
30 Nevertheless what does the Scripture [e]say? [k]*"Cast out the bondwoman and her son, for the son of the bondwoman shall not be heir with the son of the freewoman."*
31 So then, brethren, we are [l]not children of the bondwoman but of the [m]free.

5 [n]STAND fast therefore in the liberty by which Christ has made us free,* and do not be entangled again with a [o]yoke of bondage.

V. Characteristics Displayed in the Life of a Christian Justified by Faith Alone, 5:2–26

2 Indeed I, Paul, [e]say to you that [p]if you become circumcised, Christ will profit you nothing.
3 And I testify again to every man who becomes circumcised that he is a [q]debtor to keep the whole [r]law.
4 You have become [s]estranged from Christ, you who *attempt to* be [t]justified by [r]law; you have [u]fallen from [v]grace.
5 For we through the [j]Spirit eagerly [w]wait for the hope of [x]righteousness by [y]faith.
6 For in Christ Jesus neither [z]circumcision nor uncircumcision avails anything, but [y]faith [aa]working through [bb]love.
7 You ran well. Who hindered you from obeying the truth?
8 This persuasion does not *come* from Him who calls you.
9 A little [cc]leaven leavens the whole lump.
10 I have confidence in you, in the Lord, that you will have no other mind; but he who troubles you shall bear his judgment, whoever he is.
11 And I, brethren, if I still preach circumcision, why do I still suffer persecution? Then the offense of the cross has ceased.
12 I could wish that those who trouble you would even cut themselves off!
13 For you, brethren, have been called to [dd]liberty; only do not *use* liberty as an [ee]opportunity for the [ff]flesh, but through [bb]love serve one another.
14 For all the [r]law is fulfilled in one word, *even* in this: [gg]*"You shall love your neighbor as yourself."*
15 But if you [hh]bite and devour one another, beware lest you be consumed by one another!

Sanctification is through the Spirit, not the law

16 I say then: [ii]Walk in the [j]Spirit, and you shall not fulfill the lust of the [ff]flesh.

The Spirit gives victory over sin (cp. Rom. 8:2; see Rom. 7:15, note)

17 For the [ff]flesh [jj]lusts against the [j]Spirit, and the Spirit against the flesh; and these are contrary to one another, so that you [kk]do not do the things that you wish.
18 But if you are [ll]led by the [j]Spirit, you are [mm]not under the [r]law.
19 Now the [nn]works of the [ff]flesh are evident, which are:

*
4:24 NU-Text and M-Text omit *the.*
5:1 NU-Text reads *For freedom Christ has made us free; stand fast therefore.*

24
a Or *testaments.* See Ex. 19:5 and Heb. 8:8, *notes*
b Ex. 24:6–8
c 5:1
26
d Cp. Heb. 12:22
27
e Inspiration: vv. 27, 30; 5:2; Gal. 6:11. (Ex. 4:15; 2 Tim. 3:16, *note*)
f Isa. 54:1
28
g Rom. 9:8; Gal. 3:29
h Gen. 17:15–19
29
i Gen. 21:9
j Holy Spirit (NT): v. 29; 5:5, 16–18; Gal. 5:22. (Mt. 1:18; Acts 2:4, *note*)
30
k Gen. 21:10
31
l Cp. Rom. 6:14
m Lit. *free woman*
CHAPTER 5
1
n Phil. 4:1
o Acts 15:10
2
p Cp. Acts 15:1
3
q Dt. 27:26; Rom. 2:25
r Law (of Moses): vv. 3–4,14, 18; Gal. 6:13. (Ex. 19:1; Gal. 3:24, *note*)
4
s Col. 1:23
t Justification: v. 4; Ti. 3:7. (Lk. 18:14; Rom. 3:28, *note*)
u Lit. *fallen away*
v Grace: v. 4; Gal. 6:18. (Jn. 1:14; Jn. 1:17, *note*)
5
w Cp. Rom. 5:2–5
x See Rom. 10:10, *note*
y Faith: vv. 5–6; Gal. 5:22. (Gen. 3:20; Heb. 11:39, *note*)
6
z Gal. 6:15
aa 1 Th. 1:3
bb Law (of Christ): vv. 6,13; Gal. 6:2. (Jn. 13:34; 2 Jn. 5)
9
cc Leaven: v. 9. (Gen. 19:3; Mt. 13:33, *note*)
13
dd Rom. 8:2; Gal. 5:1
ee Rom. 6:1; 1 Pet. 2:16
ff Flesh: vv. 13, 16–17,19; Gal. 5:24. (Jn. 8:15; Jude 23)
14
gg Lev. 19:18; Mt. 22:39; Rom. 13:9
15
hh Cp. Jas. 3:13–16
16
ii Cp. Rom. 8:12–13
17
jj Rom. 7:22–23
kk Lit. *may not.* Cp. Rom. 7:15–25
18
ll Rom. 8:14
mm i.e. *not under bondage of effort to please God by works of the law.* Rom. 6:14
19
nn Rom. 1:26–31; Eph. 5:3,11; 2 Tim. 3:2–4

21
a 1 Cor. 6:9–10
b See Mt. 6:33, *note*
22
c See Rev. 19:8, *note*
d Holy Spirit (NT): vv. 22–23, 25; 6:8; Eph. 1:13. (Mt. 1:18; Acts 2:4, *note*)
e Faith: v. 22; Eph. 1:13. (Gen. 3:20; Heb. 11:39, *note*)
24
f Flesh: v. 24; 6:8; Eph. 2:3. (Jn. 8:15; Jude 23)
25
g Cp. Rom. 8:12–13
CHAPTER 6
1
h See Rom. 3:23, *note*
i Cp. Rom. 15:1
j Eph. 4:2; cp. 2 Th. 3:15
k Test/tempt: v. 1; 1 Th. 3:5. (Gen. 3:1; Jas. 1:14, *note*)
2
l Acts 20:35; 1 Th. 5:14
m Law (of Christ): v. 2; Eph. 1:15. (Jn. 13:34; 2 Jn. 5)
3
n Rom. 12:3

adultery,* fornication, uncleanness, lewdness,
20 idolatry, sorcery, hatred,
contentions, jealousies, outbursts of wrath, selfish ambitions, dissensions, heresies,
21 envy, murders,* drunkenness, revelries, and the like; of
which I tell you beforehand, just
as I also told *you* in time past,
that those who practice such
things will [a]not inherit the
[b]kingdom of God.

Christian character is produced by the Holy Spirit, not by self-effort (cp. Jn. 15:1–5; Gal. 2:20)

22 [1]But the [c]fruit of the
[d]Spirit is love, joy, peace, longsuffering, kindness, goodness,
[e]faithfulness,
23 gentleness, self-control.
Against such there is no law.
24 And those *who are*
Christ's have crucified the
[f]flesh with its passions and desires.
25 If we live in the [d]Spirit, let
us also [g]walk in the Spirit.
26 Let us not become con-
ceited, provoking one another,
envying one another.

VI. The Outworking of the New Life in Christ Jesus, 6:1–16

(1) The new life as a brotherhood

(a) The case of a sinning brother

6 BRETHREN, if a man is
overtaken in any [h]trespass,
you who *are* [i]spiritual restore
such a one in a spirit of [j]gentle-
ness, considering yourself lest
you also be [k]tempted.

(b) The case of a burdened brother

2 [l]Bear one another's burdens, and so fulfill the [m]law of
Christ.
3 For if anyone [n]thinks himself to be something, when he is
nothing, he [o]deceives himself.
4 But let each one [p]examine
his own work, and then he will
have rejoicing in [q]himself
alone, and not in another.
5 For each one shall [r]bear
his own load.

(c) The case of a teaching brother

6 Let him who is taught the
word [s]share in all good things
with him who teaches.

(2) The new life as a stewardship

7 [t]Do not be deceived, God
is not mocked; for [u]whatever a
man sows, that he will also
reap.
8 For he who sows to his
flesh will of the [f]flesh reap corruption, but he who sows to the
[d]Spirit will of the Spirit reap
everlasting [v]life.
9 And let us not grow
[w]weary while doing good, for in
due season we shall [x]reap if we
do not lose heart.

(3) The new life as a beneficence (cp. Acts 10:38)

10 Therefore, as we have
[y]opportunity, let us do good to
all, [z]especially to those who are
of the household of faith.

(4) The new life in sacrificial love

11 See with what [2]large letters I have [aa]written to you with
my own hand!
12 As many as desire to
make a good [bb]showing in the
flesh, these *would* compel you
to be circumcised, only that
they may not [cc]suffer persecution for the cross of Christ.
13 For not even those who
are circumcised keep the [dd]law,

o Jas. 1:22
4
p Judgments (the seven): v. 4; 1 Tim. 1:20. (1 Sam. 7:14; Rev. 20:12, *note*)
q Cp. 2 Cor. 10:12–18
5
r Cp. Rom. 14:12
6
s 1 Cor. 9:7–15; 1 Tim. 5:18
7
t Cp. 1 Cor. 6:9–10
u Cp. 1 Cor. 3:10–15
8
v Life (eternal): v. 8; Eph. 4:18. (Mt. 7:14; Rev. 22:19). Rom. 6:8
9
w 1 Cor. 15:58; 2 Th. 3:13
x Jas. 5:7–8
10
y Prov. 3:27
z Rom. 12:13
11
aa Inspiration: v. 11; Eph. 3:3. (Ex. 4:15; 2 Tim. 3:16, *note*)
12
bb Cp. Phil. 3:4
cc Gal. 5:11
13
dd Law (of Moses): v. 13; Eph. 2:15. (Ex. 19:1; Gal. 3:24, *note*)

*
5:19 NU-Text omits *adultery*.
5:21 NU-Text omits *murders*.

[1](5:22) Christian character is not mere moral or legal correctness, but the possession and manifestation of the graces of vv. 22–23. Taken together they present a moral portrait of Christ, and may be understood as the apostle's explanation of 2:20, "no longer I . . . but Christ," and as a definition of "fruit" in Jn. 15:1–8. This character is possible because of the believer's vital union with Christ (Jn. 15:5; 1 Cor. 12:12–13), and is wholly the fruit of the Spirit. "Fruit" (singular), in contrast with "works" (plural, v. 19), suggests that the Christian's life in the Spirit is unified in purpose and direction in contrast with the life in the flesh, with its inner conflicts and frustrations.

[2](6:11) Although no record is given in the NT as to what Paul's infirmity was (see 2 Cor. 12:7, *note*), it is possible that his eyes were in some way affected (e.g. 4:13–15). Perhaps this is the reason he ordinarily dictated his letters; but now, urged by the spiritual danger of his dear Galatians and having no amanuensis at hand, he writes with his own hand.

but they desire to have you circumcised that they may boast in your flesh.

(5) The new exultation of the new life

14 But God forbid that I should boast [a]except in the [b]cross of our Lord Jesus Christ, by whom* the [c]world has been crucified to me, and [d]I to the [e]world.

15 For in Christ Jesus neither circumcision nor uncircumcision avails anything, but a new [f]creation.

(6) The peace of the new life

16 And as many as walk according to this rule, peace and mercy *be* upon them, and upon the Israel of God.

Conclusion: the New Fellowship of Suffering, 6:17–18

17 From now on let no one trouble me, for I bear in my body the [g]marks of the Lord Jesus.

18 Brethren, the [h]grace of our Lord Jesus Christ *be* with your spirit. Amen.

* 6:14 Or *by which* (the cross)

14
a Cp. Phil. 3:7–9
b 1 Cor. 1:18
c Gk. *kosmos*. See Mt. 4:8, *note*
d Gal. 2:20; Col. 2:20
e Gk. *kosmos*. See Rev. 13:8, *note*

15
f 2 Cor. 5:17

17
g Lit. *brands*

18
h Grace: v. 18; Eph. 1:2. (Jn. 1:14; Jn. 1:17, *note*)

The Epistle of Paul the Apostle to the

EPHESIANS

Author: Paul *Theme:* The Church, Christ's Body *Date of writing:* c. A.D. 60

THE EPISTLE TO THE EPHESIANS, written in Rome, the first in order of the prison epistles (Acts 20—27; see Acts 28:30, *note*), was carried by Tychicus, concurrently with Colossians and Philemon. Probably the two larger letters had their occasion in the return of Onesimus to Philemon. Ephesians is the most impersonal of Paul's letters. Indeed the words "in Ephesus" are not in all manuscripts. Colossians 4:16 mentions an epistle to the Laodiceans. It has been conjectured that the letter known as Ephesians is really the Laodicean letter. Possibly it was sent to Ephesus and Laodicea without being addressed to any specific church. The letter would then be "to the saints. . . and faithful in Christ Jesus" anywhere.

The doctrine of the Epistle confirms this view. It contains the highest Church truth, but has nothing about church order. The Church here is the true Church, "His body," not the local church, as in Philippians, Corinthians, etc. Essentially, three lines of truth make up this Epistle: (1) the Christian's exalted position through grace; (2) the truth concerning the body of Christ; and (3) a life lived in accordance with that position.

There is a close spiritual affinity between Ephesians and Joshua, the "heavenly places" answering in Christian position to Canaan in Israel's experience. In both there is conflict, often failure, but also victory, rest, and possession (Josh. 21:43–45; Eph. 1:3; 3:14–19; 6:16). As befits a complete revelation, the number seven is conspicuous in the structure of Ephesians.

The Epistle may be divided as follows:

Introduction, 1:1–2.
I. The Believer's Standing in Grace, 1:3—3:21.
II. The Walk and Service of the Believer, 4:1—5:17.
III. The Walk and Warfare of the Spirit-filled Believer, 5:18—6:20.
Conclusion, 6:21–24.

CHAPTER 1

2
a Grace: vv. 2,6; Eph. 1:7. (Jn. 1:14; Jn. 1:17, *note*). See 2 Pet. 3:18, *note*

4
b Election (corporate): v. 4; Col. 3:12. (Dt. 7:6; 1 Pet. 5:13, *note*)
c Gk. *kosmos*
d Sanctification (NT): v. 4; Eph. 2:21. (Mt. 4:5; Rev. 22:11)

5
e Predestination: v. 5; Eph. 1:11. (Rom. 8:29; Eph. 1:11)
f Adoption: v. 5. (Rom. 8:15; Eph. 1:5)

Introduction (1:1–2)

1 PAUL, an apostle of Jesus
Christ by the will of God,
To the [1]saints who are in
Ephesus, and faithful [2]in Christ
Jesus:
2 [a]Grace to you and peace
from God our Father and the
Lord Jesus Christ.

I. The Believer's Standing in Grace, 1:1—3:21

(1) The believer in Christ in the heavenlies

3 Blessed *be* the God and
Father of our Lord Jesus Christ,
who has blessed us with every
spiritual blessing [3]in the heavenly *places* in Christ,
4 just as He [b]chose us in
Him before the foundation of
the [c]world, that we should be
[d]holy and without blame before
Him in love,
5 having [e]predestined us to
[4][f]adoption as sons by Jesus
Christ to Himself, according to
the good pleasure of His will,
6 to the praise of the glory of
His [a]grace, by which He made
us accepted in the Beloved.

---

[1](1:1) A saint, in the NT, is not a sinless person but a saved sinner. It is through faith in the Lord Jesus Christ that a sinner becomes a saint. See Rom. 1:7, *note.*

[2](1:1) This is the Christian's place as a member of the body of Christ, vitally united with Him by the baptism with the Holy Spirit (1 Cor. 12:12–13).

[3](1:3) The same Greek words rendered here "heavenly places" are translated "heavenly things" in Jn. 3:12. In both places the word signifies that which is heavenly in contradistinction to that which is earthly. "The heavenly places" may be defined as the sphere of the Christian's spiritual experience as identified with Christ in nature (2 Pet. 1:4); life (Col. 3:4; 1 Jn. 5:12); relationships (Jn. 20:17; Heb. 2:11); service (Mt. 28:20; Jn. 17:18); suffering (Phil. 1:29; 3:10; Col. 1:24); inheritance (Rom. 8:16–17); and future glory in the kingdom (Rom. 8:18–21; 1 Pet. 2:9; Rev. 1:6; 5:10). The Christian is a heavenly person, and a stranger and pilgrim on the earth (Heb. 3:1; 1 Pet. 2:11).

[4](1:5) "Adoption" (Gk. *huiothesia,* meaning *placing as a son*) is not so much a word of relationship as of position. In regeneration a Christian receives the nature of a child of God; in adoption he receives the position of a son of God. Every Christian obtains the place of a child and the right to be called a son the moment he believes (Gal. 3:25–26; 4:6; 1 Jn. 3:1,2).

7
a See Rom. 3:24, *note*
b *Sacrifice* (of Christ): v. 7; Eph. 2:13. (Gen. 3:15; Heb. 10:18, *note*)
c *Forgiveness:* v. 7; Eph. 4:32. (Lev. 4:20; Mt. 26:28, *note*)
d See Rom. 3:23, *note*
e *Grace:* v. 7; Eph. 2:5. (Jn. 1:14; Jn. 1:17, *note*). See 2 Pet. 3:18, *note*
9
f See Mt. 13:11, *note*
10
g Lit. *stewardship.* See Rev. 20:4, *note*
11
h *Predestination:* v. 11. (Rom. 8:29; Eph. 1:11)
i Isa. 46:10
12
j Or *hoped*
k vv. 6,14
13
l *Gospel:* v. 13; Eph. 2:17. (Gen. 12:3; Rev. 14:6)
m See Rom. 1:16, *note*
n *Faith:* vv. 13,15,19; Eph. 2:8. (Gen. 3:20; Heb. 11:39,

7 In Him we have [a]redemp-
tion through His [b]blood, the
[c]forgiveness of [d]sins, according to the riches of His [e]grace
8 which He made to abound
toward us in all wisdom and
prudence,
9 having made known to us
the [f]mystery of His will, according to His good pleasure
which He purposed in Himself,
10 that in the [g]dispensation
of the fullness of the times He
might gather together in one all
things in Christ, both* which
are in heaven and which are on
earth—in Him.
11 In Him also we have obtained an inheritance, being
[1h]predestined according to the
purpose of Him who works all
things according to the [i]coun-
sel of His will,
12 that we who first [j]trusted
in Christ should be to the
[k]praise of His glory.
13 In Him you also *trusted,*
after you heard the word of
truth, the [l]gospel of your [m]sal-
vation; in whom also, having
[n]believed, you were [2]sealed
with the [o]Holy Spirit of promise,
14 who* is the [p]guarantee of
our inheritance until the redemption of the purchased possession, to the praise of His
glory.

(2) Prayer for knowledge and power

15 Therefore I also, after I
heard of your [n]faith in the Lord
Jesus and your [q]love for all the
saints,
16 do not cease to give
thanks for you, making mention
of you in my [r]prayers:
17 that the God of our Lord
Jesus Christ, the Father of
glory, may give to you the spirit
of wisdom and revelation in the
knowledge of Him,
18 the eyes of your understanding* being enlightened;
that you may know what is the
hope of His calling, what are the
riches of the glory of His inheritance in the saints,
19 and what *is* the exceeding
greatness of His power toward
us who [n]believe, according to
the working of His mighty
power
20 which He worked in
Christ when He [s]raised Him
from the dead and seated *Him*
at His right hand in the heavenly *places,*
21 far above all principality
and power and might and dominion, and every name that is
named, not only in this [t]age but
also in that which is to come.

(3) Christ exalted as the Head of His body, the Church

22 And He [u]put all *things* under His feet, and gave Him *to be*
head over all *things* to the
[v]church,

*
1:10 NU-Text and M-Text omit *both.*
1:14 NU-Text reads *which.* 1:18 NU-Text and M-Text read *hearts.*

note)
o *Holy Spirit* (NT): v. 13; Eph. 2:18. (Mt. 1:18; Acts 2:4, *note*)
14
p *Assurance/security:* v. 14; Eph. 4:30. (Ps. 23:1; Jude 1, *note*)
15
q *Law* (of Christ): v. 15; Eph. 3:17. (Jn. 13:34; 2 Jn. 5)
16
r *Bible prayers* (NT): vv. 16–23; Eph. 3:14. (Mt. 6:9; Lk. 11:2, *note*)
20
s *Resurrection:* vv. 20–21; Phil. 3:10. (2 Ki. 4:35; 1 Cor. 15:52, *note*)
21
t Gk. *aiōn.* See Mk. 10:30, *note*
22
u Ps. 8:6
v *Church* (the true): v. 22; Eph. 1:23. (Mt. 16:18; Heb. 12:23)

The indwelling Spirit gives the realization of this in the Christian's present experience (Gal. 4:6); but the full manifestation of his sonship awaits the resurrection, change, and translation of saints, which is called "the redemption of our body" (Rom. 8:23; Eph. 1:14; 1 Th. 4:14–17; 1 Jn. 3:2).

[1](1:11) "Predestine" means *to mark out* or *determine beforehand.* In Scripture this idea is more inclusive than election. The latter is always limited to those specially chosen of God. But predestination includes the salvation of the elect and also all other acts and events in the universe, both good and evil (Acts 4:27–28, Gk.). Within the total predestined plan of God, it is necessary to distinguish between two classes of decreed events: (1) events divinely *caused,* such as the salvation of the elect; and (2) events divinely *permitted.* To say that God predestined the evil acts of men does not mean that God caused these acts, for this would make God the author of evil. Rather it means that God, foreknowing how men will act under various circumstances, determined beforehand to permit them so to act; thus making the acts certain to come to pass, as parts of His total plan, yet leaving all men fully responsible for what they do (Lk. 22:22; Acts 2:23). The Biblical truth of predestination raises difficult intellectual problems, but these cannot be escaped by rejecting predestination and affirming foreknowledge. For, if God foreknows all events, then they are just as certain as if they were predestined. See Election, 1 Pet. 5:13, *note;* Foreknowledge, 1 Pet. 1:20, *note.*

[2](1:13) The Holy Spirit is Himself the seal. In the symbolism of Scripture a seal signifies: (1) a finished transaction (Jer. 32:9–10; Jn. 17:4; 19:30); (2) ownership (Jer. 32:11–12; 2 Tim. 2:19); and (3) security (Est. 8:8; Dan. 6:17; Eph. 4:30).

23 which is His [a]body, the
fullness of Him who fills all in
all.

(4) Method of salvation

2 AND you *He* [b]*made alive,*
who were dead in [c]tres-
passes and sins,
2 in which you once walked
according to the course of this
[d]world, according to the
[e]prince of the power of the air,
the spirit who now works in the
sons of disobedience,
3 among whom also we all
once conducted ourselves in the
lusts of our [f]flesh, fulfilling the
desires of the [f]flesh and of the
mind, and were by nature children of wrath, just as the others.
4 But God, who is [g]rich in
mercy, because of His [h]great
love with which He loved us,
5 [i]even when we were
[1][j]dead in [c]trespasses, [k]made
us alive together with Christ (by
[l]grace you have been [m]saved),
6 and raised *us* up together,
and made *us* sit together in the
[n]heavenly *places* in Christ Jesus,
7 that in the ages to come
He might show the exceeding
[g]riches of His [l]grace in *His*
kindness toward us in Christ Jesus.
8 For by [l]grace you have
been [m]saved through [o]faith,
and that not of yourselves; *it is*
the [p]gift of God,
9 not of [q]works, lest anyone
should [r]boast.
10 For we are His workmanship, [s]created in Christ Jesus
for good [t]works, which God
prepared beforehand that we
should walk in them.

(5) Position of Gentiles by nature

11 Therefore remember that
you, once Gentiles in the flesh—
who are called Uncircumcision
by what is called the Circumcision made in the flesh by
hands—
12 that at that time you were
without Christ, being aliens
from the commonwealth of Israel and strangers from the
[u]covenants of promise, having
no hope and without God in the
[v]world.
13 But now in Christ Jesus
you who once were far off have
been brought near by the
[w]blood of Christ.

(6) Jew and Gentile one body in Christ

14 For He Himself is our

23
a Church (the true): vv. 22–23; Eph. 2:16. (Mt. 16:18; Heb. 12:23)

CHAPTER 2

1
b v. 5; Jn. 5:21; 6:63; 1 Cor. 15:22,36,45; 2 Cor. 3:6; 1 Tim. 6:13; 1 Pet. 3:18
c See Rom. 3:23, *note*

2
d Gk. *kosmos.* See Rev. 13:8, *note*
e Satan: v. 2; Eph. 4:27. (Gen. 3:1; Rev. 20:10). Jn. 12:31; 1 Jn. 5:19

3
f Flesh: v. 3; Phil. 3:3. (Jn. 8:15; Jude 23)

4
g Ps. 103:8–11
h Jn. 3:16; 1 Jn. 4:9–10

5
i Rom. 5:8
j Death (spiritual): v. 5; Eph. 4:18. (Gen. 2:17; Eph. 2:5, *note*)
k Eph. 2:1
l Grace: vv. 5,7–8; Eph. 3:2. (Jn. 1:14; Jn. 1:17, *note*)
m See Rom. 1:16, *note*

6
n See Eph. 1:3, *note*

8
o Faith: v. 8; Eph. 3:12. (Gen. 3:20; Heb. 11:39, *note*)
p Jn. 1:12–13

9
q Rom. 4:4–5; 11:6
r Rom. 3:27

10
s See Eph. 4:24, *note*
t See Jn. 3:3, *note*

12
u See Heb. 8:8, *note*
v Gk. *kosmos.* See Mt. 4:8, *note*

13
w Sacrifice (of Christ): vv. 13–14; Eph. 2:15. (Gen. 3:15; Heb. 10:18, *note*)

[1](2:5) Death (spiritual), Summary: Spiritual death is the state of the natural or unregenerate man as still in his sins (2:1), alienated from the life of God (4:18–19), and destitute of the Spirit (Rom. 8:9). Prolonged beyond the death of the body, spiritual death is a state of eternal separation from God in conscious suffering. This is called "the second death" (Rev. 2:11; 20:6,14, *note;* 21:8).

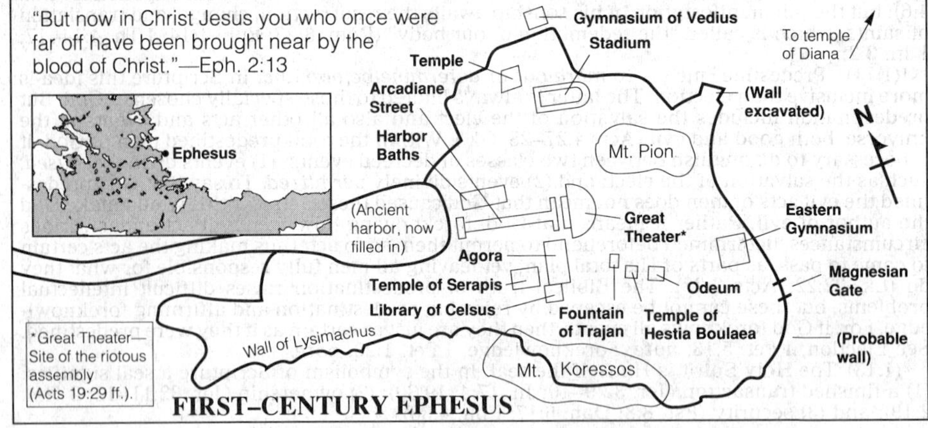

15
a Sacrifice (of Christ): vv. 13–16; Eph. 5:2. (Gen. 3:15; Heb. 10:18, *note*)
b Law (of Moses): v. 15; Phil. 3:5. (Ex. 19:1; Gal. 3:24, *note*)
16
c Reconciliation: vv. 12–18; Col. 1:20. (Rom. 5:10; Col. 1:20)
d Church (the true): vv. 15–22; 3:6,10; Eph. 3:21. (Mt. 16:18; Heb. 12:23)
17
e Christ (first advent): v. 17; Phil. 2:7. (Gen. 3:15; Acts 1:11, *note*)
f Gospel: v. 17; 3:1–10; Eph. 6:15. (Gen. 12:3; Rev. 14:6)
18
g Holy Spirit (NT): vv. 18,22; 3:5; Eph. 3:16. (Mt. 1:18; Acts 2:4, *note*)
20
h 1 Cor. 3:11
i Christ (Stone): v. 20; 1 Pet. 2:4. (Gen. 49:24; 1 Pet. 2:8)
21
j Sanctification (NT): v. 21; 3:5; Eph. 4:24. (Mt. 4:5; Rev. 22:11)
k 1 Cor. 3:16–17
22
l Jn. 17:23

peace, who has made both one,
and has broken down the middle wall of separation,
15 having abolished [a]in His
flesh the enmity, *that is,* the
[b]law of commandments *contained* in ordinances, so as to
create in Himself one [1]new man
from the two, *thus* making
peace,
16 and that He might [c]recon-
cile them both to God in one
[d]body through the [a]cross,
thereby putting to death the enmity.
17 And He [e]came and
[f]preached peace to you who
were afar off and to those who
were near.
18 For through Him we both
have access by one [g]Spirit to
the Father.

(7) The Church a temple for the habitation of God through the Spirit

19 Now, therefore, you are
no longer strangers and foreigners, but [d]fellow citizens
with the saints and members of
the household of God,
20 having been built on the
[h]foundation of the apostles and
prophets, Jesus Christ Himself
being the chief [i]corner*stone,*
21 in whom the whole building, being fitted together, grows
into a [j]holy [k]temple in the
Lord,
22 in whom you also are being built together for a [l]dwell-
ing place of God in the [g]Spirit.

(8) The Church a "mystery" hidden from past ages (cp. Col.1:24–27)

3 FOR this reason I, Paul, the
prisoner of Christ Jesus for
you Gentiles—
2 if indeed you have heard
of the [m]dispensation of the
[n]grace of God which was given
to me for you,
3 how that by revelation He
made known to me the [o]mys-
tery (as I have briefly [p]written
already,
4 by which, when you read,
you may understand my knowledge in the [o]mystery of Christ),
5 which in other [q]ages was
not made known to the sons of
men, as it has now been [p]re-
vealed by the [g]Spirit to His
[j]holy apostles and prophets:
6 [2]that the Gentiles should
be fellow heirs, of the same
[d]body, and partakers of His
promise in Christ through the
[f]gospel,
7 of which I [r]became a minister according to the gift of the
[n]grace of God given to me by
the effective working of His
[s]power.
8 To me, who am less than
the [t]least of all the [u]saints, this
[n]grace was given, that I should
[f]preach among the [v]Gentiles
the [w]unsearchable riches of
Christ,
9 and to make all see what *is*
the fellowship* of the [o]mys-
tery, which from the beginning
of the [x]ages has been hidden in
God who [y]created all things
through Jesus Christ;*
10 to the intent that now the
manifold wisdom of God might
be made known by the [d]church
to the [z]principalities and powers in the [aa]heavenly *places,*
11 [bb]according to the eternal
purpose which He accom-
plished in Christ Jesus our
Lord,
12 in whom we have [cc]bold-

*3:9 NU-Text and M-Text read *stewardship (dispensation).* • NU-Text omits *through Jesus Christ.*

CHAPTER 3
2
m Lit. *stewardship*
n Grace: vv. 2,7–8; Eph. 4:7. (Jn. 1:14; Jn. 1:17, *note*). See 2 Pet. 3:18, *note*
3
o See Mt. 13:11, *note*
p Inspiration: vv. 3–5; Eph. 4:8. (Ex. 4:15; 2 Tim. 3:16, *note*)
5
q Lit. *generations*
7
r Acts 9:15; 22:21; Gal. 1:16; 2:7–9; Eph. 3:8
s Cp. Gal. 2:7–8
8
t 1 Cor. 15:9; cp. 1 Tim. 1:15
u Cp. Rom. 1:7; 8:27; 12:13; 16:2
v See v. 6, *note;* Acts 9:15; Rom. 11:13
w vv. 18–19; Col. 2:2–3
9
x Gk. *aiōn.* See Mk. 10:30, *note*
y Jn. 1:3; Col. 1:16; Heb. 1:2
10
z Eph. 1:21
aa See Eph. 1:3, *note*
11
bb Eph. 1:4, 11
12
cc Heb. 10:19

---

[1](2:15) Here, and possibly in 4:13, the "new man" is not the individual believer but the Church, considered as the body of Christ in the sense of 1 Cor. 12:12–13; Eph. 1:22–23; cp. Col. 3:10–11; see Heb. 12:23, *note.*

[2](3:6) That Gentiles were to be saved was no mystery (Rom. 9:24–33; 10:19–21). The mystery "hidden in God" was the divine purpose to make of Jew and Gentile a wholly new thing—"the church, which is His [Christ's] body," formed by the baptism with the Holy Spirit (1 Cor. 12:12–13) and in which the earthly distinction of Jew and Gentile disappears (Eph. 2:14–15; Col. 3:10–11). The revelation of this "mystery" of the Church was foretold but not explained by Christ (Mt. 16:18). The details concerning the doctrine, position, walk, and destiny of the Church were committed to Paul and his fellow "apostles and prophets" by the Spirit (Eph. 3:5).

12
a Faith: vv. 12,17; Phil. 1:29. (Gen. 3:20; Heb. 11:39, *note*)
14
b Cp. Eph. 3:1
c Bible prayers (NT): vv. 14–21; Phil. 1:9. (Mt. 6:9; Lk. 11:2, *note*)
d Eph. 1:3
15
e Lit. *every family*
16
f Eph. 1:7; 2:4; Phil. 4:19
g Col. 1:11
h Holy Spirit (NT): v. 16; 4:3–4; Eph. 4:30. (Mt. 1:18; Acts 2:4, *note*)
17
i Jn. 14:23; cp. Col. 1:27
j Law (of Christ): vv. 17,19; 4:2; Eph. 4:15. (Jn. 13:34; 2 Jn. 5)
18
k Cp. Eph. 1:18
l Cp. Rom. 1:7; 8:27; 12:13; 16:2
m Cp. 2 Tim. 2:7
21
n Church (the true): v. 21; 4:4, 12; Eph. 4:16. (Mt. 16:18; Heb. 12:23)
o Gk. *aiōn.* See Mk. 10:30, *note*
CHAPTER 4
1
p 1 Th. 2:12

ness and access with confidence through [a]faith in Him.

(9) Prayer for apprehension

13 Therefore I ask that you
do not lose heart at my tribulations for you, which is your
glory.
14 [b]For this reason I [c]bow
my knees to the [d]Father of our
Lord Jesus Christ,*
15 from whom [e]the whole
family in heaven and earth is
named,
16 that He would grant you,
according to the [f]riches of His
glory, to be [g]strengthened with
might through His [h]Spirit in the
inner man,
17 that Christ may [i]dwell in
your hearts through [a]faith; that
you, being rooted and grounded
in [j]love,
18 may be [k]able to comprehend with all the [l]saints [m]what
is the width and length and
depth and height—
19 to know the [j]love of
Christ which passes knowledge; that you may be filled
with all the fullness of God.
20 Now to Him who is able to
do exceedingly abundantly
above all that we ask or think,
according to the power that
works in us,
21 to Him *be* glory in the
[n]church by Christ Jesus to all
generations, [o]forever and ever.
Amen.

II. The Walk and Service of the Believer, 4:1—5:17

(1) A walk worthy of high position

4 I, THEREFORE, the pris-
oner of the Lord, beseech
you to [p]walk worthy of the calling with which you were called,
2 with all lowliness and
gentleness, with longsuffering,
bearing with one another in
[j]love,
3 endeavoring to keep the
unity of the [h]Spirit in the bond
of peace.

(2) Seven unities to be kept

4 *There is* one [n]body and
one [h]Spirit, just as you were
called in one hope of your calling;
5 [q]one Lord, [r]one faith,
[s]one baptism;
6 [t]one God and Father of
all, who *is* above all, and
through all, and in you* all.

(3) The gifts of the risen Christ and their purpose (cp. 1 Cor. 12:4–11)

7 But to each one of us
[u]grace was given according to
the measure of Christ's gift.
8 Therefore He [v]says:

[w]*"When He ascended on high,*
He led captivity captive,
And gave gifts to men."

9 (Now this, *"He ascend-
ed"*—what does it mean but
that He also first* descended
into the lower parts of the
earth?
10 He who descended is also
the One who ascended far
above all the heavens, that He
might [x]fill all things.)
11 And He Himself [1]gave
[2]some *to be* apostles, some
prophets, some evangelists, and
some pastors and teachers,
12 for the equipping of the
saints for the work of ministry,
for the [y]edifying of the [n]body of
Christ,
13 till we all come to the
unity of the faith and of the
knowledge of the Son of God, to
a [z]perfect [aa]man, to the measure
of the stature of the fullness of
Christ;
14 that we should no longer

5
q 1 Cor. 1:13; 8:6
r 1 Cor. 15:1–8
s 1 Cor. 12:12–13
6
t 1 Cor. 8:6; 12:6
7
u Grace: v. 7; Eph. 4:29. (Jn. 1:14; Jn. 1:17, *note*). See 2 Pet. 3:18, *note*
8
v Inspiration: v. 8; Eph. 4:17. (Ex. 4:15; 2 Tim. 3:16, *note*)
w Ps. 68:18
10
x Eph. 1:23
12
y Rom. 14:19; 15:2; 1 Cor. 14:26; 2 Cor. 10:8; 12:19; Eph. 4:12,29
13
z See Phil. 3:12, *note*
aa See Eph. 2:15, *note*

*
3:14 NU-Text omits *of our Lord Jesus Christ.* **4:6** NU-Text omits *you;* M-Text reads *us.* **4:9** NU-Text omits *first.*

[1](4:11) In 1 Cor. 12:8–28 the Holy Spirit is seen as enduing the members of the body of Christ with spiritual gifts, or enablements for a varied service; here certain Spirit-endued men, i.e. apostles, prophets, evangelists, pastors and teachers are themselves the gifts whom the glorified Christ bestows on His body the Church. In 1 Corinthians, the gifts are spiritual enablements for specific service; in Ephesians, the gifts are men who have such enablements.

[2](4:11) The Lord, in bestowing the gifted men, determines providentially (e.g. Acts 11:22–26), or directly through the Holy Spirit (e.g. Acts 13:1–2; 16:6–7), the places of their service. Some churches or places need one gift, as, e.g. an evangelist; others need rather a pastor or teacher. Absolutely nothing in Christ's service is left to mere human judgment or self-choosing. Even an apostle was not permitted to choose his place of service (Acts 16:7–8).

be [a]children, tossed to and fro
and carried about with every
wind of doctrine, by the trickery
of men, in the cunning craftiness of deceitful plotting,
15 but, [b]speaking the truth in
[c]love, may grow up in all things
into Him who is the [d]head—
Christ—
16 from whom the whole
[e]body, joined and knit together
by what every joint supplies, according to the effective working
by which every part does its
share, causes growth of the
[e]body for the [f]edifying of itself
in [c]love.

(4) The walk of the believer as a new man in Christ

17 This I say, therefore, and
[g]testify in the Lord, that you
should no longer [h]walk as the
rest of the* Gentiles walk, in
the futility of their mind,
18 having their understanding darkened, being [i]alienated
from the [j]life of God, because
of the ignorance that is in them,
because of the blindness of their
heart;
19 who, [k]being past feeling,
have [l]given themselves over to
lewdness, to work all uncleanness with greediness.
20 But you have not so
learned Christ,
21 if indeed you have heard
Him and have been taught by
Him, as the truth is in Jesus:
22 that you [m]put off, concerning your former conduct, the
[n]old man which grows corrupt
according to the deceitful lusts,
23 and be [o]renewed in the
spirit of your mind,
24 and that you put on the
[1]new man which was created
according to God, in true [p]righ-
teousness and [q]holiness.
25 Therefore, putting away
lying, [r]*"Let each one of you*
speak truth with his neighbor,"
for we are members of one another.
26 [s]*"Be angry, and do not*
[t]*sin"*: do not let the sun go
down on your wrath,
27 [u]nor give place to the
[v]devil.
28 Let him who stole steal no
longer, but rather let him labor,
working with *his* hands what is
good, that he may have something to [w]give him who has
need.
29 Let no corrupt word proceed out of your [x]mouth, but
what is good for necessary [f]edi-
fication, that it may impart
[y]grace to the hearers.

(5) The walk of the believer as indwelt by the Spirit

30 And do not grieve the
Holy [z]Spirit of God, by whom
you [aa]were [bb]sealed for the day
of [cc]redemption.
31 Let all bitterness, wrath,
anger, clamor, and evil speaking be put away from you, with
all malice.
32 And be kind to one an-
other, tenderhearted, [dd]forgiv-
ing one another, [ee]even as God
in Christ [ff]forgave you.

(6) The walk of the believer as God's dear child

5 THEREFORE be imitators
of God as dear [gg]children.
2 And walk in [c]love, as
Christ also has [hh]loved us and
given Himself for us, an offering and a [ii]sacrifice to God for a
[jj]sweet-smelling aroma.
3 But [kk]fornication and all
[ll]uncleanness or [mm]covetous-
ness, let it not even be named
among you, as is fitting for
[nn]saints;
4 neither [oo]filthiness, nor
[pp]foolish talking, nor coarse
[qq]jesting, which are not [rr]fitting,
but rather [ss]giving of thanks.
5 For this you know,* that
no [tt]fornicator, unclean person,
nor covetous man, who is an

qq Cp. Prov. 26:19 *rr* Rom. 1:28 *ss* Phil. 4:6; Col. 3:17; 1 Th. 5:18 **5:5** *tt* 1 Cor. 5:11

*

4:17 NU-Text omits *rest of the.*
5:5 NU-Text reads *For know this.*

14
a 1 Cor. 14:20
15
b 2 Tim. 1:13
c Law (of Christ): vv. 15–16; 5:2; Eph. 5:25. (Jn. 13:34; 2 Jn. 5)
d Eph. 1:22
16
e Church (the true): v. 16; Eph. 5:23. (Mt. 16:18; Heb. 12:23)
f Rom. 14:19; 15:2; 1 Cor. 14:26; 2 Cor. 10:8; 12:19; Eph. 4:12,29
17
g Inspiration: v. 17; Eph. 5:14. (Ex. 4:15; 2 Tim. 3:16, *note*)
h Eph. 2:2
18
i Death (spiritual): v. 18; Col. 2:13. (Gen. 2:17; Eph. 2:5, *note*)
j Life (eternal): v. 18; Phil. 4:3. (Mt. 7:14; Rev. 22:19)
19
k 1 Tim. 4:2
l Cp. Rom. 1:24–32
22
m Col. 3:9–10
n See Rom. 6:6, *note*
23
o Rom. 12:2
24
p See Rom. 10:10, *note*
q Sanctification (NT): v. 24; Eph. 5:26. (Mt. 4:5; Rev. 22:11)
25
r Zech. 8:16
26
s Ps. 4:4
t See Rom. 3:23, *note*
27
u Jas. 4:7
v Satan: v. 27; Eph. 6:11. (Gen. 3:1; Rev. 20:10)
28
w Cp. Lk. 3:11
29
x Cp. Mt. 12:34–35
y Grace: v. 29; Eph. 6:24. (Jn. 1:14; Jn. 1:17, *note*). See 2 Pet. 3:18, *note*
30
z Holy Spirit (NT): v. 30; Eph. 5:18. (Mt. 1:18; Acts 2:4, *note*)
aa Assurance/security: v. 30; Phil. 1:6. (Ps. 23:1; Jude 1, *note*)
bb See Eph. 1:13, *note*
cc See Rom. 3:24, *note*
32
dd Lk. 6:37
ee Cp. Mt. 18:21–35
ff Forgiveness: v. 32; Col. 1:14. (Lev. 4:20; Mt. 26:28, *note*)
CHAPTER 5
1
gg 1 Pet. 1:14–16
2
hh Jn. 15:9; 1 Jn. 3:16
ii Sacrifice (of Christ): v. 2; Eph. 5:25. (Gen. 3:15; Heb. 10:18, *note*)
jj See Lev. 1:9, *note*
3
kk 1 Cor. 5:1; Gal. 5:19; Eph. 5:3; Col. 3:5; 1 Th. 4:3; cp. 2 Cor. 12:21; Jude 7
ll Col. 3:5–7
mm Lk. 12:15
nn Cp. Rom. 1:7; 8:27; 12:13; 16:2
4
oo Jas. 1:21
pp Ti. 3:9

[1](4:24) The "new man" is the regenerate man as distinguished from the old man (Rom. 6:6, *note*), and is a new man as having become a partaker of the divine nature and life (Col. 3:3–4; 2 Pet. 1:4), and in no sense the old man made over, or improved (2 Cor. 5:17; Gal. 6:15; Eph. 2:10; Col. 3:10). The new man is Christ "formed" in the Christian (Gal. 2:20; 4:19; Col. 1:27; 1 Jn. 4:12).

idolater, has any [a]inheritance
in the [b]kingdom of Christ and
[c]God.
6 Let no one deceive you
with empty words, for because
of these things the wrath of God
comes upon the [d]sons of disobedience.
7 Therefore do not be [e]par-
takers with them.
8 For you were once darkness, but now *you are* [f]light in
the Lord. Walk as children of
light
9 (for the fruit of the Spirit*
is in all goodness, [g]righteous-
ness, and truth),
10 [h]finding out what is acceptable to the Lord.
11 And have [i]no fellowship
with the unfruitful works of
darkness, but rather expose
them.
12 For it is shameful even to
[j]speak of those things which
are done by them in secret.
13 But all things that are exposed are [k]made manifest by
the light, for whatever makes
manifest is light.
14 Therefore He [l]says:

[m]"Awake, you who sleep,
Arise from the dead,
And Christ will give you
light."

15 See then that you walk circumspectly, not as fools but as
wise,
16 [n]redeeming the time, because the days are evil.
17 Therefore do not be unwise, but understand what the
will of the Lord *is.*

III. The Walk and Warfare
of the Spirit-filled Believer,
5:18—6:20

(1) The inner life
of the Spirit-filled believer

18 And do not be drunk with
wine, in which is dissipation;
but be filled with the [o]Spirit,
19 speaking to one another in
psalms and hymns and spiritual
songs, singing and making
[p]melody in your heart to the
Lord,
20 [q]giving thanks always for
all things to God the Father in
the name of our Lord Jesus
Christ,
21 [r]submitting to one another in the fear of God.*

(2) The married life
of Spirit-filled believers as
illustrating Christ and the Church

22 Wives, [s]submit to your
own husbands, as to the Lord.
23 For the husband is [t]head
of the wife, as also Christ is
[u]head of the [v]church; and He is
the [w]Savior of the body.
24 Therefore, just as the
[v]church is subject to Christ, so
let the wives *be* to their own
husbands in everything.
25 Husbands, [x]love your
wives, [1]just as Christ also
[y]loved the [v]church and [z]gave
Himself for [aa]her,
26 that He might [bb]sanctify
and cleanse her with the washing of water [cc]by the word,
27 that He might present
[aa]her to Himself a glorious
[v]church, not having spot or
wrinkle or any such thing, but
that she should be holy and
without blemish.
28 So husbands ought to
[x]love their own wives as their
own bodies; he who loves his
wife loves himself.
29 For no one ever hated his
own flesh, but nourishes and
cherishes it, just as [dd]the Lord
does the [v]church.
30 For [ee]we are members of
His [v]body,* of His flesh and of
His bones.
31 [ff]*"For this reason a man*
shall leave his father and
mother and be joined to his
wife, and the two shall become
one flesh."
32 This is a great [gg]mystery,
but I [l]speak concerning Christ
and the [2v]church.

*5:9 NU-Text reads *light.* 5:21 NU-Text reads *Christ.* 5:30 NU-Text omits the rest of this verse.

5 *a* 1 Cor. 6:9–10 *b Kingdom* (NT): v. 5; 1 Tim. 6:15. (Mt. 2:2; 1 Cor. 15:24, *note*) *c* See Mt. 6:33, *note*
6 *d* Eph. 2:2–3
7 *e* 1 Tim. 5:22
8 *f* 1 Th. 5:5
9 *g* See 1 Jn. 3:7, *note*
10 *h* Rom. 12:1–2
11 *i* 2 Cor. 6:14
12 *j* Cp. v. 3
13 *k* Jn. 3:21
14 *l Inspiration*: vv. 14, 32; Col. 2:4. (Ex. 4:15; 2 Tim. 3:16, *note*) *m* Isa. 26:19; 60:1
16 *n* Col. 4:5
18 *o Holy Spirit* (NT): v. 18; Eph. 6:17. (Mt. 1:18; Acts 2:4, *note*)
19 *p* Jas. 5:13
20 *q* Phil. 4:6; Col. 3:17; 1 Th. 5:18
21 *r* 1 Pet. 5:5
22 *s* Col. 3:18; 1 Pet. 3:1–6; cp. Gen. 3:16
23 *t* 1 Cor. 11:3 *u* Col. 1:18 *v Church* (the true): vv. 23–32; Col. 1:18. (Mt. 16:18; Heb. 12:23) *w* See Rom. 1:16, *note*
25 *x Law* (of Christ): vv. 25,28; Eph. 6:23. (Jn. 13:34; 2 Jn. 5) *y* Jn. 15:9; 1 Jn. 3:16 *z Sacrifice* (of Christ): v. 25; Col. 1:14. (Gen. 3:15; Heb. 10:18, *note*) *aa Bride* (of Christ): vv. 25,27; Rev. 19:7. (Jn. 3:29; Rev. 19:7, *note*)
26 *bb Sanctification* (NT): v. 26; Col. 1:22. (Mt. 4:5; Rev. 22:11) *cc* Jn. 15:3; 17:17
29 *dd* Lit. *Christ*
30 *ee* i.e. *believers*
31 *ff* Gen. 2:24
32 *gg* See Mt. 13:11, *note*

[1](5:25) Christ's labor of love on behalf of the Church is threefold: past, present, and future: (1) for love He gave Himself to redeem the Church (v. 25); (2) in love He is sanctifying the Church (v. 26); and (3) for the reward of His sacrifice and labor of love He will present the Church to Himself in flawless perfection, "one pearl of great price" (v. 27; Mt. 13:46).

[2](5:32) Verses 30–31 are quoted from Gen. 2:23–24 and exclude the interpretation that the

33 Nevertheless let each one of you in particular so love his own wife as himself, and let the wife *see* that she [a]respects *her* husband.

(3) The domestic life of Spirit-filled believers as children and servants

6 CHILDREN, [b]obey your parents in the Lord, for this is right.

2 [c]*"Honor your father and mother,"* which is the first commandment with promise:

3 *"that it may be well with you and you may live long on the earth."*

4 And you, fathers, do not [d]provoke your children to wrath, but [e]bring them up in the [f]training and admonition of the Lord.

5 [g]Bondservants, be obedient to those who are your masters according to the flesh, with fear and trembling, in sincerity of heart, as to Christ;

6 not with [h]eyeservice, as men-pleasers, but as bondservants of Christ, doing the will of God from the heart,

7 with goodwill doing service, as to the Lord, and not to men,

8 knowing that whatever good anyone does, he will [i]receive the same from the Lord, whether *he is* a slave or free.

9 And you, masters, do the same things to them, [j]giving up threatening, knowing that your own [k]Master also* is in heaven, and there is no [l]partiality with Him.

(4) The warfare of Spirit-filled believers

(a) The warrior's power

10 Finally, my [m]brethren, [n]be strong in the Lord and in the power of His might.

(b) The warrior's armor

11 Put on the whole [o]armor of God, that you may be able to stand against the wiles of the [p]devil.

(c) The warrior's foes

12 For we do not wrestle against flesh and blood, but against principalities, against powers, against the [q]rulers of the darkness of this age,* against spiritual *hosts* of wickedness in the heavenly *places.*

13 Therefore take up the whole [o]armor of God, that you may be able to withstand in the evil day, and having done all, to stand.

14 Stand therefore, having girded your [r]waist with truth, having put on the [s]breastplate of righteousness,

15 and having shod your [t]feet with the [u]preparation of the [v]gospel of peace;

16 above all, taking the [w]shield of faith with which you will be able to quench all the fiery darts of the [p]wicked one.

17 And take the [x]helmet of [y]salvation, and the [z]sword of the [aa]Spirit, which is the [v]word of God;

(d) The warrior's resource

18 [bb]praying always with all prayer and supplication in the [aa]Spirit, being watchful to this end with all perseverance and supplication for all the saints—

19 and for me, that utterance may be given to me, [cc]that I may open my mouth boldly to make known the [dd]mystery of the [v]gospel,

20 for which I am an [ee]ambassador in chains; that in it I may speak boldly, as I ought to speak.

Conclusion, 6:21–24

21 But that you also may know my affairs *and* how I am doing, [ff]Tychicus, a beloved brother and [gg]faithful minister in the Lord, will make all things known to you;

22 whom I have sent to you for this very purpose, that you

*

6:9 NU-Text reads *He who is both their Master and yours.* **6:12** NU-Text reads *rulers of this darkness.*

33
a 1 Pet. 3:1
CHAPTER 6
1
b Col. 3:20
2
c Ex. 20:12; Dt. 5:16; cp. Jer. 35:8–19
4
d Col. 3:21
e Prov. 22:6
f Or *discipline*
5
g 1 Pet. 2:18
6
h Col. 3:22
8
i Rewards: v. 8; Phil. 4:1. (Dan. 12:3; 1 Cor. 3:14, *note*)
9
j Cp. 1 Pet. 2:23
k Col. 4:1
l Acts 10:34; Rom. 2:11; Col. 3:25
10
m Mt. 23:8; Lk. 8:21; Jn. 21:23; Rom. 8:29; Heb. 2:11, 17; Rev. 12:10; 19:10
n Cp. Josh. 1:6,7,9
11
o Cp. Rom. 13:12; 2 Cor. 6:7
p Satan: vv. 11,16; 1 Th. 2:18. (Gen. 3:1; Rev. 20:10)
12
q Lit. *world rulers,* Gk. *kosmokratores*
14
r Cp. Isa. 11:5; Lk. 12:35; 1 Pet. 1:13
s Isa. 59:17; cp. 1 Th. 5:8
15
t Cp. Isa. 52:7; Rom. 10:15
u Lit. *readiness*
v Gospel: vv. 15,17,19; Phil. 1:5. (Gen. 12:3; Rev. 14:6)
16
w Cp. 1 Jn. 5:4
17
x Cp. Isa. 59:17
y See Rom. 1:16, *note*
z Cp. Heb. 4:12
aa Holy Spirit (NT): vv. 17–18; Phil. 1:19. (Mt. 1:18; Acts 2:4, *note*)
18
bb Col. 4:2; 1 Th. 5:17
19
cc Acts 4:29; Col. 4:3
dd See Mt. 13:11, *note*
20
ee 2 Cor. 5:20
21
ff Acts 20:4; 2 Tim. 4:12; Ti. 3:12
gg 1 Cor. 4:1–2; cp. Col. 1:7

reference is to the Church only as the body of Christ. Eve, taken from Adam's body, was truly "bone of [his] bones and flesh of [his] flesh," but she was also his wife, united with him in a relation which makes of "two . . . one flesh" (Mt. 19:5–6), and so a clear type of the Church as bride of Christ (cp. 2 Cor. 11:2–3). The bride types are Eve (Gen. 2:23–24), and Rebekah (Gen. 24:1–7, see *note* at v. 1). See Hos. 2:2, *note.*

may know our affairs, and *that*
he may [a]comfort your hearts.
23 Peace to the brethren, and
[b]love with faith, from God the
Father and the Lord Jesus
Christ.

24 [c]Grace *be* with all those
who love our Lord Jesus Christ
in sincerity. Amen.

22 a 2 Cor. 1:6; cp. 2 Cor. 7:13

23 b *Law* (of Christ): v. 23; Phil. 1:9. (Jn. 13:34; 2 Jn. 5)

24 c *Grace:* v. 24; Phil. 1:2. (Jn. 1:14; Jn. 1:17, *note*). See 2 Pet. 3:18, *note*

The Epistle of Paul the Apostle to the

PHILIPPIANS

Author: Paul *Theme:* Christian Experience *Date of writing:* c. A.D. 60

THE EPISTLE TO THE PHILIPPIANS, one of Paul's prison epistles, was written in Rome. It was at Philippi, which the apostle visited on his second missionary journey (Acts 16:12), that Lydia and the Philippian jailor and his family were converted to Christ (Acts 16:14–34). Now, some few years later, the church was well established, as may be inferred from its address which includes "bishops [elders] and deacons" (1:1).

The occasion of the Epistle was to acknowledge a gift of money from the church at Philippi, brought to the apostle by Epaphroditus, one of its members (4:10–18). This is a tender letter to a group of Christians who were especially close to the heart of Paul (2 Cor. 8:1–6), and comparatively little is said about doctrinal error.

The key verse is, "For to me, to live is Christ, and to die is gain" (1:21). Paul was Nero's prisoner, yet the Epistle fairly shouts with triumph, the words "joy" and "rejoice" appearing frequently (1:4,18,25,26; 2:2,28; 3:1; 4:1,4,10). Right Christian experience is the outworking, whatever our circumstances may be, of the life, nature, and mind of Christ living in us (1:6,11; 2:5,13).

Philippians reaches its pinnacle at 2:5–11 with the glorious and profound declaration regarding the humiliation and exaltation of our Lord Jesus Christ.

The Epistle may be divided as follows:

Introduction, 1:1–7.

I. Christ, the Christian's Life: Rejoicing in Spite of Suffering, 1:8–30.
II. Christ, the Christian's Pattern: Rejoicing in Lowly Service, 2:1–30.
III. Christ, Object of the Christian's Faith, Desire, and Expectation, 3:1–21.
IV. Christ, the Christian's Strength: Rejoicing through Anxiety, 4:1–19.

Conclusion, 4:20–23.

CHAPTER 1
1
a Churches (local): v. 1; Phil. 4:15. (Acts 8:3; Phil. 1:1, *note*)
b Elders: v. 1; 1 Tim. 3:1. (Acts 11:30; Ti. 1:5, *note*). 1 Tim. 3:1–7
c 1 Tim. 3:8–13
2
d Grace: vv. 2,7; Phil. 4:23. (Jn. 1:14; Jn. 1:17, *note*). See 2 Pet. 3:18, *note*
4
e Eph. 1:16; 1 Th. 1:2
5
f Gospel: vv. 5,7; Phil. 1:12. (Gen. 12:3; Rev.

Introduction:
Salutation and Thanksgiving,
1:1–7

1 PAUL and Timothy, bond-
servants of Jesus Christ,

To all the saints in Christ
Jesus [1]who are [a]in Philippi,
with the [b]bishops* and [c]dea-
cons:

2 [d]Grace to you and peace
from God our Father and the
Lord Jesus Christ.

3 I thank my God upon ev-
ery remembrance of you,
4 always in [e]every prayer
of mine making request for you
all with joy,
5 for your fellowship in the
[f]gospel from the first day until
now,
6 being confident of this
very thing, that He who has begun a good work in you will
[g]complete *it* until the [h]day of
Jesus Christ;
7 just as it is right for me to
think this of you all, because I
have you in my heart, inasmuch
as both in my chains and in the
defense and confirmation of the
[f]gospel, you all are partakers
with me of [d]grace.

I. Christ, the Christian's Life:
Rejoicing in Spite of Suffering,
1:8–30

(1) Joy triumphing over suffering

8 For God is my witness,
how greatly I long for you all
with the affection of Jesus
Christ.
9 And this I [i]pray, that your
[j]love may abound still more
and more in knowledge and all
discernment,
10 that you may approve the

*1:1 Literally *overseers*

14:6)
6
g Assurance/security: v. 6; Col. 2:2. (Ps. 23:1; Jude 1, *note*)
h Day (of Christ): v. 6; Phil 1:10. (1 Cor. 1:8. *note;* 2 Tim. 4:8)
9
i Bible prayers (NT): v. 9; Col. 1:3. (Mt. 6:9; Lk. 11:2, *note*)
j Law (of Christ): v. 9; Phil. 1:17. (Jn. 13:34; 2 Jn. 5)

---

[1](1:1) Churches (local), Summary: A local church is an assembly of professed believers in the Lord Jesus Christ, living for the most part in one locality, who meet together in His name for baptism, the Lord's Supper, worship, praise, prayer, fellowship, testimony, the ministry of the Word, discipline, and the furtherance of the Gospel (Acts 13:1–4; 20:7; 1 Cor. 5:4–5; 14:26; Phil. 4:14–18; 1 Th. 1:8; Heb. 10:25). Every such local church has Christ as its center, is a temple of God, and is indwelt by the Holy Spirit (1 Cor. 3:16–17). In organization a local church is here stated (v. 1) to be composed of "saints . . . with the bishops [elders, see 1 Tim. 3:1–13; Ti. 1:5, *note* 2] and deacons."

things that are excellent, that
you may be sincere and without
offense till the [a]day of Christ,
11 being filled with the
[b]fruits of [c]righteousness which
are by Jesus Christ, to the glory
and praise of God.
12 But I want you to know,
brethren, that the things *which*
happened to me have actually
turned out for the furtherance
of the [d]gospel,
13 so that it has become evident [e]to the whole palace
guard, and to all the rest, that
my chains are in Christ;
14 and most of the brethren
in the Lord, having become confident by my chains, [1]are much
more bold to speak the [d]word
without fear.
15 Some indeed [d]preach
Christ even from envy and
strife, and some also from goodwill:
16 The former* [d]preach
Christ from selfish ambition,
not sincerely, supposing to add
affliction to my chains;
17 but the latter out of [f]love,
knowing that I am appointed
for the defense of the [d]gospel.
18 What then? Only *that* in
every way, whether in pretense
or in truth, Christ is [d]preached;
and in this I [2][g]rejoice, yes, and
will rejoice.

(2) Paul's expectation of deliverance

19 For I know that [h]this will
turn out for my [i]deliverance
through your prayer and the
supply of the [j]Spirit of Jesus
Christ,
20 according to my earnest
expectation and hope that in
nothing I shall be ashamed, but
with all [k]boldness, as always,
so now also Christ will be magnified in my [l]body, whether by
life [m]or by death.
21 For to me, to live *is* Christ,
and to [n]die *is* gain.
22 But if *I* live on in the flesh,
this *will mean* fruit from *my* labor; yet what I shall choose I
cannot tell.
23 For* I am hard pressed
between the two, having a [o]de-
sire to depart and be with
Christ, *which is* [p]far better.
24 Nevertheless to remain in
the flesh *is* more needful for
you.
25 And being confident of
this, I know that I shall remain
and [q]continue with you all for
your progress and joy of faith,
26 that your rejoicing for me
may be more abundant in [r]Je-
sus Christ by my coming to you
again.
27 Only let your conduct be
[s]worthy of the [d]gospel of
Christ, so that whether I come
and see you or am absent, I may
hear of your affairs, that you
stand fast in [t]one spirit, with
one mind [u]striving together for
the faith of the gospel,
28 and not in any way terrified by your adversaries, which
is to them a proof of [v]perdition,
but to you of [i]salvation,* and
that from God.
29 For to you it has been
[w]granted on behalf of Christ,
not only to [x]believe in Him, but
also to [y]suffer for His sake,
30 having the same conflict
which you [z]saw in me and now
hear *is* in me.

II. Christ the Christian's Pattern: Rejoicing in Lowly Service, 2:1–30

(1) Exhortation to meekness and unity

2 THEREFORE if *there is* any
consolation in Christ, if any
comfort of [f]love, if any fellowship of the [j]Spirit, if any affection and [aa]mercy,
2 fulfill my joy by being

*1:16 NU-Text reverses the contents of verses 16 and 17. 1:23 NU-Text and M-Text read *But.* 1:28 NU-Text reads *of your salvation.*

10 *a Day* (of Christ): v. 10; Phil. 2:16. (1 Cor. 1:8, *note;* 2 Tim. 4:8)
11 *b* See Rev. 19:8, *note*
c See 1 Jn. 3:7, *note*
12 *d Gospel:* vv. 12, 14–18,27; Phil. 2:22. (Gen. 12:3; Rev. 14:6)
13 *e* Lit. *in the whole Praetorium.* Cp. Phil. 4:22
17 *f Law* (of Christ): v. 17; 2:1; Phil. 2:2. (Jn. 13:34; 2 Jn. 5)
18 *g* Cp. Lk. 9:50
19 *h* Job 13:16, LXX
i See Rom. 1:16, *note*
j Holy Spirit (NT): v. 19; 2:1; Col. 1:8. (Mt. 1:18; Acts 2:4, *note*)
20 *k* Eph. 6:19, 20
l Cp. 1 Cor. 6:20
m Rom. 14:8
21 *n Death* (physical): v. 21; Heb. 9:27. (Gen. 2:17; Heb. 9:27, *note*)
23 *o* 2 Cor. 5:2,8
p Ps. 16:11
25 *q* Cp. Phil. 2:24
26 *r* Lit. *Christ Jesus*
27 *s* Eph. 4:1
t Eph. 4:3
u Jude 3
28 *v* Cp. 2 Th. 1:4–6
29 *w* Acts 5:41; cp. Mt. 5:12
x Faith: v. 29; Phil. 3:9. (Gen. 3:20; Heb. 11:39, *note*)
y 2 Tim. 3:12
30 *z* Cp. Acts 16:19; 1 Th. 2:2
CHAPTER 2
1 *aa* Col. 3:12

[1](1:14) The grandeur of Paul's courage inspired other believers also. Thus, when his voice was muted through imprisonment, they were constrained to proclaim the Gospel boldly in his stead.

[2](1:18) The apostle could rejoice as long as Christ was being preached, even though the preaching was done insincerely and with evil motives (vv. 15–18). On the other hand, he calls for a curse upon certain teachers who perverted the Gospel message with legalism (Gal. 1:8–9). Thus he reverses that standard of values which exalts right conduct above correct doctrine.

like-minded, having the same [a]love, *being* of one accord, of [b]one mind.

3 *Let* [c]nothing *be done* through [d]selfish ambition or conceit, but in lowliness of mind let each esteem others better than himself.

4 Let each of you look out not only for [e]his own interests, but also for the interests of [f]others.

(2) The humiliation of Christ

5 Let this mind be in you which was also in [g]Christ Jesus,

6 who, being in the [1]form of God, did not consider it [h]robbery to be equal with God,

7 but [i]made Himself of no reputation, [j]taking the form of a bondservant, *and* [k]coming in the likeness of men.

8 And being found in appearance as a man, He humbled Himself and [l]became [m]obedient to *the point of* death, even the death of the cross.

(3) The exaltation of Jesus

9 [n]Therefore God also has highly exalted Him and given Him the [o]name which is above every name,

10 that at the name of Jesus [p]every knee should bow, of those in heaven, and of those on earth, and of those under the earth,

11 and *that* every tongue should confess that Jesus Christ [q]*is* Lord, to the glory of God the Father.

(4) The outworking of salvation

12 Therefore, my beloved, as you have always obeyed, not as in my presence only, but now much more in my absence, [r]work out your own [s]salvation with fear and trembling;

13 for it is [t]God who works in you both to will and to do [u]for *His* good pleasure.

14 Do all things without [v]complaining and disputing,

15 that you may become blameless and harmless, children of God without fault in the midst of a crooked and perverse [w]generation, among whom you shine as [x]lights in the [y]world,

16 holding fast the word of life, so that I may rejoice in the [z]day of Christ that I have not run in vain or labored in [aa]vain.

(5) The apostolic example

17 Yes, and if I am being [bb]poured out *as a drink offering* on the sacrifice and service of your faith, I am glad and rejoice with you all.

18 For the same reason you also be glad and rejoice with me.

19 But I [cc]trust in the Lord Jesus to send [dd]Timothy to you shortly, that I also may be encouraged when I know your state.

20 For I have no one [ee]like-minded, who will sincerely care for your state.

21 For all seek their own, not the things which are of Christ Jesus.

22 But you know his proven character, that as a son with *his* father he served with me in the [ff]gospel.

23 Therefore I hope to send him at once, as soon as I see how it goes with me.

24 But I trust in the Lord that I myself shall also [gg]come shortly.

25 Yet I considered it necessary to send to you [hh]Epaphroditus, my brother, fellow worker, and fellow soldier, but your messenger and the one who ministered to my need;

26 since he was longing for you all, and was distressed because you had heard that he was sick.

27 For indeed he was sick almost unto death; but God had

2
a Law (of Christ): vv. 1–2; Col. 1:4. (Jn. 13:34; 2 Jn. 5)
b v. 27; Phil. 4:2
3
c Gal. 5:26; Jas. 3:14
d Or *rivalry, factiousness*
4
e 1 Cor. 13:5
f Rom. 15:1–2
5
g Cp. Mt. 11:29; Jn. 13:14; Rom. 15:3; 1 Pet. 2:21
6
h Lit. *a thing to be held on to*
7
i Lit. *emptied Himself,* i.e. *divested Himself of His visible glory*
j Christ (first advent): vv. 7–8; 1 Tim. 1:15. (Gen. 3:15; Acts 1:11, *note*)
k Cp. Ps. 8:4–6
8
l Ps. 40:6–8
m Heb. 5:8
9
n Heb. 2:9
o Eph. 1:21
10
p Isa. 45:23; Rom. 14:11; Rev. 5:13
11
q Jn. 13:13; Rom. 14:9
12
r Jn. 6:27,29; Heb. 4:11; 2 Pet. 1:10
s See Rom. 1:16, *note*
13
t 1 Cor. 12:6; Heb. 13:20–21
u Eph. 1:5
14
v 1 Cor. 10:10
15
w Dt. 32:5
x Mt. 5:15–16
y Gk. *kosmos.* See Mt. 4:8, *note*
16
z Day (of Christ): v. 16; 2 Tim. 1:18. (1 Cor. 1:8, *note;* 2 Tim. 4:8)
aa Gal. 4:11; 1 Th. 3:5
17
bb Cp. 2 Tim. 4:6
19
cc Or *hope*
dd Cp. 1 Th. 3:2
20
ee 2 Tim. 3:10
22
ff Gospel: v. 22; Phil. 4:3. (Gen. 12:3; Rev. 14:6)
24
gg Cp. Phil. 1:25
25
hh Phil. 4:18

[1](2:6) This is one of the strongest assertions in the NT of the Deity of Jesus Christ. The "form" (Gk. *morphē*), is the external appearance by which a person or thing strikes the vision; yet it is an external form truly indicative of the inner nature from which it springs. Nothing in this passage teaches that the eternal Word (Jn. 1:1) emptied Himself of either His divine nature or His attributes, but only of the outward and visible manifestation of the Godhead. God may change form, but He cannot cease to be God. At all times His divine attributes could be exercised according to His will. See *notes* at Jn. 1:1 and 20:28.

mercy on him, and not only on him but on me also, lest I should have sorrow upon sorrow.

28 Therefore I sent him the more eagerly, that when you see him again you may rejoice, and I may be less sorrowful.

29 [a]Receive him therefore in the Lord with all gladness, and hold such men in esteem;

30 because for the work of Christ he came close to death, not regarding his life, to supply what was lacking in your service toward me.

III. Christ, Object of the Christian's Faith, Desire, and Expectation, 3:1–21

(1) Warning against legalizers

3 FINALLY, my brethren, [b]rejoice in the Lord. For me to write the [c]same things to you *is* not tedious, but for you *it is* safe.

2 Beware of [d]dogs, beware of [e]evil workers, beware of the mutilation!

3 For we are the [f]circumcision, who worship God in the [g]Spirit,* rejoice in Christ Jesus, and have no confidence in the [h]flesh,

(2) Warning against legal righteousness

4 though I also might have confidence in the flesh. If anyone else thinks he may have confidence in the flesh, I [i]more so:

5 circumcised the eighth day, of the stock of Israel, *of* the tribe of Benjamin, a Hebrew of the Hebrews; concerning the [j]law, a [k]Pharisee;

6 concerning zeal, [l]persecuting the [m]church; concerning the [n]righteousness which is in the [j]law, blameless.

(3) Christ, object of the believer's faith for righteousness

7 But what things were gain to me, these I have counted loss for Christ.

8 Yet indeed I also count all things loss [o]for the excellence of the knowledge of Christ Jesus my Lord, for whom I have [p]suffered the loss of all things, and count them as rubbish, that I may gain Christ

9 and be found in Him, not having my own righteousness, which *is* from the [j]law, but that which *is* through [q]faith in Christ, the [r]righteousness which is from God by faith;

(4) Christ, object of the believer's desire for fellowship in resurrection power

10 that I may know Him and the [s]power of His [t]resurrection, and the [u]fellowship of His sufferings, being conformed to His death,

11 if, by any means, I may [v]attain to the [t]resurrection [w]from the dead.

12 Not that I have already attained, or am already [1]perfected; but I press on, that I may lay hold of that for which Christ Jesus has also laid hold of me.

13 Brethren, I do not count myself to have apprehended; but one thing *I do,* [x]forgetting those things which are behind and [y]reaching forward to those things which are ahead,

*

3:3 NU-Text and M-Text read *who worship in the Spirit of God.*

29
a Cp. Mt. 10:40

CHAPTER 3

1
b 1 Th. 5:16
c Cp. 2 Pet. 1:12,15

2
d Cp. Ps. 22:16,20; Isa. 56:10–11
e Ps. 119:115

3
f Rom. 2:29
g Jn. 4:24
h Flesh: vv. 3–4; Col. 2:11. (Jn. 8:15; Jude 23)

4
i 2 Cor. 11:22–23

5
j Law (of Moses): vv. 5–6,9; 1 Tim. 1:9. (Ex. 19:1; Gal. 3:24, *note*)
k Acts 23:6

6
l Acts 8:3
m Church (visible): v. 6; 1 Tim. 3:15. (1 Cor. 10:32; 1 Tim. 3:15)
n Righteousness (OT): vv. 6,9; 2 Pet. 2:5. (Gen. 6:9; Lk. 2:25, *note*)

8
o Jer. 9:23–24; 1 Cor. 2:2; cp. Jn. 17:3
p Cp. 2 Cor. 11:25–28

9
q Faith: v. 9; 1 Th. 1:7. (Gen. 3:20; Heb. 11:39, *note*)
r See Rom. 3:21, *note*

10
s Eph. 1:19–20
t Resurrection: vv. 10–11; Col. 2:12. (2 Ki. 4:35; 1 Cor. 15:52, *note*)
u 2 Cor. 1:5; 1 Pet. 4:13

11
v Cp. Lk. 20:35
w Lit. *from among*

13
x Cp. Lk. 9:62
y Cp. 1 Cor. 9:24; 2 Tim. 4:7

---

[1](3:12) The word "perfected" or "perfect," as the Bible uses it of men, does not refer to sinless perfection. Old Testament characters described as "perfect," "blameless," or "loyal" were obviously not sinless (cp. Gen. 6:9; 1 Ki. 15:14; 2 Ki. 20:3; 1 Chr. 12:38; Job 1:1,8; Ps. 37:37). Although a number of Hebrew and Greek words are translated "perfect," the thought is usually either *completeness in all details* (Heb. *tamam*, Gk. *katartizō*), or *to reach a goal* or *achieve a purpose* (Gk. *teleioō*). Three stages of perfection are revealed: (1) Positional perfection, already possessed by every believer in Christ (Heb. 10:14). (2) Relative perfection, i.e. spiritual maturity (Phil. 3:15), especially in such aspects as the will of God (Col. 4:12), love (1 Jn. 4:17–18), holiness (2 Cor. 7:1), patience (Jas. 1:4), "every good work" (Heb. 13:21). Maturity is achieved progressively, as in 2 Cor. 7:1, "perfecting holiness," and Gal. 3:3, "are you now being made perfect?" and is accomplished through gifts of ministry bestowed (Eph. 4:12). And (3) ultimate perfection, i.e. perfection in soul, spirit, and body, "for the equipping of the saints" which Paul denies he has attained (Phil. 3:12) but which will be realized at the time of the resurrection of the dead (Phil. 3:11). For the Christian nothing short of the moral perfection of God is always the absolute standard of conduct, but Scripture recognizes that Christians do not attain sinless perfection in this life (cp. 1 Pet. 1:15–16; 1 Jn. 1:8–10).

14 I [a]press toward the goal for the prize of the upward call of God in Christ Jesus.

(5) Appeal for unity among believers

15 Therefore let us, as many as are [b]mature, have [c]this mind; and if in anything you think otherwise, [d]God will reveal even this to you.

16 Nevertheless, to *the degree* that we have already attained, let us walk by the same rule,* let us be of the same mind.

(6) No compromise for the sake of unity

17 Brethren, join in following my example, and note those who so walk, as you have us [e]for a pattern.

18 For many walk, of whom I have told you often, and now tell you even weeping, *that they are* the enemies of the cross of Christ:

19 whose [f]end *is* destruction, whose god *is their* belly, and *whose* glory *is* in their shame—who set their mind on earthly things.

(7) Christ, object of the believer's expectation

20 For our citizenship is in [g]heaven, [h]from which we also eagerly wait for the [i]Savior, the Lord Jesus Christ,

21 who will transform our [j]lowly body that it may be [k]conformed to [l]His glorious body, according to the working by which He is able even to [m]subdue all things to Himself.

IV. Christ, the Christian's Strength: Rejoicing through Anxiety, 4:1–19

(1) Exhortation to be of same mind

4 THEREFORE, my beloved and longed-for brethren, my joy and [n]crown, so stand fast in the Lord, beloved.

2 I implore Euodia and I implore Syntyche to be of the [o]same mind in the Lord.

3 And* I urge you also, true companion, help these women who labored with me in the [p]gospel, with Clement also, and the rest of my fellow workers, whose [q]names *are* in the Book of [r]Life.

(2) The secret of the peace of God

4 Rejoice in the Lord always. Again I will say, rejoice!

5 Let your gentleness be known to all men. [s]The Lord *is* at hand.

6 [t]Be anxious for nothing, but in everything by prayer and supplication, with [u]thanksgiving, let your requests be made known to God;

7 and the [v]peace of God, which surpasses all understanding, will guard your hearts and minds through Christ Jesus.

(3) The presence of the God of peace

8 Finally, brethren, whatever things are [w]true, whatever things *are* [x]noble, whatever things *are* [y]just, whatever things *are* [z]pure, whatever things *are* [aa]lovely, whatever things *are* of good report, if *there is* any [bb]virtue and if *there is* anything praiseworthy—meditate on these things.

9 The things which you learned and received and heard and saw in me, these do, and the [cc]God of peace will be with you.

(4) The believer's sufficiency through Christ

10 But I rejoiced in the Lord greatly that now at last your care for me [dd]has flourished again; though you surely did care, but you lacked opportunity.

11 Not that I speak in regard to need, for I have learned in whatever state I am, to be [ee]content:

12 I know how to be abased, and I know how to abound. Everywhere and in all things I have learned both to be full and to be hungry, both to abound and to suffer need.

13 I can do all things [ff]through Christ* who strengthens me.

14 Nevertheless you have

*

3:16 NU-Text omits *rule* and the rest of verse. **4:3** NU-Text and M-Text read *Yes.* **4:13** NU-Text reads *Him who.*

14
a Cp. Heb. 12:1–2
15
b See v. 12, *note*
c Cp. Gal. 5:10
d Hos. 6:3; Jas. 1:5
17
e 1 Cor. 4:16; Ti. 2:7–8; 1 Pet. 5:3
19
f Cp. 2 Pet. 2:1
20
g Col. 3:1
h Christ (second advent): v. 20; Col. 3:4. (Dt. 30:3; Acts 1:11, *note*)
i See Rom. 1:16, *note*
21
j Lit. *body of lowliness*
k 1 Jn. 3:2
l Lit. *the body of His glory*
m 1 Cor. 15:28
CHAPTER 4
1
n Rewards: v. 1; Col. 3:24. (Dan. 12:3; 1 Cor. 3:14, *note*)
2
o Phil. 2:2
3
p Gospel: v. 3; Phil. 4:15. (Gen. 12:3; Rev. 14:6)
q Lk. 10:20
r Life (eternal): v. 3; Col. 1:27. (Mt. 7:14; Rev. 22:19)
5
s Jas. 5:7–9; Rev. 22:7, 20; cp. Ps. 145:18
6
t Mt. 6:25; 1 Pet. 5:7
u 1 Th. 5:17–18; cp. Dan. 6:10
7
v See Mt. 10:34, *note*
8
w Eph. 4:25
x 2 Cor. 8:21
y Dt. 16:20
z Jas. 3:17
aa 1 Cor. 13:4–7
bb Or *excellence*
9
cc Heb. 13:20
10
dd Lit. *has revived*
11
ee Heb. 13:5; cp. 1 Tim. 6:6
13
ff Cp. Jn. 15:5; 2 Cor. 12:9

15
a Gospel: v. 15; Col. 1:5. (Gen. 12:3; Rev. 14:6)
b Churches (local): v. 15; Col. 1:2. (Acts 8:3; Phil. 1:1, *note*)
16
c Cp. 1 Th. 2:9
17
d Cp. Mt. 6:4
18
e Phil. 2:25
f Rom. 12:1; see Heb. 10:18, *note*

done well that you shared in my
distress.
15 Now you Philippians
know also that in the beginning
of the [a]gospel, when I departed
from Macedonia, no [b]church
shared with me concerning giving and receiving but you only.
16 For even in [c]Thessalonica
you sent *aid* once and again for
my necessities.
17 Not that I seek the gift, but
I seek the fruit that [d]abounds to
your account.
18 Indeed I have all and
abound. I am full, having received from [e]Epaphroditus the
things *sent* from you, a sweet-
smelling aroma, an acceptable
[f]sacrifice, well pleasing to God.
19 And my God shall [g]supply
all your need according to His
riches in glory by Christ Jesus.

Conclusion, 4:20–23

20 Now to our God and Fa-
ther *be* glory forever and ever.
Amen.
21 Greet every saint in Christ
Jesus. The brethren who are
with me greet you.
22 All the saints greet you,
but especially those who are of
Caesar's household.
23 The [h]grace of our Lord Jesus Christ be with you all.*
Amen.

*4:23 NU-Text reads *your spirit*.

19
g Ps. 23:1; 2 Cor. 9:8
23
h Grace: v. 23; Col. 1:2. (Jn. 1:14; Jn. 1:17, *note*)

The Epistle of Paul the Apostle to the

COLOSSIANS

Author: Paul *Theme:* Christ's Preeminence *Date of writing:* C. A.D. 60

THE EPISTLE TO THE COLOSSIANS, like the letters to the Ephesians and Philippians, was written in Rome during Paul's first imprisonment. Colosse, about 100 miles east of Ephesus, had never been visited by the apostle (1:7; 2:1). The church there may have been founded by Epaphras (1:7; 4:12,13; Phile. 23), who, with many others, had probably been converted during Paul's three-year ministry in Ephesus.

Someone had come to Colosse who taught an alluring but dangerous philosophy ultimately known as Gnosticism, the basis of much heretical teaching even today. (For further information about this error, see 2:18, *note.*) No passage in the NT more fully sets forth the eternal glory of the preexistent, omnipotent, exalted, and eternal Son of God than 1:15–23.

The Epistle may be divided as follows:

Introduction, 1:1–8.
I. The Apostle's Prayer for the Colossian Christians, 1:9–14.
II. The Preeminent Glory of Christ, 1:15–23.
III. The Apostle's Concern for the Church at Colosse, 1:24—2:23.
IV. Some Characteristics of the Abundant Life of the Christian, 3:1—4:6.
Conclusion, 4:7–18.

CHAPTER 1

2
a Churches (local): v. 2; Col. 4:15. (Acts 8:3; Phil. 1:1, *note*)
b Grace: vv. 2,6; Col. 3:16. (Jn. 1:14; Jn. 1:17, *note*)
3
c Bible prayers (NT): vv. 3, 9–11; Col. 4:12. (Mt. 6:9; Lk. 11:2, *note*)
4
d Law (of Christ): vv. 4,8; Col. 3:14. (Jn. 13:34; 2 Jn. 5)
5
e Gospel: v. 5; Col. 1:23. (Gen. 12:3; Rev. 14:6)
6
f Gk. *kosmos.* See Mt. 4:8, *note*
g Jn. 15:16
7
h Col. 4:12; Phile. 23
i 1 Cor. 4:1–2

Introduction: Greeting and Thanksgiving, 1:1–8

1 PAUL, an apostle of Jesus Christ by the will of God, and Timothy our brother,

2 To the saints and faithful brethren in Christ [a]*who are* in Colosse:

[b]Grace to you and peace from God our Father and the Lord Jesus Christ.*

3 We give thanks to the God and Father of our Lord Jesus Christ, [c]praying always for you,

4 since we heard of your faith in Christ Jesus and of your [d]love for all the saints;

5 because of the hope which is laid up for you in heaven, of which you heard before in the word of the truth of the [e]gospel,

6 which has come to you, as *it has* also in all the [f]world, and is [g]bringing forth fruit,* as *it is* also among you since the day you heard and knew the [b]grace of God in truth;

7 as you also learned from [h]Epaphras, our dear fellow servant, who is a [i]faithful minister of Christ on your behalf,

8 who also declared to us your [d]love in the [j]Spirit.

I. The Apostle's Prayer for the Colossian Christians, 1:9–14

9 For this reason we also, since the day we heard it, do not cease to [c]pray for you, and to ask that you may be filled with the [k]knowledge of His will in [l]all wisdom and spiritual understanding;

10 that you may [m]walk worthy of the Lord, fully [n]pleasing *Him,* being fruitful in every good work and increasing in the [o]knowledge of God;

11 [p]strengthened with all might, according to His glorious power, for all patience and longsuffering with [q]joy;

12 giving thanks to the Father who has qualified us to be partakers of the inheritance of the saints in the light.

13 He has delivered us from the power of darkness and conveyed *us* into the kingdom of the Son of His love,

14 in whom we have [r]redemption through His [s]blood,* the [t]forgiveness of sins.

II. The Preeminent Glory of Christ, 1:15–23

(1) The seven superiorities of Christ

15 He is the [u]image of the in-

*

1:2 NU-Text omits *and the Lord Jesus Christ.* 1:6 NU-Text and M-Text add *and growing.* 1:14 NU-Text and M-Text omit *through His blood.*

8
j Holy Spirit (NT): v. 8; 1 Th. 1:5. (Mt. 1:18; Acts 2:4, *note*)
9
k Eph. 5:17
l Eph. 1:8
10
m Eph. 4:1; 1 Th. 2:12
n 1 Th. 4:1
o 2 Pet. 3:18
11
p Eph. 3:16; 6:10
q 2 Cor. 8:2; Heb. 10:34
14
r See Rom. 3:24, *note*
s Sacrifice (of Christ): v. 14; Col. 1:20. (Gen. 3:15; Heb. 10:18, *note*)
t Forgiveness: v. 14; Col. 2:13. (Lev. 4:20; Mt. 26:28, *note*)
15
u 2 Cor. 4:4; Heb. 1:3

16
a Jn. 1:1; Heb. 1:3
b Rom. 11:36; Heb. 2:10
17
c Cp. Jn. 17:5
d Heb. 1:3
18
e Eph. 1:22
f *Church* (the true): vv. 18,24; Col. 2:19. (Mt. 16:18; Heb. 12:23)
g Rev. 1:5
19
h Jn. 1:16
20
i *Reconciliation:* vv. 20–23. (Rom. 5:10; Col. 1:20)
j *Sacrifice* (of Christ): vv. 20–22; 1 Tim. 2:6. (Gen. 3:15; Heb. 10:18, *note*)
21
k Or *estranged*
l 2 Cor. 5:18–19
22
m Eph. 2:14–16
n *Sanctification* (NT): v. 22; Col. 3:12. (Mt. 4:5; Rev. 22:11)
o Eph. 5:27
23
p 1 Cor. 15:58
q *Gospel:* v. 23; 1 Th. 1:5. (Gen.

visible God, the [1]firstborn over
all creation.
16 For [a]by Him all things
were created that are in heaven
and that are on earth, visible
and invisible, whether thrones
or dominions or principalities
or powers. [b]All things were created through Him and for Him.
17 And [c]He is before all
things, and in Him [d]all things
consist.
18 And He is the [e]head of the
body, the [f]church, who is the
beginning, the firstborn [g]from
the dead, that in all things He
may have the preeminence.
19 [2]For it pleased *the Father*
that in Him all the [h]fullness
should dwell,

(2) The reconciling work of Christ

20 and by Him to [3i]reconcile
all things to Himself, by Him,
whether things on earth or
things in heaven, having made
peace [j]through the blood of His
cross.
21 And you, who once were
[k]alienated and enemies in your
mind by wicked works, yet now
He has [l]reconciled
22 [m]in the body of His flesh
through death, to present you
[n]holy, and blameless, and above
reproach [o]in His sight—
23 if indeed you continue in
the faith, grounded and steadfast, and are [p]not moved away
from the hope of the [q]gospel
which you heard, which was
[r]preached to every creature under heaven, of which I, Paul, became a minister.

III. The Apostle's Concern for the Church at Colosse, 1:24—2:23

The church a "mystery" hidden from past ages (cp. Eph. 3:1–11)

24 I now rejoice in my sufferings for you, and fill up in my
flesh what is lacking in the [s]af-
flictions of Christ, for the sake
of His body, which is the
[f]church,
25 of which I became a minister according to the stewardship from God which was given
to me for you, to fulfill the word
of God,
26 the [t]mystery which has
been hidden from ages and
from generations, but now has
been revealed to His saints.
27 To them God willed to
make known what are the
riches of the glory of this
[t]mystery among the Gentiles:
which* is [u]Christ [v]in you, the
hope of glory.
28 Him we preach, [w]warning
every man and teaching every
man in all wisdom, that we may
present every man [x]perfect in
Christ Jesus.
29 To this *end* I also labor,
striving according to His working which works in me [y]might-
ily.

*1:27 M-Text reads *who.*

12:3; Rev. 14:6)
r Col. 1:6
24
s 2 Cor. 1:5
26
t See Mt. 13:11, *note*
27
u Rom. 8:10–11; see Eph. 4:24, *note*
v *Life* (eternal): v. 27; Col. 3:4. (Mt. 7:14; Rev. 22:19)
28
w Cp. Acts 20:20,27
x See Phil. 3:12, *note*
29
y Eph. 3:7

[1](1:15) As used of our Lord here, this term (Gk. *prōtotokos*) refers to priority of position rather than of origin. This meaning is clear in Ps. 89:27: "Also I will make him My firstborn, / The highest of the kings of the earth." The assertion in 1:15, therefore, is that Christ, as the eternal Son, holds the position of priority in relation to all creation, in that He was before all things (v. 17), He created all things (v. 16), and in Him all things consist (v. 17).

[2](1:19) "For in Him all the fullness was pleased to dwell" (lit.). God the Father was in Him (Jn. 17:21–23), and God the Holy Spirit was His in full measure (Isa. 42:1; Jn. 3:34).

[3](1:20) The word translated "reconcile" (Gk. *katallassō*) means *to change thoroughly,* and in its various forms occurs in Rom. 5:10,11; 11:15; 1 Cor. 7:11; 2 Cor. 5:18–20; Eph. 2:16; Col. 1:20–21. A study of the passages referred to above indicates that the work of God involves two distinct reconciliations: (1) The reconciliation accomplished at Calvary—"God was in Christ reconciling the world to Himself" (2 Cor. 5:19). Here God was not changed, for He had always loved the world; nor was the world changed, for it continued in sinful rebellion against God. But by the death of Christ the *relationship between God and the world* was changed: the barrier because of sin being taken away judicially, enabling God to show mercy where judgment was deserved. This reconciliation was the work of God alone, in which man had no part. And (2) there is a reconciliation wrought by God in the sinner himself, whereby he becomes changed in his rebellious attitude toward God, so that he is persuaded to receive the reconciliation already accomplished through Christ at the cross (Rom. 5:11). In this ministry of reconciling the sinner, Christians have a part, being ambassadors for Christ bearing the "word of reconciliation" committed to them (2 Cor. 5:19) and pleading with men: "Be reconciled to God" (2 Cor. 5:20).

The Godhead incarnate in Christ

(1) Christ, the fount of wisdom

2 FOR I want you to know
what a [a]great conflict I
have for you and those in Laodicea, and *for* as many as have not
seen my face in the flesh,
2 [b]that their hearts may be
encouraged, being knit together
in love, and *attaining* to all
riches of the full [c]assurance of
understanding, to the knowledge of the [1d]mystery of God,
both of the Father and* of
Christ,
3 in whom are hidden all
the treasures of [e]wisdom and
knowledge.

(2) The danger from persuasive words (cp. Rom. 16:17–18; 1 Cor. 2:4; 2 Pet. 2:3)

4 Now this I [f]say [g]lest anyone should deceive you with
persuasive words.
5 For though I am absent in
the flesh, yet I am with you in
spirit, rejoicing to [h]see your
good order and the [i]steadfast-
ness of your faith in Christ.
6 As you therefore have received Christ Jesus the Lord, so
walk in Him,
7 rooted and built up in Him
and established in the faith, as
you have been taught, abounding in it* with thanksgiving

(3) Twofold warning against false philosophy and legalism

8 Beware lest anyone cheat
you through philosophy and
empty deceit, according to the
tradition of men, according to
the basic [j]principles of the
[k]world, and not according to
Christ.

(4) The believer complete in Christ

9 For in Him [l]dwells all the
fullness of the Godhead bodily;
10 and you are complete in
Him, who is the [m]head of all
principality and power.
11 In Him you were also [n]cir-
cumcised with the circumcision
made without hands, by putting
off the body of the sins* of the
[o]flesh, by the circumcision of
Christ,
12 [p]buried with Him in baptism, in which you also were
raised with *Him* through faith in
the [q]working of God, who
[r]raised Him from the dead.
13 And you, being [s]dead in
your trespasses and the uncircumcision of your flesh, He has
[t]made alive together with Him,
having [u]forgiven you all trespasses,

(5) Law observances were abolished in Christ (cp. Mt. 5:17)

14 having [v]wiped out the
handwriting of requirements
that was against us, which was
contrary to us. And He has
taken it out of the way, having
nailed it to the cross.
15 Having [w]disarmed principalities and powers, He made a
public spectacle of them, triumphing over them in it.
16 So let no one [x]judge you
in food or in drink, or regarding
a festival or a new moon or
[y]sabbaths,
17 which are a [z]shadow of
things to come, but the substance is of Christ.

(6) Warning against false mysticism

18 Let no one cheat you of
your reward, taking delight in
false humility and worship of
[aa]angels, [2]intruding into those

*

2:2 NU-Text omits *both of the Father and*. 2:7 NU-Text omits *in it*. 2:11 NU-Text omits *of the sins*.

CHAPTER 2

1
a Phil. 1:30; Col. 1:29; 1 Th. 2:2

2
b Cp. 2 Cor. 1:6
c Assurance/security: v. 2; 1 Th. 5:23. (Ps. 23:1; Jude 1, *note*)
d See Mt. 13:11, *note*

3
e 1 Cor. 1:24, 30

4
f Inspiration: v. 4; 1 Th. 4:15. (Ex. 4:15; 2 Tim. 3:16, *note*)
g vv. 8,18; 2 Cor. 11:13; Eph. 4:14; 5:6

5
h Cp. 1 Cor. 14:40
i 1 Pet. 5:9

8
j Gal. 4:3, 9–10
k Gk. *kosmos.* See Rev. 13:8, *note*

9
l Col. 1:19; cp. Jn. 1:14

10
m Eph. 1:20–21; 1 Pet. 3:22

11
n Cp. Dt. 10:16; Jer. 4:4; Rom. 2:29; Phil. 3:3
o Flesh: v. 11; Col. 2:23. (Jn. 8:15; Jude 23)

12
p Rom. 6:4
q Eph. 1:20
r Resurrection: v. 12; 1 Th. 1:10. (2 Ki. 4:35; 1 Cor. 15:52, *note*)

13
s Death (spiritual): v. 13; Jas. 1:15. (Gen. 2:17; Eph. 2:5, *note*)
t Eph. 2:5
u Forgiveness: v. 13; Col. 3:13. (Lev. 4:20; Mt. 26:28, *note*)

14
v Eph. 2:15–16

15
w Heb. 2:14; cp. Eph. 6:12

16
x Rom. 14:3
y Sabbath: v. 16. (Gen. 2:3; Mt. 12:1, *note*)

17
z Cp. Heb. 8:5; 10:1

18
aa See Heb. 1:4, *note*

---

[1](2:2) The "mystery of God" is Christ, as incarnating the fullness of the Godhead, and all the divine wisdom and knowledge for the redemption and reconciliation of man.

[2](2:18) The error against which Paul warned the Colossians later developed into the heresy called Gnosticism (from Gk. *gnōsis,* meaning *knowledge*). This false teaching assigned to Christ a place subordinate to the true Godhead, and undervalued the uniqueness and completeness of His redemptive work. It insisted that between a holy God and this earth a host of beings, angels, etc., formed a bridge, of which host Christ was a member. This system included the worship of angels (v. 18) and a false asceticism (vv. 20–22). For all these errors, the apostle had one remedy, a knowledge (*epignōsis,* i.e. *full knowledge,* 1:9–10; 3:10) of the fullness of God in Jesus Christ. Paul is not afraid of wisdom, or knowledge, and refers to them frequently, but he does insist that the knowledge be according to divine revelation. His devastating answer to this false teaching is in 1:19 and 2:9, in which the Lord is revealed as

19
a Eph. 4:15
b Church (the true): v. 19; 3:15; 1 Th. 4:17. (Mt. 16:18; Heb. 12:23)
c Eph. 4:16
20
d Gal. 4:3, 9–10
e Gk. *kosmos.* See Rev. 13:8, *note*
22
f Or *teachings*
23
g Flesh: v. 23; 1 Pet. 3:21. (Jn. 8:15; Jude 23)
CHAPTER 3
1
h Rom. 6:5; Eph 2:6; Col. 2:12
i Rom. 8:34; Eph. 1:20
2
j Mt. 6:19–21
3
k Rom. 6:2; Gal. 2:20
4
l Life (eternal): v. 4; 1 Tim. 1:16. (Mt. 7:14; Rev. 22:19)
m Christ (second advent): v. 4; 1 Th. 1:10. (Dt. 30:3; Acts 1:11, *note*). 1 Jn. 3:2
5
n Rom. 8:13
o Cp. Eph. 5:5
6
p Rom. 1:18; Eph. 5:6
7
q Eph. 2:2; Ti. 3:3
8
r Eph. 4:22; 1 Pet. 2:1
9
s See Rom. 6:6, *note*
10
t See Eph. 4:24, *note*
u Rom. 12:2;

things which he has not* seen,
vainly puffed up by his fleshly
mind,
19 and not holding fast to the
[a]Head, from whom all the
[b]body, nourished and knit together by joints and ligaments,
[c]grows with the increase *that is*
from God.

(7) Warning against asceticism

20 Therefore,* if you died
with Christ from the basic
[d]principles of the [e]world, why,
as *though* living in the world, do
you subject yourselves to
regulations—
21 "Do not touch, do not
taste, do not handle,"
22 which all concern things
which perish with the using—
according to the commandments and [f]doctrines of men?
23 These things indeed have
an appearance of wisdom in
self-imposed religion, *false* humility, and neglect of the body,
but are of [1]no value against the
indulgence of the [g]flesh.

IV. Some Characteristics of the Abundant Life of the Christian, 3:1—4:6

The believer's union with Christ now and hereafter

3 IF then you were [h]raised
with Christ, seek those
things which are above, where
[i]Christ is, sitting at the right
hand of God.
2 Set your mind on things
above, not on things on the
[j]earth.
3 [k]For you died, and your
life is hidden with Christ in God.
4 When Christ *who is* our
[l]life [m]appears, then you also
will appear with Him in glory.

(1) Christian living

5 Therefore [n]put to death
your members which are on the
earth: fornication, uncleanness,
passion, evil desire, and covetousness, which is [o]idolatry.
6 Because of these things
the [p]wrath of God is coming
upon the sons of disobedience,
7 in which [q]you yourselves
once walked when you lived in
them.
8 [r]But now you yourselves
are to put off all these: anger,
wrath, malice, blasphemy,
filthy language out of your
mouth.
9 Do not lie to one another,
since you have put off the [s]old
man with his deeds,
10 and have put on the [t]new
man who is [u]renewed in knowledge according to the image of
Him who created him,
11 [v]where there is neither
Greek nor Jew, circumcised
nor uncircumcised, barbarian,
Scythian, slave *nor* free, but
Christ *is* all and in all.
12 Therefore, as *the* [w]elect of
God, [x]holy and beloved, [y]put
on [z]tender mercies, kindness,
humility, meekness, longsuffering;
13 bearing with one another,
and forgiving one another, if
anyone has a complaint against
another; even as Christ [aa]forgave you, so you also *must do.*
14 But [bb]above all these
things put on [cc]love, which is the
bond of [dd]perfection.
15 And let the peace of [ee]God
[ff]rule in your hearts, to which
also you were called in one
[b]body; and [gg]be thankful.
16 Let the word of Christ
dwell in you richly in all wisdom, teaching and admonishing one another in psalms and
hymns and spiritual songs,
singing with [hh]grace in your
hearts to the Lord.
17 And [ii]*whatever* you do in
word or deed, *do* all in the name
of the Lord Jesus, giving thanks
to God the Father through Him.

(2) Christian family relationships

18 Wives, submit to your
own husbands, as [jj]is fitting in
the Lord.

*
2:18 NU-Text omits *not.* 2:20 NU-Text and M-Text omit *Therefore.*

2 Cor. 4:16
11
v Gal. 3:27–28
12
w Election (corporate): v. 12; 1 Th. 1:4. (Dt. 7:6; 1 Pet. 5:13, *note*)
x Sanctification (NT): v. 12; 1 Th. 4:3. (Mt. 4:5; Rev. 22:11)
y Righteousness (garment): vv. 12–15; 1 Tim. 2:10. (Gen. 3:21; Rev. 19:8)
z Phil. 2:1–2
13
aa Forgiveness: v. 13; Heb. 9:22. (Lev. 4:20; Mt. 26:28, *note*)
14
bb 1 Pet. 4:8
cc Law (of Christ): v. 14; 1 Th. 3:6. (Jn. 13:34; 2 Jn. 5)
dd See Mt. 5:48, *note*
15
ee Or *Christ*
ff Jn. 14:27
gg 1 Th. 5:18
16
hh Grace: v. 16; Col. 4:6. (Jn. 1:14; Jn. 1:17, *note*). See 2 Pet. 3:18, *note*
17
ii 1 Cor. 10:31
18
jj Eph. 5:22

the one in whom "dwells all the fullness of the Godhead bodily." The word "fullness" (Gk. *plērōma*) is the very word Gnosticism used for the entire host of intermediary beings between God and man. The incarnate Lord, crucified, risen, and ascended is the only Mediator between God and men (1 Tim. 2:5).

[1](2:23) By creating a reputation for superior sanctity, as some did, they did not really honor God but only satisfied the flesh.

19 Husbands, [a]love your wives and do not be bitter toward them.

20 Children, obey your parents in all things, for this is well pleasing to the Lord.

21 [b]Fathers, do not provoke your children, lest they become discouraged.

(3) Servants and masters

22 [c]Bondservants, obey in all things your masters according to the flesh, not with eyeservice, as men-pleasers, but in sincerity of heart, fearing God.

23 And [d]whatever you do, do it heartily, as to the Lord and not to men,

24 knowing that from the Lord you will receive the [e]reward of the inheritance; for* you serve the Lord Christ.

25 But he who does wrong will be repaid for what he has done, and there is no partiality.

4 MASTERS, give your bondservants what is just and fair, knowing that you also have a Master in heaven.

(4) Earnest prayer; wise speech

2 Continue earnestly in prayer, being vigilant in it with thanksgiving;

3 meanwhile praying also for us, that God would open to us a door for the word, to speak the [f]mystery of Christ, for which I am also in chains,

4 that I may make it manifest, as I ought to speak.

5 [g]Walk in [h]wisdom toward those *who are* outside, redeeming the time.

6 *Let* your speech always *be* with [i]grace, seasoned with salt, that you may know how you ought to answer each one.

Conclusion: Personal Exhortations, 4:7–18

7 [j]Tychicus, a beloved brother, faithful minister, and fellow servant in the Lord, will tell you all the news about me.

19
a Eph. 5:25
21
b Eph. 6:4
22
c Eph. 6:5; 1 Tim. 6:1; Ti. 2:9; 1 Pet. 2:18
23
d Eccl. 9:10
24
e *Rewards:* v. 24; 1 Th. 2:19. (Dan. 12:3; 1 Cor. 3:14, *note*)
CHAPTER 4
3
f See Mt. 13:11, *note*
5
g Eph. 5:15
h Mt. 10:16
6
i *Grace:* vv. 6,18; 2 Th. 1:12. (Jn. 1:14; Jn. 1:17, *note*). See 2 Pet. 3:18, *note*
7
j Acts 20:4; Eph. 6:21; 2 Tim. 4:12; Ti. 3:12
8
k Cp. Eph. 6:22

8 I am sending [k]him to you for this very purpose, that he* may know your circumstances and comfort your hearts,

9 with [l]Onesimus, a faithful and beloved brother, who is *one* of you. They will make known to you all things which *are happening* here.

10 [m]Aristarchus my fellow prisoner greets you, with [n]Mark the cousin of Barnabas (about whom you received instructions: if he comes to you, welcome him),

11 and Jesus who is called Justus. These *are my* only fellow workers for the kingdom of God who are of the circumcision; they have proved to be a comfort to me.

12 [1][o]Epaphras, who is *one* of you, a bondservant of Christ, greets you, always laboring fervently for you in [p]prayers, that you may stand [q]perfect and complete* in all the will of God.

13 For I bear him witness that he has a great zeal* for you, and those who are in Laodicea, and those in Hierapolis.

14 [r]Luke the beloved physician and [s]Demas greet you.

15 Greet the brethren who are in Laodicea, and Nymphas and the [t]church that *is* in his* house.

16 Now when this epistle is [u]read among you, see that it is read also in the [t]church of the Laodiceans, and that you likewise read the epistle from Laodicea.

17 And say to [v]Archippus, "Take heed to the [w]ministry which you have received in the Lord, that you may fulfill it."

18 This salutation by my own hand—Paul. [x]Remember my chains. [i]Grace *be* with you. Amen.

9
l Phile. 10
10
m Acts 19:29; 20:4; 27:2; Phile. 24
n Acts 15:37; 2 Tim. 4:11
12
o Col. 1:7; Phile. 23
p *Bible prayers* (NT): v. 12; 1 Th. 1:2. (Mt. 6:9; Lk. 11:2, *note*)
q See Phil. 3:12, *note*
14
r 2 Tim. 4:11
s 2 Tim. 4:10; Phile. 24
15
t *Churches* (local): vv. 15–16; 1 Th. 1:1. (Acts 8:3; Phil. 1:1, *note*)
16
u Cp. 1 Th. 5:27
17
v Phile. 2
w 2 Tim. 4:5
18
x Heb. 13:3

*3:24 NU-Text omits *for.* 4:8 NU-Text reads *you may know our circumstances and he may.* 4:12 NU-Text reads *fully assured.* 4:13 NU-Text reads *concern.* 4:15 NU-Text reads *Nympha . . . her house.*

[1](4:12) Here is a touching illustration of priestly service through prayer (see 1 Pet. 2:9, *note*).

The First Epistle of Paul the Apostle to the

THESSALONIANS

Author: Paul *Theme:* Christ's Return *Date of writing:* c. A.D. 51

THE FIRST EPISTLE TO THE THESSALONIANS, written at Corinth by Paul shortly after his departure from Thessalonica (Acts 17:1–10; 18:1), was probably among the earliest of the apostle's inspired writings. Paul had visited Thessalonica on his second missionary journey, preaching in the synagogue on three successive Sabbaths (Acts 17:1–9). Because violent persecution had broken out, he was sent away for his personal safety (Acts 17:5–10).

The occasion of 1 Thessalonians was the coming of Timothy, whom Paul had sent to Thessalonica from Athens (3:1–2). Timothy's good report of the faith and love of the Thessalonians and their tender regard for the apostle prompted Paul to write this touching and intimate letter in which he commends them for their steadfastness, reminds them of truths he has taught them, and clears up certain questions about the Lord's return which Timothy had reported.

The theme of the Epistle is fourfold: (1) to confirm the young converts in Thessalonica in the foundational truths already taught them; (2) to exhort them to a life of personal holiness pleasing to the Lord; (3) to comfort them concerning those who had died; and (4) to instruct them concerning their own hope of the Lord's return. In every chapter of both 1 and 2 Thessalonians the coming of the Lord is prominent. The richness of Paul's teaching is evident in the fact that during one month the apostle had not only led them to Christ, but had taught them many of the great doctrines of the faith (cp. 1:4, *note*).

The Epistle may be divided as follows:

Introduction, 1:1–3.
I. The Model Church and the Three Tenses of the Christian Life, 1:4–10.
II. The Model Servant and His Reward, 2.
III. The Model Brother and His Sanctification, 3.
IV. The Model Life and the Believer's Hope, 4.
V. The Model Life and the Day of the Lord, 5:1–24.
Conclusion, 5:25–28.

Introduction, 1:1–4

1 PAUL, Silvanus, and Timothy,

To the [a]church of the [b]Thessalonians in God the Father and the Lord Jesus Christ:

Grace to you and peace from God our Father and the Lord Jesus Christ.*

2 We give thanks to God always for you all, making mention of you in our [c]prayers,

3 remembering without ceasing your work of faith, labor of love, and patience of hope in our Lord Jesus Christ in the sight of our God and Father,

4 knowing, beloved brethren, your [1d]election by God.

I. The Model Church and the Three Tenses of the Christian Life, 1:5–10

5 For our [e]gospel did not come to you in word only, but also in power, and in the Holy [f]Spirit and in much [g]assurance, as you know what kind of men we were among you for your sake.

6 And you became followers of us and of the Lord, having received the word in much affliction, with [h]joy of the Holy [f]Spirit,

7 so that you became examples to all in Macedonia and Achaia who [i]believe.

8 For from you the word of the Lord has [j]sounded forth, not only in Macedonia and

* 1:1 NU-Text omits *from God our Father and the Lord Jesus Christ.*

CHAPTER 1

1
a Churches (local): v. 1; 1 Th. 2:14. (Acts 8:3; Phil. 1:1, *note*)
b Acts 17:1–9

2
c Bible prayers (NT): v. 2; 1 Th. 3:10. (Mt. 6:9; Lk. 11:2, *note*)

4
d Election (corporate): v. 4; 2 Th. 2:13. (Dt. 7:6; 1 Pet. 5:13, *note*)

5
e Gospel: v. 5; 1 Th. 2:4. (Gen. 12:3; Rev. 14:6)
f Holy Spirit (NT): vv. 5–6; 1 Th. 4:8. (Mt. 1:18; Acts 2:4, *note*)
g Lit. *fulfillment*

6
h Acts 13:52

7
i Faith: v. 7; 1 Th. 2:10. (Gen. 3:20; Heb. 11:39, *note*)

8
j Rom. 10:18

---

[1](1:4) Even though Paul had ministered in Thessalonica for less than a month, many great doctrines of the Christian faith are alluded to in this Epistle: the Trinity (cp. 1:1 with vv. 5–6); the Holy Spirit (1:5–6; 4:8; 5:19); Christ's second advent (1:10; 2:19; 3:13; 4:14–17; 5:23); the Day of the Lord (5:1–3); assurance (1:5); conversion (1:9); election (1:4); resurrection (4:14–18); sanctification (4:3; 5:23); and Christian behavior (2:12; 4:1).

8
[a] 2 Th. 1:4
9
[b] Cp. 1 Cor. 12:2; Gal. 4:8
10
[c] *Christ* (second advent): v. 10; 1 Th. 2:19. (Dt. 30:3; Acts 1:11, *note*)
[d] *Resurrection:* v. 10; 1 Th. 4:14. (2 Ki. 4:35; 1 Cor. 15:52, *note*)
[e] Lit. *from among*
[f] Mt. 3:7; Rom. 5:9
CHAPTER 2
1
[g] Cp. Gal. 2:2; 4:11; Phil. 2:16
2
[h] Acts 16:12–24
[i] Acts 17:1–3
4
[j] *Gospel:* vv. 4,8–9; 1 Th. 3:2. (Gen. 12:3; Rev. 14:6)
[k] Gal. 1:10
5
[l] 2 Cor. 2:17
6
[m] Cp. Jn. 5:41,44
8
[n] Cp. Rom. 1:11
9
[o] Acts 18:3; 20:34–35; 1 Cor. 4:12;2 Th. 3:7–8; cp. Phil. 4:16

Achaia, but also [a]in every
place. Your faith toward God
has gone out, so that we do not
need to say anything.
9 For they themselves de-
clare concerning us what manner of entry we had to you, and
[1]how you turned to God [b]from
idols to serve the living and true
God,
10 and to [c]wait for His Son
from heaven, whom He [d]raised
[e]from the dead, *even* Jesus who
delivers us from the [f]wrath to
come.

II. The Model Servant and His Reward, 2

2 FOR you yourselves know,
brethren, that our coming
to you was [g]not in vain.
2 But even* after we had
suffered before and were spitefully treated at [h]Philippi, as you
know, we were [i]bold in our
God to speak to you the gospel
of God in much conflict.
3 For our exhortation *did*
not *come* from error or uncleanness, nor *was it* in deceit.
4 But as we have been ap-
proved by God to be entrusted
with the [j]gospel, even so we
speak, not as pleasing [k]men,
but God who tests our hearts.
5 For [l]neither at any time
did we use flattering words, as
you know, nor a cloak for
covetousness—God *is* witness.
6 Nor did we [m]seek glory
from men, either from you or
from others, when we might
have made demands as apostles
of Christ.
7 But we were gentle among
you, just as a nursing *mother*
cherishes her own children.
8 So, affectionately longing
for you, we were well pleased to
[n]impart to you not only the
[j]gospel of God, but also our
own lives, because you had become dear to us.
9 For you remember, brethren, our [o]labor and toil; for laboring night and day, that we
might not be a burden to any of
you, we preached to you the
[j]gospel of God.
10 You *are* witnesses, and
God *also*, how devoutly and
justly and blamelessly we behaved ourselves among you
who [p]believe;
11 as you know how we ex-
horted, and comforted, and
charged* every one of you, as a
father *does* his own children,
12 that you would walk
[q]worthy of God [r]who calls you
into His own kingdom and
glory.
13 For this reason we also
thank God without ceasing, because when you [s]received the
word of God which you heard
from us, you welcomed *it* not *as*
the word of men, but as it is in
truth, the word of God, which
also effectively [t]works in you
who [p]believe.
14 For you, brethren, became
imitators of the [u]churches of
God which are in Judea in
Christ Jesus. For you also suffered the same things from your
own countrymen, just as they
did from the Judeans,
15 who killed both the Lord
Jesus and [v]their own prophets,
and have persecuted us; and
they do not please God and are
contrary to all men,
16 [w]forbidding us to speak to
the Gentiles that they may be
[x]saved, so as always to fill up
the measure of their [y]sins; but
wrath has come upon them to
the uttermost.
17 But we, brethren, having
been taken away from you for a
short time in presence, not in
heart, endeavored more eagerly
to see your face with great desire.
18 Therefore we wanted to
come to you—even I, Paul, time
and again—but [z]Satan hindered us.
19 For what *is* our hope, or
joy, or [aa]crown of rejoicing? *Is it*

*
2:2 NU-Text and M-Text omit *even.*
2:11 NU-Text and M-Text read *implored.*

10
[p] *Faith:* vv. 10,13; 1 Th. 4:14. (Gen. 3:20; Heb. 11:39, *note*)
12
[q] Eph. 4:1
[r] 1 Cor. 1:9; 2 Th. 2:14; 2 Tim. 1:9
13
[s] Mk. 4:20
[t] 1 Pet. 1:23
14
[u] *Churches* (local): v. 14; 2 Th. 1:1. (Acts 8:3; Phil. 1:1, *note*)
15
[v] Jer. 2:30; Mt. 23:34–35; Acts 7:52; cp. Lk. 20:9–19
16
[w] Cp. Acts 17:5,13; 18:12; 22:21–22
[x] See Rom. 1:16, *note*
[y] See Rom. 3:23, *note*
18
[z] *Satan:* v. 18; 2 Th. 2:9. (Gen. 3:1; Rev. 20:10)
19
[aa] *Rewards:* v. 19; 2 Tim. 4:8. (Dan. 12:3; 1 Cor. 3:14, *note*)

[1](1:9) The tenses of the Christian's life indicated here are logical and give the true order. They occur also in v. 3. The "work of faith" is to "[turn] to God from idols" (cp. Jn. 6:28–29); the "labor of love" is to "serve the living and true God"; and the "patience of hope" is to "wait for His Son from heaven" (cp. Mt. 24:42; 25:13; Lk. 12:36–48; Acts 1:11; Phil. 3:20–21). Paul repeats this threefold sequence in Ti. 2:11–13.

not even you in the [a]presence of
our Lord Jesus Christ [b]at His
coming?
20 For you are our glory and
joy.

III. The Model Brother
and His Sanctification, 3

3 THEREFORE, when we
could no longer endure it,
we thought it good to be left in
Athens alone,
2 and sent [c]Timothy, our
brother and minister of God,
and our fellow laborer in the
[d]gospel of Christ, to establish
you and encourage you concerning your faith,
3 [e]that no one should be
shaken by these afflictions; for
you yourselves know that [f]we
are appointed to this.
4 For, in fact, we told you
before when we were with you
that we would suffer tribulation, just as it happened, and
you know.
5 For this reason, when I
could no longer endure it, I sent
to [g]know your faith, [h]lest by
some means the tempter had
[i]tempted you, and our labor
[j]might be in vain.
6 But now that Timothy has
come to us from you, and
brought us good news of your
faith and [k]love, and that you always have good remembrance
of us, greatly [l]desiring to see
us, as we also *to see* you—
7 therefore, brethren, in all
our affliction and distress we
were [m]comforted concerning
you by your faith.
8 For now we live, if you
[n]stand fast in the Lord.
9 For what thanks can we
render to God for you, for all the
joy with which we rejoice for
your sake before our God,
10 night and day [o]praying
exceedingly that we may see
your face and [p]perfect what is
lacking in your faith?
11 Now may our God and Father Himself, and our Lord Jesus Christ, direct our way to
you.
12 And may the Lord make
you increase and [q]abound [r]in
[k]love to one another and to all,
just as we *do* to you,
13 so that He may establish
[s]your hearts blameless in holiness before our God and Father
[b]at the coming of our Lord Jesus Christ with all His saints.

IV. The Model Walk and the
Believer's Hope, 4

4 FINALLY then, brethren,
we urge and exhort in the
Lord Jesus that you should
[t]abound more and more, just as
you received from us how you
ought [u]to walk and to please
God;
2 for you know what com-
mandments we gave you
through the Lord Jesus.
3 For this is the will of God,
your [v]sanctification: [w]that you
should abstain from sexual immorality;
4 that each of you should
know how to possess his own
vessel in sanctification and
honor,
5 not in passion of lust, like
the [x]Gentiles who do not know
God;
6 that no one should take
advantage of and [y]defraud his
brother in this matter, because
the Lord *is* the avenger of all
such, as we also forewarned
you and testified.
7 For God did not call us to
uncleanness, [z]but in holiness.
8 Therefore he who [aa]rejects
this does not [aa]reject man, but
God, who has also given* us
His Holy [bb]Spirit.
9 But concerning brotherly
love you have no need that I
should write to you, for you
yourselves are [cc]taught by God
to [k]love one another;
10 and indeed you do so toward all the brethren who are in
all Macedonia. But we urge you,
brethren, that you increase
more and more;
11 that you also aspire to
lead a quiet life, to [dd]mind your
own business, and to work with
your own hands, as we commanded you,
12 that you may walk [ee]prop-
erly toward those who are outside, and *that* you may lack
nothing.

* 4:8 NU-Text reads *who also gives.*

19
a Jude 24
b Christ (second advent): v. 19; 3:13; 1 Th. 4:16. (Dt. 30:3; Acts 1:11, *note*)

CHAPTER 3
2
c Cp. Acts 17:15; Phil. 2:19
d Gospel: v. 2; 2 Th. 1:8. (Gen. 12:3; Rev. 14:6)
3
e Eph. 3:13
f Jn. 16:2; Acts 9:16; 1 Cor. 4:9; 2 Tim. 3:12; 1 Pet. 2:21
5
g i.e. *ascertain*
h Cp. 2 Cor. 11:2–3
i Test/tempt: v. 5; 1 Tim. 2:14. (Gen. 3:1; Jas. 1:14, *note*)
j Cp. Gal. 2:2; 4:11; Phil. 2:16
6
k Law (of Christ): vv. 6,12; 4:9; 1 Th. 5:13. (Jn. 13:34; 2 Jn. 5)
l Cp. Phil. 1:8
7
m Cp. 2 Cor. 7:6–7
8
n Eph. 6:13–14; Phil. 4:1
10
o Bible prayers (NT): vv. 10–13; 1 Th. 5:23. (Mt. 6:9; Lk. 11:2, *note*)
p 2 Cor. 13:9; see Phil. 3:12, *note*
12
q Phil. 1:9
r Jn. 13:34–35; 1 Jn. 4:7,12
13
s 2 Th. 2:17

CHAPTER 4
1
t 1 Cor. 15:58
u Col. 1:10
3
v Sanctification (NT): v. 3; 1 Th. 5:23. (Mt. 4:5; Rev. 22:11)
w 1 Cor. 6:15–20
5
x Eph. 4:17–18
6
y Lit. *wrong*
7
z Lev. 11:44; Heb. 12:14; 1 Pet. 1:14–16
8
aa Lk. 10:16
bb Holy Spirit (NT): v. 8; 1 Th. 5:19. (Mt. 1:18; Acts 2:4, *note*)
9
cc Jn. 15:12, 17
11
dd 2 Th. 3:11; 1 Pet. 4:15
12
ee 1 Pet. 2:12

The revelation of the rapture of the Church

13 But I do not want you to be ignorant, brethren, concerning those who have fallen [a]asleep, lest you sorrow as others who have no hope.

14 For if we [b]believe that Jesus died and [c]rose again, even so God will bring with Him [d]those who sleep in Jesus.*

15 For this we [e]say to you by the word of the Lord, that we who are alive *and* remain until the coming of the Lord will by no means precede those who are asleep.

16 [f]For the Lord Himself will descend from heaven with a shout, with the voice of an archangel, and with the trumpet of God. And the dead in Christ [c]will [g]rise first.

17 [h]Then [i]we who are alive *and* remain shall be [1]caught up together with [i]them [j]in the clouds to meet the Lord in the air. And thus we shall always [k]be with the Lord.

18 Therefore [l]comfort one another with these words.

V. The Model Walk and the Day of the Lord, 5:1–24. (See Joel 1:15 and Rev. 19:19, notes)

5 BUT concerning the times and the seasons, brethren, you have no need that I should write to you.

2 For you yourselves know perfectly that the [m]day of the Lord so comes as a thief in the night.

3 For when they say, "Peace and safety!" then sudden destruction comes upon them, as labor pains upon a pregnant woman. And they shall not escape.

4 But [2n]you, brethren, are not in darkness, so that this Day should overtake you as a thief.

5 You are all sons of light and sons of the day. We are not of the night nor of darkness.

6 [o]Therefore let us not sleep, as others *do*, but let us [p]watch and be [q]sober.

7 For those who sleep, sleep at night, and those who get drunk are drunk at night.

8 But let us who are of the day be sober, putting on the [r]breastplate of faith and love, and *as* a helmet the hope of [s]salvation.

9 For God did not appoint us to wrath, but to obtain [s]salvation through our Lord Jesus Christ,

10 who died for us, that whether we wake or sleep, we should live together with Him.

11 Therefore [l]comfort each other and edify one another, just as you also are doing.

12 And we urge you, brethren, to recognize [t]those who labor among you, and are over you in the Lord and admonish you,

13 and to esteem them very highly in [u]love for their work's sake. Be at peace among yourselves.

14 Now we [v]exhort you, brethren, warn those who are unruly, comfort the fainthearted, uphold the weak, be patient with all.

15 See that no one renders evil for evil to anyone, but always pursue what is good both for yourselves and for all.

16 Rejoice always,

17 pray without ceasing,

18 in everything give thanks; for this is the will of God in Christ Jesus for you.

19 Do not quench the [w]Spirit.

20 Do not despise prophecies.

21 Test all things; hold fast what is good.

22 Abstain from every form of evil.

23 Now may the God of peace Himself [x]sanctify you completely; [y]and may your

* 4:14 Or *those who through Jesus sleep*

13
a Cp. Jn. 11:11–14
14
b *Faith:* v. 14; 2 Th. 1:10. (Gen. 3:20; Heb. 11:39, *note*)
c *Resurrection:* vv. 14, 16; 2 Tim. 2:8. (2 Ki. 4:35; 1 Cor. 15:52, *note*)
d 1 Cor. 15:20
15
e *Inspiration:* vv. 15–18; 1 Tim. 4:1. (Ex. 4:15; 2 Tim. 3:16, *note*)
16
f *Christ* (second advent): vv. 14–17; 1 Th. 5:23. (Dt. 30:3; Acts 1:11, *note*)
g Rev. 20:6
17
h 1 Cor. 15:51–53
i *Church* (the true): vv. 15–18; Heb. 2:12. (Mt. 16:18; Heb. 12:23)
j Or *in clouds*
k Jn. 14:3
18
l Or *exhort, encourage*
CHAPTER 5
2
m *Day* (of the LORD): vv. 1–4; 2 Th. 2:2. (Ps. 2:9; Rev. 19:19)
4
n Eph. 5:8; 1 Jn. 2:8
6
o Cp. Rom. 13:12–13
p Mt. 25:13; Mk. 13:35
q 1 Pet. 5:8
8
r Cp. Isa. 59:17; Eph. 6:14
s See Rom. 1:16, *note*
12
t Heb. 13:7, 17
13
u *Law* (of Christ): v. 13; 2 Th. 1:3. (Jn. 13:34; 2 Jn. 5)
14
v Or *encourage*
19
w *Holy Spirit* (NT): v. 19; 2 Th. 2:13. (Mt. 1:18; Acts 2:4, *note*)
23
x *Sanctification* (NT): v. 23; 1 Tim. 4:5. (Mt. 4:5; Rev. 22:11)
y *Bible prayers* (NT): v. 23; 2 Th. 1:11. (Mt. 6:9; Lk. 11:2, *note*)

[1](4:17) This central passage on the blessed hope of the Church includes: (1) reassurance (vv. 13–14); (2) revelation (vv. 15–17, setting forth the return of Christ, the rapture of the Church, and the reunion of all believers); and (3) comfort (v. 18).

[2](5:4) Paul's careful alternation of the pronouns "those" and "you" throughout this passage is sufficient to show that he never conceived of the Church, the body of Christ, as remaining on earth during the time of wrath in the Day of the Lord.

23
a *Assurance/security:* v. 23; 2 Th. 3:3. (Ps. 23:1; Jude 1, *note*)
b 1 Cor. 1:8–9
c *Christ* (second advent): v. 23; 2 Th. 1:7. (Dt. 30:3; Acts 1:11, *note*)
24
d 1 Cor. 10:13; 2 Th. 3:3
e Phil. 1:6
27
f Lit. *adjure,* i.e. *solemnly appeal*

whole [1]spirit, soul, and body be
[a]preserved [b]blameless at the
[c]coming of our Lord Jesus
Christ.
24 [d]He who calls you *is* faithful, who also will [e]do *it.*

Conclusion, 5:25–28

25 Brethren, pray for us.
26 Greet all the brethren with
a holy kiss.
27 I [f]charge you by the Lord
that this epistle be read to all the
holy* brethren.
28 The grace of our Lord Jesus Christ *be* with you. Amen.

*5:27 NU-Text omits *holy.*

[1](5:23) Although the words "soul" and "spirit" are sometimes used interchangeably in Scripture when referring to man (Job 7:11; 1 Cor. 5:5; Heb. 10:39), a distinction is observed in some passages. They are declared to be divisible (Heb. 4:12) and are distinguished when used in reference to the burial and resurrection of the human body. The body is buried a natural body (Gk. *sōma psuchikon—soul-body*) but raised a spiritual body (Gk. *sōma pneumatikon*) (1 Cor. 15:44). The difference between the two terms seems to be that the spirit is that which "knows" (1 Cor. 2:11) and is capable of God-consciousness and communication with God (Job 32:8; Prov. 20:27; cp. Ps. 18:28), whereas the soul is the seat of the affections, desires, emotions, and the will of man (Mt. 11:29; 26:38; Jn. 12:27). The NT word for soul (Gk. *psuchē*) corresponds to the OT soul (Heb. *nephesh;* e.g. Dt. 6:5; 14:26; 1 Sam. 18:1; 20:4,17; Job 14:22; Ps. 42:6; 84:2), whereas the NT word for spirit (Gk. *pneuma*) is the same in meaning as the OT word for spirit (Heb. *ruach;* e.g. Gen. 41:8; 1 Cor. 5:5). See Gen. 1:26, *note.*

The Second Epistle of Paul the Apostle to the

THESSALONIANS

Author: Paul *Theme:* Day of the Lord *Date of writing:* C. A.D. 51

THE SECOND EPISTLE TO THE THESSALONIANS was written by Paul shortly after he wrote his first letter to them.

The Thessalonian converts were "shaken" and "troubled," supposing, perhaps on the authority of a forged letter as from Paul, that the persecutions they were suffering were those of the "great and awesome day of the LORD." (Joel 2:31; see Joel 1:15; Rev. 19:19; and *notes*) from which they had been taught to expect deliverance at the day of Christ, that time of "our gathering together to Him" (2:1).

The present letter, then, was written to instruct the Thessalonian Christians that "our gathering together to Him [Christ]" (1 Th. 4:14–17; 2 Th. 2:1) will precede the Day of the Lord. First Thessalonians has more in view the translation of the Church; the second Epistle, "the day of the Lord" which will follow it.

The Epistle may be divided as follows:

Introduction, 1:1–4.
I. Comfort in Persecution, 1:5–12.
II. The Day of the Lord, and the Man of Sin, 2:1–12.
III. Exhortations and Instructions, 2:13—3:15.
Conclusion, 3:16–18.

Introduction: Salutation, 1:1–4

1 PAUL, Silvanus, and Timothy,

To the [a]church of the Thessalonians in God our Father and the Lord Jesus Christ:

2 Grace to you and peace from God our Father and the Lord Jesus Christ.

3 We are bound to thank God always for you, brethren, as it is fitting, because your faith grows exceedingly, and the [b]love of every one of you all abounds toward each other,

4 so that we ourselves boast of you among the [a]churches of God for your patience and faith in all your persecutions and tribulations that you endure,

I. Comfort in Persecution, 1:5–12

5 *which is* manifest evidence of the righteous judgment of God, that you may be counted worthy of the kingdom of God, for which you also suffer;

6 since *it is* a righteous thing with God to repay with tribulation those who trouble you,

7 and to *give* you who are troubled rest with us [c]when the Lord Jesus is revealed from heaven with His mighty [d]angels,

8 in flaming fire taking [e]vengeance on those who do not know God, and on those who do not obey the [f]gospel of our Lord Jesus Christ.

9 These shall be punished with everlasting destruction from the presence of the Lord and from the glory of His power,

10 when He comes, in that Day, [g]to be [h]glorified in His saints and to be admired among all those who [i]believe,* because our testimony among you was believed.

11 Therefore we also [j]pray always for you that our God would [k]count you worthy of *this* calling, and fulfill all the good pleasure of *His* goodness and the work of faith with power,

12 that the name of our Lord Jesus Christ may be glorified in you, and you in Him, according to the [l]grace of our God and the Lord Jesus Christ.

II. The Day of the Lord and the Man of Sin, 2:1–12

2 NOW, brethren, concerning the coming of our Lord Jesus Christ and our gathering together to Him, we ask you,

2 not to be soon shaken in mind or troubled, either by

*1:10 NU-Text and M-Text read *have believed.*

CHAPTER 1

1
a Churches (local): vv. 1,4; 1 Tim. 3:5. (Acts 8:3; Phil. 1:1, *note*)

3
b Law (of Christ): v. 3; 1 Tim. 1:5. (Jn. 13:34; 2 Jn. 5)

7
c Christ (second advent): v. 7; 2 Th. 2:8. (Dt. 30:3; Acts 1:11, *note*)
d See Heb. 1:4, *note*

8
e Day (of destruction): vv. 7–10; Rev. 19:20. (Job 21:30; Rev. 20:11)
f Gospel: v. 8; 2 Th. 2:14. (Gen. 12:3; Rev. 14:6)

10
g Mt. 25:31
h Jn. 17:10
i Faith: v. 10; 1 Tim. 1:16. (Gen. 3:20; Heb. 11:39, *note*)

11
j Bible prayers (NT): vv. 11–12; 2 Th. 2:16. (Mt. 6:9; Lk. 11:2, *note*)
k Col. 1:12

12
l Grace: v. 12; 2 Th. 2:16. (Jn. 1:14; Jn. 1:17, *note*). See 2 Pet. 3:18, *note.*

CHAPTER 2

2
a *Day* (of the LORD): vv. 1–12; 2 Pet. 3:10. (Ps. 2:9; Rev. 19:19). See textual note.

3
b Gk. *hē apostasia* meaning *the rebellion* or *the departure*
c *Apostasy:* vv. 1–12; 1 Tim. 4:1. (Lk. 18:8; 2 Tim. 3:1, *note*)
d *The Beast:* vv. 3–8; Rev. 13:1. (Dan. 7:8; Rev. 19:20)

4
e Cp. Isa. 14:14; Ezek. 28:2

7
f See Mt. 13:11, *note*

8
g *Day* (of the LORD): vv. 1–12; 2 Pet. 3:10. (Ps. 2:9; Rev. 19:19)
h Isa. 11:4; Rev. 19:15
i *Christ* (second advent): v. 8; 1 Tim. 6:14. (Dt. 30:3; Acts 1:11, *note*)

9
j Cp. Mt. 12:24
k *Satan:* v. 9; 1 Tim. 1:20. (Gen. 3:1; Rev. 20:10)

10
l 1 Cor. 16:22
m See Rom.

spirit or by word or by letter, as
if from us, as though the [a]day of
Christ* had come.
3 Let no one deceive you by
any means; [1]for *that Day will
not come* unless [b]the [c]falling
away comes first, and the [d]man
of sin* is revealed, the son of
perdition,
4 who opposes and [e]exalts
himself above all that is called
God or that is worshiped, so
that he sits as God* in the temple
of God, showing himself
that he is God.
5 Do you not remember that
when I was still with you I told
you these things?
6 And now you know what
is restraining, that he may be
revealed in his own time.
7 For the [f]mystery of lawlessness
is already at work;
only He* who now restrains
will do so until He* is taken out
of the way.
8 And then [d]the lawless one
will be revealed, [g]whom the
Lord will consume with the
breath of His [h]mouth and destroy
[i]with the brightness of
His coming.
9 The coming of the *lawless
one* is according to the [j]working
of [k]Satan, with all power,
signs, and lying wonders,
10 and with all unrighteous
deception among those who
perish, because they did not receive
[l]the love of the truth, that
they might be [m]saved.
11 And for this reason God
will send them strong delusion,
that they should believe the
[n]lie,
12 that they all may be condemned
who did not believe the
truth but had pleasure in unrighteousness.

III. Exhortations and Instructions, 2:13—3:15

13 But we are bound to give
thanks to God always for you,
brethren beloved by the Lord,
because God from the beginning
[o]chose you for [m]salvation
through sanctification by the
[p]Spirit and belief in the truth,
14 to which He called you by
our [q]gospel, for the obtaining of
the glory of our Lord Jesus
Christ.
15 Therefore, brethren,
stand fast and hold the [r]traditions
which you were taught,
whether by word or our epistle.
16 [s]Now may our Lord Jesus
Christ Himself, and our God
and Father, who has loved us
and given *us* everlasting consolation
and good hope by [t]grace,
17 comfort your hearts and
establish you in every good
word and work.

Prayer requested

3 FINALLY, brethren, pray
for us, that the word of the
Lord may run *swiftly* and be
glorified, just as *it is* with you,
2 and that we may be delivered
from unreasonable and
wicked men; for not all have
faith.
3 But the Lord is [u]faithful,
who will establish you and
guard *you* from the evil one.
4 And we have confidence
in the Lord concerning you,

*
2:2 NU-Text reads *the Lord.* 2:3 NU-Text reads *lawlessness.* 2:4 NU-Text omits *as God.* 2:7 Or *he* • Or *he*

1:16, *note*

11
n Cp. 1 Ki. 22:22

13
o *Election* (corporate): vv. 13–14; 2 Tim. 2:4. (Dt. 7:6; 1 Pet. 5:13, *note*)
p *Holy Spirit* (NT): v. 13; 1 Tim. 3:16. (Mt. 1:18; Acts 2:4, *note*)

14
q *Gospel:* v. 14; 1 Tim. 1:11. (Gen. 12:3; Rev. 14:6)

15
r Rom. 6:17; Jude 3

16
s *Bible prayers* (NT): v. 16; 2 Th. 3:5. (Mt. 6:9; Lk. 11:2, *note*)
t *Grace:* v. 16; 1 Tim. 1:14. (Jn. 1:14; Jn. 1:17, *note*)

CHAPTER 3

3
u *Assurance/security:* vv. 3–4; 2 Tim. 1:12. (Ps. 23:1; Jude 1, *note*)

[1](2:3) The order of events is: (1) The working of the mystery of lawlessness under divine restraint which had already begun in the apostle's time (v. 7) and which has been expanding throughout the Church Age. (2) The removal of that which restrains the mystery of lawlessness (vv. 6–7). There are various views as to the identity of the restraining influence. The use of the masculine pronoun "He" indicates that it is a person. It seems evident that it is the Holy Spirit: (a) in the OT the Holy Spirit acts as a restrainer of iniquity (Gen. 6:3); (b) the restrainer is referred to by the use of both neuter and masculine genders ("what," v. 6; "He," v. 7), as in Jn. 14:16–17; 16:12–13 concerning the coming of the Holy Spirit; and (c) it will be when the restrainer is "taken out of the way" that the man of sin will be revealed; this will be when the Church is translated and the Spirit's restraining ministry through it will cease. Observe, however, that it is not said that the restrainer will be "taken away," but "taken out of the way"; thus the Holy Spirit will continue a divine activity to the end-time, though not as a restrainer of evil through the Church. (3) The manifestation of the lawless one, the man of sin, with the resulting apostasy (vv. 3–4,8–10; Dan. 7:8; 9:27; Mt. 24:15; Rev. 13:1–18). And (4) the return of Christ to the earth in glory, which will result in the overthrow of the man of sin and the establishment of the millennial kingdom (vv. 8–10; Rev. 19:11—20:6).

both that you do and will do the
things we command you.
5 Now may the [a]Lord direct
your hearts into the love of God
and into the patience of Christ.

Christians should work while awaiting the Lord's return

6 But we command you,
brethren, in the name of our
Lord Jesus Christ, that you
[b]withdraw from every brother
who walks disorderly and not
according to the tradition which
he* received from us.
7 For you yourselves know
how you ought to [c]follow us, for
we were not disorderly among
you;
8 nor did we eat anyone's
bread free of charge, but
worked with [d]labor and toil
night and day, that we might
not be a burden to any of you,
9 not because we do not
have [e]authority, but to make
ourselves an example of how
you should [c]follow us.
10 For even when we were
with you, we commanded you
this: If anyone will not work,
neither shall he eat.
11 For we hear that there are
some who walk among you in a
disorderly manner, not working
at all, but are [f]busybodies.
12 Now those who are such
we command and exhort
through our Lord Jesus Christ
that they [g]work in quietness
and eat their own bread.
13 But *as for* you, brethren,
[h]do not grow weary *in* doing
good.
14 And if anyone does not
obey our word in this epistle,
note that person and [i]do not
keep company with him, that he
may be ashamed.
15 Yet do not count *him* as an
enemy, but [j]admonish *him* [k]as
a brother.

Conclusion: Benediction and Authentication, 3:16–18

16 Now may the [l]Lord of
peace Himself give you peace
always in every way. The Lord
be with you all.
17 The [m]salutation of Paul
with my own hand, which is a
sign in every epistle; so I write.
18 The [n]grace of our Lord Jesus Christ *be* with you all.
Amen.

* 3:6 NU-Text and M-Text read *they.*

5
a *Bible prayers* (NT): v. 5; Heb. 5:7. (Mt. 6:9; Lk. 11:2, *note*)
6
b 3:14; 1 Cor. 5:11
7
c Lit. *imitate*
8
d 1 Th. 2:9
9
e 1 Cor. 9:6–14
11
f 1 Tim. 5:13; 1 Pet. 4:15
12
g 1 Th. 4:11–12
13
h Cp. 1 Cor. 15:58; Jas. 5:7,11
14
i v. 6
15
j Cp. Ezek. 18:23; Gal. 6:1
k Lev. 19:17
16
l Jn. 14:27; Phil. 4:9
17
m 1 Cor. 16:21
18
n Rom. 16:24

The First Epistle of Paul the Apostle to

TIMOTHY

Author: Paul *Theme:* Church Order *Date of writing:* c. A.D. 64

THE FIRST EPISTLE TO TIMOTHY was written during the last few years of Paul's life. Together with 2 Timothy and Titus it is known as a Pastoral Epistle. As the first-century churches increased in number, questions of church order, soundness in the faith, and discipline arose. The apostles themselves dealt with these questions, but the approaching end of the apostolic period made necessary authoritative teaching about faith and order for the future guidance of the churches. This teaching is revealed in the Pastoral Epistles.

Timothy, to whom this Epistle and its companion letter are addressed, was intimately associated with Paul. Considerably younger than the apostle, he was the son of a Greek Gentile father and a devout Jewish mother, Eunice by name (2 Tim. 1:5). He joined Paul on the second missionary journey and was with him, e.g. in Corinth, Macedonia, Ephesus, and Jerusalem.

The key verse of the Epistle is 3:15, "so that you may know how you ought to conduct yourself in the house of God, which is the church of the living God, the pillar and ground of the truth." Particularly important is the summary of qualifications for church officers—bishops (the term is interchangeable with "elders") and deacons, 3; 5:1,17,19.

The Epistle may be divided as follows:

Introduction, 1:1–2.
I. Warning about Heresy in Doctrine and Life, 1:3–11.
II. Paul's Personal Witness and Instruction to Timothy, 1:12–20.
III. Instructions about Prayer and the Place of Women in the Church, 2.
IV. Qualifications of Bishops (Elders) and Deacons, 3.
V. The Walk of the Good Minister of Jesus Christ, 4.
VI. The Work of the Good Minister, 5.
VII. Warnings to a Good Minister, 6:1–19.
Conclusion, 6:20–21.

Introduction: Salutation, 1:1–2

1 PAUL, an apostle of [a]Jesus
Christ, by the command-
ment of God our [b]Savior and
the [a]Lord Jesus Christ, our
hope,

2 To [c]Timothy, a true [d]son
in the faith:

Grace, mercy, *and* peace
from God our Father and [a]Jesus
Christ our Lord.

I. Warning about Heresy in Doctrine and Life, 1:3–11

3 As I urged you when I
[e]went into Macedonia—remain
in Ephesus that you may charge
some that they teach no other
doctrine,
4 nor give [f]heed to fables
and endless genealogies, which
cause disputes rather than
godly edification which is in
faith.
5 Now [g]the purpose of the
commandment is [h]love from a
[i]pure heart, *from* a good conscience, and *from* sincere faith,
6 from which some, [j]hav-
ing strayed, have turned aside
to [k]idle talk,
7 desiring to be teachers of
the law, understanding neither
what they say nor the things
which they affirm.
8 But we know that the law
is [l]good if one uses it lawfully,
9 knowing this: that the
[m]law is not made for a righteous
person, but for *the* lawless and
insubordinate, for *the* ungodly
and for sinners, for *the* unholy
and profane, for murderers of
fathers and murderers of mothers, for manslayers,
10 for fornicators, for sodomites, for [n]kidnappers, for liars,
for perjurers, and if there is any
other thing that is contrary to
[o]sound doctrine,
11 according to the [p]glorious
[q]gospel of the [r]blessed God
which was [s]committed to my
trust.

II. Paul's Personal Witness and Charge to Timothy, 1:12–20

12 And I thank Christ Jesus
our Lord who has [t]enabled me,
because He counted me faithful,

CHAPTER 1
1
a Or *Christ Jesus*
b See Rom. 1:16, *note*
2
c Acts 16:1–2
d Lit. *child*
3
e Acts 20:1,3
4
f 1 Tim. 6:3–4,20
5
g Rom. 13:8–10; Gal. 5:14
h Law (of Christ): v. 5; 1 Tim. 2:15. (Jn. 13:34; 2 Jn. 5)
i Eph. 6:24
6
j Cp. 2 Tim. 4:10
k Cp. Ti. 1:10
8
l Rom. 7:12
9
m Law (of Moses): vv. 8–9; Heb. 7:19. (Ex. 19:1; Gal. 3:24, *note*)
10
n Ex. 21:16
o Cp. 2 Cor. 2:17
11
p Lit. *gospel of the glory*
q Gospel: v. 11; 2 Tim. 1:10. (Gen. 12:3; Rev. 14:6)
r 1 Tim. 6:15
s 1 Cor. 9:17
12
t 1 Cor. 15:10

12
a Col. 1:25
13
b Acts 8:3; 1 Cor. 15:9
14
c *Grace:* vv. 14–15; 2 Tim. 1:9. (Jn. 1:14; Jn. 1:17, *note*)
15
d *Christ* (first advent): v. 15; 2:6; Ti. 2:11. (Gen. 3:15; Acts 1:11, *note*)
e Gk. *kosmos.* See Mt. 4:8, *note*
f See Rom. 1:16, *note*
16
g *Faith:* v. 16; 1 Tim. 4:3. (Gen. 3:20; Heb. 11:39, *note*)
h *Life* (eternal): v. 16; 1 Tim. 4:8. (Mt. 7:14; Rev. 22:19)
17
i See Jn. 1:18, *note*
18
j Lit. *child*
20
k 2 Tim. 2:17–18
l 2 Tim. 4:14
m *Judgments* (the seven): v. 20; 2 Tim. 4:1. (1 Sam. 7:14; Rev. 20:12, *note*). 1 Cor. 5:5
n *Satan:* v. 20; 1 Tim. 3:6. (Gen. 3:1; Rev. 20:10)
CHAPTER 2
2
o Or *gravity*

[a]putting *me* into the ministry,

13 although I was [b]formerly a [1]blasphemer, a persecutor, and an insolent man; but I obtained mercy because I did *it* ignorantly in unbelief.

14 And the [c]grace of our Lord was exceedingly abundant, with faith and love which are in Christ Jesus.

15 This *is* a faithful saying and worthy of all acceptance, that Christ Jesus [d]came into the [e]world to [f]save sinners, of whom I am chief.

16 However, for this reason I obtained mercy, that in me first Jesus Christ might show all longsuffering, as a pattern to those who are going to [g]believe on Him for everlasting [h]life.

17 Now to the King eternal, immortal, [i]invisible, to God who alone is wise,* *be* honor and glory forever and ever. Amen.

18 This charge I commit to you, [j]son Timothy, according to the prophecies previously made concerning you, that by them you may wage the good warfare,

19 having faith and a good conscience, which some having rejected, concerning the faith have suffered shipwreck,

20 of whom are [k]Hymenaeus and [l]Alexander, whom I [m]delivered to [n]Satan that they may learn not to blaspheme.

III. Instructions about Prayer and the Role of Women in the Church, 2

2 THEREFORE I exhort first of all that supplications, prayers, intercessions, *and* giving of thanks be made for all men,

2 for kings and all who are in authority, that we may lead a quiet and peaceable life in all godliness and [o]reverence.

3 For this *is* good and acceptable in the sight of God our Savior,

4 who desires all men to be [f]saved and to come to the knowledge of the truth.

5 For *there is* one God and one Mediator between God and men, *the* Man Christ Jesus,

6 [d]who [p]gave Himself a ransom for all, to be testified in due time,

7 for which I was appointed a preacher and an apostle—I am speaking the truth in Christ* *and* not lying—a teacher of the Gentiles in faith and truth.

8 I desire therefore that the men pray everywhere, lifting up holy hands, without wrath and doubting;

9 in like manner also, that the women adorn themselves in modest apparel, with propriety and moderation, not with [q]braided hair or gold or pearls or costly clothing,

10 but, which is proper for women professing godliness, [r]with good works.

11 Let a woman learn in [s]silence with all [t]submission.

12 And I do not permit a woman to teach or to have authority over a man, but to be in [s]silence.

13 For Adam was formed first, then Eve.

14 And Adam was not deceived, but the woman being [u]deceived, fell into [v]transgression.

15 Nevertheless she will be saved in childbearing if they continue in faith, [w]love, and holiness, with self-control.

IV. Qualifications of Bishops (Elders) and Deacons, 3

3 THIS *is* a faithful saying: If a man desires the position of a [x]bishop, he desires a good work.

2 A [x]bishop then must be blameless, the husband of one wife, temperate, sober-minded, of good behavior, hospitable, able to teach;

3 not given to wine, not vio-

*

1:17 NU-Text reads *to the only God.*
2:7 NU-Text omits *in Christ.*

6
p *Sacrifice* (of Christ): v. 6; Ti. 2:14. (Gen. 3:15; Heb. 10:18, *note*)
9
q 1 Pet. 3:3
10
r *Righteousness* (garment): v. 10; Ti. 2:10. (Gen. 3:21; Rev. 19:8)
11
s Or *quietness.* 1 Cor. 14:34
t Cp. Gen. 3:16
14
u *Test/tempt:* v. 14; 1 Tim. 6:9. (Gen. 3:1; Jas. 1:14, *note*)
v See Rom. 3:23, *note*
15
w *Law* (of Christ): v. 15; 1 Tim. 4:12. (Jn. 13:34; 2 Jn. 5)
CHAPTER 3
1
x Or *an overseer,* also called *an elder. Elders:* vv. 1–2; 1 Tim. 5:17. (Acts 11:30; Ti. 1:5, *note*)

[1](1:13) In applying this terrible word to himself, Paul gives strong testimony to his belief in the Deity of Christ. To blaspheme is to speak injuriously of God; and surely Saul of Tarsus, the strict Pharisee, could never have spoken thus of the LORD God of Israel. But he had spoken evil of Jesus (Acts 9:4–5), and he now humbly confesses his former blasphemy.

lent, not greedy for money,* but
gentle, not quarrelsome, not
covetous;
4 one who rules his own
house well, having *his* children
in submission with all reverence
5 (for if a man does not
know how to rule his own
house, how will he take care of
the [a]church of God?);
6 not a [b]novice, lest being
puffed up with pride he fall into
the *same* condemnation as the
[c]devil.
7 Moreover he must have a
good testimony among those
who are [d]outside, lest he fall
into reproach and the [e]snare of
the [c]devil.
8 Likewise deacons *must be*
reverent, not double-tongued,
not given to much wine, not
greedy for money,
9 holding the [f]mystery of
the faith with a pure conscience.
10 But let these also first be
tested; then let them serve as
deacons, being *found* blameless.
11 [g]Likewise, *their* wives
must be reverent, not slanderers, temperate, faithful in all
things.
12 Let deacons be the husbands of one wife, ruling *their*
children and their own houses
well.
13 For those who have
served [h]well as deacons obtain
for themselves a good standing
and great boldness in the faith
which is in Christ Jesus.
14 These things I write to
you, though I hope to come to
you shortly;
15 but if I am delayed, *I write*
so that you may know how you
ought to conduct yourself in the
[a]house of God, which is the
[1i]church of the living God, the
pillar and ground of the truth.
16 And without controversy
great is the [j]mystery of godliness:

God* was manifested in
the [k]flesh,
Justified in the [l]Spirit,
Seen by [m]angels,
Preached among the
Gentiles,
Believed on in the
[n]world,
Received up in glory.

V. The Walk of the Good Minister of Jesus Christ, 4

4 NOW the [l]Spirit expressly
[o]says that in latter times
some will [p]depart from the
faith, giving heed to [2]deceiving
spirits and doctrines of demons,
2 speaking lies in hypoc-
risy, having their own conscience [q]seared with a hot iron,
3 forbidding to marry, *and*
commanding to abstain from
[r]foods which God created to be
received with thanksgiving by
those who [s]believe and know
the truth.
4 For every creature of God
is good, and nothing is to be refused if it is received with
thanksgiving;
5 for it is [t]sanctified by the
word of God and prayer.
6 If you instruct the brethren in these things, you will be
a good minister of [u]Jesus
Christ, nourished in the words
of [v]faith and of the good doctrine which you have carefully
followed.

*3:3 NU-Text omits *not greedy for money.*
3:16 NU-Text reads *Who.*

5
a *Churches* (local): vv. 5,15; Phile. 2. (Acts 8:3; Phil. 1:1, *note*)
6
b i.e. *a new or recent convert*
c *Satan:* vv. 6–7; 1 Tim. 5:15. (Gen. 3:1; Rev. 20:10)
7
d Col. 4:5; 1 Th. 4:12
e 1 Tim. 6:9; 2 Tim. 2:26
9
f v. 16; see Mt. 13:11, *note*
11
g Lit. *Women in like manner must*
13
h Mt. 25:21

15
i *Church* (visible): v. 15. (1 Cor. 10:32; 1 Tim. 3:15)
16
j See Mt. 13:11, *note*
k Jn. 1:14
l *Holy Spirit* (NT): v. 16; 4:1; 2 Tim. 1:14. (Mt. 1:18; Acts 2:4, *note*)
m See Heb. 1:4, *note*
n Gk. *kosmos.* See Mt. 4:8, *note*

CHAPTER 4
1
o *Inspiration:* v. 1; 2 Tim. 3:15. (Ex. 4:15; 2 Tim. 3:16, *note*)
p *Apostasy:* vv. 1–3; 2 Tim. 3:1. (Lk. 18:8; 2 Tim. 3:1, *note*)
2
q Eph. 4:19
3
r Col. 2:16,23
s *Faith:* v. 3; 1 Tim. 4:10. (Gen. 3:20; Heb. 11:39, *note*).
5
t *Sanctification* (NT): v. 5; Ti. 1:8. (Mt. 4:5; Rev. 22:11)
6
u Or *Christ Jesus*
v Lit. *the faith*

[1](3:15) Church (visible), Summary: The passages which speak of the Church of God (here and 1 Cor. 10:32) refer to that visible body of professed believers, called collectively "the church," though it exists under many names and divisions based upon differences in doctrine or in government. For the most part, within this historical church has existed the true Church, "which is His body, the fullness of Him who fills all in all" (Eph. 1:22–23; see Heb. 12:23, *note*), like the believing remnant within Israel (see Rom. 11:5, *note*). The predicted future of the true Church is translation and glory (1 Th. 4:14–17; Rom. 8:18–23); the future of the unsaved element of the visible church left on earth at the rapture is apostasy and divine judgment (2 Tim. 3:1–9; 2 Pet. 2:1–3).

[2](4:1) Satanic deception which caused the fall of man (cp. Gen. 3:13; 2 Cor. 11:3; 1 Tim. 2:14) will characterize the end of the age (Mt. 24:4–5,11,24; Mk. 13:6; 2 Th. 3:8–11; 1 Jn. 2:18–26; 4:1–6; 2 Jn. 7; Rev. 13:14; 19:20; 20:7–10). Satan is the one "who deceives the whole world" (Rev. 12:9) and is the power behind the beast and the false prophet (Rev. 13:4,7,12–15; 19:20; 20:3,7–10).

7 But reject profane and old wives' fables, and exercise yourself toward godliness.

8 For bodily exercise profits a little, but godliness is profitable for all things, having promise of the life that now is and of [a]that which is to come.

9 This *is* a faithful saying and worthy of all acceptance.

10 For to this *end* we both labor and suffer reproach,* because we [b]trust in the living God, who is *the* Savior of all men, especially of those who [c]believe.

11 These things command and teach.

12 Let no one despise your youth, but be an [d]example to the [c]believers in word, in conduct, in [e]love, in spirit,* in faith, in purity.

13 Till I come, give attention to reading, to exhortation, to doctrine.

14 [f]Do not neglect the gift that is in you, which was given to you by prophecy with the laying on of the hands of the [g]eldership.

15 Meditate on these things; give yourself entirely to them, that your progress may be evident to all.

16 [h]Take heed to yourself and to the doctrine. Continue in them, for in doing this you will [i]save both yourself and those who hear you.

VI. The Work of the Good Minister, 5

5 DO not rebuke an older man, but exhort *him* as a father, younger men as brothers,

2 older women as mothers, younger women as sisters, with all purity.

3 Honor widows who are really [j]widows.

4 But if any widow has children or grandchildren, let them first learn to show piety at home and to repay their [k]parents; for this is good and* acceptable before God.

5 Now she who is really a widow, and left alone, [l]trusts in God and continues in supplications and prayers night and [m]day.

6 But she who lives in pleasure is [n]dead while she lives.

7 And these things command, that they may be blameless.

8 But if anyone does not provide for his own, and [o]especially for those of his household, he has denied the faith and is worse than an unbeliever.

9 Do not let a widow under sixty years old be taken into the number, *and not unless* she has been the wife of one man,

10 well reported for [p]good works: if she has brought up children, if she has [q]lodged strangers, if she has [r]washed the saints' feet, if she has relieved the afflicted, if she has diligently followed every good work.

11 But refuse *the* younger widows; for when they have begun to grow wanton against Christ, they desire to marry,

12 having condemnation because they have cast off their first faith.

13 And besides they learn *to be* idle, wandering about from house to house, [s]and not only idle but also gossips and busybodies, saying things which they ought not.

14 Therefore I desire that *the* younger *widows* marry, bear children, manage the [t]house, give no opportunity to the adversary to speak reproachfully.

15 For some have already turned aside after [u]Satan.

16 If any [c]believing man or* woman has widows, let them relieve them, and do not let the church be burdened, that it may relieve those who are really widows.

17 [v]Let the [w]elders who rule well be counted worthy of double honor, especially those who labor in the word and doctrine.

18 For the Scripture says, [x]*"You shall not muzzle an ox while it treads out the grain,"* [y]and, "The laborer *is* worthy of his wages."

19 Do not receive an accusa-

8
a Life (eternal): v. 8; 1 Tim. 6:12. (Mt. 7:14; Rev. 22:19)
10
b Or *hope*
c Faith: vv. 10,12; 5:16; 1 Tim. 6:2. (Gen. 3:20; Heb. 11:39, *note*)
12
d Phil. 3:17; Ti. 2:7; 1 Pet. 5:3
e Law (of Christ): v. 12; 1 Tim. 6:11. (Jn. 13:34; 2 Jn. 5)
14
f 2 Tim. 1:6
g See Ti. 1:5, *note* 2
16
h Cp. Acts 20:28
i See Rom. 1:16, *note*
CHAPTER 5
3
j vv. 5,16
4
k Cp. Mt. 15:4–6
5
l Or *hopes*
m Cp. 1 Cor. 7:34

6
n Cp. Rev. 3:1
8
o 2 Cor. 12:14
10
p Cp. Acts 9:36
q Cp. Acts 16:15
r Cp. Lk. 7:44; Jn. 13:14
13
s Cp. 2 Th. 3:11
14
t i.e. *household*
15
u Satan: v. 15; 2 Tim. 2:26. (Gen. 3:1; Rev. 20:10)
17
v Cp. 1 Cor. 9:10–14; Gal. 6:6; 1 Th. 5:12–13
w Elders: v. 17; 1 Tim. 5:19. (Acts 11:30; Ti. 1:5, *note*)
18
x Dt. 25:4; 1 Cor. 9:7–9
y Lk. 10:7

*
4:10 NU-Text reads *we labor and strive.* **4:12** NU-Text omits *in spirit.* **5:4** NU-Text and M-Text omit *good and.* **5:16** NU-Text omits *man or.*

tion against an [a]elder except [b]from two or three witnesses.

20 Those who are [c]sinning rebuke in the presence of [d]all, that the rest also may fear.

21 I [e]charge *you* before God and the Lord Jesus Christ and the elect [f]angels that you observe these things without [g]prejudice, doing nothing with partiality.

22 Do not lay hands on anyone [1]hastily, nor [h]share in other people's [c]sins; keep yourself pure.

23 No longer drink only water, but use a little wine for your stomach's sake and your frequent infirmities.

24 Some men's [c]sins are [i]clearly evident, preceding *them* to judgment, but those of some *men* follow later.

25 Likewise, the good works *of some* are clearly evident, and those that are otherwise cannot be hidden.

VII. Warnings to a Good Minister, 6:1–19

6 LET as many [j]bondservants as are under the yoke count their own masters worthy of all honor, so that the name of God and *His* doctrine may not be blasphemed.

2 And those who have [k]believing masters, let them not despise *them* because they are brethren, but rather serve *them* because those who are benefited are believers and beloved. Teach and exhort these things.

3 If anyone teaches otherwise and does not consent to [l]wholesome words, *even* the words of our Lord Jesus Christ, and to the doctrine which accords with godliness,

4 he is proud, [m]knowing nothing, but is obsessed with disputes and arguments over words, from which come envy, strife, reviling, evil suspicions,

5 useless wranglings* of men of corrupt minds and destitute of the truth, who suppose that godliness is a *means of* gain. From [n]such withdraw yourself.*

6 Now godliness with [o]contentment is great gain.

7 For we brought nothing into *this* world, *and it is* [p]certain* we can carry nothing out.

8 And having food and clothing, with these we shall be [q]content.

9 But those who desire to be rich fall into [r]temptation and a snare, and *into* many foolish and harmful lusts which drown men in destruction and perdition.

10 For the love of money is a root of all *kinds of* evil, for which some have strayed from the faith in their greediness, and pierced themselves through with many sorrows.

11 But you, O man of God, [s]flee these things and pursue [t]righteousness, godliness, faith, [u]love, patience, gentleness.

12 Fight the good fight of faith, lay hold on [v]eternal life, to which you were also called and have confessed the good confession in the presence of many witnesses.

13 I urge you in the sight of God who gives life to all things, and *before* Christ Jesus [w]who witnessed the good confession before Pontius Pilate,

14 that you keep *this* commandment without spot, blameless until our Lord Jesus Christ's [x]appearing,

15 which He will manifest in His own time, *He who is* the blessed and only Potentate, the [y]King of kings and Lord of lords,

16 who alone has immortality, dwelling in unapproachable [z]light, [aa]whom no man has seen or can see, to whom *be* honor and everlasting power. Amen.

17 Command those who are rich in this present age not to be

*6:5 NU-Text and M-Text read *constant friction.* • NU-Text omits this sentence.
6:7 NU-Text omits *and it is certain.*

19
a Elders: v. 19; Ti. 1:5. (Acts 11:30; Ti. 1:5, *note*)
b Dt. 19:15; Mt. 18:16
20
c See Rom. 3:23, *note*
d Cp. Gal. 2:14
21
e Cp. 2 Tim. 4:1
f See Heb. 1:4, *note*
g Dt. 1:17
22
h Eph. 5:6–7; 2 Jn. 11
24
i Gal. 5:19–21
CHAPTER 6
1
j Eph. 6:5
2
k Faith: v. 2; 2 Tim. 1:5. (Gen. 3:20; Heb. 11:39, *note*)
3
l 2 Tim. 1:13
4
m Cp. 1 Cor. 8:2
5
n 2 Tim. 3:5
6
o Heb. 13:5; cp. Phil. 4:11
7
p Job 1:21; Ps. 49:17
8
q Prov. 30:8–9; cp. Gen. 28:20
9
r Test/tempt: v. 9; Heb. 2:18. (Gen. 3:1; Jas. 1:14, *note*)
11
s Separation: vv. 9–11; 2 Tim. 2:21. (Gen. 12:1; 2 Cor. 6:17, *note*)
t See 1 Jn. 3:7, *note*
u Law (of Christ): v. 11; 2 Tim. 1:7. (Jn. 13:34; 2 Jn. 5)
12
v Life (eternal): v. 12; 1 Tim. 6:19. (Mt. 7:14; Rev. 22:19)
13
w Jn. 18:36–37
14
x Christ (second advent): vv. 14–15; 2 Tim. 4:8. (Dt. 30:3; Acts 1:11, *note*)
15
y Kingdom (NT): v. 15; 2 Tim. 4:1. (Mt. 2:2; 1 Cor. 15:24, *note*)
16
z Dan. 2:22
aa See Jn. 1:18, *note*

[1](5:22) This injunction is as timely today as the day it was written. All too frequently immature and inexperienced Christians are placed in positions of responsibility.

haughty, nor to [a]trust in uncertain [b]riches but in the living
God, who gives us richly all
things [c]to enjoy.
18 *Let them* do good, that
they be rich in good works,
ready to give, willing to share,
19 [d]storing up for themselves
a good foundation for the time
to come, that they may lay hold
on [e]eternal life.

Conclusion: Another Charge to Timothy, 6:20–21

20 O Timothy! Guard what
was committed to your trust,
avoiding the profane *and* idle
babblings and contradictions
of what is falsely called
[1]knowledge—
21 by professing it some have
strayed concerning the faith.
Grace *be* with you. Amen.

17
a Or *hope*
b Jer. 9:23; 48:7
c Eccl. 5:18–19
19
d Mt. 6:20–21; 19:21; cp. Col. 3:1
e *Life* (eternal): v. 19; 2 Tim. 1:1. (Mt. 7:14; Rev. 22:19)

[1](6:20) Truth cannot contradict the Bible, since God, who knows all things, kept the writers of the Bible from error. If theories that rest upon mere speculation or insufficient evidence are presented as fact, in any area of knowledge, e.g. in religion, philosophy, science, etc., they deserve the description that the apostle gives here: "what is falsely called knowledge," which they are to avoid.

The Second Epistle of Paul the Apostle to

TIMOTHY

Author: Paul *Theme:* Holding the Truth *Date of writing:* c. A.D. 67

THE SECOND EPISTLE TO TIMOTHY, probably the last letter by Paul, was written toward the end of Nero's reign.

Quite different in atmosphere from the first letter to Timothy, it is less formal than the other two Pastoral Epistles and far more personal. In the earlier letter to Timothy, Paul expresses, as though he were a free man, his hope soon to be with his "son in the faith." Here in the second letter alone he speaks of the time of his departure being at hand (4:6). Paul was not only in prison, but he had been abandoned by most of his friends (1:15; 4:16).

This Epistle contains the most detailed account from Paul of conditions that will prevail upon the earth during the last days (3:1–9; 4:3–4).

The Epistle may be divided as follows:

Introduction, 1:1–2.
I. Paul's Charge to Timothy, 1:3–18.
II. The Path of an Approved Servant in a Day of Apostasy, 2.
III. The Apostasy Predicted: the Christian's Resource—the Scriptures, 3.
IV. A Faithful Servant and His Faithful Lord, 4:1–18.
Conclusion, 4:19–22.

Introduction:
Salutation, 1:1–2

1 PAUL, an apostle of Jesus
Christ* by the will of God,
according to the [a]promise of
[b]life which is in Christ Jesus,
2 To Timothy, [1]a [c]beloved
[d]son:

Grace, mercy, *and* peace
from God the Father and Christ
Jesus our Lord.

I. Paul's Charge to Timothy,
1:3–18

3 I thank God, whom I
[e]serve with a pure [f]conscience,
as *my* [g]forefathers *did,* as without ceasing I remember you in
my prayers night and day,
4 greatly [h]desiring to see
you, being mindful of your
tears, that I may be filled with
joy,
5 when I call to remem-
brance the [i]genuine [j]faith that
is in you, which dwelt first in
your grandmother Lois and
your [k]mother Eunice, and I am
persuaded is in you also.
6 Therefore I remind you to
stir up the [l]gift of God which is
in you through the laying on of
my hands.
7 For God has not given us a
spirit of [m]fear, but of [n]power
and of [o]love and of a sound
mind.
8 Therefore do not be
[p]ashamed of the testimony of
our Lord, nor of me His prisoner, but [q]share with me in the
sufferings for the gospel according to the power of God,
9 who has [r]saved us and
called *us* with a holy calling,
[s]not according to our works,
but according to His own purpose and [t]grace which was
given to us in Christ Jesus before time began,
10 but has now been revealed
by the appearing of our [r]Savior
Jesus Christ, *who* has abolished
death and brought [b]life and
[u]immortality to light through
the [v]gospel,
11 to which I was appointed a
preacher, an apostle, and a
teacher of the Gentiles.*
12 For this reason I also [2]suf-
fer these things; nevertheless I
am not ashamed, for I know
whom I have [j]believed and am

*1:1 NU-Text and M-Text read *Christ Jesus.*
1:11 NU-Text omits *of the Gentiles.*

CHAPTER 1
1
a Ti. 1:2
b Life (eternal): vv. 1, 10; Ti. 1:2. (Mt. 7:14; Rev. 22:19)
2
c 1 Tim. 1:2
d Lit. *child*
3
e Cp. Acts 23:1
f Cp. Heb. 13:18
g Acts 24:14
4
h Cp. 2 Tim. 4:9,21
5
i 1 Tim. 4:6
j Faith: vv. 5, 12; Ti. 3:8. (Gen. 3:20; Heb. 11:39, *note*)
k Acts 16:1
6
l 1 Tim. 4:14

7
m Rom. 8:15; 1 Jn. 4:18
n Cp. Acts 1:8
o Law (of Christ): v. 7; 2 Tim. 2:22. (Jn. 13:34; 2 Jn. 5)
8
p Lk. 9:26
q Cp. Col. 1:24
9
r See Rom. 1:16, *note*
s Eph. 2:8–9
t Grace: v. 9; Ti. 2:11. (Jn. 1:14; Jn. 1:17, *note*)
10
u Lit. *incorruptibility*
v Gospel: v. 10; 2 Tim. 2:8. (Gen. 12:3; Rev. 14:6)

---

[1](1:2) It was probably during Paul's first visit to Lystra that Timothy was converted (cp. Acts 16:1–3 with Acts 14:6–23).

[2](1:12) The Christian's resources in a day of general declension and apostasy are: (1) faith (1:5); (2) the Spirit (1:6–7); (3) the Word of God (1:13; 3:1–17; 4:3–4); (4) the grace of Christ (2:1); (5) separation from "vessels of . . . dishonor" (2:4,20–21); (6) the Lord's sure reward (4:7–8); and (7) the Lord's faithfulness and power (2:13,19).

persuaded that He is able to [a]keep what I have committed to Him until that Day.

13 Hold fast the pattern of [b]sound words which you have heard from me, in faith and love which are in Christ Jesus.

14 That good thing which was committed to you, keep by the Holy [c]Spirit who dwells in us.

15 This you know, that [d]all those in Asia have [e]turned away from me, among whom are Phygellus and Hermogenes.

16 The Lord grant mercy to the [f]household of Onesiphorus, for he often refreshed me, and was not ashamed of my [g]chain;

17 but when he arrived in Rome, he sought me out very zealously and found *me.*

18 The Lord [h]grant to him that he may find mercy from the Lord in that [i]Day—and you know very well how many ways he [j]ministered *to me** at Ephesus.

II. The Path of an Approved Servant in a Day of Apostasy, 2

2 YOU therefore, my [k]son, be strong in the [l]grace that is in Christ Jesus.

2 And the things that you have heard from me among many witnesses, [m]commit these to faithful men who will be able to teach others also.

The faithful servant

3 You therefore must [n]endure* hardship as a good soldier of [o]Jesus Christ.

4 No one [p]engaged in warfare entangles himself with the affairs of *this* life, that he may please him who [q]enlisted him as a soldier.

5 And also if anyone competes in athletics, he is not crowned unless he competes according to the rules.

6 The hard-working farmer must be first to partake of the crops.

7 Consider what I say, and may* the Lord [r]give you understanding in all things.

8 Remember that [s]Jesus Christ, of the seed of David, was [t]raised from the dead according to my [u]gospel,

9 for which I suffer trouble as an evildoer, *even* to the point of [v]chains; but the word of God is not [w]chained.

10 Therefore I endure all things for the sake of the [q]elect, that they also may obtain the [x]salvation which is in Christ Jesus with eternal glory.

God is faithful

11 *This is* a faithful saying:

For if we died with *Him,*
We shall also live with *Him.*

12 If we endure,
We shall also reign with *Him.*
If we [y]deny *Him,*
He also will deny us.

13 If we are faithless,
He remains faithful;
He [z]cannot deny Himself.

14 [aa]Remind *them* of these things, charging *them* before the Lord not to [bb]strive about words to no profit, to the ruin of the hearers.

15 [cc]Be diligent to present yourself approved to God, a worker who does not need to be ashamed, rightly dividing the word of truth.

16 But shun profane *and* idle babblings, for they will increase to more ungodliness.

17 And their message will spread like cancer. [dd]Hymenaeus and Philetus are of this sort,

18 who have [ee]strayed concerning the truth, [ff]saying that the [t]resurrection is already past; and they overthrow the faith of some.

God knows His servants

19 Nevertheless the solid foundation of God stands, having this seal: "The Lord [gg]knows those who are His," and, "Let everyone who names the name of Christ* depart from iniquity."

20 But in a great house there

*

1:18 *To me* is from the Vulgate and a few Greek manuscripts. 2:3 NU-Text reads *You must share.* 2:7 NU-Text reads *the Lord will give you.* 2:19 NU-Text and M-Text read *the Lord.*

12
a *Assurance/security:* v. 12; 2 Tim. 4:8. (Ps. 23:1; Jude 1, *note*)
13
b 1 Tim. 6:3
14
c *Holy Spirit* (NT): v. 14; Ti. 3:5. (Mt. 1:18; Acts 2:4, *note*)
15
d Cp. Acts 19:10
e Cp. 2 Tim. 4:10,16
16
f 2 Tim. 4:19
g Cp. Acts 28:20
18
h Mt. 6:4; Mk. 9:41
i *Day* (of Christ): v. 18; 2 Tim. 4:8. (1 Cor. 1:8, *note;* 2 Tim. 4:8)
j Heb. 6:10
CHAPTER 2
1
k Lit. *child*
l See 2 Pet. 3:18, *note*
2
m Cp. 1 Tim. 1:18
3
n 2 Tim. 4:5
o Or *Christ Jesus*
4
p Lit. *serving as a soldier.* 1 Cor. 9:25–27
q *Election* (personal): vv. 4,10; Ti. 1:1. (Dt. 7:6; 1 Pet. 5:13, *note*)
7
r Prov. 2:6
8
s Rom. 1:3–4
t *Resurrection:* vv. 8, 18; Heb. 6:2. (2 Ki. 4:35; 1 Cor. 15:52, *note*)
u *Gospel:* v. 8; Phile. 13. (Gen. 12:3; Rev. 14:6)
9
v Cp. Eph. 6:20
w Cp. Acts 28:31
10
x See Rom. 1:16, *note*
12
y Mt. 10:33
13
z Num. 23:19
14
aa Cp. 2 Pet. 1:13
bb Ti. 3:9
15
cc 1 Tim. 4:13; 2 Pet. 1:10
17
dd 1 Tim. 1:20
18
ee Cp. 1 Tim. 6:21
ff 1 Cor. 15:12
19
gg Num. 16:5; Jn. 10:14,27

are not only [a]vessels of gold
and silver, but also of wood and
clay, some for honor and some
for dishonor.
21 Therefore if anyone
[b]cleanses himself from the latter, he will be a vessel for honor,
sanctified and useful for the
Master, [c]prepared for every
good work.
22 [d]Flee also youthful lusts;
but pursue [e]righteousness,
faith, [f]love, peace with those
who call on the Lord out of a
pure heart.
23 But avoid foolish and ignorant disputes, knowing that
they generate strife.
24 And a servant of the Lord
must not quarrel but be gentle
to all, able to teach, [g]patient,
25 in [h]humility correcting
those who are in opposition, if
God [i]perhaps will grant them
[j]repentance, so that they may
know the truth,
26 and *that* they may come
to their senses *and escape* the
snare of the [k]devil, having been
taken captive by him to *do* his
will.

III. The Apostasy Predicted: the Christian's Resource—the Scriptures, 3

3 BUT [1][l]know this, [m]that in
the last days perilous times
will come:
2 [n]For men will be lovers of
themselves, lovers of money,
boasters, proud, blasphemers,
disobedient to parents, unthankful, unholy,
3 unloving, unforgiving,
slanderers, without self-
control, brutal, despisers of
good,
4 [o]traitors, headstrong,
haughty, lovers of pleasure
rather than lovers of God,
5 [p]having a form of godliness but denying its power. And
from such people [q]turn away!
6 For of this sort are those
[r]who creep into households
and make captives of gullible
women loaded down with [s]sins,
led away by various lusts,
7 always learning and never
able to come to the knowledge
of the truth.
8 Now as [t]Jannes and Jambres resisted Moses, so do these
also resist the truth: [u]men of
corrupt minds, [l]disapproved
concerning the faith;
9 but they will progress no
further, for their folly will be
manifest to all, as theirs also
was.
10 But you have carefully followed my doctrine, manner of
life, purpose, faith, longsuffering, [f]love, perseverance,
11 persecutions, afflictions,
which happened to me at [v]Anti-
och, at [w]Iconium, at Lystra—
what [x]persecutions I endured.
And out of *them* all the Lord delivered me.
12 Yes, and all who desire to
live godly in Christ Jesus will
suffer persecution.
13 But evil men and impostors will grow worse and worse,
deceiving and being deceived.
14 But you must continue in
the things which you have
learned and been assured of,
knowing from whom you have
learned *them*,
15 and that from childhood
you have known the Holy
[y]Scriptures, which are able to
[z]make you wise for [aa]salvation
through faith which is in Christ
Jesus.
16 All [y]Scripture *is* given by
[2]inspiration of God, and *is* prof-

20
a Rom. 9:21
21
b Separation: vv. 19–21; Heb. 11:25. (Gen. 12:1; 2 Cor. 6:17, *note*)
c 2 Tim. 3:17
22
d 1 Tim. 6:11
e See 1 Jn. 3:7, *note*
f Law (of Christ): v. 22; 3:10; Ti. 2:2. (Jn. 13:34; 2 Jn. 5)
24
g 1 Tim. 3:3
25
h Gal. 6:1
i Cp. Jer. 36:3; Lk. 20:13
j Repentance: v. 25; Heb. 6:1. (Mt. 3:2; Acts 17:30, *note*)
26
k Satan: v. 26; Heb. 2:14. (Gen. 3:1; Rev. 20:10)
CHAPTER 3
1
l Apostasy: vv. 1–8; 2 Tim. 4:4. (Lk. 18:8; 2 Tim. 3:1, *note*)
m 1 Tim. 4:1; 2 Pet. 3:3; 1 Jn. 2:18; Jude 17–18
2
n Cp. Rom. 1:24–32
4
o 2 Pet. 2:10

5
p Ti. 1:16; cp. Mt. 7:15
q 2 Th. 3:6
6
r Ti. 1:11
s See Rom. 3:23, *note*
8
t Ex. 7:11–12, 22; 8:7; 9:11
u 1 Tim. 6:5
11
v Acts 13:44–52
w Acts 14:1–6,19
x Cp. Jn. 15:20; 1 Th. 3:3
15
y Inspiration: vv. 15–17; Heb. 1:1. (Ex. 4:15; 2 Tim. 3:16, *note*)
z Ps. 119:97–104; Jn. 5:39
aa See Rom. 1:16, *note*

---

[1](3:1) Apostasy, Summary: Apostasy, "falling away" (2 Th. 2:3) is the act of professed Christians who deliberately reject revealed truth as to (1) the Deity of Jesus Christ, and (2) redemption through His atoning and redeeming sacrifice (1 Jn. 4:1–3; Phil. 3:18; 2 Pet. 2:1). Apostasy differs, therefore, from error concerning truth, which may be the result of ignorance (Acts 19:1–6), or heresy, which may be due to the snare of Satan (2 Tim. 2:25–26), both of which may exist with true faith. The apostate is perfectly described in 4:3–4. Apostates depart from the faith, but not from the outward profession of Christianity (3:5). Apostate teachers are described in 4:3; 2 Pet. 2:1–19; Jude 4,8,11–13,16. Apostasy in the church, as in Israel (Isa. 1:5–6; 5:5–7), is irremediable and awaits judgment (2 Th. 2:10–12; 2 Pet. 2:17,21; Jude 11–15; Rev. 3:14–16).

[2](3:16) Inspiration, Summary: Every word of Holy Scripture is inspired or "God-breathed" (Gk. *theopneustos*). Without impairing the intelligence, individuality, literary style, or personal feelings of the human authors, God supernaturally directed the writing of Scripture so

itable for doctrine, for reproof,
for correction, for instruction in
[a]righteousness,
17 that the man of God may
be [b]complete, thoroughly
equipped for every good work.

IV. A Faithful Servant
and His Faithful Lord,
4:1–18

4 I CHARGE *you* therefore
before God and the [c]Lord
Jesus Christ, who will [d]judge
the living and the dead at* His
appearing and His [e]kingdom:
2 Preach the word! Be ready
in season *and* out of season.
[f]Convince, rebuke, exhort,
with all longsuffering and
teaching.
3 For the time will come
when they will not endure
sound doctrine, but according
to their own desires, *because*
they have itching ears, they will
[g]heap up for themselves teachers;
4 [h]and they will turn *their*
ears away from the truth, and
be turned aside to fables.
5 But you be watchful in all
things, endure afflictions, do
the work of an evangelist, fulfill
your ministry.
6 For I am already being
poured out as a drink offering,
and the time of my [i]departure
is at hand.
7 I have [j]fought the good
fight, I have finished the [k]race,
I have kept the faith.
8 Finally, there is [l]laid up
for me the [m]crown of [a]righ-
teousness, which the Lord, the
righteous [n]Judge, will give to
me on that [o]Day, and not to me
only but also to all who have
loved His [p]appearing.
9 Be diligent to come to me
quickly;
10 for [q]Demas has forsaken
me, having loved this present
[r]world, and has departed for
Thessalonica—Crescens for
Galatia, Titus for Dalmatia.
11 Only Luke is with me. Get
[s]Mark and bring him with you,
for he is useful to me for ministry.
12 And [t]Tychicus I have sent
to Ephesus.
13 Bring the cloak that I left
with Carpus at Troas when you
come—and the books, espe-
cially the parchments.
14 [u]Alexander the coppersmith did me much harm. May
the Lord repay him according to
his works.
15 You also must beware of
him, for he has greatly resisted
our words.
16 At my first defense no one
stood with me, but all forsook
me. May it not be [v]charged
against them.
17 But [w]the Lord stood with
me and strengthened me, so
that the message might be

*4:1 NU-Text omits *therefore* and reads *and by* for *at.*

16
a See 1 Jn. 3:7, *note*
17
b Or *perfect.* See Phil. 3:12, *note*
CHAPTER 4
1
c Or *Christ Jesus.*
d Judgments (the seven): vv. 1,8; Heb. 9:27. (1 Sam. 7:14; Rev. 20:12, *note*)
e Kingdom (NT): v. 1; Jas. 2:5. (Mt. 2:2; 1 Cor. 15:24, *note*)
2
f Ti. 2:15
3
g Isa. 30:9–11; Jer. 5:30–31
4
h Apostasy: v. 4; Heb. 6:4. (Lk. 18:8; 2 Tim. 3:1, *note*)
6
i Cp. 2 Pet. 1:14
7
j Cp. 1 Tim. 6:12
k 1 Cor. 9:24–27; Phil. 3:13–14

8
l Assurance/security: v. 8; 2 Tim. 4:18. (Ps. 23:1; Jude 1, *note*)
m Rewards: v. 8; Heb. 11:6. (Dan. 12:3; 1 Cor. 3:14, *note*)
n Jn. 5:22
o Day (of Christ): v. 8. (1 Cor. 1:8, *note;* 2 Tim. 4:8)
p Christ (second advent): v. 8; Ti. 2:13. (Dt. 30:3; Acts 1:11, *note*)
10
q Col. 4:14; Phile. 24
r Lit. *age*
11
s Acts 12:12
12
t Acts 20:4; Ti. 3:12
14
u 1 Tim. 1:20
16
v Cp. Acts 7:60
17
w Dt. 31:6

---

that they recorded in perfect accuracy His comprehensive and infallible revelation to man. If God Himself had done the writing, the written Word would be no more accurate and authoritative than it is.

The inspiration of Scripture is attested by OT writers (2 Sam. 23:2–3; Isa. 59:21; Jer. 1:9) and by hundreds of instances where the expression "thus says the LORD" or its equivalent is used. Christ affirms the inspiration of the OT (Mt. 5:18; 22:42–43; Mk. 12:36; Jn. 10:35). The apostles bear the same testimony (Acts 1:16; 4:24–25; 28:25; Heb. 3:7; 10:15–16; 2 Pet. 1:20–21). By means of divine inspiration the writers of Scripture spoke with authority concerning the unknown past, wrote by divine guidance the historical portions, revealed the law, penned the devotional literature of the Bible, recorded the contemporary prophetic message, and prophesied the future. Inspiration extends equally to all Scripture, although only a small portion was given by direct dictation of God, e.g. Ex. 20:1; Lev. 1:1; Dt. 5:4.

The inspiration of the NT was also authenticated by Christ (see Jn. 16:12, *note*). The apostles claimed inspiration for their portions of the NT (1 Cor. 2:13; 14:37; Gal. 1:7–8; 1 Th. 4:2,15; 2 Th. 3:6,12,14). Paul quotes both Deuteronomy and Luke as Scripture (1 Tim. 5:18; cp. Dt. 25:4; Lk. 10:7). Peter declares all Paul's Epistles to be Scripture (2 Pet. 3:16). Although the NT sometimes quotes the OT loosely, in paraphrase, or interpretively, this is never done in a way to deny the authority or accuracy of the original text. The early apostolic church received the NT Scriptures as the inspired Word of God as they were written, though formal recognition of the entire canon came more slowly. Because the Scriptures are inspired, they are authoritative and without error in their original words, and constitute the infallible revelation of God to man.

preached fully through me, and
that all the Gentiles might hear.
Also I was delivered out of the
mouth of the lion.
18 And the Lord will [a]deliver
me from every evil work and
[b]preserve *me* for His heavenly
kingdom. To Him *be* glory forever and ever. Amen!

Conclusion, 4:19–22

19 Greet Prisca and [c]Aquila,
and the household of [d]Onesiph-
orus.
20 Erastus stayed in Corinth,
but [e]Trophimus I have left in
Miletus sick.
21 Do your utmost to come
before winter. Eubulus greets
you, as well as Pudens, Li-
nus, Claudia, and all the brethren.
22 The Lord Jesus Christ* be
with your spirit. Grace be with
you. Amen.

*4:22 NU-Text omits *Jesus Christ.*

18
a 2 Pet. 2:9
b Assurance/ security: v. 18; Heb. 6:11. (Ps. 23:1; Jude 1, *note*)
19
c Acts 18:2
d 2 Tim. 1:16
20
e Acts 20:4

The Epistle of Paul the Apostle to

TITUS

Author: Paul *Theme:* Church Order *Date of writing:* C. A.D. 65

THE EPISTLE TO TITUS, addressed by Paul to one of his most reliable helpers, deals chiefly with conditions in the churches located on the island of Crete. Although not mentioned in Acts, Titus is prominent in the Epistles; he was used by Paul for tasks requiring responsibility and discretion (1:5; cp. 2 Cor. 7:6–7; 8:6,16). Thus he was Paul's emissary to the church at Corinth; he was in charge of the collection for the poor in Jerusalem; and he was placed over the churches in Crete, the inhabitants of which were proverbially of low character (1:12). Later Paul sent Titus as far away as Dalmatia (Yugoslavia).

In emphasis Titus is akin to 1 Timothy. This Pastoral Epistle lists the qualifications of elders; stresses sound doctrine; states the ethical obligations of elderly men and women, young men and women, and servants; and warns against false teaching. It contains two outstanding doctrinal passages (2:1–14; 3:4–7).

The Epistle may be divided as follows:

Introduction, 1:1–4.
I. The Qualifications and Duties of Elders, 1:5–16.
II. The Pastoral Work of a True Minister, 2.
III. Exhortations to Godly Living, 3:1–11.
Conclusion, 3:12–15.

CHAPTER 1

Introduction: Salutation, 1:1–4

1 PAUL, a [a]bondservant of
God and an apostle of Jesus
Christ, according to the faith of
God's [b]elect and the acknowledgment of the truth which accords with godliness,
2 in hope of [c]eternal life
which God, who [d]cannot lie,
promised before time began,
3 but has [e]in due time manifested His word through
preaching, which was committed to me according to the
commandment of God our
[f]Savior;

4 To [g]Titus, a true [h]son in
our common faith:

Grace, mercy, *and* peace
from God the Father and the
Lord Jesus Christ* our [f]Savior.

I. The Qualifications and Duties of Elders, 1:5–16

5 For this reason I left you in
Crete, that you should set in order the things that are [1]lacking,
and appoint [2][i]elders in every
city as I commanded you—
6 if a man is blameless, the
husband of one wife, having
faithful children not accused of
dissipation or insubordination.
7 For a [i]bishop* must be
blameless, as a steward of God,
not self-willed, not quick-
tempered, not given to wine, not
violent, [j]not greedy for money,
8 but hospitable, a lover of
what is good, sober-minded,
just, [k]holy, self-controlled,
9 [l]holding fast the faithful
word as he has been taught, that

*1:4 NU-Text reads *and Christ Jesus.*
1:7 Literally *overseer*

1 *a* Or *slave* *b* *Election* (corporate): v. 1; Heb. 3:1. (Dt. 7:6; 1 Pet. 5:13, *note*)
2 *c* *Life* (eternal): v. 2; Ti. 3:7. (Mt. 7:14; Rev. 22:19) *d* Num. 23:19
3 *e* Lit. *in its own due season*, i.e. *at the proper time* *f* See Rom. 1:16, *note*
4 *g* 2 Cor. 2:13 *h* Lit. *child*
5 *i* *Elders:* vv. 5,7; Jas. 5:14. (Acts 11:30; Ti. 1:5, *note*)
7 *j* Lit. *no seeker of dishonest gain*
8 *k* *Sanctification* (NT): v. 8; Heb. 2:11. (Mt. 4:5; Rev. 22:11)
9 *l* Cp. 2 Th. 2:15

[1](1:5) It is not at all a question of the presence in the assembly of persons having the qualifications of elders, made overseers by the Holy Spirit (Acts 20:28); that such persons were in the churches of Crete is assumed. The question is altogether one of the appointment of such persons. These churches were not destitute of elders, but were at fault in having failed to duly appoint them. There is a progress of doctrine in respect to the appointing of elders.

[2](1:5) Elder (Gk. *presbuteros*) and overseer (Gk. *episkopos*) designate the same office (cp. v. 7; Acts 20:17; cp. v. 28), the former referring to the man, the latter to a function of the office. The eldership in the apostolic churches was usually plural; there is no instance of only one elder in a local church. The functions of the elders are: to rule (1 Tim. 3:4–5; 5:17); to teach (1 Tim. 5:17); to guard the body of revealed truth from perversion and error (Ti. 1:9); and to oversee the church as a shepherd his flock (Jn. 21:16; Acts 20:28; Heb. 13:17; 1 Pet. 5:2). Elders are made or set in the churches by the Holy Spirit (Acts 20:28), but great stress is laid in the NT upon their due appointment (Acts 14:23; Ti. 1:5). In Titus and 1 Timothy the qualifications of an elder become part of the Scriptures for the guidance of the churches themselves in such appointments (1 Tim. 3:1–7).

he may be able, by sound doctrine, both to exhort and convict
those who contradict.
10 For there are many insubordinate, both idle [a]talkers and
deceivers, especially those of
the circumcision,
11 whose mouths must be
stopped, who subvert whole
households, teaching things
which they ought not, [b]for the
sake of dishonest gain.
12 [c]One of them, a prophet of
their own, said, "Cretans *are* always liars, evil beasts, lazy gluttons."
13 This testimony is true.
Therefore [d]rebuke them
[e]sharply, that they may be
sound in the faith,
14 not giving heed to Jewish
fables and commandments of
men who turn from the truth.
15 [f]To the pure all things are
pure, but to those who are defiled and unbelieving nothing is
pure; but even their mind and
conscience are defiled.
16 They [g]profess to [h]know
God, but in works they deny
Him, being abominable, disobedient, and disqualified for every
good work.

II. The Pastoral Work of a True Minister, 2

2 BUT as for you, speak the
things which are proper for
sound doctrine:
2 that the older men be sober, reverent, temperate, sound
in faith, in [i]love, in patience;
3 the older women likewise,
that they be reverent in behavior, not slanderers, not given to
much wine, teachers of good
things—
4 that they admonish the
young women to love their husbands, to love their children,
5 to be discreet, chaste,
[j]homemakers, good, [k]obedient
to their own husbands, that the
word of God may not be blasphemed.
6 Likewise, exhort the
young men to be sober-minded,
7 in all things showing
yourself *to be* a [l]pattern of
good works; in doctrine *showing* integrity, reverence, incorruptibility,*
8 [m]sound speech that cannot be condemned, that one
who is an opponent may be
ashamed, having nothing evil to
say of you.*
9 *Exhort* [n]bondservants to
be obedient to their own masters, to be well pleasing in all
things, not answering back,
10 not pilfering, but showing
all good fidelity, that they may
[o]adorn the doctrine of God our
[p]Savior in all things.
11 [1]For the [q]grace of God
that brings salvation has [r]ap-
peared to all men,
12 teaching us that, denying
ungodliness and worldly lusts,
we should live soberly, righteously, and godly in the present age,
13 looking for [s]the blessed
hope and glorious appearing of
our great God and [p]Savior [t]Je-
sus Christ,
14 [r]who [u]gave Himself for
us, that He might [v]redeem us
from every lawless deed and
purify for Himself *His* own special [w]people, zealous for good
works.
15 Speak these things, exhort, and rebuke with all authority. [x]Let no one despise
you.

III. Exhortations to Godly Living, 3:1–11

3 REMIND them to be [y]sub-
ject to rulers and authorities, to obey, to be ready for every good work,
2 to speak evil of no one, to
be peaceable, gentle, showing
all humility to all men.
3 For [z]we ourselves were
also once foolish, disobedient,

*
2:7 NU-Text omits *incorruptibility.*
2:8 NU-Text and M-Text read *us.*

10
a Jas. 1:26
11
b 1 Tim. 6:5
12
c Cp. Acts 17:28
13
d 2 Tim. 4:2
e Cp. 2 Cor. 13:10
15
f Rom. 14:14, 20; cp. Lk. 11:41
16
g 2 Tim. 3:5,7
h Mt. 7:20–23; 25:12; 1 Jn. 2:4
CHAPTER 2
2
i *Law* (of Christ): v. 2; Ti. 3:15. (Jn. 13:34; 2 Jn. 5)
5
j 1 Tim. 5:14
k 1 Tim. 2:11; cp. Gen. 3:16

7
l Phil. 3:17; 1 Tim. 4:12
8
m Cp. 1 Tim. 6:3
9
n Eph. 6:5–6; 1 Tim. 6:1
10
o *Righteousness* (garment): v. 10; Ti. 3:8. (Gen. 3:21; Rev. 19:8)
p See Rom. 1:16, *note*
11
q *Grace:* v. 11; Ti. 3:7. (Jn. 1:14; Jn. 1:17, *note*)
r *Christ* (first advent): vv. 11,14; Heb. 7:27. (Gen. 3:15; Acts 1:11, *note*)
13
s *Christ* (second advent): v. 13; Heb. 9:28. (Dt. 30:3; Acts 1:11, *note*)
t Or *Christ Jesus*
14
u *Sacrifice* (of Christ): v. 14; Heb. 1:3. (Gen. 3:15; Heb. 10:18, *note*)
v See Rom. 3:24, *note*
w Dt. 14:2; 26:18; 1 Pet. 2:9
15
x Cp. 1 Tim. 4:12
CHAPTER 3
1
y Rom. 13:1; 1 Pet. 2:13
3
z 1 Cor. 6:11; 1 Pet. 4:3

[1](2:11) Verses 11–14 are notable for their perfect balance of doctrine with living. Beginning with the incarnation ("the grace of God . . . has appeared," v. 11), they relate this doctrine to a life that denies evil and practices good here and now (v. 12); that sees in the return of Christ the incentive for godly conduct ("looking for the blessed hope. . ." v. 13); and that realizes, in personal holiness and good works, the purpose of the atonement (v. 14). The passage is one of the most concise summations in the entire NT of the relation of Gospel truth to life. See also 3:4–7; Eph. 2:8–10.

deceived, serving various lusts and pleasures, living in malice and envy, hateful and hating one another.

4 But when the kindness and the love of God our [a]Savior toward man appeared,

5 [b]not by works of [c]righteousness which we have done, but according to His mercy He [a]saved us, through the washing of regeneration and renewing of the Holy [d]Spirit,

6 whom He poured out on us abundantly through Jesus Christ our [a]Savior,

7 that having been [e]justified by His [f]grace we should become heirs according to the hope of [g]eternal life.

8 This is a faithful saying, and these things I want you to affirm constantly, that those who have [h]believed in God should be careful to [i]maintain good works. These things are good and profitable to men.

9 But [j]avoid foolish disputes, genealogies, contentions, and strivings about the law; for they are unprofitable and useless.

10 Reject a divisive man after the first and second admonition,

11 knowing that such a person is warped and [k]sinning, being self-condemned.

Conclusion: Personal Remarks and Benediction, 3:12–15

12 When I send Artemas to you, or [l]Tychicus, be diligent to come to me at Nicopolis, for I have decided to spend the winter there.

13 Send Zenas the lawyer and [m]Apollos on their journey with haste, that they may lack nothing.

14 And let our *people* also learn to maintain good works, to *meet* urgent needs, that they may not be unfruitful.

15 All who *are* with me greet you. Greet those who [n]love us in the faith. Grace *be* with you all. Amen.

4
a See Rom. 1:16, *note*
5
b Eph. 2:4–9
c See Rom. 10:3, *note*
d Holy Spirit (NT): v. 5; Heb. 2:4. (Mt. 1:18; Acts 2:4, *note*)
7
e Justification: v. 7; Jas. 2:21. (Lk. 18:14; Rom. 3:28, *note*)
f Grace: v. 7; Heb. 2:9. (Jn. 1:14; Jn. 1:17, *note*)
g Life (eternal): v. 7; Heb. 7:16. (Mt. 7:14; Rev. 22:19)
8
h Faith: v. 8; Phile. 6. (Gen. 3:20; Heb. 11:39, *note*)
i Righteousness (garment): v. 8; 1 Pet. 2:12. (Gen. 3:21; Rev. 19:8)
9
j 2 Tim. 2:23
11
k See Rom. 3:23, *note*
12
l Acts 20:4; Eph. 6:21; 2 Tim. 4:12
13
m Cp. Acts 18:24
15
n Law (of Christ): v. 15; Phile. 9. (Jn. 13:34; 2 Jn. 5)

The Epistle of Paul the Apostle to

PHILEMON

Author: Paul *Theme:* Love Exemplified *Date of writing:* c. A.D. 60

THE EPISTLE TO PHILEMON, written during Paul's first imprisonment in Rome, was probably carried to Philemon, a well-to-do citizen of Colosse, by the same messenger who bore the Ephesian and Colossian letters, Tychicus. The messenger had, as his companion, Onesimus (Col. 4:9).

Onesimus, whose name means *profitable* (or *useful*), had been unprofitable to his master Philemon (v. 11); for the slave had probably robbed the master (v. 18) and had fled to Rome. There he was converted through Paul's ministry, and now Paul was sending him back accompanied by Tychicus and this letter. It is of priceless value as instruction in (1) practical righteousness; (2) Christian brotherhood; (3) Christian courtesy; and (4) the law of love.

The Epistle may be divided as follows:

Introduction, vv. 1–3.
I. The Character of Philemon, vv. 4–7.
II. Intercession for Onesimus, vv. 8–21.
Conclusion, vv. 22–25.

Introduction: Paul's Greeting, vv. 1–3

PAUL, a [a]prisoner of Christ Jesus, and Timothy *our* brother,

To Philemon our beloved *friend* and fellow laborer,

2 to the beloved* Apphia, [b]Archippus our fellow soldier, and to the [c]church in your [d]house:

3 Grace to you and peace from God our Father and the Lord Jesus Christ.

I. The Character of Philemon, vv. 4–7

4 [e]I thank my God, making mention of you always in my prayers,

5 [f]hearing of your love and faith which you have toward the Lord Jesus and toward all the saints,

6 that the sharing of your [g]faith may become [h]effective by the acknowledgment of [i]every good thing which is in you* in Christ Jesus.

7 For we have* great joy* and consolation in your love, because the hearts of the saints have been refreshed by you, brother.

II. Intercession for Onesimus, vv. 8–21

8 Therefore, though I might be very bold in Christ to command you [j]what is fitting,

9 *yet* for [k]love's sake I rather appeal *to you*—being such a one as Paul, the aged, and now also a prisoner of [l]Jesus Christ—

10 I appeal to you for my son [m]Onesimus, whom I have [n]begotten *while* in my chains,

11 who once was unprofitable to you, but now is profitable to you and to me.

12 I am sending him back.* You therefore receive him, that is, my own heart,

13 whom I wished to keep with me, that on your [o]behalf he might minister to me in my chains for the [p]gospel.

14 But without your consent I wanted to do nothing, that your good deed might not be by compulsion, as it were, but [q]voluntary.

15 For [r]perhaps he departed for a while for this *purpose,* that you might receive him forever,

16 no longer as a [s]slave but more than a [s]slave—a beloved brother, especially to me but how much more to you, both in the [t]flesh and in the Lord.

17 If then you count me as a [u]partner, receive him as *you would* me.

18 But if he has wronged you

1
a Eph. 3:1
2
b Col. 4:17
c Churches (local): v. 2; Jas. 5:14. (Acts 8:3; Phil. 1:1, *note*)
d Cp. Rom. 16:5
4
e Cp. Eph. 1:16
5
f Cp. Col. 1:3–4,9
6
g Faith: v. 6; Heb. 4:2. (Gen. 3:20; Heb. 11:39, *note*)
h Jas. 2:14–17
i 1 Th. 5:18; cp. Phil. 4:8; 2 Pet. 1:5–8
8
j v. 19
9
k Law (of Christ): v. 9; Jas. 2:8. (Jn. 13:34; 2 Jn. 5)

l Or *Christ Jesus*
10
m Col. 4:9
n Cp. 1 Cor. 4:15
13
o Cp. Phil. 2:30
p Gospel: v. 13; Heb. 4:2. (Gen. 12:3; Rev. 14:6)
14
q Cp. 2 Cor. 9:7; 1 Pet. 5:2
15
r Cp. Gen. 45:5–8
16
s 1 Cor. 7:22
t Eph. 6:5; Col. 3:22
17
u Cp. 2 Cor. 8:23

*
v. 2 NU-Text reads *to our sister Apphia.*
v. 6 NU-Text and M-Text read *us.*
v. 7 NU-Text reads *had.* • M-Text reads *thanksgiving.* v. 12 NU-Text reads *back to you in person, that is, my own heart.*

or owes anything, put that [1]on
my [a]account.
19 I, Paul, am writing with
my own [b]hand. I will repay—
not to mention to you that you
owe me even your own self besides.
20 Yes, brother, let me have
joy from you in the Lord; refresh my heart in [c]the Lord.
21 Having [d]confidence in
your obedience, I write to you,
knowing that you will do even
more than I say.

Conclusion: Personal Remarks and Benediction, vv. 22–25

22 But, meanwhile, also prepare a guest room for me, for I
[e]trust that through your prayers
I shall be granted to you.
23 [f]Epaphras, my fellow prisoner in Christ Jesus, greets you,
24 *as do* [g]Mark, [h]Aristarchus, [i]Demas, Luke, my fellow
laborers.
25 The grace of our Lord Jesus Christ *be* with your spirit.
Amen.

18 *a* Cp. Lk. 14:14
19 *b* 1 Cor. 16:21
20 *c* Or *Christ*
21 *d* Cp. 2 Cor. 7:16
22 *e* Or *hope.* Cp. Phil. 2:24
23 *f* Col. 1:7
24 *g* Acts 12:12, 25; *h* Acts 19:29; *i* 2 Tim. 4:10

[1](v. 18) Verses 17–18 perfectly illustrate imputation: "Receive him as you would me"—reckon to him my merit; "If he has wronged you or owes anything, put that on my account"—reckon to me his demerit. See Imputation, Gen. 15:6; Jas. 2:23, *note*.

The Epistle to the

HEBREWS

Author: Unknown *Theme:* Priesthood of Christ *Date of writing:* c. A.D. 68

THE EPISTLE TO THE HEBREWS is an anonymous book. Its authorship has been debated since post-apostolic days. In certain places its language is like Paul's and, on account of the personal reference to Timothy in 13:23, some scholars have attributed the letter to Paul. Although there is no conclusive proof of his authorship, Hebrews, as a part of Scripture, speaks with divine authority. The letter was composed prior to the destruction of Jerusalem, since it is evident that the temple was still standing when Hebrews was written (cp. 10:11).

The occasion of the Epistle was the need of special exhortation for Hebrew readers who had professed faith in Jesus as the Messiah, some of whom were wavering in their attitude. Hence, the exhortation is to "hold fast" (3:6) and to "go on to perfection" (6:1).

The purpose of the book, then, was (1) to confirm Jewish Christians by showing that OT Judaism had come to an end through the fulfillment by Christ of the whole purpose of the law; (2) to warn some who had identified themselves as Christians against (a) falling back into Judaism or (b) pausing short of true faith in Christ; and (3) to bring to the attention of Christians everywhere the preeminence of Jesus Christ.

The key concept throughout the book is superiority (1:4; 6:9; 7:7,19,22; 8:6; 9:23; 10:34; 11:16,35,40; 12:24). Hebrews contains a series of contrasts between the good things of Judaism and the better things of Christ. Christ is better than angels, than Moses, than Joshua, than Aaron; and the New Covenant (8:7–13) is better than the Mosaic Covenant (see Ex. 19:5, *note*).

More fully than any NT writing, Hebrews reveals the present high-priestly ministry of the Man in the glory, the Lord Jesus Christ.

The Epistle may be divided as follows:

Introduction, 1:1–3.
I. Christ as a Person Superior to All Other Persons, 1:4—4:16.
II. The Preeminence and Finality of the Priesthood of Christ, 5:1—10:18.
III. The Life of Faith, 10:19—13:19.
Conclusion, 13:20–25.

CHAPTER 1

1
a Lit. *in many portions and in many ways*
b *Inspiration:* vv. 1–2; Heb. 3:7. (Ex. 4:15; 2 Tim. 3:16, *note*)

2
c Lit. *in Son*
d Lit. *ages*

Introduction: 1:1–3

1 GOD, who [a]at various
times and in various ways
[b]spoke in time past to the fathers by the prophets,
2 has in these last days spoken to us [c]by *His* Son, whom He
has appointed heir of all things,
through whom also He made
the [d]worlds;
3 who being the [e]brightness
of *His* glory and the [f]express
[g]image of His person, and upholding all things by the word
of His power, when He had by
Himself* [h]purged our• sins,
sat down at the right hand of the
Majesty on high,

I. Christ as a Person Superior to All Others, 1:4—4:16

The Son superior to angels

4 having become so much
better than the [1]angels, as He

*1:3 NU-Text omits *by Himself*.
• NU-Text omits *our*.

3
e Or *effulgence*
f Lit. *representation of his substance*
g 2 Cor. 4:4; Col. 1:15
h *Sacrifice (of Christ):* v. 3; Heb. 7:27. (Gen. 3:15; Heb. 10:18, *note*)

---

[1](1:4) Angel, Summary: Angel, i.e. "messenger," is used of God, of men, and of an order of created spiritual beings whose chief attributes are strength and wisdom (2 Sam. 14:20; Ps. 103:20; 104:4). In the OT the expression "the Angel of the LORD" (sometimes "of God") usually implies the presence of Deity in angelic form (Gen. 16:1–13; 21:17–19; 22:11–16; 31:11–13; Ex. 3:2–4; Jud. 2:1; 6:12–16; 13:3–22). See Jud. 2:1, *note;* cp. Mal. 3:1, *note.* The word "angel" is used of men in Lk. 7:24, Gk.; Jas. 2:25, Gk.; Rev. 1:20; 2:1,8,12,18; 3:1,7,14. In Rev. 8:3–5 Christ is evidently meant. Sometimes "angel" is used of the spirit of man (Acts 12:15). Though angels are spirits (Ps. 104:4; Heb. 1:14), power is given them to become visible in the semblance of human form (Gen. 19:1, cp. v. 5; Ex. 3:2; Num. 22:22–31; Jud. 2:1; 6:11,22; 13:3,6; 1 Chr. 21:16,20; Mt. 1:20; Lk. 1:26; Jn. 20:12; Acts 7:30; 12:7–8, etc.). The word is always used in the masculine gender, though sex, in the human sense, is never ascribed to angels (Mt. 22:30; Mk. 12:25). They are exceedingly numerous (Ps. 68:17; Mt. 26:53; Heb. 12:22; Rev. 5:11). Their power is inconceivable (2 Ki. 19:35). Their place is about the throne of God (Rev. 5:11; 7:11). Their relation to believers is that of "ministering spirits sent forth to minister for those who will inherit salvation," and this ministry has reference largely to the physical safety and well-being of children of God (1 Ki. 19:5; Ps. 34:7; 91:11; Dan. 6:22; Mt. 2:13,19; 4:11; Lk. 22:43;

has by inheritance obtained a
more excellent name than they.
5 For to which of the angels
did He ever say:

"You are My [a]Son,
Today I have begotten
You"?

And again:

[b]*"I will be to Him a Father,*
And He shall be to Me a
Son"?

6 But when He again brings
the firstborn into the [c]world, He
says:

[d]*"Let all the angels of God*
*worship Him."**

7 And of the angels He says:

[e]*"Who makes His angels*
spirits
And His ministers a
flame of fire."

8 But to the Son *He says:*

"Your throne, O [f]God, is
forever and ever;
A scepter of
[g]righteousness is the
scepter of Your
kingdom.
9 *You have loved*
[h]righteousness and
hated [i]lawlessness;
Therefore God, Your
God, has anointed You
With the oil of gladness
more than Your
companions."

10 And:

[j]*"You, LORD, in the*
beginning laid the
foundation of the
earth,
And the heavens are the
work of Your hands.
11 *They will perish, but You*
remain;
And [k]they will all grow
old like a garment;
12 *Like a cloak You will*
fold them up,
And they will be
changed.
But You are the [l]same,
And Your years will not
fail."

13 But to which of the angels
has He ever said:

[m]*"Sit at My right hand,*
Till I make Your enemies
Your footstool"?

14 Are they not all ministering spirits sent forth to minister
for those who will inherit [n]sal-
vation?

Hearers warned

2 THEREFORE we must give
the more earnest heed to
the things we have heard, lest
we drift away.
2 For if the word spoken
through [o]angels proved steadfast, and every [i]transgression
and [i]disobedience received a
just reward,
3 how shall we escape if we
neglect so great a [n]salvation,
which at the first began to be
spoken by the Lord, and was
confirmed to us by those who
heard [p]Him,
4 God also bearing witness

*1:6 Psalm 97:7

5
a Ps. 2:7
b 2 Sam. 7:14
6
c Gk. *oikoumenē.* See Lk. 2:1, *note*
d Dt. 32:43, LXX
7
e Ps. 104:4
8
f vv. 8–9; Ps. 45:6–7
g Lit. *uprightness*
9
h See 1 Jn. 3:7, *note*
i See Rom. 3:23, *note*
10
j vv. 10–12; Ps. 102:25–27

11
k Isa. 50:9; 51:6
12
l Heb. 13:8
13
m Ps. 110:1; Mt. 22:44
14
n See Rom. 1:16, *note*
CHAPTER 2
2
o Acts 7:53; Gal. 3:19
3
p Lk. 1:2

Acts 5:19; 12:7–10). Comparing Heb. 1:14 with Mt. 18:10 and Ps. 91:11, it appears that this care for the heirs of salvation begins in infancy and continues through life. The angels observe us (Eccl. 5:6; 1 Cor. 4:9; Eph. 3:10), a fact which should influence conduct. Man is made "a little lower than the angels," and in incarnation Christ took "for a little while" this lower place (Ps. 8:4–5; Heb. 2:7) that He might lift the Christian into His own sphere above angels (Heb. 2:9–10). The angels are to accompany Christ in His second advent (Mt. 25:31). To them will be committed the preparation of the judgment of individual Gentiles among the nations (see Mt. 13:30,39,41–42; 25:32, *note*). The Kingdom Age is not to be subject to angels, but to Christ and those for whom He was made a little lower than the angels (Heb. 2:7). An archangel, Michael, is mentioned as having a particular relation to Israel and to the resurrections (Dan. 10:13,21; 12:1–2; 1 Th. 4:16; Jude 9). The only other angel whose name is revealed, Gabriel, was employed in the most distinguished services (Dan. 8:16; 9:21; Lk. 1:19,26).

In regard to fallen angels, two classes are mentioned: (1) "The angels who did not keep their proper domain, but left their own abode" and are chained under darkness, awaiting judgment (Jude 6; 2 Pet. 2:4; cp. Jn. 5:22; 1 Cor. 6:3). See Gen. 6:4, *note.* And (2) the angels who are not bound, but go about doing the will of Satan (see Rev. 20:10, *note*). They may be identical with the demons (see Mt. 7:22, *note*). Everlasting fire is prepared for Satan and his angels (Mt. 25:41; Rev. 20:10).

both [a]with signs and wonders,
with various miracles, and gifts
of the Holy [b]Spirit, according to
His own will?

God's purpose: the earth to be subject to humanity

5 For He has not put the
[c]world to come, of which we
speak, in subjection to angels.
6 But one testified in a certain place, saying:

[d]*"What is man that You*
are mindful of him,
Or the son of man that
You take care of him?
7 *You have made him [e]a*
little lower than the
angels;
You have crowned him
with glory and
*honor,**
And set him over the
works of Your hands.
8 *You have put all things*
in subjection under his
feet."

For in that He put all in subjection under [f]him, He left nothing
that is not put under him. But
now we do not yet see all things
put under him.

Jesus made for a little time lower than the angels

9 But we see Jesus, who was
made a little lower than the angels, for the suffering of death
crowned with glory and honor,
that He, by the [g]grace of God,
might taste death for everyone.
10 For it was fitting for Him,
[h]for whom *are* all things and by
whom *are* all things, in bringing
many sons to glory, to make the
[i]captain of their salvation [j]per-
fect through sufferings.
11 For both He who [k]sancti-
fies and those who are being
sanctified *are* all of one, for
which reason He is not
ashamed to call them brethren,
12 saying:

[l]*"I will declare Your name*
to My brethren;
In the midst of the
[m]assembly I will sing
praise to You."

13 And again:

[n]*"I will put My trust in*
*Him."**

And again:

"Here am I and the
children whom God
*has given Me."**

14 Inasmuch then as the children have partaken of flesh and
blood, He Himself likewise
shared in the same, that
through death He might destroy
him who had the power of
[o]death, that is, the [p]devil,
15 and release those who
through fear of death were all
their lifetime subject to bondage.
16 For indeed He does not
give aid to angels, but He does
give aid to the seed of Abraham.
17 Therefore, in all things He
had to be made like *His* brethren, that He might be a merciful
and faithful High [q]Priest in
things *pertaining* to God, to
make [r]propitiation for the sins
of the people.
18 For in that He Himself has
suffered, being [s]tempted, He is
able to aid those who are
tempted.

The rest of God

Christ, the Son, superior to Moses, the servant

3 THEREFORE, [k]holy brethren, partakers of the heavenly [t]calling, consider the
Apostle and High Priest of our
confession, Christ Jesus,
2 who was faithful to Him
who appointed Him, as [u]Moses
also *was faithful* in all His
house.
3 For this One has been
counted worthy of more glory
than Moses, inasmuch as He
who [v]built the house has more
honor than the house.
4 For every house is built by
someone, but He who built all
things *is* God.
5 And [u]Moses indeed *was*
faithful in all His house as a servant, for a [w]testimony of those
things which would be spoken
afterward,
6 but Christ as a Son over
His own house, whose [x]house
we are if we hold fast the confi-

*2:7 NU-Text and M-Text omit the rest of verse 7. 2:13 2 Samuel 22:3 • Isaiah 8:18

4
a Acts 2:43; 2 Cor. 12:12
b Holy Spirit (NT): v. 4; Heb. 3:7. (Mt. 1:18; Acts 2:4, *note*)
5
c Gk. *oikoumenē*. See Lk. 2:1, *note*
6
d vv. 6–8; Ps. 8:4–6
7
e Or *for a little,* i.e. *little time*
8
f 1 Cor. 15:27
9
g Grace: v. 9; Heb. 4:16. (Jn. 1:14; Jn. 1:17, *note*)
10
h Col. 1:16
i Lit. *author, originator*
j Heb. 5:8–9; see Phil. 3:12, *note*
11
k Sanctification (NT): v. 11; 3:1; Heb. 9:3. (Mt. 4:5; Rev. 22:11)
12
l Ps. 22:22
m Church (the true): v. 12; Heb. 12:23. (Mt. 16:18; Heb. 12:23)
13
n Isa. 8:17, LXX

14
o 2 Tim. 1:10
p Satan: v. 14; Jas. 4:7. (Gen. 3:1; Rev. 20:10)
17
q Heb. 5:1–10
r See Rom. 3:25, *note*
18
s Test/tempt: v. 18; Heb. 3:9. (Gen. 3:1; Jas. 1:14, *note*)
CHAPTER 3
1
t Election (corporate): v. 1; Jas. 2:5. (Dt. 7:6; 1 Pet. 5:13, *note*)
2
u Num. 12:7
3
v Zech. 6:12–13
5
w Dt. 18:15, 19
6
x Cp. Eph. 2:19

dence and the rejoicing of the hope firm to the end.*

Exhortation: the generation that came out of Egypt did not enter the Canaan rest because of unbelief

7 Therefore, as the Holy [a]Spirit [b]says:

[c]*"Today, if you will hear*
His voice,
8 *Do not harden your*
hearts as in the
rebellion,
In the day of trial in the
wilderness,
9 *Where your fathers*
tested Me, [d]tried Me,
And saw My works forty
years.
10 *Therefore I was angry*
with that generation,
And said, 'They always
go astray in their
heart,
And they have not
known My ways.'
11 *So I swore in My wrath,*
'They shall not enter My
rest.'"

12 Beware, brethren, lest there be in any of you an evil heart of unbelief in departing from the living God;

13 but exhort one another daily, while it is called *"Today,"* lest any of you be hardened through the deceitfulness of [e]sin.

14 For we have become partakers of Christ if we hold the beginning of our confidence steadfast to the end,

15 while it is said:

"Today, if you will hear
His voice,
Do not harden your
hearts as in the
rebellion."

16 For who, having heard, rebelled? Indeed, *was it* not all who came out of Egypt, *led* by Moses?

17 Now with whom was He angry forty years? *Was it* not with those who [e]sinned, whose corpses fell in the wilderness?

18 And to whom did He swear that they would not enter His rest, but to those who did not obey?

19 So we see that they could not enter in because of [f]unbelief.

The better rest for the believer

4 THEREFORE, since a promise remains of entering His rest, let us fear lest any of you seem to have come [g]short of it.

2 For indeed the [h]gospel was preached to us as well as to them; but the word which they heard did not profit them,* not being mixed with [i]faith in those who [j]heard *it.*

3 For we who have believed do enter that rest, as He has [b]said:

[k]*"So I swore in My wrath,*
'They shall not enter My
rest,'"

although the works were finished from the foundation of the world.

4 For He has [b]spoken in a certain place of the seventh *day* in this way: *"And [l]God rested on the seventh day from all His works";*

5 and again in this *place: "They shall not enter My rest."*

6 Since therefore it remains that some *must* enter it, and those to whom [m]it was first preached did not enter because of disobedience,

7 again He designates a certain day, [b]saying in David, *"Today,"* after such a long time, as it has been [n]said:

"Today, if you will hear
His voice,
Do not harden your
hearts."

8 For if Joshua had [o]given them rest, then He would not afterward have spoken of another day.

The believer rests in a perfect work of redemption

9 There remains therefore a [p]rest for the people of God.

*
3:6 NU-Text omits *firm to the end.*
4:2 NU-Text and M-Text read *profit them, since they were not united by faith with those who heeded it.*

7
a Holy Spirit (NT): v. 7; Heb. 6:4. (Mt. 1:18; Acts 2:4, *note*)
b Inspiration: v. 7; 4:3–8; Heb. 5:5. (Ex. 4:15; 2 Tim. 3:16, *note*)
c vv. 7–11; Ps. 95:7–11
9
d Test/tempt: vv. 7–9; Heb. 4:15. (Gen. 3:1; Jas. 1:14, *note*)
13
e See Rom. 3:23, *note*

19
f Num. 14:1–39; 1 Cor. 10:10–11
CHAPTER 4
1
g Cp. Heb. 12:15
2
h Gospel: v. 2; 1 Pet. 1:12. (Gen. 12:3; Rev. 14:6)
i Faith: v. 2; Heb. 10:22. (Gen. 3:20; Heb. 11:39, *note*)
j Cp. 1 Th. 2:13
3
k Ps. 95:11
4
l Gen. 2:2
6
m Lit. *the gospel*
7
n Ps. 95:7–8
8
o Josh 22:4
9
p Lit. *keeping of a sabbath*

10 For he who has entered His rest has himself also ceased from his [a]works as God *did* from His.

11 [b]Let us therefore be diligent to enter that rest, lest anyone [c]fall according to the same example of disobedience.

12 [d]For the word of God *is* [e]living and [f]powerful, and sharper than any [g]two-edged [h]sword, piercing even to the division of soul and spirit, and of joints and marrow, and is a [i]discerner of the thoughts and intents of the heart.

13 And there is no creature [j]hidden from His sight, but all things *are* [k]naked and open to the eyes of Him to whom we *must give* account.

14 Seeing then that we have a great [l]High Priest who has passed through the heavens, Jesus the Son of God, [m]let us hold fast *our* confession.

15 For we do not have a High Priest who cannot [n]sympathize with our weaknesses, but was in all *points* [o]tempted as *we are, yet* [p]without [q]sin.

16 Let us therefore come [r]boldly to the throne of [s]grace, that we may obtain mercy and find grace to help in time of need.

II. The Preeminence and Finality of the Priesthood of Christ, 5:1—10:18

The believer is kept in perfect rest by grace

The office of high priest

5 FOR every high priest taken from among men is appointed for men in things [t]*pertaining* to God, that he may offer both gifts and sacrifices for [q]sins.

2 He can have compassion on those who are ignorant and going astray, since he himself is also subject to [u]weakness.

10
a Cp. Rev. 14:13
11
b 2 Pet. 1:10
c Cp. Heb. 10:38
12
d Cp. Isa. 49:2
e 1 Pet. 1:23
f Cp. Jer. 23:29
g Rev. 2:12
h Eph. 6:17
i Cp. Jn. 12:48
13
j Ps. 33:13–15; cp. 2 Chr. 16:9
k Job 26:6; Prov. 15:11
14
l Heb. 2:17; 3:1; 5:5,10; 6:20; 7:26; 8:1; 9:11; 10:21
m Heb. 10:23
15
n Cp. Hos. 11:8
o *Test/tempt:* v. 15; Heb. 11:17. (Gen. 3:1; Jas. 1:14, *note*)
p Or *apart from*
q See Rom. 3:23, *note*
16
r Heb. 10:19, 22
s *Grace:* v. 16; Heb. 12:15. (Jn. 1:14; Jn. 1:17, *note*). See 2 Pet. 3:18, *note*
CHAPTER 5
1
t Heb. 2:17
2
u Heb. 7:28

3 Because of this he is required as for the people, so also for [v]himself, to offer *sacrifices* for [q]sins.

4 And no man takes this honor to himself, but he who is called by God, just as [w]Aaron *was.*

Christ, a high priest according to the order of Melchizedek

5 So also Christ did not glorify Himself to become [x]High Priest, *but it* was He who [y]said to Him:

> [z]*"You are My Son,*
> *Today I have begotten*
> *You."*

6 As *He* also *says* in another *place:*

> [aa]*"You are a priest forever*
> *According to the order of*
> [1]*Melchizedek"*;

7 who, in the days of His flesh, when He had offered up [bb]prayers and supplications, with vehement cries and tears to Him who was [cc]able to save Him [dd]from death, and was heard because of His godly [ee]fear,

8 though He was a Son, *yet* He learned [ff]obedience by the things which He suffered.

9 And [gg]having been perfected, He became the author of eternal [hh]salvation to all who obey Him,

10 called by God as High Priest *"according to the order of Melchizedek,"*

Appeal and warning (to 6:12)

11 of [ii]whom we have much to say, and hard to explain, since you have become dull of hearing.

12 For though by this time you ought to be teachers, you need *someone* to teach you

3
v Lev. 9:7; Heb. 9:7
4
w Ex. 28:1; Num. 16:40
5
x Heb. 2:17; 3:1; 4:14; 6:20; 7:26; 8:1; 9:11; 10:21
y *Inspiration:* vv. 5–6; Heb. 6:14. (Ex. 4:15; 2 Tim. 3:16, *note*)
z Ps. 2:7
6
aa Ps. 110:4
7
bb *Bible prayers* (NT): v. 7; Jas. 5:17. (Mt. 6:9; Lk. 11:2, *note*)
cc Mt. 26:53
dd Lit. *out of*
ee See Ps. 19:9, *note*
8
ff Phil. 2:8
9
gg Heb. 2:10
hh See Rom. 1:16, *note*
11
ii Heb. 7:1–22

[1](5:6) See Gen. 14:18, *note 4.* Melchizedek was a suitable type of Christ as High Priest, because: (1) he was a man (Heb. 7:4; 1 Tim. 2:5); (2) he was a king-priest (cp. Gen. 14:18 with Zech. 6:12–13); (3) his name means "my king is righteous" (cp. Isa. 11:5), and he was king of Salem (i.e. "peace," cp. Isa. 11:6–9); (4) he had no recorded "beginning of days" (cp. Jn. 1:1) or "end of life" (cp. Rom. 6:9; Heb. 7:23–25), nor (5) was he made a high priest by human appointment (Ps. 110:4). But the contrast between the high priesthood of Melchizedek and Aaron is only as to person, "order" (or appointment), and duration. In His work Christ follows the Aaronic pattern, the "shadow" of which Christ was the substance (Heb. 8:1–6; 9:1–28).

again the [a]first principles of the oracles of God; and you have come to need [b]milk and not solid food.

13 For everyone who partakes *only* of milk *is* unskilled in the word of righteousness, for he is a [c]babe.

14 But solid food belongs to those who are of full age, *that is,* those who by reason of use have their senses exercised to [d]discern both good and evil.

Progress toward maturity

6 THEREFORE, leaving the discussion of the elementary *principles* of Christ, let us go on to [e]perfection, not laying again [f]the foundation of [g]repentance from [h]dead works and of faith toward God,

2 of the doctrine of [i]baptisms, of laying on of hands, of [j]resurrection of the dead, and of eternal judgment.

3 And this we will* do if God permits.

4 [k]For *it is* [1]impossible for those who were once enlightened, and have tasted the heavenly gift, and have become partakers of the Holy [l]Spirit,

5 and have tasted the good word of God and the powers of the age to come,

6 if they fall away,* to renew them again to [g]repentance, since they crucify again for themselves the Son of God, and put *Him* to an open shame.

7 For the earth which drinks in the rain that often comes upon it, and bears herbs useful for those by whom it is cultivated, receives [m]blessing from God;

8 but if it bears thorns and briers, *it is* rejected and near to being cursed, whose end *is* to be burned.

9 But, beloved, we are confident of better things concerning you, yes, things that accompany [n]salvation, though we speak in this manner.

10 [o]For God *is* not unjust to forget your work and labor of* love which you have shown toward His name, *in that* you have ministered to the saints, and do [p]minister.

11 And we desire that each one of you show the same diligence to the full [q]assurance of hope until the end,

12 that you do not become sluggish, but [r]imitate those who through faith and patience inherit the promises.

The believer's High Priest within the veil assures his entrance there also

13 For when God made a promise to Abraham, because He could swear by no one greater, He swore by Himself,

14 [s]saying, [t]*"Surely bless-*

*6:3 M-Text reads *let us do.* **6:6** Or *and have fallen away.* **6:10** NU-Text omits *labor of.*

12
a Cp. Heb. 6:1–2
b 1 Cor. 3:1–3
13
c Cp. Eph. 4:14
14
d Phil. 1:9
CHAPTER 6
1
e See Phil. 3:12, *note*
f Lit. *a*
g Repentance: vv. 1, 6; Heb. 12:17. (Mt. 3:2; Acts 17:30, *note*)
h Heb. 9:14
2
i Lit. *washings.* Num. 8:7; Heb. 9:10
j Resurrection: v. 2; Heb. 11:19. (2 Ki. 4:35; 1 Cor. 15:52, *note*)
4
k Apostasy: vv. 1–9; Heb. 10:29. (Lk. 18:8; 2 Tim. 3:1, *note*)
l Holy Spirit (NT): v. 4; Heb. 9:8. (Mt. 1:18; Acts 2:4, *note*)
7
m Ps. 65:10
9
n See Rom. 1:16, *note*
10
o Cp. Mt. 25:40
p Heb. 10:32–34
11
q Assurance/security: vv. 8–12; Heb. 7:25. (Ps. 23:1; Jude 1, *note*)
12
r Heb. 13:7
14
s Inspiration: v. 14; Heb. 7:17. (Ex. 4:15; 2 Tim. 3:16, *note*)
t Gen. 22:16–17

[1](6:4) The warning in vv. 6–8 has been understood in various ways. The major interpretations are: (1) The warning is directed to some of the Jewish people who professed to be believers in Christ but stopped short of true faith in Him after advancing to the threshold of salvation. (2) The admonition presents a hypothetical case: if one could "fall away" (v. 6), it would be impossible to renew him again to repentance; for, in such an instance, it would be necessary for Christ to be crucified a second time. Obviously this will not occur (Heb. 10:12,14); thus to fall away is impossible. (3) The warning is directed toward believers who have fallen into sin to such an extent that they have crucified to themselves the Son of God all over again (v. 6) and are therefore disapproved and will lose their reward (see 1 Cor. 9:27, *note*). And (4) the warning is to those who are believers in the Lord Jesus Christ and are in danger of falling away, through unbelief or sin, and losing their salvation.

The clause rendered "who have become partakers of the Holy Spirit" (v. 4) might be paraphrased somewhat like this: "were willingly being led toward the Holy Spirit." The warning is issued to those who have been instructed and even moved by the Holy Spirit but have never committed themselves to Christ. The entire passage turns on the word "better" in v. 9. If all that is written in vv. 1–5 were equivalent to salvation, there could be nothing better. The experiences outlined may precede and even accompany salvation, but they do not always result in salvation. Scripture abundantly affirms the Christian's eternal security; therefore this passage must not be interpreted as teaching that believers in Christ can lose their salvation. See Jn. 3:15–16,36; 10:27–30; Rom. 8:35,37–39; Eph. 1:12–14; 4:30; Phil. 1:6; Heb. 10:12–14; 1 Pet. 1:3–5.

ing I will bless you, and multiplying I will multiply you."

15 And so, after he had patiently endured, he obtained the [a]promise.

16 For men indeed swear by the [b]greater, and an oath for confirmation *is* for them an end of all dispute.

17 Thus God, determining to show more abundantly to the [c]heirs of promise the [d]immutability of His counsel, [e]confirmed *it* by an oath,

18 that by two immutable things, in which it *is* impossible for God to [f]lie, we might* have strong consolation, who have fled for refuge to lay hold of the [g]hope set before *us.*

19 This *hope* we have as an anchor of the soul, both sure and steadfast, and which enters the Presence [h]*behind* the veil,

20 where the forerunner has entered for us, *even* Jesus, having become [i]High Priest forever according to the order of [j]Melchizedek.

The historic Melchizedek a type of Christ (cp. Gen. 14)

7 FOR this [j]Melchizedek, king of Salem, priest of the [k]Most High God, who met Abraham returning from the slaughter of the kings and blessed him,

2 to whom also Abraham gave a tenth part of all, first being translated "king of righteousness," and then also king of Salem, meaning "king of peace,"

3 without father, without mother, without genealogy, having neither beginning of days nor end of life, but made like the Son of God, remains a priest [1]continually.

Melchizedek high priesthood greater than Aaronic

(a) Because Aaron in Abraham paid tithes to Melchizedek

4 Now consider how great this man *was,* to whom even the patriarch Abraham gave a tenth of the spoils.

5 And indeed those who are of the [l]sons of Levi, who receive the priesthood, have a commandment to receive tithes from the people according to the law, that is, from their brethren, though they have come from the loins of Abraham;

6 but he whose genealogy is not derived from them [m]received tithes from Abraham and blessed him who had the promises.

7 Now beyond all contradiction the lesser is blessed by the better.

8 Here mortal men receive tithes, but there he *receives them,* of [n]whom it is witnessed that he lives.

9 Even Levi, who receives tithes, paid tithes through Abraham, so to speak,

10 for he was still in the loins of his father when [j]Melchizedek met him.

(b) Because the Aaronic priesthood made nothing perfect

11 [o]Therefore, if perfection were through the Levitical priesthood (for under it the people received the law), what further need *was there* that another priest should rise according to the order of [j]Melchizedek, and not be called according to the order of Aaron?

12 For the priesthood being changed, of necessity there is also a change of the law.

13 For He of whom these things are spoken belongs to another tribe, from which no man has officiated at the altar.

14 For *it is* [p]evident that our Lord arose from [q]Judah, of which tribe Moses spoke nothing concerning priesthood.*

15 And it is yet far more evident if, in the likeness of [j]Melchizedek, there arises another priest

15
a Gen. 21:5
16
b Cp. Ex. 22:10–11
17
c Rom. 8:17; Heb. 11:9
d Rom. 11:29
e Lit. *intervened with*
18
f Num. 23:19; 1 Sam. 15:29
g Col. 1:5; Heb. 7:19
19
h Lev. 16:15
20
i Heb. 2:17; 3:1; 4:14; 5:5,10; 7:26; 8:1; 9:11; 10:21
j Gen. 14:17–19; Ps. 110:4; Heb. 5:10–11
CHAPTER 7
1
k Gen. 14:18

5
l Num. 18:21–26
6
m Gen. 14:20
8
n Heb. 5:6; Rev. 1:18
11
o vv. 18–19; Rom. 7:7–14; Gal. 2:21; Heb. 8:7
14
p Gen. 49:8–10
q Mt. 1:2

*
6:18 M-Text omits *might.* 7:14 NU-Text reads *priests.*

[1](7:3) "Continually" because Melchizedek had neither "beginning of days or end of life." Cp. *note* at 5:6.

16 who has come, not according to the law of a [a]fleshly commandment, but according to the power of an [b]endless [c]life.

17 For He [d]testifies:*

"You are a priest forever
According to the order of
[e]Melchizedek."

18 For on the one hand there is an annulling of the former commandment because of its [f]weakness and unprofitableness,

19 for the [g]law made [h]nothing [i]perfect; on the other hand, *there is the* bringing in of a better [j]hope, through [k]which we draw near to God.

20 And inasmuch as *He was* not *made priest* without an oath

21 (for they have become priests without an oath, but He with an oath by Him who [d]said to Him:

[l]"The LORD has sworn
And will not relent,
'You are a priest
*forever**
According to the order of
Melchizedek'"),

22 by so much more Jesus has become a surety of a [m]better covenant.

(c) Because the Aaronic priests died; Christ lives forever

23 Also there were many priests, because they were prevented by death from continuing.

24 But He, because He continues forever, has an unchangeable priesthood.

25 Therefore He is also [n]able to [o]save [p]to the [q]uttermost those who come to God through Him, since He always lives to make [r]intercession for them.

26 For such a [s]High Priest was fitting for us, *who is* holy, harmless, undefiled, separate from [t]sinners, and has become higher than the heavens;

27 who does not need daily, as those high priests, to offer up sacrifices, first for His [u]own [t]sins and then for the people's, for this He did [v]once for all when He [w]offered up Himself.

28 For the law appoints as high priests men who have [x]weakness, but the word of the oath, which came after the law, *appoints* the Son who has been perfected forever.

(d) Because the Aaronic priests served the shadows of which Christ serves the realities

8 NOW *this is* the main point of the things we are [d]saying: We have such a High Priest, who is seated at the right hand of the throne of the Majesty in the [y]heavens,

2 a Minister of the sanctuary and of the [z]true tabernacle which the Lord erected, and not man.

3 For every high priest is appointed to offer both gifts and sacrifices. Therefore *it is* necessary that this One also have something to offer.

4 For if He were on earth, He would not be a priest, since there are priests who offer the gifts according to the law;

5 who serve the [aa]copy and [bb]shadow of the heavenly things, as Moses was divinely instructed when he was about to make the tabernacle. For He [d]said, [cc]*"See that you make all things according to the pattern shown you on the mountain."*

(e) Because Christ mediates a superior covenant

6 But now He has obtained a more excellent ministry, inasmuch as He is also Mediator of a [dd]better covenant, which was established on better promises.

The New Covenant

7 For if that [ee]first *covenant* had been [ff]faultless, then no place would have been sought for a second.

8 Because finding fault with them, He [d]says: *"Behold, the days are coming, says the [gg]LORD, when I will make a*

16
a See Rom. 7:14, *note*
b Lit. *indissoluble*
c *Life* (eternal): v. 16; Jas. 1:12. (Mt. 7:14; Rev. 22:19)
17
d *Inspiration:* vv. 17, 21; 8:1,5, 8–9; Heb. 8:10. (Ex. 4:15; 2 Tim. 3:16, *note*)
e Gen. 14:17–19; Ps. 110:4; Heb. 5:10–11
18
f Rom. 8:3; Gal. 3:21
19
g *Law* (of Moses): vv. 18–19; Heb. 10:28. (Ex. 19:1; Gal. 3:24, *note*)
h Heb. 9:9; 10:1
i See Mt. 5:48 and Phil. 3:12, *notes*
j Heb. 6:18–19
k Rom. 5:2
21
l Ps. 110:4
22
m 8:6
25
n Jude 24
o See Rom. 1:16, *note*
p i.e. *completely*
q *Assurance/security:* vv. 23–25; Heb. 8:10. (Ps. 23:1; Jude 1, *note*)
r Rom. 8:34; Heb. 9:24
26
s Heb. 2:17; 3:1; 4:14; 5:5,10; 6:20; 8:1; 9:11; 10:21
t See Rom. 3:23, *note*
27
u Lev. 16:6; Heb. 5:3

v *Christ* (first advent): v. 27; Heb. 9:28. (Gen. 3:15; Acts 1:11, *note*)
w *Sacrifice* (of Christ): v. 27; Heb. 9:12. (Gen. 3:15; Heb. 10:18, *note*)
28
x Heb. 5:2
CHAPTER 8
1
y Heb. 1:3
2
z Heb. 9:11, 24
5
aa Heb. 9:23–24
bb Col. 2:17
cc Ex. 25:40
6
dd 7:22
7
ee Ex. 3:8; 19:5
ff Cp. Heb. 7:11
8
gg vv. 8–12; Jer. 31:31–34

*
7:17 NU-Text reads *it is testified.*
7:21 NU-Text ends the quotation here.

8
a Covenant (New): vv. 8–13; Heb. 9:15. (Isa. 61:8; Heb. 8:8, *note*)
b Eight Covenants: vv. 7–8. (Gen. 2:16; Heb. 8:8)
10
c Inspiration: vv. 8–13; Heb. 10:5. (Ex. 4:15; 2 Tim. 3:16, *note*)
d Jer. 31:33
e Cp. 2 Cor. 3:3,6
f Assurance/security: vv. 10–13; Heb. 9:26. (Ps. 23:1; Jude 1, *note*)
11
g Jer. 31:34

[1a]new [2b]covenant with the
house of Israel and with the
house of Judah—
9 *"not according to the cov-*
enant that I made with their fa-
thers in the day when I took
them by the hand to lead them
out of the land of Egypt; be-
cause they did not continue in
My covenant, and I disregarded
them, says the LORD.
10 *"For this is the covenant*
that I will make with the house
of Israel after those days, [c]says
*the [d]*LORD: *I will put My laws in*
their mind and [e]write them on
their hearts; and I [f]will be their
God, and they shall be My peo-
ple.
11 *"None of them shall teach*
his neighbor, and none his
brother, saying, 'Know the
*[g]*LORD,' *for all shall know Me,*
from the least of them to the
greatest of them.
12 *"For I will be [h]merciful to*
their [i]unrighteousness, and
their [i]sins and their [i]lawless
deeds I will remember no*
more."
13 In that He says, *"A new*
covenant," He has made the
first obsolete. Now what [j]is becoming obsolete and growing
old is ready to vanish away.

(1) The ordinances and sanctuary of the Old Covenant were mere types

9 THEN indeed, even the first
covenant had ordinances of
divine service and the earthly
[k]sanctuary.
2 For a tabernacle was prepared: the first *part,* in which
was the lampstand, the table,
and the [l]showbread, which is
called the sanctuary;
3 and behind the [m]second
veil, the part of the tabernacle

* 8:12 NU-Text omits *and their lawless deeds.*

12
h Or propitious. See Rom. 3:25, *note*
i See Rom. 3:23, *note*
13
j Lit. *grows old and aged is near to disappearing*
CHAPTER 9
1
k Ex. 25:1–40
2
l See Ex. 25:30, *note*
3
m Ex. 26:31–35

[1](8:8) The New Covenant, the last of the eight great covenants of Scripture, is (1) better (cp. "more excellent" 8:6) than the Mosaic Covenant (Ex. 19:5, *note*), not morally but efficaciously (Heb. 7:19; cp. Rom. 8:3–4). (2) It is established upon "better" (i.e. unconditional) promises. In the Mosaic Covenant God said, "If you will indeed obey" (Ex. 19:5); in the New Covenant He says, "I will" (Heb. 8:10,12). (3) Under the Mosaic Covenant obedience sprang from fear (2:2; 12:25–27); under the New it issues from a willing heart and mind (8:10). (4) The New Covenant secures the personal revelation of the Lord to every believer (v. 11). (5) It assures the complete oblivion of sins (v. 12; 10:17; cp. 10:3). (6) It rests upon an accomplished redemption (Mt. 26:27–28; 1 Cor. 11:25; Heb. 9:11–12,18–23). And (7) it secures the perpetuity, future conversion, and blessing of a repentant Israel, with whom the New Covenant will yet be ratified (10:9; cp. Jer. 31:31–40; see also Kingdom (OT), Zech. 12:8, *note;* and 2 Sam. 7:8–17 with *notes*).

[2](8:8) The Eight Covenants, Summary: (1) The Edenic Covenant (Gen. 2:16, *note*) conditions the life of man in innocence. (2) The Adamic Covenant (Gen. 3:15, *note*) conditions the life of fallen men and gives promise of a Redeemer. (3) The Noahic Covenant (Gen. 9:16, *note*) establishes the principle of human government. (4) The Abrahamic Covenant (Gen. 12:2, *note*) founds the nation of Israel and confirms, with specific additions, the Adamic promise of redemption. (5) The Mosaic Covenant (Ex. 19:5, *note*) condemns all men, "for all have sinned" (Rom. 3:23; 5:12). (6) The Palestinian Covenant (Dt. 30:3, *note*) secures the final restoration and conversion of Israel. (7) The Davidic Covenant (2 Sam. 7:16, *note*) establishes the perpetuity of the Davidic family (fulfilled in Christ, Mt. 1:1; Lk. 1:31–33; Rom. 1:3), and of the Davidic kingdom over Israel and over the whole earth, to be fulfilled in and by Christ (2 Sam. 7:8–17; Zech. 12:8; Lk. 1:31–33; Acts 15:14–17; 1 Cor. 15:24). And (8) the New Covenant (Heb. 8:8, *note 1*) rests upon the sacrifice of Christ and secures the eternal blessedness, under the Abrahamic Covenant (Gal. 3:13–29), of all who believe. It is absolutely unconditional and, since no responsibility is by it committed to man, it is final and irreversible.

The relation of Christ to the eight covenants is as follows: (1) To the Edenic Covenant, Christ, as the "second Man" and the "last Adam" (1 Cor. 15:45–47), takes the place over all things which the first Adam lost (Col. 2:10; Heb. 2:7–9). (2) He is the Seed of the woman of the Adamic Covenant (Gen. 3:15; Jn. 12:31; Gal. 4:4; 1 Jn. 3:8; Rev. 20:10), and fulfilled its conditions of toil (Mk. 6:3) and obedience (Phil. 2:8; Heb. 5:8). (3) As the greatest Son of Shem, in Him was fulfilled supremely the promise to Shem in the Noahic Covenant (Gen. 9:16, *note;* Col. 2:9). (4) He is the Seed to whom the promises were made in the Abrahamic Covenant, the Son of Abraham obedient unto death (Gen. 22:18; Gal. 3:16; Phil. 2:8). (5) He lived sinlessly under the Mosaic Covenant and bore for us its curse (Gal. 3:10–13). (6) He lived obediently as a Jew in the land under the Palestinian Covenant, and will yet perform its gracious promises (Dt. 28:1—30:9). (7) He is the Seed, Heir, and King under the Davidic Covenant (Mt. 1:1; Lk. 1:31–33). And (8) His sacrifice is the foundation of the New Covenant (Mt. 26:28; 1 Cor. 11:25).

which is called the [a]Holiest of All,

4 which had the [b]golden censer and the [c]ark of the covenant overlaid on all sides with gold, in which *were* the [d]golden pot that had the manna, [e]Aaron's rod that budded, and the [f]tablets of the covenant;

5 and above it were the cherubim of glory overshadowing the mercy seat. Of these things we cannot now speak in detail.

6 Now when these things had been thus prepared, the priests [g]always went into the first part of the tabernacle, performing *the services.*

7 But into the second part the high priest *went* alone [h]once a year, not without blood, which he offered for [i]himself and *for* the people's sins *committed* in ignorance;

8 the Holy [j]Spirit indicating this, that the way into the [a]Holiest of All was not yet made manifest while the first tabernacle was still standing.

9 It *was* symbolic for the present time in which both gifts and sacrifices are offered which cannot make him who performed the service [k]perfect in regard to the conscience—

10 *concerned* only with foods and drinks, various washings, and [l]fleshly ordinances imposed until the time of [m]reformation.

(2) The sanctuary and sacrifice of the New Covenant are realities

11 But Christ came *as* [n]High Priest of the [o]good things to come,* with the greater and more perfect tabernacle not made with hands, that is, not of this creation.

12 Not with the blood of goats and calves, but [p]with His own blood He entered the [q]Most Holy Place once for all, having obtained eternal redemption.

13 For if the blood of bulls and goats and the ashes of a heifer, sprinkling the unclean, sanctifies for the purifying of the flesh,

14 how much more shall the blood of Christ, who through the eternal [j]Spirit offered Himself without spot to God, [r]cleanse your conscience from dead works to serve the living God?

15 And for this reason He is the Mediator of the [s]new covenant, [p]by means of death, for the [t]redemption of the [u]transgressions under the first covenant, that those who are called may receive the promise of the eternal inheritance.

(3) The New Covenant is the last will and testament of Christ

16 For where there *is* a [v]testament, there must also of necessity be the death of the testator.

17 For a [v]testament *is* in force after men are dead, since it has no power at all while the testator lives.

18 Therefore not even the first *covenant* was dedicated without blood.

19 For when Moses had spoken every precept to all the people according to the law, he took the blood of calves and goats, with water, scarlet wool, and hyssop, and sprinkled both the book itself and all the people,

20 saying, *"This is the blood [w]of the covenant which [x]God has commanded you."*

21 [y]Then likewise he sprinkled with blood both the tabernacle and all the vessels of the ministry.

22 And according to the law almost all things are purified with blood, and [z]without shedding of blood there is no [aa]remission.

(4) The heavenly sanctuary was purified with a better sacrifice (Lev. 16:33)

23 Therefore *it was* necessary that the [bb]copies of the things in the heavens should be purified with these, but the heavenly things themselves with better sacrifices than these.

24 For Christ has not entered the [q]holy places made with hands, *which are* copies of the

*9:11 NU-Text reads *that have come.*

3
a *Sanctification* (NT): vv. 3,8,12, 24; Heb. 9:25. (Mt. 4:5; Rev. 22:11). Also called *Most Holy Place;* see v. 12

4
b Lev. 16:12
c Ex. 25:10
d Ex. 16:33
e Num. 17:1–10
f Ex. 34:29; Dt. 10:2–5

6
g Num. 28:3

7
h Lev. 16:34
i Heb. 5:3

8
j *Holy Spirit* (NT): vv. 8,14; Heb. 10:15. (Mt. 1:18; Acts 2:4, *note*)

9
k Heb. 7:19; see Mt. 5:48 and Phil. 3:12, *notes*

10
l See Rom. 7:14, *note*
m Lit. *setting things right*

11
n Heb. 2:17; 3:1; 4:14; 5:5,10; 6:20; 7:26; 8:1; 10:21
o Eph. 1:3–11; Heb. 10:1

12
p *Sacrifice* (of Christ): vv. 12,15; Heb. 9:26. (Gen. 3:15; Heb. 10:18, *note*)
q *Sanctification* (NT): vv. 3,8,12, 24; Heb. 9:25. (Mt. 4:5; Rev. 22:11)

14
r 1 Jn. 1:7

15
s *Covenant* (New): v. 15; Heb. 12:24. (Isa. 61:8; Heb. 8:8, *note*)
t See Rom. 3:24, *note*
u See Rom. 3:23, *note*

16
v Or *covenant*

20
w Mt. 26:28
x Ex. 24:3–8

21
y Ex. 29:12, 36

22
z Lev. 17:11
aa *Forgiveness:* v. 22; Jas. 5:15. (Lev. 4:20; Mt. 26:28, *note*)

23
bb Heb. 8:5

24
a Heb. 8:2
25
b Sanctification (NT): v. 25; Heb. 10:10. (Mt. 4:5; Rev. 22:11)
26
c Assurance/security: vv. 24–26; Heb. 10:14. (Ps. 23:1; Jude 1, *note*)
d See Rom. 3:23, *note*
e Sacrifice (of Christ): v. 26; Heb. 10:10. (Gen. 3:15; Heb. 10:18, *note*)
27
f Death (physical): v. 27; 2 Pet. 1:14. (Gen. 2:17; Heb. 9:27, *note*)
g Judgments (the seven): v. 27; 1 Pet. 2:24. (1 Sam. 7:14; Rev. 20:12, *note*)
h Day (of judgment): v. 27; 2 Pet. 2:9. (Mt. 10:15; Rev. 20:11)

[a]true, but into heaven itself,
now to appear in the presence
of God for us;
25 not that He should offer
Himself often, as the high priest
enters the [b]Most Holy Place
every year with blood of another—
26 He then would have had to
suffer often since the foundation of the world; but now, once
at the end of the ages, He has
appeared to [c]put away [d]sin [e]by
the sacrifice of Himself.
27 And as it is appointed for
men to [1f]die once, but [g]after
this the [h]judgment,
28 so Christ was offered
[i]once to bear the [d]sins of many.
To those who eagerly [j]wait for
Him He will appear a [k]second
time, apart from [d]sin, for [l]sal-
vation.

(5) The one sacrifice of the New Covenant is superior to the many sacrifices of the Old

10 FOR the law, having a
[m]shadow of the good
things to come, *and* not the very
image of the things, can [n]never
with these same sacrifices,
which they offer continually
year by year, make those who
approach [o]perfect.
2 For then would they not
have ceased to be offered? For
the worshipers, once purified,
would have had no more consciousness of [d]sins.
3 But in those *sacrifices
there is* a reminder of [d]sins every year.
4 For *it is* not possible that
the blood of bulls and goats
could take away [d]sins.
5 Therefore, when He came
into the [p]world, He [q]said:

[r]*"Sacrifice and offering*
You did not desire,
But a [2]body You have
prepared for Me.
6 *In burnt offerings and*
sacrifices for [d]sin
You had no pleasure.
7 *Then I said, 'Behold, I*
have [i]come—
In the volume of the
book it is written of
Me—
To do Your will, O
God.' "

8 Previously saying, *"Sacrifice and offering, burnt offerings, and offerings for [d]sin You*

28
i Christ (first advent): v. 28; 10:5, 7; Heb. 10:9. (Gen. 3:15; Acts 1:11, *note*)
j Ti. 2:13; cp. 2 Tim. 4:8
k Christ (second advent): v. 28; Heb. 10:37. (Dt. 30:3; Acts 1:11, *note*)
l See Rom. 1:16, *note*
CHAPTER 10
1
m Heb. 8:5
n Heb. 7:19
o See Mt. 5:48, *note*
5
p Gk. *kosmos.* See Mt. 4:8, *note*
q Inspiration: v. 5; Heb. 10:15. (Ex. 4:15; 2 Tim. 3:16, *note*)
r vv. 5–7; Ps. 40:6–84

[1](9:27) Death (physical), Summary: (1) Physical death is a consequence of sin (Gen. 3:19), and the universality of death proves the universality of sin (Rom. 5:12–14). (2) Physical death affects the body only, and is not cessation of existence or of consciousness (Hab. 2:5, *note;* Lk. 16:23, *note;* Rev. 6:9–10). (3) All physical death ends in the resurrection of the body. See Resurrection, Job 19:25; 1 Cor. 15:52, *note.* (4) Because physical death is a consequence of sin, it is not inevitable to the redeemed (Gen. 5:24; 1 Cor. 15:51–52; 1 Th. 4:15–17). (5) Physical death has for the Christian a peculiar qualification. It is called "sleep," because his body may be awakened at any moment (Phil. 3:20–21; 1 Th. 4:14–18). (6) The soul and spirit live, independently of the death of the body, which is described as a "tent," in which the "I" dwells, and which may be put off (2 Cor. 5:1–8; cp. 1 Cor. 15:42–44; 2 Pet. 1:13–15). And (7) at the Christian's death he is at once "with the Lord" and his body awaits resurrection at the return of Christ (2 Cor. 5:1–8; Phil. 1:23; 1 Th. 4:13–17). Regarding the death of Christ, see Mt. 27:50, *note.*

[2](10:5) This quotation follows the LXX, with a minor variation, instead of the Hebrew text, as do many of the several hundred quotations of the OT found in the NT. Quotations are used in various ways: (1) Invariably the authors attribute unqualified divine authority to the OT, in some instances basing their argument on one word (Mt. 2:15; 22:43–45; Jn. 10:34; 19:36–37; Rom. 4:3; etc.). (2) The Septuagint is usually employed, as it is here in Hebrews, in the same way as an English translation may be quoted today (Mt. 1:23; cp. Isa. 7:14 in LXX). (3) Variations in quotations may originate in the desire to translate the original Hebrew more accurately than the LXX (1 Cor. 14:21; cp. Isa. 28:11–12 in LXX and Hebrew). (4) Many quotations were not intended to be verbatim, but are paraphrases designed to bring out the meaning or particular application (Gal. 4:30; cp. Gen. 21:10). (5) Some quotations are a summary of OT truth taken from several passages, giving the sense if not the exact words of the original (Rom. 11:26–27; cp. Isa. 59:20–21 and Isa. 27:9). (6) In some cases the quotation is only an allusion and is not intended to be an exact quotation (Rom. 9:27; cp. Isa. 10:22–23). And (7) the Holy Spirit who inspired the OT was free to reword a quotation just as a human author may restate his own writings in other words without impugning the accuracy of the original statement (Mt. 2:6; cp. Mic. 5:2). The doctrine of plenary inspiration requires only that revelation be expressed without error.

did not desire, nor had pleasure in them" (which are offered according to the law),

9 then He said, *"Behold, I have [a]come to do Your will, O God."** He takes away the first that He may establish the second.

10 By that will we have been [b]sanctified through the [c]offering of the body of Jesus Christ once *for all.*

11 And every priest stands ministering daily and offering repeatedly the same sacrifices, which can never take away [d]sins.

12 But this Man, after He had [c]offered one sacrifice for sins forever, [e]sat down [f]at the right hand of God,

13 from that time waiting till His enemies are made His footstool.

14 For by one [c]offering He has [g]perfected forever [h]those who are being [b]sanctified.

15 But the Holy [i]Spirit also witnesses to us; for after He had [j]said before,

16 *"This is the covenant that I will make with them after those days, says the [k]LORD: I will put My laws into their hearts, and in their minds I will write them,"*

17 *then He adds, "Their [d]sins and their lawless deeds I will remember no more."*

18 Now where there is remission of these, *there is* no longer an [1]offering for [d]sin.

III. The Life of Faith, 10:19—13:19

19 Therefore, brethren, having [l]boldness to enter the [b]Holiest by the blood of Jesus,

20 by a new and [m]living way which He consecrated for us, through the [n]veil, that is, His flesh,

21 and *having* a High Priest over the house of God,

22 let us [o]draw near with a true heart in full assurance of [p]faith, having our hearts sprinkled from an evil conscience and our bodies washed with pure water.

23 Let us hold fast the confession of *our* hope without wavering, for [q]He who promised *is* faithful.

24 And let us consider one another in order to stir up love and good works,

25 not forsaking the assembling of ourselves together, as *is* the manner of some, but [r]exhorting *one another,* and so much the more [s]as you see the Day [t]approaching.

The wavering warned; Jewish sacrifices have lost their efficacy; it is Christ or judgment

26 For if we [d]sin [u]willfully after we have received the knowledge of the truth, there [v]no longer remains a sacrifice for sins,

27 but a certain fearful expectation of judgment, and fiery indignation which will devour the adversaries.

28 Anyone who has rejected [w]Moses' law dies without mercy on the testimony of two or three [x]witnesses.

29 [y]Of how much worse punishment, do you suppose, will he be thought worthy [z]who has trampled the Son of God underfoot, counted the blood of the covenant by which he was [b]sanctified a common thing,

*10:9 NU-Text and M-Text omit *O God.*

9
a Christ (first advent): v. 9; 1 Pet. 2:21. (Gen. 3:15; Acts 1:11, *note*)

10
b Sanctification (NT): vv. 10,14,19, 29; Heb. 13:12. (Mt. 4:5; Rev. 22:11)
c Sacrifice (of Christ): vv. 10,12,14, 18; Heb. 11:4. (Gen. 3:15; Heb. 10:18, *note*)

11
d See Rom. 3:23, *note*

12
e Heb. 1:3
f Ps. 110:1

14
g Assurance/security: vv. 14, 16–18; 1 Pet. 1:5. (Ps. 23:1; Jude 1, *note*)
h v. 10

15
i Holy Spirit (NT): v. 15; Heb. 10:29. (Mt. 1:18; Acts 2:4, *note*)
j Inspiration: v. 15; Heb. 10:30. (Ex. 4:15; 2 Tim. 3:16, *note*)

16
k Jer. 31:33–34

19
l Heb. 4:16

20
m Jn. 14:6; Heb. 7:24–25
n Cp. Mt. 27:50–51

22
o Heb. 7:19
p Faith: v. 22; Heb. 10:38. (Gen. 3:20; Heb. 11:39, *note*)

23
q 1 Th. 5:24

25
r Or *encouraging.* Rom. 15:14
s Cp. Mt. 24:1–51
t Rom. 13:11

26
u Num. 15:30; cp. 2 Pet. 2:20–21
v Heb. 6:6

28
w Law (of Moses): v. 28; Jas. 2:10. (Ex. 19:1; Gal. 3:24, *note*)
x Dt. 17:6

29
y Cp. Heb. 2:3
z Apostasy: vv. 26–31, 38–39; 2 Pet. 2:15. (Lk. 18:8; 2 Tim. 3:1, *note*)

[1](10:18) Sacrifice, Summary: (1) The first intimation of sacrifice is at Gen. 3:21, the coats of skins having obviously come from slain animals. The first clear instance of sacrifice is in Gen. 4:4, explained in Heb. 11:4. Abel's righteousness was manifested by his sacrifice. His righteousness was not the result of his sacrifice but of his faith (11:4). (2) Before the giving of the law, the head of the family was the family priest. By the law an order of priests was established who alone could offer sacrifices. Those sacrifices were "shadows," types, expressing variously the guilt and need of the offerer in reference to God, and all pointing to Christ and fulfilled in Him. (3) As foreshadowed by the types and explained by the NT, the sacrifice of Christ is penal (Gal. 3:13; 2 Cor. 5:21); substitutionary (Lev. 1:4; Isa. 53:5–6; 2 Cor. 5:21; 1 Pet. 2:24); voluntary (Jn. 10:18); redemptive (Gal. 3:13; Eph. 1:7; cp. 1 Cor. 6:20); propitiatory (Rom. 3:25); reconciling (2 Cor. 5:18–19; Col. 1:21–22); efficacious (Jn. 12:32–33; Rom. 5:9–10; 2 Cor. 5:21; Eph. 2:13; Heb. 9:11–12,26; 10:10–17; 1 Jn. 1:7; Rev. 1:5); and revelatory (Jn. 3:16; Rom. 3:25–26; 1 Jn. 4:9–10).

and insulted the [a]Spirit of grace?

30 For we know Him who [b]said, [c]*"Vengeance is Mine, I will repay,"* says the Lord.* And again, *"The LORD will judge His people."*

31 It is a fearful thing to fall into the hands of the living God.

32 But recall the [d]former days in which, after you were illuminated, you endured a great struggle with sufferings: 33 partly while you were made a spectacle both by reproaches and tribulations, and partly while you became companions of those who were so treated; 34 for you had compassion on me* in my chains, and joyfully accepted the plundering of your goods, knowing [e]that you have a better and an enduring possession for yourselves in heaven.* 35 Therefore do not cast away your confidence, which has great reward. 36 For you have need of [f]endurance, so that after you have done the will of God, you may receive the promise:

37 *"For yet a little while,*
And He who is coming*
[g]will come and will
not [h]tarry.
38 *Now the* [i]just shall live*
by [j]faith;
But if anyone draws
back,
My soul has no pleasure
in him."

39 But we are not of those who draw back to perdition, but of those who believe to the saving of the soul.

The superiority of the way of faith

Sphere of faith

11 NOW [j]faith is the [k]substance of things hoped for, the [l]evidence of things [m]not seen. 2 For by it the elders obtained a good testimony.

3 By faith we understand that the [n]worlds were framed by the word of God, so that the things which are seen were not made of things which are visible.

Instances of faith: Abel

4 By faith [o]Abel offered to God a more excellent [p]sacrifice than Cain, through which he obtained witness that he was [q]righteous, God testifying of his gifts; and through it he being dead still [r]speaks.

Enoch

5 By faith [s]Enoch was taken away so that he did not see death, *"and was not found, because God had taken him"*; for before he was taken he had this testimony, that he pleased God. 6 But without [j]faith *it is* impossible to please *Him,* for he who comes to God must believe that He is, and *that* He is a [t]rewarder of those who diligently seek Him.

Noah

7 By faith [u]Noah, being divinely warned of things not yet seen, moved with godly fear, prepared an ark for the [v]saving of his household, by which he condemned the [w]world and became heir of the [x]righteousness which is according to faith.

Abraham and Sarah

8 By faith [y]Abraham obeyed when he was called to go out to the place which he would receive as an inheritance. And he went out, not knowing where he was going. 9 By faith he dwelt in the land of promise as *in* a foreign country, [z]dwelling in tents with Isaac and Jacob, the heirs with him of the same promise; 10 for he [aa]waited for the city which has [bb]foundations, whose builder and maker *is* God.

11 By faith [cc]Sarah herself also received strength to conceive seed, and she bore a child* when she was past the age, because she judged Him [dd]faithful who had promised. 12 Therefore from one man, and him as good as [ee]dead, were born *as many* as the [ff]stars of

---

29
a Holy Spirit (NT): v. 29; 1 Pet. 1:2. (Mt. 1:18; Acts 2:4, *note*)
30
b Inspiration: v. 30; 1 Pet. 1:11. (Ex. 4:15; 2 Tim. 3:16, *note*)
c Dt. 32:35–36
32
d Heb. 6:9–10
34
e Lit. *that you have in yourselves*
36
f Lk. 21:19; Heb. 12:1
37
g Christ (second advent): v. 37; Jas. 5:8. (Dt. 30:3; Acts 1:11, *note*)
h Rev. 22:20
38
i Hab. 2:3–4; Rom. 1:17; Gal. 3:11
j Faith: v. 38; 11:1–29; Heb. 11:30. (Gen. 3:20; Heb. 11:39, *note*)
CHAPTER 11
1
k Or *assurance*
l Lit. *conviction*
m Cp. Rom. 8:24
3
n Lit. *ages were planned*

4
o Gen. 4:3–5
p Sacrifice (typical): v. 4; Heb. 13:12. (Gen. 3:15; Heb. 10:18, *note*)
q vv. 4–7; see Rom. 10:10, *note*
r Heb. 12:24
5
s Gen. 5:22–24
6
t Rewards: v. 6; Jas. 1:12. (Dan. 12:3; 1 Cor. 3:14, *note*)
7
u Gen. 6:14–22
v See Rom. 1:16, *note*
w Gk. *kosmos.* See Mt. 4:8, *note*
x Cp. Rom. 4:13–24
8
y Gen. 12:1–4
9
z Gen. 13:3, 18
10
aa Heb. 13:14; cp. 12:22
bb Cp. Rev. 21:14
11
cc Gen. 21:1–2
dd Heb. 10:23
12
ee Rom. 4:19
ff Gen. 22:17

---

*
10:30 NU-Text omits *says the Lord.*
10:34 NU-Text reads *the prisoners* instead of *me in my chains.* • NU-Text omits *in heaven.* 10:37 Or *that which*
10:38 NU-Text reads *my just one.*
11:11 NU-Text omits *she bore a child.*

the sky in multitude—innumerable as the sand which is by the seashore.

13 These all died in faith, [a]not having received the [b]promises, but having [c]seen them afar off were assured of them,* embraced *them* and confessed that they were strangers and pilgrims on the earth.

14 For those who say such things declare plainly that they seek a homeland.

15 And truly if they had called to mind [d]that *country* from which they had come out, they would have had opportunity to [e]return.

16 But now they desire a better, that is, a heavenly *country.* Therefore God is not ashamed to be called their God, for He has [f]prepared a city for them.

17 By faith Abraham, [g]when he was [h]tested, offered up Isaac, and he who had received the promises offered up his only begotten *son,*

18 [i]of whom it was said, [j]*"In Isaac your seed shall be called,"*

19 concluding that God *was* able to [k]raise *him* up, even from the dead, from which he also received him in a [l]figurative sense.

Isaac

20 By faith [m]Isaac blessed Jacob and Esau concerning things to come.

Jacob

21 By faith [n]Jacob, when he was dying, blessed each of the sons of Joseph, and worshiped, [o]*leaning* on the top of his staff.

Joseph

22 By faith [p]Joseph, when he was dying, made mention of the departure of the children of Israel, and gave instructions concerning his bones.

The parents of Moses

23 By faith Moses, when he was born, was [q]hidden three months by his parents, because they saw *he was* a beautiful child; and they were not afraid of the king's [r]command.

13
a Heb. 11:39; cp. 10:36
b v. 39; Gen. 12:7
c Cp. Jn. 8:56
15
d Gen. 11:31
e Cp. Gen. 24:6–8; Heb. 10:38–39
16
f Jn. 14:2; Rev. 21:2
17
g Gen. 22:1–14; Jas. 2:21
h Test/tempt: v. 17; Heb. 11:37. (Gen. 3:1; Jas. 1:14, *note*)
18
i Or *to*
j Gen. 21:12
19
k Resurrection: v. 19; Heb. 11:35. (2 Ki. 4:35; 1 Cor. 15:52, *note*)
l Cp. Heb. 9:9
20
m Gen. 27:26–40
21
n Gen. 48:1–22
o Cp. Gen. 47:31
22
p Gen. 50:24–25
23
q Ex. 2:1–3
r Ex. 1:16

Moses

24 By faith [s]Moses, when he became of age, refused to be called the son of Pharaoh's daughter,

25 choosing rather to suffer affliction [t]with the people of God than to enjoy the passing pleasures of [u]sin,

26 esteeming the reproach of Christ greater riches than the treasures in* Egypt; for he looked to the [v]reward.

27 By faith he forsook Egypt, not fearing the wrath of the king; for he endured as seeing Him who is invisible.

28 By faith he kept the [w]Passover and the sprinkling of blood, lest he who destroyed the firstborn should touch them.

29 By faith [x]they passed through the Red Sea as by dry *land, whereas* the Egyptians, attempting *to do* so, were drowned.

Joshua and Israel

30 By [y]faith the [z]walls of Jericho fell down after they were encircled for seven days.

Rahab

31 By faith the harlot [aa]Rahab did not perish with those who did not believe, when she had received the spies with peace.

The many heroes of faith

32 And what more shall I say? For the time would fail me to tell of [bb]Gideon and [cc]Barak and [dd]Samson and [ee]Jephthah, also *of* [ff]David and [gg]Samuel and the prophets:

33 who through faith subdued kingdoms, worked [hh]righteousness, obtained promises, [ii]stopped the mouths of lions,

34 [jj]quenched the violence of fire, escaped the edge of the sword, out of weakness were made strong, became valiant in battle, turned to flight the armies of the aliens.

35 Women [kk]received their dead raised to life again. [1]Others were tortured, not [ll]accept-

24
s Ex. 2:11–15
25
t Separation: v. 25; Heb. 13:14. (Gen. 12:1; 2 Cor. 6:17, *note*)
u See Rom. 3:23, *note*
26
v Rom. 8:18; 2 Cor. 4:17
28
w Ex. 12:1–51
29
x Ex. 14:13–31; Jude 5
30
y Faith: vv. 1–40; Heb. 12:2. (Gen. 3:20; Heb. 11:39, *note*)
z Josh. 6:1–20
31
aa Josh. 2:1–21; 6:23; Jas. 2:25
32
bb Jud. 6:11; 7:1–25
cc Jud. 4:6–24
dd Jud. 13:24–16:31
ee Jud. 11:1–29; 12:1–7
ff 1 Sam. 16–17
gg 1 Sam. 7:9–14
33
hh See 1 Jn. 3:7, *note*
ii Dan. 6:22
34
jj Dan. 3:23–28
35
kk 1 Ki. 17:22; 2 Ki. 4:35–37
ll vv. 24–26

*

11:13 NU-Text and M-Text omit *were assured of them.* **11:26** NU-Text and M-Text read *of.*

[1](11:35) Observe that not all the heroes of faith saw their faith issue in physical triumph over

ing deliverance, that they might
obtain a better [a]resurrection.
36 Still others had trial of
mockings and scourgings, yes,
and of chains and imprisonment.
37 They were [b]stoned, they
were [1]sawn in two, were
[c]tempted,* were slain with the
sword. They wandered about in
sheepskins and goatskins, being destitute, afflicted, [d]tor-
mented—
38 of whom the [e]world was
not worthy. They wandered in
deserts and mountains, *in* dens
and caves of the earth.
39 And all these, having
obtained a good testimony
through [2]faith, did [f]not receive
the promise,
40 God having provided
something better for us, that
they should not be made [g]per-
fect [h]apart from us.

The worship and walk of the believer-priest

(1) Jesus is the perfect example

12 THEREFORE we also,
since we are surrounded
by so great a cloud of witnesses,
let [i]us lay aside every weight,
and the sin which so easily ensnares *us,* and let us [j]run with
[k]endurance the race that is set
before us,
2 looking unto Jesus, the
[l]author and [m]finisher of *our*
[n]faith, who for the joy that was
set before Him [o]endured the
cross, despising the shame, and
has sat down at the right hand
of the throne of God.

Parenthetic, to v. 17

(a) The Father's chastening

3 For [p]consider Him who
endured such hostility from
[q]sinners against Himself, lest
you become [r]weary and discouraged in your souls.
4 You have not yet resisted
to bloodshed, striving against
[q]sin.
5 And you have forgotten
the exhortation which speaks to
you as to sons:

"My son, do not despise
the chastening of the
[s]LORD,
Nor be discouraged
when you are rebuked
by Him;
6 *For whom the LORD loves*
He [t]chastens,
And scourges every son
whom He receives."

7 If* you endure chasten-
ing, God deals with you as with
[u]sons; for what [v]son is there
whom a father does not chasten?
8 But if you are without
chastening, of which [w]all have
become partakers, then you are
illegitimate and not sons.
9 Furthermore, we have had
human fathers who corrected
us, and we paid *them* respect.
Shall we not much more readily
be in subjection to the Father of
spirits and live?
10 For they indeed for a few
days chastened *us* as seemed
best to them, but He for *our*

*11:37 NU-Text omits *were tempted.*
12:7 NU-Text and M-Text read *It is for discipline that you endure; God.*

35 *a Resurrection:* v. 35; 1 Pet. 1:3. (2 Ki. 4:35; 1 Cor. 15:52, *note*)
37 *b* 2 Chr. 24:21
c Test/tempt: vv. 36–37; Jas. 1:2. (Gen. 3:1; Jas. 1:14, *note*)
d Lit. *ill-treated*
38 *e* Gk. *kosmos.* See Mt. 4:8, *note*
39 *f* Heb. 11:13; cp. 10:36
40 *g* See Mt. 5:48, *note*
h Cp. Rev. 6:11
CHAPTER 12
1 *i* Heb. 10:39
j Cp. 1 Cor. 9:24
k Heb. 10:36
2 *l* Cp. Heb. 2:10, *marg.*
m Lit. *perfecter*
n Faith: v. 2; Jas. 2:17. (Gen. 3:20; Heb. 11:39, *note*)
o Phil. 2:8
3 *p* i.e. *think about and weigh His worth.* Cp. Mt. 10:24
q See Rom. 3:23, *note*
r Cp. Gal. 6:9; Rev. 2:3
5 *s* vv. 5–6; Prov. 3:11–12
6 *t* Rev. 3:19
7 *u* Dt. 8:5; 2 Sam. 7:14
v Prov. 13:24
8 *w* Cp. 1 Pet. 5:9

---

the immediate circumstances of life. Some by faith subdued kingdoms and escaped the edge of the sword; others through faith (v. 33) were tortured and slain with the sword. "All these . . . obtained a good testimony through faith" (v. 39).

[1](11:37) According to an ancient Jewish tradition the Prophet Isaiah was sawn in two by the servants of King Manasseh.

[2](11:39) Faith, Summary: The essence of faith consists in believing and receiving what God has revealed, and may be defined as that trust in the God of the Scriptures and in Jesus Christ whom He has sent, which receives Him as Lord and Savior and impels to loving obedience and good works (Jn. 1:12; Jas. 2:14–26). The particular uses of faith give rise to its secondary definitions: (1) For salvation, faith is personal trust, apart from meritorious works, in the Lord Jesus Christ as delivered because of our offenses and raised again because of our justification (Rom. 4:5,23–25; 5:1). (2) As used in prayer, faith is the "confidence that we have in Him, that if we ask anything according to His will, He hears us" (1 Jn. 5:14–15). (3) As used in reference to unseen things of which Scripture speaks, faith gives substance to them, so that we act upon the conviction of their reality (Heb. 11:1–3). And (4) as a working principle in life, the uses of faith are illustrated in this chapter.

profit, that *we* may be partakers of His holiness.

11 Now no chastening seems to be joyful for the present, but [a]painful; nevertheless, afterward it yields the peaceable fruit of [b]righteousness to those who have been trained by it.

12 Therefore [c]strengthen the hands which hang down, and the feeble knees,

13 and make straight paths for your feet, so that what is lame may not be *dislocated,* but [d]rather be healed.

14 Pursue [e]peace with all *people,* and holiness, without which no one will see the Lord:

15 looking carefully lest anyone [f]fall short of the [g]grace of God; lest any [h]root of bitterness springing up cause trouble, and by this many become defiled;

(b) Esau a warning to professing Christians. (See Gen. 25:25,31, notes; Gen. 27:38)

16 lest there *be* any [i]fornicator or profane person like Esau, [j]who for one morsel of food sold his birthright.

17 For you know that afterward, when he wanted to inherit the blessing, he was [k]rejected, for he found no place for [l]repentance, though he sought [m]it diligently with tears.

(2) The believer-priest does not come to Mt. Sinai (the law) but to Mt. Zion (the Gospel)

18 For you have [n]not come to the [o]mountain that* may be touched and that burned with fire, and to blackness and darkness* and tempest,

19 and the sound of a trumpet and the voice of words, so that those who heard [p]*it* begged that the word should not be spoken to them anymore.

20 (For they could not endure what was commanded: *"And if so much as a beast touches the mountain, it shall be stoned* or shot with an arrow."**

21 And so terrifying was the sight *that* Moses said, *"I am exceedingly afraid* and trembling."*)

22 But you have come to Mount Zion and to the [q]city of the living God, the heavenly Jerusalem, to an innumerable company of [r]angels,

23 to the general assembly [s]and [1]church of the firstborn *who are* registered in heaven, to God the Judge of all, to the spirits of just men made [t]perfect,

24 to Jesus the [u]Mediator of the new [v]covenant, and to [w]the blood of [x]sprinkling that speaks better things than *that of* [y]Abel.

(3) Warnings and instructions: "God is a consuming fire"

25 [z]See that you do not refuse Him who speaks. For [aa]if they did not escape who refused Him who spoke on earth, much more *shall we not escape* if we turn away from Him who *speaks* from heaven,

26 whose voice then shook the earth; but now He has promised, saying, [bb]*"Yet once more I shake* not only the* [cc]*earth, but also heaven."*

27 Now this, *"Yet once more,"* indicates the [dd]removal of those things that are being shaken, as of things that are made, that the things which cannot be shaken may remain.

28 Therefore, since we are receiving a kingdom which cannot be shaken, let us have [ee]grace, by which we may* [ff]serve God acceptably with reverence and godly fear.

29 For our God *is* a consuming fire.

*
12:18 NU-Text reads *to that which.* • NU-Text reads *gloom.* **12:20** NU-Text and M-Text omit the rest of this verse. • Exodus 19:12–13 **12:21** Deuteronomy 9:19 **12:26** NU-Text reads *will shake.* **12:28** M-Text omits *may.*

11
a Cp. 1 Pet. 1:6
b See 1 Jn. 3:7, *note*
12
c Isa. 35:3
13
d Cp. Gal. 6:1
14
e Ps. 34:14
15
f Heb. 4:1
g *Grace:* v. 15; Jas. 4:6. (Jn. 1:14; Jn. 1:17, *note*)
h Dt. 29:18
16
i 1 Cor. 6:13–18
j Gen. 25:33
17
k Gen. 27:30–37
l *Repentance:* v. 17; 2 Pet. 3:9. (Mt. 3:2; Acts 17:30, *note*)
m i.e. *the blessing*
18
n Cp. 2 Cor. 3:7–13
o Ex. 19:12
19
p Ex. 20:18–26

22
q Cp. Eph. 2:19; Phil. 3:20
r See Heb. 1:4, *note*
23
s *Church* (the true): v. 23. (Mt. 16:18; Heb. 12:23)
t See Phil. 3:12, *note*
24
u Heb. 8:6
v Or *testament. Covenant* (new): v. 24; Heb. 13:20. (Isa. 61:8; Heb. 8:8, *note*)
w Ex. 24:8
x Cp. Heb. 10:22
y Heb. 11:4
25
z Cp. Acts 13:46
aa Cp. Heb. 2:2–4
26
bb Hag. 2:6
cc Cp. Ex. 19:18
27
dd Isa. 65:17
28
ee See 2 Pet. 3:18, *note*
ff Heb. 13:15

[1](12:23) Church (true), Summary: The Church, composed of the whole number of regenerate persons from Pentecost to the first resurrection (1 Cor. 15:52), united together and to Christ by the baptism with the Holy Spirit (1 Cor. 12:12–13), is the body of Christ of which He is the Head (Eph. 1:22–23). As such the Church is a holy temple for the dwelling of God through the Spirit (Eph. 2:21–22); is "one flesh" with Christ (Eph. 5:30–31); is betrothed to Him as a chaste virgin to one husband (2 Cor. 11:2–4); and will be translated to heaven at the return of the Lord in the air (1 Th. 4:13–17).

(4) The changeless Christ

13 LET brotherly love continue.

2 Do not forget to [a]entertain strangers, for by so *doing* some have [b]unwittingly entertained [c]angels.

3 Remember the [d]prisoners as if chained with them—those who are mistreated—since you yourselves are in the body also.

4 [e]Marriage *is* honorable among all, and the bed undefiled; but fornicators and adulterers God will judge.

5 *Let your* conduct *be* without [f]covetousness; *be* [g]content with such things as you have. For He Himself has [h]said, *"I will never leave you nor forsake you."**

6 So we may boldly say:

> [i]*"The LORD is my helper;*
> *I will not fear.*
> *What can man do to*
> *me?"*

7 Remember [j]those who rule over you, who have spoken the word of God to you, whose faith follow, considering the outcome of *their* conduct.

8 Jesus Christ *is* the [k]same yesterday, today, and forever.

9 Do not be carried about* with various and strange [l]doctrines. For *it is* good that the heart be established by [m]grace, not with [n]foods which have not profited those who have been occupied with them.

(5) Christian separation and worship

10 We have an [o]altar from which those who serve the tabernacle have no right to eat.

11 For the bodies of those animals, whose blood is brought into the sanctuary by the high priest for sin, are burned [p]outside the camp.

12 Therefore Jesus also, that He might [q]sanctify the people [r]with His own blood, suffered [p]outside the gate.

13 Therefore let us go forth to Him, [p]outside the camp, [s]bearing His reproach.

14 For here we have no [t]continuing city, but [u]we [v]seek the one to come.

(6) The believer-priest's sacrifice

15 Therefore by Him let us continually offer the [w]sacrifice of [x]praise to God, that is, the fruit of *our* lips, giving thanks to His name.

16 But do not forget to do good and to [y]share, for with [z]such sacrifices God is well pleased.

(7) The believer-priest's obedience

17 Obey [j]those who rule over you, and be submissive, for they [aa]watch out for your souls, as those who must give account. Let them do so with joy and not with grief, for that would be unprofitable for you.

18 Pray for us; for we are confident that we have a [bb]good conscience, in all things desiring to live honorably.

19 But I especially urge *you* to do this, that I may be restored to you the sooner.

Conclusion: Benediction and Greetings, 13:20–25

20 Now may the [cc]God of peace who brought up our Lord Jesus [dd]from the dead, that great [ee]Shepherd of the sheep, through the [ff]blood of the [gg]everlasting [hh]covenant,

21 make you [ii]complete in every good work to do His will, [jj]working in you* what is well pleasing in His sight, through Jesus Christ, to whom *be* glory forever and ever. Amen.

22 And I appeal to you, brethren, bear with the word of exhortation, for I have written to you in few words.

23 Know that *our* brother Timothy has been set free, with whom I shall see you if he comes shortly.

24 Greet all [j]those who rule over you, and all the saints. Those from Italy greet you.

25 Grace *be* with you all. Amen.

---

*
13:5 Deuteronomy 31:8; Joshua 1:5
13:9 NU-Text and M-Text read *away*.
13:21 NU-Text and M-Text read *us*.

CHAPTER 13

2
a Rom. 12:13
b Gen. 18:1–22
c See Heb. 1:4, *note*

3
d Mt. 25:36

4
e Prov. 5:18–19

5
f Lit. *love of money*
g Cp. Phil. 4:11
h Dt. 31:6

6
i Ps. 118:6

7
j Lit. *your leaders*

8
k Heb. 1:12

9
l Or *teachings*. Eph. 4:14
m See 2 Pet. 3:18, *note*
n Rom. 14:17

10
o Cp. 1 Cor. 10:18,21

11
p Cp. Jn. 19:17

12
q *Sanctification* (NT): v. 12; 1 Pet. 1:15. (Mt. 4:5; Rev. 22:11)
r *Sacrifice* (of Christ): v. 12; 1 Pet. 1:19. (Gen. 3:15; Heb. 10:18, *note*)

13
s Cp. Acts 5:41

14
t Or *lasting*. Cp. Heb. 10:34
u Cp. Heb. 11:10
v *Separation:* v. 14; 2 Jn. 10. (Gen. 12:1; 2 Cor. 6:17, *note*)

15
w *Sacrifice* (the believer-priest's); see Heb. 10:18, *note*
x Cp. Jer. 33:11

16
y Gal. 6:6
z Phil. 4:18

17
aa Cp. Ezek. 3:17

18
bb Cp. Acts 24:16

20
cc Rom. 5:1–2,10
dd Lit. *from among*
ee Jn. 10:11; 1 Pet. 5:4
ff Zech. 9:11; Heb. 10:29
gg Lit. *eternal*
hh *Covenant* (New): v. 20. (Isa. 61:8; Heb. 8:8, *note*)

21
ii See Phil. 3:12, *note*
jj Phil. 2:13

The General Epistles

THE SEVEN LETTERS—James; 1 and 2 Peter; 1, 2, and 3 John; and Jude—have been known, since the fourth century, as the Catholic or General Epistles. The designation refers to the fact that, unlike the Pauline Epistles, they are not addressed to particular churches or to individuals but rather to a wider circle and even to the Church as a whole. The earliest designation of these letters was the word "catholic" used in the sense of "universal"; "general" is a more recent term for this group of Epistles.

Some have objected that James, 1 Peter, and 2 and 3 John are not true "general" Epistles, because the direction of their teaching is too restricted. However, James, which is addressed to the Jewish Dispersion ("the twelve tribes which are scattered abroad"), is probably one of the very earliest NT books, having been written before Paul's missionary work was completed and at a time when the Church was still made up largely of Hebrew Christians. It is, therefore, validly described as a "general" Epistle. Likewise, 1 Peter, addressed to the "pilgrims" dispersed throughout five areas (Pontus, Galatia, Cappadocia, Asia, and Bithynia), is also of a "general" nature. As for 2 and 3 John, these briefest of Epistles, while addressed to individuals, are so closely related to 1 John in style and content that they may be considered appendixes to it.

Doctrinally, the General Epistles stand in relation to the Pauline Epistles as the Gospel of John does to the Synoptics—i.e. the General Epistles supplement Paul's teaching but do not conflict with it. For example, James's exposition of justification by works (Jas. 2:14–26) complements Paul's teaching of justification by faith; and Peter's teaching about "the last days" and the coming of the Lord supplements that of Paul.

The function, then, of the General Epistles may be said to round out NT doctrine by adding to the great Pauline exposition of Christianity. To state it in another way, Paul sets forth Christianity primarily for the Gentiles, while James presents it for the Jews; Peter represents a bridge between Paul and James; and John, in his Epistles, gives the universal aspect of Christianity. Paul may be thought of as the apostle of faith; James, as the apostle of works; Peter, as the apostle of hope; John, as the apostle of love; and Jude, as the apostle of the defense of the faith. Finally, in the interrelationship of the General Epistles, James and 1 Peter; 2 Peter and Jude; and the three Epistles of John have much in common.

The Epistle of

JAMES

Author: James *Theme:* Practical Christian Living *Date of writing:* A.D. 45–50

THE EPISTLE OF JAMES was written by James, the half brother of the Lord (see Mt. 4:21, *note* for the other three men in the NT named James). As head of the first Christian church, that at Jerusalem, James was a man of great authority (Acts 12:17; 15:13–29; 21:17–18). He was evidently converted by the risen Lord (1 Cor. 15:7). He writes to "the twelve tribes which are scattered abroad" (v. 1), i.e. the Christian Jews dispersed throughout the Roman Empire. The Epistle is probably one of the earliest NT books.

With its stress upon practical Christian living, the Epistle of James reflects, in its style and in its frequent references to the Sermon on the Mount, the mind and teaching of its writer's divine Brother. Although its emphasis is not theological, the Epistle is notable for moral and ethical teaching of timeless relevance for the Church. Moreover, Christ's coming again is twice referred to (5:7,8) and the new birth is clearly implied (1:18,21).

The local background of the Epistle is seen in such passages as 2:1–13; 4:1–11. James's central theme is religion (Gk. *thrēskeia*) in the high sense of devoted service for others as the outcome and proof of faith. His discussion of justification (2:14–26) does not contradict Paul's teaching on this doctrine but complements it from the practical point of view.

The book does not yield to strict analysis. It is a series of didactic sayings clustered round certain recurring themes (cp. Proverbs and Ecclesiastes). James's language is forceful and often eloquent. He gives several vivid pictures of life in the early church (e.g. 2:1–4; 5:1–6,14–16).

The Epistle may be divided as follows:

Introduction, 1:1.
I. Testing of Faith, 1:2—2:26.
II. Reality of Faith Tested by Control of the Tongue, 3.
III. Rebuke of Worldliness, 4.
IV. Rich Warned, 5:1–6.
V. Exhortations in View of the Coming of the Lord, 5:7–18.
Conclusion, 5:19–20.

Introduction, 1:1

1 JAMES, a [a]bondservant of
God and of the Lord Jesus
Christ,

To the twelve tribes which
are [b]scattered abroad:

Greetings.

I. Testing of Faith, 1:2—2:26

(1) Purpose of testing

2 My brethren, count it all
joy when you fall into various
[c]trials,
3 [d]knowing that the testing
of your faith produces patience.
4 But let patience have *its*
[e]perfect work, that you may be
perfect and complete, lacking
nothing.
5 If any of you lacks wisdom, let him ask of God, [f]who
gives to all liberally and without
reproach, and it will be given to
him.
6 [g]But let him ask in faith,
with no doubting, for he who
doubts is like a wave of the sea
driven and tossed by the wind.
7 For let not that man suppose that he will receive anything from the Lord;
8 *he is* a [h]double-minded
man, unstable in all his ways.
9 [i]Let the lowly brother
glory in his exaltation,
10 but the rich [j]in his humiliation, because as a flower of the
field he will pass away.
11 For no sooner has the sun
risen with a burning heat than it
withers the grass; its flower
falls, and its beautiful appearance perishes. So the rich man
also will fade away in his pur-
suits.
12 Blessed *is* the man who
[k]endures [c]temptation; for
when he has been approved, he
will receive the [l]crown of [m]life
which the Lord has promised to
those who love Him.

(2) Solicitation to evil not of God

13 Let no one say when he is
tempted, "I am tempted by
God"; for God cannot be
tempted by evil, nor does He
Himself tempt anyone.

CHAPTER 1

1
a Or *slave*
b Lit. *in the dispersion.* 1 Pet. 1:1
2
c Test/tempt: vv. 2–3, 12–14; 1 Pet. 1:6. (Gen. 3:1; Jas. 1:14, *note*)
3
d Rom. 5:3–5
4
e i.e. *mature and complete.* See Mt. 5:48, *note*
5
f Prov. 2:3–6
6
g Mk. 11:24
8
h Cp. Prov. 3:5–6
9
i Cp. Jas. 2:5
10
j Cp. Isa. 57:15
12
k Heb. 10:36; Jas. 5:11
l Rewards: v. 12; 1 Pet. 5:4. (Dan. 12:3; 1 Cor. 3:14, *note*)
m Life (eternal): v. 12; 1 Pet. 3:7. (Mt. 7:14; Rev. 22:19)

14 But each one is [1]tempted when he is drawn away by his own desires and enticed.

15 Then, when desire has [a]conceived, it gives birth to [b]sin; and sin, when it is full-grown, [c]brings forth [d]death.

16 Do not be deceived, my beloved brethren.

17 Every good [2]gift and every perfect gift is from [e]above, and comes down from the Father of lights, with whom there is no variation or shadow of turning.

18 [f]Of His own will He brought us forth by the [g]word of truth, that we might be a kind of [h]firstfruits of His creatures.

19 So then,* my beloved brethren, let every man be swift to hear, slow to speak, [i]slow to wrath;

20 for the wrath of man does not produce the [j]righteousness of God.

21 Therefore lay aside all filthiness and overflow of wickedness, and receive with meekness the implanted word, which is able to [k]save your souls.

(3) Test of obedience

22 But be [l]doers of the word, and not hearers only, deceiving yourselves.

23 For if anyone is a hearer of the word and not a doer, he is like a man observing his natural face in a mirror;

24 for he observes himself, goes away, and immediately forgets what kind of man he was.

25 But he who [m]looks into the perfect [n]law of liberty and continues *in it,* and is not a forgetful hearer but a doer of the work, this one will be blessed in what he does.

(4) Test of true religion

26 If anyone among you* thinks he is [o]religious, and does not bridle his [p]tongue but deceives his own heart, this one's [o]religion *is* useless.

27 [q]Pure and undefiled [o]religion before God and the Father is this: to visit orphans and [r]widows in their trouble, *and* to keep oneself unspotted from the [s]world.

(5) Test of brotherly love

2 MY brethren, do not hold the faith of our Lord Jesus Christ, *the Lord* of glory, with [3]partiality.

2 For if there should come into your assembly a man with gold rings, in fine apparel, and there should also come in a poor man in filthy clothes,

3 and you pay attention to the one wearing the fine clothes and say to him, "You sit here in a good place," and say to the poor man, "You stand there," or, "Sit here at my footstool,"

4 have you not shown partiality among yourselves, and become judges with evil thoughts?

5 Listen, my beloved brethren: [t]Has God not [u]chosen the poor of this [v]world *to be* [w]rich in faith and heirs of the [x]kingdom which He promised to those who love Him?

6 But you have dishonored the poor man. Do not the rich oppress you and drag you into the courts?

7 Do they not blaspheme that [y]noble name by which you are [z]called?

* **1:19** NU-Text reads *Know (this)* or *(This) you know.* **1:26** NU-Text omits *among you.*

15
a Ps. 7:14
b See Rom. 3:23, *note*
c Rom. 6:23
d *Death* (spiritual): v. 15; Rev. 20:12. (Gen. 2:17; Eph. 2:5, *note*)
17
e Cp. Jas. 3:15–17
18
f Jn. 1:13
g 1 Th. 2:13; 1 Pet. 1:23
h Cp. Rev. 14:4
19
i Prov. 16:32
20
j See Rom. 3:21, *note*
21
k See Rom. 1:16, *note*
22
l Mt. 7:21–28
25
m Cp. 2 Cor. 3:18
n 2:12

26
o i.e. *one who is outwardly religious.* See Gal. 1:14, *note*
p Ps. 34:13
27
q Mt. 25:34–36
r Cp. Dt. 14:29
s Gk. *kosmos.* See Rev. 13:8, *note*
CHAPTER 2
5
t 1 Cor. 1:26–28
u *Election* (corporate): v. 5; 1 Pet. 1:2. (Dt. 7:6; 1 Pet. 5:13, *note*)
v Gk. *kosmos.* See Mt. 4:8, *note*
w 1 Tim. 6:18; cp. Lk. 12:21
x *Kingdom* (NT): v. 5; Rev. 3:21. (Mt. 2:2; 1 Cor. 15:24, *note*)
7
y Or *honorable*
z Acts 11:26; 1 Pet. 4:16

[1](1:14) The concept of testing or temptation is expressed in both the OT and NT not only by the words translated "test" or "tempt," but also by the words rendered "provoke," "snare," "trials," etc. (e.g. Gen. 22:1; Ps. 7:9; 11:5; Lk. 22:28; Jas. 1:2; 1 Pet. 1:6; cp. Job 31:27; Prov. 22:25; Isa. 3:8.) The primary meaning is usually that of *proving by testing,* or *testing under trial.* Less frequently the sense is that of enticement or solicitation to evil (e.g. 1:13–14; Gen. 3:1–6; 2 Cor. 11:3–4).

[2](1:17) Two words are used in the Greek for "gift": the first in v. 17 is *dosis,* denoting *the act of giving;* the second, *dōrēma,* meaning *the thing given, the gift.*

[3](2:1) This verse contains a very strong affirmation of the Deity of the Lord Jesus Christ. It may be translated: ". . . our Lord Jesus Christ, of glory." The use of the title "Lord," and the association of our Lord with the glory of God, the Shekinah, make clear James's witness to the Lord's Deity. Furthermore, the reference to partiality indicates that all earthly distinctions disappear in the presence of Christ, the Glorious One.

8 If you really fulfill *the*
royal [a]law according to the
Scripture, [b]*"You shall love your*
neighbor as yourself," you do
well;
9 but [c]if you show partiality, you commit [d]sin, and are
convicted by the law as [e]trans-
gressors.
10 For whoever shall keep
the whole [f]law, and yet [g]stum-
ble in one *point,* he is guilty of
all.
11 For He who said, [h]*"Do not*
*commit adultery,"** also said,
*"Do not murder."** Now if you
do not commit adultery, but you
do murder, you have become a
[d]transgressor of the law.
12 So speak and so do as
those who will be judged by the
[i]law of liberty.
13 For judgment is without
mercy to the one who has
shown [j]no [k]mercy. Mercy triumphs over judgment.

(6) Test of good works

14 What *does it* profit, my
brethren, if someone says he
has faith but does not have
[l]works? Can [m]faith [n]save him?
15 If a brother or sister is naked and destitute of daily food,
16 and [o]one of you says to
them, "Depart in peace, be
warmed and filled," but you do
not give them the [p]things which
are needed for the body, what
does it profit?
17 Thus also [q]faith by itself,
if it does not have works, is
[r]dead.
18 But someone will say,
"You have faith, and I have
works." [s]Show me your faith
without your* works, and I will
show you my faith by my*
[t]works.
19 You believe that [u]there is
one God. You do well. Even the
[v]demons believe—and tremble!
20 But do you want to know,
O foolish man, that [w]faith without works is dead?*

(7) Abraham as an illustration
(cp. Rom. 4:1–25)

21 Was not Abraham our father [x]justified by works when
he offered Isaac his son on the
[y]altar?
22 Do you see that faith was
working together with his
works, and by [z]works faith was
made [aa]perfect?
23 And the Scripture was fulfilled which says, *"Abraham*
[bb]*believed God, and it was* [1cc]*ac-*
counted to him for [dd]*righteous-*
ness." And he was called the
[ee]friend of God.
24 You see then that a man is
justified by works, and not by
faith only.
25 Likewise, was not [ff]Rahab
the harlot also [x]justified by
works when she received the
messengers and sent *them* out
another way?
26 For as the body without
the spirit is dead, [gg]so faith without works is [2]dead also.

*
2:11 Deuteronomy 5:18 • Deuteronomy 5:17 2:18 NU-Text omits *your.* • NU-Text omits *my.* 2:20 NU-Text reads *useless.*

8
a Law (of Christ): v. 8; 1 Pet. 1:22. (Jn. 13:34; 2 Jn. 5)
b Lev. 19:18
9
c v. 1
d See Rom. 3:23, *note*
e Lev. 19:15; Dt. 1:17
10
f Law (of Moses): v. 10; Rev. 12:17. (Ex. 19:1; Gal. 3:24, *note*)
g Gal. 3:10; cp. Mt. 5:19
11
h Ex. 20:13–14
12
i Jas. 1:25; cp. 1 Pet. 2:16
13
j Prov. 21:13; Mt. 18:32–35
k Mic. 7:18; Mt. 5:7
14
l Mt. 7:21–23; 21:28–32
m i.e. *Can that faith save him?*
n See Rom. 1:16, *note*
16
o Cp. 1 Jn. 3:18
p Lk. 3:11
17
q Faith: vv. 17–23; Jas. 5:15. (Gen. 3:20; Heb. 11:39, *note*)
r v. 26; cp. Jn. 15:2
18
s Col. 1:6; 1 Th. 1:3; Heb. 6:10
t Gal. 5:6
19
u Or *God is one*
v Mt. 8:29; Mk. 1:24; cp. Acts 16:17; 19:15
20
w vv. 17,26
21
x Justification: vv. 21, 25. (Lk. 18:14; Rom. 3:28, *note*)
y Gen. 22:9
22
z Jn. 8:39
aa See Phil. 3:12, *note*
23
bb Gen. 15:6
cc Imputation: v. 23. (Gen. 15:6; Jas. 2:23)
dd See Rom. 3:21, *note*
ee 2 Chr. 20:7; Isa 41:8
25
ff Josh. 2:1–21; 6:25; Heb. 11:31
26
gg vv. 17,20

[1](2:23) Sometimes called "imputation," this is the act of God whereby He accounts righteousness to the believer in Christ, who has borne the believer's sins in vindication of the law. See Phile. 18, *note.*

[2](2:26) On the basis of this passage (2:14–26), James has been charged with contradicting the doctrine of justification by faith as set forth by Paul (see Rom. 4:1–5). But the supposed contradiction is merely in words rather than in underlying truth. James in this passage uses the word "faith" in the sense of intellectual orthodoxy (cp. v. 19); Paul, when he uses "faith" in a personal sense, means trust in the atoning work of Christ to the extent of full commitment to Him. For James the word "works" means the believer's works, the outward evidence of a saved life. On the other hand, Paul sometimes employs "works" to denote the deeds of the unsaved man whereby he vainly hopes to gain acceptance with God, while at other times he speaks of "good works," by which he means the fruit that the justified man must produce. Moreover, the word "justify" is for Paul a legal, positional term (see Rom. 3:28, *note*) describing a once-for-all act of God appropriated by faith alone and relating to the initial moment of the Christian life. But for James "justify" is employed of any subsequent moment of the Christian life and proves the reality of a man's faith before his fellow men.

Thus in their views of justification Paul and James complement one another (2:23); Paul stresses acceptance with God wholly by grace through faith, whereas James presents the continual evidence before men of the initial transaction. For the definitive NT statement on

II. Reality of Faith Tested by Control of the Tongue, 3

3 MY brethren, let not many of you become teachers, knowing that we shall receive a stricter judgment.

2 For we all stumble in many things. If anyone does not stumble in word, he *is* a [a]perfect man, able also to bridle the whole body.

3 Indeed,* we put [b]bits in horses' mouths that they may obey us, and we turn their whole body.

4 Look also at ships: although they are so large and are driven by fierce winds, they are turned by a very small rudder wherever the pilot desires.

5 Even so the [c]tongue is a little member and boasts great things. See how great a forest a little fire kindles!

6 [d]And the tongue *is* a fire, a world of iniquity. The tongue is so set among our members that it [e]defiles the whole body, and [f]sets on fire the course of nature; and it is set on fire by [g]hell.

7 For every kind of beast and bird, of reptile and creature of the sea, is tamed and has been tamed by mankind.

8 But no man can tame the tongue. *It is* an unruly evil, [h]full of deadly poison.

9 With it we bless our God and Father, and with it we curse men, who have been made [i]in the similitude of God.

10 Out of the same mouth proceed blessing and cursing. My brethren, these things ought not to be so.

11 Does a spring send forth fresh *water* and bitter from the same opening?

12 Can a [j]fig tree, my brethren, bear olives, or a grapevine bear figs? Thus no spring yields both salt water and fresh.*

13 Who *is* wise and understanding among you? Let him show by good conduct *that* his works *are done* in the meekness of wisdom.

14 But if you have bitter envy and self-seeking in your hearts, do not boast and lie against the truth.

15 [k]This wisdom does not descend from above, but *is* earthly, sensual, demonic.

16 For where envy and self-seeking *exist,* confusion and every evil thing *are* there.

17 But the [l]wisdom that is from above is first pure, then peaceable, gentle, willing to yield, full of mercy and good fruits, [m]without partiality and [n]without hypocrisy.

18 Now the fruit of [o]righteousness is sown in peace [p]by those who make peace.

III. Rebuke of Worldliness, 4

4 WHERE do wars and fights *come* from among you? Do *they* not *come* from your *desires for* pleasure [q]that war in your members?

2 You lust and do not have. You [r]murder and covet and cannot obtain. You fight and war. Yet* you do not have because you do not ask.

3 You ask and do not receive, [s]because you ask amiss, that you may spend *it* on your pleasures.

4 Adulterers and* adulteresses! Do you not know that [t]friendship with the [u]world is enmity with God? [v]Whoever therefore wants to be a friend of the world makes himself an enemy of God.

5 Or do you think that the Scripture says in vain, "The Spirit who dwells in us yearns jealously"?

6 But He gives more [w]grace. Therefore He says:

> [x]*"God resists the proud,*
> *But gives grace to the*
> *humble."*

7 Therefore submit to God. Resist the [y]devil and he will [z]flee from you.

8 [aa]Draw near to God and He will draw near to you. Cleanse *your* hands, *you* [bb]sin-

*

3:3 NU-Text reads *Now if.* 3:12 NU-Text reads *Neither can a salty spring produce fresh water.* 4:2 NU-Text and M-Text omit *Yet.* 4:4 NU-Text omits *Adulterers and.*

CHAPTER 3
2
a See Phil. 3:12, *note*
3
b Ps. 32:9
5
c Prov. 12:18; 15:2; Jas. 1:26
6
d Prov. 16:27
e Mt. 15:18
f Cp. Ps. 83:12–14
g Gk. *geenna.* See Mt. 5:22, *note*
8
h Cp. Ps. 140:3; Rom. 3:13
9
i Gen. 1:26; 5:1; 9:6
12
j Mt. 7:16–20
15
k Cp. Jas. 1:5,17
17
l 1 Cor. 2:6–7
m Jas. 2:1
n Rom. 12:9; 1 Pet. 1:22
18
o See 1 Jn. 3:7, *note*
p Or *for*

CHAPTER 4
1
q Rom. 7:23; Gal. 5:17; 1 Pet. 2:11
2
r Cp. 1 Jn. 3:15
3
s Cp. 1 Jn. 5:14
4
t 1 Jn. 2:15
u Gk. *kosmos.* See Rev. 13:8, *note*
v Gal. 1:4; cp. Jn. 15:19; 17:14
6
w *Grace:* v. 6; 1 Pet. 1:13. (Jn. 1:14; Jn. 1:17, *note*). See 2 Pet. 3:18, *note*
x Prov. 3:34
7
y *Satan:* v. 7; 1 Pet. 5:8. (Gen. 3:1; Rev. 20:10)
z Cp. Mt. 4:10–11
8
aa 2 Chr. 15:2; Mal. 3:7; Heb. 10:19–22
bb See Rom. 3:23, *note*

faith and works in which both views are brought together, see Eph. 2:8–10.

ners; and purify *your* hearts,
you double-minded.
9 Lament and mourn and
weep! Let your laughter be
turned to mourning and *your*
joy to gloom.
10 [a]Humble yourselves in
the sight of the Lord, and He
will lift you up.
11 [b]Do not speak evil of one
another, brethren. He who
speaks evil of a brother and
[c]judges his brother, speaks evil
of the law and judges the law.
But if you judge the law, you are
not a doer of the law but a judge.
12 There is one Lawgiver,*
[d]who is able to [e]save and to destroy. Who* are you to judge
[f]another?*
13 Come now, you who say,
"Today or tomorrow we will*
go to such and such a city,
spend a year there, buy and sell,
and make a profit";
14 whereas you do not know
what *will happen* [g]tomorrow.
For what *is* your life? [h]It is even
a vapor that appears for a little
time and then vanishes away.
15 Instead you *ought* to say,
[i]"If the Lord wills, we shall live
and do this or that."
16 But now you boast in your
arrogance. All such boasting is
evil.
17 Therefore, to him who
[j]knows to do good and does not
do *it*, to him it is [k]sin.

IV. Rich Warned, 5:1–6

5 COME now, *you* [l]rich,
weep and howl for your
miseries that are coming upon
[m]*you!*
2 Your [n]riches are cor-
rupted, and your garments are
moth-eaten.
3 Your gold and silver are
corroded, and their corrosion
will be a witness against you
and will eat your flesh like fire.
You have heaped up treasure in
the last days.
4 Indeed the wages of the laborers who mowed your fields,
which you [o]kept back by fraud,
cry out; and the [p]cries of the
reapers have reached the ears
of [q]the Lord of Sabaoth.
5 You have lived on the
earth in pleasure and [r]luxury;
you have fattened your hearts
as* in a day of slaughter.
6 You have condemned,
you have murdered the just; he
does not resist you.

V. Exhortations in View of the Coming of the Lord, 5:7–18

7 Therefore be patient,
brethren, until the coming of
the Lord. See *how* the farmer
waits for the precious fruit of
the earth, waiting patiently for
it until it receives the [s]early and
latter rain.
8 You also be patient. Establish your hearts, [t]for the
[u]coming of the Lord is at hand.
9 Do not grumble against
one another, brethren, lest you
be [v]condemned.* Behold, the
Judge is standing at the door!
10 My brethren, take the
[w]prophets, who spoke in the
name of the Lord, as an example of suffering and [x]patience.
11 Indeed we count them
[y]blessed who [z]endure. You
have heard of the [aa]persever-
ance of Job and seen the [bb]end
intended by the Lord—that the
Lord is very compassionate and
merciful.
12 But above all, my brethren, [cc]do not swear, either by
heaven or by earth or with any
other oath. But let your "Yes" be
"Yes," and *your* "No," "No," lest
you fall into judgment.*
13 Is anyone among you suffering? Let him [dd]pray. Is anyone cheerful? Let him sing
[ee]psalms.
14 Is anyone among you
sick? Let him call for the [ff]elders
of the [gg]church, and let them
pray over him, anointing him
with oil in the name of the Lord.
15 And the prayer of [hh]faith
will save the sick, and the Lord
will raise him up. And if he has
committed [k]sins, he will be
[ii]forgiven.
16 Confess *your* trespasses*
to one another, and pray for one
another, that you may be

*

4:12 NU-Text adds *and Judge.* • NU-Text and M-Text read *But who.* • NU-Text reads *a neighbor.* **4:13** M-Text reads *let us.* **5:5** NU-Text omits *as.* **5:9** NU-Text and M-Text read *judged.* **5:12** M-Text reads *hypocrisy.* **5:16** NU-Text reads *Therefore confess your sins.*

10
a Job 22:29; Lk. 14:11; 18:14; 1 Pet. 5:6
11
b Eph. 4:31; 1 Pet. 2:1–3
c Mt. 7:1–5
12
d Cp. Mt. 10:28
e See Rom. 1:16, *note*
f Rom. 14:4
14
g Prov. 27:1; cp. Lk. 12:16–20
h Job 7:7; Ps. 102:3; 1 Pet. 1:24
15
i Acts 18:21; 1 Cor. 4:19
17
j Lk. 12:47; 2 Pet. 2:21
k See Rom. 3:23, *note*
CHAPTER 5
1
l Prov. 11:28; Lk. 6:24
m Cp. Lk. 16:19–31
2
n Jer. 17:11; Mt. 6:19
4
o Lev. 19:13
p Cp. Dt. 24:15
q i.e. LORD *of hosts.* See 1 Sam. 1:3, *note*
5
r i.e. *indulgence*

7
s Cp. Dt. 11:14; Jer. 5:24; Joel 2:23
8
t Cp. 1 Cor. 7:29–31
u *Christ* (second advent): vv. 7–8; 1 Pet. 1:7. (Dt. 30:3; Acts 1:11, *note*)
9
v Mt. 7:1
10
w Cp. Mt. 5:12; Heb. 10:32
x Heb. 10:36
11
y Mt. 5:10; Jas. 1:2
z Jas. 1:12
aa Job 1:22
bb Job 42:10
12
cc Mt. 5:34
13
dd Ps. 50:14–15
ee Eph. 5:19
14
ff *Elders:* v. 14; 1 Pet. 5:1. (Acts 11:30; Ti. 1:5, *note*)
gg *Churches* (local): v. 14; 1 Pet. 5:13. (Acts 8:3; Phil. 1:1, *note*)
15
hh *Faith:* v. 15; 1 Pet. 1:5. (Gen. 3:20; Heb. 11:39, *note*)
ii *Forgiveness:* v. 15; 1 Jn. 1:9. (Lev. 4:20; Mt. 26:28, *note*)

16
[a] See Rom. 10:10, *note*
17
[b] 1 Ki. 17:1
[c] *Bible prayers* (NT): vv. 17–18; Rev. 22:20. (Mt. 6:9; Lk. 11:2, *note*)
18
[d] 1 Ki. 18:1, 42

healed. The effective, fervent
prayer of a [a]righteous man
avails much.
17 Elijah was a man with a
nature like ours, and [b]he
[c]prayed earnestly that it would
not rain; and it did not rain on
the land for three years and six
months.
18 And he prayed [d]again,
and the heaven gave rain, and
the earth produced its fruit.

Conclusion, 5:19–20

19 Brethren, if anyone
among you wanders from the
truth, and someone [e]turns him
back,
20 let him know that he who
turns a sinner from the error of
his way will save a soul* from
death and [f]cover a multitude of
[g]sins.

19
[e] Mt. 18:15; Gal. 6:1
20
[f] Prov. 10:12
[g] See Rom. 3:23, *note*

*5:20 NU-Text reads *his soul.*

The First Epistle of

PETER

Author: Peter *Theme:* Suffering and Glory *Date of writing:* C. A.D. 65

THE EPISTLE OF PETER is the fulfillment of the commission given to Peter by Christ in Lk. 22:31–32. Compare 1 Pet. 1:1 with Jas. 1:1. Peter was a minister of the circumcision (Gal. 2:9), so he writes to the dispersed Jews (1:1). He is the apostle of hope: 1:3,7,9,13; 3:9–15; 4:13; 5:4. Like Paul, Peter sets forth the doctrines of grace. There are a number of parallels in this letter to the words of the Lord recorded in the Gospels; also there are resemblances between the language of this Epistle and the speeches of Peter in Acts.

First Peter was written from Babylon (5:13). Geographical notations in 1:1 agree with Babylon as the center of writing; however, many understand the name to be a symbol of Rome. The letter is addressed to Hebrew Christians (cp. 4:3 with 1:1), with wider application to all believers in Christ.

The purpose of the Epistle is exhortation and testimony. The key thought is the suffering of the Christian. Peter pleads for steadfastness in time of suffering, in the light of the believer's hope in the resurrected Redeemer. The Epistle is full of exhortations to godly living, and is replete with quotations from and allusions to the OT.

First Peter may be divided as follows:

Introduction, 1:1–2.
I. Christian Suffering and Conduct in the Light of Complete Salvation, 1:3—2:8.
II. Christian Life in View of the Believer's Position and the Vicarious Suffering of Christ, 2:9—4:19.
III. Christian Service in the Light of the Coming of Christ, 5:1–9.
Conclusion, 5:10–14.

CHAPTER 1
1
a Jas. 1:1
2
b Election (corporate): v. 2; 1 Pet. 1:15. (Dt. 7:6; 1 Pet. 5:13, *note*)
c 2 Th. 2:13
d Holy Spirit (NT): v. 2; 1 Pet. 1:11. (Mt. 1:18; Acts 2:4, *note*)
e Rom. 1:5
f See 2 Pet. 3:18, *note*
3
g Ti. 3:5
h Resurrection: v. 3; 1 Pet. 1:21. (2 Ki. 4:35; 1 Cor. 15:52, *note*)

Introduction, 1:1–2

1 PETER, an apostle of Jesus
Christ,

To the pilgrims of the
[a]Dispersion in Pontus, Galatia,
Cappadocia, Asia, and Bi-
thynia,
2 [1b]elect according to the
foreknowledge of God the Father, in [c]sanctification of the
[d]Spirit, for [e]obedience and
sprinkling of the blood of Jesus
Christ:

[f]Grace to you and peace
be multiplied.

I. Christian Suffering and Conduct in the Light of Complete Salvation, 1:3—2:8

3 Blessed *be* the God and
Father of our Lord Jesus Christ,
who according to His abundant
[g]mercy has begotten us again to
a living hope through the [h]res-
urrection of Jesus Christ [i]from
the dead,
4 to an inheritance incorruptible and undefiled and that
does not fade away, reserved in
heaven for you,
5 who are [j]kept by the
power of God through [k]faith for
salvation ready to be revealed
in the last time.
6 In this you greatly rejoice,
though now for a little while, if
need be, you have been grieved
by various [l]trials,
7 that the genuineness of
your faith, *being* much more
precious than gold that perishes, though it is tested by fire,
[2]may be found to praise, honor,
and glory at the [m]revelation of
Jesus Christ,
8 whom having not seen*
you love. Though now you do

*1:8 M-Text reads *known*.

i Lit. *from among*
5
j Assurance/security: vv. 3–5; 2 Pet. 2:9. (Ps. 23:1; Jude 1, *note*)
k Faith: v. 5; 1 Pet. 1:8. (Gen. 3:20; Heb. 11:39, *note*)
6
l Test/tempt: vv. 6–7; 1 Pet. 4:12. (Gen. 3:1; Jas. 1:14, *note*)
7
m Christ (second advent): v. 7; 2 Pet. 3:4. (Dt. 30:3; Acts 1:11, *note*)

---

[1](1:2) In the Greek the word translated "elect" (*eklektos*) actually appears in v. 1 as a modifier of "pilgrims." The letter is addressed, therefore, "to the elect pilgrims" of the Dispersion.

[2](1:7) Suffering, in this Epistle, is set in the light of: (1) assured salvation (1:2–5); (2) glory at Christ's appearing (1:7); (3) Christ's sufferings and coming glories (1:11); (4) the Christian's association with Him in both (2:20–21; 3:17–18; 4:12–13); (5) the purifying effect of suffering (1:7; 4:1–2; 5:10); (6) the fact that Christ is now glorified in the Christian's patient suffering (4:16); and (7) the fact that suffering is disciplinary (4:17–19; cp. 1 Cor. 11:31–32; Heb. 12:5–13).

[a]not see *Him,* yet [b]believing, you rejoice with joy inexpressible and full of glory,

9 receiving the end of your [b]faith—the [c]salvation of *your* souls.

10 Of this [c]salvation the prophets have inquired and searched carefully, who prophesied of the grace *that would come* to you,

11 searching what, or what manner of time, the [d]Spirit of Christ who was in them was indicating when He [e]testified beforehand the sufferings of Christ and the glories that would follow.

12 To them it was revealed that, not to themselves, but to us* they were ministering the things which now have been reported to you through those who have preached the [f]gospel to you by the Holy [d]Spirit sent from heaven—things which [g]angels desire to look into.

13 Therefore gird up the loins of your mind, be sober, and rest *your* hope fully upon the [h]grace that is to be brought to you at the revelation of Jesus Christ;

14 as obedient children, not [i]conforming yourselves to the former lusts, *as* in your ignorance;

15 but as He who [j]called you *is* holy, you also be [k]holy in all *your* conduct,

16 because it is written, [l]*"Be* [k]*holy, for I am holy."**

17 And if you call on the Father, who [m]without partiality judges according to each one's work, conduct yourselves throughout the time of your stay *here* in fear;

18 knowing that you were not [n]redeemed with corruptible things, *like* silver or gold, from your aimless conduct *received* by tradition from your fathers,

19 but [o]with the precious blood of Christ, as of a lamb without blemish and without spot.

20 He indeed was [1][p]foreordained before the foundation of the world, but was manifest in these last times for you

21 who through Him [b]believe in God, who [q]raised Him from the dead and gave Him glory, so that your faith and hope are in God.

22 Since you have purified your souls in obeying the truth through the [d]Spirit* in sincere [r]love of the brethren, [r]love one another fervently with a pure heart,

23 having been born again, not of corruptible seed but incorruptible, through the [s]word of God which lives and abides forever,*

24 because

[t]*"All flesh is as grass,*
And all the glory of
man as the flower of*
the grass.
The grass withers,
And its flower falls
away,
25 *But the* [u]*word of the*
LORD endures forever."

Now this is the word which by the [f]gospel was preached to you.

2

THEREFORE, laying aside all malice, all deceit, hypocrisy, envy, and all evil speaking,

2 as newborn babes, desire the pure milk of the word, that you may grow thereby,*

3 if indeed you have [v]tasted that the Lord *is* gracious.

4 Coming to Him *as to* a living [w]stone, [x]rejected indeed by men, but chosen by God *and* precious,

---

8
a Jn. 20:29
b Faith: vv. 8–9,21; 1 Pet. 2:6. (Gen. 3:20; Heb. 11:39, *note*)
9
c See Rom. 1:16, *note*
11
d Holy Spirit (NT): vv. 11–12, 22; 1 Pet. 3:18. (Mt. 1:18; Acts 2:4, *note*)
e Inspiration: vv. 10–12; 2 Pet. 1:21. (Ex. 4:15; 2 Tim. 3:16, *note*)
12
f Gospel: vv. 12,25; 1 Pet. 4:6. (Gen. 12:3; Rev. 14:6)
g Eph. 3:10
13
h Grace: vv. 13, 18–19; 1 Pet. 3:7. (Jn. 1:14; Jn. 1:17, *note*)
14
i Rom. 12:2
15
j Election (corporate): v. 15; 1 Pet. 2:9. (Dt. 7:6; 1 Pet. 5:13, *note*)
k Sanctification (NT): vv. 15–16; 1 Pet. 2:5. (Mt. 4:5; Rev. 22:11)
16
l Lev. 11:44
17
m Acts 10:34
18
n See Rom. 3:24, *note*
19
o Sacrifice (of Christ): vv. 18–19; 1 Pet. 2:24. (Gen. 3:15; Heb. 10:18, *note*)
20
p Lit. *foreknown. Foreknowledge:* v. 20. (Acts 2:23; 1 Pet. 1:20)
21
q Resurrection: v. 21; 1 Pet. 3:21. (2 Ki. 4:35; 1 Cor. 15:52, *note*)
22
r Law (of Christ): v. 22; 1 Pet. 3:8. (Jn. 13:34; 2 Jn. 5)
23
s 1 Th. 2:13; Jas. 1:18
24
t Isa. 40:6–8
25
u Lit. *saying*
CHAPTER 2
3
v Ps. 34:8
4
w Christ (Stone): v. 4; 1 Pet. 2:6. (Gen. 49:24; 1 Pet. 2:8)
x Ps. 118:22

---

*
1:12 NU-Text and M-Text read *you.*
1:16 Leviticus 11:45; 19:2; 20:7
1:22 NU-Text omits *through the Spirit.*
1:23 NU-Text omits *forever.* **1:24** NU-Text reads *all its glory.* **2:2** NU-Text adds *up to salvation.*

---

[1](1:20) The sovereign choice of God in election and predestination logically originated in the divine decision based on His eternal omniscience of all possible plans of action. The order logically, not chronologically, is omniscience, divine decision (election and predestination), and foreknowledge. As God's decision is eternal, however, so also His foreknowledge is eternal. As foreknowledge extends to all events, it includes all that is embraced in election and predestination. Election is, therefore, according to foreknowledge, and foreknowledge is according to election, meaning that both are in perfect agreement. See Election, 1 Pet. 5:13, *note;* Predestination, Eph. 1:11, *note.*

5 you also, as living stones,
are being built up a spiritual
house, a [a]holy priesthood, to offer up [b]spiritual sacrifices acceptable to God through Jesus
Christ.
6 Therefore it is also contained in the Scripture,

[c]*"Behold, I lay in Zion*
A chief [d]cornerstone,
elect, precious,
And he who [e]believes on
Him will by no means
be put to shame."

7 Therefore, to you who
[e]believe, *He is* precious; but to
those who are disobedient,*

"The [d]stone which the
builders [f]rejected
Has become the chief
cornerstone,"

8 and

"A [1d]stone of stumbling
*And a rock of offense."**

They stumble, being disobedient to the word, [g]to which they
also were appointed.

II. Christian Life in View of the Believer's Position and the Vicarious Suffering of Christ, 2:9—4:19

9 But you *are* a [h]chosen
generation, a royal [2]priesthood,
a [a]holy nation, His own special
people, that you may proclaim
the [i]praises of Him who called
you out of darkness into His
marvelous light;
10 who once *were* not a people but *are* now the people of
[j]God, who had not obtained
mercy but now have obtained
mercy.
11 Beloved, I beg *you* as [k]so-
journers and pilgrims, abstain
from fleshly lusts which [l]war
against the soul,
12 having your conduct honorable among the Gentiles, that
when they speak against you as
evildoers, they may, [m]by *your*
[n]good works which they observe, glorify God in the day of
visitation.
13 Therefore [o]submit yourselves to every ordinance of
man for the Lord's sake,
whether to the king as supreme,
14 or to governors, as to
those who are sent by him for
the punishment of evildoers and
for the praise of those who do
good.
15 For this is the will of God,
that by doing good you may put

5
a Sanctification (NT): vv. 5,9; 1 Pet. 3:5. (Mt. 4:5; Rev. 22:11)
b Sacrifice (the believer-priest's); see Heb. 10:18, *note*
6
c Isa. 28:16
d Christ (Stone): vv. 6–8. (Gen. 49:24; 1 Pet. 2:8)
e Faith: vv. 6–7; 1 Jn. 3:23. (Gen. 3:20; Heb. 11:39, *note*)
7
f Ps. 118:22
8
g Cp. Rom. 9:21–24
9
h Election (corporate): v. 9; 1 Pet. 5:13. (Dt. 7:6; 1 Pet. 5:13, *note*)
i Lit. *excellencies*
10
j Hos. 1:10
11
k Ps. 119:19; cp. Lev. 25:23; Heb. 11:9–10
l Rom. 8:13; Gal. 5:17
12
m Righteousness (garment): v. 12; 1 Pet. 3:3. (Gen. 3:21; Rev. 19:8)
n Mt. 5:16
13
o Mt. 22:21; see Rom. 13:4, *note*

*
2:7 NU-Text reads *to those who disbelieve.*
2:8 Isaiah 8:14

[1](2:8) Christ is the Rock (or Stone): (1) struck that the Spirit of life may flow from Him to all who will drink (Ex. 17:6; 1 Cor. 10:4; cp. Jn. 4:13–14; 7:37–39); (2) to the Church, the foundation and chief Cornerstone (Eph. 2:20); (3) to the Jews at His first coming, a "stumbling stone" (Rom. 9:32–33; 1 Cor. 1:23); (4) to Israel at His second coming, the "capstone" of the corner (Zech. 4:7); (5) to the Gentile world power, the striking "stone . . . cut out without hands" (Dan. 2:34); (6) in the divine purpose, the Stone which, after the destruction of Gentile world power, is to grow and fill the earth (Dan. 2:35); and (7) to unbelievers, the crushing Stone of judgment that will grind those on whom it falls to powder (Mt. 21:44).

[2](2:9) The NT Priesthood, Summary: (1) Until the law was given, the head of each family was the family priest (Gen. 8:20; 26:25; 31:54). (2) When the law was proposed, the promise to perfect obedience was that Israel should be to God "a kingdom of priests" (Ex. 19:6); but Israel violated the law, and God shut up the priestly office to the Aaronic family, appointing the tribe of Levi to minister to Israel, thus constituting the typical priesthood (Ex. 28:1). (3) In the Church Age, all Christians are unconditionally constituted "kings and priests" (v. 9; Rev. 1:6), the distinction which Israel failed to achieve by works. The priesthood of the Christian is, therefore, a birthright, just as every descendant of Aaron was born to the priesthood (Heb. 5:1). (4) The chief privilege of a priest is access to God. Under law the high priest only could enter "the Holiest of All," and that but once a year (Heb. 9:7); but when Christ died, the veil, a type of Christ's human body (Heb. 10:20), was torn, so that now the believer–priests, equally with Christ the High Priest, have access to God in the Holiest (Heb. 10:19–22). The High Priest is corporeally there (Heb. 4:14–16; 9:24; 10:19–22). And (5) in the exercise of his office the NT believer-priest is (1) a sacrificer who offers a fourfold sacrifice: (a) his own living body (Rom. 12:1; Phil. 2:17; 2 Tim. 4:6; Jas. 1:27; 1 Jn. 3:16); (b) praise to God, "the fruit of our lips, giving thanks to His name," to be offered continually (Heb. 13:15; cp. Ex. 25:22, "there I will meet with you . . . above the mercy seat, from between the two cherubim which are on the ark of the Testimony"); (c) his substance (Rom. 12:13; Gal. 6:6,10; Ti. 3:14; Heb. 13:2,16; 3 Jn. 5–8); and (d) his service, i.e. "to do good" (Heb. 13:16). (2) The NT priest is also an intercessor (Col. 4:12; 1 Tim. 2:1).

to silence the ignorance of foolish men—

16 [a]as free, yet not [b]using liberty as a cloak for vice, but as [c]bondservants of God.

17 Honor all *people*. Love the brotherhood. Fear [d]God. Honor the king.

18 [e]Servants, *be* submissive to *your* masters with all fear, not only to the good and gentle, but also to the harsh.

19 For this *is* [f]commendable, if because of conscience toward God one endures grief, suffering wrongfully.

20 For [g]what credit *is it* if, when you are beaten for your [h]faults, you take it patiently? But when you do good and suffer, if you take it patiently, this *is* commendable before God.

The vicarious suffering of Christ

21 For [i]to this you were called, because Christ also suffered for us,* leaving us* an [j]example, that you should follow His steps:

22 [k]*"Who committed no* [h]*sin,*
Nor was deceit found in
His mouth";

23 who, [l]when He was reviled, did not revile in return; when He suffered, He did not threaten, but committed *Himself* to Him who judges righteously;

24 [m]who Himself [n]bore our sins in His own body on the tree, that we, having died to sins, might live for [o]righteousness—by whose stripes you were healed.

25 For you were like sheep going [p]astray, but have now returned to the [q]Shepherd and Overseer* of your souls.

Godly living in the home and in the church

3 [r]WIVES, likewise, *be* submissive to your own husbands, that even if some do not obey the word, they, without a word, may be won by the conduct of their wives,

2 when they observe your chaste conduct *accompanied* by fear.

3 Do not let your [s]adornment be *merely* outward—arranging the hair, wearing gold, or putting on *fine* apparel—

4 rather *let it be* the hidden person of the heart, with the incorruptible *beauty* of a gentle and quiet spirit, which is very precious in the sight of God.

5 For in this manner, in former times, the [t]holy women who [u]trusted in God also adorned themselves, being submissive to their own husbands,

6 as Sarah obeyed Abraham, [v]calling him lord, whose daughters you are if you do good and are not afraid with any terror.

7 [w]Husbands, likewise, dwell with *them* with understanding, giving honor to the wife, as to the weaker vessel, and as *being* heirs together of the [x]grace of [y]life, that your prayers may not be hindered.

8 Finally, all *of you be* of one mind, having compassion for one another; [z]love as brothers, *be* tenderhearted, *be* courteous;*

9 not returning evil for evil or reviling for reviling, but on the contrary [aa]blessing, knowing that you were called to this, that you may inherit a blessing.

10 For

[bb]*"He who would love life*
And see good days,
Let him refrain his
tongue from evil,
And his lips from
speaking deceit.
11 *Let him turn away from*
evil and do good;
Let him seek peace and
pursue it.
12 *For the eyes of the* LORD
are on the [o]*righteous,*
And His ears are open to
their prayers;
But the face of the LORD
is against those who
do evil."

Godly living before the world for righteousness' sake

13 And who *is* he who will harm you if you become followers of what is [cc]good?

*

2:21 NU-Text reads *you.* • NU-Text and M-Text read *you.* **2:25** Greek *Episkopos* **3:8** NU-Text reads *humble.*

16
a Rom. 6:14, 20,22
b Gal. 5:13
c Or *slaves.* 1 Cor. 6:20
17
d Prov. 24:21
18
e Eph. 6:5–8
19
f Or *grace*
20
g Lk. 6:32–34
h See Rom. 3:23, *note*
21
i Mt. 16:24; 1 Th. 3:3–4
j *Christ* (first advent): vv. 21–24; 1 Pet. 3:18. (Gen. 3:15; Acts 1:11, *note*)
22
k Isa. 53:9
23
l Isa. 53:7
24
m *Sacrifice* (of Christ): v. 24; 1 Pet. 3:18. (Gen. 3:15; Heb. 10:18, *note*)
n *Judgments* (the seven): v. 24; 1 Pet. 3:18. (1 Sam. 7:14; Rev. 20:12, *note*)
o See Rom. 10:10, *note*
25
p Isa. 53:5–6
q Ezek. 34:11; Heb. 13:20
CHAPTER 3
1
r vv. 1,5,6; Gen. 3:16; Eph. 5:22
3
s *Righteousness* (garment): vv. 3–5; 1 Pet. 5:5. (Gen. 3:21; Rev. 19:8)

5
t *Sanctification* (NT): v. 5; 1 Pet. 3:15. (Mt. 4:5; Rev. 22:11)
u Or *hoped*
6
v Gen. 18:12
7
w Eph. 5:25
x *Grace:* v. 7; 1 Pet. 5:5. (Jn. 1:14; Jn. 1:17, *note*). See 2 Pet. 3:18, *note.*
y *Life* (eternal): v. 7; 2 Pet. 1:3. (Mt. 7:14; Rev. 22:19)
8
z *Law* (of Christ): v. 8; 1 Jn. 2:10. (Jn. 13:34; 2 Jn. 5)
9
aa Mt. 5:44
10
bb Ps. 34:12–15
13
cc Prov. 16:7

14 But even if you should suffer for [a]righteousness' sake, *you are* blessed. *"And do not be afraid of their threats, nor be troubled."**

15 But [b]sanctify the Lord God* in your hearts, and always *be* [c]ready to *give* a defense to everyone who asks you a reason for the [d]hope that is in you, with meekness and fear;

16 having a good conscience, that when they defame you as evildoers, those who revile your good conduct in Christ may be ashamed.

17 For *it is* better, if it is the will of God, to suffer for doing good than for doing evil.

The vicarious suffering of Christ, preached by Christ through the Spirit in Noah (cp. 1:10–12)

18 For Christ also [e]suffered [f]once for [g]sins, the just for the unjust, that He might bring us* to God, [h]being put to death in the flesh but made alive by the [i]Spirit,

19 by [1]whom also He went and preached to the spirits in prison,

20 who formerly were disobedient, when once the Divine longsuffering waited* in the days of Noah, while *the* ark was being prepared, in which a few, that is, eight souls, were saved through water.

21 There is also an antitype which now saves us—baptism (not the removal of the filth of the [j]flesh, but the answer of a good conscience toward God), through the [k]resurrection of Jesus Christ,

22 who has gone into heaven and is at the right hand of God, [l]angels and authorities and powers having been made subject to Him.

Since Christ has suffered, why should we not suffer?

4

THEREFORE, since Christ [h]suffered for us* in the [e]flesh, arm yourselves also with the same mind, for he who has suffered in the flesh has ceased from [g]sin,

2 that he no longer should live the rest of *his* time in the flesh for the lusts of men, but for the will of God.

3 For we *have spent* enough of our past lifetime* in doing the will of the Gentiles—when we walked in lewdness, lusts, drunkenness, revelries, drinking parties, and abominable idolatries.

4 In regard to these, they think it strange that you do not run with *them* in the same flood of dissipation, speaking evil of *you.*

5 They will give an account to Him who is ready to judge the living and the dead.

6 For this reason the [m]gospel was preached also to those [n]who are dead, that they might be judged according to men in the flesh, but [o]live according to God in the spirit.

Christian conduct in the light of the times in which we live

7 But the [p]end of all things is [q]at hand; therefore be serious and watchful in your prayers.

8 And above all things have fervent love for one another, for *"love will cover a multitude of* [g]*sins."**

9 *Be* hospitable to one another without grumbling.

10 As each one has [r]received a gift, minister it to one another, as [s]good stewards of the manifold [t]grace of God.

11 [u]If anyone speaks, *let him speak* as the oracles of God. If anyone ministers, *let him do it* as with the ability which God supplies, that in [v]all things God may be glorified through Jesus Christ, to whom belong the glory and the dominion forever and ever. Amen.

14
a See 1 Jn. 3:7, *note*
15
b Sanctification (NT): v. 15; 2 Pet. 1:18. (Mt. 4:5; Rev. 22:11)
c Cp. Ps. 119:46
d Ti. 3:7
18
e Christ (first advent): v. 18; 4:1; 1 Jn. 1:1. (Gen. 3:15; Acts 1:11, *note*)
f Judgments (the seven): v. 18; 1 Pet. 4:17. (1 Sam. 7:14; Rev. 20:12, *note*)
g See Rom. 3:23, *note*
h Sacrifice (of Christ): v. 18; 4:1; 1 Jn. 1:7. (Gen. 3:15; Heb. 10:18, *note*)
i Holy Spirit (NT): v. 18; 1 Pet. 4:14. (Mt. 1:18; Acts 2:4, *note*)
21
j Flesh: v. 21; 2 Pet. 2:10. (Jn. 8:15; Jude 23)
k Resurrection: vv. 21–22; Rev. 20:5. (2 Ki. 4:35; 1 Cor. 15:52, *note*)
22
l See Heb. 1:4, *note*

CHAPTER 4
6
m Gospel: v. 6; 1 Pet. 4:17. (Gen. 12:3; Rev. 14:6)
n i.e. *it was preached then to those who are now dead*
o Rom. 8:9, 13; Gal. 5:25
7
p Jas. 5:8–9
q See Mt. 4:17, *note*
10
r Rom. 12:6–8
s 1 Cor. 4:2
t See 2 Pet. 3:18, *note*
11
u Eph. 4:29
v 1 Cor. 10:31

*
3:14 Isaiah 8:12 3:15 NU-Text reads *Christ as Lord.* 3:18 NU-Text and M-Text read *you.* 3:20 NU-Text and M-Text read *when the longsuffering of God waited patiently.* 4:1 NU-Text omits *for us.* 4:3 NU-Text reads *time.* 4:8 Proverbs 10:12

[1](3:19) This means that Christ preached by the Holy Spirit through Noah to unsaved people in OT times (cp. 1:10–11), their spirits being now in prison. The theory that the Lord Jesus, after His crucifixion, preached to the unsaved dead in Hades and gave them a second chance is not found in Scripture.

12 Beloved, do not think it strange concerning the fiery trial which is to [a]try you, as though some strange thing happened to you;

13 but rejoice [b]to the extent that you partake of Christ's sufferings, that [c]when His glory is revealed, you may also be glad with exceeding joy.

14 If you are reproached for the name of Christ, [d]blessed *are you,* for the [e]Spirit of glory and of God rests upon you.* On their part He is blasphemed, [f]but on your part He is glorified.

15 But let none of you suffer as a murderer, a thief, an evildoer, or as a busybody in other people's matters.

16 Yet if *anyone suffers* as a Christian, let him not be ashamed, but let him glorify God in this matter.*

17 For the time *has come* for [g]judgment to begin at the house of God; and if *it begins* with us first, what will *be* the end of those who do not obey the [h]gospel of God?

18 Now

"If the [i]righteous one is
[j]scarcely [k]saved,
Where will the ungodly
and the [l]sinner
*appear?"**

19 Therefore let those who suffer according to the will of God [m]commit their souls *to Him* in doing good, as to a faithful Creator.

III. Christian Service in the Light of the Coming of the Lord, 5:1–9

5 THE [n]elders who are among you I exhort, I who am a fellow elder and a [o]witness of the sufferings of Christ, and also a partaker of the [p]glory that will be revealed:

2 [q]Shepherd the flock of God which is among you, serving as overseers, not by compulsion but willingly,* not for dishonest gain but eagerly;

3 nor as being lords over those entrusted to you, but being examples to the flock;

4 and when the Chief [r]Shepherd appears, you will receive the [s]crown of glory that does not fade away.

5 Likewise you younger people, submit yourselves to *your* elders. Yes, [t]all of *you* be submissive to one another, and be [u]clothed with humility, for

[v]*"God resists the proud,*
But gives [w]grace to the
humble."

6 Therefore [x]humble yourselves under the mighty hand of God, that He may exalt you in due time,

7 casting all your care upon Him, for He cares for you.

8 Be sober, be vigilant; because* your adversary the [y]devil walks about like a roaring lion, seeking whom he may devour.

9 Resist him, steadfast in the faith, knowing that the same sufferings are experienced by your brotherhood in the [z]world.

Conclusion: Benediction and Personal Greetings, 5:10–14

10 But may* the God of all [w]grace, who called us* to His eternal glory by Christ Jesus, after you have suffered a while, [aa]perfect, establish, strengthen, and settle *you.*

11 To Him *be* the glory and the dominion forever and ever. Amen.

12 By [bb]Silvanus, our faithful brother as I consider him, I have written to you briefly, exhorting and testifying that this is the true [w]grace of God in which you stand.

13 [cc]She who is in Babylon, [1][dd]elect together with *you,*

*

4:14 NU-Text omits the rest of this verse. **4:16** NU-Text reads *name.* **4:18** Proverbs 11:31 **5:2** NU-Text adds *according to God.* **5:8** NU-Text and M-Text omit *because.* **5:10** NU-Text reads *But the God of all grace . . . will perfect, establish, strengthen, and settle you.* • NU-Text and M-Text read *you.*

12
a Test/tempt: v. 12; 2 Pet. 2:9. (Gen. 3:1; Jas. 1:14, *note*)
13
b Jas. 1:2
c 2 Tim. 2:12
14
d Mt. 5:11
e Holy Spirit (NT): v. 14; 2 Pet. 1:21. (Mt. 1:18; Acts 2:4, *note*)
f Mt. 5:16
17
g Judgments (the seven): v. 17; 2 Pet. 2:4. (1 Sam. 7:14; Rev. 20:12, *note*)
h Gospel: v. 17; Jude 3. (Gen. 12:3; Rev. 14:6)
18
i See Rom. 10:10, *note*
j i.e. *with difficulty*
k See Rom. 1:16, *note*
l See Rom. 3:23, *note*
19
m Ps. 37:5–7
CHAPTER 5
1
n Elders: vv. 1–4; 2 Jn. 1. (Acts 11:30; Ti. 1:5, *note*)
o Mt. 26:37
p Rom. 8:17–18
2
q Cp. Jn. 21:15–17

4
r Heb. 13:20; 1 Pet. 2:25; cp. Isa. 40:11
s Rewards: v. 4; 2 Jn. 8. (Dan. 12:3; 1 Cor. 3:14, *note*)
5
t Eph. 5:21
u Righteousness (garment): v. 5; Rev. 3:4. (Gen. 3:21; Rev. 19:8)
v Prov. 3:34; Jas. 4:6
w Grace: vv. 5,10,12; 2 Pet. 1:2. (Jn. 1:14; Jn. 1:17, *note*). See 2 Pet. 3:18, *note*
6
x Isa. 57:15
8
y Satan: vv. 8–9; 1 Jn. 3:8. (Gen. 3:1; Rev. 20:10)
9
z Gk. *kosmos.* See Mt. 4:8, *note*
10
aa See Phil. 3:12, *note*
12
bb 2 Cor. 1:19; 1 Th. 1:1; 2 Th. 1:1
13
cc Churches (local): v. 13; 3 Jn. 6. (Acts 8:3; Phil. 1:1, *note*)
dd Election (corporate): v. 13; 2 Pet. 1:10. (Dt. 7:6; 1 Pet. 5:13, *note*)

[1](5:13) Election, Summary: In both Testaments the Hebrew and Greek words are rendered "elect," "election" "choose," "chosen." In all cases they mean, simply, *chosen* or *to choose,* and are used of both human and divine choices. (1) In the latter use election is: (a) corporate, as of the nation of Israel, or of the Church (Isa. 45:4; Eph. 1:4); and (b) individual (1 Pet. 1:2). (2)

greets you; and *so does* Mark
my son.
14 Greet one another with a
kiss of love. Peace to you
all who are in Christ Jesus.
Amen.

Election is according to the foreknowledge of God (1:2), and wholly by grace, apart from human merit (Rom. 9:11; 11:5–6). And (3) election proceeds from the divine volition (Jn. 15:16).

Election is, therefore: (1) the sovereign act of God in grace whereby certain persons are chosen from among mankind for Himself (Jn. 15:19); and (2) the sovereign act of God whereby certain elect persons are chosen for distinctive service for Him (Lk. 6:13; Acts 9:15; 1 Cor. 1:27–28).

The Second Epistle of

PETER

Author: Peter *Theme:* Last Days *Date of writing:* c. A.D. 66

THE SECOND EPISTLE OF PETER and 2 Timothy have much in common. In both Epistles the writers are awaiting martyrdom (2 Tim. 4:6; 2 Pet. 1:14; cp. Jn. 21:18–19); both are joyful in tone; both foresee the departure from the faith that will culminate during "the last days" (2:1—3:9; 2 Tim. 3). A similar emphasis upon the peril of false teaching is found in 1 Jn. 4:1–5, in 2 Jn. 7–11, and in Jude.

The thrust of the Epistle is the eloquent and comprehensive denunciation of heresy in doctrine and life (2:1—3:3). But there are other important matters in the letter also: Peter's insistence upon the validation of the Christian's "call and election" by the practice of Christian virtues (1:4–14); his personal recollection of the transfiguration of Christ (1:15–18); his teaching about the inspired authenticity of prophecy (1:19–21) and the coming of the Lord (3:4–13); and his exhortations to spiritual diligence and steadfastness (3:14–17).

The Epistle may be divided as follows:

Introduction, 1:1–2.
I. Great Christian Virtues, 1:3–14.
II. The Transfiguration Recalled, 1:15–18.
III. Prophetic Scriptures Exalted, 1:19–21.
IV. Warnings Concerning False Teachers, 2:1—3:3.
V. The Second Coming of Christ and the Day of the Lord, 3:4–16.
Conclusion, 3:17–18.

Introduction, 1:1–2

1 SIMON Peter, a [a]bondser-
vant and [b]apostle of Jesus
Christ,

To those who have ob-
tained like precious faith with
us by the [c]righteousness of our
God and [d]Savior Jesus Christ:

2 [e]Grace and peace be multiplied to you in the knowledge
of God and of Jesus our Lord,

I. Great Christian Virtues, 1:3–14

3 as His [f]divine power has
given to us all things that *pertain* to [g]life and godliness,
through the knowledge of Him
who called us [h]by glory and virtue,

4 [i]by which have been given
to us exceedingly great and precious promises, that through
these you may be partakers of
the divine nature, having [j]es-
caped the corruption *that is* in
the [k]world through lust.

5 But also for this very reason, giving all diligence, [l]add to
your faith virtue, to virtue
knowledge,

6 to knowledge self-control,
to self-control perseverance, to
perseverance godliness,

7 to godliness brotherly

CHAPTER 1
1
a Or *slave*
b Gal. 2:8
c See Rom. 3:21, *note*
d See Rom. 1:16, *note*
2
e *Grace:* v. 2; 2 Pet. 3:18. (Jn. 1:14; Jn. 1:17, *note*)
3
f 1 Pet. 1:5
g *Life* (eternal): v. 3; 1 Jn. 1:2. (Mt. 7:14; Rev. 22:19)
h Or *by his own*
4
i 2 Cor. 1:20
j Cp. 2 Pet. 2:18–20
k Gk. *kosmos.* See Rev. 13:8, *note*
5
l Lit. *in your faith provide virtue*

kindness, and to brotherly kindness love.

8 For if these things are
yours and abound, *you will be*
neither [m]barren nor unfruitful
in the knowledge of our Lord
Jesus Christ.

9 For he who lacks these
things is [n]shortsighted, even to
blindness, and has forgotten
that he was cleansed from his
old [o]sins.

10 Therefore, brethren, be
even more diligent to make
your call and [p]election [q]sure,
[r]for if you do these things you
will never stumble;

11 for so an entrance will be
supplied to you abundantly into
the everlasting kingdom of our
Lord and Savior Jesus Christ.

12 For this reason I will not
be negligent to [s]remind you always of these things, though
you know and are established
in the present truth.

13 Yes, I think it is right, as
long as I am in this [t]tent, [u]to
stir you up by reminding *you*,

14 [v]knowing that shortly I
must [w]put off my [t]tent, just as
our Lord Jesus Christ [x]showed
me.

II. The Transfiguration Recalled, 1:15–18

15 Moreover I will be careful

8
m Lit. *idle*
9
n 1 Jn. 2:9–11
o See Rom. 3:23, *note*
10
p *Election* (personal): v. 10; 2 Jn. 1. (Dt. 7:6; 1 Pet. 5:13, *note*)
q 2 Cor. 13:5
r Cp. 1 Jn. 3:19
12
s Cp. 2 Tim. 2:14
13
t i.e. *body*
u 2 Pet. 3:1
14
v Cp. 2 Tim. 4:6
w *Death* (physical): vv. 13–14; Rev. 6:9. (Gen. 2:17; Heb. 9:27, *note*)
x Cp. Jn. 21:18–19

to ensure that you always have
a reminder of these things after
my decease.
16 For we did not follow cunningly devised [a]fables when we
made known to you the [b]power
and [c]coming of our Lord Jesus
Christ, but were [d]eyewitnesses
of His majesty.
17 For He received from God
the Father honor and glory
when such a voice came to Him
from the Excellent Glory: "This
is My beloved Son, in whom I
am well pleased."
18 And we heard this voice
which came from heaven when
we were with Him on the [1e]holy
mountain.

III. Prophetic Scriptures Exalted, 1:19–21

19 And so we have the prophetic word [2]confirmed,*
which you do well to heed as a
[f]light that shines in a dark
place, [g]until the day dawns and
the morning [h]star rises in your
[i]hearts;
20 knowing this first, that no
prophecy of Scripture is of [3]any
private interpretation,*
21 for prophecy never came
by the will of man, but [e]holy
men of God* spoke [j]*as they
were* moved by the Holy [k]Spirit.

IV. Warnings Concerning False Teachers, 2:1—3:3

They will deny redemption by blood

2 BUT there were also false
prophets among the people,
even as there will be [l]false
teachers among you, who will
secretly bring in destructive
heresies, even denying the Lord
who bought them, *and* bring on
themselves swift destruction.
2 And many will follow
their destructive ways, because
of whom the way of truth will be
blasphemed.
3 By covetousness they will
exploit you with deceptive
words; for a long time their
judgment has not been idle, and
their destruction does* not
slumber.
4 For if God did [m]not spare
the angels who sinned, but cast
them down to [n]hell and delivered *them* into chains of darkness, to be reserved for judgment;
5 and did not spare the ancient [o]world, but saved Noah,
one of eight *people,* a preacher
of [p]righteousness, bringing in
the flood on the [o]world of the
ungodly;
6 and turning the cities of
[q]Sodom and Gomorrah into
ashes, condemned *them* to destruction, making *them* an example to those who afterward
would live ungodly;
7 and delivered righteous
Lot, *who was* oppressed by the
filthy conduct of the wicked
8 (for that [p]righteous man,
dwelling among them, tor-
mented *his* [p]righteous soul
from day to day by seeing and
hearing *their* lawless deeds)—
9 *then* the Lord [r]knows
how to [s]deliver the godly out of
[t]temptations and to reserve the

16
a Cp. 2 Cor. 4:2; 1 Tim. 1:4
b Mt. 28:18; Eph. 1:19–22
c 1 Pet. 5:4
d Mt. 17:1–5; Lk. 1:2
18
e Sanctification (NT): vv. 18,21; Jude 20. (Mt. 4:5; Rev. 22:11)
19
f Jn. 1:4–5,9; cp. Ps. 119:105
g Prov. 4:18
h Rev. 2:28; 22:16
i 2 Cor. 4:5–7
21
j Inspiration: vv. 20–21; Rev. 1:1 (Ex. 4:15; 2 Tim. 3:16, *note*)
k Holy Spirit (NT): v. 21; 1 Jn. 3:24. (Mt. 1:18; Acts 2:4, *note*)
CHAPTER 2
1
l Mt. 24:5,24; 1 Tim. 4:2

4
m Judgments (the seven): v. 4; Jude 6. (1 Sam. 7:14; Rev. 20:12, *note*)
n Gk. *Tartaros,* the Greek nether world, comparable to Hades
5
o Gk. *kosmos.* See Mt. 4:8, *note*
p Righteousness (OT): vv. 5,8. (Gen. 6:9; Lk. 2:25, *note*)
6
q Gen. 19:1–26
9
r Assurance/security: v. 9; 1 Jn. 2:2. (Ps. 23:1; Jude 1, *note*)
s Ps. 34:15–19; 1 Cor. 10:13
t Test/tempt: v. 9; 2 Pet. 3:17. (Gen. 3:1; Jas. 1:14, *note*)

*
1:19 Or *We also have the more sure prophetic word.* **1:20** Or *origin* **1:21** NU-Text reads *but men spoke from God.* **2:3** M-Text reads *will not.*

[1](1:18) Where the reference is to inanimate things rather than persons the meaning of "holy," "sacred," "sanctified," or "consecrated" is, simply, *set apart for the use of God,* or *rendered sacred by the divine Presence.*

[2](1:19) Prophecy is "confirmed" by fulfillment in part. Fulfilled prophecy is a proof of inspiration because the Scripture predictions of future events were uttered so long before the events took place that no mere human sagacity or foresight could have anticipated them, and these predictions are so detailed, minute, and specific as to exclude the possibility that they were simply fortunate guesses. Hundreds of predictions concerning Israel, the land of Canaan, Babylon, Assyria, Egypt, and numerous personages—so ancient, so singular, so seemingly improbable, as well as so detailed and definite that no mortal could have anticipated them—have been fulfilled by natural elements and by men who were ignorant of them, or who utterly disbelieved them, or who struggled with frantic desperation to avoid their fulfillment. It is certain, therefore, that the Scriptures which contain them are inspired. "For prophecy never came by the will of man, but holy men of God spoke as they were moved by the Holy Spirit" (v. 21).

[3](1:20) Some suggest the basic meaning is that no prophecy is isolated from what Scripture states elsewhere; i.e. all prophecies cohere.

unjust under punishment for the [a]day of judgment,

10 and especially those who walk according to the [b]flesh in the lust of uncleanness and [c]despise authority. *They are* presumptuous, self-willed. They are not afraid to speak evil of dignitaries,

11 whereas angels, who are greater in power and might, do not bring a reviling accusation against them before the Lord.

12 But these, like [d]natural brute beasts made to be caught and destroyed, speak evil of the things they do not understand, and will utterly perish in their own corruption,

13 *and* will receive the wages of unrighteousness, *as* those who count it pleasure to carouse in the daytime. *They are* spots and blemishes, carousing in their own deceptions while they feast with you,

14 having eyes full of adultery and that cannot cease from [e]sin, enticing unstable souls. *They have* a heart trained in covetous practices, *and are* accursed children.

The marks of the false teachers

(a) They are like Balaam

15 They have [f]forsaken the right way and gone astray, following the way of [1g]Balaam the *son* of Beor, who loved the wages of unrighteousness;

16 but he was rebuked for his iniquity: a dumb donkey speaking with a man's voice restrained the madness of the prophet.

(b) They are destitute of the Spirit (cp. Jn. 4:14; 7:37–39; Rom. 8:9)

17 These are wells without water, [h]clouds* carried by a tempest, for whom is [i]reserved the blackness of darkness forever.*

(c) Their words are learned and pretentious (cp. 1 Cor. 2:1–5)

18 For when they speak great [j]swelling *words* of emptiness, they allure through the lusts of the [b]flesh, through lewdness, the ones who have actually escaped* from those who live in error.

(d) They pervert Christian liberty

19 While they promise them liberty, they themselves are [k]slaves of corruption; [l]for by whom a person is overcome, by him also he is brought into bondage.

20 For if, after they have escaped the pollutions of the [m]world through the knowledge of the Lord and [n]Savior Jesus Christ, they are [o]again entangled in them and overcome, the latter end is worse for them than the beginning.

21 For it would have been [p]better for them not to have known the way of righteousness, than having known *it,* to turn from the holy commandment delivered to them.

(e) They turn away from the faith

22 But it has happened to them according to the true [q]proverb: *"A dog returns to his own vomit,"* and, "a sow, having washed, to her wallowing in the mire."

The reason for the epistle

3 BELOVED, I now write to you this second epistle (in *both of* which I [r]stir up your pure minds by way of reminder),

2 that you may be mindful of the words [s]which were spoken before by the holy prophets, and of the commandment [t]of us,* the apostles of the Lord and [n]Savior,

3 knowing this first: that [u]scoffers will come in the last days, walking according to their own lusts,

9
a *Day (of judgment):* v. 9; 2 Pet. 3:7. (Mt. 10:15; Rev. 20:11)
10
b *Flesh:* vv. 10,18; 1 Jn. 2:16. (Jn. 8:15; Jude 23)
c Jude 8
12
d Jude 10
14
e See Rom. 3:23, *note*
15
f *Apostasy:* vv. 1–22; 1 Jn. 4:5. (Lk. 18:8; 2 Tim. 3:1, *note*)
g Num. 22:1–41
17
h Jude 12
i Jude 13
18
j Cp. Jude 18
19
k Prov. 5:22
l Jn. 8:34; Rom. 6:16
20
m Gk. *kosmos.* See Rev. 13:8, *note*
n See Rom. 1:16, *note*
o Lk. 11:26; Heb. 6:4–6
21
p Cp. Mt. 11:23–24; Lk. 12:47–48
22
q Prov. 26:11
CHAPTER 3
1
r 2 Pet. 1:13
2
s 2 Pet. 1:21
t Lit. *of the Lord and Savior by our apostles*
3
u Cp. Jude 10,18

*

2:17 NU-Text reads *and mists.* • NU-Text omits *forever.* 2:18 NU-Text reads *are barely escaping.* 3:2 NU-Text and M-Text read *commandment of the apostles of your Lord and Savior* or *commandment of your apostles of the Lord and Savior.*

[1](2:15) Balaam (see Num. 22:5, refs.) was the typical hireling prophet, anxious to make a market of his gift. This is the "way of Balaam." See the "error of Balaam," Jude 11, *note;* and the "doctrine of Balaam," Rev. 2:14, *note.*

V. The Second Coming of Christ and the Day of the Lord, 3:4–16

(1) The return of the Lord to be generally disbelieved

4 and saying, "Where is the promise of His [a]coming? For since the fathers fell asleep, all things continue as *they were* from the beginning of [b]creation."

5 For this they willfully forget: that [c]by the word of God the heavens were of old, and the earth standing out of water and in the water,

6 by which the [d]world *that* then existed [e]perished, being flooded with water.

7 But the heavens and the earth *which* are now preserved by the same word, are reserved for fire until the [f]day of judgment and [g]perdition of ungodly men.

8 But, beloved, do not forget this one thing, that with the Lord one day *is* as a thousand years, and a [h]thousand years as one day.

9 The Lord is not [i]slack concerning *His* promise, as some count slackness, but is [j]longsuffering toward us,* not [1k]willing that any should perish but that all [l]should come to [m]repentance.

(2) The purging of the heavens and the earth

10 But the [n]day of the Lord will come [o]as a thief in the night, [2]in which the [p]heavens will pass away with a great noise, and the elements will melt with fervent heat; both the earth and the works that are in it will be burned up.*

11 Therefore, since all these things will be dissolved, what manner *of persons* ought you to be in holy conduct and godliness,

12 [q]looking for and hastening the coming of the day of God, because of which the heavens will be dissolved, being on fire, and the elements will melt with fervent heat?

13 Nevertheless we, according to His [r]promise, [s]look for [t]new heavens and a [t]new earth in which [u]righteousness dwells.

14 Therefore, beloved, [s]looking forward to these things, be diligent to be found by Him in peace, without spot and [v]blameless;

15 and consider *that* the [w]longsuffering of our Lord *is* [x]salvation—as also our beloved brother Paul, according to the wisdom given to him, has written to you,

16 as also in all his [y]epistles, speaking in them of these things, in which are some things hard to understand, which untaught and unstable *people* twist to their own destruction, as *they do* also the [z]rest of the Scriptures.

Conclusion: Exhortation and Benediction, 3:17–18

17 You therefore, beloved, since you know *this* [aa]beforehand, beware [bb]lest you also fall from your own steadfastness, being led away with the error of the wicked;

18 but grow in the [3cc]grace

4
a Christ (second advent): v. 4; 1 Jn. 2:28. (Dt. 30:3; Acts 1:11, *note*)
b Gen. 6:1–7

5
c Gen. 1:6–9

6
d Gk. *kosmos.* See Mt. 4:8, *note*
e Gen. 7:21–23; Mt. 24:37–39; Lk. 17:26–27; 2 Pet. 2:5

7
f Day (of judgment): v. 7; 1 Jn. 4:17. (Mt. 10:15; Rev. 20:11)
g Lit. *destruction*

8
h Ps. 90:4

9
i Cp. Hab. 2:3
j Ps. 86:15; Isa. 30:18
k Or *desiring*
l Mt. 20:28; 1 Tim. 2:4
m Repentance: v. 9; Rev. 2:5. (Mt. 3:2; Acts 17:30, *note*)

10
n Day (of the LORD): vv. 10–13; Jude 6. (Ps. 2:9; Rev. 19:19)
o Mt. 24:42; 1 Th. 5:2; Rev. 16:15
p Gen. 1:6–8; Ps. 102:25–26; Isa. 51:6; Rev. 20:11

12
q 1 Cor. 1:7–8; Ti. 2:13–15

13
r Isa. 65:17
s Lit. *wait for*
t Rev. 21:1
u See 1 Jn. 3:7, *note*

14
v 1 Cor. 1:8; 1 Th. 5:23

15
w Ps. 86:15; Rom. 2:4
x See Rom. 1:16, *note*

16
y e.g. Rom. 8:19; 1 Cor. 15:24; 2 Th. 1:10
z 2 Tim. 3:16

17
aa Cp. Jn. 16:4
bb Test/tempt: v. 17; Rev. 2:10. (Gen. 3:1; Jas. 1:14, *note*)

18
cc Grace: v. 18; 2 Jn. 3. (Jn. 1:14; Jn. 1:17, *note*)

*3:9 NU-Text reads *you.* 3:10 NU-Text reads *laid bare* (literally *found*).

[1](3:9) Three aspects of the will of God may be observed in Scripture: (1) the sovereign will of God (Isa. 46:9–11; Dan. 4:17,35; Heb. 2:4; Rev. 17:17); (2) the moral will of God, i.e. His moral law (Mk. 3:35; Eph. 6:6; Heb. 13:21); and (3) the desires of God coming from His heart of love (Ezek. 33:11; Mt. 23:37; 2 Pet. 3:9). The sovereign will of God is certain of complete fulfillment, but the moral law is disobeyed by men, and the desires of God are fulfilled only to the extent that they are included in His sovereign will. God does not desire that any should perish, but it is clear that many will not be saved (Rev. 21:8).

[2](3:10) This refers to the close of the Day of the Lord at the end of the millennium, when the destruction of the heavens and the earth ends the Day of the Lord (Rev. 20:11; 21:1).

[3](3:18) Grace (imparted), Summary (see Grace, Jn. 1:17, *note*): Grace is the method of divine dealing in salvation and in the believer's life and service. As saved, he is "not under law but under grace" (Rom. 6:14). Having by grace brought the Christian into the highest conceivable position (Eph. 1:6), God ceaselessly works through grace, to impart to and perfect in him corresponding graces (Jn. 15:4–5; Gal. 5:22–23). Grace, therefore, stands connected with service (Rom. 12:6; 15:15–16; 1 Cor. 1:3–7; 3:10; 15:10; 2 Cor. 12:9–10; Gal. 2:9; Eph. 3:7–8; 4:7; Phil. 1:7; 2 Tim. 2:1–2; 1 Pet. 4:10); with Christian growth (2 Cor. 1:12; Eph. 4:29; Col. 3:16;

and knowledge of our Lord and Savior Jesus Christ. To Him *be* the glory both now and forever. Amen.

4:6; 2 Th. 1:12; Heb. 4:16; 12:28–29; 13:9; Jas. 4:6; 1 Pet. 1:2; 3:7; 5:5,10; 2 Pet. 3:18; Jude 4); and with giving (2 Cor. 4:15; 8:1,6–7,19; 9:14).

The First Epistle of

JOHN

Author: John *Theme:* Fellowship *Date of writing:* c. A.D. 90–95

THE FIRST EPISTLE OF JOHN, by the witness of internal evidence and comparison with the Gospel of John, was manifestly written by the Apostle John. It is a family letter from the Father to His "little children" who are in the world. With the possible exception of the Song of Solomon, it is the most intimate of the inspired writings. The sin of a Christian is treated as a child's offense against his Father, and is dealt with as a family matter (1:9; 2:1). The moral government of the universe is not in question. The child's sin as an offense against the law has been met in the cross, and "Jesus Christ the righteous" is now our "Advocate with the Father." John's Gospel leads across the threshold of the Father's house; his First Epistle makes us at home there. A tender word is used for "children" (from Gk. *teknia*), a diminutive meaning *little children, born-ones* as, e.g. the Scottish "bairns." Whereas Paul is occupied with the Christian's public position as a son, John has in mind the believer's nearness as one born of the Father.

First John may be divided as follows:

Introduction, 1:1–2.
I. Dear Children and Fellowship, 1:3—2:11.
II. Dear Children and Their Enemies, 2:12–27.
III. Dear Children and the Lord's Return, 2:28—3:3.
IV. Dear Children Contrasted with Children of Satan, 3:4–24.
V. Dear Children and False Teachers, 4:1–6.
VI. Dear Children Assured and Warned, 4:7—5:19.
Conclusion, 5:20–21.

CHAPTER 1
1
a Christ (first advent): vv. 1–3; 1 Jn. 4:2. (Gen. 3:15; Acts 1:11, *note*)
b Jn. 1:1; 1 Jn. 2:13
c Cp. Jn. 5:24; Acts 4:20
d Lk. 1:2; Jn. 1:14; 19:35
e 2 Pet. 1:16–17
f Lk. 24:39; Jn. 20:27
g Jn. 1:1,14
2
h Rom. 16:26; 1 Tim. 3:16
i Life (eternal): vv. 1–2; 1 Jn. 2:25. (Mt. 7:14; Rev. 22:19)
j Jn. 1:1,18; 16:28
3
k Jn. 17:21; 1 Cor. 1:9; 1 Jn. 2:24

Introduction: the Incarnate Word, 1:1–2

Fellowship made possible

1 THAT which [a]was [b]from
the beginning, which we
have [c]heard, which we have
[d]seen with our eyes, which we
have [e]looked upon, and our
hands have [f]handled, concerning the [g]Word of life—
2 the life was [h]manifested,
and we have seen, and bear witness, and declare to you that
[i]eternal life which was [j]with
the Father and was manifested
to us—

I. Little Children and Fellowship, 1:3—2:11

(1) Fellowship is with the Father and the Son

3 that which we have seen
and heard we declare to you,
that you also may have fellowship with us; and truly our fellowship *is* [k]with the Father and
with His Son Jesus Christ.
4 And these things we write
to you that your* [l]joy may be
full.

(2) The conditions of fellowship

(a) Their position in the light

5 This is the message which
we have heard from Him and
declare to you, that God is
[m]light and in Him is no darkness
at all.
6 If we [n]say that we have
fellowship with Him, and walk
in darkness, we lie and do not
practice the truth.
7 But if we [1o]walk in the
[p]light as He is in the light, we
have fellowship with one another, and the [q]blood of Jesus
Christ His Son cleanses us from
all sin.

(b) The recognition of indwelling sin (see 1 Cor. 11:31, note)

8 If we say that we have no
sin, we deceive ourselves, and
the truth is not in us.

* 1:4 NU-Text and M-Text read *our*.

4
l Jn. 15:11; 16:24; 1 Pet. 1:8
5
m 1 Tim. 6:16
6
n 1 Jn. 2:9–11
7
o Isa. 2:5
p See Ex. 27:20, *note*
q Sacrifice (of Christ): v. 7; Rev. 1:5. (Gen. 3:15; Heb. 10:18, *note*)

---

[1](1:7) Walking in the light is explained in vv. 8–10; Eph. 5:13. Through the Word of God the indwelling Holy Spirit shows the Christian that he (1) still possesses an old nature (v. 8), and (2) needs the forgiveness of his sins (vv. 9–10). The blood of Christ is the divine provision for both (see Advocacy, 2:1, *note*). To walk in the light is to live in fellowship with the Father and the Son. Sin interrupts fellowship but cannot change relationship. Confession restores fellowship and immediate confession keeps the fellowship unbroken.

(c) Sins confessed, forgiven, and cleansed

9 If we [a]confess our sins, He is [b]faithful and [c]just to [d]forgive us *our* sins and to cleanse us from all unrighteousness.

10 If we say that we have not sinned, we [e]make Him a liar, and His word is not in us.

(d) Fellowship maintained by Christ's advocacy

2 MY little children, these things I write to you, so that you may not sin. And if anyone [f]sins, we have an [1g]Advocate with the Father, Jesus Christ the righteous.

2 And He Himself is the [h]propitiation for our [f]sins, and not for ours only [i]but also for the whole [j]world.

(e) Recognition of God's holiness

3 Now by this we know that we know Him, if we keep His [2]commandments.

4 He who says, "I know Him," and does not keep His commandments, is a [k]liar, and the truth is not in him.

5 But whoever [l]keeps His word, truly the love of God is [m]perfected in him. By this we know that we are in Him.

6 He who says he abides in Him [n]ought himself also to walk just as He walked.

7 Brethren,* [o]I write no new commandment to you, but an old commandment which you have had [p]from the beginning. The [q]old commandment is the word which you heard from the beginning.*

8 Again, a [r]new commandment I write to you, which thing is true in Him and in you, because the darkness is passing away, and the [s]true light is already shining.

9 He who [t]says he is in the light, and hates his brother, is in darkness until now.

10 He who [u]loves his brother abides in the light, and there is no cause for stumbling in him.

11 But he who [v]hates his brother is in darkness and [w]walks in darkness, and does not know where he is going, because the darkness has blinded his eyes.

II. Little Children and Their Enemies, 2:12–27

The family addressed

12 I write to you, little children,
Because your [f]sins are [d]forgiven you for His name's sake.

13 I write to you, fathers,
Because you have known Him *who is* [x]from the beginning.
I write to you, young men,
Because you have [y]overcome the wicked one.
I write to you, [z]little children,
Because you have [aa]known the Father.

14 I have written to you, fathers,
Because you have known Him *who is* from the beginning.
I have written to you, young men,
Because you are strong, and the word of God abides in you,
And you have overcome the wicked one.

The children must not love the world

15 Do [bb]not love the [cc]world or the things in the world. [dd]If anyone loves the world, the love of the Father is not in him.

16 For all that *is* in the world—the lust of the [ee]flesh, the lust of the eyes, and the pride of life—is not of the Father but is of the world.

*2:7 NU-Text reads *Beloved.* • NU-Text omits *from the beginning.*

9
a Prov. 28:13; cp. Ps. 32:5
b Rom. 3:24–26
c Or *righteous*
d *Forgiveness:* v. 9; 2:12. (Lev. 4:20; Mt. 26:28, *note*)

10
e 1 Jn. 5:10; cp. Jn. 3:33

CHAPTER 2

1
f See Rom. 3:23, *note*
g Gk. *paraklētos,* rendered *Helper* in Jn. 14:16

2
h See Rom. 3:25, *note*
i *Assurance/security:* vv. 1–2; 1 Jn. 3:2. (Ps. 23:1; Jude 1, *note*)
j Gk. *kosmos.* See Mt. 4:8, *note*

4
k Rom. 3:4

5
l Cp. Jn. 14:23; Col. 3:16
m See Mt. 5:48, *note*

6
n Jn. 13:15; 1 Pet. 2:21

7
o Cp. 2 Jn. 5
p 1 Jn. 3:11
q Cp. Jn. 15:10

8
r Jn. 15:12
s Jn. 1:9; 8:12; 12:35

9
t v. 4; 1 Jn. 3:14

10
u *Law* (of Christ): v. 10; 1 Jn. 3:11. (Jn. 13:34; 2 Jn. 5)

11
v 1 Jn. 3:15; 4:20
w Jn. 12:35; cp. 2 Pet. 1:9

13
x 1 Jn. 1:1; Rev. 22:13
y Cp. Eph. 6:11; Heb. 2:14; 1 Jn. 4:4
z A general term for all children
aa Rom. 8:15–17; Gal. 4:6

15
bb Rom. 12:2; Gal. 1:4
cc Gk. *kosmos.* See Rev. 13:8, *note*
dd Mt. 6:24; Jas. 4:4; cp. Gal. 1:10

16
ee *Flesh:* v. 16; Jude 23. (Jn. 8:15; Jude 23)

[1](2:1) This is the advocacy of Jesus Christ for sinning believers which He carries on with the Father whereby, because of the eternal efficacy of Christ's sacrifice, He restores them to fellowship. Cp. Ps. 23:3; see Jn. 13:10, *note.*

[2](2:3) John uses "commandments" (1) in the general sense of the divine will, however revealed—"His word" (v. 5); and (2) especially of the law of Christ (Gal. 6:2; 2 Jn. 5). See also Jn. 15:10–12.

17 And the world is passing away, and the lust of it; but he who does the will of God abides forever.

The children warned against apostates

18 Little children, it is the [a]last hour; and as you have heard that the* [b]Antichrist is coming, even now many antichrists have come, by which we know that it is the [a]last hour.

19 They [1]went out from us, but they were not of us; for if they had been of us, they would have continued with us; but *they went out* [c]that they might be made manifest, that [d]none of them were of us.

20 But you have an [e]anointing from the Holy One, and you [f]know all things.*

21 I have not written to you because you do not know the truth, but [g]because you know it, and that no lie is of the truth.

22 Who is [h]a liar but he who denies that [i]Jesus is the Christ? He is [b]antichrist who denies the Father and the Son.

23 Whoever [j]denies the Son does not have the [k]Father either; he who acknowledges the Son has the Father also.

24 Therefore let that abide in you which you heard from the beginning. If what you heard from the beginning abides in you, you also will [l]abide in the Son and in the Father.

25 And this is the [m]promise that He has promised us—[n]eternal life.

26 These things I have written to you concerning those who *try to* [o]deceive you.

27 But the [p]anointing which you have received from Him abides in you, and you do not need that anyone teach you; but as the same anointing teaches you concerning all things, and is true, and is not a lie, and just as it has taught you, you will* abide in Him.

III. Little Children and the Lord's Return, 2:28—3:3

Purity exhorted

28 And now, [q]little children, abide in Him, that when* He [r]appears, we may have [s]confidence and not be ashamed before Him at His coming.

29 If you know that He is righteous, you know that everyone who practices [t]righteousness is born of Him.

3 BEHOLD [u]what manner of love the Father has bestowed on us, that we should be called children of God!* Therefore the [v]world does [w]not know us,* because it did not know Him.

2 Beloved, now we are children of God; and it has not yet been revealed what we shall be, but we [x]know that when He is [r]revealed, [y]we shall be like Him, for we shall see Him as He [z]is.

3 And everyone who has this hope in Him purifies himself, just as He is pure.

IV. Little Children Contrasted with Children of Satan, 3:4–24

Their distinguishing characteristics

4 Whoever [2]commits [aa]sin also commits lawlessness, and sin is lawlessness.

5 And you know that He was manifested to [bb]take away our [aa]sins, and [cc]in Him there is no sin.

6 Whoever abides in Him does not sin. Whoever sins has neither seen Him nor known Him.

7 [q]Little children, let no one deceive you. He who practices

*2:18 NU-Text omits *the.* 2:20 NU-Text reads *you all know.* 2:27 NU-Text reads *you abide.* 2:28 NU-Text reads *if.* 3:1 NU-Text adds *And we are.* • M-Text reads *you.*

18
a 1 Pet. 4:7
b Antichrist: vv. 18,22; 1 Jn. 4:3. (Mt. 24:5; Rev. 13:11, *note*)
19
c Cp. 1 Cor. 11:19
d Cp. Jn. 10:27–29
20
e 2 Cor. 1:21
f 1 Cor. 2:15–16
21
g Cp. 2 Pet. 3:1; Jude 5
22
h Lit. *the*
i 1 Jn. 4:3
23
j Cp. Jn. 14:9–11
k Jn. 5:23
24
l Jn. 15:5; Col. 1:23; 2 Jn. 9
25
m Jn. 3:14–16; 17:2–3
n Life (eternal): v. 25; 1 Jn. 3:15. (Mt. 7:14; Rev. 22:19)
26
o Lit. *cause you to wander, i.e. lead you astray*
27
p v. 20; Jn. 14:26; 16:13

28
q As in 2:1,12
r Christ (second advent): v. 28; 3:2–3; Jude 14. (Dt. 30:3; Acts 1:11, *note*)
s 1 Jn. 3:21; 4:17
29
t See 3:7, *note*
CHAPTER 3
1
u Eph. 2:4–7; 1 Jn. 4:10
v Gk. *kosmos.* See Mt. 4:8, *note*
w Cp. Jn. 15:18–20
2
x Assurance/security: v. 2; Jude 1. (Ps. 23:1; Jude 1, *note*)
y Rom. 8:29; 1 Cor. 15:49; Phil. 3:21
z Cp. 1 Cor. 13:10–12
4
aa See Rom. 3:23, *note*
5
bb Jn. 1:29; 2 Cor. 5:21; Heb. 9:26
cc Heb. 7:26; 1 Pet. 1:19

[1](2:19) "Went out from us," i.e. doctrinally. Doubtless then, as now, the deniers of the Son (vv. 22–23) called themselves Christians. Cp. 2 Tim. 1:15.

[2](3:4) Here and in similar places in this Epistle the Greek verb has the force of a continuous present tense (cp. 3:6,9; 5:18) and thus denotes a person's habitual attitude toward sin as expressed in his practice or non-practice of it. John is not speaking of a state of perfection in which it is impossible for a Christian ever to sin; but he is stressing the fact that a Christian cannot keep on practicing sin, because he is born of God.

[1]righteousness is righteous, just
as He is righteous.
8 He who [a]sins is of the
[b]devil, for the devil has sinned
from the beginning. For this
purpose the Son of God was
manifested, [c]that He might destroy the works of the [b]devil.
9 Whoever has been [d]born
of God does not sin, for His seed
remains in him; and he cannot
sin, because he has been born of
God.
10 In this the children of God
and the children of the [b]devil
are manifest: Whoever does not
practice [e]righteousness is not
of God, nor *is* he who does not
love his brother.
11 For this is the [f]message
that you heard from the beginning, that we should [g]love one
another,
12 not as [h]Cain *who* was of
the wicked one and murdered
his brother. And why did he
murder him? Because his works
were evil and his brother's righteous.
13 Do not marvel, my brethren, if the [i]world [j]hates you.
14 We know that we have
passed from death to life, because we [g]love the brethren. He
who does not love *his* brother*
abides in death.
15 Whoever hates his
brother is a murderer, and you
know that no murderer has
[k]eternal life abiding in him.
16 By this we know [g]love,
[l]because He laid down His life
for us. And we also ought to
[m]lay down *our* lives for the
brethren.
17 But whoever has this
world's goods, and sees his
brother in [n]need, and shuts up
his heart from him, how does
the [g]love of God [o]abide in him?
18 My little children, let us
not [g]love in word or in tongue,
but in deed and in truth.
19 And by this we know*
that we are of the truth, and
shall assure our hearts before
Him.
20 [p]For if our heart condemns us, God is greater than
our heart, and knows all things.
21 Beloved, if our heart does
not condemn us, we have [q]con-
fidence toward God.
22 And [r]whatever we ask we
receive from Him, because we
keep His commandments and
do those things that are pleasing in His sight.
23 And this is His commandment: that we should [s]believe
on the name of His Son Jesus
Christ and [g]love one another,
as He gave us* commandment.
24 Now he who keeps His
commandments [t]abides in Him,
and He in him. And by this we
know that He abides in us, by
the [u]Spirit whom He has given
us.

V. Little Children and False Teachers, 4:1–6

4 BELOVED, do not believe
every [v]spirit, but test the
spirits, whether they are of God;
because many false prophets
have gone out into the [w]world.

Marks of false teachers

(a) Erroneous doctrine concerning Christ's Person

2 By this you know the
[u]Spirit of God: Every spirit that
confesses that [x]Jesus Christ
has [y]come in the flesh is of God,
3 and every spirit that does
not confess that Jesus Christ
has [y]come in the flesh* is not of
God. And this is the *spirit* of the
[z]Antichrist, which you have
heard was coming, and is now
already in the [i]world.
4 You are of God, little children, and have overcome them,
because He who is in you is
[aa]greater than [bb]he who is in the
world.

(b) Erroneous attitude toward world

5 [cc]They are of the world.
Therefore they speak *as* of the

*
3:14 NU-Text omits *his brother.*
3:19 NU-Text reads *we shall know.*
3:23 M-Text omits *us.* 4:3 NU-Text omits *that* and *Christ has come in the flesh.*

8
a See Rom. 3:23, *note*
b Satan: vv. 8,10; Jude 9. (Gen. 3:1; Rev. 20:10)
c Heb. 2:14
9
d Jn. 3:3–6; 1 Jn. 5:18
10
e See v. 7, *note*
11
f Jn. 13:34; 1 Jn. 1:5; 2:7–11; 3:23; 4:7–12
g Law (of Christ): vv. 11,14, 16–18,23; 1 Jn. 4:7. (Jn. 13:34; 2 Jn. 5)
12
h Gen. 4:8
13
i Gk. *kosmos.* See Rev. 13:8, *note*
j Jn. 15:18–21
15
k Life (eternal): vv. 14–15; 1 Jn. 5:11. (Mt. 7:14; Rev. 22:19)
16
l Jn. 15:13; Gal. 2:20
m Cp. Rom. 16:4
17
n Cp. Lk. 3:11
o Cp. 1 Jn. 4:20
20
p Cp. 1 Cor. 4:4

21
q 1 Jn. 2:28
22
r Jn. 15:7; 1 Jn. 5:14–15
23
s Faith: v. 23; 1 Jn. 4:16. (Gen. 3:20; Heb. 11:39, *note*)
24
t Jn. 14:21
u Holy Spirit (NT): v. 24; 4:2; 1 Jn. 4:13. (Mt. 1:18; Acts 2:4, *note*)
CHAPTER 4
1
v Cp. Mt. 7:15; 2 Cor. 11:13–15
w Gk. *kosmos.* See Mt. 4:8, *note*
2
x Rom. 10:8–10; 1 Jn. 5:1
y Christ (first advent): vv. 2–3; 1 Jn. 5:20. (Gen. 3:15; Acts 1:11, *note*)
3
z Antichrist: v. 3; 2 Jn. 7. (Mt. 24:5; Rev. 13:11, *note*)
4
aa Cp. Rom. 8:31; Heb. 6:13
bb Jn. 14:30; 16:11; cp. 1 Cor. 2:12
5
cc Apostasy: vv. 1–6; Jude 4. (Lk. 18:8; 2 Tim. 3:1, *note*)

[1](3:7) "Righteousness" here, and in the passages having marginal reference to this verse, means the righteous life which is the result of salvation through Christ. By God's grace the Christian does righteously because he has been made righteous (Rom. 3:22; see Rom. 10:3, *note*).

world, and [a]the world hears them.

6 We are of God. He who knows God hears us; he who is not of God does not hear [b]us. [c]By this we know the spirit of truth and the spirit of error.

VI. Little Children Assured and Warned, 4:7—5:19

7 [d]Beloved, let us [e]love one another, for love is of God; and everyone who [f]loves is born of God and knows God.

8 He who does not love does not know God, for [g]God is love.

9 In this the love of God was [h]manifested toward us, that God has sent His only begotten [i]Son into the [j]world, that we might live through Him.

10 In this is love, [k]not that we loved God, but that He loved us and sent His Son *to be* the [l]propitiation for our sins.

God's indwelling love shown by a life of love toward Him and men

11 Beloved, if God so loved us, we also ought to [e]love one another.

12 No one has seen God at any time. If we [e]love one another, God abides in us, and His love has been [m]perfected in us.

13 By this we know that we abide in Him, and He in us, because He has given us of His [n]Spirit.

14 And we have seen and testify that the Father has sent the Son *as* [o]Savior of the [j]world.

15 Whoever [p]confesses that Jesus is the Son of God, God abides in him, and he in God.

16 And we have known and [q]believed the love that God has for us. God is love, and he who abides in love abides in God, and God [r]in him.

17 [e]Love has been perfected among us in this: that we may have [s]boldness in the [t]day of judgment; because as He is, so are we in this world.

18 There is no fear in love; but perfect love casts out fear, because fear involves torment. But he who fears has not been made [m]perfect in love.

19 [u]We love Him* because He first loved us.

20 [v]If someone says, "I love God," and hates his brother, he is a liar; for he who does not love his brother whom he has seen, how can* he love God whom he has not seen?

21 And [w]this commandment we have from Him: that he who loves God *must* [e]love his brother also.

Faith in the overcoming principle in the world conflict

5 WHOEVER [q]believes that [x]Jesus is the Christ is [y]born of God, and [z]everyone who loves Him who begot also loves him who is begotten of Him.

2 By this we know that we [e]love the children of God, when we love God and [aa]keep His commandments.

3 For this is the love of God, that we keep His commandments. And His commandments [bb]are not burdensome.

4 For whatever is born of God overcomes the [cc]world. And this is the victory that has [dd]overcome the world—our* [q]faith.

5 Who is he who overcomes the world, but he who [q]believes that Jesus is the Son of God?

6 This is He who came by [ee]water and blood—Jesus Christ; not only by water, but by water and blood. And it is the [n]Spirit who bears witness, because the [n]Spirit is truth.

7 For there are three that bear witness in heaven: the Father, the Word, and the Holy Spirit; and these three are one.

8 And there are [ff]three that bear witness on earth:* [gg]the [n]Spirit, the water, and the blood; and these three agree as one.

Blessed assurance

9 If we receive the witness of men, the witness of God is greater; for this is the [hh]witness of God which* He has testified of His Son.

10 He who [q]believes in the

*

4:19 NU-Text omits *Him.* 4:20 NU-Text reads *he cannot.* 5:4 M-Text reads *your.* 5:8 NU-Text and M-Text omit the words from *in heaven* (verse 7) through *on earth* (verse 8). Only four or five very late manuscripts contain these words in Greek. 5:9 NU-Text reads *God, that.*

5
a Jn. 15:19; 17:14
6
b Cp. Jn. 8:47
c 1 Cor. 2:12–16
7
d 1 Jn. 3:10–11,23
e Law (of Christ): vv. 7,11–12, 17,21; 5:2; 2 Jn. 5. (Jn. 13:34; 2 Jn. 5)
f 1 Jn. 3:14; 1 Th. 4:9
8
g v. 16
9
h Rom. 5:8
i Isa. 9:6–7; Jn. 3:16
j Gk. *kosmos.* See Mt. 4:8, *note*
10
k Ti. 3:5
l See Rom. 3:25, *note*
12
m See Mt. 5:48, *note*
13
n Holy Spirit (NT): v. 13; 5:6, 8; Jude 19. (Mt. 1:18; Acts 2:4, *note*)
14
o See Rom. 1:16, *note*
15
p v. 2
16
q Faith: v. 16; 5:1, 4–5,10; 1 Jn. 5:13. (Gen. 3:20; Heb. 11:39, *note*)
r Jn. 14:23
17
s 1 Jn. 2:28
t Day (of judgment): v. 17; Rev. 20:11. (Mt. 10:15; Rev. 20:11)
19
u 4:10; cp. 2 Cor. 5:14–15
20
v 1 Jn. 2:4

21
w Jn. 13:34; 15:12; 1 Jn. 3:23
CHAPTER 5
1
x 1 Jn. 4:2,15; cp. 1 Jn. 2:22–23
y Jn. 1:13
z Cp. Jn. 15:23
2
aa Jn. 15:10; 2 Jn. 6
3
bb Mt. 11:30
4
cc Gk. *kosmos.* See Rev. 13:8, *note*
dd 1 Jn. 4:4; cp. Rev. 12:11
6
ee Jn. 19:34–35; Eph. 5:26–27; cp. Jn. 15:3; 17:17
8
ff Cp. Jn. 8:17–18
gg Jn. 15:26
9
hh Jn. 5:34,37

10
a Rom. 8:16; Gal. 4:6
b Cp. 1 Jn. 1:10
11
c *Life* (eternal): vv. 11–13, 20; Jude 21. (Mt. 7:14; Rev. 22:19)
12
d Jn. 3:36; 6:47; 17:2–3
13
e *Faith:* v. 13; Rev. 2:19. (Gen. 3:20; Heb. 11:39, *note*)
f Cp. Jn. 20:31
14
g 1 Jn. 3:22
h Cp. Jas. 4:3
16
i See Rom. 3:23, *note*
j Cp. Jas. 5:15

Son of God [a]has the witness in
himself; he who does not believe God [b]has made Him a liar,
because he has not believed the
testimony that God has given of
His Son.
11 And this is the testimony:
that God has given us [c]eternal
life, and this life is in His Son.
12 He who [d]has the Son has
[c]life; he who does not have the
Son of God does not have [c]life.
13 These things I have written to you who [e]believe in the
name of the Son of God, [f]that
you may know that you have
[c]eternal life,* and that you may
continue to believe in the name
of the Son of God.
14 Now this is the confidence
that we have in Him, that [g]if we
ask anything [h]according to His
will, He hears us.
15 And if we know that He
hears us, whatever we ask, we
know that we have the petitions
that we have asked of Him.

Sober warnings

16 If anyone sees his brother
sinning a [i]sin *which does* not
lead to death, he will [j]ask, and
He will give him life for those
who commit sin not *leading* to
death. There is sin *leading* to
death. I do not say that he
should [k]pray about that.
17 [l]All unrighteousness is
sin, and there is sin not *leading*
to death.
18 We know that whoever is
[m]born of God does not sin; but
he who has been born of God
keeps himself,* and the wicked
one does not touch him.
19 We know that we are of
God, and [n]the whole world lies
under the sway of the wicked
one.

Conclusion, 5:20–21

20 And we know that the
[o]Son of God has [p]come and has
given us an understanding, that
we may know Him who is true;
and we are in Him who is true,
in His Son Jesus Christ. [q]This is
the true God and [c]eternal life.
21 Little children, [r]keep
yourselves from idols. Amen.

k Cp. Jer. 7:16
17
l 1 Jn. 3:4
18
m 1 Jn. 3:9
19
n Cp. Lk. 4:5–6; 2 Cor. 4:3–4
20
o 1 Jn. 4:2
p *Christ* (first advent): v. 20. (Gen. 3:15; Acts 1:11, *note*)
q Jn. 17:3
21
r See 2 Cor. 6:17, *note*

*
5:13 NU-Text omits the rest of this verse.
5:18 NU-Text reads *him*.

The Second Epistle of
JOHN

Author: John *Theme:* Christ's Commandment *Date of writing:* c. A.D. 90–95

THE SECOND EPISTLE OF JOHN has, on account of its salutation, occasioned much discussion. Some scholars assert that the words, "the elect lady," personify one of the first-century churches; others assume that they refer to some highly placed Christian matron with whom the Apostle John was acquainted. Brief though it is, the Epistle is not insignificant. On the contrary, its urgent message centers round the "truth" in its relation to Christian living. By the "truth" John means not only the body of revealed truth, the Scriptures, but also the Lord Jesus Christ who, as the chief Subject of the Scriptures, is Himself the Truth incarnate.

The Epistle may be divided as follows:

Introduction, vv. 1–3.
I. The Pathway of Truth and Love, vv. 4–6.
II. The Mark of a Deceiver and Antichrist, vv. 7–11.
Conclusion, vv. 12–13.

Introduction: Salutation and Invocation, vv. 1–3

THE [a]ELDER,
To the [b]elect lady and her
children, whom I love in truth,
and not only I, but also all those
who have known the truth,
2 because of the truth
[c]which abides in us and [d]will
be with us forever:

3 [e]Grace, mercy, *and* peace
will be with you* from God the
Father and from the Lord Jesus
Christ, the Son of the Father, in
truth and love.

I. The Pathway of Truth and Love, vv. 4–6

4 I [f]rejoiced greatly that I
have found *some* of your children walking in truth, as we received commandment from the
Father.
5 And now I plead with you,
lady, not as though I wrote a
new commandment to you, but
that which we have had [g]from
the beginning: [1]that we [h]love
one another.
6 [i]This is love, that we walk
according to His command-
ments. This is the commandment, that as you have heard
from the beginning, you should
walk in it.

II. The Mark of a Deceiver and Antichrist, vv. 7–11

7 For many deceivers have
gone out into the [j]world who do
not confess Jesus Christ *as*
coming in the [k]flesh. This is [l]a
deceiver and [l]an [m]antichrist.
8 Look to yourselves, that
we* do not [n]lose those things
we worked for, but *that* we*
may receive a full [o]reward.
9 Whoever [p]transgresses*
and does not abide in the [q]doc-
trine of Christ does [r]not have
God. He who abides in the doctrine of Christ has both the Father and the Son.
10 If anyone comes to you
and does [s]not bring this doctrine, do [t]not receive him into
your house nor greet him;
11 for he who greets him
shares in his evil deeds.

Conclusion, vv. 12–13

12 Having many things to
write to you, I did not wish *to do
so* with paper and ink; but I
hope to come to you and speak

---

*
v. 3 NU-Text and M-Text read *us*.
v. 8 NU-Text reads *you*. • NU-Text reads *you*. v. 9 NU-Text reads *goes ahead*.

1
a *Elders:* v. 1; 3 Jn. 1. (Acts 11:30; Ti. 1:5, *note*)
b *Election* (personal): v. 1; 2 Jn. 13. (Dt. 7:6; 1 Pet. 5:13, *note*)
2
c Cp. Col. 3:16
d Cp. 1 Pet. 1:23
3
e *Grace:* v. 3; Rev. 1:4. (Jn. 1:14; Jn. 1:17, *note*)
4
f 1 Th. 2:19–20; 3 Jn. 3–4
5
g Jn. 13:34; 1 Jn. 2:7
h *Law* (of Christ): v. 5. (Jn. 13:34; 2 Jn. 5)
6
i Jn. 14:15; 1 Jn. 5:3

7
j Gk. *kosmos.* See Mt. 4:8, *note*
k 1 Jn. 4:2
l Lit. *the*
m *Antichrist:* v. 7; Rev. 13:11. (Mt. 24:5; Rev. 13:11, *note*)
8
n Cp. Heb. 2:1; 4:1; 10:35
o *Rewards:* v. 8; Rev. 2:10. (Dan. 12:3; 1 Cor. 3:14, *note*)
9
p See Rom. 3:23, *note*
q Or *teaching*
r 1 Jn. 2:19, 24
10
s Rom. 16:17
t *Separation:* vv. 10–11; Rev. 18:4. (Gen. 12:1; 2 Cor. 6:17, *note*)

---

[1](v. 5) Law (of Christ), Summary: The new law of Christ is the divine love, as produced in the renewed heart by the Holy Spirit (Rom. 5:5; Heb. 10:16), which flows out in the energy of the Spirit, unforced and spontaneous, toward the objects of the divine love (2 Cor. 5:14–20; 1 Th. 2:7–8). It is, therefore, "the law of liberty" (Jas. 1:25; 2:12) in contrast with the external law of Moses. Moses' law demands love (Lev. 19:18; Dt. 6:5; Lk. 10:27); Christ's law is love (Rom. 5:5; 1 Jn. 4:7,19–20), and so takes the place of the external law by fulfilling it (Rom. 13:10; Gal. 5:14). It is the "law written in the heart" under the New Covenant (see Heb. 8:8, *note 1*).

12 [a]face to face, that our joy may
be full.
13 The children of your
[b]elect sister greet you. Amen.

a Cp. 3 Jn. 13–14

b Election (personal): v. 13; Jude 1. (Dt. 7:6; 1 Pet. 5:13, *note*)

The Third Epistle of

JOHN

Author: John *Theme:* Walking in Truth *Date of writing:* c. A.D. 90–95

THE THIRD EPISTLE OF JOHN, addressed by the Apostle John to his friend, Gaius, rebukes Diotrephes, who had usurped leadership in one of the churches. Slanderously rejecting John's authority, this man refused to "receive the brethren" (traveling ministers to the local church, vv. 5–8) and excommunicated those that did receive them. He stands as one of the first examples of domineering ambition in the church. In contrast with Diotrephes, two other men are briefly characterized—Gaius, notable for sound Christian living, as evidenced especially in the practice of hospitality to the itinerant ministers; and Demetrius, a believer with a lofty reputation based on living the truth. The Epistle as a whole presents a vivid glimpse of church life at the close of the first century.

Third John may be divided as follows:

Introduction, vv. 1–4.
I. Hospitality to the Traveling Ministers, vv. 5–8.
II. Domineering Diotrephes and His Evil Deeds, vv. 9–11.
III. Godly Demetrius, v. 12.
Conclusion, vv. 13–14.

Introduction: Gaius Greeted
and Characterized, vv. 1–4

THE [a]ELDER,
To the beloved Gaius,
whom I love in truth:

2 Beloved, I pray [b]that you
may prosper in all things and be
in health, just as your soul prospers.
3 For I [c]rejoiced greatly
when brethren came and testified of the truth *that is* in you,
just as you walk in the truth.
4 I have no greater [d]joy
than to hear that [e]my children
walk in [c]truth.*

I. Hospitality to Traveling
Ministers, vv. 5–8

5 Beloved, you do faithfully
whatever you do for the brethren and* for strangers,
6 who have borne witness
of your love before the [f]church.
If you send them [g]forward on
their journey in a manner worthy of God, you will do [h]well,

God's work supported
by His own people

7 because they went forth
for His name's sake, [i]taking
nothing from the Gentiles.
8 We therefore ought to [j]re-
ceive* such, that we may become fellow workers for the
truth.

II. Domineering Diotrephes
and His Evil Deeds, vv. 9–11

9 I wrote to the [f]church, but
Diotrephes, who loves to have
the [k]preeminence among them,
does not receive us.
10 Therefore, if I come, I will
call to mind his deeds which he
does, [l]prating against us with
malicious words. And not content with that, he himself does
not receive the brethren, and
forbids those who wish to, [m]put-
ting *them* out of the [f]church.
11 Beloved, do not [n]imitate
what is evil, but what is good.
He who does good is of [o]God,
but* he who does evil has not
seen [p]God.

III. Godly Demetrius, v. 12

12 Demetrius has a *good* testimony from all, and from [q]the
truth itself. And we also bear
witness, and you know that our
testimony is [r]true.

Conclusion, vv. 13–14

13 I had many things to
write, but I do not wish to write
to you with pen and ink;
14 but I hope to see you
shortly, and we shall speak
[s]face to face. Peace to you. Our
friends greet you. Greet the
friends by name.

1
a Elders: v. 1. (Acts 11:30; Ti. 1:5, *note*)
2
b Cp. Mt. 6:33
3
c 2 Jn. 4
4
d 1 Th. 2:19–20; 2 Jn. 4
e Cp. 1 Cor. 4:15
6
f Churches (local): vv. 6,9–10; Rev. 1:4. (Acts 8:3; Phil. 1:1, *note*)
g Cp. Acts 15:3
h Cp. Mt. 25:40
7
i Cp. 1 Cor. 9:15–18
8
j Mt. 10:40; Rom. 12:13; Heb. 13:2; 1 Pet. 4:9

9
k Cp. Mt. 23:8; Col. 1:18
10
l Prov. 10:8, 10; cp. 2 Pet. 2:18; Jude 10
m Cp. Mt. 23:13
11
n Ps. 37:27; Rom. 14:19; 1 Th. 5:15; 1 Tim. 6:11; 2 Tim. 2:22
o 1 Jn. 2:29
p 1 Jn. 3:10
12
q v. 4
r Cp. Jn. 21:24
14
s Cp. 2 Jn. 12

*
v. 4 NU-Text reads *the truth.*
v. 5 NU-Text adds *especially.*
v. 8 NU-Text reads *support.* v. 11 NU-Text and M-Text omit *but.*

The Epistle of

JUDE

Author: Jude *Theme:* Contending for the Faith *Date of writing:* c. A.D. 68

THE EPISTLE OF JUDE was written by Jude, who was one of the half brothers of the Lord Jesus (Mt. 13:55; Mk. 6:3). His message, one of the most severe in the NT, was occasioned by apostasy in the early church. So threatening were these heresies that the Spirit caused Jude to write this letter of warning, urging his readers to contend earnestly for the faith (v. 3) because of the prevalence of the false teachers who had already intruded into the local churches (v. 4). In burning words Jude describes these heretics, showing vividly how apostasy leads to sinful living (vv. 5–19). The Epistle concludes with a noble doxology (vv. 24–25).

Jude may be divided as follows:

Introduction, vv. 1–2.
I. Occasion of the Epistle, vv. 3–4.
II. Historical Examples of Unbelief and Rebellion, vv. 5–7.
III. False Teachers Described, vv. 8–19.
IV. Exhortations to Christians, vv. 20–23.
Conclusion, vv. 24–25.

Introduction, vv. 1–2

JUDE, a [a]bondservant of Jesus Christ, and brother of [b]James,

To those who are [c]called, sanctified* by God the Father, and [1d]preserved in Jesus Christ:

2 Mercy, peace, and love be multiplied to you.

I. Occasion of the Epistle, vv. 3–4
Warning concerning apostasy

3 Beloved, while I was very diligent to write to you concerning our common [e]salvation, [f]I found it necessary to write to you exhorting you to [g]contend earnestly for the [h]faith which was once for all delivered to the saints.

4 For certain men have crept in unnoticed, who long ago were marked out for this condemnation, ungodly men, who turn the [i]grace of our God into lewdness and [j]deny [k]the only Lord God* and our Lord Jesus Christ.

1
a Or *slave*
b See Jas. Intro. and Mt. 4:21, *note*
c Election (personal): v. 1; Rev. 17:14. (Dt. 7:6; 1 Pet. 5:13, *note*)
d Assurance/security: v. 1; Jude 24. (Ps. 23:1; Jude 1, *note*)
3
e See Rom. 1:16, *note*
f Or *I was constrained to*
g Cp. Phil. 1:27
h Gospel: v. 3; Rev. 14:6. (Gen. 12:3; Rev. 14:6)
4
i See 2 Pet. 3:18, *note*
j Apostasy: vv. 4–10; Jude 11. (Lk. 18:8; 2 Tim. 3:1, *note*)
k Lit. *our only Master, God,* *and Lord, Jesus Christ*

II. Historical Examples of Unbelief and Rebellion, vv. 5–7

5 But I want to [l]remind you, though you once knew this, that the Lord, having [e]saved the people out of the land of Egypt, afterward destroyed those who did not believe.

6 And the [m]angels who did not keep their proper domain, but left their own abode, He has reserved in everlasting chains under darkness for the [n]judgment of [o]the [2]great day;

7 as [p]Sodom and Gomorrah, and the cities around them in a similar manner to these, having given themselves over to sexual immorality and gone after strange flesh, are set forth as an example, suffering the [q]vengeance of eternal fire.

III. False Teachers Described, vv.8–19

8 Likewise also these dreamers [r]defile the flesh, reject authority, and speak evil of dignitaries.

*
v. 1 NU-Text reads *beloved.* v. 4 NU-Text omits *God.*

5
l Cp. 2 Pet. 1:12
6
m See Heb. 1:4, *note*
n Judgments (the seven): v. 6; Jude 15. (1 Sam. 7:14; Rev. 20:12, *note*)
o Day (of the LORD): v. 6; Rev. 2:27. (Ps. 2:9; Rev. 19:19)
7
p 2 Pet. 2:6
q Lit. *punishment*
8
r 2 Pet. 2:10

---

[1](v. 1) Assurance is the Christian's full conviction that, through the work of Christ alone, received by faith, he is in possession of a salvation in which he will be eternally kept. This assurance rests only upon the Scripture promises to him who believes.

[2](v. 6) The judgment of the fallen angels. The "great day" is the day of the LORD (Isa. 2:9–22, refs.). As the final judgment upon Satan occurs after the 1000 years and preceding the final judgment (Rev. 20:10), it is congruous to conclude, as to the time, that other fallen angels are judged with him (2 Pet. 2:4; Rev. 20:10). Christians are associated with Christ in this judgment (1 Cor. 6:3). See other Judgments, Rev. 20:12, *note*. Compare also Angels, Heb. 1:4, *note*.

9
[a] *Satan:* v. 9;
Rev. 2:9.
(Gen. 3:1;
Rev. 20:10)
[b] Lit. *judg-
ment*
[c] Zech. 3:2
11
[d] *Apostasy:*
vv. 1–19;
Rev. 3:15.
(Lk. 18:8;
2 Tim. 3:1,
note)
14
[e] *Christ*
(second ad-
vent):
vv. 14–15;
Rev. 1:7.
(Dt. 30:3;
Acts 1:11,
note)
15
[f] *Judgments*
(the seven):
v. 15; Rev.
20:12.
(1 Sam.
7:14; Rev.
20:12, *note*)
[g] See Rom.
3:23, *note*

9 Yet Michael the archan-
gel, in contending with the
[a]devil, when he disputed about
the body of Moses, dared not
bring against him a reviling
[b]accusation, but said, [c]"The
Lord rebuke you!"
10 But these speak evil of
whatever they do not know; and
whatever they know naturally,
like brute beasts, in these things
they corrupt themselves.
11 Woe to them! For they
have gone in the way of [1]Cain,
have [d]run greedily in the [2]error
of Balaam for profit, and
perished in the rebellion of
[3]Korah.
12 These are spots in your
love feasts, while they feast
with you without fear, serving
only themselves. *They are*
clouds without water, carried
about* by the winds; late autumn trees without fruit, twice
dead, pulled up by the roots;
13 raging waves of the sea,
foaming up their own shame;
wandering stars for whom is reserved the blackness of darkness forever.
14 Now [4]Enoch, the seventh
from Adam, prophesied about
these men also, saying, "Behold, the Lord [e]comes with ten
thousands of His saints,
15 "to execute [f]judgment on
all, to convict all who are ungodly among them of all their
ungodly deeds which they have
committed in an ungodly way,
and of all the harsh things
which ungodly [g]sinners have
spoken against Him."
16 These are grumblers,
complainers, walking according to their own lusts; and they
mouth great swelling *words*,
flattering people to gain advantage.
17 But you, beloved, remember the words which were spoken before by the apostles of
our Lord Jesus Christ:
18 how they told you that
there would be mockers in the
last time who would walk according to their own ungodly
lusts.
19 These are sensual per-
sons, who cause divisions, not
having the [h]Spirit.

IV. Exhortations to Christians, vv. 20–23

20 But you, beloved, building
yourselves up on your most
[i]holy faith, praying in the Holy
[h]Spirit,
21 keep yourselves in the
love of God, looking for the
mercy of our Lord Jesus Christ
unto [j]eternal life.
22 And on some have com-
passion, making a [5]distinc-
tion;*
23 but others save with fear,
[k]pulling *them* out of the fire,*

19
[h] *Holy
Spirit* (NT):
vv. 19–20;
Rev. 1:10.
(Mt. 1:18;
Acts 2:4,
note)
20
[i] *Sanctifica-
tion* (NT):
v. 20; Rev.
22:11. (Mt.
4:5; Rev.
22:11)
21
[j] *Life* (eter-
nal): v. 21;
Rev. 2:7.
(Mt. 7:14;
Rev. 22:19)
23
[k] Lit.
snatching

*
v. 12 NU-Text and M-Text read *along.*
v. 22 NU-Text reads *who are doubting* (or *making distinctions*). v. 23 NU-Text adds *and on some have mercy with fear* and omits *with fear* in first clause.

[1](v. 11) Compare Gen. 4:1. Cain is an example of the religious natural man who believes in God, and in "religion," but after his own will, and who rejects redemption by blood. Compelled as a teacher of religion to explain the atonement, the false teacher explains it away.

[2](v. 11) The "error of Balaam" must be distinguished from the "way of Balaam" (see 2 Pet. 2:15, *note*) and the "doctrine of Balaam" (see Rev. 2:14, *note*). Balaam's error was that, reasoning from natural morality and seeing the evil in Israel, he supposed a righteous God must curse them. He was blind to the higher morality of the cross, through which God maintains and enforces the authority and awful sanctions of His law, so that He can be just and the Justifier of a believing sinner. The "profit" of v. 11 is not necessarily money; it may be popularity, fame, or applause.

[3](v. 11) See Num. 16. The sin of Korah was denial of the authority of Moses as God's chosen spokesman, and intrusion into the priest's office.

[4](v. 14) The quotation attributed to "Enoch, the seventh from Adam" (cp. Gen. 5:19–24; Heb. 11:5–6) is similar to a passage in the noncanonical Book of Enoch (1:9), written by an unknown person who used Enoch's name for the title of the book. Jude's use of this quotation from Enoch does not suggest that he considered the Book of Enoch as authoritative. Besides, it is not impossible that Jude is the source from which the quotation eventually found its way into the Book of Enoch, since there is no evidence as to the precise contents of this apocryphal book until many centuries after the time when Jude was written. The prophecy of the godly Enoch is the earliest recorded revelation of the second coming of Christ.

[5](v. 22) Some Greek manuscripts read: "Refute those who dispute."

hating even the garment defiled by the [1a]flesh.

23 *a Flesh:* v. 23. (Jn. 8:15; Jude 23)

24 *b Assurance/security:* v. 24. (Ps. 23:1; Jude 1, *note*)

Conclusion: Doxology, vv. 24–25

24 Now to Him who is able
to [b]keep you* from
stumbling,
And to present *you*
faultless
Before the presence of
His glory with
exceeding joy,

25 To God our [c]Savior,*
Who alone is wise,*
Be glory and majesty,
Dominion and power,*
Both now and forever.
Amen.

25 c See Rom. 1:16, *note*

*
v. 24 M-Text reads *them.* v. 25 NU-Text reads *To the only God, our Savior* and omits *wise.* • NU-Text adds *through Jesus Christ our Lord.* • NU-Text adds *Before all time.*

[1](v. 23) Flesh, Summary: "Flesh," in the ethical sense, is the whole natural or unregenerate man—spirit, soul, and body—as centered upon self, prone to sin, and opposed to God (Rom. 7:18). The regenerate man is "not in the flesh but in [the sphere of] the Spirit" (Rom. 8:9); but the flesh is still in him and he may, according to his choice, "walk according to the flesh" or "the Spirit" (1 Cor. 3:1–4; Gal. 5:16–17). In the first case he is a "carnal" Christian; in the second, a "spiritual" Christian. Victory over the flesh will be the habitual experience of the Christian who walks in the Spirit (Rom. 8:2,4; Gal. 5:16–17).

THE REVELATION

of Jesus Christ

Author: John *Theme:* Consummation *Date of writing:* c. A.D. 95

REVELATION, the concluding book of the Scriptures, unfolds the great events bringing history to consummation, including the revelation of Jesus Christ at His second advent. The word "revelation," used as the title of the book, is from the late Latin *revelatio*, which means (as does the Gk. *apokalupsis*, from which the English word "apocalypse" is derived) *disclosure of that which was previously hidden or unknown.*

In the unfolding of this central theme, Jesus Christ is revealed in glory in contrast with His presentation, in the four Gospels, in His humiliation. In Revelation Christ is seen in relationship to time as He "who was and who is to come" (1:4). He is related to the Church (1:9—3:22), the tribulation (4:1—19:21), the millennial kingdom (20:1–10), and the eternal state (20:11—22:21).

Christ is presented in this book as the Ruler over the kings of the earth (1:5), the Bridegroom and Head of the Church (2:1—3:22; 19:7–9), the Lion of the tribe of Judah (5:5), the Lamb that was slain (5:6,12, etc.), the High Priest (8:3–6), and the King and Judge (19:11—20:15).

The book is a record of what the Apostle John saw and heard. Constant use is made of symbols. References to OT events and prophecies abound. Frequent shifts of locale from earth to heaven and back to earth may be observed. It is an account of divine judgment and conflict which sweeps the whole world.

Three major divisions of Revelation must be recognized. John was commanded in 1:19 to write concerning (1) things past, "the things which you have seen," i.e. the Patmos vision (1:1–20); (2) things present, "the things which are," i.e. the existing churches (2:1—3:22); and (3) things future, "the things which will take place after this," i.e. events after the Church Age ends (4:1—22:5). It is important to observe that, beginning in ch. 4, the book presents future events.

The third major division of Revelation (4:1—22:21) is characterized by series of sevens: seven seals (4:1—8:1), seven trumpets (8:2—11:19), seven bowls (15:1—16:21), seven dooms (17:1—20:15), and seven new things (21:1—22:21). Important passages which are parenthetical, supplemental, or corrective may be observed, such as the Jewish remnant and the tribulation saints (7:1–17); the angel, the little book, and the two witnesses (10:1—11:14); the Lamb, the remnant, and the proclamation of the everlasting Gospel (14:1–13); the gathering of the kings of the earth in preparation for Armageddon (16:13–16); and the four alleluias in heaven (19:1–6). These passages do not advance the prophetic narration but, looking backward and forward, sum up the past and anticipate the future. The order of the narrative is therefore not consistently chronological. The major continuity is provided by the events symbolized in the seals, trumpets, and bowls.

The main purpose of the book is to provide the setting for the revelation of Jesus Christ. Principal attention is given to the time of the tribulation (chs. 4—19), which is believed to coincide with Daniel's seventieth week (Dan. 9:24–27). The great tribulation, the latter half of that "week," is especially in view. The climax of the book begins with the revelation of the Lord Jesus Christ in ch. 19.

Interpreters of Revelation should bear in mind two passages of Scripture: 1 Pet. 1:12; 2 Pet. 1:20–21. Much that is now obscure will become clear to those for whom it was written, as the time approaches.

The book may be divided as follows:

Introduction, 1:1–3.
I. The Messages of the Ascended Lord to the Seven Churches, 1:4—3:22.
II. The Opening of the Seven-sealed Scroll, 4—6; 8:1.
III. Parenthetic: Jews and Gentiles Saved during the Tribulation, 7.
IV. The Seven Trumpet Judgments, 8:2—9:21; 11:15–19.
V. Parenthetic, 10:1—11:14.
VI. Prominent Personages, 12.
VII. The Rise and Reign of the Beast and False Prophet, 13.
VIII. Parenthetic, 14.
IX. The Seven Bowl Judgments, 15—16.
X. The Doom of Babylon, 17—18.
XI. The Battle of Armageddon and the Millennium that Follows, 19:1—20:6.
XII. The Final Judgment and the Holy City, 20:7—22:5.
XIII. The Last Message of the Bible, 22:6–19.
Conclusion, 22:20–21.

Introduction, 1:1–3

1 THE [a]Revelation of Jesus Christ, which God gave Him to show His servants—things which must shortly take place. And He [b]sent and signified *it* by His [c]angel to His servant John,

2 who bore witness to the word of God, and to the testimony of Jesus Christ, to all things that he saw.

3 Blessed *is* he who [d]reads and those who hear the words of this prophecy, and [e]keep those things which are written in it; for the time *is* [f]near.

I. The Messages of the Ascended Lord to the Seven Churches, 1:4—3:22

Things past: "The things which you have seen."

4 John, to the seven [g]churches which are in Asia:

[h]Grace to you and peace from Him who [i]is and who was and who is to come, and from the seven [j]Spirits who are before His throne,

5 and from Jesus Christ, the [k]faithful [l]witness, the firstborn from the dead, and the ruler over the kings of the earth. To Him who loved us and washed* us from our [m]sins in His own [n]blood,

6 and has made us kings* and [o]priests to His God and Father, to Him *be* glory and dominion forever and ever. Amen.

7 Behold, He is [p]coming with [q]clouds, and every eye will see Him, even they who pierced Him. And all the tribes of the earth will [r]mourn because of Him. Even so, Amen.

8 "I am the [1][s]Alpha and the Omega, *the* Beginning and *the* End,"* says the Lord,* "who is and who was and who is to come, the [t]Almighty."

Patmos vision

9 I, John, both* your brother and companion in the tribulation and kingdom and patience of Jesus Christ, was on the [2]island that is called Patmos for the word of God and for the testimony of Jesus Christ.

10 I was in the [u]Spirit on the Lord's Day, and I heard behind me a loud voice, as of a trumpet,

11 saying, "I am the [s]Alpha and the Omega, the First and the Last," and,* "What you see, write in a book and send *it* to the seven [g]churches which are in Asia:* to Ephesus, to Smyrna, to Pergamos, to Thyatira, to Sardis, to Philadelphia, and to Laodicea."

12 Then I turned to see the voice that spoke with me. And having turned I saw seven golden lampstands,

13 [v]and in the midst of the seven lampstands *One* like the Son of Man, clothed with a garment down to the feet and girded about the chest with a golden band.

14 His head and hair *were* white like wool, as white as snow, and His eyes like a flame of fire;

15 His feet *were* like fine brass, as if refined in a furnace, and His voice as the sound of many waters;

16 He had in His right hand [w]seven stars, out of His mouth went a sharp two-edged sword, and His countenance *was* like the [x]sun shining in its strength.

17 And when I saw Him, I fell at His feet as dead. But He laid His right hand on me, saying to me,* "Do not be afraid; I am the First and the Last.

18 "I *am* He who lives, and was dead, and behold, I am alive forevermore. Amen. And I

CHAPTER 1

1
a Inspiration: v. 1; Rev. 1:19. (Ex. 4:15; 2 Tim. 3:16, *note*)
b Rev. 22:6
c See Heb. 1:4, *note*

3
d Cp. 1 Th. 5:27
e Rev. 22:7
f Rev. 22:10; see Mt. 4:17, *note 4*

4
g Churches (local): vv. 4,11; Rev. 1:20. (Acts 8:3; Phil. 1:1, *note*)
h Grace: v. 4; Rev. 22:21. (Jn. 1:14; Jn. 1:17, *note*)
i Ex. 3:14
j Isa. 11:2; Rev. 3:1; 4:5; 5:6

5
k Prov. 14:5
l Isa. 55:4
m See Rom. 3:23, *note*
n Sacrifice (of Christ): vv. 5–6; Rev. 5:9. (Gen. 3:15; Heb. 10:18, *note*)

6
o 1 Pet. 2:5,9

7
p Christ (second advent): v. 7; Rev. 2:25. (Dt. 30:3; Acts 1:11, *note*)
q Mt. 24:30
r Zech. 12:10

8
s Rev. 21:6; 22:13
t Isa. 9:6

10
u Holy Spirit (NT): v. 10; Rev. 2:7. (Mt. 1:18; Acts 2:4, *note*)

13
v vv. 13–15; cp. Dan. 7:9–10; 10:5–6

16
w v. 20
x Mt. 17:2

*
1:5 NU-Text reads *loves us and freed;* M-Text reads *loves us and washed.*
1:6 NU-Text and M-Text read *a kingdom.*
1:8 NU-Text and M-Text omit *the Beginning and the End.* • NU-Text and M-Text add God.
1:9 NU-Text and M-Text omit *both.*
1:11 NU-Text and M-Text omit *I am* through third *and.* • NU-Text and M-Text omit *which are in Asia.*
1:17 NU-Text and M-Text omit *to me.*

[1](1:8) Alpha and Omega, mentioned also in Rev. 21:6 and 22:13, are the first and last letters of the Greek alphabet.

[2](1:9) In 1:1–20 John sees a vision of the risen Christ in the midst of the seven golden lampstands. From 2:1—3:22 he records the messages of our Lord to seven churches in Roman Asia. At 4:1–2 the apostle is pictured as caught up "in the Spirit" into heaven, from where he observes future things in heaven and upon the earth as recorded from 4:1—22:5.

18
a See Lk. 16:23, *note*
19
b *Inspiration:* v. 19; 2:1; Rev. 2:8. (Ex. 4:15; 2 Tim. 3:16, *note*)
c Rev. 1:9–18
d Lit. *after these things*, i.e. *after the church*. Cp. 4:1
20
e See Mt. 13:11, *note*
f *Churches* (local): v. 20; 2:1, 7; Rev. 2:8. (Acts 8:3; Phil. 1:1, *note*)
CHAPTER 2
1
g i.e. *messenger*. See Rev. 1:20, *note 1*
h Or *in*

have the keys of [a]Hades and of
Death.

Command to write

19 [b]"Write* the things
which you have [c]seen, and the
things which are, and the things
which will take place [d]after
this.
20 "The [e]mystery of the
seven stars which you saw in
My right hand, and the seven
golden lampstands: The seven
stars are the [1]angels of the
seven [f]churches, and the seven
lampstands which you saw*
are the seven [2f]churches.

Things present—seven churches: "The things which are."

(1) Message to Ephesus: the church at the end of the apostolic age

2 "TO the [g]angel of the
[f]church [h]of Ephesus [b]write,
'These things says He who
holds the seven stars in His
right hand, who walks in the
midst of the seven golden lampstands:
2 "I know your works, your
labor, your patience, and that
you cannot bear those who are
evil. And you have [i]tested
those who say they are apostles
and are not, and have found
them liars;
3 "and you have persevered
and have [j]patience, and have
labored for My name's sake and
have [k]not become weary.
4 "Nevertheless I have *this*
against you, that you have left
your first love.
5 "Remember therefore from
where you have fallen; [l]repent
and do the first works, or else I
will come to you quickly and remove your lampstand from its
place—unless you [l]repent.
6 "But this you have, that
you hate the deeds of the [3]Nico-
laitans, which I also hate.
7 "He who has an ear, let
him hear what the [m]Spirit says
to the [f]churches. To him who
overcomes I will give to eat
from the [4n]tree of [o]life, which is
in the midst of the Paradise of
God." '

2
i 1 Jn. 4:1
3
j Heb. 12:1–3
k Gal. 6:9
5
l *Repentance:* v. 5; Rev. 2:16. (Mt. 3:2; Acts 17:30, *note*)
7
m *Holy Spirit* (NT): v. 7; Rev. 2:11. (Mt. 1:18; Acts 2:4, *note*)
n Gen. 2:9; Rev. 22:2,14
o *Life* (eternal): v. 7; Rev. 2:10. (Mt. 7:14; Rev. 22:19)

*

1:19 NU-Text and M-Text read *Therefore, write.* **1:20** NU-Text and M-Text omit *which you saw.*

---

[1](1:20) Although this is the usual word for angel (Gr. *angelos*), it is often translated "messenger." The most natural explanation in this context is that these were men sent by the seven churches to ascertain the state of the aged apostle, now in exile in Patmos; but they represent any who bear God's messages to a church.

[2](1:20) The messages to the seven churches have a fourfold reference: (1) local, to the churches actually addressed; (2) admonitory, to all churches in all time as tests by which they may discern their true spiritual state in the sight of God; (3) personal, in the exhortations to him "who has an ear," and in the promises "to him who overcomes"; and (4) prophetic, as disclosing in two areas the phases in the spiritual history of the church: (a) a pattern that has been repeated again and again through the centuries; and (b) the progress of its spiritual state until the end of the Church Age. It is incredible that in a prophecy covering the church period there should be no such foreview. These messages must contain that foreview if it is in the book at all, for the Church does not appear on earth after 3:22. Again, these messages by their very terms go beyond the local assemblies mentioned. It can be seen that Ephesus (2:1–7), though a local church in the apostle's day, is typical of the first century as a whole; Smyrna (2:8–11) characterizes the church under persecution, e.g. from A.D. c. 100–316; Pergamos (2:12–17), "where Satan dwells" (2:13; cp. 2:14–15, and *notes*), is suggestive of the church mixing with the world, e.g. in the Middle Ages; Thyatira (2:18–29) reveals how evil progresses in the church and idolatry is practiced; Sardis (3:1–6) is representative of the church as dead, yet still having a minority of godly men and women, as during the Reformation; Philadelphia (3:7–13) shows revival and a state of spiritual advance; and Laodicea (3:14–19) is illustrative of the final state of apostasy which the visible church will experience.

[3](2:6,15) The name "Nicolaitans," according to early church fathers (Ignatius, Irenaeus, Clement of Alexandria, Tertullian, Hippolytus), refers to those who, while professing themselves to be Christians, lived licentiously. What in Ephesus was "deeds" (v. 6) became in Pergamos a "doctrine" (v. 15).

[4](2:7) "The tree of life" is one of the many allusions in Revelation to Genesis. In order to keep fallen man from eating of "the tree of life," God drove him from Eden and placed cherubim at the gate to guard the way to the tree (Gen. 2:9; 3:22,24). "The tree of life" appears three times in Rev. 22 (vv. 2,14,19 [Gk.]), where the new paradise is described. In the NT the word translated "tree" (Gk. *xulon*) is used of the cross (Acts 5:30; 10:39; 13:29; Gal. 3:13; 1 Pet.

(2) Message to Smyrna:
the church under persecution

8 “And to the [a]angel of the
[b]church in Smyrna [c]write,
‘These things says the
[d]First and the Last, who was
dead, and came to life:
9 “I know your works, tribulation, and poverty (but you are
rich); and *I know* the blasphemy
of those who [e]say they are Jews
and are not, but *are* a [f]syna-
gogue of [g]Satan.
10 “Do not fear any of those
things which you are about to
suffer. Indeed, the [g]devil is
about to throw *some* of you into
prison, that you may be [h]tested,
and you will have tribulation
ten days. Be faithful until death,
and I will give you the [i]crown
of [j]life.
11 “He who has an ear, let
him hear what the [k]Spirit says
to the [b]churches. He who overcomes shall not be hurt by the
[l]second death.” ’

(3) Message to Pergamos:
the church settled in the world

12 “And to the [a]angel of the
[b]church in Pergamos [c]write,
‘These things says He
who has the sharp two-edged
[m]sword:
13 “I know your works, and
where you dwell, where [g]Sa-
tan’s throne *is.* And you hold
fast to My name, and did [n]not
deny My faith even in the days
in which Antipas *was* My faithful [1]martyr, who was killed
among you, where [g]Satan
dwells.
14 “But I have a few things
against you, because you have
there those who hold the doctrine of [2]Balaam, who taught
Balak to put a stumbling block
before the [o]children of Israel, to
eat things sacrificed to idols,
and to commit sexual immorality.
15 “Thus you also have those
who hold the doctrine of the
[p]Nicolaitans, which thing I
hate.*
16 [q]“Repent, or else I will
come to you quickly and will
fight against them [r]with the
sword of My mouth.
17 “He who has an ear, let
him hear what the [k]Spirit says
to the [b]churches. To him who
overcomes I will give some of
the hidden [s]manna to eat. And
I will give him a [t]white stone,
and on the stone a [u]new name
written which no one knows except him who [v]receives *it.*” ’

(4) Message to Thyatira:
the church in idolatry

18 “And to the [a]angel of the
[b]church in Thyatira [c]write,
‘These things says the Son
of God, [w]who has eyes like a
flame of fire, and His feet like
fine brass:
19 “I know your works, love,
service, [x]faith,* and your patience; and *as* for your works,
the last *are* more than the first.
20 “Nevertheless I have a few
things against you, because you
allow* that woman* [y]Jezebel,
who calls herself a prophetess,
to teach and seduce* My servants to commit sexual immorality and eat things sacrificed
to idols.
21 “And I gave her time to
[q]repent of her sexual immorality, and she did not [q]repent.*

*

2:15 NU-Text and M-Text read *likewise* for *which thing I hate.* **2:19** NU-Text and M-Text read *faith, service.* **2:20** NU-Text and M-Text read *I have against you that you tolerate.* • M-Text reads *your wife Jezebel.* • NU-Text and M-Text read *and teaches and seduces.* **2:21** NU-Text and M-Text read *time to repent, and she does not want to repent of her sexual immorality.*

8
a i.e. *messenger.* See Rev. 1:20, *note 1*
b Churches (local): vv. 8,11–12, 17–18; Rev. 2:23. (Acts 8:3; Phil. 1:1, *note*)
c Inspiration: vv. 8, 12,18; Rev. 3:1. (Ex. 4:15; 2 Tim. 3:16, *note*)
d Rev. 1:17–18

9
e Rev. 3:9
f Cp. Jn. 8:30–47; 2 Cor. 11:14
g Satan: vv. 9–10,13; Rev. 2:24. (Gen. 3:1; Rev. 20:10)

10
h Test/tempt: v. 10; Rev. 3:10. (Gen. 3:1; Jas. 1:14, *note*)
i Rewards: v. 10; Rev. 3:11. (Dan. 12:3; 1 Cor. 3:14, *note*)
j Life (eternal): v. 10; Rev. 3:5. (Mt. 7:14; Rev. 22:19)

11
k Holy Spirit (NT): vv. 11,17; Rev. 2:29. (Mt. 1:18; Acts 2:4, *note*)
l Death (the second): v. 11; Rev. 20:6. (Jn. 8:21; Rev. 20:14, *note*)

12
m Rev. 1:16

13
n Cp. 2 Tim. 2:12

14
o Lit. *sons*

15
p See 2:6, *note*

16
q Repentance: vv. 16,21; Rev. 2:22. (Mt. 3:2; Acts 17:30, *note*)
r 2 Th. 2:8; Rev. 19:15

17
s Ex. 16:33–34; Jn. 6:49–51
t Signifying approval
u Isa. 62:2; Rev. 3:12; cp. Jn. 1:42
v Cp. Rev. 14:3

18
w Rev. 1:14–15

19
x Faith: v. 19. (Gen. 3:20; Heb. 11:39, *note*)

20
y 1 Ki. 16:31–32

2:24). It is through Christ’s death on the tree that mankind may have eternal life. He “bore our sins in His own body on the tree.”

[1](2:13) The word “martyr” derives from the Gk. *martus* (“witness”) which appears eighteen times in its various forms in this book as in 1:2,5; 3:14; 19:10; 20:4; etc.; it later came to denote *one who died because of his faithfulness in such witnessing,* as here.

[2](2:14) The “doctrine of Balaam” (see 2 Pet. 2:15 and Jude 11, *notes*) was his teaching Balak to corrupt the people who could not be cursed (Num. 31:15–16; 22:5; 23:8) by tempting them to marry women of Moab, defile their separation, and abandon their pilgrim character. It is that union of the world and the church which is spiritual unchastity (Jas. 4:4). Pergamos had lost the pilgrim character and was living (v. 13) where Satan’s throne was (v. 13), i.e. in the world (Jn. 12:31; 14:30; 16:11).

22 "Indeed I will cast her into
a sickbed, and those who commit adultery with her into great
tribulation, unless they [a]repent
of their* deeds.
23 "I will kill her children
with death, and all the
[b]churches shall know that I am
He who [c]searches the minds
and hearts. And I will give to
each one of you according to
your works.
24 "Now to you I say, and* to
the rest in Thyatira, as many as
do not have this doctrine, who
have not known the [d]depths of
[e]Satan, as they say, I will* put
on you no other burden.
25 "But hold fast what you
have [f]till I come.
26 "And he who overcomes,
and keeps My works until the
end, to him I will give [g]power
over the nations—

27 *'He shall rule them with*
a rod of iron;
They shall be dashed to
pieces like the potter's
vessels'—

[h]as [i]I also have received from
My Father;
28 "and I will give him the
morning [j]star.
29 "He who has an ear, let
him hear what the [k]Spirit says
to the [b]churches." '

(5) Message to Sardis: the church as dead, yet having a believing remnant

3 "AND to the [l]angel of the
[b]church in Sardis [m]write,
'These things says He who
[n]has the seven Spirits of God
and the seven stars: "I know
your works, that you have a
name that you are alive, but you
are dead.
2 "Be watchful, and
strengthen the things which remain, that are ready to die, for I
have not found your works
[o]perfect before God.*
3 [p]"Remember therefore
how you have received and
heard; hold fast and [q]repent.
Therefore if you will not watch,
I will come upon you [q]as a thief,
and you will not know what
hour I will come upon you.
4 "You* have a few names
even in Sardis who have not defiled their [r]garments; and
[s]they shall walk with Me in
white, for they are worthy.

*
2:22 NU-Text and M-Text read *her.*
2:24 NU-Text and M-Text omit *and.*
• NU-Text and M-Text omit *will.*
3:2 NU-Text and M-Text read *My God.*
3:4 NU-Text and M-Text read *Nevertheless you have a few names in Sardis.*

22
a Repentance: v. 22; 3:3; Rev. 3:19. (Mt. 3:2; Acts 17:30, *note*)
23
b Churches (local): vv. 23,29; 3:1; Rev. 3:6. (Acts 8:3; Phil. 1:1, *note*)
c Jer. 17:10
24
d 2 Tim. 3:1–9; cp. 1 Cor. 2:10
e Satan: v. 24; Rev. 3:9. (Gen. 3:1; Rev. 20:10)
25
f Christ (second advent): v. 25; Rev. 16:15. (Dt. 30:3; Acts 1:11, *note*)
26
g Or *authority*
27
h Ps. 2:7–9
i Day (of the LORD): v. 27; Rev. 6:17. (Ps. 2:9; Rev. 19:19)
28
j Rev. 22:16; cp. 2 Pet. 1:19
29
k Holy Spirit (NT): v. 29; Rev. 3:6. (Mt. 1:18; Acts 2:4, *note*)
CHAPTER 3
1
l i.e. *messenger.* See Rev. 1:20, *note 1*
m Inspiration: v. 1; Rev. 3:7. (Ex. 4:15; 2 Tim. 3:16, *note*)
n Rev. 1:4,16; cp. Acts 2:33
2
o See Mt. 5:48, *note*
3
p Cp. Rev. 2:5
q Rev. 16:15; cp. Mt. 24:43; 1 Th. 5:2–5
4
r Righteousness (garment): v. 4; Rev. 3:5. (Gen. 3:21; Rev. 19:8)
s Rev. 6:11

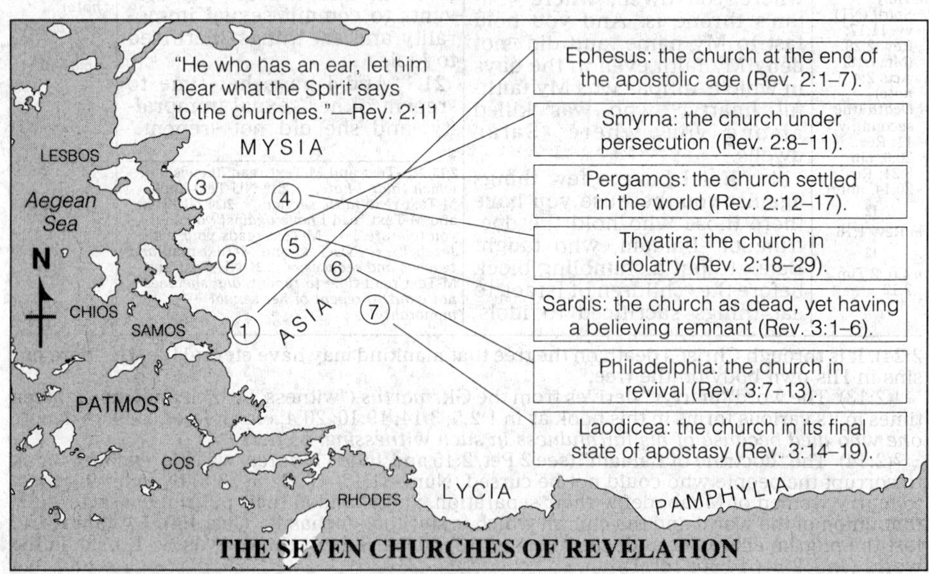
"He who has an ear, let him hear what the Spirit says to the churches."—Rev. 2:11
MYSIA
LESBOS
Aegean Sea
N
CHIOS
SAMOS
PATMOS
COS
RHODES
LYCIA
PAMPHYLIA
ASIA
1
2
3
4
5
6
7
Ephesus: the church at the end of the apostolic age (Rev. 2:1–7).
Smyrna: the church under persecution (Rev. 2:8–11).
Pergamos: the church settled in the world (Rev. 2:12–17).
Thyatira: the church in idolatry (Rev. 2:18–29).
Sardis: the church as dead, yet having a believing remnant (Rev. 3:1–6).
Philadelphia: the church in revival (Rev. 3:7–13).
Laodicea: the church in its final state of apostasy (Rev. 3:14–19).
THE SEVEN CHURCHES OF REVELATION

5 "He who overcomes shall be clothed in [a]white garments, and I will not blot out his name from the Book of [b]Life; but I will [c]confess his name before My Father and before His [d]angels.

6 "He who has an ear, let him hear what the [e]Spirit says to the [f]churches." '

(6) Message to Philadelphia: the church in revival

7 "And to the [g]angel of the [f]church in Philadelphia [h]write,

'These things says He who is [i]holy, He who is [j]true, *"He who has the [k]key of David, He who opens and no one shuts, and shuts and no one opens"*:

8 "I know your works. See, I have set before you an open door, and no one can shut it;* for you have a little strength, have kept My word, and have not denied My name.

9 "Indeed I will make *those* of the synagogue of [l]Satan, who say they are Jews and are [m]not, but lie—indeed I will make them come and worship before your feet, and to know that I have loved you.

10 "Because you have kept My command to persevere, I also will [n]keep you from the [o]hour of [p]trial which shall come upon the whole [q]world, to test those who dwell on the earth.

11 "Behold,* I am coming quickly! Hold fast what you have, that no one may take your [r]crown.

12 "He who overcomes, I will make him a [s]pillar in the temple of My God, and he shall [t]go out no more. I will [u]write on him the name of My God and the name of the city of My God, the New Jerusalem, which [v]comes down out of heaven from My God. And *I will write on him* My [w]new name.

13 "He who has an ear, let him hear what the [e]Spirit says to the [f]churches." '

(7) Message to Laodicea: the church in its final state of apostasy

14 "And to the [g]angel of the [f]church of the Laodiceans* [h]write,

'These things says the [x]Amen, the [y]Faithful and True Witness, the Beginning of the creation of God:

15 "I know your works, that [z]you are neither cold nor hot. I could wish you were cold or hot.

16 "So then, because you are lukewarm, and neither cold nor hot,* I will vomit you out of My mouth.

17 "Because you say, 'I am rich, have become wealthy, and have need of nothing'—and do not know that you are wretched, miserable, poor, blind, and naked—

18 "I counsel you to buy from Me gold refined in the fire, that you may be rich; and [a]white garments, that you may be clothed, *that* the shame of your nakedness may not be revealed; and anoint your eyes with eye salve, that you may see.

19 "As many as I love, I rebuke and [aa]chasten. Therefore be zealous and [bb]repent.

Place and attitude of Christ at the end of the Church Age

20 "Behold, I stand at the door and knock. If anyone hears My voice and opens the door, I will [cc]come in to him and dine with him, and he with Me.

21 "To him who overcomes I will grant to sit with Me on My throne, as I also overcame and sat down with My [1]Father on His [dd]throne.

22 "He who has an ear, let him hear what the [e]Spirit says to the [f]churches." ' "

5
a Righteousness (garment): vv. 5, 18; Rev. 4:4. (Gen. 3:21; Rev. 19:8)
b Life (eternal): v. 5; Rev. 13:8. (Mt. 7:14; Rev. 22:19)
c Lk. 12:8
d See Heb. 1:4, *note*

6
e Holy Spirit (NT): vv. 6,13,22; Rev. 4:2. (Mt. 1:18; Acts 2:4, *note*)
f Churches (local): vv. 6–7, 13–14,22; Rev. 22:16. (Acts 8:3; Phil. 1:1, *note*)

7
g i.e. *messenger*. See Rev. 1:20, *note* 1
h Inspiration: vv. 7, 14; Rev. 14:13. (Ex. 4:15; 2 Tim. 3:16, *note*)
i Cp. Lk. 1:35; 1 Pet. 1:16
j Jn. 14:6; Rev. 19:11
k Isa. 22:22

9
l Satan: v. 9; Rev. 12:3. (Gen. 3:1; Rev. 20:10)
m Rev. 2:9

10
n 2 Pet. 2:9
o Tribulation (the great): v. 10; Rev. 7:14. (Ps. 2:5; Rev. 7:14)
p Test/tempt: v. 10. (Gen. 3:1; Jas. 1:14, *note*)
q Gk. *oikoumene*. See Lk. 2:1, *note*

11
r Rewards: v. 11; Rev. 4:4. (Dan. 12:3; 1 Cor. 3:14, *note*)

12
s 1 Ki. 7:21; cp. Gal. 2:9
t Ps. 23:6
u Rev. 22:4
v Rev. 21:2
w Rev. 2:17

14
x 2 Cor. 1:20
y Rev. 1:5

15
z Apostasy: vv. 14–18. (Lk. 18:8; 2 Tim. 3:1, *note*)

19
aa Heb. 12:6
bb Repentance: v. 19. (Mt. 3:2; Acts 17:30, *note*)

20
cc Jn. 14:23

21
dd Kingdom (NT): v. 21; Rev. 5:1. (Mt. 2:2; 1 Cor. 15:24, *note*)

*3:8 NU-Text and M-Text read *which no one can shut.* 3:11 NU-Text and M-Text omit *Behold.* 3:14 NU-Text and M-Text read *in Laodicea.* 3:16 NU-Text and M-Text read *hot nor cold.*

1(3:21) This passage, in harmony with Lk. 1:32–33; Acts 2:30,34–35; 15:14–16, is conclusive that Christ is not now seated upon His own throne. The Davidic Covenant (see 2 Sam. 7:16, *note*) and the promises of God through the prophets and the Angel Gabriel concerning the Messianic kingdom await fulfillment. It is in a still future day that God will give to His Son, once crowned with thorns by men, the crown of His father, David.

II. The Opening of the Seven-sealed Scroll, 4—6; 8:1

Things future: "things . . . after this" (Lit. "after these things")

The scene in heaven before the breaking of the seals

CHAPTER 4

4 AFTER these things I looked, and behold, a [a]door *standing* [b]open in heaven. And the first voice which I heard *was* like a [c]trumpet speaking with me, saying, [1]"Come up here, and I will show you things which must take place [d]after this."

2 Immediately I was in the [e]Spirit; and behold, a [f]throne set in heaven, and *One* sat on the throne.

3 And He who sat there was* [g]like a jasper and a sardius stone in appearance; and *there was* a [h]rainbow around the throne, in appearance like an emerald.

Enthroned elders around the throne

4 Around the throne *were* twenty-four thrones, and on the thrones I saw twenty-four [2]elders sitting, clothed in [i]white robes; and they had [j]crowns* of gold on their heads.

5 And from the throne proceeded lightnings, thunderings, and voices.* Seven lamps of fire *were* burning before the throne, which are the* seven Spirits of God.

The four living creatures and twenty-four elders worship the Creator

6 Before the throne *there was** a [k]sea of glass, like crystal. And in the midst of the throne, and around the throne, *were* four [l]living creatures [m]full of eyes in front and in back.

7 The first [l]living creature *was* like a lion, the second [l]living creature like a calf, the third [l]living creature had a face like a man, and the fourth [l]living creature *was* like a flying eagle.

8 *The* four [l]living creatures, each having [n]six wings, were [o]full of eyes around and within. And they do not rest day or night, saying:

"Holy, holy, holy,*
Lord [p]God Almighty,
Who was and is and is to
come!"

9 Whenever the [l]living creatures give glory and honor and thanks to Him who sits on the throne, who lives forever and ever,

10 the twenty-four elders fall down before Him who sits on the throne and worship Him who lives forever and ever, and cast their [j]crowns before the throne, saying:

11 "You are worthy, O
Lord,*
To receive glory and
honor and power;
For You [q]created all
things,
And by [r]Your will they
exist* and were
created."

1
a Cp. Lk. 23:45; Heb. 10:19–20
b Ezek. 1:1
c Rev. 1:10; cp. 1 Th. 4:16
d Lit. *after these things.* Rev. 1:19
2
e Holy Spirit (NT): v. 2; Rev. 14:13. (Mt. 1:18; Acts 2:4, *note*)
f Rev. 3:21; cp. Rev. 22:3
3
g Rev. 21:11; cp. Ezek. 1:26–27
h Gen. 9:13–17; Ezek. 1:28
4
i Righteousness (garment): v. 4; Rev. 6:11. (Gen. 3:21; Rev. 19:8)
j Rewards: vv. 4,10; Rev. 11:18. (Dan. 12:3; 1 Cor. 3:14, *note*)
6
k Rev. 15:2
l See Ezek. 1:5, *note*
m Cp. Ezek. 1:18; 10:12
8
n Isa. 6:2
o Cp. Ezek. 1:18; 10;12
p Isa. 6:3
11
q Gen. 1:1; Jn. 1:3
r Col. 1:16; cp. Ps. 19:1

*
4:3 M-Text omits *And He who sat there was* (which makes the description in verse 3 modify the throne rather than God). 4:4 NU-Text and M-Text read *robes, with crowns.* 4:5 NU-Text and M-Text read *voices, and thunderings.* • M-Text omits *the.* 4:6 NU-Text and M-Text add *something like.* 4:8 M-Text has *holy* nine times. 4:11 NU-Text and M-Text read *our Lord and God.* • NU-Text and M-Text read *existed.*

[1](4:1) Beginning with 4:1 the viewpoint of John is from heaven. As the word "church" does not appear again in Revelation until 22:16, the catching up of John from earth to heaven has been taken to be a symbolic representation of the translation of the Church as occurring before the events of the tribulation described in chs. 6—19.

[2](4:4) These elders represent the Church. The very word "elder" has church significance (1 Tim. 5:17; Ti. 1:5). Crowns throughout the NT are exclusively presented as rewards for the faithful in the Church. These elders sit on thrones which are associated with the central judgment throne of God (vv. 2–4; cp. 1 Cor. 6:2–3; 2 Tim. 2:12).

The appearance of these elders, already glorified, crowned, and enthroned before the opening of the sealed book of judgment (ch. 5) and before the end-time judgments are loosed upon the world (chs. 6—18), reaffirms that the Church is not to be subjected to the judicial wrath and judgments of that time (cp. Jn. 5:24; Rom. 5:9; 1 Th. 1:10; 5:1–11; Rev. 3:10).

Seven-sealed scroll taken by Christ

5 AND I saw in the right *hand* of Him who sat on the [a]throne a scroll written inside and on the back, sealed with seven seals.

2 Then I saw a strong [b]angel proclaiming with a loud voice, [c]"Who is worthy to open the scroll and to loose its seals?"

3 And [d]no one in heaven or on the earth or under the earth was able to open the scroll, or to look at it.

4 So I wept much, because no one was found worthy to open and read* the scroll, or to look at it.

Christ in His kingly character opens the scroll (cp. Isa. 11:1; Jer. 23:5; Lk. 1:32–33)

5 But one of the elders said to me, "Do not weep. Behold, the [1e]Lion of the tribe of [f]Judah, the [g]Root of David, has [h]prevailed to open the scroll and to loose* its seven seals."

6 And I looked, and behold,* in the midst of the throne and of the four [i]living creatures, and in the midst of the elders, stood a [j]Lamb as though it had been slain, having seven [k]horns and seven [l]eyes, which are the seven [m]Spirits of God sent out into all the earth.

7 Then He [2]came and took the scroll out of the right hand of Him who sat on the throne.

The living creatures and twenty-four elders worship

8 Now when He had taken the scroll, the four [i]living creatures and the twenty-four elders [n]fell down before the Lamb, each having a harp, and golden bowls full of [o]incense, which are the [p]prayers of the saints.

9 And they sang a [q]new song, saying:

"You are worthy to take
the scroll,
And to open its seals;
For You were slain,
And have [r]redeemed us
to God [s]by Your
[t]blood
Out of every tribe and
tongue and people and
nation,
10 And have made us*
[u]kings* and [v]priests
to our God;
And we* shall [a]reign
[w]on the earth."

Angels exalt the Lamb

11 Then I looked, and I heard the voice of many angels around the throne, the [i]living creatures, and the elders; and the number of them was ten thousand times ten thousand, and thousands of thousands,

12 saying with a loud voice:

[x]"Worthy is the Lamb who
was slain
To receive power and
riches and wisdom,
And strength and honor
and glory and
blessing!"

Eventual universal adoration of the Lamb as King (cp. Phil. 2:9–11)

13 And every creature which is in heaven and on the earth and under the earth and such as are in the sea, and all that are in them, I heard saying:

"Blessing and honor and
glory and power
Be to Him who [y]sits on
the throne,
And to the [z]Lamb,
forever and ever!"*

14 Then the four [i]living creatures said, "Amen!" And the twenty-four* elders fell

CHAPTER 5

1
a *Kingdom* (NT): vv. 1–4,10; Rev. 11:15. (Mt. 2:2; 1 Cor. 15:24, *note*)

2
b See Heb. 1:4, *note*
c Rev. 4:11; 5:9; cp. Ps. 15:1

3
d Cp. Isa. 63:5

5
e Gen. 49:9
f Heb. 7:14
g Isa. 11:10; Rom. 15:12; Rev. 22:16; Mt. 1:1
h Rev. 3:21; cp. Isa. 53:12; 63:1–3

6
i See Ezek. 1:5, *note*
j Jn. 1:29
k See Dt. 33:17, *note*
l Cp. Zech. 3:8–9; 4:10
m Rev. 1:4; 3:1; 4:5

8
n Rev. 4:8–10; 19:4
o Ps. 141:2
p Rev. 8:3

9
q Rev. 4:11; 14:3; cp. Ps. 33:3; 96:1; 98:1; 149:1
r See Rom. 3:24, *note*
s Heb. 9:12; 1 Pet. 1:18–19
t *Sacrifice* (of Christ): v. 9; Rev. 7:14. (Gen. 3:15; Heb. 10:18, *note*)

10
u Ex. 19:6
v Isa. 61:6
w Or *over*

12
x v. 9; cp. Phil. 2:9–11

13
y Rev. 4:2–3; 6:16; 20:11
z v. 6; cp. Jn. 5:23

* 5:4 NU-Text and M-Text omit *and read.* 5:5 NU-Text and M-Text omit *to loose.* 5:6 NU-Text and M-Text read *I saw in the midst . . . a Lamb standing.* 5:10 NU-Text and M-Text read *them.* • NU-Text reads *a kingdom.* • NU-Text and M-Text read *they.* 5:13 M-Text adds *Amen.* 5:14 NU-Text and M-Text omit *twenty-four.*

[1](5:5) The lion is the king of beasts. Of Judah it is predicted, in Gen. 49:8–12, that his seed would hold the scepter, i.e. become king of Israel, and rule the world. Mary, the mother of Jesus, was of the tribe of Judah (Lk. 3:33).

[2](5:7) Compare Dan. 7:13–14. The two visions are identical; here is added that which was hidden from Daniel, that the kings and priests of the Church Age are to be associated with the Son of Man ("a Lamb as though it had been slain") when He "shall reign on the earth" (vv. 6–10; cp. 3:21).

down and worshiped Him who lives forever and ever.*

The seven-sealed scrolls opened

(1) First seal: false Christ

6 NOW I saw when the Lamb [a]opened one of the seals;* and I heard one of the four [b]living creatures saying with a voice like thunder, "Come and see."

2 And I looked, and behold, a white horse. He who sat on it had a bow; and a crown was given to him, and [1]he went out [c]conquering and to conquer.

(2) Second seal: war

3 When He opened the second seal, I heard the second [b]living creature saying, "Come and see."*

4 Another horse, fiery [d]red, went out. And it was granted to the one who sat on it to [e]take peace from the earth, and that *people* should kill one another; and there was given to him a great sword.

(3) Third seal: famine

5 When He opened the third seal, I heard the third [b]living creature say, "Come and see." So I looked, and behold, a [f]black horse, and he who sat on it had a pair of [g]scales in his hand.

6 And I heard a voice in the midst of the four [b]living creatures saying, "A [h]quart* of wheat for a [i]denarius,* and three quarts of barley for a denarius; and do not harm the oil and the wine."

(4) Fourth seal: death

7 When He opened the fourth seal, I heard the voice of the fourth [b]living creature saying, "Come and see."

8 So I looked, and behold, a pale horse. And the name of him who sat on it was [j]Death, and [k]Hades followed with him. And power was given to them over a fourth of the earth, to [l]kill with sword, with hunger, with death, and by the [m]beasts of the earth.

(5) Fifth seal: martyred remnant

9 When He opened the fifth seal, I saw under the altar the souls of those who had been [n]slain for the word of God and for the testimony which they held.

10 And they cried with a loud voice, saying, [o]"How long, O Lord, holy and true, until You judge and avenge our blood on those who dwell on the earth?"

11 Then a [p]white robe was given to [q]each of them; and it was said to them that they should rest a little while longer, until both *the number of* their fellow servants and their brethren, who would be killed as they *were,* was [r]completed.

(6) Sixth seal: anarchy

12 I looked when He opened the sixth seal, and behold,* there was a great [s]earthquake; and the sun became [t]black as sackcloth of hair, and the moon* became like blood.

13 And the stars of heaven [u]fell to the earth, as a fig tree drops its late figs when it is shaken by a mighty wind.

14 Then the [v]sky receded as a scroll when it is rolled up, and every [w]mountain and island was moved out of its place.

15 And the [x]kings of the earth, the great men, the rich men, the commanders,* the mighty men, every slave and every free man, [y]hid themselves in the caves and in the rocks of the mountains,

16 and said to the mountains and rocks, [z]"Fall on us and hide us from the face of Him who

CHAPTER 6

1 *a* vv. 3,5,7,9, 12; 8:1
b See Ezek. 1:5, *note*

2 *c* Mt. 24:5; cp. Dan. 7:7

4 *d* Cp. 2 Ki. 3:22–23; Nah. 2:3; Zech. 6:2
e Mt. 24:6–7

5 *f* Cp. Zech. 6:2
g Mt. 24:7; cp. Ezek. 4:16–17

6 *h* See Weights and Measures (NT), Acts 27:28, *note*
i See Coinage (NT), Mt. 5:26, *note*

8 *j* Cp. Acts 3:15; Rom. 6:23
k See Lk. 16:23, *note*
l Mt. 24:9
m Cp. Ezek. 14:21

9 *n* *Death* (physical): vv. 9–10; Rev. 9:6. (Gen. 2:17; Heb. 9:27, *note*)

10 *o* Ps. 13:1–6

11 *p* *Righteousness* (garment): vv. 9–11; Rev. 7:9. (Gen. 3:21; Rev. 19:8)
q *Remnant:* vv. 9–11; Rev. 7:3. (Isa. 1:9; Rom. 11:5, *note*)
r Cp. Heb. 11:40

12 *s* Mt. 24:7
t Joel 2:10,31

13 *u* Mt. 24:29

14 *v* Isa. 34:4
w Rev. 16:20; cp. Jer. 3:23

15 *x* Ps. 2:2–4; cp. Dan. 2:21
y Isa. 2:12,19

16 *z* Lk. 23:29–30

* • NU-Text and M-Text omit *Him who lives forever and ever.* **6:1** NU-Text and M-Text read *seven seals.* **6:3** NU-Text and M-Text omit *and see.* **6:6** Greek *choinix;* that is, approximately one quart • This was approximately one day's wage for a worker. **6:12** NU-Text and M-Text omit *behold.* • NU-Text and M-Text read *the whole moon.* **6:15** NU-Text and M-Text read *the commanders, the rich men.*

[1](6:2) The rider on the white horse is not Christ. Those who identify this rider with Him consider the passage a prophecy of conquest by the Gospel. But no crown was given to the Lord as the proclamation of the Gospel began, and the terrible world events which accompany the other three riders (vv. 3–8) do not imply an earlier conquest by Christ.

[a]sits on the throne and from the
wrath of the Lamb!
17 [b]"For the great [c]day of
His wrath has come, and who is
able to stand?"

III. Parenthetic: Jews
and Gentiles Saved
during the Tribulation, 7

7 AFTER these things I saw
four [d]angels standing at the
four corners of the earth, holding the four [e]winds of the earth,
that the wind should not blow
on the earth, on the sea, or on
any tree.
2 Then I saw another [d]angel
ascending from the east, having
the [f]seal of the living God. And
he cried with a loud voice to the
four angels to whom it was
granted to harm the earth and
the sea,
3 saying, [g]"Do not harm the
earth, the sea, or the trees till we
have [h]sealed the servants of our
God on their foreheads."

Remnant of 144,000 out of Israel

4 And I heard the number of
those who were sealed. [i]One
hundred *and* forty-four thousand of [j]all the tribes of the
children of Israel *were* sealed:

5 of the tribe of Judah
twelve thousand *were*
sealed;*
of the tribe of Reuben
twelve thousand *were*
sealed;
of the tribe of Gad
twelve thousand *were*
sealed;
6 of the tribe of Asher
twelve thousand *were*
sealed;
of the tribe of Naphtali
twelve thousand *were*
sealed;
of the tribe of Manasseh
twelve thousand *were*
sealed;
7 of the tribe of Simeon
twelve thousand *were*
sealed;
of the tribe of Levi
twelve thousand *were*
sealed;

16
a Rev. 20:11
17
b Cp. Isa. 13:6; Mt. 24:8
c *Day* (of the LORD): vv. 12–17; Rev. 16:17. (Ps. 2:9; Rev. 19:19)
CHAPTER 7
1
d See Heb. 1:4, *note*
e Cp. Dan. 7:2
2
f Cp. Eph. 1:13–14
3
g Cp. 2 Th. 2:7
h *Remnant:* vv. 3–17; Rev. 12:17. (Isa. 1:9; Rom. 11:5, *note*)
4
i *Israel* (prophecies): vv. 1–4; Rev. 12:1. (Gen. 12:2; Rom. 11:26, *note*)
j Gen. 49:1–27; cp. Dt. 33:6–25; Ezek. 48:1–7, 23–28

of the tribe of Issachar
twelve thousand *were*
sealed;
8 of the tribe of Zebulun
twelve thousand *were*
sealed;
of the tribe of Joseph
twelve thousand *were*
sealed;
of the tribe of Benjamin
twelve thousand *were*
sealed.

Gentile multitude to come out
of the great tribulation

9 After these things I
looked, and behold, [k]a great
multitude which no one could
number, of all nations, tribes,
peoples, and tongues, standing
before the throne and before the
Lamb, clothed with [l]white
robes, with [m]palm branches in
their hands,
10 and crying out with a loud
voice, saying, [n]"Salvation *be-*
longs to our God who sits on the
throne, and to the Lamb!"
11 All the [d]angels stood
around the throne and the elders and the four [o]living creatures, and fell on their faces before the throne and [p]worshiped
God,
12 saying:

"Amen! Blessing and
glory and wisdom,
Thanksgiving and honor
and power and might,
Be to our God forever
and ever.
Amen."

13 Then one of the elders answered, saying to me, "Who are
these arrayed in white robes,
and where did they come
from?"
14 And I said to him, "Sir,*
you know." So he said to me,
"These are the ones who come
out of the great [1q]tribulation,
and washed their robes and

9
k Isa. 60:1–5; cp. Rom. 11:25
l *Righteousness* (garment): vv. 9–14; Rev. 16:15. (Gen. 3:21; Rev. 19:8)
m vv. 9–10; cp. Mt. 21:8–9
10
n See Rom. 1:16, *note*
11
o See Ezek. 1:5, *note*
p Rev. 4:11; 5:9,12,14; 11:16
14
q *Tribulation* (the great): v. 14. (Ps. 2:5; Rev. 7:14)

*7:5 In NU-Text and M-Text *were sealed* is stated only in verses 5a and 8c; the words are understood in the remainder of the passage. 7:14 NU-Text and M-Text read *My lord.*

[1](7:14) Although God's people may expect tribulation throughout the present age (Jn. 16:33; Acts 14:22), the word "tribulation," as here, is also used specifically of a future time (Mt. 24:21,29; Mk. 13:24).

Since our Lord links the abomination of desolation spoken of by Daniel with this time of

14

a Rev. 22:14; cp. Isa. 1:18; Zech. 3:3–5; 1 Jn. 1:7

b *Sacrifice* (of Christ): v. 14; Rev. 12:11. (Gen. 3:15; Heb. 10:18, *note*)

15

c v. 9

16

d Lit. *scorching heat*

17

e Ezek. 34:23–24

f Rev. 21:4; cp. Isa. 25:8

CHAPTER 8

2

g See Heb. 1:4, *note*

h Angels' trumpets: cp. 1 Th. 4:16, *the trumpet of God*

made them [a]white in the [b]blood
of the Lamb.
15 "Therefore they are [c]be-
fore the throne of God, and
serve Him day and night in His
temple. And He who sits on the
throne will dwell among them.
16 "They shall neither hunger anymore nor thirst anymore; the sun shall not strike
them, nor any [d]heat;
17 "for the Lamb who is in
the midst of the throne will
[e]shepherd them and lead them
to living fountains of waters.*
And [f]God will wipe away every
tear from their eyes."

Seventh seal (cp. 4:1): composed of seven trumpets

8 WHEN He opened the sev-
enth seal, there was silence
in heaven for about half an
hour.

IV. The Seven Trumpet Judgments, 8:2—9:21; 11:15–19

Christ as high priest

2 And I saw the seven [g]an-
gels who stand before God, and
to them were given seven
[1h]trumpets.
3 Then another [g]angel, having a golden censer, came and
stood at the altar. He was given
much incense, that he should
[i]offer *it* with the [j]prayers of
all the saints upon the golden
altar which was before the
throne.
4 And the [k]smoke of the incense, with the prayers of the
saints, ascended before God
from the [g]angel's hand.
5 Then the [g]angel took the
censer, [l]filled it with fire from
the altar, and threw *it* to the
earth. And there were noises,
thunderings, [m]lightnings, and
an earthquake.
6 So the seven [g]angels who
had the seven trumpets prepared themselves to sound.

(1) First trumpet

7 The first [g]angel sounded:
And [n]hail and fire followed,
mingled with blood, and they
were thrown to the earth.* And
a [o]third of the trees were
burned up, and all [p]green grass
was burned up.

*

7:17 NU-Text and M-Text read *to fountains of the waters of life.* 8:7 NU-Text and M-Text add *And a third of the earth was burned up.*

3

i Cp. Jn. 14:13; Heb. 7:25

j Rev. 5:8

4

k Cp. Ex. 30:7–8; Ps. 141:2

5

l Cp. Lev. 16:12; Num. 16:46

m Rev. 4:5; cp. Ex. 19:18–19; Ps. 97:1–4

7

n Cp. Ex. 9:23–24; Ps. 18:13; Ezek. 38:22

o vv. 8–10; Rev. 9:15–18

p Cp. 9:4

tribulation (Mt. 24:15–21; Mk. 13:14–19), it is evident that the tribulation is to be connected with the seventieth week of Daniel (Dan. 9:27). Furthermore, the Biblical references have in common an allusion to unprecedented trouble (Jer. 30:7; Dan. 9:27; 12:1; Mt. 24:21–22).

While the seventieth week of Daniel is seven years in length (see Dan. 9:24, *note;* cp. Rev. 11:2, *note*), and the terms "tribulation" and "great tribulation," as used in the Scriptures, both have to do with the latter half of the seven years, it is customary to use "tribulation" of the whole period, and "great tribulation" of the second half of the period.

From the Scriptures we may deduce that the tribulation will begin with the signing of the covenant to permit the renewal of Jewish sacrifice (Dan. 9:27); it will be a period of unexampled trouble and judgment (see chain ref., *Tribulation,* Ps. 2:5 to Rev. 7:14), and is described in Rev. 6—19; and it will involve the whole earth (Rev. 3:10), but it is distinctively "the time of Jacob's trouble" (Jer. 30:7). The elements of the great tribulation (the latter half of the seventieth week) are: (1) the cruel reign of the "beast . . . out of the sea" (Rev. 13:1) who, at the beginning of the final three and one-half years, will break his covenant with the Jews (by virtue of which they will have re-established the temple worship, Dan. 9:27), and show himself in the temple, demanding that he be worshiped as God (Mt. 24:15; 2 Th. 2:4); (2) the active interposition of Satan "having great wrath" (Rev. 12:12), who gives his power to the beast (Rev. 13:4–5); (3) the unprecedented activity of demons (Rev. 9:2,11; cp. v. 20); and (4) the terrible bowl judgments of Rev. 16.

The tribulation will, nevertheless, be a period of salvation. An election out of Israel will be redeemed (Rev. 7:1–4) with an innumerable multitude of Gentiles (v. 9). These are said to have come "out of the great tribulation" (v. 14). They are not of the priesthood, the Church, to which they seem to stand somewhat in the relation of the Levites to the priests under the Mosaic Covenant. The great tribulation will be followed immediately by the return of Christ in glory, and the events associated therewith (Mt. 24:29–30). See Remnant (Isa. 1:9; Rom. 11:5, *note*); Beast (Dan. 7:8; Rev. 19:20, *note*); Armageddon (Rev. 16:14; 19:17, *note*).

There is a difference of opinion about the location in Revelation at which the great tribulation is first alluded to. Some suggest as early as ch. 6; others, as late as ch. 11. In any case it is described in chs. 11—18.

[1](8:2) The seven trumpets follow chronologically the opening of the seventh seal (8:1).

(2) Second trumpet

8 Then the second [a]angel sounded: And *something* like a great [b]mountain burning with fire was thrown into the sea, and a third of the sea became [c]blood.

9 And a third of the living creatures in the sea died, and a third of the [d]ships were destroyed.

(3) Third trumpet

10 Then the third [a]angel sounded: And a great [e]star [f]fell from heaven, burning like a torch, and it fell on a third of the rivers and on the [g]springs of water.

11 The name of the star is Wormwood. A third of the waters became [h]wormwood, and many men died from the water, because it was made bitter.

(4) Fourth trumpet

12 Then the fourth [a]angel sounded: And a third of the [i]sun was struck, a third of the moon, and a third of the stars, so that a third of them were darkened. A third of the day did not shine, and likewise the night.

13 And I looked, and I heard an [a]angel* flying [j]through the midst of heaven, saying with a loud voice, [k]"Woe, woe, woe to the inhabitants of the earth, because of the remaining blasts of the trumpet of the three angels who are about to sound!"

(5) Fifth trumpet

9 THEN the fifth [a]angel sounded: And I saw a [l]star fallen from heaven to the earth. To him was given the key to the [m]bottomless pit.

2 And he opened the [m]bottomless pit, and smoke arose out of the pit like the smoke of a great furnace. So the [n]sun and the air were darkened because of the smoke of the pit.

3 Then out of the smoke [o]locusts came upon the earth. And to them was given power, as the [p]scorpions of the earth have power.

4 They were commanded not to harm the grass of the earth, or any [q]green thing, or any tree, but only those men [r]who do not have the seal of God on their foreheads.

5 And they were not given *authority* to kill them, but to torment them *for* five months. Their torment *was* like the torment of a scorpion when it strikes a man.

6 In those days men will [s]seek [t]death and will not find it; they will desire to die, and death will flee from them.

7 The [u]shape of the locusts was like [v]horses prepared for battle. On their heads were [w]crowns of something like gold, and their faces *were* like the faces of men.

8 They had hair like women's hair, and their [x]teeth were like lions' *teeth*.

9 And they had [y]breastplates like breastplates of iron, and the sound of their wings *was* like the sound of [z]chariots with many horses running into battle.

10 They had tails like scorpions, [aa]and there were stings in their tails. Their power *was* to hurt men five months.

11 And they had as [bb]king over them the [a]angel of the [m]bottomless pit, whose name in Hebrew *is* [cc]Abaddon, but in Greek he has the name [cc]Apollyon.

12 One [dd]woe is past. Behold, still two more woes are coming after these things.

(6) Sixth trumpet: army from the Far East (cp. 16:12)

13 Then the sixth [a]angel sounded: And I heard a voice from the four horns of the [ee]golden altar which is before God,

14 saying to the sixth [a]angel who had the trumpet, "Release the four angels who are bound at the great river [1]Euphrates."

15 So the four [a]angels, who

* 8:13 NU-Text and M-Text read *eagle.*

8
a See Heb. 1:4, *note*
b Cp. Jer. 51:25
c Rev. 11:6; cp. Ex. 7:19–20
9
d Cp. Isa. 2:12,16
10
e 9:1; cp. Isa. 14:12
f Cp. Dan. 12:3
g Rev. 16:4; cp. Rev. 7:17
11
h Cp. Dt. 29:18; Jer. 23:15
12
i Isa. 13:10; Joel 2:31; Mt. 24:29; Rev. 6:12; cp. Ex. 10:21–23; Jn. 12:35
13
j Lit. *in mid-heaven*
k Rev. 9:12; 11:14; 12:12
CHAPTER 9
1
l 8:10; cp. Isa. 14:12–14
m Lit. *pit of the abyss*
2
n Joel 2:10; cp. Rev. 21:24
3
o Cp. Ex. 10:12–15
p Cp. Num. 21:6

4
q Cp. 8:7
r Rev. 7:2–3; cp. Rev. 13:16–17
6
s Cp. Jer. 8:3
t Death (physical): v. 6; Rev. 11:7. (Gen. 2:17; Heb. 9:27, *note*)
7
u i.e. *appearance*
v Cp. Joel 2:4
w Cp. Nah. 3:17
8
x Cp. Joel 1:6
9
y v. 17; cp. Eph. 6:14
z Cp. Joel 2:5
10
aa Or *and stings, and their power was in their tails*
11
bb Cp. Jn. 14:30; Eph. 2:2
cc Meaning *Destroyer.* Cp. Job 26:6; 1 Pet. 5:8
12
dd Rev. 8:13
13
ee Rev. 8:3

[1](9:14) The Euphrates River, mentioned in the Bible as early as the Garden of Eden (Gen. 2:14) and on which were such famous cities of the ancient world as Babylon, Nippur, and Ur, was the northeastern boundary of the land promised to Israel (Gen. 15:18; cp. Dt. 1:7; Josh.

had been prepared for the hour and day and month and year, were released to kill a [a]third of mankind.

16 Now the number of the army of the horsemen *was* two hundred million; I heard the number of them.

17 And thus I saw the horses in the vision: those who sat on them had [b]breastplates of fiery red, hyacinth blue, and sulfur yellow; and the heads of the horses *were* like the [c]heads of lions; and out of their mouths [d]came fire, smoke, and brimstone.

18 By these three *plagues* a third of mankind was killed—by the fire and the smoke and the brimstone which came out of their mouths.

19 For their power* is in their mouth and in their tails; for their [e]tails *are* like serpents, having heads; and with them they do harm.

20 But the rest of mankind, who were not killed by these plagues, did not repent of the works of their hands, that they should not [f]worship demons, and idols of gold, silver, brass, stone, and wood, which can neither [g]see nor hear nor walk.

21 And they did not repent of their murders or their [h]sorceries* or their [i]sexual immorality or their thefts.

V. Parenthetic, 10:1—11:14

Announcement by mighty angel of no further delay

10 I SAW still [j]another mighty [k]angel coming down from heaven, [l]clothed with a cloud. And a [m]rainbow *was* on his head, his [n]face *was* like the sun, and his feet like pillars of fire.

2 He had a little [o]book open in his hand. And he set his [p]right foot on the sea and *his* left *foot* on the land,

3 and cried with a loud voice, as *when* a lion roars. When he cried out, seven [q]thunders uttered their voices.

4 Now when the seven thunders uttered their voices,* I was about to write; but I heard a voice from heaven saying to me,* [r]"Seal up the things which the seven thunders uttered, and do not write them."

5 The [k]angel whom I saw standing on the sea and on the land raised up his hand* to heaven

6 and swore by Him who lives forever and ever, who [s]created heaven and the things that are in it, the earth and the things that are in it, and the sea and the things that are in it, that there should be [t]delay no longer,

7 but in the days of the sounding of the [u]seventh [k]angel, when he is about to sound, the [v]mystery of God [w]would be finished, as He declared to His servants the prophets.

John commanded to prophesy again

8 Then the [x]voice which I heard from heaven spoke to me again and said, "Go, take the little book which is open in the hand of the [k]angel who stands on the sea and on the earth."

9 So I went to the [k]angel and said to him, "Give me the little book." And he said to me, [y]"Take and eat it; and it will make your stomach bitter, but it will be as [z]sweet as honey in your mouth."

10 Then I took the little book out of the [k]angel's hand and ate it, and it was as sweet as honey in my mouth. But when I had eaten it, my stomach became bitter.

11 And he* said to me, "You

*

9:19 NU-Text and M-Text read *the power of the horses.* **9:21** NU-Text and M-Text read *drugs.* **10:4** NU-Text and M-Text read *sounded.* • NU-Text and M-Text omit *to me.* **10:5** NU-Text and M-Text read *right hand.* **10:11** NU-Text and M-Text read *they.*

15
a Rev. 8:7–9
17
b v. 9
c Cp. Isa. 5:25–30
d Cp. Ps. 27:2,12; Acts 9:1
19
e Cp. Isa. 9:15; Mic. 3:5
20
f Cp. Dt. 32:17; 1 Cor. 10:20
g Cp. Ps. 115:4–7
21
h Rev. 21:8
i Cp. Rev. 18:9
CHAPTER 10
1
j Cp. Rev. 5:2; 8:3
k See Heb. 1:4, *note*
l Cp. Acts 1:9; Rev. 1:7
m Ezek. 1:26–28; Rev. 4:3
n Rev. 1:16
2
o Cp. Rev. 5:1
p Ps. 95:5; cp. Hag. 2:6

3
q Ps. 29:3–9
4
r Cp. Dan. 8:26; 12:4–9
6
s Gen. 1:1; Rev. 4:11
t Cp. Rev. 6:11; 12:12; 16:17; 21:6
7
u Rev. 11:15
v Cp. Amos 3:7; see Mt. 13:11, *note*
w Or *also shall be completed*
8
x Cp. Rev. 4:1
9
y Cp. Ezek. 2:8–9; 3:2–3
z Cp. Ps. 19:9–10; 119:103

1:4; 1 Ki. 4:21,24; etc.) as well as the eastern boundary of the Roman Empire. It was generally considered the boundary separating the East from the West (Ezra 4:10–11; Neh. 2:9; etc.).

The army described in Rev. 9:16–19 is a military host coming from the Orient across the Euphrates River (cp. 16:12). The loosing of the angels (9:14–15) and the drying up of the Euphrates (16:12) are a preparation for the invasion of the Holy Land by the "kings from the East" (16:12) in anticipation of the battle of Armageddon (16:14–16).

must [a]prophesy [1]again about
many peoples, nations, tongues,
and kings."

"Times of the Gentiles"
to conclude in forty-two months

11 THEN I was given a
[b]reed like a measuring
rod. And the angel stood,* saying, "Rise and [c]measure the
temple of God, the altar, and
those who worship there.
2 "But leave out the court
which is outside the temple, and
do not measure it, for it has
been given to the [d]Gentiles.
And they will tread the holy
city underfoot *for* [2e]forty-two
months.

The two witnesses killed
and raised from the dead

3 "And I will give *power* to
my [f]two [3g]witnesses, and they
will prophesy one [e]thousand
two hundred and sixty days,
clothed in sackcloth."
4 [h]These are the two olive
trees and the two lampstands
standing before the God* of the
earth.
5 And if anyone wants to
harm them, [i]fire proceeds from
their mouth and devours their
enemies. And if anyone wants
to harm them, he must be killed
in this manner.
6 These have power to
[j]shut heaven, so that no rain
falls in the days of their prophecy; [k]and they have power over
waters to turn them to blood,
and to strike the earth with all
plagues, as often as they desire.
7 When they finish their testimony, the [l]beast that ascends
out of the [m]bottomless pit will
make [n]war against them, overcome them, and [o]kill them.
8 And their dead bodies *will*
lie in the street of the great [p]city
which spiritually is called
[q]Sodom and Egypt, where also
our* Lord was crucified.
9 Then *those* from the peoples, tribes, tongues, and nations will [r]see their dead bodies
three-and-a-half days, and not
allow* their dead bodies to be
put into graves.
10 And those who dwell on
the earth will [s]rejoice over
them, make merry, and send
gifts to one another, because
these two prophets tormented
those who dwell on the earth.
11 Now after the three-and-
a-half days the breath of life
from God entered them, and
they [t]stood on their feet, and
great [u]fear fell on those who
saw them.
12 And they* heard a loud
voice from heaven saying to
them, [v]"Come up here." And
they ascended to heaven in a
cloud, and their enemies [w]saw
them.
13 In the same hour there
was a great earthquake, and a
tenth of the city fell. In the
earthquake seven thousand
people were killed, and the rest
were afraid and gave glory to
the [x]God of heaven.
14 The second [y]woe is past.
Behold, the third woe is coming
quickly.

(7) Seventh trumpet
(vv. 15–19; cp. 8:2):
Christ's reign foreseen

15 Then the [z]seventh [aa]angel
sounded: And there were loud

11
a Cp. Jer. 25:15–26
CHAPTER 11
1
b See Weights and Measures (NT), Acts 27:28, *note*
c Cp. Ezek. 40:3
2
d *Times of the Gentiles:* v. 2; Rev. 16:19. (Dt. 28:49; Rev. 16:19)
e Rev. 13:5; cp. Dan. 7:25; 12:7; Rev. 12:6,14
3
f Dt. 17:6
g Cp. Isa. 43:10,12
4
h Zech. 4:2–3,14
5
i Cp. 2 Ki. 1:10,12; Jer. 5:14
6
j Cp. 1 Ki. 17:1; Jas. 5:17
k Cp. Ex. 7:10,19
7
l Cp. Rev. 13:1; 17:8
m Lit. *pit of the abyss*
n Cp. Dan. 7:21; Rev. 13:7
o *Death* (physical): v. 7; Rev. 13:3. (Gen. 2:17; Heb. 9:27, *note*)
8
p i.e. *Jerusalem*
q Cp. Isa. 1:9–10
9
r Cp. Isa. 66:23–24
10
s Cp. Ps. 79:2–4; Jn. 16:20
11
t *Miracles* (NT): v. 11. (Mt. 8:3; Acts 28:8, *note*)
u Cp. Acts 5:11
12
v Cp. Rev. 20:4–6
w Cp. v. 9
13
x Cp. Dan. 2:18
14
y Rev. 8:13
15
z Rev. 10:7
aa See Heb. 1:4, *note*

*
11:1 NU-Text and M-Text omit *And the angel stood.* 11:4 NU-Text and M-Text read *Lord.* 11:8 NU-Text and M-Text read *their.* 11:9 NU-Text and M-Text read *nations see . . . and will not allow.* 11:12 M-Text reads *I.*

[1](10:11) "Prophesy again about many peoples . . ." John is here told that he will review, with further details, those events thus far covered, especially as the events of the last three and one-half years affect the believing remnant of Israel (cp. 11:19; 12:1,2,5,17; 13:7; 14:1,3).

[2](11:2) The tribulation that is to occur at the end of this age will continue for seven years, the "one week" of Dan. 9:27 (see Rev. 7:14, *note*). This seven-year period is divided, in the prophetic writings, into two equal halves of three and one-half years each. The length of the periods is also referred to as "a time and times and half a time" (Rev. 12:14; cp. Dan. 7:25; 12:7); "forty-two months" (Rev. 11:2; 13:5); and "one thousand two hundred and sixty days" (Rev. 11:3; 12:6). The second half of this seven-year period will be characterized by increasing cruelty on the part of the world ruler, and a consequent greater intensity of persecution and suffering.

[3](11:3) Scripture does not clearly identify these two witnesses. Their power is like that of Moses and Elijah (v. 6).

voices in heaven, saying, "The
kingdoms* of this [a]world have
[1]become *the kingdoms* of our
Lord and of His Christ, and He
shall [b]reign forever and ever!"
16 And the twenty-four elders who sat before God on
their thrones fell on their faces
and [c]worshiped God,
17 saying:

"We give You thanks, O
Lord God Almighty,
The One who is and who
was and who is to
come,*
Because You have taken
Your great power and
reigned.
18 The nations were
[d]angry, and Your
wrath has come,
And the time of the
[e]dead, that they
should be judged,
And that You should
[f]reward Your servants
the prophets and the
saints,
And those who fear Your
name, small and great,
And should destroy
those who destroy the
earth."

19 [g]Then the temple of God
was [h]opened in heaven, and the
ark of His [i]covenant* was seen
in His temple. And there were
lightnings, noises, thunderings,
an earthquake, and great hail.

VI. Prominent Personages, 12

The woman, Israel, gives birth to the male Child, Christ

12 NOW a great sign appeared in heaven: a
[j]woman clothed with the sun,
with the [k]moon under her feet,
and on her head a garland of
[l]twelve stars.
2 Then being with child, she
cried out in [m]labor and in pain
to give birth.

The red dragon: Satan

3 And another sign ap-
peared in heaven: behold, a
great, fiery red [n]dragon [o]hav-
ing seven heads and [p]ten horns,
and seven [q]diadems on his
heads.
4 His tail drew a third of the
[r]stars of heaven and [s]threw
them to the earth. And the
[n]dragon stood before the
woman who was ready to give
birth, [t]to devour her Child as
soon as it was born.

The male Child: Christ

5 She bore a male Child
[u]who was to rule all nations
with a rod of iron. And her
Child was [v]caught up to God
and His throne.
6 Then the woman fled into
the [w]wilderness, where she has
a place prepared by God, that
they should feed her there one
[x]thousand two hundred and
sixty days.

The archangel: Michael

7 And war broke out in
heaven: [y]Michael and his [z]an-
gels fought with the [n]dragon;
and the dragon and his [z]angels
fought,
8 but they did not prevail,
nor was a place found for
them* in heaven any longer.
9 So the great [n]dragon was
cast out, that [n]serpent of [aa]old,
called the [n]Devil and [n]Satan,
who [bb]deceives the whole
[cc]world; he was cast to the earth,
and his [z]angels were cast out
with him.
10 Then I heard a loud voice
saying in heaven, "Now [dd]salva-
tion, and [ee]strength, and the
[ff]kingdom of our God, and [gg]the
power of His Christ have come,
for the [n]accuser of our brethren, who accused them before
our God day and night, has been
cast down.
11 "And they overcame him
by the [hh]blood of the Lamb and
by the word of their testimony,
and they did not love their lives
to the death.

15
a Gk. *kosmos.* See Rev. 13:8, *note*
b *Kingdom* (NT): v. 15; Rev. 17:14. (Mt. 2:2; 1 Cor. 15:24, *note*)
16
c vv. 16–17; Rev. 4:11; 5:9,12,14; 7:11
18
d Ps. 2:1
e Rev. 20:12–13
f *Rewards:* v. 18; Rev. 22:12. (Dan. 12:3; 1 Cor. 3:14, *note*)
19
g v. 19 is better understood when read as a part of ch. 12
h Rev. 15:5
i Cp. Ex. 37:1; Heb. 9:4
CHAPTER 12
1
j *Israel* (history): vv. 1–17; Rev. 21:12. (Gen. 12:2; Rom. 11:26, *note*)
k Cp. Gen. 37:9
l Cp. Rev. 7:4–8
2
m Isa. 66:7–10; cp. Mic. 4:10
3
n *Satan:* vv. 3–11; Rev. 12:12. (Gen. 3:1; Rev. 20:10)
o Cp. Rev. 13:1

p Cp. Dan. 7:7
q Lit. *diadems*
4
r Rev. 8:12
s Cp. Dan. 8:10
t Mt. 2:16
5
u i.e. *Christ.* Ps. 2:8–9; Rev. 2:27; 19:15; cp. Isa. 9:6–7
v Lk. 24:51; Acts 1:9–11
6
w 12:14
x Rev. 11:2,3; 13:5; cp. Dan. 9:27; see Rev. 7:14 and 11:2, *notes*
7
y Dan. 10:21; Jude 9
z See Heb. 1:4, *note*
9
aa Or *of ancient times.* Gen. 3:1; Isa. 14:12–19
bb Cp. 2 Cor. 4:4; 11:14
cc Gk. *oikoumene.* See Lk. 2:1, *note*
10
dd Lit. *the salvation.* See Rom. 1:16, *note*
ee Lit. *the power.*
ff See Rev. 20:4, *note*
gg Lit. *the authority*
11
hh *Sacrifice* (of Christ): v. 11. (Gen. 3:15; Heb. 10:18, *note*)

*
11:15 NU-Text and M-Text read *kingdom . . . has become.* 11:17 NU-Text and M-Text omit *and who is to come.* 11:19 M-Text reads *the covenant of the Lord.* 12:8 M-Text reads *him.*

[1](11:15) The seventh trumpet announces the beginning of Christ's reign on earth, when the kingdom of this world will become the kingdom of our Lord, and occurs close to the end of the great tribulation. The seven bowls (ch. 16) follow this event in rapid sequence and culminate in the second coming of Christ.

12 "Therefore rejoice, O
heavens, and you who dwell in
them! [a]Woe to the inhabitants
of the earth and the sea! For the
[b]devil has come down to you,
having great [c]wrath, because
he knows that he has a short
time."

Jewish remnant assaulted by Satan

13 Now when the [b]dragon
saw that he had been cast to
the earth, he [d]persecuted the
woman who gave birth to the
male *Child.*
14 But the woman was given
two [e]wings of a great eagle, that
she might fly into the wilderness to her [f]place, where she is
nourished for a time and times
and half a time, from the presence of the [b]serpent.
15 So the [b]serpent spewed
water out of his mouth like a
flood after the woman, that he
might cause her to be carried
away by the flood.
16 But the earth helped the
woman, and the earth opened
its mouth and swallowed up the
flood which the [b]dragon had
spewed out of his mouth.
17 And the [b]dragon was enraged with the woman, and he
went to make war with the [g]rest
of her offspring, who keep the
[h]commandments of God and
have the testimony of Jesus
Christ.*

VII. The Rise and Reign of the Beast and False Prophet, 13

The beast out of the sea: the deadly wound healed

13 THEN I* stood on the
sand of the sea. And I
saw a [1][i]beast [2]rising up out of
the sea, [j]having seven heads
and [k]ten [l]horns,* and on his
horns ten [m]crowns, and on his
heads a blasphemous [n]name.
2 Now the beast which I saw
was [3]like a leopard, his feet
were like *the feet of* a bear, and
his mouth like the mouth of a
lion. The [o]dragon gave him his
power, his throne, and great authority.
3 And *I saw* one of his heads
as if it had been [p]mortally
[4]wounded, and his deadly
wound was [q]healed. And all the
[r]world [s]marveled and followed
the beast.
4 So they worshiped the
dragon who gave authority to
the beast; and they worshiped
the beast, saying, "Who *is* like
the beast? Who is able to make
war with him?"
5 And he was given a
[t]mouth speaking great things

*
12:17 NU-Text and M-Text omit *Christ.*
13:1 NU-Text reads *he.* • NU-Text and M-Text read *ten horns and seven heads.*

12
a Rev. 8:13
b Satan: vv. 10–17; Rev. 20:2. (Gen. 3:1; Rev. 20:10)
c v. 17; cp. 1 Pet. 5:8
13
d Cp. Mt. 24:9
14
e Cp. Ex. 19:4
f v. 6; cp. Hos. 2:14–15
17
g Remnant: vv. 6,13–17; Rev. 14:5. (Isa. 1:9; Rom. 11:5, *note*)
h Law (of Moses): v. 17; Rev. 14:12. (Ex. 19:1; Gal. 3:24, *note*)

CHAPTER 13
1
i The Beast: vv. 1–8; Rev. 19:19. (Dan. 7:8; Rev. 19:20)
j Cp. Rev. 12:3
k Cp. Dan. 7:7
l See Dt. 33:17, *note*
m Lit. *diadems*
n Rev. 17:3
2
o Rev. 12:3,9
3
p Death (physical): v. 3; Rev. 18:24. (Gen. 2:17; Heb. 9:27, *note*)
q Cp. Dan. 7:8
r See v. 8, *note*
s Rev. 17:8
5
t v. 6; cp. Dan. 7:8,11, 20,25

[1](13:1) In this unveiling of conditions on the earth at the end of the age, the following factors will be manifest: (1) the world ruler is satanically energized (vv. 2,4); (2) he and his image are worshiped (vv. 4,8,12,15); (3) he is acknowledged as possessing supreme military power (v. 4); (4) he exercises a universal authority (v. 7); and (5) he persecutes the believers in Christ (vv. 6–7). The second beast is (1) a deceiver (vv. 13–14), and (2) he exercises economic dictatorship (vv. 16–17).

[2](13:1) Daniel's fourth beast (Dan. 7:26, *note*). The "ten horns" are explained in Dan. 7:24 and Rev. 17:12 to be ten kings. The whole vision is the last form of Gentile world power, a confederation of ten nations which will be a revival of the old Roman Empire. Its sphere will probably reach out beyond the old boundaries, since it is to be a world power (v. 8). For example, in Rev. 17:1–7 the woman arrayed in purple and scarlet is seen sitting on a scarlet beast. The woman is Babylon, apostate Christendom (see Rev. 18:2, *note*) and the beast is the final form of Gentile world power. Because the woman rides the beast, where one goes the other goes also; thus the world empire will embrace all the areas of Christendom, which assuredly includes the Western Hemisphere. Rev. 13:1–3 refers to the ten-kingdom power; vv. 4–10, to its ruler who is emphatically the "beast" (see Rev. 19:20, *note*).

[3](13:2) In Dan. 7:4–6 three animals—a lion, a bear, and a leopard—are seen. They are symbols of the empires which preceded the Roman Empire, the composite beast (Dan. 7:7) which combined characteristics and qualities of the first three: Babylonian voracity, Persian tenacity, and Macedonian swiftness.

[4](13:3) Fragments of the ancient Roman Empire have never ceased to exist as separate kingdoms. It was the imperial form of government which ceased; the one head "had been mortally wounded." What is written prophetically in v. 3 is the restoration of the imperial form as such, though over a federated empire of ten kingdoms. The head is "healed," i.e. restored, there is an emperor again—the beast.

and blasphemies, and he was given authority to continue* for [a]forty-two months.

6 Then he opened his mouth in blasphemy against God, to blaspheme His name, His tabernacle, and those who [b]dwell in heaven.

7 It was granted to him to make [c]war with the saints and to [1]overcome them. And authority was given him over every tribe,* tongue, and nation.

8 All who dwell on the earth will worship him, whose names have [d]not been written [e]in the Book of [f]Life of the Lamb slain from the foundation of the [2]world.

9 If anyone has an ear, let him hear.

10 He who leads into captivity shall go into captivity; he who kills with the sword must be killed with the sword. Here is the [g]patience and the faith of the saints.

The beast out of the earth: the number of a man, 666

11 Then I saw [h]another [3]beast coming up out of the earth, and he had two [i]horns [j]like a lamb and spoke like a dragon.

12 And he exercises all the authority of the first beast in his presence, and causes the earth and those who dwell in it to [k]worship the first beast, whose deadly wound was healed.

13 He performs great signs, so that he even makes [l]fire come down from heaven on the earth in the sight of men.

14 And he [m]deceives those* who dwell on the earth by those [n]signs which [o]he was granted to do in the sight of the beast, telling those who dwell on the earth to make an image to the beast who was wounded by the sword and lived.

15 [o]He was granted *power* to give breath to the image of the beast, that the image of the beast should both speak and cause as many as would not worship the image of the beast to be [p]killed.

16 He causes all, both small and great, rich and poor, free and slave, to receive [q]a mark on their right hand or on their foreheads,

17 and that no one may buy or sell except one who has the [r]mark or* the name of the beast, or the [s]number of his name.

18 Here is wisdom. Let him who has [t]understanding calculate the number of the beast, for it is the [u]number of a man: His number *is* 666.

VIII. Parenthetic, 14

The Lamb and the 144,000 on Mount Zion

14 THEN I looked, and behold, a* [v]Lamb standing on Mount Zion, and with Him one [w]hundred *and* forty-four thousand, having* His Fa-

13:5 M-Text reads *make war.*
13:7 NU-Text and M-Text add *and people.*
13:14 M-Text reads *my own people.*
13:17 NU-Text and M-Text omit *or.*
14:1 NU-Text and M-Text read *the.*
• NU-Text and M-Text add *His name and.*

5
a Rev. 11:2
6
b Cp. Rev. 12:12
7
c Cp. Dan. 7:21; Rev. 11:7
8
d Rev. 20:12–15; cp. Phil. 4:3; Rev. 3:5
e Lit. *from the foundation of the world in the book of the Lamb that was slain*
f Life (eternal): v. 8; Rev. 17:8. (Mt. 7:14; Rev. 22:19)
10
g Rev. 14:12; cp. Rev. 1:9
11
h Antichrist: vv. 11–17; Rev. 16:13. (Mt. 24:5; Rev. 13:11, *note*)
i See Dt. 33:17, *note*
j Cp. Jn. 1:29
12
k v. 8
13
l Cp. 2 Ki. 1:10
14
m Mt. 24:24; 2 Th. 2:9–12; Rev. 12:9; cp. 1 Jn. 4:1–3
n See vv. 5, 11
o Lit. *it was given him*
15
p Cp. Dan. 3:1–6
16
q Cp. Rev. 7:2–3
17
r Rev. 14:9–11
s Rev. 15:2
18
t 1 Cor. 2:14; cp. Dan. 12:10
u Cp. Ps. 9:20
CHAPTER 14
1
v Rev. 5:6
w Rev. 7:4

[1](13:7) For the assurance of victory for the people of God over all these evil forces, see Rev. 15:2.

[2](13:8) World (Gk. *kosmos*), Summary: In the sense of the present world system, the ethically bad sense of the word refers to the order or arrangement under which Satan has organized the world of unbelieving mankind upon his cosmic principles of force, greed, selfishness, ambition, and pleasure (Mt. 4:8–9; Jn. 12:31; 14:30; 18:36; Eph. 2:2; 6:12; 1 Jn. 2:15–17). This world system is imposing and powerful with military might; is often outwardly religious, scientific, cultured, and elegant; but, seething with national and commercial rivalries and ambitions, is upheld in any real crisis only by armed force, and is dominated by satanic principles. Cp. Zech. 12:1–6; see Mt. 4:8, *note.*

[3](13:11) Many identify the "beast coming up out of the earth" as the Antichrist. According to Scripture "many antichrists" (1 Jn. 2:18) and those who have the "spirit of the Antichrist" (1 Jn. 4:3) precede and prepare the way for the final Antichrist. The supreme mark of all antichrists is the denial of the incarnation of the eternal Son of God (Jn. 1:14; see Mt. 1:16, *note*). If the "beast coming up out of the earth" (vv. 11–17) is the Antichrist, he is the same as the "false prophet" of 16:13; 19:20; 20:10. Because the word "antichrist" is never directly applied to him, however, some have considered the term "antichrist," defined in the sense *against Christ,* as applying to the first beast (vv. 1–10), who is the political ruler.

ther's name [a]written on their
foreheads.
2 And I heard a voice from
heaven, like the [b]voice of many
waters, and like the voice of
loud thunder. And I heard the
sound of [c]harpists playing their
harps.
3 They sang as it were a new
song before the throne, before
the four living creatures, and
the elders; and [d]no one could
learn that song except the hundred *and* forty-four thousand
who were [e]redeemed from the
earth.
4 These are the ones who
were not defiled with women,
for they are virgins. These are
the ones who [f]follow the Lamb
wherever He goes. These were
[e]redeemed* from *among* men,
being firstfruits to God and to
the Lamb.
5 And in their mouth was
found no deceit,* for [g]they are
without fault before the throne
of God.*

Vision of the angel with the everlasting Gospel

6 Then I saw another [h]angel
flying in [i]the midst of heaven,
having the everlasting [1j]gospel
to preach to those who dwell on
the earth—to every nation,
tribe, tongue, and people—
7 saying with a loud voice,
"Fear God and give glory to
Him, for the hour of His judgment has come; and worship
Him who made heaven and
earth, the sea and springs of water."

Babylon's fall foretold

8 And another [h]angel followed, saying, "Babylon* is
[k]fallen, is fallen, that [l]great
city, because she has made all
nations drink of the wine of the
wrath of her fornication."

Doom to come on worshipers of the beast

9 Then a third [h]angel followed them, saying with a loud
voice, "If anyone worships the
beast and his [m]image, and re-

1
a Rev. 7:3; 22:4; cp. Rev. 13:16
2
b Rev. 19:6
c Cp. Rev. 15:2
3
d Cp. Rev. 5:9
e See Rom. 3:24, *note*
4
f Rev. 7:17
5
g *Remnant:* vv. 1–5; Rev. 20:4. (Isa. 1:9; Rom. 11:5, *note*)
6
h See Heb. 1:4, *note*
i Lit. *mid-heaven*
j *Gospel:* vv. 6–7. (Gen. 12:3; Rev. 14:6)
8
k Rev. 18:2
l Rev. 17:5
9
m Rev. 13:14–15

*14:4 M-Text adds *by Jesus.* 14:5 NU-Text and M-Text read *falsehood.* • NU-Text and M-Text omit *before the throne of God.* 14:8 NU-Text reads *Babylon the great is fallen, is fallen, which has made;* M-Text reads *Babylon the great is fallen. She has made.*

[1](14:6) The Gospel, Summary: The word "gospel" means *good news.* As used in the NT, the word deals with different aspects of divine revelation. Absolutely essential to man's salvation is the Gospel of the grace of God (Rom. 2:16, refs.). This is the good news that Jesus Christ died on the cross for the sins of the world, that He was raised from the dead on account of our justification, and that by Him all who believe are justified from all things. It is described as the Gospel "of God" (Rom. 1:1) because it originates in His love; "of Christ" (2 Cor. 10:14) because it flows from His sacrifice, and because He is the object of faith; "of the grace of God" (Acts 20:24) because it saves those whom the law curses; "of the glory of Christ" (2 Cor. 4:4; cp. 1 Tim. 1:11) because it concerns Him who is in the glory and who is bringing many sons to glory (Heb. 2:10); "of your salvation" (Eph. 1:13) because it is "the power of God to salvation for everyone who believes" (Rom. 1:16); and "of peace" (Eph. 6:15) because through Christ it makes peace between the believing sinner and God, and makes inward peace possible.

Another aspect of the good news is the gospel "of the kingdom" (Mt. 4:23), i.e. the good news that God purposes to set up on the earth the kingdom of Christ, the Son of David, in fulfillment of the Davidic Covenant (2 Sam. 7:16, *note*). The good news of this kingdom was announced by the OT prophets (Isa. 9:6–7), by Christ in His first coming (Mt. 9:35), and will be proclaimed during the great tribulation (Mt. 24:14).

The "everlasting gospel" (Rev. 14:6ff.) is described as the announcement of divine judgment upon the wicked in the coming great tribulation. It is good news for the suffering believers as it heralds their coming deliverance and reward (cp. v. 12). In view of this those who "dwell on the earth" are exhorted to fear God and worship Him (v. 7).

The good news of divine revelation is contrasted with "a different gospel" (2 Cor. 11:4; Gal. 1:6) which Paul states is "not another," but a perversion of the Gospel of the grace of God. We are warned against all its seductive forms which deny the sufficiency of grace alone to save, keep, and perfect. Its teachers lie under the awful anathema of God (Gal. 1:9).

The word "gospel," therefore, includes various aspects of the good news of divine revelation. But the fact that God has proclaimed the good news of the Gospel of grace, the Gospel of the coming kingdom, and the everlasting Gospel of divine judgment upon the wicked and deliverance of believers does not mean that there is more than one Gospel of salvation. Grace is the basis for salvation in all dispensations, and is under all circumstances the only way of salvation from sin.

ceives *his* [a]mark on his forehead or on his hand,

10 "he himself shall also [b]drink of the wine of the wrath of God, which is poured out full strength into the cup of His indignation. He shall be [c]tormented with fire and brimstone in the [d]presence of the holy [e]angels and in the presence of the Lamb.

11 "And the smoke of their torment ascends [f]forever and ever; and they have [g]no rest day or night, who worship the beast and his image, and whoever receives the mark of his name."

12 Here is the patience of the saints; here *are* those* who keep the [h]commandments of God and the faith of Jesus.

Blessedness of the holy dead

13 Then I heard a voice from heaven saying to me,* [i]"Write: [j]'Blessed *are* the dead who die in the Lord from now on.'" "Yes," says the [k]Spirit, "that they may rest from their labors, and their works follow [l]them."

Vision of Armageddon
(see 19:17, note)

14 Then I looked, and behold, a white cloud, and on the cloud sat *One* [m]like the Son of Man, having on His head a [n]golden crown, and in His hand a [o]sharp sickle.

15 And another [e]angel came out of the temple, crying with a loud voice to Him who sat on the cloud, "Thrust in Your sickle and reap, [p]for the time has come for You* to reap, for the harvest of the earth is ripe."

16 So He who sat on the cloud thrust in His sickle on the [q]earth, and the earth was reaped.

17 Then another [e]angel came out of the temple which is in heaven, he also having a sharp sickle.

18 And another [e]angel came out from the altar, who had [r]power over fire, and he cried with a loud cry to him who had the sharp sickle, saying, [s]"Thrust in your sharp sickle and gather the clusters of the vine of the earth, for her grapes are [t]fully ripe."

19 So the [e]angel thrust his sickle into the earth and gathered the vine of the earth, and threw *it* into the great winepress of the wrath of God.

20 And the [u]winepress was trampled outside the city, and blood came out of the winepress, up to the horses' bridles, for one thousand six hundred [v]furlongs.

IX. The Seven Bowl Judgments, 15—16

A glorious heavenly scene

15 THEN I saw another sign in heaven, great and marvelous: seven [e]angels having the [w]seven last plagues, for in them the wrath of God is complete.

2 And I saw *something* like a [x]sea of glass mingled with [y]fire, and those who have the [z]victory over the beast, over his [aa]image and over his mark* *and* over the [bb]number of his name, standing on the sea of glass, having [cc]harps of God.

3 They sing the [dd]song of Moses, the servant of God, and the song of the [ee]Lamb, saying:

[ff]"Great and marvelous *are*
Your works,
Lord God Almighty!
[gg]Just and true *are* Your
ways,
O King of the saints!*
4 Who shall not fear You,
O Lord, and glorify
Your name?
For *You* alone *are* [hh]holy.
For all nations shall
come and worship
before You,
For Your [ii]judgments
have been manifested."

5 After these things I looked, and behold,* the [jj]temple of the tabernacle of the testimony in heaven was opened.

6 And out of the temple came the seven [e]angels having the seven plagues, [kk]clothed in

*
14:12 NU-Text and M-Text omit *here are those.* 14:13 NU-Text and M-Text omit *to me.* 14:15 NU-Text and M-Text omit *for You.* 15:2 NU-Text and M-Text omit *over his mark.* 15:3 NU-Text and M-Text read *nations.* 15:5 NU-Text and M-Text omit *behold.*

9
a Rev. 13:16
10
b Ps. 75:8; Rev. 16:19; cp. Jer. 25:15
c Cp. Rev. 20:10
d 2 Th. 1:9
e See Heb. 1:4, *note*
11
f Cp. Isa. 66:23–24; Mk. 9:48; Rev. 19:3
g Cp. Rev. 4:8
12
h Law (of Moses): v. 12. (Ex. 19:1; Gal. 3:24, *note*)
13
i Inspiration: v. 13; Rev. 19:9. (Ex. 4:15; 2 Tim. 3:16, *note*)
j Cp. 1 Cor. 15:51–53; Phil. 1:23
k Holy Spirit (NT): v. 13; Rev. 17:3. (Mt. 1:18; Acts 2:4, *note*)
l 1 Cor. 3:11–15; 15:58
14
m Cp. Mt. 24:30; 26:64; Rev. 1:7
n Cp. Rev. 19:12
o Cp. Mk. 4:29
15
p Cp. Jer. 51:33
16
q Cp. Mt. 13:30,36–43; Lk. 3:17
18
r Cp. Rev. 16:8
s Joel 3:13

t Cp. 2 Th. 2:7–12
20
u Isa. 63:1–6; Rev. 19:15
v See Weights and Measures (NT), Acts 27:28, *note*
CHAPTER 15
1
w Cp. Lev. 26:21
2
x Cp. Rev. 4:6
y Cp. 1 Pet. 1:7
z Cp. Rev. 12:11
aa Rev. 13:14–15
bb Rev. 13:17
cc Cp. Ps. 150:3; Rev. 5:8
3
dd Ex. 15:1–21
ee Rev. 15:3; cp. Ps. 22:22
ff Dt. 32:3–4; Ps. 92:5; Rom. 11:33
gg Rev. 16:7
4
hh Lev. 11:44; 1 Pet. 1:16; Rev. 4:8
ii Lit. *righteous acts*
5
jj Cp. Rev. 11:19
6
kk Cp. Rev. 19:8

pure bright linen, and having
their chests [a]girded with golden
bands.
7 Then one of the four living
creatures gave to the seven [b]an-
gels seven golden bowls full of
the [c]wrath of God who lives forever and ever.
8 The temple was [d]filled
with smoke from the glory of
God and from His power, and
no one was able to enter the
temple till the seven plagues of
the seven [b]angels were completed.

(1) First bowl of wrath

16 THEN I heard a loud
voice from the temple
saying to the seven [b]angels,
"Go and [e]pour out the bowls*
of the wrath of God on the
earth."
2 So the first went and
poured out his bowl upon the
[f]earth, and a foul and loathsome [g]sore came upon the men
who had the mark of the beast
and those who worshiped his
image.

(2) Second bowl of wrath

3 Then the second [b]angel
poured out his bowl on the [h]sea,
and it became blood as of a dead
man; and every living creature
in the sea died.

(3) Third bowl of wrath

4 Then the third [b]angel
poured out his bowl on the rivers and [i]springs of water, and
they became [j]blood.
5 And I heard the angel of
the waters saying:

"You are [k]righteous, O
Lord,*
The One who is and who
was and who is to
be,*
Because You have
judged these things.
6 For they have [l]shed the
blood of saints and
prophets,
And You have given
them [m]blood to drink.
For* it is their just due."

7 And I heard another
from* the altar saying, "Even
so, Lord God Almighty, true
and righteous *are* Your judgments."

(4) Fourth bowl of wrath

8 Then the fourth [b]angel
poured out his bowl on the
[n]sun, and [o]power was given to
him to scorch men with fire.
9 And men were scorched
with great heat, and they blasphemed the name of God who
has [p]power over these plagues;
and they did not repent and give
Him glory.

(5) Fifth bowl of wrath

10 Then the fifth [b]angel
poured out his bowl on the
throne of the beast, and his
kingdom became full of [q]dark-
ness; and they gnawed their
tongues because of the pain.
11 They blasphemed the God
of heaven because of their pains
and their sores, and did not repent of their deeds.

(6) Sixth bowl of wrath

12 Then the sixth [b]angel
poured out his bowl [r]on the
great river Euphrates, and its
water was dried up, so that the
way of the kings from the east
might be prepared.

Parenthetic: Armageddon
(vv. 13–16; see 19:17, note)

13 And I saw three unclean
[s]spirits like frogs *coming* out of
the mouth of the dragon, out of
the mouth of the beast, and out
of the mouth of the [t]false
[u]prophet.
14 For they are spirits of
demons, performing [v]signs,
which go out to the kings of the
earth and* of the whole [w]world,
to gather them to the [x]battle of
that great day of God Almighty.
15 "Behold, [y]I am coming as
a thief. Blessed *is* he who
watches, and keeps his [z]gar-
ments, lest he walk naked and
they see his shame."
16 And they gathered them

*
16:1 NU-Text and M-Text read *seven bowls.* **16:5** NU-Text and M-Text omit *O Lord.* • NU-Text and M-Text read *who was, the Holy One.* **16:6** NU-Text and M-Text omit *For.* **16:7** NU-Text and M-Text omit *another from.* **16:14** NU-Text and M-Text omit *of the earth and.*

6
a Cp. Rev. 1:13
7
b See Heb. 1:4, *note*
c Cp. Jer. 25:15; Rev. 14:10
8
d Cp. Ex. 40:34–35; 1 Ki. 8:10–11; Isa. 6:4; cp. 1 Sam. 4:21–22
CHAPTER 16
1
e Cp. Ps. 79:6
2
f Cp. Rev. 8:7
g Cp. Ex. 9:8–11
3
h Cp. Rev. 8:8–9
4
i Cp. Rev. 8:10–11
j Cp. Ex. 7:17–20
5
k Cp. Rom. 3:3–6
6
l Cp. Mt. 23:35; Rev. 18:24
m Isa. 49:26

8
n Cp. Rev. 8:12
o Lit. *it was given to it*
9
p Or *authority*
10
q Cp. Ex. 10:21; Rev. 9:2
12
r Cp. Rev. 9:14
13
s Cp. Ex. 8:1–6; 1 Tim. 4:1; 1 Jn. 4:1–3
t Antichrist: v. 13; Rev. 19:20. (Mt. 24:5; Rev. 13:11, *note*)
u Cp. Rev. 13:11
14
v Cp. Rev. 13:13
w Gk. *oikoumenē.* See Lk. 2:1, *note*
x Armageddon (battle of): vv. 13–16; Rev. 19:17. (Isa. 10:27; Rev. 19:17)
15
y Christ (second advent): vv. 13–16; Rev. 19:11. (Dt. 30:3; Acts 1:11, *note*)
z Righteousness (garment): v. 15; Rev. 19:8. (Gen. 3:21; Rev. 19:8)

17
[a] See Heb. 1:4, *note*
[b] *Day* (of the LORD): vv. 12–17; Rev. 19:19. (Ps. 2:9; Rev. 19:19)
[c] Cp. Rev. 10:6–7

18
[d] Cp. Rev. 6:12; 11:13

19
[e] *Times of the Gentiles:* vv. 14, 19. (Dt. 28:49; Rev. 16:19)
[f] Rev. 17:5,18
[g] Rev. 14:8; see Isa. 13:1, *note 2*
[h] Rev. 14:10; 18:5; cp. Isa. 51:21–23

20
[i] Cp. Rev. 6:14

21
[j] Cp. Ex. 9:22–35
[k] See Weights and Measures (NT), Acts 27:28, *note*

CHAPTER 17

1
[l] Rev. 16:19
[m] Rev. 19:2
[n] Cp. Jer. 51:13

2
[o] Rev. 18:3,9
[p] Rev. 14:8

3
[q] *Holy Spirit* (NT): v. 3; Rev. 21:10. (Mt. 1:18; Acts 2:4, *note*)

together to the place called in Hebrew, [1]Armageddon.*

(7) Seventh bowl of wrath

17 Then the seventh [a]angel poured out his bowl into the air, and a loud voice came out of the temple of heaven, from the throne, saying, [b]"It is [c]done!"

18 And there were noises and thunderings and lightnings; and there was a great [d]earthquake, such a mighty and great earthquake as had not occurred since men were on the earth.

19 Now the great city was divided into three parts, and the cities of the [e]nations fell. And [f]great [2g]Babylon was remembered before God, to give her the [h]cup of the wine of the fierceness of His wrath.

20 Then every [i]island fled away, and the mountains were not found.

21 And great [j]hail from heaven fell upon men, *each hailstone* about the weight of a [k]talent. Men blasphemed God because of the plague of the hail, since that plague was exceedingly great.

X. The Doom of Babylon, 17–18

The harlot: apostate Christendom exerts power over the revived fourth world empire

17 THEN one of the seven [a]angels who had the seven bowls came and talked with me, saying to me,* "Come, I will show you the [l]judgment of the [m]great harlot who sits on many [n]waters,

2 "with whom the [o]kings of the earth committed fornication, and the inhabitants of the earth were made [p]drunk with the wine of her fornication."

3 So he carried me away in the [q]Spirit into the wilderness. And I saw a woman sitting on a scarlet beast *which was* full of [r]names of blasphemy, having seven heads and ten [s]horns.

4 The woman was [t]arrayed in purple and scarlet, and adorned with gold and precious stones and pearls, having in her hand a golden [u]cup full of abominations and the filthiness of her fornication.*

5 And on her forehead a name *was* written:

[v]MYSTERY,
[w]BABYLON THE GREAT,
THE MOTHER OF HARLOTS
AND OF THE
ABOMINATIONS OF THE
EARTH.

6 I saw the woman, drunk with the blood of the saints and with the blood of the martyrs of Jesus. And when I saw her, I marveled with great amazement.

The harlot overthrown

7 But the [a]angel said to me, "Why did you marvel? I will tell you the [v]mystery of the woman and of the beast that carries her, which has the seven heads and the ten [s]horns.

8 "The beast that you saw was, and is not, and [x]will ascend out of the [y]bottomless pit and go to perdition. And those who [z]dwell on the earth [aa]will marvel, whose names are not written in the [bb]Book of [cc]Life from the foundation of the [dd]world, when they see the beast that was, and is not, and yet [ee]is.*

9 [ff]"Here *is* the mind which has wisdom: [r]The seven heads are seven mountains on which the woman sits.

10 "There are also seven kings. Five have fallen, one is,

*

16:16 M-Text reads *Megiddo.*
17:1 NU-Text and M-Text omit *to me.*
17:4 M-Text reads *the filthiness of the fornication of the earth.* **17:8** NU-Text and M-Text read *and shall be present.*

[r] Rev. 13:1
[s] See Dt. 33:17, *note*

4
[t] Cp. Rev. 18:16
[u] Rev. 18:6

5
[v] See Mt. 13:11, *note*
[w] See Isa. 13:1, *note*

8
[x] Or *is about to*
[y] Lit. *abyss.* Rev. 9:1; 11:7
[z] Rev. 3:10
[aa] Rev. 13:3
[bb] Rev. 13:8
[cc] *Life* (eternal): v. 8; Rev. 20:12. (Mt. 7:14; Rev. 22:19)
[dd] Gk. *kosmos.* See Mt. 4:8, *note*
[ee] Cp. Rev. 13:3,13–14

9
[ff] Rev. 13:18

[1](16:16) Although the battle of Armageddon is described in ch. 19 (see 19:17, *note*), only in this verse is the location given. The word is generally interpreted as meaning *the mountain of Megiddo.* Megiddo is located on the north side of the plain of Jezreel, and is often referred to in the OT as a military stronghold (Josh. 12:21; 17:11; 2 Ki. 9:27; 23:29; see Jud. 5:19, *note*).

[2](16:19) The Times of the Gentiles, Summary: "The times of the Gentiles" (Lk. 21:24) is that long period that began with the Babylonian captivity of Judah, under Nebuchadnezzar, and is to be brought to an end by the destruction of Gentile world power by the stone "cut out without hands" (Dan. 2:34–35,44), i.e. the coming of the Lord in glory (Rev. 19:11,21). Until then Jerusalem will be, as Christ said, "trampled by Gentiles" (Lk. 21:24).

and the other has not yet come. And when he comes, he must [a]continue a short time.

11 "The [b]beast that was, and is not, is himself also the eighth, and is of the seven, and is going to perdition.

12 "The [1][c]ten [d]horns which you saw are [e]ten kings who have received no kingdom as yet, but they receive authority for [f]one hour as kings with the beast.

13 "These are of one mind, and they will give their power and authority to the beast.

Victory for the Lamb

14 "These will make [g]war with the Lamb, and the Lamb will [h]overcome them, for He is [i]Lord of lords and [j]King of kings; and those *who are* with Him *are* called, [k]chosen, and faithful."

15 Then he said to me, "The waters which you saw, where the harlot sits, are peoples, multitudes, nations, and tongues.

16 "And the ten [d]horns which you saw on* the beast, these will hate the harlot, make her [l]desolate and naked, eat her flesh and [m]burn her with fire.

17 "For God has put it into their hearts to fulfill [n]His purpose, to be of one mind, and to give their kingdom to the beast, until the words of God are fulfilled.

18 "And the woman whom you saw is that great city which reigns over the kings of the earth."

Babylon destroyed

18 AFTER these things I saw another [o]angel coming down from heaven, having great authority, and the earth was illuminated with his glory.

2 And he cried mightily* with a loud voice, saying, [2]"Babylon the great is [p]fallen, is fallen, and has become a dwelling place of demons, a prison for every foul spirit, and a cage for every unclean and hated bird!

3 "For all the nations have [q]drunk of the wine of the wrath of her fornication, the kings of the earth have committed fornication with her, and the [r]merchants of the earth have become rich through the abundance of her [s]luxury."

4 And I heard [t]another voice from heaven saying, [u]"Come out of her, my people, lest you share in her [v]sins, and lest you receive of her plagues.

5 "For her [v]sins have [w]reached* to heaven, and God has remembered her iniquities.

6 [x]"Render to her just as she rendered to you,* and repay her double according to her works; in the cup which she has mixed, mix double for her.

7 "In the measure that she glorified herself and lived luxuriously, in the same measure give her torment and sorrow;

*

17:16 NU-Text and M-Text read *saw, and the beast.* 18:2 NU-Text and M-Text omit *mightily.* 18:5 NU-Text and M-Text read *have been heaped up.* 18:6 NU-Text and M-Text omit *to you.*

10
a Rev. 13:5
11
b Rev. 13:3
12
c Rev. 13:1
d See Dt. 33:17, *note*
e Cp. Dan. 7:24
f Cp. Rev. 18:10
14
g Rev. 19:19
h Rev. 19:20; cp. 2 Th. 2:8–9
i Rev. 19:16; cp. 1 Tim. 6:15
j *Kingdom* (NT): v. 14; Rev. 19:16. (Mt. 2:2; 1 Cor. 15:24, *note*)
k *Election* (corporate): v. 14. (Dt. 7:6; 1 Pet. 5:13, *note*)
16
l Rev. 18:17
m Cp. Lev. 21:9; Jas. 4:4
17
n Cp. Rev. 18:8,20

CHAPTER 18
1
o See Heb. 1:4, *note*
2
p Rev. 14:8
3
q Cp. Jer. 51:7
r vv. 11–12
s Or *wantonness*
4
t Cp. Rev. 16:7
u *Separation:* v. 4. (Gen. 12:1; 2 Cor. 6:17, *note*)
v See Rom. 3:23, *note*
5
w Cp. Jer. 51:9
6
x Cp. Jer. 50:15,29

[1](17:12) Frequently in Scripture "ten" is the number of kings or kingdoms designated as opposed to Israel in her past history (Gen. 15:19–21; Ps. 83:1–8), or to be federated against Christ and the people of God in the future (Jer. 46—51; Dan. 2:41–42; 7:7,20,24; Rev. 12:3; 13:1).

[2](18:2) The name "Babylon," in prophecy, is sometimes used in a larger sense than mere reference to either the ancient city or nation (see Isa. 13:1, *note*). There are two forms which Babylon is to have in the end-time: political Babylon (Rev. 17:8–17) and ecclesiastical Babylon (Rev. 17:1–7,18; 18:1–24). Political Babylon is the beast's confederated empire, the last form of Gentile world dominion. Ecclesiastical Babylon is all apostate Christendom. It may very well be that this union will embrace all the religions of the world.

Although some hold to a literal rebuilding of the city of Babylon (claiming that Isa. 13:5–6,10,19–22; 14:1–6,22,25–26 necessitate future fulfillment), the evidence seems to point to the symbolic use of the name here (since Isa. 13:19–22; Jer. 51:24–26,62–64 appear to preclude such a restoration). In this latter view the reference is to Rome (cp. Rev. 18:10,16,18).

Ecclesiastical Babylon is the "great harlot" (Rev. 17:1) and is to be destroyed by political Babylon (Rev. 17:15–18), so that the beast may alone be the object of worship (2 Th. 2:3–4; Rev. 13:15). The power of political Babylon will be destroyed by the return of the Lord in glory. See Armageddon, Rev. 16:14,16; 19:17, *note*.

for she says in her heart, 'I sit *as*
[a]queen, and am no widow, and
will not see sorrow.'
8 "Therefore her plagues
will come in one day—death
and mourning and famine. And
she will be utterly burned with
fire, for [b]strong *is* the Lord God
who judges* her.

Earth dwellers lament
Babylon's destruction

9 "The [c]kings of the earth
who committed fornication and
lived luxuriously with her [d]will
weep and lament for her, when
they see the smoke of her burning,
10 "standing at a distance for
fear of her torment, saying,
'Alas, alas, that great city [e]Bab-
ylon, that mighty city! For in
[f]one hour your judgment has
come.'
11 "And the [g]merchants of
the earth will weep and [h]mourn
over her, for no one buys their
merchandise anymore:
12 "merchandise of gold and
silver, precious stones and
pearls, fine linen and purple,
silk and scarlet, every kind of
[i]citron wood, every kind of object of ivory, every kind of object of most precious wood,
bronze, iron, and marble;
13 "and cinnamon and in-
cense, fragrant oil and frankincense, wine and oil, fine flour
and wheat, cattle and sheep,
horses and chariots, and bodies
and souls of men.
14 "The fruit that your soul
longed for has [j]gone from you,
and all the things which are rich
and splendid have gone from
you,* and you shall find them
no more at all.
15 "The merchants of these
things, who became rich by her,
will [k]stand at a distance for fear
of her torment, weeping and
wailing,
16 "and saying, 'Alas, alas,
[l]that great city that was
[m]clothed in fine linen, purple,
and scarlet, and adorned with
gold and precious stones and
pearls!
17 'For in [n]one hour such
great riches came to [o]nothing.'
Every shipmaster, all who
travel by ship, sailors, and as
many as trade on the sea, stood
at a distance
18 "and cried out when they
saw the smoke of her burning,
saying, 'What *is* like this great
city?'
19 "They threw dust on their
heads and cried out, weeping
and wailing, and saying, 'Alas,
alas, that great city, in which all
who had ships on the sea became rich by her wealth! For in
one hour she is made desolate.'

Heaven rejoices over Babylon's fall

20 [p]"Rejoice over her, O
heaven, and *you* holy apostles*
and prophets, for God has
[q]avenged you on her!"
21 Then a [r]mighty angel
took up a stone like a great
[s]millstone and threw *it* into the
sea, saying, "Thus with violence
the great city Babylon shall be
thrown down, and shall not be
found anymore.
22 "The [t]sound of harpists,
musicians, flutists, and trumpeters shall not be heard in you
anymore. No craftsman of any
craft shall be found in you anymore, and the sound of a millstone shall not be heard in you
anymore.
23 "The light of a lamp shall
not shine in you anymore, and
the voice of [u]bridegroom and
bride shall not be heard in you
anymore. For your merchants
were the great men of the earth,
for by your sorcery all the nations were deceived.
24 "And in her was found the
[v]blood of prophets and saints,
and of all who were [w]slain on
the earth."

XI. The Battle of Armageddon
and the Millennium that Follows,
19:1—20:6

Rejoicing in heaven
over destruction of the harlot
(cp. 17:16–17; 18:8)

19 AFTER these things I
heard* a loud [x]voice of a
great multitude in heaven, saying, "Alleluia! [y]Salvation and

*
18:8 NU-Text and M-Text read *has judged.*
18:14 NU-Text and M-Text read *been lost to you.*
18:20 NU-Text and M-Text read *saints and apostles.*
19:1 NU-Text and M-Text add *something like.*

7
a Cp. Isa. 47:7–8
8
b Jer. 50:34; Heb. 10:31
9
c Rev. 17:2
d Cp. Jer. 50:46
10
e See Isa. 13:1, *note* 2
f vv. 17–19; cp. Rev. 17:12
11
g vv. 3,15
h Cp. Isa. 13:19
12
i Decorative and scented wood
14
j Cp. Rev. 17:16
15
k vv. 10,17
16
l Rev. 17:18
m Rev. 17:4
17
n vv. 10,19; cp. Rev. 17:12
o Rev. 17:16
20
p Rev. 12:12; cp. Isa. 44:23; Jer. 51:48
q Lit. *judged your verdict on her*
21
r Cp. Rev. 10:1
s Cp. Jer. 51:63–64
22
t Cp. Rev. 14:1–3
23
u Cp. Jer. 16:9
24
v Rev. 16:6; 17:6
w Death (physical): v. 24. (Gen. 2:17; Heb. 9:27, *note*)
CHAPTER 19
1
x v. 20; Rev. 11:15
y See Rom. 1:16, *note*

2
[a] Rev. 16:7
[b] Rev. 17:1
[c] Lk. 18:7–8; Rev. 6:10
3
[d] Rev. 18:9, 18
5
[e] Ps. 134
6
[f] Cp. Ex. 20:18
7
[g] Mt. 22:1–14; cp. Eph. 5:22–27
[h] *Bride* (of Christ): vv. 6–9; Rev. 21:9. (Jn. 3:29; Rev. 19:7, *note*)
8
[i] *Righteousness* (garment): v. 8. (Gen. 3:21; Rev. 19:8)
9
[j] *Inspiration:* v. 9; Rev. 21:5. (Ex. 4:15; 2 Tim. 3:16, *note*)
[k] Cp. Lk. 14:15

glory and honor and power *be-*
long to the Lord* our God!
2 “For true and righteous
are His [a]judgments, because He
has judged the great [b]harlot
who corrupted the earth with
her fornication; and He has
[c]avenged on her the blood of
His servants *shed* by her.”
3 Again they said, “Alleluia!
Her [d]smoke rises up forever
and ever!”
4 And the twenty-four el-
ders and the four living creatures fell down and worshiped
God who sat on the throne, saying, “Amen! Alleluia!”
5 Then a voice came from
the throne, saying, [e]“Praise our
God, all you His servants and
those who fear Him, both*
small and great!”
6 And I heard, as it were, the
voice of a great multitude, as the
sound of many waters and as
the sound of mighty [f]thunder-
ings, saying, “Alleluia! For the*
Lord God Omnipotent reigns!

Marriage of the Lamb

7 “Let us be glad and rejoice
and give Him glory, for the
[1g]marriage of the Lamb has
come, and His [h]wife has made
herself ready.”
8 And to her it was granted
to be arrayed in fine linen, clean
and bright, for the fine linen is
the [2i]righteous acts of the
saints.
9 Then he said to me,
[j]“Write: [k]‘Blessed *are* those
who are called to the marriage
supper of the Lamb!’ ” And he
said to me, “These are the true
sayings of God.”
10 And I fell at his feet to
worship him. But he said to me,
“See *that you do* not *do that!* I
am your [l]fellow servant, and of
your brethren who have the
[m]testimony of [3]Jesus. Worship
God! For the testimony of Jesus
is the spirit of prophecy.”

Second coming of Christ
in glory (cp. Mt. 24:16–30)

11 Now I [4]saw heaven
opened, and behold, a white
[n]horse. And [o]He who sat on
him *was* called [p]Faithful and
True, and in righteousness He
[5]judges and makes war.

10
[l] Heb. 1:14
[m] Lk. 24:27; Jn. 5:39; cp. Eph. 1:9–10; 1 Pet. 1:10–12
11
[n] Ps. 45:3–4; cp. Mt. 21:2–5
[o] *Christ* (second advent): vv. 11–21; Rev. 20:4. (Dt. 30:3; Acts 1:11, *note*)
[p] Rev. 3:7

*
• NU-Text and M-Text omit *the Lord.*
19:5 NU-Text and M-Text omit *both.*
19:6 NU-Text and M-Text read *our.*

[1](19:7) Bride of Christ, Summary: “The marriage of the Lamb” (lit. “the marriage supper of the Lamb”) is the consummation of the marriage of Christ and the Church as His bride. The figure is according to the oriental pattern of marriage, covering three stages: (1) the betrothal, legally binding when the individual members of the body of Christ are saved; (2) the coming of the Bridegroom for His bride at the rapture of the Church; and (3) the marriage supper of the Lamb, occurring in connection with the second coming of Christ to establish His millennial kingdom. The Lamb’s wife is to be contrasted with the harlot of 17:1; and she is also to be distinguished from Israel, the unfaithful wife of the LORD (*Jehovah*) in historic times, who is to be restored in the millennium (Isa. 54:1–10; Hos. 2:1–17).

[2](19:8) The garment in Scripture is a symbol of righteousness. In the bad ethical sense it symbolizes self-righteousness, e.g. Isa. 64:6. See Phil. 3:6–8 showing the best that a moral and religious man under law could do. In the good ethical sense the garment symbolizes (1) the basic provision of God’s salvation by grace through faith in Christ, the “garments of salvation . . . the robe of righteousness [Gk. *dikaiosunē*]” (Isa. 61:10; Rom. 3:21, *note*); and (2) the garment of “fine linen . . . the righteous acts [from Gk. *dikaiōma*] of the saints,” as here in v. 8, works of godliness and goodness produced by the Holy Spirit, as the believer judges the flesh and yields himself to God (Rom. 13:14). These are the “good works” for which we are “created in Christ Jesus” (Eph. 2:10), with which believers are to adorn themselves to bring honor to Christ’s name here (Mt. 5:16; 1 Tim. 2:10; Ti. 2:8–10; 3:8; 1 Pet. 2:12; 3:3–5; 5:5) and hereafter (Rom. 2:7,10; 1 Cor. 3:12–14, *note;* Phil. 1:10–11; 1 Pet. 1:7; Rev. 19:8).

[3](19:10) Although men, cities, and nations have a large part in Biblical prophecy, its chief subject is a Person, the Lord Jesus Christ. As John was reminded at this climactic point when he was about to see the appearance of Christ in glory, “the testimony of [witness concerning] Jesus is the spirit of prophecy.” All the prophetic themes are to be studied with care, but never in such a way as to obscure the fact of the centrality of Jesus Christ.

[4](19:11) The vision is of the departure from heaven of Christ, with the saints and angels, preparatory to the catastrophe in which Gentile world power, headed up in the beast, is struck by the stone “cut out without hands” (Dan. 2:34–35).

[5](19:11) Throughout the NT Christ is set forth as the Judge of mankind: He Himself declares this (Jn. 5:22–23,27,30). This is re-emphasized in the preaching of the apostolic church: by Peter (Acts 10:42), and by Paul in his address to the Athenians (Acts 17:31; cp. Rom. 2:16).

12 His [a]eyes *were* like a
flame of fire, and on His head
were many [b]crowns. He had* a
name written [c]that no one
knew except Himself.
13 He *was* clothed with a
robe dipped in blood, and His
name is called The [d]Word of
God.
14 And the armies in heaven,
clothed in fine linen, white and
clean,* followed Him on white
horses.
15 Now out of His [e]mouth
goes a sharp* sword, that with
it He should strike the nations.
And He Himself will [f]rule them
with a rod of iron. He Himself
[g]treads the winepress of the
fierceness and wrath of Almighty God.
16 And He has on *His* robe
and on His thigh a name written:

[h]KING OF KINGS
AND LORD OF LORDS.

Armageddon
(see note 1; cp. 16:14–16)

17 Then I saw an angel
standing in the sun; and he
cried with a loud voice, saying
to all the birds that fly in [i]the
midst of heaven, [1][j]"Come and
gather together for the [k]supper
of the great God,*
18 "that you may [l]eat the
flesh of kings, the flesh of captains, the flesh of mighty men,
the flesh of horses and of those
who sit on them, and the flesh of
all *people,* free* and slave, both
small and great."
19 And I saw the [m]beast, the
[n]kings of the earth, and their armies, gathered together to
[2][o]make war against Him [p]who
sat on the horse and against His
army.

Doom of beast and false prophet

20 Then the [3]beast was captured, and with him the [q]false
prophet who worked signs in
his presence, by which he deceived those who received the

12
a Rev. 1:14
b Lit. *diadems*
c Cp. vv. 13, 16; Mt. 11:27
13
d Jn. 1:1,14
15
e Isa. 11:4; 2 Th. 2:8; Rev. 1:16
f Ps. 2:8–9
g Isa. 63:3–6; Rev. 14:20; cp. Mt. 21:44
16
h Kingdom (NT): vv. 11–21; Rev. 20:6. (Mt. 2:2; 1 Cor. 15:24, *note*)

17
i Lit. *mid-heaven*
j Armageddon (battle of): vv. 11–21. (Isa. 10:27; Rev. 19:17)
k Cp. Ezek. 39:17–20
18
l Cp. Ezek. 32:21–31
19
m The Beast: vv. 19–20. (Dan. 7:8; Rev. 19:20)
n Rev. 16:13–16
o Day (of the LORD): vv. 11–21. (Ps. 2:9; Rev. 19:19)
p v. 11
20
q Antichrist: v. 20. (Mt. 24:5; Rev. 13:11, *note*)

*
19:12 M-Text adds *names written, and.* **19:14** NU-Text and M-Text read *pure white linen.* **19:15** M-Text adds *two-edged.* **19:17** NU-Text and M-Text read *the great supper of God.* **19:18** NU-Text and M-Text read *both free.*

Christ also will be the Judge of believers—for their works, not for salvation (Rom. 14:10; 2 Cor. 5:10). The controlling factor of judgment will be righteousness, a theme which begins at Gen. 18:25 and continues through the Scriptures to Rev. 19:11 (cp. Ps. 9:8; 50:6, etc.).

[1](19:17) Armageddon (the name itself is to be found only in 16:16) is the ancient hill and valley of Megiddo, west of the Jordan in the plain of Jezreel between Samaria and Galilee. It is the appointed place where the armies of the beast and false prophet will be destroyed by Christ's descending to earth in glory (vv. 11,15,19,21), as well as any other forces which will come against the beast in their attack on Palestine (e.g. the remainder of the Far Eastern army of 200 million men), and others (9:13–18; 16:12–14,16; cp. Joel 3:9–16; Zech. 12:1–9; 14:1–4; Mt. 24:27–30). The battle is a fulfillment of the striking-stone prophecy of Dan. 2:35, where see *note.* See also Isa. 2:12, refs.

[2](19:19) The Day of the LORD (*Jehovah*), Summary: The Day of the LORD is that period of time when God openly intervenes in the affairs of men—in judgment and in blessing. See Joel 1:15, *note.* It will begin with the translation of the Church and will terminate with the cleansing of the heavens and the earth preparatory to the bringing into being of the new heavens and the new earth.

The order of events appears to be: (1) the rapture of the Church just preceding the beginning of the Day of the LORD (1 Th. 4:13–17); (2) the fulfillment of Daniel's seventieth week (Dan. 9:27), the latter half of which is the great tribulation (Mt. 24:21; see Rev. 7:14, *note*); (3) the return of the Lord in glory to establish the millennial kingdom (Mt. 24:29–30); (4) the destruction of the beast, the false prophet, and their armies, which is the "great and awesome" aspect of the day (Rev. 19:11–21); (5) the judgment of individual Gentiles according to their treatment of Christ's brethren, the Jewish people (Zech. 14:1–9; Mt. 25:31–46) and the judgment of Israel (Ezek. 20:34–38); (6) the millennial reign of Christ on earth (Rev. 20:4–6); (7) the satanic revolt and its judgment (Rev. 20:7–10); (8) the resurrection and final judgment of the wicked (Rev. 20:11–15); (9) the destruction of the present earth and heaven by fire preparatory for the future "day of God" (2 Pet. 3:10–12); and (10) the creation of the new heavens and the new earth (Isa. 65:17–19; 66:22; 2 Pet. 3:13; Rev. 21:1).

[3](19:20) The Beast, Summary: This "beast" is the little "horn" of Dan. 7:24–26; the "one who makes desolate" of Dan. 9:27; the "abomination of desolation" of Mt. 24:15; the "man of sin" of 2 Th. 2:4–8; and earth's last and most awful tyrant, Satan's cruel instrument of wrath and hatred against God and the Jewish saints. To him Satan gives the power which he offered to Christ (Mt. 4:8–9; Rev. 13:4). See The Great Tribulation, Ps. 2:5; Rev. 7:14, *note.*

mark of the beast and those
who [a]worshiped his image.
These two were [b]cast alive into
the lake of fire burning with
brimstone.

Doom of kings and armies

21 And the rest were killed
with the sword which pro-
ceeded from the [c]mouth of Him
who sat on the horse. And all
the birds were filled with their
flesh.

Satan bound in the bottomless pit during the Kingdom Age

20 THEN I saw an angel
coming down from
heaven, having the key to the
bottomless pit and a great chain
in his hand.
2 He laid hold of the dragon,
that serpent of old, who is *the*
[d]Devil and Satan, and bound
him for a [1]thousand years;
3 and he cast him into the
bottomless pit, and shut him up,
and set a seal on him, so that he
should [e]deceive the nations no
more till the thousand years
were finished. But after these
things he must be released for a
little while.

Completion of first resurrection (see 1 Cor. 15:52, note), and the Kingdom Age

4 And I saw thrones, and
they sat on them, and judgment
was committed [f]to them. Then
I saw the souls of [g]those who
had been beheaded for their
witness to Jesus and for the
word of God, who had [h]not
worshiped the beast or his image, and had not received *his*
mark on their foreheads or on
their hands. And they [i]lived
and [j]reigned [k]with Christ for
a* [2]thousand years.
5 But the rest of the dead did
not live again until the thousand
years were finished. This *is* the
[3]first [l]resurrection.
6 [m]Blessed and holy *is* he
who has part in the first [l]resur-
rection. Over such the [n]second

*20:4 M-Text reads *the*.

20
a Rev. 13:8, 13
b *Day* (of destruction): v. 20; Rev. 20:11. (Job 21:30; Rev. 20:11)
21
c Isa. 11:4; 2 Th. 2:8; Rev. 1:16
CHAPTER 20
2
d *Satan:* v. 2; Rev. 20:7. (Gen. 3:1; Rev. 20:10)
3
e v. 8; cp. 2 Cor. 4:4; Rev. 13:14
4
f 1 Cor. 6:2
g *Remnant:* v. 4. (Isa. 1:9; Rom. 11:5, *note*)
h Cp. Rev. 13:15–17; 14:9–13
i Jn. 14:19
j v. 6; cp. 2 Tim. 2:12
k *Christ* (second advent): vv. 4–6; Rev. 22:7. (Dt. 30:3; Acts 1:11, *note*)
5
l *Resurrection:* vv. 4–6; Rev. 20:13. (2 Ki. 4:35; 1 Cor. 15:52, *note*)
6
m Cp. Rev. 14:13
n *Death* (the second): v. 6; Rev. 20:14. (Jn. 8:21; Rev. 20:14, *note*)

[1](20:2) The expression "thousand years," which occurs six times in vv. 1–7, gave rise to the term "millennium" (from the Latin *mille* meaning *thousand*, and *annus* meaning *year*). The millennium is that period of time during which Christ will reign upon the earth, a time of universal peace, prosperity, long life, and prevailing righteousness. The early church fathers, e.g. Justin Martyr and Irenaeus, interpreted this passage as referring to a future literal period of time. See Ps. 72:1–20; Isa. 9:6–7; 11:1–9; 24:22–23; 30:15–33; 35:1–10; 44:1–28; 49:1–26; 65:17–25; Jer. 23:5–6; 33:15; Mic. 4:1–4; Mt. 25:31–32; 1 Cor. 15:24–28.

[2](20:4) *The Seventh Dispensation: the Kingdom.* This is the last of the ordered ages which condition human life on the earth. It is the kingdom covenanted to David (2 Sam. 7:8–17, see v. 16, *note;* Zech. 12:8, Summary; Lk. 1:31–33; 1 Cor. 15:24, Summary). David's greater Son, the Lord Jesus Christ, will rule over the earth as King of kings and Lord of lords for 1000 years, associating with Himself in that reign His saints of all ages (Rev. 3:21; 5:9–10; 11:15–18; 15:3–4; 19:16; 20:4,6).

The Kingdom Age gathers into itself under Christ the various "times" spoken of in the Scriptures: (1) The time of oppression and misrule ends when Christ establishes His kingdom (Isa. 11:3–4). (2) The time of testimony and divine forbearance ends in judgment (Mt. 25:31–46; Acts 17:30–31; Rev. 20:7–15). (3) The time of toil ends in rest and reward (2 Th. 1:6–7). (4) The time of suffering ends in glory (Rom. 8:17–18). (5) The time of Israel's blindness and chastisement ends in restoration and conversion (Ezek. 39:25–29; Rom. 11:25–27). (6) The times of the Gentiles end in the striking down of the image and the setting up of the kingdom of the heavens (Dan. 2:34–35; Rev. 19:15–21). And (7) the time of creation's bondage ends in deliverance at the manifestation of the sons of God (Gen. 3:17; Isa. 11:6–8; Rom. 8:19–21).

At the conclusion of the thousand years, Satan is released for a little while and instigates a final rebellion which is summarily put down by the Lord. Christ casts Satan into the lake of fire to be eternally tormented, defeats the last enemy—death—and then delivers up the kingdom to the Father (see 1 Cor. 15:24, *note*, especially point 7).

For *notes* on the other dispensations, see Innocence (Gen. 1:28); Conscience or Moral Responsibility (Gen. 3:7); Human Government (Gen. 8:15); Promise (Gen. 12:1); Law (Ex. 19:1); Church (Acts 2:1).

[3](20:5) The first resurrection is the resurrection of the just (Lk. 14:14). Although it is shown in both the OT and NT that the resurrection of the just to life eternal, and the resurrection of the lost to everlasting condemnation, are distinct from one another (e.g. Dan. 12:2; Jn. 5:29), here for the first time the precise interval between the two resurrections is revealed as a period of 1000 years. See 1 Cor. 15:52, *note.*

death has no power, but they
shall be [a]priests of God and of
Christ, and shall [b]reign with
Him a thousand years.

XII. The Final Judgment and the Holy City, 20:7—22:5

Satan loosed at end of 1000 years; rebellion quelled

7 Now when the thousand
years have expired, [c]Satan will
be released from his prison
8 and will go out to deceive
the nations which are in the
four corners of the earth, [d]Gog
and Magog, to gather them together to battle, whose number
is as the sand of the sea.
9 They went up on the
breadth of the earth and surrounded the camp of the saints
and the beloved city. And fire
came down from God out of
heaven and devoured them.

Satan cast into lake of fire

10 The [1c]devil, who deceived
them, was cast into the lake of
fire and brimstone where* the
beast and the false prophet *are*.
And they will be tormented day
and night forever and ever.

Second resurrection and great white throne judgment

11 Then I saw a [2e]great white
throne and Him who sat on it,
from whose face the earth and
the heaven fled away. And
[3f]there was found no place for
them.
12 And I saw the [g]dead,
small and great, standing before God,* and [h]books were
opened. And another [i]book
was opened, which is *the Book*
of [j]Life. And the dead were
[4]judged according to their

6
a Rev. 1:6
b Kingdom (NT): v. 6; Rev. 21:5. (Mt. 2:2; 1 Cor. 15:24, *note*)
7
c Satan: vv. 7–10. (Gen. 3:1; Rev. 20:10)
8
d See Ezek. 38:2, *note*
11
e Day (of judgment): vv. 11–15. (Mt. 10:15; Rev. 20:11)
f Day (of destruction): vv. 11–15. (Job 21:30; Rev. 20:11)
12
g Death (spiritual): vv. 12–15. (Gen. 2:17; Eph. 2:5, *note*)
h Judgments (the seven): vv. 11–15; Rev. 22:12. (1 Sam. 7:14; Rev. 20:12, *note*)
i Cp. Lk. 10:20
j Life (eternal): v. 12; Rev. 20:15. (Mt. 7:14; Rev. 22:19)

*
20:10 NU-Text and M-Text add *also.*
20:12 NU-Text and M-Text read *the throne.*

[1](20:10) Satan, Summary: This fearful being, apparently created one of the cherubim (Ezek. 1:5, *note;* 28:12, *note*) and anointed for a position of great authority, perhaps over the primitive creation (Gen. 1:2, *note* 5; Ezek. 28:11–15), fell through pride (Isa. 14:12–14). His "I will" (Isa. 14:13) marks the introduction of sin into the universe. Cast out of heaven (Lk. 10:18), he makes earth and air the scene of his tireless activity (Eph. 2:2; 1 Pet. 5:8). After the creation of man he entered into the serpent (Gen. 3:1, *note*) and, beguiling Eve by his subtlety, secured the downfall of Adam and through him of the race, and the entrance of sin into the world of men (Rom. 5:12–14). The Adamic Covenant (Gen. 3:15, *note*) promised the ultimate defeat of Satan through the "Seed" of the woman. Then began Satan's long warfare against the work of God on behalf of humanity, which still continues. The present world system (Rev. 13:8), organized upon the principles of force, greed, selfishness, ambition, and sinful pleasure, is his work and was the bribe which he offered to Christ (Mt. 4:8–9). Of that world system he is ruler (Jn. 14:30; 16:11), and god (2 Cor. 4:4). As "prince of the power of the air" (Eph. 2:2) he is at the head of a vast host of demons (Mt. 7:22, *note*). To him, under God, was committed upon earth the power of death (Heb. 2:14). Cast out of heaven as his proper sphere and "position of authority," he still has access to God as the "accuser of our brethren" (Rev. 12:10) and is permitted a certain power of sifting or testing the self-confident and carnal among believers (Job 1:6–11; Lk. 22:31–32; 1 Cor. 5:5; 1 Tim. 1:20); but this is a strictly permissive and limited power, and believers so sifted are kept in faith through the advocacy of Christ (Lk. 22:31–32; 1 Jn. 2:1, *note*). At the beginning of the great tribulation Satan's privilege of access to God as accuser will be withdrawn (Rev. 12:7–12). At the return of Christ in glory Satan will be bound for 1000 years (Rev. 20:2), after which he will be "released for a little while" (Rev. 20:3,7–8) and will become the head of a final effort to overthrow the kingdom. Defeated in this, he will be cast into the lake of fire, his final doom. The notion that he reigns in hell is not biblical. He is ruler of this present world system but will be tormented in the lake of fire.

[2](20:11) The NT expressions "the judgment" and "the day of judgment," as the passages and their context show, refer to this final judgment of vv. 11–15.

[3](20:11) The "day of destruction" is that aspect of the Day of the LORD (Isa. 2:12; Joel 1:15, *note;* Rev. 19:19, Summary) which visits final and eternal judgment upon the wicked. Three such "days" are included in the Day of the LORD and are described in the marginal references beginning with Isa. 34:2.

[4](20:12) The final judgment. The subjects are the "dead." As the redeemed were raised from among the dead 1000 years before (v. 5) and have been in glory with Christ during that period, the "dead" can only be the wicked dead, from the beginning of human history to the setting up of the great white throne in space. As there are degrees in punishment (Lk. 12:47–48), the dead are judged according to their works. The Book of Life is there to answer such as plead their works for justification, e.g. Mt. 7:22–23—an awful blank where the name might have been.

The Judgments, Summary: Among the many judgments mentioned in Scripture, seven are

13
a Resurrection: vv. 12–13. (2 Ki. 4:35; 1 Cor. 15:52, *note*)
b See Lk. 16:23, *note*
14
c *Death* (the second): vv. 14–15; 21:8. (Jn. 8:21; Rev. 20:14, *note*)
15
d *Life* (eternal): v. 15; 21:6; Rev. 21:27. (Mt. 7:14; Rev. 22:19)
CHAPTER 21
1
e Cp. Isa. 65:17; 66:22; 2 Pet. 3:13
f Cp. Heb. 12:26–27; 2 Pet. 3:10–12
2
g Rev. 22:19; cp. Heb. 11:10,16
h Rev. 19:7–8; cp. Ps. 45:13–15
4
i Rev. 7:17
j Isa. 25:8; 1 Cor. 15:26
5
k *Kingdom* (NT): v. 5; 21:9–22:5. (Mt. 2:2; 1 Cor. 15:24, *note*)
l *Inspiration:* v. 5; Rev. 22:18. (Ex. 4:15; 2 Tim. 3:16, *note*)

works, by the things which
were written in the books.
13 The sea [a]gave up the dead
who were in it, and Death and
[b]Hades [a]delivered up the dead
who were in them. And they
were judged, each one according
to his works.
14 Then Death and [b]Hades
were cast into the lake of fire.
This is the [1]second [c]death.*
15 And anyone not found
written in the Book of [d]Life was
cast into the lake of fire.

The new heaven, the new earth, and the new Jerusalem

21 NOW I saw a [e]new
heaven and a new earth,
for the [f]first heaven and the
first earth had passed away.
Also there was no more sea.
2 Then I, John,* saw the
[g]holy city, [2]New Jerusalem,
coming down out of heaven
from God, prepared as a [h]bride
adorned for her husband.
3 And I heard a loud voice
from heaven saying, "Behold,
the tabernacle of God *is* with
men, and He will dwell with
them, and they shall be His people.
God Himself will be with
them *and be* their God.
4 "And God will wipe away
every [i]tear from their eyes;
there shall be no more [j]death,
nor sorrow, nor crying. There
shall be no more pain, for the
former things have passed
away."
5 Then He who sat on the
[k]throne said, "Behold, I make
all things new." And He said to
me,* "Write, [l]for these words
are true and faithful."
6 And He said to me, "It is
done!* I am the [m]Alpha and the
Omega, the Beginning and the
End. I will give of the fountain
of the water of [d]life freely to
him who thirsts.
7 "He who overcomes shall
inherit all things,* and I will be
his God and he shall be My son.
8 "But the cowardly, unbelieving,*
abominable, murderers,
sexually immoral, sorcerers,
idolaters, and all liars shall
have their part in the lake which
burns with fire and brimstone,
which is the second [c]death."

The Lamb's wife; the new Jerusalem

9 Then one of the seven angels
who had the seven bowls
filled with the seven last
plagues came to me* and talked
with me, saying, "Come, I will
show you the [n]bride, the
Lamb's wife."*•
10 And he carried me away
in the [o]Spirit to a great and high
mountain, and showed me the
great city, the holy* Jerusalem,
descending out of heaven from
God,
11 having the glory of God.
Her [p]light *was* like a most precious
stone, like a jasper stone,
clear as crystal.
12 Also she had a great and

6
m See Rev. 1:8, *note*
9
n *Bride* (of Christ): vv. 9–10. (Jn. 3:29; Rev. 19:7, *note*)
10
o *Holy Spirit* (NT): v. 10; Rev. 22:17. (Mt. 1:18; Acts 2:4, *note*)
11
p i.e. *brightness*

*20:14 NU-Text and M-Text add *the lake of fire.* 21:2 NU-Text and M-Text omit *John.* 21:5 NU-Text and M-Text omit *to me.* 21:6 M-Text omits *It is done.* 21:7 M-Text reads *overcomes, I shall give him these things.* 21:8 M-Text adds *and sinners.* 21:9 NU-Text and M-Text omit *to me.* • M-Text reads *I will show you the woman, the Lamb's bride.* 21:10 NU-Text and M-Text omit *the great* and read *the holy city, Jerusalem.*

invested with special significance. These are: (1) the judgment of the believer's sins in the cross of Christ (Jn. 12:31, *note*); (2) the believer's self-judgment (1 Cor. 11:31, *note*); (3) the judgment of the believer's works (2 Cor. 5:10, *note*); (4) the judgment of the individual Gentiles at the return of Christ to the earth (Mt. 25:32, *note*); (5) the judgment of Israel at the return of Christ to the earth (Ezek. 20:37, *note*); (6) the judgment of angels after the 1000 years (Jude 6, *note*); and (7) here, the judgment of the wicked dead with which the history of the present earth ends.

[1](20:14) Second death, Summary: "The second death" and the "lake of fire" in this verse are identical terms and are used of the eternal state of the wicked. It is "second" in relation to the preceding physical death of the wicked in unbelief and rejection of God; their eternal state is one of eternal "death" (i.e. separation from God) in sins (Jn. 8:21,24). That the second death is not annihilation is shown by a comparison of Rev. 19:20 with 20:10. After 1000 years in the lake of fire the beast and false prophet are still there, personally existing. The words "forever and ever" (*to the ages of the ages*), cp. v. 10, are used of God (1:18; 4:9,10; 10:6; 15:7), of the glory of God (Gal. 1:5, etc.) and of the dominion, the reign of God (1 Pet. 4:11; Rev. 1:6; 5:13,14; 7:12; 11:15), and plainly mean *eternal* in the sense of unending.

[2](21:2) The new Jerusalem is the dwelling place throughout eternity for the saints of all ages and fulfills the hope of Abraham for the heavenly city (Heb. 11:10–16; cp. Heb. 12:22–24).

high wall with twelve gates, and twelve [a]angels at the gates, and names written on them, which are *the names* of the [b]twelve [c]tribes of the [d]children of Israel:

13 three gates on the east, three gates on the north, three gates on the south, and three gates on the west.

14 Now the wall of the city had twelve [e]foundations, and on them were the names* of the twelve [f]apostles of the Lamb.

15 And he who talked with me had a gold [g]reed to measure the city, its gates, and its wall.

16 The city is laid out as a [h]square; its length is as great as its breadth. And he measured the city with the reed: twelve thousand [g]furlongs. Its length, breadth, and height are equal.

17 Then he measured its wall: one hundred *and* forty-four cubits, *according* to the measure of a [i]man, that is, of an [a]angel.

18 The construction of its wall was *of* jasper; and the city *was* [j]pure gold, like clear glass.

19 The [k]foundations of the wall of the city *were* adorned with all kinds of precious stones: the first foundation *was* jasper, the second sapphire, the third chalcedony, the fourth emerald,

20 the fifth sardonyx, the sixth sardius, the seventh chrysolite, the eighth beryl, the ninth topaz, the tenth chrysoprase, the eleventh jacinth, and the twelfth amethyst.

21 The twelve gates *were* twelve [l]pearls: each individual gate was of one pearl. And the [m]street of the city *was* pure gold, like transparent glass.

22 But I saw no temple in it, for the Lord God Almighty and the Lamb are its temple.

23 The city had no need of the sun or of the moon to shine in it,* for the glory* of [n]God illuminated it. The Lamb *is* its [o]light.

24 And the [p]nations of those who are [q]saved* shall walk [r]in its light, and the kings of the earth bring their glory and honor into it.*

25 Its gates shall not be [s]shut at all by day (there shall be no night there).

26 And they shall bring the glory and the honor of the nations into it.*

27 But there shall by no means [t]enter it anything that defiles, or causes* an abomination or a lie, but only those who are written in the Lamb's [u]Book of [v]Life.

The new paradise; its river and tree of life

22 AND he showed me a pure* [w]river of water of [v]life, clear as crystal, proceeding from the [x]throne of God and of the Lamb.

2 In the middle of its [y]street, and on either side of the river, *was* the [z]tree of [v]life, which bore twelve fruits, each *tree* yielding its fruit every month. The [aa]leaves of the tree *were* for the [bb]healing of the nations.

3 And there shall be [cc]no more curse, but the [dd]throne of God and of the Lamb shall be in it, and His [ee]servants shall serve Him.

4 They shall see His face, and His name *shall be* on their foreheads.

5 There shall be [ff]no night there: They need no lamp nor [gg]light of the sun, for the [n]Lord God gives them light. And they shall reign forever and ever.

XIII. The Last Message of the Bible, 22:6–19

6 Then he said to me, "These words *are* faithful and true." And the Lord God of the holy* prophets [hh]sent His angel to show His servants the things which must [ii]shortly take place.

7 "Behold, I am [jj]coming quickly! Blessed *is* he who [kk]keeps the words of the prophecy of this book."

*

21:14 NU-Text and M-Text read *twelve names.* 21:23 NU-Text and M-Text omit *in it.* • M-Text reads *the very glory.*
21:24 NU-Text and M-Text omit *of those who are saved.* • M-Text reads *the glory and honor of the nations to Him.*
21:26 M-Text adds *that they may enter in.*
21:27 NU-Text and M-Text read *anything profane, nor one who causes.*
22:1 NU-Text and M-Text omit *pure.*
22:6 NU-Text and M-Text read *spirits of the prophets.*

12
a See Heb. 1:4, *note*
b Cp. Ezek. 48:31–34
c *Israel* (prophecies): v. 12. (Gen. 12:2; Rom. 11:26, *note*)
d Lit. *sons*
14
e Cp. Heb. 11:10
f Lk. 22:29–30; cp. Eph. 2:20
15
g See Weights and Measures (NT), Acts 27:28, *note*
16
h Cp. 1 Ki. 6:20
17
i Cp. Dt. 3:11
18
j Cp. 2 Chr. 3:8
19
k Cp. Isa. 54:11
21
l Mt. 13:45–46; cp. Eph. 5:25
m Rev. 22:2
23
n Isa. 60:19
o Rev. 22:5
24
p Isa. 60:3
q See Rom. 1:16, *note*
r Lit. *by*
25
s Isa. 60:11

27
t Cp. Rev. 22:15
u Phil. 4:3; Rev. 3:5; 13:8; 20:12; 22:19; cp. Ex. 32:32; Ps. 69:28; Dan. 12:1
v *Life* (eternal): v. 27; 22:1–2; Rev. 22:14. (Mt. 7:14; Rev. 22:19)
CHAPTER 22
1
w Cp. Ezek. 47:1,12; Zech. 14:8
x Cp. Rev. 4:2–3
2
y 21:21
z Cp. Gen. 2:9; 3:22
aa Cp. Ezek. 47:12
bb Cp. Gen. 3:6–7
3
cc Cp. Gen. 3:17–19
dd v. 1
ee Rev. 7:15
5
ff Lit. *night no more*
gg Rev. 21:23
6
hh Rev. 1:1
ii Heb. 10:37
7
jj *Christ* (second advent): v. 7; Rev. 22:12. (Dt. 30:3; Acts 1:11, *note*)
kk Rev. 1:3

8 Now I, John, saw and heard* these things. And when I heard and saw, I fell down to worship before the feet of the [a]angel who showed me these things.

9 Then he said to me, "See *that you do* not *do that.* For* I am your fellow servant, and of your brethren the prophets, and of those who keep the words of this book. Worship God."

10 And he said to me, "Do [b]not seal the words of the prophecy of this book, for the time is [c]at hand.

11 "He who is unjust, let him be unjust still; he who is filthy, let him be filthy still; he who is [1]righteous, let him be righteous* still; he who is [2d]holy, let him be holy still."

12 "And behold, I am [e]coming quickly, and My [f]reward *is* with Me, to give to every one [g]according to his work.

13 "I am the [h]Alpha and the Omega, *the* Beginning and *the* End, the First and the Last."*

14 Blessed *are* those who do His commandments,* that they may have the right to the [i]tree of [j]life, and may enter through the gates into the city.

15 But* outside *are* dogs and sorcerers and sexually immoral and murderers and idolaters, and whoever loves and practices a lie.

16 "I, Jesus, have sent My angel to testify to you these things in the [k]churches. I am the Root and the Offspring of David, the Bright and Morning Star."

17 And the [l]Spirit and the bride say, "Come!" And let him who hears say, "Come!" And let him who thirsts come. Whoever desires, let him take the water of [j]life freely.

18 For* I testify to everyone who hears the [m]words of the prophecy of this book: If anyone adds to these things, God will add* to him the plagues that are written in this book;

19 and if anyone takes away from the words of the book of this prophecy, God shall take away* his part from the Book* of [3j]Life, from the holy city, and *from* the things which are written in this book.

*

22:8 NU-Text and M-Text read *am the one who heard and saw.* **22:9** NU-Text and M-Text omit *For.* **22:11** NU-Text and M-Text read *do right.* **22:13** NU-Text and M-Text read *the First and the Last, the Beginning and the End.* **22:14** NU-Text reads *wash their robes.* **22:15** NU-Text and M-Text omit *But.* **22:18** NU-Text and M-Text omit *For.* • M-Text reads *may God add.* **22:19** M-Text reads *may God take away.* • NU-Text and M-Text read *tree of life.*

8
a See Heb. 1:4, *note*
10
b Cp. Rev. 10:4
c See Mt. 4:17, *note 4*
11
d *Sanctification* (NT): v. 11. (Mt. 4:5; Rev. 22:11)
12
e *Christ* (second advent): v. 12; Rev 22:20. (Dt. 30:3; Acts 1:11, *note*)
f *Rewards:* vv. 12,14. (Dan. 12:3; 1 Cor. 3:14, *note*)
g *Judgments* (the seven): vv. 10–19. (1 Sam. 7:14; Rev. 20:12, *note*)
13
h See Rev. 1:8, *note*
14
i Prov. 11:30
j *Life* (eternal): vv. 14, 17,19. (Mt. 7:14; Rev. 22:19)
16
k *Churches* (local): v. 16. (Acts 8:3; Phil. 1:1, *note*)
17
l *Holy Spirit* (NT): v. 17. (Mt. 1:18; Acts 2:4, *note*)
18
m *Inspiration:* v. 18. (Ex. 4:15; 2 Tim. 3:16, *note*)

[1](22:11) See *notes:* OT righteousness (Lk. 2:25); NT righteousness (Rom. 3:21; 10:10); self-righteousness (Rom. 10:3); righteous living (1 Jn. 3:7); righteous garments (Rev. 19:8).

[2](22:11) Sanctification, holiness, Summary: (1) In both Testaments the same Hebrew and Greek words are rendered by the English words "sanctify," "consecrate" and "holy" in their various grammatical forms. The one uniform meaning is *to set apart for God.* (2) In both Testaments the words are used of things and of persons. (3) When sanctification is used of things, no moral quality is implied; they are consecrated or made holy because they are set apart for God. And (4) when sanctification is used of persons, it has a threefold meaning: (a) In position, believers are eternally set apart for God by redemption, "through the offering of the body of Jesus Christ once for all" (Heb. 10:10). Positionally, therefore, believers are "saints" and "holy" from the moment of believing (Phil. 1:1; Heb. 3:1). (b) In experience, believers are being sanctified by the work of the Holy Spirit through the Scriptures (Jn. 17:17; 2 Cor. 3:18; Eph. 5:25–26; 1 Th. 5:23–24). And (c) in consummation, believers' complete sanctification awaits the appearing of the Lord (Eph. 5:27; 1 Jn. 3:2). See Salvation, Rom. 1:16, *note.*

[3](22:19) Eternal life, Summary: (1) This life is called "eternal" because it is from the eternity which is past to the eternity which is to come—it is the life of God revealed in Jesus Christ, who is God (Jn. 1:4; 5:26; 1 Jn. 1:1–2). (2) This life of God, which was revealed in Christ, is imparted in a new birth by the Holy Spirit, acting upon the Word of God, to every believer in the Lord Jesus Christ (Jn. 3:3–15). (3) The life thus imparted is not a new life except in the sense of human possession; it is still "that which was from the beginning". But the recipient is a new creation (2 Cor. 5:17; Gal. 6:15). And (4) the life of God which is in the believer is an unsevered part of the life which eternally was, and eternally is, in Christ Jesus—one life in Him and in the believer; Vine and branches, Head and members (Jn. 15:1–5; 1 Cor. 6:17; 12:12–14; Gal. 2:20; Col. 1:27; 3:3–4; 1 Jn. 5:11–12).

20
a Christ (second advent): v. 20. (Dt. 30:3; Acts 1:11, *note*)

b Bible prayers (NT): v. 20. (Mt. 6:9; Lk. 11:2, *note*)

21
c Grace: v. 21. (Jn. 1:14; Jn. 1:17, *note*)

Conclusion:
Last Promise, Last Prayer,
and Last Provision,
22:20–21

20 He who testifies to these
things says, "Surely I am [a]com-
ing quickly." Amen. [b]Even so,
come, Lord Jesus!
21 The [c]grace of our Lord Jesus Christ *be* with you all.*
Amen.

*22:21 NU-Text reads *with all;* M-Text reads *with all the saints.*

Monies, Weights, and Measures

The Hebrews probably first used coins in the Persian period (500–350 B.C.). However, minting began around 700 B.C. in other nations. Prior to this, precious metals were weighed, not counted as money.

Some units appear as both measures of money and measures of weights. This comes from naming the coins after their weight. For example, the shekel was a weight long before it became the name of a coin.

It is helpful to relate biblical monies to current values. But we cannot make exact equivalents. The fluctuating value of money's purchasing power is difficult to determine in our own day. It is even harder to evaluate currencies used two to three thousand years ago.

Though there are differences of economies and standards of living, it is possible to compare monies of the biblical text to today's monies by choosing a value meaningful over time, such as a common laborer's daily wage. One day's wage corresponds to the ancient Jewish system (a silver shekel is four days' wages) as well as to the Greek and Roman systems (the drachma and the denarius were each coins representing a day's wage).

Monies

Unit	*Equivalents*	*Translations*
Jewish Weights		
Talent	3,000 shekels; 6,000 bekas	talent
Shekel	4 days' wages; 2 bekas; 20 gerahs	shekel
Beka	½ shekels; 10 gerahs	bekah
Gerah	1/20 shekel	gerah
Persian Coins		
Daric	2 days' wages; ½ Jewish silver shekel	drachma
Greek Coins		
Tetradrachma (Stater)	4 drachmas	piece of money
Didrachma	2 drachmas	tribute
Drachma	1 day's wage	piece of silver
Lepton	½ of a Roman kodrantes	mite
Roman Coins		
Aureus	25 denarii	
Denarius	1 day's wage	denarius
Assarius	1/16 of a denarius	copper coin
Kodrantes	¼ of an assarius	penny, quadrans

Weights

Unit	Weight	Equivalents	Translations
Jewish Weights			
Talent	c. 75 pounds for common talent, c. 150 pounds for royal talent	60 minas; 3,000 shekels	talent
Mina (Maneh)	1.25 pounds	50 shekels	mina
Shekel	c. .4 ounce (11.4 grams) for common shekel c. .8 ounce for royal shekel	2 bekas; 20 gerahs	shekel
Beka	c. .2 ounce (5.7 grams)	½ shekel; 10 gerahs	half a shekel
Gerah	c. .02 ounce (.57 grams)	1/20 shekel	gerah
Roman Weight			
Litra	12 ounces		pound

Measures of Length

Unit	Length	Equivalents	Translations
Day's journey	c. 20 miles		day's journey
Roman mile	4,854 feet	8 stadia	mile
Sabbath day's journey	3,637 feet	6 stadia	Sabbath day's journey
Stadion	606 feet	⅛ Roman mile	furlong
Rod	9 feet (10.5 feet in Ezekiel)	3 paces; 6 cubits	measuring reed, reed
Fathom	6 feet	4 cubits	fathom
Pace	3 feet	⅓ rod; 2 cubits	pace
Cubit	18 inches	½ pace; 2 spans	cubit
Span	9 inches	½ cubit; 3 handbreadths	span
Handbreadth	3 inches	⅓ span; 4 fingers	handbreadth
Finger	.75 inches	¼ handbreadth	finger

Liquid Measures

Unit	Measure	Equivalents	Translations
Kor	60 gallons	10 baths	kor
Metretes	10.2 gallons		gallons
Bath	6 gallons	6 hins	measure, bath
Hin	1 gallon	2 kabs	hin
Kab	2 quarts	4 logs	kab
Log	1 pint	¼ kab	log

Dry Measures

Unit	*Measure*	*Equivalents*	*Translations*
Homer	6.52 bushels	10 ephahs	homer
Kor	6.52 bushels	1 homer; 10 ephahs	kor, measure
Lethech	3.26 bushels	½ kor	half homer
Ephah	.65 bushel, 20.8 quarts	1/10 homer	ephah
Modius	7.68 quarts		basket
Seah	7 quarts	⅓ ephah	measure
Omer	2.08 quarts	1/10 ephah; 1⅘ kab	omer
Kab	1.16 quarts	4 logs	kab
Choenix	1 quart		measure
Xestes	1⅙ pints		pot
Log	.58 pint	¼ kab	log

Brief Index to Subject Chain References

BRIEF INDEX TO SUBJECT CHAIN REFERENCES

How to Use
the Complete Index to Subject Chain References

The Complete Index to Subject Chain References is an important new feature of this edition of the New Scofield Study Bible. It's simple to use. Here is an illustration using the *Adoption* chain:

At its alphabetical place in the Complete Index you will find the chain name, followed by the Summary Note location, then all of the chain references in biblical order. (Chapter numbers are listed in **boldface** type for easy scanning.)

Adoption
Summary note: Eph. 1:5
Rom. **8**:15,23.
Gal. **4**:5.
Eph. **1**:5.

The index directs you to Rom. 8:15, the first reference. In the margin you will see the chain name, the relevant verses on that page (vv. 15,23), then the next reference on a subsequent page (Gal. 4:5), then in parentheses the locations of the first reference and the Summary Note for that chain.

15 *e Adoption:* vv. 15,23; Gal. 4:5. (Rom. 8:15; Eph. 1:5) *f* Gal. 4:6	[g]heirs— heirs wi [h]suffer also be *(10) T*

The *Adoption* chain is found again at Gal. 4:5.

10:18, *note*) *i* Gal. 3:13 *j Adoption:* v. 5; Eph. 1:5. (Rom. 8:15; Eph. 1:5)	God has His Son out, [l]"A 7 Th ger a sl

This is a short chain. The last reference for *Adoption* is at Eph. 1:5. (Note that there is no next reference listed this time.)

d us to Jesus ding to is will,	Eph. 1:11) *f Adoption:* v. 5. (Rom. 8:15; Eph. 1:5)

A Summary Note for the *Adoption* chain is located at the last reference, Eph. 1:5. The note pulls together the truths that have been revealed by the verses in the chain, setting them forth in one cohesive statement.

(Heb. 3:1; 1 Pet. 2:11).
[4](1:5) "Adoption" (Gk. *hui*
relationship as of position. In
in adoption he receives the p
child and the right to be calle

For further information about Subject Chain References see p. xxi.

Complete Index to Subject Chain References

This index shows all the references within the subject chains. Thus it is an enlargement of the "Brief Index to Subject Chain References." The reader can use the references listed under each chain to locate that chain in any particular book or section of the Bible, or to follow a chain forward and backward in the Bible.

Adoption
Summary note: Eph. 1:5
Rom. **8**:15,23.
Gal. **4**:5.
Eph. **1**:5.

Angel (of the Lord)
Summary note: Jud. 2:1
Gen. **16**:7–12; **21**:17; **22**:11,15; **31**:11–13; **48**:16.
Ex. **3**:2–22; **4**:1–17; **14**:19; **23**:20–23; **32**:34–35; **33**:1–2.
Num. **22**:22–35.
Jud. **2**:1–4; **5**:23–31; **6**:11–24; **13**:3–21.
2 Sam. **24**:16–17.
1 Ki. **19**:5,7.
2 Ki. **1**:3–4,15–16; **19**:35.
1 Chr. **21**:12–20,27–30.
Ps. **34**:7; **35**:5–6.
Isa. **37**:36; **63**:9.
Zech. **1**:9,11–14,19; **2**:3; **3**:1,3,5–6; **4**:1; **5**:5,10; **6**:4–5; **12**:8.

Antichrist
Summary note: Rev. 13:11
Mt. **24**:4–5; **24**:11,23–24.
Jn. **5**:43.
2 Cor. **11**:3–4.
1 Jn. **2**:18,22; **4**:3.
2 Jn. 7.
Rev. **13**:11–17; **16**:13; **19**:20.

Apostasy
Summary note: 2 Tim. 3:1
Lk. **18**:8.
2 Th. **2**:1–12.
1 Tim. **4**:1–3.
2 Tim. **3**:1–8; **4**:4.
Heb. **6**:1–9; **10**:26–31,38–39.
2 Pet. **2**:1–22.
1 Jn. **4**:1–6.
Jude 4–19.
Rev. **3**:14–18.

Armageddon (battle of)
Summary note: Rev. 19:17
Isa. **10**:24–34; **24**:21; **26**:20–21; **34**:1–8; **63**:1–6; **66**:15–16.
Jer. **25**:29–33.
Ezek. **38**:1–23; **39**:1–24.
Joel **3**:9–14.
Obad. 15–18.
Zeph. **3**:8,15.
Zech. **10**:3; **12**:1–9; **14**:1–5.
Mt. **24**:27–28.
Lk. **17**:37.
Rev. **16**:13–16; **19**:11–21.

Assurance/security
Summary note: Jude 1
Ps. **23**:1–6; **91**:1.
Isa. **32**:17–18; **43**:1; **49**:16; **54**:17.
Hab. **3**:17–19.
Jn. **3**:16; **5**:24,29; **6**:39,51; **10**:28–29; **11**:26; **14**:19–20; **17**:11,15,24.
Acts **2**:21.
Rom. **8**:38–39; **10**:9,13.
1 Cor. **3**:22–23.
Eph. **1**:14; **4**:30.
Phil. **1**:6.
Col. **2**:2.
1 Th. **5**:23.
2 Th. **3**:3–4.
2 Tim. **1**:12; **4**:8,18.
Heb. **6**:8–12; **7**:23–25; **8**:10–13; **9**:24–26; **10**:14,16–18.
1 Pet. **1**:3–5.
2 Pet. **2**:9.
1 Jn. **2**:1–2; **3**:2.
Jude 1,24.

The Beast
Summary note: Rev. 19:20
Dan. **7**:8,11,20–26; **8**:24–25; **9**:26–27; **11**:36–45; **12**:11.
Mt. **24**:15.
Mk. **13**:14.
Jn. **5**:43.
2 Th. **2**:3–8.
Rev. **13**:1–8; **19**:19–20.

Bible prayers (OT)
Summary note: Hab. 3:1
Gen. **15**:2–3; **17**:17–18; **18**:23–33; **24**:12–14; **32**:9–12.
Ex. **32**:11–14; **33**:12–23.
Num. **6**:22–26; **10**:35–36; **11**:11–15; **12**:13; **14**:13–19; **27**:15–17.
Dt. **3**:23–25; **9**:26–29; **21**:6–8; **26**:5–10,13–15.
Josh. **7**:7–9.
Jud. **13**:8–9; **16**:28.
1 Sam. **1**:11; **2**:1.
2 Sam. **7**:18–29; **24**:17.
1 Ki. **3**:5–14; **8**:22–53; **17**:20–24; **18**:36–37; **19**:4.
2 Ki. **6**:17–18; **19**:14–19; **20**:2–3.
1 Chr. **4**:10; **29**:10–19.
2 Chr. **6**:12–42; **14**:11; **20**:6–12; **30**:18–20.
Ezra **9**:5–15.
Neh. **1**:5–11; **4**:4–5; **9**:5–38.
Ps. **51**:1–19.
Isa. **37**:14–20; **38**:3.
Jer. **14**:7–9; **32**:16–25.
Ezek. **9**:8.
Dan. **9**:3–21.
Jon. **2**:1–9.
Hab. **3**:1–19.

Bible prayers (NT)
Summary note: Lk. 11:2
Mt. **6**:9–13; **8**:2,25; **9**:18,21,27; **11**:25–26; **14**:30; **15**:22,25,27; **26**:39,42,44; **27**:46.
Mk. **5**:23,28; **7**:26; **9**:24; **10**:47–48,51; **14**:35–36,39,41; **15**:34.
Lk. **2**:28–32; **5**:12; **8**:24; **9**:38–40; **10**:21; **11**:2–4; **15**:18–19,21; **16**:24,27,30; **17**:5,13,15–16; **18**:11–13,38,41; **22**:32,42; **23**:34,42,46.
Jn. **4**:15,49; **11**:41–42; **12**:27–28; **17**:1–26.
Acts **1**:24–25; **4**:24–30; **7**:59–60; **9**:6; **22**:10,19–20.
Eph. **1**:16–23; **3**:14–21.
Phil. **1**:9.
Col. **1**:3,9–11; **4**:12.
1 Th. **1**:2; **3**:10–13; **5**:23.
2 Th. **1**:11–12; **2**:16; **3**:5.
Heb. **5**:7.
Jas. **5**:17–18.
Rev. **22**:20.

Bride (of Christ)
Summary note: Rev. 19:7
Jn. **3**:29.
Rom. **7**:4.
2 Cor. **11**:2.
Eph. **5**:25,27.
Rev. **19**:6–9; **21**:9–10.

Christ (first advent)
Summary note: Acts 1:11
Gen. **3**:15; **12**:3; **17**:19; **24**:60; **28**:14; **49**:10.
2 Sam. **7**:16.
Ps. **2**:2; **16**:10; **22**:1–18.
Isa. **7**:14; **9**:6; **28**:16; **42**:1–7; **49**:1–6; **50**:4–7; **52**:13–15; **53**:1–12; **61**:1–2.
Dan. **9**:24–26.
Hos. **11**:1.
Mic. **5**:2.
Zech. **9**:9; **11**:11–13; **13**:7.
Mal. **3**:1.
Mt. **1**:18–25; **2**:1–6; **4**:13–16; **12**:18–24; **18**:11; **21**:4–5,37; **26**:31; **27**:9–10,34–35,50; **28**:5–6.
Mk. **11**:9–10; **12**:6–8; **14**:27; **16**:6–7.
Lk. **1**:31–35; **2**:1–7,26–32; **9**:56; **19**:38; **20**:13–15.
Jn. **1**:14; **3**:13,31,34; **4**:26; **5**:43; **6**:33,38,41–42,50–51,58; **7**:29,31,42; **8**:42; **9**:39; **10**:10; **11**:27; **12**:13,46–47; **16**:27–28,30; **17**:8,18,21,23.
Acts **1**:9–11; **2**:22–32; **3**:12–15,26; **4**:10–11,26–27; **7**:52; **10**:34–43; **13**:23–25; **17**:31; **18**:5; **19**:4; **26**:23.
Rom. **1**:3–5; **8**:3; **9**:5.
Gal. **4**:4.
Eph. **2**:17.
Phil. **2**:7–8.

Lk. 18:14.
Acts 13:39.
Rom. 2:13; 3:4,20,24,26,28,30; 4:2,5,25; 5:1,9,16,18; 8:30,33.
1 Cor. 4:4; 6:11.
Gal. 2:16; 3:8,11; 3:24; 5:4.
Ti. 3:7.
Jas. 2:21,25.

Kingdom (OT)
Summary note: Zech. 12:8
Gen. 1:26–28; 9:6.
Ex. 3:1–10; 19:9; 24:12.
Num. 24:17.
Dt. 30:1–9; 33:4–5.
Josh. 1:1–5.
Jud. 2:16–18.
1 Sam. 8:1–7; 9:15–17; 10:25; 15:1–26; 16:1–13.
2 Sam. 2:1–4; 5:1–3; 7:8–16; 23:1–5.
1 Ki. 8:20; 11:9,13,30–37.
2 Ki. 25:1–7.
Ps. 2:1–9; 16:8–11; 72:1–20; 89:3–4,19–21,27–29,34–36.
Isa. 1:25–26; 2:1–4; 4:2–6; 7:14; 9:6–7; 11:1–12; 12:1–6; 14:1–2; 24:23; 32:1–2,14–18; 33:17–20; 35:1–10; 40:9–11; 62:10–12; 65:18–25.
Jer. 23:5–8; 30:7–9; 33:14–17.
Ezek. 11:14–20; 16:13–14; 20:33–44; 34:11–15,22–25; 37:21–28.
Dan. 2:34–45; 7:9,13–14.
Hos. 3:4–5.
Joel 3:12,16–21.
Amos 9:11–15.
Mic. 4:1–5; 5:2,4.
Zeph. 3:13–20.
Zech. 6:11–13; 12:6–8; 14:16–21.

Kingdom (NT)
Summary note: 1 Cor. 15:24
Mt. 2:2,5–6; 3:2; 4:17,23; 5:2–12,19–20,35; 6:10; 7:21–23; 8:11–12; 9:35; 10:7; 11:11–12; 13:3–52; 16:19,27–28; 17:1–5; 18:1–4,23–34; 19:12,14,23–24,27–28; 20:1–16,21,23; 21:1–9; 22:2–14; 23:13,39; 24:14,30–31; 25:1–46; 26:29,64; 27:37,42.
Mk. 1:14–15; 4:2–34; 9:1–4; 10:37; 11:10.
Lk. 1:32–33; 8:10; 9:26–36; 10:22; 11:2; 12:32; 13:18–21; 19:38; 22:29–30; 23:37–38,42.
Jn. 1:49–51; 12:13; 18:33–34,36–37,39; 19:3,14–15,19–22.
Acts 1:6–7; 2:30; 15:14–17; 17:7.
Rom. 15:12.
1 Cor. 15:24.
Eph. 5:5.
1 Tim. 6:15.
2 Tim. 4:1.
Jas. 2:5.
Rev. 3:21; 5:1–4,10; 11:15; 17:14; 19:11–21; 20:6; 21:5,9–27; 22:1–5.

Law (of Christ)
Summary note: 2 Jn. 5
Jn. 13:34–35; 14:15,21,23; 15:17; 17:26.
Rom. 5:5,8; 12:9–10; 13:8–14; 14:1–23; 15:1–2.
1 Cor. 4:21; 8:9–13,21; 13:1–13; 14:1; 16:14.
2 Cor. 2:4,8; 5:14; 6:6; 8:8,24; 10:5; 12:15.
Gal. 5:6,13; 6:2.
Eph. 1:15; 3:17,19; 4:2,15–16; 5:2,25,28; 6:23.
Phil. 1:9,17; 2:1–2.
Col. 1:4,8; 3:14.
1 Th. 3:6,12; 4:9; 5:13.
2 Th. 1:3.
1 Tim. 1:5; 2:15; 4:12; 6:11.
2 Tim. 1:7; 2:22; 3:10.
Ti. 2:2; 3:15.
Phile. 9.
Jas. 2:8.
1 Pet. 1:22; 3:8.
1 Jn. 2:10; 3:11,14,16–18,23; 4:7,11–12,17,21; 5:2.
2 Jn. 5.

Law (of Moses)
Summary note: Gal. 3:24
Ex. 19:1–25; 20:1–17; 31:18; 34:18–28.
Lev. 1:1–16; 16:34; 26:3; 27:1–34.
Dt. 5:1–22; 6:1–5.
Ps. 1:2; 19:7–8; 37:31; 40:8; 78:9–10; 119:1–176.
Isa. 1:10–18; 5:24–25.
Jer. 9:13–16.
Ezek. 22:26.
Dan. 9:8–13.
Mal. 4:4.
Mt. 4:4,7,10; 5:17–19,21,27,31,33,38,43; 7:12; 8:4; 11:13; 12:5; 15:3–4,6; 19:7–8,18–20; 22:24,36–40; 23:23.
Mk. 1:44; 7:8–10; 10:3–8,19–20; 12:19,26,28–31.
Lk. 1:6; 2:23–24,39; 4:4,8,12; 5:14,17; 10:26–27; 16:16–17,29,31; 18:20; 20:28; 24:27,44.
Jn. 1:17,45; 7:19,22–23,49,51; 8:5,17; 9:16; 18:31; 19:7.
Acts 3:22; 5:34; 6:13–14; 7:37,53; 10:14; 13:15,39; 15:1,5,20–21; 18:13,15; 21:20–21,24,26,28; 22:3,12; 23:3,5,29; 24:6,14; 25:8; 28:23.
Rom. 2:12–15,17–18,22–23,25–27; 3:2,19–21,27–28,31; 4:13–16; 5:13,20; 6:14–15; 7:1–9,12–14,16,22,25; 8:3–4,7; 9:4,32; 10:4–5; 13:8–10.
1 Cor. 7:19; 9:8–9,20–21; 14:21; 15:56.
2 Cor. 3:7,14–15.
Gal. 2:16,19,21; 3:2,5,10–24; 4:21; 5:3–4,14,18; 6:13.
Eph. 2:15.
Phil. 3:5–6,9.
1 Tim. 1:8–9.
Heb. 7:18–19; 10:28.
Jas. 2:10.
Rev. 12:17; 14:12.

Leaven
Summary note: Mt. 13:33
Gen. 19:3.
Ex. 12:8,15–20,34,39; 13:3,6–7; 23:15,18; 29:2,23; 34:18,25.
Lev. 2:4–5,11; 6:16–17; 7:12–13; 8:2,26; 10:12; 23:6–17.
Num. 6:15,17,19; 9:11; 28:17.
Dt. 16:3–4,8,16.
Amos 4:5.
Mt. 13:33; 16:6,11–12.
Mk. 8:15.
Lk. 12:1; 13:21.
1 Cor. 5:6–8.
Gal. 5:9.

Life (eternal)
Summary note: Rev. 22:19
Mt. 7:14; 18:8–9; 19:16–17,29; 25:46.
Mk. 10:17,30.
Lk. 10:25–28; 12:15; 18:18,30.
Jn. 1:4; 3:15–16,36; 4:14,36; 5:24–25,29,39–40; 6:27,33,35,40,47,51,54,57–58,63,68; 8:12; 10:10,28; 11:25–26; 12:25,50; 14:6; 17:2–3; 20:31.
Acts 2:28; 3:15; 5:20; 11:18; 13:46,48.
Rom. 2:7; 5:21; 6:22–23; 8:6,10.
2 Cor. 2:16; 3:6; 4:10–12; 5:4.
Gal. 2:20; 6:8.
Eph. 4:18.
Phil. 4:3.
Col. 1:27; 3:4.
1 Tim. 1:16; 4:8; 6:12,19.
2 Tim. 1:1,10.
Ti. 1:2; 3:7.
Heb. 7:16.
Jas. 1:12.
1 Pet. 3:7.
2 Pet. 1:3.
1 Jn. 1:1–2; 2:25; 3:14–15; 5:11–13,20.
Jude 21.
Rev. 2:7,10; 3:5; 13:8; 17:8; 20:12,15; 21:6,27; 22:1–2,14,17,19.

Miracles (OT)
Summary note: Jon. 1:17
Gen. 5:24; 7:11; 8:2; 11:7–9; 12:17; 15:17; 19:11,24–26; 20:17–18; 21:2.
Ex. 4:3–4,6–7; 7:10–12,20–25; 8:5–14,16–18,20–24; 9:3–6,8–11,22–26,33–35; 10:12–19,21–23; 12:29–30; 14:21–31; 15:23–25; 16:14–35; 17:5–7.
Lev. 10:1–2.
Num. 11:1–3; 16:31–35; 17:8; 20:7–11; 21:8–9.
Josh. 3:15–17; 4:15–18; 6:6–25; 10:12–14.
Jud. 14:5–6,19; 15:14–19; 16:28–30.
1 Sam. 5:3–12.
2 Sam. 6:7.
1 Ki. 13:4–6; 17:14–24; 18:30–38.
2 Ki. 1:10–12; 2:7–14,19–24; 3:16–20; 4:2–7,32–44 ; 5:10–14,27; 6:5–7,18–20; 13:21; 19:35; 20:11.
2 Chr. 26:16–21.
Isa. 37:36; 38:8.
Dan. 3:19–27; 6:16–23.
Jon. 1:17; 2:1–10.

Miracles (NT)
Summary note: Acts 28:8
Mt. 8:2–3,5–17,24–32; 9:2–7,18–25,27–30,32–35; 11:5; 12:10–13,22;

Num. **15**:32–36.
Neh. **9**:13–14.
Mt. **12**:1–13; **24**:20; **28**:1.
Mk. **2**:23–28; **3**:2–4; **6**:2; **16**:1.
Lk. **4**:16; **6**:1–7,9; **13**:10,14–16; **14**:1,3,5; **23**:54,56.
Jn. **5**:9–10,16,18; **7**:22–23; **9**:14,16; **19**:31.
Acts **13**:14,27,42,44; **15**:21; **16**:13; **17**:2; **18**:4.
Col. **2**:16.

Sacrifice (of Christ, prophetic, typical)
Summary note: Heb. 10:18
Gen. **3**:15; **4**:4; **8**:20; **12**:7–8; **13**:18; **22**:8,13.
Ex. **12**:3–11,27; **17**:15.
Lev. **1**:3–17; **2**:1–16; **3**:1–17; **4**:3–35; **5**:1–19; **6**:1–7; **16**:2–34; **17**:11.
Ps. **22**:1–18.
Isa. **52**:14–15; **53**:1–12.
Dan. **9**:26.
Zech. **12**:10.
Mt. **26**:28; **27**:33–35,38.
Mk. **14**:24; **15**:22–26.
Lk. **22**:19–20; **23**:33,46.
Jn. **1**:29,36; **3**:14,16; **6**:33,38,51; **10**:11,15,17–18; **12**:24,32–33; **19**:18,34.
Acts **13**:23,28–29; **17**:3; **20**:28; **26**:23.
Rom. **3**:25; **4**:25; **5**:6–11; **8**:3,32,34; **14**:9,15.
1 Cor. **1**:23; **5**:7; **6**:20; **7**:23; **8**:11; **10**:16; **11**:24–26; **15**:3.
2 Cor. **5**:14–15,18–19,21; **13**:4.
Gal. **1**:4; **2**:20; **3**:1,13; **4**:5.
Eph. **1**:7; **2**:13–16; **5**:2,25.
Col. **1**:14,20–22.
1 Tim. **2**:6.
Ti. **2**:14.
Heb. **1**:3; **7**:27; **9**:12,15,26; **10**:10,12,14,18; **11**:4; **13**:12.
1 Pet. **1**:18–19; **2**:24; **3**:18; **4**:1.
1 Jn. **1**:7.
Rev. **1**:5–6; **5**:9; **7**:14; **12**:11.

Sanctification (OT)
Summary note: Zech. 8:3
Gen. **2**:3.
Ex. **19**:23; **28**:1–3; **29**:37,44; **30**:30,37.
Lev. **8**:15; **27**:14–22.
Josh. **5**:15; **6**:19; **7**:13.
1 Ki. **7**:51.
2 Chr. **2**:4; **5**:1; **29**:5,17,34; **35**:6.
Ps. **2**:6; **20**:6; **89**:20.
Jer. **1**:5.
Dan. **4**:13.
Joel **1**:13–14.
Zech. **8**:3.

Sanctification (NT)
Summary note: Rev. 22:11
Mt. **4**:5; **7**:6; **23**:17,19; **24**:15; **25**:31; **27**:53.
Mk. **6**:20; **8**:38.
Lk. **1**:35,70,72,75; **2**:23; **9**:26.
Jn. **10**:36; **17**:17,19.
Acts **3**:21; **4**:27,30; **6**:13; **7**:33; **20**:32; **21**:28; **26**:18.
Rom. **1**:2,4; **6**:19,22; **7**:12; **11**:16; **12**:1–2; **15**:16.
1 Cor. **1**:2,30; **3**:17; **6**:11; **7**:14,34; **9**:13.
2 Cor. **7**:1.
Eph. **1**:4; **2**:21; **3**:5; **4**:24; **5**:26.
Col. **1**:22; **3**:12.
1 Th. **4**:3; **5**:23.
1 Tim. **4**:5.
Ti. **1**:8.
Heb. **2**:11; **3**:1; **9**:3,8,12,24–25; **10**:10,14,19,29; **13**:12.
1 Pet. **1**:15–16; **2**:5,9; **3**:5,15.
2 Pet. **1**:18,21.
Jude 20.
Rev. **22**:11.

Satan
Summary note: Rev. 20:10
Gen. **3**:1–2,4,13–14.
1 Chr. **21**:1.
Job **1**:6–9,12; **2**:1–3,6–7.
Ps. **109**:6.
Isa. **14**:12–14.
Ezek. **28**:12–15.
Zech. **3**:1–2.
Mt. **4**:1,5,8,10–11; **12**:26–27; **13**:19,38–39; **16**:23; **25**:41.
Mk. **1**:13; **3**:22–23,26; **4**:15; **8**:33.
Lk. **4**:2–13; **8**:12; **10**:18; **11**:18; **13**:16; **22**:3–6,31.
Jn. **8**:44; **12**:31; **13**:2,27; **14**:30; **17**:15.
Acts **5**:3; **10**:38; **13**:10; **26**:18.
Rom. **16**:20.
1 Cor. **5**:5; **7**:5.
2 Cor. **2**:11; **4**:4; **11**:3,14; **12**:7.
Eph. **2**:2; **4**:27; **6**:11,16.
1 Th. **2**:18.
2 Th. **2**:9.
1 Tim. **1**:20; **3**:6–7; **5**:15.
2 Tim. **2**:26.
Heb. **2**:14.
Jas. **4**:7.
1 Pet. **5**:8–9.
1 Jn. **3**:8,10.
Jude 9.
Rev. **2**:9–10,13,24; **3**:9; **12**:3–17; **20**:2,7–10.

Separation
Summary note: 2 Cor. 6:17
Gen. **12**:1–5; **13**:7–11,14–17.
Ex. **6**:6–7; **8**:25–27; **10**:8–11,24–26; **11**:7; **19**:4; **33**:16.
Lev. **20**:24–26.
Num. **6**:1–8; **16**:20–26.
Dt. **22**:10.
1 Ki. **8**:53.
Ezra **6**:21; **9**:10–12; **10**:10–11,19.
Neh. **9**:2; **13**:3.
Jn. **15**:19; **17**:6,14,16.
Rom. **12**:2.
1 Cor. **10**:20–21.
2 Cor. **6**:14–17.
1 Tim. **6**:9–11.
2 Tim. **2**:19–21.
Heb. **11**:25; **13**:14.
2 Jn. 10–11.
Rev. **18**:4.

Test/tempt
Summary note: Jas. 1:14
Gen. **3**:1–6,12–13; **22**:1.
Ex. **15**:25; **16**:4; **17**:2,7; **20**:20.
Num. **14**:22.
Dt. **6**:16; **7**:25; **8**:2,15–16; **13**:3; **33**:8–9.
Jud. **6**:39.
2 Sam. **24**:1.
1 Chr. **21**:1.
2 Chr. **32**:31.
Job. **7**:18; **23**:10; **34**:36.
Ps. **7**:9; **11**:4–5; **17**:3; **26**:2; **66**:10–12; **78**:18,41,56; **81**:7; **95**:9; **106**:14; **139**:23–24.
Prov. **1**:10; **17**:3.
Isa. **7**:12.
Jer. **9**:7; **11**:20; **12**:3; **17**:10; **20**:12.
Mal. **3**:10,15.
Mt. **4**:1,3,7; **6**:13; **16**:1; **19**:3; **22**:18,35; **26**:41.
Mk. **1**:12–13; **8**:11; **10**:2; **12**:13–15.
Lk. **4**:1–13; **8**:13; **10**:25; **11**:4,16; **20**:21–23; **22**:28,31–32,40,46.
Jn. **6**:6; **8**:6.
Acts **5**:9; **15**:10; **20**:19.
1 Cor. **7**:5; **10**:9,13.
2 Cor. **11**:3.
Gal. **4**:14; **6**:1.
1 Th. **3**:5.
1 Tim. **2**:14; **6**:9.
Heb. **2**:18; **3**:7–9; **4**:15; **11**:17,36–37.
Jas. **1**:2–3,12–14.
1 Pet. **1**:6–7; **4**:12.
2 Pet. **2**:9; **3**:17.
Rev. **2**:10; **3**:10.

Theophanies
Summary note: Gen. 12:7 (1)
Gen. **12**:7; **17**:1–22; **18**:1,17,22,33; **26**:2,24; **35**:9–13.
Josh. **5**:13–15.
Ezek. **40**:3–4.
Dan. **8**:15; **10**:4–9,16–17.

Times of the Gentiles
Summary note: Rev. 16:19
Dt. **28**:49–68.
2 Ki. **18**:9–12; **25**:1–21.
2 Chr. **36**:17–20.
Jer. **39**:7.
Dan. **2**:27–45; **4**:17,25,32; **7**:2–27.
Joel **3**:2,11–14.
Lk. **21**:24.
Rev. **11**:2; **16**:14,19.

Tribulation (the great)
Summary note: Rev. 7:14
Ps. **2**:1–5.
Isa. **24**:20.
Jer. **30**:4–7.
Dan. **12**:1.
Mt. **24**:21–22,29.
Mk. **13**:14–23.
Lk. **21**:20–26.
Rev. **3**:10; **7**:14.

"Wife" (of the LORD)
Summary note: Hos. 2:2
Isa. **54**:1–7.
Jer. **31**:32.
Hos. **2**:1–23.

Index to Annotations

ANNOTATIONS

CONCISE CONCORDANCE

Concise Concordance

To proper names, subject matter, and key words of the Bible, specially prepared for the NKJV New Scofield Study Bible

AARON
brother of Moses, the first high priest, comes out to meet Moses; can speak well. Ex. 4:14
appointed by God to be Moses' spokesman. Ex. 4:14,16,27
with Moses appeals to Pharaoh. Ex. 5:1
his rod becomes a serpent. Ex. 7:10
changes the waters into blood. Ex. 7:20
causes the plagues of frogs, lice, flies. Ex. 8:5
with Moses—the plague of boils. Ex. 9:10
with Hur holds up Moses' hands. Ex. 17:12
set apart for priest's office. Ex. 28
makes the golden calf. Ex. 32:4
consecration. Ex. 29; Lev. 8
offers sacrifice. Lev. 9
his sons: Nadab and Abihu offer profane fire. Lev. 10:1; Eleazar and Ithamar censured. Lev. 10:16
not to drink wine when going into the tabernacle. Lev. 10:8
speaks against Moses. Num. 12
rebuked by God. Num. 12:9
spoken against by Korah. Num. 16:3
makes atonement, plague stopped. Num. 16:46–48
his rod buds, and is kept in ark for a sign. Num. 17:8
for unbelief excluded from the promised land. Num. 20:12
dies on Mount Hor. Num. 20:28
chosen by God. Ps. 105:26; Heb. 5:4
his line. 1 Chr. 6:49

ABADDON
angel of the bottomless pit. Rev. 9:11

ABASED
Phil. 4:12, I know how to be *a*

ABBA
Mk. 14:36, And He said, "*A*
Rom. 8:15, whom we cry out, "*A*
Gal. 4:6, crying out, "*A*

ABED-NEGO, Dan. 1:7
saved in fiery furnace. Dan. 3. *See* Isa. 43:2

ABEL, 2 Sam. 20:14
second son of Adam. Gen. 4:2
his offering accepted. Gen. 4:4
killed by Cain. Gen. 4:8
righteous. Mt. 23:35; 1 Jn. 3:12
blood of. Lk. 11:51; Heb. 12:24
faith of. Heb. 11:4

ABHOR
Lev. 26:11, My soul shall not *a*
Job 42:6, Therefore I *a* myself
Prov. 24:24, nations will *a* him
Amos 6:8, *a* the pride of Jacob
Rom. 12:9, *A* what is evil

ABHORRED
Ps. 106:40, *a* His own inheritance
Prov. 22:14, he who is *a* by the
Zech. 11:8, and their soul also *a*

ABHORRENCE
Isa. 66:24, They shall be an *a*

ABHORRENT
Ex. 5:21, you have made us *a*

ABHORS
Job 33:20, So that his life *a*

ABIATHAR, 1 Sam. 22:20

ABIB (or Nisan)
first month of Hebrew calendar. Ex. 13:4
when passover was kept. Ex. 23:15; 34:18

ABIDE
Job 24:13, nor *a* in its paths
Ps. 15:1, LORD, who may *a*
Ps. 61:7, He shall *a* before God
Ps. 91:1, the Most High shall *a*
Jn. 8:31, Him, "If you *a*
Jn. 8:35, And a slave does not *a*
Jn. 14:16, Helper, that He may *a*
Jn. 15:4, "*A* in Me
Jn. 15:7, "If you *a* in Me
Jn. 15:9, *a* in My love
1 Cor. 13:13, And now *a* faith
1 Jn. 3:17, does the love of God *a*
1 Jn. 4:13, this we know that we *a*

ABIDES
Ps. 55:19, them, even He who *a*
Jn. 15:5, He who *a* in Me
1 Pet. 1:23, lives and *a* forever
1 Jn. 2:17, will of God *a* forever

ABIDING
Jn. 5:38, not have His word *a*
1 Jn. 3:15, has eternal life *a*

ABIEZER, Josh. 17:2
ancestor of Gideon. Jud. 6

ABIGAIL, 1 Sam. 25:14
wife of Nabal, and afterwards of David. 1 Sam. 25:39
mother of Chileab, according to 2 Sam. 3:3, or Daniel, according to 1 Chr. 3:1

ABIHU, Ex. 6:23
brother of Nadab, offers profane fire, and dies. Lev. 10:2

ABIHUD, 1 Chr. 8:3

ABIJAH, 1 Ki. 14:1
king of Judah, walked in the sins of his father. 1 Ki. 15:3
makes war against Israel. 2 Chr. 13
——— son of Jeroboam, his death foretold by Ahijah the prophet. 1 Ki. 14:12

ABIJAM
another mode of spelling Abijah. 1 Ki. 14:31

ABILITY
Dan. 1:4, understand, who had *a*
Mt. 25:15, according to his own *a*
2 Cor. 8:3, and beyond their *a*
1 Pet. 4:11, *a* which God supplies

ABIMELECH, Gen. 20:2
king of Gerar, rebuked by God about Abraham's wife. Gen. 20:3
rebukes Abraham; restores Sarah. Gen. 20:9,14
healed at Abraham's prayer. Gen. 20:17
——— (another), Isaac rebuked by, for denying his wife. Gen. 26:10
covenants with Isaac. Gen. 26:28
——— king at Shechem, son of the judge Gideon. Jud. 8:31
murders his brothers. Jud. 9:5
his death. Jud. 9:54

ABINADAB, 1 Sam. 7:1
receives the ark from Philistines. 2 Sam. 6:3

ABIRAM, Num. 16:1
with Korah and Dathan, rebels against Moses. Num. 16
his punishment. Num. 16:31; 26:10

ABISHAG, 1 Ki. 1:3
the Shunammite, serves David, cause of breach between Solomon and Adonijah. 1 Ki. 2:22

ABISHAI, 1 Sam. 26:6
brother of Joab. 1 Chr. 2:16
with David carries off Saul's spear. 1 Sam. 26:6–9
kills three hundred men. 2 Sam. 23:18

ABITUB, 1 Chr. 8:11

ABLE
Gen. 15:5, you are *a* to number
Dt. 16:17, shall give as he is *a*
1 Ki. 3:9, For who is *a* to judge
2 Chr. 25:9, "The LORD is *a*
Job 41:10, Who then is *a* to stand
Dan. 3:17, whom we serve is *a*
Mt. 3:9, God is *a* to raise up
Mt. 9:28, believe that I am *a*
Mt. 10:28, fear Him who is *a*
Mt. 20:22, Are you *a* to drink the
1 Cor. 10:13, beyond what you are *a*
2 Cor. 9:8, And God is *a* to make
Eph. 3:18, may be *a* to comprehend
2 Tim. 1:12, persuaded that He is *a*
2 Tim. 3:7, learning and never *a*
Heb. 2:18, being tempted, He is *a*
Heb. 11:19, that God was *a* to
Jude 24, to Him who is *a*

Rev. 6:17, has come, and who is *a*

ABNER, 1 Sam. 14:50
cousin of Saul, commander of his army. 1 Sam. 14:50
rebuked by David. 1 Sam. 26:5,14
makes Ishbosheth king. 2 Sam. 2:8
goes over to David. 2 Sam. 3:8
killed by Joab. 2 Sam. 3:27
mourned by David. 2 Sam. 3:31

ABODE
Jude 6, but left their own *a*

ABOLISHED
Ezek. 6:6, your works may be *a*
Eph. 2:15, having *a* in His flesh
2 Tim. 1:10, Christ, who has *a*

ABOMINABLE
Lev. 11:43, not make yourselves *a*
Ps. 14:1, They have done *a*
Isa. 14:19, your grave like an *a*
Jer. 44:4, Oh, do not do this *a*
Ti. 1:16, deny Him, being *a*
1 Pet. 4:3, and *a* idolatries
Rev. 21:8, unbelieving, *a*

ABOMINATION (of desolation)
Dan. 9:27; 11:31; 12:11; Mt. 24:15; Mk. 13:14
national. Dt. 18:9,12; Ezek. 5:11; 7; 8:5; 11:18; 16:22; Hos. 9:10
of offerings. Lev. 7:18; Dt. 17:1; 23:18; Prov. 15:8; Isa. 1:13; 41:24
prayer of the wicked. Prov. 28:9
impurity. Lev. 18:22; 20:13
defilement. Dt. 24:4; 1 Ki. 11:5; Prov. 16:12; Isa. 66:17; Ezek. 16; Rev. 21:27
falsity. Prov. 11:1; 17:15; 20:10,23
idolatry. Dt. 7:25,26; 27:15; 2 Ki. 23:13; Jer. 2:7; Ezek. 18:12; Mal. 2:11
pride. Prov. 3:32; 6:16; 11:20; 16:5

ABOMINATION
Gen. 46:34, every shepherd is an *a*
Ex. 8:26, If we sacrifice the *a*
Ps. 88:8, You have made me an *a*
Prov. 6:16, yes, seven are an *a*
Prov. 8:7, wickedness is an *a*
Prov. 11:1, Dishonest scales is an *a*
Prov. 24:9, the scoffer is an *a*
Prov. 28:9, prayer is an *a*
Prov. 29:27, An unjust man is an *a*
Isa. 1:13, incense is an *a*
Dan. 11:31, and place there the *a*
Dan. 12:11, the *a* of desolation
Mt. 24:15, the '*a* of desolation,'
Lk. 16:15, among men is an *a*

ABOMINATIONS
Dt. 18:9, to follow the *a*
Isa. 66:3, delights in their *a*
Jer. 4:1, will put away your *a*
Jer. 13:27, your harlotry, your *a*
Ezek. 8:6, you will see greater *a*
Ezek. 8:17, *a* which they commit
Ezek. 20:7, you, throw away the *a*
Ezek. 22:2, show her all her *a*
Rev. 17:4, a golden cup full of *a*
Rev. 17:5, harlots and of the *a*

ABOUND
Mt. 24:12, lawlessness will *a*
Rom. 5:20, the offense might *a*
Rom. 6:1, sin that grace may *a*
2 Cor. 4:15, thanksgiving to *a*
2 Cor. 9:8, to make all grace *a*
Phil. 4:12, and I know how to *a*
1 Th. 4:1, that you should *a*
2 Pet. 1:8, things are yours and *a*

ABOUNDED
Rom. 5:20, But where sin *a*

ABOUNDING
Ps. 103:8, and *a* in mercy
1 Cor. 15:58, immovable, always *a*

ABOVE
Ex. 20:4, that is in heaven *a*
2 Sam. 22:17, "He sent from *a*
Isa. 6:2, *A* it stood seraphim
Mt. 10:24, nor a servant *a*
Jn. 3:31, "He who comes from *a*
Jn. 8:23, I am from *a*
Jn. 19:11, given you from *a*
Eph. 4:6, of all, who is *a*
Phil. 2:9, the name which is *a*
Col. 3:1, things which are *a*
Jas. 1:17, perfect gift is from *a*

ABRAHAM, Gen. 17:5
——— (Abram), begotten by Terah. Gen. 11:27
blessed by God, and sent to Canaan. Gen. 12:5
goes down to Egypt. Gen. 12:10
causes wife to pass as sister. Gen. 12:13; 20:2
strife between him and Lot. Gen. 13:7
his descendants to be as the dust of the earth. Gen. 13:16
delivers Lot from captivity; refuses spoil. Gen. 14:16
blessed by Melchizedek. Gen. 14:19; Heb. 7:4
his faith counted for righteousness. Gen. 15:6
God's covenant with. Gen. 15:18; Ps. 105:9
he and house circumcised. Gen. 17
entertains angels. Gen. 18
pleads for Sodom. Gen. 18:23
sends away Hagar and Ishmael. Gen. 21:14
his faith in offering Isaac. Gen. 22
buys a burying place. Gen. 23
sends for a wife for his son. Gen. 24
gives his goods to Isaac. Gen. 25:5
dies (in a good old age). Gen. 25:8
his faith and works. Isa. 41:8; 51:2; Jn. 8:39; Acts 7:2; Rom. 4; Gal. 3:6; Heb. 11:8; Jas. 2:21
his posterity. Gen. 25:1

ABRAM, Gen. 11:26

ABSALOM, 2 Sam. 3:3
David's son. 2 Sam. 3:3
kills Amnon. 2 Sam. 13:28
conspires against David. 2 Sam. 15:1–12
David flees from. 2 Sam. 15:14
caught by head in a terebinth. 2 Sam. 18:9
killed by Joab. 2 Sam. 18:14
mourned by David. 2 Sam. 18:33; 19:1

ABSENT
1 Cor. 5:3, For I indeed, as *a*
2 Cor. 5:6, in the body we are *a*

ABSTAIN
Acts 15:20, we write to them to *a*
1 Th. 5:22, *A* from every form
1 Tim. 4:3, and commanding to *a*
1 Pet. 2:11, and pilgrims, *a*

ABUNDANCE
1 Ki. 18:41, is the sound of *a*
1 Chr. 22:15, workmen with you in *a*
Ps. 72:7, shall flourish, and *a*
Ps. 73:7, eyes bulge with *a*
Eccl. 5:10, nor he who loves *a*
Isa. 55:2, delight itself in *a*
Mt. 12:34, For out of the *a*
Mk. 12:44, put in out of their *a*
Lk. 12:15, not consist in the *a*
2 Cor. 8:2, of affliction the *a*
2 Cor. 12:7, above measure by the *a*
Rev. 18:3, rich through the *a*

ABUNDANT
Ps. 86:15, Longsuffering and *a*
Jon. 4:2, slow to anger and *a*
2 Cor. 11:23, in labors more *a*
1 Tim. 1:14, Lord was exceedingly *a*
1 Pet. 1:3, *a* mercy has begotten

ABUNDANTLY
Ps. 36:8, *a* satisfied with the
Jn. 10:10, may have it more *a*
Eph. 3:20, to do exceedingly *a*
Heb. 6:17, to show more *a* to the

ACACIA GROVE
place of encampment. Num. 25:1

ACCEPT
Job 42:8, For I will *a* him
Ps. 20:3, *a* your burnt
Jer. 14:12, offering, I will not *a*
Mal. 1:13, Should I *a* this from

ACCEPTABLE
Eccl. 12:10, sought to find *a*
Isa. 49:8, *a* time I have heard
Isa. 61:2, proclaim the *a* year
Lk. 4:19, proclaim the *a* year
Rom. 12:2, is that good and *a*
Eph. 5:10, finding out what is *a*
1 Tim. 2:3, For this is good and *a*
1 Pet. 2:5, spiritual sacrifices *a*

ACCEPTABLY
Heb. 12:28, we may serve God *a*

ACCEPTED
2 Cor. 6:2, Behold, now is the *a*
Eph. 1:6, which He made us *a*

ACCESS
to God, by faith. Rom. 5:2; Eph. 2:18; 3:12; Heb. 7:19; 10:19
its blessedness. Ps. 65:4; 73:28; Isa. 2:3; Jer. 31:6

ACCESS
Rom. 5:2, whom also we have *a*

Eph. 3:12, we have boldness and *a*

ACCOMPLISHED
1 Sam. 11:13, today the LORD has *a*
Prov. 13:19, A desire *a* is sweet to
Lk. 22:37, must still be *a*
Jn. 19:28, all things were now *a*

ACCORD
Josh. 9:2, and Israel with one *a*
Zeph. 3:9, serve Him with one *a*
Acts 1:14, continued with one *a*
Acts 2:46, daily with one *a*
2 Cor. 6:15, *a* has Christ with
Phil. 2:2, love, being of one *a*

ACCOUNT
Mt. 12:36, they will give *a*
Acts 1:1, The former *a* I made
Rom. 14:12, of us shall give *a*
Phile. 18, put that on my *a*
Heb. 13:17, those who must give *a*

ACCOUNTED
Gen. 15:6, in the LORD, and He *a*
Ps. 106:31, And that was *a* to him
Rom. 4:5, his faith is *a*
Rom. 8:36, *a* as sheep for the
Gal. 3:6, God, and it was *a*
Jas. 2:23, God, and it was *a*

ACCURSED
Dt. 21:23, he who is hanged is *a*
Josh. 7:1, regarding the *a*
Isa. 65:20, years old shall be *a*
Jn. 7:49, not know the law is *a*
Rom. 9:3, that I myself were *a*
1 Cor. 12:3, of God calls Jesus *a*
Gal. 1:8, to you, let him be *a*

ACCUSATION
Ezra 4:6, reign, they wrote an *a*
Mt. 27:37, over His head the *a*
Lk. 6:7, they might find an *a*
1 Tim. 5:19, Do not receive an *a*
2 Pet. 2:11, not bring a reviling *a*

ACCUSE
Lk. 3:14, anyone or *a* falsely
Lk. 23:2, they began to *a* Him
Jn. 5:45, think that I shall *a*

ACCUSED
Dan. 3:8, forward and *a* the Jews
Mt. 27:12, while He was being *a*

ACCUSER
Rev. 12:10, *a* of our brethren

ACCUSING
Rom. 2:15, their thoughts *a*

ACHAIA, Greece. Acts 18:12
Paul in. Acts 18
contribution for poor by. Rom. 15:26; 2 Cor. 9:2

ACHAN, Josh. 7:18
takes the accursed thing; is stoned. Josh. 7; 22:20; 1 Chr. 2:7

ACHISH
king of Gath, helps David. 1 Sam. 21:10; 27:2; 28:1; 29:6. *See* 1 Ki. 2:39

ACHOR, Josh. 7:24
Valley of, Achan killed there. Josh. 7:26. *See* Hos. 2:15

ACHSAH, Josh. 15:16
Caleb's daughter, won in marriage by Othniel. Jud. 1:13
asks her father's blessing. Jud. 1:15

ACKNOWLEDGE
Dt. 33:9, did he *a* his brothers
Ps. 51:3, *a* my transgressions
Prov. 3:6, in all your ways *a*
Isa. 63:16, and Israel does not *a*
Jer. 3:13, *a* your iniquity
1 Cor. 14:37, spiritual, let him *a*

ACKNOWLEDGED
Ex. 2:25, of Israel, and God *a*
Ps. 32:5, *a* my sin to You

ACKNOWLEDGES
Ps. 142:4, there is no one who *a*
1 Jn. 2:23, *a* the Son has the

ACQUAINT
Job 22:21, *a* yourself with Him

ACQUAINTANCES
Ps. 88:8, You have put away my *a*
Jer. 20:10, All my *a* watched for
Lk. 23:49, But all His *a*

ACQUAINTED
Ps. 139:3, lying down, and are *a*
Isa. 53:3, a Man of sorrows and *a*

ACQUIT
Nah. 1:3, at all *a* the wicked

ACT
Dt. 11:7, seen every great *a*
Ps. 119:126, is time for You to *a*
Isa. 28:21, His *a*, His unusual *a*
Jn. 8:4, in the very *a*

ACTIONS
1 Sam. 2:3, by Him *a* are weighed

ACTS
Jud. 5:11, LORD, the righteous *a*
Ps. 103:7, to Moses, His *a*
Ps. 145:4, declare Your mighty *a*
Ps. 145:6, of Your awesome *a*

ADAM, Gen. 2:19
created. Gen. 1
called the son of God. Lk. 3:38
blessed. Gen. 1:28
placed in Eden. Gen. 2:8
first called Adam. Gen. 2:19
creatures named by. Gen. 2:19
calls his wife Eve. Gen. 3:20
his fall and punishment. Gen. 3
hides from God. Gen. 3:8
ground cursed for his sake. Gen. 3:17
his death. Gen. 5:5
his transgression. Job 31:33; Rom. 5:14
first Adam. 1 Cor. 15:45; 1 Tim. 2:13
in, all die. 1 Cor. 15:22
——— the last. 1 Cor. 15:45

ADAR
twelfth month of Hebrew calendar, February–March. Ezra 6:15; Est. 3:7

ADD
Dt. 4:2, "You shall not *a*
Prov. 30:6, Do not *a* to His words

ADDED
Mt. 6:33, things shall be *a*
Acts 2:47, And the Lord *a* to the
Acts 11:24, many people were *a*
Gal. 3:19, It was *a* because of

ADMINISTER, 2 Cor. 8:19,20; 9:12

ADMINISTERS
Dt. 10:18, *a* justice for the

ADMIRE, 2 Th. 1:10

ADMONISH
Rom. 15:14, also to *a* one another
2 Th. 3:15, *a* him as a

ADMONISHED
Eccl. 12:12, further, my son, be *a*
Zech. 3:6, Angel of the LORD *a*

ADMONISHING
Col. 3:16, *a* one another in

ADMONITION
1 Cor. 10:11, written for our *a*
Eph. 6:4, in the training and *a*

ADONIJAH, 2 Sam. 3:4
fourth son of David, usurps the kingdom. 1 Ki. 1:5,11,25
is pardoned by Solomon. 1 Ki. 1:53
seeking to obtain Abishag, is killed. 1 Ki. 2:17–25

ADONI-ZEDEK
king of Jerusalem, resists Joshua. Josh. 10:1
his death. Josh. 10:26

ADOPTION
of the children of God. Jn. 1:12; 20:17; Rom. 8:14; 2 Cor. 6:18; Gal. 4; Eph. 1:5; Heb. 2:10; 12:5; Jas. 1:18; 1 Jn. 3:1
of the Gentiles. Isa. 66:19; Hos. 2:23; Acts 15:3; Rom. 8:15,23; 9:4; Gal. 4:5; Eph. 1:5; 2; 3; Col. 1:27

ADOPTION
Rom. 8:15, the Spirit of *a*
Rom. 8:23, waiting for the *a*
Rom. 9:4, to whom pertain the *a*
Gal. 4:5, we might receive the *a*
Eph. 1:5, *a* as sons by Jesus

ADORN
Mt. 23:29 *a* the monuments
1 Tim. 2:9, also, that the women *a*

ADORNED
Job 26:13, By His Spirit He *a*
Jer. 31:4, You shall again be *a*
Lk. 21:5, temple, how it was *a*
1 Pet. 3:5, God also *a* themselves
Rev. 21:2, prepared as a bride *a*

ADRIEL, 1 Sam. 18:19

ADRIFT
Ps. 88:5, *A* among the dead

ADULLAM, Josh. 12:15
cave of. 1 Sam. 22:1; 1 Chr. 11:15

ADULTERER
Lev. 20:10, neighbor's wife, the *a*
Job 24:15, The eye of the *a*

ADULTERERS
Jer. 23:10, the land is full of *a*

1 Cor. 6:9, nor idolaters, nor *a*
Heb. 13:4, *a* God will judge
Jas. 4:4, *A* and adulteresses

ADULTERIES
Jer. 13:27, I have seen your *a*
Hos. 2:2, her sight, and her *a*
Mk. 7:21, evil thoughts, *a*

ADULTEROUS
Mt. 12:39, *a* generation

ADULTERY
of Tamar. Gen. 38:24
of David. 2 Sam. 11:2
of Herod. Mk. 6:17
woman caught in. Jn. 8:3
in what it consists. Mt. 5:28; 15:19; 19:9; Mk. 7:21; 10:11
forbidden. Ex. 20:14; Dt. 5:18; Mt. 19:18; Rom. 13:9; Gal. 5:19
penalty of. Lev. 20:10; Mal. 3:3; 1 Cor. 6:9; Heb. 13:4
spiritual. Jer. 3; 13:27; Ezek. 16; 23; Hos. 1; 2; Rev. 2:22

ADULTERY
Ex. 20:14, You shall not commit *a*
Prov. 6:32, Whoever commits *a*
Jer. 3:8, Israel had committed *a*
Mt. 5:28, already committed *a*
Mt. 5:32, is divorced commits *a*
Mk. 10:11, another commits *a*
Jn. 8:3, a woman caught in *a*
Rev. 2:22, those who commit *a*

ADVANTAGE
Job 35:3, *a* will it be to You
Eccl. 3:19, man has no *a* over
Jn. 16:7, *a* that I go away
Rom. 3:1, What *a* then has the
2 Cor. 2:11, Satan should take *a*
1 Th. 4:6, no one should take *a*
Jude 16, people to gain *a*

ADVERSARIES
1 Sam. 2:10, The *a* of the LORD
Isa. 1:24, rid Myself of My *a*
Lk. 21:15, *a* will not be able
1 Cor. 16:9, and there are many *a*
Phil. 1:28, terrified by your *a*
Heb. 10:27, will devour the *a*

ADVERSARY
Num. 22:22, in the way as an *a*
1 Sam. 29:4, battle he become our *a*
Ps. 74:10, how long will the *a*
Lam. 1:10, *a* has spread his hand
Mt. 5:25, "Agree with your *a*
Lk. 18:3, justice for me from *a*
1 Tim. 5:14, opportunity to the *a*
1 Pet. 5:8, *a* the devil walks

ADVERSITIES
1 Sam. 10:19, you from all your *a*
Ps. 31:7, known my soul in *a*

ADVERSITY
2 Chr. 15:6, them with every *a*
Ps. 10:6, I shall never be in *a*
Ps. 94:13, from the days of *a*
Prov. 17:17, brother is born for *a*
Prov. 24:10, faint in the day of *a*
Eccl. 7:14, the day of *a* consider
Isa. 30:20, you the bread of *a*

ADVICE
1 Sam. 25:33, And blessed is your *a*
2 Cor. 8:10, in this I give my *a*

ADVOCATE
1 Jn. 2:1, sins, we have an *A*

AFAR
Ex. 24:1, and worship from *a*
Isa. 60:4, sons shall come from *a*
Jer. 23:23, and not a God *a*
Lk. 16:23, and saw Abraham *a*
Acts 2:39, to all who are *a*
Eph. 2:17, to you who were *a*
Heb. 11:13, having seen them *a*

AFFAIRS
Ps. 112:5, he will guide his *a*
Phil. 1:27, I may hear of your *a*
2 Tim. 2:4, himself with the *a*

AFFECTION
1 Cor. 7:3, to his wife the *a*
Phil. 1:8, for you all with the *a*
Phil. 2:1, the Spirit, if any *a*

AFFECTIONATE
Rom. 12:10, Be kindly *a* to one

AFFIRM
Ti. 3:8, you to *a* constantly

AFFLICT
Ex. 1:11, *a* them with their
Num. 30:13, oath to *a* her soul
Jud. 16:6, may be bound to *a* you
1 Ki. 11:39, *a* the descendants
Ps. 55:19, will hear, and *a* them
Ps. 94:5, *a* Your heritage
Isa. 58:5, a man to *a* his soul
Jer. 31:28, to destroy, and to *a*
Lam. 3:33, For He does not *a*
Zeph. 3:19, deal with all who *a*

AFFLICTED
Num. 11:11, "Why have You *a*
Ruth 1:21, and the Almighty has *a*
Job 6:14, To him who is *a*
Job 34:28, hears the cry of the *a*
Ps. 44:2, You *a* the peoples
Ps. 119:67, *a* I went astray
Ps. 119:107, I am *a* very much
Ps. 129:1, a time they have *a*
Ps. 140:12, the cause of the *a*
Prov. 15:15, days of the *a* are evil
Isa. 53:4, Smitten by God, and *a*
Isa. 53:7, oppressed and He was *a*
Isa. 54:11, "O you *a* one
Isa. 58:3, Why have we *a* our
Isa. 58:10, and satisfy the *a*
Lam. 1:4, her virgins are *a*
1 Tim. 5:10, she has relieved the *a*
Heb. 11:37, being destitute, *a*

AFFLICTING
Amos 5:12, *A* the just and taking

AFFLICTION
the result of sin. 2 Sam. 12:14; Ps. 90:7; Ezek. 6:13
foretold. Gen. 15:13; Isa. 10:12; Jer. 29:17; 42:16
man born to. Job 5:6,7
comes from God. Gen. 15:13; Num. 14:33; 2 Ki. 6:33; Job 10:15; Ps. 66:11; Isa. 9:1
sent in mercy. Gen. 50:20; Ex. 1:12; Dt. 8:16; Ps. 106:43; Ezek. 20:37; Nah. 1:12; Mt. 24:9; Acts 20:23; Rom. 8:18; Heb. 12:6; Jas. 5:10; Rev. 7:14
promises of support under. Ps. 46:5; Isa. 25:4; 43:2; Jer. 16:19; 39:17; Nah. 1:7; Mt. 11:28; Jn. 14; Acts 14:22; Heb. 2:18; Rev. 3:10
resignation under. Ps. 119:75
comfort under. Ps. 27:5; Isa. 49:13; 61:2; Jer. 31:13; Mt. 5:4; Lk. 7:13; Jn. 16:20,33; 2 Cor. 1:4; 7:6; 1 Pet. 4:13
object of. 1 Cor. 11:32; 1 Pet. 5:10
effects of. 2 Cor. 4:17
proof of God's love. Prov. 3:12; Heb. 12:6; Rev. 3:19
endurance of. 1 Sam. 3:18; 2 Sam. 12:16; Neh. 9:3; Job 1:21; 2:10; 5:17; 13:15; 34:31; Ps. 18:6; 27:4; 39:9; 50:15; 55:16,22; 56:3; 71:14; Jer. 50:4; Lam. 3:39; Lk. 21:19; Rom. 12:12; 2 Cor. 1:9; 1 Th. 4:13; 2 Th. 1:4; Heb. 12:1; Jas. 1:4; 5:10; 1 Pet. 2:20
supplication under. Jud. 4:3; 1 Sam. 1:10; 2 Sam. 24:10; 2 Ki. 19:16; 20:1,2; 2 Chr. 14:11; 20:6; Ezra 9:6; Neh. 9:32; Job 10:2; 13:23; 33:26; Ps. 66:13; Jer. 17:13; 31:18; Lam. 5:1; Dan. 9:3; Hab. 3:2; Mt. 26:39; 2 Cor. 12:8; Jas. 5:13
exhortation under. Dt. 8:3; Neh. 1:8; Prov. 3:11; Jn. 5:14
confession of sin under. Num. 21:7; Job 7:20; Ps. 32:5; Isa. 64:5,6; Jer. 31:18; Mic. 7:9
repentance under. Job 34:31; Ps. 78:34; Hos. 6:1; Lk. 15:17
support under. Dt. 4:30,31; 2 Chr. 7:13,14; Job 33:26; Ps. 73:26; Isa. 10:20
deliverances from. Ps. 34:4,19; 40:2; 126:2,3; Prov. 12:13; Isa. 63:9; Jon. 2:1,2; 2 Tim. 3:11; 4:17,18
benefits of. Job 23:10; 36:8; Ps. 66:10; 119:67,71; Eccl. 7:2; Isa. 1:25; 26:9; 48:10; Lam. 3:19,27,39; Ezek. 14:11; Hos. 2:6; 5:15; Mic. 6:9; Zech. 13:9; Jn. 15:2; Acts 14:22; Rom. 5:3; 2 Cor. 4:8; 12:7; Phil. 1:12; Heb. 12:10; 1 Pet. 2:20

AFFLICTION
Gen. 41:52, in the land of my *a*
Dt. 16:3, is, the bread of *a*
1 Sam. 1:11, indeed look on the *a*
2 Ki. 14:26, LORD saw that the *a*
Job 30:16, *a* take hold of me
Job 30:27, days of *a* confront me
Job 36:8, held in the cords of *a*
Ps. 107:10, of death, bound in *a*
Ps. 119:50, is my comfort in my *a*
Eccl. 6:2, and it is an evil *a*
Isa. 63:9, *a* He was afflicted
Jer. 16:19, refuge in the day of *a*
Lam. 1:9, "O LORD, behold my *a*
Amos 6:6, not grieved for the *a*
2 Cor. 4:17, For our light *a*
Phil. 1:16, supposing to add *a*

1 Th. 1:6, the word in much *a*

AFRAID
Gen. 3:10, garden, and I was *a*
Gen. 15:1, saying, "Do not be *a*
Ex. 3:6, his face, for he was *a*
Lev. 26:6, none will make you *a*
Dt. 7:19, of whom you are *a*
Ps. 3:6, I will not be *a*
Ps. 18:4, ungodliness made me *a*
Ps. 49:16, Do not be *a* when one
Ps. 56:3, Whenever I am *a*
Ps. 65:8, farthest parts are *a*
Isa. 8:12, a conspiracy, nor be *a*
Isa. 17:2, one will make them *a*
Isa. 51:12, that you should be *a*
Dan. 4:5, dream which made me *a*
Mt. 14:27, do not be *a*
Rom. 13:4, if you do evil, be *a*
1 Pet. 3:6, do good and are not *a*

AFTERWARD
Ex. 11:1, *A* he will let you go
Job 18:2, *a* we will speak
Ps. 73:24, *a* receive me to glory
Jn. 13:36, you shall follow Me *a*
1 Cor. 15:23, the firstfruits, *a*

AGABUS
famine and Paul's sufferings foretold by. Acts 11:28; 21:10

AGAG
spoken of by Balaam. Num. 24:7
king of Amalek, spared by Saul, killed by Samuel. 1 Sam. 15

AGAIN
Mt. 20:19, day He will rise *a*
Jn. 3:7, 'You must be born *a*
Heb. 6:6, to renew them *a*
1 Pet. 1:23, having been born *a*

AGAINST
Gen. 16:12, his hand shall be *a*
Lev. 20:3, 'I will set My face *a*
Mt. 10:35, come to 'set a man *a*
Mt. 12:25, or house divided *a*
Mt. 12:30, Me is *a* Me
Mt. 12:31, *a* the Spirit will not
Mt. 24:7, For nation will rise *a*
Mt. 26:55, out, as *a* a robber
Lk. 15:18, I have sinned *a*
Jn. 13:18, lifted up his heel *a*
Acts 4:26, LORD and *a* His Christ
Acts 9:5, to kick *a* the goads
Acts 21:28, all men everywhere *a*
Acts 23:9, let us not fight *a*
Gal. 3:21, *a* the promises of God
Eph. 6:12, we do not wrestle *a*
Rev. 2:20, I have a few things *a*

AGE
Gen. 18:11, well advanced in *a*
Gen. 48:10, Israel were dim with *a*
1 Sam. 2:33, the flower of their *a*
Job 5:26, the grave at a full *a*
Ps. 39:5, *a* is as nothing
Mk. 10:30, and in the *a* to come
Lk. 20:34, "The sons of this *a*
Jn. 9:21, He is of *a*
Heb. 5:14, who are of full *a*
Heb. 6:5, the powers of the *a*

AGED
Job 12:12, Wisdom is with *a*
Phile. 9, a one as Paul, the *a*

AGES
1 Cor. 2:7, ordained before the *a*
Eph. 3:5, *a* was not made known
Heb. 9:26, at the end of the *a*

AGONY
Christ's, in the garden. Mt. 26:36; Lk. 22:44

AGREE
Mt. 5:25, *A* with your adversary
Mt. 18:19, that if two of you *a*
Mk. 14:56, testimonies did not *a*
1 Jn. 5:8, and these three *a*

AGREED
Amos 3:3, unless they are *a*
Lk. 22:5, they were glad, and *a*

AGREEMENT
Isa. 28:15, with Sheol we are in *a*
Dan. 11:6, the North to make an *a*
2 Cor. 6:16, what *a* has the temple

AGRIPPA, Acts 25:13
Paul's defense before. Acts 25:22; 26
almost persuaded. Acts 26:28

AGUR
prophecy. Prov. 30

AHA
Ps. 35:21; 40:15; 70:3; Ezek. 25:3; 26:2; 36:2

AHAB
king of Israel. 1 Ki. 16:29
marries Jezebel; his idolatry. 1 Ki. 16:31
meets Elijah. 1 Ki. 18:17
defeats the Syrians. 1 Ki. 20
punished for sparing Ben-Hadad. 1 Ki. 20:42
takes Naboth's vineyard. 1 Ki. 21:17
his repentance. 1 Ki. 21:27
trusts false prophets, and is mortally wounded at Ramoth Gilead. 1 Ki. 22:6,34; 2 Chr. 18
——— son of Kolaiah, and Zedekiah, lying prophets. Jer. 29:21

AHASUERUS
reigns from India to Ethiopia. Est. 1:1
Vashti's disobedience, and divorce. Est. 1:12; 2:4
makes Esther queen. Est. 2:17
advances Haman. Est. 3:1
his decree to destroy the Jews. Est. 3:12
rewards Mordecai's loyalty. Est. 6
hangs Haman. Est. 7:9; 8:7
advances Mordecai. Est. 9:4; 10

AHAZ, 2 Ki. 15:38
king of Judah. 2 Ki. 16
despoils the temple. 2 Ki. 16:17
his idolatry. 2 Chr. 28:2
afflicted by Syrians. 2 Chr. 28:5
comforted by Isaiah. Isa. 7
will not ask a sign. Isa. 7:12

AHAZIAH, 1 Ki. 22:40
king of Judah, his wicked reign. 2 Ki. 8:25
goes with Joram to meet Jehu. 2 Ki. 9:21
struck by Jehu. 2 Ki. 9:27; 2 Chr. 22:9
——— king of Israel. 1 Ki. 22:40,49
his sickness and idolatry. 2 Ki. 1
his judgment by Elijah. 2 Ki. 1

AHIJAH, 1 Ki. 11:29
prophesies to Jeroboam against Solomon. 1 Ki. 11:31; against Jeroboam, and foretells his son's death. 1 Ki. 14:7

AHIKAM, 2 Ki. 22:12
protects Jeremiah. Jer. 26:24

AHIMAAZ
son of Zadok, serves David. 2 Sam. 15:27; 17:17; 18:19

AHIMELECH, 1 Sam. 21:1
slain by Saul's order, for assisting David. 1 Sam. 22:18

AHITHOPHEL, 2 Sam. 15:12
his treachery. 2 Sam. 15:31; 16:20
disgrace, and suicide. 2 Sam. 17:1,23

AHITUB, 1 Sam. 14:3

AHOLIAB, Ex. 31:6
inspired to construct the tabernacle. Ex. 35:34; 36

AHOLIBAMAH, Gen. 36:2

AI, Josh. 7:2
men of, contend with Israel. Josh. 7:5

AIDE
Acts 12:20, the king's personal *a*

AIJALON, Josh. 19:42

AIR
Gen. 1:26, the birds of the *a*
Lk. 9:58, of the *a* have nests
Eph. 2:2, of the power of the *a*
1 Cor. 9:26, as one who beats the *a*
1 Cor. 14:9, be speaking into the *a*
1 Th. 4:17, the Lord in the *a*
Rev. 16:17, his bowl into the *a*

ALARM
2 Chr. 13:12, to sound the *a* against
Zeph. 1:16, and *a* against the fortified

ALEXANDER, Mk. 15:21
——— a member of the council. Acts 4:6
——— an Ephesian Jew. Acts 19:33
——— the coppersmith. 1 Tim. 1:20; 2 Tim. 4:14

ALEXANDRIA
the city named after Alexander the Great. Acts 18:24

ALIEN
Dt. 23:7, because you were an *a*
Job 19:15, I am an *a* in their
Mal. 3:5, who turn away an *a*

ALIENATED
Ezek. 23:17, *a* herself from them

Eph. 4:18, darkened, being *a*
Col. 1:21, you, who once were *a*

ALIENS
1 Chr. 29:15, For we are *a* and
Jer. 2:25, For I have loved *a*
Hos. 7:9, *A* have devoured his
Eph. 2:12, Christ, being *a*
Heb. 11:34, the armies of the *a*

ALIKE
Eccl. 9:2, All things come *a*
Rom. 14:5, esteems every day *a*

ALIVE
Gen. 7:23, in the ark remained *a*
Num. 16:33, with them went down *a*
Dt. 4:4, LORD your God are *a*
Dt. 32:39, I kill and I make *a*
Ps. 55:15, Let them go down *a*
Ezek. 18:27, he preserves himself *a*
Mk. 16:11, heard that He was *a*
Lk. 15:24, was dead and is *a*
Acts 1:3, presented Himself *a*
Rom. 6:11, indeed to sin, but *a*
Rom. 7:9, I was *a* once without
1 Cor. 15:22, all shall be made *a*
Eph. 2:5, trespasses, made us *a*
Col. 2:13, flesh, He has made *a*
1 Th. 4:15, that we who are *a*
1 Pet. 3:18, the flesh but made *a*
Rev. 1:18, and behold, I am *a*
Rev. 3:1, a name that you are *a*
Rev. 19:20, These two were cast *a*

ALL
Eccl. 12:13, for this is man's *a*

ALLELUIA
Rev. 19:3, Again they said, "*A*

ALLOW
Ps. 16:10, *a* Your Holy One
Ps. 89:33, *a* My faithfulness
Mt. 23:13, *a* those who are
Acts 2:27, *a* Your Holy One
1 Cor. 10:13, who will not *a*

ALLOWED
Acts 14:16, bygone generations *a*

ALLURE
Hos. 2:14, behold, I will *a*
2 Pet. 2:18, of emptiness, they *a*

ALMIGHTY (God)
Gen. 17:1; Ex. 6:3; Num. 24:4; Ruth 1:20; Job 5:17; Isa. 13:6; Ezek. 1:24; Rev. 1:8. *See* GOD

ALMOND
Ex. 25:33, *a* blossoms on one
Eccl. 12:5, *a* tree blossoms

ALMOST
Ps. 73:2, for me, my feet had *a*
Acts 26:28, *a* persuade me to
Heb. 9:22, *a* all things are

ALMS
Lk. 11:41, But rather give *a*
Lk. 12:33, you have and give *a*
Acts 24:17, I came to bring *a*

ALOES
Ps. 45:8, with myrrh and *a*
Prov. 7:17, my bed with myrrh, *a*
Jn. 19:39, of myrrh and *a*

ALPHA
the first letter of the Greek alphabet. Rev. 21:6

ALPHA
Rev. 1:8, "I am the *A* and the
Rev. 22:13, "I am the *A* and the

ALPHAEUS, Mt. 10:3

ALTAR
built by Noah. Gen. 8:20; Abram. Gen. 12:7,8; 13:4,18; 22:9; Isaac. Gen. 26:25; Jacob. Gen. 33:20; 35:7; Moses. Ex. 17:15; Balaam. Num. 23:1; Reubenites, etc. Josh. 22:10; Saul. 1 Sam. 14:35; Elijah. 1 Ki. 18:30,32; Solomon. 2 Chr. 4:1
of Damascus. 2 Ki. 16:10
commanded. Gen. 35:1
how built:
of earth. Ex. 20:24
of stone. Ex. 20:25
of wood. Ex. 27:1
of incense. Ex. 30:1; 37:25
golden. Rev. 8:3; 9:13
gift brought to. Mt. 5:23
we have an. Heb. 13:10

ALTAR
Gen. 8:20, Then Noah built an *a*
Ex. 20:24, 'An *a* of earth you
Lev. 6:9, *a* shall be kept
Lev. 17:11, it to you upon the *a*
Num. 7:84, offering for the *a*
Josh. 22:34, of Gad called the *a*
Jud. 6:25, and tear down the *a*
2 Sam. 24:18, "Go up, erect an *a*
1 Ki. 13:2, out against the *a*
Ps. 43:4, I will go to the *a*
Isa. 19:19, day there will be an *a*
Lam. 2:7, Lord has spurned His *a*
Mal. 2:13, you cover the *a*
Mt. 5:23, your gift to the *a*
Mt. 23:18, swears by the *a*
Acts 17:23, I even found an *a*
1 Cor. 9:13, the offerings of the *a*
1 Cor. 10:18, partakers of the *a*
Heb. 13:10, We have an *a* from
Jas. 2:21, Isaac his son on the *a*
Rev. 8:3, and stood at the *a*

ALTARS
2 Ki. 18:22, *a* Hezekiah has taken
Ps. 84:3, Even Your *a*, O LORD
Jer. 17:1, on the horns of your *a*
Ezek. 6:4, *a* shall be broken
Hos. 8:11, has made many *a*
Hos. 12:11, *a* shall be heaps
Amos 3:14, destruction on the *a*
Rom. 11:3, and torn down Your *a*

ALTERED
Lk. 9:29, of His face was *a*

ALWAYS
Prov. 8:30, delight, Rejoicing *a*
Mt. 26:11, the poor with you *a*
Mt. 26:11, Me you do not have *a*
Mt. 28:20, lo, I am with you *a*
Lk. 15:31, 'Son, you are *a*
Lk. 18:1, to them, that men *a*
1 Cor. 15:58, immovable, *a*
Phil. 4:4, Rejoice in the Lord *a*
1 Th. 4:17, thus we shall *a*
1 Pet. 3:15, *a* be ready to give a

AM
Ex. 3:14, to Moses, "I *A* WHO I *A*
Isa. 44:6, First and I *a* the Last
Mt. 18:20, in My name, I *a*
Jn. 6:35, *a* the bread of life
Jn. 8:12, *a* the light of the
Jn. 8:23, I *a* from above
Jn. 8:58, Abraham was, I *A*
Jn. 10:9, "I *a* the door
Jn. 10:11, *a* the good shepherd
Jn. 11:25, *a* the resurrection
Jn. 14:6, to him, "I *a* the way
1 Cor. 15:10, of God I *a* what I *a*

AMALEK, Gen. 36:12
fights with Israel in Rephidim, and is defeated. Ex. 17:8,13
perpetual war declared. Ex. 17:16; Dt. 25:17
struck by: Gideon. Jud. 7:12
Saul. 1 Sam. 14:48; 15:8
David. 1 Sam. 27:9; 30:17

AMALEKITE
killed by David. 2 Sam. 1:10,15

AMASA
captain of the army of Absalom. 2 Sam. 17:25
killed by Joab. 2 Sam. 20:9,10; 1 Ki. 2:5

AMAZED
Mk. 16:8, trembled and were *a*

AMAZIAH
king of Judah, his good reign. 2 Ki. 14:1; 2 Chr. 25:1
defeats Edom. 2 Chr. 25:11
defeated by Joash king of Israel. 2 Chr. 25:21
killed at Lachish. 2 Ki. 14:19
——— priest of Bethel. Amos 7:10

AMBASSADOR
Prov. 13:17, but a faithful *a*
Eph. 6:20, for which I am an *a*

AMBASSADORS
Isa. 18:2, which sends *a* by sea
Isa. 33:7, cry outside, the *a*
2 Cor. 5:20, we are *a* for Christ

AMBITION
rebuked. Mt. 18:1; 20:25; 23:8; Lk. 22:24
punishment of. Prov. 17:19; Isa. 14:12; Ezek. 31:10
of: Babel. Gen. 11:4
Aaron and Miriam. Num. 12:10
Korah, Dathan, and Abiram. Num. 16:3
Absalom. 2 Sam. 18:9
Adonijah. 1 Ki. 1:5
Babylon. Jer. 51:53
James and John. Mt. 20:21
man of sin. 2 Th. 2:3
Diotrephes. 3 Jn. 9

AMBITION
Phil. 1:16, Christ from selfish *a*
Phil. 2:3, through selfish *a*

AMEN
1 Cor. 14:16, uninformed say "*A*
2 Cor. 1:20, are Yes, and in Him *A*
Rev. 5:14, creatures said, "*A*

AMEND
Jer. 7:3, *A* your ways and your
Jer. 35:15, from his evil way, *a*

AMISS, Dan. 3:29; Jas. 4:3

AMMINADAB, Ex. 6:23

AMMON
people of. Gen. 19:38
not to be meddled with. Dt. 2:19
not to enter the assembly. Dt. 23:3
make war on Israel, and are conquered by Jephthah. Jud. 11:4,33
killed by Saul. 1 Sam. 11:11
outrage David's servants. 2 Sam. 10
conquered by David. 2 Sam. 12:26
prophecies concerning. Jer. 25:21; 49:1; Ezek. 21:28; 25:2,3; Amos 1:13; Zeph. 2:8

AMNON
son of David. 2 Sam. 3:2
forces Tamar. 2 Sam. 13
killed by Absalom. 2 Sam. 13:28

AMON, 2 Ki. 21:18
king of Judah. 2 Ki. 21:19; 2 Chr. 33:20
his idolatry. 2 Ki. 21:21; 2 Chr. 33:23
killed by his servants. 2 Ki. 21:23

AMOS
declares God's judgment upon the nations. Amos 1:1,2
and upon Israel. Amos 3:1
his call. Amos 7:14,15
foretells Israel's restoration. Amos 9:11

AMRAM, Ex. 6:18

ANAK, Num. 13:22

ANAKIM
a tribe called after Anak. Dt. 1:28
——— giants. Num. 13:33; Dt. 9:2
cut off by Joshua. Josh. 11:21

ANANIAS
his lie and death. Acts 5:1
——— disciple, sent to Paul at Damascus. Acts 9:10; 22:12
——— high priest, Paul brought before. Acts 22:30
Paul struck by order of. Acts 23:2
rebuked by Paul. Acts 23:3

ANATHOTH, Josh. 21:18
men of, condemned for persecuting Jeremiah. Jer. 11:21. *See* 1 Ki. 2:26

ANCHOR
Heb. 6:19, hope we have as an *a*

ANCIENT
Prov. 23:10, Do not remove the *a*
Isa. 37:26, *a* times that I
Dan. 7:22, "until the *A* of Days

ANDREW, Mk. 1:29
the apostle. Mt. 4:18; Mk. 13:3; Jn. 1:40; 6:8; 12:22; Acts 1:13

ANDRONICUS
disciple at Rome. Rom. 16:7

ANGEL
Gen. 16:7, Now the *A* of the LORD
Gen. 48:16, *A* who has redeemed me
Ex. 23:20, "Behold, I send an *A*
Num. 22:23, the donkey saw the *A*
Jud. 6:22, For I have seen the *A*
Jud. 13:17, Manoah said to the *A*
1 Sam. 29:9, in my sight as an *a*
2 Sam. 24:16, *a* who was destroying
2 Ki. 19:35, night that the *a*
Isa. 63:9, the *A* of His Presence
Hos. 12:4, struggled with the *A*
Zech. 3:3, standing before the *A*
Zech. 12:8, like God, like the *A*
Mt. 1:20, things, behold, an *a*
Mt. 28:2, for an *a* of the Lord
Lk. 1:11, Then an *a* of the Lord
Lk. 2:9, And behold, an *a*
Lk. 22:43, *a* appeared to Him
Jn. 5:4, For an *a* went down at
Jn. 12:29, *a* has spoken to Him
Acts 5:19, But at night an *a*
Acts 7:35, *A* who appeared to him
Acts 12:23, immediately an *a*
Acts 23:8, and no *a* or spirit
Acts 23:9, *a* has spoken to him
Acts 27:23, by me this night an *a*
2 Cor. 11:14, himself into an *a*
Gal. 1:8, even if we, or an *a*
Rev. 5:2, Then I saw a strong *a*
Rev. 9:11, over them the *a*
Rev. 19:17, Then I saw an *a*
Rev. 22:16, Jesus, have sent My *a*

ANGEL OF THE LORD
appears to Hagar. Gen. 16:7; 21:17; Abraham. Gen. 18; Lot. Gen. 19; Moses. Ex. 3:2; Balaam. Num. 22:23; Israelites. Jud. 2; Gideon. Jud. 6:11; Manoah's wife. Jud. 13:3; Manoah. Jud. 13:11; David. 2 Sam. 24:16; 1 Chr. 21:16; Elijah. 1 Ki. 19:7; Daniel. Dan. 8:16; 9:21; 10:11; 12; Joseph. Mt. 1:20; Mary Magdalene. Mt. 28:2–7; Zacharias. Lk. 1:11; Mary. Lk. 1:26; the shepherds. Lk. 2:8–12; Peter. Acts 5:19; 12:7; Philip. Acts 8:26; Cornelius. Acts 10:3; Paul. Acts 27:23

ANGELS
nature, office, duties, and characteristics of. 2 Sam. 14:20; 1 Ki. 19:5; Neh. 9:6; Job 25:3; 38:7; Ps. 68:17; 91:11; 103:20; 104:4; 148:2; Isa. 6:2; Dan. 6:22; Mt. 13:39; 16:27; 18:10; 24:31; 25:31; Mk. 8:38; Lk. 15:7; 16:22; Acts 7:53; 12:7; 27:23; Eph. 1:21; Phil. 2:9; Col. 1:16; 2:10; 1 Th. 4:16; 2 Th. 1:7; 1 Tim. 3:16; 5:21; Heb. 1:6; 2:2; 12:22; 1 Pet. 1:12; 3:22; 2 Pet. 2:11; Jude 9; Rev. 5:2; 7; 11; 12:7; 14:6; 17
announce the nativity. Lk. 2:13
minister to Christ. Mt. 4:11; 26:53; Lk. 22:43; Jn. 1:51
saints shall judge. 1 Cor. 6:3
not to be worshiped. Col. 2:18; Rev. 19:10; 22:9
——— rebellious. 2 Pet. 2:4; Jude 6
——— of the churches. Rev. 1:20; 2; 3

ANGELS
Job 4:18, If He charges His *a*
Ps. 8:5, lower than the *a*
Ps. 91:11, He shall give His *a*
Ps. 148:2, Praise Him, all His *a*
Mt. 4:6, He shall give His *a*
Mt. 13:49, *a* will come forth
Mt. 18:10, *a* always see the face
Mt. 22:30, but are like *a*
Mt. 24:36, not even the *a*
Mt. 25:31, and all the holy *a*
Mt. 26:53, twelve legions of *a*
Lk. 15:10, the presence of the *a*
Lk. 16:22, was carried by the *a*
Lk. 20:36, are equal to the *a*
Jn. 20:12, And she saw two *a*
1 Cor. 6:3, that we shall judge *a*
1 Cor. 11:10, head, because of the *a*
Col. 2:18, and worship of *a*
2 Th. 1:7, with His mighty *a*
1 Tim. 3:16, the Spirit, seen by *a*
Heb. 1:4, much better than the *a*
Heb. 2:16, does not give aid to *a*
Heb. 12:22, company of *a*
Heb. 13:2, entertained *a*
1 Pet. 1:12, things which *a* desire
2 Pet. 2:4, did not spare the *a*
Jude 6, *a* who did not keep
Rev. 12:7, Michael and his *a*

ANGER
nature and effects of. Gen. 27:45; 44:18; 49:7; Ex. 32:19; Ps. 37:8; 69:24; Prov. 15:18; 16:32; 19:11; 21:19; 29:22; Eccl. 7:9; Isa. 13:9; 30:27; Jer. 44:6; Mt. 5:22; Ti. 1:7. *See* WRATH
remedy for. Prov. 15:1; 21:14
to be put away. Eph. 4:26,31; Col. 3:8

ANGER (divine)
Gen. 3:14; 4; Dt. 29:20; 32:19; Josh. 23:16; 2 Ki. 22:13; Ezra 8:22; Job 9:13; Ps. 7:11; 21:8; 78:21,58; 89:30; 90:7; 99:8; 106:40; Prov. 1:30; Isa. 1; 3:8; 9:13; 13:9; 47:6; Jer. 3:5; 7:19; 44:3; Nah. 1:2; Mk. 3:5; 10:14; Jn. 3:36; Rom. 1:18; 3:5; 1 Cor. 10:22; Eph. 5:6; Col. 3:6; 1 Th. 2:16; Heb. 3:18; 10:26; Rev. 21:8; 22
aroused. Ex. 4:14; Num. 11:1; 12:9; Josh. 7:1; 2 Sam. 6:7; 24:1; 2 Ki. 13:3; Jer. 17:4; Hos. 8:5; Zech. 10:3
slow. Ps. 103:8; Jon. 4:2; Nah. 1:3
deferred. Ps. 38; 103:9; Isa. 48:9; Jer. 2:35; 3:12; Hos. 14:4; Jon. 3:9,10; Col. 3:8
instances of. Gen. 19; Ex. 14:24; Job 9:13; 14:13; Ps. 76:6; 78:49; 90:7; Isa. 9:19; Jer. 7:20; 10:10; Lam. 1; Ezek. 7; 9; Nah. 1
treasured up for the wicked. Rom. 2:5; 2 Pet. 3:7
to be prayed against. Ex. 32:11; 2 Sam. 24:17; Ps. 2:12; 6; 27:9;

30:8; 38; 39:10; 74; 76:7; 79:5; 80:4; 85:4; 90:11; Isa. 64:9; Jer. 4:8; Lam. 3:39; Dan. 9:16; Mic. 7:9; Hab. 3:2; Zeph. 2:2; 3:8; Mt. 10:28; Lk. 18:13
propitiation of, by Christ. Rom. 3:25; 5:9; 2 Cor. 5:18; Eph. 2:14; Col. 1:20; 1 Th. 1:10; 1 Jn. 2:2
turned away by repentance. 1 Ki. 21:29; Job 33:27,28; Ps. 106:45; 107:13,19; Jer. 3:12; 18:7; 31:18; Joel 2:14; Lk. 15:18

ANGER
Gen. 49:7, Cursed be their *a*
Num. 25:4, sun, that the fierce *a*
Dt. 13:17, fierceness of His *a*
Dt. 29:24, of this great *a*
Jud. 10:7, So the *a* of the LORD
1 Ki. 16:2, to provoke Me to *a*
Ps. 30:5, For His *a* is but for a
Ps. 69:24, let Your wrathful *a*
Ps. 78:38, a time He turned His *a*
Ps. 78:50, made a path for His *a*
Ps. 85:5, You prolong Your *a*
Ps. 90:11, the power of Your *a*
Ps. 103:8, gracious, slow to *a*
Ps. 103:9, Nor will He keep His *a*
Prov. 15:1, harsh word stirs up *a*
Prov. 20:2, *a* sins against his own
Eccl. 7:9, *a* rests in the bosom
Isa. 1:4, *a* the Holy One of
Isa. 5:25, *a* is not turned away
Isa. 12:1, *a* is turned away
Jer. 3:12, 'I will not cause My *a*
Jer. 36:7, For great is the *a*
Ezek. 7:3, and I will send My *a*
Mic. 7:18, does not retain His *a*
Nah. 1:6, fierceness of His *a*
Zech. 10:3, *a* is kindled against
Mk. 3:5, around at them with *a*
Eph. 4:31, bitterness, wrath, *a*

ANGRY
Gen. 4:6, Cain, "Why are you *a*
Gen. 18:30, "Let not the Lord be *a*
Ps. 2:12, the Son, lest He be *a*
Ps. 7:11, judge, and God is *a*
Ps. 76:7, When once You are *a*
Ps. 79:5, Will you be *a* forever
Prov. 22:24, friendship with an *a*
Prov. 25:23, backbiting tongue an *a*
Prov. 29:22, *a* man stirs up strife
Eccl. 7:9, in your spirit to be *a*
Isa. 47:6, I was *a* with My people
Isa. 57:16, nor will I always be *a*
Isa. 57:17, covetousness I was *a*
Jon. 4:4, right for you to be *a*
Zech. 1:2, LORD has been very *a*
Zech. 1:15, I am exceedingly *a*
Mt. 5:22, you that whoever is *a*
Eph. 4:26, "Be *a*, and do not
Heb. 3:10, Therefore I was *a*
Heb. 3:17, with whom was He *a*
Rev. 11:18, The nations were *a*

ANGUISH
2 Sam. 1:9, *a* has come upon me
Job 15:24, *a* make him afraid
Ps. 38:18, I will be in *a* over my
Ps. 119:143, *a* have overtaken
Jn. 16:21, longer remembers the *a*
Rom. 2:9, tribulation and *a*

2 Cor. 2:4, much affliction and *a*

ANIMAL
Gen. 7:2, of every clean *a*
Lev. 24:18, 'Whoever kills an *a*
Prov. 12:10, the life of his *a*
Lk. 10:34, set him on his own *a*

ANIMALS
Gen. 6:20, of *a* after their kind
Ps. 66:15, sacrifices of fat *a*
Acts 10:12, of four-footed *a*
Rom. 1:23, and four-footed *a*

ANISE
Mt. 23:23, tithe of mint and *a*

ANNA
a prophetess. Lk. 2:36

ANNAS
high priest. Lk. 3:2
Christ brought to. Jn. 18:13,24
Peter and John before. Acts 4:6

ANNUL
Isa. 14:27, and who will *a*
Gal. 3:17, years later, cannot *a*

ANNULLING
Heb. 7:18, one hand there is an *a*

ANNULS
Gal. 3:15, is confirmed, no one *a*

ANOINT
Ex. 28:41, You shall *a* them
Dt. 28:40, but you shall not *a*
1 Sam. 16:3, you shall *a* for Me
2 Sam. 14:2, *a* yourself with oil
Ps. 23:5, *a* my head with oil
Isa. 21:5, Arise, you princes, *a*
Dan. 9:24, *a* the Most Holy
Mt. 6:17, when you fast, *a*
Mk. 14:8, *a* My body for burial
Mk. 16:1, they might come and *a*
Rev. 3:18, *a* your eyes with eye

ANOINTED
the (Christ). Isa. 61:1; Lk. 4:18; Acts 4:27; 10:38
the LORD's. 1 Sam. 24:10; 26:9
My. 1 Sam. 2:35; 1 Chr. 16:22; Ps. 132:10

ANOINTED
Lev. 16:32, the priest, who is *a*
1 Sam. 16:6, "Surely the LORD's *a*
2 Sam. 1:14, destroy the LORD's *a*
2 Sam. 19:21, he cursed the LORD's *a*
2 Sam. 22:51, shows mercy to His *a*
1 Chr. 16:22, "Do not touch My *a*
Ps. 20:6, the LORD saves His *a*
Isa. 61:1, because the LORD has *a*
Zech. 4:14, "These are the two *a*
Lk. 4:18, Because He has *a*
Lk. 7:46, but this woman has *a*
Jn. 9:6, *a* the eyes of the
Jn. 11:2, that Mary who *a*
Acts 4:27, Jesus, whom You *a*
2 Cor. 1:21, and has *a* us is God

ANOINTING
of Aaron and his sons as priests. Lev. 6:20; 8:10; 10:7; Saul as king. 1 Sam. 10:1; David. 1 Sam. 16:13; Solomon. 1 Ki. 1:39; Elisha. 1 Ki. 19:16; Jehu. 2 Ki. 9:6; Joash. 2 Ki. 11:12
of Christ by Mary. Mt. 26:6; Mk. 14:3; Jn. 12:3; by a woman who was a sinner. Lk. 7:37
of the Spirit. 2 Cor. 1:21; 1 Jn. 2:20

ANOINTING
Ex. 37:29, also made the holy *a*
Jas. 5:14, them pray over him, *a*
1 Jn. 2:20, But you have an *a*
1 Jn. 2:27, but as the same *a*

ANOTHER
Jn. 13:34, that you love one *a*
Jn. 14:16, and He will give you *a*
Acts 1:20, 'Let *a* take his

ANSWER
Gen. 41:16, will give Pharaoh an *a*
2 Sam. 24:13, *a* I should take back
Job 9:3, Him, he could not *a*
Job 13:22, Call, and I will *a*
Job 31:14, how shall I *a* Him
Job 40:7, and you shall *a*
Ps. 102:2, the day that I call, *a*
Ps. 143:1, In Your faithfulness *a*
Prov. 15:1, *a* turns away wrath
Prov. 15:23, A man has joy by the *a*
Prov. 24:26, He who gives a right *a*
Prov. 26:4, *a* a fool according
Isa. 50:2, was there none to *a*
Mic. 3:7, for there is no *a*
Lk. 12:11, or what you should *a*
2 Cor. 5:12, you may have an *a*
Col. 4:6, ought to *a* each one

ANSWERS
Prov. 18:13, *a* a matter before he
Prov. 18:23, but the rich *a*
Eccl. 10:19, money *a* everything

ANT
Prov. 6:6, Go to the *a*

ANTICHRIST
adversary to Christ. 1 Jn. 2:18,22; 2 Jn. 7. *See* 2 Th. 2:9; 1 Tim. 4:1

ANTICHRIST
1 Jn. 2:18, heard that the *A*
1 Jn. 2:22, *a* who denies the
1 Jn. 4:3, is the spirit of the *A*
2 Jn. 7, is a deceiver and an *a*

ANTIOCH
named in honor of Antiochus. Acts 6:5
——— (Syria), disciples first called Christians at. Acts 11:26
Barnabas and Saul called to apostleship at. Acts 13:1
Paul withstands Peter at. Gal. 2:11
——— (Pisidia), Paul's first address at. Acts 13:16
Paul and Barnabas persecuted at. Acts 13:50

ANTIPAS
martyr. Rev. 2:13

ANTITYPE
1 Pet. 3:21, *a* which now saves us

ANXIETIES
Ps. 94:19, the multitude of my *a*

Ps. 139:23, Try me, and know my *a*

ANXIETY
Prov. 12:25, *A* in the heart of man
Ezek. 12:19, eat their bread with *a*

ANXIOUS
Lk. 12:29, drink, nor have an *a*
Phil. 4:6, Be *a* for nothing

APART
Ex. 13:12, that you shall set *a*
Lev. 15:19, she shall be set *a*
Ps. 4:3, the LORD has set *a*
Rom. 3:28, justified by faith *a*

APHEK, Josh. 12:18
defeat of Saul at. 1 Sam. 29:1. *See* Josh. 13:4; 1 Sam. 4:1; 1 Ki. 20:26

APOLLOS
(another form of Apollonius or Apollodorus), eloquent and mighty in the Scriptures. Acts 18:24; 19:1; 1 Cor. 1:12; 3:4

APOLLYON, Rev. 9:11

APOSTATES
Dt. 13:13; Mt. 24:10; Lk. 8:13; Jn. 6:66; Heb. 3:12; 6:4; 2 Pet. 3:17; 1 Jn. 2
their doom. Zeph. 1:4; 2 Th. 2:8; 1 Tim. 4:1; Heb. 10:25; 2 Pet. 2:17

APOSTLE
Rom. 1:1, called to be an *a*
Rom. 11:13, inasmuch as I am an *a*
1 Cor. 9:1, Am I not an *a*
2 Cor. 12:12, the signs of an *a* were
1 Tim. 2:7, a preacher and an *a*
Heb. 3:1, consider the *A*

APOSTLES
calling of the. Mt. 4:18,21; 9:9; Mk. 1:16; Lk. 5:10; Jn. 1:38
their appointment and powers. Mt. 10; 16:19; 18:18; 28:19; Mk. 3:13; 16:15; Lk. 6:13; 9; 12:11; 24:47; Jn. 20:23; Acts 9:15,27; 20:24; 1 Cor. 5:3; 2 Th. 3:6; 2 Tim. 1:11
witnesses of Christ. Lk. 1:2; 24:33,48; Acts 1:2,22; 10:41; 1 Cor. 9:1; 15:5; 2 Pet. 1:16; 1 Jn. 1:1
their sufferings. Mt. 10:16; Lk. 21:16; Jn. 15:20; 16:2,33; Acts 4; 1 Cor. 4:9; 2 Cor. 1:4; 4:8; 11:23; Rev. 1:9
their names written in heaven. Rev. 21:14
false, condemned. 2 Cor. 11:13

APOSTLES
Mt. 10:2, of the twelve *a*
Lk. 6:13, whom He also named *a*
1 Cor. 4:9, displayed us, the *a*
1 Cor. 15:9, am the least of the *a*
2 Cor. 11:5, to the most eminent *a*
2 Cor. 11:13, themselves into *a*
Gal. 1:19, none of the other *a*
Eph. 4:11, gave some to be *a*
Rev. 2:2, who say they are *a*
Rev. 18:20, heaven, and you holy *a*

APOSTLESHIP
Acts 1:25, in this ministry and *a*
Rom. 1:5, received grace and *a*
1 Cor. 9:2, are the seal of my *a*
Gal. 2:8, in Peter for the *a*

APPAREL
exhortations concerning. Dt. 22:5; 1 Tim. 2:9; 1 Pet. 3:3
of Jewish women described. Isa. 3:16

APPAREL
Isa. 63:1, is glorious in His *a*
Zeph. 1:8, clothed with foreign *a*
Acts 1:10, by them in white *a*
1 Tim. 2:9, themselves in modest *a*
Jas. 2:2, gold rings, in fine *a*
1 Pet. 3:3, or putting on fine *a*

APPEAL
Acts 25:11, I *a* to Caesar
Phile. 9, love's sake I rather *a*

APPEAR
Gen. 1:9, and let the dry land *a*
Ex. 23:17, all your males shall *a*
Dt. 31:11, all Israel comes to *a*
Ps. 42:2, shall I come and *a*
Ps. 90:16, Let Your work *a*
Ps. 102:16, He shall *a* in His
Ezek. 21:24, doings your sins *a*
Mt. 6:16, faces that they may *a*
Mt. 23:28, also outwardly *a*
Lk. 19:11, kingdom of God would *a*
2 Cor. 5:10, For we must all *a*
Heb. 9:28, for Him He will *a*
1 Pet. 4:18, and the sinner *a*

APPEARANCE
1 Sam. 16:7, Do not look at his *a*
Lam. 4:8, *a* is blacker than soot
Lk. 9:29, As He prayed, the *a*
Jn. 7:24, judge according to *a*
2 Cor. 5:12, those who boast in *a*
2 Cor. 10:7, to the outward *a*
Phil. 2:8, found in *a* as a man
Col. 2:23, indeed have an *a*

APPEARED
Lk. 1:11, an angel of the Lord *a*
Lk. 9:31, who *a* in glory and
Ti. 2:11, brings salvation has *a*
Heb. 9:26, of the ages, He has *a*

APPEARING
1 Tim. 6:14, Lord Jesus Christ's *a*
2 Tim. 1:10, been revealed by the *a*
2 Tim. 4:1, and the dead at His *a*
2 Tim. 4:8, who have loved His *a*
Ti. 2:13, hope and glorious *a*

APPEARS
Mal. 3:2, can stand when He *a*
Col. 3:4, who is our life *a*
1 Pet. 5:4, the Chief Shepherd *a*
1 Jn. 2:28, that when He *a*

APPETITE
Job 38:39, or satisfy the *a*
Prov. 23:2, are a man given to *a*

APPHIA, Phile. 2

APPII FORUM, Acts 28:15

APPLE
Dt. 32:10, He kept him as the *a*
Prov. 7:2, And my law as the *a*
Song 2:3, Like an *a* tree among
Zech. 2:8, you touches the *a*

APPLES
Prov. 25:11, fitly spoken is like *a*
Song 2:5, refresh me with *a*

APPLIED
Eccl. 7:25, *a* my heart to know

APPOINT
Lev. 26:16, I will even *a* terror
Num. 4:19, *a* each of them to his
2 Sam. 6:21, *a* me ruler over the
Isa. 26:1, *a* salvation for walls
1 Th. 5:9, For God did not *a*
Ti. 1:5, *a* elders in every city

APPOINTED
Job 14:5, You have *a* his limits
Ps. 102:20, To release those *a*
Heb. 9:27, And as it is *a* for men

APPROACH
Lev. 18:6, *a* anyone who is near
Ps. 65:4, And cause to *a* You
Heb. 10:1, year, make those who *a*

APPROACHING
Isa. 58:2, take delight in *a* God
Heb. 10:25, as you see the Day *a*

APPROVE
Ps. 49:13, their posterity who *a*
Rom. 1:32, do the same but also *a*
Rom. 2:18, *a* the things that
Phil. 1:10, *a* the things that are

APPROVED
Rom. 14:18, to God and *a* by men
2 Tim. 2:15, to present yourself *a*
Jas. 1:12, when he has been *a*

AQUILA (and Priscilla)
go with Paul from Corinth to Ephesus. Acts 18:2,19
their constancy. Rom. 16:3; 1 Cor. 16:19
Apollos instructed by. Acts 18:26

ARAB, Josh. 15:52

ARABIA, Ps. 72:10,15; Gal. 1:17
kings of, pay tribute. 2 Chr. 9:14; 17:11; 26:7

ARARAT
ark rested on. Gen. 8:4. *See* 2 Ki. 19:37; Jer. 51:27

ARAUNAH, 2 Sam. 24:18
(Ornan), Jebusite, sells to David site for temple. 2 Sam. 24:16; 1 Chr. 21:15

ARBITRATOR
Lk. 12:14, Me a judge or an *a*

ARCHANGEL
1 Th. 4:16, the voice of an *a*
Jude 9, Yet Michael the *a*

ARCHELAUS
king of Judea, feared by Joseph. Mt. 2:22

ARCHIPPUS, Col. 4:17

ARCHITE
a native of Erech. 2 Sam. 15:32

AREOPAGITE
belonging to the Council held on Areopagus. Acts 17:34

AREOPAGUS
hill of Mars, at Athens; Paul preaches on. Acts 17:19

ARGUMENTS
Job 23:4, fill my mouth with *a*
2 Cor. 10:5, casting down *a* and

ARIEL, Ezra 8:16

ARIMATHEA
the same as Ramah. Mt. 27:57

ARISE
Ps. 12:5, needy, now I will *a*
Ps. 44:26, *A* for our help
Ps. 68:1, Let God *a*
Isa. 60:1, *A*, shine
Isa. 60:2, But the LORD will *a*
Mal. 4:2, Righteousness shall *a*
Lk. 15:18, 'I will *a* and go to
Eph. 5:14, you who sleep, *A*

ARISTARCHUS
fellow prisoner of Paul. Acts 19:29; 20:4; 27:2; Col. 4:10; Phile. 24

ARISTOBULUS
his household greeted by Paul. Rom. 16:10

ARK
of the Lord, of the Covenant, directions for making. Ex. 25:10; 37:1
passes the Jordan. Josh. 3:15; 4:11
circles Jericho. Josh. 6:11
captured by Philistines. 1 Sam. 4:5
restored. 1 Sam. 6
taken to Jerusalem. 2 Sam. 6; 15:24; 1 Chr. 13; 15; 16
brought into the temple by Solomon. 1 Ki. 8:3; 2 Chr. 5. *See* Heb. 9:4
in heaven. Rev. 11:19
——— of Noah:
ordered. Gen. 6:14; 1 Pet. 3:20
dimensions, etc. Gen. 6:15
Noah's faith in making. Heb. 11:7; 1 Pet. 3:20
——— of bulrushes. Ex. 2:3

ARK
Gen. 6:14, "Make yourself an *a*
Ex. 2:3, him, she took an *a*
Ex. 37:1, Bezalel made the *a*
Lev. 16:2, seat which is on the *a*
1 Sam. 4:3, Let us bring the *a*
Heb. 9:4, golden censer and the *a*
1 Pet. 3:20, of Noah, while the *a*
Rev. 11:19, in heaven, and the *a*

ARM
Ex. 6:6, with an outstretched *a*
Num. 11:23, "Has the LORD's *a*
2 Chr. 32:8, "With him is an *a*
Job 26:2, *a* that has no strength
Job 40:9, Have you an *a* like God
Ps. 10:15, Break the *a* of the
Ps. 89:13, You have a mighty *a*
Ps. 98:1, *a* have gained Him the
Isa. 40:10, *a* shall rule for Him
Isa. 59:16, therefore His own *a*
Lk. 1:51, strength with His *a*
Acts 13:17, with an uplifted *a*
1 Pet. 4:1, *a* yourselves also with

ARMAGEDDON
height of Megiddo. Rev. 16:16

ARMED
2 Sam. 22:40, You have *a* me with
Lk. 11:21, a strong man, fully *a*

ARMIES
Dt. 20:9, make captains of the *a*
1 Sam. 17:10, "I defy the *a*
Job 25:3, any number to His *a*
Ps. 60:10, not go out with our *a*
Mt. 22:7, And he sent out his *a*
Lk. 21:20, surrounded by *a*
Rev. 19:14, And the *a* in heaven
Rev. 19:19, the earth, and their *a*

ARMOR
Goliath's. 1 Sam. 17:5
of God. Rom. 13:12; 2 Cor. 6:7; 10:3; Eph. 6:13; 1 Th. 5:8

ARMOR
1 Sam. 17:54, but he put his *a*
Jer. 46:4, spears, put on the *a*
Rom. 13:12, let us put on the *a*
Eph. 6:11, Put on the whole *a*

ARMS
Dt. 33:27, are the everlasting *a*
Job 39:21, into the clash of *a*
Ps. 18:32, It is God who *a*
Isa. 51:5, *a* will judge the
Zech. 13:6, wounds between your *a*
Mk. 10:16, took them up in His *a*
Lk. 2:28, took Him up in his *a*

ARMY
Ps. 33:16, the multitude of an *a*
Ezek. 37:10, an exceedingly great *a*
Rev. 9:16, the number of the *a*

AROER, Dt. 2:36
built by children of Gad. Num. 32:34
boundary of Reuben. Josh. 13:16

AROMA
a soothing. (Gen. 8:21; Ex. 29:18)
type of Christ. Eph. 5:2

AROMA
Gen. 8:21, smelled a soothing *a*
2 Cor. 2:16, the one we are the *a*
Eph. 5:2, for a sweet-smelling *a*
Phil. 4:18, a sweet-smelling *a*

AROUSED
Num. 11:10, LORD was greatly *a*
Job 32:2, his wrath was *a*
Mt. 1:24, Then Joseph, being *a*

ARPAD, 2 Ki. 18:34

ARPHAXAD, Gen. 10:22

ARRAYED
Mt. 6:29, his glory was not *a*
Rev. 7:13, "Who are these *a*
Rev. 17:4, The woman was *a*

ARREST, Acts 12:4; 2 Cor. 11:32

ARROGANCE
Prov. 8:13, Pride and *a* and the
Isa. 13:11, I will halt the *a*

ARROGANT
Isa. 10:12, the fruit of the *a*
Ezek. 24:21, My sanctuary, your *a*

ARROW
2 Ki. 13:17, deliverance and the *a*
Job 41:28, *a* cannot make him flee
Ps. 11:2, make ready their *a*
Ps. 91:5, *a* that flies by day
Prov. 25:18, a sword, and a sharp *a*
Jer. 9:8, Their tongue is an *a*
Lam. 3:12, as a target for the *a*

ARROWS
2 Sam. 22:15, He sent out *a* and
Ps. 38:2, *a* pierce me deeply
Ps. 76:3, There He broke the *a*
Ps. 127:4, Like *a* in the hand of
Lam. 3:13, He has caused the *a*
Hab. 3:9, were sworn over Your *a*

ARTAXERXES, Ezra 4:8
king of Persia, oppresses the Jews. Ezra 4
——— Longimanus, permits Ezra to restore the temple. Ezra 7; and Nehemiah to rebuild Jerusalem. Neh. 2

ARTEMAS, Ti. 3:12

ASA
his good reign. 1 Ki. 15:8
wars with Baasha. 1 Ki. 15:16
his prayer against the Ethiopians. 2 Chr. 14:11
his zeal. 2 Chr. 15
seeks aid of the Syrians. 2 Chr. 16
rebuked by Hanani the seer. 2 Chr. 16:7
reigns forty years, and dies much honored. 2 Chr. 16:12

ASAHEL
his rashness; killed by Abner in self-defense. 2 Sam. 2:18; 3:27; 23:24; 1 Chr. 11:26

ASAPH, 2 Ki. 18:18
a Levite, musical composer, and leader of David's choir. 1 Chr. 6:39; 2 Chr. 5:12; 29:30; 35:15; Neh. 12:46; Ps. 50 and 73 to 83 ascribed to him

ASCEND
Ps. 24:3, Who may *a* into the
Ps. 139:8, If I *a* into heaven
Isa. 14:13, 'I will *a* into heaven
Obad. 4, *a* as high as the eagle
Jn. 6:62, see the Son of Man *a*

ASCENDED
Ps. 68:18, You have *a* on high
Prov. 30:4, Who has *a* into heaven
Jn. 3:13, "No one has *a*
Eph. 4:8, "When He *a* on high
Eph. 4:10, also the One who *a*
Rev. 11:12, And they *a* to heaven

ASCENDING
Gen. 28:12, angels of God were *a*
Jn. 1:51, the angels of God *a*

ASCENSION of Christ
from Olivet. Lk. 24:50; Jn. 14:2; 16:7; Acts 1:9; 2:33; Rom. 8:34; Eph. 4:8; 1 Pet. 3:22
typified. Lev. 16:15; Heb. 6:20; 9:7–12; Enoch. Gen. 5:24; Joseph. Gen.

41:43; Moses. Ex. 19:3; Aaron. Lev. 16:3; Elijah. 2 Ki. 2:11

ASCRIBE
Dt. 32:3, *a* greatness to our God
Job 36:3, *a* righteousness
Ps. 68:34, *A* strength to God

ASENATH
wife of Joseph. Gen. 41:45; 46:20

ASHAMED
Ezra 9:6, I am too *a* and
Ps. 6:10, all my enemies be *a*
Ps. 25:2, Let me not be *a*
Ps. 25:3, who waits on You be *a*
Jer. 8:9, The wise men are *a*
Jer. 17:13, forsake You shall be *a*
Hos. 10:6, And Israel shall be *a*
Mk. 8:38, For whoever is *a*
Rom. 1:16, am not *a* of the gospel
Phil. 1:20, nothing I shall be *a*
Heb. 11:16, Therefore God is not *a*
1 Pet. 3:16, in Christ may be *a*
1 Pet. 4:16, let him not be *a*
1 Jn. 2:28, and not be *a* before

ASHDOD, Josh. 15:46
city of Philistines; the ark carried there; men of, stricken. 1 Sam. 5
reduced by Uzziah. 2 Chr. 26:6
predictions concerning. Jer. 25:20; Amos 1:8; Zeph. 2:4; Zech. 9:6

ASHER
son of Jacob. Gen. 30:13
his descendants. Num. 1:40; 26:44; 1 Chr. 7:30; their inheritance. Josh. 19:24; Jud. 5:17
Anna, prophetess, descended from. Lk. 2:36

ASHES
Job 13:12, are proverbs of *a*
Job 30:19, become like dust and *a*
Ps. 102:9, For I have eaten *a*
Isa. 44:20, He feeds on *a*
Jon. 3:6, sackcloth and sat in *a*
Lk. 10:13, in sackcloth and *a*
Heb. 9:13, and goats and the *a*

ASHKELON
taken. Jud. 1:18; 14:19; 1 Sam. 6:17; 2 Sam. 1:20
prophecies concerning. Jer. 25:20; 47:5; Amos 1:8; Zeph. 2:4; Zech. 9:5

ASHKENAZ, Gen. 10:3

ASHTAROTH (or Ashtoreth)
statues of Ashtoreth. Josh. 9:10
idolatrous worship of, by Israel. Jud. 2:13; 1 Sam. 12:10; by Solomon. 1 Ki. 11:5,33

ASIDE
1 Cor. 16:2, lay something *a*
Jas. 1:21, lay *a* all filthiness
1 Pet. 2:1, Therefore, laying *a*

ASK
Gen. 32:29, "Why is it that you *a*
Josh. 4:6, when your children *a*
Isa. 7:11, "*A* a sign for yourself
Jer. 50:5, They shall *a* the way
Lam. 4:4, the young children *a*
Zech. 10:1, *A* the LORD for rain in
Mt. 21:22, whatever things you *a*
Lk. 11:9, *a*, and it will be
Jn. 11:22, that whatever You *a*
Jn. 14:14, *a* anything in My
Jn. 16:23, in that day you will *a*
1 Cor. 14:35, something, let them *a*
Eph. 3:20, above all that we *a*
Jas. 1:5, wisdom, let him *a*
Jas. 1:6, But let him *a* in faith
Jas. 4:2, because you do not *a*
1 Jn. 5:15, us, whatever we *a*

ASKS
Mt. 7:8, For everyone who *a*
Mt. 7:9, you who, if his son *a*
Lk. 11:11, Or if he *a* for a fish

ASLEEP
Jon. 1:5, down, and was fast *a*
Mt. 8:24, But He was *a*
1 Cor. 15:6, some have fallen *a*
1 Th. 4:15, those who are *a*
2 Pet. 3:4, the fathers fell *a*

ASSEMBLED
Ezra 9:4, of the God of Israel *a*
Ps. 48:4, behold, the kings *a*

ASSEMBLING
Heb. 10:25, not forsaking the *a*

ASSEMBLY
Ex. 16:3, to kill this whole *a*
Lev. 23:36, It is a sacred *a*
Ps. 22:22, *a* I will praise You
Ps. 26:5, I have hated the *a*
Ps. 89:5, also in the *a* of the
Ps. 89:7, to be feared in the *a*
Prov. 21:16, will rest in the *a* of
Joel 1:14, fast, call a sacred *a*
Joel 2:16, people, sanctify the *a*
Heb. 2:12, *a* I will sing praise
Heb. 12:23, to the general *a*
Jas. 2:2, come into your *a*

ASSURANCE
of faith and hope. Isa. 32:17; Col. 2:2; 1 Th. 1:5; 2 Tim. 1:12; Heb. 6:11; 10:22
confirmed by love. 1 Jn. 3:14,19; 4:18

ASSURANCE
Dt. 28:66, night, and have no *a*
Col. 2:2, riches of the full *a*
1 Th. 1:5, Spirit and in much *a*
Heb. 6:11, to the full *a* of hope
Heb. 10:22, a true heart in full *a*

ASSURE
1 Jn. 3:19, *a* our hearts before

ASSURED
Jer. 14:13, but I will give you *a*
2 Tim. 3:14, learned and been *a*

ASSYRIA
the land so named from Asshur. Gen. 2:14
Israel carried captive to. 2 Ki. 15:29; 17
army of, miraculously destroyed. 2 Ki. 19:35; Isa. 37:36
prophecies concerning. Isa. 8; 10:5; 14:24; 30:31; 31:8; Mic. 5:6; Zeph. 2:13
its glory. Ezek. 31:3

ASTONISHED
Isa. 52:14, Just as many were *a*
Mt. 7:28, that the people were *a*
Lk. 2:47, who heard Him were *a*

ASTONISHMENT
Dt. 28:37, you shall become an *a*
Jer. 8:21, *a* has taken hold

ASTRAY
Ps. 95:10, is a people who go *a*
Isa. 35:8, a fool, shall not go *a*
Amos 2:4, Their lies lead them *a*
Mt. 18:12, one of them goes *a*
Heb. 3:10, "They always go *a*
1 Pet. 2:25, like sheep going *a*

ATHALIAH
daughter of Ahab, mother of Ahaziah. 2 Ki. 8:26
kills the royal heirs, Joash only saved. 2 Ki. 11:1; 2 Chr. 22:10
killed by order of Jehoiada. 2 Ki. 11:16; 2 Chr. 23:15

ATHENIANS, Acts 17:21

ATHENS
Paul preaches to the philosophers at. Acts 17:15; 1 Th. 3:1
men of, described. Acts 17:21

ATONEMENT
under the law. Ex. 29:29; 30; Lev. 1
annual day of. Lev. 16; 23:26
made by Aaron for the plague. Num. 16:46
made by Christ. Rom. 3:24; 5:6; 2 Cor. 5:18; Gal. 1:4; 3:13; Ti. 2:14; Heb. 9:28; 1 Pet. 1:19; 2:24; 3:18; 1 Jn. 2:2; Rev. 1:5; 13:8
prophecies concerning. Isa. 53; Dan. 9:24; Zech. 13:1,7; Jn. 11:50
commemorated in the Lord's Supper. Mt. 26:26; 1 Cor. 11:23

ATONEMENT
Ex. 30:10, a year he shall make *a*
Lev. 16:30, priest shall make *a*
Lev. 17:11, the blood that makes *a*
Lev. 23:28, for it is the Day of *A*
2 Sam. 21:3, what shall I make *a*
Neh. 10:33, offerings to make *a*
Prov. 16:6, *a* is provided for
Isa. 22:14, there will be no *a*
Ezek. 16:63, I provide you an *a*

ATTAIN
Ps. 139:6, It is high, I cannot *a*
Prov. 1:5, understanding will *a*
Hos. 8:5, How long until they *a*
Lk. 20:35, worthy to *a* that age
Phil. 3:11, by any means, I may *a*

ATTALIA
so called from Attalus, the royal founder of the city, seaport. Acts 14:25

ATTEND
Ps. 17:1, just cause, O LORD, *a*
Ps. 86:6, And *a* to the voice of
Jer. 23:2, behold, I will *a*

ATTENTION
Prov. 4:20, My son, give *a* to my
1 Tim. 4:13, Till I come, give *a*
Jas. 2:3, and you pay *a* to the

ATTENTIVE
Ps. 130:2, Let Your ears be *a*
Lk. 19:48, the people were very *a*

ATTESTED
Acts 2:22, a Man *a* by God to you

AUGUSTUS, Lk. 2:1

AUSTERE
Lk. 19:21, because you are an *a*

AUTHOR
1 Cor. 14:33, For God is not the *a*
Heb. 5:9, He became the *a*
Heb. 12:2, unto Jesus, the *a*

AUTHORITIES
Rom. 13:1, *a* that exist are
1 Pet. 3:22, of God, angels and *a*

AUTHORITY
Est. 9:29, Jew, wrote with full *a*
Prov. 29:2, the righteous are in *a*
Mt. 7:29, them as one having *a*
Mt. 20:25, are great exercise *a*
Mt. 28:18, "All *a* has been given
Lk. 4:6, *a* I will give You
Jn. 5:27, and has given Him *a*
Jn. 17:2, You have given Him *a*
Acts 1:7, has put in His own *a*
Rom. 13:1, For there is no *a*
1 Cor. 11:10, to have a symbol of *a*
1 Tim. 2:2, and all who are in *a*
Ti. 2:15, and rebuke with all *a*
Jude 8, the flesh, reject *a*

AUTUMN
Jude 12, *a* trees without fruit

AVAILS
Gal. 5:6, nor uncircumcision *a*
Jas. 5:16, of a righteous man *a*

AVENGE
Dt. 32:43, for He will *a* the
Lk. 18:8, you that He will *a*
Rom. 12:19, Beloved, do not *a*
Rev. 6:10, *a* our blood on those

AVENGER
Num. 35:19, 'The *a* of blood
Ps. 8:2, the enemy and the *a*
Rom. 13:4, God's minister, an *a*
1 Th. 4:6, the Lord is the *a*

AVENGES
2 Sam. 22:48, It is God who *a*
Ps. 9:12, When He *a* blood

AWAKE
Ps. 17:15, be satisfied when I *a*
Ps. 102:7, I lie *a*
Ps. 108:2, *A*, lute and harp
Ps. 119:148, My eyes are *a*
Song 4:16, *A*, O north wind
Song 5:2, but my heart is *a*
Dan. 12:2, of the earth shall *a*
Rom. 13:11, it is high time to *a*
1 Cor. 15:34, *A* to righteousness
Eph. 5:14, "*A*, you who sleep

AWAY
Ps. 1:4, the wind drives *a*
Ps. 51:11, Do not cast me *a*
Eccl. 3:5, A time to cast *a*
Song 2:10, fair one, And come *a*
Song 2:17, and the shadows flee *a*
Mt. 1:19, minded to put her *a*
Mt. 24:35, and earth will pass *a*
Mt. 27:64, and steal Him *a*
Lk. 1:53, the rich He has sent *a*
Jn. 1:29, of God who takes *a*
Jn. 8:21, "I am going *a*
Jn. 19:15, they cried out, "*A*
Jn. 20:2, "They have taken *a*
Acts 21:36, crying out, "*A*
2 Cor. 3:14, the veil is taken *a*
Gal. 2:13, Barnabas was carried *a*
2 Th. 2:3, unless the falling *a*
2 Tim. 1:15, in Asia have turned *a*
Heb. 2:1, heard, lest we drift *a*
Heb. 6:6, if they fall *a*
Heb. 10:11, can never take *a*
1 Pet. 5:4, that does not fade *a*
1 Jn. 2:17, world is passing *a*
Rev. 20:11, and the heaven fled *a*
Rev. 22:19, if anyone takes *a*
Rev. 22:19, God shall take *a*

AWE
Ps. 33:8, the world stand in *a*
Ps. 119:161, my heart stands in *a*

AWESOME
Gen. 28:17, *a* is this place
Ex. 34:10, *a* thing that I will do
Dt. 7:21, God, the great and *a*
Dt. 10:17, God, mighty and *a*
Jud. 13:6, Angel of God, very *a*
2 Sam. 7:23, *a* deeds for Your land
Neh. 1:5, heaven, O great and *a*
Ps. 45:4, hand shall teach You *a*
Ps. 65:5, By *a* deeds in
Ps. 66:3, *a* are Your works
Ps. 66:5, He is *a* in His doing
Ps. 68:35, O God, You are more *a*
Ps. 76:12, He is *a* to the kings
Ps. 99:3, Your great and *a* name
Ps. 145:6, of the might of Your *a*
Isa. 64:3, When You did *a* things
Jer. 20:11, with me as a mighty, *a*
Lam. 1:9, her collapse was *a*
Dan. 9:4, "O Lord, great and *a*

AWL
Ex. 21:6, his ear with an *a*
Dt. 15:17, you shall take an *a*

AX
Dt. 19:5, a stroke with the *a*
Jud. 9:48, Abimelech took an *a*
2 Ki. 6:5, a tree, the iron *a*
Eccl. 10:10, If the *a* is dull
Isa. 10:15 *a* boast itself against
Mt. 3:10, And even now the *a*

AZARIAH, 2 Chr. 22:6
—— (Uzziah), king of Judah, his good reign. 2 Ki. 14:21; 2 Chr. 26
his wars. 2 Chr. 26
invades the priest's office. 2 Chr. 26:16
stricken with leprosy. 2 Ki. 15:5; 2 Chr. 26:20
—— prophet, exhorts Asa. 2 Chr. 15

AZOTUS
the Greek form of Ashdod. Acts 8:40

BAAL
worshiped. Num. 22:41; Jud. 2:13; 8:33; 1 Ki. 16:32; 18:26; 2 Ki. 17:16; 19:18; 21:3; Jer. 2:8; 7:9; 12:16; 19:5; 23:13; Hos. 2:8; 13:1
his altars and priests destroyed by Gideon. Jud. 6:25; by Elijah. 1 Ki. 18:40; by Jehu. 2 Ki. 10:18; by Jehoiada. 2 Ki. 11:18; by Josiah. 2 Ki. 23:4; 2 Chr. 34:4

BAAL-HANAN, Gen. 36:38

BAAL HAZOR, 2 Sam. 13:23

BAAL HERMON, Jud. 3:3

BAAL OF PEOR, Num. 25:3
the trespass of Israel concerning. Num. 25; Dt. 4:3; Ps. 106:28; Hos. 9:10

BAAL PERAZIM
David's victory over Philistines at. 2 Sam. 5:20

BAAL-ZEBUB
false god of Ekron, Ahaziah rebuked for sending to inquire of. 2 Ki. 1:2

BAALS, Jud. 2:11; 2 Chr. 28:2

BAASHA
king of Israel, destroys the house of Jeroboam. 1 Ki. 15:16,27
Jehu's prophecy concerning him. 1 Ki. 16:1

BABBLER
Eccl. 10:11, *b* is no different
Acts 17:18, "What does this *b*

BABBLINGS
1 Tim. 6:20, the profane and idle *b*

BABE
Lk. 1:44, the *b* leaped in my
Lk. 2:12, You will find a *B*
Heb. 5:13, for he is a *b*

BABEL
Nimrod king of. Gen. 10:10
confusion of tongues at the building of. Gen. 11:9

BABES
Ps. 8:2, Out of the mouth of *b*
Isa. 3:4, *b* shall rule over them
Mt. 11:25, revealed them to *b*
Mt. 21:16, of the mouth of *b*
Rom. 2:20, a teacher of *b*
1 Cor. 3:1, as to carnal, as to *b*
1 Pet. 2:2, as newborn *b*

BABYLON
Gen. 10:10; 2 Ki. 17:30; 20:12
ambassadors from, to Hezekiah. 2 Ki. 20:12; 2 Chr. 32:31; Isa. 39
Jewish captivity there. 2 Ki. 25; 2 Chr. 36; Jer. 39; 52
return from. Ezra 1; Neh. 2
greatness of. Dan. 4:30
taken by the Medes. Dan. 5:30

fall of. Isa. 13:14; 21:2; 47; 48; Jer. 25:12; 50; 51
church in. 1 Pet. 5:13
——— the Great. Rev. 14:8; 17; 18

BABYLONIAN, Josh. 7:21

BACA
valley of misery. Ps. 84:6

BACK
Ps. 114:3, Jordan turned *b*
Prov. 10:13, but a rod is for the *b*
Prov. 26:3, for the fool's *b*
Isa. 50:6, I gave My *b* to those
Ezek. 23:35, cast Me behind your *b*
Mt. 2:8, found Him, bring *b*
Lk. 9:62, plow, and looking *b*
Jn. 18:6, they drew *b* and fell
Phile. 12, I am sending him *b*
Heb. 10:39, of those who draw *b*
Jas. 5:19, someone turns him *b*
Rev. 5:1, inside and on the *b*

BACKBITERS
Rom. 1:30, *b*, haters of God

BACKBITING
forbidden. Ps. 15:3; Prov. 25:23; Rom. 1:30; 2 Cor. 12:20

BACKBITING
Prov. 25:23, *b* tongue an angry

BACKSLIDER
Prov. 14:14, The *b* in heart will be

BACKSLIDING
(turning from God). 1 Ki. 11:9; Mt. 18:6; 2 Cor. 11:3; Gal. 3:1; 5:4; Israel. Ex. 32; Jer. 2:19; 3:6,11; 12; 14; 22; Isa. 1; Hos. 4:16; 11:7; Saul. 1 Sam. 15:11; Solomon. 1 Ki. 11:3,4; Peter. Mt. 26:70–74; Gal. 2:14
God's displeasure at. Ps. 78:57–59
punishment of. Prov. 14:14; Jer. 2:19
pardon for, promised. 2 Chr. 7:14; Jer. 3:12; 31:20; 36:3; Hos. 14:4
restoration from. Ps. 80:3; 85:4; Lam. 5:21
healing of. Jer. 3:22; Hos. 14:4; 5:15

BACKSLIDINGS
Jer. 2:19, *b* will rebuke you
Jer. 3:22, And I will heal your *b*
Jer. 5:6, *b* have increased
Jer. 14:7, for our *b* are many

BACKWARD
1 Sam. 4:18, fell off the seat *b*
2 Ki. 20:11, shadow ten degrees *b*

BAD
Gen. 24:50, speak to you either *b*
Lev. 27:10, it, good for *b* or *b*
Mt. 7:17, *b* trees bears *b* fruit

BAG
Job 14:17, is sealed up in a *b*
Hag. 1:6, wages to put into a *b*
Mt. 10:10, "nor *b* for your

BAKE
Lev. 24:5, *b* twelve cakes with it

BAKED
Ex. 12:39, *b* unleavened cakes
1 Sam. 28:24, *b* unleavened

BAKER
Gen. 40:1, the butler and the *b*

BAKERS
Jer. 37:21, of bread from the *b*

BAKES
Isa. 44:15, kindles it and *b* bread

BALAAM, Num. 22:5
is forbidden to curse Israel. Num. 22:12
his anger. Num. 22:27
blesses Israel. Num. 23:19; 24
his prophecies. Num. 23:9,24; 24:17
his wicked counsel. Num. 31:16; Dt. 23:4. *See* Josh. 24:9; Jud. 11:25; Mic. 6:5; 2 Pet. 2:15; Jude 11; Rev. 2:14
killed. Num. 31:8; Josh. 13:22

BALAK, Num. 22:2

BALANCE
Prov. 11:1, *b* is an abomination
Isa. 40:15, small dust on the *b*

BALANCES
Amos 8:5, falsifying the *b*

BALD
Lev. 21:5, shall not make any *b*
Jer. 48:37, every head shall be *b*
Ezek. 27:31, completely *b* because

BALDHEAD
2 Ki. 2:23, Go up, you *b*

BALM
Gen. 43:11, a little *b* and a
Jer. 8:22, no *b* in Gilead

BAND
Hos. 7:1, A *b* of robbers takes
Rev. 1:13, with a golden *b*

BANDAGED
Lk. 10:34, and *b* his wounds

BANKERS
Mt. 25:27, my money with the *b*

BANNERS
Ps. 20:5, we will set up our *b*
Ps. 74:4, They set up their *b*
Song 6:4, as an army with *b*

BANQUET
Est. 5:4, *b* that I have prepared
Job 41:6, companions make a *b*
Dan. 5:10, lords, came to the *b*

BANQUETING
Song 2:4, He brought me to the *b*

BANQUETS
Amos 6:7, *b* shall be removed

BAPTISM
of John. Mt. 3:6; Mk. 1:4; Lk. 3; Jn. 1:26; Acts 19:4
by disciples, not by Christ. Jn. 4:2
Pharisees' answer concerning. Mt. 21:25; Mk. 11:29; Lk. 20:4
appointed by Christ. Mt. 28:19; Mk. 16:15; Jn. 3:22; 4:1
its signification. Acts 2:38; 19:4; 22:16; Rom. 6:3; 1 Cor. 10:2; 12:13; 15:29; Gal. 3:27; Col. 2:12; Ti. 3:5; 1 Pet. 3:21
instances of. Acts 8:12,38; 9:18; 10:48; 16:15,33; 1 Cor. 1:16
Crispus and Gaius baptized by Paul. 1 Cor. 1:14

BAPTISM
Mt. 3:7, coming to his *b*
Mt. 20:22, *b* that I am baptized
Mt. 21:25, "The *b* of John
Lk. 12:50, "But I have a *b*
Acts 19:3, said, "Into John's *b*
Rom. 6:4, with Him through *b*
Eph. 4:5, Lord, one faith, one *b*
Col. 2:12, buried with Him in *b*
1 Pet. 3:21, now saves us—*b*

BAPTISMS
Heb. 6:2, of the doctrine of *b*

BAPTIZE
Mt. 3:11, "I indeed *b* you with
Jn. 1:25, "Why then do you *b*
Jn. 4:2, Himself did not *b*
1 Cor. 1:17, did not send me to *b*

BAPTIZED
Mt. 3:14, "I need to be *b*
Mk. 16:16, *b* will be saved
Jn. 4:1, *b* more disciples
Acts 2:38, every one of you be *b*
Acts 16:33, all his family were *b*
Acts 18:8, believed and were *b*
Acts 22:16, Arise and be *b*
Rom. 6:3, were *b* into Christ
1 Cor. 1:14, I thank God that I *b*
1 Cor. 1:16, *b* the household
1 Cor. 10:2, all were *b* into Moses
1 Cor. 12:13, Spirit we were all *b*
1 Cor. 15:29, who are *b* for the dead
Gal. 3:27, of you as were *b*

BAPTIZING
Mt. 28:19, *b* them in the name of
Jn. 1:31, therefore I came *b*

BAR-JESUS (Elymas)
struck with blindness by Paul. Acts 13:6

BAR-JONAH (Simon), Mt. 16:17

BARABBAS, Mk. 15:7
a robber, released instead of Jesus. Mt. 27:16; Mk. 15:6; Lk. 23:18; Jn. 18:40

BARAK, Jud. 4:6
delivers Israel from Sisera. Jud. 4:15; Heb. 11:32

BARBARIAN
Col. 3:11, nor uncircumcised, *b*

BARBAROUS, Acts 28:2

BARE
Isa. 32:11, make yourselves *b*
Isa. 52:10, The LORD has made *b*

BARLEY
Dt. 8:8, a land of wheat and *b*
Jud. 7:13, *b* bread tumbled
Ruth 1:22, beginning of *b* harvest
Jn. 6:9, here who has five *b*
Rev. 6:6, and three quarts of *b*

BARN
Hag. 2:19, seed still in the *b*
Mt. 13:30, the wheat into my *b*
Lk. 12:24, storehouse nor *b*

BARNABAS
Levite of Cyprus, sells his lands. Acts 4:36
preaches at Antioch. Acts 11:22
accompanies Paul. Acts 11:30; 12:25; 13; 14; 15; 1 Cor. 9:6
his contention. Acts 15:36
his error. Gal. 2:13

BARNS
Prov. 3:10, *b* will be filled
Joel 1:17, *b* are broken down
Mt. 6:26, reap nor gather into *b*
Lk. 12:18, I will pull down my *b*

BARREN
Gen. 11:30, But Sarai was *b*
1 Sam. 2:5, *b* has borne seven
Ps. 113:9, He grants the *b*
Isa. 54:1, "Sing, O *b*
Lk. 23:29, 'Blessed are the *b*
Gal. 4:27, "Rejoice, O *b*
2 Pet. 1:8, you will be neither *b*

BARRENNESS
of Sarah. Gen. 11:30; 16:1; 18:1; 21; Rebekah. 25:21; Rachel. 29:31; 30:1; Manoah's wife. Jud. 13; Hannah. 1 Sam. 1; Shunammite. 2 Ki. 4:14; Elizabeth. Lk. 1

BARRENNESS
Ps. 107:34, A fruitful land into *b*

BARS
Ps. 147:13, has strengthened the *b*
Isa. 45:2, bronze and cut the *b*
Jon. 2:6, the earth with its *b*

BARSABAS, Acts 1:23

BARTHOLOMEW
the apostle. Mt. 10:3; Mk. 3:18; Lk. 6:14; Acts 1:13

BARTIMAEUS
blindness cured near Jericho. Mk. 10:46

BARUCH, Jer. 32:12
receives Jeremiah's evidence. Jer. 32:13;36
discredited by Azariah, and carried into Egypt. Jer. 43:6
God's message to. Jer. 45

BARZILLAI
loyalty to David. 2 Sam. 17:27
David's recognition of. 2 Sam. 19:31; 1 Ki. 2:7

BASE
Isa. 3:5, the elder, and the *b*
1 Cor. 1:28, and the *b* things of

BASHAN
conquered. Num. 21:33; Dt. 3:1; Ps. 68:15,22; 135:10; 136:20

BASIN
Jn. 13:5, poured water into a *b*

BASKET
Dt. 28:17, Cursed shall be your *b*
Jer. 24:2, *b* had very good figs
Mt. 5:15, and put it under a *b*
2 Cor. 11:33, I was let down in a *b*

BASKETS
Gen. 40:16, were three white *b*
Jer. 24:1, and there were two *b*
Mt. 14:20, they took up twelve *b*
Mt. 15:37, up seven large *b*

BATHED
Isa. 34:5, My sword shall be *b*
Jn. 13:10, to him, "He who is *b*

BATHSHEBA, 2 Sam. 11:3
wife of Uriah, taken by David. 2 Sam. 11; 12
appeals to David for Solomon against Adonijah. 1 Ki. 1:15
intercedes with Solomon for Adonijah. 1 Ki. 2:19

BATS
Isa. 2:20, To the moles and *b*

BATTLE
1 Sam. 17:47, *b* is the LORD's
1 Chr. 5:20, out to God in the *b*
Ps. 18:39, strength for the *b*
Prov. 21:31, for the day of *b*
Eccl. 9:11, the *b* to the strong
Isa. 28:6, who turn back the *b*
Jer. 50:22, A sound of *b* is in the
1 Cor. 14:8, prepare for *b*
Heb. 11:34, became valiant in *b*
Rev. 16:14, gather them to the *b*

BATTLES
of Israelites, etc. Gen. 14; Ex. 17; Num. 31; Josh. 8; 10; Jud. 4; 7; 8; 11; 20; 1 Sam. 4:11; 14; 17; 31; 2 Sam. 2; 10; 18; 21:15; 1 Ki. 20; 22; 2 Ki. 3; 1 Chr. 18; 19; 20; 2 Chr. 13; 14:9; 20; 25

BEAR
Gen. 4:13, greater than I can *b*
Gen. 17:21, whom Sarah shall *b*
Ex. 20:16, not *b* false witness
1 Sam. 17:37, from the paw of the *b*
Ps. 91:12, they shall *b* you up in
Prov. 18:14, *b* a broken spirit
Isa. 52:11, be clean, you who *b*
Isa. 53:11, *b* their iniquities
Jer. 44:22, LORD could no longer *b*
Hos. 13:8, *b* deprived of her cubs
Amos 5:19, lion, and a *b* met him
Zech. 6:13, He shall *b* the glory
Mt. 1:23, child, and *b* a Son
Mt. 7:18, A good tree cannot *b*
Mt. 17:17, how long shall I *b*
Mk. 15:21, by, to *b* His cross
Lk. 1:13, wife Elizabeth will *b*
Lk. 14:27, whoever does not *b*
Jn. 15:2, in Me that does not *b*
Rom. 13:4, for he does not *b*
Rom. 15:1, are strong ought to *b*
1 Cor. 10:13, you may be able to *b*
Gal. 6:2, *B* one another's
Gal. 6:17, I *b* in my body the
Heb. 9:28, *b* the sins of many
Rev. 13:2, like the feet of a *b*

BEARD
Lev. 19:27, the edges of your *b*
1 Sam. 17:35, I caught it by its *b*
2 Sam. 20:9, took Amasa by the *b*
Ps. 133:2, Running down on the *b*

BEARING
Ps. 126:6, goes forth weeping, *b*
Jn. 19:17, And He, *b* His cross
Col. 3:13, *b* with one another
Heb. 13:13, *b* His reproach

BEARS
Jn. 15:2, Every branch that *b*
1 Cor. 13:7, *b* all things
1 Jn. 5:6, it is the Spirit who *b*

BEAST
Gen. 37:20, *b* has devoured him
Ps. 36:6, You preserve man and *b*
Ps. 73:22, I was like a *b* before
Ps. 147:9, to the *b* its food
Heb. 12:20, *b* touches the mountain
Rev. 13:1, And I saw a *b* rising
Rev. 13:11, Then I saw another *b*
Rev. 19:20, the mark of the *b*

BEASTS
creation of. Gen. 1:24
power over, given to man. Gen. 1:26,28; Ps. 8:7
named by Adam. Gen. 2:20
saved from the flood. Gen. 7:2
ordinance concerning. Ex. 22:19
clean and unclean. Lev. 11; Dt. 14:4; Acts 10:12
set apart for God. Ex. 13:12; Lev. 27:9
subjects of God's care. Ps. 36:6; 104:10,11
Daniel's vision of. Dan. 7
John's vision. Rev. 13

BEASTS
Job 18:3, are we counted as *b*
Job 37:8, The *b* go into dens
Ps. 49:12, like the *b* that perish
1 Cor. 15:32, I have fought with *b*
Jude 10, like brute *b*

BEAT
Ps. 89:23, I will *b* down his foes
Prov. 23:14 You shall *b* him with a
Isa. 2:4, *b* their swords into
Mic. 4:13, you shall *b* in pieces
Mt. 26:67, spat in His face and *b*
Lk. 18:13, but *b* his breast

BEATEN
Mk. 13:9, and you will be *b*
Lk. 12:47, his will, shall be *b*
2 Cor. 11:25, Three times I was *b*
1 Pet. 2:20, it if, when you are *b*

BEAUTIFUL
Gen. 29:17, but Rachel was *b*
Ps. 48:2, *B* in elevation
Eccl. 3:11, has made everything *b*
Song 6:4, my love, you are as *b*
Isa. 4:2, of the LORD shall be *b*
Isa. 52:7, How *b* upon the
Mt. 23:27, indeed appear *b*
Acts 3:10, begging alms at the *B*
Heb. 11:23, they saw he was a *b*

BEAUTIFY
Ps. 149:4, *b* the humble with

Isa. 60:13, *b* the place of My

BEAUTY
vanity of. Ps. 39:11; Prov. 6:25; 31:30; Isa. 3:24
danger of. Gen. 12:11; 26:7; 34; 2 Sam. 11; 13
consumes away. Ps. 39:11; 49:14

BEAUTY
Ex. 28:2, for glory and for *b*
2 Sam. 1:19, "The *b* of Israel is
Ps. 27:4, To behold the *b*
Prov. 31:30, and *b* is passing
Isa. 33:17, see the King in His *b*
Isa. 53:2, no *b* that we should
Zech. 11:7, the one I called *B*
1 Pet. 3:3, Do not let your *b*
1 Pet. 3:4, the incorruptible *b*

BECAME
Gen. 2:7, *b* a living being
1 Cor. 9:20, to the Jews I *b*
Gal. 4:12, for I *b* like you

BED
Job 17:13, house, if I make my *b*
Ps. 63:6, I remember You on my *b*
Ps. 139:8, if I make my *b* in hell
Song 1:16, Also our *b* is green
Isa. 28:20, *b* is too short to stretch
Isa. 57:7, you have set your *b*
Mt. 9:6, "Arise, take up your *b*
Lk. 17:34, be two men in one *b*
Heb. 13:4, and the *b* undefiled

BEDS
Ps. 149:5, sing aloud on their *b*
Isa. 57:2, shall rest in their *b*
Amos 6:4, who lie on *b* of ivory

BEE
Isa. 7:18, Egypt, and for the *b*

BEELZEBUB
ruler of demons. Mt. 12:24; Mk. 3:22; Lk. 11:15
Christ's miracles ascribed to. Mt. 12:24

BEER LAHAI ROI, Gen. 24:62

BEERSHEBA
Abraham dwells at. Gen. 21:31; 22:19; 28:10
Hagar relieved at. Gen. 21:14
Jacob comforted at. Gen. 46:1
Elijah flees to. 1 Ki. 19:3

BEFOREHAND
Mk. 13:11, up, do not worry *b*
Mk. 13:23, told you all things *b*
Lk. 21:14, not to meditate *b*
1 Pet. 1:11, when He testified *b*

BEG
Job 9:15, I would *b* mercy of my
Lk. 16:3, I am ashamed to *b*
1 Pet. 2:11, *b* you as sojourners

BEGAN
Gen. 4:26, Then men *b* to call on
Lk. 1:70, since the world *b*

BEGETS
Prov. 17:21, *b* a scoffer does
Prov. 23:24, *b* a wise child will
Eccl. 6:3, *b* a hundred children

BEGGAR
1 Sam. 2:8, and lifts the *b*
Lk. 16:20, there was a certain *b*

BEGGARLY
Gal. 4:9, weak and *b* elements

BEGINNING
Gen. 1:1, *b* God created the
Job 8:7, Though your *b* was
Ps. 111:10, of the LORD is the *b*
Eccl. 3:11, that God does from *b*
Mt. 19:4, who made them at the *b*
Jn. 1:1, In the *b* was the Word
Jn. 2:11, This *b* of signs Jesus
Jn. 8:44, a murderer from the *b*
Jn. 15:27, with Me from the *b*
Col. 1:18, the *b*, the firstborn
Heb. 7:3, having neither *b*
Rev. 3:14, True Witness, the *B*
Rev. 21:6, and the Omega, the *B*

BEGOTTEN
Ps. 2:7, I have *b* You
Isa. 49:21, heart, 'Who has *b*
Jn. 1:14, glory as of the only *b*
1 Cor. 4:15, Christ Jesus I have *b*
1 Pet. 1:3, abundant mercy has *b*
1 Jn. 5:1, loves him who is *b*

BEGUILING
2 Pet. 2:14, *b* unstable souls

BEGUN
Gal. 3:3, Having *b* in the Spirit
Phil. 1:6, that He who has *b*

BEHALF
Job 36:2, to speak on God's *b*
2 Cor. 5:20, you on Christ's *b*
Phil. 1:29, has been granted on *b*

BEHAVE
Ps. 101:2, I will *b* wisely in a
1 Cor. 13:5, does not *b* rudely

BEHAVED
1 Sam. 18:5, sent him, and *b* wisely
1 Th. 2:10, blamelessly we *b*

BEHAVIOR
1 Tim. 3:2, of good *b*, hospitable
Ti. 2:3, they be reverent in *b*

BEHEADED
Mt. 14:10, he sent and had John *b*
Rev. 20:4, those who had been *b*

BEHEMOTH, Job 40:15

BEHOLD
Eccl. 11:7, the eyes to *b* the sun
Song 1:15, *B*, you are fair
Isa. 7:14, *B*, the virgin shall
Isa. 40:9, Judah, "*B* your God
Jn. 1:36, *B* the Lamb of God
Jn. 17:24, I am, that they may *b*
Jn. 19:5, to them, "*B* the Man
1 Jn. 3:1, *B* what manner of love

BEHOLDING
2 Cor. 3:18, with unveiled face, *b*

BEING
Gen. 2:7, man became a living *b*
Ps. 104:33, God while I have my *b*
Acts 17:28, move and have our *b*
Phil. 2:6, who, *b* in the form of

BEL
another form of Baal, an idol. Isa. 46:1; Jer. 50:2

BELIAL, 2 Cor. 6:15

BELIEF
2 Th. 2:13, by the Spirit and *b*

BELIEVE
2 Chr. 20:20, *B* in the LORD your God
Mk. 9:24, tears, "Lord, I *b*
Mk. 11:24, *b* that you receive
Mk. 16:14, because they did not *b*
Lk. 8:13, have no root, who *b*
Lk. 24:25, slow of heart to *b*
Jn. 1:12, to those who *b*
Jn. 3:12, how will you *b*
Jn. 5:38, sent, Him you do not *b*
Jn. 6:30, we may see it and *b*
Jn. 9:35, to him, "Do you *b*
Jn. 11:42, this, that they may *b*
Jn. 14:1, you *b* in God
Jn. 20:31, written that you may *b*
Acts 26:27, King Agrippa, do you *b*
Rom. 10:9, the Lord Jesus and *b*
Rom. 10:14, And how shall they *b*
1 Cor. 7:12, a wife who does not *b*
2 Cor. 4:13, I spoke," we also *b*
Gal. 3:22, given to those who *b*
Phil. 1:29, Christ, not only to *b*
Heb. 11:6, comes to God must *b*
Jas. 2:19, *b* that there is one
Jas. 2:19, Even the demons *b*
1 Jn. 4:1, Beloved, do not *b*

BELIEVED
Gen. 15:6, And he *b* in the LORD
Ps. 27:13, *b* that I would see the
Isa. 53:1, Who has *b* our report
Jn. 4:39, of that city *b* in Him
Jn. 20:29, seen Me, you have *b*
Acts 4:4, who heard the word *b*
Acts 4:32, of those who *b* were of
Acts 19:2, Holy Spirit when you *b*
Rom. 4:3, "Abraham *b* God
2 Tim. 1:12, I know whom I have *b*

BELIEVERS
1 Tim. 4:12, example to the *b*
1 Tim. 6:2, are benefited are *b*

BELIEVES
Prov. 14:15, The simple *b* every
Mk. 16:16, "He who *b* and is
Jn. 3:16, that whoever *b* in Him
Jn. 3:36, "He who *b* in the Son
Rom. 10:10, with the heart one *b*
1 Cor. 13:7, *b* all things

BELIEVING
Mt. 21:22, you ask in prayer, *b*
Gal. 3:9, blessed with *b* Abraham

BELLY
Gen. 3:14, On your *b* you shall go
Jon. 1:17, And Jonah was in the *b*
Mt. 12:40, three nights in the *b*
Phil. 3:19, whose god is their *b*

BELONG
Dan. 9:9, To the Lord our God *b*
Mk. 9:41, My name, because you *b*

BELOVED
Dt. 33:12, "The *b* of the Lord

Ps. 127:2, so He gives His *b*
Song 1:13, of myrrh is my *b*
Song 2:16, My *b* is mine
Song 5:9, *b* more than another
Song 6:1, Where has your *b*
Song 8:5, leaning upon her *b*
Isa. 5:1, a song of my *B*
Dan. 9:23, for you are greatly *b*
Mt. 3:17, "This is My *b*
Rom. 11:28, election they are *b*
Eph. 1:6, us accepted in the *B*
Col. 4:14, Luke the *b* physician
Phile. 16, than a slave as a *b*
2 Pet. 1:17, "This is My *b*
2 Pet. 3:15, our *b* brother Paul
Rev. 20:9, the saints and the *b*

BELSHAZZAR, Dan. 5:1
his profane feast, warning, and death. Dan. 5

BELT
Mt. 3:4, with a leather *b*
Acts 21:11, us, he took Paul's *b*

BELTESHAZZAR
Daniel so named. Dan. 1:7; 4:8

BEMOAN
Jer. 15:5, Or who will *b* you
Jer. 22:10, for the dead, nor *b*

BEN-AMMI, Gen. 19:38

BEN-HADAD
king of Syria, his league with Asa against Baasha. 1 Ki. 15:18
——— wars with Ahab. 1 Ki. 20
baffled by Elisha. 2 Ki. 6:8
besieges Samaria. 2 Ki. 6:24; 7
killed by Hazael. 2 Ki. 8:7
——— son of Hazael, wars with Israel. 2 Ki. 13:3

BENAIAH, 2 Sam. 8:18
valiant acts of. 2 Sam. 23:20; 1 Chr. 11:22; 27:5
proclaims Solomon king. 1 Ki. 1:32
kills Adonijah, Joab, and Shimei. 1 Ki. 2:25–46

BEND
Ps. 11:2, The wicked *b* their bow

BENEATH
Dt. 4:39, and on the earth *b*
Jn. 8:23, "You are from *b*

BENEFACTORS
Lk. 22:25, them are called "*b*

BENEFIT
Ps. 106:5, That I may see the *b*
Isa. 30:5, people who could not *b*
2 Cor. 1:15, might have a second *b*

BENJAMIN, Gen. 35:18
(first named Ben-Oni), Patriarch, youngest son of Jacob, his birth at Bethlehem. Gen. 35:16
goes into Egypt. Gen. 43:15
Joseph's stratagem to detain. Gen. 44
Jacob's prophecy concerning. Gen. 49:27
his descendants. Gen. 46:21; 1 Chr. 7:6
twice numbered. Num. 1:36; 26:38
blessed by Moses. Dt. 33:12
their inheritance. Josh. 18:11
their wickedness chastised. Jud. 20; 21
the first king chosen from. 1 Sam. 9; 10
support the house of Saul. 2 Sam. 2
afterwards adhere to that of David. 1 Ki. 12:21; 1 Chr. 11
the tribe of Paul. Phil. 3:5

BENT
Ezek. 17:7, behold, this vine *b*

BEOR, Gen. 36:32

BERACHAH, 1 Chr. 12:3
Valley of, why so named. 2 Chr. 20:26

BEREA
city of Macedonia, Paul preaches at. Acts 17:10
people 'more fair-minded'. Acts 17:11

BEREAVE
Jer. 15:7, I will *b* them of
Ezek. 36:12, no more shall you *b*
Hos. 9:12, children, yet I will *b*

BERECHIAH
1 Chr. 3:20; 6:39; Mt. 23:35

BERNICE, Acts 25:13

BESEECH
Ps. 80:14, Return, we *b* You
Rom. 12:1, *b* you therefore
Eph. 4:1, of the LORD, *b* you to

BESIDE
Ps. 23:2, He leads me *b* the
Acts 26:24, "Paul, you are *b*
2 Cor. 5:13, For if we are *b*

BEST
Amos 6:6, with the *b* ointments
Lk. 15:22, 'Bring out the *b*
1 Cor. 12:31, desire the *b*

BESTOW
Ex. 32:29, LORD, that He may *b*
1 Cor. 12:23, *b* greater honor

BESTOWED
1 Jn. 3:1, love the Father has *b*

BETH ARABAH, Josh. 15:6

BETH ARBEL, Hos. 10:14

BETH AVEN, Josh. 7:2

BETH HARAM, Josh. 13:27

BETH HARAN, Num. 32:36

BETH HORON, Josh. 10:10

BETH MAACHAH, 2 Sam. 20:14

BETH PEOR, Dt. 3:29

BETH SHEMESH, Josh. 15:10
men of, punished for looking into the ark. 1 Sam. 6:19
great battle at. 2 Ki. 14:11

BETHABARA
place where John baptized. Jn. 1:28

BETHANY
visited by Christ. Mt. 21:17; 26:6; Mk. 11:1; Lk. 19:29; Jn. 12:1
raising of Lazarus at. Jn. 11:18
ascension of Christ at. Lk. 24:50

BETHEL, Gen. 12:8
(Luz), city of Palestine, named Bethel by Jacob. Gen. 28:19; 31:13
altar built by Jacob at. Gen. 35:1
occupied by the house of Joseph. Jud. 1:22
sons of prophets resident there. 2 Ki. 2:2,3; 17:28
the king's chapel. Amos 7:13
idolatry of Jeroboam at. 1 Ki. 12:28; 13:1
reformation by Josiah at. 2 Ki. 23:15

BETHESDA
pool of, at Jerusalem, miracles wrought at. Jn. 5:2

BETHLEHEM, Gen. 35:19

BETHLEHEM IN JUDAH, Jud. 17:7

BETHLEHEM EPHRATHAH
(originally Ephratah), Naomi and Ruth return to. Ruth 1—4
David anointed at. 1 Sam. 16:13; 20:6
well of. 2 Sam. 23:15; 1 Chr. 11:17
Christ's birth at. Mt. 2:1; Lk. 2:4; Jn. 7:42; predicted. Mic. 5:2 (Ps. 132:5,6)
babies of, killed. Mt. 2:16

BETHPHAGE, Mt. 21:1

BETHSAIDA
of Galilee, native place of Philip, Peter, and Andrew. Mk. 6:45; Jn. 1:44; 12:21
blind man cured at. Mk. 8:22
condemned for unbelief. Mt. 11:21
Christ feeds the five thousand at. Lk. 9:10–17

BETHUEL, Gen. 22:22

BETRAY
Isa. 16:3, the outcasts, do not *b*
Mt. 26:21, you, one of you will *b*
Mk. 13:12, "Now brother will *b*

BETRAYED
Mt. 17:22, Man is about to be *b*
1 Cor. 11:23, in which He was *b*

BETRAYER
Mt. 26:46, See, My *b* is at

BETRAYING
Lk. 22:48, "Judas, are you *b*

BETRAYS
Jn. 21:20, who is the one who *b*

BETROTH
Dt. 28:30, "You shall *b* a wife
Hos. 2:19, "I will *b* you to Me

BETROTHAL
laws concerning. Ex. 21:8; Lev. 19:20; Dt. 20:7

BETROTHED
Lk. 1:27, to a virgin *b* to a man

2 Cor. 11:2, For I have *b* you to

BETTER
1 Sam. 15:22, *b* than sacrifice
Ps. 118:8, It is *b* to trust in
Prov. 15:16, *B* is a little with the
Prov. 17:1, *B* is a dry morsel
Prov. 19:1, *B* is the poor who
Prov. 21:19 *B* to dwell in
Prov. 27:10, *b* is a neighbor
Eccl. 4:6, *B* a handful with
Eccl. 4:9, Two are *b* than one
Eccl. 4:13, *B* a poor and wise
Eccl. 7:10, were the former days *b*
Dan. 1:15, features appeared *b*
1 Cor. 7:9, For it is *b* to marry
Phil. 1:23, Christ, which is far *b*
Heb. 1:4, *b* than the angels
Heb. 6:9, *b* things concerning
Heb. 12:24, *b* things than that

BEULAH, Isa. 62:4

BEWARE
Mt. 7:15, "*B* of false prophets
Phil. 3:2, *b* of evil workers
Col. 2:8, *B* lest anyone cheat

BEWITCHED
Gal. 3:1, *b* you that you should

BEYOND
1 Cor. 4:6, *b* what is written
2 Cor. 8:3, *b* their ability
Gal. 1:14, advanced in Judaism *b*

BEZALEL
constructs the tabernacle. Ex. 31:2; 35:30; 36—38

BILDAD, Job 2:11
his answers to Job. Job 8; 18; 25

BILHAH, Gen. 29:29
Jacob's children by. Gen. 30:5

BILLOWS
Ps. 42:7, *b* have gone over me
Jon. 2:3, all Your *b* and Your

BIND
Job 38:31, *b* the cluster of the
Job 39:10, *b* the wild ox in the
Prov. 3:3, *b* them around your
Prov. 7:3, *B* them on your fingers
Isa. 8:16, *B* up the testimony
Hos. 6:1, but He will *b* us up
Mt. 16:19, and whatever you *b*
Mt. 22:13, *B* him hand and foot
Mt. 23:4, *b* heavy burdens

BIRD
Lev. 14:52, the blood of the *b*
Job 41:5, with him as with a *b*
Ps. 11:1, soul, "Flee as a *b*
Ps. 124:7, has escaped as a *b*
Prov. 7:23, *b* hastens to the snare
Eccl. 10:20, for a *b* of the air may
Hos. 9:11, fly away like a *b*
Rev. 18:2, unclean and hated *b*

BIRDS
Gen. 40:19, *b* will eat your flesh
Ps. 104:17, *b* make their nests
Eccl. 9:12, *b* caught in a snare
Mt. 6:26, "Look at the *b*
Mt. 8:20, "Foxes have holes and *b*

BIRTH
Job 38:29, heaven, who gives it *b*
Ps. 29:9, makes the deer give *b*
Eccl. 7:1, the day of one's *b*
Isa. 66:9, bring to the time of *b*
Jer. 14:5, the deer also gave *b*
Mt. 1:18, Now the *b* of Jesus
Lk. 1:14, will rejoice at his *b*
Jn. 9:1, who was blind from *b*
Jas. 1:15, conceived, it gives *b*

BIRTHDAY
Gen. 40:20, which was Pharaoh's *b*
Mk. 6:21, *b* gave a feast for his

BIRTHRIGHT
law concerning. Dt. 21:15
despised by Esau, and obtained by Jacob. Gen. 25:31; Heb. 12:16
lost by Reuben. 1 Chr. 5:1

BIRTHRIGHT
Gen. 25:31, "Sell me your *b*
Gen. 25:34, Esau despised his *b*
Gen. 43:33, according to his *b*
Heb. 12:16, of food sold his *b*

BIRTHS, foretold
of Ishmael. Gen. 16:11
of Isaac. Gen. 18:10
of Samson. Jud. 13:3
of Samuel. 1 Sam. 1:11,17
of Josiah. 1 Ki. 13:2
of Shunammite's son. 2 Ki. 4:16
of John the Baptist. Lk. 1:13
of Messiah. Gen. 3:15; Isa. 7:14; Mic. 5; Lk. 1:31

BISHOP
1 Tim. 3:1, the position of a *b*
Ti. 1:7, *b* must be blameless

BIT
Num. 21:6, and they *b* the people
Ps. 32:9, be harnessed with *b*

BITE
Eccl. 10:11, A serpent may *b*
Gal. 5:15, But if you *b* and

BITHYNIA, Acts 16:7

BITS
Amos 6:11, the great house into *b*
Jas. 3:3, Indeed, we put *b*

BITTER
Ex. 1:14, made their lives *b*
Ex. 12:8, *b* herbs they
Prov. 31:6, to those who are *b*
Isa. 5:20, who put *b* for sweet
Col. 3:19, and do not be *b*
Jas. 3:14, But if you have *b*
Rev. 10:9, make your stomach *b*

BITTERLY
Ruth 1:20, has dealt very *b*
2 Ki. 20:3, And Hezekiah wept *b*
Mt. 26:75, went out and wept *b*

BITTERNESS
Job 21:25, man dies in the *b*
Prov. 14:10, heart knows its own *b*
Isa. 38:15, all my years in the *b*
Acts 8:23, you are poisoned by *b*
Heb. 12:15, *b* springing up cause

BLACK
Job 30:30, My skin grows *b*
Song 5:11, wavy, and *b* as a raven
Mt. 5:36, one hair white or *b*
Rev. 6:5, a *b* horse
Rev. 6:12, and the sun became *b*

BLACKNESS
Isa. 50:3, the heavens with *b*
Jude 13, whom is reserved the *b*

BLACKSMITH
Isa. 44:12, The *b* with the tongs
Isa. 54:16, I have created the *b*

BLADE
Jud. 3:22, went in after the *b*
Mk. 4:28, first the *b*

BLAME
2 Cor. 8:20, that anyone should *b*
Eph. 1:4, be holy and without *b*

BLAMELESS
Dt. 18:13, "You shall be *b*
Job 1:1, and that man was *b*
Ps. 51:4, when You speak, and *b*
Ps. 119:80, Let my heart be *b*
1 Cor. 1:8, end, that you may be *b*
Phil. 3:6, which is in the law, *b*
Col. 1:22, you holy, and *b*
1 Th. 3:13, your hearts *b* in
1 Th. 5:23, body be preserved *b*
1 Tim. 3:2, bishop then must be *b*
1 Tim. 3:10, deacons, being found *b*
2 Pet. 3:14, without spot and *b*

BLAMELESSLY
1 Th. 2:10, *b* we behaved

BLASPHEME
Ps. 74:10, *b* Your name forever
Acts 26:11, compelled them to *b*
1 Tim. 1:20, may learn not to *b*
Jas. 2:7, *b* that noble name
Rev. 13:6, God, to *b* His name

BLASPHEMED
Ps. 74:18, a foolish people has *b*
Isa. 52:5, *b* continually every
Mt. 27:39, who passed by *b* Him
Lk. 23:39, who were hanged *b*
Rom. 2:24, The name of God is *b*
1 Tim. 6:1, doctrine may not be *b*
1 Pet. 4:14, On their part He is *b*
Rev. 16:9, great heat, and they *b*

BLASPHEMER
1 Tim. 1:13, I was formerly a *b*

BLASPHEMERS
2 Tim. 3:2, boasters, proud, *b*

BLASPHEMES
Lev. 24:16, *b* the name of the
Mt. 9:3, "This Man *b*

BLASPHEMIES
Mt. 15:19, false witness, *b*
Lk. 5:21, is this who speaks *b*
Rev. 13:5, great things and *b*

BLASPHEMY
Ex. 20:7; Ps. 74:18; Isa. 52:5; Ezek. 20:27; Mt. 15:19; Lk. 22:65; Col. 3:8; Rev. 2:9; 13:5,6; 16:9
punishment of, death. Lev. 24:16; 1 Ki. 21:10

mercy for. 1 Tim. 1:13
Christ accused of. Mt. 9:3; 26:65; Mk. 2:7; Lk. 5:21; Jn. 10:33
others falsely accused of, and stoned: Naboth. 1 Ki. 21:13; Stephen. Acts 6:13; 7:54
occasion to blaspheme given by David. 2 Sam. 12:14. *See also* 1 Tim. 5:14; 6:1
against Holy Spirit. Mt. 12:31; Mk. 3:29; Lk. 12:10; 1 Jn. 5:16

BLASPHEMY
Mt. 12:31, but the *b* against
Mt. 26:65, "He has spoken *b*
Rev. 17:3, was full of names of *b*

BLAST
Job 4:9, By the *b* of God they
Isa. 25:4, for the *b* of the

BLASTED
Amos 4:9, "I *b* you with blight

BLASTUS, Acts 12:20

BLEATING
1 Sam. 15:14, "What then is this *b*

BLEMISH
Ex. 12:5, shall be without *b*
Lev. 6:6, LORD, a ram without *b*
Eph. 5:27, be holy and without *b*
1 Pet. 1:19, as of a lamb without *b*

BLEMISHED
Mal. 1:14, to the Lord what is *b*

BLESS
Gen. 12:3, *b* those who *b* you
Gen. 32:26, You go unless You *b*
Num. 6:24, "The LORD *b* you and
Ps. 34:1, *b* the LORD at all
Ps. 63:4, *b* You while I live
Ps. 103:1, *b* His holy name
Ps. 115:12, *b* the house of Israel
Ps. 115:13, *b* those who fear the
Ps. 129:8, *b* you in the name of
Ps. 132:15, I will abundantly *b*
Lk. 6:28, *b* those who curse
Rom. 12:14, *B* those who
1 Cor. 4:12, Being reviled, we *b*
Jas. 3:9, With it we *b* our God

BLESSED
those chosen, called, instructed by God. Ps. 65:4; Eph. 1:3,4.—Isa. 51:2; Rev. 19:9.—Ps. 94:12
those who trust, fear, delight in God. Ps. 2:12; 34:8; 40:4; 84:12; Jer. 17:7.—Ps. 128:1,4.—Ps. 112:1
those who hear and obey. Ps. 119:2; Mt. 13:16; Lk. 11:28; Jas. 1:25; Rev. 1:3; 22:7,14
those who know, believe, and suffer for Christ. Mt. 16:16,17.—Mt. 11:6; Lk. 1:45; Gal. 3:9.—Lk. 6:22
those who endure temptation. Jas. 1:12; watch against sin. Rev. 16:15; rebuke sinners. Prov. 24:25; die in the Lord. Rev. 14:13
the undefiled, pure, righteous, children of the righteous, upright, faithful, poor in spirit, meek, merciful, peacemakers. Ps. 119:1.—Mt. 5:8.—Ps. 5:12; Ps. 106:3; Prov. 10:6.—Prov. 20:7.—Ps. 112:2.—Prov. 28:20.—Mt. 5:3.—Mt. 5:5.—Mt. 5:7.—Mt. 5:9
the generous. Dt. 15:10; Ps. 41:1; Prov. 22:9; Lk. 14:13,14
those whose sins are forgiven. Ps. 32:1,2; Rom. 4:7

BLESSED
Gen. 1:22, And God *b* them
Gen. 12:3, the earth shall be *b*
Gen. 27:29, *b* be those who
Gen. 27:33, indeed he shall be *b*
Num. 24:9, *B* is he who
Dt. 28:4, *B* shall be the
Job 1:10, You have *b* the work of
Ps. 1:1, *B* is the man who walks
Ps. 32:2, *B* is the man to whom
Ps. 33:12, *B* is the nation whose
Ps. 41:1, *B* is he who considers
Ps. 106:3, *B* are those who keep
Ps. 118:26, *B* is he who comes
Ps. 128:4, *b* who fears the LORD
Prov. 31:28, rise up and call her *b*
Mal. 3:12, will call you *b*
Mt. 5:3, *B* are the poor in
Mt. 5:4, *B* are those who mourn
Mt. 5:5, *B* are the meek
Mt. 5:6, *B* are those who hunger
Mt. 5:7, *B* are the merciful
Mt. 5:8, *B* are the pure in
Mt. 5:9, *B* are the peacemakers
Mt. 5:10, *B* are those who are
Mt. 5:11, *B* are you when they
Mt. 11:6, *b* is he who is
Mt. 13:16, *b* are your eyes
Mt. 21:9, *b* is He who comes
Mt. 25:34, hand, 'Come, you *b*
Mt. 26:26, Jesus took bread, *b*
Lk. 1:28, *b* are you among women
Jn. 13:17, know these things, *b*
Jn. 20:29, *B* are those who have
Rom. 1:25, the Creator, who is *b*
Rom. 9:5, all, the eternally *b*
Acts 20:35, 'It is more *b* to give
Eph. 1:3, *B* be the God and
1 Tim. 1:11, *b* God which was
Heb. 7:7, the lesser is *b*
Jas. 1:25, this one will be *b*
Rev. 1:3, *B* is he who reads
Rev. 14:13, *B* are the dead who
Rev. 16:15, *B* is he who watches
Rev. 19:9, *B* are those who are
Rev. 20:6, *B* and holy is he who
Rev. 22:7, *B* is he who keeps the
Rev. 22:14, *B* are those who do His

BLESSING
and cursing the people, form of. Num. 6:22; Dt. 11:26; 27:15
and glory. Rev. 5:12,13; 7:12

BLESSING
Gen. 12:2, and you shall be a *b*
Lev. 25:21, I will command My *b*
Dt. 11:26, before you today a *b*
Job 29:13, The *b* of a perishing
Ps. 3:8, Your *b* is upon Your
Prov. 10:22, The *b* of the LORD
Ezek. 34:26, shall be showers of *b*
Joel 2:14, relent, and leave a *b*
Zech. 8:13, and you shall be a *b*
Rom. 15:29, the fullness of the *b*
1 Cor. 10:16, *b* which we bless
Gal. 3:14, that the *b* of Abraham
Eph. 1:3, with every spiritual *b*
Heb. 6:7, cultivated, receives *b*
Heb. 12:17, to inherit the *b*
Rev. 5:12, honor and glory and *b*

BLESSINGS
Josh. 8:34, of the law, the *b*
Prov. 10:6, *B* are on the head of

BLIGHT
Amos 4:9, I blasted you with *b*
Hag. 2:17, 'I struck you with *b*

BLIND
laws concerning the. Lev. 19:14; Dt. 27:18

BLIND
Job 29:15, I was eyes to the *b*
Isa. 29:9, *B* yourselves and be
Isa. 42:7, To open *b* eyes
Isa. 42:16, I will bring the *b*
Isa. 43:8, *b* people who have eyes
Isa. 56:10, His watchmen are *b*
Lam. 4:14, They wandered *b*
Mal. 1:8, when you offer the *b*
Mt. 11:5, The *b* see
Mt. 15:14, *b* leads the *b*
Lk. 4:18, of sight to the *b*
Jn. 9:40, to Him, "Are we *b*
Rev. 3:17, miserable, poor, *b*

BLINDED
Jn. 12:40, *b* their eyes and
Rom. 11:7, and the rest were *b*
2 Cor. 4:4, of this age has *b*
1 Jn. 2:11, the darkness has *b*

BLINDNESS
inflicted on: the men of Sodom. Gen. 19:11
the Syrian army. 2 Ki. 6:18
Saul of Tarsus. Acts 9:8
Elymas at Paphos. Acts 13:11
healed by Christ. Mt. 9:27; 12:22; 20:30; Mk. 8:22; 10:46; Lk. 7:21; Jn. 9 (Isa. 35:5)
spiritual. Ps. 82:5; Isa. 56:10; 59:9; Mt. 6:23; 15:14; 23:16; Jn. 1:5; 3:19; 9:39; 1 Cor. 2:14; 2 Pet. 1:9; 1 Jn. 2:9; Rev. 3:17
judicially inflicted. Ps. 69:23; Isa. 6:9; 44:18; Mt. 13:13; Jn. 12:40; cts 28:26; Rom. 11:7; 2 Cor. 3:14; 4:4
prayer for deliverance from. Ps. 13:3; 119:18
removed by Christ. Isa. 9:2; 42:7; Lk. 4:18; Jn. 8:12; 9:39; 2 Cor. 3:14; 4:6; Eph. 5:8; Col. 1:13; 1 Th. 5:4; 1 Pet. 2:9

BLINDS
Dt. 16:19, a bribe, for a bribe *b*

BLOOD
eating of, forbidden to:
man after the flood. Gen. 9:4
the Israelites under the law. Lev. 3:17; 17:10,12,13; Dt. 12:16,24; 1 Sam. 14:32,33

the Gentile Christians. Acts 15:20,29
water turned into, as a sign. Ex. 4:30, with v. 9; as a judgment. Ex. 7:17; Rev. 8:8; 11:6
law respecting. Lev. 7:26; 19:26; Dt. 12:16; Ezek. 33:25; Acts 15:29; enforced by Saul. 1 Sam. 14:32
shedding of human, forbidden. Gen. 9:5,6; Dt. 21:1–9; Ps. 106:38; Prov. 6:16,17; Isa. 59:3; Jer. 22:17; Ezek. 22:4; Mt. 27:6
of legal sacrifices. Ex. 23:18; 29:12; 30:10; 34:25; Lev. 4:7; 17:11; Heb. 9:13,19–22; 10:4
——— of the covenant. Ex. 24:8; Zech. 9:11; Heb. 10:29; 13:20
——— of Christ. 1 Cor. 10:16; Eph. 2:13; Heb. 9:14; 1 Pet. 1:19; 1 Jn. 1:7
salvation by. Heb. 9:12; 13:12; Rev. 1:5. *See* Heb. 9:22
in the Lord's Supper. Mt. 26:28; Mk. 14:24; Lk. 22:20; 1 Cor. 11:25
redemption by. Eph. 1:7; Col. 1:20; Heb. 10:19; 12:24; 1 Pet. 1:2; 1 Jn. 1:7; Rev. 1:5; 5:9; 12:11
typified, under the law. Ex. 12:13; 29:16; 30:10; Lev. 1:5; 4; 16:15; Heb. 9:7

BLOOD
Gen. 4:10, of your brother's *b*
Gen. 9:6, *b* shall be shed
Ex. 4:25, you are a husband of *b*
Lev. 17:11, *b* that makes
Lev. 17:14, *b* sustains its life
Job 16:18, do not cover my *b*
Ps. 30:9, is there in my *b*
Ps. 94:21, And condemn innocent *b*
Isa. 1:15, hands are full of *b*
Isa. 26:21, also disclose her *b*
Joel 2:31, And the moon into *b*
Mt. 26:28, For this is My *b*
Mt. 27:8, called the Field of *B*
Mt. 27:25, His *b* be on us and
Lk. 22:20, new covenant in My *b*
Jn. 1:13, were born, not of *b*
Jn. 6:54, *b* has eternal life
Acts 17:26, *b* every nation of men
Acts 20:28, with His own *b*
Rom. 3:25, propitiation by His *b*
Rom. 5:9, justified by His *b*
Eph. 1:7, through His *b*
Eph. 2:13, brought near by the *b*
Eph. 6:12, against flesh and *b*
Col. 1:20, peace through the *b*
Heb. 9:20, "This is the *b*
Heb. 9:22, are purified with *b*
Heb. 9:22, of *b* there is no
Heb. 10:19, the Holiest by the *b*
1 Pet. 1:2, sprinkling of the *b*
1 Pet. 1:19, with the precious *b*
1 Jn. 1:7, *b* of Jesus Christ His
Rev. 1:5, our sins in His own *b*
Rev. 5:9, us to God by Your *b*
Rev. 7:14, them white in the *b*
Rev. 12:11, overcame him by the *b*
Rev. 19:13, a robe dipped in *b*

BLOODSHED
Ps. 51:14, me from the guilt of *b*
Ezek. 9:9, the land is full of *b*
Mic. 3:10, build up Zion with *b*

BLOODTHIRSTY
Ps. 5:6, The LORD abhors the *b*
Ps. 55:23, *B* and deceitful men

BLOSSOM
Isa. 27:6, Israel shall *b* and bud
Isa. 35:1, and *b* as the rose
Hab. 3:17, the fig tree may not *b*

BLOT
2 Ki. 14:27, say that He would *b*
Ps. 51:9, from my sins, and *b*
Rev. 3:5, and I will not *b*

BLOTTED
Ps. 69:28, Let them be *b* out of
Isa. 44:22, I have *b* out
Acts 3:19, your sins may be *b*

BLOW
Ps. 78:26, an east wind to *b*
Song 4:16, *B* upon my garden
Jer. 14:17, with a very severe *b*

BLOWS
Prov. 20:30, *B* that hurt cleanse
Isa. 40:7, breath of the LORD *b*
Jn. 3:8, "The wind *b* where it

BOAST
1 Ki. 20:11, puts on his armor *b*
Ps. 34:2, soul shall make its *b*
Ps. 44:8, God we *b* all day long
Rom. 2:17, and make your *b*
2 Cor. 1:14, that we are your *b*
2 Cor. 10:16, you, and not to *b*
2 Cor. 11:16, that I also may *b*
Eph. 2:9, lest anyone should *b*
Jas. 3:14, your hearts, do not *b*

BOASTERS
Rom. 1:30, God, violent, proud, *b*
2 Tim. 3:2, lovers of money, *b*

BOASTFUL
Ps. 5:5, *b* shall not stand
Ps. 73:3 I was envious of the *b*

BOASTING
Rom. 3:27, Where is *b* then
1 Cor. 9:15, should make my *b*
2 Cor. 7:4, you, great is my *b*
Jas. 4:16, All such *b* is evil

BOASTS
Prov. 25:14, Whoever falsely *b*

BOAZ, Ruth 2:1
his conduct towards Ruth. Ruth 2; 3; 4
ancestor of David and Christ. Ruth 4:17,22; Mk. 1:5; Lk. 3:23,32
——— and Jachin (strength and stability), pillars of the temple. 2 Chr. 3:17

BOCHIM, Jud. 2:1
Israel rebuked by an angel at. Jud. 2:1–3
Israel repents at. Jud. 2:4,5

BODIES
Jer. 31:40, valley of the dead *b*
Rom. 12:1, *b* a living sacrifice
1 Cor. 6:15, not know that your *b*
1 Cor. 15:40, also celestial *b*
Eph. 5:28, wives as their own *b*
Rev. 18:13, and chariots, and *b*

BODILY
Lk. 3:22, *b* form like a dove
2 Cor. 10:10, *b* presence is weak
Col. 2:9, of the Godhead *b*
1 Tim. 4:8, *b* exercise

BODY (human)
not to be dishonored. Lev. 19:28; 21:5; Dt. 14:1
to be pure. Rom. 12:1; 1 Cor. 6:13; 1 Th. 4:4
of a Christian, the temple of the Holy Spirit. 1 Cor. 3:16; 6:19; 2 Cor. 6:16
dead, laws concerning. Lev. 21:11; Num. 5:2; 9:6; 19:11; Dt. 21:23; Hag. 2:13
will be raised again. Mt. 22:30; 1 Cor. 15:12; Phil. 3:21. *See* RESURRECTION

BODY of Christ
prepared by God (Heb. 10:5); Lk. 2:35; pierced by soldiers. Jn. 19:34; buried by Joseph. Mt. 27:60; Mk. 15:46; Lk. 23:53; Jn. 19:42
Church Christ's body. Rom. 12:4; 1 Cor. 10:17; 12:12; Eph. 1:22; 4:12; 5:23; Col. 1:18; 2:19; 3:15

BODY
Ps. 44:25, *b* clings to the ground
Song 5:14, *b* is carved ivory
Dan. 4:33, *b* was wet with the dew
Mt. 6:22, of the *b* is the eye
Mt. 10:28, those who kill the *b*
Mt. 26:26, this is My *b*
Mt. 27:58, and asked for the *b*
Mk. 14:51, around his naked *b*
Jn. 2:21, of the temple of His *b*
Rom. 7:24, deliver me from this *b*
Rom. 8:23, redemption of our *b*
Rom. 12:4, members in one *b*
1 Cor. 6:13, and the Lord for the *b*
1 Cor. 6:18, against his own *b*
1 Cor. 6:19, not know that your *b*
1 Cor. 6:20, glorify God in your *b*
1 Cor. 9:27, But I discipline my *b*
1 Cor. 10:17, one bread and one *b*
1 Cor. 11:24, *b* which is broken
1 Cor. 11:27, be guilty of the *b*
1 Cor. 12:12, For as the *b* is one
1 Cor. 12:13, baptized into one *b*
1 Cor. 12:14, *b* is not one member
1 Cor. 12:27, are the *b* of Christ
1 Cor. 13:3, though I give my *b*
1 Cor. 15:44, It is sown a natural *b*
Eph. 2:16, both to God in one *b*
Phil. 1:20, be magnified in my *b*
Col. 1:22, in the *b* of His flesh
Col. 2:11, by putting off the *b*
Col. 2:23, and neglect of the *b*
Col. 3:15, were called in one *b*
Heb. 10:5, *b* You have prepared
Heb. 10:10, the offering of the *b*
Jas. 2:26, For as the *b* without
1 Pet. 2:24, our sins in His own *b*

BOILS
Job 2:7, Job with painful *b*

BOLD
Prov. 28:1, the righteous are *b*
2 Cor. 11:21, whatever anyone is *b*
Phil. 1:14, are much more *b*

BOLDLY
Eph. 6:19, I may open my mouth *b*
Heb. 4:16, therefore come *b*
Heb. 13:6, So we may *b* say

BOLDNESS
through faith. Prov. 28:1; Isa. 50:7; Acts 5:29; Eph. 3:12; Heb. 10:19; 1 Jn. 4:17
exhortations to. Josh. 1:7; 2 Chr. 19:11; Jer. 1:8; Ezek. 3:9; Heb. 4:16
of Peter and John. Acts 4:13; 5:29; Stephen. Acts 7:51; Paul. Acts 9:27; 19:8; 2 Cor. 7:4; Gal. 2:11; Apollos. Acts 18:26

BOLDNESS
2 Cor. 7:4, Great is my *b* of
Eph. 3:12, in whom we have *b*
Phil. 1:20, but with all *b*
1 Tim. 3:13, standing and great *b*
Heb. 10:19, brethren, having *b*
1 Jn. 4:17, that we may have *b*

BOND
Ezek. 20:37, bring you into the *b*
Eph. 4:3, of the Spirit in the *b*
Col. 3:14, love, which is the *b*

BONDAGE
of Israel in Egypt. Ex. 1—12; Ps. 105:25; Acts 7:6
in Babylon. 2 Ki. 25; Ezra 1; 9:7; Neh. 1; Est. 3; Dan. 1
——— spiritual. Jn. 8:34; Acts 8:23; Rom. 6:16; 7:23; 8:2; Gal. 2:4; 4:3; 1 Tim. 3:7; 2 Tim. 2:26; Heb. 2:14; 2 Pet. 2:19
deliverance by Christ. Isa. 61:1; Lk. 4:18; Jn. 8:36; Rom. 8:2; Gal. 3:13

BONDAGE
Ex. 2:23, because of the *b*
Ex. 13:14, out of the house of *b*
Rom. 8:15, the spirit of *b*
Gal. 2:4, might bring us into *b*
Gal. 4:24, which gives birth to *b*
Gal. 5:1, again with a yoke of *b*
Heb. 2:15, lifetime subject to *b*
2 Pet. 2:19, he is brought into *b*

BONDS
Ps. 2:3, "Let us break Their *b*

BONDSERVANTS
Eph. 6:5, *B*, be obedient to
Col. 4:1, Masters, give your *b*
1 Pet. 2:16, for vice, but as *b*

BONDWOMAN
Gen. 21:10, "Cast out this *b*
Gal. 4:22, the one by a *b*

BONE
Gen. 2:23, "This is now *b*
Job 19:20, *b* clings to my skin
Ezek. 37:7, bonds came together, *b*

BONES
Gen. 50:25, shall carry up my *b*
Job 4:14, which made all my *b*
Job 40:18, His *b* are like beams
Ps. 22:17, I can count all My *b*
Ps. 31:10, and my *b* waste away
Ps. 32:3, I kept silent, my *b*
Eccl. 11:5, the wind, or how the *b*
Ezek. 37:4, say to them, 'O dry *b*
Ezek. 37:11, *b* are the whole house
Mt. 23:27, of dead men's *b*
Jn. 19:36, *b* shall be broken
Heb. 11:22, concerning his *b*

BOOK
of Life. Ex. 32:32; Ps. 69:28; Dan. 12:1; Phil. 4:3; Rev. 3:5; 13:8; 17:8; 21:27; opened. Rev. 20:12
——— of the Law. Dt. 28:61; 29:27; Gal. 3:10; found and read. 2 Ki. 22:8; 23:2; Neh. 8:8

BOOK
Ezra 4:15, you will find in the *b*
Neh. 8:8, distinctly from the *b*
Job 19:23, were inscribed in a *b*
Isa. 34:16, "Search from the *b*
Jer. 30:2, 'Write in a *b* for
Dan. 12:1, found written in the *b*
Mal. 3:16, so a *b* of remembrance
Gal. 3:10, are written in the *b*
Heb. 9:19, sprinkled both the *b*
Rev. 21:27, in the Lamb's *B*
Rev. 22:18, the prophecy of this *b*
Rev. 22:19, the words of the *b*

BOOKS
1 Sam. 10:25; Dan. 9:2; 2 Tim. 4:13
of various persons. 1 Chr. 29:29; 2 Chr. 9:29; 12:15; 20:34
of Solomon. 1 Ki. 4:32; 11:41
of judgment. Dan. 7:10; Rev. 20:12
burned at Ephesus. Acts 19:19

BOOKS
Eccl. 12:12, *b* there is no end
Jn. 21:25, not contain the *b*
Acts 19:19, magic brought their *b*
Rev. 20:12, and *b* were opened

BOOTH
Job 27:18, *b* which a watchman
Isa. 1:8, of Zion is left as a *b*

BORDERS
of the land determined. Num. 34; Josh. 1:4; Ezek. 47:13

BORDERS
Ex. 34:24, and enlarge your *b*
Ps. 147:14, makes peace in your *b*
Mt. 23:5, and enlarge the *b*

BORE
Gen. 4:1, conceived and *b* Cain
Isa. 51:2, And to Sarah who *b*
Isa. 53:12, *b* the sin of many
Isa. 63:9, and He *b* them and
Mt. 8:17, *b* our sicknesses
1 Pet. 2:24, who Himself *b* our sins
Rev. 12:5, *b* a male Child who was

BORN
Ex. 1:20, "Every son who is *b*
Job 5:7, yet man is *b* to
Job 14:1, "Man who is *b*
Ps. 37:4, 'This one was *b*
Eccl. 3:2, A time to be *b*
Isa. 9:6, unto us a Child is *b*
Isa. 66:8, Or shall a nation be *b*
Mt. 1:16, *b* Jesus who is called
Lk. 2:11, "For there is *b*
Jn. 3:3, unless one is *b* again
Jn. 3:6, "That which is *b*
Jn. 18:37, For this cause I was *b*
1 Cor. 15:8, me also, as by one *b*
Gal. 4:23, of the bondwoman was *b*
1 Pet. 1:23, having been *b* again
1 Jn. 4:7, who loves is *b* of God
1 Jn. 5:1, is the Christ is *b*
1 Jn. 5:18, know that whoever is *b*

BORNE
1 Cor. 15:49, And as we have *b*

BORROWER
Prov. 22:7, *b* is servant to the
Isa. 24:2, lender, so with the *b*

BORROWING
Ex. 22:14; Dt. 15:1
its evils. 2 Ki. 6:5; Prov. 22:7

BORROWS
Ps. 37:21, The wicked *b* and does

BOSOM
Prov. 6:27, man take fire to his *b*
Isa. 66:11, consolation of her *b*
Lk. 16:22, to Abraham's *b*
Jn. 1:18, Son, who is in the *b*
Jn. 13:23, leaning on Jesus' *b*

BOTTLE
See also WINESKIN. Ps. 56:8

BOTTLE
Jer. 13:12, *b* shall be filled

BOTTOMLESS
Rev. 9:1, given the key to the *b*
Rev. 17:8, ascend out of the *b*
Rev. 20:1, the key to the *b*

BOUGHS
Ps. 80:10, cedars with its *b*
Ps. 80:11, She sent out her *b*

BOUGHT
Lev. 25:28, the hand of him who *b*
Dt. 32:6, not your Father, who *b*
2 Sam. 24:24, *b* the threshing floor
Jer. 32:9, *b* the field from
Mt. 13:46, all that he had and *b*
1 Cor. 6:20, For you were *b* at a
2 Pet. 2:1, denying the Lord who *b*

BOUND
Ps. 119:61, of the wicked have *b*
Prov. 30:4, *b* the waters in a
Isa. 1:6, not been closed or *b*
Mt. 16:19, on earth will be *b*
Jn. 11:44, *b* hand and foot with
Acts 20:22, And see, now I go *b*
Acts 28:20, of Israel I am *b*
Rom. 7:2, who has a husband is *b*
1 Cor. 7:27, Are you *b* to a wife
Rev. 20:2, Devil and Satan, and *b*

BOUNDARY
Ps. 104:9, *b* that they may not

BOUNTIFUL
Isa. 32:5, the miser said to be *b*
Jer. 2:7, you into a *b* country

BOUNTIFULLY
Ps. 13:6, Because He has dealt *b*
2 Cor. 9:6, and he who sows *b*

BOW
(weapon). Gen. 48:22; Josh. 24:12; 1 Sam. 18:4; 2 Sam. 1:18,22; 2 Ki. 9:24; Ps. 44:6; 78:57; Jer. 49:35; Hos. 7:16; Rev. 6:2

BOW
Gen. 49:24, *b* remained in strength
Ex. 23:24, "You shall not *b*
Jud. 2:19, to serve them and *b*
Job 29:20, *b* is renewed in my
Ps. 44:6, will not trust in my *b*
Ps. 46:9, He breaks the *b*
Ps. 78:57, like a deceitful *b*
Ps. 95:6, let us worship and *b*
Ps. 144:5, *B* down Your heavens
Hos. 1:7, not save them by *b*
Rev. 6:2, who sat on it had a *b*

BOWED
Gen. 37:7, stood all around and *b*
2 Sam. 22:10, *b* the heavens also
1 Ki. 19:18, whose knees have not *b*
Ps. 20:8, They have *b* down and
Mt. 27:29, And they *b* the knee
Rom. 11:4, men who have not *b*

BOWL
Prov. 19:24, his hand in the *b*
Eccl. 12:6, or the golden *b*
Rev. 16:2, and poured out his *b*

BOWLS
Amos 6:6, who drink wine from *b*
Rev. 5:8, a harp, and golden *b*
Rev. 16:1, Go and pour out the *b*
Rev. 21:9, who had the seven *b*

BOWS
1 Sam. 2:4, "The *b* of the mighty

BOX
Jn. 13:29, Judas had the money *b*

BOYS
Zech. 8:5, Shall be full of *b*

BOZRAH, Gen. 36:33
prophecies concerning. Isa. 34:6; 63:1; Jer. 48:24; 49:13; Amos 1:12

BRAIDED
1 Tim. 2:9, not with *b* hair or

BRAMBLE
Lk. 6:44, gather grapes from a *b*

BRANCH (of the Lord)
prophecies concerning. Isa. 4:2; Jer. 23:5; Zech. 3:8; 6:12; Jn. 15:5; Rom. 11:16

BRANCH
Ex. 25:33, blossoms on one *b*
Job 15:32, *b* will not be green
Isa. 9:14, from Israel, palm *b*
Isa. 11:1, *B* shall grow out of
Jer. 23:5, raise to David a *B*
Jer. 33:15, grow up to David a *B*
Zech. 3:8, forth My Servant the *B*
Zech. 6:12, whose name is the *B*
Mt. 24:32, *b* has already become
Jn. 15:2, *b* that bears fruit He
Jn. 15:4, *b* cannot bear fruit
Jn. 15:6, he is cast out as a *b*

BRANCHES
Job 8:16, in the sun, and his *b*
Job 14:9, and bring forth *b*
Isa. 18:5, and cut down the *b*
Jer. 11:16, and its *b* are broken
Hos. 14:6, His *b* shall spread
Jn. 15:5, vine, you are the *b*
Rom. 11:17, *b* were broken off

BRASS
1 Cor. 13:1, become sounding *b*
Rev. 1:15, feet were like fine *b*

BRAVE
1 Cor. 16:13, in the faith, be *b*

BREACHES
Ps. 60:2, heal its *b*

BREAD
Adam's curse. Gen. 3:19
rained from heaven (manna). Ex. 16:4
miraculously supplied. 2 Ki. 4:42; Jn. 6
a type of Christ. Jn. 6:31; 1 Cor. 10:16
offered before the Lord. Ex. 25:30; Lev. 8:26; 24:5
holy, David obtains from Ahimelech. 1 Sam. 21:4
used in the Lord's Supper. Lk. 22:19; 24:30; Acts 2:42; 20:7; 1 Cor. 10:16; 11:23
unleavened. Gen. 19:3; Ex. 12:8; 1 Sam. 28:24; 2 Ki. 23:9
figuratively used. 1 Cor. 5:8

BREAD
Gen. 3:19, face you shall eat *b*
Gen. 14:18, of Salem brought out *b*
Ex. 16:4, "Behold, I will rain *b*
Ex. 23:15, shall eat unleavened *b*
Dt. 8:3, not live by *b* alone
1 Ki. 17:12, lives, I do not have *b*
2 Ki. 18:32, new wine, a land of *b*
Job 33:20, that his life abhors *b*
Ps. 14:4, people as they eat *b*
Ps. 78:20, Can He give *b* also
Ps. 127:2, up late, to eat the *b*
Ps. 132:15, her poor with *b*
Prov. 4:17, For they eat the *b*
Prov. 9:17, *b* eaten in secret is
Prov. 20:17, *B* gained by deceit is
Eccl. 9:7, Go, eat your *b* with
Eccl. 11:1, Cast your *b* upon the
Isa. 33:16, *b* will be given him
Isa. 55:2, for what is not *b*
Isa. 58:7, to share your *b*
Lam. 5:9, We get our *b* at the
Hos. 2:5, who give me my *b*
Hos. 9:4, For their *b* shall be
Amos 4:6, And lack of *b* in all
Mt. 4:3, these stones become *b*
Mt. 4:4, not live by *b* alone
Mt. 6:11, this day our daily *b*
Mt. 26:26, eating, Jesus took *b*
Mk. 6:8, no bag, no *b*
Lk. 14:15, is he who shall eat *b*
Jn. 6:32, gives you the true *b*
Jn. 6:48, "I am the *b* of life
Jn. 13:26, having dipped the *b*
1 Cor. 10:16, *b* which we break
1 Cor. 11:23, He was betrayed took *b*
1 Cor. 11:26, as you eat this *b*
2 Th. 3:8, did we eat anyone's *b*
2 Th. 3:12, and eat their own *b*

BREADTH
Rev. 21:16, is as great as its *b*

BREAK
Num. 24:6, *b* their bones and
Job 19:2, torment my soul, and *b*
Job 30:13, They *b* up my path
Ps. 58:6, *B* their teeth in their
Ps. 74:6, And now they *b* down
Ps. 89:31, *b* My statutes and do
Ps. 89:34, covenant I will not *b*
Jer. 14:21, Remember, do not *b*
Acts 20:7, together to *b* bread

BREAKING
Acts 2:42, in the *b* of bread
Acts 2:46, *b* bread from house to
Acts 21:13, weeping and *b* my heart
Rom. 2:23, dishonor God through *b*

BREAKS
Job 34:24, He *b* in pieces mighty
Ps. 119:20, My soul *b* with longing
Song 2:17, Until the day *b*
Mt. 5:19, "Whoever therefore *b*

BREAST
Jn. 13:25, back on Jesus' *b*

BREASTPLATE
of the high priest described. Ex. 28:15; 39:8
of righteousness. Eph. 6:14
of faith and love. 1 Th. 5:8

BREASTPLATE
Ex. 28:4, a *b*, an ephod
Isa. 59:17, righteousness as a *b*
Eph. 6:14, having put on the *b*

BREASTS
Gen. 49:25, blessings of the *b*
Ps. 22:9, on My mother's *b*
Prov. 5:19, doe, let her *b* satisfy
Song 4:5, Your two *b* are like
Lk. 11:27, *b* which nursed You
Lk. 23:48, done, beat their *b*

BREATH
(life), dependent upon God. Gen. 2:7; 6:17; Job 12:10; 33:4; Ps. 104:29; Ezek. 37:5; Dan. 5:23; Acts 17:25
—— of God, its power. 2 Sam. 22:16; Job 4:9; Ps. 33:6; Isa. 11:4; 30:28

BREATH
Gen. 2:7, nostrils the *b* of life
2 Sam. 22:16, a the blast of the *b*
1 Ki. 17:17, that there was no *b*
Job 4:9, perish, and by the *b*
Job 27:3, as long as my *b*
Job 33:4, has made me, and the *b*
Ps. 104:29, You take away their *b*
Ps. 144:4, Man is like a *b*
Ps. 150:6, everything that has *b*
Eccl. 3:19, they all have one *b*
Isa. 42:5, from it, who gives *b*
Ezek. 37:5, Surely I will cause *b*
Dan. 5:23, God who holds your *b*

Acts 17:25, gives to all life, *b*
2 Th. 2:8, consume with the *b*
Rev. 13:15, power to give *b*

BREATHE
Ps. 27:12, me, and such as *b*
Ezek. 37:9, winds, O breath, and *b*

BREATHES
Job 14:10, indeed he *b* his last

BRETHREN
duty of, towards each other. Gen. 13:8; Dt. 15:7; 24:14; Ps. 133; Mt. 5:22; 18:15,21; 25:40; Jn. 13:34; 15:12; Rom. 12:10; 1 Cor. 6; 8:13; Gal. 6:1; 1 Th. 4:9; 2 Th. 3:15; Heb. 13:1; 1 Pet. 1:22; 3:8; 2 Pet. 1:7; 1 Jn. 2:9; 3:17

BRETHREN
Gen. 16:12, presence of all his *b*
Dt. 17:20, be lifted above his *b*
Mt. 23:8, and you are all *b*
Mt. 25:40, least of these My *b*
Mt. 28:10, Go and tell My *b*
Rom. 8:29, firstborn among many *b*
1 Cor. 6:5, to judge between his *b*
1 Cor. 8:12, thus sin against the *b*
1 Cor. 15:6, over five hundred *b*
2 Cor. 11:26, perils among false *b*
Gal. 2:4, *b* secretly brought
Heb. 2:17, to be made like His *b*
1 Pet. 1:22, sincere love of the *b*
1 Jn. 3:14, because we love the *b*
1 Jn. 3:16, our lives for the *b*
3 Jn. 10, does not receive the *b*
Rev. 22:9, of your *b* the prophets

BRIBE
Ex. 23:8, you shall take no *b*
Dt. 16:19, *b* blinds the eyes
Eccl. 7:7, *b* debases the heart

BRIBERY
Job 15:34, consume the tents of *b*

BRIBES
Ps. 26:10, hand is full of *b*
Prov. 15:27, but he who hates *b*
Prov. 29:4, but he who receives *b*
Isa. 1:23, everyone loves *b*
Amos 5:12, the just and taking *b*

BRICK
Ex. 5:7, people straw to make *b*
Isa. 65:3, incense on altars of *b*
Nah. 3:14, Make strong the *b*

BRICKS
Gen. 11:3, "Come, let us make *b*
Ex. 5:8, *b* which they made
Ex. 5:18, deliver the quota of *b*
Isa. 9:10, *b* have fallen down

BRIDE
Isa. 49:18, them on you as a *b*
Jn. 3:29, "He who has the *b*
Rev. 21:9, I will show you the *b*
Rev. 22:17, the Spirit and the *b*

BRIDEGROOM
Isa. 61:10, righteousness, as a *b*
Isa. 62:5, and as the *b* rejoices
Mt. 9:15, mourn as long as the *b*
Mt. 9:15, *b* will be taken away
Mt. 25:1, went out to meet the *b*
Mk. 2:19, *b* fast while the
Jn. 3:29, the friend of the *b*

BRIDLE
Ps. 32:9, with bit and *b*
Jas. 3:2, *b* the whole body

BRIER
Isa. 55:13, *b* shall come up the
Ezek. 28:24, longer be a pricking *b*
Mic. 7:4, of them is like a *b*

BRIERS
Isa. 5:6, there shall come up *b*
Ezek. 2:6, their words, though *b*

BRIGHTER
Lam. 4:7, Her Nazirites were *b*
Acts 26:13, a light from heaven, *b*

BRIGHTNESS
2 Sam. 22:13, From the *b* before Him
Isa. 60:3, And kings to the *b*
Isa. 62:1, goes forth as *b*
Amos 5:20, very dark, with no *b*
Heb. 1:3, who being the *b*

BRIMSTONE
Gen. 19:24, Then the LORD rained *b*
Job 18:15, *b* is scattered on his
Rev. 9:17, fire, smoke, and *b*
Rev. 20:10, the lake of fire and *b*

BRING
Dt. 30:3, LORD your God will *b*
Job 33:30, *b* back his soul
Ps. 55:3, for they *b* down
Ps. 68:22, Lord said, "I will *b*
Isa. 41:21, *B* forth your
Isa. 42:3, *b* forth justice
Isa. 46:13, *b* My righteousness
Hos. 9:12, Though they *b* up their
Mt. 1:21, "And she will *b*
Lk. 8:14, *b* no fruit to maturity
Acts 5:28, *b* this Man's blood
Rom. 8:33, Who shall *b* a charge
Rom. 10:6, *b* Christ down from
Rom. 10:7, *b* Christ up from the
1 Th. 4:14, even so God will *b*

BROAD
Ps. 118:5, set me in a *b* place
Mt. 7:13, *b* is the way that
Mt. 23:5, their phylacteries *b*

BROKE
Ex. 32:19, *b* them at the foot of
Ps. 74:15, *b* open the fountain
Jer. 31:32, covenant which they *b*
Mt. 14:19, He blessed and *b*
Mk. 14:3, *b* the flask and poured
Jn. 19:32, *b* the legs of the

BROKEN
Gen. 17:14, he has *b* My covenant
Ps. 31:12, I am like a *b* vessel
Ps. 37:15, their bows shall be *b*
Ps. 55:20, He has *b* his covenant
Prov. 15:13, heart the spirit is *b*
Prov. 17:22, *b* spirit dries the
Prov. 18:14, but who can bear a *b*
Isa. 36:6, in the staff of this *b*
Jer. 23:9, heart within me is *b*
Hos. 5:11, is oppressed and *b*
Mt. 21:44, this stone will be *b*
Jn. 10:35, Scripture cannot be *b*
1 Cor. 11:24, My body which is *b*

BROKENHEARTED
Ps. 147:3, He heals the *b* and

BRONZE
Num. 21:9, So Moses made a *b*
Dt. 28:23, your head shall be *b*
2 Ki. 18:4, *b* serpent that Moses
Job 6:12, Or is my flesh *b*
Job 41:27, *b* as rotten wood
Ps. 107:16, broken the gates of *b*
Isa. 60:17, *b* I will bring
Jer. 1:18, *b* walls against the
Jer. 15:20, people a fortified *b*
Dan. 2:39, a third kingdom of *b*
Mic. 4:13, make your hooves *b*
Zech. 6:1, were mountains of *b*

BROOD
Isa. 14:20, The *b* of evildoers
Mt. 12:34, "*B* of vipers
Lk. 13:34, hen gathers her *b*

BROOK
1 Sam. 17:40, stones from the *b*
Ps. 110:7, shall drink of the *b*
Jn. 18:1, disciples over the *B*

BROOKS
Dt. 8:7, good land, a land of *b*
Job 6:15, *b* that pass away
Ps. 42:1, for the water *b*

BROTHER
Gen. 4:9, "Where is Abel your *b*
Ps. 35:14, he were my friend or *b*
Ps. 50:20, speak against your *b*
Prov. 17:17, and a *b* is born for
Prov. 18:19, *b* offended is harder
Eccl. 4:8, has neither son nor *b*
Jer. 9:4, and do not trust any *b*
Amos 1:11, he pursued his *b*
Mal. 1:2, "Was not Esau Jacob's *b*
Mt. 10:21, *b* will deliver up
Mt. 18:21, how often shall my *b*
Lk. 12:13, "Teacher, tell my *b*
Jn. 11:23, *b* will rise again
Rom. 14:10, do you judge your *b*
1 Cor. 6:6, *b* goes to law against
1 Cor. 8:11, shall the weak *b*
Phile. 16, slave—a beloved *b*
1 Jn. 2:10, He who loves his *b*
1 Jn. 3:12, and murdered his *b*
1 Jn. 3:15, Whoever hates his *b*
1 Jn. 5:16, *b* sinning a sin which
Rev. 1:9, I, John, both your *b*

BROTHER'S
Gen. 4:9, Am I my *b* keeper
Mt. 7:3, at the speck in your *b*

BROTHERHOOD
Amos 1:9, the covenant of *b*
Zech. 11:14, I might break the *b*
1 Pet. 2:17, Love the *b*
1 Pet. 5:9, experienced by your *b*

BROTHERLY
Rom. 12:10, to one another with *b*
Heb. 13:1, *b* love continue

BROTHERS
Job 6:15, My *b* have dealt
Ps. 69:8, a stranger to my *b*

Mk. 3:33, is My mother, or My *b*
Lk. 8:21, *b* are these who hear
Jn. 7:5, *b* did not believe
1 Pet. 3:8, love as *b*

BROUGHT
Ps. 105:48, He *b* out His people
Song 1:4, The king has *b* me into
Lk. 10:15, to heaven, will be *b*

BRUISE
Gen. 3:15, He shall *b* your head
Isa. 30:26, LORD binds up the *b*
Isa. 53:10, the LORD to *b* Him

BRUISED
Isa. 42:3, *b* reed He will not
Isa. 53:5, He was *b* for our
Mt. 12:20, *b* reed He will not

BRUTAL
Ezek. 21:31, *b* men who are

BUCKLER
Ps. 91:4, be your shield and *b*

BUD
Isa. 55:10, it bring forth and *b*

BUFFET
2 Cor. 12:7, of Satan to *b* me

BUILD
Gen. 11:4, *b* ourselves a city
2 Sam. 7:5, "Would you *b* a house
1 Ki. 8:17, *b* a temple for the name
1 Chr. 17:10, that the LORD will *b*
1 Chr. 28:6, Solomon who shall *b*
2 Chr. 2:6, able to *b* Him a temple
Ps. 127:1, labor in vain who *b*
Eccl. 3:3, down, and a time to *b*
Isa. 66:1, house that you will *b*
Jer. 24:6, I will *b* them and not
Mic. 3:10, Who *b* up Zion with
Mal. 1:4, *b* the desolate
Lk. 14:30, 'This man began to *b*
Acts 7:49, What house will you *b*
Acts 20:32, *b* you up and give you
Rom. 15:20, named, lest I should *b*
Gal. 2:18, "For if I *b* again

BUILDER
1 Cor. 3:10, me, as a wise master *b*
Heb. 11:10, foundations, whose *b*

BUILDING
1 Cor. 3:9, field, you are God's *b*
2 Cor. 5:1, destroyed, we have a *b*
Eph. 2:21, in whom the whole *b*
Jude 20, But you, beloved, *b*

BUILDS
Ps. 147:2, The LORD *b* up
Prov. 14:1, The wise woman *b*
1 Cor. 3:10, take heed how he *b*

BUILT
Prov. 9:1, Wisdom has *b* her house
Eccl. 2:4, my works great, I *b*
Dan. 4:30, Babylon, that I have *b*
Mt. 7:24, to a wise man who *b*
Mt. 7:26, a foolish man who *b*
1 Cor. 3:14, work which he has *b*
Eph. 2:20, having been *b* on the
Col. 2:7, rooted and *b* up in Him
Heb. 3:4, For every house is *b*
1 Pet. 2:5, stones, are being *b*

BUL (or Marchesvan)
eighth month of Hebrew calendar, October–November. 1 Ki. 6:38

BULL
Ps. 50:9, I will not take a *b*
Jer. 31:18, like an untrained *b*

BULLS
Isa. 1:11, in the blood of *b*
Heb. 9:13, For if the blood of *b*

BULRUSH, Ex. 2:3; Isa. 58:5

BULWARKS
Ps. 48:13, Mark well her *b*
Isa. 26:1, for walls and *b*

BUNDLE
Gen. 42:35, each man's *b* of money
Song 1:13, A *b* of myrrh is my

BURDEN
signifying prophecy. 2 Ki. 9:25; Isa. 13; 15; 17; 19; 21; 22; 23; Nah. 1:1
of affliction. Isa. 58:6; 2 Cor. 5:4
of iniquities. Ps. 38:4
of Christ, light. Mt. 11:30; Acts 15:28; Rev. 2:24

BURDEN
Num. 11:11, You have laid the *b*
2 Chr. 6:29, one knows his own *b*
Job 7:20, so that I am a *b*
Ps. 55:22, Cast your *b* on the
Eccl. 12:5, the grasshopper is a *b*
Isa. 10:27, in that day that his *b*
Zeph. 3:18, its reproach is a *b*
Mt. 11:30, easy and My *b* is light
2 Cor. 12:16, as it may, I did not *b*
1 Th. 2:9, we might not be a *b*
Rev. 2:24, on you no other *b*

BURDENED
Isa. 43:24, but you have *b* Me with

BURDENS
Ex. 2:11, and looked at their *b*
Mt. 23:4, For they bind heavy *b*
Gal. 6:2, Bear one another's *b*

BURDENSOME
Eccl. 1:13, *b* task God has given
Isa. 15:4, his life will be *b*
2 Cor. 12:13, I myself was not *b*
1 Jn. 5:3, commandments are not *b*

BURIAL
lack of, a disaster. Dt. 28:26; Ps. 79:2; Eccl. 6:3; Isa. 14:19; Jer. 7:33; 16:4; 25:33; 34:20
of Sarah. Gen. 23:19; Abraham. Gen. 25:9; Isaac. Gen. 35:29; Jacob. Gen. 50; Abner. 2 Sam. 3:31,32; Christ. Mt. 27:57; Lk. 23:50; Stephen. Acts 8:2

BURIAL
Eccl. 6:3, indeed he has no *b*
Mt. 26:12, she did it for My *b*
Jn. 12:7, for the day of My *b*
Acts 8:2, Stephen to his *b*

BURIED
Ruth 1:17, and there will I be *b*
Eccl. 8:10, I saw the wicked *b*
Mt. 14:12, away the body and *b*
Lk. 16:22, also died and was *b*
Rom. 6:4, Therefore we were *b*
1 Cor. 15:4, and that He was *b*
Col. 2:12, *b* with Him in baptism

BURN
Ex. 3:3, the bush does not *b*
Ex. 32:10, that My wrath may *b*
Josh. 11:6, *b* their chariots
Isa. 1:31, both will *b* together
Lk. 24:32, "Did not our heart *b*
Rev. 17:16, eat her flesh and *b*

BURNED
1 Cor. 3:15, If anyone's work is *b*
1 Cor. 13:3, my body to be *b*
Heb. 6:8, whose end is to be *b*
Heb. 12:18, be touched and that *b*
Heb. 13:11, are *b* outside the camp
2 Pet. 3:10, in it will be *b*
Rev. 8:7, all green grass was *b*

BURNING
Gen. 15:17, *b* torch that passed
Dt. 28:22, with severe *b* fever
Prov. 16:27, on his lips like a *b*
Jer. 20:9, *b* fire shut up in my
Ezek. 36:5, *b* jealousy against the
Amos 4:11, plucked from the *b*
Rev. 8:8, a great mountain *b*
Rev. 8:10, fell from heaven, *b*

BURNING BUSH
the Lord appears to Moses in. Ex. 3:2; Mk. 12:26; Lk. 20:37; Acts 7:35

BURNT
Gen. 22:7, lamb for a *b* offering
Ps. 51:16, delight in *b* offering
Jer. 6:20, *b* offerings are not
Amos 5:22, Though you offer Me *b*

BURNT OFFERINGS
law concerning. Lev. 1:1; 6:8
illustrations of. Gen. 8:20; 22:13; Ex. 18:12; 1 Sam. 7:9; Ezra 3:4; Job 1:5. *See* Ps. 40:6; 51:19; Isa. 40:16; Heb. 10
the continual. Ex. 29:38; Num. 28:3; 1 Chr. 16:40; 2 Chr. 13:11

BURST
Job 32:19, it is ready to *b*
Job 38:8, with doors, when it *b*
Lk. 5:37, the new wine will *b*
Acts 1:18, falling headlong, he *b*

BURY
Gen. 23:6, *b* your dead in the
Ps. 79:3, was no one to *b* them
Mt. 8:21, go and *b* my father
Mt. 8:22, and let the dead *b*

BUSH
Ex. 3:2, from the midst of a *b*
Dt. 33:16, Him who dwelt in the *b*
Acts 7:35, to him in the *b*

BUSINESS
Ps. 107:23, in ships, who do *b*
Mt. 22:5, farm, another to his *b*
Lk. 2:49, about My Father's *b*

BUSYBODIES
2 Th. 3:11, at all, but are *b*
1 Tim. 5:13, but also gossips and *b*

BUTLER
Gen. 40:23, *b* did not remember

BUTTER
Gen. 18:8, So he took *b* and milk
Ps. 55:21, were smoother than *b*
Prov. 30:33, of milk produces *b*

BUY
Gen. 41:57, in Egypt to *b* grain
Prov. 23:23, *B* the truth
Isa. 55:1, Yes, come, *b* wine and
Amos 8:6, that we may *b* the poor
Lk. 9:18, *b* food for all these
Jn. 13:29, "*B* those things we
1 Cor. 7:30, rejoice, those who *b*
Jas. 4:13, spend a year there, *b*
Rev. 3:18, "I counsel you to *b*
Rev. 13:17, and that no one may *b*

BUYER
Prov. 20:14, nothing," cries the *b*
Isa. 24:2, as with the *b*
Ezek. 7:12, 'Let not the *b*

BUYS
Prov. 31:16, a field and *b* it
Mt. 13:44, has and *b* that field
Rev. 18:11, *b* their merchandise

BYGONE
Acts 14:16, *b* generations

BYWORD
Job 17:6, But he has made me a *b*
Ps. 44:14, You make us a *b*

CAESAR, Mt. 22:17
Augustus. Lk. 2:1
Tiberius. Lk. 3:1
Claudius, time of famine. Acts 11:28
Paul appeals to. Acts 25:11
household of. Phil. 4:22

CAESAREA
named after Augustus Caesar. Acts 8:40

CAESAREA PHILIPPI
(named after Philip the tetrarch), visited by Christ. Mt. 16:13; Mk. 8:27
——— (Stratonis), Peter sent there. Acts 10
Paul visits. Acts 21:8
Paul sent to Felix there. Acts 23:23

CAGE
Jer. 5:27, *c* is full of birds
Rev. 18:2, foul spirit, and a *c*

CAIAPHAS
high priest, prophesies concerning Christ. Jn. 11:49
his counsel. Mt. 26:3
he condemns Him. Mt. 26:65; Mk. 14:63; Lk. 22:71

CAIN, Gen. 4:1
his anger. Gen. 4:5
murders Abel. Gen. 4:8; 1 Jn. 3:12
his punishment. Gen. 4:11; Jude 11

CAKE
Hos. 7:8, Ephraim is a *c*

CAKES
Song 2:5, Sustain me with *c*
Hos. 3:1, and love the raisin *c*

CALAMITIES
Ps. 57:1, refuge, until these *c*

CALAMITY
Dt. 32:35, for the day of their *c*
Prov. 1:26, will laugh at your *c*
Prov. 6:15, *c* shall come suddenly
Amos 3:6, If there is *c* in a

CALCULATED
Isa. 40:12, *c* the dust of the

CALDRON
Ezek. 11:3, this city is the *c*

CALEB
faith of. Num. 13:30; 14:6
permitted to enter Canaan. Num. 26:65; 32:12; Dt. 1:36
his request. Josh. 14:6
his possessions. Josh. 15:13
gives his daughter to Othniel as wife. Jud. 1:13

CALF
golden, Aaron's transgression in making. Ex. 32; Acts 7:40
of Samaria. Hos. 8:5,6

CALF
Ex. 32:4, and made a molded *c*
Ps. 106:19, They made a *c* in Horeb
Prov. 15:17, is, than a fatted *c*
Hos. 4:16, like a stubborn *c*
Hos. 8:5, Your *c* is rejected
Lk. 15:23, bring the fatted *c*
Rev. 4:7, creature like a *c*

CALL
of God to repentance and salvation. Ps. 49; 50; Prov. 1:20; 2—8; Isa. 1; 45:20; 55; Jer. 35:15; Hos. 6; 14; Joel 2; Jon. 3; Mt. 3; 11:28; Jn. 7:37; 12:44; Rom. 8:28; 9; 10; 11; 2 Cor. 5:20; Rev. 2:5; 3:3,19; 22:17
danger of rejecting. Ps. 50:17; Prov. 1:24; 29:1; Isa. 6:9; 66:4; Jer. 6:19; 26:4; 35:17; Mt. 22:3; Jn. 12:48; Acts 13:46; 18:6; 28:24; Rom. 11:8; 2 Th. 2:10; Heb. 2:1; 12:25; Rev. 2:5
——— of Noah. Gen. 6:13; Abraham. Gen. 12; Jacob. Gen. 28:12; Moses. Ex. 3; Gideon. Jud. 6:11; Samuel. 1 Sam. 3; Elijah. 1 Ki. 17; Elisha. 1 Ki. 19:16,19; Isaiah. Isa. 6; Jeremiah. Jer. 1; Ezekiel. Ezek. 1; Hosea. Hos. 1
of Amos. Amos 1; 7:14. *See* Mic. 1:1; Zeph. 1:1; Hag. 1:1; Zech. 1:1
of Jonah. Jon. 1
of Peter, etc. Mt. 4:18; Mk. 1:16; Lk. 5; Jn. 1:39
of Paul. Acts 9; Rom. 1:1; Gal. 1:1,11; 1 Tim. 1

CALL
1 Sam. 12:17, I will *c* to the LORD
Ps. 49:11, *c* their lands after
Prov. 8:4, To you, O men, I *c*
Isa. 55:6, *c* upon Him while He
Jer. 33:3, '*C* to Me
Zech. 13:9, They will *c* on My name
Mt. 1:21, *c* His name JESUS
Mt. 9:13, *c* the righteous
Acts 2:39, Lord our God will *c*
Rom. 9:25, *c* them My people
Rom. 10:14, then shall they *c*
1 Th. 4:7, For God did not *c*
2 Pet. 1:10, *c* and election sure

CALLED
Gen. 1:5, *c* the light Day
Gen. 3:20, *c* his wife's name Eve
Isa. 42:6, "I, the LORD, have *c*
Isa. 43:1, I have *c* you by your
Isa. 49:1, The LORD has *c* Me from
Hos. 11:1, and out of Egypt I *c*
Mt. 2:15, "Out of Egypt I *c*
Mt. 2:23, city *c* Nazareth
Mt. 20:16, For many are *c*
Rom. 8:28, to those who are the *c*
Rom. 8:30, these He also *c*
1 Cor. 7:15, But God has *c* us to
1 Pet. 2:9, praises of Him who *c*
2 Pet. 1:3, knowledge of Him who *c*
1 Jn. 3:1, *c* children of God

CALLING
Rom. 11:29, the gifts and the *c*
1 Cor. 1:26, For you see your *c*
1 Cor. 7:20, remain in the same *c*
Eph. 4:1, to walk worthy of the *c*
Eph. 4:4, in one hope of your *c*
2 Tim. 1:9, us with a holy *c*
Heb. 3:1, of the heavenly *c*

CALLS
Ps. 147:4, *c* them all by name
Isa. 64:7, there is no one who *c*
Mk. 12:37, David himself *c*
Jn. 10:3, *c* his own sheep
Rom. 10:13, For "whoever *c*

CALM
Jon. 1:12, the sea will become *c*
Mt. 8:26, there was a great *c*

CALMED
Ps. 131:2, Surely I have *c*

CALVARY, Lk. 23:33

CALVES
1 Ki. 12:28, made two *c* of gold
Job 21:10, their cow *c* without
Mal. 4:2, like stall-fed *c*
Heb. 9:12, blood of goats and *c*
Heb. 9:19, he took the blood of *c*

CAMEL
Mt. 19:24, it is easier for a *c*
Mt. 23:24, and swallow a *c*

CAMP
of Israelites. Ex. 14:19; Num. 1:52; 2; 24:5
to be kept holy. Lev. 6:11; 13:4,6; Num. 5:2; Dt. 23:10; Heb. 13:11

CAMP
Gen. 32:2, "This is God's *c*
Ex. 14:19, who went before the *c*
Heb. 13:13, to Him, outside the *c*

CAN
Phil. 4:13, I *c* do all things

CANA
Christ turns water into wine at. Jn. 2

nobleman visits Christ at. Jn. 4:47

CANAAN, Gen. 9:18; Acts 7:11
land of. Ex. 23:31; Josh. 1:4; Zeph. 2:5
promised to Abraham. Gen. 12:7; 13:14; 17:8
inhabitants of. Ex. 15:15
their wickedness at Sodom and Gomorrah. Gen. 13:13; 19
Israelites not to walk in the ways of. Lev. 18:3,24,30; 20:23
daughters of. Gen. 28:1,6,8
language of. Isa. 19:18
kingdoms of. Ps. 135:11
king of. Jud. 4:2,23,24; 5:19
wars of. Jud. 3:1
dwelling of Abraham in. Gen. 12:6; Isaac and Jacob. Gen. 28; Esau. Gen. 36; Joseph. Gen. 37
allotted to children of Israel. Josh. 14
the spies visit, and their report. Num. 13
Moses sees, from Pisgah. Num. 27:12; Dt. 3:27; 34:1
—— a son of Ham, grandson of Noah, cursed on account of his father's mockery of Noah. Gen. 9:25

CANCER
2 Tim. 2:17, will spread like *c*

CANDACE
queen of Ethiopia. Acts 8:27

CANE
Isa. 43:24, bought Me no sweet *c*
Jer. 6:20, Sheba, and sweet *c*

CANOPIES
2 Sam. 22:12, He made darkness *c*

CANOPY
Ps. 18:11, His *c* around Him was

CAPERNAUM
Christ dwells at. Mt. 4:13; Jn. 2:12
preaches at. Mt. 4:17; Mk. 1:21
performs miracles at. Mt. 8:5; 17:24; Jn. 4:46; 6:17
speaks parables at. Mt. 13:18,24; Mk. 4
condemned for impenitence. Mt. 11:23; Lk. 10:15

CAPPADOCIA, Acts 2:9; 1 Pet. 1:1

CAPSTONE
Zech. 4:7, bring forth the *c*

CAPTAIN
Prov. 6:7, which, having no *c*

CAPTIVE
Ps. 68:18, have led captivity *c*
Isa. 52:2, of your neck, O *c*
Amos 6:7, they shall now go *c*
Lk. 21:24, and be led away *c*
Eph. 4:8, He led captivity *c*

CAPTIVES
Amos 9:14, will bring back the *c*
Zeph. 2:7, and return their *c*
2 Tim. 3:6, make *c* of gullible women

CAPTIVITY
of Israelites foretold. Lev. 26:33; Dt. 28:36
of ten tribes foretold. Amos 3; 4; 7:11; fulfilled. 2 Ki. 17; 1 Chr. 5:26
of Judah foretold. Isa. 39:6; Jer. 13:19; 20:4; 25:11; 32:28; fulfilled. 2 Ki. 25; 2 Chr. 36; Ps. 137; Est. 2; Jer. 39; 52; Dan. 1
return from. Ezra 1; Neh. 2; Ps. 126

CAPTIVITY
Dt. 30:3, bring you back from *c*
Ps. 68:18, high, You have led *c*
Lam. 1:3, Judah has gone into *c*
Mt. 1:17, from David until the *c*
Rom. 7:23, and bringing me into *c*
2 Cor. 10:5, every thought into *c*
Eph. 4:8, on high, He led *c*
Rev. 13:10, shall go into *c*

CARCASS
Jud. 14:8, honey were in the *c*
Mt. 24:28, "For wherever the *c*

CARE
worldly, deprecated. Mt. 6:25; Lk. 8:14; 12:22; Jn. 6:27; 1 Cor. 7:32; Phil. 4:6; 1 Tim. 6:8; 2 Tim. 2:4; Heb. 13:5
Martha reproved for. Lk. 10:41
loving, of the Samaritan. Lk. 10:34
of Christ for His mother. Jn. 19:26
of Paul for the Corinthians. 2 Cor. 7:12; 11:28
of Titus for the Corinthians. 2 Cor. 8:16
for Paul by Philippians. Phil. 4:10

CARE
Lk. 10:40, "Lord, do You not *c*
1 Cor. 7:32, you to be without *c*
Phil. 2:20, who will sincerely *c*
1 Tim. 3:5, how will he take *c*
1 Pet. 5:7, casting all your *c*

CARED
Jn. 12:6, he said, not that he *c*

CAREFULLY
Dt. 11:22, *c* keep all these
Isa. 38:15, I shall walk *c* all my

CARELESS
Prov. 19:16, but he who is *c*

CARES
Ps. 142:4, no one *c* for my soul
Lk. 8:14, and are choked with *c*
1 Cor. 7:32, He who is unmarried *c*
1 Pet. 5:7, for He *c* for you

CARMEL, Josh. 12:22
Nabal's conduct toward David at. 1 Sam. 25
Mount, Elijah and the prophets of Baal at. 1 Ki. 18
the Shunammite woman goes to Elisha at. 2 Ki. 4:25
her child restored to life by Elisha. 2 Ki. 4:34

CARNAL
Rom. 7:14, spiritual, but I am *c*
Rom. 8:7, *c* mind is enmity
1 Cor. 3:3, for you are still *c*
2 Cor. 10:4, our warfare are not *c*

CARNALLY
Gen. 19:5, we may know them *c*
Jud. 19:22, that we may know him *c*
Rom. 8:6, *c* minded is death

CAROUSE
2 Pet. 2:13, count it pleasure to *c*

CAROUSING
Lk. 21:34, be weighed down with *c*

CARPENTER
Mk. 6:3, "Is this not the *c*

CARRIED
Dt. 1:31, the LORD your God *c*
Isa. 53:4, and *c* our sorrows
Lk. 24:51, parted from them and *c*
Rev. 17:3, *c* me away in the

CARRY
Job 5:12, their hands cannot *c*
Ps. 90:5, *c* them away like a
Mt. 3:11, I am not worthy to *c*
Jn. 5:10, for you to *c* your bed
1 Tim. 6:7, it is certain we can *c*

CARRYING
Mk. 14:13, man will meet you *c*
2 Cor. 4:10, always *c* about in the

CASE
Dt. 1:17, *c* that is too hard
Job 13:18, I have prepared my *c*
Job 23:4, I would present my *c*
Isa. 41:21, "Present your *c*
Acts 25:14, Festus laid Paul's *c*

CASSIA
Ps. 45:8, myrrh and aloes and *c*

CAST
Job 22:29, When they *c* you down
Ps. 2:3, *c* away Their
Ps. 42:5, Why are you *c* down
Ps. 44:9, But You have *c* us off
Ps. 51:11, *c* me away from Your
Ps. 78:49, He *c* on them the
Ps. 94:14, the LORD will not *c*
Ps. 102:10, me up and *c* me away
Isa. 26:19, and the earth shall *c*
Jer. 7:15, My sight, as I have *c*
Ezek. 18:31, *C* away from you all
Dan. 6:16, brought Daniel and *c*
Mic. 7:19, *c* all our sins into
Mt. 5:29, whole body to be *c*
Mt. 8:12, the kingdom will be *c*
Mt. 10:1, spirits, to *c* them out
Mk. 16:17, In My name they will *c*
Jn. 6:37, by no means *c* out
Rom. 11:1, *c* away His people
Heb. 10:35, *c* away your confidence
Rev. 4:10, *c* their crowns before
Rev. 12:9, the great dragon was *c*

CASTING
Lev. 20:23, nation which I am *c*
Mt. 4:18, Andrew his brother, *c*
2 Cor. 10:5, *c* down arguments
1 Pet. 5:7, *c* all your care

CASTOR
and Pollux, Paul's ship. Acts 28:11

CASTS
Mt. 12:26, "If Satan *c*

1 Jn. 4:18, perfect love c out

CATCH
Ps. 10:9, in wait to c the poor
Mk. 12:13, c Him in His words
Lk. 5:4, down your nets for a c
Lk. 5:10, from now on you will c

CATCHES
Jn. 10:12, and the wolf c the
1 Cor. 3:19, c the wise in their

CATERPILLAR
Ps. 78:46, their crops to the c

CATTLE
Josh. 8:2, c you shall take as
Ps. 107:38, does not let their c

CAUGHT
Gen. 22:13, behind him was a ram c
Jn. 21:3, and that night they c
Acts 8:39, Spirit of the Lord c
Rev. 12:5, her Child was c up

CAUSE
Job 5:8, I would commit my c
Ps. 7:4, my enemy without c
Ps. 35:19, hate me without a c
Ps. 67:1, c His face to shine
Ps. 143:8, C me to know the way
Prov. 18:17, one to plead his c
Isa. 51:22, God, Who pleads the c
Jer. 22:16, He judged the c
Mt. 5:22, brother without a c
Jn. 15:25, hated Me without a c
Jn. 18:37, For this c I was born

CAVES
1 Sam. 13:6, the people hid in c
Isa. 2:19, rocks, and into the c
Heb. 11:38, in dens and c of the

CEASE
Gen. 8:22, and night shall not c
Neh. 6:3, Why should the work c
Job 3:17, There the wicked c
Ps. 46:9, He makes wars c
Prov. 19:27, C listening to
Isa. 1:16, C to do evil
1 Cor. 13:8, tongues, they will c
Eph. 1:16, do not c to give
Col. 1:9, do not c to pray for

CEASED
Gen. 11:8, c building the city
Jon. 1:15, the sea, and the sea c

CEASES
Ps. 12:1, for the godly man c

CEASING
1 Th. 1:3, c your work of faith
1 Th. 2:13, thank God without c
1 Th. 5:17, pray without c

CEDAR
2 Sam. 7:2, dwell in a house of c
Ps. 92:12, He shall grow like a c
Song 1:17, of our houses are c
Jer. 22:14, it, paneling it with c
Ezek. 31:3, Indeed Assyria was a c

CEDARS
Ps. 29:5, the LORD breaks the c
Ps. 104:16, c of Lebanon which He

CELESTIAL
1 Cor. 15:40, but the glory of the c

CENCHREA
Paul shaves his head at. Acts 18:18
seaport of Corinth, church there. Rom. 16:1

CENSER
Lev. 10:1, Aaron, each took his c
Ezek. 8:11, Each man had a c
Heb. 9:4, which had the golden c
Rev. 8:5, the angel took the c

CEPHAS (Peter)
a stone. Jn. 1:42; 1 Cor. 1:12; 3:22; 9:5; 15:5; Gal. 2:9. *See* PETER

CERTAINTY
Prov. 22:21, make you know the c
Lk. 1:4, you may know the c

CERTIFICATE
Mk. 10:4, a man to write a c

CERTIFIED
Jn. 3:33, His testimony has c

CHAFF
Job 21:18, c that a storm
Ps. 1:4, c which the wind
Ps. 35:5, Let them be like c
Isa. 17:13, be chased like the c
Isa. 33:11, You shall conceive c
Zeph. 2:2, the day passes like c
Mt. 3:12, He will burn up the c

CHAIN
Lam. 3:7, He has made my c
Rev. 20:1, pit and a great c

CHAINED
2 Tim. 2:9, of God is not c
Heb. 13:3, the prisoners as if c

CHAINS
Ps. 149:8, their kings with c
Song 1:10, your neck with c
Acts 12:7, And his c fell off
Acts 26:29, am, except for these c
Col. 4:18, Remember my c
Phile. 13, minister to me in my c
2 Pet. 2:4, delivered them into c

CHALDEANS, Jer. 50:10
afflict Job. Job 1:17
besiege Jerusalem. 2 Ki. 24:2; 25:4; Jer. 37—39
wise men, preserved by Daniel. Dan. 2:24
prophecies concerning. Isa. 23:13; 43:14; 47:1; 48:14; Hab. 1:5

CHAMBERS
Job 9:9, and the c of the south
Song 1:4, brought me into his c
Jer. 22:13, and his c by injustice

CHAMPION
1 Sam. 17:4, And a c went out

CHANGE
Job 14:20, c his countenance
Job 17:12, c the night into day
Job 23:13, and who can make Him c
Ps. 55:19, Because they do not c
Ps. 102:26, a cloak You will c
Prov. 24:21, with those given to c
Jer. 13:23, Can the Ethiopian c
Dan. 7:25, c times and law
Hos. 4:7, c their glory into
Mal. 3:6, the LORD, I do not c
Gal. 4:20, now and to c my tone
Heb. 7:12, there is also a c

CHANGED
Jer. 2:11, But My people have c
Rom. 1:23, c the glory of the
1 Cor. 15:51, but we shall all be c
Heb. 7:12, the priesthood being c

CHANGERS'
Jn. 2:15, and poured out the c

CHANGES
Dan. 2:21, c the times and the

CHANNELS
Ps. 18:15, c of the sea were seen

CHARACTER
Rom. 5:4, and c, hope

CHARGE
of God to Moses and Aaron. Ex. 6:13
of Moses to Joshua. Dt. 31:7
of David to Solomon. 1 Ki. 2:1; 1 Chr. 22:6
of Jehoshaphat to the judges. 2 Chr. 19:6
of Paul to the elders of the church at Ephesus. Acts 20:17
of Paul to Timothy. 1 Tim. 5:21; 2 Tim. 4
of Peter to the elders. 1 Pet. 5

CHARGED
2 Tim. 4:16, May it not be c

CHARIOT
Ex. 14:25, He took off their c
2 Ki. 2:11, that suddenly a c
Ps. 104:3, makes the clouds His c
Acts 8:29, and overtake this c

CHARIOTS
Jud. 5:28, the clatter of his c
Ps. 20:7, Some trust in c
Ps. 68:17, The c of God are

CHARITABLE
Mt. 6:1, you do not do your c
Mt. 6:4, "that your c deed
Acts 9:36, c deeds which she

CHARM
Prov. 31:30, C is deceitful and

CHARMERS
Ps. 58:5, heed the voice of c

CHARMS
Ezek. 13:18, who sew magic c

CHASE
Lev. 26:8, Five of you shall c
Dt. 32:30, How could one c
Ps. 35:5, angel of the LORD c

CHASTE
2 Cor. 11:2, present you as a c
Ti. 2:5, to be discreet, c
1 Pet. 3:2, c conduct accompanied

CHASTEN
Prov. 19:18, C your son while there

Hos. 10:10, is My desire, I will *c*
Heb. 12:7, a father does not *c*
Rev. 3:19, I love, I rebuke and *c*

CHASTENED
Ps. 69:10, *c* my soul with fasting
Ps. 73:14, *c* every morning
Ps. 118:18, The LORD has *c* me
Jer. 2:30, In vain I have *c*
Heb. 12:10, *c* us as seemed best

CHASTENING
Dt. 11:2, have not seen the *c*
Job 5:17, do not despise the *c*
Job 34:31, 'I have borne *c*
Isa. 26:16, a prayer when Your *c*
Heb. 12:8, if you are without *c*
Heb. 12:11, Now no *c* seems to be

CHASTENS
Heb. 12:6, the LORD loves He *c*

CHASTISE
Lev. 26:28, and I, even I, will *c*
Hos. 7:12, *c* them according
Lk. 23:22, I will therefore *c*

CHASTISEMENT
Isa. 53:5, the *c* for our peace

CHATTER
Prov. 14:23, *c* leads only to

CHEAT
Lev. 19:13, 'You shall not *c*
Col. 2:8, Beware lest anyone *c*

CHEATED
1 Cor. 6:7, let yourselves be *c*
2 Cor. 7:2, we have *c* no one

CHEBAR
the river, Ezekiel's visions at. Ezek. 1; 3:15; 10:15

CHEDORLAOMER
king of Elam, takes Lot prisoner, but subdued by Abram. Gen. 14

CHEEK
Lam. 3:30, Let him give his *c*
Mic. 5:1, with a rod on the *c*
Mt. 5:39, on your right *c*

CHEEKBONE
Ps. 3:7, my enemies on the *c*

CHEEKS
Song 1:10, *c* are lovely with
Song 5:13, His *c* are like a bed
Isa. 50:6, struck Me, and My *c*

CHEER
Eccl. 11:9, and let your heart *c*
Mt. 9:2, "Son, be of good *c*

CHEERFUL
2 Cor. 9:7, for God loves a *c*
Jas. 5:13, Is anyone *c*

CHEERFULNESS
Rom. 12:8, shows mercy, with *c*

CHEESE
Job 10:10, and curdle me like *c*

CHEMOSH
god of Moab. Num. 21:29; Jud. 11:24; Jer. 48:7,13,46
worshiped by Solomon. 1 Ki. 11:7

CHERISHES
Eph. 5:29, but nourishes and *c*
1 Th. 2:7, as a nursing mother *c*

CHERUB
a man's name. Ezra 2:59

CHERUB
2 Sam. 22:11, He rode upon a *c*

CHERUBIM (plural of cherub)
in garden of Eden. Gen. 3:24
for the mercy seat and the temple. Ex. 25:18; 37:7; 1 Ki. 6:23; 2 Chr. 3:10; Ps. 80:1; Ezek. 41:18
Ezekiel's visions of. Ezek. 1; 10

CHERUBIM
Gen. 3:24, and He placed *c*
Ps. 80:1, dwell between the *c*
Ezek. 10:2, fire from among the *c*
Heb. 9:5, above it were the *c*

CHIEF
Song 5:10, is white and ruddy, *c*
1 Tim. 1:15, of whom I am *c*
1 Pet. 2:6, Zion a *c* cornerstone
1 Pet. 2:7, has become the *c*
1 Pet. 5:4, *C* Shepherd appears

CHIEF PRIESTS
consulted by Herod. Mt. 2:4
their persecution of Christ. Mt. 16:21; Mk. 14:1; 15:31; Jn. 7:32

CHILD
Ps. 131:2, like a weaned *c*
Prov. 20:11, *c* is known by his
Prov. 22:6, Train up a *c* in the
Isa. 9:6, For unto us a *C*
Isa. 11:6, *c* shall lead them
Hos. 11:1, When Israel was a *c*
Mt. 1:23, virgin shall be with *c*
Mk. 9:36, He took a little *c*
Mk. 10:15, of God as a little *c*
Lk. 1:66, kind of *c* will this be
Lk. 1:80, So the *c* grew and
1 Cor. 13:11, When I was a *c*
Rev. 12:5, She bore a male *C*

CHILDBEARING
1 Tim. 2:15, she will be saved in *c*

CHILDBIRTH
Isa. 13:8, pain as a woman in *c*

CHILDHOOD
Eccl. 11:10, from your flesh, for *c*
Mk. 9:21, And he said, "From *c*
2 Tim. 3:15, *c* you have known

CHILDLESS
Gen. 15:2, give me, seeing I go *c*
Jer. 22:30, this man down as *c*

CHILDREN
the gift of God. Gen. 33:5; Ps. 127; 128
a blessing. Prov. 10:1; 15:20; 17:6; 23:24; 27:11; 29:3
duty of. Ex. 20:12; Lev. 19:3,32; Dt. 5:16; 30:2; Prov. 1:8; 6:20; 13:1; 15:5; 19:27; 23:22; 24:21; 28:7,24; Eccl. 12:1; Eph. 6:1; Col. 3:20; 1 Tim. 5:4; Heb. 12:9; 1 Pet. 5:5
of Bethlehem, killed by Herod. Mt. 2:16 (Jer. 31:15)
blessed by Christ. Mt. 19:13; Mk. 10:13; Lk. 18:15
of God. Heb. 12:5; Eph. 5:1; 1 Pet. 1:14
of light. Lk. 16:8; Jn. 12:36; Eph. 5:8; 1 Th. 5:5

OBEDIENT
Christ. Lk. 2:51
Isaac. Gen. 22:6
Jephthah's daughter. Jud. 11:36
Samuel. 1 Sam. 2:26

WICKED
1 Sam. 2:12,25; Prov. 15:5; 17:21; 19:13,26; 28:7,24; 30:11; Isa. 3:5; Ezek. 22:7
their punishment. Ex. 21:15; Dt. 21:18; 27:16; 2 Ki. 2:23; Prov. 30:17; Mk. 7:10
of the devil. Acts 13:10

CHILDREN
Gen. 30:1, she bore Jacob no *c*
Ps. 82:6, and all of you are *c*
Ps. 127:3, *c* are a heritage
Ps. 147:13, He has blessed your *c*
Ps. 149:2, let the *c* of Zion be
Prov. 20:7, *c* are blessed after
Prov. 31:28, *c* rise up and call her
Isa. 3:12, *c* are their oppressors
Isa. 8:18, *c* whom the LORD has
Isa. 54:13, be the peace of your *c*
Isa. 63:8, they are My people, *c*
Mal. 4:6, the hearts of the *c*
Mt. 10:21, *c* will rise up against
Mt. 18:3, and become as little *c*
Mt. 19:13, *c* were brought to Him
Mt. 19:14, "Let the little *c*
Jn. 1:12, the right to become *c*
Jn. 8:39, you were Abraham's *c*
Rom. 8:16, spirit that we are *c*
1 Cor. 4:14, but as my beloved *c*
1 Cor. 14:20, Brethren, do not be *c*
2 Cor. 12:14, *c* ought not to lay up
Eph. 2:3, and were by nature *c*
Eph. 4:14, should no longer be *c*
Eph. 5:8, Walk as *c* of light
Phil. 2:15, and harmless, *c*
1 Jn. 3:2, now we are *c* of God
1 Jn. 5:2, that we love the *c*
3 Jn. 4, to hear that my *c*

CHILION, Ruth 1:2

CHINNERETH, Josh. 19:35

CHINNEROTH
plural of Chinnereth. Josh. 11:2

CHISLEV
ninth month of Hebrew calendar, November–December. Neh. 1:1; Zech. 7:1

CHLOE, 1 Cor. 1:11

CHOICE
Prov. 8:10, rather than *c* gold

CHOOSE
Dt. 30:19, therefore *c* life
Prov. 3:31, *c* none of his ways
Isa. 7:15, evil and *c* the good
Isa. 14:1, will still *c* Israel
Zech. 1:17, will again *c* Jerusalem
Jn. 15:16, "You did not *c*

Phil. 1:22, yet what I shall *c*

CHOOSES
Ps. 25:12, in the way He *c*

CHORAZIN, Mt. 11:21

CHOSE
Acts 15:7, a good while ago God *c*
Eph. 1:4, just as He *c* us in Him
2 Th. 2:13, from the beginning *c*

CHOSEN
1 Chr. 16:13, of Jacob, His *c*
Ps. 33:12, people He has *c*
Ps. 89:3, a covenant with My *c*
Ps. 119:30, *c* the way of truth
Isa. 43:10, servant whom I have *c*
Lk. 10:42, *c* that good part
Jn. 13:18, I know whom I have *c*
Acts 22:14, *c* you that you should
1 Cor. 1:27, *c* the foolish things
Jas. 2:5, Has God not *c* the poor
1 Pet. 2:9, But you are a *c*

CHRIST
the anointed, Greek for Messiah. Mt. 1:1

LORD JESUS
Mt. 1:21; Lk. 2:11; Jn. 1:41; 4:42; Acts 5:31; 11:17; 13:23; 15:11; 16:31; 20:21; Rom. 5:1,11; 6:23; 7:25; 13:14; 15:6,30; 16:13; 1 Cor. 1:2,3,7,10; 5:4; Eph. 5:23; Phil. 3:20; 1 Tim. 1:1,12; 3:13; 4:6; 5:21; 2 Tim. 1:10; Ti. 1:4; 2:13; 3:6; Phile. 3,5,25; Heb. 13:8,21; Jas. 1:1; 1 Pet. 1:3; 2 Pet. 1:1,11; 2:20; 3:2,18; 1 Jn. 4:10; Jude 1,4,17,21; Rev. 22:21
Son of God. Mt. 2:15; 3:17; 4:3,6; Lk. 1:32,35; 3:22; 4:3,9; 4:34,41; Jn. 1:34,49; 3:16,18,35,36; 5:22,23; 6:40,69; 12:26; 13:3; 14:13; 15:23; 16:27,30; 17:1; 19:7; Rom. 1:9; 5:10; 8:3,29,32; 1 Cor. 1:9; Gal. 1:16; 4:4,6; Col. 1:13; 1 Th. 1:10; Heb. 1:2,5,8; 3:6; 4:14; 5:5,8; 6:6; 7:3; 1 Jn. 4:1,3,7; 3:23; 4:9,10; 5:9
Son of Man. Ezek. 2:1; Mt. 8:20; 9:6; 10:23; 11:19; 12:8,32,40; 13:37,41; 16:13; 17:9,22; 24:27,30,44; 25:31; 26:2,24,45; Mk. 8:38; 9:12,31; 13:14; Lk. 5:24; 6:22; 9:22,26; 11:30; 12:8; 17:22; 18:8; 19:10; 21:36; 22:48; Jn. 1:51; 3:13; 5:27; 6:27,53,62; 8:28; 12:23,34; 13:31; Acts 7:56; Rev. 1:13
Immanuel. Isa. 7:14; 8:8; Mt. 1:23
Savior. Lk. 2:11; Jn. 4:42; Acts 5:31; 13:23; Eph. 5:23; 2 Pet. 1:1; 3:2; 1 Jn. 4:14; Jude 25
the Word. Jn. 1:1,14; Acts 10:36; 1 Jn. 5:7; Rev. 19:13
the Lamb of God. Jn. 1:29,36; Rev. 5:6; 6:1,16; 12:11; 13:8; 15:3; 19:7; 22:1,3
the Mediator. Gal. 3:19; 1 Tim. 2:5; Heb. 2:17; 7:25; 8:6; 9:15; 10:10; 12:2,24; 13:15
the Lord our Righteousness. Jer. 23:6; 33:16; Mal. 4:2; Acts 17:31; Rom. 5:18; Phil. 1:11; Heb. 7:2; 2 Pet. 1:1
the Lord of all. Acts 10:3,6
the Lord of glory. 1 Cor. 2:8; Jas. 2:1
King of kings, and Lord of lords. Rev. 19:16
Prophet, Priest, and King. Dt. 18:15; Isa. 49; 50; 51; 52; Nah. 1:15; Mt. 2:2; 23:36; 24:4; 25:34; Lk. 4:1,15,16,18,24; 5:3,17,32; 19:41; 21:10,25; 22:34; 23:2,27; Jn. 18:37; 19:14,19; Acts 17:7; 1 Tim. 1:17; 6:15; Heb. 1:8; 2:17; 3:1; Rev. 1:5; 11:15; 15:3; 17:14; 19:16
Alpha and Omega. Rev. 21:6; 22:13

CHRIST (the man Christ Jesus)

LIFE ON EARTH
His miraculous conception and birth predicted. Isa. 7:14; 11:1; Mt. 1:18; Lk. 1:31
accomplished at Bethlehem. Mt. 1:25; Lk. 2:7
announced to shepherds by angels. Lk. 2:9–14
wise men of the East do homage to. Mt. 2:1
circumcision of, and presentation in temple. Lk. 2:21,22
carried into Egypt. Mt. 2:13
baptism by John. Mt. 3:13; Mk. 1:9; Lk. 3:21; Jn. 1:32; 3:24
selection of disciples. Mt. 4:18; Mk. 1:16; Lk. 4:31; 5:10; Jn. 1:38
begins to preach and heal. Mt. 4:12; Mk. 1:14; Lk. 4:16
opposition of the Pharisees begins. Mt. 9:34
sufferings and death predicted. Mt. 16:17,20; Mt. 8:9,10; Lk. 9:18
transfiguration. Mt. 17; Mk. 9
institutes the Lord's Supper. Mt. 26; Mk. 14; Lk. 22 (1 Cor. 11:23)
betrayed by Judas. Mt. 26; Mk. 14; Lk. 22; Jn. 18; Acts 1
deserted by disciples. Mt. 26; Jn. 18
taken before Annas and Caiaphas, and Pilate and Herod. Mt. 26:57; 27; Mk. 14:54; 15; Lk. 23; Jn. 18:19
pronounced faultless by Pilate, yet delivered to the Jews. Mt. 27; Mk. 15; Lk. 23; Jn. 18:19
crucified. Mt. 27; Mk. 15; Lk. 23; Jn. 19
His legs not broken. Jn. 19:33
His side pierced by soldier. Jn. 19:34
His garments divided among soldiers. Mt. 27:35; Mk. 15:24; Lk. 23:34; Jn. 19:24
yields up His spirit. Mt. 27:50
buried. Mt. 27; Mk. 15; Lk. 23; Jn. 19; in a new tomb by soldiers and sealed. Mt. 27:66
His descent into lower parts of earth. Eph. 4:9
rises from the tomb. Mt. 28; Mk. 16; Lk. 24; Jn. 20:21 (1 Cor. 15:4)
appears to Mary Magdalene and disciples. Mt. 28; Mk. 16; Lk. 24; Jn. 20
shows Thomas His hands and feet. Jn. 20:27
charge to Peter to feed His lambs. Jn. 21:15
ascends into heaven. Mk. 16; Lk. 24; Acts 1:9,10
seen in heaven by Stephen. Acts 7:55
appearances after ascension:
to Paul. Acts 9:4; 18:9; 22:8
to John. Rev. 1:13

WORK ON EARTH
questions the teachers. Lk. 2:46
is tested. Mt. 4; Mk. 1:12; Lk. 4
Sermon on the Mount. Mt. 5:6,7
cleanses the temple. Ps. 69:9; Jn. 2:14
teaches Nicodemus. Jn. 3
converses with woman of Samaria. Jn. 4
the people attempt to make Him king. Jn. 6:15
taunted by His brothers. Jn. 7:4
the people's testimony. Mt. 16:13; Mk. 8:27; Lk. 9:18; Jn. 7:12
message to John the Baptist. Lk. 7:22
anointed at Simon the Pharisee's house. Lk. 7:36
pays temple tax at Capernaum. Mt. 17:24
exhorts apostles to humility. Mt. 18; Mk. 9:33; Lk. 9:49; 22:24
departs from Galilee into Judea. Mt. 19:1
teaches concerning divorce. Mt. 19:3; Lk. 16:18
reproves Herod and Jerusalem. Lk. 13:32,34
pardons woman caught in adultery. Jn. 8
compares Martha and Mary. Lk. 10:38–42
permits children to come to Him. Mt. 19:13; Mk. 10:13; Lk. 18:15
calls Zacchaeus the tax collector. Lk. 19:2
anointed by Mary at Bethany. Mt. 26:6; Mk. 14:3; Jn. 12:3
His triumphant entry into Jerusalem. Mt. 21; Mk. 11; Lk. 19; Jn. 12
drives money changers out of temple. Mt. 21:12; Mk. 11:15; Lk. 19:45
curses the fig tree. Mt. 21:19; Mk. 11:12
Greeks wish to see Jesus. Jn. 12:20
His answer. Jn. 12:23
to the chief priests. Lk. 20:3
to the Pharisees. Mt. 22:15
to the Sadducees. Mk. 12:18
glorified by the Father. Jn. 12:28
chief priests conspire to kill. Mt. 26:3; Mk. 14:1
covenant with Judas to betray. Mt. 26:13; Mk. 14:10; Lk. 22:3; Jn. 13:18
gives directions for the Passover. Mt. 26:17; Mk. 14:12; Lk. 22:7
foretells Peter's denial. Mt. 26:34; Mk. 14:29; Lk. 22:31; Jn. 13:26
love to His own. Jn. 13:1
washes His disciples' feet. Jn. 13:5

Peter's protest. Jn. 13:8
example to His disciples. Jn. 13:15
comforts His disciples. Jn. 14:1
promise to them. Jn. 14:14
leaves His peace with them. Jn. 14:27
commands them to love one another. Jn. 15:12,17
promises the Helper. Jn. 15:26; 16:7
predicts disciples' persecution. Jn. 16:2
"a little while'. Jn. 16:16
encourages prayer in His name. Jn. 16:23
prays for disciples. Jn. 17
goes over the Brook Kidron. Jn. 18:1
often went to garden. Jn. 18:2
His agony. Mt. 26:36; Lk. 22:44
betrayed by Judas. Mt. 26:47; Mk. 14:43; Lk. 22:47; Jn. 18:3
seized by the officers. Mt. 26:50; Mk. 14:46; Lk. 22:54; Jn. 18:12
forbids use of sword. Mt. 26:52; Jn. 18:11
taken before the chief priests, Pilate, and Herod; tried, found innocent, delivered to the Jews, crucifixion. *See* LIFE ON EARTH
commends His mother to the beloved disciple. Jn. 19:25
prays for His executioners. Lk. 23:34
His promise to the penitent thief. Lk. 23:43
acknowledged by centurion to be Son of God. Mt. 27:54; Mk. 15:39; to be righteous. Lk. 23:47

HIS TEACHING
preaches repentance at Galilee. Mt. 4:17; at Nazareth. Lk. 4:16
the Gospel of the kingdom. Mt. 4:23; Mk. 1:14
testimony concerning John the Baptist. Mt. 11:7; Lk. 7:24; 20:4
rebukes Chorazin, Bethsaida, Capernaum. Mt. 11:20; Lk. 10:13
speaks to the Jews concerning:
the Father and the Son. Jn. 5; 8:18,42; 10:15; 12:23
the bread of life. Jn. 6:26
descendants of Abraham. Jn. 8:31
traditions of the elders. Mt. 15:1; Mk. 7:1
answers Pharisees asking a sign. Mt. 12:38; 16:1; Mk. 8:11; Lk. 11:16; 12:54; Jn. 2:18
teaches His disciples on humility. Jn. 13:14
teaches scribes and Pharisees. Mt. 23; Mk. 12:38; Lk. 11:37; 20:45
prophesies destruction of Jerusalem, and the last times. Mt. 24; Mk. 13; Lk. 13:34; 17:20; 19:41; 21
preaches daily in the temple. Lk. 19:47
His invitation to the weary and heavy laden. Mt. 11:28
His discourses on:
suffering for the Gospel's sake. Lk. 14:26 (Mt. 10:37)
marriage. Mt. 19; Mk. 10
riches. Mt. 19:16; Mk. 10:17; Lk. 12:13; 18:18
paying taxes. Mt. 22:15; Mk. 12:13; Lk. 20:20
the resurrection. Mt. 22:23; Mk. 12:18
the two great commandments. Mt. 22:35; Mk. 12:28
the Son of David. Mt. 22:41; Mk. 12:35; Lk. 20:41
the widow's mites. Mk. 12:41; Lk. 21:1
watchfulness. Mt. 24:42; Mk. 13:33; Lk. 21:34; 12:35
the last judgment. Mt. 25:31
Sermon on the Mount: who are the blessed. Mt. 5:1; salt of the earth. 5:13; light of the world. 5:14; the righteousness of scribes and Pharisees. 5:20; anger with a brother (Raca). 5:22; you fool. 5:22; reconciliation. 5:24; adultery. 5:27; right hand and right eye. 5:29,30; divorce. 5:32,33; oaths. 5:33; eye for an eye. 5:38; love to neighbor and enemy. 5:43; be perfect. 5:48; charitable deeds. 6:1; prayer. 6:5; no vain repetitions. 6:7; Lord's Prayer. 6:9; Lk. 11:2; fasting. Mt. 6:16; treasure on earth. 6:19; bad eye. 6:23; two masters. 6:24; God and mammon. 6:24; no worry about life. 6:25; birds of the air. 6:26; being anxious, clothing, lilies of the field. 6:27; seek kingdom of God. 6:33; judge not. 7:1; plank in eye. 7:3; holy things not to be cast to dogs. 7:6; ask, seek, find. 7:7; Lk. 11:9; bread, stone, fish, serpent. Mt. 7:9,10; Lk. 11:11; narrow gate. Mt. 7:13; false prophets. 7:15; grapes, thorns, figs, thistles. 7:16; the good and bad tree. 7:17; not to be hearers but doers. 7:23,24; house on rock. 7:24; on sand. 7:27; taught as having authority. 7:29
sermon to disciples and multitudes on the level place: the blessed. Lk. 6:20–22; woe to the rich. 6:24; to the full. 6:25; to those men speak well of. 6:26; love to enemies. 6:27,35; submission under injury. 6:29; giving. 6:30,38; doing as we would be done to. 6:31; be merciful. 6:36; judge not. 6:37; hearers and doers. 6:46
letters to the seven churches in Asia. Rev. 1;2;3
discourses:
on faith, the centurion's. Mt. 8:8
to those who would follow Him. Lk. 9:23,57
on fasting. Mt. 9:14; Mk. 2:18; Lk. 5:33
on blasphemy. Mt. 12:31; Mk. 3:28; Lk. 11:15
on who are His brothers. Mt. 12:46; Mk. 3:31; Lk. 8:19

CHARACTER OF
holy. Lk. 1:35; Acts 4:27; Rev. 3:7
righteous. Isa. 53:11; Heb. 1:9
good. Mt. 19:16
faithful. Isa. 11:5; 1 Th. 5:24
true. Jn. 1:14; 7:18; 1 Jn. 5:20
just. Zech. 9:9; Jn. 5:30; Acts 22:14
guileless. Isa. 53:9; 1 Pet. 2:22
sinless. Jn. 8:46; 2 Cor. 5:21
spotless. 1 Pet. 1:19
innocent. Mt. 27:4
harmless. Heb. 7:26
resisting temptation. Mt. 4:1–10
obedient to God the Father. Ps. 40:8; Jn. 4:34; 15:10
subject to His parents. Lk. 2:51
zealous. Lk. 2:49; Jn. 2:17; 8:29
meek. Isa. 53:7; Zech. 9:9; Mt. 11:29
lowly in heart. Mt. 11:29
merciful. Heb. 2:17
patient. Isa. 53:7; Mt. 27:14
longsuffering. 1 Tim. 1:16
compassionate. Isa. 40:11; Mt. 15:32; Lk. 7:13; 19:41
benevolent. Mt. 4:23,24; 9:35; Acts 10:38
loving. Jn. 13:1; 15:13
self-denying. Mt. 8:20; 2 Cor. 8:9
humble. Lk. 22:27; Phil. 2:8
resigned. Lk. 22:42
forgiving. Lk. 23:34
saints to be conformed to. Rom. 8:29

COMPASSION OF
necessary to His priestly office. Heb. 5:2
manifested for the:
weary and heavy laden. Mt. 11:28–30
weak in faith. Isa. 40:11; 42:3, with Mt. 12:20
tempted. Heb. 2:18
afflicted. Lk. 7:13; Jn. 11:33
diseased. Mt. 14:14; Mk. 1:41
poor. Mk. 8:2
perishing sinners. Mt. 9:36; Lk. 19:41; Jn. 3:16
an encouragement to prayer. Heb. 4:15

GLORY OF
as: divine. Jn. 1:1–5; Phil. 2:6,9,10
God the Son. Mt. 3:17; Heb. 1:6,8
equal to the Father. Jn. 10:30,38
the firstborn. Col. 1:15,18; Heb. 1:6
Lord of lords, etc. Rev. 17:14
the Image of God. Col. 1:15; Heb. 1:3
Creator. Jn. 1:3; Col. 1:16; Heb. 1:2
the Blessed of God. Ps. 45:2
Mediator. 1 Tim. 2:5; Heb. 8:6
Prophet. Dt. 18:15,16, with Acts 3:22
Priest. Ps. 110:4; Heb. 4:15
King. Isa. 6:1–5, with Jn. 12:41
Judge. Mt. 16:27; 25:31,33
Shepherd. Isa. 40:10,11; Ezek. 34; Jn. 10; 11; 14
Head of the Church. Eph. 1:22
the true Light. Lk. 1:78,79; Jn. 1:4,9
the foundation of the Church. Isa. 28:16
the Way. Jn. 14:6; Heb. 10:19,20
the Truth. 1 Jn. 5:20; Rev. 3:7

the Life. Jn. 11:25; Col. 3:4; 1 Jn. 5:11
Incarnate. Jn. 1:14
in: His words. Lk. 4:22; Jn. 7:46
His works. Mt. 13:54; Jn. 2:11
His sinless perfection. Heb. 7:26–28
the fullness of His grace and truth. Ps. 45:2, with Jn. 1:14
His transfiguration. Mt. 17:2, with 2 Pet. 1:16–18
His exaltation. Acts 7:55,56; Eph. 1:21
celebrated by the redeemed. Rev. 5:8–14; 7:9–12
revealed in the Gospel. Isa. 40:5
saints shall rejoice at the revelation of. 1 Pet. 4:13
saints shall behold, in heaven. Jn. 17:24

DIVINE NATURE OF
as Lord. Col. 1:16; Isa. 6:1–3, with Jn. 12:41; Isa. 8:13,14, with 1 Pet. 2:8; Isa. 40:3, with Mt. 3:3; Isa. 40:11; 44:6, with Rev. 1:17; Isa. 48:12–16, with Rev. 22:13; Jer. 23:5,6, with 1 Cor. 1:30; Joel 2:32, with Acts 2:21, and 1 Cor. 1:2; Mal. 3:1, with Mk. 1:2, and Lk. 2:27; Heb. 13:20; Jas. 2:1
the eternal God and Creator, Judge and Savior. Ps. 45:6,7; 102:24–27, with Heb. 1:8,10–12; Isa. 9:6; Eccl. 12:14; with 1 Cor. 4:5; Jer. 10:10, with Jn. 15:20; Hos. 1:7, with Ti. 2:13; Jn. 1:1; Rom. 9:5; 2 Cor. 5:10; 2 Tim. 4:1
fellow and equal to God. Zech. 13:7; Jn. 5:17,23; 16:15; Phil. 2:6; 1 Th. 3:11; 2 Th. 2:16,17
the Lord from heaven, Lord of the Sabbath, and Lord of all. Gen. 2:3, with Mt. 12:8; Acts 10:36; Rom. 10:11–13; 1 Cor. 15:47
Son of God. Mt. 26:63–67; Jn. 1:14,18; 3:16,18; 1 Jn. 4:9
One with the Father. Jn. 10:30,38; 12:45; 14:7–10; 17:10
as sending the Spirit, equally with the Father. Jn. 14:16, with Jn. 15:26
Creator, Supporter, and Preserver of all things. Jn. 1:3; Col. 1:16,17; Heb. 1:2,3
possessing the fullness of the Godhead. Col. 2:9; Heb. 1:3
raising the dead. Jn. 5:21; 6:40,54
raising Himself from the dead. Jn. 2:19,21; 10:18
eternal, omnipresent, omnipotent, and omniscient. Ps. 45:3; Isa. 9:6; Mic. 5:2; Mt. 18:20; 28:20; Jn. 1:1; 3:13; 16:30; 21:17; Phil. 3:21; Col. 1:17; Heb. 1:8–10; Rev. 1:8
God, He redeems, purifies, and presents the Church to Himself. Eph. 5:27, with Jude 24,25; Rev. 5:9, with Ti. 2:14
acknowledged by voice from heaven. Mt. 3:17; 17:5; Jn. 12:28
His blood. Acts 20:28
object of divine worship. Acts 7:59; 2 Cor. 12:8,9; Heb. 1:6; Rev. 5:12
object of faith. Ps. 2:12, with 1 Pet. 2:6; Jer. 17:5,7, with Jn. 14:1
saints live to Him as God. Rom. 6:11, and Gal. 2:19, with 2 Cor. 5:15
acknowledged by Thomas. Jn. 20:28

HUMAN NATURE OF
proved by his:
conception. Mt. 1:18; Lk. 1:31
birth. Mt. 1:16,25; 2:2; Lk. 2:7,11
partaking of our flesh and blood. Jn. 1:14; Heb. 2:14
having a human soul. Mt. 26:38; Lk. 23:46; Acts 2:31
circumcision. Lk. 2:21
increase in wisdom and stature. Lk. 2:52
weeping. Lk. 19:41; Jn. 11:35
hungering. Mt. 4:2; 21:18
thirsting. Jn. 4:7; 19:28
sleeping. Mt. 8:24; Mk. 4:38
weariness. Jn. 4:6
Man of sorrows. Isa. 53:3,4; Lk. 22:44; Jn. 11:33; 12:27
beaten. Mt. 26:67; Lk. 22:64
enduring indignities. Lk. 23:11
scourged. Mt. 27:26; Jn. 19:1
nailed to the cross. Lk. 23:33, with Ps. 22:16
death. Jn. 19:30
pierced side. Jn. 19:34
burial. Mt. 27:59,60; Mk. 15:46
resurrection. Acts 3:15; 2 Tim. 2:8
being called like us in all things except sin. Acts 3:22; Phil. 2:7,8; Heb. 2:17; without sin. Jn. 8:46; 18:38; Heb. 4:15; 7:26,28; 1 Pet. 2:22; 1 Jn. 3:5
can be perceived by human senses. Jn. 20:27; 1 Jn. 1:1,2
necessary to His mediatorial office. Rom. 6:15,19; 1 Cor. 15:21; Gal. 4:4,5; 1 Tim. 2:5; Heb. 2:17

WAS OF THE SEED OF
the woman. Gen. 3:15; Isa. 7:14; Jer. 31:22; Lk. 1:31; Gal. 4:4
Abraham. Gen. 22:18, with Gal. 3:16; Heb. 2:16
David. 2 Sam. 7:12,16; Ps. 89:35,36; Jer. 23:5; Mt. 22:42; Mk. 10:47; Acts 2:30; 13:23; Rom. 1:3
genealogies of. Mt. 1:1; Lk. 3:23
attested by Himself. Mt. 8:20; 16:13
confession of, a test of belonging to God. 1 Jn. 4:2
acknowledged by men. Mk. 6:3; Jn. 7:27; 19:5; Acts 2:22
denied by antichrist. 1 Jn. 4:3; 2 Jn. 7

THE HEAD OF THE CHURCH
appointed by God. Eph. 1:22
declared by Himself chief cornerstone. Mt. 21:42
declared by Paul. Eph. 4:12,15; 5:23
as such has preeminence in all things. 1 Cor. 11:3; Eph. 1:22; Col. 1:18
commissioned His apostles. Mt. 10:1,7; 28:19; Jn. 20:21
instituted the sacraments. Mt. 28:19; Lk. 22:19,20
imparted gifts. Ps. 68:18, with Eph. 4:8
saints complete in. Col. 2:10

TYPES OF
Aaron. Ex. 28:1; Lev. 16:15; Heb. 4:15; 12:24
Abel. Gen. 4:8,10; Heb. 12:24
Abraham. Gen. 17:5; Eph. 3:15
Adam. Rom. 5:14; 1 Cor. 15:45
David. 2 Sam. 8:15; Ps. 89:19; Ezek.37:24; Phil. 2:9
Eliakim. Isa. 22:20
Isaac. Gen. 22:2; Heb. 11:17
Jacob. Gen. 32:28; Jn. 11:42; Heb. 7:25
Jonah. Jon. 1:17; Mt. 12:40
Joseph. Gen. 50:19,20; Heb. 7:25
Joshua. Josh. 1:5; 11:23; Acts 20:32; Heb. 4:8
Melchizedek. Gen. 14:18,20; Heb. 7:1
Moses. Num. 12:7; Dt. 18:15; Acts 3:22; 7:37; Heb. 3:2
Noah. Gen. 5:29; 2 Cor. 1:5
Samson. Jud. 16:30; Col. 2:14,15
Solomon. 2 Sam. 7:12; Lk. 1:32
Zerubbabel. Zech. 4:7,9; Heb. 12:2,3
ark. Gen. 7:16; Ex. 25:16; Ps. 40:8; Isa. 42:6; 1 Pet. 3:20,21
Jacob's ladder. Gen. 28:12; Jn. 1:51
Passover. Ex. 12; 1 Cor. 5:7
lamb. Ex. 12:3; Isa. 53:7; Jn. 1:29; Acts 8:32; 1 Pet. 1:19; Rev. 5:6; 6:1; 7:9; 12:11; 13:8; 14:1; 15:3; 17:14; 19:7; 21:9; 22:1
manna. Ex. 16:11; Jn. 6:32; Rev. 2:17
rock. Ex. 17:6; 1 Cor. 10:4
firstfruits. Ex. 22:29; 1 Cor. 15:20
golden lampstand. Ex. 25:31; Jn. 8:12
altar, bronze. Ex. 27:1,2; Heb. 13:10
laver. Ex. 30:18; Zech. 13:1; Eph. 5:26
burnt offering. Lev. 1:2; Heb. 10:10
peace offering. Lev. 3; Eph. 2:14
sin offering. Lev. 4:2; Heb. 13:11
atonement, sacrifices on day of. Lev. 16:15; Heb. 9:12
scapegoat. Lev. 16:20; Isa. 53:6
bronze serpent. Num. 21:9; Jn. 3:14
cities of refuge. Num. 35:6; Heb. 6:18
temple. 1 Ki. 6:1,38; Jn. 2:21
tabernacle. Heb. 9:8,11
veil. Heb. 10:20

CHRIST
Mt. 1:1, genealogy of Jesus C
Mt. 1:16, Jesus who is called C
Mt. 16:16, "You are the C
Mt. 26:63, if You are the C
Lk. 2:11, a Savior, who is C
Lk. 23:2, that He Himself is C
Jn. 12:34, the law that the C
Acts 9:20, he preached the C
Rom. 8:9, have the Spirit of C
Rom. 8:34, It is C who died
Rom. 15:3, C did not please
1 Cor. 1:13, Is C divided
1 Cor. 1:30, Him you are in C Jesus
Gal. 2:17, to be justified by C
Gal. 2:20, been crucified with C

Gal. 2:20, but C lives in me
Gal. 3:16, your Seed,' who is C
Gal. 3:17, before by God in C
Eph. 3:17, C may dwell in your
Eph. 5:14, C will give you
Eph. 5:23, C is head of the
Phil. 1:21, to me, to live is C
Phil. 2:11, confess that Jesus C
Phil. 4:13, C who strengthens
Col. 1:27, which is C in you
Col. 3:4, C who is our
Col. 3:11, C is all and in all
1 Tim. 2:5, and men, the Man C
Heb. 13:8, Jesus C is the same
1 Jn. 1:7, C His Son cleanses us
1 Jn. 5:1, that Jesus is the C
Rev. 12:10, of His C have come
Rev. 20:4, and reigned with C

CHRISTIAN
Acts 26:28, me to become a C
1 Pet. 4:16, anyone suffers as a C

CHRISTIANS
Acts 11:26, were first called C

CHRISTS
false, and prophets, warnings against. Mt. 7:15; 24:4,5,11,24; Mk. 13:22; Acts 20:29; 2 Th. 2:8; 1 Tim. 4:1; 2 Pet. 2:1; Rev. 13

CHURCH
of God. Acts 20:28; 1 Cor. 1:2; 10:32; 11:22; 15:9; Gal. 1:13; 1 Tim. 3:5
foundation and increase of. Mt. 16:18; Acts 2:47; Col. 1:18
authority and teaching of. Mt. 18:17; Acts 11:26,27; 1 Cor. 5:4; 12:28
organization of. Acts 14:23; 1 Cor. 4:17; 14:4,5
persecuted. Acts 8:3; 12:1; 15:9; Gal. 1:13; Phil. 3:6
greeted. Acts 18:22; Rom. 16:5; 10:16; 1 Cor. 16:19
loved by Christ. Eph. 5:25,29
edification of. 1 Cor. 14:4,19,28,34

CHURCH
Mt. 16:18, rock I will build My *c*
Mt. 18:17, them, tell it to the *c*
Acts 2:47, *c* daily those who were
Acts 14:23, elders in every *c*
1 Cor. 11:22, do you despise the *c*
Eph. 3:10, be made known by the *c*
Eph. 5:25, also loved the *c*
Eph. 5:27, Himself a glorious *c*
Eph. 5:29, as the Lord does the *c*
Col. 1:24, body, which is the *c*
1 Tim. 5:16, and do not let the *c*
Heb. 12:23, general assembly and *c*
Rev. 2:1, To the angel of the *c*

CHURCHES
the seven, in Asia. Rev. 1:4,11,20; 2:7,11,17,29; 3:6,13,22

CHURCHES
Acts 15:41, strengthening the *c*
Rom. 16:16, The *c* of Christ greet
1 Th. 2:14, imitators of the *c*
Rev. 1:4, John, to the seven *c*
Rev. 1:20, angels of the seven *c*
Rev. 22:16, these things in the *c*

CHURNING
Prov. 30:33, For as the *c* of milk

CHURNS
Hos. 11:8, My heart *c* within Me

CILICIA
disciples there. Acts 15:23,41
the country of Paul. Acts 21:39; Gal. 1:21
Paul born at Tarsus in. Acts 22:3

CIRCLE
Job 22:14, He walks above the *c*
Prov. 8:27, when He drew a *c*
Isa. 40:22, who sits above the *c*

CIRCUIT
Ps. 19:6, of heaven, and its *c*
Eccl. 1:6, comes again on its *c*

CIRCUMCISE
Dt. 10:16, *c* the foreskin of your
Dt. 30:6, LORD your God will *c*
Jer. 4:4, C yourselves to the
Acts 15:5, is necessary to *c* them

CIRCUMCISED
Gen. 17:10, among you shall be *c*
Rom. 3:30, who will justify the *c*
Rom. 4:10, While he was *c*
Gal. 2:7, the gospel for the *c*
Gal. 5:2, if you become *c*
Phil. 3:5, *c* the eighth day
Col. 2:11, In Him you were also *c*

CIRCUMCISION
the covenant of. Gen. 17:10,23,24,25
Shechemites submit to. Gen. 34:24
Zipporah resents it. Ex. 4:25
incumbent on strangers sojourning. Ex. 12:48
renewed by Joshua. Josh. 5:2
of John. Lk. 1:59
of Jesus. Lk. 2:21
of Timothy. Acts 16:3
superseded by the Gospel. Acts 15; Gal. 5:2
of heart. Dt. 10:16; 30:6
spiritual. Phil. 3:3; Col. 2:11
when profitable, and how. Rom. 2:25; 3:30; 4:9; 1 Cor. 7:19; Gal. 5:6; 6:15

CIRCUMCISION
Acts 7:8, him the covenant of *c*
Rom. 2:28, *c* that which is outward
Rom. 2:29, *c* is that of the heart
Rom. 15:8, a servant to the *c*
1 Cor. 7:19, C is nothing and
Gal. 5:6, Christ Jesus neither *c*
Phil. 3:3, For we are the *c*
Col. 2:11, circumcised with the *c*
Ti. 1:10, those of the *c*

CIRCUMSPECTLY
Eph. 5:15, then that you walk *c*

CISTERN
2 Ki. 18:31, waters of his own *c*
Prov. 5:15, from your own *c*

CITIES
Gen. 19:25, He overthrew those *c*
Isa. 61:4, repair the ruined *c*
Isa. 64:10, *c* are a wilderness
Jer. 4:7, *c* will be laid waste

Rev. 16:19, three parts, and the *c*

CITIZEN
Acts 22:28, But I was born a *c*

CITIZENS
Lk. 19:14, "But his *c* hated him
Eph. 2:19, but fellow *c* with the

CITIZENSHIP
Acts 22:28, sum I obtained this *c*
Phil. 3:20, For our *c* is in heaven

CITY
Gen. 4:17, And he built a *c*
Ps. 46:4, shall make glad the *c*
Ps. 72:16, *c* shall flourish
Ps. 107:4, They found no *c*
Ps. 122:3, *c* that is compact
Ps. 127:1, the LORD guards the *c*
Prov. 8:3, at the entry of the *c*
Isa. 1:21, *c* has become a harlot
Isa. 33:20, upon Zion, the *c*
Isa. 48:2, after the holy *c*
Lam. 1:1, How lonely sits the *c*
Jon. 4:11, Nineveh, that great *c*
Zeph. 2:15, *c* that dwelt securely
Zeph. 3:1, to the oppressing *c*
Mt. 2:23, *c* called Nazareth
Mt. 5:14, *c* that is set on a
Heb. 11:16, He has prepared a *c*
Heb. 12:22, Zion and to the *c*
Heb. 13:14, have no continuing *c*
Rev. 11:2, will tread the holy *c*
Rev. 14:8, fallen, that great *c*
Rev. 20:9, and the beloved *c*
Rev. 21:2, John, saw the holy *c*
Rev. 21:18, *c* was pure gold
Rev. 21:23, *c* had no need of the
Rev. 22:14, the gates into the *c*

CLAMOROUS
Prov. 9:13, A foolish woman is *c*

CLAP
Job 27:23, *c* their hands at him
Ps. 47:1, Oh, *c* your hands
Ps. 98:8, let the rivers *c*
Isa. 55:12, of the field shall *c*

CLAUDIA, 2 Tim. 4:21

CLAUDIUS, Acts 11:28

CLAUDIUS LYSIAS
garrison commander, rescues Paul. Acts 21:31; 22:24; 23:10
sends him to Felix. Acts 23:26

CLAY
Job 4:19, dwell in houses of *c*
Job 10:9, have made me like *c*
Job 13:12, are defenses of *c*
Job 33:6, been formed out of *c*
Job 38:14, takes on form like *c*
Ps. 40:2, pit, out of the miry *c*
Isa. 29:16, be esteemed as the *c*
Isa. 45:9, Shall the *c* say to him
Isa. 64:8, We are the *c*
Jer. 18:6, "Look, as the *c*
Dan. 2:33, iron and partly of *c*
Jn. 9:6, blind man with the *c*
Rom. 9:21, have power over the *c*

CLEAN
Gen. 7:2, seven each of every *c*

Lev. 10:10, between unclean and *c*
2 Ki. 5:12, wash in them and be *c*
Job 14:4, Who can bring a *c*
Ps. 24:4, He who has *c* hands and
Isa. 1:16, make yourselves *c*
Ezek. 36:25, Then I will sprinkle *c*
Mt. 3:12, *c* out His threshing
Mt. 8:2, You can make me *c*
Lk. 11:41, all things are *c*
Jn. 13:10, but is completely *c*
Jn. 13:11, "You are not all *c*
Jn. 15:3, "You are already *c*
Rev. 19:8, in fine linen, *c*

CLEANSE
Ex. 29:36, You shall *c* the altar
Ps. 19:12, *c* me from secret
Ps. 51:2, and *c* me from my sin
Ps. 119:9, How can a young man *c*
Ezek. 36:25, I will *c* you from all
Mt. 10:8, *c* the lepers, raise
Eph. 5:26, might sanctify and *c*
Heb. 9:14, *c* your conscience
Jas. 4:8, *C* your hands
1 Jn. 1:9, us our sins and to *c*

CLEANSED
Ps. 73:13, Surely I have *c*
Ezek. 24:13, and you were not *c*
Mt. 11:5, the lepers are *c*
Lk. 17:17, "Were there not ten *c*

CLEANSES
2 Tim. 2:21, Therefore if anyone *c*
1 Jn. 1:7, Christ His Son *c*

CLEAR
2 Sam. 23:4, *c* shining after rain
Song 6:10, fair as the moon, *c*
2 Cor. 7:11, yourselves to be *c*
Rev. 21:11, like a jasper stone, *c*
Rev. 22:1, of life, *c* as crystal

CLEFTS
Isa. 2:21, to go into the *c*
Isa. 7:19, valleys and in the *c*
Jer. 49:16, you who dwell in the *c*

CLEMENT
fellow worker of Paul. Phil. 4:3

CLEOPAS
a disciple. Lk. 24:18. *See* EMMAUS

CLERK
Acts 19:35, *c* had quieted the

CLIFF
Song 2:14, secret places of the *c*

CLIMB
Jer. 4:29, go into thickets and *c*
Joel 2:7, mighty men, they *c*
Amos 9:2, though they *c* up to

CLIMBS
Jn. 10:1, *c* up some other way

CLING
Dt. 30:20, and that you may *c*
Jn. 20:17, to her, "Do not *c*
Rom. 12:9, *C* to what is good

CLINGS
Ps. 22:15, and My tongue *c*
Ps. 119:25, My soul *c* to the dust

CLOAK
Ps. 102:26, *c* You will change them
Mt. 5:40, let him have your *c*
Heb. 1:12, *c* You will fold them
1 Pet. 2:16, using liberty as a *c*

CLODS
Job 21:33, The *c* of the valley

CLOPAS, Jn. 19:25

CLOSE
Job 19:19, *c* friends abhor me
Phil. 2:30, of Christ he came *c*

CLOSE RELATIVE
right of. Ruth 3:14; 4

CLOSED
Isa. 29:10, and has *c* your eyes
Dan. 12:9, for the words are *c*
Jon. 2:5, the deep *c* around me

CLOTH
Mt. 9:16, a piece of unshrunk *c*
Mt. 27:59, in a clean linen *c*

CLOTHE
Ex. 40:14, *c* them with tunics
Job 10:11, *c* me with skin and
Ps. 132:16, *c* her priests with
Ps. 132:18, His enemies I will *c*
Jer. 4:30, Though you *c* yourself
Mt. 6:30, He not much more *c*

CLOTHED
Gen. 3:21, of skin, and *c* them
Job 39:19, Have you *c* his neck
Ps. 30:11, off my sackcloth and *c*
Ps. 65:13, The pastures are *c*
Ps. 93:1, the LORD is *c*
Ps. 104:1, You are *c* with honor
Ps. 109:18, *c* himself with cursing
Ps. 132:9, Let Your priests be *c*
Prov. 31:21, all her household is *c*
Ezek. 16:10, *c* you with fine linen
Mt. 11:8, A man *c* in soft
Mt. 25:36, I was naked and you *c*
Mk. 5:15, legion, sitting and *c*
Mk. 15:17, And they *c* Him with
Lk. 16:19, rich man who was *c*
2 Cor. 5:2, desiring to be *c*
Rev. 3:18, that you may be *c*
Rev. 12:1, a woman *c* with the sun
Rev. 19:13, He was *c* with a robe

CLOTHES
Job 9:31, *c* will abhor me
Mk. 9:3, *c* became shining
Lk. 19:36, many spread their *c*
Acts 7:58, laid down their *c*
Acts 22:23, and tore off their *c*
Jas. 2:2, a poor man in filthy *c*

CLOTHING
Ps. 22:18, *c* they cast lots
Ps. 45:13, *c* is woven with gold
Prov. 27:26, will provide your *c*
Prov. 31:25, and honor are her *c*
Isa. 59:17, of vengeance for *c*
Mt. 6:25, the body more than *c*
Mt. 6:28, do you worry about *c*
Mt. 7:15, to you in sheep's *c*
Mt. 11:8, those who wear soft *c*
Mt. 28:3, *c* as white as snow
Jn. 19:24, *c* they cast lots

Acts 10:30, before me in bright *c*

CLOTHS
Lk. 2:12, wrapped in swaddling *c*
Jn. 20:5, in, saw the linen *c*

CLOUD
pillar of, children of Israel guided by. Ex. 13:21; 14:19; Neh. 9:19; Ps. 78:14; 105:39; 1 Cor. 10:1
appearance of the Lord in. Ex. 24:15; 34:5; Lev. 16:2; Num. 11:25; 12:5; 1 Ki. 8:10; Ezek. 10:4; Mt. 17:5; Lk. 21:27; Rev. 14:14

CLOUD
Gen. 9:13, My rainbow in the *c*
Ex. 13:21, day in a pillar of *c*
Ex. 24:15, *c* covered the mountain
Ex. 33:9, *c* descended and stood
Neh. 9:19, *c* did not depart
Ps. 78:14, He led them with the *c*
Prov. 16:15, his favor is like a *c*
Isa. 60:8, these who fly like a *c*
Hos. 6:4, like a morning *c*
Mt. 17:5, behold, a bright *c*
Lk. 21:27, of Man coming in a *c*
Acts 1:9, *c* received Him out of
1 Cor. 10:1, were under the *c*
Heb. 12:1, by so great a *c*

CLOUDS
2 Sam. 23:3, a morning without *c*
Ps. 77:17, *c* poured out water
Ps. 148:8, and hail, snow and *c*
Prov. 3:20, *c* drop down the dew
Eccl. 11:4, he who regards the *c*
Mt. 24:30, of Man coming on the *c*
1 Th. 4:17, with them in the *c*
Jude 12, are *c* without water
Rev. 1:7, He is coming with *c*

CLOUDY
Neh. 9:12, them by day with a *c*
Ps. 99:7, spoke to them in the *c*

CLOVEN
Lev. 11:3, the hoof, having *c*
Dt. 14:7, chew the cud or have *c*

CLUSTER
Song 1:14, beloved is to me a *c*
Isa. 65:8, wine is found in the *c*

COAL
Isa. 6:6, in his hand a live *c*
Isa. 47:14, it shall not be a *c*

COALS
Ps. 11:6, wicked He will rain *c*
Ps. 18:8, *c* were kindled by it
Ps. 140:10, let burning *c* fall
Prov. 6:28, Can one walk on hot *c*
Prov. 25:22, so you will heap *c*
Rom. 12:20, doing you will heap *c*

COBRA
Job 20:14, it becomes *c* venom
Ps. 58:4, *c* that stops its ear
Ps. 91:13, the lion and the *c*

COBRA'S
Isa. 11:8, shall play by the *c*

COFFIN
Gen. 50:26, and he was put in a *c*
2 Sam. 3:31, David followed the *c*

Lk. 7:14, touched the open *c*

COIN
Mt. 10:29, sold for a copper *c*
Lk. 15:8, if she loses one *c*

COLD
Gen. 8:22, and harvest, *C* and
Ps. 147:17, can stand before His *c*
Prov. 25:13, Like the *c* of snow in
Prov. 25:25, *c* water to a weary
Mt. 10:42, *c* water in the name of
Mt. 24:12, of many will grow *c*
Rev. 3:15, that you are neither *c*

COLLECTED
Lk. 19:23, coming I might have *c*

COLLECTION
2 Chr. 24:6, from Jerusalem the *c*
1 Cor. 16:1, concerning the *c*

COLOSSE
brethren at, encouraged and warned. Col. 1; 2; exhorted to holiness. Col. 3; 4

COLT
Gen. 49:11, and his donkey's *c*
Zech. 9:9, on a donkey, a *c*
Mt. 21:5, on a donkey, a *c*
Lk. 19:35, own clothes on the *c*

COME
Job 28:20, then does wisdom *c*
Ps. 24:7, of glory shall *c*
Ps. 50:3, Our God shall *c*
Ps. 65:2, You all flesh will *c*
Song 4:8, *C* with me from Lebanon
Isa. 35:4, He will *c* and save you
Isa. 55:1, who have no money, *C*
Mt. 6:10, Your kingdom *c*
Mt. 11:28, "*C* to Me
Mt. 24:5, For many will *c*
Mt. 27:42, Israel, let Him now *c*
Lk. 9:23, If anyone desires to *c*
Lk. 10:9, kingdom of God has *c*
Jn. 5:43, I have *c* in My
Jn. 7:28, and I have not *c*
Jn. 7:37, thirsts, let him *c*
Jn. 10:10, *c* that they may have
Jn. 12:46, *c* as a light into the
Jn. 14:18, I will *c* to you
Jn. 15:22, "If I had not *c*
Acts 20:29, savage wolves will *c*
1 Cor. 16:22, O Lord, *c*
Rev. 3:20, the door, I will *c*
Rev. 22:17, the bride say, "*C*

COMELINESS
Isa. 53:2, He has no form or *c*

COMES
Isa. 63:1, Who is this who *c*
Mt. 8:9, 'Come,' and he *c*
1 Cor. 11:26, Lord's death till He *c*
1 Cor. 15:24, Then *c* the end

COMFORT
Job 2:11, with him, and to *c* him
Ps. 23:4, and Your staff, they *c*
Ps. 119:82, When will you *c*
Isa. 40:1, yes, *c* My people
Isa. 51:3, For the LORD will *c*
Isa. 61:2, *c* all who mourn
Lam. 1:2, she has none to *c* her
Zech. 1:17, the LORD will again *c*
2 Cor. 1:13, and God of all *c*
2 Cor. 1:4, trouble, with the *c*
hil. 2:1, in Christ, if any *c*
1 Th. 5:11, *c* each other and edify

COMFORTED
Gen. 24:67, So Isaac was *c* after
Ps. 77:2, soul refused to be *c*
Isa. 49:13, For the LORD has *c*
Jer. 31:15, refusing to be *c*
Lk. 16:25, but now he is *c*

COMFORTER
Lam. 1:9, She had no *c*

COMFORTS
Job 29:25, the army, as one who *c*
Isa. 51:12, I, even I, am He who *c*
Isa. 57:18, him, and restore *c*
Isa. 66:13, one whom his mother *c*
2 Cor. 1:4, who *c* us in all our
2 Cor. 7:6, who *c* the downcast

COMING
Isa. 62:11, your salvation is *c*
Mal. 4:1, behold, the day is *c*
Mt. 3:11, but He who is *c*
Mt. 11:3, "Are You the *C*
Mt. 24:3, be the sign of Your *c*
Mt. 24:48, is delaying his *c*
Mk. 13:26, see the Son of Man *c*
Lk. 3:16, mightier than I is *c*
1 Cor. 15:23, are Christ's at His *c*
2 Pet. 1:16, to you the power and *c*
2 Pet. 3:4, the promise of His *c*
Rev. 3:11, Behold, I am *c*
Rev. 22:7, "Behold, I am *c*
Rev. 22:20, "Surely I am *c*

COMMAND
of God to: Adam. Gen. 2:16
Moses. Ex. 3:14
Joshua. Josh. 1:9
of Moses to the sons of Levi. Dt. 31:10
of Christ to the twelve. Mt. 10:5; Mk. 16:15; to Peter. Jn. 21:15

COMMAND
Gen. 18:19, in order that he may *c*
Dt. 28:8, "The LORD will *c*
Dt. 30:16, "in that I *c* you
Ps. 42:8, *c* His lovingkindness
Ps. 44:4, *c* victories for Jacob
Jer. 11:4, to all that I *c*
Mt. 14:28, if it is You, *c*
Lk. 9:54, *c* fire to come down
Jn. 10:18, *c* I have received
Jn. 12:50, And I know that His *c*
Jn. 15:14, if you do whatever I *c*
2 Th. 3:4, do the things we *c*

COMMANDED
Job 38:12, "Have you *c* the
Ps. 111:9, *c* His covenant forever
Ps. 133:3, For there the LORD *c*
2 Cor. 4:6, it is the God who *c*
Heb. 12:20, not endure what was *c*

COMMANDMENT
Ps. 19:8, *c* of the LORD is pure
Ps. 119:96, *c* is exceedingly broad
Prov. 6:23, For the *c* is a lamp
Isa. 29:13, Me is taught by the *c*
Mt. 22:36, which is the great *c*
Jn. 13:34, "A new *c* I give to
Jn. 14:31, the Father gave Me *c*
Rom. 7:9, law, but when the *c*
Rom. 7:13, the *c* might become
Eph. 6:2, which is the first *c*
1 Jn. 2:7, *c* is the word which
1 Jn. 3:23, And this is His *c*
2 Jn. 4, as we received *c*
2 Jn. 6, This is the *c*

COMMANDMENTS
Ex. 34:28, covenant, the Ten *C*
Dt. 6:25, to observe all these *c*
Ps. 103:18, who remember His *c*
Ps. 119:19, do not hide Your *c*
Ps. 119:47, myself in Your *c*
Ps. 119:66, for I believe Your *c*
Ps. 119:86, Your *c* are faithful
Ps. 119:127, *c* more than gold
Mt. 15:9, as doctrines the *c*
Mt. 22:40, *c* hang all the Law
Jn. 14:21, "He who has My *c*
Col. 2:22, according to the *c*
1 Jn. 3:24, Now he who keeps His *c*

COMMANDMENTS (TEN)
delivered. Ex. 20; 31:18; Dt. 5:6
two tablets of, broken. Ex. 32:19
renewed. Ex. 34:1; Dt. 10:1
fulfilled by Christ. Mt. 5:17; 19:17; 22:35; Mk. 10:17; Lk. 10:25; 18:18

COMMANDS
Mk. 1:27, with authority He *c*

COMMEND
1 Cor. 8:8, But food does not *c*

COMMENDABLE
1 Pet. 2:19, For this is *c*
1 Pet. 2:20, patiently, this is *c*

COMMENDED
Prov. 12:8, A man will be *c*
Lk. 16:8, *c* the unjust steward
Acts 14:26, where they had been *c*

COMMENDING
2 Cor. 4:2, of the truth *c*

COMMENDS
2 Cor. 10:18, but whom the Lord *c*

COMMIT
Ex. 20:14, "You shall not *c*
Prov. 16:3, *C* your works to the
Lk. 16:11, mammon, who will *c*
Lk. 23:46, into Your hands I *c*
Jn. 2:24, But Jesus did not *c*
1 Cor. 10:8, *c* sexual immorality
2 Tim. 2:2, *c* these to faithful
1 Pet. 4:19, *c* their souls to Him
1 Jn. 5:16, *c* sin not leading

COMMITS
Jn. 8:34, to you, whoever *c*
1 Jn. 3:4, sin also *c* lawlessness

COMMITTED
Jer. 2:13, For My people have *c*
Lk. 12:48, *c* things deserving
Rom. 11:32, For God has *c* them all
1 Tim. 6:20, Guard what was *c*
1 Pet. 2:22, "Who *c* no sin
1 Pet. 2:23, *c* Himself to Him who

COMMON
Lev. 4:27, of the *c* people sins
Prov. 22:2, poor have this in *c*
Mk. 12:37, *c* people heard Him
Acts 2:44, had all things in *c*
Acts 10:14, never eaten anything *c*
Acts 10:28, not call any man *c*
Ti. 1:4, a true son in our *c*
Jude 3, concerning our *c*

COMMOTION
Acts 19:23, there arose a great *c*

COMMUNED
Eccl. 1:16, I *c* with my heart

COMMUNION
of the Body and Blood of Christ. 1 Cor. 10:16
Lord's Supper instituted. Mt. 26:26; Mk. 14:22; Lk. 22:19; 1 Cor. 11:23
self-examination for. Acts 2:42; 20:7; 1 Cor. 10:21; 11:28
unworthily partaken. 1 Cor. 11:27
—— of saints. *See* FELLOWSHIP

COMMUNION
1 Cor. 10:16, bless, is it not the *c*
2 Cor. 6:14, *c* has light with
2 Cor. 13:14, *c* of the Holy Spirit

COMPANION
Ps. 55:13, a man my equal, My *c*
Ps. 119:63, I am a *c* of all who
Zech. 13:7, the Man who is My *C*
Phil. 4:3, urge you also, true *c*
Rev. 1:9, your brother and *c*

COMPANIONS
Isa. 1:23, are rebellious, and *c*
Mt. 11:16, and calling to their *c*
Heb. 1:9, more than Your *c*
Heb. 10:33, while you became *c*

COMPANY
Ps. 68:11, great was the *c*
1 Cor. 5:9, epistle not to keep *c*
1 Cor. 15:33, *c* corrupts good habits
2 Th. 3:14, and do not keep *c*
Heb. 12:22, to an innumerable *c*

COMPARE
Prov. 3:15, may desire cannot *c*
2 Cor. 10:12, *c* ourselves with

COMPARED
Ps. 89:6, the heavens can be *c*
Prov. 8:11, may desire cannot be *c*
Rom. 8:18, are not worthy to be *c*

COMPASSION
Dt. 13:17, show you mercy, have *c*
Dt. 32:36, His people and have *c*
Ps. 78:38, He, being full of *c*
Ps. 86:15, are a God full of *c*
Jer. 12:15, will return and have *c*
Lam. 3:32, yet He will show *c*
Zech. 7:9, *c* everyone to his
Mt. 9:36, He was moved with *c*
Mt. 18:33, also have had *c*
Mk. 8:2, "I have *c* on the
Rom. 9:15, whomever I will have *c*
Heb. 5:2, He can have *c* on those
1 Pet. 3:8, of one mind, having *c*
Jude 22, And on some have *c*

COMPASSIONATE
Lam. 4:10, *c* women have cooked
Jas. 5:11, the Lord is very *c*

COMPASSIONS
Lam. 3:22, because His *c* fail not

COMPEL
Lk. 14:23, *c* them to come in

COMPELLED
Acts 18:5, Macedonia, Paul was *c*

COMPELS
Job 32:18, the spirit within me *c*
Mt. 5:41, "And whoever *c*
2 Cor. 5:14, the love of Christ *c*

COMPLACENCY
Prov. 1:32, slay them, and the *c*
Zeph. 1:12, who are settled in *c*

COMPLAIN
Lam. 3:39, should a living man *c*

COMPLAINED
Dt. 1:27, and you *c* in your
Ps. 106:25, but *c* in their tents
1 Cor. 10:10, some of them also *c*

COMPLAINERS
Jude 16, These are grumblers, *c*

COMPLAINING
Phil. 2:14, all things without *c*

COMPLAINT
Job 23:3, "Even today my *c*
Ps. 142:2, I pour out my *c*
Mic. 6:2, for the LORD has a *c*
Col. 3:13, if anyone has a *c*

COMPLAINTS
Prov. 23:29, Who has *c*
Acts 25:7, laid many serious *c*

COMPLETE
2 Cor. 13:9, that you may be made *c*
Phil. 1:6, work in you will *c*
Col. 2:10, and you are *c* in Him
2 Tim. 3:17, of God may be *c*
Heb. 13:21, make you *c* in every
Rev. 15:1, the wrath of God is *c*

COMPLETELY
Jn. 7:23, I made a man *c* well
1 Th. 5:23, Himself sanctify you *c*

COMPOSED
1 Cor. 12:24, But God *c* the body

COMPREHEND
Job 37:5, which we cannot *c*
Ps. 139:3, *c* my path and my lying
Jn. 1:5, the darkness did not *c*
Eph. 3:18, may be able to *c*

CONCEAL
Job 27:11, Almighty I will not *c*
Job 33:17, *c* pride from man
Prov. 25:2, of God to *c* a matter

CONCEALED
Ps. 40:10, *c* Your lovingkindness
Prov. 27:5, than love carefully *c*

CONCEIT
Phil. 2:3, selfish ambition or *c*

CONCEITED
Gal. 5:26, Let us not become *c*

CONCEIVE
Isa. 7:14, the virgin shall *c*
Lk. 1:31, And behold, you will *c*

CONCEIVED
Ps. 51:5, in sin my mother *c*
Jas. 1:15, when desire has *c*

CONCERN
Ps. 131:1, Neither do I *c* myself
Acts 28:31, the things which *c*
2 Cor. 11:28, my deep *c* for all the

CONCERNED
1 Cor. 9:9, Is it oxen God is *c*

CONCESSION
1 Cor. 7:6, But I say this as a *c*

CONCILIATION
Eccl. 10:4, *c* pacifies great

CONCLUSION
Eccl. 12:13, Let us hear the *c*

CONDEMN
Job 10:2, say to God, 'Do not *c*
Jn. 3:17, world to *c* the world
Jn. 8:11, her, "Neither do I *c*
Rom. 2:1, judge another you *c*
1 Jn. 3:21, our heart does not *c*

CONDEMNATION
Mk. 16:16; Rom. 13:2; 2 Th. 2:12; 2 Pet. 2:3
for sin, universal. Ps. 14:3; 53:3; Rom. 3:12,19; 5:12; 6:23
for unbelief. Jn. 3:18
by the law. 2 Cor. 3:6,9
by impenitence and hypocrisy. Mt. 11:20; 23:14
according to our works. 2 Cor. 11:15
of false teachers. 2 Pet. 2:1; Jude 4
deliverance from, by Christ. Jn. 3:18; 5:24; Rom. 8:1,33
final. Mt. 25:46; Rev. 20:15

CONDEMNATION
Mt. 23:14, will receive greater *c*
Mt. 23:33, can you escape the *c*
Mk. 3:29, subject to eternal *c*
Jn. 3:19, "And this is the *c*
Jn. 5:29, the resurrection of *c*
Rom. 3:8, Their *c* is just
Rom. 8:1, therefore now no *c*
2 Cor. 3:9, of *c* had glory
1 Tim. 5:12, having *c* because they
Jude 4, marked out for this *c*

CONDEMNED
Mt. 12:37, words you will be *c*
Jn. 3:18, does not believe is *c*
Rom. 8:3, *c* sin in the flesh

CONDEMNS
Rom. 8:34, Who is he who *c*
1 Jn. 3:20, For if our heart *c*

CONDUCT
1 Sam. 4:9, *c* yourselves like men
Ps. 37:14, who are of upright *c*
1 Tim. 3:15, *c* yourself in the
Jas. 3:13, *c* that his works are
1 Pet. 1:17, to each one's work, *c*
1 Pet. 1:18, from your aimless *c*
1 Pet. 3:1, may be won by the *c*

CONFESS
Ps. 32:5, c my transgressions
Rom. 10:9, that if you c with
Rom. 14:11, every tongue shall c
Jas. 5:16, C your trespasses
1 Jn. 1:9, If we c our sins
Rev. 3:5, but I will c his name

CONFESSED
Jn. 9:22, c that He was Christ
1 Tim. 6:12, c the good confession

CONFESSES
Prov. 28:13, prosper, but whoever c
1 Jn. 4:15, c that Jesus is the

CONFESSION
of Christ unto salvation. Mt. 10:32; Mk. 8:35; Jn. 12:42; Rom. 10:9; 2 Tim. 2:12; 1 Jn. 2:23; 4:2
of sin. Lev. 5:5; Josh. 7:19; Dan. 9:20; 1 Jn. 1:9
examples of. Num. 12:11; 21:7; Josh. 7:20; 1 Sam. 7; 15:24; Ezra 9:6; Neh. 1:6; 9; Ps. 51; Dan. 9:4; Lk. 23:41
at the offering of firstfruits. Dt. 26:2
'to one another.' Jas. 5:16

CONFESSION
Josh. 7:19, of Israel, and make c
Rom. 10:10, with the mouth c
1 Tim. 6:12, confessed the good c
1 Tim. 6:13, witnessed the good c
Heb. 3:1, High Priest of our c
Heb. 4:14, let us hold fast our c

CONFIDENCE
Ps. 65:5, You who are the c
Ps. 118:8, the LORD than to put c
Isa. 30:15, c shall be your
Phil. 3:3, Jesus, and have no c
Heb. 3:6, if we hold fast the c
1 Jn. 2:28, appears, we may have c

CONFINED
Jer. 36:5, saying, "I am c
Gal. 3:22, the Scripture has c

CONFIRM
Rom. 15:8, c the promises
1 Cor. 1:8, who will also c

CONFIRMED
Gal. 3:17, covenant that was c
Heb. 2:3, by the Lord, and was c
Heb. 6:17, c it by an oath
2 Pet. 1:19, prophetic word c

CONFIRMING
Mk. 16:20, c the word through

CONFLICT
Phil. 1:30, having the same c
Col. 2:1, to know what a great c

CONFLICTS
2 Cor. 7:5, Outside were c

CONFORMED
Rom. 8:29, predestined to be c
Rom. 12:2, And do not be c
Phil. 3:10, sufferings, being c
Phil. 3:21, body that it may be c

CONFOUNDED
Ps. 69:6, who seek You be c

CONFUSE
Gen. 11:7, c their language

CONFUSED
Gen. 11:9, there the LORD c
Acts 19:32, the assembly was c

CONFUSION
Ps. 35:4, c who plot my hurt
Ps. 60:3, us drink the wine of c

CONGREGATION (of Israel)
all to keep the Passover. Ex. 12
sin offering for. Lev. 4:13; 16:17
to stone offenders. Lev. 24:14; Num. 14:10; 15:35
who not to enter. Dt. 23:1

CONGREGATION
Ps. 1:5, Nor sinners in the c
Ps. 22:16, the c of the wicked
Ps. 82:1, God stands in the c

CONIAH
contracted from Jeconiah. Jer. 22:24

CONONIAH, 2 Chr. 31:12

CONQUER
Rev. 6:2, conquering and to c

CONQUERORS
Rom. 8:37, we are more than c

CONSCIENCE
convicts of sin. Gen. 3:10; 4:13; 42:21; 1 Sam. 24:5; Prov. 20:27; Mt. 27:3; Lk. 9:7; Jn. 8:9; Rom. 2:15
purified by faith. 1 Tim. 1:19; 3:9; 2 Tim. 1:3
purified by blood of Christ. Heb. 9:14; 10:2,22
a good. Heb. 13:18; 1 Pet. 3:16
effects of a good. Acts 24:16; Rom. 13:5; 14:22; 2 Cor. 1:12; 1 Pet. 2:19
of others to be respected. Rom. 14:21; 1 Cor. 8; 10:28
seared. 1 Tim. 4:2; defiled. Ti. 1:15
ignorant. Acts 26:9; Rom. 10:2

CONSCIENCE
Jn. 8:9, convicted by their c
Acts 24:16, strive to have a c
Rom. 9:1, I am not lying, my c
Rom. 13:5, wrath but also for c
1 Cor. 10:25, no questions for c
1 Tim. 3:9, faith with a pure c
1 Tim. 4:2, having their own c
Heb. 9:14, to God, cleanse your c
Heb. 10:22, from an evil c and our
1 Pet. 3:16, having a good c

CONSECRATE
Ex. 13:2, "C to Me all the
1 Chr. 29:5, c himself this day
Joel 2:15, the trumpet in Zion, c
Mic. 4:13, c their gain to the

CONSECRATED
1 Ki. 9:3, c this house which you

CONSECRATION
of priests. Ex. 29; Lev. 8
of the Levites. Num. 8:5
of Christ. Heb. 7; 8; 10:20

CONSENT
Prov. 1:10, entice you, do not c
1 Tim. 6:3, and does not c to

CONSENTED
Ps. 50:18, you saw a thief, you c
Lk. 23:51, He had not c to their

CONSENTING
Acts 8:1, Now Saul was c to his

CONSIDER
Ps. 8:3, When I c Your heavens
Ps. 48:13, c her palaces
Prov. 23:1, c carefully what is
Eccl. 7:13, C the work of God
Isa. 1:3, My people do not c
Isa. 5:12, c the operation
Jon. 1:6, your god will c
Hag. 1:5, "C your ways
Mt. 6:28, C the lilies of the
Lk. 12:24, "C the ravens
1 Cor. 4:1, Let a man so c us
Heb. 7:4, c how great this man
Heb. 10:24, c one another in order
Heb. 12:3, c Him who endured

CONSIDERS
Ps. 33:15, c all their works

CONSIST
Col. 1:17, in Him all things c

CONSOLATION
under affliction. Dt. 33:27; Job 19:25; Ps. 10:14; 23; 34:6; 41:3; 42:5; 51:17; 55:22; 69:29; 71:9,18; 73:26; 94:19; 119:50; 126; Eccl. 7:3; Isa. 1:18; 12:1; Lam. 3:22; Ezek. 14:22; Hos. 2:14; Mic. 7:18; Zech. 1:17; Mt. 11:28; Lk. 4:18; 15; Jn. 14; 15; 16; Rom. 15:4; 16:20; 1 Cor. 10:13; 14:3; 2 Cor. 1:3; 5:1; 7:6; 12:9; Col. 1:11; 1 Th. 4:14; 5:11; 2 Th. 2:16; Heb. 4:9; 6:18; 12; Jas. 1:12; 4:7; 2 Pet. 2:9; Rev. 2:10; 7:14; 14:13

CONSOLATION
Lk. 2:25, waiting for the C
Lk. 6:24, have received your c
2 Cor. 1:5, abound in us, so our c
Phil. 2:1, if there is any c
2 Th. 2:16, given us everlasting c
Heb. 6:18, we might have strong c

CONSOLATIONS
Job 15:11, Are the c of God too

CONSOLE
Isa. 61:3, c those who mourn

CONSPIRACY
against Christ. Mt. 26:3; Mk. 3:6; 14:1; Lk. 22:2; Jn. 11:55; 13:18
against Paul. Acts 23:12

CONSPIRE
Nah. 1:9, What do you c against

CONSTANT
Acts 12:5, c prayer was

CONSULT
Ps. 62:4, They only c to cast

CONSULTED
Ps. 83:3, c together against

CONSUME
Ex. 33:3, your midst, lest I c
Dt. 5:25, this great fire will c

Ps. 59:13, C them in wrath
2 Th. 2:8, whom the Lord will c

CONSUMED
Ex. 3:2, but the bush was not c
1 Ki. 18:38, c the burnt
Ps. 90:7, For we have been c
Lam. 3:22, mercies we are not c
Gal. 5:15, beware lest you be c

CONSUMING
Ex. 24:17, the LORD was like a c
Dt. 9:3, before you as a c
Heb. 12:29, our God is a c fire

CONSUMMATION
Ps. 119:96, I have seen the c

CONSUMPTION
Dt. 28:22, will strike you with c

CONTAIN
2 Chr. 2:6, of heavens cannot c
Jn. 21:25, c the books that

CONTEMPT
Job 12:21, He pours c on princes
Prov. 18:3, wicked comes, c comes
Dan. 12:2, and everlasting c
Mk. 9:12, and be treated with c

CONTEMPTIBLE
Mal. 1:7, of the LORD is c
Mal. 2:9, also have made you c
2 Cor. 10:10, and his speech c

CONTEND
Job 10:2, show me why You c
Job 13:8, Will you c for God
Isa. 43:26, let us c together
Isa. 49:25, for I will c with him
Jer. 12:5, then how can you c
Jude 3, c earnestly for the

CONTENDED
Ex. 17:2, Therefore the people c

CONTENT
Phil. 4:11, state I am, to be c
1 Tim. 6:8, these we shall be c
Heb. 13:5, covetousness; be c

CONTENTION
Prov. 18:6, lips enter into c
Prov. 22:10, and c will leave
Jer. 15:10, strife and a man of c

CONTENTIONS
Prov. 18:18, Casting lots causes c
Gal. 5:20, sorcery, hatred, c
Ti. 3:9, genealogies, c

CONTENTIOUS
Prov. 21:19, than with a c and
Prov. 25:24, shared with a c woman
1 Cor. 11:16, anyone seems to be c

CONTENTMENT
godliness with, great gain. Ps. 37:16; Prov. 30:8; 1 Tim. 6:6
exhortations to. Ps. 37:1; Lk. 3:14; 1 Cor. 7:20; 1 Tim. 6:8; Heb. 13:5

CONTINUAL
Prov. 15:15, a merry heart has a c
Isa. 14:6, in wrath with a c
Lk. 18:5, c coming she weary me
Rom. 9:2, c grief in my heart

CONTINUALLY
Gen. 6:5, heart was only evil c
Ps. 34:1, His praise shall c
Ps. 40:11, and Your truth c
Ps. 52:1, of God endures c
Ps. 119:44, I keep Your law c
Jer. 6:7, Before Me c are grief
Hos. 12:6, and wait on your God c
Acts 6:4, will give ourselves c
Heb. 7:3, remains a priest c
Heb. 13:15, c offer the sacrifice

CONTINUE
Ps. 101:7, tells lies shall not c
Acts 13:43, persuaded them to c
Rom. 6:1, Shall we c in sin that
Gal. 3:10, who does not c in all
Col. 4:2, C earnestly in prayer
Heb. 8:9, because they did not c
Heb. 13:1, Let brotherly love c
2 Pet. 3:4, asleep, all things c

CONTINUED
Acts 2:42, c steadfastly in the
1 Jn. 2:19, us, they would have c

CONTINUES
Heb. 7:24, But He, because He c
Jas. 1:25, law of liberty and c

CONTRADICTIONS
1 Tim. 6:20, idle babblings and c

CONTRARY
Acts 18:13, to worship God c
Gal. 5:17, and these are c
1 Th. 2:15, please God and are c
1 Tim. 1:10, other thing that is c

CONTRIBUTION
Rom. 15:26, to make a certain c

CONTRITE
Ps. 34:18, saves such as have a c
Ps. 51:17, a broken and a c
Isa. 57:15, with him who has a c
Isa. 66:2, poor and of a c spirit

CONTROVERSY
Dt. 17:8, another, matters of c
Jer. 25:31, For the LORD has a c
1 Tim. 3:16, c great is

CONVERSATION
of the Lord with Moses. Ex. 33:9
of Jesus with Nicodemus. Jn. 3; with the woman of Samaria. Jn. 4:7–27; on the walk to Emmaus. Lk. 24:13
of Peter with Cornelius. Acts 10:27

CONVERSION
of sinners proceeds from God. 1 Ki. 18:37; Ps. 19:7; 78:34; Prov. 1:23; Jer. 31:18; Jn. 6:44; Acts 3:26; 11:21. *See* Ps. 51:13; Isa. 1:16; 6:10; Ezek. 18:23; 36:25; Joel 2:13; 2 Cor. 5:17; 1 Th. 1:9
call to. Isa. 1:16; Mt. 3:2; 4:17; 10:7; Acts 2:38; 17:30; Jas. 4:8
prayer for. Ps. 80:7; 85:4; Lam. 5:21
instruments of, blessed. Dan. 12:3; 1 Tim. 4:16; Jas. 5:19
of the Jews. Acts 2:41; 4:32; 6:7
of Paul. Acts 9; 22; 26
of the nations, foretold. Isa. 2:2; 11:10; 60:5; 66:12
of the Gentiles, fulfilled. Acts 8:26–40; 10; 15:3; Rom. 9—11; 1 Cor. 1; Eph. 2; 3; 1 Th. 1

CONVERTED
Mt. 18:3, unless you are c

CONVEYED
Col. 1:13, of darkness and c

CONVICT
Jn. 16:8, He has come, He will c
Ti. 1:9, c those who
Jude 15, c who are ungodly

CONVICTS
Jn. 8:46, "Which of you c

CONVINCED
Rom. 14:5, Let each be fully c

COOKED
Lam. 4:10, c their own children

COOL
Gen. 3:8, in the garden in the c
Lk. 16:24, and c my tongue

COPIES
Heb. 9:23, necessary that the c
Heb. 9:24, hands, which are c

COPPER
Dt. 8:9, hills you can dig c
Mk. 7:4, of cups, pitchers, c
Lk. 12:6, sold for two c coins

COPPERSMITH
2 Tim. 4:14, c did me much harm

COPY
Heb. 8:5, who serve the c

CORD
Josh. 2:18, this line of scarlet c
Eccl. 4:12, And a threefold c
Eccl. 12:6, before the silver c

CORDS
Ps. 129:4, in pieces the c
Prov. 5:22, he is caught in the c
Isa. 5:18, draw iniquity with c
Hos. 11:4, them with gentle c
Jn. 2:15, had made a whip of c

CORINTH
Paul and Apollos at. Acts 18; 19:1

CORINTHIANS, Acts 18:8
their divisions, etc., censured. 1 Cor. 1; 5; 11:18
their faith and graces. 2 Cor. 3
instructed concerning spiritual gifts. 1 Cor. 14; and the resurrection. 1 Cor. 15
exhorted to love, etc. 1 Cor. 13; 14:1; 2 Cor. 8; 9
their false teachers exposed. 2 Cor. 11:3,4,13
Paul commends himself to. 2 Cor. 11; 12

CORNELIUS, Acts 10:1
devout centurion, his prayer answered. Acts 10:3
sends for Peter. Acts 10:9
baptized. Acts 10:48

CORNER
Acts 26:26, was not done in a c

CORNERSTONE
Job 38:6, Or who laid its *c*
Ps. 118:22, has become the chief *c*
Isa. 28:16, stone, a precious *c*
Mt. 21:42, become the chief *c*
1 Pet. 2:6, in Zion a chief *c*

CORPSE
1 Ki. 13:24, *c* was thrown on the
Isa. 14:19, *c* trodden underfoot

CORRECT
Ps. 39:11, with rebukes You *c*
Prov. 29:17, *C* your son
Jer. 30:11, But I will *c* you in

CORRECTED
Heb. 12:9, human fathers who *c*

CORRECTION
Prov. 3:11, nor detest His *c*
Prov. 10:17, but he who refuses *c*
Prov. 12:1, but he who hates *c*
Prov. 22:15, *c* will drive it
Prov. 23:13, Do not withhold *c*
Jer. 2:30, they received no *c*
2 Tim. 3:16, for reproof, for *c*

CORRECTS
Job 5:17, is the man whom God *c*
Prov. 3:12, the LORD loves He *c*

CORRODED
Jas. 5:3, and silver are *c*

CORRUPT
Ps. 14:3, have together become *c*
Ps. 53:3, have together become *c*
Eph. 4:22, old man which grows *c*
2 Tim. 3:8, men of *c* minds
Jude 10, in these things they *c*

CORRUPTED
Gen. 6:12, for all flesh had *c*
2 Cor. 7:2, we have *c* no one
2 Cor. 11:3, so your minds may be *c*
Jas. 5:2, Your riches are *c*
Rev. 19:2, the great harlot who *c*

CORRUPTIBLE
1 Cor. 15:53, For this *c* must put on
1 Pet. 1:18, redeemed with *c* things

CORRUPTION
Ps. 16:10, Your Holy One to see *c*
Acts 13:37, God raised up saw no *c*
Rom. 8:21, from the bondage of *c*
1 Cor. 15:42, The body is sown in *c*
1 Cor. 15:50, *c* inherit incorruption
Gal. 6:8, of the flesh reap *c*
2 Pet. 1:4, having escaped the *c*
2 Pet. 2:12, perish in their own *c*

COST
Lk. 14:28, and count the *c*

COULD
Mk. 14:8, has done what she *c*
1 Cor. 13:2, *c* remove mountains
Rev. 7:9, which no one *c* number

COUNCIL
of the Jews. Mt. 26:3,59; Mk. 15:1
the apostles arraigned before. Acts 4; 5:27
Paul's discourse before. Acts 23

COUNCILS
Mk. 13:9, deliver you up to *c*

COUNSEL
advantage of good. Prov. 12:15; 13:10; 20:18; 27:9
of God, asked by: Israel. Jud. 20:18
Saul. 1 Sam. 14:37
David. 1 Sam. 23:2,10; 30:8; 1 Chr. 14:10. *See* Ps. 16:7; 33:11; 73:24; Prov. 8:14; Rev. 3:18
danger of rejecting. 2 Chr. 25:16; Prov. 1:25,26; Jer. 23:18–22; Lk. 7:30
of the wicked, condemned. Job 5:13; 10:3; 21:16; Ps. 1:1; 5:10; 33:10; 64:2–7; 81:12; 106:43; Isa. 7:5; Hos. 11:6; Mic. 6:16

COUNSEL
Job 12:13, and strength, He has *c*
Job 21:16, the *c* of the wicked is
Job 29:4, when the friendly *c*
Job 38:2, is this who darkens *c*
Ps. 1:1, who walks not in the *c*
Ps. 55:14, We took sweet *c*
Ps. 73:24, guide me with Your *c*
Prov. 1:25, you disdained all my *c*
Prov. 1:30, have none of my *c*
Prov. 11:14, Where there is no *c*
Prov. 20:5, *C* in the heart of man
Prov. 20:18, by wise *c* wage war
Isa. 40:14, whom did He take *c*
Jer. 32:19, 'You are great in *c*
Eph. 1:11, according to the *c*
Heb. 6:17, immutability of His *c*
Rev. 3:18, "I *c* you to buy from

COUNSELOR
Isa. 9:6, be called Wonderful, *C*
Isa. 41:28, but there was no *c*
Mic. 4:9, Has your *c* perished
Rom. 11:34, who has become His *c*

COUNSELORS
Prov. 11:14, *c* there is safety

COUNT
2 Sam. 24:4, *c* the people of Israel
Acts 20:24, *c* my life dear to
Phile. 17, *c* me as a partner
2 Pet. 3:9, His promise, as some *c*

COUNTED
Prov. 17:28, Even a fool is *c*
Isa. 40:15, *c* as the small dust
Rom. 4:4, the wages are not *c*
1 Tim. 1:12, He *c* me faithful
1 Tim. 5:17, who rule well be *c*

COUNTENANCE
Num. 6:26, The LORD lift up His *c*
Job 29:24, *c* they did not cast
Ps. 4:6, up the light of Your *c*
Song 5:15, His *c* is like the Lebanon
Mt. 6:16, with a sad *c*
Mt. 28:3, His *c* was like
2 Cor. 3:7, of the glory of his *c*
Rev. 1:16, sword, and His *c*

COUNTRY
Gen. 12:1, "Get out of your *c*
Prov. 25:25, good news from a far *c*
Mt. 21:33, and went into a far *c*
Heb. 11:9, as in a foreign *c*
Heb. 11:16, that is, a heavenly *c*

COUNTRYMEN
Rom. 9:3, for my brethren, my *c*

COURAGE
exhortations to. Num. 13:20; Dt. 31:6; Josh. 1:6; 10:25; 2 Sam. 10:12; 2 Chr. 19:11; Ezra 10:4; Ps. 27:14; 31:24; Isa. 41:6; 1 Cor. 16:13; Eph. 6:10
through faith: Abraham. Heb. 11:8,17; Moses. Heb. 11:25; Israelites. Heb. 11:29; Barak. Jud. 4:16; Gideon. Jud. 7:1; Jephthah. Jud. 11:29; Samson. Jud. 16:28; Jonathan. 1 Sam. 14:6; Daniel. Dan. 6:10,23; Jonah. Jon. 3:3. *See* BOLDNESS

COURAGE
Dt. 31:6, strong and of good *c*
Acts 28:15, thanked God and took *c*

COURSE
Jas. 3:6, and sets on fire the *c*

COURT
Job 9:19, appoint my day in *c*
1 Cor. 4:3, by you or by a human *c*
Gal. 4:17, They zealously *c*

COURTEOUS
1 Pet. 3:8, be tenderhearted, be *c*

COURTS
Ps. 65:4, he may dwell in Your *c*
Ps. 84:2, even faints for the *c*
Ps. 92:13, flourish in the *c*
Ps. 100:4, and into His *c*
Isa. 62:9, drink it in My holy *c*

COVENANT
Num. 18:19; 2 Chr. 13:5

COVENANT OF GOD
with Noah. Gen. 6:18; 9:8
with Abraham. Gen. 15:7,18; 17:2 (Lk. 1:72; Acts 3:25; Gal. 3:16,17)
with Isaac. Gen. 17:19; 26:3
with Jacob. Gen. 28:13 (Ex. 2:24; 6:4; 1 Chr. 16:16)
with the Israelites. Ex. 6:4; 19:5; 24; 34:27; Lev. 26:9; Dt. 5:2; 9:9; 26:16; 29; Jud. 2:1; Jer. 11; 31:33; Acts 3:25
with Phinehas. Num. 25:13
with David. 2 Sam. 23:5; Ps. 89:3,28,34. *See* Ps. 25:14
God mindful of. Dt. 7:9; 1 Ki. 8:23; Ps. 105:8; 111:5
danger of despising. Dt. 28:15; Jer. 11:2; Heb. 10:29

COVENANT
signs of: salt. Lev. 2:13; Num. 18:19; 2 Chr. 13:5; the sabbath. Ex. 31:12
Book of the. Ex. 24:7; 2 Ki. 23:2; Heb. 9:19
between: Abraham and Abimelech. Gen. 21:27
Joshua and Israelites. Josh. 24:25
David and Jonathan. 1 Sam. 18:3; 20:16; 23:18

NEW COVENANT
Jer. 31:31; Rom. 11:27; Heb. 8:8

ratified by Christ (Mal. 3:1). Lk. 1:68–80; Gal. 3:17; Heb. 8:6; 9:15; 12:24
of Christ's blood. Mt. 26:28; Mk. 14:24; Lk. 22:20; 1 Cor. 11:25; 2 Cor. 3:6; Heb. 7:22
better than the first covenant. Heb. 8:6,7; 9; 10; 12:24
a covenant of peace. Isa. 54:10; Ezek. 34:25; 37:26
unchangeable. Ps. 89:34; Isa. 54:10; 59:21
everlasting. Gen. 9:16; 17:13; Lev. 24:8; Isa. 55:3; 61:8; Ezek. 16:60,62; 37:26; Heb. 13:20

COVENANT
Gen. 6:18, I will establish My *c*
Gen. 15:18, the LORD made a *c*
Gen. 17:4, for Me, behold, My *c*
Ex. 31:16, as a perpetual *c*
Num. 18:19, it is a *c* of salt
1 Chr. 16:15, Remember His *c* forever
Job 31:1, "I have made a *c*
Ps. 25:14, will show them His *c*
Ps. 89:28, *c* shall stand firm
Ps. 132:12, sons will keep My *c*
Isa. 42:6, and give You as a *C*
Jer. 11:2, the words of this *c*
Jer. 31:31, I will make a new *c*
Jer. 34:13, 'I made a *c* with your
Zech. 11:10, I might break the *c*
Mal. 3:1, the Messenger of the *c*
Lk. 22:20, cup is the new *c*
Gal. 3:17, *c* that was confirmed
Heb. 8:6, Mediator of a better *c*
Heb. 8:7, *c* had been faultless
Heb. 8:13, He says, "A new *c*
Heb. 12:24, Mediator of the new *c*
Heb. 13:20, of the everlasting *c*

COVENANTED
2 Chr. 7:18, your kingdom, as I *c*
Hag. 2:5, to the word that I *c*

COVENANTS
Rom. 9:4, the glory, the *c*
Gal. 4:24, these are the two *c*

COVER
Ex. 33:22, the rock, and will *c*
Ps. 91:4, He shall *c* you with
Ps. 104:2, *c* Yourself with light
Isa. 11:9, LORD as the waters *c*
Isa. 26:21, and will no more *c*
Isa. 32:2, from the wind and a *c*
1 Cor. 11:7, not to *c* his head
Jas. 5:20, *c* a multitude of sins

COVERED
Ex. 15:5, The depths have *c*
Job 31:33, *c* my transgressions as
Ps. 32:1, Whose sin is *c*
Ps. 68:13, the wings of a dove *c*
Ps. 85:2, *c* all their sin
Ps. 139:13, You *c* me in my
Isa. 6:2, with two he *c* his face
Isa. 27:9, of Jacob will be *c*
Lam. 3:44, You have *c* Yourself
Mt. 10:26, For there is nothing *c*

COVERING
Ps. 105:39, spread a cloud for a *c*
Isa. 50:3, make sackcloth their *c*
1 Cor. 11:15, given to her for a *c*

COVERINGS
Gen. 3:7, and made themselves *c*

COVET
Ex. 20:17, "You shall not *c*
Mic. 2:2, *c* fields and take them
Jas. 4:2, You murder and *c*

COVETED
Acts 20:33, *c* no one's silver

COVETOUS
1 Cor. 6:10, nor thieves, nor *c*
2 Pet. 2:14, trained in *c* practices

COVETOUSNESS
described. Ps. 10:3; Prov. 21:26; Eccl. 4:8; 5:10; Ezek. 33:31; Hab. 2; Mk. 7:22; Eph. 5:5; 1 Tim. 6:10; 2 Pet. 2:14
forbidden. Ex. 20:17; Lk. 12:15; Rom. 13:9
its evil consequences. Prov. 1:18; 15:27; 27:20; Ezek. 22:13; 1 Tim. 6:9
its punishment. Job 20:15; Isa. 5:8; 57:17; Jer. 6:12; 22:17; Mic. 2:1; Hab. 2:9; 1 Cor. 5:10; 6:10; Eph. 5:5; Col. 3:5
of Laban. Gen. 31:41
of Balaam. Num. 22:21 (2 Pet. 2:15; Jude 11)
of Achan. Josh. 7:21
of Saul. 1 Sam. 15:9
of Ahab. 1 Ki. 21
of Gehazi. 2 Ki. 5:20
of Judas. Mt. 26:14
of Ananias and Sapphira. Acts 5
of Felix. Acts 24:26

COVETOUSNESS
Prov. 28:16, but he who hates *c*
Jer. 22:17, for nothing but your *c*
Lk. 12:15, heed and beware of *c*
Rom. 7:7, would not have known *c*
Eph. 5:3, all uncleanness or *c*
Heb. 13:5, conduct be without *c*

COWARDLY
Rev. 21:8, the *c*, unbelieving

CRAFTILY
Ps. 105:25, His people, to deal *c*

CRAFTINESS
Job 5:13, wise in their own *c*
2 Cor. 4:2, not walking in *c*
2 Cor. 11:3, deceived Eve by his *c*
Eph. 4:14, in the cunning *c*

CRAFTSMAN
Gen. 4:22, instructor of every *c*
Isa. 41:7, *c* encouraged the
Isa. 44:13, *c* stretches out his

CRAFTY
2 Sam. 13:3, Jonadab was a very *c*
Job 5:12, the devices of the *c*
Ps. 83:3, They have taken *c*
Prov. 7:10, of a harlot, and a *c*
2 Cor. 12:16, Nevertheless, being *c*

CRANE
Isa. 38:14, Like a *c* or a swallow

CRAVES
Isa. 29:8, and his soul still *c*

CREAM
Jud. 5:25, she brought out *c*
Job 29:6, were bathed with *c*

CREATE
Isa. 45:7, peace and *c* calamity
Isa. 65:17, For behold, I *c*

CREATED
Gen. 1:27, So God *c* man in His
Ps. 104:30, Spirit, they are *c*
Ps. 148:5, and they were *c*
Isa. 40:26, and see who has *c*
Isa. 41:20, of Israel has *c*
Jer. 31:22, For the LORD has *c*
Mal. 2:10, Has not one God *c*
1 Cor. 11:9, Nor was man *c* for the
Eph. 2:10, *c* in Christ Jesus
Eph. 3:9, hidden in God who *c*
Eph. 4:24, new man which was *c*
Col. 1:16, Him all things were *c*
1 Tim. 4:3, from foods which God *c*
Rev. 4:11, for You *c* all things

CREATION
Mk. 13:19, *c* which God
Rom. 8:20, *c* was subjected
Rom. 8:22, know that the whole *c*
2 Cor. 5:17, Christ, he is a new *c*
Gal. 6:15, anything, but a new *c*
Col. 1:15, firstborn over all *c*

CREATOR
Eccl. 12:1, Remember now your *C*
Isa. 40:28, God, the LORD, the *C*
Rom. 1:25, rather than the *C*
1 Pet. 4:19, to a faithful *C*

CREATURE
Mk. 16:15, the gospel to every *c*
1 Tim. 4:4, For every *c* of God is
Heb. 4:13, And there is no *c*
Rev. 5:13, And every *c* which is
Rev. 16:3, and every living *c*

CREATURES (living)
vision of. Ezek. 1:5; 10:10
around the heavenly throne. Rev. 4:6–9; 5:11,14; 6:1–7; 7:11; 14:3; 15:7; 20:4
Daniel's vision of. Dan. 7:3,16

CREATURES
Gen. 1:21, created great sea *c*
Jas. 1:18, firstfruits of His *c*
Rev. 4:6, were four living *c*

CREDIT
Lk. 6:32, who love you, what *c*
1 Pet. 2:20, For what *c* is it if

CREDITOR
Dt. 15:2, Every *c* who has lent
2 Ki. 4:1, *c* is coming to take my
Ps. 109:11, *c* seize all that he
Lk. 7:41, There was a certain *c*

CREEP
Ps. 104:20, of the forest *c*
2 Tim. 3:6, sort are those who *c*

CREEPING
Gen. 1:24, *c* thing and beast of
Ezek. 8:10, every sort of *c* thing

CREPT
Jude 4, For certain men have c

CRETANS, Acts 2:11; Ti. 1:12

CRETE
visited by Paul. Acts 27:7

CRIB
Isa. 1:3, donkey its master's c

CRIED
Job 29:12, the poor who c out
Ps. 22:5, They c to You
Ps. 130:1, of the depths I have c

CRIES
Gen. 4:10, your brother's blood c
Heb. 5:7, with vehement c

CRIMES
Ezek. 7:23, land is filled with c

CRIMINALS
execution of. Dt. 21:22
crucified with Christ. Lk. 23:32

CRISPUS
baptized by Paul. Acts 18:8; 1 Cor. 1:14

CROOKED
Ps. 125:5, turn aside to their c
Prov. 2:15, whose ways are c
Isa. 40:4, c places shall be made
Isa. 45:2, c places straight
Lk. 3:5, c places shall be made
Phil. 2:15, in the midst of a c

CROSS
Christ dies upon the. Mt. 27:32; Phil. 2:8; Heb. 12:2
preaching of. 1 Cor. 1:18
to be taken up, self-denial. Mt. 10:38; 16:24;
offense of. Gal. 5:11
persecution for. Gal. 6:12

CROSS
Mt. 10:38, does not take his c
Mt. 27:32, to bear His c
Mt. 27:40, down from the c
1 Cor. 1:17, lest the c of Christ
Gal. 6:12, persecution for the c
Gal. 6:14, boast except in the c
Eph. 2:16, one body through the c
Phil. 3:18, the enemies of the c
Heb. 12:2, Him endured the c

CROWD
Ex. 23:2, shall not follow a c

CROWN
and turban, high priest's. Ex. 29:6; 39:30; Lev. 8:9
of thorns. Jn. 19:5
of righteousness. 2 Tim. 4:8
of life. Jas. 1:12; Rev. 2:10
of glory. 1 Pet. 5:4
incorruptible. 1 Cor. 9:25. *See* Rev. 4:4; 9:7; 12:3; 13:1; 19:12

CROWN
Ps. 21:3, You set a c of pure
Ps. 65:11, c the year with Your
Ps. 89:39, have profaned his c
Ps. 132:18, upon Himself His c
Prov. 14:24, The c of the wise is
Prov. 16:31, head is a c of glory
Isa. 28:1, Woe to the c of pride
Isa. 28:5, hosts will be for a c
Lam. 5:16, c has fallen from our
Mt. 27:29, they had twisted a c
1 Cor. 9:25, obtain a perishable c
Phil. 4:1, brethren, my joy and c
2 Tim. 4:8, laid up for me the c
Jas. 1:12, he will receive the c
Rev. 3:11, no one may take your c
Rev. 14:14, on His head a golden c

CROWNED
Ps. 8:5, angels, and You have c
Prov. 14:18, but the prudent are c
2 Tim. 2:5, athletics, he is not c
Heb. 2:7, You have c him with glory

CROWNS
Rev. 4:4, and they had c of gold
Rev. 13:1, on his horns ten c
Rev. 19:12, His head were many c

CRUCIFIED
Mt. 27:22, "Let Him be c
Lk. 23:33, Calvary, there they c
Acts 2:23, lawless hands, have c
Rom. 6:6, that our old man was c
1 Cor. 1:13, Was Paul c for you
1 Cor. 2:2, Jesus Christ and Him c
1 Cor. 2:8, they would not have c
2 Cor. 13:4, though He was c
Gal. 2:20, "I have been c

CRUCIFY
Mk. 15:13, out again, "C Him
Jn. 19:10, I have power to c You
Heb. 6:6, since they c again

CRUEL
Gen. 49:7, wrath, for it is c
Ex. 6:9, spirit and c bondage
Ps. 25:19, hate me with c hatred
Prov. 12:10, of the wicked are c

CRUELTY
Gen. 49:5, of c are in their
Ps. 74:20, the haunts of c
Ezek. 34:4, c you have ruled

CRUSH
Job 39:15, that a foot may c
Ps. 68:23, that your foot may c
Amos 4:1, the poor, who c
Rom. 16:20, of peace will c

CRUSHED
Job 4:19, in the dust, who are c
Ps. 143:3, c my life to the
2 Cor. 4:8, every side, yet not c

CRUST
Prov. 6:26, man is reduced to a c

CRY
Ex. 2:23, and their c came up to
Job 35:9, of oppressions they c
Ps. 84:2, heart and my flesh c
Ps. 119:145, I c out with my whole
Prov. 8:1, Does not wisdom c
Isa. 40:6, "What shall I c
Jer. 7:16, nor lift up a c
Jon. 3:8, c mightily to God
Mt. 25:6, at midnight a c
Lk. 18:7, His own elect who c

CRYING
Mt. 3:3, "The voice of one c
Rev. 21:4, nor sorrow, nor c

CRYSTAL
Job 28:17, nor c can equal it
Isa. 54:12, your gates of c
Ezek. 1:22, of an awesome c
Rev. 4:6, a sea of glass, like c

CUBIT
Gen. 6:16, shall finish it to a c
Mt. 6:27, can add one c

CUCUMBERS
Num. 11:5, in Egypt, the c
Isa. 1:8, a hut in a garden of c

CUNNING
Gen. 3:1, the serpent was more c
Job 5:13, c comes quickly
Eph. 4:14, c craftiness of deceitful

CUP
Ps. 23:5, My c runs over
Ps. 73:10, waters of a full c are
Ps. 75:8, the LORD there is a c
Ps. 116:13, I will take up the c
Isa. 51:17, the dregs of the c
Jer. 16:7, men give them the c
Jer. 25:15, "Take this wine c
Hab. 2:16, The c of the LORD's
Zech. 12:2, make Jerusalem a c
Mt. 10:42, little ones only a c
Mt. 26:27, Then He took the c
Mt. 26:39, possible, let this c
Lk. 22:20, c is the new covenant
1 Cor. 10:21, cannot drink the c
1 Cor. 11:25, c is the new
Rev. 16:19, to give her the c

CURE
Mt. 17:16, but they could not c
Lk. 9:1, and to c diseases

CURES
Lk. 13:32, and perform c

CURSE
upon the earth. Gen. 3:17
upon Cain. Gen. 4:11
on Canaan. Gen. 9:25
by Job on his birth. Job.3:1; also by Jeremiah. Jer. 20:14
upon the breakers of the law. Lev. 26:14; Dt. 11:26; 27:13; 28:15; 29:19; Josh. 8:34; Prov. 3:33
Christ redeems from. Rom. 3; Gal. 3:1

CURSE
Gen. 8:21, c the ground for man's
Ex. 22:28, c a ruler of your
Lev. 19:14, 'You shall not c
Num. 22:6, c this people for me
Num. 23:25, Balaam, "Neither c
Dt. 23:5, your God turned the c
2 Sam. 16:10, said to him, 'C David
Job 2:9, C God and die
Ps. 62:4, mouth, but they c
Prov. 3:33, The c of the LORD is
Eccl. 10:20, Do not c the king
Eccl. 10:20, do not c the rich
Mal. 2:2, "I will send a c
Mal. 3:9, are cursed with a c

Gal. 3:10, law are under the *c*

CURSED
who so called. Dt. 27:15; Prov. 11:26; 27:14; Jer. 11:3; 17:5; Lam. 3:65; Zech. 5:3; Mal. 1:14; Mt. 25:41; Gal. 3:10; 2 Pet. 2:14
of God to be cut off. Ps. 37:22

CURSED
Gen. 3:14, *c* more than all cattle
Jer. 17:5, C is the man who
Jer. 48:10, *c* is he who keeps
Mt. 25:41, 'Depart from Me, you *c*
Heb. 6:8, and near to being *c*

CURSES
Gen. 12:3, I will curse him who *c*
Lev. 20:9, 'For everyone who *c*
Prov. 20:20, *c* his father or his

CURSING
forbidden. Ex. 21:17; Ps. 109:17; Prov. 30:11; Jas. 3:10
to return blessing for. Mt. 5:44; Rom. 12:14

CURSINGS
Hos. 7:16, by the sword for the *c*

CURTAIN
Ex. 26:2, of each *c* shall be
Ps. 104:2, the heavens like a *c*

CUSH (Ethiopia)
Gen. 2:13; 10:6

CUSHITE
announces Absalom's death. 2 Sam. 18:21

CUSTOM
Ps. 119:132, to me, as Your *c*
Acts 15:1, according to the *c*
1 Cor. 11:16, we have no such *c*

CUT
Job 8:14, confidence shall be *c*
Ps. 37:9, evildoers shall be *c*
Prov. 2:22, the wicked will be *c*
Mt. 5:30, causes you to sin, *c*
Mt. 24:51, and will *c* him in
Jn. 18:26, him whose ear Peter *c*
Acts 18:18, He had his hair *c*

CYMBAL
1 Cor. 13:1, or a clanging *c*

CYPRUS, Acts 4:36
disciples there. Acts 11:19
Paul and Barnabas preach there. Acts 13:4
Barnabas and Mark go there. Acts 15:39

CYRENE, Mt. 27:32
disciples of. Acts 11:20; 13:1
Simon of. Mk. 15:21

CYRUS, 2 Chr. 36:22
king of Persia, prophecies concerning. Isa. 44:28; 45:1. *See* Dan. 6:28; 10:1
his proclamation for rebuilding the temple. 2 Chr. 36:22; Ezra 1

DAGON
national idol-god of the Philistines, sacrificed to. Jud. 16:23
struck down in temple at Ashdod. 1 Sam. 5:3,4
Saul's head fastened in house of. 1 Chr. 10:10

DAILY
Ex. 16:5, much as they gather *d*
Ps. 72:15, *d* He shall be
Prov. 8:34, to me, watching *d*
Isa. 58:2, Yet they seek Me *d*
Mt. 6:11, Give us this day our *d*
Mt. 26:55, I sat *d* with you
Lk. 9:23, take up his cross *d*
Acts 17:11, the Scriptures *d*
1 Cor. 15:31, our Lord, I die *d*
Heb. 10:11, stands ministering *d*

DALMATIA, 2 Tim. 4:10

DAMASCUS, Gen. 14:15
mentioned. Gen. 15:2
subjugated by David. 2 Sam. 8:6; 1 Chr. 18:6
Elisha's prophecy there. 2 Ki. 8:7
taken by Tiglath-Pileser, king of Assyria. 2 Ki. 16:9
restored to Israel by Jeroboam. 2 Ki. 14:28
King Ahaz copies an altar there. 2 Ki. 16:10
Paul's journey to. Acts 9; 22:6
Paul restored to sight, and baptized there. Acts 9:17,18
prophecies concerning. Isa. 7:8; 8:4; 17:1; Jer. 49:23; Amos 1:3

DAN
son of Jacob, by Rachel's handmaid. Gen. 30:6
——— tribe of, numbered. Num. 1:38; 26:42
their inheritance. Josh. 19:40
blessed by Jacob. Gen. 49:16
blessed by Moses. Dt. 33:22
set up idolatry. Jud. 18:30; 1 Ki. 12:29

DANCE
Job 21:11, and their children *d*
Ps. 149:3, His name with the *d*
Eccl. 3:4, mourn, and a time to *d*
Lam. 5:15, *d* has turned into
Mt. 11:17, and you did not *d*

DANCED
2 Sam. 6:14, Then David *d* before
Mt. 14:6, daughter of Herodias *d*

DANCING
Ex. 32:19, saw the calf and the *d*
Ps. 30:11 my mourning into *d*
Lk. 15:25, he heard music and *d*

DANIEL, Dan. 1:6
(Belteshazzar), with other captives, taken from Jerusalem to Babylon. Dan. 1:3
taught the learning of the Chaldeans. Dan. 1:4
will not take the king's food or drink. Dan. 1:8
has understanding in dreams. Dan. 1:17
interprets the royal dreams. Dan. 2; 4; and handwriting on wall. Dan. 5:17
made a governor by Darius. Dan. 6:2
conspired against by the satraps. Dan. 6:4
idolatrous decree against, issued. Dan. 6:9; violation thereof. Dan. 6:10
thrown into the lion's den. Dan. 6:16; preservation in. Dan. 6:22
his vision of the four beasts. Dan. 7:3; ram and male goat. Dan. 8:3
his prayer. Dan. 9:3
promise of return from captivity. Dan. 9:20; 10:10; 12:13
name mentioned. Ezek. 14:14,20; 28:3

DARE
Rom. 5:7, someone would even *d*
1 Cor. 6:1, *D* any of you

DARIUS, Ezra 4:5
decree concerning the rebuilding of the temple. Ezra 6
——— the Median, takes Babylon. Dan. 5:31
his decree to fear the God of Daniel. Dan. 6:25

DARK
1 Ki. 8:12, dwell in the *d* cloud
Song 1:5, I am *d*
Isa. 45:19, *d* place of the earth
Lam. 3:6, *d* places like the dead
Amos 5:8, and makes the day *d*
Mic. 3:6, and the day shall be *d*
Mt. 10:27, I tell you in the *d*
Jn. 20:1, while it was still *d*
2 Pet. 1:19, shines in a *d* place

DARKENED
Ex. 10:15, so that the land was *d*
Ps. 69:23, Let their eyes be *d*
Eph. 4:18, their understanding *d*

DARKNESS
divided from light. Gen. 1:18
created by God. Isa. 45:7
supernatural. Gen. 15:12; Ex. 10:21; 14:20; Josh. 24:7; Rev. 8:12; 9:2; 16:10
at the crucifixion. Mt. 27:45; Mk. 15:33; Lk. 23:44
figurative of punishment. Mt. 8:12; 22:13; 2 Pet. 2:4,17; Jude 6
of the mind. Job 37:19; Prov. 2:13; Eccl. 2:14; Isa. 9:2; 42:7; Jn. 1:5; 3:19; 8:12; 12:35; Rom. 13:12; 1 Cor. 4:5; 2 Cor. 4:6; 6:14; Eph. 5:8; 1 Th. 5:4; 1 Pet. 2:9; 1 Jn. 1:5; 2:9
powers of. Lk. 22:53; Eph. 6:12; Col. 1:13

DARKNESS
Gen. 1:5, *d* He called Night
2 Sam. 22:29, shall enlighten my *d*
Job 22:13, through the deep *d*
Ps. 107:10, Those who sat in *d*
Ps. 139:12, *d* shall not hide
Isa. 9:2, *d* have seen a
Isa. 42:16, I will make *d* light
Isa. 60:2, and deep *d* the people
Jer. 2:31, Israel, or a land of *d*

Rom. 6:11, yourselves to be *d*
Rom. 7:8, from the law sin was *d*
Rom. 14:9, be Lord of both the *d*
1 Cor. 15:12, resurrection of the *d*
1 Cor. 15:29, baptized for the *d*
Eph. 2:1, made alive, who were *d*
1 Th. 4:16, And the *d* in Christ
1 Tim. 5:6, *d* while she lives
Jas. 2:26, without works is *d*
Rev. 20:5, *d* did not live again
Rev. 20:12, And the *d* were judged

DEADLY
Mk. 16:18, drink anything *d*
Jas. 3:8, evil, full of *d* poison
Rev. 13:3, *d* wound was healed

DEADNESS
Rom. 4:19, the *d* of Sarah's womb

DEAF
Ex. 4:11, makes the mute, the *d*
Isa. 29:18, *d* shall hear the words
Isa. 35:5, *d* shall be unstopped
Isa. 42:19, *d* as My messenger
Isa. 43:8, *d* who have ears
Mic. 7:16, their ears shall be *d*
Mt. 11:5, are cleansed and the *d*

DEAL
Dt. 32:6, Do you thus *d* with the
Isa. 52:13, My Servant shall *d*

DEATH
the consequence of Adam's sin. Gen. 2:17; 3:19; Rom. 5:12; 6:23; 1 Cor. 15:21
universal. Job 1:21; 3:17; 14:1; 21:13; Ps. 49:19; 89:48; Eccl. 5:15; 8:8; 9:5,10; 11:8; Heb. 9:27
threatened. Rom. 1:32
characterized. Gen. 3:19; Dt. 31:16 (Jn. 11:11); Job 1:21; 3:13; 10:21; 12:22; 14:2; 16:22; 24:17; Ps. 16:10; 23:4; 104:29; Eccl. 9:10; Hab. 2:5; Lk. 12:20; 2 Cor. 5:1,8; Phil. 1:23; 1 Tim. 6:7; 2 Pet. 1:14
as a punishment. Gen. 9:6; Ex. 21:12; 22:18; 31:14; 35:2; Lev. 20:2; 21:9; 1 Ki. 21:10; Mt. 15:4
vanquished by Christ. Rom. 6:9; 1 Cor. 15:26 (Hos. 13:14); 2 Tim. 1:10; Heb. 2:15; Rev. 1:18
prayers and exhortations concerning. 2 Ki. 20:1; Ps. 39; 90; Eccl. 9:10; Jn. 9:4; 1 Pet. 1:24
unknown in heaven. Lk. 20:36; Rev. 21:4
persons exempted from: Enoch. Gen. 5:24; Heb. 11:5; Elijah. 2 Ki. 2:11. *See* 1 Cor. 15:51; 1 Th. 4:17
spiritual. Isa. 9:2; Mt. 4:16; 8:22; Lk. 1:79; Jn. 6:53; Rom. 5:15; 6:13; 8:6; Eph. 2:1; 4:18; Col. 2:13; 1 Tim. 5:6; Heb. 6:1; 9:14; 1 Jn. 3:14; Rev. 3:1
deliverance from, by Christ. Jn. 5:24; Rom. 6:11; Eph. 2:5; 5:14; 1 Jn. 5:12
eternal. Prov. 14:12; Dan. 12:2; Mt. 7:13; 10:28; 23:33; 25:30,41; Mk. 9:44; Jn. 5:29; Rom. 1:32; 2:8; 6:23; 9:22; 2 Th. 1:7; Jas. 4:12; 2 Pet. 2:17
the second death. Rev. 2:11; 19:20; 20:14; 21:8
salvation from, by Christ. Jn. 3:16; 8:51; by conversion from sin. Jas. 5:20
of Christ: foretold. Isa. 53; Dan. 9:26; Zech. 13:7
voluntary. Lk. 12:50; Jn. 10:11,18; Heb. 10:7
its object. Isa. 53; Dan. 9:26; Mt. 20:28; 1 Cor. 5:7; 1 Tim. 2:6; Ti. 2:14; Heb. 9:26; 1 Pet. 1:18; Rev. 1:5
of saints. Num. 23:10; 2 Ki. 22:20; Ps. 23:4; 48:14; 116:15; Prov. 14:32; Isa. 26:19; 57:1; Dan. 12:2; Lk. 16:25; Jn. 11:11; 2 Cor. 5:8; Phil. 1:21; 2 Tim. 4:8; Heb. 11:13; Rev. 2:10
of Abraham. Gen. 25:8; Isaac. Gen. 35:29; Jacob. Gen. 49; Aaron. Num. 20:23; Moses. Dt. 34:5; Joshua. Josh. 24:29; David. 1 Ki. 2; Elisha. 2 Ki. 13:14; Stephen. Acts 7:54; Dorcas. Acts 9:37
of the wicked. Job 18:11; 21:13; 27:19; Ps. 34:16; 49:14; 73:19; Prov. 10:7; 11:7; 14:32; 29:1; Isa. 14:9; Ezek. 3:19; 18:23; Dan. 12:2; Lk. 12:20; 16:22; Jn. 8:21; Acts 1:25

DEATH
Num. 23:10, Let me die the *d*
Ruth 1:17, *d* parts you and me
Job 10:21, and the shadow of *d*
Job 30:23, You will bring me to *d*
Ps. 6:5, For in *d* there is no
Ps. 13:3, I sleep the sleep of *d*
Ps. 23:4, of the shadow of *d*
Ps. 56:13, my soul from *d*
Ps. 89:48, can live and not see *d*
Prov. 2:18, house leads down to *d*
Prov. 8:36, who hate me love *d*
Prov. 18:21, *D* and life are in the
Isa. 25:8, swallow up *d* forever
Ezek. 18:32, no pleasure in the *d*
Hos. 13:14, redeem them from *d*
Amos 5:8, turns the shadow of *d*
Mt. 16:28, who shall not taste *d*
Jn. 5:24, but has passed from *d*
Jn. 8:51, he shall never see *d*
Rom. 5:14, Nevertheless *d* reigned
Rom. 5:21, as sin reigned in *d*
Rom. 6:9, *D* no longer has
Rom. 6:23, the wages of sin is *d*
Rom. 7:5, to bear fruit to *d*
1 Cor. 11:26, proclaim the Lord's *d*
1 Cor. 15:21, since by man came *d*
1 Cor. 15:54, *D* is swallowed up in
1 Cor. 15:56, The sting of *d* is sin
2 Cor. 2:16, we are the aroma of *d*
2 Cor. 4:12, *d* is working in us
2 Cor. 7:10, the world produces *d*
Phil. 2:8, to the point of *d*
Heb. 2:9, *d* crowned with glory
Heb. 2:14, who had the power of *d*
Heb. 11:5, that he did not see *d*
Jas. 1:15, brings forth *d*
1 Pet. 3:18, to God, being put to *d*
1 Jn. 5:16, is sin leading to *d*
Rev. 2:10, Be faithful until *d*
Rev. 20:6, Over such the second *d*
Rev. 21:4, shall be no more *d*
Rev. 21:8, which is the second *d*

DEBORAH
the prophetess, judges and delivers Israel. Jud. 4
her song. Jud. 5
——— Rebekah's nurse, death of. Gen. 35:8

DEBT
censured. Ps. 37:21; Prov. 3:27; Lk. 16:5; Rom. 13:8

DEBTOR
Rom. 1:14, I am a *d* both to
Gal. 5:3, that he is a *d* to keep

DEBTORS
Mt. 6:12, as we forgive our *d*
Lk. 16:5, of his master's *d*
Rom. 8:12, brethren, we are *d*
Rom. 15:27, and they are their *d*

DECEIT
proceeds from the heart. Jer. 17:9
by false prophets. 1 Ki. 22
(and lying), work of the devil. Jn. 8:44; Acts 5:3

SOME MEMORABLE INSTANCES OF
the serpent and Eve. Gen. 3
Abram and his wife. Gen. 12:14
Isaac and his wife. Gen. 26:10
Jacob and Esau. Gen. 27
Jael and Sisera. Jud. 4:20
the old prophet. 1 Ki. 13:18
Rahab and spies at Jericho. Josh. 2:1,4,5
Gehazi and Naaman. 2 Ki. 5:20
Herod and the wise men. Mt. 2:7,8
Ananias and Sapphira. Acts 5:1. *See* LYING

DECEIT
Ps. 32:2, spirit there is no *d*
Ps. 34:13, from speaking *d*
Ps. 101:7, *d* shall not dwell
Prov. 12:20, *D* is in the heart of
Isa. 53:9, Nor was any *d* in His
Jer. 8:5, They hold fast to *d*
Jn. 1:47, in whom is no *d*
Acts 13:10, "O full of all *d*
Col. 2:8, philosophy and empty *d*
1 Pet. 2:22, no sin, nor was *d*
Rev. 14:5, mouth was found no *d*

DECEITFUL
Ps. 43:1, deliver me from the *d*
Ps. 55:23, *d* men shall not
Prov. 12:5, of the wicked are *d*
Prov. 27:6, of an enemy are *d*
Jer. 17:9, "The heart is *d*
2 Cor. 11:13, are false apostles, *d*

DECEITFULLY
Ps. 24:4, an idol, Nor sworn *d*
2 Cor. 4:2, the word of God *d*

DECEITFULNESS
Mt. 13:22, this world and the *d*
Heb. 3:13, hardened through the *d*

DECEIVE
Jer. 37:9, 'Do not *d* yourselves

Mt. 24:11, rise up and *d* many
Mt. 24:24, wonders to *d*
1 Cor. 3:18, Let no one *d* himself
Eph. 5:6, Let no one *d* you with
1 Jn. 1:8, we have no sin, we *d*

DECEIVED
Gen. 3:13, "The serpent *d*
Isa. 44:20, *d* heart has turned him
Rom. 7:11, the commandment, *d*
2 Cor. 11:3, as the serpent *d*
1 Tim. 2:14, but the woman being *d*
2 Tim. 3:13, deceiving and being *d*

DECEIVER
Mal. 1:14, "But cursed be the *d*
Mt. 27:63, how that *d* said
2 Jn. 7, This is a *d* and an

DECEIVES
Mt. 24:4, heed that no one *d*
Jas. 1:26, *d* his own heart

DECENTLY
1 Cor. 14:40, all things be done *d*

DECEPTION
Ps. 38:12, *d* all the day long

DECEPTIVE
2 Pet. 2:3, you with *d* words

DECISION
Prov. 16:33, but its every *d*
Joel 3:14, in the valley of *d*

DECLARE
Ps. 19:1, The heavens *d* the
Ps. 22:22, *d* Your name to My
Ps. 66:16, *d* what He had done
Ps. 92:15, *d* that the LORD is
Isa. 53:8, *d* His generation
Heb. 2:12, "I will *d* Your name
1 Jn. 1:3, seen and heard we *d*

DECLARED
Jn. 1:18, the Father, He has *d*
Rom. 1:4, and *d* to be the Son of

DECREE
Ps. 2:7, "I will declare the *d*
Ps. 148:6, *d* which shall not pass
Lk. 2:1, in those days that a *d*

DEDICATED
Dt. 20:5, house and has not *d*
Ezek. 44:29, every *d* thing in
Heb. 9:18, first covenant was *d*

DEDICATION
of tabernacle. Ex. 40; Lev. 8; 9; Num. 7
of temple. 1 Ki. 8; 2 Chr. 5:6
of wall of Jerusalem. Neh. 12:27

DEDICATION
Ezra 6:17, sacrifices at the *d*
Jn. 10:22, it was the Feast of *D*

DEED
Jud. 19:30, *d* has been done
Mt. 6:2, you do a charitable *d*
Col. 3:17, you do in word or *d*

DEEDS
Ps. 9:11, Declare His *d* among
Ps. 99:8, vengeance on their *d*
Ps. 106:39, harlot by their own *d*
Isa. 12:4, declare His *d* among
Jer. 5:28, they surpass the *d*
Jn. 3:19, because their *d*
Jn. 8:41, "You do the *d*
Rom. 2:6, one according to his *d*
Rom. 8:13, you put to death the *d*
2 Jn. 11, shares in his evil *d*

DEEP
Gen. 2:21, LORD God caused a *d*
Ps. 33:7, He lays up the *d*
Ps. 42:7, *D* calls unto *d*
Ps. 95:4, In his hand are the *d*
Ps. 107:24, His wonders in the *d*
Prov. 20:20, put out in *d* darkness
Isa. 63:13, led them through the *d*
Jon. 2:5, *d* closed around me
Hab. 3:10, *d* uttered its voice
Lk. 5:4, "Launch out into the *d*
2 Cor. 11:25, I have been in the *d*

DEEPER
Job 11:8, *D* than Sheol

DEEPLY
Song 5:1, Drink, yes, drink *d*
Mk. 8:12, But He sighed *d*

DEER
Gen. 49:21, "Naphtali is a *d*
Ps. 42:1, As the *d* pants for the
Isa. 35:6, shall leap like a *d*

DEFEATED
1 Sam. 4:10, and Israel was *d*

DEFECT
Lev. 21:17, who has any *d*

DEFEND
2 Ki. 19:34, 'For I will *d* this
Job 13:15, *d* my own ways before
Ps. 82:3, *D* the poor and
Isa. 1:17, *d* the fatherless
Isa. 31:5, of hosts *d* Jerusalem

DEFENDER
Ps. 68:5, a *d* of widows

DEFENSE
Eccl. 7:12, For wisdom is a *d*
Isa. 33:16, *d* will be the
Phil. 1:17, am appointed for the *d*
2 Tim. 4:16, *d* no one stood with me
1 Pet. 3:15, be ready to give a *d*

DEFILE
Mt. 15:18, the heart, and they *d*
Jude 8, also these dreamers *d*

DEFILED
Ps. 74:7, *d* the dwelling place
Isa. 59:3, For your hands are *d*
Jn. 18:28, lest they should be *d*
Ti. 1:15, to those who are *d*
Ti. 1:15, and conscience are *d*
Jude 23, even the garment *d*

DEFILES
Mt. 15:11, mouth, this *d* a man
1 Cor. 3:17, *d* the temple of God
Rev. 21:27, it anything that *d*

DEFRAUD
1 Th. 4:6, *d* his brother in this

DEGENERATE
Jer. 2:21, before Me into the *d*
Ezek. 16:30, *d* is your heart

DEGREES
2 Ki. 20:9, go forward ten *d*

DELICACIES
Ps. 141:4, let me eat of their *d*
Prov. 23:3, Do not desire his *d*
Dan. 1:5, of the king's *d*

DELICATE
Isa. 47:1, be called tender and *d*
Jer. 6:2, a lovely and *d* woman

DELIGHT
1 Sam. 15:22, the LORD as great *d*
2 Chr. 17:6, And his heart took *d*
Job 27:10, Will he *d* himself in
Ps. 1:2, But his *d* is in the
Ps. 37:4, *D* your self also in the
Ps. 40:8, I *d* to do Your will
Ps. 119:92, Your law had been my *d*
Prov. 7:18, *d* ourselves with love
Prov. 8:30, And I was daily His *d*
Prov. 12:22, truthfully are His *d*
Isa. 55:2, And let your soul *d*
Isa. 58:13, call the Sabbath a *d*
Rom. 7:22, For I *d* in the law of

DELIGHTED
Dt. 10:15, The LORD *d* only in

DELIGHTS
Song 7:6, O love, with your *d*
Isa. 62:4, For the LORD *d* in you
Mic. 7:18, forever, because He *d*

DELILAH, Jud. 16:4

DELIVER
Ex. 3:8, *d* them out of the hand
Job 5:19, He shall *d* you in six
Job 10:7, is no one who can *d*
Job 33:24, '*D* him from going down
Ps. 22:8, Let Him *d* Him
Ps. 33:19, *d* their soul from
Ps. 91:15, I will *d* him and honor
Prov. 2:16, *d* you from the immoral
Eccl. 8:8, wickedness will not *d*
Isa. 50:2, have I no power to *d*
Dan. 3:17, we serve is able to *d*
Mt. 6:13, into temptation, but *d*
Mt. 27:43, let Him *d* Him now if
1 Cor. 5:5, *d* such a one to Satan
2 Tim. 4:18, And the Lord will *d*
2 Pet. 2:9, *d* the godly out of

DELIVERANCE
Ps. 18:50, *d* He gives to His king
Prov. 21:31, but *d* is of the LORD
Heb. 11:35, not accepting *d*

DELIVERANCES
Lot. Gen. 14; 19; Moses. Ex. 2; Israel. Ex. 14; Jud. 4; 7; 15; 1 Sam. 7; 14; 17; 2 Ki. 19; 2 Chr. 14; 20; Daniel, Shadrach, Meshach, and Abed-Nego. Dan. 3:19; 6:22; the apostles. Acts 5:19; 12:7; 16:26; 28:1; 2 Tim. 4:17

DELIVERED
Job 29:12, *d* the poor who cried
Ps. 56:13, for You have *d* my soul
Jer. 20:13, For He has *d* the life
Mt. 11:27, All things have been *d*
Rom. 4:25, who was *d* up because
Rom. 7:6, But now we have been *d*

2 Cor. 1:10, who *d* us from so great
Jude 3, was once for all *d*

DELIVERER
Jud. 3:9, the LORD raised up a *d*
2 Ki. 13:5, LORD gave Israel a *d*
Rom. 11:26, *D* will come out of

DELIVERERS
Neh. 9:27, *d* who saved them

DELIVERS
1 Cor. 15:24, *d* the kingdom to God
1 Th. 1:10, even Jesus who *d*

DELUSION
2 Th. 2:11, send them strong *d*

DEMETRIUS
silversmith. Acts 19:24
disciple. 3 Jn. 12

DEMON
Mt. 17:18, Jesus rebuked the *d*
Lk. 7:33, you say, 'He has a *d*
Jn. 8:48, and have a *d*

DEMONIC
Jas. 3:15, is earthly, sensual, *d*

DEMONS
confess Jesus to be Christ. Mt. 8:29; Mk. 1:24; 3:11; 5:7; Lk. 4:34,41; Acts 19:15; Jas. 2:19
sacrifices offered to. Lev. 17:7; Dt. 32:17; Ps. 106:37; 1 Cor. 10:20; Rev. 9:20

DEMONS
Dt. 32:17, They sacrificed to *d*
Ps. 106:37, their daughters to *d*
Lk. 9:1, authority over all *d*
Lk. 10:17, the *d* are subject
1 Cor. 10:21, Lord and the cup of *d*
Jas. 2:19, Even the *d* believe
Rev. 18:2 a dwelling place of *d*

DEMONSTRATE
Rom. 3:25, faith, to *d* His

DEMONSTRATES
Rom. 5:8, *d* His own love toward

DEN
Isa. 11:8, in the viper's *d*
Jer. 7:11, by My name, become a *d*
Dan. 6:16, cast him into the *d*
Mt. 21:13, it a '*d* of thieves

DENARII
Mt. 18:28; Mk. 14:5; Lk. 7:41; 10:35

DENARIUS
Mt. 20:2, the laborers for a *d*
Mt. 22:19, they brought Him a *d*
Rev. 6:6, quart of wheat for a *d*

DENIED
Lk. 12:9, before men will be *d*
Jn. 18:27, Peter then *d* again
Acts 3:14, *d* the Holy One and the
Acts 19:36, things cannot be *d*
1 Tim. 5:8, household, he has *d*
Rev. 3:8, word, and have not *d*

DENIES
Mt. 10:33, But whoever *d*
1 Jn. 2:22, *d* that Jesus is the

DENS
Ps. 104:22, lie down in their *d*
Heb. 11:38, and mountains, in *d*

DENY
Prov. 30:9, lest I be full and *d*
Mt. 16:24, let him *d* himself
2 Tim. 2:13, He cannot *d* Himself
Ti. 1:16, in works they *d*
Jude 4, *d* the only Lord
Rev. 2:13, *d* My faith even

DENYING
2 Tim. 3:5, but *d* its power
Ti. 2:12, *d* ungodliness and
2 Pet. 2:1, *d* the Lord who bought

DEPART
Gen. 49:10, scepter shall not *d*
Job 21:14, they say to God, '*D*
Ps. 34:14, *D* from evil
Prov. 3:7, fear the LORD and *d*
Isa. 54:10, the mountains, shall *d*
Mt. 25:41, on the left hand, '*D*
1 Tim. 4:1, will *d* from the faith

DEPARTED
Dt. 9:7, the day that you *d*

DEPARTING
Heb. 3:12, heart of unbelief in *d*

DEPARTURE
Acts 20:29, *d* savage wolves will
2 Tim. 4:6, and the time of my *d*

DEPRESSION
Prov. 12:25, of man causes *d*

DEPRIVE
Eccl. 4:8, *d* myself of good
1 Cor. 7:5, *d* one another except

DEPTH
Mt. 13:5, because they had no *d*
Rom. 8:39, nor height nor *d*
Rom. 11:33, Oh, the *d* of the
Eph. 3:18, width and length and *d*

DEPTHS
Ex. 15:5, *d* have covered them
Ps. 77:16, The *d* also trembled
Ps. 86:13, my soul from the *d*
Ps. 106:9, led them through the *d*
Ps. 107:26, go down again to the *d*
Prov. 8:24, *d* I was brought forth
Mic. 7:19, our sins into the *d*
Rev. 2:24, have not known the *d*

DERANGED
Jer. 51:7, the nations are *d*

DERISION
Ps. 2:4, shall hold them in *d*
Jer. 20:7, I am in *d* daily

DESCEND
Ps. 49:17, His glory shall not *d*
Mk. 15:32, *d* now from the cross
1 Th. 4:16, Lord Himself will *d*
Jas. 3:15, This wisdom does not *d*

DESCENDANTS
Ps. 22:23, All you *d* of Jacob
Ps. 25:13, *d* shall inherit the
Isa. 45:25, In the LORD all the *d*
Jn. 8:33, "We are Abraham's *d*

DESCENDED
Ex. 19:18, because the LORD *d*
Eph. 4:9, that He also first *d*
Eph. 4:10, He who *d* is also the

DESCENDING
Gen. 28:12, were ascending and *d*
Jn. 1:32, "I saw the Spirit *d*
Jn. 1:51, God ascending and *d*
Rev. 21:10, the holy Jerusalem, *d*

DESERT
Isa. 35:1, *d* shall rejoice
Isa. 43:19, and rivers in the *d*
Mt. 24:26, 'Look, He is in the *d*

DESERTED
Mt. 14:13, *d* place by Himself

DESERTS
Isa. 48:21, led them through the *d*
Heb. 11:38, They wandered in *d*

DESERVE
Ps. 28:4, to them what they *d*
Ezek. 7:27, *d* I will judge them

DESIGN
Ex. 26:31, with an artistic *d*
Ezek. 43:11, may keep its whole *d*

DESIRABLE
Gen. 3:6, the eyes, and a tree *d*
Acts 6:2, *d* that we should leave

DESIRE
Gen. 3:16, *d* shall be for your
Job 21:14, for we do not *d*
Ps. 21:2, him his heart's *d*
Ps. 51:6, Behold, You *d* truth in
Ps. 73:25, upon earth that I *d*
Ps. 112:10, the *d* of the wicked
Ps. 145:16, and satisfy the *d*
Prov. 21:25, The *d* of the lazy
Eccl. 12:5, a burden, and *d* fails
Isa. 26:8, the *d* of our soul is
Lk. 22:15, *d* I have desired
Jn. 17:24, "Father, I *d* that
Rom. 7:8, all manner of evil *d*
Rom. 10:1, Brethren, my heart's *d*
1 Cor. 12:31, *d* the best gifts
1 Cor. 14:1, *d* spiritual gifts
Phil. 1:23, the two, having a *d*
Col. 3:5, passion, evil *d*
Jas. 1:15, *d* has conceived

DESIRED
Ps. 19:10, *d* are they than gold
Ps. 27:4, One thing I have *d*
Ps. 107:30, guides them to their *d*
Prov. 19:22, What is *d* in a man is
Eccl. 2:10, Whatever my eyes *d*
Lk. 22:15, desire I have *d*

DESIRES
Ps. 34:12, Who is the man who *d*
Ps. 37:4, shall give you the *d*
Jn. 8:44, the devil, and the *d*
Eph. 2:3, fulfulling the *d*
Jas. 4:1, not come from your *d*

DESOLATE
Ps. 25:16, on me, for I am *d*
Ps. 107:4, the wilderness in a *d*
Isa. 49:21, my children and am *d*
Isa. 62:4, any more be termed *D*

Jer. 4:7, to make your land *d*
Mt. 23:38, house is left to you *d*
Rev. 18:19, one hour she is made *d*

DESOLATION
Mt. 24:15, the 'abomination of *d*
Lk. 21:20, then know that its *d*

DESOLATIONS
Ps. 46:8, LORD, who has made *d*

DESPAIRED
Eccl. 2:20, turned my heart and *d*
2 Cor. 1:8, strength, so that we *d*

DESPERATELY
Job 27:22, he flees *d* from its

DESPISE
Lev. 26:15, if you *d* My statutes
1 Sam. 2:30, *d* Me shall be lightly
Prov. 23:22, *d* your mother when she
Amos 5:21, *d* your feast days
Mal. 1:6, to you priests who *d*
Mt. 6:24, one and *d* the other
Rom. 2:4, *d* the riches of His
1 Cor. 11:22, *d* the church of God
2 Pet. 2:10, and *d* authority

DESPISED
Eccl. 9:16, poor man's wisdom is *d*
Isa. 5:24, *d* the word of the Holy
Isa. 53:3, He is *d* and rejected
1 Cor. 1:28, the things which are *d*

DESPISERS, Acts 13:41; 2 Tim. 3:3

DESPISES
Prov. 11:12, wisdom *d* his neighbor
Prov. 13:13, *d* the word will be
Prov. 14:21, *d* his neighbor sins
Prov. 15:20, but a foolish man *d*
Ezek. 21:10, *d* the scepter of My

DESPISING
Heb. 12:2, the cross, *d* the shame

DESTINY
Lam. 1:9, did not consider her *d*

DESTITUTE
Ps. 102:17, the prayer of the *d*
1 Tim. 6:5, of corrupt minds and *d*
Jas. 2:15, sister is naked and *d*

DESTROY
Gen. 18:23, *d* the righteous
Ps. 101:8, *d* all the wicked
Ps. 118:10 of the LORD I will *d*
Ps. 145:20, the wicked He will *d*
Eccl. 7:16, Why should you *d*
Isa. 11:9, shall not hurt nor *d*
Jer. 13:14, have mercy, but will *d*
Jer. 17:18, *d* them with double
Mt. 5:17, I did not come to *d*
Mt. 10:28, Him who is able to *d*
Mt. 27:20, Barabbas and *d* Jesus
Mk. 14:58, *d* this temple
Lk. 6:9, to save life or to *d*
Lk. 9:56, *d* men's lives but to
Rom. 14:20, *d* the work of God for
1 Cor. 1:19, *d* the wisdom of the
1 Cor. 6:13, foods, but God will *d*
Jas. 4:12, able to save and to *d*

DESTROYED
Gen. 7:23, *d* all living things
2 Sam. 22:41, *d* those who hated me
Hos. 4:6, My people are *d*
Hos. 13:9, "O Israel, you are *d*
2 Cor. 5:1, house, this tent, is *d*

DESTROYER
Ps. 17:4, the paths of the *d*
Prov. 18:9, him who is a great *d*
1 Cor. 10:10, destroyed by the *d*

DESTRUCTION
Job 5:21, not be afraid of *d*
Job 26:6, *D* has no covering
Ps. 35:8, *d* come upon him
Ps. 73:18, cast them down to *d*
Ps. 90:3, You turn man to *d*
Ps. 91:6, *d* that lays waste
Ps. 103:4, your life from *d*
Prov. 10:29, *d* will come to the
Prov. 16:18, Pride goes before *d*
Prov. 18:12, *d* the heart of a man
Isa. 19:18, called the City of *D*
Isa. 60:18, neither wasting nor *d*
Jer. 46:20, heifer, but *d* comes
Rom. 9:22, wrath prepared for *d*
1 Cor. 5:5, one to Satan for the *d*
Phil. 3:19, whose end is *d*
1 Th. 5:3, then sudden *d*
2 Th. 1:9, with everlasting *d*
1 Tim. 6:9, which drown men in *d*
2 Pet. 3:16, twist to their own *d*

DESTRUCTIVE
2 Pet. 2:1, bring in *d* heresies

DETERMINED
Job 14:5, Since his days are *d*
Isa. 10:23, of hosts will make a *d*
Dan. 9:24, "Seventy weeks are *d*
Acts 17:26, *d* their preappointed
1 Cor. 2:2, For I *d* not to know

DETESTABLE
Dt. 14:3, shall not eat any *d*

DEVICE
Eccl. 9:10, there is no work or *d*

DEVICES
2 Cor. 2:11, not ignorant of his *d*

DEVIL
(Abaddon, Apollyon, Beelzebub, Belial, Satan), the adversary of God and man. 1 Pet. 5:8
ruler of: the demons. Mt. 12:24
powers of the air. Eph. 2:2
this world. Jn. 14:30
sinner from the beginning. 1 Jn. 3:8
cast out of heaven. Lk. 10:18
cast down to hell. Isa. 14:15; 2 Pet. 2:4; Jude 6
as serpent, causes the fall of man. Gen. 3:1
lies to Eve. Gen. 3:4
cursed by God. Gen. 3:14
appears before God. Job 1:6; 2:1
called Abaddon and Apollyon. Rev. 9:11; Beelzebub. Mt. 12:24; Belial. 2 Cor. 6:15; Lucifer. Isa. 14:12; Satan. Lk. 10:18
tested Christ. Mt. 4:3–10; Mk. 1:13; Lk. 4:2; Eve. Gen. 3; David. 1 Chr. 21:1; Job. Job 2:7
desired to have the apostles. Lk. 22:31
repulsed by Christ. Mt. 4:10; Lk. 4:8,12
enters into: Judas Iscariot. Lk. 22:3; Jn. 13:2
Ananias. Acts 5:3

AS RULER AND GOD OF THIS WORLD, HE
perverts the scriptures. Mt. 4:6
opposes God's work. Zech. 3:1; 1 Th. 2:18
hinders the gospel. Mt. 13:19; 2 Cor. 4:4
works lying wonders. 2 Th. 2:9; Rev. 16:14
appears as an angel of light. 2 Cor. 11:14
is the father of lies. Jn. 8:44; 1 Ki. 22:22

VANQUISHED BY CHRIST
by resisting him. Mt. 4:11
by casting out demons. Mt. 4:24; 8:31; Mk. 1:23; 5:2; Lk. 9:42; 11:20; 13:32
by giving power to exorcise. Mt. 10:1; Mk. 16:17; Lk. 9:1; Acts 16:18; 19:12
by destroying the works of. 1 Jn. 3:8
in His death. Col. 2:15; Heb. 2:14
to be resisted by believers. Rom. 16:20; 2 Cor. 2:11; 11:3; Eph. 4:27; 6:16; 2 Tim. 2:26; Jas. 4:7; 1 Pet. 5:9; 1 Jn. 2:13; Rev. 12:11

CHARACTER OF
presumptuous. Job. 1:6; Isa. 14:13–14; Mt. 4:5,6
proud. 1 Tim. 3:6
powerful. Eph. 2:2; 6:12
wicked. 1 Jn. 2:13
malignant. Job 1:9; 2:4
cunning. Gen. 3:1, with 2 Cor. 11:3
deceitful. 2 Cor. 11:14; Eph. 6:11
fierce and cruel. Lk. 8:29; 9:39,42; 1 Pet. 5:8
source of apostasy. 2 Th. 2:9; 1 Tim. 4:1
shall be condemned at the judgment. Jude 6; Rev. 20:10
everlasting fire is prepared for. Mt. 25:41

COMPARED TO
a fowler. Ps. 91:3; *birds*. Mt. 13:4; *a sower of tares*. Mt. 13:25,28; *a wolf*. Jn. 10:12; *a roaring lion*. 1 Pet. 5:8; *a serpent*. Rev. 12:9; 20:2

THE WICKED
are the children of. Mt. 13:38; Acts 13:10; 1 Jn. 3:10
turn aside after. 1 Tim. 5:15
do the desires of. Jn. 8:44
are possessed by. Lk. 22:3; Acts 5:3; Eph. 2:2
blinded by. 2 Cor. 4:4
deceived by. 1 Ki. 22:21,22; Rev. 20:7,8
ensnared by. 1 Tim. 3:7; 2 Tim. 2:26
troubled by. 1 Sam. 16:14
punished together with. Mt. 25:41

DEVIL
Mt. 4:1, to be tempted by the *d*
Mt. 25:41, prepared for the *d*

Lk. 4:2, forty days by the *d*
Lk. 8:12, then the *d* comes and
Jn. 6:70, and one of you is a *d*
Jn. 8:44, of your father the *d*
Jn. 13:2, *d* having already put
Eph. 4:27, give place to the *d*
Eph. 6:11, the wiles of the *d*
2 Tim. 2:26, the snare of the *d*
Jas. 4:7, Resist the *d* and he
1 Jn. 3:8, the works of the *d*
Jude 9, contending with the *d*
Rev. 2:10, Indeed, the *d* is about

DEVIOUS
Prov. 2:15, crooked, and who are *d*

DEVISE
Prov. 3:29, Do not *d* evil against
Mic. 2:1, Woe to those who *d*

DEVISES
Ps. 36:4, *d* wickedness on his
Prov. 6:14, he *d* evil continually
Isa. 32:7, *d* wicked plans to
Isa. 32:8, But a generous man *d*

DEVOID
Prov. 11:12, who is *d* of wisdom

DEVOTED
Lev. 27:28, *d* offering is most
Num. 18:14, "Every *d* thing in
Ps. 119:38, Your servant, who is *d*

DEVOUR
Ps. 50:3, A fire shall *d* before
Mt. 23:14, For you *d* widows'
Gal. 5:15, bite and *d* one another
1 Pet. 5:8, seeking whom he may *d*
Rev. 12:4, *d* her Child as

DEVOURED
Gen. 37:20, Some wild beast has *d*
Isa. 1:20, rebel, you shall be *d*
Isa. 24:6, the curse has *d*
Jer. 2:30, Your sword has *d*
Jer. 3:24, For shame has *d*
Hos. 7:7, have *d* their judges
Amos 4:9, trees, the locust *d*
Mt. 13:4, birds came and *d* them
Rev. 20:9, of heaven and *d* them

DEVOURER
Mal. 3:11, I will rebuke the *d*

DEVOURING
Ps. 52:4, You love all *d* words
Isa. 29:6, the flame of *d* fire

DEVOUT
Lk. 2:25, man was just and *d*
Acts 8:2, *d* men carried
Acts 10:7, *d* soldier from among
Acts 13:43, *d* proselytes

DEVOUTLY, 1 Th. 2:10

DEW
Gen. 27:28, God give you of the *d*
Dt. 33:28, shall also drop *d*
Prov. 19:12, his favor is like *d*
Isa. 26:19, your *d* is like the *d*
Hos. 6:4, like the early *d*
Mic. 5:7, many peoples, like *d*

DIADEM
Isa. 62:3, LORD, and a royal *d*

DIADEMS
Rev. 12:3, ten horns, and seven *d*

DIAMOND
in high priest's breastplate. Ex. 28:18; 39:11

DIAMOND
Jer. 17:1, *d* it is engraved

DIANA
of Ephesians, tumult concerning. Acts 19:24

DICTATES
Jer. 23:17, according to the *d*

DIE
Gen. 2:17, it you shall surely *d*
2 Chr. 25:4, but a person shall *d*
Ps. 49:10, sees wise men *d*
Ps. 118:17, I shall not *d*
Prov. 31:8, who are appointed to *d*
Eccl. 2:16, how does a wise man *d*
Eccl. 3:2, born, and a time to *d*
Eccl. 7:17, why should you *d*
Ezek. 3:19, wicked way, he shall *d*
Mt. 26:35, "Even if I have to *d*
Lk. 20:36, nor can they *d*
Jn. 6:50, eat of it and not *d*
Jn. 8:24, to you that you will *d*
Jn. 11:25, though he may *d*
Jn. 11:50, one man should *d*
Jn. 11:51, that Jesus would *d*
Jn. 19:7, our law He ought to *d*
Rom. 8:13, the flesh you will *d*
1 Cor. 15:22, For as in Adam all *d*
Phil. 1:21, and to *d* is gain
Heb. 9:27, for men to *d* once
Rev. 14:13, are the dead who *d*

DIED
Gen. 7:21, And all flesh *d*
Ex. 16:3, "Oh, that we had *d*
Lk. 16:22, was that the beggar *d*
Rom. 5:6, in due time Christ *d*
Rom. 5:8, Christ *d* for us
Rom. 6:7, For he who has *d*
Rom. 6:8, Now if we *d* with
Rom. 7:9, sin revived and I *d*
2 Cor. 5:14, that if One *d* for all
2 Cor. 5:15, and He *d* for all
Gal. 2:19, through the law *d*
1 Th. 5:10, who *d* for us
2 Tim. 2:11, for if we *d* with Him
Heb. 11:13, These all *d* in faith
1 Pet. 2:24, having *d* to sins

DIES
1 Cor. 15:36, alive unless it *d*

DIFFERS
1 Cor. 15:41, for one star *d* from

DIFFUSED
Job 38:24, By what way is light *d*

DILIGENCE
Prov. 12:27, *d* is man's
2 Cor. 7:11, *d* it produced in you
2 Cor. 8:8, of your love by the *d*

DILIGENT
Ps. 77:6, and my spirit makes *d*
Prov. 10:4, *d* makes rich
Prov. 12:24, of the *d* will rule
Prov. 13:4, *d* shall be made rich
Heb. 4:11, Let us therefore be *d*

DILIGENTLY
1 Tim. 5:10, *d* followed every good
Heb. 12:15, *d* lest anyone fall

DIM
Dt. 34:7, His eyes were not *d*
Eccl. 12:3, the windows grow *d*
Lam. 4:1, the gold has become *d*

DIMLY
1 Cor. 13:12, we see in a mirror, *d*

DINAH
Jacob's daughter. Gen. 30:21
outraged by Shechem. Gen. 34:2
avenged by Simeon and Levi. Gen. 34:25

DINE
Lk. 11:37, asked Him to *d* with
Rev. 3:20, come in to him and *d*

DINNER
Mt. 22:4, I have prepared my *d*
1 Cor. 10:27, invites you to *d*

DIOTREPHES
loves preeminence. 3 Jn. 9

DIP
Ruth 2:14, *d* your piece of bread

DIPPED
Lev. 9:9, *d* his finger in the
Jn. 13:26, of bread when I have *d*
Rev. 19:13, clothed with a robe *d*

DIRECT
Ps. 5:3, the morning I will *d*
Isa. 61:8, *d* their work in truth
2 Th. 3:5, Now may the Lord *d*

DIRT
Ps. 18:42, I cast them out like *d*
Isa. 57:20, cast up mire and *d*

DISAPPEARS
Job 14:11, As water *d* from the

DISARMED
Col. 2:15, *d* principalities

DISARMS
Job 12:21, and *d* the mighty

DISASTER
Ezek. 7:26, *D* will come upon
Zeph. 3:15, you shall see *d*
Acts 27:10, voyage will end with *d*

DISCERN
2 Sam. 19:35, Can I *d* between the
Mal. 3:18, Then you shall again *d*
Mt. 16:3, *d* the face of the sky
Heb. 5:14, senses exercised to *d*

DISCERNED
1 Cor. 2:14, they are spiritually *d*

DISCERNER
Heb. 4:12, *d* of the thoughts

DISCERNMENT
Job 12:20, and takes away the *d*

DISCERNS
Eccl. 8:5, a wise man's heart *d*

DISCIPLE
Mt. 10:24, *d* is not above his
Mt. 10:42, in the name of a *d*
Lk. 14:26, he cannot be My *d*
Jn. 21:7, *d* whom Jesus loved

DISCIPLES
OF CHRIST
the seventy sent out to work miracles and preach. Lk. 10
their names written in heaven. Lk. 10:20
three thousand added to the church. Acts 2:41
five thousand believers. Acts 4:4
called Christians at Antioch. Acts 11:26
OF JOHN
inquire of Christ. Mt. 9:14; 11:2
follow Christ. Jn. 1:37
dispute about purifying. Jn. 3:25
baptized by Paul; receive the Spirit. Acts 19:1

DISCIPLES
Mt. 9:14, but Your *d* do not fast
Mt. 15:2, *d* transgress the
Mt. 20:17, took the twelve *d*
Jn. 8:31, word, you are My *d*
Jn. 9:27, to become His *d*
Jn. 9:28, but we are Moses' *d*
Jn. 15:8, so you will be My *d*

DISCIPLINE
Prov. 15:10, Harsh *d* is for him who

DISCIPLINES
Prov. 13:24, he who loves him *d*

DISCLOSE
Ps. 49:4, *d* my dark saying

DISCORD
Prov. 6:19, and one who sows *d*

DISCOURAGED
Isa. 42:4, will not fail nor be *d*
Col. 3:21, lest they become *d*
Heb. 12:3, become weary and *d*

DISCRETION
Prov. 2:11, *d* will preserve you
Prov. 8:12, out knowledge and *d*
Prov. 11:22, woman who lacks *d*
Prov. 19:11, The *d* of a man makes
Jer. 10:12, the heavens at His *d*

DISEASES
sent by God. Ex. 9; 15:26; Num. 12:10; Dt. 28:60; 2 Ki. 1:4; 5:27; 2 Chr. 21:18; 26:21; Job 2:6,7
cured by Christ. Mt. 4:23; 9:20; Jn. 5:8
power given to His disciples to cure. Lk. 9:1; Acts 28:8; exercised. Acts 3:1; 9:34; 28:8

DISFIGURE
Mt. 6:16, *d* their faces that

DISGUISES
Job 24:15, and he *d* his face
Prov. 26:24, He who hates, *d*

DISH, Mt. 23:25; Lk. 11:39

DISHONOR
Ps. 40:14, *d* who wish me evil
Isa. 23:9, *d* the pride of all
Jn. 8:49, My Father, and you *d* Me
Rom. 1:24, *d* their bodies among
Rom. 9:21, and another for *d*
1 Cor. 15:43, It is sown in *d*
2 Tim. 2:20, honor and some for *d*

DISHONORED
Jas. 2:6, But you have *d* the

DISHONORS
Mic. 7:6, For son *d* father
1 Cor. 11:4, covered, *d* his head

DISOBEDIENCE
and its results. Lev. 26:14; Dt. 8:11; 27; 28:15; Josh. 5:6; 1 Sam. 2:30; 12:15; Ps. 78:10; Isa. 3:8; 42:24; Jer. 9:13; 18:10; 22:21; 35:14; Eph. 5:6; Ti. 1:16; 3:3; Heb. 2:2. *See* Adam and Eve. Gen. 3; Pharaoh. Ex. 5:2; Achan. Josh. 7; Saul. 1 Sam. 13:9; 15; man of God. 1 Ki. 13:21; Jonah. Jon. 1; 2

DISOBEDIENCE
Rom. 5:19, *d* many were made
Eph. 2:2, works in the sons of *d*
Heb. 2:2, *d* received a just

DISOBEDIENT
Rom. 10:21, out My hands to a *d*
Ti. 3:3, *d*, deceived, serving
1 Pet. 2:8, They stumble, being *d*
1 Pet. 3:20, who formerly were *d*

DISORDERLY
Acts 19:40, for this *d* gathering
2 Th. 3:6, brother who walks *d*

DISPENSATION
Eph. 1:10, *d* of the fullness of
Eph. 3:2, *d* of the grace of God

DISPERSE
Ezek. 20:23, *d* them throughout

DISPERSION
Jn. 7:35, intend to go to the *D*
1 Pet. 1:1, the pilgrims of the *D*

DISPLEASE
Prov. 24:18, LORD see it, and it *d*

DISPLEASED
2 Sam. 11:27, that David had done *d*
Ps. 60:1, You have been *d*
Mt. 20:24, they were greatly *d*
Mk. 10:14, it, He was greatly *d*

DISPLEASURE
Dt. 9:19; Ps. 2:5; 6:1; 38:1

DISPOSSESS
Num. 33:53; Dt. 7:17; Jud. 11:23

DISPUTE
Lk. 22:24, there was also a *d*

DISPUTER
1 Cor. 1:20, Where is the *d* of this

DISPUTES
1 Tim. 1:4, *d* rather than godly
1 Tim. 6:4, but is obsessed with *d*
2 Tim. 2:23, foolish and ignorant *d*
Ti. 3:9, But avoid foolish *d*

DISQUALIFIED
1 Cor. 9:27, myself should become *d*
2 Cor. 13:5, indeed you are *d*
2 Cor. 13:7, though we may seem *d*

DISQUIETED
Ps. 42:5, And why are you *d*

DISSENSION
Acts 15:2, had no small *d* and

DISSENSIONS
Gal. 5:20, selfish ambitions, *d*

DISSIPATION
Ti. 1:6, not accused of *d*
1 Pet. 4:4, in the same flood of *d*

DISSOLVED
Isa. 34:4, of heaven shall be *d*
2 Pet. 3:12, the heavens will be *d*

DISTINCTION
Acts 15:9, and made no *d*
Rom. 10:12, For there is no *d*
Jude 22, compassion, making a *d*

DISTRESS
Gen. 35:3, me in the day of my *d*
Dt. 4:30, "When you are in *d*
1 Ki. 1:29, my life from every *d*
Job 36:16, you out of dire *d*
Job 36:19, keep you from *d*
Ps. 2:5, *d* them in His deep
Ps. 118:5, on the LORD in *d*
Prov. 1:27, a whirlwind, when *d*
Lk. 21:25, and on the earth *d*
Rom. 8:35, tribulation, or *d*
1 Cor. 7:26, of the present *d*

DISTRESSED
Ps. 143:4, heart within me is *d*
Mk. 14:33, troubled and deeply *d*

DISTRESSES
Ps. 25:17, bring me out of my *d*

DISTRIBUTE
Lk. 18:22, that you have and *d*

DISTRIBUTED
Acts 4:35, and they *d* to each as
1 Cor. 7:17, But as God has *d*

DISTRIBUTING
Rom. 12:13, *d* to the needs of the

DITCH
Mt. 15:14, will fall into a *d*

DIVERSITIES
1 Cor. 12:4, There are *d*

DIVIDE
1 Ki. 3:25, *D* the living child
Ps. 55:9, *d* their tongues
Prov. 16:19, *d* the spoil with the
Lk. 12:13, *d* the inheritance
Lk. 22:17, "Take this and *d*

DIVIDED
Ex. 14:21, and the waters were *d*
2 Sam. 1:23, death they were not *d*
Neh. 9:11, And You *d* the sea
Job 38:25, "Who has *d* a channel
Ezek. 37:22, shall they ever be *d*
Dan. 5:28, kingdom has been *d*
Amos 7:17, your land shall be *d*
Mt. 12:25, "Every kingdom *d*
Lk. 11:17, and a house *d* against
Lk. 12:52, in one house will be *d*

Lk. 15:12, So he *d* to them his
Acts 2:3, appeared to them *d*
Acts 2:45, *d* them among all
1 Cor. 1:13, Is Christ *d*
Rev. 16:19, the great city was *d*

DIVIDES
Ps. 68:12, at home *d* the spoil

DIVIDING
2 Tim. 2:15, rightly *d* the word of

DIVINATION
Lev. 19:26, shall you practice *d*
Prov. 16:10, *D* is on
Mic. 3:6, darkness without *d*
Acts 16:16, a spirit of *d* met us

DIVINE
Ezek. 13:9, futility and who *d*
Mic. 3:11, and her prophets *d*
Heb. 9:1, *d* service and the
2 Pet. 1:3, *d* power has given

DIVINER
1 Sam. 6:2; Isa. 44:25; Jer. 27:9; 29:8

DIVINERS
Jer. 27:9, your prophets, your *d*

DIVISION
Jn. 7:43, So there was a *d*
Heb. 4:12, piercing even to the *d*

DIVISIONS
of the Levites established by David. 1 Chr. 23; 24. *See* Lk. 1:5
of the singers. 1 Chr. 25
of the porters. 1 Chr. 26
of the captains. 1 Chr. 27

DIVISIONS
Rom. 16:17, those who cause *d*
1 Cor. 1:10, and that there be no *d*
1 Cor. 3:3, envy, strife, and *d*
1 Cor. 11:18, hear that there are *d*
Jude 19, persons, who cause *d*

DIVISIVE
Ti. 3:10, Reject a *d* man after

DIVORCE
when permitted. Dt. 24:1; Mt. 5:32
condemned by Christ. Mk. 10:4

DIVORCE
Dt. 24:1, her a certificate of *d*
Isa. 50:1, of your mother's *d*
Mk. 10:4, a certificate of *d*

DO
Eccl. 8:11, set in them to *d* evil
Isa. 46:11, I will also *d* it
Mt. 7:12, men to *d* to you, *d*
Lk. 10:28, *d* this and you will
Jn. 5:19, He sees the Father *d*
Jn. 15:5, without Me you can *d*
Acts 16:30, "Sirs, what must I *d*
Rom. 3:8, *d* evil that good may
Rom. 7:15, For what I will to *d*
Rom. 7:19, good that I will to *d*
1 Cor. 10:31, or whatever you *d*, *d*
Phil. 4:13, *d* all things through
Col. 3:17, *d* in word or deed, *d*
Heb. 13:16, *d* good and to share
Jas. 4:15, and *d* this or that

DOCTRINE of Christ
Mt. 7:28,29; Mk. 4:2; Jn. 7:16; Acts 2:42; 1 Tim. 4:16; 6:3; 2 Tim. 3:16; Ti. 1:1; 2:1; Heb. 6:1; 2 Jn. 9
obedience to. Rom. 6:17
not to be blasphemed. 1 Tim. 6:1,3; Ti. 2:7,10; 2 Jn. 10
no other to be taught. 1 Tim. 1:3; 4:6,13

DOCTRINE
Job 11:4, said, 'My *d* is pure
Prov. 4:2, for I give you good *d*
Jer. 10:8, idol is a worthless *d*
Mt. 16:12, of bread, but of the *d*
Mk. 1:27, What new *d* is this
Jn. 7:16, "My *d* is not Mine
Acts 5:28, Jerusalem with your *d*
Rom. 6:17, heart that form of *d*
Eph. 4:14, with every wind of *d*
1 Tim. 1:10, is contrary to sound *d*
2 Tim. 3:10, followed my *d*
2 Tim. 3:16, is profitable for *d*
2 Tim. 4:3, not endure sound *d*
Ti. 2:7, in *d* showing
Ti. 2:10, they may adorn the *d*
2 Jn. 9, not abide in the *d*

DOCTRINES, false
Jer. 10:8; Mt. 15:9; 16:12; Eph. 4:14; 2 Th. 2:11; 1 Tim. 4:1; 2 Tim. 4:3; Heb. 13:9; Rev. 2:14
to be avoided. Jer. 23:16; 29:8; Col. 2:8; 1 Tim. 1:4; 6:20

DOCTRINES
Col. 2:22, commandments and *d*
1 Tim. 4:1, spirits and *d* of
Heb. 13:9, various and strange *d*

DOEG, 1 Sam. 21:7
the Edomite, slays the priests. 1 Sam. 22:9

DOERS
Rom. 2:13, of God, but the *d*
Jas. 1:22, But be *d* of the word

DOG
1 Sam. 17:43, to David, "Am I a *d*
Ps. 59:6, they growl like a *d*
Prov. 26:11, *d* returns to his own
Eccl. 9:4, *d* is better than a
2 Pet. 2:22, *d* returns to his own

DOGS
Isa. 56:11, Yes, they are greedy *d*
Mt. 7:6, what is holy to the *d*
Mt. 15:27, *d* eat the crumbs
Lk. 16:21, Moreover the *d* came
Rev. 22:15, But outside are *d*

DOMINION
Gen. 1:26, let them have *d*
Job 25:2, "*D* and fear belong
Ps. 8:6, made him to have *d*
Ps. 19:13, let them not have *d*
Isa. 26:13, besides You have had *d*
Dan. 4:34, *d* is an everlasting
Rom. 6:14, sin shall not have *d*
2 Cor. 1:24, Not that we have *d*
Jude 25, glory and majesty, *D*

DONKEY
Balaam rebuked by. Num. 22:28; 2 Pet. 2:16
laws concerning. Ex. 13:13; 23:4; Dt. 22:10
Christ rides on one (Zech. 9:9). Mt. 21:5; Jn. 12:14
(wild), described. Job 39:5; Hos. 8:9

DONKEY
Num. 22:23, *d* saw the Angel
Job 6:5, Does the wild *d*
Isa. 1:3, *d* its master's crib
Zech. 9:9, and riding on a *d*
Mt. 21:5, colt, the foal of a *d*
Jn. 12:14, He had found a young *d*
2 Pet. 2:16, *d* speaking with a

DONKEY'S
Job 11:12, *d* colt is born a man

DONKEYS
Ps. 104:11, *d* quench their thirst
Isa. 21:7, a chariot of *d*
Jer. 14:6, And the wild *d* stood

DOOM
Prov. 16:4, for the day of *d*

DOOR
Gen. 4:7, sin lies at the *d*
Ps. 141:3, keep watch over the *d*
Prov. 26:14, *d* turns on its hinges
Mt. 27:60, stone against the *d*
Jn. 10:7, to you, I am the *d*
1 Cor. 16:9, and effective *d*
2 Cor. 2:12, *d* was opened to me by
Col. 4:3, would open to us a *d*
Jas. 5:9, is standing at the *d*
Rev. 3:8, before you an open *d*
Rev. 3:20, I stand at the *d*
Rev. 4:1, and behold, a *d*

DOORKEEPER
Ps. 84:10, I would rather be a *d*
Jn. 10:3, "To him the *d*

DOORPOSTS
Dt. 6:9, write them on the *d*
Amos 9:1, "Strike the *d*

DOORS
Ps. 24:7, up, you everlasting *d*
Prov. 8:3, the entrance of the *d*
Eccl. 12:4, when the *d* are shut in
Mal. 1:10, who would shut the *d*

DORCAS, Acts 9:36

DOUBLE
Isa. 40:2, from the LORD's hand *d*
Jer. 16:18, first I will repay *d*
1 Tim. 5:17, worthy of *d* honor
Rev. 18:6, and repay her *d*

DOUBLE-MINDED
Ps. 119:113, I hate the *d*
Jas. 1:8, he is a *d* man
Jas. 4:8, your hearts, you *d*

DOUBT
Dt. 28:66, life shall hang in *d*
Mt. 14:31, faith, why did you *d*

DOUBTING
1 Tim. 2:8, without wrath and *d*
Jas. 1:6, in faith, with no *d*

DOUBTS
Lk. 24:38, why do *d* arise in
Gal. 4:20, for I have *d* about you

Jas. 1:6, doubting, for he who *d*

DOVE
Gen. 8:9, *d* found no resting
Ps. 55:6, I had wings like a *d*
Isa. 38:14, I mourned like a *d*
Hos. 7:11, also is like a silly *d*
Mt. 3:16, descending like a *d*

DOVES
Isa. 59:11, and moan sadly like *d*
Mt. 10:16, and harmless as *d*
Mt. 21:12, of those who sold *d*

DOWNCAST
2 Cor. 7:6, who comforts the *d*

DOWRY, Gen. 34:12; 1 Sam. 18:25

DRAGNET
Hab. 1:15, gather them in their *d*
Mt. 13:47, *d* that was cast

DRAGON
Rev. 12:3, a great, fiery red *d*
Rev. 12:7, fought with the *d*
Rev. 13:4, they worshiped the *d*
Rev. 20:2, He laid hold of the *d*

DRAIN
Ps. 75:8, wicked of the earth *d*

DRAINED
Joel 2:6, all faces are *d*

DRANK
Mk. 14:23, them, and they all *d*
1 Cor. 10:4, *d* the same spiritual

DRAW
Dt. 32:13, *d* honey from the
Ps. 73:28, me to *d* near to God
Eccl. 12:1, and the years *d*
Song 1:4, *D* me away
Isa. 5:18, Woe to those who *d*
Isa. 12:3, with joy you will *d*
Jn. 2:8, "*D* some out now
Jn. 4:11, You have nothing to *d*
Jn. 12:32, will *d* all peoples
Heb. 10:22, let us *d* near with a
Jas. 4:8, *D* near to God and He

DRAWN
Ps. 37:14, The wicked have *d*
Jas. 1:14, tempted when he is *d*

DRAWS
Ps. 88:3, and my life *d* near to
Lk. 21:28, your redemption *d*

DREAD
Gen. 9:2, fear of you and the *d*
Dt. 2:25, begin to put the *d*

DREADFUL
Mal. 4:5, of the great and *d*

DREAM
Gen. 37:5, Now Joseph had a *d*
Num. 12:6, I speak to him in a *d*
Job 20:8, will fly away like a *d*
Ps. 73:20, As a *d* when one awakes
Ps. 126:1, like those who *d*
Eccl. 5:3, For a *d* comes through
Isa. 29:7, her, shall be as a *d*
Jer. 23:28, prophet who has a *d*
Dan. 4:19, do not let the *d*
Joel 2:28, your old men shall *d*
Mt. 2:13, to Joseph in a *d*
Mt. 27:19, things today in a *d*
Acts 2:17, your old men shall *d*

DREAMERS
Jude 8, *d* defile the flesh

DREAMS
vanity of. Job 20:8; Ps. 73:20; Isa. 29:8; Jer. 23:28; 27:9; Zech. 10:2
from God. Job 33:15; Joel 2:28
of Abimelech. Gen. 20:3; Jacob. Gen. 28:12; 31:10; Laban. Gen. 31:24; Joseph. Gen. 37:5; Pharaoh's servants. Gen. 40:5; Pharaoh. Gen. 41; Midianite. Jud. 7:13; Solomon. 1 Ki. 3:5; Nebuchadnezzar. Dan. 2; 4; Joseph. Mt. 1:20; 2:13; Wise men. Mt. 2:12; Pilate's wife. Mt. 27:19

DREAMS
Eccl. 5:7, in the multitude of *d*
Isa. 29:8, when a hungry man *d*
Dan. 2:1, Nebuchadnezzar had *d*

DREGS
Ps. 75:8, *d* shall all the wicked
Jer. 48:11, has settled on his *d*

DRIED
Ps. 22:15, My strength is *d*
Mk. 5:29, of her blood was *d*
Mk. 11:20, saw the fig tree *d*
Rev. 16:12, and its water was *d*

DRIFT
Heb. 2:1, have heard, lest we *d*

DRINK
Ex. 15:24, "What shall we *d*
Lev. 10:9, "Do not *d* wine or
Job 21:20, and let him *d* of the
Ps. 69:21, gave me vinegar to *d*
Prov. 5:15, *D* water from your own
Prov. 20:1, mocker, strong *d*
Prov. 31:5, lest they *d* and forget
Prov. 31:6, Give strong *d* to him
Prov. 31:7, Let him *d* and forget
Eccl. 9:7, *d* your wine with a
Isa. 5:11, follow intoxicating *d*
Isa. 5:22, mixing intoxicating *d*
Isa. 60:16, *d* the milk of the
Isa. 65:13, My servants shall *d*
Isa. 66:11, bosom, that you may *d*
Ezek. 4:11, *d* water by measure
Amos 4:1, "Bring wine, let us *d*
Mic. 2:11, to you of wine and *d*
Mt. 25:42, and you gave Me no *d*
Mt. 26:29, that day when I *d*
Mt. 27:34, mingled with gall to *d*
Mk. 15:23, with myrrh to *d*
Jn. 4:7, to her, "Give Me a *d*
Jn. 7:37, him come to Me and *d*
Rom. 14:21, *d* wine nor do anything
1 Cor. 11:25, do, as often as you *d*
1 Cor. 12:13, all been made to *d*
1 Tim. 5:23, No longer *d* only water
Rev. 14:8, has made all nations *d*

DRINK OFFERINGS
Ex. 29:40; Lev. 23:13; Num. 6:17; 15:5 (Gen. 35:14)
to idols. Isa. 57:6; Jer. 7:18; 44:17; Ezek. 20:28

DRINKS
Jn. 4:13, to her, "Whoever *d*
Jn. 6:54, *d* My blood has
1 Cor. 11:29, he who eats and *d*
Heb. 6:7, For the earth which *d*

DRIPPING
Prov. 19:13, wife are a continual *d*
Song 5:13, His lips are lilies, *d*

DRIVE
Ps. 36:11, of the wicked *d*
Dan. 4:25, They shall *d* you from
Mk. 11:15, temple and began to *d*

DRIVEN
Job 30:5, They were *d* out from
Ps. 40:14, Let them be *d* backward
Acts 27:17, sail and so were *d*
Jas. 1:6, a wave of the sea *d*

DROP
Ps. 65:12, They *d* on the pastures
Isa. 40:15, the nations are as a *d*

DROSS
Ps. 119:119, of the earth like *d*
Prov. 25:4, Take away the *d*
Isa. 1:25, purge away your *d*
Ezek. 22:18, of Israel has become *d*

DROUGHT
Jer. 2:6, through a land of *d*
Jer. 17:8, in the year of *d*
Hag. 1:11, For I called for a *d*

DROVE
Gen. 3:24, So He *d* out the man
Mt. 21:12, temple of God and *d*
Jn. 2:15, a whip of cords, He *d*

DROWN
Song 8:7, Nor can the floods *d*
1 Tim. 6:9, harmful lusts which *d*

DROWSINESS
Prov. 23:21, *d* will clothe a

DRUNK
Gen. 9:21, of the wine and was *d*
Song 5:1, *d* my wine with my milk
Isa. 51:21, you afflicted, and *d*
Isa. 63:6, My anger, made them *d*
Jer. 46:10, be satiated and made *d*
Jn. 2:10, the guests have well *d*
Acts 2:15, For these are not *d*
1 Cor. 11:21, and another is *d*
Eph. 5:18, And do not be *d*
1 Th. 5:7, and those who get *d*
Rev. 17:2, the earth were made *d*
Rev. 17:6, I saw the woman, *d*

DRUNKARD
Dt. 29:19, *d* could be included
Prov. 26:9, *d* is a proverb in the
Isa. 24:20, to and fro like a *d*
1 Cor. 5:11, or a reviler, or a *d*

DRUNKEN
Jer. 23:9, I am like a *d* man

DRUNKENNESS
of Noah. Gen. 9:21; Lot. Gen. 19:33; Nabal. 1 Sam. 25:36; Elah. 1 Ki. 16:9; Ben-Hadad. 1 Ki. 20:16; Belshazzar. Dan. 5:4; the Corinthians. 1 Cor. 11:21

DRUNKENNESS
Ezek. 23:33, will be filled with *d*
Zech. 12:2, Jerusalem a cup of *d*
Lk. 21:34, with carousing, *d*
Rom. 13:13, not in revelry and *d*
Gal. 5:21, envy, murders, *d*
1 Pet. 4:3, lusts, *d*

DRUSILLA, Acts 24:24

DRY
Gen. 1:9, place, and let the *d*
Ex. 14:21, made the sea into *d*
Jud. 6:40, It was *d* on the fleece
Jer. 51:36, I will *d* up her sea
Ezek. 17:24, *d* tree flourish
Ezek. 30:12, will make the rivers *d*
Lk. 23:31, will be done in the *d*

DUE
Lev. 10:13, because it is your *d*
Ps. 104:27, their food in *d* season
Mt. 18:34, pay all that was *d*
Rom. 5:6, *d* time Christ died
Rom. 13:7, to whom taxes are *d*
Gal. 6:9, *d* season we shall
1 Pet. 5:6, exalt you in *d* time

DULL
Isa. 6:10, heart of this people *d*
Mt. 13:15, people have grown *d*
Heb. 5:11, you have become *d*

DUMB
Isa. 35:6, the tongue of the *d*
Mk. 9:25, "Deaf and *d* spirit

DUNGEON
Gen. 40:15; 41:14; Ex. 12:29; Jer. 38:6

DUNGHILL
Lk. 14:35, the land nor for the *d*

DUST
Gen. 2:7, formed man of the *d*
Gen. 3:19, *d* you shall return
Gen. 13:16, descendants as the *d*
Gen. 18:27, now, I who am but *d*
Num. 23:10, "Who can count the *d*
Job 22:24, lay your gold in the *d*
Job 42:6, and repent in *d*
Ps. 30:9, Will the *d* praise You
Ps. 83:13, like the whirling *d*
Ps. 102:14, show favor to her *d*
Ps. 103:14, that we are *d*
Prov. 8:26, or the primal *d*
Eccl. 3:20, all are from the *d*
Isa. 40:15, counted as the small *d*
Mic. 7:17, They shall lick the *d*
Mt. 10:14, city, shake off the *d*
1 Cor. 15:49, image of the man of *d*

DUTY
Lk. 17:10, done what was our *d*

DWELL
Ps. 4:8, O LORD, make me *d*
Ps. 15:1, Who may *d* in Your holy
Ps. 25:13, He himself shall *d*
Ps. 37:3, *d* in the land
Ps. 68:18, the LORD God might *d*
Ps. 84:10, of my God than *d*
Ps. 85:9, Him, that glory may *d*
Ps. 120:5, Woe is me, that I *d*
Isa. 33:16, he will *d* on high
Isa. 52:4, into Egypt to *d* there
Isa. 57:15, "I *d* in the high and
Lam. 4:15, "They shall no longer *d*
Mt. 12:45, they enter and *d* there
Acts 2:14, of Judea and all who *d*
2 Cor. 6:16, "I will *d* in them
Eph. 3:17, that Christ may *d*
Col. 1:19, the fullness should *d*
Col. 3:16, the word of Christ *d*
Rev. 21:3, men, and He will *d*

DWELLER
Acts 7:29, fled and became a *d*

DWELLING
Num. 23:9, A people *d* alone
Job 38:19, is the way to the *d*
Eph. 2:22, built together for a *d*
Heb. 11:9, a foreign country, *d*

DWELLS
Ps. 91:1, He who *d* in the secret
Jn. 14:10, but the Father who *d*
Rom. 7:17, do it, but sin that *d*
Rom. 8:9, the Spirit of God *d*
Rom. 8:11, from the dead *d*
1 Cor. 3:16, the Spirit of God *d*
Col. 2:9, *d* all the fullness
2 Pet. 3:13, which righteousness *d*
Rev. 2:13, you, where Satan *d*

DWELT
Ps. 105:23, Egypt, and Jacob *d*
Jn. 1:14, became flesh and *d*
Heb. 11:9, By faith he *d* in the

DYING
Acts 25:11, I do not object to *d*
2 Cor. 4:10, in the body the *d*
Heb. 11:21, Jacob, when he was *d*

EAGLE
Dt. 32:11, As an *e* stirs up its
Job 9:26, *e* swooping on its prey
Prov. 23:5, fly away like an *e*
Prov. 30:19, The way of an *e*
Jer. 49:16, nest as high as the *e*
Ezek. 1:10, had the face of an *e*
Rev. 4:7, like a flying *e*
Rev. 12:14, two wings of a great *e*

EAGLES
Isa. 40:31, up with wings like *e*
Jer. 4:13, are swifter than *e*
Mt. 24:28, *e* will be gathered

EAGLES'
Ex. 19:4, how I bore you on *e*

EAR
Ex. 21:6, shall pierce his *e*
Job 12:11, Does not the *e* test
Ps. 31:2, Bow down Your *e*
Prov. 18:15, And the *e* of the wise
Isa. 50:4, He awakens My *e*
Jer. 6:10, *e* is uncircumcised
Mt. 10:27, what you hear in the *e*
Jn. 18:10, cut off his right *e*
1 Cor. 2:9, not seen, nor *e* heard
1 Cor. 12:16, if the *e* should say
Rev. 2:7, "He who has an *e*

EARLY
Mk. 16:2, Very *e* in the morning
Lk. 24:22, arrived at the tomb *e*

EARNEST
Heb. 2:1, must give the more *e*

EARNESTLY
Dt. 11:13, if you *e* obey My
Lk. 22:44, He prayed more *e*
2 Cor. 5:2, in this we groan, *e*
Jas. 5:17, *e* that it would not
Jude 3, you to contend *e*

EARS
he who has, to hear. Mt. 11:15; 13:16; Mk. 4:9,23; 7:16
have, but do not hear. Ps. 115:6; Isa. 42:20; Ezek. 12:2; Mt. 13:12; Mk. 8:18; Rom. 11:8
the Lord's, open to prayer. 2 Sam. 22:7; Ps. 18:6; 34:15; Jas. 5:4; 1 Pet. 3:12
opened by God. Job 33:16; 36:15; Ps. 40:6; Mk. 7:35

EARS
2 Ki. 21:12, both his *e* will tingle
Prov. 21:13, Whoever shuts his *e*
Isa. 6:10, And hear with their *e*
Mt. 11:15, "He who has *e*
Mt. 13:15, *e* are hard of hearing
2 Tim. 4:3, they have itching *e*
1 Pet. 3:12, *e* are open to their

EARTH
Dt. 28:23, *e* which is under you
1 Sam. 2:8, *e* are the LORD's
1 Chr. 16:33, coming to judge the *e*
Job 7:1, service for man on *e*
Job 26:7, He hangs the *e* on
Job 38:4, foundations of the *e*
Ps. 24:1, *e* is the LORD's
Ps. 47:9, the shields of the *e*
Ps. 65:9, You visit the *e*
Ps. 90:2, You had formed the *e*
Ps. 99:1, let the *e* be moved
Ps. 148:13, glory is above the *e*
Prov. 3:19, wisdom founded the *e*
Prov. 8:23, there was ever an *e*
Prov. 30:21, For three things the *e*
Eccl. 1:4, *e* abides forever
Isa. 11:4, for the meek of the *e*
Isa. 66:1, *e* is My footstool
Ezek. 43:2, and the *e* shone with
Amos 8:9, I will darken the *e*
Hab. 2:14, *e* will be filled
Mt. 5:5, shall inherit the *e*
Mt. 5:18, heaven and *e* pass away
Mt. 6:10, *e* as it is in heaven
Mt. 6:19, treasures on *e*
Heb. 12:26, then shook the *e*
Rev. 7:3, "Do not harm the *e*
Rev. 20:11, from whose face the *e*
Rev. 21:1, heaven and a new *e*

EARTHLY
Jn. 3:12, "If I have told you *e*
2 Cor. 5:1, that if our *e* house
Phil. 3:19, their mind on *e* things
Jas. 3:15, from above, but is *e*

EARTHQUAKE
1 Ki. 19:11, after the wind an *e*
Zech. 14:5, as you fled from the *e*
Mt. 28:2, there was a great *e*
Rev. 6:12, there was a great *e*

EARTHQUAKES
Isa. 29:6; Amos 1:1; Mt. 24:7; 27:54; Mk. 13:8; Acts 16:26; Rev. 8:5;

11:13; 16:18

EASE
Job 16:12, I was at *e*
Isa. 32:9, you women who are at *e*
Amos 6:1, to you who are at *e*
Lk. 12:19, take your *e*

EASIER
Mk. 2:9, "Which is *e*, to say
Mk. 10:25, "It is *e* for a camel

EAST
Gen. 2:14, goes toward the *e*
Ex. 10:13, the LORD brought an *e*
Job 38:24, *e* wind scattered
Ps. 103:12, As far as the *e*
Isa. 43:5, descendants from the *e*
Mt. 2:1, wise men from the *E*
Mt. 8:11, many will come from *e*
Lk. 13:29, will come from the *e*
Rev. 16:12, *e* might be prepared

EAT
Gen. 2:16, you may freely *e*
Gen. 3:17, 'You shall not *e*
Ps. 53:4, my people as they *e*
Prov. 25:27, good to *e* much honey
Ezek. 3:1, *e* this scroll
Amos 6:4, on your couches, *e*
Mic. 3:3, *e* the flesh of My
Mt. 6:25, life, what you will *e*
Mt. 26:17, You to *e* the Passover
Jn. 6:52, give us His flesh to *e*
Rom. 14:2, one believes he may *e*
Rom. 14:21, *e* meat nor drink wine
1 Cor. 8:13, I will never again *e*
2 Th. 3:10, neither shall he *e*
Jas. 5:3, *e* your flesh like fire

EATEN
Gen. 3:11, Have you *e* from the
Song 5:1, *e* my honeycomb with my
Hos. 10:13, *e* the fruit of lies
Acts 12:23, he was *e* by worms

EATS
Prov. 13:25, The righteous *e*
Lk. 15:2, receives sinners and *e*
Jn. 6:54, "Whoever *e* My flesh
Jn. 6:58, *e* this bread will live
Rom. 14:3, *e* despise him who does
Rom. 14:6, He who *e*, *e* to the
1 Cor. 11:29, unworthy manner *e*

EBAL
Mount, curses delivered from. Dt. 27:13; Josh. 8:33

EBED-MELECH
Ethiopian eunuch, intercedes with King Zedekiah for Jeremiah. Jer. 38:7; 39:16

EBENEZER
Israelites defeated by Philistines at. 1 Sam. 4:1
'Thus far the LORD has helped us,' (stone raised by Samuel in memory of defeat of the Philistines). 1 Sam. 7:12

EBER, Gen. 10:21; Lk. 3:35

EDEN, Gen. 2:8
Adam driven from. Gen. 3:24
mentioned. Isa. 51:3; Ezek. 28:13; 31:9; 36:35; Joel 2:3

EDIFICATION
Rom. 15:2, his good, leading to *e*
1 Cor. 14:3, prophesies speaks *e*
1 Cor. 14:26, things be done for *e*
2 Cor. 10:8, the Lord gave us for *e*
2 Cor. 13:10, has given me for *e*
1 Tim. 1:4, rather than godly *e*

EDIFIES
1 Cor. 8:1, puffs up, but love *e*
1 Cor. 14:4, he who prophesies *e*

EDIFY
1 Cor. 10:23, but not all things *e*
1 Th. 5:11, and *e* one another

EDIFYING
Eph. 4:16, of the body for the *e*

EDOM, Gen. 25:30
(Idumea), the land of Esau. Gen. 32:3; Isa. 63:1
prophecies concerning. Isa. 34; Jer. 25:21; 49:7; Ezek. 25:13; 35; Amos 1:11; Obad. 1

EDOMITES, Gen. 36:9
the descendants of Esau. Gen. 36
deny Moses passage through Edom. Num. 20:18
their possessions. Dt. 2:5; Josh. 24:4
not to be abhorred. Dt. 23:7
subdued by David. 2 Sam. 8:14
revolt. 2 Ki. 8:20; 2 Chr. 21:8
subdued by Amaziah. 2 Ki. 14:7; 2 Chr. 11:25

EFFECTIVELY
Gal. 2:8, for He who worked *e*
1 Th. 2:13, *e* works in you who

EGG
Job 6:6, in the white of an *e*
Lk. 11:12, Or if he asks for an *e*

EGLON, Jud. 3:12
oppresses Israel. Jud. 3:14
killed by Ehud. Jud. 3:21

EGYPT
Abram goes down into. Gen. 12:10
Joseph sold into. Gen. 37:36; his advancement, fall, imprisonment, and restoration there. Gen. 39; 40; 41
Jacob's sons go to buy grain in. Gen. 42
Jacob and all his descendants go there. Gen. 46:6
children of Israel grow mighty there. Ex. 1:7; afflicted, and build treasure cities. Ex. 1:11
plagued on account of Israelites. Ex. 7—11
children of Israel depart from. Ex. 13:17
army of, pursue and perish in the Red Sea. Ex. 14
kings of, harass Judah. 1 Ki. 14:25; 2 Ki. 23:29; 2 Chr. 12:2; 35:20; 36:3; Jer. 37:5
the remnant of Judah go there. Jer. 43:7
Jesus taken to. Mt. 2:13
prophecies concerning. Gen. 15:13; Isa. 11:11; 19; 20; 27:12; 30:1; Jer. 9:26; 25:19; 43:8; 44:28; 46; Ezek. 29—32; Dan. 11:8; Hos. 9:3; 11; Joel 3:19; Zech. 10:10; 14:18

EHUD
judge, delivers Israel. Jud. 3:15

EIGHT
1 Pet. 3:20, a few, that is, *e*

EKRON, Josh. 13:3
taken. Jud. 1:18
men of, stricken with tumors. 1 Sam. 5:12
their trespass offering for recovery. 1 Sam. 6:17
prophecies concerning. Amos 1:8; Zeph. 2:4; Zech. 9:5

EL BETHEL, Gen. 35:7

EL ELOHE ISRAEL
the altar erected by Jacob at Shechem. Gen. 33:20

ELAH, Gen. 36:41
king of Israel. 1 Ki. 16:8, 10
—— Valley of, Saul draws up in battle array against the Philistines. 1 Sam. 17:2
David kills Goliath there. 1 Sam. 17:49

ELAM
son of Shem. Gen. 10:22
—— Chedorlaomer, king of. Gen. 14

ELAMITES, Ezra 4:9; Acts 2:9

ELDER
Isa. 9:15, The *e* and honorable
1 Tim. 5:19, against an *e* except
1 Pet. 5:1, I who am a fellow *e*

ELDERS
seventy. Ex. 24:1; Num. 11:16
of Israel. Lev. 4:15; Dt. 21:19; 1 Sam. 16:4; Ezra 5:5; Ps. 107:32; Ezek. 8:1
of Egypt. Gen. 50:7
of the church. Acts 14:23; 15:4,6,23; 16:4; 20:17; Ti. 1:5; Jas. 5:14; 1 Pet. 5:1
Paul's charge to. Acts 20:17
Peter's charge to. 1 Pet. 5
the twenty-four. Rev. 4:4; 7:11; 14:3

ELDERS
Ex. 24:1, and seventy of the *e*
Ps. 105:22, And teach his *e*
Ezek. 7:26, and counsel from the *e*
Mt. 15:2, the tradition of the *e*
Lk. 9:22, be rejected by the *e*
Acts 14:23, they had appointed *e*
Acts 20:17, and called for the *e*
1 Tim. 5:17, *e* who rule well be
Ti. 1:5, lacking, and appoint *e*
Heb. 11:2, *e* obtained a good
Jas. 5:14, Let him call for the *e*
1 Pet. 5:1, *e* who are among you I
Rev. 4:4, I saw twenty-four *e*

ELDERSHIP
1 Tim. 4:14, of the hands of the *e*

ELEAZAR
son of Aaron, and chief priest. Ex. 6:23; 28; 29; Lev. 8; Num. 3:2; 4:16; 16:36; 20:26,28; 27:22; 31:13; 34:17; Josh. 17:4; 24:33
—— son of Abinadab, keeps the ark. 1 Sam. 7:1
—— one of David's captains. 2 Sam. 23:9; 1 Chr. 11:12

ELECT
Isa. 42:1, whom I uphold, My *E*
Isa. 45:4, and Israel My *e*
Isa. 65:22, *e* shall long enjoy
Mt. 24:31, gather together His *e*
Rom. 11:7, *e* have obtained it
1 Pet. 1:2, *e* according to the
1 Pet. 2:6, a chief cornerstone, *e*
2 Jn. 13, *e* sister greet you

ELECTION
Rom. 9:11; 11:5
by God. 1 Th. 1:4
its privileges and duties. Mk. 13:20; Lk. 18:7; Rom. 8:29; 1 Cor. 1:27; 2 Pet. 1:10

ELECTION
Rom. 11:28, *e* they are beloved
2 Pet. 1:10, call and *e* sure

ELEMENTS
Gal. 4:9, weak and beggarly *e*
2 Pet. 3:10, *e* will melt with

ELEVEN
Gen. 32:22, and his *e* sons
Mt. 28:16, *e* disciples went away
Acts 1:26, numbered with the *e*

ELHANAN
one of David's warriors. 2 Sam. 21:19; 23:24; 1 Chr. 11:26; 20:5

ELI
Eli, Eli, lama sabachtani? Mt. 27:46; Mk. 15:34
—— high priest and judge, blesses Hannah, who bears Samuel. 1 Sam. 1:17,20
Samuel brought to. 1 Sam. 1:25
wickedness of his sons. 1 Sam. 2:22
rebuked by man of God. 1 Sam. 2:27
ruin of his house shown by God. 1 Sam. 3:11
his sons killed. 1 Sam. 4:10
his death. 1 Sam. 4:18

ELIAKIM, 2 Ki. 18:18
chief minister of Hezekiah; his conference with Rabshakeh's ambassadors; mission to Isaiah. 2 Ki. 18; 19
prefigures kingdom of Christ. Isa. 22:20–25
—— son of Josiah, made king by Pharaoh, and named Jehoiakim. 2 Ki. 23:34; 2 Chr. 36:4

ELIASHIB
high priest, builds the wall. Neh. 3:1
allied with Tobiah. Neh. 13:4

ELIEZER
Abraham's steward. Gen. 15:2
—— son of Moses. Ex. 18:4; 1 Chr. 23:15
—— prophet. 2 Chr. 20:37

ELIHU, 1 Sam. 1:1
reproves Job's friends. Job 32; and Job's impatience. Job 33:8; and self-righteousness. Job 34:5
declares God's justice. Job 33:12; 34:10; 35:13; 36; power. Job 33—37; and mercy. Job 33:23; 34:28

ELIJAH
the Tishbite, prophet, predicts great drought. 1 Ki. 17:1; Lk. 4:25; Jas. 5:17
hides at the Brook Cherith, and is fed by ravens. 1 Ki. 17:5 (19:5)
raises the widow's son. 1 Ki. 17:21
his sacrifice at Carmel. 1 Ki. 18:38
kills the prophets of Baal at the Brook Kishon. 1 Ki. 18:40
flees from Jezebel into the wilderness of Beersheba. 1 Ki. 19; Rom. 11:2
anoints Elisha. 1 Ki. 19:19
by God's command denounces Ahab in Naboth's vineyard. 1 Ki. 21:17
his prediction fulfilled. 1 Ki. 22:38; 2 Ki. 9:36; 10:10
condemns Ahaziah for inquiring of Baal-Zebub. 2 Ki. 1:3,16
two companies sent to take him burnt with fire from heaven. 2 Ki. 1:10; Lk. 9:54
divides the Jordan. 2 Ki. 2:8
taken up by chariot of fire. 2 Ki. 2:11
his mantle taken by Elisha. 2 Ki. 2:13
appears at Christ's transfiguration. Mt. 17:3; Mk. 9:4; Lk. 9:30
precursor of John the Baptist. Mal. 4:5; Mt. 11:14; 16:14; Lk. 1:17; 9:8,19; Jn. 1:21

ELIM, Ex. 15:27

ELIMELECH, Ruth 1:2

ELIPHAZ, Gen. 36:4
rebukes Job. Job 4; 5; 15; 22
God's wrath against him. Job 42:7; he offers a burnt offering and Job prays for him. Job 42:8

ELISHA
succeeds Elijah. 1 Ki. 19:16
receives his mantle, and divides the Jordan. 2 Ki. 2:13
heals the waters with salt. 2 Ki. 2:22
bears destroy the youths who mock him. 2 Ki. 2:24
his miracles: water. 2 Ki. 3:16; oil. 4:4; Shunammite's son. 4:32; death in the pot. 4:40; feeds a hundred men with twenty loaves. 4:44; Naaman's leprosy. 5:14; iron floats. 6:5; Syrians struck blind. 6:18
prophesies abundance in Samaria when besieged. 2 Ki. 7:1
sends to anoint Jehu. 2 Ki. 9:1
his death. 2 Ki. 13:20
miracle wrought by his bones. 2 Ki. 13:21

ELIZABETH
cousin of Virgin Mary, and mother of John the Baptist. Lk. 1:5
angel promises her a son. Lk. 1:13
her greeting to Mary. Lk. 1:42

ELKANAH, Ex. 6:24
Samuel's father. 1 Sam. 1

ELOI (My God), Mk. 15:34

ELON, Gen. 26:34
judges Israel. Jud. 12:11

ELOQUENT
Ex. 4:10, "O my Lord, I am not *e*
Acts 18:24, an *e* man and mighty

ELUL
sixth month of Hebrew calendar, August–September. Neh. 6:15

ELYMAS, Acts 13:8
(Bar-Jesus). Acts 13:6

EMBALM
Gen. 50:2, to *e* his father

EMBANKMENT
Lk. 19:43, will build an *e*

EMERALDS
Ezek. 27:16, for your wares *e*

EMMAUS, Lk. 24:13
Christ talks with Cleopas and another on the way to. Lk. 24:15

EMPTY
Ex. 23:15, appear before Me *e*
1 Sam. 12:21, *e* things which
Job 35:13, not listen to *e* talk
Isa. 24:1, LORD makes the earth *e*
Mt. 12:44, comes, he finds it *e*
Lk. 1:53, He has sent away *e*
Eph. 5:6, you with *e* words

EMPTY-HEADED
Job 11:12, *e* man will be wise

EN DOR, Josh. 17:11
witch of. 1 Sam. 28:7

EN GEDI
city of Judah. Josh. 15:62
David dwells there. 1 Sam. 23:29; 24:1

EN ROGEL
fountain. Josh. 15:7; 18:16; 2 Sam. 17:17; 1 Ki. 1:9

ENABLED
1 Tim. 1:12, our Lord who has *e*

ENCHANTER
Isa. 3:3, and the expert *e*

ENCHANTMENTS
forbidden. Dt. 18:9; Isa. 47:9

ENCOURAGED
Rom. 1:12, is, that I may be *e*
1 Cor. 14:31, and all may be *e*
Col. 2:2, their hearts may be *e*

END
Job 8:7, yet your latter *e*
Ps. 39:4, make me to know my *e*
Ps. 119:33, shall keep it to the *e*
Prov. 14:12, *e* is the way of death

Eccl. 4:16, There was no *e* of all
Isa. 46:10, Declaring the *e*
Lam. 4:18, Our *e* was near
Ezek. 21:25, whose iniquity shall *e*
Dan. 12:8, what shall be the *e*
Amos 8:2, *e* has come upon my
Mt. 13:39, the harvest is the *e*
Mt. 24:6, to pass, but the *e*
Mt. 28:20, always, even to the *e*
Jn. 13:1, He loved them to the *e*
Rom. 10:4, For Christ is the *e*
Heb. 3:6, the hope firm to the *e*
Heb. 9:26, but now, once at the *e*
Jas. 5:11, of Job and seen the *e*
1 Pet. 4:7, But the *e* of all
1 Pet. 4:17, what will be the *e*
2 Pet. 2:20, the latter *e* is worse
Rev. 2:26, My works until the *e*
Rev. 22:13, Beginning and the *E*

ENDANGER, Eccl. 10:9; Dan. 1:10

ENDEAVOR, Ps. 28:4

ENDEAVORING
Eph. 4:3, *e* to keep the unity

ENDLESS
1 Tim. 1:4, and *e* genealogies
Heb. 7:16, to the power of an *e*

ENDS
Ps. 22:27, All the *e* of the world
Prov. 30:4, established all the *e*
Mt. 12:42, she came from the *e*
Acts 13:47, to the *e* of the
Rom. 10:18, their words to the *e*

ENDUE, Lk. 24:49

ENDURANCE
Heb. 10:36, For you have need of *e*

ENDURE
Ps. 9:7, But the LORD shall *e*
Ps. 72:5, as the sun and moon *e*
Ps. 72:17, His name shall *e*
Prov. 27:24, nor does a crown *e*
Ezek. 22:14, "Can your heart *e*
1 Cor. 4:12, persecuted, we *e*
2 Tim. 2:10, Therefore I *e* all
Jas. 5:11, them blessed who *e*

ENDURED
2 Tim. 3:11, what persecutions I *e*
Heb. 6:15, he had patiently *e*
Heb. 11:27, *e* as seeing Him who
Heb. 12:3, consider Him who *e*

ENDURES
Ps. 100:5, And His truth *e*
Ps. 136:1, For His mercy *e*
Mt. 10:22, But he who *e* to the
Mt. 13:21, *e* only for a while
Jn. 6:27, for the food which *e*
1 Cor. 3:14, he has built on it *e*
1 Cor. 13:7, hopes all things, *e*
Jas. 1:12, is the man who *e*
1 Pet. 1:25, word of the LORD *e*

ENDURING
Ps. 19:9, the LORD is clean, *e*
Heb. 10:34, *e* possession for

ENEMIES
treatment of. Ex. 23:4; 1 Sam. 24:10; Job 31:29; Prov. 24:17; 25:21; Mt. 5:44; Lk. 6:35
David and Saul. 1 Sam. 24:10; 26:9
God delivers out of the hand of. 1 Sam. 12:11; Ezra 8:31; Ps. 18:48; 59; 61:3
of God, their punishment. Ex. 15:6; Dt. 32:41; Jud. 5:31; Est. 7; 8; Ps. 68:1; 92:9; Isa. 1:24; 37:36; 2 Th. 1:8; Rev. 21:8

ENEMIES
Num. 10:35, Your *e* be scattered
Ps. 18:48, delivers me from my *e*
Ps. 23:5, the presence of my *e*
Ps. 25:2, Let not my *e* triumph
Ps. 38:19, But my *e* are vigorous
Ps. 72:9, *e* will lick the dust
Ps. 119:98, me wiser than my *e*
Ps. 139:22, I count them my *e*
Mic. 7:6, *e* are the men of his
Mt. 5:44, to you, love your *e*
Mt. 10:36, *e* will be those
Lk. 1:71, be saved from our *e*
Rom. 5:10, *e* we were reconciled
Rom. 11:28, the gospel they are *e*
1 Cor. 15:25, till He has put all *e*
Col. 1:21, were alienated and *e*
Heb. 10:13, His *e* are made His
Rev. 11:5, and devours their *e*

ENEMY
Ex. 23:22, then I will be an *e*
Job 13:24, regard me as Your *e*
Job 33:10, He counts me as His *e*
Ps. 7:4, or have plundered my *e*
Ps. 8:2, You may silence the *e*
Ps. 41:11, *e* does not triumph
Ps. 55:12, *e* who reproaches me
Ps. 143:3, *e* has persecuted my
Prov. 25:21, If your *e* is hungry
Prov. 27:6, *e* are deceitful
Jer. 30:14, with the wound of an *e*
Mic. 7:8, rejoice over me, my *e*
Mt. 5:43, and hate your *e*
1 Cor. 15:26, last *e* that will be
Gal. 4:16, become your *e* because
2 Th. 3:15, not count him as an *e*
Jas. 4:4, makes himself an *e*

ENGRAVE
Ex. 28:9, two onyx stones and *e*
Zech. 3:9, *e* its inscription

ENJOY
Lev. 26:34, *e* its sabbaths as long
Eccl. 2:1, therefore *e* pleasure
1 Tim. 6:17, richly all things to *e*
Heb. 11:25, than to *e* the passing

ENJOYMENT
Eccl. 8:15, So I commended *e*

ENLARGES
Job 12:23, He *e* nations
Hab. 2:5, *e* his desire as hell

ENLIGHTEN
Ps. 13:3, *E* my eyes
Ps. 18:28, the LORD my God will *e*

ENLIGHTENED
Heb. 6:4, those who were once *e*

ENMITY
Gen. 3:15, And I will put *e*
Rom. 8:7, the carnal mind is *e*
Eph. 2:15, in His flesh the *e*
Eph. 2:16, putting to death the *e*
Jas. 4:4, with the world is *e*

ENOCH
son of Cain. Gen. 4:17
——— son of Jared. Gen. 5:18; his faith. Heb. 11:5; prophecy. Jude 14; translation. Gen. 5:24

ENOSH, Gen. 4:26; 1 Chr. 1:1

ENOUGH
Prov. 30:15, never say, "*E*
Mk. 14:41, It is *e*
Lk. 15:17, servants have bread *e*

ENRAGED
Acts 26:11, being exceedingly *e*
Rev. 12:17, And the dragon was *e*

ENRAPTURED
Prov. 5:19, And always be *e*

ENRICHED
1 Cor. 1:5, that you were *e*
2 Cor. 9:11, while you are *e*

ENSNARED
Prov. 12:13, The wicked is *e*

ENSNARES
Heb. 12:1, sin which so easily *e*

ENTANGLE
Mt. 22:15, how they might *e*

ENTANGLES
2 Tim. 2:4, engaged in warfare *e*

ENTER
Ps. 100:4, *E* into His gates
Ps. 143:2, Do not *e* into judgment
Isa. 2:10, *E* into the rock
Isa. 57:2, He shall *e* into peace
Mt. 5:20, you will by no means *e*
Mt. 7:13, "*E* by the narrow
Mt. 19:24, *e* the kingdom of God
Mt. 25:21, *E* into the joy of your
Mt. 26:41, and pray, lest you *e*
Lk. 13:24, "Strive to *e* through
Jn. 10:1, you, he who does not *e*
Heb. 4:3, who have believed do *e*
Heb. 10:19, *e* the Holiest by the
Rev. 15:8, *e* the temple till the
Rev. 22:14, *e* through the gates

ENTERED
Lk. 22:3, Then Satan *e* Judas
Rom. 5:12, through one man sin *e*
1 Cor. 2:9, ear heard, nor have *e*
Heb. 6:20, the forerunner has *e*
Heb. 9:12, *e* the Most Holy Place

ENTERS
Jn. 10:9, If anyone *e* by Me
Heb. 6:19, *e* the Presence behind

ENTHRONED
Ps. 22:3, You are holy, *e* in

ENTICED
Jas. 1:14, his own desires and *e*

ENTICING
Prov. 7:21, *e* speech she caused

ENTIRELY
1 Tim. 4:15, give yourself *e*

ENTRANCE
Ps. 119:130, The *e* of Your words
2 Pet. 1:11, *e* will be supplied

ENTREAT
Ruth 1:16, "*E* me not to leave you
Mal. 1:9, "But now *e* God's favor
1 Cor. 4:13, being defamed, we *e*

ENTREATED
1 Ki. 13:6, man of God *e* the LORD
Ezra 8:23, *e* our God for this

ENVIOUS
Ps. 73:3, For I was *e* of the
Prov. 24:1, Do not be *e* of evil
Acts 7:9, patriarchs, becoming *e*

ENVY
Job 5:2, *e* slays a simple
Prov. 3:31, *e* the oppressor
Prov. 14:30, *e* is rottenness
Prov. 23:17, not let your heart *e*
Eccl. 9:6, *e* have now perished
Rom. 1:29, full of *e*
Rom. 13:13, not in strife and *e*
1 Cor. 13:4, love does not *e*
Gal. 5:21, *e*, murders
Ti. 3:3, living in malice and *e*
Jas. 3:16, For where *e* and
1 Pet. 2:1, deceit, hypocrisy, *e*

EPAENETUS, Rom. 16:5

EPAPHRAS
commended. Col. 1:7; 4:12

EPAPHRODITUS
Paul's joy at his recovery. Phil. 2:25
his kindness. Phil. 4:18

EPHESIANS, Acts 19:28
Paul's epistle to. Eph. 1
election. Eph. 1:4
adoption of grace. Eph. 1:6
dead in sin, made alive. Eph. 2:1,5
Gentiles made near. Eph. 2:13
unity and kindness commanded. Eph. 4—6

EPHESUS
visited by Paul. Acts 18:19; 19:1
miracles there. Acts 19:11
tumult there. Acts 19:24
Paul's address at Miletus to the elders of. Acts 20:17
Paul fights with beasts there. 1 Cor. 15:32
tarries there. 1 Cor. 16:8

EPHPHATHA, Mk. 7:34

EPHRAIM
younger son of Joseph. Gen. 41:52
and Manasseh, blessed by Jacob. Gen. 48:14
his descendants:
numbered. Num. 1:10,32; 2:18; 26:35; 1 Chr. 7:20
their possessions. Josh. 16:5; 17:14; Jud. 1:29
attack the Midianites. Jud. 7:24
quarrel with Gideon. Jud. 8:1; and Jephthah. Jud. 12
revolt from the house of David. 1 Ki. 12:25
attack Ahaz and Judah. 2 Chr. 28:6,7
release their prisoners. 2 Chr. 28:12
carried into captivity. 2 Ki. 17:5; Ps. 78:9,67; Jer. 7:15
repenting, called God's son. Jer. 31:20
prophecies concerning. Isa. 7; 9:9; 11:13; 28:1; Hos. 5—14; Zech. 9:10; 10:7

EPHRATHAH, 1 Chr. 2:50
(Bethlehem). Ps. 132:6; Mic. 5:2
spelled Ephrath. Gen. 35:16

EPHRON, Gen. 23:8
the Hittite, sells Machpelah to Abraham. Gen. 23:10

EPICUREANS
philosophers, followers of Epicurus; encounter Paul at Athens. Acts 17:18

EPISTLE
2 Cor. 3:2, You are our *e* written
2 Cor. 3:3, you are an *e*
2 Th. 2:15, by word or our *e*
2 Th. 3:14, our word in this *e*
2 Th. 3:17, is a sign in every *e*

EPISTLES
2 Cor. 3:1, *e* of commendation to
2 Pet. 3:16, as also in all his *e*

EQUAL
Ps. 55:13, it was you, a man my *e*
Mt. 20:12, and you made them *e*
Jn. 5:18, making Himself *e*
Phil. 2:6, it robbery to be *e*

EQUALITY
2 Cor. 8:14, that there may be *e*

EQUITY
Ps. 99:4, You have established *e*
Prov. 1:3, judgment, and *e*
Isa. 59:14, and *e* cannot enter
Mic. 3:9, and pervert all *e*
Mal. 2:6, with Me in peace and *e*

ERASTUS
ministers to Paul. Acts 19:22; Rom. 16:23; 2 Tim. 4:20

ERR
Isa. 3:12, you cause you to *e*
Jer. 23:13, My people Israel to *e*

ERROR
Eccl. 5:6, God that it was an *e*
Rom. 1:27, *e* which was due
Jas. 5:20, a sinner from the *e*
2 Pet. 3:17, led away with the *e*
1 Jn. 4:6, and the spirit of *e*
Jude 11, run greedily in the *e*

ERRORS
Ps. 19:12, can understand his *e*

ESARHADDON
powerful king of Assyria. 2 Ki. 19:37; Ezra 4:2; Isa. 37:38

ESAU
son of Isaac. Gen. 25:25 (Mal. 1:2; Rom. 9:13)
sells his birthright. Gen. 25:29 (Heb. 12:16)
deprived of the blessing. Gen. 27:38
his anger against Jacob. Gen. 27:41; and reconciliation. Gen. 33
his riches and descendants. Gen. 36; 1 Chr. 1:35

ESCAPE
Gen. 19:17, *E* to the mountains
Job 11:20, and they shall not *e*
Ps. 56:7, Shall they *e* by
Prov. 19:5, speaks lies will not *e*
Isa. 20:6, and how shall we *e*
Lk. 21:36, *e* all these things
Rom. 2:3, same, that you will *e*
1 Cor. 10:13, make the way of *e*
Heb. 2:3, how shall we *e* if we
Heb. 12:25, *e* who refused Him who

ESCAPED
Job 19:20, my flesh, and I have *e*
Ps. 124:7, Our soul has *e* as a
2 Pet. 2:20, after they have *e*

ESH-BAAL, 1 Chr. 8:33

ESHCOL, Gen. 14:13
grapes of. Num. 13:23

ESTABLISH
2 Chr. 9:8, to *e* them forever
Ps. 89:4, 'Your seed I will *e*
Ps. 90:17, *e* the work of our
Ps. 119:38, *E* Your word to Your
Ezek. 16:60, *e* an everlasting
Amos 5:15, *e* justice in the gate
Rom. 10:3, seeking to *e* their own
2 Th. 3:3, faithful, who will *e*
Jas. 5:8, *E* your hearts
1 Pet. 5:10, a while, perfect, *e*

ESTABLISHED
1 Chr. 16:30, also is firmly *e*
2 Chr. 1:9, David my father be *e*
Ps. 40:2, a rock, and *e* my steps
Ps. 78:5, *e* a testimony in Jacob
Ps. 93:2, Your throne is *e*
Prov. 4:26, let all your ways be *e*
Prov. 8:28, *e* the clouds above
Prov. 12:19, lip shall be *e* forever
Isa. 2:2, house shall be *e*
Jer. 10:12, by His power, He has *e*
Col. 2:7, built up in Him and *e*
Heb. 8:6, covenant, which was *e*
Heb. 13:9, that the heart be *e*

ESTABLISHES
Prov. 29:4, The king *e* the land by
2 Cor. 1:21, Now He who *e* us with

ESTEEM
Prov. 18:11, high wall in his own *e*
Isa. 53:3, and we did not *e*
Phil. 2:3, *e* others better than
Phil. 2:29, and hold such men in *e*
1 Th. 5:13, *e* them very highly

ESTEEMED
Lk. 16:15, For what is highly *e*
1 Cor. 6:4, those who are least *e*

ESTEEMS
Rom. 14:5, One person *e* one day

ESTHER, Est. 2:7
(Hadassah), made queen in the place of Vashti. Est. 2:17
pleads for her people. Est. 7:3–4

ESTRANGED
Ps. 58:3, The wicked are *e*
Ezek. 14:5, because they are all *e*
Gal. 5:4, You have become *e*

ETERNAL
Dt. 33:27, *e* God is your refuge
Eccl. 12:5, For man goes to his *e*
Mt. 19:16, I do that I may have *e*
Mt. 19:29, and inherit *e* life
Mk. 10:30, in the age to come, *e*
Jn. 3:15, not perish but have *e*
Jn. 5:39, you think you have *e*
Jn. 10:28, I give them *e* life
Jn. 17:2, that He should give *e*
Jn. 17:3, "And this is *e* life
Rom. 2:7, *e* life to those who by
Rom. 6:23, the gift of God is *e*
2 Cor. 4:17, *e* weight of glory
2 Cor. 4:18, are not seen are *e*
2 Cor. 5:1, not made with hands, *e*
1 Tim. 6:12, lay hold on *e* life
Ti. 1:2, *e* life which God
Heb. 6:2, and of *e* judgment
1 Jn. 1:2, *e* life which was
1 Jn. 3:15, that no murderer has *e*
1 Jn. 5:11, God has given us *e*
1 Jn. 5:13, that you have *e* life
Jude 21, Jesus Christ unto *e*

ETERNITY
Eccl. 3:11, Also He has put *e*
Isa. 57:15, One who inhabits *e*

ETHIOPIANS
invading Judah, subdued by Asa. 2 Chr. 14:9. *See* Num. 12:1; 2 Ki. 19:19; Est. 1:1; Job 28:19
prophecies concerning. Ps. 68:31; 87:4; Isa. 18; 20; 43:3; 45:14; Jer. 46:9; Ezek. 30:4; 38:5; Nah. 3:9; Zeph. 3:10

EUBULUS, 2 Tim. 4:21

EUNICE
commended. Acts 16:1; 2 Tim. 1:5

EUNUCH
Acts 8:27, of Ethiopia, a *e*

EUNUCHS
Mt. 19:12, made themselves *e*

EUODIA, Phil. 4:2

EUPHRATES
river. Gen. 2:14; 15:18; Dt. 11:24; Josh. 1:4; 2 Sam. 8:3; Jer. 13:4; 46:2; 51:63
typical. Rev. 9:14; 16:12

EUROCLYDON
a wind. Acts 27:14

EUTYCHUS, Acts 20:9
restored. Acts 20:7

EVANGELIST
Acts 21:8, of Philip the *e*
2 Tim. 4:5, do the work of an *e*

EVANGELISTS
Eph. 4:11, some prophets, some *e*

EVE, Gen. 3:20
created. Gen. 1:27; 2:18
her fall and fate. Gen. 3. *See* ADAM

EVEN
Prov. 14:13, *E* in laughter the
Prov. 20:11, *E* a child is known
1 Cor. 11:14, *e* nature itself teach
2 Pet. 2:1, *e* denying the Lord who

EVENING
Ps. 59:6, At *e* they return
Ps. 90:6, *e* it is cut down and
Ps. 141:2, of my hands as the *e*
Eccl. 11:6, *e* do not withhold your
Hab. 1:8, and more fierce than *e*

EVERLASTING
1 Chr. 16:36, God of Israel from *e*
Ps. 103:17, of the LORD is from *e*
Ps. 119:142, righteousness is an *e*
Ps. 145:13, Your kingdom is an *e*
Isa. 26:4, in YAH, the LORD, is *e*
Isa. 60:19, will be to you an *e*
Isa. 63:16, from *E* is Your name
Dan. 12:2, awake, some to *e* life
Jn. 3:16, not perish but have *e*
Jn. 5:24, who sent Me has *e*
Jn. 6:27, endures to *e* life
Jn. 6:40, in Him may have *e*
Jn. 6:47, believes in Me has *e*
Acts 13:46, unworthy of *e* life
Gal. 6:8, of the Spirit reap *e*
2 Th. 1:9, *e* destruction from

EVERYONE
Jer. 25:5, said, 'Repent now *e*
Jn. 3:8, *e* who is born of the
Jn. 18:37, *E* who is of the truth

EVIDENCE
Heb. 11:1, *e* of things not seen

EVIDENT
Gal. 3:11, the sight of God is *e*
1 Tim. 5:25, of some are clearly *e*
Heb. 7:14, *e* that our Lord arose

EVIL
Gen. 2:9, of good and *e*
Gen. 3:5, knowing good and *e*
Gen. 6:5, his heart was only *e*
Gen. 47:9, *e* have been the
Ezra 4:12, rebellious and *e* city
Job 5:19, *e* shall touch you
Job 30:26, I looked for good, *e*
Ps. 5:4, nor shall *e* dwell
Ps. 23:4, I will fear no *e*
Ps. 34:21, *E* shall slay the
Ps. 36:4, he does not abhor *e*
Ps. 52:3, *e* more than good
Ps. 91:10, *e* shall befall you
Prov. 10:23, To do *e* is like sport
Prov. 12:21, shall be filled with *e*
Prov. 14:19, *e* will bow before the
Prov. 15:3, Keeping watch on the *e*
Prov. 17:13, Whoever rewards *e*
Prov. 17:13, *e* will not depart
Prov. 31:12, *e* all the days of her
Eccl. 5:13, There is a severe *e*
Eccl. 9:3, of men are full of *e*
Isa. 5:20, to those who call *e*
Isa. 57:1, is taken away from *e*
Jer. 29:11, of peace and not of *e*
Jer. 44:7, commit this great *e*
Amos 5:14, Seek good and not *e*
Mt. 6:13, deliver us from the *e*
Mt. 7:11, If you then, being *e*
Mt. 9:4, "Why do you think *e*
Mt. 12:35, *e* treasure brings
Jn. 3:20, everyone practicing *e*
Jn. 18:23, bear witness of the *e*
Rom. 7:19, *e* I will not to do
Rom. 7:21, then a law, that *e*
Rom. 9:11, done any good or *e*
Rom. 12:9, Abhor what is *e*
Rom. 12:17, Repay no one *e* for
Rom. 12:21, not be overcome by *e*
Rom. 16:19, simple concerning *e*
1 Cor. 13:5, provoked, thinks no *e*
1 Th. 5:22, from every form of *e*

EVIL-MERODACH, 2 Ki. 25:27
king of Babylon, restores Jehoiachin. 2 Ki. 25:27; Jer. 52:31

EVIL-MINDEDNESS
Rom. 1:29, strife, deceit, *e*

EVILDOER
Jn. 18:30, "If He were not an *e*
2 Tim. 2:9, suffer trouble as an *e*
1 Pet. 4:15, a thief, an *e*

EVILDOERS
Ps. 37:9, *e* shall be cut off
Ps. 119:115, depart from me, you *e*
Isa. 1:4, iniquity, A brood of *e*
Isa. 14:20, *e* shall never be
1 Pet. 2:12, against you as *e*

EVILS
Ps. 40:12, *e* have surrounded me
Jer. 2:13, have committed two *e*

EXALT
Ex. 15:2, God, and I will *e*
1 Sam. 2:10, *e* the horn of His
Ps. 34:3, *e* His name together
Ps. 99:5, *E* the LORD our God
Ps. 118:28, are my God, I will *e*
Ps. 137:6, if I do not *e*
Isa. 14:13, into heaven, I will *e*
Ezek. 21:26, *E* the humble
Dan. 8:25, and he shall *e* himself

EXALTATION
Ps. 75:6, *e* comes neither from
Isa. 13:3, who rejoice in My *e*
Jas. 1:9, brother glory in his *e*

EXALTED
2 Sam. 22:47, Let God be *e*
2 Chr. 6:2, built You an *e*
Neh. 9:5, name, which is *e*
Ps. 12:8, when vileness is *e*
Ps. 46:10, I will be *e* among the
Ps. 75:10, righteous shall be *e*
Ps. 89:17, favor our horn is *e*
Ps. 97:9, You are *e* far above
Ps. 148:13, His name alone is *e*
Prov. 11:11, upright the city is *e*
Isa. 2:11, LORD alone shall be *e*
Isa. 40:4, valley shall be *e*
Acts 5:31, "Him God has *e*
2 Cor. 12:7, And lest I should be *e*
Phil. 2:9, also has highly *e*

EXALTS
Prov. 14:34, Righteousness *e*
2 Cor. 10:5, high thing that *e*
2 Th. 2:4, *e* himself above all

EXAMINE
Ps. 26:2, *E* me, O LORD
1 Cor. 11:28, But let a man *e*
Gal. 6:4, But let each one *e*

EXAMPLE
of Christ. Mt. 11:29; Jn. 13:15; Rom. 15:3,5; Phil. 2:5; 1 Pet. 2:21
of prophets. Heb. 6:12; Jas. 5:10
of apostles. 1 Cor. 4:16; 11:1; Phil. 3:17; 4:9; 1 Th. 1:6

EXAMPLE
Mt. 1:19, to make her a public *e*
Jn. 13:15, I have given you an *e*
Phil. 3:17, in following my *e*
2 Th. 3:9, to make ourselves an *e*
1 Tim. 4:12, youth, but be an *e*
1 Pet. 2:21, us, leaving us an *e*
2 Pet. 2:6, making them an *e*
Jude 7, are set forth as an *e*

EXAMPLES
1 Cor. 10:11, happened to them as *e*
1 Th. 1:7, so that you became *e*
1 Pet. 5:3, to you, but being *e*

EXCEEDING
Eph. 2:7, He might show the *e*

EXCEEDINGLY
1 Chr. 22:5, for the LORD must be *e*
Ps. 21:6, You have made him *e*
Eccl. 7:24, is far off and *e* deep
Mt. 4:8, *e* high mountain
Mt. 5:12, "Rejoice and be *e*

EXCEEDS
Mt. 5:20, your righteousness *e*

EXCEL
Ps. 103:20, you His angels, who *e*
Prov. 31:29, but you *e* them all
1 Cor. 14:12, that you seek to *e*

EXCELLENCE
Ex. 15:7, *e* You have overthrown
1 Cor. 2:1, did not come with *e*

EXCELLENT
Job 37:23, He is *e* in power
Ps. 141:5, It shall be as *e*
Prov. 8:6, will speak of *e* things
Song 5:15, like Lebanon, *e*
Isa. 12:5, for He has done *e*
Isa. 28:29, in counsel and *e*
Dan. 5:12, "Inasmuch as an *e*
Rom. 2:18, the things that are *e*
Phil. 1:10, the things that are *e*
Heb. 11:4, *e* sacrifice than Cain
2 Pet. 1:17, came to Him from the *E*

EXCELS
Prov. 22:29, Do you see a man who *e*
Eccl. 2:13, I saw that wisdom *e*
2 Cor. 3:10, of the glory that *e*

EXCHANGE
Mt. 16:26, give in *e* for his soul

EXCHANGED
Job 28:17, Nor can it be *e*
Rom. 1:25, *e* the truth of God for
Rom. 1:26, For even their women *e*

EXCLUDE
Lk. 6:22, you, and when they *e*
Gal. 4:17, they want to *e* you

EXCUSE
Eccl. 5:6, God be angry at your *e*
Jn. 15:22, now they have no *e*
Rom. 1:20, they are without *e*
2 Cor. 12:19, do you think that we *e*

EXCUSES
Lk. 14:18, began to make *e*

EXECUTE
Ps. 149:7, *e* vengeance on the
Jer. 7:5, if you thoroughly *e*
Hos. 11:9, *e* the fierceness
Jn. 5:27, *e* judgment also
Rom. 13:4, *e* wrath on him who

EXECUTES
Ps. 9:16, by the judgment He *e*
Ps. 103:6, *e* righteousness
Ps. 146:7, *e* justice for the
Mic. 7:9, *e* justice for me

EXERCISE
Mt. 20:25, those who are great *e*
1 Tim. 4:7, *e* yourself toward
1 Tim. 4:8, *e* profits a little

EXERCISED
Heb. 5:14, have their senses *e*

EXHORT
2 Th. 3:12, we command and *e*
1 Tim. 5:1, *e* him as a father
1 Tim. 6:2, and *e* these things
Ti. 1:9, doctrine, both to *e*
Ti. 2:15, Speak these things, *e*
Heb. 3:13, *e* one another

EXHORTATION
Acts 13:15, you have any word of *e*
Rom. 12:8, he who exhorts, in *e*
1 Tim. 4:13, to reading, to *e*
Heb. 13:22, with the word of *e*

EXHORTED
Jer. 11:7, For I earnestly *e*
Acts 15:32, *e* and strengthened
1 Th. 2:11, you know how we *e*

EXILE
2 Sam. 15:19, and also an *e* from
Isa. 51:14, The captive *e* hastens

EXIST
Rom. 4:17, things which do not *e*
Rev. 4:11, by Your will they *e*

EXPECT
Lk. 12:40, an hour you do not *e*

EXPECTATION
Ps. 9:18, The *e* of the poor
Ps. 62:5, God alone, for my *e*
Lk. 3:15, the people were in *e*
Heb. 10:27, a certain fearful *e*

EXPERIENCE, Gen. 30:27

EXPERT
Isa. 3:3, and the *e* enchanter
Jer. 50:9, those of an *e* warrior
Acts 26:3, because you are *e*

EXPLAIN
Gen. 41:24, no one who could *e*
Jud. 14:14, days they could not *e*
Mt. 15:15, "*E* this parable to us
Heb. 5:11, to say, and hard to *e*

EXPLAINED
Mk. 4:34, He *e* all things to His

EXPLOIT
Isa. 58:3, *e* all your
Mal. 3:5, against those who *e*
2 Pet. 2:3, they will *e* you with

EXPLOITS, Dan. 11:32

EXPOSED
Jn. 3:20, his deeds should be *e*
Eph. 5:13, all things that are *e*

EXPOUNDED
Lk. 24:27, He *e* to them in all

EXPRESS
Eccl. 1:8, man cannot *e* it
Heb. 1:3, of His glory and the *e*

EXPRESSLY
Ezek. 1:3, of the LORD came *e*
1 Tim. 4:1, Now the Spirit *e*

EXTEND
Ps. 109:12, none to *e* mercy to him
Isa. 66:12, "Behold, I will *e*
2 Cor. 10:14, did not *e* to you

EXTINGUISHED
Job 17:1, broken, my days are *e*
Isa. 43:17, they are *e*

EXTOL
Ps. 30:1, I will *e* You
Ps. 68:4, *e* Him who rides

EXTOLLED
Isa. 52:13, shall be exalted and *e*

EXTORTION
Prov. 28:8, *e* gathers it for him
Ezek. 22:12, your neighbors by *e*
Mt. 23:25, they are full of *e*

EXTORTIONERS
1 Cor. 6:10, *e* will inherit

EXULT
Job 6:10, in anguish I would *e*

EYE
Ex. 21:24, "*e* for *e*
Job 42:5, the ear, but now my *e*
Ps. 32:8, guide you with My *e*
Ps. 33:18, Behold, the *e* of the
Ps. 94:9, He who formed the *e*
Prov. 20:12, and the seeing *e*
Prov. 22:9, who has a generous *e*
Prov. 28:22, A man with an evil *e*
Prov. 30:17, *e* that mocks his
Eccl. 1:8, *e* is not satisfied
Eccl. 4:8, labors, nor is his *e*
Isa. 52:8, for they shall see *e*
Isa. 64:4, *e* seen any God besides
Zech. 2:8, the apple of His *e*
Mt. 5:29, if your right *e*
Mt. 5:38, it was said, 'An *e*
Mt. 7:3, plank in your own *e*
Mt. 18:9, *e* causes you to sin
Mt. 20:15, Or is your *e* evil
Mk. 9:47, *e* causes you sin

Lk. 18:25, the *e* of a needle
1 Cor. 12:16, "Because I am not an *e*
1 Cor. 12:17, whole body were an *e*
1 Cor. 15:52, the twinkling of an *e*
Rev. 1:7, every *e* will see Him
Rev. 3:18, your eyes with *e* salve

EYELIDS
Ps. 11:4, His eyes behold, His *e*
Prov. 4:25, *e* look right before

EYES
Gen. 3:5, *e* will be opened
Num. 10:31, and you can be our *e*
2 Ki. 9:30, she put paint on her *e*
2 Chr. 16:9, "For the *e* of the
Job 10:4, Do You have *e* of flesh
Job 19:27, And my *e* shall behold
Job 29:15, I was *e* to the blind
Job 39:29, *e* observe from afar
Ps. 10:8, *e* are secretly fixed
Ps. 25:15, *e* are ever toward the
Ps. 34:15, The *e* of the LORD are
Ps. 69:3, *e* fail while I wait
Ps. 91:8, *e* shall you look
Ps. 121:1, I will lift up my *e*
Ps. 132:4, not give sleep to my *e*
Ps. 139:16, *e* saw my substance
Prov. 4:25, *e* look straight ahead
Prov. 17:24, but the *e* of a fool
Prov. 23:5, Will you set your *e*
Prov. 23:29, Who has redness of *e*
Prov. 26:5, be wise in his own *e*
Prov. 27:20, so the *e* of man are
Eccl. 2:14, The wise man's *e*
Eccl. 6:9, *e* than the wandering
Song 1:15, You have dove's *e*
Isa. 6:5, *e* have seen the King
Isa. 29:18, of the book, and the *e*
Isa. 38:14, *e* fail from looking
Jer. 5:3, O LORD, are not Your *e*
Jer. 5:21, Who have *e* and see
Jer. 13:17, *e* will weep bitterly
Jer. 24:6, For I will set My *e*
Ezek. 1:18, rims were full of *e*
Ezek. 10:12, full of *e* all around
Dan. 7:20, that horn which had *e*
Dan. 8:5, horn between his *e*
Hab. 1:13, You are of purer *e*
Mt. 13:16, blessed are your *e*
Jn. 9:15, "He put clay on my *e*
Acts 28:27, *e* they have closed
Rom. 11:8, *e* that they should not
Gal. 4:15, plucked out your own *e*
1 Jn. 1:1, have seen with our *e*
1 Jn. 2:16, the lust of the *e*
Rev. 1:14, as snow, and His *e*
Rev. 3:18, and anointed your *e*
Rev. 4:6, creatures full of *e*
Rev. 5:6, horns and seven *e*
Rev. 21:4, tear from their *e*

EYESERVICE
Eph. 6:6, not with *e*
Col. 3:22, the flesh, not with *e*

EYEWITNESSES
Lk. 1:2, the beginning were *e*
2 Pet. 1:16, *e* of His majesty

EZEKIEL, Ezek. 1:3
sent to house of Israel. Ezek. 2; 3; 33:7
his visions of: God's glory. Ezek. 1; 8; 10; 11:22
the Jews' abominations, etc. Ezek. 8:5
their punishment. Ezek. 9; 11
the resurrection of dry bones. Ezek. 37
the measuring of the temple. Ezek. 40
intercedes for Israel. Ezek. 9:8; 11:13
his muteness. Ezek. 3:26; 24:26; 33:22
his parables. Ezek. 15; 16; 17; 19; 23; 24
exhorts Israel against idols. Ezek. 14:1; 20:1; 33:30
relates Israel's rebellions. Ezek. 20; and the sins of the rulers and people of Jerusalem. 22; 23; 24
predicts Israel's and the nations' doom. Ezek. 21; 25

EZION GEBER
on the Red Sea. Num. 33:35; 1 Ki. 9:26

EZRA, Ezra 7:1
scribe, goes up from Babylon to Jerusalem. Ezra 7:1; 8:1
his commission from Artaxerxes to rebuild the temple. Ezra 7:11
fast ordered by. Ezra 8:21
rebukes the people. Ezra 10:9
reads the Book of the Law. Neh. 8
reforms corruptions. Ezra 10; Neh. 13

FABLES
1 Tim. 1:4, nor give heed to *f*
2 Tim. 4:4, be turned aside to *f*
2 Pet. 1:16, cunningly devised *f*

FACE
Gen. 32:30, "For I have seen God *f*
Ex. 34:29, *f* shone while he
Ex. 34:33, he put a veil on his *f*
Num. 6:25, the LORD make His *f*
2 Ki. 20:2, Then he turned his *f*
Job 1:11, curse You to Your *f*
Ps. 17:15, me, I will see Your *f*
Ps. 44:24, Why do You hide Your *f*
Ps. 67:1, and cause His *f*
Eccl. 8:1, of his *f* is changed
Isa. 59:2, sins have hidden His *f*
Ezek. 3:8, I have made your *f*
Dan. 9:7, but to us shame of *f*
Mt. 11:10, before Your *f* who
Mt. 17:2, *f* shone like the sun
Acts 2:25, always before my *f*
1 Cor. 13:12, dimly, but then *f*
2 Cor. 3:7, look steadily at the *f*
2 Cor. 3:18, with unveiled *f*
Gal. 2:11, withstood him to his *f*
Jas. 1:23, his natural *f* in a
1 Pet. 3:12, but the *f* of the LORD
Rev. 22:4, They shall see His *f*

FACES
Ps. 34:5, *f* were not ashamed
Isa. 53:3, hid, as it were, our *f*
Jer. 1:8, be afraid of their *f*
Jer. 30:6, and all *f* turned pale
Mt. 6:16, they disfigure their *f*

FACTIONS
1 Cor. 11:19, there must also be *f*

FADE
Isa. 64:6, we all *f* as a leaf
Jer. 8:13, and the leaf shall *f*
Jas. 1:11, rich man also will *f*
1 Pet. 1:4, and that does not *f*

FADES
Isa. 40:7, withers, the flower *f*

FAIL
Dt. 28:32, eyes shall look and *f*
Ps. 73:26, flesh and my heart *f*
Isa. 32:6, of the thirsty to *f*
Isa. 41:17, their tongues *f*
Isa. 58:11, whose waters do not *f*
Jer. 48:33, have caused wine to *f*
Hab. 3:17, of the olive may *f*
Mal. 3:11, nor shall the vine *f*
Lk. 16:9, that when you *f*
Lk. 16:17, tittle of the law to *f*
Lk. 22:32, faith should not *f*
1 Cor. 13:8, they will *f*
Heb. 1:12, Your years will not *f*
Heb. 11:32, For the time would *f*

FAILED
Josh. 21:45, Not a word *f* of any
Job 19:14, My relatives have *f*
Ps. 142:4, refuge has *f* me

FAILING
Lk. 21:26, men's hearts *f*

FAILS
Ps. 31:10, my strength *f* because
Ps. 143:7, my spirit *f*
Ezek. 12:22, and every vision *f*
1 Cor. 13:8, Love never *f*

FAINT
Isa. 40:30, the youths shall *f*
Isa. 40:31, shall walk and not *f*
Jer. 8:18, my heart is *f* in me
Lam. 2:11, and the infants *f*

FAINTED
Ps. 107:5, thirsty, their soul *f*

FAINTHEARTED
1 Th. 5:14, unruly, comfort the *f*

FAINTS
Ps. 84:2, longs, yes, even *f*
Ps. 119:81, My soul *f* for Your
Isa. 1:5, And the whole heart *f*
Isa. 40:28, the earth, neither *f*

FAIR
Song 1:15, Behold, you are *f*
Ezek. 18:25, of the Lord is not *f*
Acts 27:8, to a place called *F*
Col. 4:1, what is just and *f*

FAIR HAVENS, Acts 27:8

FAIR-MINDED
Acts 17:11, These were more *f*

FAIRER
Ps. 45:2, *f* than the sons

FAIREST
Song 5:9, another beloved, O *f*
Song 6:1, your beloved gone, O *f*

FAITH, Heb. 11
justification by. Rom. 3:28; 5:1,16; Gal. 2:16; purification by. Acts 15:9; sanctification by. Acts 26:18
object of, Father, Son, and Holy Spirit. Mk. 11:22; Jn. 6:29; 14:1; 20:31; Acts 20:21; 2 Cor. 13:14
given by the Spirit. 1 Cor. 2:5; 12:9
in Christ. Acts 8:12; 2 Tim. 3:15
unity of. Eph. 4:5,13; Jude 3
leads to salvation, etc. Mk. 16:16; Jn. 1:12; 3:16,36; 6:40,47; Acts 16:31; Gal. 3:11; Eph. 2:8; Heb. 11:6; 1 Pet. 1:9; 1 Jn. 5:10
works by love. 1 Cor. 13; Gal. 5:6; Col. 1:4; 1 Th. 1:3; 1 Tim. 1:5; Phile. 5; Heb. 10:23; 1 Pet. 1:22; 1 Jn. 3:14,23
without works is dead. Jas. 2:17,20
produces peace, joy, hope in believing. Rom. 5:1; 15:13; 2 Cor. 4:13; 1 Pet. 1:8
excludes boasting, etc. Rom. 3:27; 4:2; 1 Cor. 1:29; Eph. 2:9
blessings received through. Mk. 16:16; Jn. 6:40; 12:36; 20:31; Acts 10:43; 16:31; 26:18; Rom. 1:17 (Hab. 2:4); Rom. 3:21; 4:16; 5:1; 2 Cor. 5:7; Gal. 2:16; 3:14,26; Eph. 1:13; 3:12,17; 1 Tim. 1:4; Heb. 4:3; 6:12; 10:38; 1 Pet. 1:5; Jude 20
miracles performed through. Mt. 9:22; Lk. 8:50; Acts 3:16
power of. Mt. 17:20; Mk. 9:23; 11:23; Lk. 17:6
trial of. 2 Th. 1:4; Heb. 11:17; Jas. 1:3,12; 1 Pet. 1:7
overcomes the world. 1 Jn. 5:4
shield of the Christian. Eph. 6:16; 1 Th. 5:8
contend earnestly for the. Jude 3
exhortations to continue in. 1 Cor. 16:13; 2 Cor. 13:5; Eph. 6:16; Phil. 1:27; Col. 1:23; 2:7; 1 Th. 5:8; 1 Tim. 1:19; 4:12; 6:11; 2 Tim. 2:22; Ti. 1:13; Heb. 10:22
examples of: Caleb. Num. 13:30; Shadrach, Meshach, and Abed-Nego. Dan. 3:17; Daniel. Dan. 6:10; Ninevites. Jon. 3:5; Peter. Mt. 16:16; Nathanael. Jn. 1:49; Martha. Jn. 11:27; Stephen. Acts 6:5; Ethiopian eunuch. Acts 8:37; Barnabas. Acts 11:24

FAITH
Dt. 32:20, in whom is no *f*
Hab. 2:4, shall live by his *f*
Mt. 6:30, you, O you of little *f*
Mt. 8:10, not found such great *f*
Mt. 17:20, *f* as a mustard seed
Mk. 4:40, that you have no *f*
Mk. 11:22, to them, "Have *f*
Lk. 17:5, "Increase our *f*
Lk. 18:8, will He really find *f*
Acts 6:5, a man full of *f*
Acts 26:18, are sanctified by *f*
Rom. 1:5, for obedience to the *f*
Rom. 1:17, God is revealed from *f*
Rom. 3:22, God, through *f*
Rom. 3:28, *f* apart from the deeds
Rom. 4:5, his *f* is accounted for
Rom. 4:14, *f* is made void and the
Rom. 4:16, those who are of the *f*
Rom. 10:8, *f* which we preach
Rom. 10:17, *f* comes by hearing
Rom. 11:20, and you stand by *f*
Rom. 12:6, in proportion to our *f*
Rom. 14:22, Do you have *f*
Rom. 14:23, he does not eat from *f*
1 Cor. 13:2, though I have all *f*
1 Cor. 13:13, And now abide *f*
2 Cor. 5:7, For we walk by *f*
Gal. 2:20, the flesh I live by *f*
Gal. 3:2, or by the hearing of *f*
Gal. 3:7, *f* are sons of Abraham
Gal. 3:12, the law is not of *f*
Gal. 3:25, But after *f* has come
Gal. 5:6, *f* working through love
Gal. 6:10, of the household of *f*
Eph. 2:8, been saved through *f*
Eph. 4:5, one Lord, one *f*
Eph. 4:13, to the unity of the *f*
Eph. 6:16, taking the shield of *f*
1 Th. 1:3, your work of *f*
2 Th. 3:2, for not all have *f*
1 Tim. 1:19, having *f* and a good
1 Tim. 3:9, the mystery of the *f*
1 Tim. 5:8, he has denied the *f*
2 Tim. 4:7, I have kept the *f*
Ti. 1:4, in our common *f*
Heb. 4:2, not being mixed with *f*
Heb. 11:1, *f* is the substance
Heb. 11:6, without *f* it is
Jas. 2:14, someone says he has *f*
Jas. 2:18, Show me your *f*
Jas. 2:24, and not by *f* only
Jas. 5:15, *f* will save the sick
2 Pet. 1:5, add to your *f* virtue
Jude 20, on your most holy *f*
Rev. 13:10, the patience and the *f*
Rev. 14:12, of God and the *f*

FAITHFUL
Dt. 7:9, God, He is God, the *f*
Ps. 12:1, *f* disappear from among
Ps. 31:23, LORD preserves the *f*
Ps. 78:8, whose spirit was not *f*
Ps. 101:6, eyes shall be on the *f*
Prov. 11:13, *f* spirit conceals a
Prov. 20:6, But who can find a *f*
Jer. 42:5, *f* witness between us
Hos. 11:12, the Holy One who is *f*
Mt. 24:45, "Who then is a *f*
Mt. 25:23, good and *f* servant
Lk. 16:10, "He who is *f* in what
Lk. 16:12, if you have not been *f*
Acts 16:15, judged me to be *f*
1 Cor. 1:9, God is *f*
1 Cor. 4:17, is my beloved and *f*
2 Cor. 1:18, But as God is *f*
Col. 1:2, *f* brethren in Christ
1 Th. 5:24, He who calls you is *f*
1 Tim. 1:15, This is a *f* saying and
Heb. 2:17, *f* High Priest in
Heb. 3:2, as Moses also was *f*
Heb. 10:23, He who promised is *f*
1 Jn. 1:9, He is *f* and just to
Rev. 2:10, Be *f* until death
Rev. 21:5, words are true and *f*

FAITHFULLY
2 Chr. 19:9; 34:12; Jer. 23:28; 3 Jn. 5

FAITHFULNESS
commended in the service of God. 2 Ki. 12:15; 2 Chr. 31:12; Mt. 24:45; 2 Cor. 2:17; 4:2; 3 Jn. 5
towards men. Dt. 1:16; Ps. 141:5; Prov. 11:13; 13:17; 14:5; 20:6; 25:13; 27:6; 28:20; Lk. 16:10; 1 Cor. 4:2; 1 Tim. 3:11; 6:2; Ti. 2:10
of Abraham. Gen. 22; Gal. 3:9
of Joseph. Gen. 39:4,22
of Moses. Num. 12:7; Heb. 3:5
of David. 1 Sam. 22:14
of Daniel. Dan. 6:4
of Paul. Acts 20:20
of Timothy. 1 Cor. 4:17
of God. Ps. 36:5; 40:10; 88:11; 89:1; 92:2; 119:75; Isa. 25:1; Lam. 3:23

FAITHFULNESS
Ps. 40:10, I have declared Your *f*
Ps. 89:2, *f* You shall establish
Ps. 89:8, Your *f* also surrounds
Ps. 92:2, and Your *f* every night
Ps. 119:90, *f* endures to all
Ps. 143:1, In Your *f* answer me
Isa. 25:1, counsels of old are *f*
Lam. 3:23, great is Your *f*
Rom. 3:3, unbelief make the *f*

FAITHLESS
Mk. 9:19, "O *f* generation
2 Tim. 2:13, If we are *f*

FALL
Gen. 2:21, a deep sleep to *f*
2 Sam. 24:14, but do not let me *f*
Ps. 5:10, Let them *f* by their
Ps. 38:17, For I am ready to *f*
Ps. 72:11, Yes, all kings shall *f*
Prov. 24:16, righteous man may *f*
Prov. 24:16, but the wicked shall *f*
Prov. 26:27, digs a pit will *f*
Isa. 34:4, all their host shall *f*
Isa. 40:30, men shall utterly *f*
Dan. 3:5, of music, you shall *f*
Mt. 7:27, and great was its *f*
Mt. 15:14, the blind, both will *f*
Mt. 24:29, the stars will *f*
Lk. 10:18, "I saw Satan *f*
Rom. 11:11, that they should *f*
1 Cor. 10:12, take heed lest he *f*
1 Tim. 3:6, with pride he *f*
Heb. 6:6, if they *f* away
Heb. 12:15, lest anyone *f* short of
Jas. 1:2, it all joy when you *f*
Rev. 6:16, and rocks, "F on us

FALLEN
Isa. 21:9, "Babylon is *f*
Gal. 5:4, you have *f* from grace
Rev. 9:1, And I saw a star *f*
Rev. 14:8, "Babylon is *f*

FALLING
Lk. 22:44, great drops of blood *f*
2 Th. 2:3, *f* away comes first

FALLOW, Jer. 4:3; Hos. 10:12

FALLS
Eccl. 4:10, who is alone when he *f*
Mt. 21:44, "And whoever *f*
Rom. 14:4, master he stands or *f*
Jas. 1:11, its flower *f*

Rev. 11:6, so that no rain *f*

FALSE
Ex. 20:16, "You shall not bear *f*
Ps. 119:104, I hate every *f* way
Prov. 17:4, gives heed to *f* lips
Prov. 21:28, *f* witness shall perish
Zech. 8:17, and do not love a *f*
Mt. 7:15, "Beware of *f* prophets
Mt. 24:24, *f* christs and *f*
1 Cor. 15:15, and we are found *f*
2 Cor. 11:26, among *f* brethren
Gal. 2:4, of *f* brethren
1 Jn. 4:1, *f* prophets have gone
Rev. 16:13, mouth of the *f* prophet

FALSE WITNESSES
condemned. *See* DECEIT, WITNESS

FALSEHOOD
Ps. 5:6, those who speak *f*
Ps. 7:14, and brings forth *f*
Ps. 119:118, For their deceit is *f*
Prov. 30:8, remove *f* and lies far
Isa. 28:15, *f* we have
Isa. 57:4, Offspring of *f*

FALSELY
Lev. 6:3, it, and swears *f*
Ps. 44:17, nor have we dealt *f*
Jer. 5:2, surely they swear *f*
Hos. 10:4, words, swearing *f*
Mt. 5:11, of evil against you *f*
1 Tim. 6:20, *f* called knowledge

FAME
1 Ki. 10:1, Sheba heard of the *f*
Ezek. 16:14, "Your *f* went out
Zeph. 3:19, them for praise and *f*
Mt. 4:24, Then His *f* went

FAMILIAR, Ps. 41:9

FAMILIAR SPIRITS
See also MEDIUMS. Lev. 19:31; 20:27

FAMILIES
Gen. 12:3, in you all the *f*
Ps. 107:41, and makes their *f*
Jer. 31:1, the God of all the *f*
Jer. 33:24, *f* which the LORD has
Acts 3:25, in your seed all the *f*

FAMILY
Zech. 12:12, shall mourn, every *f*
Acts 16:33, *f* were baptized
Eph. 3:15, from whom the whole *f*

FAMINE
threatened. Jer. 14:15; 15:2; Ezek. 5:12; 6:11; Mt. 24:7; Acts 11:28
described. Jer. 14; Lam. 4; Joel 1
occurs in: Canaan. Gen. 12; Egypt. Gen. 41; Israel. Ruth 1:1; 2 Sam. 21:1; 1 Ki. 18:2; 2 Ki. 6:25; 7; Lk. 4:25
Shunammite forewarned of. 2 Ki. 8:1
king of Egypt warned of, by Joseph. Gen. 40
of God's word. Amos 8:11

FAMINE
Gen. 12:10, Now there was a *f*
Ps. 33:19, keep them alive in *f*
Ps. 105:16, He called for a *f*
Jer. 24:10, send the sword, the *f*
Lam. 5:10, of the fever of *f*
Ezek. 5:16, I will increase the *f*
Lk. 15:14, there arose a severe *f*

FAMINES
Mt. 24:7, And there will be *f*

FAMISH
Prov. 10:3, righteous soul to *f*

FAMISHED
Isa. 5:13, honorable men are *f*

FAMOUS
Ruth 4:14, and may his name be *f*

FAN
Jer. 4:11, not to *f* or to cleanse
Mt. 3:12, "His winnowing *f*

FANCIES
Prov. 1:31, with their own *f*

FAR
Job 19:13, removed my brothers *f*
Ps. 10:5, Your judgments are *f*
Ps. 22:11, Be not *f* from Me
Ps. 73:27, those who are *f*
Prov. 15:29, The LORD is *f* from
Eccl. 7:23, but it was *f* from me
Isa. 29:13, removed their hearts *f*
Ezek. 22:5, Those near and those *f*
Mt. 15:8, their heart is *f* from
Mk. 13:34, going to a *f* country
Acts 17:27, though He is not *f*
Eph. 2:13, you who once were *f*

FAREWELL, Lk. 9:61; 2 Cor. 13:11

FARMER
2 Tim. 2:6, The hard-working *f*
Jas. 5:7, See how the *f* waits

FASHIONED
Job 10:8, have made me and *f*

FASHIONS
Ps. 33:15, He *f* their hearts

FAST
Isa. 58:4, *f* as you do this day
Isa. 58:5, *f* that I have chosen
Mt. 6:16, "Moreover, when you *f*
Mt. 9:14, disciples do not *f*
Lk. 18:12, 'I *f* twice a week

FASTED
Isa. 58:3, 'Why have we *f*
Zech. 7:5, 'When you *f* and
Mt. 4:2, And when He had *f*

FASTENED
Job 38:6, were its foundations *f*
Isa. 22:25, 'the peg that is *f*

FASTING
turned into gladness. Zech. 8:19
Christ excuses His disciples for not. Mt. 9:14; Mk. 2:18; Lk. 5:33
of Moses (twice) for forty days. Ex. 24:18; 34:28; Dt. 9:9,18
of David. 2 Sam. 12:16
of Elijah. 1 Ki. 19:8
of Christ. Mt. 4:2
of Barnabas and Paul. Acts 14:23
recommended. 1 Cor. 7:5

FASTING
Ps. 35:13, humbled myself with *f*
Ps. 109:24, are weak through *f*
Jer. 36:6, house on the day of *f*
Mt. 17:21, except by prayer and *f*
1 Cor. 7:5, give yourselves to *f*

FASTINGS
2 Cor. 6:5, in sleeplessness, in *f*

FAT
Gen. 45:18, and you will eat the *f*
Lev. 3:16, *f* is the LORD's
Jud. 3:17, Now Eglon was a very *f*
Ps. 17:10, have closed up their *f*

FATHER
Gen. 2:24, man shall leave his *f*
Gen. 17:4, and you shall be a *f*
Job 17:14, 'You are my *f*
Job 29:16, I was a *f* to the poor
Ps. 68:5, A *f* of the fatherless
Ps. 103:13, *f* pities his children
Prov. 4:1, the instruction of a *f*
Isa. 9:6, God, Everlasting *F*
Isa. 63:16, You, O LORD, are our *F*
Jer. 3:4, time cry to Me, 'My *F*
Jer. 31:9, for I am a *F* to Israel
Mal. 1:6, "A son honors his *f*
Mal. 2:10, Have we not all one *F*
Mt. 6:9, Our *F* in heaven
Mt. 10:37, "He who loves *f*
Mt. 11:27, does anyone know the *F*
Mt. 15:4, 'He who curses *f*
Mt. 23:9, for One is your *F*
Lk. 12:53, *F* will be divided
Jn. 3:35, *F* loves the Son
Jn. 5:17, *F* has been working
Jn. 5:21, *F* raises the dead
Jn. 5:22, *F* judges no one
Jn. 6:46, He has seen the *F*
Jn. 8:18, *F* who sent Me bears
Jn. 8:41, we have one *F*
Jn. 8:44, of your *f* the devil
Jn. 10:30, "I and My *F* are one
Jn. 10:38, and believe that the *F*
Jn. 14:28, 'I am going to the *F*
Jn. 15:1, *F* is the vinedresser
Jn. 16:28, came forth from the *F*
Rom. 4:11, that he might be the *f*
Rom. 4:17, "I have made you a *f*
2 Cor. 6:18, "I will be a *F*
Eph. 4:6, one God and *F* of all
1 Tim. 5:1, but exhort him as a *f*
Heb. 1:5, "I will be to Him a *F*
Heb. 7:3, without *f*, without mother
Jas. 1:17, comes down from the *F*
1 Pet. 1:17, if you call on the *F*
1 Jn. 4:14, and testify that the *F*

FATHER'S
Mt. 26:29, you in My *F* kingdom
Lk. 2:49, I must be about My *F*
Jn. 14:2, *F* house are many
1 Cor. 5:1, that a man has his *f*

FATHERLESS
God the God of. Ps. 146:9; Jer. 49:11; Hos. 14:3; helper of. Dt. 10:18; Ps. 10:14; 146:9; Father of. Ps. 68:5
duty towards. Ex. 22:22; Dt. 14:29; 24:17; Prov. 23:10; Isa. 1:17; Jer. 7:6; Jas. 1:27
the wicked oppress. Job 6:27; 22:9; Ps. 94:6; Isa. 1:23; 10:2; Jer. 5:28;

FEATHERS, Ps. 91:4; Dan. 4:33

FED
Gen. 48:15, *f* me all my life long
Dt. 8:3, and *f* you with manna
Ezek. 34:8, but the shepherds *f*
1 Cor. 3:2, *f* you with milk and

FEEBLE
Job 4:4, strengthened the *f*
Ps. 105:37, And there was none *f*
Ps. 109:24, And my flesh is *f*
Ezek. 7:17, Every hand will be *f*
Heb. 12:12, hang down, and the *f*

FEED
1 Ki. 17:4, ravens to *f* you there
Ps. 49:14, death shall *f* on them
Prov. 10:21, of the righteous *f*
Isa. 61:5, and *f* your flocks
Jn. 21:15, to him, "*F* My lambs
Jn. 21:17, to him, "*F* My sheep
Rom. 12:20, your enemy hungers, *f*
1 Cor. 13:3, my goods to *f* the poor

FEEDS
Hos. 12:1, "Ephraim *f* on the wind
Mt. 6:26, your heavenly Father *f*

FEET
Ruth 3:14, So she lay at his *f*
2 Sam. 22:37, so my *f* did not slip
Job 28:4, *f* they hang far
Job 29:15, I was *f* to the lame
Ps. 8:6, all things under his *f*
Ps. 18:33, He makes my *f* like the
Ps. 31:8, You have set my *f*
Ps. 66:9, does not allow our *f*
Ps. 73:2, *f* had almost stumbled
Ps. 122:2, *f* have been standing
Prov. 1:16, For their *f* run to
Prov. 5:5, Her *f* go down to death
Isa. 20:2, sandals off your *f*
Isa. 41:2, called him to His *f*
Isa. 49:23, up the dust of your *f*
Isa. 52:7, mountains are the *f*
Isa. 60:13, place of My *f* glorious
Nah. 1:3, are the dust of His *f*
Zech. 14:4, in that day His *f*
Mt. 18:8, two hands or two *f*
Lk. 7:38, began to wash His *f*
Lk. 10:39, also sat at Jesus' *f*
Jn. 13:5, wash the disciples' *f*
Acts 4:35, at the apostles' *f*
Rom. 3:15, *f* are swift to shed
Rom. 10:15, beautiful are the *f*
1 Cor. 15:27, things under His *f*
Eph. 6:15, and having shod your *f*
Rev. 1:17, fell at His *f* as dead
Rev. 19:10, And I fell at his *f*

FELIX, Acts 23:24
governor of Judea, Paul sent to. Acts 23:23
Paul's defense before. Acts 24:10
trembles at Paul's preaching, but leaves him bound. Acts 24:25

FELLOW
Mt. 18:28, *f* servants who owed
Mt. 24:49, begins to beat his *f*
2 Cor. 8:23, *f* worker concerning
Eph. 2:19, *f* citizens with the
Eph. 3:6, Gentiles should be *f*
Phil. 4:3, rest of my *f* workers
Col. 4:11, These are my only *f*
3 Jn. 8, that we may become *f*
Rev. 19:10, I am your *f* servant

FELLOWSHIP
of Christ. 1 Cor. 1:9; 12:27; 2 Cor. 4:11; Phil. 3:10; *See* 1 Cor. 10:16
of the Spirit. Phil. 2:1
of the saints. Acts 2:42; 2 Cor. 8:4; Gal. 2:9; Phil. 1:5; 1 Jn. 1:3
with evil, forbidden. 1 Cor. 10:20; 2 Cor. 6:14; Eph. 5:11

FELLOWSHIP
Acts 2:42, doctrine and *f*
1 Cor. 1:9, were called into the *f*
1 Cor. 10:20, not want you to have *f*
2 Cor. 6:14, *f* has righteousness
Gal. 2:9, the right hand of *f*
Eph. 5:11, And have no *f* with the
Phil. 1:5, for your *f* in the
Phil. 2:1, of love, if any *f*
Phil. 3:10, and the *f* of His
1 Jn. 1:3, also may have *f*
1 Jn. 1:6, we say that we have *f*
1 Jn. 1:7, the light, we have *f*

FENCE
Ps. 62:3, and a tottering *f*

FENCED
Job 19:8, He has *f* up my way

FERTILIZE
Lk. 13:8, I dig around it and *f*

FERVENT
Acts 18:25, and being *f* in spirit
Jas. 5:16, *f* prayer of a
1 Pet. 4:8, all things have *f*
2 Pet. 3:10, will melt with *f*

FERVENTLY
Col. 4:12, you, always laboring *f*
1 Pet. 1:22, love one another *f*

FESTIVAL
Isa. 30:29, night when a holy *f*
Col. 2:16, or regarding a *f*

FESTUS
governor of Judea. Acts 24:27
Paul brought before. Acts 25
Paul's defense before. Acts 25:8; 26
acquits Paul. Acts 25:14; 26:31

FETCH
Job 36:3, *f* my knowledge from

FETTERS
Ps. 105:18, hurt his feet with *f*
Ps. 149:8, their nobles with *f*

FEVER
Lev. 26:16, *f* which shall
Job 30:30, my bones burn with *f*
Lk. 4:39, and rebuked the *f*

FEW
Gen. 47:9, *f* and evil have been
Job 14:1, *f* days and full of
Ps. 109:8, Let his days be *f*
Eccl. 5:2, let your words be *f*
Mt. 7:14, and there are *f*
Mt. 9:37, but the laborers are *f*
Mt. 20:16, called, but *f* chosen
Lk. 13:23, "Lord, are there *f*
1 Pet. 3:20, prepared, in which a *f*
Rev. 2:20, I have a *f* things

FIDELITY
Ti. 2:10, but showing all good *f*

FIELD
Ps. 96:12, let the *f* be joyful
Isa. 5:8, to house; they add *f*
Isa. 32:15, becomes a fruitful *f*
Mt. 13:38, "The *f* is the world
Mt. 13:44, and buys that *f*
Mt. 27:8, *f* has been called the
1 Cor. 3:9, you are God's *f*

FIELDS
Hab. 3:17, *f* yield no food
Lk. 2:8, living out in the *f*
Jn. 4:35, eyes and look at the *f*

FIERCENESS
Jer. 49:16, *f* has deceived you
Rev. 19:15, the winepress of the *f*

FIERY
Num. 21:6, LORD sent *f* serpents
Dt. 33:2, right hand came a *f*
Ps. 21:9, shall make them as a *f*
Isa. 14:29, offspring will be a *f*
Dan. 3:6, burning *f* furnace
1 Pet. 4:12, concerning the *f*
Rev. 12:3, *f* red dragon having

FIG
Gen. 3:7, *f* leaves together
1 Ki. 4:25, his vine and his *f*
Isa. 34:4, fruit falling from a *f*
Hab. 3:17, *f* tree may not blossom
Lk. 13:7, fruit on this *f*
Lk. 21:29, "Look at the *f*
Jn. 1:50, 'I saw you under the *f*
Jas. 3:12, Can a *f* tree
Rev. 6:13, *f* tree drops its late

FIG TREE
parable of. Mt. 24:32; Lk. 21:29

FIGHT
Ex. 14:14, "The LORD will *f*
1 Ki. 22:4, you go with me to *f*
Neh. 4:20, Our God will *f* for us
Jn. 18:36, My servants would *f*
Acts 23:9, to him, let us not *f*
1 Tim. 6:12, *F* the good *f*
2 Tim. 4:7, have fought the good *f*
Jas. 4:2, You *f* and war

FIGHTS
Josh. 23:10, your God is He who *f*
1 Sam. 25:28, because my lord *f*
Jas. 4:1, *f* come from among

FIGS
Song 2:13, puts forth her green *f*
Jer. 24:1, *f* set before the
Mt. 7:16, thornbushes or *f*
Lk. 6:44, men do not gather *f*
Jas. 3:12, or a grapevine bear *f*

FIGURATIVELY
1 Cor. 4:6, brethren, I have *f*

FIGURE
Jn. 16:29, and using no *f*

FILL
Gen. 1:28, *f* the earth and subdue
Prov. 8:21, wealth, that I may *f*

Jer. 23:24, "Do I not *f* heaven
Hag. 2:7, *f* this temple with
Jn. 2:7, "*F* the waterpots
Eph. 4:10, that He might *f*
1 Th. 2:16, so as always to *f*

FILLED
Ps. 72:19, the whole earth be *f*
Ps. 126:2, Then our mouth was *f*
Mt. 5:6, for they shall be *f*
Mk. 7:27, "Let the children be *f*
Lk. 15:16, would gladly have *f*
Rom. 1:29, being *f* with all
Rom. 15:14, full of goodness, *f*
Eph. 3:19, that you may be *f*
Eph. 5:18, but be *f* with the
Phil. 1:11, being *f* with the
Jas. 2:16, be warmed and *f*

FILTH
Isa. 4:4, has washed away the *f*
1 Cor. 4:13, been made as the *f*
1 Pet. 3:21, the removal of the *f*

FILTHINESS
figurative of sin. Job 15:16; Ps. 14:3; Isa. 1:6; 64:6; Ezek. 24:13
purification from. Isa. 4:4; Ezek. 22:15; 36:25; Zech. 3:3; 13:1; 1 Cor. 6:11; 2 Cor. 7:1

FILTHINESS
Ezek. 36:25, from all your *f*
2 Cor. 7:1, ourselves from all *f*
Jas. 1:21, lay aside all *f*
Rev. 17:4, abominations and the *f*

FILTHY
Job 15:16, is abominable and *f*
Zech. 3:3, with *f* garments
Col. 3:8, malice, blasphemy, *f*
Jas. 2:2, poor man in *f* clothes
2 Pet. 2:7, oppressed by the *f*
Rev. 22:11, let him be *f*

FIND
Num. 32:23, sure your sin will *f*
Job 37:23, Almighty, we cannot *f*
Prov. 4:22, life to those who *f*
Eccl. 3:11, that no on can *f*
Eccl. 11:1, waters, for you will *f*
Mt. 7:7, seek, and you will *f*
Mt. 10:39, for My sake will *f*
Mt. 24:46, when he comes, will *f*
Lk. 2:12, *f* a Babe wrapped
Lk. 23:4, *f* no fault in this Man
Rom. 7:21, I *f* then a law
Heb. 4:16, *f* grace to help in

FINDING
Jon. 9:10, great things past *f*
Lk. 11:24, and *f* none
Rom. 11:33, and His ways past *f*

FINDS
Prov. 8:35, *f* me *f* life
Prov. 18:22, *f* a wife *f* a good
Eccl. 9:10, Whatever your hand *f*
Mt. 7:8, and he who seeks *f*
Mt. 10:39, *f* his life will lose
Lk. 11:10, and he who seeks *f*

FINE
2 Sam. 22:43, Then I beat them as *f*
Ps. 19:10, gold, yea, than much *f*
Prov. 25:12, *f* gold is a wise
Song 5:15, set on bases of *f* gold
Isa. 13:12, more rare than *f*
Isa. 23:18, and for *f* clothing
Lam. 4:1, how changed the *f*
Jas. 2:2, rings, in *f* apparel
Rev. 19:8, for the *f* linen is the

FINGER
Ex. 31:18, written with the *f*
1 Ki. 12:10, *f* shall be thicker
Isa. 58:9, the pointing of the *f*
Lk. 16:24, dip the tip of his *f*
Jn. 8:6, the ground with His *f*
Jn. 20:27, "Reach your *f*

FINGERS
Ps. 8:3, the work of Your *f*
Prov. 6:13, he points with his *f*
Isa. 2:8, that which their own *f*
Mt. 23:4, with one of their *f*

FINISH
Dan. 9:24, city, to *f* the
Lk. 14:28, he has enough to *f*
Jn. 5:36, has given Me to *f*
Acts 20:24, so that I may *f*

FINISHED
Jn. 17:4, *f* the work which You
Jn. 19:30, He said, "It is *f*
2 Tim. 4:7, I have *f* the race
Rev. 20:3, thousand years were *f*

FIRE
pillar of. Ex. 13:21; Neh. 9:12
God appears by. Ex. 3:2; 13:21; 19:18; Dt. 4:12; 2 Sam. 22:13; Isa. 6:4; Ezek. 1:4; Dan. 7:10; Mal. 3:2; Mt. 3:11; Rev. 1:14; 4:5
for consuming sacrifices. Gen. 15:17; Lev. 9:24; Jud. 13:20; 1 Ki. 18:38; 2 Chr. 7:1
not to be kindled on the Sabbath. Ex. 35:3
emblem of God's Word. Jer. 23:29; Acts 2:3
instrument of judgment. Gen. 19:24; Ex. 9:23; Lev. 10; Num. 11:1; 16:35; 2 Ki. 1:10; Amos 7:4; 2 Th. 1:8; Rev. 8:8
everlasting. Dt. 32:22; Isa. 33:14; 66:24; Mk. 9:44; Jude 7; Rev. 20:10
God is a consuming. Heb. 12:29

FIRE
Gen. 19:24, rained brimstone and *f*
Ex. 3:2, to him in a flame of *f*
Ex. 40:38, by day, and *f* was over
1 Ki. 18:24, God who answers by *f*
1 Ki. 19:12, LORD was not in the *f*
Ps. 39:3, I was musing, the *f*
Ps. 66:12, we went through *f*
Ps. 74:7, they have set *f*
Ps. 97:3, *f* goes before Him
Ps. 148:8, *f* and hail
Isa. 9:18, burns as the *f*
Isa. 31:9, says the LORD, whose *f*
Isa. 43:2, you walk through the *f*
Isa. 65:5, *f* that burns all the
Dan. 3:27, on whose bodies the *f*
Amos 5:6, He break out like *f*
Amos 7:4, for conflict by *f*
Mal. 3:2, like a refiner's *f*
Mt. 3:11, the Holy Spirit and *f*
Mk. 9:44, *f* is not quenched
Lk. 12:49, "I came to send *f*
Acts 2:3, tongues, as of *f*
2 Th. 1:8, *f* taking vengeance
Heb. 12:18, and that burned with *f*
Jas. 3:6, And the tongue is a *f*
Jude 7, vengeance of eternal *f*
Rev. 20:9, *f* came down from God
Rev. 20:14, into the lake of *f*

FIREBRAND
Amos 4:11, *f* plucked from the

FIREBRANDS
Prov. 26:18, a madman who throws *f*
Isa. 7:4, two stubs of smoking *f*

FIRM
Ps. 73:4, their strength is *f*
Isa. 35:3, *f* the feeble knees
Heb. 3:6, of the hope *f* to the

FIRMAMENT
Gen. 1:7, Thus God made the *f*
Ps. 19:1, *f* shows His handiwork
Ps. 150:1, in His mighty *f*
Dan. 12:3, brightness of the *f*

FIRST
Prov. 18:17, The *f* one to plead his
Isa. 43:27, *f* father sinned
Mt. 20:27, desires to be *f*
Mk. 10:44, *f* shall be slave
Mk. 13:10, the gospel must *f*
Rom. 2:9, evil, of the Jew *f*
Rom. 11:35, "Or who has *f*
1 Cor. 15:45, *f* man Adam became
2 Cor. 8:12, *f* a willing mind
Eph. 1:12, that we who *f* trusted
1 Tim. 2:13, For Adam was formed *f*
Heb. 8:7, *f* covenant had been
1 Jn. 4:19, love Him because He *f*
Rev. 1:17, I am the *F* and the
Rev. 2:4, you have left your *f*
Rev. 20:5, is the *f* resurrection

FIRST-RIPE
Mic. 7:1, *f* fruit which my soul

FIRSTBORN
claims of the. Gen. 43:33; Dt. 21:15; 2 Chr. 21:3; Col. 1:15; Heb. 12:23
dedicated to God. Ex. 13:2,12; 22:29; 34:19; Dt. 15:19
how redeemed. Ex. 34:20; Num. 3:41; 8:18
in Egypt killed. Ex. 11:4; 12:29

FIRSTBORN
Ex. 12:29, LORD struck all the *f*
Ps. 89:27, I will make him My *f*
Mic. 6:7, Shall I give my *f*
Mt. 1:25, brought forth her *f*
Rom. 8:29, that He might be the *f*
Col. 1:15, invisible God, the *f*
Col. 1:18, the beginning, the *f*
Rev. 1:5, witness, the *f* from

FIRSTFRUIT
Rom. 11:16, For if the *f* is holy

FIRSTFRUITS
laws relating to. Ex. 22:29; 23:16; 34:26; Lev. 23:10; Num. 28:26
form of dedicating. Dt. 26:10

Isa. 40:6, is like the *f* of the
Isa. 40:7, grass withers, the *f*
1 Cor. 7:36, if she is past the *f*
1 Pet. 1:24, of man as the *f*

FLOWERS
Song 2:12, *f* appear on the earth

FLOWING
Dt. 6:3, 'a land *f* with milk
Prov. 18:4, of wisdom is a *f*
Isa. 66:12, the Gentiles like a *f*

FLUTE
Gen. 4:21, play the harp and *f*
Dan. 3:5, sound of the horn, *f*

FLUTES
Ps. 150:4, instruments and *f*

FLUTISTS
Rev. 18:22, harpists, musicians, *f*

FLY
Ps. 55:6, I would *f*
Ps. 90:10, soon cut off, and we *f*
Prov. 23:5, they *f* away like an

FOE
Ps. 18:14, and scattered the *f*

FOES
Ps. 27:2, my enemies and *f*
Ps. 89:23, I will beat down his *f*

FOLD
Jn. 10:16, are not of this *f*
Heb. 1:12, a cloak You will *f*

FOLDING
Prov. 6:10, slumber, a little *f*

FOLLOW
Dt. 16:20, *f* what is altogether
Isa. 51:1, to Me, you who *f*
Mt. 8:19, *f* You wherever You go
Mt. 9:9, He said to him, "*F*
Mk. 8:34, up his cross, and *f*
Mk. 9:38, someone who does not *f*
Jn. 10:5, will by no means *f*
Jn. 12:26, serves Me, let him *f*
1 Tim. 5:24, those of some men *f*
1 Pet. 2:21, that you should *f*
Rev. 14:4, *f* the Lamb wherever
Rev. 14:13, and their works *f*

FOLLOWED
Josh. 14:8, *f* the LORD my God
Amos 7:15, LORD took me as I *f*
Mk. 10:28, we have left all and *f*

FOLLOWS
Ps. 63:8, My soul *f* close behind
Jn. 8:12, *f* Me shall not walk

FOLLY
Job 35:15, taken much notice of *f*
Ps. 85:8, not turn back to *f*
Prov. 15:21, *F* is joy to him who is
Prov. 16:22, of fools is *f*
Eccl. 10:6, *f* is set in great

FOOD
Gen. 1:29, you it shall be for *f*
Gen. 9:3, that lives shall be *f*
Dt. 10:18, stranger, giving him *f*
Job 36:31, He give *f* in
Ps. 104:14, he may bring forth *f*
Ps. 136:25, Who gives *f* to all
Prov. 13:23, Much *f* is in the
Prov. 31:15, night, and provides *f*
Ezek. 4:10, *f* which you eat shall
Hab. 3:17, the fields yield no *f*
Mal. 3:10, that there may be *f*
Mt. 24:45, to give them *f*
Mt. 25:35, and you gave Me *f*
Lk. 3:11, and he who has *f*
Jn. 21:5, have you any *f*
Acts 2:46, they ate their *f*
Acts 14:17, our hearts with *f*
Rom. 14:15, destroy with your *f*
1 Cor. 8:13, *f* makes my brother
1 Cor. 10:3, the same spiritual *f*
2 Cor. 9:10, sower, and bread for *f*
1 Tim. 6:8, And having *f* and
Heb. 5:12, and not solid *f*
Heb. 5:14, But solid *f* belongs to
Heb. 12:16, of *f* sold his
Jas. 2:15, destitute of daily *f*

FOODS
1 Cor. 6:13, *F* for the stomach
1 Tim. 4:3, *f* which God

FOOL
Ps. 14:1, *f* has said in his
Prov. 10:23, is like sport to a *f*
Prov. 11:29, *f* will be servant
Prov. 12:15, *f* is right in his own
Prov. 13:16, *f* lays open his folly
Prov. 24:7, is too lofty for a *f*
Mt. 5:22, whoever says, 'You *f*
2 Cor. 11:23, I speak as a *f*
2 Cor. 12:11, I have become a *f*

FOOLISH
Job 2:10, of the *f* women speaks
Ps. 73:22, I was so *f* and
Prov. 14:1, *f* pulls it down with
Prov. 21:20, *f* man squanders it
Jer. 4:22, "For My people are *f*
1 Cor. 1:20, Has not God made *f*
Gal. 3:1, O *f* Galatians
Ti. 3:3, were also once *f*
Ti. 3:9, But avoid *f* disputes

FOOLISHLY
2 Cor. 11:21, I speak *f*

FOOLISHNESS
Ps. 69:5, O God, You know my *f*
Prov. 9:6, Forsake *f* and live
Prov. 12:23, of fools proclaims *f*
Prov. 19:3, The *f* of a man twists
Prov. 22:15, *F* is bound up in the
Prov. 24:9, devising of *f* is sin
Isa. 32:6, person will speak *f*
1 Cor. 1:18, of the cross is *f*
1 Cor. 1:25, Because the *f* of God

FOOLS
Prov. 1:7, *f* despise wisdom
Prov. 14:8, folly of *f* is deceit
Prov. 14:9, *F* mock at sin
Eccl. 5:4, has no pleasure in *f*
1 Cor. 4:10, We are *f* for Christ's

FOOT
Ps. 121:3, will not allow your *f*
Prov. 3:23, *f* will not stumble
Isa. 1:6, From the sole of the *f*
Isa. 58:13, you turn away your *f*
Mt. 18:8, *f* causes you to sin
Lk. 4:11, you dash your *f*
1 Cor. 12:15, If the *f* should say

FOOTMEN
Jer. 12:5, have run with the *f*

FOOTSTEPS
Ps. 77:19, *f* were not known
Ps. 85:13, and shall make His *f*

FOOTSTOOL of God
the temple called. 1 Chr. 28:2; Ps. 99:5; 132:7
the earth called. Isa. 66:1; Mt. 5:35; Acts 7:49
God's foes made. Ps. 110:1; Mt. 22:44; Heb. 10:13

FOOTSTOOL
Jas. 2:3, "Sit here at my *f*

FORBID
Mk. 9:39, said, "Do not *f*
Acts 10:47, "Can anyone *f*
1 Cor. 14:39, prophesy, and do not *f*
Gal. 6:14, *f* that I should boast

FORBIDDING
Acts 28:31, confidence, no one *f*
1 Th. 2:16, *f* us to speak to the
1 Tim. 4:3, *f* to marry

FORCE
Mt. 11:12, violent take it by *f*
Jn. 6:15, come and take Him by *f*
Heb. 9:17, a testament is in *f*

FORCEFUL
Job 6:25, *f* are right words

FORCES
Prov. 11:21, Though they join *f*

FOREFATHERS
Jer. 11:10, *f* who refused to hear
Acts 7:19, and oppressed our *f*
2 Tim. 1:3, conscience, as my *f*

FOREHEADS
Ezek. 3:8, against their *f*
Ezek. 9:4, put a mark on the *f*
Rev. 9:4, seal of God on their *f*
Rev. 20:4, his mark on their *f*

FOREIGNER
Gen. 23:4, "I am a *f* and a
Ruth 2:10, of me, since I am a *f*
Lk. 17:18, to God except this *f*
1 Cor. 14:11, who speaks will be a *f*

FOREIGNERS
Isa. 2:6, with the children of *f*
Isa. 60:10, *f* shall build up your
Acts 17:21, *f* who were there
Eph. 2:19, longer strangers and *f*

FOREKNEW
Rom. 8:29, For whom He *f*
Rom. 11:2, His people whom He *f*

FOREKNOWLEDGE
Acts 2:23, purpose and *f* of God
1 Pet. 1:2, according to the *f*

FOREORDAINED
1 Pet. 1:20, He indeed was *f*

FORERUNNER
Heb. 6:20, *f* has entered for us

FORESAW
Acts 2:25, 'I *f* the LORD

FORESEEING
Gal. 3:8, *f* that God would

FORESEES
Prov. 22:3, A prudent man *f*

FOREST
Ps. 50:10, beast of the *f* is Mine
Jas. 3:5, See how great a *f*

FORESTS
Ps. 29:9, and strips the *f*

FORETOLD
Acts 3:24, have also *f* these days
Acts 7:52, killed those who *f*

FOREVER
Gen. 3:22, and eat, and live *f*
Dt. 29:29, to our children *f*
1 Ki. 10:9, has loved Israel *f*
Job 7:16, I would not live *f*
Ps. 12:7, from this generation *f*
Ps. 29:10, LORD sits as King *f*
Ps. 44:23, Do not cast us off *f*
Ps. 45:6, throne, O God, is *f*
Ps. 110:4, "You are a priest *f*
Ps. 136:1, His mercy endures *f*
Ps. 145:1, will bless Your name *f*
Ps. 146:6, who keeps truth *f*
Ps. 146:10, The LORD shall reign *f*
Prov. 27:24, for riches are not *f*
Isa. 26:4, Trust in the LORD *f*
Isa. 40:8, of our God stands *f*
Isa. 51:6, My salvation will be *f*
Lam. 3:31, will not cast off *f*
Dan. 2:20, be the name of God *f*
Dan. 12:3, Like the stars *f*
Mic. 4:5, of the LORD our God *f*
Mt. 6:13, and the glory *f*
Jn. 12:34, the Christ remains *f*
2 Cor. 11:31, who is blessed *f*
Gal. 1:5, to whom be glory *f*
Eph. 3:21, generation, *f* and ever
Phil. 4:20, and Father be glory *f*
Heb. 1:8, throne, O God, is *f*
Heb. 7:28, has been perfected *f*
1 Pet. 1:23, lives and abides *f*
Jude 13, of darkness *f*
Jude 25, power, both now and *f*
Rev. 22:5, And they shall reign *f*

FOREVERMORE
Ps. 89:52, Blessed be the LORD *f*
Ps. 113:2, this time forth and *f*
Rev. 1:18, behold, I am alive *f*

FOREWARNED
1 Th. 4:6, all such, as we also *f*

FORGAVE
Ps. 32:5, *f* the iniquity of my
Lk. 7:42, to repay, he freely *f*
Eph. 4:32, God in Christ *f*
Col. 3:13, even as Christ *f*

FORGED
Ps. 119:69, The proud have *f*

FORGERS
Job 13:4, But you *f* of lies

FORGET
Gen. 41:51, "For God has made me *f*
Dt. 4:23, yourselves, lest you *f*
Dt. 4:31, *f* the covenant of your
Dt. 6:12, *f* the LORD who brought
Job 8:13, the paths of all who *f*
Ps. 9:17, all the nations that *f*
Ps. 50:22, this, you who *f*
Ps. 78:7, *f* the works of God
Ps. 119:16, I will not *f* Your word
Ps. 137:5, If I *f* you
Prov. 3:1, My son, do not *f*
Isa. 49:15, *f* her nursing child
Isa. 51:13, *f* the LORD your Maker
Jer. 2:32, *f* her ornaments
Heb. 6:10, *f* your work and labor

FORGETFULNESS
Ps. 88:12, in the land of *f*

FORGETS
Prov. 2:17, *f* the covenant of her
Jas. 1:24, and immediately *f*

FORGETTING
Phil. 3:13, *f* those things which

FORGIVE
1 Ki. 8:39, dwelling place, and *f*
2 Chr. 7:14, *f* their sin and heal
Ps. 86:5, good, and ready to *f*
Mt. 6:12, And *f* us our debts
Mt. 6:14, Father will also *f*
Mt. 6:15, *f* men their trespasses
Mt. 18:35, his heart, does not *f*
Mk. 2:7, Who can *f* sins but God
Jn. 20:23, *f* the sins of any
2 Cor. 2:7, you ought rather to *f*
2 Cor. 2:10, anything, I also *f*
2 Cor. 12:13, *F* me this wrong
1 Jn. 1:9, *f* us our sins and to

FORGIVEN
Ps. 32:1, transgression is *f*
Mk. 4:12, sins be *f* them
Lk. 7:47, to whom little is *f*
2 Cor. 2:10, indeed I have *f*
Col. 2:13, *f* you all trespasses
Jas. 5:15, sins, he will be *f*
1 Jn. 2:12, your sins are *f*

FORGIVENESS
mutual, commanded. Gen. 50:17; Mt. 5:23; 6:14; 18:21,35; Mk. 11:25; Lk. 11:4; 17:4; 2 Cor. 2:7; Eph. 4:32; Col. 3:13; Jas. 2:13
of enemies. Mt. 5:44; Lk. 6:27; Rom. 12:14,19
—— of sin, prayed for. Ex. 32:32; 1 Ki. 8:30; 2 Chr. 6:21; Ps. 25:18; 32; 51; 79:9; 130; Dan. 9:19; Amos 7:2; Mt. 6:12
promised. Lev. 4:20; 2 Chr. 7:14; Isa. 33:24; 55:7; Jer. 3:12; 31:20;34; 33:8; Ezek. 36:25; Hos. 14:4; Mic. 7:18; Lk. 24:47; Acts 5:31; 26:18; Eph. 1:7; Col. 1:14; Jas. 5:15; 1 Jn. 1:9

FORGIVENESS
Ps. 130:4, But there is *f* with
Dan. 9:9, God belong mercy and *f*
Acts 13:38, preached to you the *f*
Acts 26:18, they may receive *f*
Eph. 1:7, His blood, the *f*

FORGIVES
Ps. 103:3, *f* all your iniquities
Lk. 7:49, "Who is this who even *f*

FORGIVING
Eph. 4:32, tenderhearted, *f*
Col. 3:13, and *f* one another

FORGOT
Gen. 40:23, remember Joseph, but *f*
Jud. 3:7, *f* the LORD their God
Ps. 78:11, *f* His works and His
Ps. 106:13, They soon *f* His works

FORGOTTEN
Dt. 32:18, *f* the God who fathered
Ps. 42:9, "Why have You *f*
Ps. 44:20, If we had *f* the name
Eccl. 9:5, memory of them is *f*
Isa. 44:21, you will not be *f*
Isa. 49:14, and my Lord has *f*
Lam. 3:17, I have *f* prosperity
Lk. 12:6, not one of them is *f*
Heb. 12:5, *f* the exhortation
2 Pet. 1:9, *f* that he was cleansed

FORM
Gen. 1:2, earth was without *f*
Isa. 44:10, Who would *f* a god or
Isa. 45:7, *f* the light and create
Lk. 3:22, descended in bodily *f*
Jn. 5:37, time, nor seen His *f*
1 Cor. 7:31, For the *f* of this
Phil. 2:6, who, being in the *f*
1 Th. 5:22, Abstain from every *f*
2 Tim. 3:5, having a *f* of

FORMED
Gen. 2:7, And the LORD God *f*
Ps. 95:5, And His hands *f*
Ps. 139:13, *f* my inward parts
Prov. 26:10, *f* everything gives the
Isa. 29:16, say of him who *f*
Isa. 43:10, Me there was no God *f*
Isa. 43:21, This people I have *f*
Jer. 1:5, "Before I *f* you in
Rom. 9:20, Will the thing *f*
Rom. 9:20, say to him who *f*
Gal. 4:19, until Christ is *f*
1 Tim. 2:13, For Adam was *f* first

FORMER
Ps. 89:49, *f* lovingkindness
Eccl. 7:10, *f* days better than
Hos. 6:3, *f* rain to the earth
Zech. 1:4, *f* prophets preached
Gal. 1:13, *f* conduct in Judaism
Eph. 4:22, your *f* conduct
Rev. 21:4, *f* things have passed

FORMS
Isa. 45:9, clay say to him who *f*
Zech. 12:1, *f* the spirit of man

FORNICATION
denounced. Ex. 22:16; Lev. 19:20; Num. 25; Dt. 22:21; 23:17; Prov. 2:16; 5:3; 6:25; 7; 9:13; 22:14; 23:27; 29:3; 31:3; Eccl. 7:26; Hos. 4:11; Mt. 15:19; Mk. 7:21; Acts 15:20; Rom. 1:29; 1 Cor. 5:9; 6:9; 2 Cor. 12:21; Gal. 5:19; Eph. 5:5; Col. 3:5; 1 Th. 4:3; 1 Tim. 1:10; Heb. 13:4; 1 Pet. 4:3; Jude 7; Rev. 2:14; 21:8; 22:15

FORNICATION
Jn. 8:41, We were not born of *f*
Rev. 14:8, of the wrath of her *f*

FORNICATOR
Eph. 5:5, you know, that no *f*
Heb. 12:16, lest there be any *f*

FORNICATORS
Heb. 13:4, but *f* and adulterers

FORSAKE
2 Chr. 15:2, but if you *f* Him
Ps. 89:30, "If his sons *f*
Ps. 94:14, *f* His inheritance
Ps. 119:87, But I did not *f*
Prov. 1:8, father, and do not *f*
Jon. 2:8, worthless idols *f*
Lk. 14:33, of you does not *f*
Heb. 13:5, never leave you nor *f*

FORSAKEN
Ps. 22:1, My God, why have You *f*
Ps. 37:25, seen the righteous *f*
Isa. 7:16, you dread will be *f*
Isa. 17:9, cities will be as a *f*
Isa. 54:7, a mere moment I have *f*
Isa. 62:4, no longer be termed *F*
Jer. 2:13, they have *f* Me
Mt. 27:46, My God, why have You *f*
2 Cor. 4:9, persecuted, but not *f*
2 Tim. 4:10, for Demas has *f*
2 Pet. 2:15, *f* the right way

FORSAKING
Heb. 10:25, *f* the assembling

FORSOOK
Dt. 32:15, *f* God who made him
Mt. 26:56, all the disciples *f*
2 Tim. 4:16, with me, but all *f*
Heb. 11:27, By faith he *f* Egypt

FORTRESS
2 Sam. 22:2, LORD is my rock, my *f*
Ps. 31:2, my rock of refuge, a *f*

FORTY DAYS
the flood. Gen. 7:17
giving of the law. Ex. 24:18
spying Canaan. Num. 13:25
Goliath's defiance. 1 Sam. 17:16
Elijah's journey to Horeb. 1 Ki. 19:8
Jonah's warning to Nineveh. Jon. 3:4
fasting of our Lord. Mt. 4:2; Mk. 1:13; Lk. 4:2
Christ's appearances after the Resurrection. Acts 1:3

FOUL
Ps. 38:5, My wounds are *f*
Mt. 16:3, *f* weather today
Rev. 18:2, a prison for every *f*

FOUND
Gen. 2:20, *f* a helper comparable
Job 28:12, where can wisdom be *f*
Ps. 32:6, when You may be *f*
Ps. 89:20, *f* My servant David
Eccl. 7:28, a thousand I have *f*
Eccl. 7:29, this only I have *f*
Song 3:4, *f* the one I love
Isa. 55:6, LORD while He may be *f*
Hos. 14:8, your fruit is *f*
Lk. 13:6, fruit on it and *f* none
Lk. 15:24, he was lost and is *f*
Jn. 1:41, *f* the Messiah" (which
Rom. 7:10, I *f* to bring death
Phil. 3:9, and be *f* in Him
2 Pet. 3:14, be diligent to be *f*

FOUNDATION
Josh. 6:26, he shall lay its *f*
Ps. 87:1, His *f* is in the holy
Ps. 89:14, and justice are the *f*
Ps. 102:25, Of old You laid the *f*
Prov. 10:25, has an everlasting *f*
Lk. 6:48, deep and laid the *f*
Lk. 6:49, the earth without a *f*
Jn. 17:24, loved Me before the *f*
1 Cor. 3:10, I have laid the *f*
1 Cor. 3:11, *f* can anyone lay than
Eph. 1:4, us in Him before the *f*
2 Tim. 2:19, the solid *f* of God
Heb. 6:1, not laying again the *f*
Rev. 13:8, Lamb slain from the *f*
Rev. 21:19, the first *f* was jasper

FOUNDATIONS
Job 38:4, when I laid the *f*
Ps. 11:3, *f* are destroyed
Ps. 104:5, You who laid the *f*
Isa. 58:12, shall raise up the *f*
Rev. 21:19, And the *f* of the wall

FOUNDED
Ps. 24:2, For He has *f* it upon
Lk. 6:48, shake it, for it was *f*

FOUNTAIN
Jn. 4:14, will become in him a *f*

FOUNTAINS
Gen. 7:11, on that day all the *f*
Prov. 5:16, *f* be dispersed abroad
Prov. 8:24, when there were no *f*
Rev. 7:17, lead them to living *f*

FOX
Neh. 4:3, build, if even a *f*
Lk. 13:32, "Go, tell that *f*

FOXES
Jud. 15:4, caught three hundred *f*
Song 2:15, *f* that spoil the vines
Lk. 9:58, *F* have holes and birds

FRAGMENTS
Mt. 14:20, *f* that remained
Lk. 9:17, of the leftover *f*
Jn. 6:13, baskets with the *f*

FRAGRANCE
Song 4:11, garments is like the *f*
Jn. 12:3, was filled with the *f*
2 Cor. 2:15, we are to God the *f*

FRAIL
Ps. 39:4, that I may know how *f*

FRAME
Ps. 103:14, For He knows our *f*
Ps. 139:15, *f* was not hidden

FRAMED
Heb. 11:3, that the worlds were *f*

FRANKINCENSE
various uses for. Ex. 30:34; Lev. 2:1; Song 3:6; Mt. 2:11

FRAUD
Ps. 10:7; Mal. 3:5; Mk. 10:19; 1 Cor. 6:8; 1 Th. 4:6; Jas. 5:4. *See* DECEIT

FREE
Job 3:19, and the servant is *f*
Isa. 58:6, let the oppressed go *f*
Jn. 8:33, 'You will be made *f*
Jn. 8:36, if the Son makes you *f*
Rom. 6:18, And having been set *f*
Rom. 6:22, now having been set *f*
Rom. 8:2, Jesus has made me *f*
1 Cor. 9:1, Am I not *f*
Gal. 3:28, is neither slave nor *f*
Gal. 4:26, Jerusalem above is *f*
Gal. 5:1, Christ has made us *f*
Eph. 6:8, he is a slave or *f*
Rev. 13:16, poor, *f* and slave

FREED
Rom. 6:7, has died has been *f*

FREEDMAN
1 Cor. 7:22, slave is the Lord's *f*

FREEDMEN, Acts 6:9

FREELY
Gen. 2:16, the garden you may *f*
Hos. 14:4, I will love them *f*
Mt. 10:8, *F* you have received
Rom. 8:32, *f* give us all
1 Cor. 2:12, that have been *f*
Rev. 22:17, the water of life *f*

FREEWOMAN
Gal. 4:22, the other by a *f*
Gal. 4:30, with the son of the *f*

FRESH
Job 29:20, My glory is *f* within
Ps. 92:14, They shall be *f*
Jas. 3:12, both salt water and *f*

FRETS
Prov. 19:3, and his heart *f*

FRIEND
Ex. 33:11, a man speaks to his *f*
2 Chr. 20:7, of Abraham Your *f*
Ps. 35:14, though he were my *f*
Ps. 88:18, *f* You have put
Prov. 17:17, *f* loves at all times
Prov. 18:24, *f* who sticks closer
Prov. 27:10, not forsake your own *f*
Mt. 11:19, a *f* of tax collectors
Lk. 11:5, of you shall have a *f*
Jn. 11:11, *f* Lazarus sleeps
Jn. 19:12, you are not Caesar's *f*
Phile. 1, Philemon our beloved *f*
Jas. 2:23, he was called the *f*
Jas. 4:4, wants to be a *f*

FRIENDS
value of. Prov. 18:24; 27:6,9,17; Jn. 15:13
Jesus calls His disciples. Lk. 12:4; Jn. 15:14; 3 Jn. 14

FRIENDS
2 Sam. 19:6, and hate your *f*
Job 16:20, My *f* scorn me
Job 19:14, *f* have forgotten me
Prov. 14:20, the rich has many *f*
Jn. 15:13, one's life for his *f*
Jn. 15:14, "You are My *f*
Jn. 15:15, I have called you *f*
Acts 24:23, to forbid any of his *f*

FRIENDSHIP
of David and Jonathan. 1 Sam. 18:1; 19; 20; 2 Sam. 1:26
with the world, unlawful. Rom. 12:2; 2 Cor. 6:17; Jas. 4:4; 1 Jn. 2:15

FROGS
Ex. 8:2, your territory with *f*
Rev. 16:13, *f* coming out of the

FRONTLETS
Ex. 13:16, on your hand and as *f*
Dt. 6:8, and they shall be as *f*

FROZEN
Job 37:10, the broad waters are *f*

FRUIT
Num. 13:26, showed them the *f*
Dt. 28:4, Blessed shall be the *f*
Ps. 1:3, brings forth its *f*
Prov. 8:19, *f* is better than gold
Prov. 11:30, The *f* of the righteous
Prov. 12:14, with good by the *f*
Song 2:3, *f* was sweet to my
Isa. 3:10, they shall eat the *f*
Isa. 28:4, like the first *f*
Isa. 57:19, "I create the *f*
Hos. 14:8, *f* is found in Me
Mt. 3:10, does not bear good *f*
Mt. 7:17, good tree bears good *f*
Mt. 26:29, not drink of this *f*
Lk. 1:42, and blessed is the *f*
Lk. 8:14, life, and bring no *f*
Lk. 13:6, and he came seeking *f*
Lk. 13:9, 'And if it bears *f*
Jn. 15:2, branch that bears *f*
Jn. 15:8, that you bear much *f*
Jn. 15:16, should go and bear *f*
Rom. 6:21, *f* did you have then in
Rom. 6:22, God, you have your *f*
Rom. 7:4, that we should bear *f*
Gal. 5:22, But the *f* of the
Phil. 4:17, but I seek the *f*
Heb. 12:11, yields the peaceable *f*
Jas. 3:18, Now the *f* of
Jude 12, autumn trees without *f*
Rev. 22:2, tree yielding its *f*

FRUITFUL
Gen. 1:22, them, saying, "Be *f*
Gen. 49:22, a *f* bough, a *f*
Ps. 128:3, wife shall be like a *f*
Acts 14:17, heaven and *f* seasons
Col. 1:10, pleasing Him, being *f*

FRUITS
Mt. 3:8, Therefore bear *f*
Mt. 7:16, know them by their *f*
2 Cor. 9:10, and increase the *f*
Jas. 3:17, of mercy and good *f*
Rev. 22:2, which bore twelve *f*

FRUSTRATE, Ezra 4:5; Isa. 44:25

FUEL
Isa. 9:19, people shall be as *f*
Ezek. 15:4, into the fire for *f*

FULFILL
Lev. 22:21, the LORD, to *f* his vow
1 Ki. 5:9, And you shall *f*
Ps. 20:5, *f* all your petitions
Ps. 145:19, *f* the desire of those
Mt. 3:15, for us to *f* all
Gal. 6:2, *f* the law of Christ
Phil. 2:2, *f* my joy by being
2 Th. 1:11, and *f* all the good
Jas. 2:8, If you really *f*

FULFILLED
Mt. 5:18, the law till all is *f*
Lk. 21:24, of the Gentiles are *f*
Lk. 24:44, all things must be *f*
Rom. 8:4, of the law might be *f*
Rom. 13:8, loves another has *f*
Gal. 5:14, For all the law is *f*

FULFILLMENT
Lk. 1:45, for there will be a *f*
Rom. 13:10, love is the *f* of the

FULL
Ruth 1:21, "I went out *f*
Job 32:18, For I am *f* of words
Ps. 29:4, of the LORD is *f*
Ps. 127:5, who has his quiver
Prov. 30:9, Lest I be *f* and deny
Eccl. 1:7, yet the sea is not *f*
Isa. 6:3, the whole earth is *f*
Ezek. 37:1, and it was *f* of bones
Mic. 3:8, But truly I am *f*
Mt. 6:22, whole body will be *f*
Jn. 1:14, of the Father, *f*
Jn. 15:11, your joy may be *f*
Acts 6:5, chose Stephen, a man *f*
1 Cor. 4:8, You are already *f*
Phil. 4:12, learned both to be *f*
Phil. 4:18, I am *f*

FULL-GROWN
Jas. 1:15, and sin, when it is *f*

FULLNESS
Ps. 36:8, satisfied with the *f*
Jn. 1:16, *f* we have all received
Rom. 11:25, to Israel until the *f*
Gal. 4:4, But when the *f* of the
Eph. 1:10, dispensation of the *f*
Eph. 3:19, filled with all the *f*
Col. 2:9, Him dwells all the *f*

FUME
Ps. 68:16, Why do you *f* with envy

FUNCTION
Rom. 12:4, do not have the same *f*

FURIOUS
Ps. 89:38, You have been *f*
Prov. 22:24, *f* man do not go
Ezek. 5:15, fury and in *f* rebukes
Nah. 1:2, LORD avenges and is *f*
Acts 5:33, this, they were *f*

FURIOUSLY
2 Ki. 9:20, for he drives *f*

FURNACE
Dt. 4:20, you out of the iron *f*
Isa. 48:10, tested you in the *f*
Dan. 3:6, of a burning fiery *f*
Mt. 13:42, cast them into the *f*
Rev. 9:2, the smoke of a great *f*

FURNISHED
Prov. 9:2, also *f* her table
Mk. 14:15, a large upper room, *f*

FURROWS
Ps. 65:10; 129:3; Hos. 10:4; 12:11

FURY
Isa. 27:4, *F* is not in Me
Isa. 51:20, they are full of the *f*
Isa. 59:18, *f* to His adversaries
Isa. 63:5, and My own *f*
Jer. 21:5, even in anger and *f*
Ezek. 5:13, and I will cause My *f*
Ezek. 6:12, Thus will I spend My *f*
Mic. 5:15, in anger and *f* on the

FUTILE
Dt. 32:47, For it is not a *f*
Jer. 10:3, of the peoples are *f*
1 Cor. 3:20, wise, that they are *f*
1 Cor. 15:17, risen, your faith is *f*

FUTILITY
Job 7:3, allotted months of *f*
Ps. 89:47, *f* have You created all
Rom. 8:20, was subjected to *f*

FUTURE
Ps. 37:37, for the *f* of that man
Ps. 37:38, the *f* of the wicked
Jer. 29:11, to give you a *f*

GABRIEL
appears to: Daniel. Dan. 8:16; 9:21
Zacharias. Lk. 1:19
Mary. Lk. 1:26

GAD
Gen. 30:11; 46:16; 49:19; 49:10; Num. 1:24; 26:15; 32; 34:14; Dt. 27:13; 33:20; Josh. 4:12; 22:1,11

GADARENES, *see also* GERGESENES
Christ's miracle in the country of. Mk. 5:1; Lk. 8:26,37

GAIN
Prov. 3:14, *g* than fine gold
Prov. 31:11, will have no lack of *g*
Eccl. 3:6, a time to *g*
Ezek. 22:27, to get dishonest *g*
Hab. 2:9, him who covets evil *g*
Phil. 1:21, and to die is *g*
Phil. 3:8, rubbish, that I may *g*
1 Tim. 6:5, is a means of *g*
1 Tim. 6:6, contentment is great *g*
1 Pet. 5:2, for dishonest *g*

GAINED
Eccl. 1:16, *g* more wisdom than all
Mt. 25:20, *g* five more talents

GAINS
Mt. 16:26, *g* the whole world

GAIUS, Acts 19:29
his piety. 3 Jn.

GALATIA
a place colonized by Gauls. Acts 16:6

GALATIANS, Gal. 3:1
Paul visits. Acts 16:6
rebuked. Gal. 1:6; 3
exhorted. Gal. 5; 6
their love to Paul. Gal. 4:13

GALILEANS
slaughter of. Lk. 13:1
disciples so called. Acts 1:11; 2:7

GALILEE, Josh. 20:7
Isaiah's prophecy concerning. Isa. 9:1; Mt. 4:15

work of Christ there. Mt. 2:22; 15:29; 26:32; 27:55; 28:7; Mk. 1:9; Lk. 4:14; 23:5; 24:6; Acts 10:37; 13:31

GALL
Ps. 69:21, They also gave me *g*
Lam. 3:19, the wormwood and the *g*
Amos 6:12, turned justice into *g*
Mt. 27:34, wine mingled with *g*

GALLIO
dismisses Paul. Acts 18:12

GAMALIEL
Num. 1:10; Acts 5:34; 22:3

GAP
Ezek. 22:30, and stand in the *g*

GARDEN
Gen. 2:8, LORD God planted a *g*
Song 4:12, *g* enclosed is my
Isa. 58:11, like a watered *g*
Ezek. 28:13, Eden, the *g* of God
Ezek. 34:29, raise up for them a *g*
Jn. 18:1, where there was a *g*
Jn. 19:41, *g* a new tomb in

GARDENER
Jn. 20:15, Him to be the *g*

GARDENS
Eccl. 2:5, I made myself *g*
Jer. 29:5, plant *g* and eat their

GARLANDS
Acts 14:13, brought oxen and *g*

GARMENT
Josh. 7:21, beautiful Babylonia *g*
Job 13:28, *g* that is moth-eaten
Ps. 69:11, made sackcloth my *g*
Ps. 104:2, with light as with a *g*
Prov. 25:20, one who takes away a *g*
Mt. 9:20, the hem of His *g*
Mt. 22:11, have on a wedding *g*
Mk. 2:21, cloth on an old *g*
Heb. 1:11, all grow old like a *g*
Jude 23, hating even the *g*

GARMENTS
Dt. 8:4, *g* did not wear out on
Job 37:17, Why are your *g* hot
Ps. 22:18, They divide My *g*
Eccl. 9:8, *g* always be white
Isa. 9:5, *g* rolled in blood
Isa. 63:1, from Edom, with dyed *g*
Zech. 3:4, Take away the filthy *g*
Mt. 11:8, man clothed in soft *g*
Mt. 21:8, spread their *g* on the
Mt. 27:35, and divided His *g*
Lk. 24:4, by them in shining *g*
Jas. 5:2, *g* are moth-eaten
Rev. 3:5, be clothed in white *g*

GARRISON
Mt. 27:27, gathered the whole *g*
2 Cor. 11:32, Damascenes with a *g*

GATE
Ps. 118:20, This is the *g* of the
Mt. 7:13, by the narrow *g*
Jn. 5:2, by the Sheep G a pool
Acts 3:2, laid daily at the *g*
Heb. 13:12, suffered outside the *g*
Rev. 21:21, each individual *g*

GATES
Gen. 24:60, possess the *g* of those
Neh. 1:3, *g* burned with fire
Job 17:16, they go down to the *g*
Ps. 24:7, up your heads, O you *g*
Ps. 87:2, The LORD loves the *g*
Ps. 118:19, Open to me the *g*
Prov. 31:23, is known in the *g*
Isa. 62:10, go through the *g*
Mt. 16:18, and the *g* of Hades
Rev. 21:12, wall with twelve *g*
Rev. 21:21, *g* were twelve pearls
Rev. 21:25, *g* shall not be shut

GATH, Josh. 11:22
Goliath of. 1 Sam. 17:4
men of, stricken with tumors. 1 Sam. 5:8
David a refugee there. 1 Sam. 27:4
taken by David. 1 Chr. 18:1; by Hazael. 2 Ki. 12:17
Uzziah breaks down the wall of. 2 Chr. 26:6

GATHER
Ps. 26:9, *g* my soul with sinners
Ps. 50:5, *G* My saints
Eccl. 3:5, and a time to *g* stones
Isa. 40:11, *g* the lambs with His
Mt. 3:12, *g* His wheat into the
Mt. 6:26, sow nor reap nor *g*
Mt. 7:16, Do men *g* grapes from
Mt. 25:26, *g* where I have not
Mk. 13:27, *g* together His

GATHERED
Ex. 16:18, *g* little had no lack
Ps. 107:3, And *g* out of the lands
Mt. 13:47, *g* some of every kind
Mt. 25:32, the nations will be *g*

GATHERING
Gen. 1:10, *g* together of the
2 Th. 2:1, *g* together to Him

GATHERS
Ps. 33:7, *g* the waters of the
Ps. 41:6, His heart *g* iniquity
Prov. 6:8, *g* her food in the
Isa. 56:8, The Lord GOD, who *g*
Mt. 23:37, together, as a hen *g*

GAVE
Gen. 3:12, to be with me, she *g*
Mt. 21:23, *g* You this authority
Jn. 3:16, that He *g* His only
Jn. 17:12, Those whom You *g*
1 Cor. 3:6, but God *g* the increase
Gal. 1:4, *g* Himself for our sins
Gal. 2:20, *g* Himself for me
Eph. 5:25, *g* Himself for it
Rev. 20:13, The sea *g* up the dead

GAZA, Gen. 10:19
Samson carries away the gates of. Jud. 16
destruction of, foretold. Jer. 47; Amos 1:6; Zeph. 2:4; Zech. 9:5

GAZED
Acts 7:55, *g* into heaven and saw

GAZING
Acts 1:11, why do you stand *g*

GEDALIAH
governor of the remnant of Judah. 2 Ki. 25:22 (Jer. 40:5)
treacherously killed by Ishmael. 2 Ki. 25:25 (Jer. 41)

GEHAZI
servant of Elisha. 2 Ki. 4:12
his covetousness. 2 Ki. 5:20

GENEALOGIES
generations of: Adam. Gen. 5; 1 Chr. 1; Lk. 3
Noah. Gen. 10; 1 Chr. 1:4
Shem. Gen. 11:10
Terah. Gen. 11:27
Abraham. Gen. 25; 1 Chr. 1:28
Jacob. Gen. 29:31; 30; 46:8; Ex. 1:2; Num. 26; 1 Chr. 2
Esau. Gen. 36; 1 Chr. 1:35
the tribes. 1 Chr. 2; 4—7
David. 1 Chr. 3
Christ. Mt. 1; Lk. 3:23
endless. 1 Tim. 1:4

GENEALOGIES
1 Tim. 1:4, fables and endless *g*

GENEALOGY
Mt. 1:1, The book of the *g*
Heb. 7:3, mother, without *g*

GENERATION
Dt. 32:5, perverse and crooked *g*
Ps. 112:2, The *g* of the upright
Ps. 145:4, *g* shall praise Your
Prov. 30:11, *g* that curses its
Prov. 30:12, *g* that is pure in its
Eccl. 1:4, One *g* passes away
Isa. 34:10, *g* it shall lie
Isa. 53:8, who will declare His *g*
Mt. 12:39, and adulterous *g*
Mt. 24:34, this *g* will by no
Acts 2:40, from this perverse *g*
1 Pet. 2:9, But you are a chosen *g*

GENERATIONS
Ps. 45:17, be remembered in all *g*
Ps. 79:13, Your praise to all *g*
Ps. 105:8, for a thousand *g*
Lk. 1:48, *g* will call me blessed

GENEROUS
Prov. 11:25, *g* soul will be made
Prov. 22:9, *g* eye will be blessed
Isa. 32:5, no longer be called *g*
Isa. 32:8, *g* man devises *g*

GENNESARET, Mt. 14:34
a lake of Palestine, miracles performed there. Mt. 17:27; Lk. 5:1; Jn. 21:6

GENTILES
their state by nature. 1 Cor. 12:2; Eph. 4:17; 1 Th. 4:5
their conversion predicted. Isa. 42:1; 49:6 (Mt. 12:18; Lk. 2:32; Acts 13:47); Mal. 1:11
calling of. Rom. 9:24
become fellow citizens with the saints. Eph. 2:19
Christ made known to. Col. 1:27

GENTILES
Gen. 10:5, *G* were separated

Isa. 42:6, as a light to the *G*
Isa. 60:3, *G* shall come to your
Isa. 61:6, the riches of the *G*
Mt. 6:32, all these things the *G*
Mt. 10:5, into the way of the *G*
Lk. 2:32, revelation to the *G*
Lk. 21:24, *G* are fulfilled
Acts 9:15, bear My name before *G*
Acts 10:45, poured out on the *G*
Acts 13:47, a light to the *G*
Rom. 2:24, blasphemed among the *G*
Rom. 3:29, also the God of the *G*
1 Cor. 5:1, even named among the *G*
Col. 1:27, mystery among the *G*
1 Tim. 2:7, a teacher of the *G*
3 Jn. 7, nothing from the *G*

GENTLE
Prov. 25:15, *g* tongue breaks a bone
Mt. 11:29, from Me, for I am *g*
1 Th. 2:7, But we were *g* among
Ti. 3:2, to be peaceable, *g*
1 Pet. 2:18, only to the good and *g*
1 Pet. 3:4, ornament of a *g*

GENTLENESS
of Christ. 2 Cor. 10:1; Mt. 11:29 (Isa. 40:11)

GENTLENESS
Ps. 18:35, *g* has made me great
1 Cor. 4:21, love and a spirit of *g*
Gal. 5:23, *g*, self-control
Eph. 4:2, all lowliness and *g*
Phil. 4:5, Let your *g* be known to
1 Tim. 6:11, love, patience, *g*

GERAR, Gen. 10:19
herdsmen of, quarrel with those of Isaac. Gen. 26:20

GERGESENES, *see also* GADARENES
Christ's miracle in the country of. Mt. 8:28

GERIZIM
mount of blessing. Dt. 11:29; 27:12; Josh. 8:33

GERSHOM
son of Moses. Ex. 2:22; 18:3
(Gershon), son of Levi. Gen. 46:11; Num. 3:17

GERSHONITES, Num. 3:21
their duties in the service of the tabernacle. Num. 4; 7; 10:17

GESHUR, 2 Sam. 3:3; 13:37; 14:23

GETHSEMANE
garden of, our Lord's agony there. Mt. 26:36; Mk. 14:32; Lk. 22:39; Jn. 18:1

GHOST
Mk. 6:49, supposed it was a *g*

GIANTS
before the flood. Gen. 6:4
inhabit Canaan. Dt. 2:10,11,19,20; 9:2
spies discourage the people by stories of. Num. 13:33; Dt. 1:28
several killed by David and his servants. 1 Sam. 17; 2 Sam. 21:16; 1 Chr. 20:4

GIBEAH, Josh. 15:57
a city of Benjamin. Jud. 19:14
sin of its inhabitants. Jud. 19:22
their punishment. Jud. 20
the city of Saul. 1 Sam. 10:26; 11:4; 14:2; 15:34; 2 Sam. 21:6

GIBEON
its inhabitants deceive Joshua. Josh. 9
delivered by him from the five kings. Josh. 10
Saul persecutes them. 2 Sam. 21:1
David makes atonement. 2 Sam. 21:3–9
Solomon's dream at. 1 Ki. 3:5
tabernacle of the Lord kept at. 1 Chr. 16:39; 21:29

GIBEONITES, 2 Sam. 21:1

GIDEON
God appoints him to deliver Israel from the Midianites. Jud. 6:14
destroys the altar and images of Baal. Jud. 6:25,27
called Jerubbaal. Jud. 6:32
God gives him two signs. Jud. 6:36–40
his army reduced, and selected by a test of water. Jud. 7:2–7
his stratagem. Jud. 7:16
subdues the Midianites. Jud. 7:19; 8
makes an ephod of the plunder. Jud. 8:24
his death. Jud. 8:32. *See* Heb. 11:32

GIFT
Prov. 18:16, *g* makes room for him
Prov. 21:14, A *g* in secret pacifies
Eccl. 3:13, it is the *g* of God
Mk. 7:11, is Corban"—'(that is, a *g*
Jn. 4:10, If you knew the *g*
Rom. 5:15, But the free *g* is not
Rom. 6:23, but the *g* of God is
1 Cor. 7:7, each one has his own *g*
1 Cor. 13:2, though I have the *g*
Eph. 2:8, it is the *g* of God
Phil. 4:17, Not that I seek the *g*
1 Tim. 4:14, Do not neglect the *g*
2 Tim. 1:6, you to stir up the *g*
Heb. 6:4, tasted the heavenly *g*
Jas. 1:17, Every good *g* and every
1 Pet. 4:10, one has received a *g*

GIFTED
Ex. 35:25, the women who were *g*
Dan. 1:4, but good-looking, *g*

GIFTS
spiritual. Ps. 29:11; 68:18,35; 84:11; Prov. 2:6; Ezek. 11:19; Acts 11:17; Rom. 12:6; 1 Cor. 1:7; 12; 13:2; 14; Eph. 2:8; Jas. 1:5,17; 4:6
temporal. Gen. 1:26; 9:1; 27:28; Lev. 26:4; Ps. 34:10; 65:9; 104; 136:25; 145:15; 147; Isa. 30:23; Acts 14:17
Corban. Mt. 15:5; Mk. 7:11

GIFTS
Num. 18:29, *g* you shall offer
Ps. 68:18, You have received *g*
Ps. 72:10, and Seba will offer *g*
Prov. 6:35, though you give many *g*
Prov. 19:6, to one who gives *g*
Mt. 7:11, how to give good *g*
Lk. 21:1, rich putting their *g*
Rom. 12:6, *g* differing
1 Cor. 12:4, are diversities of *g*
1 Cor. 14:1, and desire spiritual *g*
Eph. 4:8, captive, and gave *g*

GILBOA, 1 Sam. 28:4
Mount, Saul killed there. 1 Sam. 31; 2 Sam. 1:21

GILEAD, Gen. 31:21
land of, granted to the Reubenites, etc. Num. 32
invaded by the Ammonites. Jud. 10:17
Jephthah made captain of. Jud. 11

GILGAL
Joshua encamps there. Josh. 4:19; 9:6
Saul made king there. 1 Sam. 10:8; 11:14
Saul sacrifices at. 1 Sam. 13:8; 15:12

GIRD
Ps. 45:3, *G* Your sword upon Your
Ps. 76:10, of wrath You shall *g*
Isa. 45:5, I will *g* you
Jn. 21:18, and another will *g*
1 Pet. 1:13, Therefore *g* up the

GIRDED
Jn. 13:4, a towel and *g* Himself
Rev. 1:13, down to the feet and *g*

GIRGASHITES
descendants of Canaan. Gen. 10:15; 15:21
communion with, forbidden. Dt. 7:1
driven out. Josh. 3:10; 24:11

GIVE
1 Chr. 16:8, *g* thanks to the LORD
2 Chr. 1:10, *g* me wisdom and
Ps. 17:1, *G* ear to my prayer
Ps. . 28:4, *G* to them according
Ps. 37:4, *g* you the desires
Ps. 85:12, Yes, the LORD will *g*
Ps. 119:34, *G* me understanding
Prov. 23:26, *g* me your heart
Mic. 7:20, You will *g* truth to
Mt. 5:42, "*G* to him who asks
Mt. 6:11, *G* us this day our
Mt. 19:21, what you have and *g*
Lk. 4:6, authority I will *g*
Jn. 10:28, *g* them eternal life
Jn. 13:34, A new commandment I *g*
Acts 3:6, but what I do have I *g*
Rom. 8:32, *g* us all things
1 Cor. 10:32, *G* no offense
2 Cor. 9:7, So let each one *g*
Eph. 4:28, *g* him who has need
2 Th. 2:13, *g* thanks to God always
1 Tim. 4:15, *g* yourself entirely
1 Tim. 6:18, good works, ready to *g*

GIVEN
Mt. 13:12, to him more will be *g*
Mt. 25:29, has, more will be *g*
Lk. 12:48, to whom much is *g*
Jn. 6:39, *g* Me I should lose
Jn. 7:39, Spirit was not yet *g*
1 Cor. 2:12, have been freely *g*

1 Tim. 3:3, not *g* to wine

GIVES
Prov. 28:27, He who *g* to the poor
Eccl. 2:26, For God *g* wisdom and
Jn. 6:33, *g* life to the world
Jn. 6:37, All that the Father *g*
Jn. 10:11, The good shepherd *g*
Jn. 14:27, not as the world *g*
1 Tim. 6:17, *g* us richly all things
Jas. 1:5, who *g* to all liberally
Jas. 4:6, But He *g* more grace
Jas. 4:6, *g* grace to the humble

GLAD
Ps. 9:2, I will be *g* and
Ps. 16:9, my heart is *g*
Ps. 32:11, Be *g* in the LORD and
Ps. 46:4, streams shall make *g*
Ps. 104:15, And wine that makes *g*
Ps. 122:1, I was *g* when they said
Lk. 15:32, make merry and be *g*
Jn. 8:56, he saw it and was *g*

GLADNESS
Num. 10:10, in the day of your *g*
Est. 9:17, day of feasting and *g*
Ps. 4:7, You have put *g* in my
Ps. 51:8, me hear joy and *g*
Ps. 100:2, Serve the LORD with *g*
Isa. 35:10, shall obtain joy and *g*
Zeph. 3:17, over you with *g*
Mk. 4:16, receive it with *g*

GLASS
Rev. 4:6, there was a sea of *g*
Rev. 21:21, like transparent *g*

GLEAN, Lev. 19:10; Jer. 6:9; 49:9

GLORIFIED
Lev. 10:3, the people I must be *g*
Mt. 15:31, and they *g* the God of
Jn. 7:39, Jesus was not yet *g*
Jn. 12:16, when Jesus was *g*
Jn. 15:8, By this My Father is *g*
Jn. 17:4, "I have *g* You on the
Acts 3:13, *g* His Servant Jesus
Rom. 8:30, these He also *g*
1 Pet. 4:11, things God may be *g*

GLORIFY
Isa. 60:7, My altar, and I will *g*
Mt. 5:16, *g* your Father in
Jn. 12:28, "Father, *g* Your name
Jn. 16:14, "He will *g* Me
Jn. 17:5, And now, O Father, *g*
Jn. 21:19, what death he would *g*
Rom. 1:21, God, they did not *g*
1 Cor. 6:20, therefore *g* God in
Heb. 5:5, also Christ did not *g*
1 Pet. 4:16, ashamed, but let him *g*

GLORIFY GOD
exhortations to. 1 Chr. 16:28; Ps. 22:23; 50:15; Rom. 15:6; 1 Cor. 6:20; 10:31; 1 Pet. 2:12; Rev. 15:4

GLORIOUS
Ps. 45:13, daughter is all *g*
Ps. 72:19, And blessed be His *g*
Ps. 87:3, *G* things are spoken
Ps. 111:3, is honorable and *g*
Ps. 145:5, *g* splendor of Your
Isa. 63:15, habitation, holy and *g*
Eph. 5:27, it to Himself a *g*
Phil. 3:21, be conformed to His *g*
Ti. 2:13, *g* appearing of our

GLORY
Ex. 33:18, "Please, show me Your *g*
1 Sam. 4:21, *g* has departed from
1 Chr. 16:10, *G* in His holy name
Ps. 3:3, a shield for me, my *g*
Ps. 8:1, who have set Your *g*
Ps. 24:8, Who is this King of *g*
Ps. 26:8, the place where Your *g*
Ps. 63:2, Your power and Your *g*
Ps. 145:11, shall speak of the *g*
Prov. 3:35, wise shall inherit *g*
Prov. 20:29, The *g* of young men is
Prov. 25:2, It is the *g* of God to
Isa. 24:16, "*G* to the righteous
Isa. 42:8, *g* I will not give
Isa. 60:2, *g* will be seen upon
Ezek. 31:18, then be likened in *g*
Hos. 4:7, I will change their *g*
Zech. 2:5, and I will be the *g*
Zech. 6:13, He shall bear the *g*
Mt. 6:2, that they may have *g*
Mt. 6:13, the power and the *g*
Mt. 6:29, *g* was not arrayed
Mt. 16:27, Man will come in the *g*
Mt. 24:30, with power and great *g*
Lk. 2:14, "*G* to God in the
Jn. 1:14, and we beheld His *g*
Jn. 2:11, and manifested His *g*
Jn. 8:50, I do not seek My own *g*
Jn. 9:24, "Give God the *g*
Jn. 17:5, *g* which I had with You
Jn. 17:22, *g* which You gave Me I
Acts 12:23, he did not give *g*
Rom. 2:7, doing good seek for *g*
Rom. 3:23, fall short of the *g*
Rom. 4:20, in faith, giving *g*
Rom. 9:4, the adoption, the *g*
Rom. 9:23, the riches of His *g*
Rom. 16:27, God, alone wise, be *g*
1 Cor. 1:31, who glories, let him *g*
1 Cor. 11:7, but woman is the *g*
2 Cor. 3:10, of the *g* that excels
2 Cor. 4:4, of the gospel of the *g*
2 Cor. 4:17, eternal weight of *g*
2 Cor. 10:17, who glories, let him *g*
Phil. 4:19, to His riches in *g*
Col. 3:4, appear with Him in *g*
1 Th. 2:20, For you are our *g*
Heb. 2:10, many sons to *g*
1 Pet. 1:24, grass, and all the *g*
1 Pet. 4:11, to whom belong the *g*
1 Pet. 4:14, for the Spirit of *g*
Jude 24, the presence of His *g*
Rev. 4:11, O Lord, to receive *g*
Rev. 21:23, *g* of God illuminated

GLORYING
1 Cor. 5:6, Your *g* is not good

GLUTTON
Prov. 23:21, *g* will come to poverty
Lk. 7:34, you say, 'Look, a *g*

GLUTTONS
Prov. 28:7, *g* shames his
Ti. 1:12, evil beasts, lazy *g*

GLUTTONY
condemned. Dt. 21:20; Prov. 23:1,20; 25:16; 1 Pet. 4:3

GNASHING
Mt. 8:12, will be weeping and *g*

GO
Gen. 32:26, He said, "Let Me *g*
Ex. 5:1, 'Let My people *g*
Ex. 33:15, Presence does not *g*
Ruth 1:16, for wherever you *g*
Job 23:8, "Look, I *g* forward
Ps. 42:4, For I used to *g*
Ps. 58:3, *g* astray as soon as
Ps. 71:16, I will *g* in the
Ps. 107:23, Those who *g* down to
Ps. 139:7, Where can I *g* from
Prov. 6:6, *G* to the ant
Eccl. 3:20, All *g* to one place
Eccl. 7:2, of mourning than to *g*
Isa. 2:3, of Zion shall *g*
Mt. 8:19, You wherever You *g*
Mt. 24:26, do not *g* out
Mk. 16:15, He said to them, "*G*
Lk. 7:8, And I say to one, '*G*
Jn. 6:67, also want to *g* away
Jn. 6:68, to whom shall we *g*
Jn. 8:21, *g* you cannot come
Jn. 14:2, I *g* to prepare a place
Jn. 14:12, will do, because I *g*
Jn. 18:8, seek Me, let these *g*
Rev. 3:12, he shall *g* out no more

GOADS
Eccl. 12:11, of the wise are like *g*
Acts 9:5, to kick against the *g*

GOAL
Phil. 3:14, I press toward the *g*

GOATS
Ps. 50:13, drink the blood of *g*
Mt. 25:32, his sheep from the *g*
Heb. 9:12, with the blood of *g*
Heb. 10:4, *g* could take away

GOD

THE LORD GOD ALMIGHTY
Gen. 17:1; Ex. 6:3; Num. 24:4; Ruth 1:20; Job 5:17; Ps. 68:14; 91:1; Isa. 13:6; Ezek. 1:24; Joel 1:15; 2 Cor. 6:18; Rev. 1:8

THE CREATOR
Gen. 1; 2; Dt. 4:19; Neh. 9:6; Job 33:4; 38; Ps. 8; 19:1; 33:6; 89:11; 94:9; 104; 136; 146:6; 148; Prov. 3:19; 8:22; Eccl. 12:1; Isa. 37:16; 40:28; 43:7,13; 45:8; Jer. 10:12; 32:17; Zech. 12:1; Jn. 1:3; Acts 17:24; Rom. 1:25; Col. 1:16; Heb. 1:10; 3:4; 11:3; 1 Pet. 4:19; Rev. 4:11

HIS DEALINGS WITH
our first parents. Gen. 3. *See* ADAM, EVE
Noah and the sinful world. Gen. 6—9
Abraham. Gen. 12—24
Lot. Gen. 19
Isaac, Jacob, and Esau. Gen. 22; 25; 26; 28
Joseph. Gen. 39
Moses and Aaron. Ex. 3; 7
Pharaoh and Egypt. Ex. 7; 8
causes the plagues of Egypt: blood. Ex. 7; frogs, lice, and flies. Ex. 8;

pestilence, boils, and hail. Ex. 9; locusts and darkness. Ex. 10; death of the firstborn. Ex. 12
Israel in Egypt: institutes the Passover. Ex. 11—13; and delivers the Israelites. Ex. 14
the children of Israel during their forty years' wandering in the wilderness (Exodus, Leviticus, Numbers, Deuteronomy):
sends manna. Ex. 16:15
gives the Ten Commandments. Ex. 20
reveals His glory to Moses, Aaron, and the elders. Ex. 24
enters into covenant with Israel. Ex. 34
directs the tabernacle to be made and erected. Ex. 35; 40
propounds the law respecting sacrificial offerings. Lev. 1; Num. 28
sanctifies Aaron. Lev. 8; 9
institutes blessings and curses. Lev. 26; Dt. 27
punishes the revolt of Korah, Dathan, and Abiram. Num. 16
causes Aaron's rod to blossom. Num. 17
excludes Moses and Aaron from the promised land for unbelief. Num. 20:12
sends fiery serpents, and heals with bronze serpent. Num. 21
Balaam and Balak. Num. 22
Joshua, at Jericho and Ai. Josh. 1; 3; 4; 6; 7; 8
kings of Canaan. Josh. 10—12
Gideon. Jud. 6; Jephthah. Jud. 11; Samson. Jud. 13
Naomi and Ruth. Ruth 1—4
Hannah, Eli, and Samuel. 1 Sam. 1—3
Saul. 1 Sam. 9—31; 1 Chr. 10
David. 1 Sam. 16—31; 2 Sam. 1—24; 1 Ki. 1—2:11; 1 Chr. 11—23; 28; 29
Solomon. 1 Ki. 1—11; 2 Chr. 1—9
Rehoboam and Jeroboam. 1 Ki. 12—15; 2 Chr. 10—12
Ahab. 1 Ki. 16—22; 2 Chr. 18
Elijah. 1 Ki. 17—22; 2 Ki. 1; 2
Elisha. 2 Ki. 2—9
Hezekiah. 2 Ki. 18—20; 2 Chr. 29—32; Isa. 36—39
Josiah. 2 Ki. 22; 23; 2 Chr. 34; 35
the captive Jews in Persia. Est. 1—10
the liberated Jews. Ezra 1—10; Neh. 1—13
Job and his friends. Job 1; 2; 38—42
Isaiah. 2 Ki. 19; 20; 2 Chr. 26; 32
Jeremiah. 2 Chr. 35; 36; Jer. 26; 34—43
Daniel at Babylon. Dan. 1—10
Shadrach, Meshach, and Abed-Nego. Dan. 3
Nebuchadnezzar. Dan. 4
Jonah at Tarshish and Nineveh. Jon. 1—4

HIS REVELATIONS TO
Isaiah, warning Judah and Israel. Isa. 1—12; warning surrounding nations. Isa. 13—23; threatening impenitent Jews. Isa. 24; 39
Jeremiah, respecting Judah's overthrow on account of sin. Jer. 1—25; 27—33; 44
Ezekiel, concerning: Judah's captivity. Ezek. 3—7; the defiled temple. Ezek. 8—11; warnings to Judah. Ezek. 12—19; impending judgments. Ezek. 20—23; Jerusalem's overthrow. Ezek. 24; judgments on other nations. Ezek. 25—32; exhortations and promises. Ezek. 32—39; the new Jerusalem. Ezek. 40—48

GOD AS A SPIRIT (Jn. 4:24; 2 Cor. 3:17)
is declared to be: omnipotent. Gen. 17:1; Ex. 6:3; glorious. Ex. 15:11; Ps. 145:5; gracious. Ex. 34:6; Ps. 116:5; merciful. Ex. 34:6,7; Ps. 86:5; longsuffering. Num. 14:18; Mic. 7:18; just. Dt. 32:4; Isa. 45:21; eternal. Dt. 33:27; Ps. 90:2; Rev. 4:8–10; jealous. Josh. 24:19; Nah. 1:2; compassionate. 2 Ki. 13:23; great. 2 Chr. 2:5; Ps. 86:10; righteous. Ezra 9:15; Ps. 145:17; unsearchable. Job 11:7; 37:23; Ps. 145:3; Isa. 40:28; Rom. 11:33; invisible. Job 23:8,9; Jn. 1:18; 5:37; Col. 1:15; 1 Tim. 1:17; good. Ps. 25:8; 119:68; upright. Ps. 25:8; 92:15; holy. Ps. 99:9; Isa. 5:16; Most High. Ps. 83:18; Acts 7:48; immutable. Ps. 102:26,27; Jas. 1:17; omniscient. Ps. 139:1–6; Prov. 5:21; omnipresent. Ps. 139:7; Jer. 23:23; light. Isa. 60:19; Jas. 1:17; 1 Jn. 1:5; true. Jer. 10:10; Jn. 17:3; perfect. Mt. 5:48; incorruptible. Rom. 1:23; wise. Rom. 16:27; 1 Tim. 1:17; faithful. 1 Cor. 10:13; 1 Pet. 4:19; immortal. 1 Tim. 1:17; 6:16; a consuming fire. Heb. 12:29; love. 1 Jn. 4:8,16
none like Him. Ex. 9:14; Dt. 33:26; 2 Sam. 7:22; Isa. 46:5,9; Jer. 10:6; beside Him. Dt. 4:35; Isa. 44:6; before Him. Isa. 43:10; none good but God. Mt. 19:17
fills heaven and earth. 1 Ki. 8:27; Jer. 23:24
should be worshiped. Jn. 4:24

HIS GLORY
exhibited in Christ. Jn. 1:14; 2 Cor. 4:6; Heb. 1:3
exhibited in His: power. Ex. 15:1,6; Rom. 6:4; holiness. Ex. 15:11; name. Dt. 28:58; Neh. 9:5; majesty. Job 37:22; Ps. 93:1; 104:1; 145:5,12; Isa. 2:10; works. Ps. 19:1; 111:3
described as: highly exalted. Ps. 8:1; 113:4; eternal. Ps. 104:31; great. Ps. 138:5; rich. Eph. 3:16
exhibited to: Moses. Ex. 34:5–7, with Ex. 33:18–23; His people. Dt. 5:24; Ps. 102:16
enlightens: His people. Isa. 60:1,2; Rev. 21:11,23; Stephen. Acts 7:55
declare. 1 Chr. 16:24; Ps. 145:5,11
magnify. Ps. 57:5
saints desire to behold. Ps. 63:2; 90:16
pleaded in prayer. Ps. 79:9
the earth is full of. Isa. 6:3
not to be given to others. Isa. 42:8
to be feared. Isa. 59:19
the knowledge of, shall fill the earth. Num. 14:21; Hab. 2:14

HIS GOODNESS
proclaimed. Ps. 25:8; Nah. 1:7; Mt. 19:17
is abundant. Ex. 34:6; Ps. 33:5; great. Neh. 9:35; Zech. 9:17; enduring. Ps. 23:6; 52:1; satisfying. Ps. 65:4; Jer. 31:12,14; rich. Ps. 104:24; Rom. 2:4; universal. Ps. 145:9; Mt. 5:45
manifested: in forgiving sins. 2 Chr. 30:18; Ps. 86:5; to His Church. Ps. 31:19; Lam. 3:25; in providing for the poor. Ps. 68:10; in doing good. Ps. 119:68; 145:9; in supplying temporal wants. Acts 14:17
leads to repentance. Rom. 2:4

HIS GIFTS
are free and abundant. Num. 14:8; Rom. 8:32
are dispensed according to His will. Eccl. 2:26; Dan. 2:21; Rom. 12:6; 1 Cor. 7:7
all blessings are. Jas. 1:17; 2 Pet. 1:3

HIS SPIRITUAL GIFTS
acknowledged. Ps. 4:7; 21:2
peace. Ps. 29:11
strength and power. Ps. 68:35
are through Christ. Ps. 68:18, with Eph. 4:7,8; Jn. 6:27
Christ the chief of. Isa. 42:6; 55:4; Jn. 3:16; 4:10; 6:32,33
a new heart. Ezek. 11:19
pray for. Mt. 7:7,11; Jn. 16:23,24
rest. Mt. 11:28; 2 Th. 1:7
the Holy Spirit. Lk. 11:13; Acts 8:20
grace. Ps. 84:11; Jas. 4:6
wisdom. Prov. 2:6; Jas. 1:5
glory. Ps. 84:11; Jn. 17:22
repentance. Acts 11:18
righteousness. Rom. 5:16,17
eternal life. Rom. 6:23
are irrevocable. Rom. 11:29
faith. Eph. 2:8; Phil. 1:29
to be used for mutual profit. 1 Pet. 4:10

HIS TEMPORAL GIFTS
rain and fruitful seasons. Gen. 27:28; Lev. 26:4,5; Isa. 30:23; Acts 14:17
peace. Lev. 26:6; 1 Chr. 22:9
should cause us to remember God. Dt. 8:18
wisdom. 2 Chr. 1:42
all good things. Ps. 34:10; 1 Tim. 6:17
all creatures partake of. Ps. 136:25; 145:15,16
life. Isa. 42:5
to be used and enjoyed. Eccl. 3:13; 5:19,20; 1 Tim. 4:4,5

pray for. Zech. 10:1; Mt. 6:11
food and clothing. Mt. 6:25–33
illustrated. Mt. 25:15–30

HIS JOY OVER HIS PEOPLE

greatness of. Zeph. 3:17
on account of: their uprightness. 1 Chr. 29:17; Prov. 11:20; fear of Him. Ps. 147:11; hope in His mercy. Ps. 147:11; meekness. Ps. 149:4; praying to Him. Prov. 15:8; repentance. Lk. 15:7,10; faith. Heb. 11:5,6
leads Him to: give them the inheritance. Num. 14:8; 1 Pet. 1:4; do them good. Dt. 28:63; Jer. 32:41; Acts 14:17; prosper them. Dt. 30:9; deliver them. 2 Sam. 22:20; comfort them. Isa. 65:19
exemplified: Solomon. 1 Ki. 10:9
illustrated. Isa. 62:5; Lk. 15:23,24

HIS LAW

is absolute and perpetual. Mk. 5:18
given: to Adam. Gen. 2:16,17 with Rom. 5:12–14; to Noah. Gen. 9:6; to the Israelites. Ex. 20:2; Ps. 78:5; through Moses. Ex. 31:18; Jn. 7:19; through the ministration of angels. Acts 7:53; Gal. 3:19; Heb. 2:2
described as: perfect. Ps. 19:7; Rom. 12:2; pure. Ps. 19:8; exceedingly broad. Ps. 119:96; truth. Ps. 119:142; holy, just, and good. Rom. 7:12; spiritual. Rom. 7:14; not burdensome. 1 Jn. 5:3
requires perfect obedience. Dt. 27:26; Gal. 3:10; Jas. 2:10
requires obedience of the heart. Ps. 51:6; Mt. 5:28; 22:37
it is man's duty to keep. Eccl. 12:13
man cannot be justified by. Acts 13:39; Rom. 3:20,28; Gal. 2:16; 3:11
conscience testifies to. Rom. 2:15
all men have transgressed. Rom. 3:9,19
gives the knowledge of sin. Rom. 3:20; 7:7
brings about wrath. Rom. 4:15
man, by nature not in subjection to. Rom. 7:5; 8:7
love is the fulfilling of. Rom. 13:8,10; Gal. 5:14; Jas. 2:8
designed to prevail until Christ. Gal. 3:24
sin is a transgression of. 1 Jn. 3:4
obedience to is: of prime importance. 1 Cor. 7:19; a test of love. 1 Jn. 5:3; a characteristic of saints. Rev. 12:17
blessedness of keeping. Ps. 119:1; Mt. 5:19; 1 Jn. 3:22,24; Rev. 22:14
Christ: magnified. Isa. 42:21; came to fulfill. Mt. 5:17; explained. Mt. 7:12; 22:37–40
the love of, produces peace. Ps. 119:165
saints should: make the subject of their conversation. Ex. 13:9; prepare their hearts to seek. Ezra 7:10; pledge themselves to walk in. Neh. 10:29; pray to understand. Ps. 119:18; pray for power to keep. Ps. 119:34; keep. Ps. 119:55; delight in. Ps. 119:77; Rom. 7:22; love. Ps. 119:97,113; lament over the violation of, by others. Ps. 119:136; have, written on their hearts. Jer. 31:33, with Heb. 8:10; remember. Mal. 4:4
saints are freed from: the bondage of. Rom. 6:14; 7:4,6; Gal. 3:13; the curse of. Gal. 3:13
the wicked: forsake. 2 Chr. 12:1; Jer. 9:13; refuse to walk in. Ps. 78:10; cast away. Isa. 5:24; refuse to hear. Isa. 30:9; Jer. 6:19; forget. Hos. 4:6; despise. Amos 2:4
punishment for disobeying. Neh. 9:26,27; Isa. 65:11–13; Jer. 9:13–16
is the rule of judgment. Rom. 2:12
is established by faith. Rom. 3:31
is the rule of life to saints. 1 Cor. 9:21; Gal. 5:13,14
to be used lawfully. 1 Tim. 1:8

HIS ATTRIBUTES

eternal. Gen. 21:33; Ex. 3:14; Dt. 32:40; 33:27; Job 10:5; 36:26; Ps. 9:7; 90:2; 92:8; 93:2; 102:12; 104:31; 135:13; 145:13; 146:6,10; Eccl. 3:14; Isa. 9:6; 40:28; 41:4; 43:13; 48:12; 57:15; 63:16; Jer. 10:10; Lam. 5:19; Dan. 4:3,34; 6:26; Mic. 5:2; Hab. 1:12; Rom. 1:20; 16:26; Eph. 3:9; 1 Tim. 1:17; 6:16; 2 Pet. 3:8; Rev. 1:8; 4:9; 22:13
immutable. Num. 23:19; 1 Sam. 15:29; Ps. 33:11; 119:89; Mal. 3:6; Acts 4:28; Eph. 1:4; Heb. 1:12; 6:17; 13:8; Jas. 1:17
omniscient. Job 26:6; 34:21; Ps. 139; Prov. 15:3; Isa. 44:7; Ezek. 11:5; Mt. 12:25; Jn. 2:24; Rom. 1:20
omnipresent. Job 23:9; 26; 28; Ps. 139; Prov. 15:3; Acts 17:27
invisible. Ex. 33:20; Job 23:8; Jn. 1:18; 4:24; 5:37; Col. 1:15; 1 Tim. 1:17; 6:16; Heb. 11:;27; 1 Jn. 4:12
unsearchable. Job 11:7; 26:14; 37:15; Ps. 145:3; Eccl. 8:17; Rom. 11:33
incomprehensible. Job 5:9; 9:10; 11:7; 26:14; 36:26; 37:5; Ps. 36:6; 40:5; 106:2; 139:6; Eccl. 3:11; 8:17; 11:5; Isa. 40:12; 45:15; Mic. 4:12; 1 Tim. 6:16
holiness. Gen. 35:2; Ex. 3:5; 14; 15; 19; 20; 28:36; 34:5; 39:30; Lev. 11:44; 21:8; Josh. 5:15; 1 Sam. 2:2; 1 Chr. 16:10; Ps. 22:3; 30:4; 60:6. *See* PSALMS. Isa. 6:3; 43:15; 49:7; 57:15; Jer. 23:9; Amos 4:2; Lk. 1:49; Acts 3:14; Rom. 7:12; 1 Jn. 2:20; Rev. 4:8; 19:1
justice, etc. Gen. 2:16; 3:8; 4:9; 6:7; 9:15; 18:17,19; Ex. 32:33; Lev. 4; 7:20; 18:4; 26:21; Num. 11; 14; 16; 17; 20; 25; 26:64; 27:12; 35; Dt. 1:34–45; 4:24; 5; 6; 9:4; 10:17; 25:17; 28:15; 31:16; 32:35,41; Josh. 7:1; Jud. 1:7; 2:14; 9:56; 1 Sam. 2:30; 3:11; 6:19; 15:17; 2 Sam. 6:7; 12:1; 22; 24:11; 1 Ki. 8:20; 2 Chr. 6:17; 19:7; Ezra 8:22; Neh. 9:33; Job 4:17; 8; 10:3; 11:11; 12:6; 13:15; 14:15; 34:10; 35:13; 37:23; 40:8. *See* PSALMS. Prov. 11:21; 15:8; 28:9; 30:5; Eccl. 5:8; 8:12; 11:9; Isa. 45:21; Jer. 5:3; 9:24; 23:20; 32:19; 50:7; 51:9; Lam. 1:18; Ezek. 7:27; 16:35; 18:10; 33:17; Dan. 4:37; 9:14; Hos. 4; 5; Nah. 1:3; Hab. 1:13; Zeph. 3:5; Mal. 2:17; 4:1; Mt. 10:15; 20:13; 23:14; Lk. 12:47; 13:27; Jn. 7:18; Acts 10:34; 17:31; Rom. 2:2; Gal. 6:7; Eph. 6:8; Col. 3:25; Jas. 1:13; 1 Jn. 1:9; Rev. 15:3; 16:7
knowledge, wisdom, and power. Gen. 1; 3; 6—9; 41:16; Ex. 4:1,11; 7:10; 12:29; 14; 15; 33:19; 34:5; 35:30; 36; Num. 11:23; 12; 22:9; 23:4; 24:16; Dt. 3; 4:32; 5:24; 6:22; 7; 10; 26; 28:58; 29:29; 32:4; Josh. 3; 6; 7:10; 23:9; 24; Jud. 2; 1 Sam. 2; 4; 5; 12:18; 14:6; 16:7; 17:37,46; 18:10; 23; 2 Sam. 7:22; 1 Ki. 8:27; 22:22; 1 Chr. 16:24; 17:4; 22:18; 28:9; 29:11; 2 Chr.6:18; 14:11; 20:6; Neh. 9:5; Job 4:9; 5:9; 9; 10:4; 11:12; 19:6; 21:17; 22:23; 26:6; 33; 34:22; 35; 41. *See* PSALMS. Prov. 3:19; 5:21; 8:22; 15:3; 16:9; 19:21; 21:30; Eccl. 3:11; 7:13; Isa. 2:10; 6:3; 12:5; 14:24; 28:29; 29:16; 30:18; 33:13; 40:29; 41:21; 42:8; 43:13; 44:6,23; 45:20; 46:5; 47:4; 48:3; 52:10; 55:11; 59:1; 60:1; 66:1; Jer. 3:14; 5:22; 10:6; 14:22; 29:23; 32:17; Lam. 3:37; Ezek. 8:12; 11:5; 22:14; Dan. 2:20; 3:17,29; 4:34; 6:26; Joel 2:11; Amos 5:12; 8:7; Hab. 2:14; Mal. 3:16; Mt. 5:48; 6:13; 9:38; 10:29; 12:25; 19:26; 22:29; Mk. 5:30; 12:15; Lk. 1:48; 12:5; 18:27; Jn. 1:14; 2:24; 5:26; 6:61; 11:25; 16:19; 18:4; 19:28; 20:17; Acts 1:24; 2:17; 7:55; 15:18; Rom. 1:20; 4:17; 8:29; 11:34; 15:19; 16:27; 1 Cor. 2:9,16; 2 Cor. 4:6; 12:9; 13:4; Gal. 2:8; Eph. 1:19; 3:7; 6:10; Phil. 1:6; 3:21; Col. 3:4; 1 Tim. 1:12,17; Heb. 1:3; 2:10; 4:12; Jas. 4:6; 1 Pet. 2:20; 1 Jn. 1:5; 3:20; Jude 1,24; Rev. 1:8; 4:11; 5:13; 11:17; 19:6; 21:3
faithfulness and truth. Num. 23:19; Dt. 7:8; Josh. 21:45; 2 Sam. 7:28; 1 Ki. 8:56; Ps. 19:9; 89:34; 105:8; 111:7; 117; 119:89,160; 146:6; Isa. 25:1; 31:2; 46:11; 65:16; Jer. 4:28; Lam. 2:17; Ezek. 12:25; Mt. 24:35; Jn. 7:28; Rom. 3:4; 1 Cor. 1:9; 15:58; 2 Cor. 1:18; 1 Th. 5:24; 2 Th. 3:3; 2 Tim. 2:13; Ti. 1:2; Heb. 6:18; 10:23; 11:11; 13:5; 2 Pet. 3:9; Rev. 1:5; 3:7; 15:3; 16:7
mercy, goodness, and love. Gen. 1:28; 3:15; 4:4; 8; 9; 15:4; 16:7; 17; 18:16; 19:12; 21:12; 22:15; 24:12; 26:24; 28:10; 29:31; 32:9,24; 39:2; 46; Ex. 1:20; 2:23; 3:7; 6; 16; 17; 20:6; 22:27; 23:20; 29:45; 32:14; 33:12; 34:6; Lev. 4:35; 26:3,40; Num. 14:18; 21:7; Dt. 4:29; 7:7; 8; 10:15; 18:15; 20:4; 23:5; 28:1; 30; 32:7,43; 33; Josh. 20; Jud. 2:16;

6:36; 10:15; 13; 15:18; 1 Sam. 2:9; 7; 25:32; 2 Sam. 7:5; 12:13; 1 Ki. 8:56; 2 Chr. 16:9; 30:9; Ezra 8:18; Neh. 2:18; 9:17; Job 5:17; 7:17; 11:6; 33:14; 36:11; 37:23; Ps. 34:8; 36:5; 69:16; Prov. 8:30; 11:20; 18:10; 28:13; Eccl. 2:26; 8:11; Isa. 25:4; 27:3; 30:18; 38:17; 40:29; 43:1; 48:9,17; 49:15; 54:7; 55:3; 63:7; Jer. 3:12; 9:24; 16:14; 17:7; 31:3,12; 32:39; 33:11; 44:28; Lam. 3:22,31; Ezek. 20:17; 33:11; Dan. 9:9; Hos. 2:19; 11:4; 13:14; 14:3; Joel 2:13; Mic. 7:18; Nah. 1:7; Hab. 3:18; Zeph. 3:17; Mal. 3:6,16; 4; Mt. 5:45; 19:17; 23:37; Lk. 1:50,78; 5:21; 6:35; 13:6; Jn. 1:4,9; 3:16; 4:10; 14; 15:9; 16:7; 17; Acts 14:17; Rom. 2:4; 3:25; 5:5; 8:32; 9:22; 11; 2 Cor. 1:3; 12:9; 13:11; Gal. 1:4; Eph. 2:4,17; 4:6; 1 Tim. 2:4; 6:17; 2 Tim. 1:9; Ti. 3:4; Heb. 12:6; Jas. 1:5,17; 5:11; 1 Pet. 1:3; 3:20; 2 Pet. 3:9,15; 1 Jn. 1; Jude 21; Rev. 2:3. *See* PSALMS

jealousy. Ex. 20:5; 34:14; Dt. 4:24; 5:9; 6:15; 29:20; 32:16; Josh. 24:19; Ps. 78:58; 79:5; Ezek. 16; 23; Hos. 1; 2; Joel 2:18; Zeph. 1:18; Zech. 1:14; 1 Cor. 10:22

HIS CHARACTERS

Disposer of events. Gen. 6—9; 11:8; 12; 14:20; 18:14; 22; 25:23; 26; Ex. 9:16; Dt. 7:7; 1 Sam. 2:6; 9:15; 13:14; 15:17; 16; 2 Sam. 7:8; 22:1; Ps. 10:16; 22:28; 24; 33; 74:12; 75; Isa. 40:23; 43—45; 64:8; Jer. 8:19; 10:10; 18; 19; Dan. 4; 5; Zech. 14:9; Lk. 10:21; Rom. 9; Eph. 1; 1 Tim. 1:17; 6:15; Jas. 4:12

Judge of all. Gen. 18:25; Dt. 32:36; Jud. 11:27; Ps. 7:11; 9:7; 50; 58:11; 68:5; 75:7; 94:2; Eccl. 3:17; 11:9; 12:14; Isa. 2:4; 3:13; Jer. 11:20; Acts 10:42; Rom. 2:16; 2 Tim. 4:8; Heb. 12:23; Jude 6; Rev. 11:18; 18:8; 19:11

Searcher of hearts. 1 Chr. 28:9; Ps. 7:9; 44:21; 139:23; Prov. 17:3; 24:12; Jer. 17:10; Acts 1:24; Rom. 8:27; Rev. 2:23

Sanctuary and refuge. Dt. 33:27; 2 Sam. 22:3; Ps. 9:9; 46:1; 57:1; 59:16; 62; 71:7; 91; 94:22; 142:5; Isa. 8:14; Ezek. 11:16; Heb. 6:18

Savior. Ps. 106:21; Isa. 43:3,11; 45:15; 49:26; 60:16; 63:8; Jer. 14:8; Hos. 13:4; Lk. 1:47

HIS NAMES

Father of lights. Jas. 1:17

YAH. Isa. 26:4

God of heaven. Ezra 5:11; Neh. 1:4; 2:4

God of hosts. Ps. 80:7,14,19

Holy One. Job 6:10; Ps. 16:10; Isa. 10:17; Hos. 11:9; Hab. 1:12; 1 Jn. 2:20

Holy One of Israel. 2 Ki. 19:22; Ps. 71:22; Isa. 1:4; Jer. 50:29; 51:5; Ezek. 39:7

I AM. Ex. 3:14

Jealous. Ex. 34:14

King of kings. 1 Tim. 6:15; Rev. 17:14

Living God. Dt. 5:26; Josh. 3:10

LORD. Ex. 6:3; Ps. 83:18; Isa. 12:2

LORD of Hosts. 1 Sam. 1:11; Isa. 1:24

Lord of lords. Dt. 10:17; 1 Tim. 6:15; Rev. 17:14

Lord of Sabaoth. Rom. 9:29; Jas. 5:4

Mighty God. Ps. 50:1; Isa. 9:6; 10:21; Jer. 32:18; Hab. 1:12

Most High. Num. 24:16; Dt. 32:8; Dt. 32:8; 2 Sam. 22:14; Ps. 7:17

God Most High. Gen. 14:18; Ps. 57:2

Most High God. Dan. 3:26

THE FATHER

Mt. 11:25; 28:19; Mk. 14:36; Lk. 10:21; 22:42; 23:34,46; Jn. 1:14; Acts 1:4; 2:33; Rom. 6:4; 8:15; 15:6; 1 Cor. 8:6; 15:24; 2 Cor. 1:3; 6:18; Gal. 1:1,3,4; 4:6; Eph. 1:17; Phil. 2:11; Col. 1:19; 2:2; 1 Th. 1:1; Heb. 12:7,9; Jas. 1:27; 3:9; 1 Pet. 1:2,17; 2 Pet. 1:17; 1 Jn. 1:2; 2 Jn. 3:4,9; Jude 1

THE SON

Mt. 11:27; Mk. 13:32; Lk. 1:32; Jn. 1:18; Acts 8:37; 9:20; Rom. 1:4; 2 Cor. 1:19; Gal. 2:20; Eph. 4:13; Heb. 4:14; 1 Jn. 2:22; Rev. 2:18. *See* CHRIST

THE HOLY SPIRIT

attributes and action:

eternal. Heb. 9:14

omnipresent. Ps. 139:7–13

omniscient. 1 Cor. 2:10

omnipotent. Lk. 1:35; Rom. 15:13,19

the Spirit of glory and of God. 1 Pet. 4:14

Author of the new birth. Jn. 3:5,6, with 1 Jn. 5:4

inspiring Scripture. 2 Tim. 3:16, with 2 Pet. 1:21

the source of wisdom. Isa. 11:2; Jn. 14:26; 16:13; 1 Cor. 12:8

the source of miraculous power. Mt. 12:28, with Lk. 11:20; Acts 19:11, with Rom. 15:19

appointing and sending ministers. Acts 13:2,4, with Mt. 9:38; Acts 20:28

directing where the Gospel should be preached. Acts 16:6,7,10

dwelling in saints. Jn. 14:17, with 1 Cor. 14:25; 3:16; with 1 Cor. 6:19

Comforter of the Church. Acts 9:31, with 2 Cor. 1:3

sanctifying the Church. Ezek. 37:28, with Rom. 15:16

the Witness. Heb. 10:15, with 1 Jn. 5:9

convicting of sin, of righteousness, and of judgment. Jn. 16:8–11

personality of:

He creates and gives life. Job 33:4

He appoints and commissions His servants. Isa. 48:16; Acts 13:2; 20:28

He directs where to preach. Acts 8:29; 10:19,20

He does not permit Paul to go to Bithynia. Acts 16:6,7

He instructs Paul what to preach. 1 Cor. 2:13

He spoke in, and by, the prophets. Acts 1:16; 1 Pet. 1:11,12; 2 Pet. 1:21

He strives with sinners. Gen. 6:3; can be grieved. Isa. 63:10; teaches. Jn. 14:26; 1 Cor. 12:13; dwells with saints. Jn. 14:17; testifies of Christ. Jn. 15:26; convicts. Jn. 16:8; guides. Jn. 16:13; glorifies Christ. Jn. 16:14; can be tested. Acts 5:9; can be resisted. Acts 7:51; comforts. Acts 9:31; helps in our weaknesses. Rom. 8:26; searches all things. Rom. 11:33,34, with 1 Cor. 2:10;11; sanctifies. Rom. 15:16; 1 Cor. 6:11; works according to His own will. 1 Cor. 12:11

as Comforter:

proceeds from the Father. Jn. 15:26

given: by Christ. Isa. 61:1; Lk. 4:18; by the Father. Jn. 14:16; through Christ's intercession. Jn. 14:16

sent in the name of Christ. Jn. 14:26

sent by Christ from the Father. Jn. 15:26; 16:7

as such He: abides forever with saints. Jn. 14:16; dwells with, and in saints. Jn. 14:17; is known by saints. Jn. 14:17; teaches saints. Jn. 14:26; testifies of Christ. Jn. 15:26

edifies the Church. Acts 9:31; imparts the love of God. Rom. 5:3–5; communicates joy to saints. Rom. 14:17; Gal. 5:22; 1 Th. 1:6; imparts hope. Rom. 15:13; Gal. 5:5

the world cannot receive. Jn. 14:17

as Teacher:

promised. Prov. 1:23

as the Spirit of wisdom. Isa. 11:2; 40:13,14

given to saints. Neh. 9:20; 1 Cor. 2:12,13

necessity for. 1 Cor. 2:9,10

as such He: directs in the way of godliness. Isa. 30:21; Ezek. 36:27; teaches saints to answer persecutors. Mk. 13:11; Lk. 12:12; reveals the future. Lk. 2:26; Acts 21:11; brings the words of Christ to remembrance. Jn. 14:26; guides into all truth. Jn. 14:26; 16:13; reveals the things of Christ. Jn. 16:14; directs the decisions of the Church. Acts 15:28; reveals the things of God. 1 Cor. 2:10,13; enables ministers to teach. 1 Cor. 12:8

the natural man will not receive the things of. 1 Cor. 2:14

all are invited to attend to the instruction of. Rev. 2:7,11,29

emblems of:

water. Jn. 3:5; 7:38,39; fertilizing. Ps. 1:3; Isa. 27:3,6; 44:3,4; 58:11; refreshing. Ps. 46:4; Isa. 41:17,18; freely given. Isa. 55:1; Jn. 4:14; Rev. 22:17; cleansing. Ezek. 16:9;

Prov. 15:3, on the evil and the *g*
Prov. 17:22, A merry heart does *g*
Eccl. 6:12, who knows what is *g*
Isa. 1:17, learn to do *g*
Isa. 40:9, Zion, you who bring *g*
Isa. 52:7, tidings of *g* things
Zech. 1:13, talked to me, with *g*
Mt. 5:16, they may see your *g*
Mt. 9:22, said, "Be of *g* cheer
Mt. 12:35, "A *g* man out of the
Mt. 19:16, "*G* Teacher, what *g*
Mt. 19:17, No one is *g* but One
Mt. 26:10, For she has done a *g*
Lk. 2:10, behold, I bring you *g*
Lk. 2:14, on earth peace, *g*
Jn. 1:46, "Can anything *g*
Jn. 7:12, Some said, "He is *g*
Jn. 10:32, *g* works I have shown
Acts 10:38, who went about doing *g*
Acts 11:24, For he was a *g* man
Acts 14:17, in that He did *g*
Rom. 5:7, *g* man someone would
Rom. 7:18, in my flesh) nothing *g*
Rom. 12:21, overcome evil with *g*
Eph. 2:10, Jesus for *g* works
Col. 1:10, fruitful in every *g*
1 Tim. 1:8, know that the law is *g*
1 Tim. 2:3, For this is *g* and
1 Tim. 3:1, bishop, he desires a *g*
1 Tim. 5:4, for this is *g* and
1 Tim. 6:18, be rich in *g* works
2 Tim. 2:21, prepared for every *g*
Heb. 6:5, and have tasted the *g*
Jas. 1:17, Every *g* gift and every
1 Pet. 2:12, *g* works which they
1 Pet. 3:17, to suffer for doing *g*

GOODNESS
Ex. 33:19, "I will make all My *g*
Ex. 34:6, and abounding in *g*
Ps. 16:2, "You are my Lord, My *g*
Ps. 23:6, Surely *g* and mercy
Ps. 27:13, that I would see the *g*
Ps. 31:19, how great is Your *g*
Ps. 52:1, The *g* of God endures
Zech. 9:17, how great is its *g*
Rom. 2:4, the riches of His *g*
Rom. 11:22, consider the *g* and
Gal. 5:22, kindness, *g*

GOODS
Eccl. 5:11, When *g* increase
Mt. 12:29, and plunder his *g*
Mt. 24:47, ruler over all his *g*
Lk. 12:19, "Soul, you have many *g*
Lk. 16:1, man was wasting his *g*
Lk. 19:8, I give half of my *g*
1 Jn. 3:17, has this world's *g*

GOSHEN
(Egypt), Israelites placed there. Gen. 45:10; 46:34; 47:4
no plagues there. Ex. 8:22; 9:26
—— (Canaan). Josh. 10:41; 11:16

GOSPEL
of Christ, its teaching and works. Mt. 4:23; 24:14; Mk. 1:14; Lk. 2:10; 20:21; Acts 13:26; 14:3; 20:21; Rom. 1:2,9,16; 2:16; 10:8; 16:25; 1 Cor. 1:18; 2:13; 15:1; 2 Cor. 4:4; 5:19; 6:7; Eph. 1:13; 3:2; 6:15; Phil. 2:16; Col. 1:5; 3:16; 1 Th. 1:5; 2:8; 3:2; 1 Tim. 1:11; 6:3; Heb. 4:2; 1 Pet. 1:12,25; 4:17
preached to Abraham. Gal. 3:8
to the poor and others. Mt. 11:5; Mk. 1:15; 13:10; 16:15; Lk. 4:18; 24:47; Acts 13:46; 14; 1 Cor. 1:17; 9:16; Gal. 2:2; Rev. 14:6
its effects. Mk. 1:15; 8:35; Lk. 2:10,14; 19:8; Acts 4:32; Rom. 1:16; 12; 13; 15:29; 16:26; 2 Cor. 8; 9; Gal. 1:16; 2:14; Eph. 4—6; Phil. 1:5,17,27; Col. 1:23; 3; 4; 1 Th. 1; 2; Ti. 2; 3; Jas. 1; 1 & 2 Pet. ; 1 Jn. 3; Jude 3
rejected by the Jews. Acts 13:26; 28:25; Rom. 9—11; 1 Th. 2:16
from whom hidden. 1 Cor. 1:23; 2:8; 2 Cor. 4:3

GOSPEL
Mk. 1:1, The beginning of the *g*
Mk. 1:15, and believe in the *g*
Mk. 13:10, *g* must first be
Acts 20:24, to testify to the *g*
Rom. 1:1, separated to the *g*
Rom. 1:16, not ashamed of the *g*
1 Cor. 9:14, should live from the *g*
2 Cor. 4:3, if our *g* is veiled
Gal. 1:6, to a different *g*
Eph. 1:13, of truth, the *g*
Eph. 6:19, the mystery of the *g*
Col. 1:23, *g* which you heard
Rev. 14:6, the everlasting *g*

GOSSIPS
1 Tim. 5:13, only idle but also *g*

GOVERNMENT
Isa. 9:6, and the *g* will be upon

GRACE
of God and Jesus Christ. Ps. 84:11; Zech. 4:7; Lk. 2:40; Jn. 1:16; Acts 20:24; Rom. 11:5; 1 Cor. 15:10; 2 Cor. 8:9; 2 Tim. 1:9; 1 Pet. 5:5
salvation through. Acts 15:11; Rom. 3:24; 4:4; Eph. 2:5; 2 Th. 2:16; Ti. 3:7; 1 Pet. 1:10
effects of. 2 Cor. 1:12; Ti. 2:11; 1 Pet. 4:10. *See* GOSPEL
prayer for. Rom. 16:20; 1 Tim. 1:2; Heb. 4:16
danger of abusing. Rom. 6; Jude 4; and departing from. Gal. 5:4
exhortations concerning. 2 Tim. 1:9; Heb. 12:15,28; 2 Pet. 3:18

GRACE
Gen. 6:8, But Noah found *g*
Ps. 45:2, *G* is poured upon Your
Ps. 84:11, The LORD will give *g*
Zech. 12:10, the Spirit of *g*
Lk. 2:40, and the *g* of God was
Jn. 1:17, *g* and truth came
Acts 4:33, And great *g* was upon
Rom. 1:7, *G* to you and peace
Rom. 5:17, receive abundance of *g*
Rom. 11:6, *g* is no longer *g*
Rom. 16:20, The *g* of our Lord
2 Cor. 8:9, For you know the *g*
2 Cor. 12:9, *g* is sufficient
2 Cor. 13:14, The *g* of the Lord
Gal. 5:4, you have fallen from *g*
Eph. 1:7, to the riches of His *g*
Eph. 2:8, *g* you have been
Eph. 3:2, dispensation of the *g*
Eph. 4:7, *g* was given according
Eph. 6:24, *G* be with all those
Heb. 12:28, shaken, let us have *g*
Jas. 4:6, But He gives more *g*
1 Pet. 5:12, this is the true *g*
2 Pet. 3:18, but grow in the *g*

GRACIOUS
Gen. 43:29, he said, "God be *g*
Ex. 33:19, I will be *g* to whom I
Job 33:24, then He is *g* to him
Eccl. 10:12, wise man's mouth are *g*
Amos 5:15, of hosts will be *g*
Jon. 4:2, know that You are a *g*
Mal. 1:9, that He may be *g*
Lk. 4:22, at the *g* words which
1 Pet. 2:3, that the Lord is *g*

GRAFTED
Rom. 11:23, in unbelief, will be *g*

GRAIN
Gen. 42:5, Israel went to buy *g*
Dt. 25:4, it treads out the *g*
Ps. 65:9, You provide their *g*
Ps. 72:16, be an abundance of *g*
Prov. 11:26, him who withholds *g*
Hos. 14:7, be revived like *g*
Zech. 9:17, *G* shall make the young
Mt. 12:1, to pluck heads of *g*
Jn. 12:24, unless a *g* of wheat
1 Cor. 9:9, it treads out the *g*

GRAIN OFFERING
Lev. 2; 3; 6:14; Num. 15; Neh. 10:33

GRANT
Ps. 85:7, and *g* us Your
Mt. 20:21, *G* that these two
Rev. 3:21, who overcomes I will *g*

GRAPES
Gen. 49:11, in the blood of *g*
Dt. 32:32, their *g* are *g*
Song 2:13, *g* give a good smell
Song 2:15, vines have tender *g*
Isa. 5:2, brought forth wild *g*
Isa. 17:6, Yet gleaning *g* will be
Jer. 8:13, "No *g* shall be
Ezek. 18:2, have eaten sour *g*
Mt. 7:16, Do men gather *g*
Rev. 14:18, *g* are fully ripe

GRASPING
Eccl. 1:14, all is vanity and *g*

GRASS
2 Ki. 19:26, they were as the *g*
Job 5:25, offspring like the *g*
Ps. 90:5, *g* which grows up
Ps. 103:15, his days are like *g*
Isa. 40:7, The *g* withers
Mt. 6:30, so clothes the *g*
Mt. 14:19, to sit down on the *g*
1 Pet. 1:24, "All flesh is as *g*

GRASSHOPPERS
Isa. 40:22, inhabitants are like *g*
Nah. 3:17, generals like great *g*

GRAVE
Job 7:9, *g* does not come
Job 17:13, for the *g* as my house

Ps. 30:3, my soul up from the *g*
Ps. 49:15, the power of the *g*
Eccl. 9:10, or wisdom in the *g*
Isa. 53:9, And they made His *g*
Hos. 13:14, the power of the *g*

GRAVES
Ex. 14:11, there were no *g*
Mt. 27:52, and the *g* were opened
Lk. 11:44, *g* which are not
Jn. 5:28, *g* will hear His voice

GRAY
Gen. 42:38, would bring down my *g*
Dt. 32:25, the man of *g* hairs
Prov. 20:29, of old men is their *g*

GREAT
Gen. 12:2, and make your name *g*
1 Sam. 6:9, He has done us this *g*
1 Chr. 16:25, For the LORD is *g*
2 Chr. 2:5, I build will be *g*
Neh. 4:19, "The work is *g*
Job 5:9, Who does *g* things
Job 32:9, *G* men are not always
Ps. 22:25, in the *g* assembly
Ps. 92:5, *g* are Your works
Ps. 104:1, my God, You are very *g*
Ps. 126:2, "the LORD has done *g*
Ps. 139:17, *g* is the sum of them
Prov. 25:6, in the place of the *g*
Isa. 12:6, *g* is the Holy One
Jer. 45:5, And do you seek *g*
Lam. 3:23, *g* is Your faithfulness
Zeph. 1:14, The *g* day of the LORD
Mt. 5:19, he shall be called *g*
Mt. 13:46, one pearl of *g* price
Mt. 20:26, desires to become *g*
Lk. 22:44, *g* drops of blood
Acts 8:9, that he was someone *g*
Acts 19:28, "*G* is Diana of the
Rom. 9:2, that I have *g* sorrow
1 Tim. 3:16, without controversy *g*
1 Tim. 6:6, with contentment is *g*
2 Tim. 2:20, But in a *g* house
Ti. 2:13, appearing of our *g*
Jas. 3:5, See how *g* a forest
Rev. 6:15, *g* men, the rich men
Rev. 17:5, BABYLON THE *G*
Rev. 20:11, Then I saw a *g* white
Rev. 20:12, the dead, small and *g*

GREATER
Gen. 41:40, the throne will I be *g*
Ex. 18:11, *g* than all the gods
Dan. 7:20, whose appearance was *g*
Mt. 11:11, kingdom of heaven is *g*
Mt. 12:6, place there is One *g*
Mt. 12:41, *g* than Jonah is here
Mt. 12:42, *g* than Solomon is here
Jn. 1:50, *g* things than these
Jn. 4:12, *g* than our father
Jn. 13:16, a servant is not *g*
Jn. 13:16, *g* than he who sent him
Jn. 15:13, *G* love has no one
Jn. 15:20, 'A servant is not *g*
1 Cor. 12:23, parts have *g* modesty
1 Cor. 14:5, he who prophesies is *g*
Heb. 6:13, swear by no one *g*
1 Jn. 3:20, condemns us, God is *g*
1 Jn. 5:9, witness of God is *g*

GREATEST
Mt. 18:4, little child is the *g*
Lk. 22:24, be considered the *g*
1 Cor. 13:13, but the *g* of these is

GREATNESS
Ex. 15:7, And in the *g* of Your
Ps. 79:11, According to the *g*
Ps. 145:3, *g* is unsearchable
Ps. 145:6, I will declare Your *g*
Eccl. 1:16, I have attained *g*
Isa. 63:1, traveling in the *g*
Eph. 1:19, is the exceeding *g*

GREECE, Acts 20:2
prophecies of. Dan. 8:21; 10:20; 11:2; Zech. 9:13
Paul preaches in. Acts 16; 20

GREED
Lk. 11:39, part is full of *g*

GREEDINESS
Eph. 4:19, all uncleanness with *g*
1 Tim. 6:10, the faith in their *g*

GREEDY
Prov. 1:19, of everyone who is *g*
1 Tim. 3:3, not violent, not *g*
Ti. 1:7, not violent, not *g*

GREEK
Jn. 19:20, written in Hebrew, *G*
Rom. 1:16, and also for the *G*
Gal. 2:3, with me, being a *G*
Gal. 3:28, is neither Jew nor *G*

GREEKS (or Hellenists), Acts 18:17
preached to at Antioch. Acts 11:20
wish to see Jesus. Jn. 12:20
believe in Him. Acts 11:21; 17:4

GREEN
Ps. 23:2, lie down in *g* pastures

GREET
Mt. 5:47, *g* your brethren only
1 Cor. 16:20, *G* one another with a
2 Jn. 1:10, into your house nor *g*
3 Jn. 14, *G* the friends by name

GREETED
Lk. 1:40, and *g* Elizabeth

GREW
Lk. 2:40, And the Child *g*
Acts 12:24, But the word of God *g*
Acts 19:20, the word of the Lord *g*

GRIEF
2 Chr 6:29, burden and his own *g*
Job 6:2, *g* were fully weighed
Job 16:6, Though I speak, my *g*
Ps. 10:14, observe trouble and *g*
Prov. 14:13, of mirth may be *g*
Eccl. 1:18, much wisdom is much *g*
Isa. 53:3, and acquainted with *g*
Heb. 13:17, joy and not with *g*

GRIEVE
Lam. 3:33, *g* the children of men
Eph. 4:30, *g* the Holy Spirit

GRIEVED
Gen. 6:6, earth, and He was *g*
Job 30:25, Has not my soul *g*
Ps. 95:10, forty years I was *g*
Isa. 54:6, a woman forsaken and *g*
Isa. 63:10, *g* His Holy Spirit
Mk. 3:5, with anger, being *g*
Jn. 21:17, Peter was *g* because

GRINDERS
Eccl. 12:3, when the *g* cease

GRINDING
Eccl. 12:4, the sound of *g* is low
Isa. 3:15, *g* the faces of the
Mt. 24:41, "Two women will be *g*

GROAN
Job 24:12, The dying *g* in the
Rom. 8:23, even we ourselves *g*
2 Cor. 5:4, who are in this tent *g*

GROANING
Ex. 2:24, So God heard their *g*
Ps. 6:6, I am weary with my *g*
Jn. 11:38, Then Jesus, again *g*

GROANINGS
Rom. 8:26, *g* which cannot

GROPE
Dt. 28:29, And you shall *g*
Job 12:25, They *g* in the dark
Isa. 59:10, We *g* for the wall like
Acts 17:27, hope that they might *g*

GROUND
Gen. 3:17, "Cursed is the *g*
Ex. 3:5, you stand is holy *g*
Jer. 4:3, up your fallow *g*
Zech. 8:12, give its fruit, the *g*
Mt. 13:8, others fell on good *g*
Lk. 14:18, bought a piece of *g*
1 Tim. 3:15, God, the pillar and *g*

GROUNDED
Eph. 3:17, being rooted and *g*

GROW
Ps. 102:26, they will all *g*
Ps. 132:17, the horn of David *g*
Isa. 51:6, the earth will *g*
Mal. 4:2, you shall go out and *g*
Eph. 4:15, truth in love, may *g*
Heb. 1:11, and they will all *g*
2 Pet. 3:18, but *g* in the grace and

GRUDGINGLY
2 Cor. 9:7, in his heart, not *g*

GRUMBLERS
Jude 16, These are *g*

GUARANTEE
2 Cor. 1:22, in our hearts as a *g*
2 Cor. 5:5, us the Spirit as a *g*
Eph. 1:14, who is the *g* of our

GUARD
Gen. 3:24, *g* the way to the tree
Isa. 52:12, will be your rear *g*
Mic. 7:5, *g* the doors of your
Gal. 3:23, we were kept under *g*
1 Tim. 6:20, *G* what was committed

GUARDIANS
Gal. 4:2, but is under *g* and

GUARDS
Ps. 127:1, Unless the LORD *g*
Mt. 28:4, And the *g* shook for

GUIDANCE
Isa. 28:29, and excellent in *g*

GUIDE
Ps. 48:14, He will be our *g*

Jer. 3:4, Father, You are the *g*
Lk. 1:79, *g* our feet into the
Jn. 16:13, has come, He will *g*
Acts 1:16, Judas, who became a *g*
Rom. 2:19, you yourself are a *g*

GUIDES
Mt. 23:16, to you, blind *g*
Acts 8:31, unless someone *g*

GUILT
Lev. 26:41, they accept their *g*
Ezra 9:6, *g* has grown up to the
Mt. 23:32, of your fathers' *g*

GUILTLESS
Ex. 20:7, *g* who takes His name
Mt. 12:7, have condemned the *g*

GUILTY
Gen. 42:21, "We are truly *g*
Ezra 9:7, we have been very *g*
Rom. 3:19, the world may become *g*
Jas. 2:10, in one point, he is *g*

GULF
Lk. 16:26, you there is a great *g*

HABAKKUK
prophet, his burden, complaint to God, God's answer, his faith. Hab. 1—3

HABITATION
Ex. 15:13, to Your holy *h*
Job 8:6, your rightful *h*
Ps. 68:5, Is God in His holy *h*
Ps. 69:25, their *h* be desolate
Ps. 91:9, the Most High, your *h*
Ps. 107:7, go to a city for *h*
Ps. 107:36, establish a city for *h*
Prov. 3:33, but He blesses the *h*
Isa. 32:18, in a peaceful *h*
Isa. 33:20, Jerusalem, a quiet *h*
Zech. 2:13, from His holy *h*
Acts 1:20, 'Let his *h* be
2 Cor. 5:2, be clothed with our *h*

HADAD, Gen. 36:35; 1 Ki. 11:14

HADADEZER
2 Sam. 8:3; 10:15; 1 Chr. 18:5

HADES
Mt. 11:23, be brought down to *H*
Mt. 16:18, *H* shall not
Lk. 16:23, being in torments in *H*
Acts 2:27, not leave my soul in *H*
Rev. 1:18, I have the keys of *H*
Rev. 20:14, *H* were cast into the

HAGAR, Gen. 16:3
mother of Ishmael, fleeing from Sarah is comforted by an angel. Gen. 16:10,11
sent away with her son. Gen. 21:14; symbolism of. Gal. 4:24

HAGGAI
prophet. Ezra 5; 6:14. *See* Hag. 1; 2

HAIL
Ex. 9:18, cause very heavy *h*
Job 38:22, seen the treasury of *h*
Ps. 147:17, He casts out His *h*
Isa. 28:17, *h* will sweep away the
Rev. 16:21, of the plague of the *h*

HAILSTONES
Ps. 18:12, clouds passed with *h*

HAIR
Gen. 42:38, bring down my gray *h*
Job 4:15, the *h* on my body stood
Song 4:1, Your *h* is like a flock
Mt. 5:36, you cannot make one *h*
Lk. 21:18, "But not a *h* of your
1 Cor. 11:15, if a woman has long *h*
1 Tim. 2:9, not with braided *h*
Rev. 9:8, *h* like women's *h*

HAIRS
Ps. 40:12, are more than the *h*
Isa. 46:4, *h* I will carry you
Hos. 7:9, yes, gray *h* are here
Mt. 10:30, "But the very *h*

HAIRY
Gen. 25:25, *h* garment all over
2 Ki. 1:8, him, "A *h* man

HALLOW
Isa. 8:13, hosts, Him you shall *h*
Isa. 29:23, *h* the Holy One of
Jer. 17:24, *h* the Sabbath day

HALLOWED
Ex. 20:11, the Sabbath day and *h*
Lev. 22:32, but I will be *h*
Isa. 5:16, who is holy shall be *h*
Mt. 6:9, heaven, *h* be Your name

HAM, Gen. 9:18
son of Noah, cursed. Gen. 9:22
his descendants. Gen. 10:6; 1 Chr. 1:8; Ps. 105:23; attacked by the Simeonites. 1 Chr. 4:40

HAMAN, Est. 3:1
his advancement. Est. 3
his anger against Mordecai. Est. 3:8
his fall. Est. 7

HAMATH
Num. 34:8; Josh. 13:5; 2 Ki. 14:28; 17:24
conquered. 2 Ki. 18:34; Isa. 37:13; Jer. 49:23

HAMMER
Jer. 23:29, *h* that breaks the rock
Jer. 50:23, How the *h* of the whole

HAMOR
Gen. 33:19; 34:2; Acts 7:16

HANANEL, Neh. 3:1

HANANIAH, 1 Chr. 3:19
false prophet. Jer. 28
his death. Jer. 28:16

HAND of God
for blessing. 2 Chr. 30:12; Ezra 7:9; 8:18; Neh. 2:18
for chastisement. Dt. 2:15; Ruth 1:13; Job 2:10; 19:21; 1 Pet. 5:6

HAND
Gen. 16:12, *h* shall be against
Ex. 21:24, tooth for tooth, *h*
1 Sam. 5:11, the *h* of God was
1 Sam. 23:16, strengthened his *h*
2 Sam. 6:6, Uzzah put out his *h*
2 Sam. 24:14, let us fall into the *h*
Ezra 8:18, Then, by the good *h*
Job 6:9, He would loose His *h*
Job 15:25, he stretches out his *h*
Job 40:14, that your own right *h*
Ps. 18:35, *h* has held me up
Ps. 31:15, My times are in Your *h*
Ps. 32:4, and night Your *h*
Ps. 48:10, Your right *h* is full
Ps. 80:17, Let Your *h* be upon the
Ps. 89:21, *h* shall be established
Ps. 110:1, "Sit at My right *h*
Prov. 3:16, days is in her right *h*
Prov. 21:1, heart is in the *h*
Eccl. 9:10, Whatever your *h*
Eccl. 10:2, is at his right *h*
Eccl. 11:6, do not withhold your *h*
Song 8:3, His left *h* is under my
Isa. 48:13, My *h* has laid the
Isa. 59:1, Behold, the LORD's *h*
Isa. 64:8, are the work of Your *h*
Jer. 23:23, Am I a God near at *h*
Mt. 3:2, of heaven is at *h*
Mt. 5:30, if your right *h*
Mt. 6:3, do not let your left *h*
Mk. 9:43, *h* causes you to sin
Mk. 14:62, sitting at the right *h*
Lk. 1:74, delivered from the *h*
Acts 7:55, at the right *h* of God
Rom. 8:34, is even at the right *h*
1 Cor. 16:21, with my own *h*
Gal. 6:11, to you with my own *h*
Phil. 4:5, The Lord is at *h*
Heb. 1:13, "Sit at My right *h*
Heb. 10:12, down at the right *h*
Rev. 2:1, stars in His right *h*

HANDIWORK
Ps. 19:1, firmament shows His *h*

HANDLE
Jer. 2:8, *h* the law did not know
Lk. 24:39, *H* Me and see
Col. 2:21, do not taste, do not *h*

HANDLED
1 Jn. 1:1, and our hands have *h*

HANDS
laying on of. Num. 8:10; 27:18; Acts 6:6; 13:3; 1 Tim. 4:14; 2 Tim. 1:6
washing, declaratory of innocence. Dt. 21:6; Ps. 26:6; Mt. 27:24
lifting up, in prayer. Ex. 17:11; Ps. 28:2; 63:4; 141:2; 143:6; 1 Tim. 2:8

HANDS
Gen. 27:22, the *h* are the *h*
Josh. 9:25, here we are, in your *h*
1 Sam. 19:5, took his life in his *h*
1 Sam. 28:21, put my life in my *h*
Job 5:18, but His *h* make whole
Job 9:30, and cleanse my *h*
Job 10:8, *h* have made me and
Ps. 22:16, They pierced My *h*
Ps. 95:5, *h* formed the dry land
Prov. 31:19, stretches out her *h*
Isa. 45:9, say, 'He has no *h*
Mt. 18:8, than having two *h*
Lk. 24:39, "Behold My *h* and
Jn. 13:9, only, but also my *h*
Jn. 20:25, *h* the print of the
Acts 20:34, know that these *h*
Eph. 4:28, his *h* what is good
1 Tim. 2:8, lifting up holy *h*

1 Tim. 4:14, the laying on of the *h*
Heb. 10:31, to fall into the *h*

HANDWRITING
Col. 2:14, having wiped out the *h*

HANGED
Dt. 21:23, for he who is *h*
Mt. 27:5, went and *h* himself

HANGS
Job 26:7, *h* the earth on nothing
Gal. 3:13, is everyone who *h*

HANNAH
her song. 1 Sam. 2
vow and prayer. 1 Sam. 1:11; answered. 1 Sam. 1:19

HANUN, 2 Sam. 10:1,4; 12:30

HAPPEN
Isa. 41:22, show us what will *h*
Dan. 10:14, understand what will *h*
Jas. 4:14, not know what will *h*

HAPPINESS
Dt. 24:5, one year, and bring *h*

HAPPY
Ps. 127:5, *H* is the man who has
Ps. 144:15, *H* are the people who
Prov. 3:13, *H* is the man who finds
Prov. 14:21, mercy on the poor, *h*
Prov. 16:20, trusts in the LORD, *h*
Prov. 29:18, *h* is he who keeps
Rom. 14:22, *H* is he who does not

HARAN, Gen. 11:27
son of Terah. Gen. 11:26
——— city of Nahor, Abram comes to. Gen. 11:31; departs from. Gen. 12:4
Jacob flees to Laban at. Gen. 27:43; 28:10; 29

HARASS
Isa. 11:13, and Judah shall not *h*
Acts 12:1, *h* some from the church

HARD
Gen. 18:14, "Is anything too *h*
Job 41:24, His heart is as *h*
Ps. 60:3, shown Your people *h*
Mt. 25:24, I knew you to be a *h*
Jn. 6:60, This is a *h* saying
2 Pet. 3:16, are some things *h*

HARDEN
Ex. 4:21, But I will *h* his heart
Ps. 95:8, Do not *h* your hearts
Heb. 3:8, *h* your hearts as

HARDENED
Ex. 8:32, But Pharaoh *h* his
Job 9:4, Who has *h* himself
Mk. 6:52, their heart was *h*
Jn. 12:40, and *h* their hearts
Heb. 3:13, lest any of you be *h*

HARDENS
Prov. 21:29, A wicked man *h* his
Prov. 28:14, *h* his heart will fall
Rom. 9:18, whom He wills He *h*

HARDSHIP
Num. 20:14, *h* that has befallen us
2 Tim. 2:3, *h* as a good soldier

HARLOT
Josh. 2:1, of a *h* named Rahab
Prov. 23:27, *h* is a deep pit
1 Cor. 6:16, *h* is one body with
Heb. 11:31, *h* Rahab did not perish
Rev. 17:1, of the great *h* who

HARLOTRIES
Jer. 3:2, the land with your *h*
Hos. 2:2, Let her put away her *h*

HARLOTRY
Jer. 3:9, through her casual *h*
Jer. 13:27, the lewdness of your *h*
Ezek. 43:9, let them put their *h*
Hos. 2:4, are the children of *h*
Hos. 5:3, Ephraim, you commit *h*
Hos. 5:4, for the spirit of *h*

HARLOTS
Gen. 34:31; Lev. 19:29; 21:7; Dt. 23:17; Isa. 57:3; Jer. 3:3; Mt. 21:32; 1 Cor. 6:15
Rahab of Jericho. Josh. 2:1
priests forbidden to marry. Lev. 21:14
Solomon's judgment. 1 Ki. 3:16
figurative. Isa. 1:21; Jer. 2:20; Ezek. 16; 23; Hos. 2; Rev. 17; 18

HARLOTS
1 Ki. 22:38, his blood while the *h*
Mt. 21:31, *h* enter the
Rev. 17:5, Great, The Mother of *H*

HARM
1 Chr. 16:22, do My prophets no *h*
Jer. 25:6, and I will not *h*
Rev. 6:6, and do not *h* the oil

HARMLESS
Phil. 2:15, become blameless and *h*
Heb. 7:26, for us, who is holy, *h*

HARMONIOUS
Ps. 92:3, the harp, with *h* sound

HARP
Gen. 4:21, those who play the *h*
Ps. 150:3, with the lute and *h*
Rev. 5:8, Lamb, each having a *h*

HARPS
Ps. 137:2, We hung our *h* upon the
Rev. 14:2, playing their *h*

HARSH
Mal. 3:13, "Your words have been *h*
1 Pet. 2:18, but also to the *h*

HARVEST
Gen. 8:22, seedtime and *h*
Isa. 9:3, to the joy of *h*
Jer. 5:17, shall eat up your *h*
Jer. 8:20, "The *h* is past
Jer. 51:33, of her *h* will come
Mt. 9:37, *h* truly is plentiful
Mt. 9:38, pray the Lord of the *h*
Mk. 4:29, sickle, because the *h*
Jn. 4:35, already white for *h*
Rev. 14:15, the *h* of the earth is

HASTE
Ex. 12:11, you shall eat it in *h*
Ps. 31:22, For I said in my *h*
Lk. 2:16, And they came with *h*
Lk. 19:5, "Zacchaeus, make *h*

HASTEN
Ps. 16:4, be multiplied who *h*
Eccl. 7:9, Do not *h* in your
Isa. 60:22, I, the LORD, will *h*

HASTENING
2 Pet. 3:12, *h* the coming of the

HASTENS
Prov. 19:2, and he sins who *h*
Prov. 28:22, with an evil eye *h*
Zeph. 1:14, is near and *h* quickly

HASTILY
Eccl. 5:2, utter anything *h*
1 Tim. 5:22, lay hands on anyone *h*

HASTY
Prov. 29:20, Do you see a man *h*

HATE
Lev. 19:17, 'You shall not *h*
Ps. 5:5, *h* all workers of
Ps. 34:21, *h* the righteous shall
Ps. 97:10, love the LORD, *h* evil
Ps. 119:104, *h* every false way
Ps. 119:113, *h* the double-minded
Ps. 119:163, I *h* and abhor lying
Eccl. 3:8, love, and a time to *h*
Isa. 61:8, *h* robbery for burnt
Mic. 3:2, You who *h* good and
Mt. 6:24, either he will *h*

HATED
Eccl. 2:17, Therefore I *h* life
Eccl. 2:18, *h* all my labor in
Mal. 1:3, but Esau I have *h*
Mt. 10:22, And you will be *h*
Jn. 15:24, have seen and also *h*
Rom. 9:13, but Esau I have *h*
Eph. 5:29, For no one ever *h*
Heb. 1:9, and *h* lawlessness

HATEFUL
Prov. 30:23, *h* woman when she is
Ti. 3:3, in malice and envy, *h*

HATERS
Ps. 81:15, The *h* of the LORD
Rom. 1:30, backbiters, *h* of God

HATES
Prov. 6:16, six things the LORD *h*
Jn. 12:25, lose it, and he who *h*
Jn. 15:18, "If the world *h*
1 Jn. 2:11, *h* his brother is

HAUGHTY
2 Sam. 22:28, Your eyes are on the *h*
Ps. 18:27, bring down *h* looks
Ps. 131:1, my heart is not *h*
Prov. 16:18, *h* spirit before a fall
Prov. 21:24, A proud and *h* man
Rom. 11:20, Do not be *h*
1 Tim. 6:17, age not to be *h*

HAUNTS
Ps. 74:20, are full of the *h*

HAVEN
Gen. 49:13, shall dwell by the *h*
Ps. 107:30, to their desired *h*

HAVOC
Acts 8:3, for Saul, he made *h*

HAZAEL
king of Syria. 1 Ki. 19:15

Elisha's prediction. 2 Ki. 8:7
kills Ben-Hadad. 2 Ki. 8:15
oppresses Israel. 2 Ki. 9:14; 10:32; 12:17; 13:22

HAZOR, Josh. 11:1
Canaan, burnt. Josh. 11:10; 15:25

HEAD
Gen. 3:15, He shall bruise your *h*
Job 16:15, my skin, and laid my *h*
Ps. 7:16, return upon his own *h*
Song 5:2, *h* is covered with dew
Isa. 1:5, The whole *h* is sick
Isa. 58:5, it to bow down his *h*
Zech. 1:21, could lift up his *h*
Mt. 5:36, you swear by your *h*
1 Cor. 11:4, having his *h* covered
Eph. 1:22, and gave Him to be *h*
Eph. 5:23, For the husband is *h*
Rev. 1:14, His *h* and his hair

HEADS
of grain. Dt. 23:25; Mt. 12:1

HEADS
Ps. 66:12, men to ride over our *h*
Mt. 27:39, Him, wagging their *h*
Rev. 12:3, dragon having seven *h*

HEAL
Dt. 32:39, I wound and I *h*
Ps. 6:2, O LORD, *h* me
Isa. 61:1, sent Me to *h* the
Jer. 3:22, *h* your backslidings
Lam. 2:13, who can *h* you
Hos. 6:1, torn, but He will *h*
Mt. 10:8, "*H* the sick
Mt. 13:15, so that I should *h*
Lk. 4:18, sent Me to *h* the
Lk. 4:23, Physician, *h* yourself

HEALED
Ps. 107:20, His word and *h* them
Isa. 6:10, and return and be *h*
Isa. 53:5, His stripes we are *h*
Jer. 6:14, *h* the hurt of My
Hos. 7:1, When I would have *h*
Mt. 4:24, and He *h* them
Acts 14:9, he had faith to be *h*
Jas. 5:16, that you may be *h*
Rev. 13:3, his deadly wound was *h*

HEALING
Isa. 58:8, *h* shall spring forth
Jer. 14:19, so that there is no *h*
Nah. 3:19, Your injury has no *h*
Mal. 4:2, shall arise with *h*
Mt. 4:23, and *h* all kinds of
Rev. 22:2, tree were for the *h*

HEALINGS
1 Cor. 12:9, to another gifts of *h*
1 Cor. 12:30, Do all have gifts of *h*

HEALS
Ps. 103:3, *h* all your diseases
Isa. 30:26, *h* the stroke of their
Acts 9:34, Jesus the Christ *h*

HEALTH
of body. Gen. 43:28; 3 Jn. 2
spiritual. Ps. 42:11; Prov. 3:8; 12:18; Isa. 58:8; Jer. 8:15; 30:17; 33:6

HEALTH
Prov. 16:24, to the soul and *h*
Jer. 8:15, and for a time of *h*
Jer. 8:22, no recovery for the *h*
3 Jn. 2, all things and be in *h*

HEAP
Job 16:4, I could *h* up words
Ps. 33:7, sea together as a *h*
2 Tim. 4:3, ears, they will *h*

HEAPS
Job 27:16, Though he *h* up silver

HEAR
Dt. 6:4, "*H*, O Israel
Dt. 18:15, Him you shall *h*
Ps. 4:1, *H* me when I call
Ps. 65:2, O You who *h* prayer
Ps. 85:8, *h* what God the LORD
Ps. 94:9, ear, shall He not *h*
Prov. 22:17, *h* the words of the
Eccl. 5:1, *h* rather than to give
Isa. 1:2, *H*, O heavens
Isa. 33:13, *H*, you who are afar
Isa. 34:1, Let the earth *h*
Isa. 65:12, I spoke, you did not *h*
Mt. 13:14, 'Hearing you will *h*
Mt. 18:16, if he will not *h*
Mk. 4:24, "Take heed what you *h*
Mk. 8:18, ears, do you not *h*
Jn. 3:8, *h* the sound of it
Jn. 9:31, that God does not *h*
Rom. 10:14, And how shall they *h*
Jas. 1:19, man be swift to *h*
Rev. 2:7, *h* what the Spirit says

HEARD
Gen. 3:8, *h* the sound of the
Ex. 3:7, *h* their cry because of
Dt. 4:12, you only *h* a voice
Ps. 66:19, certainly God has *h*
Eccl. 9:17, quietly, should be *h*
Isa. 40:21, Have you not *h*
Isa. 64:4, world men have not *h*
Isa. 66:8, Who has *h* such a thing
Jer. 31:18, *h* Ephraim bemoaning
Mt. 6:7, that they will be *h*
Acts 4:4, *h* the word believed
Rom. 10:18, I say, have they not *h*
1 Cor. 2:9, not seen, nor ear *h*
2 Cor. 12:4, *h* inexpressible
2 Tim. 2:2, things that you have *h*
Heb. 2:1, the things we have *h*
Heb. 4:2, the word which they *h*
Heb. 5:7, from death, and was *h*
1 Jn. 1:1, which we have *h*
Rev. 1:10, Lord's Day, and I *h*

HEARER
Jas. 1:23, if anyone is a *h*
Jas. 1:25, is not a forgetful *h*

HEARERS
Rom. 2:13, for not the *h* of the
Eph. 4:29, impart grace to the *h*
Jas. 1:22, of the word, and not *h*

HEARING
Ex. 24:7, and read in the *h*
Neh. 13:1, Book of Moses in the *h*
Prov. 23:9, Do not speak in the *h*
Isa. 6:9, 'Keep on *h*
Mt. 13:13, *h* they do not
Mk. 4:12, *h* they may hear
1 Cor. 12:17, If the whole were *h*
Gal. 3:2, or by the *h* of faith
Heb. 5:11, have become dull of *h*

HEARS
1 Sam. 3:9, for Your servant *h*
Ps. 34:17, out, and the LORD *h*
Lk. 10:16, He who *h* you *h* Me
Jn. 8:47, of God *h* God's words
Jn. 12:47, "And if anyone *h*
Jn. 18:37, who is of the truth *h*
1 Jn. 4:6, He who knows God *h*
Rev. 22:17, And let him who *h*

HEART
of man. Gen. 6:5; 8:21; Eccl. 8:11; 9:3; Jer. 17:9; Mt. 12:34; 15:19; Lk. 6:45; Rom. 2:5
searched and tested by God. 1 Chr. 28:9; 29:17; Ps. 44:21; 139:23; Prov. 21:2; 24:12; Jer. 12:3; 17:10; 20:12; Rev. 2:23
enlightened, etc., by Him. 2 Cor. 4:6; Ps. 27:14; Prov. 16:1; 1 Th. 3:13; 2 Pet. 1:19
a new, promised. Jer. 24:7; 31:32; 32:39; Ezek. 11:19; 36:26

HEART
Gen. 6:5, *h* was only evil
Ex. 23:9, for you know the *h*
Jud. 5:16, great searchings of *h*
1 Sam. 2:1, *h* rejoices in the LORD
1 Sam. 10:9, God gave him another *h*
1 Sam. 16:7, LORD looks at the *h*
1 Ki. 11:4, his wives turned his *h*
Job 16:13, He pierces my *h*
Job 19:27, How my *h* yearns within
Job 23:16, For God made my *h*
Job 30:27, My *h* is in turmoil and
Ps. 16:7, My *h* also instructs me
Ps. 22:26, your *h* live forever
Ps. 45:1, *h* is overflowing
Ps. 57:7, My *h* is steadfast
Ps. 73:21, Thus my *h* was grieved
Ps. 84:2, my *h* and my flesh cry
Ps. 101:4, *h* shall depart from me
Ps. 101:5, look and a proud *h*
Ps. 111:1, with my whole *h*
Ps. 131:1, *h* is not haughty
Prov. 15:13, *h* makes a cheerful
Prov. 21:1, The king's *h* is in the
Prov. 23:7, as he thinks in his *h*
Prov. 26:23, with a wicked *h*
Prov. 27:19, *h* reveals the man
Prov. 28:26, trusts in his own *h*
Eccl. 7:4, the *h* of the wise is
Eccl. 8:5, and a wise man's *h*
Song 5:4, *h* yearned for him
Isa. 1:5, and the whole *h*
Isa. 16:11, *h* shall resound
Isa. 63:15, The yearning of Your *h*
Jer. 11:20, the mind and the *h*
Jer. 17:9, *h* is deceitful above
Jer. 24:7, I will give them a *h*
Jer. 31:20, therefore My *h* yearns
Ezek. 11:19, and take the stony *h*
Ezek. 18:31, get yourselves a new *h*
Ezek. 44:7, uncircumcised in *h*
Mt. 5:8, are the pure in *h*
Mt. 6:21, is, there your *h*
Mt. 15:19, of the *h* proceed evil
Jn. 7:38, *h* will flow rivers

Jn. 14:1, "Let not your *h*
Acts 4:32, believed were of one *h*
Acts 5:3, Satan filled your *h*
Acts 8:21, *h* is not right in the
Rom. 10:9, *h* that God has raised
Eph. 6:5, in sincerity of *h*
Phile. 20, refresh my *h* in the
1 Jn. 3:17, and shuts up his *h*
1 Jn. 3:20, if our *h* condemns us

HEARTILY
Col. 3:23, you do, do it *h*

HEARTS
Ps. 7:9, God tests the *h*
Ps. 69:32, who seek God, your *h*
Ps. 105:3, let the *h* of those
Mal. 4:6, And he will turn the *h*
Lk. 21:26, *h* failing them from
Acts 15:9, purifying their *h*
Phil. 4:7, will guard your *h*
Col. 3:15, of God rule in your *h*

HEATHEN
Mt. 6:7, repetitions as the *h*
Mt. 18:17, him be to you like a *h*

HEAVE OFFERING
Ex. 29:27; Num. 15:19; 18:8,30

HEAVEN
the firmament, created. Gen. 1:1,8; Ps. 8; 19; Isa. 40:22; Rev. 10:6
dwelling place of God. 1 Ki. 8:30; Ps. 2:4; 115:3; 123:1; Isa. 6:1; 66:1; Ezek. 1; 10; Mt. 6:9; Acts 7:49; Heb. 8:1; Rev. 4
happiness of. Ps. 16:11; Isa. 49:10; Dan. 12:3; Mt. 5:12; 13:43; Lk. 12:37; Jn. 12:26; 14:1; 17:24; 1 Cor. 2:9; 13:12; 1 Pet. 1:4; Rev. 7:16; 14:13; 21:4; 22:3
who enter. Mt. 5:3; 25:34; Rom. 8:17; Heb. 12:23; 1 Pet. 1:4; Rev. 7:9,14
who do not enter. Mt. 7:21; 25:41; Lk. 13:27; 1 Cor. 6:9; Gal. 5:21; Rev. 21:8; 22:15
the new. Rev. 21:1

HEAVEN
Gen. 1:8, called the firmament *H*
Dt. 33:13, precious things of *h*
Ps. 14:2, LORD looks down from *h*
Ps. 119:89, word is settled in *h*
Eccl. 5:2, For God is in *h*
Isa. 66:1, "*H* is My throne
Jer. 31:37, "If *h* above can be
Dan. 2:38, and the birds of the *h*
Dan. 4:26, come to know that *H*
Mt. 3:2, for the kingdom of *h*
Mt. 5:16, your Father in *h*
Mt. 6:10, on earth as it is in *h*
Mt. 24:35, "*H* and earth will
Mk. 8:11, from Him a sign from *h*
Lk. 15:18, have sinned against *h*
Jn. 1:51, you shall see *h*
Jn. 3:13, one has ascended to *h*
Jn. 6:32, the true bread from *h*
Jn. 12:28, a voice came from *h*
Acts 11:5, sheet, let down from *h*
Eph. 3:15, the whole family in *h*
Col. 1:5, laid up for you in *h*
Jas. 5:18, and the *h* gave rain
Rev. 8:1, there was silence in *h*
Rev. 12:1, sign appeared in *h*
Rev. 21:1, Now I saw a new *h*

HEAVENLY
Mt. 6:14, your *h* Father will
Lk. 2:13, *h* host praising God
Jn. 3:12, if I tell you *h* things
1 Cor. 15:48, are those who are *h*
Eph. 1:3, blessing in the *h*
Heb. 6:4, and have tasted the *h*
Heb. 9:23, *h* things themselves
Heb. 11:16, a better, that is, a *h*
Heb. 12:22, the living God, the *h*

HEAVENS
Lev. 26:19, I will make your *h*
Dt. 10:14, and the highest *h*
1 Ki. 8:27, *h* cannot contain
1 Chr. 16:26, the LORD made the *h*
Job 14:12, Till the *h* are no more
Ps. 2:4, in the *h* shall laugh
Ps. 19:1, *h* declare the glory
Ps. 50:6, Let the *h* declare His
Ps. 89:6, *h* can be compared
Ps. 89:11, The *h* are Yours
Ps. 103:11, For as the *h* are high
Prov. 8:27, When He prepared the *h*
Isa. 55:9, *h* are higher than the
Isa. 65:17, behold, I create new *h*
Mt. 3:16, and behold, the *h*
Mt. 24:29, *h* will be shaken
Heb. 1:10, *h* are the work of Your
2 Pet. 3:10, *h* will pass away

HEAVINESS
Ps. 69:20, and I am full of *h*
Ps. 119:28, My soul melts from *h*

HEAVY
Neh. 5:18, the bondage was *h*

HEBER
the Kenite. Jud. 4:11
——— same as Eber. 1 Chr. 5:13

HEBREW
derived from Heber, Abraham's ancestor. Gen. 14:13
the language spoken by the Jews. Jn. 19:20
a Jew. Jer. 34:9

HEBREWS
descendants of Abraham. Gen. 40:15; 43:32; Ex. 2:6; 2 Cor. 11:22; Phil. 3:5

HEBRON (Mamre)
in Canaan, Abraham dwells there. Gen. 13:18; 23:2
the spies come to. Num. 13:22
taken. Josh. 10:36
given to Caleb. Josh. 14:13; 15:13
David reigns there. 2 Sam. 2:1; 3:2; 5:1; 1 Chr. 11; 12:38; 29:27

HEBRONITES
the people of Hebron. Num. 3:27

HEDGE
Hos. 2:6, behold, I will *h*
Mic. 7:4, sharper than a thorn *h*
Mk. 12:1, a vineyard and set a *h*

HEDGED
Job 3:23, and whom God has *h*
Ps. 139:5, You have *h* me behind
Lam. 3:7, He has *h* me in so that

HEED
Ps. 119:9, By taking *h* according
Jer. 17:24, if you *h* Me
Jer. 18:18, and let us not give *h*
1 Tim. 1:4, nor give *h* to fables
Heb. 2:1, the more earnest *h*

HEEDS
Prov. 12:15, *h* counsel is wise

HEEL
Gen. 3:15, you shall bruise His *h*
Gen. 25:26, took hold of Esau's *h*
Ps. 41:9, has lifted up his *h*
Jn. 13:18, Me has lifted up his *h*

HEIGHT
Job 22:12, "Is not God in the *h*
Ps. 102:19, looked down from the *h*
Rom. 8:39, nor *h* nor depth
Eph. 3:18, length and depth and *h*

HEIR
Jer. 49:1, Has he no *h*
Gal. 4:1, Now I say that the *h*
Gal. 4:7, if a son, then an *h*
Heb. 1:2, He has appointed *h*
Heb. 11:7, world and became *h*

HEIRS
Rom. 8:17, if children, then *h*
Rom. 8:17, of God and joint *h*
Eph. 3:6, should be fellow *h*
Jas. 2:5, be rich in faith and *h*
1 Pet. 3:7, vessel, and as being *h*

HELL
Ps. 9:17, shall be turned into *h*
Ps. 55:15, go down alive into *h*
Prov. 7:27, house is the way to *h*
Prov. 23:14, his soul from *h*
Prov. 27:20, *H* and Destruction are
Isa. 14:9, "*H* from beneath is
Mt. 5:22, be in danger of *h* fire
Mt. 18:9, to be cast into *h*
Mt. 23:33, condemnation of *h*
Lk. 12:5, power to cast into *h*
Jas. 3:6, it is set on fire by *h*

HELLENISTS, *see* GREEKS

HELMET
Isa. 59:17, a breastplate, and a *h*
Eph. 6:17, And take the *h* of
1 Th. 5:8, and love, and as a *h*

HELP
Dt. 33:29, the shield of your *h*
Job 6:13, Is my *h* not within me
Ps. 3:2, "There is no *h*
Ps. 20:2, May He send you *h*
Ps. 33:20, He is our *h* and our
Ps. 42:11, yet praise Him, the *h*
Ps. 46:1, A very present *h*
Ps. 60:11, Give us *h* from trouble
Ps. 71:12, God, make haste to *h*
Ps. 89:19, "I have given *h*
Ps. 94:17, the LORD had been my *h*
Ps. 107:12, there was none to *h*
Ps. 115:9, He is their *h* and
Ps. 124:8, Our *h* is in the name
Prov. 28:17, let no one *h* him
Mk. 9:24, *h* my unbelief

Lk. 10:40, tell her to *h* me
Heb. 4:16, and find grace to *h*

HELPED
1 Sam. 7:12, far the LORD has *h*
Ps. 118:13, fall, but the LORD *h*
Isa. 49:8, of salvation I have *h*
Lk. 1:54, *h* His servant Israel

HELPER
Gen. 2:18, I will make him a *h*
Ps. 54:4, Behold, God is my *h*
Jn. 14:16, give you another *H*
Jn. 15:26, "But when the *H*
Rom. 16:2, she has been a *h*
Heb. 13:6, "The LORD is my *h*

HELPFUL
1 Cor. 6:12, all things are not *h*

HELPS
Rom. 8:26, the Spirit also *h*
1 Cor. 12:28, gifts of healings, *h*

HEM
Mt. 9:20, and touched the *h*
Mt. 14:36, might only touch the *h*

HEPHZIBAH, 2 Ki. 21:1; Isa. 62:4

HERE
Isa. 6:8, Then I said, "*H* am I

HERESIES
deprecated. 1 Cor. 11:19; Gal. 5:20; 2 Pet. 2:1. *See* Rom. 16:17; 1 Cor. 1:10; 3:3; 14:33; Phil. 2:3; 4:2; Ti. 3:10; Jude 19

HERESIES
Gal. 5:20, dissensions, *h*
2 Pet. 2:1, in destructive *h*

HERITAGE
Ex. 6:8, give it to you as a *h*
Ps. 61:5, have given me the *h*
Eccl. 3:22, for that is his *h*
Eccl. 5:18, for it is his *h*
Isa. 54:17, This is the *h* of the
Joel 3:2, of My people, My *h*
Mic. 7:14, The flock of Your *h*

HERMAS and **HERMES,** Rom. 16:14

HERMES
Paul so called. Acts 14:12

HERMOGENES, 2 Tim. 1:15

HERMON, Dt. 3:8
Mount. Dt. 4:48; Josh. 12:5; 13:5; Ps. 89:12; 133:3

HEROD
the Great, king of Judea. Mt. 2:1
troubled at Christ's birth. Mt. 2:3
kills the babies of Bethlehem. Mt. 2:16
——— Antipas, rebuked by John the Baptist, imprisons him. Lk. 3:19; beheads him. Mt. 14; Mk. 6:14
seeks to see Christ. Lk. 9:9
scourges Him, and is reconciled to Pilate. Lk. 23:7; Acts 4:27
——— Agrippa, persecutes the church. Acts 12:1
his pride and miserable death. Acts 12:23

HERODIANS
partisans of Herod, a sect, rebuked by Christ. Mt. 22:16; Mk. 12:13
plot against him. Mk. 3:6; 8:15; 12:13

HERODIAS, Mt. 14:3
married to Herod Antipas. Mk. 6:17
plans the death of John the Baptist. Mt. 14; Mk. 6:24

HESHBON, Num. 21:25
city of Sihon, taken. Num. 21:26; Dt. 2:24; Neh. 9:22; Isa. 16:8

HETH
sons of. Gen. 10:15
their kindness to Abraham. Gen. 23:7; 25:10

HEWN
Lk. 23:53, in a tomb that was *h*

HEZEKIAH, 2 Ki. 18:1
king of Judah. 2 Ki. 16:19 (2 Chr. 28:27)
abolishes idolatry. 2 Ki. 18
attacked by the Assyrians, his prayer and deliverance. 2 Ki. 19
his life lengthened, shadow of dial goes backward, displays his treasure, Isaiah's prediction. 2 Ki. 20 (Isa. 38)
his Passover. 2 Chr. 30:13
his piety, and good reign. 2 Chr. 29
his death. 2 Ki. 20:20. *See* Zeph. 1:1

HID
Gen. 3:10, and I *h* myself

HIDDEKEL (Tigris), Gen. 2:14

HIDDEN
2 Ki. 4:27, and the LORD has *h*
Job 28:21, It is *h* from the eyes
Ps. 40:10, *h* Your righteousness
Ps. 69:5, and my sins are not *h*
Ps. 119:11, Your word I have *h*
Isa. 45:3, *h* riches of secret
Hab. 3:4, there His power was *h*
Mt. 10:26, *h* that will not
1 Cor. 2:7, the *h* wisdom which God
1 Cor. 4:5, bring to light the *h*
2 Cor. 4:2, have renounced the *h*
1 Pet. 3:4, rather let it be the *h*
Rev. 2:17, give some of the *h*

HIDE
Ps. 17:8, *H* me under the shadow
Ps. 31:20, You shall *h* them in
Ps. 55:1, O God, and do not *h*
Ps. 104:29, You *h* Your face
Ps. 139:12, darkness shall not *h*
Isa. 45:15, You are God, who *h*
Isa. 58:7, *h* yourself from your
Rev. 6:16, "Fall on us and *h*

HIDES
Ps. 10:11, He *h* His face

HIDING
Ps. 32:7, You are my *h* place
Isa. 32:2, A man will be as a *h*

HIERAPOLIS, Col. 4:13

HIGH
Gen. 14:18, priest of God Most *H*
Ps. 47:2, For the LORD Most *H*
Ps. 89:13, *h* is Your right
Ps. 92:8, are on *h* forevermore
Ps. 138:6, the LORD is on *h*
Isa. 57:15, "I dwell in the *h*
Dan. 4:17, know That the Most *H*
Obad. 3, whose habitation is *h*
Mt. 17:1, up on a *h* mountain by
Rom. 12:16, your mind on *h* things
2 Cor. 10:5, *h* thing that exalts
Heb. 2:17, and faithful *H* Priest

HIGH PLACES
forbidden. Dt. 12:2; 1 Ki. 3:2; 12:31; 13:2; 14:23; Jer. 3:6

HIGH PRIEST, Ex. 28:1
his garments. Lev. 8:7

HIGHER
Job 11:8, There are *h* than heaven
Lk. 14:10, you, 'Friend, go up *h*
Heb. 7:26, *h* than the heavens

HIGHWAY
Prov. 15:19, of the upright is a *h*
Isa. 40:3, in the desert a *h*
Isa. 62:10, up, build up the *h*

HIGHWAYS
Isa. 49:11, *h* shall be elevated
Mt. 22:9, go into the *h*

HILKIAH, 2 Ki. 18:18
finds the Book of the Law. 2 Ki. 22:8

HILL
Ps. 2:6, My King on My holy *h*
Mt. 5:14, *h* cannot be hidden
Lk. 3:5, and *h* brought low
Lk. 4:29, to the brow of the *h*

HILLS
Gen. 49:26, of the everlasting *h*
Dt. 11:11, possess is a land of *h*
Ps. 95:4, of the *h* are His also
Ps. 121:1, up my eyes to the *h*
Prov. 8:25, settled, before the *h*

HINDER
Job 9:12, takes away, who can *h*
1 Cor. 9:12, all things lest we *h*

HINDERED
Rom. 1:13, come to you (but was *h*
Gal. 5:7, Who *h* you from obeying
1 Pet. 3:7, prayers may not be *h*

HINNOM
Valley of. (Josh. 15:8); 2 Ki. 23:10; 2 Chr. 28:3; 33:6; Jer. 7:31; 19:11; 32:35. *See* TOPHET and MOLOCH

HIP
Gen. 32:25, socket of Jacob's *h*

HIRAM (Huram)
king of Tyre, sends aid to David and Solomon. 2 Sam. 5:11; 1 Ki. 5; 9:11; 10:11; 1 Chr. 14:1; 2 Chr. 2:11
——— principal metalworker to Solomon. 1 Ki. 7:13

HIRE
Mt. 20:1, *h* laborers for his

HIRED
Job 7:2, *h* man who eagerly
Lk. 15:17, *h* servants have bread

HIRELING
Jn. 10:13, "The *h* flees because

HITTITES
descendants of Heth. Gen. 15:20; Jud. 1:26; 3:5

HIVITES, Gen. 10:17; Ex. 3:8,17
deceive Joshua. Josh. 9

HOLD
Ps. 77:4, *h* my eyelids open
Ps. 139:10, right hand shall *h*
Isa. 41:13, LORD your God, will *h*
Jer. 4:19, I cannot *h* my peace
1 Cor. 15:2, *h* fast that word
Heb. 4:14, *h* fast our confession
Rev. 3:3, *h* fast and repent

HOLES
Mt. 8:20, "Foxes have *h*

HOLIER
Isa. 65:5, near me, for I am *h*

HOLIEST
Heb. 9:8, the way into the *H*
Heb. 10:19, to enter the *H* by the

HOLINESS
commanded. Ex. 19:22; Lev. 11:44; 20:7; Num. 15:40; Dt. 7:6; 26:19; 28:9; Lk. 1:75; Rom. 12:1; 2 Cor. 7:1; Eph. 1:4; 4:24; Col. 3:12; 1 Th. 2:12; 1 Tim. 2:15; Heb. 12:14; 1 Pet. 1:15; 2 Pet. 3:11; Rev. 22:11

HOLINESS
Ex. 15:11, You, glorious in *h*
Ps. 60:6, has spoken in His *h*
Ps. 89:35, I have sworn by My *h*
Ps. 93:5, *h* adorns Your house
Isa. 35:8, the Highway of *H*
Rom. 1:4, to the Spirit of *h*
2 Cor. 7:1, spirit, perfecting *h*
1 Th. 4:7, uncleanness, but in *h*
Heb. 12:10, be partakers of His *h*

HOLLOW, Jud. 15:19; Isa. 40:12

HOLY
Ex. 3:5, where you stand is *h*
Ex. 19:6, priests and a *h* nation
Ex. 20:8, day, to keep it *h*
Lev. 10:10, distinguish between *h*
Lev. 19:2, LORD your God am *h*
1 Sam. 2:2, "No one is *h*
Ezra 9:2, *h* seed is mixed
Job 5:1, *h* ones will you turn
Ps. 47:8, God sits on His *h*
Ps. 48:1, God, in His *h* mountain
Ps. 86:2, my life, for I am *h*
Isa. 6:3, "*H*, *h*, *h*
Mt. 1:18, child of the *H* Spirit
Mk. 1:8, baptize you with the *H*
Mk. 13:11, who speak, but the *H*
Lk. 1:35, *H* Spirit will come
Lk. 3:22, *H* Spirit descended
Lk. 11:13, Father give the *H*
Lk. 12:12, *H* Spirit will teach
Jn. 7:39, *H* Spirit was not
Acts 1:8, *H* Spirit has come
Acts 2:4, all filled with the *H*
Acts 8:18, apostles' hands the *H*
Acts 11:15, to speak, the *H* Spirit
Acts 15:28, good to the *H* Spirit
Acts 19:2, receive the *H* Spirit
Rom. 11:16, if the firstfruit is *h*
Rom. 14:17, peace and joy in the *H*
Rom. 16:16, one another with a *h*
1 Cor. 2:13, *H* Spirit teaches
Eph. 1:4, that we should be *h*
Eph. 1:13, were sealed with the *H*
Heb. 6:4, partakers of the *H*
Heb. 9:24, has not entered the *h*
1 Pet. 1:12, *H* Spirit sent from
1 Pet. 1:15, He who called you is *h*
1 Pet. 1:16, it is written, "Be *h*
2 Pet. 1:21, moved by the *H* Spirit
1 Jn. 2:20, anointing from the *H*
Rev. 3:7, says He who is *h*
Rev. 15:4, For You alone are *h*
Rev. 22:11, is *h*, let him be *h*

HOLY PLACE
laws concerning. Ex. 28:29; Lev. 6:16; 16:2; 2 Chr. 29:5; Heb. 9:12
measure of the Most. Ezek. 41:4

HOLY SPIRIT
See GOD THE HOLY SPIRIT

HOLY THINGS
laws respecting. Ex. 28:38; Lev. 5:15; 22:2; Num. 4:19,20; 1 Chr. 23:28; Neh. 10:33; Ezek. 20:40; 22:8

HOME
Ruth 1:21, LORD has brought me *h*
Ps. 84:3, sparrow has found a *h*
Ps. 104:17, the stork has her *h*
Eccl. 12:5, to his eternal *h*
Mk. 5:19, said to him, "Go *h*
Lk. 16:9, into an everlasting *h*
Jn. 14:23, to him and make Our *h*
Jn. 19:27, took her to his own *h*
1 Cor. 11:34, let him eat at *h*
1 Cor. 14:35, own husbands at *h*
2 Cor. 5:6, that while we are at *h*
1 Tim. 5:4, to show piety at *h*

HOMELESS
1 Cor. 4:11, and beaten, and *h*

HOMEMAKERS
Ti. 2:5, be discreet, chaste, *h*

HONEST
Gen. 42:11, we are *h* men

HONEY
Jud. 14:18, "What is sweeter than *h*
Ps. 81:16, and with *h* from the
Prov. 24:13, My son, eat *h* because
Prov. 25:27, not good to eat much *h*
Song 4:11, *h* and milk are under
Mt. 3:4, was locusts and wild *h*

HONEYCOMB
Ps. 19:10, than honey and the *h*
Prov. 16:24, words are like a *h*
Lk. 24:42, fish and some *h*

HONOR
due to God. Ps. 29:2; 71:8; 145:5; Mal. 1:6; 1 Tim. 1:17; Rev. 4:11; 5:13
granted by God. 1 Ki. 3:13; Est. 8:16; Prov. 3:16; 4:8; 8:18; 22:4; 29:23; Dan. 5:18; Jn. 12:26
due to: parents. Ex. 20:12; Dt. 5:16; Mt. 15:4; Eph. 6:2; the aged. Lev. 19:32; 1 Tim. 5:1; the king. 1 Pet. 2:17

HONOR
Ex. 20:12, *H* your father and your
1 Ki. 3:13, both riches and *h*
Est. 6:6, the king delights to *h*
Ps. 7:5, earth, and lay my *h*
Ps. 49:20, A man who is in *h*
Ps. 66:2, Sing out the *h* of His
Ps. 91:15, will deliver him and *h*
Ps. 96:6, *H* and majesty are
Ps. 149:9, *h* have all His saints
Prov. 3:9, *H* the LORD with your
Prov. 15:33, before *h* is humility
Prov. 26:1, *h* is not fitting
Prov. 29:23, spirit will retain *h*
Mal. 1:6, Father, where is My *h*
Mt. 13:57, is not without *h*
Mt. 15:4, *H* your father and your
Jn. 5:23, *h* the Son just as they
Jn. 5:41, "I do not receive *h*
Jn. 8:49, but I *h* My Father
Jn. 8:54, "If I *h* Myself
Jn. 12:26, him My Father will *h*
Rom. 9:21, make one vessel for *h*
Rom. 13:7, to whom fear, *h*
1 Cor. 12:23, we bestow greater *h*
1 Th. 4:4, sanctification and *h*
1 Tim. 1:17, alone is wise, be *h*
1 Tim. 5:17, worthy of double *h*
2 Tim. 2:20, and clay, some for *h*
Heb. 5:4, no man takes this *h*
1 Pet. 2:17, *H* the king
2 Pet. 1:17, from God the Father *h*
Rev. 4:9, give glory and *h*

HONORABLE
1 Sam. 9:6, of God, and he is an *h*
Ps. 111:3, His work is *h* and
Prov. 20:3, It is *h* for a man to
Isa. 23:8, traders are the *h*
Isa. 58:13, holy day of the LORD *h*
2 Cor. 8:21, providing *h* things
Heb. 13:4, Marriage is *h* among
1 Pet. 2:12, having your conduct *h*

HONORABLENESS
Rom. 12:17; 13:13; 2 Cor. 8:21; 13:7; Phil. 4:8; 1 Th. 4:12; 1 Tim. 2:2; Heb. 13:18

HONORS
Ps. 15:4, *h* those who fear the
Mk. 7:6, 'This people *h* Me
Jn. 8:54, It is My Father who *h*

HOOKS
Isa. 19:8, will lament who cast *h*
Mic. 4:3, spears into pruning *h*

HOPE
a good. Ps. 16:9; 31:24; Acts 24:15; 28:20; Rom. 15:13
of the wicked will perish. Job 8:13; 11:20; 27:8
comfort of. Job 11:18; Ps. 146:5; Prov. 10:28; 14:32; Jer. 17:7; Lam. 3:21; Acts 24:15; Rom. 12:12; 15:4; 1 Cor. 13:13; Eph. 1:18; 4:4; Col. 1:5; Heb. 3:6
encouragement of. Ps. 31:24; 42:5; 130:7; Lam. 3:26; Rom. 8:24; 15:13; Col. 1:23; Ti. 2:13; Heb. 3:6; 6:11;

1 Pet. 1:13
prisoners of. Zech. 9:12
effect of. Rom. 5:5; 8:24; 15:4; 1 Cor. 13:7; 1 Jn. 3:3
gift of God. Gal. 5:5; 2 Th. 2:16; Ti. 1:2; 1 Pet. 1:3
ready to give reason for. 1 Pet. 3:15

HOPE
Ruth 1:12, I should say I have *h*
Job 7:6, are spent without *h*
Job 14:19, so You destroy the *h*
Job 17:15, where then is my *h*
Job 19:10, *h* He has uprooted
Ps. 16:9, also will rest in *h*
Ps. 31:24, heart, all you who *h*
Ps. 39:7, My *h* is in You
Ps. 71:5, For You are my *h*
Ps. 119:147, I *h* in Your word
Ps. 130:7, O Israel, *h* in the
Prov. 23:18, *h* will not be cut
Prov. 26:12, There is more *h*
Eccl. 9:4, the living there is *h*
Jer. 14:8, O the *H* of Israel
Lam. 3:26, good that one should *h*
Hos. 2:15, Achor as a door of *h*
Zech. 9:12, you prisoners of *h*
Acts 24:15, "I have *h* in God
Rom. 4:18, to *h*, in *h* believed
Rom. 5:2, and rejoice in *h*
Rom. 5:5, *h* does not disappoint
Rom. 8:24, were saved in this *h*
Rom. 8:24, *h* that is seen is
Rom. 8:25, But if we *h* for what
1 Cor. 13:13, now abide faith, *h*
1 Cor. 15:19, life only we have *h*
Eph. 1:18, may know what is the *h*
Eph. 4:4, were called in one *h*
Col. 1:5, *h* which is laid
Col. 1:27, Christ in you, the *h*
1 Th. 2:19, For what is our *h*
1 Th. 4:13, others who have no *h*
1 Th. 5:8, and as a helmet the *h*
1 Tim. 1:1, Jesus Christ, our *h*
Ti. 1:2, in *h* of eternal life
Ti. 2:13, for the blessed *h*
Heb. 6:18, to lay hold of the *h*
Heb. 7:19, in of a better *h*
1 Pet. 1:3, us again to a living *h*
1 Pet. 3:15, you a reason for the *h*
1 Jn. 3:3, who has this *h* in Him

HOPED
Heb. 11:1, substance of things *h*

HOPHNI and Phinehas
sons of Eli. 1 Sam. 1:3
their sin and death. 1 Sam. 2:12,22; 4:11

HOR, Num. 20:23,25

HORAM, Josh. 10:33

HOREB (Mt. Sinai)
Ex. 3:1; 17:6; 33:6; Dt. 1:6; 4:10
law given at. Ex. 19; 20; Dt. 4:10; 5:2; 18:16; 1 Ki. 8:9; Mal. 4:4
Moses twice there for forty days. Ex. 24:18; 34:28; Dt. 9:9
Elijah there for forty days. 1 Ki. 19:8

HORN
Ps. 18:2, my shield and the *h*
Ps. 112:9, *h* will be exalted
Dan. 8:5, goat had a notable *h*
Lk. 1:69, and has raised up a *h*

HORNS
figuratively mentioned. 1 Sam. 2:1; 2 Sam. 22:3; Ps. 75:4
vision of. Dan. 7:7; 8:3; Hab. 3:4; Rev. 5:6; 12:3; 13:1; 17:3
—— of the altar. 1 Ki. 1:50; 2:28
—— of iron, made by Zedekiah. 1 Ki. 22

HORRIBLE
Jer. 5:30, *h* thing has been
Hos. 6:10, I have seen a *h*

HORROR
Gen. 15:12, and behold, *h* and
Ezek. 23:33, sorrow, the cup of *h*
Ezek. 27:36, you will become a *h*

HORSE
Ex. 15:1, The *h* and its rider He
Job 39:19, Have you given the *h*
Ps. 33:17, *h* is a vain hope
Ps. 147:10, the strength of the *h*
Prov. 21:31, *h* is prepared for the
Rev. 6:2, and behold, a white *h*
Rev. 6:5, and behold, a black *h*
Rev. 6:8, and behold, a pale *h*
Rev. 19:11, and behold, a white *h*

HORSES
Eccl. 10:7, seen servants on *h*
Jer. 4:13, *h* are swifter than
Amos 6:12, Do *h* run on rocks
Jas. 3:3, we put bits in *h*

HOSANNA
children sing, to Christ. Mt. 21:9,15; Mk. 11:9; Jn. 12:13 (Ps. 118:25,26)

HOSANNA
Mt. 21:9, *H* in the highest

HOSEA
prophet, declares God's judgment against idolatrous Israel. Hos. 1; 2; 4; and his reconciliation. Hos. 2:14; 11; 13; 14

HOSHEA, Dt. 32:44
last king of Israel, his wicked reign, defeat by the king of Assyria, and captivity. 2 Ki. 15:30; 17:1

HOSPITABLE
1 Tim. 3:2, of good behavior, *h*
1 Pet. 4:9, Be *h* to one another

HOSPITALITY
Rom. 12:13; 1 Tim. 3:2; Ti. 1:8; Heb. 13:2; 1 Pet. 4:9
instances of: Abraham. Gen. 18; Lot. Gen. 19; Laban. Gen. 24:31; Jethro. Ex. 2:20; Manoah. Jud. 13:15; Samuel. 1 Sam. 9:22; David. 2 Sam. 6:19; Barzillai, etc. 2 Sam. 17:27; 19:32; the Shunammite. 2 Ki. 4:8; Nehemiah. Neh. 5:18; Job. Job.31:17; Matthew. Lk. 5:29; Zacchaeus. Lk. 19:6; Lydia. Acts 16:15; Publius, etc. Acts 28:2; Gaius. 3 Jn. 5

HOST
the heavenly. Lk. 2:13. *See* 1 Chr. 12:22; Ps. 103:21; 148:2
of the LORD. Gen. 32:2; Josh. 5:14; 1 Chr. 9:19

HOST
Isa. 40:26, who brings out their *h*
Lk. 2:13, of the heavenly *h*

HOSTILITY
Heb. 12:3, Him who endured such *h*

HOSTS
1 Sam. 17:45, name of the LORD of *h*
1 Ki. 18:15, As the LORD of *h* lives
Ps. 46:7, The LORD of *h* is with
Ps. 103:21, LORD, all you His *h*
Ps. 148:2, praise Him, all His *h*
Isa. 39:5, word of the LORD of *h*
Isa. 47:4, LORD of *h* is His name
Eph. 6:12, against spiritual *h*

HOT
Jud. 2:14, of the LORD was *h*
Ps. 39:3, My heart was *h* within
Rev. 3:15, are neither cold nor *h*

HOUND
Ps. 56:2, My enemies would *h*

HOUR
of day: the third. Mt. 20:3; Mk. 15:25; Acts 2:15; 23:23
the sixth. Mt. 27:45; Mk. 15:33; Lk. 23:44; Jn. 4:6; 19:14; Acts 10:9
the ninth. Acts 3:1; 10:3,30
at hand, coming. Mt. 26:45; Jn. 4:21; 5:25; 12:23; 13:1; 16:21; 17:1
that very same. Mt. 8:13; 9:22; 10:19; 15:28; 17:18; Lk. 12:12; Jn. 4:53; Acts 16:18,33; 22:13; 1 Cor. 4:11; 8:7
no one knows. Mt. 24:36,42; 25:13; Mk. 13:32; Rev. 3:3
of trial. Rev. 3:10; judgment. Rev. 14:7; 18:10
figurative. Rev. 8:1; 9:15

HOUR
Mt. 10:19, *h* what you should
Mt. 24:36, day and *h* no one knows
Mt. 24:44, is coming at an *h*
Mt. 26:45, Behold, the *h* is at
Lk. 22:53, But this is your *h*
Jn. 2:4, *h* has not yet come
Jn. 4:23, "But the *h* is coming
Jn. 12:23, *h* has come that the
Jn. 12:27, save Me from this *h*
Jn. 17:1, "Father, the *h*
Rev. 3:3, will not know what *h*
Rev. 3:10, keep you from the *h*

HOURS
Jn. 11:9, Are there not twelve *h*

HOUSE of God
Gen. 28:17; Jud. 20:18; 2 Chr. 5:14; Ezra 5:8,15; 7:20,23; Neh. 6:10; Ps. 84:10; Isa. 6:11; 60:7; Ezek. 41:5,13; 43:5; Mic. 4:2; Zech. 7:2; Mt. 12:4; 1 Tim. 3:15; Heb. 10:21; 1 Pet. 4:17
heaven. Acts 7:49
altars. *See* ALTAR

for worship. *See* TEMPLE

HOUSE
Gen. 12:1, from your father's *h*
Josh. 24:15, as for me and my *h*
Job 30:23, *h* appointed for all
Ps. 42:4, with them to the *h*
Ps. 65:4, the goodness of Your *h*
Prov. 2:18, For her *h* leads down
Prov. 24:3, Through wisdom a *h*
Eccl. 7:2, better to go to the *h*
Eccl. 12:3, of the *h* tremble
Isa. 2:3, to the *h* of the God of
Isa. 5:8, to those who join *h*
Isa. 6:4, *h* was filled with
Isa. 38:1, 'Set your *h* in order
Isa. 56:7, *h* shall be called a
Mt. 7:25, and beat on that *h*
Mt. 12:25, *h* divided against
Mt. 21:13, *h* shall be called a
Lk. 14:23, *h* may be filled
Jn. 2:16, make My Father's *h*
Jn. 14:2, *h* are many mansions
Acts 20:20, publicly and from *h*
Acts 28:30, in his own rented *h*
1 Tim. 3:4, who rules his own *h*
Phile. 2, the church in your *h*
Heb. 3:4, For every *h* is built
Heb. 3:6, His own *h*, whose *h*
2 Jn. 1:10, him into your *h*

HOUSEHOLD
Prov. 31:27, over the ways of her *h*
Mt. 10:13, "If the *h* is worthy
Mt. 10:36, be those of his own *h*
Acts 16:15, *h* were baptized
Acts 16:31, saved, you and your *h*
1 Cor. 1:16, also baptized the *h*
Gal. 6:10, those who are of the *h*
Phil. 4:22, who are of Caesar's *h*

HOUSEHOLDER
Mt. 13:52, *h* who brings out of

HOUSES
Job 21:9, *h* are safe from fear
Job 22:18, Yet He filled their *h*
Ps. 49:11, is that their *h*
Prov. 19:14, *H* and riches are an
Mt. 19:29, who has left *h* or
Mt. 23:14, you devour widows' *h*
1 Cor. 11:22, Do you not have *h*

HOVERING
Gen. 1:2, Spirit of God was *h*

HOW
Lk. 1:34, "*H* can this be
Jn. 10:24, *H* long do You keep
1 Th. 1:9, *h* you turned to God

HUMAN
Heb. 12:9, we have had *h* fathers

HUMBLE
Num. 12:3, man Moses was very *h*
Dt. 8:2, *h* you and test you
Job 40:11, who is proud, and *h*
Ps. 9:12, the cry of the *h*
Ps. 10:12, Do not forget the *h*
Ps. 10:17, the desire of the *h*
Ps. 25:9, *h* He guides in justice
Ps. 34:2, *h* shall hear of it and
Ps. 147:6, LORD lifts up the *h*
Prov. 16:19, *h* spirit with the
Isa. 57:15, contrite and *h* spirit
Zeph. 3:12, a meek and *h* people
Rom. 12:16, associate with the *h*
Jas. 4:6, gives grace to the *h*
Jas. 4:10, *H* yourselves in the
1 Pet. 5:5, gives grace to the *h*
1 Pet. 5:6, *h* yourselves under the

HUMBLED
2 Chr. 33:12, *h* himself greatly
Phil. 2:8, as a man, He *h* Himself

HUMBLES
Ps. 113:6, *h* Himself to behold

HUMILIATION
Ezra 9:7, to plunder, and to *h*
Acts 8:33, *h* His justice was
Jas. 1:10, but the rich in his *h*

HUMILITY, Prov. 15:33; 18:12
commanded. Mic. 6:8; Mt. 18; 20:25; Mk. 9:33; 10:43; Lk. 9:46; 14:7; 22:24; Eph. 4:2; Col. 3:12; Phil. 2:3; Jas. 4:10; 1 Pet. 5:5
benefits of. Ps. 34:2; 69:32; Prov. 3:34; Isa. 57:15; Mt. 18:4; Lk. 14:11; Jas. 4:6
profession of. Ps. 131

HUMILITY
Prov. 22:4, By *h* and the fear of
Zeph. 2:3, righteousness, seek *h*
Acts 20:19, the Lord with all *h*
Col. 2:18, delight in false *h*
Col. 3:12, mercies, kindness, *h*
2 Tim. 2:25, *h* correcting those
Ti. 3:2, gentle, showing all *h*
1 Pet. 5:5, and be clothed with *h*

HUNGER
Dt. 8:3, you, allowed you to *h*
Ps. 34:10, lack and suffer *h*
Isa. 49:10, They shall neither *h*
Jer. 38:9, likely to die from *h*
Mt. 5:6, are those who *h*
Lk. 6:25, for you shall *h*
Jn. 6:35, to Me shall never *h*
1 Cor. 4:11, present hour we both *h*
Rev. 7:16, They shall neither *h*

HUNGRY
Job 22:7, bread from the *h*
Ps. 107:9, and fills the *h*
Ps. 146:7, gives food to the *h*
Prov. 27:7, *h* soul every bitter
Isa. 58:10, your soul to the *h*
Mt. 25:35, 'for I was *h* and you
Mt. 25:37, when did we see You *h*
1 Cor. 11:21, and one is *h* and
1 Cor. 11:34, But if anyone is *h*
Phil. 4:12, to be full and to be *h*

HUNT
1 Sam. 24:11, Yet you *h* my life to
Ps. 140:11, *h* the violent man
Ezek. 13:18, *h* the souls of My

HUNTER
Gen. 10:9, Nimrod the mighty *h*
Gen. 25:27, Esau was a skillful *h*

HUR, Ex. 17:10

HURAM
another way of spelling Hiram. 2 Chr. 2:13

HURT
Ex. 21:22, *h* a woman with child
Ps. 35:4, who plot my *h*
Prov. 23:35, but I was not *h*
Eccl. 8:9, another to his own *h*
Isa. 11:9, They shall not *h*
Jer. 8:21, of my people I am *h*
Jer. 10:19, Woe is me for my *h*
Mk. 16:18, it will by no means *h*
Rev. 2:11, shall not be *h* by the

HUSBAND
Gen. 3:6, She also gave to her *h*
Ex. 4:25, "Surely you are a *h*
Prov. 31:11, *h* safely trusts her
Isa. 54:5, your Maker is your *h*
Jer. 31:32, though I was a *h*
Jn. 4:18, now have is not your *h*
1 Cor. 7:2, woman have her own *h*
1 Cor. 7:14, For the unbelieving *h*
1 Cor. 7:16, you will save your *h*
2 Cor. 11:2, betrothed you to one *h*
Eph. 5:23, For the *h* is head of
1 Tim. 3:2, the *h* of one wife

HUSBANDS
1 Cor. 14:35, them ask their own *h*
Eph. 5:25, *H*, love your wives
1 Tim. 3:12, Let deacons be the *h*

HUSHAI, 2 Sam. 15:32; 16:16; 17:5

HYMENAEUS
1 Tim. 1:20; 2 Tim. 2:17

HYMN
Mt. 26:30, they had sung a *h*

HYMNS
Acts 16:25, praying and singing *h*
Eph. 5:19, in psalms and *h*

HYPOCRISY
Mt. 23:28, you are full of *h*
Lk. 12:1, Pharisees, which is *h*
Rom. 12:9, Let love be without *h*
Gal. 2:13, away with their *h*
Jas. 3:17, and without *h*
1 Pet. 2:1, malice, all deceit, *h*

HYPOCRITE
Job 8:13, of the *h* shall perish
Job 20:5, and the joy of the *h*
Job 27:8, is the hope of the *h*
Isa. 9:17, for everyone is a *h*
Gal. 2:13, also played the *h*

HYPOCRITES
Job 36:13, "But the *h* in heart
Ps. 26:4, will I go in with *h*
Jer. 42:20, "For you were *h*
Mt. 6:5, not be like the *h*
Mt. 22:18, do you test Me, you *h*
Mt. 23:13, and Pharisees, *h*

HYSSOP
Ps. 51:7, Purge me with *h*
Jn. 19:29, sour wine, put it on *h*
Jer. 8:21, of my people I am *h*
Jer. 10:19, Woe is me for my *h*

I AM
Ex. 3:14; Jn. 8:58; Rev. 1:18

ICE
Job 6:16, dark because of the *i*

ICHABOD, 1 Sam. 4:21; 14:3

ICONIUM
Acts 13:51; 14:1; 16:2; 2 Tim. 3:11

IDDO
1 Chr. 27:21; Ezra 8:17; Zech. 1:1

IDLE
Ex. 5:8, For they are *i*
Prov. 19:15, *i* person will suffer
Mt. 12:36, *i* word men may speak
Mt. 20:3, saw others standing *i*
1 Tim. 5:13, they learn to be *i*
Ti. 1:10, both *i* talkers and

IDOL
Isa. 66:3, if he blesses an *i*
1 Cor. 8:7, thing offered to an *i*
1 Cor. 10:19, That an *i* is anything

IDOLATER
1 Cor. 5:11, or covetous, or an *i*
Eph. 5:5, man, who is an *i*

IDOLATERS
1 Cor. 6:9, fornicators, nor *i*
Rev. 21:8, immoral, sorcerers, *i*
Rev. 22:15, and murderers and *i*

IDOLATRIES
1 Pet. 4:3, and abominable *i*

IDOLATRY
Ex. 20:2; 22:20; 23:13; Lev. 26:1; Dt. 4:15; 5:7; 11:16; 17:2; 18:9; 27:15; Ps. 97:7; Jer. 2:11; 1 Cor. 10:7,14; 1 Jn. 5:21
folly of. 1 Ki. 18:26; Ps. 115:4; 135:15; Isa. 40:19; 41; 44:9; 46:1; Jer. 2:26; 10
forbidden. Dt. 16:21; Jud. 6:25; 1 Ki. 14:15; 15:13; 16:33; 2 Ki. 17:16; 21:3; 23:4
monuments of, to be destroyed. Ex. 23:24; 34:13; Dt. 7:5
enticers to. Dt. 13:1
Israelites guilty of. Ex. 32; Num. 25; Jud. 2:11; 3:7; 8:33; 18:30; 2 Ki. 17:12; also Micah. Jud. 17; Solomon. 1 Ki. 11:5; Jeroboam. 1 Ki. 12:28; Ahab, etc. 1 Ki. 16:31; 18:19; Manasseh. 2 Ki. 21:4; Ahaz. 2 Chr. 28:2; Nebuchadnezzar, etc. Dan. 3; 5; inhabitants of Lystra. Acts 14:11; Athens. Acts 17:16; Ephesus. Acts 19:28
zeal of Asa against. 1 Ki. 15:12
of Jehoshaphat. 2 Chr. 17:6
of Hezekiah. 2 Chr. 30:13
of Josiah. 2 Chr. 34
punishment of. Dt. 17:2; Jer. 8:1; 16:1; 44:21; Hos. 8:5; 1 Cor. 6:9; Eph. 5:5; Rev. 14:9; 21:8; 22:15

IDOLATRY
1 Cor. 10:14, beloved, flee from *i*
Gal. 5:20, *i*, sorcery

IDOLS
food offered to. Rom. 14; 1 Cor. 8

IDOLS
Gen. 31:19, stolen the household *i*
Ps. 96:5, of the peoples are *i*
Ps. 115:4, *i* are silver and gold
Isa. 2:8, land is also full of *i*
Jer. 50:38, insane with their *i*
Ezek. 8:12, in the room of his *i*
Hos. 4:12, from their wooden *i*
Jon. 2:8, who regard worthless *i*
Zech. 10:2, *i* speak delusion
Acts 15:20, things polluted by *i*
Rom. 2:22, You who abhor *i*
1 Cor. 10:28, This was offered to *i*
1 Jn. 5:21, Keep yourselves from *i*
Rev. 9:20, worship demons, and *i*

IGNORANCE
Acts 3:17, that you did it in *i*
Acts 17:30, *i* God overlooked
Heb. 9:7, sins committed in *i*
1 Pet. 2:15, to silence the *i*

IGNORANT
Ps. 73:22, I was so foolish and *i*
Isa. 63:16, though Abraham was *i*
1 Cor. 12:1, not want you to be *i*
1 Cor. 14:38, But if anyone is *i*
Heb. 5:2, on those who are *i*

IGNORANTLY
1 Tim. 1:13, because I did it *i*

ILLEGITIMATE
Heb. 12:8, then you are *i*

ILLUMINATED
Heb. 10:32, after you were *i*
Rev. 18:1, and the earth was *i*
Rev. 21:23, for the glory of God *i*

ILLYRICUM, Rom. 15:19

IMAGE
Gen. 1:26, Us make man in Our *i*
Dt. 4:16, yourselves a carved *i*
Ps. 73:20, shall despise their *i*
Dan. 3:1, the king made an *i*
Mt. 22:20, to them, "Whose *i*
1 Cor. 11:7, since he is the *i*
Col. 1:15, He is the *i* of the
Heb. 10:1, and not the very *i*
Rev. 14:9, the beast and his *i*
Rev. 19:20, who worshiped his *i*

IMAGES
prohibited. Ex. 20:4; Lev. 26:1; Dt. 16:22

IMAGINATION
Lk. 1:51, the proud in the *i*

IMITATE
1 Cor. 4:16, I urge you, *i* me
1 Cor. 11:1, as I also *i* Christ
Heb. 6:12, *i* those who through

IMMANUEL
Isa. 7:14, shall call His name *I*
Mt. 1:23, shall call His name *I*

IMMEDIATELY
Mk. 1:12, *i* the Spirit
Mk. 4:15, hear, Satan comes *i*
Jas. 1:24, *i* forgets what
Rev. 4:2, *I* I was in the Spirit

IMMORAL
Prov. 22:14, *i* woman is a deep pit
Rev. 21:8, murderers, sexually *i*

IMMORALITY
Mt. 5:32, except sexual *i*
1 Cor. 5:1, *i* as is not even named
1 Th. 4:3, abstain from sexual *i*

IMMORTAL
1 Tim. 1:17, to the King eternal, *i*

IMMORTALITY
Rom. 2:7, glory, honor, and *i*
1 Cor. 15:53, mortal must put on *i*
1 Tim. 6:16, who alone has *i*
2 Tim. 1:10, and brought life and *i*

IMMOVABLE
1 Cor. 15:58, be steadfast, *i*

IMMUTABILITY
of God's counsel. Heb. 6:17

IMMUTABLE
Heb. 6:18, that by two *i* things

IMPART
Rom. 1:11, see you, that I may *i*
Eph. 4:29, that it may *i* grace

IMPENITENT
Rom. 2:5, *i* heart you are

IMPLANTED
Jas. 1:21, with meekness the *i*

IMPOSSIBLE
Mt. 17:20, and nothing will be *i*
Mt. 19:26, "With men this is *i*
Lk. 1:37, God nothing will be *i*
Heb. 11:6, without faith it is *i*

IMPOSTORS
2 Tim. 3:13, *i* will grow worse

IMPOVERISH, Jud. 6:6; Isa. 40:20

IMPRISONMENT
Heb. 11:36, and of chains and *i*

IMPRISONMENTS
2 Cor. 6:5, in stripes, in *i*

IMPUDENT
Prov. 7:13; Ezek. 2:4; 3:7

IMPULSIVE
Prov. 14:29, but he who is *i*

IMPURITY
Ezek. 18:6, a woman during her *i*

IMPUTE
2 Sam. 19:19, "Do not let my lord *i*
Ps. 32:2, the LORD does not *i*
Rom. 4:8, the LORD shall not *i*

IMPUTED
Lev. 17:4, bloodshed shall be *i*
Rom. 4:11, might be *i* to them
Rom. 4:23, alone that it was *i*
Rom. 5:13, but sin is not *i*

IMPUTES
Rom. 4:6, *i* righteousness apart

INCENSE
Ex. 30:22; 37:29; Lev. 10:1; 16:13; Num. 16:46; Rev. 5:8; 8:3

INCLINE
Josh. 24:23, *i* your heart to the
Ps. 141:4, *i* my heart to any evil

INCORRUPTIBLE
Rom. 1:23, the glory of the *i*
1 Cor. 15:52, dead will be raised *i*

1 Pet. 1:4, to an inheritance *i*
1 Pet. 1:23, corruptible seed but *i*

INCORRUPTION
1 Cor. 15:42, it is raised in *i*
1 Cor. 15:50, corruption inherit *i*
1 Cor. 15:53, must put on *i*

INCREASE
Ps. 62:10, if riches *i*
Ps. 115:14, the LORD give you *i*
Prov. 1:5, hear and *i* learning
Eccl. 5:11, When goods *i*
Isa. 9:7, Of the *i* of His
Dan. 12:4, and knowledge shall *i*
Lk. 17:5, Lord, "*I* our faith
Jn. 3:30, "He must *i*
1 Cor. 3:6, but God gave the *i*
Col. 2:19, grows with the *i*
2 Tim. 2:16, for they will *i*

INCREASED
Gen. 7:17, The waters *i* and
Gen. 19:19, *i* your mercy which you
Isa. 9:3, nation and *i* its joy
Lk. 2:52, And Jesus *i* in wisdom

INCREASES
Eccl. 1:18, *i* knowledge *i*
Isa. 40:29, who have no might He *i*

INCREDIBLE
Acts 26:8, should it be thought *i*

INCURABLE
Job 34:6, My wound is *i*
Jer. 30:12, 'Your affliction is *i*
Jer. 30:15, Your sorrow is *i*

INDEBTED
Lk. 11:4, everyone who is *i*

INDEED
Gen. 1:31, *i* it was very
1 Ki. 8:27, "But will God *i*
Jn. 1:47, "Behold, an Israelite *i*

INDIA, Est. 1:1

INDICATING
Heb. 9:8, the Holy Spirit *i*
1 Pet. 1:11, who was in them was *i*

INDIGNANT
Mt. 26:8, saw it, they were *i*

INDIGNATION
Ps. 78:49, of His anger, wrath, *i*
Ps. 119:53, *I* has taken hold
Isa. 10:5, in whose hand is My *i*
Isa. 34:2, For the *i* of the LORD
Jer. 15:17, have filled me with *i*
Nah. 1:6, can stand before His *i*
Heb. 10:27, *i* which will devour
Rev. 14:10, into the cup of His *i*

INDUCED
Jer. 20:7, O LORD, You *i* me
Ezek. 14:9, if the prophet is *i*
Ezek. 14:9, I the LORD have *i*

INDULGENCE
Col. 2:23, no value against the *i*

INEXCUSABLE
Rom. 2:1, Therefore you are *i*

INEXPRESSIBLE
2 Cor. 12:4, Paradise and heard *i*
1 Pet. 1:8, you rejoice with joy *i*

INFALLIBLE
Acts 1:3, suffering by many *i*

INFANTS
Job 3:16, *i* who never saw
Lk. 18:15, they also brought *i*

INFERIOR
Dan. 2:39, another kingdom *i*
2 Cor. 11:5, that I am not at all *i*

INFIRMITIES
Mt. 8:17, "He Himself took our *i*
2 Cor. 12:5, boast, except in my *i*
1 Tim. 5:23, and your frequent *i*

INFLAMING
Isa. 57:5, *i* yourselves with gods

INGRATITUDE
to God. Rom. 1:21
exemplified by: Israel. Dt. 32:18; Saul. 1 Sam. 15:17; David. 2 Sam. 12:7,9; Nebuchadnezzar. Dan. 5; lepers. Lk. 17
punished. Neh. 9:27; Hos. 2:8,9
characteristic of the wicked. Ps. 38:20; 2 Tim. 3:2
its penalty. Prov. 17:13; Jer. 18:20

INHABIT
Prov. 10:30, the wicked will not *i*
Amos 9:14, cities and *i* them

INHABITANT
Isa. 12:6, Cry out and shout, O *i*
Isa. 33:24, And the *i* will not say

INHABITANTS
Ps. 33:14, He looks on all the *i*
Ps. 49:1, give ear, all *i*
Isa. 42:11, Let the *i* of Sela sing
Rev. 12:12, Woe to the *i* of the

INHABITED
Prov. 8:31, rejoicing in His *i*
Isa. 44:26, 'You shall be *i*
Isa. 45:18, who formed it to be *i*

INHERIT
Job 13:26, *i* the iniquities
Ps. 25:13, descendants shall *i*
Ps. 37:29, The righteous shall *i*
Prov. 3:35, The wise shall *i*
Prov. 8:21, love me to *i* wealth
Prov. 14:18, The simple *i* folly
Prov. 28:10, the blameless will *i*
Mt. 25:34, *i* the kingdom prepared
Mk. 10:17, I do that I may *i*
1 Cor. 6:9, unrighteous will not *i*
1 Pet. 3:9, you may *i* a blessing
Rev. 21:7, who overcomes shall *i*

INHERITANCE
Num. 18:20, "You shall have no *i*
Dt. 32:9, is the place of His *i*
Ps. 16:5, the portion of my *i*
Ps. 16:6, yes, I have a good *i*
Ps. 37:18, *i* shall be forever
Ps. 47:4, He will choose our *i*
Ps. 68:9, You confirmed Your *i*
Ps. 74:2, the tribe of Your *i*
Prov. 20:21, *i* gained hastily
Jer. 32:8, right of *i* is yours
Lam. 5:2, *i* has been turned
Dan. 12:13, will arise to your *i*
Acts 7:5, God gave him no *i*
Acts 20:32, and give you an *i*
Gal. 3:18, For if the *i* is of the
Eph. 1:11, we have obtained an *i*
Col. 1:12, be partakers of the *i*
Heb. 11:8, receive as an *i*
1 Pet. 1:4, *i* incorruptible

INIQUITIES
Job 13:23, How many are my *i*
Ps. 40:12, *i* have overtaken me
Ps. 65:3, *I* prevail against me
Ps. 103:3, forgives all your *i*
Ps. 130:3, LORD, should mark *i*
Isa. 53:5, was bruised for our *i*
Isa. 53:11, He shall bear their *i*
Isa. 59:2, *i* have separated you

INIQUITY
Ex. 20:5, God, visiting the *i* of the
Num. 23:21, He has not observed *i*
Ps. 7:14, wicked brings forth *i*
Ps. 25:11, O LORD, pardon my *i*
Ps. 32:5, *i* I have not hidden
Ps. 51:5, was brought forth in *i*
Ps. 66:18, If I regard *i* in my
Ps. 69:27, Add *i* to their
Ps. 92:7, workers of *i* flourish
Ps. 94:4, *i* boast in themselves
Ps. 94:20, Shall the throne of *i*
Ps. 119:133, *i* have dominion
Prov. 22:8, *i* will reap sorrow
Isa. 1:4, a people laden with *i*
Isa. 6:7, *i* is taken away
Isa. 53:6, has laid on Him the *i*
Hos. 9:9, will remember their *i*
Mic. 2:1, to those who devise *i*
Mic. 7:18, like You, pardoning *i*
Lk. 13:27, all you workers of *i*
Jas. 3:6, a fire, a world of *i*

INJUSTICE
Ex. 22:21; 23:6; Lev. 19:15; Dt. 16:19; 24:17; Job 31:13; Ps. 82:2; Prov. 22:16; 29:7; Jer. 22:3; Lk. 16:10
results of. Prov. 11:7; 28:8; Mic. 6:10; Amos 5:11; 8:5; 1 Th. 4:6; 2 Pet. 2:9

INJUSTICE
Dt. 32:4, of truth and without *i*
Job 5:16, *i* shuts her mouth
Jer. 2:5, *i* have your fathers

INK
2 Cor. 3:3, us, written not with *i*
2 Jn. 12, do so with paper and *i*

INN
Lk. 2:7, room for them in the *i*
Lk. 10:34, brought him to an *i*

INNOCENCE
Gen. 20:5, of my heart and *i*
Ps. 73:13, washed my hands in *i*

INNOCENT
Ex. 23:7, do not kill the *i*
Dt. 27:25, a bribe to slay an *i*
Job 27:17, *i* will divide the
Ps. 15:5, a bribe against the *i*
Dan. 6:22, because I was found *i*
Mt. 27:24, saying, "I am *i*
Acts 20:26, this day that I am *i*

INNUMERABLE
Heb. 11:12, *i* as the sand which is
Heb. 12:22, *i* company of angels

INQUIRED
Jud. 20:27, children of Israel *i*
1 Sam. 23:2, Therefore David *i*
Zeph. 1:6, the LORD, nor *i* of Him
1 Pet. 1:10, the prophets have *i*

INQUIRY
Dt. 19:18, shall make careful *i*

INSANE
Jer. 50:38, images, and they are *i*
Hos. 9:7, the spiritual man is *i*

INSCRIBED
Job 19:23, Oh, that they were *i*
Isa. 49:16, See, I have *i* you on

INSPIRATION
2 Tim. 3:16, is given by *i* of God

INSTRUCT
Neh. 9:20, good Spirit to *i* them
Ps. 32:8, I will *i* you and teach
1 Cor. 2:16, LORD that he may *i*

INSTRUCTED
Job 4:3, Surely you have *i*
Isa. 40:14, counsel, and who *i*
Acts 18:25, This man had been *i*
Rom. 2:18, are excellent, being *i*
Heb. 8:5, Moses was divinely *i*

INSTRUCTION
promised. Job 33:16; Ps. 32:8; Prov. 10:17; 12:1; 13:1; Mt. 13:52; 2 Tim. 3:16
recommended. Prov. 1:2,8; 4:13; 9:9; 19:20; 23:12
hated by wicked. Ps. 50:17; Prov. 1:22; 5:12
consequence of rejecting. Prov. 13:18; 15:32

INSTRUCTION
Ps. 50:17, seeing you hate *i*
Prov. 1:7, despise wisdom and *i*
Prov. 4:13, Take firm hold of *i*
Prov. 8:33, Hear *i* and be wise
Prov. 9:9, Give *i* to a wise man
Prov. 12:1, *i* loves knowledge
Prov. 19:27, Cease listening to *i*
Prov. 23:12, Apply your heart to *i*
2 Tim. 3:16, for correction, for *i*

INSTRUCTORS
1 Cor. 4:15, have ten thousand *i*

INSTRUCTS
Ps. 16:7, My heart also *i*
Ps. 94:10, He who *i* the nations

INSTRUMENT
Ps. 33:2, to Him with an *i*
Ps. 92:3, on an *i* of ten strings

INSTRUMENTS
Gen. 49:5, *i* of cruelty are in
Ps. 150:4, with stringed *i*
Rom. 6:13, your members as *i*
Rom. 6:13, and your members as *i*

INSUBORDINATE
1 Tim. 1:9, for the lawless and *i*
Ti. 1:10, For there are many *i*

INSUBORDINATION
Ti. 1:6, of dissipation or *i*

INSULTED
Lk. 18:32, will be mocked and *i*
Heb. 10:29, *i* the Spirit of grace

INSULTS
Isa. 51:7, nor be afraid of their *i*

INTEGRITY
Gen. 20:5, In the *i* of my heart
Job 2:3, he holds fast to his *i*
Job 31:6, that God may know my *i*
Ps. 26:1, I have walked in my *i*
Ps. 41:12, You uphold me in my *i*
Prov. 11:3, The *i* of the upright
Ti. 2:7, in doctrine showing *i*

INTELLIGENT
Acts 13:7, Sergius Paulus, an *i*

INTERCEDE
1 Sam. 2:25, the LORD, who will *i*

INTERCESSION
of Christ. Lk. 23:34; Rom. 8:34; Heb. 7:25; 1 Jn. 2:1
predicted. Isa. 53:12
of the Holy Spirit. Rom. 8:26
to be made for all men. 1 Tim. 2:1; Eph. 6:18; for kings. 1 Tim. 2:2
asked for by Paul. Rom. 15:30; 2 Cor. 1:11; Col. 4:3; 1 Th. 5:25; 2 Th. 3:1; Heb. 13:18

INTERCESSION
Isa. 53:12, of many, and made *i*
Rom. 8:26, Spirit Himself makes *i*
Heb. 7:25, always lives to make *i*

INTERCESSOR
Isa. 59:16, that there was no *i*

INTEREST
Ex. 22:25, shall not charge him *i*
Jer. 15:10, men lent to me for *i*
Lk. 19:23, collected it with *i*

INTERPRET
1 Cor. 12:30, Do all *i*?
1 Cor. 14:13, pray that he may *i*
1 Cor. 14:27, in turn, and let one *i*

INTERPRETATION
(of dreams), is through God. Gen. 40:8; Prov. 1:6; Dan. 2:27

INTERPRETATION
Gen. 40:12, "This is the *i*
1 Cor. 12:10, to another the *i*
1 Cor. 14:26, a revelation, has an *i*
2 Pet. 1:20, of any private *i*

INTERPRETATIONS
Gen. 40:8, Do not *i* belong to God
Dan. 5:16, that you can give *i*

INTRIGUE
Dan. 11:21, seize the kingdom by *i*
Dan. 11:34, join with them by *i*

INVISIBLE
Rom. 1:20, of the world His *i*
Col. 1:15, is the image of the *i*
1 Tim. 1:17, eternal, immortal, *i*
Heb. 11:27, as seeing Him who is *i*

INWARD
Ps. 5:9, *i* part is destruction
Ps. 64:6, Both the *i* thought
Ps. 139:13, You have formed my *i*
Rom. 7:22, God according to the *i*
2 Cor. 4:16, *i* man is being renewed

INWARDLY
Mt. 7:15, *i* they are
Rom. 2:29, is a Jew who is one *i*

IRON
Job 41:27, He regards *i* as straw
Prov. 27:17, *i* sharpens *i*
Isa. 48:4, and your neck was an *i*
Dan. 2:33, its feet partly of *i*

ISAAC, Gen. 17:19
his birth promised. Gen. 15:4; 17:16; 18:10
born. Gen. 21:2
offered by Abraham. Gen. 22:7
marries Rebekah. Gen. 24:67
blesses his sons. Gen. 27:28; dies. Gen. 35:29

ISAIAH
prophet. Isa. 1:1; 2:1
sent to Ahaz. Isa. 7; and Hezekiah. Isa. 37:6; 38:4; 39:3
prophesies concerning various nations. Isa. 7; 8; 10; 13—23; 45—47
referred to in. Mt. 3:3; 4:14; 8:17; 12:17; 13:14; 15:7; Mk. 1:3; Lk. 3:4; 4:17; Jn. 1:23; 12:38; Acts 8:32; 28:25; Rom. 9:27; 10:16; 15:12

ISCARIOT, Judas
Mt. 10:4; Mk. 3:19
his treachery. Mt. 26:21; Mk. 14:18; Lk. 22:47; Jn. 18:3
death. Mt. 27:5; Acts 1:18

ISHBOSHETH
2 Sam. 2:8; 3:7; 4:5,8

ISHMAEL
son of Abram. Gen. 16:15; 17:20; 21:17; 25:17; his descendants. Gen. 25:12; 1 Chr. 1:29
——— son of Nethaniah, kills Gedaliah. 2 Ki. 25:25; Jer. 40:14; 41

ISRAEL
Jacob so called after wrestling with God. Gen. 32:28; 35:10; Hos. 12:3

ISRAEL
Gen. 32:28, be called Jacob, but *I*
Dt. 6:4, "Hear, O *I*
2 Sam. 7:7, shepherd My people *I*
Ps. 73:1, Truly God is good to *I*
Lk. 1:54, helped His servant *I*
Rom. 9:6, For they are not all *I*
Gal. 6:16, and upon the *I* of God

ISRAELITES
descendants of Israel. Ex. 9:7
in Egypt. Ex. 1—12
the first Passover instituted. Ex. 12
flight from Egypt. Ex. 12:31
pass through the Red Sea. Ex. 14
their journeys. Ex. 14:1,19; Num. 9:15; Ps. 78:14
fed with manna and water in the wilderness. Ex. 16:4; 17:1; Num. 11; 20

God's covenant with at Mt. Sinai. Ex. 19; 20; Dt. 29:10
their idolatry. Ex. 32. *See also* 2 Ki. 17; Ezra 9; Neh. 9; Ezek. 20; 22; 23; Acts 7:39; 1 Cor. 10:1
their rebellious conduct related by Moses. Dt. 1; 2; 9
conquer and divide Canaan under Joshua. Josh. 1; 12; 13
governed by: judges. Jud. 2; kings. 1 Sam. 10; 2 Sam.; 1 & 2 Ki.; 1 & 2 Chr.
their captivity in Assyria. 2 Ki. 17; in Babylon. 2 Ki. 25; 2 Chr. 36; Jer. 39; 52; their return. Ezra; Neh.; Hag.; Zech.
God's wrath against. Ps. 78; 106; deliverances of. Ps. 105
their sufferings our examples. 1 Cor. 10:6

ISSACHAR, Gen. 30:18; 35:23
descendants of. Gen. 46:13; Jud. 5:15; 1 Chr. 7:1. *See* Gen. 49:14; Num. 1:28; 26:23; Dt. 33:18; Josh. 19:17; Ezek. 48:33; Rev. 7:7

ITALIAN, Acts 10:1

ITALY, Acts 18:2

ITCHING
2 Tim. 4:3, they have *i* ears

ITHAMAR, Ex. 6:23; Lev. 10:6
his charge. Num. 4

ITINERANT
Acts 19:13, *i* Jewish exorcists

ITTAI, 2 Sam. 15:19; 18:2

ITUREA, Lk. 3:1

JABAL,Gen. 4:20

JABBOK
Gen. 32:22; Num. 21:24; Dt. 3:16; Josh. 12:2

JABESH, 2 Ki. 15:10

JABESH GILEAD, Jud. 21:8
inhabitants struck by Israel. Jud. 21
threatened by Ammonites. 1 Sam. 11:1; delivered by Saul. 1 Sam. 11:11

JABEZ, 1 Chr. 4:9

JABIN, Jud. 4:2
king of Hazor, conquered by Joshua. Josh. 11
—— (another), destroyed by Barak. Jud. 4

JACHIN
one of the pillars of the porch of the temple. 1 Ki. 7:21; 2 Chr. 3:17

JACINTH, Rev. 21:20

JACOB
his birth. Gen. 25:26; birthright. 25:33; blessing. 27:27
sent to Padan Aram. 27:43; 28:1
his vision of the ladder, and vow. 28:10
marriages. 29; sons. 29:31; 30
dealings with Laban. 31
his vision of God's host. 32:1
his prayer. 32:9
wrestles with an angel. 32:24; Hos. 12:4
reconciled with Esau. Gen. 33
builds an altar at Bethel. 35:1
his grief for Joseph and Benjamin. 37; 42:38; 43
goes down to Egypt. 46
brought before Pharaoh. 47:7
blesses his sons. 48; 49
his death, and burial. Gen. 49:33; 50. *See* Ps. 105:23; Mal. 1:2; Rom. 9:10; Heb. 11:21

JACOB'S WELL, Jn. 4:6

JAEL
kills Sisera. Jud. 4:17; 5:24; Neh. 7:58

JAHAZIAH, Ezra 10:15

JAHAZIEL, 1 Chr. 16:6
comforts Jehoshaphat. 2 Chr. 20:14
prophecies against Moab and Ammon. 2 Chr. 20:14

JAIR, Num. 32:41
Gileadite, judge. Jud. 10:3

JAIRUS
Mt. 9:18; Mk. 5:22; Lk. 8:41

JAMBRES, 2 Tim. 3:8

JAMES
(the English equivalent for Jacob in the New Testament)
—— apostle, son of Zebedee, called. Mt. 4:21; Mk. 1:19; Lk. 5:10
ordained one of the twelve. Mt:10:2; Mk. 3:14; Lk. 6:13
witnessed Christ's transfiguration. Mt. 17:1; Mk. 9:2; Lk. 9:28
present at the passion. Mt. 26:36; Mk. 14:33
killed by Herod. Acts 12:2
—— apostle, son of Alphaeus. Mt. 10:3; Mk. 3:18; 15:40
—— the Lord's brother. Mt. 13:55; Mk. 6:3; Acts 1:14
leader of Jerusalem church. Acts 12:17; 15:13; 21:18; Gal. 1:19; 2:9,12
his teaching. Jas. 1—5
—— the father of the Apostle Judas. Lk. 6:16; Acts 1:13

JANNES and Jambres
magicians of Egypt. 2 Tim. 3:8 (Ex. 7:11)

JAPHETH, Gen. 5:32
son of Noah, blessed. Gen. 9:27
his descendants. Gen. 10:1; 1 Chr. 1:4

JARED, 1 Chr. 1:2

JASHER
book of. Josh. 10:13; 2 Sam. 1:18

JASON, Acts 17:5; Rom. 16:21

JAVAN
son of Japheth. Gen. 10:2

JEALOUS
Ex. 20:5, your God, am a *j* God
Ex. 34:14, LORD, whose name is J
Dt. 4:24, a consuming fire, a *j*
2 Cor. 11:2, For I am *j* for you

JEALOUSY
Dt. 32:16, provoked Him to *j*
Ps. 79:5, Will Your *j* burn like
Prov. 6:34, *j* is a husband's
Song 8:6, as strong as death, *j*
Rom. 10:19, will provoke you to *j*
2 Cor. 11:2, for you with godly *j*

JEBUS, Jud. 19:10

JEBUSITES
the descendants of Jebus, the son of Canaan. Gen. 15:21; Num. 13:29; Josh. 15:63; Jud. 1:21; 19:11; 2 Sam. 5:6

JECONIAH
1 Cor. 3:16; Mt. 1:11,12

JEDAIAH, 1 Chr. 4:37; 24:7

JEDIDIAH
a name of Solomon. 2 Sam. 12:25

JEDUTHUN, 1 Chr. 16:38,41; 25:6

JEHOAHAZ
son of Jehu, king of Israel. 2 Ki. 10:35; 13:4
—— (Shallum), king of Judah, his evil reign. 2 Ki. 23:31; 2 Chr. 36:1

JEHOASH, 2 Ki. 11:21

JEHOHANAN, 1 Chr. 26:3

JEHOIACHIN
king of Judah, his defeat and captivity. 2 Ki. 24:6; 2 Chr. 36:8

JEHOIADA, 2 Sam. 8:18
high priest, deposes and kills Athaliah, and restores Joash. 2 Ki. 11:4; 2 Chr. 23
repairs the temple. 2 Ki. 12:7; 2 Chr. 24:6
abolishes idolatry. 2 Chr. 23:16

JEHOIAKIM (Eliakim)
made king of Judah by Pharaoh Necho, his evil reign and captivity. 2 Ki. 23:34; 24:1; 2 Chr. 36:4; Dan. 1:2. *See* Jer. 22:18

JEHORAM
son of Jehoshaphat, king of Judah. 1 Ki. 22:50; 2 Ki. 8:16
his cruelty and death. 2 Chr. 21:4,18
—— (Joram), king of Israel, son of Ahab. 2 Ki. 1:17; 3:1
his evil reign. 2 Ki. 3:2
killed by Jehu. 2 Ki. 9:24

JEHOSHAPHAT
king of Judah, his good reign. 1 Ki. 15:24; 2 Chr. 17
his death. 1 Ki. 22:50; 2 Chr. 21:1
—— Valley of. Joel 3:2

JEHOVAH
the Eternal One (Elohim, I AM THAT I AM). Ex. 6:3

rebukes his friends. Job 6; 7; 9; 10; 12—14; 16; 17; 19; 21; 23; 24; 26—30
solemnly protests his integrity. Job 31
humbles himself. Job 40:3; 42:1
God accepts and doubly blesses. Job 42:10

JOCHEBED
Moses' mother. Ex. 6:20; Num. 26:59

JOEL
delivers God's judgments. Joel 1—3
proclaims a fast, and declares God's mercy. Joel 1:14; 2:12; 3
quoted. Acts 2:16

JOHN, Mt. 3:1
the apostle, called. Mt. 4:21; Mk. 1:19; Lk. 5:10
ordained. Mt. 10:2; Mk. 3:17
inquires of Jesus. Mk. 13:3
rebuked. Mt. 20:20; Mk. 10:35–40; Lk. 9:50
sent to prepare the Passover. Lk. 22:8
declares the deity and humanity of Jesus Christ. Jn. 1; 1 Jn. 1; 4; 5
Christ's love for. Jn. 13:23; 19:26; 21:7,20,24
his care for Mary, the Lord's mother. Jn. 19:27
meets for prayer. Acts 1:13
accompanies Peter before the council. Acts 3; 4
exhorts to obedience and warns against false teachers. 1 Jn. 1—5
sees Christ's glory in heaven. Rev. 1:13
writes The Revelation. Rev. 1:19
forbidden to worship the angel. Rev. 19:10; 22:8
—— Mark. Acts 12:12,25. *See* MARK
—— the Baptist, his coming foretold. Isa. 40:3; Mal. 4:5; Lk. 1:17
his birth and circumcision. Lk. 1:57
office, preaching, and baptism. Mt. 3; Mk. 1; Lk. 3; Jn. 1:6; 3:26; Acts 1:5; 13:24
baptizes Christ. Mt. 3; Mk. 1; Lk. 3; Jn. 1:32; 3:26
imprisoned by Herod. Mt. 4:12; Mk. 1:14; Lk. 3:20; and beheaded. Mt. 14; Mk. 6:14
sends his disciples to Christ. Mt. 11:1; Lk. 7:18
Christ's testimony to. Mt. 11:11,14; 17:12; Mk. 9:11; Lk. 7:27
his disciples receive the Holy Spirit. Acts 18:24; 19:1

JOIN
Isa. 5:8, Woe to those who *j*
Jer. 50:5, 'Come and let us *j*
Acts 5:13, of the rest dared *j*

JOINED
Gen. 2:24, and mother and be *j*
Eccl. 9:4, for him who is *j*
Hos. 4:17, "Ephraim is *j*
Mt. 19:6, what God has *j*
1 Cor. 1:10, you be perfectly *j*
1 Cor. 6:17, But he who is *j*
Eph. 4:16, the whole body, *j*

JOINT
Gen. 32:25, *j* as He wrestled
Ps. 22:14, My bones are out of *j*
Rom. 8:17, *j* heirs with Christ
Eph. 4:16, by what every *j*

JOINTS
Col. 2:19, and knit together by *j*
Heb. 4:12, and spirit, and of *j*

JONADAB, 2 Sam. 13:3
(Jehonadab), son of Rechab. 2 Ki. 10:15

JONAH
prophet. 2 Ki. 14:25
his disobedience, punishment, prayer, and repentance. Jon. 1—4
a type of Christ. Mt. 12:39; Lk. 11:29

JONATHAN
son of Saul, defeats the Philistines. 1 Sam. 13:2; 14
his love for David. 1 Sam. 18:1; 19; 20; 23:16
killed by the Philistines. 1 Sam. 31:2
David's lamentation for. 2 Sam. 1:17
—— son of Abiathar. 2 Sam. 15:27; 1 Ki. 1:42
—— one of David's nephews, his deeds. 2 Sam. 21:21; 1 Chr. 20:7
—— a Levite, hired by Micah. Jud. 17:7; 18

JOPPA, 2 Chr. 2:16; Jon. 1:3
Tabitha raised at. Acts 9:36
Peter dwells at. Acts 10:5; 11:5

JORAM
same as Jehoram. 2 Sam. 8:10

JORDAN, Gen. 13:10
river, waters of, divided: for the Israelites. Josh. 3; 4; Ps. 114:3; by Elijah and Elisha. 2 Ki. 2:8,13
Naaman's leprosy cured at. 2 Ki. 5:10
John baptizes there. Mt. 3; Mk. 1:5; Lk. 3:3. *See* Job 40:23; Ps. 42:6; Jer. 12:5; 49:19; Zech. 11:3

JOSEPH
son of Jacob. Gen. 30:24. *See* Ps. 105:17; Acts 7:9; Heb. 11:22
his dreams, and the jealousy of his brothers. Gen. 37:5
sold to the Ishmaelites. Gen. 37:28
slave to Potiphar. Gen. 39
resists Potiphar's wife. Gen. 39:7
interprets the dreams of Pharaoh's servants. Gen. 40; and of Pharaoh, predicting famine. Gen. 41:25
made ruler of Egypt. Gen. 41:39
prepares for the famine. Gen. 41:48
receives his brothers and father. Gen. 42—46
gives direction concerning his bones. Gen. 50:25
his death. Gen. 50:26
—— son of Heli, husband of the Virgin. Mt. 1:19; 2:13,19; Lk. 1:27; 2:4; 3:23
—— of Arimathea. Mt. 27:57; Mk. 15:42; Lk. 23:50; Jn. 19:38
—— (Barsabas), Justus. Acts 1:23

JOSHUA, Num. 14:6
(also spelled Hoshea, Oshea, Jehoshua, Jeshua, and Jesus), son of Nun. 1 Chr. 7:27; Heb. 4:8
vanquishes Amalek. Ex. 17:9
ministers to Moses. Ex. 24:13; 32:17; 33:11
spies out Canaan. Num. 13:16
ordained to succeed Moses. Num. 27:18; 34:17; Dt. 1:38; 3:28; 34:9
reassured by God. Josh. 1
commands his officers. Josh. 1:10
crosses river Jordan. Josh. 3
erects memorial pillars. Josh. 4
reenacts circumcision. Josh. 5
assaults and destroys Jericho. Josh. 6
condemns Achan. Josh. 7
subdues Ai. Josh. 8
his victories. Josh. 10—12
apportions the land. Josh. 14—21; Heb. 4:8
his charge to the Reubenites. Josh. 22
exhortation to the people. Josh. 23
reminds them of God's mercies. Josh. 24
renews the covenant. Josh. 24:14
his death. Josh. 24:29; Jud. 2:8
his curse. Josh. 6:26; fulfilled. 1 Ki. 16:34
an occasion recalled. Neh. 8:17

JOSIAH, 2 Ki. 21:24
prophecy concerning. 1 Ki. 13:2; fulfilled. 2 Ki. 23:15
reigns well. 2 Ki. 22
repairs the temple. 2 Ki. 22:3
hears the words of the Book of the Law. 2 Ki. 22:8
Huldah's message from God to him. 2 Ki. 22:15
ordains the reading of the Book. 2 Ki. 23
keeps a signal Passover to the Lord. 2 Chr. 35
killed by Pharaoh Necho at Megiddo. 2 Ki. 23:29

JOT
Mt. 5:18, one *j* or one tittle

JOTHAM, Jud. 9:5
son of Gideon, his parable. Jud. 9:7
—— king of Judah. 2 Ki. 15:32; 2 Chr. 27

JOURNEY
Ex. 3:18, us go three days' *j*
1 Ki. 18:27, busy, or he is on a *j*
Lk. 13:33, Nevertheless I must *j*
Jn. 4:6, wearied from His *j*

JOY
Dt. 28:47, LORD your God with *j*
Job 29:13, heart to sing for *j*
Ps. 16:11, is fullness of *j*
Ps. 30:5, *j* comes in the morning
Ps. 43:3, To God my exceeding *j*

Isa. 9:3, You according to the *j*
Isa. 12:3, *j* you will draw
Isa. 61:3, ashes, the oil of *j*
Isa. 61:7, *j* shall be theirs
Isa. 65:14, shall sing for *j*
Jer. 15:16, word was to me the *j*
Mt. 13:20, receives it with *j*
Mt. 25:21, Enter into the *j*
Lk. 1:44, in my womb for *j*
Lk. 15:7, there will be more *j*
Lk. 24:41, did not believe for *j*
Jn. 15:11, My *j* may remain in
Jn. 17:13, they may have My *j*
Rom. 15:13, fill you with all *j*
2 Cor. 2:3, that my *j* is the *j*
Gal. 5:22, the Spirit is love, *j*
Phil. 4:1, brethren, my *j* and
Col. 1:11, longsuffering with *j*
1 Th. 2:20, are our glory and *j*
Heb. 12:2, *j* that was set before
Jas. 1:2, count it all *j*
1 Pet. 1:8, *j* inexpressible
1 Pet. 4:13, with exceeding *j*
3 Jn. 4, I have no greater *j*

JOYFUL
Ps. 35:9, And my soul shall be *j*
Ps. 100:1, Make a *j* shout to the
Eccl. 7:14, of prosperity be *j*
Isa. 56:7, and make them *j*
2 Cor. 7:4, I am exceedingly *j*

JUBAL
inventor of harp and flute. Gen. 4:21

JUDAH
son of Jacob. Gen. 29:35
his descendants. Gen. 38; 46:12; Num. 1:26; 26:19; 1 Chr. 2—4
pledges himself for Benjamin. Gen. 43:3
his interview with Joseph. Gen. 44:18—46:28
blessed by Jacob. Gen. 49:8
——— tribe of, their blessing by Moses. Dt. 33:7
their inheritance. Josh. 15
they make David king. 2 Sam. 2:4; and adhere to his house. 1 Ki. 12; 2 Chr. 10; 11. *See* JEWS

JUDAISM
Gal. 1:14, And I advanced in *J*

JUDAS, Mt. 10:4
(Jude, Lebbaeus, Thaddaeus), apostle, brother of James. Mt. 10:3; Mk. 3:18; Lk. 6:16; Acts 1:13
his question to our Lord. Jn. 14:22
enjoins perseverance. Jude 3,20
denounces false disciples. Jude 4
——— the Lord's brother. Mt. 13:55; Mk. 6:3
——— Barsabas. Acts 15:22

JUDAS ISCARIOT
Mt. 10:4; Mk. 3:19; Lk. 6:16; Jn. 6:70
betrays Jesus. Mt. 26:14,47; Mk. 14:10,43; Lk. 22:3,47; Jn. 13:26; 18:2
hangs himself. Mt. 27:5 (Acts 1:18)

JUDE
abbreviated from Judas. Jude 1

JUDGE
Gen. 16:5, The LORD *j* between
Dt. 32:36, For the LORD will *j*
1 Chr. 16:33, coming to *j* the earth
Ps. 94:2, Rise up, O *J* of the
Isa. 66:16, sword the LORD will *j*
Mt. 5:25, deliver you to the *j*
Mt. 7:1, *J* not, that you be not
Lk. 12:14, who made Me a *j*
Lk. 18:2, *j* who did not fear God
Jn. 5:30, As I hear, I *j*
Jn. 7:24, "Do not *j* according
Jn. 8:15, I *j* no one
Jn. 12:47, *j* the world but to
Rom. 2:3, this, O man, you who *j*
Rom. 3:6, then how will God *j*
Rom. 14:13, Therefore let us not *j*
2 Tim. 4:1, Christ, who will *j*
2 Tim. 4:8, Lord, the righteous *J*
Heb. 12:23, heaven, to God the *J*
Jas. 4:11, But if you *j* the law
Jas. 4:12, are you to *j* another

JUDGES
appointment of. Dt. 16:18; Ezra 7:25
their functions. Ex. 18:21; Lev. 19:15; Dt. 1:16; 17:8; 2 Chr. 19:6; Ps. 82; Prov. 18:5; 24:23
unjust. 1 Sam. 8:3; Isa. 1:23; Lk. 18:2; hateful to God. Prov. 17:15; 24:24; Isa. 10:1

JUDGES
Jud. 2:16, *j* who delivered
Ruth 1:1, in the days when the *j*
Ps. 58:11, Surely He is God who *j*
Ps. 82:1, He *j* among the gods
Isa. 40:23, He makes the *j* of the
Zeph. 3:3, *j* are evening wolves
Jn. 5:22, For the Father *j*
1 Cor. 2:15, he who is spiritual *j*
1 Cor. 4:4, *j* me is the Lord
1 Pet. 2:23, Him who *j* righteously

JUDGMENT
of angels. Mt. 25:41; 2 Pet. 2:4; Jude 6; Rev. 20:10
of Christian's life and works. 1 Cor. 3:11; 2 Cor. 5:10; Col. 3:24; 2 Tim. 4:8
of Gentile nations. Mt. 25:31
of Israel. Ps. 50; Ezek. 20:33; Mal. 3:2; 4:1
of Satan. Isa. 14:12; Mt. 25:41; Jn. 12:31; 16:11; Rev. 12:9; 20:2,3,10
of self by the Christian. 1 Cor. 11:31; Heb. 12:7
of sin. Jn. 5:24; Rom. 5:9; 8:1; Gal. 3:13
to whom committed. Jn. 5:22
final. Rev. 20:11

JUDGMENT
Dt. 1:17, show partiality in *j*
Ps. 119:66, Teach me good *j*
Isa. 28:26, him in right *j*
Isa. 53:8, from prison and from *j*
Jer. 4:12, I will also speak *j*
Dan. 7:22, *j* was made in favor of
Mt. 5:21, be in danger of the *j*
Mt. 12:42, will rise up in the *j*
Jn. 5:24, shall not come into *j*
Jn. 5:30, and My *j* is righteous
Jn. 8:16, if I do judge, My *j*
Jn. 12:31, "Now is the *j*
Rom. 1:32, the righteous *j*
Rom. 5:16, *j* which came from one
Rom. 14:10, all stand before the *j*
1 Cor. 11:29, eats and drinks *j*
2 Cor. 5:10, appear before the *j*
Heb. 9:27, after this the *j*
Jas. 2:13, For *j* is without mercy
Jas. 3:1, receive a stricter *j*
1 Pet. 4:17, time has come for *j*
2 Pet. 2:3, a long time their *j*
Jude 6, darkness for the *j*

JUDGMENTS
Ps. 19:9, The *j* of the LORD are
Ps. 36:6, *j* are a great deep
Ps. 119:39, I dread, for Your *j*
Rom. 11:33, unsearchable are His *j*
Rev. 19:2, righteous are His *j*

JULIUS, Acts 27:1

JUNIA
saluted by Paul. Rom. 16:7

JUST
Gen. 6:9, Noah was a *j* man
Ps. 17:1, Hear a *j* cause
Prov. 21:15, It is a joy for the *j*
Eccl. 7:15, *j* man who perishes
Eccl. 7:20, For there is not a *j*
Isa. 26:7, *j* is uprightness
Lam. 4:13, the blood of the *j*
Hab. 2:4, *j* shall live by his
Zech. 9:9, He is *j* and having
Mt. 1:19, her husband, being a *j*
Lk. 14:14, resurrection of the *j*
Lk. 15:7, *j* persons who need no
Acts 3:14, the Holy One and the *J*
Acts 24:15, dead, both of the *j*
Rom. 1:17, *j* shall live by faith
Rom. 3:26, that He might be *j*
Phil. 4:8, whatever things are *j*
Heb. 12:23, *j* men made perfect
Jas. 5:6, have murdered the *j*
1 Jn. 1:9, He is faithful and *j*
Rev. 15:3, *J* and true are Your

JUSTICE
of God. Dt. 32:4; Job 4:17; 8:3; 34:12; Isa. 45:21; Zeph. 3:5; 1 Jn. 1:9; Rev. 15:3
to do, commanded. Lev. 19:36; Dt. 16:18; Ps. 82:3; Prov. 3:33; 11:1; Jer. 22:3; Ezek. 18:5; 45:9; Mic. 6:8; Mt. 7:12; Phil. 4:8; Rom. 13:7; 2 Cor. 8:21; Col. 4:1

JUSTICE
Dt. 32:4, for all His ways are *j*
Job 8:3, the Almighty pervert *j*
Ps. 37:6, *j* as the noonday
Ps. 72:2, and Your poor with *j*
Ps. 72:4, He will bring *j*
Ps. 82:3, Do *j* to the afflicted
Ps. 89:14, and *j* are the
Prov. 16:8, revenues without *j*
Prov. 28:5, do not understand *j*
Isa. 28:17, *j* the measuring line
Isa. 30:18, the LORD is a God of *j*
Isa. 42:1, He will bring forth *j*
Isa. 59:4, No one calls for *j*
Isa. 59:14, *J* is turned back

Isa. 61:8, I, the LORD, love *j*
Jer. 31:23, you, O home of *j*
Ezek. 45:9, plundering, execute *j*
Dan. 4:37, truth, and His ways *j*
Hos. 12:6, observe mercy and *j*
Zech. 7:9, 'Execute true *j*
Mal. 2:17, "Where is the God of *j*
Mt. 12:18, And He will declare *j*
Acts 8:33, His humiliation His *j*

JUSTIFICATION
by faith. Hab. 2:4; Acts 13:39; Rom. 1:17; 3—5; Gal. 3:11
by works. Jas. 2:14-26

JUSTIFICATION
Rom. 4:25, because of our *j*
Rom. 5:16, offenses resulted in *j*
Rom. 5:18, men, resulting in *j*

JUSTIFIED
Job 40:8, Me that you may be *j*
Isa. 45:25, of Israel shall be *j*
Mt. 12:37, words you will be *j*
Lk. 7:35, But wisdom is *j*
Lk. 18:14, *j* rather than the
Acts 13:39, who believes is *j*
Rom. 3:4, "That You may be *j*
Rom. 3:20, law no flesh will be *j*
Rom. 3:24, *j* freely by His grace
Rom. 5:1, having been *j* by
Rom. 8:30, these He also *j*
1 Cor. 6:11, but you were *j*
Gal. 2:16, that we might be *j*
Gal. 2:16, no flesh shall be *j*
Gal. 5:4, who attempt to be *j*
1 Tim. 3:16, *j* in the Spirit
Jas. 2:24, then that a man is *j*
Jas. 2:25, the harlot also *j*

JUSTIFIER
Rom. 3:26, be just and the *j*

JUSTIFIES
Prov. 17:15, He who *j* the wicked
Rom. 8:33, It is God who *j*

JUSTIFY
Isa. 5:23, *j* the wicked for a
Lk. 10:29, wanting to *j* himself
Lk. 16:15, "You are those who *j*
Rom. 3:30, is one God who will *j*
Gal. 3:8, that God would *j*

JUSTLY
Mic. 6:8, of you but to do *j*
Lk. 23:41, "And we indeed *j*
1 Th. 2:10, how devoutly and *j*

JUSTUS, Acts 1:23

KADESH, Gen. 20:1

KADESH BARNEA, Num. 34:4
Israelites murmur against Moses and Aaron, threaten to stone Caleb and Joshua, and provoke God's anger. Num. 13; 14; Dt. 1:19; Josh. 14:6

KEDAR
son of Ishmael. Gen. 25:13; 1 Chr. 1:29; Ps. 120:5; Song 1:5; Jer. 2:10; Ezek. 27:21
—— tribe of, prophecies concerning. Isa. 21:16; 42:11; 60:7; Jer. 49:28

KEDESH, Josh. 12:22

KEEP
Gen. 28:15, *k* you wherever you
Ex. 20:8, day, to *k* it holy
Lev. 25:18, and *k* My judgments
1 Ki. 6:12, *k* all My commandments
1 Chr. 4:10, and that You would *k*
Ps. 22:29, Even he who cannot *k*
Ps. 25:20, *K* my soul
Ps. 35:22, do not *k* silence
Ps. 119:106, *k* Your righteous
Prov. 4:21, *k* them in the midst of
Prov. 4:23, *K* your heart with all
Eccl. 3:7, a time to *k* silence
Hab. 2:20, Let all the earth *k*
Mt. 19:17, *k* the commandments
Jn. 14:15, If you love Me, *k*
Jn. 17:11, *k* through Your name
Acts 21:24, orderly and *k* the law
1 Cor. 14:34, Let your women *k*
Eph. 4:3, *k* the unity of the
1 Tim. 5:22, *k* yourself pure
1 Jn. 2:3, *k* His commandments
Jude 21, *k* yourselves in the
Jude 24, *k* you from stumbling
Rev. 1:3, *k* those things

KEEPER
Gen. 4:9, Am I my brother's *k*
Ps. 121:5, The LORD is your *k*

KEEPERS
Eccl. 12:3, in the day when the *k*

KEEPS
Dt. 7:9, the faithful God who *k*
Ps. 146:6, *k* truth forever
Prov. 16:17, *k* his way preserves
Prov. 19:16, *k* the commandment
Prov. 28:7, Whoever *k* the law is a
Jn. 7:19, none of you *k* the law
1 Jn. 5:18, born of God *k* himself
Rev. 16:15, and *k* his garments

KENITES
descendants of an unknown man named Kain. Gen. 15:19
their fate foretold. Num. 24:22

KEPT
2 Sam. 22:22, For I have *k* the ways
Song 1:6, vineyard I have not *k*
Mt. 19:20, these things I have *k*
Mk. 10:20, all these things I have *k*
Lk. 2:19, *k* all these things
Jn. 15:10, love, just as I have *k*
Acts 5:2, *k* back part of the
2 Tim. 4:7, I have *k* the faith
1 Pet. 1:5, who are *k* by the power
2 Pet. 3:7, which now exist are *k*

KERIOTH
a city of Judah. Josh. 15:25; Jer. 48:24,41; Amos 2:2

KETURAH
Abraham's wife. Gen. 25; her children. 1 Chr. 1:32

KEY
of David. Isa. 22:22; Rev. 3:7
keys of: heaven. Mt. 16:19; Hades. Rev. 1:18; bottomless pit. Rev. 9:1

KEY
Isa. 22:22, The *k* of the house of
Lk. 11:52, taken away the *k*
Rev. 3:7, "He who has the *k*
Rev. 20:1, heaven, having the *k*

KEYS
Mt. 16:19, I will give you the *k*
Rev. 1:18, And I have the *k*

KICK
Acts 9:5, is hard for you to *k*

KIDNAPPERS
1 Tim. 1:10, for sodomites, for *k*

KIDNAPS
Ex. 21:16, "He who *k* a man and

KIDRON
brook and ravine, near garden of Gethsemane, frequented by our Lord. Jn. 18:1
crossed by David. 2 Sam. 15:23
idols destroyed there. 1 Ki. 15:13; 2 Ki. 23:6; 2 Chr. 29:16; Jer. 31:40

KILL
Gen. 4:14, who finds me will *k*
Ex. 12:21, *k* the Passover
Dt. 32:39, I *k* and I make alive
2 Ki. 5:7, "Am I God, to *k*
Eccl. 3:3, a time to *k*
Mk. 3:4, to save life or to *k*
Lk. 11:49, of them they will *k*
Lk. 12:4, afraid of those who *k*
Jn. 7:19, Why do you seek to *k*
Acts 10:13, *k* and eat

KILLED
Gen. 4:8, Abel his brother and *k*
Gen. 4:23, For I have *k* a man for
Ex. 13:15, LORD *k* all the
1 Sam. 17:36, "Your servant has *k*
Ps. 44:22, for Your sake we are *k*
Mt. 16:21, and scribes, and be *k*
Lk. 13:4, Siloam fell and *k* them
Acts 3:15, *k* the Prince of life
Rom. 7:11, me, and by it *k*
Rom. 8:36, For Your sake we are *k*
1 Th. 2:15, who *k* both the Lord
Rev. 2:13, martyr, who was *k*

KILLS
1 Sam. 2:6, "The LORD *k* and
Mt. 23:37, the one who *k* the
2 Cor. 3:6, for the letter *k*

KIND
Gen. 6:20, animals after their *k*
Mk. 9:29, *k* can come out by
Lk. 6:35, For He is *k* to the
1 Cor. 13:4, suffers long and is *k*
Eph. 4:32, And be *k* to one

KINDLED
Ps. 2:12, When His wrath is *k*
Ezek. 20:48, I, the LORD, have *k*
Lk. 12:49, wish it were already *k*

KINDLY
Ruth 1:8, The LORD deal *k*
Acts 27:3, Julius treated Paul *k*
Rom. 12:10, *k* affectionate to one

KINDNESS
2 Sam. 2:6, may the LORD show *k*

Neh. 9:17, anger, abundant in *k*
Ps. 31:21, me His marvelous *k*
Ps. 117:2, For His merciful *k*
Prov. 31:26, tongue is the law of *k*
Isa. 54:10, *k* shall not depart
Jer. 2:2, I remember you, the *k*
2 Cor. 6:6, by longsuffering, by *k*
Gal. 5:22, longsuffering, *k*
Ti. 3:4, But when the *k* and the
2 Pet. 1:7, and to brotherly *k*

KING
Israelites desire one. 1 Sam. 8:5

KING
Gen. 14:18, Then Melchizedek *k*
Jud. 17:6, days there was no *k*
1 Sam. 8:6, said, "Give us a *k*
1 Sam. 10:24, "Long live the *k*
2 Sam. 2:4, they anointed David *k*
Ps. 2:6, Yet I have set My *K*
Ps. 10:16, The LORD is *K* forever
Ps. 20:9, *K* answer us when we
Ps. 24:7, And the *K* of glory
Ps. 33:16, *k* is saved by the
Ps. 72:1, *k* Your judgments
Ps. 74:12, For God is my *K*
Eccl. 2:12, do who succeeds the *k*
Eccl. 4:14, out of prison to be *k*
Eccl. 10:16, when your *k* is a child
Isa. 6:1, In the year that *K*
Isa. 32:1, *k* will reign in
Isa. 33:22, the LORD is our *K*
Jer. 8:19, Is not her *K* in her
Jer. 10:10, and the everlasting *K*
Ezek. 26:7, *k* of Babylon, *k*
Hos. 13:11, I gave you a *k* in My
Zech. 14:9, the LORD shall be *K*
Mt. 2:2, who has been born *K*
Mt. 27:37, This Is Jesus the *K*
Jn. 6:15, by force to make Him *k*
Jn. 19:14, Behold your *K*
Acts 17:7, there is another *k*
1 Tim. 1:17, Now to the *K* eternal
1 Tim. 6:15, only Potentate, the *K*
Heb. 7:1, this Melchizedek, *k*
1 Pet. 2:17, Honor the *k*
Rev. 19:16, *K* of kings and Lord

KING of kings
Ps. 2:6; 10:16; 24:7; 110; Zech. 9:9; Lk. 23:2; 1 Tim. 1:17; 6:15; Rev. 15:3; 17:14

KINGDOM
of God. 1 Chr. 29:11; Ps. 22:28; 45:6; 145:11; Isa. 24:23; Dan. 2:44
of Christ. Isa. 2; 4; 9; 11; 32; 35; 52; 61; 66; Mt. 16:28; 26:29; Jn. 18:36; 2 Pet. 1:11
of heaven. Mt. 3:2; 8:11; 11:11; 13:11
who shall enter. Mt. 5:3; 7:21; Lk. 9:62; Jn. 3:3; Acts 14:22; Rom. 14:17; 1 Cor. 6:9; 15:50; 2 Th. 1:5
parables concerning. Mt. 13:24

KINGDOM
Ex. 19:6, you shall be to Me a *k*
1 Sam. 15:28, LORD has torn the *k*
1 Chr. 29:11, Yours is the *k*
Ps. 22:28, *k* is the LORD's
Ps. 45:6, the scepter of Your *k*
Ps. 103:19, in heaven, and His *k*
Ps. 145:13, is an everlasting *k*
Dan. 2:44, *k* which shall never be
Dan. 4:17, High rules in the *k*
Obad. 21, *k* shall be the LORD's
Mt. 3:2, "Repent, for the *k*
Mt. 6:13, for Yours is the *k*
Mt. 6:33, But seek first the *k*
Mt. 13:11, the mysteries of the *k*
Mt. 13:38, are the sons of the *k*
Mt. 19:14, of such is the *k*
Mk. 6:23, up to half of my *k*
Mk. 12:34, are not far from the *k*
Lk. 9:62, back, is fit for the *k*
Lk. 21:10, against nation, and *k*
Jn. 3:3, he cannot see the *k*
Jn. 3:5, he cannot enter the *k*
Jn. 18:36, If My *k* were of this
Rom. 14:17, for the *k* of God is
1 Cor. 15:24, when He delivers the *k*
Gal. 5:21, will not inherit the *k*
Heb. 1:8, the scepter of Your *k*
Heb. 12:28, we are receiving a *k*
2 Pet. 1:11, into the everlasting *k*

KINGDOMS
Nebuchadnezzar's vision of. Dan. 2:36

KINGDOMS
Ps. 46:6, the *k* were moved
Isa. 14:16, tremble, who shook *k*
Mt. 4:8, showed Him all the *k*
Rev. 11:15, have become the *k*

KINGS
chosen by God. Dt. 17:14; 1 Sam. 9:17; 1 Sam. 16:1; 1 Ki. 11:35; 1 Ki. 19:15; 1 Chr. 28:4; Dan. 2:21
duty of. Prov. 25:2; Isa. 49:23
honor due to. Prov. 24:21; 25:6; Eccl. 8:2; 10:20; Mt. 22:21; Rom. 13; 1 Pet. 2:13,17
to be prayed for. 1 Tim. 2:1
parable of the king and his servants. Mt. 18:23; of the king and his guests. Mt. 22:2

KINGS
Ps. 2:2, The *k* of the earth set
Ps. 72:11, *k* shall fall down
Ps. 76:12, He is awesome to the *k*
Prov. 8:15, By me *k* reign
Prov. 22:29, He will stand before *k*
Prov. 25:3, *k* is unsearchable
Prov. 31:3, that which destroys *k*
Prov. 31:4, it is not for *k*
Isa. 49:23, *K* shall be your foster
Hos. 8:4, "They set up *k*
Mt. 10:18, before governors and *k*
Lk. 10:24, *k* have desired to see
1 Cor. 4:8, You have reigned as *k*
Rev. 1:6, and has made us *k*
Rev. 16:12, that the way of the *k*
Rev. 19:18, may eat the flesh of *k*

KIRJATH JEARIM
Josh. 9:17; 18:14; 1 Chr. 13:6
the ark brought to. 1 Sam. 7:1
ark brought from. 1 Chr. 13:5; 2 Chr. 1:4

KIRJATHAIM
Num. 32:37; Ezek. 25:9

KISH
Saul's father. 1 Sam. 9:1

KISHON
waters of Megiddo. Jud. 4:7; 5:21; 1 Ki. 18:40

KISS
holy, greet with. Rom. 16:16; 1 Cor. 16:20; 2 Cor. 13:12; 1 Th. 5:26
of love. 1 Pet. 5:14
given as mark of affection. Gen. 27:27; 29:11; 45:15; 48:10; 1 Sam. 10:1; 20:41; Lk. 7:38; 15:20; Acts 20:37
given treacherously. 2 Sam. 20:9; Mt. 26:48; Lk. 22:48
idolatrous. 1 Ki. 19:18; Job 31:27; Hos. 13:2

KISS
Ps. 2:12, *K* the Son
Song 1:2, Let him *k* me with the
Lk. 7:45, "You gave Me no *k*
Rom. 16:16, another with a holy *k*
1 Pet. 5:14, one another with a *k*

KISSED
1 Sam. 20:41, they *k* one another
Mt. 26:49, and *k* Him
Lk. 7:38, and she *k* His feet and

KITTIM, Gen. 10:4

KNEE
Isa. 45:23, that to Me every *k*
Mt. 27:29, And they bowed the *k*
Rom. 11:4, have not bowed the *k*
Rom. 14:11, every *k* shall bow to
Phil. 2:10, of Jesus every *k*

KNEES
Isa. 35:3, make firm the feeble *k*
Isa. 66:12, be dandled on her *k*
Eph. 3:14, this reason I bow my *k*
Heb. 12:12, and the feeble *k*

KNEW
Gen. 4:1, Adam *k* Eve his wife
Jer. 1:5, in the womb I *k*
Mt. 7:23, to them, 'I never *k*
Jn. 2:25, *k* what was in man
2 Cor. 5:21, He made Him who *k*

KNIT
1 Sam. 18:1, of Jonathan was *k*
Job 10:11, *k* me together with
Col. 2:2, be encouraged, being *k*

KNOCK
Mt. 7:7, *k*, and it will be
Rev. 3:20, at the door and *k*

KNOW
Gen. 3:22, *k* good and evil
Gen. 28:16, and I did not *k*
Ex. 6:7, *k* that I am the LORD
2 Ki. 5:15, *k* that there is no God
1 Chr. 28:9, you, my son Solomon, *k*
Job 5:27, Hear it, and *k* for
Job 8:9, and *k* nothing
Job 19:25, *k* that my Redeemer
Job 22:13, 'What does God *k*
Ps. 9:10, *k* Your name will put
Ps. 46:10, *k* that I am God
Ps. 51:6, make me to *k* wisdom

Jer. 17:9, Who can *k* it
Jer. 31:34, saying, 'K the LORD
Mic. 3:1, for you to *k* justice
Mt. 24:42, *k* what hour your Lord
Mt. 26:72, an oath, "I do not *k*
Jn. 1:10, the world did not *k*
Jn. 3:11, We speak what We *k*
Jn. 4:22, *k* what we worship
Jn. 6:69, *k* that You are
Jn. 10:27, hear My voice, and I *k*
Jn. 13:17, If you *k* these things
Jn. 13:18, *k* whom I have chosen
Jn. 16:30, we are sure that You *k*
Jn. 21:15, *k* that I love You
Acts 1:7, *k* times or seasons
Acts 19:15, and said, "Jesus I *k*
1 Cor. 1:21, wisdom did not *k*
1 Cor. 2:14, nor can he *k* them
1 Cor. 13:9, For we *k* in part and
2 Cor. 12:2, *k* a man in Christ who
Eph. 3:19, *k* the love of Christ
2 Tim. 1:12, *k* whom I have believed
2 Tim. 2:25, so that they may *k*
1 Jn. 2:3, we *k* that we *k* Him
1 Jn. 2:4, He who says, "I *k*
1 Jn. 2:20, and you *k* all things
1 Jn. 3:16, By this we *k* love
1 Jn. 3:19, *k* that we are of the
1 Jn. 3:24, *k* that He abides
1 Jn. 5:19, *k* that we are of God
Rev. 2:2, "I *k* your works

KNOWLEDGE
given by God. Ex. 8:10; 18:16; 31:3; 2 Chr. 1:12; Ps. 119:66; Prov. 1:4; 2:6; Eccl. 2:26; Isa. 28:9; Jer. 24:7; 31:33; Dan. 2:21; Mt. 11:25; 13:11; 1 Cor. 1:5; 2:12; 12:8
advantages of. Ps. 89:15; Prov. 1:4,7; 3:13; 4; 9:10; 10:14; 12:1; 13:16; 18:15; Eccl. 7:12; Mal. 2:7; Eph. 3:18; 4:13; Jas. 3:13; 2 Pet. 2:20
lack of. Prov. 1:22; 19:2; Jer. 4:22; Hos. 4:6; Rom. 1:28; 1 Cor. 15:34
prayed for. Jn. 17:3; Eph. 3:18; Col. 1:9; 2 Pet. 3:18
sought. 1 Cor. 14:1; Heb. 6:1; 2 Pet. 1:5
abuse of. 1 Cor. 8:1
its responsibility. Num. 15:30; Dt. 17:12; Lk. 12:47; Jn. 15:22; Rom. 1:21; 2:21; Jas. 4:17
imperfection of human. Eccl. 1:18; Isa. 44:25; 1 Cor. 1:19; 3:19; 2 Cor. 1:12
—— of good and evil, tree of. Gen. 2:9

KNOWLEDGE
Gen. 2:9, and the tree of the *k*
1 Sam. 2:3, LORD is the God of *k*
Job 21:22, Can anyone teach God *k*
Job 36:4, who is perfect in *k*
Ps. 19:2, unto night reveals *k*
Ps. 139:6, *k* is too wonderful
Prov. 3:20, *k* the depths were
Prov. 8:10, *k* rather than
Prov. 10:14, Wise people store up *k*
Prov. 14:6, *k* is easy to him who
Prov. 17:27, *k* spares his words
Prov. 19:2, a soul to be without *k*
Eccl. 1:18, and he who increases *k*
Eccl. 7:12, *k* is that wisdom
Eccl. 9:10, no work or device or *k*
Isa. 28:9, Whom will he teach *k*
Dan. 12:4, *k* shall increase
Hos. 4:6, you have rejected *k*
Acts 24:22, having more accurate *k*
Rom. 2:20, having the form of *k*
Rom. 3:20, the law is the *k* of sin
1 Cor. 8:1, *K* puffs up
1 Cor. 13:8, whether there is *k*
Eph. 3:19, Christ which passes *k*
1 Tim. 6:20, is falsely called *k*
2 Pet. 3:18, in the grace and *k*

KNOWN
Ps. 76:1, In Judah God is *k*
Ps. 89:1, my mouth will I make *k*
Jn. 8:19, If you had *k* Me
Jn. 10:14, My sheep, and am *k*
Jn. 17:25, The world has not *k*
Rom. 3:17, peace they have not *k*
Rom. 7:7, I would not have *k*
Rom. 11:34, "For who has *k*
Gal. 4:9, after you have *k*
Phil. 4:6, requests be made *k*
2 Tim. 3:15, *k* the Holy Scriptures

KNOWS
Gen. 3:5, "For God *k* that in
Ps. 44:21, *k* the secrets of the
Jer. 9:24, he understands and *k*
Dan. 2:22, *k* what is in the
Nah. 1:7, *k* those who trust
Mt. 6:8, *k* the things you have
Mt. 24:36, and hour no one *k*
Lk. 10:22, *k* who the Son is
Lk. 16:15, God *k* your hearts
Rom. 8:27, searches the hearts *k*
1 Cor. 2:11, *k* the things of God
2 Tim. 2:19, *k* those who are His
Jas. 4:17, to him who *k* to do
1 Jn. 3:20, and *k* all things
Rev. 2:17, written which no one *k*

KOHATH
son of Levi. Gen. 46:11
his descendants. Ex. 6:18; 1 Chr. 6:2
their duties. Num. 4:15; 10:21; 2 Chr. 29:12; 34:12

KORAH, Gen. 36:14
his sedition and punishment. Num. 16; 26:9; 27:3; Jude 11

LABAN
hospitality of. Gen. 24:29
gives Jacob his two daughters. Gen. 29
envies and oppresses Jacob. Gen. 30:27; 31:1
his dream. Gen. 31:24
his covenant with Jacob. Gen. 31:43

LABOR
ordained for man. Gen. 3:19; Ps. 104:23; 1 Cor. 4:12
when blessed by God. Prov. 10:16; 13:11; Eccl. 2:24; 4:9; 5:12,19

LABOR
Ex. 20:9, Six days you shall *l*
Job 9:29, why then do I *l*
Ps. 90:10, their boast is only *l*
Prov. 10:16, The *l* of the righteous
Prov. 13:11, *l* will increase
Prov. 14:23, *l* there is profit
Eccl. 1:8, things are full of *l*
Eccl. 2:22, has man for all his *l*
Isa. 53:11, He shall see the *l*
Isa. 66:7, "Before she was in *l*
Jer. 20:18, from the womb to see *l*
Mt. 11:28, to Me, all you who *l*
Jn. 6:27, "Do not *l* for the
1 Cor. 15:58, knowing that your *l*
Eph. 4:28, but rather let him *l*
Phil. 1:22, mean fruit from my *l*
1 Th. 1:3, your work of faith, *l*
Heb. 6:10, forget your work and *l*
Rev. 2:2, your works, your *l*

LABORED
1 Cor. 15:10, *l* more abundantly
Gal. 4:11, for you, lest I have *l*

LABORERS
Mt. 9:37, but the *l* are few

LABORING
Eccl. 5:12, of a *l* man is sweet
1 Th. 2:9, *l* night and day

LABORS
Prov. 16:26, The person who *l*
Eccl. 4:8, is no end to all his *l*
Jn. 4:38, entered into their *l*
Rom. 8:22, creation groans and *l*
2 Cor. 11:23, *l* more abundant
Rev. 14:13, may rest from their *l*

LACHISH, Josh. 10:3
conquered. Josh. 10:31; 12:11
Amaziah killed at. 2 Ki. 14:19

LACK
Job 31:19, anyone perish for *l*
Ps. 34:10, the LORD shall not *l*
Prov. 28:27, to the poor will not *l*
Mt. 19:20, What do I still *l*
Mk. 10:21, "One thing you *l*

LACKED
Acts 4:34, among them who *l*

LACKING
Ti. 1:5, the things that are *l*

LADDER
Gen. 28:12, and behold, a *l*

LADEN
Isa. 1:4, nation, a people *l*
Mt. 11:28, and are heavy *l*

LADIES
Jud. 5:29, wisest *l* answered her
Est. 1:18, very day the noble *l*

LADY
Isa. 47:7, 'I shall be a *l*
2 Jn. 1, Elder, To the elect *l*

LAGGING
Rom. 12:11, not *l* in diligence

LAID
Job 14:10, But man dies and is *l*
Mk. 16:6, the place where they *l*
Jn. 11:34, Where have you *l*

LAISH, 1 Sam. 25:44
taken. Jud. 18:14

LAKE
of fire. Rev. 19:20; 20:10; 21:8

LAMB
for sacrifices. Gen. 22:7; Ex. 12:3; Lev. 3:7; Isa. 1:11

LAMB
Gen. 22:7, but where is the *l*
2 Sam. 12:4, took the poor man's *l*
Isa. 11:6, shall dwell with the *l*
Isa. 53:7, He was led as a *l*
Isa. 65:25, *l* shall feed together
Jn. 1:29, The *L* of God who
1 Pet. 1:19, of Christ, as of a *l*
Rev. 5:6, the elders, stood a *L*
Rev. 5:12, "Worthy is the *L*
Rev. 12:11, by the blood of the *L*
Rev. 13:8, Book of Life of the *L*
Rev. 19:9, supper of the *L*

LAME
the, excluded from the priest's office. Lev. 21:18
animals, not proper for sacrifices. Dt. 15:21; Mal. 1:8,13
healed by Christ. Mt. 11:5; 21:14; Lk. 7:22; by the apostles. Acts 3; 8:7

LAME
Isa. 33:23, *l* take the prey
Isa. 35:6, *l* shall leap like a
Mal. 1:8, when you offer the *l*
Mt. 11:5, blind see and the *l*
Acts 3:2, And a certain man *l*
Heb. 12:13, so that what is *l*

LAMECH
descendant of Cain. Gen. 4:18
——— father of Noah. Gen. 5:25,29

LAMENTATION
for Jacob. Gen. 50:10
of David, for Saul and Jonathan. 2 Sam. 1:17; for Abner. 2 Sam. 3:31
for Josiah. 2 Chr. 35:25
for Tyre. Ezek. 26:17; 27:30; 28:12
for Pharaoh. Ezek. 32
for Christ. Lk. 23:27
for Stephen. Acts 8:2
for Babylon. Rev. 18:10

LAMENTATION
Jer. 31:15, was heard in Ramah, *l*
Mt. 2:18, was heard in Ramah, *l*
Acts 8:2, and made great *l*

LAMENTATIONS
of Jeremiah. Lam. 1

LAMP
Job 29:3; Prov. 20:27; Isa. 62:1; Zeph. 1:12; Mt. 25:1; Mk. 4:21; Lk. 11:33; 12:35

LAMP
2 Sam. 22:29, For You are my *l*
Job 21:17, "How often is the *l*
Ps. 18:28, You will light my *l*
Ps. 119:105, Your word is a *l*
Prov. 13:9, the *l* of the wicked
Prov. 20:20, his *l* will be put out
Mt. 5:15, Nor do they light a *l*
Mt. 6:22, "The *l* of the body
Lk. 8:16, when he has lit a *l*
Lk. 11:36, *l* gives you light
Lk. 15:8, does not light a *l*
Jn. 5:35, burning and shining *l*
Rev. 18:23, *l* shall not shine
Rev. 22:5, They need no *l* nor

LAMPS
in the tabernacle. Ex. 25:37; 27:20; 30:7; Lev. 24:2; Num. 8
seen in visions. Zech. 4:2; Rev. 4:5
parable referring to. Mt. 25:1

LAMPS
Ex. 37:23, he made its seven *l*
Zeph. 1:12, Jerusalem with *l*
Mt. 25:7, and trimmed their *l*
Rev. 4:5, Seven *l* of fire

LAMPSTAND
Ex. 25:32, branches of the *l*
Zech. 4:2, and there is a *l*
Mt. 5:15, a basket, but on a *l*
Heb. 9:2, in which was the *l*
Rev. 2:5, and remove your *l*

LAND
Gen. 12:1, *l* that I will show you
Ex. 3:8, *l* flowing with milk
Josh. 1:2, *l* which I am giving
Song 2:12, is heard in our *l*
Isa. 33:17, they will see the *l*
Mt. 2:6, Bethlehem, in the *l*

LANDMARK
Dt. 19:14, your neighbor's *l*
Prov. 22:28, remove the ancient *l*
Hos. 5:10, those who remove a *l*

LANGUAGE
Gen. 11:1, whole earth had one *l*
Ps. 19:3, is no speech nor *l*
Ps. 114:1, a people of strange *l*
Zeph. 3:9, the peoples a pure *l*
Acts 2:6, speak in his own *l*
Col. 3:8, blasphemy, filthy *l*

LANGUAGES
confused at Babel. Gen. 11
gift of, by Holy Spirit. Acts 2:7,8; 10:46; 19:6; 1 Cor. 12:10

LANGUAGES
Gen. 10:20, according to their *l*
1 Cor. 14:10, be, so many kinds of *l*

LAODICEA, Col. 2:1

LAODICEANS, Rev. 1:11; 3:14
Paul's epistle to. Col. 4:16

LAST
Job 19:25, He shall stand at *l*
Isa. 44:6, First and I am the *L*
Mt. 20:14, *l* man the same as
Mt. 20:16, *l* will be first
1 Jn. 2:18, children, it is the *l*
Rev. 1:11, the First and the *L*

LATTER
Joel 2:23, former rain, and the *l*
1 Tim. 4:1, *l* times some will

LATTICE
Prov. 7:6, I looked through my *l*
Song 2:9, gazing through the *l*

LAUGH
Gen. 18:13, Why did Sarah *l*
Gen. 21:6, "God has made me *l*
Ps. 59:8, You, O LORD, shall *l*
Lk. 6:25, Woe to you who *l*

LAUGHS
Job 41:29, he *l* at the threat of
Ps. 37:13, The Lord *l* at him

LAUGHTER
Ps. 126:2, was filled with *l*
Jas. 4:9, your *l* be turned to

LAW
of God, given to Adam. Gen. 2:16; to Noah. Gen. 9:3
——— of Moses, ordained. Ex. 21; Lev. 1; Num. 3
preserved on stone. Dt. 27:1; Josh. 8:32
demands entire obedience. Dt. 27:26; Gal. 3:10; Jas. 2:10
described. Ps. 19:7; 119; Rom. 7:12
to be studied by the king. Dt. 17:18
read every seventh year. Dt. 31:9
preserved in the ark. Dt. 31:24
read by Joshua. Josh. 8:34; by Ezra. Neh. 8
Book of, discovered by Hilkiah. 2 Ki. 22:8; and read by Josiah. 2 Ki. 23:2
fulfilled by Christ. Mt. 5:17; Rom. 5:18
abolished in Christ. Acts 15:24; 28:23; Gal. 2—6; Eph. 2:15; Col. 2:14; Heb. 7
all guilty under. Rom. 3:20
Christians redeemed from curse of. Jn. 1:17; Acts 13:39; 15:24,28; Rom. 10:4; Gal. 3:13

LAW
Josh. 8:32, stones a copy of the *l*
Job 28:26, When He made a *l*
Ps. 19:7, The *l* of the LORD is
Ps. 37:31, The *l* of his God is in
Ps. 119:70, I delight in Your *l*
Ps. 119:72, The *l* of Your mouth is
Ps. 119:77, *l* is my delight
Ps. 119:97, Oh, how I love Your *l*
Ps. 119:142, And Your *l* is truth
Prov. 6:23, and the *l* a light
Isa. 2:3, shall go forth the *l*
Isa. 51:4, *l* will proceed from Me
Isa. 51:7, in whose heart is My *l*
Lam. 2:9, the *L* is no more
Mal. 2:6, The *l* of truth was in
Mt. 5:17, to destroy the *L*
Mt. 7:12, for this is the *L*
Mt. 22:40, hang all the *L* and the
Lk. 16:16, "The *l* and the
Jn. 1:17, *l* was given through
Jn. 7:51, "Does our *l* judge a
Rom. 3:20, *l* is the knowledge
Rom. 4:15, because the *l* brings
Rom. 5:13, when there is no *l*
Rom. 6:14, you are not under *l*
Rom. 7:7, Is the *l* sin
Rom. 7:14, For we know that the *l*
Rom. 7:23, warring against the *l*
Rom. 8:3, For what the *l* could
1 Cor. 9:21, who are without *l*
Gal. 2:19, *l* that I might live
Gal. 3:23, under guard by the *l*
Gal. 4:4, born under the *l*
Gal. 5:14, *l* is fulfilled in one
1 Tim. 1:9, *l* is not made for a
Jas. 1:25, into the perfect *l*

Jas. 2:8, fulfill the royal *l*

LAWFUL
Mt. 12:2, doing what is not *l*
Mt. 22:17, Is it *l* to pay taxes
1 Cor. 6:12, All things are *l*

LAWGIVER
Ps. 60:7, Judah is My *l*
Isa. 33:22, the LORD is our *L*
Jas. 4:12, There is one *L*

LAWLESS
2 Th. 2:8, *l* one will be revealed
2 Pet. 2:8, and hearing their *l*

LAWLESSNESS
Mt. 7:23, Me, you who practice *l*
2 Th. 2:7, *l* is already at work
Heb. 1:9, and hated *l*
1 Jn. 3:4, and sin is *l*

LAWSUITS
censured. 1 Cor. 6:1

LAWYERS
Christ rebukes. Lk. 10:25; 11:46; 14:3

LAWYERS
Lk. 7:30, *l* rejected the will of
Lk. 11:46, Woe to you also, *l*

LAY
Mt. 8:20, nowhere to *l* His head
Acts 8:19, *l* hands may receive
1 Tim. 5:22, Do not *l* hands on
Jas. 1:21, *l* aside all

LAZARUS
and the rich man. Lk. 16:19
——— brother of Mary and Martha, raised from the dead. Jn. 11; 12:1

LAZINESS
Prov. 19:15, *L* casts one into a
Eccl. 10:18, *l* the building decays

LAZY
Prov. 12:24, *l* man will be put to
Prov. 12:27, *l* man does not roast
Prov. 13:4, soul of a *l* man desires
Prov. 19:24, *l* man buries his hand
Prov. 24:30, by the field of the *l*
Prov. 26:16, *l* man is wiser in his
Mt. 25:26, wicked and *l* servant
Ti. 1:12, liars, evil beasts, *l*

LEAD
Ex. 15:10, they sank like *l*
Ps. 25:5, *L* me in Your truth and
Ps. 31:3, *L* me and guide me
Ps. 139:10, Your hand shall *l*
Mt. 6:13, And do not *l* us into
Lk. 6:39, "Can the blind *l*

LEADS
Ps. 23:2, He *l* me beside the
Ps. 23:3, He *l* me in the paths
Mt. 15:14, And if the blind *l*
Jn. 10:3, by name and *l* them out
Rom. 2:4, the goodness of God *l*

LEAF
Gen. 8:11, plucked olive *l*
Job 13:25, Will You frighten a *l*
Jer. 17:8, *l* will be green

LEAH
Gen. 29:16,31; 30:17; 31:4; 33:2; 49:31. *See* Ruth 4:11

LEAN
Prov. 3:5, all your heart, and *l*
Mic. 3:11, Yet they *l* on the LORD

LEANING
Jn. 13:25, Then, *l* back on Jesus'
Heb. 11:21, *l* on the top of his

LEANNESS
Ps. 106:15, request, but sent *l*
Isa. 10:16, of hosts, will send *l*

LEAP
Ps. 18:29, by my God I can *l*
Isa. 35:6, Then the lame shall *l*

LEARN
Dt. 31:13, it, may hear and *l*
Ps. 119:71, *l* Your statutes
Prov. 22:25, lest you *l* his ways
Isa. 1:17, *l* to do good
Isa. 2:4, neither shall they *l*
Mt. 11:29, My yoke upon you and *l*
1 Tim. 2:11, Let a woman *l* in
Ti. 3:14, let our people also *l*

LEARNED
Isa. 50:4, Me the tongue of the *l*
Jn. 6:45, who has heard and *l*
Eph. 4:20, have not so *l* Christ
Phil. 4:12, in all things I have *l*
Heb. 5:8, *l* obedience by the

LEARNING
Prov. 1:5, hear and increase *l*
Acts 26:24, *l* is driving you mad
Rom. 15:4, were written for our *l*

LEAST
Mt. 2:6, Judah, are not the *l*
Mt. 5:19, so, shall be called *l*
1 Cor. 15:9, For I am the *l* of the

LEAVE
Gen. 2:24, a man shall *l* his
Dt. 31:6, He will not *l* you nor
Ps. 16:10, For You will not *l*
Ps. 27:9, do not *l* me nor
Heb. 13:5, "I will never *l*

LEAVEN
forbidden at the Passover. Ex. 12:15; 13:7; and in grain offerings. Lev. 2:11; 6:17; 10:12
mentioned figuratively. Mt. 13:33; 16:6; Lk. 13:21; 1 Cor. 5:6

LEAVEN
Ex. 12:15, day you shall remove *l*
Mt. 13:33, of heaven is like *l*
Mt. 16:6, and beware of the *l*
1 Cor. 5:6, know that a little *l*
Gal. 5:9, *l* leavens the whole

LEAVES
Gen. 3:7, and they sewed fig *l*
Mt. 21:19, nothing on it but *l*
Jn. 10:12, *l* the sheep and flees
Rev. 22:2, The *l* of the tree

LEBANON, Dt. 1:7
forest and mountain. Dt. 3:25; Jud. 3:3; 1 Ki. 5:14
its cedars. 2 Ki. 14:9; 2 Chr. 2:8; Ps. 92:12; Song 3:9; Isa. 40:16; Hos. 14:5

LED
Ex. 13:18, *l* the people around by
Dt. 32:12, so the LORD alone *l*
Ps. 107:7, *l* them forth by the
Isa. 63:12, *l* them by the right
Rom. 8:14, For as many as are *l*
Eph. 4:8, *l* captivity captive
2 Tim. 3:6, *l* away by various

LEFT
Mt. 6:3, *l* hand know what your
Mt. 19:27, "See, we have *l*
Mt. 19:29, And everyone who has *l*

LEGACY
Prov. 3:35, shame shall be the *l*

LEGION
of demons. Mk. 5:9; Lk. 8:30

LEGIONS
of angels. Mt. 26:53

LEGS
Prov. 26:7, Like the *l* of the lame
Song 5:15, *l* are pillars of
Jn. 19:33, did not break His *l*

LEHI, Jud. 15:9

LEMUEL
king, his lesson. Prov. 31:1

LEND
Ex. 22:25, "If you *l* money to
Dt. 15:8, *l* him sufficient
Lk. 6:34, "And if you *l*
Lk. 11:5, *l* me three loaves

LENDER
Prov. 22:7, is servant to the *l*
Isa. 24:2, as with the *l*

LENDING
regulations for. Ex. 22:25; Lev. 25:37; Dt. 15:2; 23:19; 24:10. *See* Ps. 37:26; Lk. 6:34

LENDING
Neh. 5:10, and my servants, am *l*

LENDS
Ps. 37:26, ever merciful, and *l*
Ps. 112:5, deals graciously and *l*
Prov. 19:17, has pity on the poor *l*

LENGTH
Gen. 6:15, The *l* of the ark shall
Dt. 30:20, is your life and the *l*
Prov. 3:16, *L* of days is in her
Rev. 21:16, *l* is as great as its

LENGTHENS
Ps. 109:23, a shadow when it *l*

LEOPARD
Isa. 11:6, the *l* shall lie down
Jer. 13:23, or the *l* its spots

LEPERS
not to dwell in the camp. Lev. 13:46; Num. 5:2; 12:14
four, of Samaria. 2 Ki. 7:3

LEPERS
2 Ki. 7:8, And when these *l*

Lk. 4:27, "And many *l* were in

LEPROSY
in a house. Lev. 14:33
of Miriam. Num. 12:10
of Naaman and Gehazi. 2 Ki. 5
of Uzziah. 2 Chr. 26:19
symptoms of. Lev. 13
observances on healing. Lev. 14; 22:4; Dt. 24:8
cured by Christ. Mt. 8:3; Mk. 1:41; Lk. 5:12; 17:12

LET
Gen. 1:3, "*L* there be light"
Mt. 19:14, *L* the little

LETTER
and the Spirit. Rom. 2:29; 7:6; 2 Cor. 3:6

LETTER
Rom. 7:6, the oldness of the *l*
2 Cor. 3:6, for the *l* kills
2 Cor. 7:8, you sorry with my *l*
2 Th. 2:2, or by word or by *l*

LETTERS
of David to Joab. 2 Sam. 11:14
of Jezebel. 1 Ki. 21:9
of king of Syria. 2 Ki. 5:5
of Jehu. 2 Ki. 10:1
of Elijah to Jehoram. 2 Chr. 21:12
of Hezekiah. 2 Chr. 30:1
of Bishlam and Rehum. Ezra 4:7
of Artaxerxes. Ezra 4:17
of Tatnai. Ezra 5:6
of Sennacherib to Hezekiah. Isa. 37:10,14
of Jeremiah. Jer. 29:1
of the apostles. Acts 15:23
of Claudius Lysias to Felix. Acts 23:25

LETTERS
Jn. 7:15, does this Man know *l*
2 Cor. 3:1, to you or *l* of
2 Cor. 10:10, "For his *l*
Gal. 6:11, with what large *l*

LEVI
son of Jacob. Gen. 29:34
avenges Dinah. Gen. 34:25; 49:5
—— *See* MATTHEW

LEVIATHAN
a sea monster. Ps. 104:26

LEVIATHAN
Job 41:1, "Can you draw out *L*
Ps. 104:26, *L* which You have made

LEVITE
Ex. 4:14, "Is not Aaron the *L*
Lk. 10:32, "Likewise a *L*
Acts 4:36, a *L* of the country of

LEVITES
descendants of Levi, mentioned. Ex. 6:25; 32:26
their service. Ex. 38:21
appointed over the tabernacle. Num. 1:47
their divisions, Gershonites, Kohathites, Merarites. Num. 3
duties of. Num. 3:23; 4; 8:23; 18
their consecration. Num. 8:5
inheritance of. Num. 35; Dt. 18; Josh. 21
not to be forsaken. Dt. 12:19; 14:27
their genealogies. 1 Chr. 6; 9
charged with the temple service. 1 Chr. 23—27
twenty-four divisions, instituted by David. 1 Chr. 23:6; redivided by Ezra. Ezra 6:18
their sin censured. Mal. 1:2; Ezek. 22:26

LEVITICAL
Heb. 7:11, were through the *L*

LEWDNESS
source of. Mk. 7:21; Gal. 5:19
rebuked. 2 Cor. 12:21; Eph. 4:19; 1 Pet. 4:3; Jude 4

LEWDNESS
Mk. 7:22, wickedness, deceit, *l*
Rom. 13:13, drunkenness, not in *l*
Eph. 4:19, themselves over to *l*
1 Pet. 4:3, when we walked in *l*

LIAR
Jn. 8:44, for he is a *l* and the
Rom. 3:4, but every man a *l*
1 Jn. 1:10, we make Him a *l*
1 Jn. 2:22, Who is a *l* but he who
1 Jn. 4:20, his brother, he is a *l*
1 Jn. 5:10, God has made Him a *l*

LIARS
their doom. Rev. 21:8,27; 22:15
instances: the devil. Gen. 3:4; Cain. Gen. 4:9; Sarah. Gen. 18:15; Jacob. Gen. 27:19; Joseph's brothers. Gen. 37:31,32; Gibeonites. Josh. 9:9; Samson. Jud. 16:10; Saul. 1 Sam. 15:13; Michal. 1 Sam. 19:14; David. 1 Sam. 21:2; prophet of Bethel. 1 Ki. 13:18; Gehazi. 2 Ki. 5:22; Job's friends. Job 13:4; Ninevites. Nah. 3:1; Peter. Mt. 26:72; Ananias. Acts 5:4; Cretans. Ti. 1:12

LIARS
Ps. 116:11, "All men are *l*
Ti. 1:12, Cretans are always *l*
Rev. 2:2, and have found them *l*
Rev. 21:8, *l* shall have their

LIBERALITY
commanded. Dt. 15:14; Prov. 11:25; 2 Cor. 9:13
of the Israelites. Ex. 35:21; Num. 7
of the early Christians. Acts 2:45; 4:34
of the Macedonians. 2 Cor. 8; 9; Phil. 4:15

LIBERALITY
Rom. 12:8, he who gives, with *l*
2 Cor. 8:2, the riches of their *l*

LIBERALLY
Jas. 1:5, who gives to all *l*

LIBERTY
bestowed by the Gospel. Rom. 8:21; 2 Cor. 3:17; Gal. 5:1; Jas. 1:25; 2:12 (Isa. 61:1; Lk. 4:18)
not to be misused. 1 Cor. 8:9; Gal. 5:13; 1 Pet. 2:16; 2 Pet. 2:19

LIBERTY
Lev. 25:10, year, and proclaim *l*
Ps. 119:45, And I will walk at *l*
Isa. 61:1, to proclaim *l* to the
Lk. 4:18, to proclaim *l* to the
Rom. 8:21, into the glorious *l*
1 Cor. 10:29, For why is my *l*
2 Cor. 3:17, Lord is, there is *l*
Gal. 5:1, therefore in the *l*
Gal. 5:13, *l* as an opportunity
Jas. 1:25, the perfect law of *l*
1 Pet. 2:16, yet not using *l*

LIBNAH, Num. 33:20
subdued. Josh. 10:29; 21:13
rebels. 2 Ki. 8:22
attacked by Assyrians. 2 Ki. 19:8; Isa. 37:8

LIBYA
Jer. 46:9; Dan. 11:43; Acts 2:10

LIE
Num. 23:19, man, that He should *l*
Job 7:21, For now I will *l*
Ps. 89:35, I will not *l* to David
Col. 3:9, Do not *l* to one
Ti. 1:2, God, who cannot *l*
Jas. 3:14, do not boast and *l*
1 Jn. 2:21, know it, and that no *l*
Rev. 21:27, an abomination or a *l*

LIED
Jer. 5:12, They have *l* about the
Acts 5:4, You have not *l* to men

LIES
Gen. 4:7, sin *l* at the door
Prov. 19:5, and he who speaks *l*
1 Tim. 4:2, speaking *l* in
1 Jn. 5:19, and the whole world *l*

LIFE
the gift of God. Gen. 2:7; Job 12:10; Ps. 36:6; 66:9; Dan. 5:23; Acts 17:28
long, to whom promised. Ex. 20:12; Dt. 5:33; 6:2; Prov. 3:2; 9:11; 10:27; Eph. 6:3
its vanity and uncertainty. Job 7:1; 9:25; 14:1; Ps. 39:5; 73:19; 89:47; 90:5,9; Eccl. 6:12; Isa. 38:12; Jas. 4:14; 1 Pet. 1:24
mode of spending. Lk. 1:75; Rom. 12:18; 14:8; Phil. 1:21; 1 Pet. 1:17
of Hezekiah prolonged. 2 Ki. 20; 2 Chr. 32:24; Isa. 38

SPIRITUAL
Rom. 6:4; 8; Gal. 2:20; Eph. 2:1; Col. 3:3
imparted. Ps. 71:20; 80:18; Jn. 5:21; 6:63; Rom. 4:17; 8:11; 1 Cor. 15:45; 2 Cor. 3:6; Eph. 2:1; 1 Tim. 6:13; 1 Pet. 3:18

ETERNAL
the gift of God through Jesus Christ. (Ps. 133:3) Jn. 6:27,54; 10:28; 17:3; Rom. 2:7; 6:23; 1 Jn. 1:2; 2:25; Jude 21; Rev. 2:7; 21:6
to whom promised. Jn. 3:16; 5:24; 1 Tim. 1:16

LIFE
Gen. 2:7, the breath of *l*
Gen. 2:9, *l* was also in the
Ex. 21:23, then you shall give *l*
Lev. 17:11, 'For the *l* of the
Dt. 30:15, before you today *l*
Job 10:12, You have granted me *l*
Job 12:10, in whose hand is the *l*
Job 27:8, God takes away his *l*
Job 33:30, with the light of *l*
Ps. 72:14, He will redeem their *l*
Ps. 119:50, word has given me *l*
Prov. 2:19, regain the paths of *l*
Prov. 3:18, She is a tree of *l*
Prov. 3:22, so they will be *l*
Prov. 8:35, finds me finds *l*
Prov. 15:24, *l* winds upward for the
Prov. 29:24, thief hates his own *l*
Eccl. 7:12, is that wisdom gives *l*
Isa. 38:12, I have cut off my *l*
Jer. 21:8, you the way of *l*
Jer. 39:18, *l* shall be as a prize
Mt. 6:25, not worry about your *l*
Lk. 12:15, *l* does not consist
Lk. 12:23, *L* is more than
Jn. 1:4, *l* was the light
Jn. 5:21, so the Son gives *l*
Jn. 5:26, as the Father has *l*
Jn. 6:63, spirit, and they are *l*
Jn. 8:12, have the light of *l*
Jn. 10:15, and I lay down My *l*
Jn. 11:25, resurrection and the *l*
Jn. 13:38, you lay down your *l*
Rom. 4:17, God, who gives *l*
1 Cor. 6:3, that pertain to this *l*
2 Cor. 4:10, Lord Jesus, that the *l*
Gal. 2:20, *l* which I now live
Col. 3:3, *l* is hidden with
1 Tim. 6:13, of God who gives *l*
Jas. 4:14, For what is your *l*
2 Pet. 1:3, that pertain to *l*
1 Jn. 1:2, *l* was manifested
1 Jn. 2:16, and the pride of *l*
1 Jn. 5:11, has given us eternal *l*
1 Jn. 5:12, who has the Son has *l*
Rev. 21:27, the Lamb's Book of *L*
Rev. 22:14, right to the tree of *l*
Rev. 22:17, the water of *l* freely
Rev. 22:19, from the Book of *L*

LIFT
Ps. 63:4, I will *l* up my hands
Ps. 121:1, I will *l* up my eyes to
Isa. 58:1, *l* up your voice like a
Lam. 3:41, *l* our hearts and hands
Jas. 4:10, Lord, and He will *l*

LIFTED
Ps. 30:1, O LORD, for You have *l*
Ezek. 28:2, your heart is *l*
Lk. 16:23, in Hades, he *l* up his
Jn. 3:14, the Son of Man be *l*
Jn. 12:32, "And I, if I am *l*
Jn. 12:34, of Man must be *l*

LIGHT, Gen. 1:3; Jer. 31:35
type of God's favor. Ex. 10:23; Ps. 4:6; 27:1; 97:11; Isa. 9:2; 60:19
God's word produces. Ps. 19:8; 119:105,130; Prov. 6:23
instances of miraculous. Mt. 17:2; Acts 9:3
Christ the light of the world. Lk. 2:32; Jn. 1:4; 3:19; 8:12; 12:35; Rev. 21:23
children of, disciples. Eph. 5:8; 1 Th. 5:5
God is. 1 Tim. 6:16; 1 Jn. 1:5

LIGHT
Gen. 1:3, "Let there be *l*
Job 18:5, "The *l* of the wicked
Job 22:28, *l* will shine on your
Job 38:15, the wicked their *l*
Job 38:19, to the dwelling of *l*
Ps. 4:6, LORD, lift up the *l*
Ps. 27:1, The LORD is my *l*
Ps. 43:3, Oh, send out Your *l*
Ps. 97:11, *L* is sown for the
Ps. 118:27, and He has given us *l*
Ps. 119:105, and a *l* to my path
Prov. 13:9, The *l* of the righteous
Prov. 15:30, The *l* of the eyes
Prov. 29:13, The LORD gives *l*
Eccl. 11:7, Truly the *l* is sweet
Isa. 2:5, let us walk in the *l*
Isa. 5:30, *l* is darkened by the
Isa. 8:20, because there is no *l*
Isa. 30:26, moon will be as the *l*
Isa. 58:8, *l* shall break forth
Isa. 60:1, for your *l* has come
Isa. 60:20, be your everlasting *l*
Jer. 31:35, gives the sun for a *l*
Hos. 6:5, *l* that goes
Mt. 5:14, "You are the *l*
Mt. 5:16, "Let your *l* so shine
Mt. 6:22, body will be full of *l*
Lk. 16:8, than the sons of *l*
Jn. 1:4, and the life was the *l*
Jn. 1:9, That was the true *L*
Jn. 3:19, darkness rather than *l*
Jn. 3:20, evil hates the *l*
Jn. 3:21, truth comes to the *l*
Jn. 8:12, saying, "I am the *l*
Jn. 12:36, believe in the *l*
Jn. 12:46, "I have come as a *l*
1 Cor. 4:5, *l* the hidden
2 Cor. 4:6, God who commanded *l*
Eph. 5:8, Walk as children of *l*
1 Th. 5:5, You are all sons of *l*
2 Tim. 1:10, and immortality to *l*
1 Pet. 2:9, into His marvelous *l*
2 Pet. 1:19, do well to heed as a *l*
1 Jn. 1:5, to you, that God is *l*
1 Jn. 1:7, *l* as He is in the
1 Jn. 2:9, says he is in the *l*
Rev. 21:23, The Lamb is its *l*
Rev. 22:5, Lord God gives them *l*

LIGHTEN
1 Ki. 12:9, *L* the yoke which
Jon. 1:5, the sea, to *l* the load

LIGHTLY
2 Cor. 1:17, this, did I do it *l*

LIGHTNING
Ex. 19:16; 2 Sam. 22:15; Job 28:26; 38:25; Ps. 18:14; 144:6
about God's throne. Ezek. 1:13; Rev. 4:5

LIGHTNING
Mt. 24:27, "For as the *l*
Mt. 28:3, countenance was like *l*
Lk. 10:18, saw Satan fall like *l*

LIGHTNINGS
Ex. 19:16, were thunderings and *l*
Ps. 77:18, the *l* lit up the world
Ps. 97:4, *l* light the world
Rev. 4:5, the throne proceeded *l*

LIGHTS
Gen. 1:14, "Let there be *l*
Ps. 136:7, Him who made great *l*
Phil. 2:15, whom you shine as *l*
Jas. 1:17, from the Father of *l*

LIKE
Ex. 15:11, "Who is *l* You
Song 2:2, *L* a lily among thorns
Heb. 2:17, be made *l* His brethren

LIKE-MINDED
Rom. 15:5, grant you to be *l*
Phil. 2:20, For I have no one *l*

LIKENESS
Gen. 1:26, according to Our *l*
Ex. 20:4, carved image—any *l*
Ps. 17:15, when I awake in Your *l*
Rom. 8:3, His own Son in the *l*
Phil. 2:7, and coming in the *l*

LILY
of the valley. Song 2:1; Hos. 14:5; Mt. 6:28; Lk. 12:27

LILY
Song 2:1, the *l* of the valleys
Song 2:2, Like a *l* among thorns
Hos. 14:5, shall grow like the *l*

LIMIT
Job 15:8, Do you *l* wisdom to
Prov. 8:29, to the sea its *l*

LIMITED
Ps. 78:41, *l* the Holy One of

LINE
Ps. 19:4, *l* has gone out through
Isa. 28:10, upon precept, *l* upon
Amos 7:8, I am setting a plumb *l*

LINEAGE
Lk. 2:4, was of the house and *l*

LINEN
for sacred vestments. Ex. 28:42; Lev. 6:10; 1 Sam. 2:18; 22:18. *See* Rev. 15:6

LINEN
Prov. 31:22, her clothing is fine *l*
Mk. 15:46, wrapped Him in the *l*
Rev. 19:8, *l* is the righteous

LINGER
Prov. 23:30, Those who *l* long at
Isa. 46:13, salvation shall not *l*

LION
Gen. 49:9, he lies down as a *l*
Job 10:16, like a fierce *l*
Isa. 11:7, *l* shall eat straw
Hos. 5:14, For I will be like a *l*

LIONS
Ps. 57:4, My soul is among *l*
Heb. 11:33, the mouths of *l*

LIPS
Ex. 6:12, of uncircumcised *l*

Ps. 12:3, off all flattering *l*
Ps. 31:18, Let the lying *l*
Prov. 10:21, The *l* of the righteous
Prov. 20:15, but the *l* of knowledge
Isa. 6:5, am a man of unclean *l*
Rom. 3:13, asps is under their *l*
1 Cor. 14:21, other *l* I will speak
1 Pet. 3:10, from evil, and his *l*

LISTEN
Isa. 55:2, *L* carefully to Me
Dan. 9:19, O Lord, *l* and act
Jn. 8:43, you are not able to *l*
Jn. 10:20, Why do you *l* to Him
Acts 13:16, you who fear God, *l*

LISTENS
Prov. 1:33, but whoever *l* to me

LITTLE
Song 2:15, *l* foxes that spoil the
Song 8:8, We have a *l* sister
Isa. 28:10, upon line, here a *l*
Mic. 5:2, though you are *l*
Hag. 1:9, indeed it came to *l*
Zech. 1:15, for I was a *l* angry
Mt. 10:42, *l* ones only a cup
Mt. 14:31, "O you of *l* faith
Mt. 18:5, Whoever receives one *l*
Lk. 7:47, to whom *l* is forgiven
Lk. 19:17, faithful in a very *l*
1 Tim. 4:8, exercise profits a *l*

LIVE
Gen. 3:22, eat, and *l* forever
Lev. 18:5, a man does, he shall *l*
Job 7:16, I would not *l* forever
Eccl. 9:9, *L* joyfully with the
Isa. 38:16, by these things men *l*
Ezek. 3:21, sin, he shall surely *l*
Amos 5:4, "Seek Me and *l*
Hab. 2:4, but the just shall *l*
Mt. 4:4, *l* by bread alone
Jn. 6:57, who feeds on Me will *l*
Acts 17:28, "for in Him we *l*
Rom. 12:18, *l* peaceably with all
Gal. 2:20, the life which I now *l*
Gal. 5:25, If we *l* in the Spirit
Phil. 1:21, to me, to *l* is Christ
2 Tim. 3:12, *l* godly in Christ
Heb. 13:18, to *l* honorably
1 Pet. 4:6, *l* according to God in

LIVED
Rom. 14:9, died and rose and *l*
Rev. 20:4, And they *l* and reigned

LIVES
Dt. 8:3, but man *l* by every
Acts 15:26, have risked their *l*
Rom. 6:10, He *l* to God
Rom. 14:7, For none of us *l*
Gal. 2:20, but Christ *l* in me
1 Jn. 3:16, to lay down our *l*
Rev. 1:18, "I am He who *l*

LIVING
Gen. 2:7, and man became a *l*
Ps. 56:13, in the light of the *l*
Eccl. 7:2, *l* will take it to
Eccl. 9:5, *l* know that they will
Lam. 3:39, Why should a *l* man
Mt. 22:32, the dead, but of the *l*
Lk. 24:5, Why do you seek the *l*
Acts 10:42, to be Judge of the *l*
2 Tim. 4:1, who will judge the *l*
Heb. 4:12, the word of God is *l*
1 Pet. 4:5, ready to judge the *l*
Rev. 4:7, *l* creature was like a

LO DEBAR, 2 Sam. 9:4

LO-AMMI, Hos. 1:9

LOAD
Gal. 6:5, shall bear his own *l*

LOATHE
Job 7:16, I *l* my life
Ezek. 6:9, *l* themselves for the

LOATHSOME
Prov. 13:5, but a wicked man is *l*

LOAVES
miraculous multiplication of. Mt. 14:17; 15:32; Mk. 6:35; Lk. 9:12; Jn. 6:5

LOAVES
Mt. 14:17, have here only five *l*
Mt. 15:36, He took the seven *l*
Lk. 11:5, lend me three *l*
Jn. 6:26, you ate of the *l*

LOCUST
Joel 1:4, What the chewing *l*
Joel 1:4, left, the swarming *l*

LOCUSTS
Ex. 10:4; Dt. 28:38
used as food. Lev. 11:22; Mt. 3:4
described. Prov. 30:27; Nah. 3:17; Rev. 9:7

LOCUSTS
Jud. 7:12, as numerous as *l*
Ps. 105:34, He spoke, and *l* came
Prov. 30:27, the *l* have no king
Mt. 3:4, and his food was *l*
Mk. 1:6, waist, and he ate *l*
Rev. 9:3, out of the smoke *l*

LODGED
Acts 10:23, them in and *l* them
1 Tim. 5:10, children, if she has *l*

LOFTILY
Ps. 73:8, they speak *l*

LOFTY
Ps. 131:1, haughty, nor my eyes *l*
Prov. 24:7, Wisdom is too *l*
Prov. 30:13, *l* are their eyes
Isa. 57:15, and *L* One who

LOINS
1 Pet. 1:13, gird up the *l* of your

LOIS, 2 Tim. 1:5

LONG
Dt. 5:16, your days may be *l*
Job 3:21, who *l* for death
Job 6:8, me the thing that I *l*
Ps. 119:174, I *l* for Your salvation
Mk. 12:38, go around in *l* robes
Phil. 1:8, how greatly I *l*

LONGSUFFERING
Ps. 86:15, and gracious, *l*
Gal. 5:22, is love, joy, peace, *l*
Eph. 4:2, and gentleness, with *l*
Col. 1:11, for all patience and *l*
1 Tim. 1:16, might show all *l*
1 Pet. 3:20, when once the Divine *l*
2 Pet. 3:15, and consider that the *l*

LOOK
Gen. 19:17, Do not *l* behind you
Ps. 101:5, who has a haughty *l*
Prov. 6:17, A proud *l*
Isa. 17:7, that day a man will *l*
Isa. 33:20, *L* upon Zion
Isa. 45:22, "*L* to Me
Isa. 59:9, we *l* for light
Isa. 59:11, we *l* for justice
Zech. 12:10, *l* on Me whom they
Lk. 17:23, say to you, '*L* here
2 Cor. 3:7, of Israel could not *l*
2 Cor. 4:18, while we do not *l*
Phil. 2:4, Let each of you *l*
2 Jn. 8, *L* to yourselves

LOOKED
Job 30:26, But when I *l* for good
Ps. 34:5, They *l* to Him and were
Ps. 102:19, For He *l* down from
Isa. 5:7, He *l* for justice
Jer. 8:15, "We *l* for peace
Hag. 1:9, "You *l* for much
Lk. 22:61, the Lord turned and *l*
Heb. 11:26, for he *l* to the reward

LOOKING
Lk. 9:62, the plow, and *l* back
Ti. 2:13, *l* for the blessed hope
Heb. 12:2, *l* unto Jesus
Heb. 12:15, *l* carefully lest
Jude 21, *l* for the mercy of

LOOKS
2 Sam. 14:25, Absalom for his good *l*
Job 33:27, Then he *l* at men and
Ps. 53:2, God *l* down from heaven
Isa. 2:11, The lofty *l* of man
Mt. 5:28, to you that whoever *l*

LOOM
Jud. 16:14, and the web from the *l*
Isa. 38:12, cuts me off from the *l*

LOOSE
Isa. 45:1, *l* the armor of kings
Mt. 16:19, and whatever you *l*
Jn. 11:44, said to them, "*L* him

LOOSED
Ps. 116:16, You have *l* my bonds
Eccl. 12:6, the silver cord is *l*

LORD
Ex. 15:2, *L* is my strength
Ex. 15:3, *L* is a man of war
Dt. 6:4, *L* our God, the *L*
Dt. 17:1, *L* your God a bull
1 Ki. 8:60, may know that the *L*
1 Ki. 18:21, If the *L* is God
Neh. 9:6, You alone are the *L*
Ps. 24:10, The *L* of hosts
Ps. 89:18, belongs to the *L*
Ps. 95:1, let us sing to the *L*
Ps. 95:3, *L* is the great God
Ps. 116:5, Gracious is the *L*
Ps. 125:2, *L* surrounds His people
Ps. 129:4, The *L* is righteous
Ps. 145:18, *L* is near to all who
Isa. 30:18, *L* is a God of justice

Jer. 23:6, *L* Our Righteousness
Joel 2:21, *L* has done marvelous
Hab. 3:19, *L* God is my strength
Zech. 14:9, "The *L* is one
Mt. 4:7, shall not tempt the *L*
Mt. 4:10, shall worship the *L*
Mk. 2:28, Son of Man is also *L*
Lk. 2:11, who is Christ the *L*
Lk. 6:46, why do you call Me '*L*
Lk. 24:34, *L* is risen indeed
Jn. 13:13, call Me Teacher and *L*
Acts 10:36, He is *L* of all
Acts 26:15, 'Who are You, *L*
Rom. 10:9, with your mouth the *L*
Rom. 10:12, Greek, for the same *L*
1 Cor. 12:3, say that Jesus is *L*
1 Cor. 15:47, second Man is the *L*
2 Cor. 3:17, the Spirit of the *L*
Phil. 2:11, that Jesus Christ is *L*
Jude 4, and deny the only *L*
Rev. 19:6, *L* God Omnipotent

LORD'S DAY, Rev. 1:10

LORD'S PRAYER
Mt. 6:9; Lk. 11:2

LORD'S SUPPER, *see* COMMUNION

LORDS
1 Cor. 8:5, many gods and many *l*
1 Pet. 5:3, nor as being *l* over
Rev. 17:14, for He is Lord of *l*

LORDSHIP
Lk. 22:25, Gentiles exercise *l*

LOSE
Eccl. 3:6, gain, and a time to *l*
Mt. 16:25, save his life will *l*
Gal. 6:9, reap if we do not *l*
2 Jn. 8, that we do not *l*

LOSES
Mt. 5:13, but if the salt *l*
Mt. 16:26, and *l* his own soul
Lk. 15:8, if she *l* one coin
Lk. 17:33, *l* his life will

LOSS
1 Cor. 3:15, he will suffer *l*
Phil. 3:8, count all things *l*

LOST
Ezek. 37:11, are dry, our hope is *l*
Mt. 18:11, save that which was *l*
Lk. 15:4, the one which is *l*
Lk. 15:6, my sheep which was *l*
Lk. 15:9, the piece which I *l*
Jn. 17:12, and none of them is *l*
Jn. 18:9, You gave Me I have *l*

LOT, Gen. 11:27
Abram's nephew, separates from Abram. Gen. 13:10
captured by four kings, and rescued by Abram. Gen. 14
entertains angel visitors. Gen. 19:1
saved from Sodom. Gen. 19:16; 2 Pet. 2:7
his wife turned into a pillar of salt. Gen. 19:26; Lk. 17:28,32

LOT, the
decided by God. Lev. 16:8; Prov. 16:33
Canaan apportioned by. Num. 26:55; Josh. 15
Saul chosen king by. 1 Sam. 10:17
Jonathan taken by. 1 Sam. 14:41,42
used to divide Christ's garments. Mt. 27:35; Mk. 15:24 (Ps. 22:18)
Matthias chosen apostle by. Acts 1:26

LOT
Num. 26:55, shall be divided by *l*
Ps. 16:5, You maintain my *l*
Prov. 1:14, cast in your *l* among
Prov. 16:33, *l* is cast into the lap
2 Pet. 2:7, delivered righteous *L*

LOTS
Prov. 18:18, *l* causes contentions
Mk. 15:24, garments, casting *l*
Acts 1:26, And they cast their *l*

LOUD
Gen. 39:14, I cried out with a *l*
Ps. 150:5, Him with *l* cymbals
Mt. 27:46, cried out with a *l*
Rev. 1:10, I heard behind me a *l*

LOVE
for God commanded. Dt. 6:5; 10:12; 11:1; Josh. 22:5; Ps. 31:23; Dan. 9:4; Mt. 22:37; 1 Jn. 4; 5
blessings of. Neh. 1:5; Ps. 145:20; 1 Cor. 2:9; 8:3
brotherly. Rom. 12:9,10
of husbands. Gen. 29:20; 2 Sam. 1:26; Eph. 5:25; Ti. 2:4
for Christ. Mt. 10:37; Rev. 2:4
for our neighbor. Mk. 12:33; Rom. 13:8–10; 1 Cor. 13:1–8,13; 1 Th. 1:3; 3:6; 4:9; 1 Tim. 1:5; 4:12; 2 Tim. 3:10; Heb. 6:10; Jas. 2:8; 1 Pet. 1:22; 1 Jn. 2:10; 3:14; 4:11; Rev. 2:19
almsgiving. Prov. 19:17; Mt. 19:21; Lk. 11:41; 12:33; 18:22; Acts 10:2,4; 2 Cor. 9; 3 Jn. 6
commanded. Lev. 19:18; Dt. 10:19; Mt. 5:44; 22:39; Gal. 5:14; 6:10; Eph. 4:2; 1 Jn. 3:23; 4:7,21; 2 Jn. 5
its signs and effects. 1 Cor. 8:1; 13; Gal. 5:6,13,22; Eph. 3:17; 4:16; 5:2; Col. 3:14
evidences of. Lev. 19:11; 25:35; Isa. 58:7; Mt. 18:15; 25:35; Jn. 13:35; Rom. 12:15; 1 Cor. 12:26; Eph. 4:32; 1 Th. 5:14; Heb. 6:10; 1 Pet. 4:8; 1 Jn. 3:10,14; 4:20
exemplified by Christ. Jn. 13:34; 15:12; Eph. 5:2,25; Rev. 1:5
of the world, censured. 1 Jn. 2:15

LOVE
Lev. 19:18, *l* your neighbor as
Dt. 6:5, *l* the LORD your God
2 Sam. 1:26, your *l* to me was
Ps. 4:2, How long will you *l*
Ps. 31:23, Oh, *l* the LORD
Ps. 45:7, *l* righteousness
Ps. 91:14, he has set his *l*
Ps. 119:97, Oh, how I *l* Your law
Ps. 119:165, peace have those who *l*
Ps. 145:20, preserves all who *l*
Prov. 7:18, us take our fill of *l*
Prov. 10:12, *l* covers all sins
Eccl. 3:8, a time to *l*
Eccl. 9:1, People know neither *l*
Song 1:2, *l* is better than wine
Song 2:4, banner over me was *l*
Song 3:5, stir up nor awaken *l*
Song 7:12, I will give you my *l*
Song 8:6, *l* is as strong as
Song 8:7, waters cannot quench *l*
Ezek. 16:8, time was the time of *l*
Hos. 14:4, backsliding, I will *l*
Mic. 6:8, do justly, to *l* mercy
Mt. 5:44, to you, *l* your enemies
Mt. 5:46, *l* those who *l* you
Lk. 7:42, which of them will *l*
Jn. 5:42, you do not have the *l*
Jn. 13:35, if you have *l* for one
Jn. 14:15, "If you *l* Me
Jn. 14:23, and My Father will *l*
Jn. 15:12, *l* one another as I
Jn. 15:13, *l* has no one than this
Jn. 21:15, *l* Me more than these
Jn. 21:16, of Jonah, do you *l*
Jn. 21:16, You know that I *l*
Rom. 5:5, because the *l* of God
Rom. 12:9, Let *l* be without
Rom. 13:8, to *l* one another
Rom. 13:10, *L* does no harm to a
1 Cor. 8:1, up, but *l* edifies
1 Cor. 13:4, *L* suffers long and is
1 Cor. 13:4, *l* does not envy
1 Cor. 13:4, *l* does not parade
1 Cor. 13:8, *L* never fails
1 Cor. 13:13, greatest of these is *l*
2 Cor. 5:14, For the *l* of Christ
2 Cor. 13:11, and the God of *l*
Gal. 5:22, of the Spirit is *l*
Eph. 5:25, Husbands, *l* your wives
Col. 1:13, of the Son of His *l*
Col. 3:19, *l* your wives and do
1 Tim. 1:5, the commandment is *l*
1 Tim. 2:15, continue in faith, *l*
1 Tim. 4:12, word, in conduct, in *l*
1 Tim. 6:10, For the *l* of money is
Ti. 2:4, *l* their husbands
Heb. 13:1, Let brotherly *l*
1 Pet. 1:8, having not seen you *l*
1 Pet. 2:17, *L* the brotherhood
1 Pet. 4:8, for "*l* will cover a
1 Pet. 5:14, with a kiss of *l*
2 Pet. 1:7, brotherly kindness *l*
1 Jn. 2:15, loves the world, the *l*
1 Jn. 3:14, we *l* the brethren
1 Jn. 3:16, By this we know *l*
1 Jn. 3:17, him, how does the *l*
1 Jn. 4:7, Beloved, let us *l*
1 Jn. 4:8, know God, for God is *l*
1 Jn. 4:10, In this is *l*
1 Jn. 4:12, If we *l* one another
1 Jn. 4:17, *L* has been perfected
1 Jn. 4:18, There is no fear in *l*
1 Jn. 4:19, *l* Him because He first
1 Jn. 4:21, who loves God must *l*
1 Jn. 5:3, For this is the *l*
Rev. 2:4, have left your first *l*
Rev. 12:11, and they did not *l*

LOVED
1 Ki. 10:9, Because the LORD has *l*
Ps. 88:18, *L* one and friend You
Mal. 1:2, "I have *l* you

Mal. 1:2, Yet Jacob I have *l*
Lk. 7:47, forgiven, for she *l*
Jn. 3:16, so *l* the world that
Jn. 11:36, "See how He *l*
Jn. 13:23, whom Jesus *l*
Jn. 15:9, "As the Father *l*
Jn. 17:23, *l* them as You have
Rom. 9:13, "Jacob I have *l*
Gal. 2:20, the Son of God, who *l*
Eph. 5:25, *l* the church and gave
Heb. 1:9, *l* righteousness
1 Jn. 4:10, God, but that He *l*
1 Jn. 4:11, Beloved, if God so *l*
Rev. 1:5, To Him who *l* us and

LOVELY
Ps. 84:1, *l* is Your tabernacle
Prov. 11:22, *l* woman who lacks
Song 5:16, he is altogether *l*
Phil. 4:8, whatever things are *l*

LOVER
Ti. 1:8, a *l* of what is good

LOVERS
2 Tim. 3:2, For men will be *l*

LOVES
Ps. 33:5, *l* righteousness
Ps. 34:12, life, and *l* many days
Prov. 17:17, A friend *l* at all
Mt. 10:37, "He who *l* father or
Jn. 12:25, *l* his life will lose
Jn. 14:21, *l* Me will be loved
2 Cor. 9:7, *l* a cheerful giver
Eph. 5:28, who *l* his wife *l*
1 Jn. 2:15, If anyone *l* the world
1 Jn. 4:21, *l* God must love his
1 Jn. 5:1, *l* him who is

LOVESICK
Song 2:5, apples, for I am *l*
Song 5:8, you tell him I am *l*

LOVINGKINDNESS
Ps. 40:10, not concealed Your *l*
Ps. 63:3, *l* is better than life
Ps. 92:2, to declare Your *l*
Jer. 31:3, *l* I have drawn

LOW
1 Sam. 2:7, He brings *l* and lifts
Ps. 49:2, both *l* and high
Isa. 26:5, it *l*, He lays it *l*
Lk. 3:5, and hill brought *l*

LOWER
Ps. 8:5, made him a little *l*
Ps. 63:9, shall go into the *l*
Heb. 2:7, made him a little *l*

LOWEST
Dan. 4:17, and sets over it the *l*

LOWLINESS
Eph. 4:2, with all *l* and
Phil. 2:3, or conceit, but in *l*

LOWLY
Ps. 138:6, yet He regards the *l*
Mt. 11:29, for I am gentle and *l*
Lk. 1:48, He has regarded the *l*
Lk. 1:52, and exalted the *l*
2 Cor. 10:1, in presence am *l*
Phil. 3:21, *l* body that it may be
Jas. 1:9, *l* brother glory

LOYAL
Mt. 6:24, or else he will be *l*

LUCIFER, Isa. 14:12

LUKE
the beloved physician, companion of Paul. Col. 4:14; 2 Tim. 4:11; Phile. 24 (Acts 16:12; 20:5)

LUKEWARM
Rev. 3:16, because you are *l*

LUMP
Rom. 9:21, from the same *l*
1 Cor. 5:7, you may be a new *l*

LUST
Prov. 6:25, Do not *l* after her
Prov. 11:6, caught by their *l*
Mt. 5:28, looks at a woman to *l*
Gal. 5:16, not fulfill the *l*
1 Th. 4:5, not in passion of *l*
Jas. 4:2, You *l* and do not have
1 Jn. 2:16, the *l* of the flesh

LUSTS
Rom. 13:14, to fulfill its *l*
1 Tim. 6:9, *l* which drown men
2 Tim. 2:22, also youthful *l*
Ti. 2:12, and worldly *l*
1 Pet. 1:14, to the former *l*
1 Pet. 2:11, abstain from fleshly *l*
Jude 18, to their own ungodly *l*

LUTE
Ps. 57:8, Awake, *l* and harp
Ps. 71:22, *l* I will praise You
Ps. 81:2, harp with the *l*
Ps. 92:3, ten strings, on the *l*
Ps. 108:2, Awake, *l* and harp
Ps. 150:3, Praise Him with the *l*

LUXURIOUSLY, Rev. 18:7,9

LUXURY
Prov. 19:10, *L* is not fitting
Lk. 7:25, *l* are in kings' courts
Jas. 5:5, in pleasure and *l*
Rev. 18:3, the abundance of her *l*

LYDDA
miracle at. Acts 9:32

LYDIA
of Thyatira, piety of. Acts 16:14,40

LYING
hateful to God. Prov. 6:16,19; 12:22
forbidden. Lev. 19:11; Col. 3:9
devil father of. Jn. 8:44; Acts 5:3

LYING
Ps. 119:163, I hate and abhor *l*
Prov. 13:5, righteous man hates *l*
Jer. 7:4, not trust in these *l*
Lk. 2:12, in swaddling cloths, *l*
Jn. 20:5, saw the linen cloths *l*
Eph. 4:25, putting away *l*
2 Th. 2:9, signs, and *l* wonders

LYSTRA, Acts 14:6
miracle at. Acts 14:8
Paul and Barnabas taken for gods at. Acts 14:11
Paul stoned at, by Jews. Acts 14:19

MAACAH (or Maachah), 2 Sam. 3:3
queen, her idolatry. 1 Ki. 15:13; 2 Chr. 15:16

MACEDONIA
Paul's mission there. Acts 16:9; 17
liberality of. 2 Cor. 8; 9; 11:9; Phil. 4:15
its churches. 1 and 2 Th.

MACHPELAH, Gen. 23:9
field of. Gen. 23
patriarchs buried there. Gen. 23:19; 25:9; 35:29; 49:30; 50:12

MAD
Jn. 10:20, has a demon and is *m*
Acts 26:25, he said, "I am not *m*

MADE
Gen. 1:16, *m* the stars also
Gen. 3:21, wife the LORD God *m*
Isa. 37:26, hear long ago how I *m*
Isa. 66:2, things My hand has *m*
Jn. 1:3, All things were *m*

MADNESS
David pretends. 1 Sam. 21:13
threatened. Dt. 28:28

MADNESS
1 Sam. 21:13, before them, *m*
Eccl. 1:17, wisdom and to know *m*
Eccl. 9:3, *m* is in their hearts

MAGDALA, Mt. 15:39

MAGDALENE, Mt. 27:56

MAGIC
Ezek. 13:18, women who sew *m*
Acts 19:19, *m* brought their books

MAGICIANS
of Egypt. Ex. 7:11; 8:19
of Chaldea, preserved. Dan. 2; 4:7

MAGISTRATES, Ezra 7:25
to be obeyed. Ex. 22:8; Rom. 13; Ti. 3:1; 1 Pet. 2:14

MAGNIFICENCE
Job 31:23, *m* I cannot endure

MAGNIFIED
2 Sam. 7:26, let Your name be *m*
Ps. 35:27, "Let the LORD be *m*
Ps. 138:2, for You have *m* Your
Acts 19:17, the Lord Jesus was *m*
Phil. 1:20, also Christ will be *m*

MAGNIFIES
Lk. 1:46, "My soul *m* the Lord

MAGNIFY
Ps. 34:3, *m* the LORD with me
Dan. 11:36, *m* himself above every

MAGOG
Gen. 10:2; Ezek. 38:2; Rev. 20:8

MAHANAIM, Gen. 32:2
Jacob's vision at. Gen. 32
Ishbosheth made king at. 2 Sam. 2:8
David takes refuge from Absalom at. 2 Sam. 17:24

MAHLON
and Chilion die in Moab. Ruth 1:2

MAIDENS
Ps. 148:12, Both young men and *m*
Prov. 9:3, She has sent out her *m*

MAIDSERVANT
Ruth 3:9, "I am Ruth, your *m*
Ps. 86:16, save the son of Your *m*
Lk. 1:38, "Behold the *m*
Lk. 1:48, lowly state of His *m*

MAIDSERVANTS
Nah. 2:7, *m* shall lead her as
Acts 2:18, *m* I will pour out My

MAIMED
Mk. 9:43, to enter into life *m*
Lk. 14:21, the poor and the *m*

MAINTAIN
1 Ki. 8:45, and *m* their cause

MAINTAINED
Ps. 9:4, For You have *m* my

MAJESTY
of God. 1 Chr. 29:11; Job 37:22; Ps. 93; 96; Isa. 24:14; Nah. 1; Hab. 3. *See* GOD
of Christ. 2 Pet. 1:16. *See* CHRIST

MAJESTY
Job 37:22, with God is awesome *m*
Ps. 145:5, splendor of Your *m*
Heb. 1:3, right hand of the *M*
2 Pet. 1:16, eyewitnesses of His *m*
Jude 25, wise, be glory and *m*

MAKE
Gen. 1:26, Let Us *m* man in Our
Gen. 11:4, let us *m* a name for
Gen. 12:2, *m* you a great nation
Ex. 20:4, "You shall not *m*
Jn. 14:23, *m* Our home with him

MAKER
Job 35:10, where is God my *M*
Isa. 17:7, man will look to his *M*
Isa. 45:9, who strives with his *M*
Isa. 54:5, *M* is your husband
Hos. 8:14, has forgotten his *M*
Heb. 11:10, builder and *m* is God

MALACHI
deplores and rebukes Israel's ingratitude. Mal. 1; 2
foretells the Messiah and His messenger. Mal. 3; 4

MALCHUS
Mt. 26:51; Mk. 14:47; Lk. 22:51; Jn. 18:10

MALICE
condemned. Prov. 17:5; 24:17; 1 Cor. 5:8; 14:20; Eph. 4:31; Col. 3:8; Ti. 3:3; Jas. 5:9; 1 Pet. 2:1

MALICE
1 Cor. 14:20, in *m* be babes
Ti. 3:3, pleasures, living in *m*
1 Pet. 2:1, laying aside all *m*

MALICIOUSNESS
Rom. 1:29, covetousness, *m*

MALIGN
Prov. 30:10, *m* a servant to his

MALTA
Paul shipwrecked near, and lands at. Acts 28:1
received kindly by the people. Acts 28:2
shakes off the viper at. Acts 28:5
heals Publius's father and others at. Acts 28:8–9

MAMMON, *see* MONEY

MAMRE
Abram dwells there. Gen. 13:18; 14; 18; 23:17; 35:27

MAN
created. Gen. 1:26; 2:7
his dignity. Gen. 1:27; 2:25; Eccl. 7:29
his fall. Gen. 3
his iniquity. Gen. 6:5,12; 1 Ki. 8:46; Job 14:16; 15:14; Ps. 14; 51; Eccl. 9:3; Isa. 43:27; 53:6; Jer. 3:25; 17:9; Jn. 3:19; Rom. 3:9; 5:12; 7:18; Gal. 3:10; 5:17; Jas. 1:13; 1 Jn. 1:8
his imperfection and weakness. 2 Chr. 20:12; Mt. 6:27; Rom. 9:16; 1 Cor.3:7; 2 Cor. 3:5
liable to suffering. Job 5:7; 14:1; Ps. 39:4; Eccl. 3:2; Acts 14:22; Rom. 8:22; Rev. 7:14
his ignorance. Job 8:9; 11:12; 28:12; Prov. 16:25; 27:1; Eccl. 8:17; Isa. 59:10; 1 Cor. 1:20; 8:2 (Isa. 47:10); Jas. 4:14
his mortality. Job 14; Ps. 39; 49; 62:9; 78:39; 89:48; 103:14; 144:4; 146:3; Eccl. 1:4; 12:7; Rom. 5:12; Heb. 9:27
vanity of his life. Ps. 49; Eccl. 1; 2
his whole duty. Eccl. 12:13; Mic. 6:8; 1 Jn. 3:23
his redemption. Rom. 5; 1 Cor. 15:49; Gal. 3; 4; Eph. 3; 5:25; Phil. 3:21; Col. 1; Heb. 1; 2; Rev. 5

MAN
Gen. 1:26, "Let Us make *m*
2 Sam. 12:7, "You are the *m*
Job 7:17, "What is *m*
Job 11:12, For an empty-headed *m*
Job 15:7, "Are you the first *m*
Ps. 8:4, *m* that You are mindful
Ps. 118:6, What can *m* do to me
Mt. 24:27, coming of the Son of *M*
Jn. 19:5, "Behold the *M*
1 Cor. 11:8, *m* is not from woman
1 Cor. 15:21, since by *m* came death
2 Cor. 4:16, though our outward *m*
Eph. 2:15, in Himself one new *m*
2 Tim. 3:17, the *m* of God may
Rev. 13:18, is the number of a *m*

MANASSEH
firstborn son of Joseph. Gen. 41:51
his blessing. Gen. 48
his descendants numbered, etc. Num. 1:34; 26:29; Josh. 22:1; 1 Chr. 5:23; 7:14
their inheritance. Num. 32:33; 34:14; Josh. 13:29; 17
incline to David's cause. 1 Chr. 9:3; 12:19; 2 Chr. 15:9; 30:11
——— king of Judah, his reign. 2 Ki. 21; 2 Chr. 33

MANGER
Job 39:9, Will he bed by your *m*
Lk. 2:7, and laid Him in a *m*
Lk. 2:16, the Babe lying in a *m*

MANIFEST
Jn. 14:21, *m* Myself to him
Jn. 14:22, is it that You will *m*

MANIFESTATION
1 Cor. 12:7, But the *m* of the
2 Cor. 4:2, deceitfully, but by *m*

MANIFESTED
Jn. 17:6, "I have *m* Your name
1 Tim. 3:16, God was *m* in the flesh
1 Jn. 1:2, the life was *m*
1 Jn. 4:9, the love of God was *m*

MANIFOLD
Ps. 104:24, *m* are Your works
Eph. 3:10, the *m* wisdom of God
1 Pet. 4:10, good stewards of the *m*

MANNA
promised. Ex. 16:4
sent. Ex. 16:14; Dt. 8:3; Neh. 9:20; Ps. 78:24; Jn. 6:31
fed to Israelites in wilderness. Ex. 16:31
an omer of it laid up in the ark. Ex. 16:32; Heb. 9:4
Israelites complain about it. Num. 11:6
it ceases on entering Canaan. Josh. 5:12
——— the hidden. Rev. 2:17

MANNA
Ex. 16:35, of Israel ate *m*
Ps. 78:24, had rained down *m*
Jn. 6:31, Our fathers ate the *m*
Rev. 2:17, of the hidden *m*

MANNER
2 Sam. 7:19, Is this the *m* of man
1 Cor. 11:27, in an unworthy *m*
2 Cor. 7:11, sorrowed in a godly *m*
Heb. 10:25, as is the *m* of some
2 Pet. 3:11, what *m* of persons
1 Jn. 3:1, Behold what *m* of love
3 Jn. 6, *m* worthy of God

MANOAH
father of Samson. Jud. 13; 16:31

MANSIONS
Jn. 14:2, house are many *m*

MANSLAUGHTER
Gen. 9:6; Ex. 21:12; Num. 35:6,11,22; Dt. 4:42; 19:3,4; Josh. 20:3; 21; 1 Tim. 1:9

MANTLE
2 Ki. 2:14, Then he took the *m*

MARAH
bitter waters healed there. Ex. 15:23

MARCHED
Ps. 68:7, people, when You *m*

MARK
evangelist. Acts 12:12

goes with Paul and Barnabas. Acts 12:25; 13:5
leaves them at Perga. Acts 13:13
contention about him. Acts 15:37
approved by Paul. 2 Tim. 4:11

MARK
Gen. 4:15, And the LORD set a *m*
Ps. 37:37, *M* the blameless man
Rev. 13:16, slave, to receive a *m*
Rev. 14:11, whoever receives the *m*

MARKET
1 Cor. 10:25, is sold in the meat *m*

MARRED
Isa. 52:14, so His visage was *m*
Jer. 18:4, he made of clay was *m*

MARRIAGE
instituted. Gen. 2:18
honorable. Ps. 128; Prov. 31:10; Heb. 13:4
its obligations. Mt. 19:4; Rom. 7:2; 1 Cor. 6:16; 7:10; Eph. 5:31
parables concerning. Mt. 22; 25
belongs to this world only. Mt. 22:30; Mk. 12:23
at Cana, miracle at. Jn. 2
Paul's opinion of. 1 Cor. 7; 1 Tim. 5:14
of the Lamb, typical. Rev. 19:7
unlawful marriages. Lev. 18; Dt. 7:3; Josh. 23:12; Ezra 9; 10; Neh. 13:23

MARRIAGE
Mt. 22:30, nor are given in *m*
1 Cor. 7:38, her in *m* does well
Heb. 13:4, *M* is honorable among
Rev. 19:7, the *m* of the Lamb has

MARRIED
Jer. 3:14, "for I am *m* to you
1 Cor. 7:33, But he who is *m*
1 Cor. 7:34, But she who is *m*

MARROW
Heb. 4:12, and of joints and *m*

MARRY
Mt. 19:10, it is better not to *m*
Mt. 22:30, they neither *m* nor
1 Cor. 7:9, let them *m*
1 Tim. 4:3, forbidding to *m*
1 Tim. 5:14, the younger widows *m*

MARRYING
Mt. 24:38, and drinking, *m*

MARTHA
instructed by Christ. Jn. 11:5,21
rebuked by Him. Lk. 10:38

MARTYR
Stephen the first. Acts. 7; 22:20. *See* Rev. 2:13; 17:6

MARTYR
Acts 22:20, *m* Stephen was shed
Rev. 2:13, was My faithful *m*

MARTYRS
Rev. 17:6, the blood of the *m*

MARVEL
Jn. 5:28, "Do not *m* at this

MARVELED
Mt. 8:10, Jesus heard it, He *m*
Mt. 9:33, And the multitudes *m*
Mk. 15:5, so that Pilate *m*
Rev. 13:3, And all the world *m*
Rev. 17:6, when I saw her, I *m*

MARVELOUS
Ps. 78:12, *m* things He did
Ps. 118:23, It is *m* in our eyes
Ps. 139:14, *M* are Your works
1 Pet. 2:9, of darkness into His *m*

MARVELS
Ex. 34:10, people I will do *m*

MARY
Greek form of Miriam. Mt. 1:16
the Virgin, mother of Jesus, visited by the angel Gabriel. Lk. 1:26
believes, and magnifies the Lord. Lk. 1:38,46; Jn. 2:5
Christ born of. Mt. 1:18; Lk. 2
witnesses the miracle at Cana. Jn. 2:1
desires to speak with Christ. Mt. 12:46; Mk. 3:31; Lk. 8:19
commended to John by Christ at His crucifixion. Mt. 27:56; Jn. 19:25
——— of Bethany, sister of Martha and Lazarus. Lk. 10:39,43; Jn. 11:1,2,19; 12:3
——— mother of James, the apostle, and wife of Clopas. Mk. 15:40; Lk. 24:9,10; Jn. 19:25
——— mother of John Mark and sister of Barnabas. Acts 12:12
——— of Rome. Rom. 16:6

MARY MAGDALENE, Lk. 8:2

MASTER
Gen. 24:9, of Abraham his *m*
Mt. 10:25, a servant like his *m*
Jn. 15:20, greater than his *m*
1 Cor. 3:10, *m* builder I have laid
2 Tim. 2:21, and useful for the *M*

MASTERS
Isa. 26:13, *m* besides You have
Lk. 16:13, can serve two *m*
Col. 4:1, *M*, give your bondservants
1 Tim. 6:2, who have believing *m*

MATTER
Job 19:28, *m* is found in me
Prov. 18:13, He who answers a *m*

MATTERS
Mt. 23:23, the weightier *m*
1 Cor. 6:2, judge the smallest *m*

MATTHEW (Levi)
apostle and evangelist, called. Mt. 9:9; Mk. 2:14; Lk. 5:27
sent out. Mt. 10:3; Mk. 3:18; Lk. 6:15; Acts 1:13

MATTHIAS, Acts 1:23; 26

MATURE
1 Cor. 14:20, understanding be *m*
Phil. 3:15, us, as many as are *m*
1 Cor. 2:6, among those who are *m*

MEAN
Ex. 12:26, "What do you *m*

MEANING
Dt. 6:20, 'What is the *m*
1 Cor. 14:11, if I do not know the *m*

MEANT
Gen. 50:20, but God *m* it for good

MEASURE
Dt. 25:15, a perfect and just *m*
Job 28:25, apportion the waters by *m*
Mic. 6:10, and the short *m*
Jn. 3:34, give the Spirit by *m*
Rom. 12:3, to each one a *m*
Rev. 11:1, *m* the temple of God

MEASURED
Isa. 40:12, *m* the waters in the
Mt. 7:2, you use, it will be *m*
Rev. 21:17, Then he *m* its wall

MEASURES
Dt. 25:14, your house differing *m*
Prov. 20:10, weights and diverse *m*

MEASURING
of the holy city, and New Jerusalem. Ezek. 40; Zech. 2:1; Rev. 11:1; 21:15

MEASURING
Ezek. 40:5, the man's hand was a *m*
Zech. 2:1, behold, a man with a *m*
2 Cor. 10:12, *m* themselves by
Rev. 11:1, given a reed like a *m*

MEAT
Ps. 78:20, Can He provide *m*
Ps. 78:27, He also rained *m*
Rom. 14:21, good neither to eat *m*
1 Cor. 8:13, will never again eat *m*
1 Cor. 10:25, is sold in the *m*

MEATS
clean and unclean. Lev. 11; Dt. 14; Acts 15:29; Rom. 14; 1 Cor. 8:4; Col. 2:16; 1 Tim. 4:3

MEDDLE
2 Ki. 14:10, why should you *m*

MEDES, 2 Ki. 17:6
capture Babylon. (Isa. 21:2); Dan. 5:28,31

MEDIA, Est. 1:3
Israel taken captive to. 2 Ki. 17:6; 18:11; Est. 2:6
Daniel's prophecy of. Dan. 8:20

MEDIATE
Gal. 3:20, a mediator does not *m*

MEDIATOR
one. Gal. 3:19,20; 1 Tim. 2:5; Heb. 8:6; 9:15
Jesus the. Heb. 12:24

MEDIATOR
Job 9:33, Nor is there any *m*
Gal. 3:19, by the hand of a *m*
1 Tim. 2:5, is one God and one *M*
Heb. 8:6, as He is also *M*
Heb. 12:24, to Jesus the *M* of the

MEDICINE
Prov. 17:22, does good, like *m*

MEDICINES
Jer. 46:11, you will use many *m*

MEDITATE
Gen. 24:63, Isaac went out to *m*
Josh. 1:8, but you shall *m*
Ps. 4:4, *M* within your heart on
Ps. 77:6, I *m* within my heart
Ps. 119:15, I will *m* on Your
Isa. 33:18, Your heart will *m*
Lk. 21:14, *m* beforehand on what
Phil. 4:8, *m* on these things

MEDITATES
Ps. 1:2, in His law he *m*

MEDITATION
encouraged. Ps. 1:2; 19:14; 77:12; 107:43; 119:97
injunctions to. Josh. 1:8; Ps. 4:4; Prov. 4:26; 1 Tim. 4:15. *See* Gen. 24:63

MEDITATION
Ps. 19:14, of my mouth and the *m*
Ps. 104:34, *m* be sweet to Him
Ps. 119:97, It is my *m* all the day

MEDIUM
Lev. 20:27, a woman who is a *m*
1 Sam. 28:7, me a woman who is a *m*

MEDIUM'S
Isa. 29:4, shall be like a *m*

MEDIUMS
Isa. 8:19, Seek those who are *m*

MEEK
Isa. 11:4, with equity for the *m*
Mt. 5:5, Blessed are the *m*

MEEKNESS
Christ an example of. Mt. 11:29; Lk. 23:34; 2 Cor. 10:1 (Isa. 53:2; Jn. 18:19)
exhortations to. Zeph. 2:3; Gal. 5:23; 6:1; Eph. 4:2; Phil. 2:2; Col. 3:12; 1 Tim. 6:11; 2 Tim. 2:25; Ti. 3:2; Jas. 1:21; 3:13; 1 Pet. 3:4,15
blessed by God. Ps. 22:26; 25:9; 37:11 (Mt. 5:5); 69:32; 76:9; 147:6; 149:4; Isa. 11:4; 29:19; 61:1
examples of: Moses. Num. 12:3; David. 2 Sam. 16:9; Jeremiah. Jer. 26:14

MEEKNESS
2 Cor. 10:1, with you by the *m*
Jas. 3:13, are done in the *m*

MEET
Ps. 21:3, For You *m* him with the
Amos 4:12, prepare to *m* your God
Mt. 25:6, go out to *m* him
1 Th. 4:17, *m* the Lord in the air

MEETING
Ex. 27:21, In the tabernacle of *m*
Ps. 74:8, burned up all the *m*

MEGIDDO
Josh. 12:21; 17:11; Jud. 1:27; 5:19
Ahaziah and Josiah killed there. 2 Ki. 9:27; 23:29; Zech. 12:11

MEHETABEL
Gen. 36:39; Neh. 6:10

MELCHIZEDEK
king of Salem, blesses Abram. Gen. 14:18
his priesthood and Aaron's. Ps. 110:4; Heb. 5:6,10; 6:20; 7:1

MELODY
Isa. 23:16, make sweet *m*
Eph. 5:19, singing and making *m*

MELT
Ps. 39:11, You make his beauty *m*
Isa. 13:7, man's heart will *m*
2 Pet. 3:10, the elements will *m*

MEMBER
1 Cor. 12:14, body is not one *m*
Jas. 3:5, tongue is a little *m*

MEMBERS
Mt. 5:29, you that one of your *m*
Rom. 6:13, do not present your *m*
1 Cor. 6:15, that your bodies are *m*
Eph. 4:25, neighbor, for we are *m*

MEMORIAL
Ex. 3:15, and this is My *m*
Mt. 26:13, also be told as a *m*
Mk. 14:9, be told of as a *m*

MEMORY
Job 18:17, The *m* of him perishes
Ps. 109:15, He may cut off the *m*
Prov. 10:7, The *m* of the righteous

MEMPHIS, *see also* NOPH
in Egypt. Hos. 9:6

MEN
Gen. 4:26, *m* began to call on the
Gen. 6:2, saw the daughters of *m*
Ps. 82:7, you shall die like *m*
Isa. 31:3, the Egyptians are *m*
Mt. 4:19, make you fishers of *m*
Lk. 2:14, goodwill toward *m*
Lk. 20:4, heaven or from *m*
Rom. 1:27, Likewise also the *m*
1 Cor. 3:21, let no one boast in *m*
Eph. 6:7, the Lord, and not to *m*
1 Tim. 2:5, between God and *m*

MENAHEM
king of Israel, his evil rule. 2 Ki. 15:14,18

MENE, TEKEL, UPHARSIN
Dan. 5:25–28

MENSERVANTS
Joel 2:29, And also on My *m*
Acts 2:18, And on My *m* and on

MENTION
Ps. 71:16, I will make *m* of Your
Isa. 26:13, by You only we make *m*
Isa. 62:6, You who make *m* of the
Heb. 11:22, he was dying, made *m*

MEPHIBOSHETH
son of Jonathan, his lameness. 2 Sam. 4:4
cared for by David. 2 Sam. 9:1
slandered by Ziba. 2 Sam. 16:1; 19:24
spared by David. 2 Sam. 21:7

MERAB
Saul's daughter. 1 Sam. 14:49; 18:17
her five sons hanged. 2 Sam. 21:8

MERARITES
descendants of Levi. Ex. 6:19; 1 Chr. 6:1; 23:21; 24:26
their duties and dwellings. Num. 4:29; 7:8; 10:17; Josh. 21:7; 1 Chr. 6:63

MERCHANDISE
Prov. 31:18, perceives that her *m*
Jn. 2:16, house a house of *m*

MERCHANTS
Ezek. 17:4, set it in a city of *m*
Nah. 3:16, have multiplied your *m*
Rev. 18:23, *m* were the great men

MERCIES
2 Sam. 24:14, for His *m* are great
Ps. 145:9, and His tender *m*
Acts 13:34, give you the sure *m*
2 Cor. 1:3, the Father of *m*

MERCIFUL
Ex. 34:6, LORD, the LORD God, *m*
Ps. 37:26, He is ever *m*
Ps. 67:1, God be *m* to us and
Mt. 5:7, Blessed are the *m*
Lk. 18:13, saying, 'God be *m*
Heb. 8:12, For I will be *m*
Jas. 5:11, compassionate and *m*

MERCY
supplication for. Dt. 21:8; 1 Ki. 8:30; Neh. 9:32; Ps. 51; Dan. 9:16; Hab. 3:2; Mt. 6:12
injunctions to show. Prov. 3:3; Zech. 7:9; Lk. 6:36; Rom. 12:19 (Prov. 25:21); Phil. 2:1; Col. 3:12; Jas. 2:13
of God. Ps. 78:38; 103:9; Isa. 30:18; 54:7; Lam. 3:32

MERCY
Ex. 20:6, but showing *m* to
Num. 14:18, and abundant in *m*
1 Chr. 16:34, *m* endures forever
Ps. 25:7, to Your *m* remember me
Ps. 52:8, I trust in the *m*
Ps. 57:3, shall send forth His *m*
Ps. 62:12, You, O Lord, belongs *m*
Ps. 77:8, *m* ceased forever
Ps. 85:10, *M* and truth have met
Ps. 89:2, *M* shall be built
Ps. 89:14, *m* and truth go before
Ps. 100:5, *m* is everlasting
Ps. 101:1, I will sing of *m*
Ps. 108:4, For Your *m* is great
Ps. 119:64, is full of Your *m*
Ps. 130:7, the LORD there is *m*
Prov. 3:3, Let not *m* and truth
Prov. 14:31, who honors Him has *m*
Jer. 6:23, cruel and have no *m*
Dan. 9:9, Lord our God belong *m*
Hos. 6:6, For I desire *m* and not
Mic. 6:8, do justly, to love *m*
Mt. 9:13, 'I desire *m* and not
Lk. 1:50, And His *m* is on those
Rom. 9:15, "I will have *m*
Rom. 9:16, of God who shows *m*
Rom. 11:32, that He might have *m*
1 Cor. 7:25, *m* has made trustworthy
2 Cor. 4:1, as we have received *m*
Eph. 2:4, God, who is rich in *m*
1 Tim. 1:13, but I obtained *m*
2 Tim. 1:18, that he may find *m*

Ti. 3:5, to His *m* He saved us
Heb. 4:16, that we may obtain *m*
Jas. 2:13, judgment is without *m*
Jude 21, God, looking for the *m*

MERCY SEAT
described. Ex. 25:17; 26:34; 37:6; Lev. 16:13; 1 Chr. 28:11; Heb. 9:5

MERIBAH
Israel rebels there. Ex. 17:7; Num. 20:13; 27:14; Dt. 32:51; 33:8; Ps. 81:7

MERRY
Prov. 15:13, *m* heart makes a
Eccl. 8:15, eat, drink, and be *m*
Lk. 15:32, we should make *m*

MESHACH
Dan. 1:7. *See* SHADRACH

MESHECH
son of Japheth. Gen. 10:2
traders of. Ezek. 27:13; 32:26; 38:2; 39:1

MESOPOTAMIA
(Ur), country of the two rivers; Abram leaves. Gen. 11:31; 12:1; 24:4,10. *See* Acts 2:9; 7:2
king of, defeated by Othniel. Jud. 3:8

MESSAGE
Jer. 49:14, I have heard a *m*
1 Cor. 1:18, For the *m* of the cross

MESSENGER, Job 33:23
of the covenant. Mal. 3:1; Isa. 42:19

MESSENGER
Prov. 25:13, is a faithful *m*
Mal. 3:1, "Behold, I send My *m*
Mt. 11:10, 'Behold, I send My *m*

MESSIAH
(anointed Christ). Isa. 9:6
Prince, prophecy about. Dan. 9:25

MESSIAH
Dan. 9:25, until *M* the Prince
Jn. 1:41, "We have found the *M*

METHUSELAH, Gen. 5:21
his great age. Gen. 5:27

MICAH, Jud. 17:1
makes and worships idols. Jud. 17; 18
——— prophet (Jer. 26:18); denounces Israel's sin. Mic. 1—3; 6; 7
predicts the Messiah. Mic. 4; 5; 7

MICAIAH (or Michaiah), Neh. 12:35
forewarns Ahab. 1 Ki. 22; 2 Chr. 18; Neh. 12:35

MICHAEL, Dan. 10:13,21; 12:1
Archangel. Jude 9; Rev. 12:7

MICHAL, 1 Sam. 14:49
David's wife. 1 Sam. 18:20
given to another. 1 Sam. 25:44
restored to David. 2 Sam. 3:13
mocks his religious dancing, and is rebuked. 2 Sam. 6:16,20; 1 Chr. 15:29

MIDIAN, Gen. 25:2
sons of. Gen. 25:4
——— land of. Ex. 2:15. *See* 1 Ki. 11:18; Isa. 60:6; Hab. 3:7

MIDIANITES, Gen. 37:28
their cities destroyed by Moses. Num. 31:1
subdued by Gideon. Jud. 6—8. *See* Ps. 83:9; Isa. 9:4; 10:26

MIDST
Ps. 46:5, God is in the *m*
Joel 2:27, that I am in the *m*
Mt. 18:20, I am there in the *m*

MIDWIVES
of Egypt. Ex. 1:16,20

MIGHT
Dt. 8:17, 'My power and the *m*
Ps. 145:6, shall speak of the *m*
Isa. 40:26, the greatness of His *m*
Jer. 9:23, man glory in his *m*
Jer. 51:30, their *m* has failed
Zech. 4:6, 'Not by *m* nor by
Eph. 6:10, in the power of His *m*
2 Pet. 2:11, greater in power and *m*
Rev. 7:12, honor and power and *m*

MIGHTIER
Mt. 3:11, coming after me is *m*

MIGHTILY
Isa. 2:19, to shake the earth *m*
Col. 1:29, which works in me *m*

MIGHTY
Gen. 10:9, He was a *m* hunter
Num. 22:6, for they are too *m*
2 Sam. 1:19, How the *m* have fallen
Job 9:4, is wise in heart and *m*
Ps. 24:8, The LORD *m* in battle
Prov. 23:11, their Redeemer is *m*
Isa. 5:22, Woe to men *m* at
Jer. 32:19, great in counsel and *m*
Nah. 2:3, *m* men are made red
Lk. 1:49, *m* has done great
Lk. 1:52, He has put down the *m*
1 Cor. 1:26, the flesh, not many *m*
Eph. 1:19, the working of His *m*
2 Th. 1:7, from heaven with His *m*

MILCAH, Gen. 11:29; 22:20

MILCOM, same as Moloch
false god. 1 Ki. 11:5,33; 2 Ki. 23:13

MILETUS, Acts 20:15; 2 Tim. 4:20

MILK
and honey. Josh. 5:6; Isa. 55:1
mentioned. Song 4:11; Isa. 7:22; 1 Cor. 3:2; Heb. 5:12; 1 Pet. 2:2

MILK
Jud. 5:25, for water, she gave *m*
Song 4:11, honey and *m* are under
Isa. 55:1, come, buy wine and *m*
Lam. 4:7, and whiter than *m*
Joel 3:18, shall flow with *m*
Heb. 5:12, have come to need *m*
Heb. 5:13, *m* is unskilled in the
1 Pet. 2:2, desire the pure *m*

MILL
Mt. 24:41, be grinding at the *m*

MILLSTONE
Mt. 18:6, *m* were hung around
Rev. 18:21, a stone like a great *m*

MILLSTONES
Ex. 11:5; Mt. 24:41

MIND
Rom. 8:5; Phil. 3:16,19
devoted to God. Mt. 22:37; Mk. 12:30; Rom. 7:25
a willing. 1 Chr. 28:9; Neh. 4:6; 2 Cor. 8:12
united. 1 Cor. 1:10; 2 Cor. 13:11; Phil. 2:2; 1 Pet. 3:8. *See* Heb. 8:10

MIND
Job 38:36, put wisdom in the *m*
Isa. 26:3, perfect peace, whose *m*
Lk. 12:29, nor have an anxious *m*
Rom. 7:25, *m* I myself serve the
Rom. 11:34, who has known the *m*
Rom. 12:16, Be of the same *m*
Rom. 14:5, convinced in his own *m*
1 Cor. 2:16, "Who has known the *m*
1 Cor. 14:23, are out of your *m*
Phil. 2:5, Let this *m* be in you
1 Th. 4:11, to *m* your own
2 Tim. 1:7, love and of a sound *m*

MINDFUL
Ps. 8:4, is man that You are *m*
Ps. 115:12, The LORD has been *m*
Mt. 16:23, for you are not *m*
Heb. 2:6, is man that You are *m*

MINDS
Ex. 13:17, people change their *m*
Jer. 31:33, put My law in their *m*
2 Pet. 3:1, I stir up your pure *m*
Rev. 2:23, He who searches the *m*

MINISTER
Acts 26:16, to make you a *m*
Rom. 13:4, for he is God's *m*
1 Tim. 4:6, you will be a good *m*
Heb. 8:2, a *M* of the sanctuary

MINISTERED
1 Sam. 2:11, But the child *m*
Dan. 7:10, a thousand thousands *m*
Acts 13:2, As they *m* to the Lord

MINISTERING SPIRITS
Heb. 1:14. *See* Rom. 15:25,27

MINISTERS
God's. Ps. 103:21; 104:4; Heb. 1:7
(priests). Ex. 28; Heb. 10:11
worthy of honor and obedience. 1 Th. 5:12,13; 1 Tim. 5:17; Heb. 13:17
Christ's. 1 Cor. 3:5; 4:1; 2 Cor. 3:6; 6; Eph. 3:7; 6:21
how qualified. 1 Tim. 3; Ti. 1; 1 Pet. 5

MINISTERS
Ps. 104:4, angels spirits, His *m*
Rom. 13:6, for they are God's *m*
2 Cor. 6:4, commend ourselves as *m*
2 Cor. 11:23, Are they *m* of Christ
1 Pet. 4:11, If anyone *m*

MINISTRIES
1 Cor. 12:5, are differences of *m*

MINISTRY
of the Gospel. Acts 6:4; 20:24; Rom. 12:7; 1 Cor. 16:15; 2 Cor. 3:7; 4:1;

5:18; 9:13; Eph. 6:21; Col. 1:7; 4:17; 1 Tim. 1:12

MINISTRY
Rom. 11:13, I magnify my *m*
2 Cor. 3:7, But if the *m* of death
2 Cor. 4:1, since we have this *m*
2 Cor. 5:18, has given us the *m*
Eph. 4:12, for the work of *m*
Col. 4:17, *m* which you have
2 Tim. 4:5, fulfill your *m*
Heb. 8:6, a more excellent *m*

MINT
Mt. 23:23, For you pay tithe of *m*

MIRACLE
Ex. 7:9, saying, 'Show a *m*
Mk. 9:39, no one who works a *m*
Acts 4:16, that a notable *m*

MIRACLES
performed by: Moses and Aaron at God's command. Ex. 4:3; 7:10; 7—12; 14:21; 15:25; 17:6; Num. 16:28; 20:11; 21:8
Joshua. Josh. 3; 4; 6; 10:12
Samson. Jud. 14—16
Samuel. 1 Sam. 12:18
a prophet. 1 Ki. 13:4
Elijah. 1 Ki. 17; 18; 2 Ki. 1:10–12
Elisha. 2 Ki. 2—6; 13:21
Isaiah. 2 Ki. 20:9
the disciples. Lk. 10:17
Peter. Acts 3; 5; 9:32
Stephen. Acts 6:8
Philip. Acts 8:6
Paul. Acts 13; 14; 16; 19; 20; 28
sorcerers and evil spirits. Ex. 7:11; 8:7; Mt. 24:24; 2 Th. 2:9; Rev. 13:14; 16:14; 19:20

MIRACLES
Acts 19:11, God worked unusual *m*
1 Cor. 12:10, the working of *m*
1 Cor. 12:29, Are all workers of *m*
Heb. 2:4, with various *m*

MIRIAM
sister of Moses and Aaron. Ex. 15:20; Num. 12:1,10,15; 20:1; 26:59

MIRTH
Eccl. 2:1, I will test you with *m*
Eccl. 7:4, is in the house of *m*
Isa. 24:11, joy is darkened, the *m*

MISER
Prov. 23:6, eat the bread of a *m*

MISERABLE
Job 16:2; Mt. 21:41; Rev. 3:17

MISERIES
Jas. 5:1, *m* that are coming

MISERY
Job 11:16, would forget your *m*
Prov. 31:7, and remember his *m*

MISTREATED
Dt. 26:6, But the Egyptians *m*
Heb. 13:3, those who are *m*

MISTREATS
Prov. 19:26, *m* his father and

MITES
Lk. 21:2, widow putting in two *m*

MIZPAH (Gilead)
(a lookout), Jacob and Laban meet at. Gen. 31:49
Jephthah at. Jud. 10:17; 11:11; 20:1
Samuel at. 1 Sam. 7:5
——— (Moab). 1 Sam. 22:3

MOAB, Gen. 19:37
his descendants, and territory. Dt. 2:9,18; 34:5

MOABITES, Dt. 2:9
excluded from the congregation. Dt. 23:3
conquered by: Ehud. Jud. 3:12; David. 2 Sam. 8:2; Jehoshaphat and Jehoram. 2 Ki. 1:1; 3
their overthrow. 2 Chr. 20:23
prophecies concerning. Ex. 15:15; Num. 21:29 24:17; Ps. 60:8; 83:6; Isa. 11:14; 15; 16; 25:10; Jer. 9:26; 25:21; 48; Ezek. 25:8; Amos 2:1; Zeph. 2:8

MOABITESS, Ruth 4:5

MOAN
Isa. 59:11, *m* sadly like doves

MOCK
Prov. 1:26, I will *m* when your
Prov. 14:9, Fools *m* at sin
Mt. 20:19, to the Gentiles to *m*

MOCKED
1 Ki. 18:27, at noon, that Elijah *m*
Job 12:4, "I am one *m* by his
Mt. 27:29, knee before Him and *m*
Gal. 6:7, deceived, God is not *m*

MOCKER
Prov. 20:1, Wine is a *m*

MOCKERS
Jude 18, that there would be *m*

MOCKINGS
Heb. 11:36, others had trial of *m*

MOCKS
Prov. 17:5, He who *m* the poor

MODERATION
1 Tim. 2:9, with propriety and *m*

MOLDY, Josh. 9:5,12

MOLECH, Lev. 18:21; 20:2
worship of. 1 Ki. 11:7; 2 Ki. 23:10; Jer. 32:35

MOLOCH, Acts 7:43

MOMENT
Num. 16:21, consume them in a *m*
Job 34:20, In a *m* they die
Isa. 54:8, face from you for a *m*
1 Cor. 15:52, in a *m*, in the
2 Cor. 4:17, which is but for a *m*

MONEY
Ps. 15:5, does not put out his *m*
Eccl. 10:19, *m* answers every
Isa. 52:3, be redeemed without *m*
Isa. 55:1, and you who have no *m*
Mt. 25:18, and hid his lord's *m*
Mk. 14:11, promised to give him *m*
Lk. 10:4, "Carry neither *m*
Lk. 22:35, I sent you without *m*
Acts 8:20, be purchased with *m*
1 Tim. 3:3, not greedy for *m*
1 Tim. 6:10, *m* is a root of all
Ti. 1:7, not greedy for *m*

MONEYCHANGERS
Mt. 21:12, the tables of the *m*
Jn. 2:14, *m* doing business

MONSTER
Jer. 51:34, me up like a *m*
Ezek. 29:3, of Egypt, O great *m*

MONTHS
of the Hebrews. Ex. 12:2; 13:4; Dt. 16:1; 1 Ki. 6:1; 8:2
of the Chaldeans. Neh. 1:1; 2:1

MOON
the lesser light. Gen. 1:16
referred to. Dt. 33:14; Josh. 10:12; Ps. 8:3; 89:37; 104:19; 121:6
idolatrously worshiped. Dt. 17:3; Job 31:26; Jer. 44:17
feasts of the new. 1 Sam. 20:5; 1 Chr. 23:31; Ps. 81:3; Isa. 1:13; Hos. 2:11

MOON
Ps. 72:7, until the *m* is no more
Song 6:10, morning, fair as the *m*
Joel 2:10, sun and *m* grow dark
Mk. 13:24, *m* will not give its

MORDECAI, Est. 2:5
reveals conspiracy against King Ahasuerus. Est. 2:21
is hated by Haman. Est. 3:5
honored by the king. Est. 6
advanced. Est. 8—10 (Ezra 2:2; Neh. 7:7)

MORIAH, Gen. 22:2
Mount. Gen. 22
David's sacrifice there. 2 Sam. 24:18; 1 Chr. 21:18; 22:1
temple built on. 2 Chr. 3:1

MORNING
Job 41:18, the eyelids of the *m*
Ps. 55:17, Evening and *m* and at
Ps. 139:9, the wings of the *m*
Song 6:10, looks forth as the *m*
Isa. 14:12, Lucifer, son of the *m*
Hos. 6:3, established as the *m*
Lk. 24:1, very early in the *m*
Rev. 22:16, the Bright and *M* Star

MORSEL
Job 31:17, or eaten my *m* by
Prov. 17:1, Better is a dry *m*
Heb. 12:16, Esau, who for one *m*

MORTAL
Rom. 6:12, sin reign in your *m*
1 Cor. 15:53, and this *m* must put

MORTALITY
of man. Job 19:26; Rom. 8:11; 1 Cor. 15:53; 2 Cor. 4:11; 5:4

MORTALS
Ps. 26:4, with idolatrous *m*

MOSES
born, and hidden. Ex. 2 (Acts 7:20; Heb. 11:23)
escapes to Midian. Ex. 2:15
revelation from God. Ex. 3; confirmed by signs. Ex. 4
returns to Egypt. Ex. 4:20
intercedes with Pharaoh for Israel. Ex. 5—12
leads Israel out. Ex. 14
meets God at Mount Sinai. Ex. 19:3 (24:18)
brings the law to the people. Ex. 19:25; 20—23; 34:10; 35:1; Lev. 1; Num. 5; 6; 15; 27—30; 36; Dt. 12—26
instructed to build the tabernacle. Ex. 25—31; 35:40; Num. 4; 8—10; 18; 19
his grief at Israel's idolatry. Ex. 32:19
his intercession. Ex. 32:11 (33:12)
again meets God at the mount. Ex. 34:2
skin of his face shines. Ex. 34:29 (2 Cor. 3:7,13)
sets apart Aaron. Lev. 8; 9
numbers the people. Num. 1; 26
sends out the spies to Canaan. Num. 13
intercedes for the complaining people. Num. 14:13
Korah's sedition against. Num. 16
for his unbelief not allowed to enter Canaan. Num. 20:12; 27:12; Dt. 1:35; 3:23
his government of Israel in the wilderness. Num. 20; 21
makes the bronze serpent. Num. 21:9 (Jn. 3:14)
recounts Israel's history, and exhorts to obedience. Dt. 1; 3—12; 27—31
his charge to Joshua. Dt. 3:28; 31:7,23
his death. Dt. 34:5; his body. Jude 9
seen at Christ's transfiguration. Mt. 17:3; Mk. 9:4; Lk. 9:30
his meekness. Num. 12:3; dignity. Dt. 34:10; faithfulness. Num. 12:7; Heb. 3:2

MOST
Song 5:16, His mouth is *m* sweet
Jude 20, on your *m* holy faith

MOTH
Isa. 50:9, *m* will eat them
Mt. 6:19, where *m* and rust

MOTHER
Gen. 3:20, because she was the *m*
Ps. 113:9, like a joyful *m*
Song 6:9, the only one of her *m*
Jer. 20:17, *m* might have been my
Mt. 19:5, leave his father and *m*
Jn. 19:27, "Behold your *m*
Gal. 4:26, free, which is the *m*
Rev. 17:5, The *M* of Harlots

MOTHERS
love of. Isa. 49:15; 66:13; instances. Gen. 21:10; Ex. 2; 1 Sam. 1:22; 2 Sam. 21:10; 1 Ki. 3:26; 2 Jn.
love for, enforced. Ex. 20:12; Prov. 1:8; 19:26; 23:22; Eph. 6:1

MOUNT
Ex. 19:23, come up to *M* Sinai
Song 7:5, you like *M* Carmel
Isa. 40:31, they shall *m* up with
Gal. 4:25, for this Hagar is *M*

MOUNTAIN
Ex. 3:1, to Horeb, the *m*
Job 14:18, "But as a *m* falls
Ps. 30:7, You have made my *m*
Ps. 68:15, of many peaks is the *m*
Isa. 2:3, let us go up to the *m*
Dan. 2:35, became a great *m*
Zech. 4:7, are you, O great *m*
Mt. 17:20, you will say to this *m*
2 Pet. 1:18, with Him on the holy *m*

MOUNTAINS
Job 9:5, He removes the *m*
Job 40:20, Surely the *m* yield
Ps. 72:3, *m* will bring peace
Ps. 76:4, excellent than the *m*
Ps. 90:2, *m* were brought forth
Ps. 97:5, *m* melt like wax at the
Ps. 114:4, *m* skipped like rams
Ps. 125:2, *m* surround Jerusalem
Isa. 54:10, *m* shall depart and the
Mt. 24:16, in Judea flee to the *m*
1 Cor. 13:2, that I could remove *m*
Rev. 16:20, *m* were not found

MOURN
Prov. 5:11, and you *m* at last
Eccl. 3:4, a time to *m*
Mt. 5:4, are those who *m*
Jas. 4:9, Lament and *m* and weep
Rev. 1:7, of the earth will *m*

MOURNED
Mt. 11:17, we *m* to you
1 Cor. 5:2, and have not rather *m*

MOURNER
2 Sam. 14:2; Eccl. 12:5; Hos. 9:4

MOURNERS
comfort for. Job 29:25; Rom. 12:15; 2 Cor. 1:4; 1 Th. 4:18

MOURNING
when blessed. Eccl. 7:2; Mt. 5:4; Lk. 6:21
for the dead. Gen. 50:3; Num. 20:29; Dt. 14:1; 2 Sam. 1:17; 3:31; 12:16; 18:33; 19:1; Eccl. 12:5; Jer. 6:26; 9:17; 22:18
of the priests. Lev. 21:1; Ezek. 44:25

MOURNING
Gen. 50:11, This is a deep *m*
Ps. 38:6, *m* all the day long
Isa. 60:20, *m* shall be ended
Jer. 16:7, men break bread in *m*
Jer. 31:13, I will turn their *m*
Zech. 12:11, shall be a great *m*
Jas. 4:9, be turned to *m* and

MOURNS
Ps. 35:14, heavily, as one who *m*
Isa. 24:4, The earth *m* and fades
Zech. 12:10, for Him as one *m*

MOUTH
of God. Dt. 8:3; Mt. 4:4
of babes. Ps. 8:2; Mt. 21:16
of the wicked. Ps. 32:9; 63:11; 107:42; 109:2; 144:8; Prov. 4:24; 5:3; 6:12; 19:28; Rom. 3:14; Rev. 13:5
of the righteous, etc. Ps. 37:30; Prov. 10:31; Eccl. 10:12
of fools. Prov. 14:3; 15:2; 18:7; 26:7

MOUTH
Ex. 4:11, "Who has made man's *m*
Ps. 8:2, Out of the *m* of babes
Ps. 37:30, The *m* of the righteous
Ps. 49:3, *m* shall speak wisdom
Ps. 107:42, iniquity stops its *m*
Prov. 10:14, knowledge, but the *m*
Prov. 13:3, *m* preserves his life
Prov. 22:14, The *m* of an immoral
Prov. 26:28, and a flattering *m*
Dan. 7:8, *m* speaking pompous
Mic. 7:5, the doors of your *m*
Mt. 15:11, *m* defiles a man
Lk. 19:22, *m* I will judge you
Lk. 21:15, I will give you a *m*
Rom. 10:10, *m* confession is made
Jude 16, *m* great swelling words
Rev. 3:16, vomit you out of My *m*

MOVE
Isa. 13:13, and the earth will *m*
Zech. 14:4, the mountain shall *m*
Acts 17:28, in Him we live and *m*

MOVED
Ps. 15:5, shall never be *m*
Ps. 46:5, she shall not be *m*
2 Pet. 1:21, spoke as they were *m*

MUCH
Eccl. 12:12, *m* study is
Song 4:10, *m* better than wine is
Lk. 12:48, to whom *m* is given
Rom. 5:9, *M* more then

MULTIPLIED
Ps. 16:4, sorrows shall be *m*
Acts 6:7, of the disciples *m*
Acts 12:24, of God grew and *m*

MULTIPLY
Gen. 1:22, "Be fruitful and *m*
Gen. 16:10, *m* your descendants
Job 29:18, *m* my days as the
Jer. 33:22, *m* the descendants

MULTITUDE
Dt. 1:10, stars of heaven in *m*
Ps. 5:7, Your house in the *m*
Ps. 42:4, *m* that kept a pilgrim
Prov. 10:19, In the *m* of words sin
Prov. 14:28, In a *m* of people is a
Mt. 15:32, compassion on the *m*
Lk. 2:13, with the angel a *m*
1 Pet. 4:8, "love will cover a *m*
Rev. 7:9, and behold, a great *m*

MURDER
Gen. 9:6; Lev. 24:17; Dt. 5:17; 21:9; 1 Jn. 3:15
examples of: Gen. 4; Jud. 9; 2 Sam. 3:27; 4; 12:9; 20:8; 1 Ki. 16:9; 21; 2 Ki. 15:10; 21:23; 2 Chr. 24:21

its penalty. Gen. 4:12; 9:6; Num. 35:30; Jer. 19:4; Ezek. 16:38; Gal. 5:21; Rev. 22:15
source of. Mt. 15:19; Gal. 5:21

MURDER
Ex. 20:13, "You shall not *m*
Mt. 5:21, 'You shall not *m*
Acts 9:1, threats and *m* against
Jas. 4:2, You *m* and covet and

MURDERED
Mt. 23:31, sons of those who *m*
Acts 5:30, up Jesus whom you *m*
1 Jn. 3:12, one and *m* his brother

MURDERER
Jn. 8:44, He was a *m* from the
Acts 3:14, and asked for a *m*
1 Pet. 4:15, of you suffer as a *m*
1 Jn. 3:15, his brother is a *m*

MURDERERS
Isa. 1:21, in it, but now *m*
1 Tim. 1:9, and profane, for *m*
Rev. 21:8, abominable, *m*

MURDERS
Mt. 15:19, evil thoughts, *m*
Gal. 5:21, envy, *m*

MURMURING
rebuked. Lam. 3:39; 1 Cor. 10:10; Phil. 2:14; Jude 16
of Israel, instances of. Ex. 15:23; 16; 17; Num. 11; 16; 20; 21

MUSIC
invention of. Gen. 4:21
its effects on Saul. 1 Sam. 16:14
used for worship. 2 Sam. 6:5; 1 Chr. 15:28; 16:42; 2 Chr. 7:6; 29:25; Ps. 33; 81; 92; 108; 150; Dan. 3:5
at festivities. Isa. 5:12; 14:11; Amos 6:5; Lk. 15:25; 1 Cor. 14:7
in heaven. Rev. 5:8; 14:2

MUSIC
1 Sam. 18:10, So David played *m*
Eccl. 12:4, *m* are brought low
Lk. 15:25, the house, he heard *m*

MUSING
Ps. 39:3, while I was *m*

MUSTARD SEED
parable of. Mt. 13:31; Mk. 4:30; Lk. 13:18

MUTE
Ex. 4:11, Or who makes the *m*
Ps. 38:13, *m* who does not open
Ps. 39:2, I was *m* with silence
Ps. 39:9, I was *m*

MUTILATION
Phil. 3:2, beware of the *m*

MUTUAL
Rom. 1:12, by the *m* faith both

MUZZLE
Dt. 25:4, "You shall not *m*
1 Tim. 5:18, "You shall not *m*

MYRRH
Ex. 30:23; Est. 2:12; Ps. 45:8; Song 1:13; Mt. 2:11; Mk. 15:23; Jn. 19:39

MYSTERIES
Mt. 13:11, to you to know the *m*
1 Cor. 13:2, and understand all *m*
1 Cor. 14:2, the spirit he speaks *m*

MYSTERIOUS
Dt. 30:11, today is not too *m*

MYSTERY
of the kingdom of God made known by Christ. Mk. 4:11; Eph. 1:9; 3:3; 1 Tim. 3:16; by the disciples to the world. 1 Cor. 4:1; 13:2; Eph. 6:19; Col. 2:2
of the raising of the dead. 1 Cor. 15:51
of iniquity. 2 Th. 2:7; Rev. 17:5

MYSTERY
Mk. 4:11, given to know the *m*
1 Cor. 2:7, wisdom of God in a *m*
1 Cor. 15:51, I tell you a *m*
Eph. 1:9, made known to us the *m*
Eph. 5:32, This is a great *m*
Col. 1:26, *m* which has been
1 Tim. 3:16, the *m* of godliness

NAAMAN, 2 Ki. 5:1. *See* Lk. 4:27

NABAL, 1 Sam. 25:3

NABOTH
killed by Jezebel. 1 Ki. 21
his murder avenged. 2 Ki. 9:21

NADAB, Ex. 6:23
son of Aaron, offers profane fire. Lev. 10:1,2
——— king of Israel, killed by Baasha. 1 Ki. 14:20; 15:25,28

NAHASH
invades Jabesh Gilead. 1 Sam. 11

NAHOR, Gen. 11:22
Abram's brother. Gen. 11:26; 22:20; 24:10

NAHUM
vision of. Nah. 1:1–3

NAILED
Col. 2:14, *n* it to the cross

NAIN
miracle at. Lk. 7:11

NAIOTH, 1 Sam. 19:18
school of prophets. 1 Sam. 19:23; 20:1

NAKED
Gen. 2:25, And they were both *n*
Gen. 3:7, knew that they were *n*
Job 1:21, *N* I came from my
Isa. 20:3, Isaiah has walked *n*
Mt. 25:36, 'I was *n* and you
Mk. 14:52, and fled from them *n*
2 Cor. 5:3, shall not be found *n*
Heb. 4:13, but all things are *n*
Jas. 2:15, brother or sister is *n*
Rev. 3:17, poor, blind, and *n*

NAKEDNESS
Gen. 9:22, of Canaan, saw the *n*
Rom. 8:35, or famine, or *n*
2 Cor. 11:27, often, in cold and *n*
Rev. 3:18, *n* may not be revealed

NAME
of God. Ex. 34:5,14. *See* Ex. 6:3; 15:3; Ps. 83:18
honor due to. Ex. 20:7; Dt. 5:11; 28:58; Ps. 34:3; 72:17; 111:9; Mic. 4:5; 1 Tim. 6:1
——— of Christ, prayer in. Jn. 14:13; 16:23; Rom. 1:8; Eph. 5:20; Col. 3:17; Heb. 13:15
miracles performed in. Acts 3:6; 4:10; 19:13
responsibilities of bearing. 2 Tim. 2:19
——— given to children at circumcision. Lk. 1:59; 2:21
——— value of a good. Prov. 22:1; Eccl. 7:1

NAME
Gen. 13:4, Abram called on the *n*
Gen. 35:10, Israel shall be your *n*
Ex. 3:15, This is My *n* forever
Ex. 20:7, shall not take the *n*
Dt. 28:10, are called by the *n*
Dt. 28:58, glorious and awesome *n*
2 Chr. 7:14, by My *n* will humble
Job 18:17, and he has no *n*
Ps. 8:1, excellent is Your *n*
Ps. 9:10, *n* will put their trust
Ps. 72:19, be His glorious *n*
Ps. 76:1, *n* is great in Israel
Ps. 79:6, do not call on Your *n*
Ps. 115:1, to Your *n* give glory
Ps. 138:2, above all Your *n*
Ps. 147:4, He calls them all by *n*
Prov. 18:10, The *n* of the LORD is a
Prov. 22:1, A good *n* is to be
Prov. 30:4, what is His Son's *n*
Isa. 26:13, make mention of Your *n*
Isa. 42:8, the LORD, that is My *n*
Isa. 55:13, be to the LORD for a *n*
Isa. 62:2, be called by a new *n*
Isa. 63:16, Everlasting is Your *n*
Isa. 64:7, who calls on Your *n*
Jer. 33:9, it shall be to Me a *n*
Dan. 9:15, and made Yourself a *n*
Mic. 4:5, we will walk in the *n*
Zech. 13:9, They will call on My *n*
Mal. 1:11, *n* shall be great
Mal. 4:2, to you who fear My *n*
Mt. 1:21, you shall call His *n*
Mt. 6:9, hallowed be Your *n*
Mt. 7:22, prophesied in Your *n*
Mt. 10:41, righteous man in the *n*
Mt. 12:21, *n* Gentiles will trust
Mt. 18:20, together in My *n*
Mt. 24:5, will come in My *n*
Mk. 5:9, "My *n* is Legion
Lk. 1:27, The virgin's *n* was
Lk. 1:63, "His *n* is John
Lk. 6:22, and cast out your *n*
Jn. 1:12, who believe in His *n*
Jn. 5:43, comes in his own *n*
Jn. 10:3, his own sheep by *n*
Acts 3:16, through faith in His *n*
Acts 4:12, there is no other *n*
Acts 5:41, suffer shame for His *n*
Phil. 2:9, which is above every *n*
Col. 3:17, deed, do all in the *n*
Heb. 1:4, a more excellent *n*
Jas. 2:7, blaspheme that noble *n*

1 Pet. 4:14, reproached for the *n*
Rev. 2:13, you hold fast to My *n*
Rev. 3:1, *n* that you are alive
Rev. 14:1, having His Father's *n*
Rev. 15:4, and glorify Your *n*
Rev. 19:12, *n* written that no one

NAME'S
Ps. 106:8, saved them for His *n*
1 Jn. 2:12, forgiven you for His *n*

NAMED
Gen. 48:16, let my name be *n*
Isa. 45:4, I have *n* you

NAMES
changed: by God. Gen. 17:5,15; 32:27; 2 Sam. 12:25; by man. Dan. 1:7; by Christ. Mk. 3:16,17

NAOMI, Ruth 1:2

NAPHTALI
son of Jacob. Gen. 30:8; 35:25; 46:24; 49:21; Dt. 33:23
——— tribe of, numbered. Num. 1:42; 10:27; 13:14; 26:48; Jud. 1:33
subdue the Canaanites. Jud. 4:10; 5:18; 6:35; 7:23
carried captive. 2 Ki. 15:29. *See* Isa. 9:1; Mt. 4:13

NARROW
Mt. 7:13, "Enter by the *n* gate
Mt. 7:14, *n* is the gate and

NATHAN
the prophet. 2 Sam. 7
shows David his sin. 2 Sam. 12:1
anoints Solomon king. 1 Ki. 1:34; 1 Chr. 29:29; 2 Chr. 9:29
——— son of David. 2 Sam. 5:14; Zech. 12:12; Lk. 3:31

NATHANAEL
'Israelite indeed.' Jn. 1:45; 21:2

NATION
Gen. 12:2, make you a great *n*
Gen. 20:4, You slay a righteous *n*
Ex. 19:6, priests and a holy *n*
Ps. 147:20, dealt thus with any *n*
Prov. 14:34, exalts a *n*
Isa. 2:4, up sword against *n*
Isa. 26:2, that the righteous *n*
Isa. 60:22, a small one a strong *n*
Isa. 65:1, *n* that was not called
Jer. 2:11, *n* changed its gods
Ezek. 37:22, make them one *n*
Dan. 12:1, since there was a *n*
Mt. 24:7, *n* will rise against
Lk. 7:5, for he loves our *n*
Rom. 10:19, those who are not a *n*
Rev. 13:7, tribe, tongue, and *n*

NATIONS
origin of. Gen. 10
Gospel preached to. Mt. 24:14; 28:19; 16:26; Gal. 1:16

NATIONS
Num. 23:9, itself among the *n*
Ps. 2:1, Why do the *n* rage
Ps. 2:8, I will give You the *n*
Ps. 72:11, *n* shall serve Him
Ps. 72:17, *n* shall call Him
Ps. 102:15, *n* shall fear the name
Ps. 113:4, is high above all *n*
Isa. 40:17, All *n* before Him are
Isa. 55:5, *n* who do not know
Jer. 10:7, the wise men of the *n*
Zech. 2:11, *n* shall be joined
Mt. 28:19, disciples of all the *n*
Rev. 12:5, who was to rule all *n*
Rev. 22:2, the healing of the *n*

NATIVITY
Jer. 46:16; Ezek. 21:30; 23:15

NATURAL
Rom. 1:26, women exchanged the *n*
Rom. 1:27, the men, leaving the *n*
Rom. 11:21, did not spare the *n*
1 Cor. 2:14, *n* man does not receive
1 Cor. 15:44, It is sown a *n* body
1 Cor. 15:46, not first, but the *n*

NATURE
Rom. 1:26, for what is against *n*
1 Cor. 11:14, *n* itself teach you
Gal. 2:15, We who are Jews by *n*
Eph. 2:3, by *n* children of wrath
2 Pet. 1:4, of the divine *n*

NAVY
of Solomon. 1 Ki. 9:26; 2 Chr. 8:17
of Jehoshaphat. 1 Ki. 22:28

NAZARENE, Acts 24:5

NAZARETH, Lk. 1:26
Jesus of. Mt. 2:23; 21:11; Lk. 1:26; 2:39,51; 4:16; Jn. 1:45; 18:5; Acts 2:22; 3:6

NAZIRITES
law of the. Num. 6

NEAR
Dt. 4:7, that has God so *n*
Dt. 30:14, the word is very *n*
Ps. 145:18, The LORD is *n* to all
Isa. 55:6, upon Him while He is *n*
Mt. 24:33, know that it is *n*
Lk. 21:31, kingdom of God is *n*
Rom. 10:8, "The word is *n*
Eph. 2:17, to those who were *n*
Rev. 1:3, for the time is *n*

NEARER
Rom. 13:11, now our salvation is *n*

NEBO, Dt. 32:49

NEBUCHADNEZZAR, 2 Ki. 24:1
king of Babylon. Jer. 20; 21; 25; 27; 28; 32; 34; Ezek. 26:7; 29:19
captures Jerusalem. 2 Ki. 24; 25; 2 Chr. 36; Jer. 37—39; 52; Dan. 1:1
his dreams. Dan. 2; 4
sets up the golden image. Dan. 3
his madness. Dan. 4:33
his restoration and confession. Dan. 4:34

NEBUZARADAN, 2 Ki. 25:8
his care of Jeremiah. Jer. 39:11; 40:1

NECESSARY
Job 23:12, mouth more than my *n*
Lk. 24:46, and thus it was *n*
Acts 15:28, burden than these *n*
Jude 3, I found it *n* to write

NECESSITIES
Acts 20:34, have provided for my *n*
Phil. 4:16, and again for my *n*

NECESSITY
1 Cor. 9:16, *n* is laid upon me
2 Cor. 9:7, not grudgingly or of *n*

NECHO, 2 Ki. 23:29

NECK
Gen. 27:16, smooth part of his *n*
Prov. 3:22, and grace to your *n*
Isa. 48:4, *n* was an iron sinew
Mt. 18:6, were hung around his *n*
Lk. 15:20, ran and fell on his *n*

NECKS
Neh. 9:29, stiffened their *n*
Isa. 3:16, with outstretched *n*
Rom. 16:4, who risked their own *n*

NEED
Dt. 28:48, in nakedness, and in *n*
Prov. 24:34, a prowler, and your *n*
Mt. 6:8, the things you have *n*
Mt. 21:3, 'The Lord has *n*
Acts 4:35, each as anyone had *n*
1 Cor. 12:21, hand, "I have no *n*
Phil. 2:25, who ministered to my *n*
Phil. 4:19, supply all your *n*
Heb. 4:16, to help in time of *n*
1 Jn. 3:17, sees his brother in *n*
Rev. 21:23, The city had no *n*

NEEDFUL, Phil. 1:24

NEEDY
Dt. 15:11, your poor and your *n*
Job 24:4, They push the *n*
Ps. 9:18, *n* shall not always be
Ps. 72:12, He will deliver the *n*
Ps. 113:7, and lifts the *n*
Isa. 10:2, to rob the *n* of
Isa. 14:30, *n* will lie down in
Isa. 25:4, a strength to the *n*

NEGLECT
1 Tim. 4:14, *n* the gift that is
Heb. 2:3, if we *n* so great a

NEGLECTED
Mt. 23:23, *n* the weightier
Acts 6:1, their widows were *n*

NEGLIGENT
2 Chr. 29:11; 2 Pet. 1:12

NEHEMIAH
his grief for Jerusalem. Neh. 1
his prayer for. Neh. 1:5
his visit to. Neh. 2:5,9,17
his conduct at. Neh. 4—6; 8—10; 13

NEHUSHTAN
the bronze serpent of Moses, idolatrously used by Israelites, so called by Hezekiah, and destroyed by him. 2 Ki. 18:4

NEIGHBOR
how to treat our. Ex. 20:16; 22:26; Lev. 19:18; Dt. 15:2; 27:17; Prov. 3:28; 24:28; 25:8,17; Mk. 12:31; Rom. 13:9; Gal. 5:14; Jas. 2:8

NEIGHBOR
Lev. 19:18, you shall love your *n*

Prov. 27:10, for better is a *n*
Jer. 31:34, every man teach his *n*
Hab. 2:15, gives drink to his *n*
Mt. 5:43, You shall love your *n*
Lk. 10:29, And who is my *n*
Rom. 13:9, You shall love your *n*

NEST
Job 39:27, and make its *n*
Prov. 27:8, *n* is a man who wanders
Obad. 4, though you set your *n*
Hab. 2:9, that he may set his *n*

NET
Job 19:6, me with His *n*
Ps. 35:7, have hidden their *n*
Ps. 57:6, They have prepared a *n*
Isa. 51:20, an antelope in a *n*
Hab. 1:15, catch in their *n*
Lk. 5:5, I will let down the *n*
Jn. 21:6, to them, "Cast the *n*

NETHINIM
1 Chr. 9:2; Ezra 2:43; 7:7,24; 8:17; Neh. 10:28

NEVER
Jn. 6:35, in Me shall *n* thirst
Jn. 11:26, in Me shall *n* die
1 Cor. 13:8, Love *n* fails
Heb. 10:11, *n* take away sins
Heb. 13:5, "I will *n* leave you
2 Pet. 1:21, prophecy *n* came by

NEW
Ex. 1:8, Now there arose a *n*
Num. 16:30, the LORD creates a *n*
Jud. 5:8, They chose *n* gods
Eccl. 1:9, and there is nothing *n*
Isa. 43:19, Behold, I will do a *n*
Isa. 65:17, For behold, I create *n*
Jer. 31:31, when I will make a *n*
Lam. 3:23, *n* every morning
Mt. 9:17, wine into *n* wineskins
Mt. 26:28, of the *n* covenant
Jn. 13:34, *n* commandment I
Acts 17:21, tell or to hear some *n*
2 Cor. 5:17, he is a *n* creation
Col. 3:10, *n* man who is renewed
Heb. 8:8, when I will make a *n*
2 Pet. 3:13, *n* heavens and a *n*
Rev. 2:17, *n* name written which
Rev. 5:9, And they sang a *n*
Rev. 21:1, And I saw a *n* heaven
Rev. 21:5, I make all things *n*

NEW BIRTH
(born again). Jn. 3:3,6; 1 Pet. 1:23

NEWNESS
Rom. 6:4, also should walk in *n*
Rom. 7:6, should serve in the *n*

NEWS
Ex. 33:4, heard this bad *n*
Prov. 25:25, soul, so is good *n*
Isa. 52:7, him who brings good *n*

NICODEMUS
Pharisee and ruler, goes to Jesus by night. Jn. 3:1
takes His part. Jn. 7:50
assists at Christ's burial. Jn. 19:39

NICOLAITANS, Rev. 2:6

NIGHT, Gen. 1:5; Ps. 19:2
figurative. Jn. 9:4; Rom. 13:12; 1 Th. 5:5
none in heaven. Rev. 21:25 (Isa. 60:20)

NIGHT
Gen. 1:5, darkness He called *N*
Ex. 12:42, It is a *n* of solemn
Ex. 13:22, pillar of fire by *n*
Job 7:4, and the *n* be ended
Job 35:10, gives songs in the *n*
Ps. 19:2, *n* reveals
Ps. 119:148, awake through the *n*
Ps. 136:9, and stars to rule by *n*
Isa. 26:9, desired You in the *n*
Jon. 4:10, and perished in a *n*
Lk. 6:12, and continued all *n*
Jn. 3:2, man came to Jesus by *n*
Jn. 9:4, *n* is coming when no
Jn. 19:39, came to Jesus by *n*
Rom. 13:12, The *n* is far spent
1 Th. 5:2, as a thief in the *n*
1 Th. 5:5, We are not of the *n*
Rev. 21:25, there shall be no *n*
Rev. 22:5, there shall be no *n*

NIMROD, Gen. 10:8
mighty hunter. Gen. 10:9

NINE
Lk. 17:17, where are the *n*

NINETY-NINE
Mt. 18:12, he not leave the *n*
Lk. 15:7, *n* just persons

NINEVEH, Gen. 10:11
Jonah's mission to. Jon. 1:1; 3:2
denounced by Jonah. Jon. 3:4
repenting, is spared by God. Jon. 3:5–10 (Mt. 12:41; Lk. 11:32)
the burden of. Nah. 1:1; 2; 3

NINEVITES
inhabitants of Nineveh. Lk. 11:30

NISAN (or Abib)
first month of Hebrew calendar, March–April. Neh. 2:1; Est. 3:7

NO (ancient Thebes)
threatened. Jer. 46:25; Ezek. 30:14

NO AMON, Jer. 46:25; Nah. 3:8

NOAH
Gen. 5:29; Num. 26:33; Mt. 24:37
son of Lamech. Gen. 5:29
finds grace with God. Gen. 6:8
ordered to build the ark. Gen. 6:14
with his family and animals enters the ark. Gen. 7
flood subsiding, goes out. Gen. 8:18
God blesses and makes a covenant with. Gen. 9:1,8
is drunk, and mocked by Ham. Gen. 9:22
his death. Gen. 9:29

NOB
city of, David comes to, and eats holy bread at. 1 Sam. 21:1
struck by Saul. 1 Sam. 22:19

NOBLE
Phil. 4:8, whatever things are *n*
Jas. 2:7, not blaspheme that *n*

NOBLES
Job 29:10, voice of *n* was hushed
Eccl. 10:17, king is the son of *n*
Jer. 14:3, *n* have sent their lads
Nah. 3:18, your *n* rest in the

NOD, Gen. 4:16

NOISE
Isa. 13:4, The *n* of a multitude
Isa. 17:12, people who make a *n*
Jer. 46:17, of Egypt, is but a *n*
Lam. 2:7, They have made a *n*
2 Pet. 3:10, away with a great *n*

NOSTRILS
Gen. 2:7, *n* the breath of life
Job 27:3, breath of God in my *n*
Isa. 2:22, breath is in his *n*

NOPH, *see also* MEMPHIS
Isa. 19:13; Jer. 2:16; 46:14; Ezek. 30:13

NOTE
Rom. 16:17, urge you, brethren, *n*
Phil. 3:17, *n* those who so walk

NOTHING
Job 6:21, For now you are *n*
Prov. 13:7, rich, yet has *n*
Prov. 20:14, "It is good for *n*
Isa. 40:17, before Him are as *n*
Isa. 41:29, their works are *n*
Jn. 5:30, I can of Myself do *n*
Jn. 15:5, Me you can do *n*
Acts 5:38, men, it will come to *n*
1 Cor. 1:28, bring to *n* the things
1 Cor. 4:4, For I know of *n* against
1 Cor. 13:2, have not love, I am *n*
1 Cor. 13:3, love, it profits me *n*
Phil. 4:6, Be anxious for *n*
1 Tim. 6:7, For we brought *n*
Jas. 1:4, complete, lacking *n*
3 Jn. 7, name's sake, taking *n*

NOTORIOUS
Mt. 27:16, *n* prisoner called

NOURISHED
Isa. 1:2, "I have *n* and
Col. 2:19, *n* and knit together
1 Tim. 4:6, *n* in the words of

NOURISHES
Eph. 5:29, *n* and cherishes it

NOVICE
1 Tim. 3:6, not a *n*

NUMBER
Gen. 13:16, if a man could *n*
2 Sam. 24:2, that I may know the *n*
Job 5:9, things without *n*
Job 14:16, For now You *n* my steps
Job 38:37, *n* the clouds by wisdom
Ps. 90:12, teach us to *n* our days
Ps. 147:4, He counts the *n*
Rev. 7:9, which no one could *n*
Rev. 13:18, His *n* is 666

NUMBERED
Ps. 40:5, are more than can be *n*
Dan. 5:26, God has *n* your kingdom

Lk. 22:37, 'And He was *n* with

NUMBERING
of the people, by Moses. Num. 1:18; 26:4; by David. 2 Sam. 24; 1 Chr. 21
of the Levites. Num. 3:15; 4:34; 26:57

NUN, Ex. 33:11

OAKS
Zech. 11:2, Wail, O *o* of Bashan

OARSMEN
Ezek. 27:26, *o* brought you into

OATH
God ratifies His purpose by. Ps. 132:11; Lk. 1:73; Acts 2:30; Heb. 6:17
of the forty Jews. Acts 23:12,21

OATH
1 Sam. 14:26, people feared the *o*
Eccl. 8:2, for the sake of your *o*
Jer. 11:5, I may establish the *o*
Jer. 42:18, And you shall be an *o*
Mt. 26:72, he denied with an *o*
Lk. 1:73, *o* which He swore
Acts 23:12, themselves under an *o*

OATHS
directions about. Lev. 5:4; 6:3; 19:12; Num. 30:2; Ps. 15:4; Mt. 5:33; Jas. 5:12
examples of. Gen. 14:22; 21:31; 24:2; Josh. 14:9; 1 Sam. 20:42; 28:10; Ps. 132:2
demanded. Ex. 22:11; Num. 5:21; 1 Ki. 8:31; Ezra 10:5
rash: of Esau. Gen. 25:33
of Israel to the Gibeonites. Josh. 9:19
of Jephthah. Jud. 11:30
of Saul at Beth Aven. 1 Sam. 14:24
of Herod to Herodias' daughter. Mt. 14:7

OATHS
Mt. 5:33, shall perform your *o*
Mt. 14:9, because of the *o*

OBADIAH, Obad. 1
prophet, his prediction. Obad. 17
——— Levite, porter in the temple. Neh. 12:25
——— sent by Ahab to find water. 1 Ki. 18:3
meets Elijah. 1 Ki. 18:7
how he hid a hundred prophets. 1 Ki. 18:4,13

OBED, Ruth 4:17

OBED-EDOM
prospered while taking charge of the ark. 2 Sam. 6:10; 1 Chr. 13:14; 15:18,24; 16:5
his sons. 1 Chr. 26:4,5

OBEDIENCE
of Christ. Rom. 5:19; Phil. 2:8; Heb. 5:8
to God commanded. Ex. 19:5; 23:21; Lev. 26:3; Dt. 4—8; 11; 29; Isa. 1:19; Jer. 7:23; 26:13; 38:20; Acts 5:29; Jas. 1:25
its blessings. Ex. 23:22; Dt. 28; 30; Prov. 25:12; Isa. 1:19; Heb. 11:8; 1 Pet. 1:22; Rev. 22:14
preferred before sacrifice. 1 Sam. 15:22; Ps. 50:8; Mic. 6:6
to the faith. Rom. 1:5; 16:26; 2 Cor. 7:15; 1 Pet. 1:2
of children to parents. Eph. 6:1; Col. 3:20
to masters. Eph. 6:5; Col. 3:22; Ti. 2:9
of wives to husbands. Ti. 2:5
of people to rulers. Ti. 3:1; Heb. 13:17

OBEDIENCE
Rom. 1:5, and apostleship for *o*
Rom. 5:19, *o* many will be made
2 Cor. 10:5, captivity to the *o*
Phile. 21, confidence in your *o*
Heb. 5:8, yet He learned *o*
1 Pet. 1:2, for *o* and sprinkling

OBEDIENT
Isa. 1:19, you are willing and *o*
Acts 6:7, of the priests were *o*
Rom. 15:18, make the Gentiles *o*
Eph. 6:5, bondservants, be *o* to
Phil. 2:8, Himself and became *o*
Ti. 2:5, homemakers, good, *o*
1 Pet. 1:14, as *o* children

OBEY
Ex. 5:2, LORD, that I should *o*
Dt. 4:30, God and *o* His voice
Dt. 11:27, *o* the commandments
Josh. 24:24, His voice we will *o*
1 Sam. 15:22, *o* is better than
Ps. 18:44, they hear of me they *o*
Zech. 6:15, if you diligently *o*
Acts 5:29, *o* God rather than men
Rom. 2:8, and do not *o* the truth
Rom. 6:16, yourselves slaves to *o*
Col. 3:20, *o* your parents in all
Col. 3:22, Bondservants, *o* in all
2 Th. 1:8, those who do not *o*
Heb. 13:17, O those who rule
1 Pet. 3:1, if some do not *o*

OBEYED
Rom. 6:17, of sin, yet you *o*
Rom. 10:16, they have not all *o*
Heb. 11:8, By faith Abraham *o*
1 Pet. 3:6, as Sarah *o* Abraham

OBEYING
1 Pet. 1:22, *o* the truth through

OBSCURITY
Isa. 29:18, shall see out of *o*

OBSERVANCE
Ex. 12:42, the LORD, a solemn *o*

OBSERVATION
Lk. 17:20, does not come with *o*

OBSERVE
Ps. 37:37, man, and *o* the upright
Prov. 23:26, and let your eyes *o*
Hos. 12:6, *o* mercy and justice
Mt. 28:20, teaching them to *o* all
Gal. 4:10, *o* days and months and
1 Pet. 3:2, *o* your chaste conduct

OBSERVES
Eccl. 11:4, *o* the wind will not
Rom. 14:6, He who *o* the day

OBSERVING
Jas. 1:23, *o* his natural face

OBSESSED
1 Tim. 6:4, nothing, but is *o*

OBSOLETE
Heb. 8:13, Now what is becoming *o*

OBSTINATE
Dt. 2:30, and made his heart *o*
Isa. 48:4, I knew that you were *o*

OBTAIN
Isa. 35:10, They shall *o* joy and
Rom. 11:31, they also may *o* mercy
1 Th. 5:9, *o* salvation through
Jas. 4:2, and covet and cannot *o*

OBTAINED
Acts 1:17, *o* a part in this
Rom. 11:30, yet have now *o* mercy
Heb. 6:15, endured, he *o* the
2 Pet. 1:1, To those who have *o*

OBTAINS
Prov. 8:35, *o* favor from the LORD

OCCUPATION
Gen. 46:33; Jon. 1:8; Acts 18:3; 19:25

OFFEND
Job 34:31, I will *o* no more
Jer. 2:3, that devour him will *o*
Mt. 17:27, lest we *o* them
Lk. 17:2, than that he should *o*
Jn. 6:61, them, "Does this *o*

OFFENDED
Mt. 13:57, they were *o* at Him
Rom. 14:21, stumbles or is *o*

OFFENDER
Isa. 29:21, who make a man an *o*
Acts 25:11, "For if I am an *o*

OFFENSE
giving of, deprecated. 1 Cor. 10:32; 2 Cor. 6:3; Phil. 1:10

OFFENSE
Isa. 8:14, and a rock of *o*
Mt. 16:23, You are an *o* to Me
Rom. 5:17, by the one man's *o*
1 Cor. 10:32, Give no *o*
Gal. 5:11, the *o* of the cross
Phil. 1:10, sincere and without *o*
1 Pet. 2:8, and a rock of *o*

OFFENSES
woe because of. Mt. 18:7
how to remedy. Eccl. 10:4; Mt. 5:29; 18:8; Mk. 9:43; Rom. 16:17
Christ was delivered for our. Rom. 4:25

OFFENSES
Mt. 18:7, For *o* must come
Lk. 17:1, impossible that no *o*
Rom. 4:25, up because of our *o*

OFFER
Mal. 1:8, *o* the blind as a
Mt. 5:24, come and *o* your gift
Heb. 13:15, let us continually *o*

OFFERED
1 Cor. 8:10, to eat those things *o*
Heb. 9:14, the eternal Spirit *o*
Heb. 9:28, so Christ was *o*
Heb. 10:12, *o* one sacrifice
Heb. 11:4, By faith Abel *o*

OFFERING
of Christ. Heb. 9:14,28; 10:10,12,14

OFFERING
Lev. 1:2, you shall bring your *o*
Ps. 40:6, *o* You did not require
Isa. 53:10, You make His soul an *o*
Mal. 3:3, to the LORD an *o*
Eph. 5:2, Himself for us, an *o*
Phil. 2:17, out as a drink *o*
Heb. 10:5, *o* You did not
Heb. 10:14, *o* He has perfected
Heb. 10:18, is no longer an *o*

OFFERINGS
laws for. Lev. 1—3; 22:21; Dt. 15:21; Mal. 1:13
of the spoil. Num. 31:28

OFFERINGS
Gen. 8:20, and offered burnt *o*
Ps. 20:3, He remember all your *o*
Heb. 10:6, In burnt *o*

OFFICE
Ps. 109:8, let another take his *o*
Mt. 9:9, sitting at the tax *o*

OFFICERS
Isa. 60:17, also make your *o*

OFFSCOURING
Lam. 3:45, You have made us an *o*
1 Cor. 4:13, the *o* of all things

OFFSPRING
Isa. 44:3, My blessing on your *o*
Mal. 2:15, He seeks godly *o*
Mt. 22:24, wife and raise up *o*
Acts 17:28, we are also His *o*
Rev. 22:16, am the Root and the *O*

OFTEN
Lk. 13:34, *o* I wanted to gather
1 Cor. 11:26, as *o* as you eat this
2 Cor. 11:27, in sleeplessness *o*
Heb. 9:25, should offer Himself *o*

OG
king of Bashan. Num. 21:33; Dt. 3:1; Ps. 135:11; 136:20

OHOLAH
(Samaria), and Oholibah (Jerusalem), their adulteries. Ezek. 23:4

OHOLIBAH, Ezek. 23:4

OIL
for lamps. Ex. 27:20; Lev. 24:1
for anointing. Ex. 30:31; 37:29
used in grain offerings. Lev. 2:1
miracles of. 1 Ki. 17:12; 2 Ki. 4:1
figurative. Ps. 23:5; 141:5; Isa. 61:3; Zech. 4:12; Mt. 25:1

OIL
Ex. 25:6, for the anointing *o*
Jud. 9:9, I cease giving my *o*
1 Ki. 17:12, a bin, and a little *o*
Job 29:6, poured out rivers of *o*
Ps. 92:10, anointed with fresh *o*
Ps. 104:15, the heart of man, *o*
Ps. 133:2, like the precious *o*
Ps. 141:5, be as excellent *o*
Mic. 6:7, thousand rivers of *o*
Mt. 26:7, very costly fragrant *o*
Mt. 26:9, *o* might have been sold
Jas. 5:14, anointing him with *o*
Rev. 6:6, and do not harm the *o*

OINTMENT
Christ anointed with. Mt. 26:7; Mk. 14:3; Lk. 7:37; Jn. 11:2; 12:3

OINTMENT
Prov. 27:9, *O* and perfume delight
Song 1:3, your name is *o*

OLD
Ps. 37:25, young, and now am *o*
Song 7:13, all manner, new and *o*
Mt. 5:21, was said to those of *o*
Jn. 8:57, yet fifty years *o*
Jn. 21:18, but when you are *o*
Acts 2:17, Your *o* men shall dream
Rom. 6:6, *o* man was crucified
2 Cor. 3:14, of the *O* Testament
2 Cor. 5:17, *o* things have passed
Col. 3:9, have put off the *o* man
Heb. 8:13, obsolete and growing *o*
Rev. 20:2, that serpent of *o*

OLD AGE
Job 30:2; Ps. 90:10; Eccl. 12; Ti. 2:2
reverence to. Lev. 19:32; Prov. 23:22; 1 Tim. 5:1

OLD MAN
to put off. Rom. 6:6; Eph. 4:22; Col. 3:9

OLDER
Gen. 25:23, *o* shall serve the
Job 15:10, *o* than your father
Lk. 15:25, "Now his *o* son was
1 Tim. 5:1, not rebuke an *o* man
1 Tim. 5:2, *o* women as mothers

OLDEST
Jn. 8:9, beginning with the *o*

OLIVE
Gen. 8:11, a freshly plucked *o*
Ps. 52:8, I am like a green *o*
Hab. 3:17, of the *o* may fail
Rom. 11:24, *o* tree which is wild

OLIVET
(Olives), Mount. 2 Sam. 15:30; Mt. 21:1; 24:3; Mk. 11:1; 13:3; Lk. 21:37; Jn. 8:1; Acts 1:12

OMEGA, Rev. 1:8,11; 21:6; 22:13

OMNIPOTENT
Rev. 19:6, For the Lord God *O*

OMRI
king of Israel. 1 Ki. 16:16; Mic. 6:16

ONAM, Gen. 36:23

ONAN, Gen. 38:4

ONCE
Rom. 6:10, died, He died to sin *o*
Heb. 9:27, for men to die *o*
1 Pet. 3:18, also suffered *o*

ONE
Job 33:14, God may speak in *o* way
Eccl. 4:9, Two are better than *o*
Isa. 27:12, you will be gathered *o*
Mk. 10:21, *O* thing you lack
Lk. 10:42, *o* thing is needed
Jn. 10:30, I and My Father are *o*
Jn. 17:11, that they may be *o*
Acts 2:46, *o* accord in the temple
Gal. 3:28, for you are all *o*
Eph. 2:15, to create in Himself *o*
Eph. 4:4, *o* body and *o* Spirit
Eph. 4:4, *o* hope of your calling
Eph. 4:5, *o* Lord
Eph. 4:5, *o* faith
Eph. 4:5, *o* baptism
Eph. 4:6, *o* God and Father of
1 Tim. 2:5, For there is *o* God and
1 Tim. 2:5, *o* Mediator between God
1 Tim. 3:2, the husband of *o* wife
2 Pet. 3:8, a thousand years as *o*
1 Jn. 5:7, and these three are *o*

ONESIMUS, Col. 4:9; Phile. 10

ONESIPHORUS, 2 Tim. 1:16

OPEN
Job 11:5, *o* His lips against you
Ps. 104:28, You *o* Your hand
Prov. 31:8, *O* your mouth for the
Isa. 22:22, and no one shall *o*
Hos. 4:16, a lamb in *o* country
Jn. 10:21, Can a demon *o* the eyes
2 Cor. 6:11, our heart is wide *o*
Heb. 4:13, things are naked and *o*
Rev. 5:2, *o* the scroll and to

OPENED
Isa. 53:7, *o* not His mouth
Lk. 24:31, Then their eyes were *o*
Lk. 24:32, *o* the Scriptures
Lk. 24:45, *o* their understanding
1 Cor. 16:9, effective door has *o*
Rev. 6:1, when the Lamb *o*
Rev. 19:11, Now I saw heaven *o*

OPENS
Job 33:16, *o* the ears of men
Ps. 146:8, The LORD *o* the eyes of
Jn. 10:3, him the doorkeeper *o*
Rev. 3:7, and shuts and no one *o*

OPHIR
gold of. Gen. 10:29; 1 Ki. 9:28; 10:11; 22:48; 1 Chr. 29:4; 2 Chr. 8:18; Job 22:24; Ps. 45:9; Isa. 13:12

OPHNI, Josh. 18:24

OPINION
Job 32:6, dared not declare my *o*
Rom. 11:25, be wise in your own *o*

OPINIONS
1 Ki. 18:21, falter between two *o*

OPPORTUNITY
Rom. 7:8, But sin, taking *o*
Gal. 6:10, as we have *o*
Phil. 4:10, but you lacked *o*
Heb. 11:15, they would have had *o*

OPPOSES
2 Th. 2:4, who *o* and exalts

OPPOSITION, 2 Tim. 2:25

OPPRESS
Lev. 25:17, you shall not *o*
Job 10:3, You that You should *o*
Job 37:23, He does not *o*
Hos. 12:7, he loves to *o*
Zech. 7:10, *o* the widow or the
Jas. 2:6, Do not the rich *o*

OPPRESSED
1 Sam. 12:3, Whom have I *o*
Job 20:19, For he has *o* and
Ps. 10:18, fatherless and the *o*
Ps. 103:6, for all who are *o*
Eccl. 4:1, The tears of the *o*
Isa. 53:7, He was *o* and He was
Amos 3:9, her midst, and the *o*
Acts 10:38, healing all who were *o*
2 Pet. 2:7, Lot, who was *o* by

OPPRESSES
Prov. 14:31, *o* the poor reproaches
Prov. 22:16, *o* the poor to increase
Prov. 28:3, A poor man who *o*

OPPRESSION
forbidden by God. Ex. 22:21; Lev. 25:14; Dt. 23:16; 24:14; Ps. 12:5; 62:10; Prov. 14:31; 22:16; Eccl. 4:1; 5:8; Isa. 1:17; 10; 58:6; Jer. 22:17; Ezek. 22:7; Amos 4:1; 8:4; Mic. 2:2; Mal. 3:5; Jas. 5:4

OPPRESSION
Ex. 3:7, have surely seen the *o*
Ps. 12:5, "For the *o* of the
Ps. 62:10, Do not trust in *o*
Ps. 72:14, their life from *o*
Ps. 107:39, brought low through *o*
Ps. 119:134, Redeem me from the *o*
Eccl. 4:1, considered all the *o*
Eccl. 7:7, *o* destroys a wise
Isa. 5:7, justice, but behold, *o*
Acts 7:34, surely seen the *o*

OPPRESSIONS
Job 35:9, of *o* they cry out

OPPRESSOR
Job 3:18, the voice of the *o*
Prov. 3:31, Do not envy the *o*
Prov. 28:16, is a great *o*
Isa. 51:13, of the fury of the *o*
Zech. 9:8, No more shall an *o*

OPPRESSORS
Ps. 119:121, not leave me to my *o*
Eccl. 4:1, *o* there is power

ORACLES
(the Holy Scriptures). Acts 7:38; Rom. 3:2; Heb. 5:12; 1 Pet. 4:11. *See* 2 Sam. 16:23

ORDAINED
Ps. 8:2, infants You have *o*
Jer. 1:5, *o* you a prophet
Acts 17:31, the Man whom He has *o*

ORDER
2 Ki. 20:1, 'Set your house in *o*
Job 33:5, set your words in *o*
Ps. 50:21, you, and set them in *o*
Mt. 12:44, swept, and put in *o*
1 Cor. 14:40, done decently and in *o*
1 Cor. 15:23, each one in his own *o*
Col. 2:5, to see your good *o*
Heb. 5:6, according to the *o*

ORDERS
Ps. 50:23, *o* his conduct aright I

ORDINANCE
Rom. 13:2, resists the *o* of God
1 Pet. 2:13, yourselves to every *o*

ORDINANCES
Job 38:33, Do you know the *o*
Jer. 31:36, "If those *o* depart
Jer. 33:25, not appointed the *o*
Mal. 3:7, gone away from My *o*
Heb. 9:10, and fleshly *o* imposed

ORDINATION
mode and use of. Acts 6:6; 14:23; 1 Tim. 2:7; 3; 4:14; 5:22; 2 Tim. 2:2; Ti. 1:5

ORION, Job 9:9

ORNAMENT
Prov. 1:9, will be a graceful *o*
Prov. 25:12, of gold and an *o*
Isa. 49:18, with them all as an *o*

ORNAMENTS
Jer. 2:32, a virgin forget her *o*

ORNAN
(*See also* ARAUNAH). 1 Chr. 21:15

ORPAH, Ruth 1:4

ORPHANS
Lam. 5:3, We have become *o*
Jn. 14:18, I will not leave you *o*
Jas. 1:27, to visit *o* and widows

OSTRICHES
Isa. 13:21, *o* will dwell there
Lam. 4:3, is cruel, like *o*
Mic. 1:8, a mourning like the *o*

OTHNIEL
Josh. 15:17; Jud. 1:13; 3:9

OUGHT
1 Chr. 12:32, what Israel *o* to do
Mt. 23:23, These you *o* to have
Rom. 8:26, pray for as we *o*
1 Tim. 3:15, how you *o* to conduct
1 Tim. 5:13, which they *o* not
2 Pet. 3:11, persons *o* you to be

OUTCAST
Jer. 30:17, they called you an *o*

OUTCASTS
of Israel, promised restoration. Isa. 11:12; 16:3; 27:13; Jer. 30:17; Rom. 11

OUTCASTS
Ps. 147:2, gathers together the *o*
Isa. 11:12, will assemble the *o*
Isa. 16:3, hide the *o*
Isa. 16:4, Let My *o* dwell with

OUTCRY
Ps. 144:14, that there be no *o*

OUTGOINGS
Ps. 65:8, You make the *o* of the

OUTRAGE
Jud. 20:6, lewdness and *o* in

OUTRAN
Jn. 20:4, the other disciple *o*

OUTSIDE
Mt. 23:26, and dish, that the *o*
Lk. 11:39, Pharisees make the *o*
Col. 4:5, toward those who are *o*
Heb. 13:13, to Him, *o* the camp
Rev. 22:15, But *o* are dogs and

OUTSTRETCHED
Dt. 26:8, and with an *o* arm
Jer. 21:5, against you with an *o*

OUTWARD
1 Sam. 16:7, at the *o* appearance
1 Pet. 3:3, adornment be merely *o*

OUTWARDLY
Mt. 23:27, appear beautiful *o*
Rom. 2:28, not a Jew who is one *o*

OUTWIT
Ps. 89:22, The enemy shall not *o*

OVEN
Ps. 21:9, make them as a fiery *o*
Mal. 4:1, burning like an *o*
Mt. 6:30, is thrown into the *o*

OVERCAME
Rev. 3:21, My throne, as I also *o*
Rev. 12:11, "And they *o* him by

OVERCOME
Jn. 16:33, good cheer, I have *o*
Rom. 12:21, *o* evil with good
1 Jn. 2:13, because you have *o*
Rev. 17:14, and the Lamb will *o*

OVERCOMES
1 Jn. 5:4, of God *o* the world
Rev. 2:7, *o* I will give to eat
Rev. 2:11, *o* shall not be hurt
Rev. 21:7, *o* shall inherit all

OVERCOMING
glory and reward of. 1 Jn. 2:13; Rev. 2:7,11,17,26; 3:5,12,21; 21:7

OVERFLOWING
Ps. 45:1, My heart is *o* with a

OVERLOOK, Acts 17:30

OVERSEER
Gen. 39:4, Then he made him *o*
Prov. 6:7, having no captain, *o*
1 Pet. 2:25, to the Shepherd and *O*

OVERSEERS
Acts 20:28, Spirit has made you *o*
1 Pet. 5:2, you, serving as *o*

OVERSHADOW
Lk. 1:35, of the Highest will *o*

OVERSIGHT
Gen. 43:12; Neh. 11:16

OVERTAKE
Isa. 59:9, does righteousness *o*
Jer. 42:16, you feared shall *o*
Acts 8:29, and *o* this chariot
1 Th. 5:4, that this Day should *o*

OVERTAKEN
1 Cor. 10:13, No temptation has *o*
Gal. 6:1, if a man is *o* in any

OVERTHREW
Gen. 19:25, So He *o* those cities
Isa. 13:19, will be as when God *o*
Jer. 50:40, As God *o* Sodom and
Amos 4:11, "I *o* some of you

OVERTHROW
Ex. 23:24, you shall utterly *o*
Prov. 18:5, *o* the righteous in
Hag. 2:22, *o* the throne of
2 Tim. 2:18, *o* the faith of some

OVERTHROWN
Ps. 141:6, Their judges are *o*
Lam. 4:6, of Sodom, which was *o*
Ezek. 21:27, I will make it *o*
Jon. 3:4, and Nineveh shall be *o*

OVERTHROWS
Job 12:19, and *o* the mighty
Job 34:25, *o* them in the night
Prov. 22:12, *o* the words of the

OVERTURN, Job 9:5; 28:9

OVERTURNED
Lam. 1:20, my heart is *o* within
Mt. 21:12, *o* the tables of the
Jn. 2:15, money and *o* the tables

OVERWHELM
Job 6:27, *o* the fatherless
Job 12:15, sends them out, they *o*

OVERWHELMED
Ps. 61:2, when my heart is *o*
Ps. 77:3, and my spirit was *o*
Ps. 78:53, *o* their enemies
Ps. 124:4, waters would have *o*
Ps. 143:4, my spirit is *o* within

OVERWORK
Prov. 23:4, Do not *o* to be rich

OWE
Lk. 16:5, 'How much do you *o*
Rom. 13:8, *O* no one anything
Phile. 19, *o* me even your own

OWED
Mt. 18:24, *o* him ten thousand
Mt. 18:28, fellow servants who *o*
Lk. 7:41, *o* five hundred denarii

OWN
Jn. 1:11, He came to His *o*
Jn. 13:1, having loved His *o*
Jn. 15:19, world would love its *o*
1 Cor. 6:19, you are not your *o*
1 Cor. 7:7, But each one has his *o*
Phil. 2:21, For all seek their *o*
Rev. 1:5, from our sins in His *o*

OX
Dt. 25:4, shall not muzzle an *o*
Job 39:9, "Will the wild *o*
Job 39:10, you bind the wild *o*
Ps. 29:6, like a young wild *o*
Ps. 92:10, exalted like a wild *o*
Isa. 1:3, *o* knows its owner
Ezek. 1:10, had the face of an *o*
Lk. 13:15, Sabbath loose his *o*
1 Cor. 9:9, shall not muzzle an *o*

PACE
Prov. 30:29, are majestic in *p*

PACIFIES
Prov. 21:14, A gift in secret *p*
Eccl. 10:4, for conciliation *p*

PADAN ARAM, Gen. 25:20; 28:2

PAILS
Job 21:24, *p* are full of milk

PAIN
Gen. 3:16, *p* you shall bring
Isa. 13:8, *p* as a woman in
Isa. 21:3, are filled with *p*
Isa. 66:7, before her *p* came
Jer. 15:18, Why is my *p* perpetual
Rev. 21:4, shall be no more *p*

PAINED
Ps. 55:4, My heart is severely *p*
Jer. 4:19, I am *p* in my very

PAINFUL
Ps. 73:16, this, it was too *p*
Heb. 12:11, for the present, but *p*

PAINS
Ps. 116:3, The *p* of death
Acts 2:24, having loosed the *p*
1 Th. 5:3, upon them, as labor *p*

PAINT
2 Ki. 9:30, and she put *p* on her
Jer. 4:30, your eyes with *p*

PAINTING
Jer. 22:14, it with cedar and *p*

PALACE
the temple so called. Ps. 48:3; 122:7

PALACE
Ps. 45:15, enter the King's *p*
Isa. 25:2, a *p* of foreigners
Lk. 11:21, guards his own *p*
Phil. 1:13, evident to the whole *p*

PALACES
Ps. 45:8, out of the ivory *p*
Ps. 48:3, God is in her *p*
Jer. 9:21, has entered our *p*

PALE
Isa. 29:22, his face now grow *p*
Jer. 30:6, and all faces turned *p*
Rev. 6:8, behold, a *p* horse

PALM
tree and branches. Ex. 15:27; Lev. 23:40; Dt. 34:3; Jud. 1:16; 3:13; 2 Chr. 28:15; Jn. 12:13; Rev. 7:9

PALMS
Mt. 26:67, struck Him with the *p*

PALTI, Num. 13:9

PALTIEL, Num. 34:26; 2 Sam. 3:15

PAMPERS
Prov. 29:21, *p* his servant from

PAMPHYLIA
Paul preaches there. Acts 13:13; 14:24; 27:5

PANGS
Ps. 18:4, The *p* of death
Isa. 13:8, *P* and sorrows will
Rom. 8:22, labors with birth *p*

PANICKED
Jud. 20:41, the men of Benjamin *p*

PANT
Amos 2:7, They *p* after the dust

PANTS
Ps. 42:1, As the deer *p* for the

PAPHOS, Acts 13:6

PAPYRUS
Job 8:11, "Can the *p* grow up

PARABLE
Ps. 78:2, open my mouth in a *p*
Mt. 13:34, *p* He did not speak
Lk. 12:41, do You speak this *p*

PARABLES
remarkable ones in Old Testament. Jud. 9:8–15; 2 Sam. 12:1,4; 14:5,7; 1 Ki. 20:39; 2 Ki. 14:9; 2 Chr. 25:18
as discourses. Num. 23:7; 24:5,16; Ps. 78:2; Job 27; Prov. 26:9
of the prophets. Isa. 5:1; Jer. 13:1; 18; 24; 27; Ezek. 16; 17; 19; 23; 24; 31; 33; 37
of Christ. Mt. 13:3; 34; Mk. 3:23; 4:13; Lk. 8:10. *See* CHRIST

PARABLES
Ezek. 20:49, 'Does he not speak *p*
Mk. 4:13, understand all the *p*
Lk. 8:10, rest it is given in *p*

PARADE
1 Cor. 13:4, love does not *p*

PARADISE, Rev. 2:7
promised by Christ to the penitent thief. Lk. 23:43
Paul caught up into. 2 Cor. 12:4

PARALYSIS
cured by Christ. Mt. 4:24; 8:6; 9:2; Mk. 2:3; Lk. 5:18
by His disciples. Acts 8:7; 9:33

PARAN
Mount. Gen. 21:21; Num. 10:12; 12:16; 13:26; Dt. 33:2; Hab. 3:3

PARCHMENTS
2 Tim. 4:13, especially the *p*

PARDON
of sin. 2 Chr. 30:18; Neh. 9:17; Job 7:21; Ps. 25:11; Isa. 55:7; Jer. 33:8; 50:20

PARDON
Ex. 23:21, *p* your transgressions
Ps. 25:11, O LORD, *p* my iniquity
Isa. 55:7, He will abundantly *p*
Jer. 33:8, *p* all their iniquities

PARDONING
Mic. 7:18, is a God like You, *p*

PARENTS
duty of. Prov. 13:24; 19:18; 22:6,15; 23:13; 29:15,17; Lk. 11:13; Eph. 6:4; Col. 3:21; 1 Tim. 5:8; Ti. 2:4
duty to. *See* OBEDIENCE

PARENTS
Mt. 10:21, will rise up against *p*
Lk. 18:29, has left house or *p*

Rom. 1:30, disobedient to *p*
2 Cor. 12:14, to lay up for the *p*

PART
Josh. 22:25, You have no *p* in the
Lk. 10:42, chosen that good *p*
Jn. 13:8, you, you have no *p*
1 Cor. 13:9, For we know in *p*
2 Cor. 6:15, *p* has a believer
Rev. 22:19, shall take away his *p*

PARTAKE
1 Cor. 10:17, for we all *p* of that
1 Cor. 10:21, you cannot *p* of the

PARTAKER
Ps. 50:18, and have been a *p*
1 Cor. 9:10, in hope should be *p*
1 Pet. 5:1, Christ, and also a *p*

PARTAKERS
Rom. 15:27, Gentiles have been *p*
1 Cor. 10:18, of the sacrifices *p*
2 Cor. 1:7, know that as you are *p*
Phil. 1:7, gospel, you all are *p*
Col. 1:12, qualified us to be *p*
Heb. 3:14, For we have become *p*

PARTED
Lk. 24:51, them, that He was *p*
Acts 15:39, so sharp that they *p*

PARTHIANS, Acts 2:9

PARTIAL
Lev. 19:15, You shall not be *p*

PARTIALITY
God shows no. Dt. 10:17; 2 Chr. 19:7; Job 34:19; Acts 10:34; Rom. 2:11; Gal. 2:6; Eph. 6:9; Col. 3:25; 1 Pet. 1:17

PARTIALITY
Dt. 1:17, 'You shall not show *p*
Ps. 82:2, unjustly, and show *p*
Prov. 18:5, is not good to show *p*
Mal. 2:9, but have shown *p*
Acts 10:34, that God shows no *p*
Rom. 2:11, For there is no *p*
1 Tim. 5:21, doing nothing with *p*
Jas. 2:9, but if you show *p*
Jas. 3:17, good fruits, without *p*

PARTIES
1 Pet. 4:3, revelries, drinking *p*

PARTITION
Ex. 40:3, the Testimony, and *p*

PARTNER
Prov. 29:24, Whoever is a *p* with a
Phile. 17, you count me as a *p*

PARTRIDGE
1 Sam. 26:20, when one hunts a *p*

PARTS
Ruth 1:17, anything but death *p*
Ps. 51:6, in the inward *p*
Isa. 44:23, Shout, you lower *p*
1 Cor. 12:24, but our presentable *p*
Eph. 4:9, into the lower *p*

PASS
Ex. 12:13, I will *p* over you
Ps. 8:8, of the sea that *p*
Isa. 43:2, When you *p* through the
Ezek. 20:37, "I will make you *p*
Amos 7:8, I will not *p* by them
Mt. 24:35, and earth will *p*

PASSED
1 Ki. 19:11, And behold, the LORD *p*
Rom. 3:25, forbearance God had *p*
Heb. 4:14, High Priest who has *p*
1 Jn. 3:14, know that we have *p*

PASSES
Ps. 103:16, For the wind *p* over it
Eph. 3:19, of Christ which *p*

PASSION
1 Cor. 7:9, than to burn with *p*
Col. 3:5, uncleanness, *p*

PASSIONS
Rom. 1:26, gave them up to vile *p*

PASSOVER
ordained. Ex. 12:3,11
laws relating to. Lev. 23:4; Num. 9; 28:16; Dt. 16
kept: under Moses in Egypt. Ex. 12:12; at Sinai. Num. 9:5; under Joshua in Canaan. Josh. 5:10; by Hezekiah after the captivity of Israel. 2 Chr. 30:13; by Josiah before the captivity of Judah. 2 Ki. 23:21; 2 Chr. 35; by Ezra on return from the captivity. Ezra 6:19
kept by Christ. Mt. 26:19; Mk. 14:12; Lk. 22:7; Jn. 13
a type of Christ's death. 1 Cor. 5:7

PASSOVER
Ex. 12:11, It is the LORD's *P*
2 Ki. 23:23, of King Josiah this *P*
Mt. 26:18, I will keep the *P*
1 Cor. 5:7, indeed Christ, our *P*
Heb. 11:28, By faith he kept the *P*

PAST
Job 17:11, My days are *p*
Song 2:11, lo, the winter is *p*
Rom. 11:33, and His ways *p* finding
Heb. 1:1, ways spoke in time *p*
1 Pet. 4:3, *p* lifetime in doing

PASTORS
Eph. 4:11, and some *p* and

PASTURE
Ps. 74:1, the sheep of Your *p*
Ps. 95:7, the people of His *p*
Ezek. 34:14, feed them in good *p*
Jn. 10:9, in and out and find *p*

PASTURES
Ps. 23:2, to lie down in green *p*

PATH
Job 28:7, *p* no bird knows
Ps. 16:11, You will show me the *p*
Ps. 27:11, lead me in a smooth *p*
Prov. 4:18, But the *p* of the just
Isa. 43:16, way in the sea and a *p*

PATHROS
in Egypt. Isa. 11:11; Jer. 44:1,15; Ezek. 29:14; 30:14

PATHS
Ps. 23:3, He leads me in the *p*
Ps. 25:4, Teach me Your *p*
Prov. 3:17, and all her *p* are
Isa. 42:16, *p* they have not
Isa. 59:8, themselves crooked *p*
Mt. 3:3, Make His *p* straight
Heb. 12:13, and make straight *p*

PATIENCE
commended. Ps. 37:7; Eccl. 7:8; Isa. 30:15; 40:31; Lk. 21:19; Rom. 12:12; 1 Th. 5:14; 2 Th. 3:5; 1 Tim. 3:3; 6:11; Heb. 12:1; Jas. 1:3; 5:7; 1 Pet. 2:20; 2 Pet. 1:6
blessed results of. Rom. 5:3; 15:4; Heb. 6:12; Rev. 2:2; 3:10

PATIENCE
Mt. 18:26, 'Master, have *p*
Lk. 8:15, and bear fruit with *p*
Rom. 15:5, Now may the God of *p*
1 Th. 1:3, labor of love, and *p*
1 Tim. 6:11, faith, love, *p*
Jas. 1:3, your faith produces *p*
Jas. 1:4, *p* have its perfect
Rev. 1:9, in the kingdom and *p*
Rev. 13:10, Here is the *p* and the

PATIENT
Rom. 12:12, rejoicing in hope, *p*
1 Th. 5:14, uphold the weak, be *p*

PATIENTLY
Ps. 37:7, the LORD, and wait *p*
1 Pet. 2:20, if you take it *p*

PATMOS
place of John's exile. Rev. 1:9

PATRIARCHS
their genealogy. Gen. 5

PATRIARCHS
Acts 7:8, begot the twelve *p*

PATTERN, 1 Tim. 1:16; Ti. 2:7
of the tabernacle, etc. Ex. 25:9,40 (Ezek. 43:10); Heb. 8:5

PATTERN
Ex. 26:30, *p* which you were
Phil. 3:17, as you have us for a *p*
2 Tim. 1:13, Hold fast the *p*
Heb. 8:5, *p* shown you on the

PAUL
apostle. Acts 13:9
as a persecutor. Acts 7:58; 8:1; 9:1; 22:4; 26:9; 1 Cor. 15:9; Gal. 1:13; Phil. 3:6; 1 Tim. 1:13
as a convert to the Gospel. Acts 9:3; 22:6; 26:12
as a preacher. Acts 9:19,29; 13:1,4,14; 17:18 (2 Cor. 11:32; Gal. 1:17)
stoned at Lystra. Acts 14:8,19
contends with Barnabas. Acts 15:36
is persecuted at Philippi. Acts 16
the Holy Spirit given by his hands to John's disciples at Ephesus. Acts 19:6
restores Eutychus. Acts 20:10
his charge to the elders of Ephesus. Acts 20:17
his return to Jerusalem, and persecution there. Acts 21
his defense before: the people and the council. Acts 22; 23; before Felix. Acts 24; Festus. Acts 25; and Agrippa. Acts 26

appeals to Caesar at Rome. Acts 25
his voyage and shipwreck. Acts 27
miracles by, at Malta. Acts 28:3,8
at Rome, reasons with the Jews. Acts 28:17
his love to the churches. Rom. 1:8; 15; 1 Cor. 1:4; 4:14; 2 Cor. 1; 2; 6; 7; Phil. 1; Col. 1; 1 & 2 Th.
his sufferings. 1 Cor. 4:9; 2 Cor. 11:23; 12:7; Phil. 1:12; 2 Tim. 3:11
divine revelations to. 2 Cor. 12:1
defends his apostleship. 1 Cor. 9; 2 Cor. 11; 12; 2 Tim. 3:10
commends Timothy, etc. 1 Cor. 16:10; Phil. 2:19; 1 Th. 3:2
commends Titus. 2 Cor. 7:13; 8:23
censures Peter. Gal. 2:14
pleads for Onesimus. Phile.
his epistles mentioned by Peter. 2 Pet. 3:15

PAVILION
Ps. 27:5, shall hide me in His *p*
Ps. 31:20, them secretly in a *p*

PAWS
Job 39:21, He *p* in the valley

PAY
Prov. 22:27, with which to *p*
Mic. 3:11, priests teach for *p*
Mt. 18:26, with me, and I will *p*
Mt. 22:17, *p* taxes to Caesar
Mt. 23:23, For you *p* tithe of

PEACE
to be sought of God. Ezra 6:10; Jer. 29:7; 1 Tim. 2:2
bestowed by God. Lev. 26:6; 1 Ki. 2:33; 4:24; 2 Ki. 20:19; Prov. 16:7; Isa. 45:7; Jer. 14:13
exhortations to maintain. Ps. 34:14; Mt. 5:9; Rom. 12:18; 14:19; 1 Cor. 7:15; Eph. 4:3; 1 Th. 5:13; 2 Tim. 2:22; Jas. 3:18; 1 Pet. 3:11
spiritual, gift of God. (Jn. 14:27); Acts 10:36; Rom. 1:7; 5:1; 8:6; 14:17; Phil. 4:7; Col. 3:15; 1 Th. 5:23; 2 Th. 3:16; Rev. 1:4
proclaimed to the Gentiles. Zech. 9:10; Eph. 2:14,17; 3
produced by the Spirit. Gal. 5:22
denied to the wicked. 2 Ki. 9:31; Isa. 48:22; 59:8 (Rom. 3:17); Jer. 12:12; Ezek. 7:25
to whom promised. Ps. 29:11; 85:8; 122:6; 125:5; 128:6; 147:14; Jn. 14:27; Gal. 6:16; Eph. 6:23
on earth. Lk. 2:14
in heaven. Lk. 19:38
—— king of (Melchizedek). Heb. 7:2
—— the Prince of (Christ). Isa. 9:6

PEACE
Gen. 34:21, "These men are at *p*
Lev. 26:6, I will give *p* in the
Num. 6:26, you, and give you *p*
2 Ki. 18:31, 'Make *p* with me by a
Job 5:23, field shall be at *p*
Ps. 4:8, both lie down in *p*
Ps. 34:14, seek *p*
Ps. 85:8, for He will speak *p*
Ps. 119:165, *p* have those who
Ps. 120:7, I am for *p*
Ps. 122:6, for the *p* of Jerusalem
Ps. 122:7, *P* be within your walls
Ps. 125:5, *P* be upon Israel
Eccl. 3:8, war, and a time of *p*
Isa. 9:6, Father, Prince of *P*
Isa. 26:3, keep him in perfect *p*
Isa. 59:8, *p* they have not
Jer. 6:14, slightly, saying, '*P*
Jer. 8:15, "We looked for *p*
Jer. 14:13, give you assured *p*
Ezek. 7:25, they will seek *p*
Dan. 4:1, *P* be multiplied
Mic. 5:5, this One shall be *p*
Hag. 2:9, place I will give *p*
Mt. 10:13, is worthy, let your *p*
Mt. 10:34, that I came to bring *p*
Lk. 2:14, and on earth *p*
Lk. 10:6, if a son of *p* is there
Lk. 19:42, that make for your *p*
Jn. 14:27, leave with you, My *p*
Jn. 16:33, in Me you may have *p*
Rom. 1:7, Grace to you and *p*
Rom. 5:1, by faith, we have *p*
1 Cor. 7:15, God has called us to *p*
2 Cor. 13:11, *p* will be with you
Gal. 5:22, Spirit is love, joy, *p*
Eph. 2:14, He Himself is our *p*
Phil. 4:7, and the *p* of God
Col. 1:20, heaven, having made *p*
Col. 3:15, And let the *p* of God
1 Th. 5:13, Be at *p* among
2 Tim. 2:22, faith, love, *p*
Heb. 7:2, meaning "king of *p*,"
Jas. 3:18, is sown in *p* by those
2 Pet. 1:2, *p* be multiplied

PEACE OFFERINGS
laws pertaining to. Ex. 20:24; 24:5; Lev. 3; 6; 7:11; 19:5

PEACEABLE
1 Tim. 2:2, and *p* life in all
Jas. 3:17, is first pure, then *p*

PEACEABLY
Rom. 12:18, on you, live *p*

PEACEFUL
Isa. 32:18, in a *p* habitation

PEACEMAKERS
Mt. 5:9, Blessed are the *p*

PEARL
Mt. 13:46, had found one *p*
Rev. 21:21, gate was of one *p*

PEARLS
Mt. 7:6, nor cast your *p*
1 Tim. 2:9, hair or gold or *p*
Rev. 21:21, gates were twelve *p*

PEG
Jud. 4:21, wife, took a tent *p*
Isa. 22:23, will fasten him as a *p*

PEKAH
king of Israel. 2 Ki. 15:25
his victory over Judah. 2 Chr. 28:6
denounced in prophecy. Isa. 7:1

PEKAHIAH
king of Israel. 2 Ki. 15:22

PEN
Ps. 45:1, My tongue is the *p*
Isa. 8:1, on it with a man's *p*
3 Jn. 13, to write to you with *p*

PENIEL
(the face of God), scene of Jacob's wrestling with an angel. Gen. 32:30
Gideon's vengeance upon. Jud. 8:17

PENNY
Mt. 5:26, have paid the last *p*

PENTECOST (Feast of Weeks)
how observed. Lev. 23:15; Dt. 16:9
Holy Spirit given at. Acts 2

PENTECOST
Acts 2:1, *P* had fully come

PENUEL
old form of Peniel. Gen. 32:31

PEOPLE
Ex. 6:7, will take you as My *p*
Dt. 33:29, Who is like you, a *p*
Ruth 1:16, *p* shall be my *p*
Ps. 89:15, *p* who know the joyful
Ps. 100:3, We are His *p* and the
Ps. 144:15, Happy are the *p*
Isa. 19:25, "Blessed is Egypt My *p*
Isa. 30:9, this is a rebellious *p*
Isa. 65:3, *p* who provoke Me
Jer. 24:7, and they shall be My *p*
Hos. 1:9, for you are not My *p*
Hos. 4:9, like *p*, like priest
Lk. 1:17, to make ready a *p*
Acts 15:14, take out of them a *p*
Rom. 9:25, who were not My *p*
2 Cor. 6:16, they shall be My *p*
Ti. 2:14, His own special *p*
Heb. 10:30, LORD will judge His *p*
1 Pet. 2:10, but are now the *p*
Rev. 5:9, tribe and tongue and *p*
Rev. 21:3, they shall be His *p*

PEOR (Baal)
Num. 23:28; 25:3,18; Josh. 22:17

PERCEIVE
Dt. 29:4, given you a heart to *p*
Job 23:8, but I cannot *p*
Isa. 6:9, seeing, but do not *p*
Mk. 4:12, may see and not *p*

PERDITION
what results in. Phil. 1:28; 1 Tim. 6:9; Heb. 10:39; 2 Pet. 3:7; Rev. 17:8
the son of. Jn. 17:12; 2 Th. 2:3

PERDITION
Jn. 17:12, except the son of *p*
Phil. 1:28, to them a proof of *p*
2 Th. 2:3, revealed, the son of *p*
Heb. 10:39, who draw back to *p*
2 Pet. 3:7, day of judgment and *p*

PERES, Dan. 5:28

PEREZ
Gen. 38:29; Ruth 4:18; 1 Chr. 27:3; Lk. 3:33

PERFECT
Gen. 6:9, Noah was a just man, *p*
Job 36:4, one who is *p* in
Ps. 18:30, for God, His way is *p*
Ezek. 28:15, You were *p* in your

Mt. 5:48, Father in heaven is *p*
Mt. 19:21, "If you want to be *p*
Jn. 17:23, they may be made *p*
Rom. 12:2, and *p* will of God
1 Cor. 13:10, when that which is *p*
Col. 1:28, present every man *p*
Heb. 7:19, the law made nothing *p*
Heb. 12:23, of just men made *p*
Jas. 1:17, good gift and every *p*
Jas. 3:2, in word, he is a *p*
1 Jn. 4:18, *p* love casts out fear

PERFECTED
Lk. 13:32, third day I shall be *p*
Phil. 3:12, or am already *p*
Heb. 7:28, Son who has been *p*
1 Jn. 2:5, the love of God is *p*

PERFECTION
of God. Dt. 32:4; 2 Sam. 22:31; Job 36:4; Mt. 5:48
of Christ. Heb. 2:10; 5:9; 7:28
of God's law. Ps. 19:7; 119; Jas. 1:25
of saints. Col. 1:28; 3:14. *See* Mt. 5:48; 2 Cor. 12:9; Heb. 6:1; 11:40

PERFECTION
Ps. 50:2, the *p* of beauty
Ps. 119:96, consummation of all *p*
Heb. 6:1, let us go on to *p*

PERFECTLY, Jer. 23:20; 1 Cor. 1:10

PERFORM
Ps. 119:112, *p* Your statutes
Jer. 1:12, am ready to *p* My word
Rom. 7:18, *p* what is good I

PERGAMUM
epistle to. Rev. 1:11; 2:12

PERIL
Rom. 8:35, or nakedness, or *p*

PERILOUS
Ps. 91:3, from the *p* pestilence
2 Tim. 3:1, in the last days *p*

PERILS
2 Cor. 11:26, journeys often, in *p*

PERISH
Num. 17:12, "Surely we die, we *p*
Job 34:15, All flesh would *p*
Ps. 80:16, they *p* at the rebuke
Ps. 146:4, very day his plans *p*
Jon. 1:6, so that we may not *p*
Mt. 18:14, little ones should *p*
Lk. 13:3, will all likewise *p*
Jn. 3:16, in Him should not *p*
Jn. 10:28, they shall never *p*
Col. 2:22, concern things which *p*
2 Th. 2:10, among those who *p*
2 Pet. 3:9, that any should *p*

PERISHABLE
1 Cor. 9:25, do it to obtain a *p*

PERISHED
Job 4:7, *p* being innocent
Jer. 7:28, Truth has *p* and has
Mic. 7:2, The faithful man has *p*

PERISHING
Mt. 8:25, We are *p*
2 Cor. 4:3, to those who are *p*

PERIZZITES
Gen. 13:7; 15:20; 34:30; Jud. 1:4; 2 Chr. 8:7

PERJURER
Zech. 5:3, *p* shall be expelled

PERMIT
Acts 16:7, the Spirit did not *p*
1 Tim. 2:12, do not *p* a woman

PERMITS
1 Cor. 16:7, you, if the Lord *p*
Heb. 6:3, we will do if God *p*

PERMITTED
Ps. 105:14, *p* no one to do them

PERPETUALLY
1 Ki. 9:3; 2 Chr. 7:16; Amos 1:11

PERPETUATED
Nah. 1:14, Your name shall be *p*

PERPLEXED
Jn. 13:22, at one another, *p*
2 Cor. 4:8, we are *p*

PERPLEXITY
Isa. 22:5; Mic. 7:4; Lk. 21:25

PERSECUTE
Job 19:22, *p* me as God does
Ps. 119:86, *p* me wrongfully
Mt. 5:11, when they revile and *p*
Rom. 12:14, Bless those who *p*

PERSECUTED
Ps. 109:16, *p* the poor and needy
Mt. 5:12, *p* the prophets who
Jn. 15:20, If they *p* Me
1 Cor. 15:9, *p* the church of God
2 Cor. 4:9, *p*, but not forsaken
Gal. 1:23, *p* us now preaches the

PERSECUTES
Ps. 10:2, wicked in his pride *p*

PERSECUTION
coming of. Mt. 13:21; 23:34; Mk. 10:30; Lk. 11:49; Jn. 15:20; 2 Cor. 4:9; 2 Tim. 3:12
conduct under. Mt. 5:44; 10:22; Acts 5:41; Rom. 12:14; Phil. 1:28; Heb. 10:34; 1 Pet. 4:13–19
results of. Mt. 5:10; Lk. 6:22; 9:24; Jas. 1:2; 1 Pet. 4:14; Rev. 6:9; 7:13

PERSECUTION
Mt. 13:21, *p* arises because of
Acts 8:1, At that time a great *p*
Gal. 5:11, do I still suffer *p*

PERSECUTOR
1 Tim. 1:13, a blasphemer, a *p*

PERSEVERANCE
commanded. Mt. 24:13; Mk. 13:13; Lk. 9:62; Acts 13:43; 1 Cor. 15:58; 16:13; Eph. 6:18; Col. 1:23; 2 Th. 3:13; 1 Tim. 6:14; Heb. 3:6,13; 10:23,38; 2 Pet. 3:17; Rev. 2:10,25

PERSEVERANCE
Rom. 5:3, tribulation produces *p*
Eph. 6:18, to this end will all *p*
2 Tim. 3:10, longsuffering, love, *p*
2 Pet. 1:6, to self-control *p*

PERSEVERE
Rev. 3:10, kept My command to *p*

PERSIA
kingdom of. 2 Chr. 36:20; Est. 1:3; Ezek. 27:10; 38:5; Dan. 6
prophecies concerning. Isa. 21:2; Dan. 5:28; 8:20; 10:13; 11:2

PERSIAN, Dan. 6:28

PERSISTENCE
Lk. 11:8, *p* he will rise and

PERSON
Ps. 15:4, In whose eyes a vile *p*
Prov. 19:15, *p* will suffer hunger
Mt. 22:16, do not regard the *p*
Heb. 1:3, express image of His *p*
1 Pet. 3:4, let it be the hidden *p*

PERSUADE
Acts 26:28, "You almost *p* me
2 Cor. 5:11, the Lord, we *p* men
Gal. 1:10, For do I now *p* men

PERSUADED
Prov. 25:15, a ruler is *p*
Lk. 16:31, neither will they be *p*
2 Tim. 1:12, *p* that He is able

PERSUASIVE
1 Cor. 2:4, *p* words of human
Col. 2:4, you with *p* words

PERTAIN
Rom. 15:17; 1 Cor. 6:3; 2 Pet. 1:3

PERTAINING
Heb. 2:17, Priest in things *p*
Heb. 5:1, for men in things *p*

PERTURBED
Prov. 30:21, things the earth is *p*

PERVERSE
Num. 22:32, your way is *p*
Prov. 3:32, for the *p* person is an
Prov. 4:24, *p* lips far from you
Prov. 12:8, *p* heart will be
Prov. 16:28, *p* man sows strife
Prov. 28:18, but he who is *p*
Acts 2:40, from this *p* generation

PERVERSITY
Isa. 30:12, in oppression and *p*

PERVERT
Dt. 16:19, "You shall not *p*
Mic. 3:9, and *p* all equity
Gal. 1:7, *p* the gospel of Christ

PERVERTED PERSONS, 1 Ki. 15:12

PERVERTING
Lk. 23:2, We found this fellow *p*
Acts 13:10, will you not cease *p*

PERVERTS
Ex. 23:8, *p* the words of the
Prov. 10:9, *p* his ways will become

PESTILENCE
Ex. 5:3; 9:15; Jer. 42:17; 44:13
the penalty of disobedience. Lev. 26:25; Num. 14:12; Dt. 28:21; Jer. 14:12; 27:13; Ezek. 5:12; 6:11; 7:15; Mt. 24:7; Lk. 21:11
Israel visited with. Num. 14:37; 16:46; 25:9; 2 Sam. 24:15

removed. Num. 16:47; 2 Sam. 24:16

PESTILENCE
Ps. 91:3, from the perilous *p*
Ps. 91:6, *p* that walks in
Hab. 3:5, Before Him went *p*

PESTILENCES
Mt. 24:7, will be famines, *p*

PETER, Mt. 16:18
apostle, called. Mt. 4:18; Mk. 1:16; Lk. 5; Jn. 1:35
sent out. Mt. 10:2; Mk. 3:16; Lk. 6:14
tries to walk to Jesus on the sea. Mt. 14:29
confesses Jesus to be the Christ. Mt. 16:16; Mk. 8:29; Lk. 9:20
witnesses the Transfiguration. Mt. 17; Mk. 9; Lk. 9:28; 2 Pet. 1:16
his self-confidence rebuked. Lk. 22:31; Jn. 13:36
three times denies Christ. Mt. 26:69; Mk. 14:66; Lk. 22:57; Jn. 18:17
his repentance. Mt. 26:75; Mk. 14:72; Lk. 22:62
the assembled disciples addressed by. Acts 1:15
the Jews preached to by. Acts 2:14; 3:12
brought before the council. Acts 4
condemns Ananias and Sapphira. Acts 5
denounces Simon the sorcerer. Acts 8:18
restores Aeneas and Tabitha. Acts 9:32,40
sent for by Cornelius. Acts 10
instructed by a vision not to despise the Gentiles. Acts 10:9
imprisoned, and liberated by an angel. Acts 12
his decision about circumcision. Acts 15:7
rebuked by Paul. Gal. 2:14
bears witness to Paul's teaching. 2 Pet. 3:15
comforts the church, and exhorts to holy living by his epistles. 1 & 2 Pet.
his martyrdom foretold by Christ. Jn. 21:18; 2 Pet. 1:14

PETITION
1 Sam. 1:17, of Israel grant your *p*

PETITIONS
Ps. 20:5, fulfill all your *p*
1 Jn. 5:15, *p* that we have asked

PHANUEL, Lk. 2:36

PHARAOH
title of rulers of Egypt. Gen. 12:14; Ezek. 29:3
Abram's wife taken into house of. Gen. 12:15
Pharaoh plagued because of her. Gen. 12:17
——— patron of Joseph, his dreams, etc. Gen. 40
his hospitality to Joseph's father and brothers. Gen. 47
——— oppressor of the Israelites. Ex. 1:8
daughter preserves Moses. Ex. 2:5,10; Acts 7:21
——— of the Exodus, miracles performed before, and plagues sent. Ex. 7—10
grants Moses' request. Ex. 12:31
repenting, pursues Israel, and perishes in the Red Sea. Ex. 14 (Neh. 9:10; Ps. 135:9; 136:15; Rom. 9:17)
——— father-in-law of Solomon. 1 Ki. 3:1
shelters Hadad, Solomon's adversary. 1 Ki. 11:19

PHARAOH HOPHRA
his fate predicted. Jer. 44:30. *See* Ezek. 30—32
compared to a monster. Ezek. 29:3

PHARAOH NECHO
kills Josiah. 2 Ki. 23:29; 2 Chr. 35:20
his wars with Israel. 2 Ki. 23:33; 2 Chr. 36:3

PHARISEE
Lk. 18:10, to pray, one a *P*
Acts 23:6, and brethren, I am a *P*

PHARISEES
famous ones: Nicodemus. Jn. 3:1; Simon. Lk. 7; Gamaliel. Acts 5:34; Saul of Tarsus. Acts 23:6; 26:5; Phil. 3:5
Christ entertained by. Lk. 7:36; 11:37; 14:1
Christ utters woes against. Mt. 23:13; Lk. 11:42
Christ questioned by, about: divorce. Mt. 19:3; eating. Mt. 9:11; 15:1; Mk. 2:16; Lk. 5:30; forgiveness of sin. Lk. 5:21; Sabbath. Mt. 12:2,10; fasting. Mk. 2:18; taxes. Mt. 22:17
deride Christ. Lk. 16:14
complain against Christ. Mt. 9:34; Lk. 15:2
denounced by Christ. Mt. 5:20; 16:6; 21:43; 23:2; Lk. 11:39
people cautioned against. Mk. 8:15; Lk. 12:1
seek a sign from Christ. Mt. 12:38; 16:1
take counsel against Christ. Mt. 12:14; Mk. 3:6
Nicodemus remonstrates with. Jn. 7:51
cast out the man cured of blindness. Jn. 9:13
dissensions about. Jn. 9:16
send officers to take Christ. Jn. 7:32
contend about circumcision. Acts 15:5
their belief in the resurrection, etc. Acts 23:8
and tax collector. Lk. 18

PHILADELPHIA
church of, commended. Rev. 1:11; 3:7

PHILIP
apostle, called. Jn. 1:43
sent out. Mt. 10:3; Mk. 3:18; Lk. 6:14; Jn. 12:22; Acts 1:13
remonstrated with by Christ. Jn. 14:8
——— deacon, elected. Acts 6:5
preaches in Samaria. Acts 8:5
baptizes the eunuch. Acts 8:27
his four virgin daughters prophesy. Acts 21:8
——— brother of Herod. Mt. 14:3; Mk. 6:17; Lk. 3:1,19

PHILIPPI
(a town so called after Philip of Macedonia), Paul persecuted at. Acts 16:12
church at, commended and exhorted. Phil. 1—4

PHILIPPIANS, Phil. 4:15

PHILISTIA
Gen. 21:34; Ex. 13:17; 15:14; Josh. 13:2; 2 Ki. 8:2; Ps. 60:8; Isa. 14:29,31

PHILISTINES, Gen. 21:34
origin of. Gen. 10:14; 1 Chr. 1:12
fill up Isaac's wells. Gen. 26:15
contend with: Joshua. Josh. 13; Shamgar. Jud. 3:31; Samson. Jud. 14—16; Samuel. 1 Sam. 4; 7; Jonathan. 1 Sam. 14; Saul. 1 Sam. 17; David. 1 Sam. 18
their wars with Israel. 1 Sam. 4:1; 28; 29; 31; 2 Chr. 21:16
mentioned. Ps. 60:8; 83:7; 87:4; 108:9; Isa. 2:6; 9:12; 11:14; Jer. 25:20
their destruction predicted. Jer. 47; Ezek. 25:15; Amos 1:8; Obad. 19; Zeph. 2:5; Zech. 9:6

PHILOSOPHERS
Acts 17:18, *p* encountered him

PHILOSOPHY
Col. 2:8, cheat you through *p*

PHINEHAS, Ex. 6:25
kills Zimri and Cozbi. Num. 25:7,11; Ps. 106:30
sent against the Midianites, Reubenites, and Benjamites. Num. 31:6; Josh. 22:13; Jud. 20:28
——— son of Eli, his sin and death. 1 Sam. 1:3; 2:22; 4:11

PHOEBE, Rom. 16:1

PHOENICIA
Acts 11:19; 15:3; 21:2; 27:12

PHRYGIA, Acts 2:10; 16:6; 18:23

PHYGELLUS
and Hermogenes turned away from Paul. 2 Tim. 1:15

PHYLACTERIES
Mt. 23:5, They make their *p*

PHYSICIAN
Jer. 8:22, Gilead, is there no *p*
Mt. 9:12, have no need of a *p*
Col. 4:14, Luke the beloved *p*

PHYSICIANS
Job 13:4, are all worthless *p*
Lk. 8:43, her livelihood on *p*

PIECES
Zech. 11:12, for my wages thirty *p*
Mt. 27:9, they took the thirty *p*
Rev. 2:17, shall be dashed to *p*

PIERCE
Ex. 21:6, and his master shall *p*
Lk. 2:35, a sword will *p*

PIERCED
Ps. 22:16, *p* My hands and My feet
Zech. 12:10, whom they have *p*
Jn. 19:34, of the soldiers *p*
1 Tim. 6:10, *p* themselves through
Rev. 1:7, and they also who *p*

PIERCING
Heb. 4:12, *p* even to the division

PIETY
1 Tim. 5:4, first learn to show *p*

PILATE, Mt. 27:2
Pontius, governor of Judea during our Lord's ministry, sufferings, and death. Lk. 3:1
Christ delivered to, admonished by his wife, examines Jesus, washes his hands, but delivers Him to be crucified. Mt. 27; Mk. 15; Lk. 23; Jn. 18; 19
grants request of Joseph of Arimathea. Mt. 27:57; Mk. 15:42; Lk. 23:50; Jn. 19:38. *See* Acts 3:13; 4:27; 13:28; 1 Tim. 6:13

PILGRIMAGE
Ps. 84:5, heart is set on *p*
Ps. 119:54, In the house of my *p*

PILGRIMS
1 Chr. 29:15, we are aliens and *p*
Heb. 11:13, were strangers and *p*

PILLAR
Gen. 19:26, and she became a *p*
Ex. 13:21, and by night in a *p*
1 Tim. 3:15, the living God, the *p*

PILLARS
Ex. 34:13, break their sacred *p*
Ps. 75:3, I set up its *p* firmly
Prov. 9:1, out her seven *p*
Joel 2:30, blood and fire and *p*
Rev. 10:1, and his feet like *p*

PILLOW, Mk. 4:38

PILOT
Jas. 3:4, rudder wherever the *p*

PINE
Isa. 41:19, cypress tree and the *p*
Lam. 4:9, for these *p* away

PINNACLE
Lk. 4:9, set Him on the *p*

PISGAH, Josh. 12:3
Mount. Num. 21:20; 23:14; Dt. 3:27; 34:1

PISHON
a river in Eden. Gen. 2:11

PISIDIA, Acts 13:14; 14:24

PIT
the grave, death. Job 33:18; Ps. 28:1; 30:9; 88:4; 143:7; Isa. 14:15; 38:17; Ezek. 26:20; 32:18
as a prison. Isa. 24:22; Zech. 9:11

PIT
Gen. 37:20, cast him into some *p*
Job 33:22, soul draws near the *P*
Ps. 28:1, who go down to the *p*
Prov. 22:14, woman is a deep *p*
Prov. 23:27, a harlot is a deep *p*
Prov. 28:10, fall into his own *p*
Lam. 3:53, my life in the *p*
Ezek. 31:16, who descend into the *P*
Jon. 2:6, up my life from the *p*
Zech. 9:11, from the waterless *p*
Mt. 12:11, if it falls into a *p*
Rev. 20:3, into the bottomless *p*

PITCH
used for the ark, etc. Gen. 6:14; Ex. 2:3; Isa. 34:9

PITCHERS
Jud. 7:16, hand, with empty *p*
Mk. 7:4, the washing of cups, *p*

PITHOM (and Raamses)
cities built by Israelites in Egypt. Ex. 1:11

PITIABLE
1 Cor. 15:19, of all men the most *p*

PITS
Ps. 119:85, The proud have dug *p*

PITY
Dt. 7:16, eye shall have no *p*
Job 19:21, "Have *p* on me
Ps. 69:20, for someone to take *p*
Prov. 19:17, He who has *p* on the
Isa. 63:9, *p* He redeemed them
Joel 2:18, land, and *p* His people
Jon. 4:11, And should I not *p*
Mt. 18:33, just as I had *p*

PLACE
Job 7:10, *p* know him anymore
Eccl. 3:20, All go to one *p*
Hos. 5:15, return again to My *p*
Mt. 28:6, Come, see the *p*
Jn. 8:37, My word has no *p*
Jn. 14:2, I go to prepare a *p*
Acts 1:25, might go to his own *p*

PLACES
idolatrous. 1 Ki. 11:7; 12:31; 13; Ps. 78:58; Ezek. 16:24
destruction of. Lev. 26:30; 2 Ki. 18:4; 23; 2 Chr. 14:3; 17:6; 34:3; Ezek. 6:3

PLACES
Ps. 73:18, set them in slippery *p*
Ps. 74:20, dark *p* of the earth
Isa. 40:4, and the rough *p*
Mt. 23:6, They love the best *p*
Eph. 1:3, in the heavenly *p*

PLAGUE
Paul so called. Acts 24:5

PLAGUE
Ex. 11:1, bring yet one more *p*
Ps. 91:10, *p* come near your
Ps. 106:30, and the *p* was stopped

PLAGUES
of Egypt. *See* EGYPT
of Israel. *See* PESTILENCE

PLAGUES
Ex. 9:14, I will send all My *p*
Hos. 13:14, I will be your *p*
Rev. 22:18, *p* that are written

PLAINLY
Jn. 10:24, the Christ, tell us *p*
Jn. 16:29, now You are speaking *p*
Heb. 11:14, such things declare *p*

PLAN
Ps. 140:2, *p* evil things in their
Zech. 7:10, Let none of you *p*

PLANK
Mt. 7:5, First remove the *p*

PLANS
Ps. 33:10, He makes the *p* of the
Ps. 146:4, in that very day his *p*
Prov. 6:18, that devises wicked *p*
Prov. 16:9, A man's heart *p*
Prov. 20:18, *P* are established

PLANT
used figuratively. Ps. 128:3; 144:12; Song 4:13; Isa. 5:7; 53:2; Jer. 2:21; Ezek. 34:29; Mt. 15:13

PLANT
Eccl. 3:2, A time to *p*
Isa. 53:2, Him as a tender *p*
Isa. 65:21, they shall *p* vineyards
Jer. 2:21, *p* of an alien vine
Mt. 15:13, *p* which My heavenly

PLANTED
Ps. 1:3, shall be like a tree *p*
Ps. 80:15, Your right hand has *p*
Isa. 40:24, shall they be *p*
Lk. 17:6, by the roots and be *p*
1 Cor. 3:6, I *p*, Apollos watered

PLANTS
Ps. 144:12, our sons may be as *p*
Isa. 16:8, down its choice *p*
1 Cor. 3:7, neither he who *p*

PLATFORM
Neh. 8:4, scribe stood on a *p*

PLATTER
Mt. 14:8, head here on a *p*

PLAY
Ex. 32:6, and rose up to *p*
Ps. 33:3, *p* skillfully with a
Isa. 11:8, nursing child shall *p*
1 Cor. 10:7, and rose up to *p*

PLEAD
Jud. 6:31, the one who would *p*
Job 16:21, Oh, that one might *p*
Ps. 43:1, *p* my cause against an
Prov. 6:3, *p* with your friend
Jer. 2:35, Behold, I will *p*
Jer. 25:31, *p* His case with all

PLEADED
Ex. 32:11, Then Moses *p* with the
2 Cor. 12:8, this thing I *p* with

PLEADING
of God with Israel. Isa. 1; 3:13; 43:26; Jer. 2—6; 13; Ezek. 17:20; 20:36; 22; Hos. 2; Joel 3:2; Mic. 2
of Job with God. Job 9:19; 16:21

PLEADING
2 Cor. 5:20, though God were *p*

PLEASANT
Gen. 3:6, food, that it was *p*
Ps. 106:24, they despised the *p*
Ps. 133:1, how good and how *p*
Prov. 2:10, and knowledge is *p*
Prov. 16:24, *P* words are like a
Jer. 23:10, *p* places of the
Jer. 31:20, Is he a *p* child
Dan. 10:3, I ate no *p* food

PLEASANTNESS
Prov. 3:17, Her ways are ways of *p*

PLEASE
Prov. 16:7, When a man's ways *p*
Jn. 8:29, do those things that *p*
Rom. 8:8, in the flesh cannot *p*
Rom. 15:2, *p* his neighbor for his
1 Cor. 7:32, how he may *p* the Lord
Gal. 1:10, Or do I seek to *p* men
Heb. 11:6, is impossible to *p* Him

PLEASED
Ps. 51:19, Then You shall be *p*
Isa. 42:21, The LORD is well *p*
Mal. 1:8, Would he be *p* with you
Mt. 3:17, in whom I am well *p*
1 Cor. 10:5, God was not well *p*
Heb. 11:5, testimony, that he *p*
2 Pet. 1:17, in whom I am well *p*

PLEASES
Ps. 115:3, He does whatever He *p*
Ps. 135:6, Whatever the LORD *p*

PLEASING
Phil. 4:18, sacrifice, well *p*
Col. 3:20, for this is well *p*
Heb. 13:21, in you what is well *p*

PLEASURE
Ps. 5:4, not a God who takes *p*
Ps. 51:18, Do good in Your good *p*
Ps. 102:14, Your servants take *p*
Prov. 21:17, *p* will be a poor man
Eccl. 5:4, for He has no *p*
Isa. 44:28, shall perform all My *p*
Isa. 58:3, your fast you find *p*
Isa. 58:13, nor finding your own *p*
Ezek. 18:23, Do I have any *p*
Mal. 1:10, I have no *p* in you
Lk. 12:32, your Father's good *p*
Eph. 1:5, to the good *p* of His
2 Th. 1:11, fulfill all the good *p*
1 Tim. 5:6, *p* is dead while
Heb. 10:6, for sin You had no *p*
Heb. 10:38, My soul has no *p*
Jas. 4:1, *p* that war in your
Jas. 5:5, on the earth in *p*

PLEASURES
vanity of worldly. Eccl. 2
effects of. Lk. 8:14; Jas. 5; 2 Pet. 2:13
exhortations against. 2 Tim. 3:4; Ti. 3:3; Heb. 11:25; 1 Pet. 4

PLEASURES
Ps. 16:11, Your right hand are *p*
Lk. 8:14, cares, riches, and *p*
Heb. 11:25, to enjoy the passing *p*

PLEIADES
Job 9:9, Bear, Orion, and the *P*

PLENTIFUL
Ps. 68:9, You, O God, sent a *p*
Mt. 9:37, The harvest truly is *p*

PLENTIFULLY
Lk. 12:16, rich man yielded *p*

PLENTY
the gift of God. Gen. 27:28; Dt. 16:10; 28:11; Ps. 65:8; 68:9; 104:10; 144:13; Joel 2:26; Acts 14:17

PLENTY
Gen. 41:53, *p* which were in the
Dt. 28:11, LORD will grant you *p*
Prov. 28:19, his land will have *p*

PLIGHT
Job 9:23, He laughs at the *p*

PLOT
Ps. 2:1, and the people *p*
Acts 9:24, *p* became known to Saul

PLOTS
Ps. 37:12, The wicked *p* against

PLOTTED
Mt. 26:4, and *p* to take Jesus by
Jn. 12:10, chief priests *p*

PLOW
Prov. 20:4, lazy man will not *p*
Amos 6:12, Does one *p* there with
Lk. 9:62, put his hand to the *p*
1 Cor. 9:10, he who plows should *p*

PLOWED
Jer. 26:18, "Zion shall be *p*
Hos. 10:13, You have *p* wickedness
Mic. 3:12, of you Zion shall be *p*

PLOWMAN
Amos 9:13, *p* shall overtake the

PLOWSHARES
beaten into swords. Joel 3:10
swords to be beaten into plowshares. Isa. 2:4; Mic. 4:3

PLUCK
Dt. 23:25, grain, you may *p*
Ps. 80:12, who pass by the way *p*
Jer. 12:17, obey, I will utterly *p*
Mk. 2:23, *p* the heads of grain

PLUCKED
Job 29:17, *p* the victim from his
Isa. 50:6, cheeks to those who *p*
Lk. 6:1, And His disciples *p*
Gal. 4:15, you would have *p*

PLUMB
Amos 7:7, a *p* line, with a *p*
Zech. 4:10, rejoice to see the *p*

PLUNDER
Ex. 3:22, *p* the Egyptians
Ps. 89:41, who pass by the way *p*
Isa. 3:14, The *p* of the poor is
Jer. 30:16, *p* you shall become
Mt. 12:29, house and *p* his goods

PLUNDERED
Ps. 76:5, stouthearted were *p*
Isa. 42:22, a people robbed and *p*
Jer. 4:30, "And when you are *p*
Hab. 2:8, Because you have *p*

PLUNDERING
Isa. 22:4, me because of the *p*
Heb. 10:34, accepted the *p* of your

POETS
Acts 17:28, some of your own *p*

POISON
Ps. 140:3, the *p* of asps is under
Rom. 3:13, "The *p* of asps is
Jas. 3:8, evil, full of deadly *p*

POISONED
Acts 8:23, *p* by bitterness
Acts 14:2, *p* their minds against

POLLUTIONS
under the law. Lev. 5; 11; 13; 15; 21; 22; Num. 5; 9:6; Ezek. 22
of the Sabbath. Neh. 13:15; Isa. 56:2; Ezek. 20:13
of God's altar, etc. Ex. 20:25; 2 Chr. 33:7; 36:14; Ezek. 8:6; 44:7; Dan. 8:11; Zeph. 3:4; Mal. 1:7

POLLUTIONS
2 Pet. 2:20, have escaped the *p*

POMP
Isa. 5:14, multitude and their *p*
Isa. 14:11, *p* is brought down to
Acts 25:23, had come with great *p*

POMPOUS
Dan. 7:8, and a mouth speaking *p*

PONDER
Prov. 4:26, *P* the path of your

PONDERED
Lk. 2:19, *p* them in her heart

PONDERS
Prov. 5:21, *p* all his paths

PONTIUS, *see* PILATE

POOL
Isa. 41:18, the wilderness a *p*
Jn. 5:2, by the Sheep Gate a *p*

POOLS
Ps. 84:6, also covers it with *p*
Ps. 107:35, a wilderness into *p*
Song 7:4, your eyes like the *p*

POOR
always to be found. Dt. 15:11; 1 Sam. 2:7; Mt. 26:11; Mk. 14:7; Jn. 12:8
their condition described. Job 24:4; Prov. 13:8; 14:20; 18:23; 19:4; 30:9; Eccl. 9:15; Jas. 2
comfort for. Job 31:19; Prov. 31:6; 1 Jn. 3:17
causes of poverty. Prov. 6:11; 10:4; 13:4; 19:15; 20:13; 23:21; 28:19
oppression of, described and condemned. Ex. 22:25; Dt. 15:7; 24:12; Job 24:9; Ps. 12:5; 14:6; 82:3; Prov. 14:31; 17:5; 22:16,22; 28:3; Eccl. 5:8; Isa. 3:14; Jer. 22:3; Amos 2:6; 4; 5:11; 8:4; Zech. 7:10; Jas. 2:2
kindly treatment of. Ex. 23:11; Lev. 19:10; 23:22; 25:25; Dt. 15:7; Ps. 41:1; Prov. 14:21; Isa. 58:7; 2 Cor. 8; 9; Gal. 2:10

their right to justice. Lev. 19:15; Dt. 1:17; 16:19; Prov. 24:23; 28:21; Jas. 2
God's consideration for. Job 5:15; Ps. 9:18; 68:10; 69:33; 72:2; 102:17; 113:7; 132:15; Zech. 11:7
when blessed by God. Prov. 15:16; 16:8; 19:1; 28:6,11
to be cared for by the church. Acts 6:1; 1 Cor. 16:2; 2 Cor. 8; 9; Gal. 2:10
——— in spirit, blessed by Christ. Mt. 5:3; Lk. 6:20 (Isa. 66:2)

POOR
Ex. 30:15, *p* shall not give less
Lev. 19:15, be partial to the *p*
Dt. 15:11, *p* will never cease
Job 5:16, So the *p* have hope
Job 20:19, and forsaken the *p*
Job 29:12, I delivered the *p*
Job 30:25, soul grieved for the *p*
Ps. 22:26, *p* shall eat and be
Ps. 34:6, *p* man cried out
Ps. 40:17, But I am *p* and needy
Ps. 68:10, goodness for the *p*
Ps. 74:21, Let the *p* and needy
Ps. 107:41, yet He sets the *p*
Ps. 113:7, He raises the *p*
Prov. 10:4, slack hand becomes *p*
Prov. 14:20, *p* man is hated even
Prov. 14:21, has mercy on the *p*
Prov. 14:31, who oppresses the *p*
Prov. 17:5, *p* reproaches his Maker
Prov. 19:22, *p* man is better than a
Prov. 22:2, *p* have this in common
Prov. 22:22, Do not rob the *p*
Prov. 28:3, *p* man who oppresses
Eccl. 9:15, remembered that same *p*
Amos 2:6, for silver, and the *p*
Zech. 7:10, the alien or the *p*
Zech. 11:7, in particular the *p*
Mt. 5:3, "Blessed are the *p*
Mt. 11:5, *p* have the gospel
Mt. 26:11, For you have the *p*
2 Cor. 8:9, your sakes He became *p*
Gal. 2:10, should remember the *p*
Jas. 2:5, God not chosen the *p*
Jas. 2:6, have dishonored the *p*
Rev. 3:17, wretched, miserable, *p*

PORCIUS FESTUS, Acts 24:27

PORTION
Dt. 32:9, For the LORD's *p*
Job 20:29, This is the *p* from God
Ps. 16:5, O LORD, You, are the *p*
Ps. 73:26, heart and my *p* forever
Ps. 119:57, You are my *p*
Isa. 53:12, I will divide Him a *p*
Isa. 61:7, rejoice in their *p*
Jer. 10:16, The *P* of Jacob is not
Jer. 12:10, they have trodden My *p*
Lam. 3:24, "The LORD is my *p*
Mt. 24:51, and appoint him his *p*
Lk. 12:42, to give them their *p*
Lk. 15:12, give me the *p*

PORTRAYED
Gal. 3:1, Christ was clearly *p*

POSITION
1 Tim. 3:1, If a man desires the *p*

POSSESS
Gen. 22:17, descendants shall *p*
Josh. 1:11, *p* the land which
Lk. 21:19, By your patience *p*
1 Th. 4:4, *p* his own vessel

POSSESSED
Josh. 13:1, much land yet to be *p*
Prov. 8:22, "The LORD *p* me at
Acts 4:32, of the things he *p*

POSSESSING
2 Cor. 6:10, and yet *p* all things

POSSESSION
Gen. 17:8, as an everlasting *p*
Ps. 17:14, the rest of their *p*
Ps. 44:3, they did not gain *p*
Eph. 1:14, of the purchased *p*
Heb. 10:34, and an enduring *p*

POSSESSIONS
Ps. 104:24, is full of Your *p*
Prov. 1:13, kinds of precious *p*
Eccl. 2:7, Yes, I had greater *p*
Mk. 10:22, for he had great *p*
Lk. 15:13, and there wasted his *p*
Acts 2:45, and sold their *p*

POSSIBLE
Mt. 19:26, God all things are *p*
Heb. 10:4, *p* that the blood

POSTERITY
Gen. 45:7, to preserve a *p*
Ps. 22:30, *p* shall serve Him
Ps. 49:13, *p* who approve their

POT
Ex. 16:33, to Aaron, "Take a *p*
Job 41:20, from a boiling *p*
Prov. 17:3, The refining *p* is for
Heb. 9:4, *p* that had the manna

POTENTATE
1 Tim. 6:15, the blessed and only *P*

POTIPHAR, Gen. 37:36; 39:1

POTS
Ex. 16:3, when we sat by the *p*
Jer. 52:18, also took away the *p*
Lam. 4:2, are regarded as clay *p*

POTSHERD
Job 2:8, for himself a *p*
Ps. 22:15, is dried up like a *p*
Isa. 45:9, Let the *p* strive with

POUND, Jn. 12:3

POUR
Ps. 62:8, *p* out your heart
Ps. 79:6, *P* out Your wrath
Isa. 44:3, *p* My Spirit on your
Isa. 45:8, and let the skies *p*
Jer. 10:25, *P* out Your fury
Joel 2:28, that I will *p* out My
Zech. 12:10, "And I will *p*
Rev. 16:1, angels, "Go and *p*

POURED
Job 30:16, And now my soul is *p*
Ps. 22:14, I am *p* out like water
Ps. 45:2, grace is *p* upon Your
Song 1:3, name is ointment *p*
Isa. 26:16, visited You, they *p*
Isa. 53:12, strong, because He *p*
Jer. 7:20, and My fury will be *p*
Nah. 1:6, His fury is *p* out like
Mk. 14:3, broke the flask and *p*
Rom. 5:5, of God has been *p*
Phil. 2:17, if I am being *p*
2 Tim. 4:6, I am already being *p*
Ti. 3:6, whom He *p* out on us

POVERTY
Prov. 10:15, of the poor is their *p*
Prov. 11:24, but it leads to *p*
Prov. 13:18, *P* and shame will come
Prov. 14:23, leads only to *p*
Prov. 20:13, lest you come to *p*
Prov. 30:8, give me neither *p*
Lk. 21:4, *p* put in all the
2 Cor. 8:2, and their deep *p*
2 Cor. 8:9, *p* might become rich
Rev. 2:9, tribulation, and *p*

POWER
bestowed by God. Isa. 40:29; Acts 6:8; Rom. 15:18; 1 Cor. 5:4; 2 Cor. 12:9; Eph. 1:19

POWER
Ex. 9:16, that I may show My *p*
Ex. 15:6, become glorious in *p*
2 Chr. 25:8, for God has *p* to help
Job 26:2, him who is without *p*
Job 26:14, *p* who can understand
Ps. 62:11, *p* belongs to God
Ps. 66:3, *p* Your enemies shall
Ps. 68:35, gives strength and *p*
Eccl. 8:4, a king is, there is *p*
Eccl. 8:8, No one has *p* over the
Isa. 40:26, the strength of His *p*
Mic. 3:8, truly I am full of *p*
Nah. 1:3, anger and great in *p*
Zech. 4:6, 'Not by might nor by *p*
Mt. 6:13, the kingdom and the *p*
Mt. 9:6, the Son of Man has *p*
Mt. 9:8, who had given such *p*
Mt. 22:29, Scriptures nor the *p*
Lk. 5:17, And the *p* of the Lord
Lk. 6:19, *p* went out from Him
Lk. 24:49, are endued with *p*
Jn. 10:18, I have *p* to lay it
Jn. 19:10, not know that I have *p*
Jn. 19:11, "You could have no *p*
Acts 1:8, you shall receive *p*
Acts 3:12, as though by our own *p*
Acts 8:10, man is the great *p*
Acts 8:19, "Give me this *p*
Rom. 1:16, for it is the *p*
1 Cor. 1:18, saved it is the *p*
1 Cor. 1:24, Greeks, Christ the *p*
1 Cor. 6:12, be brought under the *p*
2 Cor. 12:9, that the *p* of Christ
Eph. 1:19, greatness of His *p*
Eph. 3:7, working of His *p*
Eph. 6:10, the Lord and in the *p*
Col. 1:11, to His glorious *p*
2 Th. 1:9, the glory of His *p*
2 Tim. 1:7, of fear, but of *p*
Heb. 1:3, by the word of His *p*
Heb. 2:14, *p* of death, that
Heb. 7:16, but according to the *p*
2 Pet. 1:3, as His divine *p*
Jude 25, dominion and *p*
Rev. 2:26, to him I will give *p*
Rev. 4:11, glory and honor and *p*

Rev. 5:13, honor and glory and *p*

POWERFUL
Ps. 29:4, of the LORD is *p*
Heb. 4:12, of God is living and *p*

POWERS
heavenly. Mt. 24:29; Eph. 3:10
earthly, to be obeyed. 1 Pet. 2:13

POWERS
Col. 2:15, principalities and *p*
Heb. 6:5, word of God and the *p*

PRAISE
God worthy of. Dt. 10:21; Jud. 5:2; Isa. 12; 25; 38:19; 42:10; Jer. 31:7; Dan. 2:23; Joel 2:26; Hab. 3:3; Lk. 1:46,68; Eph. 1:6; Rev. 19:5
of man, vanity of. Prov. 27:2; Mt. 6:1

PRAISE
Gen. 49:8, your brothers shall *p*
Dt. 10:21, "He is your *p*
Jud. 5:3, I will sing *p* to the
Ps. 22:25, *p* shall be of You in
Ps. 33:1, For *p* from the upright
Ps. 34:1, *p* shall continually be
Ps. 45:17, the people shall *p*
Ps. 50:23, Whoever offers *p*
Ps. 65:1, *P* is awaiting You
Ps. 66:2, make His *p* glorious
Ps. 67:3, let all the peoples *p*
Ps. 69:34, Let heaven and earth *p*
Ps. 71:6, *p* shall be continually
Ps. 89:5, And the heavens will *p*
Ps. 109:1, silent, O God of my *p*
Ps. 119:164, Seven times a day I *p*
Ps. 145:10, All Your works shall *p*
Ps. 145:21, shall speak the *p*
Ps. 148:1, *P* the LORD
Ps. 150:6, that has breath *p*
Prov. 27:2, Let another man *p*
Prov. 31:31, let her own works *p*
Isa. 60:18, And your gates *P*
Isa. 62:7, He makes Jerusalem a *p*
Jer. 17:14, For You are my *p*
Jer. 33:9, Me a name of joy, a *p*
Zeph. 3:20, give you fame and *p*
Mt. 21:16, You have perfected *p*
Jn. 12:43, of men more than the *p*
Rom. 2:29, *p* is not from men but
1 Cor. 4:5, Then each one's *p*
2 Cor. 8:18, the brother whose *p*
Eph. 1:12, should be to the *p*
Phil. 1:11, to the glory and *p*
Heb. 2:12, I will sing *p* to You
Heb. 13:15, the sacrifice of *p*
1 Pet. 2:14, and for the *p* of those
Rev. 19:5, saying, "*P* our God

PRAISED
2 Sam. 22:4, who is worthy to be *p*
Ps. 72:15, daily He shall be *p*
Ps. 113:3, LORD's name is to be *p*
Ps. 145:3, and greatly to be *p*
Isa. 64:11, where our fathers *p*
Dan. 4:34, the Most High and *p*

PRAISES
Ps. 22:3, enthroned in the *p*
Ps. 147:1, it is good to sing *p*
Prov. 31:28, and he *p* her
Isa. 60:6, shall proclaim the *p*
1 Pet. 2:9, you may proclaim the *p*

PRAISEWORTHY
Phil. 4:8, if there is anything *p*

PRAISING
Ps. 84:4, they will still be *p*
Lk. 2:13, of the heavenly host *p*
Lk. 24:53, in the temple *p*

PRATING
Prov. 10:8, *p* fool will fall

PRAY
1 Sam. 12:23, LORD in ceasing to *p*
Ps. 55:17, at noon I will *p*
Mt. 5:44, who hate you, and *p*
Mt. 6:5, "And when you *p*
Mt. 6:6, "But you, when you *p*
Mt. 6:9, manner, therefore, *p*
Mt. 26:41, Watch and *p*
Lk. 11:1, "Lord, teach us to *p*
Lk. 18:1, men always ought to *p*
Jn. 14:16, "And I will *p*
Jn. 17:9, I do not *p* for the
Jn. 17:20, "I do not *p* for
Rom. 8:26, know what we should *p*
1 Cor. 14:15, I will *p* with the
1 Th. 5:17, *p* without ceasing
1 Th. 5:25, Brethren, *p* for us
1 Tim. 2:8, therefore that the men *p*
Jas. 5:13, Let him *p*
Jas. 5:16, to one another, and *p*
1 Jn. 5:16, say that he should *p*
3 Jn. 2, *p* that you may prosper

PRAYED
Lk. 18:11, Pharisee stood and *p*
Lk. 22:44, *p* more earnestly
Jas. 5:17, *p* earnestly that it

PRAYER
occasions, objects, examples of. 1 Chr. 16:35; Job 33:26; Ps. 122:6; Mt. 5:44; 9:38; 26:41; Lk. 18:3,38; Rom. 15:30; 1 Cor. 7:5; Jas. 5:13; 1 Pet. 3:7; 4:7
commanded. Isa. 55:6; Mt. 7:7; 26:41; Lk. 18:1; 21:36; Eph. 6:18; Phil. 4:6; Col. 4:2; 1 Th. 5:17,25; 1 Tim. 2:1,8
encouragements to. Job 33:26; Ps. 6:9; 32:6; 66:19; Isa. 65:24; Zech. 13:9; Mt. 18:19; 21:22; Mk. 11:24; Lk. 11:9; Rom. 10:13; Jas. 1:5
God hears and answers. Ps. 10:17; 65:2; 99:6; Isa. 58:9; Jn. 11:42
how to be offered. Ps. 145:18; Prov. 15:29; Eccl. 5:2; Mt. 6:5,7; 21:22; Mk. 11:24; Lk. 11:5; 18:1; Jn. 9:31; 15:7; Rom. 12:12; Eph. 6:18; Col. 4:2; 1 Tim. 2:8; 5:5; Heb. 11:6; Jas. 1:6; 4:8
through Christ. Eph. 2:18; Heb. 10:19
in the name of Christ. Jn. 16:26
promises for. Isa. 65:24; Amos 5:4; Zech. 13:9; Mt. 6:6; Lk. 11:9; Jn. 14:13
posture for. Num. 16:22; Josh. 5:14; 1 Ki. 8:22; 1 Chr. 21:16; 2 Chr. 6:13; Ps. 28:2; 95:6; Isa. 1:15; Lam. 2:19; Mt. 26:39; Mk. 11:25; Lk. 22:41; Acts 20:36; 1 Tim. 2:8
——— public. Ex. 20:24; 2 Chr. 7:14,16; Isa. 56:7; Mt. 12:9; 18:19,20; Lk. 4:16; 11:2
instances of: Joshua. Josh. 7:6–9; David. 1 Chr. 29:10,12; 2 Sam. 6:18; Solomon. 2 Chr. 6:12; Jews. Lk. 1:10; early church. Acts 2:46; 4:24; 12:5,12; Peter and John. Acts 3:1; church at Antioch. Acts 13:3; Paul and Silas. Acts 16:16; Paul with the elders. Acts 20:36; 21:5
——— private. Ps. 55:17; 88:1; Dan. 6:10; 1 Th. 5:17
instances of: Abraham. Gen. 18:23–32; Lot. Gen. 19:19; Eliezer. Gen. 24:12; Jacob. Gen. 32:9; Gideon. Jud. 6:13,22,36,39; Hannah. 1 Sam. 1; David. 2 Sam. 7:18; 1 Chr. 29:10; Elijah. 1 Ki. 18:36; Hezekiah. 2 Ki. 20:2; Isaiah. 2 Ki. 20:11; Jabez. 1 Chr. 4:10; Manasseh. 2 Chr. 33:19; Ezra. Ezra 9:5–6; Nehemiah. Neh. 2:4; Jeremiah. Jer. 32:16; Daniel. Dan. 9:3; Jonah. Jon. 2:1; Anna. Lk. 2:37; Paul. Acts 9:11; 1 Th. 5:23; Cornelius. Acts 10:2,30; Peter. Acts 9:40; 10:9
——— of the hypocrite condemned. Ps. 109:7; Prov. 1:28; 28:9; Mt. 6:5
——— the Lord's. Mt. 6:9; Lk. 11:2
——— of criminal on the cross. Lk. 23:42

PRAYER
1 Ki. 8:45, in heaven their *p*
2 Chr. 7:15, *p* made in this place
Job 15:4, fear, and restrain *p*
Job 16:17, And my *p* is pure
Ps. 35:13, *p* would return to my
Ps. 42:8, A *p* to the God of my
Ps. 72:15, *P* also will be made
Ps. 88:2, Let my *p* come before
Ps. 102:17, He shall regard the *p*
Ps. 109:4, but I give myself to *p*
Prov. 15:8, to the LORD, but the *p*
Mt. 17:21, not go out except by *p*
Lk. 6:12, all night in *p* to God
Acts 6:4, continually to *p*
Acts 16:13, where *p* was
Rom. 12:12, steadfastly in *p*
1 Cor. 7:5, to fasting and *p*
Eph. 6:18, always with all *p*
Phil. 4:6, but in everything by *p*
1 Tim. 4:5, the word of God and *p*
Jas. 5:15, And the *p* of faith

PRAYERS
of Christ. Mt. 14:23; 26:36; 27:46; Mk. 6:46; 14:32; 15:34; Lk. 6:12; 9:28; 23:34,46; Jn. 17:9

PRAYERS
Isa. 1:15, though you make many *p*
Mt. 23:14, pretense make long *p*
Col. 4:12, fervently for you in *p*
1 Tim. 2:1, that supplications, *p*
1 Pet. 3:7, *p* may not be hindered
1 Pet. 3:12, are open to their *p*
1 Pet. 4:7, and watchful in your *p*
Rev. 5:8, which are the *p*

PREACH
Jon. 3:2, that great city, and *p*
Mt. 4:17, time Jesus began to *p*
Mt. 10:27, you hear in the ear, *p*

Lk. 4:18, *P* the gospel to the
Lk. 9:60, *p* the kingdom of God
Rom. 10:15, And how shall they *p*
1 Cor. 1:23, *p* Christ crucified
1 Cor. 9:16, is me if I do not *p*
1 Cor. 15:11, I or they, so we *p*
2 Cor. 4:5, For we do not *p*
Phil. 1:15, *p* Christ even from
2 Tim. 4:2, *P* the word

PREACHED
Mk. 6:12, *p* that people
Mk. 16:20, out and *p* everywhere
Lk. 24:47, of sins should be *p*
Acts 8:5, *p* Christ to them
Acts 13:38, through this Man is *p*
1 Cor. 9:27, lest, when I have *p*
2 Cor. 11:4, whom we have not *p*
Gal. 1:8, than what we have *p*
Phil. 1:18, in truth, Christ is *p*
Heb. 4:2, the gospel was *p*
1 Pet. 3:19, also He went and *p*

PREACHER
Eccl. 1:1, The words of the *P*
Rom. 10:14, they hear without a *p*
1 Tim. 2:7, I was appointed a *p*
2 Pet. 2:5, of eight people, a *p*

PREACHES
Acts 19:13, the Jesus whom Paul *p*
2 Cor. 11:4, *p* another Jesus
Gal. 1:9, *p* any other gospel
Gal. 1:23, *p* the faith which he

PREACHING
the Gospel of Christ. Mt. 4:17; 5; 28:19; Mk. 1:14; 16:15; Lk. 4:18 (Isa. 61:1); 9:60; 24:27; Acts 2:14; 3:12; 4:8; 10:42; 13:16. *See* Rom. 10:8; 1 Cor. 1:17; 2; 15:1; Gal. 1; Eph. 1—3
Gospel manifested through. Ti. 1,3
of repentance, by John the Baptist. Mt. 3; Mk. 1; Lk. 3
of Noah. 2 Pet. 2:5
of Jonah. Jon. 3; Mt. 12:41; Lk. 11:32

PREACHING
Acts 5:42, *p* Jesus as the
Rom. 16:25, to my gospel and the *p*
1 Cor. 15:14, not risen, then our *p*

PRECEDE
1 Th. 4:15, *p* those who are asleep

PRECEPT
Isa. 28:10, *p* must be upon *p*

PRECEPTS
Neh. 9:14, and commanded them *p*
Ps. 111:7, all His *p* are sure
Ps. 119:4, us to keep Your *p*
Ps. 119:159, how I love Your *p*
Jer. 35:18, and kept all his *p*

PRECIOUS
1 Sam. 26:21, because my life was *p*
Ps. 116:15, *P* in the sight of the
Ps. 139:17, How *p* also are Your
Prov. 3:15, She is more *p* than
Isa. 43:4, Since you were *p*
Isa. 44:9, *p* things shall not
Jer. 15:19, if you take out the *p*
Lam. 4:2, The *p* sons of Zion
Jas. 5:7, farmer waits for the *p*
1 Pet. 1:7, more *p* than gold
1 Pet. 2:7, who believe, He is *p*
1 Pet. 3:4, *p* in the sight of

PREDESTINATION
Rom. 8:29; 9—11; Eph. 1:5

PREDESTINED
Rom. 8:29, He foreknew, He also *p*
Eph. 1:5, having *p* us to
Eph. 1:11, inheritance, being *p*

PREEMINENCE
Col. 1:18, He may have the *p*
3 Jn. 9, loves to have the *p*

PREFERENCE
Rom. 12:10, in honor giving *p*

PREFERRED
Jn. 1:15, comes after me is *p*

PREJUDICE
1 Tim. 5:21, these things without *p*

PREMEDITATE
Mk. 13:11, *p* what you will

PREPARATION
Jn. 19:14, Now it was the *P*
Eph. 6:15, your feet with the *p*

PREPARE
1 Sam. 7:3, *p* your hearts for the
Ps. 23:5, *p* a table before me in
Ps. 61:7, *p* mercy and truth
Isa. 40:3, *P* the way of the LORD
Isa. 62:10, *P* the way for the
Mk. 1:3, *P* the way of the LORD
Lk. 12:47, will, and did not *p*
Jn. 14:2, *p* a place for you

PREPARED
Ex. 23:20, place which I have *p*
Ps. 80:9, You *p* room for it
Prov. 8:27, When He *p* the heavens
Zeph. 1:7, for the LORD has *p*
Mt. 20:23, for whom it is *p*
Lk. 2:31, which You have *p*
Rom. 9:23, mercy, which He had *p*
1 Cor. 2:9, things which God has *p*
2 Cor. 5:5, Now He who has *p*
Eph. 2:10, *p* beforehand that we
Heb. 11:16, God, for He has *p*

PRESCRIBE, Ezra 7:22; Isa. 10:1

PRESENCE
Gen. 3:8, themselves from the *p*
Gen. 4:16, went out from the *p*
Gen. 47:15, we die in your *p*
Ex. 33:14, *P* will go with you
Lev. 19:32, and honor the *p*
Dt. 1:17, afraid in any man's *p*
Job 23:15, am terrified at His *p*
Ps. 16:11, *p* is fullness of joy
Ps. 140:13, shall dwell in Your *p*
Jer. 5:22, not tremble at My *p*
Ezek. 38:20, shall shake at My *p*
Zeph. 1:7, Be silent in the *p*
Lk. 13:26, and drank in Your *p*
Acts 2:28, full of joy in Your *p*
2 Cor. 10:10, but his bodily *p*
Phil. 2:12, obeyed, not as in my *p*

PRESENT
Acts 10:33, we are all *p* before
Rom. 7:21, evil is *p* with me
Rom. 12:1, *p* your bodies a living
1 Cor. 3:22, or death, or things *p*
1 Cor. 5:3, absent in body but *p*
Gal. 4:18, not only when I am *p*
Eph. 5:27, that He might *p*
2 Tim. 2:15, to *p* yourself
Jude 24, *p* you faultless

PRESENTED
Mt. 2:11, treasures, they *p*
Rom. 6:19, For just as you *p*

PRESENTS
Ps. 68:29, kings will bring *p*

PRESERVE
Gen. 45:5, before you to *p* life
Ps. 32:7, You shall *p* me from
Ps. 36:6, O LORD, You *p* man and
Ps. 121:7, He shall *p* your soul
Ps. 121:8, The LORD shall *p*
Jer. 49:11, children, I will *p*
Jer. 50:20, pardon those whom I *p*
Lk. 17:33, loses his life will *p*
2 Tim. 4:18, every evil work and *p*

PRESERVED
Gen. 32:30, and my life is *p*
1 Th. 5:23, soul, and body be *p*

PRESERVES
Ps. 31:23, For the LORD *p* the
Ps. 97:10, *p* the souls of His
Ps. 116:6, The LORD *p* the simple
Prov. 13:3, who guards his mouth *p*
Prov. 16:17, he who keeps his way *p*

PRESS
Phil. 3:14, I *p* toward the goal

PRESSED
Ezek. 23:8, *p* her virgin bosom
2 Cor. 4:8, We are hard *p* on every
Phil. 1:23, For I am hard *p*

PRESUMPTION
of Israelites. Num. 14:44; Dt. 1:43; prophets. Dt. 18:20; builders of Babel. Gen. 11; Korah, etc. Num. 16; Bethshemites. 1 Sam. 6:19; Hiel of Bethel. 1 Ki. 16:34; Uzzah. 2 Sam. 6:6; Uzziah. 2 Chr. 26:16; Jewish exorcists. Acts 19:13; Diotrephes. 3 Jn. 9

PRESUMPTUOUS
sins. Num. 15:30; Dt. 17:12; Ps. 19:13; 2 Pet. 2:10

PRETENDED
1 Sam. 21:13, before them, *p* madness

PRETENSE
Jer. 3:10, whole heart, but in *p*
Mt. 23:14, *p* make long prayers

PREVAIL
1 Sam. 2:9, no man shall *p*
Ps. 12:4, our tongue we will *p*
Jer. 1:19, but they shall not *p*
Mt. 16:18, of Hades shall not *p*

PREVAILED
Ex. 17:11, hand, that Israel *p*
Hos. 12:4, with the Angel and *p*
Acts 19:20, grew mightily and *p*

PREY
Ps. 76:4, the mountains of *p*
Ps. 124:6, has not given us as *p*
Isa. 49:24, Shall the *p* be taken
Isa. 59:15, evil makes himself a *p*
Ezek. 34:22, shall no longer be a *p*
Amos 3:4, he has no *p*

PRICE
Job 28:15, be weighed for its *p*
Prov. 17:16, a fool the purchase *p*
Mt. 13:46, one pearl of great *p*
Acts 5:3, back part of the *p*
1 Cor. 6:20, you were bought at a *p*

PRIDE
1 Sam. 2:3; Prov. 6:16; 16:5; 21:4; Mk. 7:20; Rom. 12:3,16
origin of. 2 Ki. 20:13; Isa. 14:13–14; Zeph. 3:11; Lk. 18:11; 1 Cor. 8:1; 1 Tim. 3:6
evil results of. Ps. 10:2; Prov. 13:10; 21:24; 28:25; Jer. 43:2; 49:16; Obad. 3
followed by shame and destruction. Prov. 11:2; 16:18; 18:12; 29:23; Isa. 28:3
exhortations against. Isa. 28:1; Jer. 13:15

PRIDE
Ps. 36:11, *p* come against me
Ps. 73:6, *p* serves as
Prov. 8:13, *p* and arrogance and
Prov. 13:10, By *p* comes nothing
Prov. 16:18, *P* goes before
Prov. 29:23, *p* will bring him low
Ezek. 16:49, her daughter had *p*
Dan. 4:37, *p* He is able to put down
Dan. 5:20, was hardened in *p*
Amos 8:7, has sworn by the *p*
Zech. 11:3, For the *p* of the
Mk. 7:22, evil eye, blasphemy, *p*
1 Tim. 3:6, *p* he fall into the
1 Jn. 2:16, eyes, and the *p* of life

PRIEST
Gen. 14:18, he was the *p* of God
1 Sam. 2:35, Myself a faithful *p*
Ps. 110:4, *p* forever according
Isa. 28:7, the *p* and the prophet
Zech. 6:13, So He shall be a *p*
Mal. 2:17, of a *p* should keep
Heb. 2:17, and faithful High *P*
Heb. 4:14, we have a great High *P*
Heb. 5:6, *p* forever according
Heb. 9:11, Christ came as High *P*

PRIEST, HIGH
Ex. 28; 39; Lev. 8; 16

PRIESTHOOD
of Christ, Aaron, and Melchizedek. Rom. 8:34; Heb. 2:17; 3; 5; 7; 1 Jn. 2:1

PRIESTHOOD
Ex. 40:15, be an everlasting *p*
Neh. 13:29, have defiled the *p*
Heb. 7:12, *p* being changed
Heb. 7:24, has an unchangeable *p*
1 Pet. 2:5, house, a holy *p*
1 Pet. 2:9, generation, a royal *p*

PRIESTS
Levitical. Ex. 28:1; Lev. 8; their duties, offerings, rites. Lev. 1; 9; 21; 22; Num. 3; Dt. 31:9; Josh. 3; 4; 1 Ki. 8:3
eighty-five killed by command of Saul. 1 Sam. 22:17
divided by lot by David. 1 Chr. 24
denounced for unfaithfulness. Jer. 1:18; 5:31; Hos. 5; 6; Mic. 3:11; Zeph. 3:4; Mal. 2
——— of Baal, killed. 1 Ki. 18:40; 2 Ki. 10:19; 11:18
——— Christians called. 1 Pet. 2:5; Rev. 1:6; 5:10; 20:6

PRIESTS
Ex. 19:6, to Me a kingdom of *p*
Mic. 3:11, her *p* teach for pay
Rev. 1:6, made us kings and *p*
Rev. 20:6, but they shall be *p*

PRINCE
of Peace. Isa. 9:6; of life. Acts 3:15
——— of the power of the air. Eph. 2:2

PRINCE
Ex. 2:14, "Who made you a *p*
Job 21:28, is the house of the *p*
Prov. 14:28, is the downfall of a *p*
Isa. 9:6, Everlasting Father, *P*
Dan. 9:25, until Messiah the *P*
Dan. 10:21, except Michael your *p*
Hos. 3:4, days without king or *p*
Mic. 7:3, *p* asks for gifts
Acts 3:15, and killed the *P*
Acts 5:31, His right hand to be *P*
Eph. 2:2, the *p* of the power

PRINCES
Job 34:19, He is not partial to *p*
Ps. 105:22, to bind his *p* at his
Ps. 113:8, He may seat him with *p*
Ps. 118:9, to put confidence in *p*
Ps. 119:23, *P* also sit and speak
Ps. 148:11, *p* and all judges of
Prov. 17:26, good, nor to strike *p*
Eccl. 10:16, is a child, and your *p*
Eccl. 10:17, of nobles, and your *p*
Isa. 3:4, children to be their *p*
Isa. 32:1, *p* will rule with
Isa. 40:23, He brings the *p*

PRINCIPAL
Prov. 4:7, Wisdom is the *p*

PRINCIPALITIES
and powers. Eph. 6:12; Col. 2:15
Christ the head of all. Eph. 1:21; Col. 1:16; 2:10

PRINCIPLES
Col. 2:20, from the basic *p*
Heb. 5:12, again the first *p*

PRISCA, 2 Tim. 4:19

PRISCILLA
diminutive of Prisca. Acts 18:2
and Aquila. Acts 18; Rom. 16:3; 1 Cor. 16:19

PRISON
Gen. 39:20, and put him into the *p*
Ps. 142:7, Bring my soul out of *p*
Isa. 42:7, in darkness from the *p*
Isa. 61:1, the opening of the *p*
Jer. 29:26, should put him in *p*
Mt. 11:2, John had heard in *p*
Mt. 25:36, I was in *p* and you
1 Pet. 3:19, to the spirits in *p*

PRISONER
Ps. 79:11, the groaning of the *p*
Eph. 3:1, reason I, Paul, the *p*
2 Tim. 1:8, Lord, nor of me His *p*

PRISONERS
Job 3:18, *p* rest together
Ps. 69:33, does not despise His *p*
Ps. 146:7, gives freedom to the *p*
Zech. 9:12, the stronghold, you *p*
Heb. 13:3, Remember the *p* as if

PRISONS
Lk. 21:12, the synagogues and *p*
2 Cor. 11:23, *p* more frequently

PRIVATELY
Mt. 24:3; Mk. 9:28; Lk. 10:23; Gal. 2:2

PRIZE
Jer. 21:9, life shall be as a *p*
1 Cor. 9:24, but one receives the *p*
Phil. 3:14, the goal for the *p*

PROCEED
Jer. 9:3, For they *p* from evil
Jas. 3:10, of the same mouth *p*

PROCEEDED
Jn. 8:42, for I *p* forth

PROCEEDS
Dt. 8:3, by every word that *p*
Mt. 4:4, by every word that *p*
Jn. 15:26, Spirit of truth who *p*
Acts 5:2, back part of the *p*

PROCESSION
Ps. 68:24, They have seen Your *p*

PROCLAIM
Ex. 33:19, you, and I will *p*
Dt. 32:3, *p* the name of the LORD
2 Sam. 1:20, *p* it not in the
Isa. 60:6, and they shall *p*
Mk. 1:45, began to *p* it freely
Acts 17:23, knowing, Him I *p*
1 Cor. 11:26, drink this cup, you *p*

PROCLAIMED
Ps. 40:9, *p* the good news
Ps. 68:11, company of those who *p*
Lk. 8:39, he went his way and *p*
Lk. 12:3, inner rooms will be *p*

PROCLAIMER
Acts 17:18, "He seems to be a *p*

PROCLAIMS
Isa. 52:7, good news, who *p*

PROCONSUL
Acts 13:8, seeking to turn the *p*
Acts 18:12, When Gallio was *p*

PRODIGAL
Lk. 15:13, with *p* living

PRODIGAL SON
parable of. Lk. 15:11

PRODUCE
Lev. 26:4, land shall yield its *p*
Ps. 144:13, all kinds of *p*

PROFANE
Lev. 10:1, and offered *p* fire
Jer. 23:11, and priest are *p*
Mal. 1:12, "But you *p* it
Acts 24:6, tried to *p* the temple
1 Tim. 4:7, But reject *p* and old
Heb. 12:16, *p* person like Esau

PROFANED
Ps. 89:39, *p* his crown by casting
Ezek. 22:8, and *p* My Sabbaths
Mal. 2:11, *p* the LORD's holy

PROFANENESS
Jer. 23:15, of Jerusalem *p* has

PROFANING
Mal. 2:10, *p* the covenant of the

PROFANITY
Lev. 18:21; 19:12; Neh. 13:18; Ezek. 22:8; Mal. 1:12

PROFESS
Ti. 1:16, They *p* to know God

PROFESSING
Rom. 1:22, *P* to be wise
1 Tim. 2:10, is proper for women *p*

PROFIT
Ps. 30:9, *p* is there in my blood
Eccl. 1:3, *p* has a man from all
Eccl. 2:11, There was no *p* under
Isa. 57:12, for they will not *p*
Jer. 7:8, words that cannot *p*
Ezek. 22:13, *p* which you have made
Mal. 3:14, *p* is it that we have
Mt. 16:26, For what *p* is it to
Mk. 8:36, "For what will it *p*
Lk. 9:25, "For what *p* is it to
Acts 16:16, her masters much *p*
Acts 16:19, hope of *p* was gone
Acts 19:24, brought no small *p*
Rom. 3:1, what is the *p* of
1 Cor. 10:33, not seeking my own *p*
Gal. 5:2, Christ will *p* you
2 Tim. 2:14, about words to no *p*
Heb. 12:10, them, but He for our *p*
Jas. 2:14, What does it *p*
Jas. 4:13, sell, and make a *p*

PROFITABLE
Job 22:2, "Can a man be *p*
2 Cor. 12:1, It is doubtless not *p*
2 Tim. 3:16, of God, and is *p*
Ti. 3:8, things are good and *p*
Phile. 11, to you, but now is *p*

PROFITS
Job 34:9, *p* a man nothing that
1 Cor. 13:3, have not love, it *p*
1 Tim. 4:8, exercise *p* a little

PROFOUND
Ps. 131:1, with things too *p*

PROLONG
Dt. 4:26, you will not *p* your
Ps. 85:5, *p* Your anger to all
Eccl. 8:13, nor will he *p* his days

PROLONGED
Eccl. 8:12, and his days are *p*

PROLONGS
Prov. 10:27, The fear of the LORD *p*

PROMISE
1 Ki. 8:56, of all His good *p*
Lk. 24:49, Behold, I send the *P*
Acts 1:4, but to wait for the *P*
Acts 2:39, "For the *p* is to you
Acts 7:17, *p* drew near which God
Acts 26:6, for the hope of the *p*
Rom. 4:14, is made void and the *p*
Rom. 4:16, *p* might be sure
Gal. 3:18, it is no longer of *p*
Heb. 4:1, Therefore, since a *p*
Heb. 6:17, to the heirs of *p*
Heb. 11:39, did not receive the *p*
2 Pet. 2:19, they *p* them liberty
1 Jn. 2:25, *p* that He has promised

PROMISED
Dt. 1:11, bless you as He has *p*
Heb. 11:11, faithful who had *p*

PROMISES
of God. Ps. 89:3; Rom. 1:2; Eph. 3:6; 2 Tim. 1:1; Heb. 6:17; 8:6
inviolable and precious. Num. 23:19; Dt. 7:9; Josh. 23:14; 1 Ki. 8:56; Ps. 77:8; 89:3; 105:42; 2 Cor. 1:20; Gal. 3:21; Heb. 6:17; 2 Pet. 1:4
God faithful to His. Ps. 105:42; Lk. 1:54; Ti. 1:2; Heb. 10:23
pleaded in prayer. Gen. 32:9,12; 1 Chr. 17:23; Isa. 43:26
to the repentant and returning. Ex. 34:7; Ps. 65:3; 103:9,13; 130:4; Isa. 1:18; 27:5; 43:25; 44:22; 45:25; 46:13; 53; 55; Jer. 31:34; 33:8; Ezek. 33:16; 36:25; Mic. 7:18; Rom. 4; 5; 2 Cor. 6:18; 7:1; Eph. 2:13
to uphold and perfect. Ps. 23; 37:17; 42:8; 73:26; 84:11; 94:14; 103:13; Isa. 25:8; 30:18; 40:29; 41:10; 43:4; 46:3; 49:14; 63:9; Jer. 31:3; Hos. 13:10; 14:4; Zeph. 3:17; Zech. 2:8; 10; Rom. 16:20; 1 Cor. 10:13; 15:57; 2 Cor. 6:18; 12:9; Eph. 1:3; 1 Pet. 1:3; 5:7
to Adam. Gen. 3:15; to Noah. Gen. 8:21; 9:9; to Abraham. Gen. 12:7; 13:14; 15; 17; 18:10; 22:15; to Hagar. Gen. 16:10; 21:17; to Isaac. Gen. 26:2; to Jacob. Gen. 28:13; 31:3; 32:12; 35:11; 46:3; to David. 2 Sam. 7:11; 1 Chr. 17:10; to Solomon. 1 Ki. 9; 2 Chr. 1:7; 7:12
of Christ to His disciples. Mt. 6:4,33; 7:7; 10; 11:28; 12:50; 16:18,24; 17:20; 19:28; 28:20; Lk. 9—12; 12:32; 22:29; Jn. 14—16; 20:21
Gentiles partakers of. Eph. 3
fulfilled in Christ. 2 Sam. 7:12 (with Acts 13:23); Lk. 1:69–73
to the poor, fatherless, etc. Dt. 10:18; Ps. 9:8; 10:14; 12:5; 68:5; 69:33; 72:12; 102:17; 107:41; 109:31; 113:7; 146:9; Prov. 15:25; 23:10; Jer. 49:11; Hos. 14:3
of temporal blessings. Ex. 23:25; Lev. 26:6; Ps. 34:9; 37:3; 91; 102:28; 112; 121:3; 128; Prov. 3:10; Isa. 32:18; 33:16; Mt. 6:25; Phil. 4:19; 1 Tim. 4:8
exhortation concerning. Heb. 4:1

PROMISES
2 Cor. 1:20, For all the *p* of God
Gal. 3:16, his Seed were the *p*
Heb. 6:12, patience inherit the *p*
Heb. 11:13, having received the *p*
2 Pet. 1:4, great and precious *p*

PROMPTLY
Prov. 13:24, him disciplines him *p*

PROOF
Phil. 1:28, which is to them a *p*

PROOFS
Acts 1:3, by many infallible *p*

PROPER
1 Cor. 7:35, you, but for what is *p*
1 Cor. 11:13, Is it *p* for a woman to
1 Tim. 2:10, but, which is *p*

PROPERLY
Rom. 13:13, Let us walk *p*

PROPHECIES
respecting Christ, and their fulfillment: prophecy. Ps. 2:7; fulfilled. Lk. 1:32,35. Gen. 3:15—(Gal. 4:4). Gen. 17:7; 22:18—(Gal. 3:16). Gen. 21:12—(Heb. 11:17–19). Ps. 132:11; Jer. 23:5—(Acts 13:23; Rom. 1:3). Gen. 49:10; Dan. 9:24–25—(Lk. 2:1). Isa. 7:14—(Mt. 1:18; Lk. 2:7). Isa. 7:14—(Mt. 1:22–23). Mic. 5:2—(Mt. 2:1; Lk. 2:4–6). Ps. 72:10—(Mt. 2:1–11). Jer. 31:15—(Mt. 2:16–18). Hos. 11:1—(Mt. 2:15). Isa. 40:3; Mal. 3:1—(Mt. 3:1,3; Lk. 1:17). Ps. 45:7; Isa. 11:2; 61:1—(Mt. 3:16; Jn. 3:34; Acts 10:38). Dt. 18:15–18—(Acts 3:20–22). Ps. 110:4—(Heb. 5:5–6). Isa. 61:1–2—(Lk. 4:16–21,43). Isa. 9:1–2—(Mt. 4:12–16,23). Zech. 9.9—(Mt. 21:1–5). Hag. 2:7,9; Mal. 3:1—(Mt. 21:12; Lk. 2:27–32; Jn. 2:13–16). Isa. 53:2—(Mk. 6:3; Lk. 9:58). Isa. 42:2—(Mt. 12:15–16,19). Isa. 40:11; 42:3—(Mt. 12:15,20; Heb. 4:15). Isa. 53:9—(1 Pet. 2:22). Ps. 69:9—(Jn. 2:17). Ps. 78:2—(Mt. 13:34–35). Isa. 35:5–6—(Mt. 11:4–6; Jn. 11:47). Ps. 22:6; 69:7,9,20—(Rom. 15:3). Ps. 69:8; Isa. 63:3—(Jn. 1:11; 7:3). Isa. 8:14—(Rom. 9:32; 1 Pet. 2:8). Ps. 69:4; Isa. 49:7—(Jn. 15:24–25). Ps. 118:22—(Mt. 21:42; Jn. 7:48). Ps. 2:1–2—(Lk. 23:12; Acts 4:27). Ps. 41:9; 55:12–14—(Jn. 13:18,21). Zech. 13:7—(Mt. 26:31,56). Zech. 11:12—(Mt. 26:15). Zech. 11:13—(Mt. 27:7). Ps. 22:14–15—(Lk. 22:42,44). Isa. 53:4–6,12; Dan. 9:26—(Mt. 20:28). Isa. 53:7—(Mt. 26:63; 27:12–14). Mic. 5:1—(Mt. 27:30). Isa. 52:14; 53:3—(Jn. 19:5). Isa. 50:6—(Mk. 14:65; Jn. 19:1). Ps. 22:16—(Jn. 19:18; 20:25). Ps. 22:1—(Mt. 27:46). Ps. 22:7–8—(Mt. 27:39–44). Ps. 69:21—(Mt. 27:34).

Ps. 22:18—(Mt. 27:35). Isa. 53:12—(Mk. 15:28). Isa. 53:12—(Lk. 23:34). Isa. 53:12—(Mt. 27:50). Ex. 12:46; Ps. 34:20—(Jn. 19:33,36). Zech. 12:10—(Jn. 19:34,37). Isa. 53:9—(Mt. 27:57–60). Ps. 16:10—(Acts 2:31). Ps. 16:10; Isa. 26:19—(Lk. 24:6,31,34). Ps. 68:18—(Lk. 24:51; Acts 1:9). Ps. 110:1—(Heb. 1:3). Zech. 6:13—(Rom. 8:34). Isa. 28:16—(1 Pet. 2:6–7). Ps. 2:6—(Lk. 1:32; Jn. 18:33–37). Isa. 11:10; 42:1—(Mt. 1:17,21; Jn. 10:16; Acts 10:45,47). Ps. 45:6–7—(Jn. 5:30; Rev. 19:11). Ps. 72:8; Dan. 7:14—(Phil. 2:9,11). Isa. 9:7; Dan. 7:14—(Lk. 1:32–33).

PROPHECY
God author of. Isa. 44:7; 45:21; Lk. 1:70; 2 Pet. 1:19,21; Rev. 1:1
gift of Christ. Eph. 4:11; Rev. 11:3
of Holy Spirit. 1 Cor. 12:10
Christ the great subject of. Lk. 24:44; Acts 3:22–24; 10:43; 1 Pet. 1:10–11
to be received with faith and reverence. 2 Chr. 20:20; Lk. 24:25; 1 Th. 5:20; 2 Pet. 1:19
pretended, guilt of. Jer. 14:14; 23:13; Ezek. 13:3
how tested. Dt. 13:1; 18:20; Jer. 14:15; 23:16

PROPHECY
1 Cor. 12:10, to another *p*
2 Pet. 1:21, for *p* never came by
Rev. 19:10, is the spirit of *p*
Rev. 22:19, of the book of this *p*

PROPHESIED
Num. 11:25, upon them, that they *p*
Jer. 23:21, to them, yet they *p*
Mt. 7:22, Lord, have we not *p*
Mt. 11:13, prophets and the law *p*
Acts 21:9, virgin daughters who *p*
1 Cor. 14:5, even more that you *p*

PROPHESIES
Jer. 28:9, for the prophet who *p*
1 Cor. 11:5, woman who prays or *p*
1 Cor. 14:4, *p* edifies the church

PROPHESY
Isa. 30:10, prophets, "Do not *p*
Jer. 5:31, The prophets *p* falsely
Joel 2:28, your daughters shall *p*
Amos 3:8, Who can but *p*
Mt. 26:68, saying, "*P* to us
Acts 2:17, your daughters shall *p*
Rom. 12:6, if prophecy, let us *p*
1 Cor. 13:9, know in part and we *p*
1 Cor. 14:39, desire earnestly to *p*

PROPHET
Ex. 7:1, shall be your *p*
Dt. 18:15, raise up for you a *P*
Dt. 34:10, arisen in Israel a *p*
1 Ki. 18:22, "I alone am left a *p*
Ps. 74:9, is no longer any *p*
Jer. 1:5, I ordained you a *p*
Ezek. 14:9, *p* is induced to speak
Hos. 9:7, The *p* is a fool
Amos 7:14, nor was I a son of a *p*
Mal. 4:5, send you Elijah the *p*
Mt. 10:41, *p* shall receive a
Mt. 13:57, *p* is not without honor
Mk. 13:14, by Daniel the *p*
Lk. 7:28, is not a greater *p*
Lk. 13:33, it cannot be that a *p*
Lk. 24:19, who was a *P*
Jn. 1:21, "Are you the *P*
Jn. 6:14, "This is truly the *P*
Rev. 19:20, with him the false *p*

PROPHETESSES
Anna. Lk. 2:36; Deborah. Jud. 4:4; Huldah. 2 Ki. 22:14; Miriam. Ex. 15:20; Noadiah. Neh. 6:14

PROPHETIC
2 Pet. 1:19, *p* word confirmed

PROPHETS
sent by God. Isa. 58:1; Jer. 1:4; 23:28; 25:4; Ezek. 2:3
Christ predicted as a prophet. Dt. 18:15; called one. Mt. 21:11; Lk. 7:16; mocked at as. Lk. 22:64
persons so called: Aaron. Ex. 7:1; Abraham. Gen. 20:7; Agabus. Acts 21:10; Ahijah. 1 Ki. 11:29; Amos. Amos 7:14; Balaam. Num. 24:2; Daniel. Dan. 10; Mt. 24:15; David. Mt. 13:35; Acts 2:30; Eldad. Num. 11:26; Elijah. 1 Ki. 18:36; Elisha. 2 Ki. 6:12; Ezekiel. Ezek. 1:3; Gad. 1 Sam. 22:5; Habakkuk. Hab. 1:1; Haggai. Ezra 5:1; 6:14; Hag. 1:1; Hananiah. Jer. 28:17; Hosea. Hos. 1:1; Rom. 9:25; Iddo. 2 Chr. 13:22; Isaiah. 2 Ki. 20:11; Isa. 1:1; Mt. 3:3; Jehu. 1 Ki. 16:7; Jeremiah. 2 Chr. 36:12; Jer. 1:5; Joel. Joel 1:1; Acts 2:16; John the Baptist. Lk. 7:28; Joshua. 1 Ki. 16:34; Jonah. 2 Ki. 14:25; Jon. 1:1; Mt. 12:39; Malachi. Mal. 1:1; Medad. Num. 11:26; Micah. Jer. 26:18; Mic. 1:1; Moses. Dt. 34:10; Nahum. Nah. 1:1; Nathan. 1 Ki. 1:32; Obadiah. Obad. 1; Oded. 2 Chr. 15:8; Paul. Acts 13:9; 27:10; Samuel. 1 Sam. 20; Shemaiah. 2 Chr. 12:5; Zacharias. Lk. 1:67; Zechariah. Zech. 1:1; Zephaniah. Zeph. 1:1
——— false: Zedekiah. 1 Ki. 22:11; Jer. 29:21; Bar-Jesus. Acts 13:6; denounced. Dt. 13; 18:20; Isa. 9:15; Jer. 6:13; 14:13; 23:9,34; 28:15; 29:20,31; Ezek. 13:3; 14:9; Mt. 7:15; 24:11; 2 Pet. 2:1; 1 Jn. 4:1

PROPHETS
Num. 11:29, LORD's people were *p*
1 Sam. 10:12, Saul also among the *p*
1 Ki. 22:22, the mouth of all his *p*
Jer. 37:19, Where now are your *p*
Ezek. 13:2, prophesy against the *p*
Zeph. 3:4, Her *p* are insolent
Mt. 5:17, the Law or the *P*
Mt. 7:12, is the Law and the *P*
Mt. 16:14, or one of the *p*
Mt. 23:29, the tombs of the *p*
Mt. 23:34, indeed, I send you *p*
Mt. 23:37, one who kills the *p*
Mt. 24:11, Then many false *p*
Lk. 16:29, have Moses and the *p*
Acts 3:25, You are sons of the *p*
Acts 7:52, *p* did your fathers not
Acts 10:43, To Him all the *p*
Acts 26:27, do you believe the *p*
Rom. 1:2, before through His *p*
Rom. 3:21, by the Law and the *P*
Rom. 11:3, have killed Your *p*
1 Cor. 14:32, *p* are subject to the
Eph. 4:11, to be apostles, some *p*
Jas. 5:10, brethren, take the *p*
1 Pet. 1:10, this salvation the *p*
2 Pet. 2:1, were also false *p*
1 Jn. 4:1, because many false *p*
Rev. 16:6, blood of saints and *p*
Rev. 18:24, found the blood of *p*
Rev. 22:9, of your brethren the *p*

PROPITIATION
Rom. 3:25, set forth as a *p*
Heb. 2:17, to God, to make *p*
1 Jn. 2:2, He Himself is the *p*
1 Jn. 4:10, His Son to be the *p*

PROPORTION
Rom. 12:6, let us prophesy in *p*

PROPRIETY
1 Tim. 2:9, modest apparel, with *p*

PROSECUTOR
Job 31:35, answer me, that my *P*

PROSELYTE
Mt. 23:15, and sea to win one *p*

PROSELYTES
Acts 2:10, Rome, both Jews and *p*

PROSPER
Gen. 39:3, made all he did to *p*
Dt. 28:29, you shall not *p*
2 Chr. 26:5, LORD, God made him *p*
Ps. 122:6, they *p* who love you
Prov. 28:13, his sins will not *p*
Isa. 53:10, of the LORD shall *p*
Isa. 54:17, against you shall *p*
Isa. 55:11, please, and it shall *p*
Jer. 12:1, of the wicked *p*
Jer. 23:5, King shall reign and *p*
1 Cor. 16:2, storing up as he may *p*
3 Jn. 2, I pray that you may *p*

PROSPERED
Gen. 24:56, since the LORD has *p*

PROSPERING
Ps. 10:5, His ways are always *p*

PROSPERITY
of the righteous. Ps. 36:8; 37:11,18; 75:10; 84:11; 92:12; Prov. 3:2; Eccl. 8:12
of the wicked. Job 12:6; 20:5; 21:7; Ps. 17:10; 37; 73:3; 92:7; Eccl. 8:14; 9:2; Jer. 12
dangers of. Dt. 6:10; Prov. 1:32; 30:8; Lk. 6:24; 12:16; 16:19; Jas. 5:1

PROSPERITY
Dt. 23:6, *p* all your days
1 Ki. 10:7, *p* exceed the fame
Job 15:21, *p* the destroyer
Job 36:11, spend their days in *p*
Ps. 30:6, Now in my *p* I said
Ps. 35:27, has pleasure in the *p*

Ps. 73:3, When I saw the *p*
Ps. 118:25, I pray, send now *p*
Eccl. 7:14, the day of *p* be joyful
Acts 19:25, that we have our *p*

PROSPEROUS
Gen. 24:21, had made his journey *p*
Josh. 1:8, will make your way *p*

PROSPERS
Prov. 17:8, he turns, he *p*
3 Jn. 2, just as your soul *p*

PROSTRATE
Job 9:13, of the proud lie *p*

PROUD
Job 38:11, *p* waves must stop
Ps. 12:3, tongue that speaks *p*
Ps. 31:23, and fully repays the *p*
Ps. 40:4, does not respect the *p*
Ps. 101:5, a haughty look and a *p*
Ps. 138:6, *p* He knows from afar
Prov. 15:25, the house of the *p*
Prov. 16:5, Everyone *p*
Prov. 28:25, *p* heart stirs up
Eccl. 7:8, is better than the *p*
Hab. 2:5, by wine, he is a *p*
Lk. 1:51, He has scattered the *p*
1 Pet. 5:5, "God resists the *p*

PROVE
1 Ki. 2:2, *p* yourself a man
Job 6:25, does your arguing *p*
Rom. 12:2, mind, that you may *p*

PROVERB
Dt. 28:37, an astonishment, a *p*
Ps. 49:4, incline my ear to a *p*
Prov. 26:7, that hang limp is a *p*
Prov. 26:9, of a drunkard is a *p*
Mic. 2:4, one shall take up a *p*
2 Pet. 2:22, to the true *p*

PROVERBS
of Solomon, Book of Proverbs; collected under Hezekiah. Prov. 25—29
various. 1 Sam. 10:12; 24:13; Lk. 4:23; 2 Pet. 2:22

PROVERBS
1 Ki. 4:32, spoke three thousand *p*
Eccl. 12:9, in order many *p*

PROVIDE
Gen. 22:8, "My son, God will *p*
Ps. 78:20, Can He *p* meat for His
Jer. 33:9, prosperity that I *p*
Mt. 10:9, "*P* neither gold nor
1 Tim. 5:8, if anyone does not *p*

PROVIDED
Acts 20:34, these hands have *p*
Heb. 11:40, *p* something better

PROVIDES
Job 38:41, *p* food for the raven
Prov. 6:8, *p* her supplies in the

PROVISION
Ps. 132:15, abundantly bless her *p*
Rom. 13:14, no *p* for the flesh

PROVOKE
Ex. 23:21, do not *p* Him
Job 12:6, *p* God are secure
Jer. 7:19, "Do they *p* Me to
Rom. 11:11, *p* them to jealousy
Eph. 6:4, you, fathers, do not *p*

PROVOKED
Ps. 78:40, How often they *p*
Ps. 78:56, *p* the Most High
Ps. 106:29, Thus they *p* Him to
Acts 17:16, his spirit was *p*
1 Cor. 13:5, seek its own, is not *p*

PRUDENCE
Prov. 1:4, To give *p* to the
Prov. 8:12, wisdom, dwell with *p*
Eph. 1:8, us in all wisdom and *p*

PRUDENT
Prov. 12:16, *p* man covers shame
Prov. 12:23, A *p* man conceals
Prov. 14:8, The wisdom of the *p*
Prov. 14:15, *p* considers well
Prov. 16:21, heart will be called *p*
Prov. 18:15, *p* acquires knowledge
Prov. 19:14, *p* wife is from the
Prov. 22:3, *p* man foresees evil
Jer. 49:7, perished from the *p*
Amos 5:13, Therefore the *p*
Mt. 11:25, from the wise and *p*

PRUDENTLY
Isa. 52:13, Servant shall deal *p*

PRUNES
Jn. 15:2, that bears fruit He *p*

PSALM
Ps. 98:5, and the sound of a *p*
Acts 13:33, in the second *P*
1 Cor. 14:26, each of you has a *p*

PSALMIST
2 Sam. 23:1, And the sweet *p*

PSALMS
1 Chr. 16:9, Sing to Him, sing *p*
Eph. 5:19, to one another in *p*
Jas. 5:13, Let him sing *p*

PSALMS, THE
I. PSALMS OF SUPPLICATION
1. on account of sin. Ps. 6; 25; 32; 38; 51; 102; 130
2. suffering. Ps. 7; 10; 13; 17; 22; 31; 35; 41—43; 54—57; 59; 64; 69—71; 77; 86; 88; 109; 120; 140—143
3. persecution. Ps. 44; 60; 74; 79; 80; 83; 89; 94; 102; 123; 137
4. public worship. Ps. 26; 27; 42; 43; 63; 65; 84; 92; 95—100; 118; 122; 132; 144—150
5. trust in God. Ps. 3—5; 11; 12; 16; 20; 23; 27; 28; 31; 42; 43; 52; 54; 56; 57; 59; 61—64; 71; 77; 86; 108; 115; 118; 121; 125; 131; 138; 141
6. the psalmist's piety. Ps. 7; 17; 26; 35; 101; 119

II. GRATITUDE
1. the psalmist personally. Ps. 9; 18; 30; 32; 34; 40; 61—63; 75; 103; 108; 116; 118; 138; 144
2. relative to the Church. Ps. 33; 46; 47; 65; 66; 68; 75; 76; 81; 85; 87; 95; 98; 105—107; 124; 126; 129; 134—136; 149

III. ADORATION
1. of God's goodness and mercy. Ps. 3; 4; 9; 16; 18; 30—34; 36; 40; 46; 65—68; 84; 85; 91; 99; 100; 103; 107; 111; 113; 116; 117; 121; 126; 145; 146
2. of God's power, majesty, and glory. Ps. 2; 3; 8; 18; 19; 24; 29; 33; 45—48; 50; 65—68; 76; 77; 89; 91—100; 104—108; 110; 111; 113—118; 135; 136; 139; 145—150

IV. DIDACTIC
1. showing the blessings of God's people and the misery of His enemies. Ps. 1; 3—5; 7; 9—15; 17; 24; 25; 32; 34; 36; 37; 41; 50; 52; 53; 58; 62; 73; 75; 82; 84; 91; 92; 94; 101; 112; 119; 121; 125; 127—129; 133; 149
2. the excellence of God's law. Ps. 19; 119
3. the vanity of human life, etc. Ps. 14; 39; 49; 53; 73; 90

V. PROPHETIC, TYPICAL, AND HISTORICAL
Ps. 2; 16; 22; 24; 31; 35; 40; 41; 45; 50; 55; 68; 69; 72; 78; 87; 88; 102; 105; 106; 109; 110; 118; 132; 135; 136

PSALTERY
Dan. 3:10, harp, lyre, and *p*

PUBLISHED
Jon. 3:7, to be proclaimed and *p*

PUFFED
1 Cor. 4:18, Now some are *p* up
1 Cor. 13:4, itself, is not *p*
1 Tim. 3:6, a novice, lest being *p*

PUFFS
1 Cor. 8:1, Knowledge *p* up

PUL, 2 Ki. 15:19; Isa. 66:19
king of Assyria. 1 Chr. 5:26

PULL
Ps. 31:4, *P* me out of the net
Lk. 12:18, I will *p* down my barns

PUNISH
Dt. 22:18, take that man and *p*
Prov. 17:26, *p* the righteous is
Isa. 13:11, "I will *p* the world
Jer. 5:9, Shall I not *p* them for
Jer. 30:20, *p* all who oppress them
Lam. 4:22, *p* your iniquity
Hos. 4:9, So I will *p* them for

PUNISHED
Ezra 9:13, You our God have *p*
Job 35:15, because He has not *p*
Acts 26:11, *p* them often in every
2 Th. 1:9, These shall be *p*

PUNISHES
Jer. 13:21, will you say when He *p*

PUNISHMENT
Gen. 4:13, *p* is greater than I
Isa. 10:3, you do in the day of *p*
Jer. 8:12, *p* they shall be cast
Jer. 10:15, *p* they shall perish
Lam. 3:39, a man for the *p*
Lam. 4:6, The *p* of the iniquity
Hos. 9:7, days of *p* have come
Amos 1:3, not turn away its *p*
Mt. 25:46, into everlasting *p*
2 Cor. 2:6, *p* which was inflicted

Heb. 10:29, Of how much worse *p*
1 Pet. 2:14, sent by him for the *p*
2 Pet. 2:9, the unjust under *p*

PUNISHMENTS
burning. Gen. 38:24; Lev. 20:14; 21:9
hanging. Gen. 40:22; Dt. 21:23; Ezra 6:11; Est. 2:23; 7:10
scourging. Lev. 19:20; Dt. 25:1; Mt. 27:26; Acts 22:25
stoning. Lev. 20:2; 24:14; 1 Ki. 21:10; Jn. 8:59; Acts 7:58; 14:19
beheading. 2 Ki. 6:31; 10:7; Mt. 14:10. *See* Heb. 11:36
crucifying. Mt. 20:19; 27:31

PUR, Est. 3:7

PURCHASED
Acts 8:20, of God could be *p*
Eph. 1:14, of the *p* possession

PURE
Ex. 25:17, a mercy seat of *p* gold
Job 4:17, Can a man be more *p*
Job 8:6, if you were *p* and
Job 11:4, 'My doctrine is *p*
Job 15:14, that he could be *p*
Job 15:15, the heavens are not *p*
Job 25:5, the stars are not *p*
Ps. 12:6, of the LORD are *p*
Ps. 18:26, will show Yourself *p*
Ps. 73:1, To such as are *p*
Prov. 15:26, of the *p* are pleasant
Prov. 16:2, ways of a man are *p*
Prov. 20:9, my heart clean, I am *p*
Prov. 21:8, but as for the *p*
Prov. 30:12, a generation that is *p*
Mic. 6:11, Shall I count *p*
Rom. 14:20, things indeed are *p*
Phil. 4:8, whatever things are *p*
1 Tim. 5:22, keep yourself *p*
Ti. 1:15, *p* all things are *p*
Jas. 3:17, above is first *p*
1 Pet. 2:2, babes, desire the *p*
1 Jn. 3:3, just as He is *p*

PURER
Hab. 1:13, *p* eyes than to behold

PURGE
Ps. 51:7, *P* me with hyssop
Mal. 3:3, *p* them as gold and

PURGED
Isa. 6:7, away, And your sin *p*
Heb. 1:3, He had by Himself *p*

PURIFICATION
Num. 19:9, for the water of *p*
Num. 31:23, with the water of *p*

PURIFIED
Ps. 12:6, earth, *p* seven times
Heb. 9:22, all things are *p*
1 Pet. 1:22, Since you have *p*

PURIFIES
1 Jn. 3:3, hope in Him *p* himself

PURIFY
Mal. 3:3, *p* the sons of Levi
Jas. 4:8, and *p* your hearts

PURIFYING
Mk. 7:19, thus *p* all foods
Acts 15:9, *p* their hearts by

Heb 9:13, sanctifies for the *p*

PURIM, Est. 9:26
Feast of. Est. 9:20

PURITY
moral, commanded. Gal. 5:16; Eph. 5:3; Phil. 2:15; 4:8; Col. 3:5; 1 Tim. 5:22; Ti. 1:15; 1 Pet. 2:11; 2 Pet. 3:1; 1 Jn. 3:3
——— of God's word and law. Ps. 12:6; 19:8; 119:140; Prov. 30:5

PURITY
Job 22:30, be delivered by the *p*
Prov. 22:11, He who loves *p* of
2 Cor. 6:6, by *p*, by knowledge
1 Tim. 4:12, spirit, in faith, in *p*

PURPLE
Lk. 16:19, who was clothed in *p*
Jn. 19:2, they put on Him a *p*
Acts 16:14, She was a seller of *p*

PURPOSE
Ps. 20:4, and fulfill all your *p*
Eccl. 3:1, A time for every *p*
Isa. 14:26, *p* that is purposed
Jn. 12:27, But for this *p* I came
Acts 2:23, by the determined *p*
Acts 11:23, them all that with *p*
Eph. 3:11, to the eternal *p*
1 Tim. 1:5, Now the *p* of the
Rev. 17:17, to fulfill His *p*

PURPOSED
2 Sam. 17:14, For the LORD had *p*
Isa. 23:9, LORD of hosts has *p*
Dan. 1:8, But Daniel *p* in his
Eph. 1:9, pleasure which He *p*

PURPOSES
2 Cor. 9:7, each one give as he *p*

PURSE
Prov. 1:14, let us all have one *p*

PURSES
Prov. 16:30, *p* his lips and brings

PURSUE
Job 13:25, And will You *p* dry
Job 30:15, *p* my honor as the wind
Jer. 48:2, The sword shall *p*
Ezek. 33:31, but their hearts *p*
Hos. 6:3, Let us know, let us *p*
Rom. 9:30, *p* righteousness
1 Cor. 14:1, *P* love
1 Tim. 6:11, *p* righteousness
1 Pet. 3:11, him seek peace and *p*

PURSUES
Prov. 13:21, Evil *p* sinners
Prov. 28:1, flee when no one *p*

PURSUING
Rom. 9:31, but Israel, *p* the law

PUT
son of Ham. Gen. 10:6

PUT
Eccl. 3:11, Also He has *p* eternity
Dan. 4:37, pride He is able to *p* down
Mt. 6:25, what you will *p* on
Jn. 20:25, *p* my hand into His
Rom. 13:14, But *p* on the Lord

PUTREFYING
Isa. 1:6, bruises and *p* sores

QUAIL
Num. 11:31, and it brought *q*
Ps. 105:40, and He brought *q*

QUAKED
Ex. 19:18, the whole mountain *q*
Mt. 27:51, and the earth *q*

QUAKES
Joel 2:10, The earth *q* before

QUALIFIED
Col. 1:12, the Father who has *q*

QUARREL
2 Ki. 5:7, see how he seeks a *q*
Prov. 20:3, any fool can start a *q*
Mt. 12:19, He will not *q* nor cry
2 Tim. 2:24, of the Lord must not *q*

QUARRELSOME
1 Tim. 3:3, but gentle, not *q*

QUARTZ
Job 28:18, be made of coral or *q*

QUEEN
Est. 1:9, *Q* Vashti also made a
Ps. 45:9, hand stands the *q*
Jer. 44:17, burn incense to the *q*
Mt. 12:42, "The *q* of the South
Acts 8:27, under Candace the *q*
Rev. 18:7, heart, 'I sit as *q*

QUEENS
Song 6:8, There are sixty *q*
Isa. 49:23, *q* your nursing mothers

QUENCH
Song 8:7, Many waters cannot *q*
Jer. 4:4, so that no one can *q*
Mt. 12:20, flax He will not *q*
Eph. 6:16, *q* all the fiery
1 Th. 5:19, Do not *q* the Spirit

QUENCHED
Num. 11:2, LORD, the fire was *q*
Ps. 118:12, they were *q* like a
Isa. 66:24, their fire is not *q*
Mk. 9:43, that shall never be *q*
Mk. 9:44, and the fire is not *q*
Heb. 11:34, *q* the violence of fire

QUESTIONS
1 Ki. 10:1, test him with hard *q*
Lk. 2:46, and asking them *q*
1 Cor. 10:25, market, asking no *q*

QUICK-TEMPERED
Prov. 14:17, *q* man acts foolishly
Ti. 1:7, not self-willed, not *q*

QUICKLY
Ex. 32:8, have turned aside *q*
Mt. 5:25, with your adversary *q*
Jn. 13:27, "What you do, do *q*
Rev. 3:11, "Behold, I am coming *q*
Rev. 22:20, "Surely I am coming *q*

QUIET
Job 3:13, lain still and been *q*
Isa. 7:4, 'Take heed, and be *q*
Isa. 14:7, earth is at rest and *q*
Zeph. 3:17, gladness, He will *q*
Mk. 10:48, warned him to be *q*
1 Th. 4:11, aspire to lead a *q*

1 Tim. 2:2, we may lead a *q* and
1 Pet. 3:4, a gentle and *q* spirit

QUIETED
Ps. 131:2, calmed and *q* my soul
Acts 19:35, the city clerk had *q*

QUIETNESS
1 Chr. 22:9, will give peace and *q*
Job 34:29, When He gives *q*
Eccl. 4:6, a handful with *q*
Isa. 30:15, in *q* and confidence
Isa. 32:17, of righteousness, *q*
2 Th. 3:12, that they work in *q*

QUIETS
Job 37:17, *q* the earth by the

QUIVER
Job 39:23, *q* rattles against him
Ps. 127:5, the man who has his *q*
Isa. 49:2, *q* He has hidden Me
Jer. 5:16, Their *q* is like an

RAAMSES, Ex. 1:11

RABBAH, Josh. 13:25
city. 2 Sam. 11; 12:26; Jer. 49:2; Ezek. 21:20; 25:5; Amos 1:14

RABBI
Mt. 23:7, be called by men, '*R*
Mt. 23:8, do not be called '*R*

RABBONI
title addressed to Christ by Mary. Jn. 20:16

RABSARIS, 2 Ki. 18:17

RABSHAKEH, 2 Ki. 18:17
reviles Hezekiah. 2 Ki. 18:19; 19:1; Isa. 36:4

RACA
Mt. 5:22, to his brother, '*R*

RACE
Ps. 19:5, man to run its *r*
Eccl. 9:11, *r* is not to the swift
1 Cor. 9:24, who run in a *r* all run
2 Tim. 4:7, I have finished the *r*
Heb. 12:1, with endurance the *r*

RACHEL, Gen. 29:6
and Jacob. Gen. 29:10,28; 30; 31:4,19,34; 35:16

RADIANT
Ps. 34:5, to Him and were *r*

RAGE
Job 40:11, Disperse the *r* of your
Ps. 2:1, Why do the nations *r*
Acts 4:25, 'Why did the nations *r*

RAGES
Prov. 18:1, he *r* against all wise

RAGING
Ps. 89:9; Lk. 8:24; Jude 13

RAGS
Prov. 23:21, clothe a man with *r*

RAHAB, Josh. 2:1; Ps. 87:4
the harlot. Josh. 2; 6:22. *See* Mt. 1:5; Heb. 11:31; Jas. 2:25
—— Egypt. Ps. 87:4; 89:10; Isa. 51:9

RAIN
the deluge. Gen. 7; Ex. 9:34; 1 Sam. 12:17; Ps. 105:32
the gift of God. Mt. 5:45; Acts 14:17
withheld. 1 Ki. 17; Jer. 14; Zech. 14:17; Jas. 5:17
symbolic. Lev. 26:4; Dt. 32:2; 2 Sam. 23:4; Ps. 68:9; Hos. 10:12

RAIN
Gen. 2:5, had not caused it to *r*
Gen. 7:12, And the *r* was on the
Job 5:10, He gives *r* on the
Job 37:6, to the gentle *r*
Ps. 68:9, sent a plentiful *r*
Ps. 147:8, clouds, who prepares *r*
Prov. 26:1, snow in summer and *r*
Prov. 28:3, *r* which leaves no food
Eccl. 12:2, not return after the *r*
Song 2:11, the *r* is over and gone
Jer. 5:24, our God, who gives *r*
Ezek. 38:22, I will *r* down on him
Joel 2:23, given you the former *r*
Zech. 14:17, there will be no *r*
Mt. 5:45, the good, and sends *r*
Mt. 7:25, and the *r* descended
Acts 14:17, He did good, gave us *r*
Heb. 6:7, *r* that often comes
Jas. 5:17, that it would not *r*
Jas. 5:18, and the heaven gave *r*

RAINBOW
God's covenant with Noah. Gen. 9:12; Ezek. 1:28
in heaven. Rev. 4:3; 10:1

RAINED
Ps. 78:24, had *r* down manna on
Lk. 17:29, *r* fire and brimstone

RAINS
Hos. 10:12, *r* righteousness

RAISE
Hos. 6:2, third day He will *r*
Mt. 3:9, that God is able to *r*
Jn. 2:19, in three days I will *r*
Jn. 6:40, and I will *r* him up at
1 Cor. 6:14, Lord and will also *r*
Jas. 5:15, and the Lord will *r*

RAISED
Ex. 9:16, this purpose I have *r*
Mt. 16:21, be killed, and be *r*
Acts 2:24, whom God *r* up
Rom. 6:4, just as Christ was *r*
Rom. 8:11, Spirit of Him who *r*
1 Cor. 6:14, And God both *r* up the
1 Cor. 15:35, "How are the dead *r*
1 Cor. 15:52, the dead will be *r*
Eph. 2:6, and *r* us up together
Col. 3:1, then you were *r*

RAISES
Ps. 113:7, *r* the poor out of the
Ps. 146:8, *r* those who are bowed
Jn. 5:21, For as the Father *r*
2 Cor. 1:9, but in God who *r*

RAM
in sacrifices. Gen. 15:9; 22:13; Ex. 29:15; Lev. 9; Num. 5:8; typical. Dan. 8:20
—— battering. Ezek. 4:2; 21:22

RAM
Dan. 8:3, *r* which had two horns

RAMAH
Josh. 18:25; Jud. 4:5; 1 Sam. 1:19; 7:17; 8:4; 19:18; 25:1; Jer. 31:15

RAMESES, Gen. 47:11

RAMOTH, 1 Chr. 6:73

RAMOTH GILEAD
Dt. 4:43; 1 Ki. 4:13,22; 2 Ki. 8:28; 9:1; 2 Chr. 18; 22:5

RAMS
Ps. 66:15, the sweet aroma of *r*
Isa. 60:7, *r* of Nebaioth shall

RAMS' HORNS
trumpets of. Josh. 6:4

RAN
Jn. 20:4, they both *r* together
Gal. 5:7, You *r* well

RANKS
Joel 2:7; Mk. 6:40

RANSOM
Job 36:18, *r* would not help you
Ps. 49:7, nor give to God a *r*
Prov. 13:8, The *r* of a man's life
Hos. 13:14, "I will *r* them from
Mk. 10:45, to give His life a *r*
1 Tim. 2:6, who gave Himself a *r*

RANSOMED
Isa. 35:10, and the *r* of the LORD
Jer. 31:11, redeemed Jacob, and *r*

RARE
1 Sam. 3:1, of the LORD was *r*
Isa. 13:12, make a mortal more *r*

RASH
Eccl. 5:2, Do not be *r* with your

RASHLY
Ps. 106:33, so that he spoke *r*
Acts 19:36, and do nothing *r*

RAVEN
Job 38:41, food for the *r*
Song 5:11, and black as a *r*

RAVENOUS
Mt. 7:15, inwardly they are *r*

RAVENS
Gen. 8:7; Lev. 11:15; Dt. 14:14; 1 Ki. 17:4; Job 38:41

RAVENS
Ps. 147:9, and to the young *r*
Lk. 12:24, "Consider the *r*

RAVISHED
Song 4:9, You have *r* my heart
Lam. 5:11, *r* the women in Zion

RAZOR
Ps. 52:2, like a sharp *r*

REACHED
Gen. 28:12, earth, and its top *r*
Rev. 18:5, For her sins have *r*

REACHING
Phil. 3:13, *r* forward to those

READ
Mt. 21:42, "Have you never *r*
Lk. 4:16, day, and stood up to *r*
2 Cor. 3:2, hearts, known and *r*
2 Cor. 3:15, when Moses is *r*
Col. 4:16, when this epistle is *r*

READER
Mk. 13:14, Let the *r* understand

READINESS
Acts 17:11, the word with all *r*
2 Cor. 8:11, that as there was a *r*

READING
of the Law. Ex. 24:7; Josh. 8:34; 2 Ki. 23; Neh. 8; 9
—— of the Prophets. Lk. 4:16
—— of the Epistles. Col. 4:16; 1 Th. 5:27. *See* Acts 13:15

READING
Acts 8:30, *r* the prophet Isaiah
1 Tim. 4:13, give attention to *r*

READS
Hab. 2:2, that he may run who *r*
Rev. 1:3, Blessed is he who *r*

READY
Isa. 38:20, "The LORD was *r*
Mt. 25:10, and those who were *r*
Lk. 22:33, "Lord, I am *r*
2 Cor. 10:6, and being *r* to punish
2 Tim. 4:2, Be *r* in season and out
1 Pet. 3:15, and always be *r*

REAFFIRM
2 Cor. 2:8, *r* your love to him

REAP
Ps. 126:5, in tears shall *r*
Hos. 8:7, *r* the whirlwind
Mt. 6:26, they neither sow nor *r*
Mt. 25:26, you knew that I *r*
Gal. 6:7, that he will also *r*
Gal. 6:9, due season we shall *r*

REAPED
Jer. 12:13, wheat but *r* thorns
Hos. 10:13, you have *r* iniquity

REAPER
Ps. 129:7, *r* does not fill his

REAPERS
Mt. 13:30, I will say to the *r*
Mt. 13:39, *r* are the angels

REAPING
Lk. 19:22, *r* what I did not

REAPS
Jn. 4:37, one sows and another *r*

REASON
Eccl. 7:25, out wisdom and the *r*
Isa. 1:18, Come now, and let us *r*
Mt. 16:8, faith, why do you *r*
Acts 26:25, words of truth and *r*
1 Pet. 3:15, who asks you a *r*

REASONABLE, Rom. 12:1

REASONED
Acts 17:2, for three Sabbaths *r*
Acts 24:25, *r* about righteousness

REBEKAH
history of. Gen. 22:23; 24:15,67; 27:6,42; 49:31; Rom. 9:10

REBEL
Num. 14:9, "Only do not *r*
Neh. 2:19, Will you *r* against the
Job 24:13, There are those who *r*
Ps. 105:28, and they did not *r*
Isa. 1:20, if you refuse and *r*

REBELLING
Ps. 78:17, more against Him by *r*

REBELLION
1 Sam. 15:23, *r* is as the sin
Job 34:37, For he adds *r* to his
Prov. 17:11, evil man seeks only *r*
Jer. 28:16, you have taught *r*
Heb. 3:8, hearts as in the *r*
Jude 11, and perished in the *r*

REBELLIOUS
Ps. 66:7, *r* exalt themselves
Ps. 68:6, but the *r* dwell in a
Isa. 65:2, day long to a *r* people
Jer. 5:23, a defiant and *r* heart
Hos. 9:15, their princes are *r*

REBELS
Jer. 6:28, are all stubborn *r*

REBUILD
Ezra 9:9, God, to *r* its ruins
Neh. 2:5, tombs, that I may *r*
Amos 9:11, *r* it as in the days of

REBUKE
Job 13:10, He will surely *r*
Job 26:11, astonished at His *r*
Ps. 80:16, they perish at the *r*
Ps. 104:7, At Your *r* they fled
Ps. 141:5, And let him *r* me
Prov. 1:23, Turn at my *r*
Prov. 9:8, *r* a wise man
Prov. 17:10, *R* is more effective
Prov. 27:5, *r* is better than love
Eccl. 7:5, better to hear the *r*
Isa. 1:17, *r* the oppressor
Jer. 15:15, sake I have suffered *r*
Mic. 4:3, *r* strong nations
Lk. 17:3, sins against you, *r*
Lk. 19:39, *r* Your disciples
1 Tim. 5:1, Do not *r* an older man
1 Tim. 5:20, who are sinning *r*
Ti. 1:13, *r* them sharply
Jude 9, "The Lord *r* you
Rev. 3:19, As many as I love, I *r*

REBUKED
Mt. 8:26, *r* the winds and the
Mk. 16:14, *r* their unbelief
Heb. 12:5, when you are *r* by Him
2 Pet. 2:16, but he was *r* for his

REBUKES
Ps. 39:11, with *r* You correct
Prov. 9:7, *r* a wicked man
Prov. 15:31, ear that hears the *r*
Prov. 28:23, *r* a man will find more

RECALL
Heb. 10:32, *r* the former days

RECEIVE
Ps. 24:5, He shall *r* blessing
Hos. 14:2, *r* us graciously
Mt. 11:14, you are willing to *r*
Mt. 21:22, believing, you will *r*
Jn. 1:11, and His own did not *r*
Jn. 5:41, "I do not *r* honor
Jn. 14:3, will come again and *r*
Jn. 14:17, the world cannot *r*
Jn. 16:24, Ask, and you will *r*
Jn. 20:22, "*R* the Holy Spirit
Acts 7:59, "Lord Jesus, *r*
Acts 19:2, *r* the Holy Spirit
Rom. 14:1, *R* one who is weak
2 Cor. 5:10, that each one may *r*
2 Cor. 6:1, *r* the grace of God in
Gal. 3:2, *r* the Spirit by the
Phil. 2:29, *R* him therefore in the
Jas. 1:7, suppose that he will *r*
1 Jn. 3:22, whatever we ask we *r*

RECEIVED
Lk. 6:24, *r* your consolation
Lk. 16:25, in your lifetime you *r*
Jn. 1:12, But as many as *r*
Rom. 14:3, for God has *r* him
1 Cor. 11:23, For I *r* from the Lord
Col. 2:6, *r* Christ
1 Tim. 3:16, *r* up in glory
2 Pet. 1:17, For He *r* from God the

RECEIVES
Prov. 15:5, *r* correction is prudent
Mt. 10:40, *r* you *r* Me
Mt. 18:5, *r* one little child
Mk. 9:37, and whoever *r* Me

RECEIVING
Heb. 12:28, *r* a kingdom which

RECOMPENSE
Prov. 6:35, He will accept no *r*
Prov. 20:22, not say, "I will *r*
Hos. 9:7, days of *r* have come

RECOMPENSED
2 Sam. 22:21, of my hands He has *r*
2 Sam. 22:25, the LORD has *r* me

RECONCILE
Eph. 2:16, and that He might *r*
Col. 1:20, *r* all things to

RECONCILED
Mt. 5:24, First be *r* to your
Rom. 5:10, were enemies we were *r*
2 Cor. 5:20, Christ's behalf, be *r*

RECONCILIATION
with God. Isa. 53:5; Dan. 9:24; Rom. 5; 2 Cor. 5:19; Eph. 2:16; Col. 1:20; Heb. 2:17

RECONCILING
Rom. 11:15, cast away is the *r*
2 Cor. 5:19, God was in Christ *r*

RECORD
Ex. 20:24, *r* My name I will come

RED
Gen. 25:25, the first came out *r*
Isa. 1:18, though they are *r*
Isa. 63:2, Why is Your apparel *r*
Mt. 16:2, for the sky is *r*

RED SEA, Ex. 14; 15; 1 Ki. 9:26

REDEEM
Num. 18:15, man you shall surely *r*

Neh. 5:5, in our power to *r* them
Job 5:20, In famine He shall *r*
Job 6:23, *R* me from the hand of
Ps. 49:7, can by any means *r*
Ps. 49:15, But God will *r* my soul
Ps. 72:14, *r* their life from
Ps. 130:8, And He shall *r* Israel
Isa. 50:2, all that it cannot *r*
Hos. 13:14, I will *r* them from
Lk. 24:21, was going to *r* Israel
Gal. 4:5, *r* those who were
Ti. 2:14, us, that He might *r*

REDEEMED
Ex. 15:13, people whom You have *r*
Ps. 106:10, *r* them from the hand
Ps. 107:2, Let the *r* of the LORD
Isa. 35:9, *r* shall walk there
Isa. 51:10, sea a road for the *r*
Isa. 52:3, and you shall be *r*
Lk. 1:68, and *r* His people
Gal. 3:13, Christ has *r* us from
1 Pet. 1:18, that you were not *r*
Rev. 5:9, were slain, and have *r*
Rev. 14:4, These were *r* from

REDEEMER
Job 19:25, For I know that my *R*
Ps. 78:35, Most High God their *R*
Prov. 23:11, for their *R* is mighty
Isa. 41:14, the LORD and your *R*
Isa. 59:20, *R* will come to Zion
Isa. 63:16, our *R* from Everlasting
Jer. 50:34, Their *R* is strong

REDEEMING
Eph. 5:16, *r* the time

REDEMPTION
by Christ. Rom. 5; Gal. 1:4; 3; 4; Eph. 1; 2; Col. 1; Heb. 9; 10; Ti. 2:14; 1 Pet. 1:18; Rev. 5:9
——— of land, etc. Lev. 25; Neh. 5:8
of the firstborn. Ex. 13:11; Num. 3:12

REDEMPTION
Ps. 49:8, For the *r* of their
Ps. 130:7, with Him is abundant *r*
Jer. 32:7, *r* is yours to buy it
Lk. 2:38, those who looked for *r*
Lk. 21:28, your *r* draws near
Rom. 3:24, grace through the *r*
Rom. 8:23, the adoption, the *r*
1 Cor. 1:30, sanctification and *r*
Eph. 1:7, In Him we have *r*
Eph. 4:30, for the day of *r*
Heb. 9:12, obtained eternal *r*

REED
Isa. 42:3, *r* He will not break
Mt. 11:7, *r* shaken by the wind
Mk. 15:19, on the head with a *r*

REEDS
Job 8:11, *r* flourish without
Ps. 68:30, the beasts of the *r*

REFINED
Job 28:1, where gold is *r*
Ps. 66:10, us as silver is *r*

REFINER
Mal. 3:3, He will sit as a *r*

REFORMATION
Heb. 9:10, until the time of *r*

REFRAIN
2 Chr. 35:21, *R* from meddling with
1 Cor. 9:6, who have no right to *r*
1 Pet. 3:10, good days let him *r*

REFRESH
Gen. 18:5, bread, that you may *r*
Phile. 20, *r* my heart in the Lord

REFRESHED
Rom. 15:32, of God, and may be *r*
1 Cor. 16:18, *r* my spirit and yours
2 Cor. 7:13, his spirit has been *r*
2 Tim. 1:16, for he often *r*

REFRESHES
Prov. 25:13, *r* the soul of his

REFRESHING
Acts 3:19, *r* may come from the

REFUGE
the Divine. Dt. 33:27; 2 Sam. 22:3; Ps. 9:9; 46:1; 48:3; Heb. 6:18
cities of. Num. 35; Dt. 4:41; 19; Josh. 20

REFUGE
Num. 35:6, six cities of *r*
Dt. 33:27, eternal God is your *r*
Ruth 2:12, you have come for *r*
Ps. 14:6, but the LORD is his *r*
Ps. 46:1, God is our *r* and
Ps. 57:1, wings I will make my *r*
Ps. 62:8, God is a *r* for us
Ps. 71:7, You are my strong *r*
Heb. 6:18, who have fled for *r*

REFUSE
Isa. 7:15, *r* the evil and choose
Jer. 9:6, through deceit they *r*
Ezek. 2:5, hear or whether they *r*
Heb. 12:25, See that you do not *r*

REFUSED
Neh. 9:17, They *r* to obey

REFUSES
Job 6:7, My soul *r* to touch
Mt. 18:17, "And if he *r* to hear

REGARD
Job 34:19, *r* the rich more than
Ps. 66:18, *r* iniquity in my heart
Ps. 102:17, *r* the prayer of the
Lk. 18:2, did not fear God nor *r*

REGARDED
Prov. 1:24, my hand and no one *r*
Lk. 1:48, *r* the lowly state

REGARDS
Prov. 13:18, *r* a rebuke will be
Lam. 4:16, He no longer *r* them

REGENERATION
Mt. 19:28, to you, that in the *r*
Ti. 3:5, the washing of *r*

REGISTERED
Lk. 2:3, So all went to be *r*
Heb. 12:23, firstborn who are *r*

REGRETTED
Mt. 21:29, but afterward he *r*

REGULATIONS
Col. 2:20, yourselves to *r*

REHOBOAM, 1 Ki. 11:43
king of Judah. 1 Ki. 11; 12; 14; 2 Chr. 9—12

REHOBOTH, Gen. 10:11; 26:22

REIGN
1 Sam. 12:12, but a king shall *r*
Job 34:30, hypocrite should not *r*
Mic. 4:7, so the LORD will *r*
Lk. 1:33, "And He will *r*
Lk. 19:14, not have this man to *r*
Rom. 5:17, righteousness will *r*
Rom. 5:21, so grace might *r*
Rom. 6:12, do not let sin *r*
1 Cor. 15:25, For He must *r* till He
Rev. 5:10, and we shall *r* on the
Rev. 20:6, of Christ, and shall *r*

REIGNED
Rom. 5:21, so that as sin *r*
1 Cor. 4:8, You have *r* as kings
Rev. 20:4, And they lived and *r*

REIGNS
Ps. 47:8, God *r* over the nations
Ps. 93:1, The LORD *r*
Isa. 52:7, to Zion, "Your God *r*
Rev. 19:6, Lord God Omnipotent *r*

REJECT
Num. 14:11, will these people *r*
Ps. 119:118, *r* all those who stray
Mk. 7:9, "All too well you *r*
Ti. 3:10, *R* a divisive man

REJECTED
Ps. 118:22, *r* has become the chief
Isa. 53:3, He is despised and *r*
Hos. 8:3, Israel has *r* the
Mt. 21:42, *r* has become the chief
Lk. 17:25, many things and be *r*
Acts 7:35, Moses whom they *r*
1 Pet. 2:4, to a living stone, *r*
1 Pet. 2:7, *r* has become the chief

REJECTION
Num. 14:34, you shall know My *r*

REJECTS
Lk. 10:16, he who *r* Me *r*
1 Th. 4:8, *r* this does not reject

REJOICE
Dt. 28:63, so the LORD will *r*
1 Chr. 16:32, let the field *r*
2 Chr. 6:41, and let Your saints *r*
Ps. 5:11, *r* who put their trust
Ps. 14:7, people, let Jacob *r*
Ps. 33:1, *R* in the LORD
Ps. 35:26, mutual confusion who *r*
Ps. 58:10, The righteous shall *r*
Ps. 63:7, of Your wings I will *r*
Ps. 63:11, But the king shall *r*
Ps. 68:3, Let them *r* before God
Ps. 89:16, In Your name they *r*
Ps. 96:11, Let the heavens *r*
Ps. 97:1, Let the earth *r*
Ps. 107:42, righteous see it and *r*
Ps. 118:24, we will *r* and be glad
Prov. 2:14, who *r* in doing evil
Prov. 5:18, be blessed, and *r*
Prov. 31:25, she shall *r* in time to
Eccl. 11:9, *R*, O young man
Song 1:4, We will be glad and *r*

Isa. 29:19, among men shall *r*
Isa. 61:10, I will greatly *r*
Isa. 65:13, My servants shall *r*
Isa. 66:14, your heart shall *r*
Jer. 32:41, 'Yes, I will *r*
Mic. 7:8, Do not *r* over me
Zeph. 3:17, He will *r* over you
Lk. 10:20, do not *r* in this
Jn. 14:28, loved me, you would *r*
Jn. 16:20, but the world will *r*
Jn. 16:22, and your heart will *r*
Rom. 12:15, *R* with those who
Phil. 1:18, and in this I *r*
Phil. 2:17, faith, I am glad and *r*
Phil. 4:4, *R* in the Lord always
1 Th. 5:16, *R* always
1 Pet. 1:8, yet believing, you *r*

REJOICED
Dt. 30:9, for good as He *r*
Eccl. 2:10, for my heart *r*
Lk. 1:47, and my spirit has *r*
Lk. 10:21, In that hour Jesus *r*
Jn. 8:56, Your father Abraham *r*
Phil. 4:10, But I *r* in the Lord

REJOICES
Ps. 16:9, glad, and my glory *r*
1 Cor. 13:6, but *r* in the truth

REJOICING
Ps. 107:22, His works with *r*
Ps. 118:15, The voice of *r* and
Ps. 119:111, for they are the *r*
Ps. 126:6, come again with *r*
Prov. 8:31, *r* in His inhabited
Acts 8:39, he went on his way *r*
2 Cor. 6:10, yet always *r*
1 Th. 2:19, or joy, or crown of *r*
Heb. 3:6, confidence and the *r*

RELATIVES
Ps. 38:11, *r* stand afar off

RELEASE
year of. Ex. 21:2; Dt. 15:1; 31:10; Jer. 34:14

RELEASE
Mt. 27:17, do you want me to *r*
Jn. 19:10, and power to *r* You
Rev. 9:14, "*R* the four angels

RELENT
Ps. 110:4, sworn and will not *r*
Jer. 4:28, and will not *r*
Jer. 26:13, then the LORD will *r*
Joel 2:14, if He will turn and *r*
Heb. 7:21, sworn and will not *r*

RELENTED
Ex. 32:14, So the LORD *r* from the
1 Chr. 21:15, the LORD looked and *r*
Jon. 3:10, and God *r* from the

RELENTING
Jer. 15:6, I am weary of *r*

RELIEF
Ex. 8:15, saw that there was *r*
Job 32:20, that I may find *r*

RELIEVE
Job 16:5, of my lips would *r*
1 Tim. 5:16, *r* those who are really

RELIEVED
Ps. 4:1, You have *r* me when I

RELIEVES
Ps. 146:9, *r* the fatherless

RELIGION
Acts 25:19, about their own *r*
Col. 2:23, in self-imposed *r*
Jas. 1:26, heart, this one's *r*
Jas. 1:27, and undefiled *r*

RELIGIOUS
Acts 17:22, things you are very *r*
Jas. 1:26, you thinks he is *r*

RELY
Isa. 50:10, name of the LORD and *r*
Ezek. 33:26, "You *r* on your sword

REMAIN
Ex. 12:10, shall let none of it *r*
Jer. 3:5, *r* angry forever
Jer. 17:25, and this city shall *r*
Amos 6:9, that if ten men *r*
Jn. 15:11, that My joy may *r*
Jn. 15:16, your fruit should *r*
Jn. 21:22, "If I will that he *r*
1 Cor. 15:6, the greater part *r*
Phil. 1:24, Nevertheless to *r*
1 Th. 4:15, we who are alive and *r*
Rev. 3:2, the things which *r*

REMAINDER
Ps. 76:10, with the *r* of wrath
Isa. 38:10, I am deprived of the *r*

REMAINED
Eccl. 2:9, Also my wisdom *r*
Lk. 1:56, And Mary *r* with her
Jn. 1:32, like a dove, and He *r*

REMAINS
Gen. 8:22, "While the earth *r*
Jn. 9:41, Therefore your sin *r*
Heb. 4:9, There *r* therefore a
1 Jn. 3:9, sin, for His seed *r*

REMEMBER
Gen. 40:14, "But *r* me when it is
Ex. 20:8, *R* the Sabbath day
Dt. 15:15, *r* that you were a
1 Chr. 16:12, *R* His marvelous works
Ps. 20:7, but we will *r* the name
Ps. 25:7, *r* the sins of my youth
Ps. 119:55, *r* Your name in the
Eccl. 12:1, *R* now your Creator
Song 1:4, *r* your love more than
Isa. 43:18, *r* the former things
Jer. 2:2, "I *r* you
Jer. 31:34, and their sin I will *r*
Amos 1:9, *r* the covenant of
Hab. 3:2, in wrath *r* mercy
Lk. 1:72, and to *r* His holy
Lk. 17:32, "*R* Lot's wife
Acts 20:35, *r* the words of the
Col. 4:18, *R* my chains
2 Tim. 2:8, *R* that Jesus Christ
Heb. 13:7, *R* those who rule

REMEMBERED
Gen. 8:1, Then God *r* Noah
Ex. 2:24, *r* His covenant with
Ps. 77:3, I *r* God
Ps. 105:8, *r* His covenant forever
Ps. 119:52, *r* Your judgments
Ps. 136:23, Who *r* us in our lowly
Ps. 137:1, yea, we wept when we *r*

Eccl. 9:15, *r* that same poor man
Isa. 63:11, *r* the days of old
Mt. 26:75, And Peter *r* the word
Acts 11:16, *r* the word of the Lord

REMEMBERS
Lam. 3:20, My soul still *r*

REMEMBRANCE
Ps. 6:5, in death there is no *r*
Ps. 77:6, *r* my song in the night
Eccl. 1:11, There is no *r* of
Isa. 43:26, Put Me in *r*
Lk. 22:19, do this in *r* of Me
1 Cor. 11:24, do this in *r* of Me

REMIND
2 Pet. 1:12, *r* you always of these
Jude 5, But I want to *r* you

REMINDER
Heb. 10:3, there is a *r* of sins
2 Pet. 1:15, you always have a *r*
2 Pet. 3:1, pure minds by way of *r*

REMISSION
of sins. Mt. 26:28; Mk. 1:4; Lk. 24:47; Acts 2:38; 10:43; Heb. 9:22; 10:18

REMISSION
Mk. 1:4, repentance for the *r*
Acts 2:38, Jesus Christ for the *r*
Heb. 10:18, where there is *r*

REMNANT
Isa. 1:9, to us a very small *r*
Isa. 10:21, The *r* will return
Jer. 15:11, be well with your *r*
Jer. 23:3, I will gather the *r*
Jer. 44:28, and all the *r* of Judah
Ezek. 6:8, Yet I will leave a *r*
Joel 2:32, *r* whom the LORD calls
Zech. 8:11, I will not treat the *r*
Rom. 11:5, time there is a *r*

REMORSEFUL
Mt. 27:3, condemned, was *r*

REMOVE
Ps. 39:10, *R* Your plague from me
Ps. 39:13, *R* Your gaze from me
Prov. 4:27, *r* your foot from evil
Prov. 30:8, *r* falsehood and lies
Eccl. 11:10, Therefore *r* sorrow
Lk. 22:42, *r* this cup from Me
Rev. 2:5, *r* your lampstand

REMOVED
Ps. 46:2, Though the earth be *r*
Ps. 103:12, *r* our transgressions
Prov. 10:30, will never be *r*
Isa. 54:10, and the hills be *r*
Mt. 21:21, this mountain, 'Be *r*

REMOVES
Job 9:5, *r* the mountains

REND
Joel 2:13, So *r* your heart

RENDER
Ps. 116:12, What shall I *r* to the
Mt. 21:41, who will *r* to him the
Mt. 22:21, "*R* therefore to Caesar

RENEW
Ps. 51:10, *r* a steadfast
Ps. 104:30, *r* the face of the

REVENGE
deprecated. Lev. 19:18; Prov. 20:22; 24:29; Mt. 5:39; Rom. 12:19; 1 Th. 5:15; 1 Pet. 3:9

REVENGE
Jer. 20:10, and we will take our *r*

REVENUES
Prov. 16:8, than vast *r* without

REVERENCE, Ti. 2:7
to God. Ex. 3:5; Ps. 89:7; 111:9; Heb. 12:28
to God's sanctuary. Lev. 19:30

REVERENCE
Lev. 19:30, and *r* My sanctuary
Ps. 89:7, and to be held in *r*
Mal. 1:6, Master, where is My *r*
1 Tim. 3:4, submission with all *r*
Heb. 12:28, God acceptably with *r*

REVERENT
Prov. 28:14, man who is always *r*
1 Tim. 3:11, their wives must be *r*
Ti. 2:2, older men be sober, *r*

REVILE
Mt. 5:11, are you when they *r*
Acts 23:4, *r* God's high priest
1 Pet. 3:16, evildoers, those who *r*

REVILED
Mk. 15:32, crucified with Him *r*
1 Pet. 2:23, who, when He was *r*

REVILER
1 Cor. 5:11, or an idolater, or a *r*

REVILERS
1 Cor. 6:10, nor drunkards, nor *r*

REVILING
1 Tim. 6:4, come envy, strife, *r*

REVIVAL
Ezra 9:8, give us a measure of *r*

REVIVE
Ps. 71:20, troubles, shall *r*
Ps. 85:6, Will You not *r* us
Ps. 119:25, *r* me according to Your
Isa. 57:15, *r* the spirit of the
Hos. 6:2, two days He will *r*
Hab. 3:2, *r* Your work in the

REVIVED
Hos. 14:7, they shall be *r*
Rom. 7:9, came, sin *r* and I died

REVOLT
instances of: cities of the plain. Gen. 14:1; Korah, Dathan, Abiram. Num. 16:1; Israel from Mesopotamia under Othniel. Jud. 3:9; southern tribes from the Philistines. Jud. 3:31; eastern tribes from Eglon. Jud. 3:12; Deborah and Barak. Jud. 4:4; southern tribes from Midian. Jud. 6—8; southern tribes from Ammon. Jud. 11; Samson. Jud. 15; Ishbosheth. 2 Sam. 2:8; Abner. 2 Sam. 3; Absalom. 2 Sam. 15:10; Adonijah. 1 Ki. 1:5; 2:13; Hadad and Rezon. 1 Ki. 11:14,23; ten tribes. 1 Ki. 12:19; 2 Chr. 10:19; Moab. 2 Ki. 1; 3:5,7; Edom. 2 Ki. 8:20; 2 Chr. 21:8; Libnah. 2 Ki. 8:22; 2 Chr. 21:10; Jehu. 2 Ki. 9:11; Hoshea. 2 Ki. 17:4; Hezekiah. 2 Ki. 18:4; Jehoiakim. 2 Ki. 24:1; Zedekiah. 2 Ki. 24:20; 2 Chr. 36:13; Jer. 52:3; Theudas. Acts 5:36; Judas of Galilee. Acts 5:37

REVOLT
Isa. 1:5, You will *r* more and

REVOLTED
Isa. 31:6, Israel have deeply *r*
Jer. 5:23, they have *r* and

REVOLTERS
Hos. 5:2, *r* are deeply involved

REWARD
to the righteous. Gen. 15:1; Ps. 19:11; 58:11; Prov. 11:18; 25:22; Mt. 5:12; 6:1; 10:41; Lk. 6:35; 1 Cor. 3:8; Col. 2:18; 3:24; Heb. 10:35; 11:6; Rev. 22:12
threatened to the wicked. Dt. 32:41; 2 Sam. 3:39; Ps. 54:5; 91:8; 109; Obad. 15; 2 Pet. 2:13; Rev. 19:17; 20:15; 22:15
exceedingly great. Gen. 15:1

REWARD
Gen. 15:1, exceedingly great *r*
Ps. 19:11, them there is great *r*
Ps. 35:12, *r* me evil for good
Ps. 58:11, "Surely there is a *r*
Ps. 91:8, look, and see the *r*
Prov. 11:18, will a sure *r*
Prov. 25:22, and the LORD will *r*
Eccl. 2:10, and this was my *r*
Isa. 40:10, behold, His *r* is with
Hos. 4:9, *r* them for their deeds
Hos. 9:1, You have loved for *r*
Mt. 5:12, for great is your *r*
Mt. 6:1, you have no *r* from
Mt. 6:2, you, they have their *r*
Mt. 10:41, receive a prophet's *r*
Mt. 10:42, by no means lose his *r*
Lk. 6:35, *r* will be great
Lk. 23:41, we receive the due *r*
1 Cor. 3:8, will receive his own *r*
Col. 2:18, cheat you of your *r*
Heb. 11:26, for he looked to the *r*
2 Jn. 8, may receive a full *r*
Rev. 22:12, quickly, and My *r*

REWARDED
Ps. 109:5, Thus they have *r*

REWARDER
Heb. 11:6, and that He is a *r*

REWARDS
Prov. 17:13, Whoever *r* evil for
Isa. 1:23, and follows after *r*
Dan. 5:17, and give your *r*

REZIN
king of Syria. 2 Ki. 15:37; 16:5,9; Isa. 7:1

REZON
of Damascus. 1 Ki. 11:23

RHODA, Acts 12:13

RIBLAH, Num. 34:11
in Syria. 2 Ki. 23:33; 25:6; Jer. 39:5; 52:9

RICH
Gen. 13:2, Abram was very *r*
1 Sam. 2:7, makes poor and makes *r*
Job 27:19, *r* man will lie down
Ps. 45:12, the *r* among the people
Ps. 49:16, when one becomes *r*
Prov. 11:25, soul will be made *r*
Prov. 13:7, who makes himself *r*
Prov. 14:20, *r* has many friends
Prov. 22:2, The *r* and the poor
Prov. 22:7, *r* rules over the poor
Prov. 28:11, *r* man is wise in his
Eccl. 10:20, do not curse the *r*
Mt. 19:23, it is hard for a *r*
Lk. 6:24, to you who are *r*
Lk. 16:21, from the *r* man's table
Lk. 18:23, for he was very *r*
Rom. 10:12, Lord over all is *r*
1 Cor. 4:8, You are already *r*
2 Cor. 8:9, though He was *r*
1 Tim. 6:9, who desire to be *r*
Jas. 1:10, but the *r* in his
Jas. 1:11, So the *r* man also will
Jas. 2:5, of this world to be *r*
Rev. 3:17, you say, 'I am *r*

RICHES
God gives. 1 Sam. 2:7; Prov. 10:22; Eccl. 5:19
the true. Prov. 3:14; Mt. 13:44; Lk. 16:11; Eph. 3:8; Col. 2:3
earthly. Dt. 8:17; 1 Chr. 29:12; Ps. 49:6; Prov. 11:4; 15:16; 23:5; 27:24; Eccl. 4:8; 5:10; 6; Jer. 9:23; 48:36; Ezek. 7:19; Zeph. 1:18; Mt. 6:19; 13:22; 1 Tim. 6:17; Jas. 1:11; 5:2; 1 Pet. 1:18
uncertain. Prov. 23:5
dangers of. Dt. 8:13; 32:15; Neh. 9:25; Prov. 15:16; 18:23; 28:11; 30:8; Eccl. 5:12; Hos. 12:8; Mic. 6:12; Mt. 13:22; 19:23; Mk. 10:22; Lk. 12:15; 1 Tim. 6:10; Jas. 2:6; 5:1
proper use of. 1 Chr. 29:3; Job 31:16,24; Ps. 62:10; Jer. 9:23; Mt. 6:19; 19:21; Lk. 16:9; 1 Tim. 6:17; Jas. 1:9; 1 Jn. 3:17
evil use of. Job 20:15; 31:24; Ps. 39:6; 49:6; 73:12; Prov. 11:28; 13:7,11; 15:6; Eccl. 2:26; 5:10; Jas. 5:3
end of the wicked rich. Job 20:16; 21:13; 27:16; Ps. 52:7; Prov. 11:4; 22:16; Eccl. 5:14; Jer. 17:11; Mic. 2:3; Hab. 2:6; Lk. 6:24; 12:16; 16:19; Jas. 5:1

RICHES
1 Chr. 29:12, Both *r* and honor come
Job 20:15, He swallows down *r*
Ps. 39:6, he heaps up *r*
Ps. 52:7, the abundance of his *r*
Ps. 62:10, if *r* increase
Ps. 112:3, *r* will be in his house
Prov. 3:16, in her left hand *r*
Prov. 8:18, *R* and honor are
Prov. 11:4, *R* do not profit
Prov. 11:28, in his *r* will fall

Prov. 13:7, yet has great *r*
Prov. 14:24, of the wise is their *r*
Prov. 19:14, and *r* are an
Prov. 22:4, of the LORD are *r*
Prov. 27:24, *r* are not forever
Eccl. 5:13, *r* kept for their owner
Isa. 45:3, darkness and hidden *r*
Isa. 61:6, you shall eat the *r*
Jer. 17:11, so is he who gets *r*
Ezek. 28:5, have increased your *r*
Mk. 10:23, for those who have *r*
Rom. 2:4, do you despise the *r*
Rom. 9:23, might make known the *r*
Eph. 1:18, what are the *r*
Eph. 2:7, show the exceeding *r*
Eph. 3:8, the unsearchable *r*
1 Tim. 6:17, trust in uncertain *r*
Heb. 11:26, *r* than the treasures
Jas. 5:2, *r* are corrupted
Rev. 5:12, to receive power and *r*

RICHLY
Col. 3:16, Christ dwell in you *r*
1 Tim. 6:17, God, who gives us *r*

RIDDLE
Jud. 14:12, "Let me pose a *r*

RIDDLES
Prov. 1:6, the wise and their *r*

RIDE
Job 30:22, wind and cause me to *r*
Ps. 45:4, in Your majesty *r*
Ps. 66:12, have caused men to *r*

RIDER
Ex. 15:1, *r* He has thrown
Job 39:18, the horse and its *r*

RIDES
Isa. 19:1, Behold, the LORD *r*

RIDGES
Ps. 65:10, You water its *r*

RIDICULE
Ps. 22:7, those who see Me *r* Me
Isa. 57:4, Whom do you *r*

RIDICULED
Mt. 9:24, they *r* Him

RIGHT
Dt. 6:18, you shall do what is *r*
Dt. 21:17, the *r* of the firstborn
Jud. 21:25, did what was *r* in his
2 Ki. 10:15, "Is your heart *r*
Ps. 107:7, them forth by the *r*
Ps. 110:1, Lord, "Sit at My *r*
Prov. 14:12, a way which seems *r*
Prov. 21:2, way of a man is *r*
Isa. 45:19, things that are *r*
Ezek. 21:27, until He comes whose *r*
Hos. 14:9, of the LORD are *r*
Amos 3:10, do not know to do *r*
Mt. 20:4, and whatever is *r*
Mk. 5:15, clothed and in his *r*
Lk. 12:57, not judge what is *r*
Jn. 1:12, to them He gave the *r*
Acts 8:21, your heart is not *r*
1 Cor. 9:4, Do we have no *r*
Rev. 2:1, seven stars in His *r*

RIGHTEOUS
Gen. 18:23, also destroy the *r*
Dt. 25:1, and they justify the *r*
1 Sam. 24:17, "You are more *r*
Job 15:14, that he could be *r*
Job 17:9, *r* will hold to his way
Job 22:19, "The *r* see it and
Ps. 1:6, knows the way of the *r*
Ps. 5:12, LORD, will bless the *r*
Ps. 7:9, *r* God tests the hearts
Ps. 11:3, what can the *r*
Ps. 34:17, The *r* cry out
Ps. 37:17, the LORD upholds the *r*
Ps. 37:21, *r* shows mercy and
Ps. 37:25, I have not seen the *r*
Ps. 112:6, the *r* will be in
Ps. 145:17, The LORD is *r* in all
Ps. 146:8, the LORD loves the *r*
Prov. 10:3, will not allow the *r*
Prov. 10:11, *r* is a well of life
Prov. 10:16, The labor of the *r*
Prov. 10:28, *r* will be gladness
Prov. 11:8, *r* is delivered from
Prov. 11:21, *r* will be delivered
Prov. 11:28, *r* will flourish
Prov. 11:31, *r* will be recompensed
Prov. 12:10, *r* man regards the life
Prov. 12:26, *r* should choose his
Prov. 15:6, *r* there is much
Prov. 15:29, the prayer of the *r*
Prov. 18:10, the *r* run to it and
Prov. 28:1, *r* are bold as a lion
Prov. 29:2, When the *r* are in
Prov. 29:7, *r* considers the cause
Eccl. 7:16, Do not be overly *r*
Eccl. 9:2, event happens to the *r*
Isa. 3:10, *r* that it shall be
Isa. 26:2, the gates, that the *r*
Isa. 41:10, with My *r* right hand
Isa. 53:11, By His knowledge My *r*
Isa. 57:1, The *r* perishes
Isa. 60:21, people shall all be *r*
Jer. 12:1, *R* are You
Dan. 4:27, your sins by being *r*
Amos 2:6, they sell the *r*
Mt. 9:13, not come to call the *r*
Mt. 13:17, *r* men desired to see
Mt. 13:43, *r* will shine forth as
Lk. 1:6, And they were both *r*
Lk. 18:9, that they were *r*
Lk. 23:47, "Certainly this was a *r*
Rom. 3:10, "There is none *r*
Rom. 5:7, *r* man will one die
Heb. 11:4, witness that he was *r*
1 Jn. 2:1, Jesus Christ the *r*
1 Jn. 3:7, just as He is *r*
Rev. 16:7, *r* are Your
Rev. 19:8, fine linen is the *r*

RIGHTEOUSLY
Ps. 67:4, judge the people *r*
Isa. 33:15, He who walks *r* and
Ti. 2:12, should live soberly, *r*
1 Pet. 2:23, to Him who judges *r*

RIGHTEOUSNESS
by faith. Gen. 15:6; Ps. 106:31; Rom. 4:3; Gal. 3:6; Jas. 2:23
of God in Christ, imputed. Isa. 54:17; Jer. 23:6; 33:16; Hos. 2:19; Rom. 1:17; 3:22; 1 Cor. 1:30; 2 Cor. 5:21; Phil. 3:9; 2 Pet. 1:1; Mal. 4:2; Ti. 2:14
of the law and faith. Rom. 10
of man. Dt. 9:4; Isa. 64:6; Dan. 9:18; Phil. 3:9

RIGHTEOUSNESS
Gen. 15:6, it to him for *r*
Job 27:6, My *r* I hold fast
Job 29:14, I put on *r*
Job 36:3, I will ascribe *r*
Ps. 4:1, I call, O God of my *r*
Ps. 11:7, righteous, He loves *r*
Ps. 24:5, from the LORD, and *r*
Ps. 35:28, shall speak of Your *r*
Ps. 40:9, the good news of *r*
Ps. 45:7, You love *r* and hate
Ps. 50:6, heavens declare His *r*
Ps. 51:14, sing aloud of Your *r*
Ps. 85:10, *r* and peace have
Ps. 85:13, *R* will go before Him
Ps. 89:16, *r* they are exalted
Ps. 94:15, will return to *r*
Ps. 97:2, *r* and justice are the
Ps. 106:3, and he who does *r*
Ps. 111:3, *r* endures forever
Ps. 119:142, *r* is an everlasting
Prov. 10:2, *r* delivers from death
Prov. 11:5, The *r* of the blameless
Prov. 11:6, The *r* of the upright
Prov. 11:19, *r* leads to life
Prov. 12:28, the way of *r* is life
Prov. 13:6, *R* guards him whose way
Prov. 14:34, *R* exalts a nation
Prov. 16:31, found in the way of *r*
Prov. 21:21, He who follows *r*
Isa. 1:21, *r* lodged in it
Isa. 11:4, *r* He shall judge
Isa. 11:5, *R* shall be the belt
Isa. 26:10, he will not learn *r*
Isa. 28:17, and *r* the plummet
Isa. 32:17, *r* will be peace
Isa. 45:24, in the LORD I have *r*
Isa. 46:12, who are far from *r*
Isa. 51:8, *r* will be forever
Isa. 57:12, I will declare your *r*
Isa. 59:16, and His own *r*
Isa. 59:17, *r* as a breastplate
Isa. 61:3, be called trees of *r*
Isa. 62:1, *r* goes forth as
Jer. 23:6, The Lord Our *R*
Jer. 33:15, to David a Branch of *r*
Jer. 51:10, has revealed our *r*
Ezek. 18:20, The *r* of the righteous
Dan. 9:7, "O Lord, *r* belongs
Dan. 9:24, in everlasting *r*
Dan. 12:3, who turn many to *r*
Hos. 10:12, for yourselves *r*
Mt. 3:15, to fulfill all *r*
Mt. 5:20, exceeds the *r* of the
Mt. 21:32, to you in the way of *r*
Lk. 1:75, in holiness and *r*
Rom. 1:17, For in it the *r*
Rom. 3:22, even the *r* of God
Rom. 4:11, a seal of the *r*
Rom. 4:22, accounted to him for *r*
Rom. 5:17, *r* will reign in life
Rom. 5:21, might reign through *r*
Rom. 8:10, is life because of *r*
Rom. 9:30, who did not pursue *r*
Rom. 9:31, pursuing the law of *r*
Rom. 10:3, ignorant of God's *r*
2 Cor. 5:21, we might become the *r*
Gal. 2:21, *r* comes through the

Eph. 6:14, the breastplate of *r*
Phil. 3:9, not having my own *r*
1 Tim. 6:11, things and pursue *r*
Ti. 3:5, *r* which we have
Heb. 11:7, *r* which is according
Jas. 1:20, does not produce the *r*
1 Pet. 3:14, should suffer for *r*
2 Pet. 2:5, a preacher of *r*
2 Pet. 3:13, a new earth in which *r*
1 Jn. 2:29, who practices *r*
1 Jn. 3:7, He who practices *r*
1 Jn. 3:10, does not practice *r*

RIGHTLY
Prov. 15:2, wise uses knowledge *r*
Song 1:4, *R* do they love you
Lk. 10:28, "You have answered *r*
2 Tim. 2:15, *r* dividing the word

RIGHTS
Ex. 21:10, and her marriage *r*

RINGLEADER
Acts 24:5, the world, and a *r*

RINGS
Jas. 2:2, a man with gold *r*

RIPE
Jer. 24:2, figs that are first *r*

RISE
Ps. 127:2, is vain for you to *r*
Isa. 33:10, "Now I will *r*
Mt. 5:45, for He makes His sun *r*
Mt. 12:41, of Nineveh will *r*
Mt. 20:19, third day He will *r*
Mt. 24:24, false prophets will *r*
Lk. 16:31, persuaded though one *r*
Lk. 18:33, third day He will *r*
Acts 17:3, had to suffer and *r*
Acts 26:23, be the first to *r*
1 Cor. 15:15, fact the dead do not *r*
1 Th. 4:16, in Christ will *r*

RISEN
Isa. 60:1, of the LORD is *r*
Mt. 11:11, there has not *r*
Mt. 28:7, disciples that He is *r*
Lk. 24:34, "The Lord is *r*
Rom. 8:34, furthermore is also *r*
1 Cor. 15:13, then Christ is not *r*
1 Cor. 15:17, if Christ is not *r*
1 Cor. 15:20, But now Christ is *r*

RISES
Job 31:14, shall I do when God *r*
Isa. 54:17, every tongue which *r*

RISING
Isa. 45:6, may know from the *r*
Mk. 9:10, questioning what the *r*
Lk. 2:34, for the fall and *r*

RIVER
of life. Rev. 22; *see* Ps. 36:8; 46:4; 65:9; Ezek. 47
——— of Egypt (Nile). Ex. 1:22; Ezek. 29:3,10
Moses hidden in. Ex. 2:5
waters of, turned into blood. Ex. 7:15

RIVER
Job 40:23, Indeed the *r* may rage
Ps. 36:8, them drink from the *r*
Ps. 46:4, *r* whose streams shall
Ps. 65:9, the *r* of God is full
Ps. 66:6, went through the *r*
Isa. 66:12, peace to her like a *r*
Mk. 1:5, in the Jordan *R*
Rev. 22:1, he showed me a pure *r*

RIVERS
Ps. 107:33, He turns *r* into a
Ps. 119:136, *R* of water run down
Ps. 137:1, By the *r* of Babylon
Eccl. 1:7, All the *r* run into the
Isa. 33:21, us a place of broad *r*
Isa. 43:19, the wilderness and *r*
Isa. 50:2, the sea, I make the *r*
Jn. 7:38, his heart will flow *r*

ROAD
Isa. 43:19, I will even make a *r*
Isa. 51:10, depths of the sea a *r*
Acts 9:27, seen the Lord on the *r*

ROAR
1 Chr. 16:32, Let the sea *r*
Ps. 46:3, though its waters *r*
Ps. 104:21, The young lions *r*
Jer. 25:30, 'The LORD will *r*
Hos. 11:10, He will *r* like a lion
Joel 3:16, The LORD also will *r*
Amos 3:4, Will a lion *r* in the

ROARING
Prov. 19:12, wrath is like the *r*
Prov. 28:15, Like a *r* lion and a
Lk. 21:25, and the waves *r*
1 Pet. 5:8, walks about like a *r*

ROARS
Jer. 6:23, their voice *r* like the
Amos 1:2, "The LORD *r* from
Rev. 10:3, as when a lion *r*

ROB
Prov. 22:22, *r* the poor because he
Isa. 10:2, *r* the needy of justice
Mal. 3:8, "Will a man *r* God
Rom. 2:22, do you *r* temples

ROBBED
Isa. 10:13, *r* their treasuries
Isa. 42:22, But this is a people *r*
Mal. 3:8, Yet you have *r* Me
2 Cor. 11:8, *r* other churches

ROBBER
Ezek. 18:10, a son who is a *r*
Jn. 10:1, is a thief and a *r*
Jn. 18:40, Barabbas was a *r*

ROBBERS
at crucifixion. Mt. 27:38; Mk. 15:27; Lk. 23:40

ROBBERS
Isa. 42:24, and Israel to the *r*
Mk. 15:27, also crucified two *r*
Jn. 10:8, Me are thieves and *r*
Acts 19:37, here who are neither *r*
2 Cor. 11:26, waters, in perils of *r*

ROBBERY
Ps. 62:10, nor vainly hope in *r*
Isa. 61:8, I hate *r* for burnt
Phil. 2:6, did not consider it *r*

ROBE
Job 29:14, justice was like a *r*
Isa. 3:24, instead of a rich *r*
Isa. 61:10, covered me with the *r*
Lk. 15:22, 'Bring out the best *r*
Jn. 19:2, on Him a purple *r*
Rev. 6:11, Then a white *r* was

ROBES
Ps. 45:14, to the King in *r*
Isa. 63:3, have stained all My *r*
Zech. 3:4, clothe you with rich *r*
Lk. 20:46, go around in long *r*
Rev. 7:9, clothed with white *r*

ROCK
water brought out of, by Moses. Ex. 17:6; Num. 20:10. *See* 1 Cor. 10:4
figuratively used. Dt. 32:4,15; 2 Sam. 22:2; 23:3; Ps. 18:2; 28:1; 31:2; 61:2; Isa. 17:10; 26:4; 32:2

ROCK
Ex. 17:6, you shall strike the *r*
Num. 20:11, and struck the *r*
Dt. 32:18, *R* who begot you
Dt. 32:31, For their *r* is not
1 Sam. 2:2, nor is there any *r*
2 Sam. 22:2, "The LORD is my *r*
2 Sam. 22:32, And who is a *r*
2 Sam. 22:47, Blessed be my *R*
Job 14:18, away, and as a *r*
Ps. 27:5, set me high upon a *r*
Ps. 31:3, For You are my *r*
Ps. 61:2, *r* that is higher than
Ps. 94:22, and my God the *r*
Ps. 114:8, who turned the *r*
Isa. 17:10, been mindful of the *R*
Isa. 32:2, shadow of a great *r*
Mt. 7:24, his house on the *r*
Mt. 16:18, *r* I will build My
Lk. 8:6, "Some fell on *r*
Rom. 9:33, stumbling stone and *r*
1 Cor. 10:4, *R* that followed them

ROCKS
Mt. 27:51, and the *r* were split
Rev. 6:16, to the mountains and *r*

ROD
of Moses. Ex. 4
of Aaron. Num. 17; Heb. 9:4

ROD
Ex. 4:20, And Moses took the *r*
2 Sam. 7:14, chasten him with the *r*
Ps. 23:4, Your *r* and Your staff
Prov. 29:15, The *r* and rebuke give
Isa. 11:1, shall come forth a *R*
Ezek. 20:37, you pass under the *r*
1 Cor. 4:21, I come to you with a *r*
Rev. 2:27, rule them with a *r*

ROLL
Job 30:14, ruinous storm they *r*
Mk. 16:3, *r* away the stone

ROLLED
Isa. 34:4, the heavens shall be *r*
Mk. 16:4, the stone had been *r*

ROME
visitors from, at Pentecost. Acts 2:10
Jews ordered to depart from. Acts 18:2
Paul preaches there. Acts 28

ROOM
Ps. 80:9, You prepared *r* for it
Zech. 10:10, until no more *r*
Mk. 14:15, you a large upper *r*
Lk. 2:7, no *r* for them in the
Lk. 14:22, still there is *r*
Acts 1:13, into the upper *r*

ROOMS
Gen. 6:14, make *r* in the ark
Mt. 24:26, He is in the inner *r*

ROOSTER
Mt. 26:75, him, "Before the *r*

ROOT
Dt. 29:18, *r* bearing bitterness
Job 5:3, the foolish taking *r*
Job 14:8, *r* may grow old in the
Isa. 11:10, day there shall be a *R*
Isa. 37:31, shall again take *r*
Mt. 13:6, because they had no *r*
Rom. 11:16, and if the *r* is holy
1 Tim. 6:10, of money is a *r*
Heb. 12:15, lest any *r* of
Rev. 22:16, I am the *R* and the

ROOTED
Eph. 3:17, that you, being *r*
Col. 2:7, *r* and built up in Him

ROOTS
Ezek. 31:7, because its *r* reached
Hos. 14:5, and lengthen his *r*
Mk. 11:20, dried up from the *r*
Jude 12, pulled up by the *r*

ROSE
Song 2:1, I am the *r* of Sharon
Isa. 35:1, and blossom as the *r*
Rom. 14:9, end Christ died and *r*
1 Cor. 15:4, buried, and that He *r*
1 Th. 4:14, Jesus died and *r*

ROSH, Gen. 46:21; Ezek. 38:2; 39:1

RUBIES
Job 28:18, of wisdom is above *r*
Prov. 3:15, more precious than *r*
Prov. 8:11, is better than *r*
Prov. 31:10, worth is far above *r*
Isa. 54:12, your pinnacles of *r*
Lam. 4:7, ruddy in body than *r*

RUDDY
1 Sam. 16:12, Now he was *r*
Song 5:10, beloved is white and *r*

RUIN
Prov. 24:22, *r* those two can bring
Isa. 25:2, have made a city a *r*
Ezek. 18:30, will not be your *r*
Lk. 6:49, And the *r* of that
2 Tim. 2:14, to no profit, to the *r*

RUINED
Isa. 60:12, shall be utterly *r*
Zech. 11:2, the mighty trees are *r*
Lk. 5:37, wineskins will be *r*

RUINS
Isa. 61:4, rebuild the old *r*

RULE
Gen. 3:16, and he shall *r*
Ps. 89:9, *r* the raging of the
Prov. 17:2, A wise servant will *r*
Eccl. 2:19, Yet he will *r* over all
1 Cor. 15:24, puts an end to all *r*
Phil. 3:16, us walk by the same *r*
Col. 3:15, let the peace of God *r*
1 Tim. 5:17, Let the elders who *r*
Heb. 13:7, Remember those who *r*

RULER
of this world. Jn. 12:31; 14:30; 16:11
——— of demons, Christ's miracles ascribed to. Mt. 9:34; 12:24; Mk. 3:22; Lk. 11:15

RULER
2 Sam. 7:8, the sheep, to be *r*
Prov. 23:1, down to eat with a *r*
Prov. 28:15, bear is a wicked *r*
Prov. 29:12, *r* pays attention
Mic. 5:2, to Me the One to be *r*
Mt. 12:24, by Beelzebub, the *r*
Mt. 25:21, I will make you *r*
Jn. 12:31, the *r* of this world
Jn. 16:11, because the *r* of this
Acts 7:27, 'Who made you a *r*
Acts 23:5, speak evil of a *r*

RULERS
Ps. 2:2, and the *r* take counsel
Prov. 8:15, *r* decree justice
Mt. 20:25, "You know that the *r*
Jn. 7:48, "Have any of the *r*
Rom. 13:3, *r* are not a
1 Cor. 2:8, which none of the *r*
Eph. 6:12, powers, against the *r*
Ti. 3:1, to be subject to *r*

RULES
2 Sam. 23:3, 'He who *r* over men
Ps. 59:13, them know that God *r*
Ps. 66:7, He *r* by His power
Prov. 16:32, *r* his spirit than he
Dan. 4:17, that the Most High *r*
Dan. 4:32, that the Most High *r*
1 Tim. 3:4, *r* his own house well
2 Tim. 2:5, according to the *r*

RULING
1 Tim. 3:12, *r* their children

RUMOR
Ezek. 7:26, *r* will be upon *r*

RUMORS
Mt. 24:6, hear of wars and *r*
Mk. 13:7, you hear of wars and *r*

RUN
Ps. 119:32, I will *r* the course of
Isa. 40:31, *r* and not be weary
Dan. 12:4, many shall *r* to and
1 Cor. 9:26, Therefore I *r* thus
Gal. 2:2, I might *r*, or had *r*
Phil. 2:16, that I have not *r*
Heb. 12:1, us, and let us *r*
1 Pet. 4:4, that you do not *r*

RUNNER
Job 9:25, are swifter than a *r*
Jer. 51:31, *r* will run to meet

RUNS
Ps. 147:15, word *r* very swiftly
Rom. 9:16, nor of him who *r*

RUSH
Isa. 17:13, The nations will *r*

RUST, Mt. 6:19,20

RUTH, Ruth 1:4
story of. Ruth 1—4
Christ descended from. Mt. 1:5

SABACHTHANI, Mk. 15:34

SABAOTH
(Hosts), the Lord of. Rom. 9:29; Jas. 5:4

SABBATH
day of rest. Gen. 2:2 (Heb. 4:4)
to be kept holy. Ex. 16:23; 20:8; 23:12; 31:13; 34:21; 35:2; Lev. 25:3; Num. 15:32; Dt. 5:12; Neh. 10:31; 13:15; Isa. 56; 58:13; Jer. 17:21; Ezek. 20:12
offerings. Num. 28:9
the seventh year kept as. Ex. 23:10; Lev. 25:1
Christ the Lord of. Mk. 2:27; Lk. 6:5
first day of the week kept as. (*See* Mt. 28:1; Mk. 16:2,9; Jn. 20:1,19,26); Acts 20:7; 1 Cor. 16:2; Rev. 1:10

SABBATH
Ex. 16:23, 'Tomorrow is a *S*
Ex. 20:8, "Remember the *S*
Mk. 2:27, *S* was made for man
Mk. 2:28, is also Lord of the *S*
Jn. 5:18, not only broke the *S*

SABBATHS
Ex. 31:13, *S* you shall keep
Isa. 1:13, The New Moons, the *S*
Ezek. 20:12 also gave them My *S*

SACKCLOTH
Ps. 30:11, You have put off my *s*
Isa. 20:2, and remove the *s*

SACRED
Isa. 1:13, iniquity and the *s*

SACRIFICE
1 Sam. 2:29, do you kick at My *s*
Ps. 40:6, *S* and offering You did
Ps. 116:17, offer to You the *s*
Prov. 21:3, to the LORD than *s*
Isa. 34:6, For the LORD has a *s*
Jer. 33:11, who will bring the *s*
Hos. 8:13, of My offerings they *s*
Jon. 2:9, But I will *s* to You
Zeph. 1:7, LORD has prepared a *s*
Mal. 1:8, offer the blind as a *s*
Mt. 9:13, desire mercy and not *s*
Mk. 9:49, *s* will be seasoned
Eph. 5:2, an offering and a *s*
Phil. 4:18, aroma, an acceptable *s*
Heb. 9:26, put away sin by the *s*
Heb. 10:12, He had offered one *s*
Heb. 10:26, no longer remains a *s*
Heb. 11:4, God a more excellent *s*
Heb. 13:15, offer the *s* of praise

SACRIFICED
Ps. 106:37, *s* their sons and their
Rev. 2:14, to eat things *s*

SACRIFICES, Lev. 22:19; Dt. 17:1
types of Christ. Heb. 9; 10

SACRIFICES
Ps. 51:17, The *s* of God are a

Isa. 1:11, multitude of your *s*
Isa. 1:13, Bring no more futile *s*
Isa. 66:3, he who *s* a lamb
Jer. 6:20, acceptable, nor your *s*
Dan. 8:11, by him the daily *s*
Mk. 12:33, burnt offerings and *s*
Heb. 7:27, priests, to offer up *s*
Heb. 13:16, *s* God is well pleased
1 Pet. 2:5, offer up spiritual *s*

SAD
Neh. 2:2, "Why is your face *s*
Eccl. 7:3, *s* countenance the
Ezek. 13:22, whom I have not made *s*
Lk. 24:17, as you walk and are *s*

SADDUCEES
(named from Zadok, founder of the sect), their controversies: with Christ. Mt. 16:1; 22:23; Mk. 12:18; Lk. 20:27; with the apostles. Acts 4:1; with Paul. Acts 23:6
their doctrines. Mt. 22:23; Mk. 12:18; Acts 23:8

SAFE
Ps. 119:117, and I shall be *s*
Prov. 29:25, in the LORD shall be *s*
Lk. 15:27, he has received him *s*

SAFELY
Ps. 78:53, And He led them on *s*
Hos. 2:18, make them lie down *s*

SAFETY
Job 5:4, sons are far from *s*
Job 11:18, take your rest in *s*
Ps. 12:5, will set him in the *s*
1 Th. 5:3, say, "Peace and *s*

SAFETY'S
Prov. 3:29, by you for *s* sake

SAINTS
of God. Dt. 33:2; 1 Sam. 2:9; Ps. 145:10; 148:14; 149; Prov. 2:8; Dan. 7:18; Zech. 14:5
believers. Rom. 8:27; Eph. 2:19; Col. 1:12; Jude 3; Rev. 5:8
obligations of. 2 Chr. 6:41; Ps. 30:4; 31:23; 34:9; 132:9; Rom. 16:2,15; 1 Cor. 6; 2 Cor. 8; 9; Eph. 4; 6:18; Phile.; Heb. 6:10; 13:24

SAINTS
Dt. 33:2, ten thousands of *s*
1 Sam. 2:9, the feet of His *s*
Job 15:15, puts no trust in His *s*
Ps. 16:3, *s* who are on the earth
Ps. 37:28, does not forsake His *s*
Ps. 50:5, "Gather My *s*
Ps. 97:10, the souls of His *s*
Ps. 116:15, is the death of His *s*
Prov. 2:8, the way of His *s*
Dan. 7:21, war against the *s*
Dan. 7:25, shall persecute the *s*
1 Cor. 1:2, Jesus, called to be *s*
Eph. 3:8, the least of all the *s*
1 Th. 3:13, Christ with all His *s*
2 Th. 1:10, be glorified in His *s*
Jude 3, all delivered to the *s*
Rev. 15:3, ways, O King of the *s*
Rev. 16:6, shed the blood of *s*
Rev. 20:9, the camp of the *s*

SALEM, Gen. 14:18; Heb. 7:1

SALOME, Mk. 15:40; 16:1

SALT
Lot's wife becomes a pillar of. Gen. 19:26
of the earth. Mt. 5:13 (Lk. 14:34; Col. 4:6)
—— Sea (Siddim). Gen. 14:3; Num. 34:3,12; Dt. 3:17; Josh. 3:16; 12:3; 15:1,2

SALT
Lev. 2:13, shall season with *s*
Mt. 5:13, "You are the *s*
Mk. 9:50, *s* loses its flavor

SALVATION
Ex. 14:13, still, and see the *s*
2 Sam. 23:5, For this is all my *s*
1 Chr. 16:23, the good news of His *s*
Ps. 3:8, *S* belongs to the LORD
Ps. 27:1, is my light and my *s*
Ps. 67:2, on earth, Your *s*
Ps. 68:20, God is the God of *s*
Ps. 71:15, and Your *s* all the day
Ps. 85:9, Surely His *s* is near
Ps. 118:14, and He has become my *s*
Ps. 119:155, *S* is far from the
Isa. 26:1, God will appoint *s*
Isa. 45:17, with an everlasting *s*
Isa. 56:1, for My *s* is about to
Isa. 60:18, call your walls *S*
Isa. 62:1, *s* as a lamp that burns
Jer. 3:23, LORD our God is the *s*
Hab. 3:18, joy in the God of my *s*
Zech. 9:9, is just and having *s*
Lk. 1:69, raised up a horn of *s*
Lk. 2:30, eyes have seen Your *s*
Lk. 19:9, to him, "Today *s*
Jn. 4:22, what we worship, for *s*
Acts 4:12, "Nor is there *s*
Acts 13:47, you should be for *s*
Rom. 1:16, the power of God to *s*
Rom. 13:11, *s* is nearer than
2 Cor. 6:2, now is the day of *s*
Phil. 2:12, work out your own *s*
1 Th. 5:9, wrath, but to obtain *s*
2 Th. 2:13, chose you for *s*
2 Tim. 2:10, also may obtain the *s*
Ti. 2:11, of God that brings *s*
Heb. 2:3, neglect so great a *s*
1 Pet. 1:10, *s* the prophets have

SAMARIA
city of. 1 Ki. 16:24; 20:1; 2 Ki. 6:24
—— region of, visited by Christ. Lk. 17:11; Jn. 4
Gospel preached there. Acts 8

SAMARITAN
parable of the good. Lk. 10:33
miracle performed on. Lk. 17:16

SAMARITAN
Lk. 10:33, But a certain *S*
Jn. 4:9, a drink from me, a *S*

SAMARITANS, 2 Ki. 17:29

SAMSON, Jud. 13—16
delivered up to Philistines. Jud. 16:21
his death. Jud. 16:30

SAMUEL, 1 Sam. 1:20
born, and presented to the Lord. 1 Sam. 1:19,26
ministers to the Lord. 1 Sam. 3
the Lord speaks to. 1 Sam. 3:11
judges Israel. 1 Sam. 7; 8:1; Acts 13:20
anoints Saul king. 1 Sam. 10:1
rebukes Saul for sin. 1 Sam. 13:13; 15:16
anoints David. 1 Sam. 16; 19:18
his death. 1 Sam. 25:1; 28:3
his spirit consulted by Saul. 1 Sam. 28:12
as a prophet. Ps. 99:6; Acts 3:24; Heb. 11:32

SANBALLAT
Neh. 2:10; 4; 6:2; 13:28

SANCTIFICATION
by Christ. Jn. 17:19; 1 Cor. 1:2,30; 6:11; Eph. 5:26; Heb. 2:11; 10:10; Jude 1
by the Spirit. Rom. 15:16; 2 Th. 2:13; 1 Pet. 1:2

SANCTIFICATION
1 Cor. 1:30, righteousness and *s*
1 Th. 4:3, will of God, your *s*
2 Th. 2:13, salvation through *s*

SANCTIFIED
the seventh day. Gen. 2:3
the firstborn to be. Ex. 13:2
the people. Ex. 19:10; Num. 11:18; Josh. 3:5
the tabernacle. Ex. 29; 30; Lev. 8:10
the priests. Lev. 8:30; 9; 2 Chr. 5:11

SANCTIFIED
Isa. 13:3, I have commanded My *s*
Jer. 1:5, you were born I *s*
Jn. 10:36, Him whom the Father *s*
Jn. 17:19, they also may be *s*
Rom. 15:16, might be acceptable, *s*
1 Cor. 1:2, to those who are *s*
1 Cor. 6:11, washed, but you were *s*
1 Cor. 7:14, husband is *s* by the
1 Tim. 4:5, for it is *s* by the
Heb. 2:11, those who are being *s*
Heb. 10:10, will we have been *s*
Jude 1, who are called, *s*

SANCTIFIES
Mt. 23:17, or the temple that *s*
Heb. 2:11, For both He who *s*

SANCTIFY
Job 1:5, would send and *s* them
Ezek. 36:23, *s* My great name
Ezek. 37:28, that I, the LORD, *s*
Ezek. 38:23, Myself and *s* Myself
Jn. 17:17, "*S* them by Your
Jn. 17:19, for their sakes I *s*
Eph. 5:26, that He might *s*

SANCTUARY
God, of His people. Isa. 8:14; Ezek. 11:16. *See* Ps. 20:2; 63:2; 68:24; 73:17; 77:13; 78:54; 96:6; 134; 150; Heb. 8; 9. *See* TEMPLE

SANCTUARY
Ex. 25:8, let them make Me a *s*

Ps. 73:17, I went into the *s*
Ps. 74:7, set fire to Your *s*
Ps. 77:13, O God, is in the *s*
Isa. 8:14, He will be as a *s*
Lam. 2:7, He has abandoned His *s*
Ezek. 11:16, I shall be a little *s*
Dan. 9:17, to shine on Your *s*
Heb. 9:1, and the earthly *s*

SAND
Gen. 32:12, descendants as the *s*
Job 6:3, be heavier than the *s*
Ps. 139:18, in number than the *s*
Isa. 10:22, O Israel, be as the *s*
Heb. 11:12, innumerable as the *s*

SANG
Ex. 15:1; Neh. 12:42; Job 38:7

SAPPHIRA, Acts 5:1

SAPPHIRES
Job 28:6, are the source of *s*

SARAH, Gen. 17:15
Sarai. Gen. 11; 12; 20:2. *See* ABRAHAM
her death and burial. Gen. 23 (Heb. 11:11; 1 Pet. 3:6)

SARDIS
church of. Rev. 1:11; 3:1

SAT
Ps. 137:1, of Babylon, there we *s*
Song 2:3, I *s* down in his shade
Jer. 15:17, *s* alone because of
Mk. 16:19, into heaven, and *s*
Rev. 4:3, And He who *s* there was

SATAN, *see* DEVIL

SATAN
1 Chr. 21:1, *S* stood up against
Job 1:6, before the LORD, and *S*
Zech. 3:2, And the LORD said to *S*
Mt. 4:10, "Away with you, *S*
Mt. 16:23, "Get behind Me, *S*
Mk. 3:23, "How can *S* cast out
Lk. 10:18, to them, "I saw *S*
Lk. 22:31, *S* has asked for you
Acts 5:3, *S* filled your heart
1 Cor. 5:5, such a one to *S*
2 Cor. 11:14, For *S* himself
2 Th. 2:9, to the working of *S*
Rev. 2:9, are a synagogue of *S*
Rev. 2:13, you, where *S* dwells
Rev. 2:24, known the depths of *S*
Rev. 12:9, called the Devil and *S*
Rev. 20:7, years have expired, *S*

SATIATED
Jer. 31:25, *s* the weary soul
Jer. 46:10, It shall be *s* and made

SATISFIED
Ps. 17:15, I shall be *s* when I
Prov. 12:11, his land will be *s*
Prov. 14:14, a good man will be *s*
Prov. 27:7, *s* soul loathes the
Prov. 30:15, that are never *s*
Eccl. 5:10, silver will not be *s*
Isa. 9:20, left hand and not be *s*
Isa. 53:11, of His soul, and be *s*
Jer. 31:14, My people shall be *s*
Ezek. 16:28, still were not *s*
Amos 4:8, but they were not *s*
Hab. 2:5, and cannot be *s*

SATISFIES
Ps. 103:5, *s* your mouth with good
Ps. 107:9, *s* the longing soul

SATISFY
Ps. 90:14, *s* us early with Your
Ps. 91:16, long life I will *s*
Ps. 132:15, *s* her poor with bread
Isa. 55:2, for what does not *s*

SATISFYING
Prov. 13:25, eats to the *s* of his

SAUL, 1 Sam. 9:2
king of Israel, his parentage, anointing by Samuel, prophesying, and acknowledgment as king. 1 Sam. 9; 10
his disobedience, and rejection by God. 1 Sam. 14:31; 15
possessed by an evil spirit, quieted by David. 1 Sam. 16:14,15,23
favors David. 1 Sam. 18:5; seeks to kill him. 1 Sam. 18:10; pursues him. 1 Sam. 20; 23; 24; 26
kills priests for helping David. 1 Sam. 22:9
inquires of the witch of Endor. 1 Sam. 28:7
his ruin and death. 1 Sam. 28:15; 31; 1 Chr. 10
his posterity. 1 Chr. 8:33
——— of Tarsus. *See* PAUL

SAVE
1 Sam. 17:47, the LORD does not *s*
2 Sam. 22:42, there was none to *s*
Job 22:29, *s* the humble person
Ps. 6:4, Oh, *s* me for Your
Ps. 28:9, *S* Your people
Ps. 57:3, send from heaven and *s*
Ps. 72:4, *s* the children of the
Ps. 72:13, *s* the souls of the
Prov. 20:22, LORD, and He will *s*
Isa. 35:4, He will come and *s*
Isa. 38:20, LORD was ready to *s*
Isa. 49:25, *s* your children
Isa. 59:1, that it cannot *s*
Isa. 63:1, mighty to *s*
Jer. 14:9, one who cannot *s*
Jer. 15:20, *s* you and deliver you
Jer. 17:14, *s* me
Jer. 31:7, O LORD, *s* Your people
Hos. 13:10, other, that he may *s*
Hos. 14:3, Assyria shall not *s*
Zeph. 3:17, the Mighty One, will *s*
Mt. 1:21, JESUS, for He will *s*
Mt. 16:25, *s* his life will
Mt. 18:11, *s* that which was
Mk. 3:4, *s* life or to kill
Lk. 23:35, let Him *s* Himself if
Lk. 23:39, You are the Christ, *s*
Jn. 12:27, 'Father, *s* Me from
Jn. 12:47, but to *s* the world
Rom. 11:14, and *s* some of them
1 Tim. 1:15, the world to *s* sinners
1 Tim. 4:16, doing this you will *s*
Jas. 1:21, able to *s* your souls
Jas. 2:14, Can faith *s* him

SAVED
Dt. 33:29, like you, a people *s*
Ps. 44:7, But You have *s* us from
Jer. 8:20, and we are not *s*
Mt. 19:25, "Who then can be *s*
Mt. 27:42, "He *s* others
Lk. 1:71, That we should be *s*
Lk. 7:50, "Your faith has *s*
Jn. 3:17, might be *s*
Acts 2:40, them, saying, "Be *s*
Acts 16:30, what must I do to be *s*
Rom. 8:24, For we were *s* in this
Rom. 10:1, is that they may be *s*
Rom. 11:26, all Israel will be *s*
1 Cor. 5:5, his spirit may be *s*
1 Cor. 15:2, which also you are *s*
2 Cor. 2:15, those who are being *s*
Eph. 2:8, grace you have been *s*
1 Tim. 2:4, all men to be *s*
1 Tim. 2:15, she will be *s* in
Ti. 3:5, to His mercy He *s*
1 Pet. 3:20, eight souls, were *s*
Rev. 21:24, of those who are *s*

SAVES
Job 5:15, *s* the needy from the
Ps. 34:18, *s* such as have a
1 Pet. 3:21, antitype which now *s*

SAVIOR
Christ. Lk. 2:11; Jn. 4:42; Acts 5:31; 13:23; Eph. 5:23; 2 Pet. 1:1; 3:2; 1 Jn. 4:14; Jude 25
——— God. Isa. 43:3,11; Jer. 14:8; Hos. 13:4; Lk. 1:47

SAVIOR
Ps. 106:21, forgot God their *S*
Isa. 19:20, He will send them a *S*
Isa. 43:3, of Israel, your *S*
Isa. 45:21, Me, a just God and a *S*
Isa. 60:16, I, the LORD, am your *S*
Isa. 63:8, So He became their *S*
Hos. 13:4, for there is no *s*
Lk. 1:47, rejoiced in God my *S*
Lk. 2:11, the city of David a *S*
Jn. 4:42, the Christ, the *S*
Acts 5:31, to be Prince and *S*
Acts 13:23, up for Israel a *S*
Eph. 5:23, and He is the *S*
1 Tim. 1:1, of God our *S* and the
1 Tim. 4:10, God, who is the *S*
2 Tim. 1:10, of our *S* Jesus Christ
Ti. 2:13, and *S* Jesus Christ

SAVIORS
Obad. 21, *s* shall come to Mount

SAVOR
Amos 5:21, days, and I do not *s*

SAWN
Heb. 11:37, stoned, they were *s*

SAY
Mt. 5:22, "But I *s* to you that
Mt. 16:15, "But who do you *s*
1 Jn. 1:8, *s* that we have no sin

SAYING
Ps. 49:4, disclose my dark *s*
Mt. 19:11, cannot accept this *s*
Jn. 6:60, "This is a hard *s*
1 Tim. 1:15, This is a faithful *s*

SAYINGS
Ps. 78:2, I will utter dark *s*

Mt. 7:24, whoever hears these *s*

SCALES
Lev. 19:36, You shall have honest *s*
Job 31:6, be weighed on honest *s*
Hos. 12:7, deceitful *s* are in his
Rev. 6:5, on it had a pair of *s*

SCARCELY, Rom. 5:7; 1 Pet. 4:18

SCARLET
Josh. 2:18, *s* cord in the window
Song 4:3, are like a strand of *s*
Isa. 1:18, your sins are like *s*
Rev. 17:3, *s* beast which was full

SCATTER
Lev. 26:33, I will *s* you among the
Ps. 68:30, *S* the peoples who
Jer. 23:1, *s* the sheep of My
Jer. 49:32, I will *s* to all winds

SCATTERED
Gen. 11:4, lest we be *s* abroad
Ps. 92:9, of iniquity shall be *s*
Jer. 23:2, "You have *s* My flock
Jer. 31:10, *s* Israel will gather
Jer. 50:17, "Israel is like *s* sheep
Mt. 9:36, they were weary and *s*
Mk. 14:27, the sheep will be *s*
Jn. 16:32, that you will be *s*

SCATTERS
Ps. 147:16, *s* the frost like ashes
Prov. 11:24, There is one who *s*
Prov. 20:8, throne of judgment *s*
Mt. 12:30, not gather with Me *s*

SCEPTER
Gen. 49:10, *s* shall not depart
Num. 24:17, *S* shall rise out of
Ps. 45:6, a *s* of righteousness
Heb. 1:8, a *s* of righteousness

SCHEME
Ps. 64:6, perfected a shrewd *s*

SCHEMER
Prov. 24:8, will be called a *s*

SCHEMES
Ps. 37:7, who brings wicked *s*
Eccl. 7:29, sought out many *s*

SCHISM
1 Cor. 12:25, there should be no *s*

SCHOOL
Acts 19:9, daily in the *s* of

SCOFF
Ps. 73:8, They *s* and speak
Hab. 1:10, They *s* at kings

SCOFFER
Prov. 9:7, "He who corrects a *s*
Prov. 13:1, *s* does not listen
Prov. 14:6, *s* seeks wisdom and
Prov. 24:9, *s* is an abomination

SCOFFERS
Prov. 29:8, *S* ensnare a city
2 Pet. 3:3, *s* will come in the

SCORCHED
Mt. 13:6, sun was up they were *s*
Rev. 16:9, And men were *s* with

SCORN
Job 16:20, My friends *s* me
Ps. 44:13, to our neighbors, a *s*

SCORNED
Lam. 1:11, consider, for I am *s*
Hab. 1:10, and princes are *s*

SCORNS
Prov. 3:34, He *s* the scornful
Prov. 30:17, *s* obedience to his

SCORPIONS
Ezek. 2:6, and you dwell among *s*
Lk. 10:19, on serpents and *s*
Rev. 9:10, They had tails like *s*

SCOURGE
Isa. 10:26, hosts will stir up a *s*
Mt. 10:17, up to councils and *s*
Mk. 10:34, will mock Him, and *s*

SCOURGES
Heb. 12:6, *s* every son whom

SCOURGING
Lev. 19:20; Dt. 25:3; 2 Cor. 11:24
of Christ. Mt. 27:26; Lk. 23:16

SCRIBE
Isa. 33:18, "Where is the *s*

SCRIBES
2 Sam. 8:17; 20:25; 1 Ki. 4:3; 2 Ki. 19:2; 22:8; 1 Chr. 27:32; Ezra 7:6; Jer. 36:26
and Pharisees, censured by Christ. Mt. 15:3; 23:2; Mk. 2:16; 3:22; Lk. 11:15,53; 20:1
conspire against Christ. Mk. 11:18; Lk. 20:19; 22:2; 23:10
persecute Stephen. Acts 6:12

SCRIBES
Mt. 7:29, and not as the *s*
Mt. 23:13, "But woe to you, *s*
Mk. 12:38, "Beware of the *s*

SCRIPTURE
Dan. 10:21, what is noted in the *S*
Mk. 15:28, *S* was fulfilled which
Lk. 4:21, "Today this *S*
Jn. 10:35, *S* cannot be broken
Rom. 4:3, For what does the *S*
Gal. 3:22, *S* has confined all
2 Tim. 3:16, All *S* is given by
2 Pet. 1:20, that no prophecy of *S*

SCRIPTURES, the Holy
given by inspiration of God through the Holy Spirit. Acts 1:16; 2 Tim. 3:16; Heb. 3:7; 2 Pet. 1:21
Christ confirms and teaches out of. Mt. 4:4; Mk. 12:10; Lk. 24:27; Jn. 7:42
testify of Christ. Jn. 5:39; Acts 10:43; 18:28; 1 Cor. 15:3
profitable for doctrine, instruction, and rule of life. Ps. 19:7; 119:9; Jn. 17:17; Acts 20:32; Rom. 15:4; 16:26; 2 Tim. 3:16,17
make wise for salvation. 2 Tim. 3:15; Jas. 1:21
to be taught diligently. Dt. 6:9; 17:19; 1 Pet. 2:2
to be kept unaltered. Dt. 4:2; Prov. 30:6; 2 Tim. 1:13 (Jude 3); Rev. 22:18
searched. Jn. 5:39; example. Acts 17:11
formerly given by God through the prophets. Lk. 16:31; Rom. 3:2; 9:4; Heb. 1:1; in the last days through Jesus Christ. Heb. 1:2; fulfilled by Him. Mt. 5:17; Lk. 24:27; Jn. 19:24; Acts 13:29
appealed to by the apostles. Acts 2; 3; 8:32; 17:2; 18:24; 28:23
rejecters will be judged by. Jn. 12:48; Heb. 2:3; 10:28; 12:25

SCRIPTURES
Mt. 22:29, not knowing the *S*
Mk. 14:49, *S* must be fulfilled
Acts 18:24, and mighty in the *S*
2 Tim. 3:15, have known the Holy *S*
2 Pet. 3:16, also the rest of the *S*

SCROLL
the heavens compared to. Isa. 34:4; Rev. 6:14

SCROLL
Ps. 40:7, in the *s* of the book
Isa. 30:8, and note it on a *s*
Ezek. 3:1, eat this *s*
Zech. 5:1, saw there a flying *s*
Rev. 5:1, on the throne a *s*
Rev. 5:3, was able to open the *s*
Rev. 6:14, the sky receded as a *s*

SEA
Ex. 15:4, drowned in the Red *S*
Ps. 104:25, this great and wide *s*
Ps. 107:23, who go down to the *s*
Prov. 8:29, to the *s* its limit
Isa. 50:2, rebuke I dry up the *s*
Hab. 2:14, the waters cover the *s*
Mt. 8:27, and the *s* obey Him
Rev. 4:6, throne there was a *s*
Rev. 15:2, standing on the *s*
Rev. 21:1, there was no more *s*

SEAL
of righteousness. Rom. 4:11

SEAL
Song 8:6, Set me as a *s* upon
Rom. 4:11, of circumcision, a *s*
2 Tim. 2:19, stands, having this *s*
Rev. 6:3, He opened the second *s*

SEALED
believers. 2 Cor. 1:22; Eph. 1:13; 4:30; in heaven, number of. Rev. 7
scroll opened. Rev. 5:6
utterances of the seven thunders. Rev. 10:4

SEALED
Job 14:17, My transgression is *s*
2 Cor. 1:22, who also has *s* us and
Eph. 4:30, by whom you were *s*
Rev. 7:4, of those who were *s*

SEALS
Gen. 38:18; Ex. 28:11; 1 Ki. 21:8; Job 38:14; Song 8:6; Jer. 32:10; Dan. 12:4; Mt. 27:66

SEAM
Jn. 19:23, tunic was without *s*

SÉANCE
1 Sam. 28:8, "Please conduct a *s*

SEARCH
Job 11:7, "Can you *s* out the
Ps. 44:21, would not God *s*
Prov. 25:2, glory of kings is to *s*
Jer. 2:34, found it by secret *s*
Jer. 17:10, I, the LORD, *s* the
Jn. 5:39, *s* the Scriptures

SEARCHED
Ps. 139:1, O LORD, You have *s*
Acts 17:11, *s* the Scriptures
1 Pet. 1:10, and *s* carefully

SEARCHER
of hearts, God. 1 Chr. 28:9; 29:17; Ps. 7:9; Jer. 17:10

SEARCHES
1 Chr. 28:9, for the LORD *s* all
Rom. 8:27, *s* the hearts knows
1 Cor. 2:10, For the Spirit *s*
Rev. 2:23, that I am He who *s*

SEASON
Eccl. 3:1, there is a *s*
2 Tim. 4:2, Be ready in *s* and out

SEASONED
Mt. 5:13, how shall it be *s*
Mk. 9:49, "For everyone will be *s*

SEASONS
continuance of. Gen. 8:22

SEASONS
Gal. 4:10, days and months and *s*
1 Th. 5:1, the times and the *s*

SEAT
Ex. 25:17, shall make a mercy *s*
Job 23:3, I might come to His *s*
Ps. 113:8, that He may *s* him with
Mt. 23:2, sit in Moses' *s*
2 Cor. 5:10, before the judgment *s*
Heb. 9:5, the mercy *s*

SEATS
Mt. 23:6, at feasts, the best *s*
Lk. 11:43, you love the best *s*

SECOND COMING
Christ's. Acts 1:11

SECOND DEATH, Rev. 20:14

SECRET
Dt. 29:29, *s* things belong
Ps. 25:14, The *s* of the LORD is
Ps. 27:5, in the *s* place of His
Ps. 139:15, when I was made in *s*
Prov. 25:9, do not disclose the *s*
Isa. 45:19, I have not spoken in *s*
Mt. 6:6, Father who is in the *s*
Eph. 5:12, are done by them in *s*

SECRETLY
Job 4:12, "Now a word was *s*
Ps. 10:9, He lies in wait *s*

SECRETS
Job 11:6, would show you the *s*
Ps. 44:21, For He knows the *s*
Prov. 11:13, A talebearer reveals *s*
Dan. 2:28, heaven who reveals *s*
Rom. 2:16, God will judge the *s*
1 Cor. 14:25, And thus the *s* of his

SECT
Acts 5:17, him (which is the *s*
Acts 26:5, to the strictest *s*

SECURELY
Isa. 47:8, pleasures, who dwell *s*
Jer. 49:31, nation that dwells *s*

SEDUCED
Prov. 7:21, flattering lips she *s*
Ezek. 13:10, because they have *s*

SEE
Ex. 33:20, for no man shall *s*
1 Sam. 16:7, the LORD does not *s*
Job 19:26, in my flesh I shall *s*
Ps. 66:5, *s* the works of God
Isa. 6:10, lest they *s* with their
Isa. 53:10, for sin, He shall *s*
Mt. 5:8, for they shall *s* God
Mt. 13:13, seeing they do not *s*
Jn. 1:50, *s* greater things than
Jn. 8:56, rejoiced to *s* My day
Jn. 12:21, we wish to *s* Jesus
Jn. 14:19, and the world will *s*
1 Jn. 3:2, Him, for we shall *s*
Rev. 22:4, They shall *s* His face

SEED
of the woman. Gen. 3:15; Rev. 12
of the serpent. Gen. 3:15
——— parables about. Mt. 13; Lk. 8:5

SEED
Gen. 21:12, *s* shall be called
Isa. 6:13, *s* shall be its stump
Isa. 53:10, He shall see His *s*
Jer. 2:21, you a noble vine, a *s*
Lk. 8:11, *s* is the word of God
Rom. 9:29, had left us a *s*
1 Cor. 15:38, to each *s* its own body
Gal. 3:16, *S* were the promises
Gal. 3:29, you are Abraham's *s*
2 Tim. 2:8, Jesus Christ, of the *s*
1 Pet. 1:23, of corruptible *s*
1 Jn. 3:9, not sin, for His *s*

SEEDS
Mt. 13:38, the good *s* are the
Gal. 3:16, not say, "And to *s*

SEEK
Dt. 4:29, will find Him if you *s*
2 Chr. 7:14, pray and *s* My face
2 Chr. 19:3, your heart to *s* God
Ezra 4:2, *s* your God as you do
Job 3:4, may God above not *s*
Ps. 10:4, countenance does not *s*
Ps. 27:4, LORD, that will I *s*
Ps. 27:8, You said, "*S* My face
Ps. 63:1, early will I *s* You
Prov. 8:17, *s* me diligently will
Prov. 25:27, *s* one's own glory
Isa. 1:17, *s* justice
Isa. 8:19, Should they *s* the dead
Isa. 11:10, the Gentiles shall *s*
Isa. 45:19, Jacob, '*S* Me in vain
Isa. 55:6, *S* the LORD while He
Isa. 58:2, Yet they *s* Me daily
Jer. 45:5, *s* great things for
Ezek. 34:16, *s* what was lost
Amos 5:4, '*S* Me and live
Mal. 2:7, and people should *s*
Mt. 6:32, things the Gentiles *s*
Mt. 7:7, *s*, and you will find
Lk. 19:10, of Man has come to *s*
Jn. 5:30, because I do not *s*
Jn. 7:34, "You will *s* Me and
Rom. 2:7, in doing good *s*
Rom. 9:32, Because they did not *s*
1 Cor. 10:24, Let no one *s* his own
2 Cor. 12:14, for I do not *s* yours
Phil. 2:21, For all *s* their own
Col. 3:1, *s* those things which
Heb. 13:14, *s* the one to come

SEEKING
Amos 8:12, run to and fro, *s*
Lk. 13:6, and he came *s* fruit
Jn. 4:23, for the Father is *s*
1 Pet. 5:8, like a roaring lion, *s*

SEEKS
Jer. 30:17, no one *s* her
Mt. 7:8, receives, and he who *s*
Rom. 3:11, There is none who *s*

SEEMS
Prov. 14:12, There is a way which *s*
Lk. 8:18, have, even what he *s*
1 Cor. 3:18, If anyone among you *s*

SEEN
Gen. 32:30, *s* God face to face
Eccl. 8:9, All this I have *s*
Song 3:3, *s* the one I love
Isa. 66:8, Who has *s* such things
Lk. 5:26, *s* strange things today
Jn. 1:18, No one has *s* God at
Jn. 5:37, time, nor *s* His form
Jn. 8:38, I speak what I have *s*
Jn. 14:9, *s* Me has *s* the
Acts 4:20, things which we have *s*
1 Cor. 9:1, *s* Jesus Christ our
2 Cor. 4:18, things which are not *s*
1 Tim. 6:16, whom no man has *s*
1 Jn. 1:1, heard, which we have *s*

SEES
Gen. 16:13, here seen Him who *s*
Ps. 33:13, *s* all the sons of men
1 Jn. 3:17, *s* his brother in need
1 Jn. 5:16, *s* his brother sinning

SEIR
Mount, Edom, land of Esau. Gen. 14:6; 32:3; 36:8,20; Dt. 33:2; Josh. 24:4; Isa. 21:11; Ezek. 25:8
predictions about. Num. 24:18; Ezek. 35:2

SELAH
a musical direction, pause. Ps. 3:2; 4:2; 24:6; 39:5,11; 46:3; 48:8; 50:6; Hab. 3:3,9,12

SELF-CONFIDENT
Prov. 14:16, a fool rages and is *s*

SELF-CONTROL
Acts 24:25, about righteousness, *s*
1 Cor. 7:9, they cannot exercise *s*
Gal. 5:23, gentleness, *s*
2 Tim. 3:3, slanderers, without *s*
2 Pet. 1:6, to knowledge *s*

SELF-CONTROLLED
Ti. 1:8, just, holy, *s*

SELF-DENIAL
Prov. 23:2; Jer. 35; Lk. 3:11; 14:33; Acts 2:45; 20:24; Rom. 6:12; 8:13;

14:20; 15:1; Gal. 5:24; Phil. 2:4; Ti. 2:12; Heb. 11:24; 1 Pet. 2:11
Christ an example of. Mt. 4:8; 8:20; Rom. 15:3; Phil. 2:6
incumbent on His followers. Mt. 10:38; 16:24; Mk. 8:34; Lk. 9:23

SELF-EXAMINATION
commanded. Lam. 3:40; Ps. 4:4; 1 Cor. 11:28; 2 Cor. 13:5

SELF-SEEKING
Jas. 3:16, envy and *s* exist

SELF-SUFFICIENCY, Job 20:22

SELFISHNESS
Isa. 56:11; Rom. 15:1; 1 Cor. 10:24; 2 Cor. 5:15; Phil. 2:4,21; 2 Tim. 3:2; Jas. 2:8

SELL
Gen. 25:31, said, "*S* me your
Ps. 44:12, *s* Your people for
Amos 2:6, *s* the righteous
Mk. 10:21, *s* whatever you have
Lk. 22:36, no sword, let him *s*
Rev. 13:17, no one may buy or *s*

SEND
Ps. 57:3, He shall *s* from heaven
Isa. 6:8, "Whom shall I *s*
Isa. 19:20, *s* them a Savior
Mt. 10:16, "Behold, I *s* you out
Mt. 13:41, The Son of Man will *s*
Lk. 16:24, *s* Lazarus that he
Jn. 14:26, whom the Father will *s*
Jn. 20:21, has sent Me, I also *s*

SENNACHERIB
2 Ki. 18:13; 2 Chr. 32; Is. 36:37

SENSELESS
Ps. 94:8, Understand, you *s*

SENSES
Heb. 5:14, of use have their *s*

SENSIBLY
Prov. 26:16, who can answer *s*

SENSUAL
Jas. 3:15, but is earthly, *s*
Jude 19, These are *s* persons

SENT
Isa. 48:16, and His Spirit have *s*
Jer. 23:21, *s* these prophets
Jn. 20:21, As the Father has *s*
Rom. 10:15, unless they are *s*
1 Jn. 4:10, *s* His Son to be the

SEPARATE
Num. 6:3, he shall *s* himself
Ezra 10:11, *s* yourselves from the
Mt. 19:6, let not man *s*
Rom. 8:35, Who shall *s* us from
Heb. 7:26, harmless, undefiled, *s*

SEPARATED
Prov. 19:4, but the poor is *s*
Isa. 56:3, "The LORD has utterly *s*
Rom. 1:1, to be an apostle, *s*
Gal. 1:15, it pleased God, who *s*

SEPARATES
Prov. 17:9, who repeats a matter *s*

SEPARATION
Eph. 2:14, the middle wall of *s*

SERAPHIM
Isa. 6:2, Above it stood *s*

SERIOUS
1 Pet. 4:7, therefore be *s* and

SERMON
on the Mount. Mt. 5—7; Lk. 6:20. *See* CHRIST

SERPENT
cursed by God. Gen. 3:14 (2 Cor. 11:3; Rev. 12:9)

SERPENT
Gen. 3:1, *s* was more cunning
Gen. 3:13, "The *s* deceived me
Num. 21:8, "Make a fiery *s*
Ps. 58:4, like the poison of a *s*
Ps. 91:13, *s* you shall trample
Ps. 140:3, their tongues like a *s*
Prov. 30:19, air, the way of a *s*
Eccl. 10:11, *s* may bite when it is
Isa. 14:29, be a fiery flying *s*
Isa. 51:9, and wounded the *s*
Mt. 7:10, will he give him a *s*
Jn. 3:14, Moses lifted up the *s*
Rev. 12:9, was cast out, that *s*

SERPENTS
fiery, sent by God, and bronze one made by Moses. Num. 21:8 (Jn. 3:14); the latter destroyed. 2 Ki. 18:4

SERPENTS
Dt. 32:33, is the poison of *s*
Mt. 10:16, be wise as *s*
Lk. 10:19, to trample on *s*

SERVANT
Gen. 9:25, a *s* of servants he
Job 7:2, *s* who earnestly
Prov. 11:29, and the fool will be *s*
Prov. 17:2, *s* will rule over a son
Prov. 29:19, A *s* will not be
Isa. 42:19, Who is blind but My *s*
Jer. 2:14, "Is Israel a *s*
Mal. 1:6, and a *s* his master
Mt. 20:26, you, let him be your *s*
Mt. 25:21, good and faithful *s*
Mt. 25:26, "You wicked and lazy *s*
Mt. 25:30, the unprofitable *s*
Lk. 12:47, that *s* who knew his
Jn. 15:15, *s* does not know what
Acts 4:27, against Your holy *S*

SERVANTS
Job 4:18, puts no trust in His *s*
Ps. 119:91, for all your *s*
Eccl. 10:7, on the ground like *s*
Isa. 61:6, shall call you the *s*
Lam. 5:8, *S* rule over us
Lk. 17:10, are unprofitable *s*
Jn. 15:15, longer do I call you *s*
1 Cor. 4:1, so consider us, as *s*

SERVE
Dt. 6:13, LORD your God and *s*
Jer. 5:19, land, so you shall *s* aliens
Zeph. 3:9, *s* Him with one accord
Mt. 6:24, You cannot *s* God and
Mt. 20:28, to be served, but to *s*
Rom. 7:25, the mind I myself *s*
Gal. 5:13, but through love *s*
Col. 3:24, *s* the Lord Christ
Heb. 9:14, *s* the living God
Rev. 7:15, *s* Him day and night in

SERVES
Jn. 12:26, "If anyone *s* Me

SERVICE
Ex. 12:26, do you mean by this *s*
Jn. 16:2, that he offers God *s*
Rom. 12:1, is your reasonable *s*
Eph. 6:7, with goodwill doing *s*
Rev. 2:19, your works, love, *s*

SERVING
Lk. 15:29, years I have been *s*
Acts 20:19, *s* the Lord with all
Rom. 12:11, fervent in spirit, *s*
1 Pet. 5:2, you, *s* as overseers

SET
Dt. 30:15, "See, I have *s*
Ps. 16:8, *s* the LORD always
Ps. 91:14, I will *s* him on high
Gal. 2:21, *s* aside the grace

SETH
son of Adam. Gen. 4:25; 5:3

SETTLE
Lk. 21:14, "Therefore *s* it in

SETTLED
Job 29:22, and my speech *s*
Ps. 119:89, O LORD, Your word is *s*
Prov. 8:25, the mountains were *s*
Mt. 25:19, *s* accounts with them

SEVEN
Ps. 119:164, *S* times a day I praise
Lk. 11:26, *s* other spirits more
Lk. 17:4, *s* times in a day
Acts 6:3, out from among you *s*
Rev. 1:4, *s* churches which are

SEVENTY
elders, the. Ex. 18:25; 24; Num. 11:16
years' captivity foretold. Jer. 25:11
Weeks, Daniel's prophecy concerning. Dan. 9:24
disciples, Christ's charge to. Lk. 10

SEVENTY
Dan. 9:24, *S* weeks are
Mt. 18:22, up to *s* times seven
Lk. 10:17, Then the *s* returned

SEVERE
Jer. 10:19, My wound is *s*
2 Cor. 2:5, not to be too *s*

SEVERITY
Rom. 11:22, the goodness and *s*

SHADE
Song 2:3, I sat down in his *s*
Isa. 4:6, be a tabernacle for *s*
Mk. 4:32, may nest under its *s*

SHADOW
Job 3:5, May darkness and the *s*
Job 14:2, He flees like a *s*
Ps. 17:8, hide me under the *s*
Ps. 39:6, walks about like a *s*
Ps. 144:4, like a passing *s*
Eccl. 6:12, he passes like a *s*
Isa. 30:2, and to trust in the *s*
Isa. 49:2, In the *s* of His hand

Col. 2:17, which are a *s* of
Heb. 10:1, the law, having a *s*
Jas. 1:17, is no variation or *s*

SHADOWS
Job 17:7, my members are like *s*
Song 2:17, and the *s* flee away

SHADRACH, Dan. 1:7
Meshach, and Abed-Nego, their faith and sufferings, and deliverance. Dan. 1; 3

SHAKE
Job 17:3, Who is he who will *s*
Isa. 2:19, *s* the earth
Isa. 52:2, *S* yourself from the
Lam. 2:15, *s* their heads at the
Nah. 2:10, and the knees *s*
Zeph. 2:15, hiss and *s* his fist
Hag. 2:7, I will *s* all nations
Heb. 12:26, *s* not only the earth

SHAKEN
Ps. 112:6, he will never be *s*
Acts 4:31, together was *s*
2 Th. 2:2, not to be soon *s*

SHAKES
Job 9:6, *s* the earth out of its
Ps. 29:8, *s* the Wilderness

SHALMANESER, 2 Ki. 17:3
carries ten tribes captive. 2 Ki. 17; 18:9

SHAME
Ps. 4:2, you turn my glory to *s*
Ps. 83:17, let them be put to *s*
Ps. 97:7, *s* who serve carved
Ps. 129:5, hate Zion be put to *s*
Prov. 3:35, *s* shall be the
Prov. 10:5, is a son who causes *s*
Isa. 50:6, hide My face from *s*
Jer. 51:51, *S* has covered our
Hos. 4:7, their glory into *s*
Joel 2:26, never be put to *s*
Zeph. 3:5, the unjust knows no *s*
Acts 5:41, worthy to suffer *s*
Rom. 9:33, will not be put to *s*
1 Cor. 1:27, to put to *s* the wise
1 Cor. 6:5, I say this to your *s*
Phil. 3:19, glory is in their *s*
Heb. 6:6, put Him to an open *s*

SHAMEFUL
Rom. 1:27, committing what is *s*
1 Cor. 14:35, for it is *s* for women
Eph. 5:12, For it is *s* even to

SHAMMAH, Gen. 36:13
his valor. 2 Sam. 23:11

SHAPHAN
repairs the temple. 2 Ki. 22:3; 2 Chr. 34:8

SHARE
Prov. 14:10, a stranger does not *s*
Isa. 58:7, *s* your bread with the
Gal. 6:6, is taught the word *s*
1 Tim. 6:18, to give, willing to *s*
Heb. 13:16, to do good and to *s*

SHARING
2 Cor. 9:13, for your liberal *s*

SHARON, 1 Chr. 27:29
rose of. Song 2:1

SHARP
Prov. 5:4, *S* as a two-edged sword

SHARPEN
Ps. 64:3, *s* their tongue like a
Eccl. 10:10, and one does not *s*

SHARPENS
Job 16:9, My adversary *s* His

SHARPNESS
2 Cor. 13:10, I should use *s*

SHATTERED
Job 16:12, at ease, but He has *s*

SHEALTIEL, Ezra 3:2

SHEARERS
Gen. 38:12; 1 Sam. 25:7; Isa. 53:7

SHEATH
Ezek. 21:30, 'Return it to its *s*
Jn. 18:11, your sword into the *s*

SHEAVES
Ps. 126:6, bringing his *s*
Ps. 129:7, nor he who binds *s*
Mic. 4:12, gather them like *s*

SHEBA
Gen. 25:3; 2 Sam. 20:1; Job 6:19; Ps. 72:10; Jer. 6:20; Ezek. 27:22; 38:13
queen of. 1 Ki. 10; 2 Chr. 9; Mt. 12:42
——— (Benjamite), revolts. 2 Sam. 20

SHEBNA
the scribe. 2 Ki. 18:18; 19:2; Isa. 22:15; 36:3; 37:2

SHECANIAH (or Shechaniah)
1 Chr. 3:21; 24:11

SHECHEM, Gen. 34:2
the Hivite. Gen. 34
——— city of. Gen. 12:6; Josh. 17:7; Ps. 60:6
discourse of Joshua at. Josh. 24
its treachery and penalty. Jud. 9:1,41

SHED
Mt. 26:28, which is *s* for many

SHEDDING
Heb. 9:22, blood, and without *s*

SHEEP
for sacrifice. Lev. 1:10; 1 Ki. 8:63; 2 Chr. 30:24
the people spoken of as. 2 Sam. 24:17; Ps. 74:1
the church compared to. Ps. 74:1; 79:13; 95:7; 100:3; Ezek. 34; 36:38; Mic. 2:12; Mt. 15:24; 25:32; Jn. 10:2; 1 Pet. 2:25
symbol of Christ. Isa. 53:7; Acts 8:32
of His people. Ps. 95:7; Jn. 21:16

SHEEP
Ps. 119:176, astray like a lost *s*
Isa. 53:7, slaughter, and as a *s*
Jer. 12:3, Pull them out like *s*
Jer. 50:6, have been lost *s*
Ezek. 34:11, will search for My *s*
Ezek. 34:17, shall judge between *s*
Zech. 13:7, *s* will be scattered
Mt. 10:6, rather to the lost *s*
Mt. 10:16, I send you out as *s*
Mt. 25:33, And He will set the *s*
Lk. 15:4, having a hundred *s*
Jn. 10:3, and he calls his own *s*
Jn. 10:14, and I know My *s*
Jn. 10:16, *s* I have which are not
Acts 8:32, "He was led as a *s*
1 Pet. 2:25, like *s* going astray

SHEEPFOLDS
Ps. 68:13, lie down among the *s*

SHEET
Acts 10:11, object like a great *s*

SHEKEL
Gen. 23:15; Ex. 30:13; Josh. 7:21; 2 Sam. 14:26; 1 Ki. 10:16; Neh. 5:15; Jer. 32:9; Ezek. 4:10

SHELTER
Ps. 61:4, I will trust in the *s*
Ps. 143:9, in You I take *s*
Joel 3:16, the LORD will be a *s*

SHELTERS
Dt. 33:12, *s* him all the day long
Zeph. 2:6, be pastures, with *s*

SHEM
Gen. 5:32; 9:26; 10:21; 11:10; 1 Chr. 1:17

SHEMAIAH
prophet. 1 Ki. 12:22; 2 Chr. 11:2; 12:5 (Jer. 29:24)

SHEOL
Job 17:16, down to the gates of *S*
Ps. 16:10, not leave my soul in *S*
Ps. 116:3, *S* laid hold of me
Isa. 38:18, *S* cannot thank
Jon. 2:2, the belly of *S* I cried

SHEPHERD
the Good (Christ). Jn. 10:14; Heb. 13:20; 1 Pet. 2:25; 5:4; (Isa. 40:11; Zech. 11:16; 13:7)
of Israel. Ps. 23:1; 80:1; Ezek. 34:11
of His flock. Isa. 63:11
worthless. Zech. 11:17
hireling. Jn. 10:12

SHEPHERD
Gen. 46:34, *s* is an abomination
2 Sam. 5:2, *s* My people Israel
Ps. 23:1, The LORD is my *s*
Ps. 78:71, *s* Jacob His people
Isa. 40:11, His flock like a *s*
Isa. 44:28, of Cyrus, 'He is My *s*
Jer. 17:16, *s* who follows You
Ezek. 34:5, because there was no *s*
Ezek. 34:23, I will establish one *s*
Amos 3:12, "As a *s* takes from
Zech. 11:17, to the worthless *s*
Mt. 26:31, 'I will strike the *S*
Jn. 10:11, "I am the good *s*
Acts 20:28, *s* the church of God
Heb. 13:20, the dead, that great *S*
1 Pet. 5:2, *S* the flock of God
1 Pet. 5:4, when the Chief *S*
Rev. 7:17, of the throne will *s*

SHEPHERDS
Num. 14:33, your sons shall be *s*

Isa. 56:11, And they are *s* who
Jer. 3:15, And I will give you *s*
Jer. 23:1, *s* who destroy and
Jer. 23:2, *s* who feed My people
Jer. 50:6, *s* have led them astray
Ezek. 34:8, *s* fed themselves
Lk. 2:8, in the same country *s*

SHESHACH
a name for Babel. Jer. 25:26; 51:41

SHETHAR-BOZNAI, Ezra 5:3
and Tatnai oppose rebuilding of temple. Ezra 5:6

SHIBBOLETH, Jud. 12:6

SHIELD
Gen. 15:1, I am your *s*
2 Sam. 22:31, He is a *s* to all who
Ps. 18:2, my *s* and the horn of
Ps. 84:11, God is a sun and *s*
Ps. 91:4, truth shall be your *s*
Eph. 6:16, all, taking the *s*

SHILOH
Messiah. Gen. 49:10
——— site of tabernacle. Josh. 18:1; Jud. 21:19; 1 Sam. 1:3; 2:14; 3:21; Ps. 78:60; Jer. 7:12; 26:6

SHIMEI, Num. 3:18
curses David. 2 Sam. 16:5
killed by Solomon. 1 Ki. 2:36

SHINE
Num. 6:25, LORD make His face *s*
Ps. 67:1, cause His face to *s*
Ps. 80:1, the cherubim, *s*
Ps. 119:135, Make Your face *s*
Dan. 12:3, who are wise shall *s*
Mt. 13:43, the righteous will *s*
Phil. 2:15, among whom you *s*

SHINED
Isa. 9:2, them a light has *s*

SHINES
Jn. 1:5, And the light *s*
2 Pet. 1:19, heed as a light that *s*

SHINING
2 Sam. 23:4, the earth, by clear *s*
Mk. 9:3, His clothes became *s*
1 Jn. 2:8, light is already *s*
Rev. 1:16, was like the sun *s*

SHIPS
Job 9:26, pass by like swift *s*
Ps. 107:23, down to the sea in *s*
Prov. 31:14, like the merchant *s*
Jas. 3:4, Look also at *s*

SHIPWRECK
1 Tim. 1:19, faith have suffered *s*

SHISHAK, 1 Ki. 11:40
invades and spoils Jerusalem. 1 Ki. 14:25; 2 Chr. 12

SHOOT
Ps. 22:7, they *s* out the lip
Ps. 64:7, But God shall *s*

SHORT
Rom. 3:23, have sinned and fall *s*
Rom. 9:28, the work and cut it *s*

SHORTENED
Ps. 89:45, his youth You have *s*
Prov. 10:27, the wicked will be *s*
Mt. 24:22, those days were *s*

SHOT
Heb. 12:20, shall be stoned or *s*

SHOUT
Ps. 95:1, *s* joyfully to the Rock
Ps. 98:4, *S* joyfully to the LORD
Ps. 100:1, Make a joyful *s*
1 Th. 4:16, from heaven with a *s*

SHOW
Gen. 12:1, a land that I will *s*
Ps. 25:4, *S* me Your ways
Isa. 46:8, *s* yourselves men
Jn. 5:20, *s* Him greater works
Jn. 14:8, *s* us the Father

SHOWBREAD
Ex. 25:30; Lev. 24:5; Heb. 9:2
David takes. 1 Sam. 21:6 (Mt. 12:4; Mk. 2:26)

SHOWERS
Ps. 65:10, make it soft with *s*
Jer. 3:3, *s* have been withheld
Jer. 14:22, can the heavens give *s*
Mic. 5:7, from the LORD, like *s*

SHREWDLY
Lk. 16:8, because he had dealt *s*

SHRINES
Acts 19:24, who made silver *s*

SHRIVELED
Job 16:8, You have *s* me up

SHUFFLES
Prov. 6:13, with his eyes, He *s*

SHULAMITE, Song 6:13

SHUNAMMITE
1 Ki. 1:3; 2 Ki. 4:12

SHUNNED
Job 1:1, feared God and *s* evil

SHUSHAN
Artaxerxes at. Neh. 1:1; Est. 2:8; 3:15

SHUT
Job 38:8, "Or who *s* in the sea
Ps. 77:9, Has He in anger *s*
Mt. 23:13, For you *s* up the

SHUTS
Prov. 21:13, *s* his ears to the cry
Isa. 33:15, *s* his eyes from seeing
1 Jn. 3:17, brother in need, and *s*
Rev. 3:7, who opens and no one *s*

SIBBOLETH
same as Shibboleth. Jud. 12:6

SICK
Hezekiah. 2 Ki. 20:1; 2 Chr. 32:24; Lazarus. Jn. 11:1; Dorcas. Acts 9:37; Peter's wife's mother. Mt. 8:14; Mk. 1:30; Lk. 4:38
healing the. Mt. 8:16; 10:8; Mk. 16:18; Lk. 7:10
when did we see You. Mt. 25:39
unto death. Phil. 2:27

SICK
Hos. 7:5, have made him *s*
Mt. 25:36, I was *s* and you
Jn. 11:3, he whom You love is *s*
1 Cor. 11:30, many are weak and *s*
2 Tim. 4:20, have left in Miletus *s*
Jas. 5:15, faith will save the *s*

SICKLE
Joel 3:13, Put in the *s*
Rev. 14:15, "Thrust in Your *s*

SICKNESS
Lev. 26:16; Dt. 28:27; 2 Sam. 12:15; 2 Chr. 21:15
conduct under. Ps. 35:13; Isa. 38:12; Mt. 25:36; Jas. 5:14. *See* AFFLICTION

SICKNESS
Prov. 18:14, will sustain him in *s*
Jn. 11:4, "This *s* is not unto

SICKNESSES
Mt. 8:17, And bore our *s*

SIDE
Ps. 118:6, The LORD is on my *s*
Jn. 21:6, the net on the right *s*

SIDON
son of Canaan. Gen. 10:15
——— city of. Gen. 49:13; Josh. 11:8; 19:28; Jud. 10:6; 18:7; 1 Ki. 5:6; 11:1; Ezra 3:7; Lk. 4:26; Acts 12:20; 27:3
prophecies concerning. Isa. 23; Jer. 25:22; 27:3; 47:4; Ezek. 27:8; 28:21; 32:30; Joel 3:4; Zech. 9:2

SIFT
Isa. 30:28, *s* the nations with the
Amos 9:9, *s* the house of Israel
Lk. 22:31, for you, that he may *s*

SIFTS
Prov. 20:26, A wise king *s* out the

SIGH
Ps. 90:9, our years like a *s*
Isa. 24:7, the merry-hearted *s*
Ezek. 9:4, of the men who *s*

SIGHING
Job 3:24, For my *s* comes before
Ps. 38:9, *s* is not hidden

SIGHT
Ex. 3:3, and see this great *s*
Mt. 11:26, seemed good in Your *s*
2 Cor. 5:7, by faith, not by *s*

SIGN
Pharisees ask a. Mt. 12:38; Mk. 8:11

SIGN
Ps. 86:17, Show me a *s* for good
Isa. 7:14, will give you a *s*
Isa. 55:13, for an everlasting *s*
Mt. 12:38, we want to see a *s*
Mt. 12:39, seeks after a *s*
Mt. 24:3, And what will be the *s*
Lk. 2:34, *s* which will be spoken
Jn. 4:54, again is the second *s*
1 Cor. 1:22, For Jews request a *s*
Rev. 12:1, Now a great *s* appeared

SIGNIFY, Jn. 12:33

SIGNS
sun and moon. Gen. 1:14; rainbow. Gen. 9:13; circumcision. Gen.

17:10; Moses. Ex. 3:12; 4:8; Sabbath. Ex. 31:13; Jonah. Mt. 12:39; apostles. Acts 2:43; *also* 1 Ki. 13:3; Isa. 7:11; 8:18; 20:3; Ezek. 24:24
false. Dt. 13:1; Mt. 24:24; 2 Th. 2:9
of the times. Mt. 16:3

SIGNS
Gen. 1:14, and let them be for *s*
Job 21:29, you not know their *s*
Ps. 105:27, They performed His *s*
Isa. 8:18, We are for *s* and
Dan. 4:3, How great are His *s*
Mt. 16:3, cannot discern the *s*
Mk. 16:20, the accompanying *s*
Jn. 2:11, *s* Jesus did in Cana of
Jn. 3:2, no one can do these *s*
Jn. 4:48, you people see *s*
Jn. 6:26, because you saw the *s*
Jn. 9:16, is a sinner do such *s*
Jn. 11:47, this Man works many *s*
Jn. 20:30, Jesus did many other *s*
Rev. 16:14, demons, performing *s*

SIHON
king of the Amorites. Num. 21:21; Dt. 1:4; 2:26; Ps. 135:11; 136:19

SILAS
shortened form of Silvanus. Acts 15:22; 16:19; 17:4. *See* 2 Cor. 1:19; 1 Th. 1:1; 1 Pet. 5:12

SILENCE
Prov. 10:19; 11:12; 17:28
women to keep. 1 Tim. 2:11
in heaven for half an hour. Rev. 8:1

SILENCE
Ps. 8:2, that You may *s*
Ps. 39:2, I was mute with *s*
Ps. 94:17, soon have settled in *s*
Isa. 47:5, "Sit in *s*
Rev. 8:1, seal, there was *s*

SILENT
1 Sam. 2:9, the wicked shall be *s*
Ps. 22:2, season, and am not *s*
Ps. 28:1, Do not be *s* to me
Ps. 31:17, Let them be *s* in the
Zeph. 1:7, Be *s* in the presence
1 Cor. 14:34, Let your women keep *s*

SILK
Ezek. 16:10, covered you with *s*

SILLY
Jer. 4:22, They are *s* children

SILOAM, Jn. 9:7

SILVANUS, 2 Cor. 1:19

SILVER
Job 22:25, and your precious *s*
Job 27:16, Though he heaps up *s*
Ps. 12:6, *s* tried in a furnace
Ps. 66:10, have refined us as *s*
Prov. 3:14, than the profits of *s*
Prov. 16:16, chosen rather than *s*
Prov. 17:3, refining pot is for *s*
Eccl. 5:10, He who loves *s* will
Isa. 1:22, *s* has become dross
Jer. 6:30, call them rejected *s*
Amos 8:6, may buy the poor for *s*
Mt. 26:15, him thirty pieces of *s*

SIMEON
son of Jacob. Gen. 29:33; 34:7,25; 42:24
his descendants. Gen. 46:10; Ex. 6:15; Num. 1:22; 26:12; 1 Chr. 4:24; 12:25
prophecy concerning. Gen. 49:5
—— blesses Christ. Lk. 2:25

SIMILITUDE
Jas. 3:9, been made in the *s*

SIMON
brother of Christ. Mt. 13:55; Mk. 6:3
—— the Canaanite (also called the Zealot), apostle. Mt. 10:4; Mk. 3:18; Lk. 6:15
—— (Pharisee), reproved. Lk. 7:36
—— leper. Mt. 26:6; Mk. 14:3
—— of Cyrene, bears the cross of Jesus. Mt. 27:32; Mk. 15:21; Lk. 23:26
—— (a tanner), Peter's vision in his house. Acts 9:43; 10:6
—— (a sorcerer), baptized. Acts 8:9; rebuked by Peter. Acts 8:18
—— Peter. *See* PETER

SIMPLE
Ps. 19:7, making wise the *s*
Ps. 116:6, LORD preserves the *s*
Ps. 119:130, understanding to the *s*
Prov. 14:15, *s* believes every word
Rom. 16:18, the hearts of the *s*

SIMPLICITY
Prov. 1:22, ones, will you love *s*
2 Cor. 1:12, in the world in *s*
2 Cor. 11:3, corrupted from the *s*

SIN, *see also* ZIN
wilderness of. Ex. 16

SIN
what it is. Dt. 9:7; Josh. 1:18; Prov. 24:9; Rom. 14:23; Jas. 4:17; 1 Jn. 3:4; 5:17
origin of. Gen. 3:6,7; Mt. 15:19; Jn. 8:44; Rom. 5:12; 1 Jn. 3:8
characteristics of. Prov. 14:34; 15:9; 30:12; Isa. 1:18; 59:3; Jer. 44:4; Eph. 5:11; Heb. 3:13,15; 6:1; 9:14; Jas. 1:15
sting of, death. 1 Cor. 15:56
all born in, and under. Gen. 5:3; Job 15:14; 25:4; Ps. 51:5; Rom. 3:9; Gal. 3:22
Christ alone is without. 2 Cor. 5:21; Heb. 4:15; 7:26; 1 Jn. 3:5; His blood alone redeems from. Jn. 1:29; Eph. 1:7; 1 Jn. 1:7; 3:5
fountain for. Zech. 13:1
repented of, and confessed. Job 33:27; Ps. 38:18; 97:10; Prov. 28:13; Jer. 3:21; Rom. 12:9; 1 Jn. 1:9
prayed, striven against, and mortified. Ps. 4:4; 19:13; 39:1; 51:2; 139:23,24; Mt. 6:13; Rom. 8:13; Col. 3:5; Heb. 12:4
excludes from heaven. 1 Cor. 6:9; Gal. 5:19; Eph. 5:5; Rev. 21:27
wages of, death. Rom. 6:23
punishment of. Gen. 2:17; Ezek. 18:4; Rom. 5:13; Heb. 10:26; Jas. 1:15

SIN
Ex. 32:20, committed a great *s*
Num. 27:3, he died in his own *s*
Num. 32:23, and be sure your *s*
Dt. 24:16, to death for his own *s*
Job 2:10, all this Job did not *s*
Job 10:6, and search out my *s*
Ps. 4:4, Be angry, and do not *s*
Ps. 39:1, my ways, lest I *s*
Ps. 51:3, *s* is always before me
Ps. 51:5, in *s* my mother
Prov. 14:34, *s* is a reproach
Eccl. 7:20, good and does not *s*
Isa. 53:10, soul an offering for *s*
Isa. 53:12, And He bore the *s*
Jer. 31:34, *s* I will remember no
Hos. 4:8, They eat up the *s*
Hos. 13:2, Now they *s* more and
Mt. 18:6, who believe in Me to *s*
Jn. 1:29, who takes away the *s*
Jn. 5:14, *S* no more
Jn. 8:7, "He who is without *s*
Jn. 16:8, convict the world of *s*
Rom. 3:9, they are all under *s*
Rom. 5:12, *s* entered the world
Rom. 5:13, *s* is not imputed
Rom. 6:1, *s* that grace may
Rom. 6:10, died to *s* once for all
Rom. 6:14, *s* shall not have
Rom. 6:15, Shall we *s* because we
Rom. 7:17, *s* that dwells in me
2 Cor. 5:21, Him who knew no *s*
2 Th. 2:3, man of *s* is revealed
Heb. 4:15, we are, yet without *s*
Heb. 9:26, appeared to put away *s*
Heb. 10:26, *s* willfully after we
Jas. 1:15, it gives birth to *s*
Jas. 4:17, do it, to him it is *s*
1 Pet. 2:22, "Who committed no *s*
1 Jn. 1:8, say that we have no *s*
1 Jn. 2:1, that you may not *s*
1 Jn. 3:4, *s* is lawlessness
1 Jn. 3:5, in Him there is no *s*
1 Jn. 3:9, and he cannot *s*
1 Jn. 5:16, for those who commit *s*
1 Jn. 5:17, unrighteousness is *s*

SINAI, Ex. 19:1; Acts 7:30
Mount. Dt. 33:2; Jud. 5:5; Ps. 68:8,17; Gal. 4:24

SINCERE
2 Cor. 6:6, Holy Spirit, by *s* love
1 Tim. 1:5, and from *s* faith
1 Pet. 1:22, *s* love of the brethren

SINCERITY
Josh. 24:14, LORD, serve Him in *s*
1 Cor. 5:8, unleavened bread of *s*
2 Cor. 1:12, simplicity and godly *s*
Col. 3:22, men-pleasers, but in *s*

SINFUL
Isa. 1:4, Alas, *s* nation
Mk. 8:38, and *s* generation
Lk. 5:8, from me, for I am a *s*
Lk. 24:7, the hands of *s* men
Rom. 7:13, become exceedingly *s*
Rom. 8:3, likeness of *s* flesh

SING
Ex. 15:21, "*S* to the LORD

Job 29:13, the widow's heart to *s*
Ps. 66:2, *S* out the honor
Ps. 101:1, I will *s* of mercy and
Ps. 137:3, "*S* us one of the songs
Isa. 65:14, My servants shall *s*
1 Cor. 14:15, I will *s* with the
Heb. 2:12, assembly I will *s*
Jas. 5:13, Let him *s* psalms

SINGERS
Ps. 68:25, The *s* went before
Eccl. 2:8, male and female *s*

SINGING
Ps. 100:2, His presence with *s*
Ps. 126:2, and our tongue with *s*
Song 2:12, the time of *s* has come
Isa. 14:7, break forth into *s*
Isa. 35:2, even with joy and *s*
Isa. 35:10, come to Zion with *s*
Eph. 5:19, and spiritual songs, *s*

SINISTER
Dan. 8:23, who understands *s*

SINK
Ps. 69:2, I *s* in deep mire
Mt. 14:30, to *s* he cried out

SINNED
Ps. 51:4, You only, have I *s*
Lam. 1:8, Jerusalem has *s*
Lam. 5:7, Our fathers *s* and are
Lk. 15:18, "Father, I have *s*
Jn. 9:2, "Rabbi, who *s*
Rom. 2:12, For as many as have *s*
Rom. 3:23, for all have *s* and
1 Cor. 7:28, marries, she has not *s*
1 Jn. 1:10, say that we have not *s*
1 Jn. 3:8, for the devil has *s*

SINNER
Eccl. 2:26, *s* He gives the work
Eccl. 8:12, *s* does evil a hundred
Eccl. 9:18, *s* destroys much good
Lk. 7:37, the city who was a *s*
Lk. 15:7, *s* who repents than
Jn. 9:16, can a man who is a *s*
1 Pet. 4:18, the ungodly and the *s*

SINNERS
Ps. 1:1, in the path of *s*
Ps. 25:8, therefore He teaches *s*
Ps. 26:9, soul with *s*
Ps. 104:35, *s* be consumed from the
Prov. 1:10, son, if *s* entice you
Isa. 33:14, The *s* in Zion are
Mt. 9:13, the righteous, but *s*
Mt. 11:19, tax collectors and *s*
Lk. 6:32, *s* love those who love
Lk. 13:2, Galileans were worse *s*
Jn. 9:31, God does not hear *s*
Rom. 5:8, while we were still *s*
Rom. 5:19, many were made *s*
1 Tim. 1:9, the ungodly and for *s*
1 Tim. 1:15, the world to save *s*
Heb. 7:26, separate from *s*
Heb. 12:3, such hostility from *s*
Jude 15, things which ungodly *s*

SINS
Job 13:23, my iniquities and *s*
Ps. 19:13, from presumptuous *s*
Ps. 90:8, You, our secret *s*
Prov. 8:36, but he who *s* against
Isa. 59:2, *s* have hidden His face
Ezek. 18:4, the soul who *s* shall
Dan. 9:24, to make an end of *s*
Mt. 18:15, if your brother *s*
Rom. 11:27, I take away their *s*
1 Cor. 15:3, *s* according to the
1 Cor. 15:17, are still in your *s*
Eph. 1:7, the forgiveness of *s*
1 Tim. 5:24, *s* are clearly evident
Heb. 9:28, once to bear the *s*
1 Jn. 1:9, If we confess our *s*
1 Jn. 2:2, propitiation for our *s*
1 Jn. 2:12, *s* are forgiven you
1 Jn. 3:6, Whoever *s* has neither
Rev. 18:4, you share in her *s*

SINS, NATIONAL
bring judgments. Mt. 23:35–36; 27:25
denounced. Isa. 1:24; 30:1; Jer. 5:9; 6:27

SISERA
Jud. 4:2,21; 5:24; 1 Sam. 12:9; Ps. 83:9

SISTER
Job 17:14, are my mother and my *s*
Song 8:8, We have a little *s*
Mt. 12:50, is My brother and *s*
Rom. 16:1, to you Phoebe our *s*
1 Cor. 7:15, *s* is not under bondage

SIT
Ps. 69:12, Those who *s* in the
Isa. 47:1, "Come down and *s*
Jer. 8:14, "Why do we *s* still
Mt. 20:23, but to *s* on My right
Mt. 23:2, and the Pharisees *s*
Heb. 1:13, "*S* at My right hand
Jas. 2:3, say to him, "You *s*
Rev. 3:21, I will grant to *s*
Rev. 18:7, heart, 'I *s* as queen

SITS
Ps. 47:8, God *s* on His holy
Isa. 40:22, It is He who *s* above
2 Th. 2:4, so that he *s* as God
Rev. 17:15, where the harlot *s*

SITTING
Ps. 139:2, You know my *s* down and
Mk. 14:62, see the Son of Man *s*
Col. 3:1, where Christ is, *s*

SIVAN
third month of Hebrew calendar, May–June. Est. 8:9

SKILL
Ps. 137:5, hand forget its *s*
Eccl. 9:11, nor favor to men of *s*
Dan. 1:17, them knowledge and *s*
Dan. 9:22, forth to give you *s*

SKILLFUL, Ps. 33:3; Ezek. 21:31

SKILLFULNESS
Ps. 78:72, guided them by the *s*

SKIN
Gen. 3:21, God made tunics of *s*
Job 2:4, LORD and said, "*S*
Job 19:20, have escaped by the *s*
Jer. 13:23, Ethiopian change his *s*
Lam. 5:10, *s* is hot as an oven

SKIP
Ps. 29:6, He makes them also *s*

SKIPPING
Song 2:8, upon the mountains, *s*

SKULL
Mt. 27:33, to say, Place of a *S*

SKY
Rev. 6:14, *s* receded as a scroll

SLACK
Dt. 7:10, He will not be *s*
Prov. 10:4, *s* hand becomes poor
2 Pet. 3:9, The Lord is not *s*

SLAIN
1 Sam. 18:7, *s* his thousands
2 Sam. 1:19, beauty of Israel is *s*
Ps. 88:5, the dead, like the *s*
Prov. 7:26, and all who were *s*
Prov. 22:13, I shall be *s* in the
Isa. 22:2, *s* men are not *s*
Isa. 26:21, no more cover her *s*
Isa. 66:16, and the *s* of the LORD
Jer. 9:1, and night for the *s*
Lam. 4:9, Those *s* by the sword
Hos. 6:5, the prophets, I have *s*
Rev. 5:12, is the Lamb who was *s*

SLANDER
Ps. 50:20, *s* your own mother's
Prov. 10:18, whoever spreads *s*

SLANDERERS
1 Tim. 3:11, be reverent, not *s*
2 Tim. 3:3, unforgiving, *s*
Ti. 2:3, in behavior, not *s*

SLANDEROUSLY
Rom. 3:8, as we are *s* reported

SLAUGHTER
Ps. 44:22, as sheep for the *s*
Isa. 53:7, led as a lamb to the *s*
Jer. 7:32, but the Valley of *S*
Zech. 11:4, "Feed the flock for *s*
Rom. 8:36, as sheep for the *s*

SLAVE
Dt. 15:15, that you were a *s*
Jn. 8:34, commits sin is a *s*
1 Cor. 7:21, you called while a *s*
Gal. 4:7, you are no longer a *s*

SLAVES
Rom. 6:6, should no longer be *s*
Rom. 6:17, though you were *s*
Rom. 6:19, your members as *s*
1 Cor. 7:23, do not become *s*

SLAY
Gen. 18:25, *s* the righteous
Gen. 20:4, *s* a righteous nation
Ps. 34:21, Evil shall *s* the
Ps. 139:19, Oh, that You would *s*
Lk. 19:27, *s* them before me

SLEEP
Gen. 15:12; 1 Sam. 26:12; Prov. 6:4–11; 19:15
figurative. Ps. 13:3; Dan. 12:2; Mk. 13:36; Rom. 13:11; 1 Cor. 11:30; 15:20,51; 1 Th. 4:13–15

SLEEP
Gen. 2:21, God caused a deep *s*
Job 4:13, the night, when deep *s*
Ps. 13:3, my eyes, lest I *s*
Ps. 44:23, Why do You *s*

Ps. 76:5, have sunk into their *s*
Ps. 90:5, they are like a *s*
Ps. 121:4, neither slumber nor *s*
Ps. 127:2, He gives His beloved *s*
Ps. 132:4, I will not give *s*
Prov. 3:24, *s* will be sweet
Prov. 4:16, For they do not *s*
Prov. 6:10, A little *s*
Prov. 20:13, Do not love *s*
Eccl. 5:12, The *s* of a laboring
Isa. 29:10, the spirit of deep *s*
Dan. 6:18, Also his *s* went from
Dan. 8:18, me, I was in a deep *s*
Lk. 22:46, them, "Why do you *s*
1 Cor. 11:30, among you, and many *s*
1 Cor. 15:51, We shall not all *s*
Eph. 5:14, "Awake, you who *s*
1 Th. 4:14, with Him those who *s*
1 Th. 5:6, Therefore let us not *s*

SLEEPERS
Song 7:9, gently the lips of *s*

SLEEPING
Mt. 9:24, is not dead, but *s*
Mt. 26:45, "Are you still *s*
Acts 12:6, that night Peter was *s*

SLEEPLESSNESS
2 Cor. 6:5, in labors, in *s*
2 Cor. 11:27, and toil, in *s* often

SLEEPS
Prov. 10:5, wise son; he who *s*
Jn. 11:11, "Our friend Lazarus *s*

SLEPT
Ps. 3:5, I lay down and *s*
Mt. 13:25, but while men *s*

SLIGHTED
Prov. 12:9, is the one who is *s*

SLING
1 Sam. 17:40, he had, and his *s*
Prov. 26:8, *s* is he who gives

SLIP
Dt. 32:35, their foot shall *s*
Ps. 17:5, my footsteps may not *s*

SLIPPERY
Ps. 35:6, way be dark and *s*
Ps. 73:18, set them in *s* places
Jer. 23:12, be to them like *s*

SLOOPS
Isa. 2:16, all the beautiful *s*

SLOTHFULNESS
Prov. 12:24,27; 15:19; 18:9; 19:15,24; 21:25; 22:13; 24:30; 26:13–16; Eccl. 10:18; Mt. 25:26; Rom. 11:8
condemned. Prov. 6:4; Rom. 12:11; 13:11; 1 Th. 5:6; Heb. 6:12

SLOW
Ex. 4:10, but I am *s* of speech
Prov. 14:29, He who is *s* to wrath
Jas. 1:19, hear, *s* to speak, *s*

SLUGGARD
Prov. 6:9, will you slumber, O *s*

SLUMBERED
Mt. 25:5, delayed, they all *s*

SLUMBERING
Job 33:15, upon men, while *s*

SMALL
Isa. 49:20, "The place is too *s*
Jer. 49:15, I will make you *s*
Amos 7:2, may stand, for he is *s*
Obad. 2, I will make you *s*
Zech. 4:10, the day of *s* things
Rev. 20:12, And I saw the dead, *s*

SMELL
Gen. 27:27, and he smelled the *s*
Isa. 3:24, *s* there will be a

SMELLS
Job 39:25, *s* the battle from afar

SMITTEN
Isa. 53:4, Him stricken, *s*

SMOKE
Gen. 19:28, went up like the *s*
Ps. 68:2, *s* is driven away
Ps. 102:3, are consumed like *s*
Ps. 119:83, like a wineskin in *s*
Song 3:6, like pillars of *s*
Isa. 34:10, *s* shall ascend forever
Isa. 51:6, vanish away like *s*
Acts 2:19, fire and vapor of *s*
Rev. 9:2, *s* arose out of the pit
Rev. 15:8, was filled with *s*
Rev. 19:3, Her *s* rises up

SMOOTH
Isa. 30:10, speak to us *s* things
Isa. 40:4, And the rough places *s*
Jer. 12:6, though they speak *s*
Lk. 3:5, the rough ways *s*

SMOOTH-SKINNED
Gen. 27:11, man, and I am a *s*

SMYRNA, Rev. 1:11

SNAIL
Ps. 58:8, *s* which melts away as

SNARE
Ex. 23:33, it will surely be a *s*
Jud. 8:27, It became a *s* to
1 Sam. 18:21, that she may be a *s*
Job 5:5, *s* snatches their
Job 18:8, and he walks into a *s*
Ps. 69:22, their table become a *s*
Ps. 124:7, as a bird from the *s*
Eccl. 9:12, birds caught in a *s*
Isa. 24:17, and the pit and the *s*
Jer. 50:23, I have laid a *s*
Lam. 3:47, *s* have come upon us
Hos. 9:8, is a fowler's *s*
Amos 3:5, a bird fall into a *s*
Lk. 21:35, it will come as a *s*
1 Tim. 6:9, temptation and a *s*
2 Tim. 2:26, and escape the *s*

SNARED
Ps. 9:16, The wicked is *s*
Isa. 8:15, and be broken, be *s*
Isa. 42:22, all of them are *s*

SNARES
Ps. 18:5, the *s* of death
Ps. 38:12, who seek my life lay *s*
Eccl. 9:14, and built great *s*
Jer. 5:26, wait as one who sets *s*

SNATCH
Job 24:9, *s* the fatherless
Jn. 10:28, neither shall anyone *s*

SNATCHES
Mt. 13:19, *s* away what was

SNEER
Mal. 1:13, and you *s* at it

SNIFFED
Jer. 14:6, they *s* at the wind

SNORTING
Job 39:20, *s* strikes terror

SNOW
Job 24:19, and heat consume the *s*
Job 37:6, For He says to the *s*
Job 38:22, the treasury of *s*
Ps. 51:7, shall be whiter than *s*
Ps. 147:16, He gives *s* like wool
Prov. 26:1, As *s* in summer and
Prov. 31:21, She is not afraid of *s*
Isa. 1:18, shall be as white as *s*
Dan. 7:9, garment was white as *s*
Mt. 28:3, clothing as white as *s*
Rev. 1:14, wool, as white as *s*

SOAKED
Isa. 34:7, their land shall be *s*

SOAP
Jer. 2:22, lye, and use much *s*

SOBER
1 Th. 5:8, of the day be *s*
Ti. 2:2, the older men be *s*

SOBERLY
Rom. 12:3, think, but to think *s*
Ti. 2:12, we should live *s*

SODA
Prov. 25:20, and like vinegar on *s*

SODOM, Gen. 10:19
its iniquity and destruction. Gen. 13:13; 18:20; 19:4–24; Dt. 23:17; 1 Ki. 14:24; Rom. 9:29
Lot's deliverance from. Gen. 19
a warning. Dt. 29:23; 32:32; Isa. 1:9; 13:19; Lam. 4:6; Mt. 10:15; Lk. 17:29; Jude 7; Rev. 11:8

SODOMITES
1 Cor. 6:9, nor homosexuals, nor *s*
1 Tim. 1:10, for fornicators, for *s*

SOFTER
Ps. 55:21, his words were *s*

SOJOURNER
Job 31:32, no *s* had to lodge

SOJOURNERS
among the Israelites, how to be treated. Ex. 22:21; 23:9; Lev. 19:33; Dt. 1:16; 10:18; 23:7; 24:14; Mal. 3:5
regulations as to the Passover, the priest's office, marriage, and the laws concerning them. Ex. 12:43; 34:16; Lev. 17:10; 22:10; 24:16; Num. 1:51; 18:7; 19:10; 35:15; Dt. 7:3; 17:15; 25:5; 31:12; Josh. 8:33; Ezra 10:2; Neh. 13:27; Ezek. 44:9. *See* HOSPITALITY
and pilgrims. 1 Pet. 2:11

SOJOURNERS
Lev. 25:23, are strangers and *s*
1 Pet. 2:11, I beg you as *s*

SOLD
Gen. 25:33, *s* his birthright
Lev. 25:33, the house that was *s*
Dt. 32:30, their Rock had *s*
Jud. 2:14, and He *s* them into the
2 Ki. 17:17, *s* themselves to do
Est. 7:4, Had we been *s* as male
Ps. 105:17, who was *s* as a slave
Mt. 13:46, *s* all that he had
Lk. 17:28, they bought, they *s*
Acts 2:45, *s* their possessions
Rom. 7:14, but I am carnal, *s*
1 Cor. 10:25, Eat whatever is *s*

SOLDIER
2 Tim. 2:3, hardship as a good *s*
2 Tim. 2:4, enlisted him as a *s*

SOLDIERS
admonition to. Lk. 3:14
at the crucifixion. Jn. 19:2,23,32
as guards. Mt. 27:66; 28:4,12; Acts 12:4; 23:10; 27:42

SOLDIERS
Mt. 28:12, sum of money to the *s*
Lk. 23:36, The *s* also mocked
Jn. 19:2, *s* twisted a crown

SOLEMNLY
Gen. 43:3, saying, "The man *s*
Acts 28:23, *s* testified of the

SOLITARILY
Mic. 7:14, heritage, who dwell *s*

SOLITARY
Ps. 68:6, God sets the *s* in

SOLOMON, 2 Sam. 5:14
king of Israel. 2 Sam. 12:24; 1 Ki. 1; 2:24; 1 Chr. 28:9; 29
asks of God wisdom. 1 Ki. 3:5 (4:29); 2 Chr. 1:7
the wise judgment of. 1 Ki. 3:16
his treaty with Hiram for building the temple. 1 Ki. 5; 2 Chr. 2
builds the temple. (2 Sam. 7:12; 1 Chr. 17:11); 1 Ki. 6; 7; 2 Chr. 3—5; the dedication. 1 Ki. 8; 2 Chr. 6
God's covenant with. 1 Ki. 9; 2 Chr. 7:12
the queen of Sheba visits. 1 Ki. 10; 2 Chr. 9; Mt. 6:29; 12:42
David's prayer for. Ps. 72
his idolatry, rebuke, and death. 1 Ki. 11:1,9,14,31,41; 2 Chr. 9:29; Neh. 13:26
his Proverbs and Songs. Prov. 1:1; Eccl. 1:1; Song 1:1

SOMEBODY
Acts 5:36, up, claiming to be *s*

SOMETHING
Lk. 7:40, "Simon, I have *s*
Gal. 6:3, thinks himself to be *s*

SON
of God, *see* CHRIST
——— of Man. Ezek. 2:1; Mt. 8:20; Acts 7:56

SON
Ps. 2:7, Me, 'You are My *S*
Prov. 4:3, I was my father's *s*
Prov. 10:1, *s* makes a glad father
Prov. 17:25, *s* is a grief to his
Prov. 31:2, And what, *s* of my womb
Isa. 9:6, is born, unto us a *S*
Isa. 14:12, heaven, O Lucifer, *s*
Dan. 3:25, fourth is like the *S*
Hos. 13:13, He is an unwise *s*
Amos 7:14, prophet, nor was I a *s*
Mal. 1:6, *s* honors his father
Mt. 1:21, will bring forth a *S*
Mt. 3:17, "This is My beloved *S*
Mt. 8:29, Jesus, You *S* of God
Mt. 13:55, not the carpenter's *s*
Mt. 14:33, You are the *S* of God
Mt. 16:16, are the Christ, the *S*
Mt. 21:37, of all he sent his *s*
Mt. 22:42, Whose *S* is He
Mt. 22:45, 'Lord,' how is He his *S*
Mt. 23:15, him twice as much a *s*
Mt. 24:37, of the *S* of Man
Mt. 27:43, 'I am the *S* of God
Mt. 27:54, "Truly this was the *S*
Mk. 1:1, of Jesus Christ, the *S*
Lk. 1:32, called the *S* of the
Lk. 7:12, out, the only *s*
Lk. 10:6, "And if a *s* of peace
Lk. 15:19, to be called your *s*
Lk. 19:9, because he also is a *s*
Jn. 1:18, The only begotten *S*
Jn. 1:34, that this is the *S*
Jn. 3:18, of the only begotten *S*
Jn. 5:19, *S* can do nothing
Jn. 8:35, *s* abides forever
Jn. 9:35, you believe in the *S*
Jn. 10:36, I said, 'I am the *S*
Jn. 19:26, "Woman, behold your *s*
Acts 8:37, Jesus Christ is the *S*
Rom. 1:4, declared to be the *S*
Rom. 1:9, in the gospel of His *S*
Rom. 8:3, by sending His own *S*
Rom. 8:32, not spare His own *S*
1 Cor. 15:28, *S* Himself will also be
Gal. 2:20, live by faith in the *S*
Gal. 4:4, God sent forth His *S*
Gal. 4:7, longer a slave but a *s*
Eph. 4:13, the knowledge of the *S*
Phile. 10, you for my *s* Onesimus
Heb. 1:5, "You are My *S*
Heb. 3:6, but Christ as a *S* over His
Heb. 5:8, though He was a *S*
Heb. 7:3, but made like the *S*
Heb. 11:24, to be called the *s*
2 Pet. 1:17, "This is My beloved *S*
1 Jn. 2:23, Whoever denies the *S*
1 Jn. 5:10, God has given of His *S*
Rev. 1:13, One like the *S* of Man

SONG
Ex. 15:2, is my strength and *s*
Ps. 33:3, Sing to Him a new *s*
Ps. 40:3, He has put a new *s*
Ps. 42:8, in the night His *s*
Ps. 69:12, me, and I am the *s*
Ps. 137:3, asked of us a *s*
Ps. 144:9, I will sing a new *s*
Isa. 5:1, to my Well-beloved a *s*
Lam. 3:14, their taunting *s*
Lam. 3:63, I am their taunting *s*
Ezek. 33:32, as a very lovely *s*
Rev. 5:9, They sang a new *s*
Rev. 15:3, And they sing the *s*

SONGS
of Moses, at the Red Sea. Ex. 15; for water. Num. 21:17; for God's mercy. Dt. 32; and of the Lamb. Rev. 15:3
of Deborah. Jud. 5; of Hannah. 1 Sam. 2; of David. 2 Sam. 22 (*see* Psalms); of Mary. Lk. 1:46; of Zacharias. Lk. 1:68; of the angels. Lk. 2:13; of Simeon. Lk. 2:29; of the redeemed. Rev. 5:9; 19

SONGS
Job 35:10, my Maker, who gives *s*
Ps. 32:7, surround me with *s*
Ps. 119:54, have been my *s* in the
Ps. 137:3, Sing us one of the *s*
Prov. 25:20, is one who sings *s*
Eph. 5:19, and spiritual *s*

SONS
of God. Job 1:6; 38:7; Rom. 8:14; 2 Cor. 6:18; Heb. 2:10; 12:5; Jas. 1:18
obligations of. Eph. 5:1; Phil. 2:15; 1 Pet. 1:14; 2:9

SONS
Job 14:21, *s* come to honor
Ps. 45:16, shall be Your *s*
Song 2:3, my beloved among the *s*
Isa. 60:4, *s* shall come from afar
Jer. 49:1, "Has Israel no *s*
Lam. 4:2, The precious *s* of Zion
Hos. 1:10, 'You are the *s*
Mal. 3:3, He will purify the *s*
Mt. 17:26, to him, "Then the *s*
Lk. 6:35, and you will be *s*
Jn. 12:36, that you may become *s*
Acts 3:25, "You are *s* of the
Rom. 8:14, of God, these are *s*
Gal. 3:7, who are of faith are *s*
Gal. 4:5, the adoption as *s*
Gal. 4:6, because you are *s*
1 Th. 5:5, You are all *s* of light
Heb. 2:10, in bringing many *s*
Heb. 12:5, speaks to you as to *s*
Heb. 12:8, illegitimate and not *s*

SOON
Ps. 90:10, for it is *s* cut off
Ps. 106:13, *s* forgot His works

SOOTHED
Isa. 1:6, or bound up, or *s*

SORCERER
Dt. 18:10, omens, or a *s*
Acts 13:8, But Elymas the *s*

SORCERERS
Jer. 27:9, soothsayers, or your *s*
Rev. 22:15, outside are dogs and *s*

SORCERESS
Ex. 22:18, shall not permit a *s*

SORCERY
Isa. 47:9; 57:3; Acts 8:9; 13:6; Rev. 21:8; 22:15

SORCERY
Num. 23:23, For there is no *s*
Gal. 5:20, idolatry, *s*

SORES
Isa. 1:6, and putrefying *s*

Lk. 16:20, Lazarus, full of *s*

SORROW
godly. 2 Cor. 7:10
earthly. Gen. 42:38; Job 17:7; Ps. 13:2; 90:10; Prov. 10:22; Isa. 35:10; Lk. 22:45; Rom. 9:2; 1 Th. 4:13
consequence of sin. Gen. 3:16–17; Ps. 51

SORROW
Gen. 3:16, multiply your *s*
Job 41:22, *s* dances before him
Ps. 13:2, in my soul, having *s*
Ps. 38:17, *s* is continually
Ps. 116:3, I found trouble and *s*
Prov. 10:22, And He adds no *s*
Prov. 14:13, the heart may *s*
Eccl. 7:3, *S* is better than
Eccl. 11:10, Therefore remove *s*
Isa. 17:11, and desperate *s*
Isa. 65:14, you shall cry for *s*
Jer. 20:18, to see labor and *s*
Jer. 30:15, Your *s* is incurable
Jer. 45:3, added grief to my *s*
Zeph. 3:18, gather those who *s*
Lk. 22:45, them sleeping from *s*
Jn. 16:6, *s* has filled your
Jn. 16:20, *s* will be turned
Rom. 9:2, that I have great *s*
2 Cor. 7:10, *s* produces repentance
Phil. 2:27, lest I should have *s*
1 Th. 4:13, *s* as others who have
Rev. 21:4, no more death, nor *s*

SORROWFUL
1 Sam. 1:15, am a woman of *s* spirit
Ps. 69:29, But I am poor and *s*
Eccl. 2:23, For all his days are *s*
Jer. 31:25, replenished every *s*
Mt. 17:23, were exceedingly *s*
Mt. 19:22, he went away *s*
Mt. 26:38, soul is exceedingly *s*
Mk. 10:22, and went away *s*
Jn. 16:20, and you will be *s*
2 Cor. 2:2, if I make you *s*
Phil. 2:28, and I may be less *s*

SORROWS
2 Sam. 22:6, the *s* of Sheol
Job 21:17, *s* God distributes
Ps. 16:4, *s* shall be multiplied
Isa. 53:3, by men, a Man of *s*
Mt. 24:8, are the beginning of *s*
1 Tim. 6:10, through with many *s*

SORRY
Gen. 6:6, *s* that He had made man
Isa. 51:19, who will be *s* for you
Mt. 14:9, And the king was *s*
2 Cor. 7:9, For you were made *s*

SOUGHT
Ps. 34:4, I *s* the LORD
Ps. 119:10, whole heart I have *s*
Song 3:1, *s* the one I love
Isa. 62:12, you shall be called *S*
Ezek. 22:30, "So I *s* for a man
Ezek. 34:4, *s* what was lost
Hos. 12:4, *s* favor from Him
Zeph. 1:6, LORD, and have not *s*
Heb. 12:17, *s* it diligently

SOUL
Gen. 49:6, *s* enter their council
Dt. 6:5, with all your *s*
1 Sam. 18:1, was knit to the *s*
1 Chr. 22:19, your heart and your *s*
Job 10:1, "My *s* loathes my life
Job 16:4, as you do, if your *s*
Job 33:22, *s* draws near the Pit
Ps. 16:10, will not leave my *s*
Ps. 19:7, converting the *s*
Ps. 23:3, He restores my *s*
Ps. 34:2, *s* shall make its boast
Ps. 35:9, *s* shall be joyful
Ps. 42:5, you cast down, O my *s*
Ps. 62:1, *s* silently waits
Ps. 66:16, He has done for my *s*
Ps. 119:175, Let my *s* live
Ps. 139:14, *s* knows very well
Ps. 142:4, no one cares for my *s*
Prov. 6:32, so destroys his own *s*
Prov. 8:36, me wrongs his own *s*
Prov. 19:2, it is not good for a *s*
Prov. 27:7, A satisfied *s* loathes
Isa. 53:10, When You make His *s*
Isa. 55:2, *s* delight itself
Isa. 55:3, and your *s* shall live
Jer. 4:19, you have heard, O my *s*
Ezek. 18:4, the *s* of the father as
Hab. 2:4, the proud, his *s*
Mt. 10:28, able to destroy both *s*
Mt. 16:26, and loses his own *s*
Mt. 22:37, with all your *s*
Jn. 12:27, Now My *s* is troubled
Acts 4:32, of one heart and one *s*
1 Th. 5:23, your whole spirit, *s*
Heb. 10:39, to the saving of the *s*
Jas. 5:20, his way will save a *s*
2 Pet. 2:8, his righteous *s*
3 Jn. 2, health, just as your *s*

SOULS
Ps. 72:13, and will save the *s*
Prov. 11:30, and he who wins *s*
Jer. 31:12, *s* shall be like a
Jer. 38:16, who made our very *s*
Acts 15:24, unsettling your *s*
Jas. 1:21, is able to save your *s*

SOUND
Prov. 14:30, *s* heart is life
Eccl. 12:4, one rises up at the *s*
Ezek. 43:2, voice was like the *s*
Joel 2:1, *s* an alarm in My holy
Mt. 6:2, do not *s* a trumpet
2 Tim. 1:13, *s* words which you
Ti. 1:13, that they may be *s*

SOUNDNESS
Ps. 38:3, There is no *s* in my
Acts 3:16, him this perfect *s*

SOUNDS
Job 15:21, Dreadful *s* are in his
1 Cor. 14:7, a distinction in the *s*

SOW
Job 4:8, *s* trouble reap
Job 31:8, then let me *s*
Ps. 107:37, *s* fields and plant
Ps. 126:5, Those who *s* in tears
Eccl. 11:4, the wind will not *s*
Isa. 32:20, Blessed are you who *s*
Jer. 4:3, ground, and do not *s*
Hos. 8:7, "They *s* the wind
Hos. 10:12, *S* for yourselves
1 Cor. 15:36, *s* is not made alive

SOWER
Isa. 55:10, may give seed to the *s*
Mt. 13:3, "Behold, a *s* went

SOWN
Isa. 40:24, shall they be *s*
Jer. 2:2, a land not *s*
Hag. 1:6, "You have *s* much
1 Cor. 9:11, *s* spiritual things
1 Cor. 15:43, It is *s* in weakness
Jas. 3:18, of righteousness is *s*

SOWS
Prov. 11:18, *s* righteousness will
Mt. 13:37, *s* the good seed is the
Jn. 4:37, 'One *s* and another
2 Cor. 9:6, *s* sparingly will
Gal. 6:7, for whatever a man *s*

SPAIN, Rom. 15:24

SPARE
Dt. 29:20, The LORD would not *s*
Job 2:6, hand, but *s* his life
Ps. 72:13, *S* the poor and needy
Jer. 13:14, I will not pity nor *s*
Joel 2:17, say, "*S* Your people
Mal. 3:17, *s* them as a man spares
Rom. 8:32, He who did not *s*
Rom. 11:21, *s* the natural branches
Rom. 11:21, branches, He may not *s*
1 Cor. 7:28, flesh, but I would *s*
2 Pet. 2:4, if God did not *s*

SPARES
Prov. 13:24, *s* his rod hates his

SPARK
Isa. 1:31, the work of it as a *s*

SPARKLES
Prov. 23:31, it is red, when it *s*

SPARKS
Job 5:7, to trouble, as the *s*
Isa. 50:11, *s* you have kindled

SPARROW
Ps. 84:3, *s* has found a home
Ps. 102:7, awake, and am like a *s*

SPARROWS
Mt. 10:31, more value than many *s*

SPAT
Mt. 27:30, Then they *s* on Him
Mk. 7:33, in his ears, and He *s*

SPEAK
Num. 22:35, only the word that I *s*
Jud. 6:39, *s* just once more
1 Ki. 12:7, *s* good words to them
Job 11:5, oh, that God would *s*
Job 13:7, Will you *s* wickedly
Job 33:14, For God may *s* in one
Job 41:3, Will he *s* softly to
Prov. 23:9, Do not *s* in the
Eccl. 3:7, and a time to *s*
Isa. 8:20, If they do not *s*
Isa. 28:11, tongue He will *s*
Jer. 20:9, *s* anymore in His name
Hab. 2:3, at the end it will *s*
Zech. 8:16, *s* each man the truth
Mt. 10:19, or what you should *s*
Mt. 10:20, it is not you who *s*
Lk. 6:26, to you when all men *s*

Jn. 3:11, *s* what We know and
Jn. 8:38, *s* what I have seen
Jn. 16:13, He hears He will *s*
Acts 2:4, Spirit and began to *s*
1 Cor. 12:30, Do all *s* with tongues
1 Cor. 14:19, I would rather *s*
Jas. 2:12, So *s* and so do as

SPEAKING
Isa. 58:13, *s* your own words
Isa. 65:24, while they are still *s*
2 Cor. 13:3, a proof of Christ *s*
1 Pet. 2:1, envy, and all evil *s*

SPEAKS
Ex. 33:11, to face, as a man *s*
Dt. 5:24, this day that God *s*
Isa. 52:6, day that I am He who *s*
Jn. 3:34, He whom God has sent *s*
Jn. 8:44, When he *s* a lie
Heb. 11:4, he being dead still *s*
Heb. 12:24, of sprinkling that *s*

SPEAR
Jer. 6:23, lay hold on bow and *s*
Jn. 19:34, His side with a *s*

SPEARS
Ps. 57:4, whose teeth are *s*
Isa. 2:4, and their *s* into
Joel 3:10, pruninghooks into *s*

SPECIAL
people of God. Dt. 14:2; Ps. 135:4; Ti. 2:14; 1 Pet. 2:9

SPECK
Mt. 7:3, do you look at the *s*

SPECTACLE
Nah. 3:6, and make you a *s*
1 Cor. 4:9, we have been made a *s*
Col. 2:15, He made a public *s*
Heb. 10:33, you were made a *s*

SPEECH
Gen. 11:1, one language and one *s*
Dt. 32:2, drop as the rain, my *s*
Job 29:22, *s* settled on them as
Ps. 19:3, There is no *s* nor
Prov. 17:7, *s* is not becoming
Isa. 29:4, your *s* shall be low
Isa. 33:19, a people of obscure *s*
Jn. 8:43, not understand My *s*
Rom. 16:18, *s* deceive the hearts
2 Cor. 10:10, his *s* contemptible
2 Cor. 11:6, I am untrained in *s*
Col. 4:6, *s* always be with grace

SPEECHLESS
Prov. 31:8, your mouth for the *s*
Mt. 22:12, And he was *s*

SPEED
Isa. 5:26, they shall come with *s*

SPEEDILY
Ezra 7:26, judgment be executed *s*
Ps. 31:2, to me, deliver me *s*
Ps. 102:2, I call, answer me *s*

SPEND
Isa. 55:2, Why do you *s* money for
Lk. 10:35, whatever more you *s*
2 Cor. 12:15, I will very gladly *s*
Jas. 4:3, amiss, that you may *s*

SPENT
Lev. 26:20, strength shall be *s*
Ps. 31:10, For my life is *s*
Isa. 49:4, in vain, I have *s*
Lk. 15:14, "But when he had *s*

SPEW
Rev. 3:16, nor hot, I will *s*

SPIDER
Prov. 30:28, *s* skillfully grasps

SPIES
sent into Canaan, by Moses. Num. 13:3,17,26; 14:36; Dt. 1:22; Heb. 3:17
sent to Jericho, by Joshua. Josh. 2:1,4,17,23; 6:17,23

SPIES
Gen. 42:9, to them, "You are *s*
Josh. 6:23, men who had been *s*
Lk. 20:20, *s* who pretended

SPIKENARD, Song 1:12
Mary anoints Christ with. Mk. 14:3; Lk. 7:37; Jn. 12:3

SPIN
Mt. 6:28, neither toil nor *s*

SPINDLE
Prov. 31:19, her hand holds the *s*

SPIRIT
of Christ. Rom. 8:9; 1 Pet. 1:11
of Antichrist. 1 Jn. 4:3
of man. Eccl. 3:21; 12:7; Zech. 12:1; 1 Cor. 2:11
broken. Ps. 51:17; Prov. 15:13; 17:22
born of. Jn. 3:5; Gal. 4:29
fruit of. Gal. 5:22; Eph. 5:9
of truth. Jn. 14:17; 15:26; 16:13
bondage. Rom. 8:15
divination. Acts 16:16
muteness, etc. Mk. 9:17
fear. 2 Tim. 1:7
jealousy. Num. 5:14
slumber. Rom. 11:8

SPIRIT
Gen. 1:2, And the *S* of God was
Gen. 6:3, *S* shall not strive
Gen. 41:38, in whom is the *S*
Ex. 35:21, and everyone whose *s*
Num. 11:17, *S* that is upon you
Num. 11:26, And the *S* rested upon
Num. 11:29, LORD would put His *S*
Num. 14:24, he has a different *s*
Num. 27:18, in whom is the *S*
2 Ki. 2:9, portion of your *s*
2 Chr. 9:4, there was no more *s*
2 Chr. 18:20, *s* came forward and
Neh. 9:20, also gave Your good *S*
Neh. 9:30, against them by Your *S*
Job 4:15, Then a *s* passed before
Job 26:4, And whose *s* came from
Job 33:4, The *S* of God has made
Ps. 31:5, hand I commit my *s*
Ps. 78:8, *s* was not faithful
Ps. 104:30, You send forth Your *S*
Ps. 143:10, Your *S* is good
Prov. 20:27, The *s* of a man is the
Eccl. 3:21, Who knows the *s*
Eccl. 12:7, *s* will return to God
Isa. 26:9, night, yes, by my *s*
Isa. 29:10, out on you the *s*
Isa. 31:3, are flesh, and not *s*
Isa. 34:16, *S* has gathered them
Isa. 38:16, is the life of my *s*
Isa. 42:1, I have put My *S*
Isa. 48:16, and His *S* have sent Me
Isa. 57:16, *s* would fail before Me
Isa. 61:1, "The *S* of the Lord
Ezek. 2:2, *S* entered me when He
Ezek. 3:12, the *S* lifted me up
Ezek. 13:3, who follow their own *s*
Ezek. 18:31, new heart and a new *s*
Ezek. 21:7, be feeble, every *s*
Ezek. 36:27, "I will put My *S*
Dan. 4:8, in him is the *S*
Dan. 5:12, as an excellent *s*
Mic. 2:11, walk in a false *s*
Zech. 12:1, and forms the *s*
Mt. 3:16, and He saw the *S*
Mt. 12:18, I will put My *S*
Mk. 1:10, *S* descending upon Him
Mk. 1:12, Immediately the *S*
Mk. 14:38, *s* indeed is willing
Lk. 1:17, go before Him in the *s*
Lk. 4:14, in the power of the *S*
Lk. 9:55, manner of *s* you are of
Lk. 23:46, hands I commit My *s*
Lk. 24:37, they had seen a *s*
Lk. 24:39, *s* does not have flesh
Jn. 4:24, "God is *S*
Jn. 6:63, I speak to you are *s*
Jn. 13:21, He was troubled in *s*
Jn. 14:17, the *S* of truth
Jn. 16:13, when He, the *S*
Acts 23:9, but if a *s* or an angel
Rom. 1:9, whom I serve with my *s*
Rom. 8:5, according to the *S*
Rom. 8:9, the flesh but in the *S*
Rom. 8:9, does not have the *S*
Rom. 8:16, *s* that we are children
Rom. 8:27, what the mind of the *S*
1 Cor. 2:10, to us through His *S*
1 Cor. 7:40, also have the *S*
1 Cor. 12:4, gifts, but the same *S*
1 Cor. 14:14, in a tongue, my *s*
2 Cor. 3:6, but the *S* gives life
2 Cor. 3:17, Now the Lord is the *S*
2 Cor. 4:13, we have the same *s*
Gal. 3:3, Having begun in the *S*
Gal. 4:6, has sent forth the *S*
Gal. 6:8, he who sows to the *S*
Eph. 1:13, with the Holy *S*
Eph. 1:17, may give to you the *s*
Eph. 4:3, the unity of the *S*
Eph. 4:4, is one body and one *S*
Phil. 1:27, stand fast in one *s*
Col. 2:5, yet I am with you in *s*
1 Th. 5:23, and may your whole *s*
1 Tim. 4:1, *S* expressly says that
Heb. 4:12, division of soul and *s*
Heb. 9:14, through the eternal *S*
Jas. 4:5, *S* who dwells in us
1 Pet. 3:18, made alive by the *S*
1 Jn. 3:24, *S* whom He has given
1 Jn. 4:1, do not believe every *s*
1 Jn. 4:2, By this you know the *S*
1 Jn. 4:6, By this we know the *s*
1 Jn. 4:13, has given us of His *S*
1 Jn. 5:6, *S* who bears witness
Jude 19, not having the *S*

Rev. 1:10, I was in the *S* on the
Rev. 2:7, him hear what the *S*
Rev. 22:17, And the *S* and the

SPIRITS
Num. 16:22, God, the God of the *s*
Ps. 104:4, who makes His angels *s*
Prov. 16:2, the LORD weighs the *s*
Mt. 10:1, power over unclean *s*
1 Tim. 4:1, heed to deceiving *s*
Heb. 1:14, not all ministering *s*
Heb. 12:9, to the Father of *s*
1 Pet. 3:19, and preached to the *s*
1 Jn. 4:1, spirit, but test the *s*

SPIRITUAL
1 Cor. 2:15, *s* judges all things
1 Cor. 3:1, *s* people but as to
1 Cor. 14:37, to be a prophet or *s*
1 Cor. 15:46, However, the *s* is not
Gal. 6:1, *s* restore such a one

SPIRITUALLY
Rom. 8:6, *s* minded is life
1 Cor. 2:14, because they are *s*

SPITEFULLY
Mt. 5:44, for those who *s*

SPITTING
Isa. 50:6, face from shame and *s*

SPLENDOR
Ps. 145:5, on the glorious *s*
Lam. 1:6, of Zion all her *s*

SPOIL
Ps. 44:10, hate us have taken *s*
Isa. 9:3, when they divide the *s*
Isa. 53:12, He shall divide the *s*
Nah. 2:9, Take *s* of silver
Zech. 14:1, *s* will be divided

SPOILER
Isa. 54:16, I have created the *s*

SPOKE
Isa. 66:4, *s* they did not hear
Mal. 3:16, who feared the LORD *s*
Jn. 7:46, "No man ever *s*
Jn. 9:29, "We know that God *s*
1 Cor. 13:11, I was a child, I *s*
Heb. 1:1, in various ways *s*
2 Pet. 1:21, *s* as they were moved

SPOKEN
Num. 14:28, 'just as you have *s*
Ps. 62:11, God has *s* once
Isa. 45:19, I have not *s* in secret
Mal. 3:13, 'What have we *s*
1 Cor. 10:30, why am I evil *s*

SPOKESMAN
Ex. 4:16, "So he shall be your *s*

SPONGE
Mt. 27:48, them ran and took a *s*

SPOT
Song 4:7, and there is no *s*
Eph. 5:27, church, not having *s*
1 Tim. 6:14, commandment without *s*
Heb. 9:14, Himself without *s*

SPOTS
2 Pet. 2:13, They are *s* and
Jude 12, These are *s* in your

SPREAD
Ezra 9:5, fell on my knees and *s*
Ps. 140:5, they have *s* a net by
Ezek. 2:10, Then He *s* it before me
Acts 6:7, Then the word of God *s*
Acts 13:49, the Lord was being *s*
2 Tim. 2:17, their message will *s*

SPREADS
Job 9:8, He alone *s* out the
Isa. 40:22, *s* them out like a tent
Lam. 1:17, Zion *s* out her hands

SPRING
Ps. 85:11, Truth shall *s* out of
Prov. 25:26, is like a murky *s*
Song 4:12, sister, my spouse, a *s*
Isa. 42:9, *s* forth I tell you
Ezek. 29:21, of Israel to *s* forth
Hos. 13:15, *s* shall become dry
Jas. 3:11, *s* send forth fresh

SPRINGING
Jn. 4:14, a fountain of water *s*
Heb. 12:15, of bitterness *s*

SPRINGS
Job 38:16, "Have you entered the *s*
Ps. 104:10, He sends the *s* into
Isa. 35:7, and the thirsty land *s*
Isa. 41:18, and the dry land *s*

SPRINKLE
Isa. 52:15, He *s* many nations
Ezek. 36:25, "Then I will *s*

SPRINKLED
Job 2:12, *s* dust on his head
Heb. 9:19, and hyssop, and *s*
Heb. 10:22, having our hearts *s*

SPRINKLING
of blood, the Passover. Ex. 12:22; Heb. 11:28
the covenant of. Ex. 24:8; Heb. 9:13
cleansing the leper by. Lev. 14:7
of oil. Lev. 14:16
of the blood of Christ. Heb. 10:22; 12:24; 1 Pet. 1:2

SPROUT
Job 14:7, down, that it will *s*
Mk. 4:27, and the seed should *s*

SPY
Num. 13:16; Josh. 2:1; Gal. 2:4

SQUARES
Prov. 1:20, voice in the open *s*
Song 3:2, *s* I will seek the one

STABILITY
Isa. 33:6, will be the *s* of your

STAFF
Gen. 32:10, this Jordan with my *s*
Ex. 12:11, your feet, and your *s*
Ps. 23:4, Your rod and Your *s*
Isa. 14:5, LORD has broken the *s*
Jer. 48:17, 'How the strong *s*
Ezek. 29:6, they have been a *s*
Heb. 11:21, on the top of his *s*

STAGGER
Job 12:25, and He makes them *s*
Jer. 25:16, they will drink and *s*

STAGGERS
Isa. 19:14, as a drunken man *s*

STAKES
Isa. 33:20, *s* will ever be removed

STALLS
Hab. 3:17, be no herd in the *s*

STAMMERERS
Isa. 32:4, *s* will be ready

STAMMERING
Isa. 28:11, For with *s* lips and
Isa. 33:19, *s* tongue that you

STAMPING
Jer. 47:3, At the noise of the *s*

STAND
Dt. 7:24, one shall be able to *s*
1 Sam. 6:20, "Who is able to *s*
Job 8:15, but it does not *s*
Job 19:25, lives, and He shall *s*
Ps. 1:5, ungodly shall not *s*
Ps. 10:1, Why do You *s* afar off
Ps. 24:3, Or who may *s* in His
Ps. 94:16, Who will *s* up for me
Ps. 109:6, and let an accuser *s*
Prov. 22:29, he will not *s* before
Eccl. 8:3, Do not take your *s*
Isa. 7:7, "It shall not *s*
Jer. 6:16, "*S* in the ways and
Jer. 35:19, not lack a man to *s*
Jer. 44:28, whose words will *s*
Dan. 2:44, and it shall *s*
Dan. 11:17, but she shall not *s*
Nah. 1:6, Who can *s* before His
Mal. 3:2, And who can *s* when He
Mk. 3:24, that kingdom cannot *s*
Rom. 14:4, he will be made to *s*
1 Cor. 16:13, Watch, *s* fast in the
2 Cor. 1:24, for by faith you *s*
Eph. 6:13, having done all, to *s*
Eph. 6:14, *S* therefore
Phil. 4:1, *s* fast in the LORD
1 Th. 3:8, now we live, if you *s*
1 Pet. 5:12, of God in which you *s*
Rev. 3:20, "Behold, I *s* at the

STANDARD
Isa. 59:19, LORD will lift up a *s*
Jer. 4:6, Set up the *s* toward

STANDING
Zech. 3:1, the LORD, and Satan *s*
Mt. 6:5, they love to pray *s*
Acts 7:56, and the Son of Man *s*
Rev. 19:17, Then I saw an angel *s*

STANDS
Isa. 3:13, The LORD *s* up to plead
1 Cor. 10:12, him who thinks he *s*

STAR
at Christ's birth. Mt. 2:2
morning star, Christ. 2 Pet. 1:19; Rev. 22:16
great star falls from heaven. Rev. 8:10; 9:1

STAR
Num. 24:17, *S* shall come out of
Mt. 2:2, For we have seen His *s*
1 Cor. 15:41, for one *s* differs from
Rev. 2:28, give him the morning *s*

Rev. 8:10, And a great *s* fell
Rev. 22:16, Bright and Morning *S*

STARS
created. Gen. 1:16
mentioned. Gen. 15:5; 37:9; Jud. 5:20; 1 Cor. 15:41; Heb. 11:12; Jude 13; Rev. 8:12; 12:1
not to be worshiped. Dt. 4:19
morning. Job 38:7

STARS
Gen. 1:16, He made the *s* also
Job 25:5, *s* are not pure in His
Job 38:7, when the morning *s*
Ps. 8:3, the moon and the *s*
Ps. 148:3, praise Him, all you *s*
Heb. 11:12, born as many as the *s*
Jude 13, wandering *s* for whom
Rev. 12:1, a garland of twelve *s*

STARVED
Job 18:12, His strength is *s*

STATE
Ps. 39:5, man at his best *s*
Ps. 136:23, us in our lowly *s*
Mt. 12:45, and the last *s* of that
Phil. 4:11, learned in whatever *s*

STATURE
Mt. 6:27, add one cubit to his *s*
Lk. 2:52, in wisdom and *s*
Eph. 4:13, the measure of the *s*

STATUTE
Lev. 3:17, shall be a perpetual *s*

STATUTES
Ps. 19:8, the *s* of the LORD are
Ps. 119:12, Teach me Your *s*
Ps. 119:54, *s* have been my songs
Ezek. 5:6, not walked in My *s*

STAY
Prov. 7:11, her feet would not *s*
Mt. 26:38, *S* here and watch
Lk. 19:5, for today I must *s*
1 Pet. 1:17, the time of your *s*

STEADFAST
Job 11:15, yes, you could be *s*
Ps. 57:7, O God, my heart is *s*
Ps. 78:37, their heart was not *s*
Ps. 112:7, his heart is *s*
Dan. 6:26, God, and *s* forever
1 Cor. 15:58, brethren, be *s*
Col. 1:23, faith, grounded and *s*
Heb. 2:2, angels proved *s*
Heb. 3:14, of our confidence *s*
Heb. 6:19, soul, both sure and *s*
1 Pet. 5:9, Resist him, *s* in the

STEADFASTLY
Lk. 9:51, *s* set His face to go
Acts 2:42, And they continued *s*
Rom. 12:12, continuing *s* in

STEADFASTNESS
Col. 2:5, good order and the *s*
2 Pet. 3:17, from your own *s*

STEADILY
2 Cor. 3:13, could not look *s*

STEADY
Ex. 17:12, and his hands were *s*

STEAL
Ex. 20:15, "You shall not *s*
Jer. 7:9, "Will you *s*
Jer. 23:30, *s* My words every one
Mt. 6:19, thieves break in and *s*
Mt. 27:64, night and *s* Him away
Mk. 10:19, murder, 'Do not *s*
Jn. 10:10, not come except to *s*
Rom. 2:21, a man should not *s*
Eph. 4:28, Let him who stole *s*

STEEP
Ezek. 38:20, *s* places shall fall
Mic. 1:4, waters poured down a *s*
Mt. 8:32, violently down the *s*

STEM
Isa. 11:1, forth a Rod from the *s*

STENCH
Isa. 3:24, there will be a *s*
Jn. 11:39, this time there is a *s*

STEP
1 Sam. 20:3, there is but a *s*
Job 31:7, *s* has turned from the

STEPHEN
English form of Stephanas, deacon and protomartyr. Acts 6:5,8; 7:58

STEPS
Job 23:11, has held fast to His *s*
Job 31:4, and count all my *s*
Job 34:21, and He sees all his *s*
Ps. 17:5, Uphold my *s* in Your
Ps. 37:23, The *s* of a good man
Ps. 37:31, of his *s* shall slide
Ps. 40:2, and established my *s*
Ps. 56:6, hide, they mark my *s*
Ps. 73:2, *s* had nearly slipped
Ps. 119:133, Direct my *s* by Your
Prov. 4:12, *s* will not be hindered
Prov. 16:9, the LORD directs his *s*
Prov. 20:24, A man's *s* are of the
Jer. 10:23, to direct his own *s*
1 Pet. 2:21, should follow His *s*

STEWARD
Lk. 12:42, faithful and wise *s*
Lk. 16:2, you can no longer be *s*
Lk. 16:8, commended the unjust *s*
Ti. 1:7, be blameless, as a *s*

STEWARDS
1 Cor. 4:1, of Christ and *s*
1 Pet. 4:10, one another, as good *s*

STEWARDSHIP
1 Cor. 9:17, entrusted with a *s*

STICK
Job 33:21, and his bones *s*
Ezek. 37:16, 'For Joseph, the *s*

STICKS
Num. 15:32, a man gathering *s*
Ezek. 37:20, "And the *s* on which

STIFF
Dt. 31:27, rebellion and your *s*
Ps. 75:5, do not speak with a *s*

STIFF-NECKED
2 Chr. 30:8, "Now do not be *s*
Acts 7:51, "You *s* and

STILL
Ps. 4:4, on your bed, and be *s*
Ps. 65:7, *s* the noise of the
Ps. 76:8, earth feared and was *s*
Ps. 107:29, that its waves are *s*
Ps. 139:18, When I awake, I am *s*
Isa. 42:14, time, I have been *s*
Jer. 47:6, rest and be *s*
Mk. 4:39, sea, "Peace, be *s*
Rev. 22:11, let him be holy *s*

STILLBORN
Job 3:16, I not hidden like a *s*
Ps. 58:8, as it goes, like a *s*
Eccl. 6:3, burial, I say that a *s*

STINGS
Prov. 23:32, like a serpent, and *s*

STIR
Job 41:10, that he would dare *s*
Ps. 35:23, *S* up Yourself
2 Tim. 1:6, I remind you to *s*
Heb. 10:24, another in order to *s*

STIRRED
2 Chr. 36:22, fulfilled, the LORD *s*
Ps. 39:2, and my sorrow was *s*
Hag. 1:14, So the LORD *s* up the

STIRS
Job 17:8, and the innocent *s*
Isa. 14:9, it *s* up the dead for
Isa. 64:7, on Your name, who *s*

STOCKS
Job 13:27, put my feet in the *s*
Jer. 20:2, *s* that were in the

STOIC
Acts 17:18, and *S* philosophers

STOICS
philosophers whose founder taught in a famous porch or Stoa. Acts 17:18

STOMACH
Mt. 15:17, mouth goes into the *s*
Mk. 7:19, his heart but his *s*
1 Cor. 6:13, Foods for the *s*

STOMACH'S
1 Tim. 5:23, little wine for your *s*

STONE
corner, Christ is. (Ps. 118:22; Isa. 28:16); Mt. 21:42; Mk. 12:10; 1 Pet. 2:6

STONE
Gen. 35:14, him, a pillar of *s*
Ex. 15:5, to the bottom like a *s*
Josh. 24:27, *s* shall be a witness
Job 41:24, heart is as hard as *s*
Ps. 118:22, *s* which the builders
Prov. 27:3, *s* is heavy and sand is
Isa. 28:16, I lay in Zion a *s*
Isa. 28:16, foundation, a tried *s*
Ezek. 36:26, take the heart of *s*
Dan. 2:34, You watched while a *s*
Hab. 2:11, *s* will cry out from
Hab. 2:19, to silent *s*
Mt. 7:9, will give him a *s*
Mt. 21:44, *s* will be broken
Mt. 27:66, secure, sealing the *s*
Lk. 20:17, *s* which the builders

Jn. 8:7, you, let him throw a *s*
Jn. 10:32, those works do you *s*
Jn. 11:8, Jews sought to *s* You
2 Cor. 3:3, not on tablets of *s*
1 Pet. 2:4, Him as to a living *s*
Rev. 2:17, give him a white *s*
Rev. 18:21, angel took up a *s*
Rev. 21:11, like a jasper *s*

STONED
Acts 7:59, *s* Stephen as he was
2 Cor. 11:25, once I was *s*
Heb. 11:37, They were *s*

STONES
precious, in the high priest's breastplate. Ex. 28:17
in the temple. 1 Chr. 29:2; 2 Chr. 3:6
in the New Jerusalem. Rev. 21:19

STONES
Isa. 54:11, I will lay your *s*
Isa. 57:6, Among the smooth *s*
Mt. 3:9, Abraham from these *s*
Mt. 4:3, command that these *s*
Mk. 13:1, see what manner of *s*
1 Pet. 2:5, also, as living *s*
Rev. 21:19, kinds of precious *s*

STONING
Lev. 20:2; 24:14; Dt. 13:10; 17:5; 22:21
of Achan. Josh. 7:25; Naboth. 1 Ki. 21; Stephen. Acts 7:58; Paul. Acts 14:19; 2 Cor. 11:25

STONY
Ezek. 11:19, them, and take the *s*
Mk. 4:5, some fell on *s* ground

STOOPED
Jn. 8:8, And again He *s* down

STOPPED
Ps. 63:11, speak lies shall be *s*
Lk. 8:44, her flow of blood *s*

STORE
Lk. 12:17, no room to *s* my crops
2 Pet. 3:7, exist are kept in *s*

STORK
Ps. 104:17, *s* has her home in the
Jer. 8:7, "Even the *s* in the

STORM
Ps. 55:8, from the windy *s*
Ps. 107:29, He calms the *s*
Prov. 1:27, terror comes like a *s*
Isa. 4:6, for a shelter from *s*
Isa. 25:4, a refuge from the *s*
Isa. 28:2, and a destroying *s*
Ezek. 38:9, coming like a *s*
Nah. 1:3, whirlwind and in the *s*

STOUTHEARTED
Ps. 76:5, *s* were plundered

STRAIGHT
Ps. 5:8, make Your way *s*
Eccl. 7:13, for who can make *s*
Isa. 40:3, make *s* in the desert a
Ezek. 1:7, Their legs were *s*
Lk. 3:4, LORD, make His paths *s*
Acts 9:11, to the street called *S*
Heb. 12:13, and make *s* paths for

STRAIGHTFORWARD
Gal. 2:14, that they were not *s*

STRAIN
Mt. 23:24, "Blind guides, who *s*

STRAITS
Dt. 28:53, and desperate *s*

STRANGE
Hos. 8:12, were considered a *s*
Lk. 5:26, "We have seen *s*
Acts 17:20, are bringing some *s*
1 Pet. 4:4, these, they think it *s*
1 Pet. 4:12, *s* thing happened

STRANGER
Gen. 42:7, but he acted as a *s*
Ex. 2:22, "I have been a *s*
Ex. 22:21, neither mistreat a *s*
Dt. 10:18, and loves the *s*
Ps. 69:8, I have become a *s*
Prov. 11:15, *s* will suffer for it
Prov. 14:10, *s* does not share its
Jer. 14:8, should You be like a *s*
Mt. 25:35, I was a *s* and you
Lk. 24:18, "Are You the only *s*

STRANGERS, *see* SOJOURNERS

STRANGERS
Gen. 15:13, descendants will be *s*
Ps. 109:11, *s* plunder his labor
Ps. 146:9, watches over the *s*
Isa. 1:7, *s* devour your land
Isa. 61:5, *S* shall stand and feed
Jn. 10:5, know the voice of *s*
Eph. 2:12, of Israel and *s*
Eph. 2:19, you are no longer *s*
1 Tim. 5:10, if she has lodged *s*
Heb. 11:13, that they were *s*
Heb. 13:2, forget to entertain *s*
3 Jn. 5, the brethren and for *s*

STRANGLED, Acts 15:20; 21:25

STRANGLING
Job 7:15, that my soul chooses *s*

STRAP
Mk. 1:7, than I, whose sandal *s*

STRAW
Job 21:18, They are like *s*
1 Cor. 3:12, stones, wood, hay, *s*

STRAY
Ps. 119:21, the cursed, who *s*
Mic. 3:5, who make my people *s*

STRAYED
Ps. 119:110, yet I have not *s*
1 Tim. 6:10, for which some have *s*
2 Tim. 2:18, who have *s* concerning

STREAM
Isa. 30:28, like an overflowing *s*
Isa. 30:33, of the LORD, like a *s*
Isa. 66:12, like a flowing *s*

STREAMS
Job 28:11, He dams up the *s*
Ps. 78:16, He also brought *s*
Ps. 126:4, O LORD, as the *s*

STREET
Isa. 42:2, to be heard in the *s*
Acts 9:11, *s* called Straight
Rev. 21:21, And the *s* of the city
Rev. 22:2, In the middle of its *s*

STREETS
Mt. 6:5, the corners of the *s*
Lk. 13:26, You taught in our *s*
Lk. 14:21, out quickly into the *s*

STRENGTH
of Israel, the Lord. Ex. 15:2; 1 Sam. 15:29; Ps. 27:1; 28:8; 29:11; 46:1; 81:1; Isa. 26:4; Joel 3:16; Zech. 12:5
—— of sin. Rom. 7; 1 Cor. 15:56
—— made perfect in weakness. 2 Cor. 12:9; Heb. 11:34; Ps. 8:2

STRENGTH
Ex. 13:3, for by *s* of hand the
Josh. 14:11, just as my *s* was then
Jud. 5:21, my soul, march on in *s*
Jud. 8:21, a man is, so is his *s*
1 Sam. 2:9, *s* no man shall
2 Sam. 22:3, the God of my *s*
2 Sam. 22:40, have armed me with *s*
1 Chr. 16:28, the LORD glory and *s*
Job 6:12, Is my *s* the *s*
Job 12:13, Him are wisdom and *s*
Job 39:11, him because his *s*
Ps. 8:2, You have ordained *s*
Ps. 18:1, love You, O LORD, my *s*
Ps. 27:1, The LORD is the *s*
Ps. 28:8, The LORD is their *s*
Ps. 29:11, The LORD will give *s*
Ps. 33:16, delivered by great *s*
Ps. 37:39, He is their *s* in the
Ps. 43:2, are the God of my *s*
Ps. 46:1, is our refuge and *s*
Ps. 68:35, is He who gives *s*
Ps. 71:16, I will go in the *s*
Ps. 73:26, but God is the *s*
Ps. 84:7, They go from *s* to
Ps. 89:17, the glory of their *s*
Ps. 96:6, *s* and beauty are in
Ps. 138:3, made me bold with *s*
Prov. 10:29, of the LORD is *s*
Prov. 24:5, knowledge increases *s*
Prov. 31:25, *S* and honor are her
Eccl. 9:16, is better than *s*
Eccl. 10:17, for *s* and not for
Isa. 25:4, For You have been a *s*
Isa. 27:5, him take hold of My *s*
Isa. 40:26, of His might and the *s*
Isa. 40:29, might He increases *s*
Isa. 44:12, works it with the *s*
Isa. 45:24, righteousness and *s*
Isa. 52:1, Put on your *s*
Jer. 16:19, O LORD, my *s* and my
Hag. 2:22, I will destroy the *s*
Lk. 1:51, He has shown *s* with
Rom. 5:6, were still without *s*
2 Cor. 12:9, *s* is made perfect
Rev. 3:8, you have a little *s*

STRENGTHEN
Ps. 27:14, and He shall *s*
Isa. 35:3, *S* the weak hands
Zech. 10:12, "So I will *s* them in
Lk. 22:32, *s* your brethren
Heb. 12:12, *s* the hands
Rev. 3:2, *s* the things

STRENGTHENED
Ezek. 34:4, weak you have not *s*

Rom. 4:20, unbelief, but was *s*
Eph. 3:16, of His glory, to be *s*
2 Tim. 4:17, stood with me and *s*

STRENGTHENING
Acts 14:22, *s* the souls of the

STRENGTHENS
Eccl. 7:19, *s* the wise more than
Phil. 4:13, through Christ who *s*

STRETCH
Ps. 68:31, will quickly *s* out her
Mt. 12:13, said to the man, "*S*
Jn. 21:18, are old, you will *s*

STRETCHED
Ps. 88:9, I have *s* out my hands
Jer. 10:12, His wisdom, and has *s*
Rom. 10:21, "All day long I have *s*

STRETCHES
Job 15:25, For he *s* out his hand

STRICKEN
Ps. 102:4, My heart is *s* and
Isa. 53:4, yet we esteemed Him *s*
Isa. 53:8, of My people He was *s*
Jer. 5:3, You have *s* them
Hos. 6:1, He has *s*

STRIFE
Prov. 3:30; 17:14; 25:8; 26:17; 1 Cor. 3:3; Gal. 5:20; Phil. 2:3,14; 2 Tim. 2:23; Ti. 3:9; Jas. 3:14
its origin. Prov. 10:12; 13:10; 15:18; 16:28; 22:10; 23:29; 26:20; 28:25; 30:33; 2 Tim. 2:23; Jas. 4:1
its results. Lev. 24:10; Gal. 5:15; Jas. 3:16
deprecated. 1 Cor. 1:11; 3:3; 6; 11:1

STRIFE
Gen. 13:8, let there be no *s*
Ps. 80:6, You have made us a *s*
Ps. 106:32, at the waters of *s*
Prov. 10:12, Hatred stirs up *s*
Prov. 13:10, comes nothing but *s*
Prov. 15:18, man stirs up *s*
Prov. 17:19, transgression loves *s*
Jer. 15:10, borne me, a man of *s*
Rom. 13:13, and lust, not in *s*
Phil. 1:15, even from envy and *s*
1 Tim. 6:4, which come envy, *s*

STRIKE
2 Ki. 6:18, said, "*S* this people
Ps. 121:6, The sun shall not *s*
Ps. 141:5, Let the righteous *s*
Prov. 19:25, *S* a scoffer
Ezek. 21:14, *s* your hands
Zech. 10:11, *s* the waves of the sea
Zech. 13:7, "*S* the Shepherd
Mal. 4:6, *s* the earth with a
Mt. 26:31, 'I will *s* the Shepherd
Jn. 18:23, if well, why do you *s*
Rev. 7:16, the sun shall not *s*
Rev. 11:6, *s* the earth with all

STRINGED
Isa. 14:11, of your *s* instruments
Amos 5:23, of your *s* instruments

STRIP
Isa. 32:11, *S* yourselves
Hos. 2:3, *s* her naked and expose

STRIPES
Ps. 89:32, their iniquity with *s*
Isa. 53:5, *s* we are healed
Lk. 12:47, be beaten with many *s*
2 Cor. 11:24, I received forty *s*
1 Pet. 2:24, *s* you were healed

STRIVE
Gen. 6:3, My Spirit shall not *s*
Ps. 103:9, He will not always *s*
Prov. 3:30, Do not *s* with a man
Isa. 45:9, Let the potsherd *s*
Lk. 13:24, "*S* to enter through
2 Tim. 2:14, the Lord not to *s*

STRIVING
Prov. 20:3, for a man to stop *s*

STROKE
Jer. 14:17, with a mighty *s*

STRONG
1 Sam. 4:9, "Be *s* and conduct
Job 9:19, indeed He is *s*
Ps. 24:8, The LORD *s* and mighty
Ps. 60:9, bring me to the *s*
Ps. 89:13, *s* is Your hand
Prov. 24:5, A wise man is *s*
Isa. 1:31, *s* shall be as tinder
Isa. 26:1, "We have a *s* city
Joel 3:10, the weak say, 'I am *s*
Lk. 11:21, "When a *s* man
Rom. 15:1, We then who are *s*
2 Cor. 12:10, I am weak, then I am *s*
2 Cor. 13:9, are weak and you are *s*
Eph. 6:10, my brethren, be *s*
Heb. 11:34, weakness were made *s*
Rev. 18:8, *s* is the Lord God

STRONGHOLD
Ps. 18:2, of my salvation, my *s*
Prov. 21:22, down the trusted *s*

STRUCK
Num. 20:11, *s* the rock twice
Job 19:21, the hand of God has *s*
Ps. 3:7, *s* all my enemies
Ps. 78:20, Behold, He *s* the rock
Isa. 57:17, I was angry and *s*
Isa. 60:10, in My wrath I *s*
Hab. 3:13, *s* the head from the
Hag. 2:17, 'I *s* you with blight
Mt. 27:30, took the reed and *s*
Lk. 22:64, Him, they *s* Him on the

STUBBLE
Isa. 33:11, shall bring forth *s*
Isa. 41:2, his sword, as driven *s*
Isa. 47:14, they shall be as *s*
Jer. 13:24, *s* that passes
Mal. 4:1, do wickedly will be *s*

STUBBORN
Dt. 21:18, If a man has a *s*
Ezek. 2:4, and *s* children

STUBBORN-HEARTED
Isa. 46:12, "Listen to Me, you *s*

STUBBORNNESS
Dt. 9:27, do not look on the *s*

STUDIED
Jn. 7:15, having never *s*

STUMBLE
Ps. 119:165, causes them to *s*
Ps. 140:4, to make my steps *s*
Prov. 3:23, your foot will not *s*
Prov. 4:19, know what makes them *s*
Isa. 5:27, one will be weary or *s*
Isa. 8:15, among them shall *s*
Isa. 59:10, we *s* at noonday as at
Isa. 63:13, that they might not *s*
Jer. 13:16, before your feet *s*
Jer. 46:6, they will *s* and fall
Mal. 2:8, have caused many to *s*
Mt. 26:31, you will be made to *s*
Mt. 26:33, if all are made to *s*
Mk. 4:17, immediately they *s*
Mk. 9:42, who believe in Me to *s*
Jn. 11:9, the day, he does not *s*
2 Cor. 11:29, Who is made to *s*
Jas. 2:10, whole law, and yet *s*
Jas. 3:2, For we all *s* in many

STUMBLED
1 Sam. 2:4, and those who *s*
Hos. 14:1, God, for you have *s*
Rom. 11:11, *s* that they should

STUMBLES
Mt. 13:21, immediately he *s*

STUMBLING
Lev. 19:14, the deaf, nor put a *s*
Isa. 8:14, but a stone of *s*
Jer. 6:21, Behold, I will lay *s*
Jer. 20:10, watched for my *s*
Ezek. 7:19, it became their *s*
Rom. 9:32, stumbled at that *s*
Rom. 9:33, I lay in Zion a *s*
Rom. 14:13, this, not to put a *s*
1 Cor. 1:23, to the Jews a *s*
1 Cor. 8:9, of yours become a *s*
1 Pet. 2:8, and "A stone of *s*
1 Jn. 2:10, is no cause for *s*
Jude 24, to keep you from *s*

STUMBLING BLOCK
before the blind. Lev. 19:14; Dt. 27:18
figurative of offense. Isa. 8:14; Rom. 9:32; 14:21; 1 Cor. 1:23; 8:9; 1 Pet. 2:8

STUPID
Job 18:3, and regarded as *s*
Prov. 12:1, hates correction is *s*
Prov. 30:2, Surely I am more *s*

SUBDUE
Ps. 47:3, *s* the peoples under us
Dan. 7:24, shall *s* three kings
Mic. 7:19, *s* our iniquities
Phil. 3:21, *s* all things to

SUBJECT
Rom. 8:7, for it is not *s*
Rom. 13:1, Let every soul be *s*
1 Cor. 15:28, all things are made *s*
1 Cor. 15:28, Himself will also be *s*
Ti. 3:1, Remind them to be *s*
Heb. 2:15, all their lifetime *s*
1 Pet. 3:22, having been made *s*

SUBJECTED
Rom. 8:20, because of Him who *s*

SUBJECTION
Heb. 2:8, put all things in *s*
Heb. 12:9, more readily be in *s*

TAIL
Dt. 28:13, the head and not the *t*
Rev. 12:4, *t* drew a third of the

TAKE
Josh. 5:15, *T* your sandal off your
Ps. 51:11, *t* Your Holy Spirit
Ps. 119:43, *t* not the word of
Ps. 143:9, in You I *t* shelter
Hos. 14:2, *t* words with you
Mt. 11:29, "*T* My yoke upon
Mt. 20:14, *T* what is yours and
Mk. 8:34, and *t* up his cross
Mk. 14:36, *T* this cup away
Jn. 10:17, My life that I may *t*
Acts 27:22, I urge you to *t* heart

TAKEN
Prov. 6:2, you are *t* by the words
Isa. 53:8, He was *t* from prison
Mt. 24:40, one will be *t* and the
Mk. 4:25, what he has will be *t*
Acts 1:9, He was *t* up
2 Th. 2:7, until He is *t* out of
Heb. 11:5, By faith Enoch was *t* away

TALE, Lk. 24:11

TALEBEARER
Lev. 19:16, not go about as a *t*
Prov. 11:13, *t* reveals secrets

TALEBEARERS
Prov. 18:8; 26:20; Ezek. 22:9; 1 Tim. 5:13; 1 Pet. 4:15

TALENT
gold. Ex. 25:39
silver. 1 Ki. 20:39
lead. Zech. 5:7

TALENTS
parable of. Mt. 25:14

TALK
Dt. 6:7, shall *t* of them when
Job 11:2, *t* be vindicated
Job 15:3, with unprofitable *t*
Ps. 71:24, My tongue also shall *t*
Mt. 22:15, entangle Him in His *t*
Jn. 14:30, "I will no longer *t*
1 Tim. 1:6, turned aside to idle *t*

TALKED
Lk. 24:32, within us while He *t*

TALKERS
Ti. 1:10, both idle *t* and

TALKING
vain, censured. 1 Sam. 2:3; Job 11:2; Prov. 13:3; 24:2; Eccl. 10:14; Ezek. 33:30; 36:3; Eph. 5:4; Ti. 1:10. *See* TALEBEARERS

TALL
Isa. 18:2, to a nation *t* and

TAMARISK TREE
for worship. Gen. 21:33
idolatrous. *See* IDOLATRY

TAMBOURINE
Job 21:12, They sing to the *t*
Isa. 24:8, The mirth of the *t*

TARES
parable of the. Mt. 13:24

TARGET
Job 7:20, You set me as Your *t*
Lam. 3:12, and set me up as a *t*

TARRY
Jer. 14:8, who turns aside to *t*
Heb. 10:37, come and will not *t*

TARSHISH
Gen. 10:4; 1 Ki. 10:22; 2 Chr. 9:21; 20:36; Jer. 10:9; Ezek. 27:12; 38:13
Jonah going there. Jon. 1:3
prophecies concerning. Ps. 48:7; 72:10; Isa. 2:16; 23; 60:9; 66:19

TARSUS, Acts 9:11; 11:25; 21:39

TARTAN
military chief. 2 Ki. 18:17

TASK
Eccl. 1:13, this burdensome *t*

TASTE
Num. 11:8, and its *t* was like the
Ps. 34:8, Oh, *t* and see that the
Ps. 119:103, are Your words to my *t*
Song 2:3, was sweet to my *t*
Col. 2:21, Do not touch, do not *t*
Heb. 2:9, might *t* death for

TASTED
Mt. 27:34, But when He had *t*
Heb. 6:4, *t* the heavenly gift
Heb. 6:5, *t* the good word
1 Pet. 2:3, *t* that the Lord is

TATTOO, Lev. 19:28

TAUGHT
Ps. 71:17, O God, You have *t*
Isa. 40:13, as His counselor has *t*
Lk. 13:26, presence, and You *t*
Jn. 6:45, they shall all be *t*
Jn. 8:28, but as My Father *t*
Gal. 1:12, from man, nor was I *t*

TAUNT
Jer. 24:9, and a byword, a *t*

TAX
Mt. 5:46, *t* collectors do the
Mt. 17:24, received the temple *t*
Mt. 21:31, I say to you that *t*
Mt. 22:19, "Show Me the *t*

TAX COLLECTOR
parable of Pharisee and. Lk. 18:10

TAX COLLECTORS
Mt. 9:11; 11:19; 18:17; Lk. 3:12
become believers in Jesus. Mt. 21:32; Lk. 5:27; 7:29; 15:1; 19:2

TAXES
Mt. 17:25, take customs or *t*
Mt. 22:17, Is it lawful to pay *t*
Lk. 23:2, forbidding to pay *t*
Rom. 13:7, *t* to whom *t*

TEACH
Dt. 6:7, *t* them diligently
Dt. 33:10, *t* Jacob Your judgments
1 Sam. 12:23, *t* you the good and the
Job 21:22, "Can anyone *t*
Job 27:11, "I will *t* you about
Job 34:32, *t* me what I do not see
Ps. 25:4, *t* me Your paths
Ps. 27:11, *T* me Your way
Ps. 34:11, *t* you the fear of the
Ps. 45:4, *t* You awesome things
Ps. 51:13, *t* transgressors Your
Ps. 90:12, So *t* us to number our
Isa. 2:3, He will *t* us His ways
Isa. 28:9, "Whom will he *t*
Mic. 3:11, a bribe, her priests *t*
Mt. 22:16, *t* the way of God in
Jn. 14:26, in My name, He will *t*
1 Cor. 11:14, even nature itself *t*
1 Tim. 2:12, permit a woman to *t*
1 Tim. 4:11, things command and *t*
1 Tim. 6:2, *T* and exhort these
Heb. 5:12, *t* you again the first

TEACHER
Mt. 23:8, for One is your *T*
Mk. 10:17, asked Him, "Good *T*
Jn. 3:2, know that You are a *t*
Jn. 13:13, "You call me *T*
Acts 5:34, named Gamaliel, a *t*
Rom. 2:20, a *t* of babes, having
1 Tim. 2:7, a *t* of the Gentiles in

TEACHERS, false
foretold and described. Jer. 5:13; 6:13; Ezek. 14:9; 22:25; Hos. 9:7; Mic. 2:11; 3:11; Zeph. 3:4; Mt. 24:4; Acts 13:6; 20:29; 2 Cor. 11:13; 1 Tim. 1:6; 4:1; 6:3; 2 Tim. 3:8; Ti. 1:11; 2 Pet. 2; Jude 4; Rev. 2:14,20
not to be listened to. Dt. 13:1; Mt. 24:5; Col. 2:8; 1 Tim. 1:4; 4:1; Heb. 13:9; 2 Pet. 2; 1 Jn. 4:1; 2 Jn. 10; Jude; Rev. 2:14
how to be tested and avoided. Isa. 8:20; Rom. 16:17; Ti. 3:10; 1 Jn. 4:2–3; 2 Jn. 10
their condemnation. Dt. 13:1; 18:20; Isa. 8:20; 9:15; Jer. 28:15; Ezek. 13:8; 14:10; Mic. 3:6; Gal. 1:8; 2 Tim. 3:9; 2 Pet. 2:1; Jude 4,10,16

TEACHERS
Ps. 119:99, than all my *t*
Isa. 30:20, *t* will not be moved
1 Cor. 12:28, prophets, third *t*
Eph. 4:11, and some pastors and *t*
1 Tim. 1:7, desiring to be *t*
Heb. 5:12, time you ought to be *t*
Jas. 3:1, of you become *t*
2 Pet. 2:1, there will be false *t*

TEACHES
Ps. 25:8, therefore He *t* sinners
1 Cor. 2:13, the Holy Spirit *t*
1 Tim. 6:3, If anyone *t* otherwise
1 Jn. 2:27, the same anointing *t*

TEACHING
from God. Ps. 71:17; Isa. 54:13; Jer. 31:34; Jn. 6:45; Gal. 1:12; Eph. 4:21; 1 Th. 4:9; 1 Jn. 2:27
——— of Christ. Mt. 5; 7:29

TEACHING
Mt. 28:20, *t* them to observe all
Acts 5:42, they did not cease *t*
Rom. 12:7, he who teaches, in *t*
Col. 1:28, *t* every man in all
Ti. 1:11, *t* things which they
Ti. 2:12, *t* us that

TEAR
Job 18:4, *t* yourself in anger

Mt. 6:7, *t* that they will be
Jn. 5:39, *t* you have eternal
Rom. 12:3, not to *t* of himself
2 Cor. 3:5, of ourselves to *t*
Eph. 3:20, all that we ask or *t*

THINKS
Ps. 40:17, yet the LORD *t* upon me
Prov. 23:7, for as he *t* in his
1 Cor. 8:2, *t* that he knows
1 Cor. 10:12, *t* he stands take heed
Gal. 6:3, For if anyone *t*
Jas. 1:26, *t* he is religious

THIRST
Isa. 41:17, tongues fail for *t*
Mt. 5:6, those who hunger and *t*
Jn. 6:35, in Me shall never *t*
Jn. 19:28, said, "I *t*!"
1 Cor. 4:11, we both hunger and *t*
Rev. 7:16, anymore nor *t* anymore

THIRSTS
Ps. 42:2, My soul *t* for God
Jn. 7:37, saying, "If anyone *t*
Rom. 12:20, if he *t*
Rev. 21:6, freely to him who *t*
Rev. 22:17, And let him who *t*

THIRSTY
Prov. 25:21, and if he is *t*
Isa. 29:8, as when a *t* man dreams
Isa. 32:6, the drink of the *t*
Isa. 35:7, *t* land springs of
Isa. 44:3, on him who is *t*
Isa. 65:13, but you shall be *t*
Mt. 25:35, I was *t* and you gave
Mt. 25:44, we see You hungry or *t*

THISTLES
Job 31:40, *t* grow instead of
Mt. 7:16, or figs from *t*

THOMAS
apostle. Mt. 10:3; Mk. 3:18; Lk. 6:15; Acts 1:13
his zeal. Jn. 11:16
his unbelief and confession. Jn. 20:24

THORN
Prov. 26:9, *t* that goes into the
Isa. 55:13, *t* shall come up the
2 Cor. 12:7, a *t* in the flesh was

THORNBUSHES
Mt. 7:16, gather grapes from *t*

THORNS, Jud. 8:7,16
crown of, placed on Christ. Mt. 27:29; Mk. 15:17; Jn. 19:2

THORNS
Gen. 3:18, Both *t* and thistles it
Prov. 22:5, *T* and snares are
Prov. 24:31, all overgrown with *t*
Eccl. 7:6, the crackling of *t*
Song 2:2, Like a lily among *t*
Jer. 4:3, and do not sow among *t*
Jer. 12:13, wheat but reaped *t*
Mt. 13:7, some fell among *t*
Jn. 19:5, wearing the crown of *t*

THOUGHT
Ps. 49:11, *t* is that their houses
Ps. 50:21, You *t* that I was
Ps. 64:6, Both the inward *t*
Ps. 119:59, I *t* about my ways
Ps. 139:2, You understand my *t*
Isa. 14:24, "Surely, as I have *t*
Amos 4:13, to man what his *t*
Lk. 9:47, perceiving the *t*
Lk. 12:17, "And he *t* within
1 Cor. 13:11, I *t* as a child

THOUGHTS
1 Chr. 28:9, the intent of the *t*
Ps. 10:4, is in none of his *t*
Ps. 40:5, *t* toward us
Ps. 92:5, *t* are very deep
Ps. 94:11, The LORD knows the *t*
Prov. 16:3, *t* will be established
Isa. 55:7, unrighteous man his *t*
Isa. 55:8, "For My *t* are not your
Jer. 4:14, long shall your evil *t*
Mic. 4:12, they do not know the *t*
Mt. 9:4, Jesus, knowing their *t*
Mt. 15:19, heart proceed evil *t*
Rom. 1:21, futile in their *t*
1 Cor. 3:20, The LORD knows the *t*

THREAD, Gen. 14:23

THREAT
Isa. 30:17, shall flee at the *t*

THREATEN
1 Pet. 2:23, suffered, He did not *t*

THREATENING
Eph. 6:9, to them, giving up *t*

THREATS
Acts 4:29, Lord, look on their *t*
Acts 9:1, still breathing *t*

THREE
Mt. 26:34, you will deny Me *t*
1 Cor. 13:13, hope, love, these *t*
1 Jn. 5:7, and these *t* are one

THRESH
Isa. 28:28, he does not *t* it
Isa. 41:15, *t* the mountains
Jer. 51:33, it is time to *t* her
Mic. 4:13, "Arise and *t*

THRESHING
Lev. 26:5, *t* shall last till the
2 Ki. 13:7, like the dust at *t*
Isa. 21:10, Oh, my *t* and the grain

THROAT
Ps. 5:9, *t* is an open tomb
Prov. 23:2, put a knife to your *t*
Jer. 2:25, unshod, and your *t*
Rom. 3:13, *t* is an open tomb

THRONE
1 Ki. 22:19, LORD sitting on His *t*
Ps. 9:7, He has prepared His *t*
Ps. 11:4, temple, the LORD's *t*
Ps. 45:6, Your *t*, O God, is
Ps. 103:19, has established His *t*
Prov. 20:28, he upholds his *t*
Isa. 6:1, Lord sitting on a *t*
Isa. 66:1, "Heaven is My *t*
Jer. 3:17, shall be called The *T*
Jer. 14:21, do not disgrace the *t*
Jer. 17:12, A glorious high *t*
Dan. 7:9, *t* was a fiery flame
Zech. 6:13, sit and rule on His *t*
Mt. 5:34, for it is God's *t*
Lk. 1:32, will give Him the *t*
Heb. 1:8, "Your *t*, O God, is
Heb. 4:16, come boldly to the *t*
Rev. 2:13, where Satan's *t*
Rev. 3:21, My Father on His *t*
Rev. 20:11, I saw a great white *t*

THRONES
Ps. 122:5, *t* are set there
Mt. 19:28, also sit on twelve *t*
Lk. 1:52, mighty from their *t*
Col. 1:16, invisible, whether *t*
Rev. 4:4, *t* I saw twenty-four

THRONG
Ps. 55:14, house of God in the *t*

THROW
Mic. 5:11, of your land and *t*
Mt. 4:6, *t* Yourself down
Mt. 15:26, children's bread and *t*

THROWN
Isa. 34:3, their slain shall be *t*
Mk. 9:42, neck, and he were *t*

THRUST
Lk. 4:29, and rose up and *t*

THUMMIM
on high priest's breastplate. Ex. 28:30; Lev. 8:8; Dt. 33:8; Ezra 2:63; Neh. 7:65

THUNDER
Ex. 9:23; 1 Sam. 7:10; 12:18; Ps. 78:48. *See* Ex. 19:16; Rev. 4:5; 16:18

THUNDER
Job 26:14, But the *t* of His power
Ps. 77:18, The voice of Your *t*
Ps. 81:7, the secret place of *t*
Ps. 104:7, *t* they hastened away
Mk. 3:17, that is, "Sons of *T*"
Rev. 14:2, the voice of loud *t*

THUNDERED
2 Sam. 22:14, "The LORD *t* from
Ps. 18:13, The LORD *t*

THUNDERINGS
Ex. 20:18, people witnessed the *t*
Rev. 19:6, the sound of mighty *t*

THUNDERS
seven. Rev. 10

THUNDERS
Job 37:5, *t* marvelously with His
Ps. 29:3, The God of glory *t*

THYATIRA, Acts 16:14
Angel of. Rev. 1:11; 2:18

TIBERIAS, Jn. 6:1

TIBERIUS CAESAR, Lk. 3:1

TIDINGS
Ps. 112:7, be afraid of evil *t*
Lk. 2:10, I bring you good *t*
Rom. 10:15, who bring glad *t*

TIGLATH-PILESER
(1 Chr. 5:6,26); 2 Ki. 15:29; 16:7; 2 Chr. 28:20

TILL
Gen. 2:5, no man to *t* the ground

TILLER
Gen. 4:2, but Cain was a *t*

TILLS
Prov. 12:11, *t* his land will be
Prov. 28:19, *t* his land will have

TIME
redemption of. Ps. 39:4; 90:12; Eccl. 12:1; Isa. 55:6; Mt. 5:25; Lk. 19:42; Jn. 9:4; 12:35; Rom. 13:11; 2 Cor. 6:2; Gal. 6:9; Eph. 5:16; Col. 4:5
for all things. Eccl. 3

TIME
Ps. 32:6, pray to You in a *t*
Ps. 37:19, ashamed in the evil *t*
Ps. 89:47, how short my *t* is
Eccl. 3:2, A *t* to be born
Eccl. 9:11, but *t* and chance
Ezek. 16:8, your *t* was the *t*
Lk. 19:44, you did not know the *t*
Jn. 7:6, *t* has not yet come
Acts 24:25, I have a convenient *t*
Rev. 1:3, for the *t* is near

TIMES
signs of. Mt. 16:3; Acts 3:21; 1 Th. 5:1; 2 Th. 2; 1 Tim. 4:1; 2 Tim. 3:1

TIMES
1 Chr. 12:32, understanding of the *t*
Job 24:1, *t* are not hidden
Ps. 31:15, *t* are in Your hand
Mt. 16:3, the signs of the *t*
Lk. 21:24, Gentiles until the *t*
Acts 1:7, not for you to know *t*
Acts 17:26, their preappointed *t*
2 Tim. 3:1, last days perilous *t*
Heb. 1:1, God, who at various *t*

TIMOTHY
Acts 16:1–2; 17:14–15; Rom. 16:21; 1 Cor. 16:10; Phil. 2:19; 2 Cor. 1:1,19

TITHE
Gen. 14:20, And he gave him a *t*
Num. 18:26, LORD, a tenth of the *t*
Dt. 14:22, "You shall truly *t*
Dt. 14:28, shall bring out the *t*
Dt. 26:12, laying aside all the *t*
2 Chr. 31:5, in abundantly the *t*
Neh. 13:12, Judah brought the *t*
Mt. 23:23, For you pay *t* of mint

TITHES
paid by Abraham to Melchizedek. Gen. 14:20; Heb. 7:6
due to God. Gen. 28:22; Lev. 27:30; Prov. 3:9; Mal. 3:8
to the Levites. Num. 18:21; 2 Chr. 31:5; Neh. 10:37; Heb. 7:5
for the feasts, and poor. Dt. 14:23,28

TITHES
Lev. 27:31, to redeem any of his *t*
Num. 18:28, *t* which you receive
Neh. 10:37, and to bring the *t*
Neh. 12:44, firstfruits, and the *t*
Neh. 13:5, the articles, the *t*
Mal. 3:10, Bring all the *t*
Lk. 18:12, I give *t* of all that I
Heb. 7:5, to receive *t* from the
Heb. 7:8, mortal men receive *t*
Heb. 7:9, Levi, who receives *t*

TITHING
Dt. 26:12, the year of *t*

TITLE
Jn. 19:19, Now Pilate wrote a *t*

TITTLE
Mt. 5:18, away, one jot or one *t*

TITUS
Gal. 2:3; 2 Cor. 2:13; 7:6,13

TOBIAH, Ezra 2:60
the Ammonite, vexes the Jews. Neh. 4:3; 6:1,12,14; 13:4

TODAY
Ps. 2:7, *t* I have begotten You
Mt. 6:30, of the field, which *t*
Lk. 12:28, the grass, which *t*
Lk. 23:43, *t* you will be with Me
Heb. 1:5, *t* I have begotten You
Heb. 3:7, "*T*, if you will hear
Heb. 13:8, the same yesterday, *t*

TOGARMAH, Gen. 10:3

TOIL
Gen. 3:17, *t* you shall eat of
Mt. 6:28, they neither *t* nor
1 Th. 2:9, our labor and *t*

TOILED
Lk. 5:5, "Master, we have *t*

TOLD
Mt. 28:7, Behold, I have *t*
Lk. 2:18, things which were *t*
Jn. 4:29, *t* me all things that I
Jn. 8:40, *t* you the truth which
Jn. 14:2, so, I would have *t*
Jn. 14:29, "And now I have *t*

TOLERABLE
Mt. 10:15, you, it will be more *t*

TOMB
Ps. 5:9, throat is an open *t*
Jn. 19:41, in the garden a new *t*
Rom. 3:13, throat is an open *t*

TOMBS
Mt. 23:27, like whitewashed *t*
Mt. 23:29, you build the *t*
Lk. 11:47, For you build the *t*

TOMORROW
Isa. 22:13, drink, for *t* we die
Isa. 56:12, *t* will be as today
Mt. 6:30, *t* is thrown into the
Mt. 6:34, do not worry about *t*
1 Cor. 15:32, drink, for *t* we die
Jas. 4:14, what will happen *t*

TONGUE
unruly. Jas. 3
must be bridled. Ps. 39:1; Prov. 4:24; 10:10,19; 14:23; 15:4; 17:20; 18:6; Eccl. 3:7; 10:12; Mt. 5:22; 12:36; Eph. 4:29; 5:4; Col. 3:8; 4:6; 1 Th. 5:11; Ti. 1:10; 2:8; 3:2; Jas. 1:26; 3; 1 Pet. 3:10

TONGUE
Job 5:21, the scourge of the *t*
Job 20:12, hides it under his *t*
Ps. 34:13, Keep your *t* from evil
Ps. 35:28, *t* shall speak of Your
Ps. 39:1, lest I sin with my *t*
Ps. 120:3, to you, you false *t*
Ps. 126:2, laughter, and out *t*
Ps. 137:6, remember you, let my *t*
Ps. 139:4, is not a word on my *t*
Prov. 10:31, but the perverse *t*
Prov. 12:19, forever, but a lying *t*
Prov. 15:4, A wholesome *t* is a
Prov. 21:23, *t* keeps his soul
Prov. 25:15, *t* breaks a bone
Isa. 45:23, *t* shall take an oath
Isa. 50:4, GOD has given Me the *t*
Phil. 2:11, *t* should confess that
Jas. 1:26, does not bridle his *t*
Jas. 3:5, *t* is a little member
Jas. 3:6, And the *t* is a fire
Jas. 3:8, no man can tame the *t*
1 Jn. 3:18, love in word or in *t*
Rev. 14:6, every nation, tribe, *t*

TONGUES
confusion of. Gen. 11
gift of. Acts 2:3; 10:46; 19:6; 1 Cor. 12:10; 13:1; 14:2

TONGUES
Ps. 31:20, From the strife of *t*
Mk. 16:17, speak with new *t*
Acts 2:3, divided *t*, as of fire
Acts 19:6, and they spoke with *t*
1 Cor. 13:1, I speak with the *t*
1 Cor. 14:22, Therefore *t* are for a

TOOTH
Ex. 21:24, "eye for eye, *t*
Prov. 25:19, is like a bad *t*
Mt. 5:38, eye for an eye and a *t*

TOPAZ, Ex. 28:17; Rev. 21:20

TOPHET
Isa. 30:33, *T* was established
Jer. 7:31, the high places of *T*
Jer. 19:12, make this city like *T*
Jer. 19:13, like the place of *T*

TORCH
Zech. 12:6, and like a fiery *t*

TORCHES
Jud. 15:5, When he had set the *t*
Dan. 10:6, his eyes like *t*
Nah. 2:3, come with flaming *t*

TORMENT
place of. Mt. 5:22; 11:23; 13:42; 23:15; 25:41,46; Lk. 16:23; Rev. 14:10; 20:10,15
for whom reserved. Mt. 25:41; 2 Pet. 2:4,17; Jude 6,13

TORMENT
Job 19:2, "How long will you *t*
Isa. 50:11, shall lie down in *t*
Mt. 8:29, You come here to *t*
Lk. 16:28, to this place of *t*
1 Jn. 4:18, fear involves *t*
Rev. 14:11, *t* ascends forever

TORMENTED
Lk. 16:24, for I am *t* in this
Rev. 20:10, And they will be *t*

TORMENTS
Lk. 16:23, "And being in *t*

TORN
beasts not to be eaten. Ex. 22:31; Lev. 22:8; Ezek. 4:14; 44:31

TORN
Lam. 3:11, aside my ways and *t*
Hos. 6:1, for He has *t*
Mt. 27:51, of the temple was *t*

TORTURED
Heb. 11:35, Others were *t*

TOSSED
Isa. 54:11, *t* with tempest
Eph. 4:14, *t* to and fro and

TOTTER
Isa. 24:20, drunkard, and shall *t*

TOUCH
Job 5:19, seven no evil shall *t*
Isa. 52:11, *t* no unclean thing
Mt. 9:21, "If only I may *t*
Mt. 14:36, that they might only *t*
1 Cor. 7:1, a man not to *t* a woman
1 Jn. 5:18, wicked one does not *t*

TOUCHED
1 Sam. 10:26, whose hearts God had *t*
Isa. 6:7, *t* my mouth with it
Jer. 1:9, hand and *t* my mouth
Heb. 12:18, mountain that may be *t*

TOUCHES
Ps. 104:32, He *t* the hills
Zech. 2:8, *t* you *t* the

TOWER
of Babel. Gen. 11; Penuel. Jud. 8:17; Shechem. Jud. 9:46; Siloam. Lk. 13:4

TOWER
Gen. 11:4, *t* whose top is in the
Ps. 61:3, for me, a strong *t*
Ps. 144:2, my fortress, my high *t*
Song 7:4, like an ivory *t*
Isa. 21:5, a watchman in the *t*
Mt. 21:33, in it and built a *t*

TRACKED
Lam. 4:18, *t* our steps so that we

TRADERS
Isa. 23:8, are princes, whose *t*

TRADITION
Mt. 15:2, transgress the *t*
Mt. 15:6, of no effect by your *t*
Col. 2:8, according to the *t*
2 Th. 3:6, *t* which he received
1 Pet. 1:18, conduct received by *t*

TRADITIONS
Gal. 1:14, zealous for the *t*
2 Th. 2:15, *t* which you were

TRAIN
Prov. 22:6, *T* up a child in the
Isa. 6:1, *t* of His robe filled

TRAINED
Lk. 6:40, who is perfectly *t*
Heb. 12:11, those who have been *t*

TRAINING
Eph. 6:4, bring them up in the *t*

TRAITOR
Lk. 6:16, also became a *t*

TRAITORS
2 Tim. 3:4, *t*, headstrong

TRAMPLE
Ps. 44:5, Your name will be *t*
Ps. 91:13, serpent you shall *t*
Isa. 1:12, hand, to *t* My courts
Mal. 4:3, You shall *t* the wicked
Mt. 7:6, swine, lest they *t*
Lk 10:19, you the authority to *t*

TRAMPLED
Isa. 63:3, *t* them in My fury
Mic. 7:10, now she will be *t*
Hab. 3:12, *t* the nations in anger
Lk. 21:24, Jerusalem will be *t*
Heb. 10:29, *t* the Son of God
Rev. 14:20, the winepress was *t*

TRANCE
of Balaam. Num. 24:4; Peter. Acts 10:10; 11:5; Paul. Acts 22:17

TRANSFIGURATION
of Christ. Mt. 17; Mk. 9:2; Lk. 9:29; Jn. 1:14; 2 Pet. 1:16

TRANSFORM
2 Cor. 11:13,14,15

TRANSFORMED
Rom. 12:2, this world, but be *t*
2 Cor. 3:18, the Lord, are being *t*

TRANSGRESS
Num. 14:41, *t* the command of the
1 Sam. 2:24, the LORD's people *t*
Ps. 17:3, my mouth shall not *t*
Prov. 16:10, his mouth must not *t*
Prov. 28:21, of bread a man will *t*
Mt. 15:2, do Your disciples *t*

TRANSGRESSED
Josh. 7:11, *t* My covenant
Isa. 43:27, your mediators have *t*
Jer. 2:8, the rulers also *t*
Ezek. 2:3, their fathers have *t*
Dan. 9:11, Yes, all Israel has *t*
Lk. 15:29, *t* your commandment

TRANSGRESSES
Hab. 2:5, "Indeed, because he *t*
2 Jn. 9, Whoever *t* and does not

TRANSGRESSION, *see* SIN

TRANSGRESSION
Ex. 34:7, iniquity and *t* and sin
Job 13:23, Make me know my *t*
Job 14:17, *t* is sealed up in a
Ps. 19:13, be innocent of great *t*
Ps. 107:17, because of their *t*
Prov. 17:9, He who covers a *t*
Prov. 17:19, He who loves *t* loves
Isa. 58:1, tell My people their *t*
Amos 4:4, at Gilgal multiply *t*
Mic. 6:7, my firstborn for my *t*
Mic. 7:18, and passing over the *t*
Rom. 4:15, no law there is no *t*
1 Tim. 2:14, deceived, fell into *t*
Heb. 2:2, steadfast, and every *t*

TRANSGRESSIONS
Job 31:33, if I have covered my *t*
Ps. 32:5, "I will confess my *t*
Ps. 39:8, me from all my *t*
Ps. 51:1, mercies, blot out my *t*
Ps. 51:3, For I acknowledge my *t*
Ps. 103:12, has He removed our *t*
Isa. 43:25, who blots out your *t*
Isa. 53:5, was wounded for our *t*
Isa. 53:8, for the *t* of My people
Ezek. 18:31, from you all the *t*
Gal. 3:19, was added because of *t*
Heb. 9:15, redemption of the *t*

TRANSGRESSOR
Isa. 48:8, and were called a *t*
Gal. 2:18, I make myself a *t*

TRANSGRESSORS
Ps. 51:13, Then I will teach *t*
Ps. 59:5, to any wicked *t*
Isa. 53:12, numbered with the *t*
Mk. 15:28, numbered with the *t*

TRANSLATION
of Enoch. Gen. 5:24; Heb. 11:5
of Elijah. 2 Ki. 2
of Church. 1 Th. 4:15

TRAP
Isa. 8:14, of Israel, as a *t*
Amos 3:5, where there is no *t*

TRAPS
Ps. 140:5, they have set *t*
Ps. 141:9, for me, and from the *t*

TRAVEL
Mt. 23:15, you *t* land and sea

TRAVELER
Jer. 14:8, *t* who turns aside

TRAVELING
Isa. 33:8, lie waste, the *t*

TREACHEROUS
Isa. 21:2, the *t* dealer deals
Jer. 9:2, an assembly of *t* men
Zeph. 3:4, are insolent, *t*

TREACHEROUSLY
Isa. 33:1, and you who deal *t*
Jer. 12:1, happy who deal so *t*
Jer. 12:6, even they have dealt *t*
Hos. 5:7, They have dealt *t*
Mal. 2:10, Why do we deal *t*
Mal. 2:16, that you do not deal *t*
Acts 7:19, "This man dealt *t*

TREACHERY
instances of. Gen. 34:13; Jud. 9; 1 Sam. 21:7; 22:9 (Ps. 52); 2 Sam. 3:27; 11:14; 16; 20:9; 1 Ki. 21:5; 2 Ki. 10:18; Est. 3; Mt. 26:47; Mk. 14:43; Lk. 22:47; Jn. 18:3

TREAD
Job 40:12, *t* down the wicked in
Ps. 60:12, it is He who shall *t*
Ps. 91:13, You shall *t* upon the
Jer. 25:30, shout, as those who *t*
Mic. 1:3, will come down and *t*
Rev. 11:2, And they will *t*

TREADS
Isa. 63:2, like one who *t* in the
Amos 4:13, *t* the high places
1 Tim. 5:18, an ox while it *t*
Rev. 19:15, *t* the winepress

TREASURE
Dt. 28:12, to you His good *t*
Ps. 119:162, one who finds great *t*
Ps. 135:4, for His special *t*
Prov. 15:6, there is much *t*
Prov. 21:20, There is desirable *t*
Isa. 33:6, of the LORD is His *t*
Mt. 6:21, "For where your *t*
Mt. 12:35, *t* brings forth evil
Mt. 13:52, *t* things new and old
Mt. 19:21, and you will have *t*
Lk. 12:21, so is he who lays up *t*
2 Cor. 4:7, But we have this *t*
Jas. 5:3, You have heaped up *t*

TREASURED
Job 23:12, *t* the words of His

TREASURER
Rom. 16:23, Erastus, the *t* of the

TREASURES
Dt. 32:34, sealed up among My *t*
Job 3:21, it more than hidden *t*
Prov. 2:4, her as for hidden *t*
Prov. 10:2, *t* of wickedness profit
Prov. 21:6, Getting *t* by a lying
Isa. 2:7, is no end to their *t*
Isa. 45:3, I will give you the *t*
Mic. 6:10, Are there yet the *t*
Mt. 6:19, for yourselves *t*
Col. 2:3, are hidden all the *t*
Heb. 11:26, riches than the *t*

TREATY
1 Ki. 3:1, Now Solomon made a *t*

TREE
of life. Gen. 2:9; 3:22; Prov. 3:18; 11:30; Ezek. 47:7,12; Rev. 2:7; 22:2,14
of knowledge of good and evil. Gen. 2:17; 3

TREE
Gen. 2:17, "but of the *t*
Gen. 3:11, you eaten from the *t*
Job 14:7, there is hope for a *t*
Ps. 1:3, *t* planted by the
Ps. 37:35, like a native green *t*
Eccl. 11:3, *t* falls to the south
Song 2:3, Like an apple *t*
Isa. 65:22, for as the days of a *t*
Jer. 17:8, *t* planted by the
Mt. 7:17, *t* bears good fruit
1 Pet. 2:24, His own body on the *t*
Rev. 2:7, give to eat from the *t*
Rev. 22:2, the river, was the *t*

TREES
Jud. 9:8, *t* once went forth
1 Ki. 4:33, Also he spoke of *t*
Ps. 96:12, Then all the *t* of the
Ps. 104:16, The *t* of the LORD are
Eccl. 2:5, all kinds of fruit *t*
Isa. 61:3, they may be called *t*
Jer. 7:20, and on beast, on the *t*
Ezek. 31:9, so that all the *t*
Mk. 8:24, "I see men like *t*
Jude 12, late autumn *t* without
Rev. 7:3, the sea, or the *t*

TREMBLE
1 Chr. 16:30, *T* before Him
Ps. 60:2, have made the earth *t*
Ps. 99:1, let the peoples *t*
Isa. 14:16, who made the earth *t*
Isa. 64:2, That the nations may *t*
Jer. 5:22, 'Will you not *t*
Jer. 10:10, wrath the earth will *t*
Jer. 33:9, they shall fear and *t*
Dan. 6:26, my kingdom men must *t*

TREMBLED
Jud. 5:4, of Edom, the earth *t*
1 Sam. 4:13, for his heart *t*
Ezra 9:4, Then everyone who *t*
Ps. 18:7, the earth shook and *t*
Jer. 4:24, and indeed they *t*

TREMBLES
Ps. 97:4, the earth sees and *t*

TREMBLING
1 Sam. 14:15, it was a very great *t*
Ezek. 12:18, your water with *t*
1 Cor. 2:3, in fear, and in much *t*
2 Cor. 7:15, *t* you received
Eph. 6:5, flesh, with fear and *t*
Phil. 2:12, with fear and *t*

TRENCH
1 Ki. 18:32, and he made a *t*

TRESPASS
offerings, laws concerning. Lev. 5; 6; Num. 5

TRESPASSES
Ps. 68:21, still goes on in his *t*
Mt. 6:14, forgive men their *t*
2 Cor. 5:19, not imputing their *t*
Eph. 2:1, who were dead in *t*
Col. 2:13, forgiven you all *t*

TRIAL
Ps. 95:8, as in the day of *t*
Heb. 3:8, in the day of *t*
1 Pet. 4:12, concerning the fiery *t*
Rev. 3:10, *t* which shall come

TRIBE
Ps. 74:2, of old, the *t* of Your
Heb. 7:13, belongs to another *t*
Rev. 5:5, the Lion of the *t*
Rev. 5:9, blood out of every *t*

TRIBES
of Israel, blessed. Gen. 49; Num. 23:20; 24; Dt. 33
their order and numbering. Num. 1; 2; 10:14; 26; 2 Sam. 24; 1 Chr. 21
number of those sealed. Rev. 7:4
——— of the earth. Rev. 1:7; 5:9; 7:9

TRIBES
Ps. 122:4, where the *t* go up
Isa. 49:6, to raise up the *t*
Acts 26:7, promise our twelve *t*
Jas. 1:1, *t* which are scattered

TRIBULATION
Mt. 24:21, there will be great *t*
Jn. 16:33, world you will have *t*
Rom. 12:12, in hope, patient in *t*
2 Cor. 7:4, joyful in all our *t*
1 Th. 3:4, that we would suffer *t*
2 Th. 1:6, *t* those who
Rev. 2:10, and you will have *t*
Rev. 2:22, with her into great *t*
Rev. 7:14, out of the great *t*

TRIBULATIONS
Acts 14:22, *t* enter the kingdom
Rom. 5:3, but we also glory in *t*
Eph. 3:13, not lose heart at my *t*
2 Th. 1:4, *t* that you endure

TRIBUTE
Mt. 22:21; Lk. 20:25; Rom. 13:6; 1 Pet. 2:13
paid by Christ. Mt. 17:24

TRIED
Ps. 17:3, You have *t* me and have
Isa. 28:16, a *t* stone, a precious

TRIMMED
Mt. 25:7, and *t* their lamps

TRIUMPH
Ps. 25:2, Let not my enemies *t*
Ps. 92:4, I will *t* in the works
2 Cor. 2:14, always leads us in *t*

TRIUMPHED
Ex. 15:1, the LORD, for He has *t*

TROAS
Acts 16:8; 20:5; 2 Cor. 2:12; 2 Tim. 4:13

TRODDEN
Isa. 63:3, *t* the winepress alone

TROOP, 2 Sam. 22:30; Ps. 18:29

TROPHIMUS
Acts 20:4; 21:29; 2 Tim. 4:20

TROUBLE
Ex. 5:19, that they were in *t*
Job 3:26, no rest, for *t* comes
Job 14:1, few days and full of *t*
Job 38:23, for the time of *t*
Ps. 3:1, have increased who *t*
Ps. 10:7, under his tongue is *t*
Ps. 22:11, from Me, for *t* is near
Ps. 27:5, *t* He shall hide me
Ps. 31:9, O LORD, for I am in *t*
Ps. 73:5, not in *t* as other men
Ps. 91:15, will be with him in *t*
Ps. 138:7, walk in the midst of *t*
Prov. 11:8, is delivered from *t*
Prov. 15:6, of the wicked is *t*
Isa. 26:16, *t* they have
Isa. 33:2, also in the time of *t*
Jer. 8:15, and there was *t*
Jer. 14:8, Savior in time of *t*
1 Cor. 7:28, such will have *t*
Gal. 1:7, there are some who *t*

TROUBLED
Ps. 30:7, Your face, and I was *t*
Ps. 104:29, Your face, they are *t*
Isa. 57:20, wicked are like the *t*
Lk. 10:41, worried and *t*
2 Th. 1:7, to give you who are *t*
2 Th. 2:2, shaken in mind or *t*

TROUBLES
1 Sam. 11:5, "What *t* the people
Job 5:19, deliver you in six *t*
Ps. 25:17, The *t* of my heart have
Ps. 25:22, out of all their *t*
Ps. 88:3, my soul is full of *t*
Isa. 65:16, because the former *t*
Mk. 13:8, will be famines and *t*
Acts 7:10, him out of all his *t*

TROUBLING
1 Sam. 16:15, spirit from God is *t*
Job 3:17, wicked cease from *t*

TRUE
2 Sam. 7:28, and Your words are *t*
Jer. 10:10, But the LORD is the *t*
Jer. 42:5, "Let the LORD be a *t*
Mt. 22:16, we know that You are *t*
Jn. 7:28, He who sent Me is *t*
Jn. 10:41, about this Man were *t*
Rom. 3:4, Indeed, let God be *t*
Phil. 4:8, whatever things are *t*
1 Jn. 5:20, may know Him who is *t*
Rev. 3:7, is holy, He who is *t*
Rev. 19:9, "These are the *t*
Rev. 21:5, for these words are *t*

TRUMPET
Ps. 81:3, Blow the *t* at the time
Jer. 4:5, "Blow the *t* in the
Mt. 6:2, deed, do not sound a *t*
1 Cor. 14:8, *t* makes an uncertain
1 Cor. 15:52, For the *t* will sound
Rev. 1:10, loud voice, as of a *t*

TRUMPETS
their use. Num. 10; Josh. 6:4; Jud. 7:16; Ps. 81:3; Ezek. 7:14; 33:3; Joel 2:1
used in the temple. 1 Chr. 13:8; 15:24; 2 Chr. 5:12; 29:27; Ps. 98:6
Feast of. Lev. 23:24; Num. 29
the seven. Rev. 8; 9; 11

TRUST
in God. Ps. 4:5; 34; 37:3; 40:3,4; 62:8; 64:10; 84:12; 115:9; 118:8; Prov. 3:5; 16:20; Isa. 26:4; 50:10; 51:5; Jer. 17:7
exemplified. 1 Sam. 17:45; 30:6; 2 Ki. 18:5; 2 Chr. 20:12; Dan. 3:28; 2 Tim. 1:12; 4:18
blessings resulting from. Ps. 5:11; 26:1; 32:10; 33:21; 34:8,22; 37:5,40; 56:11; 112:7; 125; Prov. 16:20; 28:25; 29:25; Isa. 12:2; 26:3; 57:13; Heb. 13:6
—— in man, riches, vain. Job 31:24; Ps. 20:7; 33:16; 44:6; 49:6; 52:7; 62:10; 118:8; 146:3; Prov. 11:28; 28:26; Isa. 30; 31; Jer. 7:4; 9:4; 17:5; 46:25; 49:4; Ezek. 33:13; Mk. 10:24; 2 Cor. 1:9; 1 Tim. 6:17

TRUST
Job 8:14, *t* is a spider's web
Job 15:15, If God puts no *t*
Ps. 37:3, *T* in the LORD
Ps. 71:5, You are my *t* from my
Prov. 3:5, *T* in the LORD with all
Isa. 12:2, my salvation, I will *t*
Isa. 50:10, Let him *t* in the name
Jer. 7:4, "Do not *t* in these
Mic. 7:5, Do not *t* in a friend
Mk. 10:24, for those who *t* in riches
1 Tim. 6:20, committed to your *t*

TRUSTED
Ps. 22:8, "He *t* in the LORD
Mt. 27:43, "He *t* in God
Eph. 1:12, that we who first *t*
1 Pet. 3:5, the holy women who *t*

TRUSTS
Ps. 32:10, But he who *t* in the
Prov. 28:26, He who *t* in his own

TRUTH
of God. Ex. 34:6; Num. 23:19; Dt. 32:4; Ps. 19:9; 25:10; 33:4; 57:3,10; 85:10; 86:15; 89:14; 91:4; 96:13; 100:5; 119:160; 146:6; Isa. 25:1; 65:16; Dan. 4:37; Mic. 7:20; Jn. 17:17; 2 Cor. 1:20; Rev. 15:3; 16:7
—— the Gospel. Jn. 1:17; 4:24; 5:33; 17:17; 18:37; Rom. 2:8; 1 Cor. 13:6; 2 Cor. 4:2; Gal. 3:1; Eph. 6:14; 2 Th. 2:10; 1 Tim. 2:7; 3:15; 4:3; 6:5; 2 Tim. 3:8; 4:4; Ti. 1:1; 1 Pet. 1:22
—— word of. Ps. 119:43; 2 Cor. 6:7; Eph. 1:13; Col. 1:5; 2 Tim. 2:15; Jas. 1:18. *See* SCRIPTURES, GOSPEL

TRUTH
Gen. 24:48, led me in the way of *t*
Dt. 32:4, justice, a God of *t*
Ps. 15:2, and speaks the *t*
Ps. 40:11, *t* continually preserve
Ps. 51:6, Behold, You desire *t*
Ps. 85:11, *T* shall spring out of
Ps. 91:4, *t* shall be your shield
Ps. 119:43, *t* utterly out of my
Ps. 119:142, and Your law is *t*
Ps. 119:160, of Your word is *t*
Isa. 59:14, *t* is fallen in the
Jer. 9:3, not valiant for the *t*
Hos. 4:1, "There is no *t*
Zech. 8:3, called the City of *T*
Zech. 8:16, speak each man the *t*
Mal. 2:6, *t* was in his mouth
Jn. 8:32, you shall know the *t*
Jn. 14:6, "I am the way, the *t*
Jn. 16:13, He, the Spirit of *t*
Jn. 18:38, to Him, "What is *t*
Acts 26:25, speak the words of *t*
Rom. 1:18, who suppress the *t*
1 Cor. 5:8, of sincerity and *t*
Eph. 4:15, but, speaking the *t*
Eph. 6:14, your waist with *t*
Col. 1:5, in the word of the *t*
2 Th. 2:10, the love of the *t*
1 Tim. 2:7, I am speaking the *t*
2 Tim. 2:25, they may know the *t*
2 Tim. 3:7, the knowledge of the *t*
2 Pet. 1:12, in the present *t*
2 Pet. 2:2, way of *t* will be
1 Jn. 3:19, that we are of the *t*
1 Jn. 5:6, the Spirit is *t*
3 Jn. 3, *t* that is in you

TRUTHFULNESS
Prov. 12:17; Zech. 8:16; Eph. 4:25; 1 Jn. 1:8

TRY
Ps. 26:2, *t* my mind and my heart
Jer. 9:7, refine them and *t* them
Mal. 3:10, *t* Me now in this
1 Pet. 4:12, which is to *t* you

TUBAL
Gen. 10:2; Isa. 66:19; Ezek. 27:13; 32:26; 38; 39

TUBAL-CAIN, Gen. 4:22

TUMULT
Ps. 65:7, their waves, and the *t*
Ps. 83:2, Your enemies make a *t*

TUNIC
Gen. 37:3, Also he made him a *t*
Mt. 5:40, and take away your *t*

TUNICS
Gen. 3:21, the LORD God made *t*
Mk. 6:9, not to put on two *t*
Acts 9:39, weeping, showing the *t*

TURBAN
Job 29:14, like a robe and a *t*
Ezek. 21:26, "Remove the *t*

TURN
Dt. 17:11, you shall not *t*
Ps. 80:18, Then we will not *t*
Ps. 85:8, but let them not *t*
Ps. 119:51, yet I do not *t*
Prov. 1:23, *T* at my rebuke
Prov. 7:25, not let your heart *t*
Jer. 35:15, '*T* now everyone from
Ezek. 14:6, "Repent, *t* away from
Jon. 3:8, yes, let every one *t*
Zech. 1:4, "*T* now from your evil
Mt. 5:39, on your right cheek, *t*
Lk. 1:17, *t* the hearts of the
Acts 14:15, you that you should *t*
Acts 26:18, *t* them from darkness
1 Pet. 3:11, Let him *t* away from

TURNED
Job 23:11, kept His way and not *t*
Ps. 9:17, The wicked shall be *t*
Ps. 70:2, let them be *t* back and
Ps. 119:59, *t* my feet to Your
Isa. 1:4, of Israel, they have *t*
Acts 11:21, number believed and *t*
1 Th. 1:9, and how you *t* to God

TURNING
Gal. 1:6, marvel that you are *t*
Jas. 1:17, or shadow of *t*

TURNS
Ps. 146:9, of the wicked He *t*
Prov. 15:1, A soft answer *t*
Nah. 2:8, but no one *t* back
Jas. 5:20, that he who *t*

TURTLEDOVE
Ps. 74:19, the life of Your *t*
Song 2:12, *t* is heard in our land

TUTOR
Gal. 3:24, the law was our *t*
Gal. 3:25, no longer under a *t*

TWICE
Mk. 14:30; Lk. 18:12; Jude 12

TWIST
Ps. 56:5, All day they *t* my
2 Pet. 3:16, unstable people *t* to

TWO
Gen. 7:15, the ark to Noah, *t*
Lev. 12:8, *t* young pigeons
Eccl. 4:9, *T* are better than one
Isa. 6:2, *t* he covered his
Mt. 19:5, *t* shall become one
Lk. 2:24, *t* young pigeons
Eph. 2:15, new man from the *t*

TYCHICUS
Acts 20:4; Eph. 6:21; Col. 4:7; 2 Tim. 4:12; Ti. 3:12

TYPE
Rom. 5:14, of Adam, who is a *t*

TYRE, Josh. 19:29
its wealth. Ezek. 27
its fall. Ezek. 26:7
Christ visits coasts of. Mt. 15:21
Paul lands at. Acts 21:3

UNAFRAID
Rom. 13:3, Do you want to be *u*

UNBELIEF
sin. Jn. 16:9; Rom. 11:32; Ti. 1:15; 1 Jn. 5:10
its source. Mk. 16:14; Lk. 8:12; 24:25; Jn. 5:38; 8:45; 10:26; 12:39; Acts 19:9; 2 Cor. 4:4; Eph. 2:2; 2 Th. 2:12; Heb. 3:12
the world condemned for. Jn. 3:18; 5:24
its effects. 1 Ki. 17:18; 2 Ki. 7:2; Ps. 78:19; 106:24; Isa. 53:1; Mt. 24:11; Jn. 12:37; 16:9; Acts 14:2; 19:9; Heb. 3:12
deprecated. Mt. 17:17; Jn. 20:27,29; Heb. 3:12; 4:11
instances of. Gen. 3:4; Num. 13; 14; 20:12; Dt. 9:23; 2 Ki. 7:2,17; Ps. 78; 106; Mt. 13:58; Lk. 1:20; 22:67; Jn. 5:38; 7:5; 12:37; 20:25; Acts 14:2; 17:5; Rom. 3:3; 11:20; Heb. 3:19

UNBELIEF
Mt. 13:58, because of their *u*
Mk. 9:24, help my *u*
Mk. 16:14, and He rebuked their *u*
1 Tim. 1:13, did it ignorantly in *u*
Heb. 3:12, you an evil heart of *u*
Heb. 3:19, enter in because of *u*

UNBELIEVERS
Rom. 10:14; 16:17; 1 Cor. 1:21; 2 Cor. 6:14,15; Eph. 2:12; 4:18; 5:12; Phil. 3:2; 1 Tim. 5:8; 6:5
fate of. Mk. 16:16; Jn. 3:18; 8:24; Rom. 11:20; Eph. 5:6; 2 Th. 2:12; Heb. 3:19; 4:11; 11:6; Jas. 5; 2 Pet. 2; 3; Jude 5; Rev. 21:8

UNBELIEVERS
1 Cor. 14:22, who believe but to *u*
1 Cor. 14:23, are uninformed or *u*
2 Cor. 6:14, yoked together with *u*

UNBELIEVING
Jn. 20:27, Do not be *u*
Acts 14:2, *u* Jews stirred up the
1 Cor. 7:14, For the *u* husband is
Ti. 1:15, *u* nothing is pure
Rev. 21:8, "But the cowardly, *u*

UNCERTAIN
1 Cor. 9:26; 14:8; 1 Tim. 6:17

UNCIRCUMCISED
Acts 7:51, You stiff-necked and *u*
Rom. 2:27, not the physically *u*
Rom. 3:30, by faith and the *u*
Gal. 2:7, *u* had been committed

UNCLEAN
animals. Lev. 11; 20:25; Dt. 14:3

UNCLEAN
Gen. 7:2, of animals that are *u*
Lev. 7:21, who touches any *u*
Isa. 6:5, I am a man of *u* lips
Isa. 52:1, *u* shall no longer come
Mk. 1:27, He commands even the *u*
Mk. 9:25, He rebuked the *u*
Acts 10:28, any man common or *u*
Rom. 14:14, there is nothing *u*
2 Cor. 6:17, Do not touch what is *u*
Eph. 5:5, that no fornicator, *u*

UNCLEAN SPIRITS
Mt. 10:1; 12:43,45; Acts 5:16; Rev. 16:13

UNCLEANNESS
Lev. 5; 7; 11; 12; 15; 22; Num. 5; 19; Dt. 23:10; 24:1; Zech. 13:1

UNCLEANNESS
Mt. 23:27, men's bones and all *u*
Rom. 6:19, members as slaves of *u*
1 Th. 4:7, did not call us to *u*
2 Pet. 2:10, flesh in the lust of *u*

UNCLEANNESSES
Ezek. 36:29, from all your *u*

UNCLOTHED
2 Cor. 5:4, we want to be *u*

UNCOVER
Isa. 47:2, skirt, *u* the thigh

UNCOVERS
Job 12:22, *u* deep things out of

UNDEFILED
Ps. 119:1, Blessed are the *u*
Heb. 13:4, all, and the bed *u*
1 Pet. 1:4, incorruptible and *u*

UNDERMINE
Job 6:27, And you *u* your friend

UNDERSTAND
Gen. 11:7, *u* one another's speech
Ps. 14:2, if there are any who *u*
Ps. 106:7, in Egypt did not *u*
Prov. 14:8, is to *u* his way
Prov. 28:5, Evil men do not *u*
Isa. 6:9, hearing, but do not *u*
Dan. 1:4, and quick to *u*
Dan. 10:12, set your heart to *u*
Dan. 11:33, *u* shall instruct many
Dan. 12:10, of the wicked shall *u*
Hos. 4:14, people who do not *u*
Hos. 14:9, Let him *u* these things
Jn. 8:43, Why do you not *u*
Acts 8:30, *u* what you are reading
Acts 28:27, lest they should *u*
1 Cor. 13:2, *u* all mysteries
2 Pet. 3:16, some things hard to *u*

UNDERSTANDING
1 Ki. 3:11, asked for yourself *u*
Job 12:13, He has counsel and *u*
Job 28:12, is the place of *u*
Job 28:28, depart from evil is *u*
Job 32:8, Almighty gives him *u*
Job 39:17, not endow her with *u*
Ps. 49:3, my heart shall give *u*
Ps. 119:34, Give me *u*
Ps. 119:104, Your precepts I get *u*
Ps. 147:5, His *u* is infinite
Prov. 2:2, apply your heart to *u*
Prov. 3:5, lean not on your own *u*
Prov. 3:19, *u* He established
Prov. 9:6, and go in the way of *u*
Prov. 9:10, of the Holy One is *u*
Prov. 10:23, a man of *u* has wisdom
Prov. 16:22, *U* is a wellspring
Prov. 19:8, *u* will find good
Prov. 23:23, and instruction and *u*
Prov. 28:11, but the poor who has *u*
Isa. 11:2, Spirit of wisdom and *u*
Isa. 40:28, His *u* is unsearchable
Jer. 51:15, the heaven by His *u*
Mt. 15:16, also still without *u*
Lk. 24:45, And He opened their *u*
1 Cor. 14:15, also pray with the *u*
1 Cor. 14:19, five words with my *u*
Col. 1:9, and spiritual *u*
2 Tim. 2:7, the Lord give you *u*
Jas. 3:13, Who is wise and *u*
1 Jn. 5:20, and has given us an *u*

UNDERSTANDS
Prov. 8:9, all plain to him who *u*
Prov. 14:6, is easy to him who *u*
Rom. 3:11, there is none who *u*

UNDERSTOOD
Ps. 73:17, Then I *u* their end
Eccl. 1:16, My heart has *u* great
Isa. 40:21, Have you not *u* from
Mt. 13:51, *u* all these things
Rom. 1:20, clearly seen, being *u*

UNDESIRABLE
Zeph. 2:1, gather together, O *u*

UNDIGNIFIED
2 Sam. 6:22, I will be even more *u*

UNDISCERNING
Rom. 1:31, *u*, untrustworthy

UNDONE
Isa. 6:5, "Woe is me, for I am *u*
Mt. 23:23, leaving the others *u*

UNEDUCATED
Acts 4:13, that they were *u*

UNEQUAL, 2 Cor. 6:14

UNFAITHFUL
Prov. 2:22, *u* will be uprooted
Prov. 13:15, way of the *u* is hard

UNFAITHFULLY
Ps. 78:57, back and acted *u*

UNFORGIVING
Rom. 1:31, unloving, *u*

UNFORMED
Ps. 139:16, substance, being yet *u*

UNFRUITFUL
Mk. 4:19, and it becomes *u*
Ti. 3:14, that they may not be *u*

UNGODLINESS
Ps. 18:4, *u* made me afraid
Rom. 1:18, heaven against all *u*
Rom. 11:26, He will turn away *u*

UNGODLY
Job 16:11, delivered me to the *u*
Ps. 1:5, *u* shall not stand
Ps. 1:6, of the *u* shall perish
Ps. 43:1, my cause against an *u*
Prov. 16:27, *u* man digs up evil
Rom. 4:5, who justifies the *u*

Rom. 5:6, Christ died for the *u*
2 Pet. 3:7, and perdition of *u* men
Jude 15, convict all who are *u*

UNHOLY
Ezek. 22:26, the holy and *u*
1 Tim. 1:9, for sinners, for the *u*

UNINFORMED
1 Cor. 14:16, the place of the *u*

UNINTENTIONALLY
Dt. 4:42, kills his neighbor *u*

UNITE
Ps. 86:11, *U* my heart to fear

UNITY
of the Church. Jn. 10:16; Rom. 12:5; 1 Cor. 10:17; 12:13; Gal. 3:28; Eph. 1:10; 2:19; 4:4; 5:23,30
of brethren. Ps. 133; Jn. 17:21; Acts 2:42
enforced. Ps. 133; Rom. 12:16; 15:5; 1 Cor. 1:10; 2 Cor. 13:11; Eph. 4:3; Phil. 1:27; 2:2; 1 Pet. 3:8

UNITY
Ps. 133:1, to dwell together in *u*
Eph. 4:3, to keep the *u* of the
Eph. 4:13, we all come to the *u*

UNJUST
Prov. 11:7, hope of the *u* perishes
Zeph. 3:5, *u* knows no shame
Lk. 16:8, commended the *u*
Lk. 18:11, extortioners, *u*
Acts 24:15, of the just and the *u*
Rom. 3:5, *u* who inflicts wrath
Heb. 6:10, For God is not *u*
1 Pet. 3:18, the just for the *u*
Rev. 22:11, let him be *u* still

UNJUSTLY
Ps. 82:2, long will you judge *u*
Isa. 26:10, he will deal *u*

UNKNOWN
Prov. 22:29, not stand before *u*
Acts 17:23, To The *U* God
Gal. 1:22, And I was *u* by face to

UNLAWFUL, Acts 10:28

UNLEAVENED
bread. Ex. 12:39; 13:7; 23:18; Lev. 2:4; 7:12; 8:26; Num. 6:19 (1 Cor. 5:7)

UNLEAVENED
Ex. 12:17, the Feast of *U* Bread
Mk. 14:1, the Feast of *U* Bread
1 Cor. 5:7, since you truly are *u*

UNLOVING
Rom. 1:31, untrustworthy, *u*

UNMERCIFUL
Rom. 1:31, unforgiving, *u*

UNPREPARED
2 Cor. 9:4, with me and find you *u*

UNPRESENTABLE
1 Cor. 12:23, *u* parts have greater

UNPROFITABLE
Mt. 25:30, And cast the *u*
Lk. 17:10, 'We are *u* servants

Rom. 3:12, have together become *u*
Phile. 11, who once was *u* to you
Heb. 13:17, for that would be *u*

UNPROFITABLENESS
Heb. 7:18, of its weakness and *u*

UNPUNISHED
Prov. 11:21, wicked will not go *u*
Prov. 28:20, be rich will not go *u*

UNQUENCHABLE
Mt. 3:12, up the chaff with *u*
Lk. 3:17, He will burn with *u*

UNREASONABLE
Acts 25:27; 2 Th. 3:2

UNRESTRAINED
Ex. 32:25, that the people were *u*

UNRIGHTEOUS
Isa. 55:7, *u* man his thoughts
Lk. 16:11, been faithful in the *u*
1 Cor. 6:9, *u* will not inherit the

UNRIGHTEOUSNESS
Ps. 92:15, and there is no *u*
Jer. 22:13, builds his house by *u*
Jn. 7:18, Him is true, and no *u*
Rom. 1:18, all ungodliness and *u*
Rom. 2:8, the truth, but obey *u*
Rom. 9:14, Is there *u* with God
1 Jn. 1:9, cleanse us from all *u*
1 Jn. 5:17, All *u* is sin

UNRULY
1 Th. 5:14, those who are *u*
Jas. 3:8, It is an *u* evil

UNSEARCHABLE
Prov. 25:3, heart of kings is *u*
Rom. 11:33, *u* are His judgments

UNSKILLED
Heb. 5:13, only of milk is *u*

UNSPOTTED
Jas. 1:27, to keep oneself *u*

UNSTABLE
Gen. 49:4, *U* as water

UNSTOPPED
Isa. 35:5, of the deaf shall be *u*

UNTAUGHT
2 Pet. 3:16, which *u* and unstable

UNTHANKFUL
Lk. 6:35; 2 Tim. 3:2

UNTRUSTWORTHY
Rom. 1:31, undiscerning, *u*

UNWASHED
Mk. 7:5, eat bread with *u* hands

UNWISE
Hos. 13:13, He is an *u* son
Eph. 5:17, Therefore do not be *u*

UNWORTHY
Acts 13:46, and judge yourselves *u*
1 Cor. 11:27, *u* manner will be

UPHARSIN, Dan. 5:25

UPHOLD
Job 8:20, *u* the evildoers
Ps. 119:116, *U* me according to

Isa. 42:1, My Servant whom I *u*
Isa. 63:5, there was no one to *u*

UPHOLDING
Heb. 1:3, *u* all things by the

UPHOLDS
Ps. 63:8, Your right hand *u*
Ps. 145:14, LORD *u* all who fall

UPPER
Mk. 14:15, show you a large *u*
Acts 1:13, went up into the *u*
Acts 20:8, many lamps in the *u*

UPRIGHT
Dt. 32:4, righteous and *u* is He
Job 4:7, where were the *u*
Ps. 25:8, Good and *u* is the LORD
Ps. 49:14, *u* shall have dominion
Ps. 112:2, *u* will be blessed
Ps. 112:4, *u* there arises light
Prov. 10:29, is strength for the *u*
Prov. 11:3, *u* will guide them
Prov. 11:6, *u* will deliver them
Prov. 14:11, *u* will flourish
Prov. 15:8, *u* is His delight
Prov. 15:19, of the *u* is a highway
Eccl. 7:29, that God made man *u*
Mic. 7:2, and there is no one *u*
Hab. 2:4, his soul is not *u*

UPRIGHTNESS
Job 33:23, to show man His *u*
Ps. 143:10, me in the land of *u*
Prov. 17:26, princes for their *u*
Isa. 26:7, of the just is *u*
Isa. 26:10, land of *u* he will deal

UPROAR
Mt. 26:5; Mk. 14:2; Acts 17:5; 21:31

UPROOT
2 Chr. 7:20, then I will *u*
Ps. 52:5, *u* you from the land
Mt. 13:29, *u* the wheat with

UR
land of. Gen. 11:28; 15:7

URGE, Gen. 33:11; 2 Ki. 2:17

URGENT, Dan. 3:22

URIAH
the Hittite. 2 Sam. 11; 1 Ki. 15:5; Mt. 1:6

URIJAH
—— prophet. Jer. 26:20
—— priest. 2 Ki. 16:10,16

URIM, Ex. 28:30. *See* THUMMIM

URIM
Ex. 28:30, of judgment of *U*
Dt. 33:8, Thummim and Your *U*

US
Mt. 1:23, "God with *u*
Mk. 9:40, who is not against *u*
Rom. 8:31, If God is for *u*
1 Jn. 2:19, They went out from *u*
1 Jn. 2:19, of them were of *u*

USE
Mt. 5:44, who spitefully *u* you
Rom. 1:27, leaving the natural *u*
1 Cor. 7:31, *u* this world as not

Gal. 5:13, *u* liberty as an
1 Tim. 5:23, *u* a little wine
Heb. 5:14, *u* have their

USELESS
Isa. 44:9, all of them are *u*
Ti. 3:9, are unprofitable and *u*
Jas. 1:26, one's religion is *u*

USES
1 Tim. 1:8, if one *u* it lawfully

USING
Jn. 16:29, *u* no figure of speech
Col. 2:22, perish with the *u*
1 Pet. 2:16, *u* liberty as a

USURY
Lev. 25:36, 'Take no *u* or
Ps. 15:5, put out his money at *u*

UTTER
Job 33:3, *u* pure knowledge
Ps. 78:2, *u* dark sayings of old
Eccl. 5:2, let not your heart *u*
2 Cor. 12:4, lawful for a man to *u*

UTTERANCE
Acts 2:4, the Spirit gave them *u*
Eph. 6:19, *u* may be given to me

UTTERED
Hab. 3:10, The deep *u* its voice
Rom. 8:26, which cannot be *u*
Rev. 10:4, the seven thunders *u*

UTTERMOST
1 Th. 2:16, upon them to the *u*
Heb. 7:25, *u* those who come

UTTERS
Ps. 19:2, Day unto day *u* speech
Amos 1:2, *u* His voice from
Mic. 7:3, and the great man *u*

UZ, Gen. 10:23

UZZIAH, 2 Ki. 15:13. *See* AZARIAH

VAGABOND
Gen. 4:12, *v* you shall be on the

VAIN
Ps. 2:1, the people plot a *v*
Eccl. 6:12, *v* life which he passes
Isa. 49:4, 'I have labored in *v*
1 Cor. 15:2, you believed in *v*

VALIANT
1 Sam. 18:17, Only be *v* for me
Jer. 9:3, They are not *v* for the
Jer. 46:15, *v* men swept away

VALIANTLY
Num. 24:18, while Israel does *v*
Ps. 60:12, God we will do *v*
Ps. 118:15, of the LORD does *v*

VALLEY
Ps. 23:4, I walk through the *v*
Ps. 84:6, pass through the *V*
Song 6:11, the verdure of the *v*
Isa. 40:4, *v* shall be exalted
Ezek. 37:1, in the midst of the *v*
Lk. 3:5, *v* shall be filled

VALOR
1 Sam. 16:18, a mighty man of *v*

VALUE
Job 28:13, does not know its *v*
Mt. 6:26, of more *v* than they
Acts 19:19, they counted up the *v*

VALUED
Job 28:16, It cannot be *v* in the

VANISH
Job 6:17, when it is hot, they *v*
Isa. 51:6, For the heavens will *v*
1 Cor. 13:8, knowledge, it will *v*
Heb. 8:13, old is ready to *v* away

VANISHED
Lk. 24:31, and He *v* from their

VANITY
of worldly things. Ps. 49; 90; Eccl. 1; Isa. 40:17,23
of idolatry. Dt. 32:21; 2 Ki. 17:15; Jer. 10:8; 14:22; 18:15; Acts 14:15

VAPOR
Ps. 39:5, best state is but *v*
Ps. 39:11, surely every man is *v*
Jas. 4:14, It is even a *v* that

VARIATION
Jas. 1:17, whom there is no *v*

VASHTI, Est. 1:9

VEGETABLES
Dan. 1:12, and let them give us *v*
Rom. 14:2, is weak eats only *v*

VEHEMENT
Song 8:6, of fire, a most *v*

VEIL
of women. Gen. 24:65; Ruth 3:15; 1 Cor. 11:10
of Moses. Ex. 34:33; 2 Cor. 3:13
of the tabernacle and temple. Ex. 26:31; 36:35; 2 Cor. 3:14. *See* Heb. 6:19; 9:3; 10:20
of temple, torn at crucifixion. Mt. 27:51; Mk. 15:38; Lk. 23:45

VEIL
Ex. 34:33, he put a *v* on his face
Mt. 27:51, *v* of the temple was
2 Cor. 3:13, Moses, who put a *v*
Heb. 6:19, Presence behind the *v*

VENGEANCE
belongs to God. Dt. 32:35; Ps. 94:1; 99:8; Isa. 34:8; 35:4; Jer. 50:15; Ezek. 24; 25; Nah. 1:2; 2 Th. 1:8; Heb. 10:30; Jude 7

VENGEANCE
Lev. 19:18, 'You shall not take *v*
Dt. 32:35, *V* is Mine
Prov. 6:34, spare in the day of *v*
Isa. 35:4, God will come with *v*
Isa. 59:17, on the garments of *v*
Jer. 11:20, let me see Your *v*
Lk. 21:22, are the days of *v*
Rom. 12:19, written, "*V* is Mine
2 Th. 1:8, flaming fire taking *v*
Jude 7, suffering the *v*

VENOM
Job 20:14, It becomes cobra *v*

VESSEL
Ps. 2:9, like a potter's *v*
Jer. 18:4, *v* that he made of clay
Jer. 25:34, like a precious *v*
Jer. 48:11, been emptied from *v*
Acts 9:15, for he is a chosen *v*
Rom. 9:21, lump to make one *v*
1 Th. 4:4, to possess his own *v*
1 Pet. 3:7, to the weaker *v*

VESSELS
of temple. 1 Ki. 7:40
carried to Babylon. 2 Ki. 25:14
profaned. Dan. 5
restored. Ezra 1:7

VESSELS
Rom. 9:22, longsuffering the *v*
2 Cor. 4:7, treasure in earthen *v*
Rev. 2:27, like the potter's *v*

VEXED
Ps. 73:21, grieved, and I was *v*

VICE
1 Pet. 2:16, as a cloak for *v*

VICTIM
Job 29:17, And plucked the *v*

VICTORY
over death. Isa. 25:8; 1 Cor. 15:54
by faith. 1 Jn. 5:4

VIEW
Josh. 2:1, "Go, *v* the land

VIGILANT
Col. 4:2, in prayer, being *v*
1 Pet. 5:8, Be sober, be *v*

VIGOR
Dt. 34:7, nor his natural *v*

VILE
1 Sam. 3:13, sons made themselves *v*
Job 40:4, "Behold, I am *v*
Rom. 1:26, them up to *v* passions

VINDICATED
Job 13:18, know that I shall be *v*

VINDICATION
Ps. 17:2, Let my *v* come from

VINE
Ezek. 15; 17; Rev. 14:18
Christ as the Vine. Jn. 15

VINE
Gen. 49:11, to the choice *v*
Dt. 32:32, their *v* is of the *v*
Ps. 80:8, You have brought a *v*
Jer. 2:21, planted you a noble *v*
Jer. 8:13, grapes shall be on the *v*
Hos. 10:1, Israel empties his *v*
Mic. 4:4, shall sit under his *v*
Mt. 26:29, of this fruit of the *v*
Jn. 15:1, "I am the true *v*

VINEDRESSER
Jn. 15:1, and My Father is the *v*

VINEGAR
offered to Christ on the cross. Mt. 27:34,48; Mk. 15:36; Lk. 23:36; Jn. 19:29. *See* Ps. 69:21; Prov. 10:26; 25:20

VINES
Song 2:15, foxes that spoil the *v*
Hab. 3:17, nor fruit be on the *v*

VINEYARD
Noah's. Gen. 9:20

WAGE
Mal. 3:5, those who exploit *w*
1 Tim. 1:18, *w* the good warfare

WAGES
Ex. 2:9, I will give you your *w*
Prov. 10:16, the *w* of the wicked
Isa. 19:10, *w* will be troubled
Hag. 1:6, and he who earns *w*
Zech. 11:12, to you, give me my *w*
Mt. 20:8, and give them their *w*
Lk. 3:14, be content with your *w*
Lk. 10:7, is worthy of his *w*
Rom. 4:4, him who works, the *w*
Rom. 6:23, For the *w* of sin is
1 Tim. 5:18, is worthy of his *w*
Jas. 5:4, Indeed the *w* of the

WAIL
Jer. 48:36, My heart shall *w*
Ezek. 32:18, "Son of man, *w*

WAILING
Jer. 9:19, *w* is heard from Zion
Ezek. 27:31, of heart and bitter *w*
Mt. 13:42, There will be *w*

WAIT
Job 14:14, hard service I will *w*
Job 17:13, If I *w* for the grave
Ps. 27:14, *W* on the LORD
Ps. 37:7, *w* patiently for Him
Ps. 69:3, my eyes fail while I *w*
Ps. 104:27, These all *w* for You
Isa. 8:17, And I will *w* on the
Isa. 30:18, the LORD will *w*
Isa. 40:31, those who *w* on the
Isa. 49:23, not be ashamed who *w*
Lam. 3:26, *w* quietly for the
Mic. 7:7, I will *w* for the God
Lk. 12:36, be like men who *w*
Rom. 8:25, see, we eagerly *w*
1 Cor. 11:33, *w* for one another
Gal. 5:5, the Spirit eagerly *w*
Phil. 3:20, we also eagerly *w*
1 Th. 1:10, and to *w* for His Son
Heb. 9:28, To those who eagerly *w*

WAITED
Job 30:26, and when I *w* for light
Ps. 40:1, *w* patiently for the
Isa. 25:9, we have *w* for Him
Lk. 1:21, And the people *w*
Acts 27:33, day you have *w* and
1 Pet. 3:20, Divine longsuffering *w*

WAITING
upon God. Ps. 27:14; 37:34; Prov. 20:22; Isa. 40:31; 49:23; Jer. 14:22; Lam. 3:25; Hab. 2:3; Zeph. 3:8; Lk. 12:36; Rom. 8:25; 1 Cor. 1:7; Gal. 5:5; 1 Th. 1:10; 2 Th. 3:5

WAITING
Prov. 8:34, *w* at the posts of my
Lk. 2:25, *w* for the Consolation
Lk. 23:51, who himself was also *w*
Rom. 8:23, ourselves, eagerly *w*
Heb. 10:13, from that time *w*

WAITS
Job 24:15, of the adulterer *w*
Ps. 62:1, my soul silently *w*
Ps. 130:6, My soul *w* for the Lord
Isa. 64:4, for the one who *w*
Rom. 8:19, the creation eagerly *w*

WAKE
1 Th. 5:10, that whether we *w*

WALK
Gen. 17:1, *w* before Me and be
Ex. 18:20, in which they must *w*
Dt. 5:33, "You shall *w* in all
Ps. 23:4, Yea, though I *w*
Ps. 48:12, *W* about Zion
Ps. 81:13, that Israel would *w*
Ps. 101:2, I will *w* within my
Ps. 116:9, I will *w* before the
Ps. 138:7, Though I *w* in the
Eccl. 5:1, *W* prudently when you
Eccl. 11:9, *w* in the ways of your
Isa. 2:5, come and let us *w*
Isa. 30:21, "This is the way, *w*
Isa. 40:31, be weary, they shall *w*
Isa. 50:11, *w* in the light of your
Isa. 65:2, people, who *w* in a way
Jer. 23:14, commit adultery and *w*
Hos. 14:9, the righteous *w*
Mic. 6:8, *w* humbly with your God
Jn. 5:8, take up your bed and *w*
Jn. 12:35, *W* while you have the
Rom. 6:4, so we also should *w*
Rom. 13:13, Let us *w* properly
2 Cor. 5:7, For we *w* by faith
Gal. 5:16, *W* in the Spirit
Eph. 2:10, that we should *w*
Eph. 5:2, And *w* in love
Eph. 5:8, *W* as children of light
Phil. 3:16, attained, let us *w*
Phil. 3:17, note those who so *w*
Col. 1:10, that you may *w* worthy
Col. 2:6, Jesus the Lord, so *w*
1 Th. 4:1, us how you ought to *w*
1 Jn. 2:6, *w* just as He
Rev. 3:4, and they shall *w*

WALKED
Gen. 5:22, Methuselah, Enoch *w*
Job 29:3, by His light I *w*
Isa. 9:2, The people who *w*
Mal. 2:6, He *w* with Me in peace
Jn. 11:54, Jesus no longer *w*
2 Cor. 10:2, *w* according to the
Eph. 2:2, in which you once *w*
1 Jn. 2:6, to walk just as He *w*

WALKING
with God. Dt. 5:33; 28:9; Josh. 22:5; 1 Ki. 8:36; Ps. 1; 112; Prov. 2:7; Isa. 2:3; 30:21; Jer. 6:16; 7:23; Ezek. 37:21; of Enoch. Gen. 5:24; of Noah. Gen. 6:9
in faith, love, etc. Rom. 6:4; 8:1; 13:13; 2 Cor. 5:7; Gal. 5:16; Eph. 5:2; Phil. 3:16; Col. 1:10; 2:6; 1 Jn. 1:6; Rev. 3:4; 21:24

WALKING
Gen. 3:8, of the LORD God *w*
Dan. 3:25, see four men loose, *w*
Lk. 1:6, before God, *w* in all
Jn. 6:19, they saw Jesus *w*
Acts 9:31, And *w* in the fear of
Rom. 14:15, you are no longer *w*
2 Cor. 4:2, not *w* in craftiness
2 Jn. 1:4, of your children *w*

WALKS
Dt. 23:14, the LORD your God *w*
Ps. 1:1, is the man who *w*
Ps. 15:2, He who *w* uprightly
Prov. 10:9, He who *w* with
Prov. 13:20, He who *w* with wise men
Prov. 28:18, *w* blamelessly will be
Prov. 28:26, *w* wisely will be
Isa. 35:8, Whoever *w* the road
Isa. 50:10, Who *w* in darkness and
Jer. 10:23, it is not in man who *w*
Mic. 2:7, do good to him who *w*
Jn. 11:9, If anyone *w* in the day
Jn. 12:35, he who *w* in darkness
1 Pet. 5:8, adversary the devil *w*
1 Jn. 2:11, is in darkness and *w*

WALL
Josh. 6:5, then the *w* of the city
2 Ki. 20:2, his face toward the *w*
Ps. 62:3, like a leaning *w*
Prov. 18:11, and like a high *w*
Song 8:9, If she is a *w*
Isa. 59:10, We grope for the *w*
Acts 23:3, you whitewashed *w*
2 Cor. 11:33, a window in the *w*
Eph. 2:14, down the middle *w*
Rev. 21:14, Now the *w* of the city

WALLS
Prov. 25:28, broken down, without *w*
Isa. 26:1, salvation for *w*
Isa. 60:18, you shall call your *w*
Heb. 11:30, By faith the *w* of

WANDER
Job 12:24, and makes them *w*
Job 38:41, ones cry to God, and *w*
Ps. 55:7, Indeed, I would *w*
Ps. 119:10, Oh, let me not *w*
Jer. 14:10, they have loved to *w*

WANDERED
Lam. 4:14, *w* blind in the streets
Ezek. 34:6, "My sheep *w* through
Heb. 11:38, They *w* in deserts and

WANDERERS
Hos. 9:17, And they shall be *w*

WANDERING
1 Tim. 5:13, learn to be idle, *w*
Jude 13, *w* stars for whom is

WANDERS
Job 15:23, He *w* about for bread
Prov. 27:8, Like a bird that *w*
Jas. 5:19, if anyone among you *w*

WANT
Ps. 23:1, I shall not *w*
Lk. 15:14, he began to be in *w*

WANTING
Dan. 5:27, balances, and found *w*

WANTON
Isa. 3:16, necks and *w* eyes
1 Tim. 5:11, have begun to grow *w*

WANTONNESS
condemned. Isa. 3:16; Rom. 13:13; 2 Pet. 2:18

WAR
Ex. 32:17, There is a noise of *w*
Num. 32:20, the LORD for the *w*
2 Sam. 22:35, my hands to make *w*

Job 38:23, day of battle and *w*
Ps. 27:3, *w* may rise against
Ps. 120:7, speak, they are for *w*
Prov. 20:18, by wise counsel wage *w*
Prov. 24:6, will wage your own *w*
Isa. 2:4, shall they learn *w*
Isa. 21:15, from the distress of *w*
Jer. 42:14, we shall see no *w*
Dan. 7:21, same horn was making *w*
Mic. 2:8, men returned from *w*
Lk. 14:31, going to make *w*
1 Cor. 9:7, Who ever goes to *w*
Jas. 4:1, for pleasure that *w*
Jas. 4:2, You fight and *w*
1 Pet. 2:11, fleshly lusts which *w*
Rev. 12:7, *w* broke out in heaven
Rev. 19:11, He judges and makes *w*

WARFARE
Isa. 40:2, to her, that her *w*
2 Cor. 10:4, *w* are not carnal
1 Tim. 1:18, may wage the good *w*
2 Tim. 2:4, *w* entangles

WARM
Eccl. 4:11, they will keep *w*
Hag. 1:6, but no one is *w*

WARMED
Mk. 14:54, *w* himself at the fire
Jas. 2:16, Depart in peace, be *w*

WARMING
Mk. 14:67, when she saw Peter *w*

WARMS
Job 39:14, *w* them in the dust
Isa. 44:16, He even *w* himself and

WARN
Ezek. 3:18, *w* the wicked from his
Acts 20:31, *w* everyone night
1 Cor. 4:14, beloved children I *w*
1 Th. 5:14, *w* those who are

WARNED
Gen. 43:3, "The man solemnly *w*
Ps. 19:11, them Your servant is *w*
Mt. 2:12, Then, being divinely *w*
Mt. 3:7, Who *w* you to flee
Heb. 11:7, Noah, being divinely *w*

WARNING
Col. 1:28, *w* every man and

WARPED
Ti. 3:11, such a person is *w*

WARRING
Rom. 7:23, *w* against the law of

WARRIOR
Job 16:14, He runs at me like a *w*

WARS
Ps. 46:9, He makes *w* cease to
Mt. 24:6, you will hear of *w*
Jas. 4:1, Where do *w* and fights

WASH
Job 9:30, *w* myself with snow
Ps. 26:6, I will *w* my hands in
Ps. 51:2, *W* me thoroughly
Ps. 58:10, he shall *w* his feet in
Isa. 1:16, "*W* yourselves
Jer. 4:14, O Jerusalem, *w* your
Mt. 6:17, head and *w* your face
Mt. 15:2, For they do not *w*
Mk. 7:3, not eat unless they *w*
Lk. 7:38, *w* His feet with her
Jn. 9:7, said to him, "Go, *w*
Jn. 13:5, *w* the disciples'
Jn. 13:8, "You shall never *w*
Jn. 13:14, *w* one another's
Acts 22:16, *w* away your sins

WASHED
Ps. 73:13, and *w* my hands in
Isa. 4:4, When the Lord has *w*
Ezek. 16:4, cut, nor were you *w*
Mt. 27:24, *w* his hands before
Lk. 7:44, My feet, but she has *w*
Jn. 13:12, So when He had *w*
Acts 16:33, *w* their stripes
1 Cor. 6:11, But you were *w*
1 Tim. 5:10, if she has *w* the
Rev. 1:5, Him who loved us and *w*
Rev. 7:14, *w* their robes and made

WASHING
commanded by the law. Ex. 29:4; Lev. 6:27; 13:54; 14:8; Dt. 21:6; 2 Chr. 4:6
of the feet. Gen. 18:4; 24:32; 43:24; 1 Sam. 25:41; Lk. 7:38; 1 Tim. 5:10
of the hands. Dt. 21:6; Ps. 26:6; Mt. 27:24
of disciples' feet, by Christ. Jn. 13
superstitious, censured. Mk. 7:3; Lk. 11:38
figurative. Job 9:30; Isa. 1:16; 4:4; Ti. 3:5; Heb. 10:22; Eph. 5:26
in the blood of Christ. 1 Cor. 6:11; Rev. 1:5; 7:14

WASHING
Eph. 5:26, cleanse her with the *w*
Ti. 3:5, us, through the *w*

WASHINGS
Heb. 9:10, and drinks, various *w*

WASTE
forbidden. Jn. 6:12

WASTE
Lev. 26:39, who are left shall *w*
Isa. 6:11, the cities are laid *w*
Isa. 24:1, empty and makes it *w*
Isa. 42:15, *w* the mountains
Mt. 26:8, "Why this *w*

WASTED
Joel 1:10, The field is *w*
Mk. 14:4, this fragrant oil *w*
Lk. 15:13, *w* his possessions

WASTELAND
Isa. 35:1, *w* shall be glad

WASTING
Isa. 59:7, *w* and destruction are
Lk. 16:1, that this man was *w*

WATCH
Neh. 4:9, of them we set a *w*
Job 14:16, my steps, but do not *w*
Ps. 90:4, is past, and like a *w*
Ps. 141:3, keep *w* over the door
Isa. 29:20, and all who *w* for
Nah. 2:1, *W* the road
Mt. 24:42, "*W* therefore
Mt. 26:40, "What! Could you not *w*
Mt. 26:41, "*W* and pray
1 Cor. 16:13, *W*, stand fast in the
Heb. 13:17, submissive, for they *w*

WATCHED
Job 29:2, in the days when God *w*
Mt. 24:43, he would have *w*

WATCHES
Ps. 37:32, *w* the righteous
Prov. 31:27, She *w* over the ways of
Rev. 16:15, Blessed is he who *w*

WATCHFUL
2 Tim. 4:5, But you be *w* in all
1 Pet. 4:7, be serious and *w*

WATCHFULNESS
commanded. Mt. 24:42; 25:13; 26:41; Mk. 13:35; Lk. 12:35; 21:36; 1 Cor. 10:12; Eph. 6:18; Col. 4:2; 1 Th. 5:6; 2 Tim. 4:5; 1 Pet. 4:7; 5:8; Rev. 3:2; 16:15

WATCHING
Prov. 8:34, who listens to me, *w*
Zech. 11:11, the flock, who were *w*
Lk. 12:37, he comes, will find *w*

WATCHMAN
Ps. 127:1, guards the city, the *w*
Isa. 21:11, *W*, what of the night
Ezek. 3:17, I have made you a *w*
Mic. 7:4, the day of your *w*

WATCHMEN
their duty. 2 Sam. 18:25; 2 Ki. 9:17; Ps. 127:1; Song 3:3; 5:7; Isa. 21:5,11; 52:8; Jer. 6:17; 31:6; Ezek. 3:17; 33; Hab. 2:1
evil, described. Isa. 56:10

WATCHMEN
Song 3:3, *w* who go about the
Isa. 52:8, *w* shall lift up their
Isa. 56:10, His *w* are blind
Isa. 62:6, I have set *w* on your
Jer. 6:17, Also, I set *w* over you
Jer. 51:12, strong, set up the *w*

WATER
miracles of. Gen. 21:19; Ex. 15:23; 17:6; Num. 20:7; 2 Ki. 3:20
the trial of jealousy by. Num. 5:17
used in baptism. Mt. 3:11; Acts 8:36; 10:47
Christ walks on. Mt. 14:25; Mk. 6:48; Jn. 6:19
figuratively mentioned. Ps. 65:9; Isa. 41:17; 44:3; 55:1; Jer. 2:13; Ezek. 47; Zech. 13:1; Jn. 3:5; 4:10; 7:38; Rev. 7:17; 21:6; 22
of affliction. 1 Ki. 22:27

WATER
Gen. 2:10, Eden to *w* the garden
Gen. 49:4, Unstable as *w*
Ex. 23:25, your bread and your *w*
1 Ki. 22:27, of affliction and *w*
Job 14:11, *w* disappears from the
Job 14:19, *w* wears away stones
Job 15:16, drinks iniquity like *w*
Job 22:7, not given the weary *w*
Job 26:8, He binds up the *w*
Ps. 22:14, I am poured out like *w*
Ps. 63:1, where there is no *w*
Ps. 79:3, they have shed like *w*

Prov. 5:15, Drink *w* from your own
Prov. 9:17, "Stolen *w* is sweet
Isa. 3:1, the whole supply of *w*
Isa. 41:17, and needy seek *w*
Isa. 44:3, For I will pour *w*
Jer. 8:14, silence and given us *w*
Lam. 1:16, eye overflows with *w*
Ezek. 7:17, will be as weak as *w*
Ezek. 32:6, *w* the land with the
Lk. 7:44, you gave Me no *w*
Jn. 3:23, there was much *w*
Jn. 4:10, given you living *w*
Jn. 7:38, rivers of living *w*
Jn. 19:34, blood and *w* came out
Acts 10:47, "Can anyone forbid *w*
Eph. 5:26, with the washing of *w*
Jas. 3:12, can yield both salt *w*
1 Pet. 3:20, were saved through *w*
1 Jn. 5:6, is He who came by *w*
1 Jn. 5:8, the Spirit, the *w*
Jude 12, are clouds without *w*
Rev. 22:17, let him take the *w*

WATERED
Gen. 2:6, *w* the whole face
Gen. 13:10, that it was well *w*
1 Cor. 3:6, I planted, Apollos *w*

WATERS
of creation. Gen. 1:2,6,9
the flood. Gen. 6:17; 7:6
fountain of living. Jer. 2:13; 17:13
living fountains of. Rev. 7:17

WATERS
Ex. 7:20, and struck the *w*
Job 12:15, If He withholds the *w*
Ps. 23:2, me beside the still *w*
Ps. 46:3, though its *w* roar and
Ps. 69:1, *w* have come up to my
Ps. 124:4, then the *w* would have
Prov. 11:25, rich, and he who *w*
Prov. 30:4, Who has bound the *w*
Eccl. 11:1, your bread upon the *w*
Song 4:15, a well of living *w*
Song 8:7, *w* cannot quench love
Isa. 11:9, of the LORD as the *w*
Isa. 19:5, *w* will fail from the
Isa. 43:20, because I give *w*
Isa. 54:9, have sworn that the *w*
Isa. 55:1, thirsts, come to the *w*
Jer. 2:13, fountain of living *w*
Lam. 3:54, *w* flowed over my head
Ezek. 43:2, the sound of many *w*
Jon. 2:5, *w* surrounded me
Zech. 14:8, shall be that living *w*
2 Cor. 11:26, often, in perils of *w*
Rev. 7:17, living fountains of *w*
Rev. 8:11, *w* became wormwood

WAVE
Ps. 72:16, Its fruit shall *w*

WAVE OFFERING
Ex. 29:24; Lev. 7:30; 8:27; 23:11,20; Num. 5:25; 6:20

WAVER
Rom. 4:20, He did not *w* at the

WAVERING
Heb. 10:23, of our hope without *w*

WAVES
Job 38:11, and here your proud *w*
Ps. 42:7, all Your *w* and billows
Ps. 65:7, the noise of their *w*
Jer. 51:42, the multitude of its *w*
Mt. 8:24, was covered with the *w*
Mt. 14:24, sea, tossed by the *w*
Jude 13, raging *w* of the sea

WAX
Ps. 22:14, My heart is like *w*
Ps. 68:2, *w* melts before the
Ps. 97:5, mountains melt like *w*

WAY
Ex. 18:20, and show them the *w*
Josh. 23:14, day I am going the *w*
1 Sam. 12:23, and the right *w*
2 Sam. 22:31, As for God, His *w*
Job 3:23, to a man whose *w*
Job 23:10, But He knows the *w*
Job 38:19, "Where is the *w*
Ps. 1:6, the LORD knows the *w*
Ps. 2:12, you perish in the *w*
Ps. 27:11, Teach me Your *w*
Ps. 49:13, This is the *w* of those
Ps. 67:2, *w* may be known on
Ps. 77:19, Your *w* was in the sea
Ps. 107:40, where there is no *w*
Ps. 119:30, I have chosen the *w*
Ps. 119:104, I hate every false *w*
Ps. 139:24, in the *w* everlasting
Prov. 2:8, and preserves the *w*
Prov. 4:19, The *w* of the wicked is
Prov. 6:23, instruction are the *w*
Prov. 14:12, *w* that seems right
Eccl. 11:5, not know what is the *w*
Eccl. 12:5, of terrors in the *w*
Isa. 26:7, The *w* of the just is
Isa. 30:21, "This is the *w*
Isa. 43:16, LORD, who makes a *w*
Isa. 55:7, wicked forsake his *w*
Jer. 10:23, O LORD, I know the *w*
Jer. 32:39, one heart and one *w*
Ezek. 18:25, Israel, is it not My *w*
Ezek. 33:17, *w* which is not fair
Amos 2:7, and pervert the *w*
Nah. 1:3, the LORD has His *w*
Mal. 3:1, he will prepare the *w*
Mt. 7:13, and broad is the *w*
Mt. 7:14, and difficult is the *w*
Mt. 11:10, will prepare Your *w*
Mt. 22:16, and teach the *w*
Jn. 14:4, and the *w* you know
Jn. 14:6, to him, "I am the *w*
Acts 16:17, proclaim to us the *w*
Acts 18:26, explained to him the *w*
1 Cor. 12:31, you a more excellent *w*
Heb. 10:20, *w* which He consecrated
2 Pet. 2:15, forsaken the right *w*
2 Pet. 2:21, to have known the *w*
Jude 11, have gone in the *w*

WAYS
Dt. 32:4, for all His *w* are
Job 24:13, they do not know its *w*
Job 40:19, is the first of the *w*
Ps. 25:4, Show me Your *w*
Ps. 51:13, transgressors Your *w*
Ps. 81:13, would walk in My *w*
Ps. 119:5, *w* were directed
Ps. 119:59, I thought about my *w*
Ps. 145:17, righteous in all His *w*
Prov. 5:21, For the *w* of man are
Prov. 16:7, *w* please the LORD
Isa. 2:3, He will teach us His *w*
Isa. 55:8, nor are your *w*
Jer. 6:16, "Stand in the *w*
Jer. 7:3, "Amend your *w*
Lam. 3:40, and examine our *w*
Dan. 5:23, and owns all your *w*
Hab. 3:6, *w* are everlasting
Rom. 3:16, misery are in their *w*
Rom. 11:33, judgments and His *w*
Jas. 1:8, unstable in all his *w*
2 Pet. 2:2, their destructive *w*
Rev. 15:3, and true are Your *w*

WEAK
Jud. 16:7, then I shall become *w*
2 Sam. 3:39, "And I am *w* today
Ps. 6:2, me, O LORD, for I am *w*
Isa. 40:29, gives power to the *w*
Ezek. 7:17, knee will be as *w*
Joel 3:10, let the *w* say
Zeph. 3:16, not your hands be *w*
Mt. 26:41, but the flesh is *w*
Rom. 4:19, And not being *w*
Rom. 14:1, Receive one who is *w*
1 Cor. 1:27, God has chosen the *w*
1 Cor. 4:10, We are *w*, but you are
1 Cor. 9:22, to the *w* I became as *w*
1 Cor. 11:30, this reason many are *w*
2 Cor. 12:10, For when I am *w*

WEAKENED
Ps. 102:23, *w* my strength in the
Isa. 14:12, the ground, you who *w*

WEAKENS
Jer. 38:4, *w* the hands of the men

WEAKER
2 Sam. 3:1, house of Saul grew *w*
1 Pet. 3:7, the wife, as to the *w*

WEAKNESS
1 Cor. 1:25, than men, and the *w*
1 Cor. 2:3, I was with you in *w*
1 Cor. 15:43, It is sown in *w*
Heb. 5:2, is also subject to *w*
Heb. 11:34, *w* were made strong

WEAKNESSES
Rom. 8:26, also helps in our *w*
Heb. 4:15, sympathize with our *w*

WEALTH
Dt. 8:17, have gained me this *w*
Ruth 2:1, a man of great *w*
2 Chr. 1:11, not asked riches or *w*
Ps. 49:6, who trust in their *w*
Prov. 10:15, *w* is his strong city
Prov. 13:11, *W* gained by dishonesty
Prov. 19:4, *W* makes many friends
Isa. 60:11, may bring to you the *w*

WEALTHY
Jer. 49:31, *w* nation that dwells
Rev. 3:17, rich, have become *w*

WEANED
Isa. 11:8, *w* child shall put his
Isa. 28:9, Those just *w* from milk

WEAPON
Isa. 54:17, *w* formed against you
Ezek. 9:1, with a deadly *w*

WEAPONS
Eccl. 9:18, is better than *w*

Isa. 13:5, the LORD and His *w*
2 Cor. 10:4, For the *w* of our

WEAR
Job 27:17, but the just will *w*
Mt. 6:31, 'What shall we *w*

WEARIED
Isa. 43:24, you have *w* Me with
Isa. 57:10, You are *w* in the
Jer. 12:5, and they have *w*
Mal. 2:17, You have *w* the LORD
Jn. 4:6, therefore, being *w*

WEARINESS
Mal. 1:13, say, 'Oh, what a *w*
2 Cor. 11:27, in *w* and toil

WEARISOME
Eccl. 12:12, and much study is *w*

WEARY
Gen. 27:46, to Isaac, "I am *w*
Prov. 25:17, lest he become *w*
Prov. 25:25, As cold water to a *w*
Isa. 5:27, No one will be *w*
Isa. 28:12, you may cause the *w*
Isa. 40:31, shall run and not be *w*
Isa. 50:4, to him who is *w*
Jer. 6:11, I am *w* of holding it
Jer. 9:5, *w* themselves to commit
Jer. 20:9, I was *w* of holding it
Lk. 18:5, continual coming she *w*
Gal. 6:9, And let us not grow *w*
2 Th. 3:13, do not grow *w* in
Heb. 12:3, lest you become *w*

WEATHER
Prov. 25:20, a garment in cold *w*
Mt. 16:2, 'It will be fair *w*

WEDDING
Mt. 22:3, were invited to the *w*
Mt. 22:4, Come to the *w*
Mt. 22:9, find, invite to the *w*
Mt. 25:10, in with him to the *w*
Jn. 2:1, day there was a *w*

WEEK
Dan. 9:27, with many for one *w*
Mt. 28:1, the first day of the *w*
Acts 20:7, the first day of the *w*
1 Cor. 16:2, the first day of the *w*

WEEKS
Feast of. Dt. 16:9
Seventy, prophecy of. Dan. 9:24

WEEP
1 Sam. 1:8, "Hannah, why do you *w*
Eccl. 3:4, a time to *w*
Isa. 30:19, you shall *w* no more
Jer. 13:17, it, my soul will *w*
Jer. 22:10, *W* not for the dead
Joel 2:17, to the LORD, *w* between
Mk. 5:39, this commotion and *w*
Lk. 6:21, Blessed are you who *w*
Lk. 7:13, to her, "Do not *w*
Lk. 7:32, and you did not *w*
Lk. 23:28, of Jerusalem, do not *w*
Jn. 11:31, to the tomb to *w* there
Rom. 12:15, *w* with those who *w*
1 Cor. 7:30, those who *w* as though

WEEPING
Ps. 30:5; Mt. 22:13; Lk. 7:38; Phil. 3:18; Rev. 18:15
for the departed. Gen. 23:2; 2 Sam. 1:24; Eccl. 12:5; Jer. 9:17; 22:10; Ezek. 24:16; Amos 5:16; Mk. 5:39; Jn. 11:35; 20:13; 1 Th. 4:13
none in heaven. Rev. 21:4

WEEPING
Num. 25:6, of Israel, who were *w*
2 Sam. 15:30, *w* as they went up
Ezra 3:13, the noise of the *w*
Job 16:16, face is flushed from *w*
Ps. 6:8, the voice of my *w*
Ps. 102:9, my drink with *w*
Isa. 22:12, of hosts called for *w*
Isa. 65:19, *w* shall no longer
Jer. 31:9, They shall come with *w*
Jer. 50:4, *w* they shall come
Ezek. 8:14, were sitting there *w*
Joel 2:12, with fasting, with *w*
Mal. 2:13, with tears, with *w*
Mt. 8:12, There will be *w*
Jn. 20:11, outside by the tomb *w*
Jn. 20:13, "Woman, why are you *w*
Acts 21:13, "What do you mean by *w*

WEIGH
Ps. 58:2, You *w* out the violence
Isa. 26:7, O Most Upright, You *w*

WEIGHED
Job 28:15, nor can silver be *w*
Isa. 40:12, *W* the mountains
Dan. 5:27, You have been *w*
Lk. 21:34, lest your hearts be *w*

WEIGHS
Prov. 16:2, eyes, but the LORD *w*
Isa. 33:18, Where is he who *w*

WEIGHT
Dt. 25:15, a perfect and just *w*
Prov. 11:1, a just *w* is His delight
2 Cor. 4:17, and eternal *w* of glory
Heb. 12:1, us lay aside every *w*

WEIGHTIER
Mt. 23:23, have neglected the *w*

WEIGHTS
just, commanded. Lev. 19:35; Dt. 25:13; Prov. 11:1; 16:11; 20:10,23; Ezek. 45:10; Mic. 6:10

WEIGHTY
Prov. 27:3; 2 Cor. 10:10

WELFARE
Jer. 38:4, does not seek the *w*

WELL
those who are, have no need of a physician. Mt. 9:12; Mk. 2:17; Lk. 5:31
sick ones made. Mt. 12:13; Mk. 3:5; Lk. 6:10. *See* MIRACLES

WELL
Gen. 4:7, "If you do *w*
Dt. 4:40, that it may go *w*
Ps. 49:18, you when you do *w*
Prov. 31:29, daughters have done *w*
Eccl. 8:12, know that it will be *w*
Eccl. 12:6, wheel broken at the *w*
Isa. 3:10, that it shall be *w*
Mt. 9:12, "Those who are *w*
Mt. 25:21, said to him, '*W* done
Mk. 5:34, faith has made you *w*
Jn. 4:6, Now Jacob's *w* was
1 Tim. 5:17, the elders who rule *w*

WELL-BEING
Ps. 69:22, them, and their *w*
1 Cor. 10:24, each one the other's *w*

WELLS
of Abraham. Gen. 26:15; Isaac. Gen. 26:25; Uzziah. 2 Chr. 26:10; Jacob. Jn. 4:6

WELLS
Isa. 12:3, draw water from the *w*
2 Pet. 2:17, These are *w* without

WENT
1 Jn. 2:19, They *w* out from us

WEPT
2 Ki. 8:11, and the man of God *w*
Ezra 10:1, for the people *w*
Neh. 1:4, that I sat down and *w*
Job 30:25, Have I not *w* for him
Ps. 137:1, down, yea, we *w*
Mt. 26:75, out and *w* bitterly
Lk. 19:41, He saw the city and *w*
Jn. 11:35, Jesus *w*
Rev. 5:4, So I *w* much

WET
Job 24:8, They are *w* with the
Dan. 4:33, his body was *w* with

WHEAT
Ps. 81:16, with the finest of *w*
Amos 8:5, we may trade *w*
Amos 8:6, even sell the bad *w*
Mt. 13:30, but gather the *w*
Jn. 12:24, *w* falls into the
1 Cor. 15:37, perhaps *w* or some
Rev. 18:13, oil, fine flour and *w*

WHEEL
Prov. 20:26, brings the threshing *w*
Eccl. 12:6, the fountain, or the *w*
Ezek. 1:16, in the middle of a *w*

WHEELS
Ex. 14:25, off their chariot *w*
Jer. 47:3, the rumbling of his *w*
Ezek. 1:16, appearance of the *w*
Nah. 3:2, noise of rattling *w*

WHERE
Heb. 11:8, not knowing *w* he was

WHIP
Prov. 26:3, A *w* for the horse
Nah. 3:2, The noise of a *w*

WHIRLWIND
2 Ki. 2:11, Elijah went up by a *w*
Job 38:1, Job out of the *w*
Ps. 58:9, them away as with a *w*
Isa. 40:24, *w* will take them away
Isa. 41:16, *w* shall scatter them
Jer. 25:32, *w* shall be raised
Nah. 1:3, has His way in the *w*

WHIRLWINDS
1 Ki. 19:11; 2 Ki. 2:1; Job 37:9; Isa. 66:15; Jer. 23:19; Ezek. 1:4; Zech. 9:14

WHISPER
Job 4:12, my ear received a *w*
Isa. 8:19, and wizards, who *w*

WHISPERER
Prov. 16:28, *w* separates the best

WHISPERERS
Rom. 1:29, they are *w*

WHISPERINGS
2 Cor. 12:20, backbitings, *w*

WHITE
Song 5:10, My beloved is *w*
Dan. 11:35, and make them *w*
Dan. 12:10, be purified, made *w*
Jn. 4:35, for they are already *w*
Rev. 3:4, walk with Me in *w*
Rev. 3:5, clothed in *w* garments
Rev. 6:2, behold, a *w* horse
Rev. 7:14, and made them *w*
Rev. 20:11, Then I saw a great *w*

WHITE GARMENTS
of Christ at the transfiguration. Mt. 17:2; Mk. 9:3; Lk. 9:29
of angels. Mt. 28:3; Mk. 16:5
of the redeemed. Rev. 3:5; 4:4; 7:9; 19:8,14

WHITER, Ps. 51:7; Lam. 4:7

WHITEWASHED
Mt. 23:27; Acts 23:3

WHOLE
1 Cor. 12:17, *w* body were an eye

WHOLESOME
Prov. 15:4, *w* tongue is a tree
1 Tim. 6:3, not consent to *w* words

WHOLLY
Dt. 1:36, *w* followed the LORD
Jer. 46:28, I will not leave you *w*

WICKED
their character and doom. Dt. 32:5; Job 4:8; 5; 15; 18; 20; 21; 24; 27:13; 30; 36:12; Eccl. 8:10; Isa. 1; 22; 28; 29; 37:21; 40:18; 41:6; 44:9; 45:9; 47; 57—59; 66; Jer. 2; Ezek. 5; 16; 18; 23; Hos.—Mal.; Mt. 5—7; 13:37; 15; 16; 21:33; 25; Jn. 5:29; 10; Rom. 1:21; 3:10; 1 Cor. 5:11; Gal. 5:19; Eph. 4:17; 5:5; Phil. 3:18; Col. 3:6; 2 Th. 2; 1 Tim. 1:9; 4; 6:9; 2 Tim. 3:13; Ti. 1:10; Heb. 6:4; Jas. 4; 5; 1 Pet. 4; 2 Pet. 2; 3; 1 Jn. 2:18; 4; Jude; Rev. 9:20; 14:8; 18; 20:13; 22:15
their prosperity not to be envied. Ps. 37:1; 73; Prov. 3:31; 23:17; 24:1,19; Jer. 12
friendship with, forbidden. Gen. 28:1; Ex. 23:32; 34:12; Num. 16:26; Dt. 7:2; 13:6; Josh. 23:7; Jud. 2:2; 2 Chr. 19:2; Ezra 9:12; 10:10; Neh. 9:2; Ps. 106:35; Prov. 1:10; 4:14; 12:11; 14:7; Jer. 2:25; 51:6; Rom. 16:17; 1 Cor. 5:9; 15:33; 2 Cor. 6:14; Eph. 5:7,11; Phil. 2:15; 2 Th. 3:6; 1 Tim. 6:5; 2 Tim. 3:5; 2 Pet. 3:17; Rev. 18:4

WICKED
1 Sam. 2:9, *w* shall be silent
2 Chr. 19:2, Should you help the *w*
Job 21:7, Why do the *w* live and
Job 21:30, *w* are reserved for the
Job 34:18, to nobles, 'You are *w*
Ps. 7:11, with the *w* every day
Ps. 9:16, *w* is snared in the
Ps. 9:17, *w* shall be turned
Ps. 10:13, do the *w* renounce God
Ps. 11:2, *w* bend their bow
Ps. 11:6, *w* He will rain coals
Ps. 34:21, Evil shall slay the *w*
Ps. 37:10, *w* shall be no more
Ps. 37:32, The *w* watches the
Ps. 94:3, how long will the *w*
Ps. 104:35, and the *w* be no more
Ps. 119:155, is far from the *w*
Ps. 139:24, if there is any *w*
Prov. 2:22, *w* will be cut off from
Prov. 11:5, *w* will fall by his own
Prov. 15:29, LORD is far from the *w*
Prov. 28:1, *w* flee when no one
Eccl. 7:17, Do not be overly *w*
Eccl. 8:13, not be well with the *w*
Isa. 55:7, *w* forsake his way
Isa. 57:20, But the *w* are like the
Jer. 17:9, and desperately *w*
Dan. 12:10, *w* shall do wickedly
Nah. 1:3, at all acquit the *w*
1 Jn. 5:18, *w* one does not touch
1 Jn. 5:19, the sway of the *w*

WICKEDLY
Job 13:7, Will you speak *w*
Job 34:12, God will never do *w*
Dan. 11:32, "Those who do *w*
Mal. 4:1, yes, all who do *w*

WICKEDNESS
Gen. 6:5, LORD saw that the *w*
Gen. 39:9, can I do this great *w*
1 Sam. 24:13, '*W* proceeds from the
2 Sam. 7:10, *w* oppress them
Job 22:5, Is not your *w* great
Ps. 7:9, Oh, let the *w* of the
Ps. 55:15, alive into hell, for *w*
Ps. 84:10, in the tents of *w*
Ps. 101:4, I will not know *w*
Prov. 4:17, eat the bread of *w*
Prov. 8:7, *w* is an abomination
Eccl. 8:8, *w* will not deliver
Isa. 9:18, *w* burns as the
Isa. 47:10, have trusted in your *w*
Jer. 2:19, *w* will correct you
Jer. 6:7, wells up with her *w*
Jer. 8:6, man repented of his *w*
Ezek. 3:19, not turn from his *w*
Hos. 10:13, You have plowed *w*
Hab. 1:13, and cannot look on *w*
Mal. 3:15, for those who do *w*
Lk. 11:39, is full of greed and *w*
Rom. 1:29, sexual immorality, *w*
Eph. 6:12, spiritual hosts of *w*
Jas. 1:21, and overflow of *w*

WIDE
Dt. 15:8, shall open your hand *w*
Job 29:23, opened their mouth *w*
Prov. 13:3, *w* his lips shall have
Jer. 22:14, will build myself a *w*
Mt. 7:13, *w* is the gate and
2 Cor. 6:11, to you, our heart is *w*

WIDOW
Elijah sustained by one. 1 Ki. 17
parable of. Lk. 18:3
the widow's mites. Mk. 12:42; Lk. 21:2
figurative. Isa. 47:9; 54:4; Lam. 1:1

WIDOW
Job 24:21, does no good for the *w*
Ps. 94:6, They slay the *w*
Ps. 109:9, and his wife a *w*
Ps. 146:9, the fatherless and *w*
Isa. 1:17, plead for the *w*
Lam. 1:1, How like a *w* is she
Mk. 12:42, Then one poor *w*
1 Tim. 5:4, *w* has children or
1 Tim. 5:9, Do not let a *w* under

WIDOW'S
Job 29:13, and I caused the *w*

WIDOWS
to be honored and relieved. Ex. 22:22; Dt. 14:29; 24:17; 27:19; Job 29:13; Isa. 1:17; Jer. 7:6; Acts 6:1; 9:39; 1 Tim. 5:3; Jas. 1:27
especially under God's protection. Dt. 10:18; Ps. 68:5; 146:9; Prov. 15:25; Jer. 49:11
injurers of widows, condemned. Dt. 27:19; Ps. 94:6; Isa. 1:23; 10:2; Ezek. 22:7; Mal. 3:5; Mt. 23:14; Mk. 12:40; Lk. 20:47
laws relating to their marriages. Lev. 21:14; Dt. 25:5; Ezek. 44:22; Mk. 12:19. *See* 1 Cor. 7:8

WIDOWS
Ps. 68:5, a defender of *w*
Jer. 49:11, and let your *w* trust
Acts 6:1, *w* were neglected
1 Tim. 5:14, that the younger *w*
Jas. 1:27, visit orphans and *w*

WIFE
Gen. 2:24, and be joined to his *w*
Prov. 12:4, an excellent *w* is the
Prov. 18:22, *w* finds a good thing
Prov. 19:14, but a prudent *w*
Eccl. 9:9, *w* whom you love all
Isa. 54:6, like a youthful *w*
Hos. 1:2, "Go, take yourself a *w*
Hos. 12:12, *w* he tended sheep
Mal. 2:15, with the *w* of his
Mk. 10:11, "Whoever divorces his *w*
Lk. 14:20, 'I have married a *w*
Lk. 17:32, "Remember Lot's *w*
Lk. 20:33, all seven had her as *w*
Eph. 5:33, so love his own *w*
Ti. 1:6, the husband of one *w*
1 Pet. 3:7, giving honor to the *w*
Rev. 21:9, bride, the Lamb's *w*

WILD
Mt. 3:4, locusts and *w* honey
Rom. 11:24, olive tree which is *w*

WILDERNESS
the Israelites' journeys in. Ex. 14; Num. 10:12; 13:3; 20; 33; Dt. 1:19; 8:2; 32:10; Neh. 9:19; Ps. 78:40; 95:8; 107:4
Hagar's flight into. Gen. 16:7
Elijah's flight into. 1 Ki. 19:4

(of Judea), John the Baptist preaches in. Mt. 3

WILDERNESS
Dt. 32:10, wasteland, a howling *w*
Job 24:5, *w* yields food for them
Song 3:6, coming out of the *w*
Isa. 14:17, made the world as a *w*
Isa. 41:18, I will make the *w*
Isa. 42:11, Let the *w* and its
Jer. 2:31, Have I been a *w*
Mt. 3:3, of one crying in the *w*
Jn. 3:14, the serpent in the *w*
Acts 7:38, congregation in the *w*

WILES
Eph. 6:11, to stand against the *w*

WILL
—— of God, irresistible. Dan. 4:17,35; Jn. 1:13; Rom. 9:19; Eph. 1:5; Jas. 1:18
fulfilled by Christ. (Ps. 40:8); Mt. 26:42; Mk. 14:36; Lk. 22:42; Jn. 4:34; 5:30; Heb. 10:7
how performed. Jn. 7:17; Eph. 6:6; Col. 4:12; 1 Th. 4:3; 5:18; Heb. 13:21; 1 Pet. 2:15; 4:2; 1 Jn. 2:17; 3:23
to be submitted to. Jas. 4:15. *See* Mt. 6:10; Acts 21:14; Rom. 1:10; 15:32
—— of man. Jn. 1:13; Rom. 9:16; Eph. 2:3; 1 Pet. 4:3

WILL
Mt. 6:10, *w* be done on earth as
Mt. 7:21, but he who does the *w*
Mt. 21:31, of the two did the *w*
Lk. 2:14, on earth peace, good *w*
Lk. 22:42, nevertheless not My *w*
Jn. 1:13, flesh, nor of the *w*
Jn. 5:30, I do not seek My own *w*
Jn. 6:38, not to do My own *w*
Jn. 6:39, "This is the *w*
Jn. 7:17, wills to do His *w*
Rom. 7:18, *w* is present with me
Rom. 12:2, and perfect *w* of God
Phil. 2:13, works in you both to *w*
Col. 1:9, the knowledge of His *w*
Heb. 2:4, according to His own *w*
Heb. 10:9, come to do Your *w*
Heb. 13:21, good work to do His *w*
1 Jn. 2:17, but he who does the *w*

WILLFULLY
Heb. 10:26, For if we sin *w*
2 Pet. 3:5, For this they *w*

WILLING
Ex. 35:5, is of a *w* heart
Isa. 1:19, If you are *w* and
Mt. 8:3, him, saying, "I am *w*
Mt. 26:41, The spirit indeed is *w*
Mk. 14:38, The spirit indeed is *w*
2 Cor. 8:12, if there is first a *w*
2 Pet. 3:9, *w* that any should

WILLINGLY
Rom. 8:20, to futility, not *w*
1 Cor. 9:17, For if I do this *w*
1 Pet. 5:2, by compulsion but *w*

WILLOWS
Ps. 137:2, our harps upon the *w*

WILLS
Mt. 11:27, to whom the Son *w*
Rom. 9:16, it is not of him who *w*
Jas. 4:15, say, "If the Lord *w*

WIN
Mt. 23:15, *w* one proselyte
1 Cor. 9:19, to all, that I might *w*

WIND
miraculous effects of. Gen. 8:1; Ex. 15:10; Num. 11:31; Ezek. 37:9; Jon. 1:4
rebuked by Christ. Mt. 8:26
figuratively mentioned. Job 7:7; 8:2; Jn. 3:8; Jas. 1:6; 3:4

WIND
1 Ki. 19:11, LORD was not in the *w*
Job 27:21, *w* carries him away
Ps. 1:4, the chaff which the *w*
Ps. 147:18, He causes His *w*
Prov. 11:29, will inherit the *w*
Eccl. 11:4, He who observes the *w*
Eccl. 11:5, is the way of the *w*
Song 4:16, Awake, O north *w*
Jer. 5:13, the prophets become *w*
Jer. 51:16, He brings the *w*
Hos. 12:1, Ephraim feeds on the *w*
Amos 4:13, and creates the *w*
Mt. 11:7, reed shaken by the *w*
Mk. 4:39, And the *w* ceased and
Lk. 8:24, and rebuked the *w*
Jn. 3:8, "The *w* blows where
Acts 2:2, of a rushing mighty *w*
Eph. 4:14, about with every *w*

WINDOWS
Song 2:9, looking through the *w*
Jer. 9:21, has come through our *w*
Dan. 6:10, upper room, with his *w*
Mal. 3:10, not open for you the *w*

WINDS
Ezek. 37:9, from the four *w*
Mt. 8:27, be, that even the *w*
Rev. 7:1, holding the four *w*

WINDSTORM
Mk. 4:37, And a great *w* arose

WINE
made by Noah. Gen. 9:20
used by Abram and Melchizedek. Gen. 14:18
used in offerings. Ex. 29:40; Lev. 23:13; Num. 15:5
in the Lord's Supper. Mt. 26:29
Nazirites not to drink. Num. 6:3; Jud. 13:14
Rechabites abstain from. Jer. 35
water changed to, by Christ. Jn. 2
love of. Prov. 21:17; 23:20,30; Hos. 4:11; Hab. 2:5; Eph. 5:18
its lawful use. Jud. 9:13; 19:19; Ps. 104:15; Prov. 31:6; Eccl. 10:19; Eph. 5:18; 1 Tim. 5:23
its abuse. *See* DRUNKENNESS

WINE
Gen. 9:24, Noah awoke from his *w*
Ps. 104:15, *w* that makes glad
Prov. 20:1, *W* is a mocker
Prov. 23:31, Do not look on the *w*
Song 1:2, love is better than *w*
Isa. 5:11, *w* inflames them
Isa. 55:1, Yes, come, buy *w*
Mt. 27:34, they gave Him sour *w*
Jn. 2:3, when they ran out of *w*
Eph. 5:18, do not be drunk with *w*
1 Tim. 5:23, but use a little *w*
Ti. 2:3, not given to much *w*
Rev. 16:19, her the cup of the *w*

WINEBIBBERS
Prov. 23:20, Do not mix with *w*

WINEPRESS
of the wrath of God. Rev. 14:19; 19:15. *See* Isa. 5:2; 63:3; Lam. 1:15; Mt. 21:33

WINEPRESS
Isa. 63:3, "I have trodden the *w*
Joel 3:13, for the *w* is full
Rev. 14:19, into the great *w*
Rev. 19:15, Himself treads the *w*

WINESKIN
Ps. 119:83, I have become like a *w*

WINESKINS
Mt. 9:17, new wine into old *w*

WING
1 Ki. 6:24, One *w* of the cherub
Ezek. 16:8, so I spread My *w*

WINGS
Ruth 2:12, *w* you have come
Ps. 18:10, He flew upon the *w*
Ps. 36:7, the shadow of Your *w*
Ps. 139:9, If I take the *w*
Isa. 6:2, each one had six *w*
Mal. 4:2, with healing in His *w*
Rev. 12:14, woman was given two *w*

WINK
Job 15:12; Ps. 35:19; Prov. 6:13; 10:10

WINNOW
Isa. 41:16, You shall *w* them

WINS
Prov. 11:30, *w* souls is wise

WINTER
Ps. 74:17, have made summer and *w*
Song 2:11, For lo, the *w* is past
Zech. 14:8, *w* it shall occur
Mt. 24:20, flight may not be in *w*

WIPE
Isa. 25:8, the Lord GOD will *w*
Jn. 13:5, *w* them with the towel
Rev. 21:4, *w* away every tear

WISDOM
given by God. Ex. 31:3; 1 Ki. 3:12; 4:29; 1 Chr. 22:12; 2 Chr. 1:10; Ezra 7:25; Prov. 2:6; Eccl. 2:26; Dan. 2:20; Acts 6:10; 7:10; 2 Pet. 3:15
its characteristics. Dt. 4:6; Job 28:12; Ps. 111:10; Prov. 1:2; 9; 14:8; 24:7; 28:7; Eccl. 2:13; 7:19; 9:13; Jer. 23:24; Mt. 7:24; Jas. 3:13
to be sought for. Ps. 90:12; Mt. 10:16; Rom. 16:19; Eph. 5:15; 2 Tim. 3:15; Jas. 3:13
blessings attending it. Prov. 1:5; 3:13; 8:11; 16:16; 24:3,14; Eccl. 7:11; 9:13; 12:11; Mt. 25:1

obtained in answer to prayer by Solomon, etc. 1 Ki. 3:9; 10:6; Prov. 2:3; Dan. 2:21; Jas. 1:5
personified. Prov. 1:20; 8; 9
danger of despising. Prov. 1:24; 2:12; 3:21; 5:12; 8:36; 9:12; 10:21; 11:12
apparent in the works of God. Ps. 104:1,24; 136:5; Prov. 3:19; 6:6; Jer. 10:12; Rom. 1:20; 11:33
of Joseph. Gen. 41:39; 47:13; Solomon. 1 Ki. 4:29; Daniel, etc. Ezek. 28:3; Dan. 1:17; 5:14
worldly, vanity of. Job 5:13; 11:12; Prov. 3:7; Eccl. 2; Isa. 5:21; Jer. 8:9; Zech. 9:2; Mt. 11:25; 1 Cor. 1:17; 2:4; 3:19; 2 Cor. 1:12; Jas. 3:15. *See* Gen. 3:6

WISDOM
Dt. 4:6, for this is your *w*
Job 12:2, *w* will die with you
Ps. 51:6, will make me to know *w*
Prov. 3:13, man who finds *w*
Prov. 4:5, Get *w*! Get understanding
Prov. 4:7, *W* is the principal
Prov. 9:10, is the beginning of *w*
Prov. 16:16, to get *w* than gold
Prov. 19:8, *w* loves his own soul
Prov. 24:7, *W* is too lofty for a
Eccl. 1:18, *w* is much grief
Eccl. 9:16, *W* is better than
Mt. 11:19, *w* is justified by her
Lk. 2:52, Jesus increased in *w*
Rom. 11:33, riches both of the *w*
1 Cor. 1:17, the gospel, not with *w*
1 Cor. 1:22, Greeks seek after *w*
1 Cor. 3:19, For the *w* of this world
2 Cor. 1:12, not with fleshly *w*
Eph. 3:10, now the manifold *w*
Col. 2:3, all the treasures of *w*
Col. 4:5, Walk in *w* toward those
Jas. 1:5, If any of you lacks *w*
Rev. 5:12, power and riches and *w*
Rev. 7:12, and glory and *w*

WISE
Dt. 4:6, great nation is a *w*
Job 5:13, He catches the *w*
Job 9:4, God is *w* in heart and
Job 32:9, men are not always *w*
Ps. 94:8, when will you be *w*
Ps. 107:43, *w* will observe these
Prov. 3:7, Do not be *w* in your
Prov. 11:30, who wins souls is *w*
Prov. 16:21, The *w* in heart will be
Prov. 26:5, folly, lest he be *w*
Prov. 30:24, they are exceedingly *w*
Eccl. 12:11, The words of the *w*
Jer. 4:22, They are *w* to do evil
Mt. 10:16, Therefore be *w* as
Mt. 25:2, five of them were *w*
Rom. 1:14, barbarians, both to *w*
Rom. 16:27, to God, alone *w*
1 Cor. 1:20, Where is the *w*
1 Cor. 4:10, sake, but you are *w*
Eph. 5:15, not as fools but as *w*
2 Tim. 3:15, able to make you *w*

WISELY
Ps. 101:2, I will behave *w*
Prov. 16:20, who heeds the word *w*
Eccl. 7:10, you do not inquire *w*

WISER
1 Ki. 4:31, he was *w* than all men
Job 35:11, *w* than the birds
Ps. 119:98, *w* than my enemies
1 Cor. 1:25, of God is *w* than men

WISH
Mt. 20:15, for me to do what I *w*
Lk. 12:49, *w* it were already

WISHED
Jon. 4:8, Then he *w* death for

WITCHCRAFT
forbidden. Ex. 22:18; Lev. 19:26,31; 20:6,27; Dt. 18:10; Mic. 5:12; Mal. 3:5; Gal. 5:20; Rev. 21:8; 22:15
abolished by Josiah. 2 Ki. 23:24
practiced by: Saul. 1 Sam. 28; Manasseh. 2 Ki. 21:6; 2 Chr. 33:6; Israelites. 2 Ki. 17:17; Simon of Samaria. Acts 8:9; Philippians. Acts 16:16; Ephesians. Acts 19:19

WITCHCRAFT
1 Sam. 15:23, is as the sin of *w*

WITHDRAW
Job 9:13, God will not *w* His
Job 36:7, He does not *w* His eyes
1 Tim. 6:5, From such *w* yourself

WITHER
Ps. 1:3, also shall not *w*
Ps. 37:2, *w* as the green
Ezek. 47:12, leaves will not *w*
Mt. 21:20, How did the fig tree *w*

WITHERS
Isa. 40:7, The grass *w*
Jas. 1:11, burning heat than it *w*
1 Pet. 1:24, The grass *w*

WITHHELD
Jer. 5:25, and your sins have *w*

WITHHOLD
Ps. 40:11, *w* Your tender mercies
Ps. 84:11, good thing will He *w*
Prov. 3:27, Do not *w* good from
Lk. 6:29, your cloak, do not *w*

WITHOUT
Eph. 2:12, having no hope and *w*
1 Th. 5:17, pray *w* ceasing
1 Tim. 3:16, *w* controversy
Jas. 2:26, *w* works is dead

WITHSTAND
Acts 11:17, was I that I could *w*
Eph. 6:13, you may be able to *w*

WITHSTOOD
Gal. 2:11, I *w* him to his face

WITNESS
God invoked as. Gen. 31:50; Jud. 11:10; 1 Sam. 12:5; Jer. 42:5; Mic. 1:2; Rom. 1:9; 1 Th. 2:5
—— borne to Christ, by the Father. Mt. 3:16; Lk. 3:22; Jn. 5:37; 12:28; Heb. 2:4; 1 Jn. 5:7
by the Holy Spirit. Mt. 3:16; Lk. 3:22; Jn. 1:33; 15:26; Acts 5:32; 20:23; Heb. 10:15; 1 Jn. 5:7
by the apostles. Acts 1:8; 2:32; 4:33; 5:32; 10:41; 22:15; 26:16; 1 Pet. 5:1; Rev. 20:4
by the prophets. Acts 10:43; 1 Pet. 1:10
—— Christ the Faithful and True. Rev. 1:5; 3:14
—— false. Ex. 20:16; 23:1; Lev. 19:11; Dt. 5:20; 19:16; Prov. 6:16,19; 12:17; 19:5,9,28; 21:28; 25:18; Jer. 7:9; Zech. 5:4; Lk. 3:14
against Christ. Mt. 26:60; Mk. 14:56

WITNESS
Gen. 31:50, see, God is *w* between
Job 16:19, Surely even now my *w*
Ps. 89:37, like the faithful *w*
Prov. 14:5, *w* does not lie
Isa. 55:4, have given him as a *w*
Jer. 42:5, a true and faithful *w*
Mal. 3:5, I will be a swift *w*
Mt. 24:14, all the world as a *w*
Jn. 1:7, This man came for a *w*
Jn. 3:11, do not receive Our *w*
Jn. 5:31, "If I bear *w* of
Jn. 5:32, is another who bears *w*
Jn. 5:36, But I have a greater *w*
Acts 14:3, who was bearing *w*
Acts 22:15, For you will be His *w*
Phil. 1:8, For God is my *w*
1 Jn. 5:7, are three who bear *w*
1 Jn. 5:9, If we receive the *w*
Rev. 1:2, who bore *w* to the word
Rev. 1:5, Christ, the faithful *w*
Rev. 20:4, beheaded for their *w*

WITNESSED
Rom. 3:21, is revealed, being *w*
1 Tim. 6:13, *w* the good confession

WITNESSES
two or three required. Num. 35:30; Dt. 17:6; 19:15; Mt. 18:16; 2 Cor. 13:1; 1 Tim. 5:19
—— the two. Rev. 11

WITNESSES
Dt. 17:6, of two or three *w*
Isa. 8:2, for Myself faithful *w*
Isa. 43:10, "You are My *w*
1 Tim. 6:12, presence of many *w*
Heb. 10:15, the Holy Spirit also *w*
Heb. 12:1, so great a cloud of *w*
Rev. 11:3, give power to my two *w*

WIVES
their duties to husbands. Gen. 3:16; Ex. 20:14; Rom. 7:2; 1 Cor. 7:3; 14:34; Eph. 5:22,33; Ti. 2:4; 1 Pet. 3:1
good. Prov. 12:4; 18:22; 19:14; 31:10
Levitical laws concerning. Ex. 21:3,22; 22:16; Num. 5:12; 30; Dt. 21:10,15; 24:1; Jer. 3:1; Mt. 19:3
the wife a type of the Church. Eph. 5:23; Rev. 19:7; 21:9

WIVES
Eph. 5:25, Husbands, love your *w*
1 Tim. 3:11, *w* must be reverent

WIZARDS
Isa. 8:19, who are mediums and *w*

WOES
against wickedness, etc. Isa. 5:8; 10:1; 29:15; 31:1; 45:9; Jer. 22:13; Amos 6:1; Mic. 2:1; Hab. 2:6;

Zeph. 3:1; Zech. 11:17; Mt. 26:24; Lk. 6:24; Jude 11; Rev. 8:13; 9:12; 11:14
against unbelief. Mt. 11:21; 23:13; Lk. 10:13; 11:42

WOLF
Isa. 65:25, The *w* and the lamb
Jn. 10:12, the sheep, sees the *w*

WOLVES
Mt. 7:15, they are ravenous *w*
Lk. 10:3, out as lambs among *w*
Acts 20:29, savage *w* will come in

WOMAN
creation and fall of. Gen. 2:22; 3
Christ the Seed of. (Gen. 3:15); Gal. 4:4

WOMAN
Gen. 2:23, she shall be called *W*
Prov. 14:1, *w* builds her house
Prov. 31:30, *w* who fears the LORD
Jer. 31:22, *w* shall encompass a
Mt. 5:28, whoever looks at a *w*
Lk. 7:44, "Do you see this *w*
Jn. 4:9, Then the *w* of Samaria
Jn. 8:3, brought to Him a *w*
Jn. 19:26, "*W*, behold your
Acts 9:36, *w* was full of good
Rom. 1:27, natural use of the *w*
1 Cor. 7:1, a man not to touch a *w*
1 Cor. 11:7, *w* is the glory of man
Gal. 4:4, His Son, born of a *w*
1 Tim. 2:11, Let a *w* learn in
1 Tim. 2:12, I do not permit a *w*
1 Tim. 2:14, *w* being deceived
Rev. 12:1, *w* clothed with the sun
Rev. 12:16, the earth helped the *w*

WOMB
Gen. 25:23, nations are in your *w*
1 Sam. 1:5, LORD had closed her *w*
Ps. 22:9, took Me out of the *w*
Isa. 44:2, formed you from the *w*
Isa. 49:1, called Me from the *w*
Jer. 1:5, in the *w* I knew you
Lk. 1:42, is the fruit of your *w*
Lk. 11:27, "Blessed is the *w*

WOMEN
duty of the older. Ti. 2:3; of the young. 1 Tim. 2:9; 5:14; Ti. 2:4; 1 Pet. 3. *See* WIVES

WOMEN
Jud. 5:24, blessed is she among *w*
Ps. 45:9, among Your honorable *w*
Song 1:8, O fairest among *w*
Isa. 3:12, *w* rule over them
Zech. 9:17, new wine the young *w*
Mt. 24:41, *w* will be grinding
Lk. 1:28, are you among *w*
1 Cor. 14:34, *w* keep silent in the
Ti. 2:4, admonish the young *w*
1 Pet. 3:5, times, the holy *w*
Rev. 14:4, not defiled with *w*

WONDER
Ps. 71:7, I have become as a *w*
Isa. 29:14, marvelous work and a *w*

WONDERFUL
Jud. 13:18, name, seeing it is *w*
2 Sam. 1:26, Your love to me was *w*
Job 42:3, things too *w* for me
Ps. 119:129, Your testimonies are *w*
Isa. 9:6, name will be called *W*
Isa. 28:29, of hosts, who is *w*
Mt. 21:15, and scribes saw the *w*
Acts 2:11, our own tongues the *w*

WONDERFULLY
Ps. 139:14, fearfully and *w* made

WONDERS
Ex. 3:20, *w* which I will do
Ps. 77:14, are the God who does *w*
Ps. 88:12, Shall Your *w* be known
Ps. 136:4, who alone does great *w*
Jer. 32:21, Egypt with signs and *w*
Dan. 4:3, and how mighty His *w*
Dan. 6:27, He works signs and *w*
Joel 2:30, "And I will show *w*
Mt. 7:22, and done many *w*
2 Th. 2:9, signs, and lying *w*
Heb. 2:4, both with signs and *w*

WONDROUS
Ps. 26:7, and tell of all Your *w*
Ps. 75:1, *w* works declare that
Ps. 106:22, *w* works in the land of
Zech. 3:8, for they are a *w*

WONDROUSLY
Joel 2:26, God, Who has dealt *w*

WOOD
1 Cor. 3:12, precious stones, *w*

WOODCUTTERS
Josh. 9:21, but let them be *w*

WOOL
Isa. 1:18, they shall be as *w*
Dan. 7:9, head was like pure *w*
Rev. 1:14, hair were white like *w*

WORD
Dt. 8:3, *w* that proceeds
Dt. 30:14, *w* is very near you
Ps. 119:11, *w* I have hidden
Ps. 119:50, *w* has given me life
Ps. 119:105, *w* is a lamp to my feet
Prov. 12:25, *w* makes it glad
Prov. 15:23, *w* spoken in due season
Prov. 25:11, *w* fitly spoken is
Prov. 30:5, Every *w* of God is pure
Isa. 9:8, The LORD sent a *w*
Isa. 40:8, the *w* of our God
Isa. 45:23, *w* has gone out of My
Isa. 55:11, *w* be that goes forth
Jer. 20:9, But His *w* was in my
Jer. 23:36, *w* will be his oracle
Ezek. 12:28, *w* which I speak will
Mt. 8:8, But only speak a *w*
Mt. 12:36, for every idle *w*
Lk. 8:11, The seed is the *w*
Lk. 24:19, mighty in deed and *w*
Jn. 1:1, beginning was the *W*
Jn. 1:14, *W* became flesh and
Jn. 8:51, if anyone keeps My *w*
Jn. 14:24, *w* which you hear is
Jn. 17:17, Your *w* is truth
Acts 13:48, and glorified the *w*
1 Cor. 12:8, to one is given the *w*
Eph. 5:26, of water by the *w*
Phil. 2:16, holding fast the *w*
Col. 3:16, Let the *w* of Christ
1 Th. 1:5, come to you in *w* only
2 Th. 2:17, in every good *w*
Heb. 1:3, by the *w* of His power
Heb. 4:2, *w* which they heard did
Heb. 4:12, For the *w* of God is
Jas. 1:21, the implanted *w*
Jas. 3:2, does not stumble in *w*
1 Pet. 1:23, through the *w* of God
2 Pet. 3:5, that by the *w* of God
1 Jn. 2:5, whoever keeps His *w*
1 Jn. 3:18, let us not love in *w*
1 Jn. 5:7, the Father, the *W*
Rev. 19:13, name is called The *W*

WORD of God
a name of Christ. Jn. 1:1,14; 1 Jn. 1:1; 5:7; Rev. 19:13
——— the Scriptures. Lk. 5:1; Acts 4:31; 8:14; 13:7; 16:6

WORDS
will be judged. Eccl. 5:2; Ezek. 35:13; Mal. 2:17; 3:13; Mt. 12:37

WORDS
Ps. 5:1, Give ear to my *w*
Ps. 19:14, Let the *w* of my mouth
Ps. 119:103, How sweet are Your *w*
Prov. 7:24, pay attention to the *w*
Eccl. 12:11, The *w* of the wise are
Isa. 51:16, And I have put My *w*
Hos. 14:2, Take *w* with you
Mic. 2:7, Do not My *w* do good to
Mt. 24:35, pass away, but My *w*
Lk. 4:22, at the gracious *w*
Jn. 6:63, *w* that I speak to you
Jn. 6:68, You have the *w* of
Acts 20:35, And remember the *w*
1 Cor. 1:17, not with wisdom of *w*
Rev. 1:3, those who hear the *w*
Rev. 22:7, is he who keeps the *w*

WORK
Gen. 2:2, day God ended His *w*
Ex. 40:33, Moses finished the *w*
Neh. 4:6, people had a mind to *w*
Job 14:15, You shall desire the *w*
Job 34:19, for they are all the *w*
Ps. 8:3, the *w* of Your fingers
Ps. 101:3, I hate the *w* of those
Ps. 102:25, the heavens are the *w*
Ps. 104:23, Man goes out to his *w*
Ps. 111:3, *w* is honorable and
Prov. 11:18, man does deceptive *w*
Eccl. 8:17, then I saw all the *w*
Eccl. 9:10, for there is no *w*
Eccl. 12:14, God will bring every *w*
Isa. 28:21, that He may do His *w*
Isa. 64:8, and all we are the *w*
Jer. 22:13, him nothing for his *w*
Jer. 32:19, and mighty in *w*
Hab. 1:5, For I will *w* a *w*
Mt. 21:28, and said, 'Son, go, *w*
Mk. 6:5, could do no mighty *w*
Jn. 6:28, we do, that we may *w*
Jn. 6:29, This is the *w* of God
Jn. 9:4, "I must *w* the works
Jn. 17:4, *w* which You have given
Rom. 8:28, know that all things *w*
Rom. 9:28, He will finish the *w*
Rom. 11:6, *w* is no longer *w*
Rom. 14:20, Do not destroy the *w*
1 Cor. 3:13, *w* will become manifest

1 Cor. 9:1, Are you not my *w*
1 Cor. 15:58, abounding in the *w*
1 Th. 1:3, without ceasing your *w*
2 Th. 2:17, every good word and *w*
2 Th. 3:10, If anyone will not *w*
Jas. 1:25, but a doer of the *w*

WORKED
Neh. 4:17, with one hand they *w*
Acts 15:12, and wonders God had *w*
Eph. 1:20, which He *w* in Christ

WORKER
Mt. 10:10, *w* is worthy of his
Rom. 16:21, Timothy, my fellow *w*
2 Tim. 2:15, *w* who does not need

WORKERS
Ps. 5:5, You hate all *w* of
1 Cor. 3:9, we are God's fellow *w*
Phil. 3:2, dogs, beware of evil *w*

WORKING
Mk. 16:20, everywhere, the Lord *w*
Jn. 5:17, My Father has been *w*
Eph. 1:19, according to the *w*
Col. 2:12, through faith in the *w*
2 Th. 3:11, manner, not *w* at all

WORKMAN, Hos. 8:6

WORKMANSHIP
Eph. 2:10, For we are His *w*

WORKS
of God. Job 9; 37—41; Ps. 8; 19; 89; 104; 111; 145; 147; 148; Eccl. 8:17; Jer. 10:12
—— of the law, insufficiency of. Rom. 3:20; 4:2; Gal. 3
—— good, the evidence of faith. Acts 26:20; Jas. 2:14; necessary. Mt. 5:16; Acts 9:36; 2 Cor. 8; 9; Eph. 2:10; Phil. 2:12; 1 Th. 4:11; 2 Th. 2:17; 3:8; Heb. 10:24; 1 Pet. 2:12

WORKS
Job 37:14, the wondrous *w* of God
Ps. 40:5, are Your wonderful *w*
Ps. 66:5, Come and see the *w*
Ps. 92:5, how great are Your *w*
Ps. 104:24, manifold are Your *w*
Ps. 111:2, The *w* of the LORD are
Ps. 145:10, *w* shall praise You
Prov. 31:31, And let her own *w*
Isa. 66:18, For I know their *w*
Dan. 4:37, of whose *w* are truth
Jn. 5:20, show Him greater *w*
Jn. 10:25, *w* that I do in My
Jn. 14:12, *w* that I do he will do
Acts 10:35, *w* righteousness
Rom. 9:11, might stand, not of *w*
Rom. 13:12, let us cast off the *w*
1 Cor. 12:6, is the same God who *w*
Gal. 2:16, not justified by the *w*
Gal. 5:19, Now the *w* of the flesh
Eph. 2:2, the spirit who now *w*
Eph. 2:9, not of *w*, lest anyone
Eph. 5:11, with the unfruitful *w*
Phil. 2:13, for it is God who *w*
Ti. 1:16, *w* they deny Him
Ti. 2:14, zealous for good *w*
Heb. 6:1, repentance from dead *w*
Jas. 2:14, but does not have *w*
Jas. 2:25, also justified by *w*
1 Jn. 3:8, He might destroy the *w*
Rev. 2:2, "I know your *w*
Rev. 14:13, their *w* follow them
Rev. 20:12, according to their *w*

WORLD
Ps. 9:8, He shall judge the *w*
Ps. 50:12, For the *w* is Mine
Ps. 93:1, *w* is established
Mt. 13:38, "The field is the *w*
Lk. 16:8, *w* are more shrewd
Jn. 1:10, He was in the *w*
Jn. 3:16, For God so loved the *w*
Jn. 3:17, His Son into the *w*
Jn. 4:42, the Savior of the *w*
Jn. 7:7, *w* cannot hate you
Jn. 8:23, You are of this *w*
Jn. 12:19, Look, the *w* has gone
Jn. 14:19, *w* will see Me no more
Jn. 15:18, "If the *w* hates you
Jn. 15:19, If you were of the *w*
Jn. 16:33, I have overcome the *w*
Jn. 17:9, do not pray for the *w*
Jn. 17:25, *w* has not known You
Rom. 3:19, *w* may become guilty
Rom. 12:2, be conformed to this *w*
1 Cor. 1:27, things of the *w*
1 Cor. 3:19, *w* is foolishness
Gal. 6:14, *w* has been crucified
Eph. 2:12, without God in the *w*
2 Tim. 4:10, loved this present *w*
Heb. 2:5, He has not put the *w*
Jas. 1:27, unspotted from the *w*
Jas. 4:4, *w* is enmity with God
1 Jn. 2:15, Do not love the *w*
1 Jn. 2:16, all that is in the *w*
1 Jn. 2:17, *w* is passing away
1 Jn. 3:1, *w* does not know us
1 Jn. 4:5, They are of the *w*
1 Jn. 4:17, so are we in this *w*
Rev. 13:3, And all the *w* marveled

WORLDLY
See also EARTHLY. Ti. 2:12

WORLDS
Heb. 1:2, also He made the *w*

WORM
Job 24:20, *w* should feed sweetly
Ps. 22:6, But I am a *w*
Isa. 41:14, "Fear not, you *w*
Isa. 66:24, their *w* does not die
Mk. 9:44, *w* does not die

WORMS
Job 7:5, flesh is caked with *w*
Isa. 14:11, you, and *w* cover you
Acts 12:23, he was eaten by *w*

WORMWOOD
Prov. 5:4, end she is bitter as *w*
Amos 5:7, who turn justice to *w*
Rev. 8:11, of the star is *W*

WORRY
Mt. 6:25, to you, do not *w*
Mt. 6:31, Therefore do not *w*

WORRYING
Mt. 6:27, by *w* can add one cubit

WORSE
Jer. 7:26, *w* than their fathers

WORSHIP
to be given to God alone. Ex. 20:1; Dt. 5:7; 6:13; Mt. 4:10; Lk. 4:8; Acts 10:26; 14:15; Col. 2:18; Rev. 19:10; 22:8
mode of. Lev. 10:3; Eccl. 5; Joel 2:16; Jn. 4:24; 1 Cor. 11; 14
commanded. 2 Ki. 17:36; 1 Chr. 16:29; Ps. 29; 95:6; 99:5; 100

WORSHIP
Gen. 22:5, I will go yonder and *w*
Ps. 45:11, He is your Lord, *w*
Ps. 95:6, Oh come, let us *w*
Mt. 2:2, and have come to *w* Him
Mt. 4:9, will fall down and *w*
Mt. 15:9, And in vain they *w*
Jn. 4:22, *w* what you do not know
Jn. 4:23, true worshipers will *w*
Acts 17:23, the One whom you *w*
Acts 24:14, *w* the God of my
Col. 2:18, false humility and *w*
Heb. 1:6, the angels of God *w*
Rev. 3:9, make them come and *w*
Rev. 4:10, *w* Him who lives
Rev. 14:7, *w* Him who made

WORSHIPED
Jn. 4:20, "Our fathers *w*
Rev. 5:14, *w* Him who lives
Rev. 11:16, on their faces and *w*
Rev. 19:4, *w* God who sat on the

WORSHIPER
Jn. 9:31, if anyone is a *w*

WORTH
Job 24:25, make my speech *w*
Prov. 10:20, of the wicked is *w*

WORTHLESS
Dt. 13:13; 1 Sam. 2:12; 10:27; 25:17,25; 30:22; 2 Sam. 6:20; 16:7; 20:1; 23:6; 1 Ki. 21:10,13; 2 Chr. 13:7

WORTHLESS
Ps. 119:37, looking at *w* things
Prov. 6:12, A *w* person, a wicked man
Isa. 41:29, Indeed they are all *w*

WORTHLESSNESS
Ps. 4:2, long will you love *w*

WORTHY
Gen. 32:10, "I am not *w* of the
Mt. 3:11, sandals I am not *w*
Mt. 10:11, inquire who in it is *w*
Mt. 22:8, invited were not *w*
Lk. 7:4, should do this was *w*
Lk. 15:19, and I am no longer *w*
Rom. 8:18, present time are not *w*
1 Cor. 15:9, apostles, who am not *w*
Eph. 4:1, to walk *w* of the calling
1 Tim. 5:18, "The laborer is *w*
Heb. 11:38, the world was not *w*
Rev. 3:4, white, for they are *w*
Rev. 4:11, "You are *w*, O Lord
Rev. 5:12, "*W* is the Lamb who

WOUND
Dt. 32:39, I *w* and I heal
Job 34:6, My *w* is incurable
Ps. 68:21, But God will *w* the

Jer. 15:18, and my *w* incurable
1 Cor. 8:12, and *w* their weak
Rev. 13:3, and his deadly *w*

WOUNDED
Ps. 109:22, and my heart is *w*
Isa. 51:9, and *w* the serpent
Isa. 53:5, But He was *w* for our
Jer. 37:10, there remained only *w*
Zech. 13:6, with which I was *w*
Rev. 13:14, to the beast who was *w*

WOUNDING
Gen. 4:23, killed a man for *w*

WOUNDS
Ps. 147:3, and binds up their *w*
Prov. 27:6, Faithful are the *w*
Lk. 10:34, and bandaged his *w*

WRANGLINGS
1 Tim. 6:5, useless *w* of men of

WRATH
Job 19:29; Ps. 37:8; Prov. 12:16; 14:29; 30:33; Gal. 5:20; Jas. 1:19
of God. 2 Chr. 28:11; Job 21:20; Ps. 106:23,40; Prov. 29:8; Lk. 4:28; Rom. 2:5,8; 9:22; Rev. 6:17; 11:18; 16:1; 19:15

WRATH
Num. 16:46, *w* has gone out from
Dt. 9:22, provoked the LORD to *w*
Dt. 32:27, Had I not feared the *w*
Job 5:2, *w* kills a foolish
Ps. 2:5, speak to them in His *w*
Ps. 58:9, living and burning *w*
Ps. 76:10, Surely the *w* of man
Ps. 88:16, Your fierce *w* has gone
Ps. 89:46, Will Your *w* burn like
Ps. 90:7, *w* we are terrified
Ps. 95:11, So I swore in My *w*
Ps. 110:5, in the day of His *w*
Prov. 16:14, death is the king's *w*
Prov. 19:12, The king's *w* is like
Prov. 19:19, of great *w* will suffer
Prov. 27:3, *w* is heavier than
Prov. 27:4, *W* is cruel and anger a
Isa. 10:6, *w* I will give him
Isa. 54:8, With a little *w*
Isa. 60:10, in My *w* I struck you
Hos. 5:10, I will pour out my *w*
Hab. 3:2, *w* remember mercy
Mt. 3:7, you to flee from the *w*
Jn. 3:36, see life, but the *w*
Rom. 1:18, For the *w* of God is
Rom. 2:5, up for yourself *w*
Rom. 4:15, the law brings about *w*
Rom. 9:22, wanting to show His *w*
Rom. 12:19, rather give place to *w*
Rom. 13:5, not only because of *w*
2 Cor. 12:20, outbursts of *w*
Eph. 2:3, nature children of *w*
Eph. 4:26, sun go down on your *w*
Eph. 4:31, Let all bitterness, *w*
1 Th. 1:10, delivers us from the *w*
1 Th. 2:16, *w* has come upon them
1 Tim. 2:8, holy hands, without *w*
Heb. 3:11, So I swore in My *w*
Heb. 11:27, not fearing the *w*
Jas. 1:20, for the *w* of man
Rev. 6:16, throne and from the *w*
Rev. 12:12, to you, having great *w*
Rev. 14:8, of the wine of the *w*
Rev. 14:19, winepress of the *w*
Rev. 15:1, for in them the *w*
Rev. 16:19, fierceness of His *w*

WRATHFUL
Prov. 15:18, *w* man stirs up strife

WRESTLE
Eph. 6:12, For we do not *w*

WRETCHED
Rom. 7:24, *w* man that I am
Rev. 3:17, know that you are *w*

WRETCHEDNESS
Num. 11:15, do not let me see my *w*

WRINGING
Prov. 30:33, *w* the nose produces

WRINKLE
Eph. 5:27, not having spot or *w*

WRITE
Ex. 34:27, "*W* these words
Job 13:26, *w* bitter things
Prov. 7:3, *w* them on the tablet
Jer. 22:30, '*W* this man down as
Heb. 8:10, *w* them on their hearts
Heb. 10:16, their minds I will *w*
3 Jn. 13, I had many things to *w*

WRITING
of God. Ex. 31:18; 32:16; Dan. 5:5
on the wall, expounded. Dan. 5

WRITING
Ex. 32:16, the *w* was the *w*

WRITINGS
Jn. 5:47, do not believe his *w*

WRITTEN
Ex. 31:18, tablets of stone, *w*
Prov. 22:20, Have I not *w* to you
Lk. 10:20, your names are *w*
Jn. 19:22, "What I have *w*
2 Cor. 3:3, ministered by us, *w*
Rev. 2:17, the stone a new name *w*
Rev. 22:18, the plagues that are *w*

WRONG
2 Chr. 6:37, sinned, we have done *w*
Job 19:7, I cry out concerning *w*
Job 24:12, not charge them with *w*
Ps. 105:14, no one to do them *w*
Jer. 22:3, Do no *w* and do no
Mt. 20:13, I am doing you no *w*
Lk. 23:41, Man has done nothing *w*
Acts 7:24, of them suffer *w*
Acts 25:10, Jews I have done no *w*
2 Cor. 12:13, Forgive me this *w*
Col. 3:25, But he who does *w*

WRONGED
Job 19:6, then that God has *w*
2 Cor. 7:2, We have *w* no one
Phile. 18, But if he has *w*

WRONGFULLY
Ezek. 22:29; 1 Pet. 2:19

WRONGS
Prov. 8:36, me *w* his own soul

WROTE
Dan. 5:5, of the hand that *w*
Jn. 8:6, stooped down and *w*

WROUGHT
Ps. 139:15, And skillfully *w*

WRETCHEDNESS
Num. 11:15, let me see my *w*

WRINGING
Prov. 30:33, *w* the nose produces

WRINKLE
Eph. 5:27, not having spot or *w*

YEAR
beginning of, changed. Ex. 12:1; Lev. 23:5

YEAR
Ex. 12:2, first month of the *y*
Lev. 27:24, 'In the *Y* of Jubilee
Isa. 61:2, the acceptable *y*
Ezek. 46:17, be his until the *y*
Lk. 2:41, to Jerusalem every *y*
Heb. 9:7, went alone once a *y*
Heb. 10:3, of sins every *y*

YEARN, Gen. 43:30; 1 Ki. 3:26

YEARS
Gen. 1:14, and for days and *y*
Job 10:5, Are Your *y* like the
Job 32:7, *y* should teach
Ps. 77:10, I will remember the *y*
Ps. 90:4, For a thousand *y*
Ps. 90:10, lives are seventy *y*
Ps. 102:24, Your *y* are throughout
Ps. 102:27, *y* will have no end
Lk. 2:42, when He was twelve *y*
Jn. 8:57, are not yet fifty *y*
Heb. 1:12, *y* will not fail
Rev. 20:2, for a thousand *y*
Rev. 20:6, with Him a thousand *y*

YES
Mt. 5:37, let your '*Y*' be '*Y*,'
2 Cor. 1:19, No, but in Him was *Y*

YESTERDAY
Job 8:9, For we were born *y*

YOKE
Gen. 27:40, you shall break his *y*
Dt. 28:48, and He will put a *y*
1 Ki. 12:4, Your father made our *y*
Isa. 9:4, You have broken the *y*
Lam. 3:27, a man to bear the *y*
Mt. 11:29, "Take My *y* upon you
1 Tim. 6:1, *y* count their own

YOKED
2 Cor. 6:14, Do not be unequally *y*

YOUNG
exhortations to. Lev. 19:32; Prov. 1:8; Eccl. 12:1

YOUNG
Job 33:25, His flesh shall be *y*
Ps. 37:25, I have been *y*
Ps. 84:3, she may lay her *y*
Isa. 11:7, *y* ones shall lie
Joel 2:28, dream dreams, your *y*
Mk. 14:51, *y* man followed Him
Ti. 2:4, they admonish the *y*
1 Jn. 2:13, I write to you, *y*

YOUNGER
Job 30:1, they mock at me, men *y*
Lk. 15:13, *y* son gathered all

Lk. 22:26, let him be as the *y*
1 Tim. 5:2, *y* women as sisters
1 Pet. 5:5, Likewise you *y* people

YOUNGEST
Gen. 42:13; Josh. 6:26; 1 Ki. 16:34

YOURS
1 Ki. 20:4, all that I have are *y*
2 Chr. 20:15, the battle is not *y*
Ps. 119:94, I am *Y*, save me
Mt. 6:13, *Y* is the kingdom
Mt. 20:14, 'Take what is *y*
Lk. 6:20, *y* is the kingdom
Jn. 17:10, all Mine are *Y*
1 Cor. 3:21, For all things are *y*
2 Cor. 12:14, for I do not seek *y*

YOUTH
1 Sam. 17:42, for he was only a *y*
1 Ki. 18:12, the LORD from my *y*
Ps. 25:7, the sins of my *y*
Prov. 2:17, the companion of her *y*
Eccl. 11:9, in the days of your *y*
Eccl. 11:10, and *y* are vanity
Isa. 54:4, the shame of your *y*
Jer. 1:6, speak, for I am a *y*
Jer. 2:2, the kindness of your *y*
Mt. 19:20, I have kept from my *y*
1 Cor. 7:36, the flower of her *y*
1 Tim. 4:12, no one despise your *y*

YOUTHFUL
2 Tim. 2:22, Flee also *y* lusts

YOUTHS
Prov. 7:7, perceived among the *y*
Isa. 40:30, *y* shall faint and be

ZACCHAEUS, Lk. 19:2

ZACHARIAS
father of John the Baptist, with Elizabeth his wife, accounted righteous before God. Lk. 1:6
is promised a son. Lk. 1:13
doubting, is struck mute. Lk. 1:18,22
his recovery and song. Lk. 1:64,68

ZADOK
priest. 2 Sam. 8:17; 15:24; 20:25
anoints Solomon king. 1 Ki. 1:39

ZAREPHATH
Elijah there. 1 Ki. 17:10. *See* ELIJAH

ZEAL
Rom. 12:11; 2 Cor. 7:10–11; Rev. 3:19
of Phinehas. Num. 25:7,11; Ps. 106:30
of Jehu. 2 Ki. 10:16
of the Jews. Acts 21:20; Rom. 10:2
of Paul. Acts 22:3; Gal. 1:14; Phil. 3:6
Christ an example of. Ps. 69:9; Jn. 2:17

ZEAL
2 Ki. 19:31, The *z* of the LORD of
Ps. 119:139, *z* has consumed me
Isa. 42:13, He shall stir up His *z*
Ezek. 5:13, have spoken it in My *z*
Zech. 8:2, for Zion with great *z*
Jn. 2:17, "*Z* for Your house has
Rom. 10:2, that they have a *z*
2 Cor. 9:2, *z* has stirred up the

ZEALOT, Lk. 6:15

ZEALOUS
1 Ki. 19:10, "I have been very *z*
Zech. 8:2, 'I am *z* for Zion with
1 Cor. 14:12, since you are *z*
Gal. 4:18, But it is good to be *z*
Ti. 2:14, *z* for good works

ZEBEDEE
Greek form of Zebadiah. Mt. 4:21; Mk. 1:20

ZEBOIIM
Gen. 10:19; 14:2; Dt. 29:23; Hos. 11:8

ZEBULUN
Gen. 30:20; 35:23; 49:13; Num. 1:30; 26:26; Dt. 33:13; Josh. 19:10; Jud. 4:6; 5:14,18; 6:35; 2 Chr. 30:11,18; Ps. 68:27; Ezek. 48:26; Rev. 7:8
Christ preaches in the land of. (Isa. 9:1); Mt. 4:13

ZECHARIAH
last king of Israel of Jehu's line, as foretold by the word of the Lord, begins to reign. 2 Ki. 14:29
killed by Shallum, who succeeds him. 2 Ki. 15:10
—— 'son of Berechiah', killed 'between the temple and the altar.' Mt. 23:35; Lk. 11:51
—— son of Jehoiada, stoned in the court of the Lord's house. 2 Chr. 24:20–21
—— son of Jeberechiah. Isa. 8:2
—— the prophet, his exhortations to repentance, his visions and predictions. Zech. 1—14

ZEDEKIAH
false prophet. 1 Ki. 22:11; 2 Chr. 18:10,23
—— another. Jer. 29:22
—— (Mattaniah), king of Judah. 2 Ki. 24:17; 25; 2 Chr. 36:10–11; Jer. 37; 38; 39; 52

ZENAS, Ti. 3:13

ZEPHANIAH, 2 Ki. 25:18
priest. Jer. 29:25; 37:3
—— prophet. Zeph. 1; 2; 3

ZERUBBABEL
prince of Judah. Ezra 2:2
restores the worship of God. Ezra 3:1; Neh. 12:47; Hag. 1:1,14; 2:1; Zech. 4:6

ZEUS, Acts 19:35
Barnabas addressed as. Acts 14:12

ZIKLAG
Josh. 15:31; 1 Sam. 27:6; 30:1; 2 Sam. 1:1; 1 Chr. 12:1

ZIMRI, 1 Ki. 16:9

ZIN, *see also* SIN
wilderness of. Num. 13:21; 20; 27:14; Josh. 15:1

ZION
Mount. 2 Sam. 5:7; 1 Ki. 8:1; Rom. 11:26; Heb. 12:22; Rev. 14:1

ZIPH, 1 Chr. 4:16

ZIPPORAH, Ex. 2:21; 4:20

ZOAN, Num. 13:22; Ps. 78:12

ZOAR
Gen. 13:10; 14:2; 19:22 (Isa. 15:5); Dt. 34:3; Jer. 48:34

ZOPHAR, Job 2:11; 11; 20; 42:9

ZORAH
city of Samson. Josh. 19:41; Jud. 13:2,25; 16:31

ZUPH, 1 Sam. 1:1

ZURISHADDAI, Num. 1:6

Index to Maps

Map 1: The Nations of Genesis 10
Map 2: The Exodus from Egypt
Map 3: The Conquest of Canaan
Map 4: The Kingdom Years
Map 5: Jerusalem—From David to Christ
Map 6: Palestine in Christ's Time
Map 7: Paul's First and Second Journeys
Map 8: Paul's Third and Fourth Journeys
Map 9: The Holy Land in Modern Times

The following index is divided into two parts, one for Map 5, Jerusalem, and the other for all the other maps. Place names are usually given as shown on the maps; sometimes they are followed by alternate names and spellings, which are set in parentheses. If a place name is not given as shown on the map, it is followed, in parentheses, by the alternate name or spelling that does appear on the map (example: *Melita* (*Malta* on map)). Where a place name refers to a large area, the index gives the location of the name. Where a name refers to a river, the index gives the source and mouth of the river.

In the index to Maps 1 through 4 and 6 through 9, major political divisions, such as countries and regions, are shown in capital letters (examples: EGYPT, PALESTINE). Cities are shown in upper and lower case as usual (example: Hebron). Geographical features are shown in italics (example: *Jordan River*).

INDEX TO MAPS

Map 1: The Nations of Genesis 10
Map 2: The Exodus from Egypt
Map 3: The Conquest of Canaan
Map 4: The Kingdom Years
Map 6: Palestine in Christ's Time
Map 7: Paul's First and Second Journeys
Map 8: Paul's Third and Fourth Journeys
Map 9: The Holy Land in Modern Times

INDEX TO MAPS

INDEX TO MAPS

INDEX TO MAPS

Map 5: Jerusalem—From David to Christ

Map 1
THE NATIONS OF GENESIS 10
JAVAN Descendants of Japheth (Gen. 10:2–5)
PUT Descendants of Ham (Gen. 10:6–20)
LUD Descendants of Shem (Gen. 10:21–31)
(Lydia) Later biblical name
GOMER
TOGARMAH
ASHKENAZ
(Scythians)
HITTITES
LUD
(Lydia)
JAVAN
(Greeks)
Caspian Sea
ASSHUR
(Assyria)
MADAI
(Medes)
KITTIM
(Cyprus)
ARAM
(Syria)
Tigris
Euphrates
The Great Sea
(Mediterranean Sea)
AMORITES
CANAAN
ELAM
(Persia)
PHILISTINES
ARPHAXAD
PUT
MIZRAIM
(Egypt)
Persian Gulf
Nile
Red Sea
JOKTAN
(Arabia)
Scale of Miles
0
100
200
© Thomas Nelson, Inc., 1983

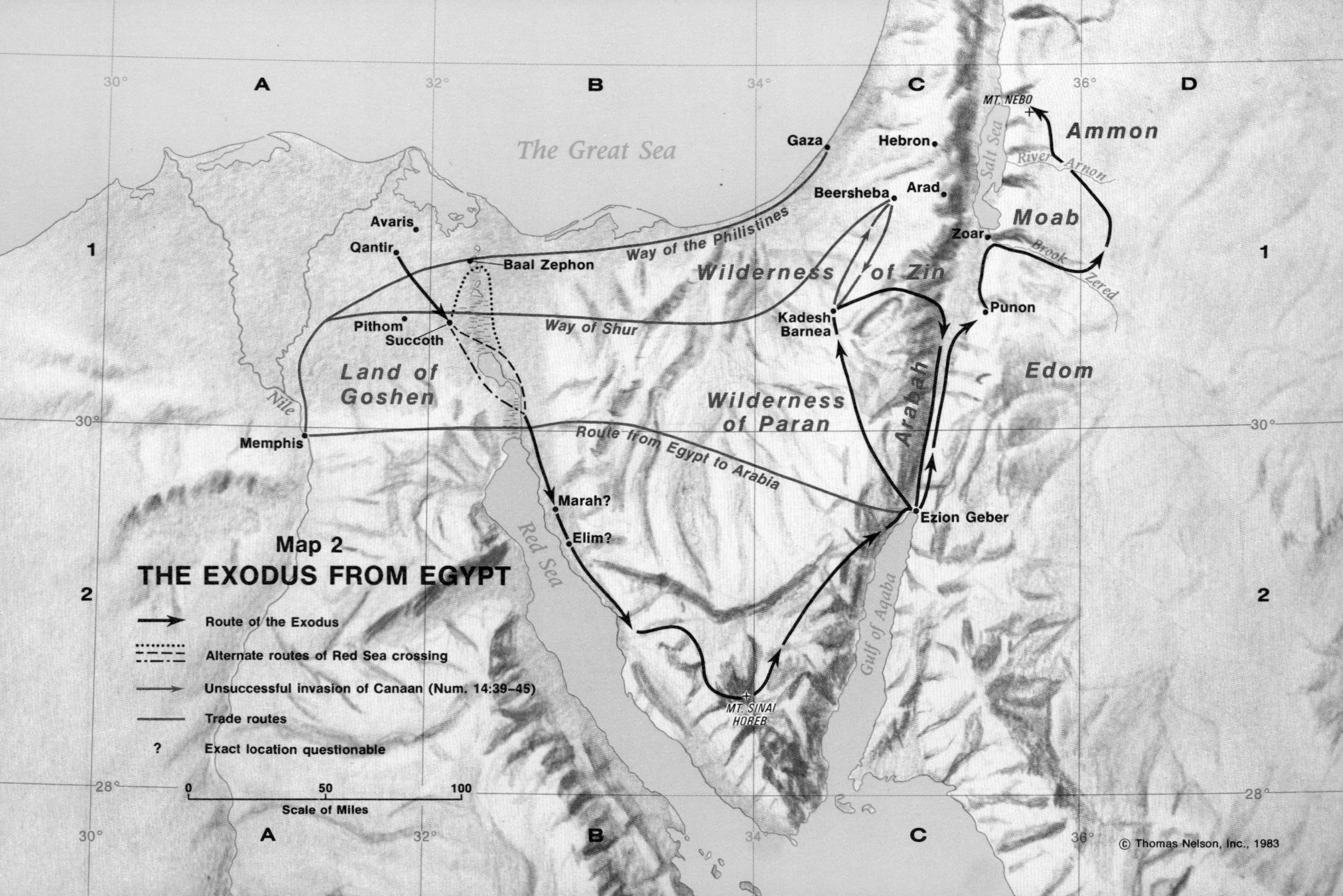
Map 2
THE EXODUS FROM EGYPT
Route of the Exodus
Alternate routes of Red Sea crossing
Unsuccessful invasion of Canaan (Num. 14:39–45)
Trade routes
? Exact location questionable
0
50
100
Scale of Miles
A
B
C
D
1
2
30°
32°
34°
36°
28°
The Great Sea
Avaris
Qantir
Baal Zephon
Way of the Philistines
Pithom
Succoth
Way of Shur
Land of Goshen
Nile
Memphis
Route from Egypt to Arabia
Marah?
Elim?
Red Sea
MT. SINAI
HOREB
Gulf of Aqaba
Wilderness of Paran
Wilderness of Zin
Kadesh Barnea
Gaza
Beersheba
Hebron
Arad
Arabah
Ezion Geber
Punon
Edom
Zoar
Salt Sea
Moab
Brook Zered
River Arnon
Ammon
MT. NEBO

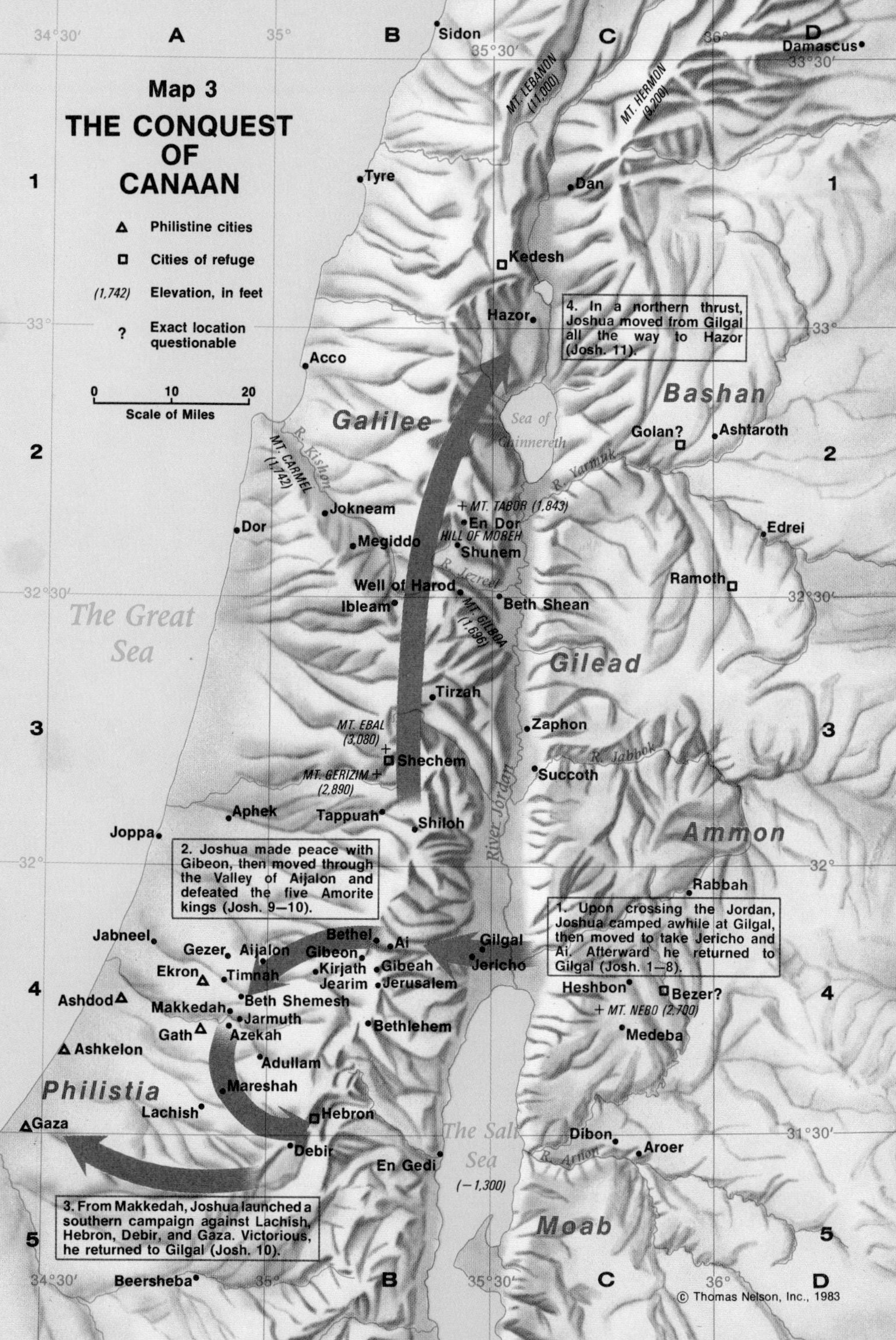
Map 3
THE CONQUEST OF CANAAN
Philistine cities
Cities of refuge
(1,742) Elevation, in feet
? Exact location questionable
0 10 20
Scale of Miles
A
B
C
D
1
2
3
4
5
34°30′
35°
35°30′
36°
33°30′
33°
32°30′
32°
31°30′
Sidon
Damascus
MT. LEBANON (11,000)
MT. HERMON (9,200)
Tyre
Dan
Kedesh
Hazor
4. In a northern thrust, Joshua moved from Gilgal all the way to Hazor (Josh. 11).
Acco
Bashan
Galilee
Sea of Chinnereth
Golan?
Ashtaroth
R. Kishon
MT. CARMEL (1,742)
R. Yarmuk
MT. TABOR (1,843)
Jokneam
En Dor
HILL OF MOREH
Shunem
Dor
Megiddo
Edrei
R. Jezreel
Well of Harod
Ramoth
Ibleam
MT. GILBOA (1,696)
Beth Shean
The Great Sea
Gilead
Tirzah
MT. EBAL (3,080)
Zaphon
R. Jabbok
Shechem
MT. GERIZIM (2,890)
River Jordan
Succoth
Aphek
Tappuah
Shiloh
Joppa
Ammon
2. Joshua made peace with Gibeon, then moved through the Valley of Aijalon and defeated the five Amorite kings (Josh. 9—10).
Rabbah
1. Upon crossing the Jordan, Joshua camped awhile at Gilgal, then moved to take Jericho and Ai. Afterward he returned to Gilgal (Josh. 1—8).
Jabneel
Bethel
Ai
Gilgal
Gezer
Aijalon
Gibeon
Jericho
Ekron
Timnah
Kirjath Jearim
Gibeah
Jerusalem
Heshbon
Bezer?
Ashdod
Beth Shemesh
Makkedah
MT. NEBO (2,700)
Jarmuth
Gath
Azekah
Bethlehem
Medeba
Ashkelon
Adullam
Philistia
Mareshah
Lachish
Hebron
Gaza
The Salt Sea
(−1,300)
Dibon
Aroer
Debir
R. Arnon
En Gedi
3. From Makkedah, Joshua launched a southern campaign against Lachish, Hebron, Debir, and Gaza. Victorious, he returned to Gilgal (Josh. 10).
Moab
Beersheba
© Thomas Nelson, Inc., 1983

Map 4
THE KINGDOM YEARS
Probable extent of Israelite control during the Kingdom of Solomon, c. 950 B.C.
The Kingdoms of Israel and Judah, c. 860 B.C.
Boundary between Israel and Judah
? Exact location questionable
0 25 50
Scale of Miles
A
B
C
1
2
3
4
5
6
34°
35°
36°
37°
33°
32°
31°
30°
Riblah
Zobah
Byblos
Phoenicia
MT. LEBANON
MT. HERMON
Sidon
Zarephath
Damascus
Tyre
Dan
Syria
Kedesh
Hazor
Acco
Sea of Chinnereth
Ashtaroth
Golan?
MT. CARMEL
The Great Sea
Jokneam
Dor
Megiddo
Ramoth Gilead
Jezreel
Taanach
MT. GILBOA
Jabesh Gilead
Dothan
Tirzah
Zaphon
Samaria
Succoth
Shechem
R. Jabbok
Jordan R.
Ammon
Aphek
Shiloh
ISRAEL
Rabbah
Joppa
Mizpah
Bethel
Jabneh
Gezer
Ramah
Heshbon
Philistia
Jerusalem
Beth Shemesh
Bethlehem
Medeba
Ashkelon
Tekoa
Adullam
Eglon?
Dibon
Gaza
Hebron
The Salt Sea
Aroer
R. Arnon
Debir
Ziklag?
Arad
Moab
Beersheba
Kir Hareseth
Zoar
R. Zered
JUDAH
Bozrah
Kadesh Barnea
Edom
Brook of Egypt
Teman
Note: Other place names significant during the time of the Kingdoms are found on Map 3.
Ezion Geber
Elath
© Thomas Nelson, Inc., 1983

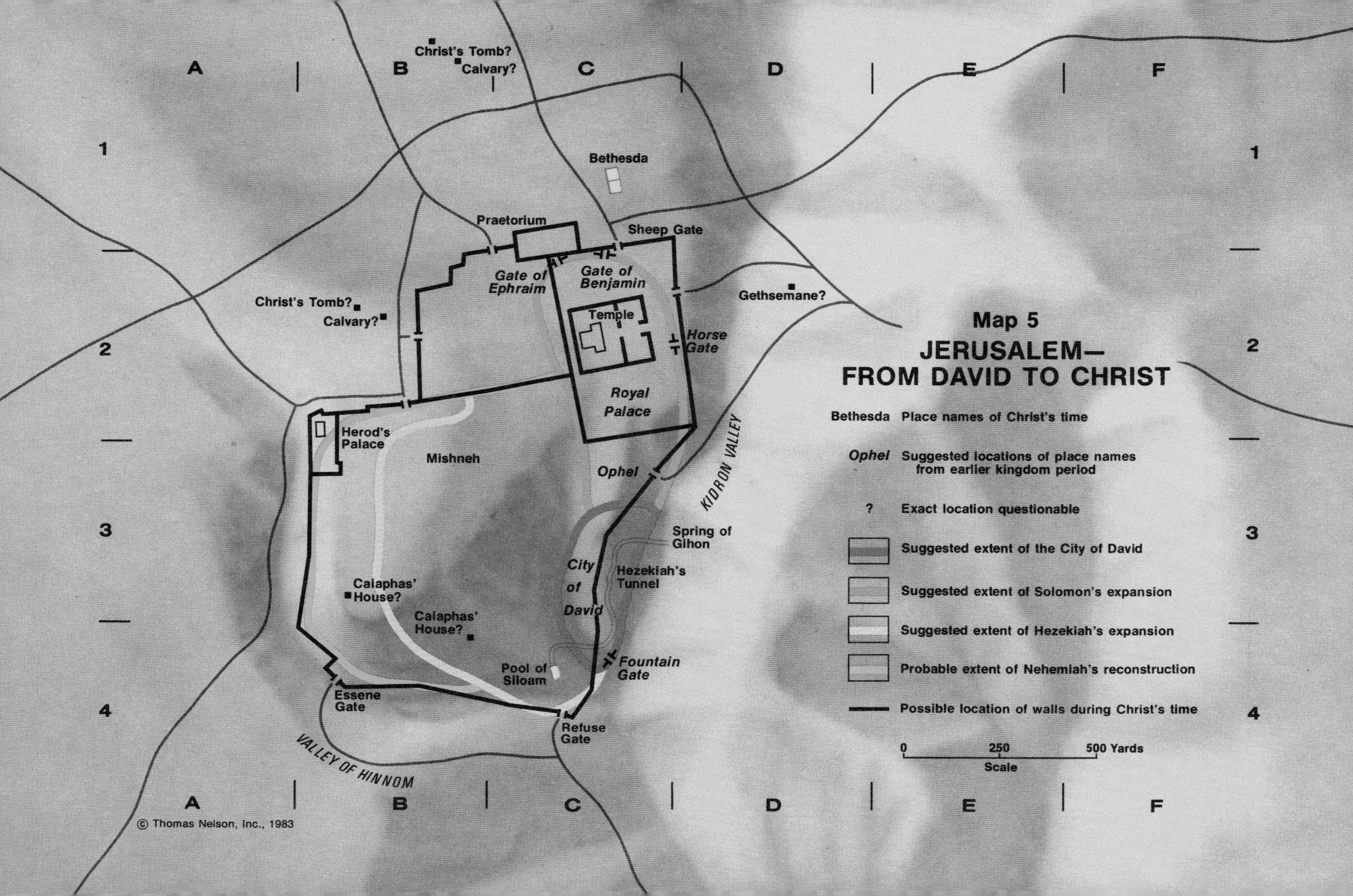
Map 5
JERUSALEM—
FROM DAVID TO CHRIST
Bethesda Place names of Christ's time
Ophel Suggested locations of place names from earlier kingdom period
? Exact location questionable
Suggested extent of the City of David
Suggested extent of Solomon's expansion
Suggested extent of Hezekiah's expansion
Probable extent of Nehemiah's reconstruction
Possible location of walls during Christ's time
0
250
500 Yards
Scale
Christ's Tomb?
Calvary?
Bethesda
Praetorium
Sheep Gate
Gate of Ephraim
Gate of Benjamin
Gethsemane?
Temple
Horse Gate
Royal Palace
Herod's Palace
Mishneh
Ophel
Kidron Valley
Spring of Gihon
City of David
Hezekiah's Tunnel
Caiaphas' House?
Pool of Siloam
Fountain Gate
Essene Gate
Refuse Gate
Valley of Hinnom
A
B
C
D
E
F
1
2
3
4

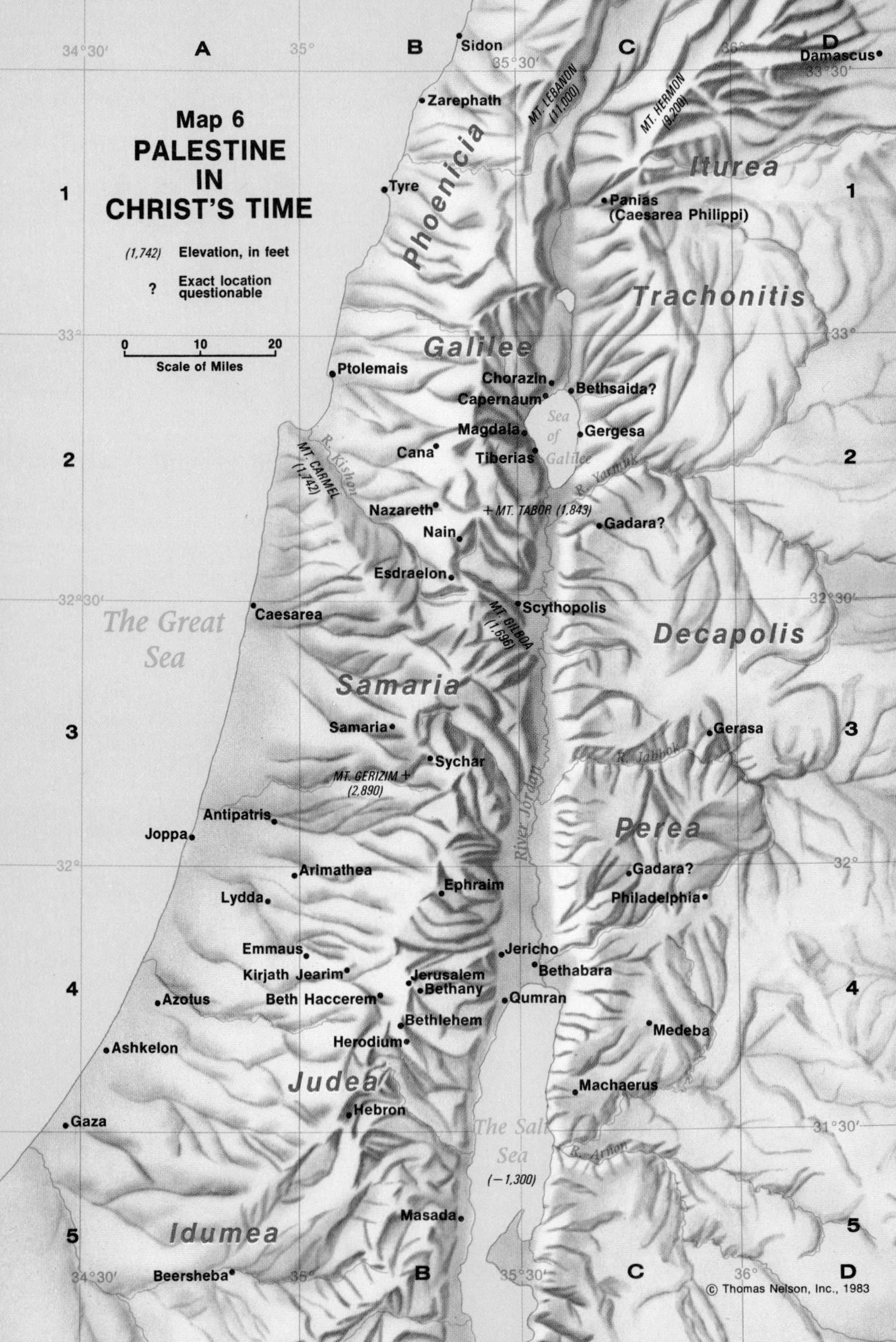

Map 6
PALESTINE IN CHRIST'S TIME
(1,742) Elevation, in feet
? Exact location questionable
0 10 20
Scale of Miles
34°30′
A
35°
B
C
D
36°
35°30′
33°30′
33°
32°30′
32°
31°30′
1
2
3
4
5
Sidon
Damascus
Zarephath
MT. LEBANON (11,000)
MT. HERMON (9,200)
Phoenicia
Iturea
Tyre
Panias
(Caesarea Philippi)
Trachonitis
Galilee
Ptolemais
Chorazin
Bethsaida?
Capernaum
Sea of Galilee
Magdala
Gergesa
Cana
Tiberias
R. Kishon
MT. CARMEL (1,742)
R. Yarmuk
Nazareth
MT. TABOR (1,843)
Gadara?
Nain
Esdraelon
Scythopolis
MT. GILBOA (1,696)
Caesarea
The Great Sea
Decapolis
Samaria
Samaria
Gerasa
Sychar
R. Jabbok
MT. GERIZIM (2,890)
River Jordan
Antipatris
Joppa
Perea
Arimathea
Gadara?
Ephraim
Lydda
Philadelphia
Emmaus
Jericho
Bethabara
Kirjath Jearim
Jerusalem
Bethany
Beth Haccerem
Qumran
Azotus
Bethlehem
Medeba
Herodium
Ashkelon
Judea
Machaerus
Hebron
Gaza
The Salt Sea
R. Arnon
(−1,300)
Masada
Idumea
Beersheba
© Thomas Nelson, Inc., 1983

A
B
C
D
1
2
16°
24°
32°
40°
Illyricum
0
150
300
Scale of Miles
Black Sea
Adriatic Sea
Italy
Macedonia
Thrace
Pontus
Bithynia
Amphipolis
Philippi
Thessalonica
Neapolis
Berea
Apollonia
Galatia
Troas
Phrygia
Cappadocia
Achaia
Athens
Antioch
Iconium
Sicily
Corinth
Ephesus
Pisidia
Lystra
Tarsus
Derbe
Perga
Attalia
Pamphylia
Lycia
Cilicia
Antioch
Seleucia
Syria
Cyprus
Crete
Salamis
Paphos
The Great Sea
Caesarea
Jerusalem
Palestine
© Thomas Nelson, Inc., 1983

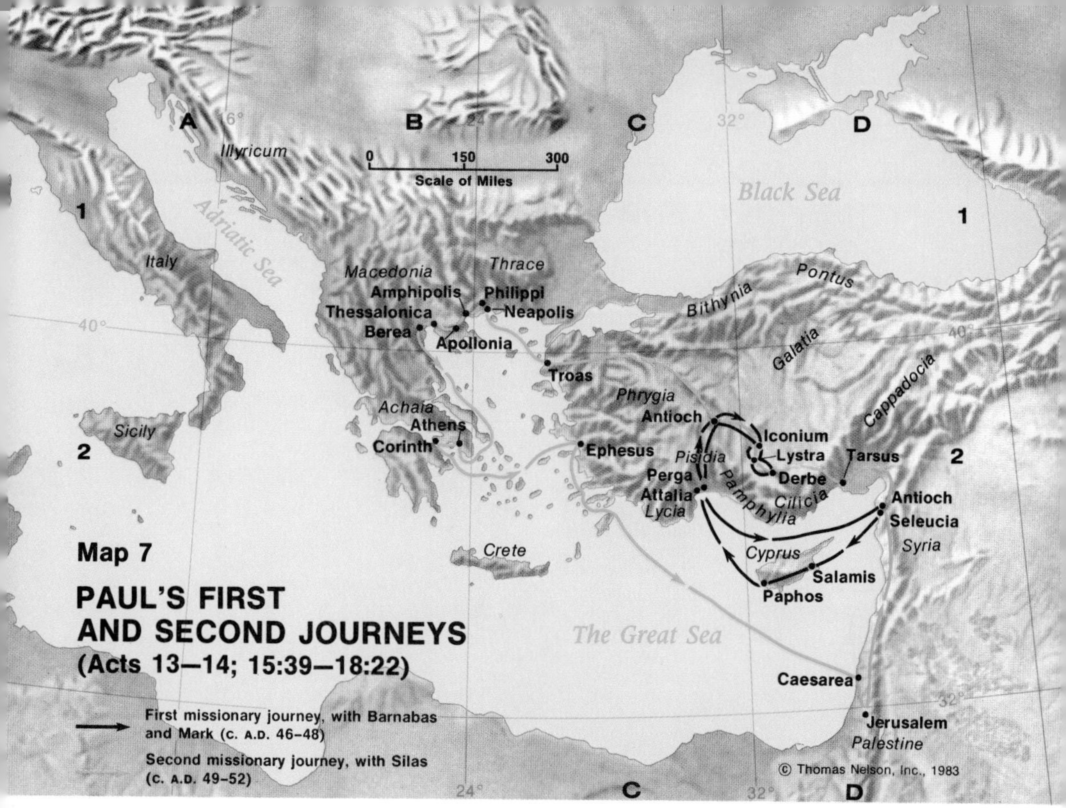

Map 7

PAUL'S FIRST AND SECOND JOURNEYS
(Acts 13–14; 15:39–18:22)

First missionary journey, with Barnabas and Mark (c. A.D. 46–48)

Second missionary journey, with Silas (c. A.D. 49–52)

A
B
C
D
1
2
16°
24°
32°
40°
Illyricum
0
150
300
Scale of Miles
Black Sea
Adriatic Sea
Rome
Three Inns
Appii Forum
Puteoli
Italy
Macedonia
Thrace
Amphipolis
Philippi
Thessalonica
Berea
Apollonia
Pontus
Bithynia
Galatia
Troas
Assos
Mitylene
Phrygia
Cappadocia
Achaia
Rhegium
Sicily
Chios
Ephesus
Antioch
Iconium
Pisidia
Corinth
Athens
Samos
Miletus
Lystra
Derbe
Tarsus
Syracuse
Pamphylia
Cilicia
Malta
Cos
Cnidus
Lycia
Myra
Antioch
Syria
Crete
Rhodes
Patara
Fair Havens
Cyprus
The Great Sea
Sidon
Tyre
Ptolemais
Caesarea
Antipatris
Jerusalem
© Thomas Nelson, Inc., 1983

Map 8

PAUL'S THIRD AND FOURTH JOURNEYS
(Acts 18:23–21:16; 27–28:16)

Third missionary journey (c. A.D. 53–57)

Fourth missionary journey (c. A.D. 59–62)

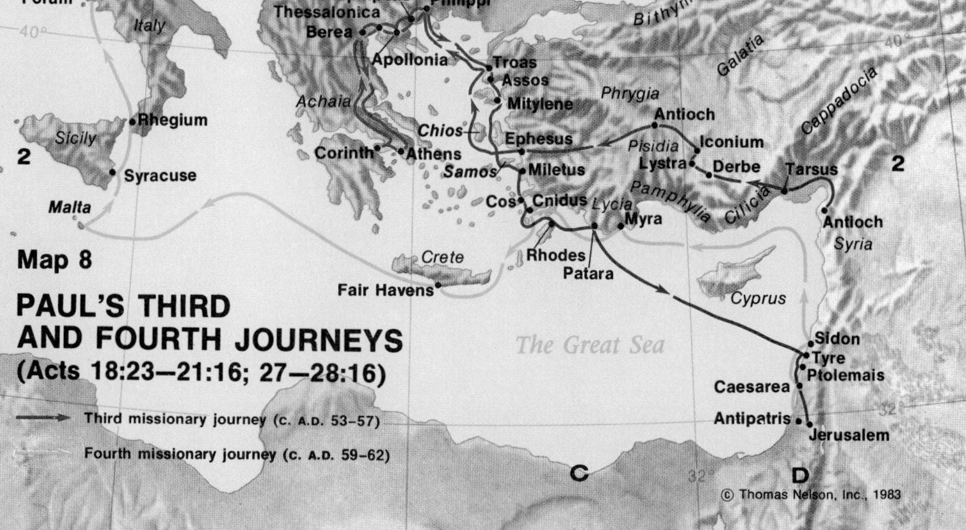

Map 9
THE HOLY LAND
IN MODERN TIMES
Area occupied by Israel since June, 1967
0
25
50
Scale of Miles
A
B
C
D
E
1
2
3
4
5
6
34°
35°
36°
37°
33°
32°
31°
30°
Tripoli
LEBANON
Beirut
LEBANON MTS.
BEKAA VALLEY
ANTI-LEBANON MTS.
Sidon
Damascus
Tyre
Dan
U.N. Buffer Zone
1973 Line
SYRIA
Qiryat Shemona
Quneitra
Nahariyya
1967 Cease-Fire Line
Safad
Golan Heights
Akko
Sea of Galilee
Haifa
Tiberias
Dera
Nazareth
Mediterranean Sea
Afula
Ramtha
Beth Shean
Hadera
Netanya
Tulkarm
Jarash
Nablus
Herzliyya
Jordan River
West Bank
Tel Aviv
Petah Tiqwa
Yafo
Amman
Rishon le Zion
Lod
Ramalah
Ramla
Ashdod
Jericho
Jerusalem
Bethlehem
Madaba
Ashqelon
Qiryat Gat
Hebron
Dead Sea
Gaza
En Gedi
Dhiban
Beersheba
Al-Arish
Karak
JORDAN
ISRAEL
EGYPT
Negev
Arabah
Sinai
Elat
Aqaba